THE OXFORD DICTIONARY OF PRONUNCIATION FOR CURRENT ENGLISH

The Oxford Dictionary of Pronunciation for Current English

Clive Upton
William A. Kretzschmar, Jr
Rafal Konopka

OXFORD
UNIVERSITY PRESS

OXFORD
UNIVERSITY PRESS

Great Clarendon Street, Oxford OX2 6DP

Oxford University Press is a department of the University of Oxford.
It furthers the University's objective of excellence in research, scholarship,
and education by publishing worldwide in

Oxford New York

Athens Auckland Bangkok Bogotá Buenos Aires Cape Town
Chennai Dar es Salaam Delhi Florence Hong Kong Istanbul Karachi
Kolkata Kuala Lumpur Madrid Melbourne Mexico City Mumbai Nairobi
Paris São Paulo Shanghai Singapore Taipei Tokyo Toronto Warsaw

with associated companies in Berlin Ibadan

Oxford is a registered trade mark of Oxford University Press
in the UK and in certain other countries

Published in the United States
by Oxford University Press Inc., New York

First published 2001

British Library Cataloguing in Publication Data
Data available

Library of Congress Cataloging in Publication Data
Data available

ISBN 0-19-863156-1

10 9 8 7 6 5 4 3 2 1

Typeset in Nimrod and Arial
by Selwood Systems
Printed in Great Britain by
T. J. International Ltd.,
Padstow, Cornwall

Contents

Dictionary team

Clive Upton

William A. Kretzschmar, Jr

Rafal Konopka

Oxford University Press

Editors
Susan Wilkin
Judith Scott

Editorial assistants
Alison Curr
Phil Gerrish
Anne McConnell

Foreign language consultants

Afrikaans
Penny Silva, *formerly* Managing editor, *Dictionary of South African English on Historical Principles*, Oxford University Press

Brazilian Portuguese
Lixia Xavier, freelance lexicographer and translator

Lusitanian Portuguese
Lia Correia-Raitt, Sub-Faculty of Portuguese, Modern Languages, Oxford University

Czech
Dr Jaromír Málek, Griffith Institute, Ashmolean Museum, Oxford

Danish
Britt-Katrin Keson, The Society for Danish Language and Literature, Copenhagen, Denmark

Dutch & Flemish
Susan Wilkin, Oxford Dictionary Department

French
Isabelle Stables, *formerly* Oxford French Dictionaries

German
Dr Michael Clark, Projects Manager, Bilingual Dictionaries, Oxford University Press

Hungarian
Dr Gábor Bátonyi, University of Bradford

Irish Gaelic
Mary O'Neill, Managing Editor, Language Engineering, Oxford University Press

Italian
Francesca Logi, freelance lexicographer and translator

Norwegian
Dr Olav Veka, Brumunddal, Norway

Polish
Danuta Padley, Oxford English Dictionary

Russian
Dr Della Thompson, Projects Manager, Bilingual Dictionaries, Oxford University Press

Spanish
Ana Cristina Llompart, freelance lexicographer and translator

Swedish
Susanne Charlett, Oxford English Dictionary

Turkish
Helen Liebeck, *formerly* Oxford Dictionary Department

Welsh
Dr Hywel Wyn Owen, University of Wales, Bangor

Preface

We are delighted to offer our models and transcriptions for the pronunciation of British and American English, in what we believe to be a new manner for the new millennium. We have developed our British and American models, not as incremental improvements upon some prior practice but as the product of our long research experience as students of language variation in Britain and America. It is perhaps ironic that specialists in accent and dialect have been called upon to decide what pronunciations are held in common as national habits or norms by British and American speakers. We believe that our wide experience with variation gives us standing to create pronunciation models which avoid slavish imitation of the dictates of self-appointed arbiters of taste or style in language, in favour of patterns which reflect the actual speech of real people.

We have of course profited from the research and scholarship on English pronunciation of those who have come before us. We cannot but admire the achievements of Daniel Jones and A. C. Gimson in Britain, or of John Kenyon and Edward Artin in America. We must acknowledge our great debt to the speakers, field workers, and our predecessors as editors of the two great national surveys of speech in Britain and American, the Survey of English Dialects and the American Linguistic Atlas Project. And we must also offer our gratitude to our colleagues in lexicography, dialectology, sociolinguistics, and other branches of the study of the English language, whether cited in the front matter or not, without whose observations and insights we could not have assessed the facts of current English pronunciation and compiled our lists.

We would also like to make a few more individual acknowledgements. We would like to thank Eric Rochester for his invaluable technical assistance. Clive Upton owes a great debt of gratitude to John Widdowson, and before him to Harold Orton and David Parry, who taught him to listen attentively and work independently; and to Lesley Upton, who herself listened and made all the right noises. William A. Kretzschmar, Jr would like to thank three people for their contributions toward this work: Virginia McDavid, for her judgement and support over many years; Lee Pederson, whose unmatched knowledge of American pronunciation, and whose friendship, provided inspiration; and Claudia Kretzschmar, who not only endured and helped to brighten the extended work on transcriptions but contributed herself, on many occasions, to their quality. Rafal Konopka would like to thank his teachers at the Jagiellonian University in Krakow, Poland, where the adventure with English began; his mentors and colleagues at the University of Georgia, without whom the adventure would not have evolved into fascination; and his family for their patience, support, and active interest.

Finally, we appeal to our readers, the living speakers of contemporary English, whether native or later acquired, to listen to the pronunciation of English around them and to revel in the endless variety of English voices and accents that they will hear. We have in this volume ascertained particular models of British and American pronunciation, and we assert their essential value for native speakers and for learners alike. Yet we will join you, our readers, in the appreciation of the multitude of accents and voices which we have not included here, and assert as well their own great value for the subtlety and richness of our English language.

CLIVE UPTON · WILLIAM A. KRETZSCHMAR, JR · RAFAL KONOPKA
October 2000

Introduction

Use of the dictionary

This dictionary presents the pronunciations of a large body of words in both British English (BR) and United States American English (AM) varieties. It is intended for use both by fluent English speakers and by learners of the language. On the one hand, it will provide those possessing a high degree of competence in English with a guide to the pronunciation of those uncommon words with which they may be unfamiliar and whose pronunciation may not immediately be apparent. On the other hand, it will give the English-language learner a comprehensive guide to the pronunciation of the core vocabulary of the two principal international English varieties.

It would of course be both impracticable and confusing to attempt to present transcriptions for even a fraction of the variety of regional and social accents which characterize British and American English. For both pragmatic and pedagogic reasons model accents have to be sought, transcriptions of which may be generally accepted as embodying the major elements of the pronunciation-types under consideration. Descriptions of the BR and AM models which have been decided upon are given below (pp. xi–xvi). In each case the choice has been for that model which, if reproduced by users of this dictionary in accordance with the principles of the International Phonetic Association, will enable them to be understood by native speakers of English without being categorized as belonging to any narrow class, age, or regional grouping.

The text of this dictionary has been so designed that reference can be made to it without careful study of a set of complicated conventions. For example, British and American pronunciations are introduced by 'BR' and 'AM' rather than by symbols. Again, when more than one transcription of a headword is thought to be necessary in either variety, complete transcriptions rather than abbreviated transcriptions are given for each alternative pronunciation. Nevertheless, given below is an explanation of the arrangement of entries for anyone wishing to study it prior to detailed use of the dictionary.

The text explained

1. Headwords

Headwords are arranged in alphabetical order.

If a word can be spelt in two or more ways, the variants are given at their respective places in the alphabetical listing. Although spelling differences are sometimes associated with written British and American English, no indication is given in this dictionary as to which spelling may be most characteristic of which accent: it is not always possible categorically to make a statement on this, and this dictionary concerns pronunciation rather than spelling. Separate headwords are created for variant spellings, regardless of whether they occupy consecutive places in the alphabetical run or are separated by other headwords.

2. The basic entry

A most basic entry consists of a headword in bold type and identical transcriptions for BR and AM:

ablaze
BR ə'bleɪz
AM ə'bleɪz

This indicates that the headword has the same pronunciations for both BR and AM, and that no derived forms need to be considered.

A simple development of this occurs when the BR and AM pronunciations differ in some way but there are still no derived forms:

afloat
BR ə'fləʊt
AM ə'floʊt

3. Several pronunciations: use of comma

Where more than one pronunciation is shown for one variety (BR or AM), those pronunciations are separated by a comma or commas:

cast
BR kɑːst, kast

digitization
AM ˌdɪdʒədə'zeɪʃən,
ˌdɪdʒəˌtaɪ'zeɪʃən

The ordering of variant pronunciations does not imply that one form is more desirable or 'correct' than another.

Commas are also used to separate transcriptions of inflectional endings: see section 6 below.

4. Added elements in transcriptions: use of parentheses

Parentheses within a phonetic transcription have two functions:

(i) they enclose optional elements in a pronunciation, the presence or absence of which will not affect the acceptability of a pronunciation.

winter
AM 'wɪn(t)ər

(ii) in BR transcriptions they enclose linking (orthographic) /r/ or intrusive (non-orthographic) /r/. See below, p. xii. Linking /r/ is shown in ordinary roman script; intrusive /r/ is italicized.

danger
BR 'deɪndʒə(r)

balsa
BR 'bɔːlsə(*r*)

5. Creation of transcriptions for derived forms: use of vertical bar

A vertical bar in a transcription denotes the place at which it should be broken in order that an inflectional ending (for example plural -s, verbal -ing) may be added (see section 6 below).

6. Inflectional form: use of comma and reverse oblique stroke

The transcription of a first or an only inflectional ending is shown immediately after transcriptions of the headword form, preceded by a hyphen and not separated from the headword transcription by any mark. Such endings are to be added either to the full headword-transcription form:

dale
deɪl, -z
(gives plural [deɪlz])

or to that part of the headword-transcription form which precedes the vertical bar, should one be in place:

eatery
BR 'iːtər|i, -ɪz
(gives plural ['iːtərɪz])

eat
AM i|t, -ts, -dɪŋ
(gives inflections [its], [idɪŋ])

Endings which frequently occur in this position are:

- nominal plural and verbal -(e)s
- verbal -ing, -ed
- comparative -er, and agent nominal -er(s)
- superlative -est

Transcriptions of different endings are separated from each other by commas. Alternative forms of the same ending, and plural -s additions to singular ending forms, are denoted by the use of the reverse oblique stroke (\):

spell
BR spɛl, -z, -ɪŋ, -d\-t
AM spɛl, -z, -ɪŋ, -d

In order to keep the presentation of entries as plain as possible, the presence of endings is not signalled at the headword nor elsewhere in the alphabetical listing. A user requiring information on a word which is derived from a headword, and which does not itself have headword status, should seek it at the end of the entry for its base form.

7. The composite symbols [ɪ] and [ʊ] (see also pp. xiii and xvii)

[ɪ] and [ʊ], when they occur in unstressed or weakly stressed syllables, are regularly reduced to [ə] by many RP (Received Pronunciation) speakers. The reduced vowel [ə] is even more a feature of AM in certain contexts for [ɪ], though less so for [ʊ]. The IPA convention of barring to signify centralization of high vowels and retraction of front vowels is a convenient way of showing this, and has been adopted for this feature. Whenever the barred symbols are used it is to be taken that both [ɪ] and [ə] for [ɨ], or [ʊ] and [ə] for [ʉ], are acceptable.

Technical discussion: transcription sets

Transcriptions in the text are broadly phonetic. That is, the transcriptions represent actual pronunciations, often with several variant forms per headword, not abstract sound units which include and hide potential variation. For instance, both [ru:m~rum] and [rʊm] are possible pronunciations of *room*, both [ɛks-] and [ɛgz-] are presented for some words beginning with ex- + vowel. A limited symbol set results in broad transcriptions, and may suggest de facto phonemicization to some readers, but our intention is always to indicate actual sounds to be produced.

No single set of vowel and consonant phonemes can represent all varieties; the following sets are appropriate to the BR and AM models used:

Vowels (BR):

	Front		Central		Back
High	i:				u:
		ɪ		ʊ	
	e		ə		
Mid					
	ɛ		ʌ		ɔ:
Low	a			ɑ:	ɒ

diphthongs: eɪ, ʌɪ, ɔɪ, aʊ, əʊ
nasality (superscript diacritic): ˜

Vowels (AM):

	Front		Central		Back
High	i				u
		ɪ		ʊ	
	e				o
Mid			ə		
	ɛ				ɔ
		æ			
Low			ɑ		

diphthongs: eɪ, aɪ, ɔɪ, aʊ, oʊ

Consonants (BR and AM):

Stops: p, b, t, d, k, g
Click: ʇ
Fricatives: æ, f, v, θ, ð, s, z, ʃ, ʒ, x, h
Lateral fricative: ɬ (=Welsh ll)
Affricates: tʃ, dʒ
Nasals: m, n, ŋ
Liquids: l (=[ʎ]), r
Semivowels: j, w
syllabic consonants: m̩-, n̩-, l̩- (the syllabic diacritic is only used in situations where ambiguity would otherwise occur)

Pronunciation models

The British English (BR) pronunciation model

An obvious model for British English pronunciation is that which is usually termed Received Pronunciation (normally abbreviated to RP), this being 'a standard of pronunciation which is generally considered correct and is also used as a model for the teaching of English to foreigners' (Upton et al., p. 4). A model labelled 'RP' has long been the norm in British English pronouncing and general dictionaries and in language-teaching classrooms. In this regard transcribers of BR, with access to a generally agreed model for description, may be considered to be more fortunate than transcribers of AM, for which no nationwide model can readily be identified (p. xiii below).

However, problems for the transcriber of BR begin rather than end with the choice of RP as the model: it is not possible to justify the choice of model for British English pronunciation simply by claiming that one has chosen RP. As Daniel Jones, like many other commentators, has made clear, RP is not and was not formerly one monolithic accent: there are variations between the pronunciations of individuals who can legitimately lay claim to an RP accent (Jones, p. 13, note 5).

Within a range of RP accents two essential trends, which have been termed 'U-RP' and 'mainstream RP' (by Wells) or 'marked' and 'unmarked' (by Honey), are to be distinguished. The one variety ('U' or 'marked') is an accent which, when heard by most native speakers of BR, leads to the user being judged old-fashioned, affected, or pretentious. The other ('mainstream' or 'unmarked') is an accent which, for native-speakers, carries connotations of education and sophistication but no especially narrow regional overtones and certainly no serious negative judgements. With obvious idiolectal variations, it is the accent we hear used by most national radio and television newsreaders and by very many middle-aged and younger professional people. It might loosely be labelled 'broadcast RP' if yet another label were to be thought desirable: it is reasonable to maintain, however, that since it is 'mainstream' and 'unmarked' it can legitimately lay claim to the RP label without qualification. This variety of the accent contrasts strongly with the 'U' or 'marked' accent of the previous generation of newsreaders and of conservative (often older) RP speakers generally.

In spite of the acknowledged existence of broadly based and more restricted RP varieties, it is the latter which have tended to characterize many descriptions of RP. Rather than being regarded as referring to a universal standard to which a large number of speakers around the country can claim at least partial access, the RP label has undeniably come to be associated restrictively with a small group of older middle- and upper-class speakers possessing close links with the south-east of England.

To correct a situation where the BR model is the possession of a small minority restricted in terms of age, class, and region, a younger, unmarked RP is that which provides the model in this dictionary. The intention is to describe for the user that accent which will be most widely acceptable, as well as most intelligible, to native BR speakers, and to which the speech of very many of them will in turn approximate closely. The model is an accent which is not regionally centred or redolent of class. Unlike the model more usually described, speech conforming to this new model can be heard spoken by a wide range of natives of many parts of the country, with a wide variety of professional backgrounds (though generally with a higher than average level of education). Note that the linking of accent to the concept of social class is avoided here. 'Class', when considered from a linguistic point of view, has rightly been described as 'a proxy variable covering distinctions in life-style, attitude and belief, as well as differential access to wealth, power and prestige' (Milroy, p. 101). Assigning social class according to accent is an increasingly unreliable procedure in Britain.

Implicit in the British English model presented here, then, is the view that a larger group of people can lay claim to possession of an RP accent than has often hitherto been acknowledged. Each word transcribed has been considered with this in mind, and each transcription is descriptive of a pronunciation which would be judged to be unexceptionable by native speakers of British English generally. As a result of this policy, certain regularly-occurring pronunciation features which have to date been ignored or marked prescriptively are allowed where they are now judged to be established features of RP. Notable examples of such features are [-tʃ-] in place of [-tj-] and [-dʒ-] in place of [-dj-] in such words as *destitute* and *reduce*: since it is considered that these are very frequent in RP, both [tʃ] and [tj], [dʒ] and [dj] transcriptions are given.

Another very significant feature judged worthy of inclusion in the model is that of 'intrusive' <r>. Intrusive <r> is a 'linking' <r> which is unhistorical and which is therefore not supported by orthography. For example, *law* in the phrase *law and order* is in BR frequently [lɔːr] (i.e. [lɔːr an(d) ɔːdə]). Long condemned by teachers of pronunciation, this is nevertheless a firmly established feature of today's mainstream RP: it is indicated in transcriptions by means of a convention similar to that for linking <r>, that is by parentheses, so that *law* is transcribed [lɔː(*r*)], but with [r] italicized. Wells (pp. 284–85) makes the point that avoidance of intrusive <r> is a feature of 'speech-conscious adoptive-RP', that is the RP of those who, not being native RP-speakers, self-consciously attempt the accent and in consequence produce a mannered and somewhat artificial variety.

The range of pronunciations 'allowable' in the description of RP presented in this dictionary is therefore somewhat greater than that in the transcriptions of more prescriptive pronouncing and general dictionaries, the criterion for inclusion being what is heard used by educated, non-regionally-marked speakers rather than what is 'allowed' by a preconceived model. In addition to requiring the inclusion of some hitherto rejected variants, this policy of recording a modern model has necessitated changes being made to existing RP transcription conventions. The principal regular points of departure from traditional RP transcription practice are discussed below.

[a] is the vowel sound in *had*, *hand*, the BR vowel having in recent years come to be articulated in a more open position than the [æ] commonly (though not universally) used by phoneticians for the RP phoneme (MacCarthy, p. 92). The use of the more open vowel is an RP change which, it has been pointed out (Wells, pp. 291–92), is carrying BR further away from AM (where [æ] is generally found).

[a] is also shown as a variant of /ɑː/, representing <a> before a voiceless fricative [s], [f], and [θ] (*brass*, *staff*, *bath*), and before a nasal [n] and [m] + consonant (*dance*, *sample*). Possession of this variant is often the one significant factor distinguishing a north-British RP speaker from her or his south-British counterpart, and RP is not to be considered as exclusively a southern-British phenomenon. This [a] is the one specifically 'northern' BR feature which has regularly been incorporated into the transcription system.

The more open /a/ can be seen to be related to our transcribing RP /e/ as [ɛ], as this reflects the lowering of this RP sound also. Gimson (p. 106) argues that /e/ once tended to be the close variety, [e], this maintaining a marked qualitative distinction between the /a/ and /e/ phonemes at a time when /a/ was [æ]. As /a/ has become lowered from the higher [æ] to the lower [a], so /e/ as [ɛ], long an acknowledged variant, has come to be the norm.

[ʌɪ] is the diphthong of *nice*, *try*. The start-point for the unmarked BR diphthong is judged to be now characteristically in the area of the vowel of *but* (half-open, back centralized), rather than the extreme low front position [a]. The notation [ʌɪ] is that first used for RP by MacCarthy.

[ɛː] is the vowel sound of *square*, *hair*. The mainstream sound is normally monophthongal, although it is sometimes attended by an off-glide, giving [ɛːə], particularly in a stressed final syllable. A full diphthong [ɛə] in this position should now be taken to be especially a feature of a marked variety of RP. The diphthong is even more rarely heard in a compound such as *hairpiece* than it is in the simplex *hair*.

Final [-i] is the vowel of -y in *happy*. This symbol, as used in this dictionary, is intended to imply both greater tension that the [ɪ] commonly used for BR in this position and also greater length. It should be noted that the shorter, less tense [ɪ] occurs in BR when, for example, the suffix *-ness* is added, and this is signalled in the transcriptions, thus:

happy
BR hap | i -ɪnɪs

In addition to these transcriptions of recent developments in RP, the two composite symbols, [ᵻ] and [ɵ], are used to represent [ɪ] or [ə] and [ʊ] or [ə] respectively (see p. x above and the discussion of vowel reduction below, p. xvii). The following are some of the major situations in which the composite symbols are used to show the possible RP choices:

-ity	[-ᵻti]	as in *falsity*, *responsibility*
-ily	[-ᵻli]	as in *happily*
-ible	[-ᵻbl]	as in *responsible*
-ibly	[-ᵻbli]	as in *terribly*
-ical	[-ᵻkl]	as in *theatrical*
-ace	[-ᵻs]	as in *pinnace*, *palace*
-is	[-ᵻs]	as in *appendicitis*
-ist	[-ᵻst]	as in *pianist*
-ful	[-fɵl]	as in *beautiful*
-ed	[-ᵻd]	as in *noted*
-es	[-ᵻz]	as in *rises*, *houses*

It should be noted that in the transcriptions the endings *-ed* and *-es* are for convenience regularly transcribed as [-ᵻd] and [-ᵻz] when they occur as derived forms under a base headword. However, although AM pronunciations are normally [-əd] and [-əz], BR pronunciations are more normally [-ɪd] and [-ɪz]. BR usage is due at least in part to the fact that pronunciations with [ə] can in certain contexts create confusing homophones in BR in such pairs as *halted* and *haltered*, *poses* and *posers* (whereas rhoticity prevents homophones being created in such pairs in AM, the <r> being pronounced in the second of each pair in that accent).

The American English (AM) pronunciation model

Unlike British English, English in the United States has no obvious standard spoken model (that is, no identifiable variety widely spoken by well-educated, cultivated residents). Education is the prime consideration in the formation of American standards, and historically different spoken standards have obtained for different regions of the country. Regional varieties of pronunciation show few signs of giving way before the mobility of the population and the omnipresence of national broadcast media. Many educated speakers from New England and from the Coastal South have accents readily identified by speakers from other parts of the country, yet speakers from the Pacific Coast also have their regional pronunciation habits, even if these are not often recognized by the public. Broadcasters with network ambitions traditionally have tried to limit the regionalisms of their accents, but the present anchorman on one network's news has achieved a certain notoriety for his preservation of certain Canadian pronunciations, and local reporters and weather forecasters often retain their regional accents. While there are indeed dialect coaches who help actors and some other people tone down their regional accents, many Americans take pride in their regional speech as a marker of cultural identity.

Since the mid 20th Century, however, there has been a trend among educated speakers, especially those of the younger generation, towards limitation of the use of marked regional features while speaking in formal settings. It is common for college students, for example, to speak without much influence of regional pronunciation in the classroom, but to use regionally marked pronunciations among friends in the hallway. Some younger educated speakers show little influence of regional speech even in informal conversation. Thus it is possible to hear a variety of voices in every American city or town. The pronunciation model adopted here follows the trend among younger educated speakers of exclusion of regional features. This model is quite similar to what one hears in the national broadcast media, since broadcasters have long participated in the more general trend of younger educated speakers.

Areas often mentioned as having regional varieties include Eastern New England (as far west as the Connecticut River valley), the Inland North (western New England to Wisconsin along the northernmost tier of states), the North Midland (the mid-Atlantic Coast through Pennsylvania to the Mississippi River, north of the Ohio River), the South Midland (the highlands extending southwest from Pennsylvania south of the Ohio River, as far as the Mississippi River and across it to Arkansas), the Coastal South (the area formerly of plantation agriculture from tidewater Virginia south through the Carolinas and Georgia and as far west as East Texas). The Western United States is variously divided: the Great Plains and Upper Midwest show a greater degree of dialect mixture owing to recent settlement; further west, the Southwest (West Texas, New Mexico, and Arizona), the Pacific Coast (California), and the Northwest (Washington, Oregon, and northern California) are often distinguished. The accents of these areas are generally not mutually exclusive in their component pronunciation features; particular features like absence of postvocalic <r> (pronunciation of an <r> sound after a vowel, before a consonant or pause) are often shared by different regions, in this case Eastern New England and the Coastal South. Rather, it is the special combination and distribution of features that distinguish a regional variety. Further, since individual speakers show idiolectal variation, the combination and distribution of features in a region are matters of statistical probabilities, not strict rules. Our AM model avoids as far as possible those pronunciation features that are strongly marked by region or are heard in only a few regions.

Canadian English preserves some differences from the speech of the United States in its eastern provinces, while the pronunciation of its western provinces is generally quite similar to what one might hear in the western states. Pronunciations which are distinctively Canadian are not included here. While Canadians would be quite right to ask that their speech not be subsumed by a model based on the speech of their southern neighbours, it is still the case that the American pronunciation model presented here will offer a fair description of Canadian English as well as that of the English of the United States.

James Hartman, author of the 'Guide to Pronunciation' for the *Dictionary of American Regional English*, classifies major regional variants under four headings: postvocalic <r>, weakened variants of diphthongs, diphthongized variants of monophthongs, and vowel alternations (Cassidy et al., pp. lviii–lxi):

Postvocalic <r> is generally not pronounced in Eastern New England and the Coastal South; the AM transcriptions always include postvocalic <r> because the various pronunciations without it (lengthening of the preceding vowel, replacement by [ə], or varying degrees of weak constriction) are regionally marked.

Weakened variants of diphthongs, whether the second element is weakly realized, e.g. [a^{ɪ}z] in *eyes*, or is absent with lengthening of the first element, e.g. [aːs] in *ice*, are characteristic of the Coastal South, the South Midland, and large parts of the Great Plains and Southwest. They are also possible for many other speakers in rapid speech. These variants are not included in the transcriptions, both because of regional marking and because this volume seeks to present pronunciations typical of the model adopted in slow to moderate speech, not all possible pronunciations.

Diphthongized variants of monophthongs, e.g. [pɪət] for *pit*, [lɑɔft] for *loft*, are possible in many regions but characteristic of the Coastal South and South Midland. According to Bronstein, it is common in all regions to realize /u/ as [ʊu] (p. 171) and /i/ as [ɪi] (p. 147), especially when positionally lengthened or under stress. These variants are not offered in the transcriptions. Possible diphthongization of vowels before <r> is shown by an optional mid-central vowel, as in [faɪ(ə)r] for *fire*, except for /ɔ/, for which no diphthongization is offered (only a weakly realized diphthong is likely for /ɔ/, e.g. [fɔ⁽ᵊ⁾r] for *four*). /e/ and /o/, however, are always represented by [eɪ] and [oʊ] in the transcriptions, since these stressed vowels are rarely heard in AM as monophthongs unless in rapid speech (see Bronstein, pp. 152, 167–68), or from Upper Midwestern speakers.

Some vowel alternations are shown in the transcription, some not.

/ɛ/ ~ /æ/ ~ /a/ – In words spelled with <a> or <e> before <r>, whether or not followed by another vowel, as in *care, carry, marry, merry, Mary*, the AM transcriptions present [ɛ], as [kɛr, kɛri, mɛri, mɛri, mɛri]. Kurath and McDavid suggest characteristic use of [ɛ] before r in the North Midland but divided usage in the Inland North and other regions (p. 16). Bronstein reports that in the Coastal South it is possible to hear *Mary* realized with [eɪ], and there and along the Atlantic Coast *carry, marry* can be realized with [æ] (pp. 152–53). We judge the pronunciations with [eɪ] and [æ] now to be recessive and regionally marked, and we do not offer them in transcriptions. In Eastern New England /æ/ is realized as [a] (or retracted to [ɑ]) before voiceless fricatives, as in *ask, path, half*, and before nasal + consonant, as in *aunt*. Outside of New England, a minority of cultivated speakers, who may view it as a prestige pronunciation, realize the vowel with [ɑ] in particular words such as *aunt* or *ask*, though not systematically. These pronunciations have not been included, because of regional and social marking. Hartman (Cassidy et al., p. lx) and Bronstein (pp. 155–56) report that /æ/ may be raised towards [ɛ] in several environments in different regions, but these pronunciations are not shown here.

/ɑ/ ~ /ɔ / – The contrast between these sounds deserves a long historical treatment that is not possible here. There is high variability and ongoing change in the realization of the stressed vowels of words historically containing either [ɑ] or [ɔ] (see Labov for detailed analysis of the regional status for merger of these sounds). We represent the merger of the two sounds in all words of the historical [ɔ] classes. Rather than present both realizations for all words with historical [ɑ], which would sanction marked regionalisms for some word classes, we have observed the following practices, though with exceptions for particular headwords: 1) short <o> words like *cot, lot* are transcribed with [ɑ]; 2) words with short <o> before <r>, with [ɔ]; 3) words with short <o> before <g, ng, nk> with [ɔ]; 4) <wa-> words like *water, wash, watch*, with [ɑ] and [ɔ]. For commentary, see Hartman in Cassidy et al., pp. lx–lxi, and Bronstein, pp. 162–67.

/o/ ~ /ɔ/ – When it occurs before <r>, this sound is indicated consistently as [ɔ] in the transcriptions, as in [fɔr], [fɔr əst] for *four, forest*. Our transcriptions thus will not distinguish between such potentially (but recessively) contrastive pairs as *horse/hoarse* or *morning/mourning*. Kurath and McDavid indicate characteristic use of [ɔ] before <r> in the North Midland but not in the Inland North or other regions (p. 16); Bronstein reports increasing use of [ɔ] before <r> (pp. 167, 169); and Hartman's later evidence indicates wide use of [ɔ] before <r> except in the Coastal South. In some words, like *forest*, the stressed vowel can sometimes be realized as [ɑ], but these pronunciations are not represented in the transcriptions.

It is quite normal in AM to simplify consonant clusters in particular environments. For example, when *-nt-* occurs intervocalically and a syllable boundary with stress does not split the cluster, it is more frequent for the <t> to be dropped than for it to be pronounced, as in ['twɛn(t)i], ['mæn(t)l] for *twenty, mantle*, but [kən'teɪn] for *contain*. Clusters are often simplified in word-final position, especially with addition of suffixes: *asked* is normally pronounced [æst], not [æskt], though *ask* is pronounced [æsk]. Substitution of [-ɪn] for [-ɪŋ] in the ending *-ing* is often thought to be characteristic of the Coastal South and South Midland, but it occurs with some frequency in the speech of all regions. It is not represented in the transcriptions.

Another normal practice in AM is to pronounce many words according to how they are spelled, even if such a pronunciation has no historical justification. Words like *calm*, *palm* often acquire an [l] sound in this manner, and even *sword* sometimes gains a [w]. Unfamiliar words are routinely pronounced as they are spelled, including many learned words and foreign words and names. Common spelling pronunciations are represented here as optional, as in *palm* [pɑ(l)m].

Vowel length is not marked in the AM transcriptions. It is only rarely minimally distinctive (e.g. *have* vs *halve*), and in AM is best considered as being environmentally conditioned. Some lengthening of vowels typically occurs before voiced consonants (*grade* vs *grate*) and before juncture, including phrase-final position.

Several variations from common transcription practices among American linguists are employed here. The schwa symbol ([ə]) has been used for both stressed and unstressed vowels. As a stressed vowel, /ə/ includes pronunciations written with [ʌ] by some American linguists, e.g. *sun* [sʌn], here transcribed [sən]; use of /ʌ/ in BR represents a more retracted and somewhat lowered sound. The [ɜ] symbol, often used to indicate a mid-central stressed vowel with r-colouring, as in *bird* [bɜd], is not used here, and neither is the symbol for a mid-central unstressed vowel with r-colouring, as in *father* [fɑðɚ]; rather, r-colouring and syllabic <r> pronunciations are always indicated by a combination of vowel + <r>, as in [bərd], [fɑðər]. The phonemes /t/ and /r/ include rather wide ranges of possible allophones, but the AM transcriptions offer only the following options: 1) intervocalic /t/, as in *latter*, is often realized as a flap [ɾ] or voiced t [t̬], but is transcribed here as [d], so that *latter* and *ladder* have identical transcriptions; 2) final <t> is often realized as a glottal stop [ʔ] or is unreleased, but is transcribed here as [t]; 3) /r/ may be realized as a trill or flap, or with varying degrees of constriction, but all allophones of /r/ are here transcribed [r]. We have not employed diacritical marks, except those for stress and syllabicity. All of these variations contribute to ease of use of the dictionary by limiting the symbol set that readers must know to read the transcriptions, without undue sacrifice in accuracy.

We have created a consistent AM model, in the absence of any actual general standard, according to the editorial policies described. The model grants us a systematic means to decide what transcriptions among many regional variants should be presented. However, we have reviewed every headword independently, and we have occasionally included pronunciations that do not fit the model when they are warranted by widespread use. If any regional or idiolectal bias can be detected among our choices for transcriptions, it is that of Kretzschmar, an Inland Northern speaker.

BR and AM stress marking

As a general rule the standard IPA stress-marking system is employed in this volume, for both primary stress (ˈ) and secondary stress (ˌ). Marks precede the stressed syllable. Absence of a mark indicates weak or tertiary stress.

BR transcriptions simply conform to this usage. AM, however, has a heavier stressing pattern than BR, with disyllabic compounds for example exhibiting both primary and secondary stress when BR characteristically exhibits only primary and weak (or tertiary) stress. Thus AM may receive two stress marks when BR exhibits only one:

baseball
BR ˈbeɪsbɔːl
AM ˈbeɪsˌbɔl

AM is also characterized by the use of secondary stress on syllables with unreduced vowels or diphthongs, where BR has an unstressed reduced vowel or an elided syllable. Thus [ˈdɪkʃəˌnɛri] is the characteristic AM pronunciation of *dictionary*, rather than BR [ˈdɪkʃnri].

Variability of the stress pattern in polysyllabic words is also characteristic of AM. To represent this fact most efficiently, we have borrowed the notation used in *Webster's Third New International Dictionary*, whereby a variably stressed syllable is marked by a combination of both stress markings (ˌˈ). In those instances where two syllables receive variable stress markings, e.g. *overbearing* [ˌˈoʊvərˌˈbɛrɪŋ], only three of the four stress permutations are possible when the word is pronounced: primary-primary, primary-secondary, and secondary-primary. Each word must have primary stress for at least one syllable.

BR and AM vowel reduction

Stress patterns exert considerable influence on the quality of unstressed vowels. In the system adopted here, there are four vowels used in unstressed syllables, [ɪ], [ə], [ɨ], and, for BR though seldom for AM, [ʉ]. The alternations of these merit explanation. Even within the limits of our models the linguistic realities do not readily lend themselves to clearly statable rules. We have, however, chosen certain principles as most representative of BR and AM:

[ɪ] is used invariably in those syllables where it precedes word-final [k], [ʃ], [dʒ], [v] in derivational suffixes, and in the participial/gerundive suffix [-ɪŋ], as in *conic*, *breakage*, *dragging*.

Similarly, [ə] is used in the suffix [-ə(r)~-ər] as in *leader*, and for AM in [-ʃ(ə)n] and [-ʒ(ə)n], as in *relation*, *equation*.

[ʉ], representing a free choice between [ʊ] and [ə], is a vowel transcription in BR adjectival ending *-ful*.

For the vowel of the inflectional suffixes plural and third-person present tense *-es*, past tense *-ed*, and superlative *-est*, and for the derivational suffix *-ist*, [ɨ] is regularly used. In these suffixes, BR usually, though not necessarily, exhibits [ɪ]. For AM, environmental factors are decisive in the selection of the unstressed variant: if the preceding syllable contains a high front vowel or a diphthong ending in a high front vowel, [ɪ] is the norm; otherwise there is a free choice in AM between [ɪ] and [ə]. The same environmental factors frequently govern the choice of vowel-sound for both varieties in the derivational suffixes *-ness* and, especially for BR, *-less*.

It must be emphasized that, while all our practices regarding unstressed vowels are generally valid, many speakers of both BR and AM alternate between the variants [ɪ] and [ə] in the environments we have considered.

Bibliography

Bronstein, Arthur J. *The Pronunciation of American English*. Englewood Cliffs, NJ: Prentice-Hall, 1960.

Cassidy, Frederic G., et al., eds. *Dictionary of American Regional English*, Vol. 1. Cambridge, Massachusetts: Belknap/Harvard Univ. Press, 1985.

Fudge, Erik. *English Word-Stress*. London: George Allen and Unwin, 1984.

Gimson, A.C. *An Introduction to the Pronunciation of English*. 4th ed., revised by Susan Ramsaran. London: Edward Arnold, 1989.

Honey, John. *Does Accent Matter?: The Pygmalion Factor*. London: Faber & Faber, 1989.

Jones, Daniel. *An Outline of English Phonetics*. 9th ed. Cambridge: Heffer, 1969.

Kurath, Hans, and Raven I. McDavid, Jr. *The Pronunciation of English in the Atlantic States*. Tuscaloosa: Univ. of Alabama Press, 1961, reprinted 1982.

Labov, William. 'The Three Dialects of English'. In P. Eckert, ed., *New Ways of Analyzing Sound Change*. San Diego: Academic Press, 1991, pp. 1–44.

MacCarthy, Peter. *The Teaching of Pronunciation*. Cambridge: Cambridge Univ. Press, 1978.

Milroy, Lesley. *Observing and Analysing Natural Language*. Oxford: Basil Blackwell, 1987.

Upton, Clive, Stewart Sanderson, and John Widdowson. *Word Maps: A Dialect Atlas of England*. London: Croom Helm, 1987.

Wells, J. C. *Accents of English*. 3 Vols. Cambridge: Cambridge Univ. Press, 1982.

Foreign pronunciations

When given in native form, a limited number of foreign headwords also have native pronunciations based on current national standards, but only where these differ significantly from the anglicized pronunciations. Foreign headwords falling within specific subject fields, e.g. culinary and musical terminology, have not been given native pronunciations. Neither have words such as 'Guignolesque' and phrases such as 'au grand sérieux', because although they contain French elements they are in fact of English coinage.

Vowels

	Front	Central	Back
High	y:		u
	ʏ		
	e(:) ø		o
Mid			
			ɔ
	œ		
		ɐ	
Low	a(:)		ɑ

/a:/	Dutch/Flemish	Waal
	German	Aachen
	Irish	Dáil, Tánaiste
/ɑ/	Danish	Dagmar
	Dutch/Flemish	Breda
	Portuguese	Beira, Carajás
/ɐ/	German	Hannover
/œ/	Danish	Ertebølle, Helsingør
	French	Verdun
	German	Götterdämmerung
	Hungarian	Fertö Tó
	Norwegian	øre
/ɔ/	Czech	Brno
	Dutch/Flemish	Concertgebouw
	French	Aix-en-Provence
	German	Worms
	Greek	Ayios Nikólaos
	Hungarian	Balaton, Magyar
/e/	Danish	Blixen
	Greek	Seféris
	Irish	feiseanna
	Norwegian	Lofoten
	Russian	Comintern
	Spanish	Algeciras
	Welsh	Betws-y-Coed
/e:/	Czech	háler
	Danish	Petersen
	Dutch/Flemish	Breda, Vermeer, Zeebrugge
	German	Dresden
	Irish	Dáil Eireann
	Swedish	Alfvén
/ø/	Dutch/Flemish	Leuven
	French	Montreux
/o/	Danish	Odense
	Dutch/Flemish	Groningen, Oostende
	French	Aubusson, Utrillo
	Italian/Spanish	mid vowel
	Brazilian Portuguese	Belo Horizonte, Estoril
	Lusitanian Portuguese	Belo Horizonte, Douro
/o:/	Norwegian	Bokmål
	Swedish	Bofors
/ʏ/	German	Baden-Württemberg, Duisburg
/y/	Afrikaans	krugerrand
	Dutch/Flemish	Rijksmuseum
	French	Althusser
/y:/	German	Zürich
	Norwegian	Nynorsk
/u/	Italian/Spanish	close back vowel
	Norwegian	Oslo
	Portuguese	Rio de Janeiro
	Russian	Godunov

Diphthongs

Dutch/Flemish	/ɛi/	Rijksmuseum
	/ɔu/	Gouda
	/œy/	Huygens
German	/ɔy/	Löwenbräu

Semivowels

/ɥ/	French	Guyenne

Consonants

Fricatives:	/β/	Spanish	Iberia
	/ʐ/	Hungarian	Magyar
	/ç/	German	Leipzig
		Polish	Łódź
	/ɣ/	Spanish	Segovia

Nasals

/ɲ/	French	Boulogne
	Spanish	Muñoz

Liquids

/ʀ/	Danish	Brahe
	Lusitanian Portuguese	Rio de Janeiro
/ʎ/	Italian	Gigli

Diacritics

~	nasality	French	Verdun
^{j}	palatalization	Irish	Dun Laoghaire Fianna Fáil
		Russian	Yekaterinburg
˺	no audible release	Danish	Aarhus

Abbreviations used in the dictionary

AFK	Afrikaans
AM	US English
B PORT	Brazilian Portuguese
BR	British English
CZ	Czech
DAN	Danish
DU	Dutch
FL	Flemish
FR	French
GER	German
GR	Greek
HU	Hungarian
IR	Irish
IT	Italian
L PORT	Lusitanian Portuguese
NO	Norwegian
POL	Polish
PORT	Brazilian and Lusitanian Portuguese
RUS	Russian
SP	Spanish
SW	Swedish
TU	Turkish
WE	Welsh

Note on trademarks and proprietary status

This dictionary includes some words which have, or are asserted to have, proprietary status as trademarks or otherwise. Their inclusion does not imply that they have acquired for legal purposes a non-proprietary or general significance, nor any other judgement concerning their legal status. In cases where the editorial staff have some evidence that a word has proprietary status this is indicated in the entry for that word by the symbol ®, but no judgement concerning the legal status of such words is made or implied thereby.

Aa

a¹
indefinite article, strong form
BR eɪ
AM eɪ
a²
indefinite article, weak form
BR ə(*r*)
AM ə
a³
letter
BR eɪ, -z
AM eɪ, -z
Aachen
BR ˈɑːk(ə)n
AM ˈɑkən
GER ˈaːxn
aah
BR ɑː(*r*), -z, -ɪŋ, -d
AM ɑ, -z, -ɪŋ, -d
Aalborg
BR ˈɑːlbɔːg
AM ˈɔlˌbɔrg, ˈɑlˌbɔrg
DAN ˈʌlˌbɔːˀ
aardvark
BR ˈɑːdvɑːk, -s
AM ˈɑrdˌvɑrk, -s
aardwolf
BR ˈɑːdwʊlf
AM ˈɑrdˌwʊlf
aardwolves
BR ˈɑːdwʊlvz
AM ˈɑrdˌwʊlvz
Aargau
BR ˈɑːgaʊ
AM ˈɑrˌgaʊ
aargh
BR ɑː(r)
AM arg
Aarhus
BR ˈɑːhuːs
AM ˈɔrˌ(h)us, ˈɑrˌ(h)us
DAN ˈɔːhuːˀs
Aaron
BR ˈɛːrən, ˈɛːrn̩
AM ˈɛrən
aasvogel
BR ˈɑːsˌfəʊgl, -z
AM ˈɑsˌfoʊgəl, -z
ab
BR ab
AM æb
aba
BR ˈabə(*r*), -z
AM ˈɑbə, əˈbɑ, -z
abaca
BR ˈabəkə(*r*), -z
AM ˈæbəkɑ, -z
abaci
BR ˈabəsʌɪ, ˈabəkʌɪ
AM ˈæbəˌsaɪ, ˈæbəˌkaɪ
aback
BR əˈbak
AM əˈbæk
abacus
BR ˈabəkəs, -ɪz
AM ˈæbəkəs, -əz
Abadan
BR ˌabəˈdɑːn, ˌabəˈdan
AM ˌɑbəˈdɑn, ˌæbəˈdæn
Abaddon
BR əˈbadn
AM əˈbædən
abaft
BR əˈbɑːft, əˈbaft
AM əˈbæft
abalone
BR ˌabəˈləʊn|i, -ɪz
AM ˈæbəˌloʊni, -z
abandon
BR əˈband|(ə)n, -(ə)nz, -ənɪŋ\-n̩ɪŋ, -(ə)nd
AM əˈbændən, -z, -ɪŋ, -d
abandonee
BR əˌbandəˈniː, -z
AM əˌbændəˈni, -z
abandoner
BR əˈbandənə(r), əˈbandn̩ə(r), -z
AM əˈbændənər, -z
abandonment
BR əˈband(ə)nm(ə)nt, -s
AM əˈbændənmənt, -s
abase
BR əˈbeɪs, -ɪz, -ɪŋ, -t
AM əˈbeɪs, -ɪz, -ɪŋ, -t
abasement
BR əˈbeɪsm(ə)nt
AM əˈbeɪsmənt
abash
BR əˈbaʃ, -ɪz, -ɪŋ, -t
AM əˈbæʃ, -əz, -ɪŋ, -t
abashment
BR əˈbaʃm(ə)nt
AM əˈbæʃmənt
abask
BR əˈbɑːsk, əˈbask
AM əˈbæsk
abatable
BR əˈbeɪtəbl
AM əˈbeɪdəbəl
abate
BR əˈbeɪt, -s, -ɪŋ, -ɪd
AM əˈbeɪ|t, -ts, -dɪŋ, -dɪd
abatement
BR əˈbeɪtm(ə)nt, -s
AM əˈbeɪtmənt, -s
abatis¹
singular
BR ˈabətɪs
AM ˈæbəˌti, ˈæbədəs
abatis²
plural
BR ˈabətiːz, ˈabətɪsɪz
AM ˈæbəˌtiz, ˈæbədəsəz
abatised
BR ˈabətɪst
AM ˈæbəˌtid, ˈæbədəst
abatises
BR ˈabətɪsɪz
AM ˈæbədəsəz
abattis¹
singular
BR əˈbatɪs
AM ˈæbəˌti, ˈæbədəs
abattis²
plural
BR əˈbatiːz, əˈbatɪsɪz
AM ˈæbəˌtiz, ˈæbədəsəz
abattised
BR əˈbatɪst
AM ˈæbəˌtid, ˈæbədəst
abattises
BR əˈbatɪsɪz
AM ˈæbədəsəz
abattoir
BR ˈabətwɑː(r), -z
AM ˈæbəˌtwɑr, -z
abaxial
BR abˈaksɪəl
AM æˈbæksiəl
abaya
BR əˈbeɪ(j)ə(*r*), -z
AM əˈbɑ(ɪ)jə, -z
abba
BR ˈabə(*r*), -z
AM ˈɑbə, əˈbɑ, -z
abbacy
BR ˈabəs|i, -ɪz
AM ˈæbəsi, -z
Abbas
BR ˈabəs
AM ˈæbəs
Abbasid
BR əˈbasɪd, ˈabəsɪd
AM əˈbæsɪd, ˈæbəsɪd
abbatial
BR əˈbeɪʃl
AM əˈbeɪʃəl
abbé
BR ˈabeɪ, -z
AM ˌæˈbeɪ, -z
abbess
BR ˈabɪs, ˈabɛs, -ɪz
AM ˈæbəs, -əz
Abbeville
BR ˈab(ɪ)vɪl
AM ˈæbiˌvɪl
Abbevillian
BR abˈvɪlɪən, ˌabɪˈvɪlɪən
AM æbˈvɪljən, ˌæbəˈvɪljən, æbˈvɪliən, ˌæbəˈvɪliən
abbey
BR ˈab|i, -ɪz
AM ˈæbi, -z
abbot
BR ˈabət, -s
AM ˈæbət, -s
abbotship
BR ˈabətʃɪp, -s
AM ˈæbətˌʃɪp, -s
Abbott
BR ˈabət
AM ˈæbət
abbreviate
BR əˈbriːvɪeɪt, -s, -ɪŋ, -ɪd
AM əˈbriviˌeɪ|t, -ts, -dɪŋ, -dɪd
abbreviation
BR əˌbriːvɪˈeɪʃn, -z
AM əˌbriviˈeɪʃən, -z
abbreviatory
BR əˈbriːvɪət(ə)ri
AM əˈbriviəˌtɔri
Abby
BR ˈabi
AM ˈæbi
Abdela
BR abˈdɛlə(*r*)
AM æbˈdɛlə
abdicable
BR ˈabdɪkəbl
AM ˈæbdəkəbəl
abdicant
BR ˈabdɪk(ə)nt, -s
AM ˈæbdəkənt, -s
abdicate
BR ˈabdɪkeɪt, -s, -ɪŋ, -ɪd
AM ˈæbdəˌkeɪ|t, -ts, -dɪŋ, -dɪd
abdication
BR ˌabdɪˈkeɪʃn, -z
AM ˌæbdəˈkeɪʃən, -z
abdicator
BR ˈabdɪkeɪtə(r), -z
AM ˈæbdəˌkeɪdər, -z
abdomen
BR ˈabdəmən, abˈdəʊmən, -z
AM ˈæbdəmən, -z
abdominal
BR abˈdɒmɪnl, əbˈdɒmɪnl
AM æbˈdɑmənəl, əbˈdɑmənəl
abdominally
BR abˈdɒmɪnl̩i, abˈdɒmɪnəli, əbˈdɒmɪnl̩i, əbˈdɒmɪnəli
AM æbˈdɑmənəli, əbˈdɑmənəli
abdominous
BR abˈdɒmɪnəs, əbˈdɒmɪnəs
AM æbˈdɑmənəs, əbˈdɑmənəs
abduct
BR əbˈdʌkt, -s, -ɪŋ, -ɪd
AM əbˈdək|(t), æbˈdək|(t), -(t)s, -tɪŋ, -təd
abduction
BR əbˈdʌkʃn, -z

AM əb'dəkʃən, æb'dəkʃən, -z

abductor
BR əb'dʌktə(r), ab'dʌktə(r), -z
AM əb'dəktər, æb'dəktər, -z

Abdul
BR 'abdʊl
AM ¦ɑb¦dʊl, ¦æb¦dʊl

Abdullah
BR ab'dʌlə(r), əb'dʌlə(r), ab'dʊlə(r), əb'dʊlə(r)
AM ɑb'dʊlə, æb'dʊlə

Abe
BR eɪb
AM eɪb

abeam
BR ə'biːm
AM ə'bim

abecedarian
BR ˌeɪbiːsiː'dɛːrɪən, -z
AM ˌeɪbisi'dɛriən, -z

abed
BR ə'bɛd
AM ə'bɛd

Abednego
BR ˌabɛd'niːgəʊ, ə'bɛdnɪgəʊ
AM ə'bɛdnəˌgoʊ

Abel
BR 'eɪbl
AM 'eɪbəl

Abelard
BR 'abɨlɑːd, 'abl̩ɑːd
AM 'æbəˌlɑrd

abele
BR ə'biːl, 'eɪbl, -z
AM ə'bil, ə'beɪl, -z

abelia
BR ə'biːlɪə(r), -z
AM ə'biljə, ə'biliə, -z

abelian
BR ə'biːlɪən
AM ə'biljən, ə'biliən

Aberaeron
BR ˌabər'ʌɪrən, ˌabər'ʌɪrn̩
AM ˌæbər'ɛrən
WE ˌaber'eɪrɒn

Aberavon
BR ˌabə(r)'avn
AM ˌæbər'eɪvən

Abercrombie
BR 'abəkrʌmbi, 'abəkrɒmbi
AM ¦æbər¦krɑmbi

Aberdare
BR ˌabə'dɛː(r)
AM ˌæbər'dɛ(ə)r

Aberdaron
BR ˌabə'darən, ˌabə'darn̩
AM ˌæbər'dɛrən

Aberdeen[1]
place in UK
BR ˌabə'diːn
AM ˌæbər'din

Aberdeen[2]
place in USA
BR 'abədiːn
AM 'æbərˌdin

Aberdonian
BR ˌabə'dəʊnɪən, -z
AM ˌæbər'doʊniən, -z

Aberdovey
BR ˌabə'dʌvi
AM ˌæbər'dəvi

Aberfan
BR ˌabə'van
AM ˌæbər'væn
WE ˌaber'van

Abergavenny
BR ˌabəgə'vɛni
AM ˌæbərgə'vɛni

Abergele
BR ˌabə'gɛli
AM ˌæbər'gɛli

Abernathy
BR ˌabə'naθ|i, -ɪz
AM 'æbərˌnæθi, -z

Abernethy
BR ˌabə'nɛθ|i, ˌabə'niːθ|i, -ɪz
AM 'æbərˌnɛθi, -z

Aberporth
BR 'abəpɔːθ, ˌabə'pɔːθ
AM ¦æbər¦pɔ(ə)rθ

aberrance
BR ə'bɛrəns, ə'bɛrn̩s
AM 'æbərəns, ə'bɛrəns

aberrancy
BR ə'bɛrənsi, ə'bɛrn̩si
AM 'æbərənsi, ə'bɛrənsi

aberrant
BR ə'bɛrənt, ə'bɛrn̩t
AM 'æbərənt, ə'bɛrənt

aberrate
BR 'abəreɪt, -s, -ɪŋ, -ɨd
AM 'æbəˌreɪ|t, -ts, -dɪŋ, -dɨd

aberration
BR ˌabə'reɪʃn, -z
AM ˌæbə'reɪʃən, -z

Abersoch
BR ˌabə'səʊk, ˌabə'sɒk
AM ˌæbər'sɑk

Abersychan
BR ˌabə'sʌk(ə)n
AM ˌæbər'sɑk(ə)n
WE ˌaber'sʌxan

Abertillery
BR ˌabətɨ'lɛːri
AM ˌæbərtə'lɛri

Aberystwyth
BR ˌabə'rɪstwɪθ
AM ˌæbə'rɪstwɪθ
WE ˌaber'ʌstwɪθ

abet
BR ə'bɛt, -s, -ɪŋ, -ɨd
AM ə'bɛ|t, -ts, -dɪŋ, -dəd

abetment
BR ə'bɛtm(ə)nt
AM ə'bɛtmənt

abetter
BR ə'bɛtə(r), -z
AM ə'bɛdər, -z

abettor
BR ə'bɛtə(r), -z
AM ə'bɛdər, -z

abeyance
BR ə'beɪəns
AM ə'beɪəns

abeyant
BR ə'beɪənt
AM ə'beɪənt

abhor
BR əb'hɔː(r), ə'bɔː(r), -z, -ɪŋ, -d
AM əb'hɔ(ə)r, æb'hɔ(ə)r, -z, -ɪŋ, -d

abhorrence
BR əb'hɒrəns, əb'hɒrn̩s, ə'bɒrəns, ə'bɒrn̩s
AM əb'hɔrəns, æb'hɔrəns

abhorrent
BR əb'hɒrənt, əb'hɒrn̩t, ə'bɒrənt, ə'bɒrn̩t
AM əb'hɔrənt, æb'hɔrənt

abhorrently
BR əb'hɒrəntli, əb'hɒrn̩tli, ə'bɒrəntli, ə'bɒrn̩tli
AM əb'hɔrən(t)li, æb'hɔrən(t)li

abhorrer
BR əb'hɔːrə(r), ə'bɔːrə(r), -z
AM əb'hɔrər, æb'hɔrər, -z

abidance
BR ə'bʌɪd(ə)ns
AM ə'baɪdns

abide
BR ə'bʌɪd, -z, -ɪŋ, -ɨd
AM ə'baɪd, -z, -ɪŋ, -ɨd

abidingly
BR ə'bʌɪdɪŋli
AM ə'baɪdɪŋli

Abidjan
BR ˌabɪ'dʒɑːn, ˌabɪ'dʒan
AM ˌæbə'dʒɑn

Abigail
BR 'abɨgeɪl
AM 'æbəˌgeɪl

Abilene
BR 'abɨliːn, 'abl̩iːn
AM 'æbəˌlin

ability
BR ə'bɪlɨt|i, -ɪz
AM ə'bɪlɨdi, -z

Abingdon
BR 'abɪŋd(ə)n
AM 'æbɪŋdən

ab initio
BR ˌab ɪ'nɪʃɪəʊ
AM ˌæb ə'nɪʃioʊ

abiogenesis
BR ˌeɪbʌɪə(ʊ)'dʒɛnɨsɪs
AM ˌeɪˌbaɪoʊ'dʒɛnəsəs

abiogenic
BR ˌeɪbʌɪəʊ'dʒɛnɪk
AM ˌeɪˌbaɪoʊ'dʒɛnɪk

abiogenically
BR ˌeɪbʌɪəʊ'dʒɛnɨkli
AM ˌeɪˌbaɪoʊ'dʒɛnək(ə)li

abiogenist
BR ˌeɪbʌɪ'ɒdʒɨnɪst, -s
AM ˌeɪˌbaɪ'ɑdʒənəst, -s

Abiola
BR ˌabɪ'əʊlə(r)
AM ˌɑbi'oʊlə

abiotic
BR ˌeɪbʌɪ'ɒtɪk
AM ˌeɪˌbaɪ'ɑdɪk

abject
BR 'abdʒɛkt
AM ¦æb¦dʒɛk(t)

abjection
BR ab'dʒɛkʃn
AM æb'dʒɛkʃən

abjectly
BR 'abdʒɛktli
AM ¦æb¦dʒɛk(t)li

abjectness
BR 'abdʒɛk(t)nəs
AM ¦æb¦dʒɛk(t)nəs

abjuration
BR ˌabdʒʊ'reɪʃn
AM ˌæbdʒə'reɪʃən

abjure
BR əb'dʒʊə(r), əb'dʒɔː(r), -z, -ɪŋ, -d
AM æb'dʒʊ(ə)r, əb'dʒʊ(ə)r, -z, -ɪŋ, -d

Abkhaz
BR ab'kaz, ab'kɑːz
AM ɑb'kɑz
RUS ab'xas

Abkhazi
BR ab'kɑːz|i, -ɪz
AM ɑb'kɑzi, -z

Abkhazia
BR ab'kɑːzɪə(r)
AM ɑb'kɑziə
RUS ab'xazʲijə

Abkhazian
BR ab'kɑːzɪən, -z
AM ɑb'kɑziən, -z

ablate
BR ə'bleɪt, -s, -ɪŋ, -ɨd
AM ə'bleɪ|t, -ts, -dɪŋ, -dɨd

ablation
BR ə'bleɪʃn
AM ə'bleɪʃən

ablatival
BR ˌablə'tʌɪvl
AM ˌæblə'taɪvəl

ablative
BR 'ablətɪv, -z
AM 'æblədɪv, ə'bleɪdɪv, -z

ablatively
BR 'ablətɪvli
AM 'æblədɪvli, ə'bleɪdɪvli

ablaut
BR 'ablaʊt, -s
AM 'æˌblaʊt, -s

ablaze
BR ə'bleɪz
AM ə'bleɪz

able
BR 'eɪbl, -ə(r), -ɪst, -d
AM 'eɪbəl, -ər, -əst, -d

ableism
BR 'eɪbl̩ɪz(ə)m
AM 'eɪbəˌlɪzəm

abloom
BR ə'bluːm
AM ə'blum

ablush
BR ə'blʌʃ
AM ə'bləʃ

ablution
BR ə'bluːʃn, -z
AM ə'bluʃən, -z

ablutionary
BR ə'bluːʃn(ə)ri
AM ə'bluʃəˌnɛri

ably
BR 'eɪbli
AM 'eɪbli, 'eɪbl̩i

abnegate
BR 'abnɪgeɪt, -s, -ɪŋ, -ɪd
AM 'æbnəˌgeɪ|t, -ts, -dɪŋ, -dɪd

abnegation
BR ˌabnɪ'geɪʃn
AM ˌæbnə'geɪʃən

abnegator
BR 'abnɪgeɪtə(r), -z
AM 'æbnəˌgeɪdər, -z

Abner
BR 'abnə(r)
AM 'æbnər

abnormal
BR ab'nɔːml, əb'nɔːml
AM æb'nɔrməl, əb'nɔrməl

abnormality
BR ˌabnə'malɪt|i, ˌabnɔː'malɪt|i, -ɪz
AM ˌæbnər'mælədi, ˌæbˌnɔr'mælədi, -z

abnormally
BR ab'nɔːml̩i, ab'nɔːməli, əb'nɔːml̩i, əb'nɔːməli
AM æb'nɔrməli, əb'nɔrməli

abnormity
BR ab'nɔːmɪt|i, əb'nɔːmɪt|i, -ɪz
AM æb'nɔrmədi, əb'nɔrmədi, -z

abo
BR 'abəʊ, -z
AM 'ɑboʊ, -z

aboard
BR ə'bɔːd
AM ə'bɔ(ə)rd

abode
BR ə'bəʊd, -z
AM ə'boʊd, -z

abolish
BR ə'bɒl|ɪʃ, -ɪʃɪz, -ɪʃɪŋ, -ɪʃt
AM ə'bɑlɪʃ, -ɪz, -ɪŋ, -t

abolishable
BR ə'bɒlɪʃəbl
AM ə'bɑləʃəbəl

abolisher
BR ə'bɒlɪʃə(r), -z
AM ə'bɑlɪʃər, -z

abolishment
BR ə'bɒlɪʃm(ə)nt
AM ə'bɑlɪʃmənt

abolition
BR ˌabə'lɪʃn
AM ˌæbə'lɪʃən

abolitionism
BR ˌabə'lɪʃn̩ɪz(ə)m, ˌabə'lɪʃənɪz(ə)m
AM ˌæbə'lɪʃəˌnɪzəm

abolitionist
BR ˌabə'lɪʃn̩ɪst, ˌabə'lɪʃənɪst, -s
AM ˌæbə'lɪʃənəst, -s

abomasa
BR ˌabə(ʊ)'meɪsə(*r*)
AM ˌæbə'meɪsə

abomasum
BR ˌabə(ʊ)'meɪsəm
AM ˌæbə'meɪsəm

abominable
BR ə'bɒm(ɪ)nəbl
AM ə'bɑm(ə)nəbəl

abominableness
BR ə'bɒm(ɪ)nəblnəs
AM ə'bɑm(ə)nəbəlnəs

abominably
BR ə'bɒm(ɪ)nəbli
AM ə'bɑm(ə)nəbli

abominate
BR ə'bɒmɪneɪt, -s, -ɪŋ, -ɪd
AM ə'bɑməˌneɪ|t, -ts, -dɪŋ, -dɪd

abomination
BR əˌbɒmɪ'neɪʃn, -z
AM əˌbɑmə'neɪʃən, -z

abominator
BR ə'bɒmɪneɪtə(r), -z
AM ə'bɑməˌneɪdər, -z

aboral
BR ab'ɔːrəl, ab'ɔːrl̩
AM æb'ɔrəl

aboriginal
BR ˌabə'rɪdʒɪnl, -z
AM ˌæbə'rɪdʒənl, ˌæbə'rɪdʒnəl, -z

aboriginality
BR ˌabəˌrɪdʒɪ'nalɪti
AM ˌæbəˌrɪdʒə'nælədi

aboriginally
BR ˌabə'rɪdʒɪnəli, ˌabə'rɪdʒɪnl̩i
AM ˌæbə'rɪdʒ(ə)nəli

aborigine
BR ˌabə'rɪdʒɪn|i, -ɪz
AM ˌæbə'rɪdʒəni, -z

aborning
BR ə'bɔːnɪŋ
AM ə'bɔrnɪŋ

abort
BR ə'bɔːt, -s, -ɪŋ, -ɪd
AM ə'bɔ(ə)rt, -ts, -'bɔrdɪŋ, -'bɔrdəd

abortifacient
BR əˌbɔːtɪ'feɪʃnt, əˌbɔːtɪ'feɪʃɪənt, -s
AM əˌbɔrdə'feɪʃənt, -s

abortion
BR ə'bɔːʃn, -z
AM ə'bɔrʃən, -z

abortionist
BR ə'bɔːʃn̩ɪst, ə'bɔːʃənɪst, -s
AM ə'bɔrʃənəst, -s

abortive
BR ə'bɔːtɪv
AM ə'bɔrdɪv

abortively
BR ə'bɔːtɪvli
AM ə'bɔrdɪvli

abortiveness
BR ə'bɔːtɪvnɪs
AM ə'bɔrdɪvnɪs

Aboukir Bay
BR ˌabʉkɪə 'beɪ
AM ˌɑbu'kɪ(ə)r 'beɪ

aboulia
BR ə'buːlɪə(*r*)
AM ə'buljə, ə'buliə

aboulic
BR ə'buːlɪk
AM ə'bulɪk

abound
BR ə'baʊnd, -z, -ɪŋ, -ɪd
AM ə'baʊnd, -z, -ɪŋ, -əd

about
BR ə'baʊt
AM ə'baʊt

above
BR ə'bʌv
AM ə'bəv

aboveboard
BR ə'bʌvbɔːd, əˌbʌv'bɔːd
AM ə'bəvˌbɔ(ə)rd

aboveground
BR ə'bʌvgraʊnd, əˌbʌv'graʊnd
AM əˌbəv'graʊnd

ab ovo
BR ˌab 'əʊvəʊ
AM æ'boʊˌvoʊ

abracadabra
BR ˌabrəkə'dabrə(*r*)
AM ˌæbrəkə'dæbrə

abrade
BR ə'breɪd, -z, -ɪŋ, -ɪd
AM ə'breɪd, -z, -ɪŋ, -ɪd

abrader
BR ə'breɪdə(r), -z
AM ə'breɪdər, -z

Abraham
BR 'eɪbrəham
AM 'eɪbrəˌhæm

Abrahams
BR 'eɪbrəhamz
AM 'eɪbrəˌhæmz

Abram[1]
name
BR 'eɪbrəm
AM 'eɪbrəm

Abram[2]
place in UK
BR 'abrəm, 'abram
AM 'eɪbrəm

Abrams
BR 'eɪbrəmz
AM 'eɪbrəmz

abrasion
BR ə'breɪʒn, -z
AM ə'breɪʒən, -z

abrasive
BR ə'breɪsɪv, ə'breɪzɪv, -z
AM ə'breɪsɪv, ə'breɪzɪv, -z

abrasively
BR ə'breɪsɪvli, ə'breɪzɪvli
AM ə'breɪsɪvli, ə'breɪzɪvli

abrasiveness
BR ə'breɪsɪvnɪs, ə'breɪzɪvnɪs
AM ə'breɪsɪvnɪs, ə'breɪzɪvnɪs

abraxus
BR ə'braksəs
AM ə'bræksəs

abreact
BR ˌabrɪ'akt, -s, -ɪŋ, -ɪd
AM ˌæbri'æk|(t), -(t)s, -tɪŋ, -təd

abreaction
BR ˌabrɪ'akʃn
AM ˌæbri'ækʃən

abreactive
BR ˌabrɪ'aktɪv
AM ˌæbri'æktɪv

abreast
BR ə'brɛst
AM ə'brɛst

abridgable
BR ə'brɪdʒəbl
AM ə'brɪdʒəbəl

abridge
BR ə'brɪdʒ, -ɪz, -ɪŋ, -d
AM ə'brɪdʒ, -ɪz, -ɪŋ, -d

abridgement
BR ə'brɪdʒm(ə)nt, -s
AM ə'brɪdʒmənt, -s

abridger
BR ə'brɪdʒə(r), -z

AM ə'brɪdʒər, -z

abroach
BR ə'brəʊtʃ
AM ə'broʊtʃ

abroad
BR ə'brɔːd
AM ə'brɔd, ə'brɑd

abrogate[1]
adjective
BR 'abrəgət
AM 'æbrəgət

abrogate[2]
verb
BR 'abrəgeɪt, -s, -ɪŋ, -ɨd
AM 'æbrəˌgeɪ|t, -ts, -dɪŋ, -dɨd

abrogation
BR ˌabrə'geɪʃn
AM ˌæbrə'geɪʃən

abrogator
BR 'abrəgeɪtə(r), -z
AM 'æbrəˌgeɪdər, -z

abrupt
BR ə'brʌpt
AM ə'brəpt

abruption
BR ə'brʌpʃn
AM ə'brəpʃən

abruptly
BR ə'brʌptli
AM ə'brəp(t)li

abruptness
BR ə'brʌp(t)nəs
AM ə'brəp(t)nəs

Abruzzi
BR ə'brʊtsi
AM ə'brutsi

Absalom
BR 'absələm, 'absl̩əm
AM 'æbsəˌlɑm

abscess
BR 'absɪs, 'absɛs, -ɨz, -t
AM 'æbˌsɛs, -əz, -t

abscisic acid
BR əbˌsɪsɪk 'asɪd, abˌsɪsɪk +
AM æb'sɪsɪk 'æsəd

abscissa
BR əb'sɪsə(*r*), ab'sɪsə(*r*), -z
AM æb'sɪsə, -z

abscissae
BR əb'sɪsiː, ab'sɪsiː
AM æb'sɪsi, æb'sɪˌsaɪ

abscission
BR əb'sɪʃn, ab'sɪʃn, -z
AM æb'sɪʒən, -z

abscond
BR əb'skɒnd, ab'skɒnd, -z, -ɪŋ, -ɨd
AM æb'skɑnd, əb'skɑnd, -z, -ɪŋ, -ɨd

absconder
BR əb'skɒndə(r) ab'skɒndə(r), -z
AM æb'skɑndər, əb'skɑndər, -z

Abse
BR 'abzi
AM 'æbsi

abseil
BR 'abseɪl, 'apseɪl, 'absʌɪl, 'apsʌɪl, -z, -ɪŋ, -d
AM 'æbˌseɪl, -z, -ɪŋ, -d

abseiler
BR 'abseɪlə(r), 'apseɪlə(r), 'absʌɪlə(r), 'apsʌɪlə(r), -z
AM 'æbˌseɪlər, -z

absence
BR 'abs(ə)ns, -ɨz
AM 'æbsəns, -əz

absent[1]
adjective
BR 'abs(ə)nt
AM 'æbsənt

absent[2]
verb
BR əb'sɛnt, ab'sɛnt, -s, -ɪŋ, -ɨd
AM æb'sɛn|t, -ts, -(t)ɪŋ, -(t)əd

absentee
BR ˌabs(ə)n'tiː, -z
AM ˌæbsən'ti, -z

absenteeism
BR ˌabs(ə)n'tiːɪz(ə)m
AM ˌæbsən'tiˌɪzəm

absently
BR 'abs(ə)ntli
AM 'æbsən(t)li

absentness
BR 'abs(ə)ntnəs
AM 'æbsən(t)nəs

absinth
BR 'absɪnθ, -s
AM 'æbˌsɪnθ, -s

absinthe
BR 'absɪnθ, -s
AM 'æbˌsɪnθ, -s

absit omen
BR ˌabsɪt 'əʊmɛn
AM ˌæbsə 'doʊmən

absolute
BR 'absəluːt, ˌabsə'luːt, -s
AM ¦æbsə¦l(j)ut, -s

absolutely
BR 'absəluːtli, ˌabsə'luːtli
AM ¦æbsə¦l(j)utli

absoluteness
BR 'absəluːtnəs, ˌabsə'luːtnəs
AM ¦æbsə¦l(j)utnəs

absolution
BR ˌabsə'luːʃn, -z
AM ˌæbsə'l(j)uʃən, -z

absolutism
BR 'absəluːtɪz(ə)m, ˌabsə'luːtɪz(ə)m
AM ¦æbsə¦l(j)uˌtɪzəm, ¦æbsə¦l(j)udɪzəm

absolutist
BR 'absəluːtɪst, ˌabsə'luːtɪst, -s
AM ¦æbsə¦l(j)udəst, -s

absolve
BR əb'zɒlv, -z, -ɪŋ, -d
AM əb'zɔlv, æb'zɔlv, əb'sɔlv, æb'sɔlv, əb'zɑlv, æb'zɑlv, əb'sɑlv, æb'sɑlv, -z, -ɪŋ, -d

absolver
BR əb'zɒlvə(r), -z
AM əb'zɔlvər, æb'zɔlvər, əb'sɔlvər, æb'sɔlvər, əb'zɑlvər, æb'zɑlvər, əb'sɑlvər, æb'sɑlvər, -z

absorb
BR əb'zɔːb, əb'sɔːb, -z, -ɪŋ, -d
AM əb'zɔ(ə)rb, æb'zɔ(ə)rb, əb'sɔ(ə)rb, æb'sɔ(ə)rb, -z, -ɪŋ, -d

absorbability
BR əbˌzɔːbə'bɪlɨti, əbˌsɔːbə'bɪlɨti
AM əbˌzɔrbə'bɪlɨdi, æbˌzɔrbə'bɪlɨdi, əbˌsɔrbə'bɪlɨdi, æbˌsɔrbə'bɪlɨdi

absorbable
BR əb'zɔːbəbl, əb'sɔːbəbl
AM əb'zɔrbəbəl, æb'zɔrbəbəl, əb'sɔrbəbəl, æb'sɔrbəbəl

absorbance
BR əb'zɔːb(ə)ns, əb'sɔːb(ə)ns
AM əb'zɔrbəns, æb'zɔrbəns, əb'sɔrbəns, æb'sɔrbəns

absorbedly
BR əb'zɔːbɨdli, əb'sɔːbɨdli
AM əb'zɔrbədli, æb'zɔrbədli, əb'sɔrbədli, æb'sɔrbədli

absorbency
BR əb'zɔːb(ə)nsi, əb'sɔːb(ə)nsi
AM əb'zɔrbənsi, æb'zɔrbənsi, əb'sɔrbənsi, æb'sɔrbənsi

absorbent
BR əb'zɔːb(ə)nt, əb'sɔːb(ə)nt
AM əb'zɔrbənt, æb'zɔrbənt, əb'sɔrbənt, æb'sɔrbənt

absorbently
BR əb'zɔːb(ə)ntli, əb'sɔːb(ə)ntli
AM əb'zɔrbən(t)li, æb'zɔrbən(t)li, əb'sɔrbən(t)li, æb'sɔrbən(t)li

absorber
BR əb'zɔːbə(r), əb'sɔːbə(r), -z
AM əb'zɔrbər, æb'zɔrbər, əb'sɔrbər, æb'sɔrbər, -z

absorbingly
BR əb'zɔːbɪŋli, əb'sɔːbɪŋli
AM əb'zɔrbɪŋli, æb'zɔrbɪŋli, əb'sɔrbɪŋli, æb'sɔrbɪŋli

absorption
BR əb'zɔːpʃn, əb'sɔːpʃn
AM əb'zɔrpʃən, æb'zɔrpʃən, əb'sɔrpʃən, æb'sɔrpʃən

absorptive
BR əb'zɔːptɪv, əb'sɔːptɪv
AM əb'zɔrptɪv, æb'zɔrptɪv, əb'sɔrptɪv, æb'sɔrptɪv

absorptiveness
BR əb'zɔːptɨvnɨs, əb'sɔːptɨvnɨs
AM əb'zɔrptɨvnɨs, æb'zɔrptɨvnɨs, əb'sɔrptɨvnɨs, æb'sɔrptɨvnɨs

absorptivity
BR ˌabzɔːp'tɪvɨti, ˌabsɔːp'tɪvɨti
AM ˌæbzɔrp'tɪvɨdi, ˌəbzɔrp'tɪvɨdi, ˌæbsɔrp'tɪvɨdi, ˌəbsɔrp'tɪvɨdi

absquatulate
BR əb'skwɒtjʉleɪt, əb'skwɒtʃʉleɪt, -s, -ɪŋ, -ɨd
AM ˌæbz'kwɑtʃəˌleɪ|t, ˌæb'skwɑtʃəˌleɪ|t, -ts, -dɪŋ, -dɨd

abstain
BR əb'steɪn, -z, -ɪŋ, -d
AM əb'steɪn, æb'steɪn, -z, -ɪŋ, -d

abstainer
BR əb'steɪnə(r) ab'steɪnə(r), -z
AM əb'steɪnər, æb'steɪnər, -z

abstemious
BR əb'stiːmɪəs
AM æb'stimiəs, əb'stimiəs

abstemiously
BR əbˈstiːmɪəsli
AM æbˈstimiəsli, əbˈstimiəsli

abstemiousness
BR əbˈstiːmɪəsnəs
AM æbˈstimiəsnəs, əbˈstimiəsnəs

abstention
BR əbˈstɛnʃn, -z
AM əbˈstɛn(t)ʃən, æbˈstɛn(t)ʃən, -z

abstentionism
BR əbˈstɛnʃn̩ɪz(ə)m, əbˈstɛnʃənɪz(ə)m
AM əbˈstɛn(t)ʃəˌnɪzəm, æbˈstɛn(t)ʃəˌnɪzəm

abstergent
BR əbˈstəːdʒ(ə)nt, abˈstəːdʒ(ə)nt, -s
AM əbˈstərdʒənt, æbˈstərdʒənt, -s

abstersion
BR əbˈstəːʃn, abˈstəːʃn, -z
AM əbˈstərʒən, æbˈstərʒən, -z

abstersive
BR əbˈstəːsɪv, abˈstəːsɪv
AM əbˈstərzɪv, æbˈstərzɪv

abstersively
BR əbˈstəːsɪvli, abˈstəːsɪvli
AM əbˈstərzɪvli, æbˈstərzɪvli

abstinence
BR ˈabstɪnəns
AM ˈæbstənəns

abstinency
BR ˈabstɪnənsi
AM ˈæbstənənsi

abstinent
BR ˈabstɪnənt
AM ˈæbstənənt

abstinently
BR ˈabstɪnəntli
AM ˈæbstənən(t)li

abstract[1]
adjective
BR ˈabstrakt
AM əbˈstræk(t), ˈæbˌstræk(t)

abstract[2]
noun
BR ˈabstrakt, -s
AM ˈæbˌstræk(t), -s

abstract[3]
verb
BR əbˈstrakt, -s, -ɪŋ, -ɪd
AM əbˈstræk|(t), ˈæbˌstræk|(t), -(t)s, -tɪŋ, -təd

abstractedly
BR əbˈstraktɪdli
AM əbˈstræktədli, æbˈstræktədli

abstractedness
BR əbˈstraktɪdnɪs
AM əbˈstræktədnəs, æbˈstræktədnəs

abstraction
BR əbˈstrakʃn, -z
AM əbˈstrækʃən, æbˈstrækʃən, -z

abstractionism
BR əbˈstrakʃn̩ɪz(ə)m, əbˈstrakʃənɪz(ə)m
AM əbˈstrækʃəˌnɪzəm, æbˈstrækʃəˌnɪzəm

abstractionist
BR əbˈstrakʃn̩ɪst, əbˈstrakʃənɪst, -s
AM əbˈstrækʃənəst, æbˈstrækʃənəst, -s

abstractive
BR əbˈstraktɪv
AM əbˈstræktɪv, æbˈstræktɪv

abstractly
BR ˈabstrak(t)li
AM əbˈstræk(t)li, æbˈstræk(t)li

abstractness
BR əbˈstrak(t)nəs
AM əbˈstræk(t)nəs, æbˈstræk(t)nəs

abstractor
BR əbˈstraktə(r), -z
AM əbˈstræktər, æbˈstræktər, -z

abstruse
BR əbˈstruːs
AM əbˈstrus, æbˈstrus

abstrusely
BR əbˈstruːsli
AM əbˈstrusli, æbˈstrusli

abstruseness
BR əbˈstruːsnəs
AM əbˈstrusnəs, æbˈstrusnəs

absurd
BR əbˈsəːd, əbˈzəːd
AM əbˈsərd, æbˈsərd, əbˈzərd, æbˈzərd

absurdism
BR əbˈsəːdɪz(ə)m, əbˈzəːdɪz(ə)m
AM əbˈsərdˌɪzəm, æbˈsərdˌɪzəm, əbˈzərdˌɪzəm, æbˈzərdˌɪzəm

absurdist
BR əbˈsəːdɪst, əbˈzəːdɪst, -s
AM əbˈsərdəst, æbˈsərdəst, əbˈzərdəst, æbˈzərdəst, -s

absurdity
BR əbˈsəːdɪt|i, əbˈzəːdɪti, -ɪz
AM əbˈsərdədi, æbˈsərdədi, əbˈzərdədi, æbˈzərdədi, -z

absurdly
BR əbˈsəːdli, əbˈzəːdli
AM əbˈsərdli, æbˈsərdli, əbˈzərdli, æbˈzərdli

absurdness
BR əbˈsəːdnəs, əbˈzəːdnəs
AM əbˈsərdnəs, æbˈsərdnəs, əbˈzərdnəs, æbˈzərdnəs

ABTA
BR ˈabtə(r)
AM ˌeɪˌbiˌtiˈeɪ, ˈæbdə

Abu Dhabi
BR ˌabuː ˈdɑːbi
AM ˌɑbu ˈdɑbi

Abuja
BR əˈbuːdʒə(r)
AM əˈbudʒə

Abukir Bay
BR ˌabʊkɪə ˈbeɪ
AM ˌɑbuˈkɪ(ə)r ˈbeɪ

abulia
BR əˈb(j)uːlɪə(r)
AM əˈbuljə, əˈbuliə

Abu Musa
BR ˌabuː ˈmuːsə(r)
AM ˌɑbu ˈmusə

abundance
BR əˈbʌnd(ə)ns
AM əˈbənd(ə)ns

abundant
BR əˈbʌnd(ə)nt
AM əˈbəndənt

abundantly
BR əˈbʌnd(ə)ntli
AM əˈbəndən(t)li

abuse[1]
noun
BR əˈbjuːs, -ɪz
AM əˈbjus, -əz

abuse[2]
verb
BR əˈbjuːz, -ɪz, -ɪŋ, -d
AM əˈbjuz, -əz, -ɪŋ, -d

abuser
BR əˈbjuːzə(r), -z
AM əˈbjuzər, -z

Abu Simbel
BR ˌabuː ˈsɪmbl
AM ˌɑbu ˈsɪmbəl

abusive
BR əˈbjuːsɪv, əˈbjuːzɪv
AM əˈbjusɪv, əˈbjuzɪv

abusively
BR əˈbjuːsɪvli, əˈbjuːzɪvli
AM əˈbjusɪvli, əˈbjuzɪvli

abusiveness
BR əˈbjuːsɪvnɪs, əˈbjuːzɪvnɪs
AM əˈbjusɪvnɪs, əˈbjuzɪvnɪs

abut
BR əˈbʌt, -s, -ɪŋ, -ɪd
AM əˈbə|t, -ts, -dɪŋ, -dəd

abutilon
BR əˈbjuːtɪlən, əˈbjuːtɪlɒn, -z
AM əˈbjudlˌɑn, -z

abutment
BR əˈbʌtm(ə)nt, -s
AM əˈbətmənt, -s

abuttal
BR əˈbʌtl
AM əˈbədl

abutter
BR əˈbʌtə(r), -z
AM əˈbədər, -z

abuzz
BR əˈbʌz
AM əˈbəz

Abydos
BR əˈbʌɪdɒs
AM əˈbaɪˌdɔs, əˈbaɪˌdɑs

abysm
BR əˈbɪz(ə)m
AM əˈbɪz(ə)m

abysmal
BR əˈbɪzml
AM əˈbɪzməl

abysmally
BR əˈbɪzml̩i, əˈbɪzməli
AM əˈbɪzməli

abyss
BR əˈbɪs, -ɪz
AM əˈbɪs, -ɪz

abyssal
BR əˈbɪsl
AM əˈbɪsəl

Abyssinia
BR ˌabɪˈsɪnɪə(r)
AM ˌæbəˈsɪniə

abzyme
BR ˈabzʌɪm, -z
AM ˈæbˌzaɪm, -z

a/c
BR əˈkaʊnt, -s
AM əˈkaʊnt, -s

acacia
BR əˈkeɪʃə(r), -z
AM əˈkeɪʃə, -z

academe
BR ˈakədiːm
AM ˈækəˌdim

academia
BR ˌakəˈdiːmɪə(r)
AM ˌækəˈdimiə

academic
BR ˌakəˈdɛmɪk, -s
AM ˌækəˈdɛmɪk, -s

academical
BR ˌakəˈdɛmɪkl, -z
AM ˌækəˈdɛməkəl, -z

academically
BR ˌakəˈdɛmɪkli
AM ˌækəˈdɛmək(ə)li

academician
BR əˌkadəˈmɪʃn, ˌakədəˈmɪʃn, -z

AM ˌækədəˈmɪʃən, əˌkædəˈmɪʃən, -z
academicism
BR ˌakəˈdɛmɪsɪz(ə)m
AM ˌækəˈdɛməˌsɪzəm
academism
BR əˈkadəmɪz(ə)m
AM əˈkædəˌmɪzəm
academy
BR əˈkadəm|i, -ɪz
AM əˈkædəmi, -z
Acadia
BR əˈkeɪdɪə(r)
AM əˈkeɪdiə
Acadian
BR əˈkeɪdɪən, -z
AM əˈkeɪdiən, -z
acaemia
BR əˈsiːmɪə(r)
AM əˈsimjə, əˈsimiə
acajau
BR ˈakəʒuː, -z
AM ˈɑkəʒu, -z
acanthi
BR əˈkanθʌɪ
AM əˈkænˌθaɪ
acanthine
BR əˈkanθʌɪn
AM əˈkænθən, əˈkænˌθaɪn
acanthus
BR əˈkanθəs, -ɪz
AM əˈkænθəs, -əz
a capella
BR ˌa kəˈpɛlə(r), ˌɑː +
AM ˌɑ kəˈpɛlə
a cappella
BR ˌa kəˈpɛlə(r), ˌɑː +
AM ˌɑ kəˈpɛlə
Acapulco
BR ˌakəˈpʊlkəʊ
AM ˌɑkəˈpʊlkoʊ, ˌɑkəˈpoʊkoʊ
acaricide
BR ˈakərɪsʌɪd, əˈkarɪsʌɪd, -z
AM əˈkɛrəˌsaɪd, -z
acarid
BR ˈakərɪd, -z
AM ˈækərəd, -z
acaroid
BR ˈakərɔɪd
AM ˈækəˌrɔɪd
acarology
BR ˌakəˈrɒlədʒi
AM ˌækəˈrɑlədʒi
acarpous
BR (ˌ)eɪˈkɑːpəs
AM eɪˈkɑrpəs
ACAS
BR ˈeɪkas
AM ˈeɪˌkæs
acatalectic
BR əˌkatəˈlɛktɪk, ˌeɪkatəˈlɛktɪk
AM ˈeɪˌkædlˈɛktɪk, əˌkædlˈɛktɪk
acatalepsy
BR əˈkatəlɛpsi, (ˌ)eɪˈkatəlɛpsi
AM eɪˈkædlˌɛpsi
acataleptic
BR əˌkatəˈlɛptɪk, ˌeɪkatəˈlɛptɪk
AM ˈeɪˌkædlˈɛptɪk, əˌkædlˈɛptɪk
acaudal
BR (ˌ)eɪˈkɔːdl
AM eɪˈkɔdəl, eɪˈkɑdəl
acaudate
BR (ˌ)eɪˈkɔːdeɪt
AM eɪˈkɔˌdeɪt, eɪˈkɑˌdeɪt
acausal
BR (ˌ)eɪˈkɔːzl
AM eɪˈkɔzəl, eɪˈkɑzəl
Accadian
BR əˈkeɪdɪən, -z
AM əˈkeɪdiən, -z
accaroid
BR ˈakərɔɪd
AM ˈækəˌrɔɪd
accede
BR əkˈsiːd, akˈsiːd, -z, -ɪŋ, -ɪd
AM ækˈsid, ə(k)ˈsid, -z, -ɪŋ, -ɪd
accelerando
BR əkˌsɛləˈrandəʊ, akˌsɛləˈrandəʊ, əˌtʃɛləˈrandəʊ
AM ɑkˌsɛləˈrɑndoʊ, ɑˌtʃɛləˈrɑndoʊ
accelerant
BR əkˈsɛlərənt, əkˈsɛlərn̩t, -s
AM əkˈsɛlərənt, ækˈsɛlərənt, -s
accelerate
BR əkˈsɛləreɪt, akˈsɛləreɪt, -s, -ɪŋ, -ɪd
AM əkˈsɛləˌreɪ|t, ækˈsɛləˌreɪ|t, -ts, -dɪŋ, -dɪd
acceleration
BR əkˌsɛləˈreɪʃn
AM əkˌsɛləˈreɪʃən, ækˌsɛləˈreɪʃən
accelerative
BR əkˈsɛl(ə)rətɪv
AM əkˈsɛlərədɪv, ækˈsɛlərədɪv, əkˈsɛləˌreɪdɪv, ækˈsɛləˌreɪdɪv
accelerator
BR əkˈsɛləreɪtə(r) akˈsɛləreɪtə(r), -z
AM əkˈsɛləˌreɪdər, ækˈsɛləˌreɪdər, -z
accelerometer
BR əkˌsɛləˈrɒmɪtə(r), akˌsɛləˈrɒmɪtə(r), -z
AM əkˌsɛləˈrɑmədər, ækˌsɛləˈrɑmədər, -z
accent¹
noun
BR ˈaks(ə)nt, -s
AM ˈækˌsɛnt, -s
accent²
verb
BR əkˈsɛnt, akˈsɛnt, -s, -ɪŋ, -ɪd
AM ˈækˈsɛn|t, -ts, -(t)ɪŋ, -(t)əd
accentor
BR əkˈsɛntə(r), akˈsɛntə(r), -z
AM ˈæksɛn(t)ər, -z
accentual
BR əkˈsɛn(t)ʃʊəl, əkˈsɛn(t)ʃ(ʊ)l, akˈsɛn(t)ʃʊəl, akˈsɛn(t)ʃ(ʊ)l, əkˈsɛntjʊəl, əkˈsɛntjʊl, akˈsɛntjʊəl, akˈsɛntjʊl
AM ækˈsɛn(t)ʃ(əw)əl, əkˈsɛn(t)ʃ(əw)əl
accentually
BR əkˈsɛn(t)ʃʊəli, əkˈsɛn(t)ʃʊli, əkˈsɛn(t)ʃl̩i, akˈsɛn(t)ʃʊəli, akˈsɛn(t)ʃʊli, akˈsɛn(t)ʃl̩i, əkˈsɛntjʊəli, əkˈsɛntjʊli, akˈsɛntjʊəli, akˈsɛntjʊli
AM ækˈsɛn(t)ʃ(əw)əli, əkˈsɛn(t)ʃ(əw)əli
accentuate
BR əkˈsɛn(t)ʃʊeɪt, akˈsɛn(t)ʃʊeɪt, əkˈsɛntjʊeɪt, akˈsɛntjʊeɪt, -s, -ɪŋ, -ɪd
AM ækˈsɛn(t)ʃəˌweɪ|t, əkˈsɛn(t)ʃəˌweɪ|t, -ts, -dɪŋ, -dɪd
accentuation
BR əkˌsɛn(t)ʃʊˈeɪʃn, akˌsɛn(t)ʃʊˈeɪʃn, əkˌsɛntjʊˈeɪʃn, akˌsɛntjʊˈeɪʃn
AM ækˌsɛn(t)ʃəˈweɪʃən, əkˌsɛn(t)ʃəˈweɪʃən
accept
BR əkˈsɛpt, akˈsɛpt, -s, -ɪŋ, -ɪd
AM əkˈsɛpt, ækˈsɛpt, -s, -ɪŋ, -əd
acceptability
BR əkˌsɛptəˈbɪlɪti, akˌsɛptəˈbɪlɪti
AM əkˌsɛptəˈbɪlɪdi, ækˌsɛptəˈbɪlɪdi
acceptable
BR əkˈsɛptəbl, akˈsɛptəbl
AM əkˈsɛptəbəl, ækˈsɛptəbəl
acceptableness
BR əkˈsɛptəblnəs, akˈsɛptəblnəs
AM əkˈsɛptəbəlnəs, ækˈsɛptəbəlnəs
acceptably
BR əkˈsɛptəbli, akˈsɛptəbli
AM əkˈsɛptəbli, ækˈsɛptəbli
acceptance
BR əkˈsɛpt(ə)ns, akˈsɛpt(ə)ns, -ɪz
AM əkˈsɛpt(ə)ns, ækˈsɛpt(ə)ns, -əz
acceptant
BR əkˈsɛpt(ə)nt, akˈsɛpt(ə)nt, -s
AM əkˈsɛptənt, ækˈsɛptənt, -s
acceptation
BR ˌaksɛpˈteɪʃn, ˌaksəpˈteɪʃn, -z
AM ˌækˌsɛpˈteɪʃən, -z
accepter
BR əkˈsɛptə(r), akˈsɛptə(r), -z
AM əkˈsɛptər, ækˈsɛptər, -z
acceptor
BR əkˈsɛptə(r), akˈsɛptə(r), -z
AM əkˈsɛptər, ækˈsɛptər, -z
access¹
noun
BR ˈaksɛs, -ɪz
AM ˈækˌsɛs, -əz
access²
verb
BR ˈaksɛs, əkˈsɛs, -ɪz, -ɪŋ, -t
AM ˈækˌsɛs, -əz, -ɪŋ, -t
accessary
BR əkˈsɛs(ə)r|i, akˈsɛs(ə)r|i, -ɪz
AM əkˈsɛs(ə)ri, ækˈsɛs(ə)ri, -z
accessibility
BR əkˌsɛsɪˈbɪlɪti, akˌsɛsɪˈbɪlɪti
AM əkˌsɛsəˈbɪlɪdi, ækˌsɛsəˈbɪlɪdi
accessible
BR əkˈsɛsɪbl, akˈsɛsɪbl
AM əkˈsɛsəbəl, ækˈsɛsəbəl
accessibly
BR əkˈsɛsɪbli, akˈsɛsɪbli
AM əkˈsɛsəbli, ækˈsɛsəbli
accession
BR əkˈsɛʃn, akˈsɛʃn
AM əkˈsɛʃən, ækˈsɛʃən
accessit
BR akˈsɛsɪt
AM ækˈsɛsət

accessorial
BR ˌaksɛˈsɔːrɪəl
AM ˌæksəˈsɔriəl

accessorise
BR əkˈsɛsərʌɪz, akˈsɛsərʌɪz, -ɪz, -ɪŋ, -d
AM əkˈsɛsəˌraɪz, ækˈsɛsəˌraɪz, -ɪz, -ɪŋ, -d

accessorize
BR əkˈsɛsərʌɪz, akˈsɛsərʌɪz, -ɪz, -ɪŋ, -d
AM əkˈsɛsəˌraɪz, ækˈsɛsəˌraɪz, -ɪz, -ɪŋ, -d

accessory
BR əkˈsɛs(ə)r|i, akˈsɛs(ə)r|i, -ɪz
AM əkˈsɛs(ə)ri, ækˈsɛs(ə)ri, -z

acciaccatura
BR əˌtʃakəˈtʊərə(r)
AM ɑˌtʃɑkəˈtʊrə

accidence
BR ˈaksɪd(ə)ns
AM ˈæksəd(ə)ns

accident
BR ˈaksɪd(ə)nt, -s
AM ˈæksədnt, -s

accidental
BR ˌaksɪˈdɛntl
AM ˌæksəˈdɛn(t)l

accidentally
BR ˌaksɪˈdɛntl̩i, ˌaksɪˈdɛntli
AM ˌæksəˈdɛn(t)li

accidie
BR ˈaksɪdi
AM ˈæksədi

accipiter
BR akˈsɪpɪtə(r), -z
AM æ(k)ˈsɪpədər, -z

acclaim
BR əˈkleɪm, -z, -ɪŋ, -d
AM əˈkleɪm, -z, -ɪŋ, -d

acclaimer
BR əˈkleɪmə(r), -z
AM əˈkleɪmər, -z

acclamation
BR ˌakləˈmeɪʃn, -z
AM ˌækləˈmeɪʃən, -z

acclamatory
BR əˈklamət(ə)ri
AM əˈklæməˌtɔri

acclimatation
BR əˌklʌɪməˈteɪʃn
AM əˌklaɪməˈteɪʃən

acclimate
BR ˈaklɪmeɪt, -s, -ɪŋ, -ɪd
AM ˈækləˌmeɪ|t, -ts, -dɪŋ, -dɪd

acclimation
BR ˌaklɪˈmeɪʃn
AM ˌækləˈmeɪʃən

acclimatisation
BR əˌklʌɪmətʌɪˈzeɪʃn
AM əˌklaɪmədəˈzeɪʃən, əˌklaɪməˌtaɪˈzeɪʃən

acclimatise
BR əˈklʌɪmətʌɪz, -ɪz, -ɪŋ, -d
AM əˈklaɪməˌtaɪz, -ɪz, -ɪŋ, -d

acclimatization
BR əˌklʌɪmətʌɪˈzeɪʃn
AM əˌklaɪmədəˈzeɪʃən, əˌklaɪməˌtaɪˈzeɪʃən

acclimatize
BR əˈklʌɪmətʌɪz, -ɪz, -ɪŋ, -d
AM əˈklaɪməˌtaɪz, -ɪz, -ɪŋ, -d

acclivitous
BR əˈklɪvɪtəs
AM əˈklɪvədəs

acclivity
BR əˈklɪvɪt|i, -ɪz
AM əˈklɪvɪdi, -z

accolade
BR ˈakəleɪd, ˌakəˈleɪd, -z
AM ˈækəˌleɪd, -z

accommodate
BR əˈkɒmədeɪt, -s, -ɪŋ, -ɪd
AM əˈkɑməˌdeɪ|t, -ts, -dɪŋ, -dɪd

accommodatingly
BR əˈkɒmədeɪtɪŋli
AM əˈkɑməˌdeɪdɪŋli

accommodation
BR əˌkɒməˈdeɪʃn, -z
AM əˌkɑməˈdeɪʃən, -z

accommodationist
BR əˌkɒməˈdeɪʃn̩ɪst, əˌkɒməˈdeɪʃənɪst, -s
AM əˌkɑməˈdeɪʃənəst, -s

accompaniment
BR əˈkʌmp(ə)nɪm(ə)nt, -s
AM əˈkəmp(ə)nimənt, əˈkəmp(ə)nəmənt, -s

accompanist
BR əˈkʌmpənɪst, əˈkʌmpn̩ɪst, -s
AM əˈkəmpənəst, -s

accompany
BR əˈkʌmp(ə)n|i, əˈkʌmpn̩|i, -ɪz, -ɪɪŋ, -ɪd
AM əˈkəmp(ə)ni, -z, -ɪŋ, -d

accompanyist
BR əˈkʌmpənɪɪst, əˈkʌmpn̩ɪɪst
AM əˈkəmp(ə)niəst

accomplice
BR əˈkʌmplɪs, əˈkɒmplɪs, -ɪz
AM əˈkɑmpləs, -əz

accomplish
BR əˈkʌmpl|ɪʃ, əˈkɒmpl|ɪʃ, -ɪʃɪz, -ɪʃɪŋ, -ɪʃt
AM əˈkɑmplɪʃ, -ɪz, -ɪŋ, -t

accomplishment
BR əˈkʌmplɪʃm(ə)nt, əˈkɒmplɪʃm(ə)nt, -s
AM əˈkɑmplɪʃmənt, -s

accompt
BR əˈkaʊnt, -s
AM əˈkaʊnt, -s

accord
BR əˈkɔːd, -z, -ɪŋ, -ɪd
AM əˈkɔ(ə)rd, -z, -ɪŋ, -əd

accordance
BR əˈkɔːdns
AM əˈkɔrdns

accordant
BR əˈkɔːdnt
AM əˈkɔrdnt

accordantly
BR əˈkɔːdntli
AM əˈkɔrdn(t)li

according
BR əˈkɔːdɪŋ
AM əˈkɔrdɪŋ

accordingly
BR əˈkɔːdɪŋli
AM əˈkɔrdɪŋli

accordion
BR əˈkɔːdɪən, -z
AM əˈkɔrdiən, -z

accordionist
BR əˈkɔːdɪənɪst, -s
AM əˈkɔrdiənəst, -s

accost
BR əˈkɒst, -s, -ɪŋ, -ɪd
AM əˈkɔst, əˈkɑst, -s, -ɪŋ, -əd

accouchement
BR əˈkuːʃmɒ̃, -z
AM ˌɑkuʃˈmɑnt, əˈkuʃmənt, -s

accoucheur
BR ˌakuːˈʃəː(r), -z
AM ˌɑkuˈʃər, -z

accoucheuse
BR ˌakuːˈʃəːz, -ɪz
AM ˌɑkuˈʃəz, -əz

account
BR əˈkaʊnt, -s, -ɪŋ, -ɪd
AM əˈkaʊn|t, -ts, -(t)ɪŋ, -(t)əd

accountability
BR əˌkaʊntəˈbɪlɪti
AM əˌkaʊn(t)əˈbɪlɪdi

accountable
BR əˈkaʊntəbl
AM əˈkaʊn(t)əbəl

accountableness
BR əˈkaʊntəblnəs
AM əˈkaʊn(t)əbəlnəs

accountably
BR əˈkaʊntəbli
AM əˈkaʊn(t)əbli

accountancy
BR əˈkaʊnt(ə)nsi
AM əˈkaʊn(t)nsi

accountant
BR əˈkaʊnt(ə)nt, -s
AM əˈkaʊn(t)ənt, -s

accounting
BR əˈkaʊntɪŋ
AM əˈkaʊn(t)ɪŋ

accouter
BR əˈkuːt|ə(r), -əz, -(ə)rɪŋ, -əd
AM əˈkudər, -z, -ɪŋ, -d

accouterment
BR əˈkuːtrɪm(ə)nt, əˈkuːtəm(ə)nt, -s
AM əˈkudərmənt, -s

accoutre
BR əˈkuːt|ə(r), -əz, -(ə)rɪŋ, -əd
AM əˈkudər, -z, -ɪŋ, -d

accoutrement
BR əˈkuːtrɪm(ə)nt, əˈkuːtəm(ə)nt, -s
AM əˈkudərmənt, -s

Accra
BR əˈkrɑː(*r*)
AM ˈækrə

accredit
BR əˈkrɛd|ɪt, -ɪts, -ɪtɪŋ, -ɪtɪd
AM əˈkrɛdə|t, -ts, -dɪŋ, -dəd

accreditation
BR əˌkrɛdɪˈteɪʃn
AM əˌkrɛdəˈdeɪʃən

accrete
BR əˈkriːt, -s, -ɪŋ, -ɪd
AM əˈkri|t, -ts, -dɪŋ, -dɪd

accretion
BR əˈkriːʃn, -z
AM əˈkriʃən, -z

accretive
BR əˈkriːtɪv
AM əˈkridɪv

Accrington
BR ˈakrɪŋt(ə)n
AM ˈækrɪŋtən

accrual
BR əˈkruːəl, -z
AM əˈkruəl, -z

accrue
BR əˈkruː, -z, -ɪŋ, -d
AM əˈkru, -z, -ɪŋ, -d

acct
BR əˈkaʊnt, -s
AM əˈkaʊnt, -s

acculturate
BR əˈkʌltʃʊreɪt, -s, -ɪŋ, -ɪd
AM əˈkəltʃəˌreɪ|t, -ts, -dɪŋ, -dɪd

acculturation
BR əˌkʌltʃʊˈreɪʃn
AM əˌkəltʃəˈreɪʃən

acculturative
BR əˈkʌltʃ(ə)rətɪv
AM əˈkəltʃ(ə)rədɪv, əˈkəltʃəˌreɪdɪv

accumulable
BR əˈkjuːmjələbl
AM əˈkjum(j)ələbəl

accumulate
BR ə'kju:mjʉleɪt, -s, -ɪŋ, -ɪd
AM ə'kjum(j)əˌleɪ|t, -ts, -dɪŋ, -dɪd

accumulation
BR əˌkju:mjʉ'leɪʃn, -z
AM əˌkjum(j)ə'leɪʃən, -z

accumulative
BR ə'kju:mjʉlətɪv
AM ə'kjum(j)ələdɪv, ə'kjum(j)əˌleɪdɪv

accumulatively
BR ə'kju:mjʉlətɪvli
AM ə'kjum(j)ələdɪvli, ə'kjum(j)əˌleɪdɪvli

accumulator
BR ə'kju:mjʉleɪtə(r), -z
AM ə'kjum(j)əˌleɪdər, -z

accuracy
BR 'akjʉrəsi
AM 'ækjərəsi

accurate
BR 'akjʉrət
AM 'ækjərət

accurately
BR 'akjʉrətli
AM 'ækjərətli

accurateness
BR 'akjʉrətnəs
AM 'ækjərətnəs

Accurist®
BR 'akjʉrɪst
AM 'ækjʊrəst

accursed
BR ə'kə:st, ə'kə:sɪd
AM ə'kərst, ə'kərsəd

accursedly
BR ə'kə:sɪdli
AM ə'kərsədli

accusal
BR ə'kju:zl, -z
AM ə'kjuzəl, -z

accusation
BR ˌakjʉ'zeɪʃn, -z
AM ˌækjə'zeɪʃən, ˌækju'zeɪʃən, -z

accusatival
BR əˌkju:zə'tʌɪvl
AM əˌkjuzə'taɪvəl

accusative
BR ə'kju:zətɪv, -z
AM ə'kjuzədɪv, -z

accusatively
BR ə'kju:zətɪvli
AM ə'kjuzədɪvli

accusatorial
BR əˌkju:zə'tɔ:rɪəl
AM əˌkjuzə'tɔriəl

accusatory
BR ə'kju:zət(ə)ri, ˌakjʉ'zeɪt(ə)ri
AM ə'kjuzəˌtɔri

accuse
BR ə'kju:z, -ɪz, -ɪŋ, -d
AM ə'kjuz, -əz, -ɪŋ, -d

accuser
BR ə'kju:zə(r), -z
AM ə'kjuzər, -z

accusingly
BR ə'kju:zɪŋli
AM ə'kjuzɪŋli

accustom
BR ə'kʌstəm, -z, -ɪŋ, -d
AM ə'kəstəm, -z, -ɪŋ, -d

ace
BR eɪs, -ɪz, -ɪŋ, -t
AM eɪs, -ɪz, -ɪŋ, -t

acedia
BR ə'si:dɪə(*r*)
AM ə'sidiə

Aceldama
BR ə'kɛldəmə(*r*), ə'sɛldəmə(*r*)
AM ə'sɛldəmə, ə'kɛldəmə

acellular
BR (ˌ)eɪ'sɛljʉlə(r)
AM eɪ'sɛljələr

acephalous
BR (ˌ)eɪ'sɛfələs, (ˌ)eɪ'sɛfl̩əs, (ˌ)eɪ'kɛfələs, (ˌ)eɪ'kɛfl̩əs
AM eɪ'sɛfələs

acer
BR 'eɪsə(r), -z
AM 'eɪsər, -z

acerb
BR ə'sə:b
AM ə'sərb

acerbic
BR ə'sə:bɪk
AM ə'sərbɪk

acerbically
BR ə'sə:bɪkli
AM ə'sərbək(ə)li

acerbity
BR ə'sə:bɪti
AM ə'sərbədi

acescence
BR ə'sɛsns
AM ə'sɛsəns

acescent
BR ə'sɛsnt
AM ə'sɛsənt

acetabula
BR ˌasɪ'tabjʉlə(*r*)
AM ˌæsə'tæbjələ

acetabulum
BR ˌasɪ'tabjʉləm
AM ˌæsə'tæbjələm

acetal
BR 'asɪtal
AM 'æsədl, 'æsəˌtæl

acetaldehyde
BR ˌasɪ'taldɪhʌɪd
AM ˌæsə'tældəˌhaɪd

acetaminophen
BR əˌsi:tə'mɪnəfɛn, əˌsɛtə'mɪnəfɛn
AM əˌsidə'mɪnəfən

acetanilide
BR ˌasɪ'tanɪlʌɪd
AM ˌæsə'tænəˌlaɪd

acetate
BR 'asɪteɪt, -s
AM 'æsəˌteɪt, -s

acetic
BR ə'si:tɪk, ə'sɛtɪk
AM ə'sidɪk

acetification
BR əˌsi:tɪfɪ'keɪʃn, əˌsɛtɪfɪ'keɪʃn
AM əˌsidəfə'keɪʃən, əˌsɛdəfə'keɪʃən

acetify
BR ə'si:tɪfʌɪ, ə'sɛtɪfʌɪ, -z, -ɪŋ, -d
AM ə'sidəˌfaɪ, ə'sɛdəˌfaɪ, -z, -ɪŋ, -d

acetone
BR 'asɪtəʊn
AM 'æsəˌtoʊn

acetose
BR 'asɪtəʊs
AM 'æsəˌtoʊs, 'æsəˌtoʊz

acetous
BR ə'si:təs, 'asɪtəs
AM ə'sidəs, 'æsədəs

acetyl
BR 'asɪtʌɪl, 'asɪtɪl
AM ə'sidl, 'æsədl

acetylcholine
BR ˌasɪtʌɪl'kəʊli:n, ˌasɪtɪl'kəʊli:n, ˌasɪtʌɪl'kəʊlɪn, ˌasɪtɪl'kəʊlɪn
AM əˌsidl'koʊˌlin, ˌæsədl'koʊˌlaɪn

acetylene
BR ə'sɛtɪli:n, ə'sɛtl̩i:n
AM ə'sɛdlən, ə'sɛdəˌlin

acetylide
BR ə'sɛtɪlʌɪd, ə'sɛtl̩ʌɪd
AM ə'sɛdlˌaɪd

acetylsalicylic
BR ˌasɪtʌɪlˌsalɪ'sɪlɪk, ˌasɪtɪlˌsalɪ'sɪlɪk
AM əˌsidlˌsælə'sɪlɪk

acey-deucey
BR ˌeɪsɪ'dju:si, ˌeɪsɪ'dʒu:si
AM ˌeɪsi'd(j)usi

acey-deucy
BR ˌeɪsɪ'dju:si, ˌeɪsɪ'dʒu:si
AM ˌeɪsi'd(j)usi

Achaea
BR ə'ki:ə(*r*)
AM ə'kiə, ə'keɪə

Achaean
BR ə'ki:ən, -z
AM ə'kiən, ə'keɪən, -z

Achaemenid
BR ə'ki:mənɪd, -z
AM ə'kimənəd, -z

acharnement
BR a'ʃɑ:nmɒ̃
AM əˌʃɑrnə'mɑn(t)

Achates
BR ə'keɪti:z
AM ə'keɪdiz

ache
BR eɪk, -s, -ɪŋ, -t
AM eɪk, -s, -ɪŋ, -t

Achebe
BR ə'tʃeɪbi
AM ə'tʃeɪbeɪ

achene
BR ə'ki:n, -z
AM ə'kin, -z

Acheron
BR 'ak(ə)rən, 'ak(ə)rn̩, 'akərɒn
AM 'ækəˌrɑn, 'ætʃəˌrɑn

Acheson
BR 'atʃɪs(ə)n
AM 'ætʃəsən

Acheulean
BR ə'(t)ʃu:lɪən, -z
AM ə'ʃuliən, -z

Acheulian
BR ə'(t)ʃu:lɪən, -z
AM ə'ʃuljən, ə'ʃuliən, -z

achievable
BR ə'tʃi:vəbl
AM ə'tʃivəbəl

achieve
BR ə'tʃi:v, -z, -ɪŋ, -d
AM ə'tʃiv, -z, -ɪŋ, -d

achievement
BR ə'tʃi:vm(ə)nt, -s
AM ə'tʃivmənt, -s

achiever
BR ə'tʃi:və(r), -z
AM ə'tʃivər, -z

achillea
BR ˌakɪ'li:ə(*r*), ə'kɪlɪə(*r*)
AM ə'kɪliə

Achilles
BR ə'kɪli:z
AM ə'kɪliz

Achinese
BR ˌatʃɪ'ni:z
AM ˌætʃə'niz, ˌɑtʃə'niz

achingly
BR 'eɪkɪŋli
AM 'eɪkɪŋli

achiral
BR eɪ'kʌɪrəl, eɪ'kʌɪrl̩
AM eɪ'kaɪrəl

achondroplasia
BR əˌkɒndrə'pleɪzɪə(*r*), ˌeɪkɒndrə'pleɪzɪə(*r*), əˌkɒndrə'pleɪʒə(*r*), ˌeɪkɒndrə'pleɪʒə(*r*)
AM ˌeɪˌkɑndrə'pleɪʒ(i)ə, ˌeɪˌkɑndrə'pleɪziə

achondroplasic
BR əˌkɒndrə'pleɪzɪk, ˌeɪkɒndrə'pleɪzɪk, -s
AM ˌeɪˌkɑndrə'pleɪʒɪk, ˌeɪˌkɑndrə'pleɪzɪk-s

achondroplastic
BR əˌkɒndrəˈplastɪk, ˌeɪkɒndrəˈplastɪk, -s
AM ˌeɪˌkɑndrəˈplæstɪk, -s

achoo
BR əˈtʃuː
AM əˈtʃu

achromat
BR ˈakrə(ʊ)mat, -s
AM ˈækrəˌmæt, -s

achromatic
BR ˌakrə(ʊ)ˈmatɪk, ˌeɪkrə(ʊ)ˈmatɪk
AM ˌækrəˈmædɪk, ˌeɪkrəˈmædɪk

achromatically
BR ˌakrə(ʊ)ˈmatɪkli, ˌeɪkrə(ʊ)ˈmatɪkli
AM ˌækrəˈmædək(ə)li, ˌeɪkrəˈmædək(ə)li

achromaticity
BR əˌkrəʊməˈtɪsɪti, ˌeɪkrəʊməˈtɪsɪti
AM eɪˌkroʊməˈtɪsɪdi, æˌkroʊməˈtɪsɪdi

achromatism
BR əˈkrəʊmətɪz(ə)m, (ˌ)eɪˈkrəʊmətɪz(ə)m
AM eɪˈkroʊməˌtɪzəm, æˈkroʊməˌtɪzəm

achromatize
BR əˈkrəʊmətʌɪz, (ˌ)eɪˈkrəʊmətʌɪz, -ɪz, -ɪŋ, -d
AM eɪˈkroʊməˌtaɪz, æˈkroʊməˌtaɪz, -ɪz, -ɪŋ, -d

achronical
BR (ˌ)eɪˈkrɒnɪkl
AM eɪˈkrɑnəkəl

achy
BR ˈeɪki
AM ˈeɪki

acicula
BR əˈsɪkjʊlə(r)
AM əˈsɪkjələ

acicular
BR əˈsɪkjʊlə(r)
AM əˈsɪkjələr

acid
BR ˈasɪd, -z
AM ˈæsəd, -z

acidic
BR əˈsɪdɪk
AM əˈsɪdɪk, æˈsɪdɪk

acidification
BR əˌsɪdɪfɪˈkeɪʃn
AM əˌsɪdəfəˈkeɪʃən, æˌsɪdəfəˈkeɪʃən

acidify
BR əˈsɪdɪfʌɪ, -z, -ɪŋ, -d
AM əˈsɪdəˌfaɪ, æˈsɪdəˌfaɪ, -z, -ɪŋ, -d

acidimeter
BR ˌasɪˈdɪmɪtə(r), -z
AM ˌæsəˈdɪmədər, -z

acidimetry
BR ˌasɪˈdɪmɪtri
AM ˌæsəˈdɪmɪtri

acidity
BR əˈsɪdɪti
AM əˈsɪdɪdi, æˈsɪdɪdi

acidly
BR ˈasɪdli
AM ˈasədli

acidness
BR ˈasɪdnɪs
AM ˈæsədnəs

acidophilic
BR ˌasɪdə(ʊ)ˈfɪlɪk
AM ˌæsədoʊˈfɪlɪk, ˌæsədəˈfɪlɪk

acidophilus
BR ˌasɪˈdɒfɪləs
AM ˌæsəˈdɑfələs

acidosis
BR ˌasɪˈdəʊsɪs
AM ˌæsəˈdoʊsəs

acidotic
BR ˌasɪˈdɒtɪk
AM ˌæsəˈdɑdɪk

acidulate
BR əˈsɪdjʊleɪt, əˈsɪdʒʊleɪt, -s, -ɪŋ, -ɪd
AM əˈsɪdʒəˌleɪ|t, -ts, -dɪŋ, -dɪd

acidulation
BR əˌsɪdjʊˈleɪʃn, əˌsɪdʒʊˈleɪʃn
AM əˌsɪdʒəˈleɪʃən

acidulous
BR əˈsɪdjʊləs, əˈsɪdʒʊləs
AM əˈsɪdʒələs

acini
BR ˈasɪnʌɪ
AM ˈæsəˌnaɪ

acinus
BR ˈasɪnəs
AM ˈæsənəs

ack
BR ak
AM æk

ack-ack
BR ˈakak
AM ˈækˌæk

ackee
BR ˈak|i, -ɪz
AM ˈæˌki, -z

ack emma
BR ˌak ˈɛmə(r)
AM ˌæk ˈɛmə

Ackerman
BR ˈakəmən
AM ˈækərmən

acknowledge
BR əkˈnɒlɪdʒ, -ɪdʒɪz, -ɪdʒɪŋ, -ɪdʒd
AM əkˈnɑlədʒ, ækˈnɑlədʒ, -əz, -ɪŋ, -d

acknowledgeable
BR əkˈnɒlɪdʒəbl
AM əkˈnɑlədʒəbəl, ækˈnɑlədʒəbəl

acknowledgement
BR əkˈnɒlɪdʒm(ə)nt, -s
AM əkˈnɑlədʒmənt, ækˈnɑlədʒmənt, -s

Ackroyd
BR ˈakrɔɪd, ˈeɪkrɔɪd
AM ˈækrɔɪd

aclinic
BR əˈklɪnɪk
AM eɪˈklɪnɪk

acme
BR ˈakm|i, -ɪz
AM ˈækmi, -z

acne
BR ˈakn|i, -ɪd
AM ˈækni, -d

acolyte
BR ˈakəlʌɪt, -s
AM ˈækəˌlaɪt, -s

Aconcagua
BR ˌak(ə)nˈkagwə(r), ˌakɒnˈkagwə(r), ˌak(ə)nˈkɑːgwə(r), ˌakɒnˈkɑːgwə(r)
AM ˌækənˈkɑgwə, ˌɑkənˈkɑgwə
SP ˌakoŋˈkaɣwa

aconite
BR ˈakənʌɪt, -s
AM ˈækəˌnaɪt, -s

aconitic
BR ˌakəˈnɪtɪk
AM ˌækəˈnɪdɪk

aconitine
BR əˈkɒnɪtiːn
AM əˈkɑnətin, əˈkɑnədən

acorn
BR ˈeɪkɔːn, -z
AM ˈeɪˌkɔ(ə)rn, -z

acotyledon
BR əˌkɒtɪˈliːd(ə)n, ˌeɪkɒtɪˈliːd(ə)n, -z
AM ˌeɪˌkɑdlˈidən, -z

acotyledonous
BR əˌkɒtɪˈliːdɪnəs, əˌkɒtɪˈliːdn̩əs, ˌeɪkɒtɪˈliːdɪnəs, ˌeɪkɒtɪˈliːdn̩əs
AM ˌeɪˌkɑdlˈidn̩əs

acoustic
BR əˈkuːstɪk, -s
AM əˈkustɪk, -s

acoustical
BR əˈkuːstɪkl
AM əˈkustəkəl

acoustically
BR əˈkuːstɪkli
AM əˈkustək(ə)li

acoustician
BR əˌkuːˈstɪʃn, ˌakuːˈstɪʃn, -z
AM əˌkuˈstɪʃən, ˌæˌkuˈstɪʃən, -z

acquaint
BR əˈkweɪnt, -s, -ɪŋ, -ɪd
AM əˈkweɪn|t, -ts, -(t)ɪŋ, -(t)ɪd

acquaintance
BR əˈkweɪnt(ə)ns, -ɪz
AM əˈkweɪn(t)ns, -əz

acquaintanceship
BR əˈkweɪnt(ə)n(s)ʃɪp, -s
AM əˈkweɪnt(ə)n(s)ˌʃɪp, -s

acquest
BR əˈkwɛst, -s
AM əˈkwɛst, -s

acquiesce
BR ˌakwɪˈɛs, -ɪz, -ɪŋ, -t
AM ˌækwiˈɛs, -əz, -ɪŋ, -t

acquiescence
BR ˌakwɪˈɛsns
AM ˌækwiˈɛsəns

acquiescent
BR ˌakwɪˈɛsnt
AM ˌækwiˈɛsənt

acquiescingly
BR ˌakwɪˈɛsɪŋli
AM ˌækwiˈɛsɪŋli

acquirable
BR əˈkwʌɪərəbl
AM əˈkwaɪ(ə)rəbəl

acquire
BR əˈkwʌɪə(r), -z, -ɪŋ, -d
AM əˈkwaɪ(ə)r, -z, -ɪŋ, -d

acquirement
BR əˈkwʌɪəm(ə)nt
AM əˈkwaɪ(ə)rmənt

acquirer
BR əˈkwʌɪərə(r), -z
AM əˈkwaɪ(ə)rər, -z

acquisition
BR ˌakwɪˈzɪʃn, -z
AM ˌækwəˈzɪʃən, -z

acquisitive
BR əˈkwɪzɪtɪv
AM əˈkwɪzɪdɪv, æˈkwɪzɪdɪv

acquisitively
BR əˈkwɪzɪtɪvli
AM əˈkwɪzɪdɪvli, æˈkwɪzɪdɪvli

acquisitiveness
BR əˈkwɪzɪtɪvnɪs
AM əˈkwɪzɪdɪvnɪs, æˈkwɪzɪdɪvnɪs

acquit
BR əˈkwɪt, -s, -ɪŋ, -ɪd
AM əˈkwɪ|t, -ts, -dɪŋ, -dɪd

acquittal
BR əˈkwɪtl, -z
AM əˈkwɪdəl, -z

acquittance
BR əˈkwɪtns, -ɪz
AM əˈkwɪtns, əˈkwɪdəns, -əz

Acre
BR ˈeɪkə(r), ˈɑːkə(r)
AM ˈeɪkər, ˈɑkər, ˈɑkrə

acre
BR ˈeɪkə(r), -z, -d
AM ˈeɪkər, -z, -d

acreage
BR ˈeɪk(ə)r|ɪdʒ, -ᵻdʒᵻz
AM ˈeɪk(ə)rɪdʒ, -ᵻz

acrid
BR ˈakrɪd
AM ˈækrəd

acridine
BR ˈakrᵻdiːn, ˈakrᵻdʌɪn
AM ˈækrəˌdin, ˈækrədən

acridity
BR əˈkrɪdᵻti
AM əˈkrɪdᵻdi, æˈkrɪdᵻdi

acridly
BR ˈakrᵻdli
AM ˈækrədli

acridness
BR ˈakrᵻdnᵻs
AM ˈækrədnəs

acriflavine
BR ˌakrᵻˈfleɪvɪn, ˌakrᵻˈfleɪviːn
AM ˌækrəˈfleɪvin

Acrilan®
BR ˈakrᵻlan
AM ˈækrəˌlæn

acrimonious
BR ˌakrᵻˈməʊnɪəs
AM ˌækrəˈmoʊniəs

acrimoniously
BR ˌakrᵻˈməʊnɪəsli
AM ˌækrəˈmoʊniəsli

acrimoniousness
BR ˌakrᵻˈməʊnɪəsnəs
AM ˌækrəˈmoʊniəsnəs

acrimony
BR ˈakrᵻməni
AM ˈækrəˌmoʊni

acrobat
BR ˈakrəbat, -s
AM ˈækrəˌbæt, -s

acrobatic
BR ˌakrəˈbatɪk, -s
AM ˌækrəˈbædɪk, -s

acrobatically
BR ˌakrəˈbatᵻkli
AM ˌækrəˈbædək(ə)li

acrocyanosis
BR ˌakrəʊsʌɪəˈnəʊsɪs
AM ˌækroʊˌsaɪəˈnoʊsɪs

acrogen
BR ˈakrədʒ(ə)n, -z
AM ˈækrədʒən, -z

acrogenous
BR əˈkrɒdʒᵻnəs, əˈkrɒdʒn̩əs
AM əˈkrɑdʒənəs

acrolect
BR ˈakrəlɛkt, -s
AM ˈækrəˌlɛkt, -s

acromegalic
BR ˌakrə(ʊ)mᵻˈɡalɪk, -s
AM ˌækroʊməˈɡælɪk, -s

acromegaly
BR ˌakrə(ʊ)ˈmɛɡəli, ˌakrə(ʊ)ˈmɛɡl̩i
AM ˌækroʊˈmɛɡəli

acronycal
BR əˈkrɒnᵻkl
AM əˈkrɑnəkəl, æˈkrɑnəkəl

acronycally
BR əˈkrɒnᵻkli
AM əˈkrɑnək(ə)li, æˈkrɑnək(ə)li

acronychal
BR əˈkrɒnᵻkl
AM əˈkrɑnəkəl, æˈkrɑnəkəl

acronychally
BR əˈkrɒnᵻkli
AM əˈkrɑnək(ə)li, æˈkrɑnək(ə)li

acronym
BR ˈakrənɪm, -z
AM ˈækrəˌnɪm, -z

acropetal
BR əˈkrɒpᵻtl
AM əˈkrɑpɛdl, æˈkrɑpɛdl

acropetally
BR əˈkrɒpᵻtl̩i
AM əˈkrɑpɛdl̩i, æˈkrɑpɛdl̩i

acrophobia
BR ˌakrə(ʊ)ˈfəʊbɪə(r)
AM ˌækrəˈfoʊbiə

acrophobic
BR ˌakrə(ʊ)ˈfəʊbɪk, -s
AM ˌækrəˈfoʊbɪk, -s

acropolis
BR əˈkrɒpəlɪs, əˈkrɒpl̩ɪs, -ᵻz
AM əˈkrɑpələs, -əz

across
BR əˈkrɒs
AM əˈkrɔs, əˈkrɑs

acrostic
BR əˈkrɒstɪk, -s
AM əˈkrɔstɪk, əˈkrɑstɪk, -s

acrylic
BR əˈkrɪlɪk
AM əˈkrɪlɪk, æˈkrɪlɪk

acrylonitrate
BR ˌakrᵻləʊˈnʌɪtreɪt
AM ˌækrəloʊˈnaɪˌtreɪt

act
BR akt, -s, -ɪŋ, -ᵻd
AM æk|(t), -(t)s, -tɪŋ, -təd

acta
BR ˈaktə(r)
AM ˈæktə

actability
BR ˌaktəˈbɪlᵻti
AM ˌæktəˈbɪlᵻdi

actable
BR ˈaktəbl
AM ˈæktəbəl

Actaeon
BR akˈtiːən
AM ækˈtiən, ˈæktiˌɑn

actin
BR ˈaktɪn
AM ˈæktən

actinia
BR akˈtiːnɪə(r)
AM ækˈtiniə

actiniae
BR akˈtiːnɪiː
AM ækˈtiniˌi, ækˈtiniˌaɪ

actinic
BR akˈtɪnɪk
AM ækˈtɪnɪk

actinide
BR ˈaktᵻnʌɪd, -z
AM ˈæktəˌnaɪd, -z

actinism
BR ˈaktᵻnɪz(ə)m
AM ˈæktəˌnɪzəm

actinium
BR akˈtɪnɪəm
AM ækˈtɪniəm

actinometer
BR ˌaktᵻˈnɒmᵻtə(r), -z
AM ˌæktəˈnɑmədər, -z

actinomorphic
BR ˌaktᵻnə(ʊ)ˈmɔːfɪk
AM ˌæktənoʊˈmɔrfɪk

Actinomycetales
BR ˌaktᵻnəʊˌmʌɪsᵻˈteɪliːz
AM ˌæktənoʊˌmaɪsəˈteɪliz

actinomycete
BR ˌaktᵻnəʊˈmʌɪsiːt, ˌaktᵻnəʊˌmʌɪˈsiːt, -s
AM ˌæktənoʊˈmaɪˌsit, ˌæktənoʊˌmaɪˈsit, -s

action
BR ˈakʃn, -z
AM ˈækʃən, -z

actionable
BR ˈakʃn̩əbl, ˈakʃ(ə)nəbl
AM ˈækʃ(ə)nəbəl

actionably
BR ˈakʃn̩əbli, ˈakʃ(ə)nəbli
AM ˈækʃ(ə)nəbli

activate
BR ˈaktᵻveɪt, -s, -ɪŋ, -ᵻd
AM ˈæktəˌveɪ|t, -ts, -dɪŋ, -dᵻd

activation
BR ˌaktᵻˈveɪʃn
AM ˌæktəˈveɪʃən

activator
BR ˈaktᵻveɪtə(r), -z
AM ˈæktəˌveɪdər, -z

active
BR ˈaktɪv
AM ˈæktɪv

actively
BR ˈaktᵻvli
AM ˈæktᵻvli

activeness
BR ˈaktᵻvnᵻs
AM ˈæktᵻvnᵻs

activism
BR ˈaktᵻvɪz(ə)m
AM ˈæktəˌvɪzəm

activist
BR ˈaktᵻvɪst, -s
AM ˈæktəvəst, -s

activity
BR akˈtɪvᵻt|i, əkˈtɪvᵻt|i, -ɪz
AM ækˈtɪvᵻdi, -z

acton
BR ˈaktən, -z
AM ˈæktən, -z

actor
BR ˈaktə(r), -z
AM ˈæktər, -z

actress
BR ˈaktrᵻs, -ᵻz
AM ˈæktrəs, -əz

actressy
BR ˈaktrᵻsi
AM ˈæktrəsi

actual
BR ˈak(t)ʃʊəl, ˈak(t)ʃ(ᵿ)l
AM ˈæk(t)ʃ(əw)əl

actualisation
BR ˌak(t)ʃʊəlʌɪˈzeɪʃn, ˌak(t)ʃᵿlʌɪˈzeɪʃn, ˌak(t)ʃl̩ʌɪˈzeɪʃn
AM ˌæk(t)ʃ(əw)əˌlaɪˈzeɪʃən, ˌæk(t)ʃ(əw)ələˈzeɪʃən

actualise
BR ˈak(t)ʃʊəlʌɪz, ˈak(t)ʃᵿlʌɪz, ˈak(t)ʃl̩ʌɪz, -z, -ɪŋ, -d
AM ˈæk(t)ʃ(əw)əˌlaɪz, -ᵻz, -ɪŋ, -d

actuality
BR ˌaktʃʊˈalᵻti
AM ˌæk(t)ʃəˈwælədi

actualization
BR ˌak(t)ʃʊəlʌɪˈzeɪʃn, ˌak(t)ʃᵿlʌɪˈzeɪʃn, ˌak(t)ʃl̩ʌɪˈzeɪʃn
AM ˌæk(t)ʃ(əw)əˌlaɪˈzeɪʃən, ˌæk(t)ʃ(əw)ələˈzeɪʃən

actualize
BR ˈak(t)ʃʊəlʌɪz, ˈak(t)ʃᵿlʌɪz, ˈak(t)ʃl̩ʌɪz, -ᵻz, -ɪŋ, -d
AM ˈæk(t)ʃ(əw)əˌlaɪz, -ᵻz, -ɪŋ, -d

actually
BR ˈak(t)ʃʊəli, ˈak(t)ʃᵿli, ˈak(t)ʃl̩i
AM ˈæk(t)ʃ(əw)əli

actuarial
BR ˌaktʃʊˈɛːrɪəl
AM ˌæk(t)ʃəˈwɛriəl

actuarially
BR ˌaktʃʊˈɛːrɪəli
AM ˌæk(t)ʃəˈwɛriəli

actuary
BR ˈaktʃʊər|i, ˈaktʃɵr|i, -ɪz
AM ˈæk(t)ʃəˌwɛri, -z
actuate
BR ˈaktʃʊeɪt, -s, -ɪŋ, -ɪd
AM ˈæk(t)ʃəˌweɪ|t, -ts, -dɪŋ, -dɪd
actuation
BR ˌaktʃʊˈeɪʃn, -z
AM ˌæk(t)ʃəˈweɪʃən, -z
actuator
BR ˈaktʃʊeɪtə(r), -z
AM ˈæk(t)ʃəˌweɪdər, -z
acuity
BR əˈkjuːɪti
AM əˈkjuədi, æˈkjuədi
aculeate
BR əˈkjuːlɪət, -s
AM əˈkjuliət, əˈkjuliˌeɪt, -s
acumen
BR ˈakjɵmən
AM əˈkjumən, æˈkjumən, ˈækjəmən, ˈækjəˌmɛn
acuminate
BR əˈkjuːmɪnət
AM əˈkjumənət, əˈkjuməˌneɪt
acupressure
BR ˈakjɵˌprɛʃə(r)
AM ˈækjəˌprɛʃər, ˈækjuˌprɛʃər
acupuncture
BR ˈakjɵpʌŋ(k)tʃə(r)
AM ˈækjəˌpəŋk(t)ʃər, ˈækjuˌpəŋk(t)ʃər
acupuncturist
BR ˈakjɵpʌŋ(k)tʃ(ə)rɪst, -s
AM ˈækjəˌpəŋ(k)(t)ʃər-əst, ˈækjuˌpəŋ(k)(t)ʃərəst, -s
acushla
BR əˈkʊʃlə(r), -z
AM əˈkʊʃlə, -z
acute
BR əˈkjuːt, -ə(r), -ɪst
AM əˈkju|t, -dər, -dəst
acutely
BR əˈkjuːtli
AM əˈkjutli
acuteness
BR əˈkjuːtnəs
AM əˈkjutnəs
acyclic
BR (ˌ)eɪˈsʌɪklɪk
AM eɪˈsaɪklɪk
acyclovir
BR (ˌ)eɪˈsʌɪkləvɪə(r)
AM eɪˈsaɪkləˌvɪ(ə)r
acyl
BR ˈeɪsʌɪl, ˈasɪl
AM ˈæsəl, ˈæˌsil
ad
BR ad
AM æd
Ada
BR ˈeɪdə(r)
AM ˈeɪdə
adage
BR ˈad|ɪdʒ, -ɪdʒɪz
AM ˈædɪdʒ, -ɪz
adagio
BR əˈdɑːdʒɪəʊ, əˈdadʒɪəʊ, -z
AM əˈdɑ(d)ʒioʊ, -z
Adam
BR ˈadəm
AM ˈædəm
adamance
BR ˈadəm(ə)ns
AM ˈædəməns
adamancy
BR ˈadəm(ə)nsi
AM ˈædəmənsi
adamant
BR ˈadəm(ə)nt
AM ˈædəmənt
adamantine
BR ˌadəˈmantʌɪn
AM ˌædəˈmænˌtaɪn, ˌædəˈmæntn, ˌædəˈmænˌtin
adamantly
BR ˈadəm(ə)ntli
AM ˈædəmən(t)li
Adamite
BR ˈadəmʌɪt, -s
AM ˈædəˌmaɪt, -s
Adams
BR ˈadəmz
AM ˈædəmz
Adamson
BR ˈadəms(ə)n
AM ˈædəmsən
adapt
BR əˈdapt, -s, -ɪŋ, -ɪd
AM əˈdæpt, -s, -ɪŋ, -əd
adaptability
BR əˌdaptəˈbɪlɪti
AM əˌdæptəˈbɪlɪdi
adaptable
BR əˈdaptəbl
AM əˈdæptəbəl
adaptableness
BR əˈdaptəblnəs
AM əˈdæptəbəlnəs
adaptably
BR əˈdaptəbli
AM əˈdæptəbli
adaptation
BR ˌadəpˈteɪʃn, ˌadapˈteɪʃn, -z
AM ˌædæpˈteɪʃən, ˌædəpˈteɪʃən, -z
adapter
BR əˈdaptə(r), -z
AM əˈdæptər, -z
adaptive
BR əˈdaptɪv
AM əˈdæptɪv
adaptively
BR əˈdaptɪvli
AM əˈdæptɪvli
adaptiveness
BR əˈdaptɪvnɪs
AM əˈdæptɪvnɪs
adaptogen
BR əˈdaptədʒ(ə)n, -z
AM əˈdæptəˌdʒɛn, əˈdæptəgən, -z
adaptogenic
BR əˌdaptəˈdʒɛnɪk
AM əˌdæptəˈdʒɛnɪk
adaptor
BR əˈdaptə(r), -z
AM əˈdæptər, -z
adat
BR ˈadat
AM ɑˈdɑt
adaxial
BR aˈdaksɪəl
AM æˈdæksiəl
ad captandum vulgus
BR ˌad kapˌtandəm ˈvʌlgəs
AM ˌæd ˌkæpˌtændəm ˈvəlgəs
Adcock
BR ˈadkɒk
AM ˈædˌkɑk
add
BR ad, -z, -ɪŋ, -ɪd
AM æd, -z, -ɪŋ, -əd
Addams
BR ˈadəmz
AM ˈædəmz
addax
BR ˈadaks, -ɪz
AM ˈæˌdæks, -əz
addenda
BR əˈdɛndə(r)
AM əˈdɛndə
addendum
BR əˈdɛndəm
AM əˈdɛndəm
adder
BR ˈadə(r), -z
AM ˈædər, -z
addict[1]
noun
BR ˈadɪkt, -s
AM ˈædɪk(t), -s
addict[2]
verb
BR əˈdɪkt, -s, -ɪŋ, -ɪd
AM əˈdɪk(t), -s, -ɪŋ, -ɪd
addictedness
BR əˈdɪktɪdnɪs
AM əˈdɪktɪdnɪs
addiction
BR əˈdɪkʃn, -z
AM əˈdɪkʃən, -z
addictive
BR əˈdɪktɪv
AM əˈdɪktɪv
addictiveness
BR əˈdɪktɪvnɪs
AM əˈdɪktɪvnɪs
Addie
BR ˈadi
AM ˈædi
Addington
BR ˈadɪŋt(ə)n
AM ˈædɪŋtən
Addis Ababa
BR ˌadɪs ˈabəbə(r)
AM ˌædəs ˈæbəbə, ˌɑdəs ˈɑbəbə
Addison
BR ˈadɪs(ə)n
AM ˈædəsən
addition
BR əˈdɪʃn
AM əˈdɪʃən
additional
BR əˈdɪʃn̩(ə)l, əˈdɪʃən(ə)l
AM əˈdɪʃənl, əˈdɪʃnəl
additionality
BR əˌdɪʃəˈnalɪti
AM əˌdɪʃəˈnælədi
additionally
BR əˈdɪʃnəli, əˈdɪʃn̩l̩i, əˈdɪʃənl̩i, əˈdɪʃ(ə)nəli
AM əˈdɪʃ(ə)nəli
additive
BR ˈadɪtɪv, -z
AM ˈædədɪv, -z
addle
BR ˈad|l, -lz, -l̩ɪŋ\-lɪŋ, -ld
AM ˈæd|əl, -əlz, -(ə)lɪŋ, -əld
address
BR əˈdrɛs, -ɪz
AM əˈdrɛs, ˈæˌdrɛs, -əz
addressable
BR əˈdrɛsəbl
AM əˈdrɛsəbəl
addressee
BR ˌadrɛˈsiː, ˌadrəˈsiː, -z
AM ˌæˌdrɛˈsi, əˌdrɛˈsi, -z
addresser
BR əˈdrɛsə(r), -z
AM əˈdrɛsər, æˈdrɛsər, -z
Addressograph®
BR əˈdrɛsəgrɑːf, əˈdrɛsəgraf, -s
AM əˈdrɛsəˌgræf, -s
adduce
BR əˈdjuːs, əˈdʒuːs, -ɪz, -ɪŋ, -t
AM əˈd(j)us, -əz, -ɪŋ, -t
adducible
BR əˈdjuːsɪbl, əˈdʒuːsɪbl
AM əˈd(j)usəbəl
adduct
BR əˈdʌkt, -s, -ɪŋ, -ɪd

AM ə'dək|(t), -(t)s, -tɪŋ, -təd

adduction
BR ə'dʌkʃn
AM ə'dəkʃən

adductive
BR ə'dʌktɪv
AM ə'dəktɪv

adductor
BR ə'dʌktə(r), -z
AM ə'dəktər, -z

Addy
BR 'adi
AM 'ædi

Adela
BR ə'deɪlə(*r*), 'adɨlə(*r*), 'adḷə(*r*)
AM ə'dɛlə

Adelaide
BR 'adɨleɪd, 'adḷeɪd
AM 'ædl,eɪd

Adele
BR ə'dɛl
AM ə'dɛl

Adélie
BR ə'deɪli
AM ə'deɪli

Adelina
BR ,adɪ'liːnə(*r*), ,adl'iːnə(*r*)
AM ,ædɛ'linə

Adeline
BR 'adɨlʌɪn, 'adḷʌɪn
AM 'ædl,aɪn

Aden
BR 'eɪdn
AM 'eɪdən

Adenauer
BR 'adənaʊə(r), 'ɑːdənaʊə(r)
AM 'æd(ə)n,aʊər

Adeney
BR 'eɪdni
AM 'æd(ə)ni

adenine
BR 'adɨniːn, 'adɨnʌɪn
AM 'ædn,in, 'ædn,aɪn

adenocarcinoma
BR ,adɨnəʊ,kɑːsɪ'nəʊmə(*r*), ,adn̩əʊ,kɑːsɪ'nəʊmə(*r*), -z
AM ,ædn̩oʊ,kɑrsə'noʊmə

adenoid
BR 'adɨnɔɪd, 'adn̩ɔɪd, -z
AM 'ædn,ɔɪd, -z

adenoidal
BR ,adɪ'nɔɪdl, ,adn'ɔɪdl
AM ,ædn'ɔɪdəl

adenoidally
BR ,adɪ'nɔɪdḷi, ,adn'ɔɪdḷi
AM ,ædn'ɔɪd(ə)li

adenoids
BR 'adɨnɔɪdz, 'adn̩ɔɪdz
AM 'ædn,ɔɪdz

adenoma
BR ,adɪ'nəʊmə(*r*), ,adn'əʊmə(*r*), -z
AM ,ædn'oʊmə, -z

adenomata
BR ,adɪ'nəʊmətə(*r*), ,adn'əʊmətə(*r*)
AM ,ædn'oʊmədə

adenopathy
BR ,adɪ'nɒpəθi, ,adn'ɒpəθi
AM ,ædn'ɑpəθi

adenosine
BR ə'dɛnə(ʊ)siːn
AM ə'dɛnə,sin, ə'dɛnəsən

adept[1]
adjective
BR 'adɛpt, ə'dɛpt
AM ə'dɛpt

adept[2]
noun
BR 'adɛpt, -s
AM ə'dɛpt, -s

adeptly
BR 'adɛptli, ə'dɛptli
AM ə'dɛp(t)li

adeptness
BR 'adɛp(t)nəs, ə'dɛp(t)nəs
AM ə'dɛp(t)nəs

adequacy
BR 'adɨkwəsi
AM 'ædəkwəsi

adequate
BR 'adɨkwət
AM 'ædəkwət

adequately
BR 'adɨkwətli
AM 'ædəkwətli

adequateness
BR 'adɨkwətnəs
AM 'ædəkwətnəs

ad eundem
BR ,ad ɪ'ʌndəm
AM ,ædi 'əndəm

à deux
BR a 'dəː(*r*), ɑː +
AM ,ɑ 'də

ad fin
BR ,ad 'fɪn
AM ,æd 'fɪn

adhere
BR əd'hɪə(r), ad'hɪə(r), -z, -ɪŋ, -d
AM æd'hɪ(ə)r, əd'hɪ(ə)r, -z, -ɪŋ, -d

adherence
BR əd'hɪərəns, əd'hɪərn̩s, ad'hɪərəns, ad'hɪərn̩s
AM æd'hɪrəns, æd'hɛrəns, əd'hɪrəns, əd'hɛrəns

adherent
BR əd'hɪərənt, əd'hɪərn̩t, ad'hɪərənt, ad'hɪərn̩t, -s
AM æd'hɪrənt, æd'hɛrənt, əd'hɪrənt, əd'hɛrənt, -s

adhesion
BR əd'hiːʒn, ad'hiːʒn
AM æd'hiʒən, əd'hiʒən

adhesive
BR əd'hiːsɪv, əd'hiːzɪv, ad'hiːsɪv, ad'hiːzɪv
AM æd'hizɪv, əd'hizɪv, æd'hisɪv, əd'hisɪv

adhesively
BR əd'hiːsɨvli, əd'hiːzɨvli, ad'hiːsɨvli, ad'hiːzɨvli
AM æd'hizɨvli, əd'hizɨvli, æd'hisɨvli, əd'hisɨvli

adhesiveness
BR əd'hiːsɨvnɨs, əd'hiːzɨvnɨs, ad'hiːsɨvnɨs, ad'hiːzɨvnɨs
AM æd'hizɨvnɨs, əd'hizɨvnɨs, æd'hisɨvnɨs, əd'hisɨvnɨs

adhibit
BR əd'hɪb|ɪt, ad'hɪb|ɪt, -ɪts, -ɨtɪŋ, -ɨtɨd
AM æd'hɪbə|t, -ts, -dɪŋ, -dəd

adhibition
BR ,ad(h)ɪ'bɪʃn, -z
AM ,æd(h)ə'bɪʃən, -z

ad hoc
BR ,ad 'hɒk
AM ,æd 'hɑk, + 'hoʊk

adhocracy
BR ad'hɒkrəsi
AM ,æd'hɑkrəsi

ad hominem
BR ,ad 'hɒmɨnɛm
AM ,æd 'hɑmənəm

adiabatic
BR ,eɪdʌɪə'batɪk, ,adɪə'batɪk
AM ,eɪ,daɪə'bædɪk, ,ædɪə'bædɪk

adiabatically
BR ,eɪdʌɪə'batɨkli, ,adɪə'batɨkli
AM ,eɪ,daɪə'bædək(ə)li, ,ædɪə'bædək(ə)li

adiantum
BR ,adɪ'antəm, -z
AM ,ædi'æn(t)əm, -z

Adidas®
BR 'adɨdas, ə'diːdas
AM ə'didəs

Adie
BR 'eɪdi
AM 'eɪdi

adieu
BR ə'djuː, ə'dʒuː, -z
AM ə'd(j)u, -z

adieux
BR ə'djuːz, ə'dʒuːz
AM ə'd(j)u

Adi Granth
BR ,ɑːdɪ 'grʌnt
AM ,ɑdi 'grɑnt

ad infinitum
BR ,ad ɪnfɪ'nʌɪtəm
AM ,æd ,ɪnfə'naɪdəm

ad initium
BR ,ad ɪn'ɪʃɪəm
AM ,æd ,ɪn'ɪʃiəm

ad interim
BR ,ad 'ɪnt(ə)rɪm
AM ,æd 'ɪn(t)ərəm

adiós
BR ,adɪ'əʊs, ,adɪ'ɒs
AM ,ɑdi'oʊs, ,ædi'oʊs
SP a'ðjos

adipocere
BR ,adɨpə'sɪə(r)
AM ,ædəpoʊ'sɪ(ə)r

adipose
BR 'adɨpəʊs, 'adɨpəʊz
AM 'ædə,poʊs, 'ædə,poʊz

adiposity
BR ,adɪ'pɒsɨti
AM ,ædə'pɑsədi

Adirondack
BR ,adɪ'rɒndak, -s
AM ,ædə'rɑn,dæk, -s

adit
BR 'adɪt, -s
AM 'ædət, -s

Adivasi
BR ,ɑːdɪ'vɑːs|i, -ɪz
AM ,ædə'vɑsi, -z

adjacency
BR ə'dʒeɪs(ə)nsi
AM ə'dʒeɪsənsi

adjacent
BR ə'dʒeɪs(ə)nt
AM ə'dʒeɪsənt

adjacently
BR ə'dʒeɪs(ə)ntli
AM ə'dʒeɪsn(t)li

adjectival
BR ,adʒɪk'tʌɪvl
AM ,ædʒə(k)'taɪvəl

adjectivally
BR ,adʒɪk'tʌɪvḷi, ,adʒɪk'tʌɪvəli
AM ,ædʒə(k)'taɪvəli

adjective
BR 'adʒɪktɪv, -z
AM 'ædʒəktɪv, -z

adjoin
BR ə'dʒɔɪn, -z, -ɪŋ, -d
AM ə'dʒɔɪn, -z, -ɪŋ, -d

adjourn
BR ə'dʒəːn, -z, -ɪŋ, -d
AM ə'dʒərn, -z, -ɪŋ, -d

adjournment
BR ə'dʒəːnm(ə)nt, -s
AM ə'dʒərnmənt, -s

adjudge
BR ə'dʒʌdʒ, -ɪz, -ɪŋ, -d
AM ə'dʒədʒ, -əz, -ɪŋ, -d

adjudgement
BR ə'dʒʌdʒm(ə)nt, -s
AM ə'dʒədʒmənt, -s

adjudicate
BR ə'dʒu:dɪkeɪt, -s, -ɪŋ, -ɪd
AM ə'dʒudə,keɪ|t, -ts, -dɪŋ, -dɪd

adjudication
BR ə,dʒu:dɪ'keɪʃn
AM ə,dʒudə'keɪʃən

adjudicative
BR ə'dʒu:dɪkətɪv
AM ə'dʒudə,keɪdɪv

adjudicator
BR ə'dʒu:dɪkeɪtə(r), -z
AM ə'dʒudə,keɪdər, -z

adjunct
BR 'adʒʌŋ(k)t, -s
AM 'æ,dʒəŋ(k)t, 'æ,dʒəŋk(t), -s

adjunctive
BR ə'dʒʌŋ(k)tɪv, -z
AM ə'dʒəŋ(k)tɪv, æ'dʒəŋ(k)tɪv, -z

adjunctively
BR ə'dʒʌŋ(k)tɪvli
AM ə'dʒəŋ(k)tɪvli, æ'dʒəŋ(k)tɪvli

adjuration
BR ,adʒʊ'reɪʃn
AM ,ædʒə'reɪʃən

adjuratory
BR ə'dʒʊərət(ə)ri, ə'dʒɔ:rət(ə)ri
AM ə'dʒʊrə,tɔri, 'ædʒərə,tɔri

adjure
BR ə'dʒʊə(r), ə'dʒɔ:(r), -z, -ɪŋ, -d
AM ə'dʒʊ(ə)r, æ'dʒʊ(ə)r, -z, -ɪŋ, -d

adjust
BR ə'dʒʌst, -s, -ɪŋ, -ɪd
AM ə'dʒəst, -s, -ɪŋ, -əd

adjustability
BR ə,dʒʌstə'bɪlɪti
AM ə,dʒəstə'bɪlɪdi

adjustable
BR ə'dʒʌstəbl
AM ə'dʒəstəbəl

adjuster
BR ə'dʒʌstə(r), -z
AM ə'dʒəstər, -z

adjustment
BR ə'dʒʌs(t)m(ə)nt, -s
AM ə'dʒəs(t)mənt, -s

adjutage
BR 'adʒʊtɪdʒ, ə'dʒu:tɪdʒ
AM 'ædʒədɪdʒ, ə'dʒudɪdʒ

adjutancy
BR 'adʒʊt(ə)nsi
AM 'ædʒədənsi, 'ædʒətnsi

adjutant
BR 'adʒʊt(ə)nt, -s
AM 'ædʒədənt, 'ædʒətnt, -s

adjuvant
BR 'adʒʊv(ə)nt, -s
AM 'ædʒəvənt, -s

Adkins
BR 'adkɪnz
AM 'ædkɪnz

Adlai
BR 'adlʌɪ
AM 'æd,laɪ

Adler
BR 'adlə(r)
AM 'ædlər

Adlerian
BR ad'lɪərɪən, -z
AM æd'lɪriən, æd'lɛriən, -z

ad lib
BR ,ad 'lɪb, -z, -ɪŋ, -d
AM ,æd 'lɪb, -z, -ɪŋ, -d

ad libitum
BR ,ad 'lɪbɪtəm
AM ,æd 'lɪbədəm

ad litem
BR ,ad 'lʌɪtəm
AM ,æd 'laɪdəm

adman
BR 'adman
AM 'æd,mæn

admass
BR 'admas
AM 'æd,mæs

admeasure
BR ad'mɛʒ|ə(r), -əz, -(ə)rɪŋ, -əd
AM æd'mɛʒər, -z, -ɪŋ, -d

admeasurement
BR ad'mɛʒəm(ə)nt, -s
AM æd'mɛʒərmənt, -s

admen
BR 'admɛn
AM 'æd,mɛn

admin
BR 'admɪn
AM 'æd,mɪn

adminicle
BR əd'mɪnɪkl, -z
AM əd'mɪnəkəl, æd'mɪnəkəl, -z

adminicular
BR ,admɪ'nɪkjʊlə(r)
AM ,ædmə'nɪkjələr

administer
BR əd'mɪnɪst|ə(r), -əz, -(ə)rɪŋ, -əd
AM əd'mɪnɪst|ər, -ərz, -(ə)rɪŋ, -ərd

administrable
BR əd'mɪnɪstrəbl
AM əd'mɪnɪstrəbəl

administrant
BR əd'mɪnɪstr(ə)nt, -s
AM əd'mɪnɪstrənt, -s

administrate
BR əd'mɪnɪstreɪt, -s, -ɪŋ, -ɪd
AM əd'mɪnɪ,streɪ|t, -ts, -dɪŋ, -dɪd

administration
BR əd,mɪnɪ'streɪʃn, -z
AM əd,mɪnə'streɪʃən, -z

administrative
BR əd'mɪnɪstrətɪv
AM əd'mɪnə,streɪdɪv, əd'mɪnəstrədɪv

administratively
BR əd'mɪnɪstrətɪvli
AM əd'mɪnə,streɪdɪvli

administrator
BR əd'mɪnɪstreɪtə(r), -z
AM əd'mɪnə,streɪdər, -z

administratorship
BR əd'mɪnɪstreɪtəʃɪp, -s
AM əd'mɪnə,streɪdər,ʃɪp, -s

administratrices
BR əd,mɪnɪ'streɪtrɪsi:z
AM əd,mɪnə'streɪtrə,siz

administratrix
BR əd'mɪnɪstreɪtrɪks, -ɪz
AM əd'mɪnə,streɪtrɪks, -ɪz

admirable
BR 'adm(ə)rəbl
AM 'ædm(ə)rəbəl

admirableness
BR 'adm(ə)rəblnəs
AM 'ædm(ə)rəbəlnəs

admirably
BR 'adm(ə)rəbli
AM 'ædm(ə)rəbli

admiral
BR 'adm(ə)rəl, 'adm(ə)rḷ, -z
AM 'ædm(ə)rəl, -z

admiralship
BR 'adm(ə)rəlʃɪp, 'adm(ə)rḷʃɪp, -s
AM 'ædm(ə)rəl,ʃɪp, -s

admiralty
BR 'adm(ə)rəlt|i, 'adm(ə)rḷt|i, -ɪz
AM 'ædm(ə)rəlti, -z

admiration
BR ,admɪ'reɪʃn
AM ,ædmə'reɪʃən

admire
BR əd'mʌɪə(r), -z, -ɪŋ, -d
AM əd'maɪ(ə)r, -z, -ɪŋ, -d

admirer
BR əd'mʌɪərə(r), -z
AM əd'maɪ(ə)rər, -z

admiringly
BR əd'mʌɪərɪŋli
AM əd'maɪ(ə)rɪŋli

admissibility
BR əd,mɪsɪ'bɪlɪti
AM əd,mɪsə'bɪlɪdi

admissible
BR əd'mɪsɪbl
AM əd'mɪsəbəl

admission
BR əd'mɪʃn, -z
AM əd'mɪʃən, -z

admissive
BR əd'mɪsɪv
AM əd'mɪsɪv

admit
BR əd'mɪt, -s, -ɪŋ, -ɪd
AM əd'mɪ|t, -ts, -dɪŋ, -dɪd

admittable
BR əd'mɪtəbl
AM əd'mɪdəbəl

admittance
BR əd'mɪt(ə)ns
AM əd'mɪtns

admittedly
BR əd'mɪtɪdli
AM əd'mɪdɪdli

admix
BR əd'mɪks, ad'mɪks, -ɪz, -ɪŋ, -t
AM æd'mɪks, -ɪz, -ɪŋ, -t

admixture
BR əd'mɪkstʃə(r), ad'mɪkstʃə(r), -z
AM æd'mɪkstʃər, -z

admonish
BR əd'mɒn|ɪʃ, -ɪʃɪz, -ɪʃɪŋ, -ɪʃt
AM əd'mɑnɪʃ, -ɪz, -ɪŋ, -t

admonishment
BR əd'mɒnɪʃm(ə)nt, -s
AM əd'mɑnɪʃmənt, -s

admonition
BR ,admə'nɪʃn, -z
AM ,ædmə'nɪʃən, -z

admonitory
BR əd'mɒnɪt(ə)ri
AM əd'mɑnə,tɔri

adnate
BR 'adneɪt
AM 'æd,neɪt

ad nauseam
BR ,ad 'nɔ:zɪam
AM ,æd 'nɔziəm, + 'nɑziəm

adnexa
BR ad'nɛksə(r)
AM æd'nɛksə

adnexal
BR ad'nɛksl
AM æd'nɛks(ə)l

adnominal
BR ad'nɒmɪnl
AM æd'nɑmənəl

ado
BR ə'du:
AM ə'du

adobe
BR ə'dəʊbi
AM ə'doʊbi
adolescence
BR ˌadə'lɛsns
AM ˌædl'ɛsəns
adolescent
BR ˌadə'lɛsnt, -s
AM ˌædl'ɛsənt, -s
adolescently
BR ˌadə'lɛsntli
AM ˌædl'ɛsn(t)li
Adonis
BR ə'dəʊnɪs, -ɪz
AM ə'dɑnəs, -əz
adopt
BR ə'dɒpt, -s, -ɪŋ, -ɪd
AM ə'dɑpt, -s, -ɪŋ, -əd
adoptee
BR əˌdɒp'tiː, -z
AM əˌdɑp'ti, -z
adopter
BR ə'dɒptə(r), -z
AM ə'dɑptər, -z
adoption
BR ə'dɒpʃn, -z
AM ə'dɑpʃən, -z
adoptive
BR ə'dɒptɪv
AM ə'dɑptɪv
adoptively
BR ə'dɒptɪvli
AM ə'dɑptɪvli
adorable
BR ə'dɔːrəbl
AM ə'dɔrəbəl
adorably
BR ə'dɔːrəbli
AM ə'dɔrəbli
adoral
BR ad'ɔːrəl ad'ɔːrl̩
AM æd'ɔrəl
adoration
BR ˌadə'reɪʃn
AM ˌædə'reɪʃən, ˌædɔ'reɪʃən
adore
BR ə'dɔː(r), -z, -ɪŋ, -d
AM ə'dɔ(ə)r, -z, -ɪŋ, -d
adorer
BR ə'dɔːrə(r), -z
AM ə'dɔrər, -z
adoringly
BR ə'dɔːrɪŋli
AM ə'dɔrɪŋli
adorn
BR ə'dɔːn, -z, -ɪŋ, -d
AM ə'dɔ(ə)rn, -z, -ɪŋ, -d
adornment
BR ə'dɔːnm(ə)nt, -s
AM ə'dɔrnmənt, -s
adown
BR ə'daʊn
AM ə'daʊn
ad personam
BR ˌad pə'səʊnam
AM ˌæd pər'soʊnəm
ad rem
BR ˌad 'rɛm
AM ˌæd 'rɛm
adrenal
BR ə'driːnl
AM ə'drinəl
adrenalin
BR ə'drɛnəlɪn, ə'drɛnl̩ɪn
AM ə'drɛnl̩ən
adrenaline
BR ə'drɛnəlɪn, ə'drɛnl̩ɪn
AM ə'drɛnl̩ən
adrenocorticotrophic
BR əˌdriːnəʊˌkɔːtɪkə(ʊ)'trɒfɪk, əˌdriːnəʊˌkɔːtɪkə(ʊ)'trəʊfɪk, əˌdrɛnəʊˌkɔːtɪkə(ʊ)'trɒfɪk, əˌdrɛnəʊˌkɔːtɪkə(ʊ)'trəʊfɪk
AM əˌdrinoʊˌkɔrdəkoʊ'trɑfɪk
adrenocorticotrophin
BR əˌdriːnəʊˌkɔːtɪkə(ʊ)'trəʊfɪn, əˌdrɛnəʊˌkɔːtɪkə(ʊ)'trəʊfɪn
AM əˌdrinoʊˌkɔrdəkoʊ'troʊfən
adrenocorticotropic
BR əˌdriːnəʊˌkɔːtɪkə(ʊ)'trɒpɪk, əˌdriːnəʊˌkɔːtɪkə(ʊ)'trəʊpɪk, əˌdrɛnəʊˌkɔːtɪkə(ʊ)'trɒpɪk, əˌdrɛnəʊˌkɔːtɪkə(ʊ)'trəʊpɪk
AM əˌdrinoʊˌkɔrdəkoʊ'trɑpɪk
Adrian
BR 'eɪdrɪən
AM 'eɪdriən
Adrianne
BR ˌadrɪ'an
AM ˌeɪdri'æn
Adriatic
BR ˌeɪdrɪ'atɪk
AM ˌeɪdri'ædɪk
Adrienne
BR ˌeɪdrɪ'ɛn, 'eɪdrɪən
AM ˌeɪdri'ɛn
adrift
BR ə'drɪft
AM ə'drɪft
adroit
BR ə'drɔɪt, -ɪst
AM ə'drɔɪ|t, -dɪst
adroitly
BR ə'drɔɪtli
AM ə'drɔɪtli
adroitness
BR ə'drɔɪtnɨs
AM ə'drɔɪtnɨs
adscititious
BR ˌadsɪ'tɪʃəs
AM ˌædsə'tɪʃəs
adsorb
BR ad'zɔːb, əd'zɔːb, ad'sɔːb, əd'sɔːb
AM æd'zɔ(ə)rb, æd'sɔ(ə)rb
adsorbable
BR ad'zɔːbəbl, əd'zɔːbəbl, ad'sɔːbəbl, əd'sɔːbəbl
AM æd'zɔrbəbəl, æd'sɔrbəbəl
adsorbate
BR ad'zɔːbət, ad'sɔːbət, ad'zɔːbeɪt, ad'sɔːbeɪt, əd'zɔːbət, əd'sɔːbət, əd'zɔːbeɪt, əd'sɔːbeɪt, -s
AM æd'zɔrbət, æd'sɔrbət, æd'zɔrˌbeɪt, æd'sɔrˌbeɪt, -s
adsorbent
BR ad'zɔːb(ə)nt, əd'zɔːb(ə)nt, ad'sɔːb(ə)nt, əd'sɔːb(ə)nt
AM æd'zɔrbənt, æd'sɔrbənt
adsorption
BR ad'zɔːpʃn, əd'zɔːpʃn, ad'sɔːpʃn, əd'sɔːpʃn
AM æd'zɔrbʃən, æd'sɔrpʃən
adsorptive
BR ad'zɔːptɪv, əd'zɔːptɪv, ad'sɔːptɪv, əd'sɔːptɪv
AM æd'zɔrptɪv, æd'sɔrptɪv
adsuki
BR ad'suːk|i, -ɪz
AM æd'suki, -z
adsum
BR 'adsʊm, 'adsʌm
AM 'ædˌsəm
adulate
BR 'adjʊleɪt, 'adʒʊleɪt, -s, -ɪŋ, -ɪd
AM 'ædʒəˌleɪ|t, 'ædjəˌleɪ|t, -ts, -dɪŋ, -dɪd
adulation
BR ˌadjʊ'leɪʃn, ˌadʒʊ'leɪʃn
AM ˌædʒə'leɪʃən, ˌædjə'leɪʃən
adulator
BR 'adjʊleɪtə(r) 'adʒʊleɪtə(r), -z
AM 'ædʒəˌleɪdər, 'ædjəˌleɪdər, -z
adulatory
BR ˌadjʊ'leɪt(ə)ri, ˌadʒʊ'leɪt(ə)ri, 'adjʊlət(ə)ri, 'adʒʊlət(ə)ri
AM 'ædʒələˌtɔri, 'ædjələˌtɔri
Adullamite
BR ə'dʌləmʌɪt, -s
AM ə'dələˌmaɪt, -s
adult
BR 'adʌlt, ə'dʌlt, -s
AM ə'dəlt, 'æˌdəlt, -s
adulterant
BR ə'dʌlt(ə)rənt, ə'dʌlt(ə)rn̩t, -s
AM ə'dəlt(ə)rənt, -s
adulterate
BR ə'dʌltəreɪt, -s, -ɪŋ, -ɪd
AM ə'dəltəˌreɪ|t, -ts, -dɪŋ, -dɪd
adulteration
BR əˌdʌltə'reɪʃn, -z
AM əˌdəltə'reɪʃən, -z
adulterator
BR ə'dʌltəreɪtə(r), -z
AM ə'dəltəˌreɪdər, -z
adulterer
BR ə'dʌlt(ə)rə(r), -z
AM ə'dəltərər, -z
adulteress
BR ə'dʌltrɪs, -ɪz
AM ə'dəlt(ə)rəs, -əz
adulterine
BR ə'dʌlt(ə)rʌɪn
AM ə'dəltərən, ə'dəltəˌrin, ə'dəltəˌraɪn
adulterous
BR ə'dʌlt(ə)rəs
AM ə'dəlt(ə)rəs
adulterously
BR ə'dʌlt(ə)rəsli
AM ə'dəlt(ə)rəsli
adulterousness
BR ə'dʌlt(ə)rəsnəs
AM ə'dəlt(ə)rəsnəs
adultery
BR ə'dʌlt(ə)r|i, -ɪz
AM ə'dəlt(ə)ri, -z
adulthood
BR 'adʌlthʊd, ə'dʌlthʊd
AM ə'dəltˌ(h)ʊd
adultly
BR 'adʌltli, ə'dʌltli
AM ə'dəltli
adultness
BR 'adʌltnəs, ə'dʌltnəs
AM ə'dəltnəs
adumbrate
BR 'adʌmbreɪt, 'adəmbreɪt, -s, -ɪŋ, -ɪd
AM 'ædəmˌbreɪ|t, ə'dəmˌbreɪ|t, -ts, -dɪŋ, -dɪd

adumbration
BR ˌadʌmˈbreɪʃn, ˌadəmˈbreɪʃn
AM ˌædəmˈbreɪʃən

adumbrative
BR ˈadʌmbreɪtɪv, ˈadəmbreɪtɪv
AM ˈædəmˌbreɪdɪv, əˈdəmbrədɪv

ad valorem
BR ˌad vəˈlɔːrɛm
AM ˌæd vəˈlɔrəm

advance
BR ədˈvɑːns, ədˈvans, -ɪz, -ɪŋ, -t
AM ədˈvæns, -əz, -ɪŋ, -t

advancement
BR ədˈvɑːnsm(ə)nt, ədˈvansm(ə)nt, -s
AM ədˈvænsmənt, -s

advancer
BR ədˈvɑːnsə(r), ədˈvansə(r), -z
AM ədˈvænsər, -z

advantage
BR ədˈvɑːnt|ɪdʒ, ədˈvant|ɪdʒ, -ɪdʒɪz, -ɪdʒɪŋ, -ɪdʒd
AM ədˈvæn(t)ɪdʒ, -ɪz, -ɪŋ, -d

advantageous
BR ˌadv(ə)nˈteɪdʒəs, ˌadvɑːnˈteɪdʒəs, ˌadvanˈteɪdʒəs
AM ˌædˌvænˈteɪdʒəs, ˌædvənˈteɪdʒəs

advantageously
BR ˌadv(ə)nˈteɪdʒəsli, ˌadvɑːnˈteɪdʒəsli, ˌadvanˈteɪdʒəsli
AM ˌædˌvænˈteɪdʒəsli, ˌædvənˈteɪdʒəsli

advantageousness
BR ˌadv(ə)nˈteɪdʒəsnəs, ˌadvɑːnˈteɪdʒəsnəs, ˌadvanˈteɪdʒəsnəs
AM ˌædˌvænˈteɪdʒəsnəs, ˌædvənˈteɪdʒəsnəs

advect
BR adˈvɛkt, ədˈvɛkt, -s, -ɪŋ, -ɪd
AM ædˈvɛk|(t), -(t)s, -tɪŋ, -təd

advection
BR adˈvɛkʃn, ədˈvɛkʃn
AM ædˈvɛkʃən

advective
BR adˈvɛktɪv, ədˈvɛktɪv
AM ædˈvɛktɪv

advent
BR ˈadv(ə)nt, ˈadvɛnt, -s
AM ˈædˌvɛnt, -s

Adventism
BR ˈadv(ə)ntɪz(ə)m
AM ˈædˌvɛnˌtɪzəm

Adventist
BR ˈadv(ə)ntɪst, -s
AM ˈædˌvɛn(t)əst, -s

adventitious
BR ˌadv(ə)nˈtɪʃəs, ˌadvɛnˈtɪʃəs
AM ˌædˌvɛnˈtɪʃəs

adventitiously
BR ˌadv(ə)nˈtɪʃəsli, ˌadvɛnˈtɪʃəsli
AM ˌædˌvɛnˈtɪʃəsli

adventure
BR ədˈvɛn(t)ʃə(r), -z
AM ədˈvɛn(t)ʃər, -z

adventurer
BR ədˈvɛn(t)ʃ(ə)rə(r), -z
AM ədˈvɛn(t)ʃərər, -z

adventuresome
BR ədˈvɛn(t)ʃəs(ə)m
AM ədˈvɛn(t)ʃərsəm

adventuress
BR ədˈvɛn(t)ʃ(ə)rɪs, -ɪz
AM ədˈvɛn(t)ʃ(ə)rəs, -əz

adventurism
BR ədˈvɛn(t)ʃərɪz(ə)m, -z
AM ədˈvɛn(t)ʃəˌrɪzəm, -z

adventurist
BR adˈvɛn(t)ʃ(ə)rɪst, -s
AM ədˈvɛn(t)ʃəˌrɪst, -s

adventurous
BR ədˈvɛn(t)ʃ(ə)rəs
AM ədˈvɛn(t)ʃ(ə)rəs

adventurously
BR ədˈvɛn(t)ʃ(ə)rəsli
AM ədˈvɛn(t)ʃ(ə)rəsli

adventurousness
BR ədˈvɛn(t)ʃ(ə)rəsnəs
AM ədˈvɛn(t)ʃ(ə)rəsnəs

adverb
BR ˈadvəːb, -z
AM ˈædˌvərb, -z

adverbial
BR ədˈvəːbɪəl, adˈvəːbɪəl, -z
AM ədˈvərbiəl, ædˈvərbiəl, -z

adverbially
BR ədˈvəːbɪəli, adˈvəːbɪəli
AM ədˈvərbiəli, ædˈvərbiəli

ad verbum
BR ˌad ˈvəːbəm
AM ˌæd ˈvərbəm, + ˈwɛrbəm

adversarial
BR ˌadvəˈsɛːrɪəl
AM ˌædvərˈsɛriəl

adversary
BR ˈadvəs(ə)r|i, ədˈvəːs(ə)r|i, -ɪz
AM ˈædvərˌsɛri, -z

adversative
BR ədˈvəːsətɪv, -z
AM ədˈvərsədɪv, -z

adversatively
BR ədˈvəːsətɪvli
AM ədˈvərsədɪvli

adverse
BR ˈadvəːs, ədˈvəːs
AM ˌædˈvərs, ədˈvərs

adversely
BR ˈadvəːsli, ədˈvəːsli
AM ˌædˈvərsli, ədˈvərsli

adverseness
BR ˈadvəːsnəs, ədˈvəːsnəs
AM ˌædˈvərsnəs, ədˈvərsnəs

adversity
BR ədˈvəːsɪt|i, -ɪz
AM ædˈvərsədi, ədˈvərsədi, -z

advert[1]
advertisement
BR ˈadvəːt, -s
AM ˈædˌvərt, -s

advert[2]
verb
BR ədˈvəːt, -s, -ɪŋ, -ɪd
AM ædˈvər|t, ədˈvər|t, -ts, -dɪŋ, -dəd

advertence
BR ədˈvəːt(ə)ns
AM ædˈvərtns, ədˈvərtns

advertency
BR ədˈvəːt(ə)nsi
AM ædˈvərtnsi, ədˈvərtnsi

advertent
BR ədˈvəːt(ə)nt
AM ædˈvərtnt, ədˈvərtnt

advertently
BR ədˈvəːt(ə)ntli
AM ædˈvərtn(t)li, ədˈvərtn(t)li

advertise
BR ˈadvətʌɪz, -ɪz, -ɪŋ, -d
AM ˈædvərˌtaɪz, -ɪz, -ɪŋ, -d

advertisement
BR ədˈvəːtɪsm(ə)nt, ədˈvəːtɪzm(ə)nt, -s
AM ˌædvərˈtaɪzmənt, ədˈvərdəzmənt, -s

advertiser
BR ˈadvətʌɪzə(r), -z
AM ˈædvərˌtaɪzər, -z

advertize
BR ˈadvətʌɪz, -ɪz, -ɪŋ, -d
AM ˈædvərˌtaɪz, -ɪz, -ɪŋ, -d

advertizer
BR ˈadvətʌɪzə(r), -z
AM ˈædvərˌtaɪzər, -z

advertorial
BR ˌadvəˈtɔːrɪəl, -z
AM ˌædvərˈtɔriəl, -z

advice
BR ədˈvʌɪs
AM ədˈvaɪs

advisability
BR ədˌvʌɪzəˈbɪlɪti
AM ədˌvaɪzəˈbɪlɪdi

advisable
BR ədˈvʌɪzəbl
AM ədˈvaɪzəbəl

advisableness
BR ədˈvʌɪzəblnəs
AM ədˈvaɪzəbəlnəs

advisably
BR ədˈvʌɪzəbli
AM ədˈvaɪzəbli

advise
BR ədˈvʌɪz, -ɪz, -ɪŋ, -d
AM ədˈvaɪz, -ɪz, -ɪŋ, -d

advisedly
BR ədˈvʌɪzɪdli
AM ədˈvaɪzɪdli

advisee
BR ədˌvʌɪˈziː, -z
AM ədˌvaɪˈzi, -z

adviser
BR ədˈvʌɪzə(r), -z
AM ədˈvaɪzər, -z

advisor
BR ədˈvʌɪzə(r), -z
AM ədˈvaɪzər, -z

advisory
BR ədˈvʌɪz(ə)ri
AM ədˈvaɪzəri

advocaat
BR ˈadvəkɑː(*r*), -z
AM ˈædvoʊˌkɑ|(t), -z\-ts

advocacy
BR ˈadvəkəsi
AM ˈædvəkəsi

advocate[1]
noun
BR ˈadvəkət, -s
AM ˈædvəkət, -s

advocate[2]
verb
BR ˈadvəkeɪt, -s, -ɪŋ, -ɪd
AM ˈædvəˌkeɪ|t, -ts, -dɪŋ, -dɪd

advocateship
BR ˈadvəkətʃɪp, -s
AM ˈædvəkətˌʃɪp, -s

advocation
BR ˌadvəˈkeɪʃn
AM ˌædvəˈkeɪʃən

advocatory
BR ədˈvɒkət(ə)ri
AM ædˈvɑkəˌtɔri

advokaat
BR ˈadvəkɑː(*r*), -z
AM ˈædvoʊˌkɑ|(t), -z\-ts

advowson
BR ədˈvaʊzn, -z
AM ədˈvaʊzn, ædˈvaʊzn, -z

advt.
BR əd'vəːtɪsm(ə)nt, əd'vəːtɪzm(ə)nt
AM ˈædvərˈtaɪzmənt, əd'vərdəzmənt

adyta
BR 'adɪtə(r)
AM 'ædədə, 'ædətə

adytum
BR 'adɪtəm
AM 'ædədəm, 'ædəˌtəm

adz
BR adz, -ɪz, -ɪŋ, -d
AM ædz, -əz, -ɪŋ, -d

adze
BR adz, -ɪz, -ɪŋ, -d
AM ædz, -əz, -ɪŋ, -d

adzuki
BR ad'zuːk|i, -ɪz
AM æd'zuki, -z

aedes
BR eɪ'iːdiːz
AM eɪ'idiz

aedile
BR 'iːdʌɪl, -z
AM 'iˌdaɪl, -z

aedileship
BR 'iːdʌɪlʃɪp, -s
AM 'iˌdaɪlˌʃɪp, -s

Aegean
BR iː'dʒiːən, ɪ'dʒiːən
AM ə'dʒiən, eɪ'dʒiən

aegis
BR 'iːdʒɪs
AM 'idʒɪs, 'eɪdʒɪs

Aegisthus
BR ɪ'dʒɪsθəs
AM ə'dʒɪsθəs, i'dʒɪsθəs

aegrotat
BR 'ʌɪgrə(ʊ)tat, 'iːgrə(ʊ)tat, -s
AM i'groʊˌtɑt, 'igroʊˌtɑt, -s

aelectasis
BR ˌatɪ'lɛktəsɪs
AM ˌædə'lɛktəsɪs

Aelfric
BR 'alfrɪk
AM 'ælfrɪk

Aeneas
BR iː'niːəs, ɪ'niːəs
AM ə'niəs

Aeneid
BR 'iːnɪɪd, iː'niːɪd, ɪ'niːɪd
AM ə'niəd

aeolian
BR ɪ'əʊlɪən, eɪ'əʊlɪən
AM i'oʊljən, eɪ'oʊljən, i'oʊliən, eɪ'oʊliən

Aeolic
BR ɪ'ɒlɪk, ɪ'əʊlɪk
AM i'oʊlɪk, eɪ'oʊlɪk

aeolotropy
BR ˌiːə(ʊ)'lɒtrəpi
AM ˌiə'lɑtrəpi

Aeolus
BR ɪ'əʊləs, 'iːələs
AM i'oʊləs, eɪ'oʊləs

aeon
BR 'iːən, 'iːɒn, -z
AM 'iən, 'iˌɑn, -z

aeonian
BR ɪ'əʊnɪən
AM i'oʊniən

aepyornis
BR ˌiːpɪ'ɔːnɪs, -ɪz
AM ˌipi'ɔrnəs, -əz

aerate
BR ɛː'reɪt, -s, -ɪŋ, -ɪd
AM 'ɛˌreɪ|t, -ts, -dɪŋ, -dɪd

aeration
BR ɛː'reɪʃn
AM ɛ'reɪʃən

aerator
BR ɛː'reɪtə(r), -z
AM 'ɛˌreɪdər, -z

aerenchyma
BR ɛː'rɛŋkɪmə(r), -z
AM ɛ'rɛŋkəmə, -z

aerial
BR 'ɛːrɪəl, -z
AM 'ɛriəl, -z

aerialist
BR 'ɛːrɪəlɪst, -s
AM 'ɛriələst, -s

aeriality
BR ˌɛːrɪ'alɪti
AM ˌɛri'ælədi

aerially
BR 'ɛːrɪəli
AM 'ɛriəli

aerie
BR 'ɪər|i, 'ɛːr|i, 'ʌɪr|i, -ɪz
AM 'ɛri, 'ɪri, 'iri, 'eɪri, -z

aeriform
BR 'ɛːrɪfɔːm
AM 'ɛrəˌfɔ(ə)rm

Aer Lingus®
BR ˌɛː 'lɪŋgəs
AM 'ɛr 'lɪŋgəs

aero
BR 'ɛːrəʊ, -z
AM 'ɛroʊ, -z

aerobatic
BR ˌɛːrə(ʊ)'batɪk, -s
AM ˌɛroʊ'bædɪk, ˌɛrə'bædɪk, -s

aerobe
BR 'ɛːrəʊb, -z
AM 'ɛˌroʊb, -z

aerobic
BR ɛː'rəʊbɪk, -s
AM ə'roʊbɪk, ɛ'roʊbɪk, -s

aerobically
BR ɛː'rəʊbɪkli
AM ə'roʊbəkli, ɛ'roʊbəkli

aerobiologist
BR ˌɛːrə(ʊ)bʌɪ'ɒlədʒɪst, -s
AM ˌɛroʊˌbaɪ'ɑlədʒəst, ˌɛrəˌbaɪ'ɑlədʒəst, -s

aerobiology
BR ˌɛːrə(ʊ)bʌɪ'ɒlədʒi
AM ˌɛroʊˌbaɪ'ɑlədʒi, ˌɛrəˌbaɪ'ɑlədʒi

aerodrome
BR 'ɛːrədrəʊm, -z
AM 'ɛroʊˌdroʊm, 'ɛrəˌdroʊm, -z

aerodynamic
BR ˌɛːrə(ʊ)dʌɪ'namɪk, -s
AM ˌɛroʊˌdaɪ'næmɪk, ˌɛrəˌdaɪ'næmɪk, -s

aerodynamically
BR ˌɛːrə(ʊ)dʌɪ'namɪkli
AM ˌɛroʊˌdaɪ'næmək(ə)li, ˌɛrəˌdaɪ'næmək(ə)li

aerodynamicist
BR ˌɛːrə(ʊ)dʌɪ'namɪsɪst, -s
AM ˌɛroʊˌdaɪ'næməsəst, ˌɛrəˌdaɪ'næməsəst, -s

aerodyne
BR 'ɛːrə(ʊ)dʌɪn, -z
AM 'ɛroʊˌdaɪn, 'ɛrəˌdaɪn, -z

aero-engine
BR 'ɛːrəʊˌɛn(d)ʒ(ɪ)n, -z
AM 'ɛroʊˌɛndʒən, 'ɛrəˌɛndʒən, -z

Aeroflot®
BR 'ɛːrə(ʊ)flɒt
AM 'ɛroʊˌflɑt, 'ɛrəˌflɑt
RUS əira'flot

aerofoil
BR 'ɛːrə(ʊ)fɔɪl, -z
AM 'ɛroʊˌfɔɪl, 'ɛrəˌfɔɪl, -z

aerogram
BR 'ɛːrə(ʊ)gram, -z
AM 'ɛroʊˌgræm, 'ɛrəˌgræm, -z

aerogramme
BR 'ɛːrə(ʊ)gram, -z
AM 'ɛroʊˌgræm, 'ɛrəˌgræm, -z

aerolite
BR 'ɛːrə(ʊ)lʌɪt, -s
AM 'ɛroʊˌlaɪt, 'ɛrəˌlaɪt, -s

aerological
BR ˌɛːrə'lɒdʒɪkl
AM ˌɛroʊ'lɑdʒəkəl, ˌɛrə'lɑdʒəkəl

aerologist
BR ɛː'rɒlədʒɪst, -s
AM ɛ'rɑlədʒəst, -s

aerology
BR ɛː'rɒlədʒi
AM ɛ'rɑlədʒi

aeromagnetic
BR ˌɛːrə(ʊ)mag'nɛtɪk
AM ˌɛroʊmæg'nɛdɪk, ˌɛrəmæg'nɛdɪk

aeronaut
BR 'ɛːrə(ʊ)nɔːt, -s
AM 'ɛroʊˌnɔt, 'ɛrəˌnɔt, 'ɛroʊˌnɑt, 'ɛrəˌnɑt, -s

aeronautic
BR ˌɛːrə(ʊ)'nɔːtɪk, -s
AM ˌɛroʊ'nɔdɪk, ˌɛrə'nɔdɪk, ˌɛroʊ'nɑdɪk, ˌɛrə'nɑdɪk, -s

aeronautical
BR ˌɛːrə(ʊ)'nɔːtɪkl
AM ˌɛroʊ'nɔdəkəl, ˌɛrə'nɔdəkəl, ˌɛroʊ'nɑdəkəl, ˌɛrə'nɑdəkəl

aeronautically
BR ˌɛːrə(ʊ)'nɔːtɪkli
AM ˌɛroʊ'nɔdək(ə)li, ˌɛrə'nɔdək(ə)li, ˌɛroʊ'nɑdək(ə)li, ˌɛrə'nɑdək(ə)li

aeronomy
BR ɛː'rɒnəmi
AM ɛ'rɑnəmi

aeroplane
BR 'ɛːrəpleɪn, -z
AM 'ɛr(ə)ˌpleɪn, 'ɛroʊˌpleɪn, -z

aerosol
BR 'ɛːrəsɒl, -z
AM 'ɛrəˌsɔl, 'ɛrəˌsɑl, -z

aerospace
BR 'ɛːrə(ʊ)speɪs
AM 'ɛroʊˌspeɪs, 'ɛrəˌspeɪs

aerostat
BR 'ɛːrə(ʊ)stat, -s
AM 'ɛroʊˌstæt, 'ɛrəˌstæt, -s

aerostatic
BR ˌɛːrə(ʊ)'statɪk
AM ˌɛroʊ'stædɪk, ˌɛrə'stædɪk

aerostatically
BR ˌɛːrə(ʊ)'statɪkli
AM ˌɛroʊ'stædək(ə)li, ˌɛrə'stædək(ə)li

aerotow
BR 'ɛːrə(ʊ)təʊ, -z, -ɪŋ, -d
AM 'ɛroʊˌtoʊ, 'ɛrəˌtoʊ, -z, -ɪŋ, -d

aerotrain
BR 'ɛːrə(ʊ)treɪn, -z
AM 'ɛroʊˌtreɪn, 'ɛrəˌtreɪn, -z

Aertex®
BR 'ɛːtɛks
AM 'ɛrˌtɛks

aeruginous
BR ɪə'ruːdʒɪnəs
AM i'rudʒənəs

aery[1]
adjective
BR 'ɛːri
AM 'ɛri, 'ɪri, 'iri, 'eɪri

aery²
noun
BR 'ɪər|i, 'ɛːr|i, 'ʌɪr|i, -ɪz
AM 'ɛri, 'ɪri, 'iri, 'eɪri, -z

Aeschines
BR 'iːskɪniːz
AM 'ɛskəniz

Aeschylean
BR ˌiːskɪ'liːən
AM ˌɛskə'liən

Aeschylus
BR 'iːskɪləs, 'iːskl̩əs
AM 'ɛskələs

Aesculapian
BR ˌiːskjʊ'leɪpɪən
AM ˌɛskə'leɪpiən

Aesop
BR 'iːsɒp
AM 'iˌsɑp, 'eɪˌsɑp

aesthete
BR 'iːsθiːt, -s
AM 'ɛsˌθit, -s

aesthetic
BR iːs'θɛtɪk, ɪs'θɛtɪk, ɛs'θɛtɪk, -s
AM ɛs'θɛdɪk, əs'θɛdɪk, -s

aesthetical
BR iːs'θɛtɪkl, ɪs'θɛtɪkl, ɛs'θɛtɪkl
AM ɛs'θɛdəkəl, əs'θɛdəkəl

aesthetically
BR iːs'θɛtɪkli, ɪs'θɛtɪkli, ɛs'θɛtɪkli
AM ɛs'θɛdək(ə)li, əs'θɛdək(ə)li

aesthetician
BR ˌiːsθɪ'tɪʃn, ˌɛsθɪ'tɪʃn
AM ˌɛsθə'tɪʃən

aestheticism
BR iːs'θɛtɪsɪz(ə)m, ɪs'θɛtɪsɪz(ə)m, ɛs'θɛtɪsɪz(ə)m
AM ɛs'θɛdəˌsɪzəm, əs'θɛdəˌsɪzəm

aestival
BR 'iːstɪvl, iːs'tʌɪvl, ɛs'tʌɪvl
AM 'ɛstəvəl, ɛs'taɪvəl

aestivate
BR 'iːstɪveɪt, 'ɛstɪveɪt, -s, -ɪŋ, ɪd
AM 'ɛstəˌveɪ|t, -ts, -dɪŋ, dɪd

aestivation
BR ˌiːstɪ'veɪʃn, ˌɛstɪ'veɪʃn
AM ˌɛstə'veɪʃən

aetatis
BR ʌɪ'tɑːtɪs, iː'teɪtɪs
AM aɪ'tɑdəs, i'tɑdəs

aether
BR 'iːθə(r)
AM 'iθər

aetiologic
BR ˌiːtɪə'lɒdʒɪk
AM ˌidiə'lɑdʒɪk

aetiological
BR ˌiːtɪə'lɒdʒɪkl
AM ˌidiə'lɑdʒəkəl

aetiologically
BR ˌiːtɪə'lɒdʒɪkli
AM ˌidiə'lɑdʒək(ə)li

aetiology
BR ˌiːtɪ'ɒlədʒi
AM ˌidi'ɑlədʒi

Afar
African people
BR 'afɑː(r), -z
AM ə'fɑr, -z

afar
BR ə'fɑː(r)
AM ə'fɑr

afeard
BR ə'fɪəd
AM ə'fɪ(ə)rd

affability
BR ˌafə'bɪlɪti
AM ˌæfə'bɪlɪdi

affable
BR 'afəbl
AM 'æfəbəl

affably
BR 'afəbli
AM 'æfəbli

affair
BR ə'fɛː(r), -z
AM ə'fɛ(ə)r, -z

affaire
BR ə'fɛː(r), -z
AM ə'fɛ(ə)r, -z

affairé
BR ə'fɛːreɪ
AM əˌfɛ'reɪ

affaire de cœur
BR əˌfɛː də 'kəː(r)
AM əˌfɛr də 'kər

affaires de cœur
BR əˌfɛː(z) də 'kəː(r)
AM əˌfɛr(z) də 'kər

affect¹
noun
BR ə'fɛkt, -s
AM 'æˌfɛk(t), ə'fɛk(t), -s

affect²
verb
BR ə'fɛkt, -s, -ɪŋ, -ɪd
AM ə'fɛk|(t), -(t)s, -tɪŋ, -təd

affectation
BR ˌafək'teɪʃn, ˌafɛk'teɪʃn, -z
AM ˌæˌfɛk'teɪʃən, -z

affectedly
BR ə'fɛktɪdli
AM ə'fɛktədli

affectingly
BR ə'fɛktɪŋli
AM ə'fɛktɪŋli

affection
BR ə'fɛkʃn, -z
AM ə'fɛkʃən, -z

affectional
BR ə'fɛkʃn̩(ə)l, ə'fɛkʃən(ə)l
AM ə'fɛkʃənl, ə'fɛkʃnəl

affectionally
BR ə'fɛkʃn̩əli, ə'fɛkʃn̩li, ə'fɛkʃənl̩i, ə'fɛkʃ(ə)nəli
AM ə'fɛkʃ(ə)nəli

affectionate
BR ə'fɛkʃənət, ə'fɛkʃn̩ət
AM ə'fɛkʃ(ə)nət

affectionately
BR ə'fɛkʃənətli, ə'fɛkʃn̩ətli
AM ə'fɛkʃ(ə)nətli

affective
BR ə'fɛktɪv
AM ə'fɛktɪv, æ'fɛktɪv

affectively
BR ə'fɛktɪvli
AM ə'fɛktɪvli, æ'fɛktɪvli

affectiveness
BR ə'fɛktɪvnɪs
AM ə'fɛktɪvnɪs, æ'fɛktɪvnɪs

affectivity
BR əˌfɛk'tɪvɪti, ˌafɛk'tɪvɪti
AM əˌfɛk'tɪvɪdi, æˌfɛk'tɪvɪdi

affenpinscher
BR 'afnˌpɪn(t)ʃə(r), -z
AM 'ɑfənˌpɪn(t)ʃər, -z

afferent
BR 'af(ə)rənt, 'af(ə)rn̩t
AM 'æf(ə)rənt

affiance
BR ə'fʌɪəns, -ɪz, -ɪŋ, -t
AM ə'faɪəns, -əz, -ɪŋ, -t

affiant
BR ə'fʌɪənt, -s
AM ə'faɪənt, -s

affiche
BR ə'fiːʃ, -ɪz
AM ə'fiʃ, -ɪz

affidavit
BR ˌafɪ'deɪvɪt, -s
AM ˌæfə'deɪvɪt, -s

affiliate¹
noun
BR ə'fɪlɪət, -s
AM ə'fɪliət, -s

affiliate²
verb
BR ə'fɪlɪeɪt, -s, -ɪŋ, -ɪd
AM ə'fɪliˌeɪ|t, -ts, -dɪŋ, -dɪd

affiliation
BR əˌfɪlɪ'eɪʃn, -z
AM əˌfɪli'eɪʃən, -z

affined
BR ə'fʌɪnd
AM ə'faɪnd

affinity
BR ə'fɪnɪt|i, -ɪz
AM ə'fɪnɪdi, -z

affirm
BR ə'fəːm, -z, -ɪŋ, -d
AM ə'fərm, -z, -ɪŋ, -d

affirmable
BR ə'fəːməbl
AM ə'fərməbəl

affirmation
BR ˌafə'meɪʃn, -z
AM ˌæfər'meɪʃən, -z

affirmative
BR ə'fəːmətɪv
AM ə'fərmədɪv

affirmatively
BR ə'fəːmətɪvli
AM ə'fərmədɪvli

affirmatory
BR ə'fəːmət(ə)ri
AM ə'fərməˌtɔri

affirmer
BR ə'fəːmə(r), -z
AM ə'fərmər, -z

affix¹
noun
BR 'afɪks, -ɪz
AM 'æˌfɪks, -ɪz

affix²
verb
BR ə'fɪks, -ɪz, -ɪŋ, -t
AM ə'fɪks, -ɪz, -ɪŋ, -t

affixture
BR ə'fɪkstʃə(r), a'fɪkstʃə(r)
AM ə'fɪkstʃər

afflatus
BR ə'fleɪtəs
AM ə'fleɪdəs

afflict
BR ə'flɪkt, -s, -ɪŋ, -ɪd
AM ə'flɪk|(t), -(t)s, -tɪŋ, -tɪd

affliction
BR ə'flɪkʃn, -z
AM ə'flɪkʃən, -z

afflictive
BR ə'flɪktɪv
AM ə'flɪktɪv

afflictively
BR ə'flɪktɪvli
AM ə'flɪktɪvli

affluence
BR 'aflʊəns
AM 'æˌfluəns, ə'fluəns

affluent
BR 'aflʊənt
AM 'æˌfluənt, ə'fluənt

affluential
BR ˌaflʊ'ɛnʃl
AM ˌæflə'wɛn(t)ʃəl

affluently
BR 'aflʊəntli
AM 'æˌfluən(t)li, ə'fluən(t)li

afflux
BR 'aflʌks, -ɪz

AM ˈæˌfləks, -əz

afforce
BR əˈfɔːs, -ɪz, -ɪŋ, -t
AM əˈfɔ(ə)rs, -əz, -ɪŋ, -t

afford
BR əˈfɔːd, -z, -ɪŋ, -ɪd
AM əˈfɔ(ə)rd, -z, -ɪŋ, -əd

affordability
BR əˌfɔːdəˈbɪlɪti
AM əˌfɔrdəˈbɪlɨdi

affordable
BR əˈfɔːdəbl
AM əˈfɔrdəbəl

affordably
BR əˈfɔːdəbli
AM əˈfɔrdəbli

afforest
BR əˈfɒrɪst, -s, -ɪŋ, -ɪd
AM əˈfɔrəst, -s, -ɪŋ, -əd

afforestation
BR əˌfɒrɪˈsteɪʃn
AM əˌfɔrəsˈteɪʃən

affranchise
BR əˈfran(t)ʃʌɪz, -ɪz, -ɪŋ, -d
AM əˈfrænˌtʃaɪz, -ɪz, -ɪŋ, -d

affray
BR əˈfreɪ, -z
AM əˈfreɪ, -z

affreightment
BR əˈfreɪtm(ə)nt
AM əˈfreɪtmənt

affricate
BR ˈafrɪkət, -s
AM ˈæfrəkət, -s

affrication
BR ˌafrɪˈkeɪʃn
AM ˌæfrəˈkeɪʃən

affricative
BR əˈfrɪkətɪv, -z
AM əˈfrɪkədɪv, ˈæfrəˌkeɪdɪv, -z

affright
BR əˈfrʌɪt, -s, -ɪŋ, -ɪd
AM əˈfraɪ|t, -ts, -dɪŋ, -dɪd

affront
BR əˈfrʌnt, -s, -ɪŋ, -ɪd
AM əˈfrən|t, -ts, -(t)ɪŋ, -(t)əd

affusion
BR əˈfjuːʒn
AM əˈfjuʒən

Afghan
BR ˈafgan, -z
AM ˈæfˌgæn, -z

Afghani
BR afˈgɑːn|i, afˈgan|i, -ɪz
AM ˌæfˈgɑni, ˌæfˈgæni, -z

Afghanistan
BR afˈganɪstɑːn, afˈganɪstan, afˌganɪˈstɑːn, afˌganɪˈstan
AM æfˈgænəˌstæn

aficionado
BR əˌfɪʃ(j)əˈnɑːdəʊ, əˌfɪsjəˈnɑːdəʊ, -z
AM əˌfɪʃəˈnɑdoʊ, əˌfɪsjəˈnɑdoʊ, -z

afield
BR əˈfiːld
AM əˈfild

afire
BR əˈfʌɪə(r)
AM əˈfaɪ(ə)r

aflame
BR əˈfleɪm
AM əˈfleɪm

aflatoxin
BR ˌafləˈtɒksɪn, -z
AM ˌæfləˈtɑks(ə)n, -z

afloat
BR əˈfləʊt
AM əˈfloʊt

aflutter
BR əˈflʌtə(r)
AM əˈflədər

afon
BR ˈav(ɒ)n
AM ˈæfən
WE ˈavɒn

afoot
BR əˈfʊt
AM əˈfʊt

afore
BR əˈfɔː(r)
AM əˈfɔ(ə)r

aforementioned
BR əˌfɔːˈmɛnʃnd, əˈfɔːˌmɛnʃnd
AM əˌfɔrˌmɛn(t)ʃənd

aforesaid
BR əˈfɔːsɛd
AM əˈfɔrˌsɛd

aforethought
BR əˈfɔːθɔːt
AM əˈfɔrˌθɔt, əˈfɔrˌθɑt

a fortiori
BR ˌeɪ ˌfɔːtɪˈɔːrʌɪ, + ˌfɔːtɪˈɔːri
AM ˌɑ ˌfɔrdiˈɔri, ˌeɪ ˌfɔrdiˈɔraɪ

afoul
BR əˈfaʊl
AM əˈfaʊl

afraid
BR əˈfreɪd
AM əˈfreɪd

afreet
BR ˈafriːt, -s
AM ˈæˌfrit, əˈfrit, -s

afresh
BR əˈfrɛʃ
AM əˈfrɛʃ

afric
BR ˈafrɪk
AM ˈæfrɪk

Africa
BR ˈafrɪkə(*r*)
AM ˈæfrəkə

African
BR ˈafrɪk(ə)n, -z
AM ˈæfrəkən, -z

Africana
BR ˌafrɪˈkɑːnə(*r*)
AM ˌæfrəˈkænə

Africander
BR ˌafrɪˈkandə(r), -z
AM ˌæfrəˈkændər, -z

africanisation
BR ˌafrɪkənʌɪˈzeɪʃn, ˌafrɪkn̩ʌɪˈzeɪʃn
AM ˌæfrəkənəˈzeɪʃən, ˌæfrəkəˌnaɪˈzeɪʃən

Africanise
BR ˈafrɪkənʌɪz, ˈafrɪkn̩ʌɪz, -ɪz, -ɪŋ, -d
AM ˈæfrəkəˌnaɪz, -ɪz, -ɪŋ, -d

Africanism
BR ˈafrɪkənɪz(ə)m, ˈafrɪkn̩ɪz(ə)m
AM ˈæfrəkəˌnɪzəm

Africanist
BR ˈafrɪkənɪst, ˈafrɪkn̩ɪst, -s
AM ˈæfrəkənəst, -s

africanization
BR ˌafrɪkənʌɪˈzeɪʃn, ˌafrɪkn̩ʌɪˈzeɪʃn
AM ˌæfrəkənəˈzeɪʃən, ˌæfrəkəˌnaɪˈzeɪʃən

Africanize
BR ˈafrɪkənʌɪz, ˈafrɪkn̩ʌɪz, -ɪz, -ɪŋ, -d
AM ˈæfrəkəˌnaɪz, -ɪz, -ɪŋ, -d

Afrikaans
BR ˌafrɪˈkɑːns, ˌafrəˈkɑːnz
AM ˌæfrəˈkɑnz

Afrika Korps
BR ˈafrɪkə ˌkɔː(r)
AM ˈæfrikə ˌkɔ(ə)r

afrikander
BR ˌafrɪˈkandə(r), -z
AM ˌæfrəˈkɑndər, -z

Afrikaner
BR ˌafrɪˈkɑːnə(r), -z
AM ˌæfrəˈkɑnər, -z

afrit
BR ˈafrɪt, -s
AM ˈæˌfrit, əˈfrit, -s

Afro
BR ˈafrəʊ
AM ˈæfroʊ

Afrocentric
BR ˌafrəʊˈsɛntrɪk
AM ˌæfroʊˈsɛntrɪk

afrormosia
BR ˌafrɔːˈməʊzɪə(*r*)
AM ˌæfrɔrˈmoʊʒ(i)ə, ˌæfrɔrˈmoʊziə

AFSCME
BR ˈafsmi
AM ˈæfsmi

aft
BR ɑːft, aft
AM æft

after
BR ˈɑːftə(r), ˈaftə(r), -z
AM ˈæftər, -z

afterbirth
BR ˈɑːftəbəːθ, ˈaftəbəːθ, -s
AM ˈæftərˌbərθ, -s

afterburner
BR ˈɑːftəˌbəːnə(r), ˈaftəˌbəːnə(r), -z
AM ˈæftərˌbərnər, -z

aftercare
BR ˈɑːftəkɛː(r), ˈaftəkɛː(r)
AM ˈæftərˌkɛ(ə)r

afterdeck
BR ˈɑːftədɛk, ˈaftədɛk, -s
AM ˈæftərˌdɛk, -s

afterglow
BR ˈɑːftəgləʊ, ˈaftəgləʊ, -z
AM ˈæftərˌgloʊ, -z

aftergrass
BR ˈɑːftəgrɑːs, ˈaftəgras
AM ˈæftərˌgræs

afterlife
BR ˈɑːftəlʌɪf, ˈaftəlʌɪf
AM ˈæftərˌlaɪf

afterlight
BR ˈɑːftəlʌɪt, ˈaftəlʌɪt
AM ˈæftərˌlaɪt

afterlives
BR ˈɑːftəlʌɪvz, ˈaftəlʌɪvz
AM ˈæftərˌlaɪvz

aftermarket
BR ˈɑːftəˌmɑːkɪt, ˈaftəˌmɑːkɪt, -s
AM ˌæftərˈmɑrkət, -s

aftermath
BR ˈɑːftəmaθ, ˈaftəmaθ, -s
AM ˈæftərˌmæθ, -s

aftermost
BR ˈɑːftəməʊst, ˈaftəməʊst
AM ˈæftərˌmoʊst

afternoon
BR ˌɑːftəˈnuːn, ˌaftəˈnuːn, -z
AM ˌæftərˈnun, -z

afterpains
BR ˈɑːftəpeɪnz, ˈaftəpeɪnz
AM ˈæftərˌpeɪnz

afterpart
BR ˈɑːftəpɑːt, ˈaftəpɑːt, -s
AM ˈæftərˌpɑrt, -s

aftershave
BR ˈɑːftəʃeɪv, ˈaftəʃeɪv, -z
AM ˈæftərˌʃeɪv, -z

aftershock
BR 'ɑːftəʃɒk, 'aftəʃɒk, -s
AM 'æftər,ʃɑk, -s

aftertaste
BR 'ɑːftəteɪst, 'aftəteɪst, -s
AM 'æftər,teɪst, -s

afterthought
BR 'ɑːftəθɔːt, 'aftəθɔːt, -s
AM 'æftər,θɔt, 'æftər,θɑt, -s

afterward
BR 'ɑːftəwəd, 'aftəwəd, -z
AM 'æftərwərd, -z

afterword
BR 'ɑːftəwəːd, 'aftəwəːd, -z
AM 'æftər,wərd, -z

afterworld
BR 'ɑːftəwəːld, 'aftəwəːld
AM 'æftər,wərld

Aga®
BR 'ɑːgə(r), -z
AM 'ɑgə, -z

Agadir
BR ,agə'dɪə(r)
AM ,ɑgə'dɪ(ə)r

Agag
BR 'eɪgag
AM 'ɑgæg

again
BR ə'gɛn, ə'geɪn
AM ə'gɛn

against
BR ə'gɛnst, ə'geɪnst
AM ə'gɛnst

Aga Khan
BR ,ɑːgə 'kɑːn
AM ,ɑgə 'kɑn

agama
BR 'agəmə(r), -z
AM ə'geɪmə, 'ægəmə, -z

Agamemnon
BR ,agə'mɛmnɒn, ,agə'mɛmnən
AM ,ægə'mɛm,nɑn

agamic
BR ə'gamɪk
AM eɪ'gæmɪk, ə'gæmɪk

agamogenesis
BR ,agəmə'dʒɛnɪsɪs
AM ,eɪ,gæmə'dʒɛnəsəs, ,ægəmoʊ'dʒɛnəsəs

agamogenetic
BR ,agəmə(ʊ)dʒɪ'nɛtɪk
AM ,eɪ,gæmədʒə'nɛdɪk, ,ægəmoʊdʒə'nɛdɪk

agamospermy
BR 'agəmə,spəːmi
AM eɪ'gæmə,spərmi, 'ægəmoʊ,spərmi

agamous
BR 'agəməs
AM 'ægəməs

agapanthus
BR ,agə'panθəs, -ɪz
AM ,ægə'pænθəs, -əz

agape[1]
adjective
BR ə'geɪp
AM ə'geɪp

agape[2]
noun
BR 'agəpeɪ, 'agəpiː, -z
AM ɑ'gɑ,peɪ, 'ɑgə,peɪ, -z

agapemone
BR ,agə'piːməni, ,agə'piːmn̩i, ,agə'pɛməni, ,agə'pɛmn̩i
AM ,ægə'pɛməni

agar
BR 'eɪgə(r), 'eɪgɑː(r)
AM 'ɑ,gɑr, 'eɪ,gɑr

agaric
BR 'ag(ə)rɪk, -s
AM 'ægərɪk, ə'gɛrɪk, -s

agate
BR 'agɪt
AM 'ægət

Agatha
BR 'agəθə(r)
AM 'ægəθə

agave
BR ə'geɪvi, ə'gɑːvi, 'ageɪv, ə'geɪvɪz\ə'gɑːvɪz\'ageɪvz
AM ə'gɑvi, -z

agaze
BR ə'geɪz
AM ə'geɪz

agba
BR 'agbə(r), -z
AM 'ægbə, -z

age
BR eɪdʒ, -ɪz, -ɪŋ, -d
AM eɪdʒ, -ɪz, -ɪŋ, -d

aged[1]
adjective
BR 'eɪdʒɪd
AM 'eɪdʒɪd

aged[2]
past tense of verb age
BR eɪdʒd
AM eɪdʒd

Agee
BR 'eɪdʒi
AM 'eɪ,dʒi

ageism
BR 'eɪdʒɪz(ə)m
AM 'eɪdʒ,ɪzəm

ageist
BR 'eɪdʒɪst, -s
AM 'eɪdʒɪst, -s

ageless
BR 'eɪdʒlɪs
AM 'eɪdʒlɪs

agelessness
BR 'eɪdʒlɪsnɪs
AM 'eɪdʒlɪsnɪs

agency
BR 'eɪdʒ(ə)ns|i, -ɪz
AM 'eɪdʒ(ə)nsi, -z

agenda
BR ə'dʒɛndə(r), -z
AM ə'dʒɛndə, -z

agendum
BR ə'dʒɛndəm
AM ə'dʒɛndəm

agent
BR 'eɪdʒ(ə)nt, -s
AM 'eɪdʒ(ə)nt, -s

agential
BR eɪ'dʒɛnʃl
AM eɪ'dʒɛn(t)ʃəl

agent provocateur
BR ,aʒɒ̃ prə,vɒkə'təː(r)
AM ,ɑʒɑn(t) prə,vɔkə'tər

agents provocateurs
BR ,aʒɒ̃ prə,vɒkə'təːz
AM ,ɑʒɑn(t)(s) prə,vɔkə'tər(z)

ager
BR 'eɪdʒə(r), -z
AM 'eɪdʒər, -z

ageratum
BR ,adʒə'reɪtəm, -z
AM ,ædʒə'reɪdəm, -z

Agfa®
BR 'agfə(r)
AM 'ægfə

Aggie
BR 'agi
AM 'ægi

aggiornamento
BR ə,dʒɔːnə'mɛntəʊ
AM ə,dʒɔrnə'mɛn,(t)oʊ

agglomerate[1]
noun, adjective
BR ə'glɒm(ə)rət, -s
AM ə'glɑmərət, -s

agglomerate[2]
verb
BR ə'glɒməreɪt, -s, -ɪŋ, -ɪd
AM ə'glɑmə,reɪ|t, -ts, -dɪŋ, -dɪd

agglomeration
BR ə,glɒmə'reɪʃn
AM ə,glɑmə'reɪʃən

agglomerative
BR ə'glɒm(ə)rətɪv
AM ə'glɑmə,reɪdɪv, ə'glɑmərədɪv

agglutinate[1]
adjective
BR ə'gluːtɪnət
AM ə'glutn̩ət

agglutinate[2]
verb
BR ə'gluːtɪneɪt, -s, -ɪŋ, -ɪd
AM ə'glutn,eɪ|t, -ts, -dɪŋ, -dɪd

agglutination
BR ə,gluːtɪ'neɪʃn
AM ə,glutn'eɪʃən

agglutinative
BR ə'gluːtɪnətɪv
AM ə'glutn̩ədɪv, ə'glutn,eɪdɪv

agglutinin
BR ə'gluːtɪnɪn, -z
AM ə'glutn̩ən, -z

aggrandise
BR ə'grandʌɪz, -ɪz, -ɪŋ, -d
AM ə'græn,daɪz, -ɪz, -ɪŋ, -d

aggrandisement
BR ə'grandɪzm(ə)nt, ə'grandʌɪzm(ə)nt, -s
AM ə'græn,daɪzmənt, -s

aggrandiser
BR ə'grandʌɪzə(r), -z
AM ə'græn,daɪzər, -z

aggrandize
BR ə'grandʌɪz, -ɪz, -ɪŋ, -d
AM ə'græn,daɪz, -ɪz, -ɪŋ, -d

aggrandizement
BR ə'grandɪzm(ə)nt, ə'grandʌɪzm(ə)nt, -s
AM ə'græn,daɪzmənt, -s

aggrandizer
BR ə'grandʌɪzə(r), -z
AM ə'græn,daɪzər, -z

aggravate
BR 'agrəveɪt, -s, -ɪŋ, -ɪd
AM 'ægrə,veɪ|t, -ts, -dɪŋ, -dɪd

aggravatingly
BR 'agrəveɪtɪŋli
AM 'ægrə,veɪdɪŋli

aggravation
BR ,agrə'veɪʃn
AM ,ægrə'veɪʃən

aggregate[1]
noun, adjective
BR 'agrɪgət, -s
AM 'ægrəgət, -s

aggregate[2]
verb
BR 'agrɪgeɪt, -s, -ɪŋ, -ɪd
AM 'ægrə,geɪ|t, -ts, -dɪŋ, -dɪd

aggregation
BR ,agrɪ'geɪʃn
AM ,ægrə'geɪʃən

aggregative
BR 'agrɪgətɪv
AM 'ægrə,geɪdɪv

aggress
BR ə'grɛs, -ɪz, -ɪŋ, -t
AM ə'grɛs, -əz, -ɪŋ, -t

aggression
BR ə'grɛʃn
AM ə'grɛʃən

aggressive
BR ə'grɛsɪv
AM ə'grɛsɪv
aggressively
BR ə'grɛsɪvli
AM ə'grɛsɪvli
aggressiveness
BR ə'grɛsɪvnɨs
AM ə'grɛsɪvnɨs
aggressor
BR ə'grɛsə(r), -z
AM ə'grɛsər, -z
aggrieve
BR ə'griːv, -z, -ɪŋ, -d
AM ə'griv, -z, -ɪŋ, -d
aggrievedly
BR ə'griːvɨdli
AM ə'grivɨdli
aggro
BR 'agrəʊ
AM 'ægroʊ
aghast
BR ə'gɑːst, ə'gast
AM ə'gæst
agile
BR 'adʒʌɪl
AM 'ædʒəl
agilely
BR 'adʒʌɪl(l)i
AM 'ædʒə(l)li
agility
BR ə'dʒɪlɪti
AM ə'dʒɪlɨdi
agin
BR ə'gɪn
AM ə'gɪn
Agincourt
BR 'a(d)ʒɪnkɔː(r), 'adʒɪnkɔːt
AM 'ædʒən,kɔ(ə)rt
aging
BR 'eɪdʒɪŋ
AM 'eɪdʒɪŋ
agio
BR 'adʒɪəʊ, -z
AM 'ædʒioʊ, -z
agiotage
BR 'adʒ(ɪ)ətɪdʒ, 'adʒ(ɪ)ətɑːʒ
AM 'ædʒədɪdʒ
agism
BR 'eɪdʒɪz(ə)m
AM 'eɪ,dʒɪzəm
agist
BR 'eɪdʒɪst, -s
AM 'eɪdʒɪst, -s
agistment
BR ə'dʒɪs(t)m(ə)nt
AM 'ədʒɪs(t)mənt
agitate
BR 'adʒɪteɪt, -s, -ɪŋ, -ɨd
AM 'ædʒə,teɪ|t, -ts, -dɪŋ, -dɨd
agitatedly
BR 'adʒɪteɪtɨdli
AM 'ædʒə,teɪdɨdli
agitation
BR ,adʒɪ'teɪʃn, -z
AM ,ædʒə'teɪʃən, -z
agitato
BR ,adʒɪ'tɑːtəʊ
AM ,ædʒə'tɑdoʊ
agitator
BR 'adʒɪteɪtə(r), -z
AM 'ædʒə,teɪdər, -z
agitprop
BR 'adʒɪtprɒp
AM 'ædʒət,prɑp
agleam
BR ə'gliːm
AM ə'glim
aglet
BR 'aglɨt, -s
AM 'æglət, -s
agley
BR ə'gleɪ, ə'gliː, ə'glʌɪ
AM ə'gleɪ, ə'gli
aglow
BR ə'gləʊ
AM ə'gloʊ
agma
BR 'agmə(*r*), -z
AM 'ægmə, -z
agnail
BR 'agneɪl, -z
AM 'æg,neɪl, -z
agnate
BR 'agneɪt, -s
AM 'æg,neɪt, -s
agnatic
BR ag'natɪk, əg'natɪk
AM æg'nædɪk
agnation
BR ag'neɪʃn, əg'neɪʃn
AM æg'neɪʃən
Agnes
BR 'agnɨs
AM 'ægnəs
Agnew
BR 'agnjuː
AM 'ægnu
Agni
BR 'agni
AM 'ægni
agnomen
BR ag'nəʊmɛn
AM æg'noʊmən
agnosia
BR ag'nəʊzɪə(*r*), ag'nəʊsɪə(*r*)
AM æg'noʊʒə
agnostic
BR ag'nɒstɪk, əg'nɒstɪk, -s
AM æg'nɑstɪk, əg'nɑstɪk, -s
agnosticism
BR ag'nɒstɪsɪz(ə)m, əg'nɒstɪsɪz(ə)m
AM æg'nɑstə,sɪzəm, əg'nɑstə,sɪzəm
Agnus Dei
BR ,agnʊs 'deɪiː
AM ¦ɑg,nʊs 'deɪ,i, ¦æg,nʊs +, ¦ɑgnəs +, ¦ægnəs +
ago
BR ə'gəʊ
AM ə'goʊ
agog
BR ə'gɒg
AM ə'gɑg
a-go-go
BR ə'gəʊgəʊ
AM ə'goʊ,goʊ
agonic
BR eɪ'gɒnɪk, ə'gɒnɪk
AM eɪ'gɑnɪk, ə'gɑnɪk
agonise
BR 'agənʌɪz, -ɨz, -ɪŋ, -d
AM 'ægə,naɪz, -ɨz, -ɪŋ, -d
agonisingly
BR 'agənʌɪzɪŋli
AM 'ægə,naɪzɪŋli
agonist
BR 'agənɪst, -s
AM 'ægənəst, -s
Agonistes
BR ,agə'nɪstiːz
AM ,ægə'nɪstiz
agonistic
BR ,agə'nɪstɪk
AM ,ægə'nɪstɪk
agonistically
BR ,agə'nɪstɪkli
AM ,ægə'nɪstɪk(ə)li
agonize
BR 'agənʌɪz, -ɨz, -ɪŋ, -d
AM 'ægə,naɪz, -ɨz, -ɪŋ, -d
agonizingly
BR 'agənʌɪzɪŋli
AM 'ægə,naɪzɪŋli
agony
BR 'agən|i, 'agn̩|i, -ɪz
AM 'ægəni, -z
agoraphobe
BR 'ag(ə)rəfəʊb, -z
AM 'æg(ə)rə,foʊb, -z
agoraphobia
BR ,ag(ə)rə'fəʊbɪə(*r*)
AM ,æg(ə)rə'foʊbiə
agoraphobic
BR ,ag(ə)rə'fəʊbɪk, -s
AM ,æg(ə)rə'foʊbɪk, -s
agouti
BR ə'guːt|i, -ɪz
AM ə'gudi, -z
Agra
BR 'ɑːgrə(*r*)
AM 'ɑgrə
agrapha
BR 'agrəfə(*r*)
AM 'ægrəfə
agraphon
BR 'agrəfɒn
AM 'ægrə,fɑn
agrarian
BR ə'grɛːrɪən
AM ə'grɛriən
agree
BR ə'griː, -z, -ɪŋ, -d
AM ə'gri, -z, -ɪŋ, -d
agreeable
BR ə'griːəbl
AM ə'griəbəl
agreeableness
BR ə'griːəblnəs
AM ə'griəbəlnəs
agreeably
BR ə'griːəbli
AM ə'griəbli
agreement
BR ə'griːm(ə)nt, -s
AM ə'grimənt, -s
agribusiness
BR 'agrɪ,bɪznɨs
AM 'ægrə,bɪznɨs
agribusinessman
BR 'agrɪ,bɪznɨsmən
AM 'ægrə,bɪznɨs,mæn
agribusinessmen
BR 'agrɪ,bɪznɨsmən
AM 'ægrə,bɪznɨs,mɛn
agrichemical
BR ,agrɪ'kɛmɪkl, -z
AM ,ægrə'kɛməkəl, -z
Agricola
BR ə'grɪkələ(*r*)
AM ə'grɪkələ
agricultural
BR ,agrɪ'kʌltʃ(ə)rəl, ,agrɪ'kʌltʃ(ə)rl̩
AM ,ægrə'kəltʃ(ə)rəl
agriculturalist
BR ,agrɪ'kʌltʃ(ə)rəlɪst, ,agrɪ'kʌltʃ(ə)rl̩ɪst, -s
AM ,ægrə'kəltʃ(ə)rələst, -s
agriculturally
BR ,agrɪ'kʌltʃ(ə)rəli, ,agrɪ'kʌltʃ(ə)rl̩i
AM ,ægrə'kəltʃ(ə)rəli
agriculture
BR 'agrɪkʌltʃə(r)
AM 'ægrə,kəltʃər
agriculturist
BR ,agrɪ'kʌltʃ(ə)rɪst, -s
AM ,ægrə'kəltʃ(ə)rəst, -s
agrimony
BR 'agrɪməni
AM 'ægrə,moʊni
Agrippa
BR ə'grɪpə(*r*)
AM ə'grɪpə
agrochemical
BR ,agrə(ʊ)'kɛmɪkl, -z
AM ,ægroʊ'kɛməkəl, ,ægrə'kɛməkəl, -z
agroforestry
BR ,agrə(ʊ)'fɒrɪstri
AM ,ægroʊ'fɔrəstri, ,ægrə'fɔrəstri
agro-industry
BR ,agrəʊ'ɪndəstri
AM ,ægroʊ'ɪndəstri

agronomic
BR ˌagrəˈnɒmɪk, -s
AM ˌæɡrəˈnɑmɪk, -s

agronomical
BR ˌagrəˈnɒmɨkl
AM ˌæɡrəˈnɑməkəl

agronomically
BR ˌagrəˈnɒmɨkli
AM ˌæɡrəˈnɑmək(ə)li

agronomist
BR əˈgrɒnəmɪst, -s
AM əˈgrɑnəməst, -s

agronomy
BR əˈgrɒnəmi
AM əˈgrɑnəmi

aground
BR əˈgraʊnd
AM əˈgraʊnd

ague
BR ˈeɪgjuː, -z, -d
AM ˈeɪˌgju, -z, -d

Aguecheek
BR ˈeɪgjuːtʃiːk
AM ˈeɪˌgjuˌtʃik

Aguilar
BR ˌagwɪˈlɑː(r)
AM ˌɑgwiˈlɑr
SP aɣiˈlar

aguish
BR ˈeɪgjuɪʃ
AM ˈeɪˌgjəwɪʃ, ˈeɪˌgjuɪʃ

Agulhas
BR əˈgʌləs
AM əˈgələs

aguti
BR əˈguːt|i, -ɪz
AM əˈgudi, -z

Agutter
BR ˈagətə(r), əˈgʌtə(r)
AM əˈgədər

ah
BR ɑː(*r*)
AM ɑ

aha
BR ɑːˈhɑː(*r*), əˈhɑː(*r*)
AM ɑˈhɑ

Ahab
BR ˈeɪhab
AM ˈeɪhæb

Ahasuerus
BR əˌhazjʊˈɪərəs, ˌeɪhazjʊˈɪərəs, əˌhazjʊˈɛːrəs, ˌeɪhazjʊˈɛːrəs
AM əˌhæzjuˈɛrəs, əˌhæʒuˈɛrəs

ahead
BR əˈhɛd
AM əˈhɛd

ahem
BR əˈhɛm, əˈhm
AM əˈhɛm, əˈhm

Aherne
BR əˈhəːn, ˈeɪhəːn
AM ˈeɪhərn

ahimsa
BR əˈhɪmsɑː(*r*)
AM əˈhɪmˌsɑ

ahistoric
BR ˌeɪhɪˈstɒrɪk
AM ˌeɪhɪsˈtɔrɪk

ahistorical
BR ˌeɪhɪˈstɒrɨkl
AM ˌeɪhɪsˈtɔrəkəl

Ahmadabad
BR ˈɑːmədəbad, ˈɑːmədəbɑːd
AM ˈɑmədəˌbɑd, ˈɑmədəˌbæd

Ahmed
BR ˈɑː(k)mɛd, ˈɑːxmɛd
AM ˈɑmɛd

ahold
BR əˈhəʊld
AM əˈhoʊld

ahoy
BR əˈhɔɪ
AM əˈhɔɪ

ahull
BR əˈhʌl
AM əˈhəl

Ahura Mazda
BR əˌhʊərə ˈmazdə(*r*)
AM əˌhʊrə ˈmɑzdə

ai
BR ʌɪ, ˈɑːɪ, -z
AM aɪ, -z

aid
BR eɪd, -z, -ɪŋ, -ɨd
AM eɪd, -z, -ɪŋ, -ɨd

Aïda
BR ʌɪˈiːdə(*r*)
AM aɪˈidə

Aidan
BR ˈeɪdn
AM ˈeɪdən

aide
BR eɪd, -z
AM eɪd, -z

aide-de-camp
BR ˌeɪddəˈkɒ̃, ˌeɪddəˈkɑ̃ː
AM ˌeɪddəˈkæmp

aide-mémoire
BR ˌeɪdmɛmˈwɑː(r), ˌeɪdˈmɛmwɑː(r), -z
AM ˌeɪdˌmɛmˈwɑr, -z

aider
BR ˈeɪdə(r), -z
AM ˈeɪdər, -z

aides-de-camp
BR ˌeɪd(z)dəˈkɒ̃, ˌeɪd(z)dəˈkɑ̃ː
AM ˌeɪdzdəˈkæmp

aides-mémoire
BR ˌeɪd(z)mɛmˈwɑː(r), ˌeɪd(z)ˈmɛmwɑː(r)
AM ˌeɪd(z)ˌmɛmˈwɑr

aides-mémoires
BR ˌeɪd(z)mɛmˈwɑːz, ˌeɪd(z)ˈmɛmwɑːz
AM ˌeɪd(z)ˌmɛmˈwɑr(z)

AIDS
BR eɪdz
AM eɪdz

aiglet
BR ˈeɪglɨt, -s
AM ˈeɪglət, -s

aigrette
BR ˈeɪgrɛt, eɪˈgrɛt, -s
AM eɪˈgrɛt, -s

Aigues-Mortes
BR ˌeɪgˈmɔːt
AM ɛgˈmɔ(ə)rt

aiguilette
BR ˌeɪgwɪˈjɛt, ˌeɪgwɪˈlɛt, -s
AM ˌeɪgwəˈlɛt, -s

aiguille
BR ˈeɪgwiː(l), eɪˈgwiː(l), -z
AM eɪˈgwil, -z

aiguillette
BR ˌeɪgwɪˈjɛt, ˌeɪgwɪˈlɛt, -s
AM ˌeɪgwəˈlɛt, -s

Aiken
BR ˈeɪk(ə)n
AM ˈeɪkɛn

aikido
BR ʌɪˈkiːdəʊ
AM aɪˈkidoʊ, ˌaɪkiˈdoʊ

ail
BR eɪl, -z, -ɪŋ, -d
AM eɪl, -z, -ɪŋ, -d

ailanthus
BR eɪˈlanθəs, -ɪz
AM eɪˈlænθəs, -əz

Aileen
BR ˈeɪliːn, ˈʌɪliːn
AM aɪˈlin

aileron
BR ˈeɪlərɒn, -z
AM ˈeɪləˌrɑn, -z

ailment
BR ˈeɪlm(ə)nt, -s
AM ˈeɪlmənt, -s

Ailsa
BR ˈeɪlsə(*r*)
AM ˈeɪlsə

ailurophile
BR ʌɪˈl(j)ʊərə(ʊ)fʌɪl, eɪˈl(j)ʊərə(ʊ)fʌɪl, ˈeɪljʉrə(ʊ)fʌɪl, -z
AM aɪˈlʊrəˌfaɪl, eɪˈlʊrəˌfaɪl, -z

ailurophobe
BR ʌɪˈl(j)ʊərə(ʊ)fəʊb, eɪˈl(j)ʊərə(ʊ)fəʊb, ˈeɪljʉrə(ʊ)fəʊb, -z
AM aɪˈlʊrəˌfoʊb, eɪˈlʊrəˌfoʊb, -z

ailurophobia
BR ʌɪˌl(j)ʊərə(ʊ)ˈfəʊbɪə(*r*), eɪˌl(j)ʊərə(ʊ)ˈfəʊbɪə(*r*)
AM aɪˌlʊrəˈfoʊbiə, eɪˌlʊrəˈfoʊbiə

aim
BR eɪm, -z, -ɪŋ, -d
AM eɪm, -z, -ɪŋ, -d

Aimée
BR ˈeɪmeɪ, ˈeɪmi
AM ɛˈmeɪ

aimless
BR ˈeɪmlɪs
AM ˈeɪmlɪs

aimlessly
BR ˈeɪmlɪsli
AM ˈeɪmlɨsli

aimlessness
BR ˈeɪmlɪsnɪs
AM ˈeɪmlɨsnɨs

ain
BR eɪn
AM eɪn

Ainsley
BR ˈeɪnzli
AM ˈeɪnzli

ain't
BR eɪnt
AM eɪnt

Aintree
BR ˈeɪntriː
AM ˈeɪntri

Ainu
BR ˈʌɪnuː, -z
AM ˈaɪˌnu, -z

aïoli
BR ʌɪˈəʊli, eɪˈəʊli
AM eɪˈoʊli

air
BR ɛː(r), -z, -ɪŋ, -d
AM ɛ(ə)r, -z, -ɪŋ, -d

airbag
BR ˈɛːbag, -z
AM ˈɛrˌbæg, -z

airbase
BR ˈɛːbeɪs, -ɪz
AM ˈɛrˌbeɪs, -ɪz

airbed
BR ˈɛːbɛd, -z
AM ˈɛrˌbɛd, -z

airborne
BR ˈɛːbɔːn
AM ˈɛrˌbɔ(ə)rn

airbrake
BR ˈɛːbreɪk, -s
AM ˈɛrˌbreɪk, -s

airbrick
BR ˈɛːbrɪk, -s
AM ˈɛrˌbrɪk, -s

airbrush
BR ˈɛːbrʌʃ, -ɪz, -ɪŋ, -t
AM ˈɛrˌbrəʃ, -əz, -ɪŋ, -t

airburst
BR ˈɛːbəːst, -s
AM ˈɛrˌbərst, -s

airbus
BR ˈɛːbʌs, -ɪz
AM ˈɛrˌbəs, -əz

aircraft
BR ˈɛːkrɑːft, ˈɛːkraft
AM ˈɛrˌkræf(t)

aircraftman
BR ˈɛːkrɑːf(t)mən, ˈɛːkraf(t)mən
AM ˈɛrˌkræf(t)mən

aircraftmen
BR ˈɛːkrɑːf(t)mən, ˈɛːkraf(t)mən
AM ˈɛrˌkræf(t)mən

aircraftsman
BR ˈɛːkrɑːf(t)smən, ˈɛːkraf(t)smən
AM ˈɛrˌkræf(t)smən

aircraftsmen
BR ˈɛːkrɑːf(t)smən, ˈɛːkraf(t)smən
AM ˈɛrˌkræf(t)smən

aircraftswoman
BR ˈɛːkrɑːf(t)sˌwʊmən, ˈɛːkraf(t)sˌwʊmən
AM ˈɛrˌkræf(t)sˌwʊmən

aircraftswomen
BR ˈɛːkrɑːf(t)sˌwɪmɪn, ˈɛːkraf(t)sˌwɪmɪn
AM ˈɛrˌkræf(t)sˌwɪmɨn

aircraftwoman
BR ˈɛːkrɑːf(t)ˌwʊmən, ˈɛːkraf(t)ˌwʊmən
AM ˈɛrˌkræf(t)ˌwʊmən

aircraftwomen
BR ˈɛːkrɑːf(t)ˌwɪmɪn, ˈɛːkraf(t)ˌwɪmɪn
AM ˈɛrˌkræf(t)ˌwɪmɨn

aircrew
BR ˈɛːkruː, -z
AM ˈɛrˌkru, -z

airdate
BR ˈɛːdeɪt
AM ˈɛrˌdeɪt

Airdrie
BR ˈɛːdri
AM ˈɛrdri

airdrop
BR ˈɛːdrɒp, -s, -ɪŋ, -t
AM ˈɛrˌdrɑp, -s, -ɪŋ, -t

Airedale
BR ˈɛːdeɪl, -z
AM ˈɛrˌdeɪl, -z

airer
BR ˈɛːrə(r), -z
AM ˈɛrər, -z

airfare
BR ˈɛːfɛː(r), -z
AM ˈɛrˌfɛ(ə)r, -z

airfield
BR ˈɛːfiːld, -z
AM ˈɛrˌfild, -z

airflow
BR ˈɛːfləʊ, -z
AM ˈɛrˌfloʊ, -z

airfoil
BR ˈɛːfɔɪl, -z
AM ˈɛrˌfɔɪl, -z

airframe
BR ˈɛːfreɪm, -z
AM ˈɛrˌfreɪm, -z

airfreight
BR ˈɛːfreɪt, -s, -ɪŋ, -ɨd
AM ˌɛrˈfreɪ|t, -ts, -dɪŋ, -dɨd

airglow
BR ˈɛːgləʊ
AM ˈɛrˌgloʊ

airgun
BR ˈɛːgʌn, -z
AM ˈɛrˌgən, -z

airhead
BR ˈɛːhɛd, -z
AM ˈɛrˌ(h)ɛd, -z

airhole
BR ˈɛːhəʊl, -z
AM ˈɛrˌ(h)oʊl, -z

airily
BR ˈɛːrɨli
AM ˈɛrəli

airiness
BR ˈɛːrɪnɨs
AM ˈɛrinɨs

airing
BR ˈɛːrɪŋ, -z
AM ˈɛrɪŋ, -z

airlane
BR ˈɛːleɪn, -z
AM ˈɛrˌleɪn, -z

airless
BR ˈɛːləs
AM ˈɛrləs

airlessly
BR ˈɛːləsli
AM ˈɛrləsli

airlessness
BR ˈɛːləsnəs
AM ˈɛrləsnəs

airlift
BR ˈɛːlɪft, -s
AM ˈɛrˌlɪft, -s

airline
BR ˈɛːlʌɪn, -z
AM ˈɛrˌlaɪn, -z

airliner
BR ˈɛːˌlʌɪnə(r), -z
AM ˈɛrˌlaɪnər, -z

airlock
BR ˈɛːlɒk, -s
AM ˈɛrˌlɑk, -s

airmail
BR ˈɛːmeɪl, -z, -ɪŋ, -d
AM ˈɛrˌmeɪl, -z, -ɪŋ, -d

airman
BR ˈɛːmən
AM ˈɛrmən

airmen
BR ˈɛːmən
AM ˈɛrmən

airmiss
BR ˈɛːmɪs, -ɨz
AM ˈɛrˌmɪs, -ɨz

airmobile
BR ˈɛːˌmə(ʊ)biːl, -z
AM ˈɛrˌmoʊbəl, -z

airplane
BR ˈɛːpleɪn, -z
AM ˈɛrˌpleɪn, -z

airplay
BR ˈɛːpleɪ, -z
AM ˈɛrˌpleɪ, -z

airpocket
BR ˈɛːˌpɒkɪt, -s
AM ˈɛrˌpɑkət, -s

airport
BR ˈɛːpɔːt, -s
AM ˈɛrˌpɔ(ə)rt, -s

airscrew
BR ˈɛːskruː, -z
AM ˈɛrˌskru, -z

airshaft
BR ˈɛːʃɑːft, ˈɛːʃaft, -s
AM ˈɛrˌʃæft, -s

airship
BR ˈɛːʃɪp, -s
AM ˈɛrˌʃɪp, -s

airsick
BR ˈɛːsɪk
AM ˈɛrˌsɪk

airsickness
BR ˈɛːˌsɪknɨs
AM ˈɛrˌsɪknɨs

airside
BR ˈɛːsʌɪd
AM ˈɛrˌsaɪd

airspace
BR ˈɛːspeɪs
AM ˈɛrˌspeɪs

airspeed
BR ˈɛːspiːd, -z
AM ˈɛrˌspid, -z

airstream
BR ˈɛːstriːm, -z
AM ˈɛrˌstrim, -z

airstrip
BR ˈɛːstrɪp, -s
AM ˈɛrˌstrɪp, -s

airtight
BR ˈɛːtʌɪt
AM ˌɛrˈtaɪt

airtime
BR ˈɛːtʌɪm
AM ˈɛrˌtaɪm

airwave
BR ˈɛːweɪv, -z
AM ˈɛrˌweɪv, -z

airway
BR ˈɛːweɪ, -z
AM ˈɛrˌweɪ, -z

airwoman
BR ˈɛːˌwʊmən
AM ˈɛrˌwʊmən

airwomen
BR ˈɛːˌwɪmɪn
AM ˈɛrˌwɪmɨn

airworthiness
BR ˈɛːˌwəːðɪnɨs
AM ˈɛrˌwərðinɨs

airworthy
BR ˈɛːˌwəːði
AM ˈɛrˌwərði

airy
BR ˈɛːr|i, -ɪə(r), -ɪɨst
AM ˈɛri, -ər, -ɨst

aisle
BR ʌɪl, -z, -d
AM aɪl, -z, -d

ait
BR eɪt, -s
AM eɪt, -s

aitch
BR eɪtʃ, -ɨz
AM eɪtʃ, -ɨz

aitchbone
BR ˈeɪtʃbəʊn, -z
AM ˈeɪtʃˌboʊn, -z

Aitchison
BR ˈeɪtʃɪs(ə)n
AM ˈeɪtʃɪsən

Aitken
BR ˈeɪ(t)kɪn
AM ˈeɪ(t)kən

Aix-en-Provence
BR ˌeɪksɒ̃prɒˈvɒ̃s
AM ˌɛksɑnproʊˈvɑns
FR ɛks ɑ̃ pʀɔvɑ̃s

Aix-la-Chapelle
BR ˌeɪksləʃəˈpɛl, ˌeɪkslaʃaˈpɛl
AM ˌɛkslɑʃɑˈpɛl
FR ɛks la ʃapɛl

Ajaccio
BR aˈdʒaksɪəʊ
AM ɑˈjɑtʃ(i)oʊ
FR aʒaksjo

ajar
BR əˈdʒɑː(r)
AM əˈdʒɑr

Ajax
BR ˈeɪdʒaks
AM ˈeɪˌdʒæks

ajuga
BR əˈdʒuːgə(*r*)
AM əˈdʒugə

aka
BR ˌeɪkeɪˈeɪ, ˈakə(*r*)
AM ˌeɪˌkeɪˈeɪ

Akai
BR ˈakʌɪ
AM ˈɑkaɪ

akala
BR ɑːˈkɑːlə(*r*), -z
AM əˈkɑlə, -z

Akbar
BR ˈakbɑː(r)
AM ˈɑkˌbɑr

akebia
BR əˈkiːbɪə(*r*)
AM əˈkibiə

akee
BR ˈak|i, -ɪz
AM æˈki, ˈæˌki, -z

akela
BR ɑːˈkeɪlə(*r*), -z
AM əˈkilə, -z

Akerman
BR ˈakəmən, ˈeɪkəmən
AM ˈækərmən

Akhenaten
BR akˈnɑːtn
AM ɑkˈnɑtn

Akhetaten
BR ˌakəˈtɑːtn
AM ˌɑkɛˈtɑtn

akimbo
BR əˈkɪmbəʊ
AM əˈkɪmboʊ

akin
BR ə'kɪn
AM ə'kɪn
Akins
BR 'eɪkɪnz
AM 'eɪkɪnz
Akita
BR ɑː'kiːtə(*r*)
AM ɑ'kidə
Akkad
BR 'akad
AM 'æk,æd, 'ɑk,ɑd
Akkadian
BR ə'keɪdɪən, a'keɪdɪən, ə'kadɪən, a'kadɪən, -z
AM ə'keɪdiən, -z
Akko
BR a'kəʊ
AM ɑ'koʊ
Akron
BR 'akrɒn, 'akr(ə)n
AM 'ækrən
Aksai Chin
BR ,aksʌɪ 'tʃɪn
AM ,æk,saɪ 'tʃɪn
Aksum
BR 'aksʊm
AM 'ɑk,sʊm
Al
BR al
AM æl
à la
BR ,a la(*r*), ,ɑː 'lɑː(*r*), + lə(*r*)
AM ,ɑ lɑ, + lə
Alabama
BR ,alə'bamə(*r*)
AM ,ælə'bæmə
Alabaman
BR ,alə'bamən, -z
AM ,ælə'bæmən, -z
Alabamian
BR ,alə'bamɪən, -z
AM ,ælə'bæmiən, -z
alabaster
BR 'aləbɑːstə(r), 'aləbastə(r)
AM 'ælə,bæstər
alabastrine
BR ,alə'bɑːstrʌɪn, ,alə'bɑːstrɪn, ,alə'bastrʌɪn, ,alə'bastrɪn
AM ,ælə'bæstrən
à la carte
BR ,a la 'kɑːt, ,a lə +, ,ɑː lɑː +
AM ,ɑ lɑ 'kɑrt, ,ɑ lə +
alack
BR ə'lak
AM ə'læk
alacrity
BR ə'lakrɪti
AM ə'lækrədi
Aladdin
BR ə'ladɪn
AM ə'lædən
Alaister
BR 'alɪstə(r)
AM 'æləstər, 'ælə,stɛ(ə)r
Alamein
BR 'aləmeɪn, ,alə'meɪn
AM ,ælə'meɪn
Alamo
BR 'aləməʊ
AM 'ælə,moʊ
à la mode
BR ,a la 'məʊd, ,a lə +, ,ɑː lɑː +
AM ,ɑ lɑ 'moʊd
Alan
BR 'alən
AM 'ælən
Alana
BR ə'lanə(*r*)
AM ə'lɑnə
alanine
BR 'aləniːn, 'alənʌɪn
AM 'ælə,nin
Alar®
BR 'eɪlɑː(r)
AM 'eɪ,lɑr
alar
BR 'eɪlə(r), 'eɪlɑː(r)
AM 'eɪlər
Alaric
BR 'alərɪk
AM 'ælərɪk
alarm
BR ə'lɑːm, -z, -ɪŋ, -d
AM ə'lɑrm, -z, -ɪŋ, -d
alarmingly
BR ə'lɑːmɪŋli
AM ə'lɑrmɪŋli
alarmism
BR ə'lɑːmɪz(ə)m
AM ə'lɑrm,ɪzəm
alarmist
BR ə'lɑːmɪst, -s
AM ə'lɑrməst, -s
alarum
BR ə'lɑːrəm, -z
AM ə'lɑrəm, -z
alas
BR ə'las, ə'lɑːs
AM ə'læs
Alasdair
BR 'aləstə(r), 'aləstɛː(r)
AM 'æləstər, 'ælə,stɛ(ə)r
Alaska
BR ə'laskə(*r*)
AM ə'læskə
Alaskan
BR ə'laskən, -z
AM ə'læskən, -z
Alastair
BR 'aləstə(r), 'aləstɛː(r)
AM 'æləstər, 'ælə,stɛ(ə)r
Alastor
BR ə'lɑːstə(r), ə'lastə(r), -z
AM ə'læstər, -z
alate
BR 'eɪleɪt, -s
AM 'eɪ,leɪt, -s
alb
BR alb, -z
AM ælb, -z
Alba
BR 'albə(*r*)
AM 'ælbə
Albacete
BR ,albə'seɪti
AM ,ælbə'seɪ,di
SP ,alβa'θete, alβa'sete
albacore
BR 'albəkɔː(r), -z
AM 'ælbə,kɔ(ə)r, -z
Alban
BR 'ɔːlbən, 'ɒlbən
AM 'ɑlbən
Albania
BR al'beɪnɪə(*r*)
AM æl'beɪniə, ɑl'beɪniə
Albanian
BR al'beɪnɪən, -z
AM æl'beɪniən, ɑl'beɪniən, -z
Albany
BR 'ɔːlbəni, 'ɒlbəni
AM 'ɔlbəni, 'ɑlbəni
albata
BR al'beɪtə(*r*)
AM æl'bædə
albatross
BR 'albətrɒs, -ɪz
AM 'ælbə,trɔs, 'ælbə,trɑs, -əz
albedo
BR al'biːdəʊ, -z
AM æl'bidoʊ, -z
Albee
BR 'ɔːlbi, 'albi
AM 'ælbi
albeit
BR ɔːl'biːɪt
AM æl'biɪt, ɔl'biɪt, ɑl'biɪt
Albemarle
BR 'albəmɑːl
AM 'ælbə,mɑr(ə)l
Albert
BR 'albət
AM 'ælbərt
Alberta
BR al'bəːtə(*r*)
AM æl'bərdə
Albertan
BR al'bəːt(ə)n, -z
AM æl'bərd(ə)n, -z
Alberti
BR al'bəːti
AM ɑl'bərdi
Albertus Magnus
BR al,bəːtəs 'magnəs
AM æl,bərdəs 'mægnəs
albescence
BR al'bɛsns
AM æl'bɛsəns
albescent
BR al'bɛsnt
AM æl'bɛsənt
Albigenses
BR ,albɪ'dʒɛnsiːz, ,albɪ'gɛnsiːz
AM ,ælbə'dʒɛnsiz
Albigensian
BR ,albɪ'dʒɛnsɪən, ,albɪ'gɛnsɪən, -z
AM ,ælbə'dʒɛn(t)siən, ,ælbə'dʒɛn(t)ʃən, -z
albinism
BR 'albɪnɪz(ə)m
AM 'ælbə,nɪzəm
albino
BR al'biːnəʊ, -z
AM æl'baɪ,noʊ, -z
Albinoni
BR ,albɪ'nəʊni
AM ,ælbə'noʊni
albinotic
BR ,albɪ'nɒtɪk
AM ,ælbə'nɑdɪk
Albion
BR 'albɪən
AM 'ælbiən
albite
BR 'albʌɪt
AM 'æl,baɪt
Ålborg
BR 'ɔːlbɔːg, 'ɑːlbɔːg
AM 'ɔl,bɔrg, 'ɑl,bɔrg
DAN 'ʌl,bɒː'
Albright
BR 'ɔːlbrʌɪt, 'ɒlbrʌɪt
AM 'ɔlbraɪt, 'ɑlbraɪt
album
BR 'albəm, -z
AM 'ælbəm, -z
albumen
BR 'albjʊmɪn
AM æl'bjumən
albumin
BR 'albjʊmɪn
AM æl'bjumən
albuminoid
BR al'bjuːmɪnɔɪd, -z
AM æl'bjumə,nɔɪd, -z
albuminous
BR al'bjuːmɪnəs
AM æl'bjumənəs
albuminuria
BR al,bjuːmɪ'njʊərɪə(*r*)
AM æl,bjumə'nʊriə
Albuquerque
BR 'albəkəːki
AM 'ælbə,kərki
alburnum
BR al'bəːnəm

AM æl'bərnəm

Albury
BR 'ɔːlb(ə)ri, 'ɒlb(ə)ri
AM 'ɔlbəri, 'ɑlbəri

Alcaeus
BR 'alsɪəs, al'siːəs
AM 'æl,siəs

alcahest
BR 'alkəhɛst
AM 'ælkə,hɛst

alcaic
BR al'keɪɪk
AM æl'keɪɪk

alcalde
BR al'kald|i, al'kɑːld|i, -ɪz
AM ɑl'kɑldi, æl'kɑldi, -z

Alcan®
BR 'alkan
AM 'ælkæn

Alcatraz
BR 'alkətraz, ,alkə'traz
AM 'ælkə,træz

Alcazar
BR ,alkə'zɑː(r), al'kazə(r)
AM ,ɑlkə,zɑr, ,æl'kæzər

Alceste
BR al'sɛst
AM ɔl'sɛst, ɑl'sɛst

Alcester
BR 'ɔːlstə(r)
AM 'ɔlsɛstər, 'ɑlsɛstər

Alcestis
BR al'sɛstɪs
AM ɔl'sɛstəs, ɑl'sɛstəs

alchemic
BR al'kɛmɪk
AM æl'kɛmɪk

alchemical
BR al'kɛmɨkl
AM æl'kɛməkəl

alchemise
BR 'alkəmʌɪz, -ɨz, -ɪŋ, -d
AM 'ælkə,maɪz, -ɨz, -ɪŋ, -d

alchemist
BR 'alkəmɪst, -s
AM 'ælkəməst, -s

alchemize
BR 'alkəmʌɪz, -ɨz, -ɪŋ, -d
AM 'ælkə,maɪz, -ɨz, -ɪŋ, -d

alchemy
BR 'alkəmi
AM 'ælkəmi

alcheringa
BR ,altʃə'rɪŋgə(r)
AM ,æltʃə'rɪŋgə

Alcibiades
BR ,alsɪ'bʌɪədiːz
AM ,ælsə'baɪədiz

alcid
BR 'alsɪd, -z
AM 'ælsəd, -z

Alcock
BR 'ɔːlkɒk, 'alkɒk
AM 'ɔl,kɑk, 'ɑl,kɑk

alcohol
BR 'alkəhɒl, -z
AM 'ælkə,hɔl, 'ælkə,hɑl, -z

alcoholic
BR ,alkə'hɒlɪk
AM ,ælkə'hɔlɪk, ,ælkə'hɑlɪk

alcoholism
BR 'alkəhɒlɪz(ə)m, 'alkəhəlɪz(ə)m
AM 'ælkə,hɔ,lɪzəm, 'ælkə,hɑ,lɪzəm

alcoholometer
BR ,alkəhɒ'lɒmɨtə(r), -z
AM ,ælkə,hɔ'lɑmədər, ,ælkə,hɑ'lɑmədər, -z

alcoholometry
BR ,alkəhɒ'lɒmɨtri
AM ,ælkə,hɔ'lɑmətri, ,ælkə,hɑ'lɑmətri

Alconbury
BR 'ɔːlk(ə)nb(ə)ri, 'ɒlk(ə)nb(ə)ri
AM 'ɔlkənbəri, 'ɑlkənbəri

Alcoran
BR ,alkə'rɑːn, 'alkəran
AM ,ɑlkoʊ'rɑn

Alcott
BR 'ɔːlkət, 'ɔːlkɒt, 'ɒlkət, 'ɒlkɒt
AM 'æl,kɑt

alcove
BR 'alkəʊv, -z
AM 'æl,koʊv, -z

Alcuin
BR 'alkwɪn
AM 'ælkwən

Aldabra
BR al'dabrə(r)
AM æl'dæbrə

Aldebaran
BR al'dɛb(ə)rən, al'dɛb(ə)rn̩
AM æl'dɛbərən

Aldeburgh
BR 'ɔːl(d)b(ə)rə(r)
AM 'ɑl(d),bəroʊ

aldehyde
BR 'aldɨhʌɪd, -z
AM 'ældə,haɪd, -z

aldehydic
BR ,aldɪ'hɪdɪk
AM ,ældə'hɪdɪk

Alden
BR 'ɔːld(ə)n, 'ɒld(ə)n
AM 'ɔldən, 'ɑldən

al dente
BR al 'dɛnti, + 'dɛnteɪ
AM ,æl 'dɛn(t)eɪ, ɑl +

alder
BR 'ɔːldə(r), 'ɒldə(r), -z
AM 'ɔldər, 'ɑldər, -z

Aldergrove
BR 'ɔːldəgrəʊv, 'ɒldəgrəʊv
AM 'ɔldər,groʊv, 'ɑldər,groʊv

alderman
BR 'ɔːldəmən, 'ɒldəmən
AM 'ɔldərmən, 'ɑldərmən

aldermanic
BR ,ɔːldə'manɪk, ,ɒldə'manɪk
AM ,ɔldər'mænɪk, ,ɑldər'mænɪk

aldermanry
BR 'ɔːldəmənri, 'ɒldəmənri
AM 'ɔldərmənri, 'ɑldərmənri

aldermanship
BR 'ɔːldəmənʃɪp, 'ɒldəmənʃɪp
AM 'ɔldərmən,ʃɪp, 'ɑldərmən,ʃɪp

Aldermaston
BR 'ɔːldəmɑːst(ə)n, 'ɔːldəmast(ə)n, 'ɒldəmɑːst(ə)n, 'ɒldəmast(ə)n
AM 'ɔldər,mæstən, 'ɑldər,mæstən

aldermen
BR 'ɔːldəmən, 'ɒldəmən
AM 'ɔldərmən, 'ɑldərmən

Alderney
BR 'ɔːldəni, 'ɒldəni
AM 'ɔldərni, 'ɑldərni

Aldersgate
BR 'ɔːldəzgeɪt, 'ɒldəzgeɪt
AM 'ɔldərs,geɪt, 'ɑldərs,geɪt

Aldershot
BR 'ɔːldəʃɒt, 'ɒldəʃɒt
AM 'ɔldər,ʃɑt, 'ɑldər,ʃɑt

Alderson
BR 'ɔːldəs(ə)n, 'ɒldəs(ə)n
AM 'ɔldərsən, 'ɑldərsən

Alderton
BR 'ɔːldət(ə)n, 'ɒldət(ə)n
AM 'ɔldərt(ə)n, 'ɑldərt(ə)n

alderwoman
BR 'ɔːldə,wʊmən, 'ɒldə,wʊmən
AM 'ɔldər,wʊmən, 'ɑldər,wʊmən

alderwomen
BR 'ɔːldə,wɪmɪn, 'ɒldə,wɪmɪn
AM 'ɔldər,wɪmɨn, 'ɑldər,wɪmɨn

Aldgate
BR 'ɔːl(d)gɨt, 'ɒl(d)gɨt, 'ɔːl(d)geɪt, 'ɒl(d)geɪt
AM 'ɔl(d),geɪt, 'ɑl(d),geɪt

Aldine
BR 'ɔːldʌɪn, 'ɔːldiːn, 'ɒldʌɪn, 'ɒldiːn
AM 'ɔl,daɪn, 'ɔldin, 'ɑl,daɪn, 'ɑldin

Aldis
BR 'ɔːldɪs, 'ɒldɪs
AM 'ɔldəs, 'ɑldəs

Aldiss
BR 'ɔːldɪs, 'ɒldɪs
AM 'ɔldəs, 'ɑldəs

aldol
BR 'aldɒl
AM 'æl,dɔl, 'æl,dɑl

aldosterone
BR al'dɒstərəʊn
AM ,æl'dɑstə,roʊn

Aldous
BR 'ɔːldəs, 'ɒldəs
AM 'ɔldəs, 'ɑldəs

Aldridge
BR 'ɔːldrɪdʒ, 'ɒldrɪdʒ
AM 'ɔldrɪdʒ, 'ɑldrɪdʒ

Aldrin
BR 'ɔːldrɪn, 'ɒldrɪn
AM 'ɔldrɪn, 'ɑldrɪn

Aldwych
BR 'ɔːldwɪtʃ, 'ɒldwɪtʃ
AM 'ɔldwɪtʃ, 'ɑldwɪtʃ

ale
BR eɪl, -z
AM eɪl, -z

aleatoric
BR ,eɪlɪə'tɒrɪk, ,alɪə'tɒrɪk
AM ,eɪliə'tɔrɪk, ,æliə'tɔrɪk

aleatory
BR ,eɪlɪ'eɪt(ə)ri, ,alɪ'eɪt(ə)ri, 'eɪlɪət(ə)ri, 'alɪət(ə)ri
AM 'eɪliə,tɔri, 'æliə,tɔri

Alec
BR 'alɪk
AM 'ælək

alecost
BR 'eɪlkɒst
AM 'eɪl,kɑst

alee
BR ə'liː
AM ə'li

alegar
BR 'eɪlɨgə(r), 'alɨgə(r)
AM 'æləgər, 'eɪləgər

alehouse
BR 'eɪlhaʊ|s, -zɨz
AM 'eɪl,(h)aʊ|s, -zəz

Aleksandrovsk
BR ˌalɪɡzanˈdrɒfsk, ˌalɪɡˈzandrɒfsk, ˌalɪksanˈdrɒfsk, ˌalɪkˈsandrɒfsk
AM ˌæləɡˈzændrɔvsk, ˌæləkˈsændrɔvsk, ˌæləɡˈzændrɑvsk, ˌæləkˈsændrɑvsk

alembic
BR əˈlɛmbɪk, -s
AM əˈlɛmbɪk, -s

alembicated
BR əˈlɛmbɪkeɪtɨd
AM əˈlɛmbəˌkeɪdɨd

alembication
BR əˌlɛmbɪˈkeɪʃn
AM əˌlɛmbəˈkeɪʃən

aleph
BR ˈalɛf, ˈɑːlɛf, ˈalɪf, ˈɑːlɪf, -s
AM ˈɑlɛf, ˈɑləf, -s

Aleppo
BR əˈlɛpəʊ
AM əˈlɛpoʊ

alert
BR əˈləːt, -s, -ɪŋ, -ɨd, -ɨst
AM əˈlər|t, -ts, -dɪŋ, -dəd, -dəst

alertly
BR əˈləːtli
AM əˈlərtli

alertness
BR əˈləːtnəs
AM əˈlərtnəs

aleuron
BR ˈaljʊərən
AM ˈæljəˌroʊn, əˈlʊroʊn

aleurone
BR ˈaljʊərəʊn
AM ˈæljəˌroʊn, əˈlʊroʊn

Aleut
BR ˈaljuːt, ˈalɪuːt, əˈl(j)uːt, -s
AM əˈlut, ˈæliˌut, -s

Aleutian
BR əˈl(j)uːʃn, -z
AM əˈl(j)uʃən, -z

alewife
BR ˈeɪlwʌɪf
AM ˈeɪlˌwaɪf

alewives
BR ˈeɪlwʌɪvz
AM ˈeɪlˌwaɪvz

Alex
BR ˈalɪks
AM ˈælɛks

Alexa
BR əˈlɛksə(r)
AM əˈlɛksə

Alexander
BR ˌalɪɡˈzɑːndə(r), ˌalɪɡˈzandə(r)
AM ˌæləɡˈzændər

alexanders
BR ˌalɪɡˈzɑːndəz, ˌalɪɡˈzandəz
AM ˌæləɡˈzændərz

Alexandra
BR ˌalɪɡˈzɑːndrə(r), ˌalɪɡˈzandrə(r)
AM ˌæləɡˈzændrə

Alexandretta
BR ˌalɪɡzɑːnˈdrɛtə(r), ˌalɪɡzanˈdrɛtə(r)
AM ˌæləɡˌzænˈdrɛdə

Alexandria
BR ˌalɪɡˈzɑːndrɪə(r), ˌalɪɡˈzandrɪə(r)
AM ˌæləɡˈzændriə

Alexandrian
BR ˌalɪɡˈzɑːndrɪən, ˌalɪɡˈzandrɪən, -z
AM ˌæləɡˈzændriən, -z

alexandrine
BR ˌalɪɡˈzɑːndrʌɪn, ˌalɪɡˈzɑːndrɪn, ˌalɪɡˈzandrʌɪn, ˌalɪɡˈzandrɪn, -z
AM ˌæləɡˈzændrən, ˌæləɡˈzænˌdrin, ˌæləɡˈzænˌdraɪn, -z

alexandrite
BR ˌalɪɡˈzɑːndrʌɪt, ˌalɪɡˈzandrʌɪt
AM ˌæləɡˈzænˌdraɪt

alexia
BR əˈlɛksɪə(r)
AM əˈlɛksiə

alexin
BR əˈlɛksɪn
AM əˈlɛksən

alexine
BR əˈlɛksiːn
AM əˈlɛkˌsin

alexipharmic
BR əˌlɛksɪˈfɑːmɪk
AM əˌlɛksəˈfɑrmɪk

Alexis
BR əˈlɛksɪs
AM əˈlɛksəs

alfa
BR ˈalfə(r), -z
AM ˈælfə, -z

Alfa-Laval
BR ˌalfələˈval
AM ˌælfələˈvɑl

alfalfa
BR alˈfalfə(r)
AM ælˈfælfə

Alfa Romeo®
BR ˌalfə rə(ʊ)ˈmeɪəʊ, + ˈrəʊmɪəʊ, -z
AM ˌælfə ˌroʊˈmeɪoʊ, -z

al-Fatah
BR alˈfatə(r), ˌalfəˈtɑː(r)
AM ˌɑlfəˈtɑ

alfisol
BR ˈalfɪsɒl
AM ˈælfəˌsɔl ˈælfəˌsɑl

Alfonso
BR alˈfɒnzəʊ, alˈfɒnsəʊ
AM ælˈfɑnˌzoʊ, ælˈfɑnˌsoʊ

Alford
BR ˈɔːlfəd, ˈɒlfəd
AM ˈɔlfərd, ˈælfərd, ˈɑlfərd

Alfred
BR ˈalfrɪd
AM ˈælfrəd

Alfreda
BR alˈfriːdə(r)
AM ælˈfrɛdə

alfresco
BR alˈfrɛskəʊ
AM ælˈfrɛskoʊ, ɑlˈfrɛskoʊ

Alfreton
BR ˈalfrɪt(ə)n, ˈɔːlfrɪt(ə)n, ˈɒlfrɪt(ə)n
AM ˈɔlfrədən, ˈælfrədən, ˈɑlfrədən, ˈɔlfrətn, ˈælfrətn, ˈɑlfrətn

Alfvén
BR ˈalfveɪn, ˈalfvən
AM ˈɑlˌveɪn
SW alˈveːn

alga
BR ˈalɡə(r)
AM ˈælɡə

algae
BR ˈaldʒiː, ˈalɡiː
AM ˈælˌdʒi

algal
BR ˈalɡl
AM ˈælɡəl

Algarve
BR alˈɡɑːv
AM ɑlˈɡɑrv
B PORT ˈɑwɡɑrvi
L PORT alˈɡarvə

algebra
BR ˈaldʒɪbrə(r)
AM ˈældʒəbrə

algebraic
BR ˌaldʒɪˈbreɪɪk
AM ˌældʒəˈbreɪɪk

algebraical
BR ˌaldʒɪˈbreɪɪkl
AM ˌældʒəˈbreɪɪkəl

algebraically
BR ˌaldʒɪˈbreɪɪkli
AM ˌældʒəˈbreɪɪk(ə)li

algebraist
BR ˈaldʒɪbreɪɪst, ˌaldʒɪˈbreɪɪst, -s
AM ˈældʒəˌbreɪɪst, ˌældʒəˈbreɪɪst, -s

Algeciras
BR ˌaldʒɪˈsɪərəs
AM ˌældʒəˈsɪrəs
SP ˌalxeˈθiras, ˌalheˈsiras

Algeo
BR ˈaldʒɪəʊ
AM ˈældʒioʊ

Alger
BR ˈaldʒə(r)
AM ˈældʒər

Algeria
BR alˈdʒɪərɪə(r)
AM ælˈdʒɪriə

Algerian
BR alˈdʒɪərɪən, -z
AM ælˈdʒɪriən, -z

Algernon
BR ˈaldʒənən, ˈaldʒn̩ən, ˈaldʒənɒn, ˈaldʒn̩ɒn
AM ˈældʒərˌnɑn

algicide
BR ˈaldʒɪsʌɪd, -z
AM ˈældʒəˌsaɪd, -z

algid
BR ˈaldʒɪd
AM ˈældʒɪd

algidity
BR alˈdʒɪdɪti
AM ælˈdʒɪdɪdi

Algie
BR ˈaldʒi
AM ˈældʒi

Algiers
BR alˈdʒɪəz
AM ælˈdʒɪ(ə)rz

alginate
BR ˈaldʒɪneɪt, ˈaldʒɪnət, -s
AM ˈældʒəˌneɪt, ˈældʒənət, -s

alginic
BR alˈdʒɪnɪk
AM ælˈdʒɪnɪk

Algipan
BR ˈaldʒɪpan
AM ˈældʒɪˌpæn

Algoa
BR alˈɡəʊə(r)
AM ælˈɡoʊə

algoid
BR ˈalɡɔɪd
AM ˈælˌɡɔɪd

Algol
BR ˈalɡɒl
AM ˈælˌɡɔl, ˈælˌɡɑl

algolagnia
BR ˌalɡə(ʊ)ˈlaɡnɪə(r)
AM ˌælɡoʊˈlæɡniə

algolagnic
BR ˌalɡə(ʊ)ˈlaɡnɪk
AM ˌælɡoʊˈlæɡnɪk

algological
BR ˌalɡəˈlɒdʒɪkl
AM ˌælɡəˈlɑdʒəkəl

algologist
BR alˈɡɒlədʒɪst, -s
AM ælˈɡɑlədʒəst, -s

algology
BR alˈɡɒlədʒi
AM ælˈɡɑlədʒi

Algonkian
BR alˈɡɒŋkɪən

AM æl'gɑŋkiən
Algonkin
BR al'gɒŋkɪn
AM æl'gɑŋkən
Algonquian
BR al'gɒŋk(w)ɪən
AM æl'gɑŋk(w)iən
Algonquin
BR al'gɒŋk(w)ɪn
AM æl'gɑŋkwən
algorithm
BR 'algərɪð(ə)m, -z
AM 'ælgəˌrɪðəm, -z
algorithmic
BR ˌalgə'rɪðmɪk
AM ˌælgə'rɪðmɪk
algorithmically
BR ˌalgə'rɪðmɨkli
AM ˌælgə'rɪðmɨk(ə)li
alguacil
BR ˌalgwə'sɪl, ˌalgwə'siːl, 'algwəsɪl, 'algwəsiːl, -z
AM ˌælgwə'sil, ˌælgwə'sɪl, -z
alguaciles
BR ˌalgwə'siːleɪz
AM ˌælgwə'sileɪz
alguazil
BR ˌalgwə'zɪl, ˌalgwə'ziːl, -z
AM ˌælgwə'zil, ˌælgwə'zɪl, -z
alguaziles
BR ˌalgwə'ziːleɪz
AM ˌælgwə'zileɪz
Algy
BR 'aldʒi
AM 'ældʒi
Alhambra
BR al'hambrə(*r*), ə'lambrə(*r*)
AM æl'hæmbrə
SP a'lambra
Alhambresque
BR ˌalham'brɛsk, ˌaləm'brɛsk
AM ˌælˌ(h)æm'brɛsk
Ali[1]
BR 'ali 'ɑːli
AM 'ɑli
Ali[2]
Muhammed, boxer
BR 'ali, ɑː'liː
AM ɑ'li
alias
BR 'eɪlɪəs, -ɪz
AM 'eɪliəs, -əz
Ali Baba
BR ˌalɪ 'bɑːbə(*r*)
AM ˌɑli 'bɑbə
alibi
BR 'alɨbʌɪ, -z
AM 'æləˌbaɪ, -z
Alicante
BR ˌalɪ'kanti
AM ˌælə'kæn(t)i, ˌɑlə'kɑn(t)i
SP ali'kante
Alice
BR 'alɪs
AM 'æləs
Alicia
BR ə'lɪʃ(ɪ)ə(*r*), ə'lɪsɪə(*r*)
AM ə'lɪʃə
Alick
BR 'alɪk
AM 'ælək
alicyclic
BR ˌalɪ'sʌɪklɪk
AM ˌælə'saɪklɪk
alidad
BR 'alɨdad, -z
AM 'æləˌdæd, -z
alidade
BR 'alɨdeɪd, -z
AM 'æləˌdeɪd, -z
alien
BR 'eɪlɪən, -z
AM 'eɪliən, 'eɪljən, -z
alienability
BR ˌeɪlɪənə'bɪlɨti
AM ˌeɪliənə'bɪlɨdi, ˌeɪljənə'bɪlɨdi
alienable
BR 'eɪlɪənəbl
AM 'eɪliənəbəl, 'eɪljənəbəl
alienage
BR 'eɪlɪənɪdʒ
AM 'eɪliənɪdʒ, 'eɪljənɪdʒ
alienate
BR 'eɪlɪəneɪt, -s, -ɪŋ, -ɨd
AM 'eɪliəˌneɪ|t, 'eɪljəˌneɪ|t, -ts, -dɪŋ, -dɨd
alienation
BR ˌeɪlɪə'neɪʃn
AM ˌeɪliə'neɪʃən, ˌeɪljə'neɪʃən
alienator
BR 'eɪlɪəneɪtə(r), -z
AM 'eɪliəˌneɪdər, 'eɪljəˌneɪdər, -z
alienism
BR 'eɪlɪənɪz(ə)m
AM 'eɪliəˌnɪzəm, 'eɪljəˌnɪzəm
alienist
BR 'eɪlɪənɪst, -s
AM 'eɪliənəst, 'eɪljənəst, -s
alienness
BR 'eɪlɪənnəs
AM 'eɪliə(n)nəs, 'eɪljə(n)nəs
aliform
BR 'eɪlɨfɔːm, 'alɨfɔːm
AM 'æləˌfɔ(ə)rm, 'eɪləˌfɔ(ə)rm
alight
BR ə'lʌɪt, -s, -ɪŋ, -ɨd
AM ə'laɪ|t, -ts, -dɪŋ, -dɨd
align
BR ə'lʌɪn, -z, -ɪŋ, -d
AM ə'laɪn, -z, -ɪŋ, -d
alignment
BR ə'lʌɪnm(ə)nt, -s
AM ə'laɪnmənt, -s
alike
BR ə'lʌɪk
AM ə'laɪk
aliment
BR 'alɨm(ə)nt, -s
AM 'æləmənt, -s
alimental
BR ˌalɪ'mɛntl
AM ˌælə'mɛn(t)l
alimentary
BR ˌalɪ'mɛnt(ə)ri
AM ˌælə'mɛn(t)əri
alimentation
BR ˌalɨmɛn'teɪʃn, ˌalɨm(ə)n'teɪʃn
AM ˌæləmən'teɪʃən
alimony
BR 'alɨmən|i, -ɪz
AM 'æləˌmoʊni, -z
aline
BR ə'lʌɪn, -z, -ɪŋ, -d
AM ə'laɪn, -z, -ɪŋ, -d
alineation
BR əˌlɪnɪ'eɪʃn, -z
AM əˌlɪni'eɪʃən, -z
alinement
BR ə'lʌɪnm(ə)nt, -s
AM ə'laɪnmənt, -s
aliphatic
BR ˌalɪ'fatɪk
AM ˌælə'fædɪk
aliquant
BR 'alɨkw(ə)nt
AM 'æləˌkwɑnt, 'æləkwənt
aliquot
BR 'alɨkwɒt
AM 'æləˌkwɑt, 'æləkwət
Alisdair
BR 'alɪstə(r), 'alɪstɛː(r)
AM 'æləstər, 'æləsˌtɛ(ə)r
Alison
BR 'alɪs(ə)n
AM 'æləsən
Alissa
BR ə'lɪsə(*r*)
AM ə'lɪsə
Alistair
BR 'alɪstə(r), 'alɪstɛː(r)
AM 'æləstər, 'æləsˌtɛ(ə)r
Alitalia®
BR ˌalɪ'talɪə(*r*)
AM ˌɑlə'tɑljə, ˌælə'tæljə, ˌɑlə'tɑliə, ˌælə'tæliə
alive
BR ə'lʌɪv
AM ə'laɪv
aliveness
BR ə'lʌɪvnɨs
AM ə'laɪvnɨs
Alix
BR 'alɪks
AM 'æləks
aliyah
BR ə'liːə(*r*)
AM ə'liə
alizarin
BR ə'lɪz(ə)rɪn
AM ə'lɪzərən
alizarine
BR ə'lɪz(ə)riːn
AM ə'lɪzərən, ə'lɪzəˌrin
alkahest
BR 'alkəhɛst
AM 'ælkəˌhɛst
alkalescence
BR ˌalkə'lɛsns
AM ˌælkə'lɛsəns
alkalescency
BR ˌalkə'lɛsnsi
AM ˌælkə'lɛsənsi
alkalescent
BR ˌalkə'lɛsnt
AM ˌælkə'lɛsənt
alkali
BR 'alkəlʌɪ, -z
AM 'ælkəˌlaɪ, -z
alkalify
BR al'kalɪfʌɪ, 'alkəlɪfʌɪ, -z, -ɪŋ, -d
AM 'ælkələˌfaɪ, -z, -ɪŋ, -d
alkalimeter
BR ˌalkə'lɪmɨtə(r), -z
AM ˌælkə'lɪmədər, -z
alkalimetry
BR ˌalkə'lɪmɨtri
AM ˌælkə'lɪmətri
alkaline
BR 'alkəlʌɪn
AM 'ælkələn, 'ælkəˌlaɪn
alkalinity
BR ˌalkə'lɪnɨti
AM ˌælkə'lɪnɨdi
alkaloid
BR 'alkəlɔɪd, -z
AM 'ælkəˌlɔɪd, -z
alkaloidal
BR ˌalkə'lɔɪdl
AM ˌælkə'lɔɪdəl
alkaloses
BR ˌalkə'ləʊsiːz
AM ˌælkə'loʊsiz
alkalosis
BR ˌalkə'ləʊsɪs
AM ˌælkə'loʊsəs
alkane
BR 'alkeɪn, -z
AM 'ælˌkeɪn, -z
alkanet
BR 'alkənɛt, -s
AM 'ælkəˌnɛt, -s

Alka-Seltzer®
BR ˌalkəˈsɛltsə(r), ˈalkəˌsɛltsə(r), -z
AM ˈælkəˌsɛl(t)sər, -z

alkene
BR ˈalkiːn, -z
AM ˈælˌkin, -z

alkyd
BR ˈalkɪd
AM ˈælˌkɪd

alkyl
BR ˈalkɪl, ˈalkʌɪl, -z
AM ˈælˌkɪl, ˈælkəl, -z

alkylate
BR ˈalkɨleɪt, -s, -ɪŋ, -ɨd
AM ˈælkəˌleɪ|t, -ts, -dɪŋ, -dɨd

alkyne
BR ˈalkʌɪn, -z
AM ˈælkaɪn, -z

all
BR ɔːl
AM ɔl, ɑl

alla breve
BR ˌalə ˈbreɪvi, ˌɑːlə +, + ˈbrɛvi, + ˈbreɪveɪ
AM ˌɑlə ˈbrɛv(ə)

alla cappella
BR ˌalə kəˈpɛlə(r), ˌɑːlə +
AM ˌɑlə kəˈpɛlə

Allah
BR ˈalə(r)
AM ˈɑlə, ˈælə

Allahabad
BR ˌaləhəˈbad, ˌaləhəˈbɑːd
AM ˌɑləhəˈbɑd, ˌæləhəˈbæd

allamanda
BR ˌaləˈmandə(r)
AM ˌæləˈmændə

Allan
BR ˈalən
AM ˈælən

allanite
BR ˈalənʌɪt
AM ˈæləˌnaɪt

allantoic
BR ˌalənˈtəʊɪk
AM ˌælənˈtoʊɪk

allantoid
BR əˈlantɔɪd
AM əˈlæntɔɪd

allantoides
BR əˈlantəʊɪdiːz
AM ˈælənˈtɔɪdiz

allantoin
BR əˈlantəʊɪn
AM əˈlæntoʊən

allantois
BR əˈlantəʊɪs
AM əˈlæntəwəs

Allaun
BR əˈlɔːn
AM ˈælɔn, ˈælɑn

allay
BR əˈleɪ, -z, -ɪŋ, -d
AM əˈleɪ, æˈleɪ, -z, -ɪŋ, -d

Allbeury
BR ɔːlˈbjʊəri
AM ˈɔlbəri, ˈɑlbəri

allegation
BR ˌalɪˈgeɪʃn, -z
AM ˌæləˈgeɪʃən, -z

allege
BR əˈlɛdʒ, -ɨz, -ɪŋ, -d
AM əˈlɛdʒ, -əz, -ɪŋ, -d

alleged
BR əˈlɛdʒ(ɨ)d
AM əˈlɛdʒ(ə)d

allegedly
BR əˈlɛdʒɨdli
AM əˈlɛdʒədli

Alleghany
BR ˌalɪˈgeɪn|i, -ɪz
AM ˌæləˈgeɪni, -z

Allegheny
BR ˌalɪˈgeɪn|i, -ɪz
AM ˌæləˈgeɪni, -z

allegiance
BR əˈliːdʒ(ə)ns, -ɨz
AM əˈlidʒəns, -əz

allegiant
BR əˈliːdʒ(ə)nt
AM əˈlidʒənt

allegoric
BR ˌalɪˈgɒrɪk
AM ˌæləˈgɔrɪk

allegorical
BR ˌalɪˈgɒrɪkl
AM ˌæləˈgɔrəkəl

allegorically
BR ˌalɪˈgɒrɪkli
AM ˌæləˈgɔrək(ə)li

allegorisation
BR ˌalɪg(ə)rʌɪˈzeɪʃn
AM ˌæləˌgɔrəˈzeɪʃən, ˌæləgəˌraɪˈzeɪʃən

allegorise
BR ˈalɪg(ə)rʌɪz, -ɨz, -ɪŋ, -d
AM ˈæləˌgɔˌraɪz, ˈæləgəˌraɪz, -ɨz, -ɪŋ, -d

allegorist
BR ˈalɪg(ə)rɪst, -s
AM ˈæləgərəst, ˈæləˌgɔrəst, -s

allegorization
BR ˌalɪg(ə)rʌɪˈzeɪʃn
AM ˌæləˌgɔrəˈzeɪʃən, ˌæləgəˌraɪˈzeɪʃən

allegorize
BR ˈalɪg(ə)rʌɪz, -ɨz, -ɪŋ, -d
AM ˈæləˌgɔˌraɪz, ˈæləgəˌraɪz, -ɨz, -ɪŋ, -d

allegory
BR ˈalɪg(ə)r|i, -ɪz
AM ˈæləˌgɔri, -z

allegretto
BR ˌalɪˈgrɛtəʊ, -z
AM ˌæləˈgrɛdoʊ, -z

allegro
BR əˈlɛgrəʊ, əˈleɪgrəʊ, -z
AM əˈlɛgroʊ, -z

allel
BR əˈlɛl, ˈalɛl, -z
AM əˈlɛl, -z

allele
BR əˈliːl, ˈaliːl, -z
AM əˈlil, -z

allelic
BR əˈliːlɪk, əˈlɛlɪk
AM əˈlilɪk, əˈlɛlɪk

allelomorph
BR əˈliːlə(ʊ)mɔːf, əˈlɛlə(ʊ)mɔːf, -s
AM əˈlɛləˌmɔ(ə)rf, əˈliləˌmɔ(ə)rf, -s

allelomorphic
BR əˌliːlə(ʊ)ˈmɔːfɪk, əˌlɛlə(ʊ)ˈmɔːfɪk
AM əˌlɛləˈmɔrfɪk, əˌliləˈmɔrfɪk

alleluia
BR ˌalɪˈluːjə(r), -z
AM ˌæləˈlujə, -z

allemande
BR ˈalɪmand, -z
AM ˈæləˌmænd, -z

Allen
BR ˈalən
AM ˈælən

Allenby
BR ˈalənbi
AM ˈælənbi

Allende
BR ʌɪˈ(j)ɛndeɪ, ʌɪˈ(j)ɛndi
AM ɑˈjɛnˌdeɪ
SP aˈjende, aˈʒende

Allentown
BR ˈaləntaʊn
AM ˈælənˌtaʊn

allergen
BR ˈalədʒɛn, ˈalədʒ(ə)n
AM ˈælərˌdʒɛn, ˈælərdʒ(ə)n

allergenic
BR ˌaləˈdʒɛnɪk
AM ˌælərˈdʒɛnɪk

allergic
BR əˈləːdʒɪk
AM əˈlərdʒɪk

allergist
BR ˈalədʒɪst, -s
AM ˈælərdʒəst, -s

allergy
BR ˈalədʒ|i, -ɪz
AM ˈælərdʒi, -z

Allerton
BR ˈalət(ə)n, ˈɒlət(ə)n
AM ˈælərt(ə)n

alleviate
BR əˈliːvɪeɪt, -s, -ɪŋ, -ɨd
AM əˈliviˌeɪ|t, -ts, -dɪŋ, -dɨd

alleviation
BR əˌliːvɪˈeɪʃn
AM əˌliviˈeɪʃən

alleviative
BR əˈliːvɪətɪv
AM əˈliviədɪv, əˈliviˌeɪdɪv

alleviator
BR əˈliːvɪeɪtə(r), -z
AM əˈliviˌeɪdər, -z

alleviatory
BR əˈliːvɪət(ə)ri
AM əˈliviəˌtɔri

alley
BR ˈal|i, -ɪz
AM ˈæli, -z

Alleyn
BR ˈalɪn
AM ˈælən

Alleyne
BR aˈleɪn, aˈliːn, ˈalɪn
AM əˈleɪn

alleyway
BR ˈalɪweɪ, -z
AM ˈæliˌweɪ, -z

alliaceous
BR ˌalɪˈeɪʃəs
AM ˌæliˈeɪʃəs

alliance
BR əˈlʌɪəns, -ɨz
AM əˈlaɪəns, -əz

allicin
BR ˈalɪsɪn, -z
AM ˈæləsən, -z

Allie
BR ˈali
AM ˈæli

allied
BR ˈalʌɪd
AM əˈlaɪd, ˈæˌlaɪd

alligator
BR ˈalɪgeɪtə(r), -z
AM ˈæləˌgeɪdər, -z

allineation
BR əˌlɪnɪˈeɪʃn, -z
AM əˌlɪniˈeɪʃən, -z

Allinson
BR ˈalɪns(ə)n
AM ˈɔlɪnsən, ˈɑlɪnsən

Allison
BR ˈalɪs(ə)n
AM ˈæləsən

alliterate
BR əˈlɪtəreɪt, -s, -ɪŋ, -ɨd
AM əˈlɪdəˌreɪ|t, -ts, -dɪŋ, -dɨd

alliteration
BR əˌlɪtəˈreɪʃn, -z
AM əˌlɪdəˈreɪʃən, -z

alliterative
BR əˈlɪt(ə)rətɪv
AM əˈlɪdərədɪv, əˈlɪdəˌreɪdɪv

allium
BR ˈalɪəm, -z
AM ˈæliəm, -z

all-nighter
BR ˌɔːlˈnʌɪtə(r), -z
AM ˌɔlˈnaɪdər, ˌɑlˈnaɪdər, -z
Alloa
BR ˈaləʊə(r)
AM ɑˈloʊə
allocable
BR ˈaləkəbl
AM ˈæləkəbəl
allocate
BR ˈaləkeɪt, -s, -ɪŋ, -ɪd
AM ˈæləˌkeɪ|t, -ts, -dɪŋ, -dɪd
allocation
BR ˌaləˈkeɪʃn, -z
AM ˌæləˈkeɪʃən, -z
allocator
BR ˈaləkeɪtə(r), -z
AM ˈæləˌkeɪdər, -z
allochthonous
BR əˈlɒkθənəs
AM əˈlɑkθənəs, æˈlɑkθənəs
allocution
BR ˌaləˈkjuːʃn
AM ˌæləˈkjuʃən
allodia
BR əˈləʊdɪə(r)
AM əˈloʊdiə
allodial
BR əˈləʊdɪəl, -z
AM əˈloʊdiəl, -z
allodium
BR əˈləʊdɪəm
AM əˈloʊdiəm
allogamy
BR əˈlɒgəmi
AM əˈlɑgəmi, æˈlɑgəmi
allograft
BR ˈaləgrɑːft, ˈaləgraft, -s
AM ˈæləˌgræft, -s
allograph
BR ˈaləgrɑːf, ˈaləgraf, -s
AM ˈæləˌgræf, -s
allographic
BR ˌaləˈgrafɪk
AM ˌæləˈgræfɪk
allomorph
BR ˈaləmɔːf, -s
AM ˈæləˌmɔ(ə)rf, -s
allomorphic
BR ˌaləˈmɔːfɪk
AM ˌæləˈmɔrfɪk
allomorphically
BR ˌaləˈmɔːfɪkli
AM ˌæləˈmɔrfək(ə)li
allopath
BR ˈaləpaθ, -s
AM ˈæləˌpæθ, -s
allopathic
BR ˌaləˈpaθɪk
AM ˌæləˈpæθɪk
allopathist
BR əˈlɒpəθɪst, -s
AM əˈlɑpəθəst, æˈlɑpəθəst, -s
allopathy
BR əˈlɒpəθi
AM əˈlɑpəθi, æˈlɑpəθi
allopatric
BR ˌaləˈpatrɪk, ˌaləˈpeɪtrɪk
AM ˌæləˈpætrɪk, ˌæləˈpeɪtrɪk
allophone
BR ˈaləfəʊn, -z
AM ˈæləˌfoʊn, -z
allophonic
BR ˌaləˈfɒnɪk
AM ˌæləˈfɑnɪk
allopolyploid
BR ˌaləˈpɒlɪplɔɪd, -z
AM ˌæləˈpɑləˌplɔɪd, -z
allot
BR əˈlɒt, -s, -ɪŋ, -ɪd
AM əˈlɑ|t, -ts, -dɪŋ, -təd
allotment
BR əˈlɒtm(ə)nt, -s
AM əˈlɑtmənt, -s
allotrope
BR ˈalətrəʊp, -s
AM ˈæləˌtroʊp, -s
allotropic
BR ˌaləˈtrɒpɪk, ˌaləˈtrəʊpɪk
AM ˌæləˈtrɑpɪk
allotropical
BR ˌaləˈtrɒpɪkl
AM ˌæləˈtrɑpəkəl
allotropy
BR əˈlɒtrəpi
AM əˈlɑtrəpi
Allott
BR ˈalət
AM ˈælət
allottee
BR alɒˈtiː, -z
AM əˌlɑˈti, ˌæləˈti, -z
allow
BR əˈlaʊ, -z, -ɪŋ, -d
AM əˈlaʊ, -z, -ɪŋ, -d
allowable
BR əˈlaʊəbl
AM əˈlaʊəbəl
allowableness
BR əˈlaʊəblnəs
AM əˈlaʊəbəlnəs
allowably
BR əˈlaʊəbli
AM əˈlaʊəbli
allowance
BR əˈlaʊəns, -ɪz
AM əˈlaʊəns, -əz
Alloway
BR ˈaləweɪ
AM ˈæləˌweɪ
allowedly
BR əˈlaʊɪdli
AM əˈlaʊədli
alloy[1]
noun
BR ˈalɔɪ, -z
AM ˈæˌlɔɪ, -z
alloy[2]
verb
BR əˈlɔɪ, -z, -ɪŋ, -d
AM ˈæˌlɔɪ, əˈlɔɪ, -z, -ɪŋ, -d
allseed
BR ˈɔːlsiːd
AM ˈɔlˌsid, ˈɑlˌsid
Allsop
BR ˈɔːlsɒp, ˈɒlsɒp
AM ˈɔlsɑp, ˈɑlsɑp
Allsopp
BR ˈɔːlsɒp, ˈɒlsɒp
AM ˈɔlsɑp, ˈɑlsɑp
allsorts
BR ˈɔːlsɔːts
AM ˈɔlˌsɔ(ə)rts, ˈɑlˌsɔ(ə)rts
allspice
BR ˈɔːlspʌɪs
AM ˈɔlˌspaɪs, ˈɑlˌspaɪs
Allston
BR ˈɔːlst(ə)n, ˈɒlst(ə)n
AM ˈɔlstən, ˈɑlstən
allude
BR əˈl(j)uːd, -z, -ɪŋ, -ɪd
AM əˈlud, -z, -ɪŋ, -əd
allure
BR əˈl(j)ʊə(r), əˈljɔː(r), -z, -ɪŋ, -d
AM əˈlu(ə)r, æˈlu(ə)r, əˈlʊr, æˈlʊr, -z, -ɪŋ, -d
allurement
BR əˈl(j)ʊəm(ə)nt, əˈljɔːm(ə)nt, -s
AM əˈlʊrmənt, -s
allusion
BR əˈl(j)uːʒn, -z
AM əˈluʒən, æˈluʒən, -z
allusive
BR əˈl(j)uːsɪv
AM əˈlusɪv, æˈlusɪv, əˈluzɪv, æˈluzɪv
allusively
BR əˈl(j)uːsɪvli
AM əˈlusɪvli, æˈlusɪvli, əˈluzɪvli, æˈluzɪvli
allusiveness
BR əˈl(j)uːsɪvnɪs
AM əˈlusɪvnɪs, æˈlusɪvnɪs, əˈluzɪvnɪs, æˈluzɪvnɪs
alluvia
BR əˈl(j)uːvɪə(r)
AM əˈluviə
alluvial
BR əˈl(j)uːvɪəl
AM əˈluviəl
alluvion
BR əˈl(j)uːvɪən
AM əˈluviən
alluvium
BR əˈl(j)uːvɪəm
AM əˈluviəm
Ally
BR ˈali
AM ˈæli
ally[1]
noun, friend
BR ˈalʌɪ, -z
AM ˈæˌlaɪ, əˈlaɪ, -z
ally[2]
noun, marble
BR ˈal|i, -ɪz
AM ˈæli, -z
ally[3]
verb
BR əˈlʌɪ, -z, -ɪŋ, -d
AM əˈlaɪ, æˈlaɪ, ˈæˌlaɪ, -z, -ɪŋ, -d
allyl
BR ˈalʌɪl, ˈalɪl, -z
AM ˈælɪl, -z
Alma
BR ˈalmə(r)
AM ˈælmə
Alma-Ata
BR alˌmɑː(r)əˈtɑː(r)
AM ɑlˌmɑɑˈtɑ
RUS alˈmaaˈta
Almagest
BR ˈalmədʒɛst
AM ˈælməˌdʒɛst
alma mater
BR ˌalmə ˈmɑːtə(r), + ˈmeɪtə(r), -z
AM ˌɑlmə ˈmɑdər, ˌælmə +, -z
almanac
BR ˈɔːlmənak, ˈɒlmənak, ˈalmənak, -s
AM ˈɔlməˌnæk, ˈælməˌnæk, ˈɑlməˌnæk, -s
almanack
BR ˈɔːlmənak, ˈɒlmənak, ˈalmənak, -s
AM ˈɔlməˌnæk, ˈælməˌnæk, ˈɑlməˌnæk, -s
almandine
BR ˈalməndiːn, ˈalməndʌɪn, -z
AM ˈɑ(l)mənˌdin, ˈæ(l)mənˌdin, -z
Alma-Tadema
BR ˈalməˈtadɪmə(r)
AM ˌɑlməˈtɑdəmə
Almería
BR ˌalməˈriːə(r)
AM ˌɑlməˈriə
almightily
BR ɔːlˈmʌɪtɪli, ɔːlˈmʌɪtḷi
AM ɔlˈmaɪdɪli, ɑlˈmaɪdɪli
almightiness
BR ɔːlˈmʌɪtɪnɪs
AM ɔlˈmaɪdinɪs, ɑlˈmaɪdinɪs

almighty
BR ɔːl'mʌɪti
AM ɔl'maɪdi, ɑl'maɪdi
almirah
BR al'mʌɪrə(r), -z
AM æl'maɪrə, -z
almond
BR 'ɑː(l)mənd, 'almənd, 'ɒlmənd, -z
AM 'ɑ(l)mənd, 'æ(l)mənd, -z
almoner
BR 'ɑː(l)mənə(r), 'almənə(r), 'ɒlmənə(r), -z
AM 'æ(l)mənər, 'ɑ(l)mənər, -z
almonry
BR 'ɑː(l)mənri, 'almənri, 'ɒlmənri
AM 'æ(l)mənri, 'ɑ(l)mənri
almost
BR 'ɔːlməʊst
AM ɔl'moʊst, 'ɔlmoʊst, ɑl'moʊst, 'ɑlmoʊst
alms
BR ɑːmz
AM ɑ(l)mz
almshouse
BR 'ɑːmzhaʊ|s, -zɪz
AM 'ɑ(l)mz,(h)aʊ|s, -zəz
almsman
BR 'ɑːmzmən
AM 'ɑ(l)mzmən
almsmen
BR 'ɑːmzmən
AM 'ɑ(l)mzmən
almucantar
BR ,alm(j)ʉ'kantə(r), -z
AM ,ælm(j)u'kæn(t)ər, -z
Alne
BR ɔː(l)n, aln
AM ɔln, ɑln
Alnmouth
BR 'alnmaʊθ
AM 'ɔlnməθ, 'ɑlnməθ
Alnwick
BR 'anɪk
AM 'ɔlnwɪk, 'ɑlnwɪk
aloe
BR 'aləʊ, -z
AM 'æloʊ, -z
aloetic
BR ,aləʊ'ɛtɪk
AM ,ɑloʊ'ɛdɪk
aloe vera
BR ,aləʊ 'vɛrə(r), + 'vɪərə(r)
AM ,æloʊ 'vɛrə
aloft
BR ə'lɒft
AM ə'lɔft, ə'lɑft
alogical
BR eɪ'lɒdʒɪkl
AM eɪ'lɑdʒəkəl
alogically
BR eɪ'lɒdʒɪkli
AM eɪ'lɑdʒək(ə)li
aloha
BR ə'ləʊ(h)ə(r)
AM ə'loʊ,(h)ɑ
alone
BR ə'ləʊn
AM ə'loʊn
aloneness
BR ə'ləʊnnəs
AM ə'loʊ(n)nəs
along
BR ə'lɒŋ
AM ə'lɔŋ, ə'lɑŋ
alongshore
BR ə'lɒŋʃɔː(r)
AM ə,lɔŋ'ʃɔ(ə)r, ə,lɑŋ'ʃɔ(ə)r
alongside
BR ə'lɒŋsʌɪd, ə,lɒŋ'sʌɪd
AM ə,lɔŋ'saɪd, ə,lɑŋ'saɪd
Alonzo
BR ə'lɒnzəʊ
AM ə'lɑnzoʊ
aloof
BR ə'luːf
AM ə'luf
aloofly
BR ə'luːfli
AM ə'lufli
aloofness
BR ə'luːfnəs
AM ə'lufnəs
alopecia
BR ,alə'piːʃ(ɪ)ə(r)
AM ,ælə'piʃ(i)ə
aloud
BR ə'laʊd
AM ə'laʊd
alow
BR ə'ləʊ
AM ə'loʊ
Aloysius
BR ,aləʊ'ɪʃəs
AM ,ælə'wɪʃɪs
alp
BR alp, -s
AM ælp, -s
alpaca
BR al'pakə(r), -z
AM æl'pækə, -z
alpargata
BR ,alpɑː'gɑːtə(r), -z
AM ,ælpər'gɑdə, -z
alpenglow
BR 'alp(ə)ngləʊ
AM 'ælpən,gloʊ
alpenhorn
BR 'alp(ə)nhɔːn, -z
AM 'ælpən,(h)ɔ(ə)rn, -z
alpenstock
BR 'alp(ə)nstɒk, -s
AM 'ælpən,stɑk, -s
alpha
BR 'alfə(r)
AM 'ælfə
alphabet
BR 'alfəbɛt, -s
AM 'ælfə,bɛt, -s
alphabetic
BR ,alfə'bɛtɪk
AM ,ælfə'bɛdɪk
alphabetical
BR ,alfə'bɛtɪkl
AM ,ælfə'bɛdəkəl
alphabetically
BR ,alfə'bɛtɪkli
AM ,ælfə'bɛdək(ə)li
alphabetisation
BR ,alfəbɛtʌɪ'zeɪʃn, ,alfəbɪtʌɪ'zeɪʃn
AM ,ælfəbə,taɪ'zeɪʃən, ,ælfə,bɛdə'zeɪʃən
alphabetise
BR 'alfəbɛtʌɪz, 'alfəbɪtʌɪz, -ɪz, -ɪŋ, -d
AM 'ælfəbə,taɪz, -ɪz, -ɪŋ, -d
alphabetization
BR ,alfəbɛtʌɪ'zeɪʃn, ,alfəbɪtʌɪ'zeɪʃn
AM ,ælfəbə,taɪ'zeɪʃən, ,ælfə,bɛdə'zeɪʃən
alphabetize
BR 'ɑːlfəbɛtʌɪz, 'alfəbətʌɪz, -ɪz, -ɪŋ, -d
AM 'ælfəbə,taɪz, -ɪz, -ɪŋ, -d
alphanumeric
BR ,alfənjuː'mɛrɪk, ,alfənjʉ'mɛrɪk
AM ,ælfən(j)u'mɛrɪk
alphanumerical
BR ,alfənjuː'mɛrɪkl, ,alfənjʉ'mɛrɪkl
AM ,ælfən(j)u'mɛrəkəl
alphanumerically
BR ,alfənjuː'mɛrɪkli, ,alfənjʉ'mɛrɪkli
AM ,ælfən(j)u'mɛrək(ə)li
Alphege
BR 'alfɪdʒ
AM 'ælfɪdʒ
Alphonso
BR al'fɒnsəʊ, al'fɒnzəʊ
AM æl'fɑnsoʊ, æl'fɑnzoʊ
alphorn
BR 'alphɔːn, -z
AM 'alp,(h)ɔ(ə)rn, -z
alpine
BR 'alpʌɪn
AM 'æl,paɪn
alpinism
BR 'alpɪnɪz(ə)m
AM 'ælpə,nɪzəm
alpinist
BR 'alpɪnɪst, -s
AM 'ælpənəst, -s
Alport
BR 'ɔːlpɔːt
AM 'ɔlpɔ(ə)rt, 'ɑlpɔ(ə)rt
alprazolam
BR al'preɪzəlam
AM æl'preɪzə,læm
already
BR ɔːl'rɛdi
AM ,ɔl'rɛdi, ,ɑl'rɛdi
Alresford
BR 'ɔːlzfəd
AM 'ɔlrɛsfɔ(ə)rd, 'ɑlrɛsfɔ(ə)rd
alright
BR ,ɔːl'rʌɪt
AM ,ɔl'raɪt, ,ɑl'raɪt
Alsace
BR al'sas
AM ,æl'sæs, ,ɑl'sæs, ,æl'sɑs, ,ɑl'sɑs
Alsager
BR 'ɔːlsədʒə(r), ɔːl'seɪdʒə(r)
AM 'ɔlsɪdʒər, 'ɑlsɪdʒər
Alsatian
BR al'seɪʃn, -z
AM æl'seɪʃən, ɑl'seɪʃən, -z
alsike
BR 'alsɪk
AM 'æl,sɪk, 'æl,saɪk
also
BR 'ɔːlsəʊ, 'ɒlsəʊ
AM 'ɔlsoʊ, 'ɑlsoʊ
Alsop
BR 'ɔːlsɒp, 'ɒlsɒp
AM 'ɔlsɑp, 'ɑlsɑp
Alston
BR 'ɔːlst(ə)n, 'ɒlst(ə)n
AM 'ɔlstən, 'ɑlstən
alstroemeria
BR ,alstrə'mɪərɪə(r), -z
AM ,ælztrə'mɪriə, ,ælstrə'mɪriə, -z
alt
BR alt
AM ɑlt
Altai
BR al'tʌɪ, ɑːl'tʌɪ
AM 'æl,taɪ, 'ɑl,taɪ
Altaic
BR al'teɪɪk
AM æl'teɪɪk, ɑl'teɪɪk
Altair
BR al'tɛː(r), 'altɛː(r)
AM 'æl,tɛ(ə)r, 'ɑl,tɛ(ə)r
Altamira
BR ,altə'mɪərə(r)
AM ,ɑltə'mɪrə
SP ,alta'mira
B PORT ,ɑwtɑ'mirɑ
L PORT altɑ'mirɑ
altar
BR 'ɔːltə(r), 'ɒltə(r), -z
AM 'ɔltər, 'ɑltər, -z

Altarnun
BR ˌɔːltəˈnʌn, ˌɒltəˈnʌn
AM ˈɔltərˌnən, ˈɑltərˌnən

altarpiece
BR ˈɔːltəpiːs, ˈɒltəpiːs, -ɪz
AM ˈɔltərˌpis, ˈɑltərˌpis, -ɪz

altazimuth
BR alˈtazɪməθ, -s
AM ælˈtæzəməθ, ɑlˈtæzəməθ, -s

Altdorfer
BR ˈaltˌdɔːfə(r)
AM ˈɑltˌdɔrfər

alter
BR ˈɔːlt|ə(r), ˈɒlt|ə(r), -əz, -(ə)rɪŋ, -əd
AM ˈɔlt|ər, ˈɑlt|ər, -ərz, -(ə)rɪŋ, -ərd

alterable
BR ˈɔːlt(ə)rəbl, ˈɒlt(ə)rəbl
AM ˈɔlt(ə)rəbəl, ˈɑlt(ə)rəbəl

alteration
BR ˌɔːltəˈreɪʃn, ˌɒltəˈreɪʃn, -z
AM ˌɔltəˈreɪʃən, ˌɑltəˈreɪʃən, -z

alterative
BR ˈɔːlt(ə)rətɪv, ˈɒlt(ə)rətɪv
AM ˈɔltəˌreɪdɪv, ˈɔltərədɪv, ˈɑltəˌreɪdɪv, ˈɑltərədɪv

altercate
BR ˈɔːltəkeɪt, ˈɒltəkeɪt, -s, -ɪŋ, -ɪd
AM ˈɔltərˌkeɪ|t, ˈɑltərˌkeɪ|t, -ts, -dɪŋ, -dɪd

altercation
BR ˌɔːltəˈkeɪʃn, ˌɒltəˈkeɪʃn, -z
AM ˌɔltərˈkeɪʃən, ˌɑltərˈkeɪʃən, -z

alter ego
BR ˌaltər ˈɛɡəʊ, ˌɔːltər +, ˌɒltə(r) +, + ˈiːɡəʊ, -z
AM ˌɔltəˈriɡoʊ, ˌɑltəˈriɡoʊ, -z

alternance
BR ˈɔːltənəns, ˈɒltənəns, -ɪz
AM ˈɔltərnəns, ˈɑltərnəns, -əz

alternant
BR ˈɔːltənənt, ˈɒltənənt, -s
AM ˈɔltərnənt, ˈɑltərnənt, -s

alternate¹
adjective
BR ɔːlˈtəːnɪt, ɒlˈtəːnɪt
AM ˈɔltərnət, ˈɑltərnət

alternate²
verb
BR ˈɔːltəneɪt, ˈɒltəneɪt, -s, -ɪŋ, -ɪd
AM ˈɔltərˌneɪ|t, ˈɑltərˌneɪ|t, -ts, -dɪŋ, -dɪd

alternately
BR ɔːlˈtəːnɪtli, ɒlˈtəːnɪtli
AM ˈɔltərnətli, ˈɑltərnətli

alternation
BR ˌɔːltəˈneɪʃn, ˌɒltəˈneɪʃn
AM ˌɔltərˈneɪʃən, ˌɑltərˈneɪʃən

alternative
BR ɔːlˈtəːnətɪv, ɒlˈtəːnətɪv, -z
AM ɔlˈtərnədɪv, ɑlˈtərnədɪv, -z

alternatively
BR ɔːlˈtəːnətɪvli, ɒlˈtəːnətɪvli
AM ɔlˈtərnədɪvli, ɑlˈtərnədɪvli

alternator
BR ˈɔːltəneɪtə(r), ˈɒltəneɪtə(r), -z
AM ˈɔltərˌneɪdər, ˈɑltərˌneɪdər, -z

Althea
BR ˈalθɪə(*r*)
AM ælˈθiə

althorn
BR ˈalt(h)ɔːn, -z
AM ˈæltˌ(h)ɔ(ə)rn, -z

although
BR ɔːlˈðəʊ, ɒlˈðəʊ
AM ɔlˈðoʊ, ɑlˈðoʊ

Althusser
BR ˌaltʉˈsɛː(r)
AM ˈɑltˌ(h)usər
FR altysɛʀ

Althusserean
BR ˌaltʉˈsɛːrɪən, -z
AM ˌɑlt(h)ʊˈsɛriən, -z

Althusserian
BR ˌaltʉˈsɛːrɪən, -z
AM ˌɑlt(h)ʊˈsɛriən, -z

altimeter
BR ˈaltɪmiːtə(r), ˈɔːltɪmiːtə(r), ˈɒltɪmiːtə(r), -z
AM ælˈtɪmədər, ɑlˈtɪmədər, -z

altimetry
BR alˈtɪmɪtri, ɔːlˈtɪmɪtri, ɒlˈtɪmɪtri
AM ælˈtɪmɪtri, ɑlˈtɪmɪtri

Altiplano
BR ˌaltɪˈplɑːnəʊ, ˌaltɪˈplanəʊ
AM ˌɔltɪˈplɑnoʊ, ˌɑltɪˈplɑnoʊ

altissimo
BR alˈtɪsɪməʊ
AM ælˈtɪsɪmoʊ, ɑlˈtɪsɪmoʊ

altitude
BR ˈaltɪtjuːd, ˈaltɪtʃuːd, -z
AM ˈældəˌt(j)ud, -z

altitudinal
BR ˈaltɪˌtjuːdɪn(ə)l, ˈaltɪˌtjuːdn̩(ə)l, ˈaltɪˌtʃuːdɪn(ə)l, ˈaltɪˌtʃuːdn̩(ə)l
AM ˌældəˈt(j)udənl, ˌældəˈt(j)udnəl

alto
BR ˈaltəʊ, -z
AM ˈæltoʊ, ˈɔltoʊ, ˈɑltoʊ, -z

altocumulus
BR ˌaltəʊˈkjuːmjʉləs
AM ˌæltoʊˈkjumjələs, ˌɔltoʊˈkjumjələs, ˌɑltoʊˈkjumjələs

altogether
BR ˌɔːltəˈɡɛðə(r)
AM ˈˌɔltəˈˌɡɛðər, ˈˌɑltəˈˌɡɛðər

Alton
BR ˈɔːlt(ə)n, ˈɒlt(ə)n
AM ˈɔldən, ˈɑldən

Altoona
BR alˈtuːnə(*r*)
AM ælˈtunə

alto-relievo
BR ˌaltəʊrɪˈliːvəʊ
AM ˌæltoʊrəˈlivoʊ, ˌɑltoʊrəˈlivoʊ

altostratus
BR ˌaltəʊˈstrɑːtəs, ˌaltəʊˈstreɪtəs
AM ˌæltoʊˈstreɪdəs, ˌæltoʊˈstrædəs, ˌɔltoʊˈstreɪdəs, ˌɔltoʊˈstrædəs, ˌɑltoʊˈstreɪdəs, ˌɑltoʊˈstrædəs

altricial
BR alˈtrɪʃl
AM ælˈtrɪʃəl

Altrincham
BR ˈɔːltrɪŋəm, ˈɒltrɪŋəm
AM ˈɔltrɪn(t)ʃəm, ˈɑltrɪn(t)ʃəm

altruism
BR ˈaltrʊɪz(ə)m
AM ˈæltrəˌwɪzəm, ˈælˌtruˌɪzəm

altruist
BR ˈaltrʊɪst, -s
AM ˈæltrəwəst, ˈælˌtruəst, -s

altruistic
BR ˌaltrʊˈɪstɪk
AM ˌæltrəˈwɪstɪk, ˌælˌtruˈɪstɪk

altruistically
BR ˌaltrʊˈɪstɪkli
AM ˌæltrəˈwɪstɪk(ə)li, ˌælˌtruˈɪstɪk(ə)li

aludel
BR ˈaljʉdɛl, -z
AM ˈæljəˌdɛl, -z

alum
BR ˈaləm, -z
AM ˈæləm, -z

alumina
BR əˈl(j)uːmɪnə(*r*)
AM əˈlumənə

aluminisation
BR əˌl(j)uːmɪnʌɪˈzeɪʃn
AM əˌluːmənəˈzeɪʃən, əˌluməˌnaɪˈzeɪʃən

aluminise
BR əˈl(j)uːmɪnʌɪz, -ɪz, -ɪŋ, -d
AM əˈluməˌnaɪz, -ɪz, -ɪŋ, -d

aluminium
BR al(j)ʉˈmɪnɪəm
AM əˈlumənəm

aluminization
BR əˌl(j)uːmɪnʌɪˈzeɪʃn
AM əˌlumənəˈzeɪʃən, əˌluməˌnaɪˈzeɪʃən

aluminize
BR əˈl(j)uːmɪnʌɪz, -ɪz, -ɪŋ, -d
AM əˈluməˌnaɪz, -ɪz, -ɪŋ, -d

aluminosilicate
BR əˌl(j)uːmɪnəʊˈsɪlɪkət, -s
AM əˌlumənəˈsɪləkət, -s

aluminous
BR əˈl(j)uːmɪnəs
AM əˈlumənəs

aluminum
BR əˈl(j)uːmɪnəm
AM əˈlumənəm

alumna
BR əˈlʌmnə(*r*)
AM əˈləmnə

alumnae
BR əˈlʌmniː
AM əˈləmˌnaɪ, əˈləmni

alumni
BR əˈlʌmnʌɪ
AM əˈləmˌnaɪ

alumnus
BR əˈlʌmnəs
AM əˈləmnəs

Alun
BR ˈalɪn
AM ˈælən

Alvar
BR ˈalvɑː(r)
AM ˈɑlˌvɑr

Alvarez
BR alˈvɑːrɛz, ˈalvərɛz
AM ˈælvəˌrɛz

alveolar
BR ˌalvɪˈəʊlə(r), alˈvɪələ(r), ˈalvɪələ(r), -z
AM ælˈvi(ə)lər, ˌælviˈoʊlər, -z

alveolarisation
BR ˌalvɪəʊlərʌɪˈzeɪʃn, alˌvɪələrəˈzeɪʃn
AM ælˌvi(ə)lərəˈzeɪʃən, ælˌvi(ə)ləˌraɪˈzeɪʃən

alveolarise
BR ˌalvɪˈəʊlərʌɪz, alˈvɪələrʌɪz, ˈalvɪələrʌɪz
AM ælˈvi(ə)ləˌraɪz

alveolarization
BR ˌalvɪə(ʊ)lərʌɪˈzeɪʃn, alˌvɪələrəˈzeɪʃn
AM ælˌvi(ə)lərəˈzeɪʃən, ælˌvi(ə)ləˌraɪˈzeɪʃən

alveolarize
BR ˌalvɪˈəʊlərʌɪz, alˈvɪələrʌɪz, ˈalvɪələrʌɪz
AM ælˈvi(ə)ləˌraɪz

alveolate
BR alˈvɪələt
AM ælˈviələt

alveole
BR ˈalvɪəʊl, -z
AM ˈælviˌoʊl, -z

alveoli
BR ˌalvɪˈəʊlʌɪ, ˌalvɪˈəʊliː, alˈvɪəlʌɪ, alˈvɪəliː, ˈalvɪəlʌɪ, ˈalvɪəliː
AM ælˈviəˌlaɪ, ælˈviəˌli

alveolus
BR ˌalvɪˈəʊləs, alˈvɪələs, ˈalvɪələs
AM ælˈviələs, ˌælviˈoʊləs

Alvin
BR ˈalvɪn
AM ˈælvən

always
BR ˈɔːlweɪz, ˈɔːlwɪz
AM ˈɔlwəz, ˈɔlˌweɪz, ˈɑlwəz, ˈɑlˌweɪz

Alwyn
BR ˈɔːlwɪn, ˈalwɪn
AM ˈɔlwɪn, ˈɑlwɪn

alyssum
BR ˈalɪs(ə)m, -z
AM əˈlɪsəm, -z

Alzheimer's
BR ˈaltshʌɪməz, ˈɔːltshʌɪməz
AM ˈɑltsˌ(h)aɪmərz

am[1]
strong form
BR am
AM æm

am[2]
weak form
BR əm, m
AM əm, m

a.m.
BR ˌeɪˈɛm
AM ˌeɪˈɛm

amadavat
BR ˈamədəvat, -s
AM ˈæmədəˌvæt, -s

amadou
BR ˈamədu:
AM ˈɑməˌdu

amah
BR ˈɑːmə(r), -z
AM ˈɑmə, -z

amain
BR əˈmeɪn
AM əˈmeɪn

Amal
BR əˈmɑːl, ˈamɑːl
AM ɑˈmɑl

Amalekite
BR əˈmaləkʌɪt
AM əˈmæləˌkaɪt

Amalfi
BR əˈmalfi
AM əˈmɑlfi, əˈmælfi

amalgam
BR əˈmalgəm, -z
AM əˈmælgəm, -z

amalgamate
BR əˈmalgəmeɪt, -s, -ɪŋ, -ɪd
AM əˈmælgəˌmeɪ|t, -ts, -dɪŋ, -dɨd

amalgamation
BR əˌmalgəˈmeɪʃn, -z
AM əˌmælgəˈmeɪʃən, -z

Amanda
BR əˈmandə(r)
AM əˈmændə

amanita
BR ˌaməˈnʌɪtə(r), ˌaməˈniːtə(r), -z
AM ˌæməˈnaɪdə, ˌæməˈnidə, -z

amanuenses
BR əˌmanjʊˈɛnsiːz
AM əˌmænjəˈwɛnˌsiz

amanuensis
BR əˌmanjʊˈɛnsɪs
AM əˌmænjəˈwɛnsəs

amaranth
BR ˈamərənθ, -s
AM ˈæməˌrænθ, -s

amaranthine
BR ˌaməˈranθʌɪn
AM ˌæməˈrænθən, ˌæməˈrænˌθaɪn

amaretti
BR ˌaməˈrɛti
AM ˌæməˈrɛdi

amaretto
BR ˌaməˈrɛtəʊ
AM ˌæməˈrɛdoʊ

Amarillo
BR ˌaməˈrɪləʊ
AM ˌæməˈrɪloʊ

amaryllis
BR ˌaməˈrɪlɪs, -ɪz
AM ˌæməˈrɪlɪs, -ɪz

amass
BR əˈmas, -ɪz, -ɪŋ, -t
AM əˈmæs, -əz, -ɪŋ, -t

amasser
BR əˈmasə(r), -z
AM əˈmæsər, -z

amassment
BR əˈmasm(ə)nt
AM əˈmæsmənt

amateur
BR ˈamət(ʃ)ə(r), ˌaməˈtəː(r), -z
AM ˈæmədər, ˈæməˌtər, ˌæməˈt(j)ʊr, -z

amateurish
BR ˈamət(ə)rɪʃ, ˈamətʃərɪʃ, ˌaməˈtəːrɪʃ
AM ˌæməˈtʃʊrɪʃ, ˌæməˌtərɪʃ, ˌæməˈt(j)ʊrɪʃ

amateurishly
BR ˈamət(ə)rɪʃli, ˈamətʃərɪʃli, ˌaməˈtəːrɪʃli
AM ˌæməˈtʃʊrɪʃli, ˌæməˈtərɪʃli, ˌæməˈt(j)ʊrɪʃli

amateurishness
BR ˈamət(ə)rɪʃnɪs, ˈamətʃərɪʃnɪs, ˌaməˈtəːrɪʃnɪs
AM ˈæməˈtʃʊrɪʃnɪs, ˈæməˈtərɪʃnɪs, ˈæməˈt(j)ʊrɪʃnɪs

amateurism
BR ˈamət(ʃ)ərɪz(ə)m, ˌaməˈtəːrɪz(ə)m
AM ˈæməˌtʃʊˌrɪzəm, ˈæmədəˌrɪzəm, ˈæməˌt(j)ʊˌrɪzəm

Amati
BR əˈmɑːt|i, aˈmɑːt|i, -ɪz
AM ɑˈmɑdi, -z

amative
BR ˈamətɪv
AM ˈæmədɪv

amativeness
BR ˈamətɪvnɪs
AM ˈæmədɪvnɪs

amatol
BR ˈamətɒl
AM ˈæməˌdɔl ˈæməˌdɑl

amatory
BR ˈamət(ə)ri
AM ˈæməˌtɔri

amauroses
BR ˌamɔːˈrəʊsiːz
AM ˌæmɔˈroʊsiz, ˌæmɑˈroʊsiz

amaurosis
BR ˌamɔːˈrəʊsɪs
AM ˌæmɔˈroʊsəs, ˌæmɑˈroʊsəs

amaurotic
BR ˌamɔːˈrɒtɪk
AM ˌæmɔˈrɑdɪk, ˌæmɑˈrɑdɪk

amaze
BR əˈmeɪz, -ɪz, -ɪŋ, -d
AM əˈmeɪz, -ɪz, -ɪŋ, -d

amazement
BR əˈmeɪzm(ə)nt
AM əˈmeɪzmənt

amazingly
BR əˈmeɪzɪŋli
AM əˈmeɪzɪŋli

amazingness
BR əˈmeɪzɪŋnɪs
AM əˈmeɪzɪŋnɪs

Amazon
BR ˈaməz(ə)n, -z
AM ˈæməˌzɑn, ˈæməzən, -z

Amazonia
BR ˌaməˈzəʊnɪə(r)
AM ˌæməˈzoʊniə

Amazonian
BR ˌaməˈzəʊnɪən, -z
AM ˌæməˈzoʊniən, -z

Amazulu
BR ˌaməˈzuːluː
AM ˌæməˈzulu

ambages
BR ˈambɪdʒɪz, amˈbeɪdʒɪz
AM ˈæmbɪdʒɪz, ˌæmˈbeɪdʒɪz

ambassador
BR amˈbasədə(r), -z
AM æmˈbæsədər, əmˈbæsədər, -z

ambassadorial
BR amˌbasəˈdɔːrɪəl, ˌambasəˈdɔːrɪəl
AM æmˌbæsəˈdɔriəl, əmˌbæsəˈdɔriəl

ambassadorship
BR amˈbasədəʃɪp, -s
AM æmˈbæsədərˌʃɪp, əmˈbæsədərˌʃɪp, -s

ambassadress
BR amˈbasədrɪs, amˌbasəˈdrɛs, -ɪz
AM æmˈbæsədrəs, əmˈbæsədrəs, -əz

ambatch
BR ˈambatʃ, -ɪz
AM ˈæmˌbætʃ, -əz

Ambato
BR amˈbɑːtəʊ
AM ɑmˈbɑdoʊ

amber
BR ˈambə(r)
AM ˈæmbər

ambergris
BR ˈambəgriːs
AM ˈæmbərˌgri(s), ˈæmbərˌgrɪs

amberjack
BR ˈambədʒak, -s
AM ˈæmbərˌdʒæk, -s

ambiance
BR 'ambɪəns, 'ɒmbɪɒns, 'ɒ̃bɪɒ̃s, -ɪz
AM 'æmbiəns, 'æmbjəns, -əz

ambidexter
BR ˌambɪ'dɛkstə(r), -z
AM ˌæmbə'dɛkstər, -z

ambidexterity
BR ˌambɪdɛk'stɛrɪti
AM ˌæmbəˌdɛks'tɛrədi

ambidextrous
BR ˌambɪ'dɛkstrəs
AM ˌæmbə'dɛkst(ə)rəs

ambidextrously
BR ˌambɪ'dɛkstrəsli
AM ˌæmbə'dɛkst(ə)rəsli

ambidextrousness
BR ˌambɪ'dɛkstrəsnəs
AM ˌæmbə'dɛkst(ə)rəsnəs

ambience
BR 'ambɪəns, 'ɒmbɪɒns, 'ɒ̃bɪɒ̃s, -ɪz
AM 'æmbiəns, 'æmbjəns, -əz

ambient
BR 'ambɪənt
AM 'æmbiənt, 'æmbjənt

ambiguous
BR am'bɪɡjʊəs
AM æm'bɪɡjəwəs

ambiguously
BR am'bɪɡjʊəsli
AM æm'bɪɡjəwəsli

ambiguousness
BR am'bɪɡjʊəsnəs
AM æm'bɪɡjəwəsnəs

ambisonics
BR ˌambɪ'sɒnɪks
AM ˌæmbə'sɑnɪks

ambit
BR 'ambɪt, -s
AM 'æmbət, -s

ambition
BR am'bɪʃn, -z
AM æm'bɪʃən, -z

ambitious
BR am'bɪʃəs
AM æm'bɪʃəs

ambitiously
BR am'bɪʃəsli
AM æm'bɪʃəsli

ambitiousness
BR am'bɪʃəsnəs
AM æm'bɪʃəsnəs

ambivalence
BR am'bɪvələns, am'bɪvəln̩s, am'bɪvl̩(ə)ns
AM æm'bɪv(ə)ləns

ambivalency
BR am'bɪvələnsi, am'bɪvəln̩si, am'bɪvl̩(ə)nsi
AM æm'bɪv(ə)lənsi

ambivalent
BR am'bɪvələnt, am'bɪvəln̩t, am'bɪvl̩(ə)nt
AM æm'bɪv(ə)lənt

ambivalently
BR am'bɪvələntli, am'bɪvəln̩tli, am'bɪvl̩(ə)ntli
AM æm'bɪvələn(t)li

ambiversion
BR ˌambɪ'vəːʃn
AM ˌæmbi'vərʒən

ambivert
BR 'ambɪvəːt, -s
AM 'æmbəˌvərt, -s

amble
BR 'amb|l, -lz, -l̩ɪŋ\-lɪŋ, -ld
AM 'æmb|əl, -əlz, -(ə)lɪŋ, -əld

ambler
BR 'amblə(r), 'ambl̩ə(r), -z
AM 'æmblər, -z

Ambleside
BR 'amblsʌɪd
AM 'æmbəlˌsaɪd

amblyopia
BR ˌamblɪ'əʊpɪə(r)
AM ˌæmbli'oʊpiə

amblyopic
BR ˌamblɪ'ɒpɪk
AM ˌæmbli'ɑpɪk

ambo
BR 'ambəʊ, -z
AM 'æmˌboʊ, -z

amboina
BR am'bɔɪnə(r)
AM æm'bɔɪnə

Amboinese
BR ˌambɔɪ'niːz
AM ˌæmˌbɔɪ'niz

ambones
BR am'bəʊniːz
AM æm'boʊniz

Ambonese
BR ˌambə(ʊ)'niːz
AM ˌæmbə'niz

amboyna
BR am'bɔɪnə(r)
AM æm'bɔɪnə

Ambrose
BR 'ambrəʊz
AM 'æmˌbroʊz

ambrosia
BR am'brəʊzɪə(r)
AM æm'broʊʒə

ambrosial
BR am'brəʊzɪəl
AM æm'broʊʒ(i)əl

ambrosian
BR am'brəʊzɪən
AM æm'broʊʒən

ambry
BR 'ambr|i, -ɪz
AM 'æmbri, -z

ambs-ace
BR 'eɪmzeɪs, 'amzeɪs, ˌamz'eɪs
AM 'eɪmˌzeɪs, 'æmˌzeɪs

ambulance
BR 'ambjʉləns, 'ambjʉln̩s, -ɪz
AM 'æmbjələns, -əz

ambulanceman
BR 'ambjʉlənsˌman, 'ɑːmbjʉln̩sˌman
AM 'æmbjələnsˌmæn

ambulancemen
BR 'ambjʉlənsˌmɛn, 'ambjʉln̩sˌmɛn
AM 'æmbjələnsˌmɛn

ambulant
BR 'ambjʉlənt, 'ambjʉln̩t
AM 'æmbjələnt

ambulate
BR 'ambjʉleɪt, -s, -ɪŋ, -ɪd
AM 'æmbjəˌleɪ|t, -ts, -dɪŋ, -dɪd

ambulation
BR ˌambjʉ'leɪʃn
AM ˌæmbjə'leɪʃən

ambulatory
BR 'ambjʉlət(ə)ri
AM 'æmbjələˌtɔri

ambuscade
BR ˌambʉ'skeɪd, -z
AM 'æmbəˌskeɪd, ˌæmbə'skeɪd, -z

ambush
BR 'ambʊʃ, -ɪz, -ɪŋ, -t
AM 'æmbʊʃ, -əz, -ɪŋ, -t

ambystoma
BR am'bɪstəmə(r), -z
AM æm'bɪstəmə, -z

Amdahl
BR 'amdɑːl
AM 'æmdɑl

ameer
BR ə'mɪə(r), -z
AM ə'mɪ(ə)r, -z

Amelia
BR ə'miːlɪə(r)
AM ə'miljə, ə'miliə

ameliorate
BR ə'miːlɪəreɪt, -s, -ɪŋ, -ɪd
AM ə'miliəˌreɪ|t, ə'miljəˌreɪ|t, -ts, -dɪŋ, -dɪd

amelioration
BR əˌmiːlɪə'reɪʃn
AM əˌmiliə'reɪʃən, əˌmiljə'reɪʃən

ameliorative
BR ə'miːlɪərətɪv, -z
AM ə'miliərədɪv, ə'miljərədɪv, ə'miliəˌreɪdɪv, ə'miljəˌreɪdɪv, -z

ameliorator
BR ə'miːlɪəreɪtə(r), -z
AM ə'miliəˌreɪdər, ə'miljəˌreɪdər, -z

amen
BR ˌɑː'mɛn, ˌeɪ'mɛn, -z
AM ˈɑˈmɛn, ˈeɪˈmɛn, -z

amenability
BR əˌmiːnə'bɪlɪti
AM əˌminə'bɪlɨdi

amenable
BR ə'miːnəbl
AM ə'minəbəl

amenableness
BR ə'miːnəblnəs
AM ə'minəbəlnəs

amenably
BR ə'miːnəbli
AM ə'minəbli

amend
BR ə'mɛnd, -z, -ɪŋ, -ɪd
AM ə'mɛnd, -z, -ɪŋ, -əd

amendable
BR ə'mɛndəbl
AM ə'mɛndəbəl

amendatory
BR ə'mɛndət(ə)ri
AM ə'mɛndəˌtɔri

amende honorable
BR aˌmɒ̃d ɒnə'rɑːbl(ə)(r), -z
AM ˌɑmɑnˌdɔnə'rɑbl, -z

amender
BR ə'mɛndə(r), -z
AM ə'mɛndər, -z

amendment
BR ə'mɛn(d)m(ə)nt, -s
AM ə'mɛn(d)mənt, -s

Amenhotep
BR ˌamɛn'həʊtɛp, a'mɛn(h)əʊtɛp
AM ˌæmən'hoʊtəp, ˌɑmən'hoʊtəp

amenity
BR ə'miːnɪt|i, ə'mɛnɪt|i, -ɪz
AM ə'mɛnədi, -z

amenorrhea
BR əˌmɛnə'riːə(r)
AM eɪˌmɛnə'riə, ɑˌmɛnə'riə

amenorrhoea
BR əˌmɛnə'riːə(r)
AM eɪˌmɛnə'riə, ɑˌmɛnə'riə

ament[1]
catkin
BR ə'mɛnt, -s
AM 'eɪˌmɛnt, 'eɪmənt, -s

ament[2]
person with amentia
BR 'eɪmɛnt, ə'mɛnt, -s
AM 'eɪˌmɛnt, 'eɪmənt, -s

amenta
BR ə'mɛntə(r)
AM ə'mɛn(t)ə

amentia
BR eɪˈmɛnʃ(ɪ)ə(*r*), əˈmɛnʃ(ɪ)ə(*r*)
AM eɪˈmɛn(t)ʃiə

amentum
BR əˈmɛntəm
AM əˈmɛn(t)əm

Amerasian
BR ˌaməˈreɪʃn, ˌaməˈreɪʒn, -z
AM ˌæmərˈeɪʒən, ˌæmərˈeɪʃən, -z

amerce
BR əˈməːs, -ɪz, -ɪŋ, -t
AM əˈmərs, -əz, -ɪŋ, -t

amercement
BR əˈməːsm(ə)nt, -s
AM əˈmərsmənt, -s

amerciable
BR əˈməːsɪəbl
AM əˈmərsiəbəl, əˈmərʃəbəl

America
BR əˈmɛrɪkə(*r*), -z
AM əˈmɛrəkə, -z

American
BR əˈmɛrɪk(ə)n, -z
AM əˈmɛr(ə)kən, -z

Americana
BR əˌmɛrɪˈkɑːnə(*r*)
AM əˌmɛrəˈkɑnə, əˌmɛrəˈkænə

Americanisation
BR əˌmɛrɪkənʌɪˈzeɪʃn, əˌmɛrɪkn̩ʌɪˈzeɪʃn
AM əˌmɛrəkənəˈzeɪʃən, əˌmɛrəkəˌnaɪˈzeɪʃən

Americanise
BR əˈmɛrɪkənʌɪz, əˈmɛrɪkn̩ʌɪz, -ɪz, -ɪŋ, -d
AM əˈmɛrəkəˌnaɪz, -ɪz, -ɪŋ, -d

Americanism
BR əˈmɛrɪkənɪz(ə)m, əˈmɛrɪkn̩ɪz(ə)m, -z
AM əˈmɛrəkəˌnɪzəm, -z

americanist
BR əˈmɛrɪkənɪst, əˈmɛrɪkn̩ɪst, -s
AM əˈmɛrəkənəst, -s

Americanization
BR əˌmɛrɪkənʌɪˈzeɪʃn, əˌmɛrɪkn̩ʌɪˈzeɪʃn
AM əˌmɛrəkənəˈzeɪʃən, əˌmɛrəkəˌnaɪˈzeɪʃən

Americanize
BR əˈmɛrɪkənʌɪz, əˈmɛrɪkn̩ʌɪz, -ɪz, -ɪŋ, -d
AM əˈmɛrəkəˌnaɪz, -ɪz, -ɪŋ, -d

americium
BR ˌaməˈrɪsɪəm, ˌaməˈrɪʃɪəm
AM æməˈrisiəm, æməˈriʃiəm

Amerind
BR ˈamərɪnd, -z
AM ˈæməˌrɪnd, -z

Amerindian
BR ˌaməˈrɪndɪən, -z
AM ˌæməˈrɪndiən, ˌæməˈrɪndjən, -z

Amerindic
BR ˌaməˈrɪndɪk
AM ˌæməˈrɪndɪk

Amersham
BR ˈaməʃ(ə)m
AM ˈæmərʃəm

Ames
BR eɪmz
AM eɪmz

Amesbury
BR ˈeɪmzb(ə)ri
AM ˈeɪmzbəri

Ameslan
BR ˈamɪslan
AM ˈæm(ə)ˌslæn

amethyst
BR ˈamɪθɪst, -s
AM ˈæməθəst, -s

amethystine
BR ˌamɪˈθɪstʌɪn
AM ˌæməˈθɪstən, ˌæməˈθɪsˌtaɪn, ˌæməˈθɪsˌtin

Amex®
BR ˈamɛks, ˈeɪmɛks
AM ˈæˌmɛks

Amharic
BR amˈharɪk
AM æmˈhɛrɪk

Amherst
BR ˈam(h)əːst
AM ˈæm(h)ərst

amiability
BR ˌeɪmɪəˈbɪlɪti
AM ˌeɪmiəˈbɪlɪdi

amiable
BR ˈeɪmɪəbl
AM ˈeɪmiəbəl

amiableness
BR ˈeɪmɪəblnəs
AM ˈeɪmiəbəlnəs

amiably
BR ˈeɪmɪəbli
AM ˈeɪmiəbli

amianthus
BR ˌamɪˈanθəs
AM ˌæmiˈænθəs

amibiguity
BR ˌambɪˈgjuːɪt|i, -ɪz
AM ˌæmbəˈgjuwədi, -z

amicability
BR ˌamɪkəˈbɪlɪti
AM ˌæməkəˈbɪlɪdi

amicable
BR ˈamɪkəbl
AM ˈæməkəbəl

amicableness
BR ˈamɪkəblnəs
AM ˈæməkəbəlnəs

amicably
BR ˈamɪkəbli
AM ˈæməkəbli

amice
BR ˈam|ɪs, -ɪsɪz
AM ˈæməs, -əz

amicus curiae
BR əˌmʌɪkʊs ˈkjʊərɪʌɪ, əˈmiːkʊs +, aˈmʌɪkʊs +, aˈmiːkʊs +, + ˈkjʊərɪiː, + ˈkjɔːrɪʌɪ, + ˈkjɔːrɪiː
AM əˌmikəs ˈk(j)ʊriˌaɪ, + ˈk(j)ʊriˌi

amid
BR əˈmɪd
AM əˈmɪd

amide
BR ˈamʌɪd, -z
AM ˈæˌmaɪd, ˈæməd, -z

Amidol®
BR ˈamɪdɒl
AM ˈæmədɔl, ˈæmədɑl

amidone
BR ˈamɪdəʊn
AM ˈæməˌdoʊn

amidships
BR əˈmɪdʃɪps
AM əˈmɪdˌʃɪps

amidst
BR əˈmɪdst
AM əˈmɪdst

Amiens
BR ˈamɪɒ̃
AM ˈɑmiən
FR amjɛ̃

Amies
BR ˈeɪmɪz
AM ˈeɪmis

amigo
BR əˈmiːgəʊ, -z
AM əˈmigoʊ, -z

Amin
BR ɑːˈmiːn, aˈmiːn
AM ɑˈmin

amine
BR ˈamiːn, ˈamɪn, əˈmiːn, -z
AM əˈmin, ˈæˌmin, -z

amino
BR əˈmiːnəʊ, əˈmʌɪnəʊ, ˈamɪnəʊ
AM əˈminoʊ

amir
BR aˈmɪə(r), əˈmɪə(r), -z
AM əˈmɪ(ə)r, -z

Amirante Islands
BR ˈamɪrant ˌʌɪlən(d)z, ˌamɪˈranti +
AM ˈæməˌrænt ˈaɪlən(d)z

amirate
BR ˈamɪrət, ˈamɪərət, aˈmɪərət, əˈmɪərət, aˈmɪəreɪt, əˈmɪəreɪt, -s
AM ˈɛmərət, -s

Amis
BR ˈeɪmɪs
AM ˈeɪmɪs

Amish
BR ˈɑːmɪʃ, ˈamɪʃ
AM ˈɑmɪʃ

amiss
BR əˈmɪs
AM əˈmɪs

amitosis
BR ˌeɪmʌɪˈtəʊsɪs, ˌamɪˈtəʊsɪs
AM ˌeɪˌmaɪˈtoʊsəs, ˌæməˈtoʊsəs

amitriptyline
BR ˌamɪˈtrɪptɪliːn
AM ˌæməˈtrɪptələn

amity
BR ˈamɪti
AM ˈæmədi

Amlwch
BR ˈamlʊx, ˈamlʊk
AM ˈæmlwɪtʃ

Amman[1]
place in Jordan
BR əˈmɑːn, aˈmɑːn, aˈman
AM ɑˈmɑn

Amman[2]
river in Wales
BR ˈamən
AM ˈæmən

ammeter
BR ˈamiːtə(r), ˈamˌmiːtə(r), -z
AM ˈæ(m)ˌmidər, -z

ammo
BR ˈaməʊ
AM ˈæmoʊ

Ammon
BR ˈamən
AM ˈæmən

ammonia
BR əˈməʊnɪə(*r*)
AM əˈmoʊnjə

ammoniac
BR əˈməʊnɪak
AM əˈmoʊniˌæk

ammoniacal
BR ˌamə(ʊ)ˈnʌɪəkl
AM ˌæməˈnaɪəkəl

ammoniated
BR əˈməʊnɪeɪtɪd
AM əˈmoʊniˌeɪdəd

ammonite
BR ˈamənʌɪt, -s
AM ˈæməˌnaɪt, -s

ammonium
BR əˈməʊnɪəm
AM əˈmoʊniəm

ammtrack
BR ˈamtrak, -s
AM ˈæmˌtræk, -s

ammunition
BR ˌamjʊˈnɪʃn
AM ˌæmjəˈnɪʃən

amnesia
BR am'ni:zɪə(r), am'ni:ʒə(r)
AM æm'niʒə

amnesiac
BR am'ni:zɪak, -s
AM æm'nizi,æk, -s

amnesic
BR am'ni:zɪk, am'ni:sɪk, -s
AM æm'nizɪk, æm'nisɪk, -s

amnesty
BR 'amnɪst|i, -ɪz
AM 'æmnəsti, 'æm,nɛsti, -z

amniocentesis
BR ,amnɪəʊsɛn'ti:sɪs
AM ,æmnioʊ,sɛn'tisɨs

amnion
BR 'amnɪən, -z
AM 'æmni,ɑn, 'æmniən, -z

amniote
BR 'amnɪəʊt, -s
AM 'æmni,oʊt, -s

amniotic
BR ,amnɪ'ɒtɪk
AM ,æmni'ɑdɪk

Amoco®
BR 'amәkәʊ
AM 'æməkoʊ

amoeba
BR ə'mi:bə(r), -z
AM ə'mibə, -z

amoebae
BR ə'mi:bi:
AM ə'mibi

amoebean
BR ə'mi:bɪən
AM ə'mibiən

amoebic
BR ə'mi:bɪk
AM ə'mibɪk

amoeboid
BR ə'mi:bɔɪd
AM ə'mi,bɔɪd

amok
BR ə'mɒk, ə'mʌk
AM ə'mək, ə'mɑk

among
BR ə'mʌŋ
AM ə'məŋ

amongst
BR ə'mʌŋst
AM ə'məŋs(t)

amontillado
BR ə,mɒntɪ'lɑ:dəʊ, -z
AM ə,mɑntə'lɑdoʊ, ə,mɑntə'jɑdoʊ, -z

amoral
BR ,eɪ'mɒrəl, ,eɪ'mɒrl̩
AM ,eɪ'mɔrəl

amoralism
BR ,eɪ'mɒrəlɪz(ə)m, ,eɪ'mɒrl̩ɪz(ə)m
AM ,eɪ'mɔrə,lɪzəm

amoralist
BR ,eɪ'mɒrəlɪst, ,eɪ'mɒrl̩ɪst, -s
AM ,eɪ'mɔrələst, -s

amorality
BR ,eɪmə'ralɪti
AM ,eɪmə'rælədi

amorally
BR ,eɪ'mɒrəli, ,eɪ'mɒrl̩i
AM ,eɪ'mɔrəli

amoretti
BR ,amə'rɛti
AM ,æmə'rɛdi

amoretto
BR ,amə'rɛtəʊ
AM ,æmə'rɛdoʊ

amorist
BR 'amərɪst, -s
AM 'æmərəst, -s

Amorite
BR 'amərʌɪt, -s
AM 'æmə,raɪt, -s

amoroso
BR ,amə'rəʊsəʊ, -z
AM ,ɑmə'roʊsoʊ, ,æmə'roʊsoʊ, -z

amorous
BR 'am(ə)rəs
AM 'æm(ə)rəs

amorously
BR 'am(ə)rəsli
AM 'æm(ə)rəsli

amorousness
BR 'am(ə)rəsnəs
AM 'æm(ə)rəsnəs

amorpha
BR ə'mɔ:fə(r), -z
AM ə'mɔrfə, -z

amorphism
BR ə'mɔ:fɪz(ə)m
AM ə'mɔr,fɪzəm, eɪ'mɔr,fɪzəm

amorphous
BR ə'mɔ:fəs
AM ə'mɔrfəs, eɪ'mɔrfəs

amorphously
BR ə'mɔ:fəsli
AM ə'mɔrfəsli, eɪ'mɔrfəsli

amorphousness
BR ə'mɔ:fəsnəs
AM ə'mɔrfəsnəs, eɪ'mɔrfəsnəs

amortisable
BR ə'mɔ:tʌɪzəbl
AM 'æmər,taɪzəbəl

amortisation
BR ə,mɔ:tʌɪ'zeɪʃn, -z
AM 'æmərdə'zeɪʃən, 'æmɔr,taɪ'zeɪʃən, -z

amortise
BR ə'mɔ:tʌɪz, -ɪz, -ɪŋ, -d
AM 'æmər,taɪz, -ɨz, -ɪŋ, -d

amortizable
BR ə'mɔ:tʌɪzəbl
AM 'æmər,taɪzəbəl

amortization
BR ə,mɔ:tʌɪ'zeɪʃn, -z
AM 'æmərdə'zeɪʃən, 'æmɔr,taɪ'zeɪʃən, -z

amortize
BR ə'mɔ:tʌɪz, -ɪz, -ɪŋ, -d
AM 'æmər,taɪz, -ɨz, -ɪŋ, -d

Amory
BR 'eɪm(ə)ri
AM 'eɪməri

Amos
BR 'eɪmɒs
AM 'eɪməs

amount
BR ə'maʊnt, -s, -ɪŋ, -ɨd
AM ə'maʊn|t, -ts, -(t)ɪŋ, -(t)əd

amour
BR ə'mʊə(r), ə'mɔ:(r), -z
AM ə'mʊ(ə)r, ɑ'mʊ(ə)r, -z

amourette
BR ,amə'rɛt, -s
AM ,æmə'rɛt, -s

amour propre
BR ,amʊə 'prɒpr(ər), ,amɔ: +
AM ,ɑmʊr 'prɔpr(ə)

Amoy
BR ə'mɔɪ
AM ɑ'mɔɪ

amp
BR amp, -s
AM æmp, -s

ampelopsis
BR ,ampɪ'lɒpsɪs
AM ,æmpə'lɑpsəs

amperage
BR 'amp(ə)rɪdʒ
AM 'æmp(ə)rɪdʒ

ampere
BR 'ampɛ:(r), -z
AM 'æm,pɪ(ə)r, 'æm,pɛ(ə)r, -z

ampersand
BR 'ampəsand, -z
AM 'æmpər,sænd, -z

Ampex®
BR 'ampɛks
AM 'æmpɛks

amphetamine
BR am'fɛtəmi:n, am'fɛtəmɪn, -z
AM æm'(p)fɛdə,min, æm'(p)fɛdəmən, -z

amphibia
BR am'fɪbɪə(r)
AM æm'(p)fɪbiə

amphibian
BR am'fɪbɪən, -z
AM æm'(p)fɪbiən, -z

amphibiology
BR am,fɪbɪ'ɒlədʒi
AM æm,(p)fɪbi'ɑlədʒi

amphibious
BR am'fɪbɪəs
AM æm'(p)fɪbiəs

amphibiously
BR am'fɪbɪəsli
AM æm'(p)fɪbiəsli

amphibole
BR 'amfɪbəʊl, -z
AM 'æm(p)fə,boʊl, -z

amphibolite
BR am'fɪbəlʌɪt, -s
AM æm'(p)fɪbə,laɪt, -s

amphibology
BR ,amfɪ'bɒlədʒ|i, -ɪz
AM ,æm(p)fə'bɑlədʒi, -z

amphibrach
BR 'amfɪbrak, -s
AM 'æm(p)fə,bræk, -s

amphibrachic
BR ,amfɪ'brakɪk
AM ,æm(p)fə'brækɪk

amphictyon
BR am'fɪktɪən, -z
AM æm'(p)fɪktiən, -z

amphictyonic
BR am,fɪktɪ'ɒnɪk
AM ,æm,(p)fɪkti'ɑnɪk

amphictyony
BR am'fɪktɪəni
AM æm'(p)fɪktiəni

amphigamous
BR am'fɪgəməs
AM æm'(p)fɪgəməs

amphigori
BR 'amfɪ,gɔ:r|i, 'amfɪg(ə)r|i, am'fɪg(ə)r|i, -ɪz
AM 'æm(p)fə,gɔri, æm'(p)fɪgəri, -z

amphigouri
BR 'amfɪ,gʊər|i, 'amfɪg(ə)r|i, am'fɪg(ə)r|i, -ɪz
AM 'æm(p)fə,guri, æm'(p)fɪgəri, -z

amphimictic
BR ,amfɪ'mɪktɪk
AM ,æm(p)fə'mɪktɪk

amphimixes
BR ,amfɪ'mɪksi:z
AM ,æm(p)fə'mɪksiz

amphimixis
BR ,amfɪ'mɪksɪs
AM ,æm(p)fə'mɪksɨs

amphioxi
BR ,amfɪ'ɒksi
AM ,æm(p)fi'ɑksi

amphioxus
BR ,amfɪ'ɒksəs
AM ,æm(p)fi'ɑksəs

amphipathic
BR ,amfɪ'paθɪk
AM ,æm(p)fə'pæθɪk

amphipod
BR 'amfɪpɒd, -z
AM 'æm(p)fə,pɑd, -z

amphipoda
BR am'fɪpədə(r)

AM æm'(p)fɪpədə

amphiprostyle
BR ˌamfɪ'prəʊstʌɪl, -z
AM ˌæm(p)fə'proʊˌstaɪl, -z

amphisbaena
BR ˌamfɪs'biːnə(r), -z
AM ˌæm(p)fəs'binə, -z

amphitheater
BR 'amfɪθɪətə(r), -z
AM 'æm(p)fəˌθiədər, -z

amphitheatre
BR 'amfɪθɪətə(r), -z
AM 'æm(p)fəˌθiədər, -z

Amphitrite
BR ˌamfɪ'trʌɪti
AM ˌæm(p)fə'traɪdi

Amphitryon
BR am'fɪtrɪən
AM æm'(p)fɪtriˌɑn

amphora
BR 'amf(ə)rə(r), -z
AM 'æm(p)fərə, æm(p)'fɔrə, -z

amphorae
BR 'amf(ə)riː
AM 'æm(p)fəˌri, æm(p)'fɔˌraɪ

amphoteric
BR ˌamfə(ʊ)'tɛrɪk
AM ˌæm(p)fə'tɛrɪk

amphotericin
BR ˌamfə(ʊ)'tɛrɪsɪn
AM ˌæm(p)fə'tɛrəsən

ampicillin
BR ˌampɪ'sɪlɪn
AM 'æmpəˌsɪlɪn

ample
BR 'ampl, -ə(r), -ɪst
AM 'æmpəl, -(ə)lər, -(ə)ləst

Ampleforth
BR 'amplfɔːθ
AM 'æmpəlˌfɔ(ə)rθ

ampleness
BR 'amplnəs
AM 'æmpəlnəs

Amplex®
BR 'amplɛks
AM 'æmplɛks

amplexicaul
BR am'plɛksɪkɔːl
AM æm'plɛksəˌkɔl, æm'plɛksəˌkɑl

amplification
BR ˌamplɪfɪ'keɪʃn
AM ˌæmpləfə'keɪʃən

amplifier
BR 'amplɪfʌɪə(r), -z
AM 'æmpləˌfaɪər, -z

amplify
BR 'amplɪfʌɪ, -z, -ɪŋ, -d
AM 'æmpləˌfaɪ, -z, -ɪŋ, -d

amplitude
BR 'amplɪtjuːd, 'amplɪtʃuːd, -z
AM 'æmpləˌt(j)ud, -z

amply
BR 'ampli
AM 'æmp(ə)li

Ampney
BR 'ampni
AM 'æmpni

ampoule
BR 'amp(j)uːl, -z
AM 'æmˌpjul, -z

Ampthill
BR 'am(p)t(h)ɪl
AM 'æm(p)t(h)ɪl

ampule
BR 'amp(j)uːl, -z
AM 'æmˌpjul, -z

ampulla
BR am'pʊlə(r)
AM æm'p(j)ʊlə, æm'pələ, 'æmˌpjʊlə

ampullae
BR am'pʊliː
AM æm'p(j)ʊˌli, æm'pəˌli

amputate
BR 'ampjʉteɪt, -s, -ɪŋ, -ɪd
AM 'æmpjəˌteɪ|t, -ts, -dɪŋ, -dɨd

amputation
BR ˌampjʉ'teɪʃn, -z
AM ˌæmpjə'teɪʃən, -z

amputator
BR 'ampjʉteɪtə(r), -z
AM 'æmpjəˌteɪdər, -z

amputee
BR ˌampjʉ'tiː, -z
AM ˌæmpjə'ti, -z

Amritsar
BR am'rɪtsə(r), am'rɪtsɑː(r)
AM ɑm'rɪtsər

Amsterdam
BR ˌam(p)stə'dam, 'am(p)stədam
AM 'æm(p)stərˌdæm

Amstrad®
BR 'amstrad
AM 'æmstræd

amtrac
BR 'amtrak, -s
AM 'æmˌtræk, -s

Amtrak®
BR 'amtrak
AM 'æmˌtræk

amuck
BR ə'mʌk
AM ə'mək

Amu Darya
BR ˌɑːmuː 'dɑːrɪə(r), aˌmuː +
AM ˌɑmu 'dɑrjə
RUS a'mu da'rʲja

amulet
BR 'amjʉlət, -s
AM 'æmjələt, 'æmjəˌlɛt, -s

Amundsen
BR 'amən(d)s(ə)n, 'amʊn(d)s(ə)n
AM 'æmən(d)sən
NO 'aːmʉnsen

Amur
BR a'muːə(r), 'amʊə(r)
AM ɑ'mu(ə)r

amuse
BR ə'mjuːz, -ɪz, -ɪŋ, -d
AM ə'mjuz, -əz, -ɪŋ, -d

amusement
BR ə'mjuːzm(ə)nt, -s
AM ə'mjuzmənt, -s

amusing
BR ə'mjuːzɪŋ
AM ə'mjuzɪŋ

amusingly
BR ə'mjuːzɪŋli
AM ə'mjuzɪŋli

amusive
BR ə'mjuːzɪv
AM ə'mjuzɪv

Amy
BR 'eɪmi
AM 'eɪmi

amygdala
BR ə'mɪgdələ(r), -z
AM ə'mɪgdələ, -z

amygdalae
BR ə'mɪgdəliː
AM ə'mɪgdəli, ə'mɪgdəˌlaɪ

amygdale
BR ə'mɪgdəliː
AM ə'mɪgdəli

amygdaloid
BR ə'mɪgdəlɔɪd
AM ə'mɪgdəˌlɔɪd

amyl
BR 'am(ɪ)l, 'eɪmʌɪl
AM 'æməl

amylase
BR 'amɪleɪz
AM 'æməˌleɪs, 'æməˌleɪz

amyloid
BR 'amɪlɔɪd
AM 'æməˌlɔɪd

amylopsin
BR 'amɪlɒpsɪn, ˌamɪ'lɒpsɪn
AM ˌæmə'lɑpsən

amyotrophy
BR ˌamɪ'ɒtrəfi
AM ˌæmi'ɑtrəfi

Amytal®
BR 'amɪtal
AM 'æməˌtɔl, 'æməˌtɑl

an¹
strong form
BR an
AM æn

an²
weak form
BR ən, n
AM ən, n

ana
BR 'ɑːnə(r), -z
AM 'ɑnə, -z

Anabaptism
BR ˌanə'baptɪz(ə)m
AM ˌænə'bæpˌtɪzəm

Anabaptist
BR ˌanə'baptɪst, -s
AM ˌænə'bæptəst, -s

anabas
BR 'anəbas
AM 'ænəbəs, 'ænəˌbæs

anabases
BR ə'nabəsiːz
AM ə'næbəˌsiz

anabasis
BR ə'nabəsɪs
AM ə'næbəsəs

anabatic
BR ˌanə'batɪk
AM ˌænə'bædɪk

anabioses
BR ˌanəbʌɪ'əʊsiːz
AM ˌænəˌbaɪ'oʊsiz

anabiosis
BR ˌanəbʌɪ'əʊsɪs
AM ˌænəˌbaɪ'oʊsəs

anabiotic
BR ˌanəbʌɪ'ɒtɪk
AM ˌænəˌbaɪ'ɑdɪk

anabolic
BR ˌanə'bɒlɪk, -s
AM ˌænə'bɑlɪk, -s

anabolism
BR ə'nabəlɪz(ə)m
AM ə'næbəˌlɪzəm, æ'næbəˌlɪzəm

anabranch
BR 'anəbrɑːn(t)ʃ, 'anəbran(t)ʃ, -ɪz
AM 'ænəˌbræŋk, -s

anachronic
BR ˌanə'krɒnɪk
AM ˌænə'krɑnɪk

anachronism
BR ə'nakrənɪz(ə)m, -z
AM ə'nækrəˌnɪzəm, -z

anachronistic
BR əˌnakrə'nɪstɪk
AM əˌnækrə'nɪstɪk

anachronistically
BR əˌnakrə'nɪstɪkli
AM əˌnækrə'nɪstək(ə)li

Anacin®
BR 'anəsɪn, -z
AM 'ænəsɪn, -z

anacolutha
BR ˌanəkə'luːθə(r)
AM ˌænəkə'luθə

anacoluthic
BR ˌanəkə'luːθɪk
AM ˌænəkə'luθɪk

anacoluthon
BR ˌanəkə'luːθ(ə)n, ˌanəkə'luːθɒn
AM ˌænəkə'luˌθɑn

anaconda
BR ˌanəˈkɒndə(r), -z
AM ˌænəˈkɑndə, -z

Anacreon
BR əˈnakrɪən
AM əˈnækriən

anacreontic
BR əˌnakrɪˈɒntɪk
AM əˌnækriˈɑn(t)ɪk

anacruses
BR ˌanəˈkruːsiːz
AM ˌænəˈkruˌsiz

anacrusis
BR ˌanəˈkruːsɪs
AM ˌænəˈkrusəs

Anadin®
BR ˈanədɪn, -z
AM ˈænədɪn, -z

anadromous
BR əˈnadrəməs
AM əˈnædrəməs, æˈnædrəməs

anaemia
BR əˈniːmɪə(r)
AM əˈnimiə

anaemic
BR əˈniːmɪk, -s
AM əˈnimɪk, -s

anaerobe
BR ˈanərəʊb, -z
AM ˈænəˌroʊb, -z

anaerobic
BR ˌanəˈrəʊbɪk, ˌanɛːˈrəʊbɪk
AM ˌænˌɛˈroʊbɪk, ˌænəˈroʊbɪk

anaesthesia
BR ˌanɪsˈθiːzɪə(r), ˌanɪsˈθiːʒə(r)
AM ˌænəsˈθiʒə

anaesthesiologist
BR ˌanɪsθiːzɪˈɒlədʒɪst, -s
AM ˌænəsˌθiziˈɑlədʒəst, -s

anaesthesiology
BR ˌanɪsθiːzɪˈɒlədʒi
AM ˌænəsˌθiziˈɑlədʒi

anaesthetic
BR ˌanɪsˈθɛtɪk, -s
AM ˌænəsˈθɛdɪk, -s

anaesthetical
BR ˌanɪsˈθɛtɪkl
AM ˌænəsˈθɛdəkəl

anaesthetically
BR ˌanɪsˈθɛtɪkli
AM ˌænəsˈθɛdək(ə)li

anaesthetisation
BR əˌniːsθɪtʌɪˈzeɪʃn
AM əˌnɛsθədəˈzeɪʃən, əˌnɛsθəˌtaɪˈzeɪʃən

anaesthetise
BR əˈniːsθɪtʌɪz, -ɪz, -ɪŋ, -d
AM əˈnɛsθəˌtaɪz, -ɪz, -ɪŋ, -d

anaesthetist
BR əˈniːsθɪtɪst, -s
AM əˈnɛsθədəst, -s

anaesthetization
BR əˌniːsθɪtʌɪˈzeɪʃn
AM əˌnɛsθədəˈzeɪʃən, əˌnɛsθəˌtaɪˈzeɪʃən

anaesthetize
BR əˈniːsθɪtʌɪz, -ɪz, -ɪŋ, -d
AM əˈnɛsθəˌtaɪz, -ɪz, -ɪŋ, -d

anaglyph
BR ˈanəglɪf, -s
AM ˈænəˌglɪf, -s

anaglyphic
BR ˌanəˈglɪfɪk
AM ˌænəˈglɪfɪk

anaglypta
BR ˌanəˈglɪptə(r), -z
AM ˌænəˈglɪptə, -z

anagnorises
BR ˌanəgˈnɒrɪsiːz
AM ˌæˌnægˈnɔrəsiz

anagnorisis
BR ˌanəgˈnɒrɪsɪs
AM ˌæˌnægˈnɔrəsəs

anagoge
BR ˈanəgɒdʒi, ˈanəgəʊdʒi
AM ˈænəˌgɑdʒi, ˈænəˌgoʊdʒi

anagogic
BR ˌanəˈgɒdʒɪk, -s
AM ˌænəˈgɑdʒɪk, -s

anagogical
BR ˌanəˈgɒdʒɪkl
AM ˌænəˈgɑdʒəkəl

anagogically
BR ˌanəˈgɒdʒɪkli
AM ˌænəˈgɑdʒək(ə)li

anagogy
BR ˈanəgɒdʒi, ˈanəgəʊdʒi
AM ˈænəˌgɑdʒi, ˈænəˌgoʊdʒi

anagram
BR ˈanəgram, -z
AM ˈænəˌgræm, -z

anagrammatic
BR ˌanəgrəˈmatɪk
AM ˌænəgrəˈmædɪk

anagrammatical
BR ˌanəgrəˈmatɪkl
AM ˌænəgrəˈmædəkəl

anagrammatically
BR ˌanəgrəˈmatɪkli
AM ˌænəgrəˈmædək(ə)li

anagrammatise
BR ˌanəˈgramətʌɪz, -ɪz, -ɪŋ, -d
AM ˌænəˈgræməˌtaɪz, -ɪz, -ɪŋ, -d

anagrammatize
BR ˌanəˈgramətʌɪz, -ɪz, -ɪŋ, -d
AM ˌænəˈgræməˌtaɪz, -ɪz, -ɪŋ, -d

Anaheim
BR ˈanəhʌɪm
AM ˈænəˌhaɪm

anal
BR ˈeɪnl
AM ˈeɪnəl

analect
BR ˈanəlɛkt, -s
AM ˈænlˌɛk|(t), -(t)s

analecta
BR ˌanəˈlɛktə(r)
AM ˌænəˈlɛktə

analemma
BR ˌanəˈlɛmə(r)
AM ˌænəˈlɛmə

analemmatic
BR ˌanəlɛˈmatɪk
AM ˌanələˈmædɪk

analeptic
BR ˌanəˈlɛptɪk
AM ˌænəˈlɛptɪk

analgesia
BR ˌanlˈdʒiːzɪə(r)
AM ˌænlˈdʒiziə, ˌænlˈdʒiʒə

analgesic
BR ˌanlˈdʒiːzɪk, -s
AM ˌænlˈdʒizɪk, -s

anally
BR ˈeɪnḷi, ˈeɪnəli
AM ˈeɪnəli

analog
BR ˈanəlɒg, ˈanḷɒg, -z
AM ˈænlˌɔg, ˈænlˌɑg, -z

analogic
BR ˌanəˈlɒdʒɪk
AM ˌænəˈlɑdʒɪk

analogical
BR ˌanəˈlɒdʒɪkl
AM ˌænəˈlɑdʒəkəl

analogically
BR ˌanəˈlɒdʒɪkli
AM ˌænəˈlɑdʒək(ə)li

analogise
BR əˈnalədʒʌɪz, -ɪz, -ɪŋ, -d
AM əˈnæləˌdʒaɪz, -ɪz, -ɪŋ, -d

analogist
BR əˈnalədʒɪst, -s
AM əˈnælədʒəst, -s

analogize
BR əˈnalədʒʌɪz, -ɪz, -ɪŋ, -d
AM əˈnæləˌdʒaɪz, -ɪz, -ɪŋ, -d

analogous
BR əˈnaləgəs
AM əˈnæləgəs

analogously
BR əˈnaləgəsli
AM əˈnæləgəsli

analogousness
BR əˈnaləgəsnəs
AM əˈnæləgəsnəs

analogue
BR ˈanəlɒg, ˈanḷɒg, -z
AM ˈænlˌɔg, ˈænlˌɑg, -z

analogy
BR əˈnalədʒ|i, -ɪz
AM əˈnælədʒi, -z

analphabetic
BR ˌanalfəˈbɛtɪk
AM ˌæˌnælfəˈbɛdɪk

analphabetical
BR ˌanalfəˈbɛtɪkl
AM ˌæˌnælfəˈbɛdəkəl

analphabetically
BR ˌanalfəˈbɛtɪkli
AM ˌæˌnælfəˈbɛdək(ə)li

analysable
BR ˈanəlʌɪzəbl, ˈanḷʌɪzəbl
AM ˌænəˈlaɪzəbəl

analysand
BR əˈnalɪsand, -z
AM əˈnæləˌsænd, əˈnæləˌzænd, -z

analyse
BR ˈanəlʌɪz, ˈanḷʌɪz, -ɪz, -ɪŋ, -d
AM ˈænlˌaɪz, -ɪz, -ɪŋ, -d

analyser
BR ˈanəlʌɪzə(r), ˈanḷʌɪzə(r), -z
AM ˈænlˌaɪzər, -z

analyses
BR əˈnalɪsiːz
AM əˈnæləˌsiz

analysis
BR əˈnalɪsɪs
AM əˈnæləsəs

analyst
BR ˈanəlɪst, ˈanḷɪst, -s
AM ˈænələst, -s

analytic
BR ˌanəˈlɪtɪk
AM ˌænəˈlɪdɪk

analytical
BR ˌanəˈlɪtɪkl
AM ˌænəˈlɪdɪkəl

analytically
BR ˌanəˈlɪtɪkli
AM ˌænəˈlɪdɪk(ə)li

analyzable
BR ˈanəlʌɪzəbl, ˈanḷʌɪzəbl
AM ˌænəˈlaɪzəbəl

analyze
BR ˈanəlʌɪz, ˈanḷʌɪz, -ɪz, -ɪŋ, -d
AM ˈænlˌaɪz, -ɪz, -ɪŋ, -d

analyzer
BR ˈanəlʌɪzə(r), ˈanḷʌɪzə(r), -z
AM ˈænlˌaɪzər, -z

anamnesis
BR ˌanəmˈniːsɪs
AM ˌænəmˈnisɪs

anamorphic
BR ˌanəˈmɔːfɪk
AM ˌænəˈmɔrfɪk

anamorphoses
BR ˌanəˈmɔːfəsiːz
AM ˌænəˈmɔrfəsiz

anamorphosis
BR ˌanəˈmɔːfəsɪs
AM ˌænəˈmɔrfəsəs

ananas
BR əˈnɑːnəs, ˈanənəs, əˈnanəs
AM ˈɑnɑˈnɑs

anandrous
BR əˈnandrəs
AM əˈnændrəs

Ananias
BR ˌanəˈnʌɪəs
AM ˌænəˈnaɪəs

anapaest
BR ˈanəpiːst, ˈanapɛst, -s
AM ˈænəˌpɛst, -s

anapaestic
BR ˌanəˈpiːstɪk, ˌanəˈpɛstɪk
AM ˌænəˈpɛstɪk

anapest
BR ˈanəpiːst, ˈanapɛst, -s
AM ˈænəˌpɛst, -s

anapestic
BR ˌanəˈpiːstɪk, ˌanəˈpɛstɪk
AM ˌænəˈpɛstɪk

anaphase
BR ˈanəfeɪz, -ɪz
AM ˈænəˌfeɪz, -ɪz

anaphor
BR ˈanəfɔː(r)
AM ˈænəˌfɔ(ə)r

anaphora
BR əˈnaf(ə)rə(*r*)
AM əˈnæf(ə)rə

anaphoric
BR ˌanəˈfɒrɪk
AM ˌænəˈfɔrɪk

anaphrodisiac
BR əˌnafrəˈdɪzɪak, -s
AM ˌæˌnəfrəˈdɪziˌæk, -s

anaphylactic
BR ˌanəfɪˈlaktɪk
AM ˌænəfəˈlæktɪk

anaphylaxis
BR ˌanəfɪˈlaksɪs
AM ˌænəfəˈlæksəs

anaptyctic
BR ˌanəpˈtɪktɪk, ˌanapˈtɪktɪk
AM ˌænæpˈtɪktɪk

anaptyxes
BR ˌanəpˈtɪksiːz, ˌanapˈtɪksiːz
AM ˌænæpˈtɪksiz

anaptyxis
BR ˌanəpˈtɪksɪs, ˌanapˈtɪksɪs
AM ˌænæpˈtɪksɪs

anarch
BR ˈanɑːk, -s
AM ˈænˌɑrk, -s

anarchic
BR əˈnɑːkɪk
AM æˈnærkɪk, əˈnærkɪk

anarchical
BR əˈnɑːkɪkl
AM æˈnɑrkəkəl, əˈnɑrkəkəl

anarchically
BR əˈnɑːkɪkli
AM æˈnɑrkək(ə)li, əˈnɑrkək(ə)li

anarchism
BR ˈanəkɪz(ə)m
AM ˈænərˌkɪzəm, ˈæˌnɑrˌkɪzəm

anarchist
BR ˈanəkɪst, -s
AM ˈænərkəst, -s

anarchistic
BR ˌanəˈkɪstɪk
AM ˌænərˈkɪstɪk

anarchy
BR ˈanəki
AM ˈænərki

Anasazi
BR ˌanəˈsɑːzi, ˌanəˈsazi
AM ˌænəˈsɑzi

Anastasia
BR ˌanəˈsteɪzɪə(*r*), ˌanəˈstɑːzɪə(*r*)
AM ˌænəˈsteɪʒə
RUS ənəstaˈsʲijə

anastigmat
BR anˈastɪgmat, ənˈastɪgmat, ˌanəˈstɪgmat, -s
AM ˌænəˈstɪgˌmæt, -s

anastigmatic
BR ˌanəstɪgˈmatɪk
AM ˌænəˌstɪgˈmædɪk

anastomose
BR əˈnastəməʊz, aˈnastəməʊz, -ɪz, -ɪŋ, -d
AM əˈnæstəˌmoʊz, əˈnæstəˌmoʊs, -əz, -ɪŋ, -d

anastomoses
BR əˌnastəˈməʊsiːz, aˌnastəˈməʊsiːz, ˌanəstəˈməʊsiːz
AM əˌnæstəˈmoʊsiz

anastomosis
BR əˌnastəˈməʊsɪs, aˌnastəˈməʊsɪs, ˌanəstəˈməʊsɪs
AM əˌnæstəˈmoʊsəs

anastrophe
BR əˈnastrəfi, aˈnastrəfi
AM əˈnæstrəfi

anathema
BR əˈnaθɪmə(*r*)
AM əˈnæθəmə

anathematisation
BR əˌnaθɪmətʌɪˈzeɪʃn
AM əˌnæθ(ə)mədəˈzeɪʃən, əˌnæθ(ə)məˌtaɪˈzeɪʃən

anathematise
BR əˈnaθɪmətʌɪz, -ɪz, -ɪŋ, -d
AM əˈnæθ(ə)məˌtaɪz, -ɪz, -ɪŋ, -d

anathematization
BR əˌnaθɪmətʌɪˈzeɪʃn
AM əˌnæθ(ə)mədəˈzeɪʃən, əˌnæθ(ə)məˌtaɪˈzeɪʃən

anathematize
BR əˈnaθɪmətʌɪz, -ɪz, -ɪŋ, -d
AM əˈnæθ(ə)məˌtaɪz, -ɪz, -ɪŋ, -d

Anatolia
BR ˌanəˈtəʊlɪə(*r*)
AM ˌænəˈtoʊljə, ˌænəˈtoʊliə

Anatolian
BR ˌanəˈtəʊlɪən, -z
AM ˌænəˈtoʊljən, ˌænəˈtoʊliən, -z

anatomic
BR ˌanəˈtɒmɪk
AM ˌænəˈtɑmɪk

anatomical
BR ˌanəˈtɒmɪkl
AM ˌænəˈtɑməkəl

anatomically
BR ˌanəˈtɒmɪkli
AM ˌænəˈtɑmək(ə)li

anatomise
BR əˈnatəmʌɪz, -ɪz, -ɪŋ, -d
AM əˈnædəˌmaɪz, -ɪz, -ɪŋ, -d

anatomist
BR əˈnatəmɪst, -s
AM əˈnædəməst, -s

anatomize
BR əˈnatəmʌɪz, -ɪz, -ɪŋ, -d
AM əˈnædəˌmaɪz, -ɪz, -ɪŋ, -d

anatomy
BR əˈnatəm|i, -ɪz
AM əˈnædəmi, -z

anatta
BR əˈnatə(*r*)
AM əˈnɑdə

anatto
BR əˈnatəʊ
AM əˈnɑdoʊ

Anaxagoras
BR ˌanakˈsag(ə)rəs, ˌanakˈsagəras
AM ˌænəkˈsægərəs

Anaximander
BR əˌnaksɪˈmandə(r)
AM əˌnæksəˈmændər

Anaximenes
BR ˌanakˈsɪmɪniːz
AM ˌænəkˈsɪməniz

anbury
BR ˈanb(ə)r|i, -ɪz
AM ˈænbəri, -z

ancestor
BR ˈansɪstə(r), ˈansɛstə(r), -z
AM ˈænˌsɛstər, -z

ancestral
BR anˈsɛstr(ə)l
AM ænˈsɛstrəl

ancestrally
BR anˈsɛstrḷi, anˈsɛstrəli
AM ænˈsɛstrəli

ancestress
BR ˈansɪstrɪs, ˈansɛstrɪs, -ɪz
AM ˈænˌsɛstrəs, -əz

ancestry
BR ˈansɪstr|i, ˈansɛstr|i, -ɪz
AM ˈænˌsɛstri, -z

Anchises
BR anˈkʌɪsiːz
AM æŋˈkaɪsiz

anchor
BR ˈaŋk|ə(r), -əz, -(ə)rɪŋ, -əd
AM ˈæŋk|ər, -ərz, -(ə)rɪŋ, -ərd

anchorage
BR ˈaŋk(ə)r|ɪdʒ, -ɪdʒɪz
AM ˈæŋk(ə)rɪdʒ, -ɪz

anchoress
BR ˈaŋk(ə)rɪs, ˈaŋkərɛs, -ɪz
AM ˈæŋk(ə)rəs, -əz

anchoretic
BR ˌaŋkəˈrɛtɪk
AM ˌæŋkəˈrɛdɪk

anchorhold
BR ˈaŋkəhəʊld, -z
AM ˈæŋkərˌ(h)oʊld, -z

anchorite
BR ˈaŋkərʌɪt, -s
AM ˈæŋkəˌraɪt, -s

anchoritic
BR ˌaŋkəˈrɪtɪk
AM ˌæŋkəˈrɪdɪk

anchorman
BR ˈaŋkəman
AM ˈæŋkərˌmæn

anchormen
BR ˈaŋkəmɛn
AM ˈæŋkərˌmɛn

anchorperson
BR ˈaŋkəˌpəːsn, -z
AM ˈæŋkərˌpərsən, -z

anchorwoman
BR ˈaŋkəˌwʊmən
AM ˈæŋkərˌwʊmən

anchorwomen
BR ˈaŋkəˌwɪmɪn
AM ˈæŋkərˌwɪmɪn

anchoveta
BR ˌantʃə(ʊ)ˈvɛtə(*r*), -z
AM ˌæntʃoʊˈvɛdə, -z

anchovy
BR ˈantʃəv|i, -ɪz
AM ˈænˈtʃoʊvi, -z

anchusa
BR aŋ'k(j)u:zə(r), an'tʃu:zə(r), -z
AM æŋ'kjuzə, æŋ'kjusə, -z

anchylose
BR 'aŋkɪləʊz, 'aŋkɪləʊs, -ɪz, -ɪŋ, -d\-t
AM 'æŋkə,loʊs, 'æŋkə,loʊz, -əz, -ɪŋ, -t\-d

ancien régime
BR ,ɒsɪã reɪ'ʒi:m, ,ɒnsɪan +, -z
AM 'ɑnsiɛn rə'ʒim, -z

ancient
BR 'eɪnʃ(ə)nt, -s
AM 'eɪn(t)ʃənt, -s

anciently
BR 'eɪnʃ(ə)ntli
AM 'eɪn(t)ʃən(t)li

ancientness
BR 'eɪnʃ(ə)ntnəs
AM 'eɪn(t)ʃən(t)nəs

ancillary
BR an'sɪlər|i, -ɪz
AM 'ænsə,lɛri, -z

ancipital
BR an'sɪpɪtl
AM æn'sɪpədl

ancon
BR 'aŋkɒn, 'aŋk(ə)n, -z
AM 'æŋ,kɑn, -z

ancones
BR aŋ'kəʊni:z
AM ,æŋ'koʊniz

Ancyra
BR an'sʌɪrə(r)
AM æn'saɪrə

and[1]
strong form
BR and
AM ænd

and[2]
weak form
BR (ə)n(d)
AM (ə)n(d)

Andalucía
BR ,andəlu:'siə(r)
AM ,ændə'luʒə, ,ændə'luʃ(i)ə
SP ,andalu'θia, ,andalu'sia

Andalusia
BR ,andə'lu:sɪə(r), ,andəlu:'si:ə(r)
AM ,ændə'luʒə, ,ændə'luʃ(i)ə

Andalusian
BR ,andə'lu:sɪən, ,andəlu:'si:ən, -z
AM ,ændə'luʒən, ,ændə'luʃən, -z

Andaman
BR 'andəmən, -z
AM 'ændəmən, -z

Andamanese
BR ,andəmə'ni:z
AM ,ændəmə'niz

andante
BR an'dant|i, an'dant|eɪ, -ɪz\-eɪz
AM ɑn'dɑn(t)eɪ, -z

andantino
BR ,andan'ti:nəʊ, -z
AM ,ɑn,dɑn'tinoʊ, -z

Andean
BR 'andɪən, an'di:ən
AM ,æn,diən

Andersen
BR 'andəs(ə)n
AM 'ændərsən

Anderson
BR 'andəs(ə)n
AM 'ændərsən

Andes
BR 'andi:z
AM 'ændiz

andesite
BR 'andɪsʌɪt, 'andɪzʌɪt
AM 'ændə,zaɪt

Andhra Pradesh
BR ,andrə prə'dɛʃ
AM ,ɑndrə prə'dɛʃ

andiron
BR 'andʌɪən, -z
AM 'æn,daɪ(ə)rn, -z

Andorra
BR an'dɔ:rə(r), an'dɒrə(r)
AM æn'dɔrə

Andorran
BR an'dɔ:rən, an'dɔ:rn̩, an'dɒrən, an'dɒrn̩, -z
AM æn'dɔrən, -z

André
BR 'ɒndreɪ, 'andreɪ, 'ɑ:ndreɪ
AM 'ɑn,dreɪ

Andrea
BR 'andrɪə(r)
AM 'ændriə, æn'dreɪə

Andreas
BR an'dreɪəs
AM æn'dreɪəs

Andrew
BR 'andru:
AM 'æn,dru

Andrews
BR 'andru:z
AM 'æn,druz

androcentric
BR ,andrə(ʊ)'sɛntrɪk
AM ,ændroʊ'sɛntrɪk

androcentrism
BR ,andrə(ʊ)'sɛntrɪz(ə)m
AM ,ændroʊ'sɛn,trɪzm

Androcles
BR 'andrəkli:z
AM 'ændrə,kliz

androecia
BR an'dri:sɪə(r)
AM æn'driʃ(i)ə

androecium
BR an'dri:sɪəm
AM æn'driʃ(i)əm

androgen
BR 'andrədʒ(ə)n, 'andrədʒɛn, -z
AM 'ændrədʒən, -z

androgenic
BR ,andrə(ʊ)'dʒɛnɪk
AM ,ændrə'dʒɛnɪk

androgyne
BR 'andrədʒʌɪn, -z
AM 'ændrə,dʒaɪn, -z

androgynous
BR an'drɒdʒɪnəs
AM æn'drɑdʒənəs

androgyny
BR an'drɒdʒɪni
AM æn'drɑdʒəni

android
BR 'andrɔɪd, -z
AM 'æn,drɔɪd, -z

Andromache
BR ən'drɒməki
AM æn'drɑməki

Andromeda
BR an'drɒmɪdə(r)
AM æn'drɑmədə

androstenedione
BR ,andrɒsti:n'dʌɪəʊn
AM ,ændrəstin'daɪoʊn

androsterone
BR ,andrə(ʊ)'stɪərəʊn an'drɒstərəʊn
AM æn'drɑstə,roʊn

Andy
BR 'andi
AM 'ændi

anear
BR ə'nɪə(r)
AM ə'ni(ə)r

anecdotage
BR 'anɪkdəʊtɪdʒ
AM 'ænək,doʊdɪdʒ

anecdotal
BR ,anɪk'dəʊtl
AM ,ænək'doʊdl

anecdotalist
BR ,anɪk'dəʊtl̩ɪst, -s
AM ,ænək'doʊdələst, -s

anecdotally
BR ,anɪk'dəʊtl̩i
AM ,ænək'doʊdəli

anecdote
BR 'anɪkdəʊt, -s
AM 'ænək,doʊt, -s

anecdotic
BR ,anɪk'dɒtɪk
AM ,ænək'dɑdɪk

anechoic
BR ,anɪ'kəʊɪk
AM ,ænə'koʊɪk

anele
BR ə'ni:l, -z, -ɪŋ, -d
AM ə'ni(ə)l, -z, -ɪŋ, -d

anemia
BR ə'ni:mɪə(r)
AM ə'nimiə

anemic
BR ə'ni:mɪk, -s
AM ə'nimɪk, -s

anemograph
BR ə'nɛməgrɑ:f, ə'nɛməgraf, -s
AM ə'nɛmə,græf, -s

anemographic
BR ə,nɛmə'grafɪk
AM ə,nɛmə'græfɪk

anemometer
BR ,anɪ'mɒmɪtə(r), -z
AM ,ænə'mɑmədər, -z

anemometric
BR ,anɪmə'mɛtrɪk
AM ,ænəmə'mɛtrɪk

anemometry
BR ,anɪ'mɒmɪtri
AM ,ænə'mɑmətri

anemone
BR ə'nɛmən|i, -ɪz
AM ə'nɛməni, -z

anemophilous
BR ,anɪ'mɒfɪləs, ,anɪ'mɒfl̩əs
AM ,ænə'mɑfələs

anencephalic
BR ,anɛnsɪ'falɪk, ,anɛŋkɛ'falɪk
AM ,æn,ɛnsə'fælɪk

anencephaly
BR ,anɛn'sɛfəli, ,anɛn'sɛfl̩i, ,anɛn'kɛfəli, ,anɛn'kɛfl̩i
AM ,æn,ɛn'sɛfəli

anent
BR ə'nɛnt
AM ə'nɛnt

aneroid
BR 'anərɔɪd
AM 'ænə,rɔɪd

anesthesia
BR ,anɪs'θi:zɪə(r), ,anɪs'θi:ʒə(r)
AM ,ænəs'θiʒə

anesthesiologist
BR ,anɪsθi:zɪ'ɒlədʒɪst, -s
AM ,ænəs,θizi'ɑlədʒəst, -s

anesthesiology
BR ,anɪsθi:zɪ'ɒlədʒi
AM ,ænəs,θizi'ɑlədʒi

anesthetic
BR ,anɪs'θɛtɪk, -s
AM ,ænəs'θɛdɪk, -s

anesthetical
BR ,anɪs'θɛtɪkl
AM ,ænəs'θɛdəkəl

anesthetically
BR ,anɪs'θɛtɪkli

AM ˌænəsˈθɛdək(ə)li

anesthetist
BR əˈniːsθɨtɪst, -s
AM əˈnɛsθədəst, -s

anesthetization
BR əˌniːsθɨtʌɪˈzeɪʃn
AM əˌnɛsθədəˈzeɪʃən, əˌnɛsθəˌtaɪˈzeɪʃən

anesthetize
BR əˈniːsθɨtʌɪz, -ɨz, -ɪŋ, -d
AM əˈnɛsθəˌtaɪz, -ɨz, -ɪŋ, -d

anestrous
BR (ˌ)anˈiːstrəs
AM ænˈɛstrəs

anestrus
BR (ˌ)anˈiːstrəs
AM ænˈɛstrəs

Aneurin
BR əˈnʌɪrɪn, əˈnʌɪrn̩
AM əˈnjərən, ˈænjərən
WE anˈeɪrɪn

aneurin
BR əˈnjʊərɪn, əˈnjɔːrɪn, ˈanjɵrɪn
AM ˈænjərən, əˈnjərən

aneurism
BR ˈanjɵrɪz(ə)m, -z
AM ˈænjəˌrɪzəm, -z

aneurysm
BR ˈanjɵrɪz(ə)m, -z
AM ˈænjəˌrɪzəm, -z

aneurysmal
BR ˌanjɵˈrɪzml
AM ˌænjəˈrɪzməl

anew
BR əˈnjuː
AM əˈn(j)u

Anfield
BR ˈanfiːld
AM ˈænˌfild

anfractuosity
BR ˌanfraktjʊˈɒsɨti, ˌanfraktʃʊˈɒsɨti
AM ænˌfræktʃəˈwɑsədi

anfractuous
BR anˈfraktjʊəs, anˈfraktʃʊəs
AM ænˈfræk(t)ʃ(əw)əs

angary
BR ˈaŋg(ə)ri
AM ˈæŋgəri

angel
BR ˈeɪn(d)ʒ(ə)l, -z
AM ˈeɪndʒəl, -z

Angela
BR ˈan(d)ʒ(ɨ)lə(r)
AM ˈændʒələ

angeldust
BR ˈeɪn(d)ʒ(ə)ldʌst
AM ˈeɪndʒəlˌdəst

angelfish
BR ˈeɪn(d)ʒ(ə)lfɪʃ
AM ˈeɪndʒəlˌfɪʃ

angelic
BR anˈdʒɛlɪk
AM ænˈdʒɛlɪk

angelica
BR anˈdʒɛlɨkə(r)
AM ænˈdʒɛləkə

angelical
BR anˈdʒɛlɨkl
AM ænˈdʒɛləkəl

angelically
BR anˈdʒɛlɨkli
AM ænˈdʒɛlək(ə)li

Angelico
BR anˈdʒɛlɨkəʊ
AM ænˈdʒɛləˌkoʊ

Angelina
BR ˌan(d)ʒɨˈliːnə(r)
AM ˌændʒəˈlinə

Angelo
BR ˈan(d)ʒɨləʊ
AM ˈændʒɛloʊ

Angelou
BR ˈan(d)ʒəluː
AM ˈændʒəlu

angelus
BR ˈan(d)ʒ(ɨ)ləs, ˈan(d)ʒl̩əs, -ɨz
AM ˈændʒələs, -əz

anger
BR ˈaŋg|ə(r), -əz, -(ə)rɪŋ, -əd
AM ˈæŋg|ər, -ərz, -(ə)rɪŋ, -ərd

Angers
BR ɒ̃ˈʒeɪ
AM ɑnˈʒɛr(z)

Angevin
BR ˈan(d)ʒɨvɪn, -z
AM ˈændʒəvən, -z
FR ɑ̃ʒvɛ̃

Angharad
BR aŋˈharəd
AM ˈæŋgəˌræd
WE aŋˈharad

Angie
BR ˈan(d)ʒi
AM ˈændʒi

angina
BR anˈdʒʌɪnə(r)
AM ænˈdʒaɪnə

angiogram
BR ˈan(d)ʒɪə(ʊ)gram, -z
AM ˈændʒioʊˌgræm, ˈændʒ(i)əˌgræm, -z

angiography
BR ˌan(d)ʒɪˈɒgrəfi
AM ˌændʒiˈɑgrəfi

angioma
BR ˌan(d)ʒɪˈəʊmə(r), -z
AM ˌændʒiˈoʊmə, -z

angiomata
BR ˌan(d)ʒɪˈəʊmətə(r)
AM ˌændʒiˈoʊmədə

angioplasty
BR ˈan(d)ʒɪə(ʊ)plasti
AM ˈændʒiəˌplæsti

angiosperm
BR ˈan(d)ʒɪə(ʊ)spəːm, -z
AM ˈændʒiəˌspərm, -z

angiospermous
BR ˌan(d)ʒɪə(ʊ)ˈspəːməs
AM ˌændʒiəˈspərməs

Angkor
BR ˈaŋkɔː(r)
AM ˈæŋkɔ(ə)r

angle
BR ˈaŋg|l, -lz, -l̩ɪŋ\-lɪŋ, -ld
AM ˈæŋg|əl, -əlz, -(ə)lɪŋ, -əld

angledozer
BR ˈaŋglˌdəʊzə(r), -z
AM ˈæŋgəlˌdoʊzər, -z

Anglepoise®
BR ˈaŋglpɔɪz
AM ˈæŋgəlˌpɔɪz

angler
BR ˈaŋglə(r), -z
AM ˈæŋglər, -z

Anglesey
BR ˈaŋglsiː
AM ˈæŋgəlsi

angleworm
BR ˈaŋglwəːm, -z
AM ˈæŋgəlˌwərm, -z

Anglia
BR ˈaŋglɪə(r)
AM ˈæŋgliə

Anglian
BR ˈaŋglɪən, -z
AM ˈæŋgliən, -z

Anglican
BR ˈaŋglɪk(ə)n, -z
AM ˈæŋgləkən, -z

Anglicanism
BR ˈaŋglɪkənɪz(ə)m, ˈaŋglɪkn̩ɪz(ə)m
AM ˈæŋgləkəˌnɪzəm

anglice
BR ˈaŋglɪsi
AM ˈæŋgləsi

Anglicisation
BR ˌaŋglɪsʌɪˈzeɪʃn
AM ˌæŋgləsəˈzeɪʃən, ˌæŋgləˌsaɪˈzeɪʃən

Anglicise
BR ˈaŋglɪsʌɪz, -ɨz, -ɪŋ, -d
AM ˈæŋgləˌsaɪz, -ɨz, -ɪŋ, -d

Anglicism
BR ˈaŋglɪsɪz(ə)m, -z
AM ˈæŋgləˌsɪzəm, -z

Anglicist
BR ˈaŋglɪsɪst, -s
AM ˈæŋgləsəst, -s

Anglicization
BR ˌaŋglɪsʌɪˈzeɪʃn
AM ˌæŋgləsəˈzeɪʃən, ˌæŋgləˌsaɪˈzeɪʃən

Anglicize
BR ˈaŋglɪsʌɪz, -ɨz, -ɪŋ, -d
AM ˈæŋgləˌsaɪz, -ɨz, -ɪŋ, -d

Anglist
BR ˈaŋglɪst, -s
AM ˈæŋgləst, -s

Anglistics
BR aŋˈglɪstɪks
AM æŋˈlɪstɪks

Anglo
BR ˈaŋgləʊ, -z
AM ˈæŋgloʊ, -z

Anglocentric
BR ˌaŋglə(ʊ)ˈsɛntrɪk
AM ˌæŋgloʊˈsɛntrɪk, ˌæŋgləˈsɛntrɪk

Anglomania
BR ˌaŋglə(ʊ)ˈmeɪnɪə(r)
AM ˌæŋgloʊˈmeɪniə, ˌæŋgləˈmeɪniə

Anglomaniac
BR ˌaŋgləʊˈmeɪnɪak, -s
AM ˌæŋgloʊˈmeɪniˌæk, ˌæŋgləˈmeɪniˌæk, -s

Anglophile
BR ˈaŋglə(ʊ)fʌɪl, -z
AM ˈæŋgloʊˌfaɪl, ˈæŋgləˌfaɪl, -z

Anglophilia
BR ˌaŋglə(ʊ)ˈfɪlɪə(r)
AM ˌæŋgloʊˈfɪljə, ˌæŋgləˈfɪljə, ˌæŋgloʊˈfɪliə, ˌæŋgləˈfɪliə

Anglophobe
BR ˈaŋglə(ʊ)fəʊb, -z
AM ˈæŋgloʊˌfoʊb, ˈæŋgləˌfoʊb, -z

Anglophobia
BR ˌaŋglə(ʊ)ˈfəʊbɪə(r)
AM ˌæŋgloʊˈfoʊbiə, ˌæŋgləˈfoʊbiə

Anglophone
BR ˈaŋgləfəʊn
AM ˈæŋgloʊˌfoʊn, ˈæŋgləˌfoʊn

Angmering
BR ˈaŋmərɪŋ
AM ˈæŋˌmɛrɪŋ

Angola
BR aŋˈgəʊlə(r)
AM æŋˈgoʊlə, ænˈgoʊlə

Angolan
BR aŋˈgəʊlən, -z
AM æŋˈgoʊlən, ænˈgoʊlən, -z

angora
BR aŋˈgɔːrə(r), -z
AM æŋˈgɔrə, -z

Angostura
BR ˌaŋgəˈstjʊərə(r), ˌaŋgəˈstjɔːrə(r), ˌaŋgəˈstʃʊərə(r), ˌaŋgəˈstʃɔːrə(r)
AM ˌæŋgəˈst(j)ʊrə

Angoulême
BR ˌɒŋgʊˈlɛm
AM ˌæŋgʊˈlɛm

angrily
BR ˈaŋgrɨli

AM 'æŋgrəli

angry
BR 'aŋgr|i, -ɪə(r), -ɪɪst
AM 'æŋgri, -ər, -ɪst

angst
BR aŋ(k)st
AM æŋ(k)st, ɑŋ(k)st

angstrom
BR 'aŋstrəm, 'aŋstrʌm, 'aŋstrɒm, -z
AM 'æŋstrəm, -z

Anguilla
BR aŋ'gwɪlə(r)
AM æŋ'gwɪlə

Anguillan
BR aŋ'gwɪlən, -z
AM æŋ'gwɪlən, -z

anguine
BR 'aŋgwɪn
AM 'æŋgwɪn

anguish
BR 'aŋgw|ɪʃ, -ɪʃɪz, -ɪʃɪŋ, -ɪʃt
AM 'æŋgwɪʃ, -əz, -ɪŋ, -t

angular
BR 'aŋgjʊlə(r)
AM 'æŋgjələr

angularity
BR ˌaŋgjʊ'larɪt|i, -ɪz
AM ˌæŋgjə'lɛrədi, -z

angularly
BR 'aŋgjʊləli
AM 'æŋgjələrli

Angus
BR 'aŋgəs
AM 'æŋgəs

angwantibo
BR əŋ'gwɒntɪbəʊ, -z
AM æŋ'(g)wɑn(t)əˌboʊ, -z

anharmonic
BR ˌanhɑː'mɒnɪk
AM ˌænhɑr'mɑnɪk

anhedral
BR an'hiːdr(ə)l, an'hɛdr(ə)l
AM æn'hidrəl

Anhui
BR 'ɑːn(h)wiː
AM 'ɑnˌ(h)wi

Anhwei
BR 'ɑːn(h)weɪ
AM 'ɑnˌ(h)weɪ

anhydride
BR an'hʌɪdrʌɪd, -z
AM æn'haɪˌdraɪd, -z

anhydrite
BR an'hʌɪdrʌɪt
AM æn'haɪˌdraɪt

anhydrous
BR an'hʌɪdrəs
AM æn'haɪdrəs

ani
BR 'ɑːn|i, -ɪz
AM 'ɑni, -z

aniconic
BR ˌanʌɪ'kɒnɪk
AM ˌæˌnaɪ'kɑnɪk

anicut
BR 'anɪkʌt, -s
AM 'ænəkət, -s

anigh
BR ə'nʌɪ
AM ə'naɪ

anil
BR 'an(ɪ)l
AM 'ænəl

anile
BR 'anʌɪl
AM 'æˌnaɪl, 'eɪˌnaɪl

aniline
BR 'anɪliːn, 'anḷiːn, 'anɪlɪn, 'anḷɪn
AM 'ænələn

anilingus
BR ˌeɪnɪ'lɪŋgəs
AM ˌeɪnɪ'lɪŋgəs

anility
BR ə'nɪlɪti
AM ə'nɪlɪdi, æ'nɪlɪdi

anima
BR 'anɪmə(r)
AM 'ænəmə

animadversion
BR ˌanɪmad'vəːʃn, ˌanɪməd'vəːʃn, ˌanɪmad'vəːʒn, ˌanɪməd'vəːʒn-z
AM ˌænəmˌæd'vərʒən, -z

animadvert
BR ˌanɪmad'vəːt, ˌanɪməd'vəːt, -s, -ɪŋ, -ɪd
AM ˌænəmˌæd'vər|t, -ts, -dɪŋ, -dəd

animal
BR 'anɪml, -z
AM 'ænəməl, -z

animalcular
BR ˌanɪ'malkjʊlə(r)
AM ˌænə'mæ(l)kjələr

animalcule
BR ˌanɪ'malkjuːl, -z
AM ˌænə'mælˌkjul, -z

animalisation
BR ˌanɪməlʌɪ'zeɪʃn, ˌanɪmḷʌɪ'zeɪʃn
AM ˌænəmələ'zeɪʃən, ˌænəməˌlaɪ'zeɪʃən

animalise
BR 'anɪməlʌɪz, 'anɪmḷʌɪz, -ɪz, -ɪŋ, -d
AM 'ænəməˌlaɪz, -ɪz, -ɪŋ, -d

animalism
BR 'anɪməlɪz(ə)m, 'anɪmḷɪz(ə)m
AM 'ænəməˌlɪzəm

animalist
BR 'anɪməlɪst, 'anɪmḷɪst, -s
AM 'ænəmələst, -s

animalistic
BR ˌanɪmə'lɪstɪk, ˌanɪml'ɪstɪk
AM ˌænəmə'lɪstɪk

animality
BR ˌanɪ'malɪti
AM ˌænə'mælədi

animalization
BR ˌanɪməlʌɪ'zeɪʃn, ˌanɪmḷʌɪ'zeɪʃn
AM ˌænəmələ'zeɪʃən, ˌænəməˌlaɪ'zeɪʃən

animalize
BR 'anɪməlʌɪz, 'anɪmḷʌɪz, -ɪz, -ɪŋ, -d
AM 'ænəməˌlaɪz, -ɪz, -ɪŋ, -d

anima mundi
BR ˌanɪmə 'mʊndi
AM ˌænəmə 'mʊndi

animate[1]
adjective
BR 'anɪmət
AM 'ænəmət

animate[2]
verb
BR 'anɪmeɪt, -s, -ɪŋ, -ɪd
AM 'ænəˌmeɪ|t, -ts, -dɪŋ, -dɪd

animatedly
BR 'anɪmeɪtɪdli
AM 'ænəˌmeɪdɪdli

animation
BR ˌanɪ'meɪʃn
AM ˌænə'meɪʃən

animator
BR 'anɪmeɪtə(r), -z
AM 'ænəˌmeɪdər, -z

animatron
BR 'anɪmətrɒn, -z
AM 'ænəməˌtrɑn, -z

animatronic
BR ˌanɪmə'trɒnɪk, -s
AM ˌænəmə'trɑnɪk, -s

animé
BR 'anɪmeɪ
AM ˌænə'meɪ

animism
BR 'anɪmɪz(ə)m
AM 'ænəˌmɪzəm

animist
BR 'anɪmɪst, -s
AM 'ænəməst, -s

animistic
BR ˌanɪ'mɪstɪk
AM ˌænə'mɪstɪk

animosity
BR ˌanɪ'mɒsɪt|i, -ɪz
AM ˌænə'mɑsədi, -z

animus
BR 'anɪməs
AM 'ænəməs

anion
BR 'anˌʌɪən, -z
AM 'ænˌaɪən, -z

anionic
BR ˌanʌɪ'ɒnɪk
AM ˌænaɪ'ɑnɪk

anis
BR a'niːs
AM ɑ'nis, ə'nis

anise
BR 'anɪs
AM 'ænəs

aniseed
BR 'anɪsiːd
AM 'ænə(s)ˌsid

anisette
BR ˌanɪ'zɛt, ˌanɪ'sɛt
AM ˌænə'sɛt, ˌænə'zɛt

anisogamy
BR ˌanʌɪ'sɒgəmi
AM ˌænˌaɪ'sɑgəmi

anisomorphic
BR anˌʌɪsə(ʊ)'mɔːfɪk, ˌanʌɪsə(ʊ)'mɔːfɪk
AM ænˌaɪsə'mɔrfɪk, ˌænˌaɪsə'mɔrfɪk

anisotropic
BR anˌʌɪsə(ʊ)'trɒpɪk, ˌanʌɪsə(ʊ)'trɒpɪk, anˌʌɪsə(ʊ)'trəʊpɪk, ˌanʌɪsə(ʊ)'trəʊpɪk
AM ænˌaɪsə'trɑpɪk, ˌænˌaɪsə'trɑpɪk

anisotropically
BR anˌʌɪsə(ʊ)'trɒpɪkli, ˌanʌɪsə(ʊ)'trɒpɪkli
AM ænˌaɪsə'trɑpək(ə)li, ˌænˌaɪsə'trɑpək(ə)li

anisotropy
BR ˌanʌɪ'sɒtrəpi
AM ˌænˌaɪ'sɑtrəpi

Anita
BR ə'niːtə(r)
AM ə'nidə

Anjou
BR ˌɑːn'ʒuː, ˌɒ̃'ʒuː
AM 'ɑnʒu

Ankara
BR 'aŋk(ə)rə(r)
AM 'æŋkərə

anker
BR 'aŋkə(r), -z
AM 'æŋkər, -z

ankerite
BR 'aŋkərʌɪt
AM 'æŋkəˌraɪt

ankh
BR aŋk, -s
AM ɑŋk, -s

ankle
BR 'aŋkl, -z
AM 'æŋkəl, -z

anklet
BR 'aŋklɪt, -s
AM 'æŋklət, -s

ankylose
BR 'aŋkɪləʊz, 'aŋkɪləʊs
AM 'æŋkəˌloʊs, 'æŋkəˌloʊz, -əz, -ɪŋ, -t\-d

ankyloses
BR ˌaŋkɪ'ləʊsiːz
AM 'æŋkəˌloʊsiz

ankylosis
BR ˌaŋkɪˈləʊsɪs
AM ˈæŋkəˌloʊsəs

ankylotic
BR ˌaŋkɪˈlɒtɪk
AM ˌæŋkəˈlɑdɪk

Anlaby
BR ˈanləbi
AM ˈænləbi

anlace
BR ˈanləs, -ɪz
AM ˈænləs, -əz

Ann
BR an
AM æn

Anna
BR ˈanə(r)
AM ˈænə

Annaba
BR aˈnɑːbə(r)
AM æ(n)ˈnɑbə

Annabel
BR ˈanəbɛl
AM ˈænəˌbɛl

Annabella
BR ˌanəˈbɛlə(r)
AM ˌænəˈbɛlə

annal
BR ˈanl, -z
AM ˈænəl, -z

annalist
BR ˈanəlɪst, ˈanl̩ɪst, -s
AM ˈænl̩əst, -s

annalistic
BR ˌanəˈlɪstɪk, ˌanlˈɪstɪk
AM ˌænlˈɪstɪk

annalistically
BR ˌanəˈlɪstɪkli, ˌanl̩ˈɪstɪkli
AM ˌænlˈɪstɪk(ə)li

Annamarie
BR ˌanəməˈriː
AM ˌænəməˈri

Annamese
BR ˌanəˈmiːz
AM ˌænəˈmiz

Annapolis
BR əˈnapəlɪs, əˈnapl̩ɪs
AM əˈnæpəlɪs, ˌænˈæpəlɪs

Annapurna
BR ˌanəˈpəːnə(r)
AM ˌænəˈpərnə

annates
BR ˈaneɪts
AM ˈæˌneɪts, ˈænəts

annatto
BR əˈnɑːtəʊ
AM əˈnɑdoʊ

Anne
BR an
AM æn

anneal
BR əˈniːl, -z, -ɪŋ, -d
AM əˈni(ə)l, -z, -ɪŋ, -d

annealer
BR əˈniːlə(r), -z
AM əˈnilər, -z

annectent
BR əˈnɛkt(ə)nt
AM əˈnɛkt(ə)nt

Anneka
BR ˈanɪkə(r)
AM ˈænɛkə

annelid
BR ˈanəlɪd, ˈanl̩ɪd, -z
AM ˈænələd, ˈænəˌlɪd, -z

annelidan
BR əˈnɛlɨd(ə)n
AM əˈnɛlədən, æˈnɛlədən

Annemarie
BR ˌanməˈriː
AM ˌænməˈri

Annesley
BR ˈan(ɪ)zli
AM ˈænzli

Annette
BR əˈnɛt, aˈnɛt
AM əˈnɛt

annex¹
noun
BR ˈanɛks, -ɪz
AM ˈæˌnɛks, -əz

annex²
verb
BR əˈnɛks, ˈanɛks, -ɪz, -ɪŋ, -t
AM əˈnɛks, æˈnɛks, -əz, -ɪŋ, -t

annexation
BR ˌanɛkˈseɪʃn, ˌanəkˈseɪʃn, -z
AM ˌæˌnɛkˈseɪʃən, ˌænəkˈseɪʃən, -z

annexe
BR ˈanɛks, -ɪz
AM ˈæˌnɛks, -əz

annexure
BR ˈanɛkʃʊə(r), -z
AM ˈænɛkˌʃʊ(ə)r, -z

annicut
BR ˈanɪkʌt, -s
AM ˈænəkət, -s

Annie
BR ˈani
AM ˈæni

Annigoni
BR ˌanɪˈgəʊni
AM ˌænəˈgoʊni, ˌænəˈgɑni

annihilate
BR əˈnʌɪəleɪt, -s, -ɪŋ, -ɪd
AM əˈnaɪəˌleɪ|t, -ts, -dɪŋ, -dɨd

annihilation
BR əˌnʌɪəˈleɪʃn
AM əˌnaɪəˈleɪʃən

annihilationism
BR əˌnʌɪəˈleɪʃn̩ɪz(ə)m, əˌnʌɪəˈleɪʃənɪz(ə)m
AM əˌnaɪəˈleɪʃəˌnɪzəm

annihilator
BR əˈnʌɪəleɪtə(r), -z
AM əˈnaɪəˌleɪdər, -z

anniversary
BR ˌanɪˈvəːs(ə)r|i, -ɪz
AM ˌænəˈvərs(ə)ri, -z

Anno Domini
BR ˌanəʊ ˈdɒmɪnʌɪ, + ˈdɒmɪniː
AM ˌænoʊ ˈdɑməni

annotatable
BR ˈanə(ʊ)teɪtəbl
AM ˈænəˌteɪdəbəl

annotate
BR ˈanə(ʊ)teɪt, -s, -ɪŋ, -ɪd
AM ˈænəˌteɪ|t, -ts, -dɪŋ, -dɨd

annotation
BR ˌanə(ʊ)ˈteɪʃn, -z
AM ˌænəˈteɪʃən, -z

annotative
BR ˈanə(ʊ)teɪtɪv
AM ˈænəˌteɪdɪv

annotator
BR ˈanə(ʊ)teɪtə(r), -z
AM ˈænəˌteɪdər, -z

announce
BR əˈnaʊns, -ɪz, -ɪŋ, -t
AM əˈnaʊns, -əz, -ɪŋ, -t

announcement
BR əˈnaʊnsm(ə)nt, -s
AM əˈnaʊnsmənt, -s

announcer
BR əˈnaʊnsə(r), -z
AM əˈnaʊnsər, -z

annoy
BR əˈnɔɪ, -z, -ɪŋ, -d
AM əˈnɔɪ, -z, -ɪŋ, -d

annoyance
BR əˈnɔɪəns, -ɪz
AM əˈnɔɪəns, -əz

annoyer
BR əˈnɔɪə(r), -z
AM əˈnɔɪər, -z

annoying
BR əˈnɔɪɪŋ
AM əˈnɔɪɪŋ

annoyingly
BR əˈnɔɪɪŋli
AM əˈnɔɪɪŋli

annoyingness
BR əˈnɔɪɪŋnɪs
AM əˈnɔɪɪŋnɪs

annual
BR ˈanjʊəl, ˈanjʉl, -z
AM ˈænj(əw)əl, -z

annualise
BR ˈanjʊəlʌɪz, ˈanjʉlʌɪz, -ɪz, -ɪŋ, -d
AM ˈænj(əw)əˌlaɪz, -ɪz, -ɪŋ, -d

annualize
BR ˈanjʊəlʌɪz, ˈanjʉlʌɪz, -ɪz, -ɪŋ, -d
AM ˈænj(əw)əˌlaɪz, -ɪz, -ɪŋ, -d

annually
BR ˈanjʊəli, ˈanjʉli
AM ˈænj(əw)əli

annuitant
BR əˈnjuːɪt(ə)nt, -s
AM əˈn(j)uədənt, əˈn(j)uətnt, -s

annuity
BR əˈnjuːɪt|i, -ɪz
AM əˈn(j)uədi, -z

annul
BR əˈnʌl, -z, -ɪŋ, -d
AM əˈnəl, -z, -ɪŋ, -d

annular
BR ˈanjʉlə(r)
AM ˈænjələr

annularly
BR ˈanjʉləli
AM ˈænjələrli

annulate
BR ˈanjʉleɪt, -s, -ɪŋ, -ɪd
AM ˈænjəˌleɪ|t, -ts, -dɪŋ, -dɨd

annulation
BR ˌanjʉˈleɪʃn
AM ˌænjəˈleɪʃən

annulet
BR ˈanjʉlɪt, -s
AM ˈænjələt, ˈænjəˌlɛt, -s

annuli
BR ˈanjʉlʌɪ
AM ˈænjəˌlaɪ

annulment
BR əˈnʌlm(ə)nt, -s
AM əˈnəlmənt, -s

annulus
BR ˈanjʉləs, -ɪz
AM ˈænjələs, -əz

annunciate
BR əˈnʌnsɪeɪt, əˈnʌnʃɪeɪt, -s, -ɪŋ, -ɪd
AM əˈnənsiˌeɪ|t, -ts, -dɪŋ, -dɨd

annunciation
BR əˌnʌnsɪˈeɪʃn, əˌnʌnʃɪˈeɪʃn, -z
AM əˌnənsiˈeɪʃən, -z

annunciator
BR əˈnʌnsɪeɪtə(r), əˈnʌnʃɪeɪtə(r), -z
AM əˈnənsiˌeɪdər, -z

annus
BR ˈanʉs
AM ˈænəs

annus horribilis
BR ˌanʉs hɒˈrɪbɪlɪs, + həˈrɪbɪlɪs
AM ˌænəs həˈrɪbələs

annus mirabilis
BR ˌanʉs mɪˈrɑːbɪlɪs
AM ˌænəs məˈrɑbələs

Anny
BR ˈani
AM ˈæni

anoa
BR əˈnəʊə(r), aˈnəʊə(r), -z

AM ə'noʊə, -z

anodal
BR a'nəʊdl
AM 'ænoʊdəl, eɪ'noʊdəl

anode
BR 'anəʊd, -z
AM 'ænoʊd, -z

anodic
BR a'nɒdɪk
AM æn'ɑdɪk

anodise
BR 'anədʌɪz, -ɨz, -ɪŋ, -d
AM 'ænəˌdaɪz, -ɨz, -ɪŋ, -d

anodiser
BR 'anədʌɪzə(r), -z
AM 'ænəˌdaɪzər, -z

anodize
BR 'anədʌɪz, -ɨz, -ɪŋ, -d
AM 'ænəˌdaɪz, -ɨz, -ɪŋ, -d

anodizer
BR 'anədʌɪzə(r), -z
AM 'ænəˌdaɪzər, -z

anodyne
BR 'anədʌɪn, -z
AM 'ænəˌdaɪn, -z

anoeses
BR ˌanəʊ'iːsiːz
AM ˌænoʊ'isiz

anoesis
BR ˌanəʊ'iːsɪs
AM ˌænoʊ'isəs

anoetic
BR ˌanəʊ'ɛtɪk
AM ˌænə'wɛdɪk

anoint
BR ə'nɔɪnt, -s, -ɪŋ, -ɨd
AM ə'nɔɪn|t, -(t)s, -(t)ɪŋ, -(t)ɨd

anointer
BR ə'nɔɪntə(r), -z
AM ə'nɔɪn(t)ər, -z

anole
BR ə'nəʊl|i, -ɪz
AM ə'noʊli, -z

anomalistic
BR əˌnɒmə'lɪstɪk
AM əˌnɑmə'lɪstɪk

anomalous
BR ə'nɒmələs, ə'nɒml̩əs
AM ə'nɑmələs

anomalously
BR ə'nɒmələsli, ə'nɒml̩əsli
AM ə'nɑmələsli

anomalousness
BR ə'nɒmələsnəs, ə'nɒml̩əsnəs
AM ə'nɑmələsnəs

anomalure
BR ə'nɒməl(j)ʊə(r), ə'nɒml̩(j)ʊə(r), -z
AM ə'nɑməˌlʊ(ə)r, -z

anomaly
BR ə'nɒməl|i, ə'nɒml̩|i, -ɪz
AM ə'nɑməli, -z

anomic
BR ə'nɒmɪk, a'nɒmɪk, ə'nəʊmɪk, a'nəʊmɪk
AM ə'nɑmɪk, ə'noʊmɪk

anomie
BR 'anəmi
AM 'ænəmi, ˌænə'mi

anomy
BR 'anəmi
AM 'ænəmi, ˌænə'mi

anon
BR ə'nɒn
AM ə'nɑn

Anona
BR ə'nəʊnə(r)
AM ə'noʊnə

anonym
BR 'anənɪm, -z
AM 'ænəˌnɪm, -z

anonymity
BR ˌanə'nɪmɨti
AM ˌænə'nɪmɨdi

anonymous
BR ə'nɒnɨməs
AM ə'nɑnəməs

anonymously
BR ə'nɒnɨməsli
AM ə'nɑnəməsli

anopheles
BR ə'nɒfɨliːz, ə'nɒfl̩iːz
AM ə'nɑfəliz

anophthalmia
BR ˌanɒf'θalmɪə(r)
AM ˌænɑf'θælmiə, ˌænɑp'θælmiə

anorak
BR 'anərak, -s
AM 'ænəˌræk, -s

anorectic
BR ˌanə'rɛktɪk, -s
AM ˌænə'rɛktɪk, -s

anorexia
BR ˌanə'rɛksɪə(r)
AM ˌænə'rɛksiə

anorexia nervosa
BR ˌanərɛksɪə nəː'vəʊsə(r), anəˌrɛksɪə +, nəː'vəʊzə(r)
AM ˌænə'rɛksiə nər'voʊsə, + nər'voʊzə

anorexic
BR ˌanə'rɛksɪk, -s
AM ˌænə'rɛksɪk, -s

anorexically
BR ˌanə'rɛksɨkli
AM ˌænə'rɛksək(ə)li

anorgasmia
BR ˌanɔː'gazmɪə(r)
AM ˌænɔr'gæzmiə

anorthite
BR ə'nɔːθʌɪt
AM ə'nɔrˌθaɪt

anorthosite
BR ə'nɔːθəsʌɪt
AM ə'nɔrθəˌsaɪt

anorthositic
BR əˌnɔːθə'sɪtɪk
AM əˌnɔrθə'sɪdɪk

anosmia
BR a'nɒzmɪə(r), a'nɒsmɪə(r)
AM æ'nɑzmiə, æ'nɑsmiə

anosmic
BR a'nɒzmɪk, a'nɒsmɪk, -s
AM æ'nɑzmɪk, æ'nɑsmɪk, -s

another
BR ə'nʌðə(r)
AM ə'nəðər

Anouilh
BR 'anʊiː, ˌanʊ'iː, a'nuːi
AM ɑ'nui, ɑ'nwi
FR anuj

anovulant
BR a'nɒvjələnt, a'nɒvjəln̩t, -s
AM ə'nɑvjələnt, -s

anoxaemia
BR ˌanɒk'siːmɪə(r)
AM ˌæˌnɑk'simiə

anoxia
BR a'nɒksɪə(r)
AM æ'nɑksiə

anoxic
BR a'nɒksɪk
AM æ'nɑksɪk

Ansafone®
BR 'ɑːnsəfəʊn, 'ansəfəʊn
AM 'ænsəˌfoʊn

Ansbacher
BR 'anzbakə(r)
AM 'ænzˌbɑkər
GER 'ansbaxɐ

Anschluss
BR 'anʃlʊs
AM 'ɑnˌʃlus

Anscombe
BR 'anskəm, 'anzkəm
AM 'ænskəmb

Ansell
BR 'ansl
AM 'æns(ɛ)l

Anselm
BR 'ansɛlm
AM 'ænsəlm

anserine
BR 'ansərʌɪn
AM 'ænsəˌraɪn, 'ænsərən, 'ænsəˌrin

Anshan
BR 'anʃan
AM 'ænˌʃæn

Anson
BR 'ansn
AM 'ænsən

Anstey
BR 'ansti
AM 'ænsti

Anstruther[1]
BR 'anstrʌðə(r)
AM 'ænstrəðər

Anstruther[2]
traditional form
BR 'anstə(r), 'eɪnstə(r)
AM 'ænstər

Ansty
BR 'ansti
AM 'ænsti

answer
BR 'ɑːns|ə(r), 'ans|ə(r), -əz, -(ə)rɪŋ, -əd
AM 'æns|ər, -ərz, -(ə)rɪŋ, -ərd

answerability
BR ˌɑːns(ə)rə'bɪlɨti, ˌans(ə)rə'bɪlɨti
AM ˌæns(ə)rə'bɪlɨdi

answerable
BR 'ɑːns(ə)rəbl, 'ans(ə)rəbl
AM 'æns(ə)rəbəl

answerably
BR 'ɑːns(ə)rəbli, 'ans(ə)rəbli
AM 'æns(ə)rəbli

answerphone
BR 'ɑːnsəfəʊn, 'ansəfəʊn, -z
AM 'ænsərˌfoʊn, -z

ant
BR ant, -s
AM ænt, -s

antacid
BR ˌant'asɪd, ˌan'tasɪd, -z
AM ˌæn(t)'æsəd, -z

Antaeus
BR an'teɪəs
AM æn'teɪəs

antagonisation
BR anˌtagənʌɪ'zeɪʃn, anˌtagn̩ʌɪ'zeɪʃn
AM ænˌtægənə'zeɪʃən, ænˌtægəˌnaɪ'zeɪʃən

antagonise
BR an'tagənʌɪz, an'tagn̩ʌɪz, -ɨz, -ɪŋ, -d
AM æn'tægəˌnaɪz, -ɨz, -ɪŋ, -d

antagonism
BR an'tagənɪz(ə)m, an'tagn̩ɪz(ə)m, -z
AM æn'tægəˌnɪzəm, -z

antagonist
BR an'tagənɪst, an'tagn̩ɪst, -s
AM æn'tægənəst, -s

antagonistic
BR anˌtagə'nɪstɪk, ˌantagə'nɪstɪk
AM ˌænˌtægə'nɪstɪk

antagonistically
BR anˌtagə'nɪstɨkli, ˌantagə'nɪstɨkli
AM ˌænˌtægə'nɪstɪk(ə)li

antagonization
BR an,tagənʌɪ'zeɪʃn, an,tagn̩ʌɪ'zeɪʃn
AM æn,tægənə'zeɪʃən, æn,tægə,naɪ'zeɪʃən

antagonize
BR an'tagənʌɪz, an'tagn̩ʌɪz, -ɪz, -ɪŋ, -d
AM æn'tægə,naɪz, -ɪz, -ɪŋ, -d

Antakya
BR an'takjə(r)
AM æn'tɑkjə
TU ʌn'tʌkjʌ

antalkali
BR ant'alkəlʌɪ, -z
AM æn'tælkəlaɪ, -z

Antalya
BR an'talɪə(r)
AM æn'tɑliə
TU ʌn'tʌljʌ

Antananarivo
BR ,antənanə'riːvəʊ
AM ,ɑn(t)ə,nɑnə'rivoʊ, ,æn(t)ə,nænə'rivoʊ

Antarctic
BR an'tɑːktɪk
AM æn'(t)ɑrktɪk, æn'(t)ɑrdɪk

Antarctica
BR an'tɑːktɪkə(r)
AM æn'(t)ɑrktəkə æn'(t)ɑrdəkə

Antares
BR an'tɛːriːz, an'tɑːriːz
AM æn'tɛriz

ante
BR 'anti
AM 'æn(t)i

anteater
BR 'ant,iːtə(r), -z
AM 'æn(t),idər, -z

antebellum
BR ,antɪ'bɛləm
AM ,æn(t)i'bɛləm, ,æn(t)ə'bɛləm

antecedence
BR ,antɪ'siːd(ə)ns, 'antɪ,siːd(ə)ns
AM ,æn(t)ə'sidns

antecedent
BR ,antɪ'siːd(ə)nt, 'antɪ,siːd(ə)nt, -s
AM ,æn(t)ə'sidnt, -s

antecedently
BR ,antɪ'siːd(ə)ntli, 'antɪ,siːd(ə)ntli
AM ,æn(t)ə'sidn(t)li

antechamber
BR 'antɪ,tʃeɪmbə(r), -z
AM 'æn(t)i,tʃeɪmbər, 'æn(t)ə,tʃeɪmbər, -z

antechapel
BR 'antɪ,tʃapl, -z
AM 'æn(t)i,tʃæpəl, 'æn(t)ə,tʃæpəl, -z

antedate
BR 'antɪdeɪt, -s, -ɪŋ, -ɪd
AM 'æn(t)ə,deɪ|t, 'æn(t)i,deɪ|t, -ts, -dɪŋ, -dɪd

antediluvial
BR ,antɪdɪ'luːvɪəl
AM ,æn(t)idə'luviəl, ,æn(t)ədə'luviəl

antediluvially
BR ,antɪdɪ'luːvɪəli
AM ,æn(t)idə'luviəli, ,æn(t)ədə'luviəli

antediluvian
BR ,antɪdɪ'luːvɪən, -z
AM ,æn(t)idə'luviən, ,æn(t)ədə'luviən, -z

antelope
BR 'antɪləʊp, -s
AM 'æn(t)ə,loʊp, 'æntl,oʊp, -s

ante-mortem
BR ,antɪ'mɔːtəm
AM ,æn(t)i'mɔrdəm, ,æn(t)ə'mɔrdəm

antemundane
BR ,antɪmʌn'deɪn
AM ,æn(t)i,mən'deɪn, ,æn(t)ə,mən'deɪn

antenatal
BR ,antɪ'neɪtl
AM ,æn(t)i'neɪdl, ,æn(t)ə'neɪdl

antenna
BR an'tɛnə(r), -z
AM æn'tɛnə, -z

antennae
BR an'tɛniː, an'tɛnʌɪ
AM æn'tɛni, æn'tɛ,naɪ

antennal
BR an'tɛnl
AM æn'tɛnəl

antennary
BR an'tɛn(ə)ri
AM æn'tɛnəri

antennule
BR an'tɛnjuːl, -z
AM æn'tɛnjul, -z

antenuptial
BR ,antɪ'nʌp(t)ʃ(ə)l
AM ,æn(t)i'nəpʃəl, ,æn(t)ə'nəpʃəl

antepartum
BR ,antɪ'pɑːtəm
AM ,æn(t)i'pɑrdəm

antependia
BR ,antɪ'pɛndɪə(r)
AM ,æn(t)i'pɛndiə, ,æn(t)ə'pɛndiə

antependium
BR ,antɪ'pɛndɪəm
AM ,æn(t)i'pɛndiəm, ,æn(t)ə'pɛndiəm

antepenult
BR ,antɪpɪ'nʌlt, -s
AM ,æn(t)i'pɛnəlt, ,æn(t)ə'pɛnəlt, ,æn(t)i'pinəlt, ,æn(t)ə'pinəlt, -s

antepenultimate
BR ,antɪpɪ'nʌltɪmət, -s
AM ,æn(t)ipə'nəltəmət, ,æn(t)əpə'nəltəmət, -s

anteprandial
BR ,antɪ'prandɪəl
AM ,æn(t)i'prændiəl, ,æn(t)ə'prændiəl

anterior
BR an'tɪərɪə(r)
AM æn'tɪriər

anteriority
BR an,tɪərɪ'ɒrɪti
AM æn,tɪri'ɔrədi

anteriorly
BR an'tɪərɪəli
AM æn'tɪriərli

anteriorness
BR an'tɪərɪənəs
AM æn'tɪriərnəs

anteroom
BR 'antɪruːm, 'antɪrʊm, -z
AM 'æn(t)i,rum, 'æn(t)i,rʊm, 'æn(t)ə,rum, 'æn(t)ə,rʊm, -z

Anthea
BR 'anθɪə(r)
AM æn'θiə

antheap
BR 'anthiːp, -s
AM 'æn(t),(h)ip, -s

anthelion
BR ant'hiːlɪən, an'θiːlɪən, -z
AM ænt'hiliən, æn'θiliən, -z

anthelminthic
BR ,anθɛl'mɪnθɪk
AM ,æn,θɛl'mɪnθɪk

anthelmintic
BR ,anθɛl'mɪntɪk
AM ,æn,θɛl'mɪntɪk

anthem
BR 'anθəm, -z
AM 'ænθəm, -z

anthemia
BR an'θiːmɪə(r)
AM æn'θimiə

anthemion
BR an'θiːmɪən
AM æn'θimiən

anther
BR 'anθə(r), -z
AM 'ænθər, -z

antheral
BR 'anθ(ə)rəl, 'anθ(ə)rl̩
AM 'ænθərəl

antheridia
BR ,anθɪ'rɪdɪə(r)
AM ,ænθə'rɪdiə

antheridium
BR ,anθɪ'rɪdɪəm
AM ,ænθə'rɪdiəm

anthill
BR 'anthɪl, -z
AM 'æn(t),(h)ɪl, -z

anthological
BR ,anθə'lɒdʒɪkl
AM ,ænθə'lɑdʒəkəl

anthologise
BR an'θɒlədʒʌɪz, -ɪz, -ɪŋ, -d
AM æn'θɑlə,dʒaɪz, -ɪz, -ɪŋ, -d

anthologist
BR an'θɒlədʒɪst, -s
AM æn'θɑlədʒəst, -s

anthologize
BR an'θɒlədʒʌɪz, -ɪz, -ɪŋ, -d
AM æn'θɑlə,dʒaɪz, -ɪz, -ɪŋ, -d

anthology
BR an'θɒlədʒ|i, -ɪz
AM æn'θɑlədʒi, -z

Anthony
BR 'antəni
AM 'ænθəni, 'æntəni

anthozoan
BR ,anθə'zəʊən, -z
AM ,ænθə'zoʊən, -z

anthracene
BR 'anθrəsiːn
AM 'ænθrə,sin

anthracic
BR an'θrasɪk
AM æn'θræsɪk

anthracite
BR 'anθrəsʌɪt
AM 'ænθrə,saɪt

anthracitic
BR ,anθrə'sɪtɪk
AM ,ænθrə'sɪdɪk

anthracnose
BR an'θraknəʊs, an'θraknəʊz
AM æn'θræk,noʊs, æn'θræk,noʊz

anthrax
BR 'anθraks
AM 'æn,θræks

anthropocentric
BR ,anθrəpə'sɛntrɪk
AM ,ænθrə,poʊ'sɛntrɪk, ,ænθrəpə'sɛntrɪk

anthropocentrically
BR ,anθrəpə'sɛntrɪkli
AM ,ænθrə,poʊ'sɛntrək(ə) ,ænθrəpə'sɛntrək(ə)li

anthropocentrism
BR ,anθrəpə(ʊ)'sɛntrɪz(ə)ı
AM ,ænθrə,poʊ'sɛn,trɪzəm ,ænθrəpə'sɛn,trɪzəm

anthropogenesis
BR ,anθrəpə'dʒɛnɪsɪs
AM ,ænθrə,poʊ'dʒɛnəsəs, ,ænθrəpə'dʒɛnəsəs

anthropogenic
BR ,anθrəpə'dʒɛnɪk
AM ,ænθrə,poʊ'dʒɛnɪk, ,ænθrəpə'dʒɛnɪk

anthropogeny
BR ˌanθrəˈpɒdʒɪni, ˌanθrəˈpɒdʒn̩i
AM ˌænθrəˈpɑdʒəni

anthropography
BR ˌanθrəˈpɒɡrəfi
AM ˌænθrəˈpɑɡrəfi

anthropoid
BR ˈanθrəpɔɪd, -z
AM ˈænθrəˌpɔɪd, -z

anthropoidal
BR ˌanθrəˈpɔɪdl
AM ˌænθrəˈpɔɪdəl

anthropological
BR ˌanθrəpəˈlɒdʒɪkl
AM ˌænθrəpəˈlɑdʒəkəl

anthropologically
BR ˌanθrəpəˈlɒdʒɪkli
AM ˌænθrəpəˈlɑdʒək(ə)li

anthropologist
BR ˌanθrəˈpɒlədʒɪst, -s
AM ˌænθrəˈpɑlədʒəst, -s

anthropology
BR ˌanθrəˈpɒlədʒi
AM ˌænθrəˈpɑlədʒi

anthropometric
BR ˌanθrəpəˈmɛtrɪk
AM ˌænθrəpəˈmɛtrɪk

anthropometry
BR ˌanθrəˈpɒmɪtri
AM ˌænθrəˈpɑmətri

anthropomorphic
BR ˌanθrəpəˈmɔːfɪk
AM ˌænθrəpəˈmɔrfɪk

anthropomorphically
BR ˌanθrəpəˈmɔːfɪkli
AM ˌænθrəpəˈmɔrfək(ə)li

anthropomorphise
BR ˌanθrəpəˈmɔːfʌɪz, -ɪz, -ɪŋ, -d
AM ˌænθrəpəˈmɔrˌfaɪz, -ɪz, -ɪŋ, -d

anthropomorphism
BR ˌanθrəpəˈmɔːfɪz(ə)m
AM ˌænθrəpəˈmɔrˌfɪzəm

anthropomorphist
BR ˌanθrəpəˈmɔːfɪst, -s
AM ˌænθrəpəˈmɔrfəst, -s

anthropomorphize
BR ˌanθrəpəˈmɔːfʌɪz, -ɪz, -ɪŋ, -d
AM ˌænθrəpəˈmɔrˌfaɪz, -ɪz, -ɪŋ, -d

anthropomorphous
BR ˌanθrəpəˈmɔːfəs
AM ˌænθrəpəˈmɔrfəs

anthroponymy
BR ˌanθrəˈpɒnɪmi
AM ˌænθrəˈpɑnəmi

anthropophagi
BR ˌanθrəˈpɒfəɡʌɪ
AM ˌænθrəˈpɑfədʒaɪ, ˌænθrəˈpɒfəɡaɪ

anthropophagous
BR ˌanθrəˈpɒfəɡəs
AM ˌænθrəˈpɑfəɡəs

anthropophagus
BR ˌanθrəˈpɒfəɡəs
AM ˌænθrəˈpɑfəɡəs

anthropophagy
BR ˌanθrəˈpɒfədʒi
AM ˌænθrəˈpɑfədʒi

anti
BR ˈant|i, -ɪz
AM ˈænˌtaɪ, ˈæn(t)i, -z

antibacterial
BR ˌantɪbakˈtɪərɪəl
AM ˌænˌtaɪˈbæktɪriəl, ˌæn(t)iˈbæktɪriəl

Antibes
BR ɒnˈtiːb, ɒ̃ˈtiːb, ɑːnˈtiːb, anˈtiːb
AM ɑnˈtib(z)

antibioses
BR ˌantɪbʌɪˈəʊsiːz
AM ˌæn(t)iˌbaɪˈoʊsiz

antibiosis
BR ˌantɪbʌɪˈəʊsɪs
AM ˌæn(t)iˌbaɪˈoʊsəs

antibiotic
BR ˌantɪbʌɪˈɒtɪk, -s
AM ˌæn(t)iˌbaɪˈɑdɪk, -s

antibiotically
BR ˌantɪbʌɪˈɒtɪkli
AM ˌæn(t)iˌbaɪˈɑdək(ə)li

antibody
BR ˈantɪˌbɒd|i, -ɪz
AM ˈæn(t)əˌbɑdi, ˈæn(t)iˌbɑdi, -z

antic
BR ˈantɪk, -s
AM ˈæn(t)ɪk, -s

anticathode
BR ˌantɪˈkaθəʊd, -z
AM ˌæn(t)əˈkæˌθoʊd, ˌæn(t)iˈkæˌθoʊd, -z

anticatholic
BR ˌantɪˈkaθ(ə)lɪk, ˌantɪˈkaθl̩ɪk, -s
AM ˌænˌtaɪˈkæθ(ə)lɪk, ˌæn(t)iˈkæθ(ə)lɪk, -s

Antichrist
BR ˈantɪkrʌɪst, -s
AM ˈænˌtaɪˌkraɪst, ˈæn(t)iˌkraɪst, ˈæn(t)əˌkraɪst, -s

antichristian
BR ˌantɪˈkrɪstʃ(ə)n, ˌantɪˈkrɪstɪən
AM ˌænˌtaɪˈkrɪstʃən, ˌæn(t)iˈkrɪstʃən, ˌæn(t)əˈkrɪstʃən

anticipant
BR anˈtɪsɪp(ə)nt, -s
AM ænˈtɪsəpənt, -s

anticipate
BR anˈtɪsɪpeɪt, -s, -ɪŋ, -ɪd
AM ænˈtɪsəˌpeɪ|t, -ts, -dɪŋ, -dɨd

anticipation
BR anˌtɪsɪˈpeɪʃn, ˌantɪsɪˈpeɪʃn, -z
AM ænˌtɪsəˈpeɪʃən, -z

anticipative
BR anˈtɪsɪpətɪv
AM ænˈtɪsəˌpeɪdɪv, ænˈtɪsəpədɪv

anticipator
BR anˈtɪsɪpeɪtə(r), -z
AM ænˈtɪsəˌpeɪdər, -z

anticipatory
BR anˈtɪsɪpət(ə)ri, ˌantɪsɪˈpeɪt(ə)ri
AM ænˈtɪsəpəˌtɔri

anticlerical
BR ˌantɪˈklɛrɪkl
AM ˌænˌtaɪˈklɛrəkəl, ˌæn(t)iˈklɛrəkəl, ˌæn(t)əˈklɛrəkəl

anticlericalism
BR ˌantɪˈklɛrɪkl̩ɪz(ə)m, ˌantɪˈklɛrɪkəlɪz(ə)m
AM ˌænˌtaɪˈklɛrəkəˌlɪzəm, ˌæn(t)iˈklɛrəkəˌlɪzəm, ˌæn(t)əˈklɛrəkəˌlɪzəm

anticlimactic
BR ˌantɪklʌɪˈmaktɪk
AM ˌænˌtaɪklaɪˈmæktɪk, ˌæn(t)iˌklaɪˈmæktɪk, ˌæn(t)əˌklaɪˈmæktɪk, ˌænˌtaɪˌklaɪˈmædɪk, ˌæn(t)iˌklaɪˈmædɪk, ˌæn(t)əˌklaɪˈmædɪk

anticlimactically
BR ˌantɪklʌɪˈmaktɪkli, ˌantɪklɪˈmaktɪkli
AM ˌænˌtaɪklaɪˈmæktək(ə)li, ˌæn(t)iˌklaɪˈmæktək(ə)li, ˌæn(t)əˌklaɪˈmæktək(ə)li, ˌænˌtaɪˌklaɪˈmædək(ə)li, ˌæn(t)iˌklaɪˈmæd(ə)k(ə)li, ˌæn(t)əˌklaɪˈmædək(ə)li

anticlimax
BR ˌantɪˈklʌɪmaks, -ɪz
AM ˌænˌtaɪˈklaɪˌmæks, ˌæn(t)iˈklaɪˌmæks, ˌæn(t)əˈklaɪˌmæks, -əz

anticlinal
BR ˈantɪklʌɪnl, ˌantɪˈklʌɪnl
AM ˌænˌtaɪˈklaɪnl, ˌæn(t)iˈklaɪnl, ˌæn(t)əˈklaɪnl

anticline
BR ˈantɪklʌɪn, -z
AM ˈænˌtaɪˌklaɪn, ˈæn(t)iˌklaɪn, ˈæn(t)əˌklaɪn, -z

anticlockwise
BR ˌantɪˈklɒkwʌɪz
AM ˌænˌtaɪˈklɑkˌwaɪz, ˌæn(t)iˈklɑkˌwaɪz, ˌæn(t)əˈklɑkˌwaɪz

anticoagulant
BR ˌantɪkəʊˈaɡjʊlənt, ˌantɪkəʊˈaɡjʊl̩nt, -s
AM ˌænˌtaɪkoʊˈæɡjələnt, ˌæn(t)ikoʊˈæɡjələnt, ˌæn(t)əkoʊˈæɡjələnt, -s

anticodon
BR ˌantɪˈkəʊdɒn, -z
AM ˌænˌtaɪˈkoʊdən, ˌæn(t)iˈkoʊdən, ˌæn(t)əˈkoʊdn, -z

anticommunist
BR ˌantɪˈkɒmjʊnɪst, -s
AM ˌænˌtaɪˈkɑmjənəst, ˌæn(t)iˈkɑmjənəst, ˌæn(t)əˈkɑmjənəst, -s

anticonstitutional
BR ˌantɪˌkɒnstɪˈtjuːʃn(ə)l, ˌantɪˌkɒnstɪˈtjuːʃən(ə)l, ˌantɪˌkɒnstɪˈtʃuːʃən(ə)l
AM ˌænˌtaɪˌkɑnstəˈt(j)uʃ(ə)nəl, ˌæn(t)iˌkɑnstəˈt(j)uʃ(ə)nəl, ˌæn(t)əˌkɑnstəˈt(j)uʃ(ə)nəl

anticonvulsant
BR ˌantɪkənˈvʌls(ə)nt, -s
AM ˌænˌtaɪkənˈvəlsənt, ˌæn(t)ikənˈvəlsənt, ˌæn(t)əkənˈvəlsənt, -s

anticyclone
BR ˌantɪˈsʌɪkləʊn, -z
AM ˌænˌtaɪˈsaɪˌkloʊn, ˌæn(t)iˈsaɪˌkloʊn, ˌæn(t)əˈsaɪˌkloʊn, -z

anticyclonic
BR ˌantɪsʌɪˈklɒnɪk
AM ˌænˌtaɪˌsaɪˈklɑnɪk, ˌæn(t)iˌsaɪˈklɑnɪk, ˌæn(t)əˌsaɪˈklɑnɪk

antidazzle
BR ˌantɪˈdazl
AM ˌænˌtaɪˈdæzəl, ˌæn(t)iˈdæzəl, ˌæn(t)əˈdæzəl

antidepressant
BR ˌantɪdɪˈprɛsnt, -s
AM ˌæn(t)ədəˈprɛsənt, ˌænˌtaɪdəˈprɛsənt, ˌæn(t)idəˈprɛsənt, -s

antidiuretic
BR ˌantɪˌdʌɪjʊˈrɛtɪk, -s
AM ˌænˌtaɪˌdaɪəˈrɛdɪk, ˌæn(t)iˌdaɪəˈrɛdɪk, ˌæn(t)əˌdaɪəˈrɛdɪk, -s

antidotal
BR ˈantɪdəʊtl, ˌantɪˈdəʊtl

AM ˌæn(t)əˈdoʊdl

antidote
BR ˈantɪdəʊt, -s
AM ˈæn(t)əˌdoʊt, -s

antielectron
BR ˌantɪɪˈlɛktrɒn
AM ˌæn(t)iəˈlɛkˌtrɑn, ˌænˌtaɪəˈlɛkˌtrɑn

anti-establishment
BR ˌantɪɪˈstablɪʃm(ə)nt, ˌantɪɛsˈtablɪʃm(ə)nt
AM ˌænˌtaɪəˈstæblɪʃmənt, ˌæn(t)iəˈstæblɪʃmənt, ˌænˌtaɪɛˈstæblɪʃmənt, ˌæn(t)iɛˈstæblɪʃmənt

Antietam
BR anˈtiːtəm
AM ænˈtidəm

anti-fascist
BR ˌantɪˈfaʃɪst, -s
AM ˌænˌtaɪˈfæʃəst, ˌæn(t)iˈfæʃəst, ˌæn(t)əˈfæʃəst, -s

antifebrile
BR ˌantɪˈfiːbrʌɪl, ˌantɪˈfɛbrʌɪl
AM ˌæn(t)əˈfɛbrəl, ˌæn(t)əˈfɛˌbraɪl

antifreeze
BR ˈantɪfriːz, -ɪz
AM ˈæn(t)əˌfriz, ˈæn(t)iˌfriz, ˈænˌtaɪˌfriz, -ɪz

anti-g
BR ˌantɪˈdʒiː
AM ˌænˌtaɪˈdʒi, ˌæn(t)iˈdʒi

antigen
BR ˈantɪdʒ(ə)n, -z
AM ˈæn(t)ədʒən, ˈæn(t)əˌdʒɛn, -z

antigenic
BR ˌantɪˈdʒɛnɪk
AM ˌæn(t)əˈdʒɛnɪk

Antigone
BR anˈtɪgəni, anˈtɪgn̩i
AM ænˈtɪgəni

anti-government
BR ˌantɪˈgʌv(ə)nm(ə)nt, ˌantɪˈgʌvəm(ə)nt
AM ˌænˌtaɪˈgəvər(n)mənt, ˌæn(t)iˈgəvər(n)mənt, ˌæn(t)əˈgəvər(n)mənt

anti-gravity
BR ˌantɪˈgravɪti
AM ˌænˌtaɪˈgrævədi, ˌæn(t)iˈgrævədi, ˌæn(t)əˈgrævədi

Antigua
BR anˈtiːg(w)ə(r)
AM ænˈtig(w)ə

Antiguan
BR anˈtiːg(w)ən, -z
AM ænˈtig(w)ən, -z

antihero
BR ˈantɪˌhɪərəʊ, -z
AM ˈænˌtaɪˌhiroʊ, ˈæn(t)iˌhiroʊ, ˈæn(t)əˌhiroʊ, -z

antihistamine
BR ˌantɪˈhɪstəmiːn, ˌantɪˈhɪstəmɪn
AM ˌæn(t)əˈhɪstəmən, ˌænˌtaɪˈhɪstəmən, ˌæn(t)iˈhɪstəmən, ˌæn(t)əˈhɪstəmin, ˌænˌtaɪˈhɪstəmin, ˌæn(t)iˈhɪstəmin

anti-inflammatory
BR ˌantɪɪnˈflamət(ə)r|i, -ɪz
AM ˌænˌtaɪənˈflæməˌtɔri, ˌæn(t)iənˈflæməˌtɔri, -z

anti-inflation
BR ˌæntɪɪnˈfleɪʃn
AM ˌænˌtaɪənˈfleɪʃən, ˌæn(t)iənˈfleɪʃən

anti-intellectual
BR ˌantɪˌɪntɪˈlɛktʃʊəl, ˌantɪˌɪntɪˈlɛktʃ(ʉ)l, ˌantɪˌɪntɪˈlɛktjʊəl, ˌantɪˌɪntɪˈlɛktjʉl, -z
AM ˌænˌtaɪˌɪn(t)əˈlɛk(t)ʃ(əw)əl, ˌæn(t)iˌɪn(t)əˈlɛk(t)ʃ(əw)əl, -z

anti-Jacobin
BR ˌantɪˈdʒakəbɪn, -z
AM ˌænˌtaɪˈdʒækəbən, ˌæn(t)iˈdʒækəbən, ˌæn(t)əˈdʒækəbən, -z

antiknock
BR ˌantɪˈnɒk
AM ˌænˌtaɪˈnɑk, ˌæn(t)iˈnɑk, ˌæn(t)əˈnɑk

Antillean
BR anˈtɪlɪən, -z
AM ænˈtɪljən, ænˈtɪliən, -z

Antilles
BR anˈtɪliːz
AM ænˈtɪliz

antilog
BR ˈantɪlɒg, -z
AM ˈænˌtaɪˌlɔg, ˈæn(t)iˌlɔg, ˈæn(t)əˌlɔg, ˈænˌtaɪˌlɑg, ˈæn(t)iˌlɑg, ˈæn(t)əˌlɑg, -z

antilogarithm
BR ˌantɪˈlɒgərɪð(ə)m, -z
AM ˌænˌtaɪˈlɔgəˌrɪðəm, ˌæn(t)iˈlɔgəˌrɪðəm, ˌæn(t)əˈlɔgəˌrɪðəm, ˌænˌtaɪˈlɑgəˌrɪðəm, ˌæn(t)iˈlɑgəˌrɪðəm, ˌæn(t)əˈlɑgəˌrɪðəm, -z

antilogy
BR anˈtɪlədʒ|i, -ɪz
AM ænˈtɪlədʒi, -z

antimacassar
BR ˌantɪməˈkasə(r), -z
AM ˌæn(t)iməˈkæsər, ˌæn(t)əməˈkæsər, -z

antimalarial
BR ˌantɪməˈlɛːrɪəl
AM ˌænˌtaɪməˈlɛriəl, ˌæn(t)iməˈlɛriəl, ˌæn(t)əməˈlɛriəl

antimasque
BR ˈantɪmɑːsk, ˈantɪmask, -s
AM ˌæn(t)iˈmæsk, ˌæn(t)əˈmæsk, -s

antimatter
BR ˈantɪˌmatə(r)
AM ˈænˌtaɪˌmædər, ˈæn(t)iˌmædər

antimetabolite
BR ˌantɪmɪˈtabəlʌɪt, ˌantɪmɪˈtabl̩ʌɪt, -s
AM ˌænˌtaɪməˈtæbəˌlaɪt, ˌæn(t)iməˈtæbəˌlaɪt, ˌæn(t)əməˈtæbəˌlaɪt, -s

antimonarchical
BR ˌantɪməˈnɑːkɪkl
AM ˌænˌtaɪməˈnɑrkəkəl, ˌæn(t)iməˈnɑrkəkəl, ˌæn(t)əməˈnɑrkəkəl

antimonial
BR ˌantɪˈməʊnɪəl
AM ˌæn(t)əˈmoʊniəl

antimonic
BR ˌantɪˈmɒnɪk
AM ˌæn(t)əˈmɑnɪk

antimonious
BR ˌantɪˈməʊnɪəs
AM ˌæn(t)əˈmoʊniəs

antimony
BR ˈantɪməni
AM ˈæn(t)əˌmoʊni

antinode
BR ˈantɪnəʊd, -z
AM ˈæn(t)iˌnoʊd, ˈæn(t)əˌnoʊd, -z

antinomian
BR ˌantɪˈnəʊmɪən, -z
AM ˈæn(t)iˌnoʊmiən, ˈæn(t)əˌnoʊmiən, -z

antinomianism
BR ˌantɪˈnəʊmɪənɪz(ə)m
AM ˌæn(t)iˈnoʊmiəˌnɪzəm, ˌæn(t)əˈnoʊmiəˌnɪzəm

antinomy
BR anˈtɪnəm|i, -ɪz
AM ænˈtɪnəmi, -z

antinovel
BR ˈantɪˌnɒvl, -z
AM ˈænˌtaɪˌnɑvəl, ˈæn(t)iˌnɑvəl, ˈæn(t)əˌnɑvəl, -z

anti-nuclear
BR ˌantɪˈn(j)uːklɪə(r)
AM ˌænˌtaɪˈn(j)ʊklɪ(ə)r, ˌæn(t)iˈn(j)ʊklɪ(ə)r, ˌæn(t)əˈn(j)ʊklɪ(ə)r

Antioch
BR ˈantɪɒk
AM ˈɑn(t)iˌɑk

Antiochus
BR anˈtʌɪəkəs
AM ænˈtaɪəkəs

antioxidant
BR ˌantɪˈɒksɪd(ə)nt, -s
AM ˈænˌtaɪˈɑksədnt, ˌæn(t)iˈɑksədnt, ˌæn(t)əˈɑksədnt, -s

antiparticle
BR ˈantɪˌpɑːtɪkl, -z
AM ˈænˌtaɪˌpɑrdəkəl, ˈæn(t)iˌpɑrdəkəl, ˈæn(t)əˌpɑrdəkəl, -z

Antipas
BR ˈantɪpas
AM ˈæn(t)əpəs

antipasto
BR ˌantɪˈpastəʊ, ˌantɪˈpɑːstəʊ, ˈantɪˌpastəʊ, ˈantɪˌpɑːstəʊ
AM ˌæn(t)əˈpɑstoʊ, ˌæn(t)əˈpæstoʊ

antipathetic
BR ˌantɪpəˈθɛtɪk, anˌtɪpəˈθɛtɪk
AM ˌæn(t)əpəˈθɛdɪk, ænˌtɪpəˈθɛdɪk

antipathetical
BR ˌantɪpəˈθɛtɪkl, anˌtɪpəˈθɛtɪkl
AM ˌæn(t)əpəˈθɛdəkəl, ænˌtɪpəˈθɛdəkəl

antipathetically
BR ˌantɪpəˈθɛtɪkli, anˌtɪpəˈθɛtɪkli
AM ˌæn(t)əpəˈθɛdək(ə)li, ænˌtɪpəˈθɛdək(ə)li

antipathic
BR ˌantɪˈpaθɪk
AM ˌæn(t)əˈpæθɪk

antipathy
BR anˈtɪpəθ|i, -ɪz
AM ænˈtipəθi, -z

antipersonnel
BR ˌantɪpəːsəˈnɛl, ˌantɪpəːsnˈɛl
AM ˌænˌtaɪˌpərsəˈnɛl, ˌæn(t)iˌpərsəˈnɛl, ˌæn(t)əˌpərsəˈnɛl

antiperspirant
BR ˌantɪˈpəːspɪrənt, ˌantɪˈpəːspɪrn̩t, -s
AM ˌæn(t)əˈpərspərənt, ˌænˌtaɪˈpərspərənt, ˌæn(t)iˈpərspərənt, -s

antiphlogistic
BR ˌantɪfləˈdʒɪstɪk
AM ˌæn(t)əfləˈdʒɪstɪk

antiphon
BR 'antɪf(ə)n, 'antɪfɒn, -z
AM 'æn(t)ifən, 'æn(t)əˌfɑn, -z
antiphonal
BR an'tɪfn̩(ə)l, an'tɪfən(ə)l
AM æn'tɪfənəl
antiphonally
BR an'tɪfn̩əli, an'tɪfn̩li, an'tɪfənl̩i, an'tɪf(ə)n(ə)li
AM æn'tɪfənəli
antiphonary
BR an'tɪfn̩ər|i, an'tɪf(ə)nər|i, -ɪz
AM æn'tɪfəˌnɛri, -z
antiphony
BR an'tɪfn̩|i, an'tɪfən|i, -ɪz
AM æn'tɪfəni, -z
antiphrasis
BR an'tɪfrəsɪs
AM æn'tɪfrəsəs
antipodal
BR an'tɪpədl
AM æn'tɪpədəl
antipode
BR 'antɪpəʊd, -z
AM 'æn(t)əˌpoʊd, -z
antipodean
BR anˌtɪpə'dɪən, ˌantɪpə'dɪən, -z
AM ænˌtɪpə'diən, -z
antipodes
BR an'tɪpədiːz
AM æn'tɪpədiz
antipole
BR 'antɪpəʊl, -z
AM ˌænˌtaɪ'poʊl, ˌæn(t)i'poʊl, ˌæn(t)ə'poʊl, -z
antipope
BR 'antɪpəʊp, -s
AM ˌænˌtaɪ'poʊp, ˌæn(t)i'poʊp, ˌæn(t)ə'poʊp, -s
antiproton
BR 'antɪˌprəʊtɒn, -z
AM 'ænˌtaɪˌproʊˌtɑn, 'æn(t)iˌproʊˌtɑn, 'æn(t)əˌproʊˌtɑn, -z
antipruritic
BR ˌantɪprʊə'rɪtɪk
AM ˌænˌtaɪprə'rɪdɪk, ˌæn(t)iˌprə'rɪdɪk, ˌæn(t)əˌprə'rɪdɪk
antipyretic
BR ˌantɪpʌɪ'rɛtɪk, -s
AM ˌænˌtaɪˌpaɪ'rɛdɪk, ˌæn(t)iˌpaɪ'rɛdɪk, ˌæn(t)əˌpaɪ'rɛdɪk, -s
antiquarian
BR ˌantɪ'kwɛːrɪən, -z
AM ˌæn(t)ə'kwɛriən, -z
antiquarianism
BR ˌantɪ'kwɛːrɪənɪz(ə)m
AM ˌæn(t)ə'kwɛriəˌnɪzəm
antiquary
BR 'antɪkwər|i, -ɪz
AM 'æn(t)əˌkwɛri, -z
antiquated
BR 'antɪkweɪtɪd
AM 'æn(t)əˌkweɪdɪd
antique
BR an'tiːk, -s, -ɪŋ, -t
AM æn'tik, -s, -ɪŋ, -t
antiquity
BR an'tɪkwɪt|i, -ɪz
AM æn'tɪkwɪdi, -z
anti-racism
BR ˌantɪ'reɪsɪz(ə)m
AM ˌænˌtaɪ'reɪˌsɪzəm, ˌæn(t)i'reɪˌsɪzəm, ˌæn(t)ə'reɪˌsɪzəm
anti-racist
BR ˌantɪ'reɪsɪst, -s
AM ˌænˌtaɪ'reɪsɪst, ˌæn(t)i'reɪsɪst, ˌæn(t)ə'reɪsɪst, -s
antirrhinum
BR ˌantɪ'rʌɪnəm, -z
AM ˌæn(t)ə'raɪnəm, ˌæn(t)i'raɪnəm, -z
antisabbatarian
BR ˌantɪˌsabə'tɛːrɪən, -z
AM ˌænˌtaɪˌsæbə'tɛriən, ˌæn(t)iˌsæbə'tɛriən, ˌæn(t)əˌsæbə'tɛriən, -z
antiscorbutic
BR ˌantɪskɔː'bjuːtɪk, -s
AM ˌænˌtaɪˌskɔr'bjudɪk, ˌæn(t)iˌskɔr'bjudɪk, ˌæn(t)əˌskɔr'bjudɪk, -s
antiscriptural
BR ˌantɪ'skrɪptʃ(ə)rəl, ˌantɪ'skrɪptʃ(ə)rl̩
AM ˌænˌtaɪ'skrɪp(t)ʃ(ə)rəl, ˌæn(t)i'skrɪp(t)ʃ(ə)rəl, ˌæn(t)ə'skrɪp(t)ʃ(ə)rəl
antisepsis
BR ˌantɪ'sɛpsɪs
AM ˌæn(t)ə'sɛpsəs, ˌæn(t)i'sɛpsəs, ˌænˌtaɪ'sɛpsəs
antiseptic
BR ˌantɪ'sɛptɪk, -s
AM ˌæn(t)ə'sɛptɪk, -s
antiseptically
BR ˌantɪ'sɛptɪkli
AM ˌæn(t)ə'sɛptək(ə)li
antisera
BR 'antɪˌsɪərə(r)
AM 'ænˌtaɪˌsɪrə, 'æn(t)iˌsɪrə
antiserum
BR 'antɪˌsɪərəm, -z
AM 'ænˌtaɪˌsɪrəm, 'æn(t)iˌsɪrəm, -z
antisocial
BR ˌantɪ'səʊʃl
AM ˌænˌtaɪ'soʊʃəl, ˌæn(t)i'soʊʃəl, ˌæn(t)ə'soʊʃəl
antisocially
BR ˌantɪ'səʊʃl̩i, ˌantɪ'səʊʃəli
AM ˌænˌtaɪ'soʊʃəli, ˌæn(t)i'soʊʃəli, ˌæn(t)ə'soʊʃəli
antispasmodic
BR ˌantɪspaz'mɒdɪk, -s
AM ˌænˌtaɪˌspæz'mɑdɪk, ˌæn(t)iˌspæz'mɑdɪk, ˌæn(t)ə'spæz'mɑdɪk, -s
antistatic
BR ˌantɪ'statɪk
AM ˌænˌtaɪ'stædɪk, ˌæn(t)i'stædɪk, ˌæn(t)ə'stædɪk
antistatically
BR ˌantɪ'statɪkli
AM ˌænˌtaɪ'stædək(ə)li, ˌæn(t)i'stædək(ə)li, ˌæn(t)ə'stædək(ə)li
Antisthenes
BR an'tɪsθɪniːz
AM æn'tɪsθəniz
antistrophe
BR an'tɪstrəf|i, -ɪz
AM æn'tɪstrəfi, -z
antistrophic
BR ˌantɪ'strɒfɪk
AM ˌæn(t)ə'strɑfɪk
antitetanus
BR ˌantɪ'tɛtənəs, ˌantɪ'tɛtn̩əs
AM ˌænˌtaɪ'tɛtnəs, ˌæn(t)i'tɛtnəs, ˌæn(t)ə'tɛtnəs
antitheism
BR ˌantɪ'θiːɪz(ə)m
AM ˌænˌtaɪ'θiˌɪzəm, ˌæn(t)i'θiˌɪzəm, ˌæn(t)ə'θiˌɪzəm
antitheist
BR ˌantɪ'θiːɪst, -s
AM ˌænˌtaɪ'θiɪst, ˌæn(t)i'θiɪst, ˌæn(t)ə'θiɪst, -s
antitheses
BR an'tɪθɪsiːz
AM æn'tɪθəˌsiz
antithesis
BR an'tɪθɪsɪs
AM æn'tɪθəsəs
antithetic
BR ˌantɪ'θɛtɪk
AM ˌæn(t)ə'θɛdɪk
antithetical
BR ˌantɪ'θɛtɪkl
AM ˌæn(t)ə'θɛdəkəl
antithetically
BR ˌantɪ'θɛtɪkli
AM ˌæn(t)ə'θɛdək(ə)li
antitoxic
BR ˌantɪ'tɒksɪk
AM ˌænˌtaɪ'tɑksɪk, ˌæn(t)i'tɑksɪk, ˌæn(t)ə'tɑksɪk
antitoxin
BR ˌantɪ'tɒksɪn, -z
AM ¦æn(t)i¦tɑksən, ¦æn(t)ə¦tɑksən, -z
antitrade
BR ˌantɪ'treɪd, -z
AM ˌænˌtaɪ'treɪd, ˌæn(t)i'treɪd, ˌæn(t)ə'treɪd, -z
antitrinitarian
BR ˌantɪˌtrɪnɪ'tɛːrɪən, -z
AM ˌænˌtaɪˌtrɪnɪ'tɛriən, ˌæn(t)iˌtrɪnɪ'tɛriən, ˌæn(t)əˌtrɪnɪ'tɛriən, -z
antitrust
BR ˌantɪ'trʌst
AM ˌænˌtaɪ'trəst, ˌæn(t)i'trəst, ˌæn(t)ə'trəst
antitype
BR 'antɪtʌɪp, -s
AM ˌænˌtaɪ'taɪp, ˌæn(t)i'taɪp, ˌæn(t)ə'taɪp, -s
antitypical
BR ˌantɪ'tɪpɪkl
AM ˌænˌtaɪ'tɪpɪkəl, ˌæn(t)i'tɪpɪkəl, ˌæn(t)ə'tɪpɪkəl
antivenene
BR ˌantɪ'vɛniːn, -z
AM ˌænˌtaɪ¦vɛnən, ˌæn(t)i¦vɛnən, ˌæn(t)ə¦vɛnən, ˌænˌtaɪ¦vinɪn, ˌæn(t)i¦vinɪn, ˌæn(t)ə¦vinɪn, -z
antivenin
BR ˌantɪ'vɛnɪn, -z
AM ˌænˌtaɪ'vɛnən, ˌæn(t)i'vɛnən, ˌæn(t)ə'vɛnən, -z
antiviral
BR ˌantɪ'vʌɪrəl, ˌantɪ'vʌɪrl̩
AM ˌænˌtaɪ'vaɪrəl, ˌæn(t)i'vaɪrəl, ˌæn(t)ə'vaɪrəl
antivirus
BR 'antɪvʌɪrəs, -ɪz
AM ˌænˌtaɪ'vaɪrəs, ˌæn(t)i'vaɪrəs, ˌæn(t)ə'vaɪrəs, -əz
antivivisection
BR ˌantɪˌvɪvɪ'sɛkʃn
AM ˌænˌtaɪˌvɪvə'sɛkʃən, ˌæn(t)iˌvɪvə'sɛkʃən, ˌæn(t)əˌvɪvə'sɛkʃən
antivivisectionism
BR ˌantɪˌvɪvɪ'sɛkʃn̩ɪz(ə)m, ˌantɪˌvɪvɪ'sɛkʃənɪz(ə)m

AM ˌænˌtaɪˌvɪvəˈsɛkʃəˌnɪzəm, ˌæn(t)iˌvɪvəˈsɛkʃəˌnɪzəm, ˌæn(t)əˌvɪvəˈsɛkʃəˌnɪzəm
antivivisectionist
BR ˌantɪˌvɪvɪˈsɛkʃn̩ɪst, ˌantɪˌvɪvɪˈsɛkʃənɪst, -s
AM ˌænˌtaɪˌvɪvəˈsɛkʃənəst ˌæn(t)iˌvɪvəˈsɛkʃənəst, ˌæn(t)əˌvɪvəˈsɛkʃənəst, -s
antler
BR ˈantlə(r), -z, -d
AM ˈæntlər, -z, -d
antlike
BR ˈantlʌɪk
AM ˈæntˌlaɪk
antlion
BR ˈantˌlʌɪən, -z
AM ˈæntˌlaɪən, -z
Antofagasta
BR ˌantəfəˈgastə(r)
AM ˌɑntoʊfəˈgɑstə
Antoine
BR anˈtwɑːn
AM ˌænˌtwɑn
Antoinette
BR ˌantwəˈnɛt
AM ˌæntwəˈnɛt
Anton
BR ˈantɒn
AM ˈænˌtɑn
Antonia
BR anˈtəʊnɪə(r)
AM ænˈtoʊniə
Antonine
BR ˈantənʌɪn, -z
AM ˈæntəˌnaɪn, -z
Antoninus
BR ˌantəˈnʌɪnəs
AM ˌæntəˈnaɪnəs
Antonio
BR anˈtəʊnɪəʊ
AM ænˈtoʊnioʊ
Antonioni
BR ˌantəʊnɪˈəʊni, anˌtəʊnɪˈəʊni
AM ˌænˌtoʊniˈoʊni
Antonius
BR anˈtəʊnɪəs
AM ænˈtoʊniəs
antonomasia
BR ˌantənəˈmeɪzɪə(r)
AM ænˌtɑnəˈmeɪʒə
Antony
BR ˈantəni
AM ˈæntəni, ˈænθəni
antonym
BR ˈantənɪm, -z
AM ˈæntəˌnɪm, -z
antonymous
BR anˈtɒnɪməs
AM ænˈtɑnəməs
antonymy
BR anˈtɒnɪmi
AM ænˈtɑnəmi
antra
BR ˈantrə(r)
AM ˈæntrə
antral
BR ˈantr(ə)l
AM ˈæntrəl
Antrim
BR ˈantrɪm
AM ˈæntrəm
Antrobus
BR ˈantrəbəs
AM ˈæntrəbəs
antrum
BR ˈantrəm, -z
AM ˈæntrəm, -z
antsy
BR ˈan(t)si
AM ˈæn(t)si
Antwerp
BR ˈantwəːp
AM ˈæntwərp
Anubis
BR əˈnjuːbɪs
AM əˈnubɪs
anuran
BR əˈnjʊərən, əˈnjʊərn̩, -z
AM əˈn(j)ʊrən, -z
anuresis
BR ˌanjʊˈriːsɪs
AM ˌænjəˈrisɪs
anus
BR ˈeɪnəs, -ɪz
AM ˈeɪnəs, -əz
Anvers
BR ɒ̃ˈvɛː(r)
AM ɑnˈvɛ(ə)r(z)
anvil
BR ˈanv(ɪ)l, -z
AM ˈænvəl, ˈænˌvɪl, -z
Anwar
BR ˈanwɑː(r)
AM ˈænwɑr
Anwen
BR ˈanwɛn, ˈanwɪn
AM ˈænwən
Anwyl
BR ˈanw(ɪ)l
AM ˈænwəl
anxiety
BR aŋˈzʌɪɪt|i, -ɪz
AM æŋˈzaɪɪdi, -z
anxious
BR ˈaŋ(k)ʃəs
AM ˈæŋ(k)ʃəs
anxiously
BR ˈaŋ(k)ʃəsli
AM ˈæŋ(k)ʃəsli
anxiousness
BR ˈaŋ(k)ʃəsnəs
AM ˈæŋ(k)ʃəsnəs
any
BR ˈɛni
AM ˈɛni
anybody
BR ˈɛnɪbɒdi, ˈɛnɪbədi
AM ˈɛniˌbɑdi, ˈɛniˌbədi
anyhow
BR ˈɛnɪhaʊ
AM ˈɛniˌhaʊ
anymore
BR ˌɛnɪˈmɔː(r)
AM ˌɛniˈmɔ(ə)r
anyone
BR ˈɛnɪwʌn
AM ˈɛniˌwən
anyplace
BR ˈɛnɪpleɪs
AM ˈɛniˌpleɪs
anything
BR ˈɛnɪθɪŋ
AM ˈɛniˌθɪŋ
anytime
BR ˈɛnɪtʌɪm
AM ˈɛniˌtaɪm
anyway
BR ˈɛnɪweɪ, -z
AM ˈɛniˌweɪ, -z
anywhere
BR ˈɛnɪwɛː(r)
AM ˈɛniˌ(h)wɛ(ə)r
anywise
BR ˈɛnɪwʌɪz
AM ˈɛniˌwaɪz
Anzac
BR ˈanzak, -s
AM ˈænˌzæk, -s
Anzio
BR ˈanzɪəʊ
AM ˈænzioʊ
ANZUS
BR ˈanzəs
AM ˈænzəs
ao dai
BR ˌaʊ ˈdʌɪ, -z
AM ˈɔˌdaɪ, ˈoʊ +, -z
A-OK
BR ˌeɪəʊˈkeɪ
AM ˈeɪˌoʊˈkeɪ
A-okay
BR ˌeɪəʊˈkeɪ
AM ˈeɪˌoʊˈkeɪ
aorist
BR ˈeɪərɪst, ˈɛːrɪst, -s
AM ˈeɪərəst, -s
aoristic
BR ˌeɪəˈrɪstɪk, ˌɛːˈrɪstɪk
AM ˌeɪəˈrɪstɪk
aorta
BR eɪˈɔːtə(r), -z
AM eɪˈɔrdə, -z
aortal
BR eɪˈɔːtl
AM eɪˈɔrdl
aortic
BR eɪˈɔːtɪk
AM eɪˈɔrdɪk
aoudad
BR ˈɑːʊdad, ˈaʊdad, -z
AM ˈɑʊˌdæd, ˈɑˌudæd, -z
à outrance
BR ˌa uːˈtrɑːns, ˌɑː +
AM ˌɑ uˈtrɑns
apace
BR əˈpeɪs
AM əˈpeɪs
Apache
BR əˈpatʃ|i, -ɪz
AM əˈpætʃi, -z
apanage
BR ˈapən|ɪdʒ, ˈapn̩|ɪdʒ, -ɪdʒɪz
AM ˈæpənɪdʒ, -ɪz
apart
BR əˈpɑːt
AM əˈpɑrt
apartheid
BR əˈpɑːteɪt, əˈpɑːtʌɪd, əˈpɑːtʌɪt
AM əˈpɑrˌteɪt, əˈpɑrˌtaɪt
apartment
BR əˈpɑːtm(ə)nt, -s
AM əˈpɑrtmənt, -s
apartness
BR əˈpɑːtnəs
AM əˈpɑrtnəs
apathetic
BR ˌapəˈθɛtɪk
AM ˌæpəˈθɛdɪk
apathetical
BR ˌapəˈθɛtɪkl
AM ˌæpəˈθɛdəkəl
apathetically
BR ˌapəˈθɛtɪkli
AM ˌæpəˈθɛdək(ə)li
apathy
BR ˈapəθi
AM ˈæpəθi
apatite
BR ˈapətʌɪt, -s
AM ˈæpəˌtaɪt, -s
ape
BR eɪp, -s, -ɪŋ, -t
AM eɪp, -s, -ɪŋ, -t
apeak
BR əˈpiːk
AM əˈpik
Apeldoorn
BR ˈapldɔːn
AM ˈæpəlˌdɔ(ə)rn
apelike
BR ˈeɪplʌɪk
AM ˈeɪpˌlaɪk
Apelles
BR əˈpɛliːz
AM əˈpɛliz
apeman
BR ˈeɪpman
AM ˈeɪpˌmæn
apemen
BR ˈeɪpmɛn
AM ˈeɪpˌmɛn
Apennines
BR ˈapɪnʌɪnz

AM ˈæpəˌnaɪnz

aperçu
BR ˌapəːˈs(j)uː, -z
AM ˌæpərˈsu, ˌɑpɛrˈs(j)u, -z

aperient
BR əˈpɪərɪənt, -s
AM əˈpɪriənt, -s

aperiodic
BR ˌeɪpɪərɪˈɒdɪk
AM ˌeɪˌpɪriˈɑdɪk

aperiodicity
BR ˌeɪpɪərɪəˈdɪsɪti
AM ˌeɪˌpɪriəˈdɪsɪdi

aperitif
BR əˌpɛrəˈtiːf, əˈpɛrətiːf, -s
AM ɑˌpɛrəˈtif, əˌpɛrəˈtif, -s

aperture
BR ˈapətʃə(r), -z
AM ˈæpərˌtʃʊ(ə)r, -z

apery
BR ˈeɪpər|i, -ɪz
AM ˈeɪpəri, -z

apetalous
BR ˌeɪˈpɛtl̩əs
AM ˌeɪˈpɛdl̩əs

apex
BR ˈeɪpɛks, -ɪz
AM ˈeɪˌpɛks, -əz

Apfelstrudel
BR ˈapf(ə)lˌstruːdl, ˈapf(ə)lˌʃtruːdl, -z
AM ˌæpfəlˈstrudəl, -z

aphaeresis
BR əˈfɪərɪsɪs, aˈfɪərɪsɪs
AM əˈfɛrəsəs, æˈfɛrəsəs

aphasia
BR əˈfeɪzɪə(r), əˈfeɪʒə(r)
AM əˈfeɪʒiə

aphasic
BR əˈfeɪzɪk
AM əˈfeɪzɪk

aphelia
BR əˈfiːlɪə(r)
AM əˈfiljə, əˈfiliə

aphelion
BR əˈfiːlɪən, apˈhiːlɪən
AM əˈfiljən, əˈfiliən

apheresis
BR əˈfɪərɪsɪs, aˈfɪərɪsɪs
AM əˈfɛrəsəs, æˈfɛrəsəs

aphesis
BR ˈafɪsɪs
AM ˈæfəsəs

aphetic
BR əˈfɛtɪk
AM əˈfɛdɪk, æˈfɛdɪk

aphetically
BR əˈfɛtɪkli
AM əˈfɛdək(ə)li, æˈfɛdək(ə)li

aphid
BR ˈeɪfɪd, -z
AM ˈeɪfɨd, -z

aphides
BR ˈeɪfɪdiːz
AM ˈeɪfɨˌdiz, ˈæfəˌdiz

aphis
BR ˈeɪfɪs, -ɪz
AM ˈeɪfɨs, ˈæfəs, -ɪz

aphonia
BR eɪˈfəʊnɪə(r)
AM ˌeɪˈfoʊniə, əˈfoʊniə

aphonic
BR eɪˈfɒnɪk, əˈfɒnɪk
AM eɪˈfɑnɪk

aphony
BR ˈafəni, ˈafn̩i
AM ˈæfəni

aphorise
BR ˈafərʌɪz, -ɪz, -ɪŋ, -d
AM ˈæfəˌraɪz, -ɪz, -ɪŋ, -d

aphorism
BR ˈafərɪz(ə)m, -z
AM ˈæfəˌrɪzəm, -z

aphorist
BR ˈaf(ə)rɪst, -s
AM ˈæfərəst, -s

aphoristic
BR ˌafəˈrɪstɪk
AM ˌæfəˈrɪstɪk

aphoristically
BR ˌafəˈrɪstɪkli
AM ˌæfəˈrɪstɪk(ə)li

aphorize
BR ˈafərʌɪz, -ɪz, -ɪŋ, -d
AM ˈæfəˌraɪz, -ɪz, -ɪŋ, -d

Aphra
BR ˈafrə(r)
AM ˈæfrə

aphrodisiac
BR ˌafrəˈdɪzɪak, -s
AM ˌæfrəˈdiziˌæk, ˌæfrəˈdiziˌæk, ˌæfrəˈdiʒiˌæk, -s

Aphrodisias
BR ˌafrəˈdɪzɪas
AM ˌæfrəˈdɪziəs, ˌæfrəˈdiziəs, ˌæfrəˈdiʒiəs

Aphrodite
BR ˌafrəˈdʌɪti
AM ˌæfroʊˈdaɪdi, ˌæfrəˈdaɪdi

aphtha
BR ˈafθə(r)
AM ˈæfθə

aphthous
BR ˈafθəs
AM ˈæfθəs

aphyllous
BR eɪˈfɪləs
AM eɪˈfɪləs

Apia
BR ɑːˈpiːə(r), əˈpiːə(r), ˈapɪə(r)
AM ˈɑpiə

apian
BR ˈeɪpɪən
AM ˈeɪpiən

apiarian
BR ˌeɪpɪˈɛːrɪən
AM ˌeɪpiˈɛriən

apiarist
BR ˈeɪpɪərɪst, -s
AM ˈeɪpiərəst, -s

apiary
BR ˈeɪpɪər|i, -ɪz
AM ˈeɪpiˌɛri, -z

apical
BR ˈapɪkl, ˈeɪpɪkl
AM ˈæpəkəl, ˈeɪpɨkəl

apically
BR ˈapɪkli, ˈeɪpɪkli
AM ˈæpək(ə)li, ˈeɪpɨk(ə)li

apices
BR ˈeɪpɪsiːz
AM ˈeɪpəˌsiz, ˈæpəˌsiz

apicultural
BR ˌeɪpɪˈkʌltʃ(ə)rəl, ˌeɪpɪˈkʌltʃ(ə)rl̩
AM ˌeɪpəˈkəltʃ(ə)rəl

apiculture
BR ˈeɪpɪˌkʌltʃə(r)
AM ˈeɪpəˌkəltʃər

apiculturist
BR ˌeɪpɪˈkʌltʃ(ə)rɪst, -s
AM ˌeɪpəˈkəltʃ(ə)rəst, -s

apiece
BR əˈpiːs
AM əˈpis

apis
BR ˈeɪpɪs
AM ˈeɪpɨs

apish
BR ˈeɪpɪʃ
AM ˈeɪpɪʃ

apishly
BR ˈeɪpɨʃli
AM ˈeɪpɨʃli

apishness
BR ˈeɪpɨʃnɪs
AM ˈeɪpɪʃnɪs

aplanat
BR ˈaplənat, -s
AM ˈæpləˌnæt, -s

aplanatic
BR ˌapləˈnatɪk
AM ˌæpləˈnædɪk

aplasia
BR əˈpleɪzɪə(r), əˈpleɪʒə(r)
AM əˈpleɪʒiə

aplastic
BR ˌeɪˈplastɪk
AM ˌeɪˈplæstɪk

aplenty
BR əˈplɛnti
AM əˈplɛn(t)i

aplomb
BR əˈplɒm
AM əˈplɑm, əˈpləm, əˈploʊm

apnea
BR ˈapnɪə(r)
AM ˈæpniə

apnoea
BR ˈapnɪə(r)
AM ˈæpniə

apocalypse
BR əˈpɒkəlɪps, -ɪz
AM əˈpɑkəˌlɪps, -ɪz

apocalyptic
BR əˌpɒkəˈlɪptɪk
AM əˌpɑkəˈlɪptɪk

apocalyptical
BR əˌpɒkəˈlɪptɪkl
AM əˌpɑkəˈlɪptɪkəl

apocalyptically
BR əˌpɒkəˈlɪptɪkli
AM əˌpɑkəˈlɪptɪk(ə)li

apocarpous
BR ˌapəˈkɑːpəs
AM ˌæpəˈkɑrpəs

apochromat
BR ˌapəˈkrəʊmat, ˈapəkrə(ʊ)mat, -s
AM ˌæpəˈkroʊmət, -s

apochromatic
BR ˌapəkrə(ʊ)ˈmatɪk
AM ˌæpəkroʊˈmædɪk

apocope
BR əˈpɒkəp|i, -ɪz
AM əˈpɑkəpi, -z

apocrine
BR ˈapəkrʌɪn, ˈapəkrɪn
AM ˈæpəkrən, ˈæpəˌkraɪn, ˈæpəˌkrin

apocrypha
BR əˈpɒkrɪfə(r), -z
AM əˈpɑkrəfə, -z

apocryphal
BR əˈpɒkrɪfl
AM əˈpɑkrəfəl

apocryphally
BR əˈpɒkrɪfl̩i, əˈpɒkrɪfəli
AM əˈpɑkrəfəli

apodal
BR ˈapədl
AM eɪˈpoʊdəl

apodeictic
BR ˌapəˈdʌɪktɪk
AM ˌæpəˈdaɪktɪk

apodeictical
BR ˌapəˈdʌɪktɪkl
AM ˌæpəˈdaɪktɨkəl

apodeictically
BR ˌapəˈdʌɪktɪkli
AM ˌæpəˈdaɪktɪk(ə)li

apodictic
BR ˌapəˈdɪktɪk
AM ˌæpəˈdɪktɪk

apodictical
BR ˌapəˈdɪktɪkl
AM ˌæpəˈdɪktɨkəl

apodictically
BR ˌapəˈdɪktɨkli
AM ˌæpəˈdɪktɪk(ə)li

apodoses
BR əˈpɒdəsiːz
AM əˈpadəsiz

apodosis
BR əˈpɒdəsɪs
AM əˈpadəsəs

apogean
BR ˌapə(ʊ)ˈdʒiːən
AM ˌæpəˈdʒiən

apogee
BR ˈapədʒiː, -z
AM ˈæpədʒi, -z

apolaustic
BR ˌapəˈlɔːstɪk
AM ˌæpəˈlɔstɪk, ˌæpəˈlastɪk

apolitical
BR ˌeɪpəˈlɪtɨkl
AM ˌeɪpəˈlɪdəkəl

apolitically
BR ˌeɪpəˈlɪtɨkli
AM ˌeɪpəˈlɪdək(ə)li

Apollinaire
BR əˌpɒlɪˈnɛː(r)
AM əˌpaləˈnɛ(ə)r

Apollinaris
BR əˌpɒlɪˈnɛːrɪs, əˌpɒlɪˈnɑːrɪs
AM əˌpaləˈnɛrəs

Apollo
BR əˈpɒləʊ
AM əˈpaloʊ

Apollonian
BR ˌapəˈləʊnɪən
AM ˌæpəˈloʊniən

Apollonius
BR ˌapəˌləʊnɪəs
AM ˌæpəˈloʊniəs

Apollyon
BR əˈpɒlɪən, əˈpɒlɪɒn
AM əˈpaliən

apologetic
BR əˌpɒləˈdʒɛtɪk, -s
AM əˌpaləˈdʒɛdɪk, -s

apologetical
BR əˌpɒləˈdʒɛtɨkl
AM əˌpaləˈdʒɛdəkəl

apologetically
BR əˌpɒləˈdʒɛtɨkli
AM əˌpaləˈdʒɛdək(ə)li

apologia
BR ˌapəˈləʊdʒ(ɪ)ə(r), -z
AM ˌapəˈloʊdʒ(i)ə, əˌpoʊləˈdʒiə, -z

apologise
BR əˈpɒlədʒʌɪz, -ɨz, -ɪŋ, -d
AM əˈpaləˌdʒaɪz, -ɨz, -ɪŋ, -d

apologist
BR əˈpɒlədʒɪst, -s
AM əˈpalədʒəst, -s

apologize
BR əˈpɒlədʒʌɪz, -ɨz, -ɪŋ, -d
AM əˈpaləˌdʒaɪz, -ɨz, -ɪŋ, -d

apologue
BR ˈapəlɒg, -z
AM ˈæpəˌlɔg, ˈæpəˌlag, -z

apology
BR əˈpɒlədʒ|i, -ɪz
AM əˈpalədʒi, -z

apolune
BR ˈapəluːn, -z
AM ˈæpəˌlun, -z

apomictic
BR ˌapəˈmɪktɪk
AM ˌæpəˈmɪktɪk

apomixis
BR ˌapəˈmɪksɪs
AM ˌæpəˈmɪksɪs

apophatic
BR ˌapəˈfatɪk
AM ˌæpəˈfædɪk

apophthegm
BR ˈapəθɛm, -z
AM ˈæpəˌθɛm, -z

apophthegmatic
BR ˌapəθɛgˈmatɪk
AM ˌæpəθəˈmædɪk

apophthegmatically
BR ˌapəθɛgˈmatɨkli
AM ˌæpəθəˈmædək(ə)li

apophyses
BR əˈpɒfɨsiːz
AM əˈpafəˌsiz

apophysis
BR əˈpɒfɨsɪs
AM əˈpafəsəs

apoplectic
BR ˌapəˈplɛktɪk
AM ˌæpəˈplɛktɪk

apoplectical
BR ˌapəˈplɛktɨkl
AM ˌæpəˈplɛktəkəl

apoplectically
BR ˌapəˈplɛktɨkli
AM ˌæpəˈplɛktək(ə)li

apoplexy
BR ˈapəplɛks|i, -ɪz
AM ˈæpəˌplɛksi, -z

aposematic
BR ˌapə(ʊ)sɪˈmatɪk
AM ˌæpəsɛˈmædɪk

aposiopeses
BR ˌapə(ʊ)sʌɪəˈpiːsiːz
AM ˌæpəˌsaɪəˈpisiz

aposiopesis
BR ˌapə(ʊ)sʌɪəˈpiːsɪs
AM ˌæpəˌsaɪəˈpisɪs

apostasy
BR əˈpɒstəs|i, -ɪz
AM əˈpastəsi, -z

apostate
BR əˈpɒsteɪt, -s
AM əˈpaˌsteɪt, əˈpastət, -s

apostatic
BR ˌapəˈstatɪk
AM ˌæpəˈstædɪk

apostatical
BR ˌapəˈstatɨkl
AM ˌæpəˈstædəkəl

apostatically
BR ˌapəˈstatɨkli
AM ˌæpəˈstædək(ə)li

apostatise
BR əˈpɒstətʌɪz, -ɨz, -ɪŋ, -d
AM əˈpastəˌtaɪz, -ɨz, -ɪŋ, -d

apostatize
BR əˈpɒstətʌɪz, -ɨz, -ɪŋ, -d
AM əˈpastəˌtaɪz, -ɨz, -ɪŋ, -d

a posteriori
BR ˌeɪ pɒˌstɛrɪˈɔːrʌɪ, ˌɑː +, + pɒˌstɪərɪˈɔːrʌɪ
AM ˌɑ ˌpaˌstɪriˈɔˌri, ˌeɪ ˌpaˌstɪriˈɔˌraɪ

apostigmat
BR ˈapəstɪgmat, -s
AM ˈæpəˌstɪgˌmæt, -s

apostil
BR əˈpɒstɪl, -z
AM əˈpastl, -z

apostille
BR əˈpɒstɪl, -z
AM əˈpastl, -z

apostle
BR əˈpɒsl, -z
AM əˈpasəl, -z

apostleship
BR əˈpɒslʃɪp, -s
AM əˈpasəlˌʃɪp, -s

apostolate
BR əˈpɒstəleɪt, əˈpɒstələt, -s
AM əˈpastəˌleɪt, əˈpastələt, -s

apostolic
BR ˌapəˈstɒlɪk
AM ˌæpəˈstalɪk

apostolical
BR ˌapəˈstɒlɨkl
AM ˌæpəˈstaləkəl

apostolically
BR ˌapəˈstɒlɨkli
AM ˌæpəˈstalək(ə)li

apostrophe
BR əˈpɒstrəf|i, -ɪz
AM əˈpastrəfi, -z

apostrophic
BR ˌapəˈstrɒfɪk
AM ˌæpəˈstrafɪk

apostrophise
BR əˈpɒstrəfʌɪz, -ɨz, -ɪŋ, -d
AM əˈpastrəˌfaɪz, -ɨz, -ɪŋ, -d

apostrophize
BR əˈpɒstrəfʌɪz, -ɨz, -ɪŋ, -d
AM əˈpastrəˌfaɪz, -ɨz, -ɪŋ, -d

apothecary
BR əˈpɒθɪk(ə)r|i, -ɪz
AM əˈpaθəˌkɛri, -z

apothegm
BR ˈapəθɛm, -z
AM ˈæpəˌθɛm, -z

apothem
BR ˈapəθɛm, -z
AM ˈæpəˌθɛm, -z

apotheoses
BR əˌpɒθɪˈəʊsiːz
AM əˌpaθiˈoʊˌsiz

apotheosis
BR əˌpɒθɪˈəʊsɪs
AM əˌpaθiˈoʊsəs

apotheosise
BR əˈpɒθɪəsʌɪz, -ɨz, -ɪŋ, -d
AM əˈpaθiəˌsaɪz, ˌæpəˈθiəˌsaɪz, -ɨz, -ɪŋ, -d

apotheosize
BR əˈpɒθɪəsʌɪz, -ɨz, -ɪŋ, -d
AM əˈpaθiəˌsaɪz, ˌæpəˈθiəˌsaɪz, -ɨz, -ɪŋ, -d

apotropaic
BR ˌapətrəˈpeɪɪk
AM ˌæpətrəˈpeɪɪk

appal
BR əˈpɔːl, -z, -ɪŋ, -d
AM əˈpɔl, əˈpal, -z, -ɪŋ, -d

Appalachia
BR ˌapəˈleɪ(t)ʃ(ɪ)ə(r)
AM ˌæpəˈleɪ(t)ʃ(i)ə, ˌæpəˈlæ(t)ʃ(i)ə

Appalachian
BR ˌapəˈleɪ(t)ʃən, ˌapəˈleɪtʃn, -z
AM ˌæpəˈleɪ(t)ʃ(i)ən, ˌæpəˈlæ(t)ʃ(i)ən, -z

appall
BR əˈpɔːl, -z, -ɪŋ, -d
AM əˈpɔl, əˈpal, -z, -ɪŋ, -d

appallingly
BR əˈpɔːlɪŋli
AM əˈpɔlɪŋli, əˈpalɪŋli

Appaloosa
BR ˌapəˈluːsə(r), -z
AM ˌæpəˈlusə, -z

appanage
BR ˈapən|ɪdʒ, ˈapn̩|ɪdʒ, -ɨdʒɨz
AM ˈæpənɪdʒ, -ɨz

apparat
BR ˌapəˈrɑːt, ˌapəˈrat, -s
AM ˈæpəˌræt, ˈɑpəˌrat, ˌæpəˈrat, -s

apparatchik
BR ˌapəˈra(t)tʃɪk, ˌapəˈrɑː(t)tʃɪk, -s

AM ˌɑpəˈrɑtʃɪk, -s

apparatus
BR ˌapəˈreɪtəs, -ɨz
AM ˌæpəˈrædəs, ˌæpəˈreɪdəs, -əz

apparel
BR əˈparəl, əˈparḷ, -z, -ɪŋ, -d
AM əˈpɛrəl, -z, -ɪŋ, -d

apparent
BR əˈparənt, əˈparṇt
AM əˈpɛrənt

apparently
BR əˈparəntli, əˈparṇtli
AM əˈpɛrən(t)li

apparentness
BR əˈparəntnəs, əˈparṇtnəs
AM əˈpɛrən(t)nəs

apparition
BR ˌapəˈrɪʃn, -z
AM ˌæpəˈrɪʃən, -z

apparitor
BR əˈparɨtə(r), -z
AM əˈpɛrədər, -z

appassionata
BR əˌpasjəˈnɑːtə(*r*)
AM əˌpɑsiəˈnɑdə, əˌpæsiəˈnɑdə

appeal
BR əˈpiːl, -z, -ɪŋ, -d
AM əˈpil, -z, -ɪŋ, -d

appealable
BR əˈpiːləbl
AM əˈpiləbəl

appealer
BR əˈpiːlə(r), -z
AM əˈpilər, -z

appealing
BR əˈpiːlɪŋ
AM əˈpilɪŋ

appealingly
BR əˈpiːlɪŋli
AM əˈpilɪŋli

appear
BR əˈpɪə(r), -z, -ɪŋ, -d
AM əˈpɪ(ə)r, -z, -ɪŋ, -d

appearance
BR əˈpɪərəns, əˈpɪərṇs, -ɨz
AM əˈpɪrəns, -əz

appease
BR əˈpiːz, -ɨz, -ɪŋ, -d
AM əˈpiz, -ɨz, -ɪŋ, -d

appeasement
BR əˈpiːzm(ə)nt
AM əˈpizmənt

appeaser
BR əˈpiːzə(r), -z
AM əˈpizər, -z

appellant
BR əˈpɛlənt, əˈpɛlṇt, -s
AM əˈpɛlənt, -s

appellate
BR əˈpɛlət
AM əˈpɛlət

appellation
BR ˌapəˈleɪʃn, -z
AM ˌæpəˈleɪʃən, -z

appellation contrôlée
BR ˌapɛlasjɒ̃ ˌkɒ̃trəʊˈleɪ
AM ɑˌpɛlɑˈsiɔn ˌkɔntrəˈleɪ

appellation d'origine contrôlée
BR ˌapɛlasjɒ̃ ˌdɒrɪˈʒiːn ˌkɒ̃trəʊˈleɪ
AM ɑˌpɛlɑˈsiɔn dɔriˌʒin ˌkɔntrəˈleɪ

appellative
BR əˈpɛlətɪv, -z
AM əˈpɛlədɪv, -z

appellatively
BR əˈpɛlətɪvli
AM əˈpɛlədɨvli

appellee
BR ˌapəˈliː, ˌapɛlˈiː, -z
AM ˌæpɛlˈi, -z

append
BR əˈpɛnd, -z, -ɪŋ, -ɨd
AM əˈpɛnd, -z, -ɪŋ, -əd

appendage
BR əˈpɛnd|ɪdʒ, -ɨdʒɨz
AM əˈpɛndɪdʒ, -ɨz

appendant
BR əˈpɛnd(ə)nt, -s
AM əˈpɛnd(ə)nt, -s

appendectomy
BR ˌapɛnˈdɛktəm|i, ˌap(ə)nˈdɛktəm|i, -ɪz
AM ˌæpənˈdɛktəmi, ˌæˌpɛnˈdɛktəmi, -z

appendicectomy
BR əˌpɛndɪˈsɛktəm|i, -ɪz
AM əˌpɛndəˈsɛktəmi, -z

appendices
BR əˈpɛndɪsiːz
AM əˈpɛndəˌsiz

appendicitis
BR əˌpɛndɪˈsʌɪtɪs
AM əˌpɛndəˈsaɪdɪs

appendix
BR əˈpɛnd|ɪks, -ɪksɪz
AM əˈpɛndɪks, -ɨz

apperceive
BR ˌapəˈsiːv, -z, -ɪŋ, -d
AM ˌæpərˈsiv, -z, -ɪŋ, -d

apperception
BR ˌapəˈsɛpʃn
AM ˌæpərˈsɛpʃən

apperceptive
BR ˌapəˈsɛptɪv
AM ˌæpərˈsɛptɪv

appertain
BR ˌapəˈteɪn, -z, -ɪŋ, -d
AM ˌæpərˈteɪn, -z, -ɪŋ, -d

appertinent
BR əˈpəːtɪnənt
AM əˈpərtnənt

appestat
BR ˈapɪstat, -s
AM ˈæpəˌstæt, -s

appetence
BR ˈapɪt(ə)ns
AM ˈæpədəns, ˈæpətns

appetency
BR ˈapɪt(ə)ns|i, -ɪz
AM ˈæpədənsi, ˈæpətnsi, -z

appetent
BR ˈapɪt(ə)nt
AM ˈæpədənt, ˈæpətnt

appetise
BR ˈapɪtʌɪz, -ɨz, -ɪŋ, -d
AM ˈæpəˌtaɪz, -ɨz, -ɪŋ, -d

appetiser
BR ˈapɪtʌɪzə(r), -z
AM ˈæpəˌtaɪzər, -z

appetisingly
BR ˈapɪtʌɪzɪŋli
AM ˈæpəˌtaɪzɪŋli

appetite
BR ˈapɪtʌɪt, -s
AM ˈæpəˌtaɪt, -s

appetitive
BR əˈpɛtɪtɪv
AM ˈæpəˌtaɪdɪv, əˈpɛdədɪv

appetize
BR ˈapɪtʌɪz, -ɨz, -ɪŋ, -d
AM ˈæpəˌtaɪz, -ɨz, -ɪŋ, -d

appetizer
BR ˈapɪtʌɪzə(r), -z
AM ˈæpəˌtaɪzər, -z

appetizing
BR ˈapɪtʌɪzɪŋ
AM ˈæpəˌtaɪzɪŋ

appetizingly
BR ˈapɪtʌɪzɪŋli
AM ˈæpəˌtaɪzɪŋli

Appian Way
BR ˌapɪən ˈweɪ
AM ˌæpiən ˈweɪ

applaud
BR əˈplɔːd, -z, -ɪŋ, -ɨd
AM əˈplɔd, əˈplɑd, -z, -ɪŋ, -əd

applause
BR əˈplɔːz
AM əˈplɔz, əˈplɑz

apple
BR ˈapl, -z
AM ˈæpəl, -z

Appleby
BR ˈaplbi
AM ˈæpəlˌbi

applecart
BR ˈaplkɑːt, -s
AM ˈæpəlˌkɑrt, -s

Appledore
BR ˈapldɔː(r)
AM ˈæpəlˌdɔ(ə)r

applejack
BR ˈapldʒak
AM ˈæpəlˌdʒæk

Appleton
BR ˈaplt(ə)n
AM ˈæpəlt(ə)n

appliable
BR əˈplʌɪəbl
AM əˈplaɪəbəl

appliableness
BR əˈplʌɪəblnəs
AM əˈplaɪəbəlnəs

appliance
BR əˈplʌɪəns, -ɨz
AM əˈplaɪəns, -əz

applicability
BR əˌplɪkəˈbɪlɨti, ˌaplɪkəˈbɪlɨti
AM ˌæpləkəˈbɪlɨdi

applicable
BR əˈplɪkəbl, ˈaplɪkəbl
AM ˈæpləkəbəl

applicableness
BR əˈplɪkəblnəs, ˈaplɪkəblnəs
AM ˈæpləkəbəlnəs

applicably
BR əˈplɪkəbli, ˈaplɪkəbli
AM ˈæpləkəbli

applicant
BR ˈaplɪk(ə)nt, -s
AM ˈæpləkənt, -s

application
BR aplɪˈkeɪʃn, -z
AM ˌæpləˈkeɪʃən, -z

applicator
BR ˈaplɪkeɪtə(r), -z
AM ˈæpləˌkeɪdər, -z

applied
BR əˈplʌɪd
AM əˈplaɪd

applier
BR əˈplʌɪə(r), -z
AM əˈplaɪər, -z

appliqué
BR əˈpliːkeɪ, -z, -ɪŋ, -d
AM ˌæpləˌkeɪ, -z, -ɪŋ, -d

apply
BR əˈplʌɪ, -z, -ɪŋ, -d
AM əˈplaɪ, -z, -ɪŋ, -d

appoggiatura
BR əˌpɒdʒ(ɪ)əˈt(j)ʊərə(*r*), -z
AM əˌpɑdʒəˈtʊrə, -z

appoint
BR əˈpɔɪnt, -s, -ɪŋ, -ɨd
AM əˈpɔɪn|t, -ts, -(t)ɪŋ, -(t)ɨd

appointee
BR əˌpɔɪnˈtiː, ˌapɔɪnˈtiː, -z
AM əˌpɔɪnˈti, -z

appointer
BR əˈpɔɪntə(r), -z
AM əˈpɔɪn(t)ər, -z

appointive
BR əˈpɔɪntɪv
AM əˈpɔɪn(t)ɪv

appointment
BR ə'pɔɪntm(ə)nt, -s
AM ə'pɔɪntmənt, -s

Appomattox
BR ˌapə'matəks
AM ˌæpə'mædəks

apport
BR ə'pɔːt
AM ə'pɔ(ə)rt

apportion
BR ə'pɔːʃ|n, -nz, -n̩ɪŋ\-ənɪŋ, -nd
AM ə'pɔrʃ|ən, -ənz, -(ə)nɪŋ, -ənd

apportionable
BR ə'pɔːʃn̩əbl, ə'pɔːʃ(ə)nəbl
AM ə'pɔrʃ(ə)nəbəl

apportionment
BR ə'pɔːʃnm(ə)nt, -s
AM ə'pɔrʃənmənt, -s

appose
BR ə'pəʊz, -ɪz, -ɪŋ, -d
AM ə'poʊz, -əz, -ɪŋ, -d

apposite
BR 'apəzɪt
AM 'æpəzət

appositely
BR 'apəzɪtli
AM 'æpəzətli

appositeness
BR 'apəzɪtnɪs
AM 'æpəzətnəs

apposition
BR ˌapə'zɪʃn, -z
AM ˌæpə'zɪʃən, -z

appositional
BR ˌapə'zɪʃn(ə)l, ˌapə'zɪʃən(ə)l
AM ˌæpə'zɪʃ(ə)nəl

appositive
BR ə'pɒzɪtɪv
AM ə'pɑzədɪv

appositively
BR ə'pɒzɪtɪvli
AM ə'pɑzədɪvli

appraisable
BR ə'preɪzəbl
AM ə'preɪzəbəl

appraisal
BR ə'preɪzl, -z
AM ə'preɪzəl, -z

appraise
BR ə'preɪz, -ɪz, -ɪŋ, -d
AM ə'preɪz, -ɪz, -ɪŋ, -d

appraisee
BR əˌpreɪ'ziː, -z
AM əˌpreɪ'zi, -z

appraisement
BR ə'preɪzm(ə)nt, -s
AM ə'preɪzmənt, -s

appraiser
BR ə'preɪzə(r), -z
AM ə'preɪzər, -z

appraisingly
BR ə'preɪzɪŋli
AM ə'preɪzɪŋli

appraisive
BR ə'preɪzɪv
AM ə'preɪzɪv

appreciable
BR ə'priːʃ(ɪ)əbl
AM ə'priʃ(i)əbəl

appreciably
BR ə'priːʃ(ɪ)əbli
AM ə'priʃ(i)əbli

appreciate
BR ə'priːʃɪeɪt, ə'priːsɪeɪt, -s, -ɪŋ, -ɨd
AM ə'priʃiˌeɪ|t, -ts, -dɪŋ, -dɨd

appreciation
BR əˌpriːʃɪ'eɪʃn, əˌpriːsɪ'eɪʃn, -z
AM əˌpriʃi'eɪʃən, -z

appreciative
BR ə'priːʃ(ɪ)ətɪv, ə'priːsɪətɪv
AM ə'priʃ(i)ədɪv

appreciatively
BR ə'priːʃ(ɪ)ətɨvli, ə'priːsɪətɨvli
AM ə'priʃ(i)ədɨvli

appreciativeness
BR ə'priːʃ(ɪ)ətɨvnɨs, ə'priːsɪətɨvnɨs
AM ə'priʃ(i)ədɨvnɨs

appreciator
BR ə'priːʃɪeɪtə(r), ə'priːsɪeɪtə(r), -z
AM ə'priʃiˌeɪdər, -z

appreciatory
BR ə'priːʃ(ɪ)ət(ə)ri, ə'priːsɪət(ə)ri
AM ə'priʃ(i)əˌtɔri

apprehend
BR ˌaprɪ'hɛnd, -z, -ɪŋ, -ɨd
AM ˌæprə'hɛnd, ˌæpri'hɛnd, -z, -ɪŋ, -əd

apprehensibility
BR ˌaprɨhɛnsɪ'bɪlɨti
AM ˌæprəˌhɛnsə'bɪlɨdi, ˌæpriˌhɛnsə'bɪlɨdi

apprehensible
BR ˌaprɪ'hɛnsɨbl
AM ˌæprə'hɛnsəbəl, ˌæpri'hɛnsəbəl

apprehension
BR ˌaprɪ'hɛnʃn, -z
AM ˌæprə'hɛn(t)ʃən, ˌæpri'hɛn(t)ʃən, -z

apprehensive
BR ˌaprɪ'hɛnsɪv
AM ˌæprə'hɛnsɪv, ˌæpri'hɛnsɪv

apprehensively
BR ˌaprɪ'hɛnsɨvli
AM ˌæprə'hɛnsɨvli, ˌæpri'hɛnsɨvli

apprehensiveness
BR ˌaprɪ'hɛnsɨvnɨs
AM ˌæprə'hɛnsɨvnɨs, ˌæpri'hɛnsɨvnɨs

apprentice
BR ə'prɛntɪs, -ɪz, -ɪŋ, -t
AM ə'prɛn(t)əs, -əz, -ɪŋ, -t

apprenticeship
BR ə'prɛntɨ(s)ʃɪp, -s
AM ə'prɛn(t)əsˌʃɪp, -s

apprise
BR ə'prʌɪz, -ɪz, -ɪŋ, -d
AM ə'praɪz, -ɪz, -ɪŋ, -d

apprize
BR ə'prʌɪz, -ɪz, -ɪŋ, -d
AM ə'praɪz, -ɪz, -ɪŋ, -d

appro
BR 'aprəʊ
AM 'æproʊ

approach
BR ə'prəʊtʃ, -ɪz, -ɪŋ, -t
AM ə'proʊtʃ, -əz, -ɪŋ, -t

approachability
BR əˌprəʊtʃə'bɪlɨti
AM əˌproʊtʃə'bɪlɨdi

approachable
BR ə'prəʊtʃəbl
AM ə'proʊtʃəbəl

approbate
BR 'aprə(ʊ)beɪt, -s, -ɪŋ, -ɨd
AM 'æprəˌbeɪ|t, 'æproʊˌbeɪ|t, -ts, -dɪŋ, -dɨd

approbation
BR ˌaprə(ʊ)'beɪʃn
AM ˌæprə'beɪʃən

approbative
BR 'aprəbeɪtɪv
AM ˌæprə'beɪdɪv, ə'proʊbədɪv

approbatory
BR ˌaprə(ʊ)'beɪt(ə)ri
AM 'æprəbəˌtɔri, ə'proʊbəˌtɔri

appropriate[1]
adjective
BR ə'prəʊprɪət
AM ə'proʊpriət

appropriate[2]
verb
BR ə'prəʊprɪeɪt, -s, -ɪŋ, -ɨd
AM ə'proʊpriˌeɪ|t, -ts, -dɪŋ, -dɨd

appropriately
BR ə'prəʊprɪətli
AM ə'proʊpriətli

appropriateness
BR ə'prəʊprɪətnəs
AM ə'proʊpriətnəs

appropriation
BR əˌprəʊprɪ'eɪʃn, -z
AM əˌproʊpri'eɪʃən, -z

appropriationist
BR əˌprəʊprɪ'eɪʃn̩ɪst, əˌprəʊprɪ'eɪʃənɪst, -s
AM əˌproʊpri'eɪʃənəst, -s

appropriative
BR ə'prəʊprɪətɪv
AM ə'proʊpriˌeɪdɪv, ə'proʊpriədɪv

appropriator
BR ə'prəʊprɪeɪtə(r), -z
AM ə'proʊpriˌeɪdər, -z

approval
BR ə'pruːvl, -z
AM ə'pruvəl, -z

approve
BR ə'pruːv, -z, -ɪŋ, -d
AM ə'pruv, -z, -ɪŋ, -d

approving
BR ə'pruːvɪŋ
AM ə'pruvɪŋ

approvingly
BR ə'pruːvɪŋli
AM ə'pruvɪŋli

approximant
BR ə'prɒksɪm(ə)nt, -s
AM ə'prɑksəmənt, -s

approximate[1]
adjective
BR ə'prɒksɪmət
AM ə'prɑksəmət

approximate[2]
verb
BR ə'prɒksɪmeɪt, -s, -ɪŋ, -ɨd
AM ə'prɑksəˌmeɪ|t, -ts, -dɪŋ, -dɨd

approximately
BR ə'prɒksɪmətli
AM ə'prɑksəmətli

approximation
BR əˌprɒksɪ'meɪʃn, -z
AM əˌprɑksə'meɪʃən, -z

approximative
BR ə'prɒksɪmətɪv
AM ə'prɑksəˌmeɪdɪv

approximatively
BR ə'prɒksɪmətɨvli
AM ə'prɑksəˌmeɪdɨvli

appurtenance
BR ə'pəːtɪnəns, ə'pəːtn̩əns, -ɪz
AM ə'pərtn̩əns, -əz

appurtenant
BR ə'pəːtɪnənt, ə'pəːtn̩ənt
AM ə'pərtn̩ənt

apraxia
BR eɪ'praksɪə(r), ə'praksɪə(r)
AM eɪ'præksiə

après-ski
BR ˌapreɪ'skiː
AM ˌɑpreɪ'ski

apricot
BR 'eɪprɪkɒt, -s
AM 'æprəˌkɑt, 'eɪprəˌkɑt, -s

April
BR 'eɪpr(ɪ)l, -z
AM 'eɪprəl, -z

a priori
BR ˌeɪ prʌɪ'ɔːrʌɪ, ˌɑː +, + prʌɪ'ɔːri, + prɪ'ɔːri

AM ˌɑ priˈɔri, ˌeɪ priˈɔri

apriorism
BR (ˌ)eɪˈprʌɪərɪz(ə)m
AM eɪˈpraɪəˌrɪzəm

aprioristic
BR ˌeɪprʌɪəˈrɪstɪk
AM ˌeɪˌpraɪəˈrɪstɪk

aprioristically
BR ˌeɪprʌɪəˈrɪstɪkli
AM ˌeɪˌpraɪəˈrɪstɪk(ə)li

apron
BR ˈeɪpr(ə)n, -z, -d
AM ˈeɪprən, -z, -d

apronful
BR ˈeɪpr(ə)nfʊl, -z
AM ˈeɪprənˌfʊl, -z

apropos
BR ˌaprəˈpəʊ, ˈaprəpəʊ
AM ˌæprəˈpoʊ

apse
BR aps, -ɪz
AM æps, -əz

apsidal
BR ˈapsɪdl
AM ˈæpsədəl

apsides
BR ˈapsɪdiːz
AM ˈæpsəˌdiz

apsis
BR ˈapsɪs
AM ˈæpsəs

Apsley
BR ˈapsli
AM ˈæpsli

apt
BR apt, -ə(r), -ɪst
AM æpt, -ər, -əst

Apted
BR ˈaptɪd
AM ˈæptəd

apterous
BR ˈapt(ə)rəs
AM ˈæptərəs

apteryx
BR ˈapt(ə)rɪks, -ɪz
AM ˈæptərɪks, -ɪz

aptitude
BR ˈaptɪtjuːd, ˈaptɪtʃuːd, -z
AM ˈæptəˌt(j)ud, -z

aptly
BR ˈaptli
AM ˈæp(t)li

aptness
BR ˈap(t)nəs
AM ˈæp(t)nəs

Apuleius
BR ˌapjʉˈliːəs, ˌapjʉˈleɪəs
AM ˌapjəˈliəs

Apulia
BR əˈpjuːlɪə(r)
AM əˈpjuljə, əˈpjuliə

Aqaba
BR ˈakəbə(r), ˈakəbɑː(r)
AM ˈɑkəˌbɑ

aqua
BR ˈakwə(r)
AM ˈɑkwə, ˈækwə

aquaculture
BR ˈakwəˌkʌltʃə(r)
AM ˈɑkwəˌkəltʃər, ˈækwəˌkəltʃər

aqua fortis
BR ˌakwə ˈfɔːtɪs
AM ˌɑkwə ˈfɔrdəs, ˌækwə +

Aqua Libra®
BR ˌakwə ˈliːbrə(r)
AM ˌɑkwə ˈlɪbrə, ˌækwə +

aqualung
BR ˈakwəlʌŋ, -z
AM ˈɑkwəˌləŋ, ˈækwəˌləŋ, -z

aquamarine
BR ˌakwəməˈriːn, -z
AM ˌɑkwəməˈrin, ˌækwəməˈrin, -z

aquanaut
BR ˈakwənɔːt, -s
AM ˈɑkwəˌnɔt, ˈækwəˌnɔt, ˈɑkwəˌnɑt, ˈækwəˌnɑt, -s

aquaphobia
BR ˌakwəˈfəʊbɪə(r)
AM ˌɑkwəˈfoʊbiə, ˌækwəˈfoʊbiə

aquaplane
BR ˈakwəpleɪn, -z, -ɪŋ, -d
AM ˈɑkwəˌpleɪn, ˈækwəˌpleɪn, -z, -ɪŋ, -d

aqua regia
BR ˌakwə ˈrɛdʒɪə(r)
AM ˌɑkwə ˈrɛdʒiə, ˌækwə +

aquarelle
BR ˌakwəˈrɛl, -z
AM ˌɑk(w)əˈrɛl, ˌæk(w)əˈrɛl, -z

aquaria
BR əˈkwɛːrɪə(r)
AM əˈkwɛriə

Aquarian
BR əˈkwɛːrɪən, -z
AM əˈkwɛriən, -z

aquarist
BR ˈakwərɪst, -s
AM əˈkwɛrəst, -s

aquarium
BR əˈkwɛːrɪəm, -z
AM əˈkwɛriəm, -z

Aquarius
BR əˈkwɛːrɪəs
AM əˈkwɛriəs

Aquarobics®
BR ˌakwəˈrəʊbɪks
AM ˌɑkwəˈroʊbɪks, ˌækwəˈroʊbɪks

Aquascutum®
BR ˌakwəˈskjuːtəm
AM ˌɑkwəˈskjudəm, ˌækwəˈskjudəm

aquatic
BR əˈkwatɪk, -s
AM əˈkwɑdɪk, əˈkwædɪk, -s

aquatint
BR ˈakwətɪnt, -s
AM ˈɑkwəˌtɪnt, ˈækwəˌtɪnt, -s

aquavit
BR ˈakwəvɪt, ˈakwəviːt
AM ˈɑkwəˌvit, ˈækwəˌvit

aqua vitae
BR ˌakwə ˈviːtʌɪ, ˈvʌɪtiː
AM ˌɑkwə ˈvaɪdi, ˌækwə +, + ˈviˌtaɪ

aqueduct
BR ˈakwɪdʌkt, -s
AM ˈɑkwəˌdək|(t), ˈækwəˌdək|(t), -(t)s

aqueous
BR ˈakwɪəs, ˈeɪkwɪəs
AM ˈɑkwiəs, ˈeɪkwiəs, ˈækwiəs

aqueously
BR ˈakwɪəsli, ˈeɪkwɪəsli
AM ˈɑkwiəsli, ˈeɪkwiəsli, ˈækwiəsli

aquiculture
BR ˈakwɪˌkʌltʃə(r)
AM ˈɑkwəˌkəltʃər, ˈækwəˌkəltʃər

aquifer
BR ˈakwɪfə(r), -z
AM ˈɑkwəfər, ˈækwəfər, -z

Aquila
BR əˈkwɪlə(r)
AM əˈk(w)ɪlə, ˈækwələ

aquilegia
BR ˌakwɪˈliːdʒ(ɪ)ə(r), -z
AM ˌækwəˈlidʒ(i)ə, -z

aquiline
BR ˈakwɪlʌɪn
AM ˈækwəˌlaɪn, ˈækwələn

Aquinas
BR əˈkwʌɪnəs
AM əˈkwaɪnəs

Aquitaine
BR ˈakwɪteɪn
AM ˈækwəˌteɪn
FR akitɛn

Aquitania
BR ˌakwɪˈteɪnɪə(r)
AM ˌækwəˈteɪniə

aquiver
BR əˈkwɪvə(r)
AM əˈkwɪvər

Arab
BR ˈarəb, -z
AM ˈɛrəb, -z

Arabella
BR ˌarəˈbɛlə(r)
AM ˌɛrəˈbɛlə

arabesque
BR ˌarəˈbɛsk, -s
AM ˌɛrəˈbɛsk, -s

Arabia
BR əˈreɪbɪə(r)
AM əˈreɪbiə

Arabian
BR əˈreɪbɪən, -z
AM əˈreɪbjən, -z

Arabic
BR ˈarəbɪk
AM ˈɛrəbɪk

Arabicism
BR əˈrabɪsɪz(ə)m, -z
AM əˈræbəˌsɪzəm, -z

arabinose
BR əˈrabɪnəʊz, əˈrabɪnəʊs
AM əˈræbəˌnoʊs, əˈræbəˌnoʊz

arabis
BR ˈarəbɪs
AM ˈɛrəbəs

Arabism
BR ˈarəbɪz(ə)m
AM ˈɛrəˌbɪzəm

Arabist
BR ˈarəbɪst, -s
AM ˈɛrəbəst, -s

arable
BR ˈarəbl
AM ˈɛrəbəl

Araby
BR ˈarəbi
AM ˈɛrəbi

Arachne
BR əˈrakni
AM əˈrækni

arachnid
BR əˈraknɪd, -z
AM əˈræknəd, -z

arachnida
BR əˈraknɪdə(r)
AM əˈræknədə

arachnidae
BR əˈraknɪdiː
AM əˈræknəˌdi, əˈræknəˌdaɪ, əˈræknəˌdeɪ

arachnidan
BR əˈraknɪd(ə)n, -z
AM əˈræknədən, -z

arachnoid
BR əˈraknɔɪd, -z
AM əˈrækˌnɔɪd, -z

arachnologist
BR ˌarəkˈnɒlədʒɪst, -s
AM ˌɛˌrækˈnɑlədʒəst, -s

arachnology
BR ˌarəkˈnɒlədʒi
AM ˌɛˌrækˈnɑlədʒi

Arafat
BR ˈarəfat
AM ˈɛrəˌfæt

Arafura
BR ˌarəˈf(j)ʊərə(r), ˌarəˈfjɔːrə(r)
AM ˌɛrəˈf(j)ʊrə

Aragon
BR ˈarəg(ə)n
AM ˈɛrəˌgɑn

arak
BR ˈarək
AM ˈɛrək, ˈɛˌræk

Arakan
BR ˌarəˈkan
AM ˌɛrəˈkɑn

Aral
BR ˈarəl, ˈarḷ
AM ˈɛrəl

Araldite®
BR ˈarəldʌɪt, ˈarḷdʌɪt
AM ˈɛrəlˌdaɪt

Aramaic
BR ˌarəˈmeɪɪk
AM ˌɛrəˈmeɪɪk

Araminta
BR ˌarəˈmɪntə(r)
AM ˌɛrəˈmɪn(t)ə

Aran
BR ˈarən, ˈarṇ
AM ˈɛrən

Aranda
BR əˈrandə(r), -z
AM əˈrændə, -z

Arapaho
BR əˈrapəhəʊ
AM əˈræpəˌhoʊ

arapaima
BR ˌarəˈpʌɪmə(r), -z
AM ˌɛrəˈpaɪmə, -z

Ararat
BR ˈarərat
AM ˈɛrəˌræt

arational
BR eɪˈraʃṇ(ə)l, eɪˈraʃən(ə)l
AM eɪˈræʃənl, eɪˈræʃnəl

Araucanian
BR ˌarɔːˈkeɪnɪən, -z
AM ˌɛˌrɔˈkeɪniən, ˌɛˌrɑˈkeɪniən, -z

araucaria
BR ˌarɔːˈkɛːrɪə(r), ˌarəˈkɛːrɪə(r), -z
AM ˌɛˌrɔˈkɛriə, ˌɛˌrɑˈkɛriə, -z

Arawak
BR ˈarəwak
AM ˈɛrəˌwɑk

arb
BR ɑːb, -z
AM ɑrb, -z

arbalest
BR ˈɑːbəlɪst, ˈɑːbḷɪst, ˈɑːbəlɛst, ˈɑːbḷɛst, -s
AM ˈɑrbələst, ˈɑrbəˌlɛst, -s

arbiter
BR ˈɑːbɨtə(r), -z
AM ˈɑrbədər, -z

arbitrage
BR ˈɑːbɨtrɑːʒ, ˌɑːbɨˈtrɑːʒ
AM ˈɑrbəˌtrɑʒ

arbitrager
BR ˈɑːbɨtrɑːʒə(r), ˌɑːbɨˈtrɑːʒə(r), -z
AM ˈɑrbəˌtrɑʒər, -z

arbitrageur
BR ˌɑːbɨtrɑːˈʒəː(r), -z
AM ˌɑrbəˌtrɑˈʒər, -z

arbitral
BR ˈɑːbɨtr(ə)l
AM ˈɑrbətrəl

arbitrament
BR ɑːˈbɪtrəm(ə)nt, -s
AM ɑrˈbɪtrəmənt, -s

arbitrarily
BR ˈɑːbɨt(rə)rɨli, ˌɑːbɨˈtrɛrɨli
AM ˌɑrbəˈtrɛrəli

arbitrariness
BR ˈɑːbɨt(rə)rɪnɪs
AM ˌɑrbəˈtrɛrinɪs

arbitrary
BR ˈɑːbɨt(rə)ri
AM ˈɑrbəˌtrɛri

arbitrate
BR ˈɑːbɨtreɪt, -s, -ɪŋ, -ɨd
AM ˈɑrbəˌtreɪ|t, -ts, -dɪŋ, -dɨd

arbitration
BR ˌɑːbɨˈtreɪʃn
AM ˌɑrbəˈtreɪʃən

arbitrator
BR ˈɑːbɨtreɪtə(r), -z
AM ˈɑrbəˌtreɪdər, -z

arbitratorship
BR ˈɑːbɨtreɪtəʃɪp, -s
AM ˈɑrbəˌtreɪdərˌʃɪp, -s

arbitress
BR ˈɑːbətrɪs, -ɨz
AM ˈɑrbətrəs, -əz

arblast
BR ˈɑːblɑːst, ˈɑːblast, -s
AM ˈɑrˌblæst, -s

arbor
BR ˈɑːbə(r), -z, -d
AM ˈɑrbər, -z, -d

arboraceous
BR ˌɑːbəˈreɪʃəs
AM ˌɑrbəˈreɪʃəs

arboreal
BR ɑːˈbɔːrɪəl
AM ɑrˈbɔriəl

arboreous
BR ɑːˈbɔːrɪəs
AM ɑrˈbɔriəs

arborescence
BR ˌɑːbəˈrɛsns
AM ˌɑrbəˈrɛsəns

arborescent
BR ˌɑːbəˈrɛsnt
AM ˌɑrbəˈrɛsənt

arboreta
BR ˌɑːbəˈriːtə(r)
AM ˌɑrbəˈridə

arboretum
BR ˌɑːbəˈriːtəm, -z
AM ˌɑrbəˈridəm, -z

arboricultural
BR ɑːˌbɔːrɨˈkʌltʃ(ə)rəl, ɑːˌbɔːrɨˈkʌltʃ(ə)rḷ, ˌɑːb(ə)rɨˈkʌltʃ(ə)rəl, ˌɑːb(ə)rɨˈkʌltʃ(ə)rḷ
AM ˌɑrbərəˈkəltʃ(ə)rəl, ɑrˈbɔrəˌkəltʃ(ə)rəl

arboriculture
BR ˈɑːb(ə)rɨˌkʌltʃə(r), ɑːˈbɔːrɨˌkʌltʃə(r)
AM ˈɑrbərəˌkəltʃər, ɑrˈbɔrəˌkəltʃər

arboriculturist
BR ɑːˌbɔːrɨˈkʌltʃ(ə)rɪst, ˌɑːb(ə)rɨˈkʌltʃ(ə)rɪst, -s
AM ˌɑrbərəˈkəltʃ(ə)rəst, ɑrˈbɔrəˌkəltʃ(ə)rəst, -s

arborisation
BR ˌɑːb(ə)rʌɪˈzeɪʃn
AM ˌɑrbərəˈzeɪʃən, ˌɑrbəˌraɪˈzeɪʃən

arborization
BR ˌɑːb(ə)rʌɪˈzeɪʃn
AM ˌɑrbərəˈzeɪʃən, ˌɑrbəˌraɪˈzeɪʃən

arbor vitae
BR ˌɑːbə ˈvʌɪtiː, + ˈviːtʌɪ
AM ˌɑrbər ˈvaɪdi, + ˈviˌtaɪ

arbour
BR ˈɑːbə(r), -z, -d
AM ˈɑrbər, -z, -d

Arbus
BR ˈɑːbəs
AM ˈɑrbəs

Arbuthnot
BR ɑːˈbʌθnət, ɑːˈbʌθnɒt
AM ˈɑrbəθnət, ˈɑrbəθˌnɑt

arbutus
BR ɑːˈbjuːtəs, -ɨz
AM ɑrˈbjudəs, -əz

arc
BR ɑːk, -s, -ɪŋ, -t
AM ɑrk, -s, -ɪŋ, -t

arcade
BR ɑːˈkeɪd, -z, -ɨd
AM ɑrˈkeɪd, -z, -ɨd

Arcadia
BR ɑːˈkeɪdɪə(r)
AM ɑrˈkeɪdiə

Arcadian
BR ɑːˈkeɪdɪən, -z
AM ɑrˈkeɪdiən, -z

Arcadianism
BR ɑːˈkeɪdɪənɪz(ə)m
AM ɑrˈkeɪdiəˌnɪzəm

arcading
BR ɑːˈkeɪdɪŋ
AM ɑrˈkeɪdɪŋ

Arcady
BR ˈɑːkədi
AM ˈɑrkədi

arcana
BR ɑːˈkeɪnə(r), ɑːˈkɑːnə(r)
AM ɑrˈkeɪnə

arcane
BR ɑːˈkeɪn
AM ɑrˈkeɪn

arcanely
BR ɑːˈkeɪnli
AM ɑrˈkeɪnli

arcanum
BR ɑːˈkeɪnəm
AM ɑrˈkeɪnəm

Arc de Triomphe
BR ˌɑːk də ˈtrɪɒmf
AM ˈɑrk də ˌtriˈɔnf

arch
BR ɑːtʃ, -ɨz, -ɪŋ, -t, -ə(r), -ɨst
AM ɑrtʃ, -əz, -ɪŋ, -t, -ər, -əst

Archaean
BR ɑːˈkiːən, -z
AM ɑrˈkiən, -z

archaeologic
BR ˌɑːkɪəˈlɒdʒɪk
AM ˌɑrkiəˈlɑdʒɪk

archaeological
BR ˌɑːkɪəˈlɒdʒɨkl
AM ˌɑrkiəˈlɑdʒəkəl

archaeologically
BR ˌɑːkɪəˈlɒdʒɨkli
AM ˌɑrkiəˈlɑdʒək(ə)li

archaeologise
BR ˌɑːkɪˈɒlədʒʌɪz, -ɨz, -ɪŋ, -d
AM ˌɑrkiˈɑləˌdʒaɪz, -ɨz, -ɪŋ, -d

archaeologist
BR ˌɑːkɪˈɒlədʒɪst, -s
AM ˌɑrkiˈɑlədʒəst, -s

archaeologize
BR ˌɑːkɪˈɒlədʒʌɪz, -ɨz, -ɪŋ, -d
AM ˌɑrkiˈɑləˌdʒaɪz, -ɨz, -ɪŋ, -d

archaeology
BR ˌɑːkɪˈɒlədʒi
AM ˌɑrkiˈɑlədʒi

archaeopteryx
BR ˌɑːkɪˈɒpt(ə)r|ɪks, -ɪksɪz
AM ˌɑrkiˈɑptərɪks, -ɨz

archaic
BR ɑːˈkeɪɪk
AM ɑrˈkeɪɪk

archaically
BR ɑːˈkeɪɪkli
AM ɑrˈkeɪɪk(ə)li

archaise
BR ˈɑːkeɪʌɪz, ˈɑːkɪʌɪz, -ɨz, -ɪŋ, -d
AM ˈɑrkiˌaɪz, ˈɑrkeɪˌaɪz, -ɨz, -ɪŋ, -d

archaism
BR ˈɑːkeɪɪz(ə)m, -z
AM ˈɑrkiˌɪzəm, ˈɑrkeɪˌɪzəm, -z

archaist
BR ˈɑːkeɪɪst, -s
AM ˈɑrkiɨst, ˈɑrkeɪɨst, -s

archaistic
BR ˌɑːkeɪˈɪstɪk
AM ˌɑrkiˈɪstɪk, ˌɑrkeɪˈɪstɪk

archaistically
BR ˌɑːkeɪˈɪstɨkli
AM ˌɑrkiˈɪstɨk(ə)li, ˌɑrkeɪˈɪstɨk(ə)li

archaize
BR ˈɑːkeɪʌɪz, ˈɑːkɪʌɪz, -ɨz, -ɪŋ, -d
AM ˈɑrkiˌaɪz, ˈɑrkeɪˌaɪz, -ɨz, -ɪŋ, -d

archangel
BR ˈɑːkeɪn(d)ʒ(ə)l, ˌɑːkˈeɪn(d)ʒ(ə)l, -z
AM ˈɑrkˌeɪndʒəl, -z

archangelic
BR ˌɑːkanˈdʒɛlɪk
AM ˌɑrkˌænˈdʒɛlɪk

archbishop
BR (ˌ)ɑːtʃˈbɪʃəp, -s
AM ˌɑrtʃˈbɪʃəp, -s

archbishopric
BR (ˌ)ɑːtʃˈbɪʃəprɪk, -s
AM ˌɑrtʃˈbɪʃəprɪk, -s

archdeacon
BR (ˌ)ɑːtʃˈdiːk(ə)n, -z
AM ˌɑrtʃˈdikən, -z

archdeaconry
BR ˌɑːtʃˈdiːk(ə)nr|i, -ɪz
AM ˌɑrtʃˈdikənri, -z

archdeaconship
BR ˌɑːtʃˈdiːk(ə)nʃɪp, -s
AM ˌɑrtʃˈdikənˌʃɪp, -s

archdiocesan
BR ˌɑːtʃdʌɪˈɒsɪsn
AM ˌɑrtʃˌdaɪˈɑsəsən

archdiocese
BR ˌɑːtʃˈdʌɪəsɪs, -ɪz
AM ˌɑrtʃˈdaɪəsɨs, ˌɑrtʃˈdaɪəˌsiz, -ɪz

archducal
BR ˌɑːtʃˈdjuːkl, ˌɑːtʃˈdʒuːkl
AM ˌɑrtʃˈd(j)ukəl

archduchess
BR ˌɑːtʃˈdʌtʃɪs, -ɪz
AM ˌɑrtʃˈdətʃəs, -əz

archduchy
BR ˌɑːtʃˈdʌtʃ|i, -ɪz
AM ˌɑrtʃˈdətʃi, -z

archduke
BR ˌɑːtʃˈdjuːk, ˌɑːtʃˈdʒuːk, -s
AM ˌɑrtʃˈd(j)uk, -s

archdukedom
BR ˌɑːtʃˈdjuːkdəm, ˌɑːtʃˈdʒuːkdəm, -z
AM ˌɑrtʃˈd(j)ukdəm, -z

archegonia
BR ˌɑːkɨˈɡəʊnɪə(*r*)
AM ˌɑrkəˈɡoʊniə

archegonium
BR ˌɑːkɨˈɡəʊnɪəm
AM ˌɑrkəˈɡoʊniəm

Archelaus
BR ˌɑːkɨˈleɪəs
AM ˌɑrkəˈleɪəs

arch-enemy
BR ˌɑːtʃˈɛnɨm|i, -ɪz
AM ˌɑrˈtʃɛnəmi, -z

archeologic
BR ˌɑːkɪəˈlɒdʒɪk
AM ˌɑrkiəˈlɑdʒɪk

archeological
BR ˌɑːkɪəˈlɒdʒɨkl
AM ˌɑrkiəˈlɑdʒəkəl

archeologically
BR ˌɑːkɪəˈlɒdʒɨkli
AM ˌɑrkiəˈlɑdʒək(ə)li

archeologist
BR ˌɑːkɪˈɒlədʒɪst, -s
AM ˌɑrkiˈɑlədʒəst, -s

archeologize
BR ˌɑːkɪˈɒlədʒʌɪz, -ɨz, -ɪŋ, -d
AM ˌɑrkiˈɑləˌdʒaɪz, -ɨz, -ɪŋ, -d

archeology
BR ˌɑːkɪˈɒlədʒi
AM ˌɑrkiˈɑlədʒi

archeopteryx
BR ˌɑːkɪˈɒpt(ə)r|ɪks, -ɨksɪz
AM ˌɑrkiˈɑptərɪks, -ɪz

archer
BR ˈɑːtʃə(r), -z
AM ˈɑrtʃər, -z

archery
BR ˈɑːtʃ(ə)ri
AM ˈɑrtʃ(ə)ri

archetypal
BR ˌɑːkɨˈtʌɪpl, ˈɑːkɨˌtʌɪpl
AM ˈɑrk(ə)ˈtaɪpəl

archetypally
BR ˌɑːkɨˈtʌɪpl̩i, ˌɑːkɨˈtʌɪpəli, ˈɑːkɨˌtʌɪpl̩i, ˈɑːkɨˌtʌɪpəli
AM ˈɑrk(ə)ˈtaɪpəli

archetype
BR ˈɑːkɨtʌɪp, -s
AM ˈɑrk(ə)ˌtaɪp, -s

archetypical
BR ˌɑːkɨˈtɪpɨkl
AM ˌɑrk(ə)ˈtɪpɨkəl

archetypically
BR ˌɑːkɨˈtɪpɨkli
AM ˌɑrk(ə)ˈtɪpɨk(ə)li

Archibald
BR ˈɑːtʃɨbɔːld, ˈɑːtʃɪb(ə)ld
AM ˈɑrtʃəˌbɔld, ˈɑrtʃəˌbɑld

archidiaconal
BR ˌɑːkɪdʌɪˈakənl, ˌɑːkɪdʌɪˈakn̩l
AM ˌɑrkəˌdaɪˈækənəl, ˌɑrkəˌdiˈækənəl

archidiaconate
BR ˌɑːkɪdʌɪˈakəneɪt, ˌɑːkɪdʌɪˈakənɨt, ˌɑːkɪdʌɪˈakn̩eɪt, ˌɑːkɪdʌɪˈakn̩ɨt, ˌɑːkɪdɪˈakəneɪt, ˌɑːkɪdɪˈakənɨt, ˌɑːkɪdɪˈakn̩eɪt, ˌɑːkɪdɪˈakn̩ɨt, -s
AM ˌɑrkəˌdaɪˈækənət, ˌɑrkəˌdiˈækənət, -s

Archie
BR ˈɑːtʃi
AM ˈɑrtʃi

archiepiscopacy
BR ˌɑːkɪɪˈpɪskəpəs|i, -ɪz
AM ˌɑrkiəˈpɪskəpəsi, -z

archiepiscopal
BR ˌɑːkɪɪˈpɪskəpl
AM ˌɑrkiəˈpɪskəpəl

archiepiscopate
BR ˌɑːkɪɪˈpɪskəpət, -s
AM ˌɑrkiəˈpɪskəpət, -s

archil
BR ˈɑːkɪl, ˈɑːtʃɪl, -z
AM ˈɑrtʃəl, -z

Archilochus
BR ˌɑːkɨˈləʊkəs
AM ˌɑrkəˈloʊkəs

archimandrite
BR ˌɑːkɨˈmandrʌɪt, -s
AM ˌɑrkəˈmænˌdraɪt, -s

Archimedean
BR ˌɑːkɨˈmiːdɪən, -z
AM ˌɑrkəˈmidiən, -z

Archimedes
BR ˌɑːkɨˈmiːdiːz
AM ˌɑrkəˈmidiz

archipelago
BR ˌɑːkɨˈpɛlɨɡəʊ, -z
AM ˌɑrkəˈpɛləˌɡoʊ, ˌɑrtʃəˈpɛləˌɡoʊ, -z

architect
BR ˈɑːkɨtɛkt, -s
AM ˈɑrkəˌtɛk|(t), -(t)s

architectonic
BR ˌɑːkɨtɛkˈtɒnɪk, -s
AM ˈɑrkəˌtɛkˈtɑnɪk, -s

architectural
BR ˌɑːkɨˈtɛktʃ(ə)rəl, ˌɑːkɨˈtɛktʃ(ə)rl̩
AM ˌɑrkəˈtɛk(t)ʃ(ə)rəl

architecturally
BR ˌɑːkɨˈtɛktʃ(ə)rəli, ˌɑːkɨˈtɛktʃ(ə)rl̩i
AM ˌɑrkəˈtɛk(t)ʃ(ə)rəli

architecture
BR ˈɑːkɨtɛktʃə(r)
AM ˈɑrkəˌtɛk(t)ʃər

architrave
BR ˈɑːkɨtreɪv, -z
AM ˈɑrkəˌtreɪv, -z

archival
BR ˈɑːkʌɪvl, ɑːˈkʌɪvl
AM ɑrˈkaɪvəl

archive
BR ˈɑːkʌɪv, -z, -ɪŋ, -d
AM ˈɑrˌkaɪv, -z, -ɪŋ, -d

archivist
BR ˈɑːkɨvɪst, -s
AM ˈɑrkəvəst, ˈɑrˌkaɪvɨst, -s

archivolt
BR ˈɑːkɨvəʊlt, -s
AM ˈɑrkəˌvoʊlt, -s

archlute
BR ˈɑːtʃl(j)uːt, -s
AM ˈɑrtʃˌlut, -s

archly
BR ˈɑːtʃli
AM ˈɑrtʃli

archness
BR ˈɑːtʃnəs
AM ˈɑrtʃnəs

archon
BR ˈɑːkɒn, ˈɑːk(ə)n, -z
AM ˈɑrˌkɑn, -z

archonship
BR ˈɑːkɒnʃɪp, ˈɑːk(ə)nʃɪp, -s
AM ˈɑrˌkɑnˌʃɪp, -s

archpriest
BR ˌɑːtʃˈpriːst, -s
AM ˌɑrtʃˈprist, -s

arch-rival
BR ˌɑːtʃˈrʌɪvl, -z
AM ˌɑrtʃˈraɪvəl, -z

archway
BR ˈɑːtʃweɪ, -z
AM ˈɑrtʃˌweɪ, -z

Archy
BR ˈɑːtʃi
AM ˈɑrtʃi

Arco
BR ˈɑːkəʊ
AM ˈɑrkoʊ

arctic
BR ˈɑːktɪk
AM ˈɑrktɪk, ˈɑrdɪk

Arcturus
BR ɑːkˈtjʊərəs
AM ˌɑrkˈt(j)ʊrəs

arcuate[1]
adjective
BR ˈɑːkjʊət
AM ˈɑrkjəwət, ˈɑrkjəˌweɪt

arcuate[2]
verb
BR ˈɑːkjʊeɪt, -s, -ɪŋ, -ɨd
AM ˈɑrkjəˌweɪ|t, -ts, -dɪŋ, -dɨd

arcus senilis
BR ˌɑːkəs sɪˈnʌɪlɪs
AM ˌɑrkəs səˈnilɨs

Ardagh
BR ˈɑːdə(*r*), ˈɑːdɑː(*r*)
AM ˈɑrdɔ

Ardèche
BR ɑːˈdɛʃ
AM ɑrˈdɛʃ
Arden
BR ˈɑːdn
AM ˈɑrdən
ardency
BR ˈɑːdnsi
AM ˈɑrdnsi
Ardennes
BR ɑːˈdɛn(z)
AM ɑrˈdɛn(z)
ardent
BR ˈɑːdnt
AM ˈɑrdnt
ardently
BR ˈɑːdntli
AM ˈɑrdn(t)li
Ardizzone
BR ˌɑːdɪˈzəʊni
AM ˌɑrdɪˈzoʊni
Ardmore
BR ɑːdˈmɔː(r)
AM ˈɑrdmɔ(ə)r
Ardnamurchan
BR ˌɑːdnəˈməːk(ə)n
AM ˌɑrdnəˈmərtʃən
ardor
BR ˈɑːdə(r), -z
AM ˈɑrdər, -z
ardour
BR ˈɑːdə(r), -z
AM ˈɑrdər, -z
Ardoyne
BR ɑːˈdɔɪn
AM ɑrˈdɔɪn
Ardrossan
BR ɑːˈdrɒsn
AM ˈɑrdrɔsən, ˈɑrdrɑsən
Ards
BR ɑːdz
AM ɑrdz
arduous
BR ˈɑːdjʊəs, ˈɑːdʒʊəs
AM ˈɑrdʒəwəs
arduously
BR ˈɑːdjʊəsli, ˈɑːdʒʊəsli
AM ˈɑrdʒəwəsli
arduousness
BR ˈɑːdjʊəsnəs, ˈɑːdʒʊəsnəs
AM ˈɑrdʒəwəsnəs
are[1]
strong form
BR ɑː(r)
AM ɑr
are[2]
unit
BR ɑː(r), -z
AM ɑr, -z
are[3]
weak form
BR ə(r)
AM ər
area
BR ˈɛːrɪə(r), -z
AM ˈɛriə, -z
areal
BR ˈɛːrɪəl
AM ˈɛriəl
areaway
BR ˈɛːrɪəweɪ, -z
AM ˈɛriəˌweɪ, -z
areca
BR ˈarɪkə(r), əˈriːkə(r), -z
AM əˈrikə, ˈɛrəkə, -z
areg
BR ˈɑːrɛg, ˈarɛg
AM ˈɑˌrɛg
arena
BR əˈriːnə(r), -z
AM əˈrinə, -z
arenaceous
BR ˌarɪˈneɪʃəs
AM ˌarəˈneɪʃəs
Arendt
BR ˈɑːrənt
AM ˈarənt
Arenig
BR aˈrɛnɪg, əˈrɛnɪg
AM ˈɛrənɪg
aren't
BR ɑːnt
AM ˈɑr(ə)nt
areola
BR əˈriːələ(r), -z
AM əˈriələ, -z
areolae
BR əˈriːəliː
AM əˈriəˌli, əˈriəˌlaɪ
areolar
BR əˈriːələ(r)
AM əˈriələr
areometer
BR ˌɛːrɪˈɒmɪtə(r), ˌarɪˈɒmɪtə(r), -z
AM ˌɛriˈɑmədər, -z
Areopagi
BR ˌarɪˈɒpəgʌɪ
AM ˌɛriˈɑpəgaɪ
Areopagite
BR ˌarɪˈɒpəgʌɪt, -s
AM ˌærɪˈɑpəˌgaɪt, -s
Areopagitica
BR ˌarɪɒpəˈdʒɪtɪkə(r)
AM ˌæriˌɑpəˈdʒɪdɪkə
Areopagus
BR ˌarɪˈɒpəgəs
AM ˌɛriˈɑpəgəs
Arequipa
BR ˌarɪˈk(w)iːpə(r)
AM ˌɛrəˈk(w)ipə
Ares
BR ˈɛːriːz
AM ˈɛriz
arête
BR əˈrɛt, aˈrɛt, -s
AM əˈreɪt, -s
Aretha
BR əˈriːθə(r)
AM əˈriθə
Arethusa
BR ˌarɪˈθjuːzə(r)
AM ˌɛrəˈθuzə
Arfon
BR ˈɑːv(ɒ)n
AM ˈɑrfən
WE ˈarvɒn
argala
BR ˈɑːgələ(r), ˈɑːgl̩ə(r), -z
AM ˈɑrgələ, -z
argali
BR ˈɑːgəli, ˈɑːgl̩i
AM ˈɑrgəli
argent
BR ˈɑːdʒ(ə)nt
AM ˈɑrdʒənt
argentiferous
BR ˌɑːdʒ(ə)nˈtɪf(ə)rəs
AM ˌɑrdʒənˈtɪf(ə)rəs
Argentina
BR ˌɑːdʒ(ə)nˈtiːnə(r)
AM ˌɑrdʒənˈtinə
SP ˌarxenˈtina
Argentine
BR ˈɑːdʒ(ə)ntʌɪn, ˈɑːdʒ(ə)ntiːn
AM ˈɑrdʒənˌtin, ˈɑrdʒənˌtaɪn
Argentinian
BR ˌɑːdʒ(ə)nˈtɪnɪən, -z
AM ˌɑrdʒənˈtɪniən, -z
Argie
BR ˈɑːdʒi, -ɪz
AM ˈɑrdʒi, -z
argil
BR ˈɑːdʒɪl
AM ˈɑrdʒəl
argilaceous
BR ˌɑːdʒɪˈleɪʃəs
AM ˌɑrdʒəˈleɪʃəs
argillaceous
BR ˌɑːdʒɪˈleɪʃəs
AM ˌɑrdʒəˈleɪʃəs
arginine
BR ˈɑːdʒɪniːn, ˈɑːdʒɪnʌɪn
AM ˈɑrdʒəˌnin, ˈɑrdʒəˌnaɪn
Argive
BR ˈɑːgʌɪv, ˈɑːdʒʌɪv
AM ˈɑrˌgaɪv
argle-bargle
BR ˌɑːglˈbɑːgl
AM ˈɑrgəlˈbɑrgəl
Argo
BR ˈɑːgəʊ
AM ˈɑrgoʊ
argol
BR ˈɑːgɒl, -z
AM ˈɑrgəl, -z
argon
BR ˈɑːgɒn, ˈɑːg(ə)n
AM ˈɑrˌgɑn
Argonaut
BR ˈɑːgənɔːt, -s
AM ˈɑrgəˌnɔt, ˈɑrgəˌnɑt, -s
Argos
BR ˈɑːgɒs
AM ˈɑrgəs, ˈɑrgɔs, ˈɑrgɑs
argosy
BR ˈɑːgəs|i, -ɪz
AM ˈɑrgəsi, -z
argot
BR ˈɑːgəʊ, -z
AM ɑrˈgoʊ, ˈɑrgət, -z
arguable
BR ˈɑːgjʊəbl
AM ˈɑrgjəwəbəl
arguably
BR ˈɑːgjʊəbli
AM ˈɑrgjəwəbli
argue
BR ˈɑːgjuː, -z, -ɪŋ, -d
AM ˈɑrgju, -z, -ɪŋ, -d
arguer
BR ˈɑːgjʊə(r), -z
AM ˈɑrgjəwər, -z
argufy
BR ˈɑːgjʉfʌɪ, -z, -ɪŋ, -d
AM ˈɑrgjəˌfaɪ, -z, -ɪŋ, -d
argument
BR ˈɑːgjʉm(ə)nt, -s
AM ˈɑrgjəmənt, -s
argumental
BR ˌɑːgjʉˈmɛntl
AM ˌɑrgjəˈmɛn(t)l
argumentation
BR ˌɑːgjʉmɛnˈteɪʃn, ˌɑːgjʉm(ə)nˈteɪʃn
AM ˌɑrgjəmənˈteɪʃən, ˌɑrgjəˌmɛnˈteɪʃən
argumentative
BR ˌɑːgjʉˈmɛntətɪv
AM ˌɑrgjəˈmɛn(t)ədɪv
argumentatively
BR ˌɑːgjʉˈmɛntətɪvli
AM ˌɑrgjəˈmɛn(t)ədɪvli
argumentativeness
BR ˌɑːgjʉˈmɛntətɪvnɪs
AM ˌɑrgjəˈmɛn(t)ədɪvnɪs
argumentum e silencio
BR ɑːgjʉˌmɛntəm eɪ sɪˈlɛntiəʊ, + sɪˈlɛnʃɪəʊ
AM ˌɑrgəˈmɛn(t)əm eɪ sɪˈlɛnsioʊ
Argus
BR ˈɑːgəs, -ɪz
AM ˈɑrgəs, -əz
argute
BR ɑːˈgjuːt
AM ɑrˈgjut
argutely
BR ɑːˈgjuːtli
AM ɑrˈgjutli
argy-bargy
BR ˌɑːdʒɪˈbɑːdʒi
AM ˈɑrdʒiˈbɑrdʒi

Argyle
BR ɑːˈgʌɪl
AM ˈɑrˌgaɪl
Argyll
BR ɑːˈgʌɪl
AM ˈɑrˌgaɪl
Argyllshire
BR ɑːˈgʌɪlʃ(ɪ)ə(r)
AM ˈɑrˌgaɪlˌʃɪ(ə)r
Århus
BR ˈɔːhuːs
AM ˈɔrˌ(h)us, ˈɑrˌ(h)us
DAN ˈɔːhuːˀs
aria
BR ˈɑːrɪə(r), -z
AM ˈɑriə, -z
Ariadne
BR ˌarɪˈadni
AM ˌɛriˈædni
Arian
BR ˈɛːrɪən, -z
AM ˈɛriən, -z
Ariane
BR ˌarɪˈan
AM ˌɛriˈæn
Arianism
BR ˈɛːrɪənɪz(ə)m
AM ˈɛriəˌnɪzəm
Arianna
BR ˌarɪˈanə(r)
AM ˌɛriˈænə
arid
BR ˈarɪd
AM ˈɛrəd
aridisol
BR əˈrɪdɪsɒl
AM əˈrɪdɪˌsɔl əˈrɪdɪˌsɑl
aridity
BR əˈrɪdɪti
AM əˈrɪdɪdi, ɛˈrɪdɪdi
aridly
BR ˈarɪdli
AM ˈɛrədli
aridness
BR ˈarɪdnɪs
AM ˈɛrədnəs
ariel
BR ˈɛːrɪəl, -z
AM ˈɛriəl, -z
Arielle
BR ˌarɪˈɛl
AM ˌɛriˈɛl
Aries
BR ˈɛːriːz
AM ˈɛˌriz, ˈeɪˌriz
arietta
BR ˌarɪˈɛtə(r)
AM ˌɑriˈɛdə, ˌɛriˈɛdə
aright
BR əˈrʌɪt
AM əˈraɪt
aril
BR ˈarɪl, ˈarl̩, -z
AM ˈɛrəl, -z
arillate
BR ˈarɪlət, ˈarɪleɪt
AM ˈɛrələt, ˈɛrəˌleɪt
Arimathaea
BR ˌarɪməˈθiːə(r)
AM ˌɛrəməˈθiə
Arimathea
BR ˌarɪməˈθiːə(r)
AM ˌɛrəməˈθiə
arioso
BR ˌarɪˈəʊzəʊ, ˌɑːrɪˈəʊzəʊ, ˌarɪˈəʊsəʊ, ˌɑːrɪˈəʊsəʊ, -z
AM ˌɑriˈoʊsoʊ, ˌɑriˈoʊzoʊ, -z
Ariosto
BR ˌarɪˈɒstəʊ
AM ˌɑriˈɑstoʊ
arise
BR əˈrʌɪz, -ɪz, -ɪŋ
AM əˈraɪz, -ɪz, -ɪŋ
arisen
BR əˈrɪzn
AM əˈrɪzn
arisings
BR əˈrʌɪzɪŋz
AM əˈraɪzɪŋz
Aristarchus
BR ˌarɪˈstɑːkəs
AM ˌɛrəˈstɑrkəs
Aristides
BR ˌarɪˈstʌɪdiːz
AM ˌɛrəˈstaɪdiz
Aristippus
BR ˌarɪˈstɪpəs
AM ˌɛrəˈstɪpəs
aristocracy
BR ˌarɪˈstɒkrəs|i, -ɪz
AM ˌɛrəˈstɑkrəsi, -z
aristocrat
BR ˈarɪstəkrat, əˈrɪstəkrat, -s
AM əˈrɪstəˌkræt, -s
aristocratic
BR ˌarɪstəˈkratɪk, əˌrɪstəˈkratɪk
AM əˌrɪstəˈkrædɪk
aristocratically
BR ˌarɪstəˈkratɪkli, əˌrɪstəˈkratɪkli
AM əˌrɪstəˈkrædək(ə)li
Aristophanes
BR ˌarɪˈstɒfəniːz, ˌarɪˈstɒfn̩iːz
AM ˌɛrəˈstɑfəniz
Aristotelian
BR ˌarɪstəˈtiːlɪən, -z
AM əˌrɪstəˈtil(i)jən, ˌɛrəstəˈtil(i)jən, -z
Aristotle
BR ˈarɪstɒtl
AM ˈɛrəsˌtɑdəl
Arita
BR əˈriːtə(r)
AM əˈridə
arithmetic[1]
adjective
BR ˌarɪθˈmɛtɪk
AM ˌɛrɪθˈmɛdɪk
arithmetic[2]
noun
BR əˈrɪθmətɪk
AM əˈrɪθməˌtɪk
arithmetical
BR ˌarɪθˈmɛtɪkl
AM ˌɛrɪθˈmɛdəkəl
arithmetically
BR ˌarɪθˈmɛtɪkli
AM ˌɛrɪθˈmɛdək(ə)li
arithmetician
BR ˌarɪθməˈtɪʃn, əˌrɪθməˈtɪʃn, -z
AM əˌrɪθməˈtɪʃən, -z
Arius
BR ˈɛːrɪəs, əˈrʌɪəs
AM ˈɛriəs, əˈraɪəs
Arizona
BR ˌarɪˈzəʊnə(r)
AM ˌɛrəˈzoʊnə
Arizonan
BR ˌarɪˈzəʊnən, -z
AM ˌɛrəˈzoʊnən, -z
ark
BR ɑːk, -s
AM ɑrk, -s
Arkansas
BR ˈɑːk(ə)nsɔː(r)
AM ˈɑrkənˌsɑ
arkose
BR ˈɑːkəʊs, ˈɑːkəʊz
AM ˈɑrˌkoʊs, ˈɑrˌkoʊz
Arkwright
BR ˈɑːkrʌɪt
AM ˈɑrkˌraɪt
Arlene
BR ˈɑːliːn
AM ɑrˈlin
Arles
BR ɑːl(z)
AM ˈɑr(ə)l(z)
Arlette
BR ɑːˈlɛt
AM ɑrˈlɛt
Arlington
BR ˈɑːlɪŋt(ə)n
AM ˈɑrlɪŋtən
arm
BR ɑːm, -z, -ɪŋ, -d
AM ɑrm, -z, -ɪŋ, -d
armada
BR ɑːˈmɑːdə(r), -z
AM ɑrˈmɑdə, -z
Armadale
BR ˈɑːmədeɪl
AM ˈɑrməˌdeɪl
armadillo
BR ˌɑːməˈdɪləʊ, -z
AM ˌɑrməˈdɪloʊ, -z
Armageddon
BR ˌɑːməˈgɛdn
AM ˌɑrməˈgɛdən
Armagh
BR ˌɑːˈmɑː(r)
AM ɑrˈmɑ
Armagnac
BR ˈɑːmənjak, -s
AM ˈɑrmənˌjæk, -s
Armalite®
BR ˈɑːməlʌɪt, -s
AM ˈɑrməˌlaɪt, -s
armament
BR ˈɑːməm(ə)nt, -s
AM ˈɑrməmənt, -s
armamentaria
BR ˌɑːməmɛnˈtɛːrɪə(r), ˌɑːməm(ə)nˈtɛːrɪə(r)
AM ˌɑrməmənˈtɛriə
armamentarium
BR ˌɑːməmɛnˈtɛːrɪəm, ˌɑːməm(ə)nˈtɛːrɪəm
AM ˌɑrməmənˈtɛriəm
Armand
BR ˈɑːmənd
AM ˈɑrmənd
Armani
BR ɑːˈmɑːni
AM ɑrˈmɑni
Armatrading
BR ˌɑːməˈtreɪdɪŋ
AM ˈɑrməˌtreɪdɪŋ
armature
BR ˈɑːmətʃ(ʊ)ə(r), ˈɑːmətjʊə(r), -z
AM ˈɑrmətʃər, ˈɑrməˌtʃʊ(ə)r, ˈɑrməˌt(j)ʊ(ə)r, -z
armband
BR ˈɑːmband, -z
AM ˈɑrmˌbænd, -z
armchair
BR ˈɑːmtʃɛː(r), ˌɑːmˈtʃɛː(r), -z
AM ˈɑrmˌtʃɛ(ə)r, -z
arme blanche
BR ˌɑːm ˈblɒ̃ʃ
AM ˌɑrm ˈblɑnʃ
Armenia
BR ɑːˈmiːnɪə(r)
AM ɑrˈminiə
Armenian
BR ɑːˈmiːnɪən, -z
AM ɑrˈminiən, -z
Armentières
BR ˌɑːm(ə)nˈtɪəz, ˈɑːm(ə)ntɪəz, ˌɑːm(ə)ntɪˈɛː(r)
AM ɑrˌməntiˈɛr(z)
FR aʀmɑ̃tjɛʀ
armeria
BR ɑːˈmɪərɪə(r)
AM ɑrˈmɪriə
armes blanches
BR ˌɑːm(z) ˈblɒ̃ʃ
AM ˌɑrm(z)ˈblɑnʃ
Armfield
BR ˈɑːmfiːld
AM ˈɑrmˌfild
armful
BR ˈɑːmfʊl, -z
AM ˈɑrmˌfʊl, -z
armhole
BR ˈɑːmhəʊl, -z
AM ˈɑrmˌ(h)oʊl, -z

Armidale
BR 'ɑːmɪdeɪl
AM 'ɑrmə,deɪl
armiger
BR 'ɑːmɪdʒə(r), -z
AM 'ɑrmədʒər, -z
armigerous
BR ɑː'mɪdʒ(ə)rəs
AM ɑr'mɪdʒ(ə)rəs
armillaria
BR ,ɑːmɪ'lɛːrɪə(r)
AM ,ɑrmə'lɛriə
armillary
BR ɑː'mɪl(ə)r|i, 'ɑːmɪl(ə)r|i, -ɪz
AM 'ɑrmə,lɛri, -z
Arminian
BR ɑː'mɪnɪən, -z
AM ɑr'mɪniən, -z
Arminianism
BR ɑː'mɪnɪənɪz(ə)m
AM ɑr'mɪniə,nɪzəm
Arminius
BR ɑː'mɪnɪəs
AM ɑr'mɪniəs
Armistead
BR 'ɑːmɪstɛd, 'ɑːmɪstɪd
AM 'ɑrmə,stɛd
armistice
BR 'ɑːmɪstɪs, -ɪz
AM 'ɑrməstəs, -əz
Armitage
BR 'ɑːmɪtɪdʒ
AM 'ɑrmədɪdʒ
armless
BR 'ɑːmləs
AM 'ɑrmləs
armlet
BR 'ɑːmlɪt, -s
AM 'ɑrmlət, -s
Armley
BR 'ɑːmli
AM 'ɑrmli
armload
BR 'ɑːmləʊd, -z
AM 'ɑrm,loʊd, -z
armlock
BR 'ɑːmlɒk, -s, -ɪŋ, -t
AM 'ɑrm,lɑk, -s, -ɪŋ, -t
armoire
BR ɑː'mwɑː(r), -z
AM ɑrm'wɑr, -z
armor
BR 'ɑːm|ə(r), -əz, -(ə)rɪŋ, -əd
AM 'ɑrmər, -z, -ɪŋ, -d
armorer
BR 'ɑːm(ə)rə(r), -z
AM 'ɑrmərər, -z
armorial
BR ɑː'mɔːrɪəl
AM ɑr'mɔriəl
Armorica
BR ɑː'mɒrɪkə(r)
AM ɑr'mɔrəkə
armorist
BR 'ɑːm(ə)rɪst, -s
AM 'ɑrmərəst, -s
armory
BR 'ɑːm(ə)r|i, -ɪz
AM 'ɑrm(ə)ri, -z
armour
BR 'ɑːm|ə(r), -əz, -(ə)rɪŋ, -əd
AM 'ɑrmər, -z, -ɪŋ, -d
armourer
BR 'ɑːm(ə)rə(r), -z
AM 'ɑrmərər, -z
armoury
BR 'ɑːm(ə)r|i, -ɪz
AM 'ɑrm(ə)ri, -z
armpit
BR 'ɑːmpɪt, -s
AM 'ɑrm,pɪt, -s
armrest
BR 'ɑːmrɛst, -s
AM 'ɑrm,rɛst, -s
Armstrong
BR 'ɑːmstrɒŋ
AM 'ɑrm,strɔŋ, 'ɑrm,strɑŋ
army
BR 'ɑːm|i, -ɪz
AM 'ɑrmi, -z
Arndale
BR 'ɑːndeɪl
AM 'ɑrn,deɪl
Arne
BR ɑːn
AM ɑrn
Arnhem
BR 'ɑːnəm
AM 'ɑrnəm, 'ɑrn,hɛm
arnica
BR 'ɑːnɪkə(r)
AM 'ɑrnəkə
Arno
BR 'ɑːnəʊ
AM 'ɑr,noʊ
Arnold
BR 'ɑːnld
AM 'ɑrnəld
aroid
BR 'ɛːrɔɪd, -z
AM 'ɛrɔɪd, -z
aroint
BR ə'rɔɪnt
AM ə'rɔɪnt
aroma
BR ə'rəʊmə(r), -z
AM ə'roʊmə, -z
aromatherapeutic
BR ə,rəʊmə,θɛrə'pjuːtɪk
AM ə,roʊmə,θɛrə'pjudɪk
aromatherapist
BR ə,rəʊmə'θɛrəpɪst, ə'rəʊmə,θɛrəpɪst, -s
AM ə,roʊmə'θɛrəpəst, -s
aromatherapy
BR ə,rəʊmə'θɛrəpi, ə'rəʊmə,θɛrəpi
AM ə,roʊmə'θɛrəpi
aromatic
BR ,arə'matɪk
AM ,ɛrə'mædɪk, ,ɛroʊ'mædɪk
aromatically
BR ,arə'matɪkli
AM ,ɛrə'mædək(ə)li, ,ɛroʊ'mædək(ə)li
aromaticity
BR ,arəmə'tɪsɪti
AM ,ɛrəmə'tɪsɪdi
aromatisation
BR ə,rəʊmətʌɪ'zeɪʃn
AM ə,roʊmədə'zeɪʃən, ə,roʊmə,taɪ'zeɪʃən
aromatise
BR ə,rəʊmətʌɪz, -ɪz, -ɪŋ, -d
AM ə'roʊmə,taɪz, -ɪz, -ɪŋ, -d
aromatization
BR ə,rəʊmətʌɪ'zeɪʃn
AM ə,roʊmədə'zeɪʃən, ə,roʊmə,taɪ'zeɪʃən
aromatize
BR ə,rəʊmətʌɪz, -ɪz, -ɪŋ, -d
AM ə'roʊmə,taɪz, -ɪz, -ɪŋ, -d
arose
BR ə'rəʊz
AM ə'roʊz
around
BR ə'raʊnd
AM ə'raʊnd
arousable
BR ə'raʊzəbl
AM ə'raʊzəbəl
arousal
BR ə'raʊzl
AM ə'raʊzəl
arouse
BR ə'raʊz, -ɪz, -ɪŋ, -d
AM ə'raʊz, -əz, -ɪŋ, -d
arouser
BR ə'raʊzə(r), -z
AM ə'raʊzər, -z
Arp
BR ɑːp
AM ɑrp
arpeggio
BR ɑː'pɛdʒɪəʊ, -z
AM ɑr'pɛdʒioʊ, -z
arquebus
BR 'ɑːkwɪbəs, -ɪz
AM 'ɑrk(w)əbəs, -əz
arquebusier
BR ,ɑːkwɪbə'siːə(r), -z
AM ,ɑrk(w)əbə'sɪ(ə)r, -z
arrack
BR 'arək
AM 'ɛrək, 'ɛ,ræk
arraign
BR ə'reɪn, -z, -ɪŋ, -d
AM ə'reɪn, -z, -ɪŋ, -d
arraignment
BR ə'reɪnm(ə)nt, -s
AM ə'reɪnmənt, -s
Arran
BR 'arən, 'arn̩
AM 'ɛrən
arrange
BR ə'reɪn(d)ʒ, -ɪz, -ɪŋ, -d
AM ə'reɪndʒ, -ɪz, -ɪŋ, -d
arrangeable
BR ə'reɪn(d)ʒəbl
AM ə'reɪndʒəbəl
arrangement
BR ə'reɪn(d)ʒm(ə)nt, -s
AM ə'reɪndʒmənt, -s
arranger
BR ə'reɪn(d)ʒə(r), -z
AM ə'reɪndʒər, -z
arrant
BR 'arənt, 'arn̩t
AM 'ɛrənt
arrantly
BR 'arəntli, 'arn̩tli
AM 'ɛrən(t)li
Arras
BR 'arəs
AM 'ɛrəs
arras
BR 'arəs, -ɪz
AM 'ɛrəs, -əz
Arrau
BR ə'raʊ
AM ə'raʊ
array
BR ə'reɪ, -z, -ɪŋ, -d
AM ə'reɪ, -z, -ɪŋ, -d
arrear
BR ə'rɪə(r), -z
AM ə'rɪ(ə)r, -z
arrearage
BR ə'rɪərɪdʒ
AM ə'rɪrɪdʒ
arrest
BR ə'rɛst, -s, -ɪŋ, -ɪd
AM ə'rɛst, -s, -ɪŋ, -əd
arrestable
BR ə'rɛstəbl
AM ə'rɛstəbəl
arrestation
BR ,arɛ'steɪʃn
AM ə,rɛs'teɪʃən
arrester
BR ə'rɛstə(r), -z
AM ə'rɛstər, -z
arresting
BR ə'rɛstɪŋ
AM ə'rɛstɪŋ
arrestingly
BR ə'rɛstɪŋli
AM ə'rɛstɪŋli
arrestment
BR ə'rɛs(t)m(ə)nt, -s
AM ə'rɛs(t)mənt, -s
arrhythmia
BR ə'rɪðmɪə(r), eɪ'rɪðmɪə(r)

AM ə'rɪðmiə, eɪ'rɪðmiə

arrière-pensée
BR ˌarɪɛː'pɒnseɪ, ˌarɪɛː'pɒ̃seɪ, ˌarɪɛːpɒn'seɪ, ˌarɪɛːpɒ̃'seɪ
AM ˌariɛrˌpɑn'seɪ

arrière-pensées
BR ˌarɪɛː'pɒnseɪ(z), ˌarɪɛː'pɒ̃seɪ(z), ˌarɪɛːpɒn'seɪ(z), ˌarɪɛːpɒ̃'seɪ(z)
AM ˌariɛrˌpɑn'seɪ(z)

arris
BR 'arɪs, -ɪz
AM 'ɛrəs, -əz

arrival
BR ə'rʌɪvl, -z
AM ə'raɪvəl, -z

arrive
BR ə'rʌɪv, -z, -ɪŋ, -d
AM ə'raɪv, -z, -ɪŋ, -d

arrivederci
BR ˌarɪvə'dɛːtʃi
AM ˌɛrəvə'dɛrtʃi, əˌrivə'dɛrtʃi

arrivisme
BR ˌariː'vɪz(ə)m
AM ˌari'vizm(ə)

arriviste
BR ˌariː'viːst, -s
AM ˌari'vist, -s

arrogance
BR 'arəg(ə)ns
AM 'ɛrəgəns

arrogancy
BR 'arəg(ə)nsi
AM 'ɛrəgənsi

arrogant
BR 'arəg(ə)nt
AM 'ɛrəgənt

arrogantly
BR 'ɛrəg(ə)ntli
AM 'ɛrəgən(t)li

arrogate
BR 'arəgeɪt, -s, -ɪŋ, -ɪd
AM 'ɛrəˌgeɪ|t, -ts, -dɪŋ, -dɪd

arrogation
BR ˌarə'geɪʃn, -z
AM ˌɛrə'geɪʃən, -z

arrondissement
BR ə'rɒndɪsm(ə)nt, əˌrɒ̃diː'smɒ̃
AM ə'rɑndəsmənt, ə'rɑndiˌsmɑn

arrondissements
BR ə'rɒndɪsm(ə)nts, əˌrɒ̃diː'smɒ̃(z)
AM ə'rɑndəsmən(ts), ə'rɑndiˌsmɑn(z)

arrow
BR 'arəʊ, -z
AM 'ɛroʊ, -z

arrowhead
BR 'arə(ʊ)hɛd, -z
AM 'ɛroʊˌ(h)ɛd, -z

arrowroot
BR 'arə(ʊ)ruːt
AM 'ɛroʊˌrut

Arrowsmith
BR 'arə(ʊ)smɪθ
AM 'ɛroʊˌsmɪθ

arrowy
BR 'arəʊi
AM 'ɛrəwi

arroyo
BR ə'rɔɪəʊ, -z
AM ə'rɔɪ(j)oʊ, -z

arrythmia
BR ə'rɪðmɪə(*r*), eɪ'rɪðmɪə(*r*)
AM ə'rɪðmiə, eɪ'rɪðmiə

arse
BR ɑːs, -ɪz
AM æs, ɑrs, -əz

arsehole
BR 'ɑːshəʊl, -z
AM 'æsˌ(h)oʊl, -z

arsenal
BR 'ɑːs(ə)nl, 'ɑːsn̩l, -z
AM 'ɑrs(ə)nəl, -z

arsenate
BR 'ɑːs(ɪ)neɪt, 'ɑːsn̩eɪt, 'ɑːs(ɪ)nɪt, 'ɑːsn̩ɪt, -s
AM 'ɑrs(ə)nət, 'ɑrs(ə)ˌneɪt, -s

arsenic[1]
adjective
BR ɑː'sɛnɪk
AM ɑr'sɛnɪk

arsenic[2]
noun
BR 'ɑːs(ə)nɪk, 'ɑːsn̩ɪk
AM 'ɑrs(ə)nɪk

arsenical
BR ɑː'sɛnɪkl
AM ɑr'sɛnəkəl

arsenically
BR ɑː'sɛnɪkli
AM ɑr'sɛnək(ə)li

arsenicum
BR ɑː'sɛnɪkəm
AM ɑr'sɛnəkəm

arsenious
BR ɑː'siːnɪəs
AM ɑr'siniəs

arses[1]
plural of arse
BR 'ɑːsɪz
AM 'æsəz, 'ɑrsəz

arses[2]
plural of arsis
BR 'ɑːsiːz
AM 'ɑrˌsiz

arsine
BR 'ɑːsiːn
AM ˌɑrˌsin

arsis
BR 'ɑːsɪs, -ɪz
AM 'ɑrsəs, -əz

arson
BR 'ɑːsn
AM 'ɑrsən

arsonist
BR 'ɑːsn̩ɪst, 'ɑːsənɪst, -s
AM 'ɑrs(ə)nəst, -s

arsphenamine
BR ɑːs'fɛnəmiːn, ɑːs'fɛnəmɪn
AM ɑr'sfɛnəmən, ɑr'sfɛnəˌmin

arsy-versy
BR ˌɑːsɪ'vəːsi
AM ˌɑrsi'vərsi

art
BR ɑːt, -s
AM ɑrt, -s

Artaxerxes
BR ˌɑːtə'zəːksiːz
AM ˌɑrdə'zərksiz

art deco
BR ˌɑːt 'dɛkəʊ
AM ˌɑrt 'dɛkoʊ

artefact
BR 'ɑːtɪfakt, -s
AM 'ɑrdəˌfæk(t), -(t)s

artefactual
BR ˌɑːtɪ'faktʃʊəl, ˌɑːtɪ'faktʃ(ʊ)l
AM ˌɑrdə'fæk(t)ʃ(əw)əl

artel
BR ɑː'tɛl, -z
AM ɑr'tɛl, -z

Artemis
BR 'ɑːtɪmɪs
AM 'ɑrdəməs

artemisia
BR ˌɑːtɪ'mɪzɪə(*r*), ˌɑːtɪ'miːzɪə(*r*), -z
AM ˌɑrdə'miʒ(i)ə, ˌɑrdə'miziə , -z

Artemus
BR 'ɑːtɪməs
AM 'ɑrdɛməs

arterial
BR ɑː'tɪərɪəl
AM ɑr'tɪriəl

arterialisation
BR ɑːˌtɪərɪəlʌɪ'zeɪʃn
AM ɑrˌtɪriələ'zeɪʃən, ɑrˌtɪriəˌlaɪ'zeɪʃən

arterialise
BR ɑː'tɪərɪəlʌɪz, -ɪz, -ɪŋ, -d
AM ɑr'tɪriəˌlaɪz, -ɪz, -ɪŋ, -d

arterialization
BR ɑːˌtɪərɪəlʌɪ'zeɪʃn
AM ɑrˌtɪriələ'zeɪʃən, ɑrˌtɪriəˌlaɪ'zeɪʃən

arterialize
BR ɑː'tɪərɪəlʌɪz, -ɪz, -ɪŋ, -d
AM ɑr'tɪriəˌlaɪz, -ɪz, -ɪŋ, -d

arteriogram
BR ɑː'tɪərɪə(ʊ)gram, -z
AM ɑr'tɪrioʊˌgræm, ɑr'tɪriəˌgræm, -z

arteriole
BR ɑː'tɪərɪəʊl, -z
AM ɑr'tɪriˌoʊl, -z

arterioscleroses
BR ɑːˌtɪərɪəʊsklɪ'rəʊsiːz
AM ɑrˌtɪrioʊsklə'roʊsiz, ɑrˌtɪriəsklə'roʊsiz

arteriosclerosis
BR ɑːˌtɪərɪəʊsklə'rəʊsɪs
AM ɑrˌtɪrioʊsklɪ'roʊsəs, ɑrˌtɪriəsklə'roʊsəs

arteriosclerotic
BR ɑːˌtɪərɪəʊsklɪ'rɒtɪk
AM ɑrˌtɪrioʊsklə'rɑdɪk, ɑrˌtɪriəsklə'rɑdɪk

arteritis
BR ˌɑːtə'rʌɪtɪs
AM ˌɑrdə'raɪdɪs

artery
BR 'ɑːt(ə)r|i, -ɪz
AM 'ɑrdəri, -z

artesian
BR ɑː'tiːzɪən, ɑː'tiːʒn
AM ɑr'tiʒən

artful
BR 'ɑːtf(ʉ)l
AM 'ɑrtfəl

artfully
BR 'ɑːtfʉli, 'ɑːtfl̩i
AM 'ɑrtfəli

artfulness
BR 'ɑːtf(ʉ)lnəs
AM 'ɑrtfəlnəs

arthritic
BR ɑː'θrɪtɪk, -s
AM ɑr'θrɪdɪk, -s

arthritis
BR ɑː'θrʌɪtɪs
AM ɑr'θraɪdɪs

arthrodesis
BR ɑː'θrɒdɪsɪs
AM ˌɑr'θrɑdəsɪs

arthropod
BR 'ɑːθrəpɒd, -z
AM 'ɑrθrəˌpɑd, -z

arthroscope
BR 'ɑːθrəskəʊp, -s
AM 'ɑrθrəˌskoʊp, -s

arthroscopic
BR ˌɑːθrə'skɒpɪk
AM ˌɑrθrə'skɑpɪk

arthroscopy
BR ɑː'θrɒskəp|i, -ɪz
AM ɑr'θrɑskəpi, -z

Arthur
BR 'ɑːθə(r)
AM 'ɑrθər

Arthurian
BR ɑː'θjʊərɪən, ɑː'θjɔːrɪən
AM ɑr'θ(j)ʊriən

artic
BR ɑː'tɪk, -s
AM ɑr'tɪk, -s

artichoke
BR 'ɑːtɪtʃəʊk, -s
AM 'ɑrdəˌtʃoʊk, -s

article
BR 'ɑːtɪk|l, -lz, -l̩ɪŋ/-lɪŋ, -ld
AM 'ɑrdəkəl, -z, -ɪŋ, -d

articulacy
BR ɑː'tɪkjʉləsi
AM ɑr'tɪkjələsi

articular
BR ɑː'tɪkjʉlə(r)
AM ɑr'tɪkjələr

articulate[1]
adjective
BR ɑː'tɪkjʉlət
AM ɑr'tɪkjələt

articulate[2]
verb
BR ɑː'tɪkjʉleɪt, -s, -ɪŋ, -ɪd
AM ɑr'tɪkjə,leɪ|t, -ts, -dɪŋ, -dɨd

articulately
BR ɑː'tɪkjʉlətli
AM ɑr'tɪkjələtli

articulateness
BR ɑː'tɪkjʉlətnəs
AM ɑr'tɪkjələtnəs

articulation
BR ɑː,tɪkjʉ'leɪʃn, -z
AM ɑr,tɪkjə'leɪʃən, -z

articulator
BR ɑː'tɪkjʉleɪtə(r), -z
AM ɑr'tɪkjə,leɪdər, -z

articulatory
BR ɑː'tɪkjʉlət(ə)ri, ɑː,tɪkjʉ'leɪt(ə)ri
AM ɑr'tɪkjələ,tɔri

artifact
BR 'ɑːtɪfakt, -s
AM 'ɑrdə,fæk(t), -(t)s

artifactual
BR ,ɑːtɪ'faktʃʊəl, ,ɑːtɪ'faktʃ(ʉ)l
AM ,ɑrdə'fæk(t)ʃ(əw)əl

artifice
BR 'ɑːtɪfɪs, -ɪz
AM 'ɑrdəfəs, -əz

artificer
BR ɑː'tɪfɪsə(r), -z
AM ɑr'tɪfəsər, 'ɑrdə,fɪsər, -z

artificial
BR ,ɑːtɪ'fɪʃl
AM ,ɑrdə'fɪʃəl

artificialise
BR ,ɑːtɪ'fɪʃəlʌɪz, ,ɑːtɪ'fɪʃl̩ʌɪz, -ɪz, -ɪŋ, -d
AM ,ɑrdə'fɪʃə,laɪz, -ɪz, -ɪŋ, -d

artificiality
BR ,ɑːtɪ,fɪʃɪ'alɪti
AM ,ɑrdə,fɪʃi'ælədi

artificialize
BR ,ɑːtɪ'fɪʃəlʌɪz, ,ɑːtɪ'fɪʃl̩ʌɪz, -ɪz, -ɪŋ, -d
AM ,ɑrdə'fɪʃə,laɪz, -ɪz, -ɪŋ, -d

artificially
BR ,ɑːtɪ'fɪʃl̩i, ,ɑːtɪ'fɪʃəli
AM ,ɑrdə'fɪʃəli

artillerist
BR ɑː'tɪl(ə)rɪst, -s
AM ɑr'tɪl(ə)rɨst, -s

artillery
BR ɑː'tɪl(ə)r|i, -ɪz
AM ɑr'tɪl(ə)ri, -z

artilleryman
BR ɑː'tɪl(ə)rɪmən
AM ɑr'tɪl(ə)rimən

artillerymen
BR ɑː'tɪl(ə)rɪmən
AM ɑr'tɪl(ə)rimən

artily
BR 'ɑːtɪli
AM 'ɑrdəli

artiness
BR 'ɑːtɪnɪs
AM 'ɑrdinɨs

artisan
BR ,ɑːtɪ'zan, -z
AM 'ɑrdəzn, 'ɑrdə,zæn, -z

artisanate
BR ,ɑːtɪ'zaneɪt
AM 'ɑrdəzə,neɪt

artist
BR 'ɑːtɪst, -s
AM 'ɑrdəst, -s

artiste
BR ɑː'tiːst, -s
AM ɑr'tist, -s

artistic
BR ɑː'tɪstɪk
AM ɑr'tɪstɪk

artistical
BR ɑː'tɪstɪkl
AM ɑr'tɪstɪkəl

artistically
BR ɑː'tɪstɪkli
AM ɑr'tɪstɪk(ə)li

artistry
BR 'ɑːtɪstri
AM 'ɑrdəstri

artless
BR 'ɑːtləs
AM 'ɑrtləs

artlessly
BR 'ɑːtləsli
AM 'ɑrtləsli

artlessness
BR 'ɑːtləsnəs
AM 'ɑrtləsnəs

art nouveau
BR ,ɑː(t) nuː'vəʊ, + nʊ'vəʊ
AM ,ɑr(t) ,nu'voʊ

Artois
BR ɑː'twɑː(r)
AM ɑr'twɑ

artsy-craftsy
BR ,ɑːtsɪ'krɑːf(t)si
AM ,ɑrtsi'kræf(t)si

artwork
BR 'ɑːtwəːk
AM 'ɑrt,wərk

arty
BR 'ɑːt|i, -ɪə(r), -ɪɪst
AM 'ɑrdi, -ər, -ɪst

arty-crafty
BR ,ɑːtɪ'krɑːfti
AM ,ɑrdi'kræfti

Aruba
BR ə'ruːbə(*r*)
AM ə'rubə

arugula
BR ə'ruːgjʉlə(*r*)
AM ə'rugələ

arum
BR 'ɛːrəm, -z
AM 'ɛrəm, -z

Arundel
BR 'arəndl, 'arn̩dl
AM ə'rəndəl, 'ɛrəndɛl

Arunta
BR ə'rʌntə(*r*), -z
AM ə'rən(t)ə, -z

arvo
BR 'ɑːvəʊ, -z
AM 'ɑr,voʊ, -z

Arwel
BR 'ɑːwɛl
AM 'ɑrwəl

Arwyn
BR 'ɑːwɪn
AM 'ɑrwɪn

Aryan
BR 'ɛːrɪən, 'ɑːrɪən, 'arɪən, -z
AM 'ɛriən, -z

aryl
BR 'arɪl, 'arl̩, -z
AM 'ɛrəl, -z

arytenoid
BR ,arɪ'tiːnɔɪd
AM ə'rɪdə,nɔɪd, ə'rɪtn̩ɔɪd, ,ɛrə'ti,nɔɪd

as[1]
strong form
BR az
AM æz

as[2]
weak form
BR əz
AM əz

Asa
BR 'eɪsə(*r*), 'eɪzə(*r*), 'ɑːsə(*r*)
AM 'eɪzə

asafoetida
BR ,asə'fɛtɪdə(*r*), ,asə'fiːtɪdə(*r*)
AM ,æsə'fɛdədə, ,æsə'fidədə

Asante
BR ə'santi
AM ə'sɑn(t)i

Asaph
BR 'asaf, 'asəf
AM 'æsæf

asbestine
BR as'bɛstʌɪn, az'bɛstʌɪn
AM æs'bɛs,tɪn, æz'bɛs,tɪn, əs'bɛs,tɪn, əz'bɛs,tɪn

asbestos
BR as'bɛstəs, as'bɛstɒs, az'bɛstəs, az'bɛstɒs
AM æs'bɛstəs, æz'bɛstəs, əs'bɛstəs, əz'bɛstəs

asbestosine
BR as'bɛstəsʌɪn, az'bɛstəsʌɪn
AM æs'bɛstə,sɪn, æz'bɛstə,sɪn

asbestosis
BR ,asbɛ'stəʊsɪs, ,azbɛ'stəʊsɪs
AM ,æs,bɛs'toʊsəs, ,æz,bɛs'toʊsəs

Asbury
BR 'asb(ə)ri
AM 'æzbəri

Ascalon
BR 'askəlɒn
AM 'ɑskə,lɑn

ASCAP
BR 'askap
AM 'æskæp

ascarid
BR 'askərɪd, -z
AM 'æskərɪd, -z

ascaris
BR 'askərɪs, -ɪz
AM 'æskərəs, -əz

ascend
BR ə'sɛnd, -z, -ɪŋ, -ɪd
AM ə'sɛnd, -z, -ɪŋ, -əd

ascendance
BR ə'sɛnd(ə)ns
AM ə'sɛnd(ə)ns, æ'sɛnd(ə)ns

ascendancy
BR ə'sɛnd(ə)nsi
AM ə'sɛnd(ə)nsi

ascendant
BR ə'sɛnd(ə)nt
AM ə'sɛnd(ə)nt

ascender
BR ə'sɛndə(r), -z
AM ə'sɛndər, -z

ascension
BR ə'sɛnʃn
AM ə'sɛn(t)ʃən

ascensional
BR ə'sɛnʃn̩(ə)l, ə'sɛnʃən(ə)l
AM ə'sɛn(t)ʃ(ə)nəl

Ascensiontide
BR ə'sɛnʃ(ə)ntʌɪd
AM ə'sɛn(t)ʃən,taɪd

ascent
BR ə'sɛnt, -s
AM ə'sɛnt, -s

ascentionist
BR ə'sɛnʃn̩ɪst, ə'sɛnʃ(ə)nɪst, -s
AM ə'sɛn(t)ʃənəst, -s

Ascentiontide
BR ə'sɛnʃntʌɪd
AM ə'sɛn(t)ʃən,taɪd

ascertain
BR ˌasə'teɪn, -z, -ɪŋ, -d
AM ˌæsər'teɪn, -z, -ɪŋ, -d

ascertainable
BR ˌasə'teɪnəbl
AM ˌæsər'teɪnəbəl

ascertainment
BR ˌasə'teɪnm(ə)nt
AM ˌæsər'teɪnmənt

asceses
BR ə'siːsiːz
AM ə'sisiz, æ'sisiz

ascesis
BR ə'siːsɪs
AM ə'sisɪs, æ'sisɪs

ascetic
BR ə'sɛtɪk
AM ə'sɛdɪk, æ'sɛdɪk

ascetically
BR ə'sɛtɨkli
AM ə'sɛdək(ə)li, æ'sɛdək(ə)li

asceticism
BR ə'sɛtɨsɪz(ə)m
AM ə'sɛdəˌsɪzəm, æ'sɛdəˌsɪzəm

Ascham
BR 'askəm
AM 'æskəm

aschelminth
BR 'aʃhɛlmɪnθ 'askhɛlmɪnθ, -s
AM 'æʃɛlˌmɪnθ 'æskɛlˌmɪnθ, -s

asci
BR 'askʌɪ, 'aski
AM 'æsˌkaɪ, 'æski

ascidian
BR ə'sɪdɪən, -z
AM ə'sɪdiən, -z

ASCII
BR 'aski
AM 'æski

ascites
BR ə'sʌɪtiːz
AM ə'saɪdiz

Asclepiad
BR ə'skliːpɪad, -z
AM ə'sklipiəd, æ'sklipiəd, -z

Asclepius
BR ə'skliːpɪəs
AM ə'sklipiəs, æ'sklipiəs

ascomycete
BR ˌaskə'mʌɪsiːt
AM ˌæskəˌmaɪˌsit

ascomycetes
BR ˌaskə'mʌɪsiːts ˌaskəmʌɪ'siːtiːz
AM ˌæskəˌmaɪˌsits ˌæskəˌmaɪˌsidiz

Ascona
BR a'skəʊnə(r)
AM æs'koʊnə

ascorbic
BR ə'skɔːbɪk
AM ə'skɔrbɪk

ascot
BR 'askət, 'askɒt, -s
AM 'æsˌkɑt, 'æskət, -s

ascribable
BR ə'skrʌɪbəbl
AM ə'skraɪbəbəl

ascribe
BR ə'skrʌɪb, -z, -ɪŋ, -d
AM ə'skraɪb, -z, -ɪŋ, -d

ascription
BR ə'skrɪpʃn
AM ə'skrɪpʃən

ascus
BR 'askəs
AM 'æskəs

Asda®
BR 'azdə(r)
AM 'æzdə

asdic
BR 'azdɪk
AM 'æzdɪk

ASEAN
BR 'asɪan
AM ə'siən

aseity
BR (ˌ)eɪ'siːɪti, ə'siːɪti
AM eɪ'siɪdi, ə'siɪdi

asepsis
BR (ˌ)eɪ'sɛpsɪs, ə'sɛpsɪs, a'sɛpsɪs
AM eɪ'sɛpsəs

aseptic
BR (ˌ)eɪ'sɛptɪk, ə'sɛptɪk, a'sɛptɪk
AM eɪ'sɛptɪk

aseptically
BR (ˌ)eɪ'sɛptɪkli, ə'sɛptɪkli, a'sɛptɪkli
AM eɪ'sɛptək(ə)li

asexual
BR (ˌ)eɪ'sɛkʃʊəl, (ˌ)eɪ'sɛkʃ(ʊ)l, (ˌ)eɪ'sɛksjʊ(ə)l
AM eɪ'sɛkʃ(əw)əl

asexuality
BR ˌeɪsɛkʃʊ'alɪti, eɪˌsɛkʃʊ'alɪti, ˌeɪsɛksjʊ'alɪti, eɪˌsɛksjʊ'alɪti
AM eɪsɛkʃə'wælədi

asexually
BR (ˌ)eɪ'sɛkʃʊəli, (ˌ)eɪ'sɛkʃʊli, (ˌ)eɪ'sɛkʃl̩i, (ˌ)eɪ'sɛksjʊ(ə)li
AM eɪ'sɛkʃ(əw)əli

Asgard
BR 'asgɑːd, 'azgɑːd
AM 'æsˌgɑrd, 'æzˌgɑrd

ash
BR aʃ, -ɪz
AM æʃ, -əz

ashamed
BR ə'ʃeɪmd
AM ə'ʃeɪmd

ashamedly
BR ə'ʃeɪmɨdli
AM ə'ʃeɪmɨdli

ashamedness
BR ə'ʃeɪm(ɨ)dnɨs
AM ə'ʃeɪmɨdnɨs, ə'ʃeɪm(d)nɪs

Ashanti
BR ə'ʃanti
AM ə'ʃɑn(t)i

ashbin
BR 'aʃbɪn, -z
AM 'æʃˌbɪn, -z

Ashby
BR 'aʃbi
AM 'æʃbi

Ashby-de-la-Zouch
BR ˌaʃbɪˌdələ'zuːʃ
AM ˌæʃˌbidələ'zuʃ

ashcan
BR 'aʃkan, -z
AM 'æʃˌkæn, -z

Ashcroft
BR 'aʃkrɒft
AM 'æʃˌkrɔft, 'æʃˌkrɑft

Ashdod
BR 'aʃdɒd
AM 'æʃˌdɑd

Ashdown
BR 'aʃdaʊn
AM 'æʃˌdaʊn

Ashe
BR aʃ
AM æʃ

ashen
BR 'aʃn
AM 'æʃən

Asher
BR 'aʃə(r)
AM 'æʃər

ashet
BR 'aʃɪt, -s
AM 'æʃət, -s

Ashford
BR 'aʃfəd
AM 'æʃfərd

ashiness
BR 'aʃɪnɪs
AM 'æʃinɪs

Ashington
BR 'aʃɪŋt(ə)n
AM 'æʃɪŋtən

Ashkelon
BR 'aʃkəlɒn
AM 'æʃkəˌlɑn

Ashkenazi
BR ˌaʃkɪ'nɑːzi
AM ˌæʃkə'nɑzi

Ashkenazic
BR ˌaʃkɪ'nɑːzɪk
AM ˌæʃkə'nɑzɪk

Ashkenazim
BR ˌaʃkɪ'nɑːzɪm
AM ˌæʃkə'nɑzɪm

Ashkenazy
BR ˌaʃkɪ'nɑːzi
AM ˌæʃkə'nɑzi
RUS əʃkʲi'nazʲi

Ashkhabad
BR 'aʃkəbad, 'aʃkəbɑːd
AM 'ɑʃkəˌbɑd, 'ɑʃkəˌbæd
RUS əʃxa'bat

ashlar
BR 'aʃlə(r), 'aʃlɑː(r)
AM 'æʃlər

ashlaring
BR 'aʃlərɪŋ, 'aʃlɑːrɪŋ
AM 'æʃlərɪŋ

Ashley
BR 'aʃli
AM 'æʃli

Ashmolean
BR aʃ'məʊlɪən
AM æʃ'moʊliən

ashore
BR ə'ʃɔː(r)
AM ə'ʃɔ(ə)r

ashpan
BR 'aʃpan, -z
AM 'æʃˌpæn, -z

ashplant
BR 'aʃplɑːnt, 'aʃplant, -s
AM 'æʃˌplænt, -s

Ashquelon
BR 'aʃkəlɒn
AM 'æʃkəˌlɑn, 'æskəˌlɑn

ashram
BR 'aʃram, 'aʃrəm, -z
AM 'ɑʃrəm, -z

ashrama
BR 'aʃrəmə(r), -z
AM 'ɑʃrəmə, -z

Ash Shariqah
BR ˌaʃ ʃə'riːkə(r)
AM æʃ ʃə'rikə

Ashton
BR 'aʃt(ə)n
AM 'æʃt(ə)n

Ashton-under-Lyne
BR ˌaʃt(ə)nˌʌndə'lʌɪn
AM ˌæʃt(ə)nˌəndər'laɪn

ashtray
BR 'aʃtreɪ, -z
AM 'æʃˌtreɪ, -z

Ashur
BR 'aʃə(r)
AM 'æʃər

Ashurbanipal
BR ˌaʃʊə'banɪpal
AM ɑˌʃʊr'bɑniˌpɑl

ashwood
BR 'aʃwʊd

AM 'æʃˌwʊd
Ashworth
BR 'aʃwə(:)θ
AM 'æʃˌwərθ
ashy
BR 'aʃ|i, -ɪə(r), -ɪɪst
AM 'æʃi, -ər, -ɪst
Asia
BR 'eɪʃə(r), 'eɪʒə(r)
AM 'eɪʒə
Asian
BR 'eɪʃ(ə)n, 'eɪʒ(ə)n, -z
AM 'eɪʒən, -z
Asiatic
BR ˌeɪzɪ'atɪk, ˌeɪsɪ'atɪk, ˌeɪʃɪ'atɪk, ˌeɪʒɪ'atɪk
AM ˌeɪʒi'ædɪk, ˌeɪzi'ædɪk
aside
BR ə'sʌɪd, -z
AM ə'saɪd, -z
Asimov
BR 'asɪmɒv, 'azɪmɒv
AM 'æzəˌmɔv, 'æzəˌmɑv
asinine
BR 'asɪnʌɪn
AM 'æsəˌnaɪn, 'æsnˌaɪn
asininity
BR ˌasɪ'nɪnɪt|i, -ɪz
AM ˌæsə'nɪnɪdi, -z
ask
BR ɑːsk, ask, -s, -ɪŋ, -t
AM æsk, -s, -ɪŋ, -t
askance
BR ə'skans, ə'skɑːns
AM ə'skæns
askari
BR ə'skɑːr|i, a'skɑːr|i, -ɪz
AM æ'skæri, ə'skɑri, -z
Askelon
BR 'askɪlɒn, 'askl̩ɒn, 'askɪlən, 'askl̩ən
AM 'æskɛˌlɑn, 'æʃkəˌlɑn
asker
BR 'ɑːskə(r), 'askə(r), -z
AM 'æskər, -z
askeses
BR ə'skɛsiːz
AM ə'skisiz
askesis
BR ə'skɛsɪs
AM ə'skisəs
Askew
surname
BR 'askjuː
AM 'æskju
askew
BR ə'skjuː
AM ə'skju
Askey
BR 'aski
AM 'æski
Askham
BR 'askəm
AM 'æskəm
Askrigg
BR 'askrɪɡ
AM 'æskrɪɡ
aslant
BR ə'slɑːnt, ə'slant
AM ə'slænt
asleep
BR ə'sliːp
AM ə'slip
ASLEF
BR 'azlɛf
AM 'æzˌlɛf
aslope
BR ə'sləʊp
AM ə'sloʊp
Asmara
BR ə'smɑːrə(r), as'mɑːrə(r), az'mɑːrə(r)
AM æs'mɛrə
asocial
BR eɪ'səʊʃl
AM eɪ'soʊʃəl
asocially
BR eɪ'səʊʃl̩i, eɪ'səʊʃəli
AM eɪ'soʊʃəli
Asoka
BR ə'səʊkə(r), ə'ʃəʊkə(r)
AM ə'soʊkə, ə'ʃoʊkə
asp
BR asp, -s
AM æsp, -s
asparagus
BR ə'sparəɡəs
AM ə'spɛrəɡəs
aspartame
BR ə'spɑːteɪm
AM 'æspɑrˌteɪm
aspartic
BR ə'spɑːtɪk
AM ə'spɑrdɪk
Aspatria
BR a'speɪtrɪə(r), ə'speɪtrɪə(r)
AM æ'speɪtriə
aspect
BR 'aspɛkt, -s
AM 'æˌspɛk|(t), -(t)s
aspected
BR a'spɛktɪd, 'aspɛktɪd
AM 'æsˌpɛktəd, æ'spɛktəd
aspectual
BR a'spɛktʃʊəl, a'spɛktʃ(ʊ)l, a'spɛktjʊəl, a'spɛktjʊl
AM æ'spɛk(t)ʃ(əw)əl
aspectually
BR a'spɛktʃʊəli, a'spɛktʃʊli, a'spɛktʃl̩i, a'spɛktjʊəli, a'spɛktjʊli
AM æ'spɛk(t)ʃ(əw)əli
Aspel
BR 'aspl
AM 'æspɛl
Aspell
BR 'aspl
AM 'æspɛl
aspen
BR 'aspən, -z
AM 'æspən, -z
asperge
BR ə'spəːdʒ, -ɪz, -ɪŋ, -d
AM ə'spərdʒ, -əz, -ɪŋ, -d
aspergill
BR 'aspədʒɪl, -z
AM 'æspərˌdʒɪl, -z
aspergilla
BR ˌaspə'dʒɪlə(r)
AM ˌæspər'dʒɪlə
aspergillum
BR ˌaspə'dʒɪləm, -z
AM ˌæspər'dʒɪləm, -z
asperity
BR ə'spɛrɪt|i, -ɪz
AM ə'spɛrədi, æ'spɛrədi, -z
asperse
BR ə'spəːs, -ɪz, -ɪŋ, -t
AM ə'spərs, æ'spərs, -əz, -ɪŋ, -t
aspersion
BR ə'spəːʃn, ə'spəːʒn, -z
AM ə'spərʒən, æ'spərʃən, -z
aspersoria
BR ˌaspə'sɔːrɪə(r)
AM ˌæspər'sɔriə
aspersorium
BR ˌaspə'sɔːrɪəm
AM ˌæspər'sɔriəm
asphalt
BR 'asfalt, 'aʃfalt, 'asfɔːlt, 'aʃfɔːlt, 'asfəlt, 'aʃfəlt
AM 'æsˌfɔlt, 'æsˌfɑlt
asphalter
BR 'asfɔːltə(r), 'aʃfɔːltə(r), 'asfəltə(r), 'aʃfəltə(r), -z
AM æs'fɔltər, æs'fɑltər, -z
asphaltic
BR as'faltɪk, aʃ'faltɪk
AM æs'fɔltɪk, æs'fɑltɪk
asphodel
BR 'asfədɛl, -z
AM 'æsfəˌdɛl, -z
asphyxia
BR əs'fɪksɪə(r)
AM æ'sfɪksiə, ə'sfɪksiə
asphyxial
BR əs'fɪksɪəl
AM æ'sfɪksiəl, ə'sfɪksiəl
asphyxiant
BR əs'fɪksɪənt, -s
AM æ'sfɪksiənt, ə'sfɪksiənt, -s
asphyxiate
BR əs'fɪksɪeɪt, -s, -ɪŋ, -ɪd
AM æ'sfɪksiˌeɪ|t, ə'sfɪksiˌeɪ|t, -ts, -dɪŋ, -dɪd
asphyxiation
BR əsˌfɪksɪ'eɪʃn
AM æˌsfɪksi'eɪʃən, əˌsfɪksi'eɪʃən
asphyxiator
BR əs'fɪksɪeɪtə(r), -z
AM æ'sfɪksiˌeɪdər, ə'sfɪksiˌeɪdər, -z
aspic
BR 'aspɪk
AM 'æspɪk
aspidistra
BR ˌaspɪ'dɪstrə(r), -z
AM ˌæspə'dɪstrə, -z
Aspinall
BR 'aspɪnl, 'aspɪnɔːl
AM 'æspəˌnɔl, 'æspəˌnɑl
aspirant
BR 'asp(ɪ)rənt, 'asp(ɪ)rn̩t, ə'spʌɪrənt, ə'spʌɪrn̩t, -s
AM 'æspərənt, ə'spaɪrənt, -s
aspirate[1]
noun, adjective
BR 'asp(ɪ)rət, -s
AM 'æsp(ə)rət, -s
aspirate[2]
verb
BR 'aspɪreɪt, -s, -ɪŋ, -ɪd
AM 'æspəˌreɪ|t, -ts, -dɪŋ, -dɪd
aspiration
BR ˌaspɪ'reɪʃn, -z
AM ˌæspə'reɪʃən, -z
aspirational
BR ˌaspɪ'reɪʃn̩(ə)l, ˌaspɪ'reɪʃən(ə)l
AM ˌæspə'reɪʃ(ə)nəl
aspirator
BR 'aspɪreɪtə(r), -z
AM 'æspəˌreɪdər, -z
aspire
BR ə'spʌɪə(r), -z, -ɪŋ, -d
AM ə'spaɪ(ə)r, -z, -ɪŋ, -d
aspirin
BR 'aspr(ɪ)n, -z
AM 'æsp(ə)rən, -z
asplenium
BR ə'spliːnɪəm, -z
AM ə'spliniəm, æ'spliniəm, -z
Aspro®
BR 'asprəʊ, -z
AM 'æsproʊ, -z
asquint
BR ə'skwɪnt

AM 'æskwɪnt

Asquith
BR 'askwɪθ
AM 'æskwəθ

ass
BR as, -ɪz
AM æs, -əz

Assad
BR a'sɑːd, a'sad
AM ɑ'sɑd, 'ɑ,sɑd

assagai
BR 'asəɡʌɪ, -z
AM 'æsə'ɡaɪ, -z

assai
BR a'sʌɪ
AM ɑ'saɪ

assail
BR ə'seɪl, -z, -ɪŋ, -d
AM ə'seɪl, -z, -ɪŋ, -d

assailable
BR ə'seɪləbl
AM ə'seɪləbəl, æ'seɪləbəl

assailant
BR ə'seɪlənt, ə'seɪlṇt, -s
AM ə'seɪlənt, -s

Assam
BR ə'sam, a'sam
AM ə'sæm, æ'sæm, 'æ,sæm

Assamese
BR ,asə'miːz
AM ,æsə'miz

assassin
BR ə'sas(ɪ)n, -z
AM ə'sæsṇ, -z

assassinate
BR ə'sasɪneɪt, -s, -ɪŋ, -ɪd
AM ə'sæsn,eɪ|t, -ts, -dɪŋ, -dɪd

assassination
BR ə,sasɪ'neɪʃn, -z
AM ə,sæsn'eɪʃən, -z

assassinator
BR ə'sasɪneɪtə(r), -z
AM ə'sæsn,eɪdər, -z

assault
BR ə'sɔːlt, ə'sɒlt, -s, -ɪŋ, -ɪd
AM ə'sɔlt, ə'sɑlt, -s, -ɪŋ, -əd

assaulter
BR ə'sɔːltə(r), ə'sɒltə(r), -z
AM ə'sɔltər, ə'sɑltər, -z

assaultive
BR ə'sɔːltɪv, ə'sɒltɪv
AM ə'sɔltɪv, ə'sɑltɪv

assay
BR ə'seɪ, 'aseɪ, -z, -ɪŋ, -d
AM 'æ,seɪ, ə'seɪ, -z, -ɪŋ, -d

assayable
BR a'seɪəbl, 'aseɪəbl, -z
AM 'æseɪəbəl, ə'seɪəbl, -z

assayer
BR ə'seɪə(r), 'aseɪə(r), -z
AM 'æseɪər, ə'seɪər, -z

assegai
BR 'asəɡʌɪ, -z
AM 'æsə'ɡaɪ, -z

assemblage
BR ə'sɛmbl|ɪdʒ, -ɪdʒɪz
AM ə'sɛmblɪdʒ, -ɪz

assemble
BR ə'sɛmb|l, -lz, -ḷɪŋ\-lɪŋ, -ld
AM ə'sɛmb|əl, -əlz, -(ə)lɪŋ, -əld

assembler
BR ə'sɛmblə(r), -z
AM ə'sɛmblər, -z

assembly
BR ə'sɛmbl|i, -ɪz
AM ə'sɛmbli, -z

assemblyman
BR ə'sɛmblɪmən
AM ə'sɛmblimən

assemblymen
BR ə'sɛmblɪmən
AM ə'sɛmblimən

assent
BR ə'sɛnt, -s, -ɪŋ, -ɪd
AM ə'sɛn|t, æ'sɛn|t, -ts, -(t)ɪŋ, -(t)əd

assenter
BR ə'sɛntə(r), -z
AM ə'sɛn(t)ər, æ'sɛn(t)ər, -z

assentient
BR ə'sɛnʃ(ə)nt
AM ə'sɛn(t)ʃənt, æ'sɛn(t)ʃənt

assentor
BR ə'sɛntə(r), -z
AM ə'sɛn(t)ər, æ'sɛn(t)ər, -z

assert
BR ə'səːt, -s, -ɪŋ, -ɪd
AM ə'sər|t, -ts, -dɪŋ, -dəd

asserter
BR ə'səːtə(r), -z
AM ə'sərdər, -z

assertion
BR ə'səːʃn, -z
AM ə'sərʃən, -z

assertive
BR ə'səːtɪv
AM ə'sərdɪv

assertively
BR ə'səːtɪvli
AM ə'sərdɪvli

assertiveness
BR ə'səːtɪvnɪs
AM ə'sərdɪvnɪs

assertor
BR ə'səːtə(r), -z
AM ə'sərdər, -z

assess
BR ə'sɛs, -ɪz, -ɪŋ, -t
AM ə'sɛs, -əz, -ɪŋ, -t

assessable
BR ə'sɛsəbl
AM ə'sɛsəbəl

assessment
BR ə'sɛsm(ə)nt, -s
AM ə'sɛsmənt, -s

assessor
BR ə'sɛsə(r), -z
AM ə'sɛsər, -z

assessorial
BR ,asə'sɔːrɪəl, ,asɛ'sɔːrɪəl
AM ,æ,sɛ'sɔriəl, ,æsə'sɔriəl

asset
BR 'asɛt, 'asɪt, -s
AM 'æ,sɛt, -s

assever
BR ə'sɛvə(r), -z, -ɪŋ, -d
AM ə'sɛvər, -z, -ɪŋ, -d

asseverate
BR ə'sɛvəreɪt, -s, -ɪŋ, -ɪd
AM ə'sɛvə,reɪ|t, -ts, -dɪŋ, -dɪd

asseveration
BR ə,sɛvə'reɪʃn, -z
AM ə,sɛvə'reɪʃən, -z

asshole
BR 'ɑːshəʊl, -z
AM 'æs,(h)oʊl, -z

assibilate
BR ə'sɪbɪleɪt, -s, -ɪŋ, -ɪd
AM ə'sɪbə,leɪ|t, -ts, -dɪŋ, -dɪd

assibilation
BR ə,sɪbɪ'leɪʃn
AM ə,sɪbə'leɪʃən

assiduity
BR ,asɪ'djuːɪt|i, ,asɪ'dʒuːɪt|i, -ɪz
AM ,æsə'd(j)uədi, -z

assiduous
BR ə'sɪdjʊəs, ə'sɪdʒʊəs
AM ə'sɪdʒəwəs

assiduously
BR ə'sɪdjʊəsli, ə'sɪdʒʊəsli
AM ə'sɪdʒ(ə)wəsli

assiduousness
BR ə'sɪdjʊəsnəs, ə'sɪdʒʊəsnəs
AM ə'sɪdʒ(əw)əsnəs

assign
BR ə'sʌɪn, -z, -ɪŋ, -d
AM ə'saɪn, -z, -ɪŋ, -d

assignable
BR ə'sʌɪnəbl
AM ə'saɪnəbəl

assignat
BR 'asɪɡnat, ,asiː'njɑː(*r*), 'asɪɡnats, ,asiː'njɑːz
AM 'æsɪɡ,næt, -s

assignation
BR ,asɪɡ'neɪʃn, -z
AM ,æsɪɡ'neɪʃən, -z

assignee
BR ,asʌɪ'niː, -z
AM ə,saɪ'ni, ,æ,saɪ'ni, -z

assigner
BR ə'sʌɪnə(r), -z
AM ə'saɪnər, -z

assignment
BR ə'sʌɪnm(ə)nt, -s
AM ə'saɪnmənt, -s

assignor
BR ə'sʌɪnə(r), -z
AM ə'saɪnər, -z

assimilable
BR ə'sɪmɪləbl
AM ə'sɪmələbəl

assimilate
BR ə'sɪmɪleɪt, -s, -ɪŋ, -ɪd
AM ə'sɪmə,leɪ|t, -ts, -dɪŋ, -dɪd

assimilation
BR ə,sɪmɪ'leɪʃn
AM ə,sɪmə'leɪʃən

assimilative
BR ə'sɪmɪlətɪv
AM ə'sɪmə,leɪdɪv, ə'sɪmələdɪv

assimilator
BR ə'sɪmɪleɪtə(r), -z
AM ə'sɪmə,leɪdər, -z

assimilatory
BR ə'sɪmɪlət(ə)ri
AM ə'sɪmɪlə,tɔri

Assisi
BR ə'siːsi, ə'siːzi
AM ə'sisi, ə'sizi

assist
BR ə'sɪst, -s, -ɪŋ, -ɪd
AM ə'sɪst, -s, -ɪŋ, -ɪd

assistance
BR ə'sɪst(ə)ns
AM ə'sɪst(ə)ns

assistant
BR ə'sɪst(ə)nt, -s
AM ə'sɪst(ə)nt, -s

assister
BR ə'sɪstə(r), -z
AM ə'sɪstər, -z

assize
BR ə'sʌɪz, -ɪz
AM ə'saɪz, -ɪz

ass-kicking
BR 'ɑːs,kɪkɪŋ
AM 'æs,kɪkɪŋ

ass-licking
BR 'ɑːs,lɪkɪŋ
AM 'æs,lɪkɪŋ

associability
BR ə,səʊʃ(ɪ)ə'bɪlɪti, ə,səʊsɪə'bɪlɪti
AM ə,soʊʃ(i)ə'bɪlɪdi

associable
BR ə'səʊʃ(ɪ)əbl, ə'səʊsɪəbl
AM ə'soʊʃ(i)əbəl

associate[1]
noun
BR ə'səʊʃ(ɪ)ət, ə'səʊsɪət, -s

AM ə'soʊsiət, ə'soʊʃ(i)ət, -s

associate²
verb
BR ə'səʊʃɪeɪt, ə'səʊsɪeɪt, -s, -ɪŋ, -ɨd
AM ə'soʊsi,eɪ|t, ə'soʊʃi,eɪ|t, -ts, -dɪŋ, -dɨd

associateship
BR ə'səʊʃɪətʃɪp, ə'səʊsɪətʃɪp, -s
AM ə'soʊsiət,ʃɪp, ə'soʊʃiət,ʃɪp, -s

association
BR ə,səʊsɪ'eɪʃn, ə,səʊʃɪ'eɪʃn, -z
AM ə,soʊsi'eɪʃən, ə,soʊʃi'eɪʃən, -z

associational
BR ə,səʊsɪ'eɪʃn̩(ə)l, ə,səʊsɪ'eɪʃən(ə)l, ə,səʊʃɪ'eɪʃn̩(ə)l, ə,səʊʃɪ'eɪʃən(ə)l
AM ə,soʊsi'eɪʃ(ə)nəl, ə,soʊʃi'eɪʃ(ə)nəl

associationist
BR ə,səʊsɪ'eɪʃn̩ɪst, ə,səʊsɪ'eɪʃənɪst, ə,səʊʃɪ'eɪʃn̩ɪst, ə,səʊʃɪ'eɪʃənɪst, -s
AM ə,soʊsi'eɪʃənəst, ə,soʊʃi'eɪʃənəst, -s

associative
BR ə'səʊʃ(ɪ)ətɪv, ə'səʊsɪətɪv
AM ə'soʊsiədɪv, ə'soʊʃədɪv, ə'soʊsi,eɪdɪv, ə'soʊʃi,eɪdɪv

associatively
BR ə'səʊʃ(ɪ)ətɪvli, ə'səʊsɪətɪvli
AM ə'soʊsiədɨvli, ə'soʊʃədɨvli, ə'soʊsi,eɪdɨvli, ə'soʊʃi,eɪdɨvli

associativity
BR ə,səʊʃ(ɪ)ə'tɪvɪti, ə,səʊsɪə'tɪvɨti
AM ə,soʊsiə'tɪvɨdi, ə,soʊʃ(i)ə'tɪvɨdi

associator
BR ə'səʊʃɪeɪtə(r), ə'səʊsɪeɪtə(r), -z
AM ə'soʊsi,eɪdər, ə'soʊʃi,eɪdər, -z

associatory
BR ə'səʊʃ(ɪ)ət(ə)ri, ə'səʊsɪət(ə)ri
AM ə'soʊsiə,tɔri, ə'soʊʃiə,tɔri

assoil
BR ə'sɔɪl, -z, -ɪŋ, -d
AM ə'sɔɪl, -z, -ɪŋ, -d

assonance
BR 'asənəns, 'asn̩əns, -ɪz
AM 'æsn̩əns, -əz

assonant
BR 'asənənt, 'asn̩ənt
AM 'æsn̩ənt

assonate
BR 'asəneɪt, 'asn̩eɪt, -s, -ɪŋ, -ɨd
AM 'æsə,neɪ|t, -ts, -dɪŋ, -dɨd

assort
BR ə'sɔːt, -s, -ɪŋ, -ɨd
AM ə'sɔ(ə)rt, -ts, -'sɔrdɪŋ, -'sɔrdəd

assortative
BR ə'sɔːtətɪv
AM ə'sɔrdədɪv

assortment
BR ə'sɔːtm(ə)nt, -s
AM ə'sɔrtmənt, -s

assuage
BR ə'sweɪdʒ, -ɪz, -ɪŋ, -d
AM ə'sweɪdʒ, -ɪz, -ɪŋ, -d

assuagement
BR ə'sweɪdʒm(ə)nt
AM ə'sweɪdʒmənt

assuager
BR ə'sweɪdʒə(r), -z
AM ə'sweɪdʒər, -z

assuasive
BR ə'sweɪsɪv, ə'sweɪzɪv
AM ə'sweɪsɪv, ə'sweɪzɪv

assumable
BR ə'sjuːməbl
AM ə'suməbəl

assume
BR ə'sjuːm, -z, -ɪŋ, -d
AM ə'sum, -z, -ɪŋ, -d

assumedly
BR ə'sjuːmɨdli
AM ə'sumədli

assuming
BR ə'sjuːmɪŋ
AM ə'sumɪŋ

assumingly
BR ə'sjuːmɪŋli
AM ə'sumɪŋli

assumpsit
BR ə'sʌm(p)sɪt
AM ə'səm(p)sət

assumption
BR ə'sʌm(p)ʃn, -z
AM ə'səm(p)ʃən, -z

assumptive
BR ə'sʌm(p)tɪv
AM ə'səm(p)tɪv

Assur
BR 'asə(r)
AM 'æsər

assurable
BR ə'ʃʊərəbl, ə'ʃɔːrəbl
AM ə'ʃʊrəbəl

assurance
BR ə'ʃʊərəns, ə'ʃʊərn̩s, ə'ʃɔːrəns, ə'ʃɔːrn̩s, -ɪz
AM ə'ʃʊrəns, -əz

assure
BR ə'ʃʊə(r), ə'ʃɔː(r), -z, -ɪŋ, -d
AM ə'ʃʊ(ə)r, -z, -ɪŋ, -d

assuredly
BR ə'ʃʊərɨdli, ə'ʃɔːrɨdli
AM ə'ʃʊr(ə)dli

assuredness
BR ə'ʃʊərɨdnɨs, ə'ʃɔːrɨdnɨs
AM ə'ʃʊr(ə)dnəs

assurer
BR ə'ʃʊərə(r), ə'ʃɔːrə(r), -z
AM ə'ʃʊrər, -z

Assyria
BR ə'sɪrɪə(*r*)
AM ə'sɪriə

Assyrian
BR ə'sɪrɪən, -z
AM ə'sɪriən, -z

Assyriologist
BR ə,sɪrɪ'ɒlədʒɪst, -s
AM ə,sɪri'ɑlədʒəst, -s

Assyriology
BR ə,sɪrɪ'ɒlədʒi
AM ə,sɪri'ɑlədʒi

astable
BR eɪ'steɪbl
AM eɪ'steɪbəl

Astaire
BR ə'stɛː(r)
AM ə'stɛ(ə)r

Astarte
BR ə'stɑːti, a'stɑːti
AM ə'stɑrdi

astatic
BR (,)eɪ'statɪk
AM eɪ'stædɪk

astatine
BR 'astətiːn, 'astətɪn
AM 'æstə,tin

Astbury
BR 'as(t)b(ə)ri
AM 'æs(t)bɛri

aster
BR 'astə(r), -z
AM 'æstər, -z

asterisk
BR 'ast(ə)rɪsk, -s, -ɪŋ, -t
AM 'æstə,rɪ|sk, 'æstə,rɪ|ks, -sks\-ksɪz, -ɪŋ, -t

asterism
BR 'ast(ə)rɪz(ə)m, -z
AM 'æstə,rɪzəm, -z

Asterix
BR 'astərɪks
AM 'æstə,rɪks

astern
BR ə'stəːn
AM ə'stərn

asteroid
BR 'astərɔɪd, -z
AM 'æstə,rɔɪd, -z

asteroidal
BR ,astə'rɔɪdl
AM ,æstə'rɔɪdəl

asthenia
BR as'θiːnɪə(*r*), əs'θiːnɪə(*r*)
AM æs'θiniə, əs'θiniə

asthenic
BR as'θɛnɪk, əs'θɛnɪk
AM æs'θɛnɪk, əs'θɛnɪk

asthenosphere
BR as'θɛnə(ʊ)sfɪə(r), əs'θɛnə(ʊ)sfɪə(r)
AM æs'θɛnə,sfɪ(ə)r, əs'θɛnə,sfɪ(ə)r

asthma
BR 'asmə(*r*)
AM 'æzmə

asthmatic
BR as'matɪk, -s
AM æz'mædɪk, -s

asthmatical
BR as'matɪkl
AM æz'mædəkəl

asthmatically
BR as'matɪkli
AM æz'mædək(ə)li

Asti
BR 'ast|i, -ɪz
AM 'ɑsti, -z

astigmatic
BR ,astɪg'matɪk
AM ,æstɪg'mædɪk

astigmatism
BR ə'stɪgmətɪz(ə)m
AM ə'stɪgmə,tɪzəm

astilbe
BR ə'stɪlb|i, -ɪz
AM ə'stɪlbi, -z

astir
BR ə'stəː(r)
AM ə'stər

Asti spumante
BR ,astɪ spjʉ'manti
AM ,ɑsti spʊ'mɑn(t)i

Astley
BR 'astli
AM 'æs(t)li

Aston
BR 'ast(ə)n
AM 'æst(ə)n

astonish
BR ə'stɒn|ɪʃ, -ɨʃɪz, -ɨʃɪŋ, -ɨʃt
AM ə'stɑnɪʃ, -ɨz, -ɪŋ, -t

astonishingly
BR ə'stɒnɨʃɪŋli
AM ə'stɑnɪʃɪŋli

astonishment
BR ə'stɒnɨʃm(ə)nt, -s
AM ə'stɑnɪʃmənt, -s

Astor
BR 'astə(*r*)
AM 'æstər

Astoria
BR ə'stɔːrɪə(*r*), a'stɔːrɪə(*r*)

AM ə'stɔriə

astound
BR ə'staʊnd, -z, -ɪŋ, -ɪd
AM ə'staʊnd, -z, -ɪŋ, -əd

astoundingly
BR ə'staʊndɪŋli
AM ə'staʊndɪŋli

astra
BR 'astrə(*r*)
AM 'æstrə

astraddle
BR ə'stradl
AM ə'strædəl

astragal
BR 'astrəg(ə)l, -z
AM 'æstrəgəl, -z

astragali
BR ə'stragəlʌɪ, ə'stragl̩ʌɪ
AM ə'strægə,laɪ

astragalus
BR ə'stragələs, ə'stragl̩əs
AM ə'strægələs

astrakhan
BR ,astrə'kan
AM 'ɑstrə,kɑn, 'æstrə,kæn

astral
BR 'astr(ə)l
AM 'æstrəl

astrally
BR 'astrəli, 'astrl̩i
AM 'æstrəli

astrantia
BR ə'strantɪə(*r*)
AM ə'stræn(t)iə

astray
BR ə'streɪ
AM ə'streɪ

Astrid
BR 'astrɪd
AM 'æstrəd

astride
BR ə'strʌɪd
AM ə'straɪd

astringency
BR ə'strɪn(d)ʒ(ə)nsi
AM ə'strɪndʒənsi

astringent
BR ə'strɪn(d)ʒ(ə)nt, -s
AM ə'strɪndʒənt, -s

astringently
BR ə'strɪn(d)ʒ(ə)ntli
AM ə'strɪndʒən(t)li

astrobiology
BR ,astrəʊbʌɪ'ɒlədʒi
AM ,æstroʊ,baɪ'ɑlədʒi

astrobotany
BR ,astrəʊ'bɒtəni, ,astrəʊ'bɒtn̩i
AM ,æstroʊ'bɑtn̩i

astrochemistry
BR ,astrəʊ'kɛmɪstri
AM ,æstroʊ'kɛməstri

astrodome
BR 'astrə(ʊ)dəʊm, -z
AM 'æstrə,doʊm, -z

astrohatch
BR 'astrə(ʊ)hatʃ, -ɪz
AM 'æstrə,hætʃ, 'æstroʊ,hætʃ, -əz

astrolabe
BR 'astrə(ʊ)leɪb, -z
AM 'æstrə,leɪb, 'æstrə,læb, -z

astrologer
BR ə'strɒlədʒə(r), -z
AM ə'strɑlədʒər, -z

astrologic
BR ,astrə'lɒdʒɪk
AM ,æstrə'lɑdʒɪk

astrological
BR ,astrə'lɒdʒɪkl
AM ,æstrə'lɑdʒəkəl

astrologically
BR ,astrə'lɒdʒɪkli
AM ,æstrə'lɑdʒək(ə)li

astrology
BR ə'strɒlədʒi
AM ə'strɑlədʒi

åstrom
BR 'ɔːstrəm, 'ɑːstrəm, -z
AM 'ɔstrəm, 'ɑstrəm, -z

astronaut
BR 'astrənɔːt, -s
AM 'æstrə,nɔt, 'æstrə,nɑt, -s

astronautical
BR ,astrə'nɔːtɪkl
AM ,æstrə'nɔdəkəl, ,æstrə'nɑdəkəl

astronautically
BR ,astrə'nɔːtɪkli
AM ,æstrə'nɔdək(ə)li, ,æstrə'nɑdək(ə)li

astronautics
BR ,astrə'nɔːtɪks
AM ,æstrə'nɔdɪks

astronomer
BR ə'strɒnəmə(r), -z
AM ə'strɑnəmər, -z

astronomic
BR ,astrə'nɒmɪk
AM ,æstrə'nɑmɪk

astronomical
BR ,astrə'nɒmɪkl
AM ,æstrə'nɑməkəl

astronomically
BR ,astrə'nɒmɪkli
AM ,æstrə'nɑmək(ə)li

astronomy
BR ə'strɒnəmi
AM ə'strɑnəmi

astrophysical
BR ,astrəʊ'fɪzɪkl
AM ,æstroʊ'fɪzəkəl

astrophysicist
BR ,astrəʊ'fɪzɪsɪst, -s
AM ,æstroʊ'fɪzəsəst, -s

astrophysics
BR ,astrəʊ'fɪzɪks
AM ¦æstroʊ¦fɪzɪks

Astroturf®
BR 'astrəʊtəːf
AM 'æstrə,tərf, 'æstroʊ,tərf

Asturias
BR a'st(j)ʊərɪas, ə'st(j)ʊərɪas, a'st(j)ʊərɪəs, ə'st(j)ʊərɪəs
AM æ'st(j)ʊriəs, ə'st(j)ʊriəs

astute
BR ə'stjuːt, ə'stʃuːt, -ə(r), -ɪst
AM ə'st(j)u|t, -dər, -dəst

astutely
BR ə'stjuːtli, ə'stʃuːtli
AM ə'st(j)utli

astuteness
BR ə'stjuːtnəs, ə'stʃuːtnəs
AM ə'st(j)utnəs

Astyanax
BR a'stʌɪənaks, ə'stʌɪənaks
AM ə'staɪə,næks

Asunción
BR a,sʊn(t)sɪ'ɒn
AM æ,sʊn(t)si'ɑn, æ,sʊn(t)si'ɔn
SP asun'θjon, asun'sjon

asunder
BR ə'sʌndə(r)
AM ə'səndər

Asur
BR 'asə(r)
AM 'æsər

Aswad
BR 'azwɒd, 'aswɒd
AM 'æswɑd

Aswan
BR ,as'wɑːn, ,as'wan, 'aswɑːn, 'aswan
AM ¦æz¦wɑn

asylum
BR ə'sʌɪləm, -z
AM ə'saɪləm, -z

asymmetric
BR ,eɪsɪ'mɛtrɪk, ,asɪ'mɛtrɪk
AM ,eɪsə'mɛtrɪk

asymmetrical
BR ,eɪsɪ'mɛtrɪkl, ,asɪ'mɛtrɪkl
AM ,eɪsə'mɛtrəkəl

asymmetrically
BR ,eɪsɪ'mɛtrɪkli, ,asɪ'mɛtrɪkli
AM ,eɪsə'mɛtrək(ə)li

asymmetry
BR eɪ'sɪmɪtri
AM eɪ'sɪmətri

asymptomatic
BR ,eɪsɪm(p)tə'matɪk
AM ,eɪ,sɪm(p)tə'mædɪk

asymptote
BR 'asɪm(p)təʊt, -s
AM 'æsəm(p),toʊt, -s

asymptotic
BR ,asɪm'tɒtɪk
AM ,æsəm(p)'tɑdɪk

asymptotically
BR ,asɪm'tɒtɪkli
AM ,æsəm(p)'tɑdək(ə)li

asynchronous
BR eɪ'sɪŋkrənəs
AM eɪ'sɪŋkrənəs

asynchronously
BR eɪ'sɪŋkrənəsli
AM eɪ'sɪŋkrənəsli

asyndetic
BR ,asɪn'dɛtɪk, ,eɪsɪn'dɛtɪk
AM ,æsn'dɛdɪk

asyndeton
BR ə'sɪndɪt(ə)n
AM ə'sɪndə,tɑn, eɪ'sɪndə,tɑn

at¹
strong form
BR at
AM æt

at²
weak form
BR ət
AM ət

Atabrine®
BR 'atəbriːn, 'atəbrɪn
AM 'ædəbrən, 'ædə,brin

Atacama
BR ,atə'kɑːmə(*r*)
AM ,ɑdə'kɑmə

Atack
BR 'eɪtak
AM 'eɪtæk

Atahualpa
BR ,atə'(h)wɑːlpə(*r*), ,atə'(h)walpə(*r*)
AM ,ɑtə'(h)wɑlpə

Atalanta
BR ,atə'lantə(*r*)
AM ,ædə'læn(t)ə

ataractic
BR ,atər'aktɪk
AM ,ædə'ræktɪk

ataraxia
BR ,atər'aksɪə(*r*)
AM ,ædə'ræksiə

ataraxic
BR ,atər'aksɪk
AM ,ædə'ræksɪk

ataraxy
BR 'atəraksi
AM 'ædə,ræksi

Atari®
BR ə'tɑːri
AM ɑ'tɑri

Atatürk
BR 'atətəːk
AM 'ædə,tərk
TU ʌtʌ'tyrk

atavism
BR 'atəvɪz(ə)m
AM 'ædə,vɪzəm

atavistic
BR ,atə'vɪstɪk
AM ,ædə'vɪstɪk

atavistically
BR ,atə'vɪstɪkli
AM ,ædə'vɪstək(ə)li

ataxia
BR ə'taksɪə(r), a'taksɪə(r)
AM ə'tæksiə, eɪ'tæksiə

ataxic
BR ə'taksɪk, -s
AM ə'tæksɪk, -s

ataxy
BR ə'taksi
AM ə'tæksi

Atchison
BR 'atʃɪs(ə)n
AM 'ætʃɪsən

atchoo
BR ə'tʃuː
AM ə'tʃu

Atco®
BR 'atkəʊ
AM 'ætkoʊ

ate
BR ɛt, eɪt
AM eɪt

Atebrin®
BR 'atɨbriːn, 'atɨbrɪn
AM 'ædəbrən, 'ædə,brin

atelier
BR ə'tɛlɪeɪ, -z
AM ,ædl'jeɪ, ə'tɛl,jeɪ, -z

a tempo
BR ,ɑː 'tɛmpəʊ
AM ,ɑ 'tɛmpoʊ

atemporal
BR eɪ'tɛmp(ə)rəl, eɪ'tɛmp(ə)rl̩
AM eɪ,tɛm'pɔrəl, eɪ'tɛmp(ə)rəl

Aten
BR 'ɑːt(ə)n
AM 'ɑtn

Athabasca
BR ,aθə'baskə(r)
AM ,æθə'bæskə

Athabascan
BR ,aθə'bask(ə)n, -z
AM ,æθə'bæskən, -z

Athanasian
BR ,aθə'neɪʃn, ,aθə'neɪʒn, ,aθə'neɪsɪən, ,aθə'neɪzɪən
AM ,æθə'neɪʒən

Athanasius
BR ,aθə'neɪʃəs, ,aθə'neɪʒəs, ,aθə'neɪsɪəs, ,aθə'neɪzɪəs
AM ,æθə'neɪʃ(i)əs, ,æθə'neɪʒ(i)əs

Athapaskan
BR ,aθə'pask(ə)n, -z
AM ,æθə'pæskən, -z

atheism
BR 'eɪθɪɪz(ə)m
AM 'eɪθi,ɪzəm

atheist
BR 'eɪθɪɪst, -s
AM 'eɪθiɨst, -s

atheistic
BR ,eɪθɪ'ɪstɪk
AM ,eɪθi'ɪstɪk

atheistical
BR ,eɪθɪ'ɪstɨkl
AM ,eɪθi'ɪstɨkəl

atheistically
BR ,eɪθɪ'ɪstɨkli
AM ,eɪθi'ɪstɨk(ə)li

atheling
BR 'aθəlɪŋ, 'aθl̩ɪŋ, -z
AM 'æθ(ə)lɪŋ, -z

Athelstan
BR 'aθəlst(ə)n, 'aθlst(ə)n, 'aθəlstan, 'aθl̩stan
AM 'æθəl,stæn

athematic
BR ,aθiː'matɪk, ,eɪθiː'matɪk, ,aθɪ'matɪk, ,eɪθɪ'matɪk
AM ,æθi'mædɪk, ,eɪθi'mædɪk

Athena
BR ə'θiːnə(r)
AM ə'θinə

athenaeum
BR ,aθɪ'niːəm, -z
AM ,æθə'niəm, -z

Athene
BR ə'θiːni
AM ə'θini

atheneum
BR ,aθɪ'niːəm, -z
AM ,æθə'niəm, -z

Athenian
BR ə'θiːnɪən, -z
AM ə'θiniən, -z

Athens
BR 'aθ(ɪ)nz
AM 'æθənz

atheoretical
BR ,eɪθɪə'rɛtɨkl
AM eɪ,θiə'rɛdəkəl

atheroma
BR ,aθə'rəʊmə(r), -z
AM ,æθə'roʊmə, -z

atheromata
BR ,aθə'rəʊmətə(r)
AM ,æθə'roʊmədə

atheroscleroses
BR ,aθ(ə)rəʊsklɪ'rəʊsiːz, ,aθ(ə)rəʊsklɛ'rəʊsiːz
AM ,æθə,roʊsklə'roʊsiz

atherosclerosis
BR ,aθ(ə)rəʊsklɪ'rəʊsɪs, ,aθ(ə)rəʊsklɛ'rəʊsɪs
AM ,æθə,roʊsklə'roʊsəs

atherosclerotic
BR ,aθ(ə)rəʊsklɪ'rɒtɪk
AM ,æθə,roʊsklə'rɑdɪk

Atherstone
BR 'aθəst(ə)n
AM 'æðər,stoʊn

Atherton
BR 'aθət(ə)n
AM 'æðərt(ə)n

athetosis
BR ,aθɪ'təʊsɪs
AM ,æθə'toʊsɪs

athirst
BR ə'θəːst
AM ə'θərst

athlete
BR 'aθliːt, -s
AM 'æθ(ə),lit, -s

athletic
BR aθ'lɛtɪk, əθ'lɛtɪk
AM æθ(ə)'lɛdɪk

athletically
BR aθ'lɛtɨkli, əθ'lɛtɨkli
AM æθ(ə)'lɛdək(ə)li

athleticism
BR aθ'lɛtɨsɪz(ə)m, əθ'lɛtɨsɪz(ə)m
AM æθ(ə)'lɛdə,sɪzəm

Athlone
BR (,)aθ'ləʊn
AM 'æθloʊn

Athol
BR 'aθɒl
AM 'æθɔl, 'æθɑl

Atholl
BR 'aθ(ɒ)l
AM 'æθɔl, 'æθɑl

Athos
BR 'aθɒs, 'eɪθɒs
AM 'ɑθ,ɑs, 'eɪ,θɑs

athwart
BR ə'θwɔːt
AM ə'θwɔ(ə)rt

atilt
BR ə'tɪlt
AM ə'tɪlt

atingle
BR ə'tɪŋgl
AM ə'tɪŋgəl

atishoo
BR ə'tɪʃuː
AM ə'tɪʃu

Ativan®
BR 'atɪvan
AM 'ædɪvæn

Atkin
BR 'atkɪn
AM 'ætkɪn

Atkins
BR 'atkɪnz
AM 'ætkɪnz

Atkinson
BR 'atkɪns(ə)n
AM 'ætkɪnsən

Atlanta
BR ət'lantə(r)
AM ə(t)'læn(t)ə

Atlantean
BR ət'lantɪən, -z
AM ,æt'læn(t)iən, -z

atlantes
BR ət'lantiːz
AM ət'læntiz, æt'læntiz

Atlantic
BR ət'lantɪk
AM ət'læn(t)ɪk

Atlanticism
BR ət'lantɪsɪz(ə)m
AM ət'læn(t)ə,sɪzəm

Atlanticist
BR ət'lantɪsɪst, -s
AM ət'læn(t)əsəst, -s

Atlantis
BR ət'lantɪs, at'lantɪs
AM ət'læn(t)əs

atlantosaurus
BR ət,lantə'sɔːrəs, -ɨz
AM ət,læn(t)ə'sɔrəs, -əz

atlas
BR 'atləs, -ɨz
AM 'ætləs, -əz

atman
BR 'ɑːtmən
AM 'ɑtmən

atmosphere
BR 'atməsfɪə(r), -z
AM 'ætmə,sfɪ(ə)r, -z

atmospheric
BR ,atməs'fɛrɪk, -s
AM ,ætmə'sfɪrɪk, -s

atmospherical
BR ,atməs'fɛrɪkl
AM ,ætmə'sfɪrɨkəl

atmospherically
BR ,atməs'fɛrɨkli
AM ,ætmə'sfɪrɨk(ə)li

atoll
BR 'atɒl, -z
AM 'æ,tɔl, 'æ,tɑl, -z

atom
BR 'atəm, -z
AM 'ædəm, -z

atomic
BR ə'tɒmɪk
AM ə'tɑmɪk

atomically
BR ə'tɒmɨkli
AM ə'tɑmək(ə)li

atomicity
BR ,atə'mɪsɨti
AM ,ædə'mɪsɨdi

atomisation
BR ,atəmʌɪ'zeɪʃn
AM ,ædəmə'zeɪʃən, ,ædə,maɪ'zeɪʃən

atomise
BR 'atəmʌɪz, -ɨz, -ɪŋ, -d
AM 'ædə,maɪz, -ɨz, -ɪŋ, -d

atomiser
BR 'atəmʌɪzə(r), -z

AM 'ædə,maɪzər, -z

atomism
BR 'atəmɪz(ə)m
AM 'ædə,mɪzəm

atomist
BR 'atəmɪst, -s
AM 'ædəməst, -s

atomistic
BR ,atə'mɪstɪk
AM ,ædə'mɪstɪk

atomistically
BR ,atə'mɪstɪkli
AM ,ædə'mɪstɪk(ə)li

atomization
BR ,atəmʌɪ'zeɪʃn
AM ,ædəmə'zeɪʃən, ,ædə,maɪ'zeɪʃən

atomize
BR 'atəmʌɪz, -ɨz, -ɪŋ, -d
AM 'ædə,maɪz, -ɨz, -ɪŋ, -d

atomizer
BR 'atəmʌɪzə(r), -z
AM 'ædə,maɪzər, -z

atomy
BR 'atəm|i, -ɪz
AM 'ædəmi, -z

atonal
BR (,)eɪ'təʊnl
AM eɪ'toʊnəl, æ'toʊnəl

atonality
BR ,eɪtə(ʊ)'nalɨti
AM ,eɪtoʊ'nælədi, ,ætoʊ'nælədi

atonally
BR (,)eɪ'təʊnl̩i, (,)eɪ'təʊnəli
AM eɪ'toʊnəli

atone
BR ə'təʊn, -z, -ɪŋ, -d
AM ə'toʊn, -z, -ɪŋ, -d

atonement
BR ə'təʊnm(ə)nt, -s
AM ə'toʊnmənt, -s

atonic
BR (,)eɪ'tɒnɪk
AM eɪ'tɑnɪk

atony
BR 'atəni
AM 'ætn̩i

atop
BR ə'tɒp
AM ə'tɑp

Atora®
BR ə'tɔːrə(*r*)
AM ə'tɔrə

atrabilious
BR ,atrə'bɪlɪəs
AM ,ætrə'bɪliəs

atrabiliousness
BR ,atrə'bɪlɪəsnəs
AM ,ætrə'bɪliəsnəs

Atreus
BR 'eɪtrɪəs, 'eɪtrɪuːs
AM 'eɪtriəs

atria
BR 'eɪtrɪə(*r*)
AM 'eɪtriə

atrial
BR 'eɪtrɪəl
AM 'eɪtriəl

atrium
BR 'eɪtrɪəm, -z
AM 'eɪtriəm, -z

atrocious
BR ə'trəʊʃəs
AM ə'troʊʃəs

atrociously
BR ə'trəʊʃəsli
AM ə'troʊʃəsli

atrociousness
BR ə'trəʊʃəsnəs
AM ə'troʊʃəsnəs

atrocity
BR ə'trɒsɪt|i, -ɪz
AM ə'trɑsədi, -z

atrophic
BR ə'trɒfɪk, (,)eɪ'trɒfɪk
AM ə'trɑfɪk

atrophy
BR 'atrəf|i, -ɪz, -ɪɪŋ, -ɪd
AM 'ætrəfi, -z, -ɪŋ, -d

atropine
BR 'atrəpiːn, 'atrəpɪn
AM 'ætrə,pin

Atropos
BR 'atrəpɒs, 'atrəpəs
AM 'ætrə,pɔs, 'ætrə,pəs, 'ætrə,pɑs

attaboy
BR 'atəbɔɪ
AM ',ædə',bɔɪ

attach
BR ə'tatʃ, -ɨz, -ɪŋ, -t
AM ə'tætʃ, -əz, -ɪŋ, -t

attachable
BR ə'tatʃəbl
AM ə'tætʃəbəl

attaché
BR ə'taʃeɪ, -z
AM ,ædə'ʃeɪ, æ,tæ'ʃeɪ, -z

attacher
BR ə'tatʃə(r), -z
AM ə'tætʃər, -z

attachment
BR ə'tatʃm(ə)nt, -s
AM ə'tætʃmənt, -s

attack
BR ə'tak, -s, -ɪŋ, -t
AM ə'tæk, -s, -ɪŋ, -t

attacker
BR ə'takə(r), -z
AM ə'tækər, -z

attain
BR ə'teɪn, -z, -ɪŋ, -d
AM ə'teɪn, -z, -ɪŋ, -d

attainability
BR ə,teɪnə'bɪlɨti
AM ə,teɪnə'bɪlɨdi

attainable
BR ə'teɪnəbl
AM ə'teɪnəbəl

attainableness
BR ə'teɪnəblnəs
AM ə'teɪnəbəlnəs

attainder
BR ə'teɪndə(r), -z
AM ə'teɪndər, -z

attainment
BR ə'teɪnm(ə)nt, -s
AM ə'teɪnmənt, -s

attaint
BR ə'teɪnt, -s, -ɪŋ, -ɨd
AM ə'teɪn|t, -ts, -(t)ɪŋ, -(t)ɨd

Attalid
BR 'atəlɪd, -z
AM 'ædl,ɪd, -z

attar
BR 'atə(r), 'atɑː(r)
AM 'ædər, 'æ,tɑr

attemper
BR ə'tɛmp|ə(r), -əz, -(ə)rɪŋ, -əd
AM ə'tɛmp|ər, -ərz, -(ə)rɪŋ, -ərd

attempt
BR ə'tɛm(p)t, -s, -ɪŋ, -ɨd
AM ə'tɛm(p)t, -s, -ɪŋ, -əd

attemptable
BR ə'tɛm(p)təbl
AM ə'tɛm(p)təbəl

Attenborough
BR 'atnb(ə)rə(*r*)
AM 'ætn,bərə

attend
BR ə'tɛnd, -z, -ɪŋ, -ɨd
AM ə'tɛnd, -z, -ɪŋ, -əd

attendance
BR ə'tɛnd(ə)ns, -ɨz
AM ə'tɛnd(ə)ns, -əz

attendant
BR ə'tɛnd(ə)nt, -s
AM ə'tɛnd(ə)nt, -s

attendee
BR ə,tɛn'diː, ,atɛn'diː, -z
AM ə,tɛn'di, ,ætɛn'di, -z

attender
BR ə'tɛndə(r), -z
AM ə'tɛndər, -z

attention
BR ə'tɛnʃn, -z
AM ə'tɛn(t)ʃən, -z

attentional
BR ə'tɛnʃn̩(ə)l, ə'tɛnʃən(ə)l
AM ə'tɛn(t)ʃ(ə)nəl

attentive
BR ə'tɛntɪv
AM ə'tɛn(t)ɪv

attentively
BR ə'tɛntɨvli
AM ə'tɛn(t)ɨvli

attentiveness
BR ə'tɛntɨvnɨs
AM ə'tɛn(t)ɨvnɨs

attenuate[1]
adjective
BR ə'tɛnjʊət
AM ə'tɛnjəwət

attenuate[2]
verb
BR ə'tɛnjʊeɪt, -s, -ɪŋ, -ɨd
AM ə'tɛnjə,weɪ|t, -ts, -dɪŋ, -dɨd

attenuation
BR ə,tɛnjʊ'eɪʃn
AM ə,tɛnjə'weɪʃən

attenuator
BR ə'tɛnjʊeɪtə(r), -z
AM ə'tɛnjə,weɪdər, -z

attest
BR ə'tɛst, -s, -ɪŋ, -ɨd
AM ə'tɛst, -s, -ɪŋ, -əd

attestable
BR ə'tɛstəbl
AM ə'tɛstəbəl

attestation
BR ,atɛ'steɪʃn, ,atə'steɪʃn, -z
AM ,æ,tɛ'steɪʃən, ,ædə'steɪʃən, -z

attestor
BR ə'tɛstə(r), -z
AM ə'tɛstər, -z

attic
BR 'atɪk, -s
AM 'ædɪk, -s

Attica
BR 'atɪkə(*r*)
AM 'ædəkə

Atticism
BR 'atɪsɪz(ə)m, -z
AM 'ædə,sɪzəm, -z

Attila
BR ə'tɪlə(*r*)
AM ə'tɪlə

attire
BR ə'tʌɪə(r), -z, -ɪŋ, -d
AM ə'taɪ(ə)r, -z, -ɪŋ, -d

Attis
BR 'atɪs
AM 'ædəs

attitude
BR 'atɪtjuːd, 'atɪtʃuːd, -z
AM 'ædə,t(j)ud, -z

attitudinal
BR ,atɪ'tjuːdɪnl, ,atɪ'tʃuːdɪnl
AM ,ædə't(j)udn̩əl

attitudinise
BR ,atɪ'tjuːdɪnʌɪz, ,atɪ'tʃuːdɪnʌɪz, -ɨz, -ɪŋ, -d
AM ,ædə't(j)udn,aɪz, -ɨz, -ɪŋ, -d

attitudinize
BR ,atɪ'tjuːdɪnʌɪz, ,atɪ'tʃuːdɪnʌɪz, -ɨz, -ɪŋ, -d
AM ,ædə't(j)udn,aɪz, -ɨz, -ɪŋ, -d

Attlee
BR 'atli
AM 'ætli

attorney
BR ə'təːn|i, -ɪz
AM ə'tərni, -z

attorneyship
BR ə'təːnɪʃɪp, -s
AM ə'tərni,ʃɪp, -s

attract
BR ə'trakt, -s, -ɪŋ, -ɪd
AM ə'træk(t), -(t)s, -tɪŋ, -təd

attractability
BR ə,traktə'bɪlɪti
AM ə,træktə'bɪlɨdi

attractable
BR ə'traktəbl
AM ə'træktəbəl

attractant
BR ə'trakt(ə)nt, -s
AM ə'træktnt, -s

attraction
BR ə'trakʃn, -z
AM ə'trækʃən, -z

attractive
BR ə'traktɪv
AM ə'træktɪv

attractively
BR ə'traktɨvli
AM ə'træktɨvli

attractiveness
BR ə'traktɨvnɪs
AM ə'træktɨvnɪs

attractor
BR ə'traktə(r), -z
AM ə'træktər, -z

attributable
BR ə'trɪbjʉtəbl
AM ə'trɪbjədəbəl

attributableness
BR ə'trɪbjʉtəblnəs
AM ə'trɪbjədəbəlnəs

attributably
BR ə'trɪbjʉtəbli
AM ə'trɪbjədəbli

attribute[1]
noun
BR 'atrɪbjuːt, -s
AM 'ætrə,bjut, -s

attribute[2]
verb
BR ə'trɪbj|uːt, -uːts, -ʊtɪŋ, -ʊtɪd
AM ə'trɪbj|ət, ə'trɪ,bj|ut, -əts\-uts, -ədɪŋ, -ədəd

attribution
BR ,atrɪ'bjuːʃn, -z
AM ,ætrə'bjuʃən, -z

attributive
BR ə'trɪbjʉtɪv
AM ə'trɪbjədɪv

attributively
BR ə'trɪbjʉtɨvli
AM ə'trɪbjədɨvli

attrition
BR ə'trɪʃn
AM ə'trɪʃən

attritional
BR ə'trɪʃn̩(ə)l, ə'trɪʃən(ə)l
AM ə'trɪʃ(ə)nəl

attune
BR ə'tjuːn, ə'tʃuːn, -z, -ɪŋ, -d
AM ə't(j)un, -z, -ɪŋ, -d

Atwell
BR 'atwɛl
AM 'ætwɛl

atwitter
BR ə'twɪtə(*r*)
AM ə'twɪdər

Atwood
BR 'atwʊd
AM 'æt,wʊd

atypical
BR (,)eɪ'tɪpɨkl
AM ,eɪ'tɪpɨkəl

atypically
BR (,)eɪ'tɪpɨkli
AM ,eɪ'tɪpɨk(ə)li

aubade
BR əʊ'bɑːd, -z
AM oʊ'bɑd, -z

auberge
BR əʊ'bɛːʒ, 'əʊbɛːʒ, -ɪz
AM oʊ'bɛrʒ, -ɪz

aubergine
BR 'əʊbəʒiːn, -z
AM 'oʊbər,ʒin, -z

Auberon
BR 'ɔːb(ə)rən, 'ɔːb(ə)rn̩, 'ɔːb(ə)rɒn, 'əʊb(ə)rən, 'əʊb(ə)rn̩, 'əʊb(ə)rɒn
AM 'oʊbə,rɑn

Aubrey
BR 'ɔːbri
AM 'ɔbri, 'ɑbri

aubrietia
BR ɔː'briːʃə(*r*), -z
AM ɔ'briʃ(i)ə, ɑ'briʃ(i)ə, -z

auburn
BR 'ɔːbən
AM 'ɔbərn, 'ɑbərn

Aubusson
BR 'əʊbjʉsɒn, -z
AM ,oʊbə'sɔn, ,oʊbə'sɑn, -z
FR obysɔ̃

Auchinleck
BR 'ɔːk(ɪ)nlɛk
AM 'ɔkɪn,lɛk, 'æfløk, 'ɑkɪn,lɛk

Auchtermuchty
BR ,ɒxtə'mʊxti, ,ɒktə'mʌkti, ,ɔːktə'mʌkti
AM 'ɔktər,məkti, 'ɑktər,məkti

Auckland
BR 'ɔːklənd
AM 'ɔklənd, 'ɑklənd

au contraire
BR ,əʊ kɒn'trɛː(r)
AM ,oʊ ,kɑn'trɛ(ə)r

au courant
BR ,əʊ kʊ'rɒ̃
AM ,oʊ 'kʊrɑnt

auction
BR 'ɔːkʃ|n, 'ɒkʃ|n, -nz, -n̩ɪŋ\-ənɪŋ, -nd
AM 'ɔkʃ|ən, 'ɑkʃ|ən, -ənz, -(ə)nɪŋ, -ənd

auctioneer
BR ,ɔːkʃə'nɪə(r), ,ɒkʃə'nɪə(r), -z
AM ,ɔkʃə'nɪ(ə)r, ,ɑkʃə'nɪ(ə)r, -z

auctioneering
BR ,ɔːkʃə'nɪərɪŋ, ,ɒkʃə'nɪərɪŋ
AM ,ɔkʃə'nɪrɪŋ, ,ɑkʃə'nɪrɪŋ

auctorial
BR ɔːk'tɔːrɪəl
AM ɔk'tɔriəl, ɑk'tɔriəl

audacious
BR ɔː'deɪʃəs
AM ɔ'deɪʃəs, ɑ'deɪʃəs

audaciously
BR ɔː'deɪʃəsli
AM ɔ'deɪʃəsli, ɑ'deɪʃəsli

audaciousness
BR ɔː'deɪʃəsnəs
AM ɔ'deɪʃəsnəs, ɑ'deɪʃəsnəs

audacity
BR ɔː'dasɪti
AM ɔ'dæsədi, ɑ'dæsədi

Auden
BR 'ɔːdn
AM 'ɔdən, 'ɑdən

Audi®
BR 'aʊd|i, -ɪz
AM 'aʊdi, -z

audibility
BR ,ɔːdɪ'bɪlɪti
AM ,ɔdə'bɪlɨdi, ,ɑdə'bɪlɨdi

audible
BR 'ɔːdɪbl
AM 'ɔdəbəl, 'ɑdəbəl

audibleness
BR 'ɔːdɪblnəs
AM 'ɔdəbəlnəs, 'ɑdəbəlnəs

audibly
BR 'ɔːdɪbli
AM 'ɔdəbli, 'ɑdəbli

Audie
BR 'ɔːdi
AM 'ɔdi, 'ɑdi

audience
BR 'ɔːdɪəns, -ɪz
AM 'ɔdiəns, 'ɑdiəns, -əz

audile
BR 'ɔːdʌɪl, -z
AM 'ɔ,daɪl, 'ɑ,daɪl, -z

audio
BR 'ɔːdɪəʊ, -z
AM 'ɔdioʊ, 'ɑdioʊ, -z

audiocassette
BR 'ɔːdɪəʊkə,sɛt, -s
AM ,ɔdioʊkə'sɛt, ,ɑdioʊkə'sɛt, -s

audiolingual
BR ,ɔːdɪəʊ'lɪŋgw(ə)l
AM ,ɔdioʊ'lɪŋgwəl, ,ɑdioʊ'lɪŋgwəl

audiological
BR ,ɔːdɪə'lɒdʒɪkl
AM ,ɔdiə'lɑdʒəkəl, ,ɑdiə'lɑdʒəkəl

audiologist
BR ,ɔːdɪ'ɒlədʒɪst, -s
AM ,ɔdi'ɑlədʒəst, ,ɑdi'ɑlədʒəst, -s

audiology
BR ,ɔːdɪ'ɒlədʒi
AM ,ɔdi'ɑlədʒi, ,ɑdi'ɑlədʒi

audiometer
BR ,ɔːdɪ'ɒmɪtə(r), -z
AM ,ɔdi'ɑmədər, ,ɑdi'ɑmədər, -z

audiometry
BR ,ɔːdɪ'ɒmɪtri
AM ,ɔdi'ɑmətri, ,ɑdi'ɑmətri

audiophile
BR 'ɔːdɪə(ʊ)fʌɪl, -z
AM 'ɔdioʊ,faɪl, 'ɑdioʊ,faɪl, -z

audiotape
BR 'ɔːdɪəʊ,teɪp, -s
AM 'ɔdioʊ,teɪp, 'ɑdioʊ,teɪp, -s

audiotyping
BR 'ɔːdɪəʊ,tʌɪpɪŋ
AM 'ɔdioʊ,taɪpɪŋ, 'ɑdioʊ,taɪpɪŋ

audiotypist
BR 'ɔːdɪəʊ,tʌɪpɪst, -s
AM 'ɔdioʊ,taɪpɪst, 'ɑdioʊ,taɪpɪst, -s

audio-visual
BR ,ɔːdɪəʊ'vɪʒʊ(ə)l, ,ɔːdɪəʊ'vɪzjʊ(ə)l, ,ɔːdɪəʊ'vɪʒ(ʉ)l, ,ɔːdɪəʊ'vɪzj(ʉ)l
AM ,ɔdioʊ'vɪʒ(ə)wəl, ,ɔdioʊ'vɪʒəl, ,ɑdioʊ'vɪʒ(ə)wəl, ,ɑdioʊ'vɪʒəl

audit
BR 'ɔːd|ɪt, -ɪts, -ɪtɪŋ, -ɪtɪd
AM 'ɔdə|t, 'ɑdə|t, -ts, -dɪŋ, -dəd

audition
BR ɔː'dɪʃ|n, -nz, -n̩ɪŋ\-ənɪŋ, -nd
AM ɔ'dɪʃ|ən, ɑ'dɪʃ|ən, -ənz, -(ə)nɪŋ, -ənd

auditive
BR 'ɔːdɪtɪv

AM 'ɔdədɪv, 'ɑdədɪv

auditor
BR 'ɔːdɪtə(r), -z
AM 'ɔdədər, 'ɑdədər, -z

auditoria
BR ˌɔːdɪ'tɔːrɪə(r)
AM ˌɔdə'tɔriə, ˌɑdə'tɔriə

auditorial
BR ˌɔːdɪ'tɔːrɪəl
AM ˌɔdə'tɔriəl, ˌɑdə'tɔriəl

auditorium
BR ˌɔːdɪ'tɔːrɪəm, -z
AM ˌɔdə'tɔriəm, ˌɑdə'tɔriəm, -z

auditory
BR 'ɔːdɪt(ə)ri
AM 'ɔdəˌtɔri, 'ɑdəˌtɔri

Audlem
BR 'ɔːdləm
AM 'ɔdləm, 'ɑdləm

Audley
BR 'ɔːdli
AM 'ɔdli, 'ɑdli

Audra
BR 'ɔːdrə(r)
AM 'ɔdrə, 'ɑdrə

Audrey
BR 'ɔːdri
AM 'ɔdri, 'ɑdri

Audubon
BR 'ɔːdəbɒn
AM 'ɔdəˌbɑn, 'ɑdəˌbɑn

au fait
BR ˌəʊ 'feɪ
AM ˌoʊ 'feɪ

au fond
BR ˌəʊ 'fɔ̃
AM ˌoʊ 'fɔnd

Augean
BR ɔː'dʒiːən
AM ɔ'dʒiən, 'ɔˌgiən, ɑ'dʒiən, 'ɑgiən

auger
BR 'ɔːgə(r), -z
AM 'ɔgər, 'ɑgər, -z

aught
BR ɔːt
AM ɔt, ɑt

augite
BR 'ɔːdʒʌɪt
AM 'ɔˌdʒaɪt, 'ɔgaɪt, 'ɑˌdʒaɪt, 'ɑgaɪt

augment
BR ɔːg'mɛnt, -s, -ɪŋ, -ɪd
AM ɔg'mɛn|t, ɑg'mɛn|t, -ts, -(t)ɪŋ, -(t)əd

augmentation
BR ˌɔːgmɛn'teɪʃn, ˌɔːgm(ə)n'teɪʃn
AM ˌɔgmən'teɪʃən, ˌɔgˌmɛn'teɪʃən, ˌɑgmən'teɪʃən, ˌɑgˌmɛn'teɪʃən

augmentative
BR ɔːg'mɛntətɪv
AM ɔg'mɛn(t)ədɪv, ɑg'mɛn(t)ədɪv

augmenter
BR ɔːg'mɛntə(r), -z
AM ɔg'mɛn(t)ər, ɑg'mɛn(t)ər, -z

au grand sérieux
BR əʊ ˌgrɒ̃ ˌsɛrɪ'əː(z)
AM ˌoʊ ˌgrɑn ˌsɛri'ə

au gratin
BR əʊ 'gratã, + 'gratan
AM ˌoʊ 'grɑtn, + 'grætn

Augsburg
BR 'aʊgzbəːg
AM 'ɔgzbərg, 'aʊgzˌbərg, 'ɑgzˌbərg
GER 'aʊksbʊrk

augur
BR 'ɔːgə(r), -z, -ɪŋ, -d
AM 'ɔgər, 'ɑgər, -z, -ɪŋ, -d

augural
BR 'ɔːgjʊrəl, 'ɔːgjʊrl̩
AM 'ɔg(j)ərəl, 'ɑg(j)ərəl

augury
BR 'ɔːgjʊr|i, -ɪz
AM 'ɔg(j)əri, 'ɑg(j)əri, -z

August[1]
forename
BR 'aʊgʊst
AM 'ɔgəst, 'ɑgəst

August[2]
month
BR 'ɔːgəst, -s
AM 'ɔgəst, 'ɑgəst, -s

august[1]
adjective
BR ɔː'gʌst, -ɪst
AM ɔ'gəst, ɑ'gəst, -əst

august[2]
clown
BR 'aʊgʊst, -s
AM 'ɔgəst, 'ɑgəst, -s

Augusta
BR ɔː'gʌstə(r), ə'gʌstə(r)
AM ə'gəstə

Augustan
BR ə'gʌst(ə)n, ɔː'gʌst(ə)n, -z
AM ɔ'gəstən, ə'gəstən, ɑ'gəstən, -z

Augustine
BR 'ɔːgəstiːn, 'ɔːgəstʌɪn, -z
AM 'ɔgəˌstin, 'ɑgəˌstin, ə'gəstən, -z

Augustinian
BR ˌɔːgə'stɪnɪən, -z
AM ˌɔgə'stɪniən, ˌɑgə'stɪniən, -z

augustly
BR ɔː'gʌstli
AM ɔ'gəs(t)li, ɑ'gəs(t)li

augustness
BR ɔː'gʌs(t)nəs
AM ɔ'gəs(t)nəs, ɑ'gəs(t)nəs

Augustus
BR ɔː'gʌstəs, ə'gʌstəs
AM ə'gəstəs

au jus
BR əʊ 'ʒuː(s)
AM oʊ 'ʒu(s)

auk
BR ɔːk, -s
AM ɔk, ɑk, -s

auklet
BR 'ɔːklɪt, -s
AM 'ɔklət, 'ɑklət, -s

auld lang syne
BR ˌɔːld laŋ 'zʌɪn, ˌəʊld +, + 'sʌɪn
AM ˌoʊ(l) ˌlæŋ 'zaɪn, ˌoʊl ˌdlæŋ +

aulic
BR 'ɔːlɪk
AM 'ɔlɪk, 'ɑlɪk

aumbry
BR 'ɔːmbr|i, -ɪz
AM 'ɔmbri, 'ɑmbri, -z

au naturel
BR əʊ ˌnatʃʊ'rɛl, + ˌnatjʊ'rɛl
AM ˌoʊ ˌnætʃə'rɛl

aunt
BR ɑːnt, -s
AM ænt, -s

auntie
BR 'ɑːnt|i, -ɪz
AM 'æn(t)i, -z

aunty
BR 'ɑːnt|i, -ɪz
AM 'æn(t)i, -z

au pair
BR ˌəʊ 'pɛː(r), -z
AM ˌoʊ 'pɛ(ə)r, -z

aura
BR 'ɔːrə(r), -z
AM 'ɔrə, -z

aural
BR 'ɔːrl̩, 'ɔːrəl
AM 'ɔrəl

aurally
BR 'ɔːrl̩i, 'ɔːrəli
AM 'ɔrəli

Aurangzeb
BR ˌɔːraŋ'zɛb
AM ɔˌræŋ'zɛb, ɑˌræŋ'zɛb

aureate
BR 'ɔːrɪeɪt, 'ɔːrɪət
AM 'ɔriət, 'ɔriˌeɪt

Aurelia
BR ɔː'riːlɪə(r)
AM ɔ'riliə, ɑ'riliə, ɔ'riljə, ɑ'riljə

Aurelian[1]
BR ɔː'riːlɪən
AM ɔ'riliən

Aurelian[2]
BR ɔː'riːlɪən
AM ɔ'riliən, ɑ'riliən, ɔ'riljən, ɑ'riljən

Aurelius
BR ɔː'riːlɪəs
AM ɔ'riliəs, ɑ'riliəs

aureola
BR ɔː'riːələ(r), ˌɔːrɪ'əʊlə(r), -z
AM ɔ'riələ, ɑ'riələ, -z

aureole
BR 'ɔːrɪəʊl, -z
AM 'ɔriˌoʊl, -z

aureomycin
BR ˌɔːrɪə(ʊ)'mʌɪsɪn
AM ˌɔrioʊ'maɪsɪn

au revoir
BR ˌəʊ rɪ'vwɑː(r), ˌɔː +
AM ˌɔ rə'vwɑr, ˌoʊ +

auric
BR 'ɔːrɪk
AM 'ɔrɪk

auricle
BR 'ɔːrɪkl, 'ɒrɪkl, -z
AM 'ɔrəkəl, -z

auricula
BR ɔː'rɪkjʊlə(r), -z
AM ɔ'rɪkjələ, ɑ'rɪkjələ, -z

auricular
BR ɔː'rɪkjʊlə(r)
AM ɔ'rɪkjələr, ɑ'rɪkjələr

auricularly
BR ɔː'rɪkjʊləli
AM ɔ'rɪkjələrli, ɑ'rɪkjələrli

auriculate[1]
adjective
BR ɔː'rɪkjʊlət
AM ɔ'rɪkjələt, ɑ'rɪkjələt

auriculate[2]
verb
BR ɔː'rɪkjʊleɪt, -s, -ɪŋ, -ɪd
AM ɔ'rɪkjəˌleɪ|t, ɑ'rɪkjəˌleɪ|t, -ts, -dɪŋ, -dɪd

auriferous
BR ɔː'rɪf(ə)rəs
AM ɔ'rɪfərəs, ɑ'rɪfərəs

Auriga
BR ɔː'rʌɪgə(r)
AM ɔ'raɪgə, ɑ'raɪgə

Aurignacian
BR ˌɔːrɪ'njeɪʃn, ˌɔːrɪg'neɪʃn, -z
AM ˌɔrə'gneɪʃən, -z

auriscope
BR 'ɔːrɪskəʊp, -s
AM 'ɔrəˌskoʊp, -s

aurist
BR 'ɔːrɪst, -s
AM 'ɔrəst, -s

aurochs
BR 'ɔːrɒks
AM 'aʊˌrɑks, 'ɔˌrɑks, 'ɑˌrɑks

aurora
BR əˈrɔːrə(r), ɔːˈrɔːrə(r)
AM əˈrɔrə, ɔˈrɔrə, ɑˈrɔrə

aurora australis
BR əˌrɔːrə(r) ɔːˈstrɑːlɪs, ɔːˌrɔːrə(r)+, + ɔːˈstreɪlɪs, + ɒˈstrɑːlɪs, + ɒˈstreɪlɪs
AM əˈrɔrə ɔˈstreɪlɪs, ɔˈrɔrə +, ɑˈrɔrə +

aurora borealis
BR əˌrɔːrə ˌbɔːrɪˈeɪlɪs, ɔːˌrɔːrə +, + ˌbɔːrɪˈɑːlɪs
AM əˈrɔrə ˌbɔriˈæləs, ɔˈrɔrə +, ɑˈrɔrə +

auroral
BR əˈrɔːrəl, əˈrɔːrl̩, ɔːˈrɔːrəl, ɔːˈrɔːrl̩
AM əˈrɔrəl, ɔˈrɔrəl, ɑˈrɔrəl

Auschwitz
BR ˈaʊʃwɪts, ˈaʊʃvɪts
AM ˈaʊʃwɪts, ˈaʊʃvɪts

auscultate
BR ˈɔːsk(ə)lteɪt, ˈɔːskʌlteɪt, -s, -ɪŋ, -ɪd
AM ˈɔskəlˌteɪ|t, ˈɑskəlˌteɪ|t, -ts, -dɪŋ, -dɪd

auscultation
BR ˌɔːsk(ə)lˈteɪʃn, ˌɔːskʌlˈteɪʃn, -z
AM ˌɔskəlˈteɪʃən, ˌɑskəlˈteɪʃən, -z

auscultatory
BR ɔːˈskʌltət(ə)ri
AM ɔˈskəltəˌtɔri, ɑˈskəltəˌtɔri

au sérieux
BR ˌəʊ sɛrɪˈəː(z)
AM ˌoʊ ˌsɛriˈə

auspicate
BR ˈɔːspɪkeɪt, -s, -ɪŋ, -ɪd
AM ˈɔspəˌkeɪ|t, ˈɑspəˌkeɪ|t, -ts, -dɪŋ, -dɪd

auspice
BR ˈɔːsp|ɪs, -ɪsɪz\-ɪsiːz
AM ˈɔspəs, ˈɑspəs, -əz

auspicious
BR ɔːˈspɪʃəs
AM ɔˈspɪʃəs, ɑˈspɪʃəs

auspiciously
BR ɔːˈspɪʃəsli
AM ɔˈspɪʃəsli, ɑˈspɪʃəsli

auspiciousness
BR ɔːˈspɪʃəsnəs
AM ɔˈspɪʃəsnəs, ɑˈspɪʃəsnəs

Aussie
BR ˈɒz|i, -ɪz
AM ˈɔsi, ˈɑsi, -z

Aust
BR ɔːst
AM ɔst, ɑst

Austell
BR ˈɔːstl, ˈɒstl
AM ˌɔsˈtɛl, ˌɑsˈtɛl

Austen
BR ˈɒstɪn, ˈɔːstɪn
AM ˈɔstən, ˈɑstən

austere
BR ɔːˈstɪə(r), ɒˈstɪə(r), -ə(r), -ɪst
AM ɔˈstɪ(ə)r, ɑˈstɪ(ə)r, -ər, -ɪst

austerely
BR ɔːˈstɪəli, ɒˈstɪəli
AM ɔˈstɪrli, ɑˈstɪrli

austereness
BR ɔːˈstɪənəs, ɒˈstɪənəs
AM ɔˈstɪrnɨs, ɑˈstɪrnɨs

austerity
BR ɔːˈstɛrɪti, ɒˈstɛrɪt|i, -ɪz
AM ɔˈstɛrədi, ɑˈstɛrədi, -z

Austerlitz
BR ˈaʊstəlɪts, ˈɔːstəlɪts
AM ˈɔstərˌlɪts, ˈaʊstərˌlɪts, ˈɑstərˌlɪts

Austick
BR ˈɔːstɪk, ˈɒstɪk
AM ˈɔstɪk, ˈɑstɪk

Austin
BR ˈɒstɪn, ˈɔːstɪn
AM ˈɔstən, ˈɑstən

austral
BR ˈɔːstr(ə)l, ˈɒstr(ə)l
AM ˈɔstrəl, ˈɑstrəl

Australasia
BR ˌɒstrəˈleɪʒə(r), ˌɒstrəˈleɪʃə(r), ˌɔːstrəˈleɪʒə(r), ˌɔːstrəˈleɪʃə(r)
AM ˌɔstrəˈleɪʒə, ˌɔstrəˈleɪʃə, ˌɑstrəˈleɪʒə, ˌɑstrəˈleɪʃə

Australasian
BR ˌɒstrəˈleɪʒn, ˌɒstrəˈleɪʃn, ˌɔːstrəˈleɪʒn, ˌɔːstrəˈleɪʃn, -z
AM ˌɔstrəˈleɪʒən, ˌɔstrəˈleɪʃən, ˌɑstrəˈleɪʒən, ˌɑstrəˈleɪʃən, -z

Australia
BR ɒˈstreɪlɪə(r), ɔːˈstreɪlɪə(r), əˈstreɪlɪə(r)
AM ɔˈstreɪljə, ɔˈstreɪliə, ɑˈstreɪljə, ɑˈstreɪliə

Australian
BR ɒˈstreɪlɪən, ɔːˈstreɪlɪən, -z
AM ɔˈstreɪljən, ɔˈstreɪliən, ɑˈstreɪljən, ɑˈstreɪliən, -z

Australianise
BR ɒˈstreɪlɪənʌɪz, ɔːˈstreɪlɪənʌɪz, -ɪz, -ɪŋ, -d
AM ɔˈstreɪljəˌnaɪz, ɔˈstreɪliəˌnaɪz, ɑˈstreɪljəˌnaɪz, ɑˈstreɪliəˌnaɪz, -ɪz, -ɪŋ, -d

Australianism
BR ɒˈstreɪlɪənɪz(ə)m, ɔːˈstreɪlɪənɪz(ə)m, -z
AM ɔˈstreɪljəˌnɪzəm, ɔˈstreɪliəˌnɪzəm, ɑˈstreɪljəˌnɪzəm, ɑˈstreɪliəˌnɪzəm, -z

Australianize
BR ɒˈstreɪlɪənʌɪz, ɔːˈstreɪlɪənʌɪz, -ɪz, -ɪŋ, -d
AM ɔˈstreɪljəˌnaɪz, ɔˈstreɪliəˌnaɪz, ɑˈstreɪljəˌnaɪz, ɑˈstreɪliəˌnaɪz, -ɪz, -ɪŋ, -d

Australoid
BR ˈɒstrəlɔɪd, ˈɔːstrəlɔɪd, -z
AM ˈɔstrəˌlɔɪd, ˈɑstrəˌlɔɪd, -z

australopithecine
BR ˌɒstrələʊˈpɪθɪsiːn, ˌɒstrələʊˈpɪθɪsʌɪn, ˌɔːstrələʊˈpɪθɪsiːn, ˌɔːstrələʊˈpɪθɪsʌɪn, -z
AM ˌɔstrəloʊˈpɪθəˌsin, ˌɑstrəloʊˈpɪθəˌsin, -z

Australopithecus[1]
BR ˌɒstrələʊˈpɪθɪkəs, ˌɔːstrələʊˈpɪθɪkəs
AM ˌɔstrəloʊˈpɪθəkəs, ˌɑstrəʊˈpɪθəkəs

Australopithecus[2]
BR ˌɒstrələʊˈpɪθɪkəs, ˌɔːstrələʊˈpɪθɪkəs
AM ˌɔstrəloʊˈpɪθəkəs, ˌɑstrəloʊˈpɪθəkəs

Austria
BR ˈɒstrɪə(r), ˈɔːstrɪə(r)
AM ˈɔstriə, ˈɑstriə

Austrian
BR ˈɒstrɪən, ˈɔːstrɪən, -z
AM ˈɔstriən, ˈɑstriən, -z

Austro-
BR ˈɒstrəʊ, ˈɔːstrəʊ
AM ˈɔstroʊ, ˈɑstroʊ

Austronesian
BR ˌɒstrəˈniːzj(ə)n, ˌɔːstrəˈniːzj(ə)n, ˌɒstrəˈniːʒn, ˌɔːstrəˈniːʒn, -z
AM ˌɔstroʊˈniʒən, ˌɔstroʊˈniʃən, ˌɑstroʊˈniʒən, ˌɑstroʊˈniʃən, -z

Austyn
BR ˈɒstɪn, ˈɔːstɪn
AM ˈɔstən, ˈɑstən

autarchic
BR ɔːˈtɑːkɪk
AM ɔˈtɑrkɪk, ɑˈtɑrkɪk

autarchical
BR ɔːˈtɑːkɪkl
AM ɔˈtɑrkəkəl, ɑˈtɑrkəkəl

autarchy
BR ˈɔːtɑːk|i, -ɪz
AM ˈɔˌtɑrki, ˈɑˌtɑrki, -z

autarkic
BR ɔːˈtɑːkɪk
AM ɔˈtɑrkɪk, ɑˈtɑrkɪk

autarkical
BR ɔːˈtɑːkɪkl
AM ɔˈtɑrkəkəl, ɑˈtɑrkəkəl

autarkist
BR ɔːˈtɑːkɪst, -s
AM ˈɔˌtɑrkəst, ˈɑˌtɑrkəst, -s

autarky
BR ˈɔːtɑːk|i, -ɪz
AM ˈɔˌtɑrki, ˈɑˌtɑrki, -z

auteur
BR ɔːˈtəː(r), əʊˈtəː(r), -z
AM oʊˈtər, ɔˈtər, ɑˈtər, -z

auteurism
BR ɔːˈtəːrɪz(ə)m, əʊˈtəːrɪz(ə)m
AM oʊˈtəˌrɪzəm, ɔˈtəˌrɪzəm, ɑˈtəˌrɪzəm

auteurist
BR ɔːˈtəːrɪst, əʊˈtəːrɪst
AM oʊˈtərəst, ɔˈtərəst, ɑˈtərəst

authentic
BR ɔːˈθɛntɪk
AM əˈθɛn(t)ɪk, ɔˈθɛn(t)ɪk, ɑˈθɛn(t)ɪk

authentically
BR ɔːˈθɛntɪkli
AM əˈθɛn(t)ək(ə)li, ɔˈθɛn(t)ək(ə)li, ɑˈθɛn(t)ək(ə)li

authenticate
BR ɔːˈθɛntɪkeɪt, -s, -ɪŋ, -ɪd
AM əˈθɛn(t)əˌkeɪ|t, ɔˈθɛn(t)əˌkeɪ|t, ɑˈθɛn(t)əˌkeɪ|t , -ts, -dɪŋ, -dɪd

authentication
BR ɔːˌθɛntɪˈkeɪʃn
AM əˌθɛn(t)əˈkeɪʃən, ɔˈθɛn(t)əˈkeɪʃən, ɑˈθɛn(t)əˈkeɪʃən

authenticator
BR ɔːˈθɛntɪkeɪtə(r), -z

AM ə'θɛn(t)ə,keɪdər, ɔ'θɛn(t)ə,keɪdər, ɑ'θɛn(t)ə,keɪdər, -z

authenticity
BR ,ɔːθɛn'tɪsɪti
AM ,ɔ,θɛn'tɪsɨdi, ,ɔθən'tɪsɨdi, ,ɑ,θɛn'tɪsɨdi, ,ɑθən'tɪsɨdi

author
BR 'ɔːθə(r), -z, -ɪŋ, -d
AM 'ɔθər, 'ɑθər, -z, -ɪŋ, -d

authoress
BR 'ɔːθ(ə)rɪs, ,ɔːθə'rɛs, -ɪz
AM 'ɔθ(ə)rəs, 'ɑθ(ə)rəs, -əz

authorial
BR ɔː'θɔːrɪəl
AM ɔ'θɔriəl, ɑ'θɔriəl

authorisation
BR ,ɔːθ(ə)rʌɪ'zeɪʃn, ,ɔːθ(ə)rɪ'zeɪʃn, -z
AM ,ɔθərə'zeɪʃən, ,ɔθə,raɪ'zeɪʃən, ,ɑθərə'zeɪʃən, ,ɑθə,raɪ'zeɪʃən, -z

authorise
BR 'ɔːθərʌɪz, -ɪz, -ɪŋ, -d
AM 'ɔθə,raɪz, 'ɑθə,raɪz, -ɪz, -ɪŋ, -d

authoritarian
BR ɔː,θɒrɪ'tɛːrɪən, ,ɔːθɒrɪ'tɛːrɪən, -z
AM ɔ,θɔrə'tɛriən, ə,θɔrə'tɛriən, ɑ,θɔrə'tɛriən, -z

authoritarianism
BR ɔː,θɒrɪ'tɛːrɪənɪz(ə)m, ,ɔːθɒrɪ'tɛːrɪənɪz(ə)m
AM ɔ,θɔrə'tɛriə,nɪzəm, ə,θɔrə'tɛriə,nɪzəm, ɑ,θɔrə'tɛriə,nɪzəm

authoritative
BR ɔː'θɒrɪtətɪv
AM ɔ'θɔrə,teɪdɪv, ə'θɔrə,teɪdɪv, ɑ'θɔrə,teɪdɪv

authoritatively
BR ɔː'θɒrɪtətɪvli
AM ɔ'θɔrə,teɪdɨvli, ə'θɔrə,teɪdɨvli, ɑ'θɔrə,teɪdɨvli

authoritativeness
BR ɔː'θɒrɪtətɪvnɪs
AM ɔ'θɔrə,teɪdɨvnɨs, ə'θɔrə,teɪdɨvnɨs, ɑ'θɔrə,teɪdɨvnɨs

authority
BR ɔː'θɒrɪt|i, -ɪz
AM ɔ'θɔrədi, ə'θɔrədi, ɑ'θɔrədi, -z

authorization
BR ,ɔːθərʌɪ'zeɪʃn, -z
AM ,ɔθərə'zeɪʃən, ,ɔθə,raɪ'zeɪʃən, ,ɑθərə'zeɪʃən, ,ɑθə,raɪ'zeɪʃən, -z

authorize
BR 'ɔːθərʌɪz, -ɪz, -ɪŋ, -d
AM 'ɔθə,raɪz, 'ɑθə,raɪz, -ɪz, -ɪŋ, -d

authorship
BR 'ɔːθəʃɪp
AM 'ɔθər,ʃɪp, 'ɑθər,ʃɪp

autism
BR 'ɔːtɪz(ə)m
AM 'ɔ,tɪzəm, 'ɑ,tɪzəm

autistic
BR ɔː'tɪstɪk
AM ɔ'tɪstɪk, ɑ'tɪstɪk

auto
BR 'ɔːtəʊ, -z
AM 'ɔdoʊ, 'ɑdoʊ, -z

Autobahn
BR 'ɔːtəbɑːn, -z
AM 'ɔdə,bɑn, 'ɔdoʊ,bɑn, 'ɑdə,bɑn, 'ɑdoʊ,bɑn, -z
GER 'autobaːn

autobiographer
BR ,ɔːtə(ʊ)bʌɪ'ɒgrəfə(r), -z
AM ,ɔdə,baɪ'ɑgrəfər, ,ɔdoʊ,baɪ'ɑgrəfər, ,ɑdə,baɪ'ɑgrəfər, ,ɑdoʊ,baɪ'ɑgrəfər, -z

autobiographic
BR ,ɔːtə(ʊ)bʌɪə'grafɪk
AM ,ɔdə,baɪə'græfɪk, ,ɔdoʊ,baɪə'græfɪk, ,ɑdə,baɪə'græfɪk, ,ɑdoʊ,baɪə'græfɪk

autobiographical
BR ,ɔːtə(ʊ)bʌɪə'grafɪkl
AM ,ɔdə,baɪə'græfəkəl, ,ɔdoʊ,baɪə'græfəkəl, ,ɑdə,baɪə'græfəkəl, ,ɑdoʊ,baɪə'græfəkəl

autobiographically
BR ,ɔːtə(ʊ)bʌɪə'grafɪkli
AM ,ɔdə,baɪə'græfək(ə)li, ,ɔdoʊ,baɪə'græfək(ə)li, ,ɑdə,baɪə'græfək(ə)li, ,ɑdoʊ,baɪə'græfək(ə)li

autobiography
BR ,ɔːtə(ʊ)bʌɪ'ɒgrəf|i, -ɪz
AM ,ɔdə,baɪ'ɑgrəfi, ,ɔdoʊ,baɪ'ɑgrəfi, ,ɑdə,baɪ'ɑgrəfi, ,ɑdoʊ,baɪ'ɑgrəfi, -z

autocade
BR 'ɔːtəkeɪd, -z
AM 'ɔdə,keɪd, 'ɔdoʊ,keɪd, 'ɑdə,keɪd, 'ɑdoʊ,keɪd, -z

autocar
BR 'ɔːtə(ʊ)kɑː(r), -z
AM 'ɔdə,kɑr, 'ɔdoʊ,kɑr, 'ɑdə,kɑr, 'ɑdoʊ,kɑr, -z

autocatalyst
BR ,ɔːtəʊ'katəlɪst, ,ɔːtəʊ'katl̩ɪst, -s
AM ,ɔdə'kædələst, ,ɔdoʊ'kædələst, ,ɑdə'kædələst, ,ɑdoʊ'kædələst, -s

autocephalous
BR ,ɔːtə'sɛf(ə)ləs, ,ɔːtə'sɛfl̩əs, ,ɔːtə'kɛf(ə)ləs, ,ɔːtə'kɛfl̩əs
AM ,ɔdə'sɛfələs, ,ɔdoʊ'sɛfələs, ,ɑdə'sɛfələs, ,ɑdoʊ'sɛfələs

autochange
BR 'ɔːtə(ʊ)tʃeɪn(d)ʒ, -ɪz
AM 'ɔdə,tʃeɪndʒ, 'ɔdoʊ,tʃeɪndʒ, 'ɑdə,tʃeɪndʒ, 'ɑdoʊ,tʃeɪndʒ, -ɨz

autochanger
BR 'ɔːtə(ʊ),tʃeɪn(d)ʒə(r), -z
AM 'ɔdə,tʃeɪndʒər, 'ɔdoʊ,tʃeɪndʒər, 'ɑdə,tʃeɪndʒər, 'ɑdoʊ,tʃeɪndʒər, -z

autochthon
BR ɔː'tɒkθ(ə)n, ɔː'tɒkθɒn, -z
AM ɔ'tɑkθən, ɔ'tɑk,θɑn, ɑ'tɑk,θɑn, -z

autochthonal
BR ɔː'tɒkθənl, ɔː'tɒkθn̩l
AM ɔ'tɑkθənəl, ɑ'tɑkθənəl

autochthonic
BR ,ɔːtɒk'θɒnɪk
AM ,ɔ,tɑk'θɑnɪk, ,ɑ,tɑk'θɑnɪk

autochthonous
BR ɔː'tɒkθənəs, ɔː'tɒkθn̩əs
AM ɔ'tɑkθənəs, ɑ'tɑkθənəs

autoclave
BR 'ɔːtə(ʊ)kleɪv, -z
AM 'ɔdə,kleɪv, 'ɔdoʊ,kleɪv, 'ɑdə,kleɪv, 'ɑdoʊ,kleɪv, -z

autocode
BR 'ɔːtə(ʊ)kəʊd, -z
AM 'ɔdə,koʊd, 'ɔdoʊ,koʊd, 'ɑdə,koʊd, 'ɑdoʊ,koʊd, -z

autocracy
BR ɔː'tɒkrəs|i, -ɪz
AM ɔ'tɑkrəsi, ɑ'tɑkrəsi, -z

autocrat
BR 'ɔːtəkrat, -s
AM 'ɔdə,kræt, 'ɔdoʊ,kræt, 'ɑdə,kræt, 'ɑdoʊ,kræt, -s

autocratic
BR ,ɔːtə'kratɪk
AM ,ɔdə'krædɪk, ,ɔdoʊ'krædɪk, ,ɑdə'krædɪk, ,ɑdoʊ'krædɪk

autocratical
BR ,ɔːtə'kratɪkl
AM ,ɔdə'krædəkəl, ,ɔdoʊ'krædəkəl, ,ɑdə'krædəkəl, ,ɑdoʊ'krædəkəl

autocratically
BR ,ɔːtə'kratɪkli
AM ,ɔdə'krædək(ə)li, ,ɔdoʊ'krædək(ə)li, ,ɑdə'krædək(ə)li, ,ɑdoʊ'krædək(ə)li

autocross
BR 'ɔːtəʊkrɒs
AM 'ɔdoʊ,krɔs, 'ɔdə,krɔs, 'ɑdoʊ,krɑs, 'ɑdə,krɑs

Autocue®
BR 'ɔːtə(ʊ)kjuː, -z
AM 'ɔdoʊ,kju, 'ɔdə,kju, 'ɑdoʊ,kju, 'ɑdə,kju, -z

autocycle
BR 'ɔːtə(ʊ),sʌɪkl, -z
AM 'ɔdə,saɪkəl, 'ɔdoʊ,saɪkəl, 'ɑdə,saɪkəl, 'ɑdoʊ,saɪkəl, -z

auto-da-fé
BR ,ɔːtə(ʊ)də'feɪ, -z
AM ,ɔdədə'feɪ, ,ɔ,toʊdə'feɪ, ,ɑdədə'feɪ, ,ɑ,toʊdə'feɪ, -z

autodestruct
BR ,ɔːtəʊdɪ'strʌkt, -s, -ɪŋ, -ɪd
AM ,ɔdədə'strək|(t), ,ɔdədi'strək|(t), ,ɔdoʊdə'strək|(t), ,ɔdoʊdi'strək|(t), ,ɑdədə'strək|(t), ,ɑdədi'strək|(t), ,ɑdoʊdə'strək|(t), ,ɑdoʊdi'strək|(t), -(t)s, -tɪŋ, -təd

autodidact
BR ,ɔːtəʊ'dʌɪdakt, -s
AM ,ɔdə'daɪ,dæk(t), ,ɔdoʊ'daɪ,dæk(t), ,ɑdə'daɪ,dæk(t), ,ɑdoʊ'daɪ,dæk(t), -s

autodidactic
BR ,ɔːtə(ʊ)dʌɪ'daktɪk
AM ,ɔdədə'dæktɪk, ,ɔdə,daɪ'dæktɪk, ,ɔdoʊdə'dæktɪk, ,ɔdoʊ,daɪ'dæktɪk, ,ɑdədə'dæktɪk, ,ɑdə,daɪ'dæktɪk,

ˌɑdoʊdəˈdæktɪk, ˌɑdoʊˌdaɪˈdæktɪk

autoerotic
BR ˌɔːtəʊɪˈrɒtɪk
AM ˌɔdoʊəˈrɑdɪk, ˌɑdoʊəˈrɑdɪk

autoeroticism
BR ˌɔːtəʊɪˈrɒtɪsɪz(ə)m
AM ˌɔdoʊəˈrɑdəˌsɪzəm, ˌɑdoʊəˈrɑdəˌsɪzəm

autofocus
BR ˈɔːtə(ʊ)ˌfəʊkəs
AM ˈɔdəˌfoʊkəs, ˈɔdoʊˌfoʊkəs, ˈɑdəˌfoʊkəs, ˈɑdoʊˌfoʊkəs

autogamous
BR ɔːˈtɒgəməs
AM ɔˈtɑgəməs, əˈtɑgəməs, ɑˈtɑgəməs

autogamy
BR ɔːˈtɒgəmi
AM ɔˈtɑgəmi, əˈtɑgəmi, ɑˈtɑgəmi

autogenic
BR ˌɔːtə(ʊ)ˈdʒɛnɪk
AM ˌɔdəˈdʒɛnɪk, ˌɔdoʊˈdʒɛnɪk, ˌɑdəˈdʒɛnɪk, ˌɑdoʊˈdʒɛnɪk

autogenous
BR ɔːˈtɒdʒɪnəs
AM ɔˈtɑdʒənəs, əˈtɑdʒənəs, ɑˈtɑdʒənəs

autogiro
BR ˌɔːtə(ʊ)ˈdʒʌɪrəʊ, ˈɔːtə(ʊ)ˌdʒʌɪrəʊ, -z
AM ˌɔdoʊˈdʒaɪroʊ, ˌɔdəˈdʒaɪroʊ, ˌɑdoʊˈdʒaɪroʊ, ˌɑdəˈdʒaɪroʊ, -z

autograft
BR ˈɔːtə(ʊ)grɑːft, ˈɔːtə(ʊ)graft, -s
AM ˈɔdəˌgræft, ˈɔdoʊˌgræft, ˈɑdəˌgræft, ˈɑdoʊˌgræft, -s

autograph
BR ˈɔːtəgrɑːf, ˈɔːtəgraf, -s, -ɪŋ, -t
AM ˈɔdəˌgræf, ˈɔdoʊˌgræf, ˈɑdəˌgræf, ˈɑdoʊˌgræf, -s, -ɪŋ, -t

autographic
BR ˌɔːtəˈgrafɪk
AM ˌɔdəˈgræfɪk, ˌɔdoʊˈgræfɪk, ˌɑdəˈgræfɪk, ˌɑdoʊˈgræfɪk

autography
BR ɔːˈtɒgrəfi
AM ɔˈtɑgrəfi, ɑˈtɑgrəfi

autogyro
BR ˌɔːtə(ʊ)ˈdʒʌɪrəʊ, ˈɔːtə(ʊ)ˌdʒʌɪrəʊ, -z
AM ˌɔdoʊˈdʒaɪroʊ, ˌɔdəˈdʒaɪroʊ, ˌɑdoʊˈdʒaɪroʊ, ˌɑdəˈdʒaɪroʊ, -z

autoharp
BR ˈɔːtəʊhɑːp, -s
AM ˈɔdəˌhɑrp, ˈɔdoʊˌhɑrp, ˈɑdəˌhɑrp, ˈɑdoʊˌhɑrp, -s

autoimmune
BR ˌɔːtəʊɪˈmjuːn
AM ˌɔdoʊəˈmjun, ˌɑdoʊəˈmjun

autoimmunity
BR ˌɔːtəʊɪˈmjuːnɪti
AM ˌɔdoʊəˈmjʊnədi, ˌɑdoʊəˈmjʊnədi, -z

autointoxication
BR ˌɔːtəʊɪnˌtɒksɪˈkeɪʃn
AM ˌɔdoʊənˌtɑksəˈkeɪʃən, ˌɑdoʊənˌtɑksəˈkeɪʃən

autologous
BR ɔːˈtɒləgəs
AM ɔˈtɑləgəs, ɑˈtɑləgəs

Autolycus
BR ɔːˈtɒlɪkəs
AM ɔˈtɑləkəs, ɑˈtɑləkəs

autolyses
BR ɔːˈtɒlɪsiːz
AM ɔˈtɑləsiz, ɑˈtɑləsiz

autolysis
BR ɔːˈtɒlɪsɪs
AM ɔˈtɑləsəs, ɑˈtɑləsəs

autolytic
BR ˌɔːtə(ʊ)ˈlɪtɪk
AM ˌɔdlˈɪdɪk, ˌɑdlˈɪdɪk

automaker
BR ˈɔːtəʊˌmeɪkə(r), -z
AM ˈɔdoʊˌmeɪkər, ˈɔdəˌmeɪkər, ˈɑdoʊˌmeɪkər, ˈɑdəˌmeɪkər, -z

automat
BR ˈɔːtəmat, -s
AM ˈɔdəˌmæt, ˈɔdoʊˌmæt, ˈɑdəˌmæt, ˈɑdoʊˌmæt, -s

automata
BR ɔːˈtɒmətə(*r*)
AM ɔˈtɑmədə, ɑˈtɑmədə

automate
BR ˈɔːtəmeɪt, -s, -ɪŋ, -ɪd
AM ˈɔdəˌmeɪ|t, ˈɔdoʊˌmeɪ|t, ˈɑdəˌmeɪ|t, ˈɑdoʊˌmeɪ|t, -ts, -dɪŋ, -dɪd

automatic
BR ˌɔːtəˈmatɪk
AM ˌɔdəˈmædɪk, ˌɔdoʊˈmædɪk, ˌɑdəˈmædɪk, ˌɑdoʊˈmædɪk

automatically
BR ˌɔːtəˈmatɪkli
AM ˌɔdəˈmædək(ə)li, ˌɔdoʊˈmædək(ə)li, ˌɑdəˈmædək(ə)li, ˌɑdoʊˈmædək(ə)li

automaticity
BR ˌɔːtəməˈtɪsɪti
AM ˌɔdəməˈtɪsɪdi, ˌɑdəməˈtɪsɪdi

automation
BR ˌɔːtəˈmeɪʃn
AM ˌɔdəˈmeɪʃən, ˌɔdoʊˈmeɪʃən, ˌɑdəˈmeɪʃən, ˌɑdoʊˈmeɪʃən

automatisation
BR ˌɔːtəmatʌɪˈzeɪʃn
AM ɔˌtɑmədəˈzeɪʃən, ɔˌtɑməˌtaɪˈzeɪʃən, əˌtɑmədəˈzeɪʃən, ɑˌtɑmədəˈzeɪʃən, ɑˌtɑməˌtaɪˈzeɪʃən

automatise
BR ˈɔːtəmətʌɪz, -ɪz, -ɪŋ, -d
AM ɔˈtɑməˌtaɪz, əˈtɑməˌtaɪz, ɑˈtɑməˌtaɪz, -ɪz, -ɪŋ, -d

automatism
BR ɔːˈtɒmətɪz(ə)m
AM ɔˈtɑməˌtɪzəm, əˈtɑməˌtɪzəm, ɑˈtɑməˌtɪzəm

automatist
BR ɔːˈtɒmətɪst, -s
AM ɔˈtɑmədəst, əˈtɑmədəst, ɑˈtɑmədəst, -s

automatization
BR ˌɔːtəmatʌɪˈzeɪʃn
AM ɔˌtɑmədəˈzeɪʃən, ɔˌtɑməˌtaɪˈzeɪʃən, əˌtɑmədəˈzeɪʃən, ɑˌtɑmədəˈzeɪʃən, ɑˌtɑməˌtaɪˈzeɪʃən

automatize
BR ˈɔːtəmətʌɪz, -ɪz, -ɪŋ, -d
AM ɔˈtɑməˌtaɪz, əˈtɑməˌtaɪz, ɑˈtɑməˌtaɪz, -ɪz, -ɪŋ, -d

automaton
BR ɔːˈtɒmət(ə)n, -z
AM ɔˈtɑmədən, ɑˈtɑmədən, ɔːtɑməˌtɑn, ɑˈtɑməˌtɑn, -z

automobile
BR ˈɔːtəmə(ʊ)biːl, -z
AM ˌɔdəmoʊˌbil, ˌɔdoʊmoʊˌbil, ˌɑdəmoʊˌbil, ˌɑdoʊmoʊˌbil, -z

automotive
BR ˌɔːtəˈməʊtɪv
AM ˌɔdəˈmoʊdɪv, ˌɔdoʊˈmoʊdɪv, ˌɑdəˈmoʊdɪv, ˌɑdoʊˈmoʊdɪv

autonomic
BR ˌɔːtəˈnɒmɪk
AM ˌɔdəˈnɑmɪk, ˌɔdoʊˈnɑmɪk, ˌɑdəˈnɑmɪk, ˌɑdoʊˈnɑmɪk

autonomist
BR ɔːˈtɒnəmɪst, -s
AM ɔˈtɑnəməst, əˈtɑnəməst, ɑˈtɑnəməst, -s

autonomous
BR ɔːˈtɒnəməs
AM ɔˈtɑnəməs, əˈtɑnəməs, ɑˈtɑnəməs

autonomously
BR ɔːˈtɒnəməsli
AM ɔˈtɑnəməsli, əˈtɑnəməsli, ɑˈtɑnəməsli

autonomy
BR ɔːˈtɒnəm|i, -ɪz
AM ɔˈtɑnəmi, əˈtɑnəmi, ɑˈtɑnəmi, -z

autopilot
BR ˈɔːtə(ʊ)ˌpʌɪlət, -s
AM ˈɔdoʊˌpaɪlət, ˈɔdəˌpaɪlət, ˈɑdoʊˌpaɪlət, ˈɑdəˌpaɪlət, -s

autopista
BR ˈɔːtə(ʊ)ˌpiːstə(*r*), -z
AM ˈɔdoʊˌpistə, ˈɑdoʊˌpistə, -z

autopolyploid
BR ˌɔːtəʊˈpɒlɪplɔɪd, -z
AM ˌɔdoʊˈpɑləˌplɔɪd, ˌɔdəˈpɑləˌplɔɪd, ˌɑdoʊˈpɑləˌplɔɪd, ˌɑdəˈpɑləˌplɔɪd, -z

autopolyploidy
BR ˌɔːtəʊˈpɒlɪplɔɪdi
AM ˌɔdoʊˈpɑləˌplɔɪdi, ˌɔdəˈpɑləˌplɔɪdi, ˌɑdoʊˈpɑləˌplɔɪdi, ˌɑdəˈpɑləˌplɔɪdi

autopsy
BR ˈɔːtɒps|i, -ɪz
AM ˈɔˌtɑpsi, ˈɑˌtɑpsi, -z

autoradiograph
BR ˌɔːtəʊˈreɪdɪə(ʊ)grɑːf, ˌɔːtəʊˈreɪdɪə(ʊ)graf
AM ˌɔdəˈreɪdiəˌgræf, ˌɔdoʊˈreɪdiəˌgræf, ˌɑdəˈreɪdiəˌgræf, ˌɑdoʊˈreɪdiəˌgræf

autoradiographic
BR ˌɔːtəʊˌreɪdɪəˈgrafɪk
AM ˌɔdəˌreɪdiəˈgræfɪk, ˌɔdoʊˌreɪdiəˈgræfɪk, ˌɑdəˌreɪdiəˈgræfɪk, ˌɑdoʊˌreɪdiəˈgræfɪk

autoradiography
BR ˌɔːtəʊˌreɪdɪˈɒgrəfi

AM ˌɔdəˌreɪdi'ɑgrəfi, ˌɔdoʊˌreɪdi'ɑgrəfi, ˌɑdəˌreɪdi'ɑgrəfi, ˌɑdoʊˌreɪdi'ɑgrəfi

autorotation
BR ˌɔːtəʊrə(ʊ)'teɪʃn, -z
AM ˌɔdoʊˌroʊ'teɪʃən, ˌɑdoʊˌroʊ'teɪʃən, -z

autoroute
BR 'ɔːtəʊruːt, -s
AM 'ɔdoʊˌrut, 'ɑdoʊˌrut, 'ɔdoʊˌrʊt, 'ɑdoʊˌrʊt, 'ɔdoʊˌraʊt, 'ɑdoʊˌraʊt, -s

autostrada
BR 'ɔːtə(ʊ)ˌstrɑːdə(*r*), -z
AM 'ɔdoʊˌstrɑdə, 'ɔdəˌstrɑdə, 'ɑdoʊˌstrɑdə, 'ɑdəˌstrɑdə, -z
IT auto'strada

autostrade
BR 'ɔːtə(ʊ)ˌstrɑːdi
AM 'ɔdoʊˌstrɑdi, 'ɔdəˌstrɑdi, 'ɑdoʊˌstrɑdi, 'ɑdəˌstrɑdi
IT auto'strade

autotelic
BR ˌɔːtə(ʊ)'tɛlɪk
AM ˌɔdoʊ'tɛlɪk, ˌɔdə'tɛlɪk, ˌɑdoʊ'tɛlɪk, ˌɑdə'tɛlɪk

autotomy
BR ɔː'tɒtəmi
AM ɔ'tɑdəmi, ɑ'tɑdəmi

autotoxic
BR ˌɔːtəʊ'tɒksɪk
AM ˌɔdoʊ'tɑksɪk, ˌɔdə'tɑksɪk, ˌɑdoʊ'tɑksɪk, ˌɑdə'tɑksɪk

autotoxin
BR 'ɔːtə(ʊ)ˌtɒksɪn, -z
AM 'ɔdoʊˌtɑksən, 'ɔdəˌtɑksən, 'ɑdoʊˌtɑksən, 'ɑdəˌtɑksən, -z

autotrophic
BR ˌɔːtə(ʊ)'trɒfɪk, ˌɔːtə(ʊ)'trəʊfɪk
AM ˌɔdoʊ'trɑfɪk, ˌɔdə'trɑfɪk, ˌɑdoʊ'trɑfɪk, ˌɑdə'trɑfɪk

autotype
BR 'ɔːtə(ʊ)tʌɪp, -s, -ɪŋ, -t
AM 'ɔdoʊˌtaɪp, 'ɔdəˌtaɪp, 'ɑdoʊˌtaɪp, 'ɑdəˌtaɪp, -s, -ɪŋ, -t

autotypography
BR ˌɔːtə(ʊ)tʌɪ'pɒgrəfi
AM ˌɔdoʊˌtaɪ'pɑgrəfi, ˌɔdəˌtaɪ'pɑgrəfi, ˌɑdoʊˌtaɪ'pɑgrəfi, ˌɑdəˌtaɪ'pɑgrəfi

autoworker
BR 'ɔːtəʊˌwəːkə(r), -z
AM 'ɔdəˌwərkər, 'ɔdoʊˌwərkər, 'ɑdəˌwərkər, 'ɑdoʊˌwərkər, -z

autoxidation
BR ˌɔːtəʊˌɒksɪ'deɪʃn
AM ˌɔdəˌɑksə'deɪʃən, ˌɔdoʊˌɑksə'deɪʃən, ˌɑdəˌɑksə'deɪʃən, ˌɑdoʊˌɑksə'deɪʃən

autumn
BR 'ɔːtəm, -z
AM 'ɔdəm, 'ɑdəm, -z

autumnal
BR ɔː'tʌmn(ə)l
AM ɔ'təmnəl, ɑ'təmnəl

autumnally
BR ɔː'tʌmn̩li, ɔː'tʌmnəli
AM ɔ'təmnəli, ɑ'təmnəli

Auty
BR 'ɔːti
AM 'ɔdi, 'ɑdi

Auvergne
BR əʊ'vɛːn, əʊ'vəːn
AM oʊ'vɛ(ə)rn, oʊ'vərn
FR ovɛʀɲ

auxanometer
BR ˌɔːksə'nɒmɪtə(r), -z
AM ˌɔgzə'nɑmədər, ˌɔksə'nɑmədər, ˌɑgzə'nɑmədər, ˌɑksə'nɑmədər, -z

auxiliary
BR ɔːg'zɪlɪər|i, ɒg'zɪlɪər|i, -ɪz
AM ɔg'zɪl(ə)ri, əg'zɪl(ə)ri, ɑg'zɪl(ə)ri, ɔg'zɪljəri, əg'zɪljəri, ɑg'zɪljəri, -z

auxin
BR 'ɔːksɪn, -z
AM 'ɔksən, 'ɑksən, -z

Ava
BR 'eɪvə(*r*)
AM 'eɪvə

avadavat
BR 'avədəvat, -s
AM 'ævədəˌvæt, -s

avail
BR ə'veɪl, -z, -ɪŋ, -d
AM ə'veɪl, -z, -ɪŋ, -d

availability
BR əˌveɪlə'bɪlɪti
AM əˌveɪlə'bɪlɪdi

available
BR ə'veɪləbl
AM ə'veɪləbəl

availableness
BR ə'veɪləblnəs
AM ə'veɪləbəlnəs

availably
BR ə'veɪləbli
AM ə'veɪlɪbli

avalanche
BR 'avəlɑːn(t)ʃ, 'avəlan(t)ʃ, -ɪz, -ɪŋ, -t
AM 'ævəˌlæn(t)ʃ, -əz, -ɪŋ, -t

Avalon
BR 'avəlɒn
AM 'ævəˌlɑn

avant-garde
BR ˌavɒ̃'gɑːd, ˌavɒŋ'gɑːd
AM ˌɑˌvɑn'gɑrd, əˌvɑn(t)'gɑrd

avant-gardism
BR ˌavɒ̃'gɑːdɪz(ə)m, ˌavɒŋ'gɑːdɪz(ə)m
AM ˌɑˌvɑn'gɑrˌdɪzəm, əˌvɑn(t)'gɑrˌdɪzəm

avant-gardist
BR ˌavɒ̃'gɑːdɪst, ˌavɒŋ'gɑːdɪst, -s
AM ˌɑˌvɑn'gɑrdəst, əˌvɑn(t)'gɑrdəst, -s

Avar
BR 'avɑː(r), -z
AM 'ɑvɑr, -z

avarice
BR 'av(ə)rɪs
AM 'ævərəs

avaricious
BR ˌavə'rɪʃəs
AM ˌævə'rɪʃəs

avariciously
BR ˌavə'rɪʃəsli
AM ˌævə'rɪʃəsli

avariciousness
BR ˌavə'rɪʃəsnəs
AM ˌævə'rɪʃəsnəs

avast
BR ə'vɑːst, ə'vast
AM ə'væst

avatar
BR 'avətɑː(r), ˌavə'tɑː(r), -z
AM 'ævəˌtɑr, ˌævə'tɑr, -z

avaunt
BR ə'vɔːnt
AM ə'vɔnt, ə'vɑnt

ave
prayer
BR 'ɑːv|i, 'ɑːv|eɪ, -ɪz\-eɪz
AM 'ɑˌveɪ, 'ɑˌvi, -z

Avebury
BR 'eɪvb(ə)ri
AM 'eɪvbəri

avenge
BR ə'vɛn(d)ʒ, -ɪz, -ɪŋ, -d
AM ə'vɛndʒ, -əz, -ɪŋ, -d

avenger
BR ə'vɛn(d)ʒə(r), -z
AM ə'vɛndʒər, -z

avens
BR 'eɪv(ɪ)nz, 'av(ɪ)nz
AM 'ævənz

aventurine
BR ə'vɛntʃərʌɪn
AM ə'vɛn(t)ʃəˌrin, ə'vɛn(t)ʃəˌraɪn

avenue
BR 'avɪnjuː, -z
AM 'ævəˌn(j)u, -z

aver
BR ə'vəː(r), -z, -ɪŋ, -d
AM ə'vər, -z, -ɪŋ, -d

average
BR 'av(ə)r|ɪdʒ, -ɪdʒɪz, -ɪdʒɪŋ, -ɪdʒd
AM 'æv(ə)rɪdʒ, -ɪz, -ɪŋ, -d

averagely
BR 'av(ə)rɪdʒli
AM 'æv(ə)rɪdʒli

avermectin
BR ˌeɪvə'mɛktɪn
AM ˌeɪvər'mɛktɪn

averment
BR ə'vəːm(ə)nt
AM ə'vərmənt

Avernus
BR ə'vəːnəs
AM ə'vərnəs

Averroës
BR ə'vɛrəʊiːz, ˌavə'rəʊiːz
AM ə'vɛroʊˌiz, ə'vɛrəwiz

averse
BR ə'vəːs
AM ə'vərs

aversely
BR ə'vəːsli
AM ə'vərsli

averseness
BR ə'vəːsnəs
AM ə'vərsnəs

aversion
BR ə'vəːʃn, -z
AM ə'vərʒən, -z

aversive
BR ə'vəːsɪv, ə'vəːzɪv
AM ə'vərsɪv, ə'vərzɪv

aversively
BR ə'vəːsɪvli, ə'vəːzɪvli
AM ə'vərsɪvli, ə'vərzɪvli

avert
BR ə'vəːt, -s, -ɪŋ, -ɪd
AM ə'vər|t, æ'vər|t, -ts, -dɪŋ, -dəd

avertable
BR ə'vəːtəbl
AM ə'vərdəbəl

avertible
BR ə'vəːtɪbl
AM ə'vərdəbəl

Avery
BR 'eɪv(ə)ri
AM 'eɪvəri

Avesta
BR ə'vɛstə(*r*)
AM ə'vɛstə

Avestan
BR ə'vɛst(ə)n, -z
AM ə'vɛstən, -z

Avestic
BR ə'vɛstɪk, -s
AM ə'vɛstɪk, -s

avgolemono
BR ˌavgə(ʊ)'lɛmənəʊ
AM ˌɑvgə'lɛmənoʊ

Avia®
BR 'eɪvɪə(r)
AM 'ɑviə

avian
BR 'eɪvɪən
AM 'eɪviən

aviary
BR 'eɪvɪər|i, -ɪz
AM 'eɪviˌɛri, -z

aviate
BR 'eɪvɪeɪt, -s, -ɪŋ, -ɨd
AM 'eɪviˌeɪ|t, -ts, -dɪŋ, -dɨd

aviation
BR ˌeɪvɪ'eɪʃn
AM ˌeɪvi'eɪʃən

aviator
BR 'eɪvɪeɪtə(r), -z
AM 'eɪviˌeɪdər, -z

aviatrices
BR ˌeɪvɪ'eɪtrɪsiːz
AM ˌeɪvɪ'eɪtrɪˌsiz

aviatrix
BR 'eɪvɪətrɪks, -ɨz
AM ˌeɪvi'eɪtrɪks, 'eɪviəˌtrɪks, -ɨz

Avicenna
BR ˌavɪ'sɛnə(r)
AM ˌævə'sɛnə

aviculture
BR 'eɪvɪˌkʌltʃə(r)
AM 'eɪvəˌkəltʃər, 'ævəˌkəltʃər

aviculturist
BR 'eɪvɪˌkʌltʃ(ə)rɪst, -s
AM 'eɪvəˌkəltʃ(ə)rəst, 'ævəˌkəltʃ(ə)rəst, -s

avid
BR 'avɪd
AM 'ævəd

avidity
BR ə'vɪdɪti
AM ə'vɪdɨdi

avidly
BR 'avɨdli
AM 'ævədli

Aviemore
BR ˌavɪ'mɔː(r), 'avɪmɔː(r)
AM 'æviˌmɔ(ə)r

avifauna
BR 'eɪvɪˌfɔːnə(r)
AM ˌeɪvi'fɔnə, ˌævi'fɔnə, ˌeɪvi'fɑnə, ˌævi'fɑnə

Avignon
BR 'aviːnjɒ̃, 'av(ɪ)njɒ̃
AM ˌævən'jɔn, ˌævən'jɑn

Ávila
BR 'avɪlə(r), 'avl̩ə(r)
AM 'ɑvilə

avionic
BR ˌeɪvɪ'ɒnɪk, -s
AM ˌeɪvi'ɑnɪk, -s

Avis®
BR 'eɪvɪs
AM 'eɪvɨs

avitaminoses
BR eɪˌvɪtəmɪ'nəʊsiːz, eɪˌvʌɪtəmɪ'nəʊsiːz
AM ˌeɪˌvaɪdəmə'noʊsiz

avitaminosis
BR eɪˌvɪtəmɪ'nəʊsɪs, eɪˌvʌɪtəmɪ'nəʊsɪs
AM ˌeɪˌvaɪdəmə'noʊsəs

avizandum
BR ˌavɪ'zandəm
AM ˌævɪ'zændəm

Avoca
BR ə'vəʊkə(r)
AM ə'voʊkə

avocado
BR ˌavə'kɑːdəʊ, -z
AM ˌævə'kɑdoʊ, ˌɑvə'kɑdoʊ, -z

avocation
BR ˌavə'keɪʃn, -z
AM ˌævə'keɪʃən, -z

avocet
BR 'avəsɛt, -s
AM 'ævəˌsɛt, -s

Avogadro
BR ˌavə(ʊ)'gadrəʊ, ˌavə(ʊ)'gɑːdrəʊ
AM ˌɑvə'gɑdroʊ

avoid
BR ə'vɔɪd, -z, -ɪŋ, -ɨd
AM ə'vɔɪd, -z, -ɪŋ, -ɨd

avoidable
BR ə'vɔɪdəbl
AM ə'vɔɪdəbəl

avoidably
BR ə'vɔɪdəbli
AM ə'vɔɪdəbli

avoidance
BR ə'vɔɪd(ə)ns, -ɨz
AM ə'vɔɪd(ə)ns, -ɨz

avoider
BR ə'vɔɪdə(r), -z
AM ə'vɔɪdər, -z

avoirdupois
BR ˌavədə'pɔɪz, ˌavwəd(j)uː'pwɑː(r)
AM ˌɑvərdə'pɔɪz, 'ɑvərdəˌpɔɪz

Avon¹
Devon river
BR 'avn
AM 'eɪˌvɑn

Avon²
English county, English Midland river
BR 'eɪvn
AM 'eɪˌvɑn

Avon³
Scottish loch and river
BR ɑːn
AM 'eɪˌvɑn

Avon⁴
tradename
BR 'eɪvɒn
AM 'eɪˌvɑn

Avonmouth
BR 'eɪvnmaʊθ
AM 'eɪˌvɑnˌmaʊθ

avouch
BR ə'vaʊtʃ, -ɨz, -ɪŋ, -t
AM ə'vaʊtʃ, -əz, -ɪŋ, -t

avouchment
BR ə'vaʊtʃm(ə)nt, -s
AM ə'vaʊtʃmənt, -s

avow
BR ə'vaʊ, -z, -ɪŋ, -d
AM ə'vaʊ, -z, -ɪŋ, -d

avowable
BR ə'vaʊəbl
AM ə'vaʊəbəl

avowal
BR ə'vaʊəl, -z
AM ə'vaʊ(ə)l, -z

avowedly
BR ə'vaʊwɨdli
AM ə'vaʊədli

Avril
BR 'avrɪl
AM 'ævrəl

avulsion
BR ə'vʌlʃn
AM ə'vəlʃən

avuncular
BR ə'vʌŋkjʊlə(r)
AM ə'vəŋkjələr

AWACS
BR 'eɪwaks
AM 'eɪˌwæks

await
BR ə'weɪt, -s, -ɪŋ, -ɨd
AM ə'weɪ|t, -ts, -dɪŋ, -dɨd

awake
BR ə'weɪk, -s, -ɪŋ
AM ə'weɪk, -s, -ɪŋ

awaken
BR ə'weɪk|(ə)n, -(ə)nz, -(ə)nɪŋ\-n̩ɪŋ, -(ə)nd
AM ə'weɪk|ən, -ənz, -(ə)nɪŋ, -ənd

award
BR ə'wɔːd, -z, -ɪŋ, -ɨd
AM ə'wɔ(ə)rd, -z, -ɪŋ, -əd

awarder
BR ə'wɔːdə(r), -z
AM ə'wɔrdər, -z

aware
BR ə'wɛː(r)
AM ə'wɛ(ə)r

awareness
BR ə'wɛːnəs, -ɨz
AM ə'wɛrnəs, -əz

awash
BR ə'wɒʃ
AM ə'wɔʃ, ə'wɑʃ

away
BR ə'weɪ
AM ə'weɪ

awe
BR ɔː(r), -z, -ɪŋ, -d
AM ɔ, ɑ, -z, -ɪŋ, -d

aweary
BR ə'wɪəri
AM ə'wɪri

aweigh
BR ə'weɪ
AM ə'weɪ

aweless
BR 'ɔːləs
AM 'ɔləs, 'ɑləs

awelessness
BR 'ɔːləsnəs
AM 'ɔləsnəs, 'ɑləsnəs

awesome
BR 'ɔːs(ə)m
AM 'ɔsəm, 'ɑsəm

awesomely
BR 'ɔːs(ə)mli
AM 'ɔsəmli, 'ɑsəmli

awesomeness
BR 'ɔːs(ə)mnəs
AM 'ɔsəmnəs, 'ɑsəmnəs

awestricken
BR 'ɔːˌstrɪk(ə)n
AM 'ɔˌstrɪkən, 'ɑˌstrɪkən

awestruck
BR 'ɔːstrʌk
AM 'ɔˌstrək, 'ɑˌstrək

awful
BR 'ɔːf(ʊ)l
AM 'ɔfəl, 'ɑfəl

awfully¹
horribly
BR 'ɔːfʊli, 'ɔːfl̩i
AM 'ɔf(ə)li, 'ɑf(ə)li

awfully²
very
BR 'ɔːfli, 'ɔːfl̩i
AM 'ɔf(ə)li, 'ɑf(ə)li

awfulness
BR 'ɔːf(ʊ)lnəs
AM 'ɔfəlnəs, 'ɑfəlnəs

awheel
BR ə'wiːl
AM ə'(h)wil

awhile
BR ə'wʌɪl
AM ə'(h)waɪl

awkward
BR 'ɔːkwəd
AM 'ɔkwərd, 'ɑkwərd

awkwardly
BR 'ɔːkwədli
AM 'ɔkwərdli, 'ɑkwərdli

awkwardness
BR 'ɔːkwədnəs, -ɨz

AM 'ɔkwərdnəs, 'ɑkwərdnəs, -əz

awl
BR ɔːl, -z
AM ɔl, ɑl, -z

awn
BR ɔːn, -z, -d
AM ɔn, ɑn, -z, -d

awning
BR 'ɔːnɪŋ, -z
AM 'ɔnɪŋ, 'ɑnɪŋ, -z

awoke
BR ə'wəʊk
AM ə'woʊk

awoken
BR ə'wəʊk(ə)n
AM ə'woʊkən

AWOL
BR 'eɪwɒl
AM 'eɪˌwɔl, 'eɪˌwɑl

awry
BR ə'rʌɪ
AM ə'raɪ

ax
BR aks, -ɪz, -ɪŋ, -t
AM æks, -əz, -ɪŋ, -t

axe
BR aks, -ɪz, -ɪŋ, -t
AM æks, -əz, -ɪŋ, -t

axel
BR 'aksl, -z
AM 'æksəl, -z

axeman
BR 'aksmən, 'aksman
AM 'æksˌmæn

axemen
BR 'aksmən, 'aksmɛn
AM 'æksˌmɛn

axes[1]
plural of axis
BR 'aksiːz
AM 'ækˌsiz

axes[2]
plural of ax, axe
BR 'aksɪz
AM 'æksəz

Axholme
BR 'akshəʊm
AM 'æks,(h)oʊm

axial
BR 'aksɪəl
AM 'æksiəl

axiality
BR ˌaksɪ'alɪti
AM ˌæksi'ælədi

axially
BR 'aksɪəli
AM 'æksiəli

axil
BR 'aks(ɪ)l, -z
AM 'æksəl, -z

axilla
BR ak'sɪlə(*r*)
AM æk'sɪlə

axillae
BR ak'sɪliː
AM æk'sɪli, æk'sɪˌlaɪ

axillary
BR ak'sɪl(ə)ri
AM æk'sɪləri

axiological
BR ˌaksɪə'lɒdʒɪkl
AM ˌæksiə'lɑdʒəkəl

axiologist
BR ˌaksɪ'ɒlədʒɪst, -s
AM ˌæksi'ɑlədʒəst, -s

axiology
BR ˌaksɪ'ɒlədʒi
AM ˌæksi'ɑlədʒi

axiom
BR 'aksɪəm, -z
AM 'æksiəm, -z

axiomatic
BR ˌaksɪə'matɪk
AM ˌæksiə'mædɪk

axiomatically
BR ˌaksɪə'matɪkli
AM ˌæksiə'mædək(ə)li

axis
BR 'aksɪs
AM 'æksəs

axle
BR 'aksl, -z, -d
AM 'æksəl, -z, -d

axman
BR 'aksmən, 'aksman
AM 'æksˌmæn

axmen
BR 'aksmən, 'aksmɛn
AM 'æksˌmɛn

Axminster
BR 'aksˌmɪnstə(r), -z
AM 'æksˌmɪnstər, -z

axolotl
BR ˌaksə'lɒtl, 'aksəlɒtl, -z
AM 'æksəˌlɑdl, -z

axon
BR 'aksɒn, -z
AM 'ækˌsɑn, -z

axonometric
BR ˌaksənə(ʊ)'mɛtrɪk, ˌaksn̩ə(ʊ)'mɛtrɪk
AM ˌæksənə'mɛtrɪk

axonometrically
BR ˌaksənə(ʊ)'mɛtrɪkli, ˌaksn̩ə(ʊ)'mɛtrɪkli
AM ˌæksənə'mɛtrək(ə)li

Axum
BR 'aksʌm
AM 'ɑkˌsʊm

ay
yes
BR ʌɪ, -z
AM aɪ, -z

Ayacucho
BR ˌʌɪ(j)ə'kuːtʃəʊ
AM ˌaɪə'kutʃoʊ

ayah
BR 'ʌɪ(j)ə(*r*), -z
AM 'aɪə, -z

ayatollah
BR ˌʌɪ(j)ə'tɒlə(*r*), -z
AM ˌaɪə'toʊlə, -z

Ayckbourn
BR 'eɪkbɔːn
AM 'aɪkˌbɔ(ə)rn

Aycliffe
BR 'eɪklɪf
AM 'aɪklɪf

aye[1]
always
BR eɪ, ʌɪ
AM eɪ

aye[2]
yes
BR ʌɪ, -z
AM aɪ, -z

aye-aye
noun
BR 'ʌɪʌɪ, -z
AM 'aɪˌaɪ, -z

aye aye
interjection
BR ˌʌɪ 'ʌɪ
AM 'aɪ 'aɪ

Ayer
BR ɛː(r)
AM ɛ(ə)r

Ayers
BR ɛːz
AM ɛ(ə)rz

Áyios Nikólaos
BR ˌʌɪ(j)ɒs ˌnɪkə'leɪɒs
AM ˌaɪəs ˌnɪkə'leɪəs
GR ˌaɪɔs niː'kɔlaɔs

Aylesbury
BR 'eɪlzb(ə)r|i, -ɪz
AM 'eɪlzbəri, -z

Aylesham
BR 'eɪlʃ(ə)m
AM 'eɪlˌʃæm, 'eɪlʃəm

Aylmer
BR 'eɪlmə(r)
AM 'eɪlmər

Aylsham
BR 'eɪlʃ(ə)m
AM 'eɪlˌʃæm, 'eɪlʃəm

Aylward
BR 'eɪlwəd, 'eɪlwɔːd
AM 'eɪlwɔ(ə)rd

Aymara
BR 'ʌɪmərɑː(*r*), -z
AM 'aɪmɑrɑ, -z

Aynho
BR 'eɪnhəʊ
AM 'eɪnhoʊ

Ayot
BR 'eɪət
AM 'eɪɑt

Ayr
BR ɛː(r)
AM ɛ(ə)r

Ayrshire
BR 'ɛːʃ(ɪ)ə(r)
AM 'ɛrˌʃɪ(ə)r

Ayrton
BR 'ɛːt(ə)n
AM 'ɛrt(ə)n

Aysgarth
BR 'eɪzgɑːθ
AM 'aɪsgɑrθ

Ayto
BR 'eɪtəʊ
AM 'eɪtu

Ayub Khan
BR ʌɪˌjuːb 'kɑːn, ˌʌɪjuːb +
AM ˌɑ'jub 'kɑn

azalea
BR ə'zeɪlɪə(*r*), -z
AM ə'zeɪljə, ə'zeɪliə, -z

Azania
BR ə'zeɪnɪə(*r*)
AM ə'zeɪniə

Azanian
BR ə'zeɪnɪən
AM ə'zeɪniən

azeotrope
BR 'eɪzɪətrəʊp, ə'ziːətrəʊp, -s
AM eɪ'ziəˌtroʊp, -s

azeotropic
BR ˌeɪzɪə'trɒpɪk, ˌeɪzɪə'trəʊpɪk, əˌziːə'trɒpɪk, əˌziːə'trəʊpɪk
AM ˌeɪˌziə'trɑpɪk

Azerbaijan
BR ˌazəbʌɪ'(d)ʒɑːn
AM ˌæzərˌbaɪ'(d)ʒɑn, ˌæʒərˌbaɪ'(d)ʒɑn

Azerbaijani
BR ˌazəbʌɪ'(d)ʒɑːn|i, -ɪz
AM ˌæzərˌbaɪ'(d)ʒɑni, ˌæʒərˌbaɪ'(d)ʒɑni, -z

Azeri
BR ə'zɛːr|i, -ɪz
AM ə'zɛri, -z

azide
BR 'eɪzʌɪd, -z
AM 'eɪˌzaɪd, -z

Azilian
BR ə'zɪlɪən
AM ə'zɪljən, ə'zɪliən

azimuth
BR 'azɪməθ, -s
AM 'æzəməθ, -s

azimuthal
BR ˌazɪ'mʌθl, ˌazɪ'mjuːθl
AM ˌæzə'məθəl

azine
BR 'eɪziːn, -z
AM 'æˌzin, 'eɪˌzin, -z

Aziz
BR a'ziːz, ə'ziːz, a'zɪz, ə'zɪz
AM ə'ziz

Aznavour
BR 'aznəvʊə(r), 'aznəvɔː(r)
AM 'æznəˌvɔ(ə)r

azobenzine
BR ˌeɪzəʊ'bɛnziːn, ˌazəʊ'bɛnziːn
AM ˌeɪzoʊ'bɛnzin, ˌæzoʊ'bɛnzin

azoic
BR eɪ'zəʊɪk, ə'zəʊɪk
AM eɪ'zoʊɪk, ə'zɔɪk

Azores
BR ə'zɔːz
AM 'eɪˌzɔ(ə)rz

Azov
BR 'azɒv, 'ɑːzɒv, 'eɪzɒv
AM 'æzɔv, 'æzɑv

Aztec
BR 'aztɛk, -s
AM 'æztɛk, -s

Aztecan
BR 'aztɛk(ə)n, az'tɛk(ə)n
AM ˌæzˈtɛkən

azuki
BR ə'zuːk|i, -ɪz
AM ə'zuki, -z

azure
BR 'aʒə(r), 'aʒj(ʊ)ə(r), 'azj(ʊ)ə(r), 'eɪʒə(r), 'eɪʒj(ʊ)ə(r), 'eɪzj(ʊ)ə(r)
AM 'æʒər

azurite
BR 'aʒərʌɪt, 'aʒj(ʊ)ərʌɪt, 'azj(ʊ)ərʌɪt, 'eɪʒərʌɪt, 'eɪʒj(ʊ)ərʌɪt, 'eɪzj(ʊ)ərʌɪt
AM 'æʒəˌraɪt

azygous
BR 'azɪɡəs
AM ˌeɪ'zaɪɡəs

Bb

b
BR biː, -z
AM bi, -z

baa
BR bɑː(r), -z, -ɪŋ, -d
AM bɑ, -z, -ɪŋ, -d

Baader-Meinhof
BR ˌbɑːdəˈmʌɪnhɒf
AM ˌbɑdərˈmaɪnˌ(h)ɔf, ˌbɑdərˈmaɪnˌ(h)ɑf

Baal
BR ˈbeɪ(ə)l, bɑːl
AM ˈbeɪ(ə)l, bɑl

Baalbek
BR ˈbɑːlbɛk
AM ˈbɑlˌbɛk

Baalim
BR ˈbeɪlɪm, ˈbɑːlɪm
AM ˈbeɪlɪm

Baalism
BR ˈbeɪlɪz(ə)m, ˈbɑːlɪz(ə)m
AM ˈbeɪˌlɪzəm

baas
BR bɑːs, -ɪz
AM bɑs, -əz

baasskap
BR ˈbɑːskap, ˈbɑːskɑːp, ˈbaskap
AM ˈbɑsˌkæp, ˈbæsˌkæp

Baath
BR bɑːθ
AM bɑs, bɑθ

Ba'ath
BR bɑːθ
AM bɑs, bɑθ

Baathist
BR ˈbɑːθɪst, -s
AM ˈbɑθəst, -s

baba
BR ˈbɑːbɑː(r), ˈbɑːbə(r), -z
AM ˈbɑˌbɑ, -z

babacoote
BR ˈbabəkuːt, ˈbɑːbəkuːt, -s
AM ˈbɑbəˌkut, -s

Babbage
BR ˈbabɪdʒ
AM ˈbæbɪdʒ

Babbitt
BR ˈbabɪt
AM ˈbæbət

Babbittry
BR ˈbabɪtri
AM ˈbæbətri

babble
BR ˈbab|l, -lz, -l̩ɪŋ\-lɪŋ, -ld
AM ˈbæb|əl, -əlz, -(ə)lɪŋ, -əld

babblement
BR ˈbablm(ə)nt
AM ˈbæbəlmənt

babbler
BR ˈbabl̩ə(r), ˈbablə(r), -z
AM ˈbæb(ə)lər, -z

babbling
BR ˈbabl̩ɪŋ, ˈbablɪŋ, -z
AM ˈbæb(ə)lɪŋ, -z

Babcock
BR ˈbabkɒk
AM ˈbæbˌkɑk

babe
BR beɪb, -z
AM beɪb, -z

Babel
BR ˈbeɪbl, -z
AM ˈbeɪbəl, ˈbæbəl, -z

babesiasis
BR ˌbɑːbɪˈzʌɪəsɪs
AM ˌbæbəˈzaɪəsɪs

babesiosis
BR bəˌbiːziˈəʊsɪs
AM ˌbæbəˈzaɪəsɪs

Babi
BR ˈbɑːb|i, -ɪz
AM ˈbɑbi, -z

babiche
BR bəˈbiːʃ
AM bəˈbiʃ

Babington
BR ˈbabɪŋt(ə)n
AM ˈbæbɪŋtən

babirusa
BR ˌbɑːbɪˈruːsə(r), -z
AM ˌbɑbəˈrusə, -z

Babism
BR ˈbɑːbɪz(ə)m
AM ˈbɑˌbɪzəm

Babist
BR ˈbɑːbɪst, -s
AM ˈbɑbəst, -s

baboo
BR ˈbɑːbuː, -z
AM ˈbɑˈbu, -z

baboon
BR bəˈbuːn, -z
AM bæˈbun, -z

Babs
BR babz
AM bæbz

babu
BR ˈbɑːbuː, -z
AM ˈbɑˈbu, -z

babushka
BR bəˈbuːʃkə(r), baˈbuːʃkə(r), bəˈbʊʃkə(r), baˈbʊʃkə(r), -z
AM bəˈbʊʃkə, -z
RUS ˈbabuʃkə

baby
BR ˈbeɪb|i, -ɪz, -ɪɪŋ, -ɪd
AM ˈbeɪbi, -z, -ɪŋ, -d

Babycham®
BR ˈbeɪbɪʃam, -z
AM ˈbeɪbiʃəm, -z

Babygro®
BR ˈbeɪbɪɡrəʊ, -z
AM ˈbeɪbiˌɡroʊ, -z

babyhood
BR ˈbeɪbɪhʊd
AM ˈbeɪbiˌ(h)ʊd

babyish
BR ˈbeɪbɪɪʃ
AM ˈbeɪbiɪʃ

babyishly
BR ˈbeɪbɪɪʃli
AM ˈbeɪbiɪʃli

babyishness
BR ˈbeɪbɪɪʃnɪs
AM ˈbeɪbiɪʃnɪs

Babylon
BR ˈbabɪlɒn, ˈbabɪlən, ˈbabl̩ən
AM ˈbæbəˌlɑn

Babylonia
BR ˌbabɪˈləʊnɪə(r)
AM ˌbæbəˈloʊniə

Babylonian
BR ˌbabɪˈləʊnɪən, -z
AM ˌbæbəˈloʊniən, -z

babysat
BR ˈbeɪbɪsat
AM ˈbeɪbiˌsæt

babysit
BR ˈbeɪbɪsɪt, -s, -ɪŋ
AM ˈbeɪbiˌsɪ|t, -ts, -dɪŋ

babysitter
BR ˈbeɪbɪˌsɪtə(r), -z
AM ˈbeɪbiˌsɪdər, -z

Bacall
BR bəˈkɔːl
AM bəˈkɔl, bəˈkɑl

Bacardi®
BR bəˈkɑːd|i, -ɪz
AM bəˈkɑrdi, -z

baccalaureate
BR ˌbakəˈlɔːrɪət, -s
AM ˌbækəˈlɔriət, -s

baccara
BR ˈbakərɑː(r), ˌbakəˈrɑː(r)
AM ˈbɑkəˈrɑ, ˈbækəˈrɑ

baccarat
BR ˈbakərɑː(r), ˌbakəˈrɑː(r)
AM ˈbɑkəˈrɑ, ˈbækəˈrɑ

baccate
BR ˈbakeɪt
AM ˈbæˌkeɪt

Bacchae
BR ˈbakiː, ˈbakʌɪ
AM ˈbɑkˌi, ˈbɑkˌaɪ, ˈbækˌi, ˈbækˌaɪ

bacchanal
BR ˌbakəˈnal, ˈbakənal, ˈbakən(ə)l, ˈbakn̩l, -z
AM ˈbɑkəˈnɑl, ˈbækəˈnæl, -z

bacchanalia
BR ˌbakəˈneɪlɪə(r)
AM ˌbɑkəˈneɪljə, ˌbækəˈneɪljə, ˌbɑkəˈneɪliə, ˌbækəˈneɪliə

bacchanalian
BR ˌbakəˈneɪlɪən, -z
AM ˌbɑkəˈneɪljən, ˌbækəˈneɪljən, ˌbɑkəˈneɪliən, ˌbækəˈneɪliən, -z

bacchant
BR ˈbak(ə)nt, -s
AM bəˈkɑnt, bəˈkænt, -s

bacchante
BR bəˈkant|i, bəˈkant, -ɪz\-s
AM bəˈkɑn(t)i, bəˈkæn(t)i, -z

bacchantic
BR bəˈkantɪk
AM bəˈkɑn(t)ɪk, bəˈkæn(t)ɪk

bacchic
BR ˈbakɪk
AM ˈbɑkɪk, ˈbækɪk

Bacchus
BR ˈbakəs
AM ˈbɑkəs, ˈbækəs

bacciferous
BR bakˈsɪf(ə)rəs
AM bɑkˈsɪf(ə)rəs, bækˈsɪf(ə)rəs

baccy
BR ˈbaki
AM ˈbɑki, ˈbæki

Bach
BR bɑːk, bɑːx
AM bɑk

Bacharach
BR ˈbakərak
AM ˈbækəˌræk, ˈbɑkəˌrɑk

bachelor
BR ˈbatʃ(ə)lə(r), ˈbatʃl̩ə(r), -z
AM ˈbætʃ(ə)lər, -z

bachelorhood
BR ˈbatʃ(ə)ləhʊd, ˈbatʃl̩əhʊd
AM ˈbætʃ(ə)lərˌ(h)ʊd

bachelorship
BR ˈbatʃ(ə)ləʃɪp, ˈbatʃl̩əʃɪp
AM ˈbætʃ(ə)lərˌʃɪp

bacillar
BR bəˈsɪlə(r), ˈbasɪlə(r)
AM bəˈsɪlər, ˈbæsələr

bacillary
BR bəˈsɪl(ə)ri, ˈbasɪl(ə)ri, ˈbasl̩(ə)ri
AM ˈbæsəˌlɛri

bacilli
BR bəˈsɪlʌɪ
AM bəˈsɪˌlaɪ

bacilliform
BR bəˈsɪlɨfɔːm
AM bəˈsɪlə,fɔ(ə)rm

bacillus
BR bəˈsɪləs
AM bəˈsɪləs

bacitracin
BR ˌbasɪˈtreɪsɪn
AM ˌbæ(k)səˈtreɪsɪn

back
BR bak, -s, -ɪŋ, -t
AM bæk, -s, -ɪŋ, -t

backache
BR ˈbakeɪk, -s
AM ˈbæk,eɪk, -s

backbench
BR ˌbakˈbɛn(t)ʃ, -ɨz
AM ˌbækˈbɛn(t)ʃ, -əz

backbencher
BR ˈbak,bɛn(t)ʃə(r), ˌbakˈbɛn(t)ʃə(r), -z
AM ˌbækˈbɛn(t)ʃər, -z

backbit
BR ˈbakbɪt
AM ˈbæk,bɪt

backbite
BR ˈbakbʌɪt, -s, -ɪŋ
AM ˈbæk,baɪ|t, -ts, -dɪŋ

backbiter
BR ˈbak,bʌɪtə(r), -z
AM ˈbæk,baɪdər, -z

backbitten
BR ˈbak,bɪtn
AM ˈbæk,bɪtn

backblocks
BR ˈbakblɒks
AM ˈbæk,blɑks

backboard
BR ˈbakbɔːd, -z
AM ˈbæk,bɔ(ə)rd, -z

backbone
BR ˈbakbəʊn, -z
AM ˈbæk,boʊn, -z

backbreaking
BR ˈbak,breɪkɪŋ
AM ˈbæk,breɪkɪŋ

backchat
BR ˈbaktʃat
AM ˈbæk,tʃæt

backcloth
BR ˈbakklɒ|θ, -θs\-ðz
AM ˈbæk,klɔ|θ, ˈbæk,klɑ|θ, -θs\-ðz

backcomb
BR ˈbakkəʊm, -z, -ɪŋ, -d
AM ˈbæk,koʊm, -z, -ɪŋ, -d

backcourt
BR ˈbakkɔːt, -s
AM ˈbæk,kɔ(ə)rt, -s

backdate
BR ˌbakˈdeɪt, -s, -ɪŋ, -ɨd
AM ˈbæk,deɪ|t, -ts, -dɪŋ, -dɨd

backdraft
BR ˈbakdrɑːft, ˈbakdraft, -s
AM ˈbæk,dræft, -s

backdrop
BR ˈbakdrɒp, -s
AM ˈbæk,drɑp, -s

backer
BR ˈbakə(r), -z
AM ˈbækər, -z

backfield
BR ˈbakfiːld, -z
AM ˈbæk,fild, -z

back-fill
BR ˈbakfɪl, -z, -ɪŋ, -d
AM ˈbæk,fɪl, -z, -ɪŋ, -d

backfire¹
noun
BR ˈbak,fʌɪə(r), -z
AM ˈbæk,faɪ(ə)r, -z

backfire²
verb
BR ˌbakˈfʌɪə(r), -z, -ɪŋ, -d
AM ˈbæk,faɪ(ə)r, -z, -ɪŋ, -d

backgammon
BR ˈbak,gamən
AM ˈbæk,gæmən

background
BR ˈbakgraʊnd, -z
AM ˈbæk,graʊnd, -z

backhand
BR ˈbakhand, -z
AM ˈbæk,(h)ænd, -z

backhanded
BR ˌbakˈhandɨd
AM ˈbæk,(h)ændəd

backhandedly
BR ˌbakˈhandɨdli
AM ˈbæk,(h)ændədli

backhander
BR ˈbak,handə(r), ˌbakˈhandə(r), -z
AM ˈbæk,(h)ændər, -z

Backhouse
BR ˈbakhaʊs
AM ˈbæk,(h)aʊs

backing
BR ˈbakɪŋ, -z
AM ˈbækɪŋ, -z

backlash
BR ˈbaklaʃ, -ɨz
AM ˈbæk,læʃ, -əz

backless
BR ˈbakləs
AM ˈbækləs

backlighting
BR ˌbakˈlʌɪtɪŋ, ˈbak,lʌɪtɪŋ
AM ˈbæk,laɪdɪŋ

backlist
BR ˈbaklɪst, -s
AM ˈbæk,lɪst, -s

backlit
BR ˌbakˈlɪt, ˈbaklɪt
AM ˈbæk,lɪt

backlog
BR ˈbaklɒg, -z
AM ˈbæk,lɔg, ˈbæk,lɑg, -z

backmarker
BR ˈbak,mɑːkə(r), -z
AM ˈbæk,mɑrkər, -z

backmost
BR ˈbakməʊst
AM ˈbæk,moʊst

backpack
BR ˈbakpak, -s, -ɪŋ, -t
AM ˈbæk,pæk, -s, -ɪŋ, -t

backpacker
BR ˈbak,pakə(r), -z
AM ˈbæk,pækər, -z

backpedal
BR ˌbakˈpɛd|l, -lz, -l̩ɪŋ\-lɪŋ, -ld
AM ˈbæk,pɛd|əl, -əlz, -(ə)lɪŋ, -əld

backrest
BR ˈbakrɛst, -s
AM ˈbæk,rɛst, -s

backroom
BR ˌbakˈruːm, ˌbakˈrʊm, ˈbakruːm, ˈbakrʊm, -z
AM ¦bæk¦rum, ¦bæk¦rʊm, -z

Backs
BR baks
AM bæks

backscratcher
BR ˈbak,skratʃə(r), -z
AM ˈbæk,skrætʃər, -z

backscratching
BR ˈbak,skratʃɪŋ
AM ˈbæk,skrætʃɪŋ

backsheesh
BR ˈbakʃiːʃ, ˌbakˈʃiːʃ
AM ˈbæk¦ʃiʃ

backside
BR ˈbaksʌɪd, ˌbakˈsʌɪd, -z
AM ˈbæk,saɪd, -z

backsight
BR ˈbaksʌɪt, -s
AM ˈbæk,saɪt, -s

backslapping
BR ˈbak,slapɪŋ, -z
AM ˈbæk,slæpɪŋ, -z

backslash
BR ˈbakslaʃ, -ɨz
AM ˈbæk,slæʃ, -əz

backslid
BR ˌbakˈslɪd
AM ˈbæk,slɪd

backslide
BR ˌbakˈslʌɪd, -z, -ɪŋ
AM ˈbæk,slaɪd, -z, -ɪŋ

backslider
BR ˈbak,slʌɪdə(r), ˌbakˈslʌɪdə(r), -z
AM ˈbæk,slaɪdər, -z

backspace¹
noun
BR ˈbakspeɪs, -ɨz
AM ˈbæk,speɪs, -ɨz

backspace²
verb
BR ˌbakˈspeɪs, -ɨz, -ɪŋ, -t
AM ˈbæk,speɪs, -ɨz, -ɪŋ, -t

backspin
BR ˈbakspɪn, -z
AM ˈbæk,spɪn, -z

backstage
BR ˌbakˈsteɪdʒ
AM ˌbækˈsteɪdʒ

backstair
adjective
BR ˌbakˈstɛː(r)
AM ˌbækˈstɛ(ə)r

backstairs
BR ˌbakˈstɛːz
AM ˌbækˈstɛ(ə)rz

backstay
BR ˈbaksteɪ, -z
AM ˈbæk,steɪ, -z

backstitch
BR ˈbakstɪtʃ, -ɨz, -ɪŋ, -t
AM ˈbæk,stɪtʃ, -ɨz, -ɪŋ, -t

backstop
BR ˈbakstɒp, -s
AM ˈbæk,stɑp, -s

backstrap
BR ˈbakstrap, -s
AM ˈbæk,stræp, -s

backstreet
BR ˈbakstriːt, -s
AM ¦bæk¦strit, -s

backstretch
BR ˈbakstrɛtʃ
AM ˈbæk,strɛtʃ

backstroke
BR ˈbakstrəʊk
AM ˈbæk,stroʊk

backtalk
BR ˈbaktɔːk
AM ˈbæk,tɔk, ˈbæk,tɑk

backtrack
BR ˈbaktrak, -s, -ɪŋ, -t
AM ˈbæk,træk, -s, -ɪŋ, -t

backtracker
BR ˈbak,trakə(r), -z
AM ˈbæk,trækər, -z

backup
BR ˈbakʌp, -s
AM ˈbæk,əp, -s

backveld
BR ˈbakvɛlt, -s
AM ˈbæk,vɛlt, -s

backvelder
BR ˈbak,vɛltə(r), ˈbak,vɛldə(r), -z
AM ˈbæk,vɛldər, -z

backward
BR ˈbakwəd
AM ˈbækwərd

backwardation
BR ˌbakwəˈdeɪʃn
AM ˌbækwərˈdeɪʃən

backwardly
BR ˈbakwədli
AM ˈbækwərdli

backwardness
BR 'bakwədnəs
AM 'bækwərdnəs

backwards
BR 'bakwədz
AM 'bækwərdz

backwash
BR 'bakwɒʃ
AM 'bæk,wɔʃ, 'bæk,wɑʃ

backwater
BR 'bak,wɔːtə(r), -z
AM 'bæk,wɔdər, 'bæk,wɑdər, -z

backwoods
BR 'bakwʊdz
AM ¦bæk'wʊdz

backwoodsman
BR 'bak,wʊdzmən
AM ,bæk'wʊdzmən

backwoodsmen
BR 'bak,wʊdzmən
AM ,bæk'wʊdzmən

backy
BR 'baki
AM 'bæki

backyard
BR ,bak'jɑːd, -z
AM ,bæk'jɑrd, -z

Bacofoil
BR 'beɪkə(ʊ)fɔɪl
AM 'bækə,fɔɪl

Bacolod
BR bə'kəʊlɒd
AM bə'koʊ,lɑd

bacon
BR 'beɪk(ə)n
AM 'beɪkən

Baconian
BR beɪ'kəʊnɪən, bə'kəʊnɪən, -z
AM bə'koʊniən, beɪ'koʊniən, -z

bacteraemia
BR ,baktə'riːmɪə(r)
AM ,bæktə'rimiə

bacteremia
BR ,baktə'riːmɪə(r)
AM ,bæktə'rimiə

bacteria
BR bak'tɪərɪə(r)
AM bæk'tɪriə

bacterial
BR bak'tɪərɪəl
AM bæk'tɪriəl

bactericidal
BR bak,tɪərɪ'sʌɪdl
AM bæk,tɪri'saɪdəl

bactericide
BR bak'tɪərɪsʌɪd, -z
AM bæk'tɪri,saɪd, -z

bacteriological
BR bak,tɪərɪə'lɒdʒɪkl
AM bæk,tɪriə'lɑdʒəkəl

bacteriologically
BR bak,tɪərɪə'lɒdʒɪkli
AM bæk,tɪriə'lɑdʒək(ə)li

bacteriologist
BR bak,tɪərɪ'ɒlədʒɪst, -s
AM bæk,tɪri'ɑlədʒəst, -s

bacteriology
BR bak,tɪərɪ'ɒlədʒi
AM bæk,tɪri'ɑlədʒi

bacteriolyses
BR bak,tɪərɪ'ɒlɪsiːz
AM bæk,tɪri'ɑləsiz

bacteriolysis
BR bak,tɪərɪ'ɒlɪsɪs
AM bæk,tɪri'ɑləsəs

bacteriolytic
BR bak,tɪərɪə'lɪtɪk
AM bæk,tɪriə'lɪdɪk

bacteriophage
BR bak'tɪərɪə,feɪdʒ, -ɪz
AM bæk'tɪriə,feɪdʒ, -ɪz

bacteriostases
BR bak,tɪərɪəʊ'steɪsiːz
AM bæk,tɪrioʊ'steɪsiz, bæk,tɪrioʊ'stæsiz, bæk,tɪri'ɑstəsiz

bacteriostasis
BR bak,tɪərɪəʊ'steɪsɪs
AM bæk,tɪrioʊ'steɪsɪs, bæk,tɪrioʊ'stæsəs, bæk,tɪri'ɑstəsəs

bacteriostatic
BR bak,tɪərɪə(ʊ)'statɪk
AM bæk,tɪriə'stædɪk

bacterium
BR bak'tɪərɪəm
AM bæk'tɪriəm

Bactria
BR 'baktrɪə(r)
AM 'bæktriə

Bactrian
BR 'baktrɪən, -z
AM 'bæktriən, -z

bad
BR bad
AM bæd

badass
BR 'badɑːs, -ɪz
AM 'bæd,æs, -əz

Baddesley
BR 'bad(ɪ)zli
AM 'bæd(ə)zli

baddish
BR 'badɪʃ
AM 'bædɪʃ

baddy
BR 'bad|i, -ɪz
AM 'bædi, -z

bade
BR bad, beɪd
AM beɪd, bæd

Badedas®
BR bə'deɪdəs, bə'deɪdas, 'bɑːdɪdas, 'badɪdas
AM 'bædədəs

Badel
BR bə'dɛl
AM 'beɪdəl, 'bædəl

Baden[1]
English surname
BR 'beɪdn
AM 'beɪdən

Baden[2]
German placename
BR 'bɑːdn
AM 'bɑdən

Baden-Baden
BR ,bɑːdn'bɑːdn
AM ¦bɑdən'bɑdən

Baden-Powell
BR ,beɪdn'paʊ(ə)l
AM ¦bɑdn'paʊəl

Baden-Württemberg
BR ,bɑːdn'wəːtəmbəːg
AM ,bɑdn'wərtəm,bərg
GER ,baːdn̩'vʏrtəmbɛrk

Bader
BR 'bɑːdə(r)
AM 'beɪdər

badge
BR badʒ, -ɪz, -ɪŋ, -d
AM bædʒ, -əz, -ɪŋ, -d

badger
BR 'badʒ|ə(r), -əz, -(ə)rɪŋ, -əd
AM 'bædʒər, -z, -ɪŋ, -d

Badian
BR 'beɪdɪən, -z
AM 'bɑdiən, -z

badinage
BR 'badɪnɑːʒ, ,badɪ'nɑːʒ
AM ,bædn'ɑʒ

badlands
BR 'badlandz
AM 'bæd,lændz

badly
BR 'badli
AM 'bædli

badminton
BR 'badmɪnt(ə)n
AM 'bæd,mɪtn, 'bæd,mɪn(t)ən

bad-mouth
BR 'badmaʊ|θ, 'babmaʊ|θ, 'badmaʊ|ð, 'babmaʊ|ð, -θs\-ðz, -θɪŋ\-ðɪŋ, -θt\-ðd
AM 'bæd,maʊ|θ, -θs\-ðz, -θɪŋ\-ðɪŋ, -θt\-ðd

badness
BR 'badnəs
AM 'bædnəs

Badon
BR 'beɪdn
AM 'beɪdən

Baedeker
BR 'beɪdɪkə(r), 'beɪ,dɛkə(r), -z
AM 'beɪdəkər, 'beɪ,dɛkə(r), -z

Baerlein
BR 'bɛːlʌɪn
AM 'bɛr,laɪn

Baez
BR 'bʌɪ(ɛ)z
AM baɪ'ɛz

Baffin
BR 'bafɪn
AM 'bæfən

baffle
BR 'baf|l, -lz, -l̩ɪŋ\-lɪŋ, -ld
AM 'bæf|əl, -əlz, -(ə)lɪŋ, -əld

baffleboard
BR 'baflbɔːd, -z
AM 'bæfəl,bɔ(ə)rd, -z

bafflement
BR 'baflm(ə)nt
AM 'bæfəlmənt

baffle-plate
BR 'baflpleɪt, -s
AM 'bæfəl,pleɪt, -s

baffler
BR 'bafl̩ə(r), 'baflə(r), -z
AM 'bæf(ə)lər, -z

bafflingly
BR 'bafl̩ɪŋli, 'baflɪŋli
AM 'bæf(ə)lɪŋli

BAFTA
BR 'baftə(r)
AM 'bæftə

bag
BR bag, -z, -ɪŋ, -d
AM bæg, -z, -ɪŋ, -d

Baganda
BR bə'gandə(r)
AM bə'gɑndə

Bagandan
BR bə'gandən, -z
AM bə'gɑndən, -z

bagarre
BR bə'gɑː(r), ba'gɑː(r), -z
AM bə'gɑr, -z

bagasse
BR bə'gas, ba'gas, bə'gɑːs, ba'gɑːs
AM bə'gɑs

bagatelle
BR ,bagə'tɛl
AM ,bægə'tɛl

Bagdad
BR ,bag'dad
AM 'bæg,dæd

Bagehot
BR 'badʒət
AM 'bædʒət

bagel
BR 'beɪgl, -z
AM 'beɪgəl, -z

bagful
BR 'bagfʊl, -z
AM 'bæg,fʊl, -z

baggage
BR 'bagɪdʒ
AM 'bægɪdʒ

baggily
BR 'bagɨli
AM 'bæɡəli

bagginess
BR 'baɡɪnɪs
AM 'bæɡinɨs

baggy
BR 'baɡ|i, -ɪə(r), -ɪɪst
AM 'bæɡi, -ər, -ɨst

Baghdad
BR ˌbag'dad
AM 'bæɡˌdæd

bagman
BR 'baɡman
AM 'bæɡˌmæn

bagmen
BR 'baɡmɛn
AM 'bæɡˌmɛn

Bagnall
BR 'baɡnl
AM 'bæɡnl

Bagnell
BR 'baɡnl
AM 'bæɡnl

bagnio
BR 'banjəʊ, 'bɑːnjəʊ, -z
AM 'bænˌjoʊ, -z

bagpipe
BR 'baɡpʌɪp, -s, -ɪŋ, -t
AM 'bæɡˌpaɪp, -s, -ɪŋ, -t

bagpiper
BR 'baɡˌpʌɪpə(r), -z
AM 'bæɡˌpaɪpər, -z

Bagshaw
BR 'baɡʃɔː(r)
AM 'bæɡˌʃɔ

Bagshot
BR 'baɡʃɒt
AM 'bæɡˌʃɑt

baguet
BR ba'ɡɛt, -s
AM bæ'ɡɛt, -s

baguette
BR ba'ɡɛt, -s
AM bæ'ɡɛt, -s

Baguley
BR 'baɡəli, 'baɡḷi
AM 'bæɡəli

bagwash
BR 'baɡwɒʃ, -ɨz
AM 'bæɡˌwɔʃ, 'bæɡˌwɑʃ, -əz

bah
BR bɑː(r)
AM bɑ

Bahai
BR bə'hʌɪ, bɑː'hʌɪ, -z
AM bɑ'haɪ, -z

Baha'i
BR bə'hʌɪ, bɑː'hʌɪ, -z
AM bɑ'haɪ, -z

Baha'ism
BR bə'hʌɪɪz(ə)m, bɑː'hʌɪɪz(ə)m
AM bɑ'haɪˌɪzəm

Baha'ist
BR bə'hʌɪɪst, bɑː'hʌɪɪst, -s
AM bɑ'haɪɨst, -s

Baha'ite
BR 'bɑːhəʌɪt, -s
AM 'bɑhaɪˌaɪt, -s

Bahamas
BR bə'hɑːməz
AM bə'hɑməs

Bahamian
BR bə'heɪmɪən, bə'hɑːmɪən, -z
AM bə'hɑmiən, bə'heɪmiən, -z

Bahasa
BR bə'hɑːsə(r)
AM bə'hɑsə

Baha Ullah
BR ˌbɑːhɑː 'ʊlɑː(r), + 'ʊlə(r), bəˌhɑː(r) ʊ'lɑː(r)
AM ˌbɑhɑ 'ʊlɑ

Bahawalpur
BR bəˌhɑːw(ə)l'pʊə(r)
AM bɑˌhɑwəl'pʊ(ə)r

Bahía
BR bə'hiːə(r)
AM bɑ'(h)iə

Bahrain
BR bɑː'reɪn
AM bɑ'reɪn

Bahraini
BR bɑː'reɪn|i, -ɪz
AM bɑ'reɪni, -z

Bahrein
BR bɑː'reɪn
AM bɑ'reɪn

Bahreini
BR bɑː'reɪn|i, -ɪz
AM bɑ'reɪni, -z

baht
BR bɑːt, -s
AM bɑt, -s

baignoire
BR 'beɪnwɑː(r), -z
AM ˌbeɪnˈwɑr, -z

Baikal
BR bʌɪ'kɑːl, bʌɪ'kal
AM baɪ'kɑl

bail
BR beɪl, -z, -ɪŋ, -d
AM beɪl, -z, -ɪŋ, -d

bailable
BR 'beɪləbl
AM 'beɪləbəl

Baildon
BR 'beɪld(ə)n
AM 'beɪldən

Baile Átha Cliath
BR ˌblɑː ˌaθə 'klɪə(r)
AM ˌbɑl ˌæθə 'kliə
IR ˌblʲaː 'kʲlʲiə

bailee
BR ˌbeɪ'liː, 'beɪliː, -z
AM beɪ'li, -z

bailer
BR 'beɪlə(r), -z
AM 'beɪlər, -z

bailey
BR 'beɪl|i, -ɪz
AM 'beɪli, -z

bailie
BR 'beɪl|i, -ɪz
AM 'beɪli, -z

bailiff
BR 'beɪlɪf, -s
AM 'beɪlɨf, -s

bailiwick
BR 'beɪlɪwɪk, -s
AM 'beɪliˌwɪk, 'beɪlɨˌwɪk, -s

Baillie
BR 'beɪli
AM 'beɪli

Bailly
BR 'beɪli
AM 'beɪli

bailment
BR 'beɪlm(ə)nt
AM 'beɪlmənt

bailor
BR 'beɪlə(r), -z
AM 'beɪlər, -z

bailout
BR 'beɪlaʊt
AM 'beɪˌlaʊt

bailsman
BR 'beɪlzmən
AM 'beɪlzmən

bailsmen
BR 'beɪlzmən
AM 'beɪlzmən

Bain
BR beɪn
AM beɪn

Bainbridge
BR 'beɪnbrɪdʒ
AM 'beɪnˌbrɪdʒ

Baines
BR beɪnz
AM beɪnz

bain-marie
BR ˌbanmə'riː, ˌba(m)mə'riː, -z
AM ˌbænmə'ri, ˌbæ(m)mə'ri

bains-marie
BR ˌbanmə'riː, ˌba(m)mə'riː, -z
AM ˌbænmə'ri, ˌbæ(m)mə'ri, -z

Bairam
BR bʌɪ'rɑːm
AM baɪ'rɑm

Baird
BR bɛːd
AM bɛ(ə)rd

bairn
BR bɛːn, -z
AM bɛ(ə)rn, -z

Bairstow
BR 'bɛːstəʊ
AM 'bɛrstoʊ

bait
BR beɪt, -s, -ɪŋ, -ɨd
AM beɪ|t, -ts, -dɪŋ, -dɨd

baize
BR beɪz
AM beɪz

Baja California
BR ˌbɑːhə ˌkalɪ'fɔːnɪə(r)
AM ˌbɑhɑ ˌkælə'fɔrniə

Bajan
BR 'beɪdʒ(ə)n, -z
AM 'bɑhən, -z

bajra
BR 'bɑːdʒrɑː(r)
AM 'bɑdʒrə

bake
BR beɪk, -s, -ɪŋ, -t
AM beɪk, -s, -ɪŋ, -t

bakehouse
BR 'beɪkhaʊ|s, -zɪz
AM 'beɪkˌ(h)aʊ|s, -zəz

Bakelite®
BR 'beɪkəlʌɪt
AM 'beɪk(ə)ˌlaɪt

baker
BR 'beɪkə(r), -z
AM 'beɪkər, -z

Bakerloo
BR ˌbeɪkə'luː
AM ˌbeɪkər'lu

bakery
BR 'beɪk(ə)r|i, -ɪz
AM 'beɪkəri, -z

Bakewell
BR 'beɪkw(ɛ)l
AM 'beɪkˌwɛl

Bakhtin
BR bak'tiːn
AM ˌbɑk'tin, ˌbæk'tin
RUS bax'tʲin

baklava
BR 'bakləvə(r)
AM ˌbɑklə'vɑ
TU bʌklʌ'vʌ

baksheesh
BR 'bakʃiːʃ, ˌbak'ʃiːʃ
AM ˌbæk'ʃiʃ

Bakst
BR bakst
AM bækst

Baku
BR 'bɑːˌkuː, bɑː'kuː
AM bɑ'ku

Bakunin
BR bə'kuːnɪn, ba'kuːnɪn
AM bə'kunɪn

Bala
BR 'balə(r), 'bɑːlə(r)
AM 'bɑlə

Balaam
BR 'beɪləm
AM 'beɪləm

balaclava
BR ˌbalə'klɑːvə(r), -z

AM ˌbæləˈklɑvə, ˌbɑləˈklɑvə, -z

balafon
BR ˈbaləfɒn, -z
AM ˈbæləˌfɑn, -z

balalaika
BR ˌbaləˈlʌɪkə(r), -z
AM ˌbɑləˈlaɪkə, ˌbæləˈlaɪkə, -z

balance
BR ˈbaləns, ˈbalṇs, -ɪz, -ɪŋ, -t
AM ˈbæləns, -əz, -ɪŋ, -t

balanceable
BR ˈbalənsəbl, ˈbalṇsəbl
AM ˈbælənsəbəl

balancer
BR ˈbalənsə(r), ˈbalṇsə(r), -z
AM ˈbælənsər, -z

Balanchine
BR ˈbalən(t)ʃiːn, ˌbalənˈ(t)ʃiːn
AM ˈbɑlænˌ(t)ʃin

balas-ruby
BR ˈbaləsˌruːb|i, -ɪz
AM ˈbæləsˌrubi, -z

balata
BR ˈbalətə(r), bəˈlɑːtə(r), -z
AM bəˈlɑdə, ˈbælədə, -z

Balaton
BR ˈbalətɒn
AM ˈbɑləˌtɑn
HU ˌbɔlɔˈtɒn

Balboa
BR balˈbəʊə(r)
AM bælˈboʊə

Balbriggan
BR balˈbrɪg(ə)n
AM bælˈbrɪgən

Balchin
BR ˈbɔːl(t)ʃɪn, ˈbɒl(t)ʃɪn
AM ˈbɔltʃɪn, ˈbɑltʃɪn

Balcomb
BR ˈbɔːlkəm, ˈbɒlkəm
AM ˈbɔlkəmb, ˈbɑlkəmb

Balcombe
BR ˈbɔːlkəm, ˈbɒlkəm
AM ˈbɔlkəmb, ˈbɑlkəmb

Balcon
BR ˈbɔːlk(ə)n, ˈbɒlk(ə)n
AM ˈbælkən

balcony
BR ˈbalkən|i, ˈbalkṇ|i, -ɪz, -ɪd
AM ˈbælkəni, -z, -d

bald
BR bɔːld, -z, -ɪŋ, -ɪd, -ə(r), -ɪst
AM bɔld, bɑld, -ər, -əst, -z, -ɪŋ, -əd

baldachin
BR ˈbɔːldəkɪn, -z
AM ˈbɔldəkən, ˈbɑldəkən, -z

baldaquin
BR ˈbɔːldəkɪn, -z
AM ˈbɔldəkən, ˈbɑldəkən, -z

Balder
BR ˈbɔːldə(r), ˈbɒldə(r)
AM ˈbɔldər, ˈbɑldər

balderdash
BR ˈbɔːldədaʃ
AM ˈbɔldərˌdæʃ, ˈbɑldərˌdæʃ

baldhead
BR ˈbɔːldhɛd, -z
AM ˈbɔldˌ(h)ɛd, ˈbɑldˌ(h)ɛd, -z

baldheaded
BR ˌbɔːldˈhɛdɪd
AM ˈbɔldˈhɛdəd, ˈbɑldˈhɛdəd

baldie
BR ˈbɔːld|i, -ɪz
AM ˈbɔldi, ˈbɑldi, -z

baldish
BR ˈbɔːldɪʃ
AM ˈbɔldɪʃ, ˈbɑldɪʃ

baldly
BR ˈbɔːldli
AM ˈbɔl(d)li, ˈbɑl(d)li

baldmoney
BR ˈbɔːldˌmʌn|i, -ɪz
AM ˈbɔl(d)ˌməni, ˈbɑl(d)ˌməni, -z

baldness
BR ˈbɔːldnəs
AM ˈbɔl(d)nəs, ˈbɑl(d)nəs

Baldock
BR ˈbɔːldɒk, ˈbɒldɒk
AM ˈbɔldɑk, ˈbɑldɑk

baldpate
BR ˈbɔːldpeɪt, -s
AM ˈbɔl(d)ˌpeɪt, ˈbɑl(d)ˌpeɪt, -s

baldric
BR ˈbɔːldrɪk, -s
AM ˈbɔldˌrɪk, ˈbɑldˌrɪk, -s

Baldry
BR ˈbɔːldri, ˈbɒldri
AM ˈbɔldri, ˈbɑldri

Baldwin
BR ˈbɔːldwɪn
AM ˈbɔldwən, ˈbɑldwən

baldy
BR ˈbɔːld|i, -ɪz
AM ˈbɔldi, ˈbɑldi, -z

bale
BR beɪl, -z, -ɪŋ, -d
AM beɪl, -z, -ɪŋ, -d

Balearic
BR ˌbalɪˈarɪk, bəˈlɪərɪk, bəˈlɛːrɪk, -s
AM ˌbæliˈɛrɪk, -s

baleen
BR bəˈliːn
AM bəˈlin

baleful
BR ˈbeɪlf(ʊ)l
AM ˈbeɪlfəl

balefully
BR ˈbeɪlfʊli, ˈbeɪlfḷi
AM ˈbeɪlfəli

balefulness
BR ˈbeɪlf(ʊ)lnəs
AM ˈbeɪlfəlnəs

Balenciaga
BR bəˌlɛnsɪˈɑːgə(r)
AM bəˈlɛnsiˈɑgə
SP ˌbalenˈθjaɣa, ˌbalenˈsjaɣa

baler
BR ˈbeɪlə(r), -z
AM ˈbeɪlər, -z

Balfour
BR ˈbalfə(r), ˈbalfɔː(r), ˌbalˈfɔː(r)
AM ˈbælˌfɔ(ə)r

Balham
BR ˈbaləm
AM ˈbɔləm, ˈbɑləm

Bali
BR ˈbɑːli
AM ˈbɑˌli

Balinese
BR ˌbɑːlɪˈniːz
AM ˌbɑləˈniz, ˌbæləˈniz

Baliol
BR ˈbeɪlɪəl
AM ˈbeɪliəl

balk
BR bɔː(l)k, -s, -ɪŋ, -t
AM bɔ(l)k, bɑ(l)k, -s, -ɪŋ, -t

Balkan
BR ˈbɔːlk(ə)n, ˈbɒlk(ə)n, -z
AM ˈbɔlkən, ˈbɑlkən, -z

Balkanisation
BR ˌbɔːlkənʌɪˈzeɪʃn, ˌbɔːlkṇʌɪˈzeɪʃn, ˌbɒlkənʌɪˈzeɪʃn, ˌbɒlkṇʌɪˈzeɪʃn
AM ˌbɔlkənəˈzeɪʃən, ˌbɔlkəˌnaɪˈzeɪʃən, ˌbɑlkənəˈzeɪʃən, ˌbɑlkəˌnaɪˈzeɪʃən

Balkanise
BR ˈbɔːlkənʌɪz, ˈbɔːlkṇʌɪz, ˈbɒlkənʌɪz, ˈbɒlkṇʌɪz, -ɪz, -ɪŋ, -d
AM ˈbɔlkəˌnaɪz, ˈbɑlkəˌnaɪz, -ɪz, -ɪŋ, -d

Balkanization
BR ˌbɔːlkənʌɪˈzeɪʃn, ˌbɔːlkṇʌɪˈzeɪʃn, ˌbɒlkənʌɪˈzeɪʃn, ˌbɒlkṇʌɪˈzeɪʃn
AM ˌbɔlkənəˈzeɪʃən, ˌbɔlkəˌnaɪˈzeɪʃən, ˌbɑlkənəˈzeɪʃən, ˌbɑlkəˌnaɪˈzeɪʃən

Balkanize
BR ˈbɔːlkənʌɪz, ˈbɔːlkṇʌɪz, ˈbɒlkənʌɪz, ˈbɒlkṇʌɪz, -ɪz, -ɪŋ, -d
AM ˈbɔlkəˌnaɪz, ˈbɑlkəˌnaɪz, -ɪz, -ɪŋ, -d

Balkhash
BR ˈbalkaʃ
AM ˈbælˌkæʃ
RUS balˈxaʃ

balky
BR ˈbɔːk|i, -ɪə(r), -ɪɪst
AM ˈbɔki, ˈbɑki, -ər, -ɪst

ball
BR bɔːl, -z, -ɪŋ, -d
AM bɔl, bɑl, -z, -ɪŋ, -d

Ballachulish
BR ˌbaləˈhuːlɪʃ
AM ˌbæləˈtʃulɪʃ

ballad
BR ˈbaləd, -z
AM ˈbæləd, -z

ballade
BR bəˈlɑːd, baˈlɑːd, -z
AM bəˈlɑd, -z

balladeer
BR ˌbaləˈdɪə(r), -z
AM ˌbæləˈdɪ(ə)r, -z

balladry
BR ˈbaləd r|i, -ɪz
AM ˈbælədri, -z

Ballantine
BR ˈbaləntʌɪn
AM ˈbælənˌtaɪn

Ballantrae
BR ˌbalənˈtreɪ
AM ˈbæləntri

Ballantyne
BR ˈbaləntʌɪn
AM ˈbælənˌtaɪn

Ballarat
BR ˈbalərat, ˌbaləˈrat
AM ˈbæləˌræt

Ballard
BR ˈbalɑːd
AM ˈbælərd

ballast
BR ˈbaləst
AM ˈbæləst

Ballater
BR ˈbalətə(r)
AM ˈbælədər

ballbearing
BR ˌbɔːlˈbɛːrɪŋ, -z
AM ˈbɔlˈbɛrɪŋ, ˈbɑlˈbɛrɪŋ, -z

ballboy
BR ˈbɔːlbɔɪ, -z
AM ˈbɔlˌbɔɪ, ˈbɑlˌbɔɪ, -z

ballcock
BR ˈbɔːlkɒk, -s
AM ˈbɔlˌkɑk, ˈbɑlˌkɑk, -s

ballerina
BR ˌbaləˈriːnə(r), -z
AM ˌbæləˈrinə, -z

Ballesteros
BR ˌbalɪˈstɛːrɒs
AM ˌbæləˈstɛˌroʊs, ˌbaɪjəsˈtɛroʊs
SP ˌbajesˈteros

ballet
BR ˈbaleɪ, -z
AM bæˈleɪ, -z

balletic
BR bəˈlɛtɪk, baˈlɛtɪk
AM bæˈlɛdɪk, bəˈlɛdɪk

balletomane
BR ˈbalɪtə(ʊ)meɪn, bəˈlɛtə(ʊ)meɪn, baˈlɛtə(ʊ)meɪn, -z
AM bəˈlɛdəˌmeɪn, bæˈlɛdəˌmeɪn, -z

balletomania
BR ˌbalɪtə(ʊ)ˈmeɪnɪə(r), bəˈlɛtəˌmeɪnɪə(r), baˈlɛtəˌmeɪnɪə(r)
AM bəˌlɛdəˈmeɪniə, bæˌlɛdəˈmeɪniə

Ballets Russes
BR ˌbaleɪ ˈruːs
AM ˌbæˌleɪ ˈrus

ballgirl
BR ˈbɔːlgəːl, -z
AM ˈbɔlˌgərl, ˈbɑlˌgərl, -z

ballhandler
BR ˈbɔːlˌhandlə(r), ˈbɔːlˌhandl̩ə(r), -z
AM ˈbɔlˌ(h)æn(də)lər, ˈbɑlˌ(h)æn(də)lər, -z

ballhawk
BR ˈbɔːlhɔːk, -s
AM ˈbɔlˌ(h)ɔk, ˈbɑlˌ(h)ɑk, -s

Balliol
BR ˈbeɪlɪəl
AM ˈbeɪliəl

ballista
BR bəˈlɪstə(r), -z
AM bəˈlɪstə, -z

ballistae
BR bəˈlɪstiː
AM bəˈlɪsti

ballistic
BR bəˈlɪstɪk, -s
AM bəˈlɪstɪk, -s

ballistically
BR bəˈlɪstɪkli
AM bəˈlɪstɪk(ə)li

ballock
BR ˈbɒlək, -s
AM ˈbɔlək, ˈbɑlək, -s

ballon d'essai
BR ˌbalɒ̃ dɛˈseɪ
AM bɑˌlɔn ˌdɛˈseɪ

ballons d'essai
BR ˌbalɒ̃ dɛˈseɪ
AM bɑˌlɔn ˌdɛˈseɪ

balloon
BR bəˈluːn, -z, -ɪŋ, -d
AM bəˈlun, -z, -ɪŋ, -d

balloonist
BR bəˈluːnɪst, -s
AM bəˈlunəst, -s

ballot
BR ˈbalət, -s, -ɪŋ, -ɨd
AM ˈbælə|t, -ts, -dɪŋ, -dɨd

ballpark
BR ˈbɔːlpɑːk, -s
AM ˈbɔlˌpɑrk, ˈbɑlˌpɑrk, -s

ballplayer
BR ˈbɔːlˌpleɪə(r), -z
AM ˈbɔlˌpleɪər, ˈbɑlˌpleɪər, -z

ballpoint
BR ˈbɔːlpɔɪnt, -s
AM ˈbɔlˌpɔɪnt, ˈbɑlˌpɔɪnt, -s

ballroom
BR ˈbɔːlruːm, ˈbɔːlrʊm, -z
AM ˈbɔlˌrum, ˈbɔlˌrʊm, ˈbɑlˌrum, ˈbɑlˌrʊm, -z

balls
verb
BR bɔːlz, -ɪz, -ɪŋ, -d
AM bɔlz, bɑlz, -əz, -ɪŋ, -d

ballsy
BR ˈbɔːlzi
AM ˈbɔlzi, ˈbɑlzi

bally
BR ˈbali
AM ˈbæli

Ballycastle
BR ˌbalɪˈkɑːsl, ˌbalɪˈkasl
AM ˈbæliˌkæsəl

ballyhoo
BR ˌbalɪˈhuː, -z
AM ˈbæliˌhu, -z

Ballymacarrett
BR ˌbalɪməˈkarət
AM ˌbæliməˈkɛrət

Ballymena
BR ˌbalɪˈmiːnə(r)
AM ˌbæliˈminə

Ballymoney
BR ˌbalɪˈmʌni
AM ˌbælɪˈməni

ballyrag
BR ˈbalɪrag, -z, -ɪŋ, -d
AM ˈbæliˌræg, -z, -ɪŋ, -d

balm
BR bɑːm, -z
AM bɑ(l)m, -z

Balmain
BR ˈbalmã
AM ˈbɔlmeɪn, ˈbɑlmeɪn

balmily
BR ˈbɑːmɪli
AM ˈbɑ(l)məli

balminess
BR ˈbɑːmɪnɪs
AM ˈbɑ(l)minɨs

Balmoral
BR balˈmɒrəl, balˈmɒrl̩
AM bælˈmɔrəl

balmy
BR ˈbɑːm|i, -ɪə(r), -ɪɪst
AM ˈbɑ(l)mi, -ər, -ɨst

balneary
BR ˈbalnɪəri
AM ˈbælniˌɛri

balneological
BR ˌbalnɪəˈlɒdʒɪkl
AM ˌbælniəˈlɑdʒəkəl

balneologist
BR ˌbalnɪˈɒlədʒɪst, -s
AM ˌbælniˈɑlədʒəst, -s

balneology
BR ˌbalnɪˈɒlədʒi
AM ˌbælniˈɑlədʒi

balniel
BR ˈbalnɪəl
AM ˈbælniəl

baloney
BR bəˈləʊni
AM bəˈloʊni

BALPA
BR ˈbalpə(r)
AM ˈbælpə

balsam
BR ˈbɔːls(ə)m, ˈbɒls(ə)m, -z
AM ˈbɔlsəm, ˈbɑlsəm, -z

balsamic
BR bɔːlˈsamɪk, bɒlˈsamɪk
AM bɔlˈsɑmɪk, bɑlˈsɑmɪk, bɔlˈsæmɪk, bɑlˈsæmɪk

balsamiferous
BR ˌbɔːlsəˈmɪf(ə)rəs, ˌbɒlsəˈmɪf(ə)rəs
AM ˌbɔlsəˈmɪf(ə)rəs, ˌbɑlsəˈmɪf(ə)rəs

balsa wood
BR ˈbɔːlsə wʊd, ˈbɒlsə +
AM ˈbɔlsə ˌwʊd, ˈbɑlsə ˌwʊd

Balt
BR bɔːlt, bɒlt, -s
AM bɔlt, bɑlt, -s

Balthasar
BR balˈθazə(r), ˈbalθəzɑː(r), ˌbalθəˈzɑː(r)
AM bælˈθæzər, bɔlˈθæzər, bɑlˈθæzər, ˈbɔlθəˌzɑr, ˈbɑlθəˌzɑr

Balthazar
BR balˈθazə(r), ˈbalθəzɑː(r), ˌbalθəˈzɑː(r)
AM bælˈθæzər, bɔlˈθæzər, bɑlˈθæzər, ˈbɔlθəˌzɑr, ˈbɑlθəˌzɑr

balti
BR ˈbɔːlt|i, ˈbɒlt|i, -ɪz
AM ˈbælti, ˈbɔlti, ˈbɑlti, -z

Baltic
BR ˈbɔːltɪk, ˈbɒltɪk
AM ˈbɔltɪk, ˈbɑltɪk

Baltimore
BR ˈbɔːltɪmɔː(r), ˈbɒltɪmɔː(r)
AM ˈbɔltəˌmɔ(ə)r, ˈbɑltəˌmɔ(ə)r

Baltistan
BR ˌbɔːltɪˈstɑːn, ˌbɔːltɪˈstan, ˌbɒltɪˈstɑːn, ˌbɒltɪˈstan
AM ˈbɔltəˌstæn, ˈbɑltəˌstæn

Baluchistan
BR bəˌluːtʃɪˈstɑːn, bəˌluːtʃɪˈstan
AM bəˈlutʃəˌstæn

balun
BR ˈbalʌn, -z
AM ˈbælən, -z

baluster
BR ˈbaləstə(r), -z, -d
AM ˈbæləstər, -z, -d

balustrade
BR ˌbaləˈstreɪd, -z, -ɪŋ, -ɨd
AM ˈbæləˌstreɪd, -z, -ɪŋ, -ɨd

Balzac
BR ˈbalzak
AM bɑlˈzɑk, bɑlˈzæk

Bamako
BR ˌbaməˈkəʊ, ˈbamakəʊ
AM bəˈmæˌkoʊ, bəˈmɑˌkoʊ

bambini
BR bamˈbiːni
AM bæmˈbini

bambino
BR bamˈbiːnəʊ, -z
AM bæmˈbinoʊ, -z

bamboo
BR ˌbamˈbuː, -z
AM ˌbæmˈbu, -z

bamboozle
BR bamˈbuːz|l, -lz, -l̩ɪŋ\-lɪŋ, -ld
AM bæmˈbuz|əl, -əlz, -(ə)lɪŋ, -əld

bamboozlement
BR bamˈbuːzlm(ə)nt
AM bæmˈbuzlmənt

bamboozler
BR bamˈbuːzl̩ə(r), bamˈbuːzlə(r), -z
AM bæmˈbuz(ə)lər, -z

Bamian
BR ˈbeɪmɪən
AM ˈbeɪmiən

ban
BR ban, -z, -ɪŋ, -d
AM bæn, -z, -ɪŋ, -d

banal
BR bə'nɑːl, bə'nal
AM 'beɪnl, bə'næl, bə'nɑl
banality
BR bə'nalɪt|i, -ɪz
AM bə'nælədi, beɪ'nælədi, -z
banally
BR bə'nɑːlli
AM 'beɪnɨli
banana
BR bə'nɑːnə(r), -z
AM bə'nænə, -z
banausic
BR bə'nɔːzɪk, bə'nɔːsɪk
AM bə'nɔzɪk, bə'nɔsɪk, bə'nɑzɪk, bə'nɑsɪk
Banbury
BR 'banb(ə)ri
AM 'bænbəri
banc
BR baŋk
AM bæŋk
Bancroft
BR 'bankrɒft, 'baŋkrɒft
AM 'bæn,krɔft, 'bæŋ,krɔft, 'bæn,krɑft, 'bæŋ,krɑft
band
BR band, -z, -ɪŋ, -ɨd
AM bænd, -z, -ɪŋ, -əd
Banda
BR 'bandə(r)
AM 'bændə
bandage
BR 'band|ɪdʒ, -ɨdʒɪz, -ɨdʒɪŋ, -ɪdʒd
AM 'bænd|ɪdʒ, -ɨdʒɪz, -ɨdʒɪŋ, -ɪdʒd
bandana
BR ban'danə(r), -z
AM bæn'dænə, -z
bandanna
BR ban'danə(r), -z
AM bæn'dænə, -z
Bandaranaike
BR ˌband(ə)rə'nʌɪɨkə(r)
AM ˌbændrə'niki
Bandar Seri Begawan
BR ˌbandɑː ˌsɛrɪ bə'gɑːwən, ˌbandə +
AM ˌbændər ˌsɛri bə'gɑwən
bandbox
BR 'ban(d)bɒks, -ɪz
AM 'bæn(d),bɑks, -əz
bandeau
BR 'bandəʊ, -z
AM ¦bæn¦doʊ, -z
bandeaux
BR 'bandəʊz
AM ¦bæn¦doʊz
banderilla
BR ˌbandə'rɪljə(r), -z
AM ˌbændə'ri(j)ə, -z
banderol
BR 'bandərəʊl, -z
AM 'bændə,roʊl, -z
banderole
BR 'bandərəʊl, -z
AM 'bændə,roʊl, -z
bandicoot
BR 'bandɪkuːt, -s
AM 'bændi,kut, -s
bandit
BR 'bandɪt, -s
AM 'bændɪt, -s
bandito
BR ban'diːtəʊ, -z
AM bæn'didoʊ, -z
banditry
BR 'bandɪtri
AM 'bændɪtri
banditti
BR ban'dɪtiː
AM bæn'didi
bandleader
BR 'band,liːdə(r), -z
AM 'bæn(d),lidər, -z
bandmaster
BR 'ban(d),mɑːstə(r), 'ban(d),mastə(r), -z
AM 'bæn(d),mæstər, -z
bandoleer
BR ˌbandə'lɪə(r), -z
AM ˌbændə'lɪ(ə)r, -z
bandolier
BR ˌbandə'lɪə(r), -z
AM ˌbændə'lɪ(ə)r, -z
bandore
BR ban'dɔː(r), 'bandɔː(r), -z
AM ¦bæn¦dɔ(ə)r, -z
bandsman
BR 'ban(d)smən
AM 'bæn(d)zmən
bandsmen
BR 'ban(d)smən
AM 'bæn(d)zmən
bandstand
BR 'ban(d)stand, -z
AM 'bæn(d),stænd, -z
Bandung
BR 'bandʊŋ, ˌban'dʊŋ
AM 'bɑn,duŋ, 'bɑn,dʊŋ
bandwagon
BR 'band,wag(ə)n, -z
AM 'bæn(d),wægən, -z
bandwidth
BR 'bandwɪdθ, 'bandwɪtθ
AM 'bæn(d),wɪdθ, 'bæn(d),wɪtθ
bandy
BR 'band|i, -ɪz, -ɪɪŋ, -ɪd, -ɪə(r), -ɪɪst
AM 'bændi, -z, -ɪŋ, -d, -ər, -ɪst
bane
BR beɪn
AM beɪn
baneberry
BR 'beɪnb(ə)r|i, -ɪz
AM 'beɪn,bɛri, -z
baneful
BR 'beɪnf(ʊ)l
AM 'beɪnfəl
banefully
BR 'beɪnfʊli, 'beɪnfḷi
AM 'beɪnfəli
banefulness
BR 'beɪnf(ʊ)lnəs
AM 'beɪnfəlnəs
Banff
BR banf
AM bænf
bang
BR baŋ, -z, -ɪŋ, -d
AM bæŋ, -z, -ɪŋ, -d
Bangalore
BR ˌbaŋgə'lɔː(r)
AM ˌbæŋgə'lɔ(ə)r
banger
BR 'baŋə(r), -z
AM 'bæŋər, -z
Bangkok
BR ˌbaŋ'kɒk
AM 'bæŋkɑk
Bangladesh
BR ˌbaŋglə'dɛʃ
AM ˌbɑŋglə'dɛʃ
Bangladeshi
BR ˌbaŋglə'dɛʃ|i, -ɪz
AM ˌbɑŋglə'dɛʃi, -z
bangle
BR 'baŋgl, -z
AM 'bæŋgəl, -z
Bangor
BR 'baŋgə(r)
AM 'bæŋgər, 'bæŋ,gɔ(ə)r
bangtail
BR 'baŋteɪl, -z
AM 'bæŋ,teɪl, -z
Bangui
BR ˌbɒŋ'giː, ˌbɑːŋ'giː, 'bɑːŋgi
AM 'bæŋgi
banian
BR 'banjan, 'banjən, -z
AM 'bænjən, -z
banish
BR 'ban|ɪʃ, -ɨʃɪz, -ɨʃɪŋ, -ɪʃt
AM 'bænɪʃ, -ɪz, -ɪŋ, -t
banishment
BR 'banɪʃm(ə)nt
AM 'bænɪʃmənt
banister
BR 'banɪstə(r), -z
AM 'bænəstər, -z
banjax
BR 'bandʒaks, -t
AM 'bæn,dʒæks, -t
banjo
BR 'bandʒəʊ, -z
AM 'bændʒoʊ, -z
banjoist
BR 'bandʒəʊɪst, -s
AM 'bændʒəwəst, -s
Banjul
BR ban'dʒuːl
AM 'bæn,dʒul
bank
BR baŋ|k, -ks, -kɪŋ, -(k)t
AM bæŋ|k, -ks, -kɪŋ, -(k)t
bankability
BR ˌbaŋkə'bɪlɨti
AM ˌbæŋkə'bɪlɨdi
bankable
BR 'baŋkəbl
AM 'bæŋkəbəl
bankbill
BR 'baŋkbɪl, -z
AM 'bæŋk,bɪl, -z
bankbook
BR 'baŋkbʊk, -s
AM 'bæŋk,bʊk, -s
banker
BR 'baŋkə(r), -z
AM 'bæŋkər, -z
banknote
BR 'baŋknəʊt, -s
AM 'bænk,noʊt, -s
bankroll
BR 'baŋkrəʊl, -z, -ɪŋ, -d
AM 'bæŋk,roʊl, -z, -ɪŋ, -d
bankrupt
BR 'baŋk,rʌpt, -s, -ɪŋ, -ɨd
AM 'bæŋk,rəpt, -s, -ɪŋ, -əd
bankruptcy
BR 'baŋkrʌp(t)s|i, -ɪz
AM 'bæŋk,rəp(t)si, -z
banksia
BR 'baŋksɪə(r), -z
AM 'bæŋksiə, -z
banner
BR 'banə(r), -z, -d
AM 'bænər, -z, -d
banneret
BR 'banərɪt, ˌbanə'rɛt, -s
AM 'bænərət, ˌbænə'rɛt, -s
bannister
BR 'banɪstə(r), -z
AM 'bænəstər, -z
bannock
BR 'banək, -s
AM 'bænək, -s
Bannockburn
BR 'banəkbəːn
AM 'bænək,bərn
banns
BR banz
AM bænz
banquet
BR 'baŋkw|ɪt, -ɪts, -ɪtɪŋ, -ɪtɨd

AM ˈbæŋkwɨ|t, -ts, -dɪŋ, -dɨd

banqueter
BR ˈbaŋkwɨtə(r), -z
AM ˈbæŋkwɨdər, -z

banquette
BR baŋˈkɛt, -s
AM bæŋˈkɛt, -s

banshee
BR ˈbanʃiː, -z
AM ˈbænʃi, -z

banshie
BR ˈbanʃiː, -z
AM ˈbænʃi, -z

bantam
BR ˈbantəm, -z
AM ˈbæn(t)əm, -z

bantamweight
BR ˈbantəmweɪt, -s
AM ˈbæn(t)əmˌweɪt, -s

banter
BR ˈbant|ə(r), -əz, -(ə)rɪŋ, -əd
AM ˈbæn(t)ər, -z, -ɪŋ, -d

banterer
BR ˈbant(ə)rə(r), -z
AM ˈbæn(t)ərər, -z

Banting
BR ˈbantɪŋ
AM ˈbæn(t)ɪŋ

Bantu
BR ˈbantuː, banˈtuː, -z
AM ˈbænˌtu, -z

Bantustan
BR ˌbantuːˈstɑːn, ˌbantuːˈstan, -z
AM ˈbænˌtuˌstæn, -z

banyan
BR ˈbanjan, ˈbanjən, -z
AM ˈbænjən, ˈbænˌjæn, -z

banzai
BR ˈbanzʌɪ
AM ˈbɑnˌzaɪ

baobab
BR ˈbeɪə(ʊ)bab, ˈbaʊbab, -z
AM ˈbaʊˌbæb, ˈbeɪəˌbæb, -z

bap
BR bap, -s
AM bæp, -s

baptise
BR bapˈtʌɪz, -ɨz, -ɪŋ, -d
AM ˌbæpˌtaɪz, ˌbæbˌtaɪz, -ɨz, -ɪŋ, -d

baptism
BR ˈbaptɪz(ə)m, -z
AM ˈbæpˌtɪzəm, ˈbæbˌtɪzəm, -z

baptismal
BR bapˈtɪzml
AM bæpˈtɪzməl, bæbˈtɪzməl

Baptist
BR ˈbaptɪst, -s
AM ˈbæptəst, ˈbæbtəst, -s

baptistery
BR ˈbaptɨst(ə)r|i, -ɪz
AM ˈbæptəstri, ˈbæbtəstri, -z

baptistry
BR ˈbaptɨstr|i, -ɪz
AM ˈbæptəstri, ˈbæbtəstri, -z

baptize
BR bapˈtʌɪz, -ɨz, -ɪŋ, -d
AM ˌbæpˌtaɪz, ˌbæbˌtaɪz, -ɨz, -ɪŋ, -d

bar
BR bɑː(r), -z, -ɪŋ, -d
AM bɑr, -z, -ɪŋ, -d

Barabbas
BR bəˈrabəs
AM bəˈræbəs

barathea
BR ˌbarəˈθiːə(r)
AM ˌbærəˈθiə

barb
BR bɑːb, -z, -ɪŋ, -d
AM bɑrb, -z, -ɪŋ, -d

Barbadian
BR bɑːˈbeɪdɪən, bɑːˈbeɪdʒ(ə)n, -z
AM bɑrˈbeɪdiən, -z

Barbados
BR bɑːˈbeɪdəs, bɑːˈbeɪdɒs
AM bɑrˈbeɪdəs, bɑrˈbeɪˌdoʊs

Barbara
BR ˈbɑːb(ə)rə(r)
AM ˈbɑrb(ə)rə

barbarian
BR bɑːˈbɛːrɪən, -z
AM bɑrˈbɛriən, -z

barbaric
BR bɑːˈbarɪk
AM bɑrˈbɛrɪk

barbarically
BR bɑːˈbarɨkli
AM bɑrˈbɛrək(ə)li

barbarisation
BR ˌbɑːb(ə)rʌɪˈzeɪʃn
AM ˌbɑrbərəˈzeɪʃən, ˌbɑrbəˌraɪˈzeɪʃən

barbarise
BR ˈbɑːbərʌɪz, -ɨz, -ɪŋ, -d
AM ˈbɑrbəˌraɪz, -ɨz, -ɪŋ, -d

barbarism
BR ˈbɑːbərɪz(ə)m, -z
AM ˈbɑrbəˌrɪzəm, -z

barbarity
BR bɑːˈbarɨt|i, -ɪz
AM bɑrˈbɛrədi, -z

barbarization
BR ˌbɑːb(ə)rʌɪˈzeɪʃn
AM ˌbɑrbərəˈzeɪʃən, ˌbɑrbəˌraɪˈzeɪʃən

barbarize
BR ˈbɑːbərʌɪz, -ɨz, -ɪŋ, -d
AM ˈbɑrbəˌraɪz, -ɨz, -ɪŋ, -d

Barbarossa
BR ˌbɑːbəˈrɒsə(r)
AM ˌbɑrbəˈroʊsə, ˌbɑrbəˈrɔsə

barbarous
BR ˈbɑːb(ə)rəs
AM ˈbɑrbərəs

barbarously
BR ˈbɑːb(ə)rəsli
AM ˈbɑrbərəsli

barbarousness
BR ˈbɑːb(ə)rəsnəs
AM ˈbɑrbərəsnəs

Barbary
BR ˈbɑːb(ə)ri
AM ˈbɑrbəri

barbate
BR ˈbɑːbeɪt
AM ˈbɑrˌbeɪt

barbecue
BR ˈbɑːbɨkjuː, -z, -ɪŋ, -d
AM ˈbɑrbəˌkju, ˈbɑrbiˌkju, -z, -ɪŋ, -d

barbel
BR ˈbɑːbl, -z
AM ˈbɑrbəl, -z

barbell
BR ˈbɑːbɛl, -z
AM ˈbɑrˌbɛl, -z

barber
BR ˈbɑːbə(r), -z
AM ˈbɑrbər, -z

barberry
BR ˈbɑːb(ə)r|i, -ɪz
AM ˈbɑrˌbɛri, -z

barbershop
BR ˈbɑːbəʃɒp, -s
AM ˈbɑrbərˌʃɑp, -s

barbet
BR ˈbɑːbɪt, -s
AM ˈbɑrbət, -s

barbette
BR bɑːˈbɛt, -s
AM bɑrˈbɛt, -s

barbican
BR ˈbɑːbɪk(ə)n, -z
AM ˈbɑrbəkən, -z

Barbirolli
BR ˌbɑːbɪˈrɒli
AM ˌbɑrbəˈroʊli

barbital
BR ˈbɑːbɪtl
AM ˈbɑrbəˌtɑl, ˈbɑrbəˌtɔl

barbitone
BR ˈbɑːbɪtəʊn
AM ˈbɑrbəˌtoʊn

barbiturate
BR bɑːˈbɪtʃ(ʊ)rɪt, bɑːˈbɪtjʊrɪt, -s
AM bɑrˈbɪtʃərət, -s

barbituric
BR ˌbɑːbɪˈtʃʊərɪk, ˌbɑːbɪˈtjʊərɪk
AM ˌbɑrbəˈtʃʊrɪk

Barbizon
BR ˈbɑːbɪzɒn
AM ˈbɑrbəˌzɑn

barbless
BR ˈbɑːbləs
AM ˈbɑrbləs

barbola
BR bɑːˈbəʊlə(r)
AM bɑrˈboʊlə

Barbour®
BR ˈbɑːbə(r), -z
AM ˈbɑrbər, -z

Barbuda
BR bɑːˈbjuːdə(r)
AM bɑrˈbjudə

Barbudan
BR bɑːˈbjuːdn, -z
AM bɑrˈbjudən, -z

barbule
BR ˈbɑːbjuːl, -z
AM ˈbɑrˌbjul, -z

barbwire
BR ˌbɑːbˈwʌɪə(r)
AM ˌbɑrbˈwaɪ(ə)r

barcarole
BR ˌbɑːkəˈrəʊl, ˈbɑːkərəʊl, -z
AM ˈbɑrkəˌroʊl, -z

barcarolle
BR ˌbɑːkəˈrəʊl, ˈbɑːkərəʊl, -z
AM ˈbɑrkəˌroʊl, -z

Barcelona
BR ˌbɑːsɪˈləʊnə(r)
AM ˌbɑrsəˈloʊnə
SP ˌbarθeˈlona, ˌbarseˈlona

Barclay
BR ˈbɑːkli, ˈbɑːkleɪ
AM ˈbɑrkli

Bar-Cochba
BR ˌbɑːˈkɒtʃbə(r)
AM ˌbɑrˈkɔtʃbə, ˌbɑrˈkɑtʃbə

barcode
BR ˈbɑːkəʊd, -z, -ɪŋ, -ɨd
AM ˈbɑrˌkoʊd, -z, -ɪŋ, -əd

bard
BR bɑːd, -z
AM bɑrd, -z

bardic
BR ˈbɑːdɪk
AM ˈbɑrdɪk

Bardo
BR ˈbɑːdəʊ
AM ˈbɑrˌdoʊ

bardolater
BR bɑːˈdɒlətə(r), -z
AM bɑrˈdɑlədər, -z

bardolatry
BR bɑːˈdɒlətri
AM bɑrˈdɑlətri

Bardot
BR bɑːˈdəʊ
AM bɑrˈdoʊ

bardy
BR 'bɑːd|i, -ɪz
AM 'bɑrdi, -z
bare
BR bɛː(r), -ə(r), -ɨst, -z, -ɪŋ, -d
AM bɛ(ə)r, -ər, -əst, -z, -ɪŋ, -d
bareback
BR 'bɛːbak
AM 'bɛrˌbæk
barebacked
BR ˌbɛː'bakt
AM 'bɛrˌbækt
barebones
BR 'bɛːbəʊnz
AM ˌbɛrˌboʊnz
barefaced
BR ˌbɛː'feɪst
AM ˌbɛrˌfeɪst
barefacedly
BR ˌbɛː'feɪstli, ˌbɛː'feɪsɨdli
AM ˌbɛrˌfeɪsɨdli, ˌbɛrˌfeɪstli
barefacedness
BR ˌbɛː'feɪstnɪs, ˌbɛː'feɪsɨdnɪs
AM ˌbɛrˌfeɪsɨdnɪs, ˌbɛrˌfeɪstnɪs
barefoot
BR 'bɛːfʊt
AM 'bɛrˌfʊt
barefooted
BR ˌbɛː'fʊtɨd
AM 'bɛrˌfʊdəd
barège
BR ba'rɛːʒ, -ɨz
AM bə'rɛʒ, -əz
bareheaded
BR ˌbɛː'hɛdɨd
AM ˌbɛrˌhɛdəd
barelegged
BR ˌbɛː'lɛg(ɨ)d
AM ˌbɛrˌlɛg(ə)d
barely
BR 'bɛːli
AM 'bɛrli
bareness
BR 'bɛːnəs
AM 'bɛrnəs
Barents
BR 'barənts, 'barn̩ts
AM 'bɛrən(t)s
barf
BR bɑːf, -s, -ɪŋ, -t
AM bɑrf, -s, -ɪŋ, -t
barfly
BR 'bɑːflʌɪ, -z
AM 'bɑrˌflaɪ, -z
bargain
BR 'bɑːg|(ɨ)n, -(ɨ)nz, -ɨnɪŋ\-n̩ɪŋ, -(ɨ)nd
AM 'bɑrgən, -z, -ɪŋ, -d
bargainer
BR 'bɑːgɨnə(r), 'bɑːgn̩ə(r), -z
AM 'bɑrgənər, -z
barge
BR bɑːdʒ, -ɨz, -ɪŋ, -d
AM bɑrdʒ, -əz, -ɪŋ, -d
bargeboard
BR 'bɑːdʒbɔːd, -z
AM 'bɑrdʒˌbɔ(ə)rd, -z
bargee
BR bɑː'dʒiː, -z
AM 'bɑrdʒi, -z
Bargello
BR bɑː'dʒɛləʊ
AM bɑr'(d)ʒɛloʊ
bargeman
BR 'bɑːdʒmən
AM 'bɑrdʒmən
bargemen
BR 'bɑːdʒmən
AM 'bɑrdʒmən
bargepole
BR 'bɑːdʒpəʊl, -z
AM 'bɑrdʒˌpoʊl, -z
bargirl
BR 'bɑːgəːl, -z
AM 'bɑrˌgərl, -z
bargraph
BR 'bɑːgrɑːf, 'bɑːgraf, -s
AM 'bɑrˌgræf, -s
Bari
BR 'bɑːri
AM 'bɑri, 'bɛri
baric
BR 'bɛːrɪk, 'barɪk
AM 'bɛrɪk
barilla
BR bə'rɪlə(r), -z
AM bə'rɪlə, -z
Barisal
BR ˌbarɨ'sɑːl
AM 'bɛrəˌsɔl, 'bɛrəˌsɑl
barite
BR 'barʌɪt, 'bɛːrʌɪt
AM 'bɛˌraɪt
baritone
BR 'barɨtəʊn, -z
AM 'bɛrəˌtoʊn, -z
barium
BR 'bɛːrɪəm
AM 'bɛriəm
bark
BR bɑːk, -s, -ɪŋ, -t
AM bɑrk, -s, -ɪŋ, -t
barkeep
BR 'bɑːkiːp, -s
AM 'bɑrˌkip, -s
barkeeper
BR 'bɑːˌkiːpə(r), -z
AM 'bɑrˌkipər, -z
barkentine
BR 'bɑːk(ə)ntiːn
AM 'bɑrkənˌtin
barker
BR 'bɑːkə(r), -z
AM 'bɑrkər, -z
Barkley
BR 'bɑːkli
AM 'bɑrkli
Barkly
BR 'bɑːkli
AM 'bɑrkli
barley
BR 'bɑːli
AM 'bɑrli
barleycorn
BR 'bɑːlɪkɔːn, -z
AM 'bɑrliˌkɔ(ə)rn, -z
barleymow
BR ˌbɑːlɪ'məʊ, -z
AM 'bɑrliˌmoʊ, -z
Barlow
BR 'bɑːləʊ
AM 'bɑrloʊ
barm
BR bɑːm
AM bɑrm
barmaid
BR 'bɑːmeɪd, -z
AM 'bɑrˌmeɪd, -z
barman
BR 'bɑːmən
AM 'bɑrmən
barmbrack
BR 'bɑːmbrak, -s
AM 'bɑrmˌbræk, -s
barmecidal
BR ˌbɑːmɨ'sʌɪdl
AM ˌbɑrmə'saɪdəl
Barmecide
BR 'bɑːmɨsʌɪd, -z
AM 'bɑrməˌsaɪd, -z
barmen
BR 'bɑːmən
AM 'bɑrmən
barmily
BR 'bɑːmɨli
AM 'bɑrməli
barminess
BR 'bɑːmɪnɪs
AM 'bɑrminɪs
bar mitzvah
BR ˌbɑː 'mɪtsvə(r), -z
AM ˌbɑr 'mɪtsvə, -z
barmy
BR 'bɑːm|i, -ɪə(r), -ɪɨst
AM 'bɑrmi, -ər, -ɨst
barn
BR bɑːn, -z
AM bɑrn, -z
Barnabas
BR 'bɑːnəbəs
AM 'bɑrnəbəs
Barnaby
BR 'bɑːnəbi
AM 'bɑrnəbi
barnacle
BR 'bɑːnəkl, -z, -d
AM 'bɑrnəkəl, -z, -d
Barnard
BR 'bɑːnɑːd
AM 'bɑrˌnɑrd
Barnardo
BR bə'nɑːdəʊ
AM bər'nɑrdoʊ
barnbrack
BR 'bɑːnbrak, -s
AM 'bɑrnˌbræk, -s
Barnes
BR bɑːnz
AM bɑrnz
Barnett
BR 'bɑːnɪt, bɑː'nɛt
AM bɑr'nɛt
Barney
BR 'bɑːni
AM 'bɑrni
barney
BR 'bɑːn|i, -ɪz, -ɪɪŋ, -ɪd
AM 'bɑrni, -z, -ɪŋ, -d
Barnsley
BR 'bɑːnzli
AM 'bɑrnzli
barnstorm
BR 'bɑːnstɔːm, -z, -ɪŋ, -d
AM 'bɑrnˌstɔ(ə)rm, -z, -ɪŋ, -d
barnstormer
BR 'bɑːnˌstɔːmə(r), -z
AM 'bɑrnˌstɔrmər, -z
Barnum
BR 'bɑːnəm
AM 'bɑrnəm
barnyard
BR 'bɑːnjɑːd, -z
AM 'bɑrnˌjɑrd, -z
Baroda
BR bə'rəʊdə(r)
AM bə'roʊdə
barograph
BR 'barəgrɑːf, 'barəgraf, -s
AM 'bɛrəˌgræf, -s
barographic
BR ˌbarə'grafɪk
AM ˌbɛrə'græfɪk
barographical
BR ˌbarə'grafɪkl
AM ˌbɛrə'græfəkəl
barographically
BR ˌbarə'grafɪkli
AM ˌbɛrə'græfək(ə)li
barometer
BR bə'rɒmɨtə(r), -z
AM bə'rɑmədər, -z
barometric
BR ˌbarə'mɛtrɪk
AM ˌbɛrə'mɛtrɪk
barometrical
BR ˌbarə'mɛtrɪkl
AM ˌbɛrə'mɛtrəkəl
barometrically
BR ˌbarə'mɛtrɪkli
AM ˌbɛrə'mɛtrək(ə)li
barometry
BR bə'rɒmɨtri
AM bə'rɑmətri
baron
BR 'barən, 'barn̩, -z
AM 'bɛrən, -z

baronage
BR ˈbarən|ɪdʒ, ˈbarn̩|ɪdʒ, -ɨdʒɪz
AM ˈbɛrənɪdʒ, -ɪz

baroness
BR ˈbarənɪs, ˈbarn̩ɪs, ˈbarənɛs, ˈbarn̩ɛs, -ɪz
AM ˈbɛrənəs, -əz

baronet
BR ˈbarənɪt, ˈbarn̩ɪt, ˈbarənɛt, ˈbarn̩ɛt, ˌbarəˈnɛt, -s
AM ˈbɛrəˌnɛt, -s

baronetage
BR ˈbarənɪt|ɪdʒ, ˈbarn̩ɪt|ɪdʒ, ˈbarənɛt|ɪdʒ, ˈbarn̩ɛt|ɪdʒ, ˌbarˈnɛt|ɪdʒ, -ɨdʒɪz
AM ˈbɛrəˌnɛdɪdʒ, ˈbɛrənədɪdʒ, -ɪz

baronetcy
BR ˈbarənɪts|i, ˈbarn̩ɪts|i, ˈbarənɛts|i, ˈbarn̩ɛts|i, -ɪz
AM ˈbɛrənɛtsi, -z

baronial
BR bəˈrəʊnɪəl
AM bəˈroʊniəl

barony
BR ˈbarən|i, ˈbarn̩|i, -ɪz
AM ˈbɛrəni, -z

baroque
BR bəˈrɒk
AM bəˈroʊk, bəˈrɑk

barouche
BR bəˈruːʃ, -ɪz
AM bəˈruʃ, -əz

barquantine
BR ˈbɑːk(ə)ntiːn, -z
AM ˈbɑrkənˌtin, -z

barque
BR bɑːk, -s
AM bɑrk, -s

barquentine
BR ˈbɑːk(ə)ntiːn, -z
AM ˈbɑrkənˌtin, -z

Barr
BR bɑː(r)
AM bɑr

barrack
BR ˈbarək, -s, -ɪŋ, -t
AM ˈbɛrək, -s, -ɪŋ, -t

barracks
BR ˈbarəks
AM ˈbɛrəks

barracoon
BR ˌbarəˈkuːn, -z
AM ˌbɛrəˈkun, -z

barracouta
BR ˌbarəˈkuːtə(*r*), -z
AM ˌbɛrəˈkudə, -z

barracuda
BR ˌbarəˈk(j)uːdə(*r*), -z
AM ˌbɛrəˈkudə, -z

barrage
BR ˈbarɑː(d)ʒ, -ɪz, -ɪŋ, -d
AM bəˈrɑ(d)ʒ, -əz, -ɪŋ, -d

barramunda
BR ˌbarəˈmʌndə(*r*), -z
AM ˌbɛrəˈməndə, -z

barramundi
BR ˌbarəˈmʌndi
AM ˌbɛrəˈməndi

barrator
BR ˈbarətə(r), -z
AM ˈbɛrədər, -z

barratrous
BR ˈbarətrəs
AM ˈbɛrətrəs

barratry
BR ˈbarətri
AM ˈbɛrətri

barre
BR bɑː(r), -z
AM bɑr, -z

barré
BR ˈbareɪ
AM bɑˈreɪ

barrel
BR ˈbarəl, ˈbarl̩, -z
AM ˈbɛrəl, -z

barrelful
BR ˈbarəlfʊl, ˈbarl̩fʊl, -z
AM ˈbɛrəlˌfʊl, -z

barrelhead
BR ˈbarəlhɛd, ˈbarl̩hɛd, -z
AM ˈbɛrəlˌ(h)ɛd, -z

barrelhouse
BR ˈbarəlhaʊ|s, ˈbarl̩haʊ|s, -zɪz
AM ˈbɛrəlˌ(h)aʊ|s, -zəz

barren
BR ˈbarən, ˈbarn̩, -ə(r), -ɪst
AM ˈbɛrən, -ər, -əst

barrenly
BR ˈbarənli, ˈbarn̩li
AM ˈbɛrənli

barrenness
BR ˈbarənnəs, ˈbarn̩nəs
AM ˈbɛrə(n)nəs

barret
BR ˈbarɪt, -s
AM ˈbɛrət, -s

barrette
BR bəˈrɛt, bɑːˈrɛt, baˈrɛt, -s
AM bəˈrɛt, -s

barricade
BR ˌbarɪˈkeɪd, ˈbarɪkeɪd, -z, -ɪŋ, -ɪd
AM ˈbɛrəˌkeɪd, -z, -ɪŋ, -ɪd

Barrie
BR ˈbari
AM ˈbɛri

barrier
BR ˈbarɪə(r), -z
AM ˈbɛriər, -z

barrio
BR ˈbarɪəʊ, -z
AM ˈbarioʊ, -z

barrister
BR ˈbarɪstə(r), -z
AM ˈbɛrəstər, -z

Barron
BR ˈbarən, ˈbarn̩
AM ˈbɛrən

barrow
BR ˈbarəʊ, -z
AM ˈbɛroʊ, -z

Barrow-in-Furness
BR ˈbarəʊɪnˈfəːnɪs
AM ˈbɛroʊənˈfərnəs

barrowload
BR ˈbarə(ʊ)ləʊd, -z
AM ˈbɛroʊˌloʊd, -z

Barry
BR ˈbari
AM ˈbɛri

Barrymore
BR ˈbarɪmɔː(r)
AM ˈbɛriˌmɔ(ə)r

Barsac
BR ˈbɑːsak, -s
AM ˈbɑrˌsæk, -s

Bart
BR bɑːt
AM bɑrt

Bart.
Baronet
BR ˈbarənɪt, ˈbarn̩ɪt, ˈbarənɛt, ˈbarn̩ɛt, ˌbarəˈnɛt
AM ˈbɛrənət

bartender
BR ˈbɑːˌtɛndə(r), -z
AM ˈbɑrˌtɛndər, -z

barter
BR ˈbɑːt|ə(r), -əz, -(ə)rɪŋ, -əd
AM ˈbɑrdər, -z, -ɪŋ, -d

barterer
BR ˈbɑːt(ə)rə(r), -z
AM ˈbɑrdərər, -z

Barth
BR bɑːθ
AM bɑrθ

Barthes
BR bɑːt
AM bɑrt

Bartholomew
BR bɑːˈθɒləmjuː
AM bɑrˈθɑləˌmju

bartizan
BR ˈbɑːtɪz(ə)n, ˌbɑːtɪˈzan, -z, -d
AM ˈbɑrdəzən, ˈbɑrdəˌzæn, -z, -d

Bartlett
BR ˈbɑːtlɪt
AM ˈbɑrtlət

Bartók
BR ˈbɑːtɒk
AM ˈbɑrˌtɑk
HU ˈbɒrtoːk

Bartolomeo
BR bɑːˌtɒləˈmeɪəʊ
AM bɑrˌtɑləˈmeɪoʊ

Barton
BR ˈbɑːtn
AM ˈbɑrt(ə)n

bartsia
BR ˈbɑːtsɪə(*r*), -z
AM ˈbɑrtsiə, -z

Baruch
BR ˈbarək
AM ˈbɑrək, bəˈruk

baryon
BR ˈbarɪɒn, -z
AM ˈbɛriˌɑn, -z

baryonic
BR ˌbarɪˈɒnɪk
AM ˌbɛriˈɑnɪk

Baryshnikov
BR bəˈrɪʃnɨkɒf, bəˈrɪʃnɨkɒv
AM bəˈrɪʃnəˌkɔv, bəˈrɪʃnəˌkɔf, bəˈrɪʃnəˌkɑv, bəˈrɪʃnəˌkɑf

barysphere
BR ˈbarɪsfɪə(r), -z
AM ˈbɛrəˌsfɪ(ə)r, -z

baryta
BR bəˈrʌɪtə(*r*)
AM bəˈraɪdə

barytes
BR bəˈrʌɪtiːz
AM bəˈraɪdiz

barytic
BR bəˈrɪtɪk
AM bəˈrɪdɪk

barytone
BR ˈbarɪtəʊn, -z
AM ˈbɛrəˌtoʊn, -z

basal
BR ˈbeɪsl
AM ˈbeɪsəl, ˈbeɪzəl

basalt
BR ˈbasɔːlt, ˈbaslt
AM bəˈsɔlt, ˈbæˌsɔlt, ˈbeɪˌsɔlt, bəˈsɑlt, ˈbæˌsɑlt, ˈbeɪˌsɑlt

basaltic
BR bəˈsɔːltɪk, bəˈsɒltɪk
AM bəˈsɔltɪk, bəˈsɑltɪk

basan
BR ˈbaz(ə)n
AM ˈbæsən, ˈbæzn

bascule
BR ˈbaskjuːl, -z
AM ˈbæsˌkjul, -z

base
BR beɪs, -ɪz, -ɪŋ, -t, -ə(r), -ɪst
AM beɪs, -ɪz, -ɪŋ, -t, -ər, -ɪst

baseball
BR ˈbeɪsbɔːl, -z
AM ˈbeɪsˌbɔl, ˈbeɪsˌbɑl, -z

baseboard
BR ˈbeɪsbɔːd, -z
AM ˈbeɪsˌbɔ(ə)rd, -z

baseborn
BR ˌbeɪs'bɔːn, 'beɪsbɔːn
AM 'beɪsˌbɔ(ə)rn

basehead
BR 'beɪshɛd, -z
AM 'beɪsˌ(h)ɛd, -z

Basel
BR 'bɑːzl
AM 'bɑzəl

baseless
BR 'beɪsləs
AM 'beɪsləs

baselessly
BR 'beɪsləsli
AM 'beɪsləsli

baselessness
BR 'beɪsləsnəs
AM 'beɪsləsnəs

baseline
BR 'beɪslʌɪn, -z
AM 'beɪˌslaɪn, -z

baseload
BR 'beɪsləʊd, -z
AM 'beɪsˌloʊd, -z

baseman
BR 'beɪsmən
AM 'beɪsmən

basemen
BR 'beɪsmən
AM 'beɪsmən

basement
BR 'beɪsm(ə)nt, -s
AM 'beɪsmənt, -s

baseness
BR 'beɪsnəs
AM 'beɪsnəs

basenji
BR bə'sɛn(d)ʒ|i, -ɪz
AM bə'sɛn(d)ʒi, -z

baseplate
BR 'beɪspleɪt, -s
AM 'beɪsˌpleɪt, -s

bases
plural of basis
BR 'beɪsiːz
AM 'beɪsiz

bash
BR baʃ, -ɪz, -ɪŋ, -t
AM bæʃ, -əz, -ɪŋ, -t

bashful
BR 'baʃf(ʊ)l
AM 'bæʃfəl

bashfully
BR 'baʃfəli, 'baʃfl̩i
AM 'bæʃfəli

bashfulness
BR 'baʃf(ʊ)lnəs
AM 'bæʃfəlnəs

bashi-bazouk
BR ˌbaʃɪbə'zuːk, -s
AM ˌbæʃibə'zuk, -s

Bashkir
BR baʃ'kɪə(r), -z
AM bæʃ'kɪ(ə)r, -z

Bashkiria
BR baʃ'kɪərɪə(*r*)
AM bæʃ'kɪriə

basho
BR 'baʃəʊ, -z
AM 'bɑʃɔ, 'bɑʃoʊ, -z

basic
BR 'beɪsɪk, -s
AM 'beɪsɪk, -s

basically
BR 'beɪsɪkli
AM 'beɪsɪk(ə)li

basicity
BR beɪ'sɪsɪt|i, -ɪz
AM beɪ'sɪsɪdi, -z

basidia
BR bə'sɪdɪə(*r*)
AM bə'sɪdiə

basidial
BR bə'sɪdɪəl
AM bə'sɪdiəl

basidium
BR bə'sɪdɪəm
AM bə'sɪdiəm

Basie
BR 'beɪsi, 'beɪzi
AM 'beɪsi

basil
BR 'bazl
AM 'bæzəl, 'beɪzəl

basilar
BR 'bazɪlə(r), 'bazl̩ə(r), 'basɪlə(r), 'basl̩ə(r)
AM 'bæzələr, 'beɪsələr

basilect
BR 'bazɪlɛkt, 'beɪsɪlɛkt, -s
AM 'bæzəˌlɛk|(t), 'beɪsəˌlɛk|(t), -(t)s

basilectal
BR ˌbazɪ'lɛktl, ˌbeɪsɪ'lɛktl
AM ˌbæzə'lɛktəl, ˌbeɪsə'lɛktəl

basilectally
BR ˌbazɪ'lɛktl̩i, ˌbeɪsɪ'lɛktəli
AM ˌbæzə'lɛktəli, ˌbeɪsə'lɛktəli

basilica
BR bə'zɪlɪkə(*r*), bə'sɪlɪkə(*r*), -z
AM bə'sɪləkə, bə'zɪləkə, -z

basilican
BR bə'zɪlɪk(ə)n, bə'sɪlɪk(ə)n
AM bə'sɪləkən, bə'zɪləkən

basilisk
BR 'bazɪlɪsk, 'basɪlɪsk, -s
AM 'bæsəˌlɪsk, 'bæzəˌlɪsk, -s

basin
BR 'beɪsn, -z
AM 'beɪsn, -z

basinet
BR ˌbasɪ'nɛt, 'basɪnɛt, 'basɪnɪt, -s
AM ˌbæsə'nɛt, -s

basinful
BR 'beɪsnfʊl, -z
AM 'beɪsnˌfʊl, -z

basipetal
BR beɪ'sɪpɪtl
AM beɪ'sɪpɪdl

basipetally
BR beɪ'sɪpɪtl̩i, beɪ'sɪpɪtəli
AM beɪ'sɪpɪdl̩i

basis
BR 'beɪsɪs
AM 'beɪsəs

bask
BR bɑːsk, bask, -s, -ɪŋ, -t
AM bæsk, -s, -ɪŋ, -t

Baskerville
BR 'baskəvɪl
AM 'bæskərˌvɪl

basket
BR 'bɑːskɪt, 'baskɪt, -s
AM 'bæskət, -s

basketball
BR 'bɑːskɪtbɔːl, 'baskɪtbɔːl, -z
AM 'bæskətˌbɔl, 'bæskətˌbɑl, -z

basketful
BR 'bɑːskɪtfʊl, 'baskɪtfʊl, -z
AM 'bæskətˌfʊl, -z

basketry
BR 'bɑːskɪtri, 'baskɪtri
AM 'bæskətri

basketwork
BR 'bɑːskɪtwəːk, 'baskɪtwəːk
AM 'bæskətˌwərk

Baskin
BR 'baskɪn
AM 'bæskən

Basle
BR bɑːl, 'bɑːzl
AM bɑl, 'bɑzəl

basmati
BR bas'mɑːti, baz'mɑːti, bas'mati, baz'mati
AM ˌbɑs'mɑdi, ˌbɑz'mɑdi

bas mitzvah
BR ˌbɑːs 'mɪtsvə(*r*), -z
AM ˌbɑs 'mɪtsvə, -z

basnet
BR 'basnɪt, -s
AM 'bæsnət, -s

basophilic
BR ˌbeɪsə(ʊ)'fɪlɪk
AM ˌbeɪsə'fɪlɪk

Basotho
BR bə'suːtuː
AM bə'soʊtoʊ, bə'soʊθoʊ

Basotholand
BR bə'suːtuːland
AM bə'soʊdoʊˌlænd, bə'soʊθoʊˌlænd

Basque
BR bask, bɑːsk, -s
AM bæsk, -s

Basra
BR 'bazrə(*r*), 'bɑːzrə(*r*)
AM 'bɑsrə

bas-relief
BR 'basrɪˌliːf, ˌbɑːrɪ'liːf, ˌbasrɪ'liːf, -s
AM ˌbɑrə'lif, -s

Bass
BR bas, -ɪz
AM bæs, -əz

bass[1]
fish
BR bas, -ɪz
AM bæs, -əz

bass[2]
music
BR beɪs, -ɪz
AM beɪs, -ɪz

basset
BR 'basɪt, -s
AM 'bæsət, -s

Bassey
BR 'basi
AM 'bæsi

bassi
BR 'basi
AM 'bæsi

bassinet
BR ˌbasɪ'nɛt, -s
AM ˌbæsə'nɛt, -s

bassinette
BR ˌbasɪ'nɛt, -s
AM ˌbæsə'nɛt, -s

bassi profondi
BR ˌbasɪ prə'fɒndi
AM ˌbæsi prə'fəndi

bassi profundi
BR ˌbasɪ prə'fʌndi
AM ˌbæsi prə'fəndi

bassist
BR 'beɪsɪst, -s
AM 'beɪsɪst, -s

basso
BR 'basəʊ
AM 'bæsoʊ

bassoon
BR bə'suːn, -z
AM bə'sun, -z

bassoonist
BR bə'suːnɪst, -s
AM bə'sunəst, -s

basso profondo
BR ˌbasəʊ prə'fɒndəʊ
AM ˌbæsoʊ prə'fəndoʊ

basso-relievo
BR ˌbasəʊrɪ'liːvəʊ, ˌbasəʊrɪ'ljeɪvəʊ, -z
AM ˌbæsoʊrə'livoʊ, ˌbæsoʊri'livoʊ, -z

basswood
BR ˈbaswʊd
AM ˈbæsˌwʊd

bast
BR bast
AM bæst

bastard
BR ˈbɑːstəd, ˈbastəd, -z
AM ˈbæstərd, -z

bastardisation
BR ˌbɑːstədʌɪˈzeɪʃn, ˌbastədʌɪˈzeɪʃn
AM ˌbæstərdəˈzeɪʃən, ˌbæstərˌdaɪˈzeɪʃən

bastardise
BR ˈbɑːstədʌɪz, ˈbastədʌɪz, -ɪz, -ɪŋ, -d
AM ˈbæstərˌdaɪz, -ɪz, -ɪŋ, -d

bastardization
BR ˌbɑːstədʌɪˈzeɪʃn, ˌbastədʌɪˈzeɪʃn
AM ˌbæstərdəˈzeɪʃən, ˌbæstərˌdaɪˈzeɪʃən

bastardize
BR ˈbɑːstədʌɪz, ˈbastədʌɪz, -ɪz, -ɪŋ, -d
AM ˈbæstərˌdaɪz, -ɪz, -ɪŋ, -d

bastardy
BR ˈbɑːstədi, ˈbastədi
AM ˈbæstərdi

baste
BR beɪst, -s, -ɪŋ, -ɨd
AM beɪst, -s, -ɪŋ, -ɨd

Bastet
BR ˈbastɪt
AM ˈbæstət

Bastia
BR ˈbastɪə(r)
AM ˈbɑstiə

Bastille
BR baˈstiːl
AM bæˈstil

bastinado
BR ˌbastɪˈnɑːdəʊ, ˌbastɪˈneɪdəʊ, -z
AM ˌbæstəˈneɪdoʊ, -z

bastion
BR ˈbastɪən, -z
AM ˈbæstʃən, ˈbæstiən, -z

Bastogne
BR baˈstəʊn(jə(r))
AM bæˈstoʊn(jə)
FR bastɔɲ

basuco
BR bəˈsuːkəʊ
AM bəˈsukoʊ

Basuto
BR bəˈsuːtəʊ
AM bəˈsudoʊ

Basutoland
BR bəˈsuːtəʊland
AM bəˈsudoʊˌlænd

bat
BR bat, -s, -ɪŋ, -ɨd
AM bæ|t, -ts, -dɪŋ, -dəd

Bata
BR ˈbɑːtə(r)
AM ˈbɑdə

batata
BR bəˈtɑːtə(r), -z
AM bəˈtɑdə, -z

Batavia
BR bəˈteɪvɪə(r)
AM bəˈteɪviə

Batavian
BR bəˈteɪvɪən, -z
AM bəˈteɪviən, -z

batch
BR batʃ, -ɪz, -ɪŋ, -t
AM bætʃ, -əz, -ɪŋ, -t

Batdambang
BR ˌbat(ə)mˈbaŋ
AM ˌbædəmˈbæŋ

bate
BR beɪt, -s, -ɪŋ, -ɨd
AM beɪ|t, -ts, -dɪŋ, -dɨd

bateau
BR ˈbatəʊ, baˈtəʊ, -z
AM bæˈtoʊ, bəˈtoʊ, ˈbædoʊ, -z

bateaux
BR ˈbatəʊz, baˈtəʊz
AM bæˈtoʊ, bəˈtoʊ, ˈbædoʊ

bateleur
BR ˈbatələː(r), ˈbatl̩əː(r), -z
AM ˌbædəˈlər, -z

Bates
BR beɪts
AM beɪts

Batesian mimicry
BR ˌbeɪtsɪən ˈmɪmɨkri
AM ˌbeɪtsiən ˈmɪməkri

Bateson
BR ˈbeɪtsn
AM ˈbeɪtsən

bath[1]
noun
BR bɑːθ, baθ, bɑːðz\bɑːθs\baθs
AM bæ|θ, -ðz\-θs

bath[2]
verb
BR bɑːθ, baθ, -s, -ɪŋ, -t
AM bæθ, -s, -ɪŋ, -t

bathe
BR beɪð, -z, -ɪŋ, -d
AM beɪð, -z, -ɪŋ, -d

bather
BR ˈbeɪðə(r), -z
AM ˈbeɪðər, -z

bathetic
BR bəˈθɛtɪk
AM bəˈθɛdɪk

bathhouse
BR ˈbɑːθhaʊ|s, ˈbaθhaʊ|s, -zɪz
AM ˈbæθˌ(h)aʊ|s, -zəz

batholith
BR ˈbaθəlɪθ, -s
AM ˈbæθəˌlɪθ, -s

bathometer
BR bəˈθɒmɪtə(r), -z
AM bəˈθɑmədər, -z

bathos
BR ˈbeɪθɒs
AM ˈbeɪˌθɑs

bathotic
BR beɪˈθɒtɪk
AM beɪˈθɑdɪk

bathrobe
BR ˈbɑːθrəʊb, ˈbaθrəʊb, -z
AM ˈbæθˌroʊb, -z

bathroom
BR ˈbɑːθruːm, ˈbaθruːm, ˈbɑːθrʊm, -z
AM ˈbæθˌrum, ˈbæθˌrʊm, -z

Bathsheba
BR ˌbaθˈʃiːbə(r), ˈbaθʃɪbə(r)
AM ˌbæθˈʃibə

bathtub
BR ˈbɑːθtʌb, ˈbaθtʌb, -z
AM ˈbæθˌtəb, -z

Bathurst
BR ˈbaθəːst
AM ˈbæθərst

bathwater
BR ˈbɑːθˌwɔːtə(r), ˈbaθˌwɔːtə(r)
AM ˈbæθˌwɔdər, ˈbæθˌwɑdər

bathyal
BR ˈbaθɪəl
AM ˈbæθiəl

bathypelagic
BR ˌbaθɪpɪˈladʒɪk
AM ˌbæθəpəˈlædʒɪk

bathyscaphe
BR ˈbaθɪskaf, -s
AM ˈbæθəˌskæf, -s

bathysphere
BR ˈbaθɪsfɪə(r), -z
AM ˈbæθəˌsfɪ(ə)r, -z

batik
BR bəˈtiːk, baˈtiːk, ˈbatɪk, -s
AM bəˈtik, ˈbædɪk, -s

Batista
BR baˈtiːstə(r), bəˈtiːstə(r)
AM bəˈtistə

batiste
BR baˈtiːst, bəˈtiːst, -s
AM bəˈtist, -s

Batman
cartoon and film hero
BR ˈbatman
AM ˈbætˌmæn

batman
army servant
BR ˈbatmən
AM ˈbætmən

batmen
army servants
BR ˈbatmən
AM ˈbætmən

baton
BR ˈbat(ə)n, ˈbatɒn, -z
AM bəˈtɑn, bæˈtɑn, -z

Baton Rouge
BR ˌbat(ə)n ˈruːʒ
AM ˌbædən ˈruʒ, ˌbætn ˈruʒ

batrachian
BR bəˈtreɪkɪən, -z
AM bəˈtreɪkiən, -z

batsman
BR ˈbatsmən
AM ˈbætsmən

batsmanship
BR ˈbatsmənʃɪp
AM ˈbætsmənˌʃɪp

batsmen
BR ˈbatsmən
AM ˈbætsmən

battalion
BR bəˈtalɪən, -z
AM bəˈtæljən, -z

Battambang
BR ˌbat(ə)mˈbaŋ
AM ˈbædəmˌbæŋ

batteau
BR ˈbatəʊ, baˈtəʊ, -z
AM bæˈtoʊ, bəˈtoʊ, ˈbædoʊ, -z

batteaux
BR ˈbatəʊz, baˈtəʊz
AM bæˈtoʊ, bəˈtoʊ, ˈbædoʊ

battels
BR ˈbatlz
AM ˈbædlz

batten
BR ˈbat|n, -nz, -n̩ɪŋ\-nɪŋ, -nd
AM ˈbætn, -z, -ɪŋ, -d

Battenberg
BR ˈbatnbəːɡ, -z
AM ˈbætnˌbərɡ, -z

batter
BR ˈbat|ə(r), -əz, -(ə)rɪŋ, -əd
AM ˈbædər, -z, -ɪŋ, -d

batterer
BR ˈbat(ə)rə(r), -z
AM ˈbædərər, -z

Battersea
BR ˈbatəsiː
AM ˈbædərˌsi

battery
BR ˈbat(ə)r|i, -ɪz
AM ˈbædəri, -z

Batticaloa
BR ˌbatɪkəˈləʊə(r)
AM ˌbædəkəˈloʊə

battily
BR ˈbatɪli
AM ˈbædəli

battiness
BR ˈbatɪnɪs
AM ˈbædinɨs

battle
BR 'bat|l, -lz, -l̩ɪŋ\-lɪŋ, -ld
AM 'bædəl, -z, -ɪŋ, -d

battleax
BR 'batl̩aks, -ɪz
AM 'bædl,æks, -əz

battleaxe
BR 'batl̩aks, -ɪz
AM 'bædl,æks, -əz

battlebus
BR 'batlbʌs, -ɪz
AM 'bædl,bəs, -əz

battlecruiser
BR 'batl,kruːzə(r), -z
AM 'bædl,kruzər, -z

battledore
BR 'batldɔː(r), -z
AM 'bædl,dɔ(ə)r, -z

battledress
BR 'batldrɛs
AM 'bædl,drɛs

battlefield
BR 'batlfiːld, -z
AM 'bædl,fild, -z

battleground
BR 'batlgraʊnd, -z
AM 'bædl,graʊnd, -z

battlegroup
BR 'batlgruːp, -s
AM 'bædl,grup, -s

battlement
BR 'batlm(ə)nt, -s, -ɪd
AM 'bædlmən|t, -ts, -(t)əd

battler
BR 'batl̩ə(r), 'batlə(r), -z
AM 'bætlər, 'bædələr, -z

battleship
BR 'batlʃɪp, -s
AM 'bædl,ʃɪp, -s

battue
BR ba't(j)uː, -z
AM bæ'tu, -z

batty
BR 'bat|i, -ɪə(r), -ɪɪst
AM 'bædi, -ər, -ɪst

batwing
BR 'batwɪŋ, -z
AM 'bæt,wɪŋ, -z

batwoman
BR 'bat,wʊmən
AM 'bæt,wʊmən

batwomen
BR 'bat,wɪmɪn
AM 'bæt,wɪmɪn

bauble
BR 'bɔːbl, -z
AM 'bɔbəl, 'bɑbəl, -z

baud
BR bɔːd, bəʊd, -z
AM bɔd, bɑd, -z

Baudelaire
BR 'bəʊdəlɛː(r), 'bəʊdl̩ɛː(r)
AM ,boʊdə'lɛ(ə)r

Bauer
BR 'baʊə(r)
AM 'baʊər

Bauhaus
BR 'baʊhaʊs
AM 'baʊ,haʊs

baulk
BR bɔː(l)k, -s, -ɪŋ, -t
AM bɔk, bɑk, -s, -ɪŋ, -t

baulker
BR 'bɔː(l)kə(r), -z
AM 'bɔkər, 'bɑkər, -z

baulkiness
BR 'bɔː(l)kɪnɪs
AM 'bɔkinɪs, 'bɑkinɪs

baulky
BR 'bɔː(l)k|i, -ɪə(r), -ɪɪst
AM 'bɔki, 'bɑki, -ər, -ɪst

Baum
BR bɔːm, baʊm
AM bɔm, bɑm, baʊm

bauxite
BR 'bɔːksʌɪt
AM 'bɑk,saɪt, 'bɔk,saɪt

bauxitic
BR bɔːk'sɪtɪk
AM ,bɑk'sɪdɪk, ,bɔk'sɪdɪk

Bavaria
BR bə'vɛːrɪə(*r*)
AM bə'vɛriə

Bavarian
BR bə'vɛːrɪən, -z
AM bə'vɛriən, -z

bawbee
BR ,bɔː'b|iː, 'bɔːb|i, -iːz\-ɪz
AM ¦bɔ,bi, ¦bɑ,bi, -z

bawd
BR bɔːd, -z
AM bɔd, bɑd, -z

bawdily
BR 'bɔːdɪli
AM 'bɔdəli, 'bɑdəli

bawdiness
BR 'bɔːdɪnɪs
AM 'bɔdinɪs, 'bɑdinɪs

bawdry
BR 'bɔːdri
AM 'bɔdri, 'bɑdri

bawdy
BR 'bɔːd|i, -ɪə(r), -ɪɪst
AM 'bɔdi, 'bɑdi, -ər, -ɪst

bawl
BR bɔːl, -z, -ɪŋ, -d
AM bɔl, bɑl, -z, -ɪŋ, -d

bawler
BR 'bɔːlə(r), -z
AM 'bɔlər, 'bɑlər, -z

Bax
BR baks
AM bæks

Baxter
BR 'bakstə(r)
AM 'bækstər

bay
BR beɪ, -z, -ɪŋ, -d
AM beɪ, -z, -ɪŋ, -d

bayadère
BR ,bʌɪə'dɪə(r), ,bʌɪə'dɛː(r)
AM ¦baɪə¦dɛ(ə)r

Bayard
BR 'beɪɑːd
AM baɪ'ɑrd

bayberry
BR 'beɪb(ə)r|i, -ɪz
AM 'beɪ,bɛri, -z

Bayer
BR 'beɪə(r)
AM 'beɪər

Bayern
BR 'bʌɪəːn
AM 'baɪərn

Bayeux Tapestry
BR ,bʌɪəː 'tapɪstri, ,beɪəː +
AM bɑ,jə 'tæpəstri

Baylis
BR 'beɪlɪs
AM 'beɪlɪs

bayonet
BR 'beɪənɪt, 'beɪənɛt, ,beɪə'nɛt, -s, -ɪŋ, -ɪd
AM ¦beɪə¦nɛ|t, -ts, -dɪŋ, -dəd

Bayonne[1]
place in France
BR bʌɪ'ɒn
AM ,bɑ'jɔn

Bayonne[2]
place in New Jersey
BR beɪ'əʊn
AM ,beɪ'joʊn

bayou
BR 'bʌɪuː, -z
AM 'baɪu, 'baɪoʊ, -z

Bayreuth
BR 'bʌɪrɔɪt, ,bʌɪ'rɔɪt
AM ¦baɪ¦rɔɪt

Baz
BR baz
AM bæz

bazaar
BR bə'zɑː(r), -z
AM bə'zɑr, -z

bazar
BR bə'zɑː(r), -z
AM bə'zɑr, -z

bazooka
BR bə'zuːkə(*r*), -z
AM bə'zukə, -z

bazuco
BR bə'zuːkəʊ
AM bə'zukoʊ

bdellium
BR 'dɛlɪəm
AM '(b)dɛliəm

be
BR biː, -ɪŋ
AM bi, -ɪŋ

Bea
BR biː
AM bi

beach
BR biːtʃ, -ɪz, -ɪŋ, -t
AM bitʃ, -ɪz, -ɪŋ, -t

beachcomber
BR 'biːtʃ,kəʊmə(r), -z
AM 'bitʃ,koʊmər, -z

beachfront
BR 'biːtʃfrʌnt, -s
AM 'bitʃ,frənt, -s

beachhead
BR 'biːtʃhɛd, -z
AM 'bitʃ,(h)ɛd, -z

Beach-la-mar
BR ,biːtʃlə'mɑː(r)
AM ,bitʃlə'mɑr

beachside
BR 'biːtʃsʌɪd
AM 'bitʃ,saɪd

beachwear
BR 'biːtʃwɛː(r)
AM 'bitʃ,wɛ(ə)r

Beachy Head
BR ,biːtʃɪ 'hɛd
AM ,bitʃi 'hɛd

beacon
BR 'biːk(ə)n, -z
AM 'bikən, -z

bead
BR biːd, -z, -ɪŋ, -ɪd
AM bid, -z, -ɪŋ, -ɪd

beadily
BR 'biːdɪli
AM 'bidɪli

beadiness
BR 'biːdɪnɪs
AM 'bidinɪs

beadle
BR 'biːdl, -z
AM 'bidəl, -z

beadleship
BR 'biːdlʃɪp, -s
AM 'bidl,ʃɪp, -s

beadsman
BR 'biːdzmən
AM 'bidzmən

beadsmen
BR 'biːdzmən
AM 'bidzmən

beadwork
BR 'biːdwəːk
AM 'bid,wərk

beady
BR 'biːd|i, -ɪə(r), -ɪɪst
AM 'bidi, -ər, -ɪst

beagle
BR 'biːg|l, -lz, -l̩ɪŋ\-lɪŋ, -ld
AM 'big|əl, -əlz, -(ə)lɪŋ, -əld

beagler
BR 'biːgl̩ə(r), 'biːglə(r), -z
AM 'big(ə)lər, -z

beak
BR biːk, -s, -t
AM bik, -s, -t
beaker
BR ˈbiːkə(r), -z
AM ˈbikər, -z
beaky
BR ˈbiːki
AM ˈbiki
Beale
BR biːl
AM bil
beam
BR biːm, -z, -ɪŋ, -d
AM bim, -z, -ɪŋ, -d
beamer
BR ˈbiːmə(r), -z
AM ˈbimər, -z
Beamon
BR ˈbiːmən
AM ˈbimən
beamy
BR ˈbiːm|i, -ɪə(r), -ɪɪst
AM ˈbimi, -ər, -ɪst
bean
BR biːn, -z
AM bin, -z
beanbag
BR ˈbiːnbag, -z
AM ˈbinˌbæg, -z
beanery
BR ˈbiːn(ə)r|i, -ɪz
AM ˈbinəri, -z
beanfeast
BR ˈbiːnfiːst, -s
AM ˈbinˌfist, -s
beanie
BR ˈbiːn|i, -ɪz
AM ˈbini, -z
beano
BR ˈbiːnəʊ, -z
AM ˈbinoʊ, -z
beanpole
BR ˈbiːnpəʊl, -z
AM ˈbinˌpoʊl, -z
beanshoot
BR ˈbiːnʃuːt, -s
AM ˈbinˌʃut, -s
beansprout
BR ˈbiːnspraʊt, -s
AM ˈbinˌspraʊt, -s
beanstalk
BR ˈbiːnstɔːk, -s
AM ˈbinˌstɔk, ˈbinˌstɑk, -s
bear
BR bɛː(r), -z, -ɪŋ
AM bɛ(ə)r, -z, -ɪŋ
bearability
BR ˌbɛːrəˈbɪlɪti
AM ˌbɛrəˈbɪlɪdi
bearable
BR ˈbɛːrəbl
AM ˈbɛrəbəl
bearably
BR ˈbɛːrəbli
AM ˈbɛrəbli
bearcat
BR ˈbɛːkat, -s
AM ˈbɛrˌkæt, -s
beard
BR bɪəd, -z, -ɪŋ, -ɪd
AM bɪ(ə)rd, -z, -ɪŋ, -ɪd
beardie
BR ˈbɪəd|i, -ɪz
AM ˈbɪrdi, -z
beardless
BR ˈbɪədləs
AM ˈbɪrdləs
beardlessness
BR ˈbɪədləsnəs
AM ˈbɪrdləsnəs
Beardsley
BR ˈbɪədzli
AM ˈbɪrdzli
bearer
BR ˈbɛːrə(r), -z
AM ˈbɛrər, -z
beargarden
BR ˈbɛːˌgɑːdn, -z
AM ˈbɛrˌgɑrdən, -z
bearing
BR ˈbɛːrɪŋ, -z
AM ˈbɛrɪŋ, -z
bearish
BR ˈbɛːrɪʃ
AM ˈbɛrɪʃ
bearishness
BR ˈbɛːrɪʃnɪs
AM ˈbɛrɪʃnəs
bearleader
BR ˈbɛːˌliːdə(r), -z
AM ˈbɛrˌlidər, -z
Béarnaise
BR ˌbɛːˈneɪz
AM ˌbɛrˈneɪz
bearpit
BR ˈbɛːpɪt, -s
AM ˈbɛrˌpɪt, -s
bearskin
BR ˈbɛːskɪn, -z
AM ˈbɛrˌskɪn, -z
Beasley
BR ˈbiːzli
AM ˈbizli
beast
BR biːst, -s
AM bist, -s
beastie
BR ˈbiːst|i, -ɪz
AM ˈbisti, -z
beastings
BR ˈbiːstɪŋz
AM ˈbistɪŋz
beastliness
BR ˈbiːs(t)lɪnɪs
AM ˈbis(t)linɪs
beastly
BR ˈbiːs(t)l|i, -ɪə(r), -ɪɪst
AM ˈbis(t)li, -ər, -ɪst
beat
BR biːt, -s, -ɪŋ
AM bi|t, -ts, -dɪŋ
beatable
BR ˈbiːtəbl
AM ˈbidəbəl
beaten
BR ˈbiːtn
AM ˈbitn
beater
BR ˈbiːtə(r), -z
AM ˈbidər, -z
beatific
BR ˌbɪəˈtɪfɪk
AM ˌbiəˈtɪfɪk
beatifically
BR ˌbɪəˈtɪfɪkli
AM ˌbiəˈtɪfɪk(ə)li
beatification
BR bɪˌatɪfɪˈkeɪʃn
AM biˌædəfəˈkeɪʃən
beatify
BR bɪˈatɪfʌɪ, -z, -ɪŋ, -d
AM biˈædəˌfaɪ, -z, -ɪŋ, -d
beating
BR ˈbiːtɪŋ, -z
AM ˈbidɪŋ, -z
beatitude
BR bɪˈatɪtjuːd, bɪˈatɪtʃuːd, -z
AM biˈædəˌt(j)ud, -z
Beatles
BR ˈbiːtlz
AM ˈbidlz
beatnik
BR ˈbiːtnɪk, -s
AM ˈbitnɪk, -s
Beaton
BR ˈbiːtn
AM ˈbitn
Beatrice
BR ˈbɪətrɪs
AM ˈbiətrɪs
Beatrix
BR ˈbɪətrɪks
AM ˈbiətrɪks
Beatty
BR ˈbiːti, ˈbeɪti
AM ˈbidi, ˈbeɪdi
beau
BR bəʊ, -z
AM boʊ, -z
Beaufort
BR ˈbəʊfət, ˈbəʊfɔːt
AM ˈboʊfərt
beau geste
BR ˌbəʊ ˈʒɛst
AM ˌboʊ ˈʒɛst
beau idéal
BR ˌbəʊ ʌɪˈdɪəl, + ˌɪdeɪˈɑːl, -z
AM ˌboʊ ɪdeɪˈɑl, -z
Beaujolais
BR ˈbəʊʒəleɪ
AM ˌboʊʒəˈleɪ
Beaujolais Nouveau
BR ˌbəʊʒəleɪ nuːˈvəʊ
AM ˌboʊʒəˌleɪ nuˈvoʊ
Beaumarchais
BR ˈbəʊmɑːʃeɪ, ˌbəʊmɑːˈʃeɪ
AM ˌboʊˌmɑrˈʃeɪ
Beaumaris
BR ˌbəʊˈmarɪs
AM ˌboʊˈmɛrəs
beau monde
BR ˌbəʊ ˈmɒnd
AM ˌboʊ ˈmɔnd
Beaumont
BR ˈbəʊmɒnt
AM ˈboʊˌmɑnt
Beaune
BR bəʊn, -z
AM boʊn, -z
beaut
BR bjuːt, -s
AM bjut, -s
beauteous
BR ˈbjuːtɪəs
AM ˈbjudiəs
beauteously
BR ˈbjuːtɪəsli
AM ˈbjudiəsli
beauteousness
BR ˈbjuːtɪəsnəs
AM ˈbjudiəsnəs
beautician
BR bjuːˈtɪʃn, -z
AM bjuˈtɪʃən, -z
beautification
BR ˌbjuːtɪfɪˈkeɪʃn
AM ˌbjudəfəˈkeɪʃən
beautifier
BR ˈbjuːtɪfʌɪə(r), -z
AM ˈbjudəˌfaɪər, -z
beautiful
BR ˈbjuːtɪf(ʊ)l
AM ˈbjudəfəl
beautifully
BR ˈbjuːtɪf(ʊ)li, ˈbjuːtɪfl̩i
AM ˈbjudəf(ə)li
beautify
BR ˈbjuːtɪfʌɪ, -z, -ɪŋ, -d
AM ˈbjudəˌfaɪ, -z, -ɪŋ, -d
beauty
BR ˈbjuːt|i, -ɪz
AM ˈbjudi, -z
Beauvais
BR bəʊˈveɪ
AM ˌboʊˈveɪ
beaux
BR bəʊ(z)
AM boʊ
beaux-arts
BR ˌbəʊˈzɑː(r)
AM ˌboʊˈzɑr
beaver
BR ˈbiːv|ə(r), -əz, -(ə)rɪŋ, -əd
AM ˈbivər, -z, -ɪŋ, -d
Beaverboard
BR ˈbiːvəbɔːd
AM ˈbivərˌbɔ(ə)rd

Beaverbrook
BR 'bi:vəbrʊk
AM 'bivər,brʊk

bebop
BR 'bi:bɒp
AM 'bi,bap

bebopper
BR 'bi:,bɒpə(r), -z
AM 'bi,bapər, -z

becalm
BR bɪ'kɑ:m, -z, -ɪŋ, -d
AM bə'kɑ(l)m, bi'kɑ(l)m, -z, -ɪŋ, -d

became
BR bɪ'keɪm
AM bə'keɪm, bi'keɪm

becard
BR 'bɛkəd, bə'kɑ:d, -z
AM bə'kard, 'bɛkərd, -z

because
BR bɪ'kɒz, bɪ'kʌz
AM bə'kəz, bi'kəz, bə'kɔz, bi'kɔz, bə'kɑz, bi'kɑz,

béchamel
BR ,beɪʃə'mɛl
AM ,beɪʃə'mɛl

bêche-de-mer
BR ,bɛʃdə'mɛ:(r)
AM ,bɛʃdə'mɛ(ə)r

Bechstein
BR 'bɛkstʌɪn, -z
AM 'bɛk,staɪn, -z

Bechuanaland
BR ,bɛtʃʊ'ɑ:nəland
AM ,bɛtʃ'wɑnə,lænd

beck
BR bɛk, -s
AM bɛk, -s

Beckenbauer
BR 'bɛk(ə)nbaʊə(r)
AM 'bɛkən,baʊər

Becker
BR 'bɛkə(r)
AM 'bɛkər

Becket
BR 'bɛkɪt
AM 'bɛkət

Beckett
BR 'bɛkɪt
AM 'bɛkət

Beckford
BR 'bɛkfəd
AM 'bɛkfərd

Beckmann
BR 'bɛkmən
AM 'bɛkmən

beckon
BR 'bɛk|(ə)n, -(ə)nz, -ənɪŋ\-n̩ɪŋ, -(ə)nd
AM 'bɛk|ən, -ənz, -(ə)nɪŋ, -ənd

Becky
BR 'bɛki
AM 'bɛki

becloud
BR bɪ'klaʊd, -z, -ɪŋ, -ɪd
AM bə'klaʊd, bi'klaʊd, -z, -ɪŋ, -əd

become
BR bɪ'kʌm, -z, -ɪŋ
AM bə'kəm, bi'kəm, -z, -ɪŋ

becoming
BR bɪ'kʌmɪŋ
AM bə'kəmɪŋ, bi'kəmɪŋ

becomingly
BR bɪ'kʌmɪŋli
AM bə'kəmɪŋli, bi'kəmɪŋli

becomingness
BR bɪ'kʌmɪŋnɪs
AM bə'kəmɪŋnɪs, bi'kəmɪŋnɪs

bed
BR bɛd, -z, -ɪŋ, -ɪd
AM bɛd, -z, -ɪŋ, -əd

bedabble
BR bɪ'dab|l, -lz, -l̩ɪŋ\-lɪŋ, -ld
AM bə'dæb|əl, bi'dæb|əl, -əlz, -(ə)lɪŋ, -əld

bedad
BR bɪ'dad
AM bə'dæd

bedaub
BR bɪ'dɔ:b, -z, -ɪŋ, -d
AM bə'dɔb, bi'dɔb, bə'dɑb, bi'dɑb, -z, -ɪŋ, -d

bedazzle
BR bɪ'daz|l, -lz, -l̩ɪŋ\-lɪŋ, -ld
AM bə'dæz|əl, bi'dæz|əl, -əlz, -(ə)lɪŋ, -əld

bedazzlement
BR bɪ'dazlm(ə)nt
AM bə'dæzlmənt, bi'dæzlmənt

bedbug
BR 'bɛdbʌg, -z
AM 'bɛd,bəg, -z

bedchamber
BR 'bɛd,tʃeɪmbə(r), -z
AM 'bɛd,tʃeɪmbər, -z

bedclothes
BR 'bɛdkləʊ(ð)z
AM 'bɛd,kloʊ(ð)z

beddable
BR 'bɛdəbl
AM 'bɛdəbəl

bedder
BR 'bɛdə(r), -z
AM 'bɛdər, -z

Beddoes
BR 'bɛdəʊz
AM 'bɛdoʊz

Bede
BR bi:d
AM bid

bedeck
BR bɪ'dɛk, -s, -ɪŋ, -t
AM bə'dɛk, bi'dɛk, -s, -ɪŋ, -t

bedeguar
BR 'bɛdɪgɑ:(r)
AM 'bɛdə,gar

bedel
BR 'bi:dl, bɪ'dɛl, -z
AM 'bidəl, -z

bedell
BR 'bi:dl, -z
AM 'bidəl, -z

bedevil
BR bɪ'dɛv|l, -lz, -l̩ɪŋ\-lɪŋ, -ld
AM bə'dɛv|əl, bi'dɛv|əl, -əlz, -(ə)lɪŋ, -əld

bedevilment
BR bɪ'dɛvlm(ə)nt
AM bə'dɛvəlmənt, bi'dɛvəlmənt

bedew
BR bɪ'dju:, bɪ'dʒu:, -z, -ɪŋ, -d
AM bə'd(j)u, bi'd(j)u, -z, -ɪŋ, -d

bedfast
BR 'bɛdfɑ:st, 'bɛdfast
AM 'bɛd,fæst

bedfellow
BR 'bɛd,fɛləʊ, -z
AM 'bɛd,fɛloʊ, -z

Bedford
BR 'bɛdfəd
AM 'bɛdfərd

Bedfordshire
BR 'bɛdfədʃ(ɪ)ə(r)
AM 'bɛdfərd,ʃɪ(ə)r

bedframe
BR 'bɛdfreɪm, -z
AM 'bɛd,freɪm, -z

bedhead
BR 'bɛdhɛd, -z
AM 'bɛd,(h)ɛd, -z

bedight
BR bɪ'dʌɪt, -s, -ɪŋ, -ɪd
AM bə'daɪ|t, bi'daɪ|t, -ts, -dɪŋ, -dɪd

bedim
BR bɪ'dɪm, -z, -ɪŋ, -d
AM bə'dɪm, bi'dɪm, -z, -ɪŋ, -d

bedizen
BR bɪ'dʌɪz|(ə)n, -(ə)nz, -ənɪŋ\-n̩ɪŋ, -(ə)nd
AM bə'daɪzən, -z, -ɪŋ, -d

bedjacket
BR 'bɛd,dʒakɪt, -s
AM 'bɛd,dʒækət, -s

bedlam
BR 'bɛdləm
AM 'bɛdləm

bedlinen
BR 'bɛd,lɪnɪn
AM 'bɛd,lɪnɪn

Bedlington
BR 'bɛdlɪŋtən, -z
AM 'bɛdlɪŋtən, -z

bedmaker
BR 'bɛd,meɪkə(r), -z
AM 'bɛd,meɪkər, -z

Bedouin
BR 'bɛdʊɪn, -z
AM 'bɛd(ə)wən, -z

bedpan
BR 'bɛdpan, -z
AM 'bɛd,pæn, -z

bedplate
BR 'bɛd,pleɪt, -s
AM 'bɛd,pleɪt, -s

bedpost
BR 'bɛdpəʊst, -s
AM 'bɛd,poʊst, -s

bedraggle
BR bɪ'drag|l, -lz, -l̩ɪŋ\-lɪŋ, -ld
AM bə'dræg|əl, bi'dræg|əl, -əlz, -(ə)lɪŋ, -əld

bedridden
BR 'bɛd,rɪdn
AM 'bɛd,rɪdən

bedrock
BR 'bɛdrɒk
AM 'bɛd,rɑk

bedroll
BR 'bɛdrəʊl, -z
AM 'bɛd,roʊl, -z

bedroom
BR 'bɛdru:m, 'bɛdrʊm, -z
AM 'bɛd,rum, 'bɛd,rʊm, -z

bedside
BR 'bɛdsʌɪd
AM 'bɛd,saɪd

bedsit
BR ,bɛd'sɪt, 'bɛdsɪt, -s
AM 'bɛd,sɪt, -s

bedsitter
BR ,bɛd'sɪtə(r), -z
AM 'bɛd,sɪdər, -z

bed-sitting room
BR ,bɛd'sɪtɪŋ ru:m, + rʊm, -z
AM ,bɛd'sɪdɪŋ ,rum + ,rʊm, -z

bedsock
BR 'bɛdsɒk, -s
AM 'bɛd,sɑk, -s

bedsore
BR 'bɛdsɔ:(r), -z
AM 'bɛd,sɔ(ə)r, -z

bedspread
BR 'bɛdsprɛd, -z
AM 'bɛd,sprɛd, -z

bedstead
BR 'bɛdstɛd, -z
AM 'bɛd,stɛd, -z

bedstraw
BR 'bɛdstrɔ:(r)
AM 'bɛd,strɔ, 'bɛd,strɑ

bedtable
BR 'bɛd,teɪbl, -z
AM 'bɛd,teɪbəl, -z

bedtime
BR 'bɛdtʌɪm, -z
AM 'bɛd,taɪm, -z

Beduin
BR 'bɛdʊɪn, -z
AM 'bɛd(ə)wən, 'bɛdə,win, -z

bee
BR biː, -z
AM bi, -z

Beeb
BR biːb
AM bib

Beebe
BR 'biːbi
AM 'bibi

beech
BR biːtʃ, -ɪz
AM bitʃ, -ɪz

Beecham
BR 'biːtʃəm
AM 'bitʃəm

beechmast
BR 'biːtʃmɑːst, 'biːtʃmast
AM 'bitʃ,mæst

beechnut
BR 'biːtʃnʌt, -s
AM 'bitʃ,nət, -s

beechwood
BR 'biːtʃwʊd
AM 'bitʃ,wʊd

beechy
BR 'biːtʃi
AM 'bitʃi

beef
BR biːf, -s, -ɪŋ, -t
AM bif, -s, -ɪŋ, -t

beefalo
BR 'biːfələʊ, -z
AM 'bifə,loʊ, -z

beefburger
BR 'biːf,bəːgə(r), -z
AM 'bif,bərgər, -z

beefcake
BR 'biːfkeɪk, -s
AM 'bif,keɪk, -s

beefeater
BR 'biːf,iːtə(r), -z
AM 'bif,idər, -z

beefheart
BR 'biːfhɑːt
AM 'bif,(h)ɑrt

beefily
BR 'biːfɪli
AM 'bifɪli

beefiness
BR 'biːfɪnɪs
AM 'bifinɪs

beefsteak
BR 'biːfsteɪk, -s
AM 'bif,steɪk, -s

beefwood
BR 'biːfwʊd, -z
AM 'bif,wʊd, -z

beefy
BR 'biːf|i, -ɪə(r), -ɪɪst
AM 'bifi, -ər, -ɪst

beehive
BR 'biːhʌɪv, -z
AM 'bi,(h)aɪv, -z

beeline
BR 'biːlʌɪn
AM 'bi,laɪn

Beelzebub
BR bɪ'ɛlzɪbʌb
AM bi'ɛlzəbəb

been
BR biːn
AM bin

beep
BR biːp, -s, -ɪŋ, -t
AM bip, -s, -ɪŋ, -t

beeper
BR 'biːpə(r), -z
AM 'bipər, -z

beer
BR bɪə(r), -z
AM bɪ(ə)r, -z

beerbelly
BR 'bɪə,bɛl|i, -ɪz
AM 'bɪr,bɛli, -z

Beerbohm
BR 'bɪəbəʊm
AM 'bɪr,boʊm

beerhouse
BR 'bɪəhaʊ|s, -zɪz
AM 'bɪr,(h)aʊ|s, -zəz

beerily
BR 'bɪərɪli
AM 'bɪrɪli

beeriness
BR 'bɪərɪnɪs
AM 'bɪrinɪs

beermoney
BR 'bɪə,mʌni
AM 'bɪr,məni

beerpot
BR 'bɪəpɒt, -s
AM 'bɪr,pɑt, -s

Beersheba
BR ,bɪə'ʃiːbə(r)
AM ,bɪr'ʃibə

beery
BR 'bɪər|i, -ɪə(r), -ɪɪst
AM 'bɪri, -ər, -ɪst

beestings
BR 'biːstɪŋz
AM 'bi,stɪŋz

beeswax
BR 'biːzwaks
AM 'biz,wæks

beeswing
BR 'biːzwɪŋ
AM 'biz,wɪŋ

beet
BR biːt, -s
AM bit, -s

Beethoven
BR 'beɪt(h)əʊvn
AM 'beɪ,toʊvən

beetle
BR 'biːt|l, -lz, -l̩ɪŋ\-lɪŋ, -ld
AM 'bidəl, -z, -ɪŋ, -d

Beeton
BR 'biːtn
AM 'bitn

beetroot
BR 'biːtruːt, -s
AM 'bit,rut, -s

beeves
BR biːvz
AM bivz

befall
BR bɪ'fɔːl, -z, -ɪŋ
AM bə'fɔl, bi'fɔl, bə'fɑl, bi'fɑl, -z, -ɪŋ

befallen
BR bɪ'fɔːlən
AM bə'fɔlən, bi'fɔlən, bə'fɑlən, bi'fɑlən

befell
BR bɪ'fɛl
AM bə'fɛl, bi'fɛl

befit
BR bɪ'fɪt, -s, -ɪŋ, -ɪd
AM bə'fɪ|t, bi'fɪ|t, -ts, -dɪŋ, -dɪd

befittingly
BR bɪ'fɪtɪŋli
AM bə'fɪdɪŋli, bi'fɪdɪŋli

befog
BR bɪ'fɒg, -z, -ɪŋ, -d
AM bə'fɑg, bi'fɑg, -z, -ɪŋ, -d

befool
BR bɪ'fuːl, -z, -ɪŋ, -d
AM bə'ful, bi'ful, -z, -ɪŋ, -d

before
BR bɪ'fɔː(r)
AM bə'fɔ(ə)r, bi'fɔ(ə)r

beforehand
BR bɪ'fɔːhand
AM bə'fɔr,(h)ænd, bi'fɔr,(h)ænd

beforetime
BR bɪ'fɔːtʌɪm
AM bə'fɔr,taɪm, bi'fɔr,taɪm

befoul
BR bɪ'faʊl, -z, -ɪŋ, -d
AM bə'faʊl, bi'faʊl, -z, -ɪŋ, -d

befriend
BR bɪ'frɛnd, -z, -ɪŋ, -ɪd
AM bə'frɛnd, bi'frɛnd, -z, -ɪŋ, -əd

befuddle
BR bɪ'fʌd|l, -lz, -l̩ɪŋ\-lɪŋ, -ld
AM bə'fədəl, bi'fəd|əl, -əlz, -(ə)lɪŋ, -əld

befuddlement
BR bɪ'fʌdlm(ə)nt
AM bə'fədəlmənt, bi'fədəlmənt

beg
BR bɛg, -z, -ɪŋ, -d
AM bɛg, -z, -ɪŋ, -d

begad
BR bɪ'gad
AM bə'gæd, bi'gæd

began
BR bɪ'gan
AM bə'gæn, bi'gæn

begat
BR bɪ'gat
AM bə'gæt, bi'gæt

beget
BR bɪ'gɛt, -s, -ɪŋ
AM bə'gɛ|t, bi'gɛ|t, -ts, -dɪŋ

begetter
BR bɪ'gɛtə(r), -z
AM bə'gɛdər, bi'gɛdər, -z

beggar
BR 'bɛgə(r), -z, -ɪŋ, -d
AM 'bɛgər, -z, -ɪŋ, -d

beggarliness
BR 'bɛgəlɪnɪs
AM 'bɛgərlinɪs

beggarly
BR 'bɛgəli
AM 'bɛgərli

beggary
BR 'bɛgəri
AM 'bɛgəri

Begin
Menachem
BR 'beɪgɪn
AM 'beɪgɪn

begin
BR bɪ'gɪn, -z, -ɪŋ
AM bə'gɪn, bi'gɪn, -z, -ɪŋ

beginner
BR bɪ'gɪnə(r), -z
AM bə'gɪnər, bi'gɪnər, -z

beginning
BR bɪ'gɪnɪŋ, -z
AM bə'gɪnɪŋ, bi'gɪnɪŋ, -z

begird
BR bɪ'gəːd, -z, -ɪŋ
AM bə'gərd, bi'gərd, -z, -ɪŋ

begirt
BR bɪ'gəːt
AM bə'gərt, bi'gərt

begone
BR bɪ'gɒn
AM bə'gɔn, bə'gɑn, bi'gɔn, bi'gɑn

begonia
BR bɪ'gəʊnɪə(r), -z
AM bə'goʊnjə, bi'goʊnjə, -z

begorra
BR bɪ'gɒrə(r)
AM bə'gɔrə, bi'gɔrə

begot
BR bɪ'gɒt
AM bə'gɑt, bi'gɑt

begotten
BR bɪ'gɒtn
AM bə'gɑtn, bi'gɑtn

begrime
BR bɪ'ɡrʌɪm, -z, -ɪŋ, -d
AM bə'ɡraɪm, bi'ɡraɪm, -z, -ɪŋ, -d

begrudge
BR bɪ'ɡrʌdʒ, -ɪz, -ɪŋ, -d
AM bə'ɡrədʒ, bi'ɡrədʒ, -əz, -ɪŋ, -d

begrudgingly
BR bɪ'ɡrʌdʒɪŋli
AM bə'ɡrədʒɪŋli, bi'ɡrədʒɪŋli

beguile
BR bɪ'ɡʌɪl, -z, -ɪŋ, -d
AM bə'ɡaɪl, bi'ɡaɪl, -z, -ɪŋ, -d

beguilement
BR bɪ'ɡʌɪlm(ə)nt
AM bə'ɡaɪlmənt, bi'ɡaɪlmənt

beguiler
BR bɪ'ɡʌɪlə(r), -z
AM bə'ɡaɪlər, bi'ɡaɪlər, -z

beguilingly
BR bɪ'ɡʌɪlɪŋli
AM bə'ɡaɪlɪŋli, bi'ɡaɪlɪŋli

beguine
BR bɪ'ɡi:n, -z
AM bə'ɡin, -z

begum
BR 'bi:ɡəm, 'beɪɡəm, -z
AM 'biɡəm, 'beɪɡəm, -z

begun
BR bɪ'ɡʌn
AM bə'ɡən, bi'ɡən

behalf
BR bɪ'hɑ:f
AM bə'hæf, bə'hɑf, bi'hæf, bi'hɑf

Behan
BR 'bi:ən
AM 'biən

behave
BR bɪ'heɪv, -z, -ɪŋ, -d
AM bə'heɪv, bi'heɪv, -z, -ɪŋ, -d

behavior
BR bɪ'heɪvjə(r), -z
AM bə'heɪvjər, bi'heɪvjər, -z

behavioral
BR bɪ'heɪvjərəl, bɪ'heɪvjər̩l
AM bə'heɪvjərəl, bi'heɪvjərəl

behavioralist
BR bɪ'heɪvjərəlɪst, bɪ'heɪvjər̩lɪst, -s
AM bə'heɪvjərələst, bi'heɪvjərələst, -s

behaviorally
BR bɪ'heɪvjərəli, bɪ'heɪvjər̩li
AM bə'heɪvjərəli, bi'heɪvjərəli

behaviorism
BR bɪ'heɪvjərɪz(ə)m
AM bə'heɪvjəˌrɪzəm, bi'heɪvjəˌrɪzəm

behaviorist
BR bɪ'heɪvjərɪst, -s
AM bə'heɪvjərəst, bi'heɪvjərəst, -s

behavioristic
BR bɪˌheɪvjə'rɪstɪk
AM bəˌheɪvjə'rɪstɪk, biˌheɪvjə'rɪstɪk

behavioristically
BR bɪˌheɪvjə'rɪstɪkli
AM bəˌheɪvjə'rɪstɪk(ə)li, biˌheɪvjə'rɪstɪk(ə)li

behaviour
BR bɪ'heɪvjə(r), -z
AM bə'heɪvjər, bi'heɪvjər, -z

behavioural
BR bɪ'heɪvjərəl, bɪ'heɪvjər̩l
AM bə'heɪvjərəl, bi'heɪvjərəl

behaviouralist
BR bɪ'heɪvjərəlɪst, bɪ'heɪvjər̩lɪst, -s
AM bə'heɪvjərələst, bi'heɪvjərələst, -s

behaviourally
BR bɪ'heɪvjərəli, bɪ'heɪvjər̩li
AM bə'heɪvjərəli, bi'heɪvjərəli

behaviourism
BR bɪ'heɪvjərɪz(ə)m
AM bə'heɪvjəˌrɪzəm, bi'heɪvjəˌrɪzəm

behaviourist
BR bɪ'heɪvjərɪst, -s
AM bə'heɪvjərɪst, bi'heɪvjərɪst, -s

behaviouristic
BR bɪˌheɪvjə'rɪstɪk
AM bəˌheɪvjə'rɪstɪk, biˌheɪvjə'rɪstɪk

behaviouristically
BR bɪˌheɪvjə'rɪstɪkli
AM bəˌheɪvjə'rɪstɪk(ə)li, biˌheɪvjə'rɪstɪk(ə)li

behead
BR bɪ'hɛd, -z, -ɪŋ, -ɪd
AM bə'hɛd, bi'hɛd, -z, -ɪŋ, -əd

beheld
BR bɪ'hɛld
AM bə'hɛld, bi'hɛld

behemoth
BR bɪ'hi:məθ, bɪ'hi:mɒθ, -s
AM bɪ'himəθ, bi'himəθ, 'biəməθ, -s

behest
BR bɪ'hɛst, -s
AM bə'hɛst, bi'hɛst, -s

behind
BR bɪ'hʌɪnd, -z
AM bə'haɪnd, bi'haɪnd, -z

behindhand
BR bɪ'hʌɪndhand
AM bə'haɪn(d)ˌ(h)ænd, bi'haɪn(d)ˌ(h)ænd

Behn
BR bɛn
AM beɪn

behold
BR bɪ'həʊld, -z, -ɪŋ
AM bə'hoʊld, bi'hoʊld, -z, -ɪŋ

beholden
BR bɪ'həʊld(ə)n
AM bə'hoʊldən, bi'hoʊldən

beholder
BR bɪ'həʊldə(r), -z
AM bə'hoʊldər, bi'hoʊldər, -z

behoof
BR bɪ'hu:f
AM bə'huf, bi'huf

behoove
BR bɪ'hu:v, -z, -ɪŋ, -d
AM bə'huv, bi'huv, -z, -ɪŋ, -d

behove
BR bɪ'həʊv, -z, -ɪŋ, -d
AM bə'huv, bi'huv, -z, -ɪŋ, -d

Behrens
BR 'bɛ:rəns, 'bɛ:rənz
AM 'bɛrəns

Behring
BR 'bɛ:rɪŋ
AM 'bɛrɪŋ

Beiderbecke
BR 'bʌɪdəbɛk
AM 'baɪdərˌbɛk

beige
BR beɪʒ
AM beɪʒ

beigel
BR 'beɪɡl, -z
AM 'beɪɡəl, -z

Beijing
BR ˌbeɪ'(d)ʒɪŋ
AM ˌbeɪ'(d)ʒɪŋ

being
BR 'bi:ɪŋ, -z
AM 'biɪŋ, -z

Beira
BR 'bʌɪrə(*r*)
AM 'baɪrə
PORT 'bejra

Beirut
BR ˌbeɪ'ru:t
AM ˌbeɪ'rut

beisa
BR 'beɪzə(*r*)
AM 'beɪzə

bejabbers
BR bɪ'dʒabəz
AM bə'dʒæbərz, bi'dʒæbərz

bejabers
BR bɪ'dʒeɪbəz
AM bə'dʒæbərz, bi'dʒæbərz

bejewel
BR bɪ'dʒu:(ə)l, -z, -ɪŋ, -d
AM bə'dʒuəl, bi'dʒuəl, -z, -ɪŋ, -d

Bekaa
BR bɛ'kɑ:(*r*), bɪ'kɑ:(*r*)
AM bə'kɑ

bel
BR bɛl, -z
AM bɛl, -z

belabor
BR bɪ'leɪb|ə(r), -əz, -(ə)rɪŋ, -əd
AM bə'leɪbər, bi'leɪbər, -z, -ɪŋ, -d

belabour
BR bɪ'leɪb|ə(r), -əz, -(ə)rɪŋ, -əd
AM bə'leɪbər, bi'leɪbər, -z, -ɪŋ, -d

Belafonte
BR ˌbɛlə'fɒnti
AM ˌbɛlə'fɑn(t)i

Belarus
BR ˌbɛlə'ru:s, ˌbɛlə'rʊs
AM ˌbɛlə'rus

belated
BR bɪ'leɪtɪd
AM bə'leɪdɪd, bi'leɪdɪd

belatedly
BR bɪ'leɪtɪdli
AM bə'leɪdɪdli, bi'leɪdɪdli

belatedness
BR bɪ'leɪtɪdnɪs
AM bə'leɪdɪdnɪs, bi'leɪdɪdnɪs

Belau
BR bɛ'laʊ, bɪ'laʊ
AM bə'laʊ

belay[1]
noun
BR 'bi:leɪ, -z
AM bə'leɪ, bi'leɪ, -z

belay[2]
verb
BR bɪ'leɪ, -z, -ɪŋ, -d
AM bə'leɪ, bi'leɪ, -z, -ɪŋ, -d

bel canto
BR ˌbɛl 'kantəʊ
AM ˌbɛl 'kɑn(t)oʊ

belch
BR bɛltʃ, -ɪz, -ɪŋ, -t
AM bɛltʃ, -əz, -ɪŋ, -t

belcher
BR 'bɛltʃə(r), -z
AM 'bɛltʃər, -z

beldam
BR 'bɛldəm, -z
AM 'bɛldəm, -z

beldame
BR 'bɛldəm, -z

AM ˈbɛldəm, ˈbɛlˌdeɪm, -z

beleaguer
BR bɪˈliːɡ|ə(r), -əz, -(ə)rɪŋ, -əd
AM bəˈliɡər, biˈliɡər, -z, -ɪŋ, -d

Belém
BR bɛˈlɛm
AM beɪˈlɛm, bɛˈlɛm

belemnite
BR ˈbɛləmnʌɪt, -s
AM ˈbɛləmˌnaɪt, -s

bel esprit
BR ˌbɛl ɛˈspriː, -z
AM ˌbɛl əˈspri, -z

Belfast
BR ˌbɛlˈfɑːst, ˌbɛlˈfast, ˈbɛlfɑːst, ˈbɛlfast
AM ˈbɛlˌfæst

belfry
BR ˈbɛlfr|i, -ɪz
AM ˈbɛlfri, -z

Belgae
BR ˈbɛlɡʌɪ, ˈbɛldʒiː, ˈbɛlɡiː
AM ˈbɛldʒi, ˈbɛlɡi, ˈbɛldʒaɪ

Belgian
BR ˈbɛldʒ(ə)n, -z
AM ˈbɛldʒən, -z

Belgic
BR ˈbɛldʒɪk
AM ˈbɛldʒɪk

Belgium
BR ˈbɛldʒəm
AM ˈbɛldʒəm

Belgrade
BR ˌbɛlˈɡreɪd
AM ˈbɛlˌɡreɪd, ˈbɛlˌɡræd

Belgravia
BR bɛlˈɡreɪvɪə(r)
AM ˌbɛlˈɡreɪviə

Belgravian
BR bɛlˈɡreɪvɪən, -z
AM ˌbɛlˈɡreɪviən, -z

Belial
BR ˈbiːlɪəl
AM ˈbiliəl, ˈbɛliəl

belie
BR bɪˈlʌɪ, -z, -ɪŋ, -d
AM bəˈlaɪ, biˈlaɪ, -z, -ɪŋ, -d

belief
BR bɪˈliːf, -s
AM bəˈlif, biˈlif, -s

believability
BR bəˌliːvəˈbɪlɪti
AM bəˌlivəˈbɪlɪdi, biˌlivəˈbɪlɪdi

believable
BR bɪˈliːvəbl
AM bəˈlivəbəl, biˈlivəbəl

believably
BR bɪˈliːvəbli
AM bəˈlivəbli, biˈlivəbli

believe
BR bɪˈliːv, -z, -ɪŋ, -d
AM bəˈliv, biˈliv, -z, -ɪŋ, -d

believer
BR bɪˈliːvə(r), -z
AM bəˈlivər, biˈlivər, -z

belike
BR bɪˈlʌɪk
AM bəˈlaɪk, biˈlaɪk

Belinda
BR bɪˈlɪndə(r)
AM bəˈlɪndə

Belisarius
BR ˌbɛlɪˈsɛːrɪəs, ˌbɛlɪˈsɑːrɪəs
AM ˌbɛləˈsɛriəs

belittle
BR bɪˈlɪt|l, -lz, -lɪŋ\-lɪŋ, -ld
AM bəˈlɪdəl, biˈlɪdəl-z, -ɪŋ, -d

belittlement
BR bɪˈlɪtlm(ə)nt
AM bəˈlɪdlmənt, biˈlɪdlmənt

belittler
BR bɪˈlɪtl̩ə(r), bɪˈlɪtlə(r), -z
AM bəˈlɪdələr, biˈlɪdələr, -z

belittlingly
BR bɪˈlɪtl̩ɪŋli, bɪˈlɪtlɪŋli
AM bəˈlɪdəlɪŋli, biˈlɪdəlɪŋli

Belize
BR bɪˈliːz, bɛˈliːz
AM bəˈliz

Belizean
BR bɪˈliːzɪən, bɛˈliːzɪən, -z
AM bəˈliziən, bəˈliʒən, -z

Belizian
BR bɪˈliːzɪən, bɛˈliːzɪən, -z
AM bəˈliziən, bəˈliʒən, -z

bell
BR bɛl, -z, -ɪŋ, -d
AM bɛl, -z, -ɪŋ, -d

Bella
BR ˈbɛlə(r)
AM ˈbɛlə

belladona
BR ˌbɛləˈdɒnə(r)
AM ˌbɛləˈdɑnə

belladonna
BR ˌbɛləˈdɒnə(r)
AM ˌbɛləˈdɑnə

Bellamy
BR ˈbɛləmi
AM ˈbɛləmi

Bellay
BR bəˈleɪ
AM bəˈleɪ

bellbird
BR ˈbɛlbəːd, -z
AM ˈbɛlˌbərd, -z

bellboy
BR ˈbɛlbɔɪ, -z
AM ˈbɛlˌbɔɪ, -z

belle
BR bɛl, -z
AM bɛl, -z

belle époque
BR ˌbɛl eɪˈpɒk, -s
AM ˌbɛl əˈpɑk, -s

belle laide
BR ˌbɛl ˈleɪd, -z
AM ˌbɛl ˈlɛd, -z

Bellerophon
BR bɪˈlɛrəfɒn, bɪˈlɛrəf(ə)n
AM bəˈlɛrəˌfɑn, bəˈlɛrəfən

belles-lettres
BR ˌbɛlˈlɛtr(ər)
AM ˌbɛlˈlɛtr(ə)

belletrism
BR ˌbɛlˈlɛtrɪz(ə)m
AM ˌbɛlˈlɛtrɪzəm

belletrist
BR ˌbɛlˈlɛtrɪst, -s
AM ˌbɛlˈlɛtrəst, -s

belletristic
BR ˌbɛləˈtrɪstɪk
AM ˌbɛləˈtrɪstɪk

bellettrist
BR ˌbɛlˈlɛtrɪst, -s
AM ˌbɛlˈlɛtrəst, -s

Bellevue
BR ˌbɛlˈvjuː
AM ˈbɛlˌvju

bellflower
BR ˈbɛlˌflaʊə(r), -z
AM ˈbɛlˌflaʊ(ə)r, -z

bellhop
BR ˈbɛlˌhɒp, -s
AM ˈbɛlˌ(h)ɑp, -s

bellicose
BR ˈbɛlɪkəʊs, ˈbɛlɪkəʊz
AM ˈbɛləˌkoʊs, ˈbɛləˌkoʊz

bellicosely
BR ˈbɛlɪkəʊsli, ˈbɛlɪkəʊzli
AM ˈbɛləˌkoʊsli, ˈbɛləˌkoʊzli

bellicosity
BR ˌbɛlɪˈkɒsɪti
AM ˌbɛləˈkɑsədi

belligerence
BR bɪˈlɪdʒ(ə)rəns, bɪˈlɪdʒ(ə)rn̩s
AM bəˈlɪdʒ(ə)rəns

belligerency
BR bɪˈlɪdʒ(ə)rənsi, bɪˈlɪdʒ(ə)rn̩si
AM bəˈlɪdʒ(ə)rənsi

belligerent
BR bɪˈlɪdʒ(ə)rənt, bɪˈlɪdʒ(ə)rn̩t, -s
AM bəˈlɪdʒ(ə)rənt, -s

belligerently
BR bɪˈlɪdʒ(ə)rəntli, bɪˈlɪdʒ(ə)rn̩tli
AM bəˈlɪdʒ(ə)rən(t)li

Bellini
BR bɛˈliːni, bəˈliːni
AM bəˈlini

bellman
BR ˈbɛlmən
AM ˈbɛlmən

bellmen
BR ˈbɛlmən
AM ˈbɛlmən

Belloc
BR ˈbɛlɒk
AM bəˈlɔk, bəˈlɑk

bellow
BR ˈbɛləʊ, -z, -ɪŋ, -d
AM ˈbɛl|oʊ, -oʊz, -əwɪŋ, -oʊd

bellpush
BR ˈbɛlpʊʃ, -ɪz
AM ˈbɛlˌpʊʃ, -əz

bellringer
BR ˈbɛlˌrɪŋə(r), -z
AM ˈbɛlˌrɪŋər, -z

bellringing
BR ˈbɛlˌrɪŋɪŋ
AM ˈbɛlˌrɪŋɪŋ

bellrope
BR ˈbɛlrəʊp, -s
AM ˈbɛlˌroʊp, -s

bellwether
BR ˈbɛlˌwɛðə(r), -z
AM ˈbɛlˌwɛðər, -z

belly
BR ˈbɛl|i, -ɪz, -ɪɪŋ, -ɪd
AM ˈbɛli, -z, -ɪŋ, -d

bellyache
BR ˈbɛlieɪk, -s, -ɪŋ, -t
AM ˈbɛliˌeɪk, -s, -ɪŋ, -t

bellyacher
BR ˈbɛlɪ ˌeɪkə(r), -z
AM ˈbɛliˌeɪkər, -z

bellyband
BR ˈbɛlɪband, -z
AM ˈbɛliˌbænd, -z

bellyflop
BR ˈbɛlɪflɒp, -s, -ɪŋ, -t
AM ˈbɛliˌflɑp, -s, -ɪŋ, -t

bellyful
BR ˈbɛlɪfʊl, -z
AM ˈbɛliˌfʊl, -z

Belmondo
BR bɛlˈmɒndəʊ
AM bɛlˈmɔndoʊ, bɛlˈmɑndoʊ

Belmont
BR ˈbɛlmɒnt
AM ˈbɛlmɑnt

Belmopan
BR ˌbɛlmə(ʊ)ˈpan
AM ˈbɛlməˌpæn

Belo Horizonte
BR ˌbɛləʊ ˌhɒrɪˈzɒnteɪ
AM ˌbɛloʊ ˌhɔrəˈzɔnˌteɪ, + ˌhɔrəˈzɑnˌteɪ
B PORT ˌbelu orizõˈtʃi
L PORT ˌbɛloriˈzõtə

belong
BR bɪˈlɒŋ, -z, -ɪŋ, -d
AM bəˈlɔŋ, biˈlɔŋ, bəˈlɑŋ, biˈlɑŋ, -z, -ɪŋ, -d

belongingness
BR bɪˈlɒŋɪŋnɪs
AM bəˈlɔŋɪŋnɪs, biˈlɔŋɪŋnɪs, bəˈlɑŋɪŋnɪs, biˈlɑŋɪŋnɪs

belongings
BR bɪˈlɒŋɪŋz
AM bəˈlɔŋɪŋz, biˈlɔŋɪŋz, bəˈlɑŋɪŋz, biˈlɑŋɪŋz

Belorussia
BR ˌbɛlə(ʊ)ˈrʌʃə(r), ˌbɛlə(ʊ)ˈruːsɪə(r)
AM ˌbɛloʊˈrəʃə

Belorussian
BR ˌbɛlə(ʊ)ˈrʌʃn, ˌbɛlə(ʊ)ˈruːsɪən, -z
AM ˌbɛloʊˈrəʃən, -z

beloved
BR bɪˈlʌv(ɨ)d
AM bəˈləv(ə)d, biˈləv(ə)d

below
BR bɪˈləʊ
AM bəˈloʊ, biˈloʊ

Bel Paese®
BR ˌbɛl pɑːˈeɪzi
AM ˌbɛl pɑˈeɪzi

Belsen
BR ˈbɛlsn
AM ˈbɛlsən

Belshazzar
BR bɛlˈʃazə(r)
AM ˈbɛlʃəˌzɑr, bɛlˈʃæzər

belt
BR bɛlt, -s, -ɪŋ, -ɨd
AM bɛlt, -s, -ɪŋ, -əd

Beltane
BR ˈbɛlteɪn
AM ˈbɛlˌteɪn

belter
BR ˈbɛltə(r), -z
AM ˈbɛltər, -z

beltman
BR ˈbɛltmən
AM ˈbɛltmən

beltmen
BR ˈbɛltmən
AM ˈbɛltmən

beluga
BR bɪˈluːgə(r), bɛˈluːgə(r), -z
AM bəˈlugə, -z

belvedere
BR ˈbɛlvɪdɪə(r), ˌbɛlvɪˈdɪə(r), -z
AM ˈbɛlvəˌdɪ(ə)r, -z

Belvoir
BR ˈbiːvə(r)
AM ˈbɛlˌvwɑr, ˈbɛlˌvɔ(ə)r

belying
BR bɪˈlʌɪɪŋ
AM bəˈlaɪɪŋ, biˈlaɪɪŋ

bema
BR ˈbiːmə(r), -z
AM ˈbimə, -z

bemata
BR ˈbiːmətə(r)
AM ˈbimədə

Bemba
BR ˈbɛmbə(r), -z
AM ˈbɛmbə, -z

Bembridge
BR ˈbɛmbrɪdʒ
AM ˈbɛmˌbrɪdʒ

bemedaled
BR bɪˈmɛdld
AM bəˈmɛdld, biˈmɛdld

bemedalled
BR bɪˈmɛdld
AM bəˈmɛdld, biˈmɛdld

bemire
BR bɪˈmʌɪə(r), -z, -ɪŋ, -d
AM bəˈmaɪ(ə)r, biˈmaɪ(ə)r, -z, -ɪŋ, -d

bemoan
BR bɪˈməʊn, -z, -ɪŋ, -d
AM bəˈmoʊn, biˈmoʊn, -z, -ɪŋ, -d

bemuse
BR bɪˈmjuːz, -ɪz, -ɪŋ, -d
AM bəˈmjuz, biˈmjuz, -əz, -ɪŋ, -d

bemusedly
BR bɪˈmjuːzɪdli
AM bəˈmjuzədli, biˈmjuzədli

bemusement
BR bɪˈmjuːzm(ə)nt
AM bəˈmjuzmənt, biˈmjuzmənt

Ben
BR bɛn
AM bɛn

Benares
BR bɪˈnɑːrɪz, bɛˈnɑːrɪz, bɪˈnɑːriːz, bɛˈnɑːriːz
AM bəˈnɑriz

Benbecula
BR ˌbɛnˈbɛkjʉlə(r)
AM ˌbɛnˈbɛkjʊlə

Ben Bella
BR ˌbɛn ˈbɛlə(r)
AM ˌbɛn ˈbɛlə

bench
BR bɛn(t)ʃ, -ɪz, -ɪŋ, -t
AM bɛn(t)ʃ, -əz, -ɪŋ, -t

bencher
BR ˈbɛn(t)ʃə(r), -z
AM ˈbɛn(t)ʃər, -z

benchmark
BR ˈbɛn(t)ʃmɑːk, -s
AM ˈbɛn(t)ʃˌmɑrk, -s

bend
BR bɛnd, -z, -ɪŋ, -ɪd
AM bɛnd, -z, -ɪŋ, -əd

bendable
BR ˈbɛndəbl
AM ˈbɛndəbəl

bender
BR ˈbɛndə(r), -z
AM ˈbɛndər, -z

Bendigo
BR ˈbɛndɪgəʊ
AM ˈbɛndəˌgoʊ

bendiness
BR ˈbɛndɪnɪs
AM ˈbɛndinɪs

Bendix®
BR ˈbɛndɪks
AM ˈbɛndɪks

bendy
BR ˈbɛnd|i, -ɪə(r), -ɪɪst
AM ˈbɛndi, -ər, -ɪst

beneath
BR bɪˈniːθ
AM bəˈniθ, biˈniθ

benedicite
BR ˌbɛnɪˈdʌɪsɪt|i, ˌbɛnɪˈdiːtʃɪt|i, -ɪz
AM ˌbɛnəˈdɪsɪdi, ˌbeɪneɪˈditʃiˌteɪ, -z

Benedick
BR ˈbɛnɪdɪk
AM ˈbɛnəˌdɪk

Benedict
BR ˈbɛnɪdɪkt
AM ˈbɛnəˌdɪk(t)

Benedictine
BR ˌbɛnɪˈdɪktiːn, -z
AM ˌbɛnəˈdɪkˌtin, -z

benediction
BR ˌbɛnɪˈdɪkʃn, -z
AM ˌbɛnəˈdɪkʃən, -z

benedictory
BR ˌbɛnɪˈdɪkt(ə)ri
AM ˌbɛnəˈdɪktəri

Benedictus
BR ˌbɛnɪˈdɪktəs
AM ˌbɛnəˈdɪktəs

benefaction
BR ˌbɛnɪˈfakʃn, -z
AM ˌbɛnəˈfækʃən, -z

benefactor
BR ˈbɛnɪfaktə(r), -z
AM ˈbɛnəˌfæktər, -z

benefactress
BR ˈbɛnɪfaktrɪs, -ɪz
AM ˈbɛnəˌfæktrəs, -əz

benefic
BR bɪˈnɛfɪk
AM bəˈnɛfɪk

benefice
BR ˈbɛnɪfɪs, -ɪz, -t
AM ˈbɛnəfəs, -əz, -t

beneficence
BR bɪˈnɛfɪs(ə)ns
AM bəˈnɛfəs(ə)ns

beneficent
BR bɪˈnɛfɪs(ə)nt
AM bəˈnɛfəs(ə)nt

beneficently
BR bɪˈnɛfɪs(ə)ntli
AM bəˈnɛfəsən(t)li

beneficial
BR ˌbɛnɪˈfɪʃl
AM ˌbɛnəˈfɪʃəl

beneficially
BR ˌbɛnɪˈfɪʃli, ˌbɛnɪˈfɪʃəli
AM ˌbɛnəˈfɪʃəli

beneficiary
BR ˌbɛnɪˈfɪʃ(ə)r|i, ˌbɛnɪˈfɪʃɪər|i, -ɪz
AM ˌbɛnəˈfɪʃiˌɛri, -z

beneficiation
BR ˌbɛnɪfɪʃɪˈeɪʃn
AM ˌbɛnəˌfɪʃiˈeɪʃən

benefit
BR ˈbɛnɪf|ɪt, -s, -ɪtɪŋ, -ɪtɪd
AM ˈbɛnəfɪ|t, -ts, -dɪŋ, -dɪd

Benelux
BR ˈbɛnɪlʌks
AM ˈbɛnlˌəks, ˈbɛnəˌləks

Benenden
BR ˈbɛnəndən
AM ˈbɛnəndən

Benetton®
BR ˈbɛnɪtɒn, ˈbɛnɪt(ə)n
AM ˈbɛnəˌtɑn, ˈbɛnətn

benevolence
BR bɪˈnɛvələns, bɪˈnɛvlņs, bɪˈnɛvḷ(ə)ns
AM bəˈnɛvəl(ə)ns

benevolent
BR bɪˈnɛvələnt, bɪˈnɛvlņt, bɪˈnɛvḷ(ə)nt
AM bəˈnɛvəl(ə)nt

benevolently
BR bɪˈnɛvələntli, bɪˈnɛvlņtli, bɪˈnɛvḷəntli
AM bəˈnɛvəl(ə)n(t)li

Benfleet
BR ˈbɛnfliːt
AM ˈbɛnˌflit

Bengal
BR ˌbɛnˈgɔːl, ˌbɛŋˈgɔːl
AM ˈbɛnˌgɑl, ˈbɛŋˌgɑl

Bengali
BR ˌbɛnˈgɔːl|i, ˌbɛŋˈgɔːl|i, -ɪz
AM ˌbɛnˈgɑli, ˌbɛŋˈgɑli, -z

Benghazi
BR ˌbɛnˈɡɑːzi, ˌbɛŋˈɡɑːzi
AM ˌbɛnˈɡɑzi, ˌbɛŋˈɡɑzi

Benguela
BR ˌbɛnˈɡweɪlə(r), ˌbɛŋˈɡweɪlə(r), ˌbɛnˈɡwɛlə(r), ˌbɛŋˈɡwɛlə(r)
AM ˌbɛnˈɡwɛlə, ˌbɛŋˈɡwɛlə
PORT bẽˈɡelɑ

Ben-Gurion
BR ˌbɛnˈɡʊərɪən
AM ˌbɛnˈɡuriən

Benidorm
BR ˈbɛnɪdɔːm
AM ˈbɛnəˌdɔ(ə)rm
SP ˌbeniˈðor(m)

benighted
BR bɪˈnʌɪtɪd
AM bəˈnaɪdɪd, biˈnaɪdɪd

benightedly
BR bɪˈnʌɪtɪdli
AM bəˈnaɪdɪdli, biˈnaɪdɪdli

benightedness
BR bɪˈnʌɪtɪdnɪs
AM bəˈnaɪdɪdnɪs, biˈnaɪdɪdnɪs

benign
BR bɪˈnʌɪn
AM bəˈnaɪn, biˈnaɪn

benignancy
BR bɪˈnɪɡnənsi
AM bəˈnɪɡnənsi

benignant
BR bɪˈnɪɡnənt
AM bəˈnɪɡnənt

benignantly
BR bɪˈnɪɡnəntli
AM bəˈnɪɡnən(t)li

benignity
BR bɪˈnɪɡnɪti
AM bəˈnɪɡnɪdi, -z

benignly
BR bɪˈnʌɪnli
AM bəˈnaɪnli, biˈnaɪnli

Benin
BR bɪˈniːn, bɛˈniːn
AM bəˈnin

Beninese
BR ˌbɛnɪˈniːz, bɪˌniːˈniːz, bɛˌniːˈniːz
AM ˌbɛnəˈniz

benison
BR ˈbɛnɪz(ə)n, ˈbɛnɪs(ə)n, -z
AM ˈbɛnəsən, ˈbɛnəzn, -z

Benito
BR bɪˈniːtəʊ, bɛˈniːtəʊ
AM bəˈnidoʊ

Benjamin
BR ˈbɛn(d)ʒəmɪn
AM ˈbɛndʒəmən

Benlate
BR ˈbɛnleɪt
AM ˈbɛnˌleɪt

Benn
BR bɛn
AM bɛn

Bennett
BR ˈbɛnɪt
AM ˈbɛnət

Ben Nevis
BR ˌbɛn ˈnɛvɪs
AM ˌbɛn ˈnɛvəs

benni
BR ˈbɛni
AM ˈbɛni

Benny
BR ˈbɛni
AM ˈbɛni

Benson
BR ˈbɛnsn
AM ˈbɛnsən

bent
BR bɛnt, -s
AM bɛnt, -s

Bentham
BR ˈbɛnθəm, ˈbɛntəm
AM ˈbɛnθəm

Benthamism
BR ˈbɛnθəmɪz(ə)m, ˈbɛntəmɪz(ə)m
AM ˈbɛnθəˌmɪzəm, ˈbɛn(t)əˌmɪzəm

Benthamite
BR ˈbɛnθəmʌɪt, ˈbɛntəmʌɪt, -s
AM ˈbɛnθəˌmaɪt, ˈbɛn(t)əˌmaɪt, -s

benthic
BR ˈbɛnθɪk
AM ˈbɛnθɪk

benthos
BR ˈbɛnθɒs
AM ˈbɛnˌθɑs

Bentley
BR ˈbɛntl|i, -ɪz
AM ˈbɛntli, -z

Benton
BR ˈbɛntən
AM ˈbɛn(t)ən

bentonite
BR ˈbɛntənʌɪt
AM ˈbɛntnˌaɪt

bentwood
BR ˈbɛntwʊd
AM ˈbɛntˌwʊd

Benue
BR ˈbɛnʊeɪ
AM ˈbeɪnwɑ

benumb
BR bɪˈnʌm, -z, -ɪŋ, -d
AM bəˈnəm, biˈnəm, -z, -ɪŋ, -d

Benz
BR bɛnz
AM bɛnz

Benzedrine®
BR ˈbɛnzɪdriːn, ˈbɛnzɪdrɪn
AM ˈbɛnzəˌdrin, ˈbɛnzədrən

benzene
BR ˈbɛnziːn, bɛnˈziːn
AM ˈbɛnˌzin

benzenoid
BR ˈbɛnzɪnɔɪd
AM ˈbɛnzəˌnɔɪd

Benzies
BR ˈbɛnjɪz
AM ˈbɛnziz

benzin
BR ˈbɛnzɪn, bɛnˈzɪn
AM ˈbɛnˌzin, ˈbɛnzən

benzine
BR ˈbɛnziːn, bɛnˈziːn
AM ˈbɛnˌzin, ˌbɛnˈzin

benzocaine
BR ˈbɛnzəkeɪn
AM ˈbɛnzəˌkeɪn

benzodiazepine
BR ˌbɛnzəʊdʌɪˈeɪzɪpiːn, ˌbɛnzəʊdʌɪˈazɪpiːn, -z
AM ˌbɛnzəˌdaɪˈæzəˌpin, -z

benzoic
BR bɛnˈzəʊɪk
AM bɛnˈzoʊɪk

benzoin
BR ˈbɛnzəʊɪn
AM ˈbɛnzəwən, ˈbɛnzəˌwin

benzol
BR ˈbɛnzɒl
AM ˈbɛnˌzɔl, ˈbɛnˌzɑl

benzole
BR ˈbɛnzəʊl
AM ˈbɛnˌzoʊl

benzoyl
BR ˈbɛnzəʊɪl
AM ˈbɛnzəwəl

benzyl
BR ˈbɛnz(ɪ)l
AM ˈbɛnˌzil, ˈbɛnzəl

Beowulf
BR ˈbeɪə(ʊ)wʊlf
AM ˈbeɪəˌwʊlf

bequeath
BR bɪˈkwiː|ð, bɪˈkwiː|θ, -ðz\-θs, -ðɪŋ\-θɪŋ, -ðd\-θt
AM bəˈkwi|ð, bəˈkwi|θ, biˈkwi|ð, biˈkwi|θ, -ðz\-θs, -ðɪŋ\-θɪŋ, -ðd\-θt

bequeather
BR bɪˈkwiːðə(r), bɪˈkwiːθə(r), -z
AM bəˈkwiðər, bəˈkwiθər, biˈkwiðər, biˈkwiθər, -z

bequest
BR bɪˈkwɛst, -s
AM bəˈkwɛst, biˈkwɛst, -s

Bequia
BR ˈbɛkwi, ˈbɛkweɪ
AM ˈbɪkwiə

berate
BR bɪˈreɪt, -s, -ɪŋ, -ɪd
AM bəˈreɪ|t, biˈreɪ|t, -ts, -dɪŋ, -dɪd

Berber
BR ˈbəːbə(r), -z
AM ˈbərbər, -z

Berbera
BR ˈbəːb(ə)rə(r)
AM ˈbərbərə

berberine
BR ˈbəːbəriːn
AM ˈbərbəˌrin

berberis
BR ˈbəːb(ə)rɪs
AM ˈbərbərəs

berceuse
BR bɛːˈsəːz, -ɪz
AM bɛrˈsəz, -əz

Bere
BR bɪə(r)
AM bɪ(ə)r

bereave
BR bɪˈriːv, -z, -ɪŋ, -d
AM bəˈriv, biˈriv, -z, -ɪŋ, -d

bereavement
BR bɪˈriːvm(ə)nt
AM bəˈrivmənt, biˈrivmənt

bereft
BR bɪˈrɛft
AM bəˈrɛft, biˈrɛft

Berengaria
BR ˌbɛr(ə)ŋˈɡɛːrɪə(r)
AM ˌbɛrəŋˈɡɛriə

Berenice
BR ˌbɛrɪˈniːs, ˌbɛrɪˈnʌɪsi, ˌbɛrɪˈniːtʃeɪ, ˌbɛrɪˈniːtʃi
AM ˌbɛrəˈnis

Beresford
BR ˈbɛrɪsfəd, ˈbɛrɪzfəd
AM ˈbɛrəsfərd

beret
BR ˈbɛr|eɪ, ˈbɛr|i, -eɪz\-ɪz
AM bəˈreɪ, bɛˈreɪ, -z

Berg
BR bəːɡ
AM bərɡ

berg
BR bəːɡ, -z
AM bərɡ, -z

bergamasque
BR ˈbəːɡəmɑːsk, ˈbəːɡəmask, -s
AM ˈbərɡəˌmæsk, -s

Bergamo
BR ˈbəːɡəməʊ, ˈbɛːɡəməʊ
AM ˈbərɡəˌmoʊ

bergamot
BR ˈbəːɡəmɒt, -s

AM 'bərgə,mɑt, -s

Bergen
BR 'bəːg(ə)n, 'bɛːg(ə)n
AM 'bərgən

bergenia
BR bə'giːnɪə(r)
AM bər'giniə

Berger
BR 'bəːgə(r), 'bəːdʒə(r)
AM 'bərgər

Bergerac
BR 'bəːʒərak
AM 'bərʒə,ræk

Bergman
BR 'bəːgmən
AM 'bərgmən
SW bɛrj'man

bergschrund
BR 'bəːgʃrʊnd, 'bəːkʃrʊnt, -s
AM 'bərk,ʃrʊnt, -s

Bergson
BR 'bəːgsn
AM 'bərgsən

beribboned
BR bɪ'rɪb(ə)nd
AM bə'rɪbənd, bi'rɪbənd

beriberi
BR ,bɛrɪ'bɛri
AM ,bɛri'bɛri

Bering
BR 'bɛːrɪŋ
AM 'bɛrɪŋ
DAN 'beʌeŋ

berk
BR bəːk, -s
AM bərk, -s

Berkeleian
BR bɑː'kliːən, -z
AM 'bərkliən, 'bɑrkliən, -z

Berkeley[1]
places and names in Britain
BR 'bɑːkli
AM 'bɑrkli

Berkeley[2]
places and names in U.S.A.
BR 'bəːkli
AM 'bərkli

berkelium
BR bəː'kiːlɪəm
AM 'bərk(i)liəm

Berkhampstead
BR 'bəːkəmstɛd
AM 'bərkəm,stɛd

Berkley
BR 'bəːkli
AM 'bərkli

Berks
abbreviation of English county
BR bɑːks
AM bərks

Berkshire
BR 'bɑːkʃ(ɪ)ə(r)
AM 'bərkʃɪ(ə)r

Berlei
BR 'bəːli
AM 'bərli

Berlin
BR bəː'lɪn
AM bər'lɪn

Berliner
BR bəː'lɪnə(r), -z
AM bər'lɪnər, -z

Berlioz
BR 'bɛːlɪəʊz
AM 'bɛrli,oʊz

Berlitz
BR 'bəːlɪts
AM ,bər'lɪts

berm
BR bəːm, -z
AM bərm, -z

berme
BR bəːm, -z
AM bərm, -z

Bermondsey
BR 'bəːmən(d)zi
AM 'bərmənzi

Bermuda
BR bə'mjuːdə(r)
AM bər'mjudə

Bermudan
BR bə'mjuːdn, -z
AM bər'mjudən, -z

Bermudas
BR bə'mjuːdəz
AM bər'mjudəz

Bermudian
BR bə'mjuːdɪən, -z
AM bər'mjudiən, -z

Bern
BR bəːn, bɛːn
AM bərn, bɛrn

Bernadette
BR ,bəːnə'dɛt
AM ,bərnə'dɛt

Bernadotte
BR ,bəːnə'dɒt
AM ,bɛrnə'dɑt

Bernard[1]
British name
BR 'bəːnəd
AM 'bərnərd

Bernard[2]
U.S. name
BR bə'nɑːd
AM bər'nɑrd

Bernardette
BR ,bəːnə'dɛt
AM ,bərnə'dɛt

Berne
BR bəːn, bɛːn
AM bərn, bɛrn

Berners
BR 'bəːnəz
AM 'bərnərz

Bernese
BR ,bəː'niːz
AM ,bər'niz

Bernhardt
BR 'bəːnhɑːt
AM 'bərn,(h)ɑrt

Bernice
BR 'bəːnɪs, bə'niːs, bəː'niːs
AM bər'nis

Bernini
BR bə(ː)'niːni
AM bər'nini

Bernouilli
BR bə(ː)'nuːli
AM bər'nuli
FR bɛʀnuji

Bernstein
BR 'bəːnstʌɪn, 'bəːnstiːn
AM 'bərnstin, 'bərnstaɪn

Berol®
BR 'biːrɒl
AM 'bɛrəl

Berra
BR 'bɛrə(r)
AM 'bɛrə

Berridge
BR 'bɛrɪdʒ
AM 'bɛrɪdʒ

berry
BR 'bɛr|i, -ɪz, -ɪɪŋ, -ɪd
AM 'bɛri, -z, -ɪŋ, -d

berserk
BR bə(ː)'zəːk, bə(ː)'səːk
AM bər'sərk, bər'zərk

berserker
BR bə(ː)'zəːkə(r), bə(ː)'səːkə(r)
AM bər'sərkər, bər'zərkər, -z

Bert
BR bəːt
AM bərt

berth
BR bəːθ, -s, -ɪŋ, -t
AM bərθ, -s, -ɪŋ, -t

Bertha
BR 'bəːθə(r)
AM 'bərθə

Bertie
BR 'bəːti
AM 'bərdi

Bertolucci
BR ,bəːtə'luːtʃi
AM ,bərdə'lutʃi

Bertram
BR 'bəːtrəm
AM 'bərtrəm

Bertrand
BR 'bəːtr(ə)nd
AM 'bərtrən(d)

Berwick
BR 'bɛrɪk
AM 'bɛrɪk

Berwickshire
BR 'bɛrɪkʃ(ɪ)ə(r)
AM 'bər(w)ɪkʃɪ(ə)r

Berwyn
BR 'bɛːwɪn, 'bəːwɪn
AM 'bərwən

beryl
BR 'bɛrɪl, 'bɛrl̩, -z
AM 'bɛrəl, -z

berylliosis
BR bɪ,rɪlɪ'əʊsɪs
AM bə,rɪli'oʊsɪs

beryllium
BR bɪ'rɪlɪəm
AM bə'rɪliəm

Berzelius
BR bə'ziːlɪəs, bə'zeɪlɪəs
AM bər'ziliəs
SW bɛr'seːlɪəs

Bes
BR bɛs
AM bɛs

Besançon
BR 'bɛz(ə)nsɒn, bɪ'zɒ̃sɒ̃
AM ,bɛzən'sɔn

Besant
BR 'bɛsnt, 'bɛznt
AM 'bɛsənt

beseech
BR bɪ'siːtʃ, -ɪz, -ɪŋ, -t
AM bə'sitʃ, bi'sitʃ, -ɪz, -ɪŋ, -t

beseem
BR bɪ'siːm, -z, -ɪŋ, -d
AM bə'sim, bi'sim, -z, -ɪŋ, -d

beset
BR bɪ'sɛt, -s, -ɪŋ
AM bə'sɛ|t, bi'sɛ|t, -ts, -dɪŋ

besetment
BR bɪ'sɛtm(ə)nt
AM bə'sɛtmənt, bi'sɛtmənt

beshrew
BR bɪ'ʃruː, -z, -ɪŋ, -d
AM bə'ʃru, bi'ʃru, -z, -ɪŋ, -d

beside
BR bɪ'sʌɪd, -z
AM bə'saɪd, bi'saɪd, -z

besiege
BR bɪ'siːdʒ, -ɪz, -ɪŋ, -d
AM bə'sidʒ, bi'sidʒ, -ɪz, -ɪŋ, -d

besieger
BR bɪ'siːdʒə(r), -z
AM bə'sidʒər, bi'sidʒər, -z

beslaver
BR bɪ'slav|ə(r), bɪ'sleɪv|ə(r), -əz, -(ə)rɪŋ, -əd
AM bə'sleɪvər, bi'sleɪvər, -z, -ɪŋ, -d

beslobber
BR bɪ'slɒb|ə(r), -əz, -(ə)rɪŋ, -əd

AM bə'slɑbər, bi'slɑbər, -z, -ɪŋ, -d

besmear
BR bɪ'smɪə(r), -z, -ɪŋ, -d
AM bə'smɪ(ə)r, bi'smɪ(ə)r, -z, -ɪŋ, -d

besmirch
BR bɪ'sməːtʃ, -ɪz, -ɪŋ, -t
AM bə'smərtʃ, bi'smərtʃ, -əz, -ɪŋ, -t

besom
BR 'biːz(ə)m, 'bɪz(ə)m, -z
AM 'bizəm, 'bɛzəm, -z

besotted
BR bɪ'sɒtɪd
AM bə'sɑdəd, bi'sɑdəd

besottedly
BR bɪ'sɒtɪdli
AM bə'sɑdədli, bi'sɑdədli

besottedness
BR bɪ'sɒtɪdnɪs
AM bə'sɑdədnəs, bi'sɑdədnəs

besought
BR bɪ'sɔːt
AM bə'sɔt, bi'sɔt, bə'sɑt, bi'sɑt

bespangle
BR bɪ'spaŋg|l, -lz, -l̩ɪŋ\-lɪŋ, -ld
AM bə'spæŋg|əl, bi'spæŋg|əl, -əlz, -(ə)lɪŋ, -əld

bespatter
BR bɪ'spat|ə(r), -əz, -(ə)rɪŋ, -əd
AM bə'spædər, bi'spædər, -z, -ɪŋ, -d

bespeak
BR bɪ'spiːk, -s, -ɪŋ
AM bə'spik, bi'spik, -s, -ɪŋ

bespectacled
BR bɪ'spɛktəkld
AM bə'spɛktəkəld, bi'spɛktəkəld

bespoke
BR bɪ'spəʊk
AM bə'spoʊk, bi'spoʊk

bespoken
BR bɪ'spəʊk(ə)n
AM bə'spoʊkən, bi'spoʊkən

besprinkle
BR bɪ'sprɪŋk|l, -lz, -l̩ɪŋ\-lɪŋ, -ld
AM bə'sprɪŋk|əl, bi'sprɪŋk|əl, -əlz, -(ə)lɪŋ, -əld

Bess
BR bɛs
AM bɛs

Bessarabia
BR ˌbɛsə'reɪbɪə(r)
AM ˌbɛsə'reɪbiə
RUS bʲisa'rabʲijə

Bessarabian
BR ˌbɛsə'reɪbɪən, -z
AM ˌbɛsə'reɪbiən, -z

Bessel
BR 'bɛsl
AM 'bɛsəl

Bessemer
BR 'bɛsɪmə(r)
AM 'bɛs(ə)mər

Bessie
BR 'bɛsi
AM 'bɛsi

best
BR bɛst, -s, -ɪŋ, -ɪd
AM bɛst, -s, -ɪŋ, -əd

bestial
BR 'bɛstɪəl, 'bɛstʃl
AM 'bistʃəl, 'bisdiəl, 'bɛstʃəl, 'bɛsdiəl

bestialise
BR 'bɛstɪəlʌɪz, 'bɛstʃl̩ʌɪz, -ɪz, -ɪŋ, -d
AM 'bistʃəˌlaɪz, 'bisdiəˌlaɪz, 'bɛstʃəˌlaɪz, 'bɛsdiəˌlaɪz, -ɪz, -ɪŋ, -d

bestialism
BR 'bɛstɪəlɪz(ə)m, 'bɛstʃl̩ɪz(ə)m
AM 'bistʃəˌlɪzəm, 'bisdiəˌlɪzəm, 'bɛstʃəˌlɪzəm, 'bɛsdiəˌlɪzəm

bestiality
BR ˌbɛstɪ'alɪt|i, ˌbɛstʃɪ'alɪt|i, -ɪz
AM ˌbistʃi'ælədi, ˌbisdi'ælədi, ˌbɛstʃi'ælədi, ˌbɛsdi'ælədi, -z

bestialize
BR 'bɛstɪəlʌɪz, 'bɛstʃl̩ʌɪz, -ɪz, -ɪŋ, -d
AM 'bɛstʃəˌlaɪz, 'bistʃəˌlaɪz, -ɪz, -ɪŋ, -d

bestially
BR 'bɛstɪəli, 'bɛstʃl̩i
AM 'bistʃəli, 'bisdiəli, 'bɛstʃəli, 'bɛsdiəli

bestiary
BR 'bɛstɪər|i, 'bɛstʃər|i, -ɪz
AM 'bisdiˌɛri, 'bistʃiˌɛri, 'bɛsdiˌɛri, 'bɛstʃiˌɛri, -z

bestir
BR bɪ'stəː(r), -z, -ɪŋ, -d
AM bə'stər, bi'stər, -z, -ɪŋ, -d

bestow
BR bɪ'stəʊ, -z, -ɪŋ, -d
AM bə'stoʊ, bi'stoʊ, -z, -ɪŋ, -d

bestowal
BR bɪ'stəʊəl
AM bə'stoʊəl, bi'stoʊəl

bestowment
BR bɪ'stəʊm(ə)nt
AM bə'stoʊmənt, bi'stoʊmənt

bestrew
BR bɪ'struː, -z, -ɪŋ, -d
AM bə'stru, bi'stru, -z, -ɪŋ, -d

bestrewn
BR bɪ'struːn
AM bə'strun, bi'strun

bestridden
BR bɪ'strɪdn
AM bə'strɪdən, bi'strɪdən

bestride
BR bɪ'strʌɪd, -z, -ɪŋ
AM bə'straɪd, bi'straɪd, -z, -ɪŋ

bestrode
BR bɪ'strəʊd
AM bə'stroʊd, bi'stroʊd

bestseller
BR ˌbɛs(t)'sɛlə(r), -z
AM ˌbɛst'sɛlər, -z

Beswick
BR 'bɛzɪk
AM 'bɛzwɪk

bet
BR bɛt, -s, -ɪŋ, -ɪd
AM bɛ|t, -ts, -dɪŋ, -dəd

beta
BR 'biːtə(r), -z
AM 'beɪdə, -z

betake
BR bɪ'teɪk, -s, -ɪŋ
AM bə'teɪk, bi'teɪk, -s, -ɪŋ

betaken
BR bɪ'teɪk(ə)n
AM bə'teɪkən, bi'teɪkən

Betamax®
BR 'biːtəmaks
AM 'beɪdəˌmæks

betatron
BR 'biːtətrɒn, -z
AM 'beɪdəˌtrɑn, -z

betcha
BR 'bɛtʃə(r)
AM 'bɛtʃə

betel
BR 'biːtl
AM 'bidl

Betelgeuse
BR 'biːtl(d)ʒəːz, 'bɛtl(d)ʒəːz, 'biːtldʒuːs
AM 'bidlˌdʒus, 'bɛdlˌdʒus, 'bidlˌdʒuz, 'bɛdlˌdʒuz

bête noire
BR ˌbɛt 'nwɑː(r)
AM ˌbeɪt 'nwɑr, ˌbɛt +

bêtes noires
BR ˌbɛt 'nwɑː(r), + 'nwɑːz
AM ˌbeɪt 'nwɑrz, ˌbɛt +

Beth
BR bɛθ
AM bɛθ

Bethan
BR 'bɛθ(ə)n
AM 'bɛθən

Bethany
BR 'bɛθəni, 'bɛθn̩i
AM 'bɛθəni

Bethel
BR 'bɛθl, -z
AM 'bɛθəl, -z

Bethesda
BR bɪ'θɛzdə(r), bɛ'θɛzdə(r)
AM bə'θɛzdə

bethink
BR bɪ'θɪŋk, -s, -ɪŋ
AM bə'θɪŋk, bi'θɪŋk, -s, -ɪŋ

Bethlehem
BR 'bɛθlɪhɛm, 'bɛθlɪəm
AM 'bɛθləˌhɛm

Bethnal Green
BR ˌbɛθnl 'griːn
AM ˌbɛθnəl 'grin

bethought
BR bɪ'θɔːt
AM bə'θɔt, bi'θɔt, bə'θɑt, bi'θɑt

Bethune
surname
BR 'biːtn, bɪ'θjuːn, bɛ'θjuːn
AM bə'θ(j)un

Béthune
place in France
BR bɪ'θjuːn, bɛ'θjuːn, bɪ't(j)uːn, bɛ't(j)uːn
AM bə't(j)un
FR betyn

betide
BR bɪ'tʌɪd, -z
AM bə'taɪd, bi'taɪd, -z

betimes
BR bɪ'tʌɪmz
AM bə'taɪmz, bi'taɪmz

bêtise
BR beɪ'tiːz, -ɪz
AM beɪ'tiz, -ɪz

Betjeman
BR 'bɛtʃɪmən
AM 'bɛtʃəmən

betoken
BR bɪ'təʊk|(ə)n, -(ə)nz, -ənɪŋ\-n̩ɪŋ, -(ə)nd
AM bə'toʊkən, bi'toʊkən, -z, -ɪŋ, -d

betony
BR 'bɛtəni, 'bɛtn̩i
AM 'bɛtn̩i

betook
BR bɪ'tʊk
AM bə'tʊk, bi'tʊk

betray
BR bɪ'treɪ, -z, -ɪŋ, -d

AM bə'treɪ, bi'treɪ, -z, -ɪŋ, -d
betrayal
BR bɪ'treɪəl, -z
AM bə'treɪ(ə)l, bi'treɪ(ə)l, -z
betrayer
BR bɪ'treɪə(r), -z
AM bə'treɪər, bi'treɪər, -z
betroth
BR bɪ'trəʊ|ð, bɪ'trəʊ|θ, -ðz\-θs, -ðɪŋ\-θɪŋ, -ðd\-θt
AM bə'troʊ|ð, bə'trɔ|θ, bə'troʊ|θ, bi'troʊ|ð, bi'trɔ|θ, bi'troʊ|θ, bə'trɑ|θ, bi'trɑ|θ, -θs\-ðz, -θɪŋ\-ðɪŋ, -θt\-ðd
betrothal
BR bɪ'trəʊðl, -z
AM bə'troʊðəl, bə'trɔθəl, bə'troʊθəl, bi'troʊðəl, bi'trɔθəl, bi'troʊθəl, bə'trɑθəl, bi'trɑθəl, -z
Betsy
BR 'bɛtsi
AM 'bɛtsi
Bette
BR bɛt
AM bɛt
better
BR 'bɛt|ə(r), -əz, -(ə)rɪŋ, -əd
AM 'bɛdər, -z, -ɪŋ, -d
betterment
BR 'bɛtəm(ə)nt
AM 'bɛdərmənt
Betterton
BR 'bɛtət(ə)n
AM 'bɛdərt(ə)n
Betteshanger
BR 'bɛt(ɪ)s,haŋ(g)ə(r)
AM 'bɛdəs,(h)æŋər
Betti
BR 'bɛti
AM 'bɛdi
Bettina
BR bɪ'tiːnə(*r*)
AM bə'tinə
bettor
BR 'bɛtə(r), -z
AM 'bɛdər, -z
Betts
BR bɛts
AM bɛts
Bettws
BR 'bɛtəs
AM 'bɛdwz
Betty
BR 'bɛti
AM 'bɛdi
between
BR bɪ'twiːn
AM bə'twin, bi'twin
betweentimes
BR bɪ'twiːntʌɪmz
AM bə'twin,taɪmz, bi'twin,taɪmz
betwixt
BR bɪ'twɪkst
AM bə'twɪkst, bi'twɪkst
Betws-y-Coed
BR ˌbɛt(ə)s ə 'kɔɪd, + 'kəʊɪd
AM ˌbɛdəs ə 'kɔɪd
WE ˌbetʊs ʌ 'kɔɪd
Beulah
BR 'bjuːlə(*r*)
AM 'bjʊlə
Bevan
BR 'bɛvn
AM 'bɛvən
bevatron
BR 'bɛvətrɒn, -z
AM 'bɛvə,trɑn, -z
bevel
BR 'bɛv|l, -lz, -l̩ɪŋ\-əlɪŋ, -ld
AM 'bɛv|əl, -əlz, -(ə)lɪŋ, -əld
beverage
BR 'bɛv(ə)r|ɪdʒ, -ɪdʒɪz
AM 'bɛv(ə)rɪdʒ, -ɪz
Beveridge
BR 'bɛv(ə)rɪdʒ
AM 'bɛv(ə)rɪdʒ
Beverley
BR 'bɛvəli
AM 'bɛvərli
Beverly
BR 'bɛvəli
AM 'bɛvərli
Bevin
BR 'bɛvɪn
AM 'bɛvən
Bevis
BR 'bɛvɪs, 'biːvɪs
AM 'bivɪs
bevvy
BR 'bɛv|i, -ɪz, -ɪd
AM 'bɛvi, -z, -d
bevy
BR 'bɛv|i, -ɪz
AM 'bɛvi, -z
bewail
BR bɪ'weɪl, -z, -ɪŋ, -d
AM bə'weɪl, bi'weɪl, -z, -ɪŋ, -d
bewailer
BR bɪ'weɪlə(r), -z
AM bə'weɪlər, bi'weɪlər, -z
beware
BR bɪ'wɛː(r)
AM bə'wɛ(ə)r, ˌbi'wɛ(ə)r
Bewdley
BR 'bjuːdli
AM 'bjudli
Bewes
BR bjuːz
AM bjuz
bewhiskered
BR bɪ'wɪskəd
AM bə'wɪskərd, bi'wɪskərd
Bewick
BR 'bjuːɪk, -s
AM 'biwɪk, -s
bewigged
BR bɪ'wɪgd
AM bə'wɪgd, bi'wɪgd
bewilder
BR bɪ'wɪld|ə(r), -əz, -(ə)rɪŋ, -əd
AM bə'wɪldər, bi'wɪldər, -z, -ɪŋ, -d
bewilderingly
BR bɪ'wɪld(ə)rɪŋli
AM bə'wɪldərɪŋli, bi'wɪldərɪŋli
bewilderment
BR bɪ'wɪldəm(ə)nt
AM bə'wɪldərmənt, bi'wɪldərmənt
bewitch
BR bɪ'wɪtʃ, -ɪz, -ɪŋ, -t
AM bə'wɪtʃ, bi'wɪtʃ, -ɪz, -ɪŋ, -t
bewitchingly
BR bɪ'wɪtʃɪŋli
AM bə'wɪtʃɪŋli, bi'wɪtʃɪŋli
Bexhill
BR ˌbɛks'hɪl
AM ˌbɛks'hɪl
Bexley
BR 'bɛksli
AM 'bɛksli
Bexleyheath
BR ˌbɛkslɪ'hiːθ
AM ˌbɛksli'hiθ
bey
BR beɪ, -z
AM beɪ, -z
Beynon
BR 'bʌɪnən
AM 'baɪnən
beyond
BR bɪ'jɒnd
AM bi'(j)ɑnd
bezant
BR 'bɛz(ə)nt, -s
AM 'bɛznt, -s
bezel
BR 'bɛzl, -z
AM 'bɛzəl, -z
bezique
BR bɪ'ziːk
AM bə'zik
bezoar
BR 'biːzɔː(r), -z
AM 'bi,zɔ(ə)r, -z
Bhagavadgita
BR ˌbagəvəd'giːtə(*r*), ˌbʌgəvəd'giːtə(*r*)
AM ˌbɑgə,vɑd'gidə
bhagwan
BR 'bagwɑːn, bʌ'gwɑːn, -z
AM 'bɑg,wɑn, -z
bhaji
BR 'bʌdʒ|i, 'bɑːdʒ|i, -ɪz
AM 'bɑdʒi, -z
bhakti
BR 'bʌkti, 'bɑːkti
AM 'bɑkti
bhang
BR baŋ
AM bæŋ
bhangra
BR 'baŋgrə(*r*), 'bɑːŋgrə(*r*)
AM 'bæŋ(g)rə
bharal
BR 'bʌrəl, 'bʌrl̩, -z
AM 'bɑrəl, -z
Bhopal
BR bə(ʊ)'pɑːl
AM boʊ'pɑl
Bhutan
BR ˌbuː'tɑːn, bʊ'tɑːn
AM ˌbu'tɑn
Bhutanese
BR ˌbuːtə'niːz
AM ˌbudə'niz
Bhutto
BR 'buːtəʊ, 'bʊtəʊ
AM 'budoʊ
bi
BR bʌɪ, -z
AM baɪ, -z
Biafra
BR bɪ'afrə(*r*)
AM bi'æfrə
Biafran
BR bɪ'afrən, -z
AM bi'æfrən, -z
bialy
BR bɪ'ɑːl|i, -ɪz
AM bi'ɑli, -z
Bianca
BR bɪ'aŋkə(*r*)
AM bi'ɑŋkə
biannual
BR (ˌ)bʌɪ'anjʊəl, (ˌ)bʌɪ'anjʉl
AM ˌbaɪ'ænj(əw)əl
biannually
BR (ˌ)bʌɪ'anjʊəli, (ˌ)bʌɪ'anjʉli
AM ˌbaɪ'ænj(əw)əli
Biarritz
BR ˌbɪə'rɪts, 'bɪərɪts
AM 'biə,rɪts
bias
BR 'bʌɪəs, -ɪz, -ɪŋ, -t
AM 'baɪəs, -əz, -ɪŋ, -t
biathlete
BR bʌɪ'aθliːt, -s
AM baɪ'æθ(ə)lit, -s
biathlon
BR bʌɪ'aθlən, bʌɪ'aθlɒn, -z

AM baɪˈæθˌlɑn, -z

biaxal
BR ˌbʌɪˈaksl
AM ˌbaɪˈæksəl

biaxial
BR ˌbʌɪˈaksɪəl
AM ˌbaɪˈæksiəl

bib
BR bɪb, -z
AM bɪb, -z

bibber
BR ˈbɪbə(r), -z
AM ˈbɪbər, -z

bibelot
BR ˈbɪb(ə)ləʊ, -z
AM ˈbɪb(ə)ˌloʊ, -z

Bible
BR ˈbʌɪbl, -z
AM ˈbaɪbəl, -z

biblical
BR ˈbɪblɨkl
AM ˈbɪblɨkəl

biblically
BR ˈbɪblɨkli
AM ˈbɪblɨk(ə)li

bibliographer
BR ˌbɪblɪˈɒɡrəfə(r), -z
AM ˌbɪbliˈɑɡrəfər, -z

bibliographic
BR ˌbɪblɪəˈɡrafɪk
AM ˌbɪbliəˈɡræfɪk

bibliographical
BR ˌbɪblɪəˈɡrafɪkl
AM ˌbɪbliəˈɡræfəkəl

bibliographically
BR ˌbɪblɪəˈɡrafɪkli
AM ˌbɪbliəˈɡræfək(ə)li

bibliographise
BR ˌbɪblɪˈɒɡrəfʌɪz, -ɪz, -ɪŋ, -d
AM ˌbɪbliˈɑɡrəˌfaɪz, -ɪz, -ɪŋ, -d

bibliographize
BR ˌbɪblɪˈɒɡrəfʌɪz, -ɪz, -ɪŋ, -d
AM ˌbɪbliˈɑɡrəˌfaɪz, -ɪz, -ɪŋ, -d

bibliography
BR ˌbɪblɪˈɒɡrəf|i, -ɪz
AM ˌbɪbliˈɑɡrəfi, -z

bibliolater
BR ˌbɪblɪˈɒlətə(r), -z
AM ˌbɪbliˈɑlədər, -z

bibliolatry
BR ˌbɪblɪˈɒlətri
AM ˌbɪbliˈɑlətri

bibliomancy
BR ˈbɪblɪəˌmansi
AM ˈbɪbliəˌmænsi

bibliomania
BR ˌbɪblɪəˈmeɪnɪə(*r*)
AM ˌbɪbliəˈmeɪniə

bibliomaniac
BR ˌbɪblɪəˈmeɪnɪak
AM ˌbɪbliəˈmeɪniˌæk, -s

bibliophil
BR ˈbɪblɪə(ʊ)fɪl, -z
AM ˈbɪbliəˌfaɪl, -z

bibliophile
BR ˈbɪblɪə(ʊ)fʌɪl, -z
AM ˈbɪbliəˌfaɪl, -z

bibliophilic
BR ˌbɪblɪəˈfɪlɪk
AM ˌbɪbliəˈfɪlɪk

bibliophily
BR ˌbɪblɪˈɒfɨli, ˌbɪblɪˈɒfl̩i
AM ˌbɪbliˈɑfəli

bibliopole
BR ˈbɪblɪə(ʊ)pəʊl, -z
AM ˈbɪbliəˌpoʊl, -z

bibliopoly
BR ˌbɪblɪˈɒpəli, ˌbɪblɪˈɒpl̩i
AM ˌbɪbliˈɑpəli

bibulous
BR ˈbɪbjʉləs
AM ˈbɪbjələs

bibulousness
BR ˈbɪbjʉləsnəs
AM ˈbɪbjələsnəs

Bic®
BR bɪk, -s
AM bɪk, -s

bicameral
BR (ˌ)bʌɪˈkam(ə)rəl, (ˌ)bʌɪˈkam(ə)rl̩
AM ˌbaɪˈkæmərəl

bicameralism
BR (ˌ)bʌɪˈkam(ə)rəlɪz(ə)m, (ˌ)bʌɪˈkam(ə)rl̩ɪz(ə)m
AM ˌbaɪˈkæmərəˌlɪzəm

bicarb
BR ˈbʌɪkɑːb
AM ˈbaɪˌkɑrb

bicarbonate
BR (ˌ)bʌɪˈkɑːbənət, (ˌ)bʌɪˈkɑːbn̩ət
AM ˌbaɪˈkɑrbənət

bice
BR bʌɪs
AM baɪs

bicentenary
BR ˌbʌɪs(ɛ)nˈtiːnər|i, ˌbʌɪs(ɛ)nˈtɛnər|i, -ɪz
AM ˌbaɪsɛnˈtɛnəri, -z

bicentennial
BR ˌbʌɪs(ɛ)nˈtɛnɪəl, -z
AM ˌbaɪsənˈtɛniəl, -z

bicephalous
BR (ˌ)bʌɪˈsɛfələs, (ˌ)bʌɪˈsɛfl̩əs, (ˌ)bʌɪˈkɛf(ə)ləs, (ˌ)bʌɪˈkɛfl̩əs
AM baɪˈsɛfələs

biceps
BR ˈbʌɪsɛps
AM ˈbaɪˌsɛps

Bicester
BR ˈbɪstə(r)
AM ˈbɪ(sɛ)stər

bichir
BR ˈbɪʃɪə(r)
AM ˈbɪʃɪ(ə)r

bichloride
BR (ˌ)bʌɪˈklɔːrʌɪd, -z
AM baɪˈklɔˌraɪd, -z

bichromate
BR (ˌ)bʌɪˈkrəʊmeɪt, -s
AM baɪˈkroʊˌmeɪt, -s

bicker
BR ˈbɪk|ə(r), -əz, -(ə)rɪŋ, -əd
AM ˈbɪkər, -z, -ɪŋ, -d

bickerer
BR ˈbɪk(ə)rə(r), -z
AM ˈbɪkərər, -z

Bickerton
BR ˈbɪkət(ə)n
AM ˈbɪkərt(ə)n

bicolor
BR ˌbʌɪˈkʌlə(r), -z
AM ˌbaɪˈkələr, -z

bicolored
BR ˌbʌɪˈkʌləd, -z
AM ˌbaɪˈkələrd, -z

bicolour
BR ˌbʌɪˈkʌlə(r), -z
AM ˌbaɪˈkələr, -z

bicoloured
BR bʌɪˈkʌləd, -z
AM ˌbaɪˈkələrd, -z

biconcave
BR (ˌ)bʌɪˈkɒŋkeɪv
AM baɪˈkɑnkeɪv

biconcavity
BR ˌbʌɪkɒnˈkavɨti, ˌbʌɪkɒŋˈkavɨti, ˌbʌɪkənˈkavɨti, ˌbʌɪkəŋˈkavɨti
AM baɪˌkɑnˈkævədi

biconvex
BR (ˌ)bʌɪˈkɒnvɛks
AM baɪˈkɑnvɛks

biconvexity
BR ˌbʌɪkɒnˈvɛksɪti, ˌbʌɪk(ə)nˈvɛksɪti
AM baɪˌkɑnˈvɛksədi

bicultural
BR ˌbʌɪˈkʌltʃ(ə)rəl, ˌbʌɪˈkʌltʃ(ə)rl̩
AM baɪˈkəltʃ(ə)rəl

bicuspid
BR ˌbʌɪˈkʌspɪd, -z
AM baɪˈkəspəd, -z

bicuspidate
BR ˌbʌɪˈkʌspɨdeɪt
AM baɪˈkəspədət, baɪˈkəspəˌdeɪt

bicycle
BR ˈbʌɪsɪk|l, -lz, -l̩ɪŋ\-lɪŋ, -ld
AM ˈbaɪsɪk|əl, ˈbaɪˌsɪk|əl, -əlz, -(ə)lɪŋ, -əld

bicycler
BR ˈbʌɪsɪklə(r), -z
AM ˈbaɪsɪk(ə)lər, ˈbaɪˌsɪk(ə)lər, -z

bicyclist
BR ˈbʌɪsɪklɪst, -s
AM ˈbaɪˌsɪk(ə)ləst, ˈbaɪsɪkləst, -s

bid
BR bɪd, -z, -ɪŋ
AM bɪd, -z, -ɪŋ

biddability
BR ˌbɪdəˈbɪlɨti
AM ˌbɪdəˈbɪlɨdi

biddable
BR ˈbɪdəbl
AM ˈbɪdəbəl

Biddell
BR ˈbɪdl, bɪˈdɛl
AM ˈbɪdəl, bɪˈdɛl

bidden
BR ˈbɪdn
AM ˈbɪd(ə)n

bidder
BR ˈbɪdə(r), -z
AM ˈbɪdər, -z

Biddie
BR ˈbɪdi
AM ˈbɪdi

Biddle
BR ˈbɪdl
AM ˈbɪdəl

Biddulph
BR ˈbɪdʌlf
AM ˈbɪdəlf

biddy
BR ˈbɪd|i, -ɪz
AM ˈbɪdi, -z

bide
BR bʌɪd, -z, -ɪŋ, -ɨd
AM baɪd, -z, -ɪŋ, -ɨd

Bideford
BR ˈbɪdɨfəd
AM ˈbɪdəfərd

bidet
BR ˈbiːdeɪ, -z
AM bəˈdeɪ, biˈdeɪ, -z

bidialectal
BR ˌbʌɪdʌɪəˈlɛkt(ə)l
AM ˌbaɪˌdaɪəˈlɛktəl

bidialectalism
BR ˌbʌɪdʌɪəˈlɛktəlɪz(ə)m, ˌbʌɪdʌɪəˈlɛktl̩ɪz(ə)m
AM ˌbaɪˌdaɪˈlɛktəˌlɪzəm

bidonville
BR ˈbɪdnvɪl, -z
AM ˈbaɪdnˌvɪl, ˈbaɪdnvəl, -z

Biedermeier
BR ˈbiːdəmʌɪə(r)
AM ˈbidərˌmaɪər

Bielefeld
BR ˈbiːləfɛld, ˈbiːləfɛlt
AM ˈbiləˌfɛld

biennia
BR bʌɪˈɛnɪə(*r*)
AM baɪˈɛniə

biennial
BR bʌɪˈɛnɪəl
AM baɪˈɛniəl

biennially
BR bʌɪˈɛnɪəli
AM baɪˈɛniəli
biennium
BR bʌɪˈɛnɪəm, -z
AM baɪˈɛniəm, -z
bier
BR bɪə(r), -z
AM bɪ(ə)r, -z
Bierce
BR bɪəs
AM bɪərs
bierwurst
BR ˈbɪəwəːst, ˈbɪəvəːst, ˈbɪəvʊəst
AM ˈbɪrˌwərst, ˈbɪrˌvʊrst
biff
BR bɪf, -s, -ɪŋ, -t
AM bɪf, -s, -ɪŋ, -t
Biffen
BR ˈbɪfɪn
AM ˈbɪfən
biffin
BR ˈbɪfɪn, -z
AM ˈbɪfɪn, -z
Biffo
BR ˈbɪfəʊ
AM ˈbɪfoʊ
bifid
BR ˈbʌɪfɪd
AM ˈbaɪfɪd
bifida
BR ˈbɪfɪdə(*r*)
AM ˈbɪfɪdə
bifidly
BR ˈbʌɪfɪdli
AM ˈbaɪfɪdli
bifocal
BR ˌbʌɪˈfəʊkl, -z
AM ˈbaɪˌfoʊkəl, -z
bifoliate
BR ˌbʌɪˈfəʊlɪeɪt, ˌbʌɪˈfəʊlɪət
AM ˌbaɪˈfoʊliˌeɪt, ˌbaɪˈfoʊliət
bifurcate¹
adjective
BR ˌbʌɪˈfəːkeɪt, ˌbʌɪˈfəːkɪt
AM baɪˈfərˌkeɪt, baɪˈfərkət
bifurcate²
verb
BR ˈbʌɪfəkeɪt, -s, -ɪŋ, -ɪd
AM ˈbaɪfərˌkeɪ|t, -ts, -dɪŋ, -dɪd
bifurcation
BR ˌbʌɪfəːˈkeɪʃn, -z
AM ˌbaɪfərˈkeɪʃən, -z
big
BR bɪɡ, -ə(r), -ɪst
AM bɪɡ, -ər, -ɪst
bigamist
BR ˈbɪɡəmɪst, -s
AM ˈbɪɡəməst, -s
bigamous
BR ˈbɪɡəməs
AM ˈbɪɡəməs
bigamously
BR ˈbɪɡəməsli
AM ˈbɪɡəməsli
bigamy
BR ˈbɪɡəmi
AM ˈbɪɡəmi
Bigelow
BR ˈbɪɡɪləʊ
AM ˈbɪɡəˌloʊ
biggie
BR ˈbɪɡ|i, -ɪz
AM ˈbɪɡi, -z
biggish
BR ˈbɪɡɪʃ
AM ˈbɪɡɪʃ
Biggles
BR ˈbɪɡlz
AM ˈbɪɡ(ə)lz
Biggleswade
BR ˈbɪɡlzweɪd
AM ˈbɪɡ(ə)lzˌweɪd
Biggs
BR bɪɡz
AM bɪɡz
bighead
BR ˈbɪɡhɛd, -z, -ɪd
AM ˈbɪɡˌ(h)ɛd, -z, -əd
bigheadedness
BR ˌbɪɡˈhɛdɪdnɪs
AM ˌbɪɡˈhɛdədnəs
bighorn
BR ˈbɪɡhɔːn, -z
AM ˈbɪɡˌ(h)ɔ(ə)rn, -z
bight
BR bʌɪt, -s
AM baɪt, -s
bigmouth
BR ˈbɪɡmaʊ|θ, -ðz
AM ˈbɪɡˌmaʊ|θ, -ðz
bigness
BR ˈbɪɡnɪs
AM ˈbɪɡnɪs
bigot
BR ˈbɪɡət, -s, -ɪd
AM ˈbɪɡə|t, -ts, -dəd
bigotry
BR ˈbɪɡətri
AM ˈbɪɡətri
bigraph
BR ˈbʌɪɡrɑːf, ˈbʌɪɡraf, -s
AM ˈbaɪˌɡræf, -s
bigwig
BR ˈbɪɡwɪɡ, -z
AM ˈbɪɡˌwɪɡ, -z
Bihar
BR bɪˈhɑː(r)
AM biˈhɑr
Bihari
BR bɪˈhɑːr|i, -ɪz
AM bəˈhɑri, -z
bijou
BR ˈbiːʒuː, -z
AM ˈbiˈʒu, -z
bijouterie
BR biːˈʒuːt(ə)ri
AM biˌʒudəˈri
bijoux
BR ˈbiːʒuː(z)
AM ˈbiˈʒu(z)
bike
BR bʌɪk, -s, -ɪŋ, -t
AM baɪk, -s, -ɪŋ, -t
biker
BR ˈbʌɪkə(r), -z
AM ˈbaɪkər, -z
bikini
BR bɪˈkiːn|i, -ɪz
AM bɪˈkini, -z
Biko
BR ˈbiːkəʊ
AM ˈbikoʊ
bilabial
BR (ˌ)bʌɪˈleɪbɪəl, -z
AM ˌbaɪˈleɪbiəl, -z
bilabially
BR (ˌ)bʌɪˈleɪbɪəli
AM ˌbaɪˈleɪbiəli
bilateral
BR (ˌ)bʌɪˈlat(ə)rəl, (ˌ)bʌɪˈlat(ə)rl
AM ˌbaɪˈlædərəl
bilateralism
BR (ˌ)bʌɪˈlat(ə)rəlɪz(ə)m, (ˌ)bʌɪˈlat(ə)rl̩ɪz(ə)m
AM ˌbaɪˈlædərəˌlɪzəm
bilaterally
BR (ˌ)bʌɪˈlat(ə)rəli, (ˌ)bʌɪˈlat(ə)rl̩i
AM ˌbaɪˈlædərəli
Bilbao
BR bɪlˈbaʊ
AM bɪlˈbaʊ
bilberry
BR ˈbɪlb(ə)r|i, -ɪz
AM ˈbɪlˌbɛri, -z
bilbo
BR ˈbɪlbəʊ, -z
AM ˈbɪlboʊ, -z
Bildungsroman
BR ˈbɪldʊŋsrə(ʊ)ˌmɑːn
AM ˈbɪldʊŋzˌroʊˌmɑn
Bildungsromane
BR ˈbɪldʊŋsrə(ʊ)ˌmɑːnə(*r*)
AM ˈbɪldʊŋzˌroʊˌmɑnə
bile
BR bʌɪl
AM baɪl
bilge
BR bɪldʒ, -ɪz
AM bɪldʒ, -ɪz
bilgepump
BR ˈbɪldʒpʌmp, -s
AM ˈbɪldʒˌpəmp, -s
bilharzia
BR bɪlˈhɑːtsɪə(*r*), bɪlˈhɑːzɪə(*r*)
AM bɪlˈhɑrziə
bilharziasis
BR ˌbɪlhɑːˈtsʌɪəsɪs, ˌbɪlhɑːˈzʌɪəsɪs
AM ˌbɪlˌ(h)ɑrˈzaɪəsəs
biliary
BR ˈbɪlɪəri
AM ˈbɪliˌɛri, ˈbɪljəri
bilingual
BR (ˌ)bʌɪˈlɪŋɡw(ə)l
AM ˌbaɪˈlɪŋɡwəl
bilingualism
BR (ˌ)bʌɪˈlɪŋɡwəlɪz(ə)m, (ˌ)bʌɪˈlɪŋɡwl̩ɪz(ə)m
AM ˌbaɪˈlɪŋɡwəˌlɪzəm
bilious
BR ˈbɪlɪəs
AM ˈbɪliəs, ˈbɪljəs
biliously
BR ˈbɪlɪəsli
AM ˈbɪliəsli, ˈbɪljəsli
biliousness
BR ˈbɪlɪəsnəs
AM ˈbɪliəsnəs, ˈbɪljəsnəs
bilirubin
BR ˌbɪlɪˈruːbɪn
AM ˈbɪliˌrubən
bilk
BR bɪlk, -s, -ɪŋ, -t
AM bɪlk, -s, -ɪŋ, -t
bilker
BR ˈbɪlkə(r), -z
AM ˈbɪlkər, -z
bill
BR bɪl, -z, -ɪŋ, -d
AM bɪl, -z, -ɪŋ, -d
billable
BR ˈbɪləbl
AM ˈbɪləbəl
billabong
BR ˈbɪləbɒŋ, -z
AM ˈbɪləˌbɔŋ, ˈbɪləˌbɑŋ, -z
billboard
BR ˈbɪlbɔːd, -z
AM ˈbɪlˌbɔ(ə)rd, -z
Billericay
BR ˌbɪləˈrɪki
AM ˌbɪləˈrɪki
billet
BR ˈbɪlɪt, -s, -ɪŋ, -ɪd
AM ˈbɪlɪ|t, -ts, -dɪŋ, -dɪd
billet-doux
BR ˌbɪleɪˈduː, ˌbɪlɪˈduː
AM ˌbɪleɪˈdu
billetee
BR ˌbɪlɪˈtiː, -z
AM ˌbɪləˈti, -z
billeter
BR ˈbɪlɪtə(r), -z
AM ˈbɪlədər, -z
billets-doux
BR ˌbɪleɪˈduːz, ˌbɪlɪˈduːz
AM ˌbɪleɪˈduz
billfold
BR ˈbɪlfəʊld, -z
AM ˈbɪlˌfoʊld, -z
billhead
BR ˈbɪlhɛd, -z
AM ˈbɪlˌ(h)ɛd, -z

billhook
BR ˈbɪlhʊk, -s
AM ˈbɪlˌ(h)ʊk, -s

billiard
BR ˈbɪljəd, -z
AM ˈbɪljərd, -z

Billie
BR ˈbɪli
AM ˈbɪli

Billingham
BR ˈbɪlɪŋəm
AM ˈbɪlɪŋˌ(h)æm

Billingsgate
BR ˈbɪlɪŋzgeɪt
AM ˈbɪlɪŋzˌgeɪt

Billingshurst
BR ˈbɪlɪŋzhəːst
AM ˈbɪlɪŋzˌ(h)ərst

billion
BR ˈbɪljən, -z
AM ˈbɪljən, -z

billionaire
BR ˌbɪljəˈnɛː(r), -z
AM ˈbɪljəˌnɛ(ə)r, -z

billionairess
BR ˌbɪljəˈnɛːrɪs, ˌbɪljəˈnɛːrɛs, -ɪz
AM ˈbɪljəˌnɛrəs, -əz

billionth
BR ˈbɪljənθ, -s
AM ˈbɪljənθ, -s

billon
BR ˈbɪlən
AM ˈbɪlən

billow
BR ˈbɪləʊ, -z, -ɪŋ, -d
AM ˈbɪl|oʊ, -oʊz, -əwɪŋ, -oʊd

billowy
BR ˈbɪləʊi
AM ˈbɪləwi

billposter
BR ˈbɪlˌpəʊstə(r), -z
AM ˈbɪlˌpoʊstər, -z

billposting
BR ˈbɪlˌpəʊstɪŋ
AM ˈbɪlˌpoʊstɪŋ

billsticker
BR ˈbɪlˌstɪkə(r), -z
AM ˈbɪlˌstɪkər, -z

billy
BR ˈbɪl|i, -ɪz
AM ˈbɪli, -z

billybong
BR ˈbɪlɪbɒŋ, -z
AM ˈbɪlɪˌbɔŋ, ˈbɪlɪˌbɑŋ, -z

billycan
BR ˈbɪlɪkan, -z
AM ˈbɪliˌkæn, -z

billycock
BR ˈbɪlɪkɒk, -s
AM ˈbɪliˌkɑk, -s

billy-o
BR ˈbɪlɪəʊ
AM ˈbɪliˌoʊ

billy-oh
BR ˈbɪlɪəʊ
AM ˈbɪliˌoʊ

bilobate
BR ˌbʌɪˈləʊbeɪt
AM baɪˈloʊˌbeɪt

bilobed
BR ˌbʌɪˈləʊbd
AM baɪˈloʊbd

Biloxi
BR bɪˈlʌksi, bɪˈlɒksi
AM bəˈləksi

biltong
BR ˈbɪltɒŋ
AM ˈbɪlˌtɔŋ, ˈbɪlˌtɑŋ

bimanal
BR (ˌ)bʌɪˈmeɪnl, ˈbɪmənl
AM baɪˈmeɪnl, ˈbɪmənəl

bimanous
BR ˈbɪmənəs
AM ˈbɪmənəs

bimbashi
BR bɪmˈbaʃ|i, -ɪz
AM bɪmˈbæʃi, -z

bimbo
BR ˈbɪmbəʊ, -z
AM ˈbɪmboʊ, -z

bi-media
BR ˌbʌɪˈmiːdɪə(r)
AM ˌbaɪˈmidiə

bimetallic
BR ˌbʌɪmɪˈtalɪk, ˌbʌɪmɛˈtalɪk
AM ˌbaɪməˈtælɪk

bimetallism
BR ˌbʌɪˈmɛtl̩ɪz(ə)m
AM ˌbaɪˈmɛdlˌɪzəm

bimetallist
BR ˌbʌɪˈmɛtl̩ɪst, -s
AM ˌbaɪˈmɛdləst, -s

bimillenary
BR ˌbʌɪmɪˈlɛn(ə)r|i, ˌbʌɪmɪˈliːn(ə)r|i, ˌbʌɪˈmɪlɪn(ə)r|i, -ɪz
AM baɪˈmɪləˌnɛri, -z

bimodal
BR (ˌ)bʌɪˈməʊdl
AM ˌbaɪˈmoʊdəl

bimodality
BR ˌbʌɪmə(ʊ)ˈdalɪti
AM ˌbaɪˌmoʊˈdælədi

bimonthly
BR (ˌ)bʌɪˈmʌnθl|i, -ɪz
AM ˌbaɪˈmənθli, -z

bin
BR bɪn, -z, -ɪŋ, -d
AM bɪn, -z, -ɪŋ, -d

binary
BR ˈbʌɪn(ə)r|i, -ɪz
AM ˈbaɪnəri, ˈbaɪˌnɛri, -z

binate
BR ˈbʌɪneɪt
AM ˈbaɪˌneɪt

binaural
BR (ˌ)bʌɪˈnɔːrəl, (ˌ)bʌɪˈnɔːrl̩
AM ˌbaɪˈnɔrəl

Binchy
BR ˈbɪn(t)ʃi
AM ˈbɪn(t)ʃi

bind
BR bʌɪnd, -z, -ɪŋ
AM baɪnd, -z, -ɪŋ

binder
BR ˈbʌɪndə(r), -z
AM ˈbaɪndər, -z

bindery
BR ˈbʌɪnd(ə)r|i, -ɪz
AM ˈbaɪnd(ə)ri, -z

bindi-eye
BR ˈbɪndɪʌɪ
AM ˈbɪn(d)iˌaɪ

binding
BR ˈbʌɪndɪŋ, -z
AM ˈbaɪndɪŋ, -z

bindweed
BR ˈbʌɪndwiːd
AM ˈbaɪn(d)ˌwid

bine
BR bʌɪn, -z
AM baɪn, -z

bin-end
BR ˈbɪnɛnd, -z
AM ˈbɪnˌɛnd, -z

Binet
BR ˈbiːneɪ
AM bəˈneɪ

bing
BR bɪŋ, -z
AM bɪŋ, -z

binge
BR bɪn(d)ʒ, -ɪz, -ɪŋ, -d
AM bɪndʒ, -ɪz, -ɪŋ, -d

Bingen
BR ˈbɪŋən
AM ˈbɪŋən

Bingham
BR ˈbɪŋəm
AM ˈbɪŋəm

Bingley
BR ˈbɪŋli
AM ˈbɪŋgli

bingo
BR ˈbɪŋgəʊ
AM ˈbɪŋgoʊ

binman
BR ˈbɪnman
AM ˈbɪnˌmæn

binmen
BR ˈbɪnmɛn
AM ˈbɪnˌmɛn

binnacle
BR ˈbɪnəkl, -z
AM ˈbɪnəkəl, -z

Binnie
BR ˈbɪni
AM ˈbɪni

Binns
BR bɪnz
AM bɪnz

binocular
adjective
BR (ˌ)bʌɪˈnɒkjʊlə(r), bɪˈnɒkjʊlə(r)
AM bəˈnɑkjələr, baɪˈnɑkjələr

binoculars
noun
BR bɪˈnɒkjʊləz
AM bəˈnɑkjələrz

binomial
BR (ˌ)bʌɪˈnəʊmɪəl
AM baɪˈnoʊmiəl

binomially
BR (ˌ)bʌɪˈnəʊmɪəli
AM baɪˈnoʊmiəli

binominal
BR (ˌ)bʌɪˈnɒmɪnl
AM baɪˈnɑmənəl

bint
BR bɪnt, -s
AM bɪnt, -s

Binyon
BR ˈbɪnjən
AM ˈbɪnjən

bio
BR ˈbʌɪəʊ
AM ˈbaɪoʊ

bioceramic
BR ˌbʌɪə(ʊ)sɪˈramɪk, -s
AM ˌbaɪoʊsəˈræmɪk, -s

biochemical
BR ˌbʌɪə(ʊ)ˈkɛmɪkl
AM ˌbaɪoʊˈkɛməkəl

biochemist
BR ˌbʌɪə(ʊ)ˈkɛmɪst, -s
AM ˌbaɪoʊˈkɛməst, ˌbaɪəˈkɛməst, -s

biochemistry
BR ˌbʌɪə(ʊ)ˈkɛmɪstri
AM ˌbaɪoʊˈkɛməstri, ˌbaɪəˈkɛməstri

biochip
BR ˈbʌɪəʊtʃɪp, -s
AM ˈbaɪoʊˌtʃɪp, -s

biocoenology
BR ˌbʌɪə(ʊ)sɪˈnɒlədʒi
AM ˌbaɪoʊsiˈnɑlədʒi, ˌbaɪəsiˈnɑlədʒi

biocoenoses
BR ˌbʌɪə(ʊ)sɪˈnəʊsiːz
AM ˌbaɪoʊsəˈnoʊsiz, ˌbaɪəsəˈnoʊsiz

biocoenosis
BR ˌbʌɪə(ʊ)sɪˈnəʊsɪs
AM ˌbaɪoʊsəˈnoʊsəs, ˌbaɪəsəˈnoʊsəs

biocoenotic
BR ˌbʌɪə(ʊ)sɪˈnɒtɪk
AM ˌbaɪoʊsəˈnɑdɪk, ˌbaɪəsəˈnɑdɪk

biocompatibility
BR ˌbʌɪəʊkəmˌpatɪˈbɪlɪti
AM ˌbaɪoʊkəmˌpædəˈbɪlɪdi, ˌbaɪəkəmˌpædəˈbɪlɪdi

biocompatible
BR ˌbʌɪə(ʊ)kəmˈpatɪbl

AM ˌbaɪoʊkəmˈpædəbəl, ˌbaɪəkəmˈpædəbəl

biocomputing
BR ˌbʌɪə(ʊ)kəmˈpjuːtɪŋ
AM ˌbaɪoʊkəmˈpjudɪŋ, ˌbaɪəkəmˈpjudɪŋ

biocontrol
BR ˌbʌɪəʊkənˈtrəʊl
AM ˌbaɪoʊkənˈtroʊl, ˌbaɪəkənˈtroʊl

biodata
BR ˈbʌɪə(ʊ)ˌdeɪtə(r)
AM ˈbaɪoʊˌdædə

biodegradability
BR ˌbʌɪə(ʊ)dɪˌgreɪdəˈbɪlɪti
AM ˌbaɪoʊdəˌgreɪdəˈbɪlɪdi, ˌbaɪoʊdiˌgreɪdəˈbɪlɪdi

biodegradable
BR ˌbʌɪə(ʊ)dɪˈgreɪdəbl
AM ˌbaɪoʊdəˈgreɪdəbəl, ˌbaɪoʊdiˈgreɪdəbəl

biodegradation
BR ˌbʌɪə(ʊ)ˌdɛgrəˈdeɪʃn
AM ˌbaɪoʊˌdɛgrəˈdeɪʃən

biodiversity
BR ˌbʌɪə(ʊ)dʌɪˈvəːsɪti
AM ˌbaɪoʊdəˈvərsədi, ˌbaɪoʊˌdaɪˈvərsədi

bioenergetic
BR ˌbʌɪəʊˌɛnəˈdʒɛtɪk
AM ˌbaɪoʊˌɛnərˈdʒɛdɪk

bioenergy
BR ˌbʌɪəʊˈɛnədʒi
AM ˌbaɪoʊˈɛnərdʒi

bioengineer
BR ˌbʌɪəʊˌɛndʒɪˈnɪə(r), -z, -ɪŋ
AM ˌbaɪoʊˈɛndʒənɪ(ə)r, -z, -ɪŋ

bioethicist
BR ˌbʌɪəʊˈɛθɪsɪst, -s
AM ˌbaɪoʊˈɛθəsəst, -s

bioethics
BR ˌbʌɪəʊˈɛθɪks
AM ˌbaɪoʊˈɛθɪks

biofeedback
BR ˌbʌɪəʊˈfiːdbak
AM ˌbaɪoʊˈfidˌbæk

bioflavonoid
BR ˌbʌɪəʊˈfleɪvɪnɔɪd
AM ˌbaɪoʊˈfleɪvəˌnɔɪd

biogas
BR ˈbʌɪə(ʊ)gas
AM ˈbaɪoʊˌgæs

biogenesis
BR ˌbʌɪə(ʊ)ˈdʒɛnɪsɪs
AM ˌbaɪoʊˈdʒɛnəsəs

biogenetic
BR ˌbʌɪə(ʊ)dʒɪˈnɛtɪk
AM ˌbaɪoʊdʒəˈnɛdɪk

biogenic
BR ˌbʌɪə(ʊ)ˈdʒɛnɪk
AM ˌbaɪoʊˈdʒɛnɪk

biogeographic
BR ˌbʌɪə(ʊ)ˌdʒɪəˈgrafɪk
AM ˌbaɪoʊˌdʒiəˈgræfɪk

biogeographical
BR ˌbʌɪə(ʊ)ˌdʒɪəˈgrafɪkl
AM ˌbaɪoʊˌdʒiəˈgræfəkəl

biogeography
BR ˌbʌɪə(ʊ)dʒɪˈɒgrəfi
AM ˌbaɪoʊdʒiˈɑgrəfi

biograph
BR ˈbʌɪə(ʊ)grɑːf, ˈbʌɪə(ʊ)graf, -s
AM ˈbaɪəˌgræf, -s

biographer
BR bʌɪˈɒgrəfə(r), -z
AM ˌbaɪˈɑgrəfər, -z

biographic
BR ˌbʌɪəˈgrafɪk
AM ˌbaɪəˈgræfɪk

biographical
BR ˌbʌɪəˈgrafɪkl
AM ˌbaɪəˈgræfəkəl

biographically
BR ˌbʌɪəˈgrafɪkli
AM ˌbaɪəˈgræfək(ə)li

biography
BR bʌɪˈɒgrəf|i, -ɪz
AM baɪˈɑgrəfi, -z

biological
BR ˌbʌɪəˈlɒdʒɪkl
AM ˌbaɪəˈlɑdʒəkəl

biologically
BR ˌbʌɪəˈlɒdʒɪkli
AM ˌbaɪəˈlɑdʒək(ə)li

biologist
BR bʌɪˈɒlədʒɪst, -s
AM baɪˈɑlədʒəst, -s

biology
BR bʌɪˈɒlədʒi
AM baɪˈɑlədʒi

bioluminescence
BR ˌbʌɪəʊˌl(j)uːmɪˈnɛsns
AM ˌbaɪəˌluməˈnɛs(ə)ns

bioluminescent
BR ˌbʌɪəʊˌl(j)uːmɪˈnɛsnt
AM ˌbaɪəˌluməˈnɛs(ə)nt

biomass
BR ˈbʌɪə(ʊ)mas
AM ˈbaɪoʊˌmæs

biomaterial
BR ˌbʌɪə(ʊ)məˈtɪərɪəl, -z
AM ˌbaɪəməˈtɪriəl, -z

biomathematics
BR ˌbʌɪə(ʊ)maθ(ɪ)ˈmatɪks
AM ˌbaɪəˌmæθˈmædɪks

biome
BR ˈbʌɪəʊm, -z
AM ˈbaɪˌoʊm, -z

biomechanics
BR ˌbʌɪə(ʊ)mɪˈkanɪks
AM ˌbaɪəməˈkænɪks

biomedical
BR ˌbʌɪə(ʊ)ˈmɛdɪkl
AM ˌbaɪəˈmɛdəkəl

biomedicine
BR ˌbʌɪəʊˈmɛd(ɪ)s(ɪ)n
AM ˌbaɪəˈmɛd(ə)sən

biometric
BR ˌbʌɪə(ʊ)ˈmɛtrɪk, -s
AM ˌbaɪoʊˈmɛtrɪk, -s

biometrical
BR ˌbʌɪə(ʊ)ˈmɛtrɪkl
AM ˌbaɪoʊˈmɛtrəkəl

biometrician
BR ˌbʌɪə(ʊ)mɪˈtrɪʃn, -z
AM ˌbaɪoʊməˈtrɪʃən, -z

biometry
BR bʌɪˈɒmɪtri
AM baɪˈɑmətri

biomorph
BR ˈbʌɪə(ʊ)mɔːf, -s
AM ˈbaɪəˌmɔ(ə)rf, -s

biomorphic
BR ˌbʌɪə(ʊ)ˈmɔːfɪk
AM ˌbaɪəˈmɔrfɪk

bionic
BR bʌɪˈɒnɪk, -s
AM baɪˈɑnɪk, -s

bionically
BR bʌɪˈɒnɪkli
AM baɪˈɑnək(ə)li

bionomic
BR ˌbʌɪə(ʊ)ˈnɒmɪk, -s
AM baɪˈnɑmɪk, -s

biophysic
BR ˌbʌɪə(ʊ)ˈfɪzɪk, -s
AM ˌbaɪoʊˈfɪzɪk, -s

biophysical
BR ˌbʌɪə(ʊ)ˈfɪzɪkl
AM ˌbaɪoʊˈfɪzɪkəl

biophysically
BR ˌbʌɪə(ʊ)ˈfɪzɪkli
AM ˌbaɪoʊˈfɪzɪkəl(ə)li

biophysicist
BR ˌbʌɪə(ʊ)ˈfɪzɪsɪst, -s
AM ˌbaɪoʊˈfɪzɪsɪst, -s

biopic
BR ˈbʌɪə(ʊ)pɪk, -s
AM ˈbaɪoʊˌpɪk, -s

biopsy
BR ˈbʌɪɒps|i, -ɪz
AM ˈbaɪˌɑpsi, -z

biorhythm
BR ˈbʌɪə(ʊ)ˌrɪðm, -z
AM ˈbaɪoʊˌrɪðəm, -z

biorhythmic
BR ˌbʌɪə(ʊ)ˈrɪðmɪk
AM ˌbaɪoʊˈrɪðmɪk

biorhythmically
BR ˌbʌɪə(ʊ)ˈrɪðmɪkli
AM ˌbaɪoʊˈrɪðmɪk(ə)li

bioscope
BR ˈbʌɪəskəʊp, -s
AM ˈbaɪəsˌkoʊp, -s

biosensor
BR ˈbʌɪə(ʊ)ˌsɛnsə(r), -z
AM ˈbaɪoʊˌsɛnsər, ˈbaɪəˌsɛnsər, -z

biosphere
BR ˈbʌɪəsfɪə(r)
AM ˈbaɪəˌsfɪ(ə)r

biosyntheses
BR ˌbʌɪə(ʊ)ˈsɪnθɪsiːz
AM ˌbaɪoʊˈsɪnθəsiz

biosynthesis
BR ˌbʌɪə(ʊ)ˈsɪnθɪsɪs
AM ˌbaɪoʊˈsɪnθəsəs

biosynthetic
BR ˌbʌɪə(ʊ)sɪnˈθɛtɪk
AM ˌbaɪoʊˌsɪnˈθɛdɪk

biota
BR bʌɪˈəʊtə(r)
AM baɪˈoʊdə

biotechnologist
BR ˌbʌɪə(ʊ)tɛkˈnɒlədʒɪst, -s
AM ˌbaɪoʊˌtɛkˈnɑlədʒəst, -s

biotechnology
BR ˌbʌɪə(ʊ)tɛkˈnɒlədʒi
AM ˌbaɪoʊˌtɛkˈnɑlədʒi

biotic
BR bʌɪˈɒtɪk
AM baɪˈɑdɪk

biotin
BR ˈbʌɪətɪn, -z
AM ˈbaɪətn, -z

biotite
BR ˈbʌɪətʌɪt, -s
AM ˈbaɪəˌtaɪt, -s

biparous
BR ˈbɪp(ə)rəs
AM ˈbɪpərəs

bipartisan
BR ˌbʌɪpɑːtɪˈzan, bʌɪˈpɑːtɪz(ə)n
AM baɪˈpɑrdəz(ə)n

bipartisanship
BR ˌbʌɪpɑːtɪˈzanʃɪp, bʌɪˈpɑːtɪz(ə)nʃɪp
AM baɪˈpɑrdəzənˌʃɪp

bipartite
BR (ˌ)bʌɪˈpɑːtʌɪt
AM baɪˈpɑrˌtaɪt

biped
BR ˈbʌɪpɛd, -z
AM ˈbaɪˌpɛd, -z

bipedal
BR ˌbʌɪˈpiːdl, ˌbʌɪˈpɛdl
AM ˌbaɪˈpɛdəl, ˌbaɪˈpidəl

bipedalism
BR ˌbʌɪˈpiːdlɪz(ə)m, ˌbʌɪˈpɛdlɪz(ə)m
AM ˌbaɪˈpɛdlˌɪzəm, ˌbaɪˈpidlˌɪzəm

bipedality
BR ˌbʌɪpɛˈdalɪti, ˌbʌɪpɪˈdalɪti
AM ˌbaɪpəˈdælədi

biphenyl
BR ˌbʌɪˈfiːnʌɪl, ˌbʌɪˈfɛnɪl, -z
AM baɪˈfɛnəl, -z

bipinnate
BR ˌbʌɪˈpɪneɪt, ˌbʌɪˈpɪnɪt
AM baɪˈpɪnɪt

biplane
BR ˈbʌɪpleɪn, -z
AM ˈbaɪˌpleɪn, -z

bipolar
BR ˌbʌɪˈpəʊlə(r)
AM baɪˈpoʊlər

bipolarity
BR ˌbʌɪpə(ʊ)ˈlarɪti
AM ˌbaɪpoʊˈlɛrədi

biquadratic
BR ˌbʌɪkwɒˈdratɪk, ˌbʌɪkwəˈdratɪk, -s
AM ˌbaɪkwɑˈdrædɪk, ˌbaɪkwəˈdrædɪk, -s

birch
BR bəːtʃ, -ɨz, -ɪŋ, -t
AM bərtʃ, -əz, -ɪŋ, -t

birchen
BR ˈbəːtʃn
AM ˈbərtʃən

birchwood
BR ˈbəːtʃwʊd
AM ˈbərtʃˌwʊd

bird
BR bəːd, -z
AM bərd, -z

birdbath
BR ˈbəːd|bɑːθ, ˈbəːd|baθ, -bɑːðz\-bɑːθs\-baθs
AM ˈbərdˌbæ|θ, -θs\-ðz

birdbrain
BR ˈbəːdbreɪn, -z, -d
AM ˈbərdˌbreɪn, -z, -d

birdcage
BR ˈbəːdkeɪdʒ, -ɨz
AM ˈbərdˌkeɪdʒ, -ɨz

birder
BR ˈbəːdə(r), -z
AM ˈbərdər, -z

birdie
BR ˈbəːd|i, -ɪz
AM ˈbərdi, -z

birdlime
BR ˈbəːdlʌɪm
AM ˈbərdˌlaɪm

birdseed
BR ˈbəːdsiːd
AM ˈbərdˌsid

Birdseye
BR ˈbəːdzʌɪ
AM ˈbərdzˌaɪ

bird's-eye
BR ˈbəːdzʌɪ
AM ˈbərdzˌaɪ

birdsong
BR ˈbəːdsɒŋ
AM ˈbərdˌsɔŋ, ˈbərdˌsɑŋ

birdtable
BR ˈbəːdˌteɪbl, -z
AM ˈbərdˌteɪbəl, -z

birdwatcher
BR ˈbəːdˌwɒtʃə(r), -z
AM ˈbərdˌwɔtʃər, ˈbərdˌwɑtʃər, -z

birdwatching
BR ˈbəːdˌwɒtʃɪŋ
AM ˈbərdˌwɔtʃɪŋ, ˈbərdˌwɑtʃɪŋ

birefringence
BR ˌbʌɪrɪˈfrɪn(d)ʒ(ə)ns
AM ˌbaɪrəˈfrɪndʒəns

birefringent
BR ˌbʌɪrɪˈfrɪn(d)ʒ(ə)nt
AM ˌbaɪrəˈfrɪndʒənt

bireme
BR ˈbʌɪriːm, -z
AM ˈbaɪˌrim, -z

biretta
BR bɪˈrɛtə(r), -z
AM bəˈrɛdə, -z

Birgitta
BR bɪəˈgɪtə(r)
AM bərˈgidə

biriani
BR ˌbɪrɪˈɑːn|i, -ɪz
AM ˌbɪriˈɑni, -z

Birkbeck
BR ˈbəːkbɛk
AM ˈbərkbɛk

Birkenhead
BR ˌbəːk(ə)nˈhɛd, ˈbəːk(ə)nhɛd
AM ˈbərkənˌ(h)ɛd

Birkenshaw
BR ˈbəːk(ɪ)nʃɔː(r)
AM ˈbərk(ə)nˌʃɔ

Birkett
BR ˈbəːkɪt
AM ˈbərkət

birl
BR bəːl, -z, -ɪŋ, -d
AM bərl, -z, -ɪŋ, -d

Birmingham[1]
place in England
BR ˈbəːmɪŋəm
AM ˈbərmɪŋˌ(h)æm

Birmingham[2]
place in USA
BR ˈbəːmɪŋham
AM ˈbərmɪŋˌ(h)æm

biro®
BR ˈbʌɪrəʊ, -z
AM ˈbɪroʊ, ˈbaɪroʊ, -z

Birobidzhan
BR ˌbɪrəbɪˈdʒɑːn, ˌbɪrəbɪˈdʒan
AM ˌbɪroʊbəˈ(d)ʒɑn

birr
BR bəː(r), -z, -ɪŋ, -d
AM bər, -z, -ɪŋ, -d

Birt
BR bəːt
AM bərt

birth
BR bəːθ, -s, -ɪŋ, -t
AM bərθ, -s, -ɪŋ, -t

birthday
BR ˈbəːθdeɪ, -z
AM ˈbərθˌdeɪ, -z

birthmark
BR ˈbəːθmɑːk, -s
AM ˈbərθˌmɑrk, -s

birthplace
BR ˈbəːθpleɪs, -ɨz
AM ˈbərθˌpleɪs, -ɨz

birthrate
BR ˈbəːθreɪt, -s
AM ˈbərθˌreɪt, -s

birthright
BR ˈbəːθrʌɪt, -s
AM ˈbərθˌraɪt, -s

birthstone
BR ˈbəːθstəʊn, -z
AM ˈbərθˌstoʊn, -z

birthweight
BR ˈbəːθweɪt
AM ˈbərθˌweɪt

Birtwistle
BR ˈbəːtwɪsl
AM ˈbərtˌwɪsəl

biryani
BR ˌbɪrɪˈɑːn|i, -ɪz
AM ˌbɪriˈɑni, -z

bis
BR bɪs
AM bɪs

Biscay
BR ˈbɪskeɪ
AM ˌbɪsˈkeɪ

Biscayne
BR bɪˈskeɪn
AM bɪsˈkeɪn

biscuit
BR ˈbɪskɪt, -s
AM ˈbɪskɨt, -s

biscuity
BR ˈbɪskɨti
AM ˈbɪskɨdi

bisect
BR bʌɪˈsɛkt, -s, -ɪŋ, -ɨd
AM baɪˈsɛk|(t), -(t)s, -tɪŋ, -təd

bisection
BR bʌɪˈsɛkʃn
AM baɪˈsɛkʃən

bisector
BR bʌɪˈsɛktə(r), -z
AM baɪˈsɛktər, -z

bisexual
BR (ˌ)bʌɪˈsɛkʃʊəl, (ˌ)bʌɪˈsɛkʃ(ʉ)l, (ˌ)bʌɪˈsɛksjʊ(ə)l, -z
AM ˌbaɪˈsɛkʃ(əw)əl, -z

bisexuality
BR ˌbʌɪsɛkʃʊˈalɪti, ˌbʌɪsɛksjʊˈalɪti
AM ˌbaɪˌsɛkʃəˈwælədi

bish
BR bɪʃ, -ɨz
AM bɪʃ, -ɨz

bishop
BR ˈbɪʃəp, -s
AM ˈbɪʃəp, -s

bishopric
BR ˈbɪʃəprɪk, -s
AM ˈbɪʃəprɪk, -s

Bishopsgate
BR ˈbɪʃəpsgeɪt
AM ˈbɪʃəpsˌgeɪt

bisk
BR bɪsk, -s
AM bɪsk, -s

Bislama
BR ˈbɪʃləmɑː(r)
AM bɪsˈlɑmə

Bisley
BR ˈbɪzli
AM ˈbɪzli

Bismarck
BR ˈbɪzmɑːk
AM ˈbɪzmɑrk

bismuth
BR ˈbɪzməθ
AM ˈbɪzməθ

bison
BR ˈbʌɪsn, -z
AM ˈbaɪsən, -z

bisque
BR bɪsk, -s
AM bɪsk, -s

Bissau
BR bɪˈsaʊ
AM bɪˈsaʊ

Bissell
BR ˈbɪsl
AM ˈbɪsəl

bissextile
BR bɪˈsɛkstʌɪl
AM baɪˈsɛkstəl

bistable
BR ˌbʌɪˈsteɪbl
AM baɪˈsteɪbəl

bister
BR ˈbɪstə(r), -d
AM ˈbɪstər, -d

Bisto®
BR ˈbɪstəʊ
AM ˈbɪstoʊ

bistort
BR ˈbɪstɔːt, -s
AM ˈbɪstɔ(ə)rt, -s

bistoury
BR ˈbɪst(ə)r|i, -ɪz
AM ˈbɪst(ə)ri, -z

bistre
BR ˈbɪstə(r), -d
AM ˈbɪstər, -d

bistro
BR ˈbɪstrəʊ, ˈbiːstrəʊ, -z
AM ˈbɪstroʊ, ˈbistroʊ, -z

bisulfate
BR ˌbʌɪˈsʌlfeɪt
AM baɪˈsəlˌfeɪt

bisulphate
BR ˌbʌɪˈsʌlfeɪt
AM baɪˈsəlˌfeɪt

bisulphite
BR ˌbʌɪˈsʌlfʌɪt
AM baɪˈsəlˌfaɪt

bit
BR bɪt, -s
AM bɪt, -s

bitch
BR bɪtʃ, -ɨz, -ɪŋ, -t
AM bɪtʃ, -ɨz, -ɪŋ, -t

bitchily
BR ˈbɪtʃɨli
AM ˈbɪtʃɨli

bitchiness
BR 'bɪtʃɪnɨs
AM 'bɪtʃinɨs

bitchy
BR 'bɪtʃ|i, -ɪə(r), -ɪɨst
AM 'bɪtʃi, -ər, -əst

bite
BR bʌɪt, -s, -ɪŋ
AM baɪ|t, -ts, -dɪŋ

biter
BR 'bʌɪtə(r), -z
AM 'baɪdər, -z

Bithynia
BR bɪ'θɪnɪə(r)
AM bə'θɪniə

bitingly
BR 'bʌɪtɪŋli
AM 'baɪdɪŋli

bitmap
BR 'bɪtmap, -s, -ɪŋ, -t
AM 'bɪtˌmæp, -s, -ɪŋ, -t

bitt
BR bɪt, -s
AM bɪt, -s

bitten
BR 'bɪtn
AM 'bɪtn

bitter
BR 'bɪt|ə(r), -əz, -(ə)rə(r), -(ə)rɨst
AM 'bɪdər, -z, -ər, -əst

bitterling
BR 'bɪtəlɪŋ, -z
AM 'bɪdərlɪŋ, -z

bitterly
BR 'bɪtəli
AM 'bɪdərli

bittern
BR 'bɪtn, 'bɪtəːn, -z
AM 'bɪdərn, -z

bitterness
BR 'bɪtənəs
AM 'bɪdərnəs

bitterroot
BR 'bɪtəruːt
AM 'bɪdərˌrut, 'bɪdərˌrʊt

bittersweet[1]
adjective
BR ˌbɪtə'swiːt
AM ˌbɪdərˌswit

bittersweet[2]
noun
BR 'bɪtəswiːt
AM ˌbɪdərˌswit

bittily
BR 'bɪtɨli
AM 'bɪdɨli

bittiness
BR 'bɪtɪnɨs
AM 'bɪdinɨs

bitty
BR 'bɪt|i, -ɪə(r), -ɪɨst
AM 'bɪdi, -ər, -ɨst

bitumen
BR 'bɪtʃʉmɪn, 'bɪtjʉmɪn
AM baɪ't(j)umən, bə't(j)umən

bituminisation
BR bɨˌtjuːmɨnʌɪ'zeɪʃn, bɨˌtʃuːmɨnʌɪ'zeɪʃn
AM baɪˌt(j)umənə'zeɪʃən, bəˌt(j)umənə'zeɪʃən, baɪˌt(j)uməˌnaɪ'zeɪʃən, bəˌt(j)uməˌnaɪ'zeɪʃən

bituminise
BR bɨ'tjuːmɨnʌɪz, bɨ'tʃuːmɨnʌɪz, -ɨz, -ɪŋ, -d
AM baɪ't(j)umənˌaɪz, bə't(j)umənˌaɪz, -ɨz, -ɪŋ, -d

bituminization
BR bɨˌtjuːmɨnʌɪ'zeɪʃn, bɨˌtʃuːmɨnʌɪ'zeɪʃn
AM baɪˌt(j)umənə'zeɪʃən, bəˌt(j)umənə'zeɪʃən, baɪˌt(j)uməˌnaɪ'zeɪʃən, bəˌt(j)uməˌnaɪ'zeɪʃən

bituminize
BR bɨ'tjuːmɨnʌɪz, bɨ'tʃuːmɨnʌɪz, -ɨz, -ɪŋ, -d
AM baɪ't(j)umənˌaɪz, bə't(j)umənˌaɪz, -ɨz, -ɪŋ, -d

bituminous
BR bɨ'tjuːmɨnəs, bɨ'tʃuːmɨnəs
AM baɪ't(j)umənəs, bə't(j)umənəs

bivalence
BR (ˌ)bʌɪ'veɪləns, (ˌ)bʌɪ'veɪlņs
AM ˌbaɪ'veɪləns

bivalency
BR (ˌ)bʌɪ'veɪlənsi, (ˌ)bʌɪ'veɪlņsi
AM ˌbaɪ'veɪlənsi

bivalent
BR (ˌ)bʌɪ'veɪlənt, ˌbʌɪ'veɪlņt
AM ˌbaɪ'veɪlənt

bivalve
BR 'bʌɪvalv, -z
AM 'baɪˌvælv, -z

bivouac
BR 'bɪvʊak, -s, -ɪŋ, -t
AM 'bɪv(ə)ˌwæk, -s, -ɪŋ, -t

bivvy
BR 'bɪv|i, -ɪz
AM 'bɪvi, -z

biweekly
BR (ˌ)bʌɪ'wiːkl|i, -ɪz
AM ˌbaɪ'wikli, -z

biyearly
BR ˌbʌɪ'jɪəli, ˌbʌɪ'jəːli
AM ˌbaɪ'jɪrli

biz
BR bɪz
AM bɪz

bizarre
BR bɨ'zɑː(r)
AM bə'zɑr

bizarrely
BR bɨ'zɑːli
AM bə'zɑrli

bizarreness
BR bɨ'zɑːnəs
AM bə'zɑrnəs

bizarrerie
BR bɨ'zɑːrəri
AM bə'zɑrəri, bəˌzɑrə'ri

Bizerta
BR bɨ'zəːtə(*r*)
AM bə'zərdə

Bizerte
BR bɨ'zəːtə(*r*)
AM bə'zərdə

Bizet
BR 'biːzeɪ
AM bi'zeɪ

Bjorn
BR bɪ'ɔːn
AM bjɔ(ə)rn
SW bjəːrn

blab
BR blab, -z, -ɪŋ, -d
AM blæb, -z, -ɪŋ, -d

blabber
BR 'blab|ə(r), -əz, -(ə)rɪŋ, -əd
AM 'blæbər, -z, -ɪŋ, -d

blabbermouth
BR 'blabəmaʊ|θ, -ðz
AM 'blæbərˌmaʊ|θ, -θs\-ðz

Blaby
BR 'bleɪbi
AM 'blæbi

black
BR blak, -s, -ɪŋ, -t, -ə(r), -ɨst
AM blæk, -s, -ɪŋ, -t, -ər, -əst

blackamoor
BR 'blakəmɔː(r), -z
AM 'blækəˌmɔ(ə)r, -z

blackball
BR 'blakbɔːl, -z, -ɪŋ, -d
AM 'blækˌbɔl, 'blækˌbɑl, -z, -ɪŋ, -d

blackbeetle
BR 'blakˌbiːtl, -z
AM 'blækˌbidəl, -z

blackberry
BR 'blakb(ə)r|i, -ɪz
AM 'blækˌbɛri, -z

blackberrying
BR 'blakˌbɛrɪɪŋ
AM 'blækˌbɛriɪŋ

blackbird
BR 'blakbəːd, -z
AM 'blækˌbərd, -z

blackboard
BR 'blakbɔːd, -z
AM 'blækˌbɔ(ə)rd, -z

blackboy
BR 'blakbɔɪ, -z
AM 'blækˌbɔɪ, -z

blackbuck
BR 'blakbʌk, -s
AM 'blækˌbək, -s

Blackburn
BR 'blakbəːn
AM 'blækbərn

blackcap
BR 'blakkap, -s
AM 'blækˌkæp, -s

blackcock
BR 'blakkɒk, -s
AM 'blækˌkɑk, -s

blackcurrant
BR ˌblak'kʌrənt, ˌblak'kʌrņt
AM ˌblæk'kərənt

blacken
BR 'blak|(ə)n, -(ə)nz, -ənɪŋ\-ņɪŋ, -(ə)nd
AM 'blæk|ən, -ənz, -(ə)nɪŋ, -ənd

Blackett
BR 'blakɪt
AM 'blækət

Blackfeet
BR 'blakfiːt
AM 'blækˌfit

blackfellow
BR 'blakˌfɛləʊ, -z
AM 'blækˌfɛloʊ, -z

blackfish
BR 'blakfɪʃ
AM 'blækˌfɪʃ

blackfly
BR 'blakflʌɪ, -z
AM 'blækˌflaɪ, -z

Blackfoot
BR 'blakfʊt
AM 'blækˌfʊt

Blackfriars
BR ˌblak'frʌɪəz, 'blakˌfrʌɪəz
AM 'blækˌfraɪərz

blackguard
BR 'blagɑːd, 'blagəd, -z
AM 'blægərd, 'blæˌgɑrd, -z

blackguardly
BR 'blagɑːdli, 'blagədli
AM 'blægərdli, 'blæˌgɑrdli

blackhead
BR 'blakhɛd, -z
AM 'blækˌ(h)ɛd, -z

Blackheath
BR ˌblak'hiːθ
AM 'blækˌ(h)iθ

Blackie
BR 'blaki, 'bleɪki
AM 'blæki

blacking
BR 'blakɪŋ
AM 'blækɪŋ

blackish
BR 'blakɪʃ
AM 'blækɪʃ

blackjack
BR 'blakdʒak
AM 'blæk,dʒæk

blacklead
BR 'blaklɛd, -z, -ɪŋ, -ɨd
AM 'blæk,lɛd, -z, -ɪŋ, -əd

blackleg
BR 'blaklɛg, -z
AM 'blæk,lɛg, -z

blacklist
BR 'blaklɪst, -s, -ɪŋ, -ɨd
AM 'blæk,lɪst, -s, -ɪŋ, -ɨd

blackly
BR 'blakli
AM 'blækli

blackmail
BR 'blakmeɪl, -z, -ɪŋ, -d
AM 'blæk,meɪl, -z, -ɪŋ, -d

blackmailer
BR 'blak,meɪlə(r), -z
AM 'blæk,meɪlər, -z

Black Maria
BR ,blak mə'rʌɪə(*r*), -z
AM ,blæk mə'riə, -z

Blackmore
BR 'blakmɔː(r)
AM 'blæk,mɔ(ə)r

blackness
BR 'blaknəs
AM 'blæknəs

blackout
BR 'blakaʊt, -s
AM 'blæk,aʊt, -s

Blackpool
BR 'blakpuːl
AM 'blæk,pul

Blackshirt
BR 'blakʃəːt, -s
AM 'blæk,ʃərt, -s

blacksmith
BR 'blaksmɪθ, -s
AM 'blæk,smɪθ, -s

blackspot
BR 'blakspɒt, -s
AM 'blæk,spɑt, -s

Blackstone
BR 'blakstəʊn, 'blakst(ə)n
AM 'blæk,stoʊn, 'blækstən

blackthorn
BR 'blakθɔːn, -z
AM 'blæk,θɔ(ə)rn, -z

blacktop
BR 'blaktɒp, -s
AM 'blæk,tɑp, -s

Blackwall
BR 'blakwɔːl
AM 'blæk,wɔl, 'blæk,wɑl

Blackwell
BR 'blakw(ɛ)l
AM 'blæk,wɛl, 'blækwəl

Blackwood
BR 'blakwʊd
AM 'blæk,wʊd

bladder
BR 'bladə(r), -z
AM 'blædər, -z

bladderwort
BR 'bladəwəːt, -s
AM 'blædər,wərt, 'blædər,wɔ(ə)rt, -s

bladderwrack
BR 'bladərak
AM 'blædə(r),ræk

blade
BR bleɪd, -z, -ɨd
AM bleɪd, -z, -ɨd

bladebone
BR 'bleɪdbəʊn, -z
AM 'bleɪd,boʊn, -z

Bladon
BR 'bleɪdn
AM 'bleɪdən

blaeberry
BR 'bleɪb(ə)r|i, -ɪz
AM 'bleɪ,bɛri, -z

Blaenau Ffestiniog
BR ,blʌɪnʌɪ fɛ'stɪnɪɒg
AM 'bleɪnaɪ fɛ'stɪnjɑg
WE ,bleɪnaɪ fe'stɪnjɒg

blag
BR blag, -z, -ɪŋ, -d
AM blæg, -z, -ɪŋ, -d

blagger
BR 'blagə(r), -z
AM 'blægər, -z

blague
BR blag
AM blɑg

blagueur
BR bla'gəː(r), -z
AM 'blɑgər, blɑ'gər, -z

blah
BR blɑː(*r*)
AM blɑ

blah-blah
BR ,blɑː'blɑː(*r*)
AM 'blɑ'blɑ

blain
BR bleɪn, -z
AM bleɪn, -z

Blair
BR blɛː(r)
AM blɛ(ə)r

Blairgowrie
BR ,blɛː'gaʊri
AM ,blɛr'gaʊri

Blaise
BR bleɪz
AM bleɪz

Blake
BR bleɪk
AM bleɪk

Blakemore
BR 'bleɪkmɔː(r)
AM 'bleɪk,mɔ(ə)r

Blakeney
BR 'bleɪkni
AM 'bleɪkni

Blakey
BR 'bleɪk|i, -ɪz
AM 'bleɪki, -z

blamable
BR 'bleɪməbl
AM 'bleɪməbəl

blamably
BR 'bleɪməbli
AM 'bleɪməbli

blame
BR bleɪm, -z, -ɪŋ, -d
AM bleɪm, -z, -ɪŋ, -d

blameable
BR 'bleɪməbl
AM 'bleɪməbəl

blameably
BR 'bleɪməbli
AM 'bleɪməbli

blameful
BR 'bleɪmf(ʊ)l
AM 'bleɪmfəl

blamefully
BR 'bleɪmfʊli, 'bleɪmfḷi
AM 'bleɪmfəli

blameless
BR 'bleɪmlɪs
AM 'bleɪmlɪs

blamelessly
BR 'bleɪmlɪsli
AM 'bleɪmlɪsli

blamelessness
BR 'bleɪmlɪsnɪs
AM 'bleɪmlɪsnɪs

blameworthiness
BR 'bleɪm,wəːðɪnɪs
AM 'bleɪm,wərðinɪs

blameworthy
BR 'bleɪm,wəːði
AM 'bleɪm,wərði

blanc
BR blɑːŋk, blɒ̃
AM blɑŋk

blanch
BR blɑːn(t)ʃ, blan(t)ʃ, -ɪz, -ɪŋ, -t
AM blæn(t)ʃ, -əz, -ɪŋ, -t

Blanchard
BR 'blan(t)ʃəd, 'blan(t)ʃɑːd
AM 'blæn(t)ʃərd

Blanche
BR blɑːn(t)ʃ, blan(t)ʃ
AM blæn(t)ʃ

blancmange
BR blə'mɒn(d)ʒ, -ɪz
AM blə'mɑn(d)ʒ, -əz

blanco
BR 'blaŋkəʊ, -z, -ɪŋ, -d
AM 'blæŋkoʊ, -z, -ɪŋ, -d

bland
BR bland, -ə(r), -ɪst
AM blænd, -ər, -əst

Blandford
BR 'blan(d)fəd
AM 'blæn(d)fərd

blandish
BR 'bland|ɪʃ, -ɪʃɪz, -ɪʃɪŋ, -ɪʃt
AM 'blændɪʃ, -ɪz, -ɪŋ, -t

blandishment
BR 'blandɪʃm(ə)nt, -s
AM 'blændɪʃmənt, -s

blandly
BR 'blandli
AM 'blæn(d)li

blandness
BR 'blan(d)nəs
AM 'blæn(d)nəs

blank
BR blaŋ|k, -ks, -kɪŋ, -(k)t, -kə(r), -kɪst
AM blæŋ|k, -ks, -kɪŋ, -(k)t, -kər, -kəst

Blankenship
BR 'blaŋk(ə)nʃɪp
AM 'blæŋkən,ʃɪp

blanket
BR 'blaŋk|ɪt, -ɪts, -ɪtɪŋ, -ɪtɪd
AM 'blæŋkə|t, -ts, -dɪŋ, -dəd

blanketweed
BR 'blaŋkɪtwiːd
AM 'blæŋkət,wid

blankety
BR 'blaŋkɪti
AM 'blæŋkədi

blankness
BR 'blaŋknəs
AM 'blæŋknəs

blanky
BR 'blaŋki
AM 'blæŋki

blanquette
BR ,blɒŋ'kɛt, ,blaŋ'kɛt, -s
AM ,blɑŋ'kɛt, -s

Blantyre
BR 'blantʌɪə(r)
AM 'blæn,taɪ(ə)r

blare
BR blɛː(r), -z, -ɪŋ, -d
AM blɛ(ə)r, -z, -ɪŋ, -d

blarney
BR 'blɑːni
AM 'blɑrni

blasé
BR 'blɑːzeɪ
AM blɑ'zeɪ

blaspheme
BR blas'fiːm, blɑːs'fiːm, -z, -ɪŋ, -d
AM ¦blæs¦fim, -z, -ɪŋ, -d

blasphemer
BR blas'fiːmə(r), blɑːs'fiːmə(r), -z
AM blæs'fimər, 'blæsfəmər, -z

blasphemous
BR ˈblasfəməs, ˈblɑːsfəməs
AM ˈblæsfəməs

blasphemously
BR ˈblasfəməsli, ˈblɑːsfəməsli
AM ˈblæsfəməsli

blasphemy
BR ˈblasfəm|i, ˈblɑːsfəmi, -ɪz
AM ˈblæsfəmi, -z

blast
BR blɑːst, blast, -s, -ɪŋ, -ɨd
AM blæst, -s, -ɪŋ, -əd

blaster
BR ˈblɑːstə(r), ˈblastə(r), -z
AM ˈblæstər, -z

blastula
BR ˈblastjʉlə(r), ˈblastʃʉlə(r), -z
AM ˈblæstʃələ, -z

blastulae
BR ˈblastjʉliː, ˈblastʃʉliː
AM ˈblæstʃəli, ˈblæstʃəˌlaɪ

blatancy
BR ˈbleɪtnsi
AM ˈbleɪtnsi

blatant
BR ˈbleɪtnt
AM ˈbleɪtnt

blatantly
BR ˈbleɪtntli
AM ˈbleɪtn(t)li

Blatchford
BR ˈblatʃfəd
AM ˈblætʃfərd

blather
BR ˈblað|ə(r), -əz, -(ə)rɪŋ, -əd
AM ˈblæðər, -z, -ɪŋ, -d

blatherer
BR ˈblað(ə)rə(r), -z
AM ˈblæðərər, -z

blatherskite
BR ˈblaðəskʌɪt, -s
AM ˈblæðərˌskaɪt, -s

Blavatsky
BR bləˈvatski
AM bləˈvætski

Blawith[1]
BR ˈbleɪwɪθ
AM ˈbleɪˌwɪθ

Blawith[2]
places in Cumbria, UK
BR blɑːð
AM ˈbleɪˌwɪθ

Blaydon
BR ˈbleɪdn
AM ˈbleɪdən

blaze
BR bleɪz, -ɪz, -ɪŋ, -d
AM bleɪz, -ɪz, -ɪŋ, -d

blazer
BR ˈbleɪzə(r), -z
AM ˈbleɪzər, -z

blazingly
BR ˈbleɪzɪŋli
AM ˈbleɪzɪŋli

blazon
BR ˈbleɪzn, -z, -ɪŋ, -d
AM ˈbleɪzən, -z, -ɪŋ, -d

blazonment
BR ˈbleɪznm(ə)nt
AM ˈbleɪzənmənt

blazonry
BR ˈbleɪznri
AM ˈbleɪzənri

Blea
BR bliː
AM bli

bleach
BR bliːtʃ, -ɪz, -ɪŋ, -t
AM blitʃ, -ɪz, -ɪŋ, -t

bleacher
BR ˈbliːtʃə(r), -z
AM ˈblitʃər, -z

bleak
BR bliːk, -ə(r), -ɨst
AM blik, -ər, -ɨst

bleakly
BR ˈbliːkli
AM ˈblikli

bleakness
BR ˈbliːknɨs
AM ˈbliknɨs

blear
BR blɪə(r)
AM blɪ(ə)r

blearily
BR ˈblɪərɨli
AM ˈblɪrɨli, ˈblirɨli

bleariness
BR ˈblɪərɪnɨs
AM ˈblɪrinɨs, ˈblirinɨs

bleary
BR ˈblɪər|i, -ɪə(r), -ɪɨst
AM ˈblɪri, ˈbliri, -ər, -ɨst

Bleasdale
BR ˈbliːzdeɪl
AM ˈblizˌdeɪl

bleat
BR bliːt, -s, -ɪŋ, -ɨd
AM bli|t, -ts, -dɪŋ, -dɨd

bleatingly
BR ˈbliːtɪŋli
AM ˈblidɪŋli

bleb
BR blɛb, -z
AM blɛb, -z

bled
BR blɛd
AM blɛd

Bleddyn
BR ˈblɛðɪn
AM ˈblɛdən

bleed
BR bliːd, -z, -ɪŋ
AM blid, -z, -ɪŋ

bleeder
BR ˈbliːdə(r), -z
AM ˈblidər, -z

bleep
BR bliːp, -s, -ɪŋ, -t
AM blip, -s, -ɪŋ, -t

bleeper
BR ˈbliːpə(r), -z
AM ˈblipər, -z

blemish
BR ˈblɛm|ɪʃ, -ɨʃɪz, -ɨʃɪŋ, -ɪʃt
AM ˈblɛmɪʃ, -ɪz, -ɪŋ, -t

Blencathra
BR blɛnˈkaθrə(r)
AM blɛnˈkæθrə

blench
BR blɛn(t)ʃ, -ɪz, -ɪŋ, -t
AM blɛn(t)ʃ, -əz, -ɪŋ, -t

blend
BR blɛnd, -z, -ɪŋ, -ɨd
AM blɛnd, -z, -ɪŋ, -əd

blende
BR blɛnd, -z
AM blɛnd, -z

blender
BR ˈblɛndə(r), -z
AM ˈblɛndər, -z

Blenheim
BR ˈblɛnɪm
AM ˈblɛnəm

Blenkinsop
BR ˈblɛŋkɪnsɒp
AM ˈblɛŋkənˌsɑp

Blennerhassett
BR ˌblɛnəˈhasɪt, ˈblɛnəhasɪt
AM ˌblɛnərˈ(h)æsət

blenny
BR ˈblɛn|i, -ɪz
AM ˈblɛni, -z

blent
BR blɛnt
AM blɛnt

blepharitis
BR ˌblɛfəˈrʌɪtɪs
AM ˌblɛfəˈraɪdɪs

Blériot
BR ˈblɛ(ː)rɪəʊ
AM ˈblɛrioʊ

blesbok
BR ˈblɛsbɒk, -s
AM ˈblɛsˌbɑk, -s

blesbuck
BR ˈblɛsbʌk, -s
AM ˈblɛsˌbək, -s

bless
BR blɛs, -ɪz, -ɪŋ, -t
AM blɛs, -əz, -ɪŋ, -t

blessed
adjective
BR blɛst, ˈblɛsɨd
AM blɛst, ˈblɛsəd

blessedly
BR ˈblɛsɨdli
AM ˈblɛsədli

blessedness
BR ˈblɛsɨdnɨs
AM ˈblɛsədnəs

blessing
BR ˈblɛsɪŋ, -z
AM ˈblɛsɪŋ, -z

Blessington
BR ˈblɛsɪŋt(ə)n
AM ˈblɛsɪŋtən

blest
BR blɛst
AM blɛst

Bletchley
BR ˈblɛtʃli
AM ˈblɛtʃli

blether
BR ˈblɛð|ə(r), -əz, -(ə)rɪŋ, -əd
AM ˈblɛθər, -əz, -(ə)rɪŋ, -əd

bletherskate
BR ˈblɛðəskeɪt, -s
AM ˈblɛθərˌskeɪt, -s

Blevins
BR ˈblɛvɪnz
AM ˈblɛvənz

blew
BR bluː
AM blu

Blewett
BR ˈbluːɪt
AM ˈbluət

blewits
BR ˈbluːɪts
AM ˈbluəts

Blewitt
BR ˈbluːɪt
AM ˈbluət

Bligh
BR blʌɪ
AM blaɪ

blight
BR blʌɪt, -s, -ɪŋ, -ɨd
AM blaɪ|t, -ts, -dɪŋ, -dɨd

blighter
BR ˈblʌɪtə(r), -z
AM ˈblaɪdər, -z

Blighty
BR ˈblʌɪti
AM ˈblaɪdi

blimey
BR ˈblʌɪmi
AM ˈblaɪmi

blimp
BR blɪmp, -s
AM blɪmp, -s

blimpery
BR ˈblɪmp(ə)ri
AM ˈblɪmp(ə)ri

blimpish
BR ˈblɪmpɪʃ
AM ˈblɪmpɪʃ

blind
BR blʌɪn|d, -(d)z, -dɪŋ, -dɨd, -də(r), -dɨst
AM blaɪn|d, -(d)z, -dɪŋ, -dɨd, -ər, -dɨst

blinder
BR 'blʌɪndə(r), -z
AM 'blaɪndər, -z
blindfold
BR 'blʌɪn(d)fəʊld, -z
AM 'blaɪn(d),foʊld, -z
blindingly
BR 'blʌɪndɪŋli
AM 'blaɪndɪŋli
blindly
BR 'blʌɪndli
AM 'blaɪn(d)li
blindness
BR 'blʌɪn(d)nɪs
AM 'blaɪn(d)nɪs
blindworm
BR 'blʌɪn(d)wəːm, -z
AM 'blaɪn(d),wərm, -z
blini
BR 'blɪn|i, -ɪz
AM 'blɪni, -z
blink
BR blɪŋ|k, -ks, -kɪŋ, -(k)t
AM blɪŋ|k, -ks, -kɪŋ, -(k)t
blinker
BR 'blɪŋk|ə(r), -əz, -(ə)rɪŋ, -əd
AM 'blɪŋkər, -z, -ɪŋ, -d
blintz
BR blɪn(t)s, -ɪz
AM blɪn(t)s, -ɪz
blip
BR blɪp, -s, -ɪŋ, -t
AM blɪp, -s, -ɪŋ, -t
bliss
BR blɪs, -ɪz, -ɪŋ, -t
AM blɪs, -əz, -ɪŋ, -t
Blissett
BR 'blɪsɪt
AM 'blɪsɪt
blissful
BR 'blɪsf(ʊ)l
AM 'blɪsfəl
blissfully
BR 'blɪsfʊli, 'blɪsfḷi
AM 'blɪsfəli
blissfulness
BR 'blɪsf(ʊ)lnəs
AM 'blɪsfəlnəs
blister
BR 'blɪst|ə(r), -əz, -(ə)rɪŋ, -əd
AM 'blɪst|ər, -ərz, -(ə)rɪŋ, -ərd
blistery
BR 'blɪst(ə)ri
AM 'blɪst(ə)ri
blithe
BR blʌɪð, -ə(r), -ɪst
AM blaɪð, -ər, -ɪst
blithely
BR 'blʌɪðli
AM 'blaɪðli
blitheness
BR 'blʌɪðnɪs
AM 'blaɪðnɪs
blithering
BR 'blɪð(ə)rɪŋ
AM 'blɪðərɪŋ
blithesome
BR 'blʌɪðs(ə)m
AM 'blaɪðsəm
blitz
BR blɪts, -ɪz, -ɪŋ, -t
AM blɪts, -ɪz, -ɪŋ, -t
Blitzkrieg
BR 'blɪtskriːg, -z
AM 'blɪts,krig, -z
Blixen
BR 'blɪksn
AM 'blɪksən
DAN 'blegsən
blizzard
BR 'blɪzəd, -z
AM 'blɪzərd, -z
bloat
BR bləʊt, -s, -ɪŋ, -ɪd
AM bloʊ|t, -ts, -dɪŋ, -dəd
bloater
BR 'bləʊtə(r), -z
AM 'bloʊdər, -z
blob
BR blɒb, -z, -ɪŋ, -d
AM blɑb, -z, -ɪŋ, -d
bloc
BR blɒk, -s
AM blɑk, -s
Bloch
BR blɒx, blɒk
AM blɑk
block
BR blɒk, -s, -ɪŋ, -t
AM blɑk, -s, -ɪŋ, -t
blockade
BR blɒ'keɪd, blə'keɪd, -z, -ɪŋ, -ɪd
AM blɑ'keɪd, -z, -ɪŋ, -ɪd
blockader
BR blɒ'keɪdə(r), blə'keɪdə(r), -z
AM blɑ'keɪdər, -z
blockage
BR 'blɒk|ɪdʒ, -ɪdʒɪz
AM 'blɑkɪdʒ, -ɪz
blockboard
BR 'blɒkbɔːd, -z
AM 'blɑk,bɔ(ə)rd, -z
blockbuster
BR 'blɒk,bʌstə(r), -z
AM 'blɑk,bəstər, -z
blockbusting
BR 'blɒk,bʌstɪŋ
AM 'blɑk,bəstɪŋ
blocker
BR 'blɒkə(r), -z
AM 'blɑkər, -z
blockhead
BR 'blɒkhɛd, -z
AM 'blɑk,(h)ɛd, -z
blockheaded
BR ,blɒk'hɛdɪd
AM 'blɑk,(h)ɛdəd
blockhouse
BR 'blɒkhaʊ|s, -zɪz
AM 'blɑk,(h)aʊ|s, -zəz
blockish
BR 'blɒkɪʃ
AM 'blɑkɪʃ
blockishly
BR 'blɒkɪʃli
AM 'blɑkɪʃli
blockishness
BR 'blɒkɪʃnɪs
AM 'blɑkɪʃnɪs
Blodwen
BR 'blɒdwɪn, 'blɒdwɛn
AM 'blɑdwən
Bloemfontein
BR 'bluːmfɒnteɪn, 'bluːmf(ə)nteɪn
AM 'blʊm,fanteɪn, 'blʊm,fanteɪn
Blofeld
BR 'bləʊfɛld
AM 'bloʊ,fɛld
Blok
BR blɒk
AM blɑk
bloke
BR bləʊk, -s
AM bloʊk, -s
Blomfield
BR 'blɒmfiːld, 'bluːmfiːld
AM 'blɑm,fild
blond
BR blɒnd, -z, -ə(r), -ɪst
AM blɑnd, -z, -ər, -əst
blonde
BR blɒnd, -z, -ə(r), -ɪst
AM blɑnd, -z, -ər, -əst
Blondel
BR blɒn'dɛl
AM ,blɑn'dɛl
blondie
BR 'blɒnd|i, -ɪz
AM 'blɑndi, -z
Blondin
BR 'blɒndɪn
AM 'blɑndən
blondness
BR 'blɒn(d)nəs
AM 'blɑn(d)nəs
blood
BR blʌd, -z, -ɪŋ, -ɪd
AM bləd, -z, -ɪŋ, -əd
bloodbath
BR 'blʌd|bɑːθ, 'blʌd|baθ, -bɑːðz\-bɑːθs\-baθs
AM 'bləd,bæθ, -s, -ðz
bloodhound
BR 'blʌdhaʊnd, -z
AM 'bləd,(h)aʊnd, -z
bloodily
BR 'blʌdɪli
AM 'blədɪli
bloodiness
BR 'blʌdɪnɪs
AM 'blədinɪs
bloodless
BR 'blʌdləs
AM 'blədləs
bloodlessly
BR 'blʌdləsli
AM 'blədləsli
bloodlessness
BR 'blʌdləsnəs
AM 'blədləsnəs
bloodletting
BR 'blʌd,lɛtɪŋ, -z
AM 'bləd,lɛdɪŋ, -z
bloodline
BR 'blʌdlʌɪn, -z
AM 'bləd,laɪn, -z
bloodlust
BR 'blʌdlʌst
AM 'bləd,ləst
bloodroot
BR 'blʌdruːt
AM 'bləd,rut, 'bləd,rʊt
bloodshed
BR 'blʌdʃɛd
AM 'bləd,ʃɛd
bloodshot
BR 'blʌdʃɒt
AM 'bləd,ʃɑt
bloodstain
BR 'blʌdsteɪn, -z, -d
AM 'bləd,steɪn, -z, -d
bloodstock
BR 'blʌdstɒk
AM 'bləd,stɑk
bloodstone
BR 'blʌdstəʊn, -z
AM 'bləd,stoʊn, -z
bloodstream
BR 'blʌdstriːm, -z
AM 'bləd,strim, -z
bloodsucker
BR 'blʌd,sʌkə(r), -z
AM 'bləd,səkər, -z
bloodsucking
BR 'blʌd,sʌkɪŋ
AM 'bləd,səkɪŋ
bloodthirstily
BR 'blʌd,θəːstɪli
AM 'bləd,θərstɪli
bloodthirstiness
BR 'blʌd,θəːstɪnɪs
AM 'bləd,θərstinɪs
bloodthirsty
BR 'blʌd,θəːst|i, -ɪə(r), -ɪɪst
AM 'bləd,θərsti, -ər, -ɪst
bloodworm
BR 'blʌdwəːm, -z
AM 'bləd,wərm, -z
bloom
BR bluːm, -z, -ɪŋ, -d
AM blum, -z, -ɪŋ, -d
bloomer
BR 'bluːmə(r), -z
AM 'blumər, -z
bloomery
BR 'bluːm(ə)r|i, -ɪz

AM 'blumǝri, -z
Bloomfield
BR 'blu:mfi:ld
AM 'blum,fild
Bloomingdale's
BR 'blu:mɪŋdeɪlz
AM 'blumɪŋ,deɪlz
Bloomsbury
BR 'blu:mzb(ǝ)ri
AM 'blumz,bɛri, 'blumzbǝri
bloop
BR blu:p, -s, -ɪŋ, -t
AM blup, -s, -ɪŋ, -t
blooper
BR 'blu:pǝ(r), -z
AM 'blupǝr, -z
blossom
BR 'blɒs|(ǝ)m, -(ǝ)mz, -(ǝ)mɪŋ\-m̩ɪŋ, -(ǝ)md
AM 'blɑsǝm, -z, -ɪŋ, -d
blossomy
BR 'blɒsǝmi, 'blɒsm̩i
AM 'blɑsǝmi
blot
BR blɒt, -s, -ɪŋ, -ɨd
AM blɑ|t, -ts, -dɪŋ, -dǝd
blotch
BR blɒtʃ, -ɨz, -ɪŋ, -t
AM blɑtʃ, -ǝz, -ɪŋ, -t
blotchily
BR 'blɒtʃɨli
AM 'blɑtʃǝli
blotchiness
BR 'blɒtʃɪnɨs
AM 'blɑtʃinɨs
blotchy
BR 'blɒtʃ|i, -ɪǝ(r), -ɪɨst
AM 'blɑtʃi, -ǝr, -ɨst
blotter
BR 'blɒtǝ(r), -z
AM 'blɑdǝr, -z
blotto
BR 'blɒtǝʊ
AM 'blɑdoʊ
Blount
BR blʌnt, blaʊnt
AM blaʊnt, blǝnt
blouse
BR blaʊz, -ɨz, -ɪŋ, -d
AM blaʊs, blaʊz, -ǝz, -ɪŋ, -d
blouson
BR 'blaʊz(ɒ)n, 'blu:z(ɒ)n, -z
AM 'blaʊzn, 'blaʊ,zɑn, 'blaʊsǝn, 'blaʊ,sɑn, -z
blow
BR blǝʊ, -z, -ɪŋ
AM bloʊ, -z, -ɪŋ
blowback
BR 'blǝʊbak, -s
AM 'bloʊ,bæk, -s
blowby
BR 'blǝʊbʌɪ
AM 'bloʊ,baɪ
blowdry
BR 'blǝʊdrʌɪ, ,blǝʊ'drʌɪ, -z, -ɪŋ, -d
AM 'bloʊ,draɪ, -z, -ɪŋ, -d
blower
BR 'blǝʊǝ(r), -z
AM 'bloʊǝr, -z
blowfish
BR 'blǝʊfɪʃ
AM 'bloʊ,fɪʃ
blowfly
BR 'blǝʊflʌɪ, -z
AM 'bloʊ,flaɪ, -z
blowgun
BR 'blǝʊgʌn, -z
AM 'bloʊ,gǝn, -z
blowhard
BR 'blǝʊhɑ:d, -z
AM 'bloʊ,hɑrd, -z
blowhole
BR 'blǝʊhǝʊl, -z
AM 'bloʊ,hoʊl, -z
blowily
BR 'blǝʊɨli
AM 'bloʊǝli
blowiness
BR 'blǝʊɪnɨs
AM 'bloʊinɨs
blowlamp
BR 'blǝʊlamp, -s
AM 'bloʊ,læmp, -s
blown
BR blǝʊn
AM bloʊn
blowout
BR 'blǝʊaʊt, -s
AM 'bloʊ,aʊt, -s
blowpipe
BR 'blǝʊpʌɪp, -s
AM 'bloʊ,paɪp, -s
blowsily
BR 'blaʊzɨli
AM 'blaʊzǝli
blowsiness
BR 'blaʊzɪnɨs
AM 'blaʊzinɨs
blowsy
BR 'blaʊz|i, -ɪǝ(r), -ɪɨst
AM 'blaʊzi, -ǝr, -ɨst
blowtorch
BR 'blǝʊtɔ:tʃ, -ɨz
AM 'bloʊ,tɔ(ǝ)rtʃ, -ɨz
blowy
BR 'blǝʊ|i, -ɪǝ(r), -ɪɨst
AM 'bloʊi, -ǝr, -ɨst
blowzily
BR 'blaʊzɨli
AM 'blaʊzǝli
blowziness
BR 'blaʊzɪnɨs
AM 'blaʊzinɨs
blowzy
BR 'blaʊz|i, -ɪǝ(r), -ɪɨst
AM 'blaʊzi, -ǝr, -ɨst
blub
BR blʌb, -z, -ɪŋ, -d
AM blǝb, -z, -ɪŋ, -d
blubber
BR 'blʌb|ǝ(r), -ǝz, -(ǝ)rɪŋ, -ǝd
AM 'blǝbǝr, -ǝz, -(ǝ)rɪŋ, -ǝd
blubberer
BR 'blʌb(ǝ)rǝ(r), -z
AM 'blǝbǝrǝr, -z
blubberingly
BR 'blʌb(ǝ)rɪŋli
AM 'blǝbǝrɪŋli
blubbery
BR 'blʌb(ǝ)ri
AM 'blǝbǝri
Blücher
BR 'blu:kǝ(r), 'blu:tʃǝ(r)
AM 'blutʃǝr, 'blukǝr
GER 'blʏçɐ
bluchers
BR 'blu:kǝz, 'blu:tʃǝz
AM 'blukǝrz, 'blutʃǝrz
bludge
BR blʌdʒ, -ɨz, -ɪŋ, -d
AM blǝdʒ, -ǝz, -ɪŋ, -d
bludgeon
BR 'blʌdʒ|(ǝ)n, -(ǝ)nz, -n̩ɪŋ\-ǝnɪŋ, -(ǝ)nd
AM 'blǝdʒǝn, -z, -ɪŋ, -d
bludger
BR 'blʌdʒǝ(r), -z
AM 'blǝdʒǝr, -z
blue
BR blu:, -z, -ɪŋ, -d, -ǝ(r), -ɨst
AM blu, -z, -ɪŋ, -d, -ǝr, -ǝst
bluebag
BR 'blu:bag, -z
AM 'blu,bæg, -z
bluebeard
BR 'blu:bɪǝd, -z
AM 'blu,bɪ(ǝ)rd, -z
bluebell
BR 'blu:bɛl, -z
AM 'blu,bɛl, -z
blueberry
BR 'blu:b(ǝ)r|i, 'blu:,bɛr|i, -ɪz
AM 'blu,bɛri, -z
bluebird
BR 'blu:bǝ:d, -z
AM 'blu,bǝrd, -z
bluebonnet
BR 'blu:,bɒnɪt, -s
AM ',blu'bɑnǝt, -s
bluebottle
BR 'blu:,bɒtl, -z
AM 'blu,bɑdǝl, -z
bluecoat
BR 'blu:kǝʊt, -s
AM 'blu,koʊt, -s
Bluecol
BR 'blu:kɒl
AM 'blukǝl, 'blukɑl
Bluefields
BR 'blu:fi:ldz
AM 'blu,fildz
bluefish
BR 'blu:fɪʃ
AM 'blu,fɪʃ
bluegill
BR 'blu:gɪl, -z
AM 'blu,gɪl, -z
bluegrass
BR 'blu:grɑ:s, 'blu:gras
AM 'blu,græs
bluegum
BR 'blu:gʌm
AM 'blu,gǝm
blueish
BR 'blu:ɪʃ
AM 'bluɪʃ
bluejacket
BR 'blu:,dʒakɪt, -s
AM 'blu,dʒækǝt, -s
bluejay
BR 'blu:dʒeɪ, -z
AM 'blu,dʒeɪ, -z
Bluemantle
BR 'blu:,mantl
AM 'blu,mæn(t)ǝl
blueness
BR 'blu:nǝs
AM 'blunǝs
blueprint
BR 'blu:prɪnt, -s
AM 'blu,prɪnt, -s
blues
BR blu:z
AM bluz
bluestocking
BR 'blu:,stɒkɪŋ, -z
AM 'blu,stɑkɪŋ, -z
bluestone
BR 'blu:stǝʊn, -z
AM 'blu,stoʊn, -z
bluesy
BR 'blu:zi
AM 'bluzi
bluet
BR 'blu:ɪt
AM 'bluǝt
bluethroat
BR 'blu:θrǝʊt, -s
AM 'blu,θroʊt, -s
bluetit
BR 'blu:tɪt, -s
AM 'blu,tɪt, -s
Bluett
BR 'blu:ɪt
AM 'bluǝt
Blue Vinney
BR ,blu: 'vɪni
AM ,blu 'vɪni
bluey
BR 'blu:|i, -ɪz
AM 'blui, -z
bluff
BR blʌf, -s, -ɪŋ, -t, -ɨst
AM blǝf, -s, -ɪŋ, -t, -ǝst
bluffer
BR 'blʌfǝ(r), -z
AM 'blǝfǝr, -z

bluffly
BR ˈblʌfli
AM ˈbləfli
bluffness
BR ˈblʌfnəs
AM ˈbləfnəs
bluing
BR ˈbluːɪŋ
AM ˈbluɪŋ
bluish
BR ˈbluːɪʃ
AM ˈbluɪʃ
Blum
BR bluːm
AM blum
Blumenbach
BR ˈbluːmənbak
AM ˈblumənˌbɑk
Blundell
BR ˈblʌndl
AM ˈbləndəl, blənˈdɛl
Blunden
BR ˈblʌndən
AM ˈbləndən
blunder
BR ˈblʌnd|ə(r), -əz, -(ə)rɪŋ, -əd
AM ˈblənd|ər, -ərz, -(ə)rɪŋ, -ərd
blunderbuss
BR ˈblʌndəbʌs, -ɪz
AM ˈbləndərˌbəs, -əz
blunderer
BR ˈblʌnd(ə)rə(r), -z
AM ˈbləndərər, -z
blunderingly
BR ˈblʌnd(ə)rɪŋli
AM ˈbləndərɪŋli
blunge
BR blʌn(d)ʒ, -ɪz, -ɪŋ, -d
AM blən(d)ʒ, -əz, -ɪŋ, -d
blunger
BR ˈblʌn(d)ʒə(r), -z
AM ˈblən(d)ʒər, -z
blunt
BR blʌnt, -s, -ɪŋ, -ɪd, -ə(r), -ɪst
AM blənt, -s, -ɪŋ, -əd, -ər, -əst
bluntly
BR ˈblʌntli
AM ˈblən(t)li
bluntness
BR ˈblʌntnəs
AM ˈblən(t)nəs
blur
BR bləː(r), -z, -ɪŋ, -d
AM blər, -z, -ɪŋ, -d
blurb
BR bləːb, -z
AM blərb, -z
blurry
BR ˈbləːr|i, -ɪə(r), -ɪɪst
AM ˈbləri, -ər, -ɪst
blurt
BR bləːt, -s, -ɪŋ, -ɪd
AM blər|t, -ts, -dɪŋ, -dəd
blush
BR blʌʃ, -ɪz, -ɪŋ, -t
AM bləʃ, -əz, -ɪŋ, -t
blusher
BR ˈblʌʃə(r), -z
AM ˈbləʃər, -z
blushful
BR ˈblʌʃf(ʊ)l
AM ˈbləʃfəl
bluster
BR ˈblʌst|ə(r), -əz, -(ə)rɪŋ, -əd
AM ˈbləstər, -əz, -(ə)rɪŋ, -əd
blusterous
BR ˈblʌst(ə)rəs
AM ˈbləst(ə)rəs
blusterously
BR ˈblʌst(ə)rəsli
AM ˈbləst(ə)rəsli
blustery
BR ˈblʌst(ə)ri
AM ˈbləstəri
Blu-Tack®
BR ˈbluːtak
AM ˈblutæk
Bly
BR blʌɪ
AM blaɪ
Blyth
BR blʌɪð, blʌɪθ, blʌɪ
AM blaɪθ, blaɪð
Blythe
BR blʌɪð
AM blaɪð
Blyton
BR ˈblʌɪtn
AM ˈblaɪtn
B.Mus.
Bachelor of Music
BR ˌbiː ˈmjuːz
AM ˌbi ˈmjuz
B'nai B'rith
BR bəˈneɪ bəˈriːθ, + ˈbrɪθ
AM bəˈneɪ ˈbrɪθ
bo
BR bəʊ, -z, -ɪŋ, -d
AM boʊ, -z, -ɪŋ, -d
boa
BR ˈbəʊə(r), -z
AM ˈboʊə, -z
Boadicea
BR ˌbəʊ(ə)dɪˈsiːə(r)
AM ˌboʊədəˈsiə
Boakes
BR bəʊks
AM boʊks
Boaks
BR bəʊks
AM boʊks
Boanerges
BR ˌbəʊəˈnəːdʒiːz, bəʊˈanədʒiːz
AM ˌboʊəˈnərˌdʒiz
boar
BR bɔː(r), -z
AM bɔ(ə)r, -z
board
BR bɔːd, -z, -ɪŋ, -ɪd
AM bɔ(ə)rd, -z, -ɪŋ, -əd
boarder
BR ˈbɔːdə(r), -z
AM ˈbɔrdər, -z
boardroom
BR ˈbɔːdruːm, ˈbɔːdrʊm, -z
AM ˈbɔrdˌrum, ˈbɔrdˌrʊm, -z
boardsailer
BR ˈbɔːdˌseɪlə(r), -z
AM ˈbɔrdˌseɪlər, -z
boardsailing
BR ˈbɔːdˌseɪlɪŋ, -z
AM ˈbɔrdˌseɪlɪŋ, -z
boardsailor
BR ˈbɔːdˌseɪlə(r), -z
AM ˈbɔrdˌseɪlər, -z
boardwalk
BR ˈbɔːdwɔːk, -s
AM ˈbɔrdˌwɔk, ˈbɔrdˌwɑk, -s
boart
BR bɔːt, -s
AM bɔ(ə)rt, -s
Boas
BR ˈbəʊaz
AM ˈboʊæz
boast
BR bəʊst, -s, -ɪŋ, -ɪd
AM boʊst, -s, -ɪŋ, -əd
boaster
BR ˈbəʊstə(r), -z
AM ˈboʊstər, -z
boastful
BR ˈbəʊs(t)f(ʊ)l
AM ˈboʊs(t)fəl
boastfully
BR ˈbəʊs(t)fʊli, ˈbəʊstfli
AM ˈboʊs(t)fəli
boastfulness
BR ˈbəʊs(t)f(ʊ)lnəs
AM ˈboʊs(t)fəlnəs
boastingly
BR ˈbəʊstɪŋli
AM ˈboʊstɪŋli
boat
BR bəʊt, -s, -ɪŋ, -ɪd
AM boʊ|t, -ts, -dɪŋ, -dəd
boatbuilder
BR ˈbəʊtˌbɪldə(r), -z
AM ˈboʊtˌbɪldər, -z
boatel
BR ˌbəʊˈtɛl, -z
AM ˌboʊˈtɛl, -z
Boateng
BR ˈbwʌtɛŋ, ˈbəʊ(ə)tɛŋ
AM ˈbwɑˌtɛŋ, ˈboʊ(ə)ˌtɛŋ
boater
BR ˈbəʊtə(r), -z
AM ˈboʊdər, -z
boatful
BR ˈbəʊtfʊl, -z
AM ˈboʊtˌfʊl, -z
boathouse
BR ˈbəʊthaʊ|s, -zɪz
AM ˈboʊtˌ(h)aʊ|s, -zəz
boatlift
BR ˈbəʊtlɪft, -s
AM ˈboʊtˌlɪft, -s
boatload
BR ˈbəʊtləʊd, -z
AM ˈboʊtˌloʊd, -z
boatman
BR ˈbəʊtmən
AM ˈboʊtmən
boatmen
BR ˈbəʊtmən
AM ˈboʊtmən
boatswain
BR ˈbəʊsn, -z
AM ˈboʊsn, -z
boatyard
BR ˈbəʊtjɑːd, -z
AM ˈboʊtˌjɑrd, -z
Boaz
BR ˈbəʊaz
AM ˈboʊæz
bob
BR bɒb, -z, -ɪŋ, -d
AM bɑb, -z, -ɪŋ, -d
Bobbie
BR ˈbɒbi
AM ˈbɑbi
bobbin
BR ˈbɒbɪn, -z
AM ˈbɑbɪn, -z
bobbinet
BR ˈbɒbɪnɪt, -s
AM ˌbɑbəˈnɛt, -s
bobble
BR ˈbɒbl̩, -z, -ɪŋ, -d
AM ˈbɑbəl, -z, -ɪŋ, -d
bobbly
BR ˈbɒbl̩i
AM ˈbɑbli
bobby
BR ˈbɒb|i, -ɪz
AM ˈbɑbi, -z
bobbysox
BR ˈbɒbɪsɒks
AM ˈbɑbiˌsɑks
bobbysoxer
BR ˈbɒbɪˌsɒksə(r), -z
AM ˈbɑbiˌsɑksər, -z
bobcat
BR ˈbɒbkat, -s
AM ˈbɑbˌkæt, -s
bobolink
BR ˈbɒbəlɪŋk, -s
AM ˈbɑbəˌlɪŋk, -s
bobsled
BR ˈbɒbslɛd, -z, -ɪŋ, -ɪd
AM ˈbɑbˌslɛd, -z, -ɪŋ, -əd
bobsleigh
BR ˈbɒbsleɪ, -z, -ɪŋ, -d
AM ˈbɑbˌsleɪ, -z, -ɪŋ, -d

bobsleigher
BR 'bɒbˌsleɪə(r), -z
AM 'bɑbˌsleɪər, -z

bobstay
BR 'bɒbsteɪ, -z
AM 'bɑbˌsteɪ, -z

bobtail
BR 'bɒbteɪl, -z, -d
AM 'bɑbˌteɪl, -z, -d

bobwhite
BR 'bɒbwʌɪt, -s
AM bɑb'(h)waɪt, -s

bocage
BR bə'kɑːʒ, bɒ'kɑːʒ
AM boʊ'kɑʒ

Boca Raton
BR ˌbəʊkə rə'təʊn
AM ˌboʊkə rə'toʊn

Boccaccio
BR bə'kɑːtʃɪəʊ, bɒ'kɑːtʃɪəʊ, bə'katʃɪəʊ, bɒ'katʃɪəʊ
AM bə'katʃioʊ

bocce
BR 'bɒtʃiː
AM 'bɑtʃi

Boccherini
BR ˌbɒkə'riːni
AM ˌbɑkə'rini

bocci
BR 'bɒtʃiː
AM 'bɑtʃi

Boche
BR bɒʃ, -ɪz
AM bɔʃ, bɑʃ, -əz

bock
BR bɒk, -s
AM bɑk, -s

bod
BR bɒd, -z
AM bɑd, -z

bodacious
BR bə'deɪʃəs
AM ˌboʊ'deɪʃəs

bodaciously
BR bə'deɪʃəsli
AM ˌboʊ'deɪʃəsli

bodaciousness
BR bə'deɪʃəsnəs
AM ˌboʊ'deɪʃəsnəs

Boddington
BR 'bɒdɪŋt(ə)n
AM 'bɑdɪŋtən

bode
BR bəʊd, -z, -ɪŋ, -ɪd
AM boʊd, -z, -ɪŋ, -əd

bodeful
BR 'bəʊdf(ʊ)l
AM 'boʊdfəl

bodega
BR bə(ʊ)'diːgə(r), -z
AM boʊ'deɪgə, -z
SP bo'deɣa

bodement
BR 'bəʊdm(ə)nt, -s
AM 'boʊdmənt, -s

bodge
BR bɒdʒ, -ɪz, -ɪŋ, -d
AM bɑdʒ, -z, -ɪŋ, -d

Bodiam
BR 'bəʊdɪəm, 'bɒdɪəm
AM 'bɑdiəm

bodice
BR 'bɒdɪs, -ɪz
AM 'bɑdəs, -əz

bodiless
BR 'bɒdɪlɪs
AM 'bɑdiləs

bodily
BR 'bɒdɪli
AM 'bɑdəli

bodkin
BR 'bɒdkɪn, -z
AM 'bɑdkən, -z

Bodleian
BR 'bɒdlɪən
AM 'bɑdliən

Bodley
BR 'bɒdli
AM 'bɑdli

Bodmer
BR 'bɒdmə(r)
AM 'bɑdmər

Bodmin
BR 'bɒdmɪn
AM 'bɑdmən

Bodnant
BR 'bɒdnant
AM 'bɑdnənt

Bodoni
BR bə'dəʊni
AM boʊ'doʊni

body
BR 'bɒd|i, -ɪz
AM 'bɑdi, -z

bodybuilder
BR 'bɒdɪˌbɪldə(r), -z
AM 'bɑdiˌbɪldər, -z

bodybuilding
BR 'bɒdɪˌbɪldɪŋ
AM 'bɑdiˌbɪldɪŋ

bodyguard
BR 'bɒdɪgɑːd, -z
AM 'bɑdiˌgɑrd, -z

bodyline
BR 'bɒdɪlʌɪn
AM 'bɑdiˌlaɪn

bodyliner
BR 'bɒdɪˌlʌɪnə(r), -z
AM 'bɑdiˌlaɪnər, -z

bodylining
BR 'bɒdɪˌlʌɪnɪŋ, -z
AM 'bɑdiˌlaɪnɪŋ, -z

bodysuit
BR 'bɒdɪs(j)uːt, -s
AM 'bɑdiˌsut, -s

bodywork
BR 'bɒdɪwəːk
AM 'bɑdiˌwərk

Boehm
BR 'bəʊ(ə)m, bəːm
AM boʊm, bʊm

Boeing®
BR 'bəʊɪŋ, -z
AM 'boʊɪŋ, -z

Boeotia
BR bɪ'əʊʃə(r)
AM bi'oʊʃə

Boeotian
BR bɪ'əʊʃn, -z
AM bi'oʊʃən, -z

Boer
BR bɔː(r), 'bəʊə(r), bʊə(r), -z
AM 'boʊ(ə)r, bɔ(ə)r, -z

Boethius
BR bəʊ'iːθɪəs
AM boʊ'iθiəs

boeuf bourgignon
BR ˌbəːf 'bɔːgɪnjɒ̃
AM ˌbʊf ˌbərgɪn'jɔn

boff
BR bɒf, -s
AM bɑf, -s

boffin
BR 'bɒfɪn, -z
AM 'bɑfən, -z

boffo
BR 'bɒfəʊ
AM 'bɑfoʊ

boffola
BR bɒ'fəʊlə(r), bə'fəʊlə(r), -z
AM bɑ'foʊlə, -z

Bofors
BR 'bəʊfəz
AM 'boʊfɔ(ə)rz
SW boː'fɒʃ

bog
BR bɒg, -z, -ɪŋ, -d
AM bɔg, bɑg, -z, -ɪŋ, -d

Bogarde
BR 'bəʊgɑːd
AM 'boʊˌgɑrd

Bogart
BR 'bəʊgɑːt
AM 'boʊ'gɑrt

bogey
BR 'bəʊg|i, -ɪz, -ɪɪŋ, -ɪd
AM 'boʊgi, -z, -ɪŋ, -d

bogeyman
BR 'bəʊgɪman
AM 'boʊgiˌmæn, 'bʊgiˌmæn

bogeymen
BR 'bəʊgɪmɛn
AM 'boʊgiˌmɛn, 'bʊgiˌmɛn

bogginess
BR 'bɒgɪnɪs
AM 'bɔginəs, 'bɑginɪs

Boggis
BR 'bɒgɪs
AM 'bɑgəs

boggle
BR 'bɒg|l, -lz, -l̩ɪŋ\-lɪŋ, -ld
AM 'bɑg|əl, -əlz, -(ə)lɪŋ, -əld

boggy
BR 'bɒg|i, -ɪə(r), -ɪɪst
AM 'bɔgi, 'bɑgi, -ər, -ɪst

bogie
BR 'bəʊg|i, -ɪz
AM 'boʊgi, -z

bogle
BR 'bəʊgl, -z
AM 'boʊgəl, -z

Bognor
BR 'bɒgnə(r)
AM 'bɑgnər

bogong
BR 'bəʊgɒŋ, -z
AM 'boʊgɑŋ, -z

Bogotá
BR ˌbɒgə'tɑː(r)
AM 'boʊgəˌtɑ

bogus
BR 'bəʊgəs
AM 'boʊgəs

bogusness
BR 'bəʊgəsnəs
AM 'boʊgəsnəs

bogy
BR 'bəʊg|i, -ɪz
AM 'boʊgi, -z

bogyman
BR 'bəʊgɪman
AM 'boʊgiˌmæn, 'bʊgiˌmæn

bogymen
BR 'bəʊgɪmɛn
AM 'boʊgiˌmɛn, 'bʊgiˌmɛn

bohea
BR bəʊ'hi
AM boʊ'hi

Bohème
BR bəʊ'ɛm, bəʊ'eɪm
AM boʊ'ɛm

Bohemia
BR bə(ʊ)'hiːmɪə(r)
AM boʊ'himiə

Bohemian
BR bə(ʊ)'hiːmɪən, -z
AM boʊ'himiən, -z

Bohemianism
BR bə(ʊ)'hiːmɪənɪz(ə)m
AM boʊ'himiəˌnɪzəm

boho
BR 'bəʊhəʊ, -z
AM 'boʊˌhoʊ, -z

Bohr
BR bɔː(r)
AM bɔ(ə)r
DAN 'boːʌ

bohunk
BR 'bəʊhʌŋk, -s
AM 'boʊˌhəŋk, -s

boil
BR bɔɪl, -z, -ɪŋ, -d
AM bɔɪl, -z, -ɪŋ, -d

Boileau
BR bwa'ləʊ, bwɑː'ləʊ
AM ˌbwɑ'loʊ

boiler
BR ˈbɔɪlə(r), -z
AM ˈbɔɪlər, -z

boilermaker
BR ˈbɔɪləˌmeɪkə(r), -z
AM ˈbɔɪlərˌmeɪkər, -z

boing
BR bɔɪŋ
AM bɔɪŋ

boink
BR bɔɪŋk
AM bɔɪŋk

Boise
BR ˈbɔɪzi
AM ˈbɔɪzi

boisterous
BR ˈbɔɪst(ə)rəs
AM ˈbɔɪst(ə)rəs

boisterously
BR ˈbɔɪst(ə)rəsli
AM ˈbɔɪst(ə)rəsli

boisterousness
BR ˈbɔɪst(ə)rəsnəs
AM ˈbɔɪst(ə)rəsnəs

Bokhara
BR bɒˈkɑːrə(r), bə(ʊ)ˈkɑːrə(r)
AM boʊˈkɑrə, boʊˈkɛrə
RUS buxaˈra

Bokmål
BR ˈbʊkmɔːl
AM ˈbʊkˌmɔl, ˈbʊkˌmɑl
NO ˈbuːkmoːl

bola
BR ˈbəʊlə(r), -z
AM ˈboʊlə, -z

Bolam
BR ˈbəʊləm
AM ˈboʊləm

bolas
BR ˈbəʊləs, -ɪz
AM ˈboʊləs, -əz

bold
BR bəʊld, -ə(r), -ɪst
AM boʊld, -ər, -əst

boldface
BR ˈbəʊldfeɪs
AM ˈboʊl(d)ˌfeɪs

boldfaced
BR ˌbəʊldˈfeɪst
AM ˈboʊl(d)ˌfeɪst

boldly
BR ˈbəʊldli
AM ˈboʊl(d)li

boldness
BR ˈbəʊldnəs
AM ˈboʊl(d)nəs

Boldre
BR ˈbəʊldə(r)
AM ˈboʊldər

Boldrewood
BR ˈbəʊldəwʊd
AM ˈboʊldərˌwʊd

bole
BR bəʊl, -z
AM boʊl, -z

Boléat
BR ˈbəʊlɪat, ˈbəʊlɪət, ˈbəʊlɪɑː(r)
AM ˈboʊliət

bolection
BR bə(ʊ)ˈlɛkʃn, -z
AM boʊˈlɛkʃən, -z

bolero¹
dance
BR bəˈlɛːrəʊ, -z
AM bəˈlɛroʊ, -z

bolero²
jacket
BR ˈbɒlərəʊ, -z
AM bəˈlɛroʊ, -z

boletus
BR bəˈliːtəs, -ɪz
AM boʊˈlidəs, -əz

Boleyn
BR bəˈlɪn, ˈbʊlɪn
AM bəˈlɪn, ˈbʊlən

bolide
BR ˈbəʊlʌɪd, ˈbəʊlɪd, -z
AM ˈboʊˌlaɪd, ˈboʊləd, -z

Bolingbroke
BR ˈbɒlɪŋbrʊk, ˈbʊlɪŋbrʊk
AM ˈbɑlɪŋˌbrʊk, ˈboʊlɪŋˌbroʊk

Bolinger
BR ˈbɒlɪn(d)ʒə(r)
AM ˈboʊlɪndʒər, ˈbɑlɪndʒər

Bolitho
BR bəˈlʌɪθəʊ
AM bəˈlaɪθoʊ

Bolívar
BR ˈbɒlɪvɑː(r), ˌbɒlɪˈvɑː(r)
AM ˈboʊləˌvɑr, ˈbɑləˌvɑr

bolivar
BR ˈbɒlɪvɑː(r), -z
AM ˈboʊləˌvɑr, ˈbɑləˌvɑr, -z

Bolivia
BR bəˈlɪvɪə(r)
AM bəˈlɪviə

Bolivian
BR bəˈlɪvɪən, -z
AM bəˈlɪviən, -z

boliviano
BR bəˌlɪvɪˈɑːnəʊ, -z
AM bəˌlɪviˈɑnoʊ, -z
SP ˌboliˈβjano

boll
BR bɒl, bəʊl, -z
AM bɑl, boʊl, -z

Bollandist
BR ˈbɒləndɪst
AM ˈbɑləndəst, ˈbələndəst

bollard
BR ˈbɒlɑːd, ˈbɒləd, -z
AM ˈbɑlərd, ˈbɑˌlɑrd, -z

Bollin
BR ˈbɒlɪn
AM ˈbɑlən

Bollinger®
BR ˈbɒlɪn(d)ʒə(r)
AM ˈbɑləndʒər, ˈbələndʒər

bollocking
BR ˈbɒləkɪŋ
AM ˈbɑləkɪŋ, ˈbələkɪŋ

bollocks
BR ˈbɒləks
AM ˈbɑləks, ˈbələks

bolo
BR ˈbəʊləʊ, -z
AM ˈboʊˌloʊ, -z

Bologna
BR bəˈlɒnjə(r)
AM bəˈloʊnjə

bologna
sausage
BR bəˈləʊni, bəˈlɒnjə(r)
AM bəˈloʊni

Bolognese
BR ˌbɒləˈn(j)eɪz
AM ˌboʊləˈniz, ˌboʊləˈneɪz

bolometer
BR bəˈlɒmɪtə(r), -z
AM boʊˈlɑmədər, bəˈlɑmədər, -z

bolometric
BR ˌbɒləˈmɛtrɪk
AM ˌboʊloʊˈmɛtrɪk, ˌboʊləˈmɛtrɪk

bolometry
BR bəˈlɒmɪtri
AM boʊˈlɑmətri, bəˈlɑmətri

boloney
BR bəˈləʊni
AM bəˈloʊni

Bolshevik
BR ˈbɒlʃɪvɪk, -s
AM ˈboʊlʃəˌvɪk, -s

Bolshevism
BR ˈbɒlʃɪvɪz(ə)m
AM ˈboʊlʃəˌvɪzəm

Bolshevist
BR ˈbɒlʃɪvɪst, -s
AM ˈboʊlʃəvəst, -s

bolshie
BR ˈbɒlʃ|i, -ɪz
AM ˈboʊlʃi, -z

bolshily
BR ˈbɒlʃɪli
AM ˈboʊlʃəli

bolshiness
BR ˈbɒlʃɪnɪs
AM ˈboʊlʃinɪs

Bolshoi
BR ˌbɒlˈʃɔɪ, ˈbɒlʃɔɪ
AM ˈboʊlˌʃɔɪ

Bolshoy
BR ˌbɒlˈʃɔɪ, ˈbɒlʃɔɪ
AM ˈboʊlˌʃɔɪ

bolshy
BR ˈbɒlʃ|i, -ɪz, -ɪə(r), -ɪɪst
AM ˈboʊlʃi, -z, -ər, -ɪst

Bolsover
BR ˈbɒlsəʊvə(r)
AM ˈboʊlˌsoʊvər

bolster
BR ˈbəʊlst|ə(r), -əz, -(ə)rɪŋ, -əd
AM ˈboʊlstər, -z, -ɪŋ, -d

bolsterer
BR ˈbəʊlst(ə)rə(r), -z
AM ˈboʊlstərər, -z

bolt
BR bəʊlt, -s, -ɪŋ, -ɪd
AM boʊlt, -s, -ɪŋ, -əd

bolter
BR ˈbəʊltə(r), -z
AM ˈboʊltər, -z

bolthole
BR ˈbəʊlthəʊl, -z
AM ˈboʊltˌ(h)oʊl, -z

Bolton
BR ˈbəʊlt(ə)n
AM ˈboʊltən

Boltzmann
BR ˈbɒltsmən
AM ˈbɔltsmən, ˈbɑltsmən

bolus
BR ˈbəʊləs, -ɪz
AM ˈboʊləs, -əz

Bolzano
BR bɒlˈzɑːnəʊ, bɒlˈtsɑːnəʊ
AM ˌbɔlˈzɑnoʊ, ˌbɑlˈzɑnoʊ

bomb
BR bɒm, -z, -ɪŋ, -d
AM bɑm, -z, -ɪŋ, -d

bombard¹
noun
BR ˈbɒmbɑːd, -z
AM ˈbɑmˌbɑrd, -z

bombard²
verb
BR bɒmˈbɑːd, -z, -ɪŋ, -ɪd
AM bɑmˈbɑrd, -z, -ɪŋ, -əd

bombarde
BR ˈbɒmbɑːd, -z
AM ˈbɑmˌbɑrd, -z

bombardier
BR ˌbɒmbəˈdɪə(r), -z
AM ˌbɑmbə(r)ˈdɪ(ə)r, -z

bombardment
BR bɒmˈbɑːdm(ə)nt, -s
AM bɑmˈbɑrdmənt, -s

bombardon
BR ˈbɒmbədən, -z
AM ˈbɑmbərdən, bɑmˈbɑrdən, -z

bombasine
BR ˈbɒmbəziːn
AM ˈbɑmbəˌzin, ˈbɑmbəˌsin

bombast
BR 'bɒmbast
AM 'bambæst

bombastic
BR bɒm'bastɪk
AM bam'bæstɪk

bombastically
BR bɒm'bastɪkli
AM bam'bæstək(ə)li

Bombay
BR ˌbɒm'beɪ
AM ˌbam'beɪ

bombazine
BR 'bɒmbəziːn, ˌbɒmbə'ziːn
AM 'bambəˌzin, 'bambəˌsin

bombe
BR bɒm(b), bɔ̃ːb, -z
AM bam(b), -z

bomber
BR 'bɒmə(r), -z
AM 'bamər, -z

bombora
BR bɒm'bɔːrə(r), -z
AM ˌbam'bɔrə, -z

bombproof
BR 'bɒmpruːf
AM 'bamˌpruf

bombshell
BR 'bɒmʃɛl, -z
AM 'bamˌʃɛl, -z

bombsight
BR 'bɒmsʌɪt, -s
AM 'bamˌsaɪt, -s

bombsite
BR 'bɒmsʌɪt, -s
AM 'bamˌsaɪt, -s

bona fide
BR ˌbəʊnə 'fʌɪdi
AM 'boʊnə ˌfaɪd, 'banə +, ˌboʊnə 'faɪdi

bona fides
BR ˌbəʊnə 'fʌɪdiːz
AM 'boʊnə ˌfaɪdz, 'banə +, ˌboʊnə 'faɪdiz

Bonaire
BR bɒn'ɛː(r)
AM bə'nɛ(ə)r

Bonallack
BR bə'nalək
AM bə'nælək

bonanza
BR bə'nanzə(r), -z
AM bə'nænzə, -z

Bonaparte
BR 'bəʊnəpɑːt
AM 'boʊnəˌpart

bona vacantia
BR ˌbəʊnə və'kantɪə(r)
AM 'boʊnə və'kan(t)iə

Bonaventura
BR ˌbɒnəvɛn'tjʊərə(r), ˌbɒnəvɛn'tjɔːrə(r), ˌbɒnəvɛn'tʃʊərə(r), ˌbɒnəvɛn'tʃɔːrə(r)
AM ˌbanəvɛn'tʃʊrə

Bonaventure
BR 'bɒnəvɛn(t)ʃə(r), ˌbɒnə'vɛn(t)ʃə(r)
AM 'banəˌvən(t)ʃər

bon-bon
BR 'bɒnbɒn, -z
AM 'banˌban, -z

bonce
BR bɒns, -ɪz
AM bans, -əz

bond
BR bɒnd, -z, -ɪŋ, -ɪd
AM band, -z, -ɪŋ, -əd

bondage
BR 'bɒndɪdʒ
AM 'bandɪdʒ

bondager
BR 'bɒndɪdʒə(r), -z
AM 'bandɪdʒər, -z

bondholder
BR 'bɒndˌhəʊldə(r), -z
AM 'ban(d)ˌ(h)oʊldər, -z

Bondi
BR 'bɒndʌɪ
AM 'bandi

bondman
BR 'bɒndmən
AM 'ban(d)mən

bondmen
BR 'bɒndmən
AM 'ban(d)mən

bondsman
BR 'bɒn(d)zmən
AM 'ban(d)zmən

bondsmen
BR 'bɒn(d)zmən
AM 'ban(d)zmən

bondstone
BR 'bɒn(d)stəʊn, -z
AM 'ban(d)ˌstoʊn, -z

bondswoman
BR 'bɒn(d)zˌwʊmən
AM 'ban(d)zˌwʊmən

bondswomen
BR 'bɒn(d)zˌwɪmɪn
AM 'ban(d)zˌwɪmɨn

bondwoman
BR 'bɒndˌwʊmən
AM 'ban(d)ˌwʊmən

bondwomen
BR 'bɒndˌwɪmɪn
AM 'ban(d)ˌwɪmɨn

bone
BR bəʊn, -z, -ɪŋ, -d
AM boʊn, -z, -ɪŋ, -d

bonefish
BR 'bəʊnfɪʃ
AM 'boʊnˌfɪʃ

bonehead
BR 'bəʊnhɛd, -z
AM 'boʊnˌ(h)ɛd, -z

boneheaded
BR ˌbəʊn'hɛdɪd
AM 'boʊnˌ(h)ɛdəd

boneless
BR 'bəʊnləs
AM 'boʊnləs

bonemeal
BR 'bəʊnmiːl
AM 'boʊnˌmil

boner
BR 'bəʊnə(r), -z
AM 'boʊnər, -z

boneshaker
BR 'bəʊnˌʃeɪkə(r), -z
AM 'boʊnˌʃeɪkər, -z

Bo'ness
BR ˌbəʊ'nɛs
AM boʊ'nɛs

bonfire
BR 'bɒnfʌɪə(r), -z
AM 'banˌfaɪ(ə)r, -z

bong
BR bɒŋ, -z, -ɪŋ, -d
AM baŋ, -z, -ɪŋ, -d

bongo
BR 'bɒŋgəʊ, -z
AM 'bɔŋgoʊ, 'baŋgoʊ, -z

Bonham
BR 'bɒnəm
AM 'banəm

Bonhoeffer
BR 'bɒnˌhəːfə(r), 'bɒnˌhɒfə(r)
AM 'banˌ(h)ɔfər, 'banˌ(h)afər

bonhomie
BR 'bɒnəmiː, 'bɒnɒmiː
AM 'banəmi, ˌbanə'mi

bonhomous
BR 'bɒnəməs
AM 'banəməs

bonier
BR 'bəʊnɪə(r)
AM 'boʊniər

boniest
BR 'bəʊnɪɪst
AM 'boʊniɨst

Boniface
BR 'bɒnɪfeɪs
AM 'banəfəs

boniness
BR 'bəʊnɪnɪs
AM 'boʊninɨs

Bonington
BR 'bɒnɪŋt(ə)n
AM 'banɪŋtən

Bonio
BR 'bəʊnɪəʊ
AM 'boʊnioʊ

bonism
BR 'bəʊnɪz(ə)m
AM 'boʊˌnɪzəm

bonist
BR 'bəʊnɪst, -s
AM 'boʊnəst, -s

Bonita
BR bə'niːtə(r)
AM bə'nidə

bonito
BR bə'niːtəʊ, -z
AM bə'nidoʊ, bə'nidə, -z

bonk
BR bɒŋ|k, -ks, -kɪŋ, -(k)t
AM baŋ|k, -ks, -kɪŋ, -(k)t

bonker
BR 'bɒŋkə(r), -z
AM 'baŋkər, -z

bon mot
BR ˌbɒn 'məʊ, ˌbɔ̃ +
AM ˌbɔn 'moʊ

Bonn
BR bɒn
AM ban

Bonnard
BR bɒ'nɑː(r)
AM bɔ'nar, ba'nar

bonne bouche
BR ˌbɒn 'buːʃ, -ɪz
AM ˌbən 'buʃ, -əz

Bonner
BR 'bɒnə(r)
AM 'banər

bonnes bouches
BR ˌbɒn 'buːʃ
AM ˌbən 'buʃ

bonnet
BR 'bɒn|ɪt, -ɪts, -ɪtɪd
AM 'banə|t, -ts, -dəd

bonnethead
BR 'bɒnɪthɛd, -z
AM 'banətˌ(h)ɛd, -z

Bonneville
BR 'bɒnəvɪl
AM 'banəˌvɪl

Bonnie
BR 'bɒni
AM 'bani

bonnily
BR 'bɒnɨli
AM 'banəli

bonniness
BR 'bɒnɪnɪs
AM 'baninɨs

bonny
BR 'bɒn|i, -ɪə(r), -ɪɪst
AM 'bani, -ər, -ɨst

bonsai
BR 'bɒnsʌɪ
AM ˌban'saɪ

Bonser
BR 'bɒnsə(r)
AM 'bansər

bons mots
BR ˌbɒn 'məʊ(z), ˌbɔ̃ +
AM ˌbɔn 'moʊz

Bonsor
BR 'bɒnsə(r)
AM 'bansər

bonspiel
BR 'bɒnspiːl, -z

AM ˈbɑnˌspil, ˈbɑnˌʃpil, -z

bons vivants
BR ˌbɒ̃ viːˈvɒ̃z, ˌbɒn viːˈvɒnz, ˌbɒn viːˈvɒnts
AM ˌbɑn viˈvɑn(t)s

bons viveurs
BR ˌbɒ̃ viːˈvəː, ˌbɒn +
AM ˌbɑn viˈvərz

bontbok
BR ˈbɒntbɒk, -s
AM ˈbɑntˌbɑk, -s

bontebok
BR ˈbɒntɨbɒk, -s
AM ˈbɑn(t)iˌbɑk, -s

bonus
BR ˈbəʊnəs, -ɨz
AM ˈboʊnəs, -ɨz

bon vivant
BR ˌbɒ̃ viːˈvɒ̃, ˌbɒn viːˈvɒn(t), -ts\-z
AM ˌbɑn viˈvɑnt, -s

bon viveur
BR ˌbɒ̃ viːˈvəː(r), ˌbɒn +, -z
AM ˌbɑn viˈvər, -z

bon voyage
BR ˌbɒn vɔɪˈɑːʒ
AM ˈbɑn ˌvɔɪˈɑʒ, ˈboʊn +

bonxie
BR ˈbɒŋks|i, -z
AM ˈbɑŋksi, -z

bony
BR ˈbəʊn|i, -ɪə(r), -ɪɨst
AM ˈboʊni, -ər, -ɨst

bonze
BR bɒnz, -ɨz
AM bɑnz, -əz

bonzer
BR ˈbɒnzə(r)
AM ˈbɑnzər

Bonzo
BR ˈbɒnzəʊ
AM ˈbɑnzoʊ

boo
BR buː, -z, -ɪŋ, -d
AM bu, -z, -ɪŋ, -d

boob
BR buːb, -z, -ɪŋ, -d
AM bub, -z, -ɪŋ, -d

booboisie
BR ˌbuːbwɑːˈziː
AM ˌbuˌbwɑˈzi

booboo
BR ˈbuːbuː, -z
AM ˈbuˌbu, -z

boobook
BR ˈbuːbʊk, -s
AM ˈbuˌbʊk, -s

booby
BR ˈbuːb|i, -ɪz
AM ˈbubi, -z

boobyish
BR ˈbuːbiɪʃ
AM ˈbubiɪʃ

boodle
BR ˈbuːdl
AM ˈbudəl

boogie
BR ˈbuːg|i, -ɪz, -ɪɪŋ, -ɪd
AM ˈbʊgi, -z, -ɪŋ, -d

boogie-woogie
BR ˌbuːgɪˈwuːgi
AM ˌbʊgiˈwʊgi

boohoo
BR ˌbuːˈhuː
AM ˈbuˈhu

book
BR bʊk, -s, -ɪŋ, -t
AM bʊk, -s, -ɪŋ, -t

bookable
BR ˈbʊkəbl
AM ˈbʊkəbəl

bookbinder
BR ˈbʊkˌbʌɪndə(r), -z
AM ˈbʊkˌbaɪndər, -z

bookbinding
BR ˈbʊkˌbʌɪndɪŋ
AM ˈbʊkˌbaɪndɪŋ

bookcase
BR ˈbʊkkeɪs, -ɨz
AM ˈbʊ(k)ˌkeɪs, -ɪz

bookend
BR ˈbʊkɛnd, -z
AM ˈbʊkˌɛnd, -z

booker
BR ˈbʊkə(r), -z
AM ˈbʊkər, -z

bookie
BR ˈbʊk|i, -ɪz
AM ˈbʊki, -z

booking
BR ˈbʊkɪŋ, -z
AM ˈbʊkɪŋ, -z

bookish
BR ˈbʊkɪʃ
AM ˈbʊkɪʃ

bookishly
BR ˈbʊkɨʃli
AM ˈbʊkɨʃli

bookishness
BR ˈbʊkɨʃnɨs
AM ˈbʊkɨʃnɨs

bookkeeper
BR ˈbʊkˌkiːpə(r), -z
AM ˈbʊ(k)ˌkipər, -z

bookkeeping
BR ˈbʊkˌkiːpɪŋ
AM ˈbʊ(k)ˌkipɪŋ

booklet
BR ˈbʊklɨt, -s
AM ˈbʊklɨt, -s

booklist
BR ˈbʊklɪst, -s
AM ˈbʊkˌlɪst, -s

bookmaker
BR ˈbʊkˌmeɪkə(r), -z
AM ˈbʊkˌmeɪkər, -z

bookmaking
BR ˈbʊkˌmeɪkɪŋ
AM ˈbʊkˌmeɪkɪŋ

bookman
BR ˈbʊkmən
AM ˈbʊkmən

bookmark
BR ˈbʊkmɑːk, -s
AM ˈbʊkˌmɑrk, -s

bookmarker
BR ˈbʊkˌmɑːkə(r), -z
AM ˈbʊkˌmɑrkər, -z

bookmen
BR ˈbʊkmən
AM ˈbʊkmən

bookmobile
BR ˈbʊkmə(ʊ)biːl, -z
AM ˈbʊkmoʊˌbil, ˈbʊkməˌbil, -z

bookplate
BR ˈbʊkpleɪt, -s
AM ˈbʊkˌpleɪt, -s

bookseller
BR ˈbʊkˌsɛlə(r), -z
AM ˈbʊkˌsɛlər, -z

bookshelf
BR ˈbʊkʃɛlf
AM ˈbʊkˌʃɛlf

bookshelves
BR ˈbʊkʃɛlvz
AM ˈbʊkˌʃɛlvz

bookshop
BR ˈbʊkʃɒp, -s
AM ˈbʊkˌʃɑp, -s

bookstall
BR ˈbʊkstɔːl, -z
AM ˈbukˌstɔl, ˈbukˌstɑl, -z

bookstand
BR ˈbʊkstand, -z
AM ˈbʊkˌstænd, -z

bookstore
BR ˈbʊkstɔː(r), -z
AM ˈbʊkˌstɔ(ə)r, -z

booksy
BR ˈbʊksi
AM ˈbʊksi

bookwork
BR ˈbʊkwəːk
AM ˈbʊkˌwərk

bookworm
BR ˈbʊkwəːm, -z
AM ˈbʊkˌwərm, -z

Boole
BR buːl
AM bul

Boolean
BR ˈbuːlɪən
AM ˈbuliən

boom
BR buːm, -z, -ɪŋ, -d
AM bum, -z, -ɪŋ, -d

boomer
BR ˈbuːmə(r), -z
AM ˈbumər, -z

boomerang
BR ˈbuːməraŋ, -z, -ɪŋ, -d
AM ˈbuməˌræŋ, -z, -ɪŋ, -d

boomlet
BR ˈbuːmlɨt, -s
AM ˈbumlət, -s

boomslang
BR ˈbuːmslaŋ, -z
AM ˈbumˌslæŋ, -z

boomtown
BR ˈbuːmtaʊn, -z
AM ˈbumˌtaʊn, -z

boon
BR buːn, -z
AM bun, -z

boondock
BR ˈbuːndɒk, -s
AM ˈbunˌdɑk, -s

boondoggle
BR ˈbuːnˌdɒg|l, -lz, -l̩ɪŋ\-lɪŋ, -ld
AM ˈbunˌdɑg|əl, -əlz, -(ə)lɪŋ, -əld

Boone
BR buːn
AM bun

boonies
BR ˈbuːnɪz
AM ˈbuniz

boor
BR bʊə(r), bɔː(r), -z
AM bʊ(ə)r, -z

boorish
BR ˈbʊərɪʃ, ˈbɔːrɪʃ
AM ˈbʊrɪʃ

boorishly
BR ˈbʊərɨʃli, ˈbɔːrɨʃli
AM ˈbʊrɨʃli

boorishness
BR ˈbʊərɪʃnɪs, ˈbɔːrɪʃnɪs
AM ˈbʊrɪʃnɪs

Boosey
BR ˈbuːzi
AM ˈbuzi

boost
BR buːst, -s, -ɪŋ, -ɨd
AM bust, -s, -ɪŋ, -ɨd

booster
BR ˈbuːstə(r), -z
AM ˈbustər, -z

boot
BR buːt, -s, -ɪŋ, -ɨd
AM bu|t, -ts, -dɪŋ, -dəd

bootblack
BR ˈbuːtblak, -s
AM ˈbutˌblæk, -s

bootboy
BR ˈbuːtbɔɪ, -z
AM ˈbutˌbɔɪ, -z

bootee
BR buːˈtiː, ˈbuːtiː, -z
AM buˈti, -z

Boötes
BR bəʊˈəʊtiːz
AM boʊˈoʊdiz

booth
BR buː|ð, buː|θ, -ðz
AM bu|θ, -ðz

Bootham
BR 'bu:ðəm
AM 'buðəm

Boothby
BR 'bu:ðbi
AM 'buθbi

Boothe
BR bu:ð, bu:θ
AM buθ

Boothia
BR 'bu:θɪə(*r*)
AM 'buθiə

Boothroyd
BR 'bu:ðrɔɪd
AM 'buθrɔɪd

bootie
BR bu:'ti:, 'bu:ti:, -z
AM 'budi, -z

bootjack
BR 'bu:tdʒak, -s
AM 'but,dʒæk, -s

bootlace
BR 'bu:tleɪs, -ɪz
AM 'but,leɪs, -ɪz

Bootle
BR 'bu:tl
AM 'budəl

bootleg
BR 'bu:tlɛg, -z, -ɪŋ, -d
AM 'but,lɛg, -z, -ɪŋ, -d

bootlegger
BR 'bu:t,lɛgə(r), -z
AM 'but,lɛgər, -z

bootless
BR 'bu:tləs
AM 'butləs

bootlicker
BR 'bu:t,lɪkə(r), -z
AM 'but,lɪkər, -z

bootstrap
BR 'bu:tstrap, -s, -ɪŋ, -t
AM 'but,stræp, -s, -ɪŋ, -t

booty
BR 'bu:ti
AM 'budi

booze
BR bu:z, -ɪz, -ɪŋ, -d
AM buz, -əz, -ɪŋ, -d

boozer
BR 'bu:zə(r), -z
AM 'buzər, -z

boozily
BR 'bu:zɪli
AM 'buzəli

booziness
BR 'bu:zɪnɪs
AM 'buzinɪs

boozy
BR 'bu:z|i, -ɪə(r), -ɪɪst
AM 'buzi, -ər, -ɪst

bop
BR bɒp, -s, -ɪŋ, -t
AM bɑp, -s, -ɪŋ, -t

Bophuthatswana
BR bə,pu:tə'tswɑ:nə(*r*), ,bɒpu:tət'swɑ:nə(*r*)
AM ,boʊ,pʊdət'swɑnə

bopper
BR 'bɒpə(r), -z
AM 'bɑpər, -z

bora
BR 'bɔ:rə(*r*), -z
AM 'bɔrə, -z

Bora-Bora
BR ,bɔ:rə'bɔ:rə(*r*)
AM ,bɔrə'bɔrə

boracic
BR bə'rasɪk
AM bə'ræsɪk

borage
BR 'bɒrɪdʒ
AM 'bɔrɪdʒ, 'bɑrɪdʒ

borak
BR 'bɔ:rak
AM 'bɔrək

borane
BR 'bɔ:reɪn, -z
AM 'bɔ,reɪn, -z

borate
BR 'bɔ:reɪt, -s
AM 'bɔ,reɪt, -s

borax
BR 'bɔ:raks
AM 'bɔ,ræks

borazon
BR 'bɔ:rəzɒn
AM 'bɔrə,zɑn

borborygmi
BR ,bɔ:bə'rɪgmi
AM ,bɔrbə'rɪgmi

borborygmic
BR ,bɔ:bə'rɪgmɪk
AM ,bɔrbə'rɪgmɪk

borborygmus
BR ,bɔ:bə'rɪgməs
AM ,bɔrbə'rɪgməs

Bordeaux
BR bɔ:'dəʊ
AM ,bɔr'doʊ

bordel
BR bɔ:'dɛl, -z
AM 'bɔrdəl, -z

bordello
BR bɔ:'dɛləʊ, -z
AM ,bɔr'dɛloʊ, -z

border
BR 'bɔ:d|ə(r), -əz, -(ə)rɪŋ, -əd
AM 'bɔrdər, -z, -ɪŋ, -d

bordereau
BR ,bɔ:də'rəʊ, -z
AM ,bɔrdə'roʊ, -z

bordereaux
BR ,bɔ:də'rəʊz
AM ,bɔrdə'roʊ(z)

borderer
BR 'bɔ:d(ə)rə(r), -z
AM 'bɔrdərər, -z

borderland
BR 'bɔ:dəland, -z
AM 'bɔrdər,lænd, -z

borderline
BR 'bɔ:dəlʌɪn, -z
AM 'bɔrdər,laɪn, -z

Bordet
BR bɔ:'deɪ
AM bɔr'deɪ

bordone
BR bɔ:'dəʊni
AM bɔr'doʊni

bordure
BR 'bɔ:djʊə(r), -z
AM 'bɔrdʒər, -z

bore
BR bɔ:(r), -z, -ɪŋ, -d
AM bɔ(ə)r, -z, -ɪŋ, -d

boreal
BR 'bɔ:rɪəl
AM 'bɔriəl

borealis
BR ,bɔ:rɪ'eɪlɪs, ,bɔ:rɪ'ɑ:lɪs
AM ,bɔri'æləs, ,bɔri'eɪlɪs

boredom
BR 'bɔ:dəm
AM 'bɔrdəm

Boreham
BR 'bɔ:rəm, 'bɔ:rm̩
AM 'bɔrəm

borehole
BR 'bɔ:həʊl, -z
AM 'bɔr,(h)oʊl, -z

borer
BR 'bɔ:rə(r), -z
AM 'bɔrər, -z

Borg
BR bɔ:g
AM bɔ(ə)rg
SW bɒrj

Borges
BR 'bɔ:xɛs, 'bɔ:gɛs
AM 'bɔr,hɛs, 'bɔrgəs

Borgia
BR 'bɔ:(d)ʒ(ɪ)ə(*r*)
AM 'bɔrʒə

boric
BR 'bɔ:rɪk, 'bɒrɪk
AM 'bɔrɪk

boring
BR 'bɔ:rɪŋ, -z
AM 'bɔrɪŋ, -z

boringly
BR 'bɔ:rɪŋli
AM 'bɔrɪŋli

boringness
BR 'bɔ:rɪŋnɪs
AM 'bɔrɪŋnɪs

Boris
BR 'bɒrɪs
AM 'bɔrəs

Bork
BR bɔ:k
AM bɔ(ə)rk

Bormann
BR 'bɔ:mən
AM 'bɔrmən

born
BR bɔ:n
AM bɔ(ə)rn

borne
BR bɔ:n
AM bɔ(ə)rn

borné
BR bɔ:'neɪ
AM bɔr'neɪ

Bornean
BR 'bɔ:nɪən, -z
AM 'bɔrniən, -z

Borneo
BR 'bɔ:nɪəʊ
AM 'bɔrnioʊ

Bornholm
BR 'bɔ:nhəʊm
AM 'bɔrn,(h)oʊm
DAN ,bɔ:n'hʌl'm

Borobudur
BR ,bɒrəbə'dʊə(r)
AM ,bɔrəbə'dʊ(ə)r

Borodin
BR 'bɒrədɪn
AM 'bɔrə,din
RUS bəra'dʲin

Borodino
BR ,bɒrə'di:nəʊ
AM ,bɔrə'dinoʊ
RUS bərədʲi'no

borofluoride
BR ,bɔ:rə(ʊ)'flʊərʌɪd, ,bɔ:rə(ʊ)'flɔ:rʌɪd
AM ,bɔrə'flʊ,raɪd, ,bɔrə'flɔ,raɪd

boron
BR 'bɔ:rɒn
AM 'bɔ,rɑn

boronia
BR bə'rəʊnɪə(*r*), -z
AM bə'roʊniə, -z

borosilicate
BR ,bɔ:rə(ʊ)'sɪlɪkeɪt, ,bɔ:rə(ʊ)'sɪlɪkət
AM ,bɔrə'sɪləkət

borough
BR 'bʌrə(*r*), -z
AM 'bəroʊ, 'bərə, -z

Borromini
BR ,bɒrə'mi:ni
AM ,bɔrə'mini

borrow
BR 'bɒrəʊ, -z, -ɪŋ, -d
AM 'bɑr|oʊ, 'bɔr|oʊ, -oʊz, -əwɪŋ, -oʊd

Borrowdale
BR 'bɒrə(ʊ)deɪl
AM 'bɑroʊ,deɪl

borrower
BR 'bɒrəʊə(r), -z
AM 'bɑrəwər, 'bɔrəwər, -z

borrowing
BR 'bɒrəʊɪŋ, -z
AM 'bɑrəwɪŋ, 'bɔrəwɪŋ, -z

Borsalino®
BR ,bɔ:sə'li:nəʊ, -z
AM ,bɔrsə'linoʊ, -z

borsch
BR bɔ:ʃ

AM bɔ(ə)rʃ

borscht
BR bɔːʃt
AM bɔ(ə)rʃt

borshcht
BR bɔːʃt
AM bɔ(ə)rʃt

Borstal
BR 'bɔːstl, -z
AM 'bɔ(ə)rstl, -z

bort
BR bɔːt
AM bɔ(ə)rt

Borth
BR bɔːθ
AM bɔ(ə)rθ

Borthwick
BR 'bɔːθwɪk
AM 'bɔrθwɪk

bortsch
BR bɔːtʃ
AM bɔ(ə)rtʃ

borzoi
BR 'bɔːzɔɪ, 'bɔːtsɔɪ, -z
AM 'bɔr,zɔɪ, -z

Bosanquet
BR 'bəʊznkɛt, 'bəʊzŋkɛt
AM 'boʊzən,kɛt

Bosc
BR bɒsk
AM bask

boscage
BR 'bɒsk|ɪdʒ, -ɨdʒɨz
AM 'baskɪdʒ, -ɨz

Boscastle
BR 'bɒs,kaːsl, 'bɒs,kasl
AM 'bɔz,kæsəl, 'baz,kæsəl

Boscawen[1]
placename
BR 'bɒsk(ə)wɪn, 'bɒskwʌɪn
AM 'baskəwən

Boscawen[2]
surname
BR bɒ'skəʊən
AM ba'skaʊən

Bosch
BR bɒʃ
AM bɔʃ, baʃ

Boscobel
BR 'bɒskəbɛl
AM 'baskə,bɛl

Bose
BR bəʊz, bəʊs
AM boʊz

bosh
BR bɒʃ
AM baʃ

bosie
BR 'bəʊz|i, -ɪz
AM 'boʊsi, -z

boskage
BR 'bɒsk|ɪdʒ, -ɨdʒɨz
AM 'baskɪdʒ, -ɨz

boskiness
BR 'bɒskɪnɨs
AM 'baskinɨs

Boskop
BR 'bɒskɒp
AM 'bas,kap

bosky
BR 'bɒski
AM 'baski

bos'n
BR 'bəʊsn, -z
AM 'boʊsn, -z

bo's'n
BR 'bəʊsn, -z
AM 'boʊsn, -z

Bosnia
BR 'bɒznɪə(r)
AM 'bazniə, 'bɔzniə

Bosnian
BR 'bɒznɪən, -z
AM 'bazniən, 'bɔzniən, -z

bosom
BR 'bʊz(ə)m, -z
AM 'bʊzəm, -z

bosomy
BR 'bʊzəmi, 'bʊzm̩i
AM 'bʊzəmi

boson
BR 'bəʊsɒn, 'bəʊzɒn
AM 'boʊ,san, 'boʊ,zan

Bosphorus
BR 'bɒsf(ə)rəs
AM 'basf(ə)rəs

Bosporus
BR 'bɒsp(ə)rəs
AM 'basp(ə)rəs

boss
BR bɒs, -ɨz, -ɪŋ, -t
AM bɔs, bas, -əz, -ɪŋ, -t

bossa nova
BR ,bɒsə 'nəʊvə(r), -z
AM ,basə 'noʊvə, -z

bossily
BR 'bɒsɨli
AM 'bɔsəli, 'basəli

bossiness
BR 'bɒsɪnɨs
AM 'bɔsinɨs, 'basinɨs

bossy
BR 'bɒs|i, -ɪə(r), -ɪɪst
AM 'bɔsi, 'basi, -ər, -ɨst

Bostik®
BR 'bɒstɪk
AM 'bastɪk

Bostock
BR 'bɒstɒk
AM 'bastək

Boston
BR 'bɒst(ə)n
AM 'bɔstən, 'bastən

Bostonian
BR bɒ'stəʊnɪən, -z
AM bɔ'stoʊniən, ba'stoʊniən, -z

bosun
BR 'bəʊsn, -z
AM 'boʊsn, -z

bo'sun
BR 'bəʊsn, -z
AM 'boʊsn, -z

Boswell
BR 'bɒzw(ɛ)l
AM 'bazwəl

Bosworth
BR 'bɒzwə(ː)θ
AM 'baz,wərθ

bot
BR bɒt, -s
AM bat, -s

botanic
BR bə'tanɪk
AM bə'tænɪk

botanical
BR bə'tanɪkl
AM bə'tænəkəl

botanically
BR bə'tanɪkli
AM bə'tænək(ə)li

botanise
BR 'bɒtənʌɪz, 'bɒtn̩ʌɪz, -ɨz, -ɪŋ, -d
AM 'batn,aɪz, -ɨz, -ɪŋ, -d

botanist
BR 'bɒtənɪst, 'bɒtn̩ɪst, -s
AM 'batn̩əst, -s

botanize
BR 'bɒtənʌɪz, 'bɒtn̩ʌɪz, -ɨz, -ɪŋ, -d
AM 'batn,aɪz, -ɨz, -ɪŋ, -d

botany
BR 'bɒtəni, 'bɒtn̩i
AM 'batn̩i

botargo
BR bə'taːgəʊ, -z
AM boʊ'targoʊ, -z

botch
BR bɒtʃ, -ɨz, -ɪŋ, -t
AM batʃ, -əz, -ɪŋ, -t

botcher
BR 'bɒtʃə(r), -z
AM 'batʃər, -z

botel
BR ,bəʊ'tɛl, -z
AM ,boʊ'tɛl, -z

botfly
BR 'bɒtflʌɪ, -z
AM 'bat,flaɪ, -z

both
BR bəʊθ
AM boʊθ

Botha
BR 'bəʊtə(r), 'bʊətə(r)
AM 'boʊθə, 'boʊdə
AFK 'bʊəta

Botham
BR 'bəʊθəm
AM 'baðəm

bother
BR 'bɒð|ə(r), -əz, -(ə)rɪŋ, -əd
AM 'bað|ər, -ərz, -(ə)rɪŋ, -ərd

botheration
BR ,bɒðə'reɪʃn
AM ,baðə'reɪʃən

bothersome
BR 'bɒðəs(ə)m
AM 'baðərsəm

Bothnia
BR 'bɒθnɪə(r)
AM 'baθniə

Bothwell
BR 'bɒθw(ɛ)l
AM 'baθwəl

bothy
BR 'bɒθ|i, -ɪz
AM 'baθi, -z

Botolph
BR 'bɒtɒlf
AM 'badəlf

botryoid
BR 'bɒtrɪɔɪd
AM 'batri,ɔɪd

botryoidal
BR ,bɒtrɪ'ɔɪdl
AM ,batri'ɔɪdəl

Botswana
BR bɒt'swaːnə(r)
AM bat'swanə

Botswanan
BR bɒt'swaːnən, -z
AM bat'swanən, -z

bott
BR bɒt, -s
AM bat, -s

Botticelli
BR ,bɒtɪ'tʃɛli
AM ,badə'tʃɛli

bottle
BR 'bɒt|l, -lz, -l̩ɪŋ\-lɪŋ, -ld
AM 'badəl, -z, -ɪŋ, -d

bottleful
BR 'bɒtlfʊl, -z
AM 'badl,fʊl, -z

bottleneck
BR 'bɒtlnɛk, -s
AM 'badl,nɛk, -s

bottlenose
BR 'bɒtlnəʊz, -ɨz, -d
AM 'badl,noʊz, -ɨz, -d

bottler
BR 'bɒtl̩ə(r), 'bɒtlə(r), -z
AM 'badl̩ər, 'badlər, -z

bottlewasher
BR 'bɒtl,wɒʃə(r), -z
AM 'badl,wɔʃər, 'badl,waʃər, -z

bottom
BR 'bɒtəm, -z, -ɪŋ, -d
AM 'badəm, -z, -ɪŋ, -d

bottomless
BR 'bɒtəmləs
AM 'badəmləs

bottomlessness
BR 'bɒtəmləsnəs
AM 'badəmləsnəs

Bottomley
BR 'bɒtəmli
AM 'bɑdəmli

bottommost
BR 'bɒtə(m)məʊst
AM 'bɑdə(m),moʊst

bottomry
BR 'bɒtəmr|i, -ɪz, -ɪɪŋ, -ɪd
AM 'bɑdəmri, -z, -ɪŋ, -d

botulinus
BR ,bɒtjʊ'lʌɪnəs, ,bɒtʃʊ'lʌɪnəs
AM ,bɑtʃə'laɪnəs

botulism
BR 'bɒtjʊlɪz(ə)m, 'bɒtʃʊlɪz(ə)m
AM 'bɑtʃə,lɪzəm

Boucher
BR 'baʊtʃə(r), 'bu:ʃeɪ
AM bu'ʃeɪ

bouclé
BR 'bu:kleɪ
AM ,bu'kleɪ

Boudicca
BR 'bu:dɪkə(r)
AM bu'dɪkə

boudoir
BR 'bu:dwɑ:(r), -z
AM ¦bud¦wɑr, -z

bouffant
BR 'bu:fɒ̃, 'bu:fɒŋ, 'bu:fɒnt
AM ¦bu¦fɑnt

bougainvillaea
BR ,bu:g(ə)n'vɪlɪə(r), -z
AM ,bugən'vɪljə, ,bugən'vɪliə, -z

Bougainville
BR 'bu:g(ə)nvɪl
AM 'bugən,vɪl

bougainvillea
BR ,bu:g(ə)n'vɪlɪə(r), -z
AM ,bugən'vɪljə, ,bugən'vɪliə, -z

Bougainvillian
BR ,bu:g(ə)n'vɪlɪən, -z
AM ,bugən'vɪljən, ,bugən'vɪliən, -z

bough
BR baʊ, -z
AM baʊ, -z

bought
BR bɔ:t
AM bɔt, bɑt

boughten
BR 'bɔ:tn
AM 'bɔtn, 'bɑtn

bougie
BR 'bu:ʒ|i, -ɪz
AM 'bu(d)ʒi, -z

bouillabaisse
BR ,bu:jə'bɛs, ,bu:jə'beɪs, 'bu:jəbɛs, 'bu:jəbeɪs
AM ¦bu(l)jə¦bɛs, ¦bu(l)jə¦beɪs

bouilli
BR 'bu:ji
AM bu'ji

bouillon
BR 'bu:jɒ̃, 'bu:jɒn, 'bwi:jɒ̃, 'bwi:jɒn
AM 'bu(l),jɑn, 'bəl,jɑn

boulder
BR 'bəʊldə(r), -z
AM 'boʊldər, -z

bouldery
BR 'bəʊld(ə)ri
AM 'boʊldəri

boule[1]
Greek legislative body
BR 'bu:l|i, 'bu:l|eɪ, -ɪz\-eɪz
AM 'buli, -z
GR vu:'li:

boule[2]
ornamental inlay
BR bu:l, -z
AM bul, -z

boules
game
BR bu:l
AM bul

boulevard
BR 'bʊləvɑ:d, 'bu:l(ə)vɑ:d, -z
AM 'bʊlə,vɑrd, -z

boulevardier
BR ,bu:ləvɑ:'djeɪ, -z
AM ,bʊl(ə)vɑr'djeɪ, -z

Boulez
BR 'bu:lɛz, 'bu:leɪ
AM bu'lɛz

boulle
BR bu:l
AM bul

Boulogne
BR bʊ'lɔɪn
AM bu'loʊn(jə)
FR bulɔɲ

boult
BR bəʊlt, -s, -ɪŋ, -ɪd
AM boʊlt, -s, -ɪŋ, -əd

Boulter
BR 'bəʊltə(r)
AM 'boʊldər

Boulting
BR 'bəʊltɪŋ
AM 'boʊltɪŋ

Boulton
BR 'bəʊlt(ə)n
AM 'boʊlt(ə)n

bounce
BR baʊns, -ɪz, -ɪŋ, -t
AM baʊns, -əz, -ɪŋ, -t

bouncer
BR 'baʊnsə(r), -z
AM 'baʊnsər, -z

bouncily
BR 'baʊnsɪli
AM 'baʊnsəli

bounciness
BR 'baʊnsɪnɪs
AM 'baʊnsinɪs

bouncy
BR 'baʊns|i, -ɪə(r), -ɪɪst
AM 'baʊnsi, -ər, -ɪst

bound
BR baʊnd, -z, -ɪŋ, -ɪd
AM baʊnd, -z, -ɪŋ, -əd

boundary
BR 'baʊnd(ə)r|i, -ɪz
AM 'baʊnd(ə)ri, -z

bounden
BR 'baʊndən
AM 'baʊndən

bounder
BR 'baʊndə(r), -z
AM 'baʊndər, -z

boundless
BR 'baʊndləs
AM 'baʊn(d)ləs

boundlessly
BR 'baʊndləsli
AM 'baʊn(d)ləsli

boundlessness
BR 'baʊndləsnəs
AM 'baʊn(d)ləsnəs

bounteous
BR 'baʊntɪəs
AM 'baʊn(t)iəs

bounteously
BR 'baʊntɪəsli
AM 'baʊn(t)iəsli

bounteousness
BR 'baʊntɪəsnəs
AM 'baʊn(t)iəsnəs

bountiful
BR 'baʊntɪf(ʊ)l
AM 'baʊn(t)ifəl

bountifully
BR 'baʊntɪfʊli, 'baʊntɪfli
AM 'baʊn(t)if(ə)li

bountifulness
BR 'baʊntɪf(ʊ)lnəs
AM 'baʊn(t)ifəlnəs

bounty
BR 'baʊnt|i, -ɪz
AM 'baʊn(t)i, -z

bouquet
BR bʊ'keɪ, bəʊ'keɪ, -z
AM boʊ'keɪ, bu'keɪ, -z

bouquet garni
BR ,bʊkeɪ gɑ:'ni:
AM ,boʊkeɪ gɑr'ni, ,bukeɪ +

bouquetin
BR 'bu:kətɪn, -z
AM ,bukə'tɛn, -z

bouquets garnis
BR ,bʊkeɪ gɑ:'ni:
AM ,boʊkeɪ gɑr'ni, ,bukeɪ +

Bourbon
French royal family
BR 'bɔ:b(ə)n, 'bɔ:bɒn, 'bʊəb(ə)n, 'bʊəbɒn
AM 'bʊrbən

bourbon
whisky
BR 'bə:b(ə)n
AM 'bərbən

bourdon
BR 'bʊəd(ə)n, 'bɔ:d(ə)n, -z
AM 'bʊrdən, -z

bourgeois[1]
middle class
BR 'bʊəʒwɑ:(r), 'bɔ:ʒwɑ:(r)
AM ¦bʊr¦ʒwɑ

bourgeois[2]
print
BR bə:'dʒɔɪs
AM bər'dʒɔɪs

bourgeoisie
BR ,bʊəʒwɑ:'zi:, ,bɔ:ʒwɑ:'zi:
AM ¦bʊrʒwɑ¦zi

Bourguiba
BR bʊə'gi:bə(r), bɔ:'gi:bə(r)
AM bʊr'gibə

Bourke
BR bə:k
AM bɔ(ə)rk

bourn
BR bɔ:n, -z
AM bɔ(ə)rn, -z

bourne
BR bɔ:n, -z
AM bɔ(ə)rn, -z

Bournemouth
BR 'bɔ:nməθ
AM 'bɔrnməθ

Bournville
BR 'bɔ:nvɪl, ,bɔ:n'vɪl
AM 'bɔrn,vɪl

Bournvita
BR ,bɔ:n'vi:tə(r)
AM ,bɔrn'vidə

bourrée
BR 'bʊreɪ, 'bʊəreɪ, -z
AM bʊ'reɪ, -z

bourse
BR bʊəs, bɔ:s, -ɪz
AM bʊ(ə)rs, -əz

Bourton
BR 'bɔ:tn
AM 'bɔrt(ə)n

boustrophedon
BR ,baʊstrə'fi:dn, ,bu:strə'fi:dn
AM ,bustrə'fi,dɑn, ,bustrə'fidən

bout
BR baʊt, -s
AM baʊt, -s

boutique
BR bu:'ti:k, -s
AM bu'tik, -s

boutonnière
BR ˌbuːtɒnɪˈɛː(r), ˌbuːtɒnˈjɛː(r), -z
AM ˌbutnˈɪ(ə)r, -z

Bouverie
BR ˈbuːv(ə)ri
AM ˈbuvəri

Bouvet
BR ˈbuːveɪ
AM ˈbuˌveɪ

bouzouki
BR bʊˈzuːk|i, -ɪz
AM bʊˈzuki, bəˈzuki, -z

Bovary
BR ˈbəʊv(ə)ri
AM ˈboʊvəri

bovate
BR ˈbəʊveɪt, -s
AM ˈboʊˌveɪt, -s

Bovey Tracy
BR ˌbʌvɪ ˈtreɪsi, ˌbɒvɪ +
AM ˌbəvi ˈtreɪsi

bovid
BR ˈbəʊvɪd, -z
AM ˈboʊvɪd, -z

bovine
BR ˈbəʊvʌɪn
AM ˈboʊˌvaɪn

bovinely
BR ˈbəʊvʌɪnli
AM ˈboʊˌvaɪnli

Bovingdon
BR ˈbɒvɪŋdən, ˈbʌvɪŋdən
AM ˈbəvɪŋd(ə)n

Bovington
BR ˈbɒvɪŋt(ə)n
AM ˈbəvɪŋt(ə)n

Bovis
BR ˈbəʊvɪs
AM ˈboʊvəs

Bovril®
BR ˈbɒvr(ɪ)l
AM ˈbɑvrəl

bovver
BR ˈbɒvə(r)
AM ˈbɑvər

Bow
BR bəʊ
AM boʊ

bow[1]
bend, submit
BR baʊ, -z, -ɪŋ, -d
AM baʊ, -z, -ɪŋ, -d

bow[2]
with violin, weapon, knot
BR bəʊ, -z, -ɪŋ, -d
AM boʊ, -z, -ɪŋ, -d

Bowater
BR ˈbəʊˌwɔːtə(r)
AM ˈboʊˌwɔdər, ˈboʊˌwɑdər

bow-compass
BR ˈbəʊˌkʌmpəs, -ɪz
AM ˈboʊˌkəmpəs, -əz

Bowden
BR ˈbaʊdn, ˈbəʊdn
AM ˈboʊdən, ˈbaʊdən

Bowdler
BR ˈbaʊdlə(r)
AM ˈbaʊdlər

bowdlerisation
BR ˌbaʊdlərʌɪˈzeɪʃn
AM ˌboʊdlərəˈzeɪʃən, ˌboʊdləˌraɪˈzeɪʃən, ˌbaʊdlərəˈzeɪʃən, ˌbaʊdləˌraɪˈzeɪʃən, ˌbɔdlərəˈzeɪʃən, ˌbɔdləˌraɪˈzeɪʃən, ˌbɑdlərəˈzeɪʃən, ˌbɑdləˌraɪˈzeɪʃən

bowdlerise
BR ˈbaʊdlərʌɪz, -ɪz, -ɪŋ, -d
AM ˈboʊdləˌraɪz, ˈbaʊdləˌraɪz, ˈbɔdləˌraɪz, ˈbɑdləˌraɪz, -ɪz, -ɪŋ, -d

bowdleriser
BR ˈbaʊdlərʌɪzə(r), -z
AM ˈboʊdləˌraɪzər, ˈbaʊdləˌraɪzər, ˈbɔdləˌraɪzər, ˈbɑdləˌraɪzər, -z

bowdlerism
BR ˈbaʊdlərɪz(ə)m, -z
AM ˈboʊdləˌrɪzəm, ˈbaʊdləˌrɪzəm, ˈbɔdləˌrɪz(ə)m, ˈbɑdləˌrɪz(ə)m, -z

bowdlerization
BR ˌbaʊdlərʌɪˈzeɪʃn
AM ˌboʊdlərəˈzeɪʃən, ˌboʊdləˌraɪˈzeɪʃən, ˌbaʊdlərəˈzeɪʃən, ˌbaʊdləˌraɪˈzeɪʃən, ˌbɔdlərəˈzeɪʃən, ˌbɔdləˌraɪˈzeɪʃən, ˌbɑdlərəˈzeɪʃən, ˌbɑdləˌraɪˈzeɪʃən

bowdlerize
BR ˈbaʊdlərʌɪz, -ɪz, -ɪŋ, -d
AM ˈboʊdləˌraɪz, ˈbaʊdləˌraɪz, ˈbɔdləˌraɪz, ˈbɑdləˌraɪz, -ɪz, -ɪŋ, -d

bowdlerizer
BR ˈbaʊdlərʌɪzə(r), -z
AM ˈboʊdləˌraɪzər, ˈbaʊdləˌraɪzər, ˈbɔdləˌraɪzər, ˈbɑdləˌraɪzər, -z

bowel
BR ˈbaʊ(ə)l, -z
AM ˈbaʊ(ə)l, -z

Bowen
BR ˈbəʊɪn
AM ˈboʊən

bower
BR ˈbaʊə(r), -z
AM ˈbaʊ(ə)r, -z

bowerbird
BR ˈbaʊəbəːd, -z
AM ˈbaʊərˌbərd, -z

Bowers
BR ˈbaʊəz
AM ˈbaʊ(ə)rz

bowery
BR ˈbaʊər|i, -ɪz
AM ˈbaʊ(ə)ri, -z

Bowes
BR bəʊz
AM boʊz

bowfin
BR ˈbəʊfɪn, -z
AM ˈboʊˌfɪn, -z

bowhead
BR ˈbəʊhɛd, -z
AM ˈboʊˌ(h)ɛd, -z

bowie
BR ˈbaʊ|i, ˈbəʊ|i, -ɪz
AM ˈboʊi, ˈbui, -z

bowie knife
BR ˈbəʊɪ nʌɪf, ˈbuːɪ +
AM ˈbui ˌnaɪf, ˈboʊi +

bowie knives
BR ˈbəʊɪ nʌɪvz, ˈbuːɪ +
AM ˈbui ˌnaɪvz, ˈboʊi +

Bowker
BR ˈbaʊkə(r)
AM ˈbaʊkər

bowl
BR bəʊl, -z, -ɪŋ, -d
AM boʊl, -z, -ɪŋ, -d

Bowlby
BR ˈbəʊlbi
AM ˈboʊlbi

bowler
BR ˈbəʊlə(r), -z
AM ˈboʊlər, -z

Bowles
BR bəʊlz
AM boʊlz

bowlful
BR ˈbəʊlfʊl, -z
AM ˈboʊlˌfʊl, -z

bowline
BR ˈbəʊlɪn, -z
AM ˈboʊlən, -z

Bowman
BR ˈbəʊmən
AM ˈboʊmən

bowman[1]
archer
BR ˈbəʊmən
AM ˈboʊmən

bowman[2]
on a boat
BR ˈbaʊmən
AM ˈbaʊmən

bowmen[1]
archers
BR ˈbəʊmən
AM ˈboʊmən

bowmen[2]
on a boat
BR ˈbaʊmən
AM ˈbaʊmən

Bowness
BR bəʊˈnɛs
AM ˈboʊnəs

Bowring
BR ˈbaʊrɪŋ
AM ˈbaʊrɪŋ, ˈboʊrɪŋ

bowsaw
BR ˈbəʊsɔː(r), -z
AM ˈboʊˌsɔ, ˈboʊˌsɑ, -z

bowser®
BR ˈbaʊzə(r), -z
AM ˈbaʊzər, -z

bowshot
BR ˈbəʊʃɒt, -s
AM ˈboʊˌʃɑt, -s

bowsprit
BR ˈbəʊsprɪt, -s
AM ˈbaʊˌsprɪt, ˈboʊˌsprɪt, -s

bowstring
BR ˈbəʊstrɪŋ, -z
AM ˈboʊˌstrɪŋ, -z

bow-wow[1]
a dog
BR ˈbaʊwaʊ, -z
AM ˈbaʊˌwaʊ, -z

bow-wow[2]
imitating a dog's bark
BR ˌbaʊˈwaʊ, -z
AM ˌbaʊˈwaʊ, -z

bowyang
BR ˈbəʊjaŋ, -z
AM ˈboʊˌjæŋ, -z

bowyer
BR ˈbəʊjə(r), -z
AM ˈboʊjər, -z

box
BR bɒks, -ɪz, -ɪŋ, -t
AM bɑks, -əz, -ɪŋ, -t

boxcalf
BR ˈbɒkskɑːf
AM ˈbɑksˌkæ|f, -vz

boxcar
BR ˈbɒkskɑː(r), -z
AM ˈbɑksˌkɑr, -z

boxer
BR ˈbɒksə(r), -z
AM ˈbɑksər, -z

boxful
BR ˈbɒksfʊl, -z
AM ˈbɑksˌfʊl, -z

boxroom
BR ˈbɒksruːm, ˈbɒksrʊm, -z
AM ˈbɑksˌrum, ˈbɑksˌrʊm, -z

boxwood
BR ˈbɒkswʊd
AM ˈbɑksˌwʊd

boxy
BR ˈbɒks|i, -ɪə(r), -ɪɪst
AM ˈbɑksi, -ər, -ɪst

boy
BR bɔɪ, -z
AM bɔɪ, -z

boyar
BR 'bɔɪɑː(r), 'bəʊjɑː(r), bəʊ'jɑː(r), -z
AM boʊ'jɑr, -z

Boyce
BR bɔɪs
AM bɔɪs

boycott
BR 'bɔɪkɒt, -s, -ɪŋ, -ɨd
AM 'bɔɪ,kɑ|t, -ts, -dɪŋ, -dəd

Boyd
BR bɔɪd
AM bɔɪd

Boyer
BR 'bɔɪə(r)
AM 'bɔɪər

boyfriend
BR 'bɔɪfrɛnd, -z
AM 'bɔɪ,frɛnd, -z

boyhood
BR 'bɔɪhʊd, -z
AM 'bɔɪ,(h)ʊd, -z

boyish
BR 'bɔɪɪʃ
AM 'bɔɪɪʃ

boyishly
BR 'bɔɪɨʃli
AM 'bɔɪɨʃli

boyishness
BR 'bɔɪɨʃnɨs
AM 'bɔɪɨʃnɨs

Boyle
BR bɔɪl
AM 'bɔɪ(ə)l

Boyne
BR bɔɪn
AM bɔɪn

boyo
BR 'bɔɪəʊ, -z
AM 'bɔɪoʊ, -z

boysenberry
BR 'bɔɪzn,bɛr|i, -ɪz
AM 'bɔɪzən,bɛri, -z

Boyson
BR 'bɔɪsn
AM 'bɔɪsən

Boz
BR bɒz
AM bɑz

bozo
BR 'bəʊzəʊ, -z
AM 'boʊ,zoʊ, -z

B.Phil.
BR ˌbiː 'fɪl, -z
AM ˌbi 'fɪl, -z

bra
BR brɑː(*r*), -z
AM brɑ, -z

braai
BR brʌɪ, -z, -ɪŋ, -d
AM braɪ, -z, -ɪŋ, -d

Brabant
BR brə'bant
AM brə'bænt
DU 'braːbɑnt
FR bʀabɑ̃

Brabazon
BR 'brabəz(ə)n
AM 'bræbə,zɑn

Brabham
BR 'brabəm
AM 'brɑbəm

Brabin
BR 'breɪbɪn
AM 'breɪbɨn

Brabourne
BR 'breɪbɔːn, 'breɪb(ə)n
AM 'breɪ,bɔrn

brace
BR breɪs, -ɨz, -ɪŋ, -t
AM breɪs, -ɨz, -ɪŋ, -t

Bracegirdle
BR 'breɪs,gəːdl
AM 'breɪs,gərdəl

bracelet
BR 'breɪslɨt, -s
AM 'breɪslət, -s

bracer
BR 'breɪsə(r), -z
AM 'breɪsər, -z

brach
BR bratʃ, -ɨz
AM brætʃ, -əz

brachial
BR 'breɪkɪəl
AM 'breɪkiəl, 'brækiəl

brachiate[1]
adjective
BR 'breɪkɪeɪt, 'breɪkɪət
AM 'breɪki,eɪt, 'breɪkiɨt

brachiate[2]
verb
BR 'breɪkɪeɪt, -s, -ɪŋ, -ɨd
AM 'breɪki,eɪ|t, -ts, -dɪŋ, -dɨd

brachiation
BR ˌbreɪkɪ'eɪʃn
AM ˌbreɪki'eɪʃən

brachiator
BR 'breɪkɪeɪtə(r), -z
AM 'breɪki,eɪdər, -z

brachiopod
BR 'brakɪəpɒd, 'breɪkɪəpɒd, -z
AM 'brækiə,pɑd, 'breɪkiə,pɑd, -z

brachiosauri
BR ˌbrakɪə(ʊ)'sɔːrʌɪ
AM ˌbrækioʊ'sɔ,raɪ

brachiosaurus
BR ˌbrakɪə'sɔːrəs, -ɪz
AM ˌbrækioʊ'sɔrəs, -əz

brachistochrone
BR brə'kɪstəkrəʊn, -z
AM bræ'kɪstə,kroʊn, brə'kɪstə,kroʊn, -z

brachycephalic
BR ˌbrakɪsɪ'falɪk, ˌbrakɪkɛ'falɪk
AM ˌbræki'sɛfəlɪk, ˌbrækə'sɛfəlɪk

brachycephalous
BR ˌbrakɪ'sɛfələs, ˌbrakɪ'sɛfl̩əs, ˌbrakɪ'kɛfələs, ˌbrakɪ'kɛfl̩əs
AM ˌbræki'sɛfələs, ˌbrækə'sɛfələs

brachycephaly
BR ˌbrakɪ'sɛfəli, ˌbrakɪ'sɛfl̩i, ˌbrakɪ'kɛfəli, ˌbrakɪ'kɛfl̩i
AM ˌbræki'sɛfəli, ˌbrækə'sɛfəli

brachylogy
BR brə'kɪlədʒi, -z
AM bræ'kɪlədʒi, brə'kɪlədʒi, -z

bracing
BR 'breɪsɪŋ
AM 'breɪsɪŋ

bracingness
BR 'breɪsɪŋnɪs
AM 'breɪsɪŋnɪs

brack
BR brak, -s
AM bræk, -s

bracken
BR 'brak(ə)n
AM 'brækən

Brackenbury
BR 'brak(ə)nb(ə)ri
AM 'brækən,bɛri, 'brækənbəri

bracket
BR 'brak|ɪt, -ɪts, -ɨtɪŋ, -ɨtɨd
AM 'bræk|ət, -əts, -ədɪŋ, -ədəd

brackish
BR 'brakɪʃ
AM 'brækɪʃ

brackishness
BR 'brakɨʃnɪs
AM 'brækɨʃnɪs

Bracknell
BR 'braknl
AM 'bræknəl

braconid
BR 'brakənɪd, -z
AM 'brækə,nɪd, -z

bract
BR brakt, -s
AM bræk|(t), -(t)s

bracteal
BR 'braktɪəl
AM 'bræktiəl

bracteate
BR 'braktɪət, -s
AM 'bræktiɨt, 'brækti,eɪt, -s

brad
BR brad, -z
AM bræd, -z

bradawl
BR 'bradɔːl, -z
AM 'bræd,ɔl, 'bræd,ɑl, -z

Bradbury
BR 'bradb(ə)ri
AM 'bræd,bɛri, 'brædbəri

Braden
BR 'breɪdn
AM 'breɪdən

Bradford
BR 'bradfəd
AM 'brædfərd

Bradley
BR 'bradli
AM 'brædli

Bradman
BR 'bradmən
AM 'brædmən

Bradshaw
BR 'bradʃɔː(*r*), -z
AM 'bræd,ʃɔ, 'bræd,ʃɑ, -z

Bradwell
BR 'bradw(ɛ)l
AM 'bræd,wɛl

Brady
BR 'breɪdi
AM 'breɪdi

bradycardia
BR ˌbradɪ'kɑːdɪə(*r*)
AM ˌbrædə'kɑrdiə

bradykinin
BR ˌbradɪ'kʌɪnɪn
AM ˌbrædi'kaɪnɨn

bradyseism
BR 'bradɪsʌɪz(ə)m
AM 'brædəsɛ,ɪzəm

brae
BR breɪ, -z
AM breɪ, -z

Braemar
BR ˌbreɪ'mɑː(r)
AM ˌbreɪ'mɑr

brag
BR brag, -z, -ɪŋ, -d
AM bræg, -z, -ɪŋ, -d

Braga
BR 'brɑːgə(*r*)
AM 'brɑgə

Braganza
BR brə'ganzə(*r*)
AM brə'gɑnzə

Bragg
BR brag
AM bræg

braggadocio
BR ˌbragə'dəʊtʃɪəʊ
AM ˌbrægə'doʊʃioʊ

braggart
BR 'bragət, -s
AM 'brægərt, -s

bragger
BR 'bragə(r), -z
AM 'brægər, -z

braggingly
BR 'bragɪŋli
AM 'brægɪŋli

Brahe
BR 'brɑːhə(*r*), 'brɑːhi

AM ˈbrɑˌhi
DAN ˈbʀɑːa

Brahma
BR ˈbrɑːmə(r), -z
AM ˈbrɑmə, -z

Brahman
BR ˈbrɑːmən, -z
AM ˈbrɑmən, -z

Brahmana
BR ˈbrɑːmənə(r)
AM ˈbrɑmənə

Brahmanic
BR brɑːˈmanɪk
AM brɑˈmænɪk

Brahmanical
BR brɑːˈmanɨkl
AM brɑˈmænəkəl

Brahmanism
BR ˈbrɑːmənɪz(ə)m
AM ˈbrɑməˌnɪzəm

Brahmaputra
BR ˌbrɑːməˈpuːtrə(r)
AM ˌbrɑməˈputrə

Brahmin
BR ˈbrɑːmɪn, -z
AM ˈbrɑmən, -z

Brahminism
BR ˈbrɑːmɨnɪz(ə)m
AM ˈbrɑməˌnɪzəm

Brahms
BR brɑːmz
AM brɑmz

braid
BR breɪd, -z, -ɪŋ, -ɨd
AM breɪd, -z, -ɪŋ, -ɨd

braider
BR ˈbreɪdə(r), -z
AM ˈbreɪdər, -z

brail
BR breɪl, -z
AM breɪl, -z

Braille
BR breɪl
AM breɪl

brain
BR breɪn, -z, -ɪŋ, -d
AM breɪn, -z, -ɪŋ, -d

brainbox
BR ˈbreɪnbɒks, -ɪz
AM ˈbreɪnˌbɑks, -əz

brainchild
BR ˈbreɪntʃʌɪld
AM ˈbreɪnˌtʃaɪld

Braine
BR breɪn
AM breɪn

brainfag
BR ˈbreɪnfag
AM ˈbreɪnˌfæg

braininess
BR ˈbreɪnɪnɨs
AM ˈbreɪninɨs

brainless
BR ˈbreɪnlɨs
AM ˈbreɪnlɨs

brainlessly
BR ˈbreɪnlɨsli
AM ˈbreɪnlɨsli

brainlessness
BR ˈbreɪnlɨsnɨs
AM ˈbreɪnlɨsnɨs

brainpan
BR ˈbreɪnpan, -z
AM ˈbreɪnˌpæn, -z

brainpower
BR ˈbreɪnˌpaʊə(r)
AM ˈbreɪnˌpaʊər

brainsick
BR ˈbreɪnsɪk
AM ˈbreɪnˌsɪk

brainstem
BR ˈbreɪnstɛm, -z
AM ˈbreɪnˌstɛm, -z

brainstorm
BR ˈbreɪnstɔːm, -z, -ɪŋ, -d
AM ˈbreɪnˌstɔ(ə)rm, -z, -ɪŋ, -d

Braintree
BR ˈbreɪntriː
AM ˈbreɪnˌtri

brainwash
BR ˈbreɪnwɒʃ, -ɨz, -ɪŋ, -t
AM ˈbreɪnˌwɔʃ, ˈbreɪnˌwɑʃ, -əz, -ɪŋ, -t

brainwave
BR ˈbreɪnweɪv, -z
AM ˈbreɪnˌweɪv, -z

brainwork
BR ˈbreɪnwəːk
AM ˈbreɪnˌwərk

brainy
BR ˈbreɪn|i, -ɪə(r), -ɪɪst
AM ˈbreɪni, -ər, -ɨst

braise
BR breɪz, -ɨz, -ɪŋ, -d
AM breɪz, -ɨz, -ɪŋ, -d

Braithwaite
BR ˈbreɪθweɪt
AM ˈbreɪθˌweɪt

brake
BR breɪk, -s, -ɪŋ, -t
AM breɪk, -s, -ɪŋ, -t

brakeless
BR ˈbreɪklɨs
AM ˈbreɪklɨs

brakeman
BR ˈbreɪkmən
AM ˈbreɪkmən

brakemen
BR ˈbreɪkmən
AM ˈbreɪkmən

brakesman
BR ˈbreɪksmən
AM ˈbreɪksmən

brakesmen
BR ˈbreɪksmən
AM ˈbreɪksmən

brakevan
BR ˈbreɪkvan, -z
AM ˈbreɪkˌvæn, -z

braless
BR ˈbrɑːləs
AM ˈbrɑləs

Bram
BR bram
AM bræm

Bramah
BR ˈbrɑːmə(r)
AM ˈbrɑmə

Bramante
BR brəˈmanti
AM brɑˈmɑn(t)i

bramble
BR ˈbrambl, -z
AM ˈbræmbəl, -z

brambling
BR ˈbramblɪŋ, -z
AM ˈbræmblɪŋ, -z

brambly
BR ˈbrambli
AM ˈbræmbli

Bramhope
BR ˈbramhəʊp
AM ˈbræmˌ(h)oʊp

Bramley
BR ˈbramli, -z
AM ˈbræmli, -z

Brampton
BR ˈbram(p)tən
AM ˈbræmt(ə)n

Bramwell
BR ˈbramw(ɛ)l
AM ˈbræmˌwɛl

bran
BR bran
AM bræn

Branagh
BR ˈbranə(r)
AM ˈbrænə

branch
BR brɑːn(t)ʃ, bran(t)ʃ, -ɨz, -ɪŋ, -t
AM bræn(t)ʃ, -əz, -ɪŋ, -t

branchia
BR ˈbraŋkɪə(r)
AM ˈbrɑŋkiə, ˈbræŋkiə

branchiae
BR ˈbraŋkɪiː
AM ˈbrɑŋkiˌi, ˈbræŋkiˌi, ˈbrɑŋkiˌaɪ, ˈbræŋkiˌaɪ

branchial
BR ˈbraŋkɪəl
AM ˈbrɑŋkiəl, ˈbræŋkiəl

branchiate
BR ˈbraŋkɪeɪt, ˈbraŋkɪət
AM ˈbrɑŋkiɪt, ˈbrɑŋkiˌeɪt, ˈbræŋkiɪt, ˈbræŋkiˌeɪt

branchlet
BR ˈbrɑːn(t)ʃlɪt, ˈbran(t)ʃlɪt, -s
AM ˈbræn(t)ʃlət, -s

branchlike
BR ˈbrɑːn(t)ʃlʌɪk, ˈbran(t)ʃlʌɪk
AM ˈbræn(t)ʃˌlaɪk

branchy
BR ˈbrɑːn(t)ʃi, ˈbran(t)ʃi
AM ˈbræn(t)ʃi

brand
BR brand, -z, -ɪŋ, -ɨd
AM brænd, -z, -ɪŋ, -əd

Brandeis
BR ˈbrandʌɪs
AM ˈbrænˌdaɪs

Brandenburg
BR ˈbrand(ə)nbəːg
AM ˈbrændənˌbərg

brander
BR ˈbrandə(r), -z
AM ˈbrændər, -z

brandish
BR ˈbrand|ɪʃ, -ɨʃɨz, -ɨʃɪŋ, -ɪʃt
AM ˈbrændɪʃ, -ɨz, -ɪŋ, -t

brandisher
BR ˈbrandɨʃə(r), -z
AM ˈbrændɪʃər, -z

brandling
BR ˈbrandlɪŋ, -z
AM ˈbræn(d)lɪŋ, -z

Brando
BR ˈbrandəʊ
AM ˈbrændoʊ

Brandon
BR ˈbrandən
AM ˈbrændən

Brandreth
BR ˈbrandrɪθ, ˈbrandrɛθ
AM ˈbrændrəθ

Brands Hatch
BR ˌbran(d)z ˈhatʃ
AM ˌbræn(d)z ˈhætʃ

Brandt
BR brant
AM brænt

brandy
BR ˈbrand|i, -ɪz
AM ˈbrændi, -z

Brangwyn
BR ˈbraŋgwɪn
AM ˈbræŋgwən

Braniff
BR ˈbranɪf
AM ˈbrænəf

Branigan
BR ˈbranɪg(ə)n
AM ˈbrænəgən

brank-ursine
BR ˌbraŋkˈəːsʌɪn
AM ˌbræŋkˈərˌsaɪn

Brannigan
BR ˈbranɪg(ə)n
AM ˈbrænəgən

Branson
BR ˈbransn
AM ˈbrænsən

Branston
BR ˈbranst(ə)n
AM ˈbrænstən

brant
BR brant
AM brænt

Braque
BR brɑːk, brak
AM brɑk

Brasenose
BR 'breɪznəʊz
AM 'breɪzˌnoʊz

brash
BR braʃ, -ə(r), -ɨst
AM bræʃ, -ər, -əst

Brasher
BR 'breɪʃə(r)
AM 'bræʃər

brashly
BR 'braʃli
AM 'bræʃli

brashness
BR 'braʃnəs
AM 'bræʃnəs

brasier
BR 'breɪzɪə(r), 'breɪʒə(r), -z
AM 'breɪʒər, 'breɪˌziər, -z

Brasília
BR brə'zɪlɪə(r)
AM brə'zɪljə, brə'zɪliə

brass
BR brɑːs, bras, -ɪz, -ɪŋ, -t
AM bræs, -əz, -ɪŋ, -t

brassage
BR 'brasɪdʒ
AM brə'sɑʒ, 'bræsɪdʒ

brassard
BR 'brasɑːd, -z
AM 'bræˌsɑrd, -z

brassbound
BR ˌbrɑːs'baʊnd, ˌbras'baʊnd
AM 'bræsˌbaʊnd

brasserie
BR 'bras(ə)r|i, -ɪz
AM ˌbræsə'ri, -z
FR bʀasʀi

Brassey
BR 'brasi
AM 'bræsi

brassica
BR 'brasɨkə(r), -z
AM 'bræsəkə, -z

brassie
BR 'brasi, -z
AM 'bræsi, -z

brassiere
BR 'brazɪə(r), -z
AM brə'zɪ(ə)r, -z

brassily
BR 'brɑːsɨli, 'brasɨli
AM 'bræsəli

brassiness
BR 'brɑːsɪnɨs, 'brasɪnɨs
AM 'bræsinɨs

Brasso®
BR 'brɑːsəʊ, 'brasəʊ
AM 'bræsoʊ

brassware
BR 'brɑːswɛː(r), 'braswɛː(r)
AM 'bræsˌwɛ(ə)r

brassy
BR 'brɑːsi, 'brasi
AM 'bræsi

brat
BR brat, -s
AM bræt, -s

Bratislava
BR ˌbratɪ'slɑːvə(r)
AM ˌbrɑdə'slɑvə
CZ 'brʌtjslʌvʌ

brattice
BR 'brat|ɪs, -ɨsɪz
AM 'brædəs, -əz

bratty
BR 'brati
AM 'brædi

bratwurst
BR 'bratwəːst, 'bratvəːst, 'bratvʊəst
AM 'brɑtˌwərst

Braun
BR brɔːn, braʊn
AM braʊn

Braunschweig
BR 'braʊnʃwʌɪg
AM 'braʊnˌʃwaɪg

braunschweiger
BR 'braʊnˌʃwʌɪgə(r)
AM 'braʊnˌʃwaɪgər

bravado
BR brə'vɑːdəʊ
AM brə'vɑˌdoʊ

brave
BR breɪv, -z, -ɪŋ, -d, -ə(r), -ɨst
AM breɪv, -z, -ɪŋ, -d, -ər, -ɨst

bravely
BR 'breɪvli
AM 'breɪvli

braveness
BR 'breɪvnɨs
AM 'breɪvnɨs

Bravington
BR 'bravɪŋt(ə)n
AM 'breɪvɪŋt(ə)n

bravo![1]
hooray!
BR (ˌ)brɑː'vəʊ, -z
AM ˈbrɑˈvoʊ, -z

bravo[2]
letter B
BR 'brɑːvəʊ
AM 'brɑvoʊ

bravura
BR brə'vjʊərə(r), brə'vjɔːrə(r)
AM brə'v(j)urə

braw
BR brɔː(r)
AM brɔ

Brawdy
BR 'brɔːdi
AM 'brɔdi, 'brɑdi

brawl
BR brɔːl, -z, -ɪŋ, -d
AM brɔl, brɑl, -z, -ɪŋ, -d

brawler
BR 'brɔːlə(r), -z
AM 'brɔlər, 'brɑlər, -z

brawn
BR brɔːn
AM brɔn, brɑn

brawniness
BR 'brɔːnɪnɨs
AM 'brɔninɨs, 'brɑninɨs

brawny
BR 'brɔːn|i, -ɪə(r), -ɪɨst
AM 'brɔni, 'brɑni, -ər, -ɨst

bray
BR breɪ, -z, -ɪŋ, -d
AM breɪ, -z, -ɪŋ, -d

braze
BR breɪz, -ɪz, -ɪŋ, -d
AM breɪz, -ɪz, -ɪŋ, -d

brazen
BR 'breɪzn
AM 'breɪzən

brazenly
BR 'breɪznli
AM 'breɪzənli

brazenness
BR 'breɪznnəs
AM 'breɪzə(n)nəs

brazer
BR 'breɪzə(r), -z
AM 'breɪzər, -z

brazier
BR 'breɪzɪə(r), 'breɪʒə(r), -z
AM 'breɪʒər, 'breɪˌziər, -z

braziery
BR 'breɪzɪəri, 'breɪʒəri, -z
AM 'breɪʒəri, 'breɪˌziəri, -z

Brazil
BR brə'zɪl
AM brə'zɪl

Brazilian
BR brə'zɪlɪən, -z
AM brə'zɪljən, brə'zɪliən, -z

Brazzaville
BR 'brazəvɪl, 'brɑːzəvɪl
AM 'brazəˌvɪl

breach
BR briːtʃ, -ɪz, -ɪŋ, -t
AM britʃ, -ɪz, -ɪŋ, -t

bread
BR brɛd, -z, -ɪŋ, -ɨd
AM brɛd, -z, -ɪŋ, -əd

Breadalbane
BR brɪ'dɔːlb(ɨ)n, brɪ'dalb(ɨ)n
AM 'brɛdəlˌbeɪn

breadbasket
BR 'brɛdˌbɑːskɪt, 'brɛdˌbaskɪt, -s
AM 'brɛdˌbæskət, -s

breadboard
BR 'brɛdbɔːd, -z
AM 'brɛdˌbɔ(ə)rd, -z

breadbox
BR 'brɛdbɒks, -ɪz
AM 'brɛdˌbɑks, -əz

breadcrumb
BR 'brɛdkrʌm, -z
AM 'brɛdˌkrəm, -z

breadfruit
BR 'brɛdfruːt, -s
AM 'brɛdˌfrut, -s

breadline
BR 'brɛdlʌɪn
AM 'brɛdˌlaɪn

breadth
BR brɛdθ, brɛtθ
AM brɛdθ, brɛtθ

breadthways
BR 'brɛdθweɪz, 'brɛtθweɪz
AM 'brɛdθˌweɪz, 'brɛtθˌweɪz

breadthwise
BR 'brɛdθwʌɪz, 'brɛtθwʌɪz
AM 'brɛdθˌwaɪz, 'brɛtθˌwaɪz

breadwinner
BR 'brɛdˌwɪnə(r), -z
AM 'brɛdˌwɪnər, -z

break
BR breɪk, -s, -ɪŋ
AM breɪk, -s, -ɪŋ

breakable
BR 'breɪkəbl, -z
AM 'breɪkəbəl, -z

breakage
BR 'breɪk|ɪdʒ, -ɨdʒɪz
AM 'breɪkɪdʒ, -ɪz

breakaway
BR 'breɪkəweɪ, -z
AM 'breɪkəˌweɪ, -z

breakdown
BR 'breɪkdaʊn, -z
AM 'breɪkˌdaʊn, -z

breaker
BR 'breɪkə(r), -z
AM 'breɪkər, -z

breakfast
BR 'brɛkfəst, -s, -ɪŋ, -ɨd
AM 'brɛkfəst, -s, -ɪŋ, -əd

breakfaster
BR 'brɛkfəstə(r), -z
AM 'brɛkfəstər, -z

breakneck
BR 'breɪknɛk
AM 'breɪkˌnɛk

breakout
BR 'breɪkaʊt, -s
AM 'breɪkˌaʊt, -s

breakpoint
BR ˈbreɪkpɔɪnt, -s
AM ˈbreɪkˌpɔɪnt, -s

Breakspear
BR ˈbreɪkspɪə(r)
AM ˈbreɪkˌspɪ(ə)r

breakthrough
BR ˈbreɪkθruː, -z
AM ˈbreɪkˌθru, -z

breakup
BR ˈbreɪkʌp, -s
AM ˈbreɪkˌəp, -s

breakwater
BR ˈbreɪkˌwɔːtə(r), -z
AM ˈbreɪkˌwɔdər, ˈbreɪkˌwɑdər, -z

bream
BR briːm
AM brim

Brearley
BR ˈbrɪəli
AM ˈbrɪrli

breast
BR brɛst, -s, -ɪŋ, -ɨd
AM brɛst, -s, -ɪŋ, -əd

breastbone
BR ˈbrɛs(t)bəʊn, -z
AM ˈbrɛs(t)ˌboʊn, -z

breastfed
BR ˈbrɛs(t)fɛd
AM ˈbrɛs(t)ˌfɛd

breastfeed
BR ˈbrɛs(t)fiːd, -z, -ɪŋ
AM ˈbrɛs(t)ˌfid, -z, -ɪŋ

breastless
BR ˈbrɛstləs
AM ˈbrɛs(t)ləs

breastplate
BR ˈbrɛs(t)pleɪt, -s
AM ˈbrɛs(t)ˌpleɪt, -s

breaststroke
BR ˈbrɛs(t)strəʊk
AM ˈbrɛs(t)ˌstroʊk

breastsummer
BR ˈbrɛs(t)ˌsʌmə(r), -z
AM ˈbrɛs(t)ˌsəmər, -z

breastwork
BR ˈbrɛstwəːk, -s
AM ˈbrɛs(t)ˌwərk, -s

breath
BR brɛθ, -s
AM brɛθ, -s

breathable
BR ˈbriːðəbl
AM ˈbriθəbəl

breathalyse
BR ˈbrɛθəlʌɪz, ˈbrɛθl̩ʌɪz, -ɨz, -ɪŋ, -d
AM ˈbrɛθəˌlaɪz, -ɨz, -ɪŋ, -d

breathalyze
BR ˈbrɛθəlʌɪz, ˈbrɛθl̩ʌɪz, -ɨz, -ɪŋ, -d
AM ˈbrɛθəˌlaɪz, -ɨz, -ɪŋ, -d

Breathalyzer®
BR ˈbrɛθəlʌɪzə(r), ˈbrɛθl̩ʌɪzə(r), -z
AM ˈbrɛθəˌlaɪzər, -z

breathe
BR briːð, -z, -ɪŋ, -d
AM brið, -z, -ɪŋ, -d

breather
BR ˈbriːðə(r), -z
AM ˈbriðər, -z

breathily
BR ˈbrɛθɨli
AM ˈbrɛθɨli

breathiness
BR ˈbrɛθɪnɨs
AM ˈbrɛθinɨs

breathless
BR ˈbrɛθləs
AM ˈbrɛθləs

breathlessly
BR ˈbrɛθləsli
AM ˈbrɛθləsli

breathlessness
BR ˈbrɛθləsnəs
AM ˈbrɛθləsnəs

breathtaking
BR ˈbrɛθˌteɪkɪŋ
AM ˈbrɛθˌteɪkɪŋ

breathtakingly
BR ˈbrɛθˌteɪkɪŋli
AM ˈbrɛθˌteɪkɪŋli

breathy
BR ˈbrɛθ|i, -ɪə(r), -ɪɨst
AM ˈbrɛθi, -ər, -ɨst

breccia
BR ˈbrɛtʃ(ɪ)ə(*r*), -z
AM ˈbrɛ(t)ʃ(i)ə, -z

brecciate
BR ˈbrɛtʃɪeɪt, -s, -ɪŋ, -ɨd
AM ˈbrɛ(t)ʃ(i)ˌeɪ|t, -ts, -dɪŋ, -dɨd

brecciation
BR ˌbrɛtʃɪˈeɪʃn
AM ˌbrɛ(t)ʃiˈeɪʃən

Brechin
BR ˈbriːkɪn, ˈbriːxɪn
AM ˈbrikɪn

Brecht
BR brɛxt, brɛkt
AM brɛkt

Brechtian
BR ˈbrɛxtɪən, ˈbrɛktɪən
AM ˈbrɛktiən

Breckenridge
BR ˈbrɛk(ə)nrɪdʒ
AM ˈbrɛkənˌrɪdʒ

Breckland
BR ˈbrɛklənd
AM ˈbrɛklənd

Brecknock
BR ˈbrɛknɒk
AM ˈbrɛkˌnɑk

Brecknockshire
BR ˈbrɛknəkʃ(ɪ)ə(r)
AM ˈbrɛkˌnɑkˌʃɪ(ə)r

Brecon
BR ˈbrɛkn
AM ˈbrɛkən

Breconshire
BR ˈbrɛknʃ(ɪ)ə(r)
AM ˈbrɛkənˌʃɪ(ə)r

bred
BR brɛd
AM brɛd

Breda
BR ˈbriːdə(*r*), ˈbreɪdə(*r*)
AM ˈbreɪdə
DU breːˈdɑ

Bredon
BR ˈbriːdn
AM ˈbridn

breech
of gun
BR briːtʃ, -ɨz, -ɪŋ, -t
AM britʃ, -ɨz, -ɪŋ, -t

breeches
trousers
BR ˈbrɪtʃɨz, ˈbriːtʃɨz
AM ˈbrɪtʃɨz, ˈbritʃɨz

breeches-buoy
BR ˌbriːtʃɨzˈbɔɪ, ˈbriːtʃɨzbɔɪ, -z
AM ˈbritʃɨzˌbɔɪ, ˈbritʃɨzˌbui, -z

breed
BR briːd, -z, -ɪŋ
AM brid, -z, -ɪŋ

breeder
BR ˈbriːdə(r), -z
AM ˈbridər, -z

breeks
BR briːks
AM briks

Breen
BR briːn
AM brin

breeze
BR briːz, -ɨz, -ɪŋ, -d
AM briz, -ɨz, -ɪŋ, -d

breezeblock
BR ˈbriːzblɒk, -s
AM ˈbrizˌblɑk, -s

breezeless
BR ˈbriːzlɨs
AM ˈbrizlɨs

breezeway
BR ˈbriːzweɪ, -z
AM ˈbrizˌweɪ, -z

breezily
BR ˈbriːzɨli
AM ˈbrizɨli

breeziness
BR ˈbriːzɪnɨs
AM ˈbrizinɨs

breezy
BR ˈbriːz|i, -ɪə(r), -ɪɨst
AM ˈbrizi, -ər, -ɨst

Bremen
BR ˈbreɪmən, ˈbrɛmən
AM ˈbreɪmən, ˈbrɛmən

Bremner
BR ˈbrɛmnə(r)
AM ˈbrɛmnər

bremsstrahlung
BR ˈbrɛmzˌʃtrɑːlʊŋ
AM ˈbrɛmˌʃtrɑləŋ

Bren
BR brɛn
AM brɛn

Brenda
BR ˈbrɛndə(*r*)
AM ˈbrɛndə

Brendan
BR ˈbrɛnd(ə)n
AM ˈbrɛndən

Brendel
BR ˈbrɛndl
AM ˈbrɛndəl

Brennan
BR ˈbrɛnən
AM ˈbrɛnən

Brenner Pass
BR ˌbrɛnə ˈpɑːs, + ˈpas
AM ˌbrɛnər ˈpæs

brent
BR brɛnt
AM brɛnt

Brentwood
BR ˈbrɛntwʊd
AM ˈbrɛntˌwʊd

Breslau
BR ˈbrɛslaʊ
AM ˈbrɛˌslaʊ

Bresson
BR ˈbrɛsn
AM ˈbrɛsən
FR bʀɛsɔ̃

Brest
BR brɛst
AM brɛst

Brest-Litovsk
BR ˌbrɛstlɪˈtɒfsk
AM ˌbrɛstˈlɪtɑfsk

brethren
BR ˈbrɛðr(ɨ)n
AM ˈbrɛð(ə)rən

Breton
BR ˈbrɛt(ə)n, ˈbrɛtɒn, -z
AM ˈbrɛtn, -z

Brett
BR brɛt
AM brɛt

Bretton
BR ˈbrɛtn
AM ˈbrɛtn

Breughel
BR ˈbrɔɪgl
AM ˈbrɔɪgəl

breve
BR briːv, -z
AM briv, brɛv, -z

brevet
BR ˈbrɛv|ɪt, -ɪts, -ɪtɪŋ, -ɪtɨd
AM brəˈvɛ|t, -ts, -dɪŋ, -dəd

breviary
BR ˈbrɛvɪər|i, ˈbriːvɪər|i, -ɪz
AM ˈbriv(j)əri, ˈbriviˌɛri, -z

breviate
BR ˈbriːvɪət, -s
AM ˈbriviət, -s

brevity
BR ˈbrɛvɨti
AM ˈbrɛvədi

brew
BR bruː, -z, -ɪŋ, -d
AM bru, -z, -ɪŋ, -d

brewer
BR ˈbruːə(r), -z
AM ˈbruər, -z

brewery
BR ˈbruːər|i, -ɪz
AM ˈbru(ə)ri, -z

Brewis
BR ˈbruːɪs
AM ˈbruɪs

brewster
BR ˈbruːstə(r), -z
AM ˈbrustər, -z

Brezel
BR ˈbrɛtsl, -z
AM ˈbrɛtsəl, -z

Brezhnev
BR ˈbrɛʒnɛv, ˈbrɛʒnɛf
AM ˈbrɛʒˌnɛv, ˈbrɛʒˌnɛf

Brian
BR ˈbrʌɪən
AM ˈbraɪən

BrianBorú
BR ˌbrʌɪən bəˈruː
AM ˌbraɪən bəˈru

briar
BR ˈbrʌɪə(r), -z
AM ˈbraɪ(ə)r, -z

Briard
BR brɪˈɑːd, -z
AM briˈɑrd, -z

briarwood
BR ˈbrʌɪəwʊd
AM ˈbraɪ(ə)rˌwʊd

bribable
BR ˈbrʌɪbəbl
AM ˈbraɪbəbəl

bribe
BR brʌɪb, -z, -ɪŋ, -d
AM braɪb, -z, -ɪŋ, -d

briber
BR ˈbrʌɪbə(r), -z
AM ˈbraɪbər, -z

bribery
BR ˈbrʌɪb(ə)ri
AM ˈbraɪb(ə)ri

bric-à-brac
BR ˈbrɪkəbrak
AM ˈbrɪkəˌbræk

Brice
BR brʌɪs
AM braɪs

brick
BR brɪk, -s, -ɪŋ, -t
AM brɪk, -s, -ɪŋ, -t

brickbat
BR ˈbrɪkbat, -s
AM ˈbrɪkˌbæt, -s

brickdust
BR ˈbrɪkdʌst
AM ˈbrɪkˌdəst

brickfield
BR ˈbrɪkfiːld, -z
AM ˈbrɪkˌfild, -z

brickfielder
BR ˈbrɪkˌfiːldə(r), -z
AM ˈbrɪkˌfildər, -z

brickie
BR ˈbrɪk|i, -ɪz
AM ˈbrɪki, -z

bricklayer
BR ˈbrɪkˌleɪə(r), -z
AM ˈbrɪkˌleɪ(ə)r, -z

bricklaying
BR ˈbrɪkˌleɪɪŋ
AM ˈbrɪkˌleɪɪŋ

brickmaker
BR ˈbrɪkˌmeɪkə(r), -z
AM ˈbrɪkˌmeɪkər, -z

brickmaking
BR ˈbrɪkˌmeɪkɪŋ
AM ˈbrɪkˌmeɪkɪŋ

brickwork
BR ˈbrɪkwəːk, -s
AM ˈbrɪkˌwərk, -s

bricky
BR ˈbrɪki
AM ˈbrɪki

brickyard
BR ˈbrɪkjɑːd, -z
AM ˈbrɪkˌjɑrd, -z

bridal
BR ˈbrʌɪdl
AM ˈbraɪdəl

bridally
BR ˈbrʌɪdl̩i
AM ˈbraɪdl̩i

bride
BR brʌɪd, -z
AM braɪd, -z

bridegroom
BR ˈbrʌɪdgruːm, -z
AM ˈbraɪdˌgrum, -z

Brideshead
BR ˈbrʌɪdzhɛd
AM ˈbraɪdzˌ(h)ɛd

bridesmaid
BR ˈbrʌɪdzmeɪd, -z
AM ˈbraɪdzˌmeɪd, -z

bridesman
BR ˈbrʌɪdzmən
AM ˈbraɪdzmən

bridesmen
BR ˈbrʌɪdzmən
AM ˈbraɪdzmən

bridewell
BR ˈbrʌɪdw(ɛ)l, -z
AM ˈbraɪdˌwɛl, ˈbraɪdwəl, -z

bridge
BR brɪdʒ, -ɨz, -ɪŋ, -d
AM brɪdʒ, -ɨz, -ɪŋ, -d

bridgeable
BR ˈbrɪdʒəbl
AM ˈbrɪdʒəbəl

bridgehead
BR ˈbrɪdʒhɛd, -z
AM ˈbrɪdʒˌ(h)ɛd, -z

Bridgeman
BR ˈbrɪdʒmən
AM ˈbrɪdʒmən

Bridgend
BR ˌbrɪdʒˈɛnd
AM ˈbrɪdʒˌɛnd

Bridgeport
BR ˈbrɪdʒpɔːt
AM ˈbrɪdʒˌpɔ(ə)rt

Bridger
BR ˈbrɪdʒə(r)
AM ˈbrɪdʒər

Bridges
BR ˈbrɪdʒɨz
AM ˈbrɪdʒɨz

Bridget
BR ˈbrɪdʒɪt
AM ˈbrɪdʒət

Bridgetown
BR ˈbrɪdʒtaʊn
AM ˈbrɪdʒˌtaʊn

Bridgewater
BR ˈbrɪdʒwɔːtə(r)
AM ˈbrɪdʒˌwɔdər, ˈbrɪdʒˌwɑdər

bridgework
BR ˈbrɪdʒwəːk
AM ˈbrɪdʒˌwərk

Bridgman
BR ˈbrɪdʒmən
AM ˈbrɪdʒmən

Bridgnorth
BR ˈbrɪdʒnɔːθ
AM ˈbrɪdʒˌnɔrθ

Bridgwater
BR ˈbrɪdʒwɔːtə(r)
AM ˈbrɪdʒˌwɔdər, ˈbrɪdʒˌwɑdər

bridle
BR ˈbrʌɪd|l, -lz, -l̩ɪŋ\-lɪŋ, -ld
AM ˈbraɪd|əl, -əlz, -(ə)lɪŋ, -əld

bridleway
BR ˈbrʌɪdlweɪ, -z
AM ˈbraɪdlˌweɪ, -z

Bridlington
BR ˈbrɪdlɪŋt(ə)n
AM ˈbrɪdlɪŋt(ə)n

bridoon
BR brɨˈduːn, -z
AM brəˈdun, -z

Bridport
BR ˈbrɪdpɔːt
AM ˈbrɪdˌpɔ(ə)rt

Brie
BR briː
AM bri

brief
BR briːf, -s, -ɪŋ, -t, -ə(r), -ɨst
AM brif, -s, -ɪŋ, -t, -ər, -ɨst

briefcase
BR ˈbriːfkeɪs, -ɨz
AM ˈbrifˌkeɪs, -ɨz

briefless
BR ˈbriːflɨs
AM ˈbriflɨs

briefly
BR ˈbriːfli
AM ˈbrifli

briefness
BR ˈbriːfnɨs
AM ˈbrifnɨs

brier
BR ˈbrʌɪə(r), -z
AM ˈbraɪ(ə)r, -z

Brierley
BR ˈbrʌɪəli, ˈbrɪəli
AM ˈbraɪ(ə)rli

Brierly
BR ˈbrʌɪəli, ˈbrɪəli
AM ˈbraɪ(ə)rli

Briers
BR ˈbrʌɪəz
AM ˈbraɪ(ə)rz

brierwood
BR ˈbrʌɪəwʊd, -z
AM ˈbraɪ(ə)rˌwʊd, -z

briery
BR ˈbrʌɪəri
AM ˈbraɪ(ə)ri

brig
BR brɪg, -z
AM brɪg, -z

brigade
BR brɨˈgeɪd, -z
AM brəˈgeɪd, -z

brigadier
BR ˌbrɪgəˈdɪə(r), -z
AM ˌbrɪgəˈdɪ(ə)r, -z

Brigadoon
BR ˌbrɪgəˈduːn
AM ˌbrɪgəˈdun

brigalow
BR ˈbrɪgələʊ, -z
AM ˈbrɪgəˌloʊ, -z

brigand
BR ˈbrɪg(ə)nd, -z
AM ˈbrɪg(ə)nd, -z

brigandage
BR ˈbrɪg(ə)ndɪdʒ
AM ˈbrɪg(ə)ndɪdʒ

brigandine
BR ˈbrɪg(ə)ndiːn, -z
AM ˈbrɪgənˌdin, -z

brigandish
BR ˈbrɪg(ə)ndɪʃ
AM ˈbrɪgəndɪʃ

brigandism
BR ˈbrɪg(ə)ndɪz(ə)m
AM ˈbrɪgənˌdɪzəm

brigandry
BR ˈbrɪg(ə)ndri

AM ˈbrɪɡəndri

brigantine
BR ˈbrɪɡ(ə)ntiːn, -z
AM ˈbrɪɡənˌtin, -z

Brigg
BR brɪɡ
AM brɪɡ

Briggs
BR brɪɡz
AM brɪɡz

Brigham
BR ˈbrɪɡəm
AM ˈbrɪɡəm

Brighouse
BR ˈbrɪɡhaʊs
AM ˈbrɪɡˌ(h)aʊs

bright
BR brʌɪt, -ə(r), -ɨst
AM braɪ|t, -dər, -dɨst

brighten
BR ˈbrʌɪt|n, -nz, -n̩ɪŋ\-nɪŋ, -nd
AM ˈbraɪtn, -z, -ɪŋ, -d

brightish
BR ˈbrʌɪtɪʃ
AM ˈbraɪdɪʃ

Brightlingsea
BR ˈbrʌɪtlɪŋsiː
AM ˈbraɪtlɪŋˌsi

brightly
BR ˈbrʌɪtli
AM ˈbraɪtli

brightness
BR ˈbrʌɪtnɨs
AM ˈbraɪtnɨs

Brighton
BR ˈbrʌɪtn
AM ˈbraɪtn

brightwork
BR ˈbrʌɪtwəːk
AM ˈbraɪtˌwərk

Brigid
BR ˈbrɪdʒɪd
AM ˈbrɪdʒəd

Brigit
BR ˈbrɪdʒɪt
AM ˈbrɪdʒət

Brigitte
BR ˈbrɪʒɪt, brɪˈʒiːt
AM ˈbrɪdʒət

brill
BR brɪl
AM brɪl

brilliance
BR ˈbrɪlj(ə)ns, ˈbrɪlɪəns
AM ˈbrɪljəns

brilliancy
BR ˈbrɪlj(ə)nsi, ˈbrɪlɪənsi
AM ˈbrɪljənsi

brilliant
BR ˈbrɪlj(ə)nt, ˈbrɪlɪənt, -s
AM ˈbrɪljənt, -s

brilliantine
BR ˈbrɪlj(ə)ntiːn
AM ˈbrɪljənˌtin

brilliantly
BR ˈbrɪlj(ə)ntli, ˈbrɪlɪəntli
AM ˈbrɪljən(t)li

brilliantness
BR ˈbrɪlj(ə)ntnəs, ˈbrɪlɪəntnəs
AM ˈbrɪljən(t)nɨs

Brillo®
BR ˈbrɪləʊ
AM ˈbrɪloʊ

brim
BR brɪm, -z, -ɪŋ, -d
AM brɪm, -z, -ɪŋ, -d

Brimble
BR ˈbrɪmbl
AM ˈbrɪmbəl

brimful
BR ˌbrɪmˈfʊl, ˈbrɪmfʊl
AM ˈbrɪmˌfʊl

brimless
BR ˈbrɪmlɨs
AM ˈbrɪmlɨs

brimstone
BR ˈbrɪmstən, ˈbrɪmstəʊn
AM ˈbrɪmzˌtoʊn, ˈbrɪmˌstoʊn

brimstony
BR ˈbrɪmstəni, ˈbrɪmstəʊni
AM ˈbrɪmzˌtoʊni, ˈbrɪmˌstoʊni

Brindisi
BR ˈbrɪndɪzi
AM ˈbrɪndɪzi

brindle
BR ˈbrɪndl, -d
AM ˈbrɪndəl, -d

Brindley
BR ˈbrɪndli
AM ˈbrɪn(d)li

brine
BR brʌɪn
AM braɪn

bring
BR brɪŋ, -z, -ɪŋ
AM brɪŋ, -z, -ɪŋ

bringer
BR ˈbrɪŋə(r), -z
AM ˈbrɪŋər, -z

brininess
BR ˈbrʌɪmɪnɨs
AM ˈbraɪmɪnɨs

brinjal
BR ˈbrɪn(d)ʒ(ə)l
AM ˈbrɪn(d)ʒəl

brink
BR brɪŋk, -s
AM brɪŋk, -s

brinkmanship
BR ˈbrɪŋkmənʃɪp
AM ˈbrɪŋkmənˌʃɪp

brinksmanship
BR ˈbrɪŋksmənʃɪp
AM ˈbrɪŋksmənˌʃɪp

Brinks-Mat®
BR ˈbrɪŋksmat
AM ˈbrɪŋksˌmæt

briny
BR ˈbrʌɪni
AM ˈbraɪni

bri-nylon
BR ˌbrʌɪˈnʌɪlɒn
AM ˌbraɪˈnaɪlən

brio
BR ˈbriːəʊ
AM ˈbrioʊ

brioche
BR ˌbriːˈɒʃ, ˈbriːɒʃ, ˌbriːˈəʊʃ, ˈbriːəʊʃ, -ɪz
AM briˈɔʃ, briˈoʊʃ, -əz

briolette
BR ˌbriːə(ʊ)ˈlɛt, -s
AM ˌbriəˈlɛt, -s

Briony
BR ˈbrʌɪəni
AM ˈbraɪəni

briquet
BR brɪˈkɛt, -s
AM brəˈkɛt, -s

briquette
BR brɪˈkɛt, -s
AM brəˈkɛt, -s

Brisbane
BR ˈbrɪzbən
AM ˈbrɪzbən, ˈbrɪzˌbeɪn

Brisco
BR ˈbrɪskəʊ
AM ˈbrɪskoʊ

Briscoe
BR ˈbrɪskəʊ
AM ˈbrɪskoʊ

brisk
BR brɪsk, -ə(r), -ɨst
AM brɪsk, -ər, -ɪst

brisken
BR ˈbrɪsk|(ə)n, -(ə)nz, -n̩ɪŋ\-ənɪŋ, -nd
AM ˈbrɪsk|n, -nz, -n̩ɪŋ, -nd

brisket
BR ˈbrɪskɪt, -s
AM ˈbrɪskɨt, -s

briskly
BR ˈbrɪskli
AM ˈbrɪskli

briskness
BR ˈbrɪsknɨs
AM ˈbrɪsknɨs

brisling
BR ˈbrɪzlɪŋ, ˈbrɪslɪŋ
AM ˈbrɪzlɪŋ, ˈbrɪslɪŋ

bristle
BR ˈbrɪs|l, -lz, -l̩ɪŋ\-lɪŋ, -ld
AM ˈbrɪs|əl, -əlz, -(ə)lɪŋ, -əld

bristletail
BR ˈbrɪslteɪl, -z
AM ˈbrɪsəlˌteɪl, -z

bristleworm
BR ˈbrɪslwəːm, -z
AM ˈbrɪsəlˌwərm, -z

bristliness
BR ˈbrɪslɪnɨs
AM ˈbrɪslinɨs, ˈbrɪsl̩inɨs

bristly
BR ˈbrɪsli
AM ˈbrɪsli, ˈbrɪsl̩i

Bristol
BR ˈbrɪstl
AM ˈbrɪstl

bristols
BR ˈbrɪstlz
AM ˈbrɪstlz

Bristow
BR ˈbrɪstəʊ
AM ˈbrɪstoʊ

Bristowe
BR ˈbrɪstəʊ
AM ˈbrɪstoʊ

Brit
BR brɪt, -s
AM brɪt, -s

Britain
BR ˈbrɪtn
AM ˈbrɪtn, ˈbrɪdn

Britannia
BR brɪˈtanjə(r)
AM brɪˈtænjə

Britannic
BR brɪˈtanɪk
AM brɪˈtænɪk

britches
BR ˈbrɪtʃɪz
AM ˈbrɪtʃɪz

Briticism
BR ˈbrɪtɪsɪz(ə)m, -z
AM ˈbrɪdəˌsɪzəm, -z

British
BR ˈbrɪtɪʃ
AM ˈbrɪdɪʃ

Britisher
BR ˈbrɪtɨʃə(r), -z
AM ˈbrɪdɪʃər, -z

Britishism
BR ˈbrɪtɨʃɪz(ə)m, -z
AM ˈbrɪdəˌʃɪzəm, -z

Britishness
BR ˈbrɪtɨʃnɨs
AM ˈbrɪdɪʃnɨs

Britoil
BR ˈbrɪtɔɪl
AM ˈbrɪdɔɪl

Briton
BR ˈbrɪtn, -z
AM ˈbrɪtn, -z

Britt
BR brɪt
AM brɪt

Brittain
BR ˈbrɪtn
AM ˈbrɪtn

Brittan
BR ˈbrɪtn
AM ˈbrɪtn

Brittany
BR ˈbrɪtəni, ˈbrɪtn̩i

AM ˈbrɪtn̩i

Britten
BR ˈbrɪtn
AM ˈbrɪtn

brittle
BR ˈbrɪtl̩, -ə(r), -ɪst
AM ˈbrɪdəl, -ər, -ɪst

brittlely
BR ˈbrɪtlli
AM ˈbrɪdl̩i

brittleness
BR ˈbrɪtlnəs
AM ˈbrɪdlnɨs

brittly
BR ˈbrɪtl̩i
AM ˈbrɪdl̩i

Britton
BR ˈbrɪtn
AM ˈbrɪtn

Britvic®
BR ˈbrɪtvɪk, -s
AM ˈbrɪtvɨk, -s

britzka
BR ˈbrɪtskə(r), -z
AM ˈbrɪtʃkə, ˈbrɪtskə, -z

Brixham
BR ˈbrɪks(ə)m
AM ˈbrɪksəm

Brize Norton
BR ˌbrʌɪz ˈnɔːtn
AM ˌbraɪz ˈnɔrtən

Brno
BR ˈbəːnəʊ, brəˈnəʊ
AM ˈbərˌnoʊ
CZ ˈbrnɔ

bro
BR brəʊ
AM broʊ

broach
BR brəʊtʃ, -ɪz, -ɪŋ, -t
AM broʊtʃ, -əz, -ɪŋ, -t

broad
BR brɔːd, -z, -ə(r), -ɪst
AM brɔd, brɑd, -z, -ər, -əst

broadband
BR ˈbrɔːdband
AM ˈbrɔdˌbænd, ˈbrɑdˌbænd

Broadbent
BR ˈbrɔːdbɛnt
AM ˈbrɔdˌbɛnt, ˈbrɑdˌbɛnt

broadbrimmed
BR ˌbrɔːdˈbrɪmd
AM ˈbrɔdˈbrɪmd, ˈbrɑdˈbrɪmd

broadcast
BR ˈbrɔːdkɑːst, ˈbrɔːdkast, -s, -ɪŋ
AM ˈbrɔdˌkæst, ˈbrɑdˌkæst, -s, -ɪŋ

broadcaster
BR ˈbrɔːdˌkɑːstə(r), ˈbrɔːdˌkastə(r), -z
AM ˈbrɔdˌkæstər, ˈbrɑdˌkæstər, -z

broadcloth
BR ˈbrɔːdklɒθ
AM ˈbrɔdˌklɔθ, ˈbrɑdˌklɑθ

broaden
BR ˈbrɔːd|n, -nz, -n̩ɪŋ\-nɪŋ, -nd
AM ˈbrɔdən, ˈbrɑdən, -z, -ɪŋ, -d

Broadhead
BR ˈbrɔːdhɛd
AM ˈbrɔdˌ(h)ɛd, ˈbrɑdˌ(h)ɛd

Broadhurst
BR ˈbrɔːdhəːst
AM ˈbrɔdˌ(h)ərst, ˈbrɑdˌ(h)ərst

broadleaf
BR ˈbrɔːdliːf
AM ˈbrɔdˌlif, ˈbrɑdˌlif

broadleaved
BR ˌbrɔːdˈliːvd
AM ˈbrɔdˌlivd, ˈbrɑdˌlivd

broadloom
BR ˈbrɔːdluːm
AM ˈbrɔdˌlum, ˈbrɑdˌlum

broadly
BR ˈbrɔːdli
AM ˈbrɔdli, ˈbrɑdli

broadminded
BR ˌbrɔːdˈmʌɪndɨd
AM ˈbrɔdˈmaɪn(d)ɨd, ˈbrɑdˈmaɪn(d)ɨd

broadmindedly
BR ˌbrɔːdˈmʌɪndɨdli
AM ˈbrɔdˈmaɪn(d)ɨdli, ˈbrɑdˈmaɪn(d)ɨdli

broadmindedness
BR ˌbrɔːdˈmʌɪndɨdnɨs
AM ˈbrɔdˈmaɪn(d)ɨdnɨs, ˈbrɑdˈmaɪn(d)ɨdnɨs

Broadmoor
BR ˈbrɔːdmɔː(r), ˈbrɔːdmʊə(r)
AM ˈbrɔdˌmɔ(ə)r, ˈbrɔdˌmʊ(ə)r, ˈbrɑdˌmɔ(ə)r, ˈbrɑdˌmʊ(ə)r

broadness
BR ˈbrɔːdnəs
AM ˈbrɔdnəs, ˈbrɑdnəs

broadsheet
BR ˈbrɔːdʃiːt, -s
AM ˈbrɔdˌʃit, ˈbrɑdˌʃit, -s

broadside
BR ˈbrɔːdsʌɪd, -z
AM ˈbrɔdˌsaɪd, ˈbrɑdˌsaɪd, -z

broadspectrum
BR ˌbrɔːdˈspɛktrəm
AM ˌbrɔdˈspɛktrəm, ˌbrɑdˈspɛktrəm

Broadstairs
BR ˈbrɔːdstɛːz
AM ˈbrɔdˌstɛrz, ˈbrɑdˌstɛrz

broadsword
BR ˈbrɔːdsɔːd, -z
AM ˈbrɔdˌsɔ(ə)rd, ˈbrɑdˌsɔ(ə)rd, -z

broadtail
BR ˈbrɔːdteɪl, -z
AM ˈbrɔdˌteɪ(ə)l, ˈbrɑdˌteɪ(ə)l, -z

Broadway
BR ˈbrɔːdweɪ
AM ˈbrɔdˌweɪ, ˈbrɑdˌweɪ

broadwise
BR ˈbrɔːdwʌɪz
AM ˈbrɔdˌwaɪz, ˈbrɑdˌwaɪz

Broadwood
BR ˈbrɔːdwʊd
AM ˈbrɔdˌwʊd, ˈbrɑdˌwʊd

Brobdingnag
BR ˈbrɒbdɪŋnag
AM ˈbrɑbdɪŋˌnæg

Brobdingnagian
BR ˌbrɒbdɪŋˈnagɪən, -z
AM ˌbrɑbdɪŋˈnægiən, -z

brocade
BR brəˈkeɪd, -z, -ɨd
AM broʊˈkeɪd, -z, -ɨd

brocatel
BR ˌbrɒkəˈtɛl
AM ˌbrɑkəˈtɛl

brocatelle
BR ˌbrɒkəˈtɛl
AM ˌbrɑkəˈtɛl

broccoli
BR ˈbrɒkəli
AM ˈbrɑk(ə)li

broch
BR brɒk, brɒx, -s
AM brɑk, -s

brochette
BR brɒˈʃɛt, -s
AM broʊˈʃɛt, -s

brochure
BR ˈbrəʊʃə(r), brəˈʃʊə(r), -z
AM broʊˈʃʊ(ə)r, -z

brock
BR brɒk, -s
AM brɑk, -s

Brockbank
BR ˈbrɒkbaŋk
AM ˈbrɑkˌbæŋk

Brocken
BR ˈbrɒk(ə)n
AM ˈbrɑkən

Brockenhurst
BR ˈbrɒk(ə)nhəːst
AM ˈbrɑkənˌ(h)ərst

brocket
BR ˈbrɒkɪt, -s
AM ˈbrɑkət, -s

Brocklebank
BR ˈbrɒklbaŋk
AM ˈbrɑkəlˌbæŋk

Broderick
BR ˈbrɒd(ə)rɪk
AM ˈbrɑd(ə)rɪk, ˈbrɔd(ə)rɪk

broderie anglaise
BR ˌbrəʊd(ə)rɪ ˌɒŋˈgleɪz, ˌbrɒd(ə)rɪ +, + ˈɒŋgleɪz
AM ˌbroʊdəriˌɑŋˈglɛz

Brodie
BR ˈbrəʊdi
AM ˈbroʊdi

Brodsky
BR ˈbrɒdski
AM ˈbrɑdski

Broederbond
BR ˈbruːdəbɒnd, ˈbruːdəbɒnt
AM ˈbroʊdərˌbɑnd

Brogan
BR ˈbrəʊg(ə)n
AM ˈbroʊgən

brogue
BR brəʊg, -z
AM broʊg, -z

broil
BR brɔɪl, -z, -ɪŋ, -d
AM brɔɪl, -z, -ɪŋ, -d

broiler
BR ˈbrɔɪlə(r), -z
AM ˈbrɔɪlər, -z

broke
BR brəʊk, -s, -ɪŋ, -t
AM broʊk, -s, -ɪŋ, -t

broken
BR ˈbrəʊk(ə)n
AM ˈbroʊk(ə)n

brokenly
BR ˈbrəʊk(ə)nli
AM ˈbroʊkənli

brokenness
BR ˈbrəʊk(ə)nnəs
AM ˈbroʊkə(n)nəs

broker
BR ˈbrəʊkə(r), -z
AM ˈbroʊkər, -z

brokerage
BR ˈbrəʊk(ə)rɪdʒ
AM ˈbroʊk(ə)rɪdʒ

Brolac
BR ˈbrəʊlak
AM ˈbroʊlæk

brolga
BR ˈbrɒlgə(r), -z
AM ˈbrɑlgə, -z

brolly
BR ˈbrɒl|i, -ɪz
AM ˈbrɑli, -z

bromate
BR ˈbrəʊmeɪt, -s
AM ˈbroʊˌmeɪt, -s

Bromberg
BR ˈbrɒmbəːg

AM 'brɑm,bərg

brome
BR brəʊm, -z
AM broʊm, -z

bromelia
BR brə(ʊ)'mi:lɪə(r), -z
AM broʊ'miljə, broʊ'mɛljə, broʊ'miliə, broʊ'mɛliə, -z

bromeliad
BR brə(ʊ)'mi:lɪad, -z
AM broʊ'mili,æd, broʊ'mɛliəd, -z

bromic
BR 'brəʊmɪk
AM 'broʊmɪk

bromide
BR 'brəʊmʌɪd, -z
AM 'broʊ,maɪd, -z

bromine
BR 'brəʊmi:n
AM 'broʊ,min

bromism
BR 'brəʊmɪz(ə)m
AM 'broʊ,mɪzəm

Bromley
BR 'brɒmli, 'brʌmli
AM 'brɑmli

bromoform
BR 'brəʊməfɔ:m
AM 'broʊmə,fɔ(ə)rm

Brompton
BR 'brɒm(p)t(ə)n, 'brʌm(p)t(ə)n
AM 'brɑm(p)tən

Bromsgrove
BR 'brɒmzgrəʊv
AM 'brɑmz,groʊv

Bromwich
BR 'brɒmɪtʃ, 'brɒmɪdʒ
AM 'brɑmwɪtʃ

Bromyard
BR 'brɒmjɑ:d
AM 'brɑmjərd, 'brɑm,jɑrd

bronc
BR brɒŋk, -s
AM brɑŋk, -s

bronchi
BR 'brɒŋkʌɪ, 'brɒŋki:
AM 'brɑŋ,kaɪ, 'brɑŋ,ki

bronchia
BR 'brɒŋkɪə(r)
AM 'brɑŋkiə

bronchiae
BR 'brɒŋkɪi:
AM 'brɑŋki,i, 'brɑŋki,aɪ

bronchial
BR 'brɒŋkɪəl
AM 'brɑŋkiəl

bronchiolar
BR ,brɒŋkɪ'əʊlə(r), 'brɒŋkɪələ(r)
AM 'brɑŋkiələr, ,brɑŋki'oʊlər

bronchiole
BR 'brɒŋkɪəʊl, -z
AM 'brɑŋki,oʊl, -z

bronchitic
BR brɒŋ'kɪtɪk
AM brɑŋ'kɪdɪk

bronchitis
BR brɒŋ'kʌɪtɪs
AM brɑŋ'kaɪdɪs, brɑn'kaɪdɪs

bronchocele
BR 'brɒŋkə(ʊ)si:l, -z
AM 'brɑŋkoʊ,sil, -z

bronchopneumonia
BR ,brɒŋkə(ʊ)nju:'məʊnɪə(r), ,brɒŋkə(ʊ)njʊ'məʊnɪə(r)
AM ,brɑŋkoʊn(j)ʊ'moʊnjə

bronchoscope
BR 'brɒŋkə(ʊ)skəʊp, -s
AM 'brɑŋkə,skoʊp, -s

bronchoscopy
BR brɒŋ'kɒskəp|i, -ɪz
AM ,brɑŋ'kɑskəpi, -z

bronchus
BR 'brɒŋkəs
AM 'brɑŋkəs

bronco
BR 'brɒŋkəʊ, -z
AM 'brɑŋkoʊ, -z

Bronski
BR 'brɒnski
AM 'brɑnski

Bronstein
BR 'brɒnsti:n
AM 'brɑn,stin, 'brɑn,staɪn

Brontë
BR 'brɒnti
AM 'brɑn(t)i

brontosaur
BR 'brɒntəsɔ:(r), -z
AM 'brɑn(t)ə,sɔ(ə)r, -z

brontosauri
BR ,brɒntə'sɔ:rʌɪ
AM ,brɑn(t)ə'sɔraɪ

brontosaurus
BR ,brɒntə'sɔ:rəs, -ɪz
AM ,brɑn(t)ə'sɔrəs, -əz

Bronwen
BR 'brɒnwən
AM 'brɑnwən

Bronx
BR brɒŋks
AM brɔŋks, brɑŋks

bronze
BR brɒnz, -ɪz, -ɪŋ, -d
AM brɑnz, -əz, -ɪŋ, -d

bronzy
BR 'brɒnzi
AM 'brɑnzi

brooch
BR brəʊtʃ, -ɪz
AM broʊtʃ, brutʃ, -əz

brood
BR bru:d, -z, -ɪŋ, -ɪd
AM brud, -z, -ɪŋ, -əd

brooder
BR 'bru:də(r), -z
AM 'brudər, -z

broodily
BR 'bru:dɪli
AM 'brudəli

broodiness
BR 'bru:dɪnɪs
AM 'brudinɪs

broodingly
BR 'bru:dɪŋli
AM 'brudɪŋli

broody
BR 'bru:d|i, -ɪə(r), -ɪɪst
AM 'brudi, -ər, -ɪst

brook
BR brʊk, -s, -ɪŋ, -t
AM brʊk, -s, -ɪŋ, -t

Brooke
BR brʊk
AM brʊk

Brookes
BR brʊks
AM brʊks

Brookfield
BR 'brʊkfi:ld
AM 'brʊk,fild

Brooking
BR 'brʊkɪŋ
AM 'brʊkɪŋ

Brooklands
BR 'brʊklən(d)z
AM 'brʊklən(d)z

brooklet
BR 'brʊklɪt, -s
AM 'brʊklət, -s

brooklime
BR 'brʊklʌɪm
AM 'brʊk,laɪm

Brooklyn
BR 'brʊklɪn
AM 'brʊklən

Brookner
BR 'brʊknə(r)
AM 'brʊknər

Brooks
BR brʊks
AM brʊks

Brookside
BR 'brʊksʌɪd, ,brʊk'sʌɪd
AM 'brʊk,saɪd

brookweed
BR 'brʊkwi:d
AM 'brʊk,wid

Brookwood
BR 'brʊkwʊd
AM 'brʊk,wʊd

broom
BR bru:m, -z
AM brum, -z

Broome
BR bru:m
AM brum

broomrape
BR 'bru:mreɪp
AM 'brum,reɪp

broomstick
BR 'bru:mstɪk, -s
AM 'brum,stɪk, -s

Brophy
BR 'brəʊfi
AM 'broʊfi

Bros
Brothers
BR brɒs, brɒz
AM 'brəðərz

brose
BR brəʊz
AM broʊz

Brosnahan
BR 'brɒznəhən
AM 'brɑznə,hæn, 'brɑznən

broth
BR brɒθ, -s
AM brɔθ, brɑθ, -s

brothel
BR 'brɒθl, -z
AM 'brɑθəl, 'brɔθəl, 'brɑðəl, 'brɔðəl, -z

brother
BR 'brʌðə(r), -z
AM 'brəðər, -z

brotherhood
BR 'brʌðəhʊd, -z
AM 'brəðər,(h)ʊd, -z

brotherliness
BR 'brʌðəlɪnɪs
AM 'brəðərlinɪs

brotherly
BR 'brʌðəli
AM 'brəðərli

Brotherton
BR 'brʌðət(ə)n
AM 'brəðərt(ə)n

Brough
BR brʌf
AM brəf

brougham
BR 'bru:əm, bru:m, -z
AM 'broʊ(ə)m, 'bru(ə)m, -z

brought
BR brɔ:t
AM brɔt, brɑt

Broughton
BR 'brɔ:tn, 'brʌft(ə)n, 'braʊtn
AM 'brɔtn, 'brɑtn

brouhaha
BR 'bru:hɑ:hɑ:(r)
AM 'bru,hɑ,hɑ

brow
BR braʊ, -z, -d
AM braʊ, -z, -d

browbeat
BR 'braʊbi:t, -s, -ɪŋ
AM 'braʊ,bi|t, -ts, -dɪŋ

browbeaten
BR 'braʊ,bi:tn

AM 'braʊˌbitn

browbeater
BR 'braʊˌbiːtə(r), -z
AM 'braʊˌbidər, -z

brown
BR braʊn, -z, -ɪŋ, -d, -ə(r), -ɨst
AM braʊn, -z, -ɪŋ, -d, -ər, -əst

Browne
BR braʊn
AM braʊn

brownfield
BR 'braʊnfiːld
AM 'braʊnˌfild

Brownhills
BR 'braʊnhɪlz
AM 'braʊnˌ(h)ɪlz

Brownian
BR 'braʊnɪən, -z
AM 'braʊnjən, -z

brownie
BR 'braʊn|i, -ɪz
AM 'braʊni, -z

Browning
BR 'braʊnɪŋ
AM 'braʊnɪŋ

brownish
BR 'braʊnɪʃ
AM 'braʊnɪʃ

Brownjohn
BR 'braʊndʒɒn
AM 'braʊnˌdʒɑn

brownness
BR 'braʊnnəs
AM 'braʊ(n)nəs

brownout
BR 'braʊnaʊt, -s
AM 'braʊnˌaʊt, -s

Brownshirt
BR 'braʊnʃəːt, -s
AM 'braʊnˌʃərt, -s

brownstone
BR 'braʊnstəʊn, -z
AM 'braʊnˌstoʊn, -z

browny
BR 'braʊni
AM 'braʊni

browse
BR braʊz, -ɪz, -ɪŋ, -d
AM braʊz, -əz, -ɪŋ, -d

browser
BR 'braʊzə(r), -z
AM 'braʊzər, -z

browze
BR braʊz, -ɨz, -ɪŋ, -d
AM braʊz, -əz, -ɪŋ, -d

browzer
BR 'braʊzə(r), -z
AM 'braʊzər, -z

Broxbourne
BR 'brɒksbɔːn
AM 'brɑksˌbɔrn

Brubeck
BR 'bruːbɛk
AM 'brubɛk

Bruce
BR bruːs
AM brus

brucellosis
BR ˌbruːsɪ'ləʊsɪs
AM ˌbrusə'loʊsəs

Bruch
BR brʊk
AM brʊk
GER brʊx

brucite
BR 'bruːsʌɪt
AM 'bruˌsaɪt

Bruckner
BR 'brʊknə(r)
AM 'bruknər

Bruegel
BR 'brɔɪɡl
AM 'brɔɪɡəl

Brueghel
BR 'brɔɪɡl
AM 'brɔɪɡəl

Bruges
BR bruːʒ
AM bruʒ

bruin
BR 'bruːɪn, -z
AM 'bruən, -z

bruise
BR bruːz, -ɨz, -ɪŋ, -d
AM bruz, -əz, -ɪŋ, -d

bruiser
BR 'bruːzə(r), -z
AM 'bruzər, -z

bruit
BR bruːt, -s, -ɪŋ, -ɨd
AM bru|t, -ts, -dɪŋ, -dəd

Brum
BR brʌm
AM brəm

brumby
BR 'brʌmb|i, -ɪz
AM 'brəmbi, -z

brume
BR bruːm
AM brum

Brummagem
BR 'brʌmədʒəm
AM 'brəmədʒəm

Brummell
BR 'brʌml
AM 'brəməl

Brummie
BR 'brʌm|i, -ɪz
AM 'brəmi, -z

Brummy
BR 'brʌm|i, -ɪz
AM 'brəmi, -z

brumous
BR 'bruːməs
AM 'brəməs

brunch
BR brʌn(t)ʃ, -ɨz, -ɪŋ, -t
AM brən(t)ʃ, -əz, -ɪŋ, -t

Brunei
BR 'bruːnʌɪ, brʊ'nʌɪ
AM ˌbru'naɪ

Bruneian
BR 'bruːnʌɪən, brʊ'nʌɪən, -z
AM ˌbru'naɪən, -z

Brunel
BR brʊ'nɛl
AM brə'nɛl

brunet
BR bruː'nɛt, brʊ'nɛt, -s
AM bru'nɛt, -s

brunette
BR bruː'nɛt, brʊ'nɛt, -s
AM bru'nɛt, -s

Brunhild
BR 'brʊnhɪld
AM 'brunˌ(h)ɪld

Brünhilde
BR ˌbrʊn'hɪldə(r), 'brʊnˌhɪldə(r)
AM ˌbrun'hɪldə

Bruno
BR 'bruːnəʊ
AM 'brunoʊ

Brunswick
BR 'brʌnzwɪk
AM 'brənzwɪk

brunt
BR brʌnt
AM brənt

Brunton
BR 'brʌnt(ə)n
AM 'brən(t)ən, 'brəntn

bruschetta
BR brʉ'skɛtə(r)
AM brʊ'skɛdə

brush
BR brʌʃ, -ɨz, -ɪŋ, -t
AM brəʃ, -əz, -ɪŋ, -t

brushfire
BR 'brʌʃfʌɪə(r), -z
AM 'brəʃˌfaɪ(ə)r, -z

brushless
BR 'brʌʃləs
AM 'brəʃləs

brushlike
BR 'brʌʃlʌɪk
AM 'brəʃˌlaɪk

brushwood
BR 'brʌʃwʊd
AM 'brəʃˌwʊd

brushwork
BR 'brʌʃwəːk
AM 'brəʃˌwərk

brushy
BR 'brʌʃi
AM 'brəʃi

brusque
BR brʊsk, bruːsk, brʌsk
AM brəsk

brusquely
BR 'brʊskli, 'bruːskli, 'brʌskli
AM 'brəskli

brusqueness
BR 'brʊsknəs, 'bruːsknəs, 'brʌsknəs
AM 'brəsknəs

brusquerie
BR 'brʊskəri, 'bruːskəri, 'brʌskəri
AM 'brəskəri

Brussels
BR 'brʌslz
AM 'brəsəlz

brut
BR bruːt
AM brut

brutal
BR 'bruːtl
AM 'brudl

brutalisation
BR ˌbruːtl̩ʌɪ'zeɪʃn
AM 'brudlə'zeɪʃən, 'brudlˌaɪ'zeɪʃən

brutalise
BR 'bruːtl̩ʌɪz, -ɨz, -ɪŋ, -d
AM 'brudlˌaɪz, -ɨz, -ɪŋ, -d

brutalism
BR 'bruːtl̩ɪz(ə)m
AM 'brudl̩ɪzəm

brutalist
BR 'bruːtl̩ɪst, -s
AM 'brudl̩əst, -s

brutality
BR bruː'talɨt|i, brʊ'talɨti, -ɪz
AM bru'tælədi, -z

brutalization
BR ˌbruːtl̩ʌɪ'zeɪʃn
AM 'brudlə'zeɪʃən, 'brudlˌaɪ'zeɪʃən

brutalize
BR 'bruːtl̩ʌɪz, -ɨz, -ɪŋ, -d
AM 'brudlˌaɪz, -ɨz, -ɪŋ, -d

brutally
BR 'bruːtl̩i
AM 'brudl̩i

brute
BR bruːt, -s
AM brut, -s

brutish
BR 'bruːtɪʃ
AM 'brudɪʃ

brutishly
BR 'bruːtɪʃli
AM 'brudɪʃli

brutishness
BR 'bruːtɪʃnɨs
AM 'brudɪʃnɨs

Brutus
BR 'bruːtəs
AM 'brudəs

bruxism
BR 'brʊksɪz(ə)m, 'brʌksɪz(ə)m
AM 'brəkˌsɪzəm

Bryan
BR ˈbrʌɪən
AM ˈbraɪən

Bryant
BR ˈbrʌɪənt
AM ˈbraɪənt

Bryce
BR brʌɪs
AM braɪs

Bryden
BR ˈbrʌɪdn
AM ˈbraɪd(ə)n

Brylcreem®
BR ˈbrɪlkriːm
AM ˈbrɪlˌkrim

Bryn
BR brɪn
AM brɪn

Brynley
BR ˈbrɪnli
AM ˈbrɪnli

Bryn Mawr
place in USA
BR ˌbrɪn ˈmɔː(r)
AM ˌbrɪn ˈmɔ(ə)r

Brynmawr
place in UK
BR ˌbrɪnˈmaʊə(r)
AM ˌbrɪnˈmaʊ(ə)r, ˈbrɪnˈmɔ(ə)r
WE ˌbrɪn ˈmaʊr

Brynmor
BR ˈbrɪnmɔː(r)
AM ˈbrɪnmɔ(ə)r

Brynner
BR ˈbrɪnə(r)
AM ˈbrɪnər

bryological
BR ˌbrʌɪəˈlɒdʒɪkl
AM ˌbraɪəˈlɑdʒəkəl

bryologist
BR brʌɪˈɒlədʒɪst, -s
AM braɪˈɑlədʒəst, -s

bryology
BR brʌɪˈɒlədʒi
AM braɪˈɑlədʒi

bryony
BR ˈbrʌɪəni
AM ˈbraɪəni

bryophyte
BR ˈbrʌɪəfʌɪt, -s
AM ˈbraɪəˌfaɪt, -s

bryophytic
BR ˌbrʌɪəˈfɪtɪk
AM ˌbraɪəˈfɪdɪk

bryozoan
BR ˌbrʌɪəˈzəʊən, -z
AM ˌbraɪəˈzoʊən, -z

bryozoology
BR ˌbrʌɪəʊzuːˈɒlədʒi, ˌbrʌɪəʊzəʊˈɒlədʒi
AM ˌbraɪəˌzuˈɑlədʒi, ˌbraɪəzəˈwɑlədʒi

Bryson
BR ˈbrʌɪsn
AM ˈbraɪs(ə)n

Brythonic
BR brɪˈθɒnɪk
AM braɪˈθɑnɪk

Brzezinski
BR brəˈʒɪnski
AM brəˈʒɪnski

BSc
BR ˌbiːɛsˈsiː, -z
AM ˌbiˌɛsˈsi, -z

bub
BR bʌb, -z
AM bəb, -z

bubal
BR ˈbjuːbl, -z
AM ˈbjubl, -z

bubble
BR ˈbʌb|l, -lz, -l̩ɪŋ\-lɪŋ, -ld
AM ˈbəb|l, -lz, -lɪŋ, -ld

bubblegum
BR ˈbʌblɡʌm
AM ˈbəblˌɡəm

bubbler
BR ˈbʌbl̩ə(r), ˈbʌblə(r), -z
AM ˈbəb(ə)lər, -z

bubbly
BR ˈbʌbl̩i, ˈbʌbli
AM ˈbəb(ə)li

bubbly-jock
BR ˈbʌblɪdʒɒk, -s
AM ˈbəb(ə)liˌdʒɑk, -s

Buber
BR ˈb(j)uːbə(r)
AM ˈbubər

bubo
BR ˈbjuːbəʊ, -z
AM ˈb(j)uˌboʊ, -z

bubonic
BR bjuːˈbɒnɪk
AM b(j)uˈbɑnɪk

bubonocele
BR bjuːˈbɒnəsiːl, -z
AM bjuˈbɑnəˌsil, -z

buccal
BR ˈbʌkl
AM ˈbəkəl

buccaneer
BR ˌbʌkəˈnɪə(r), -z, -ɪŋ
AM ˌbəkəˈnɪ(ə)r, -z, -ɪŋ

buccaneerish
BR ˌbʌkəˈnɪərɪʃ
AM ˌbəkəˈnɪrɪʃ

buccinator
BR ˈbʌksɪneɪtə(r), -z
AM ˈbəksəˌneɪdər, -z

Buccleugh
BR bəˈkluː
AM bəˈklu

Bucelas
BR bjuːˈsɛləs
AM b(j)uˈsɛləs

Bucephalus
BR bjuːˈsɛfələs, bjuːˈsɛfl̩əs
AM bjuˈsɛfələs

Buchan
BR ˈbʌk(ə)n
AM ˈbəkən

Buchanan
BR bjuːˈkanən, b(j)ʉˈkanən
AM bjuˈkænən

Bucharest
BR ˌb(j)uːkəˈrɛst
AM ˈbukəˌrɛst

Buchenwald
BR ˈbuːk(ə)nvald
AM ˈbukənˌwɑld

Buchmanism
BR ˈbʌkmənɪz(ə)m
AM ˈbəkməˌnɪzəm

Buchmanite
BR ˈbʌkmənʌɪt, -s
AM ˈbəkməˌnaɪt, -s

buchu
BR ˈbʌkuː
AM ˈbəku

buck
BR bʌk, -s, -ɪŋ, -t
AM bək, -s, -ɪŋ, -t

buckaroo
BR ˌbʌkəˈruː, -z
AM ˌbəkəˈru, -z

buckbean
BR ˈbʌkbiːn, -z
AM ˈbəkˌbin, -z

buckboard
BR ˈbʌkbɔːd, -z
AM ˈbəkˌbɔ(ə)rd, -z

Buckden
BR ˈbʌkd(ə)n
AM ˈbəkdən

bucker
BR ˈbʌkə(r), -z
AM ˈbəkər, -z

bucket
BR ˈbʌkɪt, -s
AM ˈbəkət, -s

bucketful
BR ˈbʌkɪtfʊl, -z
AM ˈbəkətˌfʊl, -z

buckeye
BR ˈbʌkʌɪ, -z
AM ˈbəkˌaɪ, -z

Buckfastleigh
BR ˌbʌkfɑːs(t)ˈliː
AM ˌbəkfəs(t)ˈli

Buckie
BR ˈbʌki
AM ˈbəki

Buckingham
BR ˈbʌkɪŋəm
AM ˈbəkɪŋˌ(h)æm

Buckinghamshire
BR ˈbʌkɪŋəmʃ(ɪ)ə(r)
AM ˈbəkɪŋəmʃɪ(ə)r

Buckland
BR ˈbʌklənd
AM ˈbəklənd

buckle
BR ˈbʌk|l, -lz, -l̩ɪŋ\-lɪŋ, -ld
AM ˈbək|əl, -z, -ɪŋ, -d

buckler
BR ˈbʌklə(r), -z
AM ˈbək(ə)lər, -z

Buckley
BR ˈbʌkli
AM ˈbəkli

buckling
BR ˈbʌklɪŋ, -z
AM ˈbəklɪŋ, -z

Buckmaster
BR ˈbʌkmɑːstə(r), ˈbʌkmastə(r)
AM ˈbəkˌmæstər

Buckminster
BR ˈbʌkmɪnstə(r)
AM ˈbəkˌmɪnstər

Bucknall
BR ˈbʌknl
AM ˈbəknəl

Bucknell
BR ˈbʌknl
AM ˌbəkˈnɛl

Buckner
BR ˈbʌknə(r)
AM ˈbəknər

bucko
BR ˈbʌkəʊ, -z
AM ˈbəkoʊ, -z

buckra
BR ˈbʌkrə(*r*), -z
AM ˈbəkrə, -z

buckram
BR ˈbʌkrəm
AM ˈbəkrəm

buck rarebit
BR ˌbʌk ˈrɛːbɪt, + ˈrabɪt
AM ˌbək ˈrɛrbɪt

Bucks.
Buckinghamshire
BR bʌks
AM bəks

bucksaw
BR ˈbʌksɔː(*r*), -z
AM ˈbəkˌsɔ, ˈbəkˌsɑ, -z

buckshee
BR ˌbʌkˈʃiː
AM ˈbəkˈʃi

buckshot
BR ˈbʌkʃɒt
AM ˈbəkˌʃɑt

buckskin
BR ˈbʌkskɪn, -z
AM ˈbəkˌskɪn, -z

buckteeth
BR ˌbʌkˈtiːθ
AM ˌbəkˈtiθ

buckthorn
BR ˈbʌkθɔːn, -z
AM ˈbəkˌθɔ(ə)rn, -z

Buckton
BR ˈbʌktən
AM ˈbəktən

bucktooth
BR ˌbʌkˈtuːθ, -t
AM ˈbəkˌtuθ, -t

buckwheat
BR ˈbʌkwiːt
AM ˈbəkˌ(h)wit
bucolic
BR bjuːˈkɒlɪk, bjʉˈkɒlɪk
AM bjuˈkɑlɪk
bucolically
BR bjuːˈkɒlɨkli, bjʉˈkɒlɨkli
AM bjuˈkɑlək(ə)li
bud
BR bʌd, -z, -ɪŋ, -ɨd
AM bəd, -z, -ɪŋ, -əd
Budapest
BR ˌb(j)uːdəˈpɛst
AM ˈbudəˌpɛst, ˈbudəˌpɛʃt
HU ˈbudapɛʃt
Buddha
BR ˈbʊdə(r), -z
AM ˈbudə, ˈbʊdə, -z
Buddhism
BR ˈbʊdɪz(ə)m
AM ˈbuˌdɪzəm, ˈbʊˌdɪzəm
Buddhist
BR ˈbʊdɪst, -s
AM ˈbudəst, ˈbʊdəst, -s
Buddhistic
BR bʊˈdɪstɪk
AM buˈdɪstɪk, bʊˈdɪstɪk
Buddhistical
BR bʊˈdɪstɨkl
AM buˈdɪstɨkəl, bʊˈdɪstɨkəl
buddleia
BR ˈbʌdlɪə(r), -z
AM ˈbədˌliə, -z
buddy
BR ˈbʌd|i, -ɪz
AM ˈbədi, -z
Bude
BR bjuːd
AM bjud
budge
BR bʌdʒ, -ɨz, -ɪŋ, -d
AM bədʒ, -ɨz, -ɪŋ, -d
budgerigar
BR ˈbʌdʒ(ə)rɪgɑː(r), -z
AM ˈbədʒəriˌgɑr, -z
budget
BR ˈbʌdʒ|ɪt, -ɪts, -ɨtɪŋ, -ɨtɨd
AM ˈbədʒə|t, -ts, -dɪŋ, -dəd
budgetary
BR ˈbʌdʒɪt(ə)ri
AM ˈbədʒəˌtɛri
budgie
BR ˈbʌdʒ|i, -ɪz
AM ˈbədʒi, -z
Budleigh
BR ˈbʌdli
AM ˈbədli
Budweiser®
BR ˈbʌdwʌɪzə(r), -z
AM ˈbədˌwaɪzər, -z
Buenos Aires
BR ˌbweɪnəs ˈʌɪ(ə)riːz, ˌbwɛnəs +, + ˈɛːriːz
AM ˌbweɪnəs ˈɛrəs, + ˈaɪrəz
Buerk
BR bəːk
AM bərk
buff
BR bʌf, -s, -ɪŋ, -t
AM bəf, -s, -ɪŋ, -t
buffalo
BR ˈbʌfələʊ, ˈbʌfl̩əʊ, -z
AM ˈbəf(ə)ˌloʊ, -z
buffer
BR ˈbʌfə(r), -z
AM ˈbəfər, -z
buffet¹
food
BR ˈbʊfeɪ, -z
AM ˌbəˈfeɪ, -z
buffet²
hit
BR ˈbʌf|ɪt, -ɪts, -ɨtɪŋ, -ɨtɨd
AM ˈbəfə|t, -ts, -dɪŋ, -dəd
bufflehead
BR ˈbʌflhɛd, -z
AM ˈbəflˌ(h)ɛd, -z
buffo
BR ˈbʊfəʊ, -z
AM ˈbufoʊ, -z
buffoon
BR bəˈfuːn, -z
AM bəˈfun, -z
buffoonery
BR bəˈfuːn(ə)r|i, -ɪz
AM bəˈfunəri, -z
buffoonish
BR bəˈfuːnɪʃ
AM bəˈfunɪʃ
Buffs
BR bʌfs
AM bəfs
bug
BR bʌg, -z, -ɪŋ, -d
AM bəg, -z, -ɪŋ, -d
bugaboo
BR ˈbʌgəbuː, -z
AM ˈbəgəˌbu, -z
Buganda
BR bʉˈgandə(r)
AM bəˈgændə
Bugandan
BR bʉˈgandən, -z
AM bəˈgændən, -z
Bugatti
BR b(j)ʉˈgat|i, -ɪz
AM b(j)ʊˈgɑdi, -z
bugbear
BR ˈbʌgbɛː(r), -z
AM ˈbəgˌbɛ(ə)r, -z
bugger
BR ˈbʌg|ə(r), -əz, -(ə)rɪŋ, -əd
AM ˈbəg|ər, -əz, -(ə)rɪŋ, -əd
buggery
BR ˈbʌg(ə)ri
AM ˈbəgəri
buggy
BR ˈbʌg|i, -ɪz
AM ˈbəgi, -z
bughouse
BR ˈbʌghaʊ|s, -zɪz
AM ˈbəgˌ(h)aʊ|s, -zəz
bugjuice
BR ˈbʌgdʒuːs
AM ˈbəgˌdʒus
bugle
BR ˈbjuːg|l, -lz, -l̩ɪŋ\-lɪŋ, -ld
AM ˈbjug|əl, -əlz, -(ə)lɪŋ, -əld
bugler
BR ˈbjuːglə(r), -z
AM ˈbjuglər, -z
buglet
BR ˈbjuːglɨt, -s
AM ˈbjuglət, -s
bugloss
BR ˈbjuːglɒs, -ɨz
AM ˈbjuˌglɑs, -əz
Bugner
BR ˈbʌgnə(r), ˈbʊgnə(r)
AM ˈbəgnər
bugrake
BR ˈbʌgreɪk, -s
AM ˈbəgˌreɪk, -s
buhl
BR buːl, -z
AM bul, -z
Buick®
BR ˈbjuːɪk, -s
AM ˈbjuɪk, -s
build
BR bɪld, -z, -ɪŋ
AM bɪld, -z, -ɪŋ
builder
BR ˈbɪldə(r), -z
AM ˈbɪldər, -z
building
BR ˈbɪldɪŋ, -z
AM ˈbɪldɪŋ, -z
built
BR bɪlt
AM bɪlt
Builth Wells
BR ˌbɪlθ ˈwɛlz
AM ˌbɪlθ ˈwɛlz
Buitoni®
BR bjʊˈtəʊni
AM bjuˈtoʊni
Bujumbura
BR ˌbʊdʒʉmˈbʊərə(r)
AM buˌdʒəmˈburə
Bukhara
BR bʊˈkɑːrə(r), bʊˈxɑːrə(r)
AM buˈkɑrə
RUS bukaˈra
Bukovina
BR ˌbʊkəˈviːnə(r)
AM ˌbukəˈvinə
Bukowski
BR bʊˈkɒfski, bʊˈkɒvski
AM buˈkaʊski
Bukta
BR ˈbʌktə(r)
AM ˈbəktə
Bulawayo
BR ˌbʊləˈweɪəʊ
AM ˌbʊləˈweɪˌoʊ
bulb
BR bʌlb, -z
AM bəlb, -z
bulbaceous
BR bʌlˈbeɪʃəs
AM ˌbəlˈbeɪʃəs
bulbar
BR ˈbʌlbə(r)
AM ˈbəlbər
bulbil
BR ˈbʌlbɪl, -z
AM ˈbəlbəl, -z
bulbous
BR ˈbʌlbəs
AM ˈbəlbəs
bulbousness
BR ˈbʌlbəsnəs
AM ˈbəlbəsnəs
bulbul
BR ˈbʊlbʊl, -z
AM ˈbʊlˌbʊl, -z
Bulgar
BR ˈbʌlgɑː(r), ˈbʊlgɑː(r), -z
AM ˈbəlgər, -z
Bulgaria
BR bʌlˈgɛːrɪə(r), bʊlˈgɛːrɪə(r)
AM ˌbəlˈgɛriə
Bulgarian
BR bʌlˈgɛːrɪən, bʊlˈgɛːrɪən, -z
AM ˌbəlˈgɛriən, -z
bulge
BR bʌldʒ, -ɨz, -ɪŋ, -d
AM bəldʒ, -əz, -ɪŋ, -d
bulghur
BR ˈbʌlgə(r)
AM ˈbəlgər
bulginess
BR ˈbʌldʒɪnɨs
AM ˈbəldʒinɨs
bulgur
BR ˈbʌlgə(r)
AM ˈbəlgər
bulgy
BR ˈbʌldʒi
AM ˈbəldʒi
bulimarexia
BR b(j)ʉˌlɪməˈrɛksɪə(r)
AM ˌbʊliməˈrɛksiə
bulimarexic
BR b(j)ʉˌlɪməˈrɛksɪk, -s

AM ˌbʊlimə'rɛksɪk, -s

bulimia
BR b(j)ʉ'lɪmɪə(r)
AM bʊ'limiə

bulimia nervosa
BR b(j)ʉˌlɪmɪə nəː'vəʊsə(r), + nəː'vəʊzə(r)
AM bʊ'limiə ˌnər'voʊsə, + ˌnər'voʊzə

bulimic
BR b(j)ʉ'lɪmɪk, -s
AM bʊ'limɪk, -s

bulk
BR bʌlk, -s, -ɪŋ, -t
AM bəlk, -s, -ɪŋ, -t

bulkhead
BR 'bʌlkhɛd, -z
AM 'bəlkˌ(h)ɛd, -z

bulkily
BR 'bʌlkɨli
AM 'bəlkəli

bulkiness
BR 'bʌlkɪnɨs
AM 'bəlkinɨs

bulkmail
BR 'bʌlkmeɪl
AM 'bəlkˌmeɪl

bulky
BR 'bʌlk|i, -ɪə(r), -ɪɨst
AM 'bəlki, -ər, -ɨst

bull
BR bʊl, -z, -ɪŋ, -d
AM bʊl, -z, -ɪŋ, -d

bulla
BR 'bʊlə(r), 'bʌlə(r)
AM 'bʊlə

bullace
BR 'bʊləs, -ɨz
AM 'bʊləs, -əz

bullae
BR 'bʊliː, 'bʌliː
AM 'bʊli, 'bʊˌlaɪ

bullate
BR 'bʊleɪt
AM 'bʊˌleɪt

bulldog
BR 'bʊldɒg, -z
AM 'bʊlˌdɔg, 'bʊlˌdɑg, -z

bulldoze
BR 'bʊldəʊz, -ɨz, -ɪŋ, -d
AM 'bʊlˌdoʊz, -əz, -ɪŋ, -d

bulldozer
BR 'bʊlˌdəʊzə(r), -z
AM 'bʊlˌdoʊzər, -z

Bullen
BR 'bʊlɪn
AM 'bʊlən

Buller
BR 'bʊlə(r)
AM 'bʊlər

bullet
BR 'bʊlɪt, -s
AM 'bʊlət, -s

bulletin
BR 'bʊlɨtɪn, -z
AM 'bʊlətn, 'bʊlədən, -z

bulletproof
BR 'bʊlɨtpruːf
AM 'bʊlətˌpruf

bullfight
BR 'bʊlfʌɪt, -s
AM 'bʊlˌfaɪt, -s

bullfighter
BR 'bʊlˌfʌɪtə(r), -z
AM 'bʊlˌfaɪdər, -z

bullfighting
BR 'bʊlˌfʌɪtɪŋ
AM 'bʊlˌfaɪdɪŋ

bullfinch
BR 'bʊlfɪn(t)ʃ, -ɨz
AM 'bʊlˌfɪn(t)ʃ, -ɨz

bullfrog
BR 'bʊlfrɒg, -z
AM 'bʊlˌfrɔg, 'bʊlˌfrɑg, -z

bullhead
BR 'bʊlhɛd, -z
AM 'bʊlˌ(h)ɛd, -z

bullhorn
BR 'bʊlhɔːn, -z
AM 'bʊlˌ(h)ɔ(ə)rn, -z

bullion
BR 'bʊlɪən
AM 'bʊljən, 'bʊliən

bullish
BR 'bʊlɪʃ
AM 'bʊlɪʃ

bullishly
BR 'bʊlɨʃli
AM 'bʊlɨʃli

bullishness
BR 'bʊlɨʃnɨs
AM 'bʊlɪʃnɨs

bullnecked
BR ˌbʊl'nɛkt
AM 'bʊlˌnɛkt

bullock
BR 'bʊlək, -s
AM 'bʊlək, -s

bullocky
BR 'bʊlək|i, -ɪz
AM 'bʊləki, -z

Bullokar
BR 'bʊləkɑː(r), 'bʊləkə(r)
AM 'bʊləkər

Bullough
BR 'bʊləʊ
AM 'bʊloʊ

bullring
BR 'bʊlrɪŋ, -z
AM 'bʊlˌrɪŋ, -z

bullshit
BR 'bʊlʃɪt, -s, -ɪŋ, -ɨd
AM 'bʊlˌʃɪ|t, -ts, -dɪŋ, -dɨd

bullshitter
BR 'bʊlˌʃɪtə(r), -z
AM 'bʊlˌʃɪdər, -z

bulltrout
BR 'bʊltraʊt, -s
AM 'bʊlˌtraʊt, -s

bullwhip
BR 'bʊlwɪp, -s, -ɪŋ, -t
AM 'bʊlˌ(h)wɪp, -s, -ɪŋ, -t

bully
BR 'bʊl|i, -ɪz, -ɪɪŋ, -ɪd
AM 'bʊli, -z, -ɪŋ, -d

bullyboy
BR 'bʊlɪbɔɪ, -z
AM 'bʊliˌbɔɪ, -z

bullyrag
BR 'bʊlɪrag, -z, -ɪŋ, -d
AM 'bʊliˌræg, -z, -ɪŋ, -d

Bulmer
BR 'bʊlmə(r)
AM 'bʊlmər

bulrush
BR 'bʊlrʌʃ, -ɨz
AM 'bʊlˌrəʃ, -əz

Bulstrode
BR 'bʊlstrəʊd
AM 'bʊlˌstroʊd

Bultitude
BR 'bʌltɨtjuːd, 'bʌltɨtʃuːd
AM 'bʊldəˌtud

bulwark
BR 'bʊlwək, 'bʌlwək, 'bʊlwəːk, 'bʌlwəːk, -s
AM 'bʊlˌwərk, -s

Bulwer-Lytton
BR ˌbʊlwə'lɪtn
AM ˌbʊlwər'lɪtn

bum
BR bʌm, -z, -ɪŋ, -d
AM bəm, -z, -ɪŋ, -d

bumbag
BR 'bʌmbag, -z
AM 'bəmˌbæg, -z

bumble
BR 'bʌmb|l, -lz, -l̩ɪŋ\-lɪŋ, -ld
AM 'bəmb|əl, -əlz, -(ə)lɪŋ, -əld

bumblebee
BR 'bʌmblbiː, -z
AM 'bəmbəlˌbi, -z

bumbledom
BR 'bʌmbldəm
AM 'bəmbəldəm

bumbler
BR 'bʌmblə(r), -z
AM 'bəmb(ə)lər, -z

bumboat
BR 'bʌmbəʊt, -s
AM 'bəmˌboʊt, -s

bumf
BR bʌmf
AM bəmf

bumiputra
BR ˌbuːmɪ'puːtrə(r), -z
AM ˌbumi'putrə, -z

bumkin
BR 'bʌmkɪn, -z
AM 'bəmkən, -z

bummalo
BR 'bʌmələʊ
AM 'bəməˌloʊ

bummaree
BR ˌbʌmə'riː, -z
AM ˌbəmə'ri, -z

bummer
BR 'bʌmə(r), -z
AM 'bəmər, -z

bump
BR bʌm|p, -ps, -pɪŋ, -(p)t
AM bəmp, -s, -ɪŋ, -t

bumper
BR 'bʌmpə(r), -z
AM 'bəmpər, -z

bumph
BR bʌmf
AM bəmf

bumpily
BR 'bʌmpɨli
AM 'bəmpəli

bumpiness
BR 'bʌmpɪnɨs
AM 'bəmpinɨs

bumpkin
BR 'bʌm(p)kɪn, -z
AM 'bəm(p)kən, -z

bumptious
BR 'bʌm(p)ʃəs
AM 'bəm(p)ʃəs

bumptiously
BR 'bʌm(p)ʃəsli
AM 'bəm(p)ʃəsli

bumptiousness
BR 'bʌm(p)ʃəsnəs
AM 'bəm(p)ʃəsnəs

bumpy
BR 'bʌmp|i, -ɪə(r), -ɪɨst
AM 'bəmpi, -ər, -ɨst

bun
BR bʌn, -z
AM bən, -z

Buna
BR 'b(j)uːnə(r)
AM 'b(j)unə

Bunbury
BR 'bʌnb(ə)ri
AM 'bənˌbɛri

bunch
BR bʌn(t)ʃ, -ɨz, -ɪŋ, -t
AM bən(t)ʃ, -əz, -ɪŋ, -t

bunchy
BR 'bʌn(t)ʃi
AM 'bən(t)ʃi

bunco
BR 'bʌŋkəʊ, -z, -ɪŋ, -d
AM 'bəŋk|oʊ, -oʊz, -əwɪŋ, -oʊd

buncombe
BR 'bʌŋkəm
AM 'bəŋkəm

bund
BR bʌnd, -z
AM bənd, -z

bunder
BR 'bʌndə(r), -z
AM 'bəndər, -z
Bundesbank
BR 'bʊndəzbaŋk
AM 'bʊndəs,bæŋk
Bundesrat
BR 'bʊndəzrɑːt
AM 'bʊndəs,rɑt
Bundestag
BR 'bʊndəztɑːg
AM 'bʊndəs,tɑg, 'bʊndə,stæg
bundle
BR 'bʌnd|l, -lz, -l̩ɪŋ\-lɪŋ, -ld
AM 'bən|dəl, -dəlz, -(d)(ə)lɪŋ, -dəld
bundler
BR 'bʌndlə(r), -z
AM 'bən(də)lər, -z
bundobust
BR 'bʌndəbʌst
AM 'bəndə,bəst
Bundy
BR 'bʌndi
AM 'bəndi
bung
BR bʌŋ, -z, -ɪŋ, -d
AM bəŋ, -z, -ɪŋ, -d
bungaloid
BR 'bʌŋgəlɔɪd
AM 'bəŋgə,lɔɪd
bungalow
BR 'bʌŋgələʊ, -z
AM 'bəŋgə,loʊ, -z
Bungay
BR 'bʌŋgi
AM 'bəŋgi
bungee
BR 'bʌndʒ|i, -ɪz
AM 'bəndʒi, -z
bunghole
BR 'bʌŋhəʊl, -z
AM 'bəŋ,(h)oʊl, -z
bungle
BR 'bʌŋg|l, -lz, -l̩ɪŋ\-lɪŋ, -ld
AM 'bəŋg|əl, -əlz, -(ə)lɪŋ, -əld
bungler
BR 'bʌŋglə(r), -z
AM 'bəŋg(ə)lər, -z
bunion
BR 'bʌnjən, -z
AM 'bənjən, -z
bunk
BR bʌŋ|k, -ks, -kɪŋ, -(k)t
AM bəŋ|k, -ks, -kɪŋ, -(k)t
bunker
BR 'bʌŋkə(r), -z, -ɪŋ, -d
AM 'bəŋkər, -z, -ɪŋ, -d
bunkhouse
BR 'bʌŋkhaʊ|s, -zɪz
AM 'bəŋk,(h)aʊ|s, -zəz

bunko
BR 'bʌŋkəʊ, -z, -ɪŋ, -d
AM 'bəŋkoʊ, -z, -ɪŋ, -d
bunkum
BR 'bʌŋkəm
AM 'bəŋkəm
bunny
BR 'bʌn|i, -ɪz
AM 'bəni, -z
Bunsen
BR 'bʌnsn
AM 'bənsən
bunt
BR bʌn|t, -(t)s, -tɪŋ, -tɪd
AM bən|t, -ts, -(t)ɪŋ, -(t)əd
buntal
BR 'bʌntl
AM bʊn'tɑl, 'bən(t)l
Bunter
BR 'bʌntə(r)
AM 'bən(t)ər
bunting
BR 'bʌntɪŋ, -z
AM 'bən(t)ɪŋ, -z
buntline
BR 'bʌntlʌɪn, -z
AM 'bənt,laɪn, -z
Bunty
BR 'bʌnti
AM 'bən(t)i
Buñuel
BR 'buːnjʊɛl, bʊn'wɛl
AM 'bʊnjəwəl, ,bʊn'wɛl
bunya
BR 'bʌnjə(*r*), -z
AM 'bənjə, -z
Bunyan
BR 'bʌnjən
AM 'bənjən
Bunyanesque
BR ,bʌnjə'nɛsk
AM ,bənjə'nɛsk
bunyip
BR 'bʌnjɪp, -s
AM 'bənjɪp, -s
Buonaparte
BR 'bəʊnəpɑːt
AM 'boʊnə,pɑrt
buoy
BR bɔɪ, -z, -ɪŋ, -d
AM buɪ, bɔɪ, -z, -ɪŋ, -d
buoyage
BR 'bɔɪɪdʒ
AM 'bɔɪɪdʒ, 'bujɪdʒ
buoyancy
BR 'bɔɪənsi
AM 'bɔɪənsi, 'bujənsi
buoyant
BR 'bɔɪənt
AM 'bɔɪənt, 'bujənt
buoyantly
BR 'bɔɪəntli
AM 'bɔɪən(t)li, 'bujən(t)li

BUPA
BR 'b(j)uːpə(*r*)
AM 'b(j)upə
buppie
BR 'bʌp|i, -ɪz
AM 'bəpi, -z
bur
BR bəː(r), -z
AM bər, -z
burb
BR bəːb, -z
AM bərb, -z
Burbage
BR 'bəːbɪdʒ
AM 'bərbɪdʒ
Burbank
BR 'bəːbaŋk
AM 'bər,bæŋk
Burberry®
BR 'bəːb(ə)r|i, -ɪz
AM 'bərbəri, 'bər,bɛri, -z
burble
BR 'bəːb|l, -lz, -l̩ɪŋ\-lɪŋ, -ld
AM 'bərb|əl, -əlz, -(ə)lɪŋ, -əld
burbler
BR 'bəːbl̩ə(r), 'bəːblə(r), -z
AM 'bərb(ə)lər, -z
burbot
BR 'bəːbət, -s
AM 'bərbət, -s
Burch
BR bəːtʃ
AM bərtʃ
Burchfield
BR 'bəːtʃfiːld
AM 'bərtʃ,fild
Burckhardt
BR 'bəːkhɑːt
AM 'bərk,(h)ɑrt
Burco
BR 'bəːkəʊ
AM 'bərkoʊ
burden
BR 'bəːd|n, -nz, -n̩ɪŋ\-nɪŋ, -nd
AM 'bərdən, -z, -ɪŋ, -d
burdensome
BR 'bəːdns(ə)m
AM 'bərdnsəm
burdensomeness
BR 'bəːdns(ə)mnəs
AM 'bərdnsəmnəs
Burdett
BR 'bəːdɛt, ,bəː'dɛt, bə'dɛt
AM bər'dɛt
burdock
BR 'bəːdɒk
AM 'bər,dɑk
Burdon
BR 'bəːdn
AM 'bərd(ə)n

bureau
BR 'bjʊərəʊ, 'bjɔːrəʊ, -z
AM 'bjuroʊ, -z
bureaucracy
BR bjʊ'rɒkrəs|i, bjɔː'rɒkrəsi, -ɪz
AM bjʊ'rɑkrəsi, -z
bureaucrat
BR 'bjʊərəkrat, 'bjɔːrəkrat, -s
AM 'bjurə,kræt, -s
bureaucratic
BR ,bjʊərə'kratɪk, ,bjɔːrə'kratɪk
AM ,bjurə'krædɪk
bureaucratically
BR ,bjʊərə'kratɪkli, ,bjɔːrə'kratɪkli
AM ,bjurə'krædək(ə)li
bureaucratisation
BR bjʊ,rɒkrətʌɪ'zeɪʃn, bjɔː,rɒkrətʌɪ'zeɪʃn
AM bju,rɑkrədə'zeɪʃən, bju,rɑkrə,taɪ'zeɪʃən
bureaucratise
BR bjʊ'rɒkrətʌɪz, bjɔː'rɒkrətʌɪz, -ɪz, -ɪŋ, -d
AM bju'rɑkrə,taɪz, -ɪz, -ɪŋ, -d
bureaucratization
BR bjʊ,rɒkrətʌɪ'zeɪʃn, bjɔː,rɒkrətʌɪ'zeɪʃn
AM bju,rɑkrədə'zeɪʃən, bju,rɑkrə,taɪ'zeɪʃən
bureaucratize
BR bjʊ'rɒkrətʌɪz, bjɔː'rɒkrətʌɪz, -ɪz, -ɪŋ, -d
AM bju'rɑkrə,taɪz, -ɪz, -ɪŋ, -d
bureaux
BR 'bjʊərəʊ(z), 'bjɔːrəʊ(z)
AM 'bjʊroʊ
buret
BR bjʊ'rɛt, -s
AM bjʊ'rɛt, -s
burette
BR bjʊ'rɛt, -s
AM bjʊ'rɛt, -s
Burford
BR 'bəːfəd
AM 'bərfərd
burg
BR bəːg, -z
AM bərg, -z
burgage
BR 'bəːg|ɪdʒ, -ɪdʒɪz
AM 'bərgɪdʒ, -ɪz
Burgas
BR 'bəːgəs
AM 'bərgəs
Burge
BR bəːdʒ
AM bərdʒ
burgee
BR 'bəːdʒiː, bəː'dʒiː, -z

AM ˌbər'dʒi, -z

burgeon
BR 'bəːdʒ|(ə)n, -(ə)nz, -n̩ɪŋ\-ənɪŋ, -(ə)nd
AM 'bərdʒən, -z, -ɪŋ, -d

burger
BR 'bəːgə(r), -z
AM 'bərgər, -z

burgess
BR 'bəːdʒɪs, -ɨz
AM 'bərdʒəs, -əz

burgh
BR 'bʌrə(r), -z
AM bərg, 'bəroʊ, -z

burghal
BR 'bəːgl
AM 'bərgəl

burgher
BR 'bəːgə(r), -z
AM 'bərgər, -z

Burghley
BR 'bəːli
AM 'bərli

burglar
BR 'bəːglə(r), -z
AM 'bərglər, -z

burglarious
BR (ˌ)bəː'glɛːrɪəs
AM ˌbər'glɛriəs

burglariously
BR (ˌ)bəː'glɛːrɪəsli
AM ˌbər'glɛriəsli

burglarise
BR 'bəːglərʌɪz, -ɨz, -ɪŋ, -d
AM 'bərgləˌraɪz, -ɨz, -ɪŋ, -d

burglarize
BR 'bəːglərʌɪz, -ɨz, -ɪŋ, -d
AM 'bərgləˌraɪz, -ɨz, -ɪŋ, -d

burglary
BR 'bəːglər|i, -ɪz
AM 'bərgləri, -z

burgle
BR 'bəːg|l, -lz, -l̩ɪŋ\-lɪŋ, -ld
AM 'bərg|əl, -əlz, -(ə)lɪŋ, -əld

burgomaster
BR 'bəːgəˌmɑːstə(r), 'bəːgəˌmaste(r), -z
AM 'bərgəˌmæstər, -z

burgoo
BR 'bəːguː, ˌbəː'guː
AM ˌbər'gu

Burgoyne
BR 'bəːgɔɪn, bəː'gɔɪn
AM ˌbər'gɔɪn

burgrave
BR 'bəːgreɪv, -z
AM 'bərˌgreɪv, -z

Burgundian
BR bə(ː)'gʌndɪən
AM bər'gəndiən

burgundy
BR 'bəːg(ə)nd|i, -ɪz
AM 'bərgəndi, -z

burhel
BR 'bʌrəl, 'bʌrl̩, -z
AM 'bərəl, -z

burial
BR 'bɛrɪəl, -z
AM 'bɛriəl, -z

burin
BR 'bjʊərɪn, 'bjɔːrɪn, -z
AM 'bjurən, -z

burk
BR bəːk, -s
AM bərk, -s

burka
BR 'bəːkə(r), -z
AM 'bərkə, -z

burke
BR bəːk, -s, -ɪŋ, -t
AM bərk, -s, -ɪŋ, -t

Burkina
BR bəː'kiːnə(r)
AM bər'kinə

Burkina Faso
BR bəːˌkiːnə 'fasəʊ
AM bərˌkinə 'fɑsoʊ

Burkinan
BR bəː'kiːnən, -z
AM bər'kinən, -z

Burkitt's lymphoma
BR ˌbəːkɪts lɪm'fəʊmə(r)
AM ˌbərkəts lɪm'foʊmə

burl
BR bəːl, -z, -ɪŋ, -d
AM bərl, -z, -ɪŋ, -d

burlap
BR 'bəːlap
AM 'bərˌlæp

Burleigh
BR 'bəːli
AM 'bərli

burlesque
BR bəː'lɛsk, -s, -ɪŋ, -t
AM ˌbər'lɛsk, -s, -ɪŋ, -t

burlesquer
BR bəː'lɛskə(r), -z
AM ˌbər'lɛskər, -z

Burley
BR 'bəːli
AM 'bərli

burliness
BR 'bəːlɪnɨs
AM 'bərlinɨs

Burlington
BR 'bəːlɪŋt(ə)n
AM 'bərlɪŋt(ə)n

burly
BR 'bəːl|i, -ɪə(r), -ɪɨst
AM 'bərli, -ər, -ɨst

Burma
BR 'bəːmə(r)
AM 'bərmə

Burman
BR 'bəːmən, -z
AM 'bərmən, -z

Burmese
BR ˌbəː'miːz
AM ˌbər'miz

burn
BR bəːn, -z, -ɪŋ, -d
AM bərn, -z, -ɪŋ, -d

Burnaby
BR 'bəːnəbi
AM 'bərnəbi

Burnaston
BR 'bəːnəst(ə)n
AM 'bərnəst(ə)n

Burne
BR bəːn
AM bərn

burner
BR 'bəːnə(r), -z
AM 'bərnər, -z

burnet
BR 'bəːnɪt, -s
AM bər'nɛt, 'bərnət, -s

Burnett
BR bə(ː)'nɛt, 'bəːnɪt
AM bər'nɛt

Burney
BR 'bəːni
AM 'bərni

Burnham
BR 'bəːnəm
AM 'bərnəm

burningly
BR 'bəːnɪŋli
AM 'bərnɪŋli

burnish
BR 'bəːn|ɪʃ, -ɪʃɪz, -ɪʃɪŋ, -ɪʃt
AM 'bərnɪʃ, -ɨz, -ɪŋ, -t

burnisher
BR 'bəːnɪʃə(r), -z
AM 'bərnɪʃər, -z

Burnley
BR 'bəːnli
AM 'bərnli

burnoose
BR bəː'nuːs, -ɨz
AM bər'nus, -əz

burnous
BR bəː'nuːs, -ɨz
AM bər'nus, -əz

burnouse
BR bəː'nuːs, -ɨz
AM bər'nus, -əz

Burns
BR bəːnz
AM bərnz

Burnside
BR 'bəːnsʌɪd
AM 'bərnˌsaɪd

burnt
BR bəːnt
AM bərnt

Burntisland
BR (ˌ)bəːnt'ʌɪlənd
AM ˌbərn(t)'aɪlənd

burp
BR bəːp, -s, -ɪŋ, -t
AM bərp, -s, -ɪŋ, -t

burr
BR bəː(r), -z, -ɪŋ, -d
AM bər, -z, -ɪŋ, -d

Burra
BR 'bʌrə(r)
AM 'bərə

burrawang
BR 'bʌrəwaŋ, -z
AM 'bərəˌwæŋ, -z

Burrell
BR 'bʌrəl, 'bʌrl̩
AM 'bərəl

Burren
BR 'bʌrən, 'bʌrn̩
AM 'bərən

burrito
BR bʊ'riːtəʊ, bʌ'riːtəʊ, -z
AM bə'ridoʊ, -z

burro
BR 'bʌrəʊ, 'bʊrəʊ, -z
AM 'bəroʊ, 'bʊroʊ, 'bərə, -z

Burrough
BR 'bʌrəʊ
AM 'bəroʊ

Burroughs
BR 'bʌrəʊz
AM 'bəroʊz

burrow
BR 'bʌrəʊ, -z, -ɪŋ, -d
AM 'bər|oʊ, -oʊz, -əwɪŋ, -oʊd

burrower
BR 'bʌrəʊə(r), -z
AM 'bərəwər, -z

Burrows
BR 'bʌrəʊz
AM 'bəroʊz

bursa
BR 'bəːsə(r), -z
AM 'bərsə, -z

bursae
BR 'bəːsiː
AM 'bərsi, 'bərˌsaɪ

bursal
BR 'bəːsl
AM 'bərsəl

bursar
BR 'bəːsə(r), -z
AM 'bərsər, 'bərˌsɑr, -z

bursarial
BR bəː'sɛːrɪəl
AM bər'sɛriəl

bursarship
BR 'bəːsəʃɪp, -s
AM 'bərsərˌʃɪp, -s

bursary
BR 'bəːs(ə)r|i, -ɪz
AM 'bərsəri, -z

burse
BR bəːs, -ɨz
AM bərs, -ɨz

bursitis
BR bəː'sʌɪtɨs
AM bər'saɪdɨs

Burslem
BR 'bəːzləm
AM 'bərzləm

burst
BR bəːst, -s, -ɪŋ
AM bərst, -s, -ɪŋ

Burstall
BR 'bəːst(ɔː)l
AM 'bər,stɔl, 'bər,stɑl

burstproof
BR 'bəːs(t)pruːf
AM 'bərs(t),prʊf

Burt
BR bəːt
AM bərt

burthen
BR 'bəːðn, -z
AM 'bərðən, -z

burton
BR 'bəːtn, -z
AM 'bərtn, -z

Burtonwood
BR ,bəːtn'wʊd
AM 'bərtn,wʊd

Burundan
BR bʉ'rʊndən, -z
AM bə'rʊndən, -z

Burundi
BR bʉ'rʊndi
AM bə'rʊndi

Burundian
BR bʉ'rʊndɪən, -z
AM bə'rʊndiən, -z

bury
BR 'bɛr|i, -ɪz, -ɪɪŋ, -ɪd
AM 'bɛri, -z, -ɪŋ, -d

Bury St Edmunds
BR ,bɛrɪ snt 'ɛdmən(d)z
AM ,bɛri ,seɪnt 'ɛdmən(d)z

bus
BR bʌs, -ɨz, -ɪŋ, -t
AM bəs, -ɨz, -ɪŋ, -t

busbar
BR 'bʌsbɑː(r), -z
AM 'bəs,bɑr, -z

busboy
BR 'bʌsbɔɪ, -z
AM 'bəs,bɔɪ, -z

busby
BR 'bʌzb|i, -ɪz
AM 'bəzbi, -z

bush
BR bʊʃ, -ɨz, -ɪŋ, -t
AM bʊʃ, -ɨz, -ɪŋ, -t

bushbaby
BR 'bʊʃ,beɪb|i, -ɪz
AM 'bʊʃ,beɪbi, -z

bushbuck
BR 'bʊʃbʌk, -s
AM 'bʊʃ,bək, -s

bushcraft
BR 'bʊʃkrɑːft, 'bʊʃkraft
AM 'bʊʃ,kræft

bushel
BR 'bʊʃl, -z
AM 'bʊʃəl, -z

bushelful
BR 'bʊʃlfʊl, -z
AM 'bʊʃəl,fʊl, -z

Bushey
BR 'bʊʃi
AM 'bʊʃi

bushfire
BR 'bʊʃ,fʌɪə(r), -z
AM 'bʊʃ,faɪ(ə)r, -z

bushido
BR bʊ'ʃiːdəʊ, ,bʊʃɪ'dəʊ
AM 'buʃi,doʊ

bushily
BR 'bʊʃɨli
AM 'bʊʃəli

bushiness
BR 'bʊʃɪnɨs
AM 'bʊʃinɨs

Bushman
BR 'bʊʃmən
AM 'bʊʃmən

bushmaster
BR 'bʊʃ,mɑːstə(r), 'bʊʃ,mastə(r), -z
AM 'bʊʃ,mæstər, -z

Bushmen
BR 'bʊʃmən
AM 'bʊʃmən

Bushnell
BR 'bʊʃnl
AM 'bʊʃ,nɛl

bushranger
BR 'bʊʃ,reɪn(d)ʒə(r), -z
AM 'bʊʃ,reɪndʒər, -z

bushveld
BR 'bʊʃvɛlt
AM 'bʊʃ,vɛlt

bushwhack
BR 'bʊʃwak, -s, -ɪŋ, -t
AM 'bʊʃ,(h)wæk, -s, -ɪŋ, -t

bushwhacker
BR 'bʊʃ,wakə(r), -z
AM 'bʊʃ,(h)wækər, -z

bushy
BR 'bʊʃ|i, -ɪə(r), -ɪɨst
AM 'bʊʃi, -ər, -ɨst

busily
BR 'bɪzɨli
AM 'bɪzɨli

business
BR 'bɪznɨs, -ɨz
AM 'bɪznɨs, 'bɪznɨz, -əz

businesslike
BR 'bɪznɨslʌɪk
AM 'bɪznɨs,laɪk, 'bɪznɨz,laɪk

businessman
BR 'bɪznɨsmən, 'bɪznɨs,man
AM 'bɪznɨs,mæn, 'bɪznɨz,mæn

businessmen
BR 'bɪznɨsmən, 'bɪznɨs,mɛn
AM 'bɪznɨs,mɛn, 'bɪznɨz,mɛn

businesswoman
BR 'bɪznɨs,wʊmən
AM 'bɪznɨs,wʊmən, 'bɪznɨz,wʊmən

businesswomen
BR 'bɪznɨs,wɪmɪn
AM 'bɪznɨs,wɪmɨn, 'bɪznɨz,wɪmɨn

busk
BR bʌsk, -s, -ɪŋ, -t
AM bəsk, -s, -ɪŋ, -t

busker
BR 'bʌskə(r), -z
AM 'bəskər, -z

buskin
BR 'bʌskɪn, -z, -d
AM 'bəskən, -z, -d

busman
BR 'bʌsmən
AM 'bəsmən

busmen
BR 'bʌsmən
AM 'bəsmən

buss
BR bʌs, -ɨz, -ɪŋ, -t
AM bəs, -əz, -ɪŋ, -t

bust
BR bʌst, -s, -ɪŋ, -ɨd
AM bəst, -s, -ɪŋ, -ɨd

bustard
BR 'bʌstəd, -z
AM 'bəstərd, -z

bustee
BR 'bʌstiː, -z
AM bəs'ti, -z

buster
BR 'bʌstə(r), -z
AM 'bəstər, -z

bustier
BR 'bʌstɪeɪ, 'bʊstɪeɪ, -z
AM 'bəstiər, -z

bustiness
BR 'bʌstɪnɨs
AM 'bəstinɨs

bustle
BR 'bʌs|l, -lz, -l̩ɪŋ\-lɪŋ, -ld
AM 'bəs|əl, -əlz, -(ə)lɪŋ, -əld

busty
BR 'bʌst|i, -ɪə(r), -ɪɨst
AM 'bəsti, -ər, -ɨst

busy
BR 'bɪz|i, -ɪə(r), -ɪɨst
AM 'bɪzi, -ər, -ɨst

busybody
BR 'bɪzɪ,bɒd|i, -ɪz
AM 'bɪzi,bɑdi, -z

busyness
BR 'bɪzɪnɨs
AM 'bɪzinɨs

busywork
BR 'bɪzɪwəːk
AM 'bɪzi,wərk

but[1]
strong form
BR bʌt, -s, -ɪŋ, -ɨd
AM bə|t, -ts, -dɪŋ, -dəd

but[2]
weak form
BR bət, -s
AM bət, -s

butadiene
BR ,bjuːtə'dʌɪiːn
AM ,bjudə'daɪ,in

but and ben
BR ,bʌt (ə)n(d) 'bɛn
AM ,bəd ən 'bɛn

butane
BR 'bjuːteɪn
AM 'bju,teɪn

butanoic
BR ,bjuːtə'nəʊɪk
AM ,bjudə'noʊɪk

butanol
BR 'bjuːtənɒl
AM 'bjudə,nɔl, 'bjudə,nɑl

butanone
BR 'bjuːtənəʊn
AM 'bjudə,noʊn

butch
BR bʊtʃ
AM bʊtʃ

butcher
BR 'bʊtʃə(r), -z, -ɪŋ, -d
AM 'bʊtʃər, -z, -ɪŋ, -d

butcherly
BR 'bʊtʃəli
AM 'bʊtʃərli

butchery
BR 'bʊtʃ(ə)r|i, -ɪz
AM 'bʊtʃəri, -z

Bute
BR bjuːt
AM bjut

butene
BR 'bjuːtiːn
AM 'bjudin

Buthelezi
BR ,buːtə'leɪzi
AM ,budə'leɪzi

butle
BR 'bʌt|l, -lz, -l̩ɪŋ\-lɪŋ, -ld
AM 'bədəl, -z, -ɪŋ, -d

butler
BR 'bʌtlə(r), -z
AM 'bətlər, -z

Butlin's
BR 'bʌtlɪnz
AM 'bətlənz

butt
BR bʌt, -s, -ɪŋ, -ɨd
AM bə|t, -ts, -dɪŋ, -dəd

butte
BR bju:t, -s
AM bjut, -s
butter
BR 'bʌt|ə(r), -əz, -(ə)rɪŋ, -əd
AM 'bədər, -əz, -(ə)rɪŋ, -əd
butterball
BR 'bʌtəbɔ:l, -z
AM 'bədər,bɔl, 'bədər,bɑl, -z
butterbur
BR 'bʌtəbə:(r), -z
AM 'bədər,bər, -z
buttercream
BR 'bʌtəkri:m
AM 'bədər,krim
buttercup
BR 'bʌtəkʌp, -s
AM 'bədər,kəp, -s
butterdish
BR 'bʌtədɪʃ, -ɪz
AM 'bədər,dɪʃ, -ɪz
butterfat
BR 'bʌtəfat
AM 'bədər,fæt
Butterfield
BR 'bʌtəfi:ld
AM 'bədər,fild
butterfingers
BR 'bʌtə,fɪŋgəz
AM 'bədər,fɪŋgərz
butterfish
BR 'bʌtəfɪʃ
AM 'bədər,fɪʃ
butterfly
BR 'bʌtəflʌɪ, -z
AM 'bədər,flaɪ, -z
butteriness
BR 'bʌt(ə)rɪnɪs
AM 'bədərinɪs
Butterkist®
BR 'bʌtəkɪst
AM 'bədər,kɪst
butterknife
BR 'bʌtənʌɪf
AM 'bədər,naɪf
butterknives
BR 'bʌtənʌɪvz
AM 'bədər,naɪvz
Buttermere
BR 'bʌtəmɪə(r)
AM 'bədər,mɪ(ə)r
buttermilk
BR 'bʌtəmɪlk
AM 'bədər,mɪlk
butternut
BR 'bʌtənʌt, -s
AM 'bədər,nət, -s
Butters
BR 'bʌtəz
AM 'bədərz
butterscotch
BR 'bʌtəskɒtʃ, -ɪz
AM 'bədər,skɑtʃ, -ɪz
butterwort
BR 'bʌtəwə:t, -s
AM 'bədər,wərt, 'bədər,wɔ(ə)rt, -s
Butterworth
BR 'bʌtəwə:θ
AM 'bədər,wərθ
buttery
BR 'bʌt(ə)r|i, -ɪz
AM 'bədəri, 'bətri, -z
buttle
BR bʌt|l, -lz, -l̩ɪŋ\-lɪŋ, -ld
AM bədəl, -z, -ɪŋ, -d
buttock
BR 'bʌtək, -s
AM 'bədək, -s
button
BR 'bʌtn̩, -z, -ɪŋ, -d
AM 'bət|n, -nz, -(ə)nɪŋ, -nd
buttonhole
BR 'bʌtnhəʊl, -z, -ɪŋ, -d
AM 'bətn,(h)oʊl, -z, -ɪŋ, -d
buttonhook
BR 'bʌtnhʊk, -s
AM 'bətn,(h)ʊk, -s
buttonless
BR 'bʌtnləs
AM 'bətnləs
Buttons
BR 'bʌtnz
AM 'bətnz
buttonwood
BR 'bʌtnwʊd, -z
AM 'bətn,wʊd, -z
buttony
BR 'bʌtn̩i
AM 'bətn̩i
buttress
BR 'bʌtrɪs, -ɪz, -ɪŋ, -t
AM 'bətrəs, -əz, -ɪŋ, -t
butty
BR 'bʌt|i, -ɪz
AM 'bədi, -z
butyl
BR 'bju:tʌɪl, 'bju:tɪl
AM 'bjudl, 'bju,tɪl
butyrate
BR 'bju:tɪreɪt
AM 'bjudə,reɪt
butyric
BR bju:'tɪrɪk
AM bju'tɪrɪk
buxom
BR 'bʌks(ə)m
AM 'bəksəm
buxomly
BR 'bʌks(ə)mli
AM 'bəksəmli
buxomness
BR 'bʌks(ə)mnəs
AM 'bəksəmnəs
Buxted
BR 'bʌkstɪd, 'bʌkstɛd
AM 'bək,stɛd
Buxtehude
BR ,bʊkstə'hu:də(*r*), 'bʊkstə,hu:də(*r*)
AM 'bəkstə,hudə
DAN ,bugsdə'hu:ðə
Buxton
BR 'bʌkstən
AM 'bəkstən
buy
BR bʌɪ, -z, -ɪŋ
AM baɪ, -z, -ɪŋ
buyable
BR 'bʌɪəbl
AM 'baɪəbəl
buyer
BR 'bʌɪə(r), -z
AM 'baɪər, -z
buyout
BR 'bʌɪaʊt, -s
AM 'baɪ,aʊt, -s
Buzby
BR 'bʌzbi
AM 'bəzbi
Buzfuz
BR 'bʌzfʌz
AM 'bəz,fəz
buzz
BR bʌz, -ɪz, -ɪŋ, -d
AM bəz, -əz, -ɪŋ, -d
buzzard
BR 'bʌzəd, -z
AM 'bəzərd, -z
buzzer
BR 'bʌzə(r), -z
AM 'bəzər, -z
buzzword
BR 'bʌzwə:d, -z
AM 'bəz,wərd, -z
bwana
BR 'bwɑ:nə(*r*), -z
AM 'bwɑnə, -z
Bwlch
BR bʊlx, bʊlk
AM bʊlk
by
BR bʌɪ
AM baɪ
Byatt
BR 'bʌɪət
AM 'baɪət
Byblos
BR 'bɪblɒs
AM 'bɪblɑs
bye
BR bʌɪ, -z
AM baɪ, -z
bye-bye
goodbye
BR ,bʌɪ'bʌɪ, -z
AM ¦baɪ¦baɪ, -z
bye-byes
sleep
BR 'bʌɪbʌɪz
AM ¦baɪ¦baɪz
byelaw
BR 'bʌɪlɔ:(*r*), -z
AM 'baɪ,lɔ, 'baɪ,lɑ, -z
Byelorussia
BR ,bjɛləʊ'rʌʃə(*r*), bɪ,ɛləʊ'rʌʃə(*r*), ,bjɛləʊ'ru:sɪə(*r*), bɪ,ɛləʊ'ru:sɪə(*r*)
AM ,bjɛlə'rəʃə
Byelorussian
BR ,bjɛləʊ'rʌʃn, bɪ,ɛləʊ'rʌʃn, ,bjɛləʊ'ru:sɪən, bɪ,ɛləʊ'ru:sɪən, -z
AM ,bjɛlə'rəʃən, -z
Byers
BR 'bʌɪəz
AM 'baɪərz
Byfield
BR 'bʌɪfi:ld
AM 'baɪ,fild
Byfleet
BR 'bʌɪfli:t
AM 'baɪ,flit
bygone
BR 'bʌɪgɒn, -z
AM 'baɪ,gɔn, 'baɪ,gɑn, -z
Bygraves
BR 'bʌɪgreɪvz
AM 'baɪ,greɪvz
Byker
BR 'bʌɪkə(r)
AM 'baɪkər
bylaw
BR 'bʌɪlɔ:(*r*), -z
AM 'baɪ,lɔ, 'baɪ,lɑ, -z
byline
BR 'bʌɪlʌɪn, -z
AM 'baɪ,laɪn, -z
byname
BR 'bʌɪneɪm, -z
AM 'baɪ,neɪm, -z
Byng
BR bɪŋ
AM bɪŋ
bypass
BR 'bʌɪpɑ:s, 'bʌɪpas, -ɪz, -ɪŋ, -t
AM 'baɪ,pæs, -əz, -ɪŋ, -t
bypath
BR 'bʌɪpɑ:|θ, 'bʌɪpa|θ, -θs\-ðz
AM 'baɪ,pæ|θ, -θs\-ðz
byplay
BR 'bʌɪpleɪ
AM 'baɪ,pleɪ
Byrd
BR bə:d
AM bərd
Byrds
BR bə:dz
AM bərdz
byre
BR 'bʌɪə(r), -z
AM 'baɪ(ə)r, -z
Byrne
BR bə:n
AM bərn
byroad
BR 'bʌɪrəʊd, -z

AM ˈbaɪˌroʊd, -z

Byron
BR ˈbʌɪrən
AM ˈbaɪrən

Byronic
BR bʌɪˈrɒnɪk
AM baɪˈrɑnɪk

Byronically
BR bʌɪˈrɒnɨkli
AM baɪˈrɑnək(ə)li

Bysshe
BR bɪʃ
AM bɪʃ

byssi
BR ˈbɪsʌɪ
AM ˈbɪˌsaɪ, ˈbɪˌsi

byssinosis
BR ˌbɪsɪˈnəʊsɪs
AM ˌbɪsɪˈnoʊsəs

byssus
BR ˈbɪsəs, -ɪz
AM ˈbɪsəs, -əz

bystander
BR ˈbʌɪˌstandə(r), -z
AM ˈbaɪˌstændər, -z

byte
BR bʌɪt, -s
AM baɪt, -s

byway
BR ˈbʌɪweɪ, -z
AM ˈbaɪˌweɪ, -z

byword
BR ˈbʌɪwəːd, -z
AM ˈbaɪˌwərd, -z

Byzantine
BR bɪˈzantʌɪn, bʌɪˈzantʌɪn, ˈbɪzntʌɪn, ˈbɪzntiːn
AM ˈbɪzənˌtin

Byzantinism
BR bɪˈzantɨnɪz(ə)m, bʌɪˈzantɨnɪz(ə)m
AM bəˈzæn(t)əˌnɪzəm

Byzantinist
BR bɪˈzantɨnɪst, bʌɪˈzantɨnɪst, -s
AM bəˈzæn(t)ənəst, -s

Byzantium
BR bɪˈzantɪəm, bʌɪˈzantɪəm
AM bəˈzæn(t)iəm, baɪˈzæn(t)iəm

Cc

c
BR siː, -z
AM si, -z

Caaba
BR 'kɑːbə(r), 'kabə(r)
AM 'kɑbə, 'kæbə

cab
BR kab, -z
AM kæb, -z

cabal
BR kə'bal, -z
AM kə'bɑl, kə'bæl, -z

cabala
BR kə'bɑːlə(r), 'kabələ(r), -z
AM kə'bɑlə, 'kæbələ, -z

cabalism
BR kə'bɑːlɪz(ə)m, 'kabəlɪz(ə)m
AM 'kæbəˌlɪzəm

cabalist
BR kə'bɑːlɪst, 'kabəlɪst, -s
AM 'kæbələst, -s

cabalistic
BR ˌkabə'lɪstɪk
AM ˌkæbə'lɪstɪk

cabalistical
BR ˌkabə'lɪstɨkl
AM ˌkæbə'lɪstɨkəl

cabalistically
BR ˌkabə'lɪstɨkli
AM ˌkæbə'lɪstək(ə)li

caballero
BR ˌkabə'lɛːrəʊ, ˌkabə'jɛːrəʊ, -z
AM ˌkæbə'jɛroʊ, ˌkæbl'ɛroʊ, ˌkɑbə'jɛroʊ, ˌkɑbl'əroʊ, -z

cabana
BR kə'bɑːnə(r), -z
AM kə'bænə, -z

cabaret
BR 'kabəreɪ, -z
AM ˌkæbəˈreɪ, -z

cabbage
BR 'kab|ɪdʒ, -ɨdʒɪz
AM 'kæbɪdʒ, -ɨz

cabbagy
BR 'kabɨdʒi
AM 'kæbɪdʒi

cabbala
BR kə'bɑːlə(r), 'kabələ(r), -z
AM kə'bɑlə, 'kæbələ, -z

cabbalism
BR kə'bɑːlɪz(ə)m, 'kabəlɪz(ə)m
AM 'kæbəˌlɪzəm

cabbalist
BR kə'bɑːlɪst, 'kabəlɪst, -s
AM 'kæbələst, -s

cabbalistic
BR ˌkabə'lɪstɪk
AM ˌkæbə'lɪstɪk

cabbalistical
BR ˌkabə'lɪstɨkl
AM ˌkæbə'lɪstɨkəl

cabbalistically
BR ˌkabə'lɪstɨkli
AM ˌkæbə'lɪstək(ə)li

cabbie
BR 'kab|i, -ɪz
AM 'kæbi, -z

cabby
BR 'kab|i, -ɪz
AM 'kæbi, -z

cabdriver
BR 'kabˌdrʌɪvə(r), -z
AM 'kæbˌdraɪvər, -z

caber
BR 'keɪbə(r), -z
AM 'kɑbər, 'keɪbər, -z

cabernet
BR 'kabəneɪ
AM ˌkæbərˈneɪ

Cabernet Franc
BR ˌkabəneɪ 'frɒ̃
AM ˌkæbər'neɪ 'frɑŋk

Cabernet Sauvignon
BR ˌkabəneɪ ˌsəʊvɪ'njɒ̃
AM ˌkæbərˈneɪ soʊvən'jɑn

cabin
BR 'kabɪn, -z
AM 'kæbən, -z

Cabinda
BR kə'bɪndə(r)
AM kə'bɪndə

cabinet
BR 'kabɪnɪt, 'kabn̩ɪt, -s
AM 'kæb(ə)nət, -s

cabinetmaker
BR 'kabɪnɨtˌmeɪkə(r), 'kabn̩ɨtˌmeɪkə(r), -z
AM 'kæb(ə)nətˌmeɪkər, -z

cabinetmaking
BR 'kabɪnɨtˌmeɪkɪŋ, 'kabn̩ɨtˌmeɪkɪŋ
AM 'kæb(ə)nətˌmeɪkɪŋ

cabinetry
BR 'kabɪnɨtri, 'kabn̩ɨtri
AM 'kæb(ə)nətri

cable
BR 'keɪb|l, -lz, -l̩ɪŋ\-lɪŋ, -ld
AM 'keɪb|əl, -əlz, -(ə)lɪŋ, -əld

cablecar
BR 'keɪblkɑː(r), -z
AM 'keɪbəlˌkɑr, -z

cablegram
BR 'keɪblgram, -z
AM 'keɪbəlˌgræm, -z

cableway
BR 'keɪblweɪ, -z
AM 'keɪbəlˌweɪ, -z

cabman
BR 'kabmən
AM 'kæbˌmæn, 'kæbmən

cabmen
BR 'kabmən
AM 'kæbˌmɛn, 'kæbmən

cabochon
BR 'kabəʃɒn
AM 'kæbəˌʃɑn

caboodle
BR kə'buːdl
AM kə'budəl

caboose
BR kə'buːs, -ɪz
AM kəˌbus, -ɪz

Cabora Bassa
BR kəˌbɔːrə 'basə(r)
AM kəˌbɔrə 'bɑsə

Caborn
BR 'keɪbɔːn
AM 'keɪˌbɔ(ə)rn

caboshed
BR kə'bɒʃt
AM kə'bɑʃt

Cabot
BR 'kabət
AM 'kæbət

cabotage
BR 'kabətɑːʒ, 'kabətɪdʒ
AM 'kæbəˌtɑʒ, 'kæbədɪdʒ

cabotin
BR 'kabətɪn, -z
AM 'kæbətn, -z

cabotine
BR 'kabətiːn, -z
AM 'kæbəˌtin, -z

cabriole
BR 'kabrɪəʊl, ˌkabrɪ'əʊl, -z
AM 'kæbrioʊl, 'kæbriəl, -z

cabriolet
BR 'kabrɪəleɪ, -z
AM ˌkæbriəˈleɪ, -z

ca'canny
BR ˌkɑː'kani, ˌkɑː'kɒni
AM kæ'kæni

cacao
BR kə'kaʊ, kə'kɑːəʊ, kə'keɪəʊ, -z
AM kə'kaʊ, kə'kɑoʊ, kə'keɪoʊ, -z

cacciatore
BR ˌkatʃə'tɔːri, ˌkɑːtʃə'tɔːri, ˌkatʃə'tɔːreɪ, ˌkɑːtʃə'tɔːreɪ
AM ˌkɑtʃə'tɔri, ˌkætʃə'tɔri

cachalot
BR 'kaʃəlɒt, -s
AM 'kæʃəˌlɑt, -s

cache
BR kaʃ, -ɪz, -ɪŋ, -t
AM kæʃ, -əz, -ɪŋ, -t

cachectic
BR kə'kɛktɪk
AM kə'kɛktɪk

cachepot
BR ˌkaʃ'pəʊ, 'kaʃpɒt
AM 'kæʃˌpɑt, 'kæʃˌpoʊ

cachet
BR 'kaʃeɪ, -z
AM kæ'ʃeɪ, -z

cachexia
BR ka'kɛksɪə(r), kə'kɛksɪə(r)
AM kə'kɛksiə

cachexy
BR ka'kɛksi, kə'kɛksi
AM kə'kɛksi

cachinnate
BR 'kakɪneɪt, -s, -ɪŋ, -ɨd
AM 'kækəˌneɪ|t, -ts, -dɪŋ, -dɨd

cachinnation
BR ˌkakɪ'neɪʃn, -z
AM ˌkækə'neɪʃən, -z

cachinnatory
BR ˌkakɪ'neɪt(ə)ri
AM 'kækənəˌtɔri

cacholong
BR 'kaʃəlɒŋ, -z
AM 'kɑʃəˌlɔŋ, 'kɑʃəˌlɑŋ, -z

cachou
BR 'kaʃuː, kə'ʃuː, -z
AM kæ'ʃu, kə'ʃu, -z

cachucha
BR kə'tʃuːtʃə(r), -z
AM kə'tʃutʃə, -z

cacique
BR ka'siːk, kə'siːk, -s
AM kə'sik, -s

caciquism
BR ka'siːkɪz(ə)m, kə'siːkɪz(ə)m
AM kə'siˌkɪzəm

cackle
BR 'kak|l, -lz, -l̩ɪŋ\-lɪŋ, -ld
AM 'kæk|əl, -əlz, -(ə)lɪŋ, -əld

cackler
BR 'kakl̩ə(r), 'kaklə(r), -z
AM 'kæk(ə)lər, -z

cacodaemon
BR ˌkakə'diːmən, -z
AM ˌkækə'dimən, -z

cacodemon
BR ˌkakə'diːmən, -z
AM ˌkækə'dimən, -z

cacodyl
BR 'kakədʌɪl, 'kakədɪl
AM 'kækəˌdɪl

cacodylic
BR ˌkakəˈdɪlɪk
AM ˌkækəˈdɪlɪk
cacoepy
BR kaˈkəʊɪpi, kəˈkəʊɪpi, ˈkakəʊpi
AM ˈkækəˌwɛpi, kəˈkɑwəpi
cacoethes
BR ˌkakəʊˈiːθiːz
AM ˌkækəˈwiðiz
cacographer
BR kaˈkɒɡrəfə(r), kəˈkɒɡrəfə(r), -z
AM kəˈkɑɡrəfər, -z
cacographic
BR ˌkakəˈɡrafɪk
AM ˌkækəˈɡræfɪk
cacographical
BR ˌkakəˈɡrafɪkl
AM ˌkækəˈɡræfɪkəl
cacography
BR kaˈkɒɡrəfi, kəˈkɒɡrəfi
AM kəˈkɑɡræfi
cacology
BR kaˈkɒlədʒi, kəˈkɒlədʒi
AM kəˈkɑlədʒi
cacomistle
BR ˈkakəˌmɪsl, -z
AM ˈkækəˌmɪsəl, -z
cacophonous
BR kəˈkɒfənəs, kəˈkɒfn̩əs, kaˈkɒfənəs, kaˈkɒfn̩əs
AM kəˈkɑfənəs
cacophony
BR kəˈkɒfən|i, kəˈkɒfn̩|i, kaˈkɒfən|i, kaˈkɒfn̩|i, -ɪz
AM kəˈkɑfəni, -z
cactaceous
BR kakˈteɪʃəs
AM kækˈteɪʃəs
cactal
BR ˈkaktl
AM ˈkæktl
cacti
BR ˈkaktʌɪ
AM ˈkækˌtaɪ
cactus
BR ˈkaktəs, -ɪz
AM ˈkæktəs, -əz
cacuminal
BR kaˈkjuːmɪnl, kəˈkjuːmɪnl
AM kəˈkjumənəl
cad
BR kad, -z
AM kæd, -z
cadastral
BR kəˈdastr(ə)l
AM kəˈdæstrəl
cadaver
BR kəˈdavə(r), kəˈdɑːvə(r), kəˈdeɪvə(r), -z
AM kəˈdævər, -z
cadaveric
BR kəˈdav(ə)rɪk
AM kəˈdæv(ə)rɪk
cadaverous
BR kəˈdav(ə)rəs
AM kəˈdæv(ə)rəs
cadaverousness
BR kəˈdav(ə)rəsnəs
AM kəˈdæv(ə)rəsnəs
Cadbury
BR ˈkadb(ə)ri
AM ˈkædbəri
CAD-CAM
BR ˈkadkam
AM ˈkædˌkæm
caddie
BR ˈkad|i, -ɪz
AM ˈkædi, -z
caddis
BR ˈkadɪs
AM ˈkædəs
caddish
BR ˈkadɪʃ
AM ˈkædɪʃ
caddishly
BR ˈkadɪʃli
AM ˈkædɪʃli
caddishness
BR ˈkadɪʃnɪs
AM ˈkædɪʃnɪs
caddy
BR ˈkad|i, -ɪz
AM ˈkædi, -z
cade
BR keɪd, -z
AM keɪd, -z
Cadell
BR kəˈdɛl, ˈkadl
AM kəˈdɛl, ˈkædəl
cadence
BR ˈkeɪdns, -ɪz, -t
AM ˈkeɪdns, -ɪz, -t
cadency
BR ˈkeɪdns|i, -ɪz
AM ˈkeɪdnsi, -z
cadential
BR keɪˈdɛnʃl
AM ˌkeɪˈdɛn(t)ʃəl
cadenza
BR kəˈdɛnzə(r), -z
AM kəˈdɛnzə, -z
Cader Idris
BR ˌkadər ˈɪdrɪs
AM ˌkɑdər ˈɪdrɪs
cadet
BR kəˈdɛt, -s
AM kəˈdɛt, -s
cadetship
BR kəˈdɛtʃɪp, -s
AM kəˈdɛtˌʃɪp, -s
cadge
BR kadʒ, -ɪz, -ɪŋ, -d
AM kædʒ, -əz, -ɪŋ, -d
cadger
BR kadʒə(r), -z
AM kædʒər, -z
cadi
BR ˈkɑːd|i, -ɪz
AM ˈkɑdi, -z
Cadillac®
BR ˈkadɪlak, ˈkadl̩ak, -s
AM ˈkædəˌlæk, -s
Cadiz
BR kəˈdɪz
AM kəˈdiz, kəˈdɪz
Cadíz
BR kəˈdɪz
AM kəˈdiz, kəˈdɪz
Cadman
BR ˈkadmən
AM ˈkædmən
Cadmean
BR kadˈmiːən
AM kædˈmi(ə)n, ˈkædmin
cadmic
BR ˈkadmɪk
AM ˈkædmɪk
cadmium
BR ˈkadmɪəm
AM ˈkædmiəm
Cadmus
BR ˈkadməs
AM ˈkædməs
Cadogan
BR kəˈdʌɡ(ə)n
AM kəˈdɑɡən
cadre
BR ˈkɑːdə(r), -z
AM ˈkædˌreɪ, ˈkædri, ˈkɑdri, ˈkɑdˌreɪ, -z
caducei
BR kəˈdjuːsɪʌɪ, kəˈdjuːʃɪʌɪ, kəˈdʒuːsɪʌɪ, kəˈdʒuːʃɪʌɪ
AM kəˈd(j)uʃiˌaɪ, kəˈd(j)usiˌaɪ
caduceus
BR kəˈdjuːsɪəs, kəˈdjuːʃɪəs, kəˈdʒuːsɪəs, kəˈdʒuːʃɪəs
AM kəˈd(j)uʃ(i)əs, kəˈd(j)usiəs
caducity
BR kəˈdjuːsɪti, kəˈdʒuːsɪti
AM kəˈd(j)usədi
caducous
BR kəˈdjuːkəs, kəˈdʒuːkəs
AM kəˈd(j)ukəs
Cadwallader
BR kadˈwɒlədə(r)
AM ˌkædˈwɑlədər
caeca
BR ˈsiːkə(r)
AM ˈsikə
caecal
BR ˈsiːkl
AM ˈsikəl
caecilian
BR sɪˈsɪlɪən, -z
AM siˈsɪljən, siˈsɪliən, -z
caecitis
BR sɪˈsʌɪtɪs
AM siˈsaɪdəs
caecum
BR ˈsiːk(ə)m
AM ˈsikəm
Caedmon
BR ˈkadmən
AM ˈkædmən
Caen
BR kɒ̃, kɑːn
AM kɑn
Caenozoic
BR ˌsiːnəˈzəʊɪk
AM ˌsinəˈzoʊɪk
Caernarfon
BR kəˈnɑːvn
AM kərˈnɑrvən
WE kaɪrˈnarvɒn
Caernarvonshire
BR kəˈnɑːvnʃ(ɪ)ə(r)
AM kərˈnɑrvənʃɪ(ə)r
Caesar
BR ˈsiːzə(r), -z
AM ˈsizər, -z
Caesarea
BR ˌsiːzəˈriːə(r)
AM sɪzəˈriə
caesarean
BR sɪˈzɛːrɪən, -z
AM sɪˈzɛriən, -z
caesarian
BR sɪˈzɛːrɪən, -z
AM sɪˈzɛriən, -z
caesious
BR ˈsiːzɪəs
AM ˈsiziəs
caesium
BR ˈsiːzɪəm
AM ˈsiziəm
caesura
BR sɪˈzjʊərə(r), sɪˈʒʊərə(r), sɪˈzjɔːrə(r), sɪˈʒɔːrə(r), -z
AM sɪˈʒurə, sɪˈzurə, -z
caesural
BR sɪˈzjʊərəl, sɪˈzjʊərl̩, sɪˈʒʊərəl, sɪˈʒʊərl̩, sɪˈzjɔːrəl, sɪˈzjɔːrl̩, sɪˈʒɔːrəl, sɪˈʒɔːrl̩
AM sɪˈʒurəl, sɪˈzurəl
cafard
BR kaˈfɑː(r)
AM ˈkæfər
café
BR ˈkaf|eɪ, ˈkaf|i, -eɪ\-ɪz
AM ˌkæˈfeɪ, kəˈfeɪ, -z
café au lait
BR ˌkafeɪ əʊ ˈleɪ, -z
AM ˈkæˌfeɪ oʊ ˈleɪ, kəˈfeɪ oʊ ˈleɪ, -z

café noir
BR ˌkafeɪ ˈnwɑː(r), -z
AM ˈkæˌfeɪ ˈnwɑr, -z

cafeteria
BR ˌkafɪˈtɪərɪə(r), -z
AM ˌkæfəˈtɪriə, -z

cafetière
BR ˌkafˈtjɛː(r), -z
AM ˌkæfˈtjɛ(ə)r, -z

caff
BR kaf, -s
AM kæf, -s

caffeine
BR ˈkafiːn
AM kæˈfin

caftan
BR ˈkaftan, -z
AM ˈkæftən, ˈkæfˌtæn, -z

cage
BR keɪdʒ, -ɪz, -ɪŋ, -d
AM keɪdʒ, -ɪz, -ɪŋ, -d

cagebird
BR ˈkeɪdʒbəːd, -z
AM ˈkeɪdʒˌbərd, -z

cagey
BR ˈkeɪdʒ|i, -ɪə(r), -ɪɪst
AM ˈkeɪdʒi, -ər, -ɪst

cageyness
BR ˈkeɪdʒɪnɪs
AM ˈkeɪdʒinɪs

cagily
BR ˈkeɪdʒɪli
AM ˈkeɪdʒɪli

caginess
BR ˈkeɪdʒɪnɪs
AM ˈkeɪdʒinɪs

Cagliari
BR ˌkalɪˈɑːri
AM ˌkælˈjɑri

Cagney
BR ˈkagni
AM ˈkægni

cagoule
BR kəˈguːl, -z
AM kəˈgul, -z

Cahill
BR ˈkɑːhɪl, ˈkeɪhɪl
AM ˈkeɪhɪl

cahoots
BR kəˈhuːts
AM kəˈhuts

Caiaphas
BR ˈkʌɪəfas
AM ˈkaɪəfəs

Caicos
BR ˈkeɪkɒs, ˈkeɪkəs
AM ˈkeɪkɔs, ˈkeɪkəs, ˈkeɪkɑs

caiman
BR ˈkeɪmən, -z
AM ˈkeɪmən, -z

Cain
BR keɪn
AM keɪn

Caine
BR keɪn
AM keɪn

Cainozoic
BR ˌkʌɪnəˈzəʊɪk
AM ˌkeɪnəˈzoʊɪk

caïque
BR kʌɪˈiːk, kɑːˈiːk, -s
AM kɑˈik, kaɪˈik, -s

cairn
BR kɛːn, -z
AM kɛ(ə)rn, -z

Cairncross
BR ˈkɛːnkrɒs
AM ˈkɛrnˌkrɔs, ˈkɛrnˌkrɑs

cairngorm
BR ˈkɛːngɔːm, -z
AM ˈkɛrnˌgɔ(ə)rm, -z

Cairngorms
BR ˈkɛːngɔːmz
AM ˈkɛrnˌgɔ(ə)rmz

Cairns
BR kɛːnz
AM kɛrnz

Cairo
BR ˈkʌɪrəʊ
AM ˈkaɪroʊ

caisson
BR ˈkeɪsn, ˈkeɪsɒn, kəˈsuːn, -z
AM ˈkeɪsɑn, ˈkeɪsən, -z

Caister
BR ˈkeɪstə(r)
AM ˈkeɪstər

Caistor
BR ˈkeɪstə(r)
AM ˈkeɪstər

Caithness
BR ˈkeɪθnɛs, ˈkeɪθnɪs, keɪθˈnɛs
AM ˈkeɪθnɪs

caitiff
BR ˈkeɪtɪf, -s
AM ˈkeɪdəf, -s

Caitlin
BR ˈkeɪtlɪn
AM ˈkeɪtˌlɪn

Caius[1]
Cambridge college
BR kiːz
AM kiz

Caius[2]
Roman name
BR ˈkʌɪəs
AM ˈkaɪəs, ˈkeɪəs

cajole
BR kəˈdʒəʊl, -z, -ɪŋ, -d
AM kəˈdʒoʊl, -z, -ɪŋ, -d

cajolement
BR kəˈdʒəʊlm(ə)nt
AM kəˈdʒoʊlmənt

cajoler
BR kəˈdʒəʊlə(r), -z
AM kəˈdʒoʊlər, -z

cajolery
BR kəˈdʒəʊl(ə)ri
AM kəˈdʒoʊləri

Cajun
BR ˈkeɪdʒ(ə)n, -z
AM ˈkeɪdʒən, -z

cake
BR keɪk, -s, -ɪŋ, -t
AM keɪk, -s, -ɪŋ, -t

cakewalk
BR ˈkeɪkwɔːk, -s
AM ˈkeɪkˌwɔk, ˈkeɪkˌwɑk, -s

Calabar
BR ˌkaləˈbɑː(r), ˈkaləbɑː(r)
AM ˌkæləˈbɑr

calabash
BR ˈkaləbaʃ, -ɪz
AM ˈkæləˌbæʃ, -ɪz

calaboose
BR ˈkaləbuːs, ˌkaləˈbuːs, -ɪz
AM ˈkæləˌbus, -ɪz

calabrese
BR ˈkaləbriːs, ˈkaləbriːz
AM ˈkæləˌbris, ˈkæləˌbriz

Calabria
BR kəˈlabrɪə(r)
AM kɑˈlɑbriə, kəˈleɪbriə

Calabrian
BR kəˈlabrɪən, -z
AM kɑˈlɑbriən, kəˈleɪbriən, -z

Calais
BR ˈkaleɪ, ˈkali
AM kæˈleɪ

calaloo
BR ˈkaləluː
AM ˈkæləˌlu

calalu
BR ˈkaləluː
AM ˈkæləˌlu

calamanco
BR ˌkaləˈmaŋkəʊ, -z
AM ˌkæləˈmæŋkoʊ, -z

calamander
BR ˈkaləmandə(r)
AM ˈkæləmændər

calamari
BR kaləˈmɑːri
AM ˌkɑləˈmɑri

calamary
BR ˈkaləmər|i, -ɪz
AM ˈkæləˌmɛri, -z

calami
BR ˈkaləmʌɪ
AM ˈkæləˌmaɪ

calamine
BR ˈkaləmʌɪn
AM ˈkæləˌmaɪn

calamint
BR ˈkaləmɪnt
AM ˈkæləˌmɪnt

calamitous
BR kəˈlamɪtəs
AM kəˈlæmədəs

calamitously
BR kəˈlamɪtəsli
AM kəˈlæmədəsli

calamitousness
BR kəˈlamɪtəsnəs
AM kəˈlæmədəsnəs

calamity
BR kəˈlamɪt|i, -ɪz
AM kəˈlæmədi, -z

calamus
BR ˈkaləməs
AM ˈkæləməs

calando
BR kəˈlandəʊ
AM kəˈlændoʊ

calash
BR kəˈlaʃ, -ɪz
AM kəˈlæʃ, -əz

calathea
BR ˌkaləˈθiːə(r)
AM ˌkæləˈθiə

calcanea
BR kalˈkeɪnɪə(r)
AM kælˈkeɪniə

calcaneal
BR kalˈkeɪnɪəl
AM kælˈkeɪniəl

calcanei
BR kalˈkeɪnɪʌɪ
AM kælˈkeɪniˌaɪ

calcaneum
BR kalˈkeɪnɪəm
AM kælˈkeɪniəm

calcaneus
BR kalˈkeɪnɪəs
AM kælˈkeɪniəs

calcareous
BR kalˈkɛːrɪəs
AM kælˈkɛriəs

calcareousness
BR kalˈkɛːrɪəsnəs
AM kælˈkɛriəsnəs

calceolaria
BR ˌkalsɪəˈlɛːrɪə(r), -z
AM ˌkælsiəˈlɛriə, -z

calceolate
BR ˈkalsɪələt
AM ˈkælsiələt

calces
BR ˈkalsiːz
AM ˈkælsiz

calciferol
BR kalˈsɪfərɒl, -z
AM kælˈsɪf(ə)rəl, -z

calciferous
BR kalˈsɪf(ə)rəs
AM kælˈsɪf(ə)rəs

calcific
BR kalˈsɪfɪk
AM ˌkælˈsɪfɪk

calcification
BR ˌkalsɪfɪˈkeɪʃn
AM ˌkælsəfəˈkeɪʃən

calcifuge
BR ˈkalsɪfjuː(d)ʒ, -ɪz
AM ˈkælsəˌfjudʒ, -əz

calcify
BR ˈkalsɨfʌɪ, -z, -ɪŋ, -d
AM ˈkælsəˌfaɪ, -z, -ɪŋ, -d

calcination
BR ˌkalsɪˈneɪʃn
AM kælsəˈneɪʃən

calcine
BR ˈkalsʌɪn, ˈkalsɪn, -z, -ɪŋ, -d
AM ˈkælˌsaɪn, ˈkælˌsin, -z, -ɪŋ, -d

calcite
BR ˈkalsʌɪt
AM ˈkælˌsaɪt

calcitic
BR kalˈsɪtɪk
AM kælˈsɪdɪk

calcium
BR ˈkalsɪəm
AM ˈkælsiəm

Calcot
BR ˈkalkət, ˈkalkɒt, ˈkɔːlkət, ˈkɔːlkɒt, ˈkɒlkət, ˈkɒlkɒt
AM ˈkælkɑt, ˈkɑlkɑt, ˈkɔlkɑt

Calcott
BR ˈkalkət, ˈkalkɒt, ˈkɔːlkət, ˈkɔːlkɒt, ˈkɒlkət, ˈkɒlkɒt
AM ˈkælkɑt, ˈkɑlkɑt, ˈkɔlkɑt

calcrete
BR ˈkalkriːt, -s
AM ˈkælˌkrit, -s

calc-sinter
BR ˌkalkˈsɪntə(r)
AM ˈkælkˌsɪn(t)ər

calcspar
BR ˈkalkspɑː(r)
AM ˈkælkˌspɑr

calc-tuff
BR ˈkalktʌf
AM ˈkælkˌtəf

calculability
BR ˌkalkjʊləˈbɪlɨti
AM ˌkælkjələˈbɪlɨdi

calculable
BR ˈkalkjʊləbl
AM ˈkælkjələbəl

calculably
BR ˈkalkjʊləbli
AM ˈkælkjələbli

calculate
BR ˈkalkjʊleɪt, -s, -ɪŋ, -ɨd
AM ˈkælkjəˌleɪ|t, -ts, -dɪŋ, -dɨd

calculatedly
BR ˈkalkjʊleɪtɨdli
AM ˈkælkjəˌleɪdɨdli

calculatingly
BR ˈkalkjʊleɪtɪŋli
AM ˈkælkjəˌleɪdɪŋli

calculation
BR ˌkalkjʊˈleɪʃn, -z
AM ˌkælkjəˈleɪʃən, -z

calculative
BR ˈkalkjʊlətɪv
AM ˈkælkjəˌleɪdɪv

calculator
BR ˈkalkjʊleɪtə(r), -z
AM ˈkælkjəˌleɪdər, -z

calculi
BR ˈkalkjʊlʌɪ
AM ˈkælkjəˌlaɪ

calculous
BR ˈkalkjʊləs
AM ˈkælkjələs

calculus
BR ˈkalkjʊləs, -ɪz
AM ˈkælkjələs, -əz

Calcutta
BR kalˈkʌtə(*r*)
AM kælˈkədə

caldaria
BR kalˈdɛːrɪə(*r*)
AM kælˈdɛriə

caldarium
BR kalˈdɛːrɪəm, -z
AM kælˈdɛriəm, -z

Caldecote
BR ˈkɔːldɨkət, ˈkɔːldɨkɒt, ˈkɒldɨkət, ˈkɒldɨkɒt
AM ˈkɔldəˌkɑt, ˈkɑldəˌkɑt

Caldecott
BR ˈkɔːldɨkɒt, ˈkɔːldɨkət, ˈkɒldɨkɒt, ˈkɒldɨkət
AM ˈkɔldəˌkɑt, ˈkɑldəˌkɑt

Calder
BR ˈkɔːldə(r), ˈkɒldə(r)
AM ˈkɔldər, ˈkɑldər

caldera
BR kalˈdɛːrə(*r*), kɔːlˈdɛːrə(*r*), ˈkɔːld(ə)rə(*r*)
AM kɔlˈdɛrə, kɑlˈdɛrə, kælˈdɛrə

Calderdale
BR ˈkɔːldədeɪl, ˈkɒldədeɪl
AM ˈkɔldərˌdeɪl, ˈkɑldəˌdeɪl

Calderón
BR ˈkaldərɒn
AM ˈkɔldəˌrɔn, ˈkɑldəˌrɔn
SP ˌkaldeˈron

caldron
BR ˈkɔːldr(ə)n, ˈkɒldr(ə)n, -z
AM ˈkɔldrən, ˈkɑldrən, -z

Caldwell
BR ˈkɔːldwɛl, ˈkɒldwɛl
AM ˈkɔldwɛl, ˈkɑldwɛl

Caldy
BR ˈkɔːldi, ˈkɒldi
AM ˈkɔldi, ˈkɑldi

Caleb
BR ˈkeɪlɛb
AM ˈkeɪləb

calebrese
BR ˈkalɨbriːs
AM ˈkæləˌbris, ˈkæləˌbriz

Caledonian
BR ˌkalɨˈdəʊnɪən, -z
AM ˌkæləˈdoʊniən, -z

calefacient
BR ˌkalɪˈfeɪʃnt
AM ˌkæləˈfeɪʃənt

calefaction
BR ˌkalɪˈfakʃn
AM ˌkæləˈfækʃən

calefactory
BR ˌkalɪˈfakt(ə)r|i, -ɪz
AM ˌkæləˈfæktɔri, -z

calendar
BR ˈkalɪndə(r), -z
AM ˈkæləndər, -z

calender
BR ˈkalɪndə(r), -z
AM ˈkæləndər, -z

calendric
BR kəˈlɛndrɪk, kaˈlɛndrɪk
AM kəˈlɛndrɪk

calendrical
BR kəˈlɛndrɪkl, kaˈlɛndrɪkl
AM kəˈlɛndrəkəl

calends
BR ˈkalɛndz, ˈkalɪndz
AM ˈkɑlɛn(d)z, ˈkælɛn(d)z

calendula
BR kəˈlɛndjʊlə(*r*), kaˈlɛndjʊlə(*r*), kəˈlɛndʒʊlə(*r*), kaˈlɛndʒʊlə(*r*)
AM kəˈlɛndʒələ

calenture
BR ˈkalɪntjʊə(r), ˈkaln̩tjʊə(r), ˈkalɪntʃə(r), ˈkaln̩tʃə(r)
AM ˈkælən(t)ʃʊ(ə)r, ˈkælən(t)ʃər

calf
BR kɑːf
AM kæf

calfhood
BR ˈkɑːfhʊd
AM ˈkæfˌ(h)ʊd

calfish
BR ˈkɑːfɪʃ
AM ˈkæfɪʃ

calf-length
BR ˌkɑːfˈlɛŋ(k)θ, ˈkɑːflɛŋ(k)θ
AM ˈkæfˌlɛŋθ

calflike
BR ˈkɑːflʌɪk
AM ˈkæfˌlaɪk

calfskin
BR ˈkɑːfskɪn, -z
AM ˈkæfˌskɪn, -z

Calgary
BR ˈkalg(ə)ri
AM ˈkælgəri

Calhoun
BR kalˈhuːn, kəˈhuːn
AM kælˈ(h)un

Cali
BR ˈkɑːli
AM ˈkɑli

Caliban
BR ˈkalɨban
AM ˈkæləˌbæn

caliber
BR ˈkalɨbə(r), -z, -d
AM ˈkæləbər, -z, -d

calibrate
BR ˈkalɨbreɪt, -s, -ɪŋ, -ɨd
AM ˈkæləbreɪ|t, -ts, -dɪŋ, -dɨd

calibration
BR ˌkalɪˈbreɪʃn
AM kæləˈbreɪʃən

calibrator
BR ˈkalɨbreɪtə(r), -z
AM ˈkæləˌbreɪdər, -z

calibre
BR ˈkalɨbə(r), -z, -d
AM ˈkæləbər, -z, -d

calices
BR ˈkeɪlɪsiːz
AM ˈkæləsiz

caliche
BR kəˈliːtʃi
AM kəˈliʃ

calicle
BR ˈkalɪkl, -z
AM ˈkæləkəl, -z

calico
BR ˈkalɪkəʊ
AM ˈkæləˌkoʊ

Calicut
BR ˈkalɪkət, ˈkalɪkʌt
AM ˈkæləkət

calif
BR ˈkeɪlɪf, ˈkalɪf, kaˈliːf, -s
AM ˈkeɪləf, ˈkæləf, -s

California
BR ˌkalɪˈfɔːnɪə(*r*)
AM ˌkæləˈfɔrnjə, ˌkæləˈfɔrniə

Californian
BR ˌkalɪˈfɔːnɪən, -z
AM ˌkæləˈfɔrnjən, ˌkæləˈfɔrniən, -z

californium
BR ˌkalɪˈfɔːnɪəm
AM ˌkæləˈfɔrniəm

Caligula
BR kəˈlɪgjʊlə(*r*)
AM kəˈlɪg(j)ʊlə

calipash
BR ˈkalɪpaʃ, -ɪz
AM ˈkæləˌpæʃ, -əz

calipee
BR ˈkalɪpiː, -z
AM ˈkæləˌpi, -z

caliper
BR 'kalɪpə(r), -z
AM 'kæləpər, -z

caliph
BR 'keɪlɪf, 'kalɪf, ka'li:f, -s
AM 'keɪləf, 'kæləf, -s

caliphate
BR 'kalɪfeɪt, 'keɪlɪfeɪt, -s
AM 'keɪlə,feɪt, 'kælə,feɪt, -s

calisthenic
BR ˌkalɪs'θɛnɪk, -s
AM ˌkæləs'θɛnɪk, -s

calix
BR 'keɪl|ɪks, -ɪksɪz
AM 'keɪlɪks, 'kælɪks, -ɪz

calk
BR kɔ:k, -s, -ɪŋ, -t
AM kɔk, kɑk, -s, -ɪŋ, -t

Calke
BR kɔ:k
AM kɔk, kɑk

calkin
BR 'kalkɪn, -z
AM 'kɔkən, 'kælkən, 'kɑkən, -z

call
BR kɔ:l, -z, -ɪŋ, -d
AM kɔl, kɑl, -z, -ɪŋ, -d

calla
BR 'kalə(r), -z
AM 'kælə, -z

Callaghan
BR 'kaləhan, 'kaləhən
AM 'kælə,hæn

Callahan
BR 'kaləhan, 'kaləhən
AM 'kælə,hæn

Callander
BR 'kaləndə(r)
AM 'kæləndər

Callas
BR 'kaləs
AM 'kæləs

callback
BR 'kɔ:lbak, -s
AM 'kɔl,bæk, 'kɑl,bæk, -s

callboy
BR 'kɔ:lbɔɪ, -z
AM 'kɔl,bɔɪ, 'kɑl,bɔɪ, -z

Callenor
BR 'tʃalənə(r)
AM 'tʃælənər

caller
BR 'kɔ:lə(r), -z
AM 'kɔlər, 'kɑlər, -z

callgirl
BR 'kɔ:lgə:l, -z
AM 'kɔl,gərl, 'kɑl,gərl, -z

calligrapher
BR kə'lɪgrəfə(r), -z
AM kə'lɪgrəfər, -z

calligraphic
BR ˌkalɪ'grafɪk
AM ˌkælə'græfɪk

calligraphical
BR ˌkalɪ'grafɪkl
AM ˌkælə'græfəkəl

calligraphically
BR ˌkalɪ'grafɪkli
AM ˌkælə'græfək(ə)li

calligraphist
BR kə'lɪgrəfɪst, -s
AM kə'lɪgrəfəst, -s

calligraphy
BR kə'lɪgrəfi
AM kə'lɪgrəfi

Callil
BR kə'lɪl
AM kə'lɪl

Callimachus
BR kə'lɪməkəs
AM kə'lɪməkəs, ˌkælə'mɑkəs

calling
BR 'kɔ:lɪŋ, -z
AM 'kɔlɪŋ, 'kɑlɪŋ, -z

calliope
BR kə'lʌɪəp|i, ka'lʌɪəp|i, -ɪz
AM kə'laɪəpi, -z

calliper
BR 'kalɪpə(r), -z
AM 'kæləpər, -z

callipygian
BR ˌkalɪ'pɪdʒɪən
AM ˌkælə'pɪdʒiən

callipygous
BR ˌkalɪ'pɪdʒɪəs
AM ˌkælə'pɪdʒiəs

callisthenic
BR ˌkalɪs'θɛnɪk, -s
AM ˌkæləs'θɛnɪk, -s

Callisto
BR kə'lɪstəʊ
AM kə'lɪstoʊ

callop
BR 'kaləp, -s
AM 'kæləp, -s

callosity
BR kə'lɒsɪt|i, -ɪz
AM kə'lɑsədi, -z

callous
BR 'kaləs, -ɪz
AM 'kæləs, -əz

callously
BR 'kaləsli
AM 'kæləsli

callousness
BR 'kaləsnəs
AM 'kæləsnəs

callow
BR 'kaləʊ, -ə(r), -ɪst
AM 'kæl|oʊ, -əwər, -əwəst

callowly
BR 'kaləʊli
AM 'kæloʊli

callowness
BR 'kaləʊnəs
AM 'kæloʊnəs

Callum
BR 'kaləm
AM 'kæləm

calluna
BR kə'lu:nə(r), -z
AM kə'l(j)unə, -z

callus
BR 'kaləs, -ɪz
AM 'kæləs, -ɪz

calm
BR kɑ:m, -z, -ɪŋ, -d, -ə(r), -ɪst
AM kɑ(l)m, -z, -ɪŋ, -d, -ər, -əst

calmative
BR 'kalmətɪv, 'kɑ:mətɪv, -z
AM 'kɑ(l)mədɪv, -z

calmly
BR kɑ:mli
AM kɑ(l)mli

calmness
BR 'kɑ:mnəs
AM kɑ(l)mnəs

calmodulin
BR kal'mɒdjʊlɪn
AM kæl'mɑdjələn

Calne
BR kɑ:n
AM kɑ(l)n

calomel
BR 'kaləmɛl
AM 'kæləməl

calor
BR 'kalə(r)
AM 'kælər

caloric
BR ka'lɒrɪk, kə'lɒrɪk, 'kal(ə)rɪk
AM kə'lɔrɪk, kə'lɑrɪk, 'kælərɪk

calorie
BR 'kal(ə)r|i, -ɪz
AM 'kæl(ə)ri, -z

calorific
BR ˌkalə'rɪfɪk
AM ˌkælə'rɪfɪk

calorifically
BR ˌkalə'rɪfɪkli
AM ˌkælə'rɪfɪk(ə)li

calorification
BR kəˌlɒrɪfɪ'keɪʃn
AM kəˌlɔrəfə'keɪʃən

calorimeter
BR ˌkalə'rɪmɪtə(r), -z
AM ˌkælə'rɪmədər, -z

calorimetric
BR ˌkal(ə)rɪ'mɛtrɪk
AM ˌkælərə'mɛtrɪk

calorimetry
BR ˌkalə'rɪmɪtri
AM ˌkælə'rɪmətri

calory
BR 'kal(ə)r|i, -ɪz
AM 'kæl(ə)ri, -z

calotte
BR kə'lɒt, -s
AM kə'lɑt, -s

Calpurnia
BR kal'pə:nɪə(r)
AM kæl'pərniə

calque
BR kalk, -s
AM kælk, -s

Calthorpe
BR 'kalθɔ:p
AM 'kæl,θɔ(ə)rp

caltrop
BR 'kaltrəp, 'kɔ:ltrəp, -s
AM 'kæltrəp, -s

Calum
BR 'kaləm
AM 'kæləm

calumet
BR 'kaljʊmɛt, -s
AM ˌkæljəˌmɛt, -s

calumniate
BR kə'lʌmnɪeɪt, -s, -ɪŋ, -ɪd
AM kə'ləmni,eɪ|t, -ts, -dɪŋ, -dɪd

calumniation
BR kəˌlʌmnɪ'eɪʃn, -z
AM kə'ləmni,eɪʃən, -z

calumniator
BR kə'lʌmnɪeɪtə(r), -z
AM kə'ləmni,eɪdər, -z

calumniatory
BR kə'lʌmnɪət(ə)ri
AM kə'ləmniə,tɔri

calumnious
BR kə'lʌmnɪəs
AM kə'ləmniəs

calumny
BR 'kaləmn|i, -ɪz
AM 'kæləmni, -z

Calvados
BR 'kalvədɒs
AM 'kælvə,doʊs

calvary
BR 'kalv(ə)r|i, -ɪz
AM 'kælv(ə)ri, -z

calve
BR kɑ:v, -z, -ɪŋ, -d
AM kæ(l)v, -z, -ɪŋ, -d

Calverley
BR 'kalvəli, 'kɑ:vəli
AM 'kælvərli

Calvert
BR 'kalvət, 'kɔ:lvət
AM 'kælvərt

calves
BR kɑ:vz
AM kævz

Calvin
BR 'kalvɪn
AM 'kælvən

Calvinise
BR 'kalvɪnʌɪz, -ɪz, -ɪŋ, -d

AM 'kælvə,naɪz, -ɪz, -ɪŋ, -d

Calvinism
BR 'kalvɪnɪz(ə)m
AM 'kælvə,nɪzəm

Calvinist
BR 'kalvɪnɪst, -s
AM 'kælvənəst, -s

Calvinistic
BR ,kalvɪ'nɪstɪk
AM ,kælvə'nɪstɪk

Calvinistical
BR ,kalvɪ'nɪstɪkl
AM ,kælvə'nɪstɪkəl

Calvinistically
BR ,kalvɪ'nɪstɪkli
AM ,kælvə'nɪstɪk(ə)li

Calvinize
BR 'kalvɪnʌɪz, -ɪz, -ɪŋ, -d
AM 'kælvə,naɪz, -ɪz, -ɪŋ, -d

calx
BR kalks, -ɪz
AM kælks, -ɪz

calyces
BR 'keɪlɪsiːz
AM 'keɪləsiz

calypso
BR kə'lɪpsəʊ, -z
AM kə'lɪpsoʊ, -z

calyx
BR 'keɪl|ɪks, 'kal|ɪks, -ɪksɪz\-ɪksiːz
AM 'keɪlɪks, -ɪz

calzone
BR kal'tsəʊn|i, -ɪz
AM kæl'zoʊn(i), -z

calzoni
BR kal'tsəʊni
AM kæl'zoʊni

cam
BR kam, -z
AM kæm, -z

camaraderie
BR ,kamə'rɑːd(ə)ri, ,kamə'rad(ə)ri
AM ,kɑm(ə)'rædəri, ,kæm(ə)'rɑdəri

Camargue
BR kə'mɑːg
AM kə'mɑrg

camarilla
BR ,kamə'rɪlə(r), ,kamə'rɪjə(r), -z
AM ,kæmə'rɪlə, -z

camaron
BR ,kamə'rəʊn, 'kam(ə)rən, 'kam(ə)rn̩, -z
AM 'kæmərən, -z

camber
BR 'kambə(r), -z
AM 'kæmbər, -z

Camberwell
BR 'kambəw(ɛ)l
AM 'kæmbər,wɛl

cambia
BR 'kambɪə(r)
AM 'kæmbiə

cambial
BR 'kambɪəl
AM 'kæmbiəl

cambist
BR 'kambɪst, -s
AM 'kæmbəst, -s

cambium
BR 'kambɪəm
AM 'kæmbiəm

Cambodia
BR kam'bəʊdɪə(r)
AM kæm'boʊdiə

Cambodian
BR kam'bəʊdɪən, -z
AM kæm'boʊdiən, -z

Camborne
BR 'kambɔːn
AM 'kæm,bɔ(ə)rn

Cambria
BR 'kambrɪə(r)
AM 'kæmbriə

Cambrian
BR 'kambrɪən, -z
AM 'kæmbriən, -z

cambric
BR 'kambrɪk
AM 'keɪmbrɪk

Cambridge
BR 'keɪmbrɪdʒ
AM 'keɪm,brɪdʒ

Cambridgeshire
BR 'keɪmbrɪdʒʃ(ɪ)ə(r)
AM 'keɪm,brɪdʒʃɪ(ə)r

Cambyses
BR kam'bʌɪsiːz
AM kæm'baɪsiz

camcorder
BR 'kam,kɔːdə(r), -z
AM 'kæm,kɔrdər, -z

Camden Town
BR ,kamdən 'taʊn
AM ,kæmdən 'taʊn

came
BR keɪm
AM keɪm

camel
BR 'kaml, -z
AM 'kæməl, -z

camelback
BR 'kamlbak
AM 'kæməl,bæk

cameleer
BR ,kamə'lɪə(r), -z
AM ,kæmə'lɪ(ə)r, -z

Camelford
BR 'kamlfəd
AM 'kæmlfərd

camelhair
BR 'kamlhɛː(r)
AM 'kæməl,(h)ɛ(ə)r

Camelia
BR kə'miːlɪə(r)
AM kə'miljə, kə'miliə

camellia
BR kə'miːlɪə(r), kə'mɛlɪə(r), -z
AM kə'miljə, kə'miliə, -z

camelopard
BR 'kamɪlə(ʊ)pɑːd, 'kaml̩ə(ʊ)pɑːd, kə'mɛləpɑːd, -z
AM kə'mɛləpɑrd, 'kæməloʊ,pɑrd, -z

Camelot
BR 'kamɪlɒt
AM 'kæməl,lɑt

camelry
BR 'kamlr|i, -ɪz
AM 'kæməlri, -z

Camembert
BR 'kaməmbɛː(r)
AM ,kæməm'bɛ(ə)r

cameo
BR 'kamɪəʊ, -z
AM 'kæmioʊ, -z

camera
BR 'kam(ə)rə(r), -z
AM 'kæm(ə)rə, -z

cameraman
BR 'kamrəman, 'kamrəmən
AM 'kæm(ə)rə,mæn, 'kæm(ə)rəmən

cameramen
BR 'kamrəmɛn, 'kamrəmən
AM 'kæm(ə)rəmən

camera obscura
BR ,kam(ə)rə(r) əb'skjʊərə(r), + ɒb'skjʊərə(r), əb'skjɔːrə(r), ɒb'skjɔːrə(r), -z
AM ,kæm(ə)rə 'ɑbskjurə, -z

camerawork
BR 'kam(ə)rəwəːk
AM 'kæm(ə)rə,wərk

camerlingo
BR ,kamə'lɪŋgəʊ, -z
AM ,kæmər'lɪŋgoʊ, -z

Cameron
BR 'kam(ə)rən, 'kam(ə)rn̩
AM 'kæm(ə)rən

Cameroon
BR ,kamə'ruːn
AM ,kæmə'run

Cameroonian
BR ,kamə'ruːnɪən, -z
AM ,kæmə'runiən, -z

camiknickers
BR 'kamɪ,nɪkəz
AM 'kæmə,nɪkərz

Camilla
BR kə'mɪlə(r)
AM kə'mɪlə

Camille
BR kə'mɪl, kə'miːl
AM kə'mil

cami-nicks
BR 'kamɪnɪks
AM 'kæmə,nɪks

camion
BR 'kamɪən, -z
AM 'kæmjən, -z

camisole
BR 'kamɪsəʊl, -z
AM 'kæmə,soʊl, -z

camomile
BR 'kaməmʌɪl
AM 'kæmə,mil, 'kæmə,maɪl

Camorra
BR kə'mɔːrə(r)
AM kə'mɔrə

camouflage
BR 'kaməflɑː(d)ʒ, -ɪz, -ɪŋ, -d
AM 'kæmə,flɑ(d)ʒ, -əz, -ɪŋ, -d

camp
BR kamp, -s, -ɪŋ, -t
AM kæmp, -s, -ɪŋ, -t

campaign
BR kam'peɪn, -z, -ɪŋ, -d
AM kæm'peɪn, -z, -ɪŋ, -d

campaigner
BR kam'peɪnə(r), -z
AM kæm'peɪnər, -z

Campania
BR kam'panɪə(r)
AM kɑm'pɑniə

campanile
BR ,kampə'niːl|i, -ɪz
AM ,kæmpə'nil(i), -z

campanologer
BR ,kampə'nɒlədʒə(r), -z
AM ,kæmpə'nɑlədʒər, -z

campanological
BR ,kampənə'lɒdʒɪkl, ,kampn̩ə'lɒdʒɪkl
AM ,kæmpənə'lɑdʒəkəl

campanologist
BR ,kampə'nɒlədʒɪst, -s
AM ,kæmpə'nɑlədʒəst, -s

campanology
BR ,kampə'nɒlədʒi
AM ,kæmpə'nɑlədʒi

campanula
BR kam'panjʉlə(r), kəm'panjʉlə(r), -z
AM kæm'pænjələ, -z

campanulate
BR kam'panjʉlət, kəm'panjʉlət
AM kæm'pænjələt, kæm'pænjə,leɪt

Campari®
BR kam'pɑːri
AM kɑm'pɑri

Campbell
BR 'kambl
AM 'kæmbəl

Campbell-Bannerman
BR 'kambl'banəmən
AM 'kæmbəl'bænər-mən

Campden
BR 'kam(p)dən
AM 'kæm(p)dən

Campeachy
BR kam'pi:tʃi
AM kæm'pitʃi

Campeche
BR kam'pi:tʃi
AM kæm'pitʃi

camper
BR 'kampə(r), -z
AM 'kæmpər, -z

campesino
BR ˌkampɪ'si:nəʊ
AM ˌkæmpə'sinoʊ

campfire
BR 'kampfʌɪə(r), -z
AM 'kæmpˌfaɪ(ə)r, -z

campground
BR 'kampgraʊnd, -z
AM 'kæmpˌgraʊnd, -z

camphor
BR 'kamfə(r)
AM 'kæmfər

camphorate
BR 'kamfəreɪt, -s, -ɪŋ, -ɪd
AM 'kæmfəˌreɪ|t, -ts, -dɪŋ, -dɪd

camphoric
BR kam'fɒrɪk
AM ˌkæm'fɔrɪk

campily
BR 'kampɨli
AM 'kæmpɨli

campiness
BR 'kampɪnɪs
AM 'kæmpinɨs

camping
BR 'kampɪŋ
AM 'kæmpɪŋ

Campion
BR 'kampɪən
AM 'kæmpiən

Campsie
BR 'kam(p)si
AM 'kæmpsi, 'kæmpzi

campsite
BR 'kampsʌɪt, -s
AM 'kæmpˌsaɪt, -s

campus
BR 'kampəs, -ɪz
AM 'kæmpəs, -əz

campy
BR 'kamp|i, -ɪə(r), -ɪɪst
AM 'kæmpi, -ər, -ɪst

campylobacter
BR 'kampɪlə(ʊ),bak-tə(r), -z
AM 'kæmpələˌbæktər, kæm'pɪləˌbæktər, -z

CAMRA
BR 'kamrə(r)
AM 'kæmrə

Camrose
BR 'kamrəʊz
AM 'kæmˌroʊz

camshaft
BR 'kamʃɑ:ft, 'kamʃaft, -s
AM 'kæmˌʃæft, -s

Camus
BR 'kamu:, ka'mu:
AM kɑ'mu

camwood
BR 'kamwʊd
AM 'kæmˌwʊd

can[1]
auxiliary verb, strong form
BR kan
AM kæn

can[2]
auxiliary verb, weak form
BR kən
AM kən

can[3]
noun, verb, put in cans
BR kan, -z, -ɪŋ, -d
AM kæn, -z, -ɪŋ, -d

Cana
BR 'keɪnə(r)
AM 'keɪnə

Canaan
BR 'keɪnən
AM 'keɪnən

Canaanite
BR 'keɪnənʌɪt, -s
AM 'keɪnəˌnaɪt, -s

Canada
BR 'kanədə(r)
AM 'kænədə

Canadian
BR kə'neɪdɪən, -z
AM kə'neɪdiən, -z

canaille
BR kə'nɑ:ɪ
AM kə'naɪ, kə'neɪl

canal
BR kə'nal, -z
AM kə'næl, -z

Canaletto
BR ˌkanə'lɛtəʊ
AM ˌkænə'lɛdoʊ

canalisation
BR ˌkanəlʌɪ'zeɪʃn, ˌkanl̩ʌɪ'zeɪʃn
AM ˌkænələ'zeɪʃən, kænəlˌaɪ'zeɪʃən

canalise
BR 'kanəlʌɪz, 'kanl̩ʌɪz, -ɪz, -ɪŋ, -d
AM 'kænəˌlaɪz, -ɪz, -ɪŋ, -d

canalization
BR ˌkanəlʌɪ'zeɪʃn, ˌkanl̩ʌɪ'zeɪʃn
AM ˌkænələ'zeɪʃən, kænəlˌaɪ'zeɪʃən

canalize
BR 'kanəlʌɪz, 'kanl̩ʌɪz, -ɪz, -ɪŋ, -d
AM 'kænəˌlaɪz, -ɪz, -ɪŋ, -d

canalside
BR kə'nalsʌɪd
AM kə'nælˌsaɪd

canapé
BR 'kanəpeɪ, -z
AM 'kænəpeɪ, 'kænəpi, -z

canard
BR kə'nɑ:d, ka'nɑ:d, 'kanɑ:d, -z
AM kə'nɑrd, -z

Canarese
BR ˌkanə'ri:z
AM ˌkɑnə'riz

Canaries
BR kə'nɛ:rɪz
AM kə'nɛriz

canary
BR kə'nɛ:r|i, -ɪz
AM kə'nɛri, -z

canasta
BR kə'nastə(r)
AM kə'næstə

canaster
BR kə'nastə(r)
AM kə'næstər, kə'næstər

Canavan
BR 'kanəv(ə)n
AM 'kænəvn

Canaveral
BR kə'nav(ə)rəl, kə'nav(ə)rl̩
AM kə'næv(ə)rəl

Canberra
BR 'kanb(ə)rə(r)
AM 'kænˌbɛrə, 'kænbərə

cancan
BR 'kankan, -z
AM 'kænˌkæn, -z

cancel
BR 'kans|l, -lz, -l̩ɪŋ\-əlɪŋ, -ld
AM 'kæns|əl, -əlz, -(ə)lɪŋ, -əld

cancelation
BR ˌkansɪ'leɪʃn, -z
AM ˌkænsə'leɪʃən, -z

canceler
BR 'kansɨlə(r), 'kansl̩ə(r), -z
AM 'kæns(ə)lər, -z

cancellation
BR ˌkansɪ'leɪʃn, -z
AM ˌkænsə'leɪʃən, -z

canceller
BR 'kansɨlə(r), 'kansl̩ə(r), -z
AM 'kæns(ə)lər, -z

cancellous
BR 'kansɨləs, 'kansl̩əs
AM 'kænsələs

cancer
BR 'kansə(r), -z
AM 'kænsər, -z

Cancerian
BR kan'sɪərɪən, kan'sɛ:rɪən, -z
AM kæn'sɛriən, -z

cancerous
BR 'kans(ə)rəs
AM 'kæns(ə)rəs

cancerously
BR 'kans(ə)rəsli
AM 'kæns(ə)rəsli

cancroid
BR 'kaŋkrɔɪd, -z
AM 'kæŋkrɔɪd, -z

Cancún
BR kaŋ'ku:n
AM kæŋ'kun

Candace
BR 'kandɪs, kan'deɪsi
AM 'kændəs

candela
BR kan'di:lə(r), kan'dɛlə(r), 'kandələ(r), -z
AM kæn'dɛlə, kæn'dilə, -z

candelabra
BR ˌkandɪ'lɑ:brə(r), -z
AM ˌkændə'lɑbrə, -z

candelabrum
BR ˌkandɪ'lɑ:brəm
AM ˌkændə'lɑbrəm

Canderel®
BR 'kandərɛl
AM 'kændərɛl

candescence
BR kan'dɛsns, kən'dɛsns
AM kæn'dɛsns, kən'dɛsəns

candescent
BR kan'dɛsnt, kən'dɛsnt
AM kæn'dɛsnt, kən'dɛsənt

Candice
BR 'kandɪs
AM 'kændəs

candid
BR 'kandɪd
AM 'kændəd

Candida
BR 'kandɪdə(r)
AM 'kændɪdə, kæn'didə

candida
BR 'kandɪdə(r), -z
AM 'kændɪdə, -z

candidacy
BR 'kandɪdəs|i, -ɪz
AM 'kæn(d)ədəsi, -z

candidate
BR 'kandɨdeɪt, 'kandɨdət, -s
AM 'kæn(d)əˌdeɪt, -s

candidature
BR 'kandɨdətʃə(r), -z
AM 'kæn(d)ədəˌtʃʊ(ə)r, 'kæn(d)əˌdeɪtʃər, -z

Candide
BR (ˌ)kɒn'diːd, kɒ̃'diːd
AM kæn'did

candidiasis
BR ˌkandɪ'dʌɪəsɪs
AM ˌkændə'daɪəsəs

candidly
BR 'kandɨdli
AM 'kændədli

candidness
BR 'kandɨdnɨs
AM 'kændədnəs

candied
BR 'kandɪd
AM 'kændid

candiru
BR ˌkandɪ'ruː, -z
AM ˌkændə'ruː, -z

candle
BR 'kandl, -z
AM 'kændəl, -z

candleholder
BR 'kandlˌhəʊldə(r), -z
AM 'kændlˌ(h)oʊldər, -z

candlelight
BR 'kandllʌɪt
AM 'kændlˌlaɪt

candlelit
BR 'kandllɪt
AM 'kændlˌlɪt

Candlemas
BR 'kandlmas, 'kandlməs
AM 'kændlməs

candlepower
BR 'kandlˌpaʊə(r)
AM 'kændlˌpaʊ(ə)r

candler
BR 'kandl̩ə(r), -z
AM 'kæn(də)lər, -z

candlestick
BR 'kandlstɪk, -s
AM 'kændlˌstɪk, -s

candlewick
BR 'kandlwɪk
AM 'kændlˌwɪk

Candlin
BR 'kandlɪn
AM 'kæn(d)lən

candor
BR 'kandə(r)
AM 'kændər

candour
BR 'kandə(r)
AM 'kændər

candy
BR 'kand|i, -ɪz, -ɪɪŋ, -ɪd
AM 'kændi, -z, -ɪŋ, -d

candyfloss
BR 'kandɪflɒs, -ɪz
AM 'kændiˌflɔs, 'kændiˌflɑs, -əz

candytuft
BR 'kandɪtʌft, -s
AM 'kændiˌtəf(t), -s

cane
BR keɪn, -z, -ɪŋ, -d
AM keɪn, -z, -ɪŋ, -d

canebrake
BR 'keɪnbreɪk, -s
AM 'keɪnˌbreɪk, -s

canebreak
BR 'keɪnbreɪk, -s
AM 'keɪnˌbreɪk, -s

caner
BR 'keɪnə(r), -z
AM 'keɪnər, -z

Canes Venatici
BR ˌkeɪniːz vɪ'natɪsʌɪ, ˌkɑːniːz +, ˌkɑːneɪz +, + vɛ'natɪsʌɪ
AM ˌkeɪniz vɛ'nɑdəsi

canicular
BR kə'nɪkjʉlə(r)
AM kə'nɪkjələr

canine
BR 'keɪnʌɪn, 'kanʌɪn, -z
AM 'keɪˌnaɪn, -z

caning
BR 'keɪnɪŋ, -z
AM 'keɪnɪŋ, -z

Canis Major
BR ˌkanɪs 'meɪdʒə(r), ˌkeɪnɪs +
AM ˌkeɪnɪs 'meɪdʒər, ˌkænɪs +

Canis Minor
BR ˌkanɪs 'mʌɪnə(r), ˌkeɪnɪs +
AM ˌkeɪnɪs 'maɪnər, ˌkænɪs +

canister
BR 'kanɪstə(r), -z
AM 'kænəstər, -z

canker
BR 'kaŋk|ə(r), -əz, -(ə)rɪŋ, -əd
AM 'kæŋkər, -z, -ɪŋ, -d

cankerous
BR 'kaŋk(ə)rəs
AM 'kæŋk(ə)rəs

cankerworm
BR 'kaŋkəwəːm, -z
AM 'kæŋkərˌwərm, -z

canna
BR 'kanə(r), -z
AM 'kænə, -z

cannabis
BR 'kanəbɪs
AM 'kænəbəs

Cannae
BR 'kaniː
AM 'kæni, 'kæˌnaɪ

cannel
BR 'kanl
AM 'kænəl

cannellini
BR ˌkanə'liːni, ˌkanl'iːni
AM ˌkænə'lini

cannelloni
BR ˌkanə'ləʊni, ˌkanl'əʊni
AM ˌkænl'oʊni

canneloni
BR ˌkanə'ləʊni, ˌkanl'əʊni
AM ˌkænl'oʊni

cannelure
BR 'kanəljʊə(r), 'kanl̩jʊə(r), -z
AM 'kænlˌ(j)ʊər, -z

canner
BR 'kanə(r), -z
AM 'kænər, -z

cannery
BR 'kan(ə)r|i, -ɪz
AM 'kænəri, -z

Cannes
BR kan
AM kæn, kɑn

cannibal
BR 'kanɨbl, -z
AM 'kænəbəl, -z

cannibalisation
BR ˌkanɨbəlʌɪ'zeɪʃn, ˌkanɨbl̩ʌɪ'zeɪʃn
AM ˌkænəbələ'zeɪʃən, ˌkænəbəˌlaɪ'zeɪʃən

cannibalise
BR 'kanɨbəlʌɪz, 'kanɨbl̩ʌɪz, -ɪz, -ɪŋ, -d
AM 'kænəbəˌlaɪz, -ɪz, -ɪŋ, -d

cannibalism
BR 'kanɨbəlɪz(ə)m, 'kanɨbl̩ɪz(ə)m
AM 'kænəbəˌlɪzəm

cannibalistic
BR ˌkanɨbə'lɪstɪk, ˌkanɨbl'ɪstɪk
AM ˌkænəbə'lɪstɪk

cannibalistically
BR ˌkanɨbə'lɪstɨkli, ˌkanɨbl'ɪstɨkli
AM ˌkænəbə'lɪstɪk(ə)li

cannibalization
BR ˌkanɨbəlʌɪ'zeɪʃn, ˌkanɨbl̩ʌɪ'zeɪʃn
AM ˌkænəbələ'zeɪʃən, ˌkænəbəlˌaɪ'zeɪʃən

cannibalize
BR 'kanɨbəlʌɪz, 'kanɨbl̩ʌɪz, -ɪz, -ɪŋ, -d
AM 'kænəbəˌlaɪz, -ɪz, -ɪŋ, -d

cannikin
BR 'kanɨkɪn, -z
AM 'kænəkən, -z

cannily
BR 'kanɨli
AM 'kænɨli

canniness
BR 'kanɪnɪs
AM 'kæninɪs

Canning
BR 'kanɪŋ
AM 'kænɪŋ

Cannizzaro
BR ˌkanɪ'zɑːrəʊ
AM ˌkænə'zɛroʊ, ˌkænə'zɑroʊ

Cannock
BR 'kanək
AM 'kænək

cannoli
BR kə'nəʊli
AM kə'noʊli

cannon
BR 'kanən, -z, -ɪŋ, -d
AM 'kænən, -z, -ɪŋ, -d

cannonade
BR ˌkanə'neɪd, -z, -ɪŋ, -ɨd
AM ˌkænə'neɪd, -z, -ɪŋ, -ɨd

cannonball
BR 'kanənbɔːl, -z
AM 'kænənˌbɔl, 'kænənˌbɑl, -z

cannoneer
BR ˌkanə'nɪə(r), -z
AM ˌkænə'nɪ(ə)r, -z

cannonry
BR 'kanənri
AM 'kænənri

cannot
BR 'kanɒt, 'kanət, ka'nɒt, kə'nɒt
AM kə'nɑt, 'kæˌnɑt

cannula
BR 'kanjʉlə(r), -z
AM 'kænjələ, -z

cannulae
BR 'kanjʉliː, 'kanjʉlʌɪ
AM 'kænjəli, 'kænjəˌlaɪ

cannulate
BR 'kanjʉleɪt, -s, -ɪŋ, -ɨd
AM 'kænjəˌleɪ|t, -ts, -dɪŋ, -dɨd

canny
BR 'kan|i, -ɪə(r), -ɪɪst
AM 'kæni, -ər, -ɨst

canoe
BR kə'nuː, -z, -ɪŋ, -d
AM kə'nu, -z, -ɪŋ, -d

canoeist
BR kə'nuːɪst, -s
AM kə'nuəst, -s

canola
BR kə'nəʊlə(r)
AM kə'noʊlə

canon
BR 'kanən, -z
AM 'kænən, -z

cañon
BR 'kanjən, -z
AM 'kænjən, -z

Canonbury
BR 'kanənb(ə)ri
AM 'kænən,bɛri, 'kænənbəri

canoness
BR ,kanə'nɛs, -ɪz
AM 'kænənəs, -əz

canonic
BR kə'nɒnɪk
AM kə'nɑnɪk

canonical
BR kə'nɒnɨkl, -z
AM kə'nɑnəkəl, -z

canonically
BR kə'nɒnɨkli
AM kə'nɑnək(ə)li

canonicate
BR kə'nɒnɨkət, -s
AM kə'nɑnə,kət, -s

canonicity
BR ,kanə'nɪsɨti
AM ,kænə'nɪsɨdi

canonisation
BR ,kanənʌɪ'zeɪʃn, -z
AM kænənə'zeɪʃn, ,kænə,naɪ'zeɪʃən, -z

canonise
BR 'kanənʌɪz, -ɨz, -ɪŋ, -d
AM 'kænə,naɪz, -ɨz, -ɪŋ, -d

canonist
BR 'kanənɪst, -s
AM 'kænənəst, -s

canonization
BR ,kanənʌɪ'zeɪʃn, -z
AM kænənə'zeɪʃn, ,kænə,naɪ'zeɪʃən, -z

canonize
BR 'kanənʌɪz, -ɨz, -ɪŋ, -d
AM 'kænə,naɪz, -ɨz, -ɪŋ, -d

canonry
BR 'kanənr|i, -ɪz
AM 'kænənri, -z

canoodle
BR kə'nu:d|l, -lz, -lɪŋ\-lɪŋ, -ld
AM kə'nud|əl, -əlz, -(ə)lɪŋ, -əld

Canopic
BR kə'nəʊpɪk, kə'nɒpɪk
AM kə'nɑpɪk

canopied
BR 'kanəpɪd
AM 'kænəpid

Canopus
BR kə'nəʊpəs
AM kə'noʊpəs

canopy
BR 'kanəp|i, -ɪz
AM 'kænəpi, -z

canorous
BR kə'nɔ:rəs
AM kə'nɔrəs

Canova
BR kə'nəʊvə(r)
AM kə'noʊvə

canst
BR kanst
AM kænst

cant
BR kant, -s, -ɪŋ, -ɨd
AM kænt, -s, -ɪŋ, -ɨd

can't
BR kɑ:nt
AM kænt

Cantab.
BR 'kantab
AM 'kæntæb

cantabile
BR kan'tɑ:bɨleɪ, kan'tɑ:bḷeɪ, kan'tɑ:bɨli, kan'tɑ:bḷi
AM kɑn'tɑbə,leɪ

Cantabria
BR kan'tabrɪə(r)
AM kən'teɪbriə

Cantabrian
BR kan'tabrɪən, -z
AM kən'teɪbriən, -z

Cantabrigian
BR ,kantə'brɪdʒɪən, -z
AM ,kæn(t)ə'brɪdʒiən, -z

cantal
BR 'kantɑ:l
AM 'kɑn(t)l

cantaloup
BR 'kantəlu:p, -s
AM 'kæn(t)l,oʊp, -s

cantaloupe
BR 'kantəlu:p, -s
AM 'kæn(t)l,oʊp, -s

cantankerous
BR kan'taŋk(ə)rəs
AM kæn'tæŋk(ə)rəs

cantankerously
BR kan'taŋk(ə)rəsli
AM kæn'tæŋk(ə)rəsli

cantankerousness
BR kan'taŋk(ə)rəsnəs
AM kæn'tæŋk(ə)rəsnəs

cantata
BR kan'tɑ:tə(r), kən'tɑ:tə(r), -z
AM kən'tɑdə, -z

cantatrice
BR 'kantətri:s, -ɨz
AM ,kɑn(t)ə'tris, -ɨz

canteen
BR kan'ti:n, -z
AM kæn'tin, -z

cantelope
BR 'kantəlu:p, -s
AM 'kæn(t)l,oʊp, -s

canter
BR 'kant|ə(r), -əz, -(ə)rɪŋ, -əd
AM 'kæntər, -z, -ɪŋ, -d

Canterbury
BR 'kantəb(ə)ri
AM 'kæn(t)ər,bɛri, 'kæn(t)ərbəri

cantharides
BR kan'θarɪdi:z
AM kæn'θɛrədiz

canthi
BR 'kanθʌɪ
AM 'kæn,θaɪ

canthus
BR 'kanθəs
AM 'kænθəs

canticle
BR 'kantɪkl, -z
AM 'kæn(t)əkəl, -z

cantilena
BR ,kantɪ'leɪnə(r), ,kantɪ'li:nə(r), -z
AM ,kæn(t)ə'linə, ,kæn(t)ə'leɪnə, -z

cantilever
BR 'kantɨli:və(r), 'kantḷi:və(r), -z
AM 'kænt(ə),livər, -z

cantillate
BR 'kantɨleɪt, 'kantḷeɪt, -s, -ɪŋ, -ɨd
AM 'kæn(t)ə,leɪ|t, -ts, -dɪŋ, -dɨd

cantillation
BR ,kantɪ'leɪʃn, ,kantl'eɪʃn
AM ,kæn(t)ə'leɪʃən

cantina
BR kan'ti:nə(r), -z
AM kæn'tinə, -z

cantle
BR 'kantl
AM 'kæn(t)əl

canto
BR 'kantəʊ, -z
AM 'kæn,toʊ, 'kæn(t)oʊ, -z

Canton[1]
China
BR ,kan'tɒn
AM 'kæn,tɑn

Canton[2]
US, Wales
BR 'kantən
AM 'kæn(t)ən

canton
BR 'kantɒn, 'kantən, -z
AM 'kæn(t)ən, 'kæn,tɑn, -z

cantonal
BR kan'tɒnl, 'kantənl, 'kantṇl
AM kæn'tɑnəl, 'kæn(t)ənəl, 'kænt(ə)nəl

Cantonese
BR ,kantə'ni:z
AM ,kæn(t)ə'niz

cantonment
BR kan'tu:nm(ə)nt, kən'tu:nm(ə)nt, -s
AM kæn'toʊnmənt, kæn'tɑnmənt, -s

cantor
BR 'kantɔ:(r), 'kantə(r), -z
AM 'kæn(t)ər, 'kæn,(t)ɔ(ə)r, -z

cantorial
BR kan'tɔ:rɪəl
AM kæn'tɔriəl

cantoris
BR kan'tɔ:rɪs
AM kæn'tɔrəs

cantrail
BR 'kantreɪl, -z
AM 'kæn,treɪl, -z

Cantrell
BR kan'trɛl
AM kæn'trɛl, 'kæntrəl

cantrip
BR 'kantrɪp, -s
AM 'kæn,trɪp, -s

Canuck
BR kə'nʌk, -s
AM kə'nək, -s

Canute
BR kə'nju:t
AM kə'n(j)ut

canvas
BR 'kanvəs, -ɨz
AM 'kænvəs, -əz

canvass
BR 'kanvəs, -ɨz, -ɪŋ, -t
AM 'kænvəs, -əz, -ɪŋ, -t

canvasser
BR 'kanvəsə(r), -z
AM 'kænvəsər, -z

Canvey
BR 'kanvi
AM 'kænvi

canyon
BR 'kanjən, -z
AM 'kænjən, -z

canzone
BR kan'tsəʊn|i, kan'zəʊn|i, -ɪz
AM kɑn'zoʊneɪ, kæn'zoʊni, -z

canzonet
BR ,kanzə'nɛt, -s
AM ,kænzə'nɛt, -s

canzonetta
BR ,kanzə'nɛtə(r), -z
AM ,kænzə'nɛdə, -z

caoutchouc
BR 'kaʊtʃʊk
AM kaʊ'tʃʊk

cap
BR kap, -s, -ɪŋ, -t
AM kæp, -s, -ɪŋ, -t

capability
BR ,keɪpə'bɪlɪt|i, -ɪz
AM ,keɪpə'bɪlɨdi, -z

Capablanca
BR 'kapə'blaŋkə(r)
AM ,kɑpə'blɑŋkə

capable
BR 'keɪpəbl
AM 'keɪpəbəl

capableness
BR 'keɪpəblnəs
AM 'keɪpəbəlnəs

capably
BR 'keɪpəbli
AM 'keɪpəbli

capacious
BR kə'peɪʃəs
AM kə'peɪʃəs

capaciously
BR kə'peɪʃəsli
AM kə'peɪʃəsli

capaciousness
BR kə'peɪʃəsnəs
AM kə'peɪʃəsnəs

capacitance
BR kə'pasɪt(ə)ns
AM kə'pæsətns

capacitate
BR kə'pasɪteɪt, -s, -ɪŋ, -ɨd
AM kə'pæsəteɪ|t, -ts, -dɪŋ, -dɨd

capacitative
BR kə'pasɪtətɪv
AM kə'pæsə,teɪdɪv

capacitive
BR kə'pasɪtɪv
AM kə'pæsədɪv

capacitor
BR kə'pasɪtə(r), -z
AM kə'pæsədər, -z

capacity
BR kə'pasɪt|i, -ɪz
AM kə'pæsədi, -z

cap-à-pie
BR ,kapə'pi:
AM ',kɑpə',pieɪ

caparison
BR kə'parɪs(ə)n, -z, -ɪŋ, -d
AM kə'pɛrəsən, -z, -ɪŋ, -d

cape
BR keɪp, -s
AM keɪp, -s

capelin
BR 'keɪplɪn, 'kaplɪn, 'keɪpl̩ɪn
AM 'keɪpələn

Capella
BR kə'pɛlə(*r*)
AM kə'pɛlə

capellini
BR ,kapə'li:ni, ,kapl'i:ni
AM ,kæpə'lini

caper
BR 'keɪp|ə(r), -əz, -(ə)rɪŋ, -əd
AM 'keɪpər, -z, -ɪŋ, -d

capercaillie
BR ,kapə'keɪl|i, -ɪz
AM ,kæpər'keɪli, -z

capercailzie
BR ,kapə'keɪl|i, -ɪz
AM ,kæpər'keɪlzi, -z

caperer
BR 'keɪp(ə)rə(r), -z
AM 'keɪpərər, -z

Capernaum
BR kə'pə:nɪəm
AM kə'pərniəm

capeskin
BR 'keɪpskɪn
AM 'keɪp,skɪn

Capet
BR 'kapɪt
AM 'keɪpɪt, 'kæpət
FR kapɛ

Capetian
BR kə'pi:ʃn, -z
AM kə'piʃən, -z

Cape Verde
BR ,keɪp 'və:d, + 'vɛ:d
AM ,keɪp 'vərd(i)

Cape Verdean
BR ,keɪp 'və:dɪən, + 'vɛ:dɪən, -z
AM ,keɪp 'vərdiən, -z

capful
BR 'kapfʊl, -z
AM 'kæp,fʊl, -z

capias
BR 'keɪpɪəs
AM 'keɪpiəs

capillarity
BR ,kapɪ'larɪti
AM kæpə'lɛrədi

capillary
BR kə'pɪl(ə)r|i, -ɪz
AM 'kæpə,lɛri, -z

Capistrano
BR ,kapɪ'strɑ:nəʊ
AM ,kæpə'strɑnoʊ

capital
BR 'kapɪtl, -z
AM 'kæpədl, -z

capitalisation
BR ,kapɪtl̩ʌɪ'zeɪʃn, ,kapɪtəlʌɪ'zeɪʃn
AM ,kæpədl̩ə'zeɪʃən, ,kæpədl,aɪ'zeɪʃən

capitalise
BR 'kapɪtl̩ʌɪz, 'kapɪtəlʌɪz, -ɨz, -ɪŋ, -d
AM 'kæpədl,aɪz, -ɨz, -ɪŋ, -d

capitalism
BR 'kapɪtl̩ɪzm, 'kapɪtəlɪzm
AM 'kæpədl,ɪzəm

capitalist
BR 'kapɪtl̩ɪst, 'kapɪtəlɪst, -s
AM 'kæpədl̩əst, -s

capitalistic
BR ,kapɪtl'ɪstɪk, ,kapɪtə'lɪstɪk
AM ,kæpədl'ɪstɪk

capitalistically
BR ,kapɪtl'ɪstɪkli, ,kapɪtə'lɪstɪkli
AM ',kæpədl'ɪstək(ə)li

capitalization
BR ,kapɪtl̩ʌɪ'zeɪʃn, ,kapɪtəlʌɪ'zeɪʃn
AM ,kæpədl̩ə'zeɪʃən, ,kæpədl,aɪ'zeɪʃən

capitalize
BR 'kapɪtl̩ʌɪz, 'kapɪtəlʌɪz, -ɨz, -ɪŋ, -d
AM 'kæpədl,aɪz, -ɨz, -ɪŋ, -d

capitally
BR 'kapɪtl̩i
AM 'kæpədl̩i

capitation
BR ,kapɪ'teɪʃn, -z
AM ,kæpə'teɪʃən, -z

capitol
BR 'kapɪt(ɒ)l, -z
AM 'kæpədl, -z

capitolian
BR ,kapɪ'təʊlɪən
AM ,kæpə'toʊljən, ,kæpə'toʊliən

Capitoline
BR kə'pɪtəlʌɪn, kə'pɪtl̩ʌɪn, 'kapɪtəlʌɪn, 'kapɪtl̩ʌɪn
AM 'kæpədə,laɪn

capitula
BR kə'pɪtjʉlə(*r*), kə'pɪtʃʉlə(*r*)
AM kə'pɪtʃələ

capitular
BR kə'pɪtjʉlə(r), kə'pɪtʃʉlə(r)
AM kə'pɪtʃələr

capitulary
BR kə'pɪtjʉlər|i, kə'pɪtʃʉlər|i, -ɪz
AM kə'pɪtʃə,lɛri, -z

capitulate
BR kə'pɪtjʉleɪt, kə'pɪtʃʉleɪt, -s, -ɪŋ, -ɨd
AM kə'pɪtʃə,leɪ|t, -ts, -dɪŋ, -dɨd

capitulation
BR kə,pɪtjʉ'leɪʃn, kə,pɪtʃʉ'leɪʃn
AM kə,pɪtʃə'leɪʃən

capitulator
BR kə'pɪtjʉleɪtə(r), kə'pɪtʃʉleɪtə(r), -z
AM kə'pɪtʃə,leɪdər, -z

capitulatory
BR kə'pɪtjʉlət(ə)ri, kə'pɪtʃʉlət(ə)ri
AM kə'pɪtʃələ,tɔri

capitulum
BR kə'pɪtjʉləm, kə'pɪtʃʉləm
AM kə'pɪtʃələm

Caplan
BR 'kaplən
AM 'kæplən

Caplet®
BR 'kaplɪt
AM 'kæplət

caplin
BR 'keɪplɪn, 'kaplɪn, -z
AM 'kæplən, -z

cap'n
captain
BR 'kapn
AM 'kæpn

capo
BR 'kapəʊ, -z
AM 'keɪpoʊ, 'kɑpoʊ, -z

Capo di Monte
BR ,kapəʊ dɪ 'mɒnti
AM 'kɑpoʊ di 'mɑn(t)i

capoeira
BR ,kapʊ'eɪrə(*r*)
AM ,kæpoʊ'eɪrə

capon
BR 'keɪpən, 'keɪpɒn, -z
AM 'keɪpɑn, 'keɪpən, -z

caponata
BR ,kapə(ʊ)'nɑ:tə(*r*)
AM ,kæpə'nɑdə

Capone
BR kə'pəʊn
AM kə'poʊn

caponier
BR ,kapə'nɪə(r), -z
AM ,keɪpə'nɪ(ə)r, -z

caponise
BR 'keɪpənʌɪz, 'keɪpn̩ʌɪz, -ɨz, -ɪŋ, -d
AM 'keɪpə,naɪz, -ɨz, -ɪŋ, -d

caponize
BR 'keɪpənʌɪz, 'keɪpn̩ʌɪz, -ɨz, -ɪŋ, -d
AM 'keɪpə,naɪz, -ɨz, -ɪŋ, -d

capot
BR kə'pɒt, -s, -ɪŋ, -ɨd
AM kə'pɑt, -z, -ɪŋ, -d

capo tasto
BR ,kapəʊ 'tastəʊ, -z
AM ,kɑpoʊ 'tɑstoʊ, -z

Capote
BR kə'pəʊti
AM kə'poʊdi

capote
BR kə'pəʊt, -s
AM kə'poʊt, -s

Cappadocia
BR ,kapə'dəʊsɪə(*r*), ,kapə'dəʊʃ(ɪ)ə(*r*)
AM ,kæpə'doʊʃə

Cappadocian
BR ,kapə'dəʊsɪən, ,kapə'dəʊʃɪən, ,kapə'dəʊʃn, -z
AM ,kæpə'doʊʃən, -z

cappuccino
BR ,kapʉ'tʃi:nəʊ, -z
AM ,kɑpə'tʃinoʊ, ,kæpə'tʃinoʊ, -z

cappuchino
BR ˌkapʊˈtʃiːnəʊ, -z
AM ˌkɑpəˈtʃinoʊ, ˌkæpəˈtʃinoʊ, -z

Capra
BR ˈkaprə(r)
AM ˈkæprə

Capri
BR kəˈpriː, ˈkapri
AM kəˈpri, ˈkæpri

capric
BR ˈkaprɪk
AM ˈkæprɪk

capriccio
BR kəˈprɪtʃɪəʊ, -z
AM kəˈpritʃioʊ, -z

capriccioso
BR kəˌprɪtʃɪˈəʊsəʊ
AM kəˌpritʃiˈoʊsoʊ

caprice
BR kəˈpriːs, -ɪz
AM kəˈpris, -ɪz

capricious
BR kəˈprɪʃəs
AM kəˈprɪʃəs, kəˈpriʃəs

capriciously
BR kəˈprɪʃəsli
AM kəˈprɪʃəsli, kəˈpriʃəsli

capriciousness
BR kəˈprɪʃəsnəs
AM kəˈprɪʃəsnəs, kəˈpriʃəsnəs

Capricorn
BR ˈkaprɪkɔːn
AM ˈkæprəˌkɔ(ə)rn

Capricornian
BR ˌkaprɪˈkɔːnɪən, -z
AM ˌkæprəˈkɔrniən, -z

Capricornus
BR ˌkaprɪˈkɔːnəs
AM ˌkæprəˈkɔrnəs

caprine
BR ˈkaprʌɪn
AM ˈkæˌpraɪn

capriole
BR ˈkaprɪəʊl, -z, -ɪŋ, -d
AM ˈkæpriˌoʊl, -z, -ɪŋ, -d

caproic
BR kəˈprəʊɪk, kaˈprəʊɪk
AM kəˈproʊɪk

caps.
capitals
BR kaps
AM kæps

Capsian
BR ˈkapsɪən, -z
AM ˈkæpsiən, -z

capsicum
BR ˈkapsɪkəm, -z
AM ˈkæpsəkəm, -z

capsid
BR ˈkapsɪd, -z
AM ˈkæpsəd, -z

capsizal
BR (ˌ)kapˈsʌɪzl
AM ˈkæpˌsaɪzəl, kæpˈsaɪzəl

capsize
BR (ˌ)kapˈsʌɪz, -ɪz, -ɪŋ, -d
AM ˈkæpˌsaɪz, kæpˈsaɪz, -ɪz, -ɪŋ, -d

capstan
BR ˈkapstən, -z
AM ˈkæpstən, -z

capstone
BR ˈkapstəʊn, -z
AM ˈkæpˌstoʊn, -z

capsular
BR ˈkapsjʊlə(r)
AM ˈkæps(j)ələr

capsulate
BR ˈkapsjʊlət
AM ˈkæps(j)ələt

capsule
BR ˈkapsjuːl, ˈkapsjʊl, ˈkaps(ə)l, -z
AM ˈkæpsəl, ˈkæpˌs(j)ul, -z

capsulise
BR ˈkapsjʊlʌɪz, -ɪz, -ɪŋ, -d
AM ˈkæps(j)əˌlaɪz, -ɪz, -ɪŋ, -d

capsulize
BR ˈkapsjʊlʌɪz, -ɪz, -ɪŋ, -d
AM ˈkæps(j)əˌlaɪz, -ɪz, -ɪŋ, -d

captain
BR ˈkapt(ɪ)n, -z, -ɪŋ, -d
AM ˈkæpt(ə)n, -z, -ɪŋ, -d

captaincy
BR ˈkapt(ɪ)ns|i, -ɪz
AM ˈkæpt(ə)nsi, -z

captainship
BR ˈkapt(ɪ)nʃɪp, -s
AM ˈkæpt(ə)nˌʃɪp, -s

caption
BR ˈkapʃn, -z
AM ˈkæpʃən, -z

captious
BR ˈkapʃəs
AM ˈkæpʃəs

captiously
BR ˈkapʃəsli
AM ˈkæpʃəsli

captiousness
BR ˈkapʃəsnəs
AM ˈkæpʃəsnəs

captivate
BR ˈkaptɪveɪt, -s, -ɪŋ, -ɪd
AM ˈkæptəˌveɪ|t, -ts, -dɪŋ, -dɪd

captivatingly
BR ˈkaptɪveɪtɪŋli
AM ˈkæptəˌveɪdɪŋli

captivation
BR ˌkaptɪˈveɪʃn
AM ˌkæptəˈveɪʃən

captive
BR ˈkaptɪv, -z
AM ˈkæptɪv, -z

captivity
BR kapˈtɪvɪti
AM kæpˈtɪvɪdi

captor
BR ˈkaptə(r), -z
AM ˈkæptər, ˈkæpˌtɔ(ə)r, -z

capture
BR ˈkaptʃə(r), -z, -ɪŋ, -d
AM ˈkæp(t)ʃər, -z, -ɪŋ, -d

capturer
BR ˈkaptʃ(ə)rə(r), -z
AM ˈkæp(t)ʃərər, -z

Capua
BR ˈkapjʊə(r)
AM ˈkæpjuə

capuche
BR kəˈpuː(t)ʃ, -ɪz
AM kəˈpu(t)ʃ, -əz

Capuchin
BR ˈkapjʊ(t)ʃɪn, kəˈpuː(t)ʃɪn, -z
AM ˈkæpjə(t)ʃən, kəˈp(j)u(t)ʃən, -z

Capulet
BR ˈkaplʊlɪt
AM ˈkæpjələt

capybara
BR ˌkapɪˈbɑːrə(r)
AM ˈkæpəˌbɛrə

car
BR kɑː(r), -z
AM kɑr, -z

Cara
BR ˈkɑːrə(r)
AM ˈkɛrə

carabid
BR ˈkarebɪd, -z
AM ˈkɛrəˌbɪd, -z

carabineer
BR ˌkarəbɪˈnɪə(r), -z
AM ˌkɛrəbəˈnɪ(ə)r, -z

carabiner
BR ˌkarəˈbiːnə(r), -z
AM ˌkɛrəˈbinər, -z

carabiniere
BR ˌkarəbɪˈnjɛːri
AM ˌkɛrəbəˈnjɛri

carabinieri
BR ˌkarəbɪˈnjɛːri
AM ˌkɛrəbəˈnjɛri

caracal
BR ˈkarəkal, -z
AM ˈkɛrəˌkæl, -z

Caracalla
BR ˌkarəˈkalə(r)
AM ˌkɛrəˈkɑlə

caracara
BR ˌkarəˈkɑːrə(r), -z
AM ˌkɛrəˈkɑrə, -z

Caracas
BR kəˈrakəs
AM kəˈrɑkəs, kəˈrækəs

caracole
BR ˈkarəkəʊl, -z
AM ˈkɛrəˌkoʊl, -z

Caractacus
BR kəˈraktəkəs
AM kəˈrɑktəkəs

caracul
BR ˈkarək(ʌ)l
AM ˈkɛrəkəl

Caradoc
BR kəˈradək, kəˈradɒk
AM ˈkɛrədɑk

Caradog
BR kəˈradɒg
AM ˈkɛrəˌdɔg, ˈkɛrəˌdɑg

carafe
BR kəˈraf, kəˈrɑːf, -s
AM kəˈræf, -s

caragana
BR ˌkarəˈgɑːnə(r)
AM ˌkɛrəˈgɑnə

Carajás
BR kəˈrɑːhəs
AM kəˈrɑhəs
PORT kɑrɑˈʒaʃ

caramba
BR kəˈrambə(r)
AM kəˈrɑmbə

carambola
BR ˌkarəmˈbəʊlə(r), ˌkarm̩ˈbəʊlə(r), -z
AM ˌkɛrəmˈboʊlə, -z

caramel
BR ˈkarəmɛl, ˈkarəm(ə)l, ˈkarm̩(ə)l, -z
AM ˈkɑrməl, ˈkɛrəməl, ˈkɛrəˌmɛl, -z

caramelisation
BR ˌkarəməlʌɪˈzeɪʃn, ˌkarm̩əlʌɪˈzeɪʃn, ˌkarəml̩ʌɪˈzeɪʃn, ˌkarm̩l̩ʌɪˈzeɪʃn
AM ˌkɑrmələˈzeɪʃən, ˌkɑrməˌlaɪˈzeɪʃən

caramelise
BR ˈkarəməlʌɪz, ˈkaraml̩ʌɪz, ˈkarm̩l̩ʌɪz, -ɪz, -ɪŋ, -d
AM ˈkɑrməˌlaɪz, -ɪz, -ɪŋ, -d

caramelization
BR ˌkarəməlʌɪˈzeɪʃn, ˌkarm̩əlʌɪˈzeɪʃn, ˌkarəml̩ʌɪˈzeɪʃn, ˌkarm̩l̩ʌɪˈzeɪʃn
AM ˌkɑrmələˈzeɪʃən, ˌkɑrməˌlaɪˈzeɪʃən

caramelize
BR ˈkarəməlʌɪz, ˈkarəml̩ʌɪz, ˈkarm̩l̩ʌɪz, -ɪz, -ɪŋ, -d
AM ˈkɑrməˌlaɪz, -ɪz, -ɪŋ, -d

carangid
BR kəˈrandʒɪd, -z

AM kə'rændʒəd, kə'ræŋgəd, -z
carapace
BR 'karəpeɪs, -ɨz
AM 'kɛrə,peɪs, -ɨz
carat
BR 'karət, -s
AM 'kɛrət, -s
Caratacus
BR kə'ratəkəs
AM kə'rɑdəkəs
Caravaggio
BR ,karə'vadʒɪəʊ
AM ,kɛrə'vɑdʒioʊ
caravan
BR 'karəvan, -z
AM 'kɛrə,væn, -z
caravanette
BR ,karəva'nɛt, ,karəvə'nɛt, -s
AM ,kɛrəvə'nɛt, -s
caravanner
BR 'karəvanə(r), -z
AM 'kɛrə,vænər, -z
caravansary
BR ,karə'vans(ə)r|i, -ɪz
AM ,kɛrə'vænsəri, -z
caravanserai
BR ,karə'van|sərʌɪ, ,karə'van|s(ə)ri, -sərʌɪz\-s(ə)rɪz
AM ,kærə'vænsə,raɪ, -z
caravansery
BR ,karə'vans(ə)r|i, -ɪz
AM ,kɛrə'vænsəri, -z
caravel
BR 'karəvɛl, ,karə'vɛl, -z
AM 'kɛrəvɛl, ,kɛrə'vɛl, -z
caraway
BR 'karəweɪ, -z
AM 'kɛrə,weɪ, -z
carb
BR kɑ:b, -z
AM karb, -z
carbamate
BR 'kɑ:bəmeɪt
AM 'karbə,meɪt
carbazole
BR 'kɑ:bəzəʊl
AM 'karbə,zoʊl
carbide
BR 'kɑ:bʌɪd, -z
AM 'kar,baɪd, -z
carbine
BR 'kɑ:bʌɪn, -z
AM 'kar,baɪn, karbin, -z
carbineer
BR ,kɑ:bɪ'nɪə(r), -z
AM ,karbə'nɪ(ə)r, -z
carbohydrate
BR ,kɑ:bə(ʊ)'hʌɪdreɪt, -s
AM ,karbə'haɪd,reɪt, -s
carbolic
BR kɑ:'bɒlɪk
AM kar'bɑlɪk
carbon
BR 'kɑ:bən, -z
AM 'karbən, -z
carbonaceous
BR ,kɑ:bə'neɪʃəs
AM ,karbə'neɪʃəs
carbonade
BR ,kɑ:bə'neɪd, ,kɑ:bə'nɑ:d, -z
AM ,karbə'neɪd, -z
carbonado
BR ,kɑ:bə'neɪdəʊ, ,kɑ:bə'nɑ:dəʊ, -z
AM ,karbə'neɪdoʊ, -z
carbonara
BR ,kɑ:bə'nɑ:rə(*r*)
AM ,karbə'nɛrə
carbonate[1]
noun
BR 'kɑ:bəneɪt, 'kɑ:bənət, -s
AM 'karbənət, -s
carbonate[2]
verb
BR 'kɑ:bəneɪt, -s, -ɪŋ, -ɨd
AM 'karbə,neɪ|t, -ts, -dɪŋ, -dɨd
carbonation
BR ,kɑ:bə'neɪʃn
AM ,karbə'neɪʃən
carbonatite
BR kɑ:'bɒnətʌɪt
AM ,kar'bɑnə,taɪt
carbonic
BR kɑ:'bɒnɪk
AM kar'bɑnɪk
carboniferous
BR ,kɑ:bə'nɪf(ə)rəs
AM ,karbə'nɪf(ə)rəs
carbonisation
BR ,kɑ:bənʌɪ'zeɪʃn, ,kɑ:bn̩ʌɪ'zeɪʃn
AM ,karbənə'zeɪʃən, ,karbə,naɪ'zeɪʃən
carbonise
BR 'kɑ:bənʌɪz, 'kɑ:bn̩ʌɪz, -ɨz, -ɪŋ, -d
AM 'karbə,naɪz, -ɨz, -ɪŋ, -d
carbonization
BR ,kɑ:bənʌɪ'zeɪʃn, ,kɑ:bn̩ʌɪ'zeɪʃn
AM ,karbənə'zeɪʃən, ,karbə,naɪ'zeɪʃən
carbonize
BR 'kɑ:bənʌɪz, 'kɑ:bn̩ʌɪz, -ɨz, -ɪŋ, -d
AM 'karbə,naɪz, -ɨz, -ɪŋ, -d
carbon monoxide
BR ,kɑ:bən mə'nɒksʌɪd, + mɒ'nɒksʌɪd
AM ,karbən mə'nɑksaɪd
carbonyl
BR 'kɑ:bənɪl, 'kɑ:bənʌɪl, -z
AM 'karbə,nɪl, -z
Carborundum®
BR ,kɑ:bə'rʌndəm
AM ,karbə'rəndəm
carboxyl
BR kɑ:'bɒksɪl, kɑ:'bɒksʌɪl, -z
AM kar'bɑksl, -z
carboxylase
BR kɑ:'bɒksɨleɪz
AM ,kar'bɑksə,leɪz
carboxylate
BR kɑ:'bɒksɨleɪt
AM ,kar'bɑksə,leɪt
carboxylic
BR ,kɑ:bɒk'sɪlɪk
AM ,kar,bɑk'sɪlɪk
carboy
BR 'kɑ:bɔɪ, -z
AM 'kar,bɔɪ, -z
carbuncle
BR 'kɑ:bʌŋkl, -z
AM 'kar,bəŋkəl, -z
carbuncular
BR kɑ:'bʌŋkjʉlə(r)
AM kar'bəŋkjələr
carburant
BR 'kɑ:bjʉrənt, 'kɑ:bjʉrn̩t, -s
AM 'karbərənt, -s
carburation
BR ,kɑ:bjʉ'reɪʃn, ,kɑ:bə'reɪʃn, ,kɑ:bjʉ'reɪʃn
AM ,karb(j)ə'reɪʃən
carburet
BR 'kɑ:bjʉrət, 'kɑ:bərət, -s, -ɨd
AM 'karbə,rɛt, -ts, -dəd
carburetor
BR ,kɑ:bə'rɛtə(r), ,kɑ:bjʉ'rɛtə(r), -z
AM 'karbə,reɪdər, -z
carburetter
BR ,kɑ:bə'rɛtə(r), ,kɑ:bjʉ'rɛtə(r), -z
AM 'karbə,reɪdər, -z
carburettor
BR ,kɑ:bə'rɛtə(r), ,kɑ:bjʉ'rɛtə(r), -z
AM 'karbə,reɪdər, -z
carcajou
BR 'kɑ:kə(d)ʒu:
AM 'karkə,(d)ʒu
carcase
BR 'kɑ:kəs, -ɨz
AM 'karkəs, -əz
carcass
BR 'kɑ:kəs, -ɨz
AM 'karkəs, -əz
Carcassonne
BR ,kɑ:kə'sɒn
AM ,karkə'sɑn
Carchemish
BR 'kɑ:kəmɪʃ, kɑ:'kɛmɪʃ, kɑ:'ki:mɪʃ
AM 'karkə,mɪʃ
carcinogen
BR kɑ:'sɪnədʒ(ə)n, 'kɑ:sɪnədʒ(ə)n, 'kɑ:sn̩ədʒ(ə)n, -z
AM kar'sɪnədʒən, 'karsn̩ə,dʒɛn, -z
carcinogenesis
BR ,kɑ:s(ɪ)nə'dʒɛnɪsɪs, ,kɑ:sn̩ə'dʒɛnɪsɪs
AM ¦kars(ə)nə'dʒɛnəsəs, ¦karsn̩oʊ'dʒɛnəsəs
carcinogenic
BR ,kɑ:s(ɪ)nə'dʒɛnɪk, ,kɑ:sn̩ə'dʒɛnɪk, kɑ:,sɪnə'dʒɛnɪk
AM ¦kars(ə)nə'dʒɛnɪk, ¦karsn̩oʊ'dʒɛnɪk
carcinogenically
BR ,kɑ:s(ɪ)nə'dʒɛnɨkli, ,kɑ:sn̩ə'dʒɛnɨkli, kɑ:,sɪnə'dʒɛnɨkli
AM ¦kars(ə)nə'dʒɛnək(ə)li ¦karsn̩oʊ'dʒɛnək(ə)li
carcinogenicity
BR ,kɑ:s(ɪ)nə(ʊ)dʒɛ'nɪsɨti, ,kɑ:sn̩ə(ʊ)dʒɛ'nɪsɨti, kɑ:,sɪnə(ʊ)dʒɛ'nɪsɨti
AM ,karsn̩oʊdʒɛ'nɪsɨdi, ,kars(ə)nədʒɛ'nɪsɨdi
carcinoma
BR ,kɑ:sɪ'nəʊmə(*r*), ,kɑ:sn'əʊmə(*r*), -z
AM ,karsə'noʊmə, -z
carcinomatous
BR ,kɑ:sɪ'nəʊmətəs, ,kɑ:sn'əʊmətəs
AM ,karsə'nɑmədəs
card
BR kɑ:d, -z, -ɪŋ, -ɨd
AM kard, -z, -ɪŋ, -əd
cardamom
BR 'kɑ:dəməm
AM 'kardəməm
cardamum
BR 'kɑ:dəməm
AM 'kardəməm
cardboard
BR 'kɑ:dbɔ:d
AM 'kard,bɔ(ə)rd
carder
BR 'kɑ:də(r), -z
AM 'kardər, -z
Cardew
BR 'kɑ:dju:, 'kɑ:dʒu:
AM 'kardju, 'kardʒu
cardholder
BR 'kɑ:d,həʊldə(r), -z
AM 'kard,(h)oʊldər, -z
cardiac
BR 'kɑ:dɪak, -s
AM 'kardi,æk, -s
cardiacal
BR kɑ:'dʌɪəkl

AM kɑr'daɪəkəl
cardie
BR 'kɑːd|i, -ɪz
AM 'kɑrdi, -z
Cardiff
BR 'kɑːdɪf
AM 'kɑrdəf
cardigan
BR 'kɑːdɪg(ə)n, -z
AM 'kɑrdəgən, -z
Cardin
BR 'kɑːdã, 'kɑːdan
AM kɑr'dæn
cardinal
BR 'kɑːdɪn(ə)l, 'kɑːdn̩(ə)l, -z
AM 'kɑrdn̩əl, 'kɑrdənəl, -z
cardinalate
BR 'kɑːdɪnələt, 'kɑːdɪnl̩ət, 'kɑːdn̩ələt, 'kɑːdn̩l̩ət, -s
AM 'kɑrdn̩ələt, 'kɑrdənələt, -s
cardinality
BR ˌkɑːdɪ'nalɪti
AM ˌkɑrdə'nælədi, ˌkɑrdn'ælədi
cardinally
BR 'kɑːdɪnl̩i, 'kɑːdɪnəli, 'kɑːdn̩l̩i, 'kɑːdn̩əli
AM 'kɑrdn̩əli, 'kɑrdənəli
cardinalship
BR 'kɑːdɪn(ə)lʃɪp, 'kɑːdn̩(ə)lʃɪp, -s
AM 'kɑrdn̩əlˌʃɪp, 'kɑrdənəlˌʃɪp, -s
cardiogram
BR 'kɑːdɪə(ʊ)gram, -z
AM 'kɑrdioʊˌgræm, 'kɑrdiəˌgræm, -z
cardiograph
BR 'kɑːdɪə(ʊ)grɑːf, 'kɑːdɪə(ʊ)graf, -s
AM 'kɑrdioʊˌgræf, 'kɑrdiəˌgræf, -s
cardiographer
BR ˌkɑːdɪ'ɒgrəfə(r), -z
AM ˌkɑrdi'ɑgrəfər, -z
cardiography
BR ˌkɑːdɪ'ɒgrəfi
AM ˌkɑrdi'ɑgrəfi
cardiologist
BR ˌkɑːdɪ'ɒlədʒɪst, -s
AM ˌkɑrdi'ɑlədʒəst, -s
cardiology
BR ˌkɑːdɪ'ɒlədʒi
AM ˌkɑrdi'ɑlədʒi
cardiometer
BR ˌkɑːdɪ'ɒmɪtə(r), -z
AM ˌkɑrdi'ɑmədər, -z
cardiopulmonary
BR ˌkɑːdɪəʊ'pʊlmən(ə)ri
AM ˌkɑrdioʊ'pʊlməˌnɛri
cardiovascular
BR ˌkɑːdɪəʊ'vaskjʉlə(r)
AM ˌkɑrdioʊ'væskjələr, ˌkɑrdiə'væskjələr
cardoon
BR ˌkɑː'duːn, -z
AM ˌkɑr'dun, -z
cardphone
BR 'kɑːdfəʊn, -z
AM 'kɑrdˌfoʊn, -z
cardpunch
BR 'kɑːdpʌn(t)ʃ, -ɪz
AM 'kɑrdˌpən(t)ʃ, -əz
cardsharp
BR 'kɑːdʃɑːp, -s
AM 'kɑrdˌʃɑrp, -s
Cardus
BR 'kɑːdəs
AM 'kɑrdəs
Cardwell
BR 'kɑːdw(ɛ)l
AM 'kɑrdˌwɛl
cardy
BR 'kɑːd|i, -ɪz
AM 'kɑrdi, -z
care
BR kɛː(r), -z, -ɪŋ, -d
AM kɛ(ə)r, -z, -ɪŋ, -d
careen
BR kə'riːn, -z, -ɪŋ, -d
AM kə'rin, -z, -ɪŋ, -d
careenage
BR kə'riːnɪdʒ
AM kə'rinɪdʒ
career
BR kə'rɪə(r), -z, -ɪŋ, -d
AM kə'rɪ(ə)r, -z, -ɪŋ, -d
careerism
BR kə'rɪərɪz(ə)m
AM kə'rɪ(ə)ˌrɪzəm
careerist
BR kə'rɪərɪst, -s
AM kə'rɪrəst, -s
carefree
BR 'kɛːfriː, ˌkɛː'friː
AM ˌkɛr'fri
carefreely
BR 'kɛːfriːli, ˌkɛː'friːli
AM ˌkɛr'frili
carefreeness
BR 'kɛːfriːnɪs, ˌkɛː'friːnɪs
AM ˌkɛr'frinɪs
careful
BR 'kɛː|f(ʊ)l, -f(ʊ)lɪst\-fl̩ɪst
AM 'kɛrfəl, -əst
carefully
BR 'kɛːf(ʊ)li, 'kɛfl̩i
AM 'kɛrf(ə)li
carefulness
BR 'kɛːf(ʊ)lnəs
AM 'kɛrfəlnəs
careless
BR 'kɛːləs
AM 'kɛrləs
carelessly
BR 'kɛːləsli
AM 'kɛrləsli
carelessness
BR 'kɛːləsnəs
AM 'kɛrləsnəs
carer
BR 'kɛːrə(r), -z
AM 'kɛrər, -z
caress
BR kə'rɛs, -ɪz, -ɪŋ, -t
AM kə'rɛs, -əz, -ɪŋ, -t
caressingly
BR kə'rɛsɪŋli
AM kə'rɛsɪŋli
caret
BR 'karɪt, -s
AM 'kɛrət, -s
caretake
BR 'kɛːteɪk, -s, -ɪŋ
AM 'kɛrˌteɪk, -s, -ɪŋ
caretaker
BR 'kɛːˌteɪkə(r), -z
AM 'kɛrˌteɪkər, -z
Carew
BR kə'ruː, 'kɛːri
AM kə'ru, 'kɛru
careworn
BR 'kɛːwɔːn
AM 'kɛrˌwɔ(ə)rn
Carey
BR 'kɛːri
AM 'kɛri
carezza
BR kə'rɛtsə(*r*)
AM kə'rɛtsə, kə'rɛzə
carfare
BR 'kɑːfɛː(r)
AM 'kɑrˌfɛ(ə)r
carfax
BR 'kɑːfaks, -ɪz
AM 'kɑrˌfæks, -əz
carferry
BR 'kɑːˌfɛr|i, -ɪz
AM 'kɑrˌfɛri, -z
carful
BR 'kɑːfʊl, -z
AM 'kɑrˌfʊl, -z
Cargill
BR 'kɑːgɪl, kɑː'gɪl
AM 'kɑrˌgɪl, 'kɑrgəl
cargo
BR 'kɑːgəʊ, -z
AM 'kɑrgoʊ, -z
carhop
BR 'kɑːhɒp, -s
AM 'kɑrˌ(h)ɑp, -s
Caria
BR 'kɛːrɪə(*r*)
AM 'kɛriə
cariama
BR ˌkarɪ'ɑːmə(*r*), -z
AM ˌkɛri'ɑmə, -z
Carian
BR 'karɪən, -z
AM 'kɛriən, -z
Carib
BR 'karɪb, -z
AM 'kɛrəb, -z
Caribbean
BR ˌkarɪ'biːən, kə'rɪbɪən
AM ˌkɛrə'biən, kə'rɪbiən
Caribbean Sea
BR ˌkarɪbiːən 'siː, kəˌrɪbɪən +
AM ˌkɛrə'biən 'si, kə'rɪbiən +
caribou
BR 'karɪbuː, -z
AM 'kɛrəˌbu, -z
caricatural
BR ˌkarɪkə'tʃʊərəl, ˌkarɪkə'tʃʊərl̩, ˌkarɪkəˌtjʊərəl, ˌkarɪkə'tjʊərl̩, ˌkarɪkə'tʃɔːrəl, ˌkarɪkə'tʃɔːrl̩, ˌkarɪkəˌtjɔːrəl, ˌkarɪkə'tjɔːrl̩
AM ˌkɛrəkə'tʃʊrəl, 'kɛrəkətʃərəl
caricature
BR 'karɪkətʃʊə(r), 'karɪkətjʊə(r), 'karɪkətʃɔː(r), 'karɪkətjɔː(r), -z, -ɪŋ, -d
AM 'kɛrəkəˌtʃʊ(ə)r, 'kɛrəkətʃər, -z, -ɪŋ, -d
caricaturist
BR 'karɪkətʃʊərɪst, 'karɪkətjʊərɪst, 'karɪkətʃɔːrɪst, 'karɪkətjɔːrɪst, -s
AM 'kɛrəkəˌtʃʊrəst, -s
CARICOM
BR 'karɪkɒm
AM 'kɛrəˌkɑm
caries
BR 'kɛːriːz
AM 'kɛriz
carillon
BR 'karɪljən, 'karl̩jən, 'karɪlɒn, 'karl̩ɒn, kə'rɪljən, kə'rɪljɒn, -z
AM 'kɛrəˌlɑn, 'kɛrələn, -z
carina
BR kə'riːnə(r), kə'rʌɪnə(*r*), -z
AM kə'rinə, kə'raɪnə, -z
carinae
BR kə'riːniː, kə'riːnʌɪ, kə'rʌɪniː, kə'rʌɪnʌɪ
AM kə'rini, kə'riˌnaɪ, kə'raɪni, kə'raɪˌnaɪ
carinal
BR kə'riːnl, kə'rʌɪnl
AM kə'rinəl, kə'raɪnəl
carinate[1]
adjective
BR 'karɪneɪt, 'karɪnət
AM 'kɛrənət, 'kɛrəˌneɪt

carinate²
verb
BR ˈkarɨneɪt, -s, -ɪŋ, -ɨd
AM ˈkɛrəˌneɪ|t, -ts, -dɪŋ, -dɨd

caring
BR ˈkɛːrɪŋ
AM ˈkɛrɪŋ

Carinthia
BR kəˈrɪnθɪə(r)
AM kəˈrɪnθiə

carioca
BR ˌkarɪˈəʊkə(r)
AM ˌkɛriˈoʊkə

cariogenic
BR ˌkarɪəˈdʒɛnɪk
AM ˌkɛriəˈdʒɛnɪk, ˌkɛrioʊˈdʒɛnɪk

carious
BR ˈkɛːrɪəs
AM ˈkɛrɪəs

Carisbrooke
BR ˈkarɨzbrʊk, ˈkarɪsbrʊk
AM ˈkɛrəsˌbrʊk

carking
BR ˈkɑːkɪŋ
AM ˈkɑrkɪŋ

Carl
BR kɑːl
AM kɑrl

Carla
BR ˈkɑːlə(r)
AM ˈkɑrlə

Carleton
BR ˈkɑːlt(ə)n
AM ˈkɑrltən

Carlin
BR ˈkɑːlɪn
AM ˈkɑrln

carline
BR ˈkɑːlʌɪn, ˈkɑːlɪn, -z
AM ˈkɑrˌlaɪn, -z

Carlisle
BR (ˌ)kɑːˈlʌɪl, ˈkɑːlʌɪl
AM ˈkɑrˈlaɪl

Carlo
BR ˈkɑːləʊ
AM ˈkɑrloʊ

carload
BR ˈkɑːləʊd, -z
AM ˈkɑrˌloʊd, -z

Carlovingian
BR ˌkɑːlə(ʊ)ˈvɪn(d)ʒɪən, ˌkɑːlə(ʊ)ˈvɪn(d)ʒ(ə)n, -z
AM ˌkɑrləˈvɪndʒ(i)ən, -z

Carlow
BR ˈkɑːləʊ
AM ˈkɑrloʊ

Carlsbad
BR ˈkɑːlzbad
AM ˈkɑrlzˌbæd, ˈkɑrlzˌbɑd

Carlsberg®
BR ˈkɑːlzbəːg
AM ˈkɑrlzˌbərg

Carlson
BR ˈkɑːlsn
AM ˈkɑrlsən

Carlton
BR ˈkɑːlt(ə)n
AM ˈkɑrltən

Carly
BR ˈkɑːli
AM ˈkɑrli

Carlyle
BR (ˌ)kɑːˈlʌɪl
AM ˈkɑrˌlaɪl

carmaker
BR ˈkɑːˌmeɪkə(r), -z
AM ˈkɑrˌmeɪkər, -z

Carman
BR ˈkɑːmən
AM ˈkɑrmən

carman
BR ˈkɑːmən
AM ˈkɑrmən

Carmarthen
BR kəˈmɑːðn
AM ˌkɑrˈmɑrðən

Carmel
BR ˈkɑːml, ˈkɑːmɛl, (ˌ)kɑːˈmɛl
AM kɑrˈmɛl

Carmelite
BR ˈkɑːmɨlʌɪt, ˈkɑːml̩ʌɪt, -s
AM ˈkɑrməˌlaɪt, -s

Carmen
BR ˈkɑːmən, ˈkɑːmɛn
AM ˈkɑrmən

carmen
BR ˈkɑːmən
AM ˈkɑrmən

Carmichael
BR kɑːˈmʌɪkl, ˈkɑːmʌɪkl
AM ˈkɑrˌmaɪkl

Carmina Burana
BR kɑːˌmiːnə bʉˈrɑːnə(r)
AM kɑrˌminə b(j)uˈrɑnə

carminative
BR ˈkɑːmɨnətɪv, ˈkɑːmn̩ətɪv, -z
AM kɑrˈmɪnədɪv, ˈkɑrməˌneɪdɪv, -z

carmine
BR ˈkɑːmʌɪn
AM ˈkɑrmaɪn

Carnaby Street
BR ˈkɑːnəbɪ striːt
AM ˈkɑrnəbi ˌstrit

Carnac
BR ˈkɑːnak
AM ˈkɑrˌnæk

carnage
BR ˈkɑːnɪdʒ
AM ˈkɑrnɪdʒ

carnal
BR ˈkɑːnl
AM ˈkɑrnəl

carnalise
BR ˈkɑːnəlʌɪz, ˈkɑːnl̩ʌɪz, -ɨz, -ɪŋ, -d
AM ˈkɑrnəˌlaɪz, -ɨz, -ɪŋ, -d

carnality
BR kɑːˈnalɨti
AM kɑrˈnælədi

carnalize
BR ˈkɑːnəlʌɪz, ˈkɑːnl̩ʌɪz, -ɨz, -ɪŋ, -d
AM ˈkɑrnəˌlaɪz, -ɨz, -ɪŋ, -d

carnally
BR ˈkɑːnəli, ˈkɑːnl̩i
AM ˈkɑrnəli

Carnap
BR ˈkɑːnap
AM ˈkɑrnəp

Carnarvon
BR kəˈnɑːvn
AM kəˈnɑrvn

carnassial
BR kɑːˈnasɪəl, -z
AM kɑrˈnæsiəl, -z

Carnatic
BR kɑːˈnatɪk
AM kɑrˈnædɪk

carnation
BR kɑːˈneɪʃn, -z
AM kɑrˈneɪʃən, -z

carnauba
BR kɑːˈnɔːbə(r), kɑːˈnaʊbə(r)
AM kɑrˈnɔbə, kɑrˈnɑbə

Carné
BR kɑːˈneɪ
AM kɑrˈneɪ

Carnegie
BR kɑːˈniːgi
AM ˈkɑrnəgi, kɑrˈneɪgi

carnelian
BR kɑːˈniːlɪən, -z
AM kɑrˈniliən, -z

carnet
BR ˈkɑːneɪ, -z
AM kɑrˈneɪ, -z

Carney
BR ˈkɑːni
AM ˈkɑrni

Carnforth
BR ˈkɑːnfɔːθ
AM ˈkɑrnˌfɔ(ə)rθ

carnival
BR ˈkɑːnɨvl, -z
AM ˈkɑrnəvəl, -z

Carnivora
BR kɑːˈnɪv(ə)rə(r)
AM kɑrˈnɪv(ə)rə

carnivore
BR ˈkɑːnɨvɔː(r), -z
AM ˈkɑrnəˌvɔ(ə)r, -z

carnivorous
BR kɑːˈnɪv(ə)rəs
AM kɑrˈnɪv(ə)rəs

carnivorously
BR kɑːˈnɪv(ə)rəsli
AM kɑrˈnɪv(ə)rəsli

carnivorousness
BR kɑːˈnɪv(ə)rəsnəs
AM kɑrˈnɪv(ə)rəsnəs

Carnot
BR ˈkɑːnəʊ
AM kɑrˈnoʊ

Carnoustie
BR kɑːˈnuːsti
AM kɑrˈnusdi

carny
BR ˈkɑːni
AM ˈkɑrni

carob
BR ˈkarəb, -z
AM ˈkɛrəb, -z

carol
BR ˈkarəl, ˈkarl̩, -z, -ɪŋ, -d
AM ˈkɛrəl, -z, -ɪŋ, -d

Carole
BR ˈkarəl, ˈkarl̩
AM ˈkɛrəl

Carolean
BR ˌkarəˈliːən, -z
AM ˈkɛrəˌlin, -z

caroler
BR ˈkarələ(r), ˈkarl̩ə(r), -z
AM ˈkɛrələr, -z

Carolina
BR ˌkarəˈlʌɪnə(r), -z
AM ˌkɛrəˈlaɪnə, -z

Caroline
BR ˈkarəlʌɪn, ˈkarəlɪn, ˈkarl̩ɪn
AM ˈkɛrəˌlaɪn, ˈkɛrələn

Carolingian
BR ˌkarəˈlɪŋgɪən, ˌkarəˈlɪn(d)ʒɪən, -z
AM ˌkɛrəˈlɪn(d)ʒ(i)ən, -z

caroller
BR ˈkarələ(r), ˈkarl̩ə(r), -z
AM ˈkɛrələr, -z

carolus
BR ˈkarələs, -ɨz
AM ˈkɛrələs, -əz

Carolyn
BR ˈkarəlɪn, ˈkarl̩ɪn
AM ˈkɛrələn

carom
BR ˈkarəm, ˈkarm̩, -z, -ɪŋ, -d
AM ˈkɛrəm, -z, -ɪŋ, -d

Caron
BR ˈkarən, ˈkarn̩, kəˈrɒn
AM ˈkɛrən

carotene
BR ˈkarətiːn
AM ˈkɛrəˌtin

carotenoid
BR kəˈrɒtɨnɔɪd
AM kəˈrɑtnˈɔɪd

Carothers
BR kə'rʌðəz
AM kə'rəðərz
carotid
BR kə'rɒtɪd
AM kə'rɑdəd
carousal
BR kə'raʊzl, -z
AM kə'raʊzəl, -z
carouse
BR kə'raʊz, -ɪz, -ɪŋ, -d
AM kə'raʊz, -əz, -ɪŋ, -d
carousel
BR ˌkarə'sɛl, -z
AM ˌkɛrə'sɛl, -z
carouser
BR kə'raʊzə(r), -z
AM kə'raʊzər, -z
carp
BR kɑːp, -s, -ɪŋ, -t
AM kɑrp, -s, -ɪŋ, -t
Carpaccio
BR kɑː'patʃɪəʊ
AM kɑr'pɑtʃ(i)oʊ
carpal
BR 'kɑːpl, -z
AM 'kɑrpəl, -z
carpark
BR 'kɑːpɑːk, -s, -ɪŋ
AM 'kɑrˌpɑrk, -s, -ɪŋ
Carpathian
BR kɑː'peɪθɪən, -z
AM kɑr'peɪθiən, -z
carpe diem
BR ˌkɑːpɪ 'diːɛm
AM ˌkɑrpə di'ɛm
carpel
BR 'kɑːpl, -z
AM 'kɑrpəl, -z
carpellary
BR 'kɑːpəl(ə)ri, 'kɑːpl̩(ə)ri
AM 'kɑrpəˌlɛri
Carpentaria
BR ˌkɑːp(ə)n'tɛːrɪə(r), ˌkɑːpɛn'tɛːrɪə(r)
AM ˌkɑrpən'tɛriə
carpenter
BR 'kɑːp(ɪ)ntə(r), -z
AM 'kɑrpən(t)ər, -z
carpentry
BR 'kɑːp(ɪ)ntri
AM 'kɑrpəntri
carper
BR 'kɑːpə(r), -z
AM 'kɑrpər, -z
carpet
BR 'kɑːp|ɪt, -ɪts, -ɪtɪŋ, -ɪtɪd
AM 'kɑrpə|t, -ts, -dɪŋ, -dəd
carpetbag
BR 'kɑːpɪtbag, -z, -ɪŋ
AM 'kɑrpətˌbæg, -z, -ɪŋ
carpetbagger
BR 'kɑːpɪtˌbagə(r), -z
AM 'kɑrpətˌbægər, -z
carpeting
BR 'kɑːpɪtɪŋ, -z
AM 'kɑrpədɪŋ, -z
carphology
BR kɑː'fɒlədʒi
AM kɑr'fɑlədʒi
carpi
BR 'kɑːpʌɪ
AM 'kɑrˌpaɪ
carpology
BR kɑː'pɒlədʒi
AM kɑr'pɑlədʒi
carport
BR 'kɑːpɔːt, -s
AM 'kɑrˌpɔ(ə)rt, -s
carpus
BR 'kɑːpəs
AM 'kɑrpəs
Carr
BR kɑː(r)
AM kɑr
carrack
BR 'karək, -s
AM 'kɛrək, -s
carrageen
BR 'karəgiːn, ˌkarə'giːn
AM ˌkɛrə'gin, 'kɛrəˌgin
carragheen
BR 'karəgiːn, ˌkarə'giːn
AM ˌkɛrə'gin, 'kɛrəˌgin
Carrara
BR kə'rɑːrə(r)
AM kə'rɑrə, kə'rɛrə
carraway
BR 'karəweɪ, -z
AM 'kɛrəˌweɪ, -z
carrel
BR 'karəl, 'karl̩, -z
AM 'kɛrəl, -z
Carreras
BR kə'rɛːrəs
AM kə'rɛrəs
carriage
BR 'kar|ɪdʒ, -ɪdʒɪz
AM 'kɛrɪdʒ, -ɪz
carriageway
BR 'karɪdʒweɪ, -z
AM 'kɛrɪdʒˌweɪ, -z
carrick
BR 'karɪk
AM 'kɛrɪk
Carrickfergus
BR ˌkarɪk'fəːgəs
AM ˌkɛrək'fərgəs
Carrie
BR 'kari
AM 'kɛri
carrier
BR 'karɪə(r), -z
AM 'kɛriər, -z
Carrington
BR 'karɪŋt(ə)n
AM 'kɛrɪŋtən
carriole
BR 'karɪəʊl, -z
AM 'kɛrioʊl, -z
carrion
BR 'karɪən
AM 'kɛriən
Carroll
BR 'karəl, 'karl̩
AM 'kɛrəl
Carron
BR 'karən, 'karn̩
AM 'kɛrən
carronade
BR ˌkarə'neɪd, -z
AM ˌkɛrə'neɪd, -z
carrot
BR 'karət, -s
AM 'kɛrət, -s
carroty
BR 'karəti
AM 'kɛrədi
carrousel
BR ˌkarə'sɛl, -z
AM ˌkɛrə'sɛl, -z
Carruthers
BR kə'rʌðəz, 'krɪðəz
AM kə'rəðərz
carry
BR 'kar|i, -ɪz, -ɪɪŋ, -ɪd
AM 'kɛri, -z, -ɪŋ, -d
carryall
BR 'karɪɔːl, -z
AM 'kɛriˌɔl, 'kɛriˌɑl, -z
carrycot
BR 'karɪkɒt, -s
AM 'kɛriˌkɑt, -s
carse
BR kɑːs, -ɪz
AM kɑrs, -əz
Carshalton
BR kɑː'ʃɔːlt(ə)n
AM kɑr'ʃɔltən, kɑr'ʃɑltən
carsick
BR 'kɑːsɪk
AM 'kɑrˌsɪk
carsickness
BR 'kɑːˌsɪknɪs
AM 'kɑrˌsɪknɪs
Carson
BR 'kɑːsn
AM 'kɑrsən
Carstairs
BR 'kɑːstɛːz
AM 'kɑrˌstɛrz
cart
BR kɑːt, -s, -ɪŋ, -ɪd
AM kɑr|t, -ts, -dɪŋ, -dəd
cartage
BR 'kɑːtɪdʒ
AM 'kɑrdɪdʒ
Cartagena
BR ˌkɑːtə'dʒiːnə(r), ˌkɑːtə'heɪnə(r)
AM ˌkɑrtə'heɪnə, ˌkɑrdə'ginə
carte
BR kɑːt
AM kɑrt
carte blanche
BR ˌkɑːt 'blɒ̃ʃ, + 'blɑːn(t)ʃ
AM 'kɑrt 'blɑn(t)ʃ
carte-de-visite
BR ˌkɑːtdəvɪ'ziːt
AM ˌkɑrtdəvɪ'zit
cartel
BR kɑː'tɛl, -z
AM kɑr'tɛl, -z
cartelisation
BR ˌkɑːtəlʌɪ'zeɪʃn, ˌkɑːtl̩ʌɪ'zeɪʃn
AM ˌkɑrˌtɛlə'zeɪʃən, 'kɑrdəˌlaɪ'zeɪʃən
cartelise
BR 'kɑːtəlʌɪz, 'kɑːtl̩ʌɪz, -ɪz, -ɪŋ, -d
AM 'kɑrdəˌlaɪz, -ɪz, -ɪŋ, -d
cartelization
BR ˌkɑːtəlʌɪ'zeɪʃn, ˌkɑːtl̩ʌɪ'zeɪʃn
AM ˌkɑrˌtɛlə'zeɪʃən, 'kɑrdəˌlaɪ'zeɪʃən
cartelize
BR 'kɑːtəlʌɪz, 'kɑːtl̩ʌɪz, -ɪz, -ɪŋ, -d
AM 'kɑrdəˌlaɪz, -ɪz, -ɪŋ, -d
carter
BR 'kɑːtə(r), -z
AM 'kɑrdər, -z
Carteret
BR 'kɑːtərɪt, 'kɑːtərɛt
AM 'kɑrdərət, ˌkɑrdər'ɛt
cartes blanches
BR ˌkɑːts 'blɒ̃ʃ, + 'blɑːn(t)ʃ
AM 'kɑrts 'blɑn(t)ʃ
cartes de visite
BR ˌkɑːt də vɪ'ziːt
AM ˌkɑrt də vɪ'zit
Cartesian
BR kɑː'tiːzɪən, kɑː'tiːʒn, -z
AM kɑr'tiʒən, -z
Cartesianism
BR kɑː'tiːzɪənɪz(ə)m
AM kɑr'tiʒəˌnɪzəm
cartful
BR 'kɑːtfʊl, -z
AM 'kɑrtˌfʊl, -z
Carthage
BR 'kɑːθɪdʒ
AM 'kɑrθədʒ
Carthaginian
BR ˌkɑːθə'dʒɪnɪən, -z
AM ˌkɑrθə'dʒɪniən, -z
carthorse
BR 'kɑːthɔːs, -ɪz
AM 'kɑrtˌ(h)ɔ(ə)rs, -ɪz
Carthusian
BR kɑː'θjuːzɪən, -z
AM kɑr'θ(j)uʒən, -z
Cartier
BR 'kɑːtɪeɪ

AM ˌkardiˌeɪ
Cartier-Bresson
BR ˌkɑːtɪeɪˈbrɛsɔ̃
AM ˌkardiˌeɪbrəˈsɔn, ˌkardiˌeɪbrəˈsɑn
cartilage
BR ˈkɑːtɪl|ɪdʒ, ˈkɑːtḷ|ɪdʒ, -ɨdʒɨz
AM ˈkardlɪdʒ, -ɨz
cartilaginoid
BR ˌkɑːtɪˈladʒɨnɔɪd, ˌkɑːtlˈadʒɨnɔɪd, ˌkɑːtɪˈladʒṇɔɪd, ˌkɑːtlˈadʒṇɔɪd
AM ˌkardlˈædʒənɔɪd
cartilaginous
BR ˌkɑːtɪˈladʒɨnəs, ˌkɑːtlˈadʒɨnəs, ˌkɑːtɪˈladʒṇəs, ˌkɑːtlˈadʒṇəs
AM ˌkardlˈædʒənəs
Cartland
BR ˈkɑːtlənd
AM ˈkartlənd
cartload
BR ˈkɑːtləʊd, -z
AM ˈkartˌloʊd, -z
Cartmel
BR ˈkɑːtm(ə)l, ˈkɑːtmɛl
AM ˈkartˌmɛl
cartogram
BR ˈkɑːtəgram, -z
AM ˈkardəˌgræm, -z
cartographer
BR kɑːˈtɒgrəfə(r), -z
AM karˈtɑgrəfər, -z
cartographic
BR ˌkɑːtəˈgrafɪk
AM ˌkardəˈgræfɪk
cartographical
BR ˌkɑːtəˈgrafɪkl
AM ˌkardəˈgræfəkəl
cartographically
BR ˌkɑːtəˈgrafɪkli
AM ˌkardəˈgræfək(ə)li
cartography
BR kɑːˈtɒgrəfi
AM karˈtɑgrəfi
cartomancy
BR ˈkɑːtə(ʊ)mansi
AM ˈkardəˌmænsi
carton
BR ˈkɑːtn, -z
AM ˈkartn, -z
cartoon
BR kɑːˈtuːn, -z, -ɪŋ
AM karˈtun, -z, -ɪŋ
cartoonish
BR kɑːˈtuːnɪʃ
AM karˈtunɪʃ
cartoonist
BR kɑːˈtuːnɪst, -s
AM karˈtunəst, -s
cartoony
BR kɑːˈtuːni
AM karˈtuni
cartophilist
BR kɑːˈtɒfɪlɪst, kɑːˈtɒfḷɪst, -s
AM karˈtɑfələst, -s
cartophily
BR kɑːˈtɒfɪli, kɑːˈtɒfḷi
AM karˈtɑfəli
cartouche
BR kɑːˈtuːʃ, -ɨz
AM karˈtuʃ, -ɨz
FR kaʀtuʃ
cartridge
BR ˈkɑːtr|ɪdʒ, -ɨdʒɨz
AM ˈkartrɪdʒ, -ɨz
cartulary
BR ˈkɑːtjʊləri, ˈkɑːtʃʊləri
AM ˈkartʃəˌlɛri
cartwheel
BR ˈkɑːtwiːl, -z, -ɪŋ, -d
AM ˈkartˌ(h)wil, -z, -ɪŋ, -d
cartwright
BR ˈkɑːtrʌɪt, -s
AM ˈkartˌraɪt, -s
caruncle
BR kəˈrʌŋkl, -z
AM kəˈrəŋkəl, -z
caruncular
BR kəˈrʌŋkjʊlə(r)
AM kəˈrəŋkjələr
Caruso
BR kəˈruːsəʊ, kəˈruːzəʊ
AM kəˈrusoʊ
Caruthers
BR kəˈrʌðəz, ˈkrɪðəz
AM kəˈrəðərz
carve
BR kɑːv, -z, -ɪŋ, -d
AM karv, -z, -ɪŋ, -d
carvel
BR ˈkɑːv(ɛ)l, -z
AM ˈkarvəl, -z
carven
BR ˈkɑːvn
AM ˈkarvən
carver
BR ˈkɑːvə(r), -z
AM ˈkarvər, -z
carvery
BR ˈkɑːv(ə)r|i, -ɪz
AM ˈkarv(ə)ri, -z
carve-up
BR ˈkɑːvʌp
AM ˈkarvəp
carving
BR ˈkɑːvɪŋ, -z
AM ˈkarvɪŋ, -z
carwash
BR ˈkɑːwɒʃ, -ɨz
AM ˈkarˌwɔʃ, ˈkarˌwɑʃ, -əz
Cary[1]
forename
BR ˈkari
AM ˈkɛri
Cary[2]
surname
BR ˈkɛːri
AM ˈkɛri
caryatid
BR ˌkarɪˈatɪd, -z
AM ˌkɛriˈædəd, ˈkɛriəˌtɪd, -z
Caryl
BR ˈkarɪl, ˈkarḷ
AM ˈkɛrəl
caryopsis
BR ˌkarɪˈɒpsɪs, -ɪz
AM ˌkɛriˈɑpsəs, -əz
carzey
BR ˈkɑːz|i, -ɪz
AM ˈkarzi, -z
casa
BR ˈkɑːsə(r), ˈkasə(r), -z
AM ˈkɑzə, ˈkɑsə, -z
Casablanca
BR ˌkasəˈblaŋkə(r)
AM ˌkɑsəˈblɑŋkə, ˌkæsəˈblæŋkə
Casals
BR kəˈsalz
AM kəˈsɑls
Casanova
BR ˌkasəˈnəʊvə(r), -z
AM ˌkæzəˈnoʊvə, ˌkæsəˈnoʊvə, -z
casbah
BR ˈkazbɑː(r), -z
AM ˈkæsˌbɑ, ˈkæzˌbɑ, -z
cascabel
BR ˈkaskəb(ə)l, -z
AM ˈkæskəbəl, -z
cascade
BR kaˈskeɪd, kəˈskeɪd, -z, -ɪŋ, -ɨd
AM kæˈskeɪd, -z, -ɪŋ, -ɨd
cascara
BR kaˈskɑːrə(r), kəˈskɑːrə(r)
AM kæˈskɛrə
cascarilla
BR ˌkaskəˈrɪlə(r)
AM ˌkæskəˈrɪlə
case
BR keɪs, -ɨz, -ɪŋ, -t
AM keɪs, -ɨz, -ɪŋ, -t
caseation
BR ˌkeɪsɪˈeɪʃn
AM ˌkeɪsiˈeɪʃən
casebook
BR ˈkeɪsbʊk, -s
AM ˈkeɪsˌbʊk, -s
casebound
BR ˈkeɪsbaʊnd
AM ˈkeɪsˌbaʊnd
casein
BR ˈkeɪsɪɪn, ˈkeɪsiːn
AM keɪˈsin, ˈkeɪsin
caseinogen
BR keɪˈsiːnədʒ(ə)n, ˌkeɪsɪˈɪnədʒ(ə)n
AM keɪˈseɪnədʒən, ˌkeɪsiˈɪnədʒən
caseload
BR ˈkeɪsləʊd, -z
AM ˈkeɪsˌloʊd, -z
casemate
BR ˈkeɪsmeɪt, -s
AM ˈkeɪsˌmeɪt, -s
casement
BR ˈkeɪsm(ə)nt, -s
AM ˈkeɪsmənt, -s
caseous
BR ˈkeɪsɪəs
AM ˈkeɪsiəs
casern
BR kəˈzəːn, -z
AM kəˈzərn, -z
casework
BR ˈkeɪswəːk
AM ˈkeɪsˌwərk
caseworker
BR ˈkeɪsˌwəːkə(r), -z
AM ˈkeɪsˌwərkər, -z
Casey
BR ˈkeɪsi
AM ˈkeɪsi
cash
BR kaʃ, -ɨz, -ɪŋ, -t
AM kæʃ, -əz, -ɪŋ, -t
cashable
BR ˈkaʃəbl
AM ˈkæʃəbəl
cashbook
BR ˈkaʃbʊk, -s
AM ˈkæʃˌbʊk, -s
cashbox
BR ˈkaʃbɒks, -ɨz
AM ˈkæʃˌbɑks, -əz
cashew
BR ˈkaʃuː, kaˈʃuː, kəˈʃuː, -z
AM ˈkæˌʃu, -z
cashflow
BR ˈkaʃfləʊ
AM ˈkæʃˌfloʊ
cashier
BR kəˈʃɪə(r), kaˈʃɪə(r), -z, -ɪŋ, -d
AM kæˈʃɪ(ə)r, -z, -ɪŋ, -d
cashless
BR ˈkaʃləs
AM ˈkæʃləs
Cashman
BR ˈkaʃmən
AM ˈkæʃmən
cashmere
BR ˈkaʃmɪə(r), ˌkaʃˈmɪə(r)
AM ˈkæʒmɪ(ə)r, kæʒˈmɪ(ə)r, ˈkæʃmɪ(ə)r, kæʃˈmɪ(ə)r
cashpoint
BR ˈkaʃpɔɪnt, -s
AM ˈkæʃˌpɔɪnt, -s
casing
BR ˈkeɪsɪŋ, -z

AM ˈkeɪsɪŋ, -z

casino
BR kəˈsiːnəʊ, -z
AM kəˈsinoʊ, -z

Casio®
BR ˈkasɪəʊ
AM ˈkæsioʊ

cask
BR kɑːsk, kask, -s
AM kæsk, -s

casket
BR ˈkɑːskɪt, ˈkaskɪt, -s
AM ˈkæskət, -s

Caslon
BR ˈkazlɒn
AM ˈkæslən

Caspar
BR ˈkaspə(r)
AM ˈkæspər

Casper
BR ˈkaspə(r)
AM ˈkæspər

Caspian Sea
BR ˌkaspɪən ˈsiː
AM ˌkæspiən ˈsi

casque
BR kask, kɑːsk, -s
AM kæsk, -s

Cassandra
BR kəˈsandrə(r), -z
AM kəˈsændrə, -z

cassareep
BR ˈkasəriːp
AM ˈkæsəˌrip

cassata
BR kəˈsɑːtə(r)
AM kəˈsɑdə

cassation
BR kaˈseɪʃn, kəˈseɪʃn, -z
AM kəˈseɪʃən, kæˈseɪʃən, -z

cassava
BR kəˈsɑːvə(r)
AM kəˈsɑvə

Cassegrain
BR ˌkasɪˈgreɪn
AM ˈkæsəˌgreɪn

Cassel
BR ˈkasl
AM ˈkæsəl

Cassell
BR ˈkasl
AM ˈkæsəl

casserole
BR ˈkasərəʊl, -z
AM ˈkæsəˌroʊl, -z

cassette
BR kəˈsɛt, -s
AM kəˈsɛt, -s

cassia
BR ˈkasɪə(r)
AM ˈkæʃə

Cassidy
BR ˈkasɪdi
AM ˈkæsədi

Cassie
BR ˈkasi
AM ˈkæsi

Cassiopeia
BR ˌkasɪə(ʊ)ˈpiːə(r)
AM ˌkæsiəˈpiə

cassis
BR kaˈsiːs, kəˈsiːs, ˈkasiːs
AM kɑˈsis, kəˈsis

cassiterite
BR kəˈsɪtərʌɪt
AM kəˈsɪdəˌraɪt

Cassius
BR ˈkasɪəs
AM ˈkæsiəs

Cassivelaunus
BR ˌkasɪvɪˈlɔːnəs
AM ˌkæsəvəˈlɔnəs, ˌkæsəvəˈlɑnəs

cassock
BR ˈkasək, -s, -t
AM ˈkæsək, -s, -t

Casson
BR ˈkasn
AM ˈkæsən

cassoulet
BR ˌkasʊˈleɪ, ˈkasʊleɪ, -z
AM ˌkæsəˈleɪ, ˌkæsʊˈleɪ, -z

cassowary
BR ˈkasəwər|i, ˈkasəwɛːr|i, -ɪz
AM ˈkæsəwɛri, -z

cast
BR kɑːst, kast, -s, -ɪŋ
AM kæst, -s, -ɪŋ

Castalia
BR kaˈsteɪlɪə(r)
AM kəˈsteɪljə, kəˈsteɪliə

Castalian
BR kaˈsteɪlɪən
AM kəˈsteɪljən, kəˈsteɪliən

castanet
BR ˌkastəˈnɛt, -s
AM ˌkæstəˈnɛt, -s

castaway
BR ˈkɑːstəweɪ, ˈkastəweɪ, -z
AM ˈkæstəˌweɪ, -z

caste
BR kɑːst, kast, -s
AM kæst, -s

casteism
BR ˈkɑːstɪz(ə)m, ˈkastɪz(ə)m
AM ˈkæstˌɪzəm

castelan
BR ˈkastələn, -z
AM ˈkæstələn, ˈkæstəˌlæn, -z

Castel Gandolfo
BR ˌkast(ɛ)l ganˈdɒlfəʊ
AM ˌkæstəl gɑnˈdɔlfoʊ, ˌkæstəl gɑnˈdɑlfoʊ

castellan
BR ˈkastələn, -z
AM ˈkæstələn, ˈkæstəˌlæn, -z

castellated
BR ˈkastɪleɪtɪd, ˈkastl̩eɪtɪd
AM ˈkæs(t)əˌleɪdɪd

castellation
BR ˌkastɪˈleɪʃn, ˌkastlˈeɪʃn, -z
AM ˌkæs(t)əˈleɪʃən, -z

caster
BR ˈkɑːstə(r), ˈkastə(r), -z
AM ˈkæstər, -z

Casterbridge
BR ˈkɑːstəbrɪdʒ, ˈkastəbrɪdʒ
AM ˈkæstərˌbrɪdʒ

castigate
BR ˈkastɪgeɪt, -s, -ɪŋ, -ɪd
AM ˈkæstəˌgeɪ|t, -ts, -dɪŋ, -dɪd

castigation
BR ˌkastɪˈgeɪʃn
AM ˌkæstəˈgeɪʃən

castigator
BR ˈkastɪgeɪtə(r), -z
AM ˈkæstəˌgeɪdər, -z

castigatory
BR ˈkastɪgeɪt(ə)ri, ˈkastɪgət(ə)ri
AM ˈkæstəgəˌtɔri

Castile
BR kaˈstiːl, kəˈstiːl
AM kæˈstil

Castilian
BR kaˈstɪlɪən, kəˈstɪlɪən, -z
AM kæˈstɪljən, kəˈstɪljən, kæˈstɪliən, kəˈstɪliən, -z

Castillo
BR kaˈstiː(j)əʊ
AM kæˈsti(j)oʊ

castle
BR ˈkɑːs|l, ˈkas|l, -lz, -l̩ɪŋ\-lɪŋ, -ld
AM ˈkæsəl, -z, -ɪŋ, -d

Castlebar
BR ˌkɑːslˈbɑː(r), ˌkaslˈbɑː(r)
AM ˌkæsəlˈbɑr

Castleford
BR ˈkaslfəd, ˈkɑːslfəd
AM ˈkæsəlfərd

Castlemaine
BR ˈkɑːslmeɪn, ˈkaslmeɪn
AM ˈkæsəlˌmeɪn

Castlereagh
BR ˈkɑːslreɪ, ˈkaslreɪ
AM ˈkæsəlreɪ

Castleton
BR ˈkaslt(ə)n, ˈkɑːslt(ə)n
AM ˈkæsəltən

Castlewellan
BR ˌkɑːslˈwɛlən, ˌkaslˈwɛlən
AM ˌkæsəlˈwɛlən

castor
BR ˈkɑːstə(r), ˈkastə(r), -z
AM ˈkæstər, -z

castrate
BR kaˈstreɪt, kəˈstreɪt, -s, -ɪŋ, -ɪd
AM ˈkæˌstreɪ|t, -ts, -dɪŋ, -dɪd

castrati
BR kaˈstrɑːtiː, kəˈstrɑːtiː
AM kæˈstrɑdi

castration
BR kaˈstreɪʃn, kəˈstreɪʃn, -z
AM kæˈstreɪʃən, -z

castrative
BR kaˈstreɪtɪv, kəˈstreɪtɪv
AM kæˈstreɪdɪv

castrato
BR kaˈstrɑːtəʊ, kəˈstrɑːtəʊ
AM kæˈstrɑdoʊ

castrator
BR kaˈstreɪtə(r), kəˈstreɪtə(r), -z
AM ˈkæˌstreɪdər, -z

castratory
BR kaˈstreɪt(ə)ri, kəˈstreɪt(ə)ri
AM ˈkæstrəˌtɔri

Castries
BR kaˈstriːz, kaˈstriːs
AM ˌkæsˌtriz

Castro
BR ˈkastrəʊ
AM ˈkæstroʊ

Castroism
BR ˈkastrəʊɪz(ə)m
AM ˈkæstrəˌwɪzəm

Castrol®
BR ˈkastrɒl, ˈkastr(ə)l
AM ˈkæsˌtrɔl, ˈkæsˌtrɑl

casual
BR ˈkaʒʊ(ə)l, ˈkaʒjʊl, ˈkaʒ(ʊ)l, ˈkazjʊ(ə)l, kazj(ʊ)l
AM ˈkæʒuəl

casually
BR ˈkaʒʊəli, ˈkaʒjʊli, ˈkaʒl̩i, ˈkazjʊli, ˈkazjl̩i
AM ˈkæʒ(əw)əli

casualness
BR ˈkaʒʊəlnəs, ˈkaʒjʊlnəs, ˈkaʒl̩nəs, ˈkazjʊlnəs, ˈkazjlnəs
AM ˈkæʒ(əw)əlnəs

casualty
BR ˈkaʒ(j)ʉlt|i, -ɪz
AM ˈkæʒ(əw)əlti, -z

casuarina
BR ˌkazjʊəˈriːnə(r), ˌkaʒjʊəˈriːnə(r), ˌkaʒʉˈriːnə(r), ˌkazjʊəˈrʌɪnə(r), ˌkaʒjʊəˈrʌɪnə(r), ˌkaʒʉˈrʌɪnə(r), -z
AM ˌkæʒuəˈrinə, ˌkæʒuəˈraɪnə, -z

casuist
BR ˈkazjʊɪst, ˈkaʒʊɪst, -s
AM ˈkæʒəwəst, -s

casuistic
BR ˌkazjʊˈɪstɪk, ˌkaʒʊˈɪstɪk
AM ˌkæʒəˈwɪstɪk

casuistical
BR ˌkazjʊˈɪstɨkl, ˌkaʒʊˈɪstɨkl
AM ˌkæʒəˈwɪstɨkəl

casuistically
BR ˌkazjʊˈɪstɨkli, ˌkaʒʊˈɪstɨkli
AM ˌkæʒəˈwɪstɨk(ə)li

casuistry
BR ˈkazjʊɪstri, ˈkaʒʊɪstri
AM ˈkæʒəwəstri

casus belli
BR ˌkɑːsəs ˈbɛliː, ˌkeɪsəs ˈbɛlʌɪ
AM ˌkɑsəs ˈbɛli, ˌkeɪsəs +

Casy
BR ˈkeɪsi
AM ˈkeɪsi

cat
BR kat, -s
AM kæt, -s

catabolic
BR ˌkatəˈbɒlɪk
AM ˌkædəˈbɔlɪk, ˌkædəˈbɑlɪk

catabolically
BR ˌkatəˈbɒlɨkli
AM ˌkædəˈbɔlək(ə)li, ˌkædəˈbɑlək(ə)li

catabolism
BR kəˈtabəlɪz(ə)m
AM kəˈtæbəˌlɪzəm

catabolize
BR kəˈtabəlʌɪz, -ɨz, -ɪŋ, -d
AM kəˈtæbəˌlaɪz, -ɨz, -ɪŋ, -d

catechesis
BR ˌkatəˈkiːsɪs
AM ˌkædəˈkisɨs

catachresis
BR ˌkatəˈkriːsɪs
AM ˌkædəˈkrisɨs

catachrestic
BR ˌkatəˈkrɛstɪk
AM ˌkædəˈkrɛstɪk

catachrestical
BR ˌkatəˈkrɛstɨkl
AM ˌkædəˈkrɛstəkəl

cataclasis
BR ˌkatəˈkleɪsɪs, -ɨz
AM ˌkædəˈkleɪsɨs, -ɨz

cataclasm
BR ˈkatəˌklaz(ə)m, -z
AM ˈkædəˌklæzəm, -z

cataclastic
BR ˌkatəˈklastɪk
AM ˌkædəˈklæstɪk

cataclysm
BR ˈkatəklɪz(ə)m, -z
AM ˈkædəˌklɪzəm, -z

cataclysmal
BR ˌkatəˈklɪzml
AM ˌkædəˈklɪzməl

cataclysmic
BR ˌkatəˈklɪzmɪk
AM ˌkædəˈklɪzmɪk

cataclysmically
BR ˌkatəˈklɪzmɨkli
AM ˌkædəˈklɪzmɨk(ə)li

catacomb
BR ˈkatəkuːm, -z
AM ˈkædəˌkoʊm, -z

catadioptric
BR ˌkatədʌɪˈɒptrɪk
AM ˌkædəˌdaɪˈɑptrɪk

catadromous
BR kəˈtadrəməs
AM kəˈtædrəməs

catafalque
BR ˈkatəfalk, -s
AM ˈkædəˌfælk, -s

Catalan
BR ˈkatəlan, ˈkatl̩an, -z
AM ˈkædlˌæn, ˈkædələn, -z

catalase
BR ˈkatəleɪz, ˈkatl̩eɪz, -ɨz
AM ˈkædlˌeɪs, ˈkædlˌeɪz, -ɨz

catalectic
BR ˌkatəˈlɛktɪk, ˌkatlˈɛktɪk
AM ˌkædəˈlɛktɪk

catalepsy
BR ˈkatəlɛpsi, ˈkatl̩ɛpsi
AM ˈkædlˌɛpsi

cataleptic
BR ˌkatəˈlɛptɪk, ˌkatlˈɛptɪk
AM ˌkædlˈɛptɪk

Catalina
BR ˌkatəˈliːnə(r)
AM ˌkædəˈlinə

catalog
BR ˈkatəlɒg, ˈkatl̩ɒg, -z, -ɪŋ, -d
AM ˈkædlˌɔg, ˈkædlˌɑg, -z, -ɪŋ, -d

catalogue
BR ˈkatəlɒg, ˈkatl̩ɒg, -z, -ɪŋ, -d
AM ˈkædlˌɔg, kædlˌɑg, -z, -ɪŋ, -d

cataloguer
BR ˈkatəlɒgə(r), ˈkatl̩ɒgə(r), -z
AM ˈkædlˌɔgər, ˈkædlˌɑgər, -z

catalogue raisonné
BR ˌkatəlɒg ˌreɪzɒˈneɪ, ˌkatl̩ɒg +
AM ˌkædlˌɔg rɛzəˈneɪ, ˌkædlˌɑg rɛzəˈneɪ

catalogues raisonnés
BR ˌkatəlɒg ˌreɪzɒˈneɪz, ˌkatl̩ɒg +
AM ˌkædlˌɔg rɛzəˈneɪz, ˌkædlˌɑg rɛzəˈneɪz

Catalonia
BR ˌkatəˈləʊnɪə(r), ˌkatl̩ˈəʊnɪə(r)
AM ˌkædlˈoʊniə

Catalonian
BR ˌkatəˈləʊnɪən, ˌkatl̩ˈəʊnɪən, -z
AM ˌkædlˈoʊniən, -z

catalpa
BR kəˈtalpə(r)
AM kəˈtælpə

catalyse
BR ˈkatəlʌɪz, ˈkatl̩ʌɪz, -ɨz, -ɪŋ, -d
AM ˈkædlˌaɪz, -ɨz, -ɪŋ, -d

catalyser
BR ˈkatəlʌɪzə(r), ˈkatl̩ʌɪzə(r)
AM ˈkædlˌaɪzər

catalysis
BR kəˈtalɪsɪs
AM kəˈtæləsəs

catalyst
BR ˈkatəlɪst, ˈkatl̩ɪst, -s
AM ˈkædl̩əst, -s

catalytic
BR ˌkatəˈlɪtɪk
AM ˌkædəˈlɪdɪk

catalyze
BR ˈkatəlʌɪz, ˈkatl̩ʌɪz, -ɨz, -ɪŋ, -d
AM ˈkædlˌaɪz, -ɨz, -ɪŋ, -d

catamaran
BR ˈkatəməˌran, ˌkatəməˈran, -z
AM ˌkædəməˌræn, -z

catamite
BR ˈkatəmʌɪt, -s
AM ˈkædəˌmaɪt, -s

catamount
BR ˈkatəmaʊnt, -s
AM ˈkædəˌmaʊnt, -s

catamountain
BR ˈkatəˌmaʊntɪn, -z
AM ˈkædəˌmaʊntn, -z

catananche
BR ˌkatəˈnaŋk|i, -ɪz
AM ˌkædəˈnæŋki, -z

Catania
BR kəˈtanɪə(r)
AM kəˈtɑniə, kəˈteɪniə

cataphora
BR kəˈtaf(ə)rə(r)
AM kəˈtæf(ə)rə

cataphoresis
BR ˌkatəfəˈriːsɪs
AM ˌkædəfəˈrisɪs

cataphoretic
BR ˌkatəfəˈrɛtɪk
AM ˌkædəfəˈrɛdɪk

cataphoretically
BR ˌkatəfəˈrɛtɨkli
AM ˌkædəfəˈrɛdək(ə)li

cataplasm
BR ˈkatəˌplaz(ə)m, -z
AM ˈkædəˌplæzəm, -z

cataplectic
BR ˌkatəˈplɛktɪk
AM ˌkædəˈplɛktɪk

cataplexy
BR ˈkatəˌplɛks|i, -ɪz
AM ˈkædəˌplɛksi, -z

catapult
BR ˈkatəpʌlt, ˈkatəpʊlt, -s, -ɪŋ, -ɨd
AM ˈkædəpəlt, ˈkædəˌpʊlt, -s, -ɪŋ, -ɨd

cataract
BR ˈkatərakt, -s
AM ˈkædəˌræk|(t), -(t)s

catarrh
BR kəˈtɑː(r), -z
AM kəˈtɑr, -z

catarrhal
BR kəˈtɑːrəl, kəˈtɑːrl̩
AM kəˈtɑrəl

catarrhine
BR ˈkatərʌɪn
AM ˈkædəˌraɪn

catastrophe
BR kəˈtastrəf|i, -ɪz
AM kəˈtæstrəfi, -z

catastrophic
BR ˌkatəˈstrɒfɪk
AM ˌkædəˈstrɑfɪk

catastrophically
BR ˌkatəˈstrɒfɨkli
AM ˌkædəˈstrɑfək(ə)li

catastrophism
BR kəˈtastrəˌfɪz(ə)m
AM kəˈtæstrəˌfɪzəm

catastrophist
BR kəˈtastrəfɪst, -s
AM kəˈtæstrəfəst, -s

catatonia
BR ˌkatəˈtəʊnɪə(r)
AM ˌkædəˈtoʊniə

catatonic
BR ˌkatəˈtɒnɪk
AM ˌkædəˈtɑnɪk

catawba
BR kəˈtɔːbə(r), -z
AM kəˈtɔbə, kəˈtɑbə, -z

catbird
BR ˈkatbəːd, -z

AM 'kæt,bərd, -z

catboat
BR 'katbəʊt, -s
AM 'kæt,boʊt, -s

catcall
BR 'katkɔːl, -z, -ɪŋ, -d
AM 'kæt,kɔl, 'kæt,kɑl, -z, -ɪŋ, -d

catch
BR katʃ, -ɨz, -ɪŋ
AM kɛtʃ, -əz, -ɪŋ

catchable
BR 'katʃəbl
AM 'kɛtʃəbəl

catchall
BR 'katʃɔːl, -z
AM 'kɛtʃ,ɔl, 'kɛtʃ,ɑl, -z

catcher
BR 'katʃə(r), -z
AM 'kɛtʃər, -z

catchfly
BR 'katʃflʌɪ, -z
AM 'kɛtʃ,flaɪ, -z

catchily
BR 'katʃɨli
AM 'kɛtʃəli

catchiness
BR 'katʃɪnɨs
AM 'kɛtʃinɨs

catchline
BR 'katʃlʌɪn, -z
AM 'kɛtʃ,laɪn, -z

catchment
BR 'katʃm(ə)nt, -s
AM 'kɛtʃmənt, -s

catchpenny
BR 'katʃ,pɛn|i, -ɪz
AM 'kɛtʃ,pɛni, -z

catchphrase
BR 'katʃfreɪz, -ɨz
AM 'kɛtʃ,freɪz, -ɨz

catchpole
BR 'katʃpəʊl, -z
AM 'kɛtʃ,poʊl, -z

catchup
BR 'kɛtʃʌp
AM 'kɛtʃəp

catchweight
BR 'katʃweɪt, -s
AM 'kætʃ,weɪt, -s

catchword
BR 'katʃwəːd, -z
AM 'kætʃ,wərd, -z

catchy
BR 'katʃ|i, -ɪə(r), -ɪɨst
AM 'kɛtʃi, -ər, -ɨst

cate
BR keɪt, -s
AM keɪt, -s

catechetic
BR ,katɪ'kɛtɪk, -s
AM ,kædə'kɛdɪk, -s

catechetical
BR ,katɪ'kɛtɪkl
AM ,kædə'kɛdəkəl

catechetically
BR ,katɪ'kɛtɪkli
AM ,kædə'kɛdək(ə)li

catechise
BR 'katɪkʌɪz, -ɨz, -ɪŋ, -d
AM 'kædə,kaɪz, -ɨz, -ɪŋ, -d

catechiser
BR 'katɪkʌɪzə(r), -z
AM 'kædə,kaɪzər, -z

catechism
BR 'katɪkɪz(ə)m, -z
AM 'kædə,kɪzəm, -z

catechismal
BR ,katɪ'kɪzml
AM ,kædə'kɪzməl

catechist
BR 'katɪkɪst, -s
AM 'kædəkəst, -s

catechize
BR 'katɪkʌɪz, -ɨz, -ɪŋ, -d
AM 'kædə,kaɪz, -ɨz, -ɪŋ, -d

catechizer
BR 'katɪkʌɪzə(r), -z
AM 'kædə,kaɪzər, -z

catechol
BR 'katɪtʃɒl, 'katɪkɒl
AM 'kædə,kɔl, 'kædə,kɑl, 'kædə,koʊl

catecholamine
BR ,katɪ'kəʊləmiːn
AM ,kædə'koʊlə,min

catechu
BR 'katɪ(t)ʃuː
AM 'kædə,tʃu, 'kædə,kju

catechumen
BR ,katɪ'kjuːmɪn, ,katɪ'kjuːmɛn, -z
AM ¦kædə¦kjumən, -z

categorial
BR ,katɪ'gɔːrɪəl
AM ,kædə'gɔriəl

categoric
BR ,katɪ'gɒrɪk
AM ,kædə'gɔrɪk

categorical
BR ,katɪ'gɒrɪkl
AM ,kædə'gɔrəkəl

categorically
BR ,katɪ'gɒrɪkli
AM ,kædə'gɔrək(ə)li

categorisation
BR ,katɪg(ə)rʌɪ'zeɪʃn
AM ,kædəg(ə)rə'zeɪʃən, ,kædəgə,raɪ'zeɪʃən

categorise
BR 'katɪgərʌɪz, -ɨz, -ɪŋ, -d
AM 'kædəgə,raɪz, 'kædəgɔ,raɪz, -ɨz, -ɪŋ, -d

categorization
BR ,katɪg(ə)rʌɪ'zeɪʃn
AM ,kædəg(ə)rə'zeɪʃən, ,kædəgə,raɪ'zeɪʃən

categorize
BR 'katɪgərʌɪz, -ɨz, -ɪŋ, -d
AM 'kædəgə,raɪz, 'kædəgɔ,raɪz, -ɨz, -ɪŋ, -d

category
BR 'katɪg(ə)r|i, -ɪz
AM 'kædə,gɔri, -z

catena
BR kə'tiːnə(*r*)
AM kə'tinə

catenae
BR kə'tiːniː
AM kə'tini, kə'ti,naɪ

catenary
BR kə'tiːn(ə)r|i, -ɪz
AM 'kædə,nɛri, 'kædn,ɛri, -z

catenate
BR 'katɪneɪt, -s, -ɪŋ, -ɨd
AM 'kædə,neɪt, 'kædn,eɪ|t, -ts, -dɪŋ, -dɨd

catenation
BR ,katɪ'neɪʃn
AM ,kædə'neɪʃən, ,kædn'eɪʃən

cater
BR 'keɪt|ə(r), -əz, -(ə)rɪŋ, -əd
AM 'keɪdər, -z, -ɪŋ, -d

cateran
BR 'kat(ə)rən, 'kat(ə)rn̩, -z
AM 'kædərən, -z

cater-cornered
BR ,keɪtə'kɔːnəd, ,katə'kɔːnəd, 'keɪtə,kɔːnəd, 'katə,kɔːnəd
AM ¦kædi¦kɔrnərd, 'kædə,kɔrnər(d), 'kɪdi,kɔrnər(d)

caterer
BR 'keɪt(ə)rə(r), -z
AM 'keɪdərər, -z

Caterham
BR 'keɪt(ə)rəm, 'keɪt(ə)rm̩
AM 'keɪdərəm

Caterina
BR ,katə'riːnə(*r*)
AM ,kædə'rinə

caterpillar
BR 'katəpɪlə(r), -z
AM 'kædər,pɪlər, -z

caterwaul
BR 'katəwɔːl, -z, -ɪŋ, -d
AM 'kædər,wɔl, 'kædər,wɑl, -z, -ɪŋ, -d

Catesby
BR 'keɪtsbi
AM 'keɪtsbi

catfish
BR 'katfɪʃ, -ɨz
AM 'kæt,fɪʃ, -ɨz

catfood
BR 'katfuːd
AM 'kæt,fud

Catford
BR 'katfəd
AM 'kætfərd

catgut
BR 'katgʌt
AM 'kæt,gət

Cath
BR kaθ
AM kæθ

Cathar
BR 'kaθɑː(r), -z
AM 'kæθɑr, -z

Catharine
BR 'kaθ(ə)rɪn, 'kaθ(ə)rn̩
AM 'kæθ(ə)rən

Catharism
BR 'kaθərɪz(ə)m, 'kaθɑːrɪz(ə)m
AM 'kæθərɪsm

Catharist
BR 'kaθərɪst, 'kaθɑːrɪst, -s
AM 'kæθərəst, -s

catharsis
BR kə'θɑːsɪs
AM kə'θɑrsəs

cathartic
BR kə'θɑːtɪk
AM kə'θɑrdɪk

cathartically
BR kə'θɑːtɪkli
AM kə'θɑrdək(ə)li

Cathay
BR (,)ka'θeɪ, kə'θeɪ
AM kə'θeɪ

Cathays
BR kə'teɪz
AM kə'teɪz

Cathcart
BR 'kaθkɑːt, ,kaθ'kɑːt
AM 'kæθ,kɑrt

cathead
BR 'kathɛd, -z
AM 'kæt,(h)ɛd, -z

cathectic
BR kə'θɛktɪk
AM kə'θɛktɪk

cathedra
BR kə'θiːdrə(*r*)
AM kə'θidrə

cathedral
BR kə'θiːdr(ə)l, -z
AM kə'θidrəl, -z

Cather
BR 'kaθə(r)
AM 'kæθər

Catherine
BR 'kaθ(ə)rɪn, 'kaθ(ə)rn̩
AM 'kæθ(ə)rɪn

catheter
BR 'kaθɪtə(r), -z
AM 'kæθədər, -z

catheterise
BR 'kaθɪtərʌɪz, -ɨz, -ɪŋ, -d

AM ˈkæθədəˌraɪz, -ɪz, -ɪŋ, -d

catheterization
BR ˌkaθɪtərʌɪˈzeɪʃn
AM ˌkæθədərəˈzeɪʃən, ˌkæθədəˌraɪˈzeɪʃən

catheterize
BR ˈkaθɪtərʌɪz, -ɪz, -ɪŋ, -d
AM ˈkæθədəˌraɪz, -ɪz, -ɪŋ, -d

cathetometer
BR ˌkaθɪˈtɒmɪtə(r), -z
AM ˌkæθəˈtɑmədər, -z

cathexis
BR kəˈθɛksɪs
AM kəˈθɛksəs

Cathie
BR ˈkaθi
AM ˈkæθi

Cathleen
BR ˈkaθliːn
AM ˌkæθˈlin

cathodal
BR kaˈθəʊdl, kəˈθəʊdl
AM kəˈθoʊdəl

cathode
BR ˈkaθəʊd, -z
AM ˈkæˌθoʊd, -z

cathodic
BR kaˈθɒdɪk, kəˈθɒdɪk
AM kəˈθɑdɪk

Catholic
BR ˈkaθ(ə)lɪk, -s
AM ˈkæθ(ə)lɪk, -s

catholic
BR ˈkaθ(ə)lɪk, -s
AM ˈkæθ(ə)lɪk, -s

catholically
BR ˈkaθ(ə)lɪkli
AM ˈkæθ(ə)lək(ə)li

Catholicise
BR kəˈθɒlɪsʌɪz, -ɪz, -ɪŋ, -d
AM kəˈθɑləˌsaɪz, -ɪz, -ɪŋ, -d

Catholicism
BR kəˈθɒlɪsɪz(ə)m
AM kəˈθɑləˌsɪzəm

Catholicity
BR ˌkaθəˈlɪsɪti
AM ˌkæθəˈlɪsɪdi

Catholicize
BR kəˈθɒlɪsʌɪz, -ɪz, -ɪŋ, -d
AM kəˈθɑləˌsaɪz, -ɪz, -ɪŋ, -d

catholicly
BR ˈkaθ(ə)lɪkli
AM ˈkæθ(ə)lək(ə)li

catholicon
BR kəˈθɒlɪkɒn, -z
AM kəˈθɑləkɑn, -z

cathouse
BR ˈkathaʊ|s, -zɪz
AM ˈkætˌ(h)aʊ|s, -zɪz

Cathryn
BR ˈkaθr(ɪ)n
AM ˈkæθrɪn

Cathy
BR ˈkaθi
AM ˈkæθi

Catiline
BR ˈkatɪlʌɪn, ˈkatḷʌɪn
AM ˈkædəˌlaɪn

cation
BR ˈkatˌʌɪən, -z
AM ˈkædˌaɪən, ˈkædˌaɪˌɑn, -z

cationic
BR ˌkatʌɪˈɒnɪk
AM ˌkædaɪˈɑnɪk

catkin
BR ˈkatkɪn, -z
AM ˈkætkən, -z

catlick
BR ˈkatlɪk, -s
AM ˈkætlɪk, -s

catlike
BR ˈkatlʌɪk
AM ˈkætˌlaɪk

Catling
BR ˈkatlɪŋ
AM ˈkætlɪŋ

catmint
BR ˈkatmɪnt
AM ˈkætˌmɪnt

catnap
BR ˈkatnap, -s, -ɪŋ, -t
AM ˈkætˌnæp, -s, -ɪŋ, -t

catnip
BR ˈkatnɪp
AM ˈkætˌnɪp

Cato
BR ˈkeɪtəʊ
AM ˈkeɪdoʊ

cat-o'-nine-tails
BR ˌkatəˈnʌɪnteɪlz
AM ˌkædəˈnaɪnˌteɪlz

catoptric
BR kaˈtɒptrɪk, kəˈtɒptrɪk, -s
AM kəˈtɑptrɪk, -s

Catrin
BR ˈkatrɪn
AM ˈkætrɪn

Catrina
BR kəˈtriːnə(*r*)
AM kəˈtrinə

Catrine
BR ˈkatriːn
AM ˈkætrən, kəˈtrin(ə)

Catriona
BR kaˈtriː(ə)nə(*r*), kəˈtriː(ə)nə(*r*), ˌkatrɪˈəʊnə(*r*)
AM kæˈtrioʊnə, ˌkætriˈoʊnə

CAT scan
BR ˈkat skan, -z
AM ˈkæt ˌskæn, -z

Catskill
BR ˈkatskɪl
AM ˈkætˌskɪl

catsuit
BR ˈkatsuːt, -s
AM ˈkætˌsut, -s

catsup
BR ˈkatsəp, ˈkatsʌp, ˈkɛtʃəp, ˈkɛtʃʌp
AM ˈkɛtʃəp, ˈkætsəp, ˈkætʃəp

cattail
BR ˈkatteɪl
AM ˈkæ(t)ˌteɪl

Catterick
BR ˈkat(ə)rɪk
AM ˈkædərɪk

cattery
BR ˈkat(ə)r|i, -ɪz
AM ˈkædəri, -z

cattily
BR ˈkatɪli
AM ˈkædəli

cattiness
BR ˈkatɪnɪs
AM ˈkædinɪs

cattish
BR ˈkatɪʃ
AM ˈkædɪʃ

cattishly
BR ˈkatɪʃli
AM ˈkædɪʃli

cattishness
BR ˈkatɪʃnɪs
AM ˈkædɪʃnɪs

cattle
BR ˈkatl
AM ˈkædəl

cattleman
BR ˈkatlmən
AM ˈkædlmən

cattlemen
BR ˈkatlmən
AM ˈkædlmən

cattlepen
BR ˈkatlpɛn, -z
AM ˈkædlˌpɛn, -z

cattleya
BR ˈkatlɪə(*r*)
AM ˈkætliə, kætˈleɪə, kætˈliə

Catto
BR ˈkatəʊ
AM ˈkædoʊ

Catton
BR ˈkatn
AM ˈkætn

catty
BR ˈkat|i, -ɪə(r), -ɪɪst
AM ˈkædi, -ər, -ɪst

Catullus
BR kəˈtʌləs
AM kəˈtələs

catwalk
BR ˈkatwɔːk, -s
AM ˈkætˌwɔk, ˈkætˌwɑk, -s

Caucasian
BR kɔːˈkeɪzɪən, kɔːˈkeɪʒn, -z
AM kɔˈkeɪʒən, kɑˈkeɪʒən, -z

Caucasoid
BR ˈkɔːkəsɔɪd, -z
AM ˈkɔkəˌsɔɪd, ˈkɑkəˌsɔɪd, -z

Caucasus
BR ˈkɔːkəsəs
AM ˈkɔkəsəs, ˈkɑkəsəs

caucus
BR ˈkɔːkəs, -ɪz
AM ˈkɔkəs, ˈkɑkəs, -əz

caudal
BR ˈkɔːdl
AM ˈkɔdəl, ˈkɑdəl

caudally
BR ˈkɔːdḷi
AM ˈkɔdəli, ˈkɑdəli

caudate
BR ˈkɔːdeɪt
AM ˈkɔˌdeɪt, ˈkɑˌdeɪt

caudillo
BR kɔːˈdiːljəʊ, kɔːˈdɪləʊ, kaʊˈdiːjəʊ, -z
AM kaʊˈdijoʊ, -z

Caughey
BR ˈkahi
AM ˈkɑhi

caught
BR kɔːt
AM kɔt, kɑt

caul
BR kɔːl, -z
AM kɔl, kɑl, -z

cauldron
BR ˈkɔːldr(ə)n, ˈkɒldr(ə)n, -z
AM ˈkɔldrən, ˈkɑldrən, -z

Caulfield
BR ˈkɔː(l)fiːld
AM ˈkɔlˌfild, ˈkɑlˌfild

cauliflower
BR ˈkɒlɪˌflaʊə(r), -z
AM ˈkɔləˌflaʊər, ˈkɑləˌflaʊər, ˈkɔliˌflaʊər, ˈkɑliˌflaʊər, -z

caulk
BR kɔːk, -s, -ɪŋ, -t
AM kɔk, kɑk, -s, -ɪŋ, -t

caulker
BR ˈkɔːkə(r), -z
AM ˈkɔkər, ˈkɑkər, -z

Caunce
BR kɔːns
AM kɔns, kɑns

causable
BR ˈkɔːzəbl
AM ˈkɔzəbəl, ˈkɑzəbəl

causal
BR ˈkɔːzl
AM ˈkɔzəl, ˈkɑzəl

causality
BR kɔː'zalɨti
AM kɔ'zælədi, kɑ'zælədi

causally
BR 'kɔːzl̩i, 'kɔːzəli
AM 'kɔzəli, 'kɑzəli

causation
BR kɔː'zeɪʃn
AM kɔ'zeɪʃən, kɑ'zeɪʃən

causative
BR 'kɔːzətɪv, -z
AM 'kɔzədɪv, 'kɑzədɪv, -z

causatively
BR 'kɔːzətɨvli
AM 'kɔzədɨvli, 'kɑzədɨvli

cause
BR kɔːz, -ɨz, -ɪŋ, -d
AM kɔz, kɑz, -əz, -ɪŋ, -d

'cause
because
BR kəz
AM kəz

cause célèbre
BR ˌkɔːz sɪ'lɛːbr(ər), + sɛ'lɛːbr(ər)
AM ˌkoʊz sə'lɛbr, ˌkɔz +

causeless
BR 'kɔːzləs
AM 'kɔzləs, 'kɑzləs

causelessly
BR 'kɔːzləsli
AM 'kɔzləsli, 'kɑzləsli

causer
BR 'kɔːzə(r), -z
AM 'kɔzər, 'kɑzər, -z

causerie
BR 'kəʊz(ə)r|i, -ɪz
AM ˌkoʊz(ə)'ri, 'koʊzəri, -z

causes célèbres
BR ˌkɔːz sɪ'lɛːbr(ər), ˌkɔːz sɛ'lɛːbr(ər)
AM ˌkoʊz sə'lɛbr, ˌkɔz sə'lɛbr

causeway
BR 'kɔːzweɪ, -z
AM 'kɔzˌweɪ, 'kɑzˌweɪ, -z

causey
BR 'kɔːz|i, 'kɔːs|i, -ɪz
AM 'kɔzi, 'kɑzi, -z

caustic
BR 'kɔːstɪk, 'kɒstɪk
AM 'kɔstɪk, 'kɑstɪk

caustically
BR 'kɔːstɨkli, 'kɒstɨkli
AM 'kɔstək(ə)li, 'kɑstək(ə)li

causticise
BR 'kɔːstɨsʌɪz, 'kɒstɨsʌɪz, -ɨz, -ɪŋ, -d
AM 'kɔstəˌsaɪz, 'kɑstəˌsaɪz, -ɨz, -ɪŋ, -d

causticity
BR kɔː'stɪsɨti, kɒ'stɪsɨti
AM kɔ'stɪsɨdi, kɑ'stɪsɨdi

causticize
BR 'kɔːstɨsʌɪz, 'kɒstɨsʌɪz, -ɨz, -ɪŋ, -d
AM 'kɔstəˌsaɪz, 'kɑstəˌsaɪz, -ɨz, -ɪŋ, -d

Caute
BR kəʊt
AM kɔt, kɑt

cauterisation
BR ˌkɔːt(ə)rʌɪ'zeɪʃn
AM ˌkɔdərə'zeɪʃən, ˌkɔdəˌraɪ'zeɪʃən, ˌkɑdərə'zeɪʃən, ˌkɑdəˌraɪ'zeɪʃən

cauterise
BR 'kɔːtərʌɪz, -ɨz, -ɪŋ, -d
AM 'kɔdəˌraɪz, 'kɑdəˌraɪz, -ɨz, -ɪŋ, -d

cauterization
BR ˌkɔːt(ə)rʌɪ'zeɪʃn
AM ˌkɔdərə'zeɪʃən, ˌkɔdəˌraɪ'zeɪʃən, ˌkɑdərə'zeɪʃən, ˌkɑdəˌraɪ'zeɪʃən

cauterize
BR 'kɔːtərʌɪz, -ɨz, -ɪŋ, -d
AM 'kɔdəˌraɪz, 'kɑdəˌraɪz, -ɨz, -ɪŋ, -d

cautery
BR 'kɔːt(ə)r|i, -ɪz
AM 'kɔdəri, 'kɑdəri, -z

Cauthen
BR 'kɔːθn
AM 'kɔθən, 'kɑθən

caution
BR 'kɔːʃ|(ə)n, -(ə)nz, -n̩ɪŋ\-ənɪŋ, -(ə)nd
AM 'kɔʃ|ən, 'kɑʃ|ən, -ənz, -(ə)nɪŋ, -ənd

cautionary
BR 'kɔːʃn̩(ə)ri, 'kɔːʃən(ə)ri
AM 'kɔʃəˌnɛri, 'kɑʃəˌnɛri

cautious
BR 'kɔːʃəs
AM 'kɔʃəs, 'kɑʃəs

cautiously
BR 'kɔːʃəsli
AM 'kɔʃəsli, 'kɑʃəsli

cautiousness
BR 'kɔːʃəsnəs
AM 'kɔʃəsnəs, 'kɑʃəsnəs

Cavafy
BR ka'vɑːfi
AM kɑ'vɑfi

cavalcade
BR ˌkavl'keɪd, 'kavlkeɪd, -z
AM ˌkævəlˌkeɪd, -z

cavalier
BR ˌkavə'lɪə(r), -z
AM ˌkævə'lɪ(ə)r, -z

cavalierly
BR ˌkavə'lɪəli
AM ˌkævə'lɪrli

cavalry
BR 'kavlr|i, -ɪz
AM 'kævəlri, -z

cavalryman
BR 'kavlrɪmən
AM 'kævəlrimən

cavalrymen
BR 'kavlrɪmən
AM 'kævəlrimən

Cavan
BR 'kavn
AM 'kævən

Cavanagh
BR 'kavənə(r), 'kavn̩ə(r), kə'vanə(r)
AM 'kævəˌnɔ, 'kævəˌnɑ

cavatina
BR ˌkavə'tiːnə(r), -z
AM ˌkævə'tinə, -z

Cave
BR keɪv
AM keɪv

cave[1]
beware!
BR 'keɪvi
AM 'keɪvi

cave[2]
noun, verb
BR keɪv, -z, -ɪŋ, -d
AM keɪv, -z, -ɪŋ, -d

caveat
BR 'kavɪat, -s
AM 'kæviˌɑt, -s

caveat emptor
BR ˌkavɪat 'ɛm(p)tɔː(r)
AM ˌkæviˌɑt 'ɛm(p)ˌtɔ(ə)r

cavelike
BR 'keɪvlʌɪk
AM 'keɪvˌlaɪk

Cavell
BR 'kavl, kə'vɛl
AM 'kævəl, kə'vɛl

caveman
BR 'keɪvman
AM 'keɪvˌmæn

cavemen
BR 'keɪvmɛn
AM 'keɪvmən, 'keɪvˌmɛn

Cavendish
BR 'kavndɪʃ
AM 'kævəndɪʃ

caver
BR 'keɪvə(r), -z
AM 'keɪvər, -z

cavern
BR 'kavn, -z, -d
AM 'kævərn, -z, -d

cavernous
BR 'kavənəs, 'kavn̩əs
AM 'kævərnəs

cavernously
BR 'kavənəsli, 'kavn̩əsli
AM 'kævərnəsli

Caversham
BR 'kavəʃ(ə)m
AM 'kævərʃəm

cavesson
BR 'kavɨsn, -z
AM 'kævəsən, -z

cavetti
BR kə'vɛti
AM kə'vɛdi

cavetto
BR kə'vɛtəʊ
AM kə'vɛdoʊ

caviar
BR 'kavɪɑː(r)
AM 'kæviˌɑr

caviare
BR 'kavɪɑː(r)
AM 'kæviˌɑr

cavil
BR 'kavl̩, 'kavɪl, -z, -ɪŋ, -d
AM 'kæv|əl, -əlz, -(ə)lɪŋ, -əld

caviller
BR 'kavl̩ə(r), -z
AM 'kævələr, -z

cavitation
BR ˌkavɨ'teɪʃn
AM ˌkævə'teɪʃən

cavity
BR 'kavɪt|i, -ɪz
AM 'kævədi, -z

cavort
BR kə'vɔːt, -s, -ɪŋ, -ɨd
AM kə'vɔ(ə)rt, -ts, -'vɔrdɪŋ, -'vɔrdəd

Cavour
BR kə'vʊə(r), kə'vɔː(r)
AM kə'vʊ(ə)r

cavy
BR 'keɪv|i, -ɪz
AM 'keɪˌvi, -z

caw
BR kɔː(r), -z, -ɪŋ, -d
AM kɔ, kɑ, -z, -ɪŋ, -d

Cawdor
BR 'kɔːdɔː(r), 'kɔːdə(r)
AM 'kɔdɔ(ə)r, 'kɑdɔ(ə)r

Cawdrey
BR 'kɔːdri
AM 'kɔdri, 'kɑdri

Cawley
BR 'kɔːli
AM 'kɔli, 'kɑli

Cawnpore
BR ˌkɔːn'pɔː(r)
AM 'kɔnˌpɔ(ə)r, 'kɑnˌpɔ(ə)r

Cawood
BR 'keɪwʊd
AM 'keɪˌwʊd

Caxton
BR ˈkakst(ə)n
AM ˈkækstən

cay
BR kiː, keɪ, -z
AM ki, keɪ, -z

cayenne
BR (ˌ)keɪˈɛn, (ˌ)kʌɪˈɛn
AM ˌkaɪˈ(j)ɛn, ˌkeɪˈ(j)ɛn

Cayley
BR ˈkeɪli
AM ˈkeɪli

cayman
BR ˈkeɪmən, -z
AM ˈkeɪmən, -z

cayuse
BR ˈkʌɪ(j)uːs, -ɪz
AM ˈkaɪˌ(j)us, -əz

Cazenove
BR ˈkazɪnəʊv
AM ˈkæzəˌnoʊv

cc
BR ˌsiːˈsiː, -z
AM ˈsiˈsi, -z

CD-ROM
BR ˌsiːdiːˈrɒm, -z
AM ˌsiˌdiˈrɑm, -z

ceanothus
BR ˌsiːəˈnəʊθəs, -ɪz
AM ˌsiəˈnoʊθəs, -əz

cease
BR siːs, -ɪz, -ɪŋ, -t
AM sis, -ɪz, -ɪŋ, -t

ceasefire
BR ˈsiːsfʌɪə(r), ˌsiːsˈfʌɪə(r), -z
AM ˈsisˌfaɪ(ə)r, -z

ceaseless
BR ˈsiːslɪs
AM ˈsislɪs

ceaselessly
BR ˈsiːslɪsli
AM ˈsislɪsli

ceaselessness
BR ˈsiːslɪsnɪs
AM ˈsislɪsnɪs

ceca
BR ˈsiːkə(*r*)
AM ˈsikə

cecal
BR ˈsiːkl
AM ˈsikəl

Cecil
BR ˈsɛs(ɪ)l, ˈsɪs(ɪ)l, ˈsiːs(ɪ)l
AM ˈsisəl, ˈsɛsəl

Cecile
BR sɪˈsiːl, sɛˈsiːl, ˈsɛsiːl
AM səˈsil

Cecilia
BR sɪˈsiːlɪə(*r*)
AM səˈsiljə, səˈsiliə

Cecily
BR ˈsɛsɪli, ˈsɛsḷi
AM ˈsɛsəli

cecitis
BR sɪˈsʌɪtɪs
AM siˈsaɪdɪs

cecity
BR ˈsiːsɪti
AM ˈsisɨdi

cecum
BR ˈsiːkəm
AM ˈsikəm

cedar
BR ˈsiːdə(r), -z
AM ˈsidər, -z

cedarn
BR ˈsiːdən
AM ˈsidərn

cedarwood
BR ˈsiːdəwʊd, -z
AM ˈsidərˌwʊd, -z

cede
BR siːd, -z, -ɪŋ, -ɪd
AM sid, -z, -ɪŋ, -ɪd

cedi
BR ˈsiːd|i, -ɪz
AM ˈseɪdi, -z

cedilla
BR sɪˈdɪlə(r), -z
AM səˈdɪlə, -z

Cedric
BR ˈsɛdrɪk, ˈsiːdrɪk
AM ˈsidrɪk

Ceefax®
BR ˈsiːfaks
AM ˈsiˌfæks

ceili
BR ˈkeɪl|i, -ɪz
AM ˈkeɪli, -z

ceilidh
BR ˈkeɪl|i, -ɪz
AM ˈkeɪli, -z

ceiling
BR ˈsiːlɪŋ, -z
AM ˈsilɪŋ, -z

Ceinwen
BR ˈkʌɪnwɛn, ˈkʌɪnwɪn
AM ˈkaɪnwən
WE ˈkeɪnwen

celadon
BR ˈsɛlədən
AM ˈsɛləˌdɑn

celandine
BR ˈsɛləndʌɪn, -z
AM ˈsɛlənˌdin, ˈsɛlənˌdaɪn, -z

Celanese®
BR ˌsɛləˈniːz
AM ˌsɛləˈniz

celeb
BR sɪˈlɛb, -z
AM səˈlɛb, -z

Celebes
BR sɪˈliːbɪz, sɛˈliːbiːz, ˈsɛlɪbiːz
AM ˈsɛləˌbiz

celebrant
BR ˈsɛlɪbr(ə)nt, -s
AM ˈsɛləbrənt, -s

celebrate
BR ˈsɛlɪbreɪt, -s, -ɪŋ, -ɪd
AM ˈsɛləˌbreɪ|t, -ts, -dɪŋ, -dɪd

celebration
BR ˌsɛlɪˈbreɪʃn, -z
AM ˌsɛləˈbreɪʃən, -z

celebrator
BR ˈsɛlɪbreɪtə(r), -z
AM ˈsɛləˌbreɪdər, -z

celebratory
BR ˌsɛlɪˈbreɪt(ə)ri, ˈsɛlɪbrət(ə)ri
AM səˈlɛbrəˌtɔri, ˈsɛləbrəˌtɔri

celebrity
BR sɪˈlɛbrɪt|i, -ɪz
AM səˈlɛbrədi, -z

celeriac
BR sɪˈlɛrɪak
AM səˈlɛriˌæk

celerity
BR sɪˈlɛrɪti
AM səˈlɛrədi

celery
BR ˈsɛləri
AM ˈsɛl(ə)ri

celesta
BR sɪˈlɛstə(*r*)
AM səˈlɛstə

celeste
BR sɪˈlɛst, -s
AM səˈlɛst, -s

celestial
BR sɪˈlɛstɪəl
AM səˈlɛstʃəl, səˈlɛsˌdiəl

celestially
BR sɪˈlɛstɪəli
AM səˈlɛstʃəli

celestine
BR ˈsɛlɪstʌɪn, ˈsɛlɪstiːn
AM ˈsɛləˈstin

Celia
BR ˈsiːlɪə(*r*)
AM ˈsiljə, ˈsiliə

celiac
BR ˈsiːlɪak
AM ˈsiliˌæk

celibacy
BR ˈsɛlɪbəsi
AM ˈsɛləbəsi

celibate
BR ˈsɛlɪbət, -s
AM ˈsɛləbət, -s

cell
BR sɛl, -z, -d
AM sɛl, -z, -d

cellar
BR ˈsɛlə(r), -z
AM ˈsɛlər, -z

cellarage
BR ˈsɛl(ə)rɪdʒ
AM ˈsɛlərɪdʒ

cellarer
BR ˈsɛl(ə)rə(r), -z
AM ˈsɛlərər, -z

cellaret
BR ˈsɛl(ə)rɪt, -s
AM ˈsɛlərət, -s

cellarman
BR ˈsɛləmən
AM ˈsɛlərmən

cellarmen
BR ˈsɛləmən
AM ˈsɛlərən

Cellini
BR tʃɛˈliːni, tʃɪˈliːni
AM ˈtʃɛlɪni

cellist
BR ˈtʃɛlɪst, -s
AM ˈtʃɛləst, -s

Cellnet®
BR ˈsɛlnɛt
AM ˈsɛlˌnɛt

cello
BR ˈtʃɛləʊ, -z
AM ˈtʃɛloʊ, -z

Cellophane®
BR ˈsɛləfeɪn
AM ˈsɛləˌfeɪn

cellphone
BR ˈsɛlfəʊn, -z
AM ˈsɛlˌfoʊn, -z

cellular
BR ˈsɛljʉlə(r)
AM ˈsɛljələr

cellularity
BR ˌsɛljʉˈlarɪti
AM ˌsɛljəˈlɛrədi

cellulase
BR ˈsɛljʉleɪz
AM ˈsɛljəˌleɪz

cellulate
BR ˈsɛljʉleɪt, -s, -ɪŋ, -ɪd
AM ˈsɛljəˌleɪ|t, -ts, -dɪŋ, -dɪd

cellulation
BR ˌsɛljʉˈleɪʃn
AM ˌsɛljəˈleɪʃən

cellule
BR ˈsɛljuːl, -z
AM ˈsɛlˌjul, -z

cellulite
BR ˈsɛljʉlʌɪt
AM ˈsɛljəˌlaɪt

cellulitis
BR ˌsɛljʉˈlʌɪtɪs
AM ˌsɛljəˈlaɪdɪs

celluloid
BR ˈsɛljʉlɔɪd
AM ˈsɛljəˌlɔɪd

cellulose
BR ˈsɛljʉləʊs, ˈsɛljʉləʊz
AM ˈsɛljəˌloʊs, ˈsɛljəˌloʊz

cellulosic
BR ˌsɛljʉˈlɒsɪk
AM ˌsɛljəˈlɑsɪk

cellulous
BR ˈsɛljʉləs
AM ˈsɛljələs

celom
BR 'si:ləm
AM 'siləm
Celsius
BR 'sɛlsɪəs
AM 'sɛlsiəs, 'sɛlʃəs
Celt
BR kɛlt, -s
AM kɛlt, sɛlt, -s
Celtic[1]
noun, adjective, language
BR 'kɛltɪk
AM 'kɛltɪk
Celtic[2]
noun, soccer team
BR 'sɛltɪk
AM 'sɛltɪk
Celticism
BR 'kɛltɨsɪz(ə)m, -z
AM 'kɛltəˌsɪzəm, 'sɛltəˌsɪzəm, -z
Celtics
basketball team
BR 'sɛltɪks
AM 'sɛltɪks
Cemaes
BR 'kɛmʌɪs, kɪ'mʌɪs
AM 'kɛmaɪs
cembalo
BR 'tʃɛmbələʊ, -z
AM 'tʃɛmbəˌloʊ, -z
cement
BR sɪ'mɛnt, -s, -ɪŋ, -ɨd
AM sə'mɛnt, -s, -ɪŋ, -əd
cementation
BR ˌsi:mɛn'teɪʃn
AM ˌsimɛn'teɪʃən
cementer
BR sɪ'mɛntə(r), -z
AM sə'mɛn(t)ər, -z
cementite
BR sɪ'mɛntʌɪt
AM sə'mɛnˌtaɪt
cementitious
BR ˌsi:mɛn'tɪʃəs
AM ˌsimɛn'tɪʃəs
cementium
BR sɪ'mɛntɪəm, sɪ'mɛnʃɪəm
AM sɪ'mɛn(t)iəm
cementum
BR sɪ'mɛntəm
AM sə'mɛn(t)əm
cemetery
BR 'sɛmɨt(ə)r|i, -ɪz
AM 'sɛməˌtɛri, -z
Cemmaes
BR 'kɛmʌɪs, kɪ'mʌɪs
AM 'kɛmaɪs
cenacle
BR 'sɛnəkl, -z
AM 'sɛnək(ə)l, -z
cenobite
BR 'si:nəbʌɪt, -s
AM 'sɛnəˌbaɪt, -s
cenotaph
BR 'sɛnətɑ:f, 'sɛnətaf, -s
AM 'sɛnəˌtæf, -s
cenote
BR sɪ'nəʊti, sɪ'nəʊteɪ
AM sɪ'noʊdi
Cenozoic
BR ˌsi:nə'zəʊɪk
AM ˌsinə'zoʊɪk, ˌsɛnə'zoʊɪk
cense
BR sɛns, -ɪz, -ɪŋ, -t
AM sɛns, -əz, -ɪŋ, -t
censer
BR 'sɛnsə(r), -z
AM 'sɛnsər, -z
censor
BR 'sɛns|ə(r), -əz, -(ə)rɪŋ, -əd
AM 'sɛns|ər, -ərz, -(ə)rɪŋ, -ərd
censorial
BR sɛn'sɔ:rɪəl
AM sɛn'sɔriəl
censorially
BR sɛn'sɔ:rɪəli
AM sɛn'sɔriəli
censorian
BR sɛn'sɔ:rɪən
AM sɛn'sɔriən
censorious
BR sɛn'sɔ:rɪəs
AM sɛn'sɔriəs
censoriously
BR sɛn'sɔ:rɪəsli
AM sɛn'sɔriəsli
censoriousness
BR sɛn'sɔ:rɪəsnəs
AM sɛn'sɔriəsnəs
censorship
BR 'sɛnsəʃɪp
AM 'sɛnsərˌʃɪp
censurable
BR 'sɛnʃ(ə)rəbl
AM 'sɛn(t)ʃ(ə)rəbəl
censure
BR 'sɛnʃ|ə(r), -əz, -(ə)rɪŋ, -əd
AM 'sɛn(t)ʃər, -z, -ɪŋ, -d
census
BR 'sɛnsəs, -ɪz
AM 'sɛnsəs, -əz
cent
BR sɛnt, -s
AM sɛnt, -s
cental
BR 'sɛntl, -z
AM 'sɛn(t)l, -z
centaur
BR 'sɛntɔ:(r), -z
AM 'sɛnˌtɔ(ə)r, -z
Centaurus
BR sɛn'tɔ:rəs
AM sɛn'tɔrəs
centaury
BR 'sɛntɔ:ri
AM 'sɛn(t)əri
centavo
BR sɛn'tɑ:vəʊ, -z
AM sɛn'tɑvoʊ, -z
centenarian
BR ˌsɛntɪ'nɛ:rɪən, -z
AM ˌsɛn(t)ə'nɛriən, -z
centenary
BR sɛn'ti:n(ə)r|i, s(ə)n'ti:n(ə)r|i, sɛn'tɛn(ə)r|i, s(ə)n'tɛn(ə)r|i, -ɪz
AM sɛn'tɛnəri, 'sɛntnˌɛri, -z
centennial
BR sɛn'tɛnɪəl, s(ə)n'tɛnɪəl, -z
AM sɛn'tɛniəl, sən'tɛniəl, -z
center
BR 'sɛnt|ə(r), -əz, -(ə)rɪŋ, -əd
AM 'sɛn(t)|ər, -ərz, -(ə)rɪŋ, -ərd
centerboard
BR 'sɛntəbɔ:d, -z
AM 'sɛn(t)ərˌbɔ(ə)rd, -z
centerfold
BR 'sɛntəfəʊld, -z
AM 'sɛn(t)ərˌfoʊld, -z
centerline
BR 'sɛntəlʌɪn, -z
AM 'sɛn(t)ərˌlaɪn, -z
centermost
BR 'sɛntəməʊst
AM 'sɛn(t)ərˌmoʊst
centerpiece
BR 'sɛntəpi:s, -ɪz
AM 'sɛn(t)ərˌpis, -ɪz
centesimal
BR sɛn'tɛsɪml
AM sɛn'tɛsəməl
centesimally
BR sɛn'tɛsɪmli, sɛn'tɛsɪməli
AM sɛn'tɛs(ə)məli
centigrade
BR 'sɛntɪgreɪd
AM 'sɛn(t)əˌgreɪd
centigram
BR 'sɛntɪgram, -z
AM 'sɛn(t)əˌgræm, -z
centigramme
BR 'sɛntɪgram, -z
AM 'sɛn(t)əˌgræm, -z
centiliter
BR 'sɛntɪˌli:tə(r), -z
AM 'sɛn(t)əˌlidər, -z
centilitre
BR 'sɛntɪˌli:tə(r), -z
AM 'sɛn(t)əˌlidər, -z
centime
BR 'sɒnti:m, 'sɑ:nti:m, -z
AM 'sɑnˌtim, ˌsɑn'tim, -z
centimeter
BR 'sɛntɪˌmi:tə(r), -z
AM 'sɛn(t)əˌmidər, -z
centimetre
BR 'sɛntɪˌmi:tə(r), -z
AM 'sɛn(t)əˌmidər, -z
centimo
BR 'sɛntɪməʊ, -z
AM 'sɛn(t)əmoʊ, -z
centipede
BR 'sɛntɪpi:d, -z
AM 'sɛn(t)əˌpid, -z
centner
BR 'sɛntnə(r), -z
AM 'sɛntnər, -z
cento
BR 'sɛntəʊ, -z
AM 'sɛnˌtoʊ, -z
centra
BR 'sɛntrə(r)
AM 'sɛntrə
central
BR 'sɛntr(ə)l
AM 'sɛntrəl
centralisation
BR ˌsɛntrəlʌɪ'zeɪʃn, ˌsɛntrl̩ʌɪ'zeɪʃn
AM ˌsɛntrələ'zeɪʃən, ˌsɛntrəˌlaɪ'zeɪʃən
centralise
BR 'sɛntrəlʌɪz, 'sɛntrl̩ʌɪz, -ɪz, -ɪŋ, -d
AM 'sɛntrəˌlaɪz, -ɪz, -ɪŋ, -d
centralism
BR 'sɛntrəlɪz(ə)m, 'sɛntrl̩ɪz(ə)m
AM 'sɛntrəˌlɪzəm
centralist
BR 'sɛntrəlɪst, 'sɛntrl̩ɪst
AM 'sɛntrələst
centrality
BR sɛn'tralɨti
AM sɛn'trælədi
centralization
BR ˌsɛntrəlʌɪ'zeɪʃn, ˌsɛntrl̩ʌɪ'zeɪʃn
AM ˌsɛntrələ'zeɪʃən, ˌsɛntrəˌlaɪ'zeɪʃən
centralize
BR 'sɛntrəlʌɪz, 'sɛntrl̩ʌɪz, -ɪz, -ɪŋ, -d
AM 'sɛntrəˌlaɪz, -ɪz, -ɪŋ, -d
centrally
BR 'sɛntrəli, 'sɛntrl̩i
AM 'sɛntrəli
centre
BR 'sɛnt|ə(r), -əz, -(ə)rɪŋ, -əd
AM 'sɛn(t)|ər, -ərz, -(ə)rɪŋ, -ərd
centreboard
BR 'sɛntəbɔ:d, -z
AM 'sɛn(t)ərˌbɔ(ə)rd, -z

centrefold
BR 'sɛntəfəʊld, -z
AM 'sɛn(t)ər,foʊld, -z
centreline
BR 'sɛntəlʌɪn, -z
AM 'sɛn(t)ər,laɪn, -z
centremost
BR 'sɛntəməʊst
AM 'sɛn(t)ər,moʊst
centrepiece
BR 'sɛntəpi:s, -ɪz
AM 'sɛn(t)ər,pis, -ɪz
centric
BR 'sɛntrɪk
AM 'sɛntrɪk
centrical
BR 'sɛntrɪkl
AM 'sɛntrəkəl
centricity
BR sɛn'trɪsɪti
AM ,sɛn'trɪsɪdi
centrifugal
BR ,sɛntrɪ'fju:gl,
sɛn'trɪfjʊgl,
s(ə)n'trɪfjʊgl
AM sɛn'trɪf(j)əgəl
centrifugally
BR ,sɛntrɪ'fju:gli,
sɛn'trɪfjʊgli,
s(ə)n'trɪfjʊgli
AM sɛn'trɪf(j)əg(ə)li
centrifugation
BR ,sɛntrɪfjʊ'geɪʃn
AM ,sɛntrə,fju'geɪʃən
centrifuge
BR 'sɛntrɪfju:(d)ʒ, -ɪz
AM 'sɛntrə,fjudʒ, -əz
centriole
BR 'sɛntrɪəʊl, -z
AM 'sɛntri,oʊl, -z
centripetal
BR ,sɛntrɪ'pi:tl,
sɛn'trɪpɪtl,
s(ə)n'trɪpɪtl
AM sɛn'trɪpɪdl
centripetally
BR ,sɛntrɪ'pi:tli,
sɛn'trɪpɪtli,
s(ə)n'trɪpɪtli
AM sɛn'trɪpədɪli
centrism
BR 'sɛntrɪz(ə)m
AM 'sɛnt,rɪzəm
centrist
BR 'sɛntrɪst, -s
AM 'sɛntrəst, -s
centroid
BR 'sɛntrɔɪd, -z
AM 'sɛntrɔɪd, -z
centromere
BR 'sɛntrə(ʊ)mɪə(r), -z
AM 'sɛntrə,mɪ(ə)r, -z
centrosome
BR 'sɛntrə(ʊ)səʊm, -z
AM 'sɛntrə,soʊm, -z
centrum
BR 'sɛntrəm
AM 'sɛntrəm
centum
BR 'kɛntəm
AM 'kɛn(t)əm
centumvirate
BR sɛn'tʌmvɪrət, -s
AM sɛn'təmvərət, -s
centuple
BR 'sɛntjʊpl, 'sɛntʃʊpl
AM sɛn't(j)upəl,
'sɛntəpəl
centurion
BR sɛn'tjʊərɪən,
sɛn'tʃʊərɪən,
sɛn'tjɔ:rɪən,
sɛn'tʃɔ:rɪən, -z
AM sɛn't(j)ʊriən, -z
century
BR 'sɛntʃ(ʊ)r|i, -ɪz
AM 'sɛn(t)ʃ(ə)ri, -z
ceorl
BR tʃə:l, -z
AM tʃərl, -z
cep
BR sɛp, -s
AM sɛp, -s
cephalic
BR sɪ'falɪk, kɛ'falɪk
AM sə'fælɪk
Cephalonia
BR ,kɛfə'ləʊnɪə(*r*),
,sɛfə'ləʊnɪə(*r*)
AM ,sɛfə'loʊniə
cephalopod
BR 'kɛf(ə)ləpɒd,
'kɛfləpɒd,
'sɛf(ə)ləpɒd,
'sɛfləpɒd, -z
AM 'sɛfələ,pɑd, -z
cephalopoda
BR ,kɛfə'lɒpədə(*r*),
,sɛfə'lɒpədə(*r*)
AM sɛfə'lɑpədə
cephalothorax
BR ,kɛf(ə)ləʊ'θɔ:raks,
,kɛfləʊ'θɔ:raks,
,sɛf(ə)ləʊ'θɔ:raks,
,sɛfləʊ'θɔ:raks, -ɪz
AM ,sɛfələ'θɔræks, -əz
cephalothoraxes
BR ,kɛfələʊ'θɔ:raksɪz,
,kɛfləʊ'θɔ:raksɪz,
,sɛf(ə)ləʊ'θɔ:raksɪz,
,sɛfləʊ'θɔ:raksɪz
AM ,sɛfələ'θɔræksiz
Cephas
BR 'si:fas
AM 'sifəs
cepheid
BR 'si:fɪɪd, 'sɛfɪɪd, -z
AM 'sifiəd, 'sɛfiəd, -z
Cepheus
BR 'si:fɪəs
AM 'sifiəs
ceramic
BR sɪ'ramɪk, -s
AM sə'ræmɪk, -s
ceramicist
BR sɪ'ramɪsɪst, -s
AM sə'ræməsəst, -s
ceramist
BR sɪ'ramɪst, -s
AM sə'ræməst, -s
cerastes
BR sɪ'rasti:z, -ɪz
AM sə'ræstiz, -ɪz
cerastium
BR sɪ'rastɪəm, -z
AM sə'ræstiəm, -z
Cerberus
BR 'sə:b(ə)rəs
AM 'sərbərəs
cercaria
BR sə'kɛ:rɪə(*r*)
AM sər'kɛriə
cercariae
BR sə:'kɛ:rɪi:
AM sər'kɛrii
cerci
BR 'sə:kʌɪ
AM 'sərkaɪ, 'sərsaɪ
cercopithecine
BR ,sə:kə(ʊ)'pɪθɪsi:n
AM ,sərkə'pɪθɪ,sin
cercopithecoid
BR ,sə:kə(ʊ)'pɪθɪkɔɪd
AM ,sərkə'pɪθɪ,kɔɪd
cercus
BR 'sə:kəs
AM 'sərkəs
cere
BR sɪə(r), -z
AM sɪ(ə)r, -z
cereal
BR 'sɪərɪəl, -z
AM 'sɪriəl, -z
cerebella
BR ,sɛrɪ'bɛlə(*r*)
AM ,sɛrə'bɛlə
cerebellar
BR ,sɛrɪ'bɛlə(r)
AM ,sɛrə'bɛlər
cerebellum
BR ,sɛrɪ'bɛləm, -z
AM ,sɛrə'bɛləm, -z
Cerebos®
BR 'sɛrɪbɒs
AM 'sɛrəbɔs, 'sɛrəbɑs
cerebra
BR sɪ'ri:brə(*r*),
'sɛrɪbrə(*r*)
AM sə'ribrə, 'sɛrəbrə
cerebral
BR sɪ'ri:br(ə)l,
'sɛrɪbr(ə)l
AM sə'ribrəl, 'sɛrəbrəl
cerebrally
BR sɪ'ri:brli,
sɪ'ri:brəli, 'sɛrɪbrli,
'sɛrɪbrəli
AM sə'ribrəli,
'sɛr(ə)brəli
cerebrate
BR 'sɛrɪbreɪt, -s, -ɪŋ, -ɪd
AM 'sɛrə,breɪ|t, -ts,
-dɪŋ, -dɪd
cerebration
BR ,sɛrɪ'breɪʃn
AM ,sɛrə'breɪʃən
cerebroside
BR 'sɛrɪbrəsʌɪd, -z
AM 'sɛrəbrə,saɪd,
sə'ribrə,saɪd, -z
cerebrospinal
BR ,sɛrɪbrəʊ'spʌɪnl,
sɪ,ri:brəʊ'spʌɪnl
AM sə,ribroʊ'spaɪnəl,
¦sɛrəbroʊ'spaɪnəl
cerebrovascular
BR ,sɛrɪbrəʊ'vaskjʊlə(r),
sɪ,ri:brəʊ'vaskjʊlə(r)
AM sə,ribroʊ'væskjələr,
¦sɛrəbroʊ'væskjələr
cerebrum
BR sɪ'ri:brəm,
'sɛrɪbrəm
AM sə'ribrəm,
'sɛrəbrəm
cerecloth
BR 'sɪəklɒ|θ, -θs\-ðz
AM 'sɪr,klɔ|θ, 'sɪr,klɑ|θ,
-θs\-ðz
Ceredigion
BR ,kɛrɪ'dɪgɪɒn
AM ,kɛrə'dɪgiən
WE ,kere'dɪgjɒn
cerement
BR 'sɪəm(ə)nt,
'sɛrɪm(ə)nt, -s
AM 'sɪrmənt, -s
ceremonial
BR ,sɛrɪ'məʊnɪəl
AM ,sɛrə'moʊniəl
ceremonialism
BR ,sɛrɪ'məʊnɪəlɪz(ə)m
AM ,sɛrə'moʊniə,lɪzəm
ceremonialist
BR ,sɛrɪ'məʊnɪəlɪst, -s
AM ,sɛrə'moʊniələst,
-s
ceremonially
BR ,sɛrɪ'məʊnɪəli
AM ,sɛrə'moʊniəli
ceremonious
BR ,sɛrɪ'məʊnɪəs
AM ,sɛrə'moʊniəs
ceremoniously
BR ,sɛrɪ'məʊnɪəsli
AM ,sɛrə'moʊniəsli
ceremoniousness
BR ,sɛrɪ'məʊnɪəsnəs
AM ,sɛrə'moʊniəsnəs
ceremony
BR 'sɛrɪmən|i, -ɪz
AM 'sɛrə,moʊni, -z
Cerenkov
BR tʃɪ'rɛŋkɒf,
tʃɪ'rɛŋkɒv
AM tʃə'rɛŋkov,
tʃə'rɛŋkɔf,
tʃə'rɛŋkɑv,
tʃə'rɛŋkɑf
Ceres
BR 'sɪəri:z

AM 'sɪriz
ceresin
BR 'sɛrɪsɪn
AM 'sɛrəsən
Ceri
BR 'kɛri
AM 'kɛri
cerif
BR 'sɛrɪf, -s
AM 'sɛrɪf, -s
cerise
BR sɪ'ri:z, sɪ'ri:s
AM sə'ris, sə'riz
cerium
BR 'sɪərɪəm
AM 'siriəm
cermet
BR 'sə:mɛt
AM 'sər,mɛt
CERN
BR sə:n
AM sərn
Cerne Abbas
BR ˌsə:n 'abəs
AM ˌsərn 'æbəs
cerography
BR sɪ'rɒgrəfi
AM sə'rɑgrəfi
ceroplastic
BR ˌsɪərəʊ'plastɪk
AM ˌsɪroʊ'plæstɪk, ˌsɛroʊ'plæstɪk
cert
BR sə:t, -s
AM sərt, -s
certain
BR 'sə:t(ɪ)n
AM 'sərtn
certainly
BR 'sə:t(ɪ)nli
AM 'sərtnli
certainty
BR 'sə:t(ɪ)nt|i, -ɪz
AM 'sərtn(t)i, -z
Cert.Ed.
BR ˌsə:t'ɛd, -z
AM ˌsərt'ɛd, -z
certes
BR 'sə:ti:z, 'sə:tɪz
AM 'sərdiz
certifiable
BR ˌsə:tɪ'fʌɪəbl, 'sə:tɪfʌɪəbl
AM ˌsərdə'faɪəbəl
certifiably
BR ˌsə:tɪ'fʌɪəbli, 'sə:tɪfʌɪəbli
AM ˌsərdə'faɪəbli
certificate[1]
noun
BR sə'tɪfɪkət, -s
AM sər'tɪfəkət, -s
certificate[2]
verb
BR sə'tɪfɪkeɪt, -s, -ɪŋ, -ɪd
AM ˌsər'tɪfəkeɪ|t, -ts, -dɪŋ, -dɪd
certification
BR ˌsə:tɪfɪ'keɪʃn, -z
AM ˌsərdəfə'keɪʃən, -z
certificatory
BR sə'tɪfɪkət(ə)ri
AM sər'tɪfəkəˌtɔri
certify
BR 'sə:tɪfʌɪ, -z, -ɪŋ, -d
AM 'sərdəˌfaɪ, -z, -ɪŋ, -d
certiorari
BR ˌsə:tɪə'rɛ:rʌɪ, ˌsə:ʃɪə'rɛ:rʌɪ, ˌsə:tɪə'rɑ:ri, ˌsə:ʃɪə'rɑ:ri
AM ˌsɛrʃ(i)ə'rɛri
certitude
BR 'sə:tɪtju:d, 'sə:tɪtʃu:d
AM 'sərdəˌt(j)ud
cerulean
BR sɪ'ru:lɪən
AM sə'ruliən
cerumen
BR sɪ'ru:mɛn, sɪ'ru:mɪn
AM sə'rumən
ceruminous
BR sɪ'ru:mɪnəs
AM sə'rumənəs
ceruse
BR 'sɪəru:s, sɪ'ru:s
AM sə'rus, 'sɪrus
Cervantes
BR sə:'vanti:z, sə:'vantɪz
AM sər'vɑnteɪs
cervelat
BR 'sə:vəlat, 'sə:vəlɑ:(r), ˌsə:və'lat, ˌsə:və'lɑ:(r)
AM 'sərvələt
cervical
BR sə(:)'vʌɪkl, 'sə:vɪkl
AM 'sərvɪkəl
cervices
BR 'sə:vɪsi:z
AM 'sərvəˌsiz
cervine
BR 'sə:vʌɪn
AM 'sərˌvaɪn
cervix
BR 'sə:v|ɪks, -ɪksɪz
AM 'sərˌvɪks, -ɪz
Cesar
BR 'seɪzɑ:(r)
AM 'sizər, 'seɪzɑr
César
BR 'seɪzɑ:(r)
AM 'seɪzɑr
cesarean
BR sɪ'zɛ:rɪən, -z
AM sə'zɛriən, -z
Cesarewitch
BR sɪ'zarɪwɪtʃ
AM sə'zɑrəwɪtʃ
cesarian
BR sɪ'zɛ:rɪən, -z
AM sə'zɛriən, -z
cesium
BR 'si:zɪəm
AM 'siziəm
cess
BR sɛs, -ɪz
AM sɛs, -əz
cessation
BR sɛ'seɪʃn, sɪ'seɪʃn, -z
AM sɛ'seɪʃən, sə'seɪʃən, -z
cesser
BR 'sɛsə(r)
AM 'sɛsər
cession
BR 'sɛʃn, -z
AM 'sɛʃən, -z
cessionary
BR 'sɛʃən(ə)r|i, 'sɛʃn̩(ə)r|i, -ɪz
AM 'sɛʃəˌnɛri, -z
Cessna®
BR 'sɛsnə(r), -z
AM 'sɛsnə, -z
cesspit
BR 'sɛspɪt, -s
AM 'sɛsˌpɪt, -s
cesspool
BR 'sɛspu:l, -z
AM 'sɛsˌpul, -z
cesta
BR 'sɛstə(r), -z
AM 'sɛstə, -z
cesti
BR 'sɛstʌɪ, 'sɛsti:
AM 'sɛsˌtaɪ, 'sɛsti
c'est la vie
BR ˌseɪ lɑ: 'vi:, + lə +
AM ˌseɪ lɑ 'vi
cestode
BR 'sɛstəʊd, -z
AM 'sɛsˌtoʊd, -z
cestoid
BR 'sɛstɔɪd, -z
AM 'sɛsˌtɔɪd, -z
cestus
BR 'sɛstəs
AM 'sɛstəs
cetacea
BR sɪ'teɪʃə(r)
AM sə'teɪʃiə
cetacean
BR sɪ'teɪʃn
AM sə'teɪʃən
cetaceous
BR sɪ'teɪʃəs
AM sə'teɪʃəs
cetane
BR 'si:teɪn
AM 'siˌteɪn
ceteris paribus
BR ˌkeɪt(ə)rɪs 'parɪbəs, ˌkɛt(ə)rɪs +, + 'pɑ:rɪbəs, + 'parɪbʊs, + 'pɑ:rɪbʊs
AM ˌkeɪdərəs 'pɛrəbəs, ˌseɪdərəs +, ˌsɛdərəs +
cetological
BR ˌsi:tə'lɒdʒɪkl
AM ˌsidə'lɑdʒəkəl
cetologist
BR sɪ'tɒlədʒɪst, si:'tɒlədʒɪst, -s
AM sə'tɑlədʒəst, si'tɑlədʒəst, -s
cetology
BR sɪ'tɒlədʒi, si:'tɒlədʒi
AM sə'tɑlədʒi, si'tɑlədʒi
Cetshwayo
BR kɛtʃ'wʌɪəʊ
AM kɛtʃ'waɪoʊ
Cetus
BR 'si:təs
AM 'sidəs
Ceuta
BR 's(j)u:tə(r)
AM 'seɪudə
Cévennes
BR sɛ'vɛn
AM sə'vɛn
Ceylon
BR sɪ'lɒn
AM seɪ'lɑn, sə'lɑn
Ceylonese
BR ˌsɛlə'ni:z
AM ˌsɛlə'niz, ˌseɪlə'niz
Cézanne
BR sɪ'zan, seɪ'zan
AM seɪ'zɑn
cha
BR tʃɑ:(r)
AM tʃɑ
Chablis
BR 'ʃabli:
AM ʃɑ'bli, ʃə'bli
Chabrier
BR 'ʃabrɪeɪ, 'ʃɑ:brɪeɪ
AM 'ʃɑbriˌeɪ
Chabrol
BR ʃa'brɒl, ʃə'brɒl
AM ʃɑ'broʊl
cha-cha
BR 'tʃɑ:tʃɑ:(r), -z, -ɪŋ
AM 'tʃɑˌtʃɑ, -z, -ɪŋ
cha-cha-cha
BR ˌtʃɑ:tʃɑ:'tʃɑ:(r)
AM ˌtʃɑˌtʃɑ'tʃɑ, 'tʃɑ'tʃɑ'tʃɑ
chacma
BR 'tʃakmə(r), -z
AM 'tʃɑkmə, -z
chaconne
BR ʃə'kɒn, ʃa'kɒn, -z
AM ʃɑ'kɔn, ʃɑ'kɑn, ʃə'kɔn, ʃə'kɑn, -z
Chad
BR tʃad
AM tʃæd
chadar
BR 'tʃɑ:də(r), -z
AM 'tʃɑdər, -z

Chadian
BR 'tʃadɪən, -z
AM 'tʃædiən, -z
Chadic
BR 'tʃadɪk
AM 'tʃædɪk
chador
BR 'tʃɑːdɔː(r), 'tʃʌdə(r)
AM 'tʃɑˌdɔ(ə)r
Chadwick
BR 'tʃadwɪk
AM 'tʃædˌwɪk
chaeta
BR 'kiːtə(*r*)
AM 'kidə
chaetae
BR 'kiːtiː
AM 'kidi
chaetognath
BR 'kiːtənaθ, -s
AM 'kidɑgˌnaθ, -s
chaetopod
BR 'kiːtəpɒd, -z
AM 'kidəˌpɑd, -z
chafe
BR tʃeɪf, -s, -ɪŋ, -t
AM tʃeɪf, -s, -ɪŋ, -t
chafer
BR 'tʃeɪfə(r), -z
AM 'tʃeɪfər, -z
chaff
BR tʃɑːf, tʃaf, -s, -ɪŋ, -t
AM tʃæf, -s, -ɪŋ, -t
chaffer
BR 'tʃaf|ə(r), -əz, -(ə)rɪŋ, -əd
AM 'tʃæfər, -z, -ɪŋ, -d
chafferer
BR 'tʃaf(ə)rə(r), -z
AM 'tʃæfərər, -z
chaffinch
BR 'tʃafɪn(t)ʃ, -ɨz
AM 'tʃæˌfɪntʃ, -ɨz
chaffiness
BR 'tʃɑːfɪnɨs, 'tʃafɪnɨs
AM 'tʃæfinɨs
chaffy
BR 'tʃɑːfi, 'tʃafi
AM 'tʃæfi
Chagall
BR ʃa'gal, ʃə'gal, ʃa'gɑːl, ʃə'gɑːl
AM ʃə'gɑl
Chagas' disease
BR 'ʃɑːgəs dɪˌziːz
AM 'ʃɑgəs dəˌziz, + dɪˌziz
Chagos Archipelago
BR ˌʃɑːgəs ˌɑːkɪ'pɛləgəʊ
AM ˌʃɑgəs ˌɑrkə'pɛləgoʊ, + ˌɑrtʃɪ'pɛləgoʊ
chagrin
BR 'ʃagr(ɨ)n, -z, -ɪŋ, -d
AM ʃə'grɪn, -z, -ɪŋ, -d
Chaim
BR xʌɪm, hʌɪm
AM kaɪ(ə)m
chain
BR tʃeɪn, -z, -ɪŋ, -d
AM tʃeɪn, -z, -ɪŋ, -d
chaingang
BR 'tʃeɪngaŋ, -z
AM 'tʃeɪnˌgæŋg, -z
chainless
BR 'tʃeɪnlɨs
AM 'tʃeɪnləs
chainmail
BR ˌtʃeɪn'meɪl, 'tʃeɪnmeɪl
AM 'tʃeɪnˌmeɪl
chainsaw
BR 'tʃeɪnsɔː(*r*), -z
AM 'tʃeɪnˌsɔ, 'tʃeɪnˌsɑ, -z
chainwork
BR 'tʃeɪnwəːk
AM 'tʃeɪnˌwərk
chair
BR tʃɛː(r), -z, -ɪŋ, -d
AM tʃɛ(ə)r, -z, -ɪŋ, -d
chairlady
BR 'tʃɛːˌleɪd|i, -ɪz
AM 'tʃɛrˌleɪdi, -z
chairlift
BR 'tʃɛːlɪft, -s
AM 'tʃɛrˌlɪft, -s
chairman
BR 'tʃɛːmən
AM 'tʃɛrmən
chairmanship
BR 'tʃɛːmənʃɪp, -s
AM 'tʃɛrmənˌʃɪp, -s
chairmen
BR 'tʃɛːmən
AM 'tʃɛrmən
chairperson
BR 'tʃɛːˌpəːsn, -z
AM 'tʃɛrˌpərsən, -z
chairwoman
BR 'tʃɛːˌwʊmən
AM 'tʃɛrˌwʊmən
chairwomen
BR 'tʃɛːˌwɪmɪn
AM 'tʃɛrˌwɪmɨn
chaise
BR ʃeɪz, -ɨz
AM ʃeɪz, -ɨz
chaise longue
BR ˌʃeɪz 'lɒŋ, -z
AM ˌʃeɪz 'lɔŋ, + 'laʊndʒ, ˌʃeɪz 'lɑŋ, -z
chakra
BR 'tʃʌkrə(*r*), 'tʃakrə(*r*), 'tʃɑːkrə(*r*), -z
AM 'tʃɑkrə, -z
chalaza
BR kə'leɪzə(*r*), -z
AM kə'leɪzə, -z
chalazae
BR kə'leɪziː
AM kə'leɪzi, kə'leɪˌzaɪ
Chalcedon
BR 'kalsɪdɒn, 'kalsɪd(ə)n
AM 'kælsəˌdɑn, kæl'sidən
Chalcedonian
BR ˌkalsɪ'dəʊnɪən, -z
AM ˌkælsə'doʊniən, -z
chalcedonic
BR ˌkalsɪ'dɒnɪk
AM ˌkælsə'dɑnɪk
chalcedony
BR kal'sɛdən|i, kal'sɛdn̩|i, -ɪz
AM kæl'sɛdn̩i, tʃæl'sɛdn̩i, 'kælsəˌdoʊni, 'tʃælsəˌdoʊni, -z
Chalcidice
BR kal'sɪdɪsi
AM kæl'sɪdɨsi
Chalcis
BR 'kalsɪs
AM 'kælsəs
chalcolithic
BR ˌkalkə'lɪθɪk
AM ˌkælkə'lɪθɪk
chalcopyrite
BR ˌkalkə(ʊ)'pʌɪrʌɪt
AM ˌkælkə'paɪˌraɪt
Chaldea
BR kal'diːə(*r*)
AM kæl'diə
Chaldean
BR kal'diːən, -z
AM kæl'diən, -z
Chaldee
BR 'kaldiː, -z
AM 'kældi, -z
chaldron
BR 'tʃɔːldr(ə)n, -z
AM 'tʃɔldrən, 'tʃɑldrən, -z
chalet
BR 'ʃal|eɪ, 'ʃal|i, -eɪz\-ɪz
AM ˌʃæ'leɪ, -z
Chalfont
BR 'tʃalf(ɒ)nt
AM 'tʃælfɑnt
Chaliapin
BR ʃal'jɑːpɪn
AM ˌʃɑl'jɑˌpɪn
chalice
BR 'tʃalɪs, -ɨz
AM 'tʃæləs, -əz
chalk
BR tʃɔːk, -s, -ɪŋ, -t
AM tʃɔk, tʃɑk, -s, -ɪŋ, -t
chalkboard
BR 'tʃɔːkbɔːd, -z
AM 'tʃɔkˌbɔ(ə)rd, 'tʃɑkˌbɔ(ə)rd, -z
Chalker
BR 'tʃɔːkə(r)
AM tʃɔkər, tʃɑkər
chalkily
BR 'tʃɔːkɪli
AM 'tʃɔkəli, 'tʃɑkəli
chalkiness
BR 'tʃɔːkɪnɪs
AM 'tʃɔkinɨs, 'tʃɑkinɨs
chalky
BR 'tʃɔːk|i, -ɪə(r), -ɪɪst
AM 'tʃɔki, 'tʃɑki, -ər, -ɨst
challah
BR 'hɑːlə(*r*), xɑː'lɑː(*r*), -z
AM 'hɑlə, -z
challenge
BR 'tʃalɪn(d)ʒ, -ɪz, -ɪŋ, -d
AM 'tʃæləndʒ, -əz, -ɪŋ, -d
challengeable
BR 'tʃalɪn(d)ʒəbl
AM 'tʃæləndʒəbəl
challenger
BR 'tʃalɪn(d)ʒə(r), -z
AM 'tʃæləndʒər, -z
challengingly
BR 'tʃalɪn(d)ʒɪŋli
AM 'tʃæləndʒɪŋli
Challes
BR 'tʃalɪs
AM 'tʃæləs
challis
BR 'ʃalɪs, 'ʃali
AM 'ʃali, 'ʃæləs
Challoner
BR 'tʃalənə(r)
AM 'tʃælənər
Chalmers
BR 'tʃɑːməz
AM 'tʃɑlmərz, 'tʃælmərz
chalumeau
BR 'ʃalʉməʊ
AM 'ʃæləˌmoʊ
chalumeaux
BR 'ʃalʉməʊ(z)
AM 'ʃæləˌmoʊ(z)
chalybeate
BR kə'lɪbɪət
AM kə'lɪbiət
cham
BR kam, -z
AM kæm, -z
chamaephyte
BR 'kamɪfʌɪt, -s
AM 'kæməˌfaɪt, -s
chamber
BR 'tʃeɪmbə(r), -z, -d
AM 'tʃeɪmbər, -z, -d
chamberlain
BR 'tʃeɪmbəlɪn, -z
AM 'tʃeɪmbərlən, -z
chamberlainship
BR 'tʃeɪmbəlɪnʃɪp
AM 'tʃeɪmbərlənˌʃɪp
chambermaid
BR 'tʃeɪmbəmeɪd, -z

AM 'tʃeɪmbər,meɪd, -z
Chambers
BR 'tʃeɪmbəz
AM 'tʃeɪmbərz
Chambertin
BR 'ʃɒ̃bətɑ̃, -z
AM ,ʃɑmbər'tɛn, -z
Chambourcy®
BR ʃam'bʊəsi
AM ʃæm'bʊrsi
chambray
BR 'ʃɒmbreɪ, 'ʃambreɪ
AM 'ʃæm,breɪ
chambré
BR 'ʃɒmbreɪ, 'ʃambreɪ
AM 'ʃæm,breɪ
chameleon
BR kə'mi:lɪən, -z
AM kə'miljən, kə'miliən, -z
chameleonic
BR kə,mi:lɪ'ɒnɪk
AM kə,mili'ɑnɪk
chamfer
BR '(t)ʃamf|ə(r), -əz, -(ə)rɪŋ, -əd
AM '(t)ʃæmfər, -z, -ɪŋ, -d
chammy
BR 'ʃam|i, -ɪz, -ɪɪŋ, -ɪd
AM 'ʃæmi, -z, -ɪŋ, -d
chamois[1]
animal
BR 'ʃamwɑ:(*r*), -z
AM 'ʃæmi, ʃæm'wɑ, -z
chamois[2]
leather
BR 'ʃam|i, -ɪz, -ɪɪŋ, -ɪd
AM 'ʃæmi, -z, -ɪŋ, -d
chamomile
BR 'kaməmʌɪl
AM 'kæmə,mil, 'kæmə,maɪl
Chamonix
BR 'ʃaməni:, 'ʃamɒni:
AM ʃɑmə'ni
champ
BR tʃamp, -s, -ɪŋ, -t
AM tʃæmp, -s, -ɪŋ, -t
champagne
BR ,ʃam'peɪn, -z
AM ,ʃæm'peɪn, -z
champaign
BR ,ʃam'peɪn, -z
AM ,ʃæm'peɪn, -z
champenoise
BR ,ʃampə'nwɑ:z
AM ,ʃæmpə'nwɑz
champers
BR 'ʃampəz
AM 'ʃæmpərz
champertous
BR 'tʃampətəs
AM 'tʃæmpərdəs
champerty
BR 'tʃampət|i, -ɪz
AM 'tʃæmpərdi, -z
champion
BR 'tʃampɪən, -z, -ɪŋ, -d
AM 'tʃæmpiən, -z, -ɪŋ, -d
championship
BR 'tʃampɪənʃɪp, -s
AM 'tʃæmpiən,ʃɪp, -s
Champlain
BR ʃam'pleɪn
AM ,ʃæm'pleɪn
champlevé
BR 'ʃampləveɪ
AM ,ʃɑm(p)lə'veɪ
Champneys
BR 'tʃampnɪz
AM 'tʃæmpniz
Champs-Élysées
BR ,ʃɒ̃zə'li:zeɪ
AM ,ʃɑnzəli'zeɪ
Chan
BR tʃan
AM tʃæn
chance
BR tʃɑ:ns, tʃans, -ɪz, -ɪŋ, -t
AM tʃæns, -əz, -ɪŋ, -t
chancel
BR 'tʃɑ:nsl, 'tʃansl, -z
AM 'tʃænsəl, -z
chancellery
BR 'tʃɑ:ns(ə)l(ə)r|i, 'tʃɑ:nsl̩(ə)r|i, 'tʃans(ə)l(ə)r|i, 'tʃansl̩(ə)r|i, -ɪz
AM 'tʃæns(ə)ləri, -z
chancellor
BR 'tʃɑ:ns(ə)lə(r), 'tʃɑ:nsl̩ə(r), 'tʃans(ə)lə(r), 'tʃansl̩ə(r), -z
AM 'tʃæns(ə)lər, -z
chancellorship
BR 'tʃɑ:ns(ə)ləʃɪp, 'tʃɑ:nsl̩əʃɪp, 'tʃans(ə)ləʃɪp, 'tʃansl̩əʃɪp, -s
AM 'tʃæns(ə)lər,ʃɪp, -s
chance-medley
BR ,tʃɑ:ns'mɛdl|i, ,tʃans'mɛdl|i, -ɪz
AM ,tʃæns'mɛdli, -z
chancer
BR 'tʃɑ:nsə(r), 'tʃansə(r), -z
AM 'tʃænsər, -z
chancery
BR 'tʃɑ:ns(ə)r|i, 'tʃans(ə)r|i, -ɪz
AM 'tʃæns(ə)ri, -z
chancily
BR 'tʃɑ:nsɪli, 'tʃansɪli
AM 'tʃænsəli
chanciness
BR 'tʃɑ:nsɪnɪs, 'tʃansɪnɪs
AM 'tʃænsinɪs
chancre
BR 'ʃaŋkə(r), -z
AM 'kæŋkər, 'ʃæŋkər, -z
chancroid
BR 'ʃaŋkrɔɪd
AM 'kæŋk,rɔɪd, 'ʃæŋk,rɔɪd
Chanctonbury
BR 'tʃaŋ(k)t(ə)nb(ə)ri
AM 'tʃæŋktən,bɛri, 'tʃæŋktənbəri
chancy
BR 'tʃɑ:ns|i, 'tʃans|i, -ɪə(r), -ɪɪst
AM 'tʃænsi, -ər, -ɪst
chandelier
BR ,ʃandə'lɪə(r), -z
AM ,ʃændə'lɪ(ə)r, -z
chandelle
BR ʃan'dɛl, ʃɑ:n'dɛl
AM ʃɑn'dɛl, ʃæn'dɛl
Chandigarh
BR ,tʃʌndɪ'gə:(r), ,tʃandɪ'gɑ:(r)
AM 'tʃəndəgər, ,tʃəndə'gər
chandler
BR 'tʃɑ:ndlə(r), 'tʃandlə(r), -z
AM 'tʃæn(d)lər, -z
chandlery
BR 'tʃɑ:ndləri, 'tʃandləri
AM 'tʃæn(d)ləri
Chandos
BR '(t)ʃandɒs
AM 'tʃændɔs, 'tʃændɑs
Chandrasekhar
BR ,tʃandrə'seɪkə(r)
AM ,ʃɑndrə'seɪkər
Chanel
BR ʃə'nɛl
AM ʃə'nɛl
Chaney
BR 'tʃeɪni
AM 'tʃeɪni
Chang
BR tʃaŋ
AM tʃæŋ
Changchun
BR 'tʃaŋ'tʃu:n
AM ,tʃæŋ'tʃun
change
BR tʃeɪn(d)ʒ, -ɪz, -ɪŋ, -d
AM tʃeɪndʒ, -ɪz, -ɪŋ, -d
changeability
BR ,tʃeɪn(d)ʒə'bɪlɪti
AM ,tʃeɪndʒə'bɪlɪdi
changeable
BR 'tʃeɪn(d)ʒəbl
AM 'tʃeɪndʒəbəl
changeableness
BR 'tʃeɪn(d)ʒəblnəs
AM 'tʃeɪndʒəbəlnəs
changeably
BR 'tʃeɪn(d)ʒəbli
AM 'tʃeɪndʒəbli
changeful
BR 'tʃeɪn(d)ʒf(ʊ)l
AM 'tʃeɪndʒfəl
changefulness
BR 'tʃeɪn(d)ʒf(ʊ)lnəs
AM 'tʃeɪndʒfəlnəs
changeless
BR 'tʃeɪn(d)ʒlɪs
AM 'tʃeɪndʒlɪs
changelessly
BR 'tʃeɪn(d)ʒlɪsli
AM 'tʃeɪndʒlɪsli
changelessness
BR 'tʃeɪn(d)ʒlɪsnɪs
AM 'tʃeɪndʒlɪsnɪs
changeling
BR 'tʃeɪn(d)ʒlɪŋ, -z
AM 'tʃeɪndʒlɪŋ, -z
changeover
BR 'tʃeɪn(d)ʒ,əʊvə(r), -z
AM 'tʃeɪndʒ,oʊvər, -z
changer
BR 'tʃeɪn(d)ʒə(r), -z
AM 'tʃeɪndʒər, -z
changeround
BR 'tʃeɪn(d)ʒraʊnd
AM 'tʃeɪndʒ,raʊnd
Changi
BR 'tʃaŋgi
AM 'tʃæŋ(g)i
Changsha
BR ,tʃaŋ'ʃɑ:(*r*)
AM 'tʃæŋ'ʃɑ
channel
BR 'tʃanl̩, -z, -ɪŋ, -d
AM 'tʃænəl, -z, -ɪŋ, -d
channelise
BR 'tʃanl̩ʌɪz, -ɪz, -ɪŋ, -d
AM 'tʃænl,aɪz, -ɪz, -ɪŋ, -d
channelize
BR 'tʃanl̩ʌɪz, -ɪz, -ɪŋ, -d
AM 'tʃænl,aɪz, -ɪz, -ɪŋ, -d
Channing
BR 'tʃanɪŋ
AM 'tʃænɪŋ
Channon
BR 'tʃanən
AM 'tʃænən
chanson
BR 'ʃɒ̃sɒ̃, 'ʃɒnsɒ̃, 'ʃɒnsɒn, -z
AM ʃɑn'sɔn, ʃɑn'sɑn +, -z
chanson de geste
BR ,ʃɒ̃sɒ̃ də 'ʒɛst, ,ʃɒnsɒ̃ +, ,ʃɒnsɒn +
AM ʃɑn'sɔn də 'ʒɛst, ʃɑn'sɑn +
chansons de geste
BR ,ʃɒ̃sɒ̃(z) də 'ʒɛst, ,ʃɒnsɒ̃(z) +, ,ʃɒnsɒn(z) +

AM ʃɑn'sɔn(z) də 'ʒɛst, ʃɑn'sɑn(z) +

chant
BR tʃɑːnt, tʃant, -s, -ɪŋ, -ɪd
AM tʃænt, -z, -ɪŋ, -əd

Chantal
BR ˌʃɒn'tal, ˌʃɑːn'tal, ˌʃan'tal, ˌʃɒn'tɑːl, ˌʃɑːn'tɑːl, ˌʃan'tɑːl
AM ˌʃæn'tɑl, ˌʃɑn'tɑl

chanter
BR 'tʃɑːntə(r), 'tʃantə(r), -z
AM 'tʃæn(t)ər, -z

chanterelle
BR ˌʃɑːntə'rɛl, ˌʃantə'rɛl, -z
AM ˌʃæn(t)ə'rɛl, ˌʃɑn(t)ə'rɛl, -z

chanteur
BR ˌʃɒn'təː(r), ˌʃɑːn'təː(r)
AM ˌʃɑn'tər

chanteurs
BR ˌʃɒn'təːz, ˌʃɑːn'təːz
AM ˌʃɑn'tərz

chanteuse
BR ˌʃɒn'təːz, ˌʃɑːn'təːz
AM ˌʃɑn'tʊz

chanteuses
BR ˌʃɒn'təːz, ˌʃɒn'təːzɪz, ˌʃɑːn'təːz, ˌʃɑːn'təːzɪz
AM ˌʃɑn'tʊz, ˌʃɑn'tʊzəz

chantey
BR 'ʃant|i, -ɪz
AM 'ʃæn(t)i, -z

chanticleer
BR 'ʃɑːntɪklɪə(r), 'ʃɒntɪklɪə(r), 'ʃantɪklɪə(r), 'tʃɑːntɪklɪə(r), 'tʃantɪklɪə(r), -z
AM 'tʃæn(t)əˌklɪ(ə)r, -z

Chantilly
BR ʃan'tɪli
AM ˌʃæn'tɪli

chantry
BR 'tʃɑːntr|i, 'tʃantr|i, -ɪz
AM 'tʃæntri, -z

chanty
BR 'ʃant|i, -ɪz
AM 'ʃæn(t)i, -z

Chanukkah
BR 'hanʊkə(r), 'xanʊkə(r), 'hɑːnʊkə(r), 'xɑːnʊkə(r)
AM 'hɑnəkə

chaology
BR keɪ'ɒlədʒi
AM keɪ'ɑlədʒi

chaos
BR 'keɪɒs
AM 'keɪˌɑs, 'keɪˌɔs

chaotic
BR keɪ'ɒtɪk
AM keɪ'ɑdɪk

chaotically
BR keɪ'ɒtɪkli
AM keɪ'ɑdək(ə)li

chap
BR tʃap, -s, -ɪŋ, -t
AM tʃæp, -s, -ɪŋ, -t

chaparejos
BR ˌ(t)ʃapə'reɪhəʊs
AM ˌʃæpə'reɪəs

chaparral
BR ˌʃapə'ral
AM ˌʃæpə'ræl

chapati
BR tʃə'pɑːt|i, tʃə'pat|i, -ɪz
AM tʃə'pɑdi, -z

chapatti
BR tʃə'pɑːt|i, tʃə'pat|i, -ɪz
AM tʃə'pɑdi, -z

chapbook
BR 'tʃapbʊk, -s
AM 'tʃæpˌbʊk, -s

chape
BR 'tʃeɪp, -s
AM 'tʃeɪp, -s

chapeau-bras
BR ˌʃapəʊ'brɑː(r), -z
AM ˌʃɑpoʊ'brɑ, -z

chapel
BR 'tʃapl, -z
AM 'tʃæpəl, -z

Chapel-en-le-Frith
BR ˌtʃaplˌɛnlə'frɪθ, ˌtʃaplˌɒnlə'frɪθ
AM ˌtʃæpələnðə'frɪθ

chapelry
BR 'tʃaplr|i, -ɪz
AM 'tʃæpəlri, -z

chaperon
BR 'ʃapərəʊn, -z, -ɪŋ, -d
AM 'ʃæpəˌroʊn, -z, -ɪŋ, -d

chaperonage
BR 'ʃapərəʊnɪdʒ
AM 'ʃæpəˌroʊnɪdʒ, ˌʃæpə'roʊnɪdʒ

chaperone
BR 'ʃapərəʊn, -z, -ɪŋ, -d
AM 'ʃæpəˌroʊn, -z, -ɪŋ, -d

chapfallen
BR 'tʃapˌfɔːlən
AM 'tʃæpˌfɔlən, 'tʃæpˌfɑlən

chaplain
BR 'tʃaplɪn, -z
AM 'tʃæplən, -z

chaplaincy
BR 'tʃaplɪns|i, -ɪz
AM 'tʃæplənsi, -z

chaplet
BR 'tʃaplɪt, -s, -ɪd
AM 'tʃæplət, -s, -əd

Chaplin
BR 'tʃaplɪn
AM 'tʃæplən

chapman
BR 'tʃapmən
AM 'tʃæpmən

chapmen
BR 'tʃapmən
AM 'tʃæpmən

chappal
BR 'tʃapl, -z
AM 'tʃæpəl, -z

Chappell
BR 'tʃapl
AM 'tʃæpəl

chappie
BR 'tʃap|i, -ɪz
AM 'tʃæpi, -z

chappy
BR 'tʃap|i, -ɪz
AM 'tʃæpi, -z

chapter
BR 'tʃaptə(r), -z
AM 'tʃæptər, -z

char
BR tʃɑː(r), -z, -ɪŋ, -d
AM tʃɑr, -z, -ɪŋ, -d

charabanc
BR 'ʃarəbaŋ, -z
AM 'ʃɛrəˌbæŋk, -z

char à bancs
BR 'ʃarəbaŋ
AM 'ʃɛrəˌbæŋk

characin
BR 'karəsɪn, -z
AM 'kɛrəsən, -z

character
BR 'karɪktə(r), -z
AM 'kɛr(ə)ktər, -z

characterful
BR 'karɪktəf(ʊ)l
AM 'kɛr(ə)ktərfəl

characterfully
BR 'karɪktəf(ʊ)li, 'karɪktəfḷi
AM 'kɛr(ə)ktərfəli

characterisation
BR ˌkarɪkt(ə)rʌɪ'zeɪʃn, -z
AM ˌkɛr(ə)ktərə'zeɪʃən, ˌkɛr(ə)ktəˌraɪ'zeɪʃən, -z

characterise
BR 'karɪktərʌɪz, -ɪz, -ɪŋ, -d
AM 'kɛr(ə)ktəˌraɪz, -ɪz, -ɪŋ, -d

characteristic
BR ˌkarɪktə'rɪstɪk, -s
AM ˌkɛr(ə)ktə'rɪstɪk, -s

characteristically
BR ˌkarɪktə'rɪstɪkli
AM ˌkɛr(ə)ktə'rɪstək(ə)li

characterization
BR ˌkarɪkt(ə)rʌɪ'zeɪʃn, -z
AM ˌkɛr(ə)ktərə'zeɪʃən, ˌkɛr(ə)ktəˌraɪ'zeɪʃən, -z

characterize
BR 'karɪktərʌɪz, -ɪz, -ɪŋ, -d
AM 'kɛr(ə)ktəˌraɪz, -ɪz, -ɪŋ, -d

characterless
BR 'karɪktələs
AM 'kɛr(ə)ktərˌləs

characterology
BR ˌkarɪktə'rɒlədʒi
AM ˌkɛr(ə)ktə'rɑlədʒi

charade
BR ʃə'rɑːd, -z
AM ʃə'reɪd, -z

charango
BR tʃə'raŋgəʊ, -z
AM tʃə'ræŋgoʊ, -z

charas
BR 'tʃɑːrəs
AM 'tʃɑrəs

charbroil
BR 'tʃɑːbrɔɪl, -z, -ɪŋ, -d
AM 'tʃɑrˌbrɔɪl, -z, -ɪŋ, -d

charcoal
BR 'tʃɑːkəʊl
AM 'tʃɑrˌkoʊl

charcuterie
BR ʃɑː'kuːt(ə)riː
AM ˌʃɑrˌkudə'ri

chard
BR tʃɑːd, -z
AM tʃɑrd, -z

Chardonnay
BR 'ʃɑːdəneɪ
AM ˌʃɑrdn'eɪ

chare
BR tʃɛː(r), -z, -ɪŋ, -d
AM tʃɛ(ə)r, -z, -ɪŋ, -d

charge
BR tʃɑːdʒ, -ɪz, -ɪŋ, -d
AM tʃɑrdʒ, -əz, -ɪŋ, -d

chargeable
BR 'tʃɑːdʒəbl
AM 'tʃɑrdʒəbəl

chargeableness
BR 'tʃɑːdʒəblnəs
AM 'tʃɑrdʒəbəlnəs

chargeably
BR 'tʃɑːdʒəbli
AM 'tʃɑrdʒəbli

chargé d'affaires
BR ˌʃɑːʒeɪ da'fɛː(r), + də'fɛː(r)
AM ˌʃɑrʒeɪ dɑ'fɛ(ə)r

chargehand
BR 'tʃɑːdʒhand, -z
AM 'tʃɑrdʒ(h)ænd, -z

charger
BR 'tʃɑːdʒə(r), -z
AM 'tʃɑrdʒər, -z

chargés d'affaires
BR ˌʃɑːʒeɪ da'fɛːz, + də'fɛːz

AM ˌʃɑrʒeɪ(z) dɑ'fɛr(z)
charily
BR 'tʃɛːrɨli
AM 'tʃɛrəli
chariness
BR 'tʃɛːrɪnɨs
AM 'tʃɛrinɨs
Charing Cross
BR ˌtʃarɪŋ 'krɒs, ˌtʃɛːrɪŋ +
AM ¦tʃɛrɪŋ 'krɔs, ¦tʃɛrɪŋ 'krɑs
chariot
BR 'tʃarɪət, -s
AM 'tʃɛriət, -s
charioteer
BR ˌtʃarɪə'tɪə(r), -z
AM ˌtʃɛriə'tɪ(ə)r, -z
charisma
BR kə'rɪzmə(r)
AM kə'rɪzmə
charismatic
BR ˌkarɪz'matɪk
AM ˌkɛrəz'mædɪk
charismatically
BR ˌkarɪz'matɨkli
AM ˌkɛrəz'mædək(ə)li
Charisse
BR ʃə'riːs
AM ʃɑ'ris
charitable
BR 'tʃarɨtəbl
AM 'tʃɛrədəbəl
charitableness
BR 'tʃarɨtəblnəs
AM 'tʃɛr(ə)dəbəlnəs
charitably
BR 'tʃarɨtəbli
AM 'tʃɛr(ə)dəbli
charity
BR 'tʃarɨt|i, -ɪz
AM 'tʃɛrədi, -z
charivari
BR ˌʃarɪ'vɑːr|i, -ɪz
AM ˌʃɪvə'ri, -z
charivaria
BR ˌʃarɪ'vɑːrɪə(r)
AM ˌʃɪvə'riə
charlady
BR 'tʃɑːˌleɪd|i, -ɪz
AM 'tʃɑrˌleɪdi, -z
charlatan
BR 'ʃɑːlət(ə)n, -z
AM 'ʃɑrlədən, 'ʃɑrlətn, -z
charlatanism
BR 'ʃɑːlətənɪz(ə)m, 'ʃɑːlətn̩ɪz(ə)m
AM 'ʃɑrlədəˌnɪzəm, 'ʃɑrlətnˌɪzəm
charlatanry
BR 'ʃɑːlət(ə)nri
AM 'ʃɑrlədənri, 'ʃɑrlətnri
Charlecote
BR 'tʃɑːlkəʊt, 'tʃɑːlkət
AM 'tʃɑrl(ə)ˌkoʊt
Charlemagne
BR 'ʃɑːləmeɪn
AM 'ʃɑrləˌmeɪn
Charlene
BR 'ʃɑːliːn
AM ˌʃɑr'lin
Charles
BR tʃɑːlz
AM tʃɑrlz
Charleston
BR 'tʃɑːlst(ə)n, -z
AM 'tʃɑrlstən, -z
charley horse
BR 'tʃɑːlɪ hɔːs
AM 'tʃɑrli ˌhɔ(ə)rs
Charlie
BR 'tʃɑːli
AM 'tʃɑrli
charlie
BR 'tʃɑːl|i, -ɪz
AM 'tʃɑrli, -z
charlock
BR 'tʃɑːlək, 'tʃɑːlɒk
AM 'tʃɑrˌlɑk, 'tʃɑrlək
charlotte
BR 'ʃɑːlət, -s
AM 'ʃɑrlət, -s
Charlottenburg
BR ʃɑː'lɒtnbəːg
AM tʃɑr'lɑdənˌbərg
charlotte russe
BR ˌʃɑːlət 'ruːs
AM ¦ʃɑrˌlɑt 'rus
charlottes russes
BR ˌʃɑːlət 'ruːs
AM ¦ʃɑrˌlɑt 'rus
Charlottetown
BR 'ʃɑːləttaʊn
AM 'ʃɑrlə(t)ˌtaʊn
Charlton
BR 'tʃɑːlt(ə)n
AM 'tʃɑrltən
charm
BR tʃɑːm, -z, -ɪŋ, -d
AM tʃɑrm, -z, -ɪŋ, -d
Charmaine
BR (ˌ)ʃɑː'meɪn
AM ˌʃɑr'meɪn
charmer
BR 'tʃɑːmə(r), -z
AM 'tʃɑrmər, -z
charmeuse
BR ʃɑː'məːz
AM ˌʃɑr'm(j)ʊz
Charmian
BR 'ʃɑːmɪən
AM 'ʃɑrmiən
charming
BR 'tʃɑːmɪŋ
AM 'tʃɑrmɪŋ
charmingly
BR 'tʃɑːmɪŋli
AM 'tʃɑrmɪŋli
charmless
BR 'tʃɑːmləs
AM 'tʃɑrmləs
charmlessly
BR 'tʃɑːmləsli
AM 'tʃɑrmləsli
charmlessness
BR 'tʃɑːmləsnəs
AM 'tʃɑrmləsnəs
charnel
BR 'tʃɑːnl, -z
AM 'tʃɑrnəl, -z
Charnock
BR 'tʃɑːnɒk, 'tʃɑːnək
AM 'tʃɑrnək
Charolais
BR 'ʃarəleɪ, -z
AM ˌʃɛrə'leɪ, -z
Charollais
BR 'ʃarəleɪ, -z
AM ˌʃɛrə'leɪ, -z
Charon
BR 'kɛːrən, 'kɛːrn̩, 'kɛːrɒn
AM 'kɛrən
charpoy
BR 'tʃɑːpɔɪ, -z
AM 'tʃɑrˌpɔɪ, -z
charr
BR tʃɑː(r)
AM tʃɑr
Charrington
BR 'tʃarɪŋt(ə)n
AM 'tʃɛrɪŋtən
charro
BR 'tʃɑːrəʊ, -z
AM 'tʃɑroʊ, -z
chart
BR tʃɑːt, -s, -ɪŋ, -ɨd
AM tʃɑr|t, -ts, -dɪŋ, -dəd
chartbuster
BR 'tʃɑːtˌbʌstə(r), -z
AM 'tʃɑrtˌbəstər, -z
charter
BR 'tʃɑːt|ə(r), -əz, -(ə)rɪŋ, -əd
AM 'tʃɑrdər, -z, -ɪŋ, -d
charterer
BR 'tʃɑːt(ə)rə(r), -z
AM 'tʃɑrdərər, -z
Charterhouse
BR 'tʃɑːtəhaʊs
AM 'tʃɑrdərˌ(h)aʊs
Charteris
BR 'tʃɑːt(ə)rɪs, 'tʃɑːtəz
AM 'tʃɑrdərəs
Chartism
BR 'tʃɑːtɪz(ə)m
AM 'tʃɑrdɪzəm
Chartist
BR 'tʃɑːtɪst, -s
AM 'tʃɑrdəst, -s
Chartres
BR 'ʃɑːtr(ər)
AM 'ʃɑrt(rə)
chartreuse
BR ʃɑː'trəːz, -ɪz
AM ʃɑr'truz, ʃɑr'trus, -əz
Chartwell
BR 'tʃɑːtw(ɛ)l
AM 'tʃɑrtˌwɛl
charwoman
BR 'tʃɑːˌwʊmən
AM 'tʃɑrˌwʊmən
charwomen
BR 'tʃɑːˌwɪmɪn
AM 'tʃɑrˌwɪmɨn
chary
BR 'tʃɛːr|i, -ɪə(r), -ɪɪst
AM 'tʃɛri, -ər, -ɨst
Charybdis
BR kə'rɪbdɪs
AM kə'rɪbdɨs, tʃə'rɪbdɨs
chase
BR tʃeɪs, -ɪz, -ɪŋ, -t
AM tʃeɪs, -ɨz, -ɪŋ, -t
chaser
BR 'tʃeɪsə(r), -z
AM 'tʃeɪsər, -z
Chasid
BR 'hasɪd, 'xasɪd
AM 'hɑsɪd
Chasidim
BR 'hasɪdɪm, 'xasɪdɪm
AM 'hɑsɪdɪm
Chasidism
BR 'hasɪdɪz(ə)m, 'xasɪdɪz(ə)m
AM 'hɑsɪˌdɪzəm
chasm
BR 'kaz(ə)m, -z
AM 'kæzəm, -z
chasmic
BR 'kazmɪk
AM 'kæzmɪk
chasse
BR ʃas, ʃɑːs, -ɪz
AM ʃɑs, -əz
chassé
BR ʃa'seɪ, 'ʃaseɪ, -z, -ɪŋ, -d
AM ʃɑ'seɪ, -z, -ɪŋ, -d
chasseur
BR ʃa'səː(r), -z
AM ʃɑ'sər, -z
chassis[1]
singular
BR 'ʃasi
AM 'tʃæsi, 'ʃæsi
chassis[2]
plural
BR 'ʃasɪz
AM 'tʃæsiz, 'ʃæsiz
chaste
BR tʃeɪst
AM tʃeɪst
chastely
BR 'tʃeɪstli
AM 'tʃeɪs(t)li
chasten
BR 'tʃeɪs|n, -nz, -n̩ɪŋ\-nɪŋ, -nd
AM 'tʃeɪs|n, -nz, -(ə)nɪŋ, -nd

chastener
BR 'tʃeɪsn̩ə(r), -z
AM 'tʃeɪsənər, -z
chasteness
BR tʃeɪstnɨs
AM tʃeɪs(t)nɨs
chastise
BR tʃa'stʌɪz, tʃə'stʌɪz, -ɨz, -ɪŋ, -d
AM 'tʃæs,taɪz, tʃæs'taɪz, -ɨz, -ɪŋ, -d
chastisement
BR tʃa'stʌɪzm(ə)nt, tʃə'stʌɪzm(ə)nt, 'tʃastɨzm(ə)nt, -s
AM tʃæs'taɪzmənt, 'tʃæs,taɪzmənt, -s
chastiser
BR tʃa'stʌɪzə(r), tʃə'stʌɪzə(r), -z
AM 'tʃæstaɪzər, -z
chastity
BR 'tʃastɨti
AM 'tʃæstədi
chasuble
BR 'tʃazjʉbl, -z
AM 'tʃæzəbəl, 'tʃæsəbəl, -z
chat
BR tʃat, -s, -ɪŋ, -ɨd
AM tʃæ|t, -ts, -dɪŋ, -dəd
Chataway
BR 'tʃatəweɪ
AM 'tʃædəweɪ
chateau
BR 'ʃatəʊ, -z
AM ʃæ'toʊ, -z
chateaubriand
BR ,ʃatəʊbrɪ'ɒn(d), ,ʃatəʊbrɪ'õ, -z
AM ʃæ,toʊbri'ɔn, ʃæ,toʊbri'ɑn, -z
chateaux
BR 'ʃatəʊ(z)
AM ʃæ'toʊ(z)
châtelaine
BR 'ʃatəleɪn, 'ʃatl̩eɪn, -z
AM ,ʃædl'ɛn, 'ʃædl,eɪn, -z
Chater
BR 'tʃeɪtə(r)
AM 'tʃeɪdər
Chatham
BR 'tʃatəm
AM 'tʃædəm
chatline
BR 'tʃatlʌɪn, -z
AM 'tʃæt,laɪn, -z
chatshow
BR 'tʃat-ʃəʊ, -z
AM 'tʃæt,ʃoʊ, -z
Chattanooga
BR ,tʃatn'u:gə(r), ,tʃatə'nu:gə(r)
AM ,tʃætn'ugə
chattel
BR 'tʃatl, -z
AM 'tʃædl, -z
chatter
BR 'tʃat|ə(r), -əz, -(ə)rɪŋ, -əd
AM 'tʃædər, -z, -ɪŋ, -d
chatterbox
BR 'tʃatəbɒks, -ɨz
AM 'tʃædər,bɑks, -əz
chatterer
BR 'tʃat(ə)rə(r), -z
AM 'tʃædərər, -z
Chatterjee
BR 'tʃatədʒi:
AM 'tʃædər,dʒi
Chatterji
BR 'tʃatədʒi:
AM 'tʃædər,dʒi
Chatterley
BR 'tʃatəli
AM 'tʃædərli
Chatterton
BR 'tʃatət(ə)n
AM 'tʃædərtən
chattery
BR 'tʃat(ə)ri
AM 'tʃædəri
chattily
BR 'tʃatɨli
AM 'tʃædəli
chattiness
BR 'tʃatɪnɨs
AM 'tʃædinɨs
Chatto
BR 'tʃatəʊ
AM 'tʃædoʊ
chatty
BR 'tʃat|i, -ɪə(r), -ɪɨst
AM 'tʃædi, -ər, -ɨst
Chatwin
BR 'tʃatwɪn
AM 'tʃæt,wɪn
Chaucer
BR 'tʃɔ:sə(r)
AM 'tʃɔsər, 'tʃɑsər
Chaucerian
BR tʃɔ:'sɪərɪən
AM tʃɔ'sɛriən, tʃɔ'sɪriən, tʃɑ'sɛriən, tʃɑ'sɪriən
chaud-froid
BR 'ʃəʊfrwɑ:(r), ,ʃəʊ'frwɑ:(r), -z
AM ,ʃoʊ'frwɑ, -z
Chaudhury
BR 'tʃaʊd(ə)ri
AM 'tʃaʊdəri
chaudron
BR 'tʃɔ:drən, -z
AM 'tʃɔdrən, 'tʃɑdrən, -z
chauds-froids
BR 'ʃəʊfrwɑ:(r)z, ,ʃəʊ'frwɑ:(r)z
AM ,ʃoʊ'frwɑz
chauffeur
BR 'ʃəʊfə(r), -z, -ɪŋ, -d
AM 'ʃoʊfər, ʃoʊ'fər, -z, -ɪŋ, -d
chauffeuse
BR ʃəʊ'fə:z, -ɨz
AM ,ʃoʊ'fəz, -əz
chaulmoogra
BR tʃɔ:l'mu:grə(r), -z
AM tʃɔl'mugrə, tʃɑl'mugrə, -z
chausses
BR ʃəʊs
AM ʃoʊs
chautauqua
BR ʃə'tɔ:kwə(r), -z
AM ʃə'tɔkwə, ʃə'tɑkwə, -z
chauvinism
BR 'ʃəʊvɪnɪz(ə)m
AM 'ʃoʊvə,nɪzəm
chauvinist
BR 'ʃəʊvɪnɪst, -s
AM 'ʃoʊvənəst, -s
chauvinistic
BR ,ʃəʊvɪ'nɪstɪk
AM ,ʃoʊvə'nɪstɪk
chauvinistically
BR ,ʃəʊvɪ'nɪstɪkli
AM ,ʃoʊvə'nɪstɪk(ə)li
Chavasse
BR ʃə'vas
AM ʃə'vɑs
Chavez
BR 'ʃavɛz
AM ,ʃɑ,vɛz
chaw
BR tʃɔ:(r), -z, -ɪŋ, -d
AM tʃɔ, tʃɑ, -z, -ɪŋ, -d
chayote
BR tʃʌɪ'əʊt|i, -ɪz
AM tʃaɪ'oʊdi, tʃi'joʊdi, -z
Chaz
BR tʃaz
AM tʃæz
Che
BR tʃeɪ
AM (t)ʃeɪ
Cheadle
BR 'tʃi:dl
AM 'tʃidəl
Cheam
BR tʃi:m
AM tʃim
cheap
BR tʃi:p, -ə(r), -ɨst
AM tʃip, -ər, -ɨst
cheapen
BR 'tʃi:p|(ə)n, -(ə)nz, -ənɪŋ\-n̩ɪŋ, -(ə)nd
AM 'tʃip|ən, -ənz, -(ə)nɪŋ, -ənd
cheapie
BR 'tʃi:p|i, -ɪz
AM 'tʃipi, -z
cheapish
BR 'tʃi:pɪʃ
AM 'tʃipɪʃ
cheapjack
BR 'tʃi:pdʒak, -s
AM 'tʃip,dʒæk, -s
cheaply
BR 'tʃi:pli
AM 'tʃipli
cheapness
BR 'tʃi:pnɨs
AM 'tʃipnɨs
cheapo
BR 'tʃi:pəʊ, -z
AM 'tʃipoʊ, -z
Cheapside
BR 'tʃi:psʌɪd
AM 'tʃip,saɪd
cheapskate
BR 'tʃi:pskeɪt, -s
AM 'tʃip,skeɪt, -s
cheat
BR tʃi:t, -s, -ɪŋ, -ɨd
AM tʃi|t, -ts, -dɪŋ, -dɨd
cheater
BR tʃi:tə(r), -z
AM tʃidər, -z
cheatingly
BR tʃi:tɪŋli
AM tʃidɪŋli
Chechen
BR 'tʃɛtʃɛn, -z
AM 'tʃɛtʃɛn, -z
Chechnya
BR 'tʃɛtʃnjɑ:(r), ,tʃɛtʃ'njɑ:(r)
AM 'tʃɛtʃniə
check
BR tʃɛk, -s, -ɪŋ, -t
AM tʃɛk, -s, -ɪŋ, -t
checkable
BR 'tʃɛkəbl
AM 'tʃɛkəbəl
checkbook
BR 'tʃɛkbʊk, -s
AM 'tʃɛk,bʊk, -s
checker
BR 'tʃɛkə(r), -z
AM 'tʃɛkər, -z
checkerberry
BR 'tʃɛkə,bɛr|i, -ɪz
AM 'tʃɛkər,bɛri, -z
checkerboard
BR 'tʃɛkəbɔ:d, -z
AM 'tʃɛkər,bɔ(ə)rd, -z
checkerman
BR 'tʃɛkəmən
AM 'tʃɛkərmən
checkermen
BR 'tʃɛkəmən
AM 'tʃɛkərmən
Checkland
BR 'tʃɛklənd
AM 'tʃɛklənd
Checkley
BR 'tʃɛkli
AM 'tʃɛkli
checklist
BR 'tʃɛklɪst, -s
AM 'tʃɛk,lɪst, -s

checkmark
BR 'tʃɛkmɑːk, -s
AM 'tʃɛkˌmɑrk, -s

checkmate
BR 'tʃɛkmeɪt, ˌtʃɛk'meɪt, -s, -ɪŋ, -ɨd
AM 'tʃɛkˌmeɪ|t, -ts, -dɪŋ, -dɨd

checkout
BR 'tʃɛkaʊt, -s
AM 'tʃɛkˌaʊt, -s

checkpoint
BR 'tʃɛkpɔɪnt, -s
AM 'tʃɛkˌpɔɪnt, -s

checkrail
BR 'tʃɛkreɪl, -z
AM 'tʃɛkˌreɪl, -z

checkrein
BR 'tʃɛkreɪn, -z
AM 'tʃɛkˌreɪn, -z

checkroom
BR 'tʃɛkruːm, 'tʃɛkrʊm, -z
AM 'tʃɛkˌrum, 'tʃɛkˌrʊm, -z

checkup
BR 'tʃɛkʌp, -s
AM 'tʃɛkˌəp, -s

check-valve
BR 'tʃɛkvalv, -z
AM 'tʃɛkˌvælv, -z

checkweighman
BR 'tʃɛkweɪmən
AM 'tʃɛkˌweɪmən

checkweighmen
BR 'tʃɛkweɪmən
AM 'tʃɛkˌweɪmən

cheddar
BR 'tʃɛdə(r), -z
AM 'tʃɛdər, -z

Chedzoy
BR 'tʃɛdzɔɪ
AM 'tʃɛdzɔɪ

cheek
BR tʃiːk, -s, -ɪŋ, -t
AM tʃik, -s, -ɪŋ, -t

cheekbone
BR 'tʃiːkbəʊn, -z
AM 'tʃikˌboʊn, -z

cheekily
BR 'tʃiːkɨli
AM 'tʃikɨli

cheekiness
BR 'tʃiːkɪnɨs
AM 'tʃikinɨs

cheeky
BR 'tʃiːk|i, -ɪə(r), -ɪɨst
AM 'tʃiki, -ər, -ɨst

cheep
BR tʃiːp, -s, -ɪŋ, -t
AM tʃip, -s, -ɪŋ, -t

cheer
BR tʃɪə(r), -z, -ɪŋ, -d
AM tʃɪ(ə)r, -z, -ɪŋ, -d

cheerful
BR 'tʃɪəf(ʊ)l
AM 'tʃɪrfəl

cheerfully
BR 'tʃɪəfʊli, 'tʃɪəfl̩i
AM 'tʃɪrfəli

cheerfulness
BR 'tʃɪəf(ʊ)lnəs
AM 'tʃɪrfəlnəs

cheerily
BR 'tʃɪərɨli
AM 'tʃɪrɨli

cheeriness
BR 'tʃɪərɪnɨs
AM 'tʃɪrinɨs

cheerio
BR ˌtʃɪərɪ'əʊ
AM ˌtʃɪri'oʊ

cheerleader
BR 'tʃɪəˌliːdə(r), -z
AM 'tʃɪrˌlidər, -z

cheerless
BR 'tʃɪələs
AM 'tʃɪrlɨs

cheerlessly
BR 'tʃɪələsli
AM 'tʃɪrlɨsli

cheerlessness
BR 'tʃɪələsnəs
AM 'tʃɪrlɨsnɨs

cheerly
BR 'tʃɪəli
AM 'tʃɪrli

cheers
BR tʃɪəz
AM tʃɪ(ə)rz

cheery
BR 'tʃɪər|i, -ɪɨst
AM 'tʃɪri, -ɨst

cheese
BR tʃiːz, -ɪz, -d
AM tʃiz, -ɨz, -d

cheeseboard
BR 'tʃiːzbɔːd, -z
AM 'tʃizˌbɔ(ə)rd, -z

cheeseburger
BR 'tʃiːzˌbəːɡə(r), -z
AM 'tʃizˌbərɡər, -z

cheesecake
BR 'tʃiːzkeɪk, -s
AM 'tʃizˌkeɪk, -s

cheesecloth
BR 'tʃiːzklɒ|θ, -θs\-ðz
AM 'tʃizˌklɔ|θ, 'tʃizˌklɑ|θ, -θs\-ðz

cheesemaker
BR 'tʃiːzˌmeɪkə(r), -z
AM 'tʃizˌmeɪkər, -z

cheesemaking
BR 'tʃiːzˌmeɪkɪŋ
AM 'tʃizˌmeɪkɪŋ

Cheeseman
BR 'tʃiːzmən
AM 'tʃizmən

cheesemonger
BR 'tʃiːzˌmʌŋɡə(r), -z
AM 'tʃizˌmɑŋɡər, 'tʃizˌməŋɡər, -z

cheeseparing
BR 'tʃiːzˌpɛːrɪŋ, -z
AM 'tʃizˌpɛrɪŋ, -z

cheesewood
BR 'tʃiːzwʊd, -z
AM 'tʃizˌwʊd, -z

Cheesewright
BR 'tʃiːzrʌɪt
AM 'tʃizˌraɪt

cheesily
BR 'tʃiːzɨli
AM 'tʃizɨli

cheesiness
BR 'tʃiːzɪnɨs
AM 'tʃizinɨs

cheesy
BR 'tʃiːzi
AM 'tʃizi

cheetah
BR 'tʃiːtə(r), -z
AM 'tʃidə, -z

Cheetham
BR 'tʃiːtəm
AM 'tʃidəm

chef
BR ʃɛf, -s
AM ʃɛf, -s

chef-d'œuvre
BR ˌʃeɪ'dəːv(rər), -z
AM ˌʃɛf'dəvr(ə), -z

chefs-d'œuvre
BR ˌʃeɪ'dəːv(rər), -z
AM ˌʃɛf 'dəvr(ə), -z

Chegwin
BR 'tʃɛɡwɪn
AM 'tʃɛɡwən

Cheka
BR 'tʃɛkə(r)
AM 'tʃɛkə
RUS tʃʲi'ka

Cheke
BR tʃiːk
AM tʃik

Chekhov
BR 'tʃɛkɒf, 'tʃɛkɒv
AM 'tʃɛkɔv, 'tʃɛkɔf, 'tʃɛkɑv, 'tʃɛkɑf

Chekhovian
BR tʃɛ'kəʊvɪən
AM tʃɛ'koʊviən

chela[1]
claw
BR 'kiːlə(r)
AM 'kilə

chela[2]
disciple
BR 'tʃeɪlə(r), -z
AM 'tʃeɪˌlɑ, -z

chelae
BR 'kiːliː
AM 'kili, 'kiˌlaɪ

chelate
BR 'kiːleɪt, -s
AM 'kiˌleɪt, -s

chelation
BR kiː'leɪʃn
AM ki'leɪʃən

chelicera
BR kə'lɪs(ə)rə(r)
AM kə'lɪsərə

chelicerae
BR kə'lɪs(ə)riː
AM kə'lɪsəri

Chelicerata
BR kəˌlɪsə'reɪtə(r)
AM kəˌlɪsə'rɑdɑ

Chellean
BR 'ʃɛlɪən
AM 'ʃɛliən

Chellian
BR 'ʃɛlɪən
AM 'ʃɛliən

Chelmer
BR 'tʃɛlmə(r)
AM 'tʃɛlmər

Chelmsford
BR 'tʃɛlmzfəd
AM 'tʃɛlmsfərd

chelonian
BR kɪ'ləʊnɪən, -z
AM kə'loʊniən, -z

Chelsea
BR 'tʃɛlsi
AM 'tʃɛlsi

Cheltenham
BR 'tʃɛltnəm, 'tʃɛltn̩əm
AM 'tʃɛltnˌhæm, 'tʃɛltnəm

Chelyabinsk
BR ˌtʃɛljə'bɪnsk
AM tʃə'ljɑbɪnsk
RUS tʃʲiˈlʲabʲinsk

chemical
BR 'kɛmɨkl, -z
AM 'kɛməkəl, -z

chemically
BR 'kɛmɨkli
AM 'kɛmək(ə)li

chemiluminescence
BR ˌkɛmɪˌluːmɪ'nɛsns
AM ˌkɛmiˌlumə'nɛsns

chemiluminescent
BR ˌkɛmɪˌluːmɪ'nɛsnt
AM ˌkɛmiˌlumə'nɛsnt

chemin de fer
BR ʃəˌman də 'fɛː(r)
AM ʃəˌmɑn də 'fɛ(ə)r

chemins de fer
BR ʃəˌman də 'fɛː(r)
AM ʃəˌmɑn(z) də 'fɛ(ə)r

chemise
BR ʃə'miːz, -ɪz
AM ʃə'miz, -ɨz

chemisorption
BR ˌkɛmɪ'sɔːpʃn
AM ˌkɛmi'sɔrpʃən

chemist
BR 'kɛmɪst, -s
AM 'kɛməst, -s

chemistry
BR 'kɛmɪstri
AM 'kɛməstri

Chemnitz
BR ˈkɛmnɪts
AM ˈkɛmnɪts

chemosyntheses
BR ˌkiːmə(ʊ)ˈsɪnθɪsiːz, ˌkɛmə(ʊ)ˈsɪnθɪsiːz
AM ˌkimoʊˈsɪnθəsiz, ˌkɛmoʊˈsɪnθəsiz

chemosynthesis
BR ˌkiːmə(ʊ)ˈsɪnθɪsɪs, ˌkɛmə(ʊ)ˈsɪnθɪsɪs
AM ˌkimoʊˈsɪnθəsəs, ˌkɛmoʊˈsɪnθəsəs

chemotaxis
BR ˌkiːmə(ʊ)ˈtaksɪs, ˌkɛmə(ʊ)ˈtaksɪs
AM ˌkimoʊˈtæksɪs, ˌkɛmoʊˈtæksɪs

chemotherapist
BR ˌkiːmə(ʊ)ˈθɛrəpɪst, ˌkɛmə(ʊ)ˈθɛrəpɪst, -s
AM ˌkimoʊˈθɛrəpəst, ˌkɛmoʊˈθɛrəpəst, -s

chemotherapy
BR ˌkiːmə(ʊ)ˈθɛrəpi, ˌkɛmə(ʊ)ˈθɛrəpi
AM ˌkimoʊˈθɛrəpi, ˌkɛmoʊˈθɛrəpi

chemurgic
BR kɛˈməːdʒɪk
AM kəˈmərdʒɪk

chemurgy
BR ˈkɛməːdʒi
AM ˈkɛmərdʒi

Chenevix
BR ˈ(t)ʃɛnəvɪks
AM ˈ(t)ʃɛnəvɪks

Cheney
BR ˈtʃeɪni, ˈtʃiːni
AM ˈtʃeɪni, ˈtʃini

chenille
BR ʃəˈniːl
AM ʃəˈnil

cheongsam
BR ˌtʃɒŋˈsam, tʃɪˌɒŋˈsam, -z
AM ˈtʃɔŋˌsɑm, ˈtʃɑŋˌsɑm, -z

Cheops
BR ˈkiːɒps
AM ˈkiˌɑps

Chepstow
BR ˈtʃɛpstəʊ
AM ˈtʃɛpstoʊ

cheque
BR tʃɛk, -s
AM tʃɛk, -s

chequebook
BR ˈtʃɛkbʊk, -s
AM ˈtʃɛkˌbʊk, -s

chequer
BR ˈtʃɛkə(r), -z, -d
AM ˈtʃɛkər, -z, -d

chequerboard
BR ˈtʃɛkəbɔːd
AM ˈtʃɛkərˌbɔ(ə)rd

Chequers
BR ˈtʃɛkəz
AM ˈtʃɛkərz

Cher
BR ʃɛː(r)
AM ʃɛ(ə)r

Cherbourg
BR ˈʃəːbɔːg, ˈʃɛːbɔːg, ˈʃəːbʊəg, ˈʃɛːbʊəg
AM ˈ(t)ʃɛrˌbʊ(ə)rg

Cherenkov
BR tʃɪˈrɛŋkɒf, tʃɪˈrɛŋkɒv
AM tʃəˈrɛŋˌkɔv, tʃəˈrɛŋˌkɔf, tʃəˈrɛŋˌkɑv, tʃəˈrɛŋˌkɑf

Chérie
BR ʃəˈriː, ʃɛˈriː
AM ʃəˈri, ˈʃɛri

cherish
BR ˈtʃɛr|ɪʃ, -ɪʃɪz, -ɪʃɪŋ, -ɪʃt
AM ˈtʃɛrəʃ, -əz, -ɪŋ, -t

cherishable
BR ˈtʃɛrɪʃəbl
AM ˈtʃɛrəʃəbəl

Chernobyl
BR tʃəˈnɒbl, tʃəˈnəʊbl, ˈtʃəːnə(ʊ)bɪl
AM tʃərˈnoʊbəl, tʃɛrˈnoʊbəl

chernozem
BR ˈtʃəːnə(ʊ)zɛm
AM ˈtʃɛrnəˌzɛm

Cherokee
BR ˈtʃɛrəkiː, ˌtʃɛrəˈkiː, -z
AM ˈtʃɛrəki, -z

cheroot
BR ʃəˈruːt, -s
AM ʃəˈrut, -s

cherry
BR ˈtʃɛr|i, -ɪz
AM ˈtʃɛri, -z

cherrystone
BR ˈtʃɛrɪstəʊn
AM ˈtʃɛrɪˌstoʊn

cherrywood
BR ˈtʃɛrɪwʊd
AM ˈtʃɛriˌwʊd

chersonese
BR ˈkəːsəniːs, ˌkəːsəˈniːs, ˈkəːsəniːz, ˌkəːsəˈniːz
AM ˈkɛrsəˌniz, ˈkɛrsəˌnis

chert
BR tʃəːt, -s
AM tʃɛ(ə)rt, -s

Chertsey
BR ˈtʃəːtsi
AM ˈtʃərtsi

cherty
BR ˈtʃəːti
AM ˈtʃɛrdi

cherub
BR ˈtʃɛrəb, -z
AM ˈtʃɛrəb, -z

cherubic
BR tʃɪˈruːbɪk, tʃɛˈruːbɪk, tʃɪˈrʊbɪk, tʃɛˈrʊbɪk
AM tʃəˈrubɪk, tʃɛˈrubɪk

cherubically
BR tʃɪˈruːbɪkli, tʃɛˈruːbɪkli, tʃɪˈrʊbɪkli, tʃɛˈrʊbɪkli
AM tʃəˈrubək(ə)li, tʃɛˈrubək(ə)li

cherubim
BR ˈtʃɛrəbɪm
AM ˈtʃɛrəbɪm

Cherubini
BR ˌkɛrʊˈbiːni
AM ˌkɛrəˈbini

chervil
BR ˈtʃəːv(ɪ)l
AM ˈtʃərvəl

Cherwell
BR ˈtʃɑːw(ɛ)l
AM ˈtʃɛrˌwɛl

Cheryl
BR ˈ(t)ʃɛrɪl, ˈ(t)ʃɛrl̩
AM ˈʃɛrəl

Chesapeake
BR ˈtʃɛsəpiːk
AM ˈtʃɛsəˌpik

Chesham
BR ˈtʃɛʃ(ə)m
AM ˈtʃɛʃəm

Cheshire
BR ˈtʃɛʃ(ɪ)ə(r)
AM ˈtʃɛʃər

Cheshunt
BR ˈtʃɛsnt
AM ˈtʃɛsnt

Chesil Beach
BR ˌtʃɛzl ˈbiːtʃ
AM ˌtʃɛzəl ˈbitʃ

Chesney
BR ˈtʃɛzni, ˈtʃɛsni
AM ˈtʃɛzni, ˈtʃɛsni

chess
BR tʃɛs
AM tʃɛs

chessboard
BR ˈtʃɛsbɔːd, -z
AM ˈtʃɛsˌbɔ(ə)rd, -z

chessel
BR ˈtʃɛsl, -z
AM ˈtʃɛsəl, -z

chessman
BR ˈʃɛsman, ˈtʃɛsmən
AM ˈtʃɛsˌmæn, ˈtʃɛsmən

chessmen
BR ˈtʃɛsmɛn, ˈtʃɛsmən
AM ˈtʃɛsmɛn, ˈtʃɛsmən

chest
BR tʃɛst, -s
AM tʃɛst, -s

Chester
BR ˈtʃɛstə(r)
AM ˈtʃɛstər

chesterfield
BR ˈtʃɛstəfiːld, -z
AM ˈtʃɛstərˌfild, -z

Chester-le-Street
BR ˌtʃɛstəlɪˈstriːt
AM ˌtʃɛstərləˈstrit

Chesterton
BR ˈtʃɛstət(ə)n
AM ˈtʃɛstərtən

chestily
BR ˈtʃɛstɪli
AM ˈtʃɛstəli

chestiness
BR ˈtʃɛstɪnɪs
AM ˈtʃɛstinɪs

chestnut
BR ˈtʃɛs(t)nʌt, -s
AM ˈtʃɛs(t)ˌnət, -s

chesty
BR ˈtʃɛst|i, -ɪə(r), -ɪɪst
AM ˈtʃɛsti, -ər, -ɪst

Chetham
BR ˈtʃiːtəm, ˈtʃɛtəm
AM ˈtʃɛdəm, ˈtʃidəm

Chetnik
BR ˈtʃɛtnɪk, -s
AM ˈtʃɛtnɪk, -s

Chetwode
BR ˈtʃɛtwʊd
AM ˈtʃɛtˌwʊd

Chetwyn
BR ˈtʃɛtwɪn
AM ˈtʃɛtwən

Chetwynd
BR ˈtʃɛtwɪnd
AM ˈtʃɛtwənd

chevalet
BR ˌʃɛvəˈleɪ
AM ˌʃɛvəˈleɪ, ʃəˈvæleɪ

cheval glass
BR ʃəˈval glɑːs, + glas, -ɪz
AM ʃəˈvæl ˌglæs, -ɪz

Chevalier
surname
BR ʃɪˈvalɪeɪ
AM ʃəˈvælˌjeɪ, ʃəˌvælˈjeɪ

chevalier
BR ˌʃɛvəˈlɪə(r), -z
AM ˌʃɛvəˈlɪ(ə)r, -z

Chevening
BR ˈtʃiːvnɪŋ
AM ˈtʃiv(ə)nɪŋ

chevet
BR ʃəˈveɪ, -z
AM ʃəˈveɪ, -z

Chevette®
BR ʃəˈvɛt, -s
AM ʃəˈvɛt, -s

Chevington
BR ˈtʃɛvɪŋt(ə)n
AM ˈtʃɛvɪŋtən

Cheviot
BR ˈtʃiːvɪət, ˈtʃɛvɪət, -s
AM ˈʃɛviət, -s

cheviot
BR 'tʃi:vɪət, 'tʃɛvɪət
AM 'ʃɛviət
chèvre
BR 'ʃɛvrə(r), -z
AM 'ʃɛvrə, -z
Chevrolet®
BR 'ʃɛvrəleɪ, -z
AM ˌʃɛvrə'leɪ, -z
chevron
BR 'ʃɛvr(ə)n, -z
AM 'ʃɛvrən, -z
chevrotain
BR 'ʃɛvrəteɪn, -z
AM 'ʃɛvrəˌteɪn, -z
Chevy
Chevrolet
BR 'ʃɛv|i, -ɪz
AM 'ʃɛvi, -z
chevy
chivvy
BR 'tʃɛv|i, -ɪz, -ɪɪŋ, -ɪd
AM 'tʃɪvi, -z, -ɪŋ, -d
chew
BR tʃu:, -z, -ɪŋ, -d
AM tʃu, -z, -ɪŋ, -d
chewable
BR 'tʃu:əbl
AM 'tʃuəbəl
chewer
BR 'tʃu:ə(r), -z
AM 'tʃuər, -z
chewiness
BR 'tʃu:ɪnɨs
AM 'tʃuinɨs
chewy
BR 'tʃu:|i, -ɪə(r), -ɪɨst
AM 'tʃui, -ər, -ɨst
Cheyenne
BR (ˌ)ʃʌɪ'an
AM ˌʃaɪ'æn, ˌʃaɪ'ɛn
Cheyne
BR 'tʃeɪni
AM 'tʃeɪni
Cheyne-Stokes
BR ˌtʃeɪn'stəʊks
AM ˌtʃeɪn(i)'stoʊks
chez
BR ʃeɪ
AM ʃeɪ
chez nous
BR ˌʃeɪ 'nu:
AM ˌʃeɪ 'nu
chi
BR kʌɪ, -z
AM kaɪ, -z
chiack
BR 'tʃʌɪak, -s, -ɪŋ, -t
AM 'tʃaɪək, -s, -ɪŋ, -t
Chiang Kai-shek
BR ˌtʃaŋ kʌɪ'ʃɛk
AM ˌ(t)ʃæŋ ˌkaɪ'ʃɛk
Chiangmai
BR tʃɪˌaŋ'mʌɪ
AM ˌ(t)ʃ(i)æŋ'maɪ
Chianti
BR kɪ'anti
AM ki'ɑn(t)i
Chiapas
BR tʃɪ'apəs
AM tʃi'ɑpəs, 'tʃɑpəs
chiaroscuro
BR kɪˌɑ:rə'sk(j)ʊərəʊ, -z
AM kjɑrə'skʊroʊ, -z
chiasma
BR kʌɪ'azmə(r)
AM kaɪ'æzmə
chiasmus
BR kʌɪ'azməs
AM kaɪ'æzməs
chiastic
BR kʌɪ'astɪk
AM kaɪ'æstɪk
Chibcha
BR 'tʃɪbtʃə(r), -z
AM 'tʃɪbtʃə, -z
Chibchan
BR 'tʃɪbtʃən
AM 'tʃɪbtʃən
chibouk
BR tʃɪ'bu:k, -s
AM ʃə'buk, ʃə'bʊk, -s
chic
BR ʃi:k
AM ʃik
Chicago
BR ʃɪ'kɑ:gəʊ
AM ʃɪ'kɔgoʊ, ʃɪ'kɑgoʊ
Chicagoan
BR ʃɪ'kɑ:gəʊən
AM ʃɪ'kɔgəwən, ʃɪ'kɑgəwən
chicana
BR (t)ʃɪ'kɑ:nə(r), -z
AM tʃɪ'kɑnɑ, -z
chicane
BR ʃɪ'keɪn, -z
AM ʃə'keɪn, -z
chicanery
BR ʃɪ'keɪn(ə)r|i, -ɪz
AM ʃə'keɪn(ə)ri, -z
chicano
BR (t)ʃɪ'kɑ:nəʊ, -z
AM (t)ʃɪ'kɑnoʊ, -z
Chichén Itzá
BR ˌtʃɪtʃ(ə)n 'ɪtsə(r)
AM tʃiˌtʃɛn it'sɑ
Chichester
BR 'tʃɪtʃɨstə(r)
AM 'tʃɪtʃəstər
Chichewa
BR tʃɪ'tʃeɪwə(r)
AM tʃə'tʃeɪwə
chichi
BR 'ʃi:ʃi:
AM 'tʃiˌtʃi
Chichimec
BR 'tʃi:tʃɨmɛk
AM 'tʃitʃəˌmɛk
chick
BR tʃɪk, -s
AM tʃɪk, -s
chickabiddy
BR 'tʃɪkəˌbɪd|i, -ɪz
AM 'tʃɪkəˌbɪdi, -z
chickadee
BR 'tʃɪkədi:, -z
AM 'tʃɪkɨdi, -z
chickaree
BR 'tʃɪkəri:, -z
AM 'tʃɪkəri, -z
Chickasaw
BR 'tʃɪkəsɔ:(r)
AM 'tʃɪkəˌsɔ, 'tʃɪkəˌsɑ
chicken
BR 'tʃɪk|(ɨ)n, -(ɨ)nz, -n̩ɪŋ\-ɨnɪŋ, -(ɨ)nd
AM 'tʃɪkən, -z
chickenfeed
BR 'tʃɪk(ɨ)nfi:d
AM 'tʃɪkənˌfid
chickenpox
BR 'tʃɪk(ɨ)npɒks
AM 'tʃɪkənˌpɑks
chickling
BR 'tʃɪklɪŋ, -z
AM 'tʃɪklɪŋ, -z
chickpea
BR 'tʃɪkpi:, -z
AM 'tʃɪkˌpi, -z
chickweed
BR 'tʃɪkwi:d
AM 'tʃɪkˌwid
chicle
BR 'tʃɪkl
AM 'tʃɪkəl
chicly
BR 'ʃi:kli
AM 'ʃikli
chicness
BR 'ʃi:knɨs
AM 'ʃiknɨs
chicory
BR 'tʃɪk(ə)ri
AM 'tʃɪkəri
chid
BR tʃɪd
AM tʃɪd
chide
BR tʃʌɪd, -z, -ɪŋ, -ɨd
AM tʃaɪd, -z, -ɪŋ, -ɨd
chider
BR 'tʃʌɪdə(r), -z
AM 'tʃaɪdər, -z
chidingly
BR 'tʃʌɪdɪŋli
AM 'tʃaɪdɪŋli
chief
BR tʃi:f, -s
AM tʃif, -s
chiefdom
BR 'tʃi:fdəm, -z
AM 'tʃifdəm, -z
chiefly
BR 'tʃi:fli
AM 'tʃifli
chieftain
BR 'tʃi:ft(ə)n, -z
AM 'tʃiftən, -z
chieftaincy
BR 'tʃi:ft(ə)ns|i, -ɪz
AM 'tʃiftənsi, -z
chieftainship
BR 'tʃi:ft(ə)nʃɪp, -s
AM 'tʃiftənˌʃɪp, -s
chiffchaff
BR 'tʃɪftʃaf, -s
AM 'tʃɪfˌtʃæf, -s
chiffon
BR 'ʃɪfɒn
AM ʃɪ'fɑn, 'ʃɪˌfɑn
chiffonier
BR ˌʃɪfə'nɪə(r), -z
AM ˌʃɪfə'nɪ(ə)r, -z
chiffonnier
BR ˌʃɪfə'nɪə(r), -z
AM ˌʃɪfə'nɪ(ə)r, -z
chifforobe
BR 'ʃɪfərəʊb, -z
AM 'ʃɪfəˌroʊb, -z
chigger
BR 'tʃɪgə(r), -z
AM 'tʃɪgər, -z
chignon
BR 'ʃi:njɒ̃, 'ʃi:njɒn, -z
AM 'ʃinjɑn, ʃin'jɑn, -z
chigoe
BR 'tʃɪgəʊ, -z
AM 'tʃigoʊ, -z
Chigwell
BR 'tʃɪgw(ɛ)l
AM 'tʃɪgˌwɛl
Chihuahua
BR tʃɪ'wɑ:wə(r), -z
AM tʃə'wɑwə
chihuahua
BR tʃɪ'wɑ:wə(r), -z
AM tʃə'wɑwə, -z
chikungunya
BR ˌtʃɪk(ə)n'gʌnjə(r)
AM ˌtʃɪkən'gənjə
chilblain
BR 'tʃɪlbleɪn, -z, -d
AM 'tʃɪlˌbleɪn, -z, -d
child
BR tʃʌɪld
AM tʃaɪld
childbearing
BR 'tʃʌɪl(d)ˌbɛ:rɪŋ
AM 'tʃaɪl(d)ˌbɛrɪŋ
childbed
BR 'tʃʌɪl(d)bɛd
AM 'tʃaɪl(d)ˌbɛd
childbirth
BR 'tʃʌɪl(d)bə:θ
AM 'tʃaɪl(d)ˌbərθ
childcare
BR 'tʃʌɪl(d)kɛ:(r)
AM 'tʃaɪl(d)ˌkɛ(ə)r
Childe
BR tʃʌɪld
AM tʃaɪld
Childermas
BR 'tʃɪldəmas
AM 'tʃɪldərˌmæs

Childers
BR 'tʃɪldəz
AM 'tʃɪldərz

childhood
BR 'tʃʌɪldhʊd, -z
AM 'tʃaɪl(d),(h)ʊd, -z

childish
BR 'tʃʌɪldɪʃ
AM 'tʃaɪldɪʃ

childishly
BR 'tʃʌɪldɪʃli
AM 'tʃaɪldɪʃli

childishness
BR 'tʃʌɪldɪʃnɨs
AM 'tʃaɪldɪʃnɨs

childless
BR 'tʃʌɪl(d)lɨs
AM 'tʃaɪl(d)lɨs

childlessly
BR 'tʃʌɪl(d)lɨsli
AM 'tʃaɪl(d)lɨsli

childlessness
BR 'tʃʌɪl(d)lɨsnɨs
AM 'tʃaɪl(d)lɨsnɨs

childlike
BR 'tʃʌɪl(d)lʌɪk
AM 'tʃaɪl(d),laɪk

childminder
BR 'tʃʌɪl(d),mʌɪndə(r), -z
AM 'tʃaɪl(d),maɪndər, -z

childproof
BR 'tʃʌɪl(d)pruːf
AM 'tʃaɪl(d),pruf

child-rearing
BR 'tʃʌɪld,rɪərɪŋ
AM 'tʃaɪl(d),rɪrɪŋ

children
BR 'tʃɪldr(ə)n
AM 'tʃɪldr(ə)n

Childs
BR tʃʌɪldz
AM tʃaɪldz

Childwall
BR 'tʃɪl(d)wɔːl
AM tʃaɪld,wɔl, tʃaɪld,wɑl

Chile
BR 'tʃɪli
AM 'tʃɪli

chile
BR 'tʃɪl|i, -ɪz
AM 'tʃɪli, -z

Chilean
BR 'tʃɪlɪən, -z
AM 'tʃɪliən, tʃə'leiən, -z

chili
BR 'tʃɪl|i, -ɪz
AM 'tʃɪli, -z

chiliad
BR 'kɪlɪad, 'kɪlɪəd, -z
AM 'kɪli,æd, -z

chiliasm
BR 'kɪlɪaz(ə)m
AM 'kɪli,æzəm

chiliast
BR 'kɪlɪast, -s
AM 'kɪli,æst, -s

chiliastic
BR ,kɪlɪ'astɪk
AM ,kɪli'æstɪk

chill
BR tʃɪl, -z, -ɪŋ, -d
AM tʃɪl, -z, -ɪŋ, -d

chiller
BR 'tʃɪlə(r), -z
AM 'tʃɪlər, -z

chilli
BR 'tʃɪl|i, -ɪz
AM 'tʃɪli, -z

chilliness
BR 'tʃɪlɪnɨs
AM 'tʃɪlinɨs

chillingly
BR 'tʃɪlɪŋli
AM 'tʃɪlɪŋli

chillness
BR 'tʃɪlnɨs
AM 'tʃɪlnɨs

chillsome
BR 'tʃɪls(ə)m
AM 'tʃɪlsəm

chillum
BR 'tʃɪləm
AM 'tʃɪləm

chilly
BR 'tʃɪl|i, -ɪə(r), -ɪɨst
AM 'tʃɪli, -ər, -ɨst

Chilpruf
BR 'tʃɪlpruːf
AM 'tʃɪl,pruf

Chiltern
BR 'tʃɪlt(ə)n, -z
AM 'tʃɪltərn, -z

Chilton
BR 'tʃɪlt(ə)n
AM 'tʃɪltən

chimaera
BR kʌɪ'mɪərə(r), kɪ'mɪərə(r), -z
AM kaɪ'mɪrə, kə'mɪrə, -z

Chimborazo
BR ,tʃɪmbə'rɑːzəʊ
AM ,tʃɪmbə'rɑzoʊ

chime
BR tʃʌɪm, -z, -ɪŋ, -d
AM tʃaɪm, -z, -ɪŋ, -d

chimer
BR 'tʃɪmə(r), -z
AM 'tʃɪmər, -z

chimera
BR kʌɪ'mɪərə(r), kɪ'mɪərə(r), -z
AM kaɪ'mɪrə, kə'mɪrə, -z

chimere
BR tʃɪ'mɪə(r), -z
AM (t)ʃə'mɪ(ə)r, -z

chimeric
BR kʌɪ'mɛrɪk, kɪ'mɛrɪk
AM kaɪ'mɛrɪk, kə'mɛrɪk

chimerical
BR kʌɪ'mɛrɪkl, kɪ'mɛrɪkl
AM kaɪ'mɛrəkəl, kə'mɛrəkəl

chimerically
BR kʌɪ'mɛrɪkli, kɪ'mɛrɪkli
AM kaɪ'mɛrək(ə)li, kə'mɛrək(ə)li

chimney
BR 'tʃɪmn|i, -ɪz
AM 'tʃɪmni, -z

chimneybreast
BR 'tʃɪmnɪbrɛst, -s
AM 'tʃɪmni,brɛst, -s

chimneypiece
BR 'tʃɪmnɪpiːs, -ɪz
AM 'tʃɪmni,pis, -ɪz

chimneypot
BR 'tʃɪmnɪpɒt, -s
AM 'tʃɪmni,pɑt, -s

chimneystack
BR 'tʃɪmnɪstak, -s
AM 'tʃɪmni,stæk, -s

chimneysweep
BR 'tʃɪmnɪswiːp, -s
AM 'tʃɪmni,swip, -s

chimp
BR tʃɪmp, -s
AM tʃɪmp, -s

chimpanzee
BR ,tʃɪmpan'ziː, ,tʃɪmpən'ziː, -z
AM ,tʃɪm,pæn'zi, ,tʃɪm'pæn,zi, -z

chin
BR tʃɪn, -z
AM tʃɪn, -z

china
BR 'tʃʌɪnə(r), -z
AM 'tʃaɪnə, -z

Chinagraph
BR 'tʃʌɪnəgrɑːf, 'tʃʌɪnəgraf, -s
AM 'tʃaɪnə,græf, -s

Chinaman
BR 'tʃʌɪnəmən
AM 'tʃaɪnəmən

Chinamen
BR 'tʃʌɪnəmən
AM 'tʃaɪnəmən

Chinatown
BR 'tʃʌɪnətaʊn, -z
AM 'tʃaɪnə,taʊn, -z

chinaware
BR 'tʃʌɪnəwɛː(r)
AM 'tʃaɪnə,wɛ(ə)r

chinch
BR tʃɪn(t)ʃ, -ɨz
AM tʃɪn(t)ʃ, -ɨz

chincherinchee
BR ,tʃɪn(t)ʃɪrɪn'tʃiː, -z
AM ,tʃɪntʃərɪn'tʃi, -z

chinchilla
BR tʃɪn'tʃɪlə(r), -z
AM tʃɪn'tʃɪlə, -z

chin-chin
BR ,tʃɪn'tʃɪn
AM ¦tʃɪn'tʃɪn

Chindit
BR 'tʃɪndɪt, -s
AM 'tʃɪndɪt, -s

Chindwin
BR 'tʃɪndwɪn
AM 'tʃɪndwən

chine
BR tʃʌɪn, -z, -ɪŋ, -d
AM tʃaɪn, -z, -ɪŋ, -d

chiné
BR ʃiː'neɪ
AM ʃə'neɪ

Chinese
BR ,tʃʌɪ'niːz
AM ,tʃaɪ'niz

Chingford
BR 'tʃɪŋfəd
AM 'tʃɪŋfərd

chink
BR tʃɪŋk, -s
AM tʃɪŋk, -s

Chinky
BR 'tʃɪŋk|i, -ɪz
AM 'tʃɪŋki, -z

chinless
BR 'tʃɪnlɨs
AM 'tʃɪnlɨs

chinlessness
BR 'tʃɪnlɨsnɨs
AM 'tʃɪnlɨsnɨs

chino
BR '(t)ʃiːnəʊ, -z
AM 'tʃinoʊ, -z

chinoiserie
BR ʃɪn'wɑːz(ə)ri, ʃiːn'wɑːz(ə)ri, ʃɪn,wɑːzə'riː
AM ,ʃin,wɑzə'ri, ,ʃin'wɑzəri

Chinook
BR tʃɪ'nʊk, tʃɪ'nuːk, -s
AM (t)ʃə'nʊk, -s

chinstrap
BR 'tʃɪnstrap, -s
AM 'tʃɪn,stræp, -s

chintz
BR tʃɪn(t)s
AM tʃɪn(t)s

chintzily
BR 'tʃɪn(t)sɪli
AM 'tʃɪn(t)sɪli

chintziness
BR 'tʃɪn(t)sɪnɨs
AM 'tʃɪn(t)sinɨs

chintzy
BR 'tʃɪn(t)s|i, -ɪə(r), -ɪɨst
AM 'tʃɪn(t)si, -ər, -ɨst

chinwag
BR 'tʃɪnwag, -z
AM 'tʃɪn,wæg, -z

chionodoxa
BR ˌkʌɪənə'dɒksə(r), kʌɪˌɒnə'dɒksə(r), -z
AM ˌkaɪənoʊ'dɑksə, ˌkaɪˌɑnə'dɑksə, -z

Chios
BR 'kʌɪɒs, 'kiːɒs
AM 'kiˌɔs, 'kiˌɑs

chip
BR tʃɪp, -s, -ɪŋ, -t
AM tʃɪp, -s, -ɪŋ, -t

chipboard
BR 'tʃɪpbɔːd
AM 'tʃɪpˌbɔ(ə)rd

chipmunk
BR 'tʃɪpmʌŋk, -s
AM 'tʃɪpˌməŋk, -s

chipolata
BR ˌtʃɪpə'lɑːtə(r), -z
AM ˌtʃɪpə'lɑdə, -z

Chippendale
BR 'tʃɪp(ə)ndeɪl
AM 'tʃɪpənˌdeɪl

Chippenham
BR 'tʃɪpənəm, 'tʃɪpn̩əm
AM 'tʃɪpənəm, 'tʃɪpənˌhæm

chipper
BR 'tʃɪpə(r), -z
AM 'tʃɪpər, -z

Chippewa
BR 'tʃɪpɨwɑː(r), 'tʃɪpɨwə(r), -z
AM 'tʃɪpəwɑ, -z

chippie
BR 'tʃɪp|i, -ɪz
AM 'tʃɪpi, -z

chippiness
BR 'tʃɪpɪnɨs
AM 'tʃɪpinɨs

chipping
BR 'tʃɪpɪŋ, -z
AM 'tʃɪpɪŋ, -z

chippy
BR 'tʃɪp|i, -ɪz
AM 'tʃɪpi, -z

Chips
BR tʃɪps
AM tʃɪps

chipshot
BR 'tʃɪpʃɒt, -s
AM 'tʃɪpˌʃɑt, -s

chiral
BR 'kʌɪrəl, 'kʌɪrl̩
AM 'kaɪrəl

chirality
BR kʌɪ'ralɨti
AM kaɪ'rælədi

chi-rho
BR 'kʌɪˌrəʊ
AM ˌkaɪˌroʊ

Chirk
BR tʃəːk
AM tʃərk

chirograph
BR 'kʌɪrəgrɑːf, 'kʌɪrəgraf, -s
AM 'kaɪrəˌgræf, -s

chirographer
BR ˌkʌɪ'rɒgrəfə(r), -z
AM ˌkaɪ'rɑgrəfər, -z

chirographic
BR ˌkʌɪrə'grafɪk
AM ˌkaɪrə'græfɪk

chirographist
BR ˌkʌɪ'rɒgrəfɪst, -s
AM ˌkaɪ'rɑgrəfəst, -s

chirography
BR ˌkaɪ'rɒgrəfi
AM ˌkaɪ'rɑgrəfi

chiromancer
BR 'kʌɪrəˌmansə(r), -z
AM 'kaɪrəˌmænsər, -z

chiromancy
BR 'kʌɪrəˌmansi
AM 'kaɪrəˌmænsi

Chiron
BR 'kʌɪrən
AM 'kaɪrən

chiropodist
BR kɨ'rɒpədɪst, ʃɨ'rɒpədɪst, -s
AM kə'rɑpədəst, -s

chiropody
BR kɨ'rɒpədi, ʃɨ'rɒpədi
AM kə'rɑpədi

chiropractic
BR ˌkʌɪrə'praktɪk, 'kʌɪrəˌpraktɪk
AM ˌkaɪrə'præktɪk

chiropractor
BR 'kʌɪrəˌpraktə(r), -z
AM 'kaɪrəˌpræktər, -z

chiropteran
BR kʌɪ'rɒpt(ə)rən, kʌɪ'rɒpt(ə)rn̩, -z
AM kaɪ'rɑptərən, -z

chiropterous
BR kʌɪ'rɒpt(ə)rəs
AM kaɪ'rɑptərəs

chirp
BR tʃəːp, -s, -ɪŋ, -t
AM tʃərp, -s, -ɪŋ, -t

chirper
BR 'tʃəːpə(r), -z
AM 'tʃərpər, -z

chirpily
BR 'tʃəːpɨli
AM 'tʃərpəli

chirpiness
BR 'tʃəːpɪnɨs
AM 'tʃərpinɨs

chirpy
BR 'tʃəːp|i, -ɪə(r), -ɪɨst
AM 'tʃərpi, -ər, -ɨst

chirr
BR tʃəː(r), -z, -ɪŋ, -d
AM tʃər, -z, -ɪŋ, -d

chirrup
BR 'tʃɪrʌp, -s, -ɪŋ, -t
AM 'tʃɪrəp, -s, -ɪŋ, -t

chirrupy
BR 'tʃɪrʌpi
AM 'tʃɪrəpi

chiru
BR 'tʃɪruː, -z
AM 'tʃɪru, -z

chisel
BR 'tʃɪz|l, -lz, -l̩ɪŋ\-lɪŋ, -ld
AM 'tʃɪz|əl, -əlz, -(ə)lɪŋ, -əld

chiseler
BR 'tʃɪzl̩ə(r), 'tʃɪzlə(r), -z
AM 'tʃɪz(ə)lər, -z

chiseller
BR 'tʃɪzl̩ə(r), 'tʃɪzlə(r), -z
AM 'tʃɪz(ə)lər, -z

Chisholm
BR 'tʃɪz(ə)m
AM 'tʃɪzəm

Chislehurst
BR 'tʃɪzlhəːst
AM 'tʃɪzlˌ(h)ərst

chi-square
BR 'kʌɪskwɛː(r), -d
AM ˌkaɪˌskwɛ(ə)r, -d

Chiswick
BR 'tʃɪzɪk
AM 'tʃɪzˌwɪk, 'tʃɪzɪk

chit
BR tʃɪt, -s
AM tʃɪt, -s

chital
BR 'tʃiːtl
AM 'tʃidl

chitchat
BR 'tʃɪttʃat
AM 'tʃɪˌtʃæt

chitin
BR 'kʌɪt(ɪ)n
AM 'kaɪtn

chitinous
BR 'kʌɪtɨnəs, 'kʌɪtn̩əs
AM 'kaɪtn̩əs

chitlins
BR 'tʃɪtlɪnz
AM 'tʃɪtlɨnz

chiton
BR 'kʌɪt(ɒ)n
AM 'kaɪˌtɑn, 'kaɪtn

Chittagong
BR 'tʃɪtəgɒŋ
AM 'tʃɪdəˌgɔŋ, 'tʃɪdəˌgɑŋ

chitterling
BR 'tʃɪtl̩ɪŋ, 'tʃɪt(ə)lɪŋ, -z
AM 'tʃɪtlɨn, -z

chitty
BR 'tʃɪt|i, -ɪz
AM 'tʃɪdi, -z

chiv
BR (t)ʃɪv, -z
AM (t)ʃɪv, -z

chivalric
BR ʃɪ'valrɪk
AM ʃə'vælrɪk

chivalrous
BR 'ʃɪvlrəs
AM 'ʃɪvəlrəs

chivalrously
BR 'ʃɪvlrəsli
AM 'ʃɪvəlrəsli

chivalrousness
BR 'ʃɪvlrəsnəs
AM 'ʃɪvəlrəsnəs

chivalry
BR 'ʃɪvlri
AM 'ʃɪvəlri

Chivas
BR 'ʃɪvas, 'ʃɪvəs, 'ʃiːvəs
AM 'ʃɪvəs

chive
BR tʃʌɪv, -z
AM tʃaɪv, -z

Chivers
BR 'tʃɪvəz
AM 'tʃɪvərz

chivvy
BR 'tʃɪv|i, -ɪz, -ɪɪŋ, -ɪd
AM 'tʃɪvi, -z, -ɪŋ, -d

chiz
BR tʃɪz
AM tʃɪz

chizz
BR tʃɪz
AM tʃɪz

chlamydia
BR klə'mɪdɪə(r)
AM klə'mɪdiə

chlamydial
BR klə'mɪdɪəl
AM klə'mɪdiəl

chlamydomonas
BR ˌklamɪdə'məʊnəs
AM ˌklæmə'dɑmənəs

Chloë
BR 'kləʊi
AM 'kloʊi

chloracne
BR klɔːr'akni
AM klɔr'ækni

chloral
BR 'klɔːrəl, 'klɔːrl̩
AM 'klɔrəl

chlorambucil
BR klɔːr'ambjʊsɪl
AM klɔr'æmbjəˌsɪl

chloramine
BR 'klɔːrəmiːn
AM 'klɔrəˌmin

chloramphenicol
BR ˌklɔːram'fɛnɪkɒl, ˌklɔːrəm'fɛnɪkɒl, -z
AM ˌklɔræm'fɛnəˌkɔl, ˌklɔrɑm'fɛnəˌkɑl, -z

chlorate
BR 'klɔːreɪt, -s
AM 'klɔˌreɪt, -s

chlordane
BR ˈklɔːdeɪn
AM ˈklɔrˌdeɪn

chlorella
BR kləˈrɛlə(r), -z
AM kləˈrɛlə, -z

chloric
BR ˈklɔːrɪk, ˈklɒrɪk
AM ˈklɔrɪk

chloride
BR ˈklɔːrʌɪd, -z
AM ˈklɔˌraɪd, -z

chlorinate
BR ˈklɔːrɪneɪt, ˈklɒrɪneɪt, -s, -ɪŋ, -ɪd
AM ˈklɔrəˌneɪ|t, -ts, -dɪŋ, -dɪd

chlorination
BR ˌklɔːrɪˈneɪʃn, ˌklɒrɪˈneɪʃn
AM ˌklɔrəˈneɪʃən

chlorinator
BR ˈklɔːrɪneɪtə(r), ˈklɒrɪneɪtə(r), -z
AM ˈklɔrəˌneɪdər, -z

chlorine
BR ˈklɔːriːn
AM ˈklɔˈrin

chlorite
BR ˈklɔːrʌɪt
AM ˈklɔˌraɪt

chloritic
BR klɔːˈrɪtɪk, klɒˈrɪtɪk, kləˈrɪtɪk
AM klɔˈrɪdɪk, kləˈrɪdɪk

chlorodyne
BR ˈklɔːrə(ʊ)dʌɪn, ˈklɒrə(ʊ)dʌɪn
AM ˈklɔrəˌdaɪn

chlorofluorocarbon
BR ˌklɔːrəʊˌflʊərəʊˈkɑːb(ə)n, ˌklɔːrəʊˌflɔːrəʊˈkɑːb(ə)n, ˌklɒrəˌflʊərəˈkɑːb(ə)n, ˌklɒrəʊˌflɔːrəʊˈkɑːb(ə)n
AM ˈklɔrəˈflɔrəˌkɑrbən, ˈklɔrəˈflʊrəˌkɑrbən

chloroform
BR ˈklɒrəfɔːm, -z, -ɪŋ, -d
AM ˈklɔrəˌfɔ(ə)rm, -z, -ɪŋ, -d

Chloromycetin®
BR ˌklɔːrəʊmʌɪˈsiːtɪn, ˌklɒrəʊmʌɪˈsiːtɪn
AM ˌklɔrəˌmaɪˈsitn

chlorophyll
BR ˈklɒrəfɪl
AM ˈklɔrəˌfɪl

chlorophyllous
BR ˌklɒrəʊˈfɪləs
AM ˌklɔrəˈfɪləs

chloroplast
BR ˈklɔːrə(ʊ)plast, ˈklɒrə(ʊ)plast, -s
AM ˈklɔrəˌplæst, -s

chloroquine
BR ˈklɔːrəkwɪn, ˈklɒrəkwɪn
AM ˈklɔrəˌkwaɪn

chlorosis
BR kləˈrəʊsɪs, klɔːˈrəʊsɪs
AM klɔˈroʊsəs

chlorotic
BR klɔːˈrɒtɪk, kləˈrɒtɪk
AM kləˈrɑdɪk, klɔˈrɑdɪk

chlorous acid
BR ˌklɔːrəs ˈasɪd
AM ˌklɔrəs ˈæsəd

chlorpromazine
BR ˌklɔːˈprəʊməziːn, ˌklɔːˈprɒməziːn
AM ˌklɔrˈprɑməˌzin

Chobham
BR ˈtʃɒb(ə)m
AM ˈtʃɑbəm

choc
BR tʃɒk, -s
AM tʃɑk, -s

choc-a-bloc
BR ˌtʃɒkəˈblɒk
AM ˈtʃɑkəˈblɑk

chocaholic
BR ˌtʃɒkəˈhɒlɪk
AM ˌtʃɔkəˈhɔlɪk, ˌtʃɑkəˈhɑlɪk

choccy
BR ˈtʃɒk|i, -ɪz
AM ˈtʃɑki, -z

chocho
BR ˈtʃəʊtʃəʊ, -z
AM ˈtʃoʊˌtʃoʊ, -z

choc-ice
BR ˌtʃɒkˈʌɪs, ˈtʃɒkʌɪs, -ɪz
AM ˈtʃɔkˌaɪs, ˈtʃɑkˌaɪs, -ɪz

chock
BR tʃɒk, -s, -ɪŋ, -t
AM tʃɑk, -s, -ɪŋ, -t

chock-a-block
BR ˌtʃɒkəˈblɒk
AM ˈtʃɑkəˈblɑk

chocker
BR ˈtʃɒkə(r), -z
AM ˈtʃɑkər, -z

chockstone
BR ˈtʃɒkstəʊn
AM ˈtʃɑkˌstoʊn

chocoholic
BR ˌtʃɒkəˈhɒlɪk, -s
AM ˌtʃɔkəˈhɔlɪk, ˌtʃɑkəˈhɑlɪk, -s

chocolate
BR ˈtʃɒk(ə)lət, -s
AM ˈtʃɔk(ə)lət, ˈtʃɑk(ə)lət, -s

chocolatey
BR ˈtʃɒk(ə)ləti
AM ˈtʃɔk(ə)lədi, ˈtʃɑk(ə)lədi

Choctaw
BR ˈtʃɒktɔː(r), -z
AM ˈtʃɔkˌtɔ, ˈtʃɑkˌtɔ, -z

choice
BR tʃɔɪs, -ɪz, -ə(r), -ɪst
AM tʃɔɪs, -ɪz, -ər, -ɪst

choicely
BR ˈtʃɔɪsli
AM ˈtʃɔɪsli

choiceness
BR ˈtʃɔɪsnɪs
AM ˈtʃɔɪsnɪs

choir
BR ˈkwʌɪə(r), -z
AM ˈkwaɪər, -z

choirboy
BR ˈkwʌɪəbɔɪ, -z
AM ˈkwaɪ(ə)rˌbɔɪ, -z

choirgirl
BR ˈkwʌɪəgəːl, -z
AM ˈkwaɪ(ə)rˌgərl, -z

choirmaster
BR ˈkwʌɪəˌmɑːstə(r), ˈkwʌɪəˌmastə(r), -z
AM ˈkwaɪ(ə)rˌmæstər, -z

choke
BR tʃəʊk, -s, -ɪŋ, -t
AM tʃoʊk, -s, -ɪŋ, -t

chokeberry
BR ˈtʃəʊkb(ə)r|i, -ɪz
AM ˈtʃoʊkˌbɛri, -z

chokecherry
BR ˈtʃəʊkˌtʃɛr|i, -ɪz
AM ˈtʃoʊkˌtʃɛri, -z

choker
BR ˈtʃəʊkə(r), -z
AM ˈtʃoʊkər, -z

chokey
BR ˈtʃəʊki
AM ˈtʃoʊki

chokily
BR ˈtʃəʊkɪli
AM ˈtʃoʊkəli

chokiness
BR ˈtʃəʊkɪnɪs
AM ˈtʃoʊkinɪs

choko
BR ˈtʃəʊkəʊ, -z
AM ˈtʃoʊkoʊ, -z

choky
BR ˈtʃəʊk|i, -ɪz, -ɪə(r), -ɪɪst
AM ˈtʃoʊki, -z, -ər, -ɪst

cholangiography
BR ˌkɒlan(d)ʒɪˈɒgrəfi
AM ˌkoʊˌlændʒiˈɑgrəfi

cholecalciferol
BR ˌkɒlɪkalˈsɪf(ə)rɒl
AM ˌkoʊləˌkælˈsɪfəˌrɔl, ˌkoʊləˌkælˈsɪfəˌrɑl

cholecystectomy
BR ˌkɒlɪsɪstˈɛktəm|i, -ɪz
AM ˌkoʊləˌsɪsˈtɛktəmi, -z

cholecystography
BR ˌkɒlɪsɪstˈɒgrəfi
AM ˌkoʊləˌsɪsˈtɑgrəfi

choler
BR ˈkɒlə(r)
AM ˈkɑlər

cholera
BR ˈkɒl(ə)rə(r)
AM ˈkɑlərə

choleraic
BR ˌkɒləˈreɪɪk
AM ˌkɑləˈreɪɪk

choleric
BR ˈkɒl(ə)rɪk, kɒˈlɛrɪk
AM ˈkɑlərɪk, kəˈlɛrɪk

cholerically
BR ˈkɒl(ə)rɪkli, kɒˈlɛrɪkli
AM ˈkɑlərək(ə)li, kəˈlɛrək(ə)li

cholesterol
BR kəˈlɛst(ə)rɒl, kɒˈlɛst(ə)rɒl, kəˈlɛstr(ə)l, kɒˈlɛstr(ə)l
AM kəˈlɛstəˌrɔl, kəˈlɛstəˌrɑl

choli
BR ˈtʃəʊl|i, -ɪz
AM ˈkoʊli, -z

choliamb
BR ˈkəʊlɪam(b), -z
AM ˈkoʊliˌæm(b), -z

choliambic
BR ˌkəʊlɪˈambɪk
AM ˌkoʊliˈæmbɪk

cholic
BR ˈkɒlɪk
AM ˈkoʊlɪk, ˈkɑlɪk

choline
BR ˈkəʊliːn
AM ˈkoʊlin

cholinergic
BR ˌkəʊlɪˈnəːdʒɪk, ˌkɒlɪˈnəːdʒɪk
AM ˌkoʊləˈnərdʒɪk

Cholmeley
BR ˈtʃʌmli
AM ˈtʃəmli

Cholmondeley
BR ˈtʃʌmli
AM ˈtʃəmli

chomp
BR tʃɒmp, -s, -ɪŋ, -t
AM tʃɔmp, tʃɑmp, -s, -ɪŋ, -t

Chomskian
BR ˈtʃɒmskɪən, -z
AM ˈtʃɑmskiən, -z

Chomsky
BR ˈtʃɒmski
AM ˈtʃɑmski

chondrite
BR ˈkɒndrʌɪt, -s
AM ˈkɑnˌdraɪt, -s

chondrocranium
BR ˌkɒndrəʊˈkreɪnɪəm, -z

AM ˌkɑndroʊˈkreɪmiəm, ˌkɑndrəˈkreɪmiəm, -z

chondroma
BR kɒnˈdrəʊmə(r), -z
AM kɑnˈdroʊmə, -z

chondromata
BR kɒnˈdrəʊmətə(r)
AM kɑnˈdroʊmədə

choochoo
BR ˈtʃuːtʃuː, -z
AM ˈtʃuˌtʃu, -z

chook
BR tʃʊk, -s
AM tʃʊk, -s

choose
BR tʃuːz, -ɪz, -ɪŋ
AM tʃuz, -əz, -ɪŋ

chooser
BR ˈtʃuːzə(r), -z
AM ˈtʃuzər, -z

choosey
BR ˈtʃuːz|i, -ɪə(r), -ɪɪst
AM ˈtʃuzi, -ər, -ɪst

choosily
BR ˈtʃuːzɪli
AM ˈtʃuzəli

choosiness
BR ˈtʃuːzɪnɪs
AM ˈtʃuzinɪs

choosy
BR ˈtʃuːz|i, -ə(r), -ɪst
AM ˈtʃuzi, -ər, -ɪst

chop
BR tʃɒp, -s, -ɪŋ, -t
AM tʃɑp, -s, -ɪŋ, -t

chopfallen
BR ˈtʃɒpˌfɔːlən
AM ˈtʃɑpˌfɔlən, ˈtʃɑpˌfɑlən

chophouse
BR ˈtʃɒphaʊ|s, -zɪz
AM ˈtʃɑpˌ(h)aʊ|s, -zəz

Chopin
BR ˈʃɒpã, ˈʃəʊpã, ˈʃəʊpan
AM ˈʃoʊˌpæn

chopper
BR ˈtʃɒpə(r), -z
AM ˈtʃɑpər, -z

choppily
BR ˈtʃɒpɪli
AM ˈtʃɑpəli

choppiness
BR ˈtʃɒpɪnɪs
AM ˈtʃɑpinɪs

choppy
BR ˈtʃɒp|i, -ɪə(r), -ɪɪst
AM ˈtʃɑpi, -ər, -ɪst

chopstick
BR ˈtʃɒpstɪk, -s
AM ˈtʃɑpˌstɪk, -s

chop suey
BR ˌtʃɒp ˈsuː|i, -ɪz
AM ˌtʃɑp ˈsui, -z

choral
BR ˈkɔːrəl, ˈkɔːrl̩, -z
AM ˈkɔrəl, -z

chorale
BR kɒˈrɑːl, kɔːˈrɑːl, -z
AM kəˈræl, kəˈrɑl, kɔˈræl, kɔˈrɑl, -z

chorally
BR ˈkɔːrəli, ˈkɔːrl̩i
AM ˈkɔrəli

chord
BR kɔːd, -z, -ɪŋ
AM kɔ(ə)rd, -z, -ɪŋ

chordal
BR ˈkɔːdl
AM ˈkɔrdəl

chordate
BR ˈkɔːdeɪt, ˈkɔːdət, -s
AM ˈkɔrdət, ˈkɔrˌdeɪt, -s

chore
BR tʃɔː(r), -z
AM tʃɔ(ə)r, -z

chorea
BR kɔːˈrɪə(r), kɒˈrɪə(r). kəˈrɪə(r)
AM kəˈriə

choreograph
BR ˈkɒrɪəgrɑːf, ˈkɒrɪəgraf, -s, -ɪŋ, -t
AM ˈkɔriəˌgræf, -s, -ɪŋ, -t

choreographer
BR ˌkɒrɪˈɒgrəfə(r), -z
AM ˌkɔriˈɑgrəfər, -z

choreographic
BR ˌkɒrɪəˈgrafɪk
AM ˌkɔriəˈgræfɪk

choreographical
BR ˌkɒrɪəˈgrafɪkl
AM ˌkɔriəˈgræfəkəl

choreographically
BR ˌkɒrɪəˈgrafɪkli
AM ˌkɔriəˈgræfək(ə)li

choreography
BR ˌkɒrɪˈɒgrəfi
AM ˌkɔriˈɑgrəfi

choreologist
BR ˌkɒrɪˈɒlədʒɪst, -s
AM ˌkɔriˈɑlədʒəst, -s

choreology
BR ˌkɒrɪˈɒlədʒi
AM ˌkɔriˈɑlədʒi

choriamb
BR ˈkɒrɪamb, -z
AM ˈkoʊriəm(b), -z

choriambi
BR ˌkɒrɪˈambʌɪ
AM ˌkoʊriˈæmˌbaɪ

choriambic
BR ˌkɒrɪˈambɪk
AM ˌkoʊriˈæmbɪk

choriambus
BR ˌkɒrɪˈambəs
AM ˌkoʊriˈæmbəs

choric
BR ˈkɒrɪk
AM ˈkɔrɪk

chorine
BR ˈkɔːriːn, -z
AM ˈkɔrən, ˈkɔrin, -z

chorion
BR ˈkɔːrɪən, ˈkɔːrɪɒn, -z
AM ˈkɔriˌɑn, -z

chorionic
BR ˌkɔːrɪˈɒnɪk
AM ˌkoʊriˈɑnɪk

chorister
BR ˈkɒrɪstə(r), -z
AM ˈkɔrəstər, -z

Chorley
BR ˈtʃɔːli
AM ˈtʃɔrli

Chorlton
BR ˈtʃɔːlt(ə)n
AM ˈtʃɔrltən

Chorlton-cum-Hardy
BR ˌtʃɔːlt(ə)nkʌmˈhɑːdi
AM ˌtʃɔrltnkəmˈhɑrdi

chorographer
BR kɔːˈrɒgrəfə(r), -z
AM kəˈrɑgrəfər, -z

chorographic
BR ˌkɔːrəˈgrafɪk, ˌkɒrəˈgrafɪk
AM ˌkoʊrəˈgræfɪk

chorographically
BR ˌkɔːrəˈgrafɪkli, ˌkɒrəˈgrafɪkli
AM ˌkoʊrəˈgræfək(ə)li

chorography
BR kɔːˈrɒgrəfi
AM kəˈrɑgəfi

choroid
BR ˈkɔːrɔɪd, ˈkɒrɔɪd
AM ˈkɔrɔɪd

chorological
BR ˌkɒrəˈlɒdʒɪkl
AM ˌkoʊrəˈlɑdʒəkəl

chorologically
BR ˌkɒrəˈlɒdʒɪkli
AM ˌkoʊrəˈlɑdʒək(ə)li

chorologist
BR kɔːˈrɒlədʒɪst, -s
AM kəˈrɑlədʒəst, -s

chorology
BR kɔːˈrɒlədʒi
AM kəˈrɑlədʒi

chorten
BR ˈtʃɔːt(ə)n, -z
AM ˈtʃɔrt(ə)n, -z

chortle
BR ˈtʃɔːt|l, -lz, -l̩ɪŋ\-lɪŋ, -ld
AM ˈtʃɔrdəl, -z, -ɪŋ, -d

chorus
BR ˈkɔːrəs, -ɪz, -ɪŋ, -t
AM ˈkɔrəs, -əz, -ɪŋ, -t

chose
BR tʃəʊz
AM tʃoʊz

chosen
BR ˈtʃəʊzn
AM ˈtʃoʊzn

chota
BR ˈtʃəʊtə(r)
AM ˈtʃoʊdə

choucroute
BR ˈʃuːkruːt
AM ˌʃuˈkrut

chough
BR tʃʌf, -s
AM tʃəf, -s

choux
BR ʃuː
AM ʃu

chow
BR tʃaʊ, -z
AM tʃaʊ, -z

chowder
BR ˈtʃaʊdə(r)
AM ˈtʃaʊdər

chowkidar
BR ˈtʃəʊkɪdɑː(r), -z
AM ˈtʃoʊkəˌdɑr, -z

chow mein
BR ˌtʃaʊ ˈmeɪn, + ˈmiːn
AM ˌtʃaʊ ˈmeɪn

chrematistic
BR ˌkrɛməˈtɪstɪk, -s
AM ˌkrɛməˈtɪstɪk, -s

chrestomathy
BR krɛˈstɒməθ|i, -ɪz
AM krɛˈstɑməθi, -z

Chris
BR krɪs
AM krɪs

chrism
BR ˈkrɪz(ə)m
AM ˈkrɪzəm

chrisom
BR ˈkrɪz(ə)m, -z
AM ˈkrɪzəm, -z

Chrissie
BR ˈkrɪsi
AM ˈkrɪsi

Chrissy
BR ˈkrɪsi
AM ˈkrɪsi

Christ
BR krʌɪst, -s
AM kraɪst, -s

Christabel
BR ˈkrɪstəbɛl
AM ˈkrɪstəˌbɛl

Christadelphian
BR ˌkrɪstəˈdɛlfɪən, -z
AM ˌkrɪstəˈdɛlfiən, -z

Christchurch
BR ˈkrʌɪs(t)tʃəːtʃ
AM ˈkrɪs(t)ˌtʃərtʃ

christen
BR ˈkrɪs|n, -nz, -n̩ɪŋ\-nɪŋ, -nd
AM ˈkrɪsn, -z, -ɪŋ, -d

Christendom
BR ˈkrɪsndəm
AM ˈkrɪsndəm

christener
BR ˈkrɪsn̩ə(r), ˈkrɪsnə(r), -z
AM ˈkrɪs(ə)nər, -z

christening
BR ˈkrɪsn̩ɪŋ, ˈkrɪsnɪŋ, -z
AM ˈkrɪs(ə)nɪŋ, -z

Christensen
BR ˈkrɪst(ə)ns(ə)n
AM ˈkrɪstənsən

Christhood
BR ˈkrʌɪsthʊd
AM ˈkraɪstˌ(h)ʊd

Christi
BR ˈkrɪsti
AM ˈkrɪsti

Christian
BR ˈkrɪstʃ(ə)n, -z
AM ˈkrɪstʃən, -z

Christiana
BR ˌkrɪst(ʃ)ɪˈɑːnə(r)
AM ˌkrɪstiˈænə

Christiania
BR ˌkrɪst(ʃ)ɪˈɑːnɪə(r)
AM ˌkrɪstiˈæniə, ˌkrɪstʃiˈæniə

Christianisation
BR ˌkrɪstʃənʌɪˈzeɪʃn, ˌkrɪstʃn̩ʌɪˈzeɪʃn
AM ˌkrɪstʃənəˈzeɪʃən, ˌkrɪstʃənˌaɪˈzeɪʃən

Christianise
BR ˈkrɪstʃənʌɪz, ˈkrɪstʃn̩ʌɪz, -ɨz, -ɪŋ, -d
AM ˈkrɪstʃəˌnaɪz, -ɨz, -ɪŋ, -d

Christianity
BR ˌkrɪst(ʃ)ɪˈanɨti
AM ˌkrɪstʃiˈænədi

Christianization
BR ˌkrɪstʃənʌɪˈzeɪʃn, ˌkrɪstʃn̩ʌɪˈzeɪʃn
AM ˌkrɪstʃənəˈzeɪʃən, ˌkrɪstʃənˌaɪˈzeɪʃən

Christianize
BR ˈkrɪstʃənʌɪz, ˈkrɪstʃn̩ʌɪz, -ɨz, -ɪŋ, -d
AM ˈkrɪstʃəˌnaɪz, -ɨz, -ɪŋ, -d

Christianly
BR ˈkrɪstʃ(ə)nli
AM ˈkrɪstʃənli

Christie
BR ˈkrɪst|i, -ɪz
AM ˈkrɪsti, -z

Christina
BR krɪsˈtiːnə(r)
AM krɪsˈtinə

Christine
BR ˈkrɪstiːn, krɪsˈtiːn
AM krɪsˈtin

Christingle
BR ˈkrɪstɪŋgl, -z
AM ˈkrɪstɪŋgəl, -z

Christlike
BR ˈkrʌɪs(t)lʌɪk
AM ˈkraɪs(t)ˌlaɪk

Christly
BR ˈkrʌɪs(t)li
AM ˈkraɪs(t)li

Christmas
BR ˈkrɪsməs, -ɨz
AM ˈkrɪsməs, -əz

Christmassy
BR ˈkrɪsməsi
AM ˈkrɪsməsi

Christmastide
BR ˈkrɪsməstʌɪd
AM ˈkrɪsməsˌtaɪd

Christmastime
BR ˈkrɪsməstʌɪm
AM ˈkrɪsməsˌtaɪm

Christobel
BR ˈkrɪstəbɛl
AM ˈkrɪstəˌbɛl

Christolatry
BR krɪˈstɒlətri
AM krɪsˈtɑlətri

Christological
BR ˌkrɪstəˈlɒdʒɨkl
AM ˌkrɪstəˈlɑdʒəkəl

Christology
BR krɪˈstɒlədʒi
AM krɪsˈtɑlədʒi

Christophany
BR krɪˈstɒfəni, krɪˈstɒfn̩i
AM krɪsˈtɑfəni

Christopher
BR ˈkrɪstəfə(r)
AM ˈkrɪstəfər

Christy
BR ˈkrɪsti
AM ˈkrɪsti

chroma
BR ˈkrəʊmə(r)
AM ˈkroʊmə

chromate
BR ˈkrəʊmeɪt, -s
AM ˈkroʊˌmeɪt, -s

chromatic
BR krə(ʊ)ˈmatɪk
AM kroʊˈmædɪk, krəˈmædɪk

chromatically
BR krə(ʊ)ˈmatɨkli
AM kroʊˈmædək(ə)li, krəˈmædək(ə)li

chromaticism
BR krə(ʊ)ˈmatɨsɪz(ə)m
AM kroʊˈmædəˌsɪzəm

chromaticity
BR ˌkrəʊməˈtɪsɨti
AM ˌkroʊməˈtɪsɨdi

chromatid
BR ˈkrəʊmətɪd, -z
AM ˈkroʊməˌtɪd, -z

chromatin
BR ˈkrəʊmətɪn
AM ˈkroʊmədən

chromatism
BR ˈkrəʊmətɪz(ə)m
AM ˈkroʊməˌtɪzəm

chromatogram
BR krə(ʊ)ˈmatəgram, -z
AM kroʊˈmædəˌgræm, -z

chromatograph
BR krə(ʊ)ˈmatəgrɑːf, krə(ʊ)ˈmatəgraf, -s
AM kroʊˈmædəˌgræf, -s

chromatographic
BR krə(ʊ)ˌmatəˈgrafɪk
AM kroʊˌmædəˈgræfɪk

chromatographically
BR krə(ʊ)ˌmatəˈgrafɨkli
AM kroʊˌmædəˈgræfək(ə)li

chromatography
BR ˌkrəʊməˈtɒgrəfi
AM ˌkroʊməˈtɑgrəfi

chromatopsia
BR ˌkrəʊməˈtɒpsɪə(r)
AM ˌkroʊməˈtɑpsiə

chrome
BR krəʊm
AM kroʊm

chromic
BR ˈkrəʊmɪk
AM ˈkroʊmɪk

chrominance
BR ˈkrəʊmɪnəns
AM ˈkroʊmənəns

chromite
BR ˈkrəʊmʌɪt, -s
AM ˈkroʊˌmaɪt, -s

chromium
BR ˈkrəʊmɪəm
AM ˈkroʊmiəm

chromium-plate
BR ˌkrəʊmɪəmˈpleɪt, -s, -ɪŋ, -ɨd
AM ˌkroʊmiəmˈpleɪ|t, -ts, -dɪŋ, -dɨd

chromo
BR ˈkrəʊməʊ, -z
AM ˈkroʊˌmoʊ, -z

chromolithograph
BR ˌkrəʊməʊˈlɪθəgrɑːf, ˌkrəʊməʊˈlɪθəgraf, -s
AM ˌkroʊmoʊˈlɪθəˌgræf, -s

chromolithographer
BR ˌkrəʊməʊlɪˈθɒgrəfə(r), -z
AM ˌkroʊmoʊlɪˈθɑgrəfər, -z

chromolithographic
BR ˌkrəʊməʊˌlɪθəˈgrafɪk
AM ˌkroʊmoʊˌlɪθəˈgræfɪk

chromolithography
BR ˌkrəʊməʊlɪˈθɒgrəfi
AM ˌkroʊmoʊlɪˈθɑgrəfi

chromoly
BR ˈkrəʊmɒli, ˌkrəʊmˈɒli
AM ˈkroʊˌmɑli

chromosomal
BR ˌkrəʊməˈsəʊml
AM ˌkroʊməˈsoʊməl

chromosome
BR ˈkrəʊməsəʊm, -z
AM ˈkroʊməˌsoʊm, -z

chromosphere
BR ˈkrəʊmə(ʊ)sfɪə(r), -z
AM ˈkroʊməˌsfɪ(ə)r, -z

chromospheric
BR ˌkrəʊmə(ʊ)ˈsfɛrɪk
AM ˌkroʊməˈsfɛrɪk

chroneme
BR ˈkrəʊniːm, -z
AM ˈkroʊnim, -z

chronemic
BR krə(ʊ)ˈniːmɪk
AM kroʊˈnimɪk

chronic
BR ˈkrɒnɪk
AM ˈkrɑnɪk

chronically
BR ˈkrɒnɨkli
AM ˈkrɑnək(ə)li

chronicity
BR krɒˈnɪsəti
AM krɑˈnɪsɨdi

chronicle
BR ˈkrɒnɪk|l, -lz, -l̩ɪŋ\-lɪŋ, -ld
AM ˈkrɑnək|əl, -əlz, -(ə)lɪŋ, -əld

chronicler
BR ˈkrɒnɪkl̩ə(r), ˈkrɒnɪklə(r), -z
AM ˈkrɑnəklər, -z

chronogram
BR ˈkrɒnəgram, -z
AM ˈkrɑnəˌgræm, -z

chronogrammatic
BR ˌkrɒnəgrəˈmatɪk
AM ˌkrɑnəgrəˈmædɪk

chronograph
BR ˈkrɒnəgrɑːf, ˈkrɒnəgraf, -s
AM ˈkrɑnəˌgræf, -s

chronographic
BR ˌkrɒnəˈgrafɪk
AM ˌkrɑnəˈgræfɪk

chronologer
BR krəˈnɒlədʒə(r), -z
AM krəˈnɑlədʒər, -z

chronologic
BR ˌkrɒnəˈlɒdʒɪk
AM ˌkrɑnəˈlɑdʒɪk

chronological
BR ˌkrɒnəˈlɒdʒɪkl
AM ˌkrɑnəˈlɑdʒəkəl

chronologically
BR ˌkrɒnəˈlɒdʒɨkli
AM ˌkrɑnəˈlɑdʒək(ə)li

chronologisation
BR krəˌnɒlədʒʌɪˈzeɪʃn
AM ˌkrɑnəˌlɑdʒəˈzeɪʃən, ˌkrɑnəˌlɑˌdʒaɪˈzeɪʃən

chronologise
BR krə'nɒlədʒʌɪz, -ɨz, -ɪŋ, -d
AM krə'nɑlə,dʒaɪz, -ɨz, -ɪŋ, -d

chronologist
BR krə'nɒlədʒɪst, -s
AM krə'nɑlədʒəst, -s

chronologization
BR krə,nɒlədʒʌɪ'zeɪʃn
AM ,krɑnə,lɑdʒə'zeɪʃən, ,krɑnə,lɑ,dʒaɪ'zeɪʃən

chronologize
BR krə'nɒlədʒʌɪz, -ɨz, -ɪŋ, -d
AM krə'nɑlə,dʒaɪz, -ɨz, -ɪŋ, -d

chronology
BR krə'nɒlədʒ|i, -ɪz
AM krə'nɑlədʒi, -z

chronometer
BR krə'nɒmɨtə(r), -z
AM krə'nɑmədər, -z

chronometric
BR ,krɒnə'mɛtrɪk
AM ,krɑnə'mɛtrɪk

chronometrical
BR ,krɒnə'mɛtrɪkl
AM ,krɑnə'mɛtrəkəl

chronometrically
BR ,krɒnə'mɛtrɪkli
AM ,krɑnə'mɛtrək(ə)li

chronometry
BR krə'nɒmɨtri
AM krə'nɑmətri

chronoscope
BR 'krɒnəskəʊp, -s
AM 'krɑnə,skoʊp, -s

chrysalid
BR 'krɪsəlɪd, 'krɪsl̩ɪd, -z
AM 'krɪsə,lɪd, -z

chrysalides
BR krɪ'salɨdiːz
AM krə'sælə,diz

chrysalis
BR 'krɪsəlɪs, 'krɪsl̩ɪs, -ɨz
AM 'krɪsələs, -ɨz

chrysanth
BR krɪ'sanθ, -s
AM krə'sænθ, -s

chrysanthemum
BR krɪ'sanθɨməm, -z
AM krɪ'sænθəməm, -z

chryselephantine
BR ,krɪsɛlɪ'fantʌɪn
AM ¦krɪs,ɛlə'fæn,tin, ¦krɪs,ɛlə'fæn,taɪn

Chrysler®
BR 'krʌɪzlə(r), -z
AM 'kraɪslər, -z

chrysoberyl
BR ,krɪsə'bɛrɨl, ,krɪsə'bɛrl̩
AM 'krɪsə,bɛrəl

chrysolite
BR 'krɪsəlʌɪt, -s
AM 'krɪsə,laɪt, -s

chrysoprase
BR 'krɪsəpreɪz, -ɨz
AM 'krɪsə,preɪz, -ɨz

Chrysostom
BR 'krɪsəstəm
AM 'krɪsəstəm

Chrystal
BR 'krɪstl
AM 'krɪstl

chthonian
BR '(k)θəʊnɪən
AM 'θoʊniən

chthonic
BR '(k)θɒnɪk
AM 'θɑnɪk

chub
BR tʃʌb, -z
AM tʃəb, -z

Chubb®
BR tʃʌb
AM tʃəb

chubbily
BR 'tʃʌbɨli
AM 'tʃəbəli

chubbiness
BR 'tʃʌbɪnɨs
AM 'tʃəbinɨs

chubby
BR 'tʃʌb|i, -ɪə(r), -ɪɨst
AM 'tʃəbi, -ər, -ɨst

chuck
BR tʃʌk, -s, -ɪŋ, -t
AM tʃək, -s, -ɪŋ, -t

chucker-out
BR ,tʃʌkər'aʊt
AM 'tʃəkər'aʊt

chuckers-out
BR ,tʃʌkəz'aʊt
AM 'tʃəkərz'aʊt

chuckhole
BR 'tʃʌkhəʊl, -z
AM 'tʃək,(h)oʊl, -z

chuckle
BR 'tʃʌk|l, -lz, -l̩ɪŋ\-lɪŋ, -ld
AM 'tʃək|əl, -əlz, -(ə)lɪŋ, -əld

chucklehead
BR 'tʃʌklhɛd, -z
AM 'tʃəkəl,(h)ɛd, -z

chuckleheaded
BR ,tʃʌkl'hɛdɪd
AM 'tʃəkəl,(h)ɛdəd

chuckler
BR 'tʃʌkl̩ə(r), 'tʃʌklə(r), -z
AM 'tʃək(ə)lər, -z

chuddar
BR 'tʃʌdə(r), -z
AM 'tʃədər, -z

chufa
BR 'tʃuːfə(r)
AM 'tʃufə

chuff
BR tʃʌf, -s, -ɪŋ, -t
AM tʃəf, -s, -ɪŋ, -t

chug
BR tʃʌg, -z, -ɪŋ, -d
AM tʃəg, -z, -ɪŋ, -d

chugalug
BR 'tʃʌgəlʌg, -z, -ɪŋ, -d
AM ¦tʃəgə¦ləg, -z, -ɪŋ, -d

chukar
BR 'tʃʊkɑː(r), -z
AM 'tʃəkər, -z

chukka
BR 'tʃʌkə(r), -z
AM 'tʃəkə, -z

chukker
BR 'tʃʌkə(r), -z
AM 'tʃəkər, -z

chum
BR tʃʌm, -z, -ɪŋ, -d
AM tʃəm, -z, -ɪŋ, -d

chummily
BR 'tʃʌmɨli
AM 'tʃəməli

chumminess
BR 'tʃʌmɪnɨs
AM 'tʃəminɨs

chummy
BR 'tʃʌm|i, -ɪə(r), -ɪɨst
AM 'tʃəmi, -ər, -ɨst

chump
BR tʃʌmp, -s
AM tʃəmp, -s

chunder
BR 'tʃʌnd|ə(r), -əz, -(ə)rɪŋ, -əd
AM 'tʃənd|ər, -ərz, -(ə)rɪŋ, -ərd

Chungking
BR ,tʃʌŋ'kɪŋ
AM ,tʃəŋ'kɪŋ

chunk
BR tʃʌŋk, -s
AM tʃəŋk, -s

chunkily
BR 'tʃʌŋkɨli
AM 'tʃəŋkəli

chunkiness
BR 'tʃʌŋkɪnɨs
AM 'tʃəŋkinɨs

chunky
BR 'tʃʌŋk|i, -ɪə(r), -ɪɨst
AM 'tʃəŋki, -ər, -ɨst

Chunnel
BR 'tʃʌnl
AM 'tʃənəl

chunter
BR 'tʃʌnt|ə(r), -əz, -(ə)rɪŋ, -əd
AM 'tʃən(t)ər, -z, -ɪŋ, -d

chupatty
BR tʃə'pɑːt|i, tʃə'pat|i, -ɪz
AM tʃə'pædi, tʃə'pɑdi, -z

church
BR tʃəːtʃ, -ɨz, -ɪŋ, -t
AM tʃərtʃ, -əz, -ɪŋ, -t

Churchdown
BR 'tʃəːtʃdaʊn
AM 'tʃərtʃ,daʊn

churchgoer
BR 'tʃəːtʃ,gəʊə(r), -z
AM 'tʃərtʃ,goʊər, -z

churchgoing
BR 'tʃəːtʃ,gəʊɪŋ
AM 'tʃərtʃ,goʊɪŋ

Churchill
BR 'tʃəːtʃ(ɪ)l
AM 'tʃərtʃəl

Churchillian
BR tʃəː'tʃɪlɪən
AM tʃər'tʃɪljən, tʃər'tʃɪliən

churchily
BR 'tʃəːtʃɨli
AM 'tʃərtʃəli

churchiness
BR 'tʃəːtʃɪnɨs
AM 'tʃərtʃinɨs

churching
BR 'tʃəːtʃɪŋ, -z
AM 'tʃərtʃɪŋ, -z

churchman
BR 'tʃəːtʃmən
AM 'tʃərtʃmən

churchmanship
BR 'tʃəːtʃmənʃɪp
AM 'tʃərtʃmən,ʃɪp

churchmen
BR 'tʃəːtʃmən
AM 'tʃərtʃmən

churchwarden
BR 'tʃəːtʃ,wɔːdn, -z
AM 'tʃərtʃ,wɔrdən, -z

churchwoman
BR 'tʃəːtʃ,wʊmən
AM 'tʃərtʃ,wʊmən

churchwomen
BR 'tʃəːtʃ,wɪmɪn
AM 'tʃərtʃwɪmɪn

churchy
BR 'tʃəːtʃ|i, -ɪə(r), -ɪɨst
AM 'tʃərtʃi, -ər, -ɨst

churchyard
BR 'tʃəːtʃjɑːd, -z
AM 'tʃərtʃ,jɑrd, -z

churinga
BR tʃʌ'rɪŋgə(r), -z
AM tʃə'rɪŋgə, -z

churl
BR tʃəːl, -z
AM tʃərl, -z

churlish
BR 'tʃəːlɪʃ
AM 'tʃərlɪʃ

churlishly
BR 'tʃəːlɨʃli
AM 'tʃərlɨʃli

churlishness
BR 'tʃəːlɨʃnɨs
AM 'tʃərlɨʃnɨs

churn
BR tʃəːn, -z, -ɪŋ, -d
AM tʃərn, -z, -ɪŋ, -d

churr
BR tʃəː(r), -z, -ɪŋ, -d

AM tʃər, -z, -ɪŋ, -d

churrasco
BR tʃʊ'raskəʊ, -z
AM tʃə'rɑskoʊ, -z

Churrigueresque
BR ˌtʃʌrɪɡər'ɛsk
AM ˌtʃʊrɪɡə'rɛsk

chute
BR ʃuːt, -s
AM ʃut, -s

chutist
BR 'ʃuːtɪst, -s
AM 'ʃudəst, -s

chutnee
BR 'tʃʌtn|i, -ɪz
AM 'tʃətni, -z

chutney
BR 'tʃʌtn|i, -ɪz
AM 'tʃətni, -z

chutzpah
BR 'hʊtspə(r), 'xʊtspə(r)
AM 'hʊtspə

Chuzzlewit
BR 'tʃʌzlwɪt
AM 'tʃəzlˌwɪt

chyack
BR 'tʃʌɪak, -s, -ɪŋ, -t
AM 'tʃaɪək, -s, -ɪŋ, -t

chyle
BR kʌɪl
AM kaɪl

chylous
BR 'kʌɪləs
AM 'kaɪləs

chyme
BR kʌɪm
AM kaɪm

chymotrypsin
BR ˌkʌɪmə(ʊ)'trɪpsɪn
AM ˌkaɪmoʊ'trɪps(ə)n

chymous
BR 'kʌɪməs
AM 'kaɪməs

chypre
BR 'ʃiːprə(r)
AM 'ʃiprə

CIA
BR ˌsiːʌɪ'eɪ
AM ˌsiˌaɪ'eɪ

ciabatta
BR tʃə'bɑːtə(r), -z
AM tʃɪ'bɑdə, -z

ciabatte
BR tʃə'bɑːtiː
AM tʃɪ'bɑdi

ciao
BR tʃaʊ
AM tʃaʊ

Ciba
BR 'siːbə(r)
AM 'sibə

Cibachrome
BR ˌsiːbəkrəʊm, -z
AM 'sibəˌkroʊm, -z

Ciba-Geigy®
BR ˌsiːbə'ɡʌɪɡi
AM ˌsibə'ɡaɪɡi

ciboria
BR sɪ'bɔːrɪə(r)
AM sə'bɔriə

ciborium
BR sɪ'bɔːrɪəm
AM sə'bɔriəm

cicada
BR sɪ'kɑːdə(r), -z
AM sə'keɪdə, sə'kɑdə, -z

cicala
BR sɪ'kɑːlə(r), -z
AM sə'kɑlə, -z

cicatrices
BR ˌsɪkə'trʌɪsiːz
AM ˌsɪkə'traɪsiz, sə'keɪtrəsiz

cicatricial
BR ˌsɪkə'trɪʃl
AM ˌsɪkə'trɪʃəl

cicatrisation
BR ˌsɪkətrʌɪ'zeɪʃn
AM ˌsɪkətrə'zeɪʃən, ˌsɪkəˌtraɪ'zeɪʃən

cicatrise
BR 'sɪkətrʌɪz, -ɪz, -ɪŋ, -d
AM 'sɪkəˌtraɪz, -ɨz, -ɪŋ, -d

cicatrix
BR 'sɪkətrɪks, -ɪz
AM 'sɪkəˌtrɪks, -ɨz

cicatrization
BR ˌsɪkətrʌɪ'zeɪʃn
AM ˌsɪkətrə'zeɪʃən, ˌsɪkəˌtraɪ'zeɪʃən

cicatrize
BR 'sɪkətrʌɪz, -ɪz, -ɪŋ, -d
AM 'sɪkəˌtraɪz, -ɨz, -ɪŋ, -d

Cicely
BR 'sɪsɨli
AM 'sɪsɨli

cicely
BR 'sɪsɪl|i, -ɪz
AM 'sɪsɨli, -z

Cicero
BR 'sɪsərəʊ
AM 'sɪsəroʊ

cicerone
BR ˌtʃɪtʃə'rəʊn|i, ˌsɪsə'rəʊn|i, -ɪz
AM ˌsɪsə'roʊni, -z

ciceroni
BR ˌtʃɪtʃə'rəʊni, ˌsɪsə'rəʊni
AM ˌsɪsə'roʊni

Ciceronian
BR ˌsɪsə'rəʊnɪən
AM ˌsɪsə'roʊniən

cichlid
BR 'sɪklɪd, -z
AM 'sɪklɨd, -z

cicisbei
BR ˌtʃɪtʃɪz'beɪiː
AM ˌtʃitʃɪz'beɪi

cicisbeo
BR ˌtʃɪtʃɪz'beɪəʊ, -z
AM ˌtʃitʃɪz'beɪoʊ, -z

Cid, El
BR ɛl 'sɪd
AM ɛl 'sɪd

cider
BR 'sʌɪdə(r), -z
AM 'saɪdər, -z

ci-devant
BR ˌsiːdə'vɒ̃
AM ˌsɪdə'vɑnt

cig
BR sɪɡ, -z
AM sɪɡ, -z

cigala
BR sɪ'ɡɑːlə(r), -z
AM sə'ɡɑlə, -z

cigar
BR sɪ'ɡɑː(r), -z
AM sə'ɡɑr, -z

cigaret
BR ˌsɪɡə'rɛt, -s
AM ˌsɪɡə'rɛt, 'sɪɡəˌrɛt, -s

cigarette
BR ˌsɪɡə'rɛt, -s
AM ˌsɪɡə'rɛt, 'sɪɡəˌrɛt, -s

cigarillo
BR ˌsɪɡə'rɪləʊ, -z
AM ˌsɪɡə'rɪloʊ, -z

ciggie
BR 'sɪɡ|i, -ɪz
AM 'sɪɡi, -z

ciggy
BR 'sɪɡ|i, -ɪz
AM 'sɪɡi, -z

ciguatera
BR ˌsɪɡwə'tɛːrə(r)
AM ˌsigwə'tɛrə, ˌsɪɡwə'tɛrə

cilantro
BR sɪ'lantrəʊ
AM sɪ'lænˌtroʊ, sɪ'lɑnˌtroʊ

cilia
BR 'sɪlɪə(r)
AM 'sɪljə, 'sɪliə

ciliary
BR 'sɪlɪəri
AM 'sɪliəri

ciliate
BR 'sɪlɪeɪt
AM 'sɪliˌeɪt, 'sɪliət

ciliated
BR 'sɪlɪeɪtɪd
AM 'sɪlieɪdɨd

ciliation
BR ˌsɪlɪ'eɪʃn
AM ˌsɪli'eɪʃən

cilice
BR 'sɪl|ɪs, -ɪsɪz
AM 'sɪləs, -əz

Cilicia
BR sʌɪ'lɪsɪə(r), sɪ'lɪsɪə(r), sʌɪ'lɪʃɪə(r), sɪ'lɪʃɪə(r)
AM sə'lɪʃə

Cilician
BR sʌɪ'lɪsɪən, sɪ'lɪsɪən, sʌɪ'lɪʃɪən, sɪ'lɪʃɪən
AM sə'lɪʃən

cilium
BR 'sɪlɪəm
AM 'sɪliəm

cill
BR sɪl, -z
AM sɪl, -z

Cilla
BR 'sɪlə(r)
AM 'sɪlə

Cimabue
BR ˌtʃɪmə'buːeɪ, ˌtʃɪmə'buːi
AM ˌtʃimə'bueɪ

cimbalom
BR 'sɪmbələm, 'sɪmbl̩əm, -z
AM 'sɪmbələm, -z

cimetadine
BR sʌɪ'mɛtədiːn
AM saɪ'mɛtəˌdin

Cimmerian
BR sɪ'mɪərɪən, sɪ'mɛrɪən, -z
AM sə'mɪriən, sə'mɛriən, -z

cinch
BR sɪn(t)ʃ, -ɪz, -ɪŋ, -t
AM sɪntʃ, -ɨz, -ɪŋ, -t

cinchona
BR sɪŋ'kəʊnə(r), -z
AM sɪŋ'koʊnə, -z

cinchonic
BR sɪŋ'kɒnɪk
AM sɪŋ'kɑnɪk

cinchonine
BR 'sɪŋkəniːn
AM 'sɪŋkəˌnin, 'ʃɪŋkənən

Cincinnati
BR ˌsɪnsɪ'nati
AM ˌsɪn(t)sə'nædi

cincture
BR 'sɪŋ(k)tʃə(r), -z
AM 'sɪŋ(kt)ʃər, -z

cinder
BR 'sɪndə(r), -z
AM 'sɪndər, -z

Cinderella
BR ˌsɪndə'rɛlə(r)
AM ˌsɪndə'rɛlə

cindery
BR 'sɪnd(ə)ri
AM 'sɪndəri

Cindy
BR 'sɪndi
AM 'sɪndi

cine
BR 'sɪni
AM 'sɪni

cineaste
BR 'sɪneɪast, 'sɪnɪast, -s
AM 'sɪni,æst, 'sɪniəst, -s
cinecamera
BR 'sɪnɪ,kam(ə)rə(r), -z
AM 'sɪni,kæm(ə)rə, -z
cinefilm
BR 'sɪnɪfɪlm, -z
AM 'sɪnə,fɪlm, -z
cinema
BR 'sɪnɨmə(r), -z
AM 'sɪnəmə, -z
CinemaScope®
BR 'sɪnɨməskəʊp
AM 'sɪnəmə,skoʊp
cinematheque
BR ,sɪnɨmə'tɛk, -s
AM 'sɪnəmə,tɛk, -s
cinematic
BR ,sɪnɪ'matɪk
AM ,sɪnə'mædɪk
cinematically
BR ,sɪnɪ'matɨkli
AM ,sɪnə'mædək(ə)li
cinematograph
BR ,sɪnɪ'matəgrɑːf, ,sɪnɪ'matəgraf, -s
AM ,sɪnə'mædəgræf, -s
cinematographer
BR ,sɪnɨmə'tɒgrəfə(r), -z
AM ,sɪnəmə'tɑgrəfər, -z
cinematographic
BR ,sɪnɨ,matə'grafɪk
AM ,sɪnə,mædə'græfɪk
cinematographically
BR ,sɪnɨ,matə'grafɨkli
AM ,sɪnə,mædə'græfək(ə)li
cinematography
BR ,sɪnɨmə'tɒgrəfi
AM ,sɪnəmə'tɑgrəfi
cinéma-vérité
BR ,sɪnɨmə'vɛrɨteɪ, ,sɪnɨmɑː'vɛrɨteɪ
AM ,sɪnəmə,vɛri'teɪ
cinephile
BR 'sɪnɪfʌɪl, -z
AM 'sɪnə,faɪl, -z
Cinerama®
BR ,sɪnə'rɑːmə(r)
AM ,sɪnə'ræmə
cineraria
BR ,sɪnə'rɛːrɪə(r)
AM ,sɪnə'rɛriə
cinerarium
BR ,sɪnə'rɛːrɪəm, -z
AM ,sɪnə'rɛriəm, -z
cinerary
BR 'sɪn(ə)rəri
AM 'sɪnə,rɛri
cinereous
BR sɪ'nɪərɪəs
AM sə'nɪriəs
Cingalese
BR ,sɪŋgə'liːz
AM ,sɪŋgə'liz
cingula
BR 'sɪŋgjʉlə(r)
AM 'sɪŋgjələ
cingulum
BR 'sɪŋgjʉləm
AM 'sɪŋgjələm
cinnabar
BR 'sɪnəbɑː(r)
AM 'sɪnə,bɑr
cinnamon
BR 'sɪnəmən
AM 'sɪnəmən
cinq
BR sɪŋk
AM sɪŋk, sæŋk
cinque
BR sɪŋk
AM sɪŋk, sæŋk
cinquecentist
BR ,tʃɪŋkwɪ'tʃɛntɪst, -s
AM ,sɪŋkwə'(t)ʃɛn(t)əst, -s
cinquecento
BR ,tʃɪŋkwɪ'tʃɛntəʊ
AM ,sɪŋkwə'(t)ʃɛnoʊ
cinquefoil
BR 'sɪŋkfɔɪl, -z
AM 'sɪŋk,fɔɪl, 'sæŋk,fɔɪl, -z
Cinque Ports
BR ,sɪŋk 'pɔːts
AM 'sɪŋk 'pɔ(ə)rts, 'sæŋk +
Cinzano®
BR tʃɪn'zɑːnəʊ, tʃɪn(t)'sɑːnəʊ, -z
AM tʃɪn'zɑnoʊ, sɪn'zɑnoʊ, -z
cion
BR 'sʌɪən, -z
AM 'saɪən, -z
cipher
BR 'sʌɪf|ə(r), -əz, -(ə)rɪŋ, -əd
AM 'saɪf|ər, -ərz, -(ə)rɪŋ, -ərd
cipolin
BR 'sɪpəlɪn
AM 'sɪpələn
Cipriani
BR ,sɪprɪ'ɑːni
AM ,sɪpri'ɑni
circa
BR 'səːkə(r)
AM 'sərkə
circadian
BR səː'keɪdɪən
AM sər'keɪdiən
Circassian
BR sə'kasɪən, səː'kasɪən, -z
AM sər'kæsiən, -z
Circe
BR 'səːsi
AM 'sərsi
Circean
BR səː'siːən
AM 'sərsiən
circinate
BR 'səːsɪneɪt, 'səːsɪnət
AM 'sərsə,neɪt, 'sərsənət
circiter
BR 'səːsɪtə(r)
AM 'sərsədər
circle
BR 'səːk|l, -lz, -l̩ɪŋ\-lɪŋ, -ld
AM 'sərk|əl, -əlz, -(ə)lɪŋ, -əld
circler
BR 'səːklə(r), -z
AM 'sərk(ə)lər, -z
circlet
BR 'səːklɪt, -s
AM 'sərklət, -s
circlip
BR 'səːklɪp, -s
AM 'sərklɪp, -s
circs
BR səːks
AM sərks
circuit
BR 'səːk|ɪt, -ɪts, -ɨtɪŋ, -ɨtɨd
AM 'sərkə|t, -ts, -dɪŋ, -dəd
circuition
BR ,səːkjʊ'ɪʃn
AM ,sərkjə'wɪʃən
circuitous
BR sə(ː)'kjuːɨtəs
AM sər'kjuədəs
circuitously
BR sə(ː)'kjuːɨtəsli
AM sər'kjuədəsli
circuitousness
BR sə(ː)'kjuːɨtəsnəs
AM sər'kjuədəsnəs
circuitry
BR 'səːkɪtri
AM 'sərkətri
circuity
BR sə(ː)'kjʊɨti
AM sər'kjuədi
circular
BR 'səːkjʉlə(r), -z
AM 'sərkjələr, -z
circularisation
BR ,səːkjʉlərʌɪ'zeɪʃn
AM ,sərkjələrə'zeɪʃən, ,sərkjələ,raɪ'zeɪʃən
circularise
BR 'səːkjʉlərʌɪz, -ɨz, -ɪŋ, -d
AM 'sərkjələ,raɪz, -ɨz, -ɪŋ, -d
circularity
BR ,səːkjʉ'larɪti
AM ,sərkjə'lɛrədi
circularization
BR ,səːkjʉlərʌɪ'zeɪʃn
AM ,sərkjələrə'zeɪʃən, ,sərkjələ,raɪ'zeɪʃən
circularize
BR 'səːkjʉlərʌɪz, -ɨz, -ɪŋ, -d
AM 'sərkjələ,raɪz, -ɨz, -ɪŋ, -d
circularly
BR 'səːkjʉləli
AM 'sərkjələrli
circulate
BR 'səːkjʉleɪt, -s, -ɪŋ, -ɨd
AM 'sərkjəleɪ|t, -ts, -dɪŋ, -dɨd
circulation
BR ,səːkjʉ'leɪʃn, -z
AM ,sərkjə'leɪʃən, -z
circulative
BR 'səːkjʉlətɪv
AM 'sərkjələdɪv, 'sərkjə,leɪdɪv
circulator
BR 'səːkjʉleɪtə(r), -z
AM 'sərkjə,leɪdər, -z
circulatory
BR 'səkjʉlət(ə)ri, ,səːkjʉ'leɪt(ə)ri
AM 'sərkjələ,tɔri
circumambience
BR ,səːkəm'ambɪəns
AM ,sərkəm'æmbiəns
circumambiency
BR ,səːkəm'ambɪənsi
AM ,sərkəm'æmbiənsi
circumambient
BR ,səːkəm'ambɪənt
AM ,sərkəm'æmbiənt
circumambulate
BR ,səːkəm'ambjʉleɪt, -s, -ɪŋ, -ɨd
AM ,sərkəm'æmbjə,leɪ|t, -ts, -dɪŋ, -dɨd
circumambulation
BR ,səːkəm,ambjʉ'leɪʃn, -z
AM ,sərkəm,æmbjə'leɪʃən, -z
circumambulatory
BR ,səːkəm'ambjʉlət(ə)ri
AM ,sərkəm'æmbjələ,tɔri
circumcircle
BR 'səːkəm,səːkl, -z
AM 'sərkəm,sərkəl, -z
circumcise
BR 'səːkəmsʌɪz, -ɨz, -ɪŋ, -d
AM 'sərkəm,saɪz, -ɨz, -ɪŋ, -d
circumcision
BR ,səːkəm'sɪʒn, -z
AM ,sərkəm'sɪʒən, -z

circumference
BR sə'kʌmf(ə)rəns, sə'kʌmf(ə)rn̩s, -ɪz
AM sər'kəmf(ə)rəns, -əz

circumferential
BR səˌkʌmfə'rɛnʃl
AM sərˌkəmfə'rɛn(t)ʃəl

circumferentially
BR səˌkʌmfə'rɛnʃl̩i, səˌkʌmfə'rɛnʃəli
AM sərˌkəmfə'rɛn(t)ʃəli

circumflex
BR 'səːkəmflɛks, -ɪz
AM 'sərkəmˌflɛks, -əz

circumfluence
BR sə'kʌmflʊəns
AM sər'kəmfluəns

circumfluent
BR sə'kʌmflʊənt
AM sər'kəmfləwənt

circumfuse
BR 'səːkəmfjuːz, -ɪz
AM 'sərkəmˌfjuz, -əz

circumjacent
BR ˌsəːkəm'dʒeɪsnt
AM ˌsərkəm'dʒeɪsənt

circumlittoral
BR ˌsəːkəm'lɪt(ə)rəl, ˌsəːkəm'lɪt(ə)rl̩
AM ˌsərkəm'lɪdərəl

circumlocution
BR ˌsəːkəmlə'kjuːʃn, -z
AM ˌsərkəmˌloʊ'kjuʃən, -z

circumlocutional
BR ˌsəːkəmlə'kjuːʃn̩(ə)l, ˌsəːkəmlə'kjuːʃən(ə)l
AM ˌsərkəmˌloʊ'kjuʃ(ə)nəl

circumlocutionary
BR ˌsəːkəmlə'kjuːʃn̩(ə)ri
AM ˌsərkəmˌloʊ'kjuʃəˌnɛri

circumlocutionist
BR ˌsəːkəmlə'kjuːʃn̩ɪst, ˌsəːkəmlə'kjuːʃənɪst, -s
AM ˌsərkəmˌloʊ'kjuʃ(ə)nəst, -s

circumlocutory
BR ˌsəːkəmlə'kjuːt(ə)ri
AM ˌsərkəm'lɑkjəˌtɔri

circumlunar
BR ˌsəːkəm'l(j)uːnə(r)
AM ˌsərkəm'lunər

circumnavigate
BR ˌsəːkəm'navɪɡeɪt, -s, -ɪŋ, -ɪd
AM ˌsərkəm'nævəˌɡeɪ|t, -ts, -dɪŋ, -dɪd

circumnavigation
BR ˌsəːkəmˌnavɪ'ɡeɪʃn, -z
AM ˌsərkəmˌnævə'ɡeɪʃən, -z

circumnavigator
BR ˌsəːkəm'navɪɡeɪtə(r), -z
AM ˌsərkəm'nævəˌɡeɪdər, -z

circumpolar
BR ˌsəːkəm'pəʊlə(r)
AM ˌsərkəm'poʊlər

circumscribable
BR 'səːkəmskrʌɪbəbl, ˌsəːkəm'skrʌɪbəbl
AM ˌsərkəm'skraɪbəbəl

circumscribe
BR 'səːkəmskrʌɪb, -z, -ɪŋ, -d
AM 'sərkəmˌskraɪb, -z, -ɪŋ, -d

circumscriber
BR 'səːkəmskrʌɪbə(r), -z
AM 'sərkəmˌskraɪbər, -z

circumscription
BR ˌsəːkəm'skrɪpʃn, -z
AM ˌsərkəm'skrɪpʃən, -z

circumsolar
BR ˌsəːkəm'səʊlə(r)
AM ˌsərkəm'soʊlər

circumspect
BR 'səːkəmspɛkt
AM 'sərkəmˌspɛk(t)

circumspection
BR ˌsəːkəm'spɛkʃn
AM ˌsərkəm'spɛkʃən

circumspectly
BR 'səːkəmspɛktli
AM 'sərkəmˌspɛk(t)li

circumspectness
BR 'səːkəmspɛk(t)nəs
AM 'sərkəmˌspɛk(t)nəs

circumstance
BR 'səːkəmst(ə)ns, 'səːkəmstɑːns, 'səːkəmstans, -ɪz, -t
AM 'sərkəmˌstæns, -əz, -t

circumstantial
BR ˌsəːkəm'stanʃl
AM ˌsərkəm'stæn(t)ʃəl

circumstantiality
BR ˌsəːkəmˌstanʃɪ'alɪti
AM ˌsərkəmˌstæn(t)ʃi'ælədi

circumstantially
BR ˌsəːkəm'stanʃl̩i, ˌsəːkəm'stanʃəli
AM ˌsərkəm'stæn(t)ʃəli

circumstantiate
BR ˌsəːkəm'stanʃɪeɪt, -s, -ɪŋ, -ɪd
AM ˌsərkəm'stæn(t)ʃiˌeɪ|t, -ts, -dɪŋ, -dɪd

circumterrestrial
BR ˌsəːkəmtɪ'rɛstrɪəl
AM ˌsərkəmtə'rɛstriəl, ˌsərkəmtə'rɛstʃəl

circumvallate
BR ˌsəːəm'valeɪt, -s, -ɪŋ, -ɪd
AM ˌsərkəm'væˌleɪ|t, -ts, -dɪŋ, -dɪd

circumvallation
BR ˌsəːkəmvə'leɪʃn, ˌsəːkəmva'leɪʃn, -z
AM ˌsərkəmvæ'leɪʃən, -z

circumvent
BR ˌsəːkəm'vɛnt, 'səːkəmvɛnt, -s, -ɪŋ, -ɪd
AM ¦sərkəm¦vɛn|t, -ts, -(t)ɪŋ, -(t)əd

circumvention
BR ˌsəːkəm'vɛnʃn, -z
AM ˌsərkəm'vɛn(t)ʃən, -z

circumvolution
BR ˌsəːkəmvə'l(j)uːʃn, -z
AM ˌsərkəmvə'luʃən, -z

circus
BR 'səːkəs, -ɪz
AM 'sərkəs, -əz

ciré
BR 'siːreɪ
AM sə'reɪ

Cirencester
BR 'sʌɪrənˌsɛstə(r), 'sʌɪrn̩ˌsɛstə(r), 'sɪsɪtə(r)
AM 'saɪrɛnˌsɛstər

cire perdue
BR ˌsɪə pəː'djuː
AM 'sir ˌpər'd(j)u

cirque
BR səːk, -s
AM sərk, -s

cirrhosis
BR sɪ'rəʊsɪs
AM sə'roʊsəs

cirrhotic
BR sɪ'rɒtɪk
AM sə'rɑdɪk

cirri
BR 'sɪrʌɪ
AM 'sɪˌraɪ

cirriped
BR 'sɪrɪpɛd, -z
AM 'sɪrəˌpɛd, -z

cirrocumulus
BR ˌsɪrə(ʊ)'kjuːmjʊləs
AM ˌsɪroʊ'kjumjələs

cirrose
BR 'sɪrəʊs
AM 'sɪroʊs

cirrostratus
BR ˌsɪrə(ʊ)'strɑːtəs, ˌsɪrə(ʊ)'streɪtəs
AM ˌsɪroʊ'strædəs, ˌsɪroʊ'streɪdəs

cirrous
BR 'sɪrəs
AM 'sɪrəs

cirrus
BR 'sɪrəs
AM 'sɪrəs

cisalpine
BR (ˌ)sɪs'alpʌɪn
AM sɪs'ælpaɪn

cisatlantic
BR ˌsɪsət'lantɪk
AM ˌsɪsət'læn(t)ɪk

cisco
BR 'sɪskəʊ, -z
AM 'sɪskoʊ, -z

Ciskei
BR ˌsɪs'kʌɪ, 'sɪskʌɪ
AM 'sɪsˌkaɪ

cislunar
BR ˌsɪs'l(j)uːnə(r)
AM sɪs'lunər

cispontine
BR ˌsɪs'pɒntʌɪn
AM sɪs'pɑnˌtin, sɪs'pɑnˌtaɪn

Cissie
BR 'sɪsi
AM 'sɪsi

cissoid
BR 'sɪsɔɪd, -z
AM 'sɪsɔɪd, -z

Cissy
BR 'sɪsi
AM 'sɪsi

cist
BR sɪst, -s
AM sɪst, -s

Cistercian
BR sɪ'stəːʃn, -z
AM sɪ'stərʃən, -z

cistern
BR 'sɪstən, -z
AM 'sɪstərn, -z

cistron
BR 'sɪstrɒn, 'sɪstrən, -z
AM 'sɪsˌtrɑn, -z

cistus
BR 'sɪstəs
AM 'sɪstəs

citable
BR 'sʌɪtəbl
AM 'saɪdəbəl

citadel
BR 'sɪtəd(ə)l, 'sɪtədɛl, -z
AM 'sɪdədəl, 'sɪdəˌdɛl, -z

citation
BR sʌɪ'teɪʃn, -z
AM saɪ'teɪʃən, -z

citatory
BR sʌɪ'teɪt(ə)ri, 'sʌɪtət(ə)ri
AM 'saɪdəˌtɔri

cite
BR sʌɪt, -s, -ɪŋ, -ɪd
AM saɪ|t, -ts, -dɪŋ, -dɪd

CITES
BR 'sʌɪtiːz
AM 'saɪdiz

cithara
BR 'sɪθ(ə)rə(r), -z
AM 'sɪθ(ə)rə, -z
cither
BR 'sɪθə(r), -z
AM 'sɪθər, -z
Citibank®
BR 'sɪtɪbaŋk
AM 'sɪdiˌbæŋk
Citicorp
BR 'sɪtɪkɔːp
AM 'sɪdiˌkɔ(ə)rp
citify
BR 'sɪtɪfʌɪ, -z, -ɪŋ, -d
AM 'sɪdɨˌfaɪ, -z, -ɪŋ, -d
citizen
BR 'sɪtɨz(ə)n, -z
AM 'sɪdɨzən, 'sɪdɨsən, -z
citizenhood
BR 'sɪtɨz(ə)nhʊd
AM 'sɪdɨzənˌ(h)ʊd, 'sɪdɨsənˌ(h)ʊd
citizenly
BR 'sɪtɨz(ə)nli
AM 'sɪdɨzənli, 'sɪdɨsənli
citizenry
BR 'sɪtɨz(ə)nri
AM 'sɪdɨzənri, 'sɪdɨsənri
citizenship
BR 'sɪtɨz(ə)nʃɪp
AM 'sɪdɨzənˌʃɪp, 'sɪdɨsənˌʃɪp
citole
BR 'sɪtəʊl, -z
AM 'sɨˌtoʊl, -z
citral
BR 'sɪtr(ə)l, 'sɪtral
AM 'sɪtrəl
citrate
BR 'sɪtreɪt, -s
AM 'sɪˌtreɪt, -s
citric
BR 'sɪtrɪk
AM 'sɪtrɪk
citrin
BR 'sɪtrɪn
AM 'sɪtrən
citrine
BR 'sɪtriːn, 'sɪtrɪn
AM 'sɪtrin, 'sɪtrən, 'sɪtraɪn
Citroën®
BR 'sɪtrəʊən, 'sɪtr(ə)n, -z
AM 'sɪtrən, -z
citron
BR 'sɪtr(ə)n, -z
AM 'sɪtrən, -z
citronella
BR ˌsɪtrə'nɛlə(r)
AM ˌsɪtrə'nɛlə
citrous
BR 'sɪtrəs
AM 'sɪtrəs
citrus
BR 'sɪtrəs
AM 'sɪtrəs
cittern
BR 'sɪtəːn, -z
AM 'sɪdərn, -z
city
BR 'sɪt|i, -ɪz
AM 'sɪdi, -z
cityfied
BR 'sɪtɪfʌɪd
AM 'sɪdɨfaɪd
cityscape
BR 'sɪtɪskeɪp, -s
AM 'sɪdiˌskeɪp, -s
cityward
BR 'sɪtɪwəd, -z
AM 'sɪdiˌwərd, -z
Ciudad
BR 'θjuːdad, θjʊ'dad, ˌθɪuː'dad, 'θjuːdɑːd, θjʊ'dɑːd, ˌθɪuː'dɑːd
AM 'siuˌdæd
civet
BR 'sɪvɪt, -s
AM 'sɪvət, -s
civic
BR 'sɪvɪk, -s
AM 'sɪvɪk, -s
civically
BR 'sɪvɨkli
AM 'sɪvɨk(ə)li
civies
BR 'sɪvɪz
AM 'sɪviz
civil
BR 'sɪvl
AM 'sɪvɨl
civilian
BR sɨ'vɪlɪən, -z
AM sə'vɪljən, sə'vɪliən, -z
civilianisation
BR sɨˌvɪljənʌɪ'zeɪʃn
AM səˌvɪljənə'zeɪʃən, səˌvɪljəˌnaɪ'zeɪʃən
civilianise
BR sɨ'vɪljənʌɪz, -ɨz, -ɪŋ, -d
AM sə'vɪljəˌnaɪz, -ɨz, -ɪŋ, -d
civilianization
BR sɨˌvɪljənʌɪ'zeɪʃn
AM səˌvɪljənə'zeɪʃən, səˌvɪljəˌnaɪ'zeɪʃən
civilianize
BR sɨ'vɪljənʌɪz, -ɨz, -ɪŋ, -d
AM sə'vɪljəˌnaɪz, -ɨz, -ɪŋ, -d
civilisable
BR 'sɪvl̩ʌɪzəbl, 'sɪvɨlʌɪzəbl
AM 'sɪvəˌlaɪzəbəl
civilisation
BR ˌsɪvl̩ʌɪ'zeɪʃn, ˌsɪvɨlʌɪ'zeɪʃn, -z
AM ˌsɪvələ'zeɪʃən, ˌsɪvəˌlaɪ'zeɪʃən, -z
civilise
BR 'sɪvl̩ʌɪz, 'sɪvɨlʌɪz, -ɨz, -ɪŋ, -d
AM 'sɪvəˌlaɪz, -ɨz, -ɪŋ, -d
civiliser
BR 'sɪvl̩ʌɪzə(r), 'sɪvɨlʌɪzə(r), -z
AM 'sɪvəˌlaɪzər, -z
civility
BR sɨ'vɪlɨt|i, -ɪz
AM sə'vɪlɨdi, -z
civilizable
BR 'sɪvl̩ʌɪzəbl, 'sɪvɨlʌɪzəbl
AM 'sɪvəˌlaɪzəbəl
civilization
BR ˌsɪvl̩ʌɪ'zeɪʃn, ˌsɪvɨlʌɪ'zeɪʃn, -z
AM ˌsɪvələ'zeɪʃən, ˌsɪvəˌlaɪ'zeɪʃən, -z
civilize
BR 'sɪvl̩ʌɪz, 'sɪvɨlʌɪz, -ɨz, -ɪŋ, -d
AM 'sɪvəˌlaɪz, -ɨz, -ɪŋ, -d
civilizer
BR 'sɪvl̩ʌɪzə(r), 'sɪvɨlʌɪzə(r), -z
AM 'sɪvəˌlaɪzər, -z
civilly
BR 'sɪvl̩i, 'sɪvɨli
AM 'sɪvɨ(l)li
civvies
BR 'sɪvɪz
AM 'sɪviz
civvy
BR 'sɪv|i, -ɪz
AM 'sɪvi, -z
clachan
BR 'klax(ə)n, 'klak(ə)n
AM 'klækən
clack
BR klak, -s, -ɪŋ, -t
AM klæk, -s, -ɪŋ, -t
clacker
BR 'klakə(r), -z
AM 'klækər, -z
Clackmannan
BR klak'manən
AM klæk'mænən
Clacton
BR 'klaktən
AM 'klæktən
clad
BR klad
AM klæd
clade
BR kleɪd, -z
AM kleɪd, -z
cladism
BR 'kleɪdɪz(ə)m
AM 'kleɪˌdɪzəm
cladistics
BR klə'dɪstɪks, kla'dɪstɪks
AM klə'dɪstɪks
cladode
BR 'kleɪdəʊd, -z
AM 'klæˌdoʊd, -z
Claiborne
BR 'kleɪbɔːn
AM 'kleɪˌbɔ(ə)rn
claim
BR kleɪm, -z, -ɪŋ, -d
AM kleɪm, -z, -ɪŋ, -d
claimable
BR 'kleɪməbl
AM 'kleɪməbəl
claimant
BR 'kleɪm(ə)nt, -s
AM 'kleɪmənt, -s
claimer
BR 'kleɪmə(r), -z
AM 'kleɪmər, -z
Clair
BR klɛː(r)
AM klɛ(ə)r
clairaudience
BR ˌklɛːr'ɔːdɪəns
AM ˌklɛ'rɔdiəns, ˌklɛ'rɑdiəns
clairaudient
BR ˌklɛːr'ɔːdɪənt, -s
AM ˌklɛ'rɔdiənt, ˌklɛ'rɑdiənt, -s
Claire
BR klɛː(r)
AM klɛ(ə)r
clairvoyance
BR klɛː'vɔɪəns
AM ˌklɛr'vɔɪəns
clairvoyant
BR klɛː'vɔɪənt, -s
AM ˌklɛr'vɔɪənt, -s
clairvoyantly
BR klɛː'vɔɪəntli
AM ˌklɛr'vɔɪən(t)li
clam
BR klam, -z, -ɪŋ, -d
AM klæm, -z, -ɪŋ, -d
clamant
BR 'kleɪm(ə)nt, 'klam(ə)nt
AM 'kleɪmənt
clamantly
BR 'kleɪm(ə)ntli, 'klam(ə)ntli
AM 'kleɪmən(t)li
clambake
BR 'klambeɪk, -s
AM 'klæmˌbeɪk, -s
clamber
BR 'klamb|ə(r), -əz, -(ə)rɪŋ, -əd
AM 'klæmbər, -z, -ɪŋ, -d
clammily
BR 'klamɨli
AM 'klæməli
clamminess
BR 'klamɪnɨs
AM 'klæminɨs
clammy
BR 'klam|i, -ɪə(r), -ɪɨst
AM 'klæmi, -ər, -ɨst

clamor
BR 'klam|ə(r), -əz, -(ə)rɪŋ, -əd
AM 'klæmər, -z, -ɪŋ, -d
clamorous
BR 'klam(ə)rəs
AM 'klæmərəs
clamorously
BR 'klam(ə)rəsli
AM 'klæm(ə)rəsli
clamorousness
BR 'klam(ə)rəsnəs
AM 'klæm(ə)rəsnəs
clamour
BR 'klam|ə(r), -əz, -(ə)rɪŋ, -əd
AM 'klæmər, -z, -ɪŋ, -d
clamp
BR klamp, -s, -ɪŋ, -t
AM klæmp, -s, -ɪŋ, -t
clampdown
BR 'klampdaʊn, -z
AM 'klæmp,daʊn, -z
clamshell
BR 'klamʃɛl, -z
AM 'klæm,ʃɛl, -z
clan
BR klan, -z
AM klæn, -z
Clancarty
BR klan'kɑːti
AM klæn'kɑrdi
Clancey
BR 'klansi
AM 'klænsi
Clancy
BR 'klansi
AM 'klænsi
clandestine
BR klan'dɛstɪn, klan'dɛstʌɪn, 'klandɪstɪn, 'klandɪstʌɪn
AM klæn'dɛstən, 'klændəs,tin
clandestinely
BR klan'dɛstɨnli, klan'dɛstʌɪnli, 'klandɪstɨnli, 'klandɪstʌɪnli
AM klæn'dɛstənli, 'klændəs,tinli
clandestinity
BR ,klandɛ'stɪnɨti, ,klandɪ'stɪnɨti
AM ,klændɛs'tɪnɨdi
clang
BR klaŋ, -z, -ɪŋ, -d
AM klæŋ, -z, -ɪŋ, -d
clanger
BR 'klaŋə(r), -z
AM 'klæŋər, -z
clangor
BR 'klaŋgə(r)
AM 'klæŋər
clangorous
BR 'klaŋg(ə)rəs
AM 'klæŋərəs
clangorously
BR 'klaŋg(ə)rəsli
AM 'klæŋərəsli
clangour
BR 'klaŋgə(r)
AM 'klæŋər
clangourous
BR 'klaŋg(ə)rəs
AM 'klæŋərəs
clangourously
BR 'klaŋg(ə)rəsli
AM 'klæŋərəsli
clank
BR klaŋ|k, -ks, -kɪŋ, -(k)t
AM klæŋ|k, -ks, -kɪŋ, -(k)t
clankingly
BR 'klaŋkɪŋli
AM 'klæŋkɪŋli
clannish
BR 'klanɪʃ
AM 'klænɪʃ
clannishly
BR 'klanɨʃli
AM 'klænɨʃli
clannishness
BR 'klanɨʃnɨs
AM 'klænɨʃnɨs
clanship
BR 'klanʃɪp
AM 'klæn,ʃɪp
clansman
BR 'klanzmən
AM 'klænzmən
clansmen
BR 'klanzmən
AM 'klænzmən
clanswoman
BR 'klanz,wʊmən
AM 'klænz,wʊmən
clanswomen
BR 'klanz,wɪmɪn
AM 'klænz,wɪmɨn
clap
BR klap, -s, -ɪŋ, -t
AM klæp, -s, -ɪŋ, -t
clapboard
BR 'klapbɔːd
AM 'klæp,bɔ(ə)rd, 'klæbərd
Clapham
BR 'klap(ə)m
AM 'klæpəm
clapper
BR 'klapə(r), -z
AM 'klæpər, -z
clapperboard
BR 'klapəbɔːd, -z
AM 'klæpər,bɔ(ə)rd, -z
Clapton
BR 'klaptən
AM 'klæptən
claptrap
BR 'klaptrap
AM 'klæp,træp
claque
BR klak, -s
AM klæk, -s
claqueur
BR 'klakə(r), -z
AM 'klæ,kər, -z
Clara
BR 'klɛːrə(*r*)
AM 'klɛrə
Clarabella
BR ,klarə'bɛlə(*r*), -z
AM ,klɛrə'bɛlə, -z
Clarabelle
BR 'klarəbɛl, -z
AM 'klɛrə,bɛl, -z
Clare
BR klɛː(r)
AM klɛ(ə)r
Claremont
BR 'klɛːmɒnt, 'klɛːm(ə)nt
AM 'klɛr,mɑnt
clarence
BR 'klarəns, 'klarn̩s, -ɪz
AM 'klɛrəns, -əz
Clarenceux
BR 'klarəns(j)uː, 'klarn̩s(j)uː, 'klarənsəʊ, 'klarn̩səʊ
AM ,klɛrən'soʊ
Clarendon
BR 'klarəndən, 'klarn̩dən
AM 'klɛrəndən
claret
BR 'klarət, -s
AM 'klɛrət, -s
Clarges
BR 'klɑːdʒɪz
AM 'klɑrdʒəs
Clarice
BR 'klarɪs
AM 'klɛrɪs, klə'ris
Claridge's
BR 'klarɪdʒɪz
AM 'klɛrɪdʒɪz
clarification
BR ,klarɪfɪ'keɪʃn
AM ,klɛrəfə'keɪʃn
clarificatory
BR ,klarɪfɪ'keɪt(ə)ri, 'klarɪfɪkət(ə)ri
AM 'klɛrəfəkə,tɔri
clarifier
BR 'klarɪfʌɪə(r), -z
AM 'klɛrə,faɪər, -z
clarify
BR 'klarɪfʌɪ, -z, -ɪŋ, -d
AM 'klɛrə,faɪ, -z, -ɪŋ, -d
Clarinda
BR klə'rɪndə(*r*)
AM klə'rɪndə
clarinet
BR ,klarɪ'nɛt, -s
AM ,klɛrə'nɛt, -s
clarinetist
BR ,klarɪ'nɛtɪst, -s
AM ,klɛrə'nɛdəst, -s
clarinettist
BR ,klarɪ'nɛtɪst, -s
AM ,klɛrə'nɛdəst, -s
clarion
BR 'klarɪən, -z
AM 'klɛriən, -z
Clarissa
BR klə'rɪsə(*r*)
AM klə'rɪsə
clarity
BR 'klarɨti
AM 'klɛrədi
Clark
BR klɑːk
AM klɑrk
Clarke
BR klɑːk
AM klɑrk
clarkia
BR 'klɑːkɪə(*r*), -z
AM 'klɑrkiə, -z
Clarkson
BR 'klɑːksn
AM 'klɑrksən
Clarrie
BR 'klari
AM 'klɛri
clart
BR klɑːt, -s
AM klɑrt, -s
clarty
BR 'klɑːti
AM 'klɑrdi
clary
BR 'klɛːr|i, -ɪz
AM 'klɛri, -z
clash
BR klaʃ, -ɪz, -ɪŋ, -t
AM klæʃ, -əz, -ɪŋ, -t
clasher
BR 'klaʃə(r), -z
AM 'klæʃər, -z
clasp
BR klɑːsp, klasp, -s, -ɪŋ, -t
AM klæsp, -s, -ɪŋ, -t
clasper
BR 'klɑːspə(r), 'klaspə(r), -z
AM 'klæspər, -z
class
BR klɑːs, klas, -ɪz, -ɪŋ, -t
AM klæs, -əz, -ɪŋ, -t
classable
BR 'klɑːsəbl, 'klasəbl
AM 'klæsəbəl
classic
BR 'klasɪk, -s
AM 'klæsɪk, -s
classical
BR 'klasɪkl
AM 'klæsəkəl
classicalism
BR 'klasɪkl̩ɪz(ə)m
AM 'klæsəkə,lɪzəm

classicalist
BR 'klasɪkl̩ɪst, -s
AM 'klæsəkələst, -s
classicality
BR ˌklasɪ'kalɨti
AM ˌklæsə'kælədi
classically
BR 'klasɪkl̩i, 'klasɪkli
AM 'klæsək(ə)li
classicalness
BR 'klasɪklnəs
AM 'klæsəkəlnəs
classicise
BR 'klasɪsʌɪz, -ɪz, -ɪŋ, -d
AM 'klæsəˌsaɪz, -ɪz, -ɪŋ, -d
classicism
BR 'klasɪsɪz(ə)m, -z
AM 'klæsəˌsɪzəm, -z
classicist
BR 'klasɪsɪst, -s
AM 'klæsəsəst, -s
classicize
BR 'klasɪsʌɪz, -ɪz, -ɪŋ, -d
AM 'klæsəˌsaɪz, -ɪz, -ɪŋ, -d
classicus
BR 'klasɪkəs
AM 'klæsəkəs
classifiable
BR 'klasɪfʌɪəbl
AM ˌklæsə'faɪəbəl
classifiably
BR 'klasɪfʌɪəbli
AM ˌklæsə'faɪəbli
classification
BR ˌklasɪfɪ'keɪʃn, -z
AM ˌklæsəfə'keɪʃən, -z
classificatory
BR ˌklasɪfɪ'keɪt(ə)ri, 'klasɪfɪkət(ə)ri
AM 'klæsəfəkəˌtɔri
classifieds
BR 'klasɪfʌɪdz
AM 'klæsəˌfaɪdz
classifier
BR 'klasɪfʌɪə(r), -z
AM 'klæsəˌfaɪər, -z
classify
BR 'klasɪfʌɪ, -z, -ɪŋ, -d
AM 'klæsəˌfaɪ, -z, -ɪŋ, -d
classily
BR 'klɑːsɪli, 'klasɪli
AM 'klæsəli
classiness
BR 'klɑːsɪnɪs, 'klasɪnɪs
AM 'klæsinɪs
classism
BR 'klɑːsɪz(ə)m, 'klasɪz(ə)m
AM 'klæˌsɪzəm
classist
BR 'klɑːsɪst, 'klasɪst, -s
AM 'klæsəst, -s
classless
BR 'klɑːsləs, 'klasləs
AM 'klæsləs
classlessness
BR 'klɑːsləsnəs, 'klasləsnəs
AM 'klæsləsnəs
classmate
BR 'klɑːsmeɪt, 'klasmeɪt, -s
AM 'klæsˌmeɪt, -s
classroom
BR 'klɑːsruːm, 'klɑːsrʊm, 'klasruːm, -z
AM 'klæsˌrum, 'klæsˌrʊm, -z
classy
BR 'klɑːs|i, 'klas|i, -ɪə(r), -ɪɪst
AM 'klæsi, -ər, -ɪst
clastic
BR 'klastɪk
AM 'klæstɪk
clathrate
BR 'klaθreɪt, -s
AM 'klæθˌreɪt, -s
clatter
BR 'klat|ə(r), -əz, -(ə)rɪŋ, -əd
AM 'klædər, -z, -ɪŋ, -d
Claud
BR klɔːd
AM klɔd, klɑd
Claude
BR klɔːd
AM klɔd, klɑd
Claudette
BR (ˌ)klɔː'dɛt
AM ˌklɔ'dɛt, ˌklɑ'dɛt
Claudia
BR 'klɔːdɪə(*r*)
AM 'klɔdiə, 'klɑdiə
Claudian
BR 'klɔːdɪən
AM 'klɔdiən, 'klɑdiən
claudication
BR ˌklɔːdɪ'keɪʃn
AM ˌklɔdə'keɪʃən, ˌklɑdə'keɪʃən
Claudine
BR (ˌ)klɔː'diːn, 'klɔːdiːn
AM ˌklɔ'din, ˌklɑ'din
Claudius
BR 'klɔːdɪəs
AM 'klɔdiəs, 'klɑdiəs
clausal
BR 'klɔːzl
AM 'klɔzəl, 'klɑzəl
clausally
BR 'klɔːzl̩i, 'klɔːzəli
AM 'klɔzəli, 'klɑzəli
clause
BR klɔːz, -ɪz
AM klɔz, klɑz, -əz
Clausewitz
BR 'klaʊzəvɪts
AM 'klaʊzəˌvɪts
claustral
BR 'klɔːstr(ə)l
AM 'klɔstrəl, 'klɑstrəl
claustrophobe
BR 'klɔːstrəfəʊb, 'klɒstrəfəʊb, -z
AM 'klɔstrəˌfoʊb, 'klɑstrəˌfoʊb, -z
claustrophobia
BR ˌklɔːstrə'fəʊbɪə(*r*), ˌklɒstrə'fəʊbɪə(*r*)
AM ˌklɔstrə'foʊbiə, ˌklɑstrə'foʊbiə
claustrophobic
BR ˌklɔːstrə'fəʊbɪk, ˌklɒstrə'fəʊbɪk
AM ˌklɔstrə'foʊbɪk, ˌklɑstrə'foʊbɪk
claustrophobically
BR ˌklɔːstrə'fəʊbɨkli, ˌklɒstrə'fəʊbɨkli
AM ˌklɔstrə'foʊbək(ə)li, ˌklɑstrə'foʊbək(ə)li
clavate
BR 'kleɪveɪt
AM 'kleɪˌveɪt
clave
BR kleɪv, -z
AM kleɪv, -z
Claverhouse
BR 'kleɪvəhaʊs
AM 'kleɪvərˌ(h)aʊs
Clavering
BR 'kleɪv(ə)rɪŋ, 'klav(ə)rɪŋ
AM 'kleɪvərɪŋ, 'klævərɪŋ
Claverton
BR 'klavət(ə)n
AM 'klævərtən
clavicembalo
BR ˌklavɪ'tʃɛmbələʊ, -z
AM ˌklævə'tʃɛmbəloʊ, -z
clavichord
BR 'klavɪkɔːd, -z
AM 'klævəˌkɔ(ə)rd, -z
clavicle
BR 'klavɪkl, -z
AM 'klævəkəl, -z
clavicular
BR klə'vɪkjʉlə(r), kla'vɪkjʉlə(r)
AM klə'vɪkjələr
clavier
BR klə'vɪə(r), 'klavɪə(r), -z
AM klə'vɪ(ə)r, -z
claviform
BR 'klavɪfɔːm
AM 'klævəˌfɔ(ə)rm
claw
BR klɔː(*r*), -z, -ɪŋ, -d
AM klɔ, klɑ, -z, -ɪŋ, -d
clawback
BR 'klɔːbak, -s
AM 'klɔˌbæk, 'klɑˌbæk, -s
clawer
BR 'klɔː(*r*)ə(r), -z
AM 'klɔər, 'klɑər, -z
clawless
BR 'klɔːləs
AM 'klɔləs, 'klɑləs
clay
BR kleɪ, -z
AM kleɪ, -z
clayey
BR 'kleɪi
AM 'kleɪi
clayiness
BR 'kleɪɪnɪs
AM 'kleɪinɪs
clayish
BR 'kleɪɪʃ
AM 'kleɪɪʃ
claylike
BR 'kleɪlʌɪk
AM 'kleɪˌlaɪk
claymore
BR 'kleɪmɔː(r), -z
AM 'kleɪˌmɔ(ə)r, -z
claypan
BR 'kleɪpan, -z
AM 'kleɪˌpæn, -z
Clayton
BR 'kleɪtn
AM 'kleɪtn
clean
BR kliːn, -z, -ɪŋ, -d, -ə(r), -ɪst
AM klin, -z, -ɪŋ, -d, -ər, -ɪst
cleanable
BR 'kliːnəbl
AM 'klinəbəl
cleaner
BR 'kliːnə(r), -z
AM 'klinər, -z
cleanish
BR 'kliːnɪʃ
AM 'klinɪʃ
cleanlily
BR 'klɛnlɨli
AM 'klɛnlɨli
cleanliness
BR 'klɛnlɪnɪs
AM 'klɛnlinɪs
cleanly[1]
adjective
BR 'klɛnl|i, -ɪə(r), -ɪɪst
AM 'klɛnli, -ər, -ɪst
cleanly[2]
adverb
BR 'kliːnli
AM 'klinli
cleanse
BR klɛnz, -ɪz, -ɪŋ, -d
AM klɛnz, -əz, -ɪŋ, -d
cleanser
BR 'klɛnzə(r), -z
AM 'klɛnzər, -z
cleanskin
BR 'kliːnskɪn, -z
AM 'klinˌskɪn, -z
Cleanthes
BR klɪ'anθiːz

AM kli'ænθiz

cleanup
BR 'kli:nʌp, -s
AM 'klin,əp, -s

clear
BR klɪə(r), -z, -ɪŋ, -d, -ə(r), -ɨst
AM klɪ(ə)r, -z, -ɪŋ, -d, -ər, -ɨst

clearable
BR 'klɪərəbl
AM 'klɪrəbəl

clearance
BR 'klɪərəns, 'klɪərn̩s, -ɨz
AM 'klɪrəns, -əz

Clearasil®
BR 'klɪərəsɪl
AM 'klɪrə,sɪl

clearcole
BR 'klɪəkəʊl
AM 'klɪr,koʊl

clearer
BR 'klɪərə(r), -z
AM 'klɪrər, -z

clearing
BR 'klɪərɪŋ, -z
AM 'klɪrɪŋ, -z

clearinghouse
BR 'klɪərɪŋhaʊ|s, -zɨz
AM 'klɪrɪŋ,(h)aʊ|s, -əz

clearly
BR 'klɪəli
AM 'klɪrli

clearness
BR 'klɪənəs
AM 'klɪrnɨs

clearout
BR 'klɪəraʊt, -s
AM 'klɪr,aʊt, -s

clearsighted
BR ,klɪə'sʌɪtɨd
AM ¦klɪr'saɪdɨd

clearsightedly
BR ,klɪə'sʌɪtɨdli
AM ¦klɪr'saɪdɨdli

clearsightedness
BR ,klɪə'sʌɪtɨdnɨs
AM ¦klɪr'saɪdɨdnɨs

clearstory
BR 'klɪə,stɔ:r|i, 'klɪəst(ə)r|i, -ɪz
AM 'klɪr,stɔri, -z

clearup
BR 'klɪərʌp, -s
AM 'klɪr,əp, -s

clearway
BR 'klɪəweɪ, -z
AM 'klɪr,weɪ, -z

Cleary
BR 'klɪəri
AM 'klɪri

cleat
BR kli:t, -s
AM klit, -s

cleavable
BR 'kli:vəbl
AM 'klivəbəl

cleavage
BR 'kli:v|ɪdʒ, -ɨdʒɨz
AM 'klivɪdʒ, -ɨz

cleave
BR kli:v, -z, -ɪŋ, -d
AM kliv, -z, -ɪŋ, -d

cleaver
BR 'kli:və(r), -z
AM 'klivər, -z

cleavers
BR 'kli:vəz
AM 'klivərz

Cleckheaton
BR (,)klɛk'hi:tn
AM klɛk'hitn

Cleddau
BR 'klɛðʌɪ
AM 'klɛðaɪ

Cledwyn
BR 'klɛdwɪn
AM 'klɛdwən

cleek
BR kli:k, -s
AM klik, -s

Cleese
BR kli:z
AM kliz

Cleethorpes
BR 'kli:θɔ:ps
AM 'kliθɔ(ə)rps

clef
BR klɛf, -s
AM klɛf, -s

cleft
BR klɛft, -s
AM klɛft, -s

cleg
BR klɛg, -z
AM klɛg, -z

Clegg
BR klɛg
AM klɛg

Cleisthenes
BR 'klʌɪsθɨni:z
AM 'klaɪsθə,niz

cleistogamic
BR ,klʌɪstə'gamɪk
AM ,klaɪstə'gæmɪk

cleistogamically
BR ,klʌɪstə'gamɨkli
AM ,klaɪstə'gæmək(ə)li

cleistogamy
BR klʌɪ'stɒgəmi
AM klaɪ'stɑgəmi

Cleland
BR 'klɛlənd, 'kli:lənd
AM 'klilənd, 'klɛlənd

Clem
BR klɛm
AM klɛm

clematis
BR 'klɛmətɪs, klɪ'meɪtɪs
AM 'klɛmədəs, klə'mædəs

Clemence
BR 'klɛməns
AM 'klɛməns

clemency
BR 'klɛm(ə)nsi
AM 'klɛmənsi

Clemens
BR 'klɛmənz
AM 'klɛməns

clement
BR 'klɛm(ə)nt
AM 'klɛmənt

Clementina
BR ,klɛm(ə)n'ti:nə(*r*)
AM ,klɛmən'tinə

clementine
BR 'klɛm(ə)ntʌɪn, -z
AM 'klɛmən,taɪn, 'klɛmən,tin, -z

clemently
BR 'klɛm(ə)ntli
AM 'klɛmən(t)li

Clements
BR 'klɛm(ə)n(t)s
AM 'klɛmən(t)s

Clemmie
BR 'klɛmi
AM 'klɛmi

clenbuterol
BR klɛn'bju:tərɒl
AM klɛn'bjudə,rɑl

clench
BR klɛn(t)ʃ, -ɨz, -ɪŋ, -t
AM klɛn(t)ʃ, -əz, -ɪŋ, -t

Cleo
BR 'klɪəʊ
AM 'klioʊ

Cleobury[1]
placename
BR 'kli:b(ə)ri, 'klɪb(ə)ri
AM 'klibəri

Cleobury[2]
surname
BR 'kli:b(ə)ri, 'kləʊb(ə)ri
AM 'klibəri

Cleopatra
BR ,kli:ə'patrə(*r*), ,kli:ə'pɑ:trə(*r*)
AM ,kliə'pætrə

clepsydra
BR 'klɛpsɨdrə(*r*), klɛp'sɪdrə(*r*), -z
AM 'klɛpsədrə, -z

clerestory
BR 'klɪə,stɔ:r|i, 'klɪəst(ə)r|i, -ɪz
AM 'klɪr,stɔri, -z

clergy
BR 'klə:dʒi
AM 'klərdʒi

clergyman
BR 'klə:dʒɪmən
AM 'klərdʒimən

clergymen
BR 'klə:dʒɪmən
AM 'klərdʒimən

cleric
BR 'klɛrɪk, -s
AM 'klɛrɪk, -s

clerical
BR 'klɛrɨkl, -z
AM 'klɛrəkəl, -z

clericalism
BR 'klɛrɨkəlɪz(ə)m, 'klɛrɨkl̩ɪz(ə)m
AM 'klɛrəkəl,ɪzəm

clericalist
BR 'klɛrɨkəlɪst, 'klɛrɨkl̩ɪst, -s
AM 'klɛrəkələst, -s

clericality
BR ,klɛrɪ'kalɨti
AM ,klɛrə'kælədi

clerically
BR 'klɛrɨkl̩i
AM 'klɛrək(ə)li

clerihew
BR 'klɛrɨhju:, -z
AM 'klɛrə,hju, -z

clerisy
BR 'klɛrɪsi
AM 'klɛrəsi

clerk
BR klɑ:k, -s, -ɪŋ, -t
AM klərk, -s, -ɪŋ, -t

clerkdom
BR 'klɑ:kdəm, -z
AM 'klərkdəm, -z

Clerkenwell
BR 'klɑ:k(ə)nw(ɛ)l
AM 'klərkən,wɛl

clerkess
BR 'klɑ:kɪs, 'klɑ:kɛs, ,klɑ:'kɛs, -ɨz
AM 'klərkəs, -əz

clerkish
BR 'klɑ:kɪʃ
AM 'klərkɪʃ

clerkly
BR 'klɑ:kli
AM 'klərkli

clerkship
BR 'klɑ:kʃɪp, -s
AM 'klərk,ʃɪp, -s

Clermont
BR 'klɛ:mɒnt, 'klə:mɒnt
AM 'klɛr,mɑnt

Clery
BR 'klɪəri
AM 'klɪri, 'klɛri

Clevedon
BR 'kli:vdən
AM 'klivdən

Cleveland
BR 'kli:vlənd
AM 'klivlən(d)

clever
BR 'klɛv|ə(r), -(ə)rə(r), -(ə)rɪst
AM 'klɛvər, -ər, -əst

cleverly
BR 'klɛvəli

AM ˈklɛvərli

cleverness
BR ˈklɛvənəs
AM ˈklɛvərnəs

clevis
BR ˈklɛv|ɪs, -ɪsɪz
AM ˈklɛvəs, -ɪz

clew
BR kluː, -z, -ɪŋ, -d
AM klu, -z, -ɪŋ, -d

Clewes
BR kluːz
AM kluz

Clews
BR kluːz
AM kluz

Cley
BR kleɪ, klʌɪ
AM kleɪ

clianthus
BR klʌɪˈanθəs, klɪˈanθəs
AM kliˈænθəs

Clibborn
BR ˈklɪb(ə)n
AM ˈklɪbərn

Cliburn
BR ˈklʌɪbəːn
AM ˈklaɪbərn

cliché
BR ˈkliːʃeɪ, -z, -d
AM kliˈʃeɪ, ˈkliˌʃeɪ, -z, -d

click
BR klɪk, -s, -ɪŋ, -t
AM klɪk, -s, -ɪŋ, -t

click-clack
BR ˈklɪklak, -s, -ɪŋ, -t
AM ˈklɪ(k)ˌklæk, -s, -ɪŋ, -t

clicker
BR ˈklɪkə(r), -z
AM ˈklikər, -z

clickety-click
BR ˌklɪkɪtɪˈklɪk
AM ˌklɪkɪdiˈklɪk

client
BR ˈklʌɪənt, -s
AM ˈklaɪənt, -s

clientele
BR ˌkliːɒnˈtɛl, ˌkliːɑːnˈtɛl, ˌkliːənˈtɛl, -z
AM ˌklaɪənˈtɛl, ˌkliənˈtɛl, -z

clientship
BR ˈklʌɪəntʃɪp, -s
AM ˈklaɪən(t)ˌʃɪp, -s

cliff
BR klɪf, -s
AM klɪf, -s

Cliffe
BR klɪf
AM klɪf

cliffhanger
BR ˈklɪfˌhaŋə(r), -z
AM ˈklɪfˌ(h)æŋər, -z

cliffhanging
BR ˈklɪfˌhaŋɪŋ
AM ˈklɪfˌ(h)æŋɪŋ

cliffiness
BR ˈklɪfɪnɪs
AM ˈklɪfinɪs

clifflike
BR ˈklɪflʌɪk
AM ˈklɪfˌlaɪk

Clifford
BR ˈklɪfəd
AM ˈklɪfərd

cliffside
BR ˈklɪfsʌɪd
AM ˈklɪfˌsaɪd

clifftop
BR ˈklɪftɒp, -s
AM ˈklɪfˌtɑp, -s

cliffy
BR ˈklɪf|i, -ɪə(r), -ɪɪst
AM ˈklɪfi, -ər, -ɪst

Clifton
BR ˈklɪft(ə)n
AM ˈklɪftən

Cliftonville
BR ˈklɪft(ə)nvɪl
AM ˈklɪftənˌvɪl

climacteric
BR ˌklʌɪmakˈtɛrɪk, klʌɪˈmakt(ə)rɪk
AM klaɪˈmæktərɪk, ˌklaɪˌmækˈtɛrɪk

climacterical
BR ˌklʌɪmakˈtɛrɪkl
AM ˌklaɪˌmækˈtɛrəkəl

climactic
BR klʌɪˈmaktɪk
AM klaɪˈmæktɪk

climactical
BR klʌɪˈmaktɪkl
AM klaɪˈmæktəkəl

climactically
BR klʌɪˈmaktɪkli
AM klaɪˈmæktək(ə)li

climate
BR ˈklʌɪmɪt, -s
AM ˈklaɪmɪt, -s

climatic
BR klʌɪˈmatɪk
AM klaɪˈmædɪk

climatical
BR klʌɪˈmatɪkl
AM klaɪˈmædəkəl

climatically
BR klʌɪˈmatɪkli
AM klaɪˈmædək(ə)li

climatologic
BR ˌklʌɪmətəˈlɒdʒɪk
AM ˌklaɪmədəˈlɑdʒɪk

climatological
BR ˌklʌɪmətəˈlɒdʒɪkl
AM ˌklaɪmədəˈlɑdʒəkəl

climatologically
BR ˌklʌɪmətəˈlɒdʒɪkli
AM ˌklaɪmədəˈlɑdʒək(ə)li

climatologist
BR ˌklʌɪməˈtɒlədʒɪst, -s
AM ˌklaɪməˈtɑlədʒəst, -s

climatology
BR ˌklʌɪməˈtɒlədʒi
AM ˌklaɪməˈtɑlədʒi

climax
BR ˈklʌɪmaks, -ɪz, -ɪŋ, -t
AM ˈklaɪˌmæks, -əz, -ɪŋ, -t

climb
BR klʌɪm, -z, -ɪŋ, -d
AM klaɪm, -z, -ɪŋ, -d

climbable
BR ˈklʌɪməbl
AM ˈklaɪməbəl

climbdown
BR ˈklʌɪmdaʊn, -z
AM ˈklaɪmˌdaʊn, -z

climber
BR ˈklʌɪmə(r), -z
AM ˈklaɪmər, -z

clime
BR klʌɪm, -z
AM klaɪm, -z

clinal
BR ˈklʌɪnl
AM ˈklaɪnl

clinch
BR klɪn(t)ʃ, -ɪz, -ɪŋ, -t
AM klɪn(t)ʃ, -ɪz, -ɪŋ, -t

clincher
BR ˈklɪn(t)ʃə(r), -z
AM ˈklɪn(t)ʃər, -z

cline
BR klʌɪn, -z
AM klaɪn, -z

cling
BR klɪŋ, -z, -ɪŋ
AM klɪŋ, -z, -ɪŋ

clinger
BR ˈklɪŋə(r), -z
AM ˈklɪŋər, -z

clingfilm
BR ˈklɪŋfɪlm
AM ˈklɪŋˌfɪlm

clingfoil
BR ˈklɪŋfɔɪl
AM ˈklɪŋˌfɔɪl

clinginess
BR ˈklɪŋɪnɪs
AM ˈklɪŋinɪs

clingingly
BR ˈklɪŋɪŋli
AM ˈklɪŋɪŋli

clingstone
BR ˈklɪŋstəʊn
AM ˈklɪŋˌstoʊn

clingy
BR ˈklɪŋ|i, -ɪə(r), -ɪɪst
AM ˈklɪŋi, -ər, -ɪst

clinic
BR ˈklɪnɪk, -s
AM ˈklɪnɪk, -s

clinical
BR ˈklɪnɪkl
AM ˈklɪnəkəl

clinically
BR ˈklɪnɪkli
AM ˈklɪnək(ə)li

clinician
BR klɪˈnɪʃn, -z
AM kləˈnɪʃən, -z

clink
BR klɪŋ|k, -ks, -kɪŋ, -(k)t
AM klɪŋ|k, -ks, -kɪŋ, -(k)t

clinker
BR ˈklɪŋkə(r), -z
AM ˈklɪŋkər, -z

clinkstone
BR ˈklɪŋkstəʊn, -z
AM ˈklɪŋkˌstoʊn, -z

clinometer
BR klɪˈnɒmɪtə(r), klʌɪˈnɒmɪtə(r), -z
AM klaɪˈnɑmədər, -z

clinometric
BR ˌklʌɪnəˈmɛtrɪk
AM ˌklaɪnəˈmɛtrɪk

clinometry
BR klɪˈnɒmɪtri, klʌɪˈnɒmɪtri
AM klaɪˈnɑmətri

clint
BR klɪnt, -s
AM klɪnt, -s

Clinton
BR ˈklɪntən
AM ˈklɪn(t)ən

Clio
BR ˈkliːəʊ, ˈklʌɪəʊ
AM ˈklaɪoʊ, ˈklioʊ

cliometric
BR ˌklʌɪə(ʊ)ˈmɛtrɪk, -s
AM ˌklaɪəˈmɛtrɪk, -s

clip
BR klɪp, -s, -ɪŋ, -t
AM klɪp, -s, -ɪŋ, -t

clipboard
BR ˈklɪpbɔːd, -z
AM ˈklɪpˌbɔ(ə)rd, -z

clip-clop
BR ˈklɪpklɒp, -s, -ɪŋ, -t
AM ˈklɪpˌklɑp, -s, -ɪŋ, -t

clippable
BR ˈklɪpəbl
AM ˈklɪpəbəl

clipper
BR ˈklɪpə(r), -z
AM ˈklɪpər, -z

clippie
BR ˈklɪp|i, -ɪz
AM ˈklɪpi, -z

clipping
BR ˈklɪpɪŋ, -z
AM ˈklɪpɪŋ, -z

Clipstone
BR ˈklɪpstəʊn
AM ˈklɪpˌstoʊn

clique
BR kliːk, -s
AM klik, -s

cliquey
BR 'kliːk|i, -ɪə(r), -ɪɨst
AM 'kliki, -ər, -ɨst

cliqueyness
BR 'kliːkɪnɨs
AM 'klikinɨs

cliquish
BR 'kliːkɪʃ
AM 'klikɪʃ

cliquishness
BR 'kliːkɨʃnɨs
AM 'klikɪʃnɨs

cliquism
BR 'kliːkɪz(ə)m
AM 'klikɪzəm

cliquy
BR 'kliːki
AM 'kliki

Clissold
BR 'klɪsəʊld
AM 'klɪsoʊld

Clitheroe
BR 'klɪðərəʊ
AM 'klɪðəroʊ

clitic
BR 'klɪtɪk, -s
AM 'klɪdɪk, -s

cliticisation
BR ˌklɪtɨsʌɪ'zeɪʃn
AM ˌklɪdəsə'zeɪʃən, ˌklɪdəˌsaɪ'zeɪʃən

cliticization
BR ˌklɪtɨsʌɪ'zeɪʃn
AM ˌklɪdəsə'zeɪʃən, ˌklɪdəˌsaɪ'zeɪʃən

cliticize
BR 'klɪtɨsʌɪz, -ɨz, -ɪŋ, -d
AM 'klɪdəˌsaɪz, -ɨz, -ɪŋ, -d

clitoral
BR 'klɪt(ə)rəl, 'klɪt(ə)rl̩
AM 'klɪdər(ə)l, klə'tɔrəl

clitoridectomy
BR ˌklɪt(ə)rɪ'dɛktəm|i, -ɪz
AM ˌklɪdərə'dɛktəmi, -z

clitoris
BR 'klɪt(ə)rɪs, -ɨz
AM 'klɪdərəs, klə'tɔrəs, -əz

Clive
BR klʌɪv
AM klaɪv

Cliveden
BR 'klɪvd(ə)n
AM 'klɪvdən

clivers
BR 'klɪvəz
AM 'klɪvərz

cloaca
BR kləʊ'eɪkə(*r*), -z
AM kloʊ'eɪkə, -z

cloacae
BR kləʊ'eɪkiː
AM kloʊ'eɪˌki, kloʊ'eɪˌkaɪ

cloacal
BR kləʊ'eɪkl
AM kloʊ'eɪkəl

cloak
BR kləʊk, -s, -ɪŋ, -t
AM kloʊk, -s, -ɪŋ, -t

cloakroom
BR 'kləʊkruːm, 'kləʊkrʊm, -z
AM 'kloʊkˌrum, 'kloʊkˌrʊm, -z

clobber
BR 'klɒb|ə(r), -əz, -(ə)rɪŋ, -əd
AM 'klɑbər, -z, -ɪŋ, -d

cloche
BR klɒʃ, -ɨz
AM kloʊʃ, klɑʃ, klɔʃ, -əz

clock
BR klɒk, -s, -ɪŋ, -t
AM klɑk, -s, -ɪŋ, -t

clockmaker
BR 'klɒkˌmeɪkə(r), -z
AM 'klɑkˌmeɪkər, -z

clockmaking
BR 'klɒkˌmeɪkɪŋ
AM 'klɑkˌmeɪkɪŋ

clockwise
BR 'klɒkwʌɪz
AM 'klɑkˌwaɪz

clockwork
BR 'klɒkwəːk
AM 'klɑkˌwərk

clod
BR klɒd, -z
AM klɑd, -z

Clodagh
BR 'kləʊdə(*r*)
AM 'kloʊdə

cloddish
BR 'klɒdɪʃ
AM 'klɑdɪʃ

cloddishly
BR 'klɒdɨʃli
AM 'klɑdɨʃli

cloddishness
BR 'klɒdɨʃnɨʃ
AM 'klɑdɨʃnɨs

cloddy
BR 'klɒdi
AM 'klɑdi

clodhopper
BR 'klɒdˌhɒpə(r), -z
AM 'klɑdˌ(h)ɑpər, -z

clodhopping
BR 'klɒdˌhɒpɪŋ
AM 'klɑdˌ(h)ɑpɪŋ

clodpoll
BR 'klɒdpɒl, -z
AM 'klɑdˌpɑl, -z

clog
BR klɒg, -z, -ɪŋ, -d
AM klɑg, -z, -ɪŋ, -d

cloggily
BR 'klɒgɨli
AM 'klɑgəli

clogginess
BR 'klɒgɪnɨs
AM 'klɑginɨs

cloggy
BR 'klɒg|i, -ɪə(r), -ɪɨst
AM 'klɑgi, -ər, -ɨst

Clogher
BR 'klɒxə(r), 'klɒhə(r)
AM 'klɔhər, 'klɑhər

cloisonné
BR klwɑː'zɒneɪ
AM ˌklɔɪzn'eɪ

cloister
BR 'klɔɪst|ə(r), -əz, -(ə)rɪŋ, -əd
AM 'klɔɪstər, -z, -ɪŋ, -d

cloistral
BR 'klɔɪstr(ə)l
AM 'klɔɪstrəl

clomiphene
BR 'kləʊmɨfiːn
AM 'kloʊməˌfin

clomp
BR klɒmp, -s, -ɪŋ, -t
AM klɑmp, -s, -ɪŋ, -t

clonal
BR 'kləʊnl
AM 'kloʊnəl

clone
BR kləʊn, -z, -ɪŋ, -d
AM kloʊn, -z, -ɪŋ, -d

Clones
BR 'kləʊnɪs
AM 'kloʊnəs

clonic
BR 'klɒnɪk
AM 'klɑnɪk

clonk
BR klɒŋ|k, -ks, -kɪŋ, -(k)t
AM klɑŋ|k, -ks, -kɪŋ, -(k)t

Clonmel
BR klɒn'mɛl
AM klɑn'mɛl

clonus
BR 'kləʊnəs, -ɨz
AM 'kloʊnəs, -əz

clop
BR klɒp, -s, -ɪŋ, -t
AM klɑp, -s, -ɪŋ, -t

cloqué
BR 'kləʊkeɪ
AM kloʊ'keɪ

closable
BR 'kləʊzəbl
AM 'kloʊzəbəl

Close
BR kləʊs
AM kloʊs, kloʊz

close[1]
noun enclosure, adjective
BR kləʊs, -ɨz, -ə(r), -ɨst
AM kloʊs, -əz, -ər, -əst

close[2]
noun end, verb
BR kləʊz, -ɨz, -ɪŋ, -d
AM kloʊz, -əz, -ɪŋ, -d

closedown
BR 'kləʊzdaʊn, -z
AM 'kloʊzˌdaʊn, -z

closely
BR 'kləʊsli
AM 'kloʊsli

closeness
BR 'kləʊsnəs
AM 'kloʊsnəs

closeout
BR 'kləʊzaʊt, -s
AM 'kloʊzˌaʊt, -s

closet
BR 'klɒz|ɪt, -ɪts, -ɨtɪŋ, -ɨtɨd
AM 'klɑzə|t, -ts, -dɪŋ, -dəd

closish
BR 'kləʊsɪʃ
AM 'kloʊsɪʃ

clostridia
BR klɒ'strɪdɪə(*r*)
AM klɔ'strɪdiə, klɑ'strɪdiə

clostridium
BR klɒ'strɪdɪəm
AM klɔ'strɪdiəm, klɑ'strɪdiəm

closure
BR 'kləʊʒə(r), -z
AM 'kloʊʒər, -z

clot
BR klɒt, -s, -ɪŋ, -ɨd
AM klɑ|t, -ts, -dɪŋ, -dəd

clotbur
BR 'klɒtbəː(r)
AM 'klɑtˌbər

cloth
BR klɒ|θ, -θs\-ðz
AM klɔ|θ, klɑ|θ, -θs\-ðz

clothbound
BR 'klɒθbaʊnd
AM 'klɔθˌbaʊnd, 'klɑθˌbaʊnd

clothe
BR kləʊð, -z, -ɪŋ, -d
AM kloʊð, -z, -ɪŋ, -d

clothes
noun
BR kləʊðz
AM kloʊ(ð)z

clothesbasket
BR 'kləʊ(ð)zˌbɑːskɪt, 'kləʊ(ð)zˌbaskɪt, -s
AM 'kloʊ(ð)zˌbæskət, -s

clothesbrush
BR 'kləʊ(ð)zbrʌʃ, -ɨz
AM 'kloʊ(ð)zˌbrəʃ, -ɨz

clotheshorse
BR ˈkləʊ(ð)zhɔːs, -ɪz
AM ˈkloʊ(ð)zˌ(h)ɔ(ə)rs, -əz

clothesline
BR ˈkləʊ(ð)zlʌɪn, -z
AM ˈkloʊ(ð)zˌlaɪn, -z

clothespeg
BR ˈkləʊ(ð)zpɛɡ, -z
AM ˈkloʊ(ð)zˌpɛɡ, -z

clothespin
BR ˈkləʊ(ð)zpɪn, -z
AM ˈkloʊ(ð)zˌpɪn, -z

clothier
BR ˈkləʊðɪə(r), -z
AM ˈkloʊðjər, ˈkloʊðiər, -z

clothing
BR ˈkləʊðɪŋ
AM ˈkloʊðɪŋ

Clotho
BR ˈkləʊθəʊ
AM ˈkloʊˌθoʊ

cloths
BR klɒθs, klɒðz
AM klɔðz, klɔθs, klɑðz, klɑθs

cloture
BR ˈkləʊtʃə(r), -z
AM ˈkloʊtʃər, -z

clou
BR kluː, -z
AM klu, -z

cloud
BR klaʊd, -z, -ɪŋ, -ɨd
AM klaʊd, -z, -ɪŋ, -əd

cloudbank
BR ˈklaʊdbaŋk, -s
AM ˈklaʊdˌbæŋk, -s

cloudberry
BR ˈklaʊdb(ə)r|i, -ɪz
AM ˈklaʊdˌbɛri, -z

cloudburst
BR ˈklaʊdbəːst, -s
AM ˈklaʊdˌbərst, -s

Cloudesley
BR ˈklaʊdzli
AM ˈklaʊdzli

cloudily
BR ˈklaʊdɪli
AM ˈklaʊdəli

cloudiness
BR ˈklaʊdɪnɪs
AM ˈklaʊdinɨs

cloudland
BR ˈklaʊdland
AM ˈklaʊdˌlænd

cloudless
BR ˈklaʊdləs
AM ˈklaʊdləs

cloudlessly
BR ˈklaʊdləsli
AM ˈklaʊdlɨsli

cloudlessness
BR ˈklaʊdləsnəs
AM ˈklaʊdləsnəs

cloudlet
BR ˈklaʊdlɨt, -s
AM ˈklaʊdlət, -s

cloudscape
BR ˈklaʊdskeɪp, -s
AM ˈklaʊdˌskeɪp, -s

cloudy
BR ˈklaʊd|i, -ɪə(r), -ɪɪst
AM ˈklaʊdi, -ər, -ɨst

Clough
place in Ireland
BR klɒx
AM klɑk

clough
BR klʌf, -s
AM kləf, kloʊ, kləfs\kloʊz

clout
BR klaʊt, -s, -ɪŋ, -ɨd
AM klaʊ|t, -ts, -dɪŋ, -dəd

Clouzot
BR ˈkluːzəʊ
AM ˌkluˈzoʊ

clove
BR kləʊv, -z
AM kloʊv, -z

Clovelly
BR kləˈvɛli
AM ˈkləvəli

cloven
BR ˈkləʊvn
AM ˈkloʊvən

clover
BR ˈkləʊvə(r), -z
AM ˈkloʊvər, -z

cloverleaf
BR ˈkləʊvəliːf, -s
AM ˈkloʊvərˌlif, -s

cloverleaves
BR ˈkləʊvəliːvz
AM ˈkloʊvərˌlivz

Clovis
BR ˈkləʊvɪs
AM ˈkloʊvəs

Clowes
BR klaʊz, kləʊz, kluːz
AM klaʊz, kloʊz, kluz

clown
BR klaʊn, -z, -ɪŋ, -d
AM klaʊn, -z, -ɪŋ, -d

clownery
BR ˈklaʊn(ə)ri
AM ˈklaʊnəri

clownish
BR ˈklaʊnɪʃ
AM ˈklaʊnɪʃ

clownishly
BR ˈklaʊnɪʃli
AM ˈklaʊnɪʃli

clownishness
BR ˈklaʊnɪʃnɪs
AM ˈklaʊnɪʃnɪs

cloy
BR klɔɪ, -z, -ɪŋ, -d
AM klɔɪ, -z, -ɪŋ, -d

cloyingly
BR ˈklɔɪɪŋli
AM ˈklɔɪɪŋli

clozapine
BR ˈkləʊzəpiːn
AM ˈkloʊzəˌpin

cloze
BR kləʊz
AM kloʊz

club
BR klʌb, -z, -ɪŋ, -d
AM kləb, -z, -ɪŋ, -d

clubbability
BR ˌklʌbəˈbɪlɨti
AM ˌkləbəˈbɪlɨdi

clubbable
BR ˈklʌbəbl
AM ˈkləbəbəl

clubbableness
BR ˈklʌbəblnəs
AM ˈkləbəbəlnəs

clubbably
BR ˈklʌbəbli
AM ˈkləbəbli

clubber
BR ˈklʌbə(r), -z
AM ˈkləbər, -z

clubby
BR ˈklʌb|i, -ɪə(r), -ɪɪst
AM ˈkləbi, -ər, -əst

clubfeet
BR ˌklʌbˈfiːt
AM ˈkləbˌfit

clubfoot
BR ˌklʌbˈfʊt
AM ˈkləbˌfʊt

clubfooted
BR ˌklʌbˈfʊtɨd
AM ˈkləbˌfʊdəd

clubhouse
BR ˈklʌbhaʊ|s, -zɪz
AM ˈkləbˌ(h)aʊ|s, -zəz

clubland
BR ˈklʌbland
AM ˈkləbˌlænd

clubman
BR ˈklʌbmən
AM ˈkləbmən

clubmen
BR ˈklʌbmən
AM ˈkləbmən

clubmoss
BR ˈklʌbmɒs, -ɪz
AM ˈkləbˌmɔs, ˈkləbˌmɑs, -əz

clubroom
BR ˈklʌbruːm, ˈklʌbrʊm, -z
AM ˈkləbˌrum, ˈkləbˌrʊm, -z

clubroot
BR ˈklʌbruːt
AM ˈkləbˌrut, ˈkləbˌrʊt

clubwoman
BR ˈklʌbˌwʊmən
AM ˈkləbˌwʊmən

clubwomen
BR ˈklʌbˌwɪmɪn
AM ˈkləbˌwɪmɨn

cluck
BR klʌk, -s, -ɪŋ, -t
AM klək, -s, -ɪŋ, -t

cluckily
BR ˈklʌkɨli
AM ˈkləkəli

cluckiness
BR ˈklʌkɪnɨs
AM ˈkləkinɨs

clucky
BR ˈklʌk|i, -ɪə(r), -ɪɪst
AM ˈkləki, -ər, -əst

cludge
BR klʌdʒ, kluːdʒ, -ɪz
AM klədʒ, kludʒ, -əz

clue
BR kluː, -z, -ɪŋ, -d
AM klu, -z, -ɪŋ, -d

clueless
BR ˈkluːləs
AM ˈkluləs

cluelessly
BR ˈkluːləsli
AM ˈkluləsli

cluelessness
BR ˈkluːləsnəs
AM ˈkluləsnəs

Cluj
BR kluːʒ
AM kluʒ

clump
BR klʌm|p, -ps, -pɪŋ, -(p)t
AM kləmp, -s, -ɪŋ, -t

clumpy
BR ˈklʌmp|i, -ə(r), -ɪɪst
AM ˈkləmpi, -ər, -əst

clumsily
BR ˈklʌmzɨli
AM ˈkləmzəli

clumsiness
BR ˈklʌmzɪnɪs
AM ˈkləmzinɨs

clumsy
BR ˈklʌmz|i, -ɪə(r), -ɪɪst
AM ˈkləmzi, -ər, -ɨst

Clun
BR klʌn
AM klən

Clunes
BR kluːnz
AM klunz

clung
BR klʌŋ
AM kləŋ

Cluniac
BR ˈkluːnɪak, -s
AM ˈkluniˌæk, -s

Clunie
BR ˈkluːni
AM ˈkluni

Clunies
BR ˈkluːnɪz
AM ˈkluniz

clunk
BR klʌŋ|k, -ks, -kɪŋ, -(k)t

AM klən|k, -ks, -kɪŋ, -(k)t
Cluny
BR 'klu:ni
AM 'kluni
clupeid
BR 'klu:pɪɪd
AM 'klupiɨd
clupeoid
BR 'klu:pɪɔɪd
AM 'klupi,ɔɪd
cluster
BR 'klʌst|ə(r), -əz, -(ə)rɪŋ, -əd
AM 'kləst|ər, -ərz, -(ə)rɪŋ, -ərd
clutch
BR klʌtʃ, -ɪz, -ɪŋ, -t
AM klətʃ, -əz, -ɪŋ, -t
clutter
BR 'klʌt|ə(r), -əz, -(ə)rɪŋ, -əd
AM 'kləd|ər, -ərz, -(ə)rɪŋ, -ərd
Clutterbuck
BR 'klʌtəbʌk
AM 'klədər,bək
Clutton
BR 'klʌtn
AM 'klətn
Clwyd
BR 'klu:ɪd
AM 'kluəd
WE klwɪd
Clwydian
BR klʊ'ɪdɪən
AM klə'wɪdiən
Clydach
BR 'klɪdəx, 'klɪdək
AM 'klɪdək
WE 'klʌdax
Clyde
BR klʌɪd
AM klaɪd
Clydebank
BR 'klʌɪdbaŋk
AM 'klaɪd,bæŋk
Clydella
BR klʌɪ'dɛlə(*r*)
AM klaɪ'dɛlə
Clydesdale
BR 'klʌɪdzdeɪl, -z
AM 'klaɪdz,deɪl, -z
Clyne
BR klʌɪn
AM klaɪn
clypeal
BR 'klɪpɪəl
AM 'klɪpiəl
clypeate
BR 'klɪpɪət
AM 'klɪpiət
clypei
BR 'klɪpɪʌɪ
AM 'klɪpi,aɪ
clypeus
BR 'klɪpɪəs
AM 'klɪpiəs
Clyro
BR 'klʌɪrəʊ
AM 'klaɪroʊ
clyster
BR 'klɪstə(r), -z
AM 'klɪstər, -z
Clytemnestra
BR ,klʌɪtɪm'nɛstrə(*r*), ,klʌɪtɛm'nɛstrə(*r*)
AM ,klaɪdəm'nɛstrə
Cnut
BR kə'nju:t
AM kə'nut
CO
Commanding Officer
BR ,si:'əʊ, -z
AM ,si'oʊ, -z
Co.
Company, County
BR kəʊ
AM koʊ
c/o
BR ,kɛ:r'ɒv, ,si:'əʊ
AM 'kɛr'əv, ,si'oʊ
co-accused
BR ,kəʊə'kju:zd
AM ,koʊə'kjuzd
coacervate
BR ,kəʊə'sə:veɪt, -s
AM ,koʊə'sərvət, koʊ'æsər,veɪt, -s
coacervation
BR kəʊ,asə'veɪʃn
AM koʊ,æsər'veɪʃən
coach
BR kəʊtʃ, -ɪz, -ɪŋ, -t
AM koʊtʃ, -əz, -ɪŋ, -t
coachbuilder
BR 'kəʊtʃ,bɪldə(r), -z
AM 'koʊtʃ,bɪldər, -z
coachhouse
BR 'kəʊtʃhaʊ|s, -zɪz
AM 'koʊtʃ,(h)aʊ|s, -zəz
coachload
BR 'kəʊtʃləʊd, -z
AM 'koʊtʃ,loʊd, -z
coachman
BR 'kəʊtʃmən
AM 'koʊtʃmən
coachmen
BR 'kəʊtʃmən
AM 'koʊtʃmən
coachwood
BR 'kəʊtʃwʊd
AM 'koʊtʃ,wʊd
coachwork
BR 'kəʊtʃwə:k
AM 'koʊtʃ,wərk
coaction
BR kəʊ'akʃn
AM koʊ'ækʃən
coactive
BR kəʊ'aktɪv
AM koʊ'æktɪv
coadjacent
BR ,kəʊə'dʒeɪsnt
AM ,koʊə'dʒeɪsənt
coadjutant
BR kəʊ'adʒʉtənt
AM ,koʊ'ædʒətənt
coadjutor
BR kəʊ'adʒʉtə(r), -z
AM koʊ'ædʒədər, ,koʊə'dʒudər, -z
coadministrator
BR ,kəʊəd'mɪnɪstreɪtə(r), -z
AM ,koʊəd'mɪnə,streɪdər, -z
coagula
BR kəʊ'agjʉlə(*r*)
AM koʊ'ægjələ
coagulable
BR kəʊ'agjʉləbl
AM koʊ'ægjələbəl
coagulant
BR kəʊ'agjʉlənt, kəʊ'agjʉln̩t, -s
AM koʊ'ægjələnt, -s
coagulate
BR kəʊ'agjʉleɪt, -s, -ɪŋ, -ɨd
AM koʊ'ægjə,leɪ|t, -ts, -dɪŋ, -dɨd
coagulation
BR kəʊ,agjʉ'leɪʃn
AM koʊ,ægjə'leɪʃən
coagulative
BR kəʊ'agjʉlətɪv
AM koʊ'ægjə,leɪdɪv
coagulator
BR kəʊ'agjʉleɪtə(r), -z
AM koʊ'ægjə,leɪdər, -z
coagulatory
BR kəʊ'agjʉlət(ə)ri
AM koʊ'ægjələ,tɔri
coagulum
BR kəʊ'agjʉləm
AM koʊ'ægjələm
Coahuila
BR ,kəʊə'wi:lə(*r*)
AM ,koʊə'wilɑ
coal
BR kəʊl, -z, -ɪŋ, -d
AM koʊl, -z, -ɪŋ, -d
Coalbrookdale
BR 'kəʊlbrʊkdeɪl, ,kəʊlbrʊk'deɪl
AM 'koʊlbrʊk,deɪl, ,koʊlbrʊk'deɪl
coalbunker
BR 'kəʊl,bʌŋkə(r), -z
AM 'koʊl,bəŋkər, -z
coaler
BR 'kəʊlə(r), -z
AM 'koʊlər, -z
coalesce
BR ,kəʊə'lɛs, -ɪz, -ɪŋ, -t
AM ,koʊə'lɛs, -əz, -ɪŋ, -t
coalescence
BR ,kəʊə'lɛsns
AM ,koʊə'lɛsəns
coalescent
BR ,kəʊə'lɛsnt
AM ,koʊə'lɛsənt
coalface
BR 'kəʊlfeɪs, -ɪz
AM 'koʊl,feɪs, -ɪz
coalfield
BR 'kəʊlfi:ld, -z
AM 'koʊl,fild, -z
coalfish
BR 'kəʊlfɪʃ
AM 'koʊl,fɪʃ
coalheaver
BR 'kəʊl,hi:və(r), -z
AM 'koʊl,(h)ivər, -z
coalhole
BR 'kəʊlhəʊl, -z
AM 'koʊl,(h)oʊl, -z
coalhouse
BR 'kəʊlhaʊ|s, -zɪz
AM 'koʊl,(h)aʊ|s, -zəz
Coalisland
BR (,)kəʊl'ʌɪlənd
AM ,koʊl'aɪlənd
Coalite®
BR 'kəʊlʌɪt
AM 'koʊlaɪt
coalition
BR ,kəʊə'lɪʃn, -z
AM ,koʊə'lɪʃən, -z
coalitionist
BR ,kəʊə'lɪʃn̩ɪst, -s
AM ,koʊə'lɪʃənəst, -s
coalman
BR 'kəʊlmən
AM 'koʊlmən
coalmen
BR 'kəʊlmən
AM 'koʊlmən
coalmice
BR 'kəʊlmʌɪs
AM 'koʊl,maɪs
coalmine
BR 'kəʊlmʌɪn, -z
AM 'koʊl,maɪn, -z
coalminer
BR 'kəʊl,mʌɪnə(r), -z
AM 'koʊl,maɪnər, -z
coalmouse
BR 'kəʊlmaʊs
AM 'koʊl,maʊs
coaloil
BR 'kəʊlɔɪl
AM 'koʊl,ɔɪl
coalowner
BR 'kəʊl,əʊnə(r), -z
AM 'koʊl,oʊnər, -z
Coalport
BR 'kəʊlpɔ:t
AM 'koʊl,pɔ(ə)rt
coalsack
BR 'kəʊlsak, -s
AM 'koʊl,sæk, -s
coalscuttle
BR 'kəʊl,skʌtl, -z
AM 'koʊl,skədəl, -z

coaly
BR 'kəʊli
AM 'koʊli

coaming
BR 'kəʊmɪŋ, -z
AM 'koʊmɪŋ, -z

coaptation
BR ˌkəʊap'teɪʃn
AM ˌkoʊæp'teɪʃən

coarctation
BR ˌkəʊɑːk'teɪʃn
AM ˌkoʊɑrk'teɪʃən

coarse
BR kɔːs, -ə(r), -ɨst
AM kɔ(ə)rs, -ər, -əst

coarsely
BR 'kɔːsli
AM 'kɔrsli

coarsen
BR 'kɔːs|n, -nz, -n̩ɪŋ\-nɪŋ, -nd
AM 'kɔrsən, -z, -ɪŋ, -d

coarseness
BR 'kɔːsnəs
AM 'kɔrsnəs

coarsish
BR 'kɔːsɪʃ
AM 'kɔrsɪʃ

coast
BR kəʊst, -s, -ɪŋ, -ɨd
AM koʊst, -s, -ɪŋ, -əd

coastal
BR 'kəʊstl
AM 'koʊstəl

coaster
BR 'kəʊstə(r), -z
AM 'koʊstər, -z

coastguard
BR 'kəʊs(t)ɡɑːd, -z
AM 'koʊs(t)ˌɡɑrd, -z

coastguardsman
BR 'kəʊs(t)ɡɑːdzmən
AM 'koʊs(t)ˌɡɑrdzmən

coastguardsmen
BR 'kəʊs(t)ɡɑːdzmən
AM 'koʊs(t)ˌɡɑrdzmən

coastland
BR 'kəʊs(t)land, -z
AM 'koʊs(t)ˌlænd, -z

coastline
BR 'kəʊs(t)lʌɪn, -z
AM 'koʊs(t)ˌlaɪn, -z

coastwise
BR 'kəʊstwʌɪz
AM 'koʊs(t)ˌwaɪz

coat
BR kəʊt, -s, -ɪŋ, -ɨd
AM koʊ|t, -ts, -dɪŋ, -dəd

Coatbridge
BR 'kəʊtbrɪdʒ
AM 'koʊtˌbrɪdʒ

coatee
BR 'kəʊtiː, ˌkəʊ'tiː, -z
AM ˌkoʊ'ti, -z

Coates
BR kəʊts
AM koʊts

coati
BR kəʊ'ɑːt|i, -ɪz
AM koʊ'ɑdi, -z

coatimundi
BR kəʊˌɑːtɪ'mʌnd|i, -ɪz
AM koʊˌɑdi'məndi, -z

coating
BR 'kəʊtɪŋ, -z
AM 'koʊdɪŋ, -z

coatless
BR 'kəʊtləs
AM 'koʊtləs

Coats
BR kəʊts
AM koʊts

coax
BR kəʊks, -ɪz, -ɪŋ, -t
AM koʊks, -əz, -ɪŋ, -t

co-ax
cable
BR 'kəʊaks
AM 'koʊˌæks

coaxer
BR 'kəʊksə(r), -z
AM 'koʊksər, -z

coaxial
BR kəʊ'aksɪəl
AM koʊ'æksiəl

coaxially
BR kəʊ'aksɪəli
AM koʊ'æksiəli

coaxingly
BR 'kəʊksɪŋli
AM 'koʊksɪŋli

cob
BR kɒb, -z
AM kɑb, -z

cobalt
BR 'kəʊbɔːlt, 'kəʊbɒlt, 'kəʊb(ə)lt
AM 'koʊˌbɔlt, 'koʊˌbɑlt

cobaltic
BR kəʊ'bɔːltɪk, kəʊ'bɒltɪk
AM koʊ'bɔldɪk, koʊ'bɑldɪk

cobaltous
BR kəʊ'bɔːltəs, kəʊ'bɒltəs
AM koʊ'bɔldəs, koʊ'bɑldəs

Cobb
BR kɒb
AM kɑb

cobber
BR 'kɒbə(r), -z
AM 'kɑbər, -z

Cobbett
BR 'kɒbɪt
AM 'kɑbət

cobble
BR 'kɒb|l, -lz, -l̩ɪŋ\-lɪŋ, -ld
AM 'kɑb|əl, -əlz, -(ə)lɪŋ, -əld

cobbler
BR 'kɒblə(r), -z
AM 'kɑblər, -z

cobblestone
BR 'kɒblstəʊn, -z
AM 'kɑbəlˌstoʊn, -z

Cobbold
BR 'kɒbəʊld
AM 'kɑboʊld

Cobden
BR 'kɒbd(ə)n
AM 'kɑbdən

Cobdenism
BR 'kɒbdənɪz(ə)m
AM 'kɑbdəˌnɪzəm

Cobham
BR 'kɒb(ə)m
AM 'kɑbəm

coble
BR 'kəʊbl, -z
AM 'koʊbəl, 'kɑbəl, -z

cobnut
BR 'kɒbnʌt, -s
AM 'kɑbnət, -s

COBOL
BR 'kəʊbɒl
AM 'koʊˌbɑl

cobra
BR 'kəʊbrə(r), 'kɒbrə(r), -z
AM 'koʊbrə, -z

coburg
BR 'kəʊbəːɡ
AM 'koʊˌbərɡ

cobweb
BR 'kɒbwɛb, -z, -d
AM 'kɑbˌwɛb, -z, -d

cobwebby
BR 'kɒbwɛbi
AM 'kɑbˌwɛbi

coca
BR 'kəʊkə(r)
AM 'koʊkə(r)

Coca-Cola®
BR ˌkəʊkə'kəʊlə(r), -z
AM ˌkoʊkə'koʊlə, -z

cocaine
BR kə(ʊ)'keɪn
AM koʊ'keɪn, 'koʊˌkeɪn

cocainism
BR kə(ʊ)'keɪnɪz(ə)m
AM koʊ'keɪˌnɪzəm, 'koʊˌkeɪˌnɪzəm

coccal
BR 'kɒkl
AM 'kɑkəl

cocci
BR 'kɒk(s)ʌɪ
AM 'kɑˌkaɪ

coccidiosis
BR ˌkɒksɪdɪ'əʊsɪs, kɒkˌsɪdɪ'əʊsɪs
AM ˌkɑkˌsɪdi'oʊsəs

coccoid
BR 'kɒk(s)ɔɪd
AM 'kɑˌkɔɪd

coccolith
BR 'kɒkəlɪθ, 'kɒkl̩ɪθ, -s
AM 'kɑkəˌlɪθ, -s

coccolithophore
BR ˌkɒkə(ʊ)'lɪθəfɔː(r), -z
AM ˌkɑkə'lɪθəˌfɔ(ə)r, -z

coccus
BR 'kɒkəs
AM 'kɑkəs

coccygeal
BR kɒk'sɪdʒɪəl
AM kɑk'sɪdʒiəl

coccyx
BR 'kɒks|ɪks, -ɨksɪz
AM 'kɑkˌsɪks, -ɨz

Coch
in Welsh placenames
BR kɒx, kɒk
AM kɑk

Cochabamba
BR ˌkəʊtʃə'bambə(r)
AM ˌkoʊtʃə'bɑmbə
SP kotʃa'βamba

cochair
BR ˌkəʊ'tʃɛː(r), -z
AM ˌkoʊ'tʃɛ(ə)r, -z

co-chairman
BR ˌkəʊ'tʃɛːmən
AM ˌkoʊ'tʃɛrmən

co-chairmen
BR ˌkəʊ'tʃɛːmən
AM ˌkoʊ'tʃɛrmən

Cochin
BR 'kəʊtʃɪn, 'kɒtʃɪn
AM 'koʊtʃɪn, 'kɑtʃɪn

Cochin-China
BR ˌkəʊtʃɪn'tʃʌɪnə(r), ˌkɒtʃɪn'tʃʌɪnə(r)
AM 'koʊtʃɪn'tʃaɪnə, 'kɑtʃɪn'tʃaɪnə

cochineal
BR ˌkɒtʃɪ'niːl, 'kɒtʃɨniːl
AM 'kɑtʃəˌniəl

Cochise
BR kəʊ'tʃiːs
AM koʊ'tʃis

cochlea
BR 'kɒklɪə(r), -z
AM 'kɑkliə, -z

cochleae
BR 'kɒklɪiː
AM 'kɑkliˌi, 'kɑkliˌaɪ

cochlear
BR 'kɒklɪə(r)
AM 'kɑkliər

Cochran
BR 'kɒkr(ə)n, 'kɒxr(ə)n
AM 'kɑkrən

Cochrane
BR 'kɒkr(ə)n, 'kɒxr(ə)n
AM 'kɑkrən

cock
BR kɒk, -s, -ɪŋ, -t
AM kɑk, -s, -ɪŋ, -t

cockade
BR kə'keɪd, kɒ'keɪd, -z, -ɨd

AM kɑ'keɪd, -z, -ɨd

cock-a-doodle-doo
BR ˌkɒkəˌduːdl'duː, -z
AM ˈkɑkəˌdudəl'du, -z

cock-a-hoop
BR ˌkɒkə'huːp
AM ˌkɑkə'hup

cock-a-leekie
BR ˌkɒkə'liːki
AM ˌkɑkə'liki

cockalorum
BR ˌkɒkə'lɔːrəm, -z
AM ˌkɑkə'lɔrəm, -z

cockamamie
BR ˌkɒkə'meɪmi
AM 'kɑkəˌmeɪmi

cockamamy
BR ˌkɒkə'meɪmi
AM 'kɑkəˌmeɪmi

cock-and-bull
BR ˌkɒk(ə)n(d)'bʊl
AM 'kɑkən'bʊl

cockateel
BR ˌkɒkə'tiːl, -z
AM 'kɑkəˌtil, -z

cockatiel
BR ˌkɒkə'tiːl, -z
AM 'kɑkəˌtil, -z

cockatoo
BR ˌkɒkə'tuː, -z
AM 'kɑkəˌtu, -z

cockatrice
BR 'kɒkətrʌɪs, 'kɒkətrɪs, -ɪz
AM 'kɑkətrəs, 'kɑkəˌtraɪs, -ɨz

cockboat
BR 'kɒkbəʊt, -s
AM 'kɑkˌboʊt, -s

Cockburn
BR 'kəʊb(ə)n, 'kəʊbəːn
AM 'kɑkˌbərn

cockchafer
BR 'kɒkˌtʃeɪfə(r), -z
AM 'kɑkˌtʃeɪfər, -z

Cockcroft
BR 'kɒkrɒft
AM 'kɑkrɔft, 'kɑkrɑft

cockcrow
BR 'kɒkkrəʊ, -z
AM 'kɑkˌkroʊ, -z

cocker
BR 'kɒkə(r), -z
AM 'kɑkər, -z

cockerel
BR 'kɒkr(ə)l, -z
AM 'kɑk(ə)rəl, -z

Cockerell
BR 'kɒkr(ə)l
AM 'kɑk(ə)rəl

Cockermouth
BR 'kɒkəmaʊθ
AM 'kɑkərˌmaʊθ

cockeyed
BR ˌkɒk'ʌɪd
AM 'kɑˌkaɪd

cockfight
BR 'kɒkfʌɪt, -s, -ɪŋ
AM 'kɑkˌfaɪ|t, -ts, -dɪŋ

Cockfosters
BR 'kɒkfɒstəz, ˌkɒk'fɒstəz
AM ˌkɑk'fɑstərz, ˌkɑk'fɔstərz

cockhorse
BR ˌkɒk'hɔːs, -ɨz
AM ˌkɑk'(h)ɔ(ə)rs, -əz

cockie-leekie
BR ˌkɒkɪ'liːki
AM ˌkɑkə'liki

cockily
BR 'kɒkɪli
AM 'kɑkəli

cockiness
BR 'kɒkɪnɪs
AM 'kɑkinɨs

cockle
BR 'kɒk|l, -lz, -l̩ɪŋ\-lɪŋ, -ld
AM 'kɑk|əl, -əlz, -(ə)lɪŋ, -əld

cocklebur
BR 'kɒklbəː(r)
AM 'kɑkəlˌbər

cockleshell
BR 'kɒklʃɛl, -z
AM 'kɑkəlˌʃɛl, -z

Cockney
BR 'kɒkn|i, -ɪz
AM 'kɑkni, -z

cockneyism
BR 'kɒknɪɪz(ə)m, -z
AM 'kɑkniˌɪzəm, -z

cockpit
BR 'kɒkpɪt, -s
AM 'kɑkˌpɪt, -s

cockroach
BR 'kɒkrəʊtʃ
AM 'kɑkˌroʊtʃ

Cockroft
BR 'kɒkrɒft, 'kəʊkrɒft
AM 'kɑkrɔft, 'kɑkrɑft

cockscomb
BR 'kɒkskəʊm, -z
AM 'kɑkˌskoʊm, -z

cocksfoot
BR 'kɒksfʊt, -s
AM 'kɑksˌfʊt, -s

cockshy
BR 'kɒkʃʌɪ, -z
AM 'kɑkˌʃaɪ, -z

cocksucker
BR 'kɒkˌsʌkə(r), -z
AM 'kɑkˌsəkər, -z

cocksure
BR ˌkɒk'ʃɔː(r), ˌkɒk'ʃʊə(r)
AM ˈkɑkˈʃʊ(ə)r

cocksurely
BR ˌkɒk'ʃʊəli, ˌkɒk'ʃɔːli
AM ˈkɑkˈʃʊrli

cocksureness
BR ˌkɒk'ʃɔːnəs, ˌkɒk'ʃʊənəs
AM ˈkɑkˈʃʊrnəs

cockswain
BR 'kɒksn, -z
AM 'kɑksən, 'kɑkˌsweɪn, -z

cocktail
BR 'kɒkteɪl, -z
AM 'kɑkˌteɪl, -z

cock-up
BR 'kɒkʌp, -s
AM 'kɑkəp, -s

cocky
BR 'kɒk|i, -ɪə(r), -ɪɪst
AM 'kɑki, -ər, -ɨst

cocky-leeky
BR ˌkɒkɪ'liːki
AM ˌkɑkə'liki

coco
BR 'kəʊkəʊ, -z
AM 'koʊkoʊ, -z

cocoa
BR 'kəʊkəʊ, -z
AM 'koʊkoʊ, -z

cocoanut
BR 'kəʊkənʌt, -s
AM 'koʊkəˌnət, -s

Cocom
BR 'kəʊkɒm
AM 'koʊˌkɑm

coconut
BR 'kəʊkənʌt, -s
AM 'koʊkəˌnət, -s

cocoon
BR kə'kuːn, -z, -ɪŋ, -d
AM kə'kun, -z, -ɪŋ, -d

cocoonery
BR kə'kuːn(ə)ri
AM kə'kunəri

Cocos Islands
BR 'kəʊkəs ˌʌɪlən(d)z, 'kəʊkɒs +
AM ˌkoʊkəs 'aɪlən(d)z

cocotte
BR kə(ʊ)'kɒt, kɒ'kɒt, -s
AM koʊ'kɑt, kə'kɑt, -s

Cocteau
BR 'kɒktəʊ
AM kɑk'toʊ

cod
BR kɒd, -z
AM kɑd, -z

coda
BR 'kəʊdə(r), -z
AM 'koʊdə(r), -z

coddle
BR 'kɒd|l, -lz, -l̩ɪŋ\-lɪŋ, -ld
AM 'kɑd|əl, -əlz, -(ə)lɪŋ, -əld

coddler
BR 'kɒdl̩ə(r), -z
AM 'kɑd(ə)lər, -z

code
BR kəʊd, -z, -ɪŋ, -ɨd
AM koʊd, -z, -ɪŋ, -əd

codeine
BR 'kəʊdiːn
AM 'koʊˌdin

codependency
BR ˌkəʊdɪ'pɛnd(ə)nsi
AM ˌkoʊdə'pɛnd(ə)nsi

codependent
BR ˌkəʊdɪ'pɛnd(ə)nt, -s
AM ˌkoʊdə'pɛnd(ə)nt, -s

coder
BR 'kəʊdə(r), -z
AM 'koʊdər, -z

codeword
BR 'kəʊdwəːd, -z
AM 'koʊdˌwərd, -z

codex
BR 'kəʊdɛks, -ɨz
AM 'koʊˌdɛks, -əz

codfish
BR 'kɒdfɪʃ, -ɨz
AM 'kɑdˌfɪʃ, -ɨz

codger
BR 'kɒdʒə(r), -z
AM 'kɑdʒər, -z

codices
BR 'kəʊdɪsiːz, 'kɒdɪsiːz
AM 'koʊdəsiz, 'kɑdəsiz

codicil
BR 'kəʊdɪsɪl, 'kɒdɪsɪl, -z
AM 'kɑdəˌsəl, -z

codicillary
BR ˌkəʊdɪ'sɪləri, ˌkɒdɪ'sɪləri
AM ˌkɑdə'sɪləri

codicological
BR ˌkəʊdɪkə'lɒdʒɪkl, ˌkɒdɪkə'lɒdʒɪkl
AM ˌkɑdəkə'lɑdʒəkəl

codicologically
BR ˌkəʊdɪkə'lɒdʒɪkli, ˌkɒdɪkə'lɒdʒɪkli
AM ˌkɑdəkə'lɑdʒəkəl

codicology
BR ˌkəʊdɪ'kɒlədʒi, ˌkɒdɪ'kɒlədʒi
AM ˌkɑdə'kɑlədʒi

codification
BR ˌkəʊdɪfɪ'keɪʃn
AM ˌkɑdəfə'keɪʃən, ˌkoʊdəfə'keɪʃən

codifier
BR 'kəʊdɪfʌɪə(r), -z
AM 'kɑdəˌfaɪər, 'koʊdəˌfaɪər, -z

codify
BR 'kəʊdɪfʌɪ, -z, -ɪŋ, -d
AM 'kɑdəˌfaɪ, 'koʊdəˌfaɪ, -z, -ɪŋ, -d

codlin
BR 'kɒdlɪn, -z
AM 'kɑdlən, -z

codling
BR 'kɒdlɪŋ, -z

AM ˈkɑdlɪŋ, -z

codliver oil
BR ˌkɒdlɪvər ˈɔɪl
AM ˈ͵kɑd͵lɪvər ˈɔɪl

codomain
BR ˌkəʊdə(ʊ)ˈmeɪn
AM ˌkoʊdəˈmeɪn, ˌkoʊˌdoʊˈmeɪn

codon
BR ˈkəʊdɒn, -z
AM ˈkoʊdən, -z

codpiece
BR ˈkɒdpiːs, -ɪz
AM ˈkɑd͵pis, -ɪz

codriver
BR ˈkəʊˌdrʌɪvə(r), -z
AM ˈkoʊˌdraɪvər, -z

codswallop
BR ˈkɒdzˌwɒləp
AM ˈkɑdzˌwɑləp

Cody
BR ˈkəʊdi
AM ˈkoʊdi

Coe
BR kəʊ
AM koʊ

coecilian
BR sɪˈsɪlɪən, -z
AM siˈsɪljən, səˈsɪljən, siˈsɪliən, səˈsɪliən, -z

Coed
in Welsh placenames
BR kɔɪd
AM kɔɪd

coed
BR ˌkəʊˈɛd, -z
AM ˈkoʊˌɛd, -z

co-editor
BR ˈkəʊˌɛdɪtə(r), -z
AM ˈ͵koʊˈ͵ɛdɪdər, -z

coeducation
BR ˌkəʊɛdjʊˈkeɪʃn, ˌkəʊɛdʒʊˈkeɪʃn
AM ˌkoʊˌɛdʒəˈkeɪʃən

coeducational
BR ˌkəʊɛdjʊˈkeɪʃn̩(ə)l, ˌkəʊɛdjʊˈkeɪʃən(ə)l, ˌkəʊɛdʒʊˈkeɪʃn̩(ə)l, ˌkəʊɛdʒʊˈkeɪʃən(ə)l
AM ˌkoʊˌɛdʒəˈkeɪʃ(ə)nəl

coefficient
BR ˌkəʊɪˈfɪʃnt
AM ˌkoʊəˈfɪʃənt

coelacanth
BR ˈsiːləkanθ, -s
AM ˈsiləˌkænθ, -s

coelenterate
BR sɪˈlɛntəreɪt, sɪˈlɛnt(ə)rət, -s
AM ˌsiˈlɛntəˌreɪt, -s

coeliac
BR ˈsiːlɪak
AM ˈsiliˌæk

coelom
BR ˈsiːləm
AM ˈsiləm

coelomate
BR ˈsiːlə(ʊ)meɪt
AM ˈsiləˌmeɪt

coelostat
BR ˈsiːlə(ʊ)stat, -s
AM ˈsiləˌstæt, -s

coemption
BR kəʊˈɛm(p)ʃn
AM ˌkoʊˈɛmpʃən

Coen
BR kəʊn
AM koʊn

coenobite
BR ˈsiːnə(ʊ)bʌɪt, -s
AM ˈsinəˌbaɪt, ˈsɛnəˌbaɪt, -s

coenobitic
BR ˌsiːnəˈbɪtɪk
AM ˌsinəˈbɪdɪk, ˌsɛnəˈbɪdɪk

coenobitical
BR ˌsiːnəˈbɪtɪkl
AM ˌsinəˈbɪdɪkl, ˌsɛnəˈbɪdəkəl

coequal
BR (ˌ)kəʊˈiːkw(ə)l, -z
AM ˌkoʊˈikwəl, -z

coequality
BR ˌkəʊɪˈkwɒlɪti
AM ˌkoʊəˈkwɑlədi, ˌkoʊəˈkwɔlədi, ˌkoʊiˈkwɑlədi, ˌkoʊiˈkwɔlədi

coerce
BR kəʊˈəːs, -ɪz, -ɪŋ, -t
AM koʊˈərs, -əz, -ɪŋ, -t

coercer
BR kəʊˈəːsə(r), -z
AM koʊˈərsər, -z

coercible
BR kəʊˈəːsɪbl
AM koʊˈərsəbəl

coercibly
BR kəʊˈəːsɪbli
AM koʊˈərsəbli

coercion
BR kəʊˈəːʃn
AM koʊˈərʃən, koʊˈərʒən

coercive
BR kəʊˈəːsɪv
AM koʊˈərsɪv

coercively
BR kəʊˈəːsɪvli
AM koʊˈərsɪvli

coerciveness
BR kəʊˈəːsɪvnɪs
AM koʊˈərsɪvnɪs

coessential
BR ˌkəʊɪˈsɛnʃl
AM koʊəˈsɛn(t)ʃəl

coeternal
BR ˌkəʊɪˈtəːnl
AM ˌkoʊəˈtərnəl

coeternally
BR ˌkəʊɪˈtəːnl̩i, ˌkəʊɪˈtəːnəli
AM ˌkoʊəˈtərnəli

Coetzee
BR kuːtˈsɪə(r), kuːtˈsiː
AM ˈkoʊtsi

Coeur d'Alene
BR ˌkɔː dəˈleɪn, + dlˈeɪn
AM ˌkər dəˈleɪn

Cœur de Lion
BR ˌkəː də ˈliːɒ̃, + ˈliːɒn, + ˈliːən
AM ˌkər də ˈliɔn

coeval
BR ˌkəʊˈiːvl
AM ˌkoʊˈivəl

coevality
BR ˌkəʊiːˈvalɪti
AM ˌkoʊiˈvælədi

coevally
BR ˌkəʊˈiːvl̩i
AM ˌkoʊˈivəli

coexist
BR ˌkəʊɪɡˈzɪst, -s, -ɪŋ, -ɪd
AM ˌkoʊəɡˈzɪst, -s, -ɪŋ, -ɪd

coexistence
BR ˌkəʊɪɡˈzɪst(ə)ns
AM ˌkoʊəɡˈzɪstns

coexistent
BR ˌkəʊɪɡˈzɪst(ə)nt
AM ˌkoʊəɡˈzɪstənt

coextend
BR ˌkəʊɪkˈstɛnd, -z, -ɪŋ, -ɪd
AM ˌkoʊəkˈstɛnd, -z, -ɪŋ, -əd

coextension
BR ˌkəʊɪkˈstɛnʃn, -z
AM ˌkoʊəkˈstɛn(t)ʃən, -z

coextensive
BR ˌkəʊɪkˈstɛnsɪv
AM ˌkoʊəkˈstɛnsɪv

C of E
BR ˌsiː əv ˈiː
AM ˌsi əv ˈi

coffee
BR ˈkɒf|i, -ɪz
AM ˈkɔfi, ˈkɑfi, -z

coffeecake
BR ˈkɒfɪkeɪk, -s
AM ˈkɔfiˌkeɪk, ˈkɑfiˌkeɪk, -s

coffee klatch
BR ˈkɒfɪ klatʃ, -ɪz
AM ˈkɔfi ˌklɑtʃ, ˈkɑfi +, -əz

coffer
BR ˈkɒfə(r), -z, -d
AM ˈkɔfər, ˈkɑfər, -z, -d

cofferdam
BR ˈkɒfədam, -z
AM ˈkɔfərˌdæm, ˈkɑfərˌdæm, -z

Coffey
BR ˈkɒfi
AM ˈkɑfi

coffin
BR ˈkɒfɪn, -z
AM ˈkɔfən, ˈkɑfən, -z

coffle
BR ˈkɒfl, -z
AM ˈkɔfəl, ˈkɑfəl, -z

cog
BR kɒɡ, -z, -d
AM kɑɡ, -z, -d

Cogan
BR ˈkəʊɡ(ə)n
AM ˈkoʊɡən

cogency
BR ˈkəʊdʒ(ə)nsi
AM ˈkoʊdʒənsi

cogent
BR ˈkəʊdʒ(ə)nt
AM ˈkoʊdʒənt

cogently
BR ˈkəʊdʒ(ə)ntli
AM ˈkoʊdʒən(t)li

Coggeshall
BR ˈkɒɡɪʃl, ˈkɒksl
AM ˈkɑɡzˌ(h)ɔl, ˈkɑɡzˌ(h)ɑl

Coghill
BR ˈkɒɡ(h)ɪl
AM ˈkɑɡ(h)ɪl

cogitable
BR ˈkɒdʒɪtəbl
AM ˈkɑdʒədəbəl

cogitate
BR ˈkɒdʒɪteɪt, -s, -ɪŋ, -ɪd
AM ˈkɑdʒəˌteɪ|t, -ts, -dɪŋ, -dɪd

cogitation
BR ˌkɒdʒɪˈteɪʃn
AM ˌkɑdʒəˈteɪʃən

cogitative
BR ˈkɒdʒɪtətɪv
AM ˈkɑdʒəˌteɪdɪv

cogitator
BR ˈkɒdʒɪteɪtə(r), -z
AM ˈkɑdʒəˌteɪdər, -z

cogito
BR ˈkɒɡɪtəʊ
AM ˈkɑɡədoʊ

cogito ergo sum
BR ˌkɒɡɪtəʊ ˌəːɡəʊ ˈsʊm, + ˈsʌm
AM ˌkɑɡədoʊ ˌərɡoʊ ˈsəm

cognac
BR ˈkɒnjak, -s
AM ˈkoʊnˌjæk, ˈkɑnˌjæk, -s

cognate
BR ˈkɒɡneɪt, -s
AM ˈkɑɡˌneɪt, -s

cognately
BR ˈkɒɡneɪtli
AM ˈkɑɡˌneɪtli

cognateness
BR ˈkɒɡneɪtnɪs
AM ˈkɑɡˌneɪtnɪs

cognatic
BR kɒɡˈnatɪk
AM ˌkɑɡˈnædɪk

cognation
BR kɒɡ'neɪʃn
AM ˌkɑɡ'neɪʃən

cognisable
BR 'kɒ(ɡ)nɪzəbl, kɒɡ'nʌɪzəbl
AM 'kɑɡnəzəbəl, ˌkɑɡ'naɪzəbəl

cognisably
BR 'kɒ(ɡ)nɪzəbli, kɒɡ'nʌɪzəbli
AM 'kɑɡnəzəbli, ˌkɑɡ'naɪzəbli

cognisance
BR 'kɒ(ɡ)nɪz(ə)ns, kɒɡ'nʌɪz(ə)ns
AM 'kɑɡnəzns

cognisant
BR 'kɒ(ɡ)nɪz(ə)nt, kɒɡ'nʌɪz(ə)nt
AM 'kɑɡnəznt

cognise
BR 'kɒɡnʌɪz, -ɪz, -ɪŋ, -d
AM 'kɑɡˌnaɪz, -ɪz, -ɪŋ, -d

cognition
BR kɒɡ'nɪʃn
AM ˌkɑɡ'nɪʃən

cognitional
BR kɒɡ'nɪʃn̩(ə)l, kɒɡ'nɪʃən(ə)l
AM ˌkɑɡ'nɪʃ(ə)nəl

cognitive
BR 'kɒɡnɪtɪv
AM 'kɑɡnədɪv

cognitively
BR 'kɒɡnɪtɪvli
AM 'kɑɡnədɪvli

cognitivism
BR 'kɒɡnɪtɪvɪz(ə)m
AM 'kɑɡnədɪˌvɪzəm

cognitivist
BR 'kɒɡnɪtɪvɪst, -s
AM 'kɑɡnədɪvɪst, -s

cognizable
BR 'kɒ(ɡ)nɪzəbl, kɒɡ'nʌɪzəbl
AM 'kɑɡnəzəbəl, ˌkɑɡ'naɪzəbəl

cognizably
BR 'kɒ(ɡ)nɪzəbli, kɒɡ'nʌɪzəbli
AM 'kɑɡnəzəbli, ˌkɑɡ'naɪzəbli

cognizance
BR 'kɒ(ɡ)nɪz(ə)ns, kɒɡ'nʌɪz(ə)ns
AM 'kɑɡnəzns

cognizant
BR 'kɒ(ɡ)nɪz(ə)nt, kɒɡ'nʌɪz(ə)nt
AM 'kɑɡnəznt

cognize
BR 'kɒɡnʌɪz, kɒɡ'nʌɪz, -ɪz, -ɪŋ, -d
AM 'kɑɡˌnaɪz, -ɪz, -ɪŋ, -d

cognomen
BR ˌkɒɡ'nəʊmɛn, ˌkɒɡ'nəʊmən, -z
AM ˌkɑɡ'noʊmən, 'kɑɡnəmən, -z

cognominal
BR ˌkɒɡ'nɒmɪnl
AM ˌkɑɡ'nɑmənəl

cognoscente
BR ˌkɒɡnə'ʃɛnti, ˌkɒnjə'ʃɛnti
AM ˌkɑɡnə'ʃɛn(t)i, ˌkɑnjoʊ'ʃɛn(t)i

cognoscenti
BR ˌkɒɡnə'ʃɛnti(:), ˌkɒnjə'ʃɛnti(:)
AM ˌkɑɡnə'ʃɛn(t)i, ˌkɑnjoʊ'ʃɛn(t)i

cogwheel
BR 'kɒɡwi:l, -z
AM 'kɑɡˌ(h)wil, -z

cohabit
BR (ˌ)kəʊ'hab|ɪt, -ɪts, -ɪtɪŋ, -ɪtɪd
AM ˌkoʊ'hæbə|t, -ts, -dɪŋ, -dəd

cohabitant
BR (ˌ)kəʊ'habɪt(ə)nt, -s
AM ˌkoʊ'hæbədənt, -s

cohabitation
BR ˌkəʊhabɪ'teɪʃn, kə(ʊ)ˌhabɪ'teɪʃn
AM ˌkoʊˌhæbə'teɪʃən

cohabitee
BR ˌkəʊhabɪ'ti:, kə(ʊ)ˌhabɪ'ti:, -z
AM ˌkoʊhæbə'ti, -z

cohabiter
BR (ˌ)kəʊ'habɪtə(r), -z
AM ˌkoʊ'hæbədər, -z

Cohan
BR 'kəʊhan
AM 'koʊˌhæn, 'koʊ(ə)n

Cohen
BR 'kəʊɪn
AM 'koʊ(ə)n

cohere
BR kə(ʊ)'hɪə(r), -z, -ɪŋ, -d
AM koʊ'hɪ(ə)r, -z, -ɪŋ, -d

coherence
BR kə(ʊ)'hɪərəns, kə(ʊ)'hɪərn̩s
AM koʊ'hɪrəns

coherency
BR kə(ʊ)'hɪərənsi, kə(ʊ)'hɪərn̩si
AM koʊ'hɪrənsi

coherent
BR kə(ʊ)'hɪərənt, kə(ʊ)'hɪərn̩t
AM koʊ'hɪrənt

coherently
BR kə(ʊ)'hɪərəntli, kə(ʊ)'hɪərn̩tli
AM koʊ'hɪrən(t)li

coherer
BR kə(ʊ)'hɪərə(r), -z
AM koʊ'hɪrər, -z

cohesion
BR kə(ʊ)'hi:ʒn
AM koʊ'hiʒən

cohesive
BR kə(ʊ)'hi:sɪv
AM koʊ'hisɪv

cohesively
BR kə(ʊ)'hi:sɪvli
AM koʊ'hisɪvli

cohesiveness
BR kə(ʊ)'hi:sɪvnɪs
AM koʊ'hisɪvnɪs

Cohn
BR kəʊn
AM koʊn

coho
BR 'kəʊhəʊ, -z
AM 'koʊˌhoʊ, -z

cohort
BR 'kəʊhɔ:t, -s
AM 'koʊˌhɔ(ə)rt, -s

cohosh
BR kə'hɒʃ
AM 'koʊˌhɑʃ

COHSE
BR 'kəʊzi
AM 'koʊzi

cohune
BR kə'hu:n, -z
AM kə'hun, -z

coif[1]
noun
BR kɔɪf, -s
AM kɔɪf, -s

coif[2]
verb
BR kwɑ:f, kwɒf, -s, -ɪŋ, -t
AM kwɑf, -s, -ɪŋ, -t

coiffeur
BR kwɑ:'fə:(r), kwɒ'fə:(r), -z
AM kwɑ'fər, -z

coiffeurs
BR kwɑ:'fə:z, kwɒ'fə:z
AM kwɑ'fərz

coiffeuse
BR kwɑ:'fə:z, kwɒ'fə:z
AM kwɑ'fʊz

coiffeuses
BR kwɑ:'fə:z, kwɒ'fə:z
AM kwɑ'fʊz

coiffure
BR kwɑ:'fjʊə(r), kwɒ'fjʊə(r), kwə'fjʊə(r), -z
AM kwɑ'fjʊ(ə)r, -z

coign
BR kɔɪn, -z
AM kɔɪn, -z

coil
BR kɔɪl, -z, -ɪŋ, -d
AM kɔɪl, -z, -ɪŋ, -d

Coimbra
BR 'kwɪmbrə(r)
AM kʊ'ɪmbrə

coin
BR kɔɪn, -z, -ɪŋ, -d
AM kɔɪn, -z, -ɪŋ, -d

coinage
BR 'kɔɪn|ɪdʒ, -ɪdʒɪz
AM 'kɔɪnɪdʒ, -ɪz

coincide
BR ˌkəʊɪn'sʌɪd, -z, -ɪŋ, -ɪd
AM ˌkoʊən'saɪd, -z, -ɪŋ, -ɪd

coincidence
BR kəʊ'ɪnsɪd(ə)ns, -ɪz
AM koʊ'ɪnsədns, -ɪz

coincident
BR kəʊ'ɪnsɪd(ə)nt
AM koʊ'ɪnsədnt, koʊ'ɪnsəˌdɛnt

coincidental
BR kəʊˌɪnsɪ'dɛntl
AM koʊˌɪnsə'dɛn(t)l

coincidentally
BR kəʊˌɪnsɪ'dɛntl̩i
AM koʊˌɪnsə'dɛn(t)əli

coincidently
BR kəʊˌɪnsɪ'dɛntli
AM koʊˌɪnsə'dɛn(t)li

coiner
BR 'kɔɪnə(r), -z
AM 'kɔɪnər, -z

co-inheritor
BR ˌkəʊɪn'hɛrɪtə(r), -z
AM ˌkoʊən'hɛrədər, -z

coin-op
BR 'kɔɪnɒp, -s
AM 'kɔɪnˌɑp, -s

cointreau
BR 'kwɒntrəʊ, 'kwɑ:ntrəʊ, 'kwantrəʊ, -z
AM kwɑn'troʊ, -z

coir
BR 'kɔɪə(r)
AM 'kɔɪ(ə)r

coit
BR kɔɪt
AM kɔɪt

coital
BR 'kəʊɪtl, 'kɔɪ(ɪ)tl
AM 'koʊədl, 'kɔɪdl

coition
BR kəʊ'ɪʃn
AM koʊ'ɪʃən

coitus
BR 'kəʊɪtəs, 'kɔɪ(ɪ)təs
AM 'koʊədəs, 'kɔɪdəs

coitus interruptus
BR ˌkəʊɪtəs ˌɪntə'rʌptəs, ˌkɔɪ(ɪ)təs +
AM ˌkoʊədəs ɪn(t)ə'rəptəs, ˌkɔɪdəs +

cojones
BR kə'həʊneɪz
AM koʊ'hoʊneɪz kə'hoʊneɪz

Coke¹®
Coca-Cola
BR kəʊk, -s
AM koʊk, -s
Coke²
surname
BR kʊk, kəʊk
AM koʊk
coke
BR kəʊk, -s, -ɪŋ, -t
AM koʊk, -s, -ɪŋ, -t
Coker
BR 'kəʊkə(r)
AM 'koʊkər
col
BR kɒl, -z
AM kɑl, -z
cola
BR 'kəʊlə(*r*), -z
AM 'koʊlə, -z
colander
BR 'kʌləndə(r), -z
AM 'kɑləndər, 'kələndər, -z
Colbert¹
French surname
BR 'kɒlbɛː(r)
AM ˌkɔl'bɛ(ə)r
Colbert²
English surname
BR 'kəʊlbəːt
AM 'koʊlbərt
Colby
BR 'kɒlbi
AM 'koʊlbi
colcannon
BR kɒl'kanən, kəl'kanən
AM kəl'kænən
Colchester
BR 'kɒltʃɪstə(r), 'kɒlˌtʃɛstər
AM 'koʊlˌtʃɛstər
colchicine
BR 'kɒltʃɪsiːn, 'kɒlkɪsiːn, -z
AM 'kɑltʃəˌsin, 'kɑlkəˌsin, -z
colchicum
BR 'kɒltʃɪkəm, 'kɒlkɪkəm
AM 'kɑltʃəkəm
Colchis
BR 'kɒlkɪs
AM 'kɔlkəs, 'kɑlkəs
cold
BR kəʊld, -z, -ə(r), -ɪst
AM koʊld, -z, -ər, -əst
cold-blooded
BR ˌkəʊl(d)'blʌdɪd
AM ¦koʊl(d)¦blədəd
cold-bloodedly
BR ˌkəʊl(d)'blʌdɪdli
AM ¦koʊl(d)¦blədədli
cold-bloodedness
BR ˌkəʊl(d)'blʌdɪdnɪs
AM ¦koʊl(d)¦blədədnəs
coldish
BR 'kəʊldɪʃ
AM 'koʊldɪʃ
Colditz
BR 'kəʊldɪts, 'kɒldɪts
AM 'koʊldɪts
coldly
BR 'kəʊldli
AM 'koʊl(d)li
coldness
BR 'kəʊldnəs
AM 'koʊl(d)nəs
coldstore
BR 'kəʊl(d)stɔː(r), -z
AM 'koʊl(d)ˌstɔ(ə)r, -z
Coldstream
BR 'kəʊl(d)striːm
AM 'koʊl(d)ˌstrim
Cole
BR kəʊl
AM koʊl
Colebrook
BR 'kəʊlbrʊk
AM 'koʊlˌbrʊk
Coleclough
BR 'kəʊlklʌf
AM 'koʊlkləf
colectomy
BR kə(ʊ)'lɛktəm|i, -ɪz
AM kə'lɛktəmi, koʊ'lɛktəmi, -z
Coleford
BR 'kəʊlfəd
AM 'koʊlfərd
Coleman
BR 'kəʊlmən
AM 'koʊlmən
colemice
BR 'kəʊlmʌɪs
AM 'koʊlˌmaɪs
colemouse
BR 'kəʊlmaʊs
AM 'koʊlˌmaʊs
Colenso
BR kə'lɛnzəʊ, kə'lɛnsəʊ
AM kə'lɛnsoʊ
Coleoptera
BR ˌkɒlɪ'ɒpt(ə)rə(*r*)
AM ˌkɑli'ɑpt(ə)rə
coleopteran
BR ˌkɒlɪ'ɒpt(ə)rən, -z
AM ˌkɑli'ɑpt(ə)rən, -z
coleopterist
BR ˌkɒlɪ'ɒpt(ə)rɪst, -s
AM ˌkɑli'ɑpt(ə)rəst, -s
coleopterous
BR ˌkɒlɪ'ɒpt(ə)rəs
AM ˌkɑli'ɑpt(ə)rəs
coleoptile
BR ˌkɒlɪ'ɒptʌɪl, -z
AM ˌkɑli'ɑpˌtaɪl, -z
Coleraine
BR ˌkəʊl'reɪn
AM 'koʊlˌreɪn, ˌkoʊl'reɪn
Coleridge
BR 'kəʊl(ə)rɪdʒ
AM 'koʊl(ə)rɪdʒ
Coles
BR kəʊlz
AM koʊlz
coleseed
BR 'kəʊlsiːd
AM 'koʊlˌsid
coleslaw
BR 'kəʊlslɔː(*r*)
AM 'koʊlˌslɔ
Colet
BR 'kɒlɪt
AM 'kɑlət
Colette
BR kɒ'lɛt, kə'lɛt
AM kə'lɛt
coleus
BR 'kəʊlɪəs
AM 'koʊliəs
coley
BR 'kəʊl|i, -ɪz
AM 'koʊli, -z
Colgate®
BR 'kəʊlgeɪt, 'kɒlgeɪt
AM 'koʊlˌgeɪt
colic
BR 'kɒlɪk
AM 'kɑlɪk
colicky
BR 'kɒlɪki
AM 'kɑləki
coliform
BR 'kəʊlɪfɔːm, 'kɒlɪfɔːm
AM 'koʊliˌfɔ(ə)rm
Colima
BR kɒ'liːmə(*r*), kə'liːmə(*r*)
AM kɔ'limə, kə'limə, kɑ'limə
Colin
BR 'kɒlɪn
AM 'kɑlən
coliseum
BR ˌkɒlɪ'siːəm, -z
AM ˌkɑlə'siəm, -z
colitis
BR kə'lʌɪtɪs, kɒ'lʌɪtɪs
AM kə'laɪdəs
Coll
BR kɒl
AM kɔl, kɑl
collaborate
BR kə'labəreɪt, -s, -ɪŋ, -ɪd
AM kə'læbəˌreɪ|t, -ts, -dɪŋ, -dɪd
collaboration
BR kəˌlabə'reɪʃn
AM kəˌlæbə'reɪʃən
collaborationist
BR kəˌlabə'reɪʃn̩ɪst, kəˌlabə'reɪʃənɪst, -s
AM kəˌlæbə'reɪʃənəst, -s
collaborative
BR kə'lab(ə)rətɪv
AM kə'læbərədɪv
collaboratively
BR kə'lab(ə)rətɪvli
AM kə'læbərədɪvli
collaborator
BR kəˌlabəreɪtə(r), -z
AM kə'læbəˌreɪdər, -z
collage
BR 'kɒlɑːʒ, kɒ'lɑːʒ, kə'lɑːʒ, -ɪz
AM kə'lɑʒ, -ɪz
collagen
BR 'kɒlədʒ(ə)n
AM 'kɑlədʒən
collagist
BR 'kɒlɑːʒɪst, kɒ'lɑːʒɪst, kə'lɑːʒɪst, -s
AM 'kɑlədʒəst, -s
collapsar
BR kə'lapsɑː(r), -z
AM kə'læpsər, -z
collapse
BR kə'laps, -ɪz, -ɪŋ, -t
AM kə'læps, -əz, -ɪn, -t
collapsibility
BR kəˌlapsɪ'bɪlɪti
AM kəˌlæpsə'bɪlɪdi
collapsible
BR kə'lapsɪbl
AM kə'læpsəbəl
collar
BR 'kɒlə(r), -z, -ɪŋ, -d
AM 'kɑlər, -z, -ɪŋ, -d
collarbone
BR 'kɒləbəʊn, -z
AM 'kɑlərˌboʊn, -z
collard
BR 'kɒləd, -z
AM 'kɑlərd, -z
collarette
BR ˌkɒlə'rɛt, -s
AM ˌkɑlə'rɛt, -s
collarless
BR 'kɒlələs
AM 'kɑlərləs
collate
BR kə'leɪt, kɒ'leɪt, -s, -ɪŋ, -ɪd
AM 'koʊˌleɪ|t, 'kɑˌleɪ|t, -ts, -dɪŋ, -dɪd
collateral
BR kə'lat(ə)rəl, kə'lat(ə)rl̩
AM kə'lædərəl, kə'lætrəl
collateralise
BR kə'lat(ə)rəlʌɪz, kə'lat(ə)rl̩ʌɪz, -ɪz, -ɪŋ, -d
AM kə'lædərəˌlaɪz, kə'lætrəˌlaɪz, -ɪz, -ɪŋ, -d
collaterality
BR kəˌlatə'ralɪti
AM kəˌlædə'rælədi

collateralize
BR kə'lat(ə)rəlʌɪz, kə'lat(ə)rl̩ʌɪz, -ɪz, -ɪŋ, -d
AM kə'lædərə,laɪz, kə'lætrə,laɪz, -ɪz, -ɪŋ, -d

collaterally
BR kə'lat(ə)rəli, kə'lat(ə)rl̩i
AM kə'lædərəli, kə'lætrəli

collation
BR kə'leɪʃn, kɒ'leɪʃn
AM kə'leɪʃən

collator
BR kə'leɪtə(r), kɒ'leɪtə(r), -z
AM 'koʊ,leɪdər, 'kɑ,leɪdər, -z

colleague
BR 'kɒliːg, -z
AM 'kɑlig, -z

collect[1]
noun, prayer
BR 'kɒlɛkt, -s
AM 'kɑlɛk(t), -s

collect[2]
verb, gather together
BR kə'lɛkt, -s, -ɪŋ, -ɪd
AM kə'lɛk|(t), -(t)s, -tɪŋ, -təd

collectability
BR kə,lɛktə'bɪlɪti
AM kə'lɛktəbɪlɨdi

collectable
BR kə'lɛktəbl, -z
AM kə'lɛktəbəl, -z

collectanea
BR ,kɒlɛk'teɪnɪə(*r*)
AM ,kɑlɛk'teɪniə

collectedly
BR kə'lɛktɨdli
AM kə'lɛktədli

collecteness
BR kə'lɛktɨdnɨs
AM kə'lɛktədnəs

collectible
BR kə'lɛktəbl, -z
AM kə'lɛktəbəl, -z

collection
BR kə'lɛkʃn, -z
AM kə'lɛkʃən, -z

collective
BR kə'lɛktɪv, -z
AM kə'lɛktɪv, -z

collectively
BR kə'lɛktɨvli
AM kə'lɛktɨvli

collectiveness
BR kə'lɛktɪvnɨs
AM kə'lɛktɪvnɨs

collectivisation
BR kə,lɛktɨvʌɪ'zeɪʃn
AM kə,lɛktəvə'zeɪʃən, kə,lɛktə,vaɪ'zeɪʃən

collectivise
BR kə'lɛktɨvʌɪz, -ɪz, -ɪŋ, -d
AM kə'lɛktə,vaɪz, -ɪz, -ɪŋ, -d

collectivism
BR kə'lɛktɨvɪz(ə)m
AM kə'lɛktə,vɪzəm

collectivist
BR kə'lɛktɨvɪst, -s
AM kə'lɛktəvəst, -s

collectivistic
BR kə,lɛktɪ'vɪstɪk
AM kə,lɛktə'vɪstɪk

collectivity
BR ,kɒlɛk'tɪvɨti
AM kə,lɛk'tɪvɨdi, ,kɑlɛk'tɪvɨdi

collectivization
BR kə,lɛktɨvʌɪ'zeɪʃn
AM kə,lɛktəvə'zeɪʃən, kə,lɛktə,vaɪ'zeɪʃən

collectivize
BR kə'lɛktɨvʌɪz, -ɪz, -ɪŋ, -d
AM kə'lɛktə,vaɪz, -ɪz, -ɪŋ, -d

collector
BR kə'lɛktə(r), -z
AM kə'lɛktər, -z

colleen
BR 'kɒliːn, kɒ'liːn, kə'liːn, -z
AM kə'lin, 'kɑlin, -z

college
BR 'kɒl|ɪdʒ, -ɪdʒɪz
AM 'kɑlɪdʒ, -ɪz

colleger
BR 'kɒlɪdʒə(r)
AM 'kɑlɪdʒər

collegia
BR kə'liːdʒɪə(*r*), kə'lɛgɪə(*r*)
AM kə'lɛgiə

collegial
BR kə'liːdʒɪəl
AM kə'lidʒ(i)əl

collegiality
BR kə,liːdʒɪ'alɪti
AM kə,lidgi'ælədi

collegian
BR kə'liːdʒɪən, -z
AM kə'lidʒən, -z

collegiate
BR kə'liːdʒɪət
AM kə'lidʒ(i)ət

collegiately
BR kə'liːdʒɪətli
AM kə'lidʒ(i)ətli

collegium
BR kə'liːdʒɪəm, kə'lɛgɪəm, -z
AM kə'lɛgiəm, -z

collenchyma
BR kə'lɛŋkɪmə(*r*)
AM kə'lɛŋkəmə

collet
BR 'kɒlɪt, -s
AM 'kɑlət, -s

Collette
BR kɒ'lɛt, kə'lɛt
AM kə'lɛt

Colley
BR 'kɒli
AM 'kɑli

collide
BR kə'lʌɪd, -z, -ɪŋ, -ɪd
AM kə'laɪd, -z, -ɪŋ, -ɪd

collider
BR kə'lʌɪdə(r), -z
AM kə'laɪdər, -z

collie
BR 'kɒl|i, -ɪz
AM 'kɑli, -z

collier
BR 'kɒlɪə(r), -z
AM 'kɑljər, -z

colliery
BR 'kɒljər|i, -ɪz
AM 'kɑljəri, -z

colligate
BR 'kɒlɪgeɪt, -s, -ɪŋ, -ɪd
AM 'kɑlə,geɪ|t, -ts, -dɪŋ, -dɪd

colligation
BR ,kɒlɪ'geɪʃn, -z
AM ,kɑlə'geɪʃən, -z

colligative
BR kə'lɪgətɪv
AM 'kɑlə,geɪdɪv

collimate
BR 'kɒlɪmeɪt, -s, -ɪŋ, -ɪd
AM 'kɑlə,meɪ|t, -ts, -dɪŋ, -dɪd

collimation
BR ,kɒlɪ'meɪʃn, -z
AM kɑlə'meɪʃən, -z

collimator
BR 'kɒlɪmeɪtə(r), -z
AM 'kɑlə,meɪdər, -z

collinear
BR kɒ'lɪnɪə(r), kə(ʊ)'lɪnɪə(r)
AM kə'lɪniər

collinearity
BR kɒ,lɪnɪ'arɪti, kə,lɪnɪ'arɪti
AM kə,lɪni'ɛrədi

collinearly
BR kɒ'lɪnɪəli, kə'lɪnɪəli
AM kə'lɪniərli

Collinge
BR 'kɒlɪn(d)ʒ
AM 'kɑlɪŋ, 'kɑləndʒ

Collingham
BR 'kɒlɪŋəm
AM 'kɑlɪŋ,(h)æm

Collingwood
BR 'kɒlɪŋwʊd
AM 'kɑlɪŋ,wʊd

collins
BR 'kɒlɪnz, -ɪz
AM 'kɑlənz, -əz

Collinson
BR 'kɒlɪns(ə)n
AM 'kɑlənsən

Collis
BR 'kɒlɪs
AM 'kɑləs

collision
BR kə'lɪʒn, -z
AM kə'lɪʒən, -z

collisional
BR kə'lɪʒn̩(ə)l, kə'lɪʒən(ə)l
AM kə'lɪʒənl, kə'lɪʒnəl

collocate[1]
noun
BR 'kɒləkət, -s
AM 'kɑləkət, -s

collocate[2]
verb
BR 'kɒləkeɪt, -s, -ɪŋ, -ɪd
AM 'kɑlə,keɪ|t, -ts, -dɪŋ, -dɪd

collocation
BR ,kɒlə'keɪʃn, -z
AM ,kɑlə'keɪʃən, -z

collocutor
BR kə(ʊ)'lɒkjʉtə(r), 'kɒləkjuːtə(r), -z
AM kə'lɑkjədər, -z

collodion
BR kə'ləʊdɪən
AM kə'loʊdiən

collodium
BR kə'ləʊdɪəm
AM kə'loʊdiəm

collogue
BR kɒ'ləʊg, kə'ləʊg, -z, -ɪŋ, -d
AM kə'loʊg, -z, -ɪŋ, -d

colloid
BR 'kɒlɔɪd, -z
AM 'kɑ,lɔɪd, -z

colloidal
BR kɒ'lɔɪdl, kə'lɔɪdl
AM kə'lɔɪdəl

collop
BR 'kɒləp, -s
AM 'kɑləp, -s

colloquia
BR kə'ləʊkwɪə(*r*)
AM kə'loʊkwiə

colloquial
BR kə'ləʊkwɪəl
AM kə'loʊkwiəl

colloquialism
BR kə'ləʊkwɪəlɪz(ə)m, -z
AM kə'loʊkwiə,lɪzəm, -z

colloquially
BR kə'ləʊkwɪəli
AM kə'loʊkwiəli

colloquium
BR kə'ləʊkwɪəm, -z
AM kə'loʊkwiəm, -z

colloquy
BR 'kɒləkw|i, -ɪz
AM 'kɑlə,kwi, -z

collotype
BR 'kɒlətʌɪp, -s
AM 'kɑləˌtaɪp, -s
collude
BR kə'l(j)uːd, -z, -ɪŋ, -ɨd
AM kə'lud, -z, -ɪŋ, -əd
colluder
BR kə'l(j)uːdə(r), -z
AM kə'ludər, -z
collusion
BR kə'l(j)uːʒn
AM kə'luʒən
collusive
BR kə'l(j)uːsɪv
AM kə'lusɪv
collusively
BR kə'l(j)uːsɨvli
AM kə'lusɨvli
collusiveness
BR kə'l(j)uːsɨvnɨs
AM kə'lusɨvnɨs
colluvia
BR kə'l(j)uːvɪə(r)
AM kə'luviə
colluvium
BR kə'l(j)uːvɪəm, -z
AM kə'luviəm, -z
colly
BR kɒli
AM 'kɑli
collyria
BR kə'lɪrɪə(r)
AM kə'lɪriə
collyrium
BR kə'lɪrɪəm
AM kə'lɪriəm
collywobbles
BR 'kɒlɪˌwɒblz
AM 'kɑlɪˌwɑblz
Colman
BR 'kəʊlmən, 'kɒlmən
AM 'koʊlmən
Colnbrook
BR 'kəʊ(l)nbrʊk
AM 'koʊ(l)nˌbrʊk
Colne
BR kəʊ(l)n
AM koʊ(l)n
colobus
BR 'kɒləbəs, -ɪz
AM 'kɑləbəs, -əz
colocynth
BR 'kɒləsɪnθ, -s
AM 'kɑləˌsɪnθ, -s
Cologne
BR kə'ləʊn
AM kə'loʊn
Colombia
BR kə'lʌmbɪə(r)
AM kə'ləmbiə
Colombian
BR kə'lʌmbɪən, -z
AM kə'ləmbiən, -z
Colombo
BR kə'lʌmbəʊ
AM kə'ləmboʊ
Colón
BR kɒ'lɒn, kə'lɒn
AM kə'loʊn
colon[1]
colonial settler
BR kɒ'lɒn, kə'lɒn, -z
AM kə'loʊn, -z
colon[2]
large intestine, punctuation mark
BR 'kəʊlən, 'kəʊlɒn, -z
AM 'koʊlən, -z
colonel
BR 'kəːnl, -z
AM 'kərnəl, -z
colonelcy
BR 'kəːnls|i, -ɪz
AM 'kərnlsi, -z
colonial
BR kə'ləʊnɪəl, -z
AM kə'loʊnjəl, kə'loʊniəl, -z
colonialism
BR kə'ləʊnɪəlɪz(ə)m
AM kə'loʊniəˌlɪzəm, kə'loʊnjəˌlɪzəm
colonialist
BR kə'ləʊnɪəlɪst, -s
AM kə'loʊniələst, kə'loʊnjələst, -s
colonially
BR kə'ləʊnɪəli
AM kə'loʊniəli, kə'loʊnjəli
colonic
BR kə'lɒnɪk
AM koʊ'lɑnɪk, kə'lɑnɪk
colonisation
BR ˌkɒlənʌɪ'zeɪʃn
AM ˌkɑlənə'zeɪʃən, ˌkɑləˌnaɪ'zeɪʃən
colonise
BR 'kɒlənʌɪz, -ɨz, -ɪŋ, -d
AM 'kɑləˌnaɪz, -ɨz, -ɪŋ, -d
coloniser
BR 'kɒlənʌɪzə(r), -z
AM 'kɑləˌnaɪzər, -z
colonist
BR 'kɒlənɪst, -s
AM 'kɑlənəst, -s
colonization
BR ˌkɒlənʌɪ'zeɪʃn
AM ˌkɑlənə'zeɪʃən, ˌkɑləˌnaɪ'zeɪʃən
colonize
BR 'kɒlənʌɪz, -ɨz, -ɪŋ, -d
AM 'kɑləˌnaɪz, -ɨz, -ɪŋ, -d
colonizer
BR 'kɒlənʌɪzə(r), -z
AM 'kɑləˌnaɪzər, -z
colonnade
BR ˌkɒlə'neɪd, -z, -ɨd
AM ˌkɑlə'neɪd, -z, -ɨd
colonoscopy
BR ˌkɒlə'nɒskəp|i, -ɪz
AM ˌkoʊlə'nɑskəpi, -z
Colonsay
BR 'kɒlənzeɪ, 'kɒlənseɪ
AM 'kɑlənzeɪ, 'kɑlənseɪ
colony
BR 'kɒlən|i, -ɪz
AM 'kɑləni, -z
colophon
BR 'kɒləfən, 'kɒləfɒn, -z
AM 'kɑləfən, 'kɑləˌfɑn, -z
colophony
BR kɒ'lɒfəni, kɒ'lɒfn̩i, kə'lɒfəni, kə'lɒfn̩i
AM kə'lɑfəni, 'kɑləˌfɑni
coloquintida
BR ˌkɒlə'kwɪntɨdə(r)
AM ˌkɑlə'kwɪn(t)ədə
color
BR 'kʌl|ə(r), -əz, -(ə)rɪŋ, -əd
AM 'kələr, -z, -ɪŋ, -d
colorable
BR 'kʌl(ə)rəbl
AM 'kələrəbəl
colorably
BR 'kʌl(ə)rəbli
AM 'kələrəbli
Coloradan
BR ˌkɒlə'rɑːd(ə)n, -z
AM ˌkɑlə'rɑd(ə)n, -z
Colorado
BR ˌkɒlə'rɑːdəʊ
AM ˌkɑlə'rɑdoʊ
colorant
BR 'kʌl(ə)rənt, 'kʌl(ə)rn̩t, -s
AM 'kələrənt, -s
coloration
BR ˌkʌlə'reɪʃn
AM ˌkələ'reɪʃən
coloratura
BR ˌkɒl(ə)rə't(j)ʊərə(r), ˌkɒl(ə)rə'tʃʊərə(r), -z
AM ˌkələrə'tʊrə, -z
colorblind
BR 'kʌləblʌɪnd
AM 'kələrˌblaɪnd
colorblindness
BR 'kʌləˌblʌɪn(d)nɨs
AM 'kələrˌblaɪn(d)nɨs
colorectal
BR ˌkəʊləʊ'rɛktl
AM ˌkoʊloʊ'rɛktl
Colored
BR 'kʌləd, -z
AM 'kələrd, -z
colorfast
BR 'kʌləfɑːst, 'kʌləfast
AM 'kələrˌfæst
colorfastness
BR 'kʌləˌfɑːs(t)nəs, 'kʌləˌfas(t)nəs
AM 'kələrˌfæs(t)nəs
colorful
BR 'kʌləf(ʊ)l
AM 'kələrfəl
colorfully
BR 'kʌləfʊli, 'kʌləfl̩i
AM 'kələrf(ə)li
colorfulness
BR 'kʌləf(ʊ)lnəs
AM 'kələrfəlnəs
colorific
BR ˌkʌlə'rɪfɪk
AM ˌkələ'rɪfɪk
colorimeter
BR ˌkʌlə'rɪmɨtə(r), -z
AM ˌkələ'rɪmədər, -z
colorimetric
BR ˌkʌlərə'mɛtrɪk
AM ˌkələrə'mɛtrɪk
colorimetry
BR ˌkʌlə'rɪmɨtri
AM ˌkələ'rɪmətri
colorist
BR 'kʌl(ə)rɪst, -s
AM 'kələrəst, -s
colorize
BR 'kʌlərʌɪz, -ɨz, -ɪŋ, -d
AM 'kələˌraɪz, -ɨz, -ɪŋ, -d
colorless
BR 'kʌlələs
AM 'kələrləs
colorlessly
BR 'kʌlələsli
AM 'kələrləsli
Coloroll®
BR 'kʌlərəʊl
AM 'kələroʊl
colorway
BR 'kʌləweɪ, -z
AM 'kələrˌweɪ, -z
colory
BR 'kʌl(ə)ri
AM 'kəl(ə)ri
colossal
BR kə'lɒsl
AM kə'lɑsəl
colossally
BR kə'lɒsl̩i
AM kə'lɑsəli
colosseum
BR ˌkɒlə'siːəm, -z
AM ˌkɑlə'siəm, -z
colossi
BR kə'lɒsʌɪ
AM kə'lɑˌsaɪ
Colossians
BR kə'lɒʃnz, kə'lɒsɪənz
AM kə'lɑsiənz
colossus
BR kə'lɒsəs
AM kə'lɑsəs
colostomy
BR kə'lɒstəm|i, -ɪz
AM kə'lɑstəmi, -z
colostrum
BR kə'lɒstrəm
AM kə'lɑstrəm

colotomy
BR kə'lɒtəm|i, -ɪz
AM kə'lɑdəmi, -z

colour
BR 'kʌl|ə(r), -əz, -(ə)rɪŋ, -əd
AM 'kələr, -z, -ɪŋ, -d

colourable
BR 'kʌl(ə)rəbl
AM 'kələrəbəl

colourably
BR 'kʌl(ə)rəbli
AM 'kələrəbli

colourant
BR 'kʌl(ə)rənt, 'kʌl(ə)rn t, -s
AM 'kələrənt, -s

colouration
BR ˌkʌlə'reɪʃn
AM ˌkələ'reɪʃən

colourblind
BR 'kʌləblʌɪnd
AM 'kələrˌblaɪn(d)

colourblindness
BR 'kʌləˌblʌɪn(d)nɪs
AM 'kələrˌblaɪn(d)nɪs

Coloured
BR 'kʌləd, -z
AM 'kələrd, -z

colourfast
BR 'kʌləfɑːst, 'kʌləfast
AM 'kələrˌfæst

colourfastness
BR 'kʌləfɑːs(t)nəs, 'kʌləfas(t)nəs
AM 'kələrˌfæs(t)nəs

colourful
BR 'kʌləf(ʊ)l
AM 'kələrfəl

colourfully
BR 'kʌləfʊli, 'kʌləfl̩i
AM 'kələrfəli

colourfulness
BR 'kʌləf(ʊ)lnəs
AM 'kələrfəlnəs

colourise
BR 'kʌlərʌɪz, -ɪz, -ɪŋ, -d
AM 'kələˌraɪz, -ɪz, -ɪŋ, -d

colourist
BR 'kʌl(ə)rɪst, -s
AM 'kələrəst, -s

colourless
BR 'kʌlələs
AM 'kələrləs

colourlessly
BR 'kʌlələsli
AM 'kələrləsli

colourwash
BR 'kʌləwɒʃ, -ɪz, -ɪŋ, -t
AM 'kələrˌwɔʃ, 'kələrˌwɑʃ, -əz, -ɪŋ, -t

colourway
BR 'kʌləweɪ, -z
AM 'kələrˌweɪ, -z

coloury
BR 'kʌl(ə)ri
AM 'kəl(ə)ri

colpitis
BR kɒl'pʌɪtɪs
AM kɑl'paɪdɪs

colporteur
BR 'kɒlˌpɔːtə(r), -z
AM 'kɑlˌpɔrdər, 'kɔlˌpɔrdər, -z

colposcope
BR 'kɒlpəskəʊp, -s
AM 'kɑlpəˌskoʊp, -s

colposcopy
BR kɒl'pɒskəp|i, -ɪz
AM kɑl'pɑskəpi, -z

colpotomy
BR kɒl'pɒtəm|i, -ɪz
AM kɑl'pɑdəmi, -z

Colquhoun
BR kə'huːn
AM kə'hun

Colson
BR 'kəʊlsn
AM 'koʊlsən

Colston
BR 'kəʊlst(ə)n
AM 'koʊlstən

colt
BR kəʊlt, -s
AM koʊlt, -s

colter
BR 'kəʊltə(r), -z
AM 'koʊltər, -z

colthood
BR 'kəʊlthʊd, -z
AM 'koʊltˌ(h)ʊd, -z

coltish
BR 'kəʊltɪʃ
AM 'koʊltɪʃ

coltishly
BR 'kəʊltɪʃli
AM 'koʊltɪʃli

coltishness
BR 'kəʊltɪʃnɪs
AM 'koʊltɪʃnɪs

Coltrane
BR kɒl'treɪn
AM 'koʊlˌtreɪn

coltsfoot
BR 'kəʊltsfʊt
AM 'koʊltsˌfʊt

colubrine
BR 'kɒljʊbrʌɪn
AM 'kɑl(j)əˌbraɪn, 'kɑl(j)əbrən

Colum
BR 'kɒləm
AM 'kɑləm

Columba
BR kə'lʌmbə(*r*)
AM kə'ləmbə

columbaria
BR ˌkɒləm'bɛːrɪə(*r*)
AM ˌkɑləm'bɛriə

columbarium
BR ˌkɒləm'bɛːrɪəm
AM ˌkɑləm'bɛriəm

Columbia
BR kə'lʌmbɪə(*r*)
AM kə'ləmbiə

Columbian
BR kə'lʌmbɪən, -z
AM kə'ləmbiən, -z

columbine
BR 'kɒləmbʌɪn, -z
AM 'kɑləmˌbaɪn, -z

columbite
BR kə'lʌmbʌɪt, 'kɒləmbʌɪt
AM 'kɑləmˌbaɪt

columbium
BR kə'lʌmbɪəm
AM kə'ləmbiəm

Columbus
BR kə'lʌmbəs
AM kə'ləmbəs

column
BR 'kɒləm, -z, -d
AM 'kɑləm, -z, -d

columnar
BR kə'lʌmnə(r), 'kɒləmnə(r)
AM kə'ləmnər

columnated
BR 'kɒləmneɪtɪd
AM 'kɑləmˌneɪdɪd

columnist
BR 'kɒləm(n)ɪst, -s
AM 'kɑləm(n)əst, -s

colure
BR kə'l(j)ʊə(r), 'kəʊl(j)ʊə(r), -z
AM kə'lʊ(ə)r, -z

Colville
BR 'kɒlvɪl
AM 'koʊlˌvɪl

Colvin
BR 'kɒlvɪn
AM 'kɔlvən, 'kɑlvən

Colwyn
BR 'kɒlwɪn
AM 'kɔlwən, 'kɑlwən

Colyer
BR 'kɒljə(r)
AM 'kɑljər, 'kɑliər

Colyton
BR 'kɒlɪt(ə)n
AM 'kɑlətn

colza
BR 'kɒlzə(*r*)
AM 'kɑlzə, 'koʊlzə

coma
BR 'kəʊmə(*r*), -z
AM 'koʊmə, -z

Comanche
BR kə'man(t)ʃ|i, -ɪz
AM kə'mæn(t)ʃi, -z

comatose
BR 'kəʊmətəʊs, 'kəʊmətəʊz
AM 'koʊməˌtoʊs, 'kɑməˌtoʊz

comatosely
BR 'kəʊmətəʊsli, 'kəʊmətəʊzli
AM 'koʊməˌtoʊsli, 'kɑməˌtoʊsli

comb
BR kəʊm, -z, -ɪŋ, -d
AM koʊm, -z, -ɪŋ, -d

combat[1]
noun
BR 'kɒmbat, 'kʌmbat, -s
AM 'kɑmˌbæt, -s

combat[2]
verb
BR 'kɒmbat, 'kʌmbat, kəm'bat, -s, -ɪŋ, -ɪd
AM kəm'bæ|t, 'kɑmˌbæ|t, -ts, -dɪŋ, -dəd

combatant
BR 'kɒmbət(ə)nt, 'kʌmbət(ə)nt, kəm'bat(ə)nt, -s
AM kəm'bætnt, kəm'bædənt, -s

combative
BR 'kɒmbətɪv, 'kʌmbətɪv, kəm'batɪv
AM kəm'bædɪv

combatively
BR 'kɒmbətɪvli, 'kʌmbətɪvli, kəm'batɪvli
AM kəm'bædɪvli

combativeness
BR 'kɒmbətɪvnɪs, 'kʌmbətɪvnɪs, kəm'batɪvnɪs
AM kəm'bædɪvnɪs

combe
BR kuːm, -z
AM kum, koʊm, -z

comber
BR 'kəʊmə(r), -z
AM 'koʊmər, -z

combinable
BR kəm'bʌɪnəbl
AM 'kɑmbənəbəl

combination
BR ˌkɒmbɪ'neɪʃn, -z
AM ˌkɑmbə'neɪʃən, -z

combinational
BR ˌkɒmbɪ'neɪʃn̩(ə)l, ˌkɒmbɪ'neɪʃən(ə)l
AM ˌkɑmbə'neɪʃənl, ˌkɑmbə'neɪʃnəl

combinative
BR 'kɒmbɪnətɪv, 'kɒmbn̩ətɪv
AM 'kɑmbəˌneɪdɪv, kəm'baɪnədɪv, 'kɑmbənədɪv

combinatorial
BR ˌkɒmbɪnə'tɔːrɪəl, ˌkɒmbn̩ə'tɔːrɪəl
AM ˌkəmbənə'tɔriəl

combinatory
BR 'kɒmbɪnət(ə)ri, 'kɒmbn̩ət(ə)ri
AM 'kɑmbənəˌtɔri

combine[1]
noun
BR 'kɒmbʌɪn, -z
AM 'kɑmˌbaɪn, -z

combine[2]
verb
BR kəm'bʌɪn, -z, -ɪŋ, -d
AM kəm'baɪn, -z, -ɪŋ, -d

combings
BR 'kəʊmɪŋz
AM 'koʊmɪŋz

combo
BR 'kɒmbəʊ, -z
AM 'kɑmboʊ, -z

Combs
BR ku:mz
AM kumz

combust
BR kəm'bʌst, -s, -ɪŋ, -ɪd
AM kəm'bəst, -s, -ɪn, -əd

combustibility
BR kəmˌbʌstɪ'bɪlɪti
AM kəmˌbəstə'bɪlɨdi

combustible
BR kəm'bʌstɪbl, -z
AM kəm'bəstəbəl, -z

combustibly
BR kəm'bʌstɪbli
AM kəm'bəstəbli

combustion
BR kəm'bʌstʃ(ə)n
AM kəm'bəstʃən

combustive
BR kəm'bʌstɪv
AM kə'bəstɪv

come
BR kʌm, -z, -ɪŋ
AM kəm, -z, -ɪŋ

come-all-ye
BR ˌkʌmɔ:l'ji:, -z
AM ˌkəmˌɔl'ji,
ˌkəmˌɑl'ji, -z

come-at-able
BR kʌm'atəbl
AM ˌkəm'ædəbəl

comeback
BR 'kʌmbak, -s
AM 'kəmˌbæk, -s

Comecon
BR 'kɒmɪkɒn
AM 'kɑməˌkɑn

comedian
BR kə'mi:dɪən, -z
AM kə'midiən, -z

comedic
BR kə'mi:dɪk
AM kə'midɪk

comedically
BR kə'mi:dɪkli
AM kə'midɪk(ə)li

comedienne
BR kəˌmi:dɪ'ɛn, -z
AM kə'midiˌɛn,
kəˌmidi'ɛn, -z

comedist
BR 'kɒmɪdɪst, -s
AM 'kɑmədəst, -s

comedo
BR 'kɒmɪdəʊ,
kə'mi:dəʊ, -z
AM 'kɑməˌdoʊ, -z

comedown
BR 'kʌmdaʊn, -z
AM 'kəmˌdaʊn, -z

comedy
BR 'kɒmɪd|i, -ɪz
AM 'kɑmədi, -z

comeliness
BR 'kʌmlɪnɪs
AM 'kəmlinɪs

comely
BR 'kʌml|i, -ɪə(r), -ɪɪst
AM 'kəmli, -ər, -ɪst

Comenius
BR kə'meɪnɪəs,
kə'mi:nɪəs,
kə'mɛnɪəs
AM kə'meɪniəs

comer
BR 'kʌmə(r), -z
AM 'kəmər, -z

comestible
BR kə'mɛstɪbl, -z
AM kə'mɛstəbəl, -z

comet
BR 'kɒmɪt, -s
AM 'kɑmət, -s

cometary
BR 'kɒmɪt(ə)ri
AM 'kɑməˌtɛri

comeuppance
BR ˌkʌm'ʌp(ə)ns, -ɪz
AM kə'məpəns, -əz

comfily
BR 'kʌmfɪli
AM 'kəmfəli

comfiness
BR 'kʌmfɪnɪs
AM 'kəmfinɪs

comfit
BR 'kʌmfɪt, 'kɒmfɪt, -s
AM 'kəmfət, 'kɑmfət, -s

comfort
BR 'kʌmfət, -s, -ɪŋ, -ɪd
AM 'kəmfər|t, -ts, -dɪŋ,
-dəd

comfortable
BR 'kʌmf(ə)təbl
AM 'kəmfərdəbəl,
'kəmftərbəl

comfortableness
BR 'kʌmf(ə)təblnəs
AM 'kəmfərdəbəlnəs,
'kəmftərbəlnəs

comfortably
BR 'kʌmf(ə)təbli
AM 'kəmfərdəbli,
'kəmftərbli

comforter
BR 'kʌmfətə(r), -z
AM 'kəmfərdər, -z

comfortingly
BR 'kʌmfətɪŋli
AM 'kəmfərdɪŋli

comfortless
BR 'kʌmfətləs
AM 'kəmfərtləs

comfrey
BR 'kʌmfri
AM 'kəmfri

comfy
BR 'kʌmfi
AM 'kəmfi

comic
BR 'kɒmɪk, -s
AM 'kɑmɪk, -s

comical
BR 'kɒmɪkl
AM 'kɑməkl

comicality
BR ˌkɒmɪ'kalɪti
AM ˌkɑmə'kælədi

comically
BR 'kɒmɪkli
AM 'kɑmək(ə)li

Cominform
BR 'kɒmɪnfɔ:m
AM 'kɑmənˌfɔ(ə)rm

coming
BR 'kʌmɪŋ, -z
AM 'kəmɪŋ, -z

Comino
BR kə'mi:nəʊ
AM kə'minoʊ

Comintern
BR 'kɒmɪntə:n
AM 'kɑmənˌtərn
RUS kəmʲin'tern

comitadji
BR ˌkɒmɪ'tadʒ|i, -ɪz
AM ˌkɑmə'tɑdʒi, -z

comity
BR 'kɒmɪt|i, -ɪz
AM 'kɑmədi, -z

comma
BR 'kɒmə(*r*), -z
AM 'kɑmə, -z

command
BR kə'mɑ:nd,
kə'mand, -z, -ɪŋ, -ɪd
AM kə'mænd, -z, -ɪŋ,
-əd

commandant
BR 'kɒməndant,
'kɒməndənt,
'kɒməndɑ:nt,
ˌkɒmən'dant,
ˌkɒmən'dɑ:nt, -s
AM 'kɑmənˌdænt,
ˈkɑmənˈdɑnt, -s

commandeer
BR ˌkɒmən'dɪə(r), -z,
-ɪŋ, -d
AM ˌkɑmən'dɪ(ə)r, -z,
-ɪŋ, -d

commander
BR kə'mɑ:ndə(r),
kə'mandə(r), -z
AM kə'mændər, -z

commandership
BR kə'mɑ:ndəʃɪp,
kə'mandəʃɪp, -s
AM kə'mændərˌʃɪp, -s

commandingly
BR kə'mɑ:ndɪŋli,
kə'mandɪŋli
AM kə'mændɪŋli

commandment
BR kə'mɑ:n(d)m(ə)nt,
kə'man(d)m(ə)nt, -s
AM kə'mæn(d)mənt, -s

commando
BR kə'mɑ:ndəʊ,
kə'mandəʊ, -z
AM kə'mænˌdoʊ, -z

comme ci, comme ça
BR kɒm ˌsi: kɒm
'sɑ:(*r*), + + +'sa(*r*)
AM kəm 'si kəm'sɑ

commedia dell'arte
BR kɒ'mɛdɪə dɛl'ɑ:teɪ
AM kə'meɪdiə də'lɑrdi

comme il faut
BR ˌkɒm i:l 'fəʊ
AM ˌkəm il 'foʊ

commemorate
BR kə'mɛməreɪt, -s,
-ɪŋ, -ɪd
AM kə'mɛməˌreɪ|t, -ts,
-dɪŋ, -dɪd

commemoration
BR kəˌmɛmə'reɪʃn, -z
AM kəˌmɛmə'reɪʃən, -z

commemorative
BR kə'mɛm(ə)rətɪv
AM kə'mɛm(ə)rədɪv,
kə'mɛməˌreɪdɪv

commemoratively
BR kə'mɛm(ə)rətɪvli
AM kə'mɛm(ə)rədɪvli,
kə'mɛməˌreɪdɪvli

commemorator
BR kə'mɛməreɪtə(r),
-z
AM kə'mɛməˌreɪdər, -z

commence
BR kə'mɛns, -ɪz, -ɪŋ, -t
AM kə'mɛns, -əz, -ɪŋ, -t

commencement
BR kə'mɛnsm(ə)nt, -s
AM kə'mɛnsmənt, -s

commend
BR kə'mɛnd, -z, -ɪŋ, -ɪd
AM kə'mɛnd, -z, -ɪŋ, -əd

commendable
BR kə'mɛndəbl
AM kə'mɛndəbəl

commendably
BR kə'mɛndəbli
AM kə'mɛndəbli

commendation
BR ˌkɒm(ə)n'deɪʃn, -z
AM ˌkɑmən'deɪʃən, -z

commendatory
BR ˌkɒm(ə)n'deɪt(ə)ri
AM kə'mɛndəˌtɔri

commensal
BR kə'mɛnsl

AM kə'mɛnsəl
commensalism
BR kə'mɛnsl̩ɪz(ə)m
AM kə'mɛnsə,lɪzəm
commensality
BR ,kɒmɛn'salɪt|i, -ɪz
AM kɑ,mɛn'sælədi, -z
commensally
BR kə'mɛnsl̩i,
kə'mɛnsəli
AM kə'mɛnsəli
commensurability
BR kə,mɛnʃ(ə)rə'bɪlɪti,
kə,mɛns(ə)rə'bɪlɪti,
kə,mɛnsjʊrə'bɪlɪti
AM kə,mɛns(ə)rə'bɪlɨdi,
kə,mɛn(t)ʃ(ə)rə'bɪlɨdi
commensurable
BR kə'mɛnʃ(ə)rəbl,
kə'mɛns(ə)rəbl,
kə'mɛnsjʊrəbl
AM kə'mɛns(ə)rəbəl,
kə'mɛn(t)ʃ(ə)rəbəl
commensurableness
BR kə'mɛnʃ(ə)rəblnəs,
kə'mɛns(ə)rəblnəs,
kə'mɛnsjʊrəblnəs
AM kə'mɛns(ə)rəbəlnəs,
kə'mɛn(t)ʃ(ə)rəbəlnəs
commensurably
BR kə'mɛnʃ(ə)rəbli,
kə'mɛns(ə)rəbli,
kə'mɛnsjʊrəbli
AM kə'mɛns(ə)rəbli,
kə'mɛn(t)ʃ(ə)rəbli
commensurate
BR kə'mɛnʃ(ə)rət,
kə'mɛns(ə)rət,
kə'mɛnsjʊrət
AM kə'mɛns(ə)rət,
kə'mɛn(t)ʃ(ə)rət
commensurately
BR kə'mɛnʃ(ə)rətli,
kə'mɛns(ə)rətli,
kə'mɛnsjʊrətli
AM kə'mɛns(ə)rətli,
kə'mɛn(t)ʃ(ə)rətli
commensurateness
BR kə'mɛnʃ(ə)rətnəs,
kə'mɛns(ə)rətnəs,
kə'mɛnsjʊrətnəs
AM kə'mɛns(ə)rətnəs,
kə'mɛn(t)ʃ(ə)rətnəs
comment
BR 'kɒmɛnt, -s, -ɪŋ, -ɨd
AM 'kɑ,mɛnt, -s, -ɪŋ, -əd
commentary
BR 'kɒm(ə)nt(ə)r|i, -ɪz
AM 'kɑmən,tɛri, -z
commentate
BR 'kɒm(ə)nteɪt, -s, -ɪŋ,
-ɨd
AM 'kɑmən,teɪ|t, -ts,
-dɪŋ, -dɨd
commentator
BR 'kɒm(ə)nteɪtə(r), -z
AM 'kɑmən,teɪdər, -z
commenter
BR 'kɒmɛntə(r), -z
AM 'kɑ,mɛn(t)ər, -z
commerce
BR 'kɒmə:s
AM 'kɑmərs
commercial
BR kə'mə:ʃl, -z
AM kə'mərʃəl, -z
commercialisation
BR kə,mə:ʃəlʌɪ'zeɪʃn,
kə,mə:ʃl̩ʌɪ'zeɪʃn
AM kə,mərʃələ'zeɪʃən,
kə,mərʃə,laɪ'zeɪʃən
commercialise
BR kə'mə:ʃəlʌɪz,
kə'mə:ʃl̩ʌɪz, -ɨz, -ɪŋ, -d
AM kə'mərʃə,laɪz, -ɨz,
-ɪŋ, -d
commercialism
BR kə'mə:ʃəlɪz(ə)m,
kə'mə:ʃl̩ɪz(ə)m
AM kə'mərʃə,lɪzəm
commerciality
BR kə,mə:ʃɪ'alɪti
AM kə,mərʃi'ælədi
commercialization
BR kə,mə:ʃəlʌɪ'zeɪʃn,
kə,mə:ʃl̩ʌɪ'zeɪʃn
AM kə,mərʃələ'zeɪʃən,
kə,mərʃə,laɪ'zeɪʃən
commercialize
BR kə'mə:ʃəlʌɪz,
kə'mə:ʃl̩ʌɪz, -ɨz, -ɪŋ, -d
AM kə'mərʃə,laɪz, -ɨz,
-ɪŋ, -d
commercially
BR kə'mə:ʃəli,
kə'mə:ʃl̩i
AM kə'mərʃəli
commère
BR 'kɒmɛ:(r), -z
AM 'kɑm,mɛ(ə)r, -z
commie
BR 'kɒm|i, -ɪz
AM 'kɑmi, -z
commination
BR ,kɒmɪ'neɪʃn, -z
AM ,kɑmə'neɪʃən, -z
comminatory
BR 'kɒmɨnət(ə)ri
AM 'kɑmənə,tɔri,
kə'mɪnə,tɔri
commingle
BR kɒ'mɪŋg|l,
kə'mɪŋg|l, -lz,
-l̩ɪŋ\-lɪŋ, -ld
AM kə'mɪŋg|əl,
kɑ'mɪŋg|əl, -əlz,
-(ə)lɪŋ, -əld
comminute
BR 'kɒmɨnju:t, -s, -ɪŋ,
-ɨd
AM 'kɑmən(j)u|t, -ts,
-dɪŋ, -dəd
comminution
BR ,kɒmɪ'nju:ʃn
AM ,kɑmə'n(j)uʃən
commis
BR 'kɒmɪs, 'kɒmi
AM kə'mi
FR kɔmi
commiserate
BR kə'mɪzəreɪt, -s, -ɪŋ,
-ɨd
AM kə'mɪzə,reɪ|t, -ts,
-dɪŋ, -dɨd
commiseration
BR kə,mɪzə'reɪʃn
AM kə,mɪzə'reɪʃən
commiserative
BR kə'mɪz(ə)rətɪv,
kə'mɪzəreɪtɪv
AM kə'mɪzərədɪv,
kə'mɪzə,reɪdɪv
commiserator
BR kə'mɪzəreɪtə(r), -z
AM kə'mɪzə,reɪdər, -z
commissar
BR ,kɒmɪ'sɑ:(r),
'kɒmɪsɑ:(r), -z
AM 'kɑməsɑr, -z
commissarial
BR ,kɒmɪ'sɛ:rɪəl
AM ,kɑmə'sɛriəl
commissariat
BR ,kɒmɪ'sɛ:rɪət, -s
AM ,kɑmə'sɛriət, -s
commissary
BR 'kɒmɪs(ə)r|i, -ɪz
AM 'kɑmə,sɛri, -z
commissaryship
BR 'kɒmɪs(ə)rɪʃɪp
AM 'kɑmə,sɛri,ʃɪp
commission
BR kə'mɪʃ|n, -nz,
-n̩ɪŋ\-nɪŋ, -nd
AM kə'mɪʃən, -z, -ɪŋ, -d
commissionaire
BR kə,mɪʃə'nɛ:(r), -z
AM kə,mɪʃə'nɛ(ə)r, -z
commissional
BR kə'mɪʃn̩(ə)l,
kə'mɪʃən(ə)l
AM kə'mɪʃ(ə)nəl
commissionary
BR kə'mɪʃn̩(ə)ri
AM kə'mɪʃə,nɛri
commissioner
BR kə'mɪʃn̩ə(r),
kə'mɪʃ(ə)nə(r), -z
AM kə'mɪʃənər, -z
commissural
BR ,kɒmɪ'sjʊərəl,
,kɒmɪ'sjʊərl̩,
,kɒmɪ'sjɔ:rəl,
,kɒmɪ'sjɔ:rl̩,
,kɒmɪ'ʃʊərəl,
,kɒmɪ'ʃʊərl̩,
,kɒmɪ'ʃɔ:rəl,
,kɒmɪ'ʃɔ:rl̩
AM kə'mɪʃʊrəl,
,kɑmə'ʃʊrəl
commissure
BR 'kɒmɪsjʊə(r),
'kɒmɪʃʊə(r), -z
AM 'kɑmə,ʃʊ(ə)r, -z
commit
BR kə'mɪt, -s, -ɪŋ, -ɨd
AM kə'mɪ|t, -ts, -dɪŋ,
-dɨd
commitment
BR kə'mɪtm(ə)nt, -s
AM kə'mɪtmənt, -s
committable
BR kə'mɪtəbl
AM kə'mɪdəbəl
committal
BR kə'mɪtl, -z
AM kə'mɪdl, -z
committee
BR kə'mɪt|i:, -ɪz
AM kə'mɪdi, -z
committeeman
BR kə'mɪtɪman
AM kə'mɪdimən
committeemen
BR kə'mɪtɪmɛn
AM kə'mɪdimən
committeewoman
BR kə'mɪtɪ,wʊmən
AM kə'mɪdi,wʊmən
committeewomen
BR kə'mɪtɪ,wɪmɪn
AM kə'mɪdi,wɪmɨn
committer
BR kə'mɪtə(r), -z
AM kə'mɪdər, -z
commix
BR kɒ'mɪks, kə'mɪks,
-ɨz, -ɪŋ, -t
AM kə'mɪks, -ɨz, -ɪŋ, -t
commixture
BR kə'mɪkstʃə(r)
AM kə'mɪk(st)ʃər
commo
BR 'kɒməʊ, -z
AM 'kɑmoʊ, -z
commode
BR kə'məʊd, -z
AM kə'moʊd, -z
commodification
BR kə,mɒdɪfɪ'keɪʃn
AM kə,mɑdəfə'keɪʃən
commodify
BR kə'mɒdɪfʌɪ, -z, -ɪŋ,
-d
AM kə'mɑdə,faɪ, -z, -ɪŋ,
-d
commodious
BR kə'məʊdɪəs
AM kə'moʊdiəs
commodiously
BR kə'məʊdɪəsli
AM kə'moʊdiəsli
commodiousness
BR kə'məʊdɪəsnəs
AM kə'moʊdiəsnəs
commodity
BR kə'mɒdɪt|i, -ɪz

AM kə'mɑdədi, -z
commodore
BR 'kɒmədɔː(r), -z
AM 'kɑməˌdɔ(ə)r, -z
common
BR 'kɒmən, -z, -ə(r), -ɨst
AM 'kɑmən, -z, -ər, -əst
commonable
BR 'kɒmənəbl
AM 'kɑmənəbəl
commonage
BR 'kɒmənɪdʒ
AM 'kɑmənɪdʒ
commonality
BR ˌkɒmə'nalɨti
AM 'kɑmənˌælədi
commonalty
BR 'kɒmənlti
AM 'kɑmənəlti
commoner
BR 'kɒmənə(r), -z
AM 'kɑmənər, -z
commonhold
BR 'kɒmənhəʊld
AM 'kɑmənˌ(h)oʊld
commonholder
BR 'kɒmənˌhəʊldə(r)
AM 'kɑmənˌ(h)oʊldər
commonly
BR 'kɒmənli
AM 'kɑmənli
commonness
BR 'kɒmənnəs
AM 'kɑmə(n)nəs
commonplace
BR 'kɒmənpleɪs
AM 'kɑmənˌpleɪs
commonplaceness
BR 'kɒmənpleɪsnɨs
AM 'kɑmənˌpleɪsnɨs
commonroom
BR 'kɒmənruːm, 'kɒmənrʊm, -z
AM 'kɑmənˌrum, 'kɑmənˌrʊm, -z
commons
BR 'kɒmənz
AM 'kɑmənz
commonsense
BR ˌkɒmən'sɛns
AM ˌkɑmən'sɛns
commonsensical
BR ˌkɒmən'sɛnsɨkl
AM ˌkɑmən'sɛnsəkəl
commonwealth
BR 'kɒmənwɛlθ, -s
AM 'kɑmənˌwɛlθ, -s
commotion
BR kə'məʊʃn, -z
AM kə'moʊʃən, -z
commotional
BR kə'məʊʃn̩(ə)l, kə'məʊʃən(ə)l
AM kə'moʊʃ(ə)nəl
comms
BR kɒmz
AM kɑmz
communal
BR 'kɒmjʊnl, kə'mjuːnl
AM kə'mjunəl
communalisation
BR ˌkɒmjʊnəlʌɪ'zeɪʃn, ˌkɒmjʊnl̩ʌɪ'zeɪʃn, kəˌmjuːnəlʌɪ'zeɪʃn, kəˌmjuːnl̩ʌɪ'zeɪʃn
AM kəˌmjunələ'zeɪʃən, kəˌmjunəˌlaɪ'zeɪʃən
communalise
BR 'kɒmjʊnəlʌɪz, 'kɒmjʊnl̩ʌɪz, kə'mjuːnəlʌɪz, kə'mjuːnl̩ʌɪz, -ɨz, -ɪŋ, -d
AM kə'mjunlˌaɪz, -ɨz, -ɪŋ, -d
communalism
BR 'kɒmjʊnəlɪz(ə)m, 'kɒmjʊnl̩ɪz(ə)m, kə'mjuːnəlɪz(ə)m, kə'mjuːnl̩ɪz(ə)m
AM kə'mjunlˌɪzəm
communalist
BR 'kɒmjʊnəlɪst, 'kɒmjʊnl̩ɪst, kə'mjuːnəlɪst, kə'mjuːnl̩ɪst, -s
AM kə'mjunl̩əst, -s
communalistic
BR ˌkɒmjʊnə'lɪstɪk, ˌkɒmjʊnl'ɪstɪk, kəˌmjuːnə'lɪstɪk, kəˌmjuːnl'ɪstɪk
AM kəˌmjunə'lɪstɪk
communalistically
BR ˌkɒmjʊnə'lɪstɨkli, ˌkɒmjʊnl'ɪstɨkli, kəˌmjuːnə'lɪstɨkli, kəˌmjuːnl̩'ɪstɨkli
AM kəˌmjunə'lɪstɪk(ə)li
communality
BR ˌkɒmjʊ'nalɨti
AM ˌkɑmjə'nælədi
communalization
BR ˌkɒmjʊnəlʌɪ'zeɪʃn, ˌkɒmjʊnl̩ʌɪ'zeɪʃn, kəˌmjuːnəlʌɪ'zeɪʃn, kəˌmjuːnl̩ʌɪ'zeɪʃn
AM kəˌmjunələ'zeɪʃən, kəˌmjunəˌlaɪ'zeɪʃən
communalize
BR 'kɒmjʊnəlʌɪz, 'kɒmjʊnl̩ʌɪz, kə'mjuːnəlʌɪz, kə'mjuːnl̩ʌɪz, -ɨz, -ɪŋ, -d
AM kə'mjunlˌaɪz, -ɨz, -ɪŋ, -d
communally
BR 'kɒmjʊnl̩i, 'kɒmjʊnəli, kə'mjuːnl̩i, kə'mjuːnəli
AM kə'mjunəli
communard
BR 'kɒmjʊnɑːd, -z
AM 'kɑmjəˌnɑrd, -z
commune[1]
noun
BR 'kɒmjuːn, -z
AM 'kɑˌmjun, -z
commune[2]
verb
BR kə'mjuːn, -z, -ɪŋ, -d
AM kə'mjun, -z, -ɪŋ, -d
communicability
BR kəˌmjuːnɨkə'bɪlɨti
AM kəˌmjunəkə'bɪlɨdi
communicable
BR kə'mjuːnɨkəbl
AM kə'mjunəkəbəl
communicably
BR kə'mjuːnɨkəbli
AM kə'mjunəkəbli
communicant
BR kə'mjuːnɨk(ə)nt, -s
AM kə'mjunəkənt, -s
communicate
BR kə'mjuːnɨkeɪt, -s, -ɪŋ, -ɨd
AM kə'mjunəˌkeɪ|t, -ts, -dɪŋ, -dɨd
communication
BR kəˌmjuːnɨ'keɪʃn, -z
AM kəˌmjunə'keɪʃən, -z
communicational
BR kəˌmjuːnɨ'keɪʃn̩(ə)l, kəˌmjuːnɨ'keɪʃən(ə)l
AM kəˌmjunə'keɪʃ(ə)nəl
communicative
BR kə'mjuːnɨkətɪv
AM kə'mjunəˌkeɪdɪv, kə'mjunəkədɪv
communicatively
BR kə'mjuːnɨkətɨvli
AM kə'mjunəˌkeɪdɨvli, kə'mjunəkədɨvli
communicativeness
BR kə'mjuːnɨkətɨvnɨs
AM kə'mjunəˌkeɪdɨvnɨs, kə'mjunəkədɨvnɨs
communicator
BR kə'mjuːnɨkeɪtə(r), -z
AM kə'mjunəˌkeɪdər, -z
communicatory
BR kə'mjuːnɨkət(ə)ri, kə'mjuːnɨkeɪt(ə)ri
AM kə'mjunəkəˌtɔri
communion
BR kə'mjuːnɪən, -z
AM kə'mjunjən, -z
communiqué
BR kə'mjuːnɨkeɪ, -z
AM kəˌmjunə'keɪ, kə'mjunəˌkeɪ, -z
communisation
BR ˌkɒmjʊnʌɪ'zeɪʃn
AM ˌkɑmjənə'zeɪʃən, ˌkɑmjəˌnaɪ'zeɪʃən
communise
BR 'kɒmjʊnʌɪz, -ɨz, -ɪŋ, -d
AM 'kɑmjəˌnaɪz, -ɨz, -ɪŋ, -d
communism
BR 'kɒmjʊnɪz(ə)m
AM 'kɑmjəˌnɪzəm
communist
BR 'kɒmjʊnɪst, -s
AM 'kɑmjənəst, -s
communistic
BR ˌkɒmjʊ'nɪstɪk
AM ˌkɑmjə'nɪstɪk
communistically
BR ˌkɒmjʊ'nɪstɨkli
AM ˌkɑmjə'nɪstɨk(ə)li
communitarian
BR kəˌmjuːnɨ'tɛːrɪən, -z
AM kəˌmjunə'tɛriən, -z
community
BR kə'mjuːnɨt|i, -ɪz
AM kə'mjunədi, -z
communization
BR ˌkɒmjʊnʌɪ'zeɪʃn
AM ˌkɑmjənə'zeɪʃən, ˌkɑmjəˌnaɪ'zeɪʃən
communize
BR 'kɒmjʊnʌɪz, -ɨz, -ɪŋ, -d
AM 'kɑmjəˌnaɪz, -ɨz, -ɪŋ, -d
commutability
BR kəˌmjuːtə'bɪlɨti
AM kəˌmjudə'bɪlɨdi
commutable
BR kə'mjuːtəbl
AM kə'mjudəbəl
commutate
BR 'kɒmjʊteɪt, -s, -ɪŋ, -ɨd
AM 'kɑmjuˌteɪ|t, -ts, -dɪŋ, -dɨd
commutation
BR ˌkɒmjʊ'teɪʃn, -z
AM ˌkɑmjə'teɪʃən, -z
commutative
BR kə'mjuːtətɪv, 'kɒmjʊtətɪv, 'kɒmjʊteɪtɪv
AM 'kɑmjəˌteɪdɪv, kə'mjudədɪv
commutator
BR 'kɒmjʊteɪtə(r), -z
AM 'kɑmjəˌteɪdər, -z
commute
BR kə'mjuːt, -s, -ɪŋ, -ɨd
AM kə'mju|t, -ts, -dɪŋ, -dəd
commuter
BR kə'mjuːtə(r), -z
AM kə'mjudər, -z
Como
BR 'kəʊməʊ
AM 'koʊmoʊ

Comorin
BR ˈkɒmərɪn
AM ˈkɑmərən
Comoro
BR ˈkɒmərəʊ
AM ˈkɑməroʊ
comose
BR ˈkəʊməʊs
AM ˈkoʊˌmoʊs, ˈkoʊˌmoʊz
comp
BR kɒmp, -s
AM kɑmp, -s
compact[1]
noun
BR ˈkɒmpakt, -s
AM ˈkɑmˌpæk(t), -s
compact[2]
verb, adjective
BR kəmˈpakt, -s, -ɪŋ, -ɨd
AM kəmˈpæk|(t), ˈkɑmˌpæk|(t), -(t)s, -tɪŋ, -təd
compaction
BR kəmˈpakʃn
AM kəmˈpækʃən
compactly
BR kəmˈpaktli
AM kəmˈpæk(t)li, ˈkɑmˌpæk(t)li
compactness
BR kəmˈpak(t)nəs
AM kəmˈpæk(t)nəs, ˈkɑmˌpæk(t)nəs
compactor
BR kəmˈpaktə(r), -z
AM ˈkɑmˌpæktər, -z
compadre
BR kəmˈpɑːdr|i, -ɪz
AM kəmˈpɑdreɪ, -z
compages
BR kəmˈpeɪdʒiːz
AM kəmˈpeɪdʒɪz
compander
BR kəmˈpandə(r), -z
AM kəmˈpændər, -z
companion
BR kəmˈpanjən, -z
AM kəmˈpænjən, -z
companionable
BR kəmˈpanjənəbl
AM kəmˈpænjənəbəl
companionableness
BR kəmˈpanjənəblnəs
AM kəmˈpænjənəbəlnəs
companionably
BR kəmˈpanjənəbli
AM kəmˈpænjənəbli
companionate
BR kəmˈpanjənət
AM kəmˈpænjənət
companionship
BR kəmˈpanjənʃɪp
AM kəmˈpænjənˌʃɪp
companionway
BR kəmˈpanjənweɪ, -z
AM kəmˈpænjənˌweɪ, -z
company
BR ˈkʌmp(ə)n|i, ˈkʌmpn̩|i, -ɪz
AM ˈkəmp(ə)ni, -z
Compaq
BR ˈkɒmpak
AM ˈkɑmpæk
comparability
BR ˌkɒmp(ə)rəˈbɪlɨti
AM ˌkɑmp(ə)rəˈbɪlɨdi
comparable
BR ˈkɒmp(ə)rəbl
AM ˈkɑmp(ə)rəbəl
comparableness
BR ˈkɒmp(ə)rəblnəs
AM ˈkɑmp(ə)rəbəlnəs
comparably
BR ˈkɒmp(ə)rəbli
AM ˈkɑmp(ə)rəbli
comparatist
BR kəmˈparətɪst, -s
AM kəmˈpɛrədəst, -s
comparative
BR kəmˈparətɪv, -z
AM kəmˈpɛrədɪv, -z
comparatively
BR kəmˈparətɨvli
AM kəmˈpɛrədɨvli
comparator
BR kəmˈparətə(r), -z
AM kəmˈpɛrədər, -z
compare
BR kəmˈpɛː(r), -z, -ɪŋ, -d
AM kəmˈpɛ(ə)r, -z, -ɪŋ, -d
comparison
BR kəmˈparɪs(ə)n, -z
AM kəmˈpɛrəsən, -z
compartment
BR kəmˈpɑːtm(ə)nt, -s
AM kəmˈpɑrtmənt, -s
compartmental
BR ˌkɒmpɑːtˈmɛntl
AM kəmˌpɑrtˈmɛn(t)l
compartmentalisation
BR ˌkɒmpɑːtˌmɛntl̩ʌɪˈzeɪʃn
AM kəmˌpɑrtˌmɛn(t)ələˈzeɪʃən, kəmˌpɑrtˌmɛn(t)əˌlaɪˈzeɪʃən
compartmentalise
BR ˌkɒmpɑːtˈmɛntl̩ʌɪz, -ɨz, -ɪŋ, -d
AM kəmˌpɑrtˈmɛn(t)lˌaɪz, -ɨz, -ɪŋ, -d
compartmentalization
BR ˌkɒmpɑːtˌmɛntl̩ʌɪˈzeɪʃn
AM kəmˌpɑrtˌmɛn(t)ələˈzeɪʃən, kəmˌpɑrtˌmɛn(t)əˌlaɪˈzeɪʃən
compartmentalize
BR ˌkɒmpɑːtˈmɛntl̩ʌɪz, -ɨz, -ɪŋ, -d
AM kəmˌpɑrtˈmɛn(t)lˌaɪz, -ɨz, -ɪŋ, -d
compartmentally
BR ˌkɒmpɑːtˈmɛntl̩i
AM kəmˌpɑrtˈmɛn(t)l̩i
compartmentation
BR ˌkɒmpɑːtmɛnˈteɪʃn
AM kəmˌpɑrtˌmɛnˈteɪʃən
compass
BR ˈkʌmpəs, -ɨz, -ɪŋ, -t
AM ˈkəmpəs, -əz, -ɪŋ, -t
compassable
BR ˈkʌmpəsəbl
AM ˈkəmpəsəbəl
compassion
BR kəmˈpaʃn, -z
AM kəmˈpæʃən, -z
compassionate
BR kəmˈpaʃn̩ət, kəmˈpaʃənət
AM kəmˈpæʃ(ə)nət
compassionately
BR kəmˈpaʃənətli, kəmˈpaʃn̩ətli
AM kəmˈpæʃ(ə)nətli
compass-saw
BR ˈkʌmpəssɔː(*r*), -z
AM ˈkəmpəsˌsɔ, ˈkəmpəsˌsɑ, -z
compatibility
BR kəmˌpatɨˈbɪlɨti
AM kəmˌpædəˈbɪlɨdi
compatible
BR kəmˈpatɨbl
AM kəmˈpædəbəl
compatibly
BR kəmˈpatɨbli
AM kəmˈpædəbli
compatriot
BR kəmˈpatrɪət, -s
AM kəmˈpeɪtriət, -s
compatriotic
BR kəmˌpatrɪˈɒtɪk
AM kəmˌpeɪtriˈɑdɪk
compeer
BR ˈkɒmpɪə(r), -z
AM ˈkɑmpɪ(ə)r, kəmˈpɪ(ə)r, -z
compel
BR kəmˈpɛl, -z, -ɪŋ, -d
AM kəmˈpɛl, -z, -ɪŋ, -d
compellable
BR kəmˈpɛləbl
AM kəmˈpɛləbəl
compellingly
BR kəmˈpɛlɪŋli
AM kəmˈpɛlɪŋli
compendia
BR kəmˈpɛndɪə(*r*)
AM kəmˈpɛndiə
compendious
BR kəmˈpɛndɪəs
AM kəmˈpɛndiəs
compendiously
BR kəmˈpɛndɪəsli
AM kəmˈpɛndiəsli
compendiousness
BR kəmˈpɛndɪəsnəs
AM kəmˈpɛndiəsnəs
compendium
BR kəmˈpɛndɪəm, -z
AM kəmˈpɛndiəm, -z
compensate
BR ˈkɒmp(ə)nseɪt, ˈkɒmpɛnseɪt, -s, -ɪŋ, -ɨd
AM ˈkɑmpənˌseɪ|t, -ts, -dɪŋ, -dɨd
compensation
BR ˌkɒmp(ə)nˈseɪʃn, ˌkɒmpɛnˈseɪʃn
AM ˌkɑmpənˈseɪʃən
compensational
BR ˌkɒmp(ə)nˈseɪʃn̩(ə)l, ˌkɒmp(ə)nˈseɪʃən(ə)l, ˌkɒmpɛnˈseɪʃn̩(ə)l, ˌkɒmpɛnˈseɪʃən(ə)l
AM ˌkɑmpənˈseɪʃ(ə)nəl
compensative
BR kəmˈpɛnsɪtɪv, ˈkɒmp(ə)nseɪtɪv, ˈkɒmpɛnseɪtɪv
AM kəmˈpɛnsədɪv, ˈkɑmpənˌseɪdɪv
compensator
BR ˈkɒmp(ə)nseɪtə(r), ˈkɒmpɛnseɪtə(r), -z
AM ˈkɑmpənˌseɪdər, -z
compensatory
BR kəmˈpɛnsət(ə)ri, ˌkɒmp(ə)nˈseɪt(ə)ri, ˌkɒmpɛnˈseɪt(ə)ri
AM kəmˈpɛnsəˌtɔri
compère
BR ˈkɒmpɛː(r), -z, -ɪŋ, -d
AM ˈkɑmˌpɛ(ə)r, -z, -ɪŋ, -d
compete
BR kəmˈpiːt, -s, -ɪŋ, -ɨd
AM kəmˈpi|t, -ts, -dɪŋ, -dɨd
competence
BR ˈkɒmpɪt(ə)ns
AM ˈkɑmpəd(ə)ns
competency
BR ˈkɒmpɪt(ə)nsi
AM ˈkɑmpəd(ə)nsi
competent
BR ˈkɒmpɪt(ə)nt
AM ˈkɑmpəd(ə)nt
competently
BR ˈkɒmpɪt(ə)ntli
AM ˈkɑmpədən(t)li
competition
BR ˌkɒmpɪˈtɪʃn, -z
AM ˌkɑmpəˈtɪʃən, -z
competitive
BR kəmˈpɛtɪtɪv
AM kəmˈpɛdədɪv

competitively
BR kəm'pɛtɨtɨvli
AM kəm'pɛdədɨvli

competitiveness
BR kəm'pɛtɨtɨvnɨs
AM kəm'pɛdədɨvnɨs

competitor
BR kəm'pɛtɨtə(r), -z
AM kəm'pɛdədər, -z

compilation
BR ˌkɒmpɨ'leɪʃn, -z
AM ˌkɑmpə'leɪʃən, -z

compile
BR kəm'pʌɪl, -z, -ɪŋ, -d
AM kəm'paɪl, -z, -ɪŋ, -d

compiler
BR kəm'pʌɪlə(r), -z
AM kəm'paɪlər, -z

complacence
BR kəm'pleɪsns
AM kəm'pleɪsəns

complacency
BR kəm'pleɪsnsi
AM kəm'pleɪsənsi

complacent
BR kəm'pleɪsnt
AM kəm'pleɪsənt

complacently
BR kəm'pleɪsntli
AM kəm'pleɪsn(t)li

complain
BR kəm'pleɪn, -z, -ɪŋ, -d
AM kəm'pleɪn, -z, -ɪŋ, -d

complainant
BR kəm'pleɪnənt, -s
AM kəm'pleɪnənt, -s

complainer
BR kəm'pleɪnə(r), -z
AM kəm'pleɪnər, -z

complainingly
BR kəm'pleɪnɪŋli
AM kəm'pleɪnɪŋli

complaint
BR kəm'pleɪnt, -s
AM kəm'pleɪnt, -s

complaisance
BR kəm'pleɪzns
AM kəm'pleɪsəns, kəm'pleɪzns

complaisant
BR kəm'pleɪznt
AM kəm'pleɪsənt

complaisantly
BR kəm'pleɪzntli
AM kəm'pleɪsn(t)li, kəm'pleɪzn(t)li

compleat
BR kəm'pliːt
AM kəm'plit

complected
BR kəm'plɛktɨd
AM kəm'plɛktəd

complement
BR 'kɒmplɨm(ə)nt, -s, -ɪŋ, -ɨd
AM 'kɑmpləmən|t, -ts, -(t)ɪŋ, -(t)əd

complemental
BR ˌkɒmplɪ'mɛntl
AM ˌkɑmplə'mɛn(t)l

complementarily
BR ˌkɒmplɪ'mɛnt(ə)rɨli
AM ˌkɑmpləmɛn'tɛrəli

complementariness
BR ˌkɒmplɪ'mɛnt(ə)rɪnɨs
AM ˌkɑmpləmɛn'tɛrinɨs

complementarity
BR ˌkɒmplɨmɛn'tarɨti, ˌkɒmplɨm(ə)n'tarɨti
AM ˌkɑmpləmɛn'tɛrədi

complementary
BR ˌkɒmplɪ'mɛnt(ə)ri
AM ˌkɑmplə'mɛn(t)əri, ˌkɑmplə'mɛntri

complementation
BR ˌkɒmplɨmɛn'teɪʃn, ˌkɒmplɨm(ə)n'teɪʃn
AM ˌkɑmpləmɛn'teɪʃən

complementizer
BR 'kɒmplɨmɛntʌɪzə(r), 'kɒmplɨm(ə)ntʌɪzə(r), -z
AM 'kɑmpləmɛnˌtaɪzər, 'kɑmpləmənˌtaɪzər, -z

complete
BR kəm'pliːt, -s, -ɪŋ, -ɨd
AM kəm'pli|t, -ts, -dɪŋ, -dɨd

completely
BR kəm'pliːtli
AM kəm'plitli

completeness
BR kəm'pliːtnɨs
AM kəm'plitnɨs

completion
BR kəm'pliːʃn, -z
AM kəm'pliʃən, -z

completist
BR kəm'pliːtɪst, -s
AM kəm'plidɪst, -s

completive
BR kəm'pliːtɪv
AM kəm'plidɪv

complex[1]
adjective
BR 'kɒmplɛks
AM ˌkɑm'plɛks

complex[2]
noun
BR 'kɒmplɛks, -ɨz
AM 'kɑmplɛks, -əz

complexation
BR ˌkɒmplɛk'seɪʃn
AM kəmˌplɛk'seɪʃən

complexion
BR kəm'plɛkʃn, -z, -d
AM kəm'plɛkʃən, -z, -d

complexionless
BR kəm'plɛkʃnləs
AM kəm'plɛkʃənləs

complexity
BR kəm'plɛksɪt|i, -ɪz
AM kəm'plɛksədi, -z

complexly
BR 'kɒmplɛksli
AM ˌkɑm'plɛksli

compliance
BR kəm'plʌɪəns
AM kəm'plaɪəns

compliancy
BR kəm'plʌɪənsi
AM kəm'plaɪənsi

compliant
BR kəm'plʌɪənt
AM kəm'plaɪənt

compliantly
BR kəm'plʌɪəntli
AM kəm'plaɪən(t)li

complicacy
BR 'kɒmplɨkəs|i, -ɪz
AM 'kɑmpləkəsi, -z

complicate
BR 'kɒmplɨkeɪt, -s, -ɪŋ, -ɨd
AM 'kɑmpləˌkeɪ|t, -ts, -dɪŋ, -dɨd

complicatedly
BR 'kɒmplɨkeɪtɨdli
AM 'kɑmpləˌkeɪdɨdli

complicatedness
BR 'kɒmplɨkeɪtɨdnɨs
AM 'kɑmpləˌkeɪdɨdnɨs

complication
BR ˌkɒmplɪ'keɪʃn, -z
AM ˌkɑmplə'keɪʃən, -z

complicit
BR kəm'plɪsɪt
AM kəm'plɪsɪt

complicity
BR kəm'plɪsɨti
AM kəm'plɪsɨdi

compliment[1]
noun
BR 'kɒmplɨm(ə)nt, -s
AM 'kɑmpləmənt, -s

compliment[2]
verb
BR 'kɒmplɨmɛnt, -s, -ɪŋ, -ɨd
AM 'kɑmpləˌmɛn|t, -ts, -(t)ɪŋ, -(t)ɨd

complimentarily
BR ˌkɒmplɪ'mɛnt(ə)rɨli
AM ˌkɑmpləˌmɛn'tɛrəli

complimentary
BR ˌkɒmplɪ'mɛnt(ə)r|i, -ɪz
AM ˌkɑmplə'mɛn(t)əri, ˌkɑmplə'mɛntri, -ɪz

complin
BR 'kɒmplɪn, -z
AM 'kɑmplɪn, -z

compline
BR 'kɒmplɪn, -z
AM 'kɑmplɪn, -z

comply
BR kəm'plʌɪ, -z, -ɪŋ, -d
AM kəm'plaɪ, -z, -ɪŋ, -d

compo
BR 'kɒmpəʊ, -z
AM 'kɑmˌpoʊ, -z

component
BR kəm'pəʊnənt, -s
AM kəm'poʊnənt, -s

componential
BR ˌkɒmpə(ʊ)'nɛnʃl
AM ˌkɑmpə'nɛn(t)ʃəl

comport
BR kəm'pɔːt, -s, -ɪŋ, -ɨd
AM kəm'pɔ(ə)rt, -ts, -'pɔrdɪŋ, -'pɔrdəd

comportment
BR kəm'pɔːtm(ə)nt
AM kəm'pɔrtmənt

compose
BR kəm'pəʊz, -ɨz, -ɪŋ, -d
AM kəm'poʊz, -əz, -ɪŋ, -d

composedly
BR kəm'pəʊzɨdli
AM kəm'poʊzədli

composer
BR kəm'pəʊzə(r), -z
AM kəm'poʊzər, -z

composite
BR 'kɒmpəzɪt, 'kɒmpəzʌɪt, 'kɒmpəsʌɪt, -s
AM kəm'pɑzət, ˌkɑm'pɑzət, -s

compositely
BR 'kɒmpəzɨtli, 'kɒmpəzʌɪtli, 'kɒmpəsʌɪtli
AM kəm'pɑzətli, ˌkɑm'pɑzətli

compositeness
BR 'kɒmpəzɨtnɨs, 'kɒmpəzʌɪtnɨs, 'kɒmpəsʌɪtnɨs
AM kəm'pɑzətnəs, ˌkɑm'pɑzətnəs

composition
BR ˌkɒmpə'zɪʃn, -z
AM ˌkɑmpə'zɪʃən, -z

compositional
BR ˌkɒmpə'zɪʃn̩(ə)l, ˌkɒmpə'zɪʃən(ə)l
AM ˌkɑmpə'zɪʃ(ə)nəl

compositionally
BR ˌkɒmpə'zɪʃn̩əli, ˌkɒmpə'zɪʃn̩l̩i, ˌkɒmpə'zɪʃənl̩i, ˌkɒmpə'zɪʃ(ə)nəli
AM ˌkɑmpə'zɪʃ(ə)nəli

compositor
BR kəm'pɒzɨtə(r), -z
AM kəm'pɑzədər, -z

compos mentis
BR ˌkɒmpəs 'mɛntɪs, ˌkɒmpɒs +
AM ˌkɑmpəs 'mɛn(t)əs

compossible
BR kəm'pɒsɨbl
AM kəm'pɑsəbəl, ˌkɑm'pɑsəbəl

compost
BR 'kɒmpɒst, -s, -ɪŋ, -ɪd
AM 'kɑm,poʊst, -s, -ɪŋ, -əd

composure
BR kəm'pəʊʒə(r)
AM kəm'poʊʒər

compote
BR 'kɒmpəʊt, 'kɒmpɒt, -s
AM 'kɑm,poʊt, -s

compound[1]
noun, adjective
BR 'kɒmpaʊnd, -z
AM 'kɑm,paʊnd, -z

compound[2]
verb
BR kəm'paʊnd, -z, -ɪŋ, -ɪd
AM kəm'paʊnd, -z, -ɪŋ, -əd

compoundable
BR kəm'paʊndəbl
AM kəm'paʊndəbəl

compounder
BR kəm'paʊndə(r), -z
AM kəm'paʊndər, -z

comprador
BR ,kɒmprə'dɔː(r), -z
AM ,kɑmprə'dɔ(ə)r, -z

compradore
BR ,kɒmprə'dɔː(r), -z
AM ,kɑmprə'dɔ(ə)r, -z

comprehend
BR ,kɒmprɪ'hɛnd, -z, -ɪŋ, -ɪd
AM ,kɑmprə'hɛnd, -z, -ɪŋ, -ɪd

comprehensibility
BR ,kɒmprɪ,hɛnsɪ'bɪlɨti
AM ,kɑmprə,hɛnsə'bɪlɨdi

comprehensible
BR ,kɒmprɪ'hɛnsɪbl
AM ,kɑmprə'hɛnsəbəl

comprehensibleness
BR ,kɒmprɪ'hɛnsɪblnəs
AM ,kɑmprə'hɛnsəbəlnəs

comprehensibly
BR ,kɒmprɪ'hɛnsɪbli
AM ,kɑmprə'hɛnsəbli

comprehension
BR ,kɒmprɪ'hɛnʃn, -z
AM ,kɑmprə'hɛn(t)ʃən, -z

comprehensive
BR ,kɒmprɪ'hɛnsɪv, -z
AM ,kɑmprə'hɛnsɪv, -z

comprehensively
BR ,kɒmprɪ'hɛnsɪvli
AM ,kɑmprə'hɛnsɪvli

comprehensiveness
BR ,kɒmprɪ'hɛnsɪvnɪs
AM ,kɑmprə'hɛnsɪvnɪs

comprehensivisation
BR ,kɒmprɪhɛnsɪvʌɪ'zeɪʃn
AM ,kɑmprə,hɛnsəvə'zeɪʃən, ,kɑmprə,hɛnsə,vaɪ'zeɪʃən

comprehensivise
BR ,kɒmprɪ'hɛnsɪvʌɪz, -ɪz, -ɪŋ, -d
AM ,kɑmprə'hɛnsə,vaɪz, -ɪz, -ɪŋ, -d

comprehensivization
BR ,kɒmprɪhɛnsɪvʌɪ'zeɪʃn
AM ,kɑmprə,hɛnsəvə'zeɪʃən, ,kɑmprə,hɛnsə,vaɪ'zeɪʃən

comprehensivize
BR ,kɒmprɪ'hɛnsɪvʌɪz, -ɪz, -ɪŋ, -d
AM ,kɑmprə'hɛnsə,vaɪz, -ɪz, -ɪŋ, -d

compress[1]
noun
BR 'kɒmprɛs, -ɪz
AM 'kɑm,prɛs, -əz

compress[2]
verb
BR kəm'prɛs, -ɪz, -ɪŋ, -t
AM kəm'prɛs, -əz, -ɪŋ, -t

compressibility
BR kəm,prɛsɪ'bɪlɨti
AM kəm,prɛsə'bɪlɨdi

compressible
BR kəm'prɛsɪbl
AM kəm'prɛsəbəl

compression
BR kəm'prɛʃn
AM kəm'prɛʃən

compressive
BR kəm'prɛsɪv
AM kəm'prɛsɪv

compressor
BR kəm'prɛsə(r), -z
AM kəm'prɛsər, -z

comprisable
BR kəm'prʌɪzəbl
AM kəm'praɪzəbəl

comprise
BR kəm'prʌɪz, -ɪz, -ɪŋ, -d
AM kəm'praɪz, -ɪz, -ɪŋ, -d

compromise
BR 'kɒmprəmʌɪz, -ɪz, -ɪŋ, -d
AM 'kɑmprə,maɪz, -ɪz, -ɪŋ, -d

compromiser
BR 'kɒmprəmʌɪzə(r), -z
AM 'kɑmprə,maɪzər, -z

compromisingly
BR 'kɒmprəmʌɪzɪŋli
AM 'kɑmprə,maɪzɪŋli

compte rendu
BR ,kɒ̃t rɒ̃'duː
AM ,kɔnt ,rɑn'd(j)u

comptes rendus
BR ,kɒ̃t rɒ̃'duː(z)
AM ,kɔnt ,rɑn'd(j)u(z)

comptometer
BR ,kɒm(p)'tɒmɨtə(r), -z
AM ,kɑm(p)'tɑmədər, -z

Compton
BR 'kɒm(p)t(ə)n, 'kʌm(p)t(ə)n
AM 'kɑm(p)tən

comptroller
BR kən'trəʊlə(r), kəmp'trəʊlə(r), ,kɒmp'trəʊlə(r), -z
AM kən'troʊlər, ,kɑm(p)'troʊlər, -z

compulsion
BR kəm'pʌlʃn, -z
AM kəm'pəlʃən, -z

compulsive
BR kəm'pʌlsɪv
AM kəm'pəlsɪv

compulsively
BR kəm'pʌlsɪvli
AM kəm'pəlsɪvli

compulsiveness
BR kəm'pʌlsɪvnɪs
AM kəm'pəlsɪvnɪs

compulsorily
BR kəm'pʌls(ə)rɨli
AM kəm'pəlsərəli

compulsoriness
BR kəm'pʌls(ə)rɪnɪs
AM kəm'pəlsərinɪs

compulsory
BR kəm'pʌls(ə)ri
AM kəm'pəlsəri

compunction
BR kəm'pʌŋ(k)ʃn
AM kəm'pəŋ(k)ʃən

compunctious
BR kəm'pʌŋ(k)ʃəs
AM kəm'pəŋ(k)ʃəs

compunctiously
BR kəm'pʌŋ(k)ʃəsli
AM kəm'pəŋ(k)ʃəsli

compurgate
BR 'kɒmpəːgeɪt, -s, -ɪŋ, -ɪd
AM 'kɑmpər,geɪ|t, -ts, -dɪŋ, -dɨd

compurgation
BR ,kɒmpəː'geɪʃn
AM ,kɑmpər'geɪʃən

compurgator
BR 'kɒmpəːgeɪtə(r), -z
AM 'kɑmpər,geɪdər, -z

compurgatory
BR kəm'pəːgət(ə)ri
AM kəm'pərgə,tɔri

computability
BR kəm,pjuːtə'bɪlɨti
AM kəm,pjudə'bɪlɨdi

computable
BR kəm'pjuːtəbl
AM kəm'pjudəbəl

computably
BR kəm'pjuːtəbli
AM kəm'pjudəbli

computation
BR ,kɒmpjʉ'teɪʃn, -z
AM ,kɑmpjə'teɪʃən, -z

computational
BR ,kɒmpjʉ'teɪʃn (ə)l, ,kɒmpjʉ'teɪʃən(ə)l
AM ,kɑmpjə'teɪʃ(ə)nəl

computationally
BR ,kɒmpjʉ'teɪʃn(ə)li, ,kɒmpjʉ'teɪʃn̩l̩i, ,kɒmpjʉ'teɪʃənl̩i, ,kɒmpjʉ'teɪʃ(ə)nəli
AM ,kɑmpjə'teɪʃ(ə)nəli

compute
BR kəm'pjuːt, -s, -ɪŋ, -ɪd
AM kəm'pju|t, -ts, -dɪŋ, -dəd

computer
BR kəm'pjuːtə(r), -z
AM kəm'pjudər, -z

computerese
BR kəm,pjuːtər'iːz
AM kəm,pjudər'iz

computerisation
BR kəm,pjuːtərʌɪ'zeɪʃn
AM kəm,pjudərə'zeɪʃən, kəm,pjudə,raɪ'zeɪʃən

computerise
BR kəm'pjuːtərʌɪz, -ɪz, -ɪŋ, -d
AM kəm'pjudə,raɪz, -ɪz, -ɪŋ, -d

computerization
BR kəm,pjuːtərʌɪ'zeɪʃn
AM kəm,pjudərə'zeɪʃən, kəm,pjudə,raɪ'zeɪʃən

computerize
BR kəm'pjuːtərʌɪz, -ɪz, -ɪŋ, -d
AM kəm'pjudə,raɪz, -ɪz, -ɪŋ, -d

comrade
BR 'kɒmreɪd, 'kɒmrəd, -z
AM 'kɑm,ræd, 'kɑmrəd, -z

comradely
BR 'kɒmreɪdli, 'kɒmrədli
AM 'kɑmrədli

comradeship
BR 'kɒmreɪdʃɪp, 'kɒmrədʃɪp
AM 'kɑmræd,ʃɪp, 'kɑmrəd,ʃɪp

Comrie
BR 'kɒmri
AM 'kɑmri

coms
BR kɒmz
AM kɑmz
Comsat®
BR 'kɒmsat
AM 'kɑm,sæt
Comstock
BR 'kɒmstɒk
AM 'kɑm,stɑk
Comte
BR kɒnt, kɔːnt
AM kɔnt, kɔmt, kɑnt, kɑmt
Comtism
BR 'kɒmtɪz(ə)m
AM 'kɑm(p),tɪzəm
Comtist
BR 'kɒmtɪst, -s
AM 'kɑm(p)təst, -s
con
BR kɒn, -z, -ɪŋ, -d
AM kɑn, -z, -ɪŋ, -d
conacre
BR 'kɒn,eɪkə(r), -z
AM 'kɑ,neɪkər, -z
Conakry
BR 'kɒnəkri
AM 'kɑnəkri
con amore
BR ,kɒn ə'mɔːreɪ, + a'mɔːreɪ
AM ,kɑn ə'mɔ,reɪ
Conan
BR 'kəʊnən
AM 'koʊnən
conation
BR kə(ʊ)'neɪʃn
AM koʊ'neɪʃən
conative
BR 'kəʊnətɪv
AM 'koʊnədɪv, 'kɑnədɪv
con brio
BR ,kɒn 'briːəʊ
AM ,kɑn 'brioʊ
Concannon
BR kɒn'kanən
AM kən'kænən
concatenate
BR kən'katɪneɪt, kəŋ'katɪneɪt, (,)kɒn'katɪneɪt, (,)kɒŋ'katɪneɪt, -s, -ɪŋ, -ɪd
AM kən'kædə,neɪ|t, -ts, -dɪŋ, -dɪd
concatenation
BR kən,katɪ'neɪʃn, kəŋ,katɪ'neɪʃn, kɒn,katɪ'neɪʃn, kɒŋ,katɪ'neɪʃn, ,kɒnkatɪ'neɪʃn, ,kɒŋkatɪ'neɪʃn, -z
AM kən,kædə'neɪʃən, -z
concatenative
BR kən'katənətɪv, kəŋ'katənətɪv, kən'katn̩ətɪv, kəŋ'katn̩ətɪv, kɒn'katɪnətɪv, kɒŋ'katɪnətɪv, kɒn'katn̩ətɪv, kɒŋ'katn̩ətɪv
AM kən'kædə,neɪdɪv, kən'kædn,eɪdɪv, kən'kæd(ə)nədɪv
concave¹
adjective
BR ,kɒn'keɪv, ,kɒŋ'keɪv
AM ,kɑn'keɪv, ,kɑŋ'keɪv
concave²
noun
BR 'kɒnkeɪv, 'kɒŋkeɪv, -z
AM 'kɑn,keɪv, 'kɑŋ,keɪv, -z
concavely
BR ,kɒn'keɪvli, ,kɒŋ'keɪvli, 'kɒnkeɪvli, 'kɒŋkeɪvli
AM ,kɑn'keɪvli, ,kɑŋ'keɪvli
concavity
BR kɒn'kavɪti, kɒŋ'kavɪti, kən'kavɪti, kəŋ'kavɪti
AM ,kɑn'kævədi, ,kɑŋ'kavədi
conceal
BR kən'siːl, -z, -ɪŋ, -d
AM kən'sil, -z, -ɪŋ, -d
concealer
BR kən'siːlə(r), -z
AM kən'silər, -z
concealment
BR kən'siːlm(ə)nt, -s
AM kən'silmənt, -s
concede
BR kən'siːd, -z, -ɪŋ, -ɪd
AM kən'sid, -z, -ɪŋ, -ɪd
conceder
BR kən'siːdə(r), -z
AM kən'sidər, -z
conceit
BR kən'siːt, -s
AM kən'sit, -s
conceited
BR kən'siːtɪd
AM kən'sidɪd
conceitedly
BR kən'siːtɪdli
AM kən'sidɪdli
conceitedness
BR kən'siːtɪdnɪs
AM kən'sidɪdnɪs
conceivability
BR kən,siːvə'bɪlɪti
AM kən,sivə'bɪlɪdi
conceivable
BR kən'siːvəbl
AM kən'sivəbəl
conceivably
BR kən'siːvəbli
AM kən'sivəbli
conceive
BR kən'siːv, -z, -ɪŋ, -d
AM kən'siv, -z, -ɪŋ, -d
concelebrant
BR ,kɒn'sɛlɪbr(ə)nt, -s
AM ,kɑn'sɛləbrənt, -s
concelebrate
BR ,kɒn'sɛlɪbreɪt, -s, -ɪŋ, -ɪd
AM ,kɑn'sɛlə,breɪ|t, -ts, -dɪŋ, -dɪd
concelebrating
BR ,kɒn'sɛlɪbreɪtɪŋ
AM ,kɑn'sɛlə,breɪdɪŋ
concelebration
BR kɒn,sɛlə'breɪʃn, -z
AM ,kɑn,sɛlə'breɪʃən, -z
concentrate
BR 'kɒns(ɛ)ntreɪt, -s, -ɪŋ, -ɪd
AM 'kɑnsən,treɪ|t, -ts, -dɪŋ, -dɪd
concentratedly
BR 'kɒns(ɛ)ntreɪtɪdli
AM 'kɑnsən,treɪdɪdli
concentration
BR ,kɒns(ɛ)n'treɪʃn
AM ,kɑnsən'treɪʃən
concentrative
BR 'kɒns(ɛ)ntreɪtɪv
AM 'kɑnsən,treɪdɪv
concentrator
BR 'kɒns(ɛ)ntreɪtə(r), -z
AM 'kɑnsən,treɪdər, -z
concentre
BR kən'sɛnt|ə(r), ,kɒn'sɛnt|ə(r), -əz, -(ə)rɪŋ, -əd
AM kən'sɛn(t)ər, -z, -ɪŋ, -d
concentric
BR kən'sɛntrɪk, ,kɒn'sɛntrɪk
AM kən'sɛntrɪk
concentrically
BR kən'sɛntrɪkli, ,kɒn'sɛntrɪkli
AM kən'sɛntrək(ə)li
concentricity
BR ,kɒnsɛn'trɪsɪti
AM kən,sɛn'trɪsɪdi
Concepción
BR ,kɒnsɛp'sjɒn
AM ,kɑn,sɛpsi'oʊn
SP ,konθep'θjon, ,konsep'sjon
concept
BR 'kɒnsɛpt, -s
AM 'kɑn,sɛpt, -s
conception
BR kən'sɛpʃn, -z
AM kən'sɛpʃən, -z
conceptional
BR kən'sɛpʃn̩(ə)l, kən'sɛpʃən(ə)l
AM kən'sɛpʃ(ə)nəl
conceptionally
BR kən'sɛpʃn̩əli, kən'sɛpʃn̩li, kən'sɛpʃənli, kən'sɛpʃ(ə)nəli
AM kən'sɛpʃ(ə)nəli
conceptive
BR kən'sɛptɪv
AM kən'sɛptɪv
conceptual
BR kən'sɛptʃʊəl, kən'sɛptʃ(ʉ)l, kən'sɛptjʊəl, kən'sɛptjʉl
AM kən'sɛp(t)ʃ(əw)əl
conceptualisation
BR kən,sɛptʃʊəlʌɪ'zeɪʃn, kən,sɛptʃʉlʌɪ'zeɪʃn, kən,sɛptʃl̩ʌɪ'zeɪʃn, kən,sɛptjʊəlʌɪ'zeɪʃn, kən,sɛptjʉlʌɪ'zeɪʃn
AM kən,sɛp(t)ʃ(əw)ələ'zeɪʃən, kən,sɛp(t)ʃ(əw)ə,laɪ'zeɪʃən
conceptualise
BR kən'sɛptʃʊəlʌɪz, kən'sɛptʃʉlʌɪz, kən'sɛptʃl̩ʌɪz, kən'sɛptjʊəlʌɪz, kən'sɛptjʉlʌɪz, -ɪz, -ɪŋ, -d
AM kən'sɛp(t)ʃ(əw)ə,laɪz, -ɪz, -ɪŋ, -d
conceptualism
BR kən'sɛptʃʊəlɪz(ə)m, kən'sɛptʃʉlɪz(ə)m, kən'sɛptʃl̩ɪz(ə)m, kən'sɛptjʊəlɪz(ə)m, kən'sɛptjʉlɪz(ə)m
AM kən'sɛp(t)ʃ(əw)ə,lɪzəm
conceptualist
BR kən'sɛptʃʊəlɪst, kən'sɛptʃʉlɪst, kən'sɛptʃl̩ɪst, kən'sɛptjʊəlɪst, kən'sɛptjʉlɪst, -s
AM kən'sɛp(t)ʃ(əw)ələst, -s
conceptualization
BR kən,sɛptʃʊəlʌɪ'zeɪʃn, kən,sɛptʃʉlʌɪ'zeɪʃn, kən,sɛptʃl̩ʌɪ'zeɪʃn, kən,sɛptjʊəlʌɪ'zeɪʃn, kən,sɛptjʉlʌɪ'zeɪʃn
AM kən,sɛp(t)ʃ(əw)ələ'zeɪʃən, kən,sɛp(t)ʃ(əw)ə,laɪ'zeɪʃən
conceptualize
BR kən'sɛptʃʊəlʌɪz, kən'sɛptʃʉlʌɪz, kən'sɛptʃl̩ʌɪz,

kən'sɛptjʊəlʌɪz, kən'sɛptjʉlʌɪz, -ɪz, -ɪŋ, -d
AM kən'sɛp(t)ʃ(əw)ə-ˌlaɪz, -ɪz, -ɪŋ, -d

conceptually
BR kən'sɛptʃʊəli, kən'sɛptʃʉli, kən'sɛptʃl̩i, kən'sɛptjʊəli, kən'sɛptjʉli
AM kən'sɛp(t)ʃ(əw)əli

conceptus
BR kən'sɛptəs
AM kən'sɛptəs

concern
BR kən'səːn, -z, -ɪŋ, -d
AM kən'sərn, -z, -ɪŋ, -d

concernedly
BR kən'səːnɪdli
AM kən'sərnədli

concernedness
BR kən'səːnɪdnɪs
AM kən'sərnədnəs

concerningly
BR kən'səːnɪŋli
AM kən'sərnɪŋli

concernment
BR kən'səːnm(ə)nt, -s
AM kən'sərnmənt, -s

concert[1]
noun, agreement
BR 'kɒnsəːt
AM 'kɑnsərt

concert[2]
noun, musical performance
BR 'kɒnsət, -s
AM 'kɑnˌsərt, -s

concert[3]
verb
BR kən'səːt, -s, -ɪŋ, -ɪd
AM kən'sər|t, -ts, -dɪŋ, -dəd

concertante
BR ˌkɒntʃə'tanteɪ, ˌkɒntʃə'tanti
AM ˌkɑntʃər'tɑnˌteɪ, ˌkɔnsər'tɑnˌteɪ, ˌkɑntʃər'tɑnˌteɪ, ˌkɑnsər'tɑnˌteɪ

concerted
BR kən'səːtɪd
AM kən'sərdəd

concertedly
BR kən'səːtɪdli
AM kən'sərdədli

Concertgebouw
BR kən'səːtgɪˌbaʊ
AM kən'sərtgəˌbaʊ
DU kɔn'sɛrtxəˌbɔʊ

concertgoer
BR 'kɒnsətˌgəʊə(r), -z
AM 'kɑnsərtˌgoʊər, -z

concerti grossi
BR kənˌtʃɛːtiː 'grɒsiː, kənˌtʃəːtiː +
AM kənˌtʃɛrˌdi 'grɔsi, kənˌsɛrˌdi +

concertina
BR ˌkɒnsə'tiːnə(r), -z, -ɪŋ, -d
AM ˌkɑnsər'tinə, -z, -ɪŋ, -d

concertino
BR ˌkɒn(t)ʃə'tiːnəʊ, -z
AM ˌkɑn(t)ʃər'tinoʊ, ˌkɑnsər'tinoʊ , -z

concertmaster
BR 'kɒnsətˌmɑːstə(r), 'kɒnsətˌmastə(r), -z
AM 'kɑnsərtˌmæstər, -z

concerto
BR kən'tʃɛːtəʊ, kən'tʃəːtəʊ, -z
AM kən'(t)ʃɛrdoʊ, -z

concerto grosso
BR kənˌtʃɛːtəʊ 'grɒsəʊ, kənˌtʃəːtəʊ +, -z
AM kənˌ(t)ʃɛrˌdoʊ 'groʊsoʊ, -z

concession
BR kən'sɛʃn, -z
AM kən'sɛʃən, -z

concessionaire
BR kənˌsɛʃə'nɛː(r), kənˌsɛʃn̩'ɛː(r), -z
AM kənˌsɛʃə'nɛ(ə)r, -z

concessionary
BR kən'sɛʃn̩(ə)ri
AM kən'sɛʃəˌnɛri

concessive
BR kən'sɛsɪv
AM kən'sɛsɪv

conch
BR kɒn(t)ʃ, kɒŋk
AM kɑntʃ, kɑŋk

concha
BR 'kɒŋkə(*r*)
AM 'kɑŋkə

conchae
BR 'kɒŋkiː
AM 'kɑŋki, 'kɑŋˌkaɪ

conches
BR 'kɒn(t)ʃɪz, kɒŋks
AM 'kɑn(t)ʃəz, kɑŋks

conchie
BR 'kɒnʃ|i, -ɪz
AM 'kɑn(t)ʃi, -z

conchoid
BR 'kɒŋkɔɪd, -z
AM 'kɑŋˌkɔɪd, -z

conchoidal
BR kɒŋ'kɔɪdl
AM ˌkɑŋ'kɔɪdəl

conchological
BR ˌkɒŋkə'lɒdʒɪkl
AM ˌkɑŋkə'lɑdʒəkəl

conchologically
BR ˌkɒŋkə'lɒdʒɪkli
AM ˌkɑŋkə'lɑdʒək(ə)li

conchologist
BR kɒŋ'kɒlədʒɪst, -s
AM ˌkɑŋ'kɑlədʒəst, -s

conchology
BR kɒŋ'kɒlədʒi
AM ˌkɑŋ'kɑlədʒi

conchy
BR 'kɒnʃ|i, -ɪz
AM 'kɑn(t)ʃi, -z

concierge
BR 'kɒnsɪɛːʒ, 'kɒ̃sɪɛːʒ, ˌkɒnsɪ'ɛːʒ, ˌkɒ̃sɪ'ɛːʒ, -ɪz
AM ˌkɑn'sɪɛr(d)ʒ, -əz

conciliar
BR kən'sɪlɪə(r)
AM kən'sɪliər

conciliate
BR kən'sɪlɪeɪt, -s, -ɪŋ, -ɪd
AM kən'sɪliˌeɪ|t, -ts, -dɪŋ, -dɪd

conciliation
BR kənˌsɪlɪ'eɪʃn
AM kənˌsɪli'eɪʃən

conciliative
BR kən'sɪlɪətɪv, kən'sɪlɪeɪtɪv
AM kən'sɪliədɪv, kən'sɪliˌeɪdɪv

conciliator
BR kən'sɪlɪeɪtə(r), -z
AM kən'sɪliˌeɪdər, -z

conciliatoriness
BR kən'sɪlɪətrɪnɪs
AM kən'sɪliəˌtɔrinɪs

conciliatory
BR kən'sɪlɪət(ə)ri
AM kən'sɪliəˌtɔri

concinnity
BR kən'sɪnɪti
AM kən'sɪnɪdi

concinnous
BR kən'sɪnəs
AM kən'sɪnəs

concise
BR kən'sʌɪs
AM kən'saɪs

concisely
BR kən'sʌɪsli
AM kən'saɪsli

conciseness
BR kən'sʌɪsnɪs
AM kən'saɪsnɪs

concision
BR kən'sɪʒn
AM kən'sɪʒən

conclave
BR 'kɒŋkleɪv, -z
AM 'kɑnˌkleɪv, 'kɑŋˌkleɪv, -z

conclude
BR kən'kluːd, kəŋ'kluːd, -z, -ɪŋ, -ɪd
AM kən'klud, -z, -ɪŋ, -əd

conclusion
BR kən'kluːʒn, kəŋ'kluːʒn, -z
AM kən'kluʒən, -z

conclusive
BR kən'kluːsɪv, kəŋ'kluːsɪv
AM kən'klusɪv

conclusively
BR kən'kluːsɪvli, kəŋ'kluːsɪvli
AM kən'klusɪvli

conclusiveness
BR kən'kluːsɪvnɪs, kəŋ'kluːsɪvnɪs
AM kən'klusɪvnɪs

concoct
BR kən'kɒkt, kəŋ'kɒkt, -s, -ɪŋ, -ɪd
AM kən'kɑk|(t), -(t)s, -tɪŋ, -təd

concocter
BR kən'kɒktə(r), kəŋ'kɒktə(r), -z
AM kən'kɑktər, -z

concoction
BR kən'kɒkʃn, kəŋ'kɒkʃn, -z
AM kən'kɑkʃən, -z

concoctor
BR kən'kɒktə(r), kəŋ'kɒktə(r), -z
AM kən'kɑktər, -z

concomitance
BR kən'kɒmɪt(ə)ns, kəŋ'kɒmɪt(ə)ns
AM kən'kɑmədəns

concomitancy
BR kən'kɒmɪt(ə)nsi, kəŋ'kɒmɪt(ə)nsi
AM kən'kɑmədənsi

concomitant
BR kən'kɒmɪt(ə)nt, kəŋ'kɒmɪt(ə)nt
AM kən'kɑmədənt

concomitantly
BR kən'kɒmɪt(ə)ntli, kəŋ'kɒmɪt(ə)ntli
AM kən'kɑmədən(t)li

concord
BR 'kɒŋkɔːd, 'kɒnkɔːd
AM 'kɑŋkərd

concordance
BR kən'kɔːd(ə)ns, kəŋ'kɔːd(ə)ns, -ɪz
AM kən'kɔrdns, -əz

concordant
BR kən'kɔːd(ə)nt, kəŋ'kɔːd(ə)nt
AM kən'kɔrdnt

concordantly
BR kən'kɔːd(ə)ntli, kəŋ'kɔːd(ə)ntli
AM kən'kɔrdn(t)li

concordat
BR kɒn'kɔːdat, kɒŋ'kɔːdat, kən'kɔːdat, kəŋ'kɔːdat, -s
AM kɑn'kɔrˌdæt, -s

Concorde
BR 'kɒŋkɔːd, -z

AM 'kaŋ,kɔ(ə)rd, 'kan,kɔ(ə)rd, -z

concourse
BR 'kɒŋkɔːs, -ɪz
AM 'kaŋ,kɔ(ə)rs, 'kan,kɔ(ə)rs, -əz

concrescence
BR kən'krɛsns, kəŋ'krɛsns
AM kən'krɛsəns

concrescent
BR kən'krɛsnt, kəŋ'krɛsnt
AM kən'krɛsənt

concrete
BR 'kɒŋkriːt
AM ,kan'krit, ,kaŋ'krit

concretely
BR 'kɒŋkriːtli
AM ,kan'kritli, ,kaŋ'kritli

concreteness
BR 'kɒŋkriːtnɨs
AM ,kan'kritnɨs, ,kaŋ'kritnɨs

concretion
BR kən'kriːʃn, kəŋ'kriːʃn, -z
AM kən'kriʃən, -z

concretionary
BR kən'kriːʃn̩(ə)ri, kəŋ'kriːʃn̩(ə)ri
AM kən'kriʃə,nɛri

concretisation
BR ,kɒŋkriːtʌɪ'zeɪʃn, ,kɒŋkrɨtʌɪ'zeɪʃn
AM ,kaŋkrə,taɪ'zeɪʃən, ,kaŋkrədə'zeɪʃən, ,kankrədə'zeɪʃən, ,kankrə,taɪ'zeɪʃən

concretise
BR 'kɒŋkriːtʌɪz, 'kɒŋkrɨtʌɪz, -ɨz, -ɪŋ, -d
AM 'kaŋkrə,taɪz, 'kankrə,taɪz, -ɨz, -ɪŋ, -d

concretization
BR ,kɒŋkriːtʌɪ'zeɪʃn, ,kɒŋkrɨtʌɪ'zeɪʃn
AM ,kaŋkrə,taɪ'zeɪʃən, ,kaŋkrədə'zeɪʃən, ,kankrədə'zeɪʃən, ,kankrə,taɪ'zeɪʃən

concretize
BR 'kɒŋkriːtʌɪz, 'kɒŋkrɨtʌɪz, -ɨz, -ɪŋ, -d
AM 'kaŋkrə,taɪz, 'kaŋkrə,taɪz, -ɨz, -ɪŋ, -d

concubinage
BR kɒn'kjuːbɨnɪdʒ, kɒŋ'kjuːbɨnɪdʒ, kən'kjuːbɨnɪdʒ, kəŋ'kjuːbɨnɪdʒ
AM kən'kjubənɪdʒ

concubinary
BR kɒn'kjuːbɨn(ə)ri, kɒŋ'kjuːbɨn(ə)ri, kən'kjuːbɨn(ə)ri, kəŋ'kjuːbɨn(ə)ri
AM kən'kjubə,nɛri

concubine
BR 'kɒŋkjʉbʌɪn, -z
AM 'kaŋkjə,baɪn, 'kankjə,baɪn, -z

concupiscence
BR kən'kjuːpɨs(ə)ns, kəŋ'kjuːpɨs(ə)ns
AM kan'kjupəsəns, ,kaŋ'kjupəsəns

concupiscent
BR kən'kjuːpɨs(ə)nt, kəŋ'kjuːpɨs(ə)nt
AM kan'kjupəsənt, ,kaŋ'kjupəsənt

concur
BR kən'kəː(r), kəŋ'kəː(r), -z, -ɪŋ, -d
AM kən'kər, -z, -ɪŋ, -d

concurrence
BR kən'kʌrəns, kən'kʌrn̩s, kəŋ'kʌrəns, kəŋ'kʌrn̩s
AM kən'kərəns

concurrent
BR kən'kʌrənt, kən'kʌrn̩t, kəŋ'kʌrənt, kəŋ'kʌrn̩t
AM kən'kərənt

concurrently
BR kən'kʌrəntli, kən'kʌrn̩tli, kəŋ'kʌrəntli, kəŋ'kʌrn̩tli
AM kən'kərən(t)li

concuss
BR kən'kʌs, kəŋ'kʌs, -ɨz, -ɪŋ, -t
AM kən'kəs, -əz, -ɪŋ, -t

concussion
BR kən'kʌʃn, kəŋ'kʌʃn
AM kən'kəʃən

concussive
BR kən'kʌsɪv, kəŋ'kʌsɪv
AM kən'kəsɪv

condemn
BR kən'dɛm, -z, -ɪŋ, -d
AM kən'dɛm, -z, -ɪŋ, -d

condemnable
BR kən'dɛmnəbl
AM kən'dɛm(n)əbəl

condemnation
BR ,kɒndɛm'neɪʃn, ,kɒndəm'neɪʃn
AM ,kandɛm'neɪʃən

condemnatory
BR kən'dɛmnət(ə)ri, ,kɒndɛm'neɪt(ə)ri, ,kɒndəm'neɪt(ə)ri
AM ,kən'dɛmnə,tɔri

condensable
BR kən'dɛnsəbl
AM kən'dɛnsəbəl

condensate
BR 'kɒndɛnseɪt, 'kɒnd(ə)nseɪt, kən'dɛnseɪt, -s
AM kən'dɛn,seɪt, -s

condensation
BR ,kɒndɛn'seɪʃn, ,kɒnd(ə)n'seɪʃn
AM ,kandɛn'seɪʃən

condense
BR kən'dɛns, -ɨz, -ɪŋ, -t
AM kən'dɛns, -əz, -ɪŋ, -t

condenser
BR kən'dɛnsə(r), -z
AM kən'dɛnsər, -z

condensery
BR kən'dɛns(ə)r|i, -ɪz
AM kən'dɛns(ə)ri, -z

condescend
BR ,kɒndɪ'sɛnd, -z, -ɪŋ, -ɨd
AM ,kandə'sɛnd, -z, -ɪŋ, -əd

condescendingly
BR ,kɒndɪ'sɛndɪŋli
AM ,kandə'sɛndɪŋli

condescension
BR ,kɒndɪ'sɛnʃn
AM ,kandə'sɛn(t)ʃən

condign
BR kən'dʌɪn, 'kɒndʌɪn
AM kən'daɪn, 'kan,daɪn

condignly
BR kən'dʌɪnli, 'kɒndʌɪnli
AM kən'daɪnli, 'kan,daɪnli

condiment
BR 'kɒndɪm(ə)nt, -s
AM 'kandəmənt, -s

condition
BR kən'dɪʃ|n, -nz, -n̩ɪŋ\-nɪŋ, -nd
AM kən'dɪʃ|ən, -nz, -(ə)nɪŋ, -nd

conditional
BR kən'dɪʃn̩(ə)l, kən'dɪʃən(ə)l
AM kən'dɪʃ(ə)nəl

conditionality
BR kən,dɪʃə'nalɨti
AM kən,dɪʃə'nælədi

conditionally
BR kən'dɪʃn̩əli, kən'dɪʃn̩l̩i, kən'dɪʃənl̩i, kən'dɪʃ(ə)nəli
AM kən'dɪʃ(ə)nəli

conditioner
BR kən'dɪʃn̩ə(r), kən'dɪʃ(ə)nə(r), -z
AM kən'dɪʃ(ə)nər, -z

condo
BR 'kɒndəʊ, -z
AM 'kandoʊ, -z

condolatory
BR kən'dəʊlət(ə)ri
AM kən'doʊlə,tɔri

condole
BR kən'dəʊl, -z, -ɪŋ, -d
AM kən'doʊl, -z, -ɪŋ, -d

condolence
BR kən'dəʊləns, kən'dəʊln̩s, -ɪz
AM kən'doʊləns, -əz

condom
BR 'kɒndəm, 'kɒndɒm, -z
AM 'kandəm, -z

condominium
BR ,kɒndə'mɪnɪəm, -z
AM ,kandə'mɪniəm, -z

condonation
BR ,kɒndə(ʊ)'neɪʃn
AM kən,doʊ'neɪʃən

condone
BR kən'dəʊn, -z, -ɪŋ, -d
AM kən'doʊn, -z, -ɪŋ, -d

condoner
BR kən'dəʊnə(r), -z
AM kən'doʊnər, -z

condor
BR 'kɒndɔː(r), -z
AM 'kan,dɔ(ə)r, -z

condottiere
BR ,kɒndɒtɪ'ɛːreɪ, ,kɒndɒtɪ'ɛːri
AM ,kan,dadi'ɛri

condottieri
BR ,kɒndɒtɪ'ɛːriː
AM ,kan,dadi'ɛri

conduce
BR kən'djuːs, kən'dʒuːs, -ɨz, -ɪŋ, -t
AM kən'd(j)us, -əz, -ɪŋ, -t

conducement
BR kən'djuːsm(ə)nt, kən'dʒuːsm(ə)nt, -s
AM kən'd(j)usmənt, -s

conducive
BR kən'djuːsɪv, kən'dʒuːsɪv
AM kən'd(j)usɪv

conducively
BR kən'djuːsɪvli, kən'dʒuːsɪvli
AM kən'd(j)usɪvli

conduciveness
BR kən'djuːsɪvnɨs, kən'dʒuːsɪvnɨs
AM kən'd(j)usɪvnɨs

conduct[1]
noun
BR 'kɒndʌkt, 'kɒndəkt
AM 'kan,dək(t)

conduct[2]
verb
BR kən'dʌkt, -s, -ɪŋ, -ɨd
AM kən'dək|(t), -(t)s, -tɪŋ, -təd

conductance
BR kən'dʌkt(ə)ns

AM kən'dəktns

conducti
BR kən'dʌktʌɪ
AM kən'dək,taɪ

conductibility
BR kən,dʌktɪ'bɪlɨti
AM kən,dəktə'bɪlɨdi

conductible
BR kən'dʌktɨbl
AM kən'dəktəbəl

conduction
BR kən'dʌkʃn
AM kən'dəkʃən

conductive
BR kən'dʌktɪv
AM kən'dəktɪv

conductively
BR kən'dʌktɨvli
AM kən'dəktɨvli

conductivity
BR ,kɒndʌk'tɪvɨti
AM ,kɑndək'tɪvɨdi

conductor
BR kən'dʌktə(r), -z
AM kən'dəktər, -z

conductorship
BR kən'dʌktəʃɪp
AM kən'dəktər,ʃɪp

conductress
BR kən'dʌktrɪs, -ɨz
AM kən'dəktrəs, -əz

conductus
BR kən'dʌktəs
AM kən'dəktəs

conduit
BR 'kɒnd(w)ɪt, 'kɒndjʊɪt, 'kʌndɪt, -s
AM 'kɑn,duət, 'kɑndwət, -s

condylar
BR 'kɒndɪlə(r)
AM 'kɑndələr

condylarth
BR 'kɒndɪlɑːθ, -s
AM 'kɑndə,lɑrθ, -s

condyle
BR 'kɒndʌɪl, 'kɒndɪl, -z
AM 'kɑn,daɪl, -z

condyloid
BR 'kɒndɪlɔɪd
AM 'kɑndə,lɔɪd

condyloma
BR ,kɒndɪ'ləʊmə(*r*), -z
AM ,kɑndə'loʊmə, -z

condylomata
BR ,kɒndɪ'ləʊmətə(*r*)
AM ,kɑndə'loʊmədə

cone
BR kəʊn, -z, -ɪŋ, -d
AM koʊn, -z, -ɪŋ, -d

conestoga
BR ,kɒnɪ'stəʊgə(*r*), -z
AM ,kɑnə'stoʊgə, -z

coney
BR 'kəʊn|i, -ɪz
AM 'koʊni, -z

confab¹
noun
BR 'kɒnfab, -z
AM 'kɑnfæb, -z

confab²
verb
BR kən'fab, -z, -ɪŋ, -d
AM kən'fæb, -z, -ɪŋ, -d

confabulate
BR kən'fabjʊleɪt, -s, -ɪŋ, -ɨd
AM kən'fæbjə,leɪ|t, -ts, -dɪŋ, -dɨd

confabulation
BR kən,fabjʊ'leɪʃn, -z
AM kən,fæbjə'leɪʃən, -z

confabulatory
BR kən'fabjʊlət(ə)ri
AM kən'fæbjələ,tɔri

confect
BR kən'fɛkt, -s, -ɪŋ, -ɨd
AM kən'fɛk|t, -s, -tɪŋ, -təd

confection
BR kən'fɛkʃn, -z
AM kən'fɛkʃən, -z

confectionary
BR kən'fɛkʃn̩(ə)r|i, kən'fɛkʃnər|i, -ɪz
AM kən'fɛkʃə,nɛri, -z

confectioner
BR kən'fɛkʃn̩ə(r), -z
AM kən'fɛkʃənər, -z

confectionery
BR kən'fɛkʃn̩(ə)r|i, kən'fɛkʃnər|i, -ɪz
AM kən'fɛkʃə,nɛri, -z

confederacy
BR kən'fɛd(ə)rəs|i, -ɪz
AM kən'fɛd(ə)rəsi, -z

confederate¹
noun, adjective
BR kən'fɛd(ə)rət, -s
AM kən'fɛd(ə)rət, -s

confederate²
verb
BR kən'fɛdəreɪt, -s, -ɪŋ, -ɨd
AM kən'fɛdə,reɪ|t, -ts, -dɪŋ, -dɨd

confederation
BR kən,fɛdə'reɪʃn, -z
AM kən,fɛdə'reɪʃən, -z

confer
BR kən'fəː(r), -z, -ɪŋ, -d
AM kən'fər, -z, -ɪŋ, -d

conferee
BR ,kɒnfə(ː)'riː, -z
AM ,kɑnfə'ri, -z

conference
BR 'kɒnf(ə)rəns, 'kɒnf(ə)rn̩s, -ɨz, -ɪŋ
AM 'kɑnf(ə)rəns, 'kɑnf(ə)rəns, -əz, -ɪŋ

conferential
BR ,kɒnfə'rɛnʃl
AM ,kɑnfə'rɛn(t)ʃəl

conferment
BR kən'fəːm(ə)nt, -s
AM kən'fərmənt, -s

conferrable
BR kən'fəːrəbl
AM kən'fərəbəl

conferral
BR kən'fəːrl̩, -z
AM kən'fərəl, -z

confess
BR kən'fɛs, -ɨz, -ɪŋ, -t
AM kən'fɛs, -əz, -ɪn, -t

confessant
BR kən'fɛsnt, -s
AM kən'fɛsənt, -s

confessedly
BR kən'fɛsɨdli
AM kən'fɛsədli

confession
BR kən'fɛʃn, -z
AM kən'fɛʃən, -z

confessional
BR kən'fɛʃn̩(ə)l, kən'fɛʃən(ə)l, -z
AM kən'fɛʃ(ə)nəl, -z

confessionary
BR kən'fɛʃn̩(ə)ri
AM kən'fɛʃə,nɛri

confessor
BR kən'fɛsə(r), -z
AM kən'fɛsər, kən'fɛ,sɔ(ə)r, -z

confetti
BR kən'fɛti
AM kən'fɛdi

confidant
BR 'kɒnfɪdant, ,kɒnfɪ'dant, -s
AM 'kɑnfə,dænt, 'kɑnfə,dɑnt, -s

confidante
BR 'kɒnfɪdant, ,kɒnfɪ'dant, -s
AM 'kɑnfə,dænt, 'kɑnfə,dɑnt, -s

confide
BR kən'fʌɪd, -z, -ɪŋ, -ɨd
AM kən'faɪd, -z, -ɪŋ, -ɨd

confidence
BR 'kɒnfɪd(ə)ns, -ɨz
AM 'kɑnfədns, -ɨz

confident
BR 'kɒnfɪd(ə)nt
AM 'kɑnfədnt

confidential
BR ,kɒnfɪ'dɛnʃl
AM ,kɑnfə'dɛn(t)ʃəl

confidentiality
BR ,kɒnfɪ,dɛnʃɪ'alɪt|i, -ɪz
AM ,kɑnfə,dɛn(t)ʃi'ælədi, -z

confidentially
BR ,kɒnfɪ'dɛnʃl̩i, ,kɒnfɪ'dɛnʃəli
AM ,kɑnfə'dɛn(t)ʃəli

confidently
BR 'kɒnfɪd(ə)ntli
AM 'kɑnfədən(t)li

confiding
BR kən'fʌɪdɪŋ
AM kən'faɪdɪŋ

confidingly
BR kən'fʌɪdɪŋli
AM kən'faɪdɪŋli

configuration
BR kən,fɪgə'reɪʃn, kən,fɪgjʊ'reɪʃn, -z
AM kən,fɪg(j)ə'reɪʃən, -z

configurational
BR kən,fɪgə'reɪʃn̩(ə)l, kən,fɪgə'reɪʃən(ə)l, kən,fɪgjʊ'reɪʃn̩(ə)l, kən,fɪgjʊ'reɪʃən(ə)l
AM kən,fɪg(j)ə'reɪʃ(ə)nəl

configure
BR kən'fɪg|ə(r), -əz, -(ə)rɪŋ, -əd
AM kən'fɪgjər, -z, -ɪŋ, -d

confine
verb
BR kən'fʌɪn, -z, -ɪŋ, -d
AM kən'faɪn, -z, -ɪŋ, -d

confinement
BR kən'fʌɪnm(ə)nt, -s
AM kən'faɪnmənt, -s

confines
noun
BR 'kɒnfʌɪnz
AM 'kɑn,faɪnz

confirm
BR kən'fəːm, -z, -ɪŋ, -d
AM kən'fərm, -z, -ɪŋ, -d

confirmand
BR 'kɒnfəmand, ,kɒnfə'mand, -z
AM ¦kɑnfər¦mænd, -z

confirmation
BR ,kɒnfə'meɪʃn, -z
AM ,kɑnfər'meɪʃən, -z

confirmative
BR kən'fəːmətɪv
AM kən'fərmədɪv

confirmatory
BR kən'fəːmət(ə)ri, ,kɒnfə'meɪt(ə)ri
AM kən'fərmə,tɔri

confiscable
BR 'kɒnfɪskəbl
AM 'kɑnfəskəbəl

confiscate
BR 'kɒnfɪskeɪt, -s, -ɪŋ, -ɨd
AM 'kɑnfə,skeɪ|t, -ts, -dɪŋ, -dɨd

confiscation
BR ,kɒnfɪ'skeɪʃn, -z
AM ,kɑnfə'skeɪʃən, -z

confiscator
BR 'kɒnfɪskeɪtə(r), -z
AM 'kɑnfə,skeɪdər, -z

confiscatory
BR kən'fɪskət(ə)ri, ˌkɒnfɪ'skeɪt(ə)ri
AM kən'fɪskəˌtɔri

confiture
BR 'kɒnfɪtjʊə(r), 'kɒnfɪtʃə(r), -z
AM 'kɑnfətʃər, -z

conflagration
BR ˌkɒnflə'greɪʃn, -z
AM ˌkɑnflə'greɪʃən, -z

conflate
BR kən'fleɪt, -s, -ɪŋ, -ɨd
AM kən'fleɪ|t, -ts, -dɪŋ, -dɨd

conflation
BR kən'fleɪʃn, -z
AM kən'fleɪʃən, -z

conflict[1]
noun
BR 'kɒnflɪkt, -s
AM 'kɑnˌflɪk(t), -s

conflict[2]
verb
BR kən'flɪkt, -s, -ɪŋ, -ɨd
AM kən'flɪk|(t), -(t)s, -tɪŋ, -tɨd

confliction
BR kən'flɪkʃn, -z
AM kən'flɪkʃən, -z

conflictual[1]
BR kən'flɪktʃʊəl, kən'flɪktʃ(ʉ)l, kən'flɪktjʊəl, kən'flɪktjʉl
AM kən'flɪk(t)ʃ(əw)əl

conflictual[2]
BR kən'flɪktʃʊəl, kən'flɪktʃ(ʊ)l, kən'flɪktjʊəl, kən'flɪktjʉl
AM kən'flɪk(t)ʃ(əw)əl

confluence
BR 'kɒnflʊəns, -ɪz
AM 'kɑnˌfluəns, kən'fluəns, -əz

confluent
BR 'kɒnflʊənt
AM 'kɑnˌfluənt, kən'fluənt

conflux
BR 'kɒnflʌks, -ɪz
AM 'kɑnˌfləks, -əz

conform
BR kən'fɔːm, -z, -ɪŋ, -d
AM kən'fɔ(ə)rm, -z, -ɪŋ, -d

conformability
BR kənˌfɔːmə'bɪlɪti
AM kən'fɔrməbɪlɨdi

conformable
BR kən'fɔːməbl
AM kən'fɔrməbəl

conformably
BR kən'fɔːməbli
AM kən'fɔrməbli

conformal
BR kən'fɔːml
AM kən'fɔrməl

conformally
BR kən'fɔːmli, kən'fɔːməli
AM kən'fɔrməli

conformance
BR kən'fɔːməns
AM kən'fɔrməns

conformation
BR ˌkɒnfɔː'meɪʃn, ˌkɒnfə'meɪʃn
AM ˌkɑnfər'meɪʃən, ˌkɑnfɔr'meɪʃən

conformer
BR kən'fɔːmə(r), -z
AM kən'fɔrmər, -z

conformism
BR kən'fɔːmɪz(ə)m
AM kən'fɔrˌmɪzəm

conformist
BR kən'fɔːmɪst, -s
AM kən'fɔrməst, -s

conformity
BR kən'fɔːmɪti
AM kən'fɔrmədi

confound
BR kən'faʊnd, -z, -ɪŋ, -ɨd
AM kən'faʊnd, -z, -ɪŋ, -əd

confoundedly
BR kən'faʊndɨdli
AM kən'faʊndədli

confraternity
BR ˌkɒnfrə'təːnɪt|i, -ɪz
AM ˌkɑnfrə'tərnədi, -z

confrère
BR 'kɒnfrɛː(r), -z
AM 'kɑnˌfrɛ(ə)r, -z

confront
BR kən'frʌnt, -s, -ɪŋ, -ɨd
AM kən'frən|t, -ts, -(t)ɪŋ, -(t)əd

confrontation
BR ˌkɒnfrʌn'teɪʃn, ˌkɒnfrən'teɪʃn, -z
AM ˌkɑnfrən'teɪʃən, -z

confrontational
BR ˌkɒnfrʌn'teɪʃn̩(ə)l, ˌkɒnfrʌn'teɪʃən(ə)l, ˌkɒnfrən'teɪʃn̩(ə)l, ˌkɒnfrən'teɪʃən(ə)l
AM ˌkɑnfrən'teɪʃ(ə)nəl

confrontationally
BR ˌkɒnfrʌn'teɪʃn̩əli, ˌkɒnfrʌn'teɪʃn̩li, ˌkɒnfrʌn'teɪʃənli, ˌkɒnfrʌn'teɪʃ(ə)nəli, ˌkɒnfrən'teɪʃn̩əli, ˌkɒnfrən'teɪʃn̩li, ˌkɒnfrən'teɪʃənli, ˌkɒnfrən'teɪʃ(ə)nəli
AM ˌkɑnfrən'teɪʃ(ə)nəli

Confucian
BR kən'fjuːʃn, -z
AM kən'fjuʃən, -z

Confucianism
BR kən'fjuːʃn̩ɪz(ə)m
AM kən'fjuʃəˌnɪzəm

Confucianist
BR kən'fjuːʃn̩ɪst, -s
AM kən'fjuʃənəst, -s

Confucius
BR kən'fjuːʃəs
AM kən'fjuʃəs

confusability
BR kənˌfjuːzə'bɪlɪti
AM kənˌfjuzə'bɪlɨdi

confusable
BR kən'fjuːzəbl
AM kən'fjuzəbəl

confusably
BR kən'fjuːzəbli
AM kən'fjuzəbli

confuse
BR kən'fjuːz, -ɪz, -ɪŋ, -d
AM kən'fjuz, -əz, -ɪŋ, -d

confusedly
BR kən'fjuːzɪdli
AM kən'fjuzədli

confusible
BR kən'fjuːzɪbl, -z
AM kən'fjuzəbəl, -z

confusing
BR kən'fjuːzɪŋ
AM kən'fjuzɪŋ

confusingly
BR kən'fjuːzɪŋli
AM kən'fjuzɪŋli

confusion
BR kən'fjuːʒn
AM kən'fjuʒən

confutable
BR kən'fjuːtəbl
AM kən'fjudəbəl

confutation
BR ˌkɒnfjʉ'teɪʃn, -z
AM ˌkɑnfjə'teɪʃən, -z

confute
BR kən'fjuːt, -s, -ɪŋ, -ɨd
AM kən'fju|t, -ts, -dɪŋ, -dəd

conga
BR 'kɒŋgə(*r*), -z
AM 'kɑŋgə, -z

congé
BR 'kɒnʒeɪ, 'kɔ̃ʒeɪ, -z
AM 'kɑnˌdʒeɪ, 'kɔnˌʒeɪ, -z

congeal
BR kən'dʒiːl, -z, -ɪŋ, -d
AM kən'dʒil, -z, -ɪŋ, -d

congealable
BR kən'dʒiːləbl
AM kən'dʒiləbəl

congealment
BR kən'dʒiːlm(ə)nt
AM kən'dʒilmənt

congelation
BR ˌkɒndʒɪ'leɪʃn, -z
AM ˌkɑndʒə'leɪʃən, -z

congener
BR kən'dʒiːnə(r), -z
AM kən'dʒinər, -z

congeneric
BR ˌkɒndʒɪ'nɛrɪk
AM ˌkɑndʒə'nɛrɪk

congenerous
BR kən'dʒɛn(ə)rəs, ˌkɒn'dʒɛn(ə)rəs
AM kən'dʒɛnərəs, kən'dʒinərəs

congenerousness
BR kən'dʒɛn(ə)rəsnəs, ˌkɒn'dʒɛn(ə)rəsnəs
AM kən'dʒɛnərəsnəs, kən'dʒinərəsnəs

congenial
BR kən'dʒiːnɪəl
AM kən'dʒinjəl, kən'dʒiniəl

congeniality
BR kənˌdʒiːnɪ'alɪti
AM kənˌdʒini'ælədi

congenially
BR kən'dʒiːnɪəli
AM kən'dʒinjəli, kən'dʒiniəli

congenital
BR kən'dʒɛnɪtl
AM kən'dʒɛnədl

congenitally
BR kən'dʒɛnɪtl̩i, kən'dʒɛnɪtəli
AM kən'dʒɛnədl̩i, kən'dʒɛnədəli

conger
BR 'kɒŋgə(r), -z
AM 'kɑŋgər, -z

congeries
BR 'kɒn(d)ʒ(ə)rɪz
AM 'kɑndʒəriz

congest
BR kən'dʒɛst, -s, -ɪŋ, -ɨd
AM kən'dʒɛst, -s, -ɪŋ, -əd

congestion
BR kən'dʒɛstʃn
AM kən'dʒɛstʃən

congestive
BR kən'dʒɛstɪv
AM kən'dʒɛstɪv

congii
BR 'kɒndʒɪʌɪ
AM 'kɑndʒiaɪ

congius
BR 'kɒndʒɪəs
AM 'kɑndʒiəs

conglomerate[1]
noun, adjective
BR kən'glɒm(ə)rət, kəŋ'glɒm(ə)rət, -s
AM kən'glɑm(ə)rət, -s

conglomerate[2]
verb
BR kən'glɒməreɪt, kəŋ'glɒməreɪt, -s, -ɪŋ, -ɨd
AM kən'glɑməˌreɪ|t, -ts, -dɪŋ, -dɨd

conglomeration
BR kən,glɒmə'reɪʃn, kəŋ,glɒmə'reɪʃn, -z
AM kən,glɑmə'reɪʃən, -z

Congo
BR 'kɒŋgəʊ
AM 'kɑŋgoʊ

Congolese
BR ˌkɒŋgə'liːz
AM ˌkɑŋgə'liz

congou
BR 'kɒŋguː, 'kɒŋgəʊ
AM 'kɑŋgoʊ, 'kɑŋgu

congrats
BR kən'grats, kəŋ'grats
AM kən'græts

congratulant
BR kən'gratʃʉlənt, kən'gratʃʉln̩t, kəŋ'gratʃʉlənt, kəŋ'gratʃʉln̩t, kən'gratjʉlənt, kən'gratjʉln̩t, kəŋ'gratjʉlənt, kəŋ'gratjʉln̩t, -s
AM kən'grætʃələnt, -s

congratulate
BR kən'gratʃʉleɪt, kəŋ'gratʃʉleɪt, kən'gratjʉleɪt, kəŋ'gratjʉleɪt, -s, -ɪŋ, -ɪd
AM kən'grætʃə,leɪ|t, -ts, -dɪŋ, -dɪd

congratulation
BR kən,gratʃʉ'leɪʃn, kəŋ,gratʃʉ'leɪʃn, kən,gratjʉ'leɪʃn, kəŋ,gratjʉ'leɪʃn, -z
AM kəngrætʃə'leɪʃən, -z

congratulative
BR kən'gratʃʉlətɪv, kəŋ'gratʃʉlətɪv, kən'gratjʉlətɪv, kəŋ'gratjʉlətɪv
AM kən'grætʃələdɪv

congratulator
BR kən'gratʃʉleɪtə(r), kəŋ'gratʃʉleɪtə(r), kən'gratjʉleɪtə(r), kəŋ'gratjʉleɪtə(r), -z
AM kən'grætʃə,leɪdər, -z

congratulatory
BR kən,gratʃʉ'leɪt(ə)ri, kəŋ,gratʃʉ'leɪt(ə)ri, kən,gratjʉ'leɪt(ə)ri, kəŋ,gratjʉ'leɪt(ə)ri, kən'gratʃʉlət(ə)ri, kəŋ'gratʃʉlət(ə)ri, kən'gratjʉlət(ə)ri, kəŋ'gratʃʉlət(ə)ri
AM kən'grætʃələ,tɔri

congregant
BR 'kɒŋgrɪg(ə)nt, -s
AM 'kɑŋgrəgənt, -s

congregate
BR 'kɒŋgrɪgeɪt, -s, -ɪŋ, -ɪd
AM 'kɑŋgrə,geɪ|t, -ts, -dɪŋ, -dɪd

congregation
BR ˌkɒŋgrɪ'geɪʃn, -z
AM ˌkɑŋgrə'geɪʃən, -z

congregational
BR ˌkɒŋgrɪ'geɪʃn̩(ə)l, ˌkɒŋgrɪ'geɪʃən(ə)l
AM ˌkɑŋgrə'geɪʃ(ə)nəl

Congregationalism
BR ˌkɒŋgrɪ'geɪʃn̩əlɪz(ə)m, ˌkɒŋgrɪ'geɪʃn̩l̩ɪz(ə)m, ˌkɒŋgrɪ'geɪʃənl̩ɪz(ə)m, ˌkɒŋgrɪ'geɪʃ(ə)nəlɪz(ə)m
AM ˌkɑŋgrə'geɪʃənl,ɪzəm, ˌkɑŋgrə'geɪʃnə,lɪzəm

Congregationalist
BR ˌkɒŋgrɪ'geɪʃn̩əlɪst, ˌkɒŋgrɪ'geɪʃn̩l̩ɪst, ˌkɒŋgrɪ'geɪʃənl̩ɪst, ˌkɒŋgrɪ'geɪʃ(ə)nəlɪst, -s
AM ˌkɑŋgrə'geɪʃənl,əst, ˌkɑŋgrə'geɪʃnə,ləst, -s

congress
BR 'kɒŋgrɛs, 'kɒŋgrɪs, -ɪz
AM 'kɑŋgrəs, -əz

congressional
BR kən'grɛʃn̩(ə)l, kən'grɛʃən(ə)l, kəŋ'grɛʃn̩(ə)l, kəŋ'grɛʃən(ə)l
AM kən'grɛʃ(ə)nəl, ˌkɑŋ'grɛʃ(ə)nəl

congressman
BR 'kɒŋgrɪsmən
AM 'kɑŋgrəsmən

congressmen
BR 'kɒŋgrɪsmən
AM 'kɑŋgrəsmən

congresswoman
BR 'kɒŋgrɪs,wʊmən
AM 'kɑŋgrəs,wʊmən

congresswomen
BR 'kɒŋgrɪs,wɪmɪn
AM 'kɑŋgrəs,wɪmɪn

Congreve
BR 'kɒŋgriːv
AM 'kɑŋ,griv

congruence
BR 'kɒŋgrʊəns, -ɪz
AM kən'gruəns, 'kɑngrəwəns, -əz

congruency
BR 'kɒŋgrʊəns|i, -ɪz
AM kən'gruənsi, 'kɑngrəwənsi, -z

congruent
BR 'kɒŋgrʊənt
AM kən'gruənt, 'kɑŋgrəwənt

congruential
BR ˌkɒŋgrʊ'ɛnʃl
AM ˌkɑŋgru'ɛn(t)ʃəl

congruently
BR 'kɒŋgrʊəntli
AM kən'gruən(t)li, 'kɑŋgrəwən(t)li

congruity
BR kən'gruːɪti, kəŋ'gruːɪt|i, (ˌ)kɒn'gruːɪti, (ˌ)kɒŋ'gruːɪti, -ɪz
AM kən'gruədi, kɑŋ'gruədi, -z

congruous
BR 'kɒŋgrʊəs
AM 'kɑŋgrəwəs

congruously
BR 'kɒŋgrʊəsli
AM 'kɑŋgrəwəsli

congruousness
BR 'kɒŋgrʊəsnəs
AM 'kɑŋgrəwəsnəs

conic
BR 'kɒnɪk, -s
AM 'kɑnɪk, -s

conical
BR 'kɒnɪkl
AM 'kɑnəkəl

conically
BR 'kɒnɪkli
AM 'kɑnək(ə)li

conidia
BR kə(ʊ)'nɪdɪə(*r*)
AM kə'nɪdiə

conidial
BR kə(ʊ)'nɪdɪəl
AM kə'nɪdiəl

conidium
BR kə(ʊ)'nɪdɪəm
AM kə'nɪdiəm

conifer
BR 'kɒnɪfə(r), 'kəʊnɪfə(r), -z
AM 'kɑnəfər, -z

coniferous
BR kə'nɪf(ə)rəs
AM kə'nɪf(ə)rəs

coniform
BR 'kɒnɪfɔːm
AM 'koʊnə,fɔ(ə)rm, 'kɑnə,fɔ(ə)rm

coniine
BR 'kəʊnɪiːn
AM 'koʊniən, 'koʊni,in

Coningsby
BR 'kɒnɪŋzbi
AM 'kɑnɪŋzbi

Conisborough
BR 'kɒnɪsb(ə)rə(*r*)
AM 'kɑnəs,bəroʊ

Conisbrough
BR 'kɒnɪsbrə(*r*)
AM 'kɑnəsbrə

Coniston
BR 'kɒnɪst(ə)n
AM 'kɑnəstən

conium
BR 'kəʊnɪəm
AM 'koʊniəm

conjecturable
BR kən'dʒɛktʃ(ə)rəbl
AM kən'dʒɛk(t)ʃ(ə)rəbəl

conjecturably
BR kən'dʒɛktʃ(ə)rəbli
AM kən'dʒɛk(t)ʃ(ə)rəbli

conjectural
BR kən'dʒɛktʃ(ə)rəl, kən'dʒɛktʃ(ə)rl̩
AM kən'dʒɛk(t)ʃ(ə)rəl

conjecturally
BR kən'dʒɛktʃ(ə)rəli, kən'dʒɛktʃ(ə)rl̩i
AM kən'dʒɛk(t)ʃ(ə)rəli

conjecture
BR kən'dʒɛktʃ|ə(r), -əz, -(ə)rɪŋ, -əd
AM kən'dʒɛk(t)ʃər, -z, -ɪŋ, -d

conjoin
BR kən'dʒɔɪn, (ˌ)kɒn'dʒɔɪn, -z, -ɪŋ, -d
AM kən'dʒɔɪn, -z, -ɪŋ, -d

conjoint
BR kən'dʒɔɪnt, (ˌ)kɒn'dʒɔɪnt
AM kən'dʒɔɪnt, ˌkɑn'dʒɔɪnt

conjointly
BR kən'dʒɔɪntli, (ˌ)kɒn'dʒɔɪntli
AM kən'dʒɔɪn(t)li, ˌkɑn'dʒɔɪn(t)li

conjugal
BR 'kɒndʒʉgl̩
AM 'kɑndʒəgəl

conjugality
BR ˌkɒndʒʉ'galɪti
AM ˌkɑndʒə'gælədi

conjugally
BR 'kɒndʒʉgl̩i, 'kɒndʒʉgəli
AM 'kɑndʒəg(ə)li

conjugate[1]
adjective
BR 'kɒndʒʉgət
AM 'kɑndʒəgət

conjugate[2]
verb
BR 'kɒndʒʉgeɪt, -s, -ɪŋ, -ɪd
AM 'kɑndʒə,geɪ|t, -ts, -dɪŋ, -dɪd

conjugately
BR 'kɒndʒʉgətli
AM 'kɑndʒəgətli

conjugation
BR ˌkɒndʒʉ'geɪʃn, -z
AM ˌkɑndʒə'geɪʃən, -z

conjugational
BR ˌkɒndʒʉ'geɪʃn̩(ə)l, ˌkɒndʒʉ'geɪʃən(ə)l

AM ˌkandʒəˈgeɪʃ(ə)nəl

conjunct¹
adjective
BR kənˈdʒʌŋ(k)t
AM kənˈdʒəŋk(t)

conjunct²
noun
BR ˈkɒndʒʌŋ(k)t, -s
AM ˈkandʒəŋk(t), -s

conjunction
BR kənˈdʒʌŋ(k)ʃn, -z
AM kənˈdʒəŋ(k)ʃən, -z

conjunctional
BR kənˈdʒʌŋ(k)ʃn̩(ə)l, kənˈdʒʌŋ(k)ʃən(ə)l
AM kənˈdʒəŋ(k)ʃ(ə)nəl

conjunctionally
BR kənˈdʒʌŋ(k)ʃn̩əli, kənˈdʒʌŋ(k)ʃn̩li, kənˈdʒʌŋ(k)ʃənl̩i, kənˈdʒʌŋ(k)ʃ(ə)nəli
AM kənˈdʒəŋ(k)ʃ(ə)nəli

conjunctiva
BR ˌkɒndʒʌŋ(k)ˈtʌɪvə(r), -z
AM ˌkandʒəŋ(k)ˈtaɪvə, -z

conjunctivae
BR ˌkɒndʒʌŋ(k)ˈtʌɪviː
AM ˌkandʒəŋ(k)ˈtaɪvi, kənˈdʒəŋ(k)təˌvaɪ

conjunctival
BR ˌkɒndʒʌŋ(k)ˈtʌɪvl
AM ˌkandʒəŋ(k)ˈtaɪvəl

conjunctive
BR kənˈdʒʌŋ(k)tɪv
AM kənˈdʒəŋ(k)tɪv

conjunctively
BR kənˈdʒʌŋ(k)tɨvli
AM kənˈdʒəŋ(k)tɨvli

conjunctivitis
BR kənˌdʒʌŋ(k)tɪˈvʌɪtɨs
AM kənˌjəŋ(k)təˈvaɪdəs

conjuncture
BR kənˈdʒʌŋ(k)tʃə(r), -z
AM kənˈdʒəŋ(kt)ʃər, -z

conjuration
BR ˌkɒndʒʊˈreɪʃn, -z
AM ˌkandʒəˈeɪʃən, -z

conjure¹
command, charge
BR kənˈdʒʊə(r), -z, -ɪŋ, -d
AM kənˈdʒʊ(ə)r, -z, -ɪŋ, -d

conjure²
invoke, use magic
BR ˈkʌn(d)ʒ|ə(r), -əz, -(ə)rɪŋ, -əd
AM ˈkandʒər, -z, -ɪŋ, -d

conjurer
BR ˈkʌn(d)ʒ(ə)rə(r), -z
AM ˈkandʒərər, -z

conjuror
BR ˈkʌn(d)ʒ(ə)rə(r), -z
AM ˈkandʒərər, -z

conk
BR kɒŋ|k, -ks, -kɪŋ, -(k)t
AM kaŋ|k, kɔŋ|k, -ks, -kɪŋ, -(k)t

conker
BR ˈkɒŋkə(r), -z
AM ˈkaŋkər, ˈkɔŋkər, -z

Conley
BR ˈkɒnli
AM ˈkanli

Conlon
BR ˈkɒnlən
AM ˈkanlən

conman
BR ˈkɒnman
AM ˈkanˌmæn

conmen
BR ˈkɒnmɛn
AM ˈkanˌmɛn

con moto
BR ˌkɒn ˈməʊtəʊ
AM ˌkan ˈmoʊdoʊ

conn
BR kɒn, -z, -ɪŋ, -d
AM kan, -z, -ɪŋ, -d

Connacht
BR ˈkɒnɔːt, ˈkɒnət
AM ˈkanət

Connah
BR ˈkɒnə(r)
AM ˈkanə

connate
BR ˈkɒneɪt, kɒˈneɪt, kəˈneɪt
AM ˈkaneɪt, kəˈneɪt

connatural
BR kəˈnatʃ(ə)rəl, kəˈnatʃ(ə)rl̩
AM kəˈnætʃ(ə)rəl

connaturally
BR kəˈnatʃ(ə)rəli, kəˈnatʃ(ə)rl̩i
AM kəˈnætʃ(ə)rəli

Connaught
BR ˈkɒnɔːt, ˈkɒnət
AM ˈkanət

connect
BR kəˈnɛkt, -s, -ɪŋ, -ɨd
AM kəˈnɛk|(t), -(t)s, -tɪŋ, -təd

connectable
BR kəˈnɛktəbl
AM kəˈnɛktəbəl

connectedly
BR kəˈnɛktɨdli
AM kəˈnɛktədli

connectedness
BR kəˈnɛktɨdnɨs
AM kəˈnɛktədnəs

connecter
BR kəˈnɛktə(r), -z
AM kəˈnɛktər, -z

connectible
BR kəˈnɛktɨbl
AM kəˈnɛktəbəl

Connecticut
BR kəˈnɛtɨkət
AM kəˈnɛdəkət

connection
BR kəˈnɛkʃn, -z
AM kəˈnɛkʃən, -z

connectional
BR kəˈnɛkʃn̩(ə)l, kəˈnɛkʃən(ə)l
AM kəˈnɛkʃ(ə)nəl

connectionism
BR kəˈnɛkʃn̩ɪz(ə)m, kəˈnɛkʃənɪz(ə)m
AM kəˈnɛkʃəˌnɪzəm

connectionist
BR kəˈnɛkʃn̩ɪst, kəˈnɛkʃənɪst, -s
AM kəˈnɛkʃənəst, -s

connective
BR kəˈnɛktɪv
AM kəˈnɛktɪv

connectivity
BR ˌkɒnɛkˈtɪvɪti, kəˌnɛkˈtɪvɪti
AM kəˌnɛkˈtɪvɨdi, ˌkanɛkˈtɪvɨdi

connector
BR kəˈnɛktə(r), -z
AM kəˈnɛktər, -z

Connell
BR ˈkɒnl, kəˈnɛl
AM ˈkanəl

Connemara
BR ˌkɒnɪˈmɑːrə(r)
AM ˌkanəˈmɑrə

Conner
BR ˈkɒnə(r)
AM ˈkan(ə)r

Connery
BR ˈkɒn(ə)ri
AM ˈkan(ə)ri

connexion
BR kəˈnɛkʃn, -z
AM kəˈnɛkʃən, -z

connexional
BR kəˈnɛkʃn̩(ə)l, kəˈnɛkʃən(ə)l
AM kəˈnɛkʃ(ə)nəl

Connie
BR ˈkɒni
AM ˈkani

conniption
BR kəˈnɪpʃ(ə)n, -z
AM kəˈnɪpʃ(ə)n, -z

connivance
BR kəˈnʌɪvns
AM kəˈnaɪvəns

connive
BR kəˈnʌɪv, -z, -ɪŋ, -d
AM kəˈnaɪv, -z, -ɪŋ, -d

conniver
BR kəˈnʌɪvə(r), -z
AM kəˈnaɪvər, -z

connoisseur
BR ˌkɒnəˈsəː(r), -z
AM ˌkanəˈsər, -z

connoisseurship
BR ˌkɒnəˈsəːʃɪp
AM ˌkanəˈsərˌʃɪp

Connolly
BR ˈkɒnəli, ˈkɒnl̩i
AM ˈkan(ə)li

Connor
BR ˈkɒnə(r)
AM ˈkanər

Connors
BR ˈkɒnəz
AM ˈkanərz

connotation
BR ˌkɒnəˈteɪʃn, -z
AM ˌkanəˈteɪʃən, -z

connotative
BR ˈkɒnəteɪtɪv
AM ˈkanəˌteɪdɪv

connotatively
BR ˈkɒnəteɪtɨvli
AM ˈkanəˌteɪdɨvli

connote
BR kəˈnəʊt, -s, -ɪŋ, -ɨd
AM kəˈnoʊ|t, -ts, -dɪŋ, -dəd

connubial
BR kəˈnjuːbɪəl
AM kəˈnubiəl

connubiality
BR kəˌnjuːbɪˈalɨti
AM kəˌnubiˈælədi

connubially
BR kəˈnjuːbɪəli
AM kəˈnubiəli

conodont
BR ˈkəʊnədɒnt, -s
AM ˈkoʊnəˌdant, ˈkanəˌdant, -s

conoid
BR ˈkəʊnɔɪd, -z
AM ˈkoʊˌnɔɪd, -z

conoidal
BR kə(ʊ)ˈnɔɪdl
AM kəˈnɔɪdəl

Conor
BR ˈkɒnə(r)
AM ˈkanər

conquer
BR ˈkɒŋk|ə(r), -əz, -(ə)rɪŋ, -əd
AM ˈkaŋkər, -z, -ɪŋ, -d

conquerable
BR ˈkɒŋk(ə)rəbl
AM ˈkaŋk(ə)rəbəl

conqueror
BR ˈkɒŋk(ə)rə(r), -z
AM ˈkaŋkərər, -z

conquest
BR ˈkɒŋkwɛst, -s
AM ˈkanˌkwɛst, ˈkaŋˌkwɛst, -s

conquistador
BR kɒnˈk(w)ɪstədɔː(r), kɒŋˈk(w)ɪstədɔː(r), kənˈk(w)ɪstədɔː(r), kəŋˈk(w)ɪstədɔː(r), -z
AM ˌkanˌk(w)ɪstəˌdɔ(ə)r, kənˌk(w)ɪstəˌdɔ(ə)r,

ˌkɑŋˈk(w)ɪstəˈdɔ(ə)r,
ˌkɑnˈk(w)ɪstəˈdɔ(ə)r,
kənˈk(w)istəˈdɔ(ə)r,
ˌkɑŋˈk(w)istəˈdɔ(ə)r,
-z

conquistadores
BR kɒnˌk(w)ɪstəˈdɔːr-eɪz,
kɒŋˌk(w)ɪstəˈdɔːreɪz,
kənˌk(w)ɪstəˈdɔːreɪz,
kəŋˌk(w)ɪstəˈdɔːreɪz
AM ˌkɑnˈk(w)ɪstəˈdɔr-eɪz,
kənˈk(w)ɪstəˈdɔreɪz,
ˌkɑŋˈk(w)ɪstəˈdɔreɪz,
ˌkɑnˈk(w)istəˈdɔreɪz,
kənˈk(w)istəˈdɔreɪz,
ˌkɑŋˈk(w)istəˈdɔreɪz

Conrad
BR ˈkɒnrad
AM ˈkɑnˌræd

Conran
BR ˈkɒnrən
AM ˈkɑnrən

con-rod
BR ˈkɒnrɒd, -z
AM ˈkɑnˌrɑd, -z

Conroy
BR ˈkɒnrɔɪ
AM ˈkɑnˌrɔɪ

consanguineous
BR ˌkɒnsaŋˈgwɪnɪəs
AM ˌkɑnsæŋˈgwɪniəs

consanguineously
BR ˌkɒnsaŋˈgwɪnɪəsli
AM ˌkɑnsæŋˈgwɪniəsli

consanguinity
BR ˌkɒnsaŋˈgwɪnɨti
AM ˌkɑnsæŋˈgwɪnɨdi

conscience
BR ˈkɒnʃns, -ɨz
AM ˈkɑnʃəns, -əz

conscienceless
BR ˈkɒnʃnsləs
AM ˈkɑnʃənsləs

conscientious
BR ˌkɒnʃɪˈɛnʃəs
AM ˌkɑntʃiˈɛn(t)ʃəs

conscientiously
BR ˌkɒnʃɪˈɛnʃəsli
AM ˌkɑntʃiˈɛn(t)ʃəsli

conscientiousness
BR ˌkɒnʃɪˈɛnʃəsnəs
AM ˌkɑntʃiˈɛn(t)ʃəsnəs

conscionable
BR ˈkɒnʃənəbl,
ˈkɒnʃn̩əbl
AM ˈkɑnʃ(ə)nəbəl

conscious
BR ˈkɒnʃəs
AM ˈkɑnʃəs

consciously
BR ˈkɒnʃəsli
AM ˈkɑnʃəsli

consciousness
BR ˈkɒnʃəsnəs
AM ˈkɑnʃəsnəs

conscribe
BR kənˈskrʌɪb, -z, -ɪŋ, -d
AM kənˈskraɪb, -z, -ɪŋ, -d

conscript[1]
noun
BR ˈkɒnskrɪpt, -s
AM ˈkɑnˌskrɪpt, -s

conscript[2]
verb
BR kənˈskrɪpt, -s, -ɪŋ, -ɨd
AM kənˈskrɪp|t, -ts, -dɪŋ, -dɨd

conscription
BR kənˈskrɪpʃn
AM kənˈskrɪpʃən

consecrate
BR ˈkɒnsɪkreɪt, -s, -ɪŋ, -ɨd
AM ˈkɑnsəˌkreɪ|t, -ts, -dɪŋ, -dɨd

consecration
BR ˌkɒnsɪˈkreɪʃn, -z
AM ˌkɑnsəˈkreɪʃən, -z

consecrator
BR ˈkɒnsɪkreɪtə(r), -z
AM ˈkɑnsəˌkreɪdər, -z

consecratory
BR ˌkɒnsɪˈkreɪt(ə)ri
AM ˈkɑnsəkrəˌtɔri

consecution
BR ˌkɒnsɪˈkjuːʃn, -z
AM ˌkɑnsəˈkjuʃən, -z

consecutive
BR kənˈsɛkjʊtɪv
AM kənˈsɛkjədɪv

consecutively
BR kənˈsɛkjʊtɪvli
AM kənˈsɛkjədɪvli

consecutiveness
BR kənˈsɛkjʊtɪvnɪs
AM kənˈsɛkjədɪvnɪs

consensual
BR kənˈsɛnsjʊəl,
kənˈsɛnsj(ʉ)l,
kənˈsɛnʃʊəl,
kənˈsɛnʃ(ʉ)l,
(ˌ)kɒnˈsɛnsjʊəl,
(ˌ)kɒnˈsɛnsj(ʉ)l,
(ˌ)kɒnˈsɛnʃʊəl,
(ˌ)kɒnˈsɛnʃ(ʉ)l
AM kənˈsɛnʃ(əw)əl

consensually
BR kənˈsɛnsjʊəli,
kənˈsɛnsjʉli,
kənˈsɛnʃʊəli,
kənˈsɛnʃʉli,
kənˈsɛnʃl̩i,
(ˌ)kɒnˈsɛnsjʊəli,
(ˌ)kɒnˈsɛnsjʉli,
(ˌ)kɒnˈsɛnʃʊəli,
(ˌ)kɒnˈsɛnʃʉli,
(ˌ)kɒnˈsɛnʃl̩i
AM kənˈsɛnʃ(əw)əli

consensus
BR kənˈsɛnsəs
AM kənˈsɛnsəs

consent
BR kənˈsɛnt, -s, -ɪŋ, -ɨd
AM kənˈsɛn|t, -ts, -(t)ɪŋ, -(t)əd

consentaneous
BR ˌkɒns(ɛ)nˈteɪnɪəs
AM ˌkɑnsənˈteɪniəs

consentient
BR kənˈsɛnʃ(ə)nt
AM kənˈsɛnʃənt

consequence
BR ˈkɒnsɪkw(ə)ns, -ɨz
AM ˈkɑnsəkwəns,
ˈkɑnsəˌkwɛns, -əz

consequent
BR ˈkɒnsɪkw(ə)nt
AM ˈkɑnsəkwənt

consequential
BR ˌkɒnsɪˈkwɛnʃl
AM ˌkɑnsəˈkwɛnʃəl

consequentialism
BR ˌkɒnsɪˈkwɛnʃl̩-ɪz(ə)m,
ˌkɒnsɪˈkwɛnʃəlɪz(ə)m
AM ˌkɑnsəˈkwɛnʃəlɪzm

consequentialist
BR ˌkɒnsɪˈkwɛnʃl̩ɪst,
ˌkɒnsɪˈkwɛnʃəlɪst, -s
AM ˌkɑnsəˈkwɛnʃələst, -s

consequentiality
BR ˌkɒnsɪˌkwɛnʃɪˈalɨti
AM ˌkɑnsəˌkwɛnʃiˈæl-ədi

consequentially
BR ˌkɒnsɪˈkwɛnʃl̩i,
ˌkɒnsɪˈkwɛnʃəli
AM ˌkɑnsəˈkwɛnʃəli

consequently
BR ˈkɒnsɪkw(ə)ntli
AM ˈkɑnsəkwən(t)li

conservancy
BR kənˈsəːvns|i, -ɪz
AM kənˈsərvənsi, -z

conservation
BR ˌkɒnsəˈveɪʃn
AM ˌkɑnsərˈveɪʃən

conservational
BR ˌkɒnsəˈveɪʃn̩(ə)l,
ˌkɒnsəˈveɪʃən(ə)l
AM ˌkɑnsərˈveɪʃ(ə)nəl

conservationist
BR ˌkɒnsəˈveɪʃn̩ɪst,
ˌkɒnsəˈveɪʃənɪst, -s
AM ˌkɑnsərˈveɪʃənəst, -s

conservatism
BR kənˈsəːvətɪz(ə)m
AM kənˈsərvədɪzəm,
kənˈsərvəˌtɪzəm

conservative
BR kənˈsəːvətɪv, -z
AM kənˈsərvədɪv, -z

conservatively
BR kənˈsəːvətɪvli
AM kənˈsərvədɪvli

conservativeness
BR kənˈsəːvətɪvnɪs
AM kənˈsərvədɪvnɪs

conservatoire
BR kənˈsəːvətwɑː(r), -z
AM kənsərvəˈtwɑr, -z

conservator
BR kənˈsəːvətə(r),
ˈkɒnsəveɪtə(r), -z
AM kənˈsərvədər, -z

conservatoria
BR kənˌsəːvəˈtɔːrɪə(*r*)
AM kənˌsərvəˈtɔriə

conservatorium
BR kənˌsəːvəˈtɔːrɪəm, -z
AM kənˌsərvəˈtɔriəm, -z

conservatory
BR kənˈsəːvət(ə)r|i, -ɪz
AM kənˈsərvəˌtɔri, -ɪz

conserve[1]
noun
BR ˈkɒnsəːv, kənˈsəːv, -z
AM ˈkɑnsərv, kənˈsərv, -z

conserve[2]
verb
BR kənˈsəːv, -z, -ɪŋ, -d
AM kənˈsərv, -z, -ɪŋ, -d

consessional
BR kənˈsɛʃn̩(ə)l,
kənˈsɛʃən(ə)l
AM kənˈsɛʃ(ə)nəl

Consett
BR ˈkɒnsɪt, ˈkɒnsɛt
AM ˈkɑnˌsɛt

consider
BR kənˈsɪd|ə(r), -əz, -(ə)rɪŋ, -əd
AM kənˈsɪdər, -z, -ɪŋ, -d

considerable
BR kənˈsɪd(ə)rəbl
AM kənˈsɪdərəbəl

considerably
BR kənˈsɪd(ə)rəbli
AM kənˈsɪdər(ə)bli

considerate
BR kənˈsɪd(ə)rət
AM kənˈsɪdərət

considerately
BR kənˈsɪd(ə)rətli
AM kənˈsɪdərətli

consideration
BR kənˌsɪdəˈreɪʃn, -z
AM kənˌsɪdərˈeɪʃən, -z

Considine
BR ˈkɒnsɪdʌɪn
AM ˈkɑnsəˌdaɪn

consign
BR kənˈsʌɪn, -z, -ɪŋ, -d
AM kənˈsaɪn, -z, -ɪŋ, -d

consignee
BR ˌkɒnsʌɪˈniː, -z
AM ˌkɑnsaɪˈni, -z

consignment
BR kən'sʌɪnm(ə)nt, -s
AM kən'saɪnmənt, -s
consignor
BR kən'sʌɪnə(r), ˌkɒnsʌɪ'nɔː(r), kənˌsʌɪ'nɔː(r), -z
AM kən'saɪnər, -z
consilience
BR kən'sɪlɪəns
AM kən'sɪliəns
consist
BR kən'sɪst, -s, -ɪŋ, -ɨd
AM kən'sɪs|t, -ts, -dɪŋ, -dɨd
consistence
BR kən'sɪst(ə)ns
AM kən'sɪstns
consistency
BR kən'sɪst(ə)ns|i, -ɪz
AM kən'sɪstnsi, -z
consistent
BR kən'sɪst(ə)nt
AM kən'sɪstənt
consistently
BR kən'sɪst(ə)ntli
AM kən'sɪstən(t)li
consistorial
BR ˌkɒnsɪ'stɔːrɪəl
AM ˌkɑnsə'stɔriəl
consistory
BR kən'sɪst(ə)r|i, -ɪz
AM kən'sɪstəri, -z
consociate
BR kɒn'səʊʃɪeɪt, kɒn'səʊsɪeɪt, -s, -ɪŋ, -ɨd
AM ˌkɑn'soʊʃieɪ|t, -ts, -dɪŋ, -dɨd
consociation
BR kənˌsəʊʃɪ'eɪʃn, kənˌsəʊsɪ'eɪʃn, -z
AM ˌkɑnˌsoʊʃi'eɪʃən, -z
consolable
BR kən'səʊləbl
AM kən'soʊləbəl
consolation
BR ˌkɒnsə'leɪʃn, -z
AM ˌkɑnsə'leɪʃən, -z
consolatory
BR kən'sɒlət(ə)ri, kən'səʊlət(ə)ri
AM kən'soʊləˌtɔri
console¹
noun
BR 'kɒnsəʊl, -z
AM 'kɑnˌsoʊl, -z
console²
verb
BR kən'səʊl, -z, -ɪŋ, -d
AM kən'soʊl, -z, -ɪŋ, -d
consoler
BR kən'səʊlə(r), -z
AM kən'soʊlər, -z
consolidate
BR kən'sɒlɪdeɪt, -s, -ɪŋ, -ɨd
AM kən'sɑlədeɪ|t, -ts, -dɪŋ, -dɨd
consolidation
BR kənˌsɒlɪ'deɪʃn, -z
AM kənˌsɑlə'deɪʃən, -z
consolidator
BR kən'sɒlɪdeɪtə(r), -z
AM kən'sɑləˌdeɪdər, -z
consolidatory
BR kənˌsɒlɪ'deɪt(ə)ri
AM kən'sɑlədəˌtɔri
consolingly
BR kən'səʊlɪŋli
AM kən'soʊlɪŋli
consols
BR 'kɒns(ɒ)lz, kən'sɒlz
AM 'kɑnsəlz, kən'sɑlz
consommé
BR kɒn'sɒmeɪ, kən'sɒmeɪ, 'kɒnsəmeɪ, -z
AM ˌkɑnsə'meɪ, 'kɑnsəˌmeɪ, -z
consonance
BR 'kɒnsənəns, 'kɒnsn̩əns
AM 'kɑnsənəns
consonant
BR 'kɒnsənənt, 'kɒnsn̩ənt, -s
AM 'kɑnsənənt, -s
consonantal
BR ˌkɒnsə'nantl
AM ˌkɑnsə'nɑn(t)l
consonantly
BR ˌkɒnsə'nantl̩i, ˌkɒnsə'nantəli
AM ˌkɑnsə'nɑn(t)əli, 'kɑnsənən(t)li
con sordino
BR ˌkɒn sɔː'diːnəʊ, + 'sɔːdɪnəʊ
AM ˌkɑn ˌsɔr'dinoʊ
consort¹
noun
BR 'kɒnsɔːt, -s
AM 'kɑnsɔ(ə)rt, -s
consort²
verb
BR kən'sɔːt, -s, -ɪŋ, -ɨd
AM kən'sɔ(ə)rt, -ts, -sɔrdɪŋ, -sɔrdɨd
consortia
BR kən'sɔːtɪə(r), kən'sɔːʃə(r)
AM kən'sɔrdiə, kən'sɔrʃ(i)ə
consortium
BR kən'sɔːtɪəm, kən'sɔːʃɪəm, -z
AM kən'sɔrdiəm, kən'sɔrʃ(i)əm, -z
conspecific
BR ˌkɒnspɪ'sɪfɪk
AM ˌkɑnspə'sɪfɪk
conspectus
BR kən'spɛktəs, -ɪz
AM kən'spɛktəs, -əz
conspicuous
BR kən'spɪʃəs
AM kən'spɪkjəwəs
conspicuously
BR kən'spɪʃəsli
AM kən'spɪkjəwəsli
conspicuousness
BR kən'spɪkjʊəsnəs
AM kən'spɪkjəwəsnəs
conspiracy
BR kən'spɪrəs|i, -ɪz
AM kən'spɪrɨsi, -z
conspirator
BR kən'spɪrətə(r), -z
AM kən'spɪrədər, -z
conspiratorial
BR kənˌspɪrə'tɔːrɪəl, ˌkɒnspɪrə'tɔːrɪəl
AM kənˌspɪrə'tɔriəl
conspiratorially
BR kənˌspɪrə'tɔːrɪəli, ˌkɒnspɪrə'tɔːrɪəli
AM kənˌspɪrə'tɔriəli
conspire
BR kən'spʌɪə(r), -z, -ɪŋ, -d
AM kən'spaɪ(ə)r, -z, -ɪŋ, -d
constable¹
BR 'kʌnstəbl, 'kɒnstəbl, -z
AM 'kɑnstəbl, -z
constable²
BR 'kʌnstəbl, 'kɒnstəbl, -z
AM 'kɑnstəbəl, -z
constabulary
BR kən'stabjʊlər|i, -ɪz
AM kən'stæbjəˌlɛri, -z
Constance
BR 'kɒnst(ə)ns
AM 'kɑnstəns
constancy
BR 'kɒnst(ə)nsi
AM 'kɑnstnsi
constant
BR 'kɒnst(ə)nt, -s
AM 'kɑnstənt, -s
constantan
BR 'kɒnst(ə)ntan
AM 'kɑnstəntən
Constantine
BR 'kɒnst(ə)ntʌɪn
AM 'kɑnstənˌtin
Constantinople
BR ˌkɒnstantɪ'nəʊpl
AM ˌkɑnˌstæn(t)ə'noʊpl
constantly
BR 'kɒnst(ə)ntli
AM 'kɑnstən(t)li
Constanza
BR kən'stanzə(r), kɒn'stanzə(r)
AM kɑn'stænzə
constatation
BR ˌkɒnstə'teɪʃn, -z
AM ˌkɑnstə'teɪʃən, -z
constellate
BR 'kɒnstɨleɪt, -s, -ɪŋ, -ɨd
AM 'kɑnstəleɪ|t, -ts, -dɪŋ, -dɨd
constellation
BR ˌkɒnstɪ'leɪʃn, -z
AM ˌkɑnstə'leɪʃən, -z
consternate
BR 'kɒnstəneɪt, -s, -ɪŋ, -ɨd
AM 'kɑnstərˌneɪ|t, -ts, -dɪŋ, -dɨd
consternation
BR ˌkɒnstə'neɪʃn
AM ˌkɑnstər'neɪʃən
constipate
BR 'kɒnstɨpeɪt, -s, -ɪŋ, -ɨd
AM 'kɑnstəˌpeɪ|t, -ts, -dɪŋ, -dɨd
constipation
BR ˌkɒnstɪ'peɪʃn
AM ˌkɑnstə'peɪʃən
constituency
BR kən'stɪtjʊəns|i, kən'stɪtʃʊəns|i, -ɪz
AM kən'stɪtʃʊənsi, -ɪz
constituent
BR kən'stɪtjʊənt, kən'stɪtʃʊənt, -s
AM kən'stɪtʃʊənt, -s
constitute
BR 'kɒnstɪtjuːt, 'kɒnstɪtʃuːt, -s, -ɪŋ, -ɨd
AM 'kɑnstəˌt(j)u|t, -ts, -dɪŋ, -dɨd
constitution
BR ˌkɒnstɪ'tjuːʃn, ˌkɒnstɪ'tʃuːʃn, -z
AM ˌkɑnstə't(j)uʃən, -z
constitutional
BR ˌkɒnstɪ'tjuːʃn̩(ə)l, ˌkɒnstɪ'tjuːʃən(ə)l, ˌkɒnstɪ'tʃuːʃn̩(ə)l, ˌkɒnstɪ'tʃuːʃən(ə)l
AM ˌkɑnstə't(j)uʃ(ə)nəl
constitutionalise
BR ˌkɒnstɪ'tjuːʃn̩əlʌɪz, ˌkɒnstɪ'tjuːʃn̩l̩ʌɪz, ˌkɒnstɪ'tjuːʃənl̩ʌɪz, ˌkɒnstɪ'tjuːʃ(ə)nəlʌɪz, ˌkɒnstɪ'tʃuːʃn̩əlʌɪz, ˌkɒnstɪ'tʃuːʃn̩l̩ʌɪz, ˌkɒnstɪ'tʃuːʃənl̩ʌɪz, ˌkɒnstɪ'tʃuːʃ(ə)nəlʌɪz, -ɪz, -ɪŋ, -d
AM ˌkɑnstə't(j)uʃnəˌlaɪz, ˌkɑnstə't(j)uʃənl̩aɪz, -ɪz, -ɪŋ, -d
constitutionalism
BR ˌkɒnstɪ'tjuːʃn̩əlɪz(ə)m, ˌkɒnstɪ'tjuːʃn̩l̩ɪz(ə)m, ˌkɒnstɪ'tjuːʃənl̩ɪz(ə)m, ˌkɒnstɪ'tjuːʃ(ə)nəlɪz(ə)m, ˌkɒnstɪ'tʃuːʃn̩əlɪz(ə)m,

ˌkɒnstɪˈtʃuːʃn̩l ɪz(ə)m, ˌkɒnstɪˈtʃuːʃənl ɪz(ə)m, ˌkɒnstɪˈtʃuːʃ(ə)nəlɪz(ə)m
AM ˌkɑnstəˈt(j)uʃnəˌlɪzm, ˌkɑnstəˈt(j)uʃənl̩ɪzm

constitutionalist
BR ˌkɒnstɪˈtjuːʃn̩əlɪst, ˌkɒnstɪˈtjuːʃn̩l̩ɪst, ˌkɒnstɪˈtjuːʃənl̩ɪst, ˌkɒnstɪˈtjuːʃ(ə)nəlɪst, ˌkɒnstɪˈtʃuːʃn̩əlɪst, ˌkɒnstɪˈtʃuːʃn̩l̩ɪst, ˌkɒnstɪˈtʃuːʃənl̩ɪst, ˌkɒnstɪˈtʃuːʃ(ə)nəlɪst, -s
AM ˌkɑnstəˈt(j)uʃnəl-əst, ˌkɑnstəˈt(j)uʃənl̩əst, -s

constitutionality
BR ˌkɒnstɪˌtjuːʃəˈnalɨti, ˌkɒnstɪˌtʃuːʃəˈnalɨti
AM ˌkɑnstəˌt(j)uʃəˈnælədi

constitutionalize
BR ˌkɒnstɪˈtjuːʃn̩əlʌɪz, ˌkɒnstɪˈtjuːʃn̩l̩ʌɪz, ˌkɒnstɪˈtjuːʃənl̩ʌɪz, ˌkɒnstɪˈtjuːʃ(ə)nəlʌɪz, ˌkɒnstɪˈtʃuːʃn̩əlʌɪz, ˌkɒnstɪˈtʃuːʃn̩l̩ʌɪz, ˌkɒnstɪˈtʃuːʃənl̩ʌɪz, ˌkɒnstɪˈtʃuːʃ(ə)nəlʌɪz, -ɨz, -ɪŋ, -d
AM ˌkɑnstəˈt(j)uʃnəˌlaɪz, ˌkɑnstəˈt(j)uʃənl̩aɪz, -ɨz, -ɪŋ, -d

constitutionally
BR ˌkɒnstɪˈtjuːʃn̩əli, ˌkɒnstɪˈtjuːʃn̩l̩i, ˌkɒnstɪˈtjuːʃənl̩i, ˌkɒnstɪˈtjuːʃ(ə)nəli, ˌkɒnstɪˈtʃuːʃn̩əli, ˌkɒnstɪˈtʃuːʃn̩l̩i, ˌkɒnstɪˈtʃuːʃənl̩i, ˌkɒnstɪˈtʃuːʃ(ə)nəli
AM ˌkɑnstəˈt(j)uʃ(ə)n-əli

constitutive
BR kənˈstɪtjʊtɪv, kənˈstɪtʃʊtɪv, ˈkɒnstɪtjuːtɪv, ˈkɒnstɪtʃuːtɪv
AM ˈkɑnstəˌt(j)udɪv

constitutively
BR kənˈstɪtjʊtɪvli, kənˈstɪtʃʊtɪvli, ˈkɒnstɪtjuːtɪvli, ˈkɒnstɪtʃuːtɪvli
AM ˈkɑnstəˌt(j)udɪvli

constitutor
BR ˈkɒnstɪtjuːtə(r), ˈkɒnstɪtʃuːtə(r)
AM ˈkɑnstəˌt(j)udər

constrain
BR kənˈstreɪn, -z, -ɪŋ, -d
AM kənˈstreɪn, -z, -ɪŋ, -d

constrainedly
BR kənˈstreɪnɨdli
AM kənˈstreɪnɨdli

constraint
BR kənˈstreɪnt, -s
AM kənˈstreɪnt, -s

constrict
BR kənˈstrɪkt, -s, -ɪŋ, -ɨd
AM kənˈstrɪk|(t), -(t)s, -tɪŋ, -tɨd

constriction
BR kənˈstrɪkʃn, -z
AM kənˈstrɪkʃən, -z

constrictive
BR kənˈstrɪktɪv
AM kənˈstrɪktɪv

constrictor
BR kənˈstrɪktə(r), -z
AM kənˈstrɪktər, -z

construable
BR kənˈstruːəbl
AM kənˈstruəbəl

construal
BR kənˈstruːəl
AM kənˈstruəl

construct[1]
noun
BR ˈkɒnstrʌkt, -s
AM ˈkɑnˌstrək(t), -s

construct[2]
BR kənˈstrʌkt, -s, -ɪŋ, -ɨd
AM kənˈstrək|(t), -(t)s, -tɪŋ, -tɨd

construction
BR kənˈstrʌkʃn, -z
AM kənˈstrəkʃən, -z

constructional
BR kənˈstrʌkʃn̩(ə)l, kənˈstrʌkʃən(ə)l
AM kənˈstrəkʃ(ə)nəl

constructionally
BR kənˈstrʌkʃn̩əli, kənˈstrʌkʃn̩l̩i, kənˈstrʌkʃənl̩i, kənˈstrʌkʃ(ə)nəli
AM kənˈstrəkʃ(ə)nəli

constructionism
BR kənˈstrʌʃn̩ɪz(ə)m, kənˈstrʌkʃənɪz(ə)m
AM kənˈstrəkʃənɪzm

constructionist
BR kənˈstrʌʃn̩ɪst, kənˈstrʌkʃənɪst, -s
AM kənˈstrəkʃənəst, -s

constructive
BR kənˈstrʌtɪv
AM kənˈstrəktɪv

constructively
BR kənˈstrʌktɪvli
AM kənˈstrəktɪvli

constructiveness
BR kənˈstrʌtɪvnɨs
AM kənˈstrəktɪvnɨs

constructivism
BR kənˈstrʌktɪvɪz(ə)m
AM kənˈstrəktɪvɪzm

constructivist
BR kənˈstrʌktɪvɪst, -s
AM kənˈstrəktɪvɪst, -s

constructor
BR kənˈstrʌtə(r), -z
AM kənˈstrəktər, -z

construe
BR kənˈstruː, -z, -ɪŋ, -d
AM kənˈstru, -z, -ɪŋ, -d

consubstantial
BR ˌkɒnsəbˈstanʃl, ˌkɒnsəbˈstɑːnʃl
AM ˌkɑnsəbˈstænʃl

consubstantiality
BR ˌkɒnsəbˌstanʃɪˈalɨti, ˌkɒnsəbˌstɑːnʃɪˈalɨti
AM ˌkɑnsəbˌstænʃiˈælədi

consubstantiate
BR ˌkɒnsəbˈstanʃɪeɪt, ˌkɒnsəbˈstansɪeɪt, ˌkɒnsəbˈstɑːnʃɪeɪt, ˌkɒnsəbˈstɑːnsɪeɪt, -s, -ɪŋ, -ɨd
AM ˌkɑnsəbˈstænʃiˌeɪ|t, -ts, -dɪŋ, -dɨd

consubstantiation
BR ˌkɒnsəbˌstanʃɪˈeɪʃn, ˌkɒnsəbˌstansɪˈeɪʃn, ˌkɒnsəbˌstɑːnʃɪˈeɪʃn, ˌkɒnsəbˌstɑːnsɪˈeɪʃn
AM ˌkɑnsəbˌstænʃiˈeɪʃən

consuetude
BR ˈkɒnswɪtjuːd, ˈkɒnswɪtʃuːd
AM ˈkɑnswəˌt(j)ud

consuetudinary
BR ˌkɒnswɪˈtjuːdn̩(ə)ri, ˌkɒnswɪˈtʃuːdn̩(ə)ri
AM ˌkɑnswəˈt(j)udənˌɛri

consul
BR ˈkɒnsl, -z
AM ˈkɑnsəl, -z

consular
BR ˈkɒnsjʊlə(r)
AM ˈkɑns(j)ələr

consulate
BR ˈkɒnsjʊlət, -s
AM ˈkɑnsələt, -s

consulship
BR ˈkɒnslʃɪp, -s
AM ˈkɑnsəlʃɪp, -s

consult
BR kənˈsʌlt, -s, -ɪŋ, -ɨd
AM kənˈsəl|t, -ts, -dɪŋ, -dɨd

consultancy
BR kənˈsʌlt(ə)nsi
AM kənˈsəltnsi

consultant
BR kənˈsʌlt(ə)nt, -s
AM kənˈsəltnt, -s

consultation
BR ˌkɒnslˈteɪʃn, ˌkɒnsʌlˈteɪʃn, -z
AM ˈkɑnsəlˈteɪʃən, -z

consultative
BR kənˈsʌltətɪv
AM kənˈsəltədɪv

consultee
BR ˌkɒnsʌlˈtiː, -z
AM ˌkɑnˌsəlˈti, -z

consumable
BR kənˈsjuːməbl, -z
AM kənˈs(j)uməbəl, -z

consume
BR kənˈsjuːm, -z, -ɪŋ, -d
AM kənˈs(j)um, -z, -ɪŋ, -d

consumer
BR kənˈsjuːmə(r), -z
AM kənˈs(j)umər, -z

consumerism
BR kənˈsjuːmərɪz(ə)m
AM kənˈs(j)umərˌɪzm

consumerist
BR kənˈsjuːmərɪst, -s
AM kənˈs(j)umərəst, -s

consumingly
BR kənˈsjuːmɪŋli
AM kənˈs(j)umɪŋli

consummate[1]
adjective
BR kənˈsʌmət
AM ˈkɑnsəmət, kənˈsəmət

consummate[2]
verb
BR ˈkɒnsjʊmeɪt, -s, -ɪŋ, -ɨd
AM ˈkɑnsəˌmeɪ|t, -ts, -dɪŋ, -dɨd

consummately
BR kənˈsʌmətli
AM ˈkɑnsəmətli, kənˈsəmətli

consummation
BR ˌkɒnsjʊˈmeɪʃn
AM ˌkɑnsəˈmeɪʃən

consummative
BR ˈkɒnsəmeɪtɪv, ˈkɒnsjʊmeɪtɪv, kənˈsʌmətɪv
AM ˈkɑnsəˌmeɪdɪv, kənˈsəmədɪv

consummator
BR ˈkɒnsjʊmeɪtə(r), -z
AM ˈkɑnsəˌmeɪdər, -z

consumption
BR kənˈsʌm(p)ʃn
AM kənˈsəm(p)ʃən

consumptive
BR kənˈsʌm(p)tɪv
AM kənˈsəm(p)tɪv

consumptively
BR kənˈsʌm(p)tɪvli
AM kənˈsəm(p)tɪvli

Contac
BR ˈkɒntak
AM ˈkɑntæk

contact
BR 'kɒntakt, -s, -ɪŋ, -ɨd
AM 'kɑntæk|(t), -(t)s, -tɪŋ, -tɨd

contactable
BR 'kɒntaktəbl, kən'taktəbl
AM 'kɑntæktəbəl

Contadora
BR ˌkɒntə'dɔːrə(r)
AM ˌkɑn(t)ə'dɔrə

contagion
BR kən'teɪdʒ(ə)n, -z
AM kən'teɪdʒən, -z

contagious
BR kən'teɪdʒəs
AM kən'teɪdʒəs

contagiously
BR kən'teɪdʒəsli
AM kən'teɪdʒəsli

contagiousness
BR kən'teɪdʒəsnəs
AM kən'teɪdʒəsnəs

contain
BR kən'teɪn, -z, -ɪŋ, -d
AM kən'teɪn, -z, -ɪŋ, -d

containable
BR kən'teɪnəbl
AM kən'teɪnəbəl

container
BR kən'teɪnə(r), -z
AM kən'teɪnər, -z

containerisation
BR kənˌteɪnərʌɪ'zeɪʃn
AM kənˌteɪnərə'zeɪʃən, kənˌteɪnəˌraɪ'zeɪʃən

containerise
BR kən'teɪnərʌɪz, -ɨz, -ɪŋ, -d
AM kən'teɪnəˌraɪz, -ɨz, -ɪŋ, -d

containerization
BR kənˌteɪnərʌɪ'zeɪʃn
AM kənˌteɪnərə'zeɪʃən, kənˌteɪnəˌraɪ'zeɪʃən

containerize
BR kən'teɪnərʌɪz, -ɨz, -ɪŋ, -d
AM kən'teɪnəˌraɪz, -ɨz, -ɪŋ, -d

containment
BR kən'teɪnm(ə)nt
AM kən'teɪnmənt

contaminant
BR kən'tamɨnənt, -s
AM kən'tæmənənt, -s

contaminate
BR kən'tamɨneɪt, -s, -ɪŋ, -ɨd
AM kən'tæməneɪ|t, -ts, -dɪŋ, -dɨd

contamination
BR kənˌtamɨ'neɪʃn
AM kənˌtæmə'neɪʃən

contaminator
BR kən'tamɨneɪtə(r), -z
AM kən'tæməˌneɪdər, -z

contango
BR kən'taŋgəʊ, kɒn'taŋgəʊ, -z
AM kən'tæŋgoʊ, -z

conte
BR kɒnt, -s
AM kont, -s

Conteh
BR 'kɒnteɪ, 'kɒnti
AM 'kanteɪ

contemn
BR kən'tɛm, -z, -ɪŋ, -d
AM kən'tɛm, -z, -ɪŋ, -d

contemner
BR kən'tɛmə(r), -z
AM kən'tɛmər, -z

contemplate
BR 'kɒntəmpleɪt, 'kɒntɛmpleɪt, -s, -ɪŋ, -ɨd
AM 'kɑn(t)əmˌpleɪ|t, -ts, -dɪŋ, -dɨd

contemplation
BR ˌkɒntəm'pleɪʃn, ˌkɒntɛm'pleɪʃn
AM ˌkɑn(t)əm'pleɪʃən

contemplative
BR kən'tɛmplətɪv, -z
AM kən'tɛmplədɪv, 'kɑn(t)əmˌpleɪdɪv, -z

contemplatively
BR kən'tɛmplətɪvli
AM kən'tɛmplədɪvli

contemplator
BR 'kɒntəmpleɪtə(r), 'kɒntɛmpleɪtə(r), -z
AM 'kɑn(t)əmˌpleɪdər, -z

contemporaneity
BR kənˌtɛmp(ə)rə'niːɨti, kənˌtɛmp(ə)rə'neɪɨti
AM kənˌtɛmpərə'niɨdi, kənˌtɛmpərə'neɪɨdi

contemporaneous
BR kənˌtɛmpə'reɪnɪəs
AM kənˌtɛmpə'reɪniəs

contemporaneously
BR kənˌtɛmpə'reɪnɪəsli
AM kənˌtɛmpə'reɪniəsli

contemporaneousness
BR kənˌtɛmpə'reɪnɪəsnəs
AM kənˌtɛmpə'reɪniəsnəs

contemporarily
BR kən'tɛmp(ə)r(ər)ɨli
AM kənˌtɛmpə'rɛrəli

contemporariness
BR kən'tɛmp(ə)r(ər)ɪnɨs
AM kən'tɛmpəˌrɛrinɨs

contemporary
BR kən'tɛmp(ə)r(ər)i
AM kən'tɛmpəˌrɛri

contemporise
BR kən'tɛmp(ə)rʌɪz, -ɨz, -ɪŋ, -d
AM kən'tɛmpəˌraɪz, -ɨz, -ɪŋ, -d

contemporize
BR kən'tɛmp(ə)rʌɪz, -ɨz, -ɪŋ, -d
AM kən'tɛmpəˌraɪz, -ɨz, -ɪŋ, -d

contempt
BR kən'tɛm(p)t, -s
AM kən'tɛm(p)t, -s

contemptibility
BR kənˌtɛm(p)tɪ'bɪlɨti
AM kənˌtɛm(p)tə'bɪlɨdi

contemptible
BR kən'tɛm(p)tɪbl
AM kən'tɛm(p)təbəl

contemptibly
BR kən'tɛm(p)tɪbli
AM kən'tɛm(p)təbli

contemptuous
BR kən'tɛm(p)tjʊəs, kən'tɛm(p)tʃʊəs
AM kən'tɛm(pt)ʃ(ʊ)əs

contemptuously
BR kən'tɛm(p)tjʊəsli, kən'tɛm(p)tʃʊəsli
AM kən'tɛm(pt)ʃ(ʊ)əsli

contemptuousness
BR kən'tɛm(p)tjʊəsnəs, kən'tɛm(p)tʃʊəsnəs
AM kən'tɛm(pt)ʃ(ʊ)əsnəs

contend
BR kən'tɛnd, -z, -ɪŋ, -ɨd
AM kən'tɛnd, -z, -ɪŋ, -ɨd

contender
BR kən'tɛndə(r), -z
AM kən'tɛndər, -z

content[1]
adjective
BR kən'tɛnt
AM kən'tɛnt

content[2]
noun
BR 'kɒntɛnt, -s
AM 'kɑntɛnt, -s

contentedly
BR kən'tɛntɨdli
AM kən'tɛn(t)ədli

contentedness
BR kən'tɛntɨdnɨs
AM kən'tɛn(t)ədnəs

contention
BR kən'tɛnʃn, -z
AM kən'tɛnʃən, -z

contentious
BR kən'tɛnʃəs
AM kən'tɛnʃəs

contentiously
BR kən'tɛnʃəsli
AM kən'tɛnʃəsli

contentiousness
BR kən'tɛnʃəsnəs
AM kən'tɛnʃəsnəs

contentment
BR kən'tɛntm(ə)nt
AM kən'tɛntmənt

conterminous
BR kɒn'təːmɨnəs, kən'təːmɨnəs
AM ˌkɑn'tərmənəs

conterminously
BR kɒn'təːmɨnəsli, kən'təːmɨnəsli
AM ˌkɑn'tərmənəsli

contessa
BR kɒn'tɛsə(r), -z
AM kən'tɛsə, -z

contest[1]
noun
BR 'kɒntɛst, -s
AM 'kɑnˌtɛst, -s

contest[2]
verb
BR kən'tɛst, 'kɒntɛst, -s, -ɪŋ, -ɨd
AM kən'tɛs|t, -ts, -dɪŋ, -dɨd

contestable
BR kən'tɛstəbl, 'kɒntɛstəbl
AM kən'tɛstəbəl

contestant
BR kən'tɛst(ə)nt, -s
AM kən'tɛstənt, -s

contestation
BR ˌkɒntɛ'steɪʃn
AM ˌkɑn(t)ə'steɪʃən, kɑnˌtɛs'teɪʃən

contester
BR kən'tɛstə(r), 'kɒntɛstə(r), -z
AM kən'tɛstər, -z

context
BR 'kɒntɛkst, -s
AM 'kɑntɛkst, -s

contextual
BR kən'tɛkstʃʊəl, kən'tɛkstʃ(ʊ)l, kən'tɛkstjʊəl, kən'tɛkstjʊl
AM kən'tɛks(t)ʃ(əw)əl

contextualisation
BR kənˌtɛkstjʊəlʌɪ'zeɪʃn, kənˌtɛkstjʊlʌɪ'zeɪʃn, kənˌtɛkstʃʊəlʌɪ'zeɪʃn, kənˌtɛkstʃʊlʌɪ'zeɪʃn, kənˌtɛkstʃl̩ʌɪ'zeɪʃn
AM kənˌtɛks(t)ʃ(əw)ələ'zeɪʃən, kənˌtɛks(t)ʃ(əw)əˌlaɪ'zeɪʃən

contextualise
BR kən'tɛkstjʊəlʌɪz, kən'tɛkstjʊlʌɪz, kən'tɛkstʃʊəlʌɪz, kən'tɛkstʃʊlʌɪz, kən'tɛkstʃl̩ʌɪz, -ɨz, -ɪŋ, -d
AM kən'tɛks(t)ʃ(əw)əˌlaɪz, -ɨz, -ɪŋ, -d

contextualist
BR kən'tɛkstjʊəlɪst, kən'tɛkstjʉlɪst, kən'tɛkstʃʊəlɪst, kən'tɛkstʃʉlɪst, kən'tɛkstʃl̩ɪst
AM kən'tɛks(t)ʃ(əw)əl-əst

contextuality
BR kən,tɛkstjʊ'alɨti, kən,tɛkstʃʊ'alɨti
AM kən,tɛks(t)ʃ(əw)-'ælədi

contextualization
BR kən,tɛkstjʊəlʌɪ-'zeɪʃn, kən,tɛkstjʉlʌɪ'zeɪʃn, kən,tɛkstʃʊəlʌɪ'zeɪʃn, kən,tɛkstʃʉlʌɪ'zeɪʃn, kən,tɛkstʃl̩ʌɪ'zeɪʃn
AM kən,tɛks(t)ʃ(əw)ələ-'zeɪʃən, kən,tɛks(t)ʃ(əw)ə,laɪ-'zeɪʃən

contextualize
BR kən'tɛkstjʊəlʌɪz, kən'tɛkstjʉlʌɪz, kən'tɛkstʃʊəlʌɪz, kən'tɛkstʃʉlʌɪz, kən'tɛkstʃl̩ʌɪz, -ɨz, -ɪŋ, -d
AM kən'tɛks(t)ʃ(əw)ə-,laɪz, -ɨz, -ɪŋ, -d

contextually
BR kən'tɛkstjʊəli, kən'tɛkstjʉli, kən'tɛkstʃʊəli, kən'tɛkstʃʉli, kən'tɛkstʃl̩i
AM kən'tɛks(t)ʃ(əw)əli

Contiboard
BR 'kɒntɪbɔːd
AM 'kɑn(t)ə,bɔ(ə)rd

contiguity
BR ,kɒntɪ'gjuːɨti
AM ,kɑn(t)ə'gjuədi

contiguous
BR kən'tɪgjʊəs
AM kən'tɪgjuəs

contiguously
BR kən'tɪgjʊəsli
AM kən'tɪgjuəsli

contiguousness
BR kən'tɪgjʊəsnəs
AM kən'tɪgjuəsnəs

continence
BR 'kɒntɨnəns
AM 'kɑnt(ə)nəns, 'kɑn(t)ənəns

continent
BR 'kɒntɨnənt, -s
AM 'kɑnt(ə)nənt, -s

continental
BR ,kɒntɪ'nɛntl
AM ,kɑntə'nɛn(t)əl

continentally
BR ,kɒntɪ'nɛntl̩i
AM ,kɑn(t)ə'nɛn(t)əli

continently
BR 'kɒntɨnəntli
AM 'kɑnt(ə)nən(t)li, 'kɑn(t)ənən(t)li

contingency
BR kən'tɪn(d)ʒ(ə)ns|i, -ɪz
AM kən'tɪndʒənsi, -ɪz

contingent
BR kən'tɪn(d)ʒ(ə)nt, -s
AM kən'tɪndʒənt, -s

contingently
BR kən'tɪn(d)ʒ(ə)ntli
AM kən'tɪndʒən(t)li

continua
BR kən'tɪnjʊə(*r*)
AM kən'tɪnjuə

continuable
BR kən'tɪnjʊəbl
AM kən'tɪnjʊəbəl

continual
BR kən'tɪnjʊəl, kən'tɪnj(ʉ)l
AM kən'tɪnj(ʊ)əl

continually
BR kən'tɪnjʊəli, kənɪtɪnjʉli
AM kən'tɪnj(ʊ)əli

continuance
BR kən'tɪnjʊəns
AM kən'tɪnj(ʊ)əns

continuant
BR kən'tɪnjʊənt, -s
AM kən'tɪnj(ʊ)ənt, -s

continuation
BR kən,tɪnjʊ'eɪʃn, -z
AM kən,tɪnjʊ'eɪʃən, -z

continuative
BR kən'tɪnjʊətɪv
AM kən'tɪnjʊədɪv

continuator
BR kən'tɪnjʊeɪtə(r), -z
AM kən'tɪnjʊ,eɪdər, -z

continue
BR kən'tɪnjuː, -z, -ɪŋ, -d
AM kən'tɪnju, -z, -ɪŋ, -d

continuer
BR kən'tɪnjʊə(r), -z
AM kən'tɪnjuər, -z

continuity
BR ,kɒntɪ'njuːɨti
AM ,kɑn(t)ə'n(j)uədi, ,kɑnt'n(j)uədi

continuo
BR kən'tɪnjʊəʊ, -z
AM kən'tɪnjuoʊ, -z

continuous
BR kən'tɪnjʊəs
AM kən'tɪnjuəs

continuously
BR kən'tɪnjʊəsli
AM kən'tɪnjuəsli

continuousness
BR kən'tɪnjʊəsnəs
AM kən'tɪnjuəsnəs

continuum
BR kən'tɪnjʊəm, -z
AM kən'tɪnjuəm, -z

contort
BR kən'tɔːt, -s, -ɪŋ, -ɨd
AM kən'tɔ(ə)rt, -ts, -'tɔrdɪŋ, -'tɔrdɨd

contortion
BR kən'tɔːʃn, -z
AM kən'tɔrʃən, -z

contortionist
BR kən'tɔːʃn̩ɪst, kən'tɔːʃənɪst, -s
AM kən'tɔrʃənəst, -s

contour
BR 'kɒntʊə(r), 'kɒntɔː(r), -z
AM 'kɑntʊ(ə)r, -z

contra
BR 'kɒntrə(*r*), -z
AM 'kɑntrə, -z

contraband
BR 'kɒntrəband
AM 'kɑntrə,bænd

contrabandist
BR 'kɒntrəbandɪst, -s
AM 'kɑntrə,bændəst, -s

contrabass
BR ,kɒntrə'beɪs, 'kɒntrəbeɪs
AM ¦kɑntrə¦beɪs

contraception
BR ,kɒntrə'sɛpʃn
AM ,kɑntrə'sɛpʃən

contraceptive
BR ,kɒntrə'sɛptɪv, -z
AM ,kɑntrə'sɛptɪv, -z

contract[1]
noun
BR 'kɒntrakt, -s
AM 'kɑntræk(t), -s

contract[2]
verb, become smaller
BR kən'trakt, -s, -ɪŋ, -ɨd
AM kən'træk|(t), -(t)s, -tɪŋ, -tɨd

contract[3]
verb, make an agreement
BR 'kɒntrakt, kən'trakt, -s, -ɪŋ, -ɨd
AM 'kɑntræk|(t), kən'træk|(t), -(t)s, -tɪŋ, -tɨd

contractable
BR kən'traktəbl
AM kən'træktəbəl

contractible
BR kən'traktɨbl
AM kən'træktəbəl

contractile
BR kən'traktʌɪl
AM kən'træktəl

contractility
BR ,kɒntrak'tɪlɨti
AM ,kɑn,træk'tɪlɨdi

contraction
BR kən'trakʃn, -z
AM kən'trækʃən, -z

contractive
BR kən'traktɪv
AM kən'træktɪv

contractor
BR kən'traktə(r), 'kɒntraktə(r), -z
AM 'kɑntræktər, -z

contractual
BR kən'traktʃʊəl, kən'traktʃ(ʉ)l, kən'traktjʊəl, kən'traktjʉl
AM kən'træk(t)ʃ(əw)əl

contractually
BR kən'traktʃʊəli, kən'traktʃʉli, kən'traktʃl̩i, kən'traktjʊəli, kən'traktjʉli
AM kən'træk(t)ʃ(əw)əli

contradict
BR ,kɒntrə'dɪkt, -s, -ɪŋ, -ɨd
AM ,kɑntrə'dɪk|(t), -(t)s, -tɪŋ, -tɨd

contradictable
BR ,kɒntrə'dɪktəbl
AM ,kɑntrə'dɪktəbəl

contradiction
BR ,kɒntrə'dɪkʃn, -z
AM ,kɑntrə'dɪkʃən, -z

contradictious
BR ,kɒntrə'dɪkʃəs
AM ,kɑntrə'dɪkʃəs

contradictor
BR ,kɒntrə'dɪktə(r), -z
AM ,kɑntrə'dɪktər, -z

contradictorily
BR ,kɒntrə'dɪkt(ə)rɨli
AM ,kɑntrə'dɪktərəli

contradictoriness
BR ,kɒntrə'dɪkt(ə)rɪnɨs
AM ,kɑntrə'dɪktərinɨs

contradictory
BR ,kɒntrə'dɪkt(ə)ri
AM ,kɑntrə'dɪktəri

contradistinction
BR ,kɒntrədɪ'stɪŋ(k)ʃn
AM ,kɑntrədə'stɪŋ(k)ʃən

contradistinguish
BR ,kɒntrədɪ'stɪŋgw|ɪʃ, -ɪʃɪz, -ɪʃɪŋ, -ɪʃt
AM ,kɑntrədə'stɪŋgwɪʃ, -ɪz, -ɪŋ, -t

contraflow
BR 'kɒntrəfləʊ, -z
AM 'kɑntrə,floʊ, -z

contrail
BR 'kɒntreɪl, -z
AM 'kɑn,treɪl, -z

contraindicate
BR ,kɒntrə'ɪndɪkeɪt, -s, -ɪŋ, -ɨd
AM ,kɑntrə'ɪndɪ,keɪ|t, -ts, -dɪŋ, -dɨd

contraindication
BR ,kɒntrə,ɪndɪ'keɪʃn, -z

AM ˌkantrəˌɪndɪ'keɪʃən, -z

contralto
BR kən'trɑːltəʊ, kən'traltəʊ, -z
AM kən'træltoʊ, -z

contraposition
BR ˌkɒntrəpə'zɪʃn, -z
AM ˌkantrəpə'zɪʃən, -z

contrapositive
BR ˌkɒntrə'pɒzɪtɪv
AM ˌkantrə'pazədɪv

contraption
BR kən'trapʃn, -z
AM kən'træpʃən, -z

contrapuntal
BR ˌkɒntrə'pʌntl
AM ˌkantrə'pən(t)əl

contrapuntally
BR ˌkɒntrə'pʌntl̩i
AM ˌkantrə'pən(t)əli

contrapuntist
BR ˌkɒntrə'pʌntɪst, 'kɒntrəˌpʌntɪst, -s
AM ˌkantrə'pən(t)əst, -s

contrarian
BR kən'trɛːrɪən, -z
AM kən'trɛriən, ˌkan'trɛriən, -z

contrariety
BR ˌkɒntrə'rʌɪɪt|i, -ɪz
AM ˌkantrə'raɪɪdi, -z

contrarily
BR kən'trɛːrɨli
AM 'kantrɛrəli, kən'trɛrəli

contrariness
BR kən'trɛːrɪnɪs
AM 'kantrɛrinəs, kən'trɛrinəs

contrariwise
BR kən'trɛːrɪwʌɪz
AM 'kantrɛriˌwaɪz, kən'trɛriˌwaɪz

contrary[1]
opposite
BR 'kɒntrəri
AM 'kantrɛri

contrary[2]
perverse
BR kən'trɛːri
AM 'kantrɛri, kən'trɛri

contrast[1]
noun
BR 'kɒntrɑːst, 'kɒntrast, -s
AM 'kanˌtræst, -s

contrast[2]
verb
BR kən'trɑːst, kən'trast, 'kɒntrɑːst, 'kɒntrast, -s, -ɪŋ, -ɨd
AM 'kanˌtræst, kən'træst, -s, -ɪŋ, -ɨd

contrastingly
BR kən'trɑːstɪŋli, kən'trastɪŋli, 'kɒntrɑːstɪŋli, 'kɒntrastɪŋli
AM 'kanˌtræstɪŋli, kən'træstɪŋli

contrastive
BR kən'trɑːstɪv, kən'trastɪv, 'kɒntrɑːstɪv, 'kɒntrastɪv
AM kən'træstɪv, 'kanˌtræstɪv

contrasty
BR 'kɒntrɑːsti, 'kɒntrasti
AM 'kanˌtræsti, kən'træsti

contravene
BR ˌkɒntrə'viːn, -z, -ɪŋ, -d
AM ˌkantrə'vin, -z, -ɪŋ, -d

contravener
BR ˌkɒntrə'viːnə(r), -z
AM ˌkantrə'vinər, -z

contravention
BR 'kɒntrə'vɛnʃn, -z
AM ˌkantrə'vɛnʃən, -z

contretemps
BR 'kɒntrətɒ̃, 'kɒ̃trətɒ̃, -z
AM 'kantrəˌtɔm(p), 'kantrəˌtam(p), -z

contribute
BR kən'trɪbjuːt, 'kɒntrɪbjuːt, -s, -ɪŋ, -ɨd
AM kən'trɪbju|t, -ts, -dɪŋ, -dɨd

contribution
BR ˌkɒntrɪ'bjuːʃn, -z
AM ˌkantrə'bjuʃən, -z

contributive
BR kən'trɪbjʉtɪv
AM kən'trɪbjudɪv

contributor
BR kən'trɪbjʉtə(r), 'kɒntrɪbjuːtə(r), -z
AM kən'trɪbjudər, -z

contributory
BR kən'trɪbjʉt(ə)ri, ˌkɒntrɪ'bjuːt(ə)ri
AM kən'trɪbjəˌtɔri

con-trick
BR 'kɒntrɪk, -s
AM 'kanˌtrɪk, -s

contrite
BR 'kɒntrʌɪt, kən'trʌɪt
AM kən'traɪt

contritely
BR 'kɒntrʌɪtli, kən'trʌɪtli
AM kən'traɪtli

contrition
BR kən'trɪʃn
AM kən'trɪʃən

contrivable
BR kən'trʌɪvəbl
AM kən'traɪvəbəl

contrivance
BR kən'trʌɪvns, -ɪz
AM kən'traɪvəns, -ɪz

contrive
BR kən'trʌɪv, -z, -ɪŋ, -d
AM kən'traɪv, -z, -ɪŋ, -d

contriver
BR kən'trʌɪvə(r), -z
AM kən'traɪvər, -z

control
BR kən'trəʊl, -z, -ɪŋ, -d
AM kən'troʊl, -z, -ɪŋ, -d

controllability
BR kənˌtrəʊlə'bɪlɨti
AM kənˌtroʊlə'bɪlɨdi

controllable
BR kən'trəʊləbl
AM kən'troʊləbəl

controllably
BR kən'trəʊləbli
AM kən'troʊləbli

controller
BR kən'trəʊlə(r), -z
AM kən'troʊlər, -z

controllership
BR kən'trəʊləʃɪp
AM kən'troʊlərˌʃip

controversial
BR ˌkɒntrə'vəːʃl
AM ˌkantrə'vərsiəl, ˌkantrə'vərʃəl

controversialism
BR ˌkɒntrə'vəːʃl̩ɪz(ə)m, ˌkɒntrə'vəːʃəlɪz(ə)m
AM ˌkantrə'vərsiəlɪzm, ˌkantrə'vərʃəlɪzm

controversialist
BR ˌkɒntrə'vəːʃlɪst, ˌkɒntrə'vəːʃəlɪst, -s
AM ˌkantrə'vərsiələst, ˌkantrə'vərʃələst, -s

controversially
BR ˌkɒntrə'vəːʃl̩i, ˌkɒntrə'vəːʃəli
AM ˌkantrə'vərsiəli, ˌkantrə'vərʃəli

controversy
BR 'kɒntrəvəːs|i, kən'trɒvəs|i, -ɪz
AM 'kantrəˌvərsi, -ɪz

controvert
BR ˌkɒntrə'vəːt, 'kɒntrəvəːt, -s, -ɪŋ, -ɨd
AM ˌkantrə'vər|t, -ts, -dɪŋ, -dɨd

controvertible
BR ˌkɒntrə'vəːtɪbl
AM ˌkantrə'vərdəbəl

contumacious
BR ˌkɒntjʉ'meɪʃəs, ˌkɒntʃʉ'meɪʃəs
AM ˌkant(j)ʊ'meɪʃəs

contumaciously
BR ˌkɒntjʉ'meɪʃəsli, ˌkɒntʃʉ'meɪʃəsli
AM ˌkant(j)ʊ'meɪʃəsli

contumacy
BR 'kɒntjʉməsi, 'kɒntʃʉməsi
AM 'kant(j)ʊməsi

contumelious
BR ˌkɒntjʉ'miːlɪəs, ˌkɒntʃʉ'miːlɪəs
AM ˌkant(j)ʊ'miliəs

contumeliously
BR ˌkɒntjʉ'miːlɪəsli, ˌkɒntʃʉ'miːlɪəsli
AM ˌkant(j)ʊ'miliəsli

contumely
BR 'kɒntjuːm(ɪ)li, 'kɒntjʉm(ɪ)li, 'kɒntʃʉm(ɪ)li
AM 'kant(j)ʊm(ə)li, 'kantəmli

contuse
BR kən'tjuːz, kən'tʃuːz, -ɪz, -ɪŋ, -d
AM kən'tuz, -ɪz, -ɪŋ, -d

contusion
BR kən'tjuːʒn, kən'tʃuːʒn, -z
AM kən'tuʒən, -z

conundrum
BR kə'nʌndrəm, -z
AM kə'nəndrəm, -z

conurbation
BR ˌkɒnə(ː)'beɪʃn, -z
AM ˌkanər'beɪʃən, -z

conure
BR 'kɒnjʊə(r), -z
AM 'kan(j)ʊ(ə)r, -z

Convair
BR 'kɒnvɛː(r)
AM 'kanˌvɛ(ə)r

convalesce
BR ˌkɒnvə'lɛs, -ɪz, -ɪŋ, -t
AM ˌkanvə'lɛs, -ɪz, -ɪŋ, -t

convalescence
BR ˌkɒnvə'lɛsns, -ɪz
AM ˌkanvə'lɛsəns, -ɪz

convalescent
BR ˌkɒnvə'lɛsnt, -s
AM ˌkanvə'lɛsənt, -s

convection
BR kən'vɛkʃn
AM kən'vɛkʃən

convectional
BR kən'vɛkʃn̩(ə)l, kən'vɛkʃən(ə)l
AM kən'vɛkʃ(ə)nəl

convective
BR kən'vɛktɪv
AM kən'vɛktɪv

convector
BR kən'vɛktə(r), -z
AM kən'vɛktər, -z

convenable
BR kən'viːnəbl
AM kən'vinəbəl

convenance
BR 'kɒnvənɑːns, -ɪz
AM 'kanvənəns, -ɪz

convene
BR kən'viːn, -z, -ɪŋ, -d
AM kən'vin, -z, -ɪŋ, -d

convener
BR kən'viːnə(r), -z
AM kən'vinər, -z

convenience
BR kən'viːnɪəns, -ɪz
AM kən'vinjəns, -ɪz

convenient
BR kən'viːnɪənt
AM kən'vinjənt

conveniently
BR kən'viːnɪəntli
AM kən'vinjən(t)li

convenor
BR kən'viːnə(r), -z
AM kən'vinər, -z

convent
BR 'kɒnv(ə)nt, -s
AM 'kɑnˌvɛnt, -s

conventicle
BR kən'vɛntɨkl, -z
AM kən'vɛn(t)əkl, -z

convention
BR kən'vɛnʃn, -z
AM kən'vɛn(t)ʃən, -z

conventional
BR kən'vɛnʃn̩(ə)l, kən'vɛnʃən(ə)l
AM kən'vɛn(t)ʃ(ə)nəl

conventionalise
BR kən'vɛnʃn̩əlʌɪz, kən'vɛnʃn̩l̩ʌɪz, kən'vɛnʃənl̩ʌɪz, kən'vɛnʃ(ə)nəlʌɪz, -ɪz, -ɪŋ, -d
AM kən'vɛn(t)ʃənl̩ˌaɪz, kən'vɛn(t)ʃnəlˌaɪz, -ɪz, -ɪŋ, -d

conventionalism
BR kən'vɛnʃn̩əlɪz(ə)m, kən'vɛnʃn̩l̩ɪz(ə)m, kən'vɛnʃənl̩ɪz(ə)m, kən'vɛnʃ(ə)nəlɪz(ə)m
AM kən'vɛn(t)ʃənl̩ˌɪzəm, kən'vɛn(t)ʃnəlˌɪzəm

conventionalist
BR kən'vɛnʃn̩əlɪst, kən'vɛnʃn̩l̩ɪst, kən'vɛnʃənl̩ɪst, kən'vɛnʃ(ə)nəlɪst, -s
AM kən'vɛn(t)ʃənl̩əst, kən'vɛn(t)ʃnələst, -s

conventionality
BR kənˌvɛnʃə'nalɪt|i, -ɪz
AM kənˌvɛn(t)ʃə'nælədi, -z

conventionalize
BR kən'vɛnʃn̩əlʌɪz, kən'vɛnʃn̩l̩ʌɪz, kən'vɛnʃənl̩ʌɪz, kən'vɛnʃ(ə)nəlʌɪz, -ɪz, -ɪŋ, -d
AM kən'vɛn(t)ʃənl̩ˌaɪz, kən'vɛn(t)ʃnəlˌaɪz, -ɪz, -ɪŋ, -d

conventionally
BR kən'vɛnʃn̩əli, kən'vɛnʃn̩l̩i, kən'vɛnʃənl̩i, kən'vɛnʃ(ə)nəli
AM kən'vɛn(t)ʃ(ə)nəli

conventioneer
BR kənˌvɛnʃə'nɪə(r), -z
AM kən'vɛn(t)ʃəˌnɪ(ə)r, -z

conventual
BR kən'vɛn(t)ʃʊəl, kəm'vɛn(t)ʃ(ʉ)l, kən'vɛntjʊəl, kən'vɛntjʉl, -z
AM kən'vɛn(t)ʃ(əw)əl, -z

converb
BR 'kɒnvəːb, -z
AM 'kɑnˌvərb, -z

converge
BR kən'vəːdʒ, -ɪz, -ɪŋ, -d
AM kən'vərdʒ, -ɪz, -ɪŋ, -d

convergence
BR kən'vəːdʒ(ə)ns, -ɪz
AM kən'vərdʒəns, -əz

convergency
BR kən'vəːdʒ(ə)nsi
AM kən'vərdʒənsi

convergent
BR kən'vəːdʒ(ə)nt
AM kən'vərdʒənt

conversance
BR kən'vəːsns
AM kən'vərsəns

conversancy
BR kən'vəːsnsi
AM kən'vərsənsi

conversant
BR kən'vəːsnt
AM kən'vərsənt

conversation
BR ˌkɒnvə'seɪʃn, -z
AM ˌkɑnvər'seɪʃən, -z

conversational
BR ˌkɒnvə'seɪʃn̩(ə)l, ˌkɒnvə'seɪʃən(ə)l
AM ˌkɑnvər'seɪʃ(ə)nəl

conversationalist
BR ˌkɒnvə'seɪʃn̩əlɪst, ˌkɒnvə'seɪʃn̩l̩ɪst, ˌkɒnvə'seɪʃənl̩ɪst, ˌkɒnvə'seɪʃ(ə)nəlɪst, -s
AM ˌkɑnvər'seɪʃənl̩əst, ˌkɑnvər'seɪʃnələst, -s

conversationally
BR ˌkɒnvə'seɪʃn̩əli, ˌkɒnvə'seɪʃn̩l̩i, ˌkɒnvə'seɪʃənl̩i, ˌkɒnvə'seɪʃ(ə)nəli
AM ˌkɑnvər'seɪʃ(ə)nəli

conversationist
BR ˌkɒnvə'seɪʃn̩ɪst, ˌkɒnvə'seɪʃənɪst, -s
AM ˌkɑnvər'seɪʃənəst, -s

conversazione
BR ˌkɒnvəsatzɪ'əʊn|i, -ɪz
AM ˌkɑnvərˌsɑtsi'oʊni, -z

conversazioni
BR ˌkɒnvəsatzɪ'əʊniː
AM ˌkɑnvərˌsɑtsi'oʊni

converse[1]
adjective
BR 'kɒnvəːs, kən'vəːs
AM 'kɑnˌvərs, kən'vərs

converse[2]
noun
BR 'kɒnvəːs
AM 'kɑnˌvərs

converse[3]
verb
BR kən'vəːs, -ɪz, -ɪŋ, -t
AM kən'vərs, -əz, -ɪŋ, -t

conversely
BR 'kɒnvəːsli, kən'vəːsli
AM 'kɑnˌvərsli, kən'vərsli

converser
BR kən'vəːsə(r), -z
AM kən'vərsər, -z

conversion
BR kən'vəːʃn, -z
AM kən'vərʒən, -z

convert[1]
noun
BR 'kɒnvəːt, -s
AM 'kɑnˌvərt, -s

convert[2]
verb
BR kən'vəːt, -s, -ɪŋ, -ɪd
AM kən'vər|t, -ts, -dɪŋ, -dəd

converter
BR kən'vəːtə(r), -z
AM kən'vərdər, -z

convertibility
BR kənˌvəːtɪ'bɪlɪti
AM kənˌvərdə'bɪlɨdi

convertible
BR kən'vəːtɪbl, -z
AM kən'vərdəbəl, -z

convertibly
BR kən'vəːtɪbli
AM kən'vərdəbli

convertor
BR kən'vəːtə(r), -z
AM kən'vərdər, -z

convex
BR ˌkɒn'vɛks, 'kɒnvɛks
AM ˌkɑn'vɛks

convexity
BR kən'vɛksɪt|i, -ɪz
AM kən'vɛksədi, -z

convexly
BR ˌkɒn'vɛksli, 'kɒnvɛksli
AM ˌkɑn'vɛksli

convey
BR kən'veɪ, -z, -ɪŋ, -d
AM kən'veɪ, -z, -ɪŋ, -d

conveyable
BR kən'veɪəbl
AM kən'veɪəbəl

conveyance
BR kən'veɪəns, -ɪz, -ɪŋ, -t
AM kən'veɪəns, -ɪz, -ɪŋ, -t

conveyancer
BR kən'veɪənsə(r), -z
AM kən'veɪənsər, -z

conveyancing
BR kən'veɪənsɪŋ
AM kən'veɪənsɪŋ

conveyer
BR kən'veɪə(r), -z
AM kən'veɪər, -z

conveyor
BR kən'veɪə(r), -z
AM kən'veɪər, -z

convict[1]
noun
BR 'kɒnvɪkt, -s
AM 'kɑnˌvɪk(t), -s

convict[2]
verb
BR kən'vɪkt, -s, -ɪŋ, -ɪd
AM kən'vɪk|(t), -(t)s, -dɪŋ, -dɪd

conviction
BR kən'vɪkʃn, -z
AM kən'vɪkʃən, -z

convictive
BR kən'vɪktɪv
AM kən'vɪktɪv

convince
BR kən'vɪns, -ɪz, -ɪŋ, -t
AM kən'vɪns, -ɪz, -ɪŋ, -t

convincement
BR kən'vɪnsm(ə)nt
AM kən'vɪnsmənt

convincer
BR kən'vɪnsə(r), -z
AM kən'vɪnsər, -z

convincible
BR kən'vɪnsɪbl
AM kən'vɪnsəbəl

convincibly
BR kən'vɪnsɪbli
AM kən'vɪnsəbli

convincingly
BR kən'vɪnsɪŋli
AM kən'vɪnsɪŋli

convivial
BR kən'vɪvɪəl
AM kən'vɪviəl, kən'vɪvjəl

conviviality
BR kənˌvɪvɪ'alɪti
AM kənˌvɪvi'ælədi

convivially
BR kən'vɪvɪəli
AM kən'vɪviəli, kən'vɪvjəli

convocation
BR ˌkɒnvə'keɪʃn
AM ˌkɑnvə'keɪʃən

convocational
BR ˌkɒnvə'keɪʃn̩(ə)l, ˌkɒnvə'keɪʃən(ə)l
AM ˌkɑnvə'keɪʃ(ə)nəl

convoke
BR kən'vəʊk, -s, -ɪŋ, -t
AM kən'voʊk, -s, -ɪŋ, -t

convoluted
BR 'kɒnvəl(j)uːtɪd, ˌkɒnvə'l(j)uːtɪd
AM ¦kɑnvə¦ludəd

convolutedly
BR 'kɒnvəl(j)uːtɪdli, ˌkɒnvə'l(j)uːtɪdli
AM ¦kɑnvə¦ludədli

convolution
BR ˌkɒnvə'l(j)uːʃn, -z
AM ˌkɑnvə'luʃən, -z

convolutional
BR ˌkɒnvə'l(j)uːʃn̩(ə)l, ˌkɒnvə'l(j)uːʃən(ə)l
AM ˌkɑnvə'luʃ(ə)nəl

convolve
BR kən'vɒlv, -z, -ɪŋ, -d
AM kən'vɑlv, -z, -ɪŋ, -d

convolvulus
BR kən'vɒlvjʊləs, kən'vʌlvjʊləs, -ɪz
AM kən'vɑlvjəˌləs, -əz

convoy
BR 'kɒnvɔɪ, -z, -ɪŋ, -d
AM 'kɑnˌvɔɪ, -z, -ɪŋ, -d

convulsant
BR kən'vʌlsnt, -s
AM kən'vəlsənt, -s

convulse
BR kən'vʌls, -ɪz, -ɪŋ, -t
AM kən'vəlz, -əz, -ɪŋ, -d

convulsion
BR kən'vʌlʃn, -z
AM kən'vəlʃən, -z

convulsionary
BR kən'vʌlʃn̩(ə)ri
AM kən'vəlʃəˌnɛri

convulsive
BR kən'vʌlsɪv
AM kən'vəlsɪv

convulsively
BR kən'vʌlsɪvli
AM kən'vəlsɪvli

Conway
BR 'kɒnweɪ
AM 'kɑnweɪ

Conwy
BR 'kɒnwi
AM 'kɑnwi

cony
BR 'kəʊn|i, -ɪz
AM 'koʊni, -z

Conybeare
BR 'kɒnɪbɪə(r), 'kʌnɪbɪə(r)
AM 'kɑniˌbɛ(ə)r

coo
BR kuː, -z, -ɪŋ, -d
AM ku, -z, -ɪŋ, -d

Coober Pedy
BR ˌkuːbə 'piːdi
AM ˌkubər 'pidi

co-occur
BR ˌkəʊə'kəː(r), -z, -ɪŋ, -d
AM ˌkoʊə'kər, -z, -ɪŋ, -d

co-occurrence
BR ˌkəʊə'kʌrəns, ˌkəʊə'kʌrn̩s, -ɪz
AM ˌkoʊə'kərəns, -əz

Cooder
BR 'kuːdə(r)
AM 'kudər

cooee
BR 'kuːiː, ˌkuː'iː, -z, -ɪŋ, -d
AM 'kuˌi, ˌku'i, -z, -ɪŋ, -d

cooey
BR 'kuːiː, ˌkuː'iː, -z, -ɪŋ, -d
AM 'kuˌi, ˌku'i, -z, -ɪŋ, -d

cooingly
BR 'kuːɪŋli
AM 'kuɪŋli

cook
BR kʊk, -s, -ɪŋ, -t
AM kʊk, -s, -ɪŋ, -t

cookability
BR ˌkʊkə'bɪlɪti
AM ˌkʊkə'bɪlɪdi

cookable
BR 'kʊkəbl
AM 'kʊkəbəl

cookbook
BR 'kʊkbʊk, -s
AM 'kʊkˌbʊk, -s

cookchill
BR ˌkʊk'tʃɪl
AM ¦kʊk¦tʃɪl

Cooke
BR kʊk
AM kʊk

cooker
BR 'kʊkə(r), -z
AM 'kʊkər, -z

cookery
BR 'kʊk(ə)ri
AM 'kʊk(ə)ri

cookhouse
BR 'kʊkhaʊ|s, -zɪz
AM 'kʊkˌ(h)aʊ|s, -zəz

cookie
BR 'kʊk|i, -ɪz
AM 'kʊki, -z

cookout
BR 'kʊkaʊt, -s
AM 'kʊkˌaʊt, -s

cookshop
BR 'kʊkʃɒp, -s
AM 'kʊkˌʃɑp, -s

Cookson
BR 'kʊksn
AM 'kʊksən

cookstone
BR 'kʊkstəʊn, -z
AM 'kʊkˌstoʊn, -z

cookware
BR 'kʊkwɛː(r), -z
AM 'kʊkˌwɛ(ə)r, -z

cooky
BR 'kʊk|i, -ɪz
AM 'kʊki, -z

cool
BR kuːl, -z, -ɪŋ, -d
AM kul, -z, -ɪŋ, -d

coolabah
BR 'kuːləbɑː(r), -z
AM 'kuləˌbɑ, -z

coolant
BR 'kuːlənt, -s
AM 'kulənt, -s

cooler
BR 'kuːlə(r), -z
AM 'kulər, -z

Cooley
BR 'kuːli
AM 'kuli

Coolgardie
BR kuːl'gɑːdi
AM ˌkul'gɑrdi

coolibah
BR 'kuːlɪbɑː(r), -z
AM 'kuləˌbɑ, -z

coolibar
BR 'kuːlɪbɑː(r), -z
AM 'kuləˌbɑr, -z

Coolidge
BR 'kuːlɪdʒ
AM 'kulɪdʒ

coolie
BR 'kuːl|i, -ɪz
AM 'kuli, -z

coolish
BR 'kuːlɪʃ, -z
AM 'kulɪʃ, -z

coolly
BR 'kuːl(l)i
AM 'ku(ə)li

coolness
BR 'kuːlnəs
AM 'kulnəs

coolth
BR kuːlθ
AM kulθ

coomb
BR kuːm, -z
AM kum, -z

coombe
BR kuːm, -z
AM kum, -z

Coombes
BR kuːmz
AM kumz

Coombs
BR kuːmz
AM kumz

Coomes
BR kuːmz
AM kumz

coon
BR kuːn, -z
AM kun, -z

Cooney
BR 'kuːni
AM 'kuni

coonskin
BR 'kuːnskɪn, -z
AM 'kunˌskɪn, -z

coop
BR kuːp, -s, -ɪŋ, -t
AM kup, -s, -ɪŋ, -t

co-op
BR 'kəʊɒp, -s
AM 'koʊˌɑp, -s

Coope
BR kuːp
AM kup

cooper
BR 'kuːpə(r), -z
AM 'kupər, -z

cooperage
BR 'kuːp(ə)rɪdʒ
AM 'kup(ə)rɪdʒ

cooperant
BR kəʊ'ɒp(ə)rənt, kəʊ'ɒp(ə)rn̩t
AM koʊ'ɑpərənt

cooperate
BR kəʊ'ɒpəreɪt, -s, -ɪŋ, -ɪd
AM koʊ'ɑpəˌreɪ|t, -ts, -dɪŋ, -dɪd

cooperation
BR kəʊˌɒpə'reɪʃn, -z
AM koʊˌɑpə'reɪʃən, -z

cooperative
BR kəʊ'ɒp(ə)rətɪv, -z
AM koʊ'ɑp(ə)rədɪv, -z

cooperatively
BR kəʊ'ɒp(ə)rətɪvli
AM koʊ'ɑp(ə)rədɪvli

cooperativeness
BR kəʊ'ɒp(ə)rətɪvnɪs
AM koʊ'ɑp(ə)rədɪvnɪs

cooperator
BR kəʊ'ɒpəreɪtə(r), -z
AM koʊ'ɑpəˌreɪdər, -z

Cooperstown
BR 'kuːpəztaʊn
AM 'kupərzˌtaʊn

coopt
BR ˌkəʊ'ɒpt, -s, -ɪŋ, -ɪd
AM ˌkoʊ'ɑpt, -s, -ɪŋ, -ɪd

cooptation
BR ˌkəʊɒp'teɪʃn
AM ˌkoʊˌɑp'teɪʃən

cooption
BR ˌkəʊ'ɒpʃn, -z
AM ˌkoʊ'ɑpʃən, -z

cooptive
BR ˌkəʊ'ɒptɪv
AM ˌkoʊ'ɑptɪv

coordinate¹
noun, adjective
BR kəʊˈɔːdɪnət, -s
AM koʊˈɔrdənət, -s

coordinate²
verb
BR kəʊˈɔːdɪneɪt, -s, -ɪŋ, -ɪd
AM koʊˈɔrdəˌneɪ|t, -ts, -dɪŋ, -dɪd

coordinately
BR kəʊˈɔːdɪnətli
AM koʊˈɔrdənətli

coordination
BR kəʊˌɔːdɪˈneɪʃn, -z
AM koʊˌɔrdəˈneɪʃən, -z

coordinative
BR kəʊˈɔːdɪnətɪv
AM koʊˈɔrdəˌneɪdɪv, koʊˈɔrdənədɪv

coordinator
BR kəʊˈɔːdɪneɪtə(r), -z
AM koʊˈɔrdəˌneɪdər, -z

Coors®
BR kɔːz
AM kʊ(ə)rz, kɔ(ə)rz

coot
BR kuːt, -s
AM kut, -s

Coote
BR kuːt
AM kut

cootie
BR ˈkuːt|i, -ɪz
AM ˈkudi, -z

co-own
BR ˌkəʊˈəʊn, -z, -ɪŋ, -d
AM ˌkoʊˈoʊn, -z, -ɪŋ, -d

co-owner
BR ˌkəʊˈəʊnə(r), -z
AM ˌkoʊˈoʊnər, -z

co-ownership
BR ˌkəʊˈəʊnəʃɪp
AM ˌkoʊˈoʊnərˌʃɪp

cop
BR kɒp, -s, -ɪŋ, -t
AM kɑp, -s, -ɪŋ, -t

Copacabana
BR ˌkəʊpəkəˈbanə(r), ˌkəʊpəkəˈbɑːnə(r)
AM ˌkoʊpəkəˈbænə

copacetic
BR ˌkəʊpəˈsɛtɪk, ˌkəʊpəˈsiːtɪk
AM ˌkoʊpəˈsɛdɪk, ˌkoʊpəˈsidɪk

copaiba
BR kə(ʊ)ˈpʌɪbə(r)
AM koʊˈpaɪbə

copal
BR ˈkəʊpl
AM ˈkoʊpəl

cope
BR kəʊp, -s, -ɪŋ, -t
AM koʊp, -s, -ɪŋ, -t

copeck
BR ˈkəʊpɛk, -s
AM ˈkoʊˌpɛk, -s

Copeland
BR ˈkəʊplənd
AM ˈkoʊplən(d)

Copenhagen
BR ˌkəʊp(ə)nˈheɪɡ(ə)n, ˌkəʊp(ə)nˈhɑːɡ(ə)n
AM ˈkoʊpənˌ(h)ɑɡən, ˈkoʊpənˌ(h)eɪɡən

copepod
BR ˈkəʊpɪpɒd, -z
AM ˈkoʊpəˌpɑd, -z

coper
BR ˈkəʊpə(r), -z
AM ˈkoʊpər, -z

Copernican
BR kəˈpəːnɪk(ə)n
AM kəˈpərnəkən

Copernicus
BR kəˈpəːnɪkəs
AM kəˈpərnəkəs

Copestake
BR ˈkəʊpsteɪk
AM ˈkoʊpˌsteɪk

copestone
BR ˈkəʊpstəʊn, -z
AM ˈkoʊpˌstoʊn, -z

copiable
BR ˈkɒpɪəbl
AM ˈkɑpiəbəl

copier
BR ˈkɒpɪə(r), -z
AM ˈkɑpiər, -z

copilot
BR ˈkəʊˌpʌɪlət, -s
AM ˈkoʊˌpaɪlət, -s

coping
BR ˈkəʊpɪŋ, -z
AM ˈkoʊpɪŋ, -z

copingstone
BR ˈkəʊpɪŋstəʊn, -z
AM ˈkoʊpɪŋˌstoʊn, -z

copious
BR ˈkəʊpɪəs
AM ˈkoʊpiəs

copiously
BR ˈkəʊpɪəsli
AM ˈkoʊpiəsli

copiousness
BR ˈkəʊpɪəsnəs
AM ˈkoʊpiəsnəs

copita
BR kə(ʊ)ˈpiːtə(r), -z
AM koʊˈpidə, -z

coplanar
BR kəʊˈpleɪnə(r)
AM ˌkoʊˈpleɪnər

coplanarity
BR ˌkəʊpleɪˈnarɪti
AM ˌkoʊˌpleɪˈnɛrədi

Copland
BR ˈkəʊplənd
AM ˈkoʊplən(d)

Copley
BR ˈkɒpli
AM ˈkoʊpli

copolymer
BR ˌkəʊˈpɒlɪmə(r), -z
AM ˌkoʊˈpɑləmər, -z

copolymerisation
BR ˌkəʊˌpɒlɪmərʌɪˈzeɪʃn
AM ˌkoʊˌpɑləmərəˈzeɪʃən, ˌkoʊpəˌlɪmərəˈzeɪʃən, ˌkoʊˌpɑləməˌraɪˈzeɪʃən, ˌkoʊpəˌlɪməˌraɪˈzeɪʃən

copolymerise
BR ˌkəʊˈpɒlɪmərʌɪz, -ɪz, -ɪŋ, -d
AM ˌkoʊˈpɑləməˌraɪz, ˌkoʊpəˈlɪməˌraɪz, -ɪz, -ɪŋ, -d

copolymerization
BR ˌkəʊˌpɒlɪmərʌɪˈzeɪʃn
AM ˌkoʊˌpɑləmərəˈzeɪʃən, ˌkoʊpəˌlɪmərəˈzeɪʃən, ˌkoʊˌpɑləməˌraɪˈzeɪʃən, ˌkoʊpəˌlɪməˌraɪˈzeɪʃən

copolymerize
BR ˌkəʊˈpɒlɪmərʌɪz, -ɪz, -ɪŋ, -d
AM ˌkoʊˈpɑləməˌraɪz, ˌkoʊpəˈlɪməˌraɪz, -ɪz, -ɪŋ, -d

copout
BR ˈkɒpaʊt, -s
AM ˈkɑpˌaʊt, -s

copper
BR ˈkɒpə(r), -z
AM ˈkɑpər, -z

copperas
BR ˈkɒp(ə)rəs
AM ˈkɑp(ə)rəs

Copperbelt
BR ˈkɒpəbɛlt
AM ˈkɑpərˌbɛlt

Copperfield
BR ˈkɒpəfiːld
AM ˈkɑpərˌfild

copperhead
BR ˈkɒpəhɛd, -z
AM ˈkɑpərˌ(h)ɛd, -z

coppermine
BR ˈkɒpəmʌɪn, -z
AM ˈkɑpərˌmaɪn, -z

copperplate
BR ˈkɒpəpleɪt
AM ˈkɑpərˈpleɪt

coppersmith
BR ˈkɒpəsmɪθ, -s
AM ˈkɑpərˌsmɪθ, -s

coppery
BR ˈkɒp(ə)ri
AM ˈkɑpəri

coppice
BR ˈkɒp|ɪs, -ɪsɪz, -ɪsɪŋ, -ɪst
AM ˈkɑpəs, -əz, -ɪŋ, -t

Coppola
BR ˈkɒpələ(r)
AM ˈkɑpələ

copra
BR ˈkɒprə(r)
AM ˈkɑprə

coprocessor
BR ˌkəʊˈprəʊsɛsə(r), ˈkəʊˌprəʊsɛsə(r), -z
AM ˌkoʊˈprɑsɛsər, -z

coprolite
BR ˈkɒprəlʌɪt
AM ˈkɑprəˌlaɪt

coprology
BR kɒˈprɒlədʒi, kəˈprɒlədʒi
AM kəˈprɑlədʒi

coprophagous
BR kɒˈprɒfəɡəs, kəˈprɒfəɡəs
AM kəˈprɑfəɡəs

coprophilia
BR ˌkɒprəˈfɪlɪə(r)
AM ˈkɑprəˈfɪljə, ˈkɑprəˈfɪliə

coprophiliac
BR ˌkɒprəˈfɪlɪak, -s
AM ˌkɑprəˈfɪliˌæk, ˌkɑprəˈfɪliˌæk, -s

coprosma
BR kəˈprɒzmə(r), -z
AM kəˈprɑzmə, -z

copse
BR kɒps, -ɪz
AM kɑps, -əz

copsewood
BR ˈkɒpswʊd
AM ˈkɑpsˌwʊd

copsy
BR ˈkɒpsi
AM ˈkɑpsi

Copt
BR kɒpt, -s
AM kɑpt, -s

'copter
BR ˈkɒptə(r), -z
AM ˈkɑptər, -z

Coptic
BR ˈkɒptɪk
AM ˈkɑptɪk

copula
BR ˈkɒpjʊlə(r), -z
AM ˈkɑpjələ, ˈkoʊpjələ, -z

copular
BR ˈkɒpjʊlə(r)
AM ˈkɑpjələr, ˈkoʊpjələr

copulate
BR ˈkɒpjʊleɪt, -s, -ɪŋ, -ɪd
AM ˈkɑpjəˌleɪ|t, ˈkoʊpjəˌleɪ|t, -ts, -dɪŋ, -dɪd

copulation
BR ˌkɒpjʊˈleɪʃn
AM ˌkɑpjəˈleɪʃən, ˌkoʊpjəˈleɪʃən

copulative
BR ˈkɒpjʊlətɪv, -z

AM 'kɑpjələdɪv, 'koʊpjələdɪv, 'kɑpjəˌleɪdɪv, 'koʊpjəˌleɪdɪv, -z

copulatively
BR 'kɒpjʉlətɨvli
AM 'kɑpjəˌleɪdɨvli, 'koʊpjəˌleɪdɨvli, 'kɑpjələdɨvli, 'koʊpjələdɨvli

copulatory
BR 'kɒpjʉlət(ə)ri
AM 'kɑpjələˌtɔri, 'koʊpjələˌtɔri

copy
BR 'kɒp|i, -ɪz, -ɪɪŋ, -ɪd
AM 'kɑpi, -z, -ɪŋ, -d

copybook
BR 'kɒpɪbʊk, -s
AM 'kɑpiˌbʊk, -s

copyboy
BR 'kɒpɪbɔɪ, -z
AM 'kɑpiˌbɔɪ, -z

copycat
BR 'kɒpɪkat, -s
AM 'kɑpiˌkæt, -s

copydesk
BR 'kɒpɪdɛsk, -s
AM 'kɑpiˌdɛsk, -s

Copydex®
BR 'kɒpɪdɛks
AM 'kɑpiˌdɛks

copyhold
BR 'kɒpɪhəʊld, -z
AM 'kɑpiˌ(h)oʊld, -z

copyholder
BR 'kɒpɪˌhəʊldə(r), -z
AM 'kɑpiˌ(h)oʊldər, -z

copyist
BR 'kɒpɪɪst, -s
AM 'kɑpiəst, -s

copyread
BR 'kɒpɪriːd, -z, -ɪŋ
AM 'kɑpiˌrid, -z, -ɪŋ

copyreader
BR 'kɒpɪˌriːdə(r), -z
AM 'kɑpiˌridər, -z

copyright
BR 'kɒpɪrʌɪt, -s, -ɪŋ, -ɨd
AM 'kɑpiˌraɪ|t, -ts, -dɪŋ, -dɨd

copywriter
BR 'kɒpɪˌrʌɪtə(r), -z
AM 'kɑpɪˌraɪdər, -z

copywriting
BR 'kɒpɪˌrʌɪtɪŋ
AM 'kɑpɪˌraɪdɪŋ

coq au vin
BR ˌkɒk əʊ 'vã, + 'van
AM ˌkɑk oʊ 'væn

coquet
BR kɒ'kɛt, kə'kɛt, -s, -ɪŋ, -ɨd
AM koʊ'kɛ|t, -ts, -dɪŋ, -dəd

coquetry
BR 'kɒkɪtri
AM 'koʊkətri

coquette
BR kɒ'kɛt, kə'kɛt, -s
AM koʊ'kɛt, -s

coquettish
BR kɒ'kɛtɪʃ, kə'kɛtɪʃ
AM koʊ'kɛdɪʃ

coquettishly
BR kɒ'kɛtɪʃli, kə'kɛtɪʃli
AM koʊ'kɛdɪʃli

coquettishness
BR kɒ'kɛtɪʃnɪs, kə'kɛtɪʃnɪs
AM koʊ'kɛdɪʃnɪs

coquille
BR kɒ'kiː
AM koʊ'ki(l)

coquilles
BR kɒ'kiː
AM koʊ'ki(l)

coquina
BR kəʊ'kiːnə(r)
AM koʊ'kinə

coquito
BR kə(ʊ)'kiːtəʊ, -z
AM koʊ'kidoʊ, -z

cor
BR kɔː(r)
AM kɔ(ə)r

Cora
BR 'kɔːrə(r)
AM 'kɔrə

coracle
BR 'kɒrəkl, -z
AM 'kɔrəkl, 'kɑrəkl, -z

coracoid
BR 'kɔːrəkɔɪd, -z
AM 'kɔrəˌkɔɪd, -z

coral
BR 'kɒrəl, 'kɒrḷ, -z
AM 'kɔrəl, -z

Coralie
BR 'kɔːrəli
AM 'kɔrəli

coralline
BR 'kɒrəlʌɪn, -z
AM 'kɔrələn, 'kɔrəˌlin, -z

corallita
BR ˌkɒrə'liːtə(r)
AM ˌkɔrə'lidə

corallite
BR 'kɒrəlʌɪt, -s
AM 'kɔrəˌlaɪt, -s

coralloid
BR 'kɒrəlɔɪd, -z
AM 'kɔrəˌlɔɪd, -z

Coram
BR 'kɔːrəm
AM 'kɔrəm

coram populo
BR ˌkɔːrəm 'pɒpjʉləʊ
AM ˌkoʊrəm 'pɑpjəloʊ

cor anglais
BR ˌkɔːr 'ɑːŋgleɪ, + 'ɒŋgleɪ
AM ˌkɔ(ə)r ɔŋ'gleɪ

corbel
BR 'kɔːb(ə)l, -z
AM 'kɔrbl, -z

Corbet
BR 'kɔːbɪt
AM 'kɔrbət

Corbett
BR 'kɔːbɪt
AM 'kɔrbət

corbicula
BR kɔː'bɪkjʉlə(r)
AM ˌkɔr'bɪkjələ

corbiculae
BR kɔː'bɪkjʉliː
AM ˌkɔr'bɪkjəli

corbie
BR 'kɔːb|i, -ɪz
AM 'kɔrbi, -z

Corbin
BR 'kɔːbɪn
AM 'kɔrbɪn

Corbishley
BR 'kɔːbɪʃli
AM 'kɔrbɪʃli

cor blimey!
BR ˌkɔː 'blʌɪmi
AM ˌkɔ(ə)r 'blaɪmi

Corbridge
BR 'kɔːbrɪdʒ
AM 'kɔrˌbrɪdʒ

Corby
BR 'kɔːbi
AM 'kɔrbi

Corcoran
BR 'kɔːk(ə)rən, 'kɔːk(ə)rn̩
AM 'kɔrk(ə)rən

Corcyra
BR kɔː'sʌɪrə(r)
AM kɔr'sɪrə

cord
BR kɔːd, -z, -ɪŋ
AM kɔ(ə)rd, -z, -ɪŋ

cordage
BR 'kɔːdɪdʒ
AM 'kɔrdɪdʒ

cordate
BR 'kɔːdeɪt
AM 'kɔrˌdeɪt

Corday
BR 'kɔːdeɪ
AM kɔr'deɪ

Cordelia
BR kɔː'diːlɪə(r)
AM ˌkɔr'diljə, ˌkɔr'diliə

Cordelier
BR ˌkɔːdɪ'lɪə(r), -z
AM ˌkɔrdə'lɪ(ə)r, -z

Cordell
BR ˌkɔː'dɛl
AM kɔr'dɛl

cordial
BR 'kɔːdɪəl
AM 'kɔrdʒəl

cordiality
BR ˌkɔːdɪ'alɪti
AM ˌkɔrdʒi'ælədi

cordially
BR 'kɔːdɪəli
AM 'kɔrdʒəli

cordillera
BR ˌkɔːdɪ'ljɛːrə(r)
AM ˌkɔrdl'(j)ɛrə

cordite
BR 'kɔːdʌɪt
AM 'kɔrˌdaɪt

cordless
BR 'kɔːdləs
AM 'kɔrdləs

cordlessness
BR 'kɔːdləsnəs
AM 'kɔrdləsnəs

cordlike
BR 'kɔːdlʌɪk
AM 'kɔrˌlaɪk

Córdoba
BR 'kɔːdəbə(r)
AM 'kɔrdəbə, kɔr'doʊbə

cordon
BR 'kɔːdn, -z, -ɪŋ, -d
AM 'kɔrdən, -z, -ɪŋ, -d

cordon-bleu
BR ˌkɔːdɒn 'bləː(r), ˌkɔːdɔ̃ +
AM ˌkɔrdɔn 'blə, ˌkɔrdn 'blu

cordon sanitaire
BR ˌkɔːdɒn ˌsanɪ'tɛː(r), ˌkɔːdɔ̃ +, -z
AM ˌkɔrdɔn ˌsɑni'tɛ(ə)r, -z

Cordova
BR 'kɔːdəvə(r)
AM 'kɔrdəvə, kɔr'doʊvə

cordovan
BR 'kɔːdəvn
AM 'kɔrdəvən

corduroy
BR 'kɔːdərɔɪ, 'kɔːdjʉrɔɪ, 'kɔːdʒʉrɔɪ, -z
AM 'kɔrdəˌrɔɪ, -z

cordwain
BR 'kɔːdweɪn
AM 'kɔrdˌweɪn

cordwainer
BR 'kɔːdˌweɪnə(r), -z
AM 'kɔrdˌweɪnər, -z

cordwood
BR 'kɔːdwʊd
AM 'kɔrdˌwʊd

CORE
BR kɔː(r)
AM kɔ(ə)r

core
BR kɔː(r), -z, -ɪŋ, -d
AM kɔ(ə)r, -z, -ɪŋ, -d

co-referential
BR ˌkəʊrɛfə'rɛnʃl
AM ˌkoʊrɛfə'rɛnʃəl

corelation
BR ˌkɒrɪˈleɪʃn, -z
AM ˌkɔrəˈleɪʃən, -z

co-religionist
BR ˌkəʊrɪˈlɪdʒənɪst, ˌkəʊrɪˈlɪdʒn̩ɪst, -s
AM ˌkoʊrəˈlɪdʒənəst, -s

corella
BR kəˈrɛlə(r), kɒˈrɛlə(r), -z
AM kəˈrɛlə, -z

Corelli
BR kəˈrɛli, kɒˈrɛli
AM kəˈrɛli

Coren
BR ˈkɔːrən, ˈkɔːrn̩
AM ˈkɔrən

coreopsis
BR ˈkɒrɪˈɒpsɪs
AM ˌkɔriˈɑpsəs

corer
BR ˈkɔːrə(r), -z
AM ˈkɔrər, -z

co-respondent
BR ˌkəʊrɪˈspɒnd(ə)nt, -s
AM ˌkoʊrəˈspɑndənt, -s

Corey
BR ˈkɔːri
AM ˈkɔri

corf
BR kɔːf, -s
AM kɔ(ə)rf, -s

Corfe
BR kɔːf
AM kɔ(ə)rf

Corfu
BR ˌkɔːˈf(j)uː
AM kɔrˈfu, ˈkɔrf(j)u

corgi
BR ˈkɔːɡ|i, -ɪz
AM ˈkɔrɡi, -z

coria
BR ˈkɔːrɪə(r)
AM ˈkɔriə

coriaceous
BR ˌkɒrɪˈeɪʃəs
AM ˌkɔriˈeɪʃəs

coriander
BR ˌkɒrɪˈandə(r), ˈkɒrɪandə(r)
AM ˈkɔrɪˌændər

Corin
BR ˈkɒrɪn
AM ˈkɔrən

Corinna
BR kəˈrɪnə(r)
AM kəˈrɪnə

Corinne
BR kəˈrɪn
AM kəˈrɪn

Corinth
BR ˈkɒr(ɪ)nθ
AM ˈkɔrənθ

Corinthian
BR kəˈrɪnθɪən, -z
AM kəˈrɪnθiən, -z

Coriolanus
BR ˌkɒrɪəˈleɪnəs
AM ˌkɔriəˈleɪnəs

Coriolis
BR ˌkɒrɪˈəʊlɪs
AM ˌkɔriˈoʊləs

corium
BR ˈkɔːrɪəm
AM ˈkɔriəm

cork
BR kɔːk, -s, -ɪŋ, -t
AM kɔ(ə)rk, -s, -ɪŋ, -t

corkage
BR ˈkɔːkɪdʒ
AM ˈkɔrkɪdʒ

corker
BR ˈkɔːkə(r), -z
AM ˈkɔrkər, -z

corkiness
BR ˈkɔːkɪnɪs
AM ˈkɔrkinɪs

corklike
BR ˈkɔːklʌɪk
AM ˈkɔrkˌlaɪk

corkscrew
BR ˈkɔːkskruː, -z
AM ˈkɔrkˌskru, -z

corkwood
BR ˈkɔːkwʊd
AM ˈkɔrkˌwʊd

corky
BR ˈkɔːk|i, -ɪə(r), -ɪɪst
AM ˈkɔrki, -ər, -ɪst

Corley
BR ˈkɔːli
AM ˈkɔrli

corm
BR kɔːm, -z
AM kɔ(ə)rm, -z

Cormac
BR ˈkɔːmak, ˈkɔːmək
AM ˈkɔrmək

cormorant
BR ˈkɔːm(ə)rənt, ˈkɔːm(ə)rn̩t, -s
AM ˈkɔrmərənt, -s

corn
BR kɔːn, -z, -d
AM kɔ(ə)rn, -z, -d

cornball
BR ˈkɔːnbɔːl, -z
AM ˈkɔrnˌbɔl, -z

cornbrash
BR ˈkɔːnbraʃ
AM ˈkɔrnˌbræʃ

cornbread
BR ˈkɔːnbrɛd
AM ˈkɔrnˌbrɛd

corncob
BR ˈkɔːnkɒb, -z
AM ˈkɔrnˌkɑb, -z

corncockle
BR ˈkɔːnˌkɒkl, -z
AM ˈkɔrnˌkɑkəl, -z

corncrake
BR ˈkɔːnkreɪk, -s
AM ˈkɔrnˌkreɪk, -s

corncrib
BR ˈkɔːnkrɪb, -z
AM ˈkɔrnˌkrɪb, -z

cornea
BR ˈkɔːnɪə(r), kɔːˈniːə(r), -z
AM ˈkɔrniə, -z

corneal
BR ˈkɔːnɪəl, kɔːˈniːəl
AM ˈkɔrniəl

cornel
BR ˈkɔːnl, -z
AM ˈkɔrnəl, -z

Cornelia
BR kɔːˈniːlɪə(r)
AM kɔrˈniljə, kɔrˈniliə

cornelian
BR kɔːˈniːlɪən, -z
AM kɔrˈniljən, kɔrˈniliən, -z

Cornelius
BR kɔːˈniːlɪəs
AM kɔrˈniljəs, kɔrˈniliəs

Cornell
BR kɔːˈnɛl
AM kɔrˈnɛl

corneous
BR ˈkɔːnɪəs
AM ˈkɔrniəs

corner
BR ˈkɔːn|ə(r), -əz, -(ə)rɪŋ, -əd
AM ˈkɔrnər, -z, -ɪŋ, -d

cornerback
BR ˈkɔːnəbak, -s
AM ˈkɔrnərˌbæk, -s

cornerstone
BR ˈkɔːnəstəʊn, -z
AM ˈkɔrnərˌstoʊn, -z

cornerways
BR ˈkɔːnəweɪz
AM ˈkɔrnərˌweɪz

cornerwise
BR ˈkɔːnəwʌɪz
AM ˈkɔrnərˌwaɪz

cornet
BR ˈkɔːnɪt, -s
AM ˌkɔrˈnɛt, -s

cornetcy
BR ˈkɔːnɪtsi
AM ˌkɔrˈnɛtsi

cornetist
BR kɔːˈnɛtɪst, -s
AM ˌkɔrˈnɛdəst, -s

cornett
BR ˈkɔːnɪt, -s
AM ˌkɔrˈnɛt, -s

cornetti
BR kɔːˈnɛtiː
AM kɔrˈnɛdi

cornettist
BR kɔːˈnɛtɪst, -s
AM ˌkɔrˈnɛdəst, -s

cornetto
BR kɔːˈnɛtəʊ, -z
AM kɔrˈnɛdoʊ, -z

cornfield
BR ˈkɔːnfiːld, -z
AM ˈkɔrnˌfild, -z

cornflake
BR ˈkɔːnfleɪk, -s
AM ˈkɔrnˌfleɪk, -s

cornflour
BR ˈkɔːnˌflaʊə(r)
AM ˈkɔrnˌflaʊər

cornflower
BR ˈkɔːnˌflaʊə(r), -z
AM ˈkɔrnˌflaʊər, -z

Cornhill
BR ˌkɔːnˈhɪl, ˈkɔːnhɪl
AM ˈkɔrnˌ(h)ɪl

cornhusk
BR ˈkɔːnhʌsk, -s
AM ˈkɔrnˌ(h)əsk, -s

cornice
BR ˈkɔːn|ɪs, -ɪsɪz, -ɪst
AM ˈkɔrnɪs, -ɪz, -ɪst

corniced
BR ˈkɔːnɪst
AM ˈkɔrnɪst

corniche
BR ˈkɔːniːʃ, (ˌ)kɔːˈniːʃ, -ɪz
AM kɔrˈnɪʃ, kɔrˈniʃ, -ɪz

cornily
BR ˈkɔːnɪli
AM ˈkɔrnəli

corniness
BR ˈkɔːnɪnɪs
AM ˈkɔrninɪs

Corning
BR ˈkɔːnɪŋ
AM ˈkɔrnɪŋ

Cornish
BR ˈkɔːnɪʃ
AM ˈkɔrnɪʃ

Cornishman
BR ˈkɔːnɪʃmən
AM ˈkɔrnɪʃmən

Cornishmen
BR ˈkɔːnɪʃmən
AM ˈkɔrnɪʃmən

Cornishwoman
BR ˈkɔːnɪʃˌwʊmən
AM ˈkɔrnɪʃˌwʊmən

Cornishwomen
BR ˈkɔːnɪʃˌwɪmɪn
AM ˈkɔrnɪʃˌwɪmɪn

cornmeal
BR ˈkɔːnmiːl
AM ˈkɔrnˌmil

cornrows
BR ˈkɔːnrəʊz
AM ˈkɔrnˌroʊz

cornstalk
BR ˈkɔːnstɔːk, -s
AM ˈkɔrnˌstɔk, ˈkɔrnˌstɑk, -s

cornstarch
BR ˈkɔːnstɑːtʃ
AM ˈkɔrnˌstɑrtʃ

cornstone
BR 'kɔːnstəʊn
AM 'kɔrn,stoʊn
cornucopia
BR ,kɔːnjʊ'kəʊpɪə(r), -z
AM ,kɔrn(j)ə'koʊpiə, -z
cornucopian
BR ,kɔːnjʊ'kəʊpɪən
AM ,kɔrn(j)ə'koʊpiən
Cornwall
BR 'kɔːnwɔːl, 'kɔːnw(ə)l
AM 'kɔrn,wɔl, 'kɔrn,wɑl
Cornwallis
BR (,)kɔːn'wɒlɪs
AM ,kɔrn'wɑləs
corny
BR 'kɔːn|i, -ɪə(r), -ɪɪst
AM 'kɔrni, -ər, -ɪst
corolla
BR kə'rɒlə(r), -z
AM kə'rɑlə, kə'roʊlə, -z
corollary
BR kə'rɒl(ə)r|i, -ɪz
AM 'kɔrə,lɛri, 'kɑrə,lɛri, -z
Coromandel
BR ,kɒrə(ʊ)'mandl
AM ,kɔrə'mændəl
corona
BR kə'rəʊnə(r), -z
AM kə'roʊnə, -z
Corona Borealis
BR kə,rəʊnə ,bɔːrɪ'eɪlɪs, + ,bɔːrɪ'ɑːlɪs
AM kə'roʊnə bɔri'æləs, + ,bɔri'eɪlɪs
coronach
BR 'kɒrənəx, 'kɒrənək, -s
AM 'kɔrənək, -s
coronae
BR kə'rəʊniː
AM kə'roʊni, kə'roʊ,naɪ
coronagraph
BR kə'rəʊnəgrɑːf, kə'rəʊnəgraf, -s
AM kə'roʊnə,græf, -s
coronal
BR 'kɒrənl, 'kɒrn̩l
AM 'kɔrənəl, kə'roʊnəl
coronary
BR 'kɒrən(ə)r|i, 'kɒrn̩(ə)r|i, -ɪz
AM 'kɔrə,nɛri, -z
coronation
BR ,kɒrə'neɪʃn, -z
AM ,kɔrə'neɪʃən, -z
coroner
BR 'kɒrənə(r), 'kɒrn̩ə(r), -z
AM 'kɔrənər, -z
coronership
BR 'kɒrənəʃɪp, 'kɒrn̩əʃɪp
AM 'kɔrənər,ʃɪp
coronet
BR 'kɒrənɪt, 'kɒrənɛt, ,kɒrə'nɛt, -s, -ɪd
AM ¦kɔrə¦nɛ|t, -ts, -dəd
Corot
BR 'kɒrəʊ
AM kə'roʊ
corozo
BR kə'rəʊzəʊ, -z
AM kə'roʊzoʊ, -z
Corp.
BR kɔːp
AM kɔrp
corpora
BR 'kɔːp(ə)rə(r)
AM 'kɔrp(ə)rə
corpora delicti
BR ,kɔːp(ə)rə dɪ'lɪktʌɪ
AM ,kɔrpərə də'lɪk,taɪ
corporal
BR 'kɔːp(ə)rəl, 'kɔːp(ə)rl̩, -z
AM 'kɔrp(ə)rəl, -z
corporality
BR ,kɔːpə'ralɪti
AM ,kɔrpə'rælədi
corporally
BR 'kɔːp(ə)rəli, 'kɔːp(ə)rli
AM 'kɔrp(ə)rəli
corpora lutea
BR ,kɔːpərə 'luːtɪə(r)
AM ,kɔrpərə 'ludiə
corporate
BR 'kɔːp(ə)rət
AM 'kɔrp(ə)rət
corporately
BR 'kɔːp(ə)rətli
AM 'kɔrp(ə)rətli
corporateness
BR 'kɔːp(ə)rətnəs
AM 'kɔrp(ə)rətnəs
corporation
BR ,kɔːpə'reɪʃn, -z
AM ,kɔrpə'reɪʃən, -z
corporatism
BR 'kɔːp(ə)rətɪz(ə)m
AM 'kɔrp(ə)rə,tɪzəm
corporatist
BR 'kɔːp(ə)rətɪst
AM 'kɔrp(ə)rədəst
corporative
BR 'kɔːp(ə)rətɪv
AM 'kɔrp(ə)rədɪv
corporativism
BR 'kɔːp(ə)rətɪvɪz(ə)m
AM 'kɔrp(ə)rədə,vɪzəm
corporativist
BR 'kɔːp(ə)rətɪvɪst, -s
AM 'kɔrp(ə)rədəvəst, -s
corporeal
BR kɔː'pɔːrɪəl
AM kɔr'pɔriəl
corporeality
BR kɔː,pɔːrɪ'alɪti
AM kɔr,pɔri'ælədi
corporeally
BR kɔː'pɔːrɪəli
AM kɔr'pɔriəli
corporeity
BR ,kɔːpə'riːɪti, ,kɔːpə'reɪɪti
AM kɔrpə'riɪdi, kɔrpə'reɪɪdi
corposant
BR 'kɔːpəs(ə)nt, -s
AM 'kɔrpə,sænt, 'kɔrpəsənt, -s
corps
BR kɔː(r), -z
AM kɔ(ə)r, -z
corps de ballet
BR ,kɔː də 'baleɪ
AM ,kɔr də bæ'leɪ
corps d'élite
BR ,kɔː deɪ'liːt
AM ,kɔr deɪ'lit
corps diplomatique
BR ,kɔː ,dɪpləma'tiːk
AM ,kɔr ,dɪpləmə'tik
corpse
BR kɔːps, -ɪz
AM kɔ(ə)rps, -əz
corpulence
BR 'kɔːpjʊləns
AM 'kɔrpjələns
corpulency
BR 'kɔːpjʊlənsi
AM 'kɔrpjələnsi
corpulent
BR 'kɔːpjʊlənt, 'kɔːpjʊln̩t
AM 'kɔrpjələnt
corpus
BR 'kɔːpəs, -ɪz
AM 'kɔrpəs, -əz
Corpus Christi
BR ,kɔːpəs 'krɪsti
AM ,kɔrpəs 'krɪsti
corpuscle
BR 'kɔːpʌsl, -z
AM 'kɔr,pəsəl, -z
corpuscular
BR kɔː'pʌskjʊlə(r)
AM kɔr'pəskjələr
corpus delicti
BR ,kɔːpəs dɪ'lɪktʌɪ
AM ,kɔrpəs də'lɪktaɪ
corpus luteum
BR ,kɔːpəs 'luːtɪəm
AM ,kɔrpəs 'ludiəm
corral
BR kə'rɑːl, kə'ral, -z, -ɪŋ, -d
AM kə'ræl, -z, -ɪŋ, -d
corrasion
BR kə'reɪʒn
AM kə'reɪʒən
correct
BR kə'rɛkt, -s, -ɪŋ, -ɪd
AM kə'rɛk|(t), -(t)s, -dɪŋ, -dəd
correction
BR kə'rɛkʃn, -z
AM kə'rɛkʃən, -z
correctional
BR kə'rɛkʃn̩(ə)l, kə'rɛkʃən(ə)l
AM kə'rɛkʃ(ə)nəl
correctitude
BR kə'rɛktɪtjuːd, kə'rɛktɪtʃuːd
AM kə'rɛktə,tud
corrective
BR kə'rɛktɪv
AM kə'rɛktɪv
correctively
BR kə'rɛktɪvli
AM kə'rɛktɪvli
correctly
BR kə'rɛktli
AM kə'rɛk(t)li
correctness
BR kə'rɛk(t)nəs
AM kə'rɛk(t)nəs
corrector
BR kə'rɛktə(r), -z
AM kə'rɛktər, -z
Correggio
BR kə'rɛdʒɪəʊ
AM kə'rɛdʒioʊ
correlate[1]
noun
BR 'kɒrɪleɪt, 'kɒrɪlət, 'kɒrl̩ət, -s
AM 'kɔrələt, -s
correlate[2]
verb
BR 'kɒrɪleɪt, -s, -ɪŋ, -ɪd
AM 'kɔrə,leɪ|t, -ts, -dɪŋ, -dɪd
correlation
BR ,kɒrɪ'leɪʃn
AM ,kɔrə'leɪʃən
correlational
BR ,kɒrɪ'leɪʃn̩(ə)l, ,kɒrɪ'leɪʃən(ə)l
AM ,kɔrə'leɪʃ(ə)nəl
correlative
BR kə'rɛlətɪv, -z
AM kə'rɛlədɪv, -z
correlatively
BR kə'rɛlətɪvli
AM kə'rɛlədɪvli
correlativity
BR kə,rɛlə'tɪvɪti
AM kə,rɛlə'tɪvɪdi
correspond
BR ,kɒrɪ'spɒnd, -z, -ɪŋ, -ɪd
AM ,kɔrə'spɑnd, -z, -ɪŋ, -əd
correspondence
BR ,kɒrɪ'spɒnd(ə)ns, -ɪz

AM ˌkɔrə'spɑnd(ə)ns, -əz

correspondent
BR ˌkɒrɪ'spɒnd(ə)nt, -s
AM ˌkɔrə'spɑndənt, -s

correspondently
BR ˌkɒrɪ'spɒnd(ə)ntli
AM ˌkɔrə'spɑndən(t)li

corresponding
BR ˌkɒrɪ'spɒndɪŋ
AM ˌkɔrə'spɑndɪŋ

correspondingly
BR ˌkɒrɪ'spɒndɪŋli
AM ˌkɔrə'spɑndɪŋli

corrida
BR kɒ'riːdə(r), kə'riːdə(r), -z
AM kɔ'ridə, -z

corridor
BR 'kɒrɪdɔː(r), -z
AM 'kɔrədər, 'kɔrəˌdɔ(ə)r, -z

corrie
BR 'kɒr|i, -ɪz
AM 'kɔri, 'kɑri, -z

Corrigan
BR 'kɒrɪg(ə)n
AM 'kɔrəgən

corrigenda
BR ˌkɒrɪ'dʒɛndə(r), ˌkɒrɪ'gɛndə(r)
AM ˌkɔrə'dʒɛndə, ˌkɔrə'gɛndə

corrigendum
BR ˌkɒrɪ'dʒɛndəm, ˌkɒrɪ'gɛndəm
AM ˌkɔrə'dʒɛndəm, ˌkɔrə'gɛndəm

corrigible
BR 'kɒrɪdʒɪbl
AM 'kɔrədʒəbəl

corrigibly
BR 'kɒrɪdʒɪbli
AM 'kɔrədʒəbli

Corris
BR 'kɒrɪs
AM 'kɔrəs

corroborate
BR kə'rɒbəreɪt, -s, -ɪŋ, -ɪd
AM kə'rɑbəˌreɪ|t, -ts, -dɪŋ, -dɪd

corroboration
BR kəˌrɒbə'reɪʃn
AM kəˌrɑbə'reɪʃən

corroborative
BR kə'rɒb(ə)rətɪv
AM kə'rɑbər(ə)dɪv

corroborator
BR kə'rɒbəreɪtə(r), -z
AM kə'rɑbəˌreɪdər, -z

corroboratory
BR kə'rɒb(ə)rət(ə)ri
AM kə'rɑb(ə)rəˌtɔri

corroboree
BR kə'rɒbəriː, kəˌrɒbə'riː, -z
AM kəˌrɑbə'ri, -z

corrode
BR kə'rəʊd, -z, -ɪŋ, -ɪd
AM kə'roʊd, -z, -ɪŋ, -əd

corrodible
BR kə'rəʊdɪbl
AM kə'roʊdəbəl

corrosion
BR kə'rəʊʒn
AM kə'roʊʒən

corrosive
BR kə'rəʊsɪv
AM kə'roʊsɪv

corrosively
BR kə'rəʊsɪvli
AM kə'roʊsɪvli

corrosiveness
BR kə'rəʊsɪvnɪs
AM kə'roʊsɪvnɪs

corrugate
BR 'kɒrəgeɪt, -s, -ɪŋ, -ɪd
AM 'kɔrəˌgeɪ|t, -ts, -dɪŋ, -dɪd

corrugation
BR ˌkɒrə'geɪʃn, -z
AM ˌkɔrə'geɪʃən, -z

corrugator
BR 'kɒrəgeɪtə(r), -z
AM 'kɔrəˌgeɪdər, -z

corrupt
BR kə'rʌpt, -s, -ɪŋ, -ɪd
AM kə'rəpt, -s, -ɪŋ, -əd

corrupter
BR kə'rʌptə(r), -z
AM kə'rəptər, -z

corruptibility
BR kəˌrʌptɪ'bɪlɪti
AM kəˌrəptə'bɪlɪdi

corruptible
BR kə'rʌptɪbl
AM kə'rəptəbəl

corruptibleness
BR kə'rʌptɪblnəs
AM kə'rəptəbəlnəs

corruptibly
BR kə'rʌptɪbli
AM kə'rəptəbli

corruption
BR kə'rʌpʃn, -z
AM kə'rəpʃən, -z

corruptive
BR kə'rʌptɪv
AM kə'rəptɪv

corruptly
BR kə'rʌptli
AM kə'rəp(t)li

corruptness
BR kə'rʌptnəs
AM kə'rəp(t)nəs

corsac
BR 'kɔːsak, -s
AM 'kɔrˌsæk, kɔr'sæk, -s

corsage
BR 'kɔːsɑːʒ, -ɪz
AM kɔr'sɑʒ, -əz

corsair
BR 'kɔːsɛː(r), -z
AM ˈkɔrˈsɛ(ə)r, -z

corsak
BR 'kɔːsak, -s
AM ˈkɔrˈsæk, -s

corse
BR kɔːs, -ɪz
AM kɔ(ə)rs, -əz

corselet
BR 'kɔːslɪt, -s
AM 'kɔrslət, -s

corselette
BR 'kɔːslɪt, -s
AM 'kɔrslət, -s

corset
BR 'kɔːs|ɪt, -ɪts, -ɪtɪd
AM 'kɔrsət, -s, -əd

corsetière
BR ˌkɔːsɪ'tɪə(r), -z
AM ˌkɔrsə'tɪ(ə)r, -z

corsetry
BR 'kɔːsɪtri
AM 'kɔrsətri

Corsica
BR 'kɔːsɪkə(r)
AM 'kɔrsəkə

Corsican
BR 'kɔːsɪkən, -z
AM 'kɔrsəkən, -z

corslet
BR 'kɔːslɪt, -s
AM 'kɔrslət, -s

Corstorphine
BR kə'stɔːfɪn
AM kər'stɔrfən

Cort
BR kɔːt
AM kɔ(ə)rt

cortège
BR (ˌ)kɔː'teɪʒ, (ˌ)kɔː'tɛʒ, 'kɔːteɪʒ, 'kɔːtɛʒ, -ɪz
AM kɔr'tɛʒ, -əz

Cortes
parliament
BR 'kɔːtɛz, 'kɔːtɛs, 'kɔːtɪz
AM 'kɔrtɛz

Cortés
Hernando
BR 'kɔːtɛz, kɔː'tɛz
AM kɔr'tɛz

cortex
BR 'kɔːtɛks, -ɪz
AM 'kɔrˌtɛks, -əz

Corti
BR 'kɔːti
AM 'kɔrdi

cortical
BR 'kɔːtɪkl
AM 'kɔrdəkl

corticate
BR 'kɔːtɪkeɪt
AM 'kɔrdəˌkeɪt, 'kɔrdəkət

corticated
BR 'kɔːtɪkeɪtɪd
AM 'kɔrdəˌkeɪdɪd

cortices
BR kɔːtɪsiːz
AM 'kɔrdəˌsiz

corticotrophic
BR ˌkɔːtɪkə(ʊ)'trɒfɪk, ˌkɔːtɪkə(ʊ)'trəʊfɪk
AM ˌkɔrdəˌkoʊ'trɑfɪk

corticotrophin
BR ˌkɔːtɪkə(ʊ)'trəʊfɪn
AM ˌkɔrdəˌkoʊ'troʊfən

corticotropic
BR ˌkɔːtɪkə(ʊ)'trɒpɪk, ˌkɔːtɪkə(ʊ)'trəʊpɪk
AM ˌkɔrdəˌkoʊ'trɑpɪk

corticotropin
BR ˌkɔːtɪkə(ʊ)'trəʊpɪn
AM ˌkɔrdəˌkoʊ'troʊpən

Cortina®
BR kɔː'tiːnə(r)
AM kɔr'tinə

cortisone
BR 'kɔːtɪzəʊn
AM 'kɔrdəˌsoʊn

Corton
BR 'kɔːtn
AM 'kɔrtən

corundum
BR kə'rʌndəm
AM kə'rəndəm

Corunna
BR kə'rʌnə(r)
AM kə'rənə

coruscate
BR 'kɒrəskeɪt, -s, -ɪŋ, -ɪd
AM 'kɔrəˌskeɪ|t, -ts, -dɪŋ, -dɪd

coruscation
BR ˌkɒrə'skeɪʃn, -z
AM kɔrə'skeɪʃən, -z

corvée
BR 'kɔːveɪ, -z
AM 'kɔrˌveɪ, -z

corves
BR kɔːvz
AM kɔrvz

corvette
BR kɔː'vɛt, -s
AM kɔr'vɛt, -s

corvine
BR 'kɔːvʌɪn
AM 'kɔrˌvaɪn

Corwen
BR 'kɔːwɛn, 'kɔːwən
AM 'kɔrwən

Cory
BR 'kɔːri
AM 'kɔri

corybant
BR 'kɒrɪbant, -s
AM 'kɔrəˌbænt, -s

corybantic
BR ˌkɒrɪ'bantɪk
AM ˌkɔrə'bæn(t)ɪk

Corydon
BR 'kɒrɪd(ə)n
AM 'kɔrəd(ə)n

corymb
BR 'kɒrɪm(b)
AM 'kɔrɪm(b), 'kɑrɪm(b)

corymbose
BR 'kɒrɪmbəʊs
AM 'kɔrɪm,boʊs, 'kɑrɪm,boʊs, kə'rɪmboʊs

corynebacteria
BR ,kɒrɪnɪbak'tɪərɪə(r), kə,rɪnɪbak'tɪərɪə(r)
AM ,kɔrənibæk'tɪriə, kə,rɪnəbæk'tɪriə

corynebacterium
BR ,kɒrɪnɪbak'tɪərɪəm, kə,rɪnɪbak'tɪərɪəm
AM ,kɔrənibæk'tɪriəm, kə,rɪnəbæk'tɪriəm

coryphaei
BR ,kɒrɪ'fiːʌɪ
AM ,kɔrə'fi,aɪ

coryphaeus
BR ,kɒrɪ'fiːəs
AM ,kɔrə'fiəs

coryphée
BR 'kɒrɪfeɪ, -z
AM ¦kɔrə¦feɪ, ¦kɑrə¦feɪ, -z

Coryton
BR 'kɒrɪt(ə)n
AM 'kɔrət(ə)n

coryza
BR kə'rʌɪzə(r)
AM kə'raɪzə

Cos
BR kɒs
AM kɑs, kɔs

cos¹
cosine
BR kɒz, kɒs
AM kɔs

cos²
lettuce
BR kɒs
AM kɑs

'cos
because
BR kəz
AM kəz

Cosa Nostra
BR ,kəʊzə 'nɒstrə(r)
AM ,koʊsə 'noʊstrə, ,koʊzə +

cosec
cosecant
BR 'kəʊsɛk, -s
AM 'koʊsɛk, -s

cosecant
BR ,kəʊ'siːk(ə)nt, -s
AM koʊ'sikənt, -s

coseismal
BR kəʊ'seɪzml, -z
AM koʊ'saɪsməl, -z

coset
BR 'kəʊsɛt, -s
AM 'koʊ,sɛt, -s

Cosford
BR 'kɒsfəd
AM 'kɑsfərd, 'kɔsfərd

Cosgrave
BR 'kɒzgreɪv
AM 'kɑz,greɪv, 'kɔz,greɪv

cosh¹
weapon, hit
BR kɒʃ, -ɪz, -ɪŋ, -t
AM kɑʃ, -əz, -ɪŋ, -t

cosh²
hyperbolic cosine
BR kɒʃ, kɒs'eɪtʃ
AM kɔs, kɑʃ, kɔs'eɪtʃ, kɑs'eɪtʃ

cosher
BR 'kɒʃə(r), -z
AM 'kɑʃər, -z

cosies
BR 'kəʊzɪz
AM 'koʊziz

Così Fan Tutte
BR ,kəʊsɪ ,fan 'tʊti
AM ,koʊzi ,fɑn 'tudi

cosignatory
BR ,kəʊ'sɪgnət(ə)r|i, -ɪz
AM koʊ'sɪgnə,tɔri, -z

cosigner
BR 'kəʊ,sʌɪnə(r), -z
AM 'koʊ,saɪnər, -z

cosily
BR 'kəʊzɪli
AM 'koʊzəli

cosine
BR 'kəʊsʌɪn
AM 'koʊ,saɪn

cosiness
BR 'kəʊzɪnɪs
AM 'koʊzinɨs

CoSIRA
BR kə(ʊ)'sʌɪrə(r)
AM kə'saɪrə

cosmea
BR 'kɒzmɪə(r)
AM 'kɑzmiə

cosmetic
BR kɒz'mɛtɪk, -s
AM kɑz'mɛdɪk, -s

cosmetically
BR kɒz'mɛtɪkli
AM kɑz'mɛdək(ə)li

cosmetician
BR ,kɒzmɪ'tɪʃn, -z
AM ,kɑzmə'tɪʃən, -z

cosmetologist
BR ,kɒzmɪ'tɒlədʒɪst, -s
AM ,kɑzmə'tɑlədʒəst, -s

cosmetology
BR ,kɒzmɪ'tɒlədʒi
AM ,kɑzmə'tɑlədʒi

cosmic
BR 'kɒzmɪk
AM 'kɑzmɪk

cosmical
BR 'kɒzmɪkl
AM 'kɑzməkəl

cosmically
BR 'kɒzmɪkli
AM 'kɑzmək(ə)li

Cosmo
BR 'kɒzməʊ
AM 'kɑzmoʊ

cosmogonic
BR ,kɒzmə'gɒnɪk
AM ,kɑzmə'gɑnɪk

cosmogonical
BR ,kɒzmə'gɒnɪkl
AM ,kɑzmə'gɑnəkəl

cosmogonist
BR kɒz'mɒgənɪst, kɒz'mɒgn̩ɪst, -s
AM kɑz'mɑgənəst, -s

cosmogony
BR kɒz'mɒgəni, kɒz'mɒgn̩i
AM kɑz'mɑgəni

cosmographer
BR kɒz'mɒgrəfə(r), -z
AM kɑz'mɑgrəfər, -z

cosmographic
BR ,kɒzmə'grafɪk
AM ,kɑzmə'græfɪk

cosmographical
BR ,kɒzmə'grafɪkl
AM ,kɑzmə'græfəkəl

cosmography
BR kɒz'mɒgrəfi
AM kɑz'mɑgrəfi

cosmological
BR ,kɒzmə'lɒdʒɪkl
AM ,kɑzmə'lɑdʒəkəl

cosmologist
BR kɒz'mɒlədʒɪst, -s
AM kɑz'mɑlədʒəst, -s

cosmology
BR kɒz'mɒlədʒi
AM kɑz'mɑlədʒi

cosmonaut
BR 'kɒzmənɔːt, -s
AM 'kɔzmə,nɔt, 'kɑzmə,nɑt, -s

cosmopolis
BR kɒz'mɒpəlɪs
AM kɑz'mɑpələs

cosmopolitan
BR ,kɒzmə'pɒlɪt(ə)n, -z
AM ,kɑzmə'pɑlətn, ,kɑzmə'pɑlədən, -z

cosmopolitanise
BR ,kɒzmə'pɒlɪtənʌɪz, ,kɒzmə'pɒlɪtn̩ʌɪz, -ɪz, -ɪŋ, -d
AM ,kɑzmə'pɑlətn,aɪz, ,kɑzmə'pɑlədə,naɪz, -ɪz, -ɪŋ, -d

cosmopolitanism
BR ,kɒzmə'pɒlɪtənɪz(ə)m, ,kɒzmə'pɒlɪtn̩ɪz(ə)m
AM ,kɑzmə'pɑlətn,ɪzəm, ,kɑzmə'pɑlədə,nɪzəm

cosmopolitanize
BR ,kɒzmə'pɒlɪtənʌɪz, ,kɒzmə'pɒlɪtn̩ʌɪz, -ɪz, -ɪŋ, -d
AM ,kɑzmə'pɑlətn ,aɪz, ,kɑzmə'pɑlədə,naɪz, -ɪz, -ɪŋ, -d

cosmopolite
BR kɒz'mɒpəlʌɪt, kɒz'mɒpl̩ʌɪt, -s
AM kɑz'mɑpə,laɪt, -s

cosmos
BR 'kɒzmɒs, -ɪz
AM 'kɑzməs, 'kɑz,moʊs, -əz

co-sponsor
BR ,kəʊ'spɒns|ə(r), -əz, -(ə)rɪŋ, -əd
AM ¦koʊ¦spɑns|ər, -ərz, -(ə)rɪŋ, -ərd

Cossack
BR 'kɒsak, -s
AM 'kɔsæk, 'kɑsæk, -s

cosset
BR 'kɒs|ɪt, -ɪts, -ɪtɪŋ, -ɪtɪd
AM 'kɑsə|t, -ts, -dɪŋ, -dəd

cossie
BR 'kɒz|i, -ɪz
AM 'kɑzi, -z

cost
BR kɒst, -s, -ɪŋ
AM kɔst, kɑst, -s, -ɪŋ

Costa
BR 'kɒstə(r)
AM 'kɔstə, 'kɑstə

Costa Blanca
BR ,kɒstə 'blaŋkə(r)
AM ,kɔstə 'blæŋkə, ,kɑstə 'blæŋkə

Costa Brava
BR ,kɒstə 'brɑːvə(r)
AM ,kɔstə 'brɑvə, ,kɑstə 'brɑvə

Costa del Sol
BR ,kɒstə dɛl 'sɒl
AM ,kɔstə ,dɛl 'sɔl, ,kɑstə ,dɛl 'sɔl

Costain
BR 'kɒsteɪn, kɒ'steɪn
AM 'kɑsteɪn

costal
BR 'kɒstl
AM 'kɑstəl

co-star
BR 'kəʊstɑː(r), -z, -ɪŋ, -d
AM 'koʊ,stɑr, -z, -ɪŋ, -d

costard
BR 'kɒstəd, 'kʌstəd, -z
AM 'kɑstərd, -z

Costa Rica
BR ,kɒstə 'riːkə(r)
AM ,koʊstə 'rikə, ,kɔstə +, ,kɑstə +

Costa Rican
BR ,kɒstə 'riːkən, -z

AM ˌkoʊstə ˈrikən, ˌkɒstə +, ˌkɑstə +, -z

costate
BR ˈkɒsteɪt
AM ˈkɑˌsteɪt

Costello
BR kɒˈstɛləʊ, ˈkɒstɪləʊ, ˈkɒstl̩əʊ
AM ˌkɑsˈtɛloʊ

coster
BR ˈkɒstə(r), -z
AM ˈkɑstər, -z

costermonger
BR ˈkɒstəˌmʌŋgə(r), -z
AM ˈkɑstərˌmɑŋgər, ˈkɑstərˌməŋgər, -z

costing
BR ˈkɒstɪŋ, -z
AM ˈkɑstɪŋ, -z

costive
BR ˈkɒstɪv
AM ˈkɑstɪv

costively
BR ˈkɒstɪvli
AM ˈkɑstɪvli

costiveness
BR ˈkɒstɪvnɪs
AM ˈkɑstɪvnɪs

costliness
BR ˈkɒs(t)lɪnɪs
AM ˈkɔs(t)linɪs, ˈkɑs(t)linɪs

costly
BR ˈkɒs(t)l|i, -ɪə(r), -ɪɪst
AM ˈkɔs(t)li, ˈkɑs(t)li, -ər, -ɪst

costmary
BR ˈkɒstˌmɛːr|i, -ɪz
AM ˈkɔs(t)ˌmɛri, ˈkɑs(t)ˌmɛri, -z

Costner
BR ˈkɒs(t)nə(r)
AM ˈkɔs(t)nər, ˈkɑs(t)nər

costume
BR ˈkɒstjuːm, ˈkɒstʃuːm, -z
AM ˈkɑsˌt(j)um, -z

costumier
BR kɒˈstjuːmɪə(r), kəˈstjuːmɪə(r), kɒˈstʃuːmɪə(r), kəˈstʃuːmɪə(r), -z
AM ˌkɑstəmˈjeɪ, kɑˈst(j)uˌmɪ(ə)r, -z

cosy
BR ˈkəʊz|i, -ɪz, -ɪə(r), -ɪɪst
AM ˈkoʊzi, -z, -ər, -ɪst

cot
BR kɒt
AM kɑt

cotangent
BR kəʊˈtan(d)ʒ(ə)nt, -s
AM ˌkoʊˈtændʒənt, -s

cote
BR kəʊt, -s
AM koʊt, -s

Côte d'Azur
BR ˌkəʊt dəˈzjʊə(r), + daˈzjʊə(r)
AM ˌkoʊt dəˈzʊ(ə)r

coterie
BR ˈkəʊt(ə)r|i, -ɪz
AM ˈkoʊdəri, -z

coterminous
BR (ˌ)kəʊˈtəːmɪnəs
AM koʊˈtərmənəs

coterminously
BR (ˌ)kəʊˈtəːmɪnəsli
AM koʊˈtərmənəsli

coth
hyperbolic cotangent
BR kɒθ, ˌkɒtˈeɪtʃ
AM kɑθ

cotherni
BR kə(ʊ)ˈθəːnʌɪ
AM koʊˈθərˌnaɪ

cothernus
BR kə(ʊ)ˈθəːnəs
AM koʊˈθərnəs

Cothi
BR ˈkɒθi
AM ˈkɑθi

cotillion
BR kə(ʊ)ˈtɪlɪən, kɒˈtɪlɪən, -z
AM kəˈtɪljən, -z

Cotman
BR ˈkɒtmən
AM ˈkɑtmən

Coton
BR ˈkəʊtn
AM ˈkoʊtn

cotoneaster
BR kəˌtəʊnɪˈastə(r), -z
AM kəˈtoʊniˌæstər, -z

Cotopaxi
BR ˌkəʊtəˈpaksi
AM ˌkoʊdəˈpæksi

Cotswold
BR ˈkɒtswəʊld, -z
AM ˈkɑtsˌwoʊld, -z

cotta
BR ˈkɒtə(*r*), -z
AM ˈkɑdə, -z

cottage
BR ˈkɒt|ɪdʒ, -ɪdʒɪz
AM ˈkɑdɪdʒ, -ɪz

cottager
BR ˈkɒtɪdʒə(r), -z
AM ˈkɑdɪdʒər, -z

cottagey
BR ˈkɒtɪdʒi
AM ˈkɑdɪdʒi

cottaging
BR ˈkɒtɪdʒɪŋ
AM ˈkɑdɪdʒɪŋ

cottar
BR ˈkɒtə(r), -z
AM ˈkɑdər, -z

Cottbus
BR ˈkɒtbʊs
AM ˈkɑtˌbʊs

cotter
BR ˈkɒtə(r), -z
AM ˈkɑdər, -z

Cotterell
BR ˈkɒt(ə)rɪl, ˈkɒtrl̩
AM ˈkɑdərəl

Cotterill
BR ˈkɒt(ə)rɪl, ˈkɒtrl̩
AM ˈkɑdərəl

Cottesloe
BR ˈkɒt(ɨ)sləʊ, ˈkɒtɪzləʊ
AM ˈkɑdəsloʊ

Cottesmore
BR ˈkɒtsmɔː(r)
AM ˈkɑdəsˌmɔ(ə)r

cottier
BR ˈkɒtɪə(r), -z
AM ˈkɑdiər, -z

cottise
BR ˈkɒt|ɪs, -ɪsɪz
AM ˈkɑdəs, -əz

Cottle
BR ˈkɒtl
AM ˈkɑdəl

cotton
BR ˈkɒtn̩, -z, -ɪŋ, -d
AM ˈkɑtn, -z, -ɪŋ, -d

cottonseed
BR ˈkɒtnsiːd, -z
AM ˈkɑtnˌsid, -z

cottontail
BR ˈkɒtnteɪl, -z
AM ˈkɑtnˌteɪl, -z

cottonwood
BR ˈkɒtnwʊd, -z
AM ˈkɑtnˌwʊd, -z

cottony
BR ˈkɒtn̩i
AM ˈkɑtn̩i

Cottrell
BR ˈkɒtr(ə)l
AM kəˈtrɛl

cotyledon
BR ˌkɒtɪˈliːdn, -z
AM ˌkɑdəˈlidən, -z

cotyledonary
BR ˌkɒtɪˈliːdn̩(ə)ri
AM ˌkɑdəˈlidnˌɛri

cotyledonous
BR ˌkɒtɪˈliːdn̩əs
AM ˌkɑdəˈlidn̩əs

coucal
BR ˈkuːkl, ˈkʊkɑːl, -z
AM ˈkukəl, -z

Couch
BR kuːtʃ
AM kaʊtʃ

couch[1]
sofa, lie down, choice of words
BR kaʊtʃ, -ɪz, -ɪŋ, -t
AM kaʊtʃ, -əz, -ɪŋ, -t

couch[2]
grass
BR kaʊtʃ, kuːtʃ
AM kaʊtʃ, kʊtʃ

couchant
BR ˈkaʊtʃ(ə)nt, ˈkuːʃnt
AM ˈkaʊtʃənt, ˈkuʃnt

couchette
BR kuːˈʃɛt, -s
AM kuˈʃɛt, -s

coudé
BR kuːˈdeɪ, -z
AM kuˈdeɪ, -z

Coué
BR ˈkuːeɪ
AM kuˈeɪ

Couéism
BR ˈkuːeɪɪz(ə)m
AM kuˈeɪˌɪzəm

cougar
BR ˈkuːgə(r), ˈkuːgɑː(r), -z
AM ˈkugər, -z

cough
BR kɒf, -s, -ɪŋ, -t
AM kɔf, kɑf, -s, -ɪŋ, -t

cougher
BR ˈkɒfə(r), -z
AM ˈkɔfər, ˈkɑfər, -z

Coughlan
BR ˈkɒxlən, ˈkɒklən, ˈkɒflən
AM ˈkɔflən, ˈkɑflən

Coughton
BR ˈkəʊtn, ˈkaʊtn, ˈkɔːtn
AM ˈkɔdən, ˈkɑdən, ˈkɔtn

could[1]
strong form
BR kʊd
AM kʊd

could[2]
weak form
BR kəd
AM kəd

couldn't
BR kʊdnt
AM kʊdnt

couldst
BR kʊdst
AM kʊdst

coulée
BR ˈkuːl|i, ˈkuːl|eɪ, -ɪz\-eɪz
AM ˌkuˈleɪ, -z

coulisse
BR kuːˈliːs, -ɪz
AM kuˈlis, -ɪz

couloir
BR ˈkuːlwɑː(r), -z
AM ˌkulˈwɑr, -z

coulomb
BR ˈkuːlɒm, -z
AM ˈkuˌlɑm, ˈkuˌloʊm, -z

coulometric
BR ˌkuːləˈmɛtrɪk
AM ˌkuləˈmɛtrɪk

coulometry
BR kuːˈlɒmɪtri
AM kuˈlɑmətri

Coulsdon
BR 'ku:lzd(ə)n, 'kəʊlzd(ə)n
AM 'kulzdən

Coulson
BR 'ku:lsn, 'kəʊlsn
AM 'koʊlsən

Coulston
BR 'ku:lst(ə)n
AM 'koʊlstən

coulter
BR 'kəʊltə(r), -z
AM 'koʊltər, -z

Coulthard
BR 'ku:ltɑ:d, 'ku:lθɑ:d
AM 'koʊltɑrd, 'koʊlθɑrd

coumarin
BR 'ku:m(ə)rɪn
AM 'kumərən

coumarone
BR 'ku:mərəʊn
AM 'kumə,roʊn

council
BR 'kaʊnsl, -z
AM 'kaʊnsəl, -z

councillor
BR 'kaʊns(ɪ)lə(r), -z
AM 'kaʊns(ə)lər, -z

councillorship
BR 'kaʊns(ɪ)ləʃɪp
AM 'kaʊns(ə)lər,ʃɪp

councilman
BR 'kaʊnslmən
AM 'kaʊnsəlmən

councilmen
BR 'kaʊnslmən
AM 'kaʊnsəlmən

councilwoman
BR 'kaʊnsl,wʊmən
AM 'kaʊnsəl,wʊmən

councilwomen
BR 'kaʊnsl,wɪmɪn
AM 'kaʊnsəl,wɪmɨn

counsel
BR 'kaʊns|l, -lz, -l̩ɪŋ\-əlɪŋ, -ld
AM 'kaʊns|əl, -əlz, -(ə)lɪŋ, -əld

counsellor
BR 'kaʊns(ɪ)lə(r), -z
AM 'kaʊns(ə)lər, -z

counselor
BR 'kaʊns(ɪ)lə(r), -z
AM 'kaʊns(ə)lər, -z

count
BR kaʊnt, -s, -ɪŋ, -ɨd
AM kaʊn|t, -ts, -(t)ɪŋ, -(t)əd

countable
BR 'kaʊntəbl
AM 'kaʊn(t)əbəl

countdown
BR 'kaʊntdaʊn, -z
AM 'kaʊn(t),daʊn, -z

countenance
BR 'kaʊntɪnəns, 'kaʊntn̩əns, -ɨz, -ɪŋ, -t
AM 'kaʊnt(ə)nəns, 'kaʊn(t)ənəns, -əz, -ɪŋ, -t

counter
BR 'kaʊnt|ə(r), -əz, -(ə)rɪŋ, -əd
AM 'kaʊn(t)ər, -z, -ɪŋ, -d

counteract
BR ,kaʊntər'akt, -s, -ɪŋ, -ɨd
AM ,kaʊn(t)ər'æk|(t), -(t)s, -tɪŋ, -təd

counteraction¹
action taken in reply
BR 'kaʊntər,akʃn, -z
AM 'kaʊn(t)ər,ækʃən, -z

counteraction²
counteracting
BR ,kaʊntər'akʃn, -z
AM ,kaʊn(t)ər'ækʃən, -z

counteractive
BR ,kaʊntər'aktɪv
AM ,kaʊn(t)ər'æktɪv

counterattack
BR 'kaʊnt(ə)rə,tak, ,kaʊnt(ə)rə'tak, -s, -ɪŋ, -t
AM 'kaʊn(t)ərə,tæk, -s, -ɪŋ, -t

counterattraction
BR 'kaʊnt(ə)rə,trakʃn, ,kaʊnt(ə)rə'trakʃn, -z
AM ¦kaʊn(t)ərə¦trækʃən, -z

counterbalance¹
noun
BR 'kaʊntə,baləns, -ɨz
AM 'kaʊn(t)ər,bæləns, -əz

counterbalance²
verb
BR ,kaʊntə'baləns, -ɨz, -ɪŋ, -t
AM ,kaʊn(t)ər'bæləns, -əz, -ɪŋ, -t

counterblast
BR 'kaʊntəblɑ:st, 'kaʊntəblast, -s
AM 'kaʊn(t)ər,blæst, -s

counterblow
BR 'kaʊntəbləʊ, -z
AM 'kaʊn(t)ər,bloʊ, -z

counterchange
BR ,kaʊntə'tʃeɪn(d)ʒ, -ɨz, -ɪŋ, -d
AM ¦kaʊn(t)ər¦tʃeɪndʒ, -ɨz, -ɪŋ, -d

countercharge
BR 'kaʊntətʃɑ:dʒ, -ɨz
AM 'kaʊn(t)ər,tʃɑrdʒ, -əz

countercheck
BR ,kaʊntə'tʃɛk, -s, -ɪŋ, -t
AM ¦kaʊn(t)ər¦tʃɛk, -s, -ɪŋ, -t

counterclaim
noun
BR 'kaʊntəkleɪm, -z
AM 'kaʊn(t)ər,kleɪm, -z

counter-claim
verb
BR ,kaʊntə'kleɪm, -z, -ɪŋ, -d
AM ,kaʊn(t)ər'kleɪm, -z, -ɪŋ, -d

counterclockwise
BR ,kaʊntə'klɒkwʌɪz
AM ,kaʊn(t)ər'klɑk,waɪz

counterculture
BR 'kaʊntə,kʌltʃə(r), -z
AM 'kaʊn(t)ər,kəltʃər, -z

counterespionage
BR ,kaʊntər'ɛspɪənɑ:ʒ
AM ,kaʊn(t)ər'ɛspɪə,nɑʒ

counterfeit
BR 'kaʊntəfɪt, 'kaʊntəfi:t, -s, -ɪŋ, -ɨd
AM 'kaʊn(t)ər,fɪ|t, -ts, -dɪŋ, -dɨd

counterfeiter
BR 'kaʊntəfɪtə(r), 'kaʊntəfi:tə(r), -z
AM 'kaʊn(t)ər,fɪdər, -z

counterfoil
BR 'kaʊntəfɔɪl, -z
AM 'kaʊn(t)ər,fɔɪl, -z

counterinsurgency
BR ,kaʊnt(ə)rɪn'sə:dʒ(ə)nsi
AM ,kaʊn(t)ərɪn'sərdʒənsi

counterintelligence
BR ,kaʊnt(ə)rɪn'tɛlɪdʒ(ə)ns
AM ,kaʊn(t)ərɪn'tɛlədʒəns

counterirritant
BR ,kaʊntər'ɪrɪt(ə)nt, -s
AM ,kaʊn(t)ər'ɪrədnt, -s

counterirritation
BR ,kaʊntər,ɪrɪ'teɪʃn
AM ,kaʊn(t)ər,ɪrə'teɪʃən

countermand
BR 'kaʊntəmɑ:nd, 'kaʊntəmand, ,kaʊntə'mɑ:nd, ,kaʊntə'mand, -z, -ɪŋ, -ɨd
AM ,kaʊn(t)ər'mænd, 'kaʊn(t)ər,mænd, -z, -ɪŋ, -əd

countermarch
BR 'kaʊntəmɑ:tʃ, -ɨz, -ɪŋ, -t
AM 'kaʊn(t)ər,mɑrtʃ, -əz, -ɪŋ, -t

countermeasure
BR 'kaʊntə,mɛʒə(r), -z
AM 'kaʊn(t)ər,mɛʒər, -z

countermine
BR 'kaʊntəmʌɪn, -z, -ɪŋ, -d
AM 'kaʊn(t)ər,maɪn, -z, -ɪŋ, -d

countermove
BR 'kaʊntəmu:v, -z, -ɪŋ, -d
AM 'kaʊn(t)ər,muv, -z, -ɪŋ, -d

countermovement
BR 'kaʊntə,mu:vm(ə)nt, -s
AM 'kaʊn(t)ər,muvmənt, -s

counteroffensive
BR 'kaʊnt(ə)rə,fɛnsɪv, -z
AM 'kaʊn(t)ərə,fɛnsɪv, -z

counteroffer
BR 'kaʊntər,ɒfə(r), -z
AM 'kaʊn(t)ər,ɔfər, 'kaʊn(t)ər,ɑfər, -z

counterpane
BR 'kaʊntəpeɪn, -z
AM 'kaʊn(t)ər,peɪn, -z

counterpart
BR 'kaʊntəpɑ:t, -s
AM 'kaʊn(t)ər,pɑrt, -s

counterplot
BR 'kaʊntəplɒt, -s, -ɪŋ, -ɨd
AM 'kaʊn(t)ər,plɑ|t, -ts, -dɪŋ, -dəd

counterpoint
BR 'kaʊntəpɔɪnt, -s
AM 'kaʊn(t)ər,pɔɪnt, -s

counterpoise
BR 'kaʊntəpɔɪz, -ɨz, -ɪŋ, -d
AM 'kaʊn(t)ər,pɔɪz, -ɨz, -ɪŋ, -d

counterproductive
BR ,kaʊntəprə'dʌktɪv
AM ,kaʊn(t)ərprə'dəktɪv

counterproductively
BR ,kaʊntəprə'dʌktɪvli
AM ,kaʊn(t)ərprə'dəktɪvli

counterproductiveness
BR ,kaʊntəprə'dʌktɪvnɪs
AM ,kaʊn(t)ərprə'dəktɪvnɪs

counter-proposal
BR 'kaʊntəprəˌpəʊzl, -z
AM 'kaʊn(t)ərprəˌpoʊzəl, -z

counterpunch
BR 'kaʊntəpʌn(t)ʃ, -ɨz
AM 'kaʊn(t)ərˌpən(t)ʃ, -əz

counterrevolution
BR ˌkaʊntəˌrɛvə'l(j)uːʃn, -z
AM ˌkaʊn(t)ərˌrɛvə'luʃən, -z

counterrevolutionary
BR ˌkaʊntəˌrɛvə'l(j)uːʃn̩(ə)r|i, -ɪz
AM ˌkaʊn(t)ərˌrɛvə'luʃəˌnɛri, -z

countersank
BR 'kaʊntəsaŋk
AM 'kaʊn(t)ərˌsæŋk

counterscarp
BR 'kaʊntəskɑːp, -s
AM 'kaʊn(t)ərˌskɑrp, -s

countershaft
BR 'kaʊntəʃɑːft, 'kaʊntəʃaft, -s
AM 'kaʊn(t)ərˌʃaft, -s

countersign
BR 'kaʊntəsʌɪn, -z, -ɪŋ, -d
AM 'kaʊn(t)ərˌsaɪn, -z, -ɪŋ, -d

countersignature
BR 'kaʊntəˌsɪgnətʃə(r), -z
AM ˌkaʊn(t)ər'signəˌtʃʊ(ə)r, ˌkaʊn(t)ər'signətʃər, -z

countersigner
BR 'kaʊntəsʌɪnə(r), -z
AM 'kaʊn(t)ərˌsaɪnər, -z

countersink
BR 'kaʊntəsɪŋk, -s, -ɪŋ
AM 'kaʊn(t)ərˌsɪŋk, -s, -ɪŋ

counterspy
BR 'kaʊntəspʌɪ, -z
AM 'kaʊn(t)ərˌspaɪ, -z

counterstroke
BR 'kaʊntəstrəʊk, -s
AM 'kaʊn(t)ərˌstroʊk, -s

countersunk
BR 'kaʊntəsʌŋk
AM 'kaʊn(t)ərˌsəŋk

countertenor
BR 'kaʊntəˌtɛnə(r), -z
AM 'kaʊn(t)ərˌtɛnər, -z

counter-transference
BR 'kaʊntəˌtransf(ə)rəns, 'kaʊntəˌtransf(ə)rn̩s, 'kaʊntəˌtrɑːnsf(ə)rəns, 'kaʊntəˌtrɑːnsf(ə)rn̩s, 'kaʊntəˌtranzf(ə)rəns, 'kaʊntəˌtranzf(ə)rn̩s, 'kaʊntəˌtrɑːnzf(ə)rəns, 'kaʊntəˌtrɑːnzf(ə)rn̩s
AM 'kaʊn(t)ərˌtrænsf(ə)rəns

countervail
BR ˌkaʊntə'veɪl, -z, -ɪŋ, -d
AM ˌkaʊn(t)ər'veɪl, -z, -ɪŋ, -d

countervalue
BR 'kaʊntəˌvaljuː, -z
AM 'kaʊn(t)ərˌvælju, -z

counterweight
BR 'kaʊntəweɪt, -s
AM 'kaʊn(t)ərˌweɪt, -s

countess
BR 'kaʊntɨs, 'kaʊntɛs, ˌkaʊn'tɛs, -ɨz
AM 'kaʊn(t)əs, -əz

countinghouse
BR 'kaʊntɪŋhaʊ|s, -zɪz
AM 'kaʊn(t)ɪŋˌ(h)aʊ|s, -zəz

countless
BR 'kaʊntləs
AM 'kaʊn(t)ləs

countrified
BR 'kʌntrɪfʌɪd
AM 'kəntriˌfaɪd

country
BR 'kʌntr|i, -ɪz
AM 'kəntri, -z

countryfied
BR 'kʌntrɪfʌɪd
AM 'kəntrəˌfaɪd

countryfolk
BR 'kʌntrɪfəʊk
AM 'kəntriˌfoʊk

countryman
BR 'kʌntrɪmən
AM 'kəntrimən

countrymen
BR 'kʌntrɪmən
AM 'kəntrimən

countryside
BR 'kʌntrɪsʌɪd
AM 'kəntriˌsaɪd

countrywoman
BR 'kʌntrɪˌwʊmən
AM 'kəntriˌwʊmən

countrywomen
BR 'kʌntrɪˌwɪmɪn
AM 'kəntriˌwɪmɨn

countship
BR 'kaʊntʃɪp, -s
AM 'kaʊntˌʃɪp, -s

county
BR 'kaʊnt|i, -ɪz
AM 'kaʊn(t)i, -z

coup
BR kuː, -z
AM ku, -z

coup de grâce
BR ˌkuː də 'grɑːs, + 'gras
AM ˌku də 'grɑs

coup de main
BR ˌkuː də 'meɪn
AM ˌku də 'meɪn

coup d'état
BR ˌkuː deɪ'tɑː(*r*)
AM ˌku deɪ'tɑ

coup de théâtre
BR ˌkuː də teɪ'ɑːtr, + teɪ'ɑːtrə(*r*)
AM ˌku də ˌteɪ'ætr(ə), + ˌteɪ'ɑtr(ə)

coupé
BR 'kuːpeɪ, -z
AM ku'peɪ, -z

Couper
BR 'kuːpə(r)
AM 'kupər

Couperin
BR 'kuːpəran, 'kuːpərã
AM ˌkupə'rɛn

Coupland
BR 'kuːplənd, 'kəʊplənd
AM 'kuplənd, 'koʊplən(d)

couple
BR 'kʌp|l, -lz, -l̩ɪŋ\-lɪŋ, -ld
AM 'kəp|əl, -əlz, -(ə)lɪŋ, -əld

coupler
BR 'kʌplə(r), -z
AM 'kəplər, -z

couplet
BR 'kʌplɪt, -s
AM 'kəplət, -s

coupling
BR 'kʌplɪŋ, -z
AM 'kəplɪŋ, -z

coupon
BR 'kuːpɒn, -z
AM 'k(j)uˌpɑn, -z

coups de grâce
BR ˌkuː də 'grɑːs, + 'gras
AM ˌku də 'grɑs

coups de main
BR ˌkuː də 'meɪn
AM ˌku də 'meɪn

coups d'état
BR ˌkuː deɪ'tɑː(*r*)
AM ˌku deɪˌtɑ

coups de théâtre
BR ˌkuː də teɪ'ɑːtr, + teɪ'ɑːtrə(*r*)
AM ˌku də ˌteɪ'ætr(ə), + ˌteɪ'ɑtr(ə)

courage
BR 'kʌrɪdʒ
AM 'kərɪdʒ

courageous
BR kə'reɪdʒəs
AM kə'reɪdʒəs

courageously
BR kə'reɪdʒəsli
AM kə'reɪdʒəsli

courageousness
BR kə'reɪdʒəsnəs
AM kə'reɪdʒəsnəs

courante
BR kʊ'rɑːnt, -s
AM ku'rɑnt, -s

courgette
BR (ˌ)kɔː'ʒɛt, (ˌ)kʊə'ʒɛt, -s
AM ˌkʊr'ʒɛt, -s

courier
BR 'kʊrɪə(r), 'kʌrɪə(r), -z
AM 'kʊriər, 'kəriər, -z

courlan
BR 'kʊəlan, -z
AM 'kʊrlən, kʊr'lɑn, -z

Courland
BR 'kʊələnd
AM 'kʊrlənd

Courrèges
BR kʊ'rɛʒ, kʊ'reɪʒ
AM kʊ'rɛʒ

course
BR kɔːs, -ɨz, -ɪŋ, -t
AM kɔ(ə)rs, -əz, -ɪŋ, -t

courser
BR 'kɔːsə(r), -z
AM 'kɔrsər, -z

coursework
BR 'kɔːswəːk
AM 'kɔrsˌwərk

court
BR kɔːt, -s, -ɪŋ, -ɨd
AM kɔ(ə)r|t, -ts, -dɪŋ, -dəd

Courtauld
BR 'kɔːtəʊld
AM kɔr'toʊld

court-bouillon
BR ˌkɔːt 'buː(l)jɒn, ˌkʊə buː(l)'jɔ̃
AM 'kʊr ˌbʊ(l)jɔn, 'kɔr(t) ˌbʊ(l)jɔn

Courtelle®
BR (ˌ)kɔː'tɛl
AM kɔr'tɛl

courteous
BR 'kəːtɪəs
AM 'kərdiəs

courteously
BR 'kəːtɪəsli
AM 'kərdiəsli

courteousness
BR 'kəːtɪəsnɨs
AM 'kərdiəsnəs

courtesan
BR ˌkɔːtɪ'zan, 'kɔːtɪzan, -z
AM ˌkɔrdə'zæn, 'kɔrdəzn, -z

courtesy
BR 'kəːtɪs|i, -ɪz
AM 'kərdəsi, -z

courthouse
BR ˈkɔːthaʊ|s, -zɪz
AM ˈkɔrt,(h)aʊ|s, -zəz

courtier
BR ˈkɔːtɪə(r), ˈkɔːtjə(r), -z
AM ˈkɔrdiər, -z

courtliness
BR ˈkɔːtlɪnɪs
AM ˈkɔrtlinɪs

courtly
BR ˈkɔːtl|i, -ɪə(r), -ɪɪst
AM ˈkɔrtli, -ər, -ɪst

court-martial
BR ˌkɔːtˈmɑːʃ|l, -lz, -l̩ɪŋ\-əlɪŋ, -ld
AM ˈkɔrt,mɑrʃ|əl, -əlz, -(ə)lɪŋ, -əld

Courtney
BR ˈkɔːtni
AM ˈkɔrtni

courtroom
BR ˈkɔːtruːm, ˈkɔːtrʊm, -z
AM ˈkɔrt,rum, ˈkɔrt,rʊm, -z

courts-bouillons
BR ˌkɔːt ˈbuː(l)jɒn, ˌkʊə buː(l)ˈjɒ̃
AM ˈkʊr ˌbʊ(l)jɔn, ˈkɔr(t) ˌbʊ(l)jɔn

courtship
BR ˈkɔːtʃɪp, -s
AM ˈkɔrt,ʃɪp, -s

courts-martial
BR ˌkɔːtsˈmɑːʃl
AM ˌkɔrtsˈmɑrʃəl

courtyard
BR ˈkɔːtjɑːd, -z
AM ˈkɔrt,jɑrd, -z

Courvoisier®
BR (ˌ)kʊəˈvwazɪeɪ, (ˌ)kʊəˈvwɒzɪeɪ, (ˌ)kɔːˈvwazɪeɪ, (ˌ)kɔːˈvwɒzɪeɪ
AM kər,vwɑziˈeɪ

couscous
BR ˈkuːskuːs
AM ˈkus,kus

cousin
BR kʌzn, -z
AM kəzn, -z

cousinhood
BR ˈkʌznhʊd
AM ˈkəzn,(h)ʊd

cousinly
BR ˈkʌznli
AM ˈkəznli

Cousins
BR ˈkʌznz
AM ˈkəzənz

cousinship
BR ˈkʌznʃɪp
AM ˈkəzn,ʃɪp

Cousteau
BR ˈkuːstəʊ, kuːˈstəʊ
AM kuˈstoʊ

couth
BR kuːθ
AM kuθ

couture
BR kʉˈtjʊə(r), kʉˈtʃʊə(r)
AM kuˈtʊ(ə)r

couturier
BR kʉˈtjʊərɪeɪ, kʉˈtʃʊərɪeɪ, kʉˈtjʊərɪə(r), kʉˈtʃʊərɪə(r), -z
AM kuˈtʊriər, kuˈtʊri,eɪ, -z

couturière
BR kʉˈtjʊərɪɛː(r), kʉˈtʃʊərɪɛː(r), kʉˈtjʊərɪə(r), kʉˈtʃʊərɪə(r), -z
AM kuˈtʊriər, kuˈtʊri,ɛ(ə)r, -z

couvade
BR (ˌ)kuːˈvɑːd, -z
AM kuˈvɑd, -z

couvert
BR (ˌ)kuːˈvɛː(r), -z
AM kuˈvɛ(ə)r, -z

couverture
BR ˈkuːvətjʊə(r), ˈkuːvətʃʊə(r), ˈkuːvətʃə(r), -z
AM ˈkuvər,tʃ(ʊ)ər, -z

covalence
BR ˌkəʊˈveɪləns, ˌkəʊˈveɪln̩s
AM ˌkoʊˈveɪləns

covalency
BR ˌkəʊˈveɪləns|i, ˌkəʊˈveɪln̩si, -ɪz
AM ˌkoʊˈveɪlənsi, -z

covalent
BR ˌkəʊˈveɪlənt, ˌkəʊˈveɪln̩t
AM ˌkoʊˈveɪlənt

covalently
BR ˌkəʊˈveɪləntli, kəʊˈveɪln̩tli
AM ˌkoʊˈveɪlən(t)li

covariance
BR ˌkəʊˈvɛːrɪəns
AM ˌkoʊˈvɛriəns

cove
BR kəʊv, -z
AM koʊv, -z

covellite
BR kəʊˈvɛlʌɪt
AM koʊˈvɛ,laɪt, ˈkoʊvə,laɪt

coven
BR ˈkʌvn, -z
AM ˈkəvən, -z

covenant
BR ˈkʌvənənt, ˈkʌvn̩ənt, -s, -ɪŋ, -ɪd
AM ˈkəvənənt, -s, -ɪŋ, -əd

covenantal
BR ˌkʌvəˈnantl
AM ˌkəvəˈnən(t)l

covenanter
BR ˈkʌv(ə)nəntə(r), ˈkʌvn̩əntə(r), -z
AM ˈkəvənən(t)ər, -z

covenantor
BR ˈkʌv(ə)nəntə(r), ˈkʌvn̩əntə(r), -z
AM ˈkəvənən(t)ər, -z

Covent Garden
BR ˌkɒvnt ˈgɑːdn, ˌkʌvnt +
AM ˌkəvən(t) ˈgɑrdən

Coventry
BR ˈkɒvntri, ˈkʌvntri
AM ˈkəvəntri

cover
BR ˈkʌv|ə(r), -əz, -(ə)rɪŋ, -əd
AM ˈkəv|ər, -ərz, -(ə)rɪŋ, -ərd

coverable
BR ˈkʌv(ə)rəbl
AM ˈkəv(ə)rəbəl

Coverack
BR ˈkʌvərak
AM ˈkəvəræk

coverage
BR ˈkʌv(ə)rɪdʒ
AM ˈkəv(ə)rɪdʒ

coverall
BR ˈkʌvərɔːl, -z
AM ˈkəvər,ɔl, ˈkəvər,ɑl, -z

covercharge
BR ˈkʌvətʃɑːdʒ, -ɪz
AM ˈkəvər,tʃɑrdʒ, -əz

Coverdale
BR ˈkʌvədeɪl
AM ˈkəvər,deɪl

coverer
BR ˈkʌv(ə)rə(r), -z
AM ˈkəv(ə)rər, -z

covering
BR ˈkʌv(ə)rɪŋ, -z
AM ˈkəv(ə)rɪŋ, -z

coverlet
BR ˈkʌvəlɪt, -s
AM ˈkəvərlət, -s

Coverley
BR ˈkʌvəli
AM ˈkəvərli

covert¹
secret
BR ˈkʌvət, ˈkəʊvəːt
AM ˈkoʊˌvərt

covert²
undergrowth
BR ˈkʌvət, -s
AM ˈkəvərt, -s

covertly
BR ˈkʌvətli, ˈkəʊvəːtli
AM ˈkoʊˌvərtli

covertness
BR ˈkʌvətnəs, ˈkəʊvəːtnəs
AM ˈkoʊˌvərtnəs

coverture
BR ˈkʌvətjʊə(r), ˈkʌvətʃʊə(r), ˈkʌvətʃə(r), -z
AM ˈkəvər,tʃ(ʊ)ər, ˈkəvərtʃər, -z

covet
BR ˈkʌvɪt, -s, -ɪŋ, -ɪd
AM ˈkəvə|t, -ts, -dɪŋ, -dəd

covetable
BR ˈkʌvɪtəbl
AM ˈkəvədəbəl

covetous
BR ˈkʌvɪtəs
AM ˈkəvədəs

covetously
BR ˈkʌvɪtəsli
AM ˈkəvədəsli

covetousness
BR ˈkʌvɪtəsnəs
AM ˈkəvədəsnəs

covey
BR ˈkʌv|i, -ɪz
AM ˈkəvi, -z

covin
BR ˈkʌvɪn, -z
AM ˈkəvən, ˈkoʊvən, -z

coving
BR ˈkəʊvɪŋ
AM ˈkoʊvɪŋ

cow
BR kaʊ, -z, -ɪŋ, -d
AM kaʊ, -z, -ɪŋ, -d

cowage
BR ˈkaʊɪdʒ
AM ˈkaʊɪdʒ

Cowan
BR ˈkaʊən
AM ˈkaʊən

coward
BR ˈkaʊəd, -z
AM ˈkaʊərd, -z

cowardice
BR ˈkaʊədɪs
AM ˈkaʊərdəs

cowardliness
BR ˈkaʊədlɪnɪs
AM ˈkaʊərdlinɪs

cowardly
BR ˈkaʊədli
AM ˈkaʊərdli

cowbane
BR ˈkaʊbeɪn
AM ˈkaʊ,beɪn

cowbell
BR ˈkaʊbɛl, -z
AM ˈkaʊ,bɛl, -z

cowberry
BR ˈkaʊb(ə)r|i, -ɪz
AM ˈkaʊ,bɛri, -z

cowbird
BR ˈkaʊbəːd, -z
AM ˈkaʊ,bərd, -z

cowboy
BR ˈkaʊbɔɪ, -z
AM ˈkaʊ,bɔɪ, -z

Cowbridge
BR 'kaʊbrɪdʒ
AM 'kaʊ͵brɪdʒ
cowcatcher
BR 'kaʊ͵katʃə(r), -z
AM 'kaʊ͵kɛtʃər, -z
Cowdenbeath
BR ͵kaʊdn'biːθ
AM 'kaʊdən͵biθ
Cowdray
BR 'kaʊdri, 'kaʊdreɪ
AM 'kaʊdri, 'kaʊdreɪ
Cowdrey
BR 'kaʊdri, 'kaʊdreɪ
AM 'kaʊdri, 'kaʊdreɪ
Cowell
BR 'kaʊ(ə)l
AM 'kaʊəl
Cowen
BR 'kaʊɪn, 'kəʊɪn
AM 'kaʊən, 'koʊən
cower
BR 'kaʊə(r), -z, -ɪŋ, -d
AM 'kaʊər, -z, -ɪŋ, -d
Cowes
BR kaʊz
AM kaʊz
Cowgill
BR 'kaʊgɪl
AM 'kaʊ͵gɪl
cowgirl
BR 'kaʊgəːl, -z
AM 'kaʊ͵gərl, -z
cowhage
BR 'kaʊɪdʒ
AM 'kaʊɪdʒ
cowhand
BR 'kaʊhand, -z
AM 'kaʊ͵(h)ænd, -z
cowheel
BR ͵kaʊ'hiːl, 'kaʊhiːl, -z
AM 'kaʊ͵(h)il, -z
cowherd
BR 'kaʊhəːd, -z
AM 'kaʊ͵(h)ərd, -z
cowhide
BR 'kaʊhʌɪd
AM 'kaʊ͵(h)aɪd
Cowie
BR 'kaʊi
AM 'kaʊi
cowl
BR kaʊl, -z, -d
AM kaʊl, -z, -d
Cowley
BR 'kaʊli
AM 'kaʊli
cowlick
BR 'kaʊlɪk, -s
AM 'kaʊlɪk, -s
cowling
BR 'kaʊlɪŋ, -z
AM 'kaʊlɪŋ, -z
cowman
BR 'kaʊmən
AM 'kaʊmən
cowmen
BR 'kaʊmən
AM 'kaʊmən
cowpat
BR 'kaʊpat, -s
AM 'kaʊ͵pæt, -s
cowpea
BR 'kaʊpiː, -z
AM 'kaʊ͵pi, -z
Cowper
BR 'kuːpə(r), 'kaʊpə(r)
AM 'kaʊpər, 'kupər
cowpoke
BR 'kaʊpəʊk, -s
AM 'kaʊ͵poʊk, -s
cowpox
BR 'kaʊpɒks
AM 'kaʊ͵pɑks
cowpuncher
BR 'kaʊ͵pʌn(t)ʃə(r), -z
AM 'kaʊ͵pən(t)ʃər, -z
cowrie
BR 'kaʊr|i, -ɪz
AM 'kaʊri, -z
cowry
BR 'kaʊr|i, -ɪz
AM 'kaʊri, -z
cowshed
BR 'kaʊʃɛd, -z
AM 'kaʊ͵ʃɛd, -z
cowslip
BR 'kaʊslɪp, -s
AM 'kaʊ͵slɪp, -s
cowtown
BR 'kaʊtaʊn, -z
AM 'kaʊ͵taʊn, -z
cox
BR kɒks, -ɪz, -ɪŋ, -t
AM kɑks, -əz, -ɪŋ, -t
coxa
BR 'kɒksə(*r*)
AM 'kɑksə
coxae
BR 'kɒksiː
AM 'kɑksi, 'kɑk͵saɪ
coxal
BR 'kɒksl
AM 'kɑksəl
coxalgia
BR kɒk'saldʒ(ɪ)ə(*r*)
AM kɑk'sældʒ(i)ə
coxcomb
BR 'kɒkskəʊm, -z
AM 'kɑks͵koʊm, -z
coxcombry
BR 'kɒkskəʊmr|i, -ɪz
AM 'kɑks͵koʊmri, -z
Coxe
BR kɒks
AM kɑks
coxless
BR 'kɒksləs
AM 'kɑksləs
Coxsackie
BR kɒk'saki, kʊk'saki
AM kɑk'sæki
coxswain
BR 'kɒksn, -z
AM 'kɑksn, -z
coxswainship
BR 'kɒksnʃɪp
AM 'kɑksn͵ʃɪp
coy
BR kɔɪ
AM kɔɪ
coyly
BR 'kɔɪli
AM 'kɔɪli
coyness
BR 'kɔɪnɨs
AM 'kɔɪnɨs
coyote
BR kɔɪ'əʊt|i, kʌɪ'əʊt|i, -ɪz
AM 'kaɪ͵oʊt, kaɪ'oʊdi, 'kaɪ͵oʊts\kaɪ'oʊdiz
coypu
BR 'kɔɪp(j)uː, -z
AM 'kɔɪ͵pu, -z
coz
BR kʌz
AM kəz
cozen
BR 'kʌzn̩, -z, -ɪŋ, -d
AM 'kəzən, -z, -ɪŋ, -d
cozenage
BR 'kʌzn̩ɪdʒ
AM 'kəzənədʒ
Cozens
BR 'kʌznz
AM 'kəzənz
Cozumel
BR 'kəʊzʊmɛl
AM 'koʊzʊ͵mɛl
SP ͵koθu'mel, ͵kosu'mel
cozy
BR 'kəʊz|i, -ɪə(r), -ɪɨst
AM 'koʊzi, -ər, -ɨst
cozzie
BR 'kɒz|i, -ɪz
AM 'kɑzi, -z
crab
BR krab, -z, -ɪŋ, -d
AM kræb, -z, -ɪŋ, -d
Crabbe
BR krab
AM kræb
crabbedly
BR 'krabɨdli
AM 'kræbədli
crabbedness
BR 'krabɨdnɨs
AM 'kræb(əd)nəs
crabbily
BR 'krabɨli
AM 'kræbəli
crabbiness
BR 'krabɪnɨs
AM 'kræbinɨs
crabby
BR 'krab|i, -ɪə(r), -ɪɨst
AM 'kræbi, -ər, -ɨst
crabgrass
BR 'krabgrɑːs, 'krabgras
AM 'kræb͵græs
crablike
BR 'krablʌɪk
AM 'kræb͵laɪk
crabmeat
BR 'krabmiːt
AM 'kræb͵mit
Crabtree
BR 'krabtriː
AM 'kræb͵tri
crabways
BR 'krabweɪz
AM 'kræb͵weɪz
crabwise
BR 'krabwʌɪz
AM 'kræb͵waɪz
crack
BR krak, -s, -ɪŋ, -t
AM kræk, -s, -ɪŋ, -t
crackbrained
BR 'krakbreɪnd
AM 'kræk͵breɪn(d)
crackdown
BR 'krakdaʊn, -z
AM 'kræk͵daʊn, -z
cracker
BR 'krakə(r), -z
AM 'krækər, -z
cracker-barrel
BR 'krakə͵barəl, 'krakə͵barl̩, -z
AM 'krækər͵bɛrəl, -z
crackerjack
BR 'krakədʒak, -s
AM 'krækər͵dʒæk, -s
crackiness
BR 'krakɪnɨs
AM 'krækinɨs
crack-jaw
BR 'krakdʒɔː(*r*)
AM 'kræk͵dʒɔ
crackle
BR 'krak|l, -lz, -l̩ɪŋ\-lɪŋ, -ld
AM 'kræk|əl, -əlz, -(ə)lɪŋ, -əld
crackling
noun
BR 'kraklɪŋ, -z
AM 'kræk(ə)lɪŋ, -z
crackly
BR 'krakli
AM 'kræk(ə)li
cracknel
BR 'kraknl, -z
AM 'kræknəl, -z
crackpot
BR 'krakpɒt, -s
AM 'kræk͵pɑt, -s
cracksman
BR 'kraksmən
AM 'kræksmən
cracksmen
BR 'kraksmən

AM 'kræksmən

crackup
BR 'krakʌp, -s
AM 'kræk,əp, -s

cracky
BR 'kraki
AM 'kræki

Cracow
BR 'krakɒf, 'krakɒv, 'krakaʊ
AM 'krɑkaʊ, 'krɑkɔf, 'krɑkɑf

Craddock
BR 'kradək
AM 'krædək

cradle
BR 'kreɪd|l, -lz, -lɪŋ\-lɪŋ, -ld
AM 'kreɪd|əl, -əlz, -(ə)lɪŋ, -əld

Cradley
BR 'kreɪdli, 'kradli
AM 'krædli

craft
BR krɑːft, kraft, -s, -ɪŋ, -ɪd
AM kræft, -s, -ɪŋ, -əd

craftily
BR 'krɑːftɨli, 'kraftɨli
AM 'kræftəli

craftiness
BR 'krɑːftɪnɪs, 'kraftɪnɪs
AM 'kræftinɪs

craftsman
BR 'krɑːf(t)smən, 'kraf(t)smən
AM 'kræf(t)smən

craftsmanship
BR 'krɑːf(t)smənʃɪp, 'kraf(t)smənʃɪp
AM 'kræf(t)smən,ʃɪp

craftsmen
BR 'krɑːf(t)smən, 'kraf(t)smən
AM 'kræf(t)smən

craftspeople
plural noun
BR 'krɑːf(t)s,piːpl, 'kraf(t)s,piːpl
AM 'kræf(t)s,pipl

craftsperson
BR 'krɑːf(t)s,pəːsn, 'kraf(t)s,pəːsn
AM 'kræf(t)s,pərsən

craftswoman
BR 'krɑːf(t)s,wʊmən, 'kraf(t)s,wʊmən
AM 'kræf(t)s,wʊmən

craftswomen
BR 'krɑːf(t)s,wɪmɪn, 'kraf(t)s,wɪmɪn
AM 'kræf(t)s,wɪmɨn

craftwork
BR 'krɑːftwəːk, 'kraftwəːk
AM 'kræf(t),wərk

craftworker
BR 'krɑːft,wəːkə(r), 'kraft,wəːkə(r), -z
AM 'kræf(t),wərkər, -z

crafty
BR 'krɑːft|i, 'kraft|i, -ɪə(r), -ɪɪst
AM 'kræfti, -ər, -ɨst

crag
BR krag, -z
AM kræg, -z

craggily
BR 'kragɨli
AM 'krægəli

cragginess
BR 'kragɪnɪs
AM 'kræginɪs

craggy
BR 'krag|i, -ɪə(r), -ɪɪst
AM 'krægi, -ər, -ɨst

cragsman
BR 'kragsmən
AM 'krægsmən

cragsmen
BR 'kragsmən
AM 'krægsmən

cragswoman
BR 'krags,wʊmən
AM 'krægs,wʊmən

cragswomen
BR 'krags,wɪmɪn
AM 'krægs,wɪmɨn

Craig
BR kreɪg
AM krɛg

Craigie
BR 'kreɪgi
AM 'kreɪgi

crake
BR kreɪk, -s
AM kreɪk, -s

cram
BR kram, -z, -ɪŋ, -d
AM kræm, -z, -ɪŋ, -d

crambo
BR 'krambəʊ
AM 'kræmboʊ

Cramden
BR 'kramd(ə)n
AM 'kræmd(ə)n

Cramer
BR 'kreɪmə(r)
AM 'kreɪmər

crammer
BR 'kramə(r), -z
AM 'kræmər, -z

cramp
BR kramp, -s, -ɪŋ, -t
AM kræmp, -s, -ɪŋ, -t

crampon
BR 'krampɒn, 'krampən, -z
AM 'kræm,pɑn, -z

cran
BR kran, -z
AM kræn, -z

cranage
BR 'kreɪnɪdʒ
AM 'kreɪnɪdʒ

cranberry
BR 'kranb(ə)r|i, -ɪz
AM 'kræn,bɛri, -z

Cranborne
BR 'kranbɔːn
AM 'kræn,bɔ(ə)rn

Cranbourn
BR 'kranbɔːn
AM 'kræn,bɔ(ə)rn

Cranbourne
BR 'kranbɔːn
AM 'kræn,bɔ(ə)rn

Cranbrook
BR 'kranbrʊk
AM 'kræn,brʊk

crane
BR kreɪn, -z, -ɪŋ, -d
AM kreɪn, -z, -ɪŋ, -d

cranesbill
BR 'kreɪnzbɪl, -z
AM 'kreɪnz,bɪl, -z

Cranfield
BR 'kranfiːld
AM 'kræn,fild

crania
BR 'kreɪnɪə(r)
AM 'kreɪniə

cranial
BR 'kreɪnɪəl
AM 'kreɪniəl

cranially
BR 'kreɪnɪəli
AM 'kreɪniəli

craniate
BR 'kreɪnɪət, -s
AM 'kreɪniə,eɪt 'kreɪniət, -s

craniological
BR ,kreɪnɪə'lɒdʒɪkl
AM ,kreɪni'ɑlədʒəkəl

craniologist
BR ,kreɪnɪ'ɒlədʒɪst, -s
AM ,kreɪni'ɑlədʒəst, -s

craniology
BR ,kreɪnɪ'ɒlədʒi
AM ,kreɪni'ɑlədʒi

craniometric
BR ,kreɪnɪə'mɛtrɪk
AM ,kreɪniə'mɛtrɪk

craniometry
BR ,kreɪnɪ'ɒmɨtri
AM ,kreɪni'ɑmətri

craniotomy
BR ,kreɪnɪ'ɒtəmi, -ɪz
AM ,kreɪni'ɑdəmi, -z

cranium
BR ,kreɪnɪəm, -z
AM 'kreɪniəm, -z

crank
BR kraŋ|k, -ks, -kɪŋ, -(k)t
AM kræŋ|k, -ks, -kɪŋ, -(k)t

crankcase
BR 'kraŋkkeɪs, -ɪz
AM 'kræŋ,keɪs, -ɪz

crankily
BR 'kraŋkɨli
AM 'kræŋkəli

crankiness
BR 'kraŋkɪnɪs
AM 'kræŋkinɪs

crankpin
BR 'kraŋkpɪn, -z
AM 'kræŋk,pɪn, -z

crankshaft
BR 'kraŋkʃɑːft, 'kraŋkʃaft, -s
AM 'kræŋk,ʃæft, -s

cranky
BR 'kraŋk|i, -ɪə(r), -ɪɪst
AM 'kræŋki, -ər, -ɨst

Cranleigh
BR 'kranli
AM 'krænli

Cranley
BR 'kranli
AM 'krænli

Cranmer
BR 'kranmə(r)
AM 'krænmər

crannied
BR 'kranɪd
AM 'krænid, 'krænəd

crannog
BR 'kranəg, -z
AM 'krænəg, -z

cranny
BR 'kran|i, -ɪz
AM 'kræni, -z

Cranston
BR 'kranst(ə)n
AM 'krænstən

Cranwell
BR 'kranw(ɛ)l
AM 'kræn,wɛl

crap
BR krap, -s, -ɪŋ, -t
AM kræp, -s, -ɪŋ, -t

crape
BR kreɪp, -s
AM kreɪp, -s

crapper
BR 'krapə(r), -z
AM 'kræpər, -z

crappie
BR 'krap|i, -ɪz
AM 'krɑpi, 'kræpi, -z

crappily
BR 'krapɨli
AM 'kræpəli

crappiness
BR 'krapɪnɪs
AM 'kræpinɪs

crappy
BR 'krap|i, -ɪə(r), -ɪɪst
AM 'kræpi, -ər, -ɨst

craps
BR kraps
AM kræps

crapshooter
BR ˈkrapˌʃuːtə(r), -z
AM ˈkræpˌʃudər, -z
crapulence
BR ˈkrapjʉləns, ˈkrapjʉln̩s
AM ˈkræpjələns
crapulent
BR ˈkrapjʉlənt, ˈkrapjʉln̩t
AM ˈkræpjələnt
crapulently
BR ˈkrapjʉləntli, ˈkrapjʉln̩tli
AM ˈkræpjələn(t)li
crapulous
BR ˈkrapjʉləs
AM ˈkræpjələs
crapy
BR ˈkreɪpi
AM ˈkreɪpi
craquelure
BR ˈkrakl̩(j)ʊə(r)
AM ˈkrækəˌlʊ(ə)r
crases
BR ˈkreɪsiːz
AM ˈkreɪsiz
crash
BR kraʃ, -ɨz, -ɪŋ, -t
AM kræʃ, -ɨz, -ɪŋ, -t
Crashaw
BR ˈkraʃɔː(*r*)
AM ˈkræʃɔ, ˈkreɪʃɔ, ˈkræʃɑ, ˈkreɪʃɑ
crash-dove
BR ˈkraʃdəʊv, ˌkraʃˈdəʊv
AM ˈkræʃˈdoʊv
crasis
BR ˈkreɪsɪs
AM ˈkreɪsɨs
crass
BR kras
AM kræs
crassitude
BR ˈkrasɨtjuːd, ˈkrasɨtʃuːd
AM ˈkræsəˌt(j)ud
crassly
BR ˈkrasli
AM ˈkræsli
crassness
BR ˈkrasnəs
AM ˈkræsnəs
Crassus
BR ˈkrasəs
AM ˈkræsəs
cratch
BR kratʃ, -ɨz
AM krætʃ, -əz
Cratchit
BR ˈkratʃɪt
AM ˈkrætʃət
crate
BR kreɪt, -s, -ɪŋ, -ɨd
AM kreɪ|t, -ts, -dɪŋ, -dɨd
crateful
BR ˈkreɪtfʊl, -z
AM ˈkreɪtˌfʊl, -z
crater
BR ˈkreɪt|ə(r), -əz, -(ə)rɪŋ, -əd
AM ˈkreɪdər, -z, -ɪŋ, -d
craterous
BR ˈkreɪt(ə)rəs
AM ˈkreɪdərəs
Crathorn
BR ˈkreɪθɔːn
AM ˈkreɪˌθɔ(ə)rn
Crathorne
BR ˈkreɪθɔːn
AM ˈkreɪˌθɔ(ə)rn
cravat
BR krəˈvat, -s
AM krəˈvæt, -s
cravatted
BR krəˈvatɨd
AM krəˈvædəd
crave
BR kreɪv, -z, -ɪŋ, -d
AM kreɪv, -z, -ɪŋ, -d
craven
BR ˈkreɪv(ə)n
AM ˈkreɪvən
cravenly
BR ˈkreɪv(ə)nli
AM ˈkreɪvənli
cravenness
BR ˈkreɪv(ə)nnəs
AM ˈkreɪvə(n)nəs
craver
BR ˈkreɪvə(r), -z
AM ˈkreɪvər, -z
craving
BR ˈkreɪvɪŋ, -z
AM ˈkreɪvɪŋ, -z
craw
BR krɔː(*r*), -z
AM krɔ, krɑ, -z
crawdad
BR ˈkrɔːdad, -z
AM ˈkrɔˌdæd, ˈkrɑˌdæd, -z
crawfish
BR ˈkrɔːfɪʃ, -ɨz
AM ˈkrɔˌfɪʃ, ˈkrɑˌfɪʃ, -ɨz
Crawford
BR ˈkrɔːfəd
AM ˈkrɔfərd, ˈkrɑfərd
crawl
BR krɔːl, -z, -ɪŋ, -d
AM krɔl, krɑl, -z, -ɪŋ, -d
crawler
BR ˈkrɔːlə(r), -z
AM ˈkrɔlər, ˈkrɑlər, -z
crawlingly
BR ˈkrɔːlɪŋli
AM ˈkrɔlɪŋli, ˈkrɑlɪŋli
crawly
BR ˈkrɔːl|i, -ɪz
AM ˈkrɔli, ˈkrɑli, -z
Crawshaw
BR ˈkrɔːʃɔː(*r*)
AM ˈkrɔʃɔ, ˈkrɑʃɑ
Crawshay
BR ˈkrɔːʃeɪ
AM ˈkrɔʃeɪ, ˈkrɑʃeɪ
Cray
BR kreɪ, -z
AM kreɪ, -z
crayfish
BR ˈkreɪfɪʃ, -ɨz
AM ˈkreɪˌfɪʃ, -ɨz
Crayford
BR ˈkreɪfəd
AM ˈkreɪfərd
Crayola®
BR kreɪˈəʊlə(*r*)
AM kreɪˈoʊlə
crayon
BR ˈkreɪɒn, ˈkreɪən, -z, -ɪŋ, -d
AM ˈkreɪˌɑn, -z, -ɪŋ, -d
craze
BR kreɪz, -ɨz, -ɪŋ, -d
AM kreɪz, -ɨz, -ɪŋ, -d
crazily
BR ˈkreɪzɨli
AM ˈkreɪzɨli
craziness
BR ˈkreɪzɪnɨs
AM ˈkreɪzinɨs
crazy
BR ˈkreɪz|i, -ɪə(r), -ɪɨst
AM ˈkreɪzi, -ər, -ɨst
creak
BR kriːk, -s, -ɪŋ, -t
AM krik, -s, -ɪŋ, -t
creakily
BR ˈkriːkɨli
AM ˈkrikɨli
creakiness
BR ˈkriːkɪnɨs
AM ˈkrikinɨs
creakingly
BR ˈkriːkɪŋli
AM ˈkrikɪŋli
creaky
BR ˈkriːk|i, -ɪə(r), -ɪɨst
AM ˈkriki, -ər, -ɨst
cream
BR kriːm, -z, -ɪŋ, -d
AM krim, -z, -ɪŋ, -d
creamer
BR ˈkriːmə(r), -z
AM ˈkrimər, -z
creamery
BR ˈkriːm(ə)r|i, -ɪz
AM ˈkrim(ə)ri, -z
creamily
BR ˈkriːmɨli
AM ˈkrimɨli
creaminess
BR ˈkriːmɪnɨs
AM ˈkriminɨs
creamware
BR ˈkriːmwɛː(r)
AM ˈkrimˌwɛ(ə)r
creamy
BR ˈkriːm|i, -ɪə(r), -ɪɨst
AM ˈkrimi, -ər, -ɨst
creance
BR ˈkriːəns, -ɨz
AM ˈkriəns, -əz
crease
BR kriːs, -ɨz, -ɪŋ, -t
AM kris, -ɨz, -ɪŋ, -t
Creasey
BR ˈkriːsi
AM ˈkrisi
Creasy
BR ˈkriːsi
AM ˈkrisi
creatable
BR krɪˈeɪtəbl
AM kriˈeɪdəbəl
create
BR krɪˈeɪt, -s, -ɪŋ, -ɨd
AM kriˈeɪ|t, -ts, -dɪŋ, -dɨd
creatine
BR ˈkriːətiːn
AM ˈkriəˌtin, ˈkriədən
creation
BR krɪˈeɪʃn, -z
AM kriˈeɪʃən, -z
creationism
BR krɪˈeɪʃn̩ɪz(ə)m, krɪˈeɪʃənɪz(ə)m
AM kriˈeɪʃəˌnɪzəm
creationist
BR krɪˈeɪʃn̩ɪst, krɪˈeɪʃənɪst, -s
AM kriˈeɪʃənəst, -s
creative
BR krɪˈeɪtɪv
AM kriˈeɪdɪv
creatively
BR krɪˈeɪtɨvli
AM kriˈeɪdɨvli
creativeness
BR krɪˈeɪtɨvnɨs
AM kriˈeɪdɨvnɨs
creativity
BR ˌkriːeɪˈtɪvɨti
AM ˌkrieɪˈtɪvɨdi
creator
BR krɪˈeɪtə(r), -z
AM kriˈeɪdər, -z
creatrices
BR krɪˈeɪtrɨsiːz
AM kriˈeɪtrɨsiz
creatrix
BR krɪˈeɪtrɪks, -ɨz
AM kriˈeɪtrɪks, -ɨz
creature
BR ˈkriːtʃə(r), -z
AM ˈkritʃər, -z
creaturely
BR ˈkriːtʃəli
AM ˈkritʃərli
crèche
BR kreɪʃ, krɛʃ, -ɨz
AM krɛʃ, -əz
Crecy
BR ˈkrɛsi
AM ˈkrɛsi

Crécy
BR 'krɛsi
AM 'kreɪsi

cred
BR krɛd
AM krɛd

Creda®
BR 'kriːdə(r)
AM 'kridə

credal
BR 'kriːdl
AM 'kridəl

credence
BR 'kriːdns
AM 'kridns

credential
BR krɪ'dɛnʃl, -z
AM krə'dɛn(t)ʃəl, -z

credenza
BR krɪ'dɛnzə(r), -z
AM krə'dɛnzə, -z

credibility
BR ˌkrɛdɪ'bɪlɪti
AM ˌkrɛdə'bɪlɪdi

credible
BR 'krɛdɪbl
AM 'krɛdəbəl

credibly
BR 'krɛdɪbli
AM 'krɛdəbli

credit
BR 'krɛd|ɪt, -ɪts, -ɪtɪŋ, -ɪtɪd
AM 'krɛdə|t, -ts, -dɪŋ, -dɪd

creditability
BR ˌkrɛdɪtə'bɪlɪti
AM ˌkrɛdədə'bɪlɪdi

creditable
BR 'krɛdɪtəbl
AM 'krɛdədəbəl

creditably
BR 'krɛdɪtəbli
AM 'krɛdədəbli

Crediton
BR 'krɛdɪt(ə)n
AM 'krɛdət(ə)n

creditor
BR 'krɛdɪtə(r), -z
AM 'krɛdədər, -z

creditworthiness
BR 'krɛdɪtˌwəːðɪnɪs
AM 'krɛdətˌwərðinɪs

creditworthy
BR 'krɛdɪtˌwəːði
AM 'krɛdətˌwərði

credo
BR 'kriːdəʊ, 'kreɪdəʊ, -z
AM 'kriˌdoʊ, 'kreɪˌdoʊ, -z

credulity
BR krɪ'djuːlɪti, krɪ'dʒuːlɪti
AM krə'd(j)ulədi

credulous
BR 'krɛdjʊləs, 'krɛdʒʊləs
AM 'krɛdʒələs

credulously
BR 'krɛdjʊləsli, 'krɛdʒʊləsli
AM 'krɛdʒələsli

credulousness
BR 'krɛdjʊləsnəs, 'krɛdʒʊləsnəs
AM 'krɛdʒələsnəs

Cree
BR kriː, -z
AM kri, -z

creed
BR kriːd, -z
AM krid, -z

creedal
BR 'kriːdl
AM 'kridəl

creek
BR kriːk, -s
AM krik, krɪk, -s

creel
BR kriːl, -z
AM kril, -z

Creeley
BR 'kriːli
AM 'krili

creep
BR kriːp, -s, -ɪŋ
AM krip, -s, -ɪŋ

creeper
BR 'kriːpə(r), -z
AM 'kripər, -z

creepie
BR 'kriːp|i, -ɪə(r), -ɪɪst
AM 'kripi, -ər, -ɪst

creepily
BR 'kriːpɪli
AM 'kripəli

creepiness
BR 'kriːpɪnɪs
AM 'kripinɪs

creepy
BR 'kriːp|i, -ɪə(r), -ɪɪst
AM 'kripi, -ər, -ɪst

creepy-crawly
BR ˌkriːpɪ'krɔːl|i, -ɪz
AM ˈkripiˈkrɔli, ˈkripiˈkrɑli, -z

creese
BR kriːs, -ɪz
AM kris, -ɪz

Creighton
BR 'krʌɪtn, 'kreɪtn
AM 'kreɪtn

cremate
BR krɪ'meɪt, -s, -ɪŋ, -ɪd
AM 'kriˌmeɪ|t, -ts, -dɪŋ, -dɪd

cremation
BR krɪ'meɪʃn, -z
AM kri'meɪʃən, krə'meɪʃən, -z

cremator
BR krɪ'meɪtə(r), -z
AM 'kriˌmeɪdər, -z

crematoria
BR ˌkrɛmə'tɔːrɪə(r)
AM ˌkrimə'tɔriə

crematorium
BR ˌkrɛmə'tɔːrɪəm, -z
AM ˌkrimə'tɔriəm, -z

crematory
BR 'krɛmət(ə)r|i, -ɪz
AM 'kriməˌtɔri, -z

crème brûlée
BR ˌkrɛm bruː'leɪ
AM ˌkrɛm bru'leɪ

crème caramel
BR ˌkrɛm ˌkarə'mɛl, -z
AM ˌkrɛm ˌkɛrə'mɛl, -z

crème de cassis
BR ˌkrɛm də ka'siːs
AM ˌkrɛm də kə'si(s)

crème de la crème
BR ˌkrɛm də la 'krɛm
AM ˌkrɛm də lə 'krɛm

crème de menthe
BR ˌkrɛm də 'mɒnθ
AM ˌkrim də 'mɛnθ

crème fraîche
BR ˌkrɛm 'frɛʃ
AM ˌkrɛm 'frɛʃ

crèmes brûlées
BR ˌkrɛm bruː'leɪz
AM ˌkrɛm bru'leɪz

Cremona
BR krɪ'məʊnə(r)
AM krə'moʊnə

crenate
BR 'kriːneɪt, -ɪd
AM 'kriˌneɪ|t, -dɪd

crenation
BR krɪ'neɪʃn
AM kri'neɪʃən, krɛ'neɪʃən, krə'neɪʃən

crenature
BR 'krɛnətjʊə(r), 'kriːnətjʊə(r), 'krɛnətʃʊə(r), 'kriːnətʃʊə(r), 'krɛnətʃə(r), 'kriːnətʃə(r)
AM 'krɛnətʃər, 'krinətʃər

crenel
BR 'krɛnl, -z
AM 'krɛnəl, -z

crenelate
BR 'krɛnəleɪt, 'krɛnl̩eɪt, -s, -ɪŋ, -ɪd
AM 'krɛnəˌleɪ|t, -ts, -dɪŋ, -dɪd

crenelation
BR ˌkrɛnə'leɪʃn, ˌkrɛnl'eɪʃn, -z
AM ˌkrɛnə'leɪʃən, -z

crenellate
BR 'krɛnəleɪt, 'krɛnl̩eɪt, -s, -ɪŋ, -ɪd
AM 'krɛnəˌleɪ|t, -ts, -dɪŋ, -dɪd

crenellation
BR ˌkrɛnə'leɪʃn, ˌkrɛnl'eɪʃn, -z
AM ˌkrɛnə'leɪʃən, -z

crenelle
BR krɪ'nɛl, -z
AM krə'nɛl, -z

Creole
BR 'kriːəʊl, -z
AM 'kriˌoʊl, -z

creole
BR 'kriːəʊl, -z
AM 'kriˌoʊl, -z

creolisation
BR ˌkriːəlʌɪ'zeɪʃn
AM ˌkriələ'zeɪʃən, ˌkriəˌlaɪ'zeɪʃən

creolise
BR 'kriːəlʌɪz, -ɪz, -ɪŋ, -d
AM 'kriəˌlaɪz, -ɪz, -ɪŋ, -d

creolization
BR ˌkriːəlʌɪ'zeɪʃn
AM ˌkriələ'zeɪʃən, ˌkriəˌlaɪ'zeɪʃən

creolize
BR 'kriːəlʌɪz, -ɪz, -ɪŋ, -d
AM 'kriəˌlaɪz, -ɪz, -ɪŋ, -d

Creon
BR 'kriːɒn, 'kriːən
AM 'kriˌɑn

creosote
BR 'kriːəsəʊt
AM 'kriəˌsoʊt

crêpe
BR kreɪp, krɛp, -s
AM kreɪp, krɛp, -s

crêpe de Chine
BR ˌkreɪp də 'ʃiːn, ˌkrɛp +
AM ˌkreɪp də 'ʃin

crêpes suzette
BR ˌkreɪp(s) sʊ'zɛt, ˌkrɛp(s) +
AM ˌkreɪps su'zɛt

crêpe suzette
BR ˌkreɪp sʊ'zɛt, ˌkrɛp +
AM ˌkreɪp su'zɛt

crêpey
BR 'kreɪpi
AM 'kreɪpi

crepitant
BR 'krɛpɪtnt
AM 'krɛpədnt

crepitate
BR 'krɛpɪteɪt, -s, -ɪŋ, -ɪd
AM 'krɛpəˌteɪ|t, -ts, -dɪŋ, -dɪd

crepitation
BR ˌkrɛpɪ'teɪʃn, -z
AM ˌkrɛpə'teɪʃən, -z

crepitus
BR 'krɛpɪtəs

AM 'krɛpədəs

crept
BR krɛpt
AM krɛpt

crepuscular
BR krɪ'pʌskjʉlə(r)
AM krə'pəskjələr

crêpy
BR 'kreɪpi
AM 'kreɪpi

crescendo
BR krɪ'ʃɛndəʊ, -z
AM krə'ʃɛndoʊ, -z

crescent[1]
increasing
BR 'krɛsnt
AM 'krɛs(ə)nt

crescent[2]
shape
BR 'krɛznt, 'krɛsnt, -s
AM 'krɛs(ə)nt, -s

crescentic
BR krɪ'sɛntɪk
AM krə'sɛn(t)ɪk

cresol
BR 'kriːsɒl
AM 'kriˌsɔl, 'kriˌsɑl

cress
BR krɛs
AM krɛs

cresset
BR 'krɛsɪt, -s
AM 'krɛsət, -s

Cressida
BR 'krɛsɪdə(r)
AM 'krɛsədə

Cresswell
BR 'krɛsw(ɛ)l, 'krɛzw(ɛ)l
AM 'krɛsˌwɛl, 'krɛzˌwɛl

crest
BR krɛst, -s, -ɪd
AM krɛst, -s, -əd

crestfallen
BR 'krɛstˌfɔːlən
AM 'krɛs(t)ˌfɔlən, 'krɛs(t)ˌfɑlən

crestless
BR 'krɛstləs
AM 'krɛs(t)ləs

Creswell
BR 'krɛsw(ɛ)l, 'krɛzw(ɛ)l
AM 'krɛsˌwɛl, 'krɛzˌwɛl

cresyl
BR 'kriːsʌɪl, 'kriːsɪl
AM 'krɛsəl, 'krisəl

Cretaceous
BR krɪ'teɪʃəs
AM krə'teɪʃəs

Cretan
BR 'kriːtn, -z
AM 'kritn, -z

Crete
BR kriːt
AM krit

cretic
BR 'kriːtɪk, -s
AM 'kridɪk, -s

cretin
BR 'krɛt(ɪ)n, -z
AM 'kritn, -z

cretinise
BR 'krɛtɪnʌɪz, 'krɛtn̩ʌɪz, -ɪz, -ɪŋ, -d
AM 'kritnˌaɪz, -ɪz, -ɪŋ, -d

cretinism
BR 'krɛtɪnɪz(ə)m, 'krɛtn̩ɪz(ə)m
AM 'kritnˌɪzəm

cretinize
BR 'krɛtɪnʌɪz, 'krɛtn̩ʌɪz, -ɪz, -ɪŋ, -d
AM 'kritnˌaɪz, -ɪz, -ɪŋ, -d

cretinous
BR 'krɛtɪnəs, 'krɛtn̩əs
AM 'kritn̩əs

cretinously
BR 'krɛtɪnəsli, 'krɛtn̩əsli
AM 'kritn̩əsli

cretonne
BR krɪ'tɒn, krɛ'tɒn, 'krɛtɒn, -z
AM 'kriˌtɑn, krə'tɑn, -z

Creutzfeldt-Jakob disease
BR ˌkrɔɪtsfɛlt'jakɒb dɪˌziːz
AM ˌkrɔɪtsˌfɛld'dʒɑkəb dəˌziz

crevasse
BR krɪ'vas, -ɪz
AM krə'væs, -əz

crevice
BR 'krɛv|ɪs, -ɪsɪz
AM 'krɛvəs, -əz

crew
BR kruː, -z, -ɪŋ, -d
AM kru, -z, -ɪŋ, -d

crewcut
BR 'kruːkʌt, -s
AM 'kruˌkət, -s

Crewe
BR kruː
AM kru

crewel
BR 'kruːəl, -z
AM 'kruwəl, -z

crewelwork
BR 'kruːəlwəːk
AM 'kruwəlˌwərk

Crewkerne
BR 'kruːkəːn
AM 'kruˌkərn

crewman
BR 'kruːmən
AM 'krumən

crewmen
BR 'kruːmən
AM 'krumən

cri
BR kriː
AM kri

crib
BR krɪb, -z, -ɪŋ, -d
AM krɪb, -z, -ɪŋ, -d

cribbage
BR 'krɪbɪdʒ
AM 'krɪbɪdʒ

cribber
BR 'krɪbə(r), -z
AM 'krɪbər, -z

cribella
BR krɪ'bɛlə(r)
AM krə'bɛlə

cribellum
BR krɪ'bɛləm
AM krə'bɛləm

cribo
BR 'kriːbəʊ, -z
AM 'kriˌboʊ, -z

cribriform
BR 'krɪbrɪfɔːm
AM 'krɪbrəˌfɔ(ə)rm

cribwork
BR 'krɪbwəːk
AM 'krɪbˌwərk

Criccieth
BR 'krɪkɪəθ, 'krɪkɪɛθ
AM 'krɪkiəθ

Crich
BR krʌɪtʃ
AM kraɪtʃ

Crichton
BR 'krʌɪtn
AM 'kraɪtn

crick
BR krɪk, -s, -ɪŋ, -t
AM krɪk, -s, -ɪŋ, -t

cricket
BR 'krɪkɪt, -s
AM 'krɪkɪt, -s

cricketer
BR 'krɪkɪtə(r), -z
AM 'krɪkədər, -z

Crickhowell
BR krɪk'haʊ(ə)l
AM krɪk'haʊəl

cricoid
BR 'krʌɪkɔɪd, -z
AM 'kraɪˌkɔɪd, -z

cri de cœur
BR ˌkriː də 'kəː(r)
AM ˌkri də 'kər

cried
BR krʌɪd
AM kraɪd

Crieff
BR kriːf
AM krif

crier
BR 'krʌɪə(r), -z
AM 'kraɪər, -z

crikey!
BR 'krʌɪki
AM 'kraɪki

crim
BR krɪm, -z
AM krɪm, -z

crime
BR krʌɪm, -z
AM kraɪm, -z

Crimea
BR krʌɪ'mɪə(r)
AM kraɪ'miə

Crimean
BR krʌɪ'mɪən, -z
AM kraɪ'miən, -z

crime passionnel
BR ˌkriːm ˌpasjə'nɛl, -z
AM ˌkrim ˌpæsjə'nɛl, -z

crimes passionnels
BR ˌkriːm ˌpasjə'nɛlz
AM ˌkrim ˌpæsjə'nɛl(z)

criminal
BR 'krɪmɪnl
AM 'krɪmənl, 'krɪmnəl

criminalisation
BR ˌkrɪmɪnəlʌɪ'zeɪʃn, ˌkrɪmɪnl̩ʌɪ'zeɪʃn
AM ˌkrɪm(ə)nələ'zeɪʃən, ˌkrɪm(ə)nəˌlaɪ'zeɪʃən

criminalise
BR 'krɪmɪnəlʌɪz, 'krɪmɪnl̩ʌɪz, -ɪz, -ɪŋ, -d
AM 'krɪm(ə)nəˌlaɪz, -ɪz, -ɪŋ, -d

criminalistic
BR ˌkrɪmɪnə'lɪstɪk, ˌkrɪmɪnl'ɪstɪk, -s
AM ˌkrɪm(ə)nə'lɪstɪk, -s

criminality
BR ˌkrɪmɪ'nalɪti
AM ˌkrɪmə'nælədi

criminalization
BR ˌkrɪmɪnəlʌɪ'zeɪʃn, ˌkrɪmɪnl̩ʌɪ'zeɪʃn
AM ˌkrɪmənələ'zeɪʃən, ˌkrɪm(ə)nəˌlaɪ'zeɪʃən

criminalize
BR 'krɪmɪnəlʌɪz, 'krɪmɪnl̩ʌɪz, -ɪz, -ɪŋ, -d
AM 'krɪm(ə)nəˌlaɪz, -ɪz, -ɪŋ, -d

criminally
BR 'krɪmɪnl̩i, 'krɪmɪnəli
AM 'krɪm(ə)nəli

criminate
BR 'krɪmɪneɪt, -s, -ɪŋ, -ɪd
AM 'krɪməˌneɪ|t, -ts, -dɪŋ, -dɪd

crimination
BR ˌkrɪmɪ'neɪʃn, -z
AM ˌkrɪmə'neɪʃən, -z

criminative
BR 'krɪmɪnətɪv, -z
AM 'krɪməˌneɪdɪv, -z

criminatory
BR 'krɪmɪnət(ə)ri
AM 'krɪmənəˌtɔri

criminological
BR ˌkrɪmɪnə'lɒdʒɪkl

AM ˌkrɪmənəˈlɑdʒəkəl
criminologist
BR ˌkrɪmɪˈnɒlədʒɪst, -s
AM ˌkrɪməˈnɑlədʒəst, -s
criminology
BR ˌkrɪmɪˈnɒlədʒi
AM ˌkrɪməˈnɑlədʒi
Crimond
BR ˈkrɪmənd
AM ˈkrɪmənd
crimp
BR krɪm|p, -ps, -pɪŋ, -(p)t
AM krɪm|p, -ps, -pɪŋ, -(p)t
crimper
BR ˈkrɪmpə(r), -z
AM ˈkrɪmpər, -z
crimpily
BR ˈkrɪmpɪli
AM ˈkrɪmpɪli
crimpiness
BR ˈkrɪmpɪnɪs
AM ˈkrɪmpinɪs
crimplene®
BR ˈkrɪmpliːn
AM ˈkrɪmpˌlin
crimpy
BR ˈkrɪmpi
AM ˈkrɪmpi
crimson
BR ˈkrɪmzn̩, -z, -ɪŋ, -d
AM ˈkrɪmzn, -z, -ɪŋ, -d
cringe
BR krɪn(d)ʒ, -ɪz, -ɪŋ, -d
AM krɪndʒ, -ɪz, -ɪŋ, -d
cringer
BR ˈkrɪn(d)ʒə(r), -z
AM ˈkrɪndʒər, -z
cringle
BR ˈkrɪŋgl, -z
AM ˈkrɪŋgəl, -z
crinkle
BR ˈkrɪŋk|l, -lz, -l̩ɪŋ\-lɪŋ, -ld
AM ˈkrɪŋk|əl, -əlz, -(ə)lɪŋ, -əld
crinkliness
BR ˈkrɪŋklɪnɪs
AM ˈkrɪŋk(ə)linɪs
crinkly
BR ˈkrɪŋkl|i, -ɪə(r), -ɪɪst
AM ˈkrɪŋk(ə)li, -ər, -ɪst
crinoid
BR ˈkrʌɪnɔɪd, ˈkrɪnɔɪd
AM ˈkraɪˌnɔɪd, ˈkrɪˌnɔɪd
crinoidal
BR krʌɪˈnɔɪdl, krɪˈnɔɪdl
AM ˌkraɪˈnɔɪdəl, ˌkrɪˈnɔɪdəl
crinoline
BR ˈkrɪnəlɪn, ˈkrɪnl̩ɪn, -z
AM ˈkrɪn(ə)lɪn, ˈkrɪn(ə)ˌlin, -z
criolla
BR krɪˈəʊlə(r), -z
AM kriˈoʊlə, -z
criollo
BR krɪˈəʊləʊ, -z
AM kriˈoʊˌloʊ, -z
cripes!
BR krʌɪps
AM kraɪps
Crippen
BR ˈkrɪp(ɪ)n
AM ˈkrɪpən
cripple
BR ˈkrɪp|l, -lz, -l̩ɪŋ\-lɪŋ, -ld
AM ˈkrɪp|əl, -əlz, -(ə)lɪŋ, -əld
crippledom
BR ˈkrɪpldəm
AM ˈkrɪpəldəm
cripplehood
BR ˈkrɪplhʊd
AM ˈkrɪpəlˌ(h)ʊd
crippler
BR ˈkrɪplə(r), ˈkrɪpl̩ə(r), -z
AM ˈkrɪp(ə)lər, -z
cripplingly
BR ˈkrɪplɪŋli
AM ˈkrɪp(ə)lɪŋli
Cripps
BR krɪps
AM krɪps
Cris
BR kriːs, -ɪz
AM krɪs, -ɪz
cris de coeur
BR ˌkriː də ˈkəː(r)
AM ˌkri də ˈkər
crises
BR ˈkrʌɪsiːz
AM ˈkraɪˌsiz
crisis
BR ˈkrʌɪsɪs
AM ˈkraɪsɪs
crisp
BR krɪsp, -s, -ɪŋ, -t, -ə(r), -ɪst
AM krɪsp, -s, -ɪŋ, -t, -ər, -ɪst
crispate
BR ˈkrɪspeɪt
AM ˈkrɪsˌpeɪt
crispbread
BR ˈkrɪspbrɛd, -z
AM ˈkrɪs(p)ˌbrɛd, -z
crisper
BR ˈkrɪspə(r), -z
AM ˈkrɪspər, -z
Crispian
BR ˈkrɪspɪən
AM ˈkrɪspiən
Crispin
BR ˈkrɪspɪn
AM ˈkrɪspən
crispiness
BR ˈkrɪspɪnɪs
AM ˈkrɪspinɪs
crisply
BR ˈkrɪspli
AM ˈkrɪs(p)li
crispness
BR ˈkrɪspnɪs
AM ˈkrɪs(p)nɪs
crispy
BR ˈkrɪspi
AM ˈkrɪspi
crisscross
BR ˈkrɪskrɒs, -ɪz, -ɪŋ, -t
AM ˈkrɪsˌkrɔs, ˈkrɪsˌkrɑs, -əz, -ɪŋ, -t
crista
BR ˈkrɪstə(*r*)
AM ˈkrɪstə
cristae
BR ˈkrɪstiː
AM ˈkrɪsˌteɪ, ˈkrɪsˌtaɪ, ˈkrɪsti
cristate
BR ˈkrɪsteɪt
AM ˈkrɪˌsteɪt
cristobalite
BR krɪˈstəʊbəlʌɪt
AM krɪˈstoʊbəˌlaɪt
crit
BR krɪt, -s
AM krɪt, -s
Critchley
BR ˈkrɪtʃli
AM ˈkrɪtʃli
criteria
BR krʌɪˈtɪərɪə(*r*)
AM kraɪˈtɪriə
criterial
BR krʌɪˈtɪərɪəl
AM kraɪˈtɪriəl
criterion
BR krʌɪˈtɪərɪən, -z
AM kraɪˈtɪriən, -z
critic
BR ˈkrɪtɪk, -s
AM ˈkrɪdɪk, -s
critical
BR ˈkrɪtɪkl
AM ˈkrɪdəkəl
criticality
BR ˌkrɪtɪˈkalɪt|i, -ɪz
AM ˌkrɪdəˈkælədi, -z
critically
BR ˈkrɪtɪk(ə)li, ˈkrɪtɪkl̩i
AM ˈkrɪdək(ə)li
criticalness
BR ˈkrɪtɪklnəs
AM ˈkrɪdəkəlnəs
criticaster
BR ˌkrɪtɪˈkastə(r), ˈkrɪtɪkastə(r), -z
AM ˈkrɪdəˌkæstər, -z
criticisable
BR ˈkrɪtɪsʌɪzəbl
AM ˈkrɪdəˌsaɪzəbəl
criticise
BR ˈkrɪtɪsʌɪz, -ɪz, -ɪŋ, -d
AM ˈkrɪdəˌsaɪz, -ɪz, -ɪŋ, -d
criticiser
BR ˈkrɪtɪsʌɪzə(r), -z
AM ˈkrɪdəˌsaɪzər, -z
criticism
BR ˈkrɪtɪsɪz(ə)m, -z
AM ˈkrɪdəˌsɪzəm, -z
criticizable
BR ˈkrɪtɪsʌɪzəbl
AM ˈkrɪdəˌsaɪzəbəl
criticize
BR ˈkrɪtɪsʌɪz, -ɪz, -ɪŋ, -d
AM ˈkrɪdəˌsaɪz, -ɪz, -ɪŋ, -d
criticizer
BR ˈkrɪtɪsʌɪzə(r), -z
AM ˈkrɪdəˌsaɪzər, -z
critique
BR krɪˈtiːk, -s
AM krɪˈtik, -s
Crittall
BR ˈkrɪtɔːl
AM ˈkrɪdɔl, ˈkrɪdɑl
critter
BR ˈkrɪtə(r), -z
AM ˈkrɪdər, -z
croak
BR krəʊk, -s, -ɪŋ, -t
AM kroʊk, -s, -ɪŋ, -t
croaker
BR ˈkrəʊkə(r), -z
AM ˈkroʊkər, -z
croakily
BR ˈkrəʊkɪli
AM ˈkroʊkəli
croakiness
BR ˈkrəʊkɪnɪs
AM ˈkroʊkinɪs
croaky
BR ˈkrəʊk|i, -ɪə(r), -ɪɪst
AM ˈkroʊki, -ər, -ɪst
Croat
BR ˈkrəʊat, -s
AM ˈkroʊˌɑt, -s
Croatia
BR krəʊˈeɪʃə(*r*)
AM kroʊˈeɪʃə
Croatian
BR krəʊˈeɪʃn, -z
AM kroʊˈeɪʃən, -z
croc
BR krɒk, -s
AM krɑk, -s
Croce
BR ˈkrəʊtʃeɪ
AM ˈkroʊtʃeɪ
croceate
BR ˈkrəʊsɪeɪt
AM ˈkroʊtʃiət
crochet
BR ˈkrəʊʃeɪ, -z, -ɪŋ, -d

AM kroʊ'ʃeɪ, -z, -ɪŋ, -d
crocheter
BR 'krəʊʃeɪə(r), -z
AM kroʊ'ʃeɪər, -z
croci
BR 'krəʊkʌɪ, 'krəʊki:
AM 'kroʊˌsaɪ, 'kroʊki
crocidolite
BR krə(ʊ)'sɪdəlʌɪt
AM kroʊ'sɪdəˌlaɪt
crock
BR krɒk, -s
AM krɑk, -s
Crocker
BR 'krɒkə(r)
AM 'krɑkər
crockery
BR 'krɒk(ə)ri
AM 'krɑk(ə)ri
crocket
BR 'krɒkɪt, -s
AM 'krɑkət, -s
Crockett
BR 'krɒkɪt
AM 'krɑkət
Crockford
BR 'krɒkfəd
AM 'krɑkfərd
crocodile
BR 'krɒkədʌɪl, -z
AM 'krɑkəˌdaɪl, -z
crocodilian
BR ˌkrɒkə'dɪlɪən, -z
AM ˌkrɑkə'dɪljən, ˌkrɑkə'dɪliən, -z
crocus
BR 'krəʊkəs, -ɪz
AM 'kroʊkəs, -ɪz
Croesus
BR 'kri:səs
AM 'krisəs
croft[1]
BR krɒft, -s
AM krɔft, -s
croft[2]
BR krɒft, -s
AM krɔft, krɑft, -s
crofter
BR krɒftə(r), -z
AM krɔftər, krɑftər, -z
Crofton
BR 'krɒft(ə)n
AM 'krɑft(ə)n
Crohn's disease
BR 'krəʊnz dɪˌzi:z
AM 'kroʊnz dəˌziz
croissant
BR 'k(r)wasɒ̃, 'k(r)wɑ:sɒ̃, -z
AM ˈk(r)wɑˈsɑn(t), -z
Croker
BR 'krəʊkə(r)
AM 'kroʊkər
Cro-Magnon
BR krəʊ'manjɒ̃, krəʊ'manjɒn, krəʊ'magnən
AM kroʊ'mægnən, kroʊ'mænjən
Cromartie
BR 'krɒməti
AM ˌkroʊ'mɑrdi
Cromarty
BR 'krɒməti
AM ˌkroʊ'mɑrdi
crombec
BR 'krɒmbɛk, -s
AM 'krɑmˌbɛk, -s
Crombie
BR 'krɒmbi, 'krʌmbi
AM 'krɑmbi
Crome
BR krəʊm
AM kroʊm
Cromer
BR 'krəʊmə(r)
AM 'kroʊmər
Cromford
BR 'krɒmfəd
AM 'krɑmfərd
cromlech
BR 'krɒmləx, 'krɒmlək, -s
AM 'krɑmˌlɛk, -s
Crompton
BR 'krɒm(p)t(ə)n, 'krʌm(p)t(ə)n
AM 'krɑmtən
Cromwell
BR 'krɒmw(ɛ)l
AM 'krɑmwəl, 'krɑmˌwɛl
Cromwellian
BR krɒm'wɛlɪən
AM ˌkrɑm'wɛljən, ˌkrɑm'wɛliən
crone
BR krəʊn, -z
AM kroʊn, -z
Cronenberg
BR 'krɒnənbə:g
AM 'krɑnənˌbərg
Cronin
BR 'krəʊnɪn
AM 'kroʊnən
cronk
BR krɒŋk
AM krɑŋk
Cronus
BR 'krəʊnəs
AM 'kroʊnəs
crony
BR 'krəʊn|i, -ɪz
AM 'kroʊni, -z
cronyism
BR 'krəʊnɪɪz(ə)m
AM 'kroʊniˌɪzəm
crook
BR krʊk, -s, -ɪŋ, -t
AM krʊk, -s, -ɪŋ, -t
crookback
BR 'krʊkbak, -s
AM 'krʊkˌbæk, -s
Crooke
BR krʊk
AM krʊk
crooked
adjective
BR 'krʊkɪd, -ə(r), -ɪst
AM 'krʊkəd, -ər, -əst
crookedly
BR 'krʊkɪdli
AM 'krʊkədli
crookedness
BR 'krʊkɪdnɪs
AM 'krʊkədnəs
crookery
BR 'krʊk(ə)ri
AM 'krʊkəri
Crookes
BR krʊks
AM krʊks
Croom
BR kru:m
AM krum
Croome
BR kru:m
AM krum
croon
BR kru:n, -z, -ɪŋ, -d
AM krun, -z, -ɪŋ, -d
crooner
BR 'kru:nə(r), -z
AM 'krunər, -z
crop
BR krɒp, -s, -ɪŋ, -t
AM krɑp, -s, -ɪŋ, -t
cropper
BR 'krɒpə(r), -z
AM 'krɑpər, -z
croquet
BR 'krəʊkeɪ, 'krəʊki
AM ˌkroʊ'keɪ
croquette
BR krɒ'kɛt, krə'kɛt, -s
AM ˌkroʊ'kɛt, -s
crore
BR krɔ:(r), -z
AM krɔ(ə)r, -z
Crosbie
BR 'krɒzbi
AM 'krɔzbi, 'krɑzbi
Crosby
BR 'krɒzbi, 'krɒsbi
AM 'krɔzbi, 'krɑzbi
crosier
BR 'krəʊzɪə(r), 'krəʊʒə(r), -z
AM 'kroʊʒər, -z
Crosland
BR 'krɒslənd
AM 'krɔslənd, 'krɑslənd
cross
BR krɒs, -ɪz, -ɪŋ, -t
AM krɔs, krɑs, -əs, -ɪŋ, -t
crossbar
BR 'krɒsbɑ:(r), -z
AM 'krɔsˌbɑr, 'krɑsˌbɑr, -z
crossbeam
BR 'krɒsbi:m, -z
AM 'krɔsˌbim, 'krɑsˌbim, -z
crossbench
BR 'krɒsbɛn(t)ʃ, -ɪz
AM 'krɔsˌbɛn(t)ʃ, 'krɑsˌbɛn(t)ʃ, -əz
cross-bencher
BR 'krɒsˌbɛn(t)ʃə(r), -z
AM 'krɔsˌbɛn(t)ʃər, 'krɑsˌbɛn(t)ʃər, -z
crossbill
BR 'krɒsbɪl, -z
AM 'krɔsˌbɪl, 'krɑsˌbɪl, -z
crossbones
BR 'krɒsbəʊnz
AM 'krɔsˌboʊnz, 'krɑsˌboʊnz
crossbow
BR 'krɒsbəʊ, -z
AM 'krɔsˌboʊ, 'krɑsˌboʊ, -z
crossbowman
BR 'krɒsbəʊmən
AM 'krɔsˌboʊmən, 'krɑsˌboʊmən
crossbowmen
BR 'krɒsbəʊmən
AM 'krɔsˌboʊmən, 'krɑsˌboʊmən
crossbred
BR ˌkrɒs'brɛd, 'krɒsbrɛd
AM ˈkrɔsˈbrɛd, ˈkrɑsˈbrɛd
crossbreed
BR 'krɒsbri:d, -z, -ɪŋ
AM ˈkrɔsˈbrid, ˈkrɑsˈbrid, -z, -ɪŋ
crosscheck
BR ˌkrɒs'tʃɛk, 'krɒstʃɛk, -s, -ɪŋ, -t
AM 'krɔsˌtʃɛk, 'krɑsˌtʃɛk, -s, -ɪŋ, -t
crosscurrent
BR 'krɒsˌkʌrənt, 'krɒsˌkʌrn̩t, -s
AM 'krɔsˌkərənt, 'krɑsˌkərənt, -s
crosscut[1]
adjective, verb
BR 'krɒskʌt, ˌkrɒs'kʌt, -s, -ɪŋ
AM ˈkrɔsˈkə|t, ˈkrɑsˈkə|t, -ts, -dɪŋ
crosscut[2]
noun
BR 'krɒskʌt, -s
AM 'krɔsˌkət, 'krɑsˌkət, -s
crosse
BR krɒs, -ɪz
AM krɔs, krɑs, -əz

crossfield
BR ˌkrɒsˈfiːld
AM ˈkrɔsˌfild, ˈkrɑsˌfild

crossfire
BR ˈkrɒsfʌɪə(r)
AM ˈkrɔsˌfaɪ(ə)r, ˈkrɑsˌfaɪ(ə)r

crosshatch[1]
noun
BR ˈkrɒshatʃ, -ɪz
AM ˈkrɔsˌ(h)ætʃ, ˈkrɑsˌ(h)ætʃ, -əz

crosshatch[2]
verb
BR ˌkrɒsˈhatʃ, -ɪz, -ɪŋ, -t
AM ˈkrɔsˌ(h)ætʃ, ˈkrɑsˌ(h)ætʃ, -əz, -ɪŋ, -t

crossing
BR ˈkrɒsɪŋ, -z
AM ˈkrɔsɪŋ, ˈkrɑsɪŋ, -z

Crossland
BR ˈkrɒslənd
AM ˈkrɔslənd, ˈkrɑslənd

cross-legged
BR ˌkrɒsˈlɛg(ɪ)d
AM ˈkrɔsˌlɛg(ə)d

Crossley
BR ˈkrɒsli
AM ˈkrɔsli, ˈkrɑsli

crossly
BR ˈkrɒsli
AM ˈkrɔsli, ˈkrɑsli

Crossmaglen
BR ˌkrɒsməˈglɛn
AM ˌkrɔsməˈglɛn, ˌkrɑsməˈglɛn

Crossman
BR ˈkrɒsmən
AM ˈkrɔsmən, ˈkrɑsmən

crossmatch
BR ˌkrɒsˈmatʃ, -ɪz, -ɪŋ, -t
AM ˈkrɔsˌmætʃ, ˈkrɑsˌmætʃ, -əz, -ɪŋ, -t

crossness
BR ˈkrɒsnəs
AM ˈkrɔsnəs, ˈkrɑsnəs

crossover
BR ˈkrɒsəʊvə(r), -z
AM ˈkrɔsˌoʊvər, ˈkrɑsˌoʊvər, -z

crosspatch
BR ˈkrɒspatʃ, -ɪz
AM ˈkrɔsˌpætʃ, ˈkrɑsˌpætʃ, -əz

crosspiece
BR ˈkrɒspiːs, -ɪz
AM ˈkrɔsˌpis, ˈkrɑsˌpis, -ɪz

crossply
BR ˈkrɒsplʌɪ, -z
AM ˈkrɔsˌplaɪ, ˈkrɑsˌplaɪ, -z

crossrail
BR ˈkrɒsreɪl, -z
AM ˈkrɔsˌreɪl, ˈkrɑsˌreɪl, -z

crossroad
BR ˈkrɒsrəʊd, -z
AM ˈkrɔsˌroʊd, ˈkrɑsˌroʊd, -z

crosstab
BR ˈkrɒstab, -z
AM ˈkrɔsˌtæb, ˈkrɑsˌtæb, -z

crosstalk
BR ˈkrɒstɔːk
AM ˈkrɔsˌtɔk, ˈkrɑsˌtɑk

crosstie
BR ˈkrɒstʌɪ, -z
AM ˈkrɔsˌtaɪ, ˈkrɑsˌtaɪ, -z

crosstown
BR ˌkrɒsˈtaʊn
AM ˌkrɔsˈtaʊn, ˌkrɑsˈtaʊn

crosstree
BR ˈkrɒstriː, -z
AM ˈkrɔsˌtri, ˈkrɑsˌtri, -z

crosswalk
BR ˈkrɒswɔːk, -s
AM ˈkrɔsˌwɔk, ˈkrɑsˌwɑk, -s

crossways
BR ˈkrɒsweɪz
AM ˈkrɔsˌweɪz, ˈkrɑsˌweɪz

crosswind
BR ˈkrɒswɪnd, -z
AM ˈkrɔsˌwɪnd, ˈkrɑsˌwɪnd, -z

crosswise
BR ˈkrɒswʌɪz
AM ˈkrɔsˌwaɪz, ˈkrɑsˌwaɪz

crossword
BR ˈkrɒswəːd, -z
AM ˈkrɔswərd, ˈkrɑswərd, -z

crotch
BR krɒtʃ, -ɪz
AM krɑtʃ, -əz

crotchet
BR ˈkrɒtʃɪt, -s
AM ˈkrɑtʃət, -s

crotchetiness
BR ˈkrɒtʃɪtɪnɪs
AM ˈkrɑtʃədinɪs

crotchety
BR ˈkrɒtʃɪti
AM ˈkrɑtʃədi

croton
BR ˈkrəʊtn, -z
AM ˈkroʊtn, -z

crouch
BR kraʊtʃ, -ɪz, -ɪŋ, -t
AM kraʊtʃ, -əz, -ɪŋ, -t

croup
BR kruːp, -s
AM krup, -s

croupier
BR ˈkruːpɪeɪ, ˈkruːpɪə(r), -z
AM ˈkrupiˌeɪ, ˈkrupiər, -z

croupy
BR ˈkruːpi
AM ˈkrupi

croustade
BR krʊˈstɑːd, -z
AM ˌkrʊˈstɑd, -z

croûton
BR ˈkruːtɒn, -z
AM ˈkruˌtɑn, -z

crow
BR krəʊ, -z, -ɪŋ, -d
AM kroʊ, -z, -ɪŋ, -d

crowbar
BR ˈkrəʊbɑː(r), -z
AM ˈkroʊˌbɑr, -z

crowberry
BR ˈkrəʊb(ə)r|i, -ɪz
AM ˈkroʊˌbɛri, -z

Crowborough
BR ˈkrəʊb(ə)rə(*r*)
AM ˈkroʊˌbəroʊ, ˈkroʊbərə

crowd
BR kraʊd, -z, -ɪŋ, -ɪd
AM kraʊd, -z, -ɪŋ, -əd

crowdedness
BR ˈkraʊdɪdnɪs
AM ˈkraʊdədnɪs

crowd-pleaser
BR ˈkraʊdˌpliːzə(r), -z
AM ˈkraʊdˌplizər, -z

Crowe
BR krəʊ
AM kroʊ

crowfoot
BR ˈkrəʊfʊt, -s
AM ˈkroʊˌfʊt, -s

Crowley
BR ˈkrəʊli
AM ˈkraʊli

crown
BR kraʊn, -z, -ɪŋ, -d
AM kraʊn, -z, -ɪŋ, -d

crownpiece
BR ˈkraʊnpiːs, -ɪz
AM ˈkraʊnˌpis, -ɪz

Crowther
BR ˈkraʊðə(r)
AM ˈkraʊðər

Crowthorne
BR ˈkrəʊθɔːn
AM ˈkroʊˌθɔ(ə)rn

Croydon
BR ˈkrɔɪdn
AM ˈkrɔɪdən

crozier
BR ˈkrəʊzɪə(r), ˈkrəʊʒə(r), -z
AM ˈkroʊʒər, -z

cru
BR kruː, -z
AM kru, -z

cruces
BR ˈkruːsiːz
AM ˈkrusiz

crucial
BR ˈkruːʃl
AM ˈkruʃəl

cruciality
BR ˌkruːʃɪˈalɪti
AM ˌkruʃiˈælədi

crucially
BR ˈkruːʃḷi, ˈkruːʃəli
AM ˈkruʃəli

crucian
BR ˈkruːʃn
AM ˈkruʃən

cruciate
BR ˈkruːʃɪət, ˈkruːʃɪeɪt
AM ˈkruʃ(i)ət, ˈkruʃieɪt

crucible
BR ˈkruːsɪbl, -z
AM ˈkrusəbəl, -z

crucifer
BR ˈkruːsɪfə(r), -z
AM ˈkrusəfər, -z

cruciferous
BR kruːˈsɪf(ə)rəs
AM kruˈsɪf(ə)rəs

crucifier
BR ˈkruːsɪfʌɪə(r), -z
AM ˈkrusəˌfaɪər, -z

crucifix
BR ˈkruːsɪfɪks, -ɪz
AM ˈkrusəˌfɪks, -ɪz

crucifixion
BR ˌkruːsɪˈfɪkʃn, -z
AM ˌkrusəˈfɪkʃən, -z

cruciform
BR ˈkruːsɪfɔːm
AM ˈkrusəˌfɔ(ə)rm

crucify
BR ˈkruːsɪfʌɪ, -z, -ɪŋ, -d
AM ˈkrusəˌfaɪ, -z, -ɪŋ, -d

cruck
BR krʌk, -s
AM krək, -s

crud
BR krʌd
AM krəd

cruddy
BR ˈkrʌd|i, -ɪə(r), -ɪɪst
AM ˈkrədi, -ər, -ɪst

crude
BR kruːd, -ə(r), -ɪst
AM krud, -ər, -əst

crudely
BR ˈkruːdli
AM ˈkrudli

crudeness
BR ˈkruːdnəs
AM ˈkrudnəs

crudités
BR ˌkruːdɪˈteɪ
AM ˌkrudəˈteɪ

crudity
BR ˈkruːdɪt|i, -ɪz
AM ˈkrudədi, -z

cruel
BR 'kru:(ə)l, -ə(r), -ɨst
AM 'kru(ə)l, -ər, -əst
cruelly
BR 'kru:(ə)li
AM 'kru(ə)li
cruelness
BR 'kru:(ə)lnəs
AM 'kru(ə)lnəs
cruelty
BR 'kru:(ə)lt|i, -ɪz
AM 'kru(ə)lti, -z
cruet
BR 'kru:ɪt, -s
AM 'kruət, -s
Crufts
BR krʌfts
AM krəf(t)s
Cruikshank
BR 'krʊkʃaŋk
AM 'krʊk,ʃæŋk
cruise
BR kru:z, -ɪz, -ɪŋ, -d
AM kruz, -əz, -ɪn, -d
cruiser
BR 'kru:zə(r), -z
AM 'kruzər, -z
cruiserweight
BR 'kru:zəweɪt, -s
AM 'kruzər,weɪt, -s
cruiseway
BR 'kru:zweɪ, -z
AM 'kruz,weɪ, -z
cruller
BR 'krʌlə(r), -z
AM 'krələr, -z
crumb
BR krʌm, -z
AM krəm, -z
crumble
BR 'krʌmb|l, -lz, -l̩ɪŋ\-lɪŋ, -ld
AM 'krəmb|əl, -əlz, -(ə)lɪŋ, -əld
crumbliness
BR 'krʌmblɪnɪs
AM 'krəmblinɪs
crumbly
BR 'krʌmbli
AM 'krəmbli
crumby
BR 'krʌm|i, -ɪə(r), -ɪɪst
AM 'krəmi, -ər, -ɨst
crumhorn
BR 'krʌmhɔ:n, -z
AM 'krəm,(h)ɔ(ə)rn, -z
Crumlin
BR 'krʌmlɪn
AM 'krəmlən
crummily
BR 'krʌmɨli
AM 'krəməli
crumminess
BR 'krʌmɪnɪs
AM 'krəminɪs
crummy
BR 'krʌm|i, -ɪə(r), -ɪɪst
AM 'krəmi, -ər, -ɨst
crump
BR 'krʌm|p, -ps, -pɪŋ, -(p)t
AM 'krəm|p, -ps, -pɪŋ, -(p)t
crumpet
BR 'krʌmpɪt, -s
AM 'krəmpət, -s
crumple
BR 'krʌmp|l, -lz, -l̩ɪŋ\-lɪŋ, -ld
AM 'krəmp|əl, -əlz, -(ə)lɪŋ, -əld
crumply
BR 'krʌmpl|i, -ɪə(r), -ɪɪst
AM 'krəmp(ə)li, -ər, -ɨst
crunch
BR krʌn(t)ʃ, -ɪz, -ɪŋ, -t
AM krən(t)ʃ, -əz, -ɪŋ, -t
cruncher
BR 'krʌn(t)ʃə(r), -z
AM 'krən(t)ʃər, -z
Crunchie®
BR 'krʌ(t)ʃ|i, -ɪz
AM 'krən(t)ʃi, -z
crunchily
BR 'krʌn(t)ʃɨli
AM 'krən(t)ʃəli
crunchiness
BR 'krʌn(t)ʃɪnɪs
AM 'krən(t)ʃinɪs
crunchy
BR 'krʌn(t)ʃ|i, -ɪə(r), -ɪɪst
AM 'krən(t)ʃi, -ər, -ɨst
crupper
BR 'krʌpə(r), -z
AM 'krəpər, -z
crural
BR 'krʊərəl, 'krʊərl̩
AM 'krʊrəl
crusade
BR kru:'seɪd, -z, -ɪŋ, -ɨd
AM kru'seɪd, -z, -ɪŋ, -ɨd
crusader
BR kru:'seɪdə(r), -z
AM kru'seɪdər, -z
cruse
BR kru:z, -ɪz
AM kruz, -əz
crush
BR krʌʃ, -ɪz, -ɪŋ, -t
AM krəʃ, -əz, -ɪŋ, -t
crushable
BR 'krʌʃəbl
AM 'krəʃəbəl
crusher
BR 'krʌʃə(r), -z
AM 'krəʃər, -z
crushingly
BR 'krʌʃɪŋli
AM 'krəʃɪŋli
Crusoe
BR 'kru:səʊ
AM 'krusoʊ
crust
BR krʌst, -s
AM krəst, -s
crustacea
BR krʌ'steɪʃə(r)
AM krə'steɪʃə
crustacean
BR krʌ'steɪʃn, -z
AM krə'steɪʃən, -z
crustaceology
BR krʌ,steɪʃɪ'ɒlədʒi
AM krə,steɪʃi'ɑlədʒi
crustaceous
BR krʌ'steɪʃəs
AM krə'steɪʃəs
crustal
BR 'krʌstl
AM 'krəstəl
crustily
BR 'krʌstɨli
AM 'krəstəli
crustiness
BR 'krʌstɪnɪs
AM 'krəstinɪs
crustose
BR 'krʌstəʊs
AM 'krəs,toʊs
crusty
BR 'krʌst|i, -ɪə(r), -ɪɪst
AM 'krəsti, -ər, -ɨst
crutch
BR krʌtʃ, -ɪz
AM krətʃ, -əz
Cruttenden
BR 'krʌtndən
AM 'krətnd(ə)n
crux
BR krʌks, -ɪz
AM krəks, -əz
Cruyff
BR krɔɪf
AM krɔɪf
DU krœyf
Cruz
BR kru:z
AM kruz
cruzado
BR krʊ'zɑ:dəʊ, -z
AM krʊ'zɑdoʊ, -z
cruzeiro
BR krʊ'zɛ:rəʊ, -z
AM krʊ'zɛroʊ, -z
cry
BR krʌɪ, -z, -ɪŋ, -d
AM kraɪ, -z, -ɪŋ, -d
crybaby
BR 'krʌɪ,beɪb|i, -ɪz
AM 'kraɪ,beɪbi, -z
cryer
BR 'krʌɪə(r), -z
AM 'kraɪ(ə)r, -z
cryobiological
BR ,krʌɪəʊ,bʌɪə'lɒdʒɪkl
AM ,kraɪoʊ,baɪə'lɑdʒəkəl
cryobiologist
BR ,krʌɪəʊbʌɪ'ɒlədʒɪst, -s
AM ,kraɪoʊ,baɪ'ɑlədʒəst, -s
cryobiology
BR ,krʌɪəʊbʌɪ'ɒlədʒi
AM ,kraɪoʊ,baɪ'ɑlədʒi
cryogen
BR 'krʌɪə(ʊ)dʒ(ə)n, 'krʌɪə(ʊ)dʒɛn, -z
AM 'kraɪədʒən, -z
cryogenic
BR ,krʌɪə(ʊ)'dʒɛnɪk, -s
AM ,kraɪoʊ'dʒɛnɪk, -s
cryolite
BR 'krʌɪə(ʊ)lʌɪt
AM 'kraɪə,laɪt
cryonics
BR krʌɪ'ɒnɪks
AM ,kraɪ'ɑnɪks
cryopump
BR 'krʌɪə(ʊ)pʌmp, -s
AM 'kraɪə,pəmp, -s
cryostat
BR 'krʌɪə(ʊ)stat, -s
AM 'kraɪə,stæt, -s
cryosurgery
BR ,krʌɪəʊ'sə:dʒ(ə)ri
AM ,kraɪoʊ'sərdʒ(ə)ri
crypt
BR krɪpt, -s
AM krɪpt, -s
cryptanalysis
BR ,krɪptə'nalɪsɪs
AM ,krɪptə'næləsəs
cryptanalyst
BR ,krɪpt'anəlɪst, -s
AM ,krɪpt'ænələst, -s
cryptanalytic
BR ,krɪptanə'lɪtɪk
AM ,krɪpt,ænə'lɪdɪk
cryptanalytical
BR ,krɪptanə'lɪtɪkl
AM ,krɪpt,ænə'lɪdəkəl
cryptic
BR 'krɪptɪk
AM 'krɪptɪk
cryptically
BR 'krɪptɪkli
AM 'krɪptək(ə)li
crypto
BR 'krɪptəʊ, 'krɪptə(r), -z
AM 'krɪp,toʊ, -z
cryptocrystalline
BR ,krɪptəʊ'krɪstəlʌɪn, ,krɪptəʊ'krɪstl̩ʌɪn
AM ,krɪp,toʊ'krɪstə,laɪn, ,krɪptə'krɪstə,laɪn, ,krɪp,toʊ'krɪstələn, ,krɪptə'krɪstələn
cryptogam
BR 'krɪptəgam, -z
AM 'krɪptə,gæm, -z
cryptogamic
BR ,krɪptə'gamɪk
AM ,krɪptə'gæmɪk

cryptogamous
BR krɪp'tɒgəməs
AM krɪp'tɑgəməs

cryptogram
BR 'krɪptəgram, -z
AM 'krɪptə,græm, -z

cryptographer
BR krɪp'tɒgrəfə(r)
AM krɪp'tɑgrəfər

cryptographic
BR ,krɪptə'grafɪk
AM ,krɪptə'græfɪk

cryptographically
BR ,krɪptə'grafɨkli
AM ,krɪptə'græfək(ə)li

cryptography
BR krɪp'tɒgrəfi
AM krɪp'tɑgrəfi

cryptologist
BR krɪp'tɒlədʒɪst, -s
AM krɪp'tɑlədʒəst, -s

cryptology
BR krɪp'tɒlədʒi
AM krɪp'tɑlədʒi

cryptomeria
BR ,krɪptə'mɪərɪə(r), -z
AM ,krɪptə'mɪriə, -z

cryptosporidia
BR ,krɪptəʊspə'rɪdɪə(r)
AM ,krɪptəspə'rɪdiə

cryptosporidium
BR ,krɪptəʊspə'rɪdɪəm
AM ,krɪptəspə'rɪdiəm

cryptozoic
BR ,krɪptə(ʊ)'zəʊɪk
AM ,krɪptə'zoʊɪk

crystal
BR 'krɪstl, -z
AM 'krɪstl, -z

crystalline
BR 'krɪstəlʌɪn, 'krɪstl̩ʌɪn
AM 'krɪstələn, 'krɪstə,laɪn

crystallinity
BR ,krɪstə'lɪnɨti
AM ,krɪstə'lɪnɨdi

crystallisable
BR 'krɪstəlʌɪzəbl, 'krɪstl̩ʌɪzəbl
AM ¦krɪstə¦laɪzəbəl

crystallisation
BR ,krɪstəlʌɪ'zeɪʃn, ,krɪstl̩ʌɪ'zeɪʃn
AM ,krɪstələ'zeɪʃən, ,krɪstə,laɪ'zeɪʃən

crystallise
BR 'krɪstəlʌɪz, 'krɪstl̩ʌɪz, -ɨz, -ɪŋ, -d
AM 'krɪstə,laɪz, -ɨz, -ɪŋ, -d

crystallite
BR 'krɪstəlʌɪt, 'krɪstl̩ʌɪt, -s
AM 'krɪstə,laɪt, -s

crystallizable
BR 'krɪstəlʌɪzəbl, 'krɪstl̩ʌɪzəbl
AM ¦krɪstə¦laɪzəbəl

crystallization
BR ,krɪstəlʌɪ'zeɪʃn, ,krɪstl̩ʌɪ'zeɪʃn
AM ,krɪstələ'zeɪʃən, ,krɪstə,laɪ'zeɪʃən

crystallize
BR 'krɪstəlʌɪz, 'krɪstl̩ʌɪz, -ɨz, -ɪŋ, -d
AM 'krɪstə,laɪz, -ɨz, -ɪŋ, -d

crystallographer
BR ,krɪstə'lɒgrəfə(r), ,krɪstl'ɒgrəfə(r), -z
AM ,krɪstə'lɑgrəfər, -z

crystallographic
BR ,krɪstələ'grafɪk, ,krɪstl̩ə'grafɪk
AM ,krɪstələ'græfɪk

crystallography
BR ,krɪstə'lɒgrəfi, ,krɪstl'ɒgrəfi
AM ,krɪstə'lɑgrəfi

crystalloid
BR 'krɪstəlɔɪd, 'krɪstl̩ɔɪd, -z
AM 'krɪstə,lɔɪd, -z

csárdás
BR 'tʃɑːdaʃ, -ɨz
AM 'tʃɑrdɑʃ, -əz
HU 'tʃɑːrdɑːʃ

ctenoid
BR 'tiːnɔɪd, 'tɛnɔɪd
AM 'ti,nɔɪd, 'tɛ,nɔɪd

ctenophore
BR 'tiːnəfɔː(r), 'tɛnəfɔː(r), -z
AM 'tɛnə,fɔ(ə)r, -z

Ctesiphon
BR 'tɛsɨfɒn
AM 'tɛsə,fɑn

cuadrilla
BR kwɒ'driː(l)jə(r), -z
AM kwə'dri(l)jə, -z

cub
BR kʌb, -z, -ɪŋ, -d
AM kəb, -z, -ɪŋ, -d

Cuba
BR 'kjuːbə(r)
AM 'kjubə

Cuban
BR 'kjuːbən, -z
AM 'kjubən, -z

Cubango
BR kjuː'baŋgəʊ
AM kju'bæŋgoʊ

cubby
BR 'kʌb|i, -ɪz
AM 'kəbi, -z

cubbyhole
BR 'kʌbɪhəʊl, -z
AM 'kəbi,(h)oʊl, -z

cube
BR kjuːb, -z, -ɪŋ, -d
AM kjub, -z, -ɪŋ, -d

cubeb
BR 'kjuːbɛb, -z
AM 'kju,bɛb, -z

cuber
BR 'kjuːbə(r), -z
AM 'kjubər, -z

cubhood
BR 'kʌbhʊd
AM 'kəb,(h)ʊd

cubic
BR 'kjuːbɪk
AM 'kjubɪk

cubical
BR 'kjuːbɨkl
AM 'kjubəkəl

cubically
BR 'kjuːbɨkli
AM 'kjubək(ə)li

cubicle
BR 'kjuːbɨkl, -z
AM 'kjubəkəl, -z

cubiform
BR 'kjuːbɪfɔːm
AM 'kjubə,fɔ(ə)rm

cubism
BR 'kjuːbɪz(ə)m
AM 'kju,bɪzəm

cubist
BR 'kjuːbɪst, -s
AM 'kjubəst, -s

cubit
BR 'kjuːbɪt, -s
AM 'kjubət, -s

cubital
BR 'kjuːbɨtl
AM 'kjubədl

Cubitt
BR 'kjuːbɪt
AM 'kjubɪt

cuboid
BR 'kjuːbɔɪd
AM 'kju,bɔɪd

cuboidal
BR kjuː'bɔɪdl
AM kju'bɔɪdəl

cuce
cucumber
BR kjuːk, -s
AM kjuk, -s

Cúchulainn
BR kuː'kʌlən, kuː'xʌlən
AM ku'kələn
IR kuː'xulʲən

Cuckfield
BR 'kʌkfiːld
AM 'kək,fild

cucking-stool
BR 'kʌkɪŋstuːl, -z
AM 'kəkɪŋ,stul, -z

Cuckney
BR 'kʌkni
AM 'kəkni

cuckold
BR 'kʌkəʊld, 'kʌk(ə)ld, -z, -ɪŋ, -ɨd
AM 'kəkəld, -z, -ɪŋ, -əd

cuckoldry
BR 'kʌk(ə)ldri
AM 'kəkəldri

cuckoo
BR 'kʊkuː, -z
AM 'ku,ku, 'kʊ,ku, -z

cuckoo-spit
BR 'kʊkuːspɪt
AM 'kuku,spɪt, 'kʊku,spɪt

cucumber
BR 'kjuːkʌmbə(r), -z
AM 'kju,kəmbər, -z

cucurbit
BR kjuː'kəːbɪt, -s
AM kju'kərbət, -s

cucurbitaceous
BR kjuː,kəːbɪ'teɪʃəs
AM kju,kərbə'teɪʃəs

cud
BR kʌd
AM kəd

cudbear
BR 'kʌdbɛː(r)
AM 'kəd,bɛ(ə)r

cuddle
BR 'kʌd|l, -lz, -l̩ɪŋ\-lɪŋ, -ld
AM 'kəd|əl, -əlz, -(ə)lɪŋ, -əld

cuddlesome
BR 'kʌdls(ə)m
AM 'kədlsəm

cuddliness
BR 'kʌdlɪnɨs
AM 'kəd(ə)linɨs

cuddly
BR 'kʌdl|i, -ɪə(r), -ɪɪst
AM 'kəd(ə)li, -ər, -ɨst

cuddy
BR 'kʌdi
AM 'kədi

cudgel
BR 'kʌdʒ|(ə)l, -(ə)lz, -l̩ɪŋ\-əlɪŋ, -(ə)ld
AM 'kədʒ|əl, -əlz, -(ə)lɪŋ, -əld

Cudlipp
BR 'kʌdlɪp
AM 'kəd,lɪp

cudweed
BR 'kʌdwiːd
AM 'kəd,wid

cue
BR kjuː, -z, -ɪŋ, -d
AM kju, -z, -ɪŋ, -d

cueball
BR 'kjuːbɔːl, -z
AM 'kju,bɔl, 'kju,bɑl, -z

cueist
BR 'kjuːɪst, -s
AM 'kjuəst, -s

Cuenca
BR 'kwɛŋkə(r)
AM 'kwɛŋkə

cuesta
BR 'kwɛstə(r), -z

AM ˈkwɛstə, -z

cuff
BR kʌf, -s, -ɪŋ, -t
AM kəf, -s, -ɪŋ, -t

Cuffley
BR ˈkʌfli
AM ˈkəfli

cufflink
BR ˈkʌflɪŋk, -s
AM ˈkəfˌlɪŋk, -s

Cufic
BR ˈkjuːfɪk
AM ˈk(j)ufɪk

cui bono?
BR ˌkuːɪ ˈbəʊnəʊ, ˌkwiː +
AM ˌkwi ˈboʊnoʊ

Cuillin
BR ˈkuːlɪn, -z
AM ˈkulən, -z

cuirass
BR kwɪˈras, kjʊˈras, -ɪz
AM kwɪˈræs, kwiˈræs, -əz

cuirassier
BR ˌkwɪrəˈsɪə(r), ˌkjʊrəˈsɪə(r), -z
AM ˌkwɪrəˈsɪ(ə)r, ˌkjʊrəˈsɪ(ə)r, -z

cuish
BR kwɪʃ, -ɪz
AM kwɪʃ, -ɪz

cuisine
BR kwɪˈziːn
AM kwəˈzin, kwiˈzin

cuisse
BR kwɪs, -ɪz
AM kwɪs, -ɪz

Culbertson
BR ˈkʌlbəts(ə)n
AM ˈkəlbərts(ə)n

Culceth
BR ˈkʌltʃɪθ
AM ˈkəltʃəθ

Culdees
BR ˈkʌldiːz
AM ˈkəlˌdiz

cul-de-sac
BR ˈkʌldəsak, ˈkʊldəsak, -s
AM ˈkəldəˈsæk, -s

culinarily
BR ˈkʌlɪn(ə)rɪli
AM ˌkələˈnɛrəli, ˌkjuləˈnɛrəli

culinary
BR ˈkʌlɪn(ə)ri
AM ˈkələˌnɛri, ˈkjuləˌnɛri

cull
BR kʌl, -z, -ɪŋ, -d
AM kəl, -z, -ɪŋ, -d

Cullen
BR ˈkʌlɪn
AM ˈkələn

cullender
BR ˈkʌlɪndə(r), -z
AM ˈkələndər, -z

culler
BR ˈkʌlə(r), -z
AM ˈkələr, -z

cullet
BR ˈkʌlɪt
AM ˈkələt

Cullinan
BR ˈkʌlɪnən
AM ˈkələnən

Culloden
BR kəˈlɒdn
AM kəˈlɑdən

Cullompton
BR kəˈlʌm(p)t(ə)n
AM kəˈləm(p)tən

culm
BR kʌlm
AM kəlm

culmiferous
BR kʌlˈmɪf(ə)rəs
AM kəlˈmɪf(ə)rəs

culminant
BR ˈkʌlmɪnənt
AM ˈkəlmənənt

culminate
BR ˈkʌlmɪneɪt, -s, -ɪŋ, -ɪd
AM ˈkəlməˌneɪ|t, -ts, -dɪŋ, -dɪd

culmination
BR ˌkʌlmɪˈneɪʃn, -z
AM ˌkəlməˈneɪʃən, -z

culminative
BR ˈkʌlmɪnətɪv
AM ˈkəlməˌneɪdɪv, ˈkəlmənədɪv

culminatively
BR ˈkʌlmɪnətɪvli
AM ˈkəlməˌneɪdɪvli, ˈkəlmənədɪvli

culotte
BR kjʊˈlɒt, kjuːˈlɒt, -s
AM ˈk(j)uˌlɑt, -s

culpability
BR ˌkʌlpəˈbɪlɪti
AM ˌkəlpəˈbɪlɪdi

culpable
BR ˈkʌlpəbl
AM ˈkəlpəbəl

culpably
BR ˈkʌlpəbli
AM ˈkəlpəbli

Culpeper
BR ˈkʌlˌpɛpə(r)
AM ˈkəlˌpɛpər

Culpepper
BR ˈkʌlˌpɛpɛ(r)
AM ˈkəlˌpɛpər

culprit
BR ˈkʌlprɪt, -s
AM ˈkəlprət, -s

cult
BR kʌlt, -s
AM kəlt, -s

cultic
BR ˈkʌltɪk
AM ˈkəltɪk

cultigen
BR ˈkʌltɪdʒɛn, ˈkʌltɪdʒ(ə)n, -z
AM ˈkəltəˌdʒɛn, ˈkəltidʒən, -z

cultism
BR ˈkʌltɪz(ə)m
AM ˈkəlˌtɪzəm

cultist
BR ˈkʌltɪst, -s
AM ˈkəltəst, -s

cultivable
BR ˈkʌltɪvəbl
AM ˈkəltəvəbəl

cultivar
BR ˈkʌltɪvɑː(r), -z
AM ˈkəltəˌvɑr, -z

cultivatable
BR ˈkʌltɪveɪtəbl
AM ˈkəltəˌveɪdəbəl

cultivate
BR ˈkʌltɪveɪt, -s, -ɪŋ, -ɪd
AM ˈkəltəˌveɪ|t, -ts, -dɪŋ, -dɪd

cultivation
BR ˌkʌltɪˈveɪʃn
AM ˌkəltəˈveɪʃən

cultivator
BR ˈkʌltɪveɪtə(r), -z
AM ˈkəltəˌveɪdər, -z

cultural
BR ˈkʌltʃ(ə)rəl, ˈkʌltʃ(ə)rl̩
AM ˈkəltʃ(ə)rəl

culturalism
BR ˈkʌltʃ(ə)rəlɪz(ə)m, ˈkʌltʃ(ə)rl̩ɪz(ə)m
AM ˈkəltʃ(ə)rəˌlɪzəm

culturalist
BR ˈkʌltʃ(ə)rəlɪst, ˈkʌltʃ(ə)rl̩ɪst, -s
AM ˈkəltʃ(ə)rələst, -s

culturally
BR ˈkʌltʃ(ə)rəli, ˈkʌltʃ(ə)rl̩i
AM ˈkəltʃ(ə)rəli

culture
BR ˈkʌltʃə(r), -z, -d
AM ˈkəltʃər, -z, -d

cultus
BR ˈkʌltəs, -ɪz
AM ˈkəltəs, -əz

Culver
BR ˈkʌlvə(r)
AM ˈkəlvər

culverin
BR ˈkʌlv(ə)rɪn, -z
AM ˈkəlv(ə)rən, -z

culvert
BR ˈkʌlvət, -s, -ɪŋ, -ɪd
AM ˈkəlvər|t, -ts, -dɪŋ, -dəd

cum
BR kʌm
AM kəm

cumber
BR ˈkʌmb|ə(r), -əz, -(ə)rɪŋ, -əd
AM ˈkəmbər, -z, -ɪŋ, -d

Cumberland
BR ˈkʌmbələnd
AM ˈkəmbərlənd

Cumberledge
BR ˈkʌmbəlɪdʒ, ˈkʌmbəlɛdʒ
AM ˈkəmbərlədʒ

Cumbernauld
BR ˈkʌmbənɔːld, ˌkʌmbəˈnɔːld
AM ˈkəmbərˌnɔld, ˈkəmbərˌnɑld

cumbersome
BR ˈkʌmbəs(ə)m
AM ˈkəmbərsəm

cumbersomely
BR ˈkʌmbəs(ə)mli
AM ˈkəmbərsəmli

cumbersomeness
BR ˈkʌmbəs(ə)mnəs
AM ˈkəmbərsəmnəs

cumbia
BR ˈkʊmbɪə(r)
AM ˈkəmbiə

Cumbria
BR ˈkʌmbrɪə(r)
AM ˈkəmbriə

Cumbrian
BR ˈkʌmbrɪən, -z
AM ˈkəmbriən, -z

cumbrous
BR ˈkʌmbrəs
AM ˈkəmbrəs

cumbrously
BR ˈkʌmbrəsli
AM ˈkəmbrəsli

cumbrousness
BR ˈkʌmbrəsnəs
AM ˈkəmbrəsnəs

cum grano salis
BR kʌm ˌgrɑːnəʊ ˈseɪlɪs, kʊm +, + ˌgreɪnəʊ +, + ˈsɑːlɪs, + ˈsalɪs
AM ˌkəm ˌgrɑnoʊ ˈseɪlɪs, + ˈsæləs

cumin
BR ˈkʌmɪn, ˈk(j)uːmɪn
AM ˈkəmən, ˈk(j)umən

cummerbund
BR ˈkʌməbʌnd, -z
AM ˈkəmərˌbənd, -z

cummin
BR ˈkʌmɪn
AM ˈkəmən

Cumming
BR ˈkʌmɪŋ
AM ˈkəmɪŋ

Cummings
BR ˈkʌmɪŋz
AM ˈkəmɪŋz

Cummins
BR ˈkʌmɪnz
AM ˈkəmənz

Cumnock
BR 'kʌmnək
AM 'kəmnək

Cumnor
BR 'kʌmnə(r)
AM 'kəmnər

cumquat
BR 'kʌmkwɒt, -s
AM 'kəm,kwat, -s

cumulate
BR 'kju:mjʉleɪt, -s, -ɪŋ, -ɨd
AM 'kjumjə,leɪ|t, -ts, -dɪŋ, -dɨd

cumulation
BR ,kju:mjʉ'leɪʃn, -z
AM ,kjumjə'leɪʃən, -z

cumulative
BR 'kju:mjʉlətɪv
AM 'kjumjələdɪv, 'kjumjə,leɪdɪv

cumulatively
BR 'kju:mjʉlətɨvli
AM 'kjumjələdɨvli, 'kjumjə,leɪdɨvli

cumulativeness
BR 'kju:mjʉlətɨvnɨs
AM 'kjumjələdɨvnɨs, 'kjumjə,leɪdɨvnɨs

cumulonimbus
BR ,kju:mjʉləʊ'nɪmbəs
AM ,kjumjəloʊ'nɪmbəs

cumulostratus
BR ,kju:jʉləʊ'strɑ:təs, ,kju:mjʉləʊ'streɪtəs
AM ,kjumjəloʊ'streɪdəs, ,kjumjəloʊ'strædəs

cumulous
BR 'kju:mjʉləs
AM 'kjumjələs

cumulus
BR 'kju:mjʉləs
AM 'kjumjələs

Cunard
BR kju:'nɑ:d, kjʉ'nɑ:d, 'kju:nɑ:d
AM kju'nɑrd

cunctation
BR ,kʌŋ(k)'teɪʃn, -z
AM ,kəŋk'teɪʃən, -z

cunctator
BR 'kʌŋ(k)teɪtə(r), -z
AM 'kəŋ(k),teɪdər, -z

cuneal
BR 'kju:nɪəl
AM 'kjuniəl

cuneate
BR 'kju:nɪeɪt, 'kju:nɪət
AM 'kjuni,eɪt, 'kjuniət

cuneiform
BR 'kju:nɪfɔ:m
AM kju'niə,fɔ(ə)rm, 'kjuniə,fɔ(ə)rm, 'kjunə,fɔ(ə)rm

Cunene
BR ku:'neɪnə(r)
AM ku'neɪnə

Cuningham
BR 'kʌnɪŋəm
AM 'kənɪŋ,(h)æm

Cuninghame
BR 'kʌnɪŋəm
AM 'kənɪŋ,(h)æm

cunjevoi
BR 'kʌn(d)ʒɪvɔɪ, -z
AM 'kəndʒə,vɔɪ, -z

cunnilinctus
BR ,kʌnɪ'lɪŋ(k)təs
AM ,kənə'lɪŋ(k)təs

cunnilingus
BR ,kʌnɪ'lɪŋgəs
AM ,kənə'lɪŋgəs

cunning
BR 'kʌnɪŋ
AM 'kənɪŋ

Cunningham
BR 'kʌnɪŋəm
AM 'kənɪŋ,(h)æm

cunningly
BR 'kʌnɪŋli
AM 'kənɪŋli

cunningness
BR 'kʌnɪŋnɨs
AM 'kənɪŋnɨs

Cunobelinus
BR ,kju:nə(ʊ)bɪ'lʌɪnəs, ,kju:nə(ʊ)bɪ'li:nəs
AM ,kjunoʊbə'linəs

cunt
BR kʌnt, -s
AM kən|t, -(t)s

cup
BR kʌp, -s, -ɪŋ, -t
AM kəp, -s, -ɪŋ, -t

Cupar
BR 'ku:pə(r)
AM 'k(j)upər

cupbearer
BR 'kʌp,bɛ:rə(r), -z
AM 'kəp,bɛrər, -z

cupboard
BR 'kʌbəd, -z
AM 'kəbərd, -z

cupcake
BR 'kʌpkeɪk, -s
AM 'kəp,keɪk, -s

cupel
BR 'kju:pl, -z
AM kju'pɛl, 'kjupəl, -z

cupellation
BR ,kju:pɪ'leɪʃn
AM ,kjupə'leɪʃən

cupful
BR 'kʌpfʊl, -z
AM 'kəp,fʊl, -z

Cupid
BR 'kju:pɪd
AM 'kjupəd

cupid
BR 'kju:pɪd, -z
AM 'kjupəd, -z

cupidity
BR kju:'pɪdɨti, kjʉ'pɪdɨti
AM kju'pɪdɨdi

Cupit
BR 'kju:pɪt
AM 'kjupɪt

Cupitt
BR 'kju:pɪt
AM 'kjupɪt

cupola
BR 'kju:pələ(r), 'kju:pl̩ə(r), -z, -d
AM 'k(j)upələ, 'kəpələ, -z, -d

cupola-furnace
BR 'kju:pələ,fə:nɪs, 'kju:pl̩ə,fə:nɪs, -ɨz
AM 'k(j)upələ,fərnəs, 'kəpələ,fərnəs, -əz

cuppa
BR 'kʌpə(r), -z
AM 'kəpə, -z

cuprammonium
BR ,kju:prə'məʊnɪəm
AM ,k(j)uprə'moʊniəm

cupreous
BR 'kju:prɪəs
AM 'k(j)upriəs

cupric
BR 'kju:prɪk
AM 'k(j)uprɪk

cupriferous
BR kju:'prɪf(ə)rəs
AM k(j)u'prɪf(ə)rəs

Cuprinol®
BR 'kju:prɪnɒl
AM 'k(j)upri,nɑl

cupronickel
BR ,kju:prəʊ'nɪkl
AM ,k(j)uproʊ'nɪkəl

cuprous
BR 'kju:prəs
AM 'k(j)uprəs

cupule
BR 'kju:pju:l, -z
AM 'kjupjul, -z

cur
BR kə:(r), -z
AM kər, -z

curability
BR ,kjʊərə'bɪlɨti, ,kjɔ:rə'bɪlɨti
AM ,kjʊrə'bɪlɨdi

curable
BR 'kjʊərəbl, 'kjɔ:rəbl
AM 'kjʊrəbəl

curably
BR 'kjʊərəbli, 'kjɔ:rəbli
AM 'kjʊrəbli

Curacao
BR 'kjʊərəsəʊ, 'kjɔ:rəsəʊ, ,kjʊərə'səʊ, ,kjɔ:rə'səʊ
AM ¦k(j)ʊrə¦saʊ, ¦k(j)ʊrə¦soʊ

Curaçao
BR 'kjʊərəsəʊ, 'kjɔ:rəsəʊ, ,kjʊərə'səʊ, ,kjɔ:rə'səʊ
AM ¦k(j)ʊrə¦saʊ, ¦k(j)ʊrə¦soʊ

curacy
BR 'kjʊərəs|i, 'kjɔ:rəs|i, -ɪz
AM 'kjʊrəsi, -z

curare
BR kjʉ'rɑ:ri
AM kjʊ'rɑri

curari
BR kjʉ'rɑ:ri
AM kjʊ'rɑri

curarine
BR 'kjʊərəri:n, 'kjɔ:rəri:n, kjʉ'rɑ:ri:n
AM kjʊ'rɑ,rin, 'kjʊrɑrən

curarise
BR 'kjʊərərʌɪz, 'kjɔ:rərʌɪz, -ɨz, -ɪŋ, -d
AM 'kjʊrə,raɪz, -ɨz, -ɪŋ, -d

curarize
BR 'kjʊərərʌɪz, 'kjɔ:rərʌɪz, -ɨz, -ɪŋ, -d
AM 'kjʊrə,raɪz, -ɨz, -ɪŋ, -d

curassow
BR 'kjʊərəsəʊ, 'kjɔ:rəsəʊ, -z
AM ¦k(j)ʊrə¦saʊ, ¦k(j)ʊrə¦soʊ, -z

curate
BR 'kjʊərət, 'kjɔ:rət, -s
AM 'kjʊrət, -s

curation
BR kjʉ'reɪʃn
AM kjə'reɪʃən

curative
BR 'kjʊərətɪv, 'kjɔ:rətɪv
AM 'kjʊrədɪv

curator
BR kjʉ'reɪtə(r), -z
AM 'kjʊ,reɪdər, -z

curatorial
BR ,kjʊərə'tɔ:rɪəl, ,kjɔ:rə'tɔ:rɪəl
AM ,kjʊrə'tɔriəl

curatorship
BR kjʉ'reɪtəʃɪp, -s
AM 'kjʊ,reɪdər,ʃɪp, -s

curb
BR kə:b, -z, -ɪŋ, -d
AM kərb, -z, -ɪŋ, -d

curbside
BR 'kə:bsʌɪd
AM 'kərb,saɪd

curbstone
BR 'kə:bstəʊn, -z
AM 'kərb,stoʊn, -z

curcuma
BR 'kə:kjʉmə(r), -z
AM 'kərkjəmə, -z

curd
BR kəːd, -z
AM kərd, -z

curdle
BR 'kəːd|l, -lz, -l̩ɪŋ\-lɪŋ, -ld
AM 'kərd|əl, -əlz, -(ə)lɪŋ, -əld

curdler
BR 'kəːdlə(r), -z
AM 'kərd(ə)lər, -z

curdy
BR 'kəːdi
AM 'kərdi

cure
BR 'kjʊə(r), kjɔː(r), -z, -ɪŋ, -d
AM 'kjʊ(ə)r, -z, -ɪŋ, -d

curé
BR 'kjʊəreɪ, 'kjɔːreɪ, -z
AM kjə'reɪ, kjʊ'reɪ, -z

curer
BR 'kjʊərə(r), 'kjɔːrə(r), -z
AM 'kjʊrər, -z

curettage
BR kjʉ'rɛtɪdʒ, ˌkjʊərɪ'tɑːʒ, ˌkjɔːrɪ'tɑːʒ
AM ˌkjʊrə'tɑʒ

curette
BR kjʉ'rɛt, -s
AM kjʊ'rɛt, -s

curfew
BR 'kəːfjuː, -z
AM 'kərˌfju, -z

curia
BR 'kjʊərɪə(r), 'kjɔːrɪə(r)
AM 'kjʊriə

Curial
BR 'kjʊərɪəl, 'kjɔːrɪəl
AM 'kjʊriəl

curie
BR 'kjʊər|i, 'kjɔːr|i, -ɪz
AM 'kjʊri, -z

curio
BR 'kjʊərɪəʊ, 'kjɔːrɪəʊ, -z
AM 'kjʊrioʊ, -z

curiosa
BR ˌkjʊərɪ'əʊsə(r), ˌkjʊərɪ'əʊzə(r), ˌkjɔːrɪ'əʊzə(r), ˌkjɔːrɪ'əʊzə(r)
AM ˌkjʊri'oʊsə, ˌkjʊri'oʊzə

curiosity
BR ˌkjʊərɪ'ɒsɪt|i, ˌkjɔːrɪ'ɒsɪt|i, -ɪz
AM ˌkjʊri'ɑsədi, -z

curious
BR 'kjʊərɪəs, 'kjɔːrɪəs
AM 'kjʊriəs

curiously
BR 'kjʊərɪəsli, 'kjɔːrɪəsli
AM 'kjʊriəsli

curiousness
BR 'kjʊərɪəsnəs, 'kjɔːrɪəsnəs
AM 'kjʊriəsnəs

Curitiba
BR ˌkjʊərɪ'tiːbə(r), ˌkjɔːrɪ'tiːbə(r)
AM ˌkjuri'tibə

curium
BR 'kjʊərɪəm, 'kjɔːrɪəm
AM 'kjʊriəm

curl
BR kəːl, -z, -ɪŋ, -d
AM kərl, -z, -ɪŋ, -d

curler
BR 'kəːlə(r), -z
AM 'kərlər, -z

curlew
BR 'kəːl(j)uː, -z
AM 'kərˌlu, -z

Curley
BR 'kəːli
AM 'kərli

curlicue
BR 'kəːlɪkjuː, -z
AM 'kərliˌkju, -z

curliness
BR 'kəːlɪnɪs
AM 'kərlinɪs

curly
BR 'kəːl|i, -ɪə(r), -ɪɪst
AM 'kərli, -ər, -ɪst

curlycue
BR 'kəːlɪkjuː, -z
AM 'kərliˌkju, -z

curmudgeon
BR kə'mʌdʒ(ə)n, -z
AM kər'mədʒən, -z

curmudgeonly
BR kə'mʌdʒ(ə)nli
AM kər'mədʒənli

curmugeon
BR kə'mʌdʒ(ə)n, -z
AM kər'mədʒən, -z

currach
BR 'kʌrə(r), 'kʌrəx, 'kʌrəz\'kʌrəxs
AM 'kərə(k), -z

curragh
BR 'kʌrə(r), 'kʌrəx
AM 'kərə(k), -z

currajong
BR 'kʌrədʒɒŋ, -z
AM 'kərəˌdʒɑŋ, -z

Curran
BR 'kʌrən, 'kʌrn̩
AM 'kərən

currant
BR 'kʌrənt, 'kʌrn̩t, -s
AM 'kərənt, -s

currawong
BR 'kʌrəwɒŋ, -z
AM 'kərəˌwɑŋ, -z

currency
BR 'kʌrəns|i, 'kʌrn̩s|i, -ɪz
AM 'kərənsi, -z

current
BR 'kʌrənt, 'kʌrn̩t, -s
AM 'kərənt, -s

currently
BR 'kʌrəntli, 'kʌrn̩tli
AM 'kərən(t)li

currentness
BR 'kʌrəntnəs, 'kʌrn̩tnəs
AM 'kərən(t)nəs

curricle
BR 'kʌrɪkl, -z
AM 'kərəkəl, -z

curricula
BR kə'rɪkjʉlə(r)
AM kə'rɪkjələ

curricular
BR kə'rɪkjʉlə(r)
AM kə'rɪkjələr

curriculum
BR kə'rɪkjʉləm, -z
AM kə'rɪkjələm, -z

curriculum vitae
BR kəˌrɪkjʉləm 'viːtʌɪ
AM kəˌrɪkjələm 'viˌtaɪ, + 'vaɪˌdi

Currie
BR 'kʌri
AM 'kəri

currier
BR 'kʌrɪə(r), -z
AM 'kəriər, -z

currish
BR 'kəːrɪʃ
AM 'kərɪʃ

currishly
BR 'kəːrɪʃli
AM 'kərɪʃli

currishness
BR 'kəːrɪʃnɪs
AM 'kərɪʃnɪs

curry
BR 'kʌr|i, -ɪz, -ɪɪŋ, -ɪd
AM 'kəri, -z, -ɪŋ, -d

curse
BR kəːs, -ɪz, -ɪŋ, -t
AM kərs, -əz, -ɪn, -t

cursed
adjective
BR 'kəːsɪd, kəːst
AM 'kərsəd, kərst

cursedly
BR 'kəːsɪdli
AM 'kərsədli

cursedness
BR 'kəːsɪdnɪs
AM 'kərsədnəs

curser
BR 'kəːsə(r), -z
AM 'kərsər, -z

cursillo
BR kʊə'siː(l)jəʊ, -z
AM kər'sɪloʊ, -z

cursive
BR 'kəːsɪv
AM 'kərsɪv

cursively
BR 'kəːsɪvli
AM 'kərsɪvli

cursiveness
BR 'kəːsɪvnɪs
AM 'kərsɪvnɪs

cursor
BR 'kəːsə(r), -z
AM 'kərsər, -z

cursorial
BR kəː'sɔːrɪəl
AM kər'sɔriəl

cursorily
BR 'kəːs(ə)rəli
AM 'kərs(ə)rəli

cursoriness
BR 'kəːs(ə)rɪnɪs
AM 'kərs(ə)rinɪs

cursory
BR 'kəːs(ə)ri
AM 'kərs(ə)ri

curst
BR kəːst
AM kərst

curt
BR kəːt
AM kərt

curtail
BR kə(ː)'teɪl, -z, -ɪŋ, -d
AM kər'teɪl, -z, -ɪŋ, -d

curtailment
BR kə(ː)'teɪlm(ə)nt, -s
AM kər'teɪlmɪnt, -s

curtain
BR 'kəːtn, -z, -ɪŋ, -d
AM 'kərtn̩, -z, -ɪŋ, -d

curtain wall
BR ˌkəːtn 'wɔːl, -z
AM 'kərtnˌwɔl, 'kərtnˌwɑl, -z

curtana
BR kəː'tɑːnə(r), kəː'teɪnə(r), -z
AM kər'tɑnə, -z

curtilage
BR 'kəːtɪlɪdʒ, 'kəːtl̩ɪdʒ, -ɪz
AM 'kərdl̩ɪdʒ, -ɪz

Curtin
BR 'kəːt(ɪ)n
AM 'kərtn

Curtis
BR 'kəːtɪs
AM 'kərdəs

Curtiss
BR 'kəːtɪs
AM 'kərdəs

curtly
BR 'kəːtli
AM 'kərtli

curtness
BR 'kəːtnəs
AM 'kərtnəs

curtsey
BR 'kəːts|i, -ɪz, -ɪɪŋ, -ɪd
AM 'kərtsi, -z, -ɪŋ, -d

curtsy
BR 'kəːts|i, -ɪz, -ɪɪŋ, -ɪd
AM 'kərtsi, -z, -ɪŋ, -d
curule
BR 'kjʊər(j)uːl
AM 'kjuˌrul
curvaceous
BR kəː'veɪʃəs
AM kər'veɪʃəs
curvaceously
BR kəː'veɪʃəsli
AM kər'veɪʃəsli
curvacious
BR kəː'veɪʃəs
AM kər'veɪʃəs
curvaciously
BR kəː'veɪʃəsli
AM kər'veɪʃəsli
curvature
BR 'kəːvətʃə(r), 'kəːvətjʊə(r), -z
AM 'kərvətʃər, 'kərvəˌtʃʊ(ə)r, -z
curve
BR kəːv, -z, -ɪŋ, -d
AM kərv, -z, -ɪŋ, -d
curvet
BR kəː'vɛt, -s, -ɪŋ, -ɨd
AM kərˌvɛ|t, -ts, -dɪŋ, -dəd
curvifoliate
BR ˌkəːvɪ'fəʊlɪət
AM ˌkərvə'foʊliət
curviform
BR 'kəːvɪfɔːm
AM 'kərvəˌfɔ(ə)rm
curvilinear
BR ˌkəːvɪ'lɪnɪə(r)
AM ˌkərvə'lɪniər
curvilinearly
BR ˌkəːvɪ'lɪnɪəli
AM ˌkərvə'lɪniərli
curviness
BR 'kəːvɪnɨs
AM 'kərvinɨs
curvirostral
BR ˌkəːvɪ'rɒstr(ə)l
AM ˌkərvə'rɑstrəl
curvy
BR 'kəːv|i, -ɪə(r), -ɪɨst
AM 'kərvi, -ər, -ɨst
Curzon
BR 'kəːzn
AM 'kərzən, 'kərˌzɑn
Cusack
BR 'kjuːsak, 'kjuːzak
AM 'kjusæk, 'kjuzæk
cuscus
BR 'kʌskʌs, -ɨz
AM 'kʊskʊs, 'kəskəs, -əz
cusec
BR 'kjuːsɛk, -s
AM 'kjuˌsɛk, -s
cush
BR kʊʃ, -ɨz
AM kʊʃ, -əz
cushat
BR 'kʊʃət, -s
AM 'kʊʃət, -s
cush-cush
BR 'kʊʃkʊʃ, -ɨz
AM 'kʊʃˌkʊʃ, -əz
cushily
BR 'kʊʃɨli
AM 'kʊʃəli
cushiness
BR 'kʊʃɪnɨs
AM 'kʊʃinɨs
Cushing
BR 'kʊʃɪŋ
AM 'kʊʃɪŋ
cushion
BR 'kʊʃ|n, -nz, -n̩ɪŋ\-(ə)nɪŋ, -nd
AM 'kʊʃ|ən, -ənz, -(ə)nɪŋ, -ənd
cushiony
BR 'kʊʃn̩i, 'kʊʃəni
AM 'kʊʃəni
Cushitic
BR kʊ'ʃɪtɪk
AM kə'ʃɪdɪk
cushy
BR 'kʊʃ|i, -ɪə(r), -ɪɨst
AM 'kʊʃi, -ər, -ɨst
cusp
BR kʌsp, -s, -t
AM kəsp, -s, -t
cuspate
BR 'kʌspeɪt
AM 'kəspət, 'kəsˌpeɪt
cuspid
BR 'kʌspɪd, -z
AM 'kəspəd, -z
cuspidal
BR 'kʌspɪdl
AM 'kəspədəl
cuspidate
BR 'kʌspɪdeɪt
AM 'kəspəˌdeɪt
cuspidor
BR 'kʌspɪdɔː(r), -z
AM 'kəspəˌdɔ(ə)r, -z
cuss
BR kʌs, -ɨz, -ɪŋ, -t
AM kəs, -əz, -ɪŋ, -t
cussed
adjective
BR 'kʌsɪd
AM 'kəsəd
cussedly
BR 'kʌsɪdli
AM 'kəsədli
cussedness
BR 'kʌsɪdnɨs
AM 'kəsədnəs
Cusson
BR 'kʌsn
AM 'kəsən
custard
BR 'kʌstəd, -z
AM 'kəstərd, -z
Custer
BR 'kʌstə(r)
AM 'kəstər
custodial
BR kʌ'stəʊdɪəl, kə'stəʊdɪəl
AM kəs'toʊdiəl
custodian
BR kʌ'stəʊdɪən, kə'stəʊdɪən, -z
AM kəs'toʊdiən, -z
custodianship
BR kʌ'stəʊdɪənʃɪp, kə'stəʊdɪənʃɪp
AM kəs'toʊdiənˌʃɪp
custody
BR 'kʌstədi
AM 'kəstədi
custom
BR 'kʌstəm, -z
AM 'kəstəm, -z
customable
BR 'kʌstəməbl
AM 'kəstəməbəl
customarily
BR 'kʌstəm(ə)rɨli, 'kʌstəm(ə)rl̩i
AM ˌkəstə'mɛrəli
customariness
BR 'kʌstəm(ə)rɪnɨs
AM 'kəstəˌmɛrinəs
customary
BR 'kʌstəm(ə)ri
AM 'kəstəˌmɛri
customer
BR 'kʌstəmə(r), -z
AM 'kəstəmər, -z
customise
BR 'kʌstəmʌɪz, -ɨz, -ɪŋ, -d
AM 'kəstəˌmaɪz, -ɨz, -ɪŋ, -d
customize
BR 'kʌstəmʌɪz, -ɨz, -ɪŋ, -d
AM 'kəstəˌmaɪz, -ɨz, -ɪŋ, -d
cut
BR kʌt, -s, -ɪŋ
AM kə|t, -ts, -dɪŋ
cutaneous
BR kjuː'teɪnɪəs
AM kju'teɪniəs
cutaway
BR 'kʌtəweɪ, -z
AM 'kədəˌweɪ, -z
cutback
BR 'kʌtbak, -s
AM 'kətˌbæk, -s
cutch
BR kʌtʃ
AM kətʃ
cutdown
BR ˌkʌt'daʊn
AM 'kətˌdaʊn
cute
BR kjuːt, -ə(r), -ɨst
AM kju|t, -dər, -dəst
cutely
BR 'kjuːtli
AM 'kjutli
cuteness
BR 'kjuːtnəs
AM 'kjutnəs
Cutex
BR 'kjuːtɛks
AM 'kjuˌtɛks
cutey
BR 'kjuːt|i, -ɪz
AM 'kjudi, -z
Cutforth
BR 'kʌtfɔːθ, 'kʌtfəθ
AM 'kətˌfɔ(ə)rθ
Cuthbert
BR 'kʌθbət
AM 'kəθbərt
Cuthbertson
BR 'kʌθbəts(ə)n
AM 'kəθbərtsən
cuticle
BR 'kjuːtɪkl, -z
AM 'kjudəkəl, -z
cuticular
BR kjuː'tɪkjʉlə(r)
AM kju'dɪkjələr
Cuticura®
BR ˌkjuːtɪ'kjʊərə(r), ˌkjuːtɪ'kjɔːrə(r)
AM ˌkjudə'kjʊrə
cutie
BR 'kjuːt|i, -z
AM 'kjudi, -z
cutis
BR 'kjuːtɪs
AM 'kjudəs
cutlass
BR 'kʌtləs, -ɨz
AM 'kətləs, -ɨz
cutler
BR 'kʌtlə(r), -z
AM 'kətlər, -z
cutlery
BR 'kʌtləri
AM 'kətləri
cutlet
BR 'kʌtlɨt, -s
AM 'kətlət, -s
cutoff
BR 'kʌtɒf, -s
AM 'kədˌɔf, 'kədˌɑf, -s
cutout
BR 'kʌtaʊt, -s
AM 'kədˌaʊt, -s
cutpurse
BR 'kʌtpəːs, -ɨz
AM 'kətˌpərs, -ɨz
cutter
BR 'kʌtə(r), -z
AM 'kədər, -z
cutthroat
BR 'kʌtθrəʊt, -s
AM 'kətˌθroʊt, -s
cutting
BR 'kʌtɪŋ, -z
AM 'kədɪŋ, -z

cuttingly
BR 'kʌtɪŋli
AM 'kədɪŋli
cuttle
BR 'kʌtl, -z
AM 'kədəl, -z
cuttlebone
BR 'kʌtlbəʊn, -z
AM 'kədl,boʊn, -z
cuttlefish
BR 'kʌtlfɪʃ
AM 'kədl,fɪʃ
cutty
BR 'kʌti, -ɪz
AM 'kədi, -z
Cutty Sark
BR ,kʌtɪ 'sɑːk
AM ¦kədi ¦sɑrk
cutup
BR 'kʌtʌp, -s
AM 'kəd,əp, -s
cutwater
BR 'kʌt,wɔːtə(r), -z
AM 'kət,wɔdər, 'kət,wɑdər, -z
cutworm
BR 'kʌtwəːm, -z
AM 'kət,wərm, -z
cuvée
BR kjuː'veɪ, -z
AM k(j)u'veɪ, -z
cuvette
BR kjuː'vɛt, -s
AM kju'vɛt, -s
Cuvier
BR 'kjuːvɪeɪ
AM kuvi'eɪ
Cuxhaven
BR 'kʊks,hɑːvn
AM 'kʊks,(h)ɑvən
Cuyahoga
BR ,kʌɪə'həʊgə(r)
AM ,kaɪə'hoʊgə
Cuzco
BR 'kʊskəʊ
AM 'kuskoʊ, 'kʊzkoʊ
cwm
BR kʊm, -z
AM kʊm, -z
Cy
BR sʌɪ
AM saɪ
cyan
BR 'sʌɪən, 'sʌɪan
AM 'saɪən
cyanamid
BR sʌɪ'anəmɪd
AM saɪ'ænəməd
cyanamide
BR sʌɪ'anəmʌɪd
AM saɪ'ænə,maɪd
cyanic
BR sʌɪ'anɪk
AM saɪ'ænɪk
cyanide
BR 'sʌɪənʌɪd
AM 'saɪə,naɪd
cyano
BR 'sʌɪənəʊ, sʌɪ'anəʊ
AM 'saɪə,noʊ
cyanobacteria
BR ,sʌɪənəʊ,bak'tɪərɪə(r), sʌɪ,anəʊbak'tɪərɪə(r)
AM ,saɪənoʊ,bæk'tɪriə
cyanobacterium
BR ,sʌɪənəʊ,bak'tɪərɪəm, sʌɪ,anəʊbak'tɪərɪəm
AM ,saɪənoʊ,bæk'tɪriəm
cyanocobalamin
BR ,sʌɪənəʊkə'baləmɪn, sʌɪ,anəʊkə'baləmɪn, -z
AM ,saɪənoʊ,koʊ'bæləmən, ¦saɪənoʊ,koʊ'bælə,mɪn, -z
cyanogen
BR sʌɪ'anədʒ(ə)n, -z
AM saɪ'ænədʒən, saɪ'ænə,dʒɛn, -z
cyanogenic
BR ,sʌɪənə'dʒɛnɪk
AM ,saɪənoʊ'dʒɛnɪk
cyanoses
BR ,sʌɪə'nəʊsiːz
AM ,saɪə'noʊsiz
cyanosis
BR ,sʌɪə'nəʊsɪs
AM ,saɪə'noʊsəs
cyanotic
BR ,sʌɪə'nɒtɪk
AM ,saɪə'nɑdɪk
Cybele
BR 'sɪbɨli, 'sɪbḷi
AM 'sɪbəli, 'sɪbəl
cybercafé
BR 'sʌɪbə,kaf|eɪ, 'sʌɪbə,kaf|i, -eɪz\-ɪz
AM 'saɪbər,kæ,feɪ, -z
cybernate
BR 'sʌɪbəneɪt, -s, -ɪŋ, -ɨd
AM 'saɪbər,neɪ|t, -ts, -dɪŋ, -dɨd
cybernation
BR ,sʌɪbə'neɪʃn
AM ,saɪbər'neɪʃən
cybernetic
BR ,sʌɪbə'nɛtɪk, -s
AM ,saɪbər'nɛdɪk, -s
cybernetician
BR ,sʌɪbənə'tɪʃn, -z
AM ,saɪbərnə'tɪʃən, -z
cyberneticist
BR ,sʌɪbə'nɛtɪsɪst, -s
AM ,saɪbər'nɛdəsəst, -s
cyberpunk
BR 'sʌɪbəpʌŋk, -s
AM 'saɪbər,pəŋk, -s
cyborg
BR 'sʌɪbɔːg, -z
AM 'saɪ,bɔrg, -z
cycad
BR 'sʌɪkad, 'sʌɪkəd, -z
AM 'saɪkəd, 'saɪ,kæd, -z
Cyclades
BR 'sɪklədiːz
AM 'sɪklə,diz
Cycladic
BR sɪ'kladɪk, sʌɪ'kladɪk
AM saɪ'klɑdɪk, sə'klɑdɪk
cyclamate
BR 'sɪkləmeɪt, 'sʌɪkləmeɪt, -s
AM 'saɪklə,meɪt, -s
cyclamen
BR 'sɪkləmən
AM 'saɪkləmən, 'sɪkləmən
cycle
BR 'sʌɪkl, -z, -ɪŋ, -d
AM 'saɪk|əl, -əlz, -(ə)lɪŋ, -əld
cyclic
BR 'sʌɪklɪk, 'sɪklɪk
AM 'sɪklɪk, 'saɪklɪk
cyclical
BR 'sɪklɨkl, 'sʌɪklɨkl
AM 'sɪkləkəl, 'saɪkləkəl
cyclically
BR 'sɪklɨkli, 'sʌɪklɨkli
AM 'sɪklək(ə)li, 'saɪklək(ə)li
cyclist
BR 'sʌɪklɪst, -s
AM 'saɪkləst, -s
cycloalkane
BR ,sʌɪkləʊ'alkeɪn, -z
AM ,saɪkloʊ'æl,keɪn, -z
cyclo-cross
BR 'sʌɪklə(ʊ)krɒs
AM 'saɪkloʊ,krɔs, 'saɪkloʊ,krɑs
cyclodextrin
BR ,sʌɪkləʊ'dɛkstrɪn, -z
AM ,saɪkloʊ'dɛkstrən, -z
cyclograph
BR 'sʌɪklə(ʊ)grɑːf, 'sʌɪklə(ʊ)graf, -s
AM 'saɪkloʊ,græf, 'saɪklə,græf, -s
cyclohexane
BR ,sʌɪkləʊ'hɛkseɪn, -z
AM ,saɪkloʊ'hɛk,seɪn, -z
cycloid
BR 'sʌɪklɔɪd, -z
AM 'saɪ,klɔɪd, -z
cycloidal
BR sʌɪ'klɔɪdl
AM saɪ'klɔɪdəl
cyclometer
BR sʌɪ'klɒmɪtə(r), -z
AM saɪ'klɑmədər, -z
cyclone
BR 'sʌɪkləʊn, -z
AM 'saɪ,kloʊn, -z
cyclonic
BR sʌɪ'klɒnɪk
AM saɪ'klɑnɪk
cyclonically
BR sʌɪ'klɒnɪkli
AM saɪ'klɑnək(ə)li
cyclopaedia
BR ,sʌɪklə(ʊ)'piːdɪə(r), -z
AM ,saɪklə'pidiə, -z
cyclopaedic
BR ,sʌɪklə(ʊ)'piːdɪk
AM ,saɪklə'pidɪk
cyclopaedically
BR ,sʌɪlə(ʊ)'piːdɨkli
AM ,saɪklə'pidɪk(ə)li
cycloparaffin
BR ,sʌɪkləʊ'parəfɪn
AM ,saɪkloʊ'pɛrəfən
Cyclopean
BR ,sʌɪklə(ʊ)'piːən, sʌɪ'kləʊpɪən
AM ,saɪklə'piən, saɪ'kloʊpiən
cyclopedia
BR ,sʌɪklə(ʊ)'piːdɪə(r), -z
AM ,saɪklə'pidiə, -z
cyclopedic
BR ,sʌɪklə(ʊ)'piːdɪk
AM ,saɪklə'pidɪk
cyclopedically
BR ,sʌɪlə(ʊ)'piːdɨkli
AM ,saɪklə'pidək(ə)li
cyclopropane
BR ,sʌɪklə(ʊ)'prəʊpeɪn
AM ,saɪkloʊ'proʊ,peɪn
cyclopropyl
BR ,sʌɪklə(ʊ)'prɒp(ɪ)l, ,sʌɪklə(ʊ)'prəʊp(ɪ)l
AM ,saɪkloʊ'proʊpəl
Cyclops
BR 'sʌɪklɒps
AM 'saɪ,klɑps
cyclorama
BR ,sʌɪklə'rɑːmə(r), -z
AM ,saɪklə'ræmə, -z
cycloramic
BR ,sʌɪklə'ramɪk
AM ,saɪklə'ræmɪk
cyclosporin
BR ,sʌɪklə(ʊ)'spɔːrɪn
AM ,saɪkloʊ'spɔrən
cyclostomate
BR ,sʌɪklə(ʊ)'stəʊmeɪt
AM saɪ'klɑstəmət, ,saɪkloʊ'stoʊmeɪt
cyclostome
BR 'sʌɪkləstəʊm, -z
AM 'saɪklə,stoʊm, -z
cyclostyle
BR 'sʌɪkləstʌɪl, -z, -ɪŋ, -d
AM 'saɪklə,staɪl, -z, -ɪŋ, -d
cyclothymia
BR ,sʌɪklə(ʊ)'θʌɪmɪə(r)
AM ,saɪklə'θaɪmiə

cyclothymic
BR ˌsʌɪklə(ʊ)ˈθʌɪmɪk
AM ˌsaɪkləˈθaɪmɪk

cyclotron
BR ˈsʌɪklətrɒn, -z
AM ˈsaɪkləˌtrɑn, -z

cyder
BR ˈsʌɪdə(r), -z
AM ˈsaɪdər, -z

cygnet
BR ˈsɪgnɨt, -s
AM ˈsɪgnət, -s

Cygnus
BR ˈsɪgnəs
AM ˈsɪgnəs

cylinder
BR ˈsɪlɨndə(r), -z
AM ˈsɪləndər, -z

cylindrical
BR sɪˈlɪndrɪkl
AM səˈlɪndrəkəl

cylindrically
BR sɪˈlɪndrɨkli
AM səˈlɪndrək(ə)li

cyma
BR ˈsʌɪmə(r)
AM ˈsaɪmə

cymbal
BR ˈsɪmbl, -z
AM ˈsɪmbəl, -z

cymbalist
BR ˈsɪmbl̩ɪst, -s
AM ˈsɪmbələst, -s

cymbalo
BR ˈsɪmbələʊ, -z
AM ˈsɪmbəˌloʊ, -z

Cymbeline
BR ˈsɪmbɨliːn
AM ˈsɪmbəˌlin

cymbidium
BR ˌsɪmˈbɪdɪəm, -z
AM ˌsɪmˈbɪdiəm, -z

cymbiform
BR ˈsɪmbɨfɔːm
AM ˈsɪmbəˌfɔ(ə)rm

cyme
BR sʌɪm, -z
AM saɪm, -z

cymose
BR ˈsʌɪməʊs
AM ˈsaɪˌmoʊs, ˈsaɪˌmoʊz

Cymric
BR ˈkʌmrɪk, ˈkɪmrɪk
AM ˈkəmrɪk

Cymru
BR ˈkʌmri, ˈkʊmri
AM ˈkəmri

Cynan
BR ˈkʌnən
AM ˈkənən

Cyncoed
BR kɪnˈkɔɪd, kɪŋˈkɔɪd
AM ˌkɪŋˈkɔɪd

Cynewulf
BR ˈkɪnɨwʊlf
AM ˈkɪnəˌwʊlf

cynghanedd
BR kʌŋˈhanəð
AM kəŋˈhɑnəð
WE kʌŋˈhaneð

cynic
BR ˈsɪnɪk, -s
AM ˈsɪnɪk, -s

cynical
BR ˈsɪnɨkl
AM ˈsɪnəkəl

cynically
BR ˈsɪnɨkli
AM ˈsɪnək(ə)li

cynicism
BR ˈsɪnɨsɪz(ə)m, -z
AM ˈsɪnəˌsɪzəm, -z

cynocephali
BR ˌsʌɪnə(ʊ)ˈsɛfəlʌɪ, ˌsɪnə(ʊ)ˈsɛfl̩ʌɪ, ˈsʌɪnə(ʊ)ˈkɛfəlʌɪ, ˌsʌɪnə(ʊ)ˈkɛfl̩ʌɪ
AM ¦saɪnoʊˈsɛfəˌlaɪ, ¦saɪnəˈsɛfəˌlaɪ, ¦sɪnoʊˈsɛfəˌlaɪ, ¦sɪnəˈsɛfəˌlaɪ

cynocephalus
BR ˌsʌɪnə(ʊ)ˈsɛfələs, ˌsɪnə(ʊ)ˈsɛfl̩əs, ˈsʌɪnə(ʊ)ˈkɛfələs, ˌsʌɪnə(ʊ)ˈkɛfl̩əs
AM ¦saɪnoʊˈsɛfələs, ¦saɪnəˈsɛfələs, ¦sɪnoʊˈsɛfələs, ¦sɪnəˈsɛfələs

cynosure
BR ˈsʌɪnəʃʊə(r), ˈsʌɪnəzjʊə(r), ˈsʌɪnəʒʊə(r), ˈsɪnəʃʊə(r), ˈsɪnəzjʊə(r), ˈsɪnəʒʊə(r), -z
AM ˈsaɪnəˌʃʊ(ə)r, -z

Cynthia
BR ˈsɪnθɪə(r)
AM ˈsɪnθiə

cypher
BR ˈsʌɪf|ə(r), -əz, -(ə)rɪŋ, -əd
AM ˈsaɪfər, -z, -ɪŋ, -d

cy pres
BR ˌsiː ˈpreɪ
AM si ˈpreɪ

cypress
BR ˈsʌɪprɪs, -ɪz
AM ˈsaɪprəs, -əz

Cyprian
BR ˈsɪprɪən, -z
AM ˈsɪpriən, -z

cyprinoid
BR ˈsɪprɪnɔɪd, -z
AM ˈsɪprəˌnɔɪd, -z

Cypriot
BR ˈsɪprɪət, -s
AM ˈsɪpriət, ˈsɪpriˌɑt, -s

cypripedium
BR ˌsɪprɪˈpiːdɪəm, -z
AM ˌsɪprəˈpidiəm, -z

Cyprus
BR ˈsʌɪprəs
AM ˈsaɪprəs

cypsela
BR ˈsɪpsɪlə(r)
AM ˈsɪpsələ

cypselae
BR ˈsɪpsɪliː
AM ˈsɪpsəˌli, ˈsɪpsəˌlaɪ

Cyrano de Bergerac
BR ˌsɪrənəʊ də ˈbəːʒərak, sɪˌrɑːnəʊ +, + ˈbɛːʒərak
AM ˌsɪrənoʊ də ˈbərʒəˌræk

Cyrenaic
BR ˌsɪrɪˈneɪɪk, -s
AM ˌsɪrəˈneɪɪk, -s

Cyrenaica
BR ˌsɪrɪˈneɪɪkə(r), ˌsɪrɪˈnʌɪɪkə(r), ˌsʌɪrɪˈneɪɪkə(r), ˌsʌɪrɪˈnʌɪɪkə(r)
AM ˌsɪrəˈneɪɪkə

Cyrene
BR sʌɪˈriːni
AM kaɪˈrini, saɪˈrini

Cyrenian
BR sʌɪˈriːnɪən, -z
AM kaɪˈriniən, saɪˈriniən, -z

Cyril
BR ˈsɪrɪl, ˈsɪrl̩
AM ˈsɪrəl

Cyrillic
BR sɪˈrɪlɪk
AM səˈrɪlɪk

Cyrus
BR ˈsʌɪrəs
AM ˈsaɪrəs

cyst
BR sɪst, -s
AM sɪst, -s

cystectomy
BR sɪˈstɛktəm|i, -ɪz
AM sɪsˈtɛktəmi, -z

cysteine
BR ˈsɪstɪiːn, ˈsɪsteɪn
AM ˈsɪˌstin

cystic
BR ˈsɪstɪk
AM ˈsɪstɪk

cystine
BR ˈsɪstiːn
AM ˈsɪˌstin

cystitis
BR sɪˈstʌɪtɪs
AM sɪsˈtaɪdəs

cystoscope
BR ˈsɪstəskəʊp, -s
AM ˈsɪstəˌskoʊp, -s

cystoscopic
BR ˌsɪstəˈskɒpɪk
AM ˌsɪstəˈskɑpɪk

cystoscopy
BR sɪˈstɒskəp|i, -ɪz
AM sɪˈstɑskəpi, -z

cystotomy
BR sɪˈstɒtəm|i, -ɪz
AM sɪˈstɑdəmi, -z

Cythera
BR sɪˈθɪərə(r)
AM səˈθɪrə

Cytherea
BR ˌsɪθəˈriːə(r)
AM səˈθɪriə

cytidine
BR ˈsʌɪtɪdiːn
AM ˈsɪdəˌdin

cytochrome
BR ˈsʌɪtə(ʊ)krəʊm, -z
AM ˈsaɪdəˌkroʊm, -z

cytogenetic
BR ˌsʌɪtə(ʊ)dʒɪˈnɛtɪk, -s
AM ˌsaɪdədʒəˈnɛdɪk, -s

cytogenetical
BR ˌsʌɪtə(ʊ)dʒɪˈnɛtɪkl
AM ˌsaɪdədʒəˈnɛdəkəl

cytogenetically
BR ˌsʌɪtə(ʊ)dʒɪˈnɛtɪkli
AM ˌsaɪdədʒəˈnɛdək(ə)li

cytogeneticist
BR ˌsʌɪtə(ʊ)dʒɪˈnɛtɪsɪst, -s
AM ˌsaɪdədʒəˈnɛdəsəst, -s

cytogenic
BR ˌsʌɪtə(ʊ)ˈdʒɛnɪk, -s
AM ˌsaɪdəˈdʒɛnɪk, -s

cytological
BR ˌsʌɪtəˈlɒdʒɪkl
AM ˌsaɪdəˈlɑdʒəkəl

cytologically
BR ˌsʌɪtəˈlɒdʒɪkli
AM ˌsaɪdəˈlɑdʒək(ə)li

cytologist
BR sʌɪˈtɒlədʒɪst, -s
AM saɪˈtɑlədʒəst, -s

cytology
BR sʌɪˈtɒlədʒi
AM saɪˈtɑlədʒi

cytoplasm
BR ˈsʌɪtə(ʊ)plaz(ə)m
AM ˈsaɪdəˌplæzəm

cytoplasmic
BR ˌsʌɪtə(ʊ)ˈplazmɪk
AM ˌsaɪdəˈplæzmɪk

cytosine
BR ˈsʌɪtə(ʊ)siːn
AM ˈsaɪdəˌsin

cytotoxic
BR ˌsʌɪtə(ʊ)ˈtɒksɪk
AM ˌsaɪdəˈtɑksɪk

cytotoxin
BR ˌsʌɪtə(ʊ)ˈtɒksɪn, -z
AM ˌsaɪdəˈtɑksən, -z

czar
BR zɑː(r), tsɑː(r), -z
AM zɑr, -z

czardas
BR ˈtʃɑːdaʃ
AM ˈtʃɑrdaʃ

czarevich
BR 'zɑːrəvɪtʃ, 'tsɑːrəvɪtʃ, -ɪz
AM 'zɑrəˌvɪtʃ, -ɪz

czarevitch
BR 'zɑːrəvɪtʃ, 'tsɑːrəvɪtʃ, -ɪz
AM 'zɑrəˌvɪtʃ, -ɪz

czarevna
BR zɑː'rɛvnə(r), tsɑː'rɛvnə(r), -z
AM zɑ'rɛvnə, -z

czarina
BR zɑː'riːnə(r), tsɑː'riːnə(r), -z
AM zɑ'rinə, -z

czarism
BR 'zɑːrɪz(ə)m, 'tsɑːrɪz(ə)m
AM 'zɑrˌɪzəm

czarist
BR 'zɑːrɪst, 'tsɑːrɪst, -s
AM 'zɑrəst, -s

Czech
BR tʃɛk, -s
AM tʃɛk, -s

Czechoslovak
BR ˌtʃɛkə'sləʊvak, -s
AM ˌtʃɛkə'sloʊˌvæk, ˌtʃɛkoʊ'sloʊˌvæk, ˌtʃɛkə'sloʊˌvɑk, ˌtʃɛkoʊ'sloʊˌvɑk, -s

Czechoslovakia
BR ˌtʃɛkəslə'vakɪə(r), ˌtʃɛkəslə'vɑːkɪə(r)
AM ˌtʃɛkəˌsloʊ'vɑkiə, ˌtʃɛkoʊˌsloʊ'vɑkiə

Czechoslovakian
BR ˌtʃɛkəslə'vakɪən, ˌtʃɛkəslə'vɑːkɪən
AM ˌtʃɛkəˌsloʊ'vɑkiən, ˌtʃɛkoʊˌsloʊ'vɑkiən

Czerny
BR 'tʃəːni
AM 'tʃərni

Dd

d
BR diː, -z
AM di, -z

'd
had, would
BR d
AM d

DA
BR ˌdiːˈeɪ, -z
AM ˌdiˈeɪ, -z

dab
BR dab, -z, -ɪŋ, -d
AM dæb, -z, -ɪŋ, -d

dabber
BR ˈdabə(r), -z
AM ˈdæbər, -z

dabble
BR ˈdab|l, -lz, -l̩ɪŋ\-lɪŋ, -ld
AM ˈdæb|əl, -əlz, -(ə)lɪŋ, -əld

dabbler
BR ˈdabl̩ə(r), ˈdablə(r), -z
AM ˈdæb(ə)lər, -z

dabbling
BR ˈdabl̩ɪŋ, ˈdablɪŋ, -z
AM ˈdæb(ə)lɪŋ, -z

dabchick
BR ˈdabtʃɪk, -s
AM ˈdæbˌtʃɪk, -s

dabster
BR ˈdabstə(r), -z
AM ˈdæbstər, -z

da capo
BR ˌdɑː ˈkɑːpəʊ, də +
AM dɑ ˈkɑpoʊ, də +

Dacca
BR ˈdakɑː(r), ˈdakə(r)
AM ˈdɑkɑ

dace
BR deɪs, -ɪz
AM deɪs, -ɪz

dacha
BR ˈdatʃə(r), -z
AM ˈdɑ(t)ʃə, -z

Dachau
BR ˈdakaʊ, ˈdaxaʊ
AM ˈdɑkaʊ

dachshund
BR ˈdaks(ə)nd, -z
AM ˈdɑksˌ(h)ʊn|t, ˈdɑksˌ(h)ʊn|d, ˈdɑksˌ(h)aʊn|d, -ts\-dz

Dacia
BR ˈdeɪsɪə(r), ˈdeɪʃə(r)
AM ˈdeɪʃə

Dacian
BR ˈdeɪsɪən, ˈdeɪʃ(ə)n, -z
AM ˈdeɪʃən, -z

dacite
BR ˈdeɪsʌɪt, -s
AM ˈdeɪˌsaɪt, -s

dacoit
BR dəˈkɔɪt, -s
AM dəˈkɔɪt, -s

Dacre
BR ˈdeɪkə(r)
AM ˈdeɪkər

Dacron®
BR ˈdakrɒn
AM ˈdeɪˌkrɑn, ˈdæˌkrɑn

dactyl
BR ˈdakt(ɪ)l, -z
AM ˈdæktl, -z

dactylic
BR dakˈtɪlɪk
AM dækˈtɪlɪk

dactylography
BR ˌdaktɪˈlɒɡrəfi
AM ˌdæktəˈlɑɡrəfi

dactylology
BR ˌdaktɪˈlɒlədʒi
AM ˌdæktəˈlɑlədʒi

dad
BR dad, -z
AM dæd, -z

Dada
BR ˈdɑːdɑː(r)
AM ˈdɑdɑ

Dadaism
BR ˈdɑːdɑː(r)ɪz(ə)m, ˈdɑːdə(r)ɪz(ə)m
AM ˈdɑdɑˌɪzəm

Dadaist
BR ˈdɑːdɑː(r)ɪst, ˈdɑːdə(r)ɪst, -s
AM ˈdɑdɑəst, -s

Dadaistic
BR ˌdɑːdɑː(r)ˈɪstɪk, ˌdɑːdə(r)ˈɪstɪk
AM ˌdɑdɑˈɪstɪk

daddie
BR ˈdad|i, -ɪz
AM ˈdædi, -z

daddy
BR ˈdad|i, -ɪz
AM ˈdædi, -z

daddy-long-legs
BR ˌdadɪˈlɒŋlɛɡz, -ɪz
AM ˌdædiˈlɔŋˌlɛɡz, ˌdædiˈlɑŋˌlɛɡz, -əz

dado
BR ˈdeɪdəʊ, -z
AM ˈdeɪˌdoʊ, -z

Daedalian
BR dɪˈdeɪlɪən, -z
AM diˈdeɪljən, diˈdeɪliən, -z

Daedalus
BR ˈdiːdələs, ˈdiːdl̩əs
AM ˈdɛdələs

daemon
BR ˈdiːmən, -z
AM ˈdimən, -z

daemonic
BR dɪˈmɒnɪk
AM dəˈmɑnɪk, diˈmɑnɪk

daemonological
BR ˌdiːmənəˈlɒdʒɪkl
AM ˌdimənəˈlɑdʒəkəl

DAF®
BR daf, -s
AM dæf, ˌdiˌeɪˈɛf, -s

daff
BR daf, -s
AM dæf, -s

daffily
BR ˈdafɨli
AM ˈdæfəli

daffiness
BR ˈdafɪnɪs
AM ˈdæfinɨs

daffodil
BR ˈdafədɪl, -z
AM ˈdæfəˌdɪl, -z

daffy
BR ˈdaf|i, -ɪə(r), -ɪɪst
AM ˈdæfi, -ər, -ɨst

daft
BR dɑːft, daft, -ə(r), -ɨst
AM dæft, -ər, -əst

daftly
BR ˈdɑːftli, ˈdaftli
AM ˈdæf(t)li

daftness
BR ˈdɑːftnəs, ˈdaftnəs
AM ˈdæf(t)nəs

Dafydd
BR ˈdavɪð
AM ˈdævɪð

dag
BR daɡ, -z
AM dæɡ, -z

Dagenham
BR ˈdaɡən(ə)m, ˈdaɡn̩(ə)m
AM ˈdæɡənəm

Dagestan
BR ˌdaɡɪˈstɑːn
AM ˈdɑɡəˌstæn

dagga
BR ˈdɑːɡə(r), ˈdaɡə(r), ˈdaxə(r), -z
AM ˈdæɡə, ˈdɑɡə, -z

dagger
BR ˈdaɡə(r), -z
AM ˈdæɡər, -z

daggerboard
BR ˈdaɡəbɔːd, -z
AM ˈdæɡərˌbɔ(ə)rd, -z

daglock
BR ˈdaɡlɒk, -s
AM ˈdæɡˌlɑk, -s

Dagmar
BR ˈdaɡmɑː(r)
AM ˈdæɡmɑr
DAN ˈdɑwmɑ

dag-nab
BR ˌdaɡˈnab
AM ˌdæɡˈnæb

dago
BR ˈdeɪɡəʊ, -z
AM ˈdeɪɡoʊ, -z

Dagon
BR ˈdeɪɡɒn
AM ˈdeɪˌɡɑn

Daguerre
BR dəˈɡɛː(r)
AM dəˈɡɛ(ə)r

daguerreotype
BR dəˈɡɛːrə(ʊ)tʌɪp, -s
AM dəˈɡɛrəˌtaɪp, -s

daguerrotype
BR dəˈɡɛːrə(ʊ)tʌɪp, -s
AM dəˈɡɛrəˌtaɪp, -s

Dagwood
BR ˈdaɡwʊd
AM ˈdæɡˌwʊd

dah
BR dɑː(r)
AM dɑ

dahl
BR dɑːl
AM dɑl

dahlia[1]
BR ˈdeɪlɪə(r), -z
AM ˈdɑljə, ˈdæljə, -z

dahlia[2]
BR ˈdeɪlɪə(r), -z
AM ˈdɑljə, ˈdæljə, ˈdɑliə, ˈdæliə , -z

Dahomey
BR dəˈhəʊmi
AM dəˈhoʊmi

Dahrendorf
BR ˈdarəndɔːf, ˈdarn̩dɔːf
AM ˈdɑrəndɔ(ə)rf

Dai
BR dʌɪ
AM daɪ

Daihatsu®
BR dʌɪˈhatsuː
AM daɪˈhɑtsu

Dáil
BR dɔɪl
AM dɔɪl
IR ˈdaːlʲ

Dáil Eireann
BR ˌdɔɪl ˈɛːrən, + ˈɛːrn̩
AM ˌdɔɪl ˈɛrən
IR ˌdaːlʲ ˈeːrʲən

Dailey
BR ˈdeɪli
AM ˈdeɪli

daily
BR ˈdeɪl|i, -ɪz
AM ˈdeɪli, -z

Daimler®
BR ˈdeɪmlə(r), -z
AM ˈdaɪmlər, -z

daimon
BR ˈdʌɪməʊn, -z
AM ˈdaɪˌmoʊn, -z

daimonic
BR dʌɪˈmɒnɪk, dʌɪˈməʊnɪk

AM daɪ'moʊnɪk, daɪ'mɑnɪk

daintily
BR 'deɪntɨli
AM 'deɪn(t)əli

daintiness
BR 'deɪntɪnɨs
AM 'deɪn(t)inɨs

dainty
BR 'deɪnt|i, -ɪz, -ɪə(r), -ɪɨst
AM 'deɪn(t)i, -z, -ər, -ɨst

daiquiri
BR 'dʌɪk(ɨ)r|i, 'dak(ɨ)r|i, -ɪz
AM 'dækəri, -z

Dairen
BR dʌɪ'rɛn
AM daɪ'rɛn

dairy
BR 'dɛːr|i, -ɪz, -ɪɪŋ
AM 'dɛri, -z, -ɪŋ

dairying
BR 'dɛːrɪɪŋ
AM 'dɛriɪŋ

dairymaid
BR 'dɛːrɪmeɪd, -z
AM 'dɛri,meɪd, -z

dairyman
BR 'dɛːrɪmən, 'dɛːrɪman
AM 'dɛrimən, 'dɛri,mæn

dairymen
BR 'dɛːrɪmən, 'dɛːrɪmɛn
AM 'dɛrimən, 'dɛri,mɛn

dais
BR 'deɪɪs, deɪs, -ɨz
AM 'deɪəs, 'daɪəs, -ɨz

daisy
BR 'deɪz|i, -ɪz
AM 'deɪzi, -z

Dakar
BR 'dakɑː(r), 'dakə(r)
AM dɑ'kɑr

Dakin
BR 'deɪkɪn
AM 'deɪkɨn

Dakota
BR də'kəʊtə(r)
AM də'koʊdə

Dakotan
BR də'kəʊt(ə)n, -z
AM də'koʊtn, -z

DAKS
BR daks
AM dæks

dal
BR dɑːl
AM dɑl

Dalai Lama
BR ˌdalʌɪ 'lɑːmə(r), -z
AM 'dɑ,laɪ 'lɑmə, 'dæ,laɪ +, -z

dalasi
BR də'lɑːsi
AM də'lɑsi

dale
BR deɪl, -z
AM deɪl, -z

Dalek
BR 'dɑːlɛk, -s
AM 'dɑlək, -s

dalesfolk
BR 'deɪlzfəʊk
AM 'deɪlz,foʊk

dalesman
BR 'deɪlzmən
AM 'deɪlzmən

daleswoman
BR 'deɪlz,wʊmən
AM 'deɪlz,wʊmən

daleswomen
BR 'deɪlz,wɪmɪn
AM 'deɪlz,wɪmɨn

daleth
BR 'dɑːlɪt
AM 'dɑlɪt

Daley
BR 'deɪli
AM 'deɪli

Dalgetty
BR dal'gɛti
AM dæl'gɛdi

Dalgleish
BR dal'gliːʃ
AM dæl'gliʃ

Dalglish
BR dal'gliːʃ
AM dæl'gliʃ

Dalhousie
BR dal'haʊzi, dal'huːzi
AM dæl'huzi

Dali
BR 'dɑːli
AM 'dɑli

Dalian
BR 'dɑːlɪən
AM 'dɑljən, 'dɑliən

Dalkeith
BR dal'kiːθ
AM dæl'kiθ

Dallapiccola
BR ˌdalə'pɪkələ(r), ˌdalə'pɪkl̩ə(r)
AM ˌdɑlə'pɪkələ

Dallas
BR 'daləs
AM 'dæləs

dalliance
BR 'dalɪəns
AM 'dæliəns, 'dæljəns

dallier
BR 'dalɪə(r), -z
AM 'dæliər, -z

dally
BR 'dal|i, -ɪz, -ɪɪŋ, -ɪd
AM 'dæli, -z, -ɪŋ, -d

Dalmatia
BR dal'meɪʃə(r)
AM dæl'meɪʃə, dɑl'meɪʃə

Dalmatian
BR dal'meɪʃ(ə)n, -z
AM dæl'meɪʃən, dɑl'meɪʃən, -z

dalmatic
BR dal'matɪk
AM dæl'mædɪk

Dalriada
BR ˌdalrɪ'ɑːdə(r)
AM ˌdɑlri'ɑdə

Dalrymple
BR dal'rɪmpl, 'dalrɪmpl
AM 'dæl,rɪmpəl

dal segno
BR dal 'seɪnjəʊ, dɑːl +
AM ˌdɑl 'seɪnjoʊ

Dalston
BR 'dɔːlst(ə)n, 'dɒlst(ə)n
AM dɔlstən, dɑlstən

Dalton
BR 'dɔːlt(ə)n, 'dɒlt(ə)n
AM 'dɔltən, 'dɑltən

Daltonise
BR 'dɔːltənʌɪz, 'dɒltənʌɪz, 'dɔːltn̩ʌɪz, 'dɒltn̩ʌɪz, -ɨz, -ɪŋ, -d
AM 'dɔltə,naɪz, 'dɑltə,naɪz, -ɨz, -ɪŋ, -d

daltonism
BR 'dɔːltənɪz(ə)m, 'dɒltənɪz(ə)m, 'dɔːltn̩ɪz(ə)m, 'dɒltn̩ɪz(ə)m
AM 'dɔltə,nɪzəm, 'dɑltə,nɪzəm

Daltonize
BR 'dɔːltənʌɪz, 'dɒltənʌɪz, 'dɔːltn̩ʌɪz, 'dɒltn̩ʌɪz, -ɨz, -ɪŋ, -d
AM 'dɔltə,naɪz, 'dɑltə,naɪz, -ɨz, -ɪŋ, -d

Dalwhinnie
BR dal'wɪni
AM dæl'wɪni

Daly
BR 'deɪli
AM deɪli

Dalyell
BR dɪ'ɛl, dʌɪ'ɛl, 'dalj(ə)l
AM 'dæl,jɛl, daɪ'ɛl

Dalzell
BR dɪ'ɛl, dʌɪ'ɛl, 'dalzɛl
AM dæl'zɛl, daɪ'ɛl

Dalziel
BR dɪ'ɛl, dʌɪ'ɛl, 'dalziːl
AM 'dælzi(ə)l, daɪ'ɛl

dam
BR dam, -z, -ɪŋ, -d
AM dæm, -z, -ɪŋ, -d

damage
BR 'dam|ɪdʒ, -ɨdʒɨz, -ɨdʒɪŋ, -ɨdʒd
AM 'dæmɪdʒ, -ɨz, -ɪŋ, -d

damageable
BR 'damɨdʒəbl
AM 'dæmədʒəbəl

damagingly
BR 'damɨdʒɪŋli
AM 'dæmədʒɪŋli

Damara
BR də'mɑːrə(r), -z
AM də'mɑrə, -z

Damaraland
BR də'mɑːrəland
AM 'dɑmərə,lænd, də'mɑrə,lænd

damascene
BR 'daməsiːn
AM 'dæmə,sin, ˌdæmə'sin

Damascus
BR də'maskəs, də'mɑːskəs
AM də'mæskəs

damask
BR 'daməsk
AM 'dæməsk

Dambuster
BR 'dam,bʌstə(r), -z
AM 'dæm,bəstər, -z

dame
BR deɪm, -z
AM deɪm, -z

Damian
BR 'deɪmɪən
AM 'deɪmiən

dammar
BR 'damə(r), -z
AM 'dæmər, -z

dammit
BR 'damɪt
AM 'dæmət

damn
BR dam, -z, -ɪŋ, -d
AM dæm, -z, -ɪŋ, -d

damna
BR 'damnə(r)
AM 'dæmnə

damnable
BR 'damnəbl
AM 'dæm(n)əbəl

damnably
BR 'damnəbli
AM 'dæm(n)əbli

damnation
BR dam'neɪʃn
AM dæm'neɪʃən

damnatory
BR 'damnət(ə)ri
AM 'dæm(n)ə,tɔri

damnedest
BR 'damdɪst
AM 'dæmdəst, 'dæmnəst

damn fool
adjective
BR ˌdam 'fuːl
AM ˌdæm ˌful

damnification
BR ˌdamnɪfɪ'keɪʃn

AM ˌdæm(n)əfəˈkeɪʃən, ˌdæmnəˌfaɪˈkeɪʃən

damnify
BR ˈdamnɪfʌɪ, -z, -ɪŋ, -d
AM ˈdæm(n)əˌfaɪ, -z, -ɪŋ, -d

damningly
BR ˈdamɪŋli
AM ˈdæmɪŋli

damnum
BR ˈdamnəm
AM ˈdæmnəm

Damocles
BR ˈdaməkliːz
AM ˈdæməkliz

Damon
BR ˈdeɪmən
AM ˈdeɪmən

damosel
BR ˌdaməˈzɛl, -z
AM ˌdæm(ə)ˈzɛl, -z

damozel
BR ˌdaməˈzɛl, -z
AM ˌdæm(ə)ˈzɛl, -z

damp
BR damp, -ə(r), -ɪst
AM dæmp, -ər, -əst

dampen
BR ˈdamp|(ə)n, -(ə)nz, -n̩ɪŋ\-nɪŋ, -(ə)nd
AM ˈdæmp|ən, -ənz, -(ə)nɪŋ, -ənd

dampener
BR ˈdamp(ə)nə(r), -z
AM ˈdæmpənər, -z

damper
BR ˈdampə(r), -z
AM ˈdæmpər, -z

Dampier
BR ˈdampɪə(r)
AM ˈdæmpɪ(ə)r

dampish
BR ˈdampɪʃ
AM ˈdæmpɪʃ

damply
BR ˈdampli
AM ˈdæmpli

dampness
BR ˈdampnəs
AM ˈdæmpnəs

damsel
BR ˈdamzl, -z
AM ˈdæmzəl, -z

damselfish
BR ˈdamzlfɪʃ, -ɪz
AM ˈdæmzəlˌfɪʃ, -ɪz

damselfly
BR ˈdamzlflʌɪ, -z
AM ˈdæmzəlˌflaɪ, -z

damson
BR ˈdamzn, -z
AM ˈdæmzn, ˈdæmsən, -z

dan
BR dan, -z
AM dæn, -z

Dana
BR ˈdɑːnə(r), ˈdeɪnə(r)
AM ˈdeɪnə

Danae
BR ˈdanɪiː, ˈdaneɪiː
AM ˈdæneɪˌi, ˈdæˌnaɪ

Danaides
BR dəˈneɪɪdiːz
AM dəˈneɪəˌdiz

Dan-Air®
BR ˌdanˈɛː(r)
AM ˈdænˈɛ(ə)r

Danakil
BR ˈdanəkɪl
AM ˈdænəˌkɪl

Da Nang
BR ˌdɑː ˈnaŋ
AM ˈdɑ ˈnæŋ

Danbury
BR ˈdanb(ə)ri
AM ˈdænˌbɛri

Danby
BR ˈdanbi
AM ˈdænbi

dance
BR dɑːns, dans, -ɪz, -ɪŋ, -t
AM dæns, -əz, -ɪŋ, -t

danceable
BR ˈdɑːnsəbl, ˈdansəbl
AM ˈdænsəbəl

dancer
BR ˈdɑːnsə(r), ˈdansə(r), -z
AM ˈdænsər, -z

dancewear
BR ˈdɑːnswɛː(r), ˈdanswɛː(r)
AM ˈdænsˌwɛ(ə)r

dandelion
BR ˈdandɪlʌɪən, -z
AM ˈdændlˌaɪən, ˈdændiˌlaɪən, -z

dander
BR ˈdandə(r), -z
AM ˈdændər, -z

dandify
BR ˈdandɪfʌɪ, -z, -ɪŋ, -d
AM ˈdændəˌfaɪ, -z, -ɪŋ, -d

Dandini
BR danˈdiːni
AM dænˈdini

dandle
BR ˈdand|l, -lz, -l̩ɪŋ\-lɪŋ, -ld
AM ˈdæn|dəl, -dəlz, -(d)(ə)lɪŋ, -dəld

Dando
BR ˈdandəʊ
AM ˈdændoʊ

dandruff
BR ˈdandrʌf
AM ˈdændrəf

dandy
BR ˈdand|i, -ɪz
AM ˈdændi, -z

dandyish
BR ˈdandɪɪʃ
AM ˈdændiɪʃ

dandyism
BR ˈdandɪɪz(ə)m
AM ˈdændiˌɪzəm

Dane
BR deɪn, -z
AM deɪn, -z

Danegeld
BR ˈdeɪngɛld
AM ˈdeɪnˌgɛld

Danelaugh
BR ˈdeɪnlɔː(r)
AM ˈdeɪnˌlɔ

Danelaw
BR ˈdeɪnlɔː(r)
AM ˈdeɪnˌlɔ

daneweed
BR ˈdeɪnwiːd
AM ˈdeɪnˌwid

danewort
BR ˈdeɪnwəːt
AM ˈdeɪnˌwərt, ˈdeɪnˌwɔ(ə)rt

dang
BR daŋ
AM dæŋ

danger
BR ˈdeɪn(d)ʒə(r), -z
AM ˈdeɪndʒər, -z

Dangerfield
BR ˈdeɪn(d)ʒəfiːld
AM ˈdeɪndʒərˌfild

dangerous
BR ˈdeɪn(d)ʒ(ə)rəs
AM ˈdeɪndʒ(ə)rəs

dangerously
BR ˈdeɪn(d)ʒ(ə)rəsli
AM ˈdeɪndʒ(ə)rəsli

dangerousness
BR ˈdeɪn(d)ʒ(ə)rəsnəs
AM ˈdeɪndʒ(ə)rəsnəs

dangle
BR ˈdaŋg|l, -lz, -l̩ɪŋ\-lɪŋ, -ld
AM ˈdæŋg|əl, -əlz, -(ə)lɪŋ, -əld

dangler
BR ˈdaŋglə(r), -z
AM ˈdæŋglər, -z

dangly
BR ˈdaŋgli
AM ˈdæŋgli

Daniel
BR ˈdanjəl
AM ˈdænjəl

Daniela
BR ˌdanɪˈɛlə(r), ˌdanˈjɛlə(r)
AM ˌdænˈjɛlə

Daniell
BR ˈdanjəl
AM ˈdænjəl

Danielle
BR ˌdanɪˈɛl, ˌdanˈjɛl
AM ˌdænˈjɛl

Daniels
BR ˈdanjəlz
AM ˈdænjəlz

Danish
BR ˈdeɪnɪʃ
AM ˈdeɪnɪʃ

dank
BR daŋk, -ə(r), -ɪst
AM dæŋk, -ər, -əst

dankly
BR ˈdaŋkli
AM ˈdæŋkli

dankness
BR ˈdaŋknəs
AM ˈdæŋknəs

Dankworth
BR ˈdaŋkwə(ː)θ
AM ˈdæŋkˌwərθ

Dannimac
BR ˈdanɪmak
AM ˈdænəmæk

Danny
BR ˈdani
AM ˈdæni

danse macabre
BR ˌdɑːns məˈkɑːbr(ər), -z
AM ˈdɑns məˈkɑbr(ə), -z

danses macabres
BR ˌdɑːns məˈkɑːbr(ər)z
AM ˈdɑns məˈkɑbr(ə)z

Dansette
BR danˈsɛt, -s
AM dænˈsɛt, -s

danseur
BR dɒnˈsəː(r), dɑːnˈsəː(r), danˈsəː(r), -z
AM dænˈsər, -z

danseuse
BR dɒnˈsəːz, dɑːnˈsəːz, danˈsəːz, -z
AM dænˈsʊz, -z

Dante
BR ˈdanti, ˈdɑːnti, ˈdanteɪ, ˈdɑːnteɪ
AM ˈdɑnteɪ, ˈdænteɪ

Dantean
BR ˈdantɪən, ˈdɑːntɪən, danˈtiːən, dɑːnˈtiːən
AM ˈdɑn(t)iən, ˈdæn(t)iən

Dantesque
BR danˈtɛsk, dɑːnˈtɛsk
AM dɑnˈtɛsk, dænˈtɛsk

danthonia
BR danˈθəʊnɪə(r)
AM dænˈθoʊniə

Danton
BR ˈdantɒn, dɒ̃ˈtɒ̃
AM ˈdæn(t)ən

Danube
BR ˈdanjuːb
AM ˈdænˌjub

Danubian
BR da'nju:bɪən, də'nju:bɪən, -z
AM də'njubiən, -z

Danvers
BR 'danvəz
AM 'dænvərz

Danzig
BR 'dan(t)zɪɡ
AM 'dæn(t)zɪɡ

Dão
BR daʊ, 'dɑ:əʊ
AM 'dɑ,oʊ, daʊ
PORT dɐ̃w

dap
BR dap, -s
AM dæp, -s

daphne
BR 'dafni
AM 'dæfni

daphnia
BR 'dafnɪə(r)
AM 'dæfniə

Daphnis
BR 'dafnɪs
AM 'dæfnəs

dapper
BR 'dap|ə(r), -(ə)rɪst
AM 'dæpər, -əst

dapperly
BR 'dapəli
AM 'dæpərli

dapperness
BR 'dapənəs
AM 'dæpərnəs

dapple
BR 'dap|l, -lz, -ḷɪŋ\-lɪŋ, -ld
AM 'dæpəl, -z, -ɪŋ, -d

dapsone
BR 'dapsəʊn
AM 'dæp,soʊn

daquiri
BR 'dak(ɨ)r|i, -ɪz
AM 'dækəri, -z

Darbishire
BR 'dɑ:bɪʃ(ɪ)ə(r)
AM 'dɑrbiʃɪ(ə)r

Darby
BR 'dɑ:bi
AM 'dərbi

Darcy
BR 'dɑ:si
AM 'dɑrsi

Dardanelles
BR ˌdɑ:də'nɛlz, ˌdɑ:dn'ɛlz
AM ˌdɑrdn'ɛlz

dare
BR dɛ:(r), -z, -ɪŋ, -d
AM dɛ(ə)r, -z, -ɪŋ, -d

daredevil
BR 'dɛ:ˌdɛvl, -z
AM 'dɛrˌdɛvəl, -z

daredevilry
BR 'dɛ:ˌdɛvlri
AM 'dɛrˌdɛv(ə)lri

Darell
BR 'darəl, 'darḷ
AM 'dɛrəl

Daren
BR 'darən, 'darṇ
AM 'dɛrən

daren't
BR dɛ:nt
AM dɛr(ə)nt

darer
BR 'dɛ:rə(r), -z
AM 'dɛ(r)ər, -z

daresay
BR ˌdɛ:'seɪ, 'dɛ:seɪ
AM 'dɛrˌseɪ

Dar es Salaam
BR ˌdɑ:r ɛs sə'lɑ:m, + ɪs +, + ɛz +, + ɪz +
AM ˌdɑr ɛs sə'lɑm

Darfur
BR ˌdɑ:'fə:(r)
AM 'dɑrfʊr

darg
BR dɑ:ɡ, -z
AM dɑrɡ, -z

dargah
BR 'dɑ:ɡə(r), -z
AM 'dɑrɡə, -z

Dari
BR 'dɛ:ri
AM 'dɛri

daric
BR 'darɪk, -s
AM 'dɛrɪk, -s

Darien
BR 'dɛ:rɪən, 'darɪən
AM ˌdɛri'ɛn, 'dɑriˌɛn

Darin
BR 'darɪn, 'darən, 'darṇ
AM 'dɛrən

daring
BR 'dɛ:rɪŋ
AM 'dɛrɪŋ

daringly
BR 'dɛ:rɪŋli
AM 'dɛrɪŋli

dariole
BR 'darɪəʊl, -z
AM 'dɛrioʊl, -z

Darius¹
forename
BR 'dɛ:rɪəs, 'darɪəs
AM 'dɛriəs

Darius²
Persian king
BR də'rʌɪəs
AM də'raɪəs, 'dɛriəs

Darjeeling
BR dɑ:'dʒi:lɪŋ
AM dɑr'dʒilɪŋ

dark
BR dɑ:k
AM dɑrk

darken
BR 'dɑ:k|(ə)n, -(ə)nz, -ənɪŋ\-ṇɪŋ, -(ə)nd
AM 'dɑrk|ən, -ənz, -(ə)nɪŋ, -ənd

darkener
BR 'dɑ:k(ə)nə(r), 'dɑ:kṇə(r), -z
AM 'dɑrk(ə)nər, -z

darkey
BR 'dɑ:k|i, -ɪz
AM 'dɑrki, -z

darkie
BR 'dɑ:k|i, -ɪz
AM 'dɑrki, -z

darkish
BR 'dɑ:kɪʃ
AM 'dɑrkɪʃ

darkling
BR 'dɑ:klɪŋ
AM 'dɑrklɪŋ

darkly
BR 'dɑ:kli
AM 'dɑrkli

darkness
BR 'dɑ:knəs, -ɪz
AM 'dɑrknəs, -əz

darkroom
BR 'dɑ:kru:m, 'dɑ:krʊm, -z
AM 'dɑrkˌrum, 'dɑrkˌrʊm, -z

darksome
BR 'dɑ:ks(ə)m
AM 'dɑrksəm

darky
BR 'dɑ:k|i, -ɪz
AM 'dɑrki, -z

Darlene
BR 'dɑ:li:n
AM dɑr'lin

darling
BR 'dɑ:lɪŋ, -z
AM 'dɑrlɪŋ, -z

Darlington
BR 'dɑ:lɪŋt(ə)n
AM 'dɑrlɪŋtən

Darmstadt
BR 'dɑ:mstat, 'dɑ:mʃtat
AM 'dɑrmˌstæt, 'dɑrmˌʃtæt

darn
BR dɑ:n, -z, -ɪŋ, -d
AM dɑrn, -z, -ɪŋ, -d

darnedest
BR 'dɑ:ndɪst
AM 'dɑrndəst

darnel
BR 'dɑ:nl, -z
AM 'dɑrnəl, -z

darner
BR 'dɑ:nə(r), -z
AM 'dɑrnər, -z

Darnley
BR 'dɑ:nli
AM 'dɑrnli

Darrell
BR 'darəl, 'darḷ
AM 'dɛrəl

Darren
BR 'darən, 'darṇ
AM 'dɛrən

Darrow
BR 'darəʊ
AM 'dɛroʊ

Darryl
BR 'darəl, 'darḷ
AM 'dɛrəl

dart
BR dɑ:t, -s, -ɪŋ, -ɪd
AM dɑr|t, -ts, -dɪŋ, -dəd

d'Artagnan
BR dɑ:'tanjən
AM dɑr'tænjən

dartboard
BR 'dɑ:tbɔ:d, -z
AM 'dɑrtˌbɔ(ə)rd, -z

darter
BR 'dɑ:tə(r), -z
AM 'dɑrdər, -z

Dartford
BR 'dɑ:tfəd
AM 'dɑrtfərd

Darth Vader
BR ˌdɑ:θ 'veɪdə(r)
AM ˌdɑrθ 'veɪdər

Dartmoor
BR 'dɑ:tmʊə(r), 'dɑ:tmɔ:(r)
AM 'dɑrtˌmɔ(ə)r, 'dɑrtˌmʊ(ə)r

Dartmouth
BR 'dɑ:tməθ
AM 'dɑrtməθ

dartre
BR 'dɑ:tə(r)
AM 'dɑrdər

Darwen
BR 'dɑ:wɪn
AM 'dɑrwən

Darwin
BR 'dɑ:wɪn
AM 'dɑrwən

Darwinian
BR dɑ:'wɪnɪən
AM dɑr'wɪniən

Darwinism
BR 'dɑ:wɪnɪz(ə)m
AM 'dɑrwənˌɪzəm

Darwinist
BR 'dɑ:wɪnɪst, -s
AM 'dɑrwənəst, -s

Daryl
BR 'darəl, 'darḷ
AM 'dɛrəl

dash
BR daʃ, -ɪz, -ɪŋ, -t
AM dæʃ, -əz, -ɪŋ, -t

dashboard
BR 'daʃbɔ:d, -z
AM 'dæʃˌbɔ(ə)rd, -z

dashiki
BR da'ʃɪk|i, 'dɑ:ʃɪki, -ɪz
AM də'ʃɪki, -z

dashing
BR 'daʃɪŋ

AM ˈdæʃɪŋ
dashingly
BR ˈdaʃɪŋli
AM ˈdæʃɪŋli
dashingness
BR ˈdaʃɪŋnɨs
AM ˈdæʃɪŋnɨs
dashpot
BR ˈdaʃpɒt, -s
AM ˈdæʃˌpɑt, -s
dassie
BR ˈdas|i, -ɪz
AM ˈdæsi, -z
dastard
BR ˈdastəd, -z
AM ˈdæstərd, -z
dastardliness
BR ˈdastədlɪnɨs
AM ˈdæstərdlinɨs
dastardly
BR ˈdastədli
AM ˈdæstərdli
dastur
BR daˈstʊə(r),
dəˈstʊə(r), -z
AM dæˈstʊ(ə)r,
dəˈstʊ(ə)r, -z
dasyure
BR ˈdasɪjʊə(r), -z
AM ˈdæsiˌjʊ(ə)r, -z
data
BR ˈdeɪtə(*r*), ˈdɑːtə(*r*)
AM ˈdædə, ˈdeɪdə
databank
BR ˈdeɪtəbaŋk,
ˈdɑːtəbaŋk, -s
AM ˈdædəˌbæŋk,
ˈdeɪdəˌbæŋk, -s
database
BR ˈdeɪtəbeɪs,
ˈdɑːtəbeɪs, -ɨz
AM ˈdædəˌbeɪs,
ˈdeɪdəˌbeɪs, -ɨz
datable
BR ˈdeɪtəbl
AM ˈdeɪdəbəl
datafile
BR ˈdeɪtəfʌɪl,
ˈdɑːtəfʌɪl, -z
AM ˈdædəˌfaɪl,
ˈdeɪdəˌfaɪl, -z
Datapost®
BR ˈdeɪtəpəʊst,
ˈdɑːtəpəʊst
AM ˈdædəˌpoʊst,
ˈdeɪdəˌpoʊst
Datchet
BR ˈdatʃɪt
AM ˈdætʃət
date
BR deɪt, -s, -ɪŋ, -ɨd
AM deɪ|t, -ts, -dɪŋ, -dɨd
dateless
BR ˈdeɪtlɨs
AM ˈdeɪtlɨs
dateline
BR ˈdeɪtlʌɪn, -z
AM ˈdeɪtˌlaɪn, -z
datival
BR deɪˈtʌɪvl
AM deɪˈtaɪvəl,
dəˈtaɪvəl
datively
BR deɪˈtʌɪvəli,
deɪˈtʌɪvl̩i
AM deɪˈtaɪvəli,
dəˈtaɪvəli
dative
BR ˈdeɪtɪv, -z
AM ˈdeɪdɪv, -z
Datsun®
BR ˈdats(ə)n, -z
AM ˈdɑtsən, -z
datum
BR ˈdeɪtəm, ˈdɑːtəm
AM ˈdædəm, ˈdeɪdəm
datura
BR dəˈtjʊərə(*r*),
dəˈtʃʊərə(*r*), -z
AM dəˈt(j)ʊrə,
dəˈtʃʊrə, -z
daub
BR dɔːb, -z, -ɪŋ, -d
AM dɔb, dɑb, -z, -ɪŋ, -d
daube
BR dəʊb, -z
AM doʊb, -z
dauber
BR ˈdɔːbə(r), -z
AM ˈdɔbər, ˈdɑbər, -z
Daubigny
BR ˈdɔːbɪnji
AM ˌdɔbiˈnji, ˌdɑbiˈnji
daubster
BR ˈdɔːbstə(r), -z
AM ˈdɔbstər, ˈdɑbstər,
-z
dauby
BR ˈdɔːbi
AM ˈdɔbi, ˈdɑbi
Daudet
BR ˈdəʊdeɪ
AM dɔˈdeɪ, dɑˈdeɪ
Daugherty
BR ˈdɒkəti, ˈdɒxəti
AM ˈdɔrdi
daughter
BR ˈdɔːtə(r), -z
AM ˈdɔdər, ˈdɑdər, -z
daughterhood
BR ˈdɔːtəhʊd
AM ˈdɔdərˌ(h)ʊd,
ˈdɑdərˌ(h)ʊd
daughterly
BR ˈdɔːtəli
AM ˈdɔdərli, ˈdɑdərli
daunt
BR dɔːnt, -s, -ɪŋ, -ɨd
AM dɔn|t, dɑn|t, -ts,
-(t)ɪŋ, -(t)əd
dauntingly
BR ˈdɔːntɪŋli
AM ˈdɔn(t)ɪŋli,
ˈdɑn(t)ɪŋli
dauntless
BR ˈdɔːntləs
AM ˈdɔn(t)ləs,
ˈdɑn(t)ləs
dauntlessly
BR ˈdɔːntləsli
AM ˈdɔn(t)ləsli,
ˈdɑn(t)ləsli
dauntlessness
BR ˈdɔːntləsnəs
AM ˈdɔn(t)ləsnəs,
ˈdɑn(t)ləsnəs
dauphin
BR ˈdəʊfã, ˈdɔːfɪn, -z
AM ˈdɔfən, ˈdɑfən, -z
dauphine
BR ˈdəʊfiːn, ˈdɔːfiːn, -z
AM ˈdɔfin, ˈdɑfin, -z
Dave
BR deɪv
AM deɪv
davenport
BR ˈdavnpɔːt, -s
AM ˈdævənˌpɔ(ə)rt, -s
Daventry¹
older, local form
BR ˈdeɪntri
AM ˈdævəntri
Daventry²
BR ˈdavntri
AM ˈdævəntri
Davey
BR ˈdeɪvi
AM ˈdeɪvi
David
BR ˈdeɪvɪd
AM ˈdeɪvəd
Davidson
BR ˈdeɪvɪds(ə)n
AM ˈdeɪvɪdsən
Davie
BR ˈdeɪvi
AM ˈdeɪvi
Davies
BR ˈdeɪvɪs
AM ˈdeɪviz
da Vinci
BR də ˈvɪn(t)ʃi
AM də ˈvɪn(t)ʃi
Davis
BR ˈdeɪvɪs
AM ˈdeɪvəs
Davison
BR ˈdeɪvɪsn
AM ˈdeɪvɪsən
Davisson
BR ˈdeɪvɪsn
AM ˈdeɪvɪsən
davit
BR ˈdavɪt, -s
AM ˈdeɪvɪt, ˈdævət, -s
Davos
BR daˈvəʊs
AM dɑˈvoʊs
Davy
BR ˈdeɪvi
AM ˈdeɪvi
daw
BR dɔː(*r*), -z
AM dɔ, dɑ, -z
dawdle
BR ˈdɔːd|l, -lz, -l̩ɪŋ\-lɪŋ,
-ld
AM ˈdɔd|əl, ˈdɑd|əl, -əlz,
-(ə)lɪŋ, -əld
dawdler
BR ˈdɔːdlə(r),
ˈdɔːdl̩ə(r), -z
AM ˈdɔd(ə)lər,
ˈdɑd(ə)lər, -z
Dawe
BR dɔː(*r*)
AM dɔ
Dawes
BR dɔːz
AM dɔz, dɑz
Dawkins
BR ˈdɔːkɪnz
AM ˈdɔkənz, ˈdɑkənz
Dawlish
BR ˈdɔːlɪʃ
AM ˈdɔləʃ, ˈdɑləʃ
dawn
BR dɔːn, -z, -ɪŋ, -d
AM dɔn, dɑn, -z, -ɪŋ, -d
dawning
BR ˈdɔːnɪŋ, -z
AM ˈdɔnɪŋ, ˈdɑnɪŋ, -z
Dawson
BR ˈdɔːsn
AM ˈdɔsən, ˈdɑsən
day
BR deɪ, -z
AM deɪ, -z
Dayak
BR ˈdʌɪak, -s
AM ˈdaɪæk, -s
Dayan
BR dʌɪˈan, dʌɪˈɑːn
AM dɑˈjɑn
daybed
BR ˈdeɪbɛd, -z
AM ˈdeɪˌbɛd, -z
daybook
BR ˈdeɪbʊk, -s
AM ˈdeɪˌbʊk, -s
daybreak
BR ˈdeɪbreɪk
AM ˈdeɪˌbreɪk
daydream
BR ˈdeɪdriːm, -z, -ɪŋ, -d
AM ˈdeɪˌdrim, -z, -ɪŋ, -d
daydreamer
BR ˈdeɪˌdriːmə(r), -z
AM ˈdeɪˌdrimər, -z
Day-Glo®
BR ˈdeɪgləʊ
AM ˈdeɪˌgloʊ
dayless
BR ˈdeɪlɨs
AM ˈdeɪlɨs
daylight
BR ˈdeɪlʌɪt
AM ˈdeɪˌlaɪt

dayroom
BR 'deɪruːm, 'deɪrʊm, -z
AM 'deɪˌrum, 'deɪˌrʊm, -z

daysack
BR 'deɪsak, -s
AM 'deɪˌsæk, -s

dayside
BR 'deɪsʌɪd
AM 'deɪˌsaɪd

daystar
BR 'deɪstɑː(r), -z
AM 'deɪˌstɑr, -z

daytime
BR 'deɪtʌɪm
AM 'deɪˌtaɪm

Daytona
BR deɪ'təʊnə(r)
AM deɪ'toʊnə

daywork
BR 'deɪwəːk
AM 'deɪˌwərk

Daz®
BR daz
AM dɑz

daze
BR deɪz, -ɪz, -ɪŋ, -d
AM deɪz, -ɪz, -ɪŋ, -d

dazedly
BR 'deɪzɨdli
AM 'deɪzɨdli

dazzle
BR 'daz|l, -lz, -l̩ɪŋ\-lɪŋ, -ld
AM 'dæz|əl, -əlz, -(ə)lɪŋ, -əld

dazzlement
BR 'dazlm(ə)nt
AM 'dæzəlmənt

dazzler
BR 'dazlə(r), 'dazl̩ə(r)
AM 'dæzlər

dazzlingly
BR 'dazlɪŋli, 'dazl̩ɪŋli
AM 'dæz(ə)lɪŋli

dBase
BR 'diːbeɪs
AM 'diˌbeɪs

deaccession
BR ˌdiːək'sɛʃ|n, -nz, -ənɪŋ\-n̩ɪŋ, -nd
AM ˌdiə(k)'sɛʃən, -z, -ɪŋ, -d

deacon
BR 'diːk(ə)n, -z
AM 'dikən, -z

deaconate
BR 'diːkənət, 'diːkn̩ət, -s
AM 'dikənət, -s

deaconess
BR ˌdiːkə'nɛs, -ɪz
AM 'dikənəs, -əz

deaconship
BR 'diːk(ə)nʃɪp, -s
AM 'dikənʃɪp, -s

deactivate
BR dɪ'aktɨveɪt, ˌdiː'aktɨveɪt, -s, -ɪŋ, -ɨd
AM di'æktəˌveɪ|t, -ts, -dɪŋ, -dɨd

deactivation
BR dɪˌaktɪ'veɪʃn, ˌdiːaktɪ'veɪʃn
AM diˌæktə'veɪʃən

deactivator
BR dɪ'aktɨveɪtə(r), ˌdiː'aktɨveɪtə(r), -z
AM di'æktəˌveɪdər, -z

dead
BR dɛd, -ə(r), -ɨst
AM dɛd, -ər, -əst

deadbeat
noun
BR 'dɛdbiːt, -s
AM 'dɛdˌbit, -s

dead-beat
adjective
BR ˌdɛd'biːt
AM 'dɛd'bit

deadbolt
BR 'dɛdbəʊlt, -s
AM 'dɛdˌboʊlt, -s

deaden
BR 'dɛd|n, -nz, -n̩ɪŋ\-nɪŋ, -nd
AM 'dɛdən, -z, -ɪŋ, -d

deadener
BR 'dɛdn̩ə(r), -z
AM 'dɛdn̩ər, -z

deadeye
BR 'dɛdʌɪ
AM 'dɛdˌaɪ

deadfall
BR 'dɛdfɔːl, -z
AM 'dɛdˌfɔl, 'dɛdˌfɑl, -z

deadhead
BR 'dɛdhɛd, -z, -ɪŋ, -ɨd
AM 'dɛdˌ(h)ɛd, -z, -ɪŋ, -əd

deadlight
BR 'dɛdlʌɪt, -s
AM 'dɛdˌlaɪt, -s

deadline
BR 'dɛdlʌɪn, -z
AM 'dɛdˌlaɪn, -z

deadliness
BR 'dɛdlɪnɨs
AM 'dɛdlinɨs

deadlock
BR 'dɛdlɒk, -s, -t
AM 'dɛdˌlɑk, -s, -t

deadly
BR 'dɛdl|i, -ɪə(r), -ɪɪst
AM 'dɛdli, -ər, -ɨst

deadness
BR 'dɛdnəs
AM 'dɛdnəs

deadpan
BR 'dɛdpan
AM 'dɛdˌpæn

deadstock
BR 'dɛdstɒk
AM 'dɛdˌstɑk

de-aerate
BR ˌdiː'ɛːreɪt, -s, -ɪŋ, -ɨd
AM di'ɛˌreɪ|t, -ts, -dɪŋ, -dɨd

de-aeration
BR ˌdiːɛː'reɪʃn
AM diˌɛr'eɪʃən

deaf
BR dɛf, -ə(r), -ɨst
AM dɛf, -ər, -əst

deafen
BR 'dɛf|n, -nz, -n̩ɪŋ\-nɪŋ, -nd
AM 'dɛf|ən, -ənz, -(ə)nɪŋ, -ənd

deafeningly
BR 'dɛfn̩ɪŋli, 'dɛfnɪŋli
AM 'dɛf(ə)nɪŋli

deafly
BR 'dɛfli
AM 'dɛfli

deafness
BR 'dɛfnəs
AM 'dɛfnəs

Deakin
BR 'diːkɪn
AM 'dikɪn

deal
BR diːl, -z, -ɪŋ
AM dil, -z, -ɪŋ

dealer
BR 'diːlə(r), -z
AM 'dilər, -z

dealership
BR 'diːləʃɪp, -s
AM 'dilərˌʃɪp, -s

dealing
BR 'diːlɪŋ, -z
AM 'dilɪŋ, -z

dealt
BR dɛlt
AM dɛlt

deambulation
BR dɪˌambjʉ'leɪʃn
AM ˌdiˌæmbjə'leɪʃən

deambulatory
BR dɪ'ambjʉlət(ə)ri
AM di'æmbjələˌtɔri

deamination
BR dɪˌamɪ'neɪʃn
AM diˌæmə'neɪʃən

dean
BR diːn, -z
AM din, -z

deanery
BR 'diːn(ə)r|i, -ɪz
AM 'dinəri, -z

Deanna
BR dɪ'anə(r), 'diːnə(r)
AM di'ænə, 'dinə

dear
BR dɪə(r), -z, -ə(r), -ɨst
AM dɪ(ə)r, -z, -ər, -ɨst

Deare
BR dɪə(r)
AM dɪ(ə)r

dearie
BR 'dɪər|i, -ɪz
AM 'dɪri, -z

dearly
BR 'dɪəli
AM 'dɪrli

Dearne
BR dəːn
AM dərn

dearness
BR 'dɪənəs
AM 'dɪrnɨs

dearth
BR dəːθ, -s
AM dərθ, -s

deary
BR 'dɪər|i, -ɪz
AM 'dɪri, -z

deasil
BR 'dɛsl, 'djɛʃl
AM 'dizəl

death
BR dɛθ, -s
AM dɛθ, -s

deathbed
BR 'dɛθbɛd, -z
AM 'dɛθˌbɛd, -z

deathblow
BR 'dɛθbləʊ, -z
AM 'dɛθˌbloʊ, -z

De'ath, DeAth
BR dɪ'aθ
AM di'ɑθ

deathless
BR 'dɛθləs
AM 'dɛθləs

deathlessly
BR 'dɛθləsli
AM 'dɛθləsli

deathlessness
BR 'dɛθləsnəs
AM 'dɛθləsnəs

deathlike
BR 'dɛθlʌɪk
AM 'dɛθˌlaɪk

deathliness
BR 'dɛθlɪnɨs
AM 'dɛθlinɨs

deathly
BR 'dɛθl|i, -ɪə(r), -ɪɪst
AM 'dɛθli, -ər, -ɨst

deathtrap
BR 'dɛθtrap, -s
AM 'dɛθˌtræp, -s

deathwatch
BR 'dɛθwɒtʃ
AM 'dɛθ'wɑtʃ, 'dɛθ'wɔtʃ

deattribute
BR ˌdiːə'trɪbjuːt, -s, -ɪŋ, -ɨd
AM ˌdiə'trɪbju|t, -ts, -dɪŋ, -dəd

deattribution
BR dɪˌatrɪ'bjuːʃn, ˌdiːatrɪ'bjuːʃn, -z
AM diˌætrə'bjuʃən, -z

Deauville
BR ˈdəʊvɪl
AM ˈdoʊˌvɪl

deb
BR dɛb, -z
AM dɛb, -z

débâcle
BR deɪˈbɑːkl, dɪˈbɑːkl, -z
AM dəˈbækəl, dəˈbɑkəl, ˈdɛbəkəl, -z

debag
BR ˌdiːˈbag, -z, -ɪŋ, -d
AM diˈbæg, -z, -ɪŋ, -d

debar
BR dɪˈbɑː(r), (ˌ)diːˈbɑː(r), -z, -ɪŋ, -d
AM diˈbɑr, -z, -ɪŋ, -d

debark
BR dɪˈbɑːk, ˌdiːˈbɑːk, -s, -ɪŋ, -t
AM diˈbɑrk, -s, -ɪŋ, -t

debarkation
BR ˌdiːbɑːˈkeɪʃn, -z
AM ˌdibɑrˈkeɪʃən, -z

debarkment
BR dɪˈbɑːkm(ə)nt, ˌdiːˈbɑːkm(ə)nt, -s
AM diˈbɑrkmənt, -s

debase
BR dɪˈbeɪs, -ɪz, -ɪŋ, -t
AM diˈbeɪs, dəˈbeɪs, -ɪz, -ɪŋ, -t

debasement
BR dɪˈbeɪsm(ə)nt
AM diˈbeɪsmənt, dəˈbeɪsmənt

debaser
BR dɪˈbeɪsə(r), -z
AM diˈbeɪsər, dəˈbeɪsər, -z

debatable
BR dɪˈbeɪtəbl
AM dəˈbeɪdəbəl, diˈbeɪdəbəl

debatably
BR dɪˈbeɪtəbli
AM dəˈbeɪdəbli, diˈbeɪdəbli

debate
BR dɪˈbeɪt, -s, -ɪŋ, -ɪd
AM dəˈbeɪ|t, diˈbeɪ|t, -ts, -dɪŋ, -dɪd

debater
BR dɪˈbeɪtə(r), -z
AM dəˈbeɪdər, diˈbeɪdər, -z

debauch
BR dɪˈbɔːtʃ, -ɪz, -ɪŋ, -t
AM dəˈbɔtʃ, diˈbɔtʃ, diˈbɑtʃ, dəˈbɑtʃ, -əz, -ɪŋ, -t

debauchee
BR ˌdɛbɔːˈ(t)ʃiː, ˌdɪbɔːˈ(t)ʃiː, dɪˌbɔːˈ(t)ʃiː, -z
AM dəˌbɔˈtʃi, dəˌbɑˈtʃi, diˌbɔˈtʃi, diˌbɔˈtʃi, -z

debaucher
BR dɪˈbɔːtʃə(r), -z
AM dəˈbɔtʃər, diˈbɔtʃər, diˈbɑtʃər, dəˈbɑtʃər, -z

debauchery
BR dɪˈbɔːtʃ(ə)r|i, -ɪz
AM dəˈbɔtʃəri, diˈbɔtʃ(ə)ri, diˈbɑtʃ(ə)ri, dəˈbɑtʃəri, -z

Debbie
BR ˈdɛbi
AM ˈdɛbi

debeak
BR ˌdiːˈbiːk, -s, -ɪŋ, -t
AM diˈbik, -s, -ɪŋ, -t

de Beauvoir
BR də ˌbəʊvˈwɑː(r)
AM də ˌboʊvˈwɑr

De Beers
BR də ˈbɪəz
AM də ˈbɪ(ə)rz

Debenhams
BR ˈdɛbənəmz, ˈdɛbn̩əmz
AM ˈdɛbənəmz

debenture
BR dɪˈbɛn(t)ʃə(r), -z
AM dəˈbɛntʃər, diˈbɛntʃər, -z

debilitate
BR dɪˌbɪlɪteɪt, -s, -ɪŋ, -ɪd
AM dəˈbɪləˌteɪ|t, diˈbɪləˌteɪ|t, -ts, -dɪŋ, -dɪd

debilitatingly
BR dɪˌbɪlɪteɪtɪŋli
AM dəˈbɪləˌteɪdɪŋli, diˈbɪləˌteɪdɪŋli

debilitation
BR dɪˌbɪlɪˈteɪʃn
AM dəˌbɪləˈteɪʃən, diˌbɪləˈteɪʃən

debilitative
BR dɪˈbɪlɪtətɪv
AM dəˈbɪləˌteɪdɪv, diˈbɪləˌteɪdɪv

debility
BR dɪˈbɪlɪt|i, -ɪz
AM dəˈbɪlɪdi, -z

debit
BR ˈdɛb|ɪt, -ɪts, -ɪtɪŋ, -ɪtɪd
AM ˈdɛbɪ|t, -ts, -dɪŋ, -dɪd

debonair
BR ˌdɛbəˈnɛː(r)
AM ˌdɛbəˈnɛ(ə)r

debonaire
BR ˌdɛbəˈnɛː(r)
AM ˌdɛbəˈnɛ(ə)r

debonairly
BR ˌdɛbəˈnɛːli
AM ˌdɛbəˈnɛrli

de-bond
BR ˌdiːˈbɒnd, -z, -ɪŋ, -ɪd
AM diˈbɑnd, -z, -ɪŋ, -əd

de-bonder
BR ˌdiːˈbɒndə(r), -z
AM diˈbɑndər, -z

debone
BR ˌdiːˈbəʊn, -z, -ɪŋ, -d
AM ˌdiˈboʊn, -z, -ɪŋ, -d

Deborah
BR ˈdɛb(ə)rə(r)
AM ˈdɛb(ə)rə

debouch
BR dɪˈbaʊtʃ, dɪˈbuːʃ, (ˌ)diːˈbaʊtʃ, (ˌ)diːˈbuːʃ, -ɪz, -ɪŋ, -t
AM dəˈbuʃ, diˈbuʃ, dəˈbaʊtʃ, diˈbaʊtʃ, -əz, -ɪŋ, -t

debouchment
BR dɪˈbaʊtʃm(ə)nt, dɪˈbuːʃm(ə)nt, (ˌ)diːˈbaʊtʃm(ə)nt, (ˌ)diːˈbuːʃm(ə)nt
AM dəˈbuʃmənt, diˈbuʃmənt, dəˈbaʊtʃmənt, diˈbaʊtʃmənt

Debra
BR ˈdɛbrə(r)
AM ˈdɛbrə

Debrett
BR dəˈbrɛt
AM dəˈbrɛt

debridement
BR deɪˈbriːdmɒ̃, dɪˈbriːdm(ə)nt
AM dəˈbridmənt, deɪˈbridmənt

debrief
BR ˌdiːˈbriːf, -s, -ɪŋ, -t
AM diˈbrif, ˌdəˈbrif, -s, -ɪŋ, -t

debriefing
BR ˌdiːˈbriːfɪŋ, -z
AM diˈbrifɪŋ, ˌdəˈbrifɪŋ, -z

débris
BR ˈdɛbriː, ˈdeɪbriː
AM dəˈbri, ˈdeɪˈbri

debt
BR dɛt, -s
AM dɛt, -s

debtor
BR ˈdɛtə(r), -z
AM ˈdɛdər, -z

debug
BR ˌdiːˈbʌg, -z, -ɪŋ, -d
AM ˌdiˈbəg, -z, -ɪŋ, -d

debugger
BR ˌdiːˈbʌgə(r), -z
AM ˌdiˈbəgər, -z

debunk
BR (ˌ)diːˈbʌŋ|k, -ks, -kɪŋ, -(k)t
AM ˌdiˈbəŋ|k, -ks, -kɪŋ, -(k)t

debunker
BR (ˌ)diːˈbʌŋkə(r), -z
AM ˌdiˈbəŋkər, -z

debus
BR ˌdiːˈbʌs, -ɪz, -ɪŋ, -t
AM dəˈbəs, diˈbəs, -əz, -ɪŋ, -t

Debussy
BR dəˈb(j)uːsi
AM ˌdɛbjʊˈsi

début
BR ˈdɛbjuː, ˈdeɪbjuː, -z, -ɪŋ, -d
AM deɪˈbju, ˈdeɪˌbju, -z, -ɪŋ, -d

débutant
BR ˈdɛbjʉtɑːnt, -s
AM ˈdɛbjuˌtɑnt, ˈdɛbjəˌtɑnt, -s

débutante
BR ˈdɛbjʉtɑːnt, -s
AM ˈdɛbjuˌtɑnt, ˈdɛbjəˌtɑnt, -s

DEC
BR dɛk
AM dɛk

decadal
BR ˈdɛkədl
AM ˈdɛkədəl

decade
BR ˈdɛkeɪd, dɪˈkeɪd, -z
AM ˈdɛˌkeɪd, -z

decadence
BR ˈdɛkəd(ə)ns
AM ˈdɛkədns

decadent
BR ˈdɛkəd(ə)nt, -s
AM ˈdɛkəd(ə)nt, -s

decadentism
BR ˈdɛkəd(ə)ntɪz(ə)m
AM ˈdɛkəd(ə)nˌtɪzəm

decadently
BR ˈdɛkəd(ə)ntli
AM ˈdɛkəd(ə)ntli, ˈdɛkədən(t)li

decadic
BR dɪˈkadɪk
AM dəˈkædɪk

decaf
BR ˈdiːkaf
AM ˈdiˌkæf

decaffeinate
BR ˌdiːˈkafɪneɪt, dɪˈkafɪneɪt, -s, -ɪŋ, -ɪd
AM ˌdiˈkæfəˌneɪ|t, dəˈkæfəˌneɪ|t, -ts, -dɪŋ, -dɪd

decagon
BR ˈdɛkəg(ə)n, ˈdɛkəgɒn, -z
AM ˈdɛkəˌgɑn, -z

decagonal
BR dɪˈkagənl, dɪˈkagn̩l
AM dəˈkægənəl

decagynous
BR dɪˈkadʒɪnəs, dɛˈkadʒɪnəs
AM dəˈkædʒənəs

decahedra
BR ˌdɛkəˈhiːdrə(r)

AM ˌdɛkə'hidrə

decahedral
BR ˌdɛkə'hiːdr(ə)l
AM ˌdɛkə'hidrəl

decahedron
BR ˌdɛkə'hiːdr(ə)n, -z
AM ˌdɛkə'hidrən, -z

decal
BR 'diːkal, dɪ'kal, -z
AM 'diˌkæl, də'kæl, -z

decalcification
BR ˌdiːkalsɪfɪ'keɪʃn, diːˌkalsɪfɪ'keɪʃn
AM ˌdiˌkælsəfə'keɪʃən

decalcifier
BR ˌdiː'kalsɪfʌɪə(r), -z, -ɪŋ, -d
AM ˌdi'kælsəˌfaɪ(ə)r, -z, -ɪŋ, -d

decalcify
BR ˌdiː'kalsɪfʌɪ, -z, -ɪŋ, -d
AM ˌdi'kælsəˌfaɪ, -z, -ɪŋ, -d

decalcomania
BR ˌdiːkalkə'meɪnɪə(r), -z
AM ˌdiˌkælkə'meɪniə, -z

decaliter
BR 'dɛkəˌliːtə(r), -z
AM 'dɛkəˌlidər, -z

decalitre
BR 'dɛkəˌliːtə(r), -z
AM 'dɛkəˌlidər, -z

Decalogue
BR 'dɛkəlɒg
AM 'dɛkəˌlɔg, 'dɛkəˌlɑg

Decameron
BR dɪ'kam(ə)rən, di'kæmərən, dɪ'kam(ə)rn̩, di'kæməˌrɑn
AM də'kæmərən, di'kæməˌrɑn

decameter
BR 'dɛkəˌmiːtə(r), -z
AM 'dɛkəˌmidər, -z

decametre
BR 'dɛkəˌmiːtə(r), -z
AM 'dɛkəˌmidər, -z

decamp
BR ˌdiː'kamp, dɪ'kamp, -s, -ɪŋ, -t
AM di'kæmp, də'kæmp, -s, -ɪŋ, -t

decampment
BR ˌdiː'kampm(ə)nt, dɪ'kampm(ə)nt
AM di'kæmpmənt, də'kæmpmənt

decanal
BR dɪ'keɪnl, 'dɛkənl
AM ˌdə'keɪnəl, 'dɛkənəl

decanally
BR dɪ'keɪnl̩i, dɪ'keɪnəli, 'dɛkənl̩i, 'dɛkənəli
AM ˌdə'keɪnəli, 'dɛkənəli

decandrous
BR dɪ'kandrəs
AM də'kændrəs

decane
BR 'dɛkeɪn
AM 'dɛkeɪn

decani
BR dɪ'keɪnʌɪ
AM də'keɪˌnaɪ

decant
BR dɪ'kant, ˌdiː'kant, -s, -ɪŋ, -ɪd
AM də'kæn|t, di'kæn|t, -ts, -(t)ɪŋ, -(t)əd

decanter
BR dɪ'kantə(r), -z
AM də'kæn(t)ər, di'kæn(t)ər, -z

decapitate
BR dɪ'kapɪteɪt, (ˌ)diː'kapɪteɪt, -s, -ɪŋ, -ɪd
AM də'kæpəˌteɪ|t, di'kæpəˌteɪ|t, -ts, -dɪŋ, -dɪd

decapitation
BR dɪˌkapɪ'teɪʃn, ˌdiːkapɪ'teɪʃn, -z
AM dəˌkæpə'teɪʃən, diˌkæpə'teɪʃən, -z

decapitator
BR dɪ'kapɪteɪtə(r), (ˌ)diː'kapɪteɪtə(r), -z
AM də'kæpəˌteɪdər, di'kæpəˌteɪdər, -z

decapod
BR 'dɛkəpɒd, -z
AM 'dɛkəˌpɑd, -z

decapodan
BR dɪ'kapəd(ə)n
AM də'kæpədən

decarbonisation
BR ˌdiːkɑːbənʌɪ'zeɪʃn, ˌdiːkɑːbn̩ʌɪ'zeɪʃn
AM ˌdiˌkɑrbənə'zeɪʃən, ˌdiˌkɑrbəˌnaɪ'zeɪʃən

decarbonise
BR (ˌ)diː'kɑːbənʌɪz, (ˌ)diː'kɑːbn̩ʌɪz, -ɪz, -ɪŋ, -d
AM di'kɑrbəˌnaɪz, -ɪz, -ɪŋ, -d

decarbonization
BR ˌdiːkɑːbənʌɪ'zeɪʃn, ˌdiːkɑːbn̩ʌɪ'zeɪʃn, diːˌkɑːbənʌɪ'zeɪʃn, diːˌkɑːbn̩ʌɪ'zeɪʃn
AM ˌdiˌkɑrbənə'zeɪʃən, ˌdiˌkɑrbəˌnaɪ'zeɪʃən

decarbonize
BR (ˌ)diː'kɑːbənʌɪz, (ˌ)diː'kɑːbn̩ʌɪz, -ɪz, -ɪŋ, -d
AM di'kɑrbəˌnaɪz, -ɪz, -ɪŋ, -d

decastyle
BR 'dɛkəstʌɪl, -z
AM 'dɛkəˌstaɪl, -z

decasualisation
BR ˌdiːkaʒ(j)ʊəlʌɪ'zeɪʃn, ˌdiːkaʒ(j)ʉlʌɪ'zeɪʃn, ˌdiːkazjʊəlʌɪ'zeɪʃn, ˌdiːkazjʉlʌɪ'zeɪʃn, diːˌkaʒ(j)ʊəlʌɪ'zeɪʃn, diːˌkaʒ(j)ʉlʌɪ'zeɪʃn, diːˌkazjʊəlʌɪ'zeɪʃn, diːˌkazjʉlʌɪ'zeɪʃn
AM ˌdiˌkæʒ(əw)ələ'zeɪʃən, ˌdiˌkæʒ(əw)əˌlaɪ'zeɪʃən

decasualise
BR (ˌ)diː'kaʒ(j)ʊəlʌɪz, (ˌ)diː'kaʒ(j)ʉlʌɪz, (ˌ)diː'kazjʊəlʌɪz, (ˌ)diː'kazjʉlʌɪz, -ɪz, -ɪŋ, -d
AM ˌdi'kæʒ(əw)əˌlaɪz, -ɪz, -ɪŋ, -d

decasualization
BR ˌdiːkaʒ(j)ʊəlʌɪ'zeɪʃn, ˌdiːkaʒ(j)ʉlʌɪ'zeɪʃn, ˌdiːkazjʊəlʌɪ'zeɪʃn, ˌdiːkazjʉlʌɪ'zeɪʃn, diːˌkaʒ(j)ʊəlʌɪ'zeɪʃn, diːˌkaʒ(j)ʉlʌɪ'zeɪʃn, diːˌkazjʊəlʌɪ'zeɪʃn, diːˌkazjʉlʌɪ'zeɪʃn
AM ˌdiˌkæʒ(əw)ələ'zeɪʃən, ˌdiˌkæʒ(əw)əˌlaɪ'zeɪʃən

decasualize
BR (ˌ)diː'kaʒ(j)ʊəlʌɪz, (ˌ)diː'kaʒ(j)ʉlʌɪz, (ˌ)diː'kazjʊəlʌɪz, (ˌ)diː'kazjʉlʌɪz, -ɪz, -ɪŋ, -d
AM ˌdi'kæʒ(əw)əˌlaɪz, -ɪz, -ɪŋ, -d

decasyllabic
BR ˌdɛkəsɪ'labɪk
AM ˌdɛkəsɪ'læbɪk

decasyllable
BR 'dɛkəˌsɪləbl, ˌdɛkə'sɪləbl, -z
AM 'dɛkəˌsɪləbəl, -z

decathlete
BR dɪ'kaθliːt, -s
AM də'kæθ(ə)lit, di'kæθ(ə)lit, -s

decathlon
BR dɪ'kaθlɒn, dɪ'kaθlən, -z
AM də'kæθ(ə)ˌlɑn, di'kæθ(ə)ˌlɑn, də'kæθ(ə)lən, di'kæθ(ə)lən, -z

Decatur
BR dɪ'keɪtə(r)
AM də'keɪdər, di'keɪdər

decay
BR dɪ'keɪ, -z, -ɪŋ, -d
AM də'keɪ, di'keɪ, -z, -ɪŋ, -d

decayable
BR dɪ'keɪəbl
AM də'keɪəbəl, di'keɪəbəl

Decca
BR 'dɛkə(*r*)
AM 'dɛkə

Deccan
BR 'dɛk(ə)n
AM 'dɛkən

decease
BR dɪ'siːs, -ɪz, -ɪŋ, -t
AM də'sis, di'sis, -ɪz, -ɪŋ, -t

decedent
BR dɪ'siːdnt, -s
AM də'sidnt, di'sidnt, -s

deceit
BR dɪ'siːt
AM də'sit, di'sit

deceitful
BR dɪ'siːtf(ʉ)l
AM də'sitfəl, di'sitfəl

deceitfully
BR dɪ'siːtfʉli, dɪ'siːtfl̩i
AM də'sitfəli, di'sitfəli

deceitfulness
BR dɪ'siːtf(ʉ)lnəs
AM də'sitfəlnəs, di'sitfəlnəs

deceivable
BR dɪ'siːvəbl
AM də'sivəbəl, di'sivəbəl

deceive
BR dɪ'siːv, -z, -ɪŋ, -d
AM də'siv, di'siv, -z, -ɪŋ, -d

deceiver
BR dɪ'siːvə(r), -z
AM də'sivər, di'sivər, -z

decelerate
BR ˌdiː'sɛləreɪt, dɪ'sɛləreɪt, -s, -ɪŋ, -ɪd
AM ˌdi'sɛləˌreɪ|t, -ts, -dɪŋ, -dɪd

deceleration
BR ˌdiːsɛlə'reɪʃn, dɪˌsɛlə'reɪʃn
AM diˌsɛlə'reɪʃən, ˌdisɛlə'reɪʃən

decelerator
BR ˌdiː'sɛləreɪtə(r), dɪ'sɛləreɪtə(r), -z
AM ˌdi'sɛləˌreɪdər, -z

decelerometer
BR ˌdiːsɛlə'rɒmɪtə(r), -z
AM ˌdiˌsɛlə'rɑmədər, -z

December
BR dɪˈsɛmbə(r), -z
AM dəˈsɛmbər, diˈsɛmbər, -z

Decembrist
BR dɪˈsɛmbrɪst, -s
AM dəˈsɛmbrəst, diˈsɛmbrəst, -s

decency
BR ˈdiːsns|i, -ɪz
AM ˈdisənsi, -z

decennia
BR dɪˈsɛnɪə(*r*)
AM dəˈsɛniə

decennial
BR dɪˈsɛnɪəl
AM dəˈsɛniəl

decennially
BR dɪˈsɛnɪəli
AM dəˈsɛniəli

decennium
BR dɪˈsɛnɪəm
AM dəˈsɛniəm

decent
BR ˈdiːsnt
AM ˈdisənt

decenter
BR ˌdiːˈsɛnt|ə(r), -əz, -(ə)rɪŋ, -əd
AM ˌdiˈsɛn(t)ər, -z, -ɪŋ, -d

decently
BR ˈdiːs(ə)ntli
AM ˈdisn(t)li

decentralisation
BR ˌdiːsɛntrəlʌɪˈzeɪʃn, ˌdiːsɛntrl̩ʌɪˈzeɪʃn, diːˌsɛntrəlʌɪˈzeɪʃn, diːˌsɛntrl̩ʌɪˈzeɪʃn
AM ˈdiˌsɛntrələˈzeɪʃən, ˈdiˌsɛntrəˌlaɪˈzeɪʃən

decentralise
BR (ˌ)diːˈsɛntrəlʌɪz, (ˌ)diːˈsɛntrl̩ʌɪz, -ɪz, -ɪŋ, -d
AM diˈsɛntrəˌlaɪz, -ɪz, -ɪŋ, -d

decentralist
BR (ˌ)diːˈsɛntrəlɪst, (ˌ)diːˈsɛntrl̩ɪst, -s
AM diˈsɛntrələst, -s

decentralization
BR ˌdiːsɛntrəlʌɪˈzeɪʃn, ˌdiːsɛntrl̩ʌɪˈzeɪʃn, diːˌsɛntrəlʌɪˈzeɪʃn, diːˌsɛntrl̩ʌɪˈzeɪʃn
AM ˈdiˌsɛntrələˈzeɪʃən, ˈdiˌsɛntrəˌlaɪˈzeɪʃən

decentralize
BR (ˌ)diːˈsɛntrəlʌɪz, (ˌ)diːˈsɛntrl̩ʌɪz, -ɪz, -ɪŋ, -d
AM diˈsɛntrəˌlaɪz, -ɪz, -ɪŋ, -d

decentre
BR ˌdiːˈsɛnt|ə(r), -əz, -(ə)rɪŋ, -əd
AM ˌdiˈsɛn(t)|ər, -ərz, -(ə)rɪŋ, -ərd

deception
BR dɪˈsɛpʃn, -z
AM dəˈsɛpʃən, diˈsɛpʃən, -z

deceptive
BR dɪˈsɛptɪv
AM dəˈsɛptɪv, diˈsɛptɪv

deceptively
BR dɪˈsɛptɪvli
AM dəˈsɛptəvli, diˈsɛptəvli

deceptiveness
BR dɪˈsɛptɪvnɪs
AM dəˈsɛptɪvnɪs, diˈsɛptɪvnɪs

decerebrate
BR ˌdiːˈsɛrɪbreɪt, -s, -ɪŋ, -ɪd
AM ˌdiˈsɛrəˌbreɪ|t, -ts, -dɪŋ, -dɪd

decertify
BR (ˌ)diːˈsəːtɪfʌɪ, -z, -ɪŋ, -d
AM diˈsərdəˌfaɪ, -z, -ɪŋ, -d

dechlorinate
BR (ˌ)diːˈklɒrɪneɪt, -s, -ɪŋ, -ɪd
AM diˈklɔrəˌneɪ|t, -ts, -dɪŋ, -dɪd

dechlorination
BR ˌdiːklɒrɪˈneɪʃn, -z
AM ˌdiˌklɔrəˈneɪʃən, -z

dechristianization
BR ˌdiːkrɪstʃənʌɪˈzeɪʃn, ˌdiːkrɪstʃn̩ʌɪˈzeɪʃn
AM diˌkrɪstʃənəˈzeɪʃən, diˌkrɪstʃəˌnaɪˈzeɪʃən

dechristianize
BR (ˌ)diːˈkrɪstʃənʌɪz, (ˌ)diːˈkrɪstʃn̩ʌɪz, -ɪz, -ɪŋ, -d
AM diˈkrɪstʃəˌnaɪz, -ɪz, -ɪŋ, -d

Decian
BR ˈdiːʃɪən
AM ˈdiʃ(i)ən

decibel
BR ˈdɛsɪb(ɛ)l, -z
AM ˈdɛsəbəl, ˈdɛsəˌbɛl, -z

decidable
BR dɪˈsʌɪdəbl
AM dəˈsaɪdəbəl, diˈsaɪdəbəl

decide
BR dɪˈsʌɪd, -z, -ɪŋ, -ɪd
AM dəˈsaɪd, diˈsaɪd, -z, -ɪŋ, -ɪd

decidedly
BR dɪˈsʌɪdɪdli
AM dəˈsaɪdɪdli, diˈsaɪdɪdli

decidedness
BR dɪˈsʌɪdɪdnɪs
AM dəˈsaɪdɪdnɪs, diˈsaɪdɪdnɪs

decider
BR dɪˈsʌɪdə(r), -z
AM dəˈsaɪdər, diˈsaɪdər, -z

deciduous
BR dɪˈsɪdjʊəs, dɪˈsɪdʒʊəs
AM dəˈsɪdʒəwəs, diˈsɪdʒəwəs

deciduousness
BR dɪˈsɪdjʊəsnəs, dɪˈsɪdʒʊəsnəs
AM dəˈsɪdʒəwəsnəs, diˈsɪdʒəwəsnəs

decigram
BR ˈdɛsɪgram, -z
AM ˈdɛsəˌgræm, -z

decigramme
BR ˈdɛsɪgram, -z
AM ˈdɛsəˌgræm, -z

decile
BR ˈdɛsʌɪl, ˈdɛsɪl, -z
AM ˈdɛˌsaɪl, -z

deciliter
BR ˈdɛsɪˌliːtə(r), -z
AM ˈdɛsəˌlidər, -z

decilitre
BR ˈdɛsɪˌliːtə(r), -z
AM ˈdɛsəˌlidər, -z

decimal
BR ˈdɛsɪml, -z
AM ˈdɛs(ə)məl, -z

decimalisation
BR ˌdɛsɪməlʌɪˈzeɪʃn, ˌdɛsɪml̩ʌɪˈzeɪʃn
AM ˌdɛs(ə)mələˈzeɪʃən, ˌdɛs(ə)məˌlaɪˈzeɪʃən

decimalise
BR ˈdɛsɪməlʌɪz, ˈdɛsɪml̩ʌɪz, -ɪz, -ɪŋ, -d
AM ˈdɛs(ə)məˌlaɪz, -ɪz, -ɪŋ, -d

decimalization
BR ˌdɛsɪməlʌɪˈzeɪʃn, ˌdɛsɪml̩ʌɪˈzeɪʃn
AM ˌdɛs(ə)mələˈzeɪʃən, ˌdɛs(ə)məˌlaɪˈzeɪʃən

decimalize
BR ˈdɛsɪməlʌɪz, ˈdɛsɪml̩ʌɪz, -ɪz, -ɪŋ, -d
AM ˈdɛsəməˌlaɪz, -ɪz, -ɪŋ, -d

decimally
BR ˈdɛsɪməli, ˈdɛsɪml̩i
AM ˈdɛsəməli

decimate
BR ˈdɛsɪmeɪt, -s, -ɪŋ, -ɪd
AM ˈdɛsəˌmeɪ|t, -ts, -dɪŋ, -dɪd

decimation
BR ˌdɛsɪˈmeɪʃn
AM ˌdɛsəˈmeɪʃən

decimator
BR ˈdɛsɪmeɪtə(r), -z
AM ˈdɛsəˌmeɪdər, -z

decimeter
BR ˈdɛsɪˌmiːtə(r), -z
AM ˈdɛsəˌmidər, -z

decimetre
BR ˈdɛsɪˌmiːtə(r), -z
AM ˈdɛsəˌmidər, -z

Decimus
BR ˈdɛsɪməs
AM ˈdɛsəməs

decipher
BR dɪˈsʌɪf|ə(r), -əz, -(ə)rɪŋ, -əd
AM dəˈsaɪf|ər, diˈsaɪfər, -ərz, -(ə)rɪŋ, -ərd

decipherable
BR dɪˈsʌɪf(ə)rəbl
AM dəˈsaɪf(ə)rəbəl, diˈsaɪf(ə)rəbəl

decipherment
BR dɪˈsʌɪfəm(ə)nt
AM dəˈsaɪfərmənt, diˈsaɪfərmənt

decision
BR dɪˈsɪʒn, -z
AM dəˈsɪʒən, diˈsiʒən, -z

decisive
BR dɪˈsʌɪsɪv
AM dəˈsaɪsɪv, diˈsaɪsɪv

decisively
BR dɪˈsʌɪsɪvli
AM dəˈsaɪsɪvli, diˈsaɪsɪvli

decisiveness
BR dɪˈsʌɪsɪvnɪs
AM dəˈsaɪsɪvnɪs, diˈsaɪsɪvnɪs

deck
BR dɛk, -s, -ɪŋ, -t
AM dɛk, -s, -ɪŋ, -t

deckchair
BR ˈdɛktʃɛː(r), -z
AM ˈdɛkˌtʃɛ(ə)r, -z

decker
BR ˈdɛkə(r), -z
AM ˈdɛkər, -z

deckhand
BR ˈdɛkhand, -z
AM ˈdɛkˌ(h)ænd, -z

deckhouse
BR ˈdɛkhaʊ|s, -zɪz
AM ˈdɛkˌ(h)aʊ|s, -zəz

deckle
BR ˈdɛkl, -d
AM ˈdɛkəl, -d

declaim
BR dɪˈkleɪm, -z, -ɪŋ, -d
AM dəˈkleɪm, diˈkleɪm, -z, -ɪŋ, -d

declaimer
BR dɪˈkleɪmə(r), -z
AM dəˈkleɪmər, diˈkleɪmər, -z

declamation
BR ˌdɛkləˈmeɪʃn, -z
AM ˌdɛkləˈmeɪʃən, -z

declamatory
BR dɪ'klamət(ə)ri
AM də'klæmə,tɔri, di'klæmə,tɔri

Declan
BR 'dɛklən
AM 'dɛklən

declarable
BR dɪ'klɛːrəbl
AM də'klɛrəbəl, di'klɛrəbəl

declarant
BR dɪ'klɛːrənt, dɪ'klɛːrn̩t, -s
AM də'klɛrənt, di'klɛrənt, -s

declaration
BR ,dɛklə'reɪʃn, -z
AM ,dɛklə'reɪʃən, -z

declarative
BR dɪ'klarətɪv, -z
AM də'klɛrədɪv, -z

declaratively
BR dɪ'klarətɨvli
AM də'klɛrədɨvli

declarativeness
BR dɪ'klarətɨvnɨs
AM də'klɛrədɨvnɨs

declaratory
BR dɪ'klarət(ə)ri
AM də'klɛrə,tɔri

declare
BR dɪ'klɛː(r), -z, -ɪŋ, -d
AM də'klɛ(ə)r, di'klɛ(ə)r, -z, -ɪŋ, -d

declaredly
BR dɪ'klɛːrɨdli
AM də'klɛrədli

declarer
BR dɪ'klɛːrə(r), -z
AM də'klɛrər, di'klɛrər, -z

declass
BR (,)diː'klɑːs, (,)diː'klas, -ɨz, -ɪŋ, -t
AM di'klæs, də'klæs, -əz, -ɪŋ, -t

déclassé
BR deɪ'klaseɪ, ,deɪkla'seɪ
AM ,deɪklɑ'seɪ

déclassée
BR deɪ'klaseɪ, ,deɪkla'seɪ
AM ,deɪklɑ'seɪ

declassification
BR ,diːklasɪfɪ'keɪʃn, diː,klasɪfɪ'keɪʃn
AM di,klæsəfə'keɪʃən

declassify
BR (,)diː'klasɪfʌɪ, -z, -ɪŋ, -d
AM ,di'klæsə,faɪ, -z, -ɪŋ, -d

de-claw
BR ,diː'klɔː(r), -z, -ɪŋ, -d
AM ,di'klɔ, ,di'klɑ, -z, -ɪŋ, -d

declension
BR dɪ'klɛnʃn, -z
AM də'klɛn(t)ʃən, di'klɛn(t)ʃən, -z

declensional
BR dɪ'klɛnʃn̩(ə)l, dɪ'klɛnʃən(ə)l
AM də'klɛn(t)ʃ(ə)nəl, di'klɛn(t)ʃ(ə)nəl

declinable
BR dɪ'klʌɪnəbl
AM də'klaɪnəbəl, di'klaɪnəbəl

declination
BR ,dɛklɪ'neɪʃn, -z
AM ,dɛklə'neɪʃən, -z

declinational
BR ,dɛklɪ'neɪʃn̩(ə)l, ,dɛklɪ'neɪʃən(ə)l
AM ,dɛklə'neɪʃ(ə)nəl

decline
BR dɪ'klʌɪn, -z, -ɪŋ, -d
AM də'klaɪn, di'klaɪn, -z, -ɪŋ, -d

decliner
BR dɪ'klʌɪnə(r), -z
AM də'klaɪnər, di'klaɪnər, -z

declinometer
BR ,dɛklɪ'nɒmɨtə(r), -z
AM ,dɛklə'nɑmədər, -z

declivitous
BR dɪ'klɪvɨtəs
AM də'klɪvədəs

declivity
BR dɪ'klɪvɨt|i, -ɪz
AM də'klɪvɨdi, -z

declutch
BR (,)diː'klʌtʃ, dɪ'klʌtʃ, -ɨz, -ɪŋ, -t
AM di'klətʃ, -əz, -ɪŋ, -t

deco
BR 'dɛkəʊ
AM 'dɛkoʊ

decoct
BR dɪ'kɒkt, -s, -ɪŋ, -ɨd
AM də'kɑk|(t), di'kɑk|(t), -(t)s, -tɪŋ, -tɨd

decoction
BR dɪ'kɒkʃn, -z
AM də'kɑkʃən, di'kɑkʃən, -z

decodable
BR (,)diː'kəʊdəbl, dɪ'kəʊdəbl
AM ,di'koʊdəbəl, də'koʊdəbəl

decode
BR (,)diː'kəʊd, dɪ'kəʊd, -z, -ɪŋ, -ɨd
AM ,di'koʊd, -z, -ɪŋ, -əd

decoder
BR (,)diː'kəʊdə(r), dɪ'kəʊdə(r), -z
AM ,di'koʊdər, də'koʊdər, -z

decoke[1]
noun
BR 'diːkəʊk, -s
AM 'di,koʊk, -s

decoke[2]
verb
BR ,diː'kəʊk, dɪ'kəʊk, -s, -ɪŋ, -t
AM ,di'koʊk, də'koʊk, -s, -ɪŋ, -t

decollate
BR 'dɛkəleɪt, -s, -ɪŋ, -ɨd
AM 'dɛkə,leɪ|t, -ts, -dɪŋ, -dɨd

decollation
BR ,dɛkə'leɪʃn, -z
AM ,dɛkə'leɪʃən, -z

décolletage
BR ,deɪkɒl(ɪ)'tɑːʒ, deɪ'kɒltɑːʒ
AM deɪ,kɑlə'tɑʒ, dɛ,kɑlə'tɑʒ, deɪ,kɔlə'tɑʒ, dɛ,kɔlə'tɑʒ

décolleté
BR deɪ'kɒl(ɪ)teɪ, ,deɪkɒl(ɪ)'teɪ
AM deɪ,kɑlə'teɪ, dɛ,kɑlə'teɪ, deɪ,kɔlə'teɪ, dɛ,kɔlə'teɪ

décolletée
BR deɪ'kɒl(ɪ)teɪ, ,deɪkɒl(ɪ)'teɪ
AM deɪ,kɑlə'teɪ, dɛ,kɑlə'teɪ, deɪ,kɔlə'teɪ, dɛ,kɔlə'teɪ

decolonisation
BR ,diːkɒlənʌɪ'zeɪʃn, diː,kɒlənʌɪ'zeɪʃn
AM di,kɑlənə'zeɪʃən, di,kɑlə,naɪ'zeɪʃən

decolonise
BR (,)diː'kɒlənʌɪz, -ɨz, -ɪŋ, -d
AM di'kɑlə,naɪz, -ɨz, -ɪŋ, -d

decolonization
BR ,diːkɒlənʌɪ'zeɪʃn, diː,kɒlənʌɪ'zeɪʃn
AM di,kɑlənə'zeɪʃən, di,kɑlə,naɪ'zeɪʃən

decolonize
BR (,)diː'kɒlənʌɪz, -ɨz, -ɪŋ, -d
AM di'kɑlə,naɪz, -ɨz, -ɪŋ, -d

decolorant
BR ,diː'kʌl(ə)rənt, ,diː'kʌl(ə)rn̩t, -s
AM di'kələrənt, -s

decolorisation
BR ,diːkʌlərʌɪ'zeɪʃn, diː,kʌlərʌɪ'zeɪʃn
AM ,di,kələrə'zeɪʃən, ,di,kələ,raɪ'zeɪʃən

decolorise
BR ,diː'kʌlərʌɪz, -ɨz, -ɪŋ, -d
AM di'kələ,raɪz, -ɨz, -ɪŋ, -d

decolorization
BR ,diːkʌlərʌɪ'zeɪʃn, diː,kʌlərʌɪ'zeɪʃn
AM ,di,kələrə'zeɪʃən, ,di,kələ,raɪ'zeɪʃən

decolorize
BR ,diː'kʌlərʌɪz, -ɨz, -ɪŋ, -d
AM di'kələ,raɪz, -ɨz, -ɪŋ, -d

decommission
BR ,diːkə'mɪʃ|n, -nz, -n̩ɪŋ\-nɪŋ, -nd
AM ,dikə'mɪʃən, -z, -ɪŋ, -d

decommunisation
BR ,diːkɒmjʉnʌɪ'zeɪʃn, diː,kɒmjʉnʌɪ'zeɪʃn
AM ,di,kɑmjunə'zeɪʃən, ,di,kɑmju,naɪ'zeɪʃən

decommunise
BR ,diː'kɒmjʉnʌɪz, -ɨz, -ɪŋ, -d
AM ,di'kɑmju,naɪz, -ɨz, -ɪŋ, -d

decommunization
BR ,diːkɒmjʉnʌɪ'zeɪʃn, diː,kɒmjʉnʌɪ'zeɪʃn
AM ,di,kɑmjunə'zeɪʃən, ,di,kɑmju,naɪ'zeɪʃən

decommunize
BR ,diː'kɒmjʉnʌɪz, -ɨz, -ɪŋ, -d
AM ,di'kɑmju,naɪz, -ɨz, -ɪŋ, -d

decomposable
BR ,diːkəm'pəʊzəbl
AM ,dikəm'poʊzəbəl

decompose
BR ,diːkəm'pəʊz, -ɨz, -ɪŋ, -d
AM ,dikəm'poʊz, -əz, -ɪŋ, -d

decomposition
BR ,diːkɒmpə'zɪʃn, -z
AM ¦di,kɑmpə¦zɪʃən, -z

decompound[1]
noun
BR 'diː,kɒmpaʊnd, -z
AM ,di'kɑm,paʊnd, -z

decompound[2]
verb
BR ,diːkəm'paʊnd, -z, -ɪŋ, -ɨd
AM ,dikəm'paʊnd, -z, -ɪŋ, -əd

decompress
BR ,diːkəm'prɛs, -ɨz, -ɪŋ, -t
AM ¦dikəm'prɛs, -əz, -ɪŋ, -t

decompression
BR ,diːkəm'prɛʃn

AM ˌdikəm'prɛʃən

decompressor
BR ˌdiːkəm'prɛsə(r), -z
AM ˌdikəm'prɛsər, -z

decongestant
BR ˌdiːk(ə)n'dʒɛst(ə)nt, -s
AM ˌdikən'dʒɛstənt, -s

deconsecrate
BR ˌdiː'kɒnsɪkreɪt, -s, -ɪŋ, -ɪd
AM di'kɑnsəˌkreɪ|t, -ts, -dɪŋ, -dɪd

deconsecration
BR ˌdiːkɒnsɪ'kreɪʃn, diːˌkɒnsɪ'kreɪʃn
AM ˌdikɑnsə'kreɪʃən

deconstruct
BR ˌdiːk(ə)n'strʌkt, -s, -ɪŋ, -ɪd
AM ˌdikən'strək|(t), -(t)s, -tɪŋ, -təd

deconstruction
BR ˌdiːk(ə)n'strʌkʃn
AM ˌdikən'strəkʃən

deconstructionism
BR ˌdiːk(ə)n'strʌkʃn̩ɪz(ə)m, ˌdiːk(ə)n'strʌkʃənɪz(ə)m
AM ˌdik(ə)n'strəkʃəˌnɪzəm

deconstructionist
BR ˌdiːk(ə)n'strʌkʃn̩ɪst, ˌdiːk(ə)n'strʌkʃənɪst, -s
AM ˌdikən'strəkʃənəst, -s

deconstructive
BR ˌdiːk(ə)n'strʌktɪv
AM ˌdikən'strəktɪv

decontaminate
BR ˌdiːk(ə)n'tamɪneɪt, -s, -ɪŋ, -ɪd
AM ˌdikən'tæməˌneɪ|t, -ts, -dɪŋ, -dɪd

decontamination
BR ˌdiːk(ə)ntamɪ'neɪʃn
AM ˌdikənˌtæmə'neɪʃən

decontextualise
BR ˌdiːk(ə)n'tɛkstjʊəlʌɪz, ˌdiːk(ə)n'tɛkstjʉlʌɪz, ˌdiːk(ə)n'tɛkstʃʊəlʌɪz, ˌdiːk(ə)n'tɛkstʃʉlʌɪz, ˌdiːk(ə)n'tɛkstʃl̩ʌɪz, -ɪz, -ɪŋ, -d
AM ˌdikən'tɛks(t)ʃ(əw)əˌlaɪz, -ɪz, -ɪŋ, -d

decontextualize
BR ˌdiːk(ə)n'tɛkstjʊəlʌɪz, ˌdiːk(ə)n'tɛkstjʉlʌɪz, ˌdiːk(ə)n'tɛkstʃʊəlʌɪz, ˌdiːk(ə)n'tɛkstʃʉlʌɪz, ˌdiːk(ə)n'tɛkstʃl̩ʌɪz, -ɪz, -ɪŋ, -d
AM ˌdikən'tɛks(t)ʃ(əw)əˌlaɪz, -ɪz, -ɪŋ, -d

decontrol
BR ˌdiːk(ə)n'trəʊl, -z, -ɪŋ, -d
AM ˌdikən'troʊl, -z, -ɪŋ, -d

décor
BR 'deɪkɔː(r), 'dɛkɔː(r), -z
AM ˌdeɪˌkɔ(ə)r, də'kɔ(ə)r, -z

decorate
BR 'dɛkəreɪt, -s, -ɪŋ, -ɪd
AM 'dɛkəˌreɪ|t, -ts, -dɪŋ, -dɪd

decoration
BR ˌdɛkə'reɪʃn, -z
AM ˌdɛkə'reɪʃən, -z

decorative
BR 'dɛk(ə)rətɪv
AM 'dɛk(ə)rədɪv, 'dɛkəˌreɪdɪv

decoratively
BR 'dɛk(ə)rətɪvli
AM 'dɛk(ə)rədɪvnli, 'dɛkəˌreɪdɪvli

decorativeness
BR 'dɛk(ə)rətɪvnɪs
AM 'dɛk(ə)rədɪvnɪs, 'dɛkəˌreɪdɪvnɪs

decorator
BR 'dɛkəreɪtə(r), -z
AM 'dɛkəˌreɪdər, -z

decorous
BR 'dɛk(ə)rəs
AM 'dɛk(ə)rəs

decorously
BR 'dɛk(ə)rəsli
AM 'dɛk(ə)rəsli

decorousness
BR 'dɛk(ə)rəsnəs
AM 'dɛk(ə)rəsnəs

decorticate
BR ˌdiː'kɔːtɪkeɪt, -s, -ɪŋ, -ɪd
AM di'kɔrdəˌkeɪ|t, də'kɔrdəˌkeɪ|t, -ts, -dɪŋ, -dɪd

decortication
BR ˌdiːkɔːtɪ'keɪʃn
AM diˌkɔrdə'keɪʃən

decorum
BR dɪ'kɔːrəm
AM də'kɔrəm, di'kɔrəm

découpage
BR ˌdeɪkuː'pɑːʒ, ˌdeɪkʊ'pɑːʒ
AM ˌdeɪku'pɑʒ

decouple
BR (ˌ)diː'kʌp|l, -lz, -l̩ɪŋ\-lɪŋ, -ld
AM di'kəpəl, -z, -ɪŋ, -d

De Courcy
BR də 'kɔːsi, + 'kəːsi, + 'kʊəsi
AM də 'kərsi

decoy¹
noun
BR 'diːkɔɪ, -z
AM 'diˌkɔɪ, -z

decoy²
verb
BR dɪ'kɔɪ, -z, -ɪŋ, -d
AM də'kɔɪ, di'kɔɪ, -z, -ɪŋ, -d

decrease¹
noun
BR 'diːkriːs, -ɪz
AM də'kris, 'diˌkris, -ɪz

decrease²
verb
BR dɪ'kriːs, -ɪz, -ɪŋ, -t
AM də'kris, di'kris, -ɪz, -ɪŋ, -t

decreasingly
BR dɪ'kriːsɪŋli
AM də'krisɪŋli, di'krisɪŋli

decree
BR dɪ'kriː, -z, -ɪŋ, -d
AM də'kri, di'kri, -z, -ɪŋ, -d

decrement¹
noun
BR 'dɛkrɪm(ə)nt, -s
AM 'dɛkrəmənt, -s

decrement²
verb
BR 'dɛkrɪmɛnt, -s, -ɪŋ, -ɪd
AM 'dɛkrəˌmɛn|t, -ts, -(t)ɪŋ, -(t)əd

decreolization
BR ˌdiːkriːəlʌɪ'zeɪʃn, diːˌkriːəlʌɪ'zeɪʃn
AM ˌdiˌkriələ'zeɪʃən, ˌdiˌkriəˌlaɪ'zeɪʃən

decreolize
BR ˌdiː'kriːəlʌɪz, -ɪz, -ɪŋ, -d
AM di'kriəˌlaɪz, -ɪz, -ɪŋ, -d

decrepit
BR dɪ'krɛpɪt
AM də'krɛpət, di'krɛpət

decrepitate
BR dɪ'krɛpɪteɪt, -s, -ɪŋ, -ɪd
AM di'krɛpəˌteɪ|t, -ts, -dɪŋ, -dɪd

decrepitation
BR dɪˌkrɛpɪ'teɪʃn
AM dəˌkrɛpə'teɪʃən, diˌkrɛpə'teɪʃən

decrepitness
BR dɪ'krɛpɪtnɪs
AM də'krɛpətnəs, di'krɛpətnəs

decrepitude
BR dɪ'krɛpɪtjuːd, dɪ'krɛpɪtʃuːd
AM də'krɛpəˌt(j)ud, di'krɛpəˌt(j)ud

decrescendo
BR ˌdiːkrɪ'ʃɛndəʊ, -z
AM ˌdikrə'ʃɛndoʊ, -z

decrescent
BR dɪ'krɛsnt
AM də'krɛsənt, di'krɛsənt

decretal
BR dɪ'kriːtl
AM də'kridəl

decrial
BR dɪ'krʌɪəl
AM də'kraɪəl, di'kraɪəl

decrier
BR dɪ'krʌɪə(r), -z
AM də'kraɪər, di'kraɪər, -z

decriminalisation
BR ˌdiːkrɪmɪnəlʌɪ'zeɪʃn, ˌdiːkrɪmɪnl̩ʌɪ'zeɪʃn, diːˌkrɪmɪnəlʌɪ'zeɪʃn, diːˌkrɪmɪnl̩ʌɪ'zeɪʃn
AM ˌdiˌkrɪm(ə)nələ'zeɪʃən, ˌdiˌkrɪm(ə)nəˌlaɪ'zeɪʃən

decriminalise
BR (ˌ)diː'krɪmɪnəlʌɪz, (ˌ)diː'krɪmɪnl̩ʌɪz, -ɪz, -ɪŋ, -d
AM di'krɪmɪnəlaɪz, -ɪz, -ɪŋ, -d

decriminalization
BR ˌdiːkrɪmɪnəlʌɪ'zeɪʃn, ˌdiːkrɪmɪnl̩ʌɪ'zeɪʃn, diːˌkrɪmɪnəlʌɪ'zeɪʃn, diːˌkrɪmɪnl̩ʌɪ'zeɪʃn
AM ˌdiˌkrɪm(ə)nələ'zeɪʃən, ˌdiˌkrɪm(ə)nəˌlaɪ'zeɪʃən

decriminalize
BR (ˌ)diː'krɪmɪnəlʌɪz, (ˌ)diː'krɪmɪnl̩ʌɪz, -ɪz, -ɪŋ, -d
AM di'krɪmɪnəlaɪz, -ɪz, -ɪŋ, -d

decry
BR dɪ'krʌɪ, -z, -ɪŋ, -d
AM də'kraɪ, di'kraɪ, -z, -ɪŋ, -d

decrypt
BR (ˌ)diː'krɪpt, -s, -ɪŋ, -ɪd
AM di'krɪpt, -s, -ɪŋ, -ɪd

decryption
BR (ˌ)diː'krɪpʃn
AM də'krɪpʃən, di'krɪpʃən

decubitus
BR dɪ'kjuːbɪtəs
AM də'kjubədəs

decumbent
BR dɪ'kʌmb(ə)nt
AM də'kəmbənt, di'kəmbənt

decuple
BR 'dɛkjʉp|l, -lz, -l̩ɪŋ\-lɪŋ, -ld

AM ˈdɛkjəp|əl, -əlz, -(ə)lɪŋ, -əld

decuplet
BR ˈdɛkjʊplɪt, -s
AM ˈdɛkjəplət, -s

decurvature
BR ˌdiːˈkəːvətʃə(r), -z
AM diˈkərvətʃʊ(ə)r, diˈkərvətʃər, -z

decurve
BR ˌdiːˈkəːv, -z, -ɪŋ, -d
AM diˈkərv, -z, -ɪŋ, -d

decussate
BR dɪˈkʌseɪt, ˈdɛkəseɪt, -s, -ɪŋ, -ɨd
AM diˈkəsət, ˈdɛkəˌseɪ|t, -ts, -dɪŋ, -dɨd

decussation
BR ˌdɛkəˈseɪʃn
AM ˌdɛkəˈseɪʃən

dedans
BR dəˈdɒ̃, -z
AM dəˈdɑn(z), -z

dedicate
BR ˈdɛdɪkeɪt, -s, -ɪŋ, -ɨd
AM ˈdɛdəˌkeɪ|t, -ts, -dɪŋ, -dɨd

dedicated
BR ˈdɛdɪkeɪtɨd
AM ˈdɛdəˌkeɪdɨd

dedicatedly
BR ˈdɛdɪkeɪtɨdli
AM ˈdɛdəˌkeɪdɨdli

dedicatee
BR ˌdɛdɪkəˈtiː, -z
AM ˌdɛdəkeɪˈti, -z

dedication
BR ˌdɛdɪˈkeɪʃn, -z
AM ˌdɛdəˈkeɪʃən, -z

dedicative
BR ˈdɛdɪkətɪv
AM ˈdɛdəkədɪv, ˈdɛdəˌkeɪdɪv

dedicator
BR ˈdɛdɪkeɪtə(r), -z
AM ˈdɛdəˌkeɪdər, -z

dedicatory
BR ˈdɛdɪkət(ə)ri, ˈdɛdɪkeɪt(ə)ri
AM ˈdɛdəkəˌtɔri

deduce
BR dɪˈdjuːs, dɪˈdʒuːs, -ɨz, -ɪŋ, -t
AM dəˈd(j)us, diˈd(j)us, -əz, -ɪŋ, -t

deducible
BR dɪˈdjuːsɨbl, dɪˈdʒuːsɨbl
AM dəˈd(j)usəbəl, diˈd(j)usəbəl

deduct
BR dɪˈdʌkt, -s, -ɪŋ, -ɨd
AM dəˈdək|(t), diˈdək|(t), -(t)s, -tɪŋ, -təd

deductibility
BR dɪˌdʌktɪˈbɪlɪti
AM dəˌdəktəˈbɪlɨdi, diˌdəktəˈbɪlɨdi

deductible
BR dɪˈdʌktɨbl
AM dəˈdəktəbəl, diˈdəktəbəl

deduction
BR dɪˈdʌkʃn, -z
AM dəˈdəkʃən, diˈdəkʃən, -z

deductive
BR dɪˈdʌktɪv
AM dəˈdəktɪv, diˈdəktɪv

deductively
BR dɪˈdʌktɨvli
AM dəˈdəktɨvli, diˈdəktɨvli

Dee
BR diː
AM di

dee
BR diː, -z
AM di, -z

deed
BR diːd, -z
AM did, -z

deejay
BR ˌdiːˈdʒeɪ, -z
AM ˈdiˌdʒeɪ, -z

deem
BR diːm, -z, -ɪŋ, -d
AM dim, -z, -ɪŋ, -d

Deeming
BR ˈdiːmɪŋ
AM ˈdimɪŋ

de-emphasise
BR ˌdiːˈɛmfəsʌɪz, -ɨz, -ɪŋ, -d
AM ˌdiˈɛmfəˌsaɪz, -ɨz, -ɪŋ, -d

de-emphasize
BR ˌdiːˈɛmfəsʌɪz, -ɨz, -ɪŋ, -d
AM ˌdiˈɛmfəˌsaɪz, -ɨz, -ɪŋ, -d

deemster
BR ˈdiːmstə(r), -z
AM ˈdimstər, -z

deep
BR diːp, -ə(r), -ɨst
AM dip, -ər, -əst

deepen
BR ˈdiːp|(ə)n, -(ə)nz, -ənɪŋ\-n̩ɪŋ, -(ə)nd
AM ˈdipən, -z, -ɪŋ, -d

deeping
BR ˈdiːpɪŋ
AM ˈdipɪŋ

deeply
BR ˈdiːpli
AM ˈdipli

deepness
BR ˈdiːpnɨs
AM ˈdipnɨs

deer
BR dɪə(r)
AM dɪ(ə)r

Deere
BR dɪə(r)
AM dɪ(ə)r

deerfly
BR ˈdɪəflʌɪ, -z
AM ˈdɪrˌflaɪ, -z

deerhound
BR ˈdɪəhaʊnd, -z
AM ˈdɪrˌ(h)aʊnd, -z

deerskin
BR ˈdɪəskɪn, -z
AM ˈdɪrˌskɪn, -z

deerstalker
BR ˈdɪəˌstɔːkə(r), -z
AM ˈdɪrˌstɔkər, ˈdɪrˌstɑkər, -z

de-escalate
BR (ˌ)diːˈɛskəleɪt, -s, -ɪŋ, -ɨd
AM ˌdiˈɛskəˌleɪ|t, -ts, -dɪŋ, -dɨd

de-escalation
BR (ˌ)diːɛskəˈleɪʃn, diːˌɛskəˈleɪʃn
AM ˌdiˌɛskəˈleɪʃən

Deeside
BR ˈdiːsʌɪd
AM ˈdiˌsaɪd

def
BR dɛf
AM dɛf

deface
BR dɪˈfeɪs, -ɨz, -ɪŋ, -t
AM dəˈfeɪs, diˈfeɪs, -ɨz, -ɪŋ, -t

defaceable
BR dɪˈfeɪsəbl
AM dəˈfeɪsəbəl, diˈfeɪsəbəl

defacement
BR dɪˈfeɪsm(ə)nt, -s
AM dəˈfeɪsmənt, diˈfeɪsmənt, -s

defacer
BR dɪˈfeɪsə(r), -z
AM dəˈfeɪsər, diˈfeɪsər, -z

de facto
BR ˌdeɪ ˈfaktəʊ
AM ˌdi ˈfæktoʊ, ˌdeɪ ˈfæktoʊ, də ˈfæktoʊ

defalcate
BR ˈdiːfalkeɪt, ˈdiːfɔːlkeɪt, -s, -ɪŋ, -ɨd
AM dəˈfælˌkeɪ|t, diˈfælˌkeɪ|t, ˈdiˌfælˌkeɪ|t, dəˈfɔlˌkeɪ|t, diˈfɔlˌkeɪ|t, ˈdiˌfɔlˌkeɪ|t, dəˈfɑlˌkeɪ|t, diˈfɑlˌkeɪ|t, ˈdiˌfɑlˌkeɪ|t, -ts, -dɪŋ, -dɨd

defalcation
BR ˌdiːfalˈkeɪʃn, ˌdiːfɔːlˈkeɪʃn
AM diˌfælˈkeɪʃən, dəˌfælˈkeɪʃən, diˌfɔlˈkeɪʃən, dəˌfɔlˈkeɪʃən, diˌfɑlˈkeɪʃən, dəˌfɑlˈkeɪʃən

defalcator
BR ˈdiːfalkeɪtə(r), ˈdiːfɔːlkeɪtə(r), -z
AM dəˈfælˌkeɪdər, diˈfælˌkeɪdər, ˈdiˌfælˌkeɪdər, dəˈfɔlˌkeɪdər, diˈfɔlˌkeɪdər, ˈdiˌfɔlˌkeɪdər, dəˈfɑlˌkeɪdər, diˈfɑlˌkeɪdər, ˈdiˌfɑlˌkeɪdər, -z

De Falla
BR də ˈfʌɪjə(r)
AM də ˈfaɪjə

defamation
BR ˌdɛfəˈmeɪʃn
AM ˌdɛfəˈmeɪʃən

defamatory
BR dɪˈfamət(ə)ri
AM dəˈfæməˌtɔri, diˈfæməˌtɔri

defame
BR dɪˈfeɪm, -z, -ɪŋ, -d
AM dəˈfeɪm, diˈfeɪm, -z, -ɪŋ, -d

defamer
BR dɪˈfeɪmə(r), -z
AM dəˈfeɪmər, diˈfeɪmər, -z

defat
BR ˌdiːˈfat, -s, -ɪŋ, -ɨd
AM diˈfæ|t, -ts, -dɪŋ, -dəd

default
BR dɪˈfɔːlt, -s, -ɪŋ, -ɨd
AM dəˈfɔlt, diˈfɔlt, dəˈfɑlt, diˈfɑlt, -s, -ɪŋ, -əd

defaulter
BR dɪˈfɔːltə(r), -z
AM dəˈfɔltər, diˈfɔltər, dəˈfɑltər, diˈfɑltər, -z

defeasance
BR dɪˈfiːzns
AM dəˈfizns, diˈfizns

defeasibility
BR dɪˌfiːzɪˈbɪlɪti
AM dəˌfizəˈbɪlɨdi, diˌfizəˈbɪlɨdi

defeasible
BR dɪˈfiːzɨbl
AM dəˈfizəbəl, diˈfizəbəl

defeasibly
BR dɪˈfiːzɨbli
AM dəˈfizəbli, diˈfizəbli

defeat
BR dɪˈfiːt, -s, -ɪŋ, -ɨd
AM dəˈfi|t, diˈfi|t, -ts, -dɪŋ, -dɨd

defeatism
BR dɪˈfiːtɪz(ə)m
AM dəˈfidɪzəm, diˈfidɪzəm

defeatist
BR dɪˈfiːtɪst, -s
AM dəˈfidəst, diˈfidəst, -s

defecate
BR ˈdɛfɪkeɪt, ˈdiːfɪkeɪt, -s, -ɪŋ, -ɨd
AM ˈdɛfəˌkeɪ|t, -ts, -dɪŋ, -dɨd

defecation
BR ˌdɛfɪˈkeɪʃn, ˌdiːfɪˈkeɪʃn
AM ˌdɛfəˈkeɪʃən

defecator
BR ˈdɛfɪkeɪtə(r), ˈdiːfɪkeɪtə(r), -z
AM ˈdɛfəˌkeɪdər, -z

defect[1]
noun
BR ˈdiːfɛkt, -s
AM ˈdifɛk(t), -s

defect[2]
verb
BR dɪˈfɛkt, -s, -ɪŋ, -ɨd
AM dəˈfɛk|(t), diˈfɛk|(t), -(t)s, -tɪŋ, -təd

defection
BR dɪˈfɛkʃn, -z
AM dəˈfɛkʃən, diˈfɛkʃən, -z

defective
BR dɪˈfɛktɪv, -z
AM dəˈfɛktɪv, diˈfɛktɪv, -z

defectively
BR dɪˈfɛktɪvli
AM dəˈfɛktɪvli, diˈfɛktɪvli

defectiveness
BR dɪˈfɛktɪvnɪs
AM dəˈfɛktɪvnɪs, diˈfɛktɪvnɪs

defector
BR dɪˈfɛktə(r), -z
AM dəˈfɛktər, diˈfɛktər, -z

defence
BR dɪˈfɛns, -ɪz
AM dəˈfɛns, diˈfɛns, ˈdiˌfɛns, -əz

defenceless
BR dɪˈfɛnsləs
AM dəˈfɛnsləs, diˈfɛnsləs

defencelessly
BR dɪˈfɛnsləsli
AM dəˈfɛnsləsli, diˈfɛnsləsli

defencelessness
BR dɪˈfɛnsləsnəs
AM dəˈfɛnsləsnəs, diˈfɛnsləsnəs

defend
BR dɪˈfɛnd, -z, -ɪŋ, -ɨd
AM dəˈfɛnd, diˈfɛnd, -z, -ɪŋ, -əd

defendable
BR dɪˈfɛndəbl
AM dəˈfɛndəbəl, diˈfɛndəbəl

defendant
BR dɪˈfɛnd(ə)nt, -s
AM dəˈfɛndənt, diˈfɛndənt, -s

defender
BR dɪˈfɛndə(r), -z
AM dəˈfɛndər, diˈfɛndər, -z

defenestrate
BR (ˌ)diːˈfɛnɪstreɪt, -s, -ɪŋ, -ɨd
AM diˈfɛnəˌstreɪ|t, -ts, -dɪŋ, -dɨd

defenestration
BR ˌdiːfɛnɪˈstreɪʃn, diːˌfɛnɪˈstreɪʃn
AM diˌfɛnəˈstreɪʃən

defense
BR dɪˈfɛns, -ɪz
AM dəˈfɛns, diˈfɛns, ˈdiˌfɛns, -əz

defenseless
BR dɪˈfɛnsləs
AM dəˈfɛnsləs, diˈfɛnsləs

defenselessly
BR dɪˈfɛnsləsli
AM dəˈfɛnsləsli, diˈfɛnsləsli

defenselessness
BR dɪˈfɛnsləsnəs
AM dəˈfɛnsləsnəs, diˈfɛnsləsnəs

defensibility
BR dɪˌfɛnsɪˈbɪlɨti
AM dəˌfɛnsəˈbɪlɨdi, diˌfɛnsəˈbɪlɨdi

defensible
BR dɪˈfɛnsɪbl
AM dəˈfɛnsəbəl, diˈfɛnsəbəl

defensibly
BR dɪˈfɛnsɪbli
AM dəˈfɛnsəbli, diˈfɛnsəbli

defensive
BR dɪˈfɛnsɪv
AM dəˈfɛnsɪv, diˈfɛnsɪv

defensively
BR dɪˈfɛnsɪvli
AM dəˈfɛnsɪvli, diˈfɛnsɪvli

defensiveness
BR dɪˈfɛnsɪvnɪs
AM dəˈfɛnsɪvnɪs, diˈfɛnsɪvnɪs

defer
BR dɪˈfəː(r), -z, -ɪŋ, -d
AM dəˈfər, diˈfɛ(ə)r, -z, -ɪŋ, -d

deference
BR ˈdɛf(ə)rəns, ˈdɛf(ə)rn̩s
AM ˈdɛf(ə)rəns

deferens
BR ˈdɛfərɛnz
AM ˈdɛf(ə)rənz

deferent
BR ˈdɛf(ə)rənt, ˈdɛf(ə)rn̩t
AM ˈdɛf(ə)rənt

deferential
BR ˌdɛfəˈrɛnʃl
AM ˌdɛfəˈrɛn(t)ʃəl

deferentially
BR ˌdɛfəˈrɛnʃəli, ˌdɛfəˈrɛnʃli
AM ˌdɛfəˈrɛn(t)ʃəli

deferment
BR dɪˈfəːm(ə)nt, -s
AM dəˈfərmənt, diˈfərmənt, -s

deferrable
BR dɪˈfəːrəbl
AM dəˈfərəbəl, diˈfərəbəl

deferral
BR dɪˈfəːrəl, dɪˈfəːrl̩, -z
AM dəˈfərəl, diˈfərəl, -z

deferrer
BR dɪˈfəːrə(r), -z
AM dəˈfərər, diˈfərər, -z

defiance
BR dɪˈfʌɪəns
AM dəˈfaɪəns, diˈfaɪəns

defiant
BR dɪˈfʌɪənt
AM dəˈfaɪənt, diˈfaɪənt

defiantly
BR dɪˈfʌɪəntli
AM dəˈfaɪən(t)li, diˈfaɪən(t)li

defibrillate
BR (ˌ)diːˈfɪbrɪleɪt, -s, -ɪŋ, -ɨd
AM dəˈfɪbrəˌleɪ|t, -ts, -dɪŋ, -dɨd

defibrillation
BR ˌdiːfɪbrɪˈleɪʃn, diːˌfɪbrɪˈleɪʃn, -z
AM dəˌfɪbrəˈleɪʃən, diˌfɪbrəˈleɪʃən, -z

defibrillator
BR (ˌ)diːˈfɪbrɪleɪtə(r), -z
AM dəˈfɪbrəˌleɪdər, diˈfɪbrəˌleɪdər, -z

deficiency
BR dɪˈfɪʃ(ə)ns|i, -ɪz
AM dəˈfɪʃənsi, diˈfɪʃənsi, -z

deficient
BR dɪˈfɪʃ(ə)nt
AM dəˈfɪʃənt, diˈfɪʃənt

deficiently
BR dɪˈfɪʃ(ə)ntli
AM dəˈfɪʃən(t)li, diˈfɪʃən(t)li

deficit
BR ˈdɛfɪsɪt, -s
AM ˈdɛfəsət, -s

defier
BR dɪˈfʌɪə(r), -z
AM dəˈfaɪər, diˈfaɪər, -z

defilade
BR ˌdɛfɪˈleɪd, ˈdɛfɪleɪd, -z, -ɪŋ, -ɨd
AM ˌdɛfəˈleɪd, ˈdɛfəˌleɪd, -z, -ɪŋ, -ɨd

defile[1]
noun
BR ˈdiːfʌɪl, -z
AM ˈdiˌfaɪl, dəˈfaɪl, -z

defile[2]
verb
BR dɪˈfʌɪl, -z, -ɪŋ, -d
AM dəˈfaɪl, diˈfaɪl, -z, -ɪŋ, -d

defilement
BR dɪˈfʌɪlm(ə)nt
AM dəˈfaɪlmənt, diˈfaɪlmənt

defiler
BR dɪˈfʌɪlə(r), -z
AM dəˈfaɪlər, diˈfaɪlər, -z

definable
BR dɪˈfʌɪnəbl
AM dəˈfaɪnəbəl, diˈfaɪnəbəl

definably
BR dɪˈfʌɪnəbli
AM dəˈfaɪnəbli, diˈfaɪnəbli

define
BR dɪˈfʌɪn, -z, -ɪŋ, -d
AM dəˈfaɪn, diˈfaɪn, -z, -ɪŋ, -d

definer
BR dɪˈfʌɪnə(r), -z
AM dəˈfaɪnər, diˈfaɪnər, -z

definite
BR ˈdɛf(ɪ)nɪt
AM ˈdɛf(ə)nət

definitely
BR ˈdɛf(ɪ)nɪtli
AM ˈdɛf(ə)nətli

definiteness
BR ˈdɛf(ɪ)nɪtnɪs
AM ˈdɛf(ə)nətnəs

definition
BR ˌdɛfɪˈnɪʃn, -z
AM ˌdɛfəˈnɪʃən, -z

definitional
BR ˌdɛfɪˈnɪʃn̩(ə)l, ˌdɛfɪˈnɪʃən(ə)l
AM ˌdɛfəˈnɪʃ(ə)nəl

definitionally
BR ˌdɛfɪˈnɪʃn̩əli, ˌdɛfɪˈnɪʃn̩l̩i, ˌdɛfɪˈnɪʃənl̩i, ˌdɛfɪˈnɪʃ(ə)nəli
AM ˌdɛfəˈnɪʃ(ə)nəli

definitive
BR dɪˈfɪnɪtɪv

AM də'fɪnədɪv, di'fɪnədɪv

definitively
BR dɪ'fɪnɪtɪvli
AM də'fɪnəˌtɪvli, di'fɪnəˌtɪvli

definitiveness
BR dɪ'fɪnɪtɪvnɪs
AM də'fɪnədɪvnɪs, di'fɪnədɪvnɪs

deflagrate
BR 'dɛfləgreɪt, -s, -ɪŋ, -ɪd
AM 'dɛfləˌgreɪ|t, -ts, -dɪŋ, -dɪd

deflagration
BR ˌdɛflə'greɪʃn
AM ˌdɛflə'greɪʃən

deflagrator
BR 'dɛfləgreɪtə(r), -z
AM 'dɛfləˌgreɪdər, -z

deflate
BR dɪ'fleɪt, -s, -ɪŋ, -ɪd
AM də'fleɪ|t, di'fleɪ|t, -ts, -dɪŋ, -dɪd

deflation
BR ˌdiː'fleɪʃn, dɪ'fleɪʃn
AM də'fleɪʃən, di'fleɪʃən

deflationary
BR ˌdiː'fleɪʃn̩(ə)ri, ˌdiː'fleɪʃən(ə)ri, dɪ'fleɪʃn̩(ə)ri, dɪ'fleɪʃən(ə)ri
AM di'fleɪʃəˌnɛri, də'fleɪʃəˌnɛri

deflationist
BR ˌdiː'fleɪʃn̩ɪst, ˌdiː'fleɪʃənɪst, dɪ'fleɪʃn̩ɪst, dɪ'fleɪʃənɪst, -s
AM di'fleɪʃənəst, də'fleɪʃənəst, -s

deflator
BR dɪ'fleɪtə(r), -z
AM di'fleɪdər, də'fleɪdər, -z

deflect
BR dɪ'flɛkt, -s, -ɪŋ, -ɪd
AM də'flɛk|(t), di'flɛk|(t), -(t)s, -tɪŋ, -təd

deflection
BR dɪ'flɛkʃn, -z
AM də'flɛkʃən, di'flɛkʃən, -z

deflector
BR dɪ'flɛktə(r), -z
AM də'flɛktər, di'flɛktər, -z

deflexion
BR dɪ'flɛkʃn, -z
AM də'flɛkʃən, di'flɛkʃən, -z

defloration
BR ˌdiːflɔː'reɪʃn, ˌdiːflə'reɪʃn, ˌdɛflə'reɪʃn
AM ˌdɛflə'reɪʃən

deflower
BR ˌdiː'flaʊə(r), -z, -ɪŋ, -d
AM di'flaʊ(ə)r, də'flaʊ(ə)r, -z, -ɪŋ, -d

defocus
BR ˌdiː'fəʊkəs, -ɪz, -ɪŋ, -t
AM di'foʊkəs, -əz, -ɪŋ, -t

defocussing
BR ˌdiː'fəʊkəsɪŋ
AM di'foʊkəsɪŋ

Defoe
BR dɪ'fəʊ
AM də'foʊ

defogger
BR ˌdiː'fɒgə(r), -z
AM də'fɔgər, di'fɔgər, də'fɑgər, di'fɔgər, -z

defoliant
BR (ˌ)diː'fəʊlɪənt, -s
AM di'foʊliənt, -s

defoliate
BR (ˌ)diː'fəʊlɪeɪt, -s, -ɪŋ, -ɪd
AM di'foʊliˌeɪ|t, -ts, -dɪŋ, -dɪd

defoliation
BR diːˌfəʊlɪ'eɪʃn, ˌdiːfəʊlɪ'eɪʃn
AM diˌfoʊlɪ'eɪʃən

defoliator
BR (ˌ)diː'fəʊlɪeɪtə(r), -z
AM di'foʊliˌeɪdər, -z

deforest
BR ˌdiː'fɒrɪst, -s, -ɪŋ, -ɪd
AM di'fɔrəst, -s, -ɪŋ, -əd

deforestation
BR ˌdiːfɒrɪ'steɪʃn, diːˌfɒrɪ'steɪʃn
AM ˈdiˌfɔrə'steɪʃən

deform
BR dɪ'fɔːm, -z, -ɪŋ, -d
AM də'fɔ(ə)rm, di'fɔ(ə)rm, -z, -ɪŋ, -d

deformable
BR dɪ'fɔːməbl
AM də'fɔrməbəl, di'fɔrməbəl

deformation
BR ˌdiːfɔː'meɪʃn
AM ˌdiˌfɔr'meɪʃən, ˌdɛfər'meɪʃən

deformational
BR ˌdiːfɔː'meɪʃn̩(ə)l, ˌdiːfɔː'meɪʃən(ə)l
AM ˌdiˌfɔr'meɪʃ(ə)nəl, ˌdɛfər'meɪʃ(ə)nəl

deformity
BR dɪ'fɔːmɪt|i, -ɪz
AM də'fɔrmədi, di'fɔrmədi, -z

defraud
BR dɪ'frɔːd, -z, -ɪŋ, -ɪd
AM də'frɔd, di'frɔd, də'frɑd, di'frɑd, -z, -ɪŋ, -əd

defrauder
BR dɪ'frɔːdə(r), -z
AM də'frɔdər, di'frɔdər, də'frɑdər, di'frɑdər, -z

defray
BR dɪ'freɪ, -z, -ɪŋ, -d
AM də'freɪ, di'freɪ, -z, -ɪŋ, -d

defrayable
BR dɪ'freɪəbl
AM də'freɪəbəl, di'freɪəbəl

defrayal
BR dɪ'freɪəl
AM də'freɪ(ə)l, di'freɪ(ə)l

defrayment
BR dɪ'freɪm(ə)nt
AM də'freɪmənt, di'freɪmənt

De Freitas
BR də 'freɪtəs
AM də 'fraɪdəs

defrock
BR ˌdiː'frɒk, -s, -ɪŋ, -t
AM di'frɑk, -s, -ɪŋ, -t

defrost
BR ˌdiː'frɒst, dɪ'frɒst, -s, -ɪŋ, -ɪd
AM də'frɔst, di'frɔst, də'frɑst, di'frɑst, -s, -ɪŋ, -əd

defroster
BR ˌdiː'frɒstə(r), dɪ'frɒstə(r), -z
AM də'frɔstər, di'frɔstər, də'frɑstər, di'frɑstər, -z

deft
BR dɛft, -ə(r), -ɪst
AM dɛft, -ər, -əst

deftly
BR 'dɛftli
AM 'dɛf(t)li

deftness
BR 'dɛf(t)nəs
AM 'dɛf(t)nəs

defumigate
BR ˌdiː'fjuːmɪgeɪt, -s, -ɪŋ, -ɪd
AM di'fjuməˌgeɪ|t, -ts, -dɪŋ, -dɪd

defunct
BR dɪ'fʌŋ(k)t
AM də'fəŋ(k)t, di'fəŋ(k)t, də'fəŋk(t), di'fəŋk(t)

defunctness
BR dɪ'fʌŋ(k)tnəs, dɪ'fʌŋk(t)nəs
AM də'fəŋk(t)nəs, də'fəŋ(k)tnəs, di'fəŋk(t)nəs, di'fəŋ(k)tnəs

defuse
BR ˌdiː'fjuːz, dɪ'fjuːz, -ɪz, -ɪŋ, -d
AM də'fjuz, di'fjuz, -əz, -ɪŋ, -d

defy
BR dɪ'fʌɪ, -z, -ɪŋ, -d
AM də'faɪ, di'faɪ, -z, -ɪŋ, -d

dégagé
BR ˌdeɪgɑː'ʒeɪ, ˌdeɪgɑ'ʒeɪ
AM ˌdeɪgɑ'ʒeɪ

dégagée
BR ˌdeɪgɑː'ʒeɪ, ˌdeɪgɑ'ʒeɪ
AM ˌdeɪgɑ'ʒeɪ

Deganwy
BR dɪ'ganwi
AM də'gænwi

Degas
BR 'deɪgɑː(r)
AM deɪ'gɑ

degas
BR ˌdiː'gas, -ɪz, -ɪŋ, -t
AM di'gæs, -əz, -ɪŋ, -t

de Gaulle
BR də 'gɔːl
AM də 'gɔl, də 'gɑl

degauss
BR ˌdiː'gaʊs, -ɪz, -ɪŋ, -t
AM di'gaʊs, -əz, -ɪŋ, -t

degausser
BR ˌdiː'gaʊsə(r), -z
AM di'gaʊsər, -z

degeminate
BR ˌdiː'dʒɛmɪneɪt, -s, -ɪŋ, -ɪd
AM di'dʒɛməˌneɪ|t, -ts, -dɪŋ, -dɪd

degemination
BR ˌdiːdʒɛmɪ'neɪʃn
AM diˌdʒɛmə'neɪʃən

degeneracy
BR dɪ'dʒɛn(ə)rəsi
AM də'dʒɛn(ə)rəsi, di'dʒɛn(ə)rəsi

degenerate[1]
noun, adjective
BR dɪ'dʒɛn(ə)rət, -s
AM də'dʒɛn(ə)rət, di'dʒɛn(ə)rət, -s

degenerate[2]
verb
BR dɪ'dʒɛnəreɪt, -s, -ɪŋ, -ɪd
AM də'dʒɛn(ə)ˌreɪ|t, di'dʒɛn(ə)ˌreɪ|t, -ts, -dɪŋ, -dɪd

degenerately
BR dɪ'dʒɛn(ə)rətli
AM də'dʒɛn(ə)rətli, di'dʒɛn(ə)rətli

degeneration
BR dɪˌdʒɛnə'reɪʃn
AM dəˌdʒɛnə'reɪʃən, diˌdʒɛnə'reɪʃən

degenerative
BR dɪ'dʒɛn(ə)rətɪv
AM də'dʒɛnərədɪv, di'dʒɛnərədɪv

deglaze
BR ˌdiːˈgleɪz, -ɪz, -ɪŋ, -d
AM diˈgleɪz, -ɪz, -ɪŋ, -d

degradability
BR dɪˌgreɪdəˈbɪlɪti
AM dəˌgreɪdəˈbɪlɨdi, diˌgreɪdəˈbɪlɨdi

degradable
BR dɪˈgreɪdəbl
AM dəˈgreɪdəbəl, diˈgreɪdəbəl

degradation
BR ˌdɛgrəˈdeɪʃn
AM ˌdɛgrəˈdeɪʃən

degradative
BR dɪˈgreɪdətɪv
AM dɛˈgreɪdədɪv, ˈdɛgrəˌdeɪdɪv

degrade
BR dɪˈgreɪd, -z, -ɪŋ, -ɪd
AM dəˈgreɪd, diˈgreɪd, -z, -ɪŋ, -ɪd

degrader
BR dɪˈgreɪdə(r), -z
AM dəˈgreɪdər, diˈgreɪdər, -z

degradingly
BR dɪˈgreɪdɪŋli
AM dəˈgreɪdɪŋli, diˈgreɪdɪŋli

degranulate
BR ˌdiːˈgranjʊleɪt, -s, -ɪŋ, -ɪd
AM diˈgrænjəˌleɪ|t, -ts, -dɪŋ, -dɪd

degranulation
BR ˌdiːgranjʊˈleɪʃn, diːˌgranjʊˈleɪʃn
AM diˌgrænjəˈleɪʃən

degrease
BR ˌdiːˈgriːs, -ɪz, -ɪŋ, -t
AM diˈgris, -ɪz, -ɪŋ, -t

degreaser
BR ˌdiːˈgriːsə(r), -z
AM diˈgrisər, -z

degree
BR dɪˈgriː, -z
AM dəˈgri, diˈgri, -z

degreeless
BR dɪˈgriːlɨs
AM dəˈgrilɨs, diˈgrilɨs

degressive
BR dɪˈgrɛsɪv
AM dəˈgrɛsɪv, diˈgrɛsɪv

degum
BR ˌdiːˈgʌm, -z, -ɪŋ, -d
AM diˈgəm, -z, -ɪŋ, -d

de haut en bas
BR də ˌəʊt ɒ̃ ˈbɑː
AM də ˌoʊt ɑn ˈbɑ

de Havilland
BR də ˈhavɪlənd, + ˈhavl̩nd
AM də ˈhævələn(d)

dehisce
BR dɪˈhɪs
AM dəˈhɪs, diˈhɪs

dehiscence
BR dɪˈhɪsns
AM dəˈhɪsns, diˈhɪsns

dehiscent
BR dɪˈhɪsnt
AM dəˈhɪsnt, diˈhɪsnt

dehistoricise
BR ˌdiːhɪˈstɒrɪsʌɪz, -ɪz, -ɪŋ, -d
AM diˌhɪˈstɔrəˌsaɪz, -ɪz, -ɪŋ, -d

dehistoricize
BR ˌdiːhɪˈstɒrɪsʌɪz, -ɪz, -ɪŋ, -d
AM diˌhɪˈstɔrəˌsaɪz, -ɪz, -ɪŋ, -d

dehorn
BR ˌdiːˈhɔːn, -z, -ɪŋ, -d
AM diˈhɔ(ə)rn, -z, -ɪŋ, -d

dehumanisation
BR ˌdiːhjuːmənʌɪˈzeɪʃn, diːˌhjuːmənʌɪˈzeɪʃn
AM ˌdiˌ(h)jumənəˈzeɪʃən, dəˌ(h)jumənəˈzeɪʃən, ˌdiˌ(h)juməˌnaɪˈzeɪʃən, dəˌ(h)juməˌnaɪˈzeɪʃən

dehumanise
BR (ˌ)diːˈhjuːmənʌɪz, -ɪz, -ɪŋ, -d
AM diˈ(h)juməˌnaɪz, dəˈ(h)juməˌnaɪz, -ɪz, -ɪŋ, -d

dehumanization
BR ˌdiːhjuːmənʌɪˈzeɪʃn, diːˌhjuːmənʌɪˈzeɪʃn
AM ˌdiˌ(h)jumənəˈzeɪʃən, dəˌ(h)jumənəˈzeɪʃən, ˌdiˌ(h)juməˌnaɪˈzeɪʃən, dəˌ(h)juməˌnaɪˈzeɪʃən

dehumanize
BR (ˌ)diːˈhjuːmənʌɪz, -ɪz, -ɪŋ, -d
AM diˈ(h)juməˌnaɪz, dəˈ(h)juməˌnaɪz, -ɪz, -ɪŋ, -d

dehumidification
BR ˌdiːhjuːˌmɪdɪfɪˈkeɪʃn
AM ˌdi(h)juˌmɪdəfəˈkeɪʃən

dehumidifier
BR ˌdiːhjuːˈmɪdɪfʌɪə(r), -z
AM ˌdi(h)juˈmɪdəˌfaɪər, -z

dehumidify
BR ˌdiːhjuːˈmɪdɪfʌɪ, -z, -ɪŋ, -d
AM ˌdi(h)juˈmɪdəˌfaɪ, -z, -ɪŋ, -d

dehydrate
BR ˌdiːhʌɪˈdreɪt, -s, -ɪŋ, -ɪd
AM diˈhaɪˌdreɪ|t, -ts, -dɪŋ, -dɪd

dehydration
BR ˌdiːhʌɪˈdreɪʃn
AM ˌdiˌhaɪˈdreɪʃən

dehydrator
BR ˌdiːhʌɪˈdreɪtə(r), -z
AM diˈhaɪˌdreɪdər, -z

dehydrogenate
BR ˌdiːhʌɪˈdrɒdʒɪneɪt, -s, -ɪŋ, -ɪd
AM diˌhaɪˈdrɑdʒəˌneɪ|t, -ts, -dɪŋ, -dɪd

dehydrogenation
BR ˌdiːhʌɪdrɒdʒɪˈneɪʃn
AM ˈdihaɪˌdrɑdʒəˈneɪʃən

Deianira
BR ˌdeɪəˈnʌɪrə(r)
AM ˌdijəˈnaɪrə

de-ice
BR ˌdiːˈʌɪs, -ɪz, -ɪŋ, -t
AM ˌdiˈaɪs, -ɪz, -ɪŋ, -t

de-icer
BR ˌdiːˈʌɪsə(r), -z
AM ˌdiˈaɪsər, -z

deicide
BR ˈdeɪɪsʌɪd, ˈdiːɪsʌɪd, -z
AM ˈdiəˌsaɪd, -z

deictic
BR ˈdʌɪktɪk, ˈdeɪktɪk
AM ˈdaɪktɪk

deification
BR ˌdeɪɪfɪˈkeɪʃn, ˌdiːɪfɪˈkeɪʃn
AM ˌdiəfəˈkeɪʃən

deiform
BR ˈdeɪɪfɔːm, ˈdiːɪfɔːm
AM ˈdiəˌfɔ(ə)rm

deify
BR ˈdeɪɪfʌɪ, ˈdiːɪfʌɪ, -z, -ɪŋ, -d
AM ˈdiəˌfaɪ, -z, -ɪŋ, -d

Deighton
BR ˈdeɪtn
AM ˈdeɪtn

deign
BR deɪn, -z, -ɪŋ, -d
AM deɪn, -z, -ɪŋ, -d

Dei gratia
BR ˌdeɪiː ˈgrɑːtɪə(r), ˌdiːʌɪ ˈgreɪʃɪə(r)
AM ˌdeɪi ˈgrɑtsiə

Deimos
BR ˈdeɪmɒs, ˈdʌɪmɒs
AM ˈdaɪˌmɑs

de-industrialisation
BR ˌdiːɪnˌdʌstrɪəlʌɪˈzeɪʃn
AM ˈdiɪnˌdəstriələˌzeɪʃən, ˈdiɪnˌdəstriəˌlaɪˌzeɪʃən

de-industrialization
BR ˌdiːɪnˌdʌstrɪəlʌɪˈzeɪʃn
AM ˈdiɪnˌdəstriələˌzeɪʃən, ˈdiɪnˌdəstriəˌlaɪˌzeɪʃən

deinonychus
BR dʌɪˈnɒnɨkəs, -ɪz
AM daɪˈnɑnəkəs, -əz

deinstitutionalisation
BR ˌdiːɪnstɪˌtjuːʃn̩əlʌɪˈzeɪʃ, ˌdiːɪnstɪˌtjuːʃn̩l̩ʌɪˈzeɪʃn, ˌdiːɪnstɪˌtjuːʃənl̩ʌɪˈzeɪʃn, ˌdiːɪnstɪˌtjuːʃ(ə)nəlʌɪˈzeɪʃ, ˌdiːɪnstɪˌtʃuːʃn̩əlʌɪˈzeɪʃn, ˌdiːɪnstɪˌtʃuːʃn̩l̩ʌɪˈzeɪʃn, ˌdiːɪnstɪˌtʃuːʃənl̩ʌɪˈzeɪʃn, ˌdiːɪnstɪˌtʃuːʃ(ə)nəlʌɪˈzeɪʃ
AM ˈdiˌɪnstəˌt(j)uʃənl̩əˈzeɪ, ˈdiˌɪnstəˌt(j)uʃənlˌaɪˈzeɪʃə, ˈdiˌɪnstəˌt(j)uʃnələˈzeɪʃən, ˈdiˌɪnstəˌt(j)uʃənəˌlaɪˈzeɪʃ

deinstitutionalise
BR ˌdiːɪnstɪˈtjuːʃn̩əlʌɪz, ˌdiːɪnstɪˈtjuːʃn̩l̩ʌɪz, ˌdiːɪnstɪˈtjuːʃənl̩ʌɪz, ˌdiːɪnstɪˈtjuːʃ(ə)nəlʌɪz, ˌdiːɪnstɪˈtʃuːʃn̩əlʌɪz, ˌdiːɪnstɪˈtʃuːʃn̩l̩ʌɪz, ˌdiːɪnstɪˈtʃuːʃənl̩ʌɪz, ˌdiːɪnstɪˈtʃuːʃ(ə)nəlʌɪz, -ɪz, -ɪŋ, -d
AM ˈdiˌɪnstəˈt(j)uʃənlˌaɪz, ˈdiˌɪnstəˈt(j)uʃnəˌlaɪz, -ɪz, -ɪŋ, -d

deinstitutionalizatio
BR ˌdiːɪnstɪˌtjuːʃn̩əlʌɪˈzeɪʃ, ˌdiːɪnstɪˌtjuːʃn̩l̩ʌɪˈzeɪʃn, ˌdiːɪnstɪˌtjuːʃənl̩ʌɪˈzeɪʃn, ˌdiːɪnstɪˌtjuːʃ(ə)nəlʌɪˈzeɪʃ, ˌdiːɪnstɪˌtʃuːʃn̩əlʌɪˈzeɪʃn, ˌdiːɪnstɪˌtʃuːʃn̩l̩ʌɪˈzeɪʃn, ˌdiːɪnstɪˌtʃuːʃənl̩ʌɪˈzeɪʃn, ˌdiːɪnstɪˌtʃuːʃ(ə)nəlʌɪˈzeɪ
AM ˈdiˌɪnstəˌt(j)uʃənl̩əˈzeɪ, ˈdiˌɪnstəˌt(j)uʃənlˌaɪˈzeɪʃə, ˈdiˌɪnstəˌt(j)uʃnələˈzeɪʃən, ˈdiˌɪnstəˌt(j)uʃənəlaɪˈzeɪʃ

deinstitutionalize
BR ˌdiːɪnstɪˈtjuːʃn̩əlʌɪz, ˌdiːɪnstɪˈtjuːʃn̩l̩ʌɪz, ˌdiːɪnstɪˈtjuːʃənl̩ʌɪz, ˌdiːɪnstɪˈtjuːʃ(ə)nəlʌɪz, ˌdiːɪnstɪˈtʃuːʃn̩əlʌɪz, ˌdiːɪnstɪˈtʃuːʃn̩l̩ʌɪz, ˌdiːɪnstɪˈtʃuːʃənl̩ʌɪz, ˌdiːɪnstɪˈtʃuːʃ(ə)nəlʌɪz, -ɪz, -ɪŋ, -d
AM ˈdiˌɪnstəˈt(j)uʃənlˌaɪz, ˈdiˌɪnstəˈt(j)uʃnəˌlaɪz, -ɪz, -ɪŋ, -d

deionisation
BR ˌdiːʌɪənʌɪˈzeɪʃn, diːˌʌɪənʌɪˈzeɪʃn
AM diˌaɪənəˈzeɪʃən, diˌaɪəˌnaɪˈzeɪʃən

deionise
BR ˌdiːˈʌɪənʌɪz, -ɪz, -ɪŋ, -d
AM diˈaɪəˌnaɪz, -ɪz, -ɪŋ, -d

deioniser
BR ˌdiːˈʌɪənʌɪzə(r), -z
AM diˈaɪəˌnaɪzər, -z

deionization
BR ˌdiːʌɪənʌɪˈzeɪʃn, diːˌʌɪənʌɪˈzeɪʃn

AM di,aɪənə'zeɪʃən, di,aɪə,naɪ'zeɪʃən

deionize
BR ,di:'ʌɪənʌɪz, -ɪz, -ɪŋ, -d
AM di'aɪə,naɪz, -ɪz, -ɪŋ, -d

deionizer
BR ,di:'ʌɪənʌɪzə(r), -z
AM di'aɪə,naɪzər, -z

deipnosophist
BR dʌɪp'nɒsəfɪst, -s
AM daɪp'nɑsəfəst, -s

Deirdre
BR 'dɪədri, 'dɪədrə(*r*)
AM 'dɪr,drə

deism
BR 'deɪɪz(ə)m, 'di:ɪz(ə)m
AM 'di,ɪzəm, 'deɪ,ɪzəm

deist
BR 'deɪɪst, 'di:ɪst, -s
AM 'diɪst, 'deɪɪst, -s

deistic
BR deɪ'ɪstɪk, di:'ɪstɪk
AM di'ɪstɪk, deɪ'ɪstɪk

deistical
BR deɪ'ɪstɪkl, di:'ɪstɪkl
AM di'ɪstɪkəl, deɪ'ɪstɪkəl

deistically
BR deɪ'ɪstɪkli, di:'ɪstɪkli
AM di'ɪstɪk(ə)li, deɪ'ɪstɪk(ə)li

deity
BR 'deɪɪt|i, 'di:ɪt|i, -ɪz
AM 'diədi, 'deɪɪdi, -z

deixis
BR 'dʌɪksɪs, 'deɪksɪs
AM 'daɪksəs

déjà vu
BR ,deɪʒɑ: 'vu:
AM ,deɪʒɑ 'v(j)u

deject
BR dɪ'dʒɛkt, -s, -ɪŋ, -ɪd
AM də'dʒɛk|(t), di'dʒɛk|(t), -(t)s, -tɪŋ, -təd

dejectedly
BR dɪ'dʒɛktɪdli
AM də'dʒɛktədli, di'dʒɛktədli

dejection
BR dɪ'dʒɛkʃn
AM də'dʒɛkʃən, di'dʒɛkʃən

de jure
BR ,di: 'dʒʊəri, ,deɪ 'jʊəreɪ
AM di 'dʒʊri, deɪ 'jʊ,reɪ

De Kalb
BR də 'ka(l)b
AM də 'kæ(l)b

Dekker
BR 'dɛkə(r)
AM 'dɛkər

dekko
BR 'dɛkəʊ, -z
AM 'dɛkoʊ, -z

de Klerk
BR də 'klɛ:k
AM də 'klɛrk

de Kooning
BR də 'ku:nɪŋ
AM də 'kunɪŋ

Delacourt
BR 'dɛləkɔ:t
AM 'dɛlə,kɔ(ə)rt

Delacroix
BR 'dɛləkrwɑ:(*r*), ,dɛlə'krwɑ:(*r*)
AM ,dɛlə'k(r)wɑ

Delafield
BR 'dɛləfi:ld
AM 'dɛlə,fild

Delagoa
BR ,dɛlə'gəʊə(r)
AM ,dɛlə'goʊə

Delahaye
BR 'dɛləheɪ
AM 'dɛlə,heɪ

delaine
BR dɪ'leɪn
AM də'leɪn, di'leɪn

de la Mare
BR də la 'mɛ:(r), ,dɛlə +
AM də lɑ 'mɛ(ə)r

Delamere
BR 'dɛləmɪə(r)
AM 'dɛləmɪ(ə)r

Delaney
BR dɪ'leɪni
AM də'leɪni

de la Rue
BR də la 'ru:, ,dɛlə +
AM də lɑ 'ru

delate
BR dɪ'leɪt, -s, -ɪŋ, -ɪd
AM də'leɪ|t, di'leɪ|t, -ts, -dɪŋ, -dɪd

delation
BR dɪ'leɪʃn
AM də'leɪʃən, di'leɪʃən

delator
BR dɪ'leɪtə(r), -z
AM də'leɪdər, di'leɪdər, -z

Delaware
BR 'dɛləwɛ:(r)
AM 'dɛlə,wɛ(ə)r

delay
BR dɪ'leɪ, -z, -ɪŋ, -d
AM də'leɪ, di'leɪ, -z, -ɪŋ, -d

delayer
BR dɪ'leɪə(r), -z
AM də'leɪər, di'leɪər, -z

Delbert
BR 'dɛlbət
AM 'dɛlbərt

Delbridge
BR 'dɛlbrɪdʒ
AM 'dɛl,brɪdʒ

del credere
BR dɛl 'kreɪdəri, + 'krɛdəri
AM dɛl 'kreɪdəri

Delderfield
BR 'dɛldəfi:ld
AM 'dɛldər,fild

dele
BR 'di:l|i, -ɪz, -ɪɪŋ, -ɪd
AM 'dili, -z, -ɪŋ, -d

delectability
BR dɪ,lɛktə'bɪlɪti
AM də,lɛktə'bɪlɪdi, di,lɛktə'bɪlɪdi

delectable
BR dɪ'lɛktəbl
AM də'lɛktəbəl, di'lɛktəbəl

delectably
BR dɪ'lɛktəbli
AM də'lɛktəbli, di'lɛktəbli

delectation
BR ,di:lɛk'teɪʃn
AM ,dilɛk'teɪʃən, ,dɪlɛk'teɪʃən, ,dɛlɛk'teɪʃən

delegable
BR 'dɛlɪgəbl
AM 'dɛləgəbəl

delegacy
BR 'dɛlɪgəs|i, -ɪz
AM 'dɛləgəsi, -z

delegate[1]
noun
BR 'dɛlɪgət, -s
AM 'dɛləgət, 'dɛlə,geɪt, -s

delegate[2]
verb
BR 'dɛlɪgeɪt, -s, -ɪŋ, -ɪd
AM 'dɛlə,geɪ|t, -ts, -dɪŋ, -dɪd

delegation
BR ,dɛlɪ'geɪʃn, -z
AM ,dɛlə'geɪʃən, -z

delegator
BR 'dɛlɪgeɪtə(r), -z
AM 'dɛlə,geɪdər, -z

delete
BR dɪ'li:t, -s, -ɪŋ, -ɪd
AM də'li|t, di'li|t, -ts, -dɪŋ, -dɪd

deleterious
BR ,dɛlɪ'tɪərɪəs
AM ,dɛlə'tɪriəs

deleteriously
BR ,dɛlɪ'tɪərɪəsli
AM ,dɛlə'tɪriəsli

deleteriousness
BR ,dɛlɪ'tɪərɪəsnəs
AM ,dɛlə'tɪriəsnəs

deletion
BR dɪ'li:ʃn, -z
AM də'liʃən, di'liʃən, -z

Delfont
BR 'dɛlfɒnt
AM dɛl'fɑnt

Delft
BR dɛlft
AM dɛlft

delftware
BR 'dɛlftwɛ:(r)
AM 'dɛlf(t),wɛ(ə)r

Delgado
BR dɛl'gɑ:dəʊ
AM dɛl'gɑdoʊ

Delhi
BR 'dɛli
AM 'dɛli

deli
BR 'dɛl|i, -ɪz
AM 'dɛli, -z

Delia
BR 'di:lɪə(*r*)
AM 'diljə, 'diliə

Delian
BR 'di:lɪən, -z
AM 'diliən, -z

deliberate[1]
adjective
BR dɪ'lɪb(ə)rət
AM də'lɪb(ə)rət, di'lɪb(ə)rət

deliberate[2]
verb
BR dɪ'lɪbəreɪt, -s, -ɪŋ, -ɪd
AM də'lɪbə,reɪ|t, dɪ'lɪbə,reɪ|t, -ts, -dɪŋ, -dɪd

deliberately
BR dɪ'lɪb(ə)rətli
AM də'lɪb(ə)rətli, di'lɪb(ə)rətli

deliberateness
BR dɪ'lɪb(ə)rətnəs
AM də'lɪb(ə)rətnəs, di'lɪb(ə)rətnəs

deliberation
BR dɪ,lɪbə'reɪʃn, -z
AM də,lɪbə'reɪʃən, di,lɪbə'reɪʃən, -z

deliberative
BR dɪ'lɪb(ə)rətɪv
AM də'lɪbərədɪv, di'lɪbərədɪv, də'lɪbə,reɪdɪv, di'lɪbə,reɪdɪv

deliberatively
BR dɪ'lɪb(ə)rətɪvli
AM də'lɪbərədɪvli, di'lɪbərədɪvli, də'lɪbə,reɪdɪvli, di'lɪbə,reɪdɪvli

deliberativeness
BR dɪ'lɪb(ə)rətɪvnɪs
AM də'lɪbərədɪvnɪs, di'lɪbərədɪvnɪs, də'lɪbə,reɪdɪvnɪs, di'lɪbə,reɪdɪvnɪs

deliberator
BR dɪ'lɪbəreɪtə(r), -z
AM də'lɪbə,reɪdər, di'lɪbə,reɪdər, -z

Delibes
BR dɪ'li:b
AM də'lib
delicacy
BR 'dɛlɪkəs|i, -ɪz
AM 'dɛləkəsi, -z
delicate
BR 'dɛlɪkət
AM 'dɛlɪkət
delicately
BR 'dɛlɪkətli
AM 'dɛlɪkətli
delicateness
BR 'dɛlɪkətnəs
AM 'dɛlɪkətnəs
delicatessen
BR ˌdɛlɪkə'tɛsn, -z
AM ˌdɛlɪkə'tɛsən, -z
delicious
BR dɪ'lɪʃəs
AM də'lɪʃəs, di'lɪʃəs
deliciously
BR dɪ'lɪʃəsli
AM də'lɪʃəsli, di'lɪʃəsli
deliciousness
BR dɪ'lɪʃəsnəs
AM də'lɪʃəsnəs, di'lɪʃəsnəs
delict
BR dɪ'lɪkt, 'di:lɪkt, -s
AM də'lɪk|(t), di'lɪk|(t), -(t)s
delight
BR dɪ'lʌɪt, -s, -ɪŋ, -ɨd
AM də'laɪ|t, di'laɪ|t, -ts, -dɪŋ, -dɨd
delightedly
BR dɪ'lʌɪtɨdli
AM də'laɪdɨdli, di'laɪtɨdli
delightful
BR dɪ'lʌɪtf(ʊ)l
AM də'laɪtfəl, di'laɪtfəl
delightfully
BR dɪ'lʌɪtfʊli, dɪ'lʌɪtfl̩i
AM də'laɪtfəli, di'laɪtfəli
delightfulness
BR dɪ'lʌɪtf(ʊ)lnəs
AM də'laɪtfəlnəs, di'laɪtfəlnəs
Delilah
BR dɪ'lʌɪlə(r)
AM də'laɪlə, di'laɪlə
delimit
BR ˌdi:'lɪm|ɪt, dɪ'lɪm|ɪt, -s, -ɨtɪŋ, -ɨdɨd
AM də'lɪmɨ|t, di'lɪmɨ|t, -ts, -dɪŋ, -dɨd
delimitate
BR dɪ'lɪmɨteɪt, -s, -ɪŋ, -ɨd
AM də'lɪməˌteɪ|t, di'lɪməˌteɪ|t, -ts, -dɪŋ, -dɨd
delimitation
BR dɪˌlɪmɪ'teɪʃn
AM dəˌlɪmə'teɪʃən, diˌlɪmə'teɪʃən
delimitative
BR dɪ'lɪmɨtətɪv
AM də'lɪməˌteɪdɪv, də'lɪmədədɪv, di'lɪməˌteɪdɪv, di'lɪmədədɪv
delimiter
BR ˌdi:'lɪmɨtə(r), dɪ'lɪmɨtə(r), -z
AM də'lɪmɨdər, di'lɪmɨdər, -z
delineate
BR dɪ'lɪnɪeɪt, -s, -ɪŋ, -ɨd
AM də'lɪniˌeɪ|t, di'lɪniˌeɪ|t, -ts, -dɪŋ, -dɨd
delineation
BR dɪˌlɪnɪ'eɪʃn, -z
AM dəˌlɪni'eɪʃən, diˌlɪni'eɪʃən, -z
delineator
BR dɪ'lɪnɪeɪtə(r), -z
AM də'lɪniˌeɪdər, di'lɪniˌeɪdər, -z
delinquency
BR dɪ'lɪŋkw(ə)ns|i, -ɪz
AM də'lɪŋkwənsi, -z
delinquent
BR dɪ'lɪŋkw(ə)nt, -s
AM də'lɪŋkwənt, -s
delinquently
BR dɪ'lɪŋkw(ə)ntli
AM də'lɪŋkwən(t)li
deliquesce
BR ˌdɛlɪ'kwɛs, -ɨz, -ɪŋ, -t
AM ˌdɛlə'kwɛs, -əz, -ɪŋ, -t
deliquescence
BR ˌdɛlɪ'kwɛsns
AM ˌdɛlə'kwɛsəns
deliquescent
BR ˌdɛlɪ'kwɛsnt
AM ˌdɛlə'kwɛsənt
deliria
BR dɪ'lɪrɪə(r), dɪ'lɪərɪə(r)
AM də'lɪriə
delirious
BR dɪ'lɪrɪəs, dɪ'lɪərɪəs
AM də'lɪriəs
deliriously
BR dɪ'lɪrɪəsli, dɪ'lɪərɪəsli
AM də'lɪriəsli
delirium
BR dɪ'lɪrɪəm, dɪ'lɪərɪəm
AM də'lɪriəm
delirium tremens
BR dɪˌlɪrɪəm 'trɛmɛnz, dɪˌlɪərɪəm +
AM dəˌlɪriəm 'trɛmənz
De Lisle
BR də 'lʌɪl
AM də 'laɪl, + 'lil
Delius
BR 'di:lɪəs
AM 'diliəs
deliver
BR dɪ'lɪv|ə(r), -əz, -(ə)rɪŋ, -əd
AM də'lɪv|ər, di'lɪv|ər, -ərz, -(ə)rɪŋ, -ərd
deliverable
BR dɪ'lɪv(ə)rəbl
AM də'lɪv(ə)rəbəl, di'lɪv(ə)rəbəl
deliverance
BR dɪ'lɪv(ə)rəns, dɪ'lɪv(ə)rn̩s
AM də'lɪv(ə)rəns, di'lɪv(ə)rəns
deliverer
BR dɪ'lɪv(ə)rə(r), -z
AM də'lɪv(ə)rər, di'lɪv(ə)rər, -z
delivery
BR dɪ'lɪv(ə)r|i, -ɪz
AM də'lɪv(ə)ri, di'lɪv(ə)ri, -z
deliveryman
BR dɪ'lɪv(ə)rɪˌman, dɪ'lɪv(ə)rɪmən
AM də'lɪv(ə)riˌmæn, di'lɪv(ə)riˌmæn
deliverymen
BR dɪ'lɪv(ə)rɪˌmɛn, dɪ'lɪv(ə)rɪmən
AM də'lɪv(ə)riˌmɛn, di'lɪv(ə)riˌmɛn
dell
BR dɛl, -z
AM dɛl, -z
Della
BR 'dɛlə(r)
AM 'dɛlə
Della Cruscan
BR ˌdɛlə 'krʌsk(ə)n, -z
AM ˌdɛlə 'kruʃən, -z
Della Robbia
BR ˌdɛlə 'rɒbɪə(r)
AM ˌdɛlə 'roʊbiə
delly
BR 'dɛl|i, -ɪz
AM 'dɛli, -z
Del Mar
BR dɛl 'mɑ:(r)
AM dɛl 'mɑr
Del Monte
BR dɛl 'mɒnti, + 'mɒnteɪ
AM dɛl 'mɑn(t)i
delocalisation
BR ˌdi:ləʊkəlʌɪ'zeɪʃn, ˌdi:ləʊkl̩ʌɪ'zeɪʃn, di:ˌləʊkəlʌɪ'zeɪʃn, di:ˌləʊkl̩ʌɪ'zeɪʃn
AM diˌloʊkələ'zeɪʃən, diˌloʊkəˌlaɪ'zeɪʃən
delocalise
BR (ˌ)di:'ləʊkəlʌɪz, (ˌ)di:'ləʊkl̩ʌɪz, -ɨz, -ɪŋ, -d
AM di'loʊkəˌlaɪz, -ɨz, -ɪŋ, -d
delocalization
BR ˌdi:ləʊkəlʌɪ'zeɪʃn, ˌdi:ləʊkl̩ʌɪ'zeɪʃn, di:ˌləʊkəlʌɪ'zeɪʃn, di:ˌləʊkl̩ʌɪ'zeɪʃn
AM diˌloʊkələ'zeɪʃən, diˌloʊkəˌlaɪ'zeɪʃən
delocalize
BR (ˌ)di:'ləʊkəlʌɪz, (ˌ)di:'ləʊkl̩ʌɪz, -ɨz, -ɪŋ, -d
AM di'loʊkəˌlaɪz, -ɨz, -ɪŋ, -d
Delorean
BR də'lɔ:rɪən, -z
AM də 'lɔriən, -z
Delores
BR də'lɔ:rɪz
AM də'lɔrəs
Delors
BR də'lɔ:(r)
AM də'lɔ(ə)r
Delos
BR 'di:lɒs
AM 'dilɑs
delouse
BR ˌdi:'laʊs, -ɨz, -ɪŋ, -t
AM di'laʊs, də'laʊs, -əz, -ɪŋ, -t
Delphi
BR 'dɛlfʌɪ, 'dɛlfi
AM 'dɛlˌfaɪ
Delphian
BR 'dɛlfɪən, -z
AM 'dɛlfiən, -z
Delphic
BR 'dɛlfɪk
AM 'dɛlfɪk
Delphine
BR 'dɛlfi:n
AM 'dɛlˌfin
delphinia
BR dɛl'fɪnɪə(r)
AM dɛl'fɪniə
delphinium
BR dɛl'fɪnɪəm, -z
AM dɛl'fɪniəm, -z
delphinoid
BR 'dɛlfɪnɔɪd, -z
AM 'dɛlfəˌnɔɪd, -z
Delphinus
BR dɛl'fʌɪnəs
AM dɛl'faɪnəs
Delsey
BR 'dɛlsi
AM 'dɛlsi
delta
BR 'dɛltə(r), -z
AM 'dɛltə, -z
deltaic
BR dɛl'teɪɪk
AM dɛl'teɪɪk
deltiologist
BR ˌdɛltɪ'ɒlədʒɪst, -s
AM ˌdɛlti'ɑlədʒəst, -s

deltiology
BR ˌdɛltɪˈɒlədʒi
AM ˌdɛltiˈɑlədʒi

deltoid
BR ˈdɛltɔɪd
AM ˈdɛlˌtɔɪd

delude
BR dɪˈl(j)uːd, -z, -ɪŋ, -ɨd
AM dəˈlud, diˈlud, -z, -ɪŋ, -əd

deluder
BR dɪˈl(j)uːdə(r), -z
AM dəˈludər, diˈludər, -z

deluge
BR ˈdɛljuː(d)ʒ, -ɨz, -ɪŋ, -d
AM ˈdɛlˌjudʒ, -əz, -ɪŋ, -d

delusion
BR dɪˈl(j)uːʒn, -z
AM dəˈluʒən, diˈluʒən, -z

delusional
BR dɪˈl(j)uːʒn̩(ə)l, dɪˈl(j)uːʒən(ə)l
AM dəˈluʒ(ə)nəl, diˈluʒ(ə)nəl

delusive
BR dɪˈl(j)uːsɪv
AM dəˈlusɪv, diˈlusɪv

delusively
BR dɪˈl(j)uːsɪvli
AM dəˈlusɪvli, diˈlusɪvli

delusiveness
BR dɪˈl(j)uːsɪvnɨs
AM dəˈlusɪvnɨs, diˈlusɪvnɨs

delusory
BR dɪˈl(j)uːs(ə)ri, dɪˈl(j)uːz(ə)ri
AM dəˈlus(ə)ri, diˈlus(ə)ri, dəˈluz(ə)ri, diˈluz(ə)ri

deluster
BR ˌdiːˈlʌst|ə(r), -əz, -(ə)rɪŋ, -əd
AM dəˈləstər, diˈləstər, -z, -ɪŋ, -d

delustre
BR ˌdiːˈlʌst|ə(r), -əz, -(ə)rɪŋ, -əd
AM dəˈləstər, diˈləstər, -z, -ɪŋ, -d

deluxe
BR dɪˈlʌks
AM dəˈləks, diˈləks

de luxe
BR dɪˈlʌks
AM dəˈləks, diˈləks

delve
BR dɛlv, -z, -ɪŋ, -d
AM dɛlv, -z, -ɪŋ, -d

delver
BR ˈdɛlvə(r), -z
AM ˈdɛlvər, -z

delving
BR ˈdɛlvɪŋ, -z
AM ˈdɛlvɪŋ, -z

Delwyn
BR ˈdɛlwɪn
AM ˈdɛlwən

Delyth
BR ˈdɛlɪθ
AM ˈdɛləθ

demagnetisation
BR ˌdiːmagnɨtʌɪˈzeɪʃn, diːˌmagnɨtʌɪˈzeɪʃn
AM ¦diˌmægnədəˈzeɪʃən, ¦diˌmægnəˌtaɪˈzeɪʃən

demagnetise
BR (ˌ)diːˈmagnɨtʌɪz, -ɨz, -ɪŋ, -d
AM diˈmægnəˌtaɪz, -ɨz, -ɪŋ, -d

demagnetiser
BR (ˌ)diːˈmagnɨtʌɪzə(r), -z
AM diˈmægnəˌtaɪzər, -z

demagnetization
BR ˌdiːmagnɨtʌɪˈzeɪʃn, diːˌmagnɨtʌɪˈzeɪʃn
AM ¦diˌmægnədəˈzeɪʃən, ¦diˌmægnəˌtaɪˈzeɪʃən

demagnetize
BR (ˌ)diːˈmagnɨtʌɪz, -ɨz, -ɪŋ, -d
AM diˈmægnəˌtaɪz, -ɨz, -ɪŋ, -d

demagnetizer
BR (ˌ)diːˈmagnɨtʌɪzə(r), -z
AM diˈmægnəˌtaɪzər, -z

demagogic
BR ˌdɛməˈgɒgɪk, ˌdɛməˈgɒdʒɪk
AM ˌdɛməˈgɑdʒɪk, ˌdɛməˈgɑgɪk

demagogical
BR ˌdɛməˈgɒgɪkl, ˌdɛməˈgɒdʒɪkl
AM ˌdɛməˈgɑdʒəkəl, ˌdɛməˈgɑgəkəl

demagogically
BR ˌdɛməˈgɒgɪkli, ˌdɛməˈgɒdʒɪkli
AM ˌdɛməˈgɑdʒək(ə)li, ˌdɛməˈgɑgək(ə)li

demagogue
BR ˈdɛməgɒg, -z
AM ˈdɛməˌgɑg, -z

demagoguery
BR ˈdɛməgɒg(ə)ri, ˌdɛməˈgɒg(ə)ri
AM ˈdɛməˌgɑg(ə)ri, ¦dɛməˌgɑg(ə)ri

demagogy
BR ˈdɛməgɒgi, ˈdɛməgɒdʒi
AM ˈdɛməˌgɑdʒi, ˈdɛməˌgɑgi

deman
BR ˌdiːˈman, -z, -ɪŋ, -d
AM diˈmæn, -z, -ɪŋ, -d

demand
BR dɪˈmɑːnd, dɪˈmand, -z, -ɪŋ, -ɨd
AM dəˈmænd, diˈmænd, -z, -ɪŋ, -əd

demandable
BR dɪˈmɑːndəbl, dɪˈmandəbl
AM dəˈmændəbəl, diˈmændəbəl

demandant
BR dɪˈmɑːnd(ə)nt, dɪˈmand(ə)nt, -s
AM dəˈmændnt, diˈmændnt, -s

demander
BR dɪˈmɑːndə(r), dɪˈmandə(r), -z
AM dəˈmændər, diˈmændər, -z

demandingly
BR dɪˈmɑːndɪŋli, dɪˈmandɪŋli
AM dəˈmændɪŋli, diˈmændɪŋli

demantoid
BR dɪˈmantɔɪd, -z
AM dəˈmænˌtɔɪd, diˈmænˌtɔɪd, -z

demarcate
BR ˈdiːmɑːkeɪt, -s, -ɪŋ, -ɨd
AM dəˈmɑrˌkeɪ|t, diˈmɑrˌkeɪ|t, ˈdimɑrˌkeɪ|t, -ts, -dɪŋ, -dɨd

demarcation
BR ˌdiːmɑːˈkeɪʃn, -z
AM ˌdimɑrˈkeɪʃən, -z

demarcator
BR ˈdiːmɑːkeɪtə(r), -z
AM dəˈmɑrˌkeɪdər, diˈmɑrˌkeɪdər, ˈdimɑrˌkeɪdər, -z

démarche
BR deɪˈmɑːʃ, ˈdeɪmɑːʃ, -ɨz
AM deɪˈmɑrʃ, -əz

dematerialisation
BR ˌdiːməˌtɪərɪəlʌɪˈzeɪʃn
AM ¦diməˌtɪriələˈzeɪʃən, ¦diməˌtɪriəˌlaɪˈzeɪʃən

dematerialise
BR ˌdiːməˈtɪərɪəlʌɪz, -ɨz, -ɪŋ, -d
AM ¦diməˈtɪriəˌlaɪz, -ɨz, -ɪŋ, -d

dematerialization
BR ˌdiːməˌtɪərɪəlʌɪˈzeɪʃn
AM ¦diməˌtɪriələˈzeɪʃən, ¦diməˌtɪriəˌlaɪˈzeɪʃən

dematerialize
BR ˌdiːməˈtɪərɪəlʌɪz, -ɨz, -ɪŋ, -d
AM ¦diməˈtɪriəˌlaɪz, -ɨz, -ɪŋ, -d

Demavend
BR ˈdɛməvɛnd
AM ˈdɛməˌvɛnd

deme
BR diːm, -z
AM dim, -z

demean
BR dɪˈmiːn, -z, -ɪŋ, -d
AM dəˈmin, diˈmin, -z, -ɪŋ, -d

demeanor
BR dɪˈmiːnə(r), -z
AM dəˈminər, diˈminər, -z

demeanour
BR dɪˈmiːnə(r), -z
AM dəˈminər, diˈminər, -z

Demelza
BR dəˈmɛlzə(r)
AM dəˈmɛlzə

dement
BR dɪˈmɛnt, -s, -ɨd
AM dəˈmɛn|t, diˈmən|t, -ts, -(t)əd

dementedly
BR dɪˈmɛntɨdli
AM dəˈmɛn(t)ədli, diˈmɛn(t)ədli

dementedness
BR dɪˈmɛntɨdnɨs
AM dəˈmɛn(t)ədnəs, diˈmɛn(t)ədnəs

démenti
BR ˌdeɪˈmɒ̃tiː
AM ˌdeɪmɑnˈti

dementia
BR dɪˈmɛnʃə(r)
AM dəˈmɛn(t)ʃ(i)ə

dementia praecox
BR dɪˌmɛnʃə ˈpriːkɒks
AM dəˈmɛn(t)ʃ(i)ə ˈpriˌkɑks

démentis
BR ˌdeɪˈmɒ̃tiː(z)
AM ˌdeɪmɑnˈtiz

Demerara
BR ˌdɛməˈrɛːrə(r)
AM ˌdɛməˈrɛrə

demerge
BR ˌdiːˈməːdʒ, -ɨz, -ɪŋ, -d
AM diˈmərdʒ, -əz, -ɪŋ, -d

demerger
BR ˌdiːˈməːdʒə(r), -z
AM ˌdiˈmərdʒər, -z

demerit
BR (ˌ)diːˈmɛrɪt, -s
AM dəˈmɛrət, diˈmɛrət, -s

demeritorious
BR ˌdiːmɛrɪˈtɔːrɪəs
AM diˌmɛrəˈtɔriəs

demersal
BR dɪˈməːsl

AM də'mərsəl

demesne
BR dɪ'meɪn, -z
AM də'meɪn, -z

Demeter
BR dɪ'mi:tə(r)
AM də'midər

Demetrius
BR dɪ'mi:trɪəs
AM də'mitriɪs

demigod
BR 'dɛmɪgɒd, -z
AM 'dɛmi,gɑd, -z

demigoddess
BR 'dɛmɪ,gɒdɪs, 'dɛmɪ,gɒdɛs, -ɪz
AM 'dɛmi,gɑdəs, -əz

demijohn
BR 'dɛmɪdʒɒn, -z
AM 'dɛmi,dʒɑn, -z

demilitarisation
BR ,di:mɪlɪt(ə)rʌɪ'zeɪʃn, di:,mɪlɪt(ə)rʌɪ'zeɪʃn
AM ¦di,mɪlədərə'zeɪʃən, də,mɪlədərə'zeɪʃən, ¦di,mɪlədə,raɪ'zeɪʃən, də,mɪlədə,raɪ'zeɪʃən

demilitarise
BR (,)di:'mɪlɪt(ə)rʌɪz, -ɪz, -ɪŋ, -d
AM də'mɪlədə,raɪz, di'mɪlədə,raɪz, -ɪz, -ɪŋ, -d

demilitarization
BR ,di:mɪlɪt(ə)rʌɪ'zeɪʃn, di:,mɪlɪt(ə)rʌɪ'zeɪʃn
AM ¦di,mɪlədərə'zeɪʃən, də,mɪlədərə'zeɪʃən, ¦di,mɪlədə,raɪ'zeɪʃən, də,mɪlədə,raɪ'zeɪʃən

demilitarize
BR (,)di:'mɪlɪt(ə)rʌɪz, -ɪz, -ɪŋ, -d
AM də'mɪlədə,raɪz, di'mɪlədə,raɪz, -ɪz, -ɪŋ, -d

de Mille
BR də 'mɪl
AM də 'mɪl

demi-mondaine
BR ,dɛmɪmɒn'deɪn, -z
AM ¦dɛmi,mɑn'deɪn, -z

demi-monde
BR ,dɛmɪ'mɒnd, 'dɛmɪmɒnd
AM ¦dɛmi¦mɑnd

demineralisation
BR ,di:mɪn(ə)rəlʌɪ'zeɪʃn, ,di:mɪn(ə)rl̩ʌɪ'zeɪʃn, di:,mɪn(ə)rəlʌɪ'zeɪʃn, di:,mɪn(ə)rl̩ʌɪ'zeɪʃn
AM di,minərələ'zeɪʃən, də,mɪnərələ'zeɪʃən, di:,mɪnərə,laɪ'zeɪʃən, də,mɪnərə,laɪ'zeɪʃn

demineralise
BR (,)di:'mɪn(ə)rəlʌɪz, (,)di:'mɪn(ə)rl̩ʌɪz, -ɪz, -ɪŋ, -d
AM də'mɪnərə,laɪz, di'mɪnərə,laɪz, -ɪz, -ɪŋ, -d

demineralization
BR ,di:mɪn(ə)rəlʌɪ'zeɪʃn, ,di:mɪn(ə)rl̩ʌɪ'zeɪʃn, di:,mɪn(ə)rəlʌɪ'zeɪʃn, di:,mɪn(ə)rl̩ʌɪ'zeɪʃn
AM di,minərələ'zeɪʃən, də,mɪnərələ'zeɪʃən, di:,mɪnərə,laɪ'zeɪʃən, də,mɪnərə,laɪ'zeɪʃn

demineralize
BR (,)di:'mɪn(ə)rəlʌɪz, (,)di:'mɪn(ə)rl̩ʌɪz, -ɪz, -ɪŋ, -d
AM də'mɪnərə,laɪz, di'mɪnərə,laɪz, -ɪz, -ɪŋ, -d

demi-pension
BR ,dɛmɪ'pɒ̃sjɒ̃
AM ,dɛmi'pɛn(t)ʃən

demirep
BR 'dɛmɪrɛp, -s
AM ,dɛmi'rɛp, -s

demise
BR dɪ'mʌɪz
AM də'maɪz, di'maɪz

demisemiquaver
BR 'dɛmɪsɛmɪ,kweɪvə(r), ,dɛmɪ'sɛmɪkweɪvə(r), -z
AM ¦dɛmi¦sɛmaɪ,kweɪvər, -z

demission
BR dɪ'mɪʃn, -z
AM də'mɪʃən, di'mɪʃən, -z

demist
BR ,di:'mɪst, dɪ'mɪst, -s, -ɪŋ, -ɪd
AM di'mɪst, də'mɪst, -s, -ɪŋ, -ɪd

demister
BR ,di:'mɪstə(r), dɪ'mɪstə(r), -z
AM di'mɪstər, də'mɪstər, -z

demit
BR ,di:'mɪt, dɪ'mɪt, -s, -ɪŋ, -ɪd
AM di'mɪ|t, də'mɪ|t, -ts, -dɪŋ, -dɪd

demitasse
BR 'dɛmɪtas, 'dɛmɪtɑ:s, -ɪz
AM 'dɛmi,tɑs, 'dɛmi,tæs -əz

demiurge
BR 'dɛmɪə:dʒ, 'di:mɪə:dʒ, -ɪz
AM 'dɛmi,ərdʒ, -əz

demiurgic
BR ,dɛmɪ'ə:dʒɪk, ,di:mɪ'ə:dʒɪk
AM ,dɛmi'ərdʒɪk

demi-vierge
BR ,dɛmɪvɪ'ɛ:ʒ, -z
AM ,dɛmivi'ɛrʒ, -z

demo
BR 'dɛməʊ, -z
AM 'dɛmoʊ, -z

demob
BR (,)di:'mɒb, dɪ'mɒb, -z, -ɪŋ, -d
AM di'mɑb, də'mɑb, -z, -ɪŋ, -d

demobilisation
BR dɪ,məʊbɪlʌɪ'zeɪʃn, dɪ,məʊbl̩ʌɪ'zeɪʃn, di:,məʊbɪlʌɪ'zeɪʃn, di:,məʊbl̩ʌɪ'zeɪʃn, ,di:məʊbɪlʌɪ'zeɪʃn, ,di:məʊbl̩ʌɪ'zeɪʃn
AM di,moʊbələ'zeɪʃən, də,moʊbələ'zeɪʃən, di,moʊbə,laɪ'zeɪʃən, də,moʊbə,laɪ'zeɪʃən

demobilise
BR dɪ'məʊbɪlʌɪz, dɪ'məʊbl̩ʌɪz, (,)di:'məʊbɪlʌɪz, (,)di:'məʊbl̩ʌɪz, -ɪz, -ɪŋ, -d
AM di'moʊbə,laɪz, də'moʊbə,laɪz, -ɪz, -ɪŋ, -d

demobilization
BR dɪ,məʊbɪlʌɪ'zeɪʃn, dɪ,məʊbl̩ʌɪ'zeɪʃn, di:,məʊbɪlʌɪ'zeɪʃn, di:,məʊbl̩ʌɪ'zeɪʃn, ,di:məʊbɪlʌɪ'zeɪʃn, ,di:məʊbl̩ʌɪ'zeɪʃn
AM di,moʊbələ'zeɪʃən, də,moʊbələ'zeɪʃən, di,moʊbə,laɪ'zeɪʃən, də,moʊbə,laɪ'zeɪʃən

demobilize
BR dɪ'məʊbɪlʌɪz, dɪ'məʊbl̩ʌɪz, (,)di:'məʊbɪlʌɪz, (,)di:'məʊbl̩ʌɪz, -ɪz, -ɪŋ, -d
AM di'moʊbə,laɪz, də'moʊbə,laɪz, -ɪz, -ɪŋ, -d

democracy
BR dɪ'mɒkrəs|i, -ɪz
AM də'mɑkrəsi, -z

democrat
BR 'dɛməkrat, -s
AM 'dɛmə,kræt, -s

democratic
BR ,dɛmə'kratɪk
AM ,dɛmə'krædɪk

democratically
BR ,dɛmə'kratɪkli
AM ,dɛmə'krædək(ə)li

democratisation
BR dɪ,mɒkrətʌɪ'zeɪʃn
AM də,mɑkrədə'zeɪʃən, di,mɑkrədə'zeɪʃən, də,mɑkrə,taɪ'zeɪʃən, di,mɑkrə,taɪ'zeɪʃən

democratise
BR dɪ'mɒkrətʌɪz, -ɪz, -ɪŋ, -d
AM də'mɑkrə,taɪz, di'mɑkrə,taɪz, -ɪz, -ɪŋ, -d

democratism
BR dɪ'mɒkrətɪz(ə)m
AM də'mɑkrə,tɪzəm, di'mɑkrə,tɪzəm

democratization
BR dɪ,mɒkrətʌɪ'zeɪʃn
AM də,mɑkrədə'zeɪʃən, di,mɑkrədə'zeɪʃən, də,mɑkrə,taɪ'zeɪʃən, di,mɑkrə,taɪ'zeɪʃən

democratize
BR dɪ'mɒkrətʌɪz, -ɪz, -ɪŋ, -d
AM də'mɑkrə,taɪz, di'mɑkrə,taɪz, -ɪz, -ɪŋ, -d

Democritus
BR dɪ'mɒkrɪtəs
AM də'mɑkrədəs, di'mɑkrədəs

démodé
BR ,deɪ'məʊdeɪ
AM ,deɪmoʊ'deɪ

demodectic
BR ,di'mə(ʊ)'dɛktɪk
AM ,dimə'dɛktɪk

demodulate
BR ,di:'mɒdjʉleɪt, ,di:'mɒdʒʉleɪt, -s, -ɪŋ, -ɪd
AM di'mɑdʒə,leɪ|t, di'mɑdjʊ,leɪ|t, -ts, -dɪŋ, -dɪd

demodulation
BR ,di:mɒdjʉ'leɪʃn, ,di:mɒdʒʉ'leɪʃn
AM di,mɑdʒə'leɪʃən

demodulator
BR ,di:'mɒdjʉleɪtə(r), ,di:'mɒdʒʉleɪtə(r), -z
AM di'mɑdʒə,leɪdər, -z

demographer
BR dɪ'mɒgrəfə(r), -z
AM də'mɑgrəfər, -z

demographic
BR ,dɛmə'grafɪk, -s
AM ,dɛmə'græfɪk, -s

demographical
BR ,dɛmə'grafɪkl
AM ,dɛmə'græfəkəl

demographically
BR ,dɛmə'grafɪkli
AM ,dɛmə'græfək(ə)li

demography
BR dɪ'mɒgrəfi
AM də'mɑgrəfi

demoiselle
BR ˌdɛmwɑːˈzɛl, ˌdɛm(w)əˈzɛl, -z
AM ˌdɛm(w)ɑˈzɛl, -z

demolish
BR dɪˈmɒl|ɪʃ, -ɪʃɪz, -ɪʃɪŋ, -ɪʃt
AM dəˈmɑlɪʃ, diˈmɑlɪʃ, -ɪz, -ɪŋ, -t

demolisher
BR dɪˈmɒlɪʃə(r), -z
AM dəˈmɑlɪʃər, diˈmɑlɪʃər, -z

demolition
BR ˌdɛməˈlɪʃn, -z
AM ˌdɛməˈlɪʃən, ˌdiməˈlɪʃən, -z

demolitionist
BR ˌdɛməˈlɪʃn̩ɪst, ˌdɛməˈlɪʃənɪst, -s
AM ˌdɛməˈlɪʃənəst, ˌdiməˈlɪʃənəst, -s

demon
BR ˈdiːmən, -z
AM ˈdimən, -z

demonetisation
BR ˌdiːmʌnɨtʌɪˈzeɪʃn, diːˌmʌnɨtʌɪˈzeɪʃn
AM diˌmɑnədəˈzeɪʃən, diˌmɑnəˌtaɪˈzeɪʃən

demonetise
BR (ˌ)diːˈmʌnɨtʌɪz, -ɨz, -ɪŋ, -d
AM diˈmɑnəˌtaɪz, -ɨz, -ɪŋ, -d

demonetization
BR ˌdiːmʌnɨtʌɪˈzeɪʃn, diːˌmʌnɨtʌɪˈzeɪʃn
AM diˌmɑnədəˈzeɪʃən, diˌmɑnəˌtaɪˈzeɪʃən

demonetize
BR (ˌ)diːˈmʌnɨtʌɪz, -ɨz, -ɪŋ, -d
AM diˈmɑnəˌtaɪz, -ɨz, -ɪŋ, -d

demoniac
BR dɪˈməʊnɪak, -s
AM dəˈmoʊniˌæk, ˌdiməˈnaɪək, -s

demoniacal
BR ˌdiːməˈnʌɪəkl
AM ˌdiməˈnaɪəkəl

demoniacally
BR ˌdiːməˈnʌɪəkli
AM ˌdiməˈnaɪək(ə)li

demonic
BR dɪˈmɒnɪk, diːˈmɒnɪk
AM dəˈmɑnɪk, diˈmɑnɪk

demonical
BR dɪˈmɒnɪkl, diːˈmɒnɪkl
AM dəˈmɑnəkəl, diˈmɑnəkəl

demonically
BR dɪˈmɒnɪkli, diːˈmɒnɪkli
AM dəˈmɑnək(ə)li, diˈmɑnək(ə)li

demonisation
BR ˌdiːmənʌɪˈzeɪʃn
AM ˌdimənəˈzeɪʃən, ˌdiməˌnaɪˈzeɪʃən

demonise
BR ˈdiːmənʌɪz, -ɨz, -ɪŋ, -d
AM ˈdiməˌnaɪz, -ɨz, -ɪŋ, -d

demonism
BR ˈdiːmənɪz(ə)m
AM ˈdiməˌnɪzəm

demonization
BR ˌdiːmənʌɪˈzeɪʃn
AM ˌdimənəˈzeɪʃən, ˌdiməˌnaɪˈzeɪʃən

demonize
BR ˈdiːmənʌɪz, -ɨz, -ɪŋ, -d
AM ˈdiməˌnaɪz, -ɨz, -ɪŋ, -d

demonolatry
BR ˌdiːməˈnɒlətri
AM ˌdiməˈnɑlətri

demonological
BR ˌdiːmənəˈlɒdʒɪkl
AM ˌdimənəˈlɑdʒəkəl

demonologist
BR ˌdiːməˈnɒlədʒɪst, -s
AM ˌdiməˈnɑlədʒəst, -s

demonology
BR ˌdiːməˈnɒlədʒi
AM ˌdiməˈnɑlədʒi

demonstrability
BR dɪˌmɒnstrəˈbɪlɨti
AM dəˌmɑnstrəˈbɪlɨdi

demonstrable
BR dɪˈmɒnstrəbl
AM dəˈmɑnstrəbəl, diˈmɑnstrəbəl

demonstrably
BR dɪˈmɒnstrəbli
AM dəˈmɑnstrəbli, diˈmɑnstrəbli

demonstrate
BR ˈdɛmənstreɪt, -s, -ɪŋ, -ɨd
AM ˈdɛmənˌstreɪ|t, -ts, -dɪŋ, -dɨd

demonstration
BR ˌdɛmənˈstreɪʃn, -z
AM ˌdɛmənˈstreɪʃən, -z

demonstrational
BR ˌdɛmənˈstreɪʃn̩(ə)l, ˌdɛmənˈstreɪʃən(ə)l
AM ˌdɛmənˈstreɪʃ(ə)nəl

demonstrative
BR dɪˈmɒnstrətɪv, -z
AM dəˈmɑnstrədɪv, diˈmɑnstrədɪv, -z

demonstratively
BR dɪˈmɒnstrətɪvli
AM dəˈmɑnstrədɪvli, diˈmɑnstrədɪvli

demonstrativeness
BR dɪˈmɒnstrətɪvnɪs
AM dəˈmɑnstrədɪvnɪs, diˈmɑnstrədɪvnɪs

demonstrator
BR ˈdɛmənstreɪtə(r), -z
AM ˈdɛmənˌstreɪdər, -z

de Montfort
BR də ˈmɒntfət, + ˈmɒntfɔːt
AM də ˈmɑn(t)fərt, + ˈmɑn(t)ˌfɔ(ə)rt

demoralisation
BR dɪˌmɒrəlʌɪˈzeɪʃn, dɪˌmɒrl̩ʌɪˈzeɪʃn
AM dəˌmɔrələˈzeɪʃən, diˌmɔrələˈzeɪʃən, dəˌmɔrəˌlaɪˈzeɪʃən, diˌmɔrəˌlaɪˈzeɪʃən

demoralise
BR dɪˈmɒrəlʌɪz, dɪˈmɒrl̩ʌɪz, -ɨz, -ɪŋ, -d
AM dəˈmɔrəˌlaɪz, diˈmɔrəˌlaɪz, -ɨz, -ɪŋ, -d

demoralisingly
BR dɪˈmɒrəlʌɪzɪŋli, dɪˈmɒrl̩ʌɪzɪŋli
AM dəˈmɔrəˌlaɪzɪŋli, diˈmɔrəˌlaɪzɪŋli

demoralization
BR dɪˌmɒrəlʌɪˈzeɪʃn, dɪˈmɒrl̩ʌɪˈzeɪʃn
AM dəˌmɔrələˈzeɪʃən, diˌmɔrələˈzeɪʃən, dəˌmɔrəˌlaɪˈzeɪʃən, diˌmɔrəˌlaɪˈzeɪʃən

demoralize
BR dɪˈmɒrəlʌɪz, dɪˈmɒrl̩ʌɪz, -ɨz, -ɪŋ, -d
AM dəˈmɔrəˌlaɪz, diˈmɔrəˌlaɪz, -ɨz, -ɪŋ, -d

demoralizingly
BR dɪˈmɒrəlʌɪzɪŋli, dɪˈmɒrl̩ʌɪzɪŋli
AM dəˈmɔrəˌlaɪzɪŋli, diˈmɔrəˌlaɪzɪŋli

Demos
BR ˈdiːmɒs
AM ˈdiˌmɑs, ˈdiˌmɔs

Demosthenes
BR dɪˈmɒsθɨniːz
AM dəˈmɑsθəˌniz

demote
BR dɪˈməʊt, ˌdiːˈməʊt, -s, -ɪŋ, -ɨd
AM dəˈmoʊ|t, diˈmoʊ|t, -ts, -dɪŋ, -dəd

demotic
BR dɪˈmɒtɪk
AM dəˈmɑdɪk

demotion
BR dɪˈməʊʃn, ˌdiːˈməʊʃn, -z
AM dəˈmoʊʃən, diˈmoʊʃən, -z

demotivate
BR ˌdiːˈməʊtɪveɪt, -s, -ɪŋ, -ɨd
AM diˈmoʊdəˌveɪ|t, -ts, -dɪŋ, -dɨd

demotivation
BR ˌdiːməʊtɪˈveɪʃn
AM diˌmoʊdəˈveɪʃən

demount
BR ˌdiːˈmaʊnt, -s, -ɪŋ, -ɨd
AM diˈmaʊn|t, -ts, -(t)ɪŋ, -(t)əd

demountable
BR ˌdiːˈmaʊntəbl
AM diˈmaʊn(t)əbəl

Dempsey
BR ˈdɛm(p)si
AM ˈdɛm(p)si

Dempster
BR ˈdɛm(p)stə(r)
AM ˈdɛm(p)stər

demulcent
BR dɪˈmʌlsnt, -s
AM dəˈməlsənt, diˈməlsənt, -s

demur
BR dɪˈməː(r), -z, -ɪŋ, -d
AM dəˈmər, diˈmər, -z, -ɪŋ, -d

demure
BR dɪˈmjʊə(r), dɪˈmjɔː(r)
AM dəˈmjʊ(ə)r, diˈmjʊ(ə)r

demurely
BR dɪˈmjʊəli, dɪˈmjɔːli
AM dəˈmjʊrli, diˈmjʊrli

demureness
BR dɪˈmjʊənəs, dɪˈmjɔːnəs
AM dəˈmjʊrnəs, diˈmjʊrnəs

demurrable
BR dɪˈməːrəbl
AM dəˈmjʊrəbəl, diˈmjʊrəbəl

demurrage
BR dɪˈmʌrɪdʒ
AM dəˈmərɪdʒ

demurral
BR dɪˈmʌrəl, dɪˈmʌrl̩
AM dəˈmərəl

demurrer[1]
dissent
BR dɪˈmʌrə(r), -z
AM dəˈmərər, diˈmərər, -z

demurrer[2]
person who demurs
BR dɪˈməːrə(r), -z
AM dəˈmərər, diˈmərər, -z

demy
BR dɪˈmʌɪ, -z
AM dəˈmaɪ, -z

demystification
BR ˌdiːmɪstɪfɪˈkeɪʃn, diːˌmɪstɪfɪˈkeɪʃn
AM ˌdiˌmɪstəfəˈkeɪʃən

demystify
BR (ˌ)diːˈmɪstɪfʌɪ, -z, -ɪŋ, -d
AM diˈmɪstɪˌfaɪ, -z, -ɪŋ, -d

demythologisation
BR ˌdiːmɪˌθɒlədʒʌɪˈzeɪʃn
AM ˌdiməθɑlədʒəˈzeɪʃən, ˌdiməθɑləˌdʒaɪˈzeɪʃən

demythologise
BR ˌdiːmɪˈθɒlədʒʌɪz, -ɪz, -ɪŋ, -d
AM ˌdiməˈθɑləˌdʒaɪz, -ɪz, -ɪŋ, -d

demythologization
BR ˌdiːmɪˌθɒlədʒʌɪˈzeɪʃn
AM ˌdiməθɑlədʒəˈzeɪʃən, ˌdiməθɑləˌdʒaɪˈzeɪʃən

demythologize
BR ˌdiːmɪˈθɒlədʒʌɪz, -ɪz, -ɪŋ, -d
AM ˌdiməˈθɑləˌdʒaɪz, -ɪz, -ɪŋ, -d

den
BR dɛn, -z
AM dɛn, -z

denarii
BR dɪˈnɛːrɪʌɪ, dɪˈnɛːriiː, dɪˈnɑːrɪʌɪ, dɪˈnɑːriiː
AM dəˈnɛriˌi, dəˈnɑriˌaɪ

denarius
BR dɪˈnɛːrɪəs, dɪˈnɑːrɪəs
AM dəˈnɛriəs, dəˈnɑriəs

denary
BR ˈdiːn(ə)ri, ˈdɛn(ə)ri
AM ˈdɛnəri, ˈdinəri

denationalisation
BR ˌdiːnaʃn̩əlʌɪˈzeɪʃn, ˌdiːnaʃn̩l̩ʌɪˈzeɪʃn, ˌdiːnaʃənl̩ʌɪˈzeɪʃn, ˌdiːnaʃ(ə)nəlʌɪˈzeɪʃn, diːˌnaʃn̩əlʌɪˈzeɪʃn, diːˌnaʃn̩l̩ʌɪˈzeɪʃn, diːˌnaʃənl̩ʌɪˈzeɪʃn, diːˌnaʃ(ə)nəlʌɪˈzeɪʃn, -z
AM ˌdinæʃ(ə)nələˈzeɪʃn, ˌdinæʃ(ə)nəˌlaɪˈzeɪʃən, dəˌnæʃ(ə)nəˌlaɪˈzeɪʃən, dəˌnæʃ(ə)nələˈzeɪʃən, -z

denationalise
BR (ˌ)diːˈnaʃn̩əlʌɪz, (ˌ)diːˈnaʃn̩l̩ʌɪz, (ˌ)diːˈnaʃənl̩ʌɪz, (ˌ)diːˈnaʃ(ə)nəlʌɪz, -ɪz, -ɪŋ, -d
AM diˈnæʃ(ə)nəˌlaɪz, dəˈnæʃ(ə)nəˌlaɪz, -ɪz, -ɪŋ, -d

denationalization
BR ˌdiːnaʃn̩əlʌɪˈzeɪʃn, ˌdiːnaʃn̩l̩ʌɪˈzeɪʃn, ˌdiːnaʃənl̩ʌɪˈzeɪʃn, ˌdiːnaʃ(ə)nəlʌɪˈzeɪʃn, diːˌnaʃn̩əlʌɪˈzeɪʃn, diːˌnaʃn̩l̩ʌɪˈzeɪʃn, diːˌnaʃənl̩ʌɪˈzeɪʃn, diːˌnaʃ(ə)nəlʌɪˈzeɪʃn, -z
AM ˌdinæʃ(ə)nələˈzeɪʃn, ˌdinæʃ(ə)nəˌlaɪˈzeɪʃən, dəˌnæʃ(ə)nəˌlaɪˈzeɪʃən, dəˌnæʃ(ə)nələˈzeɪʃən, -z

denationalize
BR (ˌ)diːˈnaʃn̩əlʌɪz, (ˌ)diːˈnaʃn̩l̩ʌɪz, (ˌ)diːˈnaʃənl̩ʌɪz, (ˌ)diːˈnaʃ(ə)nəlʌɪz, -ɪz, -ɪŋ, -d
AM diˈnæʃ(ə)nəˌlaɪz, dəˈnæʃ(ə)nəˌlaɪz, -ɪz, -ɪŋ, -d

denaturalisation
BR ˌdiːnatʃ(ə)rəlʌɪˈzeɪʃn, ˌdiːnatʃ(ə)rl̩ʌɪˈzeɪʃn, diːˌnatʃ(ə)rəlʌɪˈzeɪʃn, diːˌnatʃ(ə)rl̩ʌɪˈzeɪʃn
AM diˌnætʃ(ə)rələˈzeɪʃən, diˌnætʃ(ə)rəˌlaɪˈzeɪʃən

denaturalise
BR (ˌ)diːˈnatʃ(ə)rəlʌɪz, (ˌ)diːˈnatʃ(ə)rl̩ʌɪz, -ɪz, -ɪŋ, -d
AM diˈnætʃ(ə)rəˌlaɪz, dəˈnætʃ(ə)rəˌlaɪz, -ɪz, -ɪŋ, -d

denaturalization
BR ˌdiːnatʃ(ə)rəlʌɪˈzeɪʃn, ˌdiːnatʃ(ə)rl̩ʌɪˈzeɪʃn, diːˌnatʃ(ə)rəlʌɪˈzeɪʃn, diːˌnatʃ(ə)rl̩ʌɪˈzeɪʃn
AM diˌnætʃ(ə)rələˈzeɪʃən, diˌnætʃ(ə)rəˌlaɪˈzeɪʃən

denaturalize
BR (ˌ)diːˈnatʃ(ə)rəlʌɪz, (ˌ)diːˈnatʃ(ə)rl̩ʌɪz, -ɪz, -ɪŋ, -d
AM diˈnætʃ(ə)rəˌlaɪz, dəˈnætʃ(ə)rəˌlaɪz, -ɪz, -ɪŋ, -d

denaturant
BR ˌdiːˈneɪtʃ(ə)rənt, ˌdiːˈneɪtʃ(ə)rn̩t, -s
AM diˈneɪtʃ(ə)rənt, dəˈneɪtʃ(ə)rənt, -s

denaturation
BR ˌdiːneɪtʃəˈreɪʃn, diːˌneɪtʃəˈreɪʃn
AM diˌneɪtʃəˈreɪʃən, dəˌneɪtʃəˈreɪʃən

denature
BR ˌdiːˈneɪtʃə(r), -z, -ɪŋ, -d
AM diˈneɪtʃər, dəˈneɪtʃər, -z, -ɪŋ, -d

denazification
BR ˌdiːnɑːtsɪfɪˈkeɪʃn, ˌdiːnɑːzɪfɪˈkeɪʃn, diːˌnɑːtsɪfɪˈkeɪʃn, diːˌnɑːzɪfɪˈkeɪʃn
AM diˌnɑtsəfəˈkeɪʃən

denazify
BR ˌdiːˈnɑːtsɪfʌɪ, ˌdiːˈnɑːzɪfʌɪ, -z, -ɪŋ, -d
AM diˈnɑtsəˌfaɪ, -z, -ɪŋ, -d

Denbigh
BR ˈdɛnbi
AM ˈdɛnbi

Denby
BR ˈdɛnbi
AM ˈdɛnbi

Dench
BR ˈdɛn(t)ʃ
AM ˈdɛn(t)ʃ

dendrite
BR ˈdɛndrʌɪt, -s
AM ˈdɛnˌdraɪt, -s

dendritic
BR dɛnˈdrɪtɪk
AM dɛnˈdrɪdɪk

dendritically
BR dɛnˈdrɪtɪkli
AM dɛnˈdrɪdɪk(ə)li

dendrochronological
BR ˌdɛndrəʊˌkrɒnəˈlɒdʒɪkl
AM ˌdɛndroʊˌkrɑnəˈlɑdʒəkəl

dendrochronologist
BR ˌdɛndrəʊkrəˈnɒlədʒɪst, -s
AM ˌdɛndroʊkrəˈnɑlədʒəst, -s

dendrochronology
BR ˌdɛndrəʊkrəˈnɒlədʒi
AM ˌdɛndroʊkrəˈnɑlədʒi

dendrogram
BR ˈdɛndrə(ʊ)gram, -z
AM ˈdɛndrəˌgræm, -z

dendroid
BR ˈdɛndrɔɪd
AM ˈdɛndrɔɪd

dendrological
BR ˌdɛndrəˈlɒdʒɪkl
AM ˌdɛndroʊˈlɑdʒəkəl

dendrologist
BR dɛnˈdrɒlədʒɪst, -s
AM dɛnˈdrɑlədʒəst, -s

dendrology
BR dɛnˈdrɒlədʒi
AM dɛnˈdrɑlədʒi

Dene[1]
North American people
BR ˈdɛni, ˈdɛneɪ
AM ˈdɛneɪ

Dene[2]
surname
BR diːn
AM din

dene
BR diːn, -z
AM din, -z

Deneb
BR ˈdɛnɛb
AM ˈdɛnˌɛb

de-net
BR ˌdiːˈnɛt, -s, -ɪŋ, -ɪd
AM diˈnɛ|t, -ts, -dɪŋ, -dəd

Deneuve
BR dəˈnəːv
AM dəˈnʊv

dengue
BR ˈdɛŋgi
AM ˈdɛŋgi

Den Haag
BR dɛn ˈhɑːg
AM deɪn ˈhɑg

Denham
BR ˈdɛnəm
AM ˈdɛnəm

Denholm
BR ˈdɛnəm
AM ˈdɛnəm

Denholme[1]
Yorkshire, England
BR ˈdɛnhɒlm
AM ˈdɛnhɔ(l)m, ˈdɛnhoʊ(l)m

Denholme[2]
BR ˈdɛnəm
AM ˈdɛnəm

deniability
BR dɪˌnʌɪəˈbɪlɪti
AM dəˌnaɪbəˈbɪlɪdi

deniable
BR dɪˈnʌɪəbl
AM dəˈnaɪəbəl

deniably
BR dɪˈnʌɪəbli
AM dəˈnaɪəbli

denial
BR dɪˈnʌɪəl, -z
AM dəˈnaɪ(ə)l, diˈnaɪ(ə)l, -z

denier[1]
cloth, coin
BR ˈdɛnɪə(r), ˈdɛnɪeɪ
AM dəˈnɪ(ə)r, ˈdɛnjər

denier[2]
person or thing that denies
BR dɪˈnʌɪə(r), -z
AM dəˈnaɪər, diˈnaɪər, -z

denigrate
BR ˈdɛnɪgreɪt, -s, -ɪŋ, -ɪd
AM ˈdɛnəˌgreɪ|t, -ts, -dɪŋ, -dɪd

denigration
BR ˌdɛnɪˈgreɪʃn
AM ˌdɛnəˈgreɪʃən

denigrator
BR ˈdɛnɪgreɪtə(r), -z
AM ˈdɛnəˌgreɪdər, -z

denigratory
BR ˌdɛnɪˈgreɪt(ə)ri

AM 'dɛnəgrəˌtɔri

denim
BR 'dɛnɪm, -z
AM 'dɛnəm, -z

De Niro
BR də 'nɪərəʊ
AM də'niroʊ

Denis
BR 'dɛnɪs
AM 'dɛnəs

Denise
BR dɪ'ni:z, dɪ'ni:s
AM də'nis

denitrification
BR ˌdi:nʌɪtrɪfɪ'keɪʃn, di:ˌnʌɪtrɪfɪ'keɪʃn
AM dəˌnaɪtrəfə'keɪʃən, diˌnaɪtrəfə'keɪʃən

denitrify
BR (ˌ)di:'nʌɪtrɪfʌɪ, -z, -ɪŋ, -d
AM də'naɪtrəˌfaɪ, di'naɪtrəˌfaɪ, -z, -ɪŋ, -d

denizen
BR 'dɛnɪz(ə)n, -z
AM 'dɛnəzən, -z

Denmark
BR 'dɛnmɑ:k
AM 'dɛnmɑrk

Denning
BR 'dɛnɪŋ
AM 'dɛnɪŋ

Dennis
BR 'dɛnɪs
AM 'dɛnəs

Dennison
BR 'dɛnɪs(ə)n
AM 'dɛnəsən

Denny
BR 'dɛni
AM 'dɛni

denominate
BR dɪ'nɒmɪneɪt, -s, -ɪŋ, -ɪd
AM də'nɑməˌneɪ|t, di'nɑməˌneɪ|t, -ts, -dɪŋ, -dɪd

denomination
BR dɪˌnɒmɪ'neɪʃn, -z
AM dəˌnɑmə'neɪʃən, diˌnɑmə'neɪʃən, -z

denominational
BR dɪˌnɒmɪ'neɪʃn̩(ə)l, dɪˌnɒmɪ'neɪʃən(ə)l
AM dəˌnɑmə'neɪʃ(ə)nəl, diˌnɑmə'neɪʃ(ə)nəl

denominationalism
BR dɪˌnɒmɪ'neɪʃn̩əlɪz(ə)m, dɪˌnɒmɪ'neɪʃn̩l̩ɪz(ə)m, dɪˌnɒmɪ'neɪʃənl̩ɪz(ə)m, dɪˌnɒmɪ'neɪʃ(ə)nəlɪz(ə)m
AM dəˌnɑmə'neɪʃənəˌlɪzəm, diˌnɑmə'neɪʃənəˌlɪzəm

denominationalist
BR dɪˌnɒmɪ'neɪʃn̩əlɪst, dɪˌnɒmɪ'neɪʃn̩l̩ɪst, dɪˌnɒmɪ'neɪʃənl̩ɪst, dɪˌnɒmɪ'neɪʃ(ə)nəlɪst, -s
AM dəˌnɑmə'neɪʃənələst, diˌnɑmə'neɪʃənələst, -s

denominationally
BR dɪˌnɒmɪ'neɪʃn̩əli, dɪˌnɒmɪ'neɪʃn̩l̩i, dɪˌnɒmɪ'neɪʃənl̩i, dɪˌnɒmɪ'neɪʃ(ə)nəli
AM dəˌnɑmə'neɪʃ(ə)nəli, diˌnɑmə'neɪʃ(ə)nəli

denominative
BR dɪ'nɒmɪnətɪv
AM də'nɑməˌneɪdɪv, də'nɑmənədɪv, di'nɑməˌneɪdɪv, di'nɑmənədɪv

denominator
BR dɪ'nɒmɪneɪtə(r), -z
AM də'nɑməˌneɪdər, di'nɑməˌneɪdər, -z

de nos jours
BR də ˌnəʊ 'ʒʊə(r)
AM də ˌnoʊ 'ʒʊ(ə)r

denotation
BR ˌdi:nə(ʊ)'teɪʃn
AM ˌdinoʊ'teɪʃən

denotative
BR dɪ'nəʊtətɪv, 'di:nə(ʊ)teɪtɪv
AM 'dinoʊˌteɪdɪv, də'noʊdədɪv, di'noʊdədɪv

denotatively
BR dɪ'nəʊtətɪvli, 'di:nə(ʊ)teɪtɪvli
AM 'dinoʊˌteɪdɪvli, də'noʊdədɪvli, di'noʊdədɪvli

denote
BR dɪ'nəʊt, -s, -ɪŋ, -ɪd
AM də'noʊ|t, di'noʊ|t, -ts, -dɪŋ, -dəd

dénouement
BR deɪ'n(j)u:mɒ̃, -z
AM ˌdeɪnu'mɑn, -z

denounce
BR dɪ'naʊns, -ɪz, -ɪŋ, -t
AM də'naʊns, di'naʊns, -əz, -ɪŋ, -t

denouncement
BR dɪ'naʊnsm(ə)nt, -s
AM də'naʊnsmənt, di'naʊnsmənt, -s

denouncer
BR dɪ'naʊnsə(r), -z
AM də'naʊnsər, di'naʊnsər, -z

de nouveau
BR də ˌnu:'vəʊ
AM də ˌnu'voʊ

Denovo
BR dɪ'nəʊvəʊ
AM də'noʊvoʊ

de novo
BR deɪ 'nəʊvəʊ, di: +
AM də 'noʊvoʊ, di +

dense
BR dɛns, -ə(r), -ɪst
AM dɛns, -ər, -əst

densely
BR 'dɛnsli
AM 'dɛnsli

denseness
BR 'dɛnsnəs
AM 'dɛnsnəs

densitometer
BR ˌdɛnsɪ'tɒmɪtə(r), -z
AM ˌdɛnsə'tɑmədər, -z

density
BR 'dɛnsɪt|i, -ɪz
AM 'dɛnsədi, -z

dent
BR dɛnt, -s, -ɪŋ, -ɪd
AM dɛn|t, -(t)s, -(t)ɪŋ, -(t)əd

dental
BR 'dɛntl
AM 'dɛn(t)l

dentalia
BR dɛn'teɪlɪə(r)
AM dɛn'teɪljə, dɛn'teɪliə

dentalise
BR 'dɛntl̩ʌɪz, 'dɛntəlʌɪz, -ɪz, -ɪŋ, -d
AM 'dɛn(t)lˌaɪz, -ɪz, -ɪŋ, -d

dentalium
BR dɛn'teɪlɪəm
AM dɛn'teɪliəm

dentalize
BR 'dɛntl̩ʌɪz, 'dɛntəlʌɪz, -ɪz, -ɪŋ, -d
AM 'dɛn(t)lˌaɪz, -ɪz, -ɪŋ, -d

dentate
BR 'dɛnteɪt
AM 'dɛnˌteɪt

denticle
BR 'dɛntɪkl, -z
AM 'dɛn(t)əkəl, -z

denticulate
BR dɛn'tɪkjʊlət, dɛn'tɪkjʊleɪt
AM dɛn'tɪkjələt

dentifrice
BR 'dɛntɪfrɪs, -ɪz
AM 'dɛn(t)əfrəs, -ɪz

dentil
BR 'dɛnt(ɪ)l, -z
AM 'dɛn(t)l, 'dɛnˌtɪl, -z

dentilingual
BR ˌdɛntɪ'lɪŋgwəl
AM ˌdɛn(t)ə'lɪŋgwəl

dentin
BR 'dɛnti:n
AM 'dɛnˌtɪn, dɛn'tɪn

dentinal
BR 'dɛntɪnl
AM dɛn'tinəl, 'dɛn(t)ənəl

dentine
BR 'dɛnti:n
AM 'dɛnˌtin, dɛn'tin

dentist
BR 'dɛntɪst, -s
AM 'dɛn(t)ɪst, -s

dentistry
BR 'dɛntɪstri
AM 'dɛn(t)ɪstri

dentition
BR dɛn'tɪʃn
AM dɛn'tɪʃən

Denton
BR 'dɛnt(ə)n
AM 'dɛn(t)ən

denture
BR 'dɛntʃə(r), -z
AM 'dɛn(t)ʃər, -z

denuclearisation
BR ˌdi:nju:klɪərʌɪ'zeɪʃn, di:ˌnju:klɪərʌɪ'zeɪʃn
AM diˌn(j)uklɪ(ə)rə'zeɪʃən, diˌn(j)uklɪ(ə)ˌraɪ'zeɪʃən

denuclearise
BR ˌdi:'nju:klɪərʌɪz, -ɪz, -ɪŋ, -d
AM di'n(j)uklɪəˌraɪz, -ɪz, -ɪŋ, -d

denuclearization
BR ˌdi:nju:klɪərʌɪ'zeɪʃn, di:ˌnju:klɪərʌɪ'zeɪʃn
AM diˌn(j)uklɪ(ə)rə'zeɪʃən, diˌn(j)uklɪ(ə)ˌraɪ'zeɪʃən

denuclearize
BR ˌdi:'nju:klɪərʌɪz, -ɪz, -ɪŋ, -d
AM di'n(j)uklɪəˌraɪz, -ɪz, -ɪŋ, -d

denudation
BR ˌdi:njʊ'deɪʃn
AM ˌdin(j)u'deɪʃən, ˌdɛnjə'deɪʃən

denudative
BR dɪ'nju:dətɪv
AM di'n(j)udədɪv

denude
BR dɪ'nju:d, -z, -ɪŋ, -ɪd
AM də'n(j)ud, di'n(j)ud, -z, -ɪŋ, -əd

denumerability
BR dɪˌnju:m(ə)rə'bɪlɪti
AM diˌn(j)umərə'bɪlɪdi

denumerable
BR dɪ'nju:m(ə)rəbl
AM di'n(j)um(ə)rəbəl

denumerably
BR dɪ'nju:m(ə)rəbli
AM di'n(j)um(ə)rəbli

denunciate
BR dɪ'nʌnsɪeɪt, -s, -ɪŋ, -ɪd
AM də'nənsiˌeɪ|t, di'nənsiˌeɪ|t, -ts, -dɪŋ, -dɪd

denunciation
BR dɪˌnʌnsɪˈeɪʃn, -z
AM dəˌnənsiˈeɪʃən, diˌnənsiˈeɪʃən, -z

denunciative
BR dɪˈnʌnsɪətɪv
AM dəˈnənsiˌeɪdɪv, dəˈnənsiədɪv, diˈnənsiˌeɪdɪv, diˈnənsiədɪv

denunciator
BR dɪˈnʌnsɪeɪtə(r), -z
AM dəˈnənsiˌeɪdər, diˈnənsiˌeɪdər, -z

denunciatory
BR dɪˈnʌnsɪət(ə)ri
AM dəˈnənsiəˌtɔri, diˈnənsiəˌtɔri

Denver
BR ˈdɛnvə(r)
AM ˈdɛnvər

deny
BR dɪˈnʌɪ, -z, -ɪŋ, -d
AM dəˈnaɪ, diˈnaɪ, -z, -ɪŋ, -d

Denys
BR ˈdɛnɪs
AM ˈdɛnəs

Denzil
BR ˈdɛnzl
AM ˈdɛnzəl

Deo
BR ˈdeɪəʊ
AM ˈdeɪoʊ

deoch an doris
BR ˌdɒx (ə)n ˈdɒrɪs, ˌdɒk +
AM ˌd(j)ɑkənˈdɔrəs

deodand
BR ˈdiːə(ʊ)dand, -z
AM ˈdiəˌdænd, -z

deodar
BR ˈdɪə(ʊ)dɑː(r)
AM ˈdiəˌdɑr

deodorant
BR dɪˈəʊd(ə)rənt, dɪˈəʊd(ə)rn̩t, -s
AM diˈoʊdərənt, -s

deodorisation
BR dɪˌəʊd(ə)rʌɪˈzeɪʃn
AM diˌoʊdərəˈzeɪʃən, diˌoʊdəˌraɪˈzeɪʃən

deodorise
BR dɪˈəʊd(ə)rʌɪz, -ɪz, -ɪŋ, -d
AM diˈoʊdəˌraɪz, -ɪz, -ɪŋ, -d

deodoriser
BR dɪˈəʊd(ə)rʌɪzə(r)
AM diˈoʊdəˌraɪzər

deodorization
BR dɪˌəʊd(ə)rʌɪˈzeɪʃn
AM diˌoʊdərəˈzeɪʃən, diˌoʊdəˌraɪˈzeɪʃən

deodorize
BR dɪˈəʊd(ə)rʌɪz, -ɪz, -ɪŋ, -d
AM diˈoʊdəˌraɪz, -ɪz, -ɪŋ, -d

deodorizer
BR dɪˈəʊd(ə)rʌɪzə(r), -z
AM diˈoʊdəˌraɪzər, -z

Deo gratias
BR ˌdeɪəʊ ˈɡrɑːtɪəs, + ˈɡrɑːʃɪəs
AM ˈdeɪoʊ ˈɡrɑtsiəs

deontic
BR dɪˈɒntɪk
AM diˈɑn(t)ɪk

deontological
BR dɪˌɒntəˈlɒdʒɪkl, ˌdiːɒntəˈlɒdʒɪkl
AM diˌɑn(t)əˈlɑdʒəkəl

deontologist
BR ˌdiːɒnˈtɒlədʒɪst, -s
AM diˌɑnˈtɑlədʒəst, -s

deontology
BR ˌdiːɒnˈtɒlədʒi
AM diˌɑnˈtɑlədʒi

Deo volente
BR ˌdeɪəʊ vɒˈlɛnteɪ
AM ˈdeɪoʊ vəˈlɛn(t)i

deoxygenate
BR ˌdiːˈɒksɪdʒəneɪt, dɪˈɒksɪdʒəneɪt, -s, -ɪŋ, -ɪd
AM diˈɑksədʒəˌneɪ|t, -ts, -dɪŋ, -dɪd

deoxygenation
BR diːˌɒksɪdʒəˈneɪʃn, dɪˌɒksɪdʒəˈneɪʃn
AM diˌɑksədʒəˈneɪʃən

deoxyribonucleic
BR dɪˌɒksɪˌrʌɪbəʊnjuːˈkliːɪk, dɪˌɒksɪˌrʌɪbəʊnjuːˈkleɪɪk
AM diˌɑksiˌraɪboʊn(j)uˈkliɪk, diˌɑksiˌraɪboʊˌn(j)uˈkleɪɪk

depart
BR dɪˈpɑːt, -s, -ɪŋ, -ɪd
AM dəˈpɑr|t, diˈpɑr|t, -ts, -dɪŋ, -dəd

department
BR dɪˈpɑːtm(ə)nt, -s
AM dəˈpɑrtmənt, diˈpɑrtmənt, -s

departmental
BR ˌdiːpɑːtˈmɛntl
AM dəˌpɑrtˈmɛn(t)l, diˌpɑrtˈmɛn(t)l

departmentalisation
BR ˌdiːpɑːtˌmɛntl̩ʌɪˈzeɪʃn, ˌdiːpɑːtˌmɛntəlʌɪˈzeɪʃn
AM dəˌpɑrtˌmɛn(t)ləˈzeɪʃən, diˌpɑrtˌmɛn(t)ləˈzeɪʃən, dəˌpɑrtˌmɛn(t)lˌaɪˈzeɪʃən, diˌpɑrtˌmɛn(t)lˌaɪˈzeɪʃən

departmentalise
BR ˌdiːpɑːtˈmɛntl̩ʌɪz, ˌdiːpɑːtˈmɛntəlʌɪz, -ɪz, -ɪŋ, -d
AM dəˌpɑrtˈmɛn(t)lˌaɪz, diˌpɑrtˈmɛn(t)lˌaɪz, -ɪz, -ɪŋ, -d

departmentalism
BR ˌdiːpɑːtˈmɛntl̩ɪz(ə)m, ˌdiːpɑːtˈmɛntəlɪz(ə)m
AM dəˌpɑrtˈmɛn(t)lˌɪzəm, diˌpɑrtˈmɛn(t)lˌɪzəm

departmentalization
BR ˌdiːpɑːtˌmɛntl̩ʌɪˈzeɪʃn, ˌdiːpɑːtˌmɛntəlʌɪˈzeɪʃn
AM dəˌpɑrtˌmɛn(t)ləˈzeɪʃən, diˌpɑrtˌmɛn(t)ləˈzeɪʃən, dəˌpɑrtˌmɛn(t)lˌaɪˈzeɪʃən, diˌpɑrtˌmɛn(t)lˌaɪˈzeɪʃən

departmentalize
BR ˌdiːpɑːtˈmɛntl̩ʌɪz, ˌdiːpɑːtˈmɛntəlʌɪz, -ɪz, -ɪŋ, -d
AM dəˌpɑrtˈmɛn(t)lˌaɪz, diˌpɑrtˈmɛn(t)lˌaɪz, -ɪz, -ɪŋ, -d

departmentally
BR ˌdiːpɑːtˈmɛntl̩i, ˌdiːpɑːtˈmɛntəli
AM dəˌpɑrtˈmɛn(t)l̩i, diˌpɑrtˈmɛn(t)l̩i

departure
BR dɪˈpɑːtʃə(r), -z
AM dəˈpɑrtʃər, diˈpɑrtʃər, -z

depasturage
BR ˌdiːˈpɑːstʃ(ə)rɪdʒ, ˌdiːˈpastʃ(ə)rɪdʒ, ˌdiːˈpɑːstjʊrɪdʒ, ˌdiːˈpastjʊrɪdʒ
AM dəˈpastʃərɪdʒ, diˈpastʃərɪdʒ

depasture
BR ˌdiːˈpɑːstʃ|ə(r), ˌdiːˈpastʃ|ə(r), -əz, -(ə)rɪŋ, -əd
AM dəˈpastʃər, diˈpastʃər, -z, -ɪŋ, -d

dépaysé
BR ˌdeɪpeɪˈzeɪ
AM ˈdeɪˌpeɪˈzeɪ

dépaysée
BR ˌdeɪpeɪˈzeɪ
AM ˈdeɪˌpeɪˈzeɪ

depend
BR dɪˈpɛnd, -z, -ɪŋ, -ɪd
AM dəˈpɛnd, diˈpɛnd, -z, -ɪŋ, -əd

dependability
BR dɪˌpɛndəˈbɪlɪti
AM dəˌpɛndəˈbɪlɪdi, diˌpɛndəˈbɪlɪdi

dependable
BR dɪˈpɛndəbl
AM dəˈpɛndəbəl, diˈpɛndəbəl

dependableness
BR dɪˈpɛndəblnəs
AM dəˈpɛndəbəlnəs, diˈpɛndəbəlnəs

dependably
BR dɪˈpɛndəbli
AM dəˈpɛndəbli, diˈpɛndəbli

dependant
BR dɪˈpɛnd(ə)nt, -s
AM dəˈpɛnd(ə)nt, diˈpɛnd(ə)nt, -s

dependence
BR dɪˈpɛnd(ə)ns
AM dəˈpɛnd(ə)ns, diˈpɛnd(ə)ns

dependency
BR dɪˈpɛnd(ə)ns|i, -ɪz
AM dəˈpɛnd(ə)nsi, diˈpɛnd(ə)nsi, -z

dependent
BR dɪˈpɛnd(ə)nt
AM dəˈpɛnd(ə)nt, diˈpɛnd(ə)nt

dependently
BR dɪˈpɛnd(ə)ntli
AM dəˈpɛnd(ə)n(t)li, diˈpɛnd(ə)n(t)li

depersonalisation
BR ˌdiːpəːsn̩əlʌɪˈzeɪʃn, ˌdiːpəːs(ə)nəlʌɪˈzeɪʃn, ˌdiːpəːsn̩l̩ʌɪˈzeɪʃn, diːˌpəːsn̩əlʌɪˈzeɪʃn, diːˌpəːs(ə)nəlʌɪˈzeɪʃn, diːˌpəːsn̩l̩ʌɪˈzeɪʃn
AM dəˌpərsənəˌlaɪˈzeɪʃən, diˌpərsənəˌlaɪˈzeɪʃən, dəˌpərsənələˈzeɪʃən, diˌpərsənələˈzeɪʃən

depersonalise
BR ˌdiːˈpəːsn̩əlʌɪz, ˌdiːˈpəːs(ə)nəlʌɪz, ˌdiːˈpəːsn̩l̩ʌɪz, -ɪz, -ɪŋ, -d
AM dəˈpərsənəˌlaɪz, diˈpərsənəˌlaɪz, -ɪz, -ɪŋ, -d

depersonalization
BR ˌdiːpəːsn̩əlʌɪˈzeɪʃn, ˌdiːpəːs(ə)nəlʌɪˈzeɪʃn, ˌdiːpəːsn̩l̩ʌɪˈzeɪʃn, diːˌpəːsn̩əlʌɪˈzeɪʃn, diːˌpəːs(ə)nəlʌɪˈzeɪʃn, diːˌpəːsn̩l̩ʌɪˈzeɪʃn
AM dəˌpərsənəˌlaɪˈzeɪʃən, diˌpərsənəˌlaɪˈzeɪʃən, dəˌpərsənələˈzeɪʃən, diˌpərsənələˈzeɪʃən

depersonalize
BR ˌdiːˈpəːsn̩əlʌɪz, ˌdiːˈpəːs(ə)nəlʌɪz,

ˌdiːˈpəːsn̩lʌɪz, -ɪz, -ɪŋ, -d
AM dəˈpərsənəˌlaɪz, diˈpərsənəˌlaɪz, -ɪz, -ɪŋ, -d

depict
BR dɪˈpɪkt, -s, -ɪŋ, -ɪd
AM dəˈpɪk|(t), diˈpɪk|(t), -(t)s, -tɪŋ, -tɪd

depicter
BR dɪˈpɪktə(r), -z
AM dəˈpɪktər, diˈpɪktər, -z

depiction
BR dɪˈpɪkʃn
AM dəˈpɪkʃən, diˈpɪkʃən

depictive
BR dɪˈpɪktɪv
AM dəˈpɪktɪv, diˈpɪktɪv

depictor
BR dɪˈpɪktə(r), -z
AM dəˈpɪktər, diˈpɪktər, -z

depilate
BR ˈdɛpɪleɪt, -s, -ɪŋ, -ɪd
AM ˈdɛpəˌleɪ|t, -ts, -dɪŋ, -dɪd

depilation
BR ˌdɛpɪˈleɪʃn
AM ˌdɛpəˈleɪʃən

depilatory
BR dɪˈpɪlət(ə)r|i, -ɪz
AM dəˈpɪləˌtɔri, diˈpɪləˌtɔri, -z

deplane
BR ˌdiːˈpleɪn, -z, -ɪŋ, -d
AM diˈpleɪn, -z, -ɪŋ, -d

deplete
BR dɪˈpliːt, -s, -ɪŋ, -ɪd
AM dəˈpli|t, diˈpli|t, -ts, -dɪŋ, -dɪd

depletion
BR dɪˈpliːʃn
AM dəˈpliʃən, diˈpliʃən

deplorable
BR dɪˈplɔːrəbl
AM dəˈplɔrəbəl, diˈplɔrəbəl

deplorably
BR dɪˈplɔːrəbli
AM dəˈplɔrəbli, diˈplɔrəbli

deplore
BR dɪˈplɔː|(r), -z, -rɪŋ, -d
AM dəˈplɔ(ə)r, diˈplɔ(ə)r, -z, -rɪŋ, -d

deploringly
BR dɪˈplɔːrɪŋli
AM dəˈplɔrɪŋli, diˈplɔrɪŋli

deploy
BR dɪˈplɔɪ, -z, -ɪŋ, -d
AM dəˈplɔɪ, diˈplɔɪ, -z, -ɪŋ, -d

deployment
BR dɪˈplɔɪm(ə)nt, -s
AM dəˈplɔɪmənt, diˈplɔɪmənt, -s

deplume
BR ˌdiːˈpluːm, -z, -ɪŋ, -d
AM diˈplum, -z, -ɪŋ, -d

depolarisation
BR ˌdiːpəʊlərʌɪˈzeɪʃn, diːˌpəʊlərʌɪˈzeɪʃn
AM diˌpoʊlərəˈzeɪʃən, diˌpoʊləˌraɪˈzeɪʃən, dəˌpoʊləˌraɪˈzeɪʃən, dəˌpoʊlərəˈzeɪʃən

depolarise
BR ˌdiːˈpəʊlərʌɪz, -ɪz, -ɪŋ, -d
AM diˈpoʊləˌraɪz, dəˈpoʊləˌraɪz, -ɪz, -ɪŋ, -d

depolarization
BR ˌdiːpəʊlərʌɪˈzeɪʃn, diːˌpəʊlərʌɪˈzeɪʃn
AM diˌpoʊlərəˈzeɪʃən, diˌpoʊləˌraɪˈzeɪʃən, dəˌpoʊləˌraɪˈzeɪʃən, dəˌpoʊlərəˈzeɪʃən

depolarize
BR ˌdiːˈpəʊlərʌɪz, -ɪz, -ɪŋ, -d
AM diˈpoʊləˌraɪz, dəˈpoʊləˌraɪz, -ɪz, -ɪŋ, -d

depoliticisation
BR ˌdiːpəˌlɪtɪsʌɪˈzeɪʃn
AM dipəˌlɪdəsəˈzeɪʃən, dipəˌlɪdəˌsaɪˈzeɪʃən

depoliticise
BR ˌdiːpəˈlɪtɪsʌɪz, -ɪz, -ɪŋ, -d
AM dipəˈlɪdəˌsaɪz, -əz, -ɪŋ, -d

depoliticization
BR ˌdiːpəˌlɪtɪsʌɪˈzeɪʃn
AM dipəˌlɪdəsəˈzeɪʃən, dipəˌlɪdəˌsaɪˈzeɪʃən

depoliticize
BR ˌdiːpəˈlɪtɪsʌɪz, -ɪz, -ɪŋ, -d
AM dipəˈlɪdəˌsaɪz, -əz, -ɪŋ, -d

depolymerisation
BR ˌdiːpɒlɪm(ə)rʌɪˈzeɪʃn, diːˌpɒlɪm(ə)rʌɪˈzeɪʃn
AM diˌpɑləˌmərəˈzeɪʃən, diˌpɑləməˌraɪˈzeɪʃən

depolymerise
BR ˌdiːˈpɒlɪm(ə)rʌɪz, -ɪz, -ɪŋ, -d
AM diˈpɑləməˌraɪz, -ɪz, -ɪŋ, -d

depolymerization
BR ˌdiːpɒlɪm(ə)rʌɪˈzeɪʃn, diːˌpɒlɪm(ə)rʌɪˈzeɪʃn
AM diˌpɑləˌmərəˈzeɪʃən, diˌpɑləməˌraɪˈzeɪʃən

depolymerize
BR ˌdiːˈpɒlɪm(ə)rʌɪz, -ɪz, -ɪŋ
AM diˈpɑləməˌraɪz, -ɪz, -ɪŋ

deponent
BR dɪˈpəʊnənt, -s
AM dəˈpoʊnənt, diˈpoʊnənt, -s

Depo-Provera®
BR ˌdɛpəʊprə(ʊ)ˈvɪərə(*r*)
AM ˌdɛpoʊproʊˈvɪrə

depopulate
BR ˌdiːˈpɒpjʉleɪt, -s, -ɪŋ, -ɪd
AM ˌdiˈpɑpjəˌleɪ|t, -ts, -dɪŋ, -dɪd

depopulation
BR ˌdiːpɒpjʉˈleɪʃn
AM ˌdiˌpɑpjəˈleɪʃən

deport
BR dɪˈpɔːt, -s, -ɪŋ, -ɪd
AM dəˈpɔ(ə)rt, diˈpɔ(ə)rt, -ts, -ˈpɔrdɪŋ, -ˈpɔrdəd

deportable
BR dɪˈpɔːtəbl
AM dəˈpɔrdəbəl, diˈpɔrdəbəl

deportation
BR ˌdiːpɔːˈteɪʃn, -z
AM ˌdiˌpɔrˈteɪʃən, -z

deportee
BR ˌdiːpɔːˈtiː, -z
AM ˌdiˌpɔrˈti, dəˌpɔrˈti, -z

deportment
BR dɪˈpɔːtm(ə)nt
AM dəˈpɔrtmənt, diˈpɔrtmənt

deposal
BR dɪˈpəʊzl, -z
AM dəˈpoʊzəl, diˈpoʊzəl, -z

depose
BR dɪˈpəʊz, -ɪz, -ɪŋ, -d
AM dəˈpoʊz, diˈpoʊz, -əz, -ɪŋ, -d

deposit
BR dɪˈpɒz|ɪt, -ɪts, -ɪtɪŋ, -ɪtɪd
AM dəˈpɑzə|t, diˈpɑzə|t, -ts, -dɪŋ, -dəd

depositary
BR dɪˈpɒzɪt(ə)ri, -ɪz
AM dəˈpɑzəˌtɛri, -z

deposition
BR ˌdɛpəˈzɪʃn, ˌdiːpəˈzɪʃn, -z
AM ˌdɛpəˈzɪʃən, ˌdipəˈzɪʃən, -z

depositional
BR ˌdɛpəˈzɪʃn̩(ə)l, ˌdɛpəˈzɪʃən(ə)l, ˌdiːpəˈzɪʃn̩(ə)l, ˌdiːpəˈzɪʃən(ə)l
AM ˌdɛpəˈzɪʃ(ə)nəl, ˌdipəˈzɪʃ(ə)nəl

depositor
BR dɪˈpɒzɪtə(r), -z
AM dəˈpɑzədər, -z

depository
BR dɪˈpɒzɪt(ə)r|i, -ɪz
AM dəˈpɑzəˌtɔri, -z

depot
BR ˈdɛpəʊ, -z
AM ˈdɛˌpoʊ, ˈdiˌpoʊ, -z

depravation
BR ˌdɛprəˈveɪʃn
AM ˌdɛprəˈveɪʃən

deprave
BR dɪˈpreɪv, -z, -ɪŋ, -d
AM dəˈpreɪv, diˈpreɪv, -z, -ɪŋ, -d

depravity
BR dɪˈpravɪt|i, -ɪz
AM dəˈprævədi, diˈprævədi, -z

deprecate
BR ˈdɛprɪkeɪt, -s, -ɪŋ, -ɪd
AM ˈdɛprəˌkeɪ|t, -ts, -dɪŋ, -dɪd

deprecatingly
BR ˈdɛprɪkeɪtɪŋli
AM ˈdɛprəˌkeɪdɪŋli

deprecation
BR ˌdɛprɪˈkeɪʃn
AM ˌdɛprəˈkeɪʃən

deprecative
BR ˈdɛprɪkətɪv
AM ˈdɛprəˌkeɪdɪv

deprecator
BR ˈdɛprɪkeɪtə(r), -z
AM ˈdɛprəˌkeɪdər, -z

deprecatory
BR ˈdɛprɪkət(ə)ri, ˈdɛprɪkeɪt(ə)ri, ˌdɛprɪˈkeɪt(ə)ri
AM ˈdɛprəkəˌtɔri

depreciate
BR dɪˈpriːʃɪeɪt, -s, -ɪŋ, -ɪd
AM dəˈpriʃiˌeɪ|t, diˈpriʃiˌeɪ|t, -ts, -dɪŋ, -dɪd

depreciatingly
BR dɪˈpriːʃɪeɪtɪŋli
AM dəˈpriʃiˌeɪdɪŋli, diˈpriʃiˌeɪdɪŋli

depreciation
BR dɪˌpriːʃɪˈeɪʃn
AM dəˌpriʃiˈeɪʃən, diˌpriʃiˈeɪʃən

depreciatory
BR dɪˈpriːʃ(ɪ)ət(ə)ri
AM dəˈpriʃ(i)əˌtɔri, diˈpriʃ(i)əˌtɔri

depredate
BR ˈdɛprɪdeɪt, -s, -ɪŋ, -ɪd
AM ˈdɛprəˌdeɪ|t, -ts, -dɪŋ, -dɪd

depredation
BR ˌdɛprɪˈdeɪʃn, -z
AM ˌdɛprəˈdeɪʃən, -z

depredator
BR ˈdɛprɪdeɪtə(r), -z

AM ˈdɛprəˌdeɪdər, -z
depredatory
BR dɪˈprɛdət(ə)ri, ˌdɛprɪˈdeɪt(ə)ri, ˈdɛprɪdeɪt(ə)ri
AM dəˈprɛdəˌtɔri
depress
BR dɪˈprɛs, -ɪz, -ɪŋ, -t
AM dəˈprɛs, diˈprɛs, -əz, -ɪŋ, -t
depressant
BR dɪˈprɛsnt, -s
AM dəˈprɛsənt, diˈprɛsənt, -s
depressible
BR dɪˈprɛsɪbl
AM dəˈprɛsəbəl, diˈprɛsəbəl
depressing
BR dɪˈprɛsɪŋ
AM dəˈprɛsɪŋ, diˈprɛsɪŋ
depressingly
BR dɪˈprɛsɪŋli
AM dəˈprɛsɪŋli, diˈprɛsɪŋli
depression
BR dɪˈprɛʃn, -z
AM dəˈprɛʃən, diˈprɛʃən, -z
depressive
BR dɪˈprɛsɪv, -z
AM dəˈprɛsɪv, diˈprɛsɪv, -z
depressor
BR dɪˈprɛsə(r), -z
AM dəˈprɛsər, diˈprɛsər, -z
depressurisation
BR ˌdiːprɛʃ(ə)rʌɪˈzeɪʃn, diːˌprɛʃ(ə)rʌɪˈzeɪʃn
AM diˌprɛʃərəˈzeɪʃən, diˌprɛʃəˌraɪˈzeɪʃən
depressurise
BR (ˌ)diːˈprɛʃərʌɪz, -ɪz, -ɪŋ, -d
AM diˈprɛʃəˌraɪz, -ɪz, -ɪŋ, -d
depressurization
BR ˌdiːprɛʃ(ə)rʌɪˈzeɪʃn, diːˌprɛʃ(ə)rʌɪˈzeɪʃn
AM diˌprɛʃərəˈzeɪʃən, diˌprɛʃəˌraɪˈzeɪʃən
depressurize
BR (ˌ)diːˈprɛʃərʌɪz, -ɪz, -ɪŋ, -d
AM diˈprɛʃəˌraɪz, -ɪz, -ɪŋ, -d
deprivable
BR dɪˈprʌɪvəbl
AM dəˈpraɪvəbəl, diˈpraɪvəbəl
deprival
BR dɪˈprʌɪvl
AM dəˈpraɪvəl, diˈpraɪvəl
deprivation
BR ˌdɛprɪˈveɪʃn, -z
AM ˌdɛprəˈveɪʃən, -z
deprive
BR dɪˈprʌɪv, -z, -ɪŋ, -d
AM dəˈpraɪv, diˈpraɪv, -z, -ɪŋ, -d
de profundis
BR ˌdeɪ prəˈfʊndɪs
AM ˌdeɪ prəˈfʊndəs
deprogram
BR ˌdiːˈprəʊɡram, -z, -ɪŋ, -d
AM diˈproʊˌɡræm, -z, -ɪŋ, -d
Deptford
BR ˈdɛtfəd
AM ˈdɛtfərd
depth
BR dɛpθ, -s
AM dɛpθ, -s
depthless
BR ˈdɛpθləs
AM ˈdɛpθləs
depurate
BR ˈdɛpjʉreɪt, -s, -ɪŋ, -ɪd
AM ˈdɛpjəˌreɪ|t, -ts, -dɪŋ, -dɪd
depuration
BR ˌdɛpjʉˈreɪʃn
AM ˌdɛpjəˈreɪʃən
depurative
BR dɪˈpjʊərətɪv, dɪˈpjɔːrətɪv, -z
AM dəˈpjərədɪv, -z
depurator
BR ˈdɛpjʉreɪtə(r), -z
AM ˈdɛpjəˌreɪdər, -z
deputation
BR ˌdɛpjʉˈteɪʃn, -z
AM ˌdɛpjəˈteɪʃən, -z
depute
BR dɪˈpjuːt, -s, -ɪŋ, -ɪd
AM dəˈpju|t, diˈpju|t, -ts, -dɪŋ, -dəd
deputise
BR ˈdɛpjʉtʌɪz, -ɪz, -ɪŋ, -d
AM ˈdɛpjəˌtaɪz, -ɪz, -ɪŋ, -d
deputize
BR ˈdɛpjʉtʌɪz, -ɪz, -ɪŋ, -d
AM ˈdɛpjəˌtaɪz, -ɪz, -ɪŋ, -d
deputy
BR ˈdɛpjʉt|i, -ɪz
AM ˈdɛpjədi, -z
deputyship
BR ˈdɛpjʉtɪʃɪp, -s
AM ˈdɛpjədiˌʃɪp, -s
De Quincey
BR də ˈkwɪnsi
AM də ˈkwɪnsi
deracinate
BR dɪˈrasɪneɪt, dɪˈrasn̩eɪt, -s, -ɪŋ, -ɪd
AM dəˈræsnˌeɪ|t, diˈræsnˌeɪ|t, -ts, -dɪŋ, -dɪd
deracination
BR dɪˌrasɪˈneɪʃn, dɪˌrasn̩ˈeɪʃn
AM dəˌræsnˈeɪʃən, diˌræsnˈeɪʃən
derail
BR (ˌ)diːˈreɪl, dɪˈreɪl, -z, -ɪŋ, -d
AM dəˈreɪl, diˈreɪl, -z, -ɪŋ, -d
derailleur
BR dɪˈreɪl(j)ə(r)
AM dəˈreɪlər
derailment
BR (ˌ)diːˈreɪlm(ə)nt, dɪˈreɪlm(ə)nt, -s
AM dəˈreɪlmənt, diˈreɪlmənt, -s
derange
BR dɪˈreɪn(d)ʒ, -ɪz, -ɪŋ, -d
AM dəˈreɪndʒ, diˈreɪndʒ, -ɪz, -ɪŋ, -d
derangement
BR dɪˈreɪn(d)ʒm(ə)nt
AM dəˈreɪndʒmənt
derate
BR ˌdiːˈreɪt, -s, -ɪŋ, -ɪd
AM diˈreɪ|t, -ts, -dɪŋ, -dɪd
deration
BR ˌdiːˈraʃ|n, -nz, -n̩ɪŋ\-nɪŋ, -nd
AM diˈreɪʃ|ən, -ənz, -(ə)nɪŋ, -ənd
derby
BR ˈdɑːb|i, -ɪz
AM ˈdərbi, -z
Derbyshire
BR ˈdɑːbɪʃ(ɪ)ə(r)
AM ˈdərbiˌʃɪ(ə)r
derecognition
BR ˌdiːrɛkəɡˈnɪʃn
AM ˈdiˌrɛkəɡˈnɪʃən
deregister
BR ˌdiːˈrɛdʒɪst|ə(r), -əz, -(ə)rɪŋ, -əd
AM diˈrɛdʒəst|ər, -ərz, -(ə)rɪŋ, -ərd
deregistration
BR ˌdiːrɛdʒɪˈstreɪʃn, -z
AM diˌrɛdʒəˈstreɪʃən, -z
deregulate
BR ˌdiːˈrɛɡjʉleɪt, -s, -ɪŋ, -ɪd
AM dəˈrɛɡjʊˌleɪ|t, diˈrɛɡjʊˌleɪ|t, -ts, -dɪŋ, -dɪd
deregulation
BR ˌdiːrɛɡjʉˈleɪʃn
AM dəˌrɛɡjʊˈleɪʃən, diˌrɛɡjʊˈleɪʃən
Dereham
BR ˈdɪərəm
AM ˈdɪrəm
Derek
BR ˈdɛrɪk
AM ˈdɛrək
derelict
BR ˈdɛrɪlɪkt, -s
AM ˈdɛrəˌlɪk|(t), -(t)s
dereliction
BR ˌdɛrɪˈlɪkʃn, -z
AM ˌdɛrəˈlɪkʃən, -z
derequisition
BR ˌdiːrɛkwɪˈzɪʃn
AM diˌrɛkwəˈzɪʃən
derestrict
BR ˌdiːrɪˈstrɪkt, -s, -ɪŋ, -ɪd
AM diˌrəˈstrɪk|(t), -(t)s, -tɪŋ, -tɪd
derestriction
BR ˌdiːrɪˈstrɪkʃn
AM diˌrəˈstrɪkʃən
deride
BR dɪˈrʌɪd, -z, -ɪŋ, -ɪd
AM dəˈraɪd, diˈraɪd, -z, -ɪŋ, -ɪd
derider
BR dɪˈrʌɪdə(r), -z
AM dəˈraɪdər, diˈraɪdər, -z
deridingly
BR dɪˈrʌɪdɪŋli
AM dəˈraɪdɪŋli, diˈraɪdɪŋli
de-rigging
BR ˌdiːˈrɪɡɪŋ
AM diˈrɪɡɪŋ
de rigueur
BR də rɪˈɡəː(r)
AM ˌdə rɪˈɡər
derisible
BR dɪˈrʌɪsəbl
AM dəˈraɪsəbəl, diˈraɪsəbəl
derision
BR dɪˈrɪʒn
AM dəˈrɪʒən, diˈrɪʒən
derisive
BR dɪˈrʌɪsɪv, dɪˈrʌɪzɪv, dɪˈrɪzɪv
AM dəˈraɪsɪv, diˈraɪsɪv
derisively
BR dɪˈrʌɪsɪvli, dɪˈrʌɪzɪvli, dɪˈrɪzɪvli
AM dəˈraɪsɪvli, diˈraɪsɪvli
derisiveness
BR dɪˈrʌɪsɪvnɪs, dɪˈrʌɪzɪvnɪs, dɪˈrɪzɪvnɪs
AM dəˈraɪsɪvnɪs, diˈraɪsɪvnɪs
derisorily
BR dɪˈrʌɪs(ə)rɪli, dɪˈrʌɪz(ə)rɪli
AM dəˈraɪs(ə)rəli, diˈraɪs(ə)rəli, dəˈrɪzərəli

derisory
BR dɪ'rʌɪs(ə)ri, dɪ'rʌɪz(ə)ri
AM də'raɪs(ə)ri, di'raɪs(ə)ri, də'rɪzəri

derivable
BR dɪ'rʌɪvəbl
AM də'raɪvəbəl

derivation
BR ˌdɛrɪ'veɪʃn
AM ˌdɛrə'veɪʃən

derivational
BR ˌdɛrɪ'veɪʃn̩(ə)l, ˌdɛrɪ'veɪʃən(ə)l
AM ˌdɛrə'veɪʃ(ə)nəl

derivative
BR dɪ'rɪvətɪv, -z
AM də'rɪvədɪv, -z

derivatively
BR dɪ'rɪvətɪvli
AM də'rɪvədɪvli

derive
BR dɪ'rʌɪv, -z, -ɪŋ, -d
AM də'raɪv, di'raɪv, -z, -ɪŋ, -d

d'Erlanger
BR 'dɛːlɒ̃ʒeɪ
AM 'dɛrˌlæŋər

derm
BR dəːm
AM dərm

derma
BR 'dəːmə(r)
AM 'dərmə

dermal
BR 'dəːml
AM 'dərməl

Dermaptera
BR dəː'mapt(ə)rə(r)
AM dər'mæptərə

dermapteran
BR dəː'mapt(ə)rən, dəː'mapt(ə)rn̩, -z
AM dər'mæptərən, -z

dermapterous
BR dəː'mapt(ə)rəs
AM dər'mæptərəs

dermatitis
BR ˌdəːmə'tʌɪtɪs
AM ˌdərmə'taɪdəs

dermatoglyphic
BR ˌdəːmətə'glɪfɪk, -s
AM ˌdərmədə'glɪfɪk, dərˌmædə'glɪfɪk, -s

dermatoglyphically
BR ˌdəːmətə'glɪfɪkli
AM ˌdərmədə'glɪfək(ə)li, dərˌmædə'glɪfək(ə)li

dermatoid
BR 'dəːmətɔɪd
AM 'dərməˌtɔɪd

dermatological
BR ˌdəːmətə'lɒdʒɪkl
AM ˌdərmədə'lɑdʒəkəl

dermatologically
BR ˌdəːmətə'lɒdʒɪkli
AM ˌdərmədə'lɑdʒək(ə)li

dermatologist
BR ˌdəːmə'tɒlədʒɪst, -s
AM ˌdərmə'tɑlədʒəst, -s

dermatology
BR ˌdəːmə'tɒlədʒi
AM ˌdərmə'tɑlədʒi

dermic
BR 'dəːmɪk
AM 'dərmɪk

dermis
BR 'dəːmɪs
AM 'dərməs

Dermot
BR 'dəːmət
AM 'dərmət

Dermott
BR 'dəːmət
AM 'dərmət

dernier cri
BR ˌdɛːnjeɪ 'kriː, ˌdəːnjeɪ +
AM ˌdɛrnˌjeɪ 'kri

derogate
BR 'dɛrəgeɪt, -s, -ɪŋ, -ɪd
AM 'dɛrəˌgeɪ|t, -ts, -dɪŋ, -dɪd

derogation
BR ˌdɛrə'geɪʃn
AM ˌdɛrə'geɪʃən

derogative
BR dɪ'rɒgətɪv
AM də'rɑgədɪv

derogatorily
BR dɪ'rɒgət(ə)rɪli
AM də'rɑgəˌtɔrəli, di'rɑgəˌtɔrəli

derogatory
BR dɪ'rɒgət(ə)ri
AM də'rɑgəˌtɔri, di'rɑgəˌtɔri

Deronda
BR də'rɒndə(r)
AM də'rɑndə

derrick
BR 'dɛrɪk, -s
AM 'dɛrɪk, -s

Derrida
BR də'riːdə(r)
AM dəri'dɑ

Derridean
BR də'rɪdɪən
AM də'rɪdiən

derrière
BR ˌdɛrɪ'ɛː(r), -z
AM ˌdɛri'ɛ(ə)r, -z

derring-do
BR ˌdɛrɪŋ'duː
AM ˌdɛrɪŋ'du

derringer
BR 'dɛrɪn(d)ʒə(r), 'dɛrn̩(d)ʒə(r), -z
AM 'dɛrən(d)ʒər, -z

derris
BR 'dɛrɪs
AM 'dɛrəs

Derry
BR 'dɛri
AM 'dɛri

derv
BR dəːv
AM dərv

dervish
BR 'dəːv|ɪʃ, -ɪʃɪz
AM 'dərvɪʃ, -ɪz

Derwent
BR 'dəːwənt
AM 'dərwənt

Derwentwater
BR 'dəːwəntˌwɔːtə(r)
AM 'dərwəntˌwɔdər, 'dərwəntˌwɑdər

Deryck
BR 'dɛrɪk
AM 'dɛrək

Desai
BR dɪ'sʌɪ, dɛ'sʌɪ
AM də'saɪ

desalinate
BR (ˌ)diː'salɪneɪt, -s, -ɪŋ, -ɪd
AM di'sæləˌneɪ|t, -ts, -dɪŋ, -dɪd

desalination
BR ˌdiːsalɪ'neɪʃn
AM diˌsælə'neɪʃən

desalinisation
BR ˌdiːsalɪnʌɪ'zeɪʃn, diːˌsalɪnʌɪ'zeɪʃn
AM diˌsælənə'zeɪʃən, diˌsæləˌnaɪ'zeɪʃən

desalinise
BR (ˌ)diː'salɪnʌɪz, -ɪz, -ɪŋ, -d
AM ˌdi'sæləˌnaɪz, -ɪz, -ɪŋ, -d

desalinization
BR ˌdiːsalɪnʌɪ'zeɪʃn, diːˌsalɪnʌɪ'zeɪʃn
AM diˌsælənə'zeɪʃən, diˌsæləˌnaɪ'zeɪʃən

desalinize
BR (ˌ)diː'salɪnʌɪz, -ɪz, -ɪŋ, -d
AM ˌdi'sæləˌnaɪz, -ɪz, -ɪŋ, -d

desalt
BR ˌdiː'sɔːlt, ˌdiː'sɒlt, -s, -ɪŋ, -ɪd
AM ˌdi'sɔlt, ˌdi'sɑlt, -s, -ɪŋ, -əd

desaparecido
BR ˌdɛsəparə'siːdəʊ, -z
AM ˌdɛzəˌpɛrə'sidoʊ, -z

descale
BR ˌdiː'skeɪl, -z
AM ˌdi'skeɪl, -z

descant
BR 'dɛskant, -s, -ɪŋ, -ɪd
AM 'dɛˌskænt, -s, -ɪŋ, -əd

Descartes
BR 'deɪkɑːt, deɪ'kɑːt
AM deɪ'kɑrt

descend
BR dɪ'sɛnd, -z, -ɪŋ, -ɪd
AM də'sɛnd, di'sɛnd, -z, -ɪŋ, -əd

descendant
BR dɪ'sɛnd(ə)nt, -s
AM də'sɛnd(ə)nt, di'sɛnd(ə)nt, -s

descendent
BR dɪ'sɛnd(ə)nt
AM də'sɛnd(ə)nt, di'sɛnd(ə)nt

descender
BR dɪ'sɛndə(r), -z
AM də'sɛndər, di'sɛndər, -z

descendeur
BR dɪ'sɛndə(r), -z
AM də'sɛndər, -z

descendible
BR dɪ'sɛndɪbl
AM də'sɛndəbəl, di'sɛndəbəl

descent
BR dɪ'sɛnt, -s
AM də'sɛnt, di'sɛnt, -s

descramble
BR ˌdiː'skramb|l, -lz, -l̩ɪŋ\-lɪŋ, -ld
AM di'skræmb|əl, -əlz, -(ə)lɪŋ, -əld

descrambler
BR ˌdiː'skramblə(r), ˌdiː'skrambl̩ə(r), -z
AM di'skræmb(ə)lər, -z

describable
BR dɪ'skrʌɪbəbl
AM də'skraɪbəbəl, di'skraɪbəbəl

describe
BR dɪ'skrʌɪb, -z, -ɪŋ, -d
AM də'skraɪb, di'skraɪb, -z, -ɪŋ, -d

describer
BR dɪ'skrʌɪbə(r), -z
AM də'skraɪbər, di'skraɪbər, -z

description
BR dɪ'skrɪpʃn, -z
AM də'skrɪpʃən, di'skrɪpʃən, -z

descriptive
BR dɪ'skrɪptɪv
AM də'skrɪptɪv, di'skrɪptɪv

descriptively
BR dɪ'skrɪptɪvli
AM də'skrɪptɪvli, di'skrɪptɪvli

descriptiveness
BR dɪ'skrɪptɪvnɪs
AM də'skrɪptɪvnɪs, di'skrɪptɪvnɪs

descriptivism
BR dɪ'skrɪptɪvɪz(ə)m

AM də'skrɪptɨ,vɪzəm, di'skrɪptɨ,vɪzəm

descriptor
BR dɪ'skrɪptə(r), -z
AM də'skrɪptər, di'skrɪptər, -z

descry
BR dɪ'skrʌɪ, -z, -ɪŋ, -d
AM də'skraɪ, di'skraɪ, -z, -ɪŋ, -d

Desdemona
BR ˌdɛzdɪ'məʊnə(r)
AM ˌdɛsdə'moʊnə

desecrate
BR 'dɛsɨkreɪt, -s, -ɪŋ, -ɨd
AM 'dɛsəˌkreɪ|t, -ts, -dɪŋ, -dɨd

desecration
BR ˌdɛsɪ'kreɪʃn
AM ˌdɛsə'kreɪʃən

desecrator
BR 'dɛsɨkreɪtə(r), -z
AM 'dɛsəˌkreɪdər, -z

deseed
BR ˌdiː'siːd, -z, -ɪŋ, -ɨd
AM di'sid, -z, -ɪŋ, -ɨd

desegregate
BR (ˌ)diː'sɛgrɨgeɪt, -s, -ɪŋ, -ɨd
AM ˌdi'sɛgrəˌgeɪ|t, -ts, -dɪŋ, -dɨd

desegregation
BR ˌdiːsɛgrɪ'geɪʃn
AM ˌdiˌsɛgrə'geɪʃən

deselect
BR ˌdiːsɪ'lɛkt, -s, -ɪŋ, -ɨd
AM ˌdisə'lɛk|(t), -(t)s, -tɪŋ, -təd

deselection
BR ˌdiːsɪ'lɛkʃn
AM ˌdisə'lɛkʃən

desensitisation
BR ˌdiːsɛnsɪtʌɪ'zeɪʃn, diːˌsɛnsɪtʌɪ'zeɪʃn
AM ˌdiˌsɛnsədə'zeɪʃən, ˌdiˌsɛnsəˌtaɪ'zeɪʃən, dəˌsɛnsədə'zeɪʃən, dəˌsɛnsəˌtaɪ'zeɪʃən

desensitise
BR (ˌ)diː'sɛnsɪtʌɪz, -ɨz, -ɪŋ, -d
AM di'sɛnsəˌtaɪz, də'sɛnsəˌtaɪz, -ɨz, -ɪŋ, -d

desensitiser
BR (ˌ)diː'sɛnsɪtʌɪzə(r), -z
AM di'sɛnsəˌtaɪzər, də'sɛnsəˌtaɪzər, -z

desensitization
BR ˌdiːsɛnsɪtʌɪ'zeɪʃn, diːˌsɛnsɪtʌɪ'zeɪʃn
AM ˌdiˌsɛnsədə'zeɪʃən, ˌdiˌsɛnsəˌtaɪ'zeɪʃən, dəˌsɛnsədə'zeɪʃən, dəˌsɛnsəˌtaɪ'zeɪʃən

desensitize
BR (ˌ)diː'sɛnsɪtʌɪz, -ɨz, -ɪŋ, -d
AM di'sɛnsəˌtaɪz, də'sɛnsəˌtaɪz, -ɨz, -ɪŋ, -d

desensitizer
BR (ˌ)diː'sɛnsɪtʌɪzə(r), -z
AM di'sɛnsəˌtaɪzər, də'sɛnsəˌtaɪzər, -z

desert[1]
noun
BR 'dɛzət, -s
AM 'dɛzərt, -s

desert[2]
verb
BR dɪ'zəːt, -s, -ɪŋ, -ɨd
AM də'zər|t, di'zər|t, -ts, -dɪŋ, -dəd

deserter
BR dɪ'zəːtə(r), -z
AM də'zərdər, di'zərdər, -z

desertification
BR dɪˌzəːtɨfɪ'keɪʃn
AM dəˌzərdəfə'keɪʃən

desertion
BR dɪ'zəːʃn, -z
AM də'zərʃən, di'zərʃən, -z

deserts
things deserved
BR dɪ'zəːts
AM də'zərts, di'zərts

deserve
BR dɪ'zəːv, -z, -ɪŋ, -d
AM də'zərv, di'zərv, -z, -ɪŋ, -d

deservedly
BR dɪ'zəːvɨdli
AM də'zərvədli, di'zərvədli

deservedness
BR dɪ'zəːvɨdnɨs
AM də'zərvədnəs, di'zərvədnəs

deserver
BR dɪ'zəːvə(r), -z
AM də'zərvər, di'zərvər, -z

deserving
BR dɪ'zəːvɪŋ
AM də'zərvɪŋ

deservingly
BR dɪ'zəːvɪŋli
AM də'zərvɪŋli

deservingness
BR dɪ'zəːvɪŋnɨs
AM də'zərvɪŋnɨs

desex
BR ˌdiː'sɛks, -ɨz, -ɪŋ, -t
AM di'sɛks, -əz, -ɪn, -t

desexualisation
BR ˌdiːsɛkʃʊəlʌɪ'zeɪʃn, ˌdiːsɛkʃʉlʌɪ'zeɪʃn, ˌdiːsɛkʃl̩ʌɪ'zeɪʃn, ˌdiːsɛksjʊ(ə)lʌɪ'zeɪʃn, diːˌsɛkʃʊəlʌɪ'zeɪʃn, diːˌsɛkʃʉlʌɪ'zeɪʃn, diːˌsɛkʃl̩ʌɪ'zeɪʃn, diːˌsɛksjʊ(ə)lʌɪ'zeɪʃn
AM diˌsɛkʃ(əw)ələ'zeɪʃən, diˌsɛkʃ(əw)əˌlaɪ'zeɪʃən

desexualise
BR ˌdiː'sɛkʃʊəlʌɪz, ˌdiː'sɛkʃʉlʌɪz, ˌdiː'sɛkʃl̩ʌɪz, ˌdiː'sɛkjʊ(ə)lʌɪz, -ɨz, -ɪŋ, -d
AM di'sɛkʃ(əw)əˌlaɪz, -ɨz, -ɪŋ, -d

desexualization
BR ˌdiːsɛkʃʊəlʌɪ'zeɪʃn, ˌdiːsɛkʃʉlʌɪ'zeɪʃn, ˌdiːsɛkʃl̩ʌɪ'zeɪʃn, ˌdiːsɛksjʊ(ə)lʌɪ'zeɪʃn, diːˌsɛkʃʊəlʌɪ'zeɪʃn, diːˌsɛkʃʉlʌɪ'zeɪʃn, diːˌsɛkʃl̩ʌɪ'zeɪʃn, diːˌsɛksjʊ(ə)lʌɪ'zeɪʃn
AM diɨsɛkʃ(əw)ələ'zeɪʃən, diˌsɛkʃ(əw)əˌlaɪ'zeɪʃən

desexualize
BR ˌdiː'sɛkʃʊəlʌɪz, ˌdiː'sɛkʃʉlʌɪz, ˌdiː'sɛkʃl̩ʌɪz, ˌdiː'sɛkjʊ(ə)lʌɪz, -ɨz, -ɪŋ, -d
AM di'sɛkʃ(əw)əˌlaɪz, -ɨz, -ɪŋ, -d

déshabillé
BR ˌdɛza'biːeɪ, ˌdeɪza'biːeɪ, ˌdɛzə'biːl, ˌdeɪzə'biːl
AM ˌdeɪzɑbi'eɪ

desiccant
BR 'dɛsɪk(ə)nt, -s
AM 'dɛsəkənt, -s

desiccate
BR 'dɛsɪkeɪt, -s, -ɪŋ, -ɨd
AM 'dɛsəˌkeɪ|t, -ts, -dɪŋ, -dɨd

desiccation
BR ˌdɛsɪ'keɪʃn
AM ˌdɛsə'keɪʃən

desiccative
BR 'dɛsɪkətɪv
AM 'dɛsəˌkeɪdɪv

desiccator
BR 'dɛsɪkeɪtə(r), -z
AM 'dɛsəˌkeɪdər, -z

desiderata
BR dɪˌzɪdə'rɑːtə(r)
AM dəˌzɪdə'rɑdə

desiderate[1]
adjective, noun
BR dɪ'zɪd(ə)rət, dɪ'sɪd(ə)rət
AM də'zɪdərət, də'sɪdərət

desiderate[2]
verb
BR dɪ'zɪdəreɪt, dɪ'sɪdəreɪt, -s, -ɪŋ, -ɨd
AM də'zɪdəˌreɪ|t, də'sɪdəˌreɪ|t, -ts, -dɪŋ, -dɨd

desiderative
BR dɪ'zɪd(ə)rətɪv, dɪ'sɪd(ə)rətɪv
AM də'zɪdəˌr(ə)dɪv

desideratum
BR dɪˌzɪdə'rɑːtəm
AM dəˌzɪdə'rɑdəm

design
BR dɪ'zʌɪn, -z, -ɪŋ, -d
AM də'zaɪn, di'zaɪn, -z, -ɪŋ, -d

designate[1]
adjective
BR 'dɛzɪgnət, 'dɛzɪgneɪt
AM 'dɛzɪgˌneɪt, 'dɛzɪgnət

designate[2]
verb
BR 'dɛzɪgneɪt, -s, -ɪŋ, -ɨd
AM 'dɛzɪgˌneɪ|t, -ts, -dɪŋ, -dɨd

designation
BR ˌdɛzɪg'neɪʃn, -z
AM ˌdɛzɪg'neɪʃən, -z

designator
BR 'dɛzɪgneɪtə(r), -z
AM 'dɛzɪgˌneɪdər, -z

designedly
BR dɪ'zʌɪnɨdli
AM də'zaɪnədli, di'zaɪnədli

designer
BR dɪ'zʌɪnə(r), -z
AM də'zaɪnər, di'zaɪnər, -z

designing
BR dɪ'zʌɪnɪŋ
AM də'zaɪnɪŋ, di'zaɪnɪŋ

designingly
BR dɪ'zʌɪnɪŋli
AM də'zaɪnɪŋli, di'zaɪnɪŋli

desinence
BR 'dɛzɪnəns, 'dɛzn̩əns, 'dɛsɪnəns, 'dɛsn̩əns
AM 'dɛsənəns, 'dɛzənəns

desirability
BR dɪˌzʌɪərə'bɪlɨti
AM dəˌzaɪrə'bɪlɨdi

desirable
BR dɪ'zʌɪərəbl
AM də'zaɪrəbəl

desirableness
BR dɪ'zʌɪərəblnəs
AM də'zaɪrəbəlnəs

desirably
BR dɪ'zʌɪərəbli

AM də'zaɪrəbli

desire
BR dɪ'zʌɪə(r), -z, -ɪŋ, -d
AM də'zaɪ(ə)r, di'zaɪ(ə)r, -z, -ɪŋ, -d

Desirée
BR dɪ'zɪəreɪ, dɛ'zɪəreɪ
AM ˌdɛzəˌreɪ

desirous
BR dɪ'zʌɪərəs
AM də'zaɪrəs

desist
BR dɪ'zɪst, dɪ'sɪst, -s, -ɪŋ, -ɨd
AM də'zɪst, də'sɪst, di'zɪst, di'sɪst, -s, -ɪŋ, -ɨd

desk
BR dɛsk, -s
AM dɛsk, -s

deskill
BR ˌdiː'skɪl, -z, -ɪŋ, -d
AM ˌdi'skɪl, -z, -ɪŋ, -d

deskilled
BR ˌdiː'skɪld
AM ˌdi'skɪld

deskilling
BR ˌdiː'skɪlɪŋ
AM ˌdi'skɪlɪŋ

desktop
BR 'dɛsktɒp, -s
AM 'dɛs(k)ˌtɑp, -s

deskwork
BR 'dɛskwəːk
AM 'dɛs(k)ˌwərk

desman
BR 'dɛzmən, -z
AM 'dɛzmən, -z

desmid
BR 'dɛzmɪd, -z
AM 'dɛzmɪd, -z

Des Moines
BR də 'mɔɪn
AM də 'mɔɪn

Desmond
BR 'dɛzm(ə)nd
AM 'dɛzmən(d)

desolate[1]
adjective
BR 'dɛs(ə)lət
AM 'dɛsələt, 'dɛzələt

desolate[2]
verb
BR 'dɛsəleɪt, -s, -ɪŋ, -ɨd
AM 'dɛsəˌleɪ|t, -ts, -dɪŋ, -dɨd

desolately
BR 'dɛs(ə)lətli
AM 'dɛsələtli, 'dɛzələtli

desolateness
BR 'dɛs(ə)lətnəs
AM 'dɛsələtnəs, 'dɛzələtnəs

desolation
BR ˌdɛsə'leɪʃn
AM ˌdɛzə'leɪʃən, ˌdɛsə'leɪʃən

desolator
BR 'dɛsəleɪtə(r), -z
AM 'dɛsəˌleɪdər, -z

desorb
BR ˌdiː'sɔːb, -z, -ɪŋ, -d
AM di'zɔ(ə)rb, -z, -ɪŋ, -d

desorbent
BR ˌdiː'sɔːb(ə)nt, -s
AM di'zɔrbənt, -s

desorption
BR ˌdiː'sɔːpʃn, -z
AM di'zɔrpʃən, -z

Desoutter
BR dɪ'suːtə(r)
AM də'sudər

De Souza
BR də 'suːzə(*r*)
AM də 'suzə

despair
BR dɪ'spɛː(r), -z, -ɪŋ, -d
AM də'spɛ(ə)r, di'spɛ(ə)r, -z, -ɪŋ, -d

despairingly
BR dɪ'spɛːrɪŋli
AM də'spɛrɪŋli, di'spɛrɪŋli

despatch
BR dɪ'spatʃ, -ɨz, -ɪŋ, -t
AM də'spætʃ, -əz, -ɪŋ, -t

Despenser
BR dɪ'spɛnsə(r)
AM də'spɛnsər

desperado
BR ˌdɛspə'rɑːdəʊ, -z
AM ˌdɛspə'rɑdoʊ, -z

desperate
BR 'dɛsp(ə)rət
AM 'dɛsp(ə)rət

desperately
BR 'dɛsp(ə)rətli
AM 'dɛsp(ə)rətli

desperateness
BR 'dɛsp(ə)rətnəs
AM 'dɛsp(ə)rətnəs

desperation
BR ˌdɛspə'reɪʃn
AM ˌdɛspə'reɪʃən

despicability
BR dɪˌspɪkə'bɪlɪti, ˌdɛspɪkə'bɪlɪti
AM dəˌspɪkə'bɪlɨdi, ˌdɛspəkə'bɪlɨdi

despicable
BR dɪ'spɪkəbl, 'dɛspɪkəbl
AM də'spɪkəbəl, 'dɛspəkəbəl, di'spɪkəbəl

despicably
BR dɪ'spɪkəbli, 'dɛspɪkəbli
AM də'spɪkəbli, 'dɛspəkəbli, di'spɪkəbli

despise
BR dɪ'spʌɪz, -ɨz, -ɪŋ, -d
AM də'spaɪz, di'spaɪz, -ɨz, -ɪŋ, -d

despiser
BR dɪ'spʌɪzə(r), -z
AM də'spaɪzər, di'spaɪzər, -z

despite
BR dɪ'spʌɪt
AM də'spaɪt

despiteful
BR dɪ'spʌɪtf(ʊ)l
AM də'spaɪtfəl

despitefully
BR dɪ'spʌɪtfʊli, dɪ'spʌɪtfl̩i
AM də'spaɪtfəli

despitefulness
BR dɪ'spʌɪtf(ʊ)lnəs
AM də'spaɪtfəlnəs

despoil
BR dɪ'spɔɪl, -z, -ɪŋ, -d
AM də'spɔɪl, di'spɔɪl, -z, -ɪŋ, -d

despoiler
BR dɪ'spɔɪlə(r)
AM də'spɔɪlər, di'spɔɪlər

despoilment
BR dɪ'spɔɪlm(ə)nt
AM də'spɔɪlmənt, di'spɔɪlmənt

despoliation
BR dɪˌspəʊlɪ'eɪʃn
AM dəˌspoʊli'eɪʃən, diˌspoʊli'eɪʃən

despond
BR dɪ'spɒnd, -z, -ɪŋ, -ɨd
AM də'spɑnd, di'spɑnd, -z, -ɪŋ, -əd

despondence
BR dɪ'spɒnd(ə)ns
AM də'spɑndəns, di'spɑndns

despondency
BR dɪ'spɒnd(ə)nsi
AM də'spɑndənsi, di'spɑndənsi

despondent
BR dɪ'spɒnd(ə)nt
AM də'spɑnd(ə)nt, di'spɑnd(ə)nt

despondently
BR dɪ'spɒnd(ə)ntli
AM də'spɑndən(t)li, di'spɑndən(t)li

despot
BR 'dɛspɒt, -s
AM 'dɛspət, 'dɛsˌpɑt, -s

despotic
BR dɪ'spɒtɪk
AM də'spɑdɪk

despotically
BR dɪ'spɒtɨkli
AM də'spɑdək(ə)li

despotism
BR 'dɛspətɪz(ə)m
AM 'dɛspəˌtɪzəm

desquamate
BR 'dɛskwəmeɪt, -s, -ɪŋ, -ɨd
AM 'dɛskwəˌmeɪ|t, -ts, -dɪŋ, -dɨd

desquamation
BR ˌdɛskwə'meɪʃn
AM ˌdɛskwə'meɪʃən

desquamative
BR dɪ'skwamətɪv
AM də'skwɑmədɪv

desquamatory
BR dɪ'skwamət(ə)ri
AM dɛ'skwɑməˌtɔri

des res
BR ˌdɛz 'rɛz, -ɨz
AM dəz 'rɛz, -əz

Dessau
BR 'dɛsaʊ
AM 'dɛsaʊ

dessert
BR dɪ'zəːt, -s
AM də'zərt, di'zərt, -s

dessertspoon
BR dɪ'zəːtspuːn, -z
AM də'zərtˌspun, di'zərtˌspun, -z

dessertspoonful
BR dɪ'zəːtspuːnfʊl, -z
AM də'zərtˌspunˌfʊl, di'zərtˌspunˌfəl, -z

destabilisation
BR ˌdiːsteɪbl̩ʌɪ'zeɪʃn, ˌdiːsteɪbəlʌɪ'zeɪʃn, diːˌsteɪbl̩ʌɪ'zeɪʃn, diːˌsteɪbəlʌɪ'zeɪʃn
AM diˌsteɪbələ'zeɪʃən, diˌsteɪbəˌlaɪ'zeɪʃən

destabilise
BR ˌdiː'steɪbl̩ʌɪz, ˌdiː'steɪbəlʌɪz, -ɨz, -ɪŋ, -d
AM di'steɪbəˌlaɪz, -ɨz, -ɪŋ, -d

destabilization
BR ˌdiːsteɪbl̩ʌɪ'zeɪʃn, ˌdiːsteɪbəlʌɪ'zeɪʃn, diːˌsteɪbl̩ʌɪ'zeɪʃn, diːˌsteɪbəlʌɪ'zeɪʃn
AM diˌsteɪbələ'zeɪʃən, diˌsteɪbəˌlaɪ'zeɪʃən

destabilize
BR ˌdiː'steɪbl̩ʌɪz, ˌdiː'steɪbəlʌɪz, -ɨz, -ɪŋ, -d
AM di'steɪbəˌlaɪz, -ɨz, -ɪŋ, -d

de-stalinisation
BR ˌdiːstɑːlɪnʌɪ'zeɪʃn, diːˌstɑːlɪnʌɪ'zeɪʃn
AM diˌstɑlənə'zeɪʃən, diˌstɑləˌnaɪ'zeɪʃən

de-stalinization
BR ˌdiːstɑːlɪnʌɪ'zeɪʃn, diːˌstɑːlɪnʌɪ'zeɪʃn
AM diˌstɑlənə'zeɪʃən, diˌstɑləˌnaɪ'zeɪʃən

De Stijl
BR də 'stʌɪl
AM də 'staɪl

destination
BR ˌdɛstɪˈneɪʃn, -z
AM ˌdɛstəˈneɪʃən, -z
destine
BR ˈdɛstɪn, -z, -ɪŋ, -d
AM ˈdɛstɪn, -z, -ɪŋ, -d
destiny
BR ˈdɛstɪn|i, -ɪz
AM ˈdɛstɪni, -z
destitute
BR ˈdɛstɪtjuːt, ˈdɛstɪtʃuːt
AM ˈdɛstəˌt(j)ut
destitution
BR ˌdɛstɪˈtjuːʃn, ˌdɛstɪˈtʃuːʃn
AM ˌdɛstəˈt(j)uʃən
destock
BR ˌdiːˈstɒk, -s, -ɪŋ, -t
AM diˈstɑk, -s, -ɪŋ, -t
destrier
BR ˈdɛstrɪə(r), dɛˈstriːə(r), -z
AM ˈdɛstriər, -z
destroy
BR dɪˈstrɔɪ, -z, -ɪŋ, -d
AM dəˈstrɔɪ, diˈstrɔɪ, -z, -ɪŋ, -d
destroyable
BR dɪˈstrɔɪəbl
AM dəˈstrɔɪəbəl, diˈstrɔɪəbəl
destroyer
BR dɪˈstrɔɪə(r), -z
AM dəˈstrɔɪər, diˈstrɔɪər, -z
destruct
BR dɪˈstrʌkt, -s, -ɪŋ, -ɪd
AM dəˈstrək|(t), diˈstrək|(t), -(t)s, -tɪŋ, -təd
destructibility
BR dɪˌstrʌktɪˈbɪlɪti
AM dəˌstrəktəˈbɪlɨdi, diˌstrəktəˈbɪlɨdi
destructible
BR dɪˈstrʌktɪbl
AM dəˈstrəktəbəl, diˈstrəktəbəl
destruction
BR dɪˈstrʌkʃn
AM dəˈstrəkʃən, diˈstrəkʃən
destructive
BR dɪˈstrʌktɪv
AM dəˈstrəktɪv, diˈstrəktɪv
destructively
BR dɪˈstrʌktɪvli
AM dəˈstrəktɪvli, diˈstrəktɪvli
destructiveness
BR dɪˈstrʌktɪvnɪs
AM dəˈstrəktɪvnɪs, diˈstrəktɪvnɪs
destructor
BR dɪˈstrʌktə(r), -z
AM dəˈstrəktər, diˈstrəktər, -z
Destry
BR ˈdɛstri
AM ˈdɛstri
desuetude
BR ˈdɛswɪtjuːd, ˈdɛswɪtʃuːd, dɪˈsjuːɪtjuːd, dɪˈsjuːɪtʃuːd
AM ˈdɛswiˌt(j)ud, ˈdɛswəˌt(j)ud, dəˈs(j)uəˌt(j)ud
desulfurisation
BR ˌdiːsʌlf(ə)rʌɪˈzeɪʃn, diːˌsʌlf(ə)rʌɪˈzeɪʃn
AM diˌsəlfərəˈzeɪʃən, diˌsəlfəˌraɪˈzeɪʃən
desulfurization
BR ˌdiːsʌlf(ə)rʌɪˈzeɪʃn, diːˌsʌlf(ə)rʌɪˈzeɪʃn
AM diˌsəlfərəˈzeɪʃən, diˌsəlfəˌraɪˈzeɪʃən
desulphurisation
BR ˌdiːsʌlf(ə)rʌɪˈzeɪʃn, diːˌsʌlf(ə)rʌɪˈzeɪʃn
AM diˌsəlfərəˈzeɪʃən, diˌsəlfəˌraɪˈzeɪʃən
desulphurization
BR ˌdiːsʌlf(ə)rʌɪˈzeɪʃn, diːˌsʌlf(ə)rʌɪˈzeɪʃn
AM diˌsəlfərəˈzeɪʃən, diˌsəlfəˌraɪˈzeɪʃən
desultorily
BR ˈdɛs(ə)ltrɪli, ˈdɛz(ə)ltrɪli
AM ˈdɛsəlˌtɔrəli
desultoriness
BR ˈdɛs(ə)ltrɪnɪs, ˈdɛz(ə)ltrɪnɪs
AM ˈdɛsəlˌtɔrinɪs
desultory
BR ˈdɛs(ə)lt(ə)ri, ˈdɛz(ə)lt(ə)ri
AM ˈdɛsəlˌtɔri, dəˈsəltəri
detach
BR dɪˈtatʃ, -ɪz, -ɪŋ, -t
AM dəˈtætʃ, diˈtætʃ, -əz, -ɪŋ, -t
detachable
BR dɪˈtatʃəbl
AM dəˈtætʃəbəl, diˈtætʃəbəl
detachedly
BR dɪˈtatʃɨdli
AM dəˈtætʃədli, diˈtætʃədli
detachment
BR dɪˈtatʃm(ə)nt, -s
AM dəˈtætʃmənt, diˈtætʃmənt, -s
detail
BR ˈdiːteɪl, -z, -ɪŋ, -d
AM dəˈteɪl, ˈdiˌteɪl, -z, -ɪŋ, -d
detain
BR dɪˈteɪn, -z, -ɪŋ, -d
AM dəˈteɪn, diˈteɪn, -z, -ɪŋ, -d
detainee
BR ˌdiːteɪˈniː, dɪˌteɪˈniː, -z
AM dəˌteɪˈni, diˌteɪˈni, ˌdiˌteɪˈni, -z
detainer
BR dɪˈteɪnə(r), -z
AM dəˈteɪnər, diˈteɪnər, -z
detainment
BR dɪˈteɪnm(ə)nt
AM dəˈteɪnmənt, diˈteɪnmənt
detect
BR dɪˈtɛkt, -s, -ɪŋ, -ɪd
AM dəˈtɛk|(t), diˈtɛk|(t), -(t)s, -tɪŋ, -təd
detectable
BR dɪˈtɛktəbl
AM dəˈtɛktəbəl, diˈtɛktəbəl
detectably
BR dɪˈtɛktəbli
AM dəˈtɛktəbli, diˈtɛktəbli
detection
BR dɪˈtɛkʃn
AM dəˈtɛkʃən, diˈtɛkʃən
detective
BR dɪˈtɛktɪv, -z
AM dəˈtɛktɪv, diˈtɛktɪv, -z
detector
BR dɪˈtɛktə(r), -z
AM dəˈtɛktər, diˈtɛktər, -z
detectorist
BR dɪˈtɛkt(ə)rɪst, -s
AM dəˈtɛktərɪst, diˈtɛktərɪst, -s
detent
BR dɪˈtɛnt, -s
AM dəˈtɛnt, diˈtɛnt, -s
détente
BR deɪˈtɑːnt, deɪˈtɒnt, -s
AM deɪˈtɑnt, -s
detention
BR dɪˈtɛnʃn, -z
AM dəˈtɛn(t)ʃən, diˈtɛn(t)ʃən, -z
deter
BR dɪˈtəː(r), -z, -ɪŋ, -d
AM dəˈtər, diˈtər, -z, -ɪŋ, -d
detergent
BR dɪˈtəːdʒ(ə)nt, -s
AM dəˈtərdʒənt, diˈtərdʒənt, -s
deteriorate
BR dɪˈtɪərɪəreɪt, -s, -ɪŋ, -ɪd
AM dəˈtɪriəˌreɪ|t, diˈtɪriəˌreɪ|t, -ts, -dɪŋ, -dɨd
deterioration
BR dɪˌtɪərɪəˈreɪʃn
AM dəˌtɪriəˈreɪʃən, diˌtɪriəˈreɪʃən
deteriorative
BR dɪˈtɪərɪərətɪv
AM dəˈtɪriəˌreɪdɪv, diˈtɪriəˌreɪdɪv
determent
BR dɪˈtəːm(ə)nt
AM dəˈtərmənt, diˈtərmənt
determinable
BR dɪˈtəːmɪnəbl
AM dəˈtərmənəbəl, diˈtərmənəbəl
determinacy
BR dɪˈtəːmɪnəsi
AM dəˈtərmənəsi, diˈtərmənəsi
determinant
BR dɪˈtəːmɪnənt, -s
AM dəˈtərmənənt, diˈtərmənənt, -s
determinate
BR dɪˈtəːmɪnət
AM dəˈtərmənət, diˈtərmənət
determinately
BR dɪˈtəːmɪnətli
AM dəˈtərmənətli, diˈtərmənətli
determinateness
BR dɪˈtəːmɪnətnəs
AM dəˈtərmənətnəs, diˈtərmənətnəs
determination
BR dɪˌtəːmɪˈneɪʃn
AM dəˌtərməˈneɪʃən
determinative
BR dɪˈtəːmɪnətɪv, -z
AM dəˈtərməˌneɪdɪv, dəˈtərmənədɪv, -z
determinatively
BR dɪˈtəːmɪnətɪvli
AM dəˈtərməˌneɪdɨvli, dəˈtərmənədɪvli
determinativeness
BR dɪˈtəːmɪnətɪvnɪs
AM dəˈtərməˌneɪdɪvnɪs, dəˈtərmənədɪvnɪs
determine
BR dɪˈtəːmɪn, -z, -ɪŋ, -d
AM dəˈtərm|ən, diˈtərm|ən, -ənz, -(ə)nɪŋ, -ənd
determinedly
BR dɪˈtəːmɪndli
AM dəˈtərməndli, diˈtərməndli
determinedness
BR dɪˈtəːmɪn(d)nɪs
AM dəˈtərmən(d)nəs, diˈtərmən(d)nəs

determiner
BR dɪ'tə:mɪnə(r), -z
AM də'tərmənər, di'tərmənər, -z

determinism
BR dɪ'tə:mɪnɪz(ə)m
AM də'tərməˌnɪzəm, di'tərməˌnɪzəm

determinist
BR dɪ'tə:mɪnɪst, -s
AM də'tərmənəst, di'tərmənəst, -s

deterministic
BR dɪˌtə:mɪ'nɪstɪk
AM dəˌtərmə'nɪstɪk, diˌtərmə'nɪstɪk

deterministically
BR dɪˌtə:mɪ'nɪstɪkli
AM dəˌtərmə'nɪstək(ə)li, diˌtərmə'nɪstək(ə)li

deterrence
BR dɪ'tɛrəns, dɪ'tɛrn̩s
AM də'tərəns, di'tərəns, də'tɛrəns, di'tɛrəns

deterrent
BR dɪ'tɛrənt, dɪ'tɛrn̩t, -s
AM də'tərənt, di'tərənt, də'tɛrənt, di'tɛrənt, -s

detest
BR dɪ'tɛst, -s, -ɪŋ, -ɪd
AM də'tɛst, di'tɛst, -s, -ɪŋ, -əd

detestable
BR dɪ'tɛstəbl
AM də'tɛstəbəl, di'tɛstəbəl

detestably
BR dɪ'tɛstəbli
AM də'tɛstəbli, di'tɛstəbli

detestation
BR ˌdi:tɛ'steɪʃn
AM ˌdiˌtɛ'steɪʃən

detester
BR dɪ'tɛstə(r), -z
AM də'tɛstər, di'tɛstər, -z

dethrone
BR ˌdi:'θrəʊn, dɪ'θrəʊn, -z, -ɪŋ, -d
AM də'θroʊn, di'θroʊn, -z, -ɪŋ, -d

dethronement
BR dɪ'θrəʊnm(ə)nt, ˌdi:'θrəʊnm(ə)nt, -s
AM də'θroʊnmənt, di'θroʊnmənt, -s

Detmold
BR 'dɛtməʊld
AM 'dɛtˌmoʊld

detonate
BR 'dɛtəneɪt, 'dɛtn̩eɪt, -s, -ɪŋ, -ɪd
AM 'dɛtnˌeɪ|t, 'dɛdəˌneɪ|t, -ts, -dɪŋ, -dɪd

detonation
BR ˌdɛtə'neɪʃn, ˌdɛtn'eɪʃn, -z
AM ˌdɛtn'eɪʃn, ˌdɛdə'neɪʃən, -z

detonative
BR 'dɛtənətɪv, 'dɛtn̩ətɪv
AM 'dɛtnˌeɪdɪv, 'dɛtn̩ədɪv, 'dɛdəˌneɪdɪv, 'dɛdənədɪv

detonator
BR 'dɛtəneɪtə(r), 'dɛtneɪtə(r), -z
AM 'dɛtnˌeɪdər, 'dɛdəˌneɪdər, -z

detour
BR 'di:tʊə(r), 'di:tɔ:(r), 'deɪtʊə(r), 'deɪtɔ:(r), -z, -ɪŋ, -d
AM 'diˌtʊ(ə)r, -z, -ɪŋ, -d

détour
BR 'di:tʊə(r), 'di:tɔ:(r), 'deɪtʊə(r), 'deɪtɔ:(r), -z, -ɪŋ, -d
AM 'diˌtʊ(ə)r, 'deɪˌtʊ(ə)r, -z, -ɪŋ, -d

detox
BR ˌdi:'tɒks, -ɪz, -ɪŋ, -t
AM ˈdiˌtɑks, -əs, -ɪŋ, -t

detoxicate
BR ˌdi:'tɒksɪkeɪt, dɪ'tɒksɪkeɪt, -s, -ɪŋ, -ɪd
AM di'tɑksəˌkeɪ|t, -ts, -dɪŋ, -dɪd

detoxication
BR ˌdi:tɒksɪ'keɪʃn, dɪˌtɒksɪ'keɪʃn
AM dəˌtɑksə'keɪʃən, diˌtɑksə'keɪʃən

detoxification
BR ˌdi:tɒksɪfɪ'keɪʃn, di:ˌtɒksɪfɪ'keɪʃn, dɪˌtɒksɪfɪ'keɪʃn
AM dəˌtɑksəfə'keɪʃən, diˌtɑksəfə'keɪʃən

detoxify
BR (ˌ)di:'tɒksɪfʌɪ, dɪ'tɒksɪfʌɪ, -z, -ɪŋ, -d
AM də'tɑksəˌfaɪ, di'tɑksəˌfaɪ, -z, -ɪŋ, -d

detract
BR dɪ'trakt, -s, -ɪŋ, -ɪd
AM də'træk|(t), di'træk|(t), -(t)s, -tɪŋ, -təd

detraction
BR dɪ'trakʃn, -z
AM də'trækʃən, di'trækʃən, -z

detractive
BR dɪ'traktɪv
AM də'træktɪv, di'træktɪv

detractor
BR dɪ'traktə(r), -z
AM də'træktər, di'træktər, -z

detrain
BR ˌdi:'treɪn, -z, -ɪŋ, -d
AM ˌdi'treɪn, -z, -ɪŋ, -d

detrainment
BR ˌdi:'treɪnm(ə)nt
AM ˌdi'treɪnmənt

detribalisation
BR ˌdi:trʌɪbəlʌɪ'zeɪʃn, ˌdi:trʌɪbl̩ʌɪ'zeɪʃn, di:ˌtrʌɪbəlʌɪ'zeɪʃn, di:ˌtrʌɪbl̩ʌɪ'zeɪʃn
AM diˌtraɪbələ'zeɪʃən, diˌtraɪbəˌlaɪ'zeɪʃən

detribalise
BR (ˌ)di:'trʌɪbəlʌɪz, (ˌ)di:'trʌɪbl̩ʌɪz, -ɪz, -ɪŋ, -d
AM di'traɪbəˌlaɪz, -ɪz, -ɪŋ, -d

detribalization
BR ˌdi:trʌɪbəlʌɪ'zeɪʃn, ˌdi:trʌɪbl̩ʌɪ'zeɪʃn, di:ˌtrʌɪbəlʌɪ'zeɪʃn, di:ˌtrʌɪbl̩ʌɪ'zeɪʃn
AM diˌtraɪbələ'zeɪʃən, diˌtraɪbəˌlaɪ'zeɪʃən

detribalize
BR (ˌ)di:'trʌɪbəlʌɪz, (ˌ)di:'trʌɪbl̩ʌɪz, -ɪz, -ɪŋ, -d
AM di'traɪbəˌlaɪz, -ɪz, -ɪŋ, -d

detriment
BR 'dɛtrɪm(ə)nt
AM 'dɛtrɪm(ə)nt

detrimental
BR ˌdɛtrɪ'mɛntl
AM ˌdɛtrə'mɛn(t)l

detrimentally
BR ˌdɛtrɪ'mɛntl̩i, ˌdɛtrɪ'mɛntəli
AM ˌdɛtrə'mɛn(t)l̩i

detrital
BR dɪ'trʌɪtl
AM də'traɪdəl, di'traɪdəl

detrited
BR dɪ'trʌɪtɪd
AM də'traɪdɪd, di'traɪdɪd

detrition
BR dɪ'trɪʃn
AM də'trɪʃən, di'trɪʃən

detritivore
BR dɪ'trɪtɪvɔ:(r), -z
AM də'trɪdɪˌvɔ(ə)r, -z

detritus
BR dɪ'trʌɪtəs
AM də'traɪdəs, di'traɪdəs, 'dɛtrədəs

Detroit
BR dɪ'trɔɪt
AM də'trɔɪt, di'trɔɪt

de trop
BR də 'trəʊ, deɪ +
AM də 'troʊ

Dettol®
BR 'dɛtɒl
AM 'dɛdɑl

detumescence
BR ˌdi:tjʊ'mɛsns, ˌdi:tʃʊ'mɛsns
AM ˌdit(j)u'mɛsəns

detumescent
BR ˌdi:tjʊ'mɛsnt, ˌdi:tʃʊ'mɛsnt
AM ˌdit(j)u'mɛsənt

detune
BR ˌdi:'tju:n, ˌdi:'tʃu:n, -z, -ɪŋ, -d
AM də't(j)un, di't(j)un, -z, -ɪŋ, -d

Deucalion
BR dju:'keɪlɪən
AM d(j)u'keɪliən

deuce
BR dju:s, dʒu:s, -ɪz
AM d(j)us, -əz

deuced
BR 'dju:sɪd, 'dʒu:sɪd, dju:st, dʒu:st
AM 'd(j)usəd, d(j)ust

deucedly
BR 'dju:sɪdli, 'dʒu:sɪdli, dju:stli, dʒu:stli
AM 'd(j)usədli, d(j)us(t)li

deus ex machina
BR ˌdeɪəs ɛks mə'ʃi:nə(r), + 'makɪnə(r), -z
AM ˈdeɪəs ˌɛks 'mɑkənə, -z

deuteragonist
BR ˌdju:tə'ragənɪst, ˌdju:tə'ragn̩ɪst, ˌdʒu:tə'ragənɪst, ˌdʒu:tə'ragn̩ɪst, -s
AM ˌd(j)udə'rægənəst, -s

deuterate
BR 'dju:təreɪt, 'dʒu:təreɪt, -s, -ɪŋ, -ɪd
AM 'd(j)udəˌreɪ|t, -ts, -dɪŋ, -dɪd

deuteration
BR ˌdju:tə'reɪʃn, ˌdʒu:tə'reɪʃn
AM ˌd(j)udə'reɪʃən

deuteric
BR 'dju:t(ə)rɪk, 'dʒu:t(ə)rɪk
AM 'd(j)udərɪk, d(j)u'tɛrɪk

deuterium
BR dju:'tɪərɪəm, dʒu:'tɪərɪəm
AM d(j)u'tɛriəm

Deutero-Isaiah
BR ˌdjuːtərəʊʌɪˈzʌɪə(r), ˌdʒuːtərəʊʌɪˈzʌɪə(r)
AM ˈd(j)udəroʊˌaɪˈzeɪə

deuteron
BR ˈdjuːtərɒn, ˈdʒuːtərɒn, -z
AM ˈd(j)udərən, ˈd(j)udəˌrɑn, -z

Deuteronomic
BR ˌdjuːt(ə)rəˈnɒmɪk, ˌdʒuːt(ə)rəˈnɒmɪk
AM ˌd(j)udərəˈnɑmɪk

Deuteronomical
BR ˌdjuːt(ə)rəˈnɒmɨkl, ˌdʒuːt(ə)rəˈnɒmɨkl
AM ˌd(j)udərəˈnɑməkəl

Deuteronomist
BR ˌdjuːtəˈrɒnəmɪst, ˌdʒuːtəˈrɒnəmɪst, -s
AM ˌd(j)udəˈrɑnəməst, -s

Deuteronomy
BR ˌdjuːtəˈrɒnəmi, ˌdʒuːtəˈrɒnəmi
AM ˌd(j)udəˈrɑnəmi

deuteronope
BR ˈdjuːt(ə)rənəʊp, ˈdʒuːt(ə)rənəʊp, -s
AM ˈd(j)udərəˌnoʊp, -s

deuteronopia
BR ˌdjuːt(ə)rəˈnəʊpɪə(r), ˌdʒuːt(ə)rəˈnəʊpiə(r)
AM ˌd(j)udərəˈnoʊpiə

Deutschmark
BR ˈdɔɪtʃmɑːk, -s
AM ˈdɔɪtʃˌmɑrk, -s

deutzia
BR ˈdjuːtsɪə(r), ˈdɔɪtsɪə(r), -z
AM ˈd(j)ʊtʃ(i)ə, ˈdɔɪtsiə, -z

deva
BR ˈdeɪvə(r), ˈdiːvə(r), -z
AM ˈdivə, ˈdeɪvə, -z

de Valera
BR ˌdɛ vəˈlɛːrə(r), də +
AM də vəˈlɛrə

de Valois
BR də ˈvalwɑː(r)
AM də vɑˈlwɑ, də væˈlwɑ

devaluate
BR ˌdiːˈvaljʊeɪt, -s, -ɪŋ, -ɨd
AM diˈvæljəˌweɪ|t, -ts, -dɪŋ, -dɨd

devaluation
BR ˌdiːvaljʊˈeɪʃn, dɪˌvaljʊˈeɪʃn, -z
AM ˌdiˌvæljʊˈeɪʃən, ˌdiˌvæljəˈweɪʃən, -z

devalue
BR ˌdiːˈvaljuː, -z, -ɪŋ, -d
AM diˈvælju, -z, -ɪŋ, -d

Devanagari
BR ˌdeɪvəˈnɑːg(ə)ri, ˌdɛvəˈnɑːg(ə)ri
AM ˌdeɪvəˈnɑgəri

devastate
BR ˈdɛvəsteɪt, -s, -ɪŋ, -ɨd
AM ˈdɛvəˌsteɪ|t, -ts, -dɪŋ, -dɨd

devastatingly
BR ˈdɛvəsteɪtɪŋli
AM ˈdɛvəˌsteɪdɪŋli

devastation
BR ˌdɛvəˈsteɪʃn
AM ˌdɛvəˈsteɪʃən

devastator
BR ˈdɛvəsteɪtə(r), -z
AM ˈdɛvəˌsteɪdər, -z

develop
BR dɪˈvɛləp, -s, -ɪŋ, -t
AM dəˈvɛləp, diˈvɛləp, -s, -ɪŋ, -t

developable
BR dɪˈvɛləpəbl
AM dəˈvɛləpəbəl, diˈvɛləpəbəl

developer
BR dɪˈvɛləpə(r), -z
AM dəˈvɛləpər, diˈvɛləpər, -z

development
BR dɪˈvɛləpm(ə)nt
AM dəˈvɛləpmənt, diˈvɛləpmənt

developmental
BR dɪˌvɛləpˈmɛntl̩
AM dəˌvɛləpˈmən(t)l, diˌvɛləpˈmən(t)l

developmentally
BR dɪˌvɛləpˈmɛntl̩i, dɪˌvɛləpˈmɛntəli
AM dəˌvɛləpˈmən(t)l̩i, diˌvɛləpˈmən(t)l̩i

De Vere
BR də ˈvɪə(r)
AM də ˈvɪ(ə)r

Devereux
BR ˈdɛv(ə)rəʊ, ˈdɛv(ə)rə(r), ˈdɛv(ə)ruː, ˈdɛv(ə)ruːks
AM ˈdɛvəroʊ

Devi
BR ˈdeɪvi
AM ˈdeɪvi

deviance
BR ˈdiːvɪəns
AM ˈdiviəns

deviancy
BR ˈdiːvɪəns|i, -ɪz
AM ˈdiviənsi, -z

deviant
BR ˈdiːvɪənt
AM ˈdiviənt

deviate
BR ˈdiːvɪeɪt, -s, -ɪŋ, -ɨd
AM ˈdiviˌeɪ|t, -ts, -dɪŋ, -dɨd

deviation
BR ˌdiːvɪˈeɪʃn, -z
AM ˌdiviˈeɪʃən, -z

deviational
BR ˌdiːvɪˈeɪʃn̩(ə)l, ˌdiːvɪˈeɪʃən(ə)l
AM ˌdiviˈeɪʃ(ə)nəl

deviationism
BR ˌdiːvɪˈeɪʃn̩ɪz(ə)m, ˌdiːvɪˈeɪʃənɪz(ə)m
AM ˌdiviˈeɪʃəˌnɪzəm

deviationist
BR ˌdiːvɪˈeɪʃn̩ɪst, ˌdiːvˈeɪʃənɪst, -s
AM ˌdiviˈeɪʃənəst, -s

deviator
BR ˈdiːvɪeɪtə(r), -z
AM ˈdiviˌeɪdər, -z

deviatory
BR ˈdiːvɪət(ə)ri
AM ˈdiviəˌtɔri

device
BR dɪˈvʌɪs, -ɪz
AM dəˈvaɪs, diˈvaɪs, -ɪz

devil
BR ˈdɛvl, -z
AM ˈdɛvəl, -z

devildom
BR ˈdɛvldəm
AM ˈdɛvəldəm

devilfish
BR ˈdɛvlfɪʃ, -ɪz
AM ˈdɛvəlˌfɪʃ, -ɪz

devilish
BR ˈdɛvl̩ɪʃ, ˈdɛv(ɪ)lɪʃ
AM ˈdɛv(ə)lɪʃ

devilishly
BR ˈdɛvl̩ɪʃli, ˈdɛv(ɪ)lɪʃli
AM ˈdɛv(ə)lɪʃli

devilishness
BR ˈdɛvl̩ɪʃnɪs, ˈdɛv(ɪ)lɪʃnɪs
AM ˈdɛv(ə)lɪʃnɪs

devilism
BR ˈdɛvl̩ɪz(ə)m, ˈdɛvɪlɪz(ə)m
AM ˈdɛvəˌlɪzəm

de Villiers
BR də ˈvɪljəz, + ˈvɪlɪəz
AM də ˈvɪljərz

devil-may-care
BR ˌdɛvlmeɪˈkɛː(r), ˈdɛvlmeɪkɛː(r)
AM ˈdɛvəlˌmeɪˈkɛ(ə)r

devilment
BR ˈdɛvlm(ə)nt
AM ˈdɛvəlmənt

devilry
BR ˈdɛvlri
AM ˈdɛvəlri

deviltry
BR ˈdɛvltri
AM ˈdɛvəltri

Devine
BR dɪˈvʌɪn, dɪˈviːn
AM dəˈvaɪn

devious
BR ˈdiːvɪəs
AM ˈdiviəs, ˈdivjəs

deviously
BR ˈdiːvɪəsli
AM ˈdiviəsli, ˈdivjəsli

deviousness
BR ˈdiːvɪəsnəs
AM ˈdiviəsnəs, ˈdivjəsnəs

devisable
BR dɪˈvʌɪzəbl
AM dəˈvaɪzəbəl, diˈvaɪzəbəl

devise
BR dɪˈvʌɪz, -ɪz, -ɪŋ, -d
AM dəˈvaɪz, diˈvaɪz, -ɪz, -ɪŋ, -d

devisee
BR dɪˌvʌɪˈziː, -z
AM dəˌvaɪˈzi, diˌvaɪˈzi, -z

deviser
BR dɪˈvʌɪzə(r), -z
AM dəˈvaɪzər, diˈvaɪzər, -z

devisor
BR dɪˈvʌɪzə(r), -z
AM dəˈvaɪzər, diˈvaɪzər, -z

devitalisation
BR ˌdiːvʌɪtl̩ʌɪˈzeɪʃn, ˌdiːvʌɪtəlʌɪˈzeɪʃn, diːˌvʌɪtl̩ʌɪˈzeɪʃn, diːˌvʌɪtəlʌɪˈzeɪʃn
AM ˈdiˌvaɪdləˈzeɪʃən, ˈdiˌvaɪdlˌaɪˈzeɪʃən

devitalise
BR (ˌ)diːˈvʌɪtl̩ʌɪz, (ˌ)diːˈvʌɪtəlʌɪz, -ɪz, -ɪŋ, -d
AM diˈvaɪdl̩aɪz, -ɪz, -ɪŋ, -d

devitalization
BR ˌdiːvʌɪtl̩ʌɪˈzeɪʃn, ˌdiːvʌɪtəlʌɪˈzeɪʃn, diːˌvʌɪtl̩ʌɪˈzeɪʃn, diːˌvʌɪtəlʌɪˈzeɪʃn
AM ˈdiˌvaɪdləˈzeɪʃən, ˈdiˌvaɪdlˌaɪˈzeɪʃən

devitalize
BR (ˌ)diːˈvʌɪtl̩ʌɪz, (ˌ)diːˈvʌɪtəlʌɪz, -ɪz, -ɪŋ, -d
AM diˈvaɪdl̩aɪz, -ɪz, -ɪŋ, -d

devitrification
BR ˌdiːvɪtrɪfɪˈkeɪʃn, diːˌvɪtrɪfɪˈkeɪʃn
AM ˈdiˌvɪtrəfəˈkeɪʃən

devitrify
BR (ˌ)diːˈvɪtrɪfʌɪ, -z, -ɪŋ, -d
AM diˈvɪtrəˌfaɪ, -z, -ɪŋ, -d

Devizes
BR dɪˈvʌɪzɪz
AM dəˈvizɪz

Devlin
BR 'dɛvlɪn
AM 'dɛvlən
devoice
BR (ˌ)diː'vɔɪs, -ɪz, -ɪŋ, -t
AM di'vɔɪs, -ɪz, -ɪŋ, -t
devoid
BR dɪ'vɔɪd
AM də'vɔɪd, di'vɔɪd
devoir
BR də'vwɑː(r), -z
AM dəv'wɑr, -z
devolute
BR 'diːvəl(j)uːt, 'dɛvəl(j)uːt, -s, -ɪŋ, -ɪd
AM 'dɛvəˌl(j)u|t, -ts, -dɪŋ, -dəd
devolution
BR ˌdiːvə'l(j)uːʃn, ˌdɛvə'l(j)uːʃn
AM ˌdɛvə'l(j)uʃən
devolutionary
BR ˌdiːvə'l(j)uːʃn̩(ə)ri, ˌdɛvə'l(j)uːʃn̩(ə)ri
AM ˌdɛvə'l(j)uʃəˌnɛri
devolutionist
BR ˌdiːvə'l(j)uːʃn̩ɪst, ˌdiːvə'l(j)uːʃənɪst, ˌdɛvə'l(j)uːʃn̩ɪst, ˌdɛvə'l(j)uːʃənɪst, -s
AM ˌdɛvə'l(j)uʃənəst, -s
devolve
BR dɪ'vɒlv, -z, -ɪŋ, -d
AM də'vɑlv, di'vɑlv, -z, -ɪŋ, -d
devolvement
BR dɪ'vɒlvm(ə)nt, -s
AM də'vɑlvmənt, di'vɑlvmənt, -s
Devon
BR 'dɛvn
AM 'dɛvən
Devonian
BR dɪ'vəʊnɪən, -z
AM də'voʊniən, -z
Devonport
BR 'dɛvnpɔːt
AM 'dɛvənˌpɔ(ə)rt
Devonshire
BR 'dɛvnʃ(ɪ)ə(r)
AM 'dɛvənˌʃɪ(ə)r
dévot
BR deɪ'vəʊ, -z
AM deɪ'voʊ, -z
devote
BR dɪ'vəʊt, -s, -ɪŋ, -ɪd
AM də'voʊ|t, di'voʊ|t, -ts, -dɪŋ, -dəd
dévote
BR deɪ'vɒt, -s
AM deɪ'voʊt, -s
devotedly
BR dɪ'vəʊtɪdli
AM də'voʊdədli, di'voʊdədli
devotedness
BR dɪ'vəʊtɪdnɪs
AM də'voʊdədnəs, di'voʊdədnəs
devotee
BR ˌdɛvə'tiː, -z
AM ˌdɛvə'ti, ˌdɛvoʊ'ti, -z
devotement
BR dɪ'vəʊtm(ə)nt
AM də'voʊtmənt, di'voʊtmənt
devotion
BR dɪ'vəʊʃn, -z
AM də'voʊʃən, di'voʊʃən, -z
devotional
BR dɪ'vəʊʃn̩(ə)l, dɪ'vəʊʃən(ə)l
AM də'voʊʃ(ə)nəl, di'voʊʃ(ə)nəl
devotionally
BR dɪ'vəʊʃn̩əli, dɪ'vəʊʃn̩li, dɪ'vəʊʃənl̩i, dɪ'vəʊʃ(ə)nəli
AM də'voʊʃ(ə)nəli, di'voʊʃ(ə)nəli
devour
BR dɪ'vaʊə(r), -z, -ɪŋ, -d
AM də'vaʊ(ə)r, di'vaʊ(ə)r, -z, -ɪŋ, -d
devourer
BR dɪ'vaʊərə(r), -z
AM də'vaʊrər, di'vaʊrər, -z
devouringly
BR dɪ'vaʊərɪŋli
AM də'vaʊrɪŋli, di'vaʊrɪŋli
devout
BR dɪ'vaʊt, -ə(r), -ɪst
AM də'vaʊ|t, di'vaʊ|t, -dər, -dəst
devoutly
BR dɪ'vaʊtli
AM də'vaʊtli, di'vaʊtli
devoutness
BR dɪ'vaʊtnəs
AM də'vaʊtnəs, di'vaʊtnəs
de Vries
BR də 'vriːs, + 'vriːz
AM də 'vris
dew
BR djuː
AM d(j)u
dewan
BR dɪ'wɑːn, -z
AM də'wɑn, -z
Dewar
BR 'djuːə(r)
AM 'duwər
dewar
BR 'djuːə(r), -z
AM 'duwər, -z
dewberry
BR 'djuːb(ə)r|i, -ɪz
AM 'd(j)uˌbɛri, -z
dewclaw
BR 'djuːklɔː(r), -z
AM 'd(j)uˌklɔ, 'd(j)uˌklɑ, -z
dewdrop
BR 'djuːdrɒp, -s
AM 'd(j)uˌdrɑp, -s
Dewey
BR 'djuːi
AM 'd(j)ui
dewfall
BR 'djuːfɔːl
AM 'd(j)uˌfɔl, 'd(j)uˌfɑl
Dewhurst
BR 'djuːhəːst, 'dʒuːhəːst
AM 'd(j)uˌ(h)ərst
Dewi
BR 'dɛwi
AM 'deɪwi
WE 'dewi
dewily
BR 'djuːɪli
AM 'd(j)uəli
dewiness
BR 'djuːɪnɪs
AM 'd(j)uinɪs
dewlap
BR 'djuːlap, -s
AM 'd(j)uˌlæp, -s
dewpoint
BR 'djuːpɔɪnt, -s
AM 'd(j)uˌpɔɪnt, -s
dewpond
BR 'djuːpɒnd, -z
AM 'd(j)uˌpɑnd, -z
Dewsbury
BR 'djuːzb(ə)ri, 'dʒuːzb(ə)ri
AM 'd(j)uzˌbɛri
dewy
BR 'djuː|i, -ɪə(r), -ɪɪst
AM 'd(j)ui, -ər, -ɪst
Dexedrine
BR 'dɛksɪdriːn, 'dɛksədrɪn
AM 'dɛksəˌdrin, 'dɛksədrən
dexter
BR 'dɛkstə(r)
AM 'dɛkstər
dexterity
BR dɛk'stɛrɪti
AM dɛk'stɛrədi
dexterous
BR 'dɛkst(ə)rəs
AM 'dɛkst(ə)rəs
dexterously
BR 'dɛkst(ə)rəsli
AM 'dɛkst(ə)rəsli
dexterousness
BR 'dɛkst(ə)rəsnəs
AM 'dɛkst(ə)rəsnəs
dextral
BR 'dɛkstr(ə)l
AM 'dɛkstrəl
dextrality
BR dɛk'stralɪti
AM dɛk'strælədi
dextrally
BR 'dɛkstrl̩i, 'dɛkstrəli
AM 'dɛkstrəli
dextran
BR 'dɛkstrən, -z
AM 'dɛkstrən, -z
dextrin
BR 'dɛkstrɪn
AM 'dɛkstrən
dextrorotation
BR ˌdɛkstrəʊrə(ʊ)'teɪʃn
AM ˌdɛkstrəˌroʊ'teɪʃən
dextrorotatory
BR ˌdɛkstrəʊ'rəʊtət(ə)ri
AM ˌdɛkstrə'roʊdəˌtɔri
dextrorse
BR 'dɛkstrɔːs
AM 'dɛkstrɔ(ə)rs
dextrose
BR 'dɛkstrəʊz, 'dɛkstrəʊs
AM 'dɛkstroʊs
dextrous
BR 'dɛkstrəs
AM 'dɛkst(ə)rəs
dextrously
BR 'dɛkstrəsli
AM 'dɛkst(ə)rəsli
dextrousness
BR 'dɛkstrəsnəs
AM 'dɛkst(ə)rəsnəs
dey
BR deɪ, -z
AM deɪ, -z
Dhahran
BR ˌdɑː'rɑːn, ˌdɑː'ran
AM ˌdɑ'rɑn
Dhaka
BR 'dakə(r)
AM 'dɑkə
dhal
BR dɑːl
AM dɑl
dharma
BR 'dɑːmə(r)
AM 'dɑrmə
Dhekelia
BR dɪ'keɪlɪə(r)
AM də'keɪljə, də'keɪliə
dhobi
BR 'dəʊb|i, -ɪz
AM 'doʊbi, -z
Dhofar
BR ˌdəʊ'fɑː(r)
AM ˌdoʊ'fɑr
dhole
BR dəʊl, -z
AM doʊl, -z
dhoti
BR 'dəʊt|i, -ɪz
AM 'doʊdi, -z
dhow
BR daʊ, -z

AM daʊ, -z

dhurrie
BR ˈdʌr|i, -ɪz
AM ˈdəri, -z

Di
BR dʌɪ
AM daɪ

diabetes
BR ˌdʌɪəˈbiːtiːz, ˌdʌɪəˈbiːtɪs
AM ˌdaɪəˈbidiz, ˌdaɪəˈbidɪs, ˌdaɪəˈbiˌtiz

diabetic
BR ˌdʌɪəˈbɛtɪk, -s
AM ˌdaɪəˈbɛdɪk, -s

diablerie
BR dɪˈɑːbləri, dɪˈabləri
AM diˈɑbləri

diabolic
BR ˌdʌɪəˈbɒlɪk
AM ¦daɪəˈbɑlɪk

diabolical
BR ˌdʌɪəˈbɒlɪkl
AM ¦daɪəˈbɑləkəl

diabolically
BR ˌdʌɪəˈbɒlɪkli
AM ¦daɪəˈbɑlək(ə)li

diabolise
BR dʌɪˈabəlʌɪz, -ɪz, -ɪŋ, -d
AM daɪˈæbəˌlaɪz, -ɪz, -ɪŋ, -d

diabolism
BR dʌɪˈabəlɪz(ə)m
AM daɪˈæbəˌlɪzəm

diabolist
BR dʌɪˈabəlɪst, -s
AM daɪˈæbələst, -s

diabolize
BR dʌɪˈabəlʌɪz, -ɪz, -ɪŋ, -d
AM daɪˈæbəˌlaɪz, -ɪz, -ɪŋ, -d

diabolo
BR dɪˈabələʊ, dʌɪˈabələʊ
AM diˈɑb(ə)loʊ

diachronic
BR ˌdʌɪəˈkrɒnɪk
AM ˌdaɪəˈkrɑnɪk

diachronically
BR ˌdʌɪəˈkrɒnɪkli
AM ˌdaɪəˈkrɑnək(ə)li

diachronism
BR ˌdʌɪˈakrənɪz(ə)m
AM ˌdaɪəˈkrɑˌnɪzəm

diachronistic
BR ˌdʌɪəkrəˈnɪstɪk
AM ˌdaɪəˌkrəˈnɪstɪk

diachronous
BR dʌɪˈakrənəs
AM daɪˈækrənəs

diachrony
BR dʌɪˈakrəni
AM daɪˈækrəni

diaconal
BR dʌɪˈakənl, dʌɪˈakn̩l
AM daɪˈækənəl, diˈækənəl

diaconate
BR dʌɪˈakəneɪt, dʌɪˈakn̩eɪt, dʌɪˈakənət, dʌɪˈakn̩ət, -s
AM daɪˈækənət, diˌækənət, -s

diacritic
BR ˌdʌɪəˈkrɪtɪk, -s
AM ¦daɪəˌkrɪdɪk, -s

diacritical
BR ˌdʌɪəˈkrɪtɪkl
AM ¦daɪəˌkrɪdɪkəl

diacritically
BR ˌdʌɪəˈkrɪtɪkli
AM ¦daɪəˌkrɪdɪk(ə)li

diadelphous
BR ˌdʌɪəˈdɛlfəs
AM ˌdaɪəˈdɛlfəs

diadem
BR ˈdʌɪədɛm, -z, -d
AM ˈdaɪəˌdɛm, -z, -d

Diadochi
BR dʌɪˈadəkʌɪ, dʌɪˈadəki
AM daɪˈædəˌki

diaereses
BR dʌɪˈɪərɪsiːz, dʌɪˈɛrɪsiːz
AM daɪˈɛrəˌsiz

diaeresis
BR dʌɪˈɪərɪsɪs, dʌɪˈɛrɪsɪs
AM daɪˈɛrəsəs

diageneses
BR ˌdʌɪəˈdʒɛnɪsiːz
AM ˌdaiəˈdʒɛnəsiz

diagenesis
BR ˌdʌɪəˈdʒɛnɪsɪs
AM ˌdaiəˈdʒɛnəsəs

Diaghilev
BR dɪˈagɪlɛf
AM diˈɑgələv

diagnosable
BR ˌdʌɪəgˈnəʊzəbl, ˈdʌɪəgnəʊzəbl
AM ˌdaɪəgˈnoʊsəbəl, ˌdaɪəgˈnoʊzəbəl

diagnose
BR ˌdʌɪəgˈnəʊz, ˈdʌɪəgnəʊz, -ɪz, -ɪŋ, -d
AM ˌdaɪəgˈnoʊz, ˌdaɪəgˈnoʊs, ˈdaɪəgˌnoʊs, ˈdaɪəgˌnoʊz, -əz, -ɪŋ, -d

diagnoseable
BR ˌdʌɪəgˈnəʊzəbl, ˈdʌɪəgnəʊzəbl
AM ˌdaɪəgˈnoʊzəbəl, ˌdaɪəgˈnoʊsəbəl

diagnoses
BR ˌdʌɪəgˈnəʊsiːz
AM ˌdaɪəgˈnoʊˌsiz

diagnosis
BR ˌdʌɪəgˈnəʊsɪs
AM ˌdaɪəgˈnoʊsəs

diagnostic
BR ˌdʌɪəgˈnɒstɪk, -s
AM ˌdaɪəgˈnɑstɪk, -s

diagnostically
BR ˌdʌɪəgˈnɒstɪkli
AM ˌdaɪəgˈnɑstək(ə)li

diagnostician
BR ˌdʌɪəgnɒˈstɪʃn, -z
AM ˌdaɪəgˌnɑsˈtɪʃən, -z

diagonal
BR dʌɪˈag(ə)nl, dʌɪˈagn̩l, -z
AM daɪˈægənəl, -z

diagonally
BR dʌɪˈag(ə)nl̩i, dʌɪˈagn̩l̩i, dʌɪˈag(ə)nəli, dʌɪˈagn̩əli
AM daɪˈæg(ə)nəli

diagram
BR ˈdʌɪəgram, -z
AM ˈdaɪəˌgræm, -z

diagrammatic
BR ˌdʌɪəgrəˈmatɪk
AM ˌdaɪəgrəˈmædɪk

diagrammatically
BR ˌdʌɪəgrəˈmatɪkli
AM ˌdaɪəgrəˈmædək(ə)li

diagrammatise
BR ˌdʌɪəˈgramətʌɪz, -ɪz, -ɪŋ, -d
AM ˌdaɪəˈgræməˌtaɪz, -ɪz, -ɪŋ, -d

diagrammatize
BR ˌdʌɪəˈgramətʌɪz, -ɪz, -ɪŋ, -d
AM ˌdaɪəˈgræməˌtaɪz, -ɪz, -ɪŋ, -d

diagrid
BR ˈdʌɪəgrɪd, -z
AM ˈdaɪəˌgrɪd, -z

diakinesis
BR ˌdʌɪəkɪˈniːsɪs
AM ˌdaɪəkəˈnisɪs

dial
BR ˈdʌɪəl, -z, -ɪŋ, -d
AM ˈdaɪ(ə)l, -z, -ɪŋ, -d

dialect
BR ˈdʌɪəlɛkt, -s
AM ˈdaɪəˌlɛk|(t), -(t)s

dialectal
BR ˌdʌɪəˈlɛktl
AM daɪəˈlɛkt(ə)l

dialectic
BR ˌdʌɪəˈlɛktɪk, -s
AM ˌdaɪəˈlɛktɪk, -s

dialectical
BR ˌdʌɪəˈlɛktɪkl
AM ˌdaɪəˈlɛktəkəl

dialectically
BR ˌdʌɪəˈlɛktɪkli
AM ˌdaɪəˈlɛktək(ə)li

dialectician
BR ˌdʌɪəlɛkˈtɪʃn, -z
AM ˌdaɪlɛkˈtɪʃən, -z

dialectologist
BR ˌdʌɪəlɛkˈtɒlədʒɪst, -s
AM ˌdaɪəlɛkˈtɑlədʒəst, -s

dialectology
BR ˌdʌɪəlɛkˈtɒlədʒi
AM ˌdaɪəlɛkˈtɑlədʒi

dialer
BR ˈdʌɪələ(r), -z
AM ˈdaɪlər, -z

dialler
BR ˈdʌɪələ(r), -z
AM ˈdaɪlər, -z

dialog
BR ˈdʌɪəlɒg, -z
AM ˈdaɪəˌlɔg, ˈdaɪəˌlɑg, -z

dialogic
BR ˌdʌɪəˈlɒdʒɪk
AM ˌdaɪəˈlɑdʒɪk

dialogist
BR dʌɪˈalədʒɪst, -s
AM daɪˈælədʒəst, ˈdaɪəˌlɔgəst, ˈdaɪəˌlɑgəst, -s

dialogue
BR ˈdʌɪəlɒg, -z
AM ˈdaɪəˌlɔg, ˈdaɪəˌlɑg, -z

dialyse
BR ˈdʌɪəlʌɪz, -ɪz, -ɪŋ, -d
AM ˈdaɪəˌlaɪz, -ɪz, -ɪŋ, -d

dialyses
pl of dialysis
BR dʌɪˈalɪsiːz
AM daɪˈæləsiz

dialysis
BR dʌɪˈalɪsɪs
AM daɪˈæləsəs

dialytic
BR ˌdʌɪəˈlɪtɪk
AM ˌdaɪəˈlɪdɪk

dialyze
BR ˈdʌɪəlʌɪz, -ɪz, -ɪŋ, -d
AM ˈdaɪəˌlaɪz, -ɪz, -ɪŋ, -d

diamagnetic
BR ˌdʌɪəmagˈnɛtɪk, -s
AM ˌdaɪəˌmægˈnɛdɪk, -s

diamagnetically
BR ˌdʌɪəmagˈnɛtɪkli
AM ˌdaɪəˌmægˈnɛdək(ə)li

diamagnetism
BR ˌdʌɪəˈmagnɪtɪz(ə)m
AM ˌdaɪəˈmægnəˌtɪzəm

diamanté
BR dɪəˈmɒnteɪ, dʌɪəˈmɒnteɪ, dɪəˈmanti, dʌɪəˈmanti
AM ˌdiəˌmɑnˈteɪ

diamantiferous
BR ˌdʌɪəmanˈtɪf(ə)rəs
AM ˌdaɪəmənˈtɪfərəs

diamantine
BR ˌdʌɪəˈmantiːn, ˌdʌɪəˈmantʌɪn

AM ˈdaɪəˈmæn,taɪn, ˈdaɪəˈmæn,tin, ˈdaɪəˈmæntn

diameter
BR dʌɪˈamɨtə(r), -z
AM daɪˈæmədər, -z

diametral
BR dʌɪˈamɨtr(ə)l
AM daɪˈæmətrəl

diametric
BR ˌdʌɪəˈmɛtrɪk
AM ˈdaɪəˈmɛtrɪk

diametrical
BR ˌdʌɪəˈmɛtrɨkl
AM ˈdaɪəˈmɛtrəkəl

diametrically
BR ˌdʌɪəˈmɛtrɨkli
AM ˌdaɪəˈmɛtrək(ə)li

diamond
BR ˈdʌɪəmənd, -z
AM ˈdaɪ(ə)mən(d), -z

diamondback
BR ˈdʌɪəmən(d)bak, -s
AM ˈdaɪmən,bæk, -s

diamondiferous
BR ˌdʌɪəmənˈdɪf(ə)rəs
AM ˌdaɪmənˈdɪfərəs

Diana
BR dʌɪˈanə(r)
AM daɪˈænə, diˈænə

diandrous
BR dʌɪˈandrəs
AM daɪˈændrəs

Diane
BR dʌɪˈan
AM daɪˈæn

Dianetics
BR ˌdʌɪəˈnɛtɪks
AM ˌdaɪəˈnɛdɪks

dianthus
BR dʌɪˈanθəs, -ɨz
AM daɪˈænθəs, -əz

diapason
BR ˌdʌɪəˈpeɪsn, ˌdʌɪəˈpeɪzn, -z
AM ˌdaɪəˈpeɪzn, ˌdaɪəˈpeɪsən, -z

diapause
BR ˈdʌɪəpɔːz, -ɨz
AM ˈdaɪə,pɔz, ˈdaɪə,pɑz, -əz

diaper
BR ˈdʌɪəpə(r), -z
AM ˈdaɪ(ə)pər, -z

diaphanous
BR dʌɪˈafənəs, dʌɪˈafn̩əs
AM daɪˈæfənəs

diaphanously
BR dʌɪˈafənəsli, dʌɪˈafn̩əsli
AM daɪˈæfənəsli

diaphone
BR ˈdʌɪəfəʊn, -z
AM ˈdaɪə,foʊn, -z

diaphoneme
BR ˈdʌɪə,fəʊniːm, -z
AM ˈdaɪə,foʊnim, -z

diaphonemic
BR ˌdʌɪəfəˈniːmɪk
AM ˌdaɪəfəˈnimɪk

diaphonemically
BR ˌdʌɪəfəˈniːmɨkli
AM ˌdaɪəfəˈnimɨk(ə)li

diaphonic
BR ˌdʌɪəˈfɒnɪk
AM ˌdaɪəˈfɑnɪk

diaphonically
BR ˌdʌɪəˈfɒnɨkli
AM ˌdaɪəˈfɑnək(ə)li

diaphoreses
BR ˌdʌɪəfəˈriːsiːz
AM ˌdaɪəfəˈrisiz

diaphoresis
BR ˌdʌɪəfəˈriːsɪs
AM ˌdaɪəfəˈrisɪs

diaphoretic
BR ˌdʌɪəfəˈrɛtɪk, -s
AM ˌdaɪəfəˈrɛdɪk, -s

diaphragm
BR ˈdʌɪəfram, -z
AM ˈdaɪə,fræm, -z

diaphragmatic
BR ˌdʌɪəfrə(g)ˈmatɪk
AM ˌdaɪəfrə(g)ˈmædɪk

diapositive
BR ˌdʌɪəˈpɒzɨtɪv, -z
AM ˌdaɪəˈpɑzədɪv, -z

diarchal
BR dʌɪˈɑːkl
AM daɪˈɑrkəl

diarchic
BR dʌɪˈɑːkɪk
AM daɪˈɑrkɪk

diarchy
BR ˈdʌɪɑːk|i, -ɪz
AM ˈdaɪ,ɑrki, -z

diarise
BR ˈdʌɪərʌɪz, -ɨz, -ɪŋ, -d
AM ˈdaɪə,raɪz, -ɨz, -ɪŋ, -d

diarist
BR ˈdʌɪərɪst, -s
AM ˈdaɪərəst, -s

diaristic
BR ˌdʌɪəˈrɪstɪk
AM ˌdaɪəˈrɪstɪk

diarize
BR ˈdʌɪərʌɪz, -ɨz, -ɪŋ, -d
AM ˈdaɪə,raɪz, -ɨz, -ɪŋ, -d

diarrhea
BR ˌdʌɪəˈrɪə(r)
AM ˌdaɪəˈriə

diarrheal
BR ˌdʌɪəˈrɪəl
AM ˌdaɪəˈriəl

diarrhoea
BR ˌdʌɪəˈrɪə(r)
AM ˌdaɪəˈriə

diarrhoeal
BR ˌdʌɪəˈrɪəl
AM ˌdaɪəˈriəl

diarrhoeic
BR ˌdʌɪəˈriːɪk
AM ˌdaɪəˈriɪk

diary
BR ˈdʌɪər|i, -ɪz
AM ˈdaɪ(ə)ri, -z

diascope
BR ˈdʌɪəskəʊp, -s
AM ˈdaɪə,skoʊp, -s

Diaspora
BR dʌɪˈasp(ə)rə(r)
AM daɪˈæsp(ə)rə, diˈæsp(ə)rə

diaspore
BR ˈdʌɪəspɔː(r)
AM ˈdaɪə,spɔ(ə)r

diastalsis
BR ˌdʌɪəˈstalsɪs
AM ˌdaɪəˈstɑlsəs

diastase
BR ˈdʌɪəsteɪz
AM ˈdaɪə,steɪs, ˈdaɪə,steɪz

diastasic
BR ˌdʌɪəˈsteɪsɪk
AM ˌdaɪəˈstæsɪk

diastatic
BR ˌdʌɪəˈstatɪk
AM ˌdaɪəˈstædɪk

diastole
BR dʌɪˈastəli, dʌɪˈastl̩i
AM daɪˈæstəli

diastolic
BR ˌdʌɪəˈstɒlɪk
AM daɪəˈstɑlɪk

diatessaron
BR ˌdʌɪəˈtɛs(ə)rɒn, -z
AM ˌdaɪəˈtɛsərən, daɪəˈtɛsə,rɑn, -z

diathermancy
BR ˌdʌɪəˈθəːm(ə)nsi
AM ˌdaɪəˈθərmənsi

diathermanous
BR ˌdʌɪəˈθəːmənəs
AM ˌdaɪəˈθərmənəs

diathermic
BR ˌdʌɪəˈθəːmɪk
AM ˌdaɪəˈθərmɪk

diathermous
BR ˌdʌɪəˈθəːməs
AM ˌdaɪəˈθərməs

diathermy
BR ˈdʌɪə,θəːmi
AM ˈdaɪə,θərmi

diatheses
BR dʌɪˈaθɨsiːz
AM daɪˈæθəsiz

diathesis
BR dʌɪˈaθɨsɪs
AM daɪˈæθəsəs

diatom
BR ˈdʌɪətəm, ˈdʌɪətɒm, -z
AM ˈdaɪə,tɑm, -z

diatomaceous
BR ˌdʌɪətəˈmeɪʃəs
AM ˌdaɪədəˈmeɪʃəs

diatomic
BR ˌdʌɪəˈtɒmɪk
AM ˌdʌɪəˈtɑmɪk

diatomite
BR dʌɪˈatəmʌɪt
AM daɪˈædə,maɪt

diatonic
BR ˌdʌɪəˈtɒnɪk
AM ˌdaɪəˈtɑnɪk

diatonically
BR ˌdʌɪəˈtɒnɨkli
AM ˌdaɪəˈtɑnək(ə)li

diatribe
BR ˈdʌɪətrʌɪb, -z
AM ˈdaɪə,traɪb, -z

Díaz
BR ˈdiːas, ˈdiːaθ
AM ˈdi,æz, ˈdiəs

diazepam
BR dʌɪˈeɪzɨpam, dʌɪˈazɨpam
AM daɪˈæzə,pæm

diazo
BR dʌɪˈazəʊ, dʌɪˈeɪzəʊ, -z
AM daɪˈazoʊ, daɪˈeɪzoʊ, -z

diazotype
BR dʌɪˈazə(ʊ)tʌɪp, dʌɪˈeɪzə(ʊ)tʌɪp, -s
AM daɪˈazoʊ,taɪp, daɪˈeɪzoʊ,taɪp, -s

dib
BR dɪb, -z
AM dɪb, -z

dibasic
BR dʌɪˈbeɪsɪk
AM daɪˈbeɪsɪk

dibatag
BR ˈdɪbətag, -z
AM ˈdɪbə,tæg, -z

dibber
BR ˈdɪbə(r), -z
AM ˈdɪbər, -z

dibble
BR ˈdɪb|l, -lz, -l̩ɪŋ\-lɪŋ, -ld
AM ˈdɪb|əl, -əlz, -(ə)lɪŋ, -əld

dice
BR dʌɪs, -ɨz, -ɪŋ, -t
AM daɪs, -ɨz, -ɪŋ, -t

dicentra
BR dʌɪˈsɛntrə(r)
AM daɪˈsɛntrə

dicentric
BR dʌɪˈsɛntrɪk
AM daɪˈsɛntrɪk

dicer
BR ˈdʌɪsə(r), -z
AM ˈdaɪsər, -z

dicey
BR ˈdʌɪs|i, -ɪə(r), -ɪɪst
AM ˈdaɪsi, -ər, -ɨst

dichotic
BR dʌɪˈkɒtɪk, dɪˈkɒtɪk
AM daɪˈkɑdɪk

dichotomic
BR ˌdʌɪkəˈtɒmɪk
AM ˌdaɪkəˈtɑmɪk

dichotomise
BR dʌɪˈkɒtəmʌɪz, dɪˈkɒtəmʌɪz, -ɪz, -ɪŋ, -d
AM daɪˈkɑdəˌmaɪz, -ɪz, -ɪŋ, -d

dichotomize
BR dʌɪˈkɒtəmʌɪz, dɪˈkɒtəmʌɪz, -ɪz, -ɪŋ, -d
AM daɪˈkɑdəˌmaɪz, -ɪz, -ɪŋ, -d

dichotomous
BR dʌɪˈkɒtəməs, dɪˈkɒtəməs
AM daɪˈkɑdəməs

dichotomy
BR dʌɪˈkɒtəm|i, dɪˈkɒtəmi, -ɪz
AM daɪˈkɑdəmi, -z

dichroic
BR dʌɪˈkrəʊɪk
AM daɪˈkroʊɪk

dichroism
BR dʌɪˈkrəʊɪz(ə)m
AM daɪˈkroʊˌɪzəm

dichromate
BR dʌɪˈkrəʊmeɪt
AM daɪˈkroʊˌmeɪt

dichromatic
BR ˌdʌɪkrə(ʊ)ˈmatɪk
AM ˌdaɪkrəˈmædɪk, ˌdaɪkroʊˈmædɪk

dichromatism
BR dʌɪˈkrəʊmətɪz(ə)m
AM daɪˈkroʊməˌtɪzəm

dicily
BR ˈdʌɪsɪli
AM ˈdaɪsɪli

diciness
BR ˈdʌɪsɪnɪs
AM ˈdaɪsinɪs

dick
BR dɪk, -s
AM dɪk, -s

dickcissel
BR dɪkˈsɪsl, ˈdɪksɪsl, -z
AM dɪkˈsɪsəl

dicken
BR ˈdɪk(ɪ)n
AM ˈdɪkən

Dickens
BR ˈdɪkɪnz
AM ˈdɪkənz

Dickensian
BR dɪˈkɛnziən, -z
AM dəˈkɛnziən, -z

Dickensianly
BR dɪˈkɛnziənli
AM dəˈkɛnziənli

dicker
BR ˈdɪk|ə(r), -əz, -(ə)rɪŋ, -əd
AM ˈdɪk|ər, -ərz, -(ə)rɪŋ, -ərd

dickerer
BR ˈdɪk(ə)rə(r), -z
AM ˈdɪk(ə)rər, -z

Dickerson
BR ˈdɪkəs(ə)n
AM ˈdɪkərsən

dickey
BR ˈdɪk|i, -ɪz
AM ˈdɪki, -z

dickhead
BR ˈdɪkhɛd, -z
AM ˈdɪkˌ(h)ɛd, -z

Dickie
BR ˈdɪki
AM ˈdɪki

dickie
BR ˈdɪk|i, -ɪz
AM ˈdɪki, -z

Dickins
BR ˈdɪkɪnz
AM ˈdɪkɪnz

Dickinson
BR ˈdɪkɪns(ə)n
AM ˈdɪkənsən

Dickon
BR ˈdɪk(ə)n
AM ˈdɪkɪn

Dickson
BR ˈdɪksn
AM ˈdɪksən

Dicky
BR ˈdɪki
AM ˈdɪki

dicky
BR ˈdɪk|i, -ɪə(r), -ɪɪst
AM ˈdɪki, -ər, -ɪst

dickybird
BR ˈdɪkɪbəːd, -z
AM ˈdɪkiˌbərd, -z

dicot
BR ˈdʌɪkɒt, -s
AM ˈdaɪˌkɑt, -s

dicotyledon
BR ˌdʌɪkɒtɪˈliːdn, -z
AM ˌdaɪˌkɑdlˈidn, -z

dicotyledonous
BR ˌdʌɪkɒtɪˈliːdn̩əs, ˌdʌɪkɒtɪˈliːdənəs, dʌɪˌkɒtɪˈliːdn̩əs, dʌɪˌkɒtɪˈliːdənəs
AM ˌdaɪˌkɑdlˈidənəs

dicrotic
BR dʌɪˈkrɒtɪk
AM daɪˈkrɑdɪk

dicta
BR ˈdɪktə(*r*)
AM ˈdɪktə

dictaphone
BR ˈdɪktəfəʊn, -z
AM ˈdɪktəˌfoʊn, -z

dictate[1]
noun
BR ˈdɪkteɪt, -s
AM ˈdɪkˌteɪt, -s

dictate[2]
verb
BR dɪkˈteɪt, -s, -ɪŋ, -ɪd
AM ˈdɪkˌteɪ|t, -ts, -dɪŋ, -dɪd

dictation
BR dɪkˈteɪʃn
AM dɪkˈteɪʃən

dictator
BR dɪkˈteɪtə(r), -z
AM ˈdɪkˌteɪdər, -z

dictatorial
BR ˌdɪktəˈtɔːrɪəl
AM ˌdɪktəˈtɔriəl

dictatorially
BR ˌdɪktəˈtɔːrɪəli
AM ˌdɪktəˈtɔriəli

dictatorship
BR dɪkˈteɪtəʃɪp, -s
AM ˈdɪkteɪdərˌʃɪp, dɪkˈteɪdərˌʃɪp, -s

diction
BR ˈdɪkʃn
AM ˈdɪkʃən

dictionary
BR ˈdɪkʃn̩(ə)r|i, ˈdɪkʃən(ə)r|i, -ɪz
AM ˈdɪkʃəˌnɛri, -z

Dictograph®
BR ˈdɪktəgraf
AM ˈdɪktəˌgræf

dictum
BR ˈdɪktəm, -z
AM ˈdɪktəm, -z

dicty
BR ˈdɪkti
AM ˈdɪkti

Dictyoptera
BR ˌdɪktɪˈɒpt(ə)rə(*r*)
AM ˌdɪktiˈɑptərə

dictyopteran
BR ˌdɪktɪˈɒpt(ə)rən, -z
AM ˌdɪktiˈɑptərən, -z

dictyopterous
BR ˌdɪktɪˈɒpt(ə)rəs
AM ˌdɪktiˈɑptərəs

dicynodont
BR dʌɪˈsɪnədɒnt, -s
AM daɪˈsɪnəˌdɑnt, -s

did
BR dɪd
AM dɪd

didactic
BR dʌɪˈdaktɪk
AM dəˈdæktɪk, daɪˈdæktɪk

didactically
BR dʌɪˈdaktɪkli
AM dəˈdæktək(ə)li, daɪˈdæktək(ə)li

didacticism
BR dʌɪˈdaktɪsɪz(ə)m
AM dəˈdæktəˌsɪzəm, daɪˈdæktəˌsɪzəm

didakai
BR ˈdɪdəkʌɪ, -z
AM ˈdɪdəˌkaɪ, -z

Didcot
BR ˈdɪdkət, ˈdɪdkɒt
AM ˈdɪdkət

diddicoy
BR ˈdɪdɪkɔɪ, -z
AM ˈdɪdiˌkɔɪ, -z

diddle
BR ˈdɪd|l, -lz, -l̩ɪŋ\-lɪŋ, -ld
AM ˈdɪd|əl, -əlz, -(ə)lɪŋ, -əld

diddler
BR ˈdɪdl̩ə(r), ˈdɪdlə(r), -z
AM ˈdɪd(ə)lər, -z

diddly-squat
BR ˈdɪdlɪskwɒt, ˈdɪdl̩ɪskwɒt
AM ˈdɪdliˌskwɔt, ˈdɪdl̩iˌskwɔt, ˈdɪdliˌskwɑt, ˈdɪdl̩iˌskwɑt

diddums
BR ˈdɪdəmz
AM ˈdɪdəmz

diddy
BR ˈdɪdi
AM ˈdɪdi

Diderot
BR ˈdiːdərəʊ
AM ˌdidəˈroʊ

didgeridoo
BR ˌdɪdʒərɪˈduː, -z
AM ˌdɪdʒəriˈdu, -z

didicoi
BR ˈdɪdɪkɔɪ, -z
AM ˈdɪdiˌkɔɪ, -z

didicoy
BR ˈdɪdɪkɔɪ, -z
AM ˈdɪdiˌkɔɪ, -z

didn't
BR ˈdɪdnt
AM ˈdɪdn(t)

Dido
BR ˈdʌɪdəʊ
AM ˈdaɪˌdoʊ

dido
BR ˈdʌɪdəʊ, -z
AM ˈdaɪˌdoʊ, -z

didst
BR dɪdst
AM dɪdst

didy
BR ˈdʌɪd|i, -ɪz
AM ˈdaɪdi, -z

didymium
BR dɪˈdɪmɪəm
AM daɪˈdɪmiəm

die
BR dʌɪ, -z, -ɪŋ, -d
AM daɪ, -z, -ɪŋ, -d

dieback
BR ˈdʌɪbak
AM ˈdaɪˌbæk

dieffenbachia
BR ˌdiːf(ə)nˈbakɪə(*r*), -z
AM ˌdifənˈbɑkiə, ˈdifənˌbɑkiə, -z

Diego
BR dɪˈeɪgəʊ
AM diˈeɪgoʊ

diehard
BR ˈdʌɪhɑːd, -z

AM 'daɪˌhɑrd, -z

Diekirch
BR 'dʌɪkɑːk
AM 'daɪkərk
GER 'diːkɪrç

dieldrin
BR 'diːldr(ɪ)n
AM 'dɪldrən

dielectric
BR ˌdʌɪə'lɛktrɪk
AM ˌdaɪə'lɛktrɪk

dielectrically
BR ˌdʌɪə'lɛktrɪkli
AM ˌdaɪə'lɛktrək(ə)li

diene
BR 'dʌɪiːn
AM 'daɪˌin

Dieppe
BR dɪ'ɛp
AM di'ɛp

diereses
BR dʌɪ'ɪərɪsiːz, dʌɪ'ɛrɪsiːz
AM daɪ'ɛrəˌsiz

dieresis
BR dʌɪ'ɪərɪsɪs, dʌɪ'ɛrɪsɪs
AM daɪ'ɛrəsəs

diesel
BR 'diːzl, -z
AM 'dizəl, 'disəl, -z

dieselise
BR 'diːzl̩ʌɪz, -ɪz, -ɪŋ, -d
AM 'dizəˌlaɪz, 'disəˌlaɪz, -ɪz, -ɪŋ, -d

dieselize
BR 'diːzl̩ʌɪz, -ɪz, -ɪŋ, -d
AM 'dizəˌlaɪz, 'disəˌlaɪz, -ɪz, -ɪŋ, -d

Dies Irae
BR ˌdiːeɪz 'ɪəreɪ, + 'ɪərʌɪ
AM ˌdieɪs 'ɪreɪ

dies non
BR ˌdʌɪiːz 'nɒn
AM ˌdieɪs 'nɑn

diet
BR 'dʌɪət, -s, -ɪŋ, -ɪd
AM 'daɪə|t, -ts, -dɪŋ, -dəd

dietary
BR 'dʌɪət(ə)ri
AM 'daɪəˌtɛri

Dieter
BR 'diːtə(r)
AM 'didər

dieter
BR 'dʌɪətə(r), -z
AM 'daɪədər, -z

dietetic
BR ˌdʌɪə'tɛtɪk, -s
AM ˌdaɪə'tɛdɪk, -s

dietetically
BR ˌdʌɪə'tɛtɪkli
AM ˌdaɪə'tɛdək(ə)li

diethyl
BR dʌɪ'iːθ(ɪ)l, dʌɪ'ɛθ(ɪ)l
AM daɪ'ɛθəl

dietician
BR ˌdʌɪə'tɪʃn, -z
AM ˌdaɪə'tɪʃən, -z

dietitian
BR ˌdʌɪə'tɪʃn, -z
AM ˌdaɪə'tɪʃən, -z

Dietrich
BR 'diːtrɪk, 'diːtrɪx
AM 'ditrɪk

differ
BR 'dɪf|ə(r), -əz, -(ə)rɪŋ, -əd
AM 'dɪf|ər, -ərz, -(ə)rɪŋ, -ərd

difference
BR 'dɪf(ə)rəns, 'dɪf(ə)rn̩s, -ɪz
AM 'dɪf(ə)rəns, 'dɪfər(ə)ns, -əz

different
BR 'dɪf(ə)rənt, 'dɪf(ə)rn̩t
AM 'dɪf(ə)r(ə)nt, 'dɪfərnt

differentia
BR ˌdɪfə'rɛnʃ(ɪ)ə(*r*)
AM ˌdɪfə'rɛnʃ(i)ə

differentiae
BR ˌdɪfə'rɛnʃɪiː
AM ˌdɪfə'rɛnʃiˌi, ˌdɪfə'rɛnʃiˌaɪ

differential
BR ˌdɪfə'rɛnʃl, -z
AM ˌdɪfə'rɛn(t)ʃəl, -z

differentially
BR ˌdɪfə'rɛnʃl̩i, ˌdɪfə'rɛnʃəli
AM ˌdɪfə'rɛn(t)ʃəli

differentiate
BR ˌdɪfə'rɛnʃɪeɪt, -s, -ɪŋ, -ɪd
AM ˌdɪfə'rɛn(t)ʃiˌeɪ|t, -ts, -dɪŋ, -dɪd

differentiation
BR ˌdɪfərɛnʃɪ'eɪʃn
AM ˌdɪfəˌrɛn(t)ʃi'eɪʃən

differentiator
BR ˌdɪfə'rɛnʃɪeɪtə(r), -z
AM ˌdɪfə'rɛn(t)ʃiˌeɪdər, -z

differently
BR 'dɪf(ə)rn̩tli, 'dɪf(ə)rəntli
AM 'dɪf(ə)rən(t)li, 'dɪfərn̩(t)li

differentness
BR 'dɪf(ə)rn̩tnəs, 'dɪf(ə)rəntnəs
AM 'dɪf(ə)rən(t)nəs, 'dɪfərn̩(t)nəs

difficult
BR 'dɪfɪklt
AM 'dɪfəkəlt

difficultly
BR 'dɪfɪkltli
AM 'dɪfəkəltli

difficultness
BR 'dɪfɪkltnəs
AM 'dɪfəkəltnəs

difficulty
BR 'dɪfɪklt|i, -ɪz
AM 'dɪfəkəlti, -z

diffidence
BR 'dɪfɪd(ə)ns
AM 'dɪfəd(ə)ns

diffident
BR 'dɪfɪd(ə)nt
AM 'dɪfəd(ə)nt

diffidently
BR 'dɪfɪd(ə)ntli
AM 'dɪfəd(ə)n(t)li

diffract
BR dɪ'frakt, -s, -ɪŋ, -ɪd
AM də'fræk|(t), -(t)s, -tɪŋ, -təd

diffraction
BR dɪ'frakʃn
AM də'frækʃən

diffractive
BR dɪ'fraktɪv
AM də'fræktɪv

diffractively
BR dɪ'fraktɪvli
AM də'fræktəvli

diffractometer
BR ˌdɪfrak'tɒmɪtə(r), -z
AM ˌdɪfræk'tɑmədər, -z

diffuse[1]
adjective
BR dɪ'fjuːs
AM də'fjus

diffuse[2]
verb
BR dɪ'fjuːz, -ɪz, -ɪŋ, -d
AM də'fjuz, -əz, -ɪŋ, -d

diffusely
BR dɪ'fjuːsli
AM də'fjusli

diffuseness
BR dɪ'fjuːsnəs
AM də'fjusnəs

diffuser
BR dɪ'fjuːzə(r), -z
AM də'fjuzər, -z

diffusible
BR dɪ'fjuːsɪbl
AM də'fjuzəbəl

diffusion
BR dɪ'fjuːʒn
AM də'fjuʒən

diffusionist
BR dɪ'fjuːʒn̩ɪst, dɪ'fjuːʒənɪst, -s
AM də'fjuʒənəst, -s

diffusive
BR dɪ'fjuːsɪv
AM də'fjusɪv

diffusively
BR dɪ'fjuːsɪvli
AM də'fjusəvli

diffusiveness
BR dɪ'fjuːsɪvnɪs
AM də'fjusɪvnɪs

diffusivity
BR ˌdɪfjuː'sɪvɪti, ˌdɪfjʊ'sɪvɪti
AM ˌdɪfju'sɪvɪdi

dig
BR dɪg, -z, -ɪŋ
AM dɪg, -z, -ɪŋ

Digambara
BR diː'gʌmb(ə)rə(*r*), -z
AM dɪ'gɑmbərə, -z

digamist
BR 'dɪgəmɪst, -s
AM 'dɪgəməst, -s

digamma
BR 'dʌɪˌgamə(*r*), dʌɪ'gamə(*r*), -z
AM ˈdaɪˌgæmə, -z

digamous
BR 'dɪgəməs
AM 'dɪgəməs

digamy
BR 'dɪgəm|i, -ɪz
AM 'dɪgəmi, -z

digastric
BR dʌɪ'gastrɪk
AM daɪ'gæstrɪk

Digbeth
BR 'dɪgbəθ
AM 'dɪgbəθ

Digby
BR 'dɪgbi
AM 'dɪgbi

digest[1]
noun
BR 'dʌɪdʒɛst, -s
AM 'daɪˌdʒɛst, -s

digest[2]
verb
BR dʌɪ'dʒɛst, dɪ'dʒɛst, -s, -ɪŋ, -ɪd
AM daɪ'dʒɛst, də'dʒɛst, -s, -ɪŋ, -əd

digester
BR dʌɪ'dʒɛstə(r), dɪ'dʒɛstə(r), -z
AM daɪ'dʒɛstər, də'dʒɛstər, -z

digestibility
BR dʌɪˌdʒɛstɪ'bɪlɪti, dɪˌdʒɛstɪ'bɪlɪti
AM dəˌdʒɛstə'bɪlɪdi, daɪˌdʒɛstə'bɪlɪdi

digestible
BR dʌɪ'dʒɛstɪbl, dɪ'dʒɛstɪbl
AM də'dʒɛstəbəl, daɪ'dʒɛstəbəl

digestion
BR dʌɪ'dʒɛstʃ(ə)n, dɪ'dʒɛstʃ(ə)n, -z
AM də'dʒɛstʃən, daɪ'dʒɛstʃən, -z

digestive
BR dʌɪ'dʒɛstɪv, dɪ'dʒɛstɪv
AM də'dʒɛstɪv, daɪ'dʒɛstɪv, -z

digestively
BR dʌɪ'dʒɛstɨvli, dɪ'dʒɛstɨvli
AM də'dʒɛstəvli, daɪ'dʒɛstəvli

digger
BR 'dɪɡə(r), -z
AM 'dɪɡər, -z

digging
BR 'dɪɡɪŋ, -z
AM 'dɪɡɪŋ, -z

dight
BR dʌɪt
AM daɪt

digit
BR 'dɪdʒɪt, -s
AM 'dɪdʒɨt, -s

digital
BR 'dɪdʒɨtl, -z
AM 'dɪdʒɨdl, -z

digitalin
BR ˌdɪdʒɪ'teɪlɪn
AM ˌdɪdʒɪ'tælən

digitalis
BR ˌdɪdʒɪ'teɪlɪs
AM ˌdɪdʒɪ'tæləs

digitalise
BR 'dɪdʒɨtl̩ʌɪz, 'dɪdʒɨtəlʌɪz, -ɨz, -ɪŋ, -d
AM 'dɪdʒɨdlˌaɪz, -ɨz, -ɪŋ, -d

digitalize
BR 'dɪdʒɨtl̩ʌɪz, 'dɪdʒɨtəlʌɪz, -ɨz, -ɪŋ, -d
AM 'dɪdʒɨdlˌaɪz, -ɨz, -ɪŋ, -d

digitally
BR 'dɪdʒɨtl̩i, 'dɪdʒɨtəli
AM 'dɪdʒɨdl̩i

digitate
BR 'dɪdʒɨteɪt, -s, -ɪŋ, -ɨd
AM 'dɪdʒɨˌteɪ|t, -ts, -dɪŋ, -dɨd

digitately
BR 'dɪdʒɨtətli
AM 'dɪdʒɨˌteɪtli

digitation
BR ˌdɪdʒɪ'teɪʃn
AM ˌdɪdʒɪ'teɪʃən

digitigrade
BR 'dɪdʒɨtɪɡreɪd, -z
AM 'dɪdʒɨdəˌɡreɪd, -z

digitisation
BR ˌdɪdʒɨtʌɪ'zeɪʃn
AM ˌdɪdʒədə'zeɪʃən, ˌdɪdʒəˌtaɪ'zeɪʃən

digitise
BR 'dɪdʒɨtʌɪz, -ɨz, -ɪŋ, -d
AM 'dɪdʒəˌtaɪz, -ɨz, -ɪŋ, -d

digitization
BR ˌdɪdʒɨtʌɪ'zeɪʃn
AM ˌdɪdʒədə'zeɪʃən, ˌdɪdʒəˌtaɪ'zeɪʃən

digitize
BR 'dɪdʒɨtʌɪz, -ɨz, -ɪŋ, -d
AM 'dɪdʒəˌtaɪz, -ɨz, -ɪŋ, -d

diglossia
BR dʌɪ'ɡlɒsɪə(r)
AM daɪ'ɡlɔsiə, daɪ'ɡlɑsiə

diglossic
BR dʌɪ'ɡlɒsɪk
AM daɪ'ɡlɔsɪk, daɪ'ɡlɑsɪk

dignified
BR 'dɪɡnɨfʌɪd
AM 'dɪɡnəˌfaɪd

dignifiedly
BR 'dɪɡnɨfʌɪdli
AM 'dɪɡnəˌfaɪ(ə)dli

dignify
BR 'dɪɡnɨfʌɪ, -z, -ɪŋ, -d
AM 'dɪɡnəˌfaɪ, -z, -ɪŋ, -d

dignitary
BR 'dɪɡnɨt(ə)r|i, -ɪz
AM 'dɪɡnəˌtɛri, -z

dignity
BR 'dɪɡnɨt|i, -ɪz
AM 'dɪɡnɨdi, -z

digraph
BR 'dʌɪɡrɑːf, 'dʌɪɡraf, -s
AM 'daɪˌɡræf, -s

digraphic
BR dʌɪ'ɡrafɪk
AM daɪ'ɡræfɪk

digress
BR dʌɪ'ɡrɛs, -ɨz, -ɪŋ, -t
AM daɪ'ɡrɛs, -əz, -ɪŋ, -t

digresser
BR dʌɪ'ɡrɛsə(r), -z
AM daɪ'ɡrɛsər, -z

digression
BR dʌɪ'ɡrɛʃn, -z
AM daɪ'ɡrɛʃən, -z

digressive
BR dʌɪ'ɡrɛsɪv
AM daɪ'ɡrɛsɪv

digressively
BR dʌɪ'ɡrɛsɨvli
AM daɪ'ɡrɛsəvli

digressiveness
BR dʌɪ'ɡrɛsɪvnɨs
AM daɪ'ɡrɛsɪvnɨs

dihedral
BR dʌɪ'hiːdr(ə)l
AM daɪ'hidrəl

dihydric
BR dʌɪ'hʌɪdrɪk
AM daɪ'hidrɪk

Dijon
BR 'diːʒɒ̃
AM di'ʒɑn

dik-dik
BR 'dɪkdɪk, -s
AM 'dɪkˌdɪk, -s

dike
BR dʌɪk, -s, -ɪŋ, -t
AM daɪk, -s, -ɪŋ, -t

diktat
BR 'dɪktat
AM dɪk'tɑt, 'dɪktɑt

dilapidate
BR dɪ'lapɨdeɪt, -s, -ɪŋ, -ɨd
AM də'læpəˌdeɪ|t, -ts, -dɪŋ, -dɨd

dilapidation
BR dɨˌlapɪ'deɪʃn, -z
AM dəˌlæpə'deɪʃən, -z

dilatable
BR dʌɪ'leɪtəbl, dɪ'leɪtəbl
AM 'daɪˌleɪdəbəl, daɪ'leɪdəbəl, də'leɪdəbəl

dilatation
BR ˌdʌɪleɪ'teɪʃn, ˌdʌɪlə'teɪʃn, ˌdɪlə'teɪʃn
AM ˌdɪlə'teɪʃən, ˌdaɪlə'teɪʃən

dilate
BR dʌɪ'leɪt, dɪ'leɪt, -s, -ɪŋ, -ɨd
AM 'daɪˌleɪ|t, daɪ'leɪ|t, də'leɪ|t, -ts, -dɪŋ, -dɨd

dilation
BR dʌɪ'leɪʃn, dɪ'leɪʃn
AM daɪ'leɪʃən, də'leɪʃən

dilator
BR dʌɪ'leɪtə(r), dɪ'leɪtə(r), -z
AM 'daɪˌleɪdər, daɪ'leɪdər, də'leɪdər, -z

dilatorily
BR 'dɪlət(ə)rɨli
AM ˌdɪlə'tɔrəli

dilatoriness
BR 'dɪlət(ə)rɪnɨs
AM 'dɪləˌtɔrinɨs

dilatory
BR 'dɪlət(ə)ri
AM 'dɪləˌtɔri

dildo
BR 'dɪldəʊ, -z
AM 'dɪlˌdoʊ, -z

dildoe
BR 'dɪldəʊ, -z
AM 'dɪlˌdoʊ, -z

dilemma
BR dɪ'lɛmə(r), -z
AM də'lɛmə, daɪ'lɛmə, -z

dilettante
BR ˌdɪlɪ'tant|i, -ɪz
AM 'dɪləˌtɑnt, -s

dilettanti
BR ˌdɪlɪ'tanti
AM ˌdɪlə'tɑn(t)i

dilettantism
BR ˌdɪlɪ'tantɪz(ə)m
AM 'dɪləˌtɑn(t)izəm

Dili
BR 'dɪli
AM 'dɪli

diligence
BR 'dɪlɨdʒ(ə)ns
AM 'dɪlədʒəns

diligent
BR 'dɪlɨdʒ(ə)nt
AM 'dɪlədʒənt

diligently
BR 'dɪlɨdʒ(ə)ntli
AM 'dɪlədʒən(t)li

Dilke
BR dɪlk
AM 'dɪlk(ə)

dill
BR dɪl
AM dɪl

Dillard
BR 'dɪlɑːd
AM 'dɪlərd

Dillon
BR 'dɪlən
AM 'dɪlɨn

Dillwyn
BR 'dɪlwɪn
AM 'dɪlwɨn

dilly
BR 'dɪl|i, -ɪz
AM 'dɪli, -z

dillybag
BR 'dɪlɪbaɡ, -z
AM 'dɪliˌbæɡ, -z

dilly-dally
BR ˌdɪlɪ'dal|i, 'dɪlɪˌdal|i, -ɪz, -ɪɪŋ, -ɪd
AM 'dɪliˌdæli, -z, -ɪŋ, -d

diluent
BR 'dɪljʊənt, -s
AM 'dɪljəwənt, -s

dilute
BR dʌɪ'l(j)uːt, dɪ'l(j)uːt, -s, -ɪŋ, -ɨd
AM də'lu|t, daɪ'lu|t, -ts, -dɪŋ, -dəd

dilutee
BR ˌdʌɪl(j)uː'tiː, -z
AM dəˌlu'ti, daɪ'lu'ti, -z

diluter
BR dʌɪ'l(j)uːtə(r), dɪ'l(j)uːtə(r), -z
AM də'ludər, daɪ'ludər, -z

dilution
BR dʌɪ'l(j)uːʃn, dɪ'l(j)uːʃn, -z
AM də'luʃən, daɪ'luʃn, -z

diluvia
BR dʌɪ'l(j)uːvɪə(r), dɪ'l(j)uːvɪə(r)
AM də'luviə

diluvial
BR dʌɪ'l(j)uːvɪəl, dɪ'l(j)uːvɪəl
AM də'luviəl

diluvialist
BR dʌɪ'l(j)uːvɪəlɪst, dɪ'l(j)uːvɪəlɪst, -s
AM də'luviələst, -s

diluvian
BR dʌɪ'l(j)uːvɪən, dɪ'l(j)uːvɪən
AM də'luviən

diluvium
BR dʌɪ'l(j)uːvɪəm, dɪ'l(j)uːvɪəm
AM də'luviəm

Dilwyn
BR 'dɪlwɪn
AM 'dɪlwɪn

Dilys
BR 'dɪlɪs
AM 'dɪlɨs

dim
BR dɪm, -z, -ɪŋ, -d, -ə(r), -əst
AM dɪm, -z, -ɪŋ, -d, -ər, -ɨst

DiMaggio
BR dɪ'madʒɪəʊ
AM di'mædʒioʊ

Dimbleby
BR 'dɪmblbi
AM 'dɪmbəlbi

dime
BR dʌɪm, -z
AM daɪm, -z

dimension
BR dʌɪ'mɛnʃn, dɪ'mɛnʃn, -z
AM də'mɛn(t)ʃən, -z

dimensional
BR dʌɪ'mɛnʃn̩(ə)l, dʌɪ'mɛnʃən(ə)l, dɪ'mɛnʃn̩(ə)l, dɪ'mɛnʃən(ə)l
AM də'mɛn(t)ʃ(ə)nəl

dimensionality
BR dʌɪˌmɛnʃə'nalɨti, dɪˌmɛnʃə'nalɨti
AM dəˌmɛn(t)ʃə'nælədi, dəˌmɛn(t)ʃn'ælədi, daɪˌmɛn(t)ʃə'nælədi, daɪˌmɛn(t)ʃn'ælədi

dimensionally
BR dʌɪ'mɛnʃn̩əli, dʌɪ'mɛnʃn̩l̩i, dʌɪ'mɛnʃənl̩i, dʌɪ'mɛnʃ(ə)nəli, dɪ'mɛnʃn̩əli, dɪ'mɛnʃn̩l̩i, dɪ'mɛnʃənl̩i, dɪ'mɛnʃ(ə)nəli
AM də'mɛn(t)ʃ(ə)nəli

dimensionless
BR dʌɪ'mɛnʃnləs, dʌɪ'mɛnʃənləs, dɪ'mɛnʃnləs, dɪ'mɛnʃənləs
AM də'mɛn(t)ʃənləs

dimer
BR 'dʌɪmə(r), -z
AM 'daɪmər, -z

dimeric
BR dʌɪ'mɛrɪk
AM daɪ'mɛrɪk

dimerous
BR 'dɪm(ə)rəs
AM 'dɪm(ə)rəs

dimeter
BR 'dɪmɨtə(r), -z
AM 'dɪmədər, -z

dimidiate
BR dɪ'mɪdɪət
AM də'mɪdiˌeɪt

diminish
BR dɪ'mɪn|ɪʃ, -ɨʃɨz, -ɨʃɪŋ, -ɪʃt
AM də'mɪnɪʃ, -ɨs, -ɪŋ, -t

diminishable
BR dɪ'mɪnɨʃəbl
AM də'mɪnəʃəbəl

diminuendo
BR dɪˌmɪnjʊ'ɛndəʊ, -z
AM dəˌmɪn(j)ə'wɛndoʊ, -z

diminution
BR ˌdɪmɪ'njuːʃn, -z
AM ˌdɪmə'n(j)uʃən, -z

diminutival
BR dɪˌmɪnjʉ'tʌɪvl
AM dəˌmɪnjə'taɪvəl

diminutive
BR dɪ'mɪnjʉtɪv
AM də'mɪnjədɪv

diminutively
BR dɪ'mɪnjʉtɨvli
AM də'mɪnjədəvli

diminutiveness
BR dɪ'mɪnjʉtɨvnɨs
AM də'mɪnjədɪvnɨs

dimissory
BR 'dɪmɨs(ə)ri
AM 'dɪməˌsɔri

dimity
BR 'dɪmɨti
AM 'dɪmɨdi

dimly
BR 'dɪmli
AM 'dɪmli

dimmer
BR 'dɪmə(r), -z
AM 'dɪmər, -z

dimmish
BR 'dɪmɪʃ
AM 'dɪmɪʃ

Dimmock
BR 'dɪmək
AM 'dɪmək

dimness
BR 'dɪmnɨs
AM 'dɪmnɨs

dimorphic
BR dʌɪ'mɔːfɪk
AM daɪ'mɔrfɪk

dimorphism
BR dʌɪ'mɔːfɪz(ə)m
AM daɪ'mɔrfɪzəm

dimorphous
BR dʌɪ'mɔːfəs
AM daɪ'mɔrfəs

dimple
BR 'dɪmpl, -z
AM 'dɪmpəl, -z

Dimplex®
BR 'dɪmplɛks
AM 'dɪmˌplɛks

dimply
BR 'dɪmpl̩|i, 'dɪmpl|i, -ɪə(r), -ɪɨst
AM 'dɪmpli, -ər, -ɨst

Dimpna
BR 'dɪmpnə(*r*)
AM 'dɪm(p)nə

dim sum
BR ˌdɪm 'sʌm, + 'sʊm
AM ˌdɪm 'səm

dimwit
BR 'dɪmwɪt, -s
AM 'dɪmˌwɪt, -s

DIN
BR dɪn
AM dɪn, ˌdiˌaɪ'ɛn

din
BR dɪn, -z, -ɪŋ, -d
AM dɪn, -z, -ɪŋ, -d

Dinah
BR 'dʌɪnə(*r*)
AM 'daɪnə

dinar
BR 'diːnɑː(r), -z
AM 'diˌnɑr, də'nɑr, di'nɑr, -z

Dinaric
BR dɨˌnarɪk
AM də'nɛrɪk

Dinas
BR 'diːnas
AM 'dinɨs

dine
BR dʌɪn, -z, -ɪŋ, -d
AM daɪn, -z, -ɪŋ, -d

Dineen
BR dɪ'niːn
AM dɪ'nin

diner
BR 'dʌɪnə(r), -z
AM 'daɪnər, -z

dinero
BR dɪ'nɛːrəʊ
AM də'nɛroʊ

dinette
BR dʌɪ'nɛt, -s
AM daɪ'nɛt, -s

ding
BR dɪŋ, -z, -ɪŋ, -d
AM dɪŋ, -z, -ɪŋ, -d

Dingaan
BR 'dɪŋgɑːn
AM 'dɪŋgɪn

dingaling
BR ˌdɪŋə'lɪŋ, 'dɪŋəlɪŋ, -z
AM 'dɪŋəˌlɪŋ, -z

Ding an sich
BR ˌdɪŋ an 'zɪk, + 'zɪx
AM ˌdɪŋ ˌɑn'sɪk

dingbat
BR 'dɪŋbat, -s
AM 'dɪŋˌbæt, -s

dingdong
BR 'dɪŋdɒŋ, ˌdɪŋ'dɒŋ, -z
AM 'dɪŋˌdɔŋ, 'dɪŋˌdɑŋ, -z

dinge
BR dɪn(d)ʒ, -ɨz
AM dɪn(d)ʒ, -ɨz

dinghy
BR 'dɪŋ(g)|i, -ɪz
AM 'dɪŋi, -z

dingily
BR 'dɪn(d)ʒɨli
AM 'dɪndʒɨli

dinginess
BR 'dɪn(d)ʒɪnɨs
AM 'dɪndʒinɨs

dingle
BR 'dɪŋgl, -z
AM 'dɪŋgəl, -z

Dingley
BR 'dɪŋli
AM 'dɪŋli

dingo
BR 'dɪŋgəʊ, -z
AM 'dɪŋgoʊ, -z

dingus
BR 'dɪŋgəs, -ɨz
AM 'dɪŋgəs, -əz

Dingwall
BR 'dɪŋwɔːl, 'dɪŋw(ə)l
AM 'dɪŋˌwɔl, 'dɪŋwəl, 'dɪŋˌwɑl

dingy
BR 'dɪn(d)ʒ|i, -ɪə(r), -ɪɨst
AM 'dɪndʒi, -ər, -ɨst

dink
BR dɪŋk
AM dɪŋk

dinkily
BR 'dɪŋkɨli
AM 'dɪŋkɨli

dinkiness
BR 'dɪŋkɪnɨs
AM 'dɪŋkinɨs

dinkum
BR 'dɪŋkəm
AM 'dɪŋkəm

dinky
BR 'dɪŋk|i, -ɪə(r), -ɪɨst
AM 'dɪŋki, -ər, -ɨst

dinner
BR 'dɪnə(r), -z
AM 'dɪnər, -z

dinnertime
BR 'dɪnətʌɪm, -z
AM 'dɪnərˌtaɪm, -z

dinnerware
BR 'dɪnəwɛː(r)
AM 'dɪnərˌwɛ(ə)r

Dinorwic
BR dɪ'nɔːwɪk
AM 'dɪnərˌwɪk

WE dɪn'ɒrwɪg
dinosaur
BR 'dʌɪnəsɔː(r), -z
AM 'daɪnə,sɔ(ə)r, -z
dinosaurian
BR ,dʌɪnə'sɔːrɪən
AM ,daɪnə'sɔriən
dinothere
BR 'dʌɪnə(ʊ)θɪə(r), -z
AM 'daɪnə,θɪ(ə)r, -z
dint
BR dɪnt, -s
AM dɪnt, -s
Dinwiddie
BR dɪn'wɪdi, 'dɪnwɪdi
AM 'dɪn,wɪdi
Dinwiddy
BR dɪn'wɪdi, 'dɪnwɪdi
AM 'dɪn,wɪdi
diocesan
BR dʌɪ'ɒsɪs(ə)n, dʌɪ'ɒsɪz(ə)n
AM daɪ'ɑsəsən
diocese
BR 'dʌɪəsɪs, 'dʌɪəsiːz, -ɪz
AM 'daɪə,siz, 'daɪəsəs, -ɪz
Diocletian
BR ,dʌɪə'kliːʃn
AM ,daɪə'kliʃən
diode
BR 'dʌɪəʊd, -z
AM 'daɪ,oʊd, -z
dioecious
BR dʌɪ'iːʃəs
AM daɪ'iʃəs
dioeciously
BR dʌɪ'iːʃəsli
AM daɪ'iʃəsli
Diogenes
BR dʌɪ'ɒdʒɪniːz
AM daɪ'ɑdʒəniz
diol
BR 'dʌɪɒl, -z
AM 'daɪ,ɔl, 'daɪ,ɑl, -z
Diomede
BR 'dʌɪəmiːd
AM 'daɪə,mid
Diomedes
BR ,dʌɪə'miːdiːz
AM ,daɪə'midiz
Dione
BR 'dʌɪəʊn, dʌɪ'əʊni
AM 'daɪ,oʊn
Dionysiac
BR ,dʌɪə'nɪzɪak, ,dʌɪə'nɪsɪak
AM ,daɪə'nɪsi,æk, ,daɪə'nɪzi,æk
Dionysian
BR ,dʌɪə'nɪzɪən, ,dʌɪə'nɪsɪən, ,dʌɪə'nʌɪsɪən
AM ,daɪə'nɪsiən, ,daɪə'nɪziən, ,daɪə'nɪʒ(i)ən
Dionysius
BR ,dʌɪə'nɪzɪəs, ,dʌɪə'nɪsɪəs
AM ,daɪə'nɪsiəs, ,daɪə'nɪziəs
Dionysus
BR ,dʌɪə'nʌɪsəs
AM ,daɪə'naɪsəs
Diophantine
BR ,dʌɪə(ʊ)'fantʌɪn
AM ,daɪə'fæn,taɪn
Diophantus
BR ,dʌɪə(ʊ)'fantəs
AM ,daɪə'fæn(t)əs
diopside
BR dʌɪ'ɒpsʌɪd
AM daɪ'ɑp,saɪd
diopter
BR dʌɪ'ɒptə(r), 'dʌɪɒptə(r), -z
AM ¦daɪ¦ɑptər, -z
dioptre
BR dʌɪ'ɒptə(r), 'dʌɪɒptə(r), -z
AM ¦daɪ¦ɑptər, -z
dioptric
BR dʌɪ'ɒptrɪk, -s
AM daɪ'ɑptrɪk, -s
Dior
BR 'diːɔː(r), dɪ'ɔː(r)
AM di'ɔ(ə)r
diorama
BR ,dʌɪə'rɑːmə(*r*), -z
AM ,daɪə'ræmə, ,daɪə'rɑmə, -z
dioramic
BR ,dʌɪə'ramɪk
AM ,daɪə'ræmɪk, ,daɪə'rɑmɪk
diorite
BR 'dʌɪərʌɪt
AM 'daɪə,raɪt
dioritic
BR ,dʌɪə'rɪtɪk
AM ,daɪə'rɪdɪk, ,daɪə'rɪdɪk
Dioscuri
BR dʌɪ'ɒskjʊri, dʌɪ'ɒskjʊrʌɪ, ,dʌɪə'skjʊəri, ,dʌɪə'skjʊərʌɪ
AM ,daɪə'sk(j)ʊri
diotic
BR dʌɪ'ɒtɪk, dʌɪ'əʊtɪk
AM daɪ'oʊdɪk, daɪ'ɑdɪk
dioxan
BR dʌɪ'ɒks(ə)n
AM daɪ'ɑksən
dioxane
BR dʌɪ'ɒkseɪn
AM daɪ'ɑk,seɪn
dioxide
BR dʌɪ'ɒksʌɪd, -z
AM daɪ'ɑk,saɪd, -z
dioxin
BR dʌɪ'ɒksɪn
AM daɪ'ɑksən
DIP
BR dɪp
AM dɪp
dip
BR dɪp, -s, -ɪŋ, -t
AM dɪp, -s, -ɪŋ, -t
Dip. Ed.
Diploma in Education
BR ,dɪp 'ɛd
AM ,dɪp 'ɛd
dipeptide
BR dʌɪ'pɛptʌɪd, -z
AM daɪ'pɛp,taɪd, -z
diphone
BR 'dʌɪfəʊn, -z
AM 'daɪ,foʊn, -z
diphtheria
BR dɪp'θɪərɪə(*r*), dɪf'θɪərɪə(*r*)
AM dɪp'θɪriə, dɪf'θɪriə
diphtherial
BR dɪp'θɪərɪəl, dɪf'θɪərɪəl
AM dɪp'θɪriəl, dɪf'θɪriəl
diphtheric
BR dɪf'θɛrɪk, dɪp'θɛrɪk
AM dɪp'θɪrɪk, dɪf'θɪrɪk
diphtheritic
BR ,dɪfθə'rɪtɪk, ,dɪpθə'rɪtɪk
AM ,dɪpθə'rɪdɪk, ,dɪfθə'rɪdɪk
diphtheroid
BR 'dɪfθərɔɪd, 'dɪpθərɔɪd
AM 'dɪpθə,rɔɪd, 'dɪfθə,rɔɪd
diphthong
BR 'dɪfθɒŋ, 'dɪpθɒŋ, -z
AM 'dɪp,θɔŋ, 'dɪf,θɔŋ, 'dɪp,θɑŋ, 'dɪf,θɑŋ, -z
diphthongal
BR dɪf'θɒŋgl, dɪp'θɒŋgl
AM dɪp'θɔŋ(g)əl, dɪf'θɔŋ(g)əl, dɪp'θɑŋ(g)əl, dɪf'θɑŋ(g)əl
diphthongally
BR dɪf'θɒŋgḷi, dɪf'θɒŋgəli, dɪp'θɒŋgḷi, dɪp'θɒŋgəli
AM dɪp'θɔŋ(g)əli, dɪf'θɔŋ(g)əli, dɪp'θɑŋ(g)əli, dɪf'θɑŋ(g)əli
diphthongisation
BR ,dɪfθɒŋgʌɪ'zeɪʃn, ,dɪpθɒŋgʌɪ'zeɪʃn
AM ,dɪpθɔŋ,(g)ə'zeɪʃən, ,dɪpθɔŋ,(g)aɪ'zeɪʃən, ,dɪfθɔŋ,(g)ə'zeɪʃən, ,dɪfθɔŋ,(g)aɪ'zeɪʃən, ,dɪpθɑŋ,(g)ə'zeɪʃən, ,dɪpθɑŋ,(g)aɪ'zeɪʃən, ,dɪfθɑŋ,(g)ə'zeɪʃən, ,dɪfθɑŋ,(g)aɪ'zeɪʃən
diphthongise
BR 'dɪfθɒŋgʌɪz, 'dɪpθɒŋgʌɪz, -ɪz, -ɪŋ, -d
AM 'dɪpθɔŋ,(g)aɪz, 'dɪfθɔŋ,(g)aɪz, 'dɪpθɑŋ,(g)aɪz, 'dɪfθɑŋ,(g)aɪz, -ɪz, -ɪŋ, -d
diphthongization
BR ,dɪfθɒŋgʌɪ'zeɪʃn, ,dɪpθɒŋgʌɪ'zeɪʃn
AM ,dɪpθɔŋ,(g)ə'zeɪʃən, ,dɪpθɔŋ,(g)aɪ'zeɪʃən, ,dɪfθɔŋ,(g)ə'zeɪʃən, ,dɪfθɔŋ,(g)aɪ'zeɪʃən, ,dɪpθɑŋ,(g)ə'zeɪʃən, ,dɪpθɑŋ,(g)aɪ'zeɪʃən, ,dɪfθɑŋ,(g)ə'zeɪʃən, ,dɪfθɑŋ,(g)aɪ'zeɪʃən
diphthongize
BR 'dɪfθɒŋgʌɪz, 'dɪpθɒŋgʌɪz, -ɪz, -ɪŋ, -d
AM 'dɪpθɔŋ,(g)aɪz, 'dɪfθɔŋ,(g)aɪz, 'dɪpθɑŋ,(g)aɪz, 'dɪfθɑŋ,(g)aɪz, -ɪz, -ɪŋ, -d
diphycercal
BR ,dɪfɪ'səːkl
AM ,dɪfɪ'sərkəl
Diplock
BR 'dɪplɒk
AM 'dɪp,lɑk
diplococci
BR ,dɪplə(ʊ)'kɒk(s)ʌɪ, ,dɪplə(ʊ)'kɒk(s)iː
AM ,dɪploʊ'kɑ,kaɪ, ,dɪploʊ'kɑki, ,dɪploʊ'kɑsaɪ, ,dɪploʊ'kɑksi
diplococcus
BR ,dɪplə(ʊ)'kɒkəs
AM ,dɪploʊ'kɑkəs
diplodoci
BR dɪ'plɒdəkʌɪ, ,dɪplə(ʊ)'dəʊkʌɪ
AM də'plɑdə,kaɪ
diplodocus
BR dɪ'plɒdəkəs, ,dɪplə(ʊ)'dəʊkəs, -ɪz
AM də'plɑdəkəs, -əz
diploid
BR 'dɪplɔɪd, -z
AM 'dɪplɔɪd, -z
diploidy
BR 'dɪplɔɪdi
AM 'dɪplɔɪdi
diploma
BR dɪ'pləʊmə(*r*), -z, -d
AM də'ploʊmə, -z, -d
diplomacy
BR dɪ'pləʊməsi
AM də'ploʊməsi
diplomat
BR 'dɪpləmat, -s
AM 'dɪplə,mæt, -s

diplomate
BR ˈdɪpləmeɪt, -s
AM ˈdɪpləˌmeɪt, -s

diplomatic
BR ˌdɪpləˈmatɪk
AM ˌdɪpləˈmædɪk

diplomatically
BR ˌdɪpləˈmatɨkli
AM ˌdɪpləˈmædək(ə)li

diplomatise
BR dɪˈpləʊmətʌɪz, -ɨz, -ɪŋ, -d
AM ˈdɪpləməˌtaɪz, -ɨz, -ɪŋ, -d

diplomatist
BR dɪˈpləʊmətɪst, -s
AM dəˈploʊmədəst, -s

diplomatize
BR dɪˈpləʊmətʌɪz, -ɨz, -ɪŋ, -d
AM ˈdɪpləməˌtaɪz, -ɨz, -ɪŋ, -d

diplont
BR ˈdɪplɒnt, -s
AM ˈdɪˌplɑnt, -s

Diplopoda
BR ˌdɪpləˈpəʊdə(r)
AM ˌdɪpləˈpoʊdə

diplotene
BR ˈdɪplə(ʊ)tiːn, -z
AM ˈdɪploʊˌtin, -z

dipolar
BR dʌɪˈpəʊlə(r)
AM daɪˈpoʊlər

dipole
BR ˈdʌɪpəʊl, -z
AM ˈdaɪˌpoʊl, -z

dipper
BR ˈdɪpə(r), -z
AM ˈdɪpər, -z

dippy
BR ˈdɪp|i, -ɪə(r), -ɪɪst
AM ˈdɪpi, -ər, -ɨst

dipso
BR ˈdɪpsəʊ, -z
AM ˈdɪpsoʊ, -z

dipsomania
BR ˌdɪpsə(ʊ)ˈmeɪnɪə(r)
AM ˌdɪpsəˈmeɪniə, ˌdɪpsoʊˈmeɪniə

dipsomaniac
BR ˌdɪpsə(ʊ)ˈmeɪnɪak, -s
AM ˌdɪpsəˈmeɪniˌæk, ˌdɪpsoʊˈmeɪniˌæk, -s

dipstick
BR ˈdɪpstɪk, -s
AM ˈdɪpˌstɪk, -s

dipswitch
BR ˈdɪpswɪtʃ, -ɨz
AM ˈdɪpˌswɪtʃ, -ɨz

Diptera
BR ˈdɪpt(ə)rə(r)
AM ˈdɪpt(ə)rə

dipteral
BR ˈdɪpt(ə)rəl, ˈdɪpt(ə)rl̩
AM ˈdɪpt(ə)rəl

dipteran
BR ˈdɪptərən, ˈdɪptərn̩, ˈdɪptr(ə)n, -z
AM ˈdɪpt(ə)rən, -z

dipterist
BR ˈdɪpt(ə)rɪst, -s
AM ˈdɪpt(ə)rəst, -s

dipterous
BR ˈdɪpt(ə)rəs
AM ˈdɪpt(ə)rəs

diptych
BR ˈdɪptɪk, -s
AM ˈdɪptɪk, -s

Dirac
BR dɪˈrak
AM dəˈrɑk

dire
BR ˈdʌɪə(r), -ɨst
AM ˈdaɪ(ə)r, -ɨst

direct
BR dɪˈrɛkt, dʌɪˈrɛkt, -s, -ɪŋ, -ɨd
AM dəˈrɛk|(t), daɪˈrɛk|(t), -(t)s, -tɪŋ, -təd

direction
BR dɪˈrɛkʃn, dʌɪˈrɛkʃn, -z
AM dəˈrɛkʃən, daɪˈrɛkʃən, -z

directional
BR dɪˈrɛkʃn̩(ə)l, dɪˈrɛkʃən(ə)l, dʌɪˈrɛkʃn̩(ə)l, dʌɪˈrɛkʃən(ə)l
AM dəˈrɛkʃ(ə)nəl, daɪˈrɛkʃ(ə)nəl

directionality
BR dɪˌrɛkʃəˈnalɨti, dʌɪˌrɛkʃəˈnalɨti
AM dəˌrɛkʃəˈnælədi, daɪˌrɛkʃəˈnælədi

directionally
BR dɪˈrɛkʃn̩əli, dɪˈrɛkʃn̩l̩i, dɪˈrɛkʃənl̩i, dɪˈrɛkʃ(ə)nəli, dʌɪˈrɛkʃn̩əli, dʌɪˈrɛkʃn̩l̩i, dʌɪˈrɛkʃənl̩i, dʌɪˈrɛkʃ(ə)nəli
AM dəˈrɛkʃ(ə)nəli, daɪˈrɛkʃ(ə)nəli

directionless
BR dɪˈrɛkʃnləs, dʌɪˈrɛkʃnləs
AM dəˈrɛkʃənləs, daɪˈrɛkʃənləs

directive
BR dɪˈrɛktɪv, dʌɪˈrɛktɪv, -z
AM dəˈrɛktɪv, -z

directly
BR dɪˈrɛktli, dʌɪˈrɛktli
AM dəˈrɛk(t)li, daɪˈrɛk(t)li

directness
BR dɪˈrɛk(t)nəs, dʌɪˈrɛk(t)nəs
AM dəˈrɛk(t)nəs

Directoire
BR ˌdɪrɛkˈtwɑː(r), ˌdiːrɛkˈtwɑː(r), dɪˈrɛktwɑː(r)
AM dəˌrɛkˈtwɑr

director
BR dɪˈrɛktə(r), dʌɪˈrɛktə(r), -z
AM dəˈrɛktər, daɪˈrɛktər, -z

directorate
BR dɪˈrɛkt(ə)rət, dʌɪˈrɛkt(ə)rət, -s
AM dəˈrɛkt(ə)rət, -s

directorial
BR ˌdʌɪrɛkˈtɔːrɪəl, dɪˌrɛkˈtɔːrɪəl
AM dəˌrɛkˈtɔriəl, ˌdaɪrɛkˈtɔriəl

directorship
BR dɪˈrɛktəʃɪp, dʌɪˈrɛktəʃɪp, -s
AM dəˈrɛktərˌʃɪp, -s

directory
BR dɪˈrɛkt(ə)r|i, dʌɪˈrɛkt(ə)r|i, -ɪz
AM dəˈrɛkt(ə)ri, daɪˈrɛkt(ə)ri, -z

directress
BR dɪˈrɛktrɪs, dʌɪˈrɛktrɪs, -ɨz
AM dəˈrɛktrəs, daɪˈrɛktrəs, -əz

directrices
BR dɪˈrɛktrɪsiːz
AM dəˈrɛktrəˌsiz, daɪˈrɛktrəˌsiz

directrix
BR dɪˈrɛktrɪks, dʌɪˈrɛktrɪks, -ɨz
AM dəˈrɛktrɪks, daɪˈrɛktrɪks, -ɨz

direful
BR ˈdʌɪəf(ʊ)l
AM ˈdaɪ(ə)rfəl

direfully
BR ˈdʌɪəfʊli, ˈdʌɪəfl̩i
AM ˈdaɪ(ə)rf(ə)li

direly
BR ˈdʌɪəli
AM ˈdaɪ(ə)rli

direness
BR ˈdʌɪənəs
AM ˈdaɪ(ə)rnəs

dirge
BR dəːdʒ, -ɨz
AM dərdʒ, -əz

dirgeful
BR ˈdəːdʒf(ʊ)l
AM ˈdərdʒfəl

dirham
BR ˈdɪəram, ˈdɪərəm, -z
AM ˈdɪrəm, -z

dirigible
BR ˈdɪrɪdʒɪbl, -z
AM dəˈrɪdʒəbəl, ˈdɪrədʒəbəl, -z

dirigisme
BR ˈdɪrɪʒiːz(ə)m
AM ˌdiriˈʒizm
FR diʀiʒism

dirigiste
BR ˌdɪrɪˈʒiːst, -s
AM ˌdiriˈʒist, -s
FR diʀiʒist

diriment
BR ˈdɪrɪm(ə)nt
AM ˈdɪrəmənt

dirk
BR dəːk, -s
AM dərk, -s

dirndl
BR ˈdəːndl, -z
AM ˈdərndl, -z

dirt
BR dəːt
AM dərt

dirtily
BR ˈdəːtɨli
AM ˈdərdəli

dirtiness
BR ˈdəːtɪnɪs
AM ˈdərdinɪs

dirty
BR ˈdəːt|i, -ɪz, -ɪɪŋ, -ɪd, -ɪə(r), -ɪɪst
AM ˈdərdi, -z, -ɪŋ, -d, -ər, -ɨst

disability
BR ˌdɪsəˈbɪlɪt|i, -ɪz
AM ˌdɪsəˈbɪlɨdi, -z

disable
BR dɪsˈeɪb|l, -lz, -l̩ɪŋ\-lɪŋ, -ld
AM dəˈseɪb|əl, -əlz, -(ə)lɪŋ, -əld

disablement
BR dɪsˈeɪblm(ə)nt, -s
AM dəˈseɪbəlmənt, -s

disablist
BR dɪˈseɪblɪst
AM dəˈseɪb(ə)ləst

disabuse
BR ˌdɪsəˈbjuːz, -ɨz, -ɪŋ, -d
AM ˌdɪsəˈbjuz, -əz, -ɪŋ, -d

disaccord
BR ˌdɪsəˈkɔːd, -z, -ɪŋ, -ɨd
AM ˌdɪsəˈkɔ(ə)rd, -z, -ɪŋ, -əd

disaccustom
BR ˌdɪsəˈkʌstəm, -z, -ɪŋ, -d
AM ˌdɪsəˈkəstəm, -z, -ɪŋ, -d

disadvantage
BR ˌdɪsədˈvɑːnt|ɪdʒ, ˌdɪsədˈvant|ɪdʒ, -ɪdʒɪz
AM ˌdɪsədˈvæn(t)ɪdʒ, -ɨz

disadvantageous
BR ˌdɪsadv(ə)nˈteɪdʒəs, ˌdɪsadvanˈteɪdʒəs
AM ˌdɪsˌædvənˈteɪdʒəs
disadvantageously
BR ˌdɪsadv(ə)nˈteɪdʒəsli, ˌdɪsadvanˈteɪdʒəsli
AM ˌdɪsˌædvənˈteɪdʒəsli
disadvantageousness
BR ˌdɪsadv(ə)nˈteɪdʒəsnəs, ˌdɪsadvanˈteɪdʒəsnəs
AM ˌdɪsˌædvənˈteɪdʒəsnəs
disaffected
BR ˌdɪsəˈfɛktɨd
AM ˈˌdɪsəˈfɛktəd
disaffectedly
BR ˌdɪsəˈfɛktɨdli
AM ˈˌdɪsəˈfɛktədli
disaffection
BR ˌdɪsəˈfɛkʃn
AM ˈˌdɪsəˈfɛkʃən
disaffiliate
BR ˌdɪsəˈfɪlɪeɪt, -s, -ɪŋ, -ɨd
AM ˈˌdɪsəˈfɪlieɪ|t, -ts, -dɪŋ, -dɨd
disaffiliation
BR ˌdɪsəfɪlɪˈeɪʃn
AM ˈˌdɪsəˌfɪliˈeɪʃən
disaffirm
BR ˌdɪsəˈfəːm, -z, -ɪŋ, -d
AM ˈˌdɪsəˈfərm, -z, -ɪŋ, -d
disaffirmation
BR ˌdɪsafəˈmeɪʃn
AM ˈˌdɪsəˌfərˈmeɪʃən, ˈˌdɪsˌæfərˈmeɪʃən
disafforest
BR ˌdɪsəˈfɒrɪst, -s, -ɪŋ, -ɨd
AM ˌdɪsəˈfɔrəst, -s, -ɪŋ, -əd
disafforestation
BR ˌdɪsəfɒrɪˈsteɪʃn
AM ˈˌdɪsəˌfɔrəˈsteɪʃən
disaggregate
BR dɪsˈagrɪgeɪt, -s, -ɪŋ, -ɨd
AM ˌdɪsˈægrəgeɪ|t, -ts, -dɪŋ, -dɨd
disaggregation
BR ˌdɪsagrɪˈgeɪʃn
AM ˈˌdɪsˌægrəˈgeɪʃən
disagree
BR ˌdɪsəˈgriː, -z, -ɪŋ, -d
AM ˈˌdɪsəˈgri, -z, -ɪŋ, -d
disagreeable
BR ˌdɪsəˈgriːəbl
AM ˈˌdɪsəˈgriəbəl
disagreeableness
BR ˌdɪsəˈgriːəblnəs
AM ˈˌdɪsəˈgriəbəlnəs
disagreeably
BR ˌdɪsəˈgriːəbli
AM ˈˌdɪsəˈgriəbli
disagreement
BR ˌdɪsəˈgriːm(ə)nt, -s
AM ˈˌdɪsəˈgrimənt, -s
disallow
BR ˌdɪsəˈlaʊ, -z, -ɪŋ, -d
AM ˈˌdɪsəˈlaʊ, -z, -ɪŋ, -d
disallowance
BR ˌdɪsəˈlaʊəns, -ɨz
AM ˈˌdɪsəˈlaʊəns, -əz
disambiguate
BR ˌdɪsamˈbɪgjʊeɪt, -s, -ɪŋ, -ɨd
AM ˌdɪsæmˈbɪgjəˌweɪ|t, -ts, -dɪŋ, -dɨd
disambiguation
BR ˌdɪsambɪgjʊˈeɪʃn
AM ˌdɪsamˌbɪgjəˈweɪʃən
disamenity
BR ˌdɪsəˈmiːnɨti, ˌdɪsəˈmɛnɨti, -ɪz
AM ˈˌdɪsəˈmɛnədi, -z
disannul
BR ˌdɪsəˈnʌl, -z, -ɪŋ, -d
AM ˈˌdɪsəˈnəl, -z, -ɪŋ, -d
disannulment
BR ˌdɪsəˈnʌlm(ə)nt
AM ˈˌdɪsəˈnəlmənt
disappear
BR ˌdɪsəˈpɪə(r), -z, -ɪŋ, -d
AM ˈˌdɪsəˌpɪ(ə)r, -z, -ɪŋ, -d
disappearance
BR ˌdɪsəˈpɪərəns, ˌdɪsəˈpɪərns, -ɨz
AM ˌdɪsəˈpɪrəns, -əz
disappoint
BR ˌdɪsəˈpɔɪnt, -s, -ɪŋ, -ɨd
AM ˌdɪsəˈpɔɪn|t, -ts, -(t)ɪŋ, -(t)əd
disappointedly
BR ˌdɪsəˈpɔɪntɨdli
AM ˌdɪsəˈpɔɪn(t)ədli
disappointing
BR ˌdɪsəˈpɔɪntɪŋ
AM ˌdɪsəˈpɔɪn(t)ɪŋ
disappointingly
BR ˌdɪsəˈpɔɪntɪŋli
AM ˌdɪsəˈpɔɪn(t)ɪŋli
disappointment
BR ˌdɪsəˈpɔɪntm(ə)nt, -s
AM ˌdɪsəˈpɔɪntmənt, -s
disapprobation
BR ˌdɪsaprəˈbeɪʃn, dɪsˌaprəˈbeɪʃn
AM dɪsˌæprəˈbeɪʃən
disapprobative
BR ˌdɪsaprəˈbeɪtɪv, dɪsˌaprəˈbeɪtɪv
AM ˈˌdɪsəˈproʊbədɪv
disapprobatory
BR ˌdɪsaprəˈbeɪt(ə)ri
AM ˈˌdɪsəˈproʊbəˌtɔri
disapproval
BR ˌdɪsəˈpruːvl
AM ˈˌdɪsəˈpruvəl
disapprove
BR ˌdɪsəˈpruːv, -z, -ɪŋ, -d
AM ˈˌdɪsəˈpruv, -z, -ɪŋ, -d
disapprover
BR ˌdɪsəˈpruːvə(r), -z
AM ˈˌdɪsəˈpruvər, -z
disapprovingly
BR ˌdɪsəˈpruːvɪŋli
AM ˈˌdɪsəˈpruvɪŋli
disarm
BR dɪsˈɑːm, -z, -ɪŋ, -d
AM dɪsˈɑrm, -z, -ɪŋ, -d
disarmament
BR dɪsˈɑːməm(ə)nt
AM dɪsˈɑrməmənt
disarmer
BR dɪsˈɑːmə(r), -z
AM dɪsˈɑrmər, -z
disarming
BR dɪsˈɑːmɪŋ
AM dɪsˈɑrmɪŋ
disarmingly
BR dɪsˈɑːmɪŋli
AM dɪsˈɑrmɪŋli
disarrange
BR ˌdɪsəˈreɪn(d)ʒ, -ɨz, -ɪŋ, -d
AM ˈˌdɪsəˈreɪndʒ, -ɨz, -ɪŋ, -d
disarrangement
BR ˌdɪsəˈreɪn(d)ʒm(ə)nt
AM ˈˌdɪsəˈreɪndʒmənt
disarray
BR ˌdɪsəˈreɪ
AM ˈˌdɪsəˈreɪ
disarticulate
BR ˌdɪsɑːˈtɪkjʉleɪt, -s, -ɪŋ, -ɨd
AM ˈˌdɪsɑrˈtɪkjəˌleɪ|t, -ts, -dɪŋ, -dɨd
disarticulation
BR ˌdɪsɑːtɪkjʉˈleɪʃn
AM ˌdɪsɑrˌtɪkjəˈleɪʃən
disassemble
BR ˌdɪsəˈsɛmb|l, -lz, -l̩ɪŋ\-lɪŋ, -ld
AM ˌdɪsəˈsɛmb|əl, -əlz, -(ə)lɪŋ, -əld
disassembly
BR ˌdɪsəˈsɛmbli
AM ˌdɪsəˈsɛmbli
disassociate
BR ˌdɪsəˈsəʊʃɪeɪt, ˌdɪsəˈsəʊsɪeɪt, -s, -ɪŋ, -ɨd
AM ˈˌdɪsəˈsoʊʃiˌeɪ|t, ˈˌdɪsəˈsoʊsiˌeɪ|t, -ts, -dɪŋ, -dɨd
disassociation
BR ˌdɪsəsəʊʃɪˈeɪʃn, ˌdɪsəsəʊsɪˈeɪʃn
AM ˈˌdɪsəˌsoʊʃiˈeɪʃən, ˈˌdɪsəˌsoʊsiˈeɪʃən
disaster
BR dɪˈzɑːstə(r), dɪˈzastə(r), -z
AM dəˈzæstər, -z
disastrous
BR dɪˈzɑːstrəs, dɪˈzastrəs
AM dəˈzæstrəsli
disastrously
BR dɪˈzɑːstrəsli, dɪˈzastrəsli
AM dəˈzæstrəs
disastrousness
BR dɪˈzɑːstrəsnəs, dɪˈzastrəsnəs
AM dəˈzæstrəsnəs
disavow
BR ˌdɪsəˈvaʊ, -z, -ɪŋ, -d
AM ˈˌdɪsəˈvaʊ, -z, -ɪŋ, -d
disavowal
BR ˌdɪsəˈvaʊəl
AM ˈˌdɪsəˈvaʊ(ə)l
disband
BR dɪsˈband, -z, -ɪŋ, -ɨd
AM dɪsˈbænd, -z, -ɪn, -əd
disbandment
BR dɪsˈban(d)m(ə)nt
AM dɪsˈbæn(d)mənt
disbar
BR dɪsˈbɑː(r), -z, -ɪŋ, -d
AM dɪsˈbɑr, -z, -ɪŋ, -d
disbarment
BR dɪsˈbɑːm(ə)nt
AM dɪsˈbɑrmənt
disbelief
BR ˌdɪsbɪˈliːf
AM ˌdɪsbəˈlif
disbelieve
BR ˌdɪsbɪˈliːv, -z, -ɪŋ, -d
AM ˌdɪsbəˈliv, -z, -ɪŋ, -d
disbeliever
BR ˌdɪsbɪˈliːvə(r), -z
AM ˌdɪsbəˈlivər, -z
disbelievingly
BR ˌdɪsbɪˈliːvɪŋli
AM ˌdɪsbəˈlivɪŋli
disbenefit
BR ˌdɪsˈbɛnɪfɪt, -s
AM ˌdɪsˈbɛnəfɪt, -s
disbound
BR dɪsˈbaʊnd, -z, -ɪŋ, -ɨd
AM dɪsˈbaʊnd, -z, -ɪŋ, -əd
disbud
BR (ˌ)dɪsˈbʌd, -z, -ɪŋ, -ɨd
AM dɪsˈbəd, -z, -ɪŋ, -əd
disburden
BR dɪsˈbəːd|n, -nz, -n̩ɪŋ\-nɪŋ, -nd
AM dɪsˈbərd|ən, -ənz, -(ə)nɪŋ, -ənd
disbursal
BR dɪsˈbəːsl
AM dɪsˈbərs(ə)l
disburse
BR dɪsˈbəːs, -ɨz, -ɪŋ, -t
AM dɪsˈbərs, -əz, -ɪŋ, -t
disbursement
BR dɪsˈbəːsm(ə)nt, -s
AM dɪsˈbərsmənt, -s

disburser
BR dɪs'bəːsə(r), -z
AM dɪs'bərsər, -z

disc
BR dɪsk, -s
AM dɪsk, -s

discalced
BR dɪs'kalst
AM də'skælst

discard[1]
noun
BR 'dɪskɑːd, -z
AM 'dɪsˌkɑrd, -z

discard[2]
verb
BR dɪs'kɑːd, -z, -ɪŋ, -ɨd
AM də'skɑrd, -z, -ɪŋ, -ɨd

discardable
BR dɪs'kɑːdəbl
AM də'skɑrdəbəl

discarnate
BR dɪs'kɑːnət
AM də'skɑrnət, də'skɑrˌneɪt

discern
BR dɪ'səːn, -z, -ɪŋ, -d
AM də'sərn, -z, -ɪŋ, -d

discerner
BR dɪ'səːnə(r), -z
AM də'sərnər, -z

discernible
BR dɪ'səːnɪbl
AM də'sərnəbəl

discernibly
BR dɪ'səːnɪbli
AM də'sərnəbli

discerning
BR dɪ'səːnɪŋ
AM də'sərnɪŋ

discerningly
BR dɪ'səːnɪŋli
AM də'sərnɪŋli

discernment
BR dɪ'səːnm(ə)nt
AM də'sərnmənt

discerptibility
BR dɪˌsəːptɪ'bɪlɪti
AM dəˌsərptə'bɪlɨdi

discerptible
BR dɪ'səːptɪbl
AM də'sərptəbəl

discerption
BR dɪ'səːpʃn, -z
AM də'sərpʃən, -z

discharge[1]
noun
BR 'dɪstʃɑːdʒ, -ɨz
AM 'dɪsˌtʃɑrdʒ, -əz

discharge[2]
verb
BR dɪs'tʃɑːdʒ, -ɨz, -ɪŋ, -d
AM dɪs'tʃɑrdʒ, -əz, -ɪŋ, -d

dischargeable
BR dɪs'tʃɑːdʒəbl
AM dɪs'tʃɑrdʒəbəl

discharger
BR dɪs'tʃɑːdʒə(r), -z
AM dɪs'tʃɑrdʒər, -z

dischuff
BR ˌdɪs'tʃʌf, -s, -ɪŋ, -t
AM dəs'tʃəf, -s, -ɪŋ, -t

disciple
BR dɪ'sʌɪpl, -z
AM də'saɪpəl, -z

discipleship
BR dɪ'sʌɪplʃɪp
AM də'saɪpəlˌʃɪp

disciplinable
BR 'dɪsɪplɨnəbl
AM 'dɪsɪˌplɨnəbəl

disciplinal
BR 'dɪsɪplɨnl
AM 'dɪsɪplɨnəl

disciplinarian
BR ˌdɪsɪplɪ'nɛːrɪən, -z
AM ˌdɪsəplə'nɛriən, -z

disciplinary
BR ˌdɪsɪ'plɪn(ə)ri, 'dɪsɪplɪn(ə)ri
AM 'dɪsəpləˌnɛri

discipline
BR 'dɪsɪplɪn, -z, -ɪŋ, -d
AM 'dɪsɪplɪn, -z, -ɪŋ, -d

discipular
BR dɪ'sɪpjʉlə(r)
AM də'sɪpjələr

disclaim
BR dɪs'kleɪm, -z, -ɪŋ, -d
AM dɪs'kleɪm, -z, -ɪŋ, -d

disclaimer
BR dɪs'kleɪmə(r), -z
AM dɪs'kleɪmər, -z

disclose
BR dɪs'kləʊz, -ɨz, -ɪŋ, -d
AM də'sklouz, -əz, -ɪŋ, -d

discloser
BR dɪs'kləʊzə(r), -z
AM də'sklouzər, -z

disclosure
BR dɪs'kləʊʒə(r), -z
AM də'sklouʒər, -z

disco
BR 'dɪskəʊ, -z
AM 'dɪskoʊ, -z

discoboli
BR dɪ'skɒbəlʌɪ, dɪ'skɒbl̩ʌɪ, dɪ'skɒbəliː, dɪ'skɒbl̩iː
AM də'skɑbəˌlaɪ

discobolus
BR dɪ'skɒbələs, dɪ'skɒbl̩əs
AM də'skɑbələs

discographer
BR dɪs'kɒgrəfə(r), -z
AM dɪs'kɑgrəfər, -z

discography
BR dɪs'kɒgrəf|i, -ɪz
AM dɪs'kɑgrəfi, -z

discoid
BR 'dɪskɔɪd
AM 'dɪsˌkɔɪd

discolor
BR dɪs'kʌl|ə(r), -əz, -(ə)rɪŋ, -əd
AM dɪs'kələr, -z, -ɪŋ, -d

discoloration
BR dɪsˌkʌlə'reɪʃn, ˌdɪskʌlə'reɪʃn
AM dɪsˌkələ'reɪʃən, ˈdɪsˌkələ'reɪʃən

discolour
BR dɪs'kʌlə(r), -z, -ɪŋ, -d
AM dɪs'kələr, -z, -ɪŋ, -d

discolouration
BR dɪsˌkʌlə'reɪʃn, ˌdɪskʌlə'reɪʃn
AM dɪsˌkələ'reɪʃən, ˈdɪsˌkələ'reɪʃən

discombobulate
BR ˌdɪskəm'bɒbjʉleɪt, -s, -ɪŋ, -ɨd
AM ˌdɪskəm'bɑbjəˌleɪ|t, -ts, -dɪŋ, -dɨd

discomfit
BR dɪs'kʌmfɪt, -s, -ɪŋ, -ɨd
AM dɪs'kəmfə|t, -ts, -dɪŋ, -dəd

discomfiture
BR dɪs'kʌmfɪtʃə(r)
AM dɪs'kəmfəˌtʃʊ(ə)r, dɪs'skəmfətʃər

discomfort
BR dɪs'kʌmfət, -s
AM dɪs'kəmfərt, -s

discommode
BR ˌdɪskə'məʊd, -z, -ɪŋ, -ɨd
AM ˈdɪskə'moʊd, -z, -ɪŋ, -əd

discommodious
BR ˌdɪskə'məʊdɪəs
AM ˈdɪskə'moʊdiəs

discompose
BR ˌdɪskəm'pəʊz, -ɨz, -ɪŋ, -d
AM ˈdɪskəm'poʊz, -əz, -ɪŋ, -d

discomposure
BR ˌdɪskəm'pəʊʒə(r)
AM ˈdɪskəm'poʊʒər

disconcert
BR ˌdɪskən'səːt, -s, -ɪŋ, -ɨd
AM ˈdɪskən'sər|t, -ts, -dɪŋ, -dəd

disconcertedly
BR ˌdɪskən'səːtɨdli
AM ˈdɪskən'sərdədli

disconcerting
BR ˌdɪskən'səːtɪŋ
AM ˈdɪskən'sərdɪŋ

disconcertingly
BR ˌdɪskən'səːtɪŋli
AM ˈdɪskən'sərdɪŋli

disconcertion
BR ˌdɪskən'səːʃn
AM ˌdɪskən'sərʃən

disconcertment
BR ˌdɪskən'səːtm(ə)nt
AM ˈdɪskən'sərtmənt

disconfirm
BR ˌdɪskən'fəːm, -z, -ɪŋ, -d
AM ˈdɪskən'fərm, -z, -ɪŋ, -d

disconfirmation
BR ˌdɪskɒnfəː'meɪʃn
AM ˈdɪsˌkɑnfər'meɪʃən

disconformity
BR ˌdɪskən'fɔːmɪt|i, -ɪz
AM ˈdɪskən'fɔrmədi, -z

disconnect
BR ˌdɪskə'nɛkt, -s, -ɪŋ, -ɨd
AM ˈdɪskə'nɛk|(t), -(t)s, -tɪŋ, -təd

disconnected
BR ˌdɪskə'nɛktɨd
AM ˈdɪskə'nɛktəd

disconnectedly
BR ˌdɪskə'nɛktɨdli
AM ˈdɪskə'nɛktədli

disconnectedness
BR ˌdɪskə'nɛktɨdnɨs
AM ˈdɪskə'nɛktədnəs

disconnection
BR ˌdɪskə'nɛkʃn, -z
AM ˈdɪskə'nɛkʃən, -z

disconnexion
BR ˌdɪskə'nɛkʃn, -z
AM ˈdɪskə'nɛkʃən, -z

disconsolate
BR dɪs'kɒnsələt, dɪs'kɒnsl̩ət
AM dɪs'kɑns(ə)lət

disconsolately
BR dɪs'kɒnsələtli, dɪs'kɒnsl̩ətli
AM dɪs'kɑns(ə)lətli

disconsolateness
BR dɪs'kɒnsələtnəs, dɪs'kɒnsl̩ətnəs
AM dɪs'kɑns(ə)lətnəs

disconsolation
BR ˌdɪskɒnsə'leɪʃn, dɪˌskɒnsə'leɪʃn
AM ˈdɪsˌkɑnsə'leɪʃən

discontent
BR ˌdɪskən'tɛnt, -s
AM ˈdɪskən'tɛnt, -s

discontented
BR ˌdɪskən'tɛntɨd
AM ˈdɪskən'tɛn(t)əd

discontentedly
BR ˌdɪskən'tɛntɨdli
AM ˈdɪskən'tɛn(t)ədli

discontentedness
BR ˌdɪskən'tɛntɨdnɨs
AM ˈdɪskən'tɛn(t)ədnəs

discontently
BR ˌdɪskən'tɛntli
AM ˈdɪskən'tɛn(t)li

discontentment
BR ˌdɪskənˈtɛntm(ə)nt, -s
AM ˈˌdɪskənˈtɛntmənt, -s

discontinuance
BR ˌdɪskənˈtɪnjʊəns
AM ˈˌdɪskənˈtɪnjəwəns

discontinuation
BR ˌdɪskəntɪnjʊˈeɪʃn
AM ˈˌdɪskənˌtɪnjəˈweɪʃən

discontinue
BR ˌdɪskənˈtɪnjuː, -z, -ɪŋ, -d
AM ˈˌdɪskənˈtɪnju, -z, -ɪŋ, -d

discontinuity
BR ˌdɪskɒntᵻˈnjuːɪti
AM ˈˌdɪsˌkɑntn̩ˈ(j)uədi, ˈˌdɪsˌkɑntəˈn(j)uədi

discontinuous
BR ˌdɪskənˈtɪnjʊəs
AM ˈˌdɪskənˈtɪnjəwəs

discontinuously
BR ˌdɪskənˈtɪnjʊəsli
AM ˈˌdɪskənˈtɪnjəwəsli

discord
BR ˈdɪskɔːd
AM ˈdɪsˌkɔ(ə)rd

discordance
BR dɪsˈkɔːdns
AM ˌdɪsˈkɔrdəns

discordancy
BR dɪsˈkɔːdns|i, -ɪz
AM ˌdɪsˈkɔrdənsi, -z

discordant
BR dɪsˈkɔːdnt
AM ˌdɪsˈkɔrdənt

discordantly
BR dɪsˈkɔːdntli
AM ˌdɪsˈkɔrdən(t)li

discothèque
BR ˈdɪskətɛk, -s
AM ˈdɪskəˌtɛk, -s

discount¹
noun, verb, reduce price
BR ˈdɪskaʊnt, -s, -ɪŋ, -ᵻd
AM ˈdɪsˌkaʊn|t, -ts, -(t)ɪŋ, -(t)əd

discount²
verb, treat as untrue
BR dɪsˈkaʊnt, -s, -ɪŋ, -ᵻd
AM ˌdɪsˈkaʊn|t, -ts, -(t)ɪŋ, -(t)əd

discountable
adjective, to be treated as untrue
BR dɪsˈkaʊntəbl
AM ˌdɪsˈkaʊn(t)əbəl

discountenance
BR dɪsˈkaʊntᵻnəns, -ᵻz, -ɪŋ, -t
AM dɪsˈkaʊnt(ə)nəns, dɪsˈkaʊn(t)ənəns, -əz, -ɪŋ, -t

discounter
someone who treats something as untrue
BR dɪsˈkaʊntə(r), -z
AM ˌdɪsˈkaʊn(t)ər, -z

discourage
BR dɪsˈkʌr|ɪdʒ, dᵻˈskʌr|ɪdʒ, -ᵻdʒɪz, -ᵻdʒɪŋ, -ɪdʒd
AM dəˈskərɪdʒ, -ɪz, -ɪŋ, -d

discouragement
BR dɪsˈkʌrᵻdʒm(ə)nt, dᵻˈskʌrᵻdʒm(ə)nt, -s
AM dəˈskərɪdʒmənt, -s

discouraging
BR dɪsˈkʌrᵻdʒɪŋ, dᵻˈskʌrᵻdʒɪŋ
AM dəˈskərɪdʒɪŋ

discouragingly
BR dɪsˈkʌrᵻdʒɪŋli, dᵻˈskʌrᵻdʒɪŋli
AM dəˈskərɪdʒɪŋli

discourse¹
noun
BR ˈdɪskɔːs, -ɪz
AM ˈdɪsˌkɔ(ə)rs, -əz

discourse²
verb
BR dɪsˈkɔːs, -ɪz, -ɪŋ, -t
AM dɪsˈkɔ(ə)rs, -əz, -ɪŋ, -t

discourteous
BR dɪsˈkəːtɪəs
AM dɪsˈkərdiəs

discourteously
BR dɪsˈkəːtɪəsli
AM dɪsˈkərdiəsli

discourteousness
BR dɪsˈkəːtɪəsnəs
AM dɪsˈkərdiəsnəs

discourtesy
BR dɪsˈkəːtəsi, -ɪz
AM dɪsˈkərdəsi, -z

discover
BR dᵻˈskʌv|ə(r), -əz, -(ə)rɪŋ, -əd
AM dəˈskəv|ər, -ərz, -(ə)rɪŋ, -ərd

discoverable
BR dᵻˈskʌv(ə)rəbl
AM dəˈskəv(ə)rəbəl

discoverer
BR dᵻˈskʌv(ə)rə(r), -z
AM dəˈskəv(ə)rər, -z

discovery
BR dᵻˈskʌv(ə)r|i, -ɪz
AM dəˈskəv(ə)ri, -z

discredit
BR (ˌ)dɪsˈkrɛd|ɪt, -s, -ɪtɪŋ, -ɪtᵻd
AM dɪsˈkrɛdə|t, -ts, -dɪŋ, -dəd

discreditable
BR (ˌ)dɪsˈkrɛdɪtəbl
AM dɪsˈkrɛdədəbəl

discreditably
BR (ˌ)dɪsˈkrɛdɪtəbli
AM dɪsˈkrɛdədəbli

discreet
BR dᵻˈskriːt, -ɪst
AM dəˈskri|t, -dɪst

discreetly
BR dᵻˈskriːtli
AM dəˈskritli

discreetness
BR dᵻˈskriːtnɪs
AM dəˈskritnɪs

discrepancy
BR dᵻˈskrɛpns|i, -ɪz
AM dəˈskrɛpənsi, -z

discrepant
BR dᵻˈskrɛpnt
AM dəˈskrɛpənt

discrete
BR dᵻˈskriːt
AM dəˈskrit

discretely
BR dᵻˈskriːtli
AM dəˈskritli

discreteness
BR dᵻˈskriːtnɪs
AM dəˈskritnɪs

discretion
BR dᵻˈskrɛʃn
AM dəˈskrɛʃən

discretionary
BR dᵻˈskrɛʃn̩(ə)ri
AM dəˈskrɛʃəˌnɛri

discriminant
BR dᵻˈskrɪmᵻnənt
AM dəˈskrɪm(ə)nənt

discriminate¹
adjective
BR dᵻˈskrɪmᵻnət
AM dəˈskrɪm(ə)nət

discriminate²
verb
BR dᵻˈskrɪmᵻneɪt, -s, -ɪŋ, -ᵻd
AM dəˈskrɪməˌneɪ|t, -ts, -dɪŋ, -dᵻd

discriminately
BR dᵻˈskrɪmᵻnətli
AM dəˈskrɪm(ə)nətli

discriminatingly
BR dᵻˈskrɪmᵻneɪtɪŋli
AM dəˈskrɪməˌneɪdɪŋli

discrimination
BR dᵻˌskrɪmᵻˈneɪʃn
AM dəˌskrɪməˈneɪʃən

discriminative
BR dᵻˈskrɪmᵻnətɪv
AM dəˈskrɪməˌneɪdɪv, dəˈskrɪmənədɪv

discriminator
BR dᵻˈskrɪmᵻneɪtə(r), -z
AM dəˈskrɪməˌneɪdər, -z

discriminatory
BR dᵻˈskrɪmᵻnət(ə)ri
AM dəˈskrɪmənəˌtɔri

discursive
BR dɪsˈkəːsɪv
AM dəˈskərsɪv

discursively
BR dɪsˈkəːsɪvli
AM dəˈskərsɪvli

discursiveness
BR dɪsˈkəːsɪvnɪs
AM dəˈskərsɪvnɪs

discus
BR ˈdɪskəs, -ɪz
AM ˈdɪskəs, -əz

discuss
BR dᵻˈskʌs, -ɪz, -ɪŋ, -t
AM dəˈskəs, -əz, -ɪŋ, -t

discussable
BR dᵻˈskʌsəbl
AM dəˈskəsəbəl

discussant
BR dᵻˈskʌsnt, -s
AM dəˈskəsənt, -s

discusser
BR dᵻˈskʌsə(r), -z
AM dəˈskəsər, -z

discussible
BR dᵻˈskʌsɪbl
AM dəˈskəsəbəl

discussion
BR dᵻˈskʌʃn, -z
AM dəˈskəʃən, -z

disdain
BR dɪsˈdeɪn, -z, -ɪŋ, -d
AM dɪsˈdeɪn, -z, -ɪŋ, -d

disdainful
BR dɪsˈdeɪnf(ʊ)l
AM dɪsˈdeɪnfəl

disdainfully
BR dɪsˈdeɪnfʊli, dɪsˈdeɪnfl̩i
AM dɪsˈdeɪnfəli

disdainfulness
BR dɪsˈdeɪnf(ʊ)lnəs
AM dɪsˈdeɪnfəlnəs

disease
BR dᵻˈziːz, -ɪz, -d
AM dəˈziz, -ɪz, -d

diseconomy
BR ˌdɪsɪˈkɒnəmi
AM ˈˌdɪsɪˈkɑnəmi

disembark
BR ˌdɪs(ɪ)mˈbɑːk, ˌdɪsɛmˈbɑːk, -s, -ɪŋ, -t
AM ˈˌdɪsɛmˈbɑrk, -s, -ɪŋ, -t

disembarkation
BR ˌdɪsɛmbɑːˈkeɪʃn, ˌdɪs(ɪ)mbɑːˈkeɪʃn
AM dɪsˌɛmbɑrˈkeɪʃən

disembarrass
BR ˌdɪs(ɪ)mˈbarəs, ˌdɪsɛmˈbarəs, -ɪz, -ɪŋ, -t
AM ˈˌdɪsəmˈbɛrəs, -əz, -ɪŋ, -t

disembarrassment
BR ˌdɪs(ɪ)mˈbarəsm(ə)nt, ˌdɪsɛmˈbarəsm(ə)nt
AM ˈˌdɪsəmˈbɛrəsmənt

disembodied
BR ˌdɪs(ɪ)m'bɒdɪd, ˌdɪsɛm'bɒdɪd
AM ˈdɪsəm'bɑdid

disembodiment
BR ˌdɪs(ɪ)m'bɒdɪm(ə)nt, ˌdɪsɛm'bɒdɪm(ə)nt
AM ˈdɪsəm'bɑdimənt

disembody
BR ˌdɪs(ɪ)m'bɒd|i, ˌdɪsɛm'bɒd|i, -ɪz, -ɪɪŋ, -ɪd
AM ˈdɪsəm'bɑdi, -z, -ɪŋ, -d

disembogue
BR ˌdɪs(ɪ)m'bəʊg, ˌdɪsɛm'bəʊg, -z, -ɪŋ, -d
AM ˈdɪsəm'boʊg, -z, -ɪŋ, -d

disembowel
BR ˌdɪs(ɪ)m'baʊ(ə)l, ˌdɪsɛm'baʊ(ə)l, -z, -ɪŋ, -d
AM ˈdɪsəm'baʊ(ə)l, -z, -ɪŋ, -d

disembowelment
BR ˌdɪs(ɪ)m'baʊ(ə)lm(ə)nt, ˌdɪsɛm'baʊ(ə)lm(ə)nt
AM ˈdɪsəm'baʊlmənt

disembroil
BR ˌdɪs(ɪ)m'brɔɪl, ˌdɪsɛm'brɔɪl, -z, -ɪŋ, -d
AM ˈdɪsəm'brɔɪl, -z, -ɪŋ, -d

disempower
BR ˌdɪs(ɪ)m'paʊ|ə(r), ˌdɪsɛm'paʊ|ə(r), -əz, -(ə)rɪŋ, -əd
AM ˈdɪsəm'paʊ|(ə)r, -ərd, -(ə)rɪŋ, -ərd

disenchant
BR ˌdɪs(ɪ)n'tʃɑːnt, ˌdɪs(ɪ)n'tʃant, ˌdɪsɛn'tʃɑːnt, ˌdɪsɛn'tʃant, -s, -ɪŋ, -ɪd
AM ˈdɪsən'tʃæn|t, -ts, -(t)ɪŋ, -(t)əd

disenchantingly
BR ˌdɪs(ɪ)n'tʃɑːntɪŋli, ˌdɪs(ɪ)n'tʃantɪŋli, ˌdɪsɛn'tʃɑːntɪŋli, ˌdɪsɛn'tʃantɪŋli
AM ˈdɪsən'tʃæn(t)ɪŋli

disenchantment
BR ˌdɪs(ɪ)n'tʃɑːntm(ə)nt, ˌdɪs(ɪ)n'tʃantm(ə)nt, ˌdɪsɛn'tʃɑːntm(ə)nt, ˌdɪsɛn'tʃantm(ə)nt, -s
AM ˈdɪsən'tʃæntmənt, -s

disencumber
BR ˌdɪs(ɪ)n'kʌmb|ə(r), ˌdɪsɛn'kʌmb|ə(r), -əz, -(ə)rɪŋ, -əd
AM ˈdɪsən'kəmb|ər, -ərd, -(ə)rɪŋ, -ərd

disendow
BR ˌdɪs(ɪ)n'daʊ, ˌdɪsɛn'daʊ, -z, -ɪŋ, -d
AM ˈdɪsən'daʊ, -z, -ɪŋ, -d

disendowment
BR ˌdɪs(ɪ)n'daʊm(ə)nt, ˌdɪsɛn'daʊm(ə)nt
AM ˈdɪsən'daʊmənt

disenfranchise
BR ˌdɪs(ɪ)n'frantʃʌɪz, ˌdɪsɛn'frantʃʌɪz, -ɪz, -ɪŋ, -d
AM ˈdɪsən'fræn,tʃaɪz, -ɪz, -ɪŋ, -d

disenfranchisement
BR ˌdɪs(ɪ)n'frantʃɪzm(ə)nt, ˌdɪsɛn'frantʃɪzm(ə)nt
AM ˈdɪsən'fræn,tʃaɪzmənt, ˈdɪsən'fræntʃəzmənt

disengage
BR ˌdɪs(ɪ)n'geɪdʒ, ˌdɪsɛn'geɪdʒ, -ɪz, -ɪŋ, -d
AM ˈdɪsən'geɪdʒ, -ɪz, -ɪŋ, -d

disengagement
BR ˌdɪs(ɪ)n'geɪdʒm(ə)nt, ˌdɪsɛn'geɪdʒm(ə)nt
AM ˈdɪsən'geɪdʒmənt

disentail
BR ˌdɪs(ɪ)n'teɪl, ˌdɪsɛn'teɪl, -z, -ɪŋ, -d
AM ˈdɪsən'teɪl, -z, -ɪŋ, -d

disentangle
BR ˌdɪs(ɪ)n'taŋg|l, ˌdɪsɛn'taŋg|l, -lz, -l̩ɪŋ\-lɪŋ, -ld
AM ˈdɪsən'tæŋg|əl, -əlz, -(ə)lɪŋ, -əld

disentanglement
BR ˌdɪs(ɪ)n'taŋglm(ə)nt, ˌdɪsɛn'taŋglm(ə)nt
AM ˈdɪsən'tæŋgəlmənt

disenthral
BR ˌdɪs(ɪ)n'θrɔːl, ˌdɪsɛn'θrɔːl, -z, -d
AM ˈdɪsən'θrɔl, ˈdɪsən'θrɑl, -z, -d

disenthralment
BR ˌdɪs(ɪ)n'θrɔːlm(ə)nt, ˌdɪsɛn'θrɔːlm(ə)nt
AM ˈdɪsən'θrɔlmənt, ˈdɪsən'θrɑlmənt

disentitle
BR ˌdɪs(ɪ)n'tʌɪt|l, ˌdɪsɛn'tʌɪt|l, -lz, -l̩ɪŋ\-lɪŋ, -ld
AM ˈdɪsən'taɪdəl, -z, -ɪŋ, -d

disentitlement
BR ˌdɪs(ɪ)n'tʌɪtlm(ə)nt, ˌdɪsɛn'tʌɪtlm(ə)nt
AM ˈdɪsən'taɪdlmənt

disentomb
BR ˌdɪs(ɪ)n'tuːm, ˌdɪsɛn'tuːm, -z, -ɪŋ, -d
AM ˈdɪsən'tum, -z, -ɪŋ, -d

disentombment
BR ˌdɪs(ɪ)n'tuːmm(ə)nt, ˌdɪsɛn'tuːmm(ə)nt
AM ˈdɪsən'tu(m)mənt

disequilibria
BR ˌdɪsɛkwɪ'lɪbrɪə(r), ˌdɪsiːkwɪ'lɪbrɪə(r)
AM dɪsˌɛkwə'lɪbriə, dɪsˌikwə'lɪbriə

disequilibrium
BR ˌdɪsɛkwɪ'lɪbrɪəm, ˌdɪsiːkwɪ'lɪbrɪəm
AM dɪsˌɛkwə'lɪbriəm, dɪsˌikwə'lɪbriəm

disestablish
BR ˌdɪsɪ'stabl|ɪʃ, ˌdɪsɛ'stabl|ɪʃ, -ɪʃɪz, -ɪʃɪŋ, -ɪʃt
AM ˈdɪsə'stæblɪʃ, -ɪz, -ɪŋ, -t

disestablishment
BR ˌdɪsɪ'stablɪʃm(ə)nt, ˌdɪsɛ'stablɪʃm(ə)nt
AM ˈdɪsə'stæblɪʃmənt

disesteem
BR ˌdɪsɪ'stiːm, ˌdɪsɛ'stiːm, -z, -ɪŋ, -d
AM ˈdɪsə'stim, -z, -ɪŋ, -d

diseur
BR diː'zəː(r), -z
AM di'zər, -z

diseuse
BR diː'zəːz, -ɪz
AM di'zʊz, -əz

disfavor
BR dɪs'feɪv|ə(r), -əz, -(ə)rɪŋ, -əd
AM dɪs'feɪv|ər, -ərd, -(ə)rɪŋ, -ərd

disfavour
BR dɪs'feɪv|ə(r), -əz, -(ə)rɪŋ, -əd
AM dɪs'feɪv|ər, -ərd, -(ə)rɪŋ, -ərd

disfigure
BR dɪs'fɪg|ə(r), -əz, -(ə)rɪŋ, -əd
AM dɪs'fɪgjər, -z, -ɪŋ, -d

disfigurement
BR dɪs'fɪgəm(ə)nt, -s
AM dɪs'fɪgjərmənt, -s

disforest
BR dɪs'fɒr|ɪst, -ɪsts, -ɪstɪŋ, -ɪstɪd
AM dɪs'fɔrəst, -s, -ɪŋ, -əd

disforestation
BR ˌdɪsfɒrɪ'steɪʃn, dɪsˌfɒrɪ'steɪʃn
AM dɪsˌfɔrə'steɪʃən, ˈdɪsˌfɔrə'steɪʃən

disfranchise
BR dɪs'fran(t)ʃʌɪz, -ɪz, -ɪŋ, -d
AM dɪs'fræn,tʃaɪz, -ɪz, -ɪŋ, -d

disfranchisement
BR dɪs'fran(t)ʃɪzm(ə)nt
AM dɪs'fræn,tʃaɪzmənt

disfrock
BR dɪs'frɒk, -s, -ɪŋ, -t
AM dɪs'frɑk, -s, -ɪŋ, -t

disgorge
BR dɪs'gɔːdʒ, -ɪz, -ɪŋ, -d
AM dɪs'gɔrdʒ, -əz, -ɪŋ, -d

disgorgement
BR dɪs'gɔːdʒm(ə)nt, -s
AM dɪs'gɔrdʒmənt, -s

disgrace
BR dɪs'greɪs, dɪz'greɪs, -ɪz, -ɪŋ, -t
AM dɪs'greɪs, -ɪz, -ɪŋ, -t

disgraceful
BR dɪs'greɪsf(ʊ)l, dɪz'greɪsf(ʊ)l
AM dɪs'greɪsfəl

disgracefully
BR dɪs'greɪsf(ʊ)li, dɪs'greɪsfl̩i, dɪz'greɪsf(ʊ)li, dɪz'greɪsfl̩i
AM dɪs'greɪsfəli

disgruntled
BR dɪs'grʌntld
AM dɪs'grəntld

disgruntlement
BR dɪs'grʌntlm(ə)nt
AM dɪs'grəntlmənt

disguise
BR dɪs'gʌɪz, dɪz'gʌɪz, -ɪz, -ɪŋ, -d
AM də'skaɪz, dɪs'gaɪz, -ɪz, -ɪŋ, -d

disguisement
BR dɪs'gʌɪzm(ə)nt, dɪz'gʌɪzm(ə)nt
AM dɪs'gaɪzmənt

disgust
BR dɪs'gʌst, dɪz'gʌst
AM də'skəst, dɪs'gəst

disgustedly
BR dɪs'gʌstɪdli, dɪz'gʌstɪdli
AM də'skəstədli, dɪs'gəstədli

disgustful
BR dɪs'gʌs(t)f(ʊ)l, dɪz'gʌs(t)f(ʊ)l
AM də'skəstfəl, dɪs'gəstfəl

disgusting
BR dɪs'gʌstɪŋ, dɪz'gʌstɪŋ
AM də'skəstɪŋ, dɪs'gəstɪŋ

disgustingly
BR dɪs'gʌstɪŋli, dɪz'gʌstɪŋli

AM də'skəstɪŋli, dɪs'gəstɪŋli

disgustingness
BR dɪs'gʌstɪŋnɨs, dɪz'gʌstɪŋnɨs
AM də'skəstɪŋnɨs, dɪs'gəstɪŋnɨs

dish
BR dɪʃ, -ɨz, -ɪŋ, -t
AM dɪʃ, -ɨz, -ɪŋ, -t

dishabille
BR ˌdɪsə'biːl
AM ˌdɪsə'bi(ə)l

dishabituation
BR ˌdɪsəbɪtjʊ'eɪʃn, ˌdɪsəbɪtʃʊ'eɪʃn
AM ¦dɪsəˌbɪtʃə'weɪʃən

disharmonious
BR ˌdɪshɑː'məʊnɪəs
AM ¦dɪsˌ(h)ɑr'moʊniəs

disharmoniously
BR ˌdɪshɑː'məʊnɪəsli
AM ¦dɪsˌ(h)ɑr'moʊniəsli

disharmonise
BR (ˌ)dɪs'hɑːmənʌɪz, -ɨz, -ɪŋ, -d
AM ¦dɪs'hɑrməˌnaɪz, -ɨz, -ɪŋ, -d

disharmonize
BR (ˌ)dɪs'hɑːmənʌɪz, -ɨz, -ɪŋ, -d
AM ¦dɪs'hɑrməˌnaɪz, -ɨz, -ɪŋ, -d

disharmony
BR (ˌ)dɪs'hɑːməni
AM ¦dɪs'hɑrməni

dishcloth
BR 'dɪʃklɒ|θ, -θs\-ðz
AM 'dɪʃˌklɔ|θ, 'dɪʃˌklɑ|θ, -θs\-ðz

dishearten[1]
BR dɪs'hɑːt|n, -nz, -n̩ɪŋ\-nɪŋ, -nd
AM dɪs'hɑrtn̩, -z, -ɪŋ, -d

dishearten[2]
BR dɪs'hɑːt|n, -nz, -n̩ɪŋ\-nɪŋ, -nd
AM dɪs'hɑrtn̩, -z, -ɪŋ, -d

dishearteningly
BR dɪs'hɑːtn̩ɪŋli
AM dɪs'hɑrtn̩ɪŋli

disheartenment
BR dɪs'hɑːtnm(ə)nt, -s
AM dɪs'hɑrtnmənt, -s

dishevel
BR dɪ'ʃɛvl, -z, -d
AM də'ʃɛvəl, -z, -d

dishevelment
BR dɪ'ʃɛvlm(ə)nt
AM də'ʃɛvəlmənt

Dishforth
BR 'dɪʃfəθ, 'dɪʃfɔːθ
AM 'dɪʃfərθ

dishful
BR 'dɪʃfʊl, -z
AM 'dɪʃˌfʊl, -z

dishily
BR 'dɪʃɨli
AM 'dɪʃɨli

dishiness
BR 'dɪʃɪnɨs
AM 'dɪʃinɨs

dishlike
BR 'dɪʃlʌɪk
AM 'dɪʃˌlaɪk

dishonest
BR dɪs'ɒnɪst
AM dɪs'ɑnəst

dishonestly
BR dɪs'ɒnɪstli
AM dɪs'ɑnəs(t)li

dishonesty
BR dɪs'ɒnɪsti
AM dɪs'ɑnəsti

dishonor
BR dɪs'ɒn|ə(r), -əz, -(ə)rɪŋ, -əd
AM dɪs'ɑnər, -z, -ɪŋ, -d

dishonorable
BR dɪs'ɒn(ə)rəbl
AM dɪs'ɑn(ə)rəbəl

dishonorableness
BR dɪs'ɒn(ə)rəblnəs
AM dɪs'ɑn(ə)rəbəlnəs

dishonorably
BR dɪs'ɒn(ə)rəbli
AM dɪs'ɑn(ə)rəbli

dishonour
BR dɪs'ɒn|ə(r), -əz, -(ə)rɪŋ, -əd
AM dɪs'ɑnər, -z, -ɪŋ, -d

dishonourable
BR dɪs'ɒn(ə)rəbl
AM dɪs'ɑn(ə)r(ə)bəl

dishonourableness
BR dɪs'ɒn(ə)rəblnəs
AM dɪs'ɑn(ə)rəbəlnəs

dishonourably
BR dɪs'ɒn(ə)rəbli
AM dɪs'ɑn(ə)rəbli

dishpan
BR 'dɪʃpan, -z
AM 'dɪʃˌpæn, -z

dishrag
BR 'dɪʃrag, -z
AM 'dɪʃˌræg, -z

dishwasher
BR 'dɪʃˌwɒʃə(r), -z
AM 'dɪʃˌwɔʃər, 'dɪʃˌwɑʃər, -z

dishwater
BR 'dɪʃˌwɔːtə(r)
AM 'dɪʃˌwɔdər, 'dɪʃˌwɑdər

dishy
BR 'dɪʃ|i, -ɪə(r), -ɪɪst
AM 'dɪʃi, -ər, -ɨst

disillusion
BR ˌdɪsɪ'l(j)uːʒ|n, -nz, -n̩ɪŋ\-ənɪŋ, -nd
AM ˌdɪsə'luʒən, -z, -ɪŋ, -d

disillusionise
BR ˌdɪsɪ'l(j)uːʒn̩ʌɪz, ˌdɪsɪ'l(j)uːʒənʌɪz, -ɨz, -ɪŋ, -d
AM ˌdɪsə'luʒəˌnaɪz, -ɨz, -ɪŋ, -d

disillusionize
BR ˌdɪsɪ'l(j)uːʒn̩ʌɪz, ˌdɪsɪ'l(j)uːʒənʌɪz, -ɨz, -ɪŋ, -d
AM ˌdɪsə'luʒəˌnaɪz, -ɨz, -ɪŋ, -d

disillusionment
BR ˌdɪsɪ'l(j)uːʒnm(ə)nt, -s
AM ˌdɪsə'luʒənmənt, -s

disincentive
BR ˌdɪs(ɨ)n'sɛntɪv, -z
AM ˌdɪsən'sɛn(t)ɪv, -z

disinclination
BR ˌdɪsɪnklɪ'neɪʃn, ˌdɪsɪŋklɪ'neɪʃn
AM ˌdɪsəŋklə'neɪʃən, dɪsˌɪŋklə'neɪʃən

disincline
BR ˌdɪs(ɨ)n'klʌɪn, ˌdɪsɪŋ'klʌɪn, -z, -ɪŋ, -d
AM ˌdɪsən'klaɪn, -z, -ɪŋ, -d

disincorporate
BR ˌdɪs(ɨ)n'kɔːpəreɪt, ˌdɪsɪŋ'kɔːpəreɪt, -s, -ɪŋ, -ɨd
AM ˌdɪsən'kɔrpəˌreɪ|t, -ts, -dɪŋ, -dɨd

disinfect
BR ˌdɪs(ɨ)n'fɛkt, -s, -ɪŋ, -ɨd
AM ˌdɪsən'fɛk|(t), -(t)s, -tɪŋ, -təd

disinfectant
BR ˌdɪs(ɨ)n'fɛkt(ə)nt, -s
AM ˌdɪsən'fɛktnt, -s

disinfection
BR ˌdɪs(ɨ)n'fɛkʃn, -z
AM ˌdɪsən'fɛkʃən, -z

disinfest
BR ˌdɪs(ɨ)n'fɛst, -s, -ɪŋ, -ɨd
AM ˌdɪsən'fɛst, -s, -ɪŋ, -əd

disinfestation
BR ˌdɪs(ɨ)nfɛ'steɪʃn
AM ˌdɪsənˌfɛs'teɪʃən, dɪsˌɪnfɛs'teɪʃən

disinflation
BR ˌdɪs(ɨ)n'fleɪʃn
AM ˌdɪsən'fleɪʃən

disinflationary
BR ˌdɪs(ɨ)n'fleɪʃn̩(ə)ri
AM ˌdɪsən'fleɪʃəˌnɛri

disinformation
BR ˌdɪsɪnfə'meɪʃn
AM ˌdɪsənfər'meɪʃən, dɪsˌɪnfər'meɪʃən

disingenuous
BR ˌdɪs(ɨ)n'dʒɛnjʊəs
AM ˌdɪsən'dʒɛnjəwəs

disingenuously
BR ˌdɪs(ɨ)n'dʒɛnjʊəsli
AM ˌdɪsən'dʒɛnjəwəsli

disingenuousness
BR ˌdɪs(ɨ)n'dʒɛnjʊəsnəs
AM ˌdɪsən'dʒɛnjəwəsnəs

disinherit
BR ˌdɪs(ɨ)n'hɛrɪt, -s, -ɪŋ, -ɨd
AM ˌdɪsən'hɛrɪ|t, -ts, -dɪŋ, -dɨd

disinheritance
BR ˌdɪs(ɨ)n'hɛrɪt(ə)ns
AM ˌdɪsən'hɛrətns

disintegrate
BR dɪs'ɪntɨgreɪt, -s, -ɪŋ, -ɨd
AM dɪs'ɪn(t)əˌgreɪ|t, -ts, -dɪŋ, -dɨd

disintegration
BR dɪsˌɪntɪ'greɪʃn
AM dɪsˌɪn(t)ə'greɪʃən

disintegrative
BR dɪs'ɪntɨgrətɪv
AM dɪs'ɪn(t)əˌgreɪdɪv

disintegrator
BR dɪs'ɪntɨgreɪtə(r), -z
AM dɪs'ɪn(t)əˌgreɪdər, -z

disinter
BR ˌdɪs(ɨ)n'təː(r), -z, -ɪŋ, -d
AM ˌdɪsən'tər, dɪsˌɪn'tər, -z, -ɪŋ, -d

disinterest
BR (ˌ)dɪs'ɪntrɪst, (ˌ)dɪs'ɪnt(ə)rɛst, -ɨd
AM dɪs'ɪnt(ə)rəst, -əd

disinterestedly
BR (ˌ)dɪs'ɪntrɪstɨdli, (ˌ)dɪs'ɪnt(ə)rɛstɨdli
AM dɪs'ɪnt(ə)rəstədli

disinterestedness
BR (ˌ)dɪs'ɪntrɪstɨdnɨs, (ˌ)dɪs'ɪnt(ə)rɛstɨdnɨs
AM dɪs'ɪn(t)ərəstədnəs, dɪs'ɪn(t)əˌrɛstədnəs

disinterment
BR ˌdɪs(ɨ)n'təːm(ə)nt, -s
AM ˌdɪsən'tərmənt, dɪsˌɪn'tərmənt, -s

disinvest
BR ˌdɪs(ɨ)n'vɛst, -s, -ɪŋ, -ɨd
AM ˌdɪsən'vɛst, -s, -ɪŋ, -əd

disinvestment
BR ˌdɪs(ɨ)n'vɛs(t)m(ə)nt
AM ˌdɪsən'vɛstmənt

disjecta membra
BR dɪsˌdʒɛktə 'mɛmbrə(r)
AM dəsˌdʒɛktə 'mɛmbrə

disjoin
BR dɪs'dʒɔɪn, -z, -ɪŋ, -d

AM dɪs'dʒɔɪn, -z, -ɪŋ, -d

disjoint
BR dɪs'dʒɔɪnt, -s, -ɪŋ, -ɨd
AM dɪs'dʒɔɪn|t, -ts, -(t)ɪŋ, -(t)ɨd

disjointedly
BR dɪs'jɔɪntɨdli
AM dɪs'dʒɔɪn(t)ɨdli

disjointedness
BR dɪs'jɔɪntɨdnɨs
AM dɪs'dʒɔɪn(t)ɨdnɨs

disjunct[1]
adjective
BR dɪs'dʒʌŋ(k)t
AM dɪs'dʒəŋ(k)t

disjunct[2]
noun
BR 'dɪsdʒʌŋ(k)t, -s
AM 'dɪsˌdʒəŋ(k)t, -s

disjunction
BR dɪs'dʒʌŋ(k)ʃn, -z
AM dɪs'dʒəŋ(k)ʃən, -z

disjunctive
BR dɪs'dʒʌŋ(k)tɪv
AM dɪs'dʒəŋ(k)tɪv

disjunctively
BR dɪs'dʒʌŋ(k)tɨvli
AM dɪs'dʒəŋ(k)təvli

disjuncture
BR dɪs'dʒʌŋ(k)tʃə(r), -z
AM dɪs'dʒəŋ(kt)ʃər, -z

disk
BR dɪsk, -s
AM dɪsk, -s

diskette
BR dɪ'skɛt, ˌdɪsk'ɛt, -s
AM dɪs'kɛt, -s

diskless
BR 'dɪsklɨs
AM 'dɪskləs

Disko
BR 'dɪskəʊ
AM 'dɪskoʊ

Disley
BR 'dɪzli
AM 'dɪzli

dislikable
BR dɪs'lʌɪkəbl
AM dɪs'laɪkəbəl

dislike
BR dɪs'lʌɪk, -s, -ɪŋ, -t
AM dɪs'laɪk, -s, -ɪŋ, -t

dislikeable
BR dɪs'lʌɪkəbl
AM dɪs'laɪkəbəl

dislocate
BR 'dɪsləkeɪt, -s, -ɪŋ, -ɨd
AM dɪs'loʊˌkeɪ|t, 'dɪsləˌkeɪ|t, -ts, -dɪŋ, -dɨd

dislocation
BR ˌdɪslə'keɪʃn, -z
AM ˌdɪsloʊ'keɪʃən, ˌdɪslə'keɪʃən, -z

dislodge
BR dɪs'lɒdʒ, -ɨz, -ɪŋ, -d
AM dɪs'lɑdʒ, -əz, -ɪŋ, -d

dislodgement
BR dɪs'lɒdʒm(ə)nt
AM dɪs'lɑdʒmənt

disloyal
BR (ˌ)dɪs'lɔɪ(ə)l
AM dɪs'lɔɪ(ə)l

disloyalist
BR (ˌ)dɪs'lɔɪ(ə)lɪst, -s
AM dɪs'lɔɪ(ə)ləst, -s

disloyally
BR (ˌ)dɪs'lɔɪ(ə)li
AM dɪs'lɔɪ(ə)li

disloyalty
BR (ˌ)dɪs'lɔɪ(ə)lt|i, -ɪz
AM dɪs'lɔɪ(ə)lti, -z

dismal
BR 'dɪzm(ə)l
AM 'dɪzməl

dismally
BR 'dɪzml̩i, 'dɪzməli
AM 'dɪzməli

dismalness
BR 'dɪzm(ə)lnəs
AM 'dɪzməlnəs

dismantle
BR dɪs'mant|l, -lz, -l̩ɪŋ\-lɪŋ, -ld
AM dɪs'mæn(t)əl, -z, -ɪŋ, -d

dismantlement
BR dɨs'mantlm(ə)nt
AM dɪs'mæn(t)lmənt

dismantler
BR dɪs'mantl̩ə(r), dɪs'mantlə(r), -z
AM dɪs'mæn(t)l̩ər, -z

dismast
BR ˌdɪs'mɑːst, ˌdɪs'mast, -s, -ɪŋ, -ɨd
AM dɪs'mæst, -s, -ɪŋ, -əd

dismay
BR dɪs'meɪ, -z, -ɪŋ, -d
AM də'smeɪ, -z, -ɪŋ, -d

dismember
BR (ˌ)dɪs'mɛmb|ə(r), -əz, -(ə)rɪŋ, -əd
AM dɪs'mɛmb|ər, -ərd, -(ə)rɪŋ, -ərd

dismemberment
BR (ˌ)dɪs'mɛmbəm(ə)nt, -s
AM dɪs'mɛmbərmənt, -s

dismiss
BR dɪs'mɪs, -ɨz, -ɪŋ, -t
AM də'smɪs, -ɨz, -ɪŋ, -t

dismissal
BR dɪs'mɪsl, -z
AM də'smɪsəl, -z

dismissible
BR dɪs'mɪsɨbl
AM də'smɪsəbəl

dismission
BR dɪs'mɪʃn
AM də'smɪʃən

dismissive
BR dɪs'mɪsɪv
AM də'smɪsɪv

dismissively
BR dɪs'mɪsɨvli
AM də'smɪsɨvli

dismissiveness
BR dɪs'mɪsɨvnɨs
AM də'smɪsɪvnɨs

dismount
BR (ˌ)dɪs'maʊnt, -s, -ɪŋ, -ɨd
AM dɪs'maʊn|t, -ts, -(t)ɪŋ, -(t)əd

Disney
BR 'dɪzni
AM 'dɪzni

Disneyesque
BR ˌdɪznɪ'ɛsk
AM ˈdɪzni'ɛsk

Disneyland®
BR 'dɪznɪland
AM 'dɪzniˌlænd

disobedience
BR ˌdɪsə'biːdɪəns
AM ˈdɪsə'bidiəns

disobedient
BR ˌdɪsə'biːdɪənt
AM ˈdɪsə'bidiənt

disobediently
BR ˌdɪsə'biːdɪəntli
AM ˈdɪsə'bidiən(t)li

disobey
BR ˌdɪsə'beɪ, -z, -ɪŋ, -d
AM ˈdɪsə'beɪ, -z, -ɪŋ, -d

disobeyer
BR ˌdɪsə'beɪə(r), -z
AM ˈdɪsə'beɪər, -z

disoblige
BR ˌdɪsə'blʌɪdʒ, -ɨz, -ɪŋ, -d
AM ˈdɪsə'blaɪdʒ, -ɨz, -ɪŋ, -d

disobligingly
BR ˌdɪsə'blʌɪdʒɪŋli
AM ˈdɪsə'blaɪdʒɪŋli

disorder
BR dɪs'ɔːd|ə(r), -əz, -(ə)rɪŋ, -əd
AM dɪ'sɔrdər, -z, -ɪŋ, -d

disorderliness
BR dɪs'ɔːdəlɪnɨs
AM dɪ'sɔrdərlinɨs

disorderly
BR dɪs'ɔːdəli
AM dɪ'sɔrdərli

disorganisation
BR dɪsˌɔːgənʌɪ'zeɪʃn, dɪsˌɔːgn̩ʌɪ'zeɪʃn
AM dɪˌsɔrg(ə)nə'zeɪʃən, dɪˌsɔrgəˌnaɪ'zeɪʃən

disorganise
BR dɪs'ɔːgənʌɪz, dɪs'ɔːgn̩ʌɪz, -ɨz, -ɪŋ, -d
AM dɪ'sɔrgəˌnaɪz, -ɨz, -ɪŋ, -d

disorganization
BR dɪsˌɔːgənʌɪ'zeɪʃn, dɪsˌɔːgn̩ʌɪ'zeɪʃn
AM dɪˌsɔrg(ə)nə'zeɪʃən, dɪˌsɔrgəˌnaɪ'zeɪʃən

disorganize
BR dɪs'ɔːgənʌɪz, dɪs'ɔːgn̩ʌɪz, -ɨz, -ɪŋ, -d
AM dɪ'sɔrgəˌnaɪz, -ɨz, -ɪŋ, -d

disorient
BR (ˌ)dɪs'ɔːrɪɛnt, (ˌ)dɪs'ɔːrɪənt, -s, -ɪŋ, -ɨd
AM dɪs'ɔriən|t, -ts, -(t)ɪŋ, -(t)əd

disorientate
BR (ˌ)dɪs'ɔːrɪənteɪt, (ˌ)dɪs'ɔːrɪɛnteɪt, -s, -ɪŋ, -ɨd
AM dɪs'ɔriənˌteɪ|t, -ts, -dɪŋ, -dɨd

disorientation
BR dɪsˌɔːrɪən'teɪʃn, dɪsˌɔːrɪɛn'teɪʃn
AM dɪsˌɔriən'teɪʃən

disown
BR (ˌ)dɪs'əʊn, -z, -ɪŋ, -d
AM də'soʊn, -z, -ɪŋ, -d

disowner
BR (ˌ)dɪs'əʊnə(r), -z
AM də'soʊnər, -z

disparage
BR dɪ'spar|ɪdʒ, -ɨdʒɨz, -ɨdʒɪŋ, -ɪdʒd
AM də'spɛrɪdʒ, -ɨz, -ɪŋ, -d

disparagement
BR dɪ'sparɪdʒm(ə)nt
AM də'spɛrɨdʒmənt

disparagingly
BR dɪ'sparɪdʒɪŋli
AM də'spɛrɨdʒɪŋli

disparate
BR 'dɪsp(ə)rət
AM 'dɪspərət, də'spɛrət

disparately
BR 'dɪsp(ə)rətli
AM 'dɪspərətli, də'spɛrətli

disparateness
BR 'dɪsp(ə)rətnəs
AM 'dɪspərətnəs, də'spɛrətnəs

disparity
BR dɪ'sparɪt|i, -ɪz
AM də'spɛrədi, -z

dispassionate
BR dɪs'paʃn̩ət, dɪs'paʃənət
AM dɪs'pæʃ(ə)nət

dispassionately
BR dɪs'paʃn̩ətli, dɪs'paʃənətli
AM dɪs'pæʃ(ə)nətli

dispassionateness
BR dɪs'paʃn̩ətnəs, dɪs'paʃənətnəs
AM dɪs'pæʃ(ə)nətnəs
dispatch
BR dɪ'spatʃ, -ɪz, -ɪŋ, -t
AM də'spætʃ, -əz, -ɪŋ, -t
dispatcher
BR dɪ'spatʃə(r), -z
AM də'spætʃər, -z
dispel
BR dɪ'spɛl, -z, -ɪŋ, -d
AM də'spɛl, -z, -ɪŋ, -d
dispeller
BR dɪ'spɛlə(r), -z
AM də'spɛlər, -z
dispensability
BR dɪˌspɛnsə'bɪlɪti
AM dəˌspɛnsə'bɪlɨdi
dispensable
BR dɪ'spɛnsəbl
AM də'spɛnsəbəl
dispensary
BR dɪ'spɛns(ə)r|i, -ɪz
AM də'spɛns(ə)ri, -z
dispensation
BR ˌdɪsp(ə)n'seɪʃn, ˌdɪspɛn'seɪʃn, -z
AM ˌdɪspən'seɪʃən, -z
dispensational
BR ˌdɪsp(ə)n'seɪʃn̩(ə)l, ˌdɪsp(ə)n'seɪʃən(ə)l, ˌdɪspɛn'seɪʃn̩(ə)l, ˌdɪspɛn'seɪʃən(ə)l
AM ˌdɪspən'seɪʃ(ə)nəl
dispensatory
BR dɪ'spɛnsət(ə)ri
AM də'spɛnsəˌtɔri
dispense
BR dɪ'spɛns, -ɪz, -ɪŋ, -t
AM də'spɛns, -əz, -ɪŋ, -t
dispenser
BR dɪ'spɛnsə(r), -z
AM də'spɛnsər, -z
dispersable
BR dɪ'spəːsəbl
AM də'spərsəbəl
dispersal
BR dɪ'spəːsl, -z
AM də'spərsəl, -z
dispersant
BR dɪ'spəːs(ə)nt, -s
AM də'spərsənt, -s
disperse
BR dɪ'spəːs, -ɪz, -ɪŋ, -t
AM də'spərs, -əz, -ɪŋ, -t
disperser
BR dɪ'spəːsə(r), -z
AM də'spərsər, -z
dispersible
BR dɪ'spəːsɪbl
AM də'spərsəbəl
dispersion
BR dɪ'spəːʃn
AM də'spərʒən, də'spərʃən
dispersive
BR dɪ'spəːsɪv
AM də'spərsɪv
dispirit
BR dɪ'spɪr|ɪt, -ɪts, -ɪtɪŋ, -ɪtɪd
AM də'spɪrɨ|t, -ts, -dɪŋ, -dɨd
dispiritedly
BR dɪ'spɪrɪtɪdli
AM də'spɪrɨdɨdli
dispiritedness
BR dɪ'spɪrɪtɪdnɪs
AM də'spɪrɨdɨdnɨs
dispiritingly
BR dɪ'spɪrɪtɪŋli
AM də'spɪrɨdɪŋli
displace
BR dɪs'pleɪs, -ɪz, -ɪŋ, -t
AM dɪs'pleɪs, -ɪz, -ɪŋ, -t
displacement
BR dɪs'pleɪsm(ə)nt, -s
AM dɪs'pleɪsmənt, -s
display
BR dɪ'spleɪ, -z, -ɪŋ, -d
AM də'spleɪ, -z, -ɪŋ, -d
displayer
BR dɪ'spleɪə(r), -z
AM də'spleɪər, -z
displease
BR (ˌ)dɪs'pliːz, -ɪz, -ɪŋ, -d
AM də'spliz, dɪ'spliz, -ɪz, -ɪŋ, -d
displeasingly
BR (ˌ)dɪs'pliːzɪŋli
AM də'splizɪŋli, dɪ'splizɪŋli
displeasure
BR (ˌ)dɪs'plɛʒə(r)
AM dɪs'plɛʒər
disport
BR dɪ'spɔːt, -s, -ɪŋ, -ɪd
AM də'spɔ(ə)rt, -ts, -'spɔrdɪŋ, -'spɔrdəd
disposability
BR dɪˌspəʊzə'bɪlɪti
AM dəˌspoʊzə'bɪlɨdi
disposable
BR dɪ'spəʊzəbl
AM də'spoʊzəbəl
disposal
BR dɪ'spəʊzl
AM də'spoʊzəl
dispose
BR dɪ'spəʊz, -ɪz, -ɪŋ, -d
AM də'spoʊz, -əz, -ɪŋ, -d
disposer
BR dɪ'spəʊzə(r), -z
AM də'spoʊzər, -z
disposition
BR ˌdɪspə'zɪʃn, -z
AM ˌdɪspə'zɪʃən, -z
dispossess
BR ˌdɪspə'zɛs, -ɪz, -ɪŋ, -t
AM ¦dɪspə'zɛs, -əz, -ɪŋ, -t
dispossession
BR ˌdɪspə'zɛʃn
AM ¦dɪspə'zɛʃən
dispraise
BR dɪs'preɪz, -ɪz, -ɪŋ, -d
AM dɪs'preɪz, -ɪz, -ɪŋ, -d
Disprin®
BR 'dɪsprɪn
AM 'dɪsprɪn
disproof
BR (ˌ)dɪs'pruːf
AM dɪs'pruf
disproportion
BR ˌdɪsprə'pɔːʃn
AM ¦dɪsprə'pɔrʃən
disproportional
BR ˌdɪsprə'pɔːʃn̩(ə)l, ˌdɪsprə'pɔːʃən(ə)l
AM ¦dɪsprə'pɔrʃ(ə)nəl
disproportionally
BR ˌdɪsprə'pɔːʃn̩əli, ˌdɪsprə'pɔːʃən̩li, ˌdɪsprə'pɔːʃənli, ˌdɪsprə'pɔːʃ(ə)nəli
AM ¦dɪsprə'pɔrʃ(ə)nəli
disproportionate
BR ˌdɪsprə'pɔːʃənət, ˌdɪsprə'pɔːʃn̩ət
AM ¦dɪsprə'pɔrʃ(ə)nət
disproportionately
BR ˌdɪsprə'pɔːʃənətli, ˌdɪsprə'pɔːʃn̩ətli
AM ¦dɪsprə'pɔrʃ(ə)nətli
disproportionateness
BR ˌdɪsprə'pɔːʃənətnəs, ˌdɪsprə'pɔːʃn̩ətnəs
AM ¦dɪsprə'pɔrʃ(ə)nətnəs
disproportioned
BR ˌdɪsprə'pɔːʃnd
AM ¦dɪsprə'pɔrʃənd
disprovable
BR (ˌ)dɪs'pruːvəbl
AM dɪs'pruvəbəl
disproval
BR (ˌ)dɪs'pruːvl, -z
AM dɪs'pruvəl, -z
disprove
BR (ˌ)dɪs'pruːv, -z, -ɪŋ, -d
AM dɪs'pruv, -z, -ɪŋ, -d
disputable
BR dɪ'spjuːtəbl
AM də'spjudəbəl, 'dɪspjədəbəl
disputably
BR dɪ'spjuːtəbli
AM də'spjudəbli, 'dɪspjədəbli
disputant
BR 'dɪspjʊt(ə)nt, dɪ'spjuːt(ə)nt, -s
AM də'spjutnt, -s
disputation
BR ˌdɪspjʊ'teɪʃn, -z
AM ˌdɪspjə'teɪʃən, ˌdɪspju'teɪʃən, -z
disputatious
BR ˌdɪspjʊ'teɪʃəs
AM ˌdɪspjə'teɪʃəs, ˌdɪspju'teɪʃəs
disputatiously
BR ˌdɪspjʊ'teɪʃəsli
AM ˌdɪspjə'teɪʃəsli, ˌdɪspju'teɪʃəsli
disputatiousness
BR ˌdɪspjʊ'teɪʃəsnəs
AM ˌdɪspjə'teɪʃəsnəs, ˌdɪspju'teɪʃəsnəs
dispute[1]
noun
BR dɪ'spjuːt, 'dɪspjuːt, -s
AM də'spjut, 'dɪˌspjut, -s
dispute[2]
verb
BR dɪ'spjuːt, -s, -ɪŋ, -ɪd
AM də'spju|t, -ts, -dɪŋ, -dəd
disputer
BR dɪ'spjuːtə(r), -z
AM də'spjudər, -z
disqualification
BR dɪsˌkwɒlɪfɪ'keɪʃn, -z
AM ¦dɪsˌkwɑləfə'keɪʃən, də'skwɑləfəˌkeɪʃən, -z
disqualify
BR dɪs'kwɒlɪfʌɪ, -z, -ɪŋ, -d
AM də'skwɑləˌfaɪ, dɪs'skwɑləˌfaɪ, -z, -ɪŋ, -d
disquiet
BR dɪs'kwʌɪət, -s, -ɪŋ, -ɪd
AM dɪs'kwaɪə|t, də'skwaɪə|t, -ts, -dɪŋ, -dəd
disquieting
BR dɪs'kwʌɪətɪŋ
AM dɪs'kwaɪədɪŋ, də'skwaɪədɪŋ
disquietingly
BR dɪs'kwʌɪətɪŋli
AM dɪs'kwaɪədɪŋli, də'skwaɪədɪŋli
disquietude
BR dɪs'kwʌɪɪtjuːd, dɪs'kwʌɪɪtʃuːd
AM dɪs'kwaɪəˌt(j)ud, də'skwaɪəˌt(j)ud
disquisition
BR ˌdɪskwɪ'zɪʃn, -z
AM ˌdɪskwə'zɪʃən, -z
disquisitional
BR ˌdɪskwɪ'zɪʃn̩(ə)l, ˌdɪskwɪ'zɪʃən(ə)l
AM ˌdɪskwə'zɪʃ(ə)nəl
Disraeli
BR dɪz'reɪli
AM dɪz'reɪli

disrate
BR (ˌ)dɪsˈreɪt, -s, -ɪŋ, -ɨd
AM dɪsˈreɪ|t, dəˈsreɪ|t, -ts, -dɪŋ, -dɨd
disregard
BR ˌdɪsrɪˈɡɑːd, -z, -ɪŋ, -ɨd
AM ˌdɪsrəˈɡɑrd, ˌdɪsriˈɡɑrd, -z, -ɪŋ, -əd
disregardful
BR ˌdɪsrɪˈɡɑːdf(ʊ)l
AM ˌdɪsrəˈɡɑrdfəl, ˌdɪsriˈɡɑrdfəl
disregardfully
BR ˌdɪsrɪˈɡɑːdfʊli, ˌdɪsrɪˈɡɑːdfl̩i
AM ˌdɪsrəˈɡɑrdfəli, ˌdɪsriˈɡɑrdfəli
disrelish
BR (ˌ)dɪsˈrɛl|ɪʃ, -ɪʃɨz, -ɪʃɪŋ, -ɪʃt
AM dɪsˈrɛlɪʃ, -ɨz, -ɪŋ, -t
disremember
BR ˌdɪsrɪˈmɛmb|ə(r), -əz, -(ə)rɪŋ, -əd
AM ˌdɪsrəˈmɛmbər, -z, -ɪŋ, -d
disrepair
BR ˌdɪsrɪˈpɛː(r)
AM ˌdɪsrəˈpɛ(ə)r
disreputable
BR dɪsˈrɛpjʊtəbl
AM dɪsˈrɛpjədəbəl
disreputableness
BR dɪsˈrɛpjʊtəblnəs
AM dɪsˈrɛpjədəbəlnəs
disreputably
BR dɪsˈrɛpjʊtəbli
AM dɪsˈrɛpjədəbli
disrepute
BR ˌdɪsrɪˈpjuːt
AM ˌdɪsrəˈpjut
disrespect
BR ˌdɪsrɪˈspɛkt
AM ˌdɪsrəˈspɛk(t)
disrespectful
BR ˌdɪsrɪˈspɛk(t)f(ʊ)l
AM ˌdɪsrəˈspɛk(t)fəl
disrespectfully
BR ˌdɪsrɪˈspɛk(t)fʊli, ˌdɪsrɪˈspɛk(t)fl̩i
AM ˌdɪsrəˈspɛk(t)fəli
disrobe
BR (ˌ)dɪsˈrəʊb, -z, -ɪŋ, -d
AM dɪsˈroʊb, -z, -ɪŋ, -d
disrupt
BR dɪsˈrʌpt, -s, -ɪŋ, -ɨd
AM dɪsˈrəpt, -s, -ɪŋ, -əd
disrupter
BR dɪsˈrʌptə(r), -z
AM dɪsˈrəptər, -z
disruption
BR dɪsˈrʌpʃn
AM dɪsˈrəpʃən
disruptive
BR dɪsˈrʌptɪv
AM dɪsˈrəptɪv
disruptively
BR dɪsˈrʌptɨvli
AM dɪsˈrəptəvli
disruptiveness
BR dɪsˈrʌptɨvnɨs
AM dɪsˈrəptɪvnɨs
Diss
BR dɪs
AM dɪs
dissatisfaction
BR dɪ(s)ˌsatɪsˈfakʃn, ˌdɪsatɪsˈfakʃn
AM dɪ(s)ˌsædəsˈfækʃən
dissatisfactory
BR dɪ(s)ˌsatɪsˈfakt(ə)ri, ˌdɪsatɪsˈfakt(ə)ri
AM dɪ(s)ˌsædəsˈfækˌtɔri
dissatisfiedly
BR dɪ(s)ˈsatɪsfʌɪdli
AM dɪ(s)ˈsædəsˌfaɪ(ə)dli
dissatisfy
BR dɪ(s)ˈsatɪsfʌɪ, -z, -ɪŋ, -d
AM dɪ(s)ˈsædəsˌfaɪ, -z, -ɪŋ, -d
dissect
BR dɪˈsɛkt, dʌɪˈsɛkt, -s, -ɪŋ, -ɨd
AM dəˈsɛk|(t), daɪˈsɛk|(t), -(t)s, -tɪŋ, -təd
dissection
BR dɪˈsɛkʃn, dʌɪˈsɛkʃn, -z
AM dəˈsɛkʃən, daɪˈsɛkʃən, -z
dissector
BR dɪˈsɛktə(r), dʌɪˈsɛktə(r), -z
AM dəˈsɛktər, daɪˈsɛktər, -z
disseise
BR dɪ(s)ˈsiːz, -ɨz, -ɪŋ, -d
AM də(s)ˈsiz, dɪ(s)ˈsiz, -ɨz, -ɪŋ, -d
disseisin
BR dɪ(s)ˈsiːz(ɪ)n
AM də(s)ˈsizn, dɪ(s)ˈsizn
disseize
BR dɪ(s)ˈsiːz, -ɨz, -ɪŋ, -d
AM də(s)ˈsiz, dɪ(s)ˈsiz, -ɨz, -ɪŋ, -d
disseizin
BR dɪ(s)ˈsiːz(ɪ)n
AM də(s)ˈsizn, dɪ(s)ˈsizn
dissemblance
BR dɪˈsɛmbləns
AM dɪ(s)ˈsɛmbləns
dissemble
BR dɪˈsɛmb|l, -lz, -l̩ɪŋ\-lɪŋ, -ld
AM dəˈsɛmb|əl, -əlz, -(ə)lɪŋ, -əld
dissembler
BR dɪˈsɛmblə(r), -z
AM dəˈsɛmb(ə)lər, -z
dissemblingly
BR dɪˈsɛmblɪŋli, dɪˈsɛmbl̩ɪŋli
AM dəˈsɛmb(ə)lɪŋli
disseminate
BR dɪˈsɛmɪneɪt, -s, -ɪŋ, -ɨd
AM dəˈsɛməˌneɪ|t, -ts, -dɪŋ, -dɨd
dissemination
BR dɪˌsɛmɪˈneɪʃn
AM dəˌsɛməˈneɪʃən
disseminator
BR dɪˈsɛmɪneɪtə(r), -z
AM dəˈsɛməˌneɪdər, -z
dissension
BR dɪˈsɛnʃn, -z
AM dəˈsɛn(t)ʃən, -z
dissent
BR dɪˈsɛnt, -s, -ɪŋ, -ɨd
AM dəˈsɛn|t, -ts, -(t)ɪŋ, -(t)əd
dissenter
BR dɪˈsɛntə(r), -z
AM dəˈsɛn(t)ər, -z
dissentient
BR dɪˈsɛnʃ(ɪ)ənt, dɪˈsɛnʃnt, -s
AM dəˈsɛn(t)ʃiənt, -s
dissentingly
BR dɪˈsɛntɪŋli
AM dəˈsɛn(t)ɪŋli
dissepement
BR dɪˈsɛpɪm(ə)nt, -s
AM dəˈsɛpəmənt, -s
dissertate
BR ˈdɪsəteɪt, -s, -ɪŋ, -ɨd
AM ˈdɪsərˌteɪ|t, -ts, -dɪŋ, -dɨd
dissertation
BR ˌdɪsəˈteɪʃn, -z
AM ˌdɪsərˈteɪʃən, -z
dissertational
BR ˌdɪsəˈteɪʃn̩(ə)l, ˌdɪsəˈteɪʃən(ə)l
AM ˌdɪsərˈteɪʃ(ə)nəl
disserve
BR ˌdɪsˈsəːv, dɪ(s)ˈsəːv, -z, -ɪŋ, -d
AM dɪ(s)ˈsərv, -z, -ɪŋ, -d
disservice
BR ˌdɪsˈsəːvɪs, dɪ(s)ˈsəːvɪs
AM dɪ(s)ˈsərvɪs
dissever
BR dɪˈsɛvə(r), -z, -ɪŋ, -d
AM dəˈsɛvər, -z, -ɪŋ, -d
disseverance
BR dɪˈsɛv(ə)rəns, dɪˈsɛv(ə)rn̩s
AM dəˈsɛv(ə)rəns
disseverment
BR dɪˈsɛvəm(ə)nt
AM dəˈsɛvərmənt
dissidence
BR ˈdɪsɪd(ə)ns
AM ˈdɪsədns
dissident
BR ˈdɪsɪd(ə)nt, -s
AM ˈdɪsədnt, -s
dissimilar
BR ˌdɪ(s)ˈsɪmɪlə(r), ˌdɪ(s)ˈsɪml̩ə(r), dɪ(s)ˈsɪmɪlə(r), dɪˈsɪml̩ə(r)
AM dɪ(s)ˈsɪmɪlər
dissimilarity
BR ˌdɪsɪmɪˈlarɪti, dɪ(s)ˌsɪmɪˈlarɪt|i, -ɪz
AM ˌdɪ(s)ˌsɪməˈlɛrədi, -z
dissimilarly
BR ˌdɪ(s)ˈsɪmɪləli, dɪ(s)ˈsɪmɪləli
AM dɪ(s)ˈsɪmɪlərli
dissimilate
BR dɪˈsɪmɪleɪt, -s, -ɪŋ, -ɨd
AM dɪˈsɪməˌleɪ|t, -ts, -dɪŋ, -dɨd
dissimilation
BR dɪˌsɪmɪˈleɪʃn, -z
AM dəˌsɪməˈleɪʃən, ˌdɪˌsɪməˈleɪʃən, -z
dissimilatory
BR dɪˈsɪmɪlət(ə)ri
AM dɪˈsɪmələˌtɔri
dissimilitude
BR ˌdɪsɪˈmɪlɪtjuːd, ˌdɪsɪˈmɪlɪtʃuːd
AM ˌdɪsɪˈmɪləˌt(j)ud
dissimulate
BR dɪˈsɪmjʊleɪt, -s, -ɪŋ, -ɨd
AM dɪˈsɪmjəˌleɪ|t, -ts, -dɪŋ, -dɨd
dissimulation
BR dɪˌsɪmjʊˈleɪʃn, -z
AM dəˌsɪmjəˈleɪʃən, ˌdɪˌsɪmjəˈleɪʃən, -z
dissimulator
BR dɪˈsɪmjʊleɪtə(r), -z
AM dɪˈsɪmjəˌleɪdər, -z
dissipate
BR ˈdɪsɪpeɪt, -s, -ɪŋ, -ɨd
AM ˈdɪsəˌpeɪ|t, -ts, -dɪŋ, -dɨd
dissipater
BR ˈdɪsɪpeɪtə(r), -z
AM ˈdɪsəˌpeɪdər, -z
dissipation
BR ˌdɪsɪˈpeɪʃn
AM ˌdɪsəˈpeɪʃən
dissipative
BR ˈdɪsɪpeɪtɪv
AM ˈdɪsəˌpeɪdɪv
dissipator
BR ˈdɪsɪpeɪtə(r), -z
AM ˈdɪsəˌpeɪdər, -z
dissociate
BR dɪˈsəʊʃɪeɪt, dɪˈsəʊsɪeɪt, -s, -ɪŋ, -ɨd
AM dɪˈsoʊʃiˌeɪ|t, dɪˈsoʊsiˌeɪ|t, -ts, -dɪŋ, -dɨd

dissociation
BR dɪˌsəʊʃɪˈeɪʃən, dɪˌsəʊsɪˈeɪʃn
AM dɪˌsoʊʃiˈeɪʃən, dɪˌsoʊsiˈeɪʃən

dissociative
BR dɪˈsəʊʃɪətɪv, dɪˈsəʊsɪətɪv
AM dɪˈsoʊʃiˌeɪdɪv, dɪˈsoʊsiˌeɪdɪv

dissolubility
BR dɪˌsɒljʉˈbɪlɨti
AM dəˌsɑljəˈbɪlɨdi

dissoluble
BR dɪˈsɒljʉbl
AM dəˈsɑljəbəl

dissolubly
BR dɪˈsɒljʉbli
AM dəˈsɑljəbli

dissolute
BR ˈdɪsəl(j)uːt
AM ˈdɪsəˌlut, ˈdɪsəlˌjut

dissolutely
BR ˈdɪsəl(j)uːtli
AM ˈdɪsəˌlutli, ˈdɪsəlˌjutli

dissoluteness
BR ˈdɪsəl(j)uːtnəs
AM ˈdɪsəˌlutnəs, ˈdɪsəlˌjutnəs

dissolution
BR ˌdɪsəˈl(j)uːʃn
AM ˌdɪsəˈluʃən, ˌdɪsəlˈjuʃən

dissolutionary
BR ˌdɪsəˈl(j)uːʃn̩(ə)ri
AM ˌdɪsəˈluʃəˌnɛri, ˌdɪsəlˈjuʃəˌnɛri

dissolvable
BR dɪˈzɒlvəbl
AM dəˈzɔlvəbəl, dəˈzɑlvəbəl

dissolve
BR dɪˈzɒlv, -z, -ɪŋ, -d
AM dəˈzɔlv, dəˈzɑlv, -z, -ɪŋ, -d

dissolvent
BR dɪˈzɒlv(ə)nt, -s
AM dəˈzɔlvənt, dəˈzɑlvənt, -s

dissonance
BR ˈdɪsənəns
AM ˈdɪsənəns

dissonant
BR ˈdɪsənənt
AM ˈdɪsənənt

dissonantly
BR ˈdɪsənəntli
AM ˈdɪsənən(t)li

dissuade
BR dɪˈsweɪd, -z, -ɪŋ, -ɨd
AM dəˈsweɪd, -z, -ɪŋ, -ɨd

dissuader
BR dɪˈsweɪdə(r), -z
AM dəˈsweɪdər, -z

dissuasion
BR dɪˈsweɪʒn
AM dəˈsweɪʒən

dissuasive
BR dɪˈsweɪsɪv
AM dəˈsweɪsɪv

dissyllabic
BR ˌdʌɪsɪˈlabɪk, ˌdɪsɪˈlabɪk
AM ˈdaɪsəˈlæbɪk, ˈdɪsəˈlæbɪk

dissyllable
BR ˈdʌɪˌsɪləbl, ˌdʌɪˈsɪləbl, -z
AM daɪˈsɪləbəl, dɪˈsɪləbəl, -z

dissymmetrical
BR ˌdɪ(s)sɪˈmɛtrɨkl
AM ˈdɪ(s)sɪˈmətrəkəl

dissymmetry
BR dɪ(s)ˈsɪmɨtr|i, -ɪz
AM də(s)ˈsɪmətri, dɪ(s)ˈsɪmətri, -z

distaff
BR ˈdɪstɑːf, ˈdɪstaf, -s
AM ˈdɪˌstæf, -s

distal
BR ˈdɪstl
AM ˈdɪstl

distally
BR ˈdɪstl̩i, ˈdɪstəli
AM ˈdɪstl̩i

distance
BR ˈdɪst(ə)ns, -ɨz, -ɪŋ, -t
AM ˈdɪstəns, -əz, -ɪŋ, -t

distant
BR ˈdɪst(ə)nt
AM ˈdɪstənt

distantly
BR ˈdɪst(ə)ntli
AM ˈdɪstən(t)li

distantness
BR ˈdɪst(ə)ntnəs
AM ˈdɪstən(t)nəs

distaste
BR (ˌ)dɪsˈteɪst
AM dɪsˈteɪst

distasteful
BR (ˌ)dɪsˈteɪs(t)f(ʊ)l
AM dɪsˈteɪs(t)fəl

distastefully
BR (ˌ)dɪsˈteɪs(t)fʊli, (ˌ)dɪsˈteɪs(t)fl̩i
AM dɪsˈteɪs(t)fəli

distastefulness
BR (ˌ)dɪsˈteɪs(t)f(ʊ)lnəs
AM dɪsˈteɪs(t)fəlnəs

distemper
BR dɪˈstɛmp|ə(r), -əz, -(ə)rɪŋ, -əd
AM dɪsˈtɛmpər, -z, -ɪŋ, -d

distend
BR dɪˈstɛnd, -z, -ɪŋ, -ɨd
AM dəˈstɛnd, -z, -ɪŋ, -əd

distensibility
BR dɪˌstɛnsɪˈbɪlɨti
AM dəˌstɛnsəˈbɪlɨdi

distensible
BR dɪˈstɛnsɪbl
AM dəˈstɛnsəbəl

distension
BR dɪˈstɛnʃn
AM dəˈstɛnʃən

distich
BR ˈdɪstɪk, -s
AM ˈdɪstɪk, -s

distichous
BR ˈdɪstɪkəs
AM ˈdɪstɪkəs

distil
BR dɪˈstɪl, -z, -ɪŋ, -d
AM dəˈstɪl, -z, -ɪŋ, -d

distill
BR dɪˈstɪl, -z, -ɪŋ, -d
AM dəˈstɪl, -z, -ɪŋ, -d

distillate
BR ˈdɪstɨlət, ˈdɪstl̩ət, ˈdɪstɨleɪt, -s
AM ˈdɪstɨlət, ˈdɪstəˌleɪt, -s

distillation
BR ˌdɪstɪˈleɪʃn
AM ˌdɪstəˈleɪʃən

distillatory
BR dɪˈstɪlət(ə)ri
AM dəˈstɪləˌtɔri

distiller
BR dɪˈstɪlə(r), -z
AM dəˈstɪlər, -z

distillery
BR dɪˈstɪl(ə)r|i, -ɪz
AM dəˈstɪl(ə)ri, -z

distinct
BR dɪˈstɪŋ(k)t
AM dəˈstɪŋ(k)t, dəˈstɪŋk(t)

distinction
BR dɪˈstɪŋ(k)ʃn, -z
AM dəˈstɪŋ(k)ʃən, -z

distinctive
BR dɪˈstɪŋ(k)tɪv
AM dəˈstɪŋ(k)tɪv

distinctively
BR dɪˈstɪŋ(k)tɨvli
AM dəˈstɪŋ(k)tɨvli

distinctiveness
BR dɪˈstɪŋ(k)tɨvnɨs
AM dəˈstɪŋ(k)tɪvnɨs

distinctly
BR dɪˈstɪŋ(k)tli
AM dəˈstɪŋ(k)tli, dəˈstɪŋk(t)li

distinctness
BR dɪˈstɪŋ(k)tnɨs, dɪˈstɪŋk(t)nɨs
AM dəˈstɪŋ(k)tnɨs, dəˈstɪŋk(t)nɨs

distingué
BR dɪˈstaŋgeɪ
AM dəˌstɪŋˈgeɪ

distinguée
BR dɪˌstɪŋˈgeɪ
AM dəˌstɪŋˈgeɪ

distinguish
BR dɪˈstɪŋgw|ɪʃ, -ɪʃɪz, -ɪʃɪŋ, -ɪʃt
AM dəˈstɪŋgwɪʃ, -ɨz, -ɪŋ, -t

distinguishable
BR dɪˈstɪŋgwɪʃəbl
AM dəˈstɪŋgwɪʃəbəl

distinguishably
BR dɪˈstɪŋgwɪʃəbli
AM dəˈstɪŋgwɪʃəbli

distort
BR dɪˈstɔːt, -s, -ɪŋ, -ɨd
AM dəˈstɔ(ə)rt, -ts, -ˈstɔrdɪŋ, -ˈstɔrdəd

distortedly
BR dɪˈstɔːtɨdli
AM dəˈstɔrdədli

distortedness
BR dɪˈstɔːtɨdnɨs
AM dəˈstɔrdədnəs

distorter
BR dɪˈstɔːtə(r), -z
AM dəˈstɔrdər, -z

distortion
BR dɪˈstɔːʃn, -z
AM dəˈstɔrʃən, -z

distortional
BR dɪˈstɔːʃn̩(ə)l, dɪˈstɔːʃən(ə)l
AM dəˈstɔrʃ(ə)nəl

distortionless
BR dɪˈstɔːʃnləs
AM dəˈstɔrʃənləs

distract
BR dɪˈstrakt, -s, -ɪŋ, -ɨd
AM dəˈstræk|(t), -(t)s, -tɪŋ, -təd

distracted
BR dɪˈstraktɨd
AM dəˈstræktəd

distractedly
BR dɪˈstraktɨdli
AM dəˈstræktədli

distractedness
BR dɪˈstraktɨdnɨs
AM dəˈstræktədnəs

distraction
BR dɪˈstrakʃn, -z
AM dəˈstrækʃən, -z

distractor
BR dɪˈstraktə(r), -z
AM dəˈstræktər, -z

distrain
BR dɪˈstreɪn, -z, -ɪŋ, -d
AM dəˈstreɪn, -z, -ɪŋ, -d

distrainee
BR dɪˌstreɪˈniː, ˌdɪstreɪˈniː, -z
AM dəˈstreɪˈni, -z

distrainer
BR dɪˈstreɪnə(r), -z
AM dəˈstreɪnər, -z

distrainment
BR dɪˈstreɪnm(ə)nt
AM dəˈstreɪnmənt

distrainor
BR dɪˈstreɪnə(r), -z
AM dəˈstreɪnər, -z

distraint
BR dɪˈstreɪnt
AM dəˈstreɪnt

distrait
BR dɪ'streɪ, 'dɪstreɪ
AM də'streɪ, di'streɪ
distraite
BR dɪ'streɪt, 'dɪstreɪt
AM də'streɪt, di'streɪt
distraught
BR dɪ'strɔːt
AM də'strɔt, də'strɑt
distress
BR dɪ'strɛs, -ɪz, -ɪŋ, -t
AM də'strɛs, -əz, -ɪŋ, -t
distressful
BR dɪ'strɛsf(ʊ)l
AM də'strɛsfəl
distressfully
BR dɪ'strɛsfʊli, dɪ'strɛsfl̩i
AM də'strɛsfəli
distressing
BR dɪ'strɛsɪŋ
AM də'strɛsɪŋ
distressingly
BR dɪ'strɛsɪŋli
AM də'strɛsɪŋli
distributable
BR dɪ'strɪbjʊtəbl, 'dɪstrɪbjuːtəbl
AM də'strɪbjudəbəl
distributary
BR dɪ'strɪbjʊt(ə)r|i, 'dɪstrɪbjuːt(ə)r|i, -ɪz
AM də'strɪbjuˌtɛri, -z
distribute
BR dɪ'strɪbjuːt, 'dɪstrɪbjuːt, -s, -ɪŋ, -ɪd
AM də'strɪbju|t, -ts, -dɪŋ, -dəd
distribution
BR ˌdɪstrɪ'bjuːʃn, -z
AM ˌdɪstrə'bjuʃən, -z
distributional
BR ˌdɪstrɪ'bjuːʃn(ə)l, ˌdɪstrɪ'bjuːʃən(ə)l
AM ˌdɪstrə'bjuʃ(ə)nəl
distributive
BR dɪ'strɪbjʊtɪv
AM də'strɪbjədɪv
distributively
BR dɪ'strɪbjʊtɪvli
AM də'strɪbjədɪvli
distributor
BR dɪ'strɪbjʊtə(r), 'dɪstrɪbjuːtə(r), -z
AM də'strɪbjədər, -z
district
BR 'dɪstrɪkt, -s
AM 'dɪstrɪk(t), -s
distrust
BR (ˌ)dɪs'trʌst, -s, -ɪŋ, -ɪd
AM dɪs'trəst, -s, -ɪŋ, -əd
distruster
BR (ˌ)dɪs'trʌstə(r), -z
AM dɪs'trəstər, -z
distrustful
BR (ˌ)dɪs'trʌs(t)f(ʊ)l
AM dɪs'trəs(t)fəl
distrustfully
BR (ˌ)dɪs'trʌs(t)fʊli, (ˌ)dɪs'trʌs(t)fl̩i
AM dɪs'trəs(t)fəli
distrustfulness
BR (ˌ)dɪs'trʌstf(ʊ)lnəs
AM dɪs'trəs(t)fəlnəs
disturb
BR dɪ'stəːb, -z, -ɪŋ, -d
AM də'stərb, -z, -ɪŋ, -d
disturbance
BR dɪ'stəːb(ə)ns, -ɪz
AM də'stərbəns, -əz
disturber
BR dɪ'stəːbə(r), -z
AM də'stərbər, -z
disturbingly
BR dɪ'stəːbɪŋli
AM də'stərbɪŋli
disulphide
BR dʌɪ'sʌlfʌɪd, -z
AM daɪ'səlˌfaɪd, -z
disunion
BR (ˌ)dɪs'juːnɪən
AM dɪs'junjən
disunite
BR ˌdɪsjʊ'nʌɪt, -s, -ɪŋ, -ɪd
AM ˌdɪsju'naɪ|t, ˌdɪʃ(j)u'naɪ|t, -ts, -dɪŋ, -dɪd
disunity
BR (ˌ)dɪs'juːnɪti
AM dɪs'junədi, -z
disuse[1]
noun
BR (ˌ)dɪs'juːs
AM dɪs'jus
disuse[2]
verb
BR ˌdɪs'juːz, -ɪz, -ɪŋ, -d
AM dɪs'juz, -əz, -ɪŋ, -d
disutility
BR ˌdɪsjʊ'tɪlɪti
AM ˌdɪsju'tɪlɪdi
disyllabic
BR ˌdʌɪsɪ'labɪk, ˌdɪsɪ'labɪk
AM ˌdaɪsə'læbɪk, ˌdɪsə'læbɪk
disyllable
BR 'dʌɪˌsɪləbl, ˌdʌɪ'sɪləbl, -z
AM daɪ'sɪləbəl, dɪ'sɪləbəl, -z
dit
BR dɪt, -s
AM dɪt, -s
ditch
BR dɪtʃ, -ɪz, -ɪŋ, -t
AM dɪtʃ, -ɪz, -ɪŋ, -t
ditcher
BR 'dɪtʃə(r), -z
AM 'dɪtʃər, -z
ditchwater
BR 'dɪtʃˌwɔːtə(r)
AM 'dɪtʃˌwɔdər, 'dɪtʃˌwɑdər
ditheism
BR 'dʌɪˌθiːɪz(ə)m, ˌdʌɪ'θiːɪz(ə)m
AM 'daɪθiˌɪzəm, daɪ'θiˌɪzəm
ditheist
BR 'dʌɪˌθiːɪst, ˌdʌɪ'θiːɪst, -s
AM 'daɪθiɪst, daɪ'θiɪst, -s
dither
BR 'dɪð|ə(r), -əz, -(ə)rɪŋ, -əd
AM 'dɪð|ər, -ərz, -(ə)rɪŋ, -ərd
ditherer
BR 'dɪð(ə)rə(r), -z
AM 'dɪðərər, -z
dithery
BR 'dɪð(ə)ri
AM 'dɪð(ə)ri
dithionite
BR dʌɪ'θʌɪənʌɪt
AM daɪ'θaɪəˌnaɪt
dithyramb
BR 'dɪθɪram(b)
AM dɪθəˌræm, 'dɪθiˌræm
dithyrambi
BR ˌdɪθɪ'rambʌɪ
AM ˌdɪθə'ræmˌbaɪ
dithyrambic
BR ˌdɪθɪ'rambɪk, -s
AM ˌdɪθə'ræmbɪk, ˌdɪθi'ræmbɪk, -s
dithyrambus
BR ˌdɪθɪ'rambəs
AM ˌdɪθə'ræmbəs
ditsy
BR 'dɪts|i, -ɪə(r), -ɪɪst
AM 'dɪtsi, -ər, -ɪst
dittander
BR dɪ'tandə(r)
AM də'tændər
dittany
BR 'dɪtəni, 'dɪtn̩i
AM 'dɪtəni
ditto
BR 'dɪtəʊ, -z
AM 'dɪdoʊ, -z
dittographic
BR ˌdɪtə(ʊ)'grafɪk
AM ˌdɪdoʊ'græfɪk
dittography
BR dɪ'tɒgrəf|i, -ɪz
AM dɪ'tɑgrəfi, -z
Ditton
BR 'dɪtn
AM 'dɪtn
ditty
BR 'dɪt|i, -ɪz
AM 'dɪdi, -z
ditzy
BR 'dɪts|i, -ɪə(r), -ɪɪst
AM 'dɪtsi, -ər, -ɪst
Diu
BR 'diːuː
AM 'diu
diuresis
BR ˌdʌɪjʊ'riːsɪs
AM ˌdaɪjə'risəs
diuretic
BR ˌdʌɪjʊ'rɛtɪk, -s
AM ˌdaɪjə'rɛdɪk, -s
diurnal
BR dʌɪ'əːnl
AM daɪ'ərnəl
diurnally
BR dʌɪ'əːnl̩i, dʌɪ'əːnəli
AM daɪ'ərnəli
diva
BR 'diːvə(r), -z
AM 'divə, -z
divagate
BR 'dʌɪvəgeɪt, -s, -ɪŋ, -ɪd
AM 'daɪvəˌgeɪ|t, 'dɪvəˌgeɪ|t, -ts, -dɪŋ, -dɪd
divagation
BR ˌdʌɪvə'geɪʃn, -z
AM ˌdaɪvə'geɪʃən, ˌdɪvə'geɪʃən, -z
divalency
BR (ˌ)dʌɪ'veɪlənsi, (ˌ)dʌɪ'veɪln̩si
AM daɪ'veɪlənsi
divalent
BR (ˌ)dʌɪ'veɪlənt, (ˌ)dʌɪ'veɪln̩t
AM daɪ'veɪlənt
divan
BR dɪ'van, -z
AM 'daɪˌvæn, də'væn, -z
divaricate
BR dʌɪ'varɪkeɪt, dɪ'varɪkeɪt, -s, -ɪŋ, -ɪd
AM daɪ'vɛrəˌkeɪ|t, də'vɛrəˌkeɪ|t, -ts, -dɪŋ, -dɪd
divarication
BR dʌɪˌvarɪ'keɪʃn, dɪˌvarɪ'keɪʃn
AM daɪˌvɛrə'keɪʃən, dəˌvɛrə'keɪʃən
dive
BR dʌɪv, -z, -ɪŋ, -d
AM daɪv, -z, -ɪŋ, -d
diver
BR 'dʌɪvə(r), -z
AM 'daɪvər, -z
diverge
BR dʌɪ'vəːdʒ, dɪ'vəːdʒ, -ɪz, -ɪŋ, -d
AM də'vərdʒ, daɪ'vərdʒ, -əz, -ɪŋ, -d
divergence
BR dʌɪ'vəːdʒ(ə)ns, dɪ'vəːdʒ(ə)ns, -ɪz
AM də'vərdʒəns, daɪ'vərdʒəns, -əz
divergency
BR dʌɪ'vəːdʒ(ə)ns|i, dɪ'vəːdʒ(ə)ns|i, -ɪz

AM də'vərdʒənsi, daɪ'vərdʒənsi, -z

divergent
BR dʌɪ'vəːdʒ(ə)nt, dɪ'vəːdʒ(ə)nt
AM də'vərdʒənt, daɪ'vərdʒənt

divergently
BR dʌɪ'vəːdʒ(ə)ntli, dɪ'vəːdʒ(ə)ntli
AM də'vərdʒən(t)li, daɪ'vərdʒən(t)li

divers
BR 'dʌɪvə(ː)z
AM 'daɪvərz

diverse
BR dʌɪ'vəːs
AM də'vərs, daɪ'vərs

diversely
BR dʌɪ'vəːsli
AM də'vərsli, daɪ'vərsli

diversifiable
BR dʌɪ'vəːsɪfʌɪəbl
AM də'vərsəˌfaɪəbəl, daɪ'vərsəˌfaɪəbəl

diversification
BR dʌɪˌvəːsɪfɪ'keɪʃn, dɪˌvəːsɪfɪ'keɪʃn
AM dəˌvərsəfə'keɪʃən, daɪˌvərsəfə'keɪʃən

diversify
BR dʌɪ'vəːsɪfʌɪ, -z, -ɪŋ, -d
AM də'vərsəˌfaɪ, daɪ'vərsəˌfaɪ, -z, -ɪŋ, -d

diversion
BR dʌɪ'vəːʃn, dɪ'vəːʃn, -z
AM də'vərʒən, daɪ'vərʒən, -z

diversional
BR dʌɪ'vəːʃn̩(ə)l, dʌɪ'vəːʃən(ə)l, dɪ'vəːʃn̩(ə)l, dɪ'vəːʃən(ə)l
AM də'vərʒ(ə)nəl, daɪ'vərʒ(ə)nəl

diversionary
BR dʌɪ'vəːʃn̩(ə)ri, dɪ'vəːʃn̩(ə)ri
AM də'vərʒəˌnɛri, daɪ'vərʒəˌnɛri

diversionist
BR dʌɪ'vəːʃn̩ɪst, dʌɪ'vəːʃənɪst, dɪ'vəːʃn̩ɪst, dɪ'vəːʃənɪst, -s
AM də'vərʒənəst, daɪ'vərʒənəst, -s

diversity
BR dʌɪ'vəːsɪt|i, dɪ'vəːsɪt|i, -ɪz
AM də'vərsədi, daɪ'vərsədi, -z

divert
BR dʌɪ'vəːt, dɪ'vəːt, -s, -ɪŋ, -ɪd
AM də'vər|t, daɪ'vər|t, -ts, -dɪŋ, -dəd

diverticula
BR ˌdʌɪvə'tɪkjʊlə(r)
AM ˌdaɪvər'tɪkjələ

diverticular
BR ˌdʌɪvə'tɪkjʊlə(r)
AM ˌdaɪvər'tɪkjələr

diverticulitis
BR ˌdʌɪvətɪkjʊ'lʌɪtɪs
AM ˌdaɪvərˌtɪkjə'laɪdəs

diverticulosis
BR ˌdʌɪvətɪkjʊ'ləʊsɪs
AM ˌdaɪvərˌtɪkjə'loʊsəs

diverticulum
BR ˌdʌɪvə'tɪkjʊləm
AM ˌdaɪvər'tɪkjələm

divertimenti
BR dɪˌvəːtɪ'mɛntiː
AM dəˌvərdə'mɛn(t)i

divertimento
BR dɪˌvəːtɪ'mɛntəʊ, -z
AM dəˌvərdə'mɛn(t)oʊ, -z

divertingly
BR dʌɪ'vəːtɪŋli, dɪ'vəːtɪŋli
AM də'vərdɪŋli, daɪ'vərdɪŋli

divertissement
BR ˌdiːvɛː'tiːsmɒ̃, dɪ'vəːtɪsm(ə)nt, -s
AM də'vərdəsmənt, -s

Dives
BR 'dʌɪviːz
AM 'daɪˌviz

divest
BR dʌɪ'vɛst, dɪ'vɛst, -s, -ɪŋ, -ɪd
AM daɪ'vɛst, də'vɛst, -s, -ɪŋ, -əd

divestiture
BR dʌɪ'vɛstɪtʃə(r), dɪ'vɛstɪtʃə(r)
AM daɪ'vɛstəˌtʃ(ʊ)ər, də'vɛstəˌtʃ(ʊ)ər

divestment
BR dʌɪ'vɛs(t)m(ə)nt, dɪ'vɛs(t)m(ə)nt, -s
AM daɪ'vɛstmənt, də'vɛstmənt, -s

divesture
BR dʌɪ'vɛstʃə(r), dɪ'vɛstʃə(r)
AM daɪ'vɛstʃ(ʊ)ər, də'vɛstʃ(ʊ)ər

divi
BR 'dɪv|i, -ɪz
AM 'dɪvi, -z

divide
BR dɪ'vʌɪd, -z, -ɪŋ, -ɪd
AM də'vaɪd, -z, -ɪŋ, -ɪd

dividend
BR 'dɪvɪdɛnd, 'dɪvɪd(ə)nd, -z
AM 'dɪvəˌdɛnd, -z

divider
BR dɪ'vʌɪdə(r), -z
AM də'vaɪdər, -z

divi-divi
BR ˌdɪvɪ'dɪv|i, -ɪz
AM 'dɪvi'dɪvi, -z

divination
BR ˌdɪvɪ'neɪʃn, -z
AM ˌdɪvə'neɪʃən, -z

divinatory
BR dɪ'vɪnət(ə)ri
AM də'vɪnəˌtɔri, 'dɪvɪnəˌtɔri, də'vaɪnəˌtɔri

divine
BR dɪ'vʌɪn, -ə(r), -ɪst
AM də'vaɪn, -ər, -ɪst

divinely
BR dɪ'vʌɪnli
AM də'vaɪnli

divineness
BR dɪ'vʌɪnnɪs
AM də'vaɪ(n)nɪs

diviner
BR dɪ'vʌɪnə(r), -z
AM də'vaɪnər, -z

divingboard
BR 'dʌɪvɪŋbɔːd, -z
AM 'daɪvɪŋˌbɔ(ə)rd, -z

divinity
BR dɪ'vɪnɪti
AM də'vɪnɪdi, -z

divinize
BR 'dɪvɪnʌɪz, -ɪz, -ɪŋ, -d
AM 'dɪvɪˌnaɪz, -əz, -ɪŋ, -d

Divis
BR 'dɪvɪs
AM 'dɪvɪs

divisi
BR dɪ'viːsi
AM də'visi

divisibility
BR dɪˌvɪzɪ'bɪlɪti
AM dəˌvɪzə'bɪlɪdi

divisible
BR dɪ'vɪzɪbl
AM də'vɪzəbəl

divisibly
BR dɪ'vɪzɪbli
AM də'vɪzəbli

division
BR dɪ'vɪʒn, -z
AM də'vɪʒən, -z

divisional
BR dɪ'vɪʒn̩(ə)l, dɪ'vɪʒən(ə)l
AM də'vɪʒ(ə)nəl

divisionally
BR dɪ'vɪʒn̩əli, dɪ'vɪʒn̩li, dɪ'vɪʒənl̩i, dɪ'vɪʒ(ə)nəli
AM də'vɪʒ(ə)nəli

divisionary
BR dɪ'vɪʒn̩(ə)ri
AM də'vɪʒəˌnɛri

divisionism
BR dɪ'vɪʒn̩ɪz(ə)m, dɪ'vɪʒənɪz(ə)m
AM də'vɪʒəˌnɪzəm

divisive
BR dɪ'vʌɪsɪv
AM də'vaɪsɪv, dɪ'vɪzɪv

divisively
BR dɪ'vʌɪsɪvli
AM də'vaɪsɪvli, dɪ'vɪzɪvli

divisiveness
BR dɪ'vʌɪsɪvnɪs
AM də'vaɪsɪvnɪs, dɪ'vɪzɪvnɪs

divisor
BR dɪ'vʌɪzə(r), -z
AM də'vaɪzər, -z

divorce
BR dɪ'vɔːs, -ɪz, -ɪŋ, -t
AM də'vɔ(ə)rs, -əz, -ɪŋ, -t

divorcé
BR dɪˌvɔː'siː, ˌdɪvɔː'siː, -z
AM dəˌvɔr'seɪ, -z

divorcée
BR dɪˌvɔː'siː, ˌdɪvɔː'siː, -z
AM dəˌvɔr'seɪ, dəˌvɔr'si, -z

divorcement
BR dɪ'vɔːsm(ə)nt
AM də'vɔrsmənt

divot
BR 'dɪvət, -s
AM 'dɪvət, -s

divulgation
BR ˌdʌɪvʌl'geɪʃn, ˌdɪvʌl'geɪʃn
AM daɪˌvəl'geɪʃən, dəˌvəl'geɪʃən, ˌdɪvəl'geɪʃən

divulge
BR dʌɪ'vʌldʒ, dɪ'vʌldʒ, -ɪz, -ɪŋ, -d
AM də'vəldʒ, daɪ'vəldʒ, -əz, -ɪŋ, -d

divulgement
BR dʌɪ'vʌldʒm(ə)nt, dɪ'vʌldʒm(ə)nt
AM də'vəldʒmənt, daɪ'vəldʒmənt

divulgence
BR dʌɪ'vʌldʒ(ə)ns, dɪ'vʌldʒ(ə)ns
AM də'vəldʒəns, daɪ'vəldʒəns

divvy
BR 'dɪv|i, -ɪz
AM 'dɪvi, -z

Diwali
BR dɪ'wɑːli
AM də'wɑli

Dixey
BR 'dɪksi
AM 'dɪksi

dixie
BR 'dɪks|i, -ɪz
AM 'dɪksi, -z

Dixieland
BR 'dɪksɪland
AM 'dɪksi,lænd

Dixon
BR 'dɪksn
AM 'dɪksən

dizzily
BR 'dɪzɨli
AM 'dɪzɨli

dizziness
BR 'dɪzɪnɨs
AM 'dɪzinɨs

dizzy
BR 'dɪz|i, -ɪə(r), -ɪɪst
AM 'dɪzi, -ər, -ɨst

Djakarta
BR dʒə'kɑːtə(r)
AM dʒə'kardə

djellaba
BR 'dʒɛləbə(r), dʒə'lɑːbə(r), -z
AM dʒə'lɑbə, -z

djellabah
BR 'dʒɛləbə(r), dʒə'lɑːbə(r), -z
AM dʒə'lɑbə, -z

Djerba
BR 'dʒəːbə(r)
AM 'dʒərbə

djibah
BR 'dʒɪbə(r), -z
AM 'dʒɪbə, -z

djibba
BR 'dʒɪbə(r), -z
AM 'dʒɪbə, -z

Djibouti
BR dʒɪ'buːti
AM dʒə'budi

Djiboutian
BR dʒɪ'buːtɪən, -z
AM dʒə'budiən, -z

djinn
BR dʒɪn, -z
AM dʒɪn, -z

D.Litt.
Doctor of Literature
BR ˌdiː'lɪt, -s
AM ˌdi'lɪt, -s

D.Mus.
Doctor of Music
BR ˌdiː'mʌz, -ɨz
AM ˌdi 'mjuz, -əz

Dnieper
BR '(d)niːpə(r)
AM 'nipər, də'njɛpər

Dniester
BR '(d)niːstə(r)
AM 'nistər, də'njɛstər

do
BR duː
AM du, doʊ

doable
BR 'duːəbl
AM 'duəbəl

dob
BR dɒb, -z, -ɪŋ, -d
AM dɑb, -z, -ɪŋ, -d

dobbin
BR 'dɒbɪn
AM 'dɑbən

dobe
BR 'dəʊb|i, -ɪz
AM 'doʊbi, -z

Dobell
BR dəʊ'bɛl
AM doʊ'bɛl

Dobermann
BR 'dəʊbəmən, -z
AM 'doʊbərmən, -z

Dobson
BR 'dɒbsn
AM 'dɑbsən

doc
BR dɒk, -s
AM dɑk, -s

docent
BR 'dəʊs(ə)nt, -s
AM 'doʊsənt, -s

Docetae
BR də(ʊ)'siːtiː
AM doʊ'sidi

Docetic
BR də(ʊ)'siːtɪk
AM doʊ'sidɪk

Docetism
BR də(ʊ)'siːtɪz(ə)m
AM doʊ'si,tɪzəm

Docetist
BR də(ʊ)'siːtɪst, -s
AM doʊ'sidɨst, -s

doch-an-dorris
BR ˌdɒx(ə)n'dɒrɪs, ˌdɒk(ə)n'dɒrɪs, -ɨz
AM ˌdɑkən'dɔrəs, -əz

Docherty
BR 'dɒxəti, 'dɒkəti
AM 'dɑkərdi

docile
BR 'dəʊsʌɪl
AM 'dɑsəl, 'doʊ,saɪl

docilely
BR 'dəʊsʌɪlli
AM 'dɑsə(l)li

docility
BR də(ʊ)'sɪlɨti
AM dɑ'sɪlɨdi

dock
BR dɒk, -s, -ɪŋ, -t
AM dɑk, -s, -ɪŋ, -t

dockage
BR 'dɒkɪdʒ
AM 'dɒkɪdʒ

docker
BR 'dɒkə(r), -z
AM 'dɒkər, -z

docket
BR 'dɒk|ɪt, -s, -ɨtɪŋ, -ɨtɨd
AM 'dɑkət, -s, -ɪŋ, -əd

dockland
BR 'dɒklənd, 'dɒkland, -z
AM 'dɑk,lænd, -z

dockominium
BR ˌdɒkə'mɪnɪəm, -z
AM ˌdɑkə'mɪniəm, -z

dockside
BR 'dɒksʌɪd, -z
AM 'dɑk,saɪd, -z

dockyard
BR 'dɒkjɑːd, -z
AM 'dɑk,jɑrd, -z

doctor
BR 'dɒkt|ə(r), -əz, -(ə)rɪŋ, -əd
AM 'dɑkt|ər, -ərz, -(ə)rɪŋ, -ərd

doctoral
BR 'dɒkt(ə)rəl, 'dɒkt(ə)rl
AM 'dɑkt(ə)rəl

doctorate
BR 'dɒkt(ə)rət, -s
AM 'dɑkt(ə)rət, -s

doctorhood
BR 'dɒktəhʊd
AM 'dɑktər(h)ʊd

doctorial
BR dɒk'tɔːrɪəl
AM dɑk'tɔriəl

doctorly
BR 'dɒktəli
AM 'dɑktərli

doctorship
BR 'dɒktəʃɪp, -s
AM 'dɑktər,ʃɪp, -s

doctrinaire
BR ˌdɒktrɪ'nɛː(r)
AM ˌdɑktrə'nɛ(ə)r

doctrinairism
BR ˌdɒktrɪ'nɛːrɪz(ə)m
AM ˌdɑktrə'nɛ,rɪzəm

doctrinal
BR dɒk'trʌɪnl
AM 'dɑktrənl, dɑk'traɪnəl

doctrinally
BR dɒk'trʌɪnl̩i, dɒk'trʌɪnəli
AM 'dɑktrənəli, dɑk'traɪnəli

doctrinarian
BR ˌdɒktrɪ'nɛːrɪən
AM ˌdɑktrə'nɛriən

doctrine
BR 'dɒktr(ɪ)n, -z
AM 'dɑktrən, -z

doctrinism
BR 'dɒktrɪnɪz(ə)m
AM 'dɑktrə,nɪzəm

doctrinist
BR 'dɒktrɪnɪst, -s
AM 'dɑktrənəst, -s

docudrama
BR 'dɒkjʊ,drɑːmə(r), -z
AM 'dɑkjə,drɑmə, -z

document¹
noun
BR 'dɒkjʊm(ə)nt, -s
AM 'dɑkjəmənt, -s

document²
verb
BR 'dɒkjʊmɛnt, -s, -ɪŋ, -ɨd
AM 'dɑkjə,mɛn|t, -ts, -(t)ɪŋ, -(t)əd

documental
BR ˌdɒkjʊ'mɛntl
AM ˌdɑkjə'mɛn(t)l

documentalist
BR ˌdɒkjʊ'mɛntəlɪst, ˌdɒkjʊ'mɛntl̩ɪst, -s
AM ˌdɑkjə'mɛn(t)ləst, -s

documentarily
BR ˌdɒkjʊ'mɛnt(ə)rɨli
AM ˌdɑkjə'mɛnt(ə)rəli, ˌdɑkjə'mɛn(t)ərəli

documentarist
BR ˌdɒkjʊ'mɛnt(ə)rɪst, -s
AM ˌdɑkjə'mɛnt(ə)rəst, ˌdɑkjə'mɛn(t)ərəst, -s

documentary
BR ˌdɒkjʊ'mɛnt(ə)r|i, -ɪz
AM ˌdɑkjə'mɛnt(ə)ri, ˌdɑkjə'mɛn(t)əri, -z

documentation
BR ˌdɒkjʊm(ə)n'teɪʃn, ˌdɒkjʊmɛn'teɪʃn
AM ˌdɑkjəmən'teɪʃən

Dodd
BR dɒd
AM dɑd

dodder
BR 'dɒd|ə(r), -əz, -(ə)rɪŋ, -əd
AM 'dɑdər, -z, -ɪŋ, -d

dodderer
BR 'dɒd(ə)rə(r), -z
AM 'dɑdərər, -z

dodderiness
BR 'dɒd(ə)rɪnɪs
AM 'dɑdərinɨs

doddery
BR 'dɒd(ə)ri
AM 'dɑdəri

doddle
BR 'dɒdl, -z
AM 'dɑdəl, -z

Dodds
BR dɒdz
AM dɑdz

dodecagon
BR dəʊ'dɛkəgɒn, -z
AM doʊ'dɛkə,gɑn, -z

dodecahedral
BR ˌdəʊdɛkə'hiːdr(ə)l
AM doʊ,dɛkə'hidrəl

dodecahedron
BR ˌdəʊdɛkə'hiːdr(ə)n, -z
AM doʊ,dɛkə'hidrən, -z

Dodecanese
BR ˌdəʊdɛkəˈniːz, ˌdəʊdɪkəˈniːz
AM doʊˌdɛkəˈniz

dodecaphonic
BR ˌdəʊdɛkəˈfɒnɪk, ˌdəʊdɪkəˈfɒnɪk
AM doʊˌdɛkəˈfɑnɪk

dodge
BR dɒdʒ, -ɪz, -ɪŋ, -d
AM dɑdʒ, -əz, -ɪŋ, -d

dodgem
BR ˈdɒdʒ(ə)m, -z
AM ˈdɑdʒəm, -z

dodger
BR ˈdɒdʒə(r), -z
AM ˈdɑdʒər, -z

dodgily
BR ˈdɒdʒɪli
AM ˈdɑdʒəli

dodginess
BR ˈdɒdʒɪnɪs
AM ˈdɑdʒinɪs

Dodgson
BR ˈdɒdʒsn
AM ˈdɑdʒsən

dodgy
BR ˈdɒdʒ|i, -ɪə(r), -ɪɪst
AM ˈdɑdʒi, -ər, -ɪst

dodo
BR ˈdəʊdəʊ, -z
AM ˈdoʊˌdoʊ, -z

Dodoma
BR ˈdəʊdəmə(*r*)
AM ˈdoʊdəmə, doʊˈdɑmə

Dodson
BR dɒdsn
AM ˈdɑdsən

doe
BR dəʊ, -z
AM doʊ, -z

doek
BR dʊk, -s
AM dʊk, -s

Doenitz
BR ˈdəːnɪts
AM ˈdənɪts

doer
BR ˈduːə(r), -z
AM ˈduər, -z

does
from do
BR dʌz
AM dəz

doeskin
BR ˈdəʊskɪn, -z
AM ˈdoʊˌskɪn, -z

doesn't
BR ˈdʌznt
AM ˈdəznt

doest
BR ˈduːɪst
AM ˈduəst

doeth
BR ˈduːɪθ
AM ˈduəθ

doff
BR dɒf, -s, -ɪŋ, -t
AM dɔf, dɑf, -s, -ɪŋ, -t

dog
BR dɒg, -z, -ɪŋ, -d
AM dɔg, dɑg, -z, -ɪŋ, -d

dogberry
BR ˈdɒgb(ə)r|i, -ɪz
AM ˈdɔgˌbɛri, ˈdɑgˌbɛri, -z

dogcart
BR ˈdɒgkɑːt, -s
AM ˈdɔgˌkɑrt, ˈdɑgˌkɑrt, -s

dogcatcher
BR ˈdɒgˌkatʃə(r), -z
AM ˈdɔgˌkɛtʃər, ˈdɑgˌkɛtʃər, -z

doge
BR dəʊ(d)ʒ, -ɪz
AM doʊʒ, -əz

dogface
BR ˈdɒgfeɪs, -ɪz
AM ˈdɔgˌfeɪs, ˈdɑgˌfeɪs, -ɪz

dogfight
BR ˈdɒgfʌɪt, -s
AM ˈdɔgˌfaɪt, ˈdɑgˌfaɪt, -s

dogfighter
BR ˈdɒgfʌɪtə(r), -z
AM ˈdɔgˌfaɪdər, ˈdɑgˌfaɪdər, -z

dogfighting
BR ˈdɒgfʌɪtɪŋ
AM ˈdɔgˌfaɪdɪŋ, ˈdɑgˌfaɪdɪŋ

dogfish
BR ˈdɒgfɪʃ, -ɪz
AM ˈdɔgˌfɪʃ, ˈdɑgˌfɪʃ, -ɪz

dogged
adjective
BR ˈdɒgɪd
AM ˈdɔgəd, ˈdɑgəd

doggedly
BR ˈdɒgɪdli
AM ˈdɔgədli, ˈdɑgədli

doggedness
BR ˈdɒgɪdnɪs
AM ˈdɔgədnəs, ˈdɑgədnəs

dogger
BR ˈdɒgə(r), -z
AM ˈdɔgər, ˈdɑgər, -z

doggerel
BR ˈdɒg(ə)rəl, ˈdɒg(ə)rl̩
AM ˈdɔg(ə)rəl, ˈdɑg(ə)rəl

doggie
BR ˈdɒg|i, -ɪz
AM ˈdɔgi, ˈdɑgi, -z

dogginess
BR ˈdɒgɪnɪs
AM ˈdɔginɪs, ˈdɑginɪs

doggish
BR ˈdɒgɪʃ
AM ˈdɔgɪʃ, ˈdɑgɪʃ

doggishly
BR ˈdɒgɪʃli
AM ˈdɔgɪʃli, ˈdɑgɪʃli

doggishness
BR ˈdɒgɪʃnɪs
AM ˈdɔgɪʃnɪs, ˈdɑgɪʃnɪs

doggo
BR ˈdɒgəʊ
AM ˈdɔgoʊ, ˈdɑgoʊ

doggone
BR ˈdɒgɒn
AM ˈdɔ(g)ˌgɔn, ˈdɑ(g)ˌgɑn

doggy
BR ˈdɒg|i, -ɪz
AM ˈdɔgi, ˈdɑgi, -z

doghouse
BR ˈdɒghaʊ|s, -zɪz
AM ˈdɔgˌ(h)aʊ|s, ˈdɑgˌ(h)aʊ|s, -zəz

dogie
BR ˈdəʊg|i, -ɪz
AM ˈdoʊgi, -z

dogleg
BR ˈdɒglɛg, -z
AM ˈdɔgˌlɛg, ˈdɑgˌlɛg, -z

doglike
BR ˈdɒglʌɪk
AM ˈdɔgˌlaɪk, ˈdɑgˌlaɪk

dogma
BR ˈdɒgmə(*r*), -z
AM ˈdɔgmə, ˈdɑgmə, -z

dogman
BR ˈdɒgmən, ˈdɒgman
AM ˈdɔgmən, ˈdɔgˌmæn, ˈdɑgmən, ˈdɑgˌmæn

dogmatic
BR dɒgˈmatɪk, -s
AM dɔgˈmædɪk, dɑgˈmædɪk, -s

dogmatically
BR dɒgˈmatɪkli
AM dɔgˈmædək(ə)li, dɑgˈmædək(ə)li

dogmatise
BR ˈdɒgmətʌɪz, -ɪz, -ɪŋ, -d
AM ˈdɔgməˌtaɪz, ˈdɑgməˌtaɪz, -ɪz, -ɪŋ, -d

dogmatism
BR ˈdɒgmətɪz(ə)m
AM ˈdɔgməˌtɪzəm, ˈdɑgməˌtɪzəm

dogmatist
BR ˈdɒgmətɪst, -s
AM ˈdɔgmədəst, ˈdɑgmədəst, -s

dogmatize
BR ˈdɒgmətʌɪz, -ɪz, -ɪŋ, -d
AM ˈdɔgməˌtaɪz, ˈdɑgməˌtaɪz, -ɪz, -ɪŋ, -d

dogmen
BR ˈdɒgmən, ˈdɒgmɛn
AM ˈdɔgmən, ˈdɔgˌmɛn, ˈdɑgmən, ˈdɑgˌmɛn

do-gooder
BR ˌduːˈgʊdə(r), -z
AM ˈduˌgʊdər, -z

do-goodery
BR ˌduːˈgʊd(ə)ri
AM ˌduˈgʊdəri

do-goodism
BR ˌduːˈgʊdɪz(ə)m
AM ˌduˈgʊˌdɪzəm

dogsbody
BR ˈdɒgzbɒd|i, -ɪz
AM ˈdɔgzˌbɑdi, ˈdɑgzˌbɑdi, -z

dogshore
BR ˈdɒgʃɔː(r), -z
AM ˈdɔgzˌʃɔ(ə)r, -z

dogskin
BR ˈdɒgskɪn
AM ˈdɔgzˌskɪn, ˈdɑgzˌskɪn

dogtag
BR ˈdɒgtag, -z
AM ˈdɔgˌtæg, ˈdɑgˌtæg, -z

dogteeth
BR ˈdɒgtiːθ
AM ˈdɔgˌtiθ, ˈdɑgˌtiθ

dogtooth
BR ˈdɒgtuːθ
AM ˈdɔgˌtuθ, ˈdɑgˌtuθ

dogtrot
BR ˈdɒgtrɒt
AM ˈdɔgˌtrɑt, ˈdɑgˌtrɑt

dogwatch
BR ˈdɒgwɒtʃ, -ɪz
AM ˈdɔgˌwɔtʃ, ˈdɑgˌwɑtʃ, -əz

dogwood
BR ˈdɒgwʊd
AM ˈdɔgˌwʊd, ˈdɑgˌwʊd

doh
BR dəʊ
AM doʊ

Doha
BR ˈdəʊhɑː(*r*), ˈdəʊə(*r*)
AM ˈdoʊˌhɑ

Doherty
BR ˈdɒxəti, ˈdɒhəti, ˈdəʊəti
AM ˈdɔ(ə)rdi

doily
BR ˈdɔɪl|i, -ɪz
AM ˈdɔɪli, -z

doing
BR ˈduːɪŋ, -z
AM ˈduɪŋ, -z

doit
BR dɔɪt, -s
AM dɔɪt, -s

dojo
BR ˈdəʊdʒəʊ, -z
AM ˈdoʊˌdʒoʊ, -z

Dolan
BR dəʊlən
AM ˈdoʊlən

Dolby®
BR ˈdɒlbi

AM 'doʊlbi, 'dɔlbi

dolce far niente
BR ˌdɒltʃɪ fɑː nɪ'ɛnti, ˌdɒltʃeɪ +, + nɪ'ɛnteɪ
AM ˌdoʊltʃə ˌfɑr ni'ɛnti

Dolcelatte®
BR ˌdɒltʃɪ'lati(r)
AM ˌdoʊltʃə'lædi

dolce vita
BR ˌdɒltʃɪ 'viːtə(r), ˌdɒltʃeɪ +
AM ˌdoʊltʃə 'vidə

Dolcis®
BR 'dɒlsɪs
AM 'doʊlsəs

doldrums
BR 'dɒldrəmz, 'dəʊldrəmz
AM 'doʊldrəmz, 'dɑldrəmz

dole
BR dəʊl, -z, -ɪŋ, -d
AM doʊl, -z, -ɪŋ, -d

dole-bludger
BR 'dəʊlˌblʌdʒə(r), -z
AM 'doʊlˌblədʒər, -z

doleful
BR 'dəʊlf(ʊ)l
AM 'doʊlfəl

dolefully
BR 'dəʊlfʊli, 'dəʊlfḷi
AM 'doʊlfəli

dolefulness
BR 'dəʊlf(ʊ)lnəs
AM 'doʊlfəlnəs

dolerite
BR 'dɒlərʌɪt
AM 'dɑləˌraɪt

Dolgellau
BR dɒl'gɛɬi, dɒl'gɛθli, dɒl'gɛḷʌɪ, dɒl'gɛθlʌɪ
AM dɔl'gɛli, dɑl'gɛli
WE dɒl'geɬaɪ

dolichocephalic
BR ˌdɒlɪkəʊsɪ'falɪk, ˌdɒlɪkəʊkɛ'falɪk
AM ˌdɑləkoʊsə'fælɪk

dolichocephalous
BR ˌdɒlɪkəʊ'sɛf(ə)ləs, ˌdɒlɪkəʊ'sɛfḷəs, ˌdɒlɪkəʊ'kɛf(ə)ləs, ˌdɒlɪkəʊ'kɛfḷəs
AM ˌdɑləkoʊ'sɛfələs

dolichocephaly
BR ˌdɒlɪkəʊ'sɛfəli, ˌdɒlɪkəʊ'sɛfḷi, ˌdɒlɪkəʊ'kɛfəli, ˌdɒlɪkəʊ'kɛfḷi
AM ˌdɑləkoʊ'sɛfəli

dolichosauri
BR ˌdɒlɪkə(ʊ)'sɔːrʌɪ
AM ˌdɑləkə'sɔˌraɪ

dolichosaurus
BR ˌdɒlɪkə'sɔːrəs, -ɪz
AM ˌdɑləkə'sɔrəs, -əz

Dolin
BR 'dɒlɪn
AM 'doʊlən

dolina
BR də(ʊ)'liːnə(r), -z
AM də'linə, -z

doline
BR də(ʊ)'liːnə(r), -z
AM də'linə, -z

Dolittle
BR 'duːlɪtl
AM 'duˌlɪdəl

doll
BR dɒl, -z, -ɪŋ, -d
AM dɑl, -z, -ɪŋ, -d

dollar
BR 'dɒlə(r), -z
AM 'dɑlər, -z

Dollfuss
BR 'dɒlfəs
AM 'dɑlfəs

dollhouse
BR 'dɒlhaʊ|s, -zɪz
AM 'dɑlˌ(h)aʊ|s, -zəz

dollie
BR 'dɒl|i, -ɪz
AM 'dɑli, -z

Dollond
BR 'dɒlənd
AM 'dɔlənd, 'dɑlənd

dollop
BR 'dɒləp, -s
AM 'dɑləp, -s

dolly
BR 'dɒl|i, -ɪz
AM 'dɑli, -z

Dolly Varden
BR ˌdɒlɪ 'vɑːdn, -z
AM ˌdɑli 'vɑrdən, -z

dolma
BR 'dɒlmə(r)
AM 'dɑlmə

dolman
BR 'dɒlmən, -z
AM 'doʊlmən, -z

dolmen
BR 'dɒlmən, -z
AM 'doʊlmən, -z

Dolmetsch
BR 'dɒlmɛtʃ
AM 'dɔlˌmɛtʃ, 'dɑlˌmɛtʃ

dolomite
BR 'dɒləmʌɪt
AM 'dɑləˌmaɪt, 'doʊləˌmaɪt, -s

dolomitic
BR ˌdɒlə'mɪtɪk
AM ˌdɑlə'mɪdɪk, ˌdoʊlə'mɪdɪk

dolor
BR 'dɒlə(r), -z
AM 'doʊlər, -z

Dolores
BR də'lɔːrɪs, də'lɔːrɪz
AM də'lɔrəs

doloroso
BR ˌdɒlə'rəʊsəʊ, ˌdɒlə'rəʊzəʊ
AM ˌdoʊlə'roʊsoʊ

dolorous
BR 'dɒl(ə)rəs
AM 'doʊlərəs

dolorously
BR 'dɒl(ə)rəsli
AM 'doʊlərəsli

dolorousness
BR 'dɒl(ə)rəsnəs
AM 'doʊlərəsnəs

dolour
BR 'dɒlə(r), -z
AM 'doʊlər, -z

dolphin
BR 'dɒlfɪn, -z
AM 'dɔlfən, 'dɑlfən, -z

dolphinarium
BR ˌdɒlfɪ'nɛːrɪəm, -z
AM ˌdɔlfə'nɛriəm, ˌdɑlfə'nɛriəm, -z

Dolphus
BR 'dɒlfəs
AM 'dɔlfəs, 'dɑlfəs

dolt
BR dəʊlt, -s
AM doʊlt, -s

doltish
BR 'dəʊltɪʃ
AM 'doʊltɪʃ

doltishly
BR 'dəʊltɪʃli
AM 'doʊltɪʃli

doltishness
BR 'dəʊltɪʃnɪs
AM 'doʊltɪʃnɪs

dom
BR dɒm, -z
AM dɑm, -z

domain
BR də(ʊ)'meɪn, -z
AM doʊ'meɪn, də'meɪn, -z

domaine
BR də(ʊ)'meɪn, -z
AM doʊ'meɪn, də'meɪn, -z

domanial
BR də(ʊ)'meɪnɪəl
AM doʊ'meɪniəl, də'meɪniəl

Dombey
BR 'dɒmbi
AM 'dɔmbi, 'dɑmbi

dome
BR dəʊm, -z, -d
AM doʊm, -z, -d

domelike
BR 'dəʊmlʌɪk
AM 'doʊmˌlaɪk

Domesday
BR 'duːmzdeɪ
AM 'dumzˌdeɪ

domestic
BR də'mɛstɪk, -s
AM də'mɛstɪk, -s

domesticable
BR də'mɛstɪkəbl
AM də'mɛstəkəbəl

domestically
BR də'mɛstɪkli
AM də'mɛstək(ə)li

domesticate
BR də'mɛstɪkeɪt, -s, -ɪŋ, -ɪd
AM də'mɛstəˌkeɪ|t, -ts, -dɪŋ, -dɪd

domestication
BR dəˌmɛstɪ'keɪʃn
AM dəˌmɛstə'keɪʃən

domesticity
BR ˌdɒmɪ'stɪsɪti, ˌdɒmɛ'stɪsɪti
AM ˌdoʊˌmɛ'stɪsɪdi

Domestos®
BR də'mɛstɒs
AM də'mɛstəs

domicile
BR 'dɒmɪsʌɪl, -z, -d
AM 'dɑməˌsaɪl, 'doʊməˌsaɪl, 'dɑməsəl, -z, -d

domiciliary
BR ˌdɒmɪ'sɪl(ɪ)əri
AM ˌdɑmə'sɪliˌɛri, ˌdoʊmə'sɪliˌɛri, ˌdɑmə'sɪljəri, ˌdoʊmə'sɪljəri

dominance
BR 'dɒmɪnəns
AM 'dɑmənəns

dominant
BR 'dɒmɪnənt
AM 'dɑmənənt

dominantly
BR 'dɒmɪnəntli
AM 'dɑmənən(t)li

dominate
BR 'dɒmɪneɪt, -s, -ɪŋ, -ɪd
AM 'dɑməˌneɪ|t, -ts, -dɪŋ, -dɪd

domination
BR ˌdɒmɪ'neɪʃn
AM ˌdɑmə'neɪʃən

dominator
BR 'dɒmɪneɪtə(r), -z
AM 'dɑməˌneɪdər, -z

dominatrices
BR ˌdɒmɪ'neɪtrɪsiːz
AM ˌdɑmə'neɪtrəsiz

dominatrix
BR ˌdɒmɪ'neɪtrɪks, -ɪz
AM ˌdɑmə'neɪtrɪks, -ɪz

dominee
BR 'duːmɪni, 'dʊəmɪni
AM 'duməni

domineer
BR ˌdɒmɪ'nɪə(r), -z, -ɪŋ, -d
AM ˌdɑmə'nɪ(ə)r, -z, -ɪŋ, -d

domineeringly
BR ˌdɒmɪ'nɪərɪŋli
AM ˌdɑmə'nɪrɪŋli

Domingo
BR də'mɪŋɡəʊ
AM də'mɪŋɡoʊ

Dominic
BR 'dɒmɨnɪk
AM 'dɑmənɪk

Dominica
BR ˌdɒmɨ'niːkə(r), də'mɪnɨkə(r)
AM ˌdɑmə'nikə

dominical
BR də'mɪnɨkl
AM də'mɪnɨkl

Dominican[1]
of Dominica
BR ˌdɒmɨ'niːk(ə)n, də'mɪnɨk(ə)n, -z
AM ˌdɑmə'nikən, -z

Dominican[2]
of the Dominican Republic or religious order
BR də'mɪnɨk(ə)n, -z
AM də'mɪnəkən, -z

Dominick
BR 'dɒmɨnɪk
AM 'dɔmənɪk, 'dɑmənɪk

dominie
BR 'dɒmɨn|i, -ɪz
AM 'dɑməni, -z

dominion
BR də'mɪnɪən, -z
AM də'mɪnjən, -z

Dominique
BR ˌdɒmɨ'niːk
AM ˌdɑmə'nik

domino
BR 'dɒmɨnəʊ, -z
AM 'dɑməˌnoʊ, -z

Domitian
BR də(ʊ)'mɪʃn, də(ʊ)'mɪʃɪən
AM də'mɪʃən, doʊ'mɪʃən

don
BR dɒn, -z, -ɪŋ, -d
AM dɑn, -z, -ɪŋ, -d

dona
BR 'dəʊnə(r), -z
AM 'dɑnə, 'doʊnə, -z

doña
BR 'dɒnjə(r)
AM 'dɑnjə, 'doʊnjə

donah
BR 'dəʊnə(r), -z
AM 'dɑnə, 'doʊnə, -z

Donahue
BR 'dɒnəhjuː
AM 'dɑnəˌhju

Donal
BR 'dəʊnl
AM 'dɔnəl, 'dɑnəl

Donald
BR 'dɒnld
AM 'dɔnəl(d), 'dɑnəl(d)

Donaldson
BR 'dɒnldz(ə)n
AM 'dɔnəl(d)sən, 'dɑnəl(d)sən

Donat
BR 'dəʊnat
AM 'doʊˌnɑt

donate
BR də(ʊ)'neɪt, -s, -ɪŋ, -ɨd
AM 'doʊˌneɪ|t, doʊ'neɪ|t, -ts, -dɪŋ, -dɨd

Donatello
BR ˌdɒnə'tɛləʊ
AM ˌdɑnə'tɛloʊ

donation
BR də(ʊ)'neɪʃn, -z
AM doʊ'neɪʃən, -z

Donatism
BR 'dəʊnətɪz(ə)m
AM 'doʊnəˌtɪzəm, 'dɑnəˌtɪzəm

Donatist
BR 'dəʊnətɪst, -s
AM 'doʊnədəst, 'dɑnədəst, -s

donative
BR 'dəʊnətɪv, -z
AM 'doʊnədɪv, 'dɑnədɪv, -z

donator
BR də(ʊ)'neɪtə(r), -z
AM 'doʊˌneɪdər, -z

Donatus
BR də(ʊ)'neɪtəs
AM ˌdoʊ'nɑdəs

Donau
BR 'dəʊnaʊ
AM 'doʊˌnaʊ

Donbas
BR 'dɒnbas
AM 'dɑnˌbæs

Donbass
BR 'dɒnbas
AM 'dɑnˌbæs

Doncaster
BR 'dɒŋkəstə(r), 'dɒŋkastə(r), 'dɒŋkɑːstə(r)
AM 'dɔnˌkæstər, 'dɑnˌkæstər

done
BR dʌn
AM dən

donee
BR dəʊ'niː, -z
AM doʊ'ni, -z

Donegal
BR ˌdɒnɪ'ɡɔːl
AM ˌdɑnə'ɡɔl, ˌdɑnə'ɡɑl

Donelly
BR 'dɒnəli, 'dɒnl̩i
AM 'dɔn(ə)li, 'dɑn(ə)li

Doner
BR 'dɒnə(r)
AM 'dɔnər, 'dɑnər

Donets Basin
BR dəˌnɛts 'beɪsn
AM də'nɛts 'beɪsn

Donetsk
BR də'nɛtsk
AM də'nɛtsk

dong
BR dɒŋ, -z
AM dɔŋ, dɑŋ, -z

donga
BR 'dɒŋɡə(r), -z
AM 'dɑŋɡə, 'dɔŋɡə, -z

Don Giovanni
BR ˌdɒn dʒə(ʊ)'vɑːni, + dʒə(ʊ)'vani
AM ˌdɔn dʒ(i)ə'vɑni, ˌdɑn dʒ(i)ə'vɑni

dongle
BR 'dɒŋɡl, -z
AM 'dɑŋɡəl, -z

Donington
BR 'dɒnɪŋt(ə)n
AM 'dɔnɪŋtən, 'dɑnɪŋtən

Donizetti
BR ˌdɒnɪ'zɛti
AM ˌdɑnə'zɛdi
IT donid'dzetti

donjon
BR 'dɒn(d)ʒ(ə)n, 'dʌn(d)ʒ(ə)n, -z
AM 'dɑndʒən, 'dəndʒən, -z

Don Juan
BR ˌdɒn 'dʒʊən, + '(h)wɑːn, -z
AM ˌdɑn '(h)wɑn, -z

donkey
BR 'dɒŋk|i, -ɪz
AM 'dɔŋki, 'dɑŋki, -z

donkeywork
BR 'dɒŋkɪwəːk
AM 'dɔŋkiˌwərk, 'dɑŋkiˌwərk

Donkin
BR 'dɒnkɪn
AM 'dɑnkən

Donleavy
BR dɒn'liːvi
AM 'dɔnˌlivi, 'dənˌlivi, ˌdɔn'livi, ˌdən'livi

Donlevy
BR dɒn'liːvi
AM 'dɔnˌlivi, 'dənˌlivi, ˌdɔn'livi, ˌdən'livi

donna
BR 'dɒnə(r), -z
AM 'dɑnə, -z

Donne
BR dʌn
AM dən

donné
BR 'dɒneɪ, -z
AM də'neɪ, -z

donnée
BR 'dɒneɪ, -z
AM də'neɪ, -z

Donnegan
BR 'dɒnɪɡ(ə)n
AM 'dɔnəɡən, 'dɑnəɡən

Donnell
BR 'dɒnl
AM 'dɔnəl, 'dɑnəl

Donnelly
BR 'dɒnəli, 'dɒnl̩i
AM 'dɔn(ə)li, 'dɑn(ə)li

donnish
BR 'dɒnɪʃ
AM 'dɑnɪʃ

donnishly
BR 'dɒnɨʃli
AM 'dɑnɨʃli

donnishness
BR 'dɒnɨʃnɨs
AM 'dɑnɪʃnɨs

donnybrook
BR 'dɒnɪbrʊk, -s
AM 'dɑniˌbrʊk, -s

Donoghue
BR 'dɒnəhjuː
AM 'dɔnəˌhju, 'dɑnəˌhju

Donohoe
BR 'dɒnəhəʊ
AM 'dɔnəˌhoʊ, 'dɑnəˌhoʊ

Donohue
BR 'dɒnəhjuː
AM 'dɔnəˌhju, 'dɑnəˌhju

donor
BR 'dəʊnə(r), -z
AM 'doʊnər, -z

Donovan
BR 'dɒnəv(ə)n
AM 'dɑnəvən

Don Pasquale
BR ˌdɒn pa'skɑːleɪ, + pa'skwɑːli
AM ˌdɔn pɑs'kwɑli, ˌdɑn pɑs'kwɑli

Don Quixote
BR ˌdɒn 'kwɪksət, + kɪ'(h)əʊti
AM ˌdɑn ki'hoʊdi, + 'kwɪksət

don't
BR dəʊnt
AM doʊnt

donut
BR 'dəʊnʌt, -s
AM 'doʊˌnət, -s

doodad
BR 'duːdad, -z
AM 'duˌdæd, -z

doodah
BR 'duːdɑː(r), -z
AM 'duˌdɑ, -z

doodle
BR 'duːd|l, -lz, -l̩ɪŋ\-lɪŋ, -ld
AM 'dud|əl, -əlz, -(ə)lɪŋ, -əld

doodlebug
BR 'duːdlbʌɡ, -z
AM 'dudlˌbəɡ, -z

doodler
BR 'du:dḷə(r), 'du:dlə(r), -z
AM 'dud(ə)lər, -z

doodling
BR 'du:dḷɪŋ, 'du:dlɪŋ, -z
AM 'dudḷɪŋ, 'dudlɪŋ, -z

doohickey
BR 'du:ˌhɪk|i, -ɪz
AM 'duˌhɪki, -z

Doolan
BR 'du:lən
AM 'dulən

Dooley
BR 'du:li
AM 'duli

Doolittle
BR 'du:lɪtl
AM 'duˌlɪdəl

doom
BR du:m, -z, -ɪŋ, -d
AM dum, -z, -ɪŋ, -d

doomsday
BR 'du:mzdeɪ
AM 'dumzˌdeɪ

doomster
BR 'du:mstə(r), -z
AM 'dumstər, -z

doomwatch
BR 'du:mwɒtʃ, -ɪz
AM 'dumˌwɑtʃ, 'dumˌwɔtʃ, -ə

doomwatcher
BR 'du:mˌwɒtʃə(r), -z
AM 'dumˌwɑtʃər, 'dumˌwɔtʃər, -z

Doone
BR du:n
AM dun

Doonesbury
BR 'du:nzb(ə)ri
AM 'dunzˌbɛri

door
BR dɔ:(r), -z, -d
AM dɔ(ə)r, -z, -d

doorbell
BR 'dɔ:bɛl, -z
AM 'dɔrˌbɛl, -z

doorcase
BR 'dɔ:keɪs, -ɪz
AM 'dɔrˌkeɪs, -ɪz

do-or-die
BR ˌdu:ɔ:'dʌɪ
AM 'duər'daɪ

doorframe
BR 'dɔ:freɪm, -z
AM 'dɔrˌfreɪm, -z

doorjamb
BR 'dɔ:dʒam, -z
AM 'dɔrˌdʒæm, -z

doorkeeper
BR 'dɔ:ˌki:pə(r), -z
AM 'dɔrˌkipər, -z

doorknob
BR 'dɔ:nɒb, -z
AM 'dɔrˌnɑb, -z

doorknocker
BR 'dɔ:ˌnɒkə(r), -z
AM 'dɔrˌnɑkər, -z

doorman
BR 'dɔ:mən
AM 'dɔrmən, 'dɔrˌmæn

doormat
BR 'dɔ:mat, -s
AM 'dɔrˌmæt, -s

doormen
BR 'dɔ:mən
AM 'dɔrmən, 'dɔrˌmən

doornail
BR 'dɔ:neɪl
AM 'dɔrˌneɪl

doorplate
BR 'dɔ:pleɪt, -s
AM 'dɔrˌpleɪt, -s

doorpost
BR 'dɔ:pəʊst, -s
AM 'dɔrˌpoʊst, -s

doorstep
BR 'dɔ:stɛp, -s, -ɪŋ, -t
AM 'dɔrˌstɛp, -s, -ɪŋ, -t

doorstop
BR 'dɔ:stɒp, -s
AM 'dɔrˌstɑp, -s

doorstopper
BR 'dɔ:ˌstɒpə(r), -z
AM 'dɔrˌstɑpər, -z

doorway
BR 'dɔ:weɪ, -z
AM 'dɔrˌweɪ, -z

dooryard
BR 'dɔ:jɑ:d, -z
AM 'dɔrˌjɑrd, -z

doozy
BR 'du:z|i, -ɪz
AM 'duzi, -z

dop
BR dɒp, -s
AM dɑp, -s

dopa
BR 'dəʊpə(r)
AM 'doʊpə

dopamine
BR 'dəʊpəmi:n
AM 'doʊpəˌmin

dopant
BR 'dəʊp(ə)nt, -s
AM 'doʊpənt, -s

dope
BR dəʊp, -s, -ɪŋ, -t
AM doʊp, -s, -ɪŋ, -t

doper
BR 'dəʊpə(r), -z
AM 'doʊpər, -z

dopesheet
BR 'dəʊpʃi:t, -s
AM 'doʊpˌʃit, -s

dopester
BR 'dəʊpstə(r), -z
AM 'doʊpstər, -z

dopey
BR 'dəʊp|i, -ɪə(r), -ɪɪst
AM 'doʊpi, -ər, -ɪst

dopiaza
BR 'dəʊpɪɑ:zə(r), ˌdəʊpɪ'ɑ:zə(r)
AM ˌdoʊpi'ɑzə

dopily
BR 'dəʊpɨli
AM 'doʊpəli

dopiness
BR 'dəʊpɪnɪs
AM 'doʊpinɨs

doppelgänger
BR 'dɒplˌgaŋə(r), -z
AM 'dɑpəlˌgæŋər, -z

Dopper
BR 'dɒpə(r), -z
AM 'dɑpər, -z

Doppler
BR 'dɒplə(r)
AM 'dɑplər

dopy
BR 'dəʊp|i, -ɪə(r), -ɪɪst
AM 'doʊpi, -ər, -ɪst

Dora
BR 'dɔ:rə(r)
AM 'dɔrə

Dorado
BR də'rɑ:dəʊ
AM də'rɑdoʊ

Doran
BR 'dɔ:rən, 'dɔ:rṇ
AM 'dɔrən

Dorcas
BR 'dɔ:kəs
AM 'dɔrkəs

Dorchester
BR 'dɔ:tʃɛstə(r)
AM 'dɔrˌtʃɛstər

Dordogne
BR dɔ:'dɔɪn
AM dɔr'doʊn
FR dɔʀdɔɲ

Dordrecht
BR 'dɔ:drɛkt, 'dɔ:drɛxt
AM 'dɔrˌdrɛkt

Doré
BR 'dɔ:reɪ
AM dɔ'reɪ

Doreen
BR 'dɔ:ri:n, də'ri:n
AM 'dɔrin

Dorian
BR 'dɔ:rɪən
AM 'dɔriən

Doric
BR 'dɒrɪk
AM 'dɔrɪk, 'dɑrɪk

Dorinda
BR də'rɪndə(r)
AM də'rɪndə

Doris
BR 'dɒrɪs
AM 'dɔrəs

dork
BR dɔ:k, -s
AM dɔ(ə)rk, -s

Dorking
BR 'dɔ:kɪŋ
AM 'dɔrkɪŋ

dorm
BR dɔ:m, -z
AM dɔ(ə)rm, -z

dormancy
BR 'dɔ:mənsi
AM 'dɔrmənsi

dormant
BR 'dɔ:m(ə)nt
AM 'dɔrmənt

dormer
BR 'dɔ:mə(r), -z
AM 'dɔrmər, -z

dormice
BR 'dɔ:mʌɪs
AM 'dɔrˌmaɪs

dormition
BR dɔ:'mɪʃn
AM dɔr'mɪʃən

dormitory
BR 'dɔ:mɪt(ə)r|i, -ɪz
AM 'dɔrməˌtɔri, -z

Dormobile®
BR 'dɔ:mə(ʊ)bi:l, -z
AM 'dɔrməˌbil, -z

dormouse
BR 'dɔ:maʊs
AM 'dɔrˌmaʊs

dormy
BR 'dɔ:mi
AM 'dɔrmi

Dornoch
BR 'dɔ:nɒk, 'dɔ:nɒx, 'dɔ:nək, 'dɔ:nəx
AM 'dɔrnɑk

doronicum
BR də'rɒnɪkəm
AM də'rɑnəkəm

Dorothea
BR ˌdɒrə'θɪə(r), ˌdɒrə'θi:ə(r)
AM ˌdɔrə'θiə

Dorothy
BR 'dɒrəθi
AM 'dɔrəθi

dorp
BR dɔ:p, -s
AM dɔ(ə)rp, -s

Dors
BR dɔ:z
AM dɔ(ə)rz

dorsa
BR 'dɔ:sə(r)
AM 'dɔrsə

dorsal
BR 'dɔ:sl
AM 'dɔrsəl

dorsally
BR 'dɔ:sḷi, 'dɔ:səli
AM 'dɔrsəli

Dorset
BR 'dɔ:sɪt
AM 'dɔrsət

Dorsey
BR 'dɔ:si
AM 'dɔrsi

dorsiflex
BR ˈdɔːsɪflɛks
AM ˈdɔrsəˌflɛks
dorsum
BR ˈdɔːsəm
AM ˈdɔrsəm
Dortmund
BR ˈdɔːtmənd, ˈdɔːtmʊnd
AM ˈdɔrtmənd
dory
BR ˈdɔːr|i, -ɪz
AM ˈdɔri, -z
DOS
BR dɒs
AM dɔs, dɑs
do's
BR duːz
AM duz
dos-à-dos
BR ˌdəʊzɑːˈdəʊ, -z
AM ˌdoʊzəˈdoʊ, -z
dosage
BR ˈdəʊs|ɪdʒ, -ɪdʒɪz
AM ˈdoʊsɪdʒ, -ɪz
dose
BR dəʊs, -ɪz, -ɪŋ, -t
AM doʊs, -əz, -ɪŋ, -t
do-se-do
BR ˌdəʊsɪˈdəʊ, -z
AM ˌdoʊˌsiˈdoʊ, -z
dosh
BR dɒʃ
AM dɑʃ
do-si-do
BR ˌdəʊsɪˈdəʊ, -z
AM ˌdoʊˌsiˈdoʊ, -z
dosimeter
BR dəʊˈsɪmɪtə(r)
AM doʊˈsɪmədər
dosimetric
BR ˌdəʊsɪˈmɛtrɪk
AM ˌdoʊsiˈmɛtrɪk
dosimetry
BR dəʊˈsɪmɪtri
AM doʊˈsɪmətri
Dos Passos
BR dɒs ˈpasɒs
AM ˌdɑs ˈpæˌsoʊs
doss
BR dɒs, -ɪz, -ɪŋ, -t
AM dɑs, -əz, -ɪŋ, -t
dossal
BR ˈdɒsl
AM ˈdɑsəl
dosser
BR ˈdɒsə(r), -z
AM ˈdɑsər, -z
dosshouse
BR ˈdɒshaʊ|s, -zɪz
AM ˈdɔsˌ(h)aʊ|s, ˈdɑsˌ(h)aʊs, -zəz
dossier
BR ˈdɒsɪə(r), ˈdɒsɪeɪ, -z
AM ˈdɔsiˌeɪ, ˈdɑsiˌeɪ, -z
dost
BR dʌst
AM dəst
Dostoevsky
BR ˌdɒstɔɪˈɛfski
AM ˌdɑstəˈjɛfski, ˌdɔstəˈjɛfski
Dostoyevsky
BR ˌdɒstɔɪˈɛfski
AM ˌdɑstəˈjɛfski, ˌdɔstəˈjɛfski
dot
BR dɒt, -s, -ɪŋ, -ɪd
AM dɑ|t, -ts, -dɪŋ, -dəd
dotage
BR ˈdəʊtɪdʒ
AM ˈdoʊdɪdʒ
dotard
BR ˈdəʊtəd, -z
AM ˈdoʊdərd, -z
dote
BR dəʊt, -s, -ɪŋ, -ɪd
AM doʊ|t, -ts, -dɪŋ, -dəd
doter
BR ˈdəʊtə(r), -z
AM ˈdoʊdər, -z
doth
BR dʌθ
AM dəθ, dɔθ, dɑθ
Dotheboys
BR ˈduːðəbɔɪz
AM ˈduðəˌbɔɪz
dotingly
BR ˈdəʊtɪŋli
AM ˈdoʊdɪŋli
Dotrice
BR dəˈtriːs, dɒˈtriːs
AM ˈdɑtrəs
Dotson
BR ˈdɒtsn
AM ˈdɑtsən
dotter
BR ˈdɒtə(r), -z
AM ˈdɑdər, -z
dotterel
BR ˈdɒtr(ə)l, -z
AM ˈdɑtrəl, -z
dottily
BR ˈdɒtɪli
AM ˈdɑdəli
dottiness
BR ˈdɒtɪnɪs
AM ˈdɑdinɪs
dottle
BR ˈdɒtl
AM ˈdɑdəl
dotty
BR ˈdɒt|i, -ɪə(r), -ɪɪst
AM ˈdɑdi, -ər, -ɪst
Douai¹
French town
BR ˈduːeɪ
AM duˈeɪ
FR dwɛ
Douai²
BR ˈdaʊeɪ, ˈdaʊi
AM duˈeɪ
Douala
BR duːˈɑːlə(*r*)
AM duˈ(w)ɑlə
douane
BR duːˈɑːn, -z
AM dwɑn, -z
Douay
BR ˈdaʊeɪ, ˈdaʊi, ˈduːeɪ
AM dwaɪ, duˈeɪ
double
BR ˈdʌb|l, -lz, -lɪŋ\-lɪŋ, -ld
AM ˈdəb|əl, -əlz, -(ə)lɪŋ, -əld
Doubleday
BR ˈdʌbldeɪ
AM ˈdəblˌdeɪ
double entendre
BR ˌduːbl ɒnˈtɒndrə(*r*), + ɒ̃ˈtɒ̃drə(*r*)
AM ˌdubəˌlɑnˈtɑndrə
double-ganger
BR ˈdʌblˌgaŋə(r)
AM ˈdəbəlˌgæŋ(g)ər
doubleheader
BR ˌdʌblˈhɛdə(r), -z
AM ˌdəbəlˈhɛdər, -z
doubleness
BR ˈdʌblnəs
AM ˈdəbəlnəs
doubler
BR ˈdʌblə(r), -z
AM ˈdəblər, -z
doublespeak
BR ˈdʌblspiːk
AM ˈdəbəlˌspik
doublet
BR ˈdʌblɪt, -s
AM ˈdəblət, -s
doublethink
BR ˈdʌblθɪŋk
AM ˈdəbəlˌθɪŋk
doubleton
BR ˈdʌblt(ə)n, -z
AM ˈdəbəltən, -z
doubletree
BR ˈdʌbltriː, -z
AM ˈdəbəlˌtri, -z
doubloon
BR dəˈbluːn, -z
AM dəˈblun, -z
doublure
BR dəˈblʊə(r), duːˈblʊə(r), -z
AM dəˈblʊ(ə)r, -z
doubly
BR ˈdʌbli
AM ˈdəbli
doubt
BR daʊt, -s, -ɪŋ, -ɪd
AM daʊ|t, -ts, -dɪŋ, -dəd
doubtable
BR ˈdaʊtəbl
AM ˈdaʊdəbəl
doubter
BR ˈdaʊtə(r), -z
AM ˈdaʊdər, -z
doubtful
BR ˈdaʊtf(ʊ)l
AM ˈdaʊtfəl
doubtfully
BR ˈdaʊtfəli, ˈdaʊtfl̩i
AM ˈdaʊtfəli
doubtfulness
BR ˈdaʊtf(ʊ)lnəs
AM ˈdaʊtfəlnəs
doubtingly
BR ˈdaʊtɪŋli
AM ˈdaʊdɪŋli
doubtless
BR ˈdaʊtləs
AM ˈdaʊtləs
doubtlessly
BR ˈdaʊtləsli
AM ˈdaʊtləsli
douce
BR duːs
AM dus
douceur
BR duːˈsəː(r), -z
AM duˈsər, -z
douche
BR duːʃ, -ɪz
AM duʃ, -əz
Doug
BR dʌg
AM dəg
Dougal
BR ˈdʊgl
AM ˈdugəl
Dougall
BR ˈduːgl
AM ˈdugəl
Dougan
BR ˈduːg(ə)n
AM ˈdugən
dough
BR dəʊ
AM doʊ
doughboy
BR ˈdəʊbɔɪ, -z
AM ˈdoʊˌbɔɪ, -z
Dougherty
BR ˈdɒxəti, ˈdɒkəti, ˈdəʊəti
AM ˈdɔrdi
doughiness
BR ˈdəʊɪnɪs
AM ˈdoʊinɪs
doughnut
BR ˈdəʊnʌt, -s
AM ˈdoʊˌnət, -s
doughtily
BR ˈdaʊtɪli
AM ˈdaʊdəli
doughtiness
BR ˈdaʊtɪnɪs
AM ˈdaʊdinɪs
doughty
BR ˈdaʊt|i, -ɪə(r), -ɪɪst
AM ˈdaʊdi, -ər, -ɪst
doughy
BR ˈdəʊ|i, -ɪə(r), -ɪɪst
AM ˈdoʊi, -ər, -ɪst

Dougie
BR ˈdʌgi
AM ˈdəgi

Douglas[1]
BR ˈdʌgləs
AM ˈdəgləs

Douglas[2]
traditionally
BR ˈduːgləs
AM ˈdəgləs

Douglass
BR ˈdʌgləs
AM ˈdəgləs

Doulton®
BR ˈdəʊlt(ə)n
AM ˈdɔltən, ˈdoʊltən

doum
BR duːm, -z
AM dum, daʊm, -z

Dounreay
BR ˌduːnˈreɪ
AM ˌdunˈreɪ

dour
BR ˈdʊə(r), daʊə(r)
AM ˈdaʊ(ə)r, ˈdʊ(ə)r

dourly
BR ˈdʊəli, ˈdaʊəli
AM ˈdaʊ(ə)rli, ˈdʊrli

dourness
BR ˈdʊənəs, ˈdaʊənəs
AM ˈdaʊ(ə)rnəs, ˈdʊrnəs

Douro
BR ˈdʊərəʊ
AM ˈduˌroʊ
PORT ˈdoru

douroucouli
BR ˌdʊərʊˈkuːl|i, -ɪz
AM ˌdurəˈkuli, -z

douse
BR daʊs, -ɪz, -ɪŋ, -t
AM daʊ|s, daʊ|z, -sɪz\-zɪz, -sɪŋ\-zɪŋ, -st\-zd

dove[1]
bird
BR dʌv, -z
AM dəv, -z

dove[2]
past tense of dive
BR dəʊv
AM doʊv

dovecote
BR ˈdʌvkɒt, ˈdʌvkəʊt, -s
AM ˈdəvˌkoʊt, -s

Dovedale
BR ˈdʌvdeɪl
AM ˈdəvˌdeɪl

dovelike
BR ˈdʌvlʌɪk
AM ˈdəvˌlaɪk

Dover
BR ˈdəʊvə(r)
AM ˈdoʊvər

Dovercourt
BR ˈdəʊvəkɔːt
AM ˈdoʊvərˌkɔ(ə)rt

Doveridge
BR ˈdʌv(ə)rɪdʒ
AM ˈdoʊvərɪdʒ, ˈdəvərɪdʒ

dovetail
BR ˈdʌvteɪl, -z, -ɪŋ, -d
AM ˈdəvˌteɪl, -z, -ɪŋ, -d

Dovey
BR ˈdʌvi
AM ˈdəvi

Dow
BR daʊ
AM daʊ

dowager
BR ˈdaʊɪdʒə(r), -z
AM ˈdaʊədʒər, -z

dowdily
BR ˈdaʊdɪli
AM ˈdaʊdəli

dowdiness
BR ˈdaʊdɪnɪs
AM ˈdaʊdinɪs

Dowding
BR ˈdaʊdɪŋ
AM ˈdaʊdɪŋ

dowdy
BR ˈdaʊd|i, -ɪə(r), -ɪɪst
AM ˈdaʊdi, -ər, -ɪst

dowel
BR ˈdaʊ(ə)l, -z, -ɪŋ
AM ˈdaʊ(ə)l, -z, -ɪŋ

Dowell
BR ˈdaʊ(ə)l
AM ˈdaʊəl

dower
BR ˈdaʊə(r), -z, -ɪŋ, -d
AM ˈdaʊər, -z, -ɪŋ, -d

dowerless
BR ˈdaʊələs
AM ˈdaʊərləs

Dowlais
BR ˈdaʊlʌɪs, ˈdaʊləs
AM ˈdaʊləs

Dowland
BR ˈdaʊlənd
AM ˈdaʊlən(d)

Dowling
BR ˈdaʊlɪŋ
AM ˈdaʊlɪŋ

down
BR daʊn, -z, -ɪŋ, -d
AM daʊn, -z, -ɪŋ, -d

down-and-out[1]
adjective
BR ˌdaʊnən(d)ˈaʊt
AM ˈdaʊnənˈaʊt

down-and-out[2]
noun
BR ˈdaʊnən(d)aʊt, -s
AM ˈdaʊnənˌaʊt, -s

downbeat
BR ˈdaʊnbiːt, -s
AM ˈdaʊnˌbit, -s

downcast
BR ˈdaʊnkɑːst, ˈdaʊnkast
AM ˈdaʊnˌkæst

downcomer
BR ˈdaʊnˌkʌmə(r), -z
AM ˈdaʊnˌkəmər, -z

downdraft
BR ˈdaʊndrɑːft, ˈdaʊndraft, -s
AM ˈdaʊnˌdræft, -s

downer
BR ˈdaʊnə(r), -z
AM ˈdaʊnər, -z

Downes
BR daʊnz
AM daʊnz

Downey
BR ˈdaʊni
AM ˈdaʊni

downfall
BR ˈdaʊnfɔːl, -z
AM ˈdaʊnˌfɔl, ˈdaʊnˌfɑl, -z

downfold
BR ˈdaʊnfəʊld, -z
AM ˈdaʊnˌfoʊld, -z

downgrade
verb
BR ˌdaʊnˈgreɪd, ˈdaʊngreɪd, -z, -ɪŋ, -ɪd
AM ˈdaʊnˈgreɪd, -z, -ɪŋ, -ɪd

down grade
noun
BR ˈdaʊn greɪd, -z
AM ˈdaʊn ˈgreɪd, -z

Downham
BR ˈdaʊnəm
AM ˈdaʊnəm

downhaul
BR ˈdaʊnhɔːl, -z
AM ˈdaʊnˌ(h)ɔl, ˈdaʊnˌ(h)ɑl, -z

downhearted
BR ˌdaʊnˈhɑːtɪd
AM ˈdaʊnˈhɑrdəd

downheartedly
BR ˌdaʊnˈhɑːtɪdli
AM ˈdaʊnˈhɑrdədli

downheartedness
BR ˌdaʊnˈhɑːtɪdnɪs
AM ˈdaʊnˈhɑrdədnəs

downhill
BR ˌdaʊnˈhɪl
AM ˈdaʊnˈhɪl

downhiller
BR ˈdaʊnˌhɪlə(r), -z
AM ˈdaʊnˌ(h)ɪlər, -z

Downie
BR ˈdaʊni
AM ˈdaʊni

downily
BR ˈdaʊnɪli
AM ˈdaʊnəli

downiness
BR ˈdaʊnɪnɪs
AM ˈdaʊninɪs

Downing
BR ˈdaʊnɪŋ
AM ˈdaʊnɪŋ

downland
BR ˈdaʊnland, ˈdaʊnlənd, -z
AM ˈdaʊnˌlænd, -z

downlighter
BR ˈdaʊnˌlʌɪtə(r), -z
AM ˈdaʊnˌlaɪdər, -z

download
BR ˌdaʊnˈləʊd, ˈdaʊnləʊd, -z, -ɪŋ, -ɪd
AM ˈdaʊnˈloʊd, -z, -ɪŋ, -əd

downmarket
BR ˌdaʊnˈmɑːkɪt
AM ˈdaʊnˈmɑrkət

downmost
BR ˈdaʊnməʊst
AM ˈdaʊnˌmoʊst

Downpatrick
BR ˌdaʊnˈpatrɪk
AM ˌdaʊnˈpætrək

downpipe
BR ˈdaʊnpʌɪp, -s
AM ˈdaʊnˌpaɪp, -s

downplay
BR ˌdaʊnˈpleɪ, -z, -ɪŋ, -d
AM ˈdaʊnˌpleɪ, -z, -ɪŋ, -d

downpour
BR ˈdaʊnpɔː(r), -z
AM ˈdaʊnˌpɔ(ə)r, -z

downright
BR ˈdaʊnrʌɪt
AM ˈdaʊnˌraɪt

downrightness
BR ˈdaʊnrʌɪtnɪs
AM ˈdaʊnˌraɪtnɪs

downriver
BR ˌdaʊnˈrɪvə(r)
AM ˈdaʊnˈrɪvər

Downs
BR daʊnz
AM daʊnz

downscale
BR ˌdaʊnˈskeɪl, -z, -ɪŋ, -d
AM ˈdaʊnˌskeɪl, -z, -ɪŋ, -d

downshaft
BR ˈdaʊnʃɑːft, ˈdaʊnʃaft, -s, -ɪŋ, -ɪd
AM ˈdaʊnˌʃæft, -s, -ɪŋ, -əd

downshift
BR ˈdaʊnʃɪft, -s, -ɪŋ, -ɪd
AM ˈdaʊnˌʃɪft, -s, -ɪŋ, -ɪd

downside
BR ˈdaʊnsʌɪd, -z
AM ˈdaʊnˌsaɪd, -z

downsize
BR ˌdaʊnˈsʌɪz, -ɪz, -ɪŋ, -d
AM ˈdaʊnˌsaɪz, -əz, -ɪŋ, -d

Downson
BR ˈdaʊns(ə)n
AM ˈdaʊnsən

downspout
BR ˈdaʊnspaʊt, -s

AM ˈdaʊnˌspaʊt, -s
downstage
BR ˌdaʊnˈsteɪdʒ
AM ˈdaʊnˈsteɪdʒ
downstairs
BR ˌdaʊnˈstɛːz
AM ˈdaʊnˈstɛrz
downstate
BR ˌdaʊnˈsteɪt
AM ˈdaʊnˈsteɪt
downstream
BR ˌdaʊnˈstriːm
AM ˈdaʊnˈstrim
downstroke
BR ˈdaʊnstrəʊk, -s
AM ˈdaʊnˌstroʊk, -s
downswing
BR ˈdaʊnswɪŋ, -z
AM ˈdaʊnˌswɪŋ, -z
downthrew
BR ˌdaʊnˈθruː
AM ˈdaʊnˌθru
downthrow
BR ˌdaʊnˈθrəʊ, -z, -ɪŋ
AM ˈdaʊnˌθroʊ, -z, -ɪŋ
downthrown
BR ˌdaʊnˈθrəʊn
AM ˈdaʊnˌθroʊn
downtime
BR ˈdaʊntʌɪm
AM ˈdaʊnˌtaɪm
downtown
BR ˌdaʊnˈtaʊn
AM ˈdaʊnˈtaʊn
downtrodden
BR ˈdaʊnˌtrɒdn
AM ˈdaʊnˈtrɑdən
downturn
BR ˈdaʊntəːn, -z
AM ˈdaʊnˌtərn, -z
downward
BR ˈdaʊnwəd, -z
AM ˈdaʊnwərd, -z
downwardly
BR ˈdaʊnwədli
AM ˈdaʊnwərdli
downwards
BR ˈdaʊnwədz
AM ˈdaʊnwərdz
downwarp
BR ˈdaʊnwɔːp, -s
AM ˈdaʊnwɔ(ə)rp, -s
downwind
BR ˌdaʊnˈwɪnd
AM ˈdaʊnˈwɪnd
downy
BR ˈdaʊn|i, -ɪə(r), -ɪɪst
AM ˈdaʊni, -ər, -ɨst
dowry
BR ˈdaʊ(ə)r|i, -ɪz
AM ˈdaʊ(ə)ri, -z
dowse¹
to wet
BR daʊs, -ɪz, -ɪŋ, -t
AM daʊ|s, daʊ|z, -səz\-zəz, -sɪŋ\-zɪŋ, -st\-zd

dowse²
to search for water etc
BR daʊz, -ɪz, -ɪŋ, -d
AM daʊ|z, daʊ|s, -zəz\-səz, -zɪŋ\-sɪŋ, -zd\-st
dowser¹
water pourer
BR ˈdaʊsə(r), -z
AM ˈdaʊsər, ˈdaʊzər, -z
dowser²
water searcher
BR ˈdaʊzə(r), -z
AM ˈdaʊzər, ˈdaʊsər, -z
Dowsing
BR ˈdaʊzɪŋ
AM ˈdaʊzɪŋ
dowsing rod
BR ˈdaʊzɪŋ rɒd, -z
AM ˈdaʊzɪŋ ˌrɑd, ˈdaʊsɪŋ +, -z
doxastic
BR dɒkˈsastɪk
AM dɑkˈsæstɪk
doxological
BR ˌdɒksəˈlɒdʒɪkl
AM ˌdɑksəˈlɑdʒəkəl
doxology
BR dɒkˈsɒlədʒ|i, -ɪz
AM dɑkˈsɑlədʒi, -z
doxy
BR ˈdɒks|i, -ɪz
AM ˈdɑksi, -z
doyen
BR ˈdɔɪən, ˈdɔɪɛn, -z
AM dɔɪˈ(j)ɛn, ˈdɔjən, -z
doyenne
BR ˌdɔɪˈɛn, -z
AM dɔɪˈ(j)ɛn, dɔˈjɛn, -z
Doyle
BR dɔɪl
AM dɔɪl
doyley
BR ˈdɔɪl|i, -ɪz
AM ˈdɔɪli, -z
doyly
BR ˈdɔɪl|i, -ɪz
AM ˈdɔɪli, -z
D'Oyly Carte
BR ˌdɔɪlɪ ˈkɑːt
AM ˈdɔɪli ˈkɑrt
doze
BR dəʊz, -ɪz, -ɪŋ, -d
AM doʊz, -əz, -ɪŋ, -d
dozen
BR ˈdʌzn, -z
AM ˈdəzən, -z
dozenth
BR ˈdʌznθ, -s
AM ˈdəzənθ, -s
dozer
BR ˈdəʊzə(r), -z
AM ˈdoʊzər, -z
dozily
BR ˈdəʊzɪli
AM ˈdoʊzəli

doziness
BR ˈdəʊzɪnɪs
AM ˈdoʊzinɪs
dozy
BR ˈdəʊz|i, -ɪə(r), -ɪɪst
AM ˈdoʊzi, -ər, -ɨst
D.Phil.
Doctor of Philosophy
BR ˌdiːˈfɪl
AM ˌdi ˈfɪl
Dr
BR ˈdɒktə(r), -z
AM ˈdɑktər, -z
drab
BR drab, -z, -ə(r), -ɪst
AM dræb, -z, -ər, -əst
drabble
BR ˈdrab|l, -lz, -l̩ɪŋ\-lɪŋ, -ld
AM ˈdræb|əl, -əld, -(ə)lɪŋ, -əld
drably
BR ˈdrabli
AM ˈdræbli
drabness
BR ˈdrabnəs
AM ˈdræbnəs
drachm
BR dram, -z
AM dræm, -z
drachma
BR ˈdrakmə(r), -z
AM ˈdrɑkmə, -z
drachmae
BR ˈdrakmiː, ˈdrakmeɪ
AM ˈdrɑkmi, ˈdrɑkmeɪ
drack
BR drak
AM dræk
Draco
BR ˈdreɪkəʊ
AM ˈdreɪkoʊ, ˈdrɑkoʊ
draconian
BR drəˈkəʊnɪən
AM drəˈkoʊniən, dreɪˈkoʊniən
draconic
BR drəˈkɒnɪk
AM drəˈkɑnɪk
draconically
BR drəˈkɒnɪkli
AM drəˈkɑnək(ə)li
Dracula
BR ˈdrakjʉlə(r)
AM ˈdrækjələ
draff
BR draf
AM dræf
draft
BR drɑːft, draft, -s, -ɪŋ, -ɪd
AM dræft, -s, -ɪŋ, -əd
draftee
BR ˌdrɑːfˈtiː, ˌdrafˈtiː, -z
AM ˌdræfˈti, -z

drafter
BR ˈdrɑːftə(r), ˈdraftə(r), -z
AM ˈdræftər, -z
drafthorse
BR ˈdrɑːfthɔːs, ˈdrafthɔːs, -ɪz
AM ˈdræf(t),(h)ɔ(ə)rs, -əz
draftily
BR ˈdrɑːftɪli, ˈdraftɪli
AM ˈdræftəli
draftiness
BR ˈdrɑːftɪnɪs, ˈdraftɪnɪs
AM ˈdræftinɪs
draftsman
BR ˈdrɑːf(t)smən, ˈdraf(t)smən
AM ˈdræf(t)smən
draftsmanship
BR ˈdrɑːf(t)smənʃɪp, ˈdraf(t)smənʃɪp
AM ˈdræf(t)smənˌʃɪp
draftsmen
BR ˈdrɑːf(t)smən, ˈdraf(t)smən
AM ˈdræf(t)smən
draftswoman
BR ˈdrɑːf(t)sˌwʊmən, ˈdraf(t)sˌwʊmən
AM ˈdræf(t)sˌwʊmən
draftswomen
BR ˈdrɑːf(t)sˌwɪmɪn, ˈdraf(t)sˌwɪmɪn
AM ˈdræf(t)sˌwɪmɨn
drafty
BR ˈdrɑːft|i, ˈdraft|i, -ɪə(r), -ɪɪst
AM ˈdræfti, -ər, -ɨst
drag
BR drag, -z, -ɪŋ, -d
AM dræg, -z, -ɪŋ, -d
dragée
BR ˈdraʒeɪ, ˈdrɑːʒeɪ, -z
AM drɑˈʒeɪ, -z
draggle
BR ˈdrag|l, -lz, -l̩ɪŋ\-lɪŋ, -ld
AM ˈdræg|əl, -əld, -(ə)lɪŋ, -əld
draggletail
BR ˈdragltel, -z
AM ˈdrægəlˌteɪl, -z
draggle-tailed
BR ˈdraglteɪld
AM ˈdrægəlˌteɪld
draggy
BR ˈdrag|i, -ɪə(r), -ɪɪst
AM ˈdrægi, -ər, -ɨst
dragline
BR ˈdraglʌɪn, -z
AM ˈdrægˌlaɪn, -z
dragnet
BR ˈdragnɛt, -s
AM ˈdrægˌnɛt, -s

dragoman
BR 'dragə(ʊ)mən, -z
AM 'drægəmən, -z

dragon
BR 'drag(ə)n, -z
AM 'drægən, -z

dragonet
BR 'dragənɨt, 'dragn̩ɨt, -s
AM 'drægənət, -s

dragonfish
BR 'drag(ə)nfɪʃ, -z
AM 'drægən,fɪʃ, -z

dragonfly
BR 'drag(ə)nflʌɪ, -z
AM 'drægən,flaɪ, -z

dragonish
BR 'dragənɪʃ, 'dragn̩ɪʃ
AM 'drægənɪʃ

dragonlady
BR 'drag(ə)n,leɪd|i, -ɪz
AM 'drægən,leɪdi, -z

dragonnade
BR ,dragə'neɪd, -z, -ɪŋ, -ɨd
AM ,drægə'neɪd, -z, -ɪŋ, -ɨd

dragoon
BR drə'gu:n, -z, -ɪŋ, -d
AM drə'gun, dræ'gun, -z, -ɪŋ, -d

dragster
BR 'dragstə(r), -z
AM 'drægztər, 'drægstər, -z

drail
BR dreɪl, -z
AM dreɪl, -z

drain
BR dreɪn, -z, -ɪŋ, -d
AM dreɪn, -z, -ɪŋ, -d

drainage
BR 'dreɪnɪdʒ
AM 'dreɪnɪdʒ

drainboard
BR 'dreɪnbɔ:d, -z
AM 'dreɪn,bɔ(ə)rd, -z

draincock
BR 'dreɪnkɒk, -s
AM 'dreɪn,kɑk, -s

drainer
BR 'dreɪnə(r), -z
AM 'dreɪnər, -z

drainpipe
BR 'dreɪnpʌɪp, -s
AM 'dreɪn,paɪp, -s

drake
BR dreɪk, -s
AM dreɪk, -s

Drakensberg
BR 'drak(ə)nzbə:g
AM 'dreɪkənz,bərg

Dralon®
BR 'dreɪlɒn
AM 'dreɪ,lɑn

DRAM
dynamic random access memory
BR 'di:ram
AM 'di,ræm

dram
BR dram, -z
AM dræm, -z

drama
BR 'drɑ:mə(*r*), -z
AM 'drɑmə, -z

dramadoc
BR ,drɑ:mə'dɒk, -s
AM 'drɑmə,dɑk, -s

Dramamine®
BR 'draməmi:n, -z
AM 'dræmə,min, -z

dramatic
BR drə'matɪk, -s
AM drə'mædɪk, -s

dramatically
BR drə'matɨkli
AM drə'mædək(ə)li

dramatisation
BR ,dramətʌɪ'zeɪʃn, -z
AM ,drɑmədə'zeɪʃən, ,drɑmə,taɪ'zeɪʃən, ,dræmədə'zeɪʃən, ,dræmə,taɪ'zeɪʃən, -z

dramatise
BR 'dramətʌɪz, -ɨz, -ɪŋ, -d
AM 'drɑmə,taɪz, 'dræmə,taɪz, -ɨz, -ɪŋ, -d

dramatis personae
BR drə,matɪs pə:'səʊnʌɪ, 'dramətɪs +, + pə:'səʊni:
AM drə,mɑdəs pər'soʊni, ,drɑmədəs +, + pər'soʊnaɪ

dramatist
BR 'dramətɪst, -s
AM 'drɑmədəst, 'dræmədəst, -s

dramatization
BR ,dramətʌɪ'zeɪʃn, -z
AM ,drɑmədə'zeɪʃən, ,drɑmə,taɪ'zeɪʃən, ,dræmədə'zeɪʃən, ,dræmə,taɪ'zeɪʃən, -z

dramatize
BR 'dramətʌɪz, -ɨz, -ɪŋ, -d
AM 'drɑmə,taɪz, 'dræmə,taɪz, -ɨz, -ɪŋ, -d

dramaturge
BR 'dramətə:dʒ, 'drɑ:mətə:dʒ, -ɨz
AM 'drɑmə,tərdʒ, 'dræmə,tərdʒ, -əz

dramaturgic
BR ,dramə'tə:dʒɪk, ,drɑ:mə'tə:dʒɪk
AM ,drɑmə'tərdʒɪk, ,dræmə'tərdʒɪk

dramaturgical
BR ,dramə'tə:dʒɨkl, ,drɑ:mə'tə:dʒɨkl
AM ,drɑmə'tərdʒəkəl, ,dræmə'tərdʒəkəl

dramaturgy
BR 'dramətə:dʒi, 'drɑ:mətə:dʒi
AM 'drɑmə,tərdʒi, 'dræmə,tərdʒi

Drambuie®
BR dram'b(j)u:|i, -ɪz
AM dræm'bui, -z

Drammen
BR 'dramən
AM 'dræmən

drank
BR draŋk
AM dræŋk

drape
BR dreɪp, -s, -ɪŋ, -t
AM dreɪp, -s, -ɪŋ, -t

draper
BR 'dreɪpə(r), -z
AM 'dreɪpər, -z

drapery
BR 'dreɪp(ə)r|i, -ɪz
AM 'dreɪp(ə)ri, -z

drastic
BR 'drastɪk, 'drɑ:stɪk
AM 'dræstɪk

drastically
BR 'drastɨkli, 'drɑ:stɨkli
AM 'dræstək(ə)li

drat
BR drat
AM dræt

dratted
BR 'dratɨd
AM 'drædəd

draught
BR drɑ:ft, draft, -s
AM dræft, -s

draughtboard
BR 'drɑ:f(t)bɔ:d, 'draf(t)bɔ:d, -z
AM 'dræf(t),bɔ(ə)rd, -z

draughthorse
BR 'drɑ:fthɔ:s, 'drafthɔ:s, -ɨz
AM 'dræf(t),(h)ɔ(ə)rs, -əz

draughtily
BR 'drɑ:ftɨli, 'draftɨli
AM 'dræftəli

draughtiness
BR 'drɑ:ftɪnɨs, 'draftɪnɨs
AM 'dræftinɨs

draughts
BR drɑ:fts, drafts
AM dræf(t)s

draughtsman
BR 'drɑ:f(t)smən, 'draf(t)smən
AM 'dræf(t)smən

draughtsmanship
BR 'drɑ:f(t)smənʃɪp, 'draf(t)smənʃɪp
AM 'dræf(t)smən,ʃɪp

draughtsmen
BR 'drɑ:f(t)smən, 'draf(t)smən
AM 'dræf(t)smən

draughtswoman
BR 'drɑ:f(t)s,wʊmən, 'draf(t)s,wʊmən
AM 'dræf(t)s,wʊmən

draughtswomen
BR 'drɑ:ft,wɪmɪn, 'draf(t)s,wɪmɪn
AM 'dræf(t)s,wɪmɨn

draughty
BR 'drɑ:ft|i, 'draft|i, -ɪə(r), -ɪɨst
AM 'dræfti, -ər, -ɨst

Dravidian
BR drə'vɪdɪən, -z
AM drə'vɪdiən, -z

draw
BR drɔ:(*r*), -z, -ɪŋ
AM drɔ, drɑ, -z, -ɪŋ

drawback
BR 'drɔ:bak, -s
AM 'drɔ,bæk, 'drɑ,bæk, -s

drawbridge
BR 'drɔ:brɪdʒ, -ɨz
AM 'drɔ,brɪdʒ, 'drɑ,brɪdʒ, -ɨz

drawcord
BR 'drɔ:kɔ:d, -z
AM 'drɔ,kɔ(ə)rd, 'drɑ,kɔ(ə)rd, -z

drawee
BR drɔ:(*r*)'i:, -z
AM drɔ'(w)i, drɑ'(w)i, -z

drawer[1]
in furniture
BR drɔ:(r), -z
AM 'drɔ(ə)r, 'drɑ(ə)r, -z

drawer[2]
person who draws
BR 'drɔ:(*r*)ə(r), -z
AM 'drɔ(w)ər, 'drɑ(w)ər, -z

drawerful
BR 'drɔ:fʊl, -z
AM 'drɔr,fʊl, -z

drawers
underclothes
BR drɔ:z
AM 'drɔ(ə)rz, 'drɑ(ə)rz

drawing
BR 'drɔ:(*r*)ɪŋ, -z
AM 'drɔɪŋ, 'drɑɪŋ, -z

drawl
BR drɔ:l, -z, -ɪŋ, -d
AM drɔl, drɑl, -z, -ɪŋ, -d

drawler
BR 'drɔ:lə(r), -z
AM 'drɔlər, 'drɑlər, -z

drawn
BR drɔːn
AM drɔn, drɑn
drawstring
BR ˈdrɔːstrɪŋ, -z
AM ˈdrɔˌstrɪŋ, ˈdrɑˌstrɪŋ, -z
Drax
BR draks
AM dræks
dray
BR dreɪ, -z
AM dreɪ, -z
Draycott
BR ˈdreɪkət, ˈdreɪkɒt
AM ˈdreɪˌkɑt
drayman
BR ˈdreɪmən
AM ˈdreɪmən
draymen
BR ˈdreɪmən
AM ˈdreɪmən
Drayton
BR ˈdreɪtn
AM ˈdreɪtn
dread
BR drɛd, -z, -ɪŋ, -ɨd
AM drɛd, -z, -ɪŋ, -əd
dreadful
BR ˈdrɛdf(ʊ)l
AM ˈdrɛdfəl
dreadfully
BR ˈdrɛdfʊli, ˈdrɛdfḷi
AM ˈdrɛdfəli
dreadfulness
BR ˈdrɛdf(ʊ)lnəs
AM ˈdrɛdfəlnəs
dreadlocked
BR ˈdrɛdlɒkt
AM ˈdrɛdˌlɑkt
dreadlocks
BR ˈdrɛdlɒks
AM ˈdrɛdˌlɑks
dreadnought
BR ˈdrɛdnɔːt, -s
AM ˈdrɛdˌnɔt, ˈdrɛdˌnɑt, -s
dream
BR driːm, -z, -ɪŋ
AM drim, -z, -ɪŋ
dreamboat
BR ˈdriːmbəʊt, -s
AM ˈdrimˌboʊt, -s
dreamed
BR drɛmt, driːmd
AM drimd
dreamer
BR ˈdriːmə(r), -z
AM ˈdrimər, -z
dreamful
BR ˈdriːmf(ʊ)l
AM ˈdrimfəl
dreamily
BR ˈdriːmɨli
AM ˈdrimɨli
dreaminess
BR ˈdriːmɪnɨs
AM ˈdriminɨs
dreamland
BR ˈdriːmland, -z
AM ˈdrimˌlænd, -z
dreamless
BR ˈdriːmlɨs
AM ˈdrimlɨs
dreamlessly
BR ˈdriːmlɨsli
AM ˈdrimlɨsli
dreamlessness
BR ˈdriːmlɨsnɨs
AM ˈdrimlɨsnɨs
dreamlike
BR ˈdriːmlʌɪk
AM ˈdrimˌlaɪk
dreamt
BR drɛmt
AM drɛmt
dreamtime
BR ˈdriːmtʌɪm
AM ˈdrimˌtaɪm
dreamworld
BR ˈdriːmwəːld, -z
AM ˈdrimˌwərld, -z
dreamy
BR ˈdriːm|i, -ɪə(r), -ɪɨst
AM ˈdrimi, -ər, -ɨst
drear
BR ˈdrɪə(r)
AM ˈdrɪ(ə)r
drearily
BR ˈdrɪərɨli
AM ˈdrɪrɨli, ˈdrirɨli
dreariness
BR ˈdrɪərɪnɨs
AM ˈdrɪrinɨs, ˈdririnɨs
dreary
BR ˈdrɪər|i, -ɪə(r), -ɪɨst
AM ˈdrɪri, ˈdriri, -ər, -ɨst
dreck
BR drɛk
AM drɛk
dredge
BR drɛdʒ, -ɨz, -ɪŋ, -d
AM drɛdʒ, -əz, -ɪŋ, -d
dredger
BR ˈdrɛdʒə(r), -z
AM ˈdrɛdʒər, -z
dree
BR driː, -z, -ɪŋ, -d
AM dri, -z, -ɪŋ, -d
Dreft
BR drɛft
AM drɛft
dreg
BR drɛg, -z
AM drɛg, -z
dreggy
BR ˈdrɛgi
AM ˈdrɛgi
Dreiser
BR ˈdrʌɪzə(r)
AM ˈdraɪzər
drench
BR drɛn(t)ʃ, -ɨz, -ɪŋ, -t
AM drɛn(t)ʃ, -əz, -ɪŋ, -t
Dresden
BR ˈdrɛzd(ə)n
AM ˈdrɛzdən
GER ˈdreːzdn
dress
BR drɛs, -ɨz, -ɪŋ, -t
AM drɛs, -əz, -ɪŋ, -t
dressage
BR ˈdrɛsɑː(d)ʒ
AM drəˈsɑʒ
dresser
BR ˈdrɛsə(r), -z
AM ˈdrɛsər, -z
dressily
BR ˈdrɛsɨli
AM ˈdrɛsəli
dressiness
BR ˈdrɛsɪnɨs
AM ˈdrɛsinɨs
dressing
BR ˈdrɛsɪŋ, -z
AM ˈdrɛsɪŋ, -z
dressmaker
BR ˈdrɛsˌmeɪkə(r), -z
AM ˈdrɛsˌmeɪkər, -z
dressmaking
BR ˈdrɛsˌmeɪkɪŋ
AM ˈdrɛsˌmeɪkɪŋ
dressy
BR ˈdrɛs|i, -ɪə(r), -ɪɨst
AM ˈdrɛsi, -ər, -ɨst
drew
BR druː
AM dru
Drexel
BR ˈdrɛksl
AM ˈdrɛksəl
drey
BR dreɪ, -z
AM dreɪ, -z
Dreyfus
BR ˈdreɪfəs, ˈdrʌɪfəs
AM ˈdreɪfəs, ˈdraɪfəs
dribble
BR ˈdrɪb|l, -lz, -ḷɪŋ\-lɪŋ, -ld
AM ˈdrɪb|əl, -əlz, -(ə)lɪŋ, -əld
dribbler
BR ˈdrɪbḷə(r), ˈdrɪblə(r), -z
AM ˈdrɪb(ə)lər, -z
dribbly
BR ˈdrɪbḷi, ˈdrɪbli
AM ˈdrɪbḷi, ˈdrɪbli
driblet
BR ˈdrɪblɨt, -s
AM ˈdrɪblət, -s
dribs and drabs
BR ˌdrɪbz (ə)n ˈdrabz
AM ˌdrɪbz ən ˈdræbz
dried
BR drʌɪd
AM draɪd
drier
BR ˈdrʌɪə(r), -z
AM ˈdraɪ(ə)r, -z
Driffield
BR ˈdrɪfiːld
AM ˈdrɪfild
drift
BR drɪft, -s, -ɪŋ, -ɨd
AM drɪft, -s, -ɪŋ, -ɨd
driftage
BR ˈdrɪftɪdʒ
AM ˈdrɪftɪdʒ
drifter
BR ˈdrɪftə(r), -z
AM ˈdrɪftər, -z
driftnet
BR ˈdrɪf(t)nɛt, -s
AM ˈdrɪf(t)ˌnɛt, -s
driftwood
BR ˈdrɪf(t)wʊd
AM ˈdrɪf(t)ˌwʊd
Drighlington
BR ˈdrɪglɪŋt(ə)n
AM ˈdrɪglɪŋtən
drill
BR drɪl, -z, -ɪŋ, -d
AM drɪl, -z, -ɪŋ, -d
driller
BR ˈdrɪlə(r), -z
AM ˈdrɪlər, -z
drillmaster
BR ˈdrɪlˌmɑːstə(r), ˈdrɪlˌmastə(r), -z
AM ˈdrɪlˌmæstər, -z
drillstock
BR ˈdrɪlstɒk, -s
AM ˈdrɪlˌstɑk, -s
drily
BR ˈdrʌɪli
AM ˈdraɪli
drink
BR drɪŋk, -s, -ɪŋ
AM drɪŋk, -s, -ɪŋ
drinkable
BR ˈdrɪŋkəbl
AM ˈdrɪŋkəbəl
drinker
BR ˈdrɪŋkə(r), -z
AM ˈdrɪŋkər, -z
Drinkwater
BR ˈdrɪŋkwɔːtə(r)
AM ˈdrɪŋkˌwɔdər, ˈdrɪŋkˌwɑdər
drip
BR drɪp, -s, -ɪŋ, -t
AM drɪp, -s, -ɪŋ, -t
dripfed
BR ˈdrɪpfɛd, ˌdrɪpˈfɛd
AM ˈdrɪpˌfɛd
dripfeed
BR ˈdrɪpfiːd, ˌdrɪpˈfiːd, -z, -ɪŋ
AM ˈdrɪpˌfid, -z, -ɪŋ
dripgrind
BR ˈdrɪpgrʌɪnd, ˌdrɪpˈgrʌɪnd, -z, -ɪŋ, -ɨd
AM ˈdrɪpˌgraɪnd, -z, -ɪŋ, -ɨd

drippily
BR 'drɪpɨli
AM 'drɪpɨli
drippiness
BR 'drɪpɪnɪs
AM 'drɪpinɨs
dripping
BR 'drɪpɪŋ
AM 'drɪpɪŋ
drippy
BR 'drɪp|i, -ɪə(r), -ɪɪst
AM 'drɪpi, -ər, -ɨst
Driscoll
BR 'drɪskl
AM 'drɪskəl
drivable
BR 'drʌɪvəbl
AM 'draɪvəbəl
drive
BR drʌɪv, -z, -ɪŋ
AM draɪv, -z, -ɪŋ
driveable
BR 'drʌɪvəbl
AM 'draɪvəbəl
drivel
BR 'drɪv|l, -lz, -ḷɪŋ\-lɪŋ, -ld
AM 'drɪvəl, -z, -ɪŋ, -d
driveller
BR 'drɪvḷə(r), 'drɪvlə(r), -z
AM 'drɪvələr, -z
driven
BR 'drɪvn
AM 'drɪvən
driver
BR 'drʌɪvə(r), -z
AM 'draɪvər, -z
driverless
BR 'drʌɪvələs
AM 'draɪvərləs
driveshaft
BR 'drʌɪvʃɑːft, 'drʌɪvʃaft, -s
AM 'draɪv,ʃæft, -s
driveway
BR 'drʌɪvweɪ, -z
AM 'draɪv,weɪ, -z
drizzle
BR 'drɪz|l, -lz, -ḷɪŋ\-lɪŋ, -ld
AM 'drɪz|əl, -əlz, -(ə)lɪŋ, -əld
drizzly
BR 'drɪzl|i, -ɪə(r), -ɪɪst
AM 'drɪzli, 'drɪzḷi, -ər, -ɨst
Drogheda
BR 'drɔɪɪdə(r)
AM 'drɔ(ɪ)ədə, 'drɑ(h)ədə
drogue
BR drəʊg, -z
AM droʊg, -z
droit
BR drɔɪt, -s
AM drɔɪt, -s
droit de seigneur
BR ˌdrwɑː də seɪn'jəː(r), + sɛn'jəː(r)
AM ˌdrwɑ də seɪn'jər
droit du seigneur
BR ˌdrwɑː də seɪn'jəː(r), + sɛn'jəː(r)
AM ˌdrwɑ də seɪn'jər
Droitwich
BR 'drɔɪtwɪtʃ
AM 'drɔɪtwɪtʃ
droll
BR drəʊl, -ə(r), -ɨst
AM droʊl, -ər, -əst
drollery
BR 'drəʊl(ə)r|i, -ɪz
AM 'droʊl(ə)ri, -z
drollness
BR 'drəʊlnəs
AM 'droʊlnəs
drolly
BR 'drəʊl(l)i
AM 'droʊ(l)li
drome
BR drəʊm, -z
AM droʊm, -z
dromedary
BR 'drɒmɪd(ə)r|i, -ɪz
AM 'drɑməˌdɛri, -z
dromoi
BR 'drɒmɔɪ
AM 'drɔmɔɪ, 'drɑmɔɪ
dromond
BR 'drɒmənd, 'drʌmənd, -z
AM 'drɑmənd, 'drəmənd, -z
Dromore
BR drə'mɔː(r)
AM drə'mɔ(ə)r
dromos
BR 'drɒmɒs
AM 'drɔmɔs, 'drɑmɑs
GR 'drɔmɔs
drone
BR drəʊn, -z, -ɪŋ, -d
AM droʊn, -z, -ɪŋ, -d
Dronfield
BR 'drɒnfiːld
AM 'drɑnˌfild
drongo
BR 'drɒŋgəʊ, -z
AM 'drɑŋgoʊ, -z
droob
BR druːb, -z
AM drub, -z
drool
BR druːl, -z, -ɪŋ, -d
AM drul, -z, -ɪŋ, -d
droop
BR druːp, -s, -ɪŋ, -t
AM drup, -s, -ɪŋ, -t
droopily
BR 'druːpɨli
AM 'drupəli
droopiness
BR 'druːpɪnɨs
AM 'drupinɨs
droop-snoot
BR 'druːpsnuːt, -s
AM 'drupˌsnut, -s
droopy
BR 'druːp|i, -ɪə(r), -ɪɪst
AM 'drupi, -ər, -ɨst
drop
BR drɒp, -s, -ɪŋ, -t
AM drɑp, -s, -ɪŋ, -t
drophead
BR 'drɒphɛd, -z
AM 'drɑpˌ(h)ɛd, -z
dropkick
BR 'drɒpkɪk, -s, -ɪŋ, -t
AM 'drɑpˌkɪk, -s, -ɪŋ, -t
dropleaf
BR 'drɒpliːf
AM 'drɑpˌlif
droplet
BR 'drɒplɨt, -s
AM 'drɑplət, -s
dropout
BR 'drɒpaʊt, -s
AM 'drɑpˌaʊt, -s
dropper
BR 'drɒpə(r), -z
AM 'drɑpər, -z
dropping
BR 'drɒpɪŋ, -z
AM 'drɑpɪŋ, -z
dropsical
BR 'drɒpsɨkl
AM 'drɑpsəkəl
dropsy
BR 'drɒpsi
AM 'drɑpsi
dropwort
BR 'drɒpwəːt
AM 'drɑpˌwərt, 'drɑpˌwɔ(ə)rt
droshky
BR 'drɒʃk|i, -ɪz
AM 'drɔʃki, 'drɑʃki, -z
RUS 'droʃkʲi
drosophila
BR drə'sɒfɨlə(r), drɒ'sɒfɨlə(r), -z
AM drə'sɑfələ, -z
dross
BR drɒs
AM drɔs, drɑs
drossy
BR 'drɒs|i, -ɪə(r), -ɪɪst
AM 'drɔsi, 'drɑsi, -ər, -ɨst
drought
BR draʊt, -s
AM draʊt, -s
droughty
BR 'draʊti
AM 'draʊdi
drouth
BR draʊθ
AM draʊθ
Drouzhba
BR 'druːʒbə(r)
AM 'druʒbə
drove
BR drəʊv, -z, -ɪŋ
AM droʊv, -z, -ɪŋ
drover
BR 'drəʊvə(r), -z
AM 'droʊvər, -z
drown
BR draʊn, -z, -ɪŋ, -d
AM draʊn, -z, -ɪŋ, -d
drowning
BR 'draʊnɪŋ, -z
AM 'draʊnɪŋ, -z
drowse
BR draʊz, -ɪz, -ɪŋ, -d
AM draʊz, -əz, -ɪŋ, -d
drowsily
BR 'draʊzɨli
AM 'draʊzəli
drowsiness
BR 'draʊzɪnɪs
AM 'draʊzinɨs
drowsy
BR 'draʊz|i, -ɪə(r), -ɪɪst
AM 'draʊzi, -ər, -ɨst
drowze
BR draʊz, -ɪz, -ɪŋ, -d
AM draʊz, -əz, -ɪŋ, -d
Droylsden
BR 'drɔɪlzd(ə)n
AM 'drɔɪlzdən
drub
BR drʌb, -z, -ɪŋ, -d
AM drəb, -z, -ɪŋ, -d
drudge
BR drʌdʒ, -ɪz, -ɪŋ, -d
AM drədʒ, -əz, -ɪŋ, -d
drudgery
BR 'drʌdʒ(ə)ri
AM 'drədʒ(ə)ri
drug
BR drʌg, -z, -ɪŋ, -d
AM drəg, -z, -ɪŋ, -d
drugget
BR 'drʌgɪt, -s
AM 'drəgət, -s
druggist
BR 'drʌgɪst, -s
AM 'drəgəst, -s
druggy
BR 'drʌg|i, -ɪə(r), -ɪɪst
AM 'drəgi, -ər, -ɨst
drugstore
BR 'drʌgstɔː(r), -z
AM 'drəgˌstɔ(ə)r, -z
Druid
BR 'druːɪd, -z
AM 'druəd, -z
Druidess
BR ˌdruːɪ'dɛs, -ɪz
AM 'druədəs, -əz
Druidic
BR druː'ɪdɪk
AM dru'ɪdɪk

Druidical
BR druːˈɪdɨkl
AM druˈɪdɨkəl
Druidism
BR ˈdruːɪdɪz(ə)m
AM ˈdruəd,ɪzəm
drum
BR drʌm, -z, -ɪŋ, -d
AM drəm, -z, -ɪŋ, -d
Drumalbyn
BR drʌmˈalbɪn
AM drəmˈælbən
drumbeat
BR ˈdrʌmbiːt, -s
AM ˈdrəm,bit, -s
drumfire
BR ˈdrʌmfʌɪə(r)
AM ˈdrəm,faɪ(ə)r
drumhead
BR ˈdrʌmhɛd, -z
AM ˈdrəm,(h)ɛd, -z
drumlin
BR ˈdrʌmlɪn, -z
AM ˈdrəmlən, -z
drumlinoid
BR ˈdrʌmlɨnɔɪd
AM ˈdrəmlə,nɔɪd
drummer
BR ˈdrʌmə(r), -z
AM ˈdrəmər, -z
Drummond
BR ˈdrʌm(ə)nd
AM ˈdrəmən(d)
Drumnadrochit
BR ,drʌmnəˈdrɒxɪt, ,drʌmnəˈdrɒkɪt
AM ,drəmnəˈdrɑkət
drumstick
BR ˈdrʌmstɪk, -s
AM ˈdrəm,stɪk, -s
drunk
BR drʌŋk, -s
AM drəŋk, -s
drunkard
BR ˈdrʌŋkəd, -z
AM ˈdrəŋkərd, -z
drunken
BR ˈdrʌŋk(ə)n
AM ˈdrəŋkən
drunkenly
BR ˈdrʌŋk(ə)nli
AM ˈdrəŋkənli
drunkenness
BR ˈdrʌŋk(ə)nnəs
AM ˈdrəŋkə(n)nəs
drupaceous
BR druːˈpeɪʃəs
AM druˈpeɪʃəs
drupe
BR druːp, -s
AM drup, -s
drupel
BR ˈdruːpl, -z
AM ˈdrupəl, -z
drupelet
BR ˈdruːplɨt, -s
AM ˈdruplət, -s
Drury
BR ˈdrʊəri
AM ˈdrʊri
Druse
BR druːz, -ɨz
AM druz, -əz
Drusilla
BR drʊˈsɪlə(r)
AM druˈsɪlə
druthers
BR ˈdrʌðəz
AM ˈdrəðərz
Druzba
BR ˈdruːzbə(r), ˈdruːʒbə(r)
AM ˈdruzbə, ˈdruʒbə
Druze
BR druːz, -ɨz
AM druz, -əz
dry
BR drʌɪ, -z, -ɪŋ, -d, -ə(r), -ɨst
AM draɪ, -z, -ɪŋ, -d, -ər, -ɨst
dryad
BR ˈdrʌɪad, ˈdrʌɪəd, -z
AM ˈdraɪəd, ˈdraɪ,æd, -z
dryas
BR ˈdrʌɪəs
AM ˈdraɪəs
Dryden
BR ˈdrʌɪdn
AM ˈdraɪdən
dryer
BR ˈdrʌɪə(r), -z
AM ˈdraɪər, -z
dryish
BR ˈdrʌɪɪʃ
AM ˈdraɪɪʃ
dryland
BR ˈdrʌɪlənd, -z
AM ˈdraɪlənd, ˈdraɪ,lænd, -z
dryly
BR ˈdrʌɪli
AM ˈdraɪli
dryness
BR ˈdrʌɪnɨs
AM ˈdraɪnɨs
dryopithecine
BR ,drʌɪəʊˈpɪθɨsiːn
AM ,draɪoʊˈpɪθə,sin
Dryopithecus
BR ,drʌɪəʊˈpɪθɨkəs
AM ,draɪoʊˈpɪθəkəs
Drysdale
BR ˈdrʌɪzdeɪl
AM ˈdraɪz,deɪl
drystone
BR ˈdrʌɪstəʊn
AM ˈdraɪ,stoʊn
drysuit
BR ˈdrʌɪs(j)uːt, -s
AM ˈdraɪ,sut, -s
drywall
BR ,drʌɪˈwɔːl
AM ˈdraɪ,wɔl, ˈdraɪ,wɑl
dual
BR djuːəl, dʒuːəl
AM d(j)uəl
dualise
BR ˈdjuːəlʌɪz, ˈdʒuːəlʌɪz, -ɨz, -ɪŋ, -d
AM ˈd(j)uə,laɪz, -ɨz, -ɪŋ, -d
dualism
BR ˈdjuːəlɪz(ə)m, ˈdʒuːəlɪz(ə)m
AM ˈd(j)uə,lɪzəm
dualist
BR ˈdjuːəlɪst, ˈdʒuːəlɪst, -s
AM ˈd(j)uələst, -s
dualistic
BR ,djuːəˈlɪstɪk, ,dʒuːəˈlɪstɪk
AM ,d(j)uəˈlɪstɪk
dualistically
BR ,djuːəˈlɪstɨkli, ,dʒuːəˈlɪstɨkli
AM ,d(j)uəˈlɪstɨk(ə)li
duality
BR djuːˈalɨt|i, dʒuːˈalɨt|i, -ɪz
AM d(j)uˈælədi, -z
dualize
BR ˈdjuːəlʌɪz, ˈdʒuːəlʌɪz, -ɨz, -ɪŋ, -d
AM ˈd(j)uə,laɪz, -ɨz, -ɪŋ, -d
dually
BR ˈdjuːəl(l)i, ˈdʒuːəl(l)i
AM ˈd(j)uəli
Duane
BR dweɪn, duːˈeɪn
AM dweɪn
dub
BR dʌb, -z, -ɪŋ, -d
AM dəb, -z, -ɪŋ, -d
Dubai
BR ,duːˈbʌɪ, dʊˈbʌɪ
AM duˈbaɪ
dubbin
BR ˈdʌb|ɪn, -ɪnz, -ɨnɪŋ, -ɪnd
AM ˈdəbən, -z, -ɪŋ, -d
Dubček
BR ˈdʊbtʃɛk
AM ˈdub,tʃɛk
dubiety
BR djuːˈbʌɪɨti, dʒuːˈbʌɪɨti
AM d(j)uˈbaɪɨdi
dubious
BR ˈdjuːbɪəs, ˈdʒuːbɪəs
AM ˈd(j)ubiəs
dubiously
BR ˈdjuːbɪəsli, ˈdʒuːbɪəsli
AM ˈd(j)ubiəsli
dubiousness
BR ˈdjuːbɪəsnəs, ˈdʒuːbɪəsnəs
AM ˈd(j)ubiəsnəs
dubitation
BR ,djuːbɨˈteɪʃn, ,dʒuːbɨˈteɪʃn
AM ,d(j)ubəˈteɪʃən
dubitative
BR ˈdjuːbɨtətɪv, ˈdʒuːbɨtətɪv
AM ˈd(j)ubə,teɪdɪv
dubitatively
BR ˈdjuːbɨtətɨvli, ˈdʒuːbɨtətɨvli
AM ˈd(j)ubə,teɪdɨvli
Dublin
BR ˈdʌblɪn
AM ˈdəblən
Dubliner
BR ˈdʌblɨnə(r), -z
AM ˈdəblənər, -z
Du Bois
BR dʊ ˈbwɑː(r)
AM du ˈbwɑ
Dubonnet®
BR d(j)ʊˈbɒneɪ
AM ,dubəˈneɪ
Dubrovnik
BR dʊˈbrɒvnɪk
AM duˈbrɔvnɪk, duˈbrɑvnɪk
Dubuque
BR dəˈbjuːk
AM dəˈbjuk
ducal
BR ˈdjuːkl, ˈdʒuːkl
AM ˈd(j)ukəl
ducat
BR ˈdʌkət, -s
AM ˈdəkət, -s
Duce
BR ˈduːtʃeɪ
AM ˈdutʃeɪ
Duchamp
BR dʊˈʃɒ̃
AM duˈʃɑm(p)
Duchenne
BR d(j)ʊˈʃɛn
AM d(j)uˈʃɛn
Duchesne
BR d(j)ʊˈʃeɪn
AM duˈʃeɪn, duˈkeɪn
duchess
BR ˈdʌtʃɪs, -ɪz
AM ˈdətʃəs, -əz
duchesse
BR d(j)ʊˈʃɛs, -ɨz
AM d(j)uˈʃɛs, -əz
duchy
BR ˈdʌtʃ|i, -ɪz
AM ˈdətʃi, -z
duck
BR dʌk, -s, -ɪŋ, -t
AM dək, -s, -ɪŋ, -t
duckbill
BR ˈdʌkbɪl, -z
AM ˈdək,bɪl, -z
duckboard
BR ˈdʌkbɔːd, -z
AM ˈdək,bɔ(ə)rd, -z

duckegg
BR 'dʌkɛg, -z
AM 'dək,ɛg, -z

ducker
BR 'dʌkə(r), -z
AM 'dəkər, -z

Duckett
BR 'dʌkɪt
AM 'dəkət

Duckham
BR 'dʌkəm
AM 'dəkəm

duckie
BR 'dʌk|i, -ɪz
AM 'dəki, -z

duckily
BR 'dʌkɨli
AM 'dəkəli

duckiness
BR 'dʌkɪnɨs
AM 'dəkinɨs

duckling
BR 'dʌklɪŋ, -z
AM 'dəklɪŋ, -z

ducktail
BR 'dʌkteɪl, -z
AM 'dək,teɪl, -z

duckweed
BR 'dʌkwiːd
AM 'dək,wid

Duckworth
BR 'dʌkwəθ, 'dʌkwəːθ
AM 'dək,wərθ

ducky
BR 'dʌk|i, -ɪz, -ɪə(r), -ɪɪst
AM 'dəki, -z, -ər, -ɨst

duct
BR dʌkt, -s, -ɪŋ, -ɨd
AM dək|(t), -(t)s, -tɪŋ, -təd

ductile
BR 'dʌktʌɪl
AM 'dəktl, 'dək,taɪl

ductility
BR dʌk'tɪlɨti
AM dək'tɪlɨdi

ductless
BR 'dʌktləs
AM 'dək(t)ləs

dud
BR dʌd, -z
AM dəd, -z

dude
BR djuːd, -z
AM dud, -z

dudgeon
BR 'dʌdʒ(ə)n
AM 'dədʒən

dudish
BR 'djuːdɪʃ
AM 'dudɪʃ

Dudley
BR 'dʌdli
AM 'dədli

due
BR djuː, dʒuː, -z
AM d(j)u, -z

duel
BR 'djuːəl, 'dʒuːəl, -z, -ɪŋ, -d
AM 'd(j)uəl, -z, -ɪŋ, -d

duelist
BR 'djuːəlɪst, 'dʒuːəlɪst, -s
AM 'd(j)uələst, -s

dueller
BR 'djuːələ(r), 'dʒuːələ(r), -z
AM 'd(j)uələr, -z

duellist
BR 'djuːəlɪst, 'dʒuːəlɪst, -s
AM 'd(j)uələst, -s

duende
BR dʊ'ɛndeɪ, -z
AM du'ɛn,deɪ, 'dwɛndeɪ, -z

duenna
BR d(j)ʊ'ɛnə(r), dʒʊ'ɛnə(r), -z
AM d(j)u'ɛnə, -z

duet
BR djʊ'ɛt, dʒʊ'ɛt, -s
AM d(j)u'ɛt, -s

duettist
BR djʊ'ɛtɪst, dʒʊ'ɛtɪst, -s
AM d(j)u'ɛdəst, -s

Dufay
BR dʊ'feɪ
AM du'feɪ

duff
BR dʌf, -s, -ɪŋ, -t
AM dəf, -s, -ɪŋ, -t

duffel
BR 'dʌfl
AM 'dəfəl

duffer
BR 'dʌfə(r), -z
AM 'dəfər, -z

Duffield
BR 'dʌfiːld
AM 'dəfild

duffle
BR 'dʌfl
AM 'dəfəl

Duffy
BR 'dʌfi
AM 'dəfi

Dufy
BR 'duːfi
AM du'fi

dug
BR dʌg
AM dəg

Duggan
BR 'dʌg(ə)n
AM 'dəgən

Duggleby
BR 'dʌglbi
AM 'dəgəlbi

dugite
BR 'djuːgʌɪt, -s
AM 'd(j)u,gaɪt, -s

dugong
BR 'd(j)uːgɒŋ, -z
AM 'du,gaŋ, 'du,gɔŋ, -z

dugout
BR 'dʌgaʊt, -s
AM 'dəg,aʊt, -s

duiker
BR 'dʌɪkə(r), -z
AM 'daɪkər, -z
AFK 'dœɪkər

Duisburg
BR 'djuːzbəːg, 'djuːsbəːg
AM 'duz,bərg
GER 'dʏɪsbʊrk

Dukakis
BR d(j)ʊ'kɑːkɪs
AM də'kɑkəs, d(j)ʊ'kɑkəs

duke
BR djuːk, dʒuːk, -s
AM d(j)uk, dʒuk, -s

dukedom
BR 'djuːkdəm, 'dʒuːkdəm, -z
AM 'd(j)ukdəm, -z

Dukhobor
BR 'duːkə(ʊ)bɔː(r), -z
AM 'dukə,bɔ(ə)r, -z

DUKW
BR dʌk, -s
AM dək, -s

Dulais
BR 'dɪlʌɪs, 'dɪləs
AM 'dɪləs

dulcet
BR 'dʌlsɪt
AM 'dəlsət

Dulcie
BR 'dʌlsi
AM 'dəlsi

dulcification
BR ˌdʌlsɪfɪ'keɪʃn
AM ˌdəlʃəfə'keɪʃən

dulcify
BR 'dʌlsɪfʌɪ, -z, -ɪŋ, -d
AM 'dəlsə,faɪ, -z, -ɪŋ, -d

dulcimer
BR 'dʌlsɪmə(r), -z
AM 'dəlsəmər, -z

dulcitone
BR 'dʌlsɪtəʊn
AM 'dəlsə,toʊn

dulia
BR 'djuːlɪə(r), 'dʒuːlɪə(r), d(j)ʊ'lʌɪə(r), dʒʊ'lʌɪə(r)
AM d(j)u'laɪə

dull
BR dʌl, -z, -ɪŋ, -d, -ə(r), -ɨst
AM dəl, -z, -ɪŋ, -d, -ər, -əst

dullard
BR 'dʌləd, -z
AM 'dələrd, -z

Dulles
BR 'dʌlɪs
AM 'dələs

dullish
BR 'dʌlɪʃ
AM 'dəlɪʃ

dullness
BR 'dʌlnəs
AM 'dəlnəs

dully
BR 'dʌl(l)i
AM 'dəli

dulse
BR dʌls
AM dəls

Duluth
BR dʉ'luːθ
AM də'luθ

Dulux®
BR 'djuːlʌks, 'dʒuːlʌks
AM 'd(j)uləks

Dulverton
BR 'dʌlvət(ə)n
AM 'dəlvərtən

Dulwich
BR 'dʌlɪtʃ, 'dʌlɪdʒ
AM 'dəl(w)ɪtʃ

duly
BR 'djuːli, 'dʒuːli
AM 'd(j)uli

Duma
BR 'd(j)uːmə(r), -z
AM 'dumə, -z

Dumas
BR dʊ'mɑː(r), 'd(j)uːmɑː(r)
AM du'mɑ(s)

Du Maurier
BR d(j)ʊ 'mɒrɪeɪ
AM du 'mɔri,eɪ

dumb
BR dʌm, -ə(r), -ɨst
AM dəm, -ər, -əst

Dumbarton
BR dʌm'bɑːtn
AM 'dəm,bɑrtən

dumbfound
BR (ˌ)dʌm'faʊnd, -z, -ɪŋ, -ɨd
AM ˌdəm'faʊnd, -z, -ɪŋ, -əd

dumbhead
BR 'dʌmhɛd, -z
AM 'dəm,(h)ɛd, -z

dumbly
BR 'dʌmli
AM 'dəmli

dumbness
BR 'dʌmnəs
AM 'dəmnəs

dumbo
BR 'dʌmbəʊ, -z
AM 'dəmboʊ, -z

dumbshow
BR 'dʌmʃəʊ, -z
AM 'dəm,ʃoʊ, -z

dumbstricken
BR ˈdʌmˌstrɪk(ə)n
AM ˈdəmˌstrɪkən
dumbstruck
BR ˈdʌmstrʌk
AM ˈdəmˈstrək
dumbwaiter
BR ˌdʌmˈweɪtə(r), -z
AM ˈdəmˌweɪdər, -z
dumdum
BR ˈdʌmdʌm, -z
AM ˈdəmˌdəm, -z
dumfound
BR (ˌ)dʌmˈfaʊnd, -z, -ɪŋ, -ɨd
AM ˌdəmˈfaʊnd, -z, -ɪŋ, -əd
Dumfries
BR dʌmˈfriːs
AM ˈdəmfriz
Dummkopf
BR ˈdʌmkɒpf, ˈdʊmkɒpf, -s
AM ˈdəmˌkɔ(p)f, -s
dummy
BR ˈdʌm|i, -ɪz
AM ˈdəmi, -z
dummy run
BR ˌdʌmɪ ˈrʌn, -z
AM ˌdəmi ˈrən, -z
dump
BR dʌm|p, -ps, -pɪŋ, -(p)t
AM dəmp, -s, -ɪŋ, -t
dumper
BR ˈdʌmpə(r), -z
AM ˈdəmpər, -z
dumpily
BR ˈdʌmpɨli
AM ˈdəmpəli
dumpiness
BR ˈdʌmpɪnɨs
AM ˈdəmpinɨs
dumpling
BR ˈdʌmplɪŋ, -z
AM ˈdəmplɪŋ, -z
dumpster
BR ˈdʌm(p)stə(r), -z
AM ˈdəm(p)stər, -z
dumpy
BR ˈdʌmp|i, -ɪə(r), -ɪɨst
AM ˈdəmpi, -ər, -ɨst
dun
BR dʌn
AM dən
Dunaj
BR ˈduːnʌɪ
AM ˈduˌnaɪ
Dunbar
BR dʌnˈbɑː(r)
AM ˈdənˌbɑr
Dunblane
BR dʌnˈbleɪn
AM dənˈbleɪn
Duncan
BR ˈdʌŋk(ə)n
AM ˈdəŋkən
dunce
BR dʌns, -ɪz
AM dəns, -əz
duncecap
BR ˈdʌnskap, -s
AM ˈdənsˌkæp, -s
Dunciad
BR ˈdʌnsɪad
AM ˈdənsiˌæd
Dundalk[1]
place in Ireland
BR dʌnˈdɔːk
AM dənˈdɔ(l)k
Dundalk[2]
place in US
BR ˈdʌndɔːk
AM dənˈdɔk, dənˈdɑk
Dundas
BR ˈdʌndəs
AM ˈdəndəs
Dundee
BR dʌnˈdiː
AM dənˈdi
dunderhead
BR ˈdʌndəhɛd, -z
AM ˈdəndərˌ(h)ɛd, -z
dunderheaded
BR ˌdʌndəˈhɛdɪd
AM ˈdəndərˌ(h)ɛdəd
Dundonald
BR dʌnˈdɒnld
AM dənˈdɑnəl(d)
dune
BR djuːn, dʒuːn, -z
AM d(j)un, -z
Dunedin
BR dʌnˈiːd(ɪ)n
AM dənˈidən
Dunfermline
BR dʌnˈfəːmlɪn
AM dənˈfərmlən
dung
BR dʌŋ
AM dəŋ
Dungannon
BR dʌnˈganən
AM dənˈgænən
dungaree
BR ˌdʌŋgəˈriː, -z
AM ˌdəŋgəˈri, -z
Dungarvan
BR dʌnˈgɑːv(ə)n
AM dənˈgɑrvən
Dungeness
BR ˌdʌn(d)ʒ(ə)ˈnɛs
AM ˈdəndʒənəs
dungeon
BR ˈdʌn(d)ʒ(ə)n, -z
AM ˈdəndʒən, -z
dunghill
BR ˈdʌŋhɪl, -z
AM ˈdəŋˌ(h)ɪl, -z
Dunhill
BR ˈdʌnhɪl
AM ˈdənˌ(h)ɪl
dunk
BR dʌŋ|k, -ks, -kɪŋ, -(k)t
AM dəŋ|k, -ks, -kɪŋ, -(k)t
Dunkeld
BR dʌnˈkɛld
AM dənˈkɛld
Dunkirk
BR dʌnˈkəːk, dʌŋˈkəːk
AM ˈdənˌkərk, dənˈkərk
Dunkley
BR ˈdʌŋkli
AM ˈdəŋkli
Dun Laoghaire
BR dʌn ˈlɪəri, duːn +, + ˈlɛːrə(r)
AM ˌdən ˈlɪri, + ˈlɛrə
IR duːn ˈliːrʲə
Dunlap
BR ˈdʌnlap
AM ˈdənləp, ˈdənlæp, ˈdənlɑp
dunlin
BR ˈdʌnlɪn, -z
AM ˈdənlən, -z
Dunlop[1]
traditional
BR dənˈlɒp
AM ˈdənlɑp
Dunlop[2]
BR ˈdʌnlɒp
AM ˈdənlɑp
Dunmow
BR ˈdʌnməʊ
AM ˈdənˌmoʊ
Dunn
BR dʌn
AM dən
dunnage
BR ˈdʌnɪdʒ
AM ˈdənɪdʒ
Dunne
BR dʌn
AM dən
Dunnet Head
BR ˌdʌnɪt ˈhɛd
AM ˌdənət ˈhɛd
dunno
BR dəˈnəʊ, dʌˈnəʊ, -z
AM dəˈnoʊ, -z
dunnock
BR ˈdʌnək, -s
AM ˈdənək, -s
dunny
BR ˈdʌn|i, -ɪz
AM ˈdəni, -z
Dunoon
BR dəˈnuːn, dʌnˈuːn
AM dəˈnun
Dunsinane[1]
in Scotland
BR dʌnˈsɪnən
AM ˈdənsənən
Dunsinane[2]
in Shakespeare's 'Macbeth'
BR ˈdʌnsɪneɪn, ˌdʌnsɪˈneɪn
AM ˌdənsəˈneɪn
Duns Scotus
BR ˌdʌnz ˈskəʊtəs, + ˈskɒtəs
AM ˈdənz ˈskoʊdəs
Dunstable
BR ˈdʌnstəbl
AM ˈdənstəbəl
Dunstan
BR ˈdʌnst(ə)n
AM ˈdənstən
Dunwoody
BR dʌnˈwʊdi
AM ˈdənˌwʊdi
duo
BR ˈdjuːəʊ, ˈdʒuːəʊ, -z
AM ˈd(j)uoʊ, -z
duodecimal
BR ˌdjuːə(ʊ)ˈdɛsɪml, ˌdʒuːə(ʊ)ˈdɛsɪml
AM ˌd(j)uəˈdɛsəməl, ˌd(j)uoʊˈdɛsəməl
duodecimally
BR ˌdjuːə(ʊ)ˈdɛsɪmļi, ˌdjuː(ʊ)ˈdɛsɪməli, ˌdʒuːə(ʊ)ˈdɛsɪmļi, ˌdʒuːə(ʊ)ˈdɛsɪməli
AM ˌd(j)uəˈdɛsəməli, ˌd(j)uoʊˈdɛsəməli
duodecimo
BR ˌdjuːə(ʊ)ˈdɛsɪməʊ, ˌdʒuːə(ʊ)ˈdɛsɪməʊ
AM ˌd(j)uəˈdɛsəmoʊ, ˌd(j)uoʊˈdɛsəmoʊ
duodena
BR ˌdjuːəˈdiːnə(r), ˌdʒuːəˈdiːnə(r)
AM ˌd(j)uəˈdinə, d(j)uˈɑdņə
duodenal
BR ˌdjuːəˈdiːnl, ˌdʒuːəˈdiːnl
AM ˌd(j)uəˈdinəl, d(j)uˈɑdņl
duodenary
BR ˌdjuːəˈdiːn(ə)ri, ˌdʒuːəˈdiːn(ə)ri
AM ˌd(j)uˈɑdəˌnɛri, ˌd(j)uəˈdɛnɛri
duodenitis
BR ˌdjuːəd(ɪ)nˈʌɪtɪs, ˌdʒuːəd(ɪ)nˈʌɪtɪs
AM ˌd(j)uədņˈaɪdɪs
duodenum
BR ˌdjuːəˈdiːnəm, ˌdʒuːəˈdiːnəm, -z
AM ˌd(j)uəˈdinəm, d(j)uˈɑdņm, -z
duolog
BR ˈdjuːəlɒg, ˈdʒuːəlɒg, -z
AM ˈd(j)uəˌlɔg, ˈd(j)uəˌlɑg, -z

duologue
BR 'dju:əlɒg, 'dʒu:əlɒg, -z
AM 'd(j)uə,lɔg, 'd(j)uə,lɑg, -z

duomo
BR 'dwəʊməʊ, -z
AM 'dwoʊmoʊ, -z

duopoly
BR djʊ'ɒpəl|i, djʊ'ɒpl̩|i, dʒʊ'ɒpəl|i, dʒʊ'ɒpl̩|i, -ɪz
AM d(j)u'ɑpəli, -z

duotone
BR 'dju:ə(ʊ)təʊn, 'dʒu:ə(ʊ)təʊn
AM 'd(j)uə,toʊn

dupable
BR 'dju:pəbl, 'dʒu:pəbl
AM 'd(j)upəbəl

dupe
BR dju:p, dʒu:p, -s, -ɪŋ, -t
AM d(j)up, -s, -ɪŋ, -t

duper
BR 'dju:pə(r), 'dʒu:pə(r), -z
AM 'd(j)upər, -z

dupery
BR 'dju:p(ə)r|i, 'dʒu:p(ə)r|i, -ɪz
AM 'd(j)upəri, -z

dupion
BR 'dju:pɪɒn, 'dʒu:pɪɒn, -z
AM 'dupi,ɑn, -z

duple
BR 'dju:pl, 'dʒu:pl
AM 'd(j)upəl

duplex
BR 'dju:plɛks, 'dʒu:plɛks, -ɪz
AM 'd(j)u,plɛks, -əz

duplicable
BR 'dju:plɨkəbl, 'dʒu:plɨkəbl
AM 'd(j)upləkəbəl

duplicate[1]
noun, adjective
BR 'dju:plɨkət, 'dʒu:plɨkət, -s
AM 'd(j)upləkət, -s

duplicate[2]
verb
BR 'dju:plɨkeɪt, 'dʒu:plɨkeɪt, -s, -ɪŋ, -ɨd
AM 'd(j)uplə,keɪ|t, -ts, -dɪŋ, -dɨd

duplication
BR ,dju:plɨ'keɪʃn, ,dʒu:plɨ'keɪʃn, -z
AM ,d(j)uplə'keɪʃən, -z

duplicator
BR 'dju:plɨkeɪtə(r), 'dʒu:plɨkeɪtə(r), -z
AM 'd(j)uplə,keɪdər, -z

duplicitous
BR djʊ'plɪsɨtəs, dʒʊ'plɪsɨtəs
AM d(j)u'plɪsədəs

duplicity
BR djʊ'plɪsɨti, dʒʊ'plɪsɨti
AM d(j)u'plɪsɨdi

Du Pont
BR d(j)ʊ 'pɒnt
AM d(j)u'pɑnt

duppy
BR 'dʌp|i, -ɪz
AM 'dəpi, -z

du Pré
BR d(j)ʊ 'preɪ, + 'pri:
AM du 'preɪ

Duquesne
BR d(j)ʊ'keɪn
AM du'keɪn

dura
BR 'djʊərə(*r*), 'dʒʊərə(*r*), -z
AM 'd(j)ʊrə, -z

durability
BR ,djʊərə'bɪlɨti, ,dʒʊərə'bɪlɨti, ,djɔ:rə'bɪlɨti, ,dʒɔ:rə'bɪlɨti
AM ,d(j)ʊrə'bɪlɨdi

durable
BR 'djʊərəbl, 'dʒʊərəbl, 'djɔ:rəbl, 'dʒɔ:rəbl, -z
AM 'd(j)ʊrəbəl, -z

durableness
BR 'djʊərəblnəs, 'dʒʊərəblnəs, 'djɔ:rəblnəs, 'dʒɔ:rəblnəs
AM 'd(j)ʊrəbəlnəs

durably
BR 'djʊərəbli, 'dʒʊərəbli, 'djɔ:rəbli, 'dʒɔ:rəbli
AM 'd(j)ʊrəbli

Duracell®
BR 'djʊərəsɛl, 'dʒʊərəsɛl, 'djɔ:rəsɛl, 'dʒɔ:rəsɛl
AM 'dərə,sɛl

Duraglit®
BR 'djʊərəglɪt, 'dʒʊərəglɪt, 'djɔ:rəglɪt, 'dʒɔ:rəglɪt
AM 'dərə,glɪt

Duralumin®
BR djʊ'raljʉmɪn, dʒʊ'raljʉmɪn
AM d(j)ə'ræljəmən, d(j)ʊ'ræljəmən, ,d(j)ʊrə'lumən

dura mater
BR ,djʊərə 'meɪtə(r), ,dʒʊərə +, + 'mɑ:tə(r), -z
AM 'd(j)ʊrə ,mɑdər, + ,meɪdər, -z

duramen
BR djʊ'reɪmən, dʒʊ'reɪmən
AM d(j)ʊ'reɪmən

durance
BR 'djʊərəns, 'djʊərn̩s, 'djɔ:rəns, 'djɔ:rn̩s, 'dʒʊərəns, 'dʒʊərn̩s, 'dʒɔ:rəns, 'dʒɔ:rn̩s
AM 'd(j)ʊrəns

Durango
BR d(j)ʊ'raŋgəʊ, dʒʊ'raŋgəʊ
AM də'ræŋgoʊ

Durante
BR də'ran(t)i
AM də'ræn(t)i

duration
BR djʊ'reɪʃn, dʒʊ'reɪʃn
AM də'reɪʃən

durational
BR djʊ'reɪʃn̩(ə)l, djʊ'reɪʃən(ə)l, dʒʊ'reɪʃn̩(ə)l, dʒʊ'reɪʃən(ə)l
AM də'reɪʃ(ə)nəl

durative
BR 'djʊərətɪv, 'dʒʊərətɪv, 'djɔ:rətɪv, 'dʒɔ:rətɪv
AM 'd(j)ʊrədɪv

Durban
BR 'də:b(ə)n
AM 'dərbən

durbar
BR də:bɑ:(r), -z
AM 'dər,bɑr, -z

Dürer
BR 'd(j)ʊərə(r)
AM 'dʊrər

duress
BR djʊ'rɛs, dʒʊ'rɛs
AM də'rɛs

Durex®
BR 'djʊərɛks, 'dʒʊərɛks, 'djɔ:rɛks, 'dʒɔ:rɛks, -ɨz
AM 'd(j)ʊ,rɛks, -əz

Durham
BR 'dʌrəm
AM 'dərəm

durian
BR 'd(j)ʊərɪən, 'dʒʊərɪən, -z
AM 'dʊriən, -z

during
BR 'djʊərɪŋ, 'dʒʊərɪŋ
AM 'd(j)ʊrɪŋ

Durkheim
BR 'də:khʌɪm
AM 'dərk,(h)aɪm

Durkheimian
BR ,də:k'hʌɪmɪən
AM ¦dərk¦(h)aɪmiən

durmast
BR 'də:mɑ:st, 'də:mast, -s
AM 'dər,mæst, -s

durn
BR də:n, -d
AM dərn, -d

Durocher
BR də'rəʊʃə(r)
AM də'roʊʃər

durra
BR 'dʊ(ə)rə(*r*), -z
AM 'dʊrə, -z

Durrant
BR 'dʌrənt, 'dʌrn̩t, də'rant
AM dʊ'rænt

Durrell
BR 'dʌrəl, 'dʌrl̩
AM dʊ'rɛl

Dürrenmatt
BR 'd(j)ʊərənmat, 'd(j)ʊərn̩mat
AM 'd(j)ʊrən,mæt

durrie
BR 'dʌr|i, -ɪz
AM 'dəri, -z

durry
BR 'dʌr|i, -ɪz
AM 'dəri, -z

durst
BR də:st
AM dərst

durum
BR 'dʌrəm
AM 'dərəm

durzi
BR 'də:z|i, -ɪz
AM 'dərzi, dər'zi, -z

Dushanbe
BR ,du:ʃan'beɪ
AM ,d(j)uʃɑm'beɪ

dusk
BR dʌsk, -s
AM dəsk, -s

duskily
BR 'dʌskɨli
AM 'dəskəli

duskiness
BR 'dʌskɪnɨs
AM 'dəskinɨs

dusky
BR 'dʌsk|i, -ɪə(r), -ɪɨst
AM 'dəski, -ər, -ɨst

Düsseldorf
BR 'dʊsldɔ:f
AM 'dʊsəl,dɔ(ə)rf

dust
BR dʌst, -s, -ɪŋ, -ɨd
AM dəst, -s, -ɪŋ, -əd

dustbin
BR 'dʌs(t)bɪn, -z
AM 'dəs(t),bɪn, -z

dustbowl
BR 'dʌs(t)bəʊl, -z
AM 'dəs(t),boʊl, -z

dustcart
BR 'dʌs(t)kɑ:t, -s
AM 'dəs(t),kɑrt, -s

duster
BR 'dʌstə(r), -z
AM 'dəstər, -z
dustily
BR 'dʌstɨli
AM 'dəstəli
Dustin
BR 'dʌstɪn
AM 'dəstən
dustiness
BR 'dʌstɪnɨs
AM 'dəstinɨs
dustless
BR 'dʌstləs
AM 'dəs(t)ləs
dustman
BR 'dʌs(t)mən
AM 'dəs(t)mən
dustmen
BR 'dʌs(t)mən
AM 'dəs(t)mən
dustpan
BR 'dʌs(t)pan, -z
AM 'dəs(t),pæn, -z
dustsheet
BR 'dʌs(t)ʃi:t, -s
AM 'dəs(t),ʃit, -s
dusty
BR 'dʌst|i, -ɪə(r), -ɪɨst
AM 'dəsti, -ər, -ɪst
Dutch
BR dʌtʃ
AM dətʃ
Dutchman
BR 'dʌtʃmən
AM 'dətʃmən
Dutchmen
BR 'dʌtʃmən
AM 'dətʃmən
Dutchwoman
BR 'dʌtʃ,wʊmən
AM 'dətʃ,wʊmən
Dutchwomen
BR 'dʌtʃ,wɪmɪn
AM 'dətʃ,wɪmɨn
duteous
BR 'dju:tɪəs, 'dʒu:tɪəs
AM 'd(j)udiəs
duteously
BR 'dju:tɪəsli, 'dʒu:tɪəsli
AM 'd(j)udiəsli
duteousness
BR 'dju:tɪəsnəs, 'dʒu:tɪəsnəs
AM 'd(j)udiəsnəs
dutiable
BR 'dju:tɪəbl, 'dʒu:tɪəbl
AM 'd(j)udiəbəl
dutiful
BR 'dju:tɪf(ʊ)l, 'dʒu:tɪf(ʊ)l
AM 'd(j)udəfəl, 'd(j)udifəl
dutifully
BR 'dju:tɪfʊli, 'dju:tɪfl̩i, 'dʒu:tɪfʊli, 'dʒu:tɪfl̩i
AM 'd(j)udəfəli, 'd(j)udifəli
dutifulness
BR 'dju:tɪf(ʊ)lnəs, 'dʒu:tɪf(ʊ)lnəs
AM 'd(j)udəfəlnəs, 'd(j)udifəlnəs
Du Toit
BR d(j)ʊ 'twɑ:(*r*)
AM du 'twɑ
Dutton
BR 'dʌtn
AM 'dətn
duty
BR 'dju:t|i, 'dʒu:t|i, -ɪz
AM 'd(j)udi, -z
duumvir
BR djʊ'ʌmvə(r), dʒʊ'ʌmvə(r), -z
AM d(j)u'əmvər, d(j)u'əm,vɪ(ə)r, -z
duumvirate
BR djʊ'ʌmv(ɪ)rət, dʒʊ'ʌmv(ɪ)rət
AM d(j)u'əmvərət
Duvalier
BR d(j)ʊ'valɪeɪ
AM du,vɑl'jeɪ
duvet
BR 'du:veɪ, -z
AM 'd(j)u,veɪ, -z
dux
BR dʌks
AM dəks
duyker
BR 'dʌɪkə(r), -z
AM 'daɪkər, -z
Dvořák
BR '(d)vɔ:ʒak
AM 'dvɔr,(ʒ)ɑk
dwale
BR dweɪl
AM dweɪl
Dwane
BR dweɪn
AM dweɪn
dwarf
BR dwɔ:f, -s, -ɪŋ, -t
AM d(w)ɔ(ə)rf, -s, -ɪŋ, -t
dwarfish
BR 'dwɔ:fɪʃ
AM 'd(w)ɔrfɪʃ
dwarfism
BR 'dwɔ:fɪz(ə)m
AM 'd(w)ɔr,fɪzəm
dwarves
BR dwɔ:vz
AM d(w)ɔ(ə)rvz
dweeb
BR dwi:b, -z
AM dwib, -z
dwell
BR dwɛl, -z, -ɪŋ, -d
AM dwɛl, -z, -ɪŋ, -d
dweller
BR 'dwɛlə(r), -z
AM 'dwɛlər, -z
dwelling
BR 'dwɛlɪŋ, -z
AM 'dwɛlɪŋ, -z
dwelt
BR dwɛlt
AM dwɛlt
Dwight
BR dwʌɪt
AM dwaɪt
dwindle
BR 'dwɪnd|l, -lz, -l̩ɪŋ\-lɪŋ, -ld
AM 'dwɪn|dəl, -dəlz, -(d)(ə)lɪŋ, -dəld
Dworkin
BR 'dwɔ:kɪn
AM 'dwɔrkən
Dwyer
BR 'dwʌɪə(r)
AM 'dwaɪər
dyad
BR 'dʌɪad, -z
AM 'daɪ,æd, -z
dyadic
BR dʌɪ'adɪk
AM daɪ'ædɪk
Dyak
BR 'dʌɪak, -s
AM 'daɪ,æk, -s
dyarchy
BR 'dʌɪɑ:k|i, -ɪz
AM 'daɪ,ɑrki, -z
dybbuk
BR 'dɪbʊk, di:'bu:k, -s
AM 'dɪbək, -s
dye
BR dʌɪ, -z, -ɪŋ, -d
AM daɪ, -z, -ɪŋ, -d
dyeable
BR 'dʌɪəbl
AM 'daɪəbəl
dyer
BR 'dʌɪə(r), -z
AM 'daɪər, -z
dyestuff
BR 'dʌɪstʌf, -s
AM 'daɪ,stəf, -s
dyeworks
BR 'dʌɪwə:ks
AM 'daɪ,wərks
Dyfed
BR 'dʌvɪd
AM 'dəvəd
WE 'dʌved
Dyffryn
BR 'dʌfr(ɪ)n
AM 'daɪfrɪn
dying
BR 'dʌɪɪŋ
AM 'daɪɪŋ
dyke
BR dʌɪk, -s, -ɪŋ, -t
AM daɪk, -s, -ɪŋ, -t
Dylan[1]
surname, as in Bob Dylan
BR 'dɪlən
AM 'dɪlən
Dylan[2]
Welsh forename
BR 'dɪlən, 'dʌlən
AM 'dɪlən
WE 'dʌlan
Dymchurch
BR 'dɪmtʃə:tʃ
AM 'dɪm,tʃərtʃ
Dymo
BR 'dʌɪməʊ
AM 'daɪmoʊ
Dymock
BR 'dɪmək
AM 'dɪmək
Dymond
BR 'dʌɪm(ə)nd
AM 'dɪmənd
Dymont
BR 'dʌɪm(ə)nt
AM 'daɪmənt
Dympna
BR 'dɪmpnə(*r*)
AM 'dɪm(p)nə
dynamic
BR dʌɪ'namɪk, -s
AM daɪ'næmɪk, -s
dynamical
BR dʌɪ'namɪkl
AM daɪ'næməkəl
dynamically
BR dʌɪ'namɪkli
AM daɪ'næmək(ə)li
dynamicist
BR dʌɪ'namɪsɪst, -s
AM daɪ'næməsəst, -s
dynamisation
BR ,dʌɪnəmʌɪ'zeɪʃn
AM daɪ,næmə'zeɪʃən, daɪnə,maɪ'zeɪʃən
dynamise
BR 'dʌɪnəmʌɪz, -ɪz, -ɪŋ, -d
AM 'daɪnə,maɪz, -ɪz, -ɪŋ, -d
dynamism
BR 'dʌɪnəmɪz(ə)m
AM 'daɪnə,mɪzəm
dynamist
BR 'dʌɪnəmɪst, -s
AM 'daɪnəməst, -s
dynamite
BR 'dʌɪnəmʌɪt
AM 'daɪnə,maɪt
dynamiter
BR 'dʌɪnəmʌɪtə(r), -z
AM 'daɪnə,maɪdər, -z
dynamization
BR ,dʌɪnəmʌɪ'zeɪʃn
AM daɪ,næmə'zeɪʃən, daɪnə,maɪ'zeɪʃən
dynamize
BR 'dʌɪnəmʌɪz, -ɪz, -ɪŋ, -d

AM 'daɪnə,maɪz, -ɨz, -ɪŋ, -d

dynamo
BR 'dʌɪnəməʊ, -z
AM 'daɪnə,moʊ, -z

dynamometer
BR ,dʌɪnə'mɒmɨtə(r), -z
AM ,daɪnə'mɑmədər, -z

dynast
BR 'dɪnəst, 'dʌɪnəst, 'dɪnast, 'dʌɪnast, -s
AM 'daɪ,næst, 'daɪnəst, -s

dynastic
BR dɪ'nastɪk, dʌɪ'nastɪk
AM daɪ'næstɪk, də'næstɪk

dynastically
BR dɪ'nastɨkli, dʌɪ'nastɨkli
AM daɪ'næstək(ə)li, də'næstək(ə)li

dynasty
BR 'dɪnəst|i, -ɪz
AM 'daɪnəsti, -z

dynatron
BR 'dʌɪnətrɒn, -z
AM 'daɪnə,trɑn, -z

dyne
BR dʌɪn, -z
AM daɪn, -z

Dynefor
BR dɪ'nɛvə(r), 'dɪnɨvə(r)
AM 'dɪnɨvər

Dysart
BR 'dʌɪsət, 'dʌɪsɑːt, 'dʌɪzɑːt
AM 'daɪ,sɑrt

dyscalculia
BR ,dɪskal'kjuːlɪə(r)
AM ,dɪskæl'kjuliə

dyscrasia
BR dɪs'kreɪzɪə(r)
AM dɪs'kreɪziə

dyscrasic
BR dɪs'kreɪzɪk
AM dɪs'kreɪzɪk

dysenteric
BR ,dɪs(ə)n'tɛrɪk
AM ,dɪsn'tɛrɪk

dysentery
BR 'dɪs(ə)nt(ə)ri
AM 'dɪsn,tɛri

dysfunction
BR (,)dɪs'fʌŋ(k)ʃn
AM dɪs'fəŋkʃən

dysfunctional
BR (,)dɪs'fʌŋ(k)ʃn̩(ə)l, (,)dɪs'fʌŋ(k)ʃən(ə)l
AM dɪs'fəŋkʃ(ə)nəl

dysgenic
BR dɪs'dʒɛnɪk
AM dɪs'dʒɛnɪk

dysgraphia
BR dɪs'grafɪə(r)
AM dɪs'græfiə

dysgraphic
BR dɪs'grafɪk
AM dɪs'græfɪk

dyslalia
BR dɪs'leɪlɪə(r)
AM dɪs'leɪljə, dɪs'leɪliə

dyslectic
BR dɪs'lɛktɪk, -s
AM dəs'lɛktɪk, -s

dyslexia
BR dɪs'lɛksɪə(r)
AM dəs'lɛksiə

dyslexic
BR dɪs'lɛksɪk, -s
AM dəs'lɛksɪk, -s

dyslogistic
BR ,dɪslə'dʒɪstɪk
AM ,dɪslə'dʒɪstɪk

dyslogistically
BR ,dɪslə'dʒɪstɨkli
AM ,dɪslə'dʒɪstək(ə)li

dysmenorrhoea
BR ,dɪsmɛnə'rɪə(r)
AM ',dɪs,mɛnə'riə

Dyson
BR 'dʌɪsn
AM 'daɪsən

dyspepsia
BR dɪs'pɛpsɪə(r)
AM dɪs'pɛpsiə, dɪs'pɛpʃə

dyspeptic
BR dɪs'pɛptɪk, -s
AM dɪs'pɛptɪk, -s

dysphagia
BR dɪs'feɪdʒ(ɪ)ə(r)
AM dɪs'feɪdʒ(i)ə

dysphasia
BR dɪs'feɪzɪə(r), dɪs'feɪʒə(r)
AM dɪs'feɪʒ(i)ə, dɪs'feɪziə

dysphasic
BR dɪs'feɪzɪk
AM dɪs'feɪzɪk

dysphemism
BR 'dɪsfɨmɪz(ə)m, -z
AM dɪs'fɛmɪzəm, -z

dysphoria
BR dɪs'fɔːrɪə(r)
AM dɪs'fɔriə

dysphoric
BR dɪs'fɒrɪk
AM dɪs'fɔrɪk

dysplasia
BR dɪs'pleɪzɪə(r), dɪs'pleɪʒə(r)
AM dɪs'pleɪʒ(i)ə, dɪs'pleɪziə

dysplastic
BR dɪs'plastɪk
AM dɪs'plæstɪk

dyspnea
BR dɪsp'niːə(r)
AM 'dɪs(p)niə

dyspneic
BR dɪsp'niːɪk
AM dɪs(p)'niɪk

dyspnoea
BR dɪsp'niːə(r)
AM 'dɪs(p)niə

dyspnoeic
BR dɪsp'niːɪk
AM dɪs(p)'niɪk

dyspraxia
BR dɪs'praksɪə(r)
AM dɪs'præksiə

dysprosium
BR dɪs'prəʊzɪəm
AM də'sproʊziəm

dysthymia
BR dɪs'θʌɪmɪə(r)
AM dɪs'θaɪmiə

dystocia
BR dɪs'təʊʃ(ɪ)ə(r)
AM də'stoʊʃ(i)ə

dystopia
BR dɪs'təʊpɪə(r), -z
AM də'stoʊpiə, -z

dystopian
BR dɪs'təʊpɪən, -z
AM də'stoʊpiən, -z

dystrophic
BR dɪs'trɒfɪk, dɪs'trəʊfɪk
AM dɪs'trɑfɪk

dystrophy
BR 'dɪstrəfi
AM 'dɪstrəfi

dysuria
BR dɪs'jʊərɪə(r), ,dɪsjʊ'riːə(r)
AM də'ʃʊriə

Dzerzhinsky
BR dʒəː'ʒɪnski
AM dʒər'ʒɪnski

dzho
BR ʒəʊ, zəʊ, -z
AM dʒoʊ, -z

dziggetai
BR '(d)zɪgətʌɪ, 'dʒɪgətʌɪ, -z
AM '(d)zɪgə,taɪ, -z

dzo
BR ʒəʊ, zəʊ, -z
AM (d)zoʊ, -z

Dzongkha
BR 'zɒŋkə(r)
AM 'zɔŋkə, 'zɑŋkə

Ee

e
BR iː, -z
AM i, -z

ea.
each
BR iːtʃ
AM itʃ

each
BR iːtʃ
AM itʃ

Eadie
BR ˈiːdi
AM ˈidi

eager
BR ˈiːɡə(r)
AM ˈiɡər

eagerly
BR ˈiːɡəli
AM ˈiɡərli

eagerness
BR ˈiːɡənəs
AM ˈiɡərnəs

eagle
BR ˈiːɡl, -z
AM ˈiɡəl, -z

eaglet
BR ˈiːɡlɪt, -s
AM ˈiɡlət, -s

eagre
BR ˈiːɡə(r), -z
AM ˈiɡər, -z

Eakins
BR ˈeɪkɪnz
AM ˈeɪkɪnz

Ealing
BR ˈiːlɪŋ
AM ˈilɪŋ

Eames
BR iːmz
AM imz

Eamon
BR ˈeɪmən
AM ˈeɪmən

ear
BR ɪə(r), -z, -d
AM ɪ(ə)r, -z, -d

earache
BR ˈɪəreɪk, -s
AM ˈɪrˌeɪk, -s

earbash
BR ˈɪəbaʃ, -ɪz, -ɪŋ, -t
AM ˈɪrˌbæʃ, -əz, -ɪŋ, -t

earbasher
BR ˈɪəˌbaʃə(r), -z
AM ˈɪrˌbæʃər, -z

Eardley
BR ˈəːdli
AM ˈərdli

eardrop
BR ˈɪədrɒp, -s
AM ˈɪrˌdrɑp, -s

eardrum
BR ˈɪədrʌm, -z
AM ˈɪrˌdrəm, -z

eared
BR ɪəd
AM ɪ(ə)rd

earflap
BR ˈɪəflap, -s
AM ˈɪrˌflæp, -s

earful
BR ˈɪəfʊl, -z
AM ˈɪrˌfʊl, ˈɪrfəl, -z

Earhart
BR ˈɛːhɑːt
AM ˈɛrˌ(h)ɑrt

earhole
BR ˈɪəhəʊl, -z
AM ˈɪrˌ(h)oʊl, -z

earing
BR ˈɪərɪŋ, -z
AM ˈɪrɪŋ, -z

earl
BR əːl, -z
AM ˈər(ə)l, -z

earldom
BR ˈəːldəm, -z
AM ˈərldəm, -z

Earle
BR əːl
AM ərl

earless
BR ˈɪələs
AM ˈɪrləs

Earley
BR ˈəːli
AM ˈərli

earliness
BR ˈəːlɪnɨs
AM ˈərlinɨs

earlobe
BR ˈɪələʊb, -z
AM ˈɪrˌloʊb, -z

early
BR ˈəːl|i, -ɪə(r), -ɪɪst
AM ˈərli, -ər, -ɨst

earmark
BR ˈɪəmɑːk, -s, -ɪŋ, -t
AM ˈɪrˌmɑrk, -s, -ɪŋ, -t

earmuff
BR ˈɪəmʌf, -s
AM ˈɪrˌməf, -s

earn
BR əːn, -z, -ɪŋ, -d\-t
AM ərn, -z, -ɪŋ, -d\-t

earner
BR ˈəːnə(r), -z
AM ˈərnər, -z

earnest
BR ˈəːnɪst
AM ˈərnəst

earnestly
BR ˈəːnɪstli
AM ˈərnəs(t)li

earnestness
BR ˈəːnɪs(t)nəs
AM ˈərnəs(t)nəs

earnings
BR ˈəːnɪŋz
AM ˈərnɪŋz

Earnshaw
BR ˈəːnʃɔː(*r*)
AM ˈərnˌʃɔ

EAROM
BR ˈiːrɒm
AM ˈiˌrɑm

Earp
BR əːp
AM ərp

earphone
BR ˈɪəfəʊn, -z
AM ˈɪrˌfoʊn, -z

earpiece
BR ˈɪəpiːs, -ɪz
AM ˈɪrˌpis, -ɪz

earplug
BR ˈɪəplʌɡ, -z
AM ˈɪrˌpləɡ, -z

earring
BR ˈɪərɪŋ, -z
AM ˈɪr(r)ɪŋ, -z

earshot
BR ˈɪəʃɒt
AM ˈɪrˌʃɑt

earth
BR əːθ, -s, -ɪŋ, -t
AM ərθ, -s, -ɪŋ, -t

Eartha
BR ˈəːθə(*r*)
AM ˈərθə

earthbound
BR ˈəːθbaʊnd
AM ˈərθˌbaʊnd

earthen
BR ˈəːθn, ˈəːðn
AM ˈərθən

earthenware
BR ˈəːθnwɛː(r), ˈəːðnwɛː(r)
AM ˈərθənˌwɛ(ə)r

earthily
BR ˈəːθɪli
AM ˈərθəli

earthiness
BR ˈəːθɪnɪs
AM ˈərθinɨs

earthliness
BR ˈəːθlɪnɪs
AM ˈərθlinɨs

earthling
BR ˈəːθlɪŋ, -z
AM ˈərθlɪŋ, -z

earthly
BR ˈəːθl|i, -ɪə(r), -ɪɪst
AM ˈərθli, -ər, -ɨst

earthman
BR ˈəːθman
AM ˈərθˌmæn

earthmen
BR ˈəːθmɛn
AM ˈərθˌmɛn

earthnut
BR ˈəːθnʌt, -s
AM ˈərθˌnət, -s

earthquake
BR ˈəːθkweɪk, -s
AM ˈərθˌkweɪk, -s

earthshaking
BR ˈəːθˌʃeɪkɪŋ
AM ˈərθˌʃeɪkɪŋ

earthshattering
BR ˈəːθˌʃat(ə)rɪŋ
AM ˈərθˌʃædərɪŋ

earthshatteringly
BR ˈəːθˌʃat(ə)rɪŋli
AM ˈərθˌʃædərɪŋli

earthshine
BR ˈəːθʃʌɪn
AM ˈərθˌʃaɪn

earthstar
BR ˈəːθstɑː(r), -z
AM ˈərθˌstɑr, -z

earthward
BR ˈəːθwəd, -z
AM ˈərθwərd, -z

earthwork
BR ˈəːθwəːk, -s
AM ˈərθˌwərk, -s

earthworm
BR ˈəːθwəːm, -z
AM ˈərθˌwərm, -z

earthy
BR ˈəːθ|i, -ɪə(r), -ɪɪst
AM ˈərθi, -ər, -ɨst

earwax
BR ˈɪəwaks
AM ˈɪrˌwæks

earwig
BR ˈɪəwɪɡ, -z
AM ˈɪrˌwɪɡ, -z

ease
BR iːz, -ɪz, -ɪŋ, -d
AM iz, -ɪz, -ɪŋ, -d

easeful
BR ˈiːzf(ʊ)l
AM ˈizfəl

easefully
BR ˈiːzfʊli, ˈiːzfl̩i
AM ˈizfəli

easefulness
BR ˈiːzf(ʊ)lnəs
AM ˈizfəlnəs

easel
BR ˈiːzl, -z
AM ˈizəl, -z

easement
BR ˈiːzm(ə)nt, -s
AM ˈizmənt, -s

easer
BR ˈiːzə(r), -z
AM ˈizər, -z

easily
BR ˈiːzɪli
AM ˈiz(ə)li

easiness
BR ˈiːzɪnɪs
AM ˈizinɨs

Easington
BR ˈiːzɪŋt(ə)n
AM ˈizɪŋtən

east
BR iːst, -s
AM ist, -s
eastabout
BR ˈiːstəbaʊt
AM ˈistəˌbaʊt
eastbound
BR ˈiːs(t)baʊnd
AM ˈis(t)ˌbaʊnd
Eastbourne
BR ˈiːs(t)bɔːn
AM ˈis(t)ˌbɔ(ə)rn
Eastcheap
BR ˈiːs(t)tʃiːp
AM ˈis(t)ˌtʃip
Easter
BR ˈiːstə(r), -z
AM ˈistər, -z
easterly
BR ˈiːstəl|i, -ɪz
AM ˈistərli, -z
eastern
BR ˈiːst(ə)n
AM ˈistərn
easterner
BR ˈiːstənə(r), ˈiːstn̩ə(r), -z
AM ˈistərnər, -z
easternmost
BR ˈiːst(ə)nməʊst
AM ˈistərnˌmoʊst
Eastertide
BR ˈiːstətʌɪd
AM ˈistərˌtaɪd
easting
BR ˈiːstɪŋ, -z
AM ˈistɪŋ, -z
Eastleigh
BR ˌiːs(t)ˈliː, ˈiːs(t)liː
AM ˈis(t)li
Eastman
BR ˈiːs(t)mən
AM ˈis(t)mən
Easton
BR ˈiːst(ə)n
AM ˈistən
eastward
BR ˈiːstwəd, -z
AM ˈis(t)wərd, -z
eastwardly
BR ˈiːstwədli
AM ˈis(t)wərdli
East-West
BR ˌiːs(t)ˈwɛst
AM ˌis(t)ˈwɛst
Eastwood
BR ˈiːstwʊd
AM ˈis(t)ˌwʊd
easy
BR ˈiːz|i, -ɪə(r), -ɪɪst
AM ˈizi, -ər, -ɨst
easygoing
BR ˌiːzɪˈɡəʊɪŋ
AM ˌiziˈɡoʊɪŋ
easy-peasy
BR ˌiːzɪˈpiːzi
AM ˈiziˈpizi

eat
BR iːt, -s, -ɪŋ
AM i|t, -ts, -dɪŋ
eatable
BR ˈiːtəbl, -z
AM ˈidəbəl, -z
eater
BR ˈiːtə(r), -z
AM ˈidər, -z
eatery
BR ˈiːt(ə)r|i, -ɪz
AM ˈidəri, -z
Eaton
BR ˈiːtn
AM ˈitn
eats
BR iːts
AM its
eau de Cologne
BR ˌəʊ də kəˈləʊn
AM ˌoʊ də kəˈloʊn
eau-de-Nil
BR ˌəʊ də ˈniːl
AM ˌoʊ də ˈnil
eau de toilette
BR ˌəʊ də twɑːˈlɛt
AM ˌoʊ də twɑˈlɛt
eau-de-vie
BR ˌəʊ də ˈviː
AM ˌoʊ də ˈvi
eaves
BR iːvz
AM ivz
eavesdrop
BR ˈiːvzdrɒp, -s, -ɪŋ, -t
AM ˈivzˌdrɑp, -s, -ɪŋ, -t
eavesdropper
BR ˈiːvzdrɒpə(r), -z
AM ˈivzˌdrɑpər, -z
eavestrough
BR ˈiːvztrɒf, -s
AM ˈivzˌtrɔf, ˈivzˌtrɑf, -s
ebb
BR ɛb, -z, -ɪŋ, -d
AM ɛb, -z, -ɪŋ, -d
ebb-tide
BR ˌɛbˈtʌɪd, ˈɛbtʌɪd, -z
AM ˈɛbˌtaɪd, -z
Ebbw Vale
BR ˌɛbʉ ˈveɪl
AM ˌɛbu ˈveɪl
Ebenezer
BR ɛbɪˈniːzə(r)
AM ɛbəˈnizər
Ebla
BR ˈɛblə(r)
AM ˈɛblə, ˈiblə
Ebola
BR ɪˈbəʊlə(r)
AM iˈboʊlə, əˈboʊlə
ebon
BR ˈɛb(ə)n
AM ˈɛbən
Ebonics
BR ɛˈbɒnɪks
AM iˈbɑnɪks

ebonise
BR ˈɛbənʌɪz, -ɪz, -ɪŋ, -d
AM ˈɛbəˌnaɪz, -ɨz, -ɪŋ, -d
ebonite
BR ˈɛbənʌɪt
AM ˈɛbəˌnaɪt
ebonize
BR ˈɛbənʌɪz, -ɪz, -ɪŋ, -d
AM ˈɛbəˌnaɪz, -ɨz, -ɪŋ, -d
ebony
BR ˈɛbəni, ˈɛbn̩i
AM ˈɛbəni
Ebor
BR ˈiːbɔː(r)
AM ˈibɔ(ə)r
Eboricum
BR ɪˈbɒrəkəm
AM iˈbɔrəkəm
Ebro
BR ˈiːbrəʊ, ˈɛbrəʊ
AM ˈiˌbroʊ
ebullience
BR ɪˈbʌlɪəns, ɪˈbʊlɪəns
AM əˈbʊljəns, iˈbʊljəns, əˈbəljəns, iˈbəljəns
ebulliency
BR ɪˈbʌlɪənsi, ɪˈbʊlɪənsi
AM əˈbʊljənsi, iˈbʊljənsi, əˈbəljənsi, iˈbəljənsi
ebullient
BR ɪˈbʌlɪənt, ɪˈbʊlɪənt
AM əˈbʊliənt, iˈbʊljənt, əˈbəljənt, iˈbəljənt
ebulliently
BR ɪˈbʌlɪəntli, ɪˈbʊlɪəntli
AM əˈbʊliən(t)li, iˈbʊljən(t)li, əˈbəljən(t)li, iˈbəljən(t)li
ebullition
BR ˌɛbəˈlɪʃn, -z
AM ˌɛbəˈlɪʃən, -z
Ebury
BR ˈiːb(ə)ri
AM ˈibəri
ecad
BR ˈiːkad, -z
AM ˈiˌkæd, ˈɛˌkæd, -z
écarté
BR eɪˈkɑːteɪ
AM ˌeɪkarˈteɪ
Ecce Homo
BR ˌɛkɪ ˈhəʊməʊ, ˌɛtʃeɪ +, ˌɛksɪ +, + ˈhɒməʊ
AM ˌɛtʃeɪ ˈhoʊˌmoʊ, ˌɛtʃə +
eccentric
BR ɪkˈsɛntrɪk, ɛkˈsɛntrɪk
AM ɪkˈsɛntrɪk

eccentrically
BR ɪkˈsɛntrɪkli, ɛkˈsɛntrɪkli
AM ɪkˈsɛntrək(ə)li
eccentricity
BR ˌɛksɛnˈtrɪsɪt|i, ˌɛks(ə)nˈtrɪsɪt|i, -ɪz
AM ˌɛkˌsɛnˈtrɪsɨdi, -z
Eccles
BR ˈɛklz
AM ˈɛkəlz
ecclesia
BR ɪˈkliːzɪə(r)
AM əˈkliziə, əˈkliʒiə
ecclesial
BR ɪˈkliːzɪəl
AM əˈkliziəl
Ecclesiastes
BR ɪˌkliːzɪˈastiːz
AM əˌkliziˈæstiz
ecclesiastic
BR ɪˌkliːzɪˈastɪk, -s
AM əˌkliziˈæstɪk, -s
ecclesiastical
BR ɪˌkliːzɪˈastɪkl
AM əˌkliziˈæstəkəl
ecclesiastically
BR ɪˌkliːzɪˈastɪkli
AM əˌkliziˈæstək(ə)li
ecclesiasticism
BR ɪˌkliːzɪˈastɪsɪz(ə)m
AM əˌkliziˈæstəˌsɪzəm
Ecclesiasticus
BR ɪˌkliːzɪˈastɪkəs
AM əˌkliziˈæstəkəs
ecclesiological
BR ɪˌkliːzɪəˈlɒdʒɪkl
AM əˌkliziəˈlɑdʒəkəl
ecclesiologist
BR ɪˌkliːzɪˈɒlədʒɪst, -s
AM əˌkliziˈɑlədʒəst, -s
ecclesiology
BR ɪˌkliːzɪˈɒlədʒi
AM əˌkliziˈɑlədʒi
Ecclestone
BR ˈɛklst(ə)n
AM ˈɛklstən
eccrine
BR ˈɛkrʌɪn, ˈɛkrɪn
AM ˈɛkrən, ˈɛˌkraɪn, ˈɛˌkrin
ecdysiast
BR ɛkˈdɪzɪast, -s
AM ɛkˈdiziəst, -s
ecdysis
BR ˈɛkdɪsɪs
AM ˈɛkdəsəs
echelon
BR ˈɛʃəlɒn, -z, -ɪŋ, -d
AM ˈɛ(t)ʃəˌlɑn, -z, -ɪŋ, -d
echeveria
BR ˌɛtʃɪˈvɪərɪə(r), -z
AM ˌɛtʃəvəˈriə, ˌɛtʃəvəˈraɪə, -z
echidna
BR ɪˈkɪdnə(r), -z
AM əˈkɪdnə, -z

echinite
BR ˈɛkənʌɪt, ɪˈkʌɪnʌɪt, -s
AM ˈɛkəˌnaɪt, əˈkaɪˌnaɪt, iˈkaɪˌnaɪt, -s

echinoderm
BR ɪˈkʌɪnə(ʊ)dəːm, ɪˈkɪnə(ʊ)dəːm, -z
AM əˈkaɪnəˌdərm, əˈkɪnəˌdərm, -z

echinoid
BR ɪˈkʌɪnɔɪd, ˈɛkɪnɔɪd, ˈɛkn̩ɔɪd, -z
AM ˈɛkəˌnɔɪd, əˈkaɪˌnɔɪd, iˈkaɪˌnɔɪd, -z

echinus
BR ɪˈkʌɪnəs, ˈɛkɪnəs, ˈɛkn̩əs, -ɪz
AM əˈkaɪnəs, iˈkaɪnəs, -əz

echo
BR ˈɛkəʊ, -z, -ɪŋ, -d
AM ˈɛkoʊ, -z, -ɪŋ, -d

echocardiogram
BR ˌɛkəʊˈkɑːdɪəgram, -z
AM ˌɛkoʊˈkardiəˌgræm, -z

echocardiograph
BR ˌɛkəʊˈkɑːdɪəgrɑːf, ˌɛkəʊˈkɑːdɪəgraf, -s
AM ˌɛkoʊˈkardiəˌgræf, -s

echocardiographer
BR ˌɛkəʊkɑːdɪˈɒgrəfə(r), -z
AM ˌɛkoʊˌkardiˈɑgrəfər, ˌɛkoʊˈkardiəˌgræfər, -z

echocardiography
BR ˌɛkəʊkɑːdɪˈɒgrafli, -ɪz
AM ˌɛkoʊˌkardiˈɑgrəfi, -z

echoencephalogram
BR ˌɛkəʊɛnˈsɛf(ə)lə(ʊ)gram, ˌɛkəʊɛnˈsɛfl̩ə(ʊ)gram, ˌɛkəʊɛnˈkɛf(ə)lə(ʊ)gram, ˌɛkəʊɛnˈkɛfl̩ə(ʊ)gram, -z
AM ˌɛkoʊˌɛnˈsɛfələˌgræm, -z

echoencephalography
BR ˌɛkəʊɛnˌsɛfəˈlɒgrafi, ˌɛkəʊɛnˌsɛfl̩ˈɒgrəfi, ˌɛkəʊɛnˌkɛfəˈlɒgrəfi, ˌɛkəʊɛnˌkɛfl̩ˈɒgrəfi
AM ¦ɛkoʊˌɛnˌsɛfəˈlɑgrəfi

echoer
BR ˈɛkəʊə(r), -z
AM ˈɛkoʊər, -z

echoey
BR ˈɛkəʊi
AM ˈɛkoʊi

echogram
BR ˈɛkəʊgram, -z
AM ˈɛkoʊˌgræm, -z

echograph
BR ˈɛkəʊgrɑːf, ˈɛkəʊgraf, -s
AM ˈɛkoʊˌgræf, -s

echoic
BR ɛˈkəʊɪk, ɪˈkəʊɪk
AM əˈkoʊɪk, ɛˈkoʊɪk

echoically
BR ɛˈkəʊɪkli, ɪˈkəʊɪkli
AM əˈkoʊək(ə)li, ɛˈkoʊək(ə)li

echoism
BR ˈɛkəʊəɪz(ə)m
AM ˈɛkoʊˌɪzəm

echolalia
BR ˌɛkə(ʊ)ˈleɪlɪə(r)
AM ˌɛkoʊˈleɪljə, ˌɛkoʊˈleɪliə

echoless
BR ˈɛkəʊləs
AM ˈɛkoʊləs

echolocate
BR ˈɛkəʊlə(ʊ)ˌkeɪt, -s, -ɪŋ, -ɪd
AM ˌɛkoʊˈloʊˌkeɪ|t, -ts, -dɪŋ, -dɪd

echolocation
BR ˌɛkəʊlə(ʊ)ˈkeɪʃn, ˈɛkəʊlə(ʊ)ˌkeɪʃn
AM ˌɛkoʊˌloʊˈkeɪʃən

echovirus
BR ˈɛkəʊˌvʌɪrəs
AM ˈɛkoʊˌvaɪrəs

echt
BR ɛxt, ɛkt
AM ɛkt

Eckersley
BR ˈɛkəzli
AM ˈɛkərzli

Eckert
BR ˈɛkəːt
AM ˈɛkərt

Eckhart
BR ˈɛkhɑːt
AM ˈɛkərt

éclair
BR ɪˈklɛː(r), eɪˈklɛː(r), -z
AM eɪˈklɛ(ə)r, ɪˈklɛ(ə)r, -z

éclaircissement
BR eɪˈklɛːsiːsmɒ̃
AM eɪˌklɛrsisˈmɑnt

eclampsia
BR ɪˈklam(p)sɪə(r)
AM ɪˈklæm(p)siə

eclamptic
BR ɪˈklam(p)tɪk
AM ɪˈklæm(p)tɪk

éclat
BR eɪˈklɑː(r), ɛˈklɑː(r), ˈeɪklɑː(r), ˈɛklɑː(r)
AM eɪˈklɑ

eclectic
BR ɪˈklɛktɪk
AM iˈklɛktɪk, əˈklɛktɪk

eclectically
BR ɪˈklɛktɪkli
AM iˈklɛktək(ə)li, əˈklɛktək(ə)li

eclecticism
BR ɪˈklɛktɪsɪz(ə)m
AM iˈklɛktəˌsɪzəm, əˈklɛktəˌsɪzəm

eclipse
BR ɪˈklɪps, -ɪz, -ɪŋ, -t
AM əˈklɪps, iˈklɪps, -ɪz, -ɪŋ, -t

eclipser
BR ɪˈklɪpsə(r), -z
AM əˈklɪpsər, iˈklɪpsər, -z

ecliptic
BR ɪˈklɪptɪk, -s
AM əˈklɪptɪk, iˈklɪptɪk, -s

ecliptically
BR ɪˈklɪptɪkli
AM əˈklɪptək(ə)li, iˈklɪptək(ə)li

eclogue
BR ˈɛklɒg, -z
AM ˈɛˌklɔg, ˈɛˌklɑg, -z

eclosion
BR ɪˈkləʊʒn
AM əˈkloʊʒən, iˈkloʊʒən

Eco
BR ˈɛkəʊ
AM ˈɛkoʊ

ecoclimate
BR ˈiːkəʊˌklʌɪmɪt, ˈɛkəʊˌklʌɪmɪt, -s
AM ˈɛkoʊˌklaɪmət, ˈikoʊˌklaɪmət, -s

eco-friendly
BR ˌiːkəʊˈfrɛn(d)li, ˌɛkəʊˈfrɛn(d)li
AM ˈɛkoʊˌfrɛndli, ˈikoʊˌfrɛndli

eco-label
BR ˈiːkəʊˌleɪbl, ˈɛkəʊˌleɪbl, -z
AM ˈɛkoʊˌleɪbəl, ˈikoʊˌleɪbəl, -z

eco-labelling
BR ˈiːkəʊˌleɪbl̩ɪŋ, ˈiːkəʊˌleɪblɪŋ, ˈɛkəʊˌleɪbl̩ɪŋ, ˈɛkəʊˌleɪblɪŋ
AM ˈɛkoʊˌleɪb(ə)lɪŋ, ˈikoʊˌleɪb(ə)lɪŋ

E. coli
BR ˌiː ˈkəʊlʌɪ
AM i ˈkoʊlaɪ

ecological
BR ˌiːkəˈlɒdʒɪkl, ˌɛkəˈlɒdʒɪkl
AM ¦ɛkəˈlɑdʒəkəl, ¦ikəˈlɑdʒəkəl

ecologically
BR ˌiːkəˈlɒdʒɪkli, ˌɛkəˈlɒdʒɪkli
AM ¦ɛkəˈlɑdʒək(ə)li, ¦ikəˈlɑdʒək(ə)li

ecologist
BR ɪˈkɒlədʒɪst, -s
AM iˈkɑlədʒəst, əˈkɑlədʒəst, -s

ecology
BR ɪˈkɒlədʒi
AM iˈkɑlədʒi, əˈkɑlədʒi

econometric
BR ɪˌkɒnəˈmɛtrɪk, -s
AM əˌkɑnəˈmɛtrɪk, iˌkɑnəˈmɛtrɪk, -s

econometrical
BR ɪˌkɒnəˈmɛtrɪkl
AM əˌkɑnəˈmɛtrəkəl, iˌkɑnəˈmɛtrəkəl

econometrically
BR ɪˌkɒnəˈmɛtrɪkli
AM əˌkɑnəˈmɛtrək(ə)li, iˌkɑnəˈmɛtrək(ə)li

econometrician
BR ɪˌkɒnəməˈtrɪʃn, -z
AM əˌkɑnəməˈtrɪʃən, -z

econometrist
BR ɪˌkɒnəˈmɛtrɪst, -s
AM əˌkɑnəˈmɛtrəst, iˌkɑnəˈmɛtrəst, -s

economic
BR ˌiːkəˈnɒmɪk, ˌɛkəˈnɒmɪk, -s
AM ¦ɛkəˈnɑmɪk, ¦ikəˈnɑmɪk, -s

economical
BR ˌiːkəˈnɒmɪkl, ˌɛkəˈnɒmɪkl
AM ¦ɛkəˈnɑməkəl, ¦ikəˈnɑməkəl

economically
BR ˌiːkəˈnɒmɪkli, ˌɛkəˈnɒmɪkli
AM ¦ɛkəˈnɑmək(ə)li, ¦ikəˈnɑmək(ə)li

economisation
BR ɪˌkɒnəmʌɪˈzeɪʃn
AM əˌkɑnəməˈzeɪʃən, iˌkɑnəˌmaɪˈzeɪʃən, iˌkɑnəməˈzeɪʃən, əˌkɑnəˌmaɪˈzeɪʃən, ˈˌɛkəˌnɑməˈzeɪʃən, ˈˌikəˌnɑməˈzeɪʃən

economise
BR ɪˈkɒnəmʌɪz, -ɪz, -ɪŋ, -d
AM iˈkɑnəˌmaɪz, əˈkɑnəˌmaɪz, -ɪz, -ɪŋ, -d

economiser
BR ɪˈkɒnəmʌɪzə(r), -z
AM iˈkɑnəˌmaɪzər, əˈkɑnəˌmaɪzər, -z

economist
BR ɪˈkɒnəmɪst, -s

AM i'kɑnəməst, ə'kɑnəməst, -s

economization
BR ɪˌkɒnəmʌɪ'zeɪʃn
AM əˌkɑnəmə'zeɪʃən, iˌkɑnəˌmaɪ'zeɪʃən, iˌkɑnəmə'zeɪʃən, əˌkɑnəˌmaɪ'zeɪʃən, ˈˌɛkəˌnɑmə'zeɪʃən, ˈˌikəˌnɑmə'zeɪʃən

economize
BR ɪ'kɒnəmʌɪz, -ɪz, -ɪŋ, -d
AM i'kɑnəˌmaɪz, ə'kɑnəˌmaɪz, -ɪz, -ɪŋ, -d

economizer
BR ɪ'kɒnəmʌɪzə(r), -z
AM i'kɑnəˌmaɪzər, ə'kɑnəˌmaɪzər, -z

economy
BR ɪ'kɒnəm|i, -ɪz
AM i'kɑnəmi, ə'kɑnəmi, -z

écorché
BR ˌeɪkɔː'ʃeɪ
AM ˌeɪkɔr'ʃeɪ

ecosphere
BR 'iːkəʊsfɪə(r), 'ɛkəʊsfɪə(r)
AM 'ikoʊˌsfɪ(ə)r, 'ɛkoʊˌsfɪ(ə)r

écossaise
BR ˌeɪkɒ'seɪz, ˌɛkɒ'seɪz
AM eɪˌkoʊ'seɪz

écossaises
BR ˌeɪkɒ'seɪz, ˌɛkɒ'seɪz, ˌeɪkɒ'seɪzɪz, ˌɛkɒ'seɪzɪz
AM eɪˌkoʊ'seɪz(ɪz)

ecosystem
BR 'iːkəʊˌsɪstɪm, 'ɛkəʊˌsɪstɪm, -z
AM 'ikoʊˌsɪstəm, 'ɛkoʊˌsɪstəm, -z

eco-terrorism
BR 'iːkəʊˌtɛrərɪz(ə)m, 'ɛkəʊˌtɛrərɪz(ə)m
AM 'ɛkoʊˌtɛrəˌrɪzəm, 'ikoʊˌtɛrəˌrɪzəm

eco-terrorist
BR 'iːkəʊˌtɛrərɪst, 'ɛkəʊˌtɛrərɪst, -s
AM 'ɛkoʊˌtɛrərəst, 'ikoʊˌtɛrərəst, -s

écru
BR 'eɪkruː, ɛ'kruː
AM 'ɛkru, 'eɪkru

ecstasise
BR 'ɛkstəsʌɪz, -ɪz, -ɪŋ, -d
AM 'ɛkstəˌsaɪz, -ɪz, -ɪŋ, -d

ecstasize
BR 'ɛkstəsʌɪz, -ɪz, -ɪŋ, -d
AM 'ɛkstəˌsaɪz, -ɪz, -ɪŋ, -d

ecstasy
BR 'ɛkstəs|i, -ɪz
AM 'ɛkstəsi, -z

ecstatic
BR ɪk'statɪk, ɛk'statɪk
AM ɛk'stædɪk

ecstatically
BR ɪk'statɪkli, ɛk'statɪkli
AM ɛk'stædək(ə)li

ectoblast
BR 'ɛktə(ʊ)blɑːst, 'ɛktə(ʊ)blast, -s
AM 'ɛktəˌblæst, -s

ectoblastic
BR ˌɛktə(ʊ)'blastɪk
AM ˌɛktə'blæstɪk

ectoderm
BR 'ɛktə(ʊ)dəːm, -z
AM 'ɛktəˌdərm, -z

ectodermal
BR ˌɛktə(ʊ)'dəːml
AM ˌɛktə'dərməl

ectogenesis
BR ˌɛktə(ʊ)'dʒɛnɪsɪs, -s
AM ˌɛktə'dʒɛnəsəs, -s

ectogenetic
BR ˌɛktə(ʊ)dʒɪ'nɛtɪk
AM ˌɛktədʒə'nɛdɪk

ectogenetically
BR ˌɛktə(ʊ)dʒɪ'nɛtɪkli
AM ˌɛktədʒə'nɛdək(ə)li

ectogenic
BR ˌɛktə(ʊ)'dʒɛnɪk, -s
AM ˌɛktə'dʒɛnɪk, -s

ectogenically
BR ˌɛktə(ʊ)'dʒɛnɪkli
AM ˌɛktə'dʒɛnək(ə)li

ectogenous
BR ɛk'tɒdʒɪnəs
AM ɛk'tɑdʒənəs

ectomorph
BR 'ɛktə(ʊ)mɔːf, -s
AM 'ɛktəˌmɔ(ə)rf, -s

ectomorphic
BR ˌɛktə(ʊ)'mɔːfɪk
AM ˌɛktə'mɔrfɪk

ectomorphy
BR 'ɛktə(ʊ)mɔːfi
AM 'ɛktəˌmɔrfi

ectoparasite
BR 'ɛktə(ʊ)ˌparəsʌɪt, -s
AM ˌɛktə'pɛrəˌsaɪt, -s

ectopic
BR ɛk'tɒpɪk
AM ɛk'tɑpɪk

ectoplasm
BR 'ɛktə(ʊ)plaz(ə)m
AM 'ɛktəˌplæzəm

ectoplasmic
BR ˌɛktə(ʊ)'plazmɪk
AM ˌɛktə'plæzəmɪk

ectozoon
BR ˌɛktə(ʊ)'zuːɒn, ˌɛktə(ʊ)'zəʊɒn, -z
AM ˌɛktə'zoʊən, ˌɛktə'zuən, -z

ecu
BR 'ɛkjuː, 'eɪkjuː, -z
AM eɪ'k(j)u, -z

Ecuador
BR 'ɛkwədɔː(r)
AM 'ɛkwəˌdɔ(ə)r
SP ˌekwa'ðor

Ecuadoran
BR ˌɛkwə'dɔːrən, -z
AM ˌɛkwə'dɔrən, -z

Ecuadorean
BR ˌɛkwə'dɔːrɪən, -z
AM ˌɛkwə'dɔr(i)ən, -z

Ecuadorian
BR ˌɛkwə'dɔːrɪən, -z
AM ˌɛkwə'dɔriən, -z

ecumenical
BR ˌiːkjʊ'mɛnɪkl, ˌɛkjʊ'mɛnɪkl
AM ˌɛkjə'mɛnəkəl

ecumenicalism
BR ˌiːkjʊ'mɛnɪkəlɪz(ə)m, ˌiːkjʊ'mɛnɪklɪz(ə)m, ˌɛkjʊ'mɛnɪkəlɪz(ə)m, ˌɛkjʊ'mɛnɪklɪzəm
AM ˌɛkjə'mɛnəkəˌlɪzəm

ecumenically
BR ˌiːkjʊ'mɛnɪkli, ˌɛkjʊ'mɛnɪkli
AM ˈˌɛkjə'mɛnək(ə)li

ecumenicism
BR ˌiːkjʊ'mɛnɪsɪz(ə)m, ˌɛkjʊ'mɛnɪsɪzəm
AM ˌɛkjə'mɛnəˌsɪzəm

ecumenicity
BR ɪˌkjuːmə'nɪsɪti
AM ˌɛkjəmə'nɪsɪdi

ecumenism
BR ɪ'kjuːmənɪz(ə)m
AM 'ɛkjəməˌnɪzəm, ɛ'kjuməˌnɪzəm

eczema
BR 'ɛks(ɪ)mə(*r*), 'ɛgzɪmə(*r*)
AM 'ɛksəmə, 'ɛgzəmə, ɛg'zimə, ɪg'zimə

eczematous
BR ɛk'sɛmətəs, ɪk'sɛmətəs, ɛk'zɛmətəs, ɪk'zɛmətəs
AM ɛg'zɛmədəs, ɛg'zimədəs, ɪg'zimədəs, ɪg'zɛmədəs

Ed
BR ɛd
AM ɛd

edacious
BR ɪ'deɪʃəs
AM ə'deɪʃəs, i'deɪʃəs

edacity
BR ɪ'dasɪti
AM ə'dæsədi, i'dæsədi

Edale
BR 'iːdeɪl
AM 'iˌdeɪl

Edam
BR 'iːdam
AM 'idəm

edaphic
BR ɪ'dafɪk
AM ə'dæfɪk, i'dæfɪk

Edda
BR 'ɛdə(*r*), -z
AM 'ɛdə, -z

Eddic
BR 'ɛdɪk
AM 'ɛdɪk

Eddie
BR 'ɛdi
AM 'ɛdi

Eddington
BR 'ɛdɪŋt(ə)n
AM 'ɛdɪŋtən

eddo
BR 'ɛdəʊ, -z
AM 'ɛˌdoʊ, -z

eddy
BR 'ɛd|i, -ɪz, -ɪɪŋ, -ɪd
AM 'ɛdi, -z, -ɪŋ, -d

Eddystone
BR 'ɛdɪst(ə)n
AM 'ɛdiˌstoʊn

edelweiss
BR 'eɪdlvʌɪs
AM 'eɪdlˌwaɪs, 'eɪdlˌvaɪs

edema
BR ɪ'diːmə(*r*), -z
AM ə'dimə, -z

edematose
BR ɪ'diːmətəʊs, iː'diːmətəʊs
AM ə'diməˌtoʊs, i'diməˌtoʊs, ə'diməˌtoʊz, i'diməˌtoʊz

edematous
BR ɪ'diːmətəs
AM ə'dɛmədəs

Eden
BR 'iːdn
AM 'idən

edentate
BR ɪ'dɛnteɪt
AM ə'dɛnˌteɪt

Edessa
BR ɪ'dɛsə(*r*)
AM ə'dɛsə

Edgar
BR 'ɛdgə(r)
AM 'ɛdgər

Edgbaston
BR 'ɛdʒbəst(ə)n, 'ɛdʒbast(ə)n
AM 'ɛdʒˌbæstən

edge
BR ɛdʒ, -ɪz, -ɪŋ, -d
AM ɛdʒ, -əz, -ɪŋ, -d

Edgecomb
BR 'ɛdʒkəm
AM 'ɛdʒkəm

Edgecombe
BR 'ɛdʒkəm
AM 'ɛdʒkəm

Edgehill¹
place in UK
BR ˌɛdʒ'hɪl
AM ˌɛdʒ'hɪl

Edgehill²
surname
BR 'ɛdʒhɪl
AM 'ɛdʒˌ(h)ɪl

edgeless
BR 'ɛdʒləs
AM 'ɛdʒləs

edger
BR 'ɛdʒə(r), -z
AM 'ɛdʒər, -z

Edgerton
BR 'ɛdʒət(ə)n
AM 'ɛdʒərtən

edgeways
BR 'ɛdʒweɪz
AM 'ɛdʒˌweɪz

edgewise
BR 'ɛdʒwʌɪz
AM 'ɛdʒˌwaɪz

Edgeworth
BR 'ɛdʒwə(ː)θ
AM 'ɛdʒˌwərθ

edgily
BR 'ɛdʒɨli
AM 'ɛdʒəli

edginess
BR 'ɛdʒɪnɪs
AM 'ɛdʒinɪs

edging
BR 'ɛdʒɪŋ, -z
AM 'ɛdʒɪŋ, -z

Edgware
BR 'ɛdʒwɛː(r)
AM 'ɛdʒˌwɛ(ə)r

edgy
BR 'ɛdʒ|i, -ɪə(r), -ɪɪst
AM 'ɛdʒi, -ər, -ɨst

edh
BR ɛð, -z
AM ɛð, -z

edibility
BR ˌɛdɪ'bɪlɨti
AM ˌɛdə'bɪlɨdi

edible
BR 'ɛdɨbl, -z
AM 'ɛdəbəl, -z

edibleness
BR 'ɛdɨblnəs
AM 'ɛdəbəlnəs

edict
BR 'iːdɪkt, -s
AM 'idɪk|(t), -(t)s

edictal
BR ɪ'dɪktl
AM ə'dɪktl, i'dɪktl

Edie
BR 'iːdi
AM 'idi

edification
BR ˌɛdɨfɪ'keɪʃn
AM ˌɛdəfə'keɪʃən

edifice
BR 'ɛdɨfɪs, -ɪz
AM 'ɛdəfəs, -əz

edify
BR 'ɛdɨfʌɪ, -z, -ɪŋ, -d
AM 'ɛdəˌfaɪ, -z, -ɪŋ, -d

edifyingly
BR 'ɛdɨfʌɪɪŋli
AM 'ɛdəˌfaɪɪŋli

Edinburgh
BR 'ɛd(ɨ)nb(ə)rə(r)
AM 'ɛdənbərə

Edington
BR 'ɛdɪŋt(ə)n
AM 'ɛdɪŋtən

Edison
BR 'ɛdɪs(ə)n
AM 'ɛdəsən

edit
BR 'ɛd|ɪt, -ɪts, -ɨtɪŋ, -ɨtɨd
AM 'ɛdə|t, -ts, -dɪŋ, -dəd

Edith
BR 'iːdɪθ
AM 'idɪθ

edition
BR ɪ'dɪʃn, -z
AM ə'dɪʃən, i'dɪʃən, -z

editiones principes
BR ɪˌdɪʃɪ'əʊniːz 'prɪnsɪpiːz
AM eɪˌdɪdi'oʊniz 'prɪŋkəˌpeɪs, əˌdɪʃi'oʊniz 'prɪnsəˌpiz

editio princeps
BR ɪˌdɪʃɪəʊ 'prɪnsɛps
AM eɪ'dɪdioʊ 'prɪnˌkɛps, + 'prɪnˌsɛps

editor
BR 'ɛdɨtə(r), -z
AM 'ɛdədər, -z

editorial
BR ˌɛdɪ'tɔːrɪəl, -z
AM ˌɛdə'tɔriəl, -z

editorialise
BR ˌɛdɪ'tɔːrɪəlʌɪz, -ɨz, -ɪŋ, -d
AM ˌɛdə'tɔriəˌlaɪz, -ɨz, -ɪŋ, -d

editorialist
BR ˌɛdɪ'tɔːrɪəlɪst, -s
AM ˌɛdə'tɔriələst, -s

editorialize
BR ˌɛdɪ'tɔːrɪəlʌɪz, -ɨz, -ɪŋ, -d
AM ˌɛdə'tɔriəˌlaɪz, -ɨz, -ɪŋ, -d

editorially
BR ˌɛdɪ'tɔːrɪəli
AM ˌɛdə'tɔriəli

editorship
BR 'ɛdɨtəʃɪp, -s
AM 'ɛdədərˌʃɪp, -s

Edmond
BR 'ɛdmənd
AM 'ɛdmən(d)

Edmonds
BR 'ɛdmən(d)z
AM 'ɛdmən(d)z

Edmondson
BR 'ɛdmən(d)s(ə)n
AM 'ɛdmən(d)sən

Edmonton
BR 'ɛdmənt(ə)n
AM 'ɛdmənt(ə)n

Edmund
BR 'ɛdmənd
AM 'ɛdmən(d)

Edmunds
BR 'ɛdmən(d)z
AM 'ɛdmən(d)z

Edmundson
BR 'ɛdmən(d)s(ə)n
AM 'ɛdmən(d)sən

Edna
BR 'ɛdnə(r)
AM 'ɛdnə

Edo
BR 'ɛdəʊ
AM 'idoʊ, 'ɛdoʊ

Edom
BR 'iːdəm
AM 'idəm

Edomite
BR 'iːdəmʌɪt, -s
AM 'idəˌmaɪt, -s

EDP
BR ˌiːdiː'piː
AM ˌidi'pi

Edrich
BR 'ɛdrɪtʃ
AM 'ɛdrɪtʃ

Edridge
BR 'ɛdrɪdʒ
AM 'ɛdrɪdʒ

Edsel
BR 'ɛdsl
AM 'ɛdzəl, 'ɛdsəl

educability
BR ˌɛdjʊkə'bɪlɨti, ˌɛdʒʊkə'bɪlɨti
AM ˌɛdʒəkə'bɪlɨdi

educable
BR 'ɛdjʊkəbl, 'ɛdʒʊkəbl
AM 'ɛdʒəkəbəl

educatable
BR 'ɛdjʊkeɪtəbl, 'ɛdʒʊkeɪtəbl
AM 'ɛdʒəˌkeɪdəbəl

educate
BR 'ɛdjʊkeɪt, 'ɛdʒʊkeɪt, -s, -ɪŋ, -ɨd
AM 'ɛdʒəˌkeɪ|t, -ts, -dɪŋ, -dɨd

education
BR ˌɛdjʊ'keɪʃn, ˌɛdʒʊ'keɪʃn
AM ˌɛdʒə'keɪʃən

educational
BR ˌɛdjʊ'keɪʃn̩(ə)l, ˌɛdjʊ'keɪʃən(ə)l, ˌɛdʒʊ'keɪʃn̩(ə)l, ˌɛdʒʊ'keɪʃən(ə)l
AM ˌɛdʒə'keɪʃ(ə)nəl

educationalist
BR ˌɛdjʊ'keɪʃn̩əlɪst, ˌɛdjʊ'keɪʃn̩lɪst, ˌɛdjʊ'keɪʃənl̩ɪst, ˌɛdjʊ'keɪʃ(ə)nəlɪst, ˌɛdʒʊ'keɪʃn̩əlɪst, ˌɛdʒʊ'keɪʃn̩lɪst, ˌɛdʒʊ'keɪʃənl̩ɪst, ˌɛdʒʊ'keɪʃ(ə)nəlɪst, -s
AM ˌɛdʒə'keɪʃənl̩əst, ˌɛdʒə'keɪʃnələst, -s

educationally
BR ˌɛdjʊ'keɪʃn̩əli, ˌɛdjʊ'keɪʃn̩li, ˌɛdjʊ'keɪʃənl̩i, ˌɛdjʊ'keɪʃ(ə)nəli, ˌɛdʒʊ'keɪʃn̩əli, ˌɛdʒʊ'keɪʃn̩li, ˌɛdʒʊ'keɪʃənl̩i, ˌɛdʒʊ'keɪʃ(ə)nəli
AM ˌɛdʒə'keɪʃ(ə)nəli

educationist
BR ˌɛdjʊ'keɪʃn̩ɪst, ˌɛdjʊ'keɪʃənɪst, ˌɛdʒʊ'keɪʃn̩ɪst, ˌɛdʒʊ'keɪʃənɪst, -s
AM ˌɛdʒə'keɪʃ(ə)nəst, -s

educative
BR 'ɛdjʊkətɪv, 'ɛdʒʊkətɪv
AM 'ɛdʒəˌkeɪdɪv

educator
BR 'ɛdjʊkeɪtə(r), 'ɛdʒʊkeɪtə(r), -z
AM 'ɛdʒəˌkeɪdər, -z

educe
BR ɪ'djuːs, ɪ'dʒuːs, -ɨz, -ɪŋ, -t
AM i'd(j)us, ɪ'd(j)us, -əz, -ɪŋ, -t

educible
BR ɪ'djuːsɨbl, ɪ'dʒuːsɨbl
AM i'd(j)usəbəl, ɪ'd(j)usəbəl

eduction
BR ɪ'dʌkʃn
AM i'dəkʃən, ɪ'dəkʃən

eductive
BR ɪ'dʌktɪv
AM i'dəktɪv, ɪ'dəktɪv

edulcorate
BR ɪ'dʌlkəreɪt, -s, -ɪŋ, -ɨd
AM ə'dəlkəˌreɪ|t, i'dəlkəʒˌreɪ|t, -ts, -dɪŋ, -dɨd

edulcoration
BR ɪˌdʌlkə'reɪʃn
AM əˌdəlkə'reɪʃən, iˌdəlkə'reɪʃən

edutainment
BR ˌɛdjʊ'teɪnm(ə)nt, ˌɛdʒʊ'teɪnm(ə)nt

AM ˌɛdʒəˈteɪnmənt
Edward
BR ˈɛdwəd
AM ˈɛdwərd
Edwardes
BR ˈɛdwədz
AM ˈɛdwərdz
Edwardian
BR ɛdˈwɔːdɪən, -z
AM ɛdˈwardiən, -z
Edwardiana
BR ɛdˌwɔːdɪˈɑːnə(r)
AM ˌɛdˌwardiˈænə
Edwards
BR ˈɛdwədz
AM ˈɛdwərdz
Edwin
BR ˈɛdwɪn
AM ˈɛdwən
Edwina
BR ɛdˈwiːnə(r)
AM ɛdˈwɪnə, ɛdˈwinə
Edwinstowe
BR ˈɛdwɪnstəʊ
AM ˈɛdwɪnˌstoʊ
eegit
BR ˈiːdʒɪt, -s
AM ˈidʒɪt, -s
eejit
BR ˈiːdʒɪt, -s
AM ˈidʒɪt, -s
eel
BR iːl, -z
AM il, -z
Eelam
BR ˈiːlam
AM ˈilæm
eelgrass
BR ˈiːlgrɑːs, ˈiːlgras
AM ˈilˌgræs
eelpout
BR ˈiːlpaʊt, -s
AM ˈilˌpaʊt, -s
eelworm
BR ˈiːlwəːm, -z
AM ˈilˌwərm, -z
eely
BR ˈiːli
AM ˈili
e'en
BR iːn
AM in
eeny meeny miny mo
BR ˌiːnɪ ˌmiːnɪ ˌmʌɪnɪ ˈməʊ
AM ˌini ˌmini ˌmaɪni ˈmoʊ
e'er
BR ɛː(r)
AM ɛ(ə)r
eerie
BR ˈɪəri
AM ˈɪri, ˈiri
eerily
BR ˈɪərɨli
AM ˈɪrɨli
eeriness
BR ˈɪərɪnɨs
AM ˈɪrinɨs
Eeyore
BR ˈiːɔː(r)
AM ˈiɔ(ə)r
eff
BR ɛf, -s, -ɪŋ, -t
AM ɛf, -s, -ɪŋ, -t
effable
BR ˈɛfəbl
AM ˈɛfəbəl
efface
BR ɪˈfeɪs, -ɨz, -ɪŋ, -t
AM əˈfeɪs, ɛˈfeɪs, iˈfeɪs, -əz, -ɪŋ, -t
effaceable
BR ɪˈfeɪsəbl
AM əˈfeɪsəbəl, ɛˈfeɪsəbəl, iˈfeɪsəbəl
effacement
BR ɪˈfeɪsm(ə)nt
AM əˈfeɪsmənt, ɛˈfeɪsmənt, iˈfeɪsmənt
effect
BR ɪˈfɛkt, -s, -ɪŋ, -ɨd
AM əˈfɛk|(t), iˈfɛk|(t), -(t)s, -tɪŋ, -təd
effective
BR ɪˈfɛktɪv, -z
AM əˈfɛktɪv, iˈfɛktɪv, -z
effectively
BR ɪˈfɛktɨvli
AM əˈfɛktəvli, iˈfɛktəvli
effectiveness
BR ɪˈfɛktɨvnɨs
AM əˈfɛktɪvnɨs, iˈfɛktɪvnɨs
effectivity
BR ˌɛfəkˈtɪvɨti, ˌɪfɛkˈtɪvɨti
AM ˌɛfəkˈtɪvɨdi, ˌifəkˈtɪvɨdi
effector
BR ɪˈfɛktə(r), -z
AM əˈfɛktər, iˈfɛktər, -z
effectual
BR ɪˈfɛktʃʊəl, ɪˈfɛktʃ(ʉ)l, ɪˈfɛktjʊəl, ɪˈfɛktjʉl
AM əˈfɛk(t)ʃ(əw)əl, iˈfɛk(t)ʃ(əw)əl
effectuality
BR ɪˈfɛktʃʊˈalɨti, ɪˌfɛktjʊˈalɨti
AM əˌfɛk(t)ʃəˈwælədi, iˌfɛk(t)ʃəˈwælədi
effectually
BR ɪˈfɛktʃʊəli, ɪˈfɛktʃʉli, ɪˈfɛktʃl̩i, ɪˈfɛkjʊəli, ɪˈfɛktjʉli
AM əˈfɛk(t)ʃ(əw)əli, iˈfɛk(t)ʃ(əw)əli
effectualness
BR ɪˈfɛktʃʊəlnəs, ɪˈfɛktʃ(ʉ)lnəs, ɪˈfɛktjʊəlnəs, ɪˈfɛktjʉlnəs
AM əˈfɛk(t)ʃ(əw)əlnəs, iˈfɛk(t)ʃ(əw)əlnəs
effectuate
BR ɪˈfɛktʃʊeɪt, ɪˈfɛktjʊeɪt, -s, -ɪŋ, -ɨd
AM əˈfɛk(t)ʃəˌweɪ|t, iˈfɛk(t)ʃəˌweɪ|t, -ts, -dɪŋ, -dɨd
effectuation
BR ɪˌfɛktʃʊˈeɪʃn, ɪˌfɛktjʊˈeɪʃn
AM əˌfɛk(t)ʃəˈweɪʃən, iˌfɛk(t)ʃəˈweɪʃən
effeminacy
BR ɪˈfɛmɨnəsi
AM əˈfɛmənəsi, iˈfɛmənəsi
effeminate
BR ɪˈfɛmɨnət
AM əˈfɛmənət, iˈfɛmənət
effeminately
BR ɪˈfɛmɨnətli
AM əˈfɛmənətli, iˈfɛmənətli
effendi
BR ɪˈfɛnd|i, ɛˈfɛnd|i, -ɪz
AM əˈfɛndi, ɛˈfɛndi, -z
efference
BR ˈɛf(ə)rəns, ˈɛf(ə)rn̩s
AM ˈɛfərəns
efferent
BR ˈɛf(ə)rənt, ˈɛf(ə)rn̩t
AM ˈɛfərənt
effervesce
BR ˌɛfəˈvɛs, -ɨz, -ɪŋ, -t
AM ˌɛfərˈvɛs, -əz, -ɪŋ, -t
effervescence
BR ˌɛfəˈvɛsns
AM ˌɛfərˈvɛsəns
effervescency
BR ˌɛfəˈvɛsnsi
AM ˌɛfərˈvɛsənsi
effervescent
BR ˌɛfəˈvɛsnt
AM ˌɛfərˈvɛsənt
effervescently
BR ˌɛfəˈvɛsntli
AM ˌɛfərˈvɛsn(t)li
effete
BR ɪˈfiːt
AM əˈfit, iˈfit
effeteness
BR ɪˈfiːtnɨs
AM əˈfitnɨs, iˈfitnɨs
efficacious
BR ˌɛfɪˈkeɪʃəs
AM ˌɛfəˈkeɪʃəs
efficaciously
BR ˌɛfɪˈkeɪʃəsli
AM ˌɛfəˈkeɪʃəsli
efficaciousness
BR ˌɛfɪˈkeɪʃəsnəs
AM ˌɛfəˈkeɪʃəsnəs
efficacity
BR ˌɛfɪˈkasɪti
AM ˌɛfəˈkæsədi
efficacy
BR ˈɛfɨkəsi
AM ˈɛfəkəsi
efficiency
BR ɪˈfɪʃnsi
AM əˈfɪʃənsi, iˈfɪʃənsi
efficient
BR ɪˈfɪʃnt
AM əˈfɪʃənt, iˈfɪʃənt
efficiently
BR ɪˈfɪʃntli
AM əˈfɪʃən(t)li, iˈfɪʃən(t)li
Effie
BR ˈɛfi
AM ˈɛfi
effigy
BR ˈɛfɨdʒ|i, -ɪz
AM ˈɛfɨdʒi, -z
Effingham
BR ˈɛfɪŋəm
AM ˈɛfɪŋəm, ˈɛfɪŋˌhæm
effleurage
BR ˌɛflʉˈrɑːʒ, -ɨz, -ɪŋ, -d
AM ˌɛfləˈrɑʒ, ˌɛflʊˈrɑʒ, -əz, -ɪŋ, -d
effloresce
BR ˌɛfləˈrɛs, -ɨz, -ɪŋ, -t
AM ˌɛfləˈrɛs, -əz, -ɪŋ, -t
efflorescence
BR ˌɛfləˈrɛsns
AM ˌɛfləˈrɛsəns
efflorescent
BR ˌɛfləˈrɛsnt
AM ˌɛfləˈrɛsnt
effluence
BR ˈɛflʊəns
AM ˈɛˌflʊəns
effluent
BR ˈɛflʊənt, -s
AM ˈɛˌfluənt, ˈɛfləwənt, -s
effluvia
BR ɪˈfluːvɪə(r)
AM ɛˈfluviə, əˈfluviə
effluvium
BR ɪˈfluːvɪəm
AM ɛˈfluviəm, əˈfluviəm
efflux
BR ˈɛflʌks, -ɨz
AM ˈɛˌfləks, -əz
effluxion
BR ɪˈflʌkʃn, ɛˈflʌkʃn, -z
AM ɛˈflәkʃən, -z
effort
BR ˈɛfət, -s
AM ˈɛfərt, -s
effortful
BR ˈɛfətf(ʉ)l
AM ˈɛfərtfəl
effortfully
BR ˈɛfətfʉli, ˈɛfətfl̩i
AM ˈɛfərtfəli
effortless
BR ˈɛfətləs

AM 'ɛfərtləs

effortlessly
BR 'ɛfətləsli
AM 'ɛfərtləsli

effortlessness
BR 'ɛfətləsnəs
AM 'ɛfərtləsnəs

effrontery
BR ɪ'frʌnt(ə)r|i, -ɪz
AM ə'frəntəri, i'frəntəri, -z

effulgence
BR ɪ'fʌldʒ(ə)ns
AM ə'fʊldʒəns, i'fʊldʒəns, ə'fəldʒəns, i'fəldʒəns

effulgent
BR ɪ'fʌldʒ(ə)nt
AM ə'fʊldʒənt, ə'fəldʒənt, i'fʊldʒənt, i'fəldʒənt

effulgently
BR ɪ'fʌldʒ(ə)ntli
AM ə'fʊldʒən(t)li, ə'fəldʒən(t)li, i'fʊldʒən(t)li, i'fəldʒən(t)li

effuse
BR ɪ'fjuːz, -ɪz, -ɪŋ, -d
AM ə'fjuz, i'fjuz, -əz, -ɪŋ, -d

effusion
BR ɪ'fjuːʒn, -z
AM ə'fjuʒən, i'fjuʒən, -z

effusive
BR ɪ'fjuːsɪv
AM ə'fjusɪv, i'fjusɪv, ə'fjuzɪv, i'fjuzɪv

effusively
BR ɪ'fjuːsɨvli
AM ə'fjusəvli, i'fjusəvli, ə'fjuzəvli, i'fjuzəvli

effusiveness
BR ɪ'fjuːsɨvnɨs
AM ə'fjusɪvnɨs, i'fjusɪvnɨs, ə'fjuzɪvnɨs, i'fjuzɪvnɨs

Efik
BR 'ɛfɪk
AM 'ɛfɪk

eft
BR ɛft, -s
AM ɛft, -s

EFTA
BR 'ɛftə(*r*)
AM 'ɛftə

e.g.
BR ˌiː'dʒiː
AM ˌi'dʒi

egad
BR ɪ'gad
AM ˈi'gæd

egalitarian
BR ɪˌgalɪ'tɛːrɪən
AM iˌgælə'tɛriən, əˌgælə'tɛriən

egalitarianism
BR ɪˌgalə'tɛːrɪənɪz(ə)m
AM iˌgælə'tɛriəˌnɪzəm, əˌgælə'tɛriəˌnɪzəm

Egan
BR 'iːg(ə)n
AM 'igɨn

Egbert
BR 'ɛgbət
AM 'ɛgbərt

Egerton
BR 'ɛdʒət(ə)n
AM 'ɛdʒərtən

egest
BR ɪ'dʒɛst, -s, -ɪŋ, -ɨd
AM i'dʒɛst, ə'dʒɛst, -s, -ɪŋ, -əd

egg
BR ɛg, -z, -ɪŋ, -d
AM ɛg, -z, -ɪŋ, -d

eggar
BR 'ɛgə(r), -z
AM 'ɛgər, -z

eggcup
BR 'ɛgkʌp, -s
AM 'ɛgˌkəp, -s

egger
BR 'ɛgə(r), -z
AM 'ɛgər, -z

egghead
BR 'ɛghɛd, -z
AM 'ɛgˌ(h)ɛd, -z

egginess
BR 'ɛgɪnɨs
AM 'ɛginɨs

eggless
BR 'ɛgləs
AM 'ɛgləs

eggnog
BR 'ɛgnɒg, -z
AM 'ɛgˌnɔg, 'ɛgˌnɑg, -z

eggplant
BR 'ɛgplɑːnt, 'ɛgplant, -s
AM 'ɛgˌplænt, -s

eggshell
BR 'ɛgʃɛl, -z
AM 'ɛgˌʃɛl, -z

eggwhisk
BR 'ɛgwɪsk, -s
AM 'ɛgˌwɪsk, -s

eggy
BR 'ɛg|i, -ɪə(r), -ɪɨst
AM 'ɛgi, -ər, -ɨst

Egham
BR 'ɛgəm
AM 'ɛgəm

egis
BR 'iːdʒɪs
AM 'idʒəs

eglantine
BR 'ɛgləntʌɪn, 'ɛgləntiːn
AM 'ɛglənˌtin, 'ɛglənˌtaɪn

Egmont
BR 'ɛgmɒnt
AM 'ɛgˌmɑnt, 'ɛgmənt

ego
BR 'iːgəʊ, -z
AM 'igoʊ, -z

egocentric
BR ˌɛgə(ʊ)'sɛntrɪk, ˌiːgə(ʊ)'sɛntrɪk
AM ˌigoʊ'sɛntrɪk, ˌigə'sɛntrɪk

egocentrically
BR ˌɛgə(ʊ)'sɛntrɪkli, ˌiːgə(ʊ)'sɛntrɪkli
AM ˌigoʊ'sɛntrək(ə)li, ˌigə'sɛntrək(ə)li

egocentricity
BR ˌɛgə(ʊ)sɛn'trɪsɨti, ˌɛgə(ʊ)s(ə)n'trɪsɨti, ˌiːgə(ʊ)sɛn'trɪsɨti, ˌiːgə(ʊ)s(ə)n'trɪsɨti
AM ˌigoʊsɛn'trɪsɨdi, ˌigoʊsən'trɪsɨdi

egocentrism
BR ˌɛgə(ʊ)'sɛntrɪz(ə)m, ˌiːgə(ʊ)'sɛntrɪz(ə)m
AM ˌigoʊ'sɛnˌtrɪzəm, ˌigə'sɛnˌtrɪzəm

egoism
BR 'ɛgəʊɪz(ə)m, 'iːgəʊɪz(ə)m
AM 'igəˌwɪzəm, 'igoʊˌɪzəm

egoist
BR 'ɛgəʊɪst, 'iːgəʊɪst, -s
AM 'igəwəst, 'igoʊəst, -s

egoistic
BR ˌɛgəʊ'ɪstɪk, ˌiːgəʊ'ɪstɪk
AM ˌigə'wɪstɪk, ˌigoʊ'ɪstɪk

egoistical
BR ˌɛgəʊ'ɪstɪkl, ˌiːgəʊ'ɪstɪkl
AM ˌigə'wɪstɪkəl, ˌigoʊ'ɪstɪkəl

egoistically
BR ˌɛgəʊ'ɪstɪkli, ˌiːgəʊ'ɪstɪkli
AM ˌigə'wɪstɪkəli, ˌigoʊ'ɪstɪkəli

egomania
BR ˌɛgə(ʊ)'meɪnɪə(*r*), ˌiːgə(ʊ)'meɪnɪə(*r*)
AM ˌigoʊ'meɪniə

egomaniac
BR ˌɛgə(ʊ)'meɪnɪak, ˌiːgə(ʊ)'meɪnɪak, -s
AM ˌigoʊ'meɪniˌæk, -s

egomaniacal
BR ˌɛgə(ʊ)mə'nʌɪəkl, ˌiːgə(ʊ)mə'nʌɪəkl
AM ˌigoʊmə'naɪəkəl

egotise
BR 'ɛgətʌɪz, 'iːgətʌɪz, -ɪz, -ɪŋ, -d
AM 'igəˌtaɪz, 'igoʊˌtaɪz, -ɪz, -ɪŋ, -d

egotism
BR 'ɛgətɪz(ə)m, 'iːgətɪz(ə)m
AM 'igəˌtɪzəm, 'igoʊˌtɪzəm

egotist
BR 'ɛgətɪst, 'iːgətɪst, -s
AM 'igədəst, 'igətəst, 'igoʊtəst, -s

egotistic
BR ˌɛgə'tɪstɪk, ˌiːgə'tɪstɪk
AM ˌigə'tɪstɪk, ˌigoʊ'tɪstɪk

egotistical
BR ˌɛgə'tɪstɪkl, ˌiːgə'tɪstɪkl
AM ˌigə'tɪstəkəl, ˌigoʊ'tɪstəkəl

egotistically
BR ˌɛgə'tɪstɪkli, ˌiːgə'tɪstɪkli
AM ˌigə'tɪstɪk(ə)li, ˌigoʊ'tɪstɪk(ə)li

egotize
BR 'ɛgətʌɪz, 'iːgətʌɪz, -ɪz, -ɪŋ, -d
AM 'igəˌtaɪz, 'igoʊˌtaɪz, -ɪz, -ɪŋ, -d

egregious
BR ɪ'griːdʒəs
AM ə'gridʒəs, i'gridʒəs

egregiously
BR ɪ'griːdʒəsli
AM ə'gridʒəsli, i'gridʒəsli

egregiousness
BR ɪ'griːdʒəsnəs
AM ə'gridʒəsnəs, i'gridʒəsnəs

Egremont
BR 'ɛgrɪmɒnt, 'ɛgrɪm(ə)nt
AM 'ɛgrəˌmɑnt

egress
BR 'iːgrɛs, -ɪz
AM 'iˌgrɛs, -əz

egression
BR ɪ'grɛʃn, iː'grɛʃn
AM ə'grɛʃən, i'grɛʃən

egressive
BR ɪ'grɛsɪv, iː'grɛsɪv
AM ə'grɛsɪv, i'grɛsɪv

egret
BR 'iːgrɪt, -s
AM 'igrət, 'iˌgrɛt, -s

Egypt
BR 'iːdʒɪpt
AM 'idʒəp(t)

Egyptian
BR ɪ'dʒɪpʃn, -z
AM ə'dʒɪpʃən, -z

Egyptianisation
BR ɪˌdʒɪpʃn̩ʌɪ'zeɪʃn, ɪˌdʒɪpʃənʌɪ'zeɪʃn

AM ə,dʒɪpʃənə'zeɪʃən, ə,dʒɪpʃə,naɪ'zeɪʃən

Egyptianise
BR ɪ'dʒɪpʃn̩ʌɪz, ɪ'dʒɪpʃənʌɪz, -ɪz, -ɪŋ, -d
AM ə'dʒɪpʃə,naɪz, -ɪz, -ɪŋ, -d

Egyptianization
BR ɪ,dʒɪpʃn̩ʌɪ'zeɪʃn, ɪ,dʒɪpʃənʌɪ'zeɪʃn
AM ə,dʒɪpʃənə'zeɪʃən, ə,dʒɪpʃə,naɪ'zeɪʃən

Egyptianize
BR ɪ'dʒɪpʃn̩ʌɪz, ɪ'dʒɪpʃənʌɪz, -ɪz, -ɪŋ, -d
AM ə'dʒɪpʃə,naɪz, -ɪz, -ɪŋ, -d

Egyptologist
BR ,iːdʒɪp'tɒlədʒɪst, -s
AM ¦i,dʒɪp'tɑlədʒəst, -s

Egyptology
BR ,iːdʒɪp'tɒlədʒi
AM ¦i,dʒɪp'tɑlədʒi

eh
BR eɪ
AM eɪ, ɛ

Ehrlich
BR 'ɛːlɪk, 'ɛːlɪx
AM 'ɛrlɪk

Eichmann
BR 'ʌɪkmən, 'ʌɪxmən
AM 'aɪkmən

Eid
BR iːd
AM id

eider
BR 'ʌɪdə(r), -z
AM 'aɪdər, -z

eiderdown
BR 'ʌɪdədaʊn, -z
AM 'aɪdər,daʊn, -z

eidetic
BR ʌɪ'dɛtɪk
AM aɪ'dɛdɪk

eidetically
BR ʌɪ'dɛtɨkli
AM aɪ'dɛdək(ə)li

eidola
BR ʌɪ'dəʊlə(*r*)
AM aɪ'doʊlə

eidolon
BR ʌɪ'dəʊlɒn, -z
AM aɪ'doʊlən, -z

Eifel
BR 'ʌɪfl
AM 'aɪfəl

Eiffel
BR 'ʌɪfl
AM 'aɪfəl

eigenfrequency
BR 'ʌɪg(ə)n,friːkw(ə)ns|i, -ɪz
AM 'aɪgən,frikwənsi, -z

eigenfunction
BR 'ʌɪg(ə)n,fʌŋ(k)ʃn, -z
AM 'aɪgən,fəŋkʃən, -z

eigenvalue
BR 'ʌɪg(ə)n,valjuː, -z
AM 'aɪgən,vælju, -z

Eiger
BR 'ʌɪgə(r)
AM 'aɪgər

Eigg
BR ɛg
AM ɛg

eight
BR eɪt, -s
AM eɪt, -s

eighteen
BR ,eɪ'tiːn
AM ¦eɪ(t)¦tin

eighteenmo
BR ,eɪ'tiːnməʊ
AM ,eɪ(t)'tin,moʊ

eighteenth
BR ,eɪ'tiːnθ
AM ¦eɪ(t)¦tinθ

eightfold
BR 'eɪtfəʊld
AM 'eɪt¦foʊld

eighth
BR 'eɪtθ, -s
AM 'eɪ(t)θ, -s

eighthly
BR 'eɪtθli
AM 'eɪ(t)θli

eightieth
BR 'eɪtɪɨθ
AM 'eɪdiəθ

eightsome
BR 'eɪts(ə)m, -z
AM 'eɪtsəm, -z

eighty
BR 'eɪt|i, -ɪz
AM 'eɪdi, -z

eightyfold
BR 'eɪtɪfəʊld
AM 'eɪdi,foʊld

Eilat
BR eɪ'lɑːt, eɪ'lat
AM 'eɪ,lɑt

Eileen
BR 'ʌɪliːn
AM aɪ'lin

Eilidh
BR 'eɪli
AM 'eɪli

Eindhoven
BR 'ʌɪnd,həʊvn
AM 'aɪn(d),(h)oʊvən

einkorn
BR 'ʌɪnkɔːn
AM 'aɪn,kɔ(ə)rn

Einstein
BR 'ʌɪnstʌɪn
AM 'aɪn,staɪn

einsteinium
BR ʌɪn'stʌɪnɪəm
AM aɪn'staɪniəm

Éire
BR 'ɛːrə(*r*)
AM 'ɛrə
IR 'eːrʲə

eirenic
BR ʌɪ'riːnɪk, ʌɪ'rɛnɪk
AM aɪ'rɛnɪk, aɪ'rinɪk

eirenical
BR ʌɪ'riːnɨkl, ʌɪ'rɛnɨkl
AM aɪ'rinɨkl

eirenicon
BR ʌɪ'riːnɨkɒn, ʌɪ'rɛnɨkɒn, -z
AM aɪ'rɛnə,kɑn, aɪ'rɛnəkən, -z

Eirlys
BR 'ʌɪəlɪs
AM 'aɪrləs

Eisenhower
BR 'ʌɪznhaʊə(r)
AM 'aɪzən,(h)aʊər

Eisenstadt
BR 'ʌɪznstat
AM 'aɪzən,stæt

Eisenstein
BR 'ʌɪznstʌɪn, 'ʌɪznʃtʌɪn
AM 'aɪzən,staɪn, 'aɪzən,ʃtaɪn

eisteddfod
BR ʌɪ'stɛðvɒd, ʌɪ'stɛdfəd, -z
AM aɪ'stɛð,vɔd, aɪ'stɛð,vɑd, -z
WE eɪ'steðvɒd

eisteddfodau
BR ,ʌɪstɛð'vɒdʌɪ
AM ,aɪstɛð'vɑdaɪ
WE eɪ'steðvɒdaɪ

eisteddfodic
BR ,ʌɪstɛð'vɒdɪk, ,ʌɪstɛd'fɒdɪk
AM aɪ¦stɛð¦vɔdɪk, aɪ¦stɛð¦vɑdɪk

either
BR 'ʌɪðə(r), 'iːðə(r)
AM 'iðər, 'aɪðər

either/or
BR ,ʌɪðər'ɔː(r), ,iːðər'ɔː(r)
AM ¦iðər'ɔ(ə)r, ¦aɪðər'ɔ(ə)r

Eithne
BR 'ɛθni
AM 'ɛθni

ejaculate[1]
noun
BR ɪ'dʒakjʉlət
AM i'dʒækjələt, ə'dʒækjələt

ejaculate[2]
verb
BR ɪ'dʒakjʉleɪt, -s, -ɪŋ, -ɨd
AM ə'dʒækjə,leɪ|t, i'dʒækjə,leɪ|t, -ts, -dɪŋ, -dɨd

ejaculation
BR ɪ,dʒakjʉ'leɪʃn, -z
AM ə,dʒækjə'leɪʃən, i,dʒækjə'leɪʃən, -z

ejaculator
BR ɪ'dʒakjʉleɪtə(r), -z
AM ə'dʒækjə,leɪdər, i'dʒækjə,leɪdər, -z

ejaculatory
BR ɪ'dʒakjʉlət(ə)ri
AM ə'dʒækjələ,tɔri, i'dʒækjələ,tɔri

eject
BR ɪ'dʒɛkt, -s, -ɪŋ, -ɨd
AM ə'dʒɛk|(t), i'dʒɛk|(t), -(t)s, -tɪŋ, -təd

ejecta
BR ɪ'dʒɛktə(*r*)
AM ə'dʒɛktə, i'dʒɛktə

ejection
BR ɪ'dʒɛkʃn
AM ə'dʒɛkʃən, i'dʒɛkʃən

ejective
BR ɪ'dʒɛktɪv
AM ə'dʒɛktɪv, i'dʒɛktɪv

ejectment
BR ɪ'dʒɛk(t)m(ə)nt
AM ə'dʒɛk(t)mənt, i'dʒɛk(t)mənt

ejector
BR ɪ'dʒɛktə(r), -z
AM ə'dʒɛktər, i'dʒɛktər, -z

Ekaterinburg
BR ɪ'kat(ə)rɪnbəːg
AM i'kædərən,bərg
RUS jikatʲirʲin'burk

Ekco
BR 'ɛkəʊ
AM 'ɛkoʊ

eke
BR iːk, -s, -ɪŋ, -t
AM ik, -s, -ɪŋ, -t

ekistics
BR ɪ'kɪstɪks, iː'kɪstɪks
AM ə'kɪstɪks, i'kɪstɪks

ekka
BR 'ɛkə(r), -z
AM 'ɛ,kɑ, 'ɛkə, -z

Ektachrome®
BR 'ɛktəkrəʊm
AM 'ɛktə,kroʊm

el
BR ɛl, -z
AM ɛl, -z

elaborate[1]
adjective
BR ɪ'lab(ə)rət
AM ə'læb(ə)rət, i'læb(ə)rət

elaborate[2]
verb
BR ɪ'labəreɪt, -s, -ɪŋ, -ɨd
AM ə'læbə,reɪ|t, i'læbə,reɪ|t, -ts, -dɪŋ, -dɨd

elaborately
BR ɪ'lab(ə)rətli
AM ə'læb(ə)rətli, i'læb(ə)rətli

elaborateness
BR ɪ'lab(ə)rətnəs
AM ə'læb(ə)rətnəs, i'læb(ə)rətnəs
elaboration
BR ɪˌlabə'reɪʃn, -z
AM əˌlæbə'reɪʃən, iˌlæbə'reɪʃən, -z
elaborative
BR ɪ'lab(ə)rətɪv
AM ə'læbəˌreɪdɪv, ə'læbəreɪdɪv, i'læbəˌreɪdɪv, i'læbərədɪv
elaborator
BR ɪ'labəreɪtə(r), -z
AM ə'læbəˌreɪdər, i'læbəˌreɪdər, -z
Elaine
BR ɪ'leɪn
AM ə'leɪn, i'leɪn
Elam
BR 'iːlam
AM 'iˌlæm, 'iləm
Elamite
BR 'iːləmʌɪt, -s
AM 'iləˌmaɪt, -s
Elan¹
car name
BR ɪ'lan
AM ə'læn
Elan²
place in Wales
BR 'iːlən
AM 'ilən
WE 'elan
élan
BR eɪ'lan, eɪ'lɒ̃
AM eɪ'lɑn, eɪ'læn
eland
BR 'iːlənd, -z
AM 'ilənd, -z
elapid
BR 'ɛləpɪd, -z
AM 'ɛləpəd, -z
elapse
BR ɪ'laps, -ɪz, -ɪŋ, -t
AM ə'læps, i'læps, -əz, -ɪŋ, -t
elasmobranch
BR ɪ'lazməbraŋk, -s
AM ə'læzməˌbræŋk, -s
elasmosaurus
BR ɪˌlazmə'sɔːrəs, -ɪz
AM əˌlæzmə'sɔrəs, -əz
elastane
BR ɪ'lasteɪn
AM i'læsˌteɪn, ə'læsˌteɪn
elastase
BR ɪ'lasteɪz
AM i'læsˌteɪz, ə'læsˌteɪz
elastic
BR ɪ'lastɪk
AM ə'læstɪk, i'læstɪk
elastically
BR ɪ'lastɨkli
AM ə'læstək(ə)li, i'læstək(ə)li
elasticated
BR ɪ'lastɪkeɪtɨd
AM ə'læstəˌkeɪdɨd, i'læstəˌkeɪdɨd
elasticise
BR ɪ'lastɪsʌɪz, -ɪz, -ɪŋ, -d
AM ə'læstəˌsaɪz, i'læstəˌsaɪz, -ɪz, -ɪŋ, -d
elasticity
BR ˌiːla'stɪsɨti, ˌɛla'stɪsɨti
AM əˌlæ'stɪsɨdi, iˌlæ'stɪsɨdi
elasticize
BR ɪ'lastɪsʌɪz, -ɪz, -ɪŋ, -d
AM ə'læstəˌsaɪz, i'læstəˌsaɪz, -ɪz, -ɪŋ, -d
elastomer
BR ɪ'lastəmə(r), -z
AM ə'læstəmər, i'læstəmər, -z
elastomeric
BR ɪˌlastə'mɛrɪk
AM əˌlæstə'mɛrɪk, iˌlæstə'mɛrɪk
Elastoplast®
BR ɪ'lastəplɑːst, ɪ'lastəplast, -s
AM ə'læstəˌplæst, i'læstəˌplæst, -s
elate
BR ɪ'leɪt, -s, -ɪŋ, -ɨd
AM ə'leɪ|t, i'leɪ|t, -ts, -dɪŋ, -dɨd
elated
BR ɪ'leɪtɨd
AM ə'leɪdɨd, i'leɪdɨd
elatedly
BR ɪ'leɪtɨdli
AM ə'leɪdɨdli, i'leɪdɨdli
elatedness
BR ɪ'leɪtɨdnɨs
AM ə'leɪdɨdnɨs, i'leɪdɨdnɨs
elater
BR ɪ'leɪtə(r), -z
AM ə'leɪdər, i'leɪdər, -z
elation
BR ɪ'leɪʃn
AM ə'leɪʃən, i'leɪʃən
Elba
BR 'ɛlbə(*r*)
AM 'ɛlbə
Elbe
BR ɛlb
AM ɛlb
GER 'ɛlbə
Elbert
BR 'ɛlbət
AM 'ɛlbərt
elbow
BR 'ɛlbəʊ, -z
AM 'ɛlˌboʊ, -z
elbowroom
BR 'ɛlbəʊruːm, 'ɛlbəʊrʊm
AM 'ɛlboʊˌrum, 'ɛlboʊˌrʊm
Elche
BR 'ɛltʃeɪ
AM 'ɛlˌtʃeɪ
eld
BR ɛld
AM ɛld
elder
BR 'ɛldə(r), -z
AM 'ɛldər, -z
elderberry
BR 'ɛldəˌbɛr|i, 'ɛldəb(ə)r|i, -ɪz
AM 'ɛldərˌbɛri, -z
elderflower
BR 'ɛldəˌflaʊə(r), -z
AM 'ɛldərˌflaʊər, -z
elderliness
BR 'ɛldəlɪnɨs
AM 'ɛldərlinɨs
elderly
BR 'ɛldəli
AM 'ɛldərli
eldership
BR 'ɛldəʃɪp
AM 'ɛldərˌʃɪp
eldest
BR 'ɛldɨst
AM 'ɛldəst
Eldon
BR 'ɛld(ə)n
AM 'ɛldən
eldorado
BR ˌɛldə'rɑːdəʊ, -z
AM ˌɛldə'rɑdoʊ, ˌɛldə'rædoʊ, -z
eldrich
BR 'ɛldrɪtʃ
AM 'ɛldrɪtʃ
Eldridge
BR 'ɛldrɪdʒ
AM 'ɛldrɪdʒ
eldritch
BR 'ɛldrɪtʃ
AM 'ɛldrɪtʃ
Eleanor
BR 'ɛlənə
AM 'ɛlənər
Eleanora
BR ˌɛlə'nɔːrə(*r*)
AM ˌɛlə'nɔrə
Eleatic
BR ˌɛlɪ'atɪk, ˌiːlɪ'atɪk, -s
AM ˌɛli'ædɪk, -s
elecampane
BR ˌɛlɪkam'peɪn, -z
AM ˌɛləˌkæm'peɪn, ˌɛliˌkæm'peɪn, ˌɛlə'kæmˌpeɪn, ˌɛli'kæmˌpeɪn, -z
elect
BR ɪ'lɛkt, -s, -ɪŋ, -ɨd
AM ə'lɛk|(t), i'lɛk|(t), -(t)s, -tɪŋ, -təd
electable
BR ɪ'lɛktəbl
AM ə'lɛktəbəl, i'lɛktəbəl
election
BR ɪ'lɛkʃn, -z
AM ə'lɛkʃən, i'lɛkʃən, -z
electioneer
BR ɪˌlɛkʃə'nɪə(r), -z, -ɪŋ, -d
AM əˌlɛkʃə'nɪ(ə)r, iˌlɛkʃə'nɪ(ə)r, -z, -ɪŋ, -d
electioneering
BR ɪˌlɛkʃə'nɪərɪŋ
AM əˌlɛkʃə'nɪrɪŋ, iˌlɛkʃə'nɪrɪŋ
elective
BR ɪ'lɛktɪv, -z
AM ə'lɛktɪv, i'lɛktɪv, -z
electively
BR ɪ'lɛktɨvli
AM ə'lɛktəvli, i'lɛktəvli
elector
BR ɪ'lɛktə(r), -z
AM ə'lɛktər, i'lɛktər, ə'lɛkˌtɔ(ə)r, i'lɛkˌtɔ(ə)r, -z
electoral
BR ɪ'lɛkt(ə)rəl, ɪ'lɛkt(ə)rl̩
AM ə'lɛkt(ə)rəl, i'lɛkt(ə)rəl
electorally
BR ɪ'lɛkt(ə)rəli, ɪ'lɛkt(ə)rl̩i
AM ə'lɛkt(ə)rəli, i'lɛkt(ə)rəli
electorate
BR ɪ'lɛkt(ə)rət, -s
AM ə'lɛkt(ə)rət, i'lɛkt(ə)rət, -s
electorship
BR ɪ'lɛktəʃɪp, -s
AM ə'lɛktərˌʃɪp, i'lɛktərˌʃɪp, -s
Electra
BR ɪ'lɛktrə(*r*)
AM ə'lɛktrə, i'lɛktrə
Electress
BR ɪ'lɛktrɪs, -ɪz
AM ə'lɛktrəs, i'lɛktrəs, -əz
electret
BR ɪ'lɛktrɪt, -s
AM ə'lɛktrət, i'lɛktrət, -s
electric
BR ɪ'lɛktrɪk
AM ə'lɛktrɪk, i'lɛktrɪk
electrical
BR ɪ'lɛktrɪkl, -z
AM ə'lɛktrəkəl, i'lɛktrəkəl, -z
electrically
BR ɪ'lɛktrɪkli
AM ə'lɛktrək(ə)li, i'lɛktrək(ə)li

electrician
BR ɪˌlɛkˈtrɪʃn, -z
AM əˌlɛkˈtrɪʃən, iˌlɛkˈtrɪʃən, -z

electricity
BR ɪˌlɛkˈtrɪsɪti, ˌɛlɛkˈtrɪsɪti, ˌɛlɪkˈtrɪsɪti, ˌɪlɛkˈtrɪsɪti, ˌiːlɛkˈtrɪsɪti
AM əˌlɛkˈtrɪsɪdi, iˌlɛkˈtrɪsɪdi

electrification
BR ɪˌlɛktrɪfɪˈkeɪʃn
AM əˌlɛktrəfəˈkeɪʃən, iˌlɛktrəfəˈkeɪʃən

electrifier
BR ɪˈlɛktrɪfʌɪə(r), -z
AM əˈlɛktrəˌfaɪər, iˈlɛktrəˌfaɪər, -z

electrify
BR ɪˈlɛktrɪfʌɪ, -z, -ɪŋ, -d
AM əˈlɛktrəˌfaɪ, iˈlɛktrəˌfaɪ, -z, -ɪŋ, -d

electro
BR ɪˈlɛktrəʊ, -z
AM əˈlɛktroʊ, iˈlɛktroʊ, -z

electrobiology
BR ɪˌlɛktrəʊbʌɪˈɒlədʒi
AM əˌlɛktroʊbaɪˈɑlədʒi, iˌlɛktroʊbaɪˈɑlədʒi, əˌlɛktrəbaɪˈɑlədʒi, iˌlɛktrəbaɪˈɑlədʒi

electrocardiogram
BR ɪˌlɛktrəʊˈkɑːdɪəgram, -z
AM əˌlɛktroʊˈkɑrdiəˌgræm, əˌlɛktroʊˈkɑrdioʊˌgræm, əˌlɛktrəˈkɑrdiəˌgræm, iˌlɛktroʊˈkɑrdiəˌgræm, iˌlɛktroʊˈkɑrdioʊˌgræm, iˌlɛktrəˈkɑrdiəˌgræm, -z

electrocardiograph
BR ɪˌlɛktrəʊˈkɑːdɪəgrɑːf, ɪˌlɛktrəʊˈkɑːdɪəgraf, -s
AM əˌlɛktroʊˈkɑrdɪəˌgræf, əˌlɛktroʊˈkɑrdioʊˌgræf, əˌlɛktrəˈkɑrdiəˌgræf, iˌlɛktroʊˈkɑrdiəˌgræf, iˌlɛktroʊˈkɑrdioʊˌgræf, iˌlɛktrəˈkɑrdiəˌgræf, -s

electrocardiographic
BR ɪˌlɛktrəʊˌkɑːdɪəˈgrafɪk
AM əˌlɛktroʊˌkɑrdɪəˈgræfɪk, əˌlɛktroʊˌkɑrdioʊˈgræfɪk, əˌlɛktrəˌkɑrdiəˈgræfɪk, iˌlɛktroʊˌkɑrdiəˈgræfɪk, iˌlɛktroʊˌkɑrdioʊˈgræfɪk, iˌlɛktrəˌkɑrdiəˈgræfɪk

electrocardiography
BR ɪˌlɛktrəʊˈkɑːdɪˈɒgrəfi
AM əˌlɛktroʊˌkɑrdiˈɑgrəfi, əˌlɛktrəˌkɑrdiˈɑgrəfi, iˌlɛktrəˌkɑrdiˈɑgrəfi, iˌlɛktroʊˌkɑrdiˈɑgrəfi

electrochemical
BR ɪˌlɛktrəʊˈkɛmɪkl
AM əˌlɛktroʊˈkɛməkəl, əˌlɛktrəˈkɛməkəl, iˌlɛktrəˈkɛməkəl, iˌlɛktroʊˈkɛməkəl

electrochemically
BR ɪˌlɛktrəʊˈkɛmɪkli
AM əˌlɛktroʊˈkɛmək(ə)li, əˌlɛktrəˈkɛmək(ə)li, iˌlɛktrəˈkɛmək(ə)li, iˌlɛktroʊˈkɛmək(ə)li

electrochemist
BR ɪˌlɛktrəʊˈkɛmɪst, -s
AM əˌlɛktroʊˈkɛməst, əˌlɛktrəˈkɛməst, iˌlɛktrəˈkɛməst, iˌlɛktroʊˈkɛməst, -s

electrochemistry
BR ɪˌlɛktrəʊˈkɛmɪstri
AM əˌlɛktroʊˈkɛməstri, əˌlɛktrəˈkɛməstri, iˌlɛktrəˈkɛməstri, iˌlɛktroʊˈkɛməstri

electroconvulsive
BR ɪˌlɛktrəʊkənˈvʌlsɪv
AM əˌlɛktroʊkənˈvəlsɪv, əˌlɛktrəkənˈvəlsɪv, iˌlɛktrəkənˈvəlsɪv, iˌlɛktroʊkənˈvəlsɪv

electrocute
BR ɪˈlɛktrəkjuːt, -s, -ɪŋ, -ɪd
AM əˈlɛktrəˌkju|t, iˈlɛktrəˌkju|t, -ts, -dɪŋ, -dəd

electrocution
BR ɪˌlɛktrəˈkjuːʃn, -z
AM əˌlɛktrəˈkjuʃən, iˈlɛktrəˈkjuʃən, -z

electrode
BR ɪˈlɛktrəʊd, -z
AM əˈlɛktroʊd, iˈlɛktroʊd, -z

electrodialysis
BR ɪˌlɛtrə(ʊ)dʌɪˈalɪsɪs
AM əˌlɛktroʊˌdaɪˈæləsəs, əˌlɛktrəˌdaɪˈæləsəs, iˌlɛktroʊˌdaɪˈæləsəs, iˌlɛktrəˌdaɪˈæləsəs

electrodynamic
BR ɪˌlɛtrə(ʊ)dʌɪˈnamɪk, -s
AM əˌlɛktroʊˌdaɪˈnæmɪk, əˌlɛktrəˌdaɪˈnæmɪk, iˌlɛktroʊˌdaɪˈnæmɪk, iˌlɛktrəˌdaɪˈnæmɪk, -s

electrodynamically
BR ɪˌlɛtrə(ʊ)dʌɪˈnamɪkli
AM əˌlɛktroʊˌdaɪˈnæmək(ə)li, əˌlɛktrəˌdaɪˈnæmək(ə)li, iˌlɛktroʊˌdaɪˈnæmək(ə)li, iˌlɛktrəˌdaɪˈnæmək(ə)li

electroencephalogram
BR ɪˌlɛktrəʊɪnˈsɛf(ə)ləgram, ɪˌlɛktrəʊɪnˈsɛfl̩əgram, ɪˌlɛktrəʊɛnˈsɛf(ə)ləgram, ɪˌlɛktrəʊɛnˈsɛfl̩əgram, ɪˌlɛktrəʊɪnˈkɛf(ə)ləgram, ɪˌlɛktrəʊɪnˈkɛfl̩əgram, ɪˌlɛktrəʊɛnˈkɛf(ə)ləgram, ɪˌlɛktrəʊɛnˈkɛfl̩əgram, -z
AM əˌlɛktroʊənˈsɛfələgræm, iˌlɛktroʊənˈsɛfələgræm, -z

electroencephalograph
BR ɪˌlɛktrəʊɪnˈsɛf(ə)ləgrɑːf, ɪˌlɛktrəʊɛnˈsɛf(ə)ləgrɑːf, ɪˌlɛktrəʊɪnˈkɛf(ə)ləgrɑːf, ɪˌlɛktrəʊɛnˈkɛf(ə)ləgrɑːf, ɪˌlɛktrəʊɪnˈsɛf(ə)ləgraf, ɪˌlɛktrəʊɛnˈsɛf(ə)ləgraf, ɪˌlɛktrəʊɪnˈkɛf(ə)ləgraf, ɪˌlɛktrəʊɛnˈkɛf(ə)ləgraf, -s
AM əˌlɛktroʊənˈsɛfələgræf, iˌlɛktroʊənˈsɛfələgræf, -s

electroencephalography
BR ɪˌlɛktrəʊɪnˌsɛfəˈlɒgrəfi, ɪˌlɛktrəʊɛnˌsɛfəˈlɒgrəfi, ɪˌlɛktrəʊɪnˌkɛfəˈlɒgrəfi, ɪˌlɛktrəʊɛnˌkɛfəˈlɒgrəfi
AM əˌlɛktroʊˌɛnˌsɛfəˈlɑgrəfi, iˌlɛktroʊˌɛnˌsɛfəˈlɑgrəfi

electroluminescence
BR ɪˌlɛktrəʊˌluːmɪˈnɛsns
AM əˌlɛktroʊˌluməˈnɛsəns, iˌlɛktroʊˌluməˈnɛsəns

electroluminescent
BR ɪˌlɛktrəʊˌluːmɪˈnɛsnt
AM əˌlɛktroʊˌluməˈnɛsənt, iˌlɛktroʊˌluməˈnɛsənt

Electrolux®
BR ɪˈlɛktrə(ʊ)lʌks
AM əˈlɛktrəˌləks

electrolyse
BR ɪˈlɛktrəlʌɪz, -ɪz, -ɪŋ, -d
AM əˈlɛktrəˌlaɪz, iˈlɛktrəˌlaɪz, -ɪz, -ɪŋ, -d

electrolyser
BR ɪˈlɛktrəlʌɪzə(r), -z
AM əˈlɛktrəˌlaɪzər, iˈlɛktrəˌlaɪzər, -z

electrolysis
BR ɪˌlɛkˈtrɒlɪsɪs, ˌɛlɛkˈtrɒlɪsɪs, ˌɛlɪkˈtrɒlɪsɪs, ˌɪlɛkˈtrɒlɪsɪs, ˌiːlɛkˈtrɒlɪsɪs
AM əˌlɛkˈtrɑləsəs, iˌlɛkˈtrɑləsəs

electrolyte
BR ɪˈlɛktrəlʌɪt, -s
AM əˈlɛktrəˌlaɪt, iˈlɛktrəˌlaɪt, -s

electrolytic
BR ɪˌlɛktrəˈlɪtɪk
AM əˌlɛktrəˈlɪdɪk, iˌlɛktrəˈlɪdɪk

electrolytical
BR ɪˌlɛktrəˈlɪtɪkl
AM əˌlɛktrəˈlɪdɪkəl, iˌlɛktrəˈlɪdɪkəl

electrolytically
BR ɪˌlɛktrəˈlɪtɪkli
AM əˌlɛktrəˈlɪdɪk(ə)li, iˌlɛktrəˈlɪdɪk(ə)li

electrolyze
BR ɪˈlɛktrəlʌɪz, -ɪz, -ɪŋ, -d
AM əˈlɛktrəˌlaɪz, iˈlɛktrəˌlaɪz, -ɪz, -ɪŋ, -d

electrolyzer
BR ɪˈlɛktrəlʌɪzə(r), -z
AM əˈlɛktrəˌlaɪzər, iˈlɛktrəˌlaɪzər, -z

electromagnet
BR ɪˌlɛktrə(ʊ)ˈmagnɪt, -s
AM əˌlɛktrəˈmægnət, iˌlɛktrəˈmægnət, -s

electromagnetic
BR ɪˌlɛktrə(ʊ)magˈnɛtɪk
AM əˌlɛktrəˌmægˈnɛdɪk, iˌlɛktrəˌmægˈnɛdɪk

electromagnetically
BR ɪˌlɛktrə(ʊ)magˈnɛtɪkli
AM əˌlɛktrəˌmægˈnɛdək(ə)li, iˌlɛktrəˌmægˈnɛdək(ə)li

electromagnetism
BR ɪˌlɛktrə(ʊ)ˈmagnɪtɪz(ə)m

AM ə,lɛktrə'mægnə,tɪzəm, i,lɛktrə'mægnə,tɪzəm

electromechanical
BR ɪ,lɛktrə(ʊ)mɪ'kanɪkl
AM ə,lɛktrəmə'kænəkəl, i,lɛktrəmə'kænəkəl

electrometer
BR ɪ,lɛk'trɒmɪtə(r), -z
AM ə,lɛk'trɑmədər, i,lɛk'trɑmədər, -z

electrometric
BR ɪ,lɛktrə(ʊ)'mɛtrɪk
AM ə,lɛktrə'mɛtrɪk, i,lɛktrə'mɛtrɪk

electrometry
BR ɪ,lɛk'trɒmɪtri, ,ɛlɛk'trɒmɪtri, ,ɛlɪk'trɒmɪtri, ,ɪlɛk'trɒmɪtri, ,i:lɛk'trɒmɪtri
AM ə,lɛk'trɑmətri, i,lɛk'trɑmətri

electromotive
BR ɪ,lɛktrə(ʊ)'məʊtɪv
AM ə,lɛktrə'moʊdɪv, i,lɛktrə'moʊdɪv

electron
BR ɪ'lɛktrɒn, -z
AM ə'lɛk,trɑn, i'lɛk,trɑn, -z

electronegative
BR ɪ,lɛktrə(ʊ)'nɛgətɪv
AM ə,lɛktrə'nɛgədɪv, i,lɛktrə'nɛgədɪv

electronic
BR ɪ,lɛk'trɒnɪk, ,ɛlɛk'trɒnɪk, ,ɛlɪk'trɒnɪk, ,ɪlɛk'trɒnɪk, ,i:lɛk'trɒnɪk, -s
AM ə,lɛk'trɑnɪk, i,lɛk'trɑnɪk, -s

electronically
BR ɪ,lɛk'trɒnɪkli, ,ɛlɛk'trɒnɪkli, ,ɪlɛk'trɒnɪkli, ,i:lɛk'trɒnɪkli
AM ə,lɛk'trɑnək(ə)li, i,lɛk'trɑnək(ə)li

electronvolt
BR ɪ'lɛktrɒn,vəʊlt, -s
AM ə'lɛktrɑn,voʊlt, i'lɛktrɑn,voʊlt, -s

electrophile
BR ɪ'lɛktrə(ʊ)fʌɪl, -z
AM ə'lɛktrə,faɪl, i'lɛktrə,faɪl, -z

electrophilic
BR ɪ,lɛktrə(ʊ)'fɪlɪk
AM ə,lɛktrə'fɪlɪk, i,lɛktrə'fɪlɪk

electrophonic
BR ɪ,lɛtrə(ʊ)'fɒnɪk
AM ə,lɛktrə'fɑnɪk

electrophoreses
BR ɪ,lɛktrə(ʊ)fə'ri:si:z
AM ə,lɛktrəfə'risiz, i,lɛktrəfə'risiz

electrophoresic
BR ɪ,lɛktrə(ʊ)fə'ri:sɪk
AM ə,lɛktrəfə'risɪk, i,lɛktrəfə'risɪk

electrophoresis
BR ɪ,lɛktrə(ʊ)fə'ri:sɪs
AM ə,lɛktrəfə'risɪs, i,lɛktrəfə'risɪs

electrophoretic
BR ɪ,lɛktrə(ʊ)fə'rɛtɪk
AM ə,lɛktrəfə'rɛdɪk, i,lɛktrəfə'rɛdɪk

electrophorus
BR ɪ,lɛk'trɒf(ə)rəs, ,ɛlɛk'trɒf(ə)rəs, ,ɛlɪk'trɒf(ə)rəs, ,ɪlɛk'trɒf(ə)rəs, ,i:lɛk'trɒf(ə)rəs
AM ə,lɛk'trɑf(ə)rəs, i,lɛk'trɑf(ə)rəs

electrophysiological
BR ɪ,lɛktrəʊ,fɪzɪə'lɒdʒɪkl
AM ə,lɛktrə,fɪziə'lɑdʒəkəl, i,lɛktrə,fɪziə'lɒdʒəkəl

electrophysiology
BR ɪ,lɛktrəʊ,fɪzɪ'ɒlədʒi
AM ə,lɛktrə,fɪzi'ɑlədʒi, i,lɛktrə,fɪzi'ɑlədʒi

electroplate
BR ɪ'lɛktrə(ʊ)pleɪt, ɪ,lɛtrə(ʊ)'pleɪt, -s, -ɪŋ, -ɪd
AM ə'lɛktrə,pleɪ|t, i'lɛktrə,pleɪ|t, -ts, -dɪŋ, -dɪd

electroplater
BR ɪ'lɛktrə(ʊ)pleɪtə(r), ɪ,lɛktrə(ʊ)'pleɪtə(r), -z
AM ə'lɛktrə,pleɪdər, i'lɛktrə,pleɪdər, -z

electroplexy
BR ɪ'lɛktrə(ʊ)plɛksi
AM ə'lɛktrə,plɛksi, i'lɛktrə,plɛksi

electropositive
BR ɪ,lɛktrəʊ'pɒzɪtɪv
AM ə,lɛktrə'pɑzədɪv, i,lɛktrə'pɑzədɪv

electroscope
BR ɪ'lɛktrəskəʊp, -s
AM ə'lɛktrə,skoʊp, i'lɛktrə,skoʊp, -s

electroscopic
BR ɪ,lɛktrə(ʊ)'skɒpɪk
AM ə,lɛktrə'skɑpɪk, i,lɛktrə'skɑpɪk

electrostatic
BR ɪ,lɛktrə(ʊ)'statɪk, -s
AM ə,lɛktrə'stædɪk, i,lɛktrə'stædɪk, -s

electrotechnic
BR ɪ,lɛktrəʊ'tɛknɪk, -s
AM ə,lɛktrə'tɛknɪk, i,lɛktrə'tɛknɪk, -s

electrotechnical
BR ɪ,lɛktrəʊ'tɛknɪkl
AM ə,lɛktrə'tɛknəkəl, i,lɛktrə'tɛknəkəl

electrotechnology
BR ɪ,lɛktrəʊtɛk'nɒlədʒi
AM ə,lɛktrə,tɛk'nɑlədʒi, i,lɛktrə,tɛk'nɑlədʒi

electrotherapeutic
BR ɪ,lɛktrəʊ,θɛrə'pju:tɪk
AM ə,lɛktrə,θɛrə'pjudɪk, i,lɛktrə,θɛrə'pjudɪk

electrotherapeutical
BR ɪ,lɛktrəʊ,θɛrə'pju:tɪkl
AM ə,lɛktrə,θɛrə'pjudəkəl, i,lɛktrə,θɛrə'pjudəkəl

electrotherapist
BR ɪ,lɛktrəʊ'θɛrəpɪst, -s
AM ə,lɛktrə'θɛrəpəst, i,lɛktrə'θɛrəpəst, -s

electrotherapy
BR ɪ,lɛktrəʊ'θɛrəpi
AM ə,lɛktrə'θɛrəpi, i,lɛktrə'θɛrəpi

electrothermal
BR ɪ,lɛktrəʊ'θə:ml
AM ə,lɛktrə'θərməl, i,lɛktrə'θərməl

electrotype
BR ɪ'lɛktrə(ʊ)tʌɪp, -s
AM ə'lɛktrə,taɪp, i'lɛktrə,taɪp, -s

electrotyper
BR ɪ'lɛktrə(ʊ),tʌɪpə(r), -z
AM ə'lɛktrə,taɪpər, i'lɛktrə,taɪpər, -z

electrovalence
BR ɪ,lɛktrəʊ'veɪləns, ɪ,lɛktrəʊ'veɪlṇs
AM ə,lɛktrə'veɪləns, i,lɛktrə'veɪləns

electrovalency
BR ɪ,lɛktrəʊ'veɪlənsi, ɪ,lɛktrəʊ'veɪlṇsi
AM ə,lɛktrə'veɪlənsi, i,lɛktrə'veɪlənsi

electrovalent
BR ɪ,lɛktrəʊ'veɪlənt, ɪ,lɛktrəʊ'veɪlṇt
AM ə,lɛktrə'veɪlənt, i,lɛktrə'veɪlənt

electrum
BR ɪ'lɛktrəm
AM ə'lɛktrəm, i'lɛktrəm

electuary
BR ɪ'lɛktjʊər|i, ɪ'lɛktʃʊər|i, ɪ'lɛktʃ(ʊ)r|i, -ɪz
AM ə'lɛktʃə,wɛri, i'lɛktʃə,wɛri, -z

eleemosynary
BR ,ɛl(ɪ)i:'mɒs(ɪ)nəri, ,ɛl(ɪ)i:'mɒsṇəri
AM ,ɛlə'mɑsṇəri

elegance
BR 'ɛlɪg(ə)ns
AM 'ɛləgəns

elegant
BR 'ɛlɪg(ə)nt
AM 'ɛləgənt

elegantly
BR 'ɛlɪg(ə)ntli
AM 'ɛləgən(t)li

elegiac
BR ,ɛlɪ'dʒʌɪək, -s
AM ,ɛlə'dʒaɪək, -s

elegiacal
BR ,ɛlɪ'dʒʌɪəkl
AM ,ɛlə'dʒaɪəkəl

elegiacally
BR ,ɛlɪ'dʒʌɪəkli
AM ,ɛlə'dʒaɪək(ə)li

elegise
BR 'ɛlɪdʒʌɪz, -ɪz, -ɪŋ, -d
AM 'ɛlə,dʒaɪz, -ɪz, -ɪŋ, -d

elegist
BR 'ɛlɪdʒɪst, -s
AM 'ɛlədʒəst, -s

elegize
BR 'ɛlɪdʒʌɪz, -ɪz, -ɪŋ, -d
AM 'ɛlə,dʒaɪz, -ɪz, -ɪŋ, -d

elegy
BR 'ɛlədʒ|i, -ɪz
AM 'ɛlədʒi, -z

element
BR 'ɛlɪm(ə)nt, -s
AM 'ɛləmənt, -s

elemental
BR ,ɛlɪ'mɛntl, -z
AM ,ɛlə'mɛn(t)l, -z

elementalism
BR ,ɛlɪ'mɛntəlɪz(ə)m, ,ɛlɪ'mɛntḷɪz(ə)m
AM ,ɛlə'mɛn(t)l,ɪzəm

elementally
BR ,ɛlɪ'mɛntəli, ,ɛlɪ'mɛntḷi
AM ,ɛlə'mɛn(t)ḷi

elementarily
BR ,ɛlɪ'mɛnt(ə)rɪli
AM ,ɛlə'mɛnt(ə)rəli

elementariness
BR ,ɛlɪ'mɛnt(ə)rɪnɪs
AM ,ɛlə'mɛnt(ə)rinɪs

elementary
BR ,ɛlɪ'mɛnt(ə)ri
AM ,ɛlə'mɛnt(ə)ri

elemi
BR 'ɛləm|i, -ɪz
AM 'ɛləmi, -z

elenchus
BR ɪ'lɛŋkəs
AM ə'lɛŋkəs, i'lɛŋkəs

elenctic
BR ɪ'lɛŋktɪk

AM ə'lɛŋktɪk, i'lɛŋktɪk

Eleonora
BR ˌɛlɪə'nɔːrə(r)
AM ˌɛlə'nɔrə

elephant
BR 'ɛlɨf(ə)nt, -s
AM 'ɛləfənt, -s

elephantiasis
BR ˌɛlɨf(ə)n'tʌɪəsɪs
AM ˌɛləfən'taɪəsəs

elephantine
BR ˌɛlɨ'fantʌɪn
AM ˌɛlə'fænˌtin, ˌɛlə'fænˌtaɪn, 'ɛləfənˌtin, 'ɛləfənˌtaɪn

elephantoid
BR ˌɛlɨ'fantɔɪd
AM ˌɛlə'fænˌtɔɪd, 'ɛləfənˌtɔɪd

Eleusinian
BR ˌɛljʊ'sɪnɪən
AM ˌɛl(j)u'sɪniən

Eleusis
BR ɪ'ljuːsɪs
AM ə'l(j)usɪs

elevate
BR 'ɛlɨveɪt, -s, -ɪŋ, -ɨd
AM 'ɛləˌveɪ|t, -ts, -dɪŋ, -dɨd

elevation
BR ˌɛlɨ'veɪʃn, -z
AM ˌɛlə'veɪʃən, -z

elevational
BR ˌɛlɨ'veɪʃn̩(ə)l, ˌɛlɨ'veɪʃən(ə)l
AM ˌɛlə'veɪʃ(ə)nəl

elevator
BR 'ɛlɨveɪtə(r), -z
AM 'ɛləˌveɪdər, -z

elevatory
BR ˌɛlɨ'veɪt(ə)ri
AM 'ɛləvəˌtɔri

eleven
BR ɪ'lɛvn
AM ə'lɛvən, i'lɛvən

elevenfold
BR ɪ'lɛvnfəʊld
AM ə'lɛvənˌfoʊld, i'lɛvənˌfoʊld

elevenses
BR ɪ'lɛvnzɪz
AM ə'lɛvənzəz, i'lɛvənzəz

eleventh
BR ɪ'lɛvnθ
AM ə'lɛvənθ, i'lɛvənθ

elevon
BR 'ɛlɨvɒn, -z
AM 'ɛləˌvɑn, -z

elf
BR ɛlf
AM ɛlf

Elfed
BR 'ɛlvɛd
AM 'ɛlvɛd

elfin
BR 'ɛlfɪn
AM 'ɛlfən

elfish
BR 'ɛlfɪʃ
AM 'ɛlfɪʃ

elfishly
BR 'ɛlfɨʃli
AM 'ɛlfɨʃli

elfishness
BR 'ɛlfɪʃnɨs
AM 'ɛlfɪʃnɨs

elfland
BR 'ɛlfland
AM 'ɛlˌflænd

elflock
BR 'ɛlflɒk, -s
AM 'ɛlˌflɑk, -s

Elfreda
BR ɛl'friːdə(r)
AM ˌɛl'fridə

Elfrida
BR ɛl'friːdə(r)
AM ˌɛl'fridə

Elgar
BR 'ɛlgɑː(r), 'ɛlgə(r)
AM 'ɛlgɑr

Elgin
BR 'ɛlgɪn
AM 'ɛlgən

El Giza
BR ˌɛl 'giːzə(r)
AM ˌɛl 'gizə

Elgon
BR 'ɛlgɒn
AM 'ɛlˌgɑn

El Greco
BR ˌɛl 'grɛkəʊ
AM ˌɛl 'grɛkoʊ

Eli
BR 'iːlʌɪ
AM 'iˌlaɪ

Elia
BR 'iːlɪə(r)
AM 'iljə, 'iliə

Elias
BR ɪ'lʌɪəs
AM ə'laɪəs, i'laɪəs

elicit
BR ɪ'lɪs|ɪt, -ɪts, -ɨtɪŋ, -ɨtɨd
AM ə'lɪsə|t, i'lɪsə|t, -ts, -dɪŋ, -dəd

elicitation
BR ɪˌlɪsɨ'teɪʃn, -z
AM əˌlɪsə'teɪʃən, iˌlɪsə'teɪʃən, -z

elicitor
BR ɪ'lɪsɨtə(r), -z
AM ə'lɪsədər, i'lɪsədər, -z

elide
BR ɪ'lʌɪd, -z, -ɪŋ, -ɨd
AM ə'laɪd, i'laɪd, -z, -ɪŋ, -ɨd

eligibility
BR ˌɛlɨdʒɨ'bɪlɨti
AM ˌɛlədʒə'bɪlɨdi

eligible
BR 'ɛlɨdʒɨbl
AM 'ɛlədʒəbəl

eligibly
BR 'ɛlɨdʒɨbli
AM 'ɛlədʒəbli

Elihu
BR ɪ'lʌɪhjuː, ɛ'lʌɪhjuː
AM 'ɛləh(j)u

Elijah
BR ɪ'lʌɪdʒə(r)
AM ə'laɪ(d)ʒə, i'laɪ(d)ʒə

Elim
BR 'iːlɪm
AM 'ilɨm

eliminable
BR ɪ'lɪmɨnəbl
AM ə'lɪmənəbəl, i'lɪmənəbəl

eliminate
BR ɪ'lɪmɨneɪt, -s, -ɪŋ, -ɨd
AM ə'lɪməˌneɪ|t, i'lɪməˌneɪ|t, -ts, -dɪŋ, -dɨd

elimination
BR ɪˌlɪmɨ'neɪʃn
AM əˌlɪmə'neɪʃən, iˌlɪmə'neɪʃən

eliminator
BR ɪ'lɪmɨneɪtə(r), -z
AM ə'lɪməˌneɪdər, i'lɪməˌneɪdər, -z

eliminatory
BR ɪ'lɪmɨnət(ə)ri
AM ə'lɪmənəˌtɔri, i'lɪmənəˌtɔri

Elinor
BR 'ɛlɨnə(r)
AM 'ɛlənər

ELINT
electronic intelligence
BR ɪ'lɪnt
AM 'ɛˌlɪnt

Eliot
BR 'ɛlɪət
AM 'ɛliət

Elisabeth
BR ɪ'lɪzəbəθ
AM ə'lɪz(ə)bəθ

Elisabethville
BR ɪ'lɪzəbəθvɪl
AM ə'lɪz(ə)bəθˌvɪl

Elisha
BR ɪ'lʌɪʃə(r)
AM ə'laɪʃə

elision
BR ɪ'lɪʒn, -z
AM ə'lɪʒən, -z

élite
BR ɪ'liːt, eɪ'liːt, -s
AM ə'lit, eɪ'lit, -s

élitism
BR ɪ'liːtɪz(ə)m, eɪ'liːtɪz(ə)m
AM ə'lidɪzəm, eɪ'lidɪzəm

élitist
BR ɪ'liːtɪst, eɪ'liːtɪst, -s
AM ə'lidəst, eɪ'lidəst, -s

elixir
BR ɪ'lɪks(ɪ)ə(r), -z
AM ə'lɪksər, i'lɪksər, -z

Eliza
BR ɪ'lʌɪzə(r)
AM ə'laɪzə

Elizabeth
BR ɪ'lɪzəbəθ
AM ə'lɪz(ə)bəθ

Elizabethan
BR ɪˌlɪzə'biːθn, -z
AM əˌlɪzə'biθən, iˌlɪzə'biθən, -z

elk
BR ɛlk, -s
AM ɛlk, -s

elkhound
BR 'ɛlkhaʊnd, -z
AM 'ɛlkˌ(h)aʊnd, -z

Elkie
BR 'ɛlki
AM 'ɛlki

Elkins
BR 'ɛlkɪnz
AM 'ɛlkənz

ell
BR ɛl, -z
AM ɛl, -z

Ella
BR 'ɛlə(r)
AM 'ɛlə

Elland
BR 'ɛlənd
AM 'ɛlənd

Ellen
BR 'ɛlən
AM 'ɛlən

Ellery
BR 'ɛl(ə)ri
AM 'ɛləri

Ellesmere
BR 'ɛlzmɪə(r)
AM 'ɛlzˌmɪ(ə)r

Ellice
BR 'ɛlɪs
AM 'ɛləs

Ellie
BR 'ɛli
AM 'ɛli

Ellington
BR 'ɛlɪŋt(ə)n
AM 'ɛlɪŋtən

Elliot
BR 'ɛlɪət
AM 'ɛliət

Elliott
BR 'ɛlɪət
AM 'ɛliət

ellipse
BR ɪ'lɪps, -ɪz
AM ə'lɪps, i'lɪps, -ɪz

ellipses
plural of ellipsis
BR ɪ'lɪpsiːz

AM ə'lɪpsiz, i'lɪpsiz
ellipsis
BR ɪ'lɪpsɪs
AM ə'lɪpsɨs, i'lɪpsɨs
ellipsoid
BR ɪ'lɪpsɔɪd
AM ə'lɪpsɔɪd, i'lɪpsɔɪd
ellipsoidal
BR ˌɛlɪp'sɔɪdl, ˌɪlɪp'sɔɪdl, ɪˌlɪp'sɔɪdl
AM ˌɛləp'sɔɪdəl, ˌiləp'sɔɪdəl
ellipt
BR ɪ'lɪpt, -s, -ɪŋ, -ɨd
AM ə'lɪpt, i'lɪpt, -s, -ɪŋ, -ɨd
elliptic
BR ɪ'lɪptɪk
AM ə'lɪptɪk, i'lɪptɪk
elliptical
BR ɪ'lɪptɨkl
AM ə'lɪptɨkl, i'lɪptɨkl
elliptically
BR ɪ'lɪptɨkli
AM ə'lɪptɨk(ə)li, i'lɪptɨk(ə)li
ellipticity
BR ˌɛlɪp'tɪsɨti, ˌɪlɪp'tɪsɨti, ɪˌlɪp'tɪsɨti
AM əˌlɪp'tɪsɨdi, iˌlɪp'tɪsɨdi
Ellis
BR 'ɛlɪs
AM 'ɛləs
Ellison
BR 'ɛlɪs(ə)n
AM 'ɛləsən
Ellsworth
BR 'ɛlzwəːθ
AM 'ɛlzˌwərθ
Ellul
BR 'iːlʌl, 'ɛlʌl
AM 'ɛləl
elm
BR ɛlm, -z
AM ɛlm, -z
Elmer
BR 'ɛlmə(r)
AM 'ɛlmər
Elmet
BR 'ɛlmɪt
AM 'ɛlmət
Elmo
BR 'ɛlməʊ
AM 'ɛlmoʊ
Elmwood
BR 'ɛlmwʊd
AM 'ɛlmˌwʊd
elmy
BR 'ɛlmi
AM 'ɛlmi
El Niño
BR ɛl 'niːnjəʊ
AM ˌɛl 'ninjoʊ
elocution
BR ˌɛlə'kjuːʃn
AM ˌɛlə'kjuʃən
elocutionary
BR ˌɛlə'kjuːʃn̩(ə)ri
AM ˌɛlə'kjuʃəˌnɛri
elocutionist
BR ˌɛlə'kjuːʃnɪst, ˌɛlə'kjuːʃənɪst, -s
AM ˌɛlə'kjuʃənəst, -s
Elohim
BR ɛ'ləʊhɪm, ɪ'ləʊhɪm, ˌɛləʊ'hiːm
AM ɛ'loʊˌhɪm, ə'loʊˌhɪm, ˌɛloʊ'him
Elohist
BR ɛ'ləʊhɪst, ɪ'ləʊhɪst, -s
AM ɛ'loʊ(h)əst, ə'loʊ(h)əst, -s
Eloise
BR ˌɛləʊ'iːz, 'ɛləʊiːz
AM 'ɛləˌwiz
elongate
BR 'iːlɒŋgeɪt, -s, -ɪŋ, -ɨd
AM ə'lɔŋˌgeɪ|t, i'lɔŋˌgeɪ|t, i'lɑŋˌgeɪ|t, ə'lɑŋˌgeɪ|t, -ts, -dɪŋ, -dɨd
elongation
BR ˌiːlɒŋ'geɪʃn, -z
AM əˌlɔŋ'geɪʃən, iˌlɔŋ'geɪʃən, iˌlɑŋ'geɪʃən, əˌlɑŋ'geɪʃən, -z
elope
BR ɪ'ləʊp, -s, -ɪŋ, -t
AM ə'loʊp, i'loʊp, -s, -ɪŋ, -t
elopement
BR ɪ'ləʊpm(ə)nt, -s
AM ə'loʊpmənt, i'loʊpmənt, -s
eloper
BR ɪ'ləʊpə(r), -z
AM ə'loʊpər, i'loʊpər, -z
eloquence
BR 'ɛləkw(ə)ns
AM 'ɛləkwəns
eloquent
BR 'ɛləkw(ə)nt
AM 'ɛləkwənt
eloquently
BR 'ɛləkw(ə)ntli
AM 'ɛləkwən(t)li
El Paso
BR ɛl 'pasəʊ
AM ˌɛl 'pæsoʊ
Elphick
BR 'ɛlfɪk
AM 'ɛlfɪk
Elroy
BR 'ɛlrɔɪ
AM 'ɛlrɔɪ
Elsa
BR 'ɛlsə(r)
AM 'ɛlzə, 'ɛlsə
Elsan®
BR 'ɛlsan
AM 'ɛlzən, 'ɛlsən
Elsbeth
BR 'ɛlsbəθ
AM 'ɛlzbəθ
else
BR ɛls
AM ɛls
elsewhere
BR ɛls'wɛː(r), 'ɛlswɛː(r)
AM 'ɛlsˌ(h)wɛ(ə)r
Elsie
BR 'ɛlsi
AM 'ɛlsi
Elsinore
BR 'ɛlsɪnɔː(r)
AM 'ɛlsəˌnɔ(ə)r
Elspeth
BR 'ɛlspəθ
AM 'ɛlspəθ
Elstree
BR 'ɛlstriː
AM 'ɛlsˌtri
Elsworthy
BR 'ɛlzwəːði
AM 'ɛlzˌwərði
Eltham
BR 'ɛltəm
AM 'ɛltəm
Elton
BR 'ɛlt(ə)n
AM 'ɛltən
eluant
BR 'ɛljʊənt, -s
AM 'ɛl(j)əwənt, -s
eluate
BR 'ɛljʊət, -s
AM 'ɛl(j)əwət, 'ɛl(j)əˌweɪt, -s
elucidate
BR ɪ'l(j)uːsɪdeɪt, -s, -ɪŋ, -ɨd
AM ə'lusəˌdeɪ|t, i'lusəˌdeɪ|t, -ts, -dɪŋ, -dɨd
elucidation
BR ɪˌl(j)uːsɪ'deɪʃn
AM əˌlusə'deɪʃən, iˌlusə'deɪʃən
elucidative
BR ɪ'l(j)uːsɪdeɪtɪv
AM ə'lusəˌdeɪdɪv, i'lusəˌdeɪdɪv
elucidator
BR ɪ'l(j)uːsɪdeɪtə(r), -z
AM ə'lusəˌdeɪdər, i'lusəˌdeɪdər, -z
elucidatory
BR ɪ'l(j)uːsɪdeɪt(ə)ri, ɪˌl(j)uːsɪ'deɪt(ə)ri
AM ə'lusədəˌtɔri, i'lusədəˌtɔri
elude
BR ɪ'l(j)uːd, -z, -ɪŋ, -ɨd
AM ə'lud, i'lud, -z, -ɪŋ, -əd
eluent
BR 'ɛljʊənt, -s
AM 'ɛl(j)əwənt, -s
Elul
BR 'iːlʌl, 'ɛlʌl
AM 'ɛləl
Eluned
BR ɛ'lɪnɛd
AM ə'lɪnəd
WE e'lɪned
elusive
BR ɪ'l(j)uːsɪv
AM ə'lusɪv, i'lusɪv
elusively
BR ɪ'l(j)uːsɨvli
AM ə'lusɨvli, i'lusɨvli
elusiveness
BR ɪ'l(j)uːsɪvnɨs
AM ə'lusɪvnɨs, i'lusɪvnɨs
elusory
BR ɪ'l(j)uːs(ə)ri
AM i'luzəri, ə'luzəri, ə'lusəri, i'lusəri
elute
BR ɪ'l(j)uːt, -s, -ɪŋ, -ɨd
AM ə'lu|t, i'lu|t, -ts, -dɪŋ, -dəd
elution
BR ɪ'l(j)uːʃn
AM ə'luʃən, i'luʃən
elutriate
BR ɪ'l(j)uːtrɪeɪt, -s, -ɪŋ, -ɨd
AM ə'lutriˌeɪ|t, i'lutriˌeɪ|t, -ts, -dɪŋ, -dɨd
elutriation
BR ɪˌl(j)uːtrɪ'eɪʃn
AM əˌlutri'eɪʃən, iˌlutri'eɪʃən
elver
BR 'ɛlvə(r), -z
AM 'ɛlvər, -z
elves
BR ɛlvz
AM ɛlvz
Elvira
BR ɛl'vɪərə(r), ɛl'vʌɪrə(r)
AM ɛl'vaɪrə
Elvis
BR 'ɛlvɪs
AM 'ɛlvəs
elvish
BR 'ɛlvɪʃ
AM 'ɛlvɪʃ
elvishly
BR 'ɛlvɨʃli
AM 'ɛlvɨʃli
elvishness
BR 'ɛlvɪʃnɨs
AM 'ɛlvɪʃnɨs
Elwes
BR 'ɛlwɪz
AM 'ɛlwəz
Ely[1]
forename
BR 'iːlʌɪ
AM 'iˌlaɪ

Ely²
place in UK
BR 'iːli
AM 'ili

Elyot
BR 'ɛlɪət
AM 'ɛliɪt

Élysée
BR ɪ'liːzeɪ, eɪ'liːzeɪ
AM ˌeli'zeɪ

Elysian
BR ɪ'lɪzɪən
AM ə'lɪʒ(i)ən, ɛ'lɪʒ(i)ən, i'lɪʒ(i)ən

Elysium
BR ɪ'lɪzɪəm
AM ə'lɪʒiəm, ə'lɪziəm, ɛ'lɪʒiəm, ɛ'lɪziəm, i'lɪʒiəm, i'lɪziəm

elytra
BR 'ɛlɪtrə(r)
AM 'ɛlətrə

elytron
BR 'ɛlɪtrɒn, 'ɛlɪtr(ə)n
AM 'ɛləˌtrɑn

Elzevir
BR 'ɛlzɪvɪə(r)
AM 'ɛlzəˌvɪ(ə)r

em
BR ɛm, -z
AM ɛm, -z

'em
BR əm, m
AM əm, m

emaciate
BR ɪ'meɪsɪeɪt, ɪ'meɪʃɪeɪt, -s, -ɪŋ, -ɪd
AM ə'meɪʃiˌeɪ|t, i'meɪʃiˌeɪ|t, -ts, -dɪŋ, -dɪd

emaciation
BR ɪˌmeɪsɪ'eɪʃn
AM əˌmeɪʃi'eɪʃən, iˌmeɪʃi'eɪʃən

email
BR 'iːmeɪl, -z, -ɪŋ, -d
AM 'iˌmeɪl, -z, -ɪŋ, -d

e-mail
BR 'iːmeɪl, -z, -ɪŋ, -d
AM 'iˌmeɪl, -z, -ɪŋ, -d

emanate
BR 'ɛməneɪt, -s, -ɪŋ, -ɪd
AM 'ɛməˌneɪ|t, -ts, -dɪŋ, -dɪd

emanation
BR ˌɛmə'neɪʃn, -z
AM ˌɛmə'neɪʃən, -z

emanative
BR 'ɛməneɪtɪv, 'ɛmənətɪv
AM 'ɛməˌneɪdɪv

emancipate
BR ɪ'mansɪpeɪt, -s, -ɪŋ, -ɪd
AM ə'mænsəˌpeɪ|t, i'mænsəˌpeɪ|t, -ts, -dɪŋ, -dɪd

emancipation
BR ɪˌmansɪ'peɪʃn
AM əˌmænsə'peɪʃən, iˌmænsə'peɪʃən

emancipationist
BR ɪˌmansɪ'peɪʃn̩ɪst, ɪˌmansɪ'peɪʃənɪst, -s
AM əˌmænsə'peɪʃənəst, iˌmænsə'peɪʃənəst, -s

emancipator
BR ɪ'mansɪpeɪtə(r), -z
AM ə'mænsəˌpeɪdər, i'mænsəˌpeɪdər, -z

emancipatory
BR ɪ'mansɪpət(ə)ri, ɪˌmansɪ'peɪt(ə)ri
AM ə'mænsəpəˌtɔri, i'mænsəpəˌtɔri

Emanuel
BR ɪ'manjʊ(ə)l
AM ə'mænjəwəl

emasculate
BR ɪ'maskjʊleɪt, -s, -ɪŋ, -ɪd
AM ə'mæskjəˌleɪ|t, i'mæskjəˌleɪ|t, -ts, -dɪŋ, -dɪd

emasculation
BR ɪˌmaskjʊ'leɪʃn
AM əˌmæskjə'leɪʃən, iˌmæskjə'leɪʃən

emasculator
BR ɪ'maskjʊleɪtə(r), -z
AM ə'mæskjəˌleɪdər, i'mæskjəˌleɪdər, -z

emasculatory
BR ɪ'maskjʊlət(ə)ri
AM ə'mæskjələˌtɔri, i'mæskjələˌtɔri

embalm
BR ɪm'bɑːm, ɛm'bɑːm, -z, -ɪŋ, -d
AM əm'bɑ(l)m, ɛm'bɑ(l)m, -z, -ɪŋ, -d

embalmer
BR ɪm'bɑːmə(r), ɛm'bɑːmə(r), -z
AM əm'bɑ(l)mər, ɛm'bɑ(l)mər, -z

embalmment
BR ɪm'bɑːmm(ə)nt, ɛm'bɑːmm(ə)nt
AM əm'bɑ(m)mənt, ɛm'bɑ(m)mənt, əm'bɑ(l)mənt, ɛm'bɑ(l)mənt

embank
BR ɪm'baŋ|k, ɛm'baŋ|k, -ks, -kɪŋ, -(k)t
AM əm'bæŋ|k, ɛm'bæŋ|k, -ks, -kɪŋ, -(k)t

embankment
BR ɪm'baŋkm(ə)nt, ɛm'baŋkm(ə)nt, -s
AM əm'bæŋkmənt, ɛm'bæŋkmənt, -s

embarcation
BR ˌɛmbɑː'keɪʃn, -z
AM ˌɛmˌbɑr'keɪʃən, -z

embargo
BR ɪm'bɑːgəʊ, ɛm'bɑːgəʊ, -z, -ɪŋ, -d
AM əm'bɑrgoʊ, ɛm'bɑrgoʊ, -z, -ɪŋ, -d

embark
BR ɪm'bɑːk, ɛm'bɑːk, -s, -ɪŋ, -t
AM əm'bɑrk, ɛm'bɑrk, -s, -ɪŋ, -t

embarkation
BR ˌɛmbɑː'keɪʃn, -z
AM ˌɛmˌbɑr'keɪʃən, -z

embarras de choix
BR ɒmˌbarɑː də 'ʃwɑː(r)
AM ˌɑmbɑ'rɑ də 'ʃwɑ

embarras de richesse
BR ɒmˌbarɑː də rɪ'ʃɛs
AM ˌɑmbɑ'rɑ də ri'ʃɛs

embarrass
BR ɪm'barəs, ɛm'barəs, -ɪz, -ɪŋ, -t
AM əm'bɛrəs, ɛm'bɛrəs, -əz, -ɪŋ, -t

embarrassedly
BR ɪm'barəstli, ɛm'barəstli, ɪm'barəsɪdli, ɛm'barəsɪdli
AM əm'bɛrəstli, ɛm'bɛrəstli, əm'bɛrəsədli, ɛm'bɛrəsədli

embarrassing
BR ɪm'barəsɪŋ, ɛm'barəsɪŋ
AM əm'bɛrəsɪŋ, ɛm'bɛrəsɪŋ

embarrassingly
BR ɪm'barəsɪŋli, ɛm'barəsɪŋli
AM əm'bɛrəsɪŋli, ɛm'bɛrəsɪŋli

embarrassment
BR ɪm'barəsm(ə)nt, ɛm'barəsm(ə)nt, -s
AM əm'bɛrəsmənt, ɛm'bɛrəsmənt, -s

embassy
BR 'ɛmbəs|i, -ɪz
AM 'ɛmbəsi, -z

embattle
BR ɪm'bat|l, ɛm'bat|l, -lz, -l̩ɪŋ\-lɪŋ, -ld
AM əm'bædəl, ɛm'bædəl, -z, -ɪŋ, -d

embattled
BR ɪm'batld, ɛm'batld
AM əm'bædld, ɛm'bædld

embay
BR ɪm'beɪ, ɛm'beɪ, -z, -ɪŋ, -d
AM əm'beɪ, ɛm'beɪ, -z, -ɪŋ, -d

embayment
BR ɪm'beɪm(ə)nt, ɛm'beɪm(ə)nt
AM əm'beɪmənt, ɛm'beɪmənt

embed
BR ɪm'bɛd, ɛm'bɛd, -z, -ɪŋ, -ɪd
AM əm'bɛd, ɛm'bɛd, -z, -ɪn, -əd

embedment
BR ɪm'bɛdm(ə)nt, ɛm'bɛdm(ə)nt
AM əm'bɛdmənt, ɛm'bɛdmənt

embellish
BR ɪm'bɛl|ɪʃ, ɛm'bɛl|ɪʃ, -ɪʃɪz, -ɪʃɪŋ, -ɪʃt
AM əm'bɛlɪʃ, ɛm'bɛlɪʃ, -ɪz, -ɪŋ, -t

embellisher
BR ɪm'bɛlɪʃə(r), ɛm'bɛlɪʃə(r), -z
AM əm'bɛlɪʃər, ɛm'bɛlɪʃər, -z

embellishment
BR ɪm'bɛlɪʃm(ə)nt, ɛm'bɛlɪʃm(ə)nt, -s
AM əm'bɛlɪʃmənt, ɛm'bɛlɪʃmənt, -s

ember
BR 'ɛmbə(r), -z
AM 'ɛmbər, -z

embezzle
BR ɪm'bɛz|l, ɛm'bɛz|l, -lz, -l̩ɪŋ\-lɪŋ, -ld
AM əm'bɛz|əl, ɛm'bɛz|əl, -əlz, -(ə)lɪŋ, -əld

embezzlement
BR ɪm'bɛzlm(ə)nt, ɛm'bɛzlm(ə)nt, -s
AM əm'bɛzəlmənt, ɛm'bɛzəlmənt, -s

embezzler
BR ɪm'bɛzlə(r), ɛm'bɛzlə(r), -z
AM əm'bɛzlər, ɛm'bɛzlər, əm'bɛzl̩ər, ɛm'bɛzl̩ər, -z

embitter
BR ɪm'bɪt|ə(r), ɛm'bɪt|ə(r), -əz, -(ə)rɪŋ, -əd
AM əm'bɪdər, ɛm'bɪdər, -z, -ɪŋ, -d

embitterment
BR ɪm'bɪtəm(ə)nt, ɛm'bɪtəm(ə)nt
AM əm'bɪdərmənt, ɛm'bɪdərmənt

emblazon
BR ɪm'bleɪz|n, ɛm'bleɪz|n, -nz, -n̩ɪŋ\-ənɪŋ, -nd
AM əm'bleɪzən, ɛm'bleɪzən, -z, -ɪŋ, -d

emblazonment
BR ɪm'bleɪznm(ə)nt, ɛm'bleɪznm(ə)nt
AM əm'bleɪzənmənt, ɛm'bleɪzənmənt

emblazonry
BR ɪm'bleɪznri, ɛm'bleɪznri
AM əm'bleɪzənri, ɛm'bleɪzənri

emblem
BR 'ɛmbləm, -z
AM 'ɛmbləm, -z

emblematic
BR ˌɛmblə'matɪk
AM ˌɛmblə'mædɪk

emblematical
BR ˌɛmblə'matɪkl
AM ˌɛmblə'mædəkəl

emblematically
BR ˌɛmblə'matɪkli
AM ˌɛmblə'mædək(ə)li

emblematise
BR ɛm'blɛmətʌɪz, -ɪz, -ɪŋ, -d
AM ɛm'blɛməˌtaɪz, -ɪz, -ɪŋ, -d

emblematize
BR ɛm'blɛmətʌɪz, -ɪz, -ɪŋ, -d
AM ɛm'blɛməˌtaɪz, -ɪz, -ɪŋ, -d

emblements
BR 'ɛmblɪm(ə)nts
AM ɛm'blɛmən(t)s

embodiment
BR ɪm'bɒdɪm(ə)nt, ɛm'bɒdɪm(ə)nt, -s
AM əm'bɑdəmənt, ɛm'bɑdəmənt, əm'bɑdimənt, ɛm'bɑdimənt, -s

embody
BR ɪm'bɒd|i, ɛm'bɒd|i, -ɪz, -ɪɪŋ, -ɪd
AM əm'bɑdi, -z, -ɪŋ, -d

embolden
BR ɪm'bəʊld|(ə)n, ɛm'bəʊld|(ə)n, -(ə)nz, -ənɪŋ\-n̩ɪŋ, -(ə)nd
AM əm'boʊld|ən, ɛm'boʊld|ən, -ənz, -(ə)nɪŋ, -ənd

emboli
BR 'ɛmbəlʌɪ, 'ɛmbəliː
AM 'ɛmbəˌlaɪ

embolic
BR ɛm'bɒlɪk
AM ɛm'bɑlɪk

embolism
BR 'ɛmbəlɪz(ə)m, -z
AM 'ɛmbəˌlɪzəm, -z

embolismic
BR ˌɛmbə'lɪzmɪk
AM ˌɛmbə'lɪzmɪk

embolus
BR 'ɛmbələs
AM 'ɛmbələs

embonpoint
BR ˌɒmbɒn'pwa(r), ˌɒ̃bɒ̃'pwɒ̃(r)
AM ˌɑmbɔn'pwɑn

embosom
BR ɪm'bʊz|(ə)m, ɛm'bʊz|(ə)m, -(ə)mz, -əmɪŋ\-m̩ɪŋ, -(ə)md
AM əm'bʊzəm, ɛm'bʊzəm, -z, -ɪŋ, -d

emboss
BR ɪm'bɒs, ɛm'bɒs, -ɪz, -ɪŋ, -t
AM əm'bɔs, ɛm'bɔs, əm'bɑs, ɛm'bɑs, -əz, -ɪŋ, -t

embosser
BR ɪm'bɒsə(r), ɛm'bɒsə(r), -z
AM əm'bɔsər, ɛm'bɑsər, əm'bɔsər, ɛm'bɑsər, -z

embossment
BR ɪm'bɒsm(ə)nt, ɛm'bɒsm(ə)nt, -s
AM əm'bɔsmənt, ɛm'bɔsmənt, əm'bɑsmənt, ɛm'bɑsmənt, -s

embouchure
BR ˌɒmbʉ'ʃʊə(r), -z
AM ˌɑmbu'ʃʊ(ə)r, -z

embowel
BR ɪm'baʊəl, ɛm'baʊəl, -z, -ɪŋ, -d
AM əm'baʊəl, ɛm'baʊəl, -z, -ɪŋ, -d

embower
BR ɪm'baʊə(r), ɛm'baʊə(r), -z, -ɪŋ, -d
AM əm'baʊər, ɛm'baʊər, -z, -ɪŋ, -d

embrace
BR ɪm'breɪs, ɛm'breɪs, -ɪz, -ɪŋ, -t
AM əm'breɪs, ɛm'breɪs, -ɪz, -ɪŋ, -t

embraceable
BR ɪm'breɪsəbl, ɛm'breɪsəbl
AM əm'breɪsəbəl, ɛm'breɪsəbəl

embracement
BR ɪm'breɪsm(ə)nt, ɛm'breɪsm(ə)nt, -s
AM əm'breɪsmənt, ɛm'breɪsmənt, -s

embracer
BR ɪm'breɪsə(r), ɛm'breɪsə(r), -z
AM əm'breɪsər, ɛm'breɪsər, -z

embranchment
BR ɪm'bran(t)ʃm(ə)nt, ɛm'bran(t)ʃm(ə)nt, -s
AM əm'bræn(t)ʃmənt, ɛm'bræn(t)ʃmənt, -s

embrangle
BR ɪm'braŋgl, ɛm'braŋgl, -z, -ɪŋ, -d
AM əm'bræŋg|əl, ɛm'bræŋg|əl, -əlz, -(ə)lɪŋ, -əld

embranglement
BR ɪm'braŋglm(ə)nt, ɛm'braŋglm(ə)nt
AM əm'bræŋglmənt, ɛm'bræŋglmənt

embrasure
BR ɪm'breɪʒə(r), ɛm'breɪʒə(r), -z, -d
AM əm'breɪʒər, ɛm'breɪʒər, -z, -d

embrittle
BR ɪm'brɪt|l, ɛm'brɪt|l, -lz, -l̩ɪŋ\-lɪŋ, -ld
AM əm'brɪdəl, ɛm'brɪdəl, -z, -ɪŋ, -d

embrittlement
BR ɪm'brɪtlm(ə)nt, ɛm'brɪtlm(ə)nt
AM əm'brɪdlmənt, ɛm'brɪdlmənt

embrocation
BR ˌɛmbrə'keɪʃn, -z
AM ˌɛmbrə'keɪʃən, -z

embroider
BR ɪm'brɔɪd|ə(r), ɛm'brɔɪd|ə(r), -əz, -(ə)rɪŋ, -əd
AM əm'brɔɪdər, ɛm'brɔɪdər, -z, -ɪŋ, -d

embroiderer
BR ɪm'brɔɪd(ə)rə(r), ɛm'brɔɪd(ə)rə(r), -z
AM əm'brɔɪdərər, ɛm'brɔɪdərər, -z

embroidery
BR ɪm'brɔɪd(ə)ri, ɛm'brɔɪd(ə)ri
AM əm'brɔɪd(ə)ri, ɛm'brɔɪd(ə)ri

embroil
BR ɪm'brɔɪl, ɛm'brɔɪl, -z, -ɪŋ, -d
AM əm'brɔɪl, ɛm'brɔɪl, -z, -ɪŋ, -d

embroilment
BR ɪm'brɔɪlm(ə)nt, ɛm'brɔɪlm(ə)nt, -s
AM əm'brɔɪlmənt, ɛm'brɔɪlmənt, -s

embrown
BR ɪm'braʊn, ɛm'braʊn, -z, -ɪŋ, -d
AM əm'braʊn, ɛm'braʊn, -z, -ɪŋ, -d

embryo
BR 'ɛmbrɪəʊ, -z
AM 'ɛmbriˌoʊ, -z

embryogenesis
BR ˌɛmbrɪəʊ'dʒɛnɪsɪs
AM ˌɛmbrioʊ'dʒɛnəsəs

embryoid
BR 'ɛmbrɪɔɪd
AM 'ɛmbriˌɔɪd

embryologic
BR ˌɛmbrɪə'lɒdʒɪk
AM ˌɛmbriə'lɑdʒɪk

embryological
BR ˌɛmbrɪə'lɒdʒɪkl
AM ˌɛmbriə'lɑdʒəkəl

embryologically
BR ˌɛmbrɪə'lɒdʒɪkli
AM ˌɛmbriə'lɑdʒək(ə)li

embryologist
BR ˌɛmbrɪ'ɒlədʒɪst, -s
AM ˌɛmbri'ɑlədʒəst, -s

embryology
BR ˌɛmbrɪ'ɒlədʒi
AM ˌɛmbri'ɑlədʒi

embryonal
BR ɪm'brʌɪənl, ɛm'brʌɪənl
AM ɛm'braɪənəl

embryonic
BR ˌɛmbrɪ'ɒnɪk
AM ˌɛmbri'ɑnɪk

embryonically
BR ˌɛmbrɪ'ɒnɪkli
AM ˌɛmbri'ɑnək(ə)li

Embury
BR 'ɛmb(ə)ri, 'ɛmbjʊri
AM 'ɛmbəri

embus
BR ɪm'bʌs, ɛm'bʌs, -ɪz, -ɪŋ, -t
AM əm'bəs, ɛm'bəs, -əz, -ɪŋ, -t

emcee
BR ˌɛm'siː, -z
AM ˌɛm'si, -z

Emeline
BR 'ɛmɪliːn
AM 'ɛməˌlaɪn

emend
BR ɪ'mɛnd, iː'mɛnd, -z, -ɪŋ, -ɪd
AM ə'mɛnd, i'mɛnd, -z, -ɪŋ, -əd

emendation
BR ˌiːmɛn'deɪʃn, -z
AM ˌimən'deɪʃən, ˌɛmən'deɪʃən, -z

emendator
BR 'iːmɛndeɪtə(r), -z
AM 'imɛnˌdeɪdər, 'ɛmənˌdeɪdər, -z

emendatory
BR ɪ'mɛndət(ə)ri
AM ə'mɛndəˌtɔri

Emeny
BR 'ɛməni
AM 'ɛməni

emerald
BR 'ɛm(ə)rəld, 'ɛm(ə)rl̩d, -z

AM ˈɛm(ə)rəld, -z
emeraldine
BR ˈɛm(ə)rəldiːn, ˈɛmr̩diːn
AM ˈɛm(ə)rəlˌdin, ˈɛm(ə)rəlˌdaɪn
emerge
BR ɪˈməːdʒ, -ɪz, -ɪŋ, -d
AM əˈmərdʒ, iˈmərdʒ, -əz, -ɪŋ, -d
emergence
BR ɪˈməːdʒ(ə)ns
AM əˈmərdʒəns, iˈmərdʒəns
emergency
BR ɪˈməːdʒ(ə)ns|i, -ɪz
AM əˈmərdʒənsi, iˈmərdʒənsi, -z
emergent
BR ɪˈməːdʒ(ə)nt
AM əˈmərdʒənt, iˈmərdʒənt
emergently
BR ɪˈməːdʒ(ə)ntli
AM əˈmərdʒən(t)li, iˈmərdʒən(t)li
emeritus
BR ɪˈmɛrɪtəs
AM əˈmɛrədəs, iˈmɛrədəs
emerse
BR ɪˈməːs, -t
AM əˈmərs, iˈmərs, -t
emersion
BR ɪˈməːʃn
AM əˈmərʒən, iˈmərʒn
Emerson
BR ˈɛməs(ə)n
AM ˈɛmərsən
emery
BR ˈɛm(ə)ri
AM ˈɛm(ə)ri
emesis
BR ˈɛməsɪs
AM ˈɛməsəs
emetic
BR ɪˈmɛtɪk, -s
AM əˈmɛdɪk, iˈmɛdɪk, -s
émeute
BR eɪˈməːt, -s
AM eɪˈmʊt, -s
emigrant
BR ˈɛmɪgr(ə)nt, -s
AM ˈɛməgrənt, -s
emigrate
BR ˈɛmɪgreɪt, -s, -ɪŋ, -ɪd
AM ˈɛməˌgreɪ|t, -ts, -dɪŋ, -dɪd
emigration
BR ˌɛmɪˈgreɪʃn
AM ˌɛməˈgreɪʃən
emigratory
BR ˈɛmɪgreɪt(ə)ri
AM ˈɛməgrəˌtɔri
emigré
BR ˈɛmɪgreɪ, -z
AM ˈɛməˌgreɪ, -z
émigré
BR ˈɛmɪgreɪ, -z
AM ˈɛməˌgreɪ, -z
Emil
BR ɛˈmiːl
AM ˈeɪmɨl
Emile
BR ɛˈmiːl
AM əˈmil
Emily
BR ˈɛmɪli, ˈɛml̩i
AM ˈɛm(ə)li
eminence
BR ˈɛmɪnəns, -ɪz
AM ˈɛmənəns, -əz
éminence grise
BR ˌɛmɪnəns ˈgriːz
AM ˌɛmənəns ˈgriz
eminent
BR ˈɛmɪnənt
AM ˈɛmənənt
eminently
BR ˈɛmɪnəntli
AM ˈɛmənən(t)li
emir
BR ɛˈmɪə(r), ɪˈmɪə(r), eɪˈmɪə(r), -z
AM əˈmɪ(ə)r, eɪˈmɪ(ə)r, -z
emirate
BR ˈɛmɪrət, ˈɛmɪərət, ɛˈmɪərət, ɛˈmɪəreɪt, -s
AM əˈmɪˌreɪt, əˈmɪrət, ˈɛməˌreɪt, ˈɛmərət, -s
emissary
BR ˈɛmɪs(ə)r|i, -ɪz
AM ˈɛməˌsɛri, -z
emission
BR ɪˈmɪʃn, -z
AM əˈmɪʃən, iˈmɪʃən, -z
emissive
BR ɪˈmɪsɪv
AM əˈmɪsɪv, iˈmɪsɪv
emissivity
BR ˌiːmɪˈsɪvɪti, ˌɪmɪˈsɪvɪti, ˌɛmɪˈsɪvɪti
AM ˌɛməˈsɪvɨdi, ˌiməˈsɪvɨdi
emit
BR ɪˈmɪt, -s, -ɪŋ, -ɪd
AM əˈmɪ|t, iˈmɪ|t, -ts, -dɪŋ, -dɪd
emitter
BR ɪˈmɪtə(r), -z
AM əˈmɪdər, iˈmɪdər, -z
Emley
BR ˈɛmli
AM ˈɛmli
Emlyn
BR ˈɛmlɪn
AM ˈɛmlən
Emma
BR ˈɛmə(*r*)
AM ˈɛmə
Emmanuel
BR ɪˈmanjʊəl, ɪˈmanjʉl
AM əˈmænjə(wə)l
Emmaus
BR ɪˈmeɪəs
AM əˈmeɪəs
Emmeline
BR ˈɛməliːn
AM ˈɛmɛˌlaɪn
Emmental
BR ˈɛməntɑːl
AM ˈɛmənˌtɑl
Emmentaler
BR ˈɛməntɑːlə(r)
AM ˈɛmənˌtɑlər
Emmenthal
BR ˈɛməntɑːl
AM ˈɛmənˌtɑl
Emmenthaler
BR ˈɛməntɑːlə(r)
AM ˈɛmənˌtɑlər
emmer
BR ˈɛmə(r)
AM ˈɛmər
Emmerson
BR ˈɛməs(ə)n
AM ˈɛmərsən
emmet
BR ˈɛmɪt, -s
AM ˈɛmət, -s
emmetropia
BR ˌɛmɪˈtrəʊpɪə(*r*)
AM ˌɛməˈtroʊpiə
emmetropic
BR ˌɛmɪˈtrɒpɪk, ˌɛmɪˈtrəʊpɪk
AM ˌɛməˈtrɑpɪk
Emmy
BR ˈɛm|i, -ɪz
AM ˈɛmi, -z
emollience
BR ɪˈmɒlɪəns
AM əˈmɑljəns, iˈmɑljəns
emollient
BR ɪˈmɒlɪənt, -s
AM əˈmɑljənt, iˈmɑljənt, -s
emolument
BR ɪˈmɒljʉm(ə)nt
AM əˈmɑljəmənt, iˈmɑljəmənt
Emory
BR ˈɛm(ə)ri
AM ˈɛməri
emote
BR ɪˈməʊt, -s, -ɪŋ, -ɪd
AM əˈmoʊ|t, iˈmoʊ|t, -ts, -dɪŋ, -dəd
emoter
BR ɪˈməʊtə(r), -z
AM əˈmoʊdər, iˈmoʊdər, -z
emoticon
BR ɪˈmɒtɪkɒn, ɪˈməʊtɪkɒn, -z
AM əˈmoʊdəˌkɑn, iˈmoʊdəˌkɑn, -z
emotion
BR ɪˈməʊʃn, -z
AM əˈmoʊʃən, iˈmoʊʃən, -z
emotional
BR ɪˈməʊʃn̩(ə)l, ɪˈməʊʃən(ə)l
AM əˈmoʊʃ(ə)nəl
emotionalise
BR ɪˈməʊʃn̩əlʌɪz, ɪˈməʊʃn̩lʌɪz, ɪˈməʊʃənl̩ʌɪz, ɪˈməʊʃ(ə)nəlʌɪz, -ɪz, -ɪŋ, -d
AM əˈmoʊʃənəˌlaɪz, iˈmoʊʃənəˌlaɪz, -ɪz, -ɪŋ, -d
emotionalism
BR ɪˈməʊʃn̩əlɪz(ə)m, ɪˈməʊʃn̩l̩ɪz(ə)m, ɪˈməʊʃənl̩ɪz(ə)m, ɪˈməʊʃ(ə)nəlɪz(ə)m
AM əˈmoʊʃənlˌɪzəm, əˈmoʊʃnəˌlɪzəm, iˈmoʊʃənlˌɪzəm, iˈmoʊʃnəˌlɪzəm
emotionalist
BR ɪˈməʊʃn̩əlɪst, ɪˈməʊʃn̩l̩ɪst, ɪˈməʊʃənl̩ɪst, ɪˈməʊʃ(ə)nəlɪst, -s
AM əˈmoʊʃənələst, əˈmoʊʃnələst, -s
emotionality
BR ɪˌməʊʃəˈnalɪti
AM əˌmoʊʃəˈnælədi, iˌmoʊʃəˈnælədi
emotionalize
BR ɪˈməʊʃn̩əlʌɪz, ɪˈməʊʃn̩lʌɪz, ɪˈməʊʃənl̩ʌɪz, ɪˈməʊʃ(ə)nəlʌɪz, -ɪz, -ɪŋ, -d
AM əˈmoʊʃənəˌlaɪz, iˈmoʊʃənəˌlaɪz, -ɪz, -ɪŋ, -d
emotionally
BR ɪˈməʊʃn̩əli, ɪˈməʊʃn̩l̩i, ɪˈməʊʃənl̩i, ɪˈməʊʃ(ə)nəli
AM əˈmoʊʃ(ə)nəli
emotionless
BR ɪˈməʊʃnləs
AM əˈmoʊʃənləs
emotive
BR ɪˈməʊtɪv
AM əˈmoʊdɪv, iˈmoʊdɪv
emotively
BR ɪˈməʊtɪvli
AM əˈmoʊdəvli, iˈmoʊdəvli
emotiveness
BR ɪˈməʊtɪvnɪs
AM əˈmoʊdɪvnɪs, iˈmoʊdɪvnɪs
emotivity
BR ɪˌməʊˈtɪvɪti

AM əˌmoʊ'tɪvɨdi, iˌmoʊ'tɪvɨdi

empanel
BR ɪm'panl, ɛm'panl, -z, -ɪŋ, -d
AM əm'pænl, -z, -ɪŋ, -d

empanelment
BR ɪm'panlm(ə)nt
AM əm'pænlmənt

empathetic
BR ˌɛmpə'θɛtɪk
AM ˌɛmpə'θɛdɪk

empathetically
BR ˌɛmpə'θɛtɨkli
AM ˌɛmpə'θɛdək(ə)li

empathic
BR ɪm'paθɪk, ɛm'paθɪk
AM əm'pæθɪk, ɛm'pæθɪk

empathically
BR ɪm'paθɨkli, ɛm'paθɨkli
AM əm'pæθək(ə)li, ɛm'pæθək(ə)li

empathise
BR 'ɛmpəθʌɪz, -ɨz, -ɪŋ, -d
AM 'ɛmpəˌθaɪz, -ɨz, -ɪŋ, -d

empathist
BR 'ɛmpəθɪst, -s
AM 'ɛmpəθəst, -s

empathize
BR 'ɛmpəθʌɪz, -ɨz, -ɪŋ, -d
AM 'ɛmpəˌθaɪz, -ɨz, -ɪŋ, -d

empathy
BR 'ɛmpəθi
AM 'ɛmpəθi

Empedocles
BR ɛm'pɛdəkliːz
AM ɛm'pɛdəˌkliz

empennage
BR ɪm'pɛnɪdʒ, ɛm'pɛnɪdʒ, -ɪz
AM ˌɑmpə'nɑʒ, ˌɛmpə'nɑ(d)ʒ, -əz

emperor
BR 'ɛmp(ə)rə(r), -z
AM 'ɛmp(ə)rər, -z

emperorship
BR 'ɛmp(ə)rəʃɪp, -s
AM 'ɛmp(ə)rərˌʃɪp, -s

emphases
BR 'ɛmfəsiːz
AM 'ɛmfəˌsiz

emphasis
BR 'ɛmfəsɪs
AM 'ɛmfəsəs

emphasise
BR 'ɛmfəsʌɪz, -ɨz, -ɪŋ, -d
AM 'ɛmfəˌsaɪz, -ɨz, -ɪŋ, -d

emphasize
BR 'ɛmfəsʌɪz, -ɨz, -ɪŋ, -d
AM 'ɛmfəˌsaɪz, -ɨz, -ɪŋ, -d

emphatic
BR ɪm'fatɪk, ɛm'fatɪk
AM əm'fædɪk, ɛm'fædɪk

emphatically
BR ɪm'fatɨkli, ɛm'fatɨkli
AM əm'fædək(ə)li, ɛm'fædək(ə)li

emphysema
BR ˌɛmfɪ'siːmə(*r*)
AM ˌɛmfə'simə, ˌɛmfə'zimə

empire
BR 'ɛmpʌɪə(r), -z
AM 'ɛmˌpaɪ(ə)r, -z

Empire State Building
BR ˌɛmpʌɪə ˌsteɪt 'bɪldɪŋ
AM 'ɛmˌpaɪ(ə)r 'steɪt ˌbɪldɪŋ

empiric
BR ɪm'pɪrɪk, ɛm'pɪrɪk
AM əm'pɪrɪk, ɛm'pɪrɪk

empirical
BR ɪm'pɪrɨkl, ɛm'pɪrɨkl
AM əm'pɪrɨkəl, ɛm'pɪrɨkəl

empirically
BR ɪm'pɪrɨkli, ɛm'pɪrɨkli
AM əm'pɪrɨk(ə)li, ɛm'pɪrɨk(ə)li

empiricism
BR ɪm'pɪrɨsɪz(ə)m, ɛm'pɪrɨsɪz(ə)m
AM əm'pɪrəˌsɪzəm, ɛm'pɪrəˌsɪzəm

empiricist
BR ɪm'pɪrɨsɪst, ɛm'pɪrɨsɪst, -s
AM əm'pɪrəsəst, ɛm'pɪrəsəst, -s

emplacement
BR ɪm'pleɪsm(ə)nt, ɛm'pleɪsm(ə)nt, -s
AM əm'pleɪsmənt, ɛm'pleɪsmənt, -s

emplane
BR ɪm'pleɪn, ɛm'pleɪn, -z, -ɪŋ, -d
AM əm'pleɪn, ɛm'pleɪn, -z, -ɪŋ, -d

employ
BR ɪm'plɔɪ, ɛm'plɔɪ, -z, -ɪŋ, -d
AM əm'plɔɪ, ɛm'plɔɪ, -z, -ɪŋ, -d

employability
BR ɪmˌplɔɪə'bɪlɨti, ɛmˌplɔɪə'bɪlɨti
AM əmˌplɔɪə'bɪlɨdi, ɛmˌplɔɪə'bɪlɨdi

employable
BR ɪm'plɔɪəbl, ɛm'plɔɪəbl
AM əm'plɔɪəbəl, ɛm'plɔɪəbəl

employee
BR ˌɛmplɔɪ'iː, ɪm'plɔɪiː, ɛm'plɔɪiː, -z
AM əmˌplɔ(ɪ)'i, əm'plɔˌi, əm'plɔ(ɪ)ˌi, 'ɛmˌplɔɪ'i, -z

employer
BR ɪm'plɔɪə(r), ɛm'plɔɪə(r), -z
AM əm'plɔɪ(j)ər, ɛm'plɔɪ(j)ər, əm'plɔjər, ɛm'plɔjər, -z

employment
BR ɪm'plɔɪm(ə)nt, ɛm'plɔɪm(ə)nt, -s
AM əm'plɔɪmənt, ɛm'plɔɪmənt, -s

empolder
BR ɪm'pəʊld|ə(r), ɛm'pəʊld|ə(r), -əz, -(ə)rɪŋ, -əd
AM əm'poʊldər, ɛm'poʊldər, -d, -ɪŋ, -d

emporia
BR ɪm'pɔːrɪə(*r*), ɛm'pɔːrɪə(*r*)
AM əm'pɔriə, ɛm'pɔriə

emporium
BR ɪm'pɔːrɪəm, ɛm'pɔːrɪəm, -z
AM əm'pɔriəm, ɛm'pɔriəm, -z

empower
BR ɪm'paʊ|ə(r), ɛm'paʊ|ə(r), -əz, -(ə)rɪŋ, -əd
AM əm'paʊ|ər, ɛm'paʊ|ər, -ərd, -(ə)rɪŋ, -ərd

empowerment
BR ɪm'paʊəm(ə)nt, ɛm'paʊəm(ə)nt
AM əm'paʊərmənt, ɛm'paʊərmənt

empress
BR 'ɛmprɪs, -ɪz
AM 'ɛmprəs, -əz

Empson
BR 'ɛm(p)sn
AM 'ɛm(p)sən

emptily
BR 'ɛm(p)tɨli
AM 'ɛm(p)təli

emptiness
BR 'ɛm(p)tɪnɨs
AM 'ɛm(p)tinɨs

empty
BR 'ɛm(p)t|i, -ɪz, -ɪɪŋ, -ɪd, -ɪə(r), -ɪɪst
AM 'ɛm(p)ti, -z, -ɪŋ, -d, -ər, -ɪst

empurple
BR ɪm'pəːp|l, ɛm'pəːp|l, -lz, -l̩ɪŋ\-lɪŋ, -ld

AM əm'pərpəl, ɛm'pərpəl, -z, -ɪŋ, -d

empyema
BR ˌɛmpʌɪ'iːmə(*r*)
AM ˌɛmpaɪ'imə

empyreal
BR ˌɛmpɪ'riːəl, ˌɛmpʌɪ'riːəl, ɛm'pɪrɪəl
AM ɛm'pɪriəl, ˌɛmpaɪ'riəl

empyrean
BR ˌɛmpɪ'riːən, ˌɛmpʌɪ'riːən, ɛm'pɪrɪən
AM ɛm'pɪriən, ˌɛmpaɪ'riən

Emrys
BR 'ɛmrɪs
AM 'ɛmrəs

Emsworth
BR 'ɛmzwəθ, 'ɛmzwəːθ
AM 'ɛmzˌwərθ

emu
BR 'iːmjuː, -z
AM 'im(j)u, -z

emulate
BR 'ɛmjʉleɪt, -s, -ɪŋ, -ɪd
AM 'ɛmjəˌleɪ|t, -ts, -dɪŋ, -dɪd

emulation
BR ˌɛmjʉ'leɪʃn
AM ˌɛmjə'leɪʃən

emulative
BR 'ɛmjʉlətɪv
AM 'ɛmjəˌleɪdɪv

emulator
BR 'ɛmjʉleɪtə(r), -z
AM 'ɛmjəˌleɪdər, -z

emulous
BR 'ɛmjʉləs
AM 'ɛmjələs

emulously
BR 'ɛmjʉləsli
AM 'ɛmjələsli

emulousness
BR 'ɛmjʉləsnəs
AM 'ɛmjələsnəs

emulsifiable
BR ɪ'mʌlsɪfʌɪəbl
AM ə'məlsəˌfaɪəbəl, i'məlsəˌfaɪəbəl

emulsification
BR ɪˌmʌlsɪfɪ'keɪʃn
AM əˌməlsəfə'keɪʃən, iˌməlsəfə'keɪʃən

emulsifier
BR ɪ'mʌlsɪfʌɪə(r), -z
AM ə'məlsəˌfaɪər, i'məlsəˌfaɪər, -z

emulsify
BR ɪ'mʌlsɪfʌɪ, -z, -ɪŋ, -d
AM ə'məlsəˌfaɪ, i'məlsəˌfaɪ, -z, -ɪŋ, -d

emulsion
BR ɪ'mʌlʃn, -z
AM ə'məlʃən, i'məlʃən, -z

emulsionise
BR ɪ'mʌlʃn̩ʌɪz, ɪ'mʌlʃənʌɪz, -ɪz, -ɪŋ, -d
AM ə'məlʃə,naɪz, i'məlʃə,naɪz, -ɪz, -ɪŋ, -d

emulsionize
BR ɪ'mʌlʃn̩ʌɪz, ɪ'mʌlʃənʌɪz, -ɪz, -ɪŋ, -d
AM ə'məlʃə,naɪz, i'məlʃə,naɪz, -ɪz, -ɪŋ, -d

emulsive
BR ɪ'mʌlsɪv
AM ə'məlsɪv, i'məlsɪv

Emyr
BR 'ɛmɪə(r)
AM 'ɛmɪ(ə)r

en
BR ɛn, -z
AM ɛn, -z

Ena
BR 'iːnə(r)
AM 'inə

enable
BR ɪn'eɪb|l, ɛn'eɪb|l, -lz, -lɪŋ\-lɪŋ, -ld
AM ɪ'neɪb|əl, ɛ'neɪb|əl, -əlz, -(ə)lɪŋ, -əld

enablement
BR ɪn'eɪblm(ə)nt, ɛn'eɪblm(ə)nt
AM ɪ'neɪbəlmənt, ɛ'neɪbəlmənt

enabler
BR ɪn'eɪblə(r), ɛn'eɪblə(r), -z
AM ɪ'neɪblər, ɛ'neɪblər, -z

enact
BR ɪn'akt, ɛn'akt, -s, -ɪŋ, -ɪd
AM ɪ'næk|(t), ɛ'næk|(t), -(t)s, -tɪŋ, -təd

enactable
BR ɪn'aktəbl, ɛn'aktəbl
AM ɪ'næktəbəl, ɛ'næktəbəl

enaction
BR ɪn'akʃn, ɛn'akʃn
AM ɪ'nækʃən, ɛ'nækʃən

enactive
BR ɪn'aktɪv, ɛn'aktɪv
AM ɪ'næktɪv, ɛ'næktɪv

enactment
BR ɪn'aktm(ə)nt, ɛ'naktm(ə)nt, -s
AM ɪ'næk(t)mənt, ɛ'næk(t)mənt, -s

enactor
BR ɪn'aktə(r), ɛn'aktə(r), -z
AM ɪ'næktər, ɛ'næktər, -z

enactory
BR ɪn'akt(ə)ri, ɛn'akt(ə)ri
AM ɪ'næk,tɔri, ɛ'næk,tɔri

enamel
BR ɪ'nam|l, -lz, -lɪŋ\-əlɪŋ, -ld
AM ɪ'næm|əl, ɛ'næm|əl, -əlz, -(ə)lɪŋ, -əld

enameller
BR ɪ'naml̩ə(r), ɪ'namələ(r), -z
AM ɪ'næm(ə)lər, ɛ'næm(ə)lər, -z

enamelling
BR ɪ'naml̩ɪŋ, ɪ'namәlɪŋ
AM ɪ'næm(ə)lɪŋ, ɛ'næm(ə)lɪŋ

enamelware
BR ɪ'namlwɛː(r)
AM ɪ'næməl,wɛ(ə)r, ɛ'næməl,wɛ(ə)r

enamelwork
BR ɪ'namlwəːk
AM ɪ'næməl,wərk, ɛ'næməl,wərk

enamor
BR ɪ'nam|ə(r), ɛ'nam|ə(r), -əz, -(ə)rɪŋ, -əd
AM ɪ'næmər, ɛ'næmər, -d, -ɪŋ, -d

enamored
BR ɪ'naməd, ɛ'naməd
AM ɪ'næmərd, ɛ'næmərd

enamour
BR ɪ'nam|ə(r), ɛ'nam|ə(r), -əz, -(ə)rɪŋ, -əd
AM ɪ'næmər, ɛ'næmər, -d, -ɪŋ, -d

enanthema
BR ,ɛnan'θiːmə(r), -z
AM ɛ,næn'θimə, -z

enantiomer
BR ɪ'nantɪə(ʊ)mə(r), ɛ'nantɪə(ʊ)mə(r), -z
AM ə'næntioʊmər, ɛ'næntioʊmər, -z

enantiomeric
BR ɪ,nantɪə(ʊ)'mɛrɪk, ɛ,nantɪə(ʊ)'mɛrɪk
AM ə,næntioʊ'mɛrɪk, ɛ,næntioʊ'mɛrɪk

enantiomorph
BR ə'nantɪə(ʊ)mɔːf, -s
AM ə'næntioʊ,mɔ(ə)rf, ɛ'næntioʊ,mɔ(ə)rf, -s

enantiomorphic
BR ɪ,nantɪə(ʊ)'mɔːfɪk, ɛ,nantɪə(ʊ)'mɔːfɪk
AM ə,næntioʊ'mɔrfɪk, ɛ,næntioʊ'mɔrfɪk

enantiomorphism
BR ɪ,nantɪə(ʊ)'mɔːfɪz(ə)m, ɛ,nantɪə(ʊ)'mɔːfɪz(ə)m
AM ə,næntioʊ'mɔr,fɪzəm, ɛ,næntioʊ'mɔr,fɪzəm

enantiomorphous
BR ɪ,nantɪə(ʊ)'mɔːfəs, ɛ,nantɪə(ʊ)'mɔːfəs
AM ə,næntioʊ'mɔrfəs, ɛ,næntioʊ'mɔrfəs

enarthroses
BR ,ɛnɑː'θrəʊsiːz
AM ,ɛnɑr'θroʊsiz

enarthrosis
BR ,ɛnɑː'θrəʊsɪs
AM ,ɛnɑr'θroʊsəs

en bloc
BR ,ɒ̃ 'blɒk, ,ɒn +
AM ɑn 'blɑk

en brosse
BR ,ɒ̃ 'brɒs, ,ɒn +
AM ɑn 'brɔs, ɑn 'brɑs

encaenia
BR ɪn'siːnɪə(r), ɛn'siːnɪə(r), -z
AM ɛn'siniə, ɪn'siniə, -z

encage
BR ɪn'keɪdʒ, ɛn'keɪdʒ, ɪŋ'keɪdʒ, ɛŋ'keɪdʒ, -ɪz, -ɪŋ, -d
AM ɪn'keɪdʒ, ɛn'keɪdʒ, -ɪz, -ɪŋ, -d

encamp
BR ɪn'kamp, ɛn'kamp, ɪŋ'kamp, ɛŋ'kamp, -s, -ɪŋ, -t
AM ɪn'kæmp, ɛn'kæmp, ɪŋ'kæmp, ɛŋ'kæmp, -s, -ɪŋ, -t

encampment
BR ɪn'kampm(ə)nt, ɛn'kampm(ə)nt, ɪŋ'kampm(ə)nt, ɛŋ'kampm(ə)nt, -s
AM ɪn'kæmpmənt, ɛn'kæmpmənt, ɪŋ'kæmpmənt, ɛŋ'kæmpmənt, -s

encapsulate
BR ɪn'kapsjʊleɪt, ɛn'kapsjʊleɪt, ɪŋ'kapsjʊleɪt, ɛŋ'kapsjʊleɪt, -s, -ɪŋ, -ɪd
AM ɪn'kæps(j)ə,leɪ|t, ɛn'kæps(j)ə,leɪ|t, ɪŋ'kæps(j)ə,leɪt, ɛŋ'kæps(j)ə,leɪt, -ts, -dɪŋ, -dɪd

encapsulation
BR ɪn,kapsjʊ'leɪʃn, ɛn,kapsjʊ'leɪʃn, ɪŋ,kapsjʊ'leɪʃn, ɛŋ,kapsjʊ'leɪʃn
AM ɪn,kæps(j)ə'leɪʃən, ɛn,kæps(j)ə'leɪʃən, ɪŋ,kæps(j)ə'leɪʃən, ɛŋ,kæps(j)'leɪʃən

encase
BR ɪn'keɪs, ɛn'keɪs, ɪŋ'keɪs, ɛŋ'keɪs, -ɪz, -ɪŋ, -t
AM ɪn'keɪs, ɛn'keɪs, ɪŋ'keɪs, ɛŋ'keɪs, -ɪz, -ɪŋ, -t

encasement
BR ɪn'keɪsm(ə)nt, ɛn'keɪsmənt, ɪŋ'keɪsm(ə)nt, ɛŋ'keɪsmənt, -s
AM ɪn'keɪsmənt, ɛn'keɪsmənt, ɪŋ'keɪsmənt, ɛŋ'keɪsmənt, -s

encash
BR ɪn'kaʃ, ɛn'kaʃ, ɪŋ'kaʃ, ɛŋ'kaʃ, -ɪz, -ɪŋ, -t
AM ɪn'kæʃ, ɛn'kæʃ, ɪŋ'kæʃ, ɛŋ'kæʃ, -əz, -ɪŋ, -t

encashable
BR ɪn'kaʃəbl, ɛn'kaʃəbl, ɪŋ'kaʃəbl, ɛŋ'kaʃəbl
AM ɪn'kæʃəbəl, ɛn'kæʃəbəl, ɪŋ'kæʃəbəl, ɛŋ'kæʃəbəl

encashment
BR ɪn'kaʃm(ə)nt, ɛn'kaʃm(ə)nt, ɪŋ'kaʃm(ə)nt, ɛŋ'kaʃm(ə)nt, -s
AM ɪn'kæʃmənt, ɛn'kæʃmənt, ɪŋ'kæʃmənt, ɛŋ'kæʃmənt, -s

encaustic
BR ɪn'kɔːstɪk, ɛn'kɔːstɪk, ɪŋ'kɔːstɪk, ɛŋ'kɔːstɪk, -s
AM ɪn'kɔstɪk, ɛn'kɔstɪk, ɪn'kɑstɪk, ɛn'kɑstɪk, ɪŋ'kɔstɪk, ɛŋ'kɔstɪk, ɪŋ'kɑstɪk, ɛŋ'kɑstɪk, -s

encaustically
BR ɪn'kɔːstɪkli, ɛn'kɔːstɪkli, ɪŋ'kɔːstɪkli, ɛŋ'kɔːstɪkli
AM ɪn'kɔstək(ə)li, ɛn'kɔstək(ə)li, ɪn'kɑstək(ə)li, ɛn'kɑstək(ə)li, ɪŋ'kɔstɪk(ə)li, ɛŋ'kɔstɪk(ə)li, ɪŋ'kɑstɪk(ə)li, ɛŋ'kɑstɪk(ə)li

enceinte
BR ɒ̃'sãt, ɒn'sant
AM ɑn'sænt

Enceladus
BR ɪn'sɛlədəs, ɛn'sɛlədəs

AM ən'sɛlədəs, ɛn'sɛlədəs

encephalic
BR ˌɛnsɪ'falɪk, ˌɛnkɛ'falɪk, ˌɛŋkɛ'falɪk
AM ˌɛnsə'fælɪk

encephalin
BR ɛn'sɛfəlɪn, ɛn'sɛfl̩ɪn, ɛn'kɛfəlɪn, ɛn'kɛfl̩ɪn, ɛŋ'kɛfəlɪn, ɛŋ'kɛfl̩ɪn
AM ɛn'sɛfələn, ɛn'sɛfəˌlin

encephalitic
BR ɛnˌsɛfə'lɪtɪk, ɛnˌkɛfə'lɪtɪk, ɛŋˌkɛfə'lɪtɪk, ˌɛnsɛfə'lɪtɪk, ˌɛnkɛfə'lɪtɪk, ˌɛŋkɛfə'lɪtɪk
AM ɛnˌsɛfə'lɪdɪk

encephalitis
BR ɛnˌsɛfə'lʌɪtɨs, ɛnˌkɛfə'lʌɪtɨs, ɛŋˌkɛfə'lʌɪtɨs, ˌɛnsɛfə'lʌɪtɨs, ˌɛnkɛfə'lʌɪtɨs, ˌɛŋkɛfə'lʌɪtɨs
AM ɪnˌsɛfə'laɪdəs, ɛnˌsɛfə'laɪdəs

encephalogram
BR ɛn'sɛfələgram, ɛn'sɛfl̩əgram, ɛn'kɛfələgram, ɛn'kɛfl̩əgram, ɛŋ'kɛfələgram, ɛŋ'kɛfl̩əgram, -z
AM ɪn'sɛfələˌgræm, ɛn'sɛfələˌgræm, -z

encephalograph
BR ɛn'sɛfələgrɑːf, ɛn'sɛfələgraf, ɛn'kɛfələgrɑːf, ɛn'kɛfələgraf, ɛŋ'kɛfələgrɑːf, ɛŋ'kɛfələgraf, -s
AM ɪn'sɛfələˌgræf, ɛn'sɛfələˌgræf, -s

encephalomyelitis
BR ɛnˌsɛfələʊˌmʌɪə'lʌɪtɨs, ɛnˌsɛfl̩əʊˌmʌɪə'lʌɪtɨs, ɛnˌkɛfələʊˌmʌɪə'lʌɪtɨs, ɛnˌkɛfl̩əʊˌmʌɪə'lʌɪtɨs, ɛŋˌkɛfələʊˌmʌɪə'lʌɪtɨs, ɛŋˌkɛfl̩əʊˌmʌɪə'lʌɪtɨs, -ɨz
AM ɪnˌsɛfələˌmaɪə'laɪdɨs, ɛnˌsɛfələˌmaɪə'laɪdɨs, -ɨz

encephalon
BR ɛn'sɛfəlɒn, ɛn'sɛfl̩ɒn, ɛn'kɛfəlɒn, ɛn'kɛfl̩ɒn, ɛŋ'kɛfəlɒn, ɛŋ'kɛfl̩ɒn, -z
AM ɪn'sɛfəˌlɑn, ɛn'sɛfəˌlɑn, ɪn'sɛfələn, ɛn'sɛfələn, -z

encephalopathy
BR ɛnˌsɛfə'lɒpəθi, ɛnˌkɛfə'lɒpəθi, ɛŋˌkɛfə'lɒpəθi
AM ɪnˌsɛfə'lɑpəθi, ɛnˌsɛfə'lɑpəθi

enchain
BR ɪn'tʃeɪn, ɛn'tʃeɪn, -z, -ɪŋ, -d
AM ɪn'tʃeɪn, ɛn'tʃeɪn, -z, -ɪŋ, -d

enchainment
BR ɪn'tʃeɪnm(ə)nt, ɛn'tʃeɪnm(ə)nt
AM ɪn'tʃeɪnmənt, ɛn'tʃeɪnmənt

enchant
BR ɪn'tʃɑːnt, ɪn'tʃant, ɛn'tʃɑːnt, ɛn'tʃant, -s, -ɪŋ, -ɨd
AM ɪn'tʃæn|t, ɛn'tʃæn|t, -ts, -(t)ɪŋ, -(t)əd

enchantedly
BR ɪn'tʃɑːntɨdli, ɪn'tʃantɨdli, ɛn'tʃɑːntɨdli, ɛn'tʃantɨdli
AM ɪn'tʃæn(t)ədli, ɛn'tʃæn(t)ədli

enchanter
BR ɪn'tʃɑːntə(r), ɪn'tʃantə(r), ɛn'tʃɑːntə(r), ɛn'tʃantə(r), -z
AM ɪn'tʃæn(t)ər, ɛn'tʃæn(t)ər, -z

enchanting
BR ɪn'tʃɑːntɪŋ, ɪn'tʃantɪŋ, ɛn'tʃɑːntɪŋ, ɛn'tʃantɪŋ
AM ɪn'tʃæn(t)ɪŋ, ɛn'tʃæn(t)ɪŋ

enchantingly
BR ɪn'tʃɑːntɪŋli, ɪn'tʃantɪŋli, ɛn'tʃɑːntɪŋli, ɛn'tʃantɪŋli
AM ɪn'tʃæn(t)ɪŋli, ɛn'tʃæn(t)ɪŋli

enchantment
BR ɪn'tʃɑːntm(ə)nt, ɪn'tʃantm(ə)nt, ɛn'tʃɑːntm(ə)nt, ɛn'tʃantm(ə)nt, -s
AM ɪn'tʃæntmənt, ɛn'tʃæntmənt, -s

enchantress
BR ɪn'tʃɑːntrɪs, ɪn'tʃantrɪs, ɛn'tʃɑːntrɪs, ɛn'tʃantrɪs, -ɨz
AM ɪn'tʃæntrəs, ɛn'tʃæntrəs, -əz

enchase
BR ɪn'tʃeɪs, ɛn'tʃeɪs, -ɨz, -ɪŋ, -t
AM ɪn'tʃeɪs, ɛn'tʃeɪs, -ɨz, -ɪŋ, -t

enchilada
BR ˌɛntʃɪ'lɑːdə(r), -z
AM ˌɛntʃə'lɑdə, -z

enchiridia
BR ˌɛnkʌɪ'rɪdɪə(r), ˌɛŋkʌɪ'rɪdɪə(r)
AM ˌɛŋkə'rɪdiə, ˌɛnˌkaɪ'rɪdiə

enchiridion
BR ˌɛnkʌɪ'rɪdɪən, ˌɛŋkʌɪ'rɪdɪən, -z
AM ˌɛŋkə'rɪdiən, ˌɛnˌkaɪ'rɪdiən, -z

encipher
BR ɪn'sʌɪf|ə(r), ɛn'sʌɪf|ə(r), -əz, -(ə)rɪŋ, -əd
AM ɪn'saɪf|ər, ɛn'saɪf|ər, -ərz, -(ə)rɪŋ, -ərd

encipherment
BR ɪn'sʌɪfəm(ə)nt, ɛn'sʌɪfəm(ə)nt
AM ɪn'saɪfərmənt, ɛn'saɪfərmənt

encircle
BR ɪn'səːk|l, ɛn'səːk|l, -lz, -l̩ɪŋ\-lɪŋ, -ld
AM ɪn'sərk|əl, ɛn'sərk|əl, -əlz, -(ə)lɪŋ, -əld

encirclement
BR ɪn'səːklm(ə)nt, ɛn'səːklm(ə)nt
AM ɪn'sərkəlmənt, ɛn'sərkəlmənt

en clair
BR ˌɒ̃ 'klɛː(r), ˌɒn +
AM ɑn 'klɛ(ə)r

enclasp
BR ɪn'klɑːsp, ɪn'klasp, ɛn'klɑːsp, ɛn'klasp, ɪŋ'klɑːsp, ɪŋ'klasp, ɛŋ'klɑːsp, ɛŋ'klasp, -s, -ɪŋ, -t
AM ɪn'klæsp, ɛn'klæsp, ɪŋ'klæsp, ɛŋ'klæsp, -s, -ɪŋ, -t

enclave
BR 'ɛnkleɪv, 'ɛŋkleɪv, 'ɒŋkleɪv, -z
AM 'ɛnˌkleɪv, 'ɑŋˌkleɪv, -z

enclitic
BR ɪn'klɪtɪk, ɛn'klɪtɪk, ɪŋ'klɪtɪk, ɛŋ'klɪtɪk, -s
AM ɛn'klɪdɪk, ɪn'klɪdɪk, ɛŋ'klɪdɪk, ɪŋ'klɪdɪk, -s

enclitically
BR ɪn'klɪtɨkli, ɛn'klɪtɨkli, ɪŋ'klɪtɨkli, ɛŋ'klɪtɨkli
AM ɛn'klɪdək(ə)li, ɪn'klɪdək(ə)li, ɛŋ'klɪdɪk(ə)li, ɪŋ'klɪdɪk(ə)li

enclose
BR ɪn'kləʊz, ɛn'kləʊz, ɪŋ'kləʊz, ɛŋ'kləʊz, -ɨz, -ɪŋ, -d
AM ɪn'kloʊz, ɛn'kloʊz, ɪŋ'kloʊz, ɛŋ'kloʊz, -əz, -ɪŋ, -d

enclosure
BR ɪn'kləʊʒə(r), ɛn'kləʊʒə(r), ɪŋ'kləʊʒə(r), ɛŋ'kləʊʒə(r), -z
AM ɪn'kloʊʒər, ɛn'kloʊʒər, ɪŋ'kloʊʒər, ɛŋ'kloʊʒər, -z

encode
BR ɪn'kəʊd, ɛn'kəʊd, ɪŋ'kəʊd, ɛŋ'kəʊd, -z, -ɪŋ, -ɨd
AM ɪn'koʊd, ɛn'koʊd, ɪŋ'koʊd, ɛŋ'koʊd, -z, -ɪŋ, -əd

encoder
BR ɪn'kəʊdə(r), ɛn'kəʊdə(r), ɪŋ'kəʊdə(r), ɛŋ'kəʊdə(r), -z
AM ɪn'koʊdər, ɛn'koʊdər, ɪŋ'koʊdər, ɛŋ'koʊdər, -z

encomia
BR ɪn'kəʊmɪə(r), ɛn'kəʊmɪə(r), ɪŋ'kəʊmɪə(r), ɛŋ'kəʊmɪə(r)
AM ɪn'koʊmiə, ɛn'koʊmiə, ɪŋ'koʊmiə, ɛŋ'koʊmiə

encomiast
BR ɪn'kəʊmɪast, ɛn'kəʊmɪast, ɪŋ'kəʊmɪast, ɛŋ'kəʊmɪast, -s
AM ɪn'koʊmiˌæst, ɛn'koʊmiˌæst, ɪŋ'koʊmiˌæst, ɛŋ'koʊmiˌæst, -s

encomiastic
BR ɪnˌkəʊmɪ'astɪk, ɛnˌkəʊmɪ'astɪk, ɪŋˌkəʊmɪ'astɪk, ɛŋˌkəʊmɪ'astɪk
AM ɪnˌkoʊmi'æstɪk, ɛnˌkoʊmiˌæstɪk, ɪŋˌkoʊmi'æstɪk, ɛŋˌkoʊmiˌæstɪk

encomium
BR ɪn'kəʊmɪəm, ɛn'kəʊmɪəm, ɪŋ'kəʊmɪəm, ɛŋ'kəʊmɪəm, -z
AM ɪn'koʊmiəm, ɛn'koʊmiəm,

ɪŋ'koʊmiəm, ɛŋ'koʊmiəm, -z

encompass
BR ɪn'kʌmpəs, ɛn'kʌmpəs, ɪŋ'kʌmpəs, ɛŋ'kʌmpəs, -ɪz, -ɪŋ, -t
AM ɪn'kəmpəs, ɛn'kəmpəs, ɪŋ'kəmpəs, ɛŋ'kəmpəs, -əz, -ɪŋ, -t

encompassment
BR ɪn'kʌmpəsm(ə)nt, ɛn'kʌmpəsm(ə)nt, ɪŋ'kʌmpəsm(ə)nt, ɛŋ'kʌmpəsm(ə)nt
AM ɪn'kəmpəsmənt, ɛn'kəmpəsmənt, ɪŋ'kəmpəsmənt, ɛŋ'kəmpəsmənt

encore
BR 'ɒŋkɔː(r), -z, -ɪŋ, -d
AM 'ɑnˌkɔ(ə)r, 'ɑŋˌkɔ(ə)r, -z, -ɪŋ, -d

encounter
BR ɪn'kaʊnt|ə(r), ɛn'kaʊnt|ə(r), ɪŋ'kaʊnt|ə(r), ɛŋ'kaʊnt|ə(r), -əz, -(ə)rɪŋ, -əd
AM ɪn'kaʊn(t)ər, ɛn'kaʊn(t)ər, ɪŋ'kaʊn(t)ər, ɛŋ'kaʊn(t)ər, -z, -ɪŋ, -d

encourage
BR ɪn'kʌr|ɪdʒ, ɛn'kʌr|ɪdʒ, ɪŋ'kʌr|ɪdʒ, ɛŋ'kʌr|ɪdʒ, -ɪdʒɪz, -ɪdʒɪŋ, -ɪdʒd
AM ɪn'kərɪdʒ, ɛn'kərɪdʒ, ɪŋ'kərɪdʒ, ɛŋ'kərɪdʒ, -əz, -ɪŋ, -d

encouragement
BR ɪn'kʌrɪdʒm(ə)nt, ɛn'kʌrɪdʒm(ə)nt, ɪŋ'kʌrɪdʒm(ə)nt, ɛŋ'kʌrɪdʒm(ə)nt, -s
AM ɪn'kərɪdʒmənt, ɛn'kərɪdʒmənt, ɪŋ'kərɪdʒmənt, ɛŋ'kərɪdʒmənt, -s

encourager
BR ɪn'kʌrɪdʒə(r), ɛn'kʌrɪdʒə(r), ɪŋ'kʌrɪdʒə(r), ɛŋ'kʌrɪdʒə(r), -z
AM ɪn'kərɪdʒər, ɛn'kərɪdʒər, ɪŋ'kərɪdʒər, ɛŋ'kərɪdʒər, -z

encouragingly
BR ɪn'kʌrɪdʒɪŋli, ɛn'kʌrɪdʒɪŋli, ɪŋ'kʌrɪdʒɪŋli, ɛŋ'kʌrɪdʒɪŋli
AM ɪn'kərɪdʒɪŋli, ɛn'kərɪdʒɪŋli, ɪŋ'kərɪdʒɪŋli, ɛŋ'kərɪdʒɪŋli

encrinite
BR 'ɛŋkrɪnʌɪt, -s
AM 'ɛŋkrəˌnaɪt, -s

encroach
BR ɪn'krəʊtʃ, ɛn'krəʊtʃ, ɪŋ'krəʊtʃ, ɛŋ'krəʊtʃ, -ɪz, -ɪŋ, -t
AM ɪn'kroʊtʃ, ɛn'kroʊtʃ, ɪŋ'kroʊtʃ, ɛŋ'kroʊtʃ, -əz, -ɪŋ, -t

encroacher
BR ɪn'krəʊtʃə(r), ɛn'krəʊtʃə(r), ɪŋ'krəʊtʃə(r), ɛŋ'krəʊtʃə(r), -z
AM ɪn'kroʊtʃər, ɛn'kroʊtʃər, ɪŋ'kroʊtʃər, ɛŋ'kroʊtʃər, -z

encroachment
BR ɪn'krəʊtʃm(ə)nt, ɛn'krəʊtʃm(ə)nt, ɪŋ'krəʊtʃm(ə)nt, ɛŋ'krəʊtʃm(ə)nt, -s
AM ɪn'kroʊtʃmənt, ɛn'kroʊtʃmənt, ɪŋ'kroʊtʃmənt, ɛŋ'kroʊtʃmənt, -s

encrust
BR ɪn'krʌst, ɛn'krʌst, ɪŋ'krʌst, ɛŋ'krʌst, -s, -ɪŋ, -ɪd
AM ɪn'krəst, ɛn'krəst, ɪŋ'krəst, ɛŋ'krəst, -s, -ɪŋ, -əd

encrustation
BR ˌɪnkrʌ'steɪʃn, ˌɛnkrʌ'steɪʃn, ˌɪŋkrʌ'steɪʃn, ˌɛŋkrʌ'steɪʃn
AM ɪnˌkrəs'teɪʃən, ɛnˌkrəs'teɪʃən, ɪŋˌkrəs'teɪʃən, ɛŋˌkrəs'teɪʃən

encrustment
BR ɪn'krʌs(t)m(ə)nt, ɛn'krʌs(t)m(ə)nt, ɪŋ'krʌs(t)m(ə)nt, ɛŋ'krʌs(t)m(ə)nt
AM ɪn'krəs(t)mənt, ɛn'krəs(t)mənt, ɪŋ'krəs(t)mənt, ɛŋ'krəs(t)mənt

encrypt
BR ɪn'krɪpt, ɛn'krɪpt, ɪŋ'krɪpt, ɛŋ'krɪpt, -s, -ɪŋ, -ɪd
AM ɪn'krɪpt, ɛn'krɪpt, ɪŋ'krɪpt, ɛŋ'krɪpt, -s, -ɪŋ, -ɪd

encryption
BR ɪn'krɪpʃn, ɛn'krɪpʃn, ɪŋ'krɪpʃn, ɛŋ'krɪpʃn, -z
AM ɪn'krɪpʃən, ɛn'krɪpʃən, ɪŋ'krɪpʃən, ɛŋ'krɪpʃən, -z

encumber
BR ɪn'kʌmb|ə(r), ɛn'kʌmb|ə(r), ɪŋ'kʌmb|ə(r), ɛŋ'kʌmb|ə(r), -əz, -(ə)rɪŋ, -əd
AM ɪn'kəmb|ər, ɛn'kəmb|ər, ɪŋ'kəmb|ər, ɛŋ'kəmb|ər, -ərz, -(ə)rɪŋ, -ərd

encumberment
BR ɪn'kʌmbəm(ə)nt, ɛn'kʌmbəm(ə)nt, ɪŋ'kʌmbəm(ə)nt, ɛŋ'kʌmbəm(ə)nt
AM ɪn'kəmbərmənt, ɛn'kəmbərmənt, ɪŋ'kəmbərmənt, ɛŋ'kəmbərmənt

encumbrance
BR ɪn'kʌmbr(ə)ns, ɛn'kʌmbr(ə)ns, ɪŋ'kʌmbr(ə)ns, ɛŋ'kʌmbr(ə)ns, -ɪz
AM ɪn'kəmb(ə)rəns, ɛn'kʌmb(ə)rəns, ɪŋ'kəmb(ə)rəns, ɛŋ'kʌmb(ə)rəns, -əz

encyclic
BR ɪn'sʌɪklɪk, ɛn'sʌɪklɪk, ɪn'sɪklɪk, ɛn'sɪklɪk
AM ɪn'sɪklɪk, ɛn'sɪklɪk

encyclical
BR ɪn'sɪklɪkl, ɛn'sɪklɪkl, -z
AM ɪn'sɪklәkәl, ɛn'sɪklәkәl, -z

encyclopaedia
BR ɪnˌsʌɪklə(ʊ)'piːdɪə(*r*), ɛnˌsʌɪklə(ʊ)'piːdɪə(*r*), -z
AM ɪnˌsaɪklə'pidiə, ɛnˌsaɪklə'pidiə, -z

encyclopaedic
BR ɪnˌsʌɪklə'piːdɪk, ɛnˌsʌɪklə'piːdɪk
AM ɪnˈsaɪklə'pidɪk, ɛnˈsaɪklə'pidɪk

encyclopaedically
BR ɪnˌsʌɪklə'piːdɪkli, ɛnˌsʌɪklə'piːdɪkli
AM ɪnˈsaɪklə'pidɪk(ə)li, ɛnˈsaɪklə'pidɪk(ə)li

encyclopaedism
BR ɪnˌsʌɪklə'piːdɪz(ə)m, ɛnˌsʌɪklə'piːdɪz(ə)m
AM ɪnˌsaɪklə'piˌdɪzəm, ɛnˌsaɪklə'piˌdɪzəm

encyclopaedist
BR ɪnˌsʌɪklə'piːdɪst, ɛnˌsʌɪklə'piːdɪst, -s
AM ɪnˌsaɪklə'pidɪst, ɛnˌsaɪklə'pidɪst, -s

encyclopedia
BR ɪnˌsʌɪklə(ʊ)'piːdɪə(*r*), ɛnˌsʌɪklə(ʊ)'piːdɪə(*r*), -z
AM ɪnˌsaɪklə'pidiə, ɛnˌsaɪklə'pidiə, -z

encyclopedic
BR ɪnˌsʌɪklə'piːdɪk, ɛnˌsʌɪklə'piːdɪk
AM ɪnˌsaɪklə'pidɪk, ɛnˌsaɪklə'pidɪk

encyclopedically
BR ɪnˌsʌɪklə'piːdɪkli, ɛnˌsʌɪklə'piːdɪkli
AM ɪnˈsaɪklə'pidɪk(ə)li, ɛnˈsaɪklə'pidɪk(ə)li

encyclopedism
BR ɪnˌsʌɪklə'piːdɪz(ə)m, ɛnˌsʌɪklə'piːdɪz(ə)m
AM ɪnˌsaɪklə'piˌdɪzəm, ɛnˌsaɪklə'piˌdɪzəm

encyclopedist
BR ɪnˌsʌɪklə'piːdɪst, ɛnˌsʌɪklə'piːdɪst, -s
AM ɪnˌsaɪklə'pidɪst, ɛnˌsaɪklə'pidɪst, -s

encyst
BR ɛn'sɪst, -s, -ɪŋ, -ɪd
AM ɛn'sɪst, -s, -ɪŋ, -ɪd

encystation
BR ˌɛnsɪ'steɪʃn
AM ˌɛnsə'steɪʃən

encystment
BR ɛn'sɪs(t)m(ə)nt
AM ɛn'sɪs(t)mənt

end
BR ɛnd, -z, -ɪŋ, -ɪd
AM ɛnd, -z, -ɪŋ, -əd

endanger
BR ɪn'deɪn(d)ʒ|ə(r), ɛn'deɪn(d)ʒ|ə(r), -əz, -(ə)rɪŋ, -əd
AM ɪn'deɪndʒ|ər, ɛn'deɪndʒ|ər, -ərz, -(ə)rɪŋ, -ərd

endangerment
BR ɪn'deɪn(d)ʒəm(ə)nt, ɛn'deɪn(d)ʒəm(ə)nt
AM ɪn'deɪndʒərmənt, ɛn'deɪndʒərmənt

endear
BR ɪn'dɪə(r), ɛn'dɪə(r), -z, -ɪŋ, -d
AM ɪn'dɪ(ə)r, ɛn'dɪ(ə)r, -z, -ɪŋ, -d

endearingly
BR ɪn'dɪərɪŋli, ɛn'dɪərɪŋli
AM ɪn'dɪrɪŋli, ɛn'dɪrɪŋli

endearment
BR ɪn'dɪəm(ə)nt, ɛn'dɪəm(ə)nt, -s
AM ɪn'dɪrmənt, ɛn'dɪrmənt, -s

endeavor
BR ɪn'dɛv|ə(r), ɛn'dɛv|ə(r), -əz, -(ə)rɪŋ, -əd
AM ən'dɛv|ər, ɛn'dɛv|ər, -ərz, -(ə)rɪŋ, -ərd

endeavour
BR ɪn'dɛv|ə(r), ɛn'dɛv|ə(r), -əz, -(ə)rɪŋ, -əd
AM ən'dɛv|ər, ɛn'dɛv|ər, -ərz, -(ə)rɪŋ, -ərd

endemic
BR ɛn'dɛmɪk, ɪn'dɛmɪk
AM ɛn'dɛmɪk

endemically
BR ɛn'dɛmɪkli, ɪn'dɛmɪkli
AM ɛn'dɛmək(ə)li

endemicity
BR ˌɛndɪ'mɪsɪti
AM ˌɛndə'mɪsɪdi

endemism
BR 'ɛndɪmɪz(ə)m
AM 'ɛndəˌmɪzəm

ender
BR 'ɛndə(r), -z
AM 'ɛndər, -z

Enderby
BR 'ɛndəbi
AM 'ɛndərbi

endermic
BR ɛn'də:mɪk
AM ɛn'dərmɪk

endermically
BR ɛn'də:mɪkli
AM ɛn'dərmək(ə)li

Enders
BR 'ɛndəz
AM 'ɛndərz

endgame
BR 'ɛn(d)geɪm, -z
AM 'ɛn(d)ˌgeɪm, -z

ending
BR 'ɛndɪŋ, -z
AM 'ɛndɪŋ, -z

endite
BR 'ɛndʌɪt, -s
AM 'ɛndaɪt, -s

endive
BR 'ɛndɪv, 'ɛndʌɪv, -z
AM 'ɛnˌdaɪv, -z

endless
BR 'ɛndləs
AM 'ɛn(d)ləs

endlessly
BR 'ɛndləsli
AM 'ɛn(d)ləsli

endlessness
BR 'ɛndləsnəs
AM 'ɛn(d)ləsnəs

endlong
BR 'ɛndlɒŋ
AM 'ɛn(d)ˌlɔŋ, 'ɛn(d)ˌlɑŋ

endmost
BR 'ɛn(d)məʊst
AM 'ɛn(d)ˌmoʊst

endnote
BR 'ɛn(d)nəʊt, -s
AM 'ɛn(d)ˌnoʊt, -s

endocardia
BR ˌɛndə(ʊ)'kɑ:dɪə(*r*)
AM ˌɛndoʊ'kɑrdiə

endocarditic
BR ˌɛndə(ʊ)kɑ:'dɪtɪk
AM ˌɛndoʊˌkɑr'dɪdɪk

endocarditis
BR ˌɛndəʊkɑ:'dʌɪtɪs
AM ˌɛndoʊˌkɑr'daɪdɪs

endocardium
BR ˌɛndə(ʊ)'kɑ:dɪəm
AM ˌɛndoʊ'kɑrdiəm

endocarp
BR 'ɛndə(ʊ)kɑ:p, -s
AM 'ɛndoʊˌkɑrp, -s

endocarpic
BR ˌɛndə(ʊ)'kɑ:pɪk
AM ˌɛndoʊ'kɑrpɪk

endocentric
BR ˌɛndə(ʊ)'sɛntrɪk
AM ˌɛndoʊ'sɛntrɪk

endocentrically
BR ˌɛndə(ʊ)'sɛntrɪkli
AM ˌɛndə'sɛntrək(ə)li, ˌɛndoʊ'sɛntrək(ə)li

endocrine
BR 'ɛndə(ʊ)krʌɪn, 'ɛndə(ʊ)krɪn
AM 'ɛndəkrən, 'ɛndəˌkrin, 'ɛndəˌkraɪn

endocrinological
BR ˌɛndə(ʊ)krɪnə'lɒdʒɪkl
AM ˌɛndəkrənə'lɑdʒəkəl

endocrinologist
BR ˌɛndə(ʊ)krɪ'nɒlədʒɪst, -s
AM ˌɛndəkrə'nɑlədʒəst, ˌɛndoʊkrə'nɑlədʒəst, -s

endocrinology
BR ˌɛndə(ʊ)krɪ'nɒlədʒi
AM ˌɛndəkrə'nɑlədʒi, ˌɛndoʊkrə'nɑlədʒi

endoderm
BR 'ɛndə(ʊ)də:m, -z
AM 'ɛndəˌdərm, -z

endodermal
BR ˌɛndə(ʊ)'də:ml
AM ˌɛndə'dərməl, ˌɛndoʊ'dərməl

endodermic
BR ˌɛndə(ʊ)'də:mɪk
AM ˌɛndə'dərmɪk, ˌɛndoʊ'dərmɪk

endogamous
BR ɛn'dɒgəməs
AM ɛn'dɑgəməs

endogamy
BR ɛn'dɒgəmi
AM ɛn'dɑgəmi

endogen
BR 'ɛndədʒ(ə)n, -z
AM 'ɛndədʒən, -z

endogenesis
BR ˌɛndə(ʊ)'dʒɛnɪsɪs
AM ˌɛndə'dʒɛnəsəs, ˌɛndoʊ'dʒɛnəsəs

endogenous
BR ɛn'dɒdʒɪnəs, ɛn'dɒdʒn̩əs
AM ɛn'dɑdʒənəs

endogeny
BR ɛn'dɒdʒəni, ɛn'dɒdʒn̩i
AM ɛn'dɑdʒəni

endolymph
BR 'ɛndə(ʊ)lɪmf
AM 'ɛndəˌlɪmf, 'ɛndoʊˌlɪmf

endometria
BR ˌɛndə(ʊ)'mi:trɪə(*r*)
AM ˌɛndə'mitriə, ˌɛndoʊ'mitriə

endometrial
BR ˌɛndə(ʊ)'mi:trɪəl
AM ˌɛndə'mitriəl, ˌɛndoʊ'mitriəl

endometriosis
BR ˌɛndə(ʊ)mi:trɪ'əʊsɪs
AM ˌɛndoʊˌmitri'oʊsəs

endometritis
BR ˌɛndəʊmɪ'trʌɪtɪs
AM ˌɛndəmə'traɪdɪs, ˌɛndoʊmə'traɪdɪs

endometrium
BR ˌɛndə(ʊ)'mi:trɪəm
AM ˌɛndə'mitriəm, ˌɛndoʊ'mitriəm

endomorph
BR 'ɛndə(ʊ)mɔ:f, -s
AM 'ɛndəˌmɔ(ə)rf, -s

endomorphic
BR ˌɛndə(ʊ)'mɔ:fɪk
AM ˌɛndə'mɔrfɪk, ˌɛndoʊ'mɔrfɪk

endomorphy
BR 'ɛndə(ʊ)mɔ:fi
AM 'ɛndəˌmɔrfi, 'ɛndoʊˌmɔrfi

endoparasite
BR ˌɛndəʊ'parəsʌɪt, -s
AM ɛndə'pɛrəˌsaɪt, ˌɛndoʊ'pɛrəˌsaɪt, -s

endoplasm
BR 'ɛndə(ʊ)plaz(ə)m
AM 'ɛndəˌplæz(ə)m, 'ɛndoʊˌplæzəm

endorphin
BR ɛn'dɔ:fɪn, -z
AM ˌɛn'dɔrfin, -z

endorsable
BR ɪn'dɔ:səbl, ɛn'dɔ:səbl
AM ɪn'dɔrsəbəl, ɛn'dɔrsəbəl

endorse
BR ɪn'dɔ:s, ɛn'dɔ:s, -ɪz, -ɪŋ, -t
AM ɪn'dɔ(ə)rs, ɛn'dɔ(ə)rs, -əz, -ɪŋ, -t

endorsee
BR ɪnˌdɔ:'si:, ɛnˌdɔ:'si:, -z
AM ɪnˌdɔr'si, ɛnˌdɔr'si, -z

endorsement
BR ɪn'dɔ:sm(ə)nt, ɛn'dɔ:sm(ə)nt, -s
AM ɪn'dɔrsmənt, ɛn'dɔrsmənt, -s

endorser
BR ɪn'dɔ:sə(r), ɛn'dɔ:sə(r), -z
AM ɪn'dɔrsər, ɛn'dɔrsər, -z

endoscope
BR 'ɛndəskəʊp, -s
AM 'ɛndəˌskoʊp, -s

endoscopic
BR ˌɛndə'skɒpɪk
AM ˌɛndə'skɑpɪk

endoscopically
BR ˌɛndə'skɒpɪkli
AM ˌɛndə'skɑpək(ə)li

endoscopist
BR ɛn'dɒskəpɪst, -s
AM ɛn'dɑskəpəst, -s

endoscopy
BR ɛn'dɒskəp|i, -ɪz
AM ɛn'dɑskəpi, -z

endoskeleton
BR 'ɛndəʊˌskɛlɪt(ə)n, -z
AM 'ɛndəˌskɛlətn, 'ɛndoʊˌskɛlətn, -z

endosperm
BR 'ɛndə(ʊ)spə:m, -z
AM 'ɛndəˌspərm, 'ɛndoʊˌspərm, -z

endospore
BR 'ɛndə(ʊ)spɔ:(r), -z
AM 'ɛndəˌspɔ(ə)r, 'ɛndoʊˌspɔ(ə)r, -z

endothelia
BR ˌɛndə(ʊ)'θi:lɪə(*r*)
AM ˌɛndə'θiliə, ˌɛndoʊ'θiliə

endothelial
BR ˌɛndə(ʊ)'θi:lɪəl
AM ˌɛndə'θiliəl, ˌɛndoʊ'θiliəl

endothelium
BR ˌɛndə(ʊ)'θi:lɪəm
AM ˌɛndə'θiliəm, ˌɛndoʊ'θiliəm

endothermic
BR ˌɛndə(ʊ)'θə:mɪk
AM ˌɛndə'θərmɪk, ˌɛndoʊ'θərmɪk

endothermically
BR ˌɛndə(ʊ)'θə:mɪkli
AM ˌɛndə'θərmək(ə)li, ˌɛndoʊ'θərmək(ə)li

endothermy
BR 'ɛndə(ʊ)ˌθə:mi
AM 'ɛndəˌθərmi, 'ɛndoʊˌθərmi

endow
BR ɪn'daʊ, ɛn'daʊ, -z, -ɪŋ, -d

AM ɪn'daʊ, ɛn'daʊ, -z, -ɪŋ, -d

endower
BR ɪn'daʊə(r), ɛn'daʊə(r), -z
AM ɪn'daʊər, ɛn'daʊər, -z

endowment
BR ɪn'daʊm(ə)nt, ɛn'daʊm(ə)nt, -s
AM ɪn'daʊmənt, ɛn'daʊmənt, -s

endpaper
BR 'ɛn(d),peɪpə(r), -z
AM 'ɛn(d),peɪpər, -z

endplay
BR 'ɛn(d)pleɪ, -z, -ɪŋ, -d
AM 'ɛn(d),pleɪ, -z, -ɪŋ, -d

endpoint
BR 'ɛn(d)pɔɪnt, -s
AM 'ɛn(d),pɔɪnt, -s

endrun
BR 'ɛndrʌn, -z
AM ˌɛn(d)ˈrən, -z

endue
BR ɪn'dju:, ɛn'dju:, ɪn'dʒu:, ɛn'dʒu:, -z, -ɪŋ, -d
AM ɪn'd(j)u, ɛn'd(j)u, -z, -ɪŋ, -d

endurability
BR ɪn,djʊərə'bɪlɨti, ɛn,djʊərə'bɪlɨti, ɪn,dʒʊərə'bɪlɨti, ɛn,dʒʊərə'bɪlɨti, ɪn,djɔ:rə'bɪlɨti, ɛn,djɔ:rə'bɪlɨti, ɪn,dʒɔ:rə'bɪlɨti, ɛn,dʒɔ:rə'bɪlɨti
AM ɪn,d(j)urə'bɪlɨdi, ɛn,d(j)urə'bɪlɨdi

endurable
BR ɪn'djʊərəbl, ɛn'djʊərəbl, ɪn'dʒʊərəbl, ɛn'dʒʊərəbl, ɪn'djɔ:rəbl, ɛn'djɔ:rəbl, ɪn'dʒɔ:rəbl, ɛn'dʒɔ:rəbl
AM ɪn'd(j)urəbəl, ɛn'd(j)urəbəl

endurance
BR ɪn'djʊərn̩s, ɛn'djʊərn̩s, ɪn'dʒʊərn̩s, ɛn'dʒʊərn̩s, ɪn'djɔ:rn̩s, ɛn'djɔ:rn̩s, ɪn'dʒɔ:rn̩s, ɛn'dʒɔ:rn̩s
AM ɪn'd(j)ʊrəns, ɛn'd(j)ʊrəns

endure
BR ɪn'djʊə(r), ɛn'djʊə(r), ɪn'dʒʊə(r), ɛn'dʒʊə(r), ɪn'djɔ:(r), ɛn'djɔ:(r), ɪn'dʒɔ:(r), ɛn'dʒɔ:(r), -z, -ɪŋ, -d
AM ɪn'd(j)ʊ(ə)r, ɛn'd(j)ʊ(ə)r, -z, -ɪŋ, -d

enduringly
BR ɪn'djʊərɪŋli, ɛn'djʊərɪŋli, ɪn'dʒʊərɪŋli, ɛn'dʒʊərɪŋli, ɪn'djɔ:rɪŋli, ɛn'djɔ:rɪŋli, ɪn'dʒɔ:rɪŋli, ɛn'dʒɔ:rɪŋli
AM ɪn'd(j)ʊrɪŋli, ɛn'd(j)ʊrɪŋli

enduro
BR ɪn'djʊərəʊ, ɛn'djʊərəʊ, ɪn'dʒʊərəʊ, ɛn'dʒʊərəʊ, ɪn'djɔ:rəʊ, ɛn'djɔ:rəʊ, ɪn'dʒɔ:rəʊ, ɛn'dʒɔ:rəʊ, -z
AM ɪn'd(j)ʊroʊ, ɛn'd(j)ʊroʊ, -z

endways
BR 'ɛndweɪz
AM 'ɛn(d),weɪz

endwise
BR 'ɛndwʌɪz
AM 'ɛn(d),waɪz

Endymion
BR ɛn'dɪmɪən
AM ɛn'dɪmiən

endzone
BR 'ɛn(d)zəʊn, -z
AM 'ɛn(d),zoʊn, -z

Eneas
BR i:'ni:əs, ɪ'ni:əs
AM ə'niəs, eɪ'niəs

Eneid
BR 'i:nɪɪd, i:'ni:ɪd, ɪ'ni:ɪd
AM ə'niəd, eɪ'niəd

enema
BR 'ɛnɪmə(*r*), -z
AM 'ɛnəmə, -z

enemy
BR 'ɛnɪm|i, -ɪz
AM 'ɛnəmi, -z

Energen
BR 'ɛnədʒ(ə)n
AM 'ɛnərdʒən

energetic
BR ˌɛnə'dʒɛtɪk, -s
AM ˌɛnər'dʒɛdɪk, -s

energetically
BR ˌɛnə'dʒɛtɪkli
AM ˌɛnər'dʒɛdək(ə)li

energise
BR 'ɛnədʒʌɪz, -ɨz, -ɪŋ, -d
AM 'ɛnər,dʒaɪz, -ɨz, -ɪŋ, -d

energiser
BR 'ɛnədʒʌɪzə(r), -z
AM 'ɛnər,dʒaɪzər, -z

energize
BR 'ɛnədʒʌɪz, -ɨz, -ɪŋ, -d
AM 'ɛnər,dʒaɪz, -ɨz, -ɪŋ, -d

energizer
BR 'ɛnədʒʌɪzə(r), -z
AM 'ɛnər,dʒaɪzər, -z

energumen
BR ˌɛnə'gju:mən, -z
AM ˌɛnər'gjumən, -z

energy
BR 'ɛnədʒ|i, -ɪz
AM 'ɛnərdʒi, -z

enervate
BR 'ɛnəveɪt, -s, -ɪŋ, -ɨd
AM 'ɛnər,veɪ|t, -ts, -dɪŋ, -dɨd

enervation
BR ˌɛnə'veɪʃn
AM ˌɛnər'veɪʃən

Enesco
BR ɪ'nɛskəʊ
AM ə'nɛskoʊ

Enewetak
BR ˌɛnɪ'wi:tak
AM ˌɛnə'wi,tɑk

en famille
BR ˌɒ̃ fa'mi:, ˌɒn +
AM ˌɑn fɑ'mi

enfant gâté
BR ˌɒ̃fɒ̃ ga'teɪ, ˌɒnfɒn ga'teɪ, ˌɑ:nfɑ:n ga'teɪ
AM ˌɑnfɑn gɑ'teɪ

enfants gâtés
BR ˌɒ̃fɒ̃ ga'teɪ, ˌɒnfɒn +, ˌɑ:nfɑ:n +
AM ˌɑnfɑn gɑ'teɪ

enfants terribles
BR ˌɒ̃fɒ̃ tɛ'ri:blə(*r*), ˌɒnfɒn +, ˌɑ:nfɑ:n +
AM ˌɑnfɑn tɛ'ribl(ə)

enfant terrible
BR ˌɒ̃fɒ̃ tə'ri:blə(*r*), ˌɒnfɒn +, ˌɑ:nfɑ:n +
AM ˌɑnfɑn tɛ'ribl(ə)

enfeeble
BR ɪn'fi:b|l, ɛn'fi:b|l, -lz, -l̩ɪŋ\-lɪŋ, -ld
AM ɪn'fib|əl, ɛn'fib|əl, -əlz, -(ə)lɪŋ, -əld

enfeeblement
BR ɪn'fi:blm(ə)nt, ɛn'fi:blm(ə)nt
AM ɪn'fibəlmənt, ɛn'fibəlmənt

enfeoff
BR ɪn'fi:f, ɛn'fi:f, ɪn'fɛf, ɛn'fɛf, -s, -ɪŋ, -t
AM ɪn'fif, ɛn'fif, -s, -ɪŋ, -t

enfeoffment
BR ɪn'fi:fm(ə)nt, ɛn'fi:fm(ə)nt, ɪn'fɛfm(ə)nt, ɛn'fɛfm(ə)nt
AM ɪn'fifmənt, ɛn'fifmənt

en fête
BR ˌɒ̃ 'fɛt, ˌɒn +, + 'feɪt
AM ˌɑn 'feɪt, + 'fɛt

enfetter
BR ɪn'fɛt|ə(r), ɛn'fɛt|ə(r), -əz, -(ə)rɪŋ, -əd
AM ɪn'fɛdər, ɛn'fɛdər, -z, -ɪŋ, -t

Enfield
BR 'ɛnfi:ld
AM 'ɛn,fild

enfilade[1]
noun
BR 'ɛnfɨleɪd, -z
AM ˈɛnfəˈlɑd, ˈɛnfəˈleɪd, -z

enfilade[2]
verb
BR ˌɛnfɨ'leɪd, 'ɛnfɨleɪd, -z, -ɪŋ, -ɨd
AM ˈɛnfəˈlɑd, ˈɛnfəˈleɪd, -z, -ɪŋ, -ɨd\-əd

enfold
BR ɪn'fəʊld, ɛn'fəʊld, -z, -ɪŋ, -ɨd
AM ɪn'foʊld, ɛn'foʊld, -z, -ɪŋ, -əd

enforce
BR ɪn'fɔ:s, ɛn'fɔ:s, -ɨz, -ɪŋ, -t
AM ɪn'fɔ(ə)rs, ɛn'fɔ(ə)rs, -əz, -ɪŋ, -t

enforceability
BR ɪn,fɔ:sə'bɪlɨti, ɛn'fɔ:sə'bɪlɨti
AM ɪn,fɔrsə'bɪlɨdi, ɛn,fɔrsə'bɪlɨdi

enforceable
BR ɪn'fɔ:səbl, ɛn'fɔ:səbl
AM ɪn'fɔrsəbəl, ɛn'fɔrsəbəl

enforceably
BR ɪn'fɔ:səbli, ɛn'fɔ:səbli
AM ɪn'fɔrsəbli, ɛn'fɔrsəbli

enforcedly
BR ɪn'fɔ:sɨdli, ɛn'fɔ:sɨdli
AM ɪn'fɔrsədli, ɛn'fɔrsədli

enforcement
BR ɪn'fɔ:sm(ə)nt, ɛn'fɔ:sm(ə)nt
AM ɪn'fɔrsmənt, ɛn'fɔrsmənt

enforcer
BR ɪn'fɔ:sə(r), ɛn'fɔ:sə(r), -z
AM ɪn'fɔrsər, ɛn'fɔrsər, -z

enfranchise
BR ɪn'fran(t)ʃʌɪz, ɛn'fran(t)ʃʌɪz, -ɨz, -ɪŋ, -d
AM ɪn'fræn,tʃaɪz, ɛn'fræn,tʃaɪz, -ɨz, -ɪŋ, -d

enfranchisement
BR ɪn'fran(t)ʃɪzm(ə)nt, ɛn'fran(t)ʃɪzm(ə)nt
AM ən'fræn,tʃaɪzmənt

Engadine
BR 'ɛŋɡədiːn, ,ɛŋɡə'diːn
AM 'ɛŋɡə,din

engage
BR ɪn'ɡeɪdʒ, ɛn'ɡeɪdʒ, ɪŋ'ɡeɪdʒ, ɛŋ'ɡeɪdʒ, -ɪz, -ɪŋ, -d
AM ɪn'ɡeɪdʒ, ɛn'ɡeɪdʒ, ɪŋ'ɡeɪdʒ, ɛŋ'ɡeɪdʒ, -ɪz, -ɪŋ, -d

engagé
BR ,ɒŋɡa'ʒeɪ
AM ,ɑnɡɑ'ʒeɪ, ,ɑŋɡɑ'ʒeɪ

engagement
BR ɪn'ɡeɪdʒm(ə)nt, ɛn'ɡeɪdʒm(ə)nt, ɪŋ'ɡeɪdʒm(ə)nt, ɛŋ'ɡeɪdʒm(ə)nt, -s
AM ɪn'ɡeɪdʒmənt, ɛn'ɡeɪdʒmənt, ɪŋ'ɡeɪdʒmənt, ɛŋ'ɡeɪdʒmənt, -s

engager
BR ɪn'ɡeɪdʒə(r), ɛn'ɡeɪdʒə(r), ɪŋ'ɡeɪdʒə(r), ɛŋ'ɡeɪdʒə(r), -z
AM ɪn'ɡeɪdʒər, ɛn'ɡeɪdʒər, ɪŋ'ɡeɪdʒər, ɛn'ɡeɪdʒər, -z

engaging
BR ɪn'ɡeɪdʒɪŋ, ɛn'ɡeɪdʒɪŋ, ɪŋ'ɡeɪdʒɪŋ, ɛŋ'ɡeɪdʒɪŋ
AM ɪn'ɡeɪdʒɪŋ, ɛn'ɡeɪdʒɪŋ, ɪŋ'ɡeɪdʒɪŋ, ɛŋ'ɡeɪdʒɪŋ

engagingly
BR ɪn'ɡeɪdʒɪŋli, ɛn'ɡeɪdʒɪŋli, ɪŋ'ɡeɪdʒɪŋli, ɛŋ'ɡeɪdʒɪŋli
AM ɪn'ɡeɪdʒɪŋli, ɛn'ɡeɪdʒɪŋli, ɪŋ'ɡeɪdʒɪŋli, ɛŋ'ɡeɪdʒɪŋli

engagingness
BR ɪn'ɡeɪdʒɪŋnɪs, ɛn'ɡeɪdʒɪŋnɪs, ɪŋ'ɡeɪdʒɪŋnɪs, ɛŋ'ɡeɪdʒɪŋnɪs
AM ɪn'ɡeɪdʒɪŋnɪs, ɛn'ɡeɪdʒɪŋnɪs, ɪŋ'ɡeɪdʒɪŋnɪs, ɛŋ'ɡeɪdʒɪŋnɪs

en garde
BR ,ɒ̃ 'ɡɑːd, ,ɒn +
AM ,ɑn 'ɡɑrd

engarland
BR ɪn'ɡɑːlənd, ɛn'ɡɑːlənd, ɪŋ'ɡɑːlənd, ɛŋ'ɡɑːlənd, -z, -ɪŋ, -ɪd
AM ɪn'ɡɑrlənd, ɛn'ɡɑrlənd, ɪŋ'ɡɑrlənd, ɛŋ'ɡɑrlənd, -z, -ɪŋ, -əd

Engelbert
BR 'ɛŋɡlbəːt
AM 'ɛŋɡəl,bərt

Engels
BR 'ɛŋɡlz
AM 'ɛŋɡəlz

engender
BR ɪn'dʒɛnd|ə(r), ɛn'dʒɛnd|ə(r), -əz, -(ə)rɪŋ, -əd
AM ən'dʒɛnd|ər, -ərz, -(ə)rɪŋ, -ərd

engine
BR 'ɛn(d)ʒ(ɪ)n, -z
AM 'ɛndʒən, -z

engineer
BR ,ɛn(d)ʒɪ'nɪə(r), -z, -ɪŋ, -d
AM ,ɛndʒə'nɪ(ə)r, -z, -ɪŋ, -d

engineering
BR ,ɛn(d)ʒɪ'nɪərɪŋ
AM ,ɛndʒə'nɪrɪŋ

engineership
BR ,ɛn(d)ʒɪ'nɪəʃɪp
AM ,ɛndʒə'nɪr,ʃɪp

engineless
BR 'ɛn(d)ʒ(ɪ)nlɪs
AM 'ɛndʒənləs

enginery
BR 'ɛn(d)ʒɪn(ə)ri, 'ɛn(d)ʒn̩(ə)ri
AM 'ɛndʒənri

engird
BR ɪn'ɡəːd, ɛn'ɡəːd, ɪŋ'ɡəːd, ɛŋ'ɡəːd, -z, -ɪŋ, -ɪd
AM ɪn'ɡərd, ɛn'ɡərd, ɪŋ'ɡərd, ɛŋ'ɡərd, -z, -ɪŋ, -əd

engirdle
BR ɪn'ɡəːd|l, ɛn'ɡəːd|l, ɪŋ'ɡəːd|l, ɛŋ'ɡəːd|l, -lz, -l̩ɪŋ\-lɪŋ, -ld
AM ɪn'ɡərdəl, ɛn'ɡərd|əl, ɪŋ'ɡərdəl, ɛŋ'ɡərd|əl, -əlz, -(ə)lɪŋ, -əld

England
BR 'ɪŋɡlənd
AM 'ɪŋ(ɡ)lənd

Englefield
BR 'ɛŋɡlfiːld
AM 'ɛŋɡəl,fild

Englewood
BR 'ɛŋɡlwʊd
AM 'ɛŋɡəl,wʊd

English
BR 'ɪŋɡlɪʃ
AM 'ɪŋ(ɡ)lɪʃ

Englishman
BR 'ɪŋɡlɪʃmən
AM 'ɪŋ(ɡ)lɪʃmən

Englishmen
BR 'ɪŋɡlɪʃmən
AM 'ɪŋ(ɡ)lɪʃmən

Englishness
BR 'ɪŋɡlɪʃnɪs
AM 'ɪŋ(ɡ)lɪʃnɪs

Englishwoman
BR 'ɪŋɡlɪʃ,wʊmən
AM 'ɪŋ(ɡ)lɪʃ,wʊmən

Englishwomen
BR 'ɪŋɡlɪʃ,wɪmɪn
AM 'ɪŋ(ɡ)lɪʃ,wɪmɪn

engorge
BR ɪn'ɡɔːdʒ, ɛn'ɡɔːdʒ, ɪŋ'ɡɔːdʒ, ɛŋ'ɡɔːdʒ, -ɪz, -ɪŋ, -d
AM ɪn'ɡɔrdʒ, ɛn'ɡɔrdʒ, ɪŋ'ɡɔrdʒ, ɛŋ'ɡɔrdʒ, -əz, -ɪŋ, -t

engorgement
BR ɪn'ɡɔːdʒm(ə)nt, ɛn'ɡɔːdʒm(ə)nt, ɪŋ'ɡɔːdʒm(ə)nt, ɛŋ'ɡɔːdʒm(ə)nt
AM ɪn'ɡɔrdʒmənt, ɛn'ɡɔrdʒmənt, ɪŋ'ɡɔrdʒmənt, ɛŋ'ɡɔrdʒmənt

engraft
BR ɪn'ɡrɑːft, ɛn'ɡrɑːft, ɪn'ɡraft, ɛn'ɡraft, ɪŋ'ɡrɑːft, ɛŋ'ɡrɑːft, ɪŋ'ɡraft, ɛŋ'ɡraft, -s, -ɪŋ, -ɪd
AM ɪn'ɡræft, ɛn'ɡræft, ɪŋ'ɡræft, ɛŋ'ɡræft, -s, -ɪŋ, -əd

engraftment
BR ɪn'ɡrɑːf(t)m(ə)nt, ɛn'ɡrɑːf(t)m(ə)nt, ɪn'ɡraf(t)m(ə)nt, ɛn'ɡraf(t)m(ə)nt, ɪŋ'ɡrɑːf(t)m(ə)nt, ɛŋ'ɡrɑːf(t)m(ə)nt, ɪŋ'ɡraf(t)m(ə)nt, ɛŋ'ɡraf(t)m(ə)nt
AM ɪn'ɡræf(t)mənt, ɛn'ɡræf(t)mənt, ɪŋ'ɡræf(t)mənt, ɛŋ'ɡræf(t)mənt

engrail
BR ɪn'ɡreɪl, ɛn'ɡreɪl, ɪŋ'ɡreɪl, ɛŋ'ɡreɪl, -z, -ɪŋ, -d
AM ɪn'ɡreɪl, ɛn'ɡreɪl, ɪŋ'ɡreɪl, ɛŋ'ɡreɪl, -z, -ɪŋ, -d

engrain
BR ɪn'ɡreɪn, ɛn'ɡreɪn, ɪŋ'ɡreɪn, ɛŋ'ɡreɪn, -z, -ɪŋ, -d
AM ɪn'ɡreɪn, ɛn'ɡreɪn, ɪŋ'ɡreɪn, ɛŋ'ɡreɪn, -z, -ɪŋ, -d

engram
BR 'ɛnɡram, 'ɛŋɡram, -z
AM 'ɛnɡræm, 'ɛŋɡræm, -z

engrammatic
BR ,ɛnɡrə'matɪk, ,ɛŋɡrə'matɪk
AM ,ɪnɡrə'mædɪk, ,ɛnɡrə'mædɪk, ,ɪŋɡrə'mædɪk, ,ɛŋɡrə'mædɪk

engrave
BR ɪn'ɡreɪv, ɛn'ɡreɪv, ɪŋ'ɡreɪv, ɛŋ'ɡreɪv, -z, -ɪŋ, -d
AM ɪn'ɡreɪv, ɛn'ɡreɪv, ɪŋ'ɡreɪv, ɛŋ'ɡreɪv, -z, -ɪŋ, -d

engraver
BR ɪn'ɡreɪvə(r), ɛn'ɡreɪvə(r), ɪŋ'ɡreɪvə(r), ɛŋ'ɡreɪvə(r), -z
AM ɪn'ɡreɪvər, ɛn'ɡreɪvər, ɪŋ'ɡreɪvər, ɛŋ'ɡreɪvər, -z

engraving
BR ɪn'ɡreɪvɪŋ, ɛn'ɡreɪvɪŋ, ɪŋ'ɡreɪvɪŋ, ɛŋ'ɡreɪvɪŋ, -z
AM ɪn'ɡreɪvɪŋ, ɛn'ɡreɪvɪŋ, ɪŋ'ɡreɪvɪŋ, ɛŋ'ɡreɪvɪŋ, -z

engross
BR ɪn'ɡrəʊs, ɛn'ɡrəʊs, ɪŋ'ɡrəʊs, ɛŋ'ɡrəʊs, -ɪz, -ɪŋ, -t
AM ɪn'ɡroʊs, ɛn'ɡroʊs, ɪŋ'ɡroʊs, ɛŋ'ɡroʊs, -əz, -ɪŋ, -t

engrossment
BR ɪn'ɡrəʊsm(ə)nt, ɛn'ɡrəʊsm(ə)nt, ɪŋ'ɡrəʊsm(ə)nt, ɛŋ'ɡrəʊsm(ə)nt
AM ɪn'ɡroʊsmənt, ɛn'ɡroʊsmənt, ɪŋ'ɡroʊsmənt, ɛŋ'ɡroʊsmənt

engulf
BR ɪn'ɡʌlf, ɛn'ɡʌlf, ɪŋ'ɡʌlf, ɛŋ'ɡʌlf, -s, -ɪŋ, -t
AM ɪn'ɡəlf, ɛn'ɡəlf, ɪŋ'ɡəlf, ɛŋ'ɡəlf, -s, -ɪŋ, -t

engulfment
BR ɪn'ɡʌlfm(ə)nt, ɛn'ɡʌlfm(ə)nt, ɪŋ'ɡʌlfm(ə)nt, ɛŋ'ɡʌlfm(ə)nt
AM ɪn'ɡəlfmənt, ɛn'ɡəlfmənt, ɪŋ'ɡəlfmənt, ɛŋ'ɡəlfmənt

enhance
BR ɪn'hɑːns, ɛn'hɑːns, ɪn'hans, ɛn'hans, -ɪz, -ɪŋ, -t

AM ɪn'hæns, ɛn'hæns, -əz, -ɪŋ, -t

enhancement
BR ɪn'hɑːnsm(ə)nt, ɛn'hɑːnsm(ə)nt, ɪn'hansm(ə)nt, ɛn'hansm(ə)nt, -s
AM ɪn'hænsmənt, ɛn'hænsmənt, -s

enhancer
BR ɪn'hɑːnsə(r), ɛn'hɑːnsə(r), ɪn'hansə(r), ɛn'hansə(r), -z
AM ɪn'hænsər, ɛn'hænsər, -z

enharmonic
BR ˌɛnhɑː'mɒnɪk
AM ɪnˌ(h)ɑr'mɑnɪk, ɛnˌ(h)ɑr'mɑnɪk

enharmonically
BR ˌɛnhɑː'mɒnɪkli
AM ɪnˌ(h)ɑr'mɑnək(ə)li, ɛnˌ(h)ɑr'mɑnɪək(ə)li

Enid
BR 'iːnɪd
AM 'inɨd, 'eɪnɨd

enigma
BR ɪ'nɪgmə(r), ɛ'nɪgmə(r), -z
AM ɪ'nɪgmə, ɛ'nɪgmə, -z

enigmatic
BR ˌɛnɪg'matɪk
AM ˌɛnɪg'mædɪk

enigmatical
BR ˌɛnɪg'matɨkl
AM ˌɛnɪg'mædəkəl

enigmatically
BR ˌɛnɪg'matɨkli
AM ˌɛnɪg'mædək(ə)li

enigmatise
BR ɪ'nɪgmətʌɪz, ɛ'nɪgmətʌɪz, -ɨz, -ɪŋ, -d
AM ɪ'nɪgməˌtaɪz, ɛ'nɪgməˌtaɪz, -ɨz, -ɪŋ, -d

enigmatize
BR ɪ'nɪgmətʌɪz, ɛ'nɪgmətʌɪz, -ɨz, -ɪŋ, -d
AM ɪ'nɪgməˌtaɪz, ɛ'nɪgməˌtaɪz, -ɨz, -ɪŋ, -d

Eniwetok
BR ˌɛnɪ'wiːtɒk
AM ˌɛnə'wiˌtɑk

enjambment
BR ɪn'dʒam(b)m(ə)nt, ɛn'dʒam(b)m(ə)nt, -s
AM ɪn'dʒæm(b)mənt, ɛn'dʒæm(b)mənt, -s

enjoin
BR ɪn'dʒɔɪn, ɛn'dʒɔɪn, -z, -ɪŋ, -d
AM ɪn'dʒɔɪn, ɛn'dʒɔɪn, -z, -ɪŋ, -d

enjoinment
BR ɪn'dʒɔɪnm(ə)nt, ɛn'dʒɔɪnm(ə)nt
AM ɪn'dʒɔɪnmənt, ɛn'dʒɔɪnmənt

enjoy
BR ɪn'dʒɔɪ, ɛn'dʒɔɪ, -z, -ɪŋ, -d
AM ɪn'dʒɔɪ, ɛn'dʒɔɪ, -z, -ɪŋ, -d

enjoyability
BR ɪnˌdʒɔɪə'bɪlɨti, ɛnˌdʒɔɪə'bɪlɨti
AM ɪnˌdʒɔɪə'bɪlɨdi, ɛnˌdʒɔɪə'bɪlɨdi

enjoyable
BR ɪn'dʒɔɪəbl, ɛn'dʒɔɪəbl
AM ɪn'dʒɔɪəbəl, ɛn'dʒɔɪəbəl

enjoyableness
BR ɪn'dʒɔɪəblnəs, ɛn'dʒɔɪəblnəs
AM ɪn'dʒɔɪəbəlnəs, ɛn'dʒɔɪəbəlnəs

enjoyably
BR ɪn'dʒɔɪəbli, ɛn'dʒɔɪəbli
AM ɪn'dʒɔɪəbli, ɛn'dʒɔɪəbli

enjoyer
BR ɪn'dʒɔɪə(r), ɛn'dʒɔɪə(r), -z
AM ɪn'dʒɔɪər, ɛn'dʒɔɪər, -z

enjoyment
BR ɪn'dʒɔɪm(ə)nt, ɛn'dʒɔɪm(ə)nt, -s
AM ɪn'dʒɔɪmənt, ɛn'dʒɔɪmənt, -s

enkephalin
BR ɛn'kɛfəlɪn, ɛn'kɛfl̩ɪn, ɛŋ'kɛfəlɪn, ɛŋ'kɛfl̩ɪn, -z
AM ɛn'kɛfələn, ɛn'kɛfəˌlɪn, -z

enkindle
BR ɪn'kɪnd|l, ɛn'kɪnd|l, ɪŋ'kɪnd|l, ɛŋ'kɪnd|l, -lz, -l̩ɪŋ\-lɪŋ, -ld
AM ɪn'kɪndəl, ɛn'kɪndəl, ɪŋ'kɪndəl, ɛŋ'kɪndəl, -lz, -lɪŋ, -ld

enlace
BR ɪn'leɪs, ɛn'leɪs, -ɨz, -ɪŋ, -t
AM ɪn'leɪs, ɛn'leɪs, -ɨz, -ɪŋ, -t

enlacement
BR ɪn'leɪsm(ə)nt, ɛn'leɪsm(ə)nt
AM ɪn'leɪsmənt, ɛn'leɪsmənt

enlarge
BR ɪn'lɑːdʒ, ɛn'lɑːdʒ, -ɨz, -ɪŋ, -d
AM ɪn'lɑrdʒ, ɛn'lɑrdʒ, -əz, -ɪŋ, -t

enlargeable
BR ɪn'lɑːdʒəbl, ɛn'lɑːdʒəbl
AM ɪn'lɑrdʒəbəl, ɛn'lɑrdʒəbəl

enlargement
BR ɪn'lɑːdʒm(ə)nt, ɛn'lɑːdʒm(ə)nt, -s
AM ɪn'lɑrdʒmənt, ɛn'lɑrdʒmənt, -s

enlarger
BR ɪn'lɑːdʒə(r), ɛn'lɑːdʒə(r), -z
AM ɪn'lɑrdʒər, ɛn'lɑrdʒər, -z

enlighten
BR ɪn'lʌɪt|n, ɛn'lʌɪt|n, -nz, -n̩ɪŋ\-nɪŋ, -nd
AM ɪn'laɪtn, ɛn'laɪtn, -z, -ɪŋ, -d

enlightener
BR ɪn'lʌɪtn̩ə(r), ɛn'lʌɪtn̩ə(r), -z
AM ɪn'laɪtn̩ər, ɛn'laɪtn̩ər, -z

enlightenment
BR ɪn'lʌɪtn̩m(ə)nt, ɛn'lʌɪtn̩m(ə)nt, -s
AM ɪn'laɪtnmənt, ɛn'laɪtnmənt, -s

enlist
BR ɪn'lɪst, ɛn'lɪst, -s, -ɪŋ, -ɨd
AM ɪn'lɪst, ɛn'lɪst, -s, -ɪŋ, -ɨd

enlister
BR ɪn'lɪstə(r), ɛn'lɪstə(r), -z
AM ɪn'lɪstər, ɛn'lɪstər, -z

enlistment
BR ɪn'lɪs(t)m(ə)nt, ɛn'lɪs(t)m(ə)nt
AM ɪn'lɪs(t)mənt, ɛn'lɪs(t)mənt

enliven
BR ɪn'lʌɪv|n, ɛn'lʌɪv|n, -nz, -n̩ɪŋ\-nɪŋ, -nd
AM ɪn'laɪv|ən, ɛn'laɪv|ən, -ənz, -(ə)nɪŋ, -ənd

enlivener
BR ɪn'lʌɪvn̩ə(r), ɛn'lʌɪvn̩ə(r), -z
AM ɪn'laɪv(ə)nər, ɛn'laɪv(ə)nər, -z

enlivenment
BR ɪn'lʌɪvnm(ə)nt, ɛn'lʌɪvnm(ə)nt
AM ɪn'laɪvənmənt, ɛn'laɪvənmənt

en masse
BR ˌɒ̃ 'mas, ˌɒn +, ˌɒm +
AM ˌɑn 'mæs, ˌɛn 'mæs

enmesh
BR ɪn'mɛʃ, ɛn'mɛʃ, -ɨz, -ɪŋ, -t
AM ɪn'mɛʃ, ɛn'mɛʃ, -əz, -ɪŋ, -t

enmeshment
BR ɪn'mɛʃm(ə)nt, ɛn'mɛʃm(ə)nt
AM ɪn'mɛʃmənt, ɛn'mɛʃmənt

enmity
BR 'ɛnmɨt|i, -ɪz
AM 'ɛnmədi, -z

Ennals
BR 'ɛnlz
AM 'ɛnəlz

ennead
BR 'ɛnɪad, -z
AM 'ɛniˌæd, 'ɛniəd, -z

Ennis
BR 'ɛnɪs
AM 'ɛnəs

Enniskillen
BR ˌɛnɪ'skɪlɪn
AM ˌɛnə'skɪlən

Ennius
BR 'ɛnɪəs
AM 'ɛniəs

ennoble
BR ɪ'nəʊb|l, ɛ'nəʊb|l, -lz, -l̩ɪŋ\-lɪŋ, -ld
AM ə'noʊb|əl, ɛ'noʊb|əl, -əlz, -(ə)lɪŋ, -əld

ennoblement
BR ɪ'nəʊblm(ə)nt, ɛ'nəʊblm(ə)nt
AM ə'noʊbəlmənt, ɛ'noʊbəlmənt

ennui
BR ɒn'wiː, 'ɒnwiː
AM ɑn'wi

Eno®
BR 'iːnəʊ
AM 'inoʊ

Enoch
BR 'iːnɒk
AM 'inək, 'iˌnɑk

enologist
BR iː'nɒlədʒɪst, -s
AM i'nɑlədʒəst, -s

enology
BR iː'nɒlədʒi
AM i'nɑlədʒi

enormity
BR ɪ'nɔːmɨt|i, -ɪz
AM ɪ'nɔrmədi, -z

enormous
BR ɪ'nɔːməs
AM ɪ'nɔrməs

enormously
BR ɪ'nɔːməsli
AM ɪ'nɔrməsli

enormousness
BR ɪ'nɔːməsnəs
AM ɪ'nɔrməsnəs

enosis
BR 'ɛnə(ʊ)sɪs, ɪ'nəʊsɪs
AM ə'noʊsəs, i'noʊsəs, ɛ'noʊsəs

enough
BR ɪ'nʌf
AM ɪ'nəf, i'nəf

enounce
BR ɪ'naʊns, -ɪz, -ɪŋ, -t
AM ɪ'naʊns, i'naʊns, -əz, -ɪŋ, -t

enouncement
BR ɪ'naʊnsm(ə)nt
AM ɪ'naʊnsmənt, i'naʊnsmənt

en passant
BR ˌɒ̃ pa'sɒ̃, ˌɒn +, + pa'sɑːnt, ˌɒn pa'sɑːnt
AM ˌɑn pɑ'sɑn(t)

en pension
BR ˌɒ̃ pɒ̃'sjɒ̃
AM ˌɑn pɑn'sjɔn, ˌɑn pɑn'sjɑn

enplane
BR ɪn'pleɪn, ɛn'pleɪn, -z, -ɪŋ, -d
AM ɪn'pleɪn, ɛn'pleɪn, -z, -ɪŋ, -d

enprint
BR 'ɛnprɪnt, -s
AM ɪn'prɪnt, ɛn'prɪnt, -s

enquire
BR ɪn'kwʌɪə(r), ɛn'kwʌɪə(r), ɪŋ'kwʌɪə(r), ɛŋ'kwʌɪə(r), -z, -ɪŋ, -d
AM ɪn'kwaɪ(ə)r, ɛn'kwaɪ(ə)r, -z, -ɪŋ, -d

enquirer
BR ɪn'kwʌɪərə(r), ɛn'kwʌɪərə(r), ɪŋ'kwʌɪərə(r), ɛŋ'kwʌɪərə(r), -z
AM ɪn'kwaɪ(ə)rər, ɛn'kwaɪ(ə)rər, -z

enquiringly
BR ɪn'kwʌɪərɪŋli, ɛn'kwʌɪərɪŋli, ɪŋ'kwʌɪərɪŋli, ɛŋ'kwʌɪərɪŋli
AM ɪn'kwaɪ(ə)rɪŋli, ɛn'kwaɪ(ə)rɪŋli

enquiry
BR ɪn'kwʌɪər|i, ɛn'kwʌɪər|i, ɪŋ'kwʌɪər|i, ɛŋ'kwʌɪər|i, -ɪz
AM ən'kwaɪ(ə)ri, 'ɪnˌkwaɪ(ə)ri, 'ɛnˌkwaɪ(ə)ri, -z

enrage
BR ɪn'reɪdʒ, ɛn'reɪdʒ, -ɪz, -ɪŋ, -d
AM ɪn'reɪdʒ, ɛn'reɪdʒ, -ɪz, -ɪŋ, -d

enragement
BR ɪn'reɪdʒm(ə)nt, ɛn'reɪdʒm(ə)nt
AM ɪn'reɪdʒmənt, ɛn'reɪdʒmənt

en rapport
BR ˌɒ̃ ra'pɔː(r), ˌɒn +
AM ˌɑn rɑ'pɔ(ə)r(t)

enrapt
BR ɪn'rapt, ɛn'rapt
AM ɪn'ræpt, ɛn'ræpt

enrapture
BR ɪn'raptʃə(r), ɛn'raptʃə(r), -z, -ɪŋ, -d
AM ɪn'ræptʃər, ɛn'ræptʃər, -z, -ɪŋ, -d

enrich
BR ɪn'rɪtʃ, ɛn'rɪtʃ, -ɪz, -ɪŋ, -t
AM ɪn'rɪtʃ, ɛn'rɪtʃ, -ɪz, -ɪŋ, -t

enrichment
BR ɪn'rɪtʃm(ə)nt, ɛn'rɪtʃm(ə)nt, -s
AM ɪn'rɪtʃmənt, ɛn'rɪtʃmənt, -s

Enright
BR 'ɛnrʌɪt
AM 'ɛnˌraɪt

enrobe
BR ɪn'rəʊb, ɛn'rəʊb, -z, -ɪŋ, -d
AM ɪn'roʊb, ɛn'roʊb, -z, -ɪŋ, -d

enrol
BR ɪn'rəʊl, ɛnrəʊl, -z, -ɪŋ, -d
AM ɪn'roʊl, ɛn'roʊl, -z, -ɪŋ, -d

enroll
BR ɪn'rəʊl, ɛnrəʊl, -z, -ɪŋ, -d
AM ɪn'roʊl, ɛn'roʊl, -z, -ɪŋ, -d

enrollee
BR ˌɪnrəʊ'liː, ˌɛnrəʊ'liː, -z
AM ɪnˌroʊ'li, ɛnˌroʊ'li, -z

enroller
BR ɪn'rəʊlə(r), ɛnrəʊlə(r), -z
AM ɪn'roʊlər, ɛn'roʊlər, -z

enrollment
BR ɪn'rəʊlm(ə)nt, ɛn'rəʊlm(ə)nt, -s
AM ɪn'roʊlmənt, ɛn'roʊlmənt, -s

enrolment
BR ɪn'rəʊlm(ə)nt, ɛn'rəʊlm(ə)nt, -s
AM ɪn'roʊlmənt, ɛn'roʊlmənt, -s

en route
BR ˌɒ̃ 'ruːt, ˌɒn +
AM ˌɑn 'rut, ˌɑn 'rʊt

ENSA
BR 'ɛnsə(*r*)
AM 'ɛnsə

ensanguined
BR ɪn'saŋgwɪnd, ɛn'saŋgwɪnd
AM ən'sæŋgwənd, ɛn'sæŋgwənd

ensconce
BR ɪn'skɒns, ɛn'skɒns, -ɪz, -ɪŋ, -t
AM ənz'kɑns, ən'skɑns, ɛnz'kɑns, ɛn'skɑns, -əz, -ɪŋ, -t

ensemble
BR ɒ̃'sɒ̃bl, ɑ̃ː'sɑ̃ːbl, ɒn'sɒmbl, -z
AM ɑn'sɑmbəl, -z

enshrine
BR ɪn'ʃrʌɪn, ɛn'ʃrʌɪn, -z, -ɪŋ, -d
AM ɪn'ʃraɪn, ɛn'ʃraɪn, -z, -ɪŋ, -d

enshrinement
BR ɪn'ʃrʌɪnm(ə)nt, ɛn'ʃrʌɪnm(ə)nt
AM ɪn'ʃraɪnmənt, ɛn'ʃraɪnmənt

enshroud
BR ɪn'ʃraʊd, ɛn'ʃraʊd, -z, -ɪŋ, -ɪd
AM ɪn'ʃraʊd, ɛn'ʃraʊd, -z, -ɪŋ, -əd

ensiform
BR 'ɛnsɪfɔːm
AM 'ɛnsəˌfɔ(ə)rm

ensign[1]
flag
BR 'ɛnsn, -z
AM 'ɛnsən, -z

ensign[2]
officer
BR 'ɛnsʌɪn, 'ɛnsn, -z
AM 'ɛnsən, -z

ensigncy
BR 'ɛnsʌɪns|i, -ɪz
AM 'ɛnsənsi, -z

ensilage
BR 'ɛnsɪl|ɪdʒ, 'ɛnsḷ|ɪdʒ, ɪn'sʌɪl|ɪdʒ, ɛn'sʌɪl|ɪdʒ, -ɪdʒɪz, -ɪdʒɪŋ, -ɪdʒd
AM 'ɛnsəlɪdʒ, -ɪz, -ɪŋ, -d

ensile
BR ɪn'sʌɪl, ɛn'sʌɪl, -z, -ɪŋ, -d
AM ɪn'saɪl, ɛn'saɪl, -z, -ɪŋ, -d

enslave
BR ɪn'sleɪv, ɛn'sleɪv, -z, -ɪŋ, -d
AM ɪn'sleɪv, ɛn'sleɪv, -z, -ɪŋ, -d

enslavement
BR ɪn'sleɪvm(ə)nt, ɛn'sleɪvm(ə)nt
AM ɪn'sleɪvmənt, ɛn'sleɪvmənt

enslaver
BR ɪn'sleɪvə(r), ɛn'sleɪvə(r), -z
AM ɪn'sleɪvər, ɛn'sleɪvər, -z

ensnare
BR ɪn'snɛː(r), ɛn'snɛː(r), -z, -ɪŋ, -d
AM ən'snɛ(ə)r, ɛn'snɛ(ə)r, -z, -ɪŋ, -d

ensnarement
BR ɪn'snɛːm(ə)nt, ɛn'snɛːm(ə)nt
AM ən'snɛrmənt, ɛn'snɛrmənt

ensnarl
BR ɪn'snɑːl, ɛn'snɑːl, -z, -ɪŋ, -d
AM ən'snɑrl, ɛn'snɑrl, -z, -ɪŋ, -d

Ensor
BR 'ɛnsɔː(r)
AM 'ɛnˌsɔ(ə)r

enstatite
BR 'ɛnstətʌɪt
AM 'ɛnstəˌtaɪt

ensue
BR ɪn'sjuː, ɛn'sjuː, -z, -ɪŋ, -d
AM ɪn'su, ɛn'su, -z, -ɪŋ, -d

en suite
BR ˌɒ̃ 'swiːt, ˌɒn +
AM ˌɑn 'swit

ensure
BR ɪn'ʃʊə(r), ɛn'ʃʊə(r), ɪn'ʃɔː(r), ɛn'ʃɔː(r), -z, -ɪŋ, -d
AM ɪn'ʃʊ(ə)r, ɛn'ʃʊ(ə)r, -z, -ɪŋ, -d

ensurer
BR ɪn'ʃʊərə(r), ɛn'ʃʊərə(r), ɪn'ʃɔːrə(r), ɛn'ʃɔːrə(r), -z
AM ɪn'ʃʊrər, ɛn'ʃʊrər, -z

enswathe
BR ɪn'sweɪð, ɛn'sweɪð, -z, -ɪŋ, -d
AM ən'swɑð, ɛn'swɑð, -z, -ɪŋ, -d

enswathement
BR ɪn'sweɪðm(ə)nt, ɛn'sweɪðm(ə)nt
AM ən'swɑðmənt, ɛn'swɑðmənt

entablature
BR ɪn'tablətʃə(r), ɛn'tablətʃə(r), -z
AM ən'tæbləˌtʃʊ(ə)r, ən'tæblətʃər, ən'tæbləˌtjʊ(ə)r, -z

entablement
BR ɪn'teɪblm(ə)nt, ɛn'teɪblm(ə)nt
AM ən'teɪbəlmənt, ɛn'teɪbəlmənt

entail[1]
noun
BR ɪn'teɪl, ɛn'teɪl, -z
AM 'ɛnˌteɪl, -z

entail[2]
verb
BR ɪn'teɪl, ɛn'teɪl, -z, -ɪŋ, -d

AM ɪn'teɪl, ɛn'teɪl, -z, -ɪŋ, -d

entailment
BR ɪn'teɪlm(ə)nt, ɛn'teɪlm(ə)nt, -s
AM ɪn'teɪlmənt, ɛn'teɪlmənt, -s

entangle
BR ɪn'taŋg|l, ɛn'taŋg|l, -lz, -l̩ɪŋ\-lɪŋ, -ld
AM ɪn'tæŋg|əl, ɛn'tæŋg|əl, -əlz, -(ə)lɪŋ, -əld

entanglement
BR ɪn'taŋglm(ə)nt, ɛn'taŋglm(ə)nt, -s
AM ɪn'tæŋgəlmənt, ɛn'tæŋgəlmənt, -s

entases
BR 'ɛntəsiːz
AM 'ɛn(t)əsiz

entasis
BR 'ɛntəsɪs
AM 'ɛn(t)əsəs

Entebbe
BR ɛn'tɛbi, ɪn'tɛbi
AM ɛn'tɛbi

entelechy
BR ɛn'tɛləki, ɪn'tɛləki
AM ən'tɛləki, ɛn'tɛləki

entellus
BR ɪn'tɛləs, ɛn'tɛləs, -ɪz
AM ən'tɛləs, ɛn'tɛləs, -əz

entendre
BR ɒn'tɒndrə(r), ɒ̃'tɒ̃drə(r), -z
AM ɑn'tɑndrə, -z

entente
BR ɑːn'tɑːnt, ɒn'tɒnt, ɒ̃'tɒ̃t, -s
AM ɑn'tɑnt, -s

entente cordiale
BR ɑːn,tɑːnt ,kɔːdɪ'ɑːl, ɒn'tɒnt +, ɒ̃,tɒ̃t +
AM ɑn'tɑnt ,kɔrd(ʒ)i'ɑl

enter
BR 'ɛnt|ə(r), -əz, -(ə)rɪŋ, -əd
AM 'ɛn|(t)ər, -(t)ərz, -t(ə)rɪŋ\-ərɪŋ, -(t)ərd

enterable
BR 'ɛnt(ə)rəbl
AM 'ɛn(t)ərəbəl

enterer
BR 'ɛnt(ə)rə(r), -z
AM 'ɛn(t)ərər, -z

enteric
BR ɛn'tɛrɪk
AM ɛn'tɛrɪk

enteritis
BR ,ɛntə'rʌɪtɪs
AM ,ɛn(t)ə'raɪdɪs

enterostomy
BR ,ɛntə'rɒstəm|i, -ɪz
AM ,ɛn(t)ə'rɑstəmi, -z

enterotomy
BR ,ɛntə'rɒtəm|i, -ɪz
AM ,ɛn(t)ə'rɑdəmi, -z

enterovirus
BR 'ɛnt(ə)rəʊ,vʌɪrəs, -ɪz
AM 'ɛn(t)əroʊ,vaɪrəs, -əz

enterprise
BR 'ɛntəprʌɪz, -ɪz
AM 'ɛn(t)ər,praɪz, -ɪz

enterpriser
BR 'ɛntəprʌɪzə(r), -z
AM 'ɛn(t)ər,praɪzər, -z

enterprising
BR 'ɛntəprʌɪzɪŋ
AM 'ɛn(t)ər,praɪzɪŋ

enterprisingly
BR 'ɛntəprʌɪzɪŋli
AM 'ɛn(t)ər,praɪzɪŋli

entertain
BR ,ɛntə'teɪn, -z, -ɪŋ, -d
AM ,ɛn(t)ər'teɪn, -z, -ɪŋ, -d

entertainer
BR ,ɛntə'teɪnə(r), -z
AM ,ɛn(t)ər'teɪnər, -z

entertaining
BR ,ɛntə'teɪnɪŋ
AM ,ɛn(t)ər'teɪnɪŋ

entertainingly
BR ,ɛntə'teɪnɪŋli
AM ,ɛn(t)ər'teɪnɪŋli

entertainment
BR ,ɛntə'teɪnm(ə)nt, -s
AM ,ɛn(t)ər'teɪ(n)mənt, -s

enthalpy
BR 'ɛnθalpi, 'ɛnθ(ə)lpi, ɛn'θalpi, ɪn'θalpi
AM 'ɛn,θælpi, ən'θælpi, ɛn'θælpi

enthral
BR ɪn'θrɔːl, ɛn'θrɔːl, -z, -ɪŋ, -d
AM ɪn'θrɔl, ɛn'θrɔl, ɪn'θrɑl, ɛn'θrɑl, -z, -ɪŋ, -d

enthrall
BR ɪn'θrɔːl, ɛn'θrɔːl, -z, -ɪŋ, -d
AM ɪn'θrɔl, ɛn'θrɔl, ɪn'θrɑl, ɛn'θrɑl, -z, -ɪŋ, -d

enthrallment
BR ɪn'θrɔːlm(ə)nt, ɛn'θrɔːlm(ə)nt
AM ɪn'θrɔlmənt, ɛn'θrɔlmənt, ɪn'θrɑlmənt, ɛn'θrɑlmənt

enthralment
BR ɪn'θrɔːlm(ə)nt, ɛn'θrɔːlm(ə)nt
AM ɪn'θrɔlmənt, ɛn'θrɔlmənt, ɪn'θrɑlmənt, ɛn'θrɑlmənt

enthrone
BR ɪn'θrəʊn, ɛn'θrəʊn, -z, -ɪŋ, -d
AM ən'θroʊn, ɛn'θroʊn, -z, -ɪŋ, -d

enthronement
BR ɪn'θrəʊnm(ə)nt, ɛn'θrəʊnm(ə)nt, -s
AM ən'θroʊnmənt, ɛn'θroʊnmənt, -s

enthronisation
BR ɪn,θrəʊnʌɪ'zeɪʃn, ɛn,θrəʊnʌɪ'zeɪʃn
AM ən,θroʊnə'zeɪʃən, ɛn,θroʊnə'zeɪʃən, ən,θroʊ,naɪ'zeɪʃən, ɛn,θroʊ,naɪ'zeɪʃən

enthronization
BR ɪn,θrəʊnʌɪ'zeɪʃn, ɛn,θrəʊnʌɪ'zeɪʃn
AM ən,θroʊnə'zeɪʃən, ɛn,θroʊnə'zeɪʃən, ən,θroʊ,naɪ'zeɪʃən, ɛn,θroʊ,naɪ'zeɪʃən

enthuse
BR ɪn'θjuːz, ɛn'θjuːz, -ɪz, -ɪŋ, -d
AM ɪn'θ(j)uz, ɛn'θ(j)uz, -əz, -ɪŋ, -t

enthusiasm
BR ɪn'θjuːzɪaz(ə)m, ɛn'θjuːzɪaz(ə)m, -z
AM ɪn'θ(j)uzi,æzəm, ɛn'θ(j)uzi,æzəm, -z

enthusiast
BR ɪn'θjuːzɪast, ɛn'θjuːzɪast, -s
AM ɪn'θ(j)uzi,æst, ɛn'θ(j)uzi,æst, -s

enthusiastic
BR ɪn,θjuːzɪ'astɪk, ɛn,θjuːzɪ'astɪk
AM ən,θ(j)uzi'æstɪk, ɛn,θ(j)uzi'æstɪk

enthusiastically
BR ɪn,θjuːzɪ'astɪkli, ɛn,θjuːzɪ'astɪkli
AM ən,θ(j)uzi'æstək(ə)li, ɛn,θ(j)uzi'æstək(ə)li

enthymeme
BR 'ɛnθɪmiːm
AM 'ɛnθə,mim

entice
BR ɪn'tʌɪs, ɛn'tʌɪs, -ɪz, -ɪŋ, -t
AM ɪn'taɪs, ɛn'taɪs, -ɪz, -ɪŋ, -t

enticement
BR ɪn'tʌɪsm(ə)nt, ɛn'tʌɪsm(ə)nt, -s
AM ɪn'taɪsmənt, ɛn'taɪsmənt, -s

enticer
BR ɪn'tʌɪsə(r), ɛn'tʌɪsə(r), -z
AM ɪn'taɪsər, ɛn'taɪsər, -z

enticing
BR ɪn'tʌɪsɪŋ, ɛn'tʌɪsɪŋ
AM ɪn'taɪsɪŋ, ɛn'taɪsɪŋ

enticingly
BR ɪn'tʌɪsɪŋli, ɛn'tʌɪsɪŋli
AM ɪn'taɪsɪŋli, ɛn'taɪsɪŋli

entire
BR ɪn'tʌɪə(r), ɛn'tʌɪə(r)
AM ən'taɪ(ə)r, ɛn'taɪ(ə)r

entirely
BR ɪn'tʌɪəli, ɛn'tʌɪəli
AM ən'taɪ(ə)rli, ɛn'taɪ(ə)rli

entirety
BR ɪn'tʌɪərɪti, ɛn'tʌɪərɪti
AM ɪn'taɪrədi, ɪn'taɪ(ə)rdi, ɛn'taɪrədi, ɛn'taɪ(ə)rdi

entitative
BR 'ɛntɪtətɪv
AM 'ɛn(t)ə,teɪdɪv, 'ɛn(t)ədədɪv

entitle
BR ɪn'tʌɪt|l, ɛn'tʌɪt|l, -lz, -l̩ɪŋ\-lɪŋ, -ld
AM ɪn'taɪdəl, ɛn'taɪdəl, -z, -ɪŋ, -d

entitlement
BR ɪn'tʌɪtlm(ə)nt, ɛn'tʌɪtlm(ə)nt, -s
AM ɪn'taɪdlmənt, ɛn'taɪdlmənt, -s

entity
BR 'ɛntɪt|i, -ɪz
AM 'ɛn(t)ədi, -z

entomb
BR ɪn'tuːm, ɛn'tuːm, -z, -ɪŋ, -d
AM ɪn'tum, ɛn'tum, -z, -ɪŋ, -d

entombment
BR ɪn'tuːmm(ə)nt, ɛn'tuːmm(ə)nt, -s
AM ɪn'tu(m)mənt, ɛn'tu(m)mənt, -s

entomic
BR ɛn'tɒmɪk
AM ɛn'tɑmɪk

entomological
BR ,ɛntəmə'lɒdʒɪkl
AM ,ɛn(t)əmə'lɑdʒəkəl

entomologically
BR ,ɛntəmə'lɒdʒɪkli
AM ,ɛn(t)əmə'lɑdʒək(ə)li

entomologist
BR ,ɛntə'mɒlədʒɪst, -s
AM ,ɛn(t)ə'mɑlədʒəst, -s

entomology
BR ,ɛntə'mɒlədʒi
AM ,ɛn(t)ə'mɑlədʒi

entomophagous
BR ˌɛntəˈmɒfəgəs
AM ˌɛn(t)əˈmɑfəgəs

entomophilous
BR ˌɛntəˈmɒfɪləs
AM ˌɛn(t)əˈmɑfələs

entoparasite
BR ˌɛntəʊˈparəsʌɪt, -s
AM ˌɛn(t)oʊˈpɛrəˌsaɪt, -s

entophyte
BR ˈɛntəfʌɪt, -s
AM ˈɛn(t)əˌfaɪt, -s

entourage
BR ˈɒntʊrɑːʒ, ˈɒ̃tʊrɑːʒ, -ɪz
AM ˈɑntəˌrɑʒ, ˈɑntʊˌrɑʒ, -əz

entr'acte
BR ˈɒntrakt, ɒnˈtrakt, ˈɒ̃trakt, ɒ̃ˈtrakt, -s
AM ˈɑnˌtrækt, ˈɑnˌtrɑkt, -s

entrails
BR ˈɛntreɪlz
AM ˈɛntrəlz, ˈɛntreɪlz

entrain
BR ɪnˈtreɪn, ɛnˈtreɪn, -z, -ɪŋ, -d
AM ɪnˈtreɪn, ɛnˈtreɪn, -z, -ɪŋ, -d

entrainment
BR ɪnˈtreɪnm(ə)nt, ɛnˈtreɪnm(ə)nt
AM ɪnˈtreɪnmənt, ɛnˈtreɪnmənt

entrammel
BR ɪnˈtram|l, ɛnˈtram|l, -lz, -l̩ɪŋ \-əlɪŋ, -ld
AM ɪnˈtræməl, ɛnˈtræməl, -z, -ɪŋ, -d

entrance¹
noun
BR ˈɛntr(ə)ns, -ɪz
AM ˈɛntrəns, -əz

entrance²
verb
BR ɪnˈtrɑːns, ɛnˈtrɑːns, ɪnˈtrans, ɛnˈtrans, -ɪz, -ɪŋ, -t
AM ɪnˈtræns, ɛnˈtræns, -əz, -ɪŋ, -t

entrancement
BR ɪnˈtrɑːnsm(ə)nt, ɛnˈtrɑːnsm(ə)nt, ɪnˈtransm(ə)nt, ɛnˈtransm(ə)nt
AM ɪnˈtrænsmənt, ɛnˈtrænsmənt

entrancingly
BR ɪnˈtrɑːnsɪŋli, ɛnˈtrɑːnsɪŋli, ɪnˈtransɪŋli, ɛnˈtransɪŋli
AM ɪnˈtrænsɪŋli, ɛnˈtrænsɪŋli

entrant
BR ˈɛntr(ə)nt, -s
AM ˈɛntrənt, -s

entrap
BR ɪnˈtrap, ɛnˈtrap, -s, -ɪŋ, -t
AM ɪnˈtræp, ɛnˈtræp, -s, -ɪŋ, -t

entrapment
BR ɪnˈtrapm(ə)nt, ɛnˈtrapm(ə)nt, -s
AM ɪnˈtræpmənt, ɛnˈtræpmənt, -s

entrapper
BR ɪnˈtrapə(r), ɛnˈtrapə(r), -z
AM ɪnˈtræpər, ɛnˈtræpər, -z

entreat
BR ɪnˈtriːt, ɛnˈtriːt, -s, -ɪŋ, -ɪd
AM ɪnˈtri|t, ɛnˈtri|t, -ts, -dɪŋ, -dɪd

entreatingly
BR ɪnˈtriːtɪŋli, ɛnˈtriːtɪŋli
AM ɪnˈtridɪŋli, ɛnˈtridɪŋli

entreaty
BR ɪnˈtriːt|i, ɛnˈtriːt|i, -ɪz
AM ɪnˈtridi, ɛnˈtridi, -z

entrechat
BR ˈɒ̃trəʃɑː(r), ˈɒntrəʃɑː(r), ˈɑːntrəʃɑː(r), -z
AM ˌɑntrəˈʃɑ, -z

entrecôte
BR ˈɒntrəkəʊt, ˈɒ̃trəkəʊt, -s
AM ˈɑntrəˌkoʊt, -s

entrée¹
dinner
BR ˈɒntreɪ, ˈɒ̃treɪ, -z
AM ˈɑnˌtreɪ, -z

entrée²
introduction
BR ˈɒntreɪ, ˈɒ̃treɪ, -z
AM ˌɑnˈtreɪ, ˈɑnˌtreɪ, -z

entremets
BR ˈɒntrəmeɪ, ˈɒ̃trəmeɪ, -z
AM ˈɑntrəˌmeɪ, -z

entrench
BR ɪnˈtrɛn(t)ʃ, ɛnˈtrɛn(t)ʃ, -ɪz, -ɪŋ, -t
AM ɪnˈtrɛn(t)ʃ, ɛnˈtrɛn(t)ʃ, -əz, -ɪŋ, -t

entrenchment
BR ɪnˈtrɛn(t)ʃm(ə)nt, ɛnˈtrɛn(t)ʃm(ə)nt, -s
AM ɪnˈtrɛn(t)ʃmənt, ɛnˈtrɛn(t)ʃmənt, -s

entre nous
BR ˌɒntrə ˈnuː, ɒ̃trə +, ˈɑːntrə +
AM ˈɑntrə ˈnu

entrepôt
BR ˈɒntrəpəʊ, ˈɒ̃trəpəʊ, -z
AM ˈɑntrəˌpoʊ, -z

entrepreneur
BR ˌɒntrəprəˈnəː(r), ˌɒ̃trəprəˈnəː(r), ˌɑːntrəprəˈnəː(r), -z
AM ˌɑntrəprəˈnʊ(ə)r, ˌɑntrəprəˈnər, -z

entrepreneurial
BR ˌɒntrəprəˈnəːrɪəl, ˌɒ̃trəprəˈnəːrɪəl, ˌɑːntrəprəˈnəːrɪəl
AM ˌɑntrəprəˈnəriəl, ˌɑntrəprəˈnʊriəl

entrepreneurialism
BR ˌɒntrəprəˈnəːrɪəlɪz(ə)m, ˌɒ̃trəprəˈnəːrɪəlɪz(ə)m, ˌɑːntrəprəˈnəːeɪəlɪz(ə)m
AM ˌɑntrəprəˈnəriəˌlɪzəm, ˌɑntrəprəˈnʊriəˌlɪzəm

entrepreneurially
BR ˌɒntrəprəˈnəːrɪəli, ˌɒ̃trəprəˈnəːrɪəli, ˌɑːntrəprəˈnəːrɪəli
AM ˌɑntrəprəˈnəriəli, ˌɑntrəprəˈnʊriəli

entrepreneurship
BR ˌɒntrəprəˈnəːʃɪp, ˌɒ̃trəprəˈnəːʃɪp, ˌɑːntrəprəˈnəːʃɪp
AM ˌɑntrəprəˈnərˌʃɪp, ˌɑntrəprəˈnʊrˌʃɪp

entresol
BR ˈɒntrəsɒl, ˈɒ̃trəsɒl, -z
AM ˈɛn(t)ərˌsɑl, ˈɑntrəˌsɑl, -z

entrism
BR ˈɛntrɪz(ə)m
AM ˈɛnˌtrɪzəm

entrist
BR ˈɛntrɪst, -s
AM ˈɛntrəst, -s

entropic
BR ɛnˈtrɒpɪk, ɛnˈtrəʊpɪk
AM ɛnˈtrɑpɪk

entropically
BR ɛnˈtrɒpɪkli
AM ɛnˈtrɑpək(ə)li

entropy
BR ˈɛntrəpi
AM ˈɛntrəpi

entrust
BR ɪnˈtrʌst, ɛnˈtrʌst, -s, -ɪŋ, -ɪd
AM ənˈtrəst, ɛnˈtrəst, -s, -ɪŋ, -əd

entrustment
BR ɪnˈtrʌs(t)m(ə)nt, ɛnˈtrʌs(t)m(ə)nt
AM ənˈtrəs(t)mənt, ɛnˈtrəs(t)mənt

entry
BR ˈɛntr|i, -ɪz
AM ˈɛntri, -z

entryism
BR ˈɛntrɪɪz(ə)m
AM ˈɛntriˌɪzəm

entryist
BR ˈɛntrɪɪst, -s
AM ˈɛntriɪst, -s

entryphone®
BR ˈɛntrɪfəʊn, -z
AM ˈɛntriˌfoʊn, -z

entryway
BR ˈɛntrɪweɪ, -z
AM ˈɛntriˌweɪ, -z

entwine
BR ɪnˈtwʌɪn, ɛnˈtwʌɪn, -z, -ɪŋ, -d
AM ənˈtwaɪn, ɛnˈtwaɪn, -z, -ɪŋ, -d

entwinement
BR ɪnˈtwʌɪnm(ə)nt, ɛnˈtwʌɪnm(ə)nt
AM ənˈtwaɪnmənt, ɛnˈtwaɪnmənt

enucleate
BR ɪˈnjuːklɪeɪt, -s, -ɪŋ, -ɪd
AM əˈn(j)ukliˌeɪ|t, iˈn(j)ukliˌeɪ|t, -ts, -dɪŋ, -dɪd

enucleation
BR ɪˌnjuːklɪˈeɪʃn
AM əˌn(j)ukliˈeɪʃən, iˌn(j)ukliˈeɪʃən

Enugu
BR ɪˈnuːguː, ɛˈnuːguː
AM əˈnugu

enumerable
BR ɪˈnjuːm(ə)rəbl
AM əˈn(j)umərəbəl, iˈn(j)umərəbəl

enumerate
BR ɪˈnjuːməreɪt, -s, -ɪŋ, -ɪd
AM əˈn(j)uməˌreɪ|t, iˈn(j)uməˌreɪ|t, -ts, -dɪŋ, -dɪd

enumeration
BR ɪˌnjuːməˈreɪʃn, -z
AM əˌn(j)uməˈreɪʃən, iˌn(j)uməˈreɪʃən, -z

enumerative
BR ɪˈnjuːm(ə)rətɪv
AM əˈn(j)umərədɪv, iˈn(j)umərədɪv, əˈn(j)uməˌreɪdɪv, iˈn(j)uməˌreɪdɪv

enumerator
BR ɪˈnjuːməreɪtə(r), -z
AM əˈn(j)uməˌreɪdər, iˈn(j)uməˌreɪdər, -z

enunciate
BR ɪˈnʌnsɪeɪt, ɪˈnʌnʃɪeɪt, -s, -ɪŋ, -ɪd
AM iˈnənsiˌeɪ|t, əˈnənsiˌeɪ|t, -ts, -dɪŋ, -dɪd

enunciation
BR ɪˌnʌnsɪˈeɪʃn, ɪˌnʌnʃɪˈeɪʃn, -z
AM iˌnənsiˈeɪʃən, əˌnənsiˈeɪʃən, -z

enunciative
BR ɪˈnʌnsɪətɪv, ɪˈnʌnʃɪətɪv, ɪˈnʌnsɪeɪtɪv, ɪˈnʌnʃɪeɪtɪv
AM iˈnənsiədɪv, əˈnənsiədɪv, iˈnənsiˌeɪdɪv, əˈnənsiˌeɪdɪv

enunciatively
BR ɪˈnʌnsɪətɨvli, ɪˈnʌnʃɪətɨvli
AM iˈnənsiəˌtɨvli, əˈnənsiəˌtɨvli, iˈnənsiˌeɪdɨvli, əˈnənsiˌeɪdɨvli

enunciator
BR ɪˈnʌnsɪeɪtə(r), -z
AM iˈnənsiˌeɪdər, əˈnənsiˌeɪdər, -z

enure
BR ɪˈnjʊə(r), ɪˈnjɔː(r), -z, -ɪŋ, -d
AM əˈn(j)ʊər, -z, -ɪŋ, -d

enuresis
BR ˌɛnjʊˈriːsɪs
AM ˌɛnjəˈrisəs

enuretic
BR ˌɛnjʊˈrɛtɪk, -s
AM ˌɛnjəˈrɛdɪk, -s

envelop
BR ɪnˈvɛləp, ɛnˈvɛləp, -s, -ɪŋ, -t
AM ənˈvɛləp, ɛnˈvɛləp, -s, -ɪŋ, -t

envelope
BR ˈɛnvələʊp, ˈɒnvələʊp, -s
AM ˈɛnvəˌloʊp, ˈɑnvəˌloʊp, -s

envelopment
BR ɪnˈvɛləpm(ə)nt, ɛnˈvɛləpm(ə)nt, -s
AM ənˈvɛləpmənt, ɛnˈvɛləpmənt, -s

envenom
BR ɪnˈvɛnəm, ɛnˈvɛnəm, -z, -ɪŋ, -d
AM ənˈvɛnəm, ɛnˈvɛnəm, -z, -ɪŋ, -d

enviable
BR ˈɛnvɪəbl
AM ˈɛnviəbəl

enviably
BR ˈɛnvɪəbli
AM ˈɛnviəbli

envier
BR ˈɛnvɪə(r), -z
AM ˈɛnviər, -z

envious
BR ˈɛnvɪəs
AM ˈɛnviəs

enviously
BR ˈɛnvɪəsli
AM ˈɛnviəsli

environ
BR ɪnˈvʌɪrən, ɪnˈvʌɪrn̩, ɛnˈvʌɪrən, ɛnˈvʌɪrn̩, -z, -ɪŋ, -d
AM ənˈvaɪrən, ənˈvaɪ(ə)rn, ɛnˈvaɪrən, ɛnˈvaɪ(ə)rn, -z, -ɪŋ, -d

environment
BR ɪnˈvʌɪrənm(ə)nt, ɪnˈvʌɪrn̩m(ə)nt, ɛnˈvʌɪrənm(ə)nt, ɛnˈvʌɪrn̩m(ə)nt, -s
AM ənˈvaɪrənmənt, ənˈvaɪ(ə)rnmənt, ɛnˈvaɪrənmənt, ɛnˈvaɪ(ə)rnmənt, -s

environmental
BR ɪnˌvʌɪrənˈmɛntl, ɪnˌvʌɪrn̩ˈmɛntl, ɛnˌvʌɪrənˈmɛntl, ɛnˌvʌɪrn̩ˈmɛntl
AM ənˌvaɪrənˈmɛn(t)l, ənˌvaɪ(ə)rnˈmɛn(t)l, ɛnˌvaɪrənˈmɛn(t)l, ɛnˌvaɪ(ə)rnˈmɛn(t)l

environmentalism
BR ɪnˌvʌɪrənˈmɛntl̩ɪz(ə)m, ɪnˌvʌɪrn̩ˈmɛntl̩ɪz(ə)m, ɛnˌvʌɪrənˈmɛntl̩ɪz(ə)m, ɛnˌvʌɪrn̩ˈmɛntl̩ɪz(ə)m
AM ənˌvaɪrənˈmɛn(t)lˌɪzəm, ənˌvaɪ(ə)rnˈmɛn(t)lˌɪzəm, ɛnˌvaɪrənˈmɛn(t)lˌɪzəm, ɛnˌvaɪ(ə)rnˈmɛn(t)lˌɪzəm

environmentalist
BR ɪnˌvʌɪrənˈmɛntl̩ɪst, ɪnˌvʌɪrn̩ˈmɛntl̩ɪst, ɛnˌvʌɪrənˈmɛntl̩ɪst, ɛnˌvʌɪrn̩ˈmɛntl̩ɪst, -s
AM ənˌvaɪrənˈmɛn(t)l̩əst, ənˌvaɪ(ə)rnˈmɛn(t)l̩əst, ɛnˌvaɪrənˈmɛn(t)l̩əst, ɛnˌvaɪ(ə)rnˈmɛn(t)l̩əst, -s

environmentally
BR ɪnˌvʌɪrənˈmɛntl̩i, ɪnˌvʌɪrn̩ˈmɛntl̩i, ɛnˌvʌɪrənˈmɛntl̩i, ɛnˌvʌɪrn̩ˈmɛntl̩i, ɪnˌvʌɪrənˈmɛntəli, ɪnˌvʌɪrn̩ˈmɛntəli, ɛnˌvʌɪrənˈmɛntəli, ɛnˌvʌɪrn̩ˈmɛntəli
AM ənˌvaɪrənˈmɛn(t)l̩i, ənˌvaɪ(ə)rnˈmɛn(t)l̩i, ɛnˌvaɪrənˈmɛn(t)l̩i, ɛnˌvaɪ(ə)rnˈmɛn(t)l̩i

environs
plural noun
BR ɪnˈvʌɪrənz, ɪnˈvʌɪrn̩z, ɛnˈvʌɪrənz, ɛnˈvʌɪrn̩z
AM ənˈvaɪrənz, ənˈvaɪ(ə)rnz, ɛnˈvaɪrənz, ɛnˈvaɪ(ə)rnz

envisage
BR ɪnˈvɪz|ɪdʒ, ɛnˈvɪz|ɪdʒ, -ɨdʒɪz, -ɨdʒɪŋ, -ɪdʒd
AM ənˈvɪzɪdʒ, ɛnˈvɪzɪdʒ, -ɪz, -ɪŋ, -d

envisagement
BR ɪnˈvɪzɨdʒm(ə)nt, ɛnˈvɪzɨdʒm(ə)nt
AM ənˈvɪzɪdʒmənt, ɛnˈvɪzɪdʒmənt

envision
BR ɪnˈvɪʒ|n, ɛnˈvɪʒ|n, -ənz, -n̩ɪŋ\-nɪŋ, -ənd
AM ənˈvɪʒən, ɛnˈvɪʒən, -d, -ɪŋ, -d

envoi
BR ˈɛnvɔɪ, -z
AM ˈɛnˌvɔɪ, ˈɑnˌvɔɪ, -z

envoy
BR ˈɛnvɔɪ, -z
AM ˈɛnˌvɔɪ, ˈɑnˌvɔɪ, -z

envoyship
BR ˈɛnvɔɪʃɪp, -s
AM ˈɛnˌvɔɪˌʃɪp, ˈɑnˌvɔɪˌʃɪp, -s

envy
BR ˈɛnv|i, -ɪz, -ɪɪŋ, -ɪd
AM ˈɛnvi, -z, -ɪŋ, -d

enweave
BR ɪnˈwiːv, ɛnˈwiːv, -z, -ɪŋ
AM ənˈwiv, ɛnˈwiv, -z, -ɪŋ

enwind
BR ɪnˈwʌɪnd, ɛnˈwʌɪnd, -z, -ɪŋ, -ɨd
AM ənˈwaɪn|d, ɛnˈwaɪnd, -z, -ɪŋ, -ɨd

enwove
BR ɪnˈwəʊv, ɛnˈwəʊv
AM ənˈwoʊv, ɛnˈwoʊv

enwoven
BR ɪnˈwəʊvn, ɛnˈwəʊvn
AM ənˈwoʊvən, ɛnˈwoʊvən

enwrap
BR ɪnˈrap, ɛnˈrap, -s, -ɪŋ, -t
AM ənˈræp, ɛnˈræp, -s, -ɪŋ, -t

enwreathe
BR ɪnˈriːð, ɛnˈriːð, -z, -ɪŋ, -d
AM ənˈrið, ɛnˈrið, -z, -ɪŋ, -d

Enzed
BR ɛnˈzɛd
AM ɛnˈzɛd

Enzedder
BR ɛnˈzɛdə(r), -z
AM ɛnˈzɛdər, -z

enzootic
BR ˌɛnzuːˈɒtɪk, ˌɛnzəʊˈɒtɪk
AM ˌɛnzəˈwɑdɪk, ˌɛnzoʊˈɑdɪk

enzymatic
BR ˌɛnzʌɪˈmatɪk
AM ˌɛnzəˈmædɪk, ˌɛnˌzaɪˈmædɪk

enzyme
BR ˈɛnzʌɪm, -z
AM ˈɛnˌzaɪm, -z

enzymic
BR ɛnˈzʌɪmɪk
AM ɛnˈzaɪmɪk, ɛnˈzɪmɪk

enzymology
BR ˌɛnzʌɪˈmɒlədʒi
AM ˌɛnzəˈmɑlədʒi, ˌɛnzaɪˈmɑlədʒi

Eocene
BR ˈiːə(ʊ)siːn
AM ˈiəˌsin

eohippus
BR ˌiːəʊˈhɪpəs
AM ˌioʊˈhɪpəs

EOKA
BR eɪˈəʊkə(*r*)
AM ˌiˌoʊˌkeɪˈeɪ

Eolian
BR ɪˈəʊlɪən, eɪˈəʊlɪən
AM iˈoʊljən, iˈoʊliən

eolith
BR ˈiːəlɪθ, -s
AM ˈiəˌlɪθ, -s

Eolithic
BR ˌiːə(ʊ)ˈlɪθɪk
AM ˌiəˈlɪθɪk

eon
BR ˈiːən, ˈiːɒn, -z
AM ˈiən, ˈiˌɑn, -z

Eos
BR ˈiːɒs
AM ˈiəs, ˈiˌɑs

eosin
BR ˈiːə(ʊ)sɪn
AM ˈiəsən

eosinophil
BR ˌiːə(ʊ)ˈsɪnə(ʊ)fɪl, -z
AM ˌiəˈsɪnəˌfɪl, -z

eosinophile
BR ˌiːə(ʊ)ˈsɪnə(ʊ)fʌɪl, -z
AM ˌiəˈsɪnəˌfaɪl, -z

epact
BR ˈiːpakt, ˈɛpakt, -s
AM ˈiˌpæk|(t), ˈɛˌpæk|(t), -(t)s

Epaminondas
BR ɪˌpamɪˈnɒndas, ɛˌpamɪˈnɒndas
AM əˌpɑməˈnɑndəs

eparch
BR 'ɛpɑːk, -s
AM 'ɛ,pɑrk, -s

eparchy
BR 'ɛpɑːk|i, -ɪz
AM 'ɛ,pɑrki, -z

epaulet
BR ,ɛpə'lɛt, -s
AM ¦ɛpə¦lɛt, -s

epaulette
BR ,ɛpə'lɛt, -s
AM ¦ɛpə¦lɛt, -s

Epcot®
BR 'ɛpkɒt
AM 'ɛp,kɑt

épée
BR 'ɛpeɪ, -z
AM ,ɛ'peɪ, -z

epeirogeneses
BR ɪ,pʌɪrə(ʊ)'dʒɛnɪsiːz
AM ə,paɪroʊ'dʒɛnəsiz

epeirogenesis
BR ɪ,pʌɪrə(ʊ)'dʒɛnɪsɪs
AM ə,paɪroʊ'dʒɛnəsəs

epeirogenic
BR ɪ,pʌɪrə(ʊ)'dʒɛnɪk
AM ə,paɪroʊ'dʒɛnɪk

epeirogeny
BR ,ɛpʌɪ'rɒdʒɪni, ,ɛpʌɪ'rɒdʒn̩i
AM ɛ,paɪ'rɑdʒəni

epentheses
BR ɪ'pɛnθɪsiːz, ɛ'pɛnθɪsiːz
AM ə'pɛnθə,siz, ɛ'pɛnθə,siz

epenthesis
BR ɪ'pɛnθɪsɪs, ɛ'pɛnθɪsɪs
AM ə'pɛnθəsəs, ɛ'pɛnθəsəs

epenthetic
BR ,ɛpɛn'θɛtɪk
AM ,ɛpɛn'θɛdɪk

epergne
BR ɪ'pəːn, ɛ'pəːn, -z
AM ə'pərn, i'pərn, eɪ'pərn, -z

epexegeses
BR ɛ,pɛksɪ'dʒiːsiːz, ɪ,pɛksɪ'dʒiːsiːz
AM ɛ,pɛksə'dʒisiz

epexegesis
BR ɛ,pɛksɪ'dʒiːsɪs, ɪ,pɛksɪ'dʒiːsɪs
AM ɛ,pɛksə'dʒisɪs

epexegetic
BR ɛ,pɛksɪ'dʒɛtɪk, ɪ,pɛksɪ'dʒɛtɪk
AM ɛ,pɛksə'dʒɛdɪk

epexegetical
BR ɛ,pɛksɪ'dʒɛtɪkl, ɪ,pɛksɪ'dʒɛtɪkl
AM ɛ,pɛksə'dʒɛdəkəl

epexegetically
BR ɛ,pɛksɪ'dʒɛtɪkli, ɪ,pɛksɪ'dʒɛtɪkli
AM ɛ,pɛksə'dʒɛdək(ə)li

ephebe
BR 'ɛfiːb, ɛ'fiːb, ɪ'fiːb, -z
AM 'ɛ,fib, ə'fib, ɛ'fib, -z

ephebic
BR ɛ'fiːbɪk, ɪ'fiːbɪk
AM ə'fibɪk, ɛ'fibɪk

ephedra
BR ɛ'fɛdrə(r), ɪ'fɛdrə(r), 'ɛfɪdrə(r), -z
AM ə'fɛdrə, 'ɛfədrə, -z

ephedrine
BR 'ɛfɪdriːn, 'ɛfɪdrɪn, ɪ'fɛdrɪn
AM ə'fɛdrən, ɛ'fɛdrən, 'ɛfədrən, 'ɛfə,drin

ephemera
BR ɪ'fɛm(ə)rə(r), ɛ'fɛm(ə)rə(r)
AM ə'fɛm(ə)rə

ephemeral
BR ɪ'fɛm(ə)rəl, ɪ'fɛm(ə)rl̩, ɛ'fɛm(ə)rəl, ɛ'fɛm(ə)rl̩
AM ə'fɛm(ə)rəl, i'fɛm(ə)rəl

ephemerality
BR ɪ,fɛmə'ralɪti, ɛ,fɛmə'ralɪti
AM ə,fɛm(ə)'rælədi, i,fɛm(ə)'rælədi

ephemerally
BR ɪ'fɛm(ə)rl̩i, ɪ'fɛm(ə)rəli, ɛ'fɛm(ə)rl̩i, ɛ'fɛm(ə)rəli
AM ə'fɛm(ə)rəli, i'fɛm(ə)rəli

ephemeralness
BR ɪ'fɛm(ə)rl̩nəs, ɪ'fɛm(ə)rəlnəs, ɛ'fɛm(ə)rl̩nəs, ɛ'fɛm(ə)rəlnəs
AM ə'fɛm(ə)rəlnəs, i'fɛm(ə)rəlnəs

ephemeris
BR ɪ'fɛm(ə)rɪs, ɛ'fɛm(ə)rɪs, -ɪz
AM ə'fɛm(ə)rəs, i'fɛm(ə)rəs, -ɪz

ephemerist
BR ɪ'fɛm(ə)rɪst, ɛ'fɛm(ə)rɪst, -s
AM ə'fɛm(ə)rəst, i'fɛm(ə)rəst, -s

ephemeron
BR ɪ'fɛm(ə)rɒn, ɛ'fɛm(ə)rɒn
AM ə'fɛmə,rɑn

Ephemeroptera
BR ɪ,fɛmə'rɒpt(ə)rə(r), ɛ,fɛmə'rɒpt(ə)rə(r)
AM ə,fɛmə'rɑptərə

ephemeropteran
BR ɪ,fɛmə'rɒpt(ə)rən, ɪ,fɛmə'rɒpt(ə)rn̩, ɛ,fɛmə'rɒpt(ə)rən, ɛ,fɛmə'rɒpt(ə)rn̩, -z
AM ə,fɛmə'rɑptərən, -z

ephemeropterous
BR ɪ,fɛmə'rɒpt(ə)rəs, ɛ,fɛmə'rɒpt(ə)rəs
AM ə,fɛmə'rɑptərəs

Ephesian
BR ɪ'fiːʒn, -z
AM ə'fiʒən, -z

Ephesus
BR 'ɛfɪsəs
AM 'ɛfəsəs

ephod
BR 'iːfɒd, 'ɛfɒd, -z
AM 'ɛ,fɑd, 'i,fɑd, 'ɛfəd, -z

ephor
BR 'iːfɔː(r), 'ɛfɔː(r), -z
AM 'ɛ,fɔ(ə)r, 'ɛfər, 'i,fɔ(ə)r, -z

ephorate
BR 'iːf(ə)rət, 'ɛf(ə)rət, -s
AM 'ɛfə,reɪt, 'ɛfərət, -s

ephori
BR 'iːfərʌɪ, 'ɛfərʌɪ
AM 'ɛfə,raɪ

ephorship
BR 'iːfəʃɪp, 'ɛfəʃɪp
AM 'ɛfər,ʃɪp, 'ɛ,fɔr,ʃɪp, 'i,fɔr,ʃɪp

Ephraim
BR 'iːfreɪm
AM 'ifrəm

epiblast
BR 'ɛpɪblɑːst, 'ɛpɪblast, -s
AM 'ɛpə,blæst, -s

epic
BR 'ɛpɪk, -s
AM 'ɛpɪk, -s

epical
BR 'ɛpɪkl
AM 'ɛpəkəl

epically
BR 'ɛpɪkli
AM 'ɛpək(ə)li

epicanthic
BR ,ɛpɪ'kanθɪk
AM ,ɛpə'kænθɪk, ,ɛpi'kænθɪk

epicarp
BR 'ɛpɪkɑːp, -s
AM 'ɛpə,kɑrp, -s

epicedia
BR ,ɛpɪ'siːdɪə(r)
AM ,ɛpə'sidiə

epicedian
BR ,ɛpɪ'siːdɪən
AM ,ɛpə'sidiən

epicedium
BR ,ɛpɪ'siːdɪəm
AM ,ɛpə'sidiəm

epicene
BR 'ɛpɪsiːn, -z
AM 'ɛpə,sin, -z

epicenter
BR 'ɛpɪ,sɛntə(r), -z
AM 'ɛpə,sɛn(t)ər, 'ɛpi,sɛn(t)ər, -z

epicentral
BR ,ɛpɪ'sɛntr(ə)l
AM ,ɛpə'sɛntrəl, ,ɛpi'sɛntrəl

epicentre
BR 'ɛpɪ,sɛntə(r), -z
AM 'ɛpə,sɛn(t)ər, 'ɛpi,sɛn(t)ər, -z

epicleses
BR ,ɛpɪ'kliːsiːz
AM ,ɛpə'klisiz

epiclesis
BR ,ɛpɪ'kliːsɪs
AM ,ɛpə'klisɪs

epicondilitis
BR ,ɛpɪkɒndɪ'lʌɪtɪs
AM ,ɛpəkɑndə'laɪdɪs

epicontinental
BR ,ɛpɪkɒntɪ'nɛntl
AM ,ɛpə,kɑn(t)ə'nɛn(t)l, ,ɛpi,kɑn(t)ə'nɛn(t)l

epicotyl
BR 'ɛpɪkɒtl, -z
AM 'ɛpə,kɑdl, -z

Epictetus
BR ,ɛpɪk'tiːtəs
AM ,ɛpək'tidəs

epicure
BR 'ɛpɪkjʊə(r), 'ɛpɪkjɔː(r), -z
AM 'ɛpə,kjʊ(ə)r, 'ɛpi,kjʊ(ə)r, -z

epicurean
BR ,ɛpɪkjʊ'riːən, -z
AM ,ɛpəkjə'riən, ,ɛpə'kjʊriən, -z

Epicureanism
BR ,ɛpɪkjʊ'riːənɪz(ə)m
AM ,ɛpəkjə'riə,nɪzəm, ,ɛpə'kjʊriə,nɪzəm

epicurism
BR 'ɛpɪkjʊrɪz(ə)m
AM 'ɛpə,kjʊ,rɪzəm, ɛpə'kjʊ,rɪzəm

Epicurus
BR ,ɛpɪ'kjʊərəs, ,ɛpɪ'kjɔːrəs
AM 'ɛpə,kjʊrəs, ,ɛpə'kjʊrəs

epicycle
BR 'ɛpɪ,sʌɪkl, -z
AM 'ɛpə,saɪkəl, -z

epicyclic
BR ,ɛpɪ'sʌɪklɪk
AM ,ɛpə'saɪklɪk, ,ɛpə'sɪklɪk

epicycloid
BR ,ɛpɪ'sʌɪklɔɪd, -z
AM ,ɛpə'saɪ,klɔɪd, -z

epicycloidal
BR ,ɛpɪsʌɪ'klɔɪdl
AM ,ɛpə,saɪ'klɔɪdəl

Epidaurus
BR ,ɛpɪ'dɔːrəs
AM ,ɛpə'dɔrəs

epideictic
BR ˌɛpɪˈdʌɪktɪk
AM ˌɛpəˈdaɪktɪk

epidemic
BR ˌɛpɪˈdɛmɪk, -s
AM ˌɛpəˈdɛmɪk, -s

epidemical
BR ˌɛpɪˈdɛmɪkl
AM ˌɛpəˈdɛməkəl

epidemically
BR ˌɛpɪˈdɛmɪkli
AM ˌɛpəˈdɛmək(ə)li

epidemiological
BR ˌɛpɪdiːmɪəˈlɒdʒɪkl
AM ˌɛpəˌdimiəˈlɑdʒəkəl

epidemiologist
BR ˌɛpɪdiːmɪˈɒlədʒɪst, -s
AM ˌɛpəˌdimiˈɑlədʒəst, -s

epidemiology
BR ˌɛpɪdiːmɪˈɒlədʒi
AM ˌɛpəˌdimiˈɑlədʒi

epidermal
BR ˌɛpɪˈdəːml
AM ˌɛpəˈdərməl

epidermic
BR ˌɛpɪˈdəːmɪk
AM ˌɛpəˈdərmɪk

epidermis
BR ˌɛpɪˈdəːmɪs
AM ˌɛpəˈdərmɪs

epidermoid
BR ˌɛpɪˈdəːmɔɪd
AM ˌɛpəˈdərˌmɔɪd

epidiascope
BR ˌɛpɪˈdʌɪəskəʊp, -s
AM ˌɛpəˈdaɪəˌskoʊp, -s

epididymides
BR ˌɛpɪˈdɪdɪmɪdiːz, ˌɛpɪdɪˈdɪmɪdiːz
AM ˌɛpəˈdɪdəməˌdiz, ˌɛpədəˈdɪməˌdiz, ˌɛpəˌdaɪˈdɪməˌdiz

epididymis
BR ˌɛpɪˈdɪdɪmɪs, -ɪz
AM ˌɛpəˈdɪdəməs, -əz

epidural
BR ˌɛpɪˈdjʊərəl, ˌɛpɪˈdjʊərl̩, ˌɛpɪˈdʒʊərəl, ˌɛpɪˈdʒʊərl̩, ˌɛpɪˈdjɔːrəl, ˌɛpɪˈdjɔːrl̩, ˌɛpɪˈdʒɔːrəl, ˌɛpɪˈdʒɔːrl̩, -z
AM ˌɛpəˈd(j)ʊrəl, ˌɛpiˈd(j)ʊrəl, -z

epifauna
BR ˈɛpɪˌfɔːnə(r)
AM ˌɛpəˈfɔnə, ˌɛpəˈfɑnə

epigastria
BR ˌɛpɪˈgastrɪə(r)
AM ˌɛpəˈgæstriə

epigastric
BR ˌɛpɪˈgastrɪk
AM ˌɛpəˈgæstrɪk

epigastrium
BR ˌɛpɪˈgastrɪəm
AM ˌɛpəˈgæstriəm

epigeal
BR ˌɛpɪˈdʒiːəl
AM ˌɛpəˈdʒiəl

epigene
BR ˈɛpɪdʒiːn
AM ˈɛpəˌdʒin

epigenesis
BR ˌɛpɪˈdʒɛnɪsɪs
AM ˌɛpəˈdʒɛnəsəs

epigenetic
BR ˌɛpɪdʒɪˈnɛtɪk
AM ˌɛpədʒəˈnɛdɪk

epiglottal
BR ˌɛpɪˈglɒtl
AM ˌɛpəˈglɑdl

epiglottic
BR ˌɛpɪˈglɒtɪk
AM ˌɛpəˈglɑdɪk

epiglottis
BR ˌɛpɪˈglɒtɪs, -ɪz
AM ˌɛpəˈglɑdəs, -əz

epigone
BR ˈɛpɪgəʊn, -z
AM ˈɛpəˌgoʊn, -z

epigram
BR ˈɛpɪgram, -z
AM ˈɛpəˌgræm, -z

epigrammatic
BR ˌɛpɪgrəˈmatɪk
AM ˌɛpəgrəˈmædɪk

epigrammatically
BR ˌɛpɪgrəˈmatɪkli
AM ˌɛpəgrəˈmædək(ə)li

epigrammatise
BR ˌɛpɪˈgramətʌɪz, -ɪz, -ɪŋ, -d
AM ˌɛpəˈgræməˌtaɪz, -ɪz, -ɪŋ, -d

epigrammatist
BR ˌɛpɪˈgramətɪst, -s
AM ˌɛpəˈgræmədəst, -s

epigrammatize
BR ˌɛpɪˈgramətʌɪz, -ɪz, -ɪŋ, -d
AM ˌɛpəˈgræməˌtaɪz, -ɪz, -ɪŋ, -d

epigraph
BR ˈɛpɪgrɑːf, ˈɛpɪgraf, -s
AM ˈɛpəˌgræf, -s

epigraphic
BR ˌɛpɪˈgrafɪk
AM ˌɛpəˈgræfɪk

epigraphical
BR ˌɛpɪˈgrafɪkl
AM ˌɛpəˈgræfəkəl

epigraphically
BR ˌɛpɪˈgrafɪkli
AM ˌɛpəˈgræfək(ə)li

epigraphist
BR ɪˈpɪgrəfɪst, ɛˈpɪgrəfɪst, -s
AM əˈpɪgrəfəst, ɛˈpɪgrəfəst, -s

epigraphy
BR ɪˈpɪgrəfi, ɛˈpɪgrəfi
AM əˈpɪgrəfi, ɛˈpɪgrəfi

epilate
BR ˈɛpɪleɪt, -s, -ɪŋ, -ɪd
AM ˈɛpəˌleɪ|t, -ts, -dɪŋ, -dɪd

epilation
BR ˌɛpɪˈleɪʃn
AM ˌɛpəˈleɪʃən

epilepsy
BR ˈɛpɪlɛpsi
AM ˈɛpəˌlɛpsi

epileptic
BR ˌɛpɪˈlɛptɪk, -s
AM ˌɛpəˈlɛptɪk, -s

epilimnia
BR ˌɛpɪˈlɪmnɪə(r)
AM ˌɛpəˈlɪmniə

epilimnion
BR ˌɛpɪˈlɪmnɪən, ˌɛpɪˈlɪmnɪɒn
AM ˌɛpəˈlɪmniˌɑn, ˌɛpəˈlɪmniən

epilog
BR ˈɛpɪlɒg, -z
AM ˈɛpəˌlɔg, ˈɛpəˌlɑg, ˈɛpiˌlɑg, -z

epilogist
BR ɪˈpɪlədʒɪst, ɛˈpɪlədʒɪst, ˈɛpɪləgɪst, -s
AM əˈpɪlədʒəst, ɛˈpɪlədʒəst, ˈɛpəˌlɔgəst, ˈɛpəˌlɑgəst, -s

epilogue
BR ˈɛpɪlɒg, -z
AM ˈɛpəˌlɔg, ˈɛpəˌlɑg, ˈɛpiˌlɑg, -z

epimer
BR ˈɛpɪmə(r), -z
AM ˈɛpəmər, -z

epimeric
BR ˌɛpɪˈmɛrɪk
AM ˌɛpəˈmɛrɪk

epimerise
BR ɪˈpɪmərʌɪz, ɛˈpɪmərʌɪz, ˈɛpɪmərʌɪz, -ɪz, -ɪŋ, -d
AM ˈɛpəməˌraɪz, -ɪz, -ɪŋ, -d

epimerism
BR ɪˈpɪmərɪz(ə)m, ɛˈpɪmərɪz(ə)m, ˈɛpɪmərɪz(ə)m
AM ˈɛpəməˌrɪzəm

epimerize
BR ɪˈpɪmərʌɪz, ɛˈpɪmərʌɪz, ˈɛpɪmərʌɪz, -ɪz, -ɪŋ, -d
AM ˈɛpəməˌraɪz, -ɪz, -ɪŋ, -d

epinasty
BR ˈɛpɪnasti
AM ˈɛpəˌnæsti

epinephrine
BR ˌɛpɪˈnɛfrɪn, ˌɛpɪˈnɛfriːn
AM ˌɛpəˈnɛfrən

epiphanic
BR ˌɛpɪˈfanɪk
AM ˌɛpəˈfænɪk

epiphany
BR ɪˈpɪfəni, ɪˈpɪfn̩i
AM əˈpɪfəni, iˈpɪfəni

epiphenomena
BR ˌɛpɪfɪˈnɒmɪnə(r)
AM ˌɛpəfəˈnɑmənə, ˌɛpifəˈnɑmənə

epiphenomenal
BR ˌɛpɪfɪˈnɒmɪnl
AM ˌɛpəfəˈnɑmənəl, ˌɛpifəˈnɑmənəl

epiphenomenon
BR ˌɛpɪfɪˈnɒmɪnən
AM ˌɛpəfəˈnɑmənən, ˌɛpifəˈnɑmənən

epiphyses
BR ɪˈpɪfɪsiːz, ɛˈpɪfɪsiːz
AM əˈpɪfəsiz

epiphysis
BR ɪˈpɪfɪsɪs, ɛˈpɪfɪsɪs
AM əˈpɪfəsəs

epiphytal
BR ˌɛpɪˈfʌɪtl
AM ˌɛpəˈfaɪdl

epiphyte
BR ˈɛpɪfʌɪt, -s
AM ˈɛpəˌfaɪt, -s

epiphytic
BR ˌɛpɪˈfɪtɪk
AM ˌɛpəˈfɪdɪk

epirogenic
BR ɪˌpʌɪrə(ʊ)ˈdʒɛnɪk
AM əˌpaɪroʊˈdʒɛnɪk

epirogeny
BR ˌɛpʌɪˈrɒdʒɪni
AM ɛˌpaɪˈrɑdʒəni

Epirot
BR ɛˈpʌɪrət, ɪˈpʌɪrət, -s
AM ˈɛpəˌrɑt, əˈpaɪrət, iˈpaɪrət, -s

Epirote
BR ɛˈpʌɪrəʊt, ɪˈpʌɪrəʊt, -s
AM ˈɛpəˌrɑt, ɛˈpaɪroʊt, iˈpaɪroʊt, -s

Epirus
BR ɛˈpʌɪrəs, ɪˈpʌɪrəs
AM ˈɛpərəs, əˈpaɪrəs, iˈpaɪrəs

episcopacy
BR ɪˈpɪskəpəs|i, -ɪz
AM əˈpɪskəpəsi, iˈpɪskəpəsi, -z

episcopal
BR ɪˈpɪskəpl
AM əˈpɪskəpəl, iˈpɪskəpəl

episcopalian
BR ɪˌpɪskəˈpeɪlɪən, -z
AM əˌpɪskəˈpeɪljən, iˌpɪskəˈpeɪljən,

ə,pɪskə'peɪliən, i,pɪskə'peɪliən, -z
episcopalianism
BR ɪ,pɪskə'peɪlɪənɪz(ə)m
AM ə,pɪskə'peɪljə,nɪzəm, i,pɪskə'peɪljə,nɪzəm, ə,pɪskə'peɪliə,nɪzəm, i,pɪskə'peɪliə,nɪzəm
episcopalism
BR ɪ'pɪskəpl̩ɪz(ə)m, ɪ'pɪskəpəlɪz(ə)m
AM ə'pɪskəpə,lɪzəm, i'pɪskəpə,lɪzəm
episcopally
BR ɪ'pɪskəpl̩i, ɪ'pɪskəpəli
AM ə'pɪskəp(ə)li, i'pɪskəp(ə)li
episcopate
BR ɪ'pɪskəpət, -s
AM ə'pɪskəpət, ə'pɪskə,peɪt, i'pɪskəpət, i'pɪskə,peɪt, -s
episcope[1]
projector
BR 'ɛpɪskəʊp, -s
AM 'ɛpə,skoʊp, -s
episcope[2]
supervision by a bishop
BR ɪ'pɪskəpi
AM ə'pɪskəpi, i'pɪskəpi
episematic
BR ,ɛpɪsɪ'matɪk
AM ,ɛpəsə'mædɪk, ,ɛpisə'mædɪk
episiotomy
BR ɪ,pi:zɪ'ɒtəm|i, -ɪz
AM ə'pizi,ɑdəmi, -z
episode
BR 'ɛpɪsəʊd, -z
AM 'ɛpə,soʊd, -z
episodic
BR ,ɛpɪ'sɒdɪk
AM ,ɛpə'sɑdɪk
episodically
BR ,ɛpɪ'sɒdɪkli
AM ,ɛpə'sɑdək(ə)li
epistaxes
BR ,ɛpɪ'staksi:z
AM ,ɛpə'stæksiz
epistaxis
BR ,ɛpɪ'staksɪs
AM ,ɛpə'stæksəs
epistemic
BR ,ɛpɪ'sti:mɪk
AM ,ɛpə'stɛmɪk, ,ɛpə'stimɪk
epistemically
BR ,ɛpɪ'sti:mɪkli
AM ,ɛpə'stɛmək(ə)li, ,ɛpə'stimɪk(ə)li
epistemological
BR ɪ,pɪstəmə'lɒdʒɪkl
AM ə,pɪstəmə'lɑdʒəkəl
epistemologically
BR ɪ,pɪstəmə'lɒdʒɪkli
AM ə,pɪstəmə'lɑdʒək(ə)li
epistemologist
BR ɪ,pɪstə'mɒlədʒɪst, -s
AM ə,pɪstə'mɑlədʒɪst, ɛ,pɪstə'mɑlədʒəst, i,pɪstə'mɑlədʒəst, -s
epistemology
BR ɪ,pɪstə'mɒlədʒi
AM ə,pɪstə'mɑlədʒi, ɛ,pɪstə'mɑlədʒi, i'pɪstə'mɑlədʒi
epistle
BR ɪ'pɪsl, -z
AM ə'pɪsəl, i'pɪsəl, -z
epistolary
BR ɪ'pɪstəl(ə)ri, ɪ'pɪstl̩(ə)ri
AM ə'pɪstə,lɛri, i'pɪstə,lɛri
epistoler
BR ɪ'pɪstələ(r), ɪ'pɪstl̩ə(r), -z
AM ə'pɪstələr, i'pɪstələr, -z
epistrophe
BR ɪ'pɪstrəf|i, -ɪz
AM ə'pɪstrəfi, -z
epistyle
BR 'ɛpɪstʌɪl, -z
AM 'ɛpə,staɪl, -z
epitaph
BR 'ɛpɪtɑ:f, 'ɛpɪtaf, -s
AM 'ɛpə,tæf, -s
epitaxial
BR ,ɛpɪ'taksɪəl
AM ,ɛpə'tæksiəl
epitaxy
BR 'ɛpɪtaksi
AM 'ɛpə,tæksi, ,ɛpə'tæksi
epithalamia
BR ,ɛpɪθə'leɪmɪə(*r*)
AM ,ɛpəθə'leɪmiə
epithalamial
BR ,ɛpɪθə'leɪmɪəl
AM ,ɛpəθə'leɪmiəl
epithalamic
BR ,ɛpɪθə'lamɪk
AM ,ɛpəθə'læmɪk
epithalamium
BR ,ɛpɪθə'leɪmɪəm, -z
AM ,ɛpə'θælmiəm, -z
epithelia
BR ,ɛpɪ'θi:lɪə(*r*)
AM ,ɛpə'θiliə
epithelial
BR ,ɛpɪ'θi:lɪəl
AM ,ɛpə'θiliəl
epithelium
BR ,ɛpɪ'θi:lɪəm
AM ,ɛpə'θiliəm
epithet
BR 'ɛpɪθɛt, -s
AM 'ɛpə,θɛt, -s
epithetic
BR ,ɛpɪ'θɛtɪk
AM ,ɛpə'θɛdɪk
epithetical
BR ,ɛpɪ'θɛtɪkl
AM ,ɛpə'θɛdəkəl
epithetically
BR ,ɛpɪ'θɛtɪkli
AM ,ɛpə'θɛdək(ə)li
epitome
BR ɪ'pɪtəmi
AM ə'pɪdəmi, i'pɪdəmi
epitomisation
BR ɪ,pɪtəmʌɪ'zeɪʃn
AM ə,pɪdəmə'zeɪʃən, i,pɪdəmə'zeɪʃən, ə,pɪdə,maɪ'zeɪʃən, 'i,pɪdə,maɪ'zeɪʃən
epitomise
BR ɪ'pɪtəmʌɪz, -ɪz, -ɪŋ, -d
AM ə'pɪdə,maɪz, i'pɪdə,maɪz, -ɪz, -ɪŋ, -d
epitomist
BR ɪ'pɪtəmɪst, -s
AM ə'pɪdəməst, i'pɪdəməst, -s
epitomization
BR ɪ,pɪtəmʌɪ'zeɪʃn
AM ə,pɪdəmə'zeɪʃən, i,pɪdəmə'zeɪʃən, ə,pɪdə,maɪ'zeɪʃən, 'i,pɪdə,maɪ'zeɪʃən
epitomize
BR ɪ'pɪtəmʌɪz, -ɪz, -ɪŋ, -d
AM ə'pɪdə,maɪz, i'pɪdə,maɪz, -ɪz, -ɪŋ, -d
epizoa
BR ,ɛpɪ'zəʊə(*r*)
AM ,ɛpə'zoʊə
epizoon
BR ,ɛpɪ'zu:ɒn, ,ɛpɪ'zəʊɒn
AM ,ɛpə'zoʊ,ɑn
epizootic
BR ,ɛpɪzu:'ɒtɪk, ,ɛpɪzəʊ'ɒtɪk
AM ,ɛpəzə'wɑdɪk
epoch
BR 'i:pɒk, -s
AM 'ɛpək, 'i,pɑk, -s
epochal
BR 'ɛpəkl, 'ɛpɒkl, 'i:pɒkl, i:'pɒkl
AM 'ɛpəkəl
epode
BR 'ɛpəʊd, -z
AM 'ɛ,poʊd, -z
eponym
BR 'ɛpənɪm, -z
AM 'ɛpə,nɪm, -z
eponymous
BR ɪ'pɒnɪməs
AM ə'pɑnəməs, ɛ'pɑnəməs
EPOS
BR 'i:pɒs, 'i:pɒz
AM 'i,pɑs, ,i,pi,oʊ'ɛs
epoxide
BR ɪ'pɒksʌɪd, -z
AM ə'pɑk,saɪd, -z
epoxy
BR ɪ'pɒksi
AM ə'pɑksi
Epping
BR 'ɛpɪŋ
AM 'ɛpɪŋ
EPROM
BR 'ɛprɒm, 'i:prɒm, -z
AM 'i,prɑm, -z
epsilon
BR 'ɛpsɪlɒn, 'ɛpsɪlən, ɛp'sʌɪlən, -z
AM 'ɛpsɪ,lɑn, -z
Epsom
BR 'ɛps(ə)m
AM 'ɛpsəm
Epson
BR 'ɛpsɒn, 'ɛps(ə)n
AM 'ɛpsən
Epstein
BR 'ɛpstʌɪn
AM 'ɛp,staɪn
epyllia
BR ɪ'pɪlɪə(*r*), ɛ'pɪlɪə(*r*)
AM ə'pɪljə, ə'pɪliə
epyllion
BR ɪ'pɪlɪən, ɛ'pɪlɪən
AM ə'pɪljən, ə'pɪli,ɑn
equability
BR ,ɛkwə'bɪlɪti
AM ,ɛkwə'bɪlɪdi, ,ikwə'bɪlɪdi
equable
BR 'ɛkwəbl
AM 'ɛkwəbəl, 'ikwəbəl
equableness
BR 'ɛkwəblnəs
AM 'ɛkwəbəlnəs, 'ikwəbəlnəs
equably
BR 'ɛkwəbli
AM 'ɛkwəbli, 'ikwəbli
equal
BR 'i:kw|(ə)l, -(ə)lz, -əlɪŋ\-l̩ɪŋ, -(ə)ld
AM 'ikwəl, -z, -ɪŋ, -d
equalisation
BR ,i:kwəlʌɪ'zeɪʃn, ,i:kwl̩ʌɪ'zeɪʃn
AM ,ikwələ'zeɪʃən, ,ikwə,laɪ'zeɪʃən
equalise
BR 'i:kwəlʌɪz, 'i:kwl̩ʌɪz, -ɪz, -ɪŋ, -d
AM 'ikwə,laɪz, -ɪz, -ɪŋ, -d
equaliser
BR 'i:kwəlʌɪzə(r), 'i:kwl̩ʌɪzə(r), -z
AM 'ikwə,laɪzər, -z
equalitarian
BR ɪ,kwɒlɪ'tɛ:rɪən
AM i,kwɑlə'tɛriən, ə,kwɑlə'tɛriən

equalitarianism
BR ɪˌkwɒlɪˈtɛːrɪənɪz(ə)m
AM iˌkwɑləˈtɛriəˌnɪzəm, əˌkwɑləˈtɛriəˌnɪzəm

equality
BR ɪˈkwɒlɪti
AM iˈkwɑlədi, əˈkwɑlədi, iˈkwɔlədi, əˈkwɔlədi

equalization
BR ˌiːkwəlʌɪˈzeɪʃn, ˌiːkwl̩ʌɪˈzeɪʃn
AM ˌikwələˈzeɪʃən, ˌikwəˌlaɪˈzeɪʃən

equalize
BR ˈiːkwəlʌɪz, ˈiːkwl̩ʌɪz, -ɪz, -ɪŋ, -d
AM ˈikwəˌlaɪz, -ɪz, -ɪŋ, -d

equalizer
BR ˈiːkwəlʌɪzə(r), ˈiːkwl̩ʌɪzə(r), -z
AM ˈikwəˌlaɪzər, -z

equally
BR ˈiːkwl̩i, ˈiːkwəli
AM ˈikwəli

equanimity
BR ˌiːkwəˈnɪmɪti, ˌɛkwəˈnɪmɪti
AM ˌɛkwəˈnɪmɪdi, ˌikwəˈnɪmɪdi

equanimous
BR iːˈkwanɪməs, ɪˈkwanɪməs, ɛˈkwanɪməs
AM iˈkwɑnəməs, əˈkwɑnəməs

equatable
BR ɪˈkweɪtəbl
AM əˈkweɪdɪbəl

equatably
BR ɪˈkweɪtəbli
AM əˈkweɪdɪbli

equate
BR ɪˈkweɪt, -s, -ɪŋ, -ɪd
AM əˈkweɪ|t, iˈkweɪ|t, -ts, -dɪŋ, -dɪd

equation
BR ɪˈkweɪʒn, -z
AM əˈkweɪʒən, iˈkweiʒən, -z

equational
BR ɪˈkweɪʒn̩(ə)l, ɪˈkweɪʒən(ə)l
AM əˈkweɪʒ(ə)nəl, iˈkweiʒ(ə)nəl

equator
BR ɪˈkweɪtə(r), -z
AM əˈkweɪdər, iˈkweɪdər, -z

equatorial
BR ˌɛkwəˈtɔːrɪəl
AM ˌɛkwəˈtɔriəl

equatorially
BR ˌɛkwəˈtɔːrɪəli
AM ˌɛkwəˈtɔriəli

equerry
BR ˈɛkwər|i, ɪˈkwɛr|i, -ɪz
AM ˈɛkwəri, əˈkwɛri, iˈkwɛri, ɛˈkwɛri, -z

eques
BR ˈɛkweɪz
AM ˈɛkweɪz, ˈɛkwiz

equestrian
BR ɪˈkwɛstrɪən, -z
AM əˈkwɛstriən, iˈkwɛstriən, -z

equestrianism
BR ɪˈkwɛstrɪənɪz(ə)m
AM əˈkwɛstriəˌnɪzəm, iˈkwɛstriəˌnɪzəm

equestrienne
BR ɪˌkwɛstrɪˈɛn, -z
AM əˌkwɛstriˈɛn, iˌkwɛstriˈɛn, -z

equiangular
BR ˌiːkwɪˈaŋgjʉlə(r), ˌɛkwɪˈaŋgjʉlə(r)
AM ˌɛkwəˈæŋgjələr, ˌɛkwiˈæŋgjələr, ˌikwəˈæŋgjələr, ˌikwiˈæŋgjələr

equid
BR ˈɛkwɪd, -z
AM ˈɛkwɪd, -z

equidistant
BR ˌiːkwɪˈdɪst(ə)nt, ˌɛkwɪˈdɪst(ə)nt
AM ˌɛkwəˈdɪstnt, ˌɛkwiˈdɪstnt, ˌikwəˈdɪstnt, ˌikwiˈdɪstnt

equidistantly
BR ˌiːkwɪˈdɪst(ə)ntli, ˌɛkwɪˈdɪst(ə)ntli
AM ˌɛkwəˈdɪstən(t)li, ˌɛkwiˈdɪstən(t)li, ˌikwəˈdɪstən(t)li, ˌikwiˈdɪstən(t)li

equilateral
BR ˌiːkwɪˈlat(ə)rəl, ˌiːkwɪˈlat(ə)rl̩, ˌɛkwɪˈlat(ə)rəl, ɛkwɪˈlat(ə)rl̩
AM ˌɛkwəˈlædərəl, ˌɛkwiˈlædərəl, ˌikwəˈlædərəl, ˌikwiˈlædərəl, ˌikwəˈlætrəl, ˌikwiˈlætrəl, ˌɛkwəˈlætrəl, ˌɛkwiˈlætrəl

equilibrate
BR ˌiːkwɪˈlʌɪbreɪt, ˌɛkwɪˈlʌɪbreɪt, ˌiːkwɪˈlɪbreɪt, ˌɛkwɪˈlɪbreɪt, iːˈkwɪlɪbreɪt, ɪˈkwɪlɪbreɪt, -s, -ɪŋ, -ɪd
AM əˈkwɪləˌbreɪ|t, ɛˈkwɪləˌbreɪ|t, iˈkwɪləˌbreɪ|t, -ts, -dɪŋ, -dɪd

equilibration
BR ˌiːkwɪlʌɪˈbreɪʃn, ˌɛkwɪlʌɪˈbreɪʃn, ˌiːkwɪlɪˈbreɪʃn, ˌɛkwɪlɪˈbreɪʃn, iːˌkwɪlɪˈbreɪʃn, ɪˌkwɪlɪˈbreɪʃn
AM əˌkwɪləˈbreɪʃən, ɛˌkwɪləˈbreɪʃən, iˌkwɪləˈbreɪʃən

equilibrator
BR ˌiːkwɪˈlʌɪbreɪtə(r), ˌɛkwɪˈlʌɪbreɪtə(r), ˌiːkwɪˈlɪbreɪtə(r), ˌɛkwɪˈlɪbreɪtə(r), iːˈkwɪlɪbreɪtə(r), ɪˈkwɪlɪbreɪtə(r), -z
AM əˈkwɪləˌbreɪdər, ɛˈkwɪləˌbreɪdər, iˈkwɪləˌbreɪdər, -z

equilibrist
BR ˌiːkwɪˈlɪbrɪst, ˌɛkwɪˈlɪbrɪst, ɪˈkwɪlɪbrɪst, ɛˈkwɪlɪbrɪst, -s
AM ˌikwəˈlɪbrɪst, ˌɛkwəˈlɪbrɪst, əˈkwɪləbrəst, -s

equilibrium
BR ˌiːkwɪˈlɪbrɪəm, ˌɛkwɪˈlɪbrɪəm
AM ˌɛkwəˈlɪbriəm, ˌikwəˈlɪbriəm

equine
BR ˈɛkwʌɪn, ˈiːkwʌɪn
AM ˈɛkwaɪn, ˈikwaɪn

equinoctial
BR ˌiːkwɪˈnɒkʃl, ˌɛkwɪˈnɒkʃl
AM ˌɛkwəˈnɑkʃəl, ˌikwəˈnɑkʃəl

equinox
BR ˈiːkwɪnɒks, ˈɛkwɪnɒks, -ɪz
AM ˈɛkwəˌnɑks, ˈikwəˌnɑks, -əz

equip
BR ɪˈkwɪp, -s, -ɪŋ, -t
AM əˈkwɪp, iˈkwɪp, -s, -ɪŋ, -t

equipage
BR ˈɛkwɪpɪdʒ
AM ˈɛkwəpɪdʒ

equipartition
BR ˌiːkwɪpɑːˈtɪʃn, ˌɛkwɪpɑːˈtɪʃn
AM ˌɛkwəˌpɑrˈtɪʃən, ˌikwəˌpɑrˈtɪʃən

equipment
BR ɪˈkwɪpm(ə)nt
AM əˈkwɪpmənt, iˈkwɪpmənt

equipoise
BR ˈɛkwɪpɔɪz
AM ˈɛkwəˌpɔɪz

equipollence
BR ˌiːkwɪˈpɒləns, ˌiːkwɪˈpɒln̩s, ˌɛkwɪˈpɒləns, ˌɛkwɪˈpɒln̩s
AM ˌɛkwəˈpɑləns, ˌikwəˈpɑləns

equipollency
BR ˌiːkwɪˈpɒlənsi, ˌiːkwɪˈpɒln̩si, ˌɛkwɪˈpɒlənsi, ˌɛkwɪˈpɒln̩si
AM ˌɛkwəˈpɑlənsi, ˌikwəˈpɑlənsi

equipollent
BR ˌiːkwɪˈpɒlənt, ˌiːkwɪˈpɒln̩t, ˌɛkwɪˈpɒlənt, ˌɛkwɪˈpɒln̩t, -s
AM ˌɛkwəˈpɑlənt, ˌikwəˈpɑlənt, -s

equiponderant
BR ˌiːkwɪˈpɒnd(ə)rənt, ˌiːkwɪˈpɒnd(ə)rn̩t, ˌɛkwɪˈpɒnd(ə)rənt, ˌɛkwɪˈpɒnd(ə)rn̩t
AM ˌɛkwəˈpɑndərənt, ˌikwəˈpɑndərənt

equiponderate
BR ˌiːkwɪˈpɒndəreɪt, ˌɛkwɪˈpɒndəreɪt, -s, -ɪŋ, -ɪd
AM ˌɛkwəˈpɑndəˌreɪ|t, ˌikwəˈpɑndəˌreɪ|t, -ts, -dɪŋ, -dɪd

equipotential
BR ˌiːkwɪpəˈtɛnʃl, ˌɛkwɪpəˈtɛnʃl
AM ˌɛkwəpəˈtɛn(t)ʃəl, ˌikwəpəˈtɛn(t)ʃəl

equipper
BR ɪˈkwɪpə(r), -z
AM əˈkwɪpər, iˈkwɪpər, -z

equiprobability
BR ˌiːkwɪˌprɒbəˈbɪlɪti, ˌɛkwɪˌprɒbəˈbɪlɪti
AM ˌɛkwəˌprɑbəˈbɪlɪdi, ˌikwəˌprɑbəˈbɪlɪdi

equiprobable
BR ˌiːkwɪˈprɒbəbl, ˌɛkwɪˈprɒbəbl
AM ˌɛkwəˈprɑbəbəl, ˌikwəˈprɑbəbəl

equitable
BR ˈɛkwɪtəbl
AM ˈɛkwədəbəl

equitableness
BR ˈɛkwɪtəblnəs
AM ˈɛkwədəbəlnəs

equitably
BR ˈɛkwɪtəbli
AM ˈɛkwədəbli

equitant
BR ˈɛkwɪt(ə)nt
AM ˈɛkwədənt

equitation
BR ˌɛkwɪˈteɪʃn
AM ˌɛkwəˈteɪʃən

equites
BR ˈɛkwɪteɪz

AM 'ɛkwəˌteɪz, 'ɛkwəˌtiz

equity
BR 'ɛkwɪt|i, -ɪz
AM 'ɛkwədi, -z

equivalence
BR ɪ'kwɪvələns, ɪ'kwɪvəlṇs, ɪ'kwɪvḷ(ə)ns
AM ə'kwɪv(ə)ləns, i'kwɪv(ə)ləns

equivalency
BR ɪ'kwɪvələns|i, ɪ'kwɪvəlṇsi, ɪ'kwɪvḷ(ə)nsi, -ɪz
AM ə'kwɪv(ə)lənsi, i'kwɪv(ə)lənsi, -z

equivalent
BR ɪ'kwɪvələnt, ɪ'kwɪvəlṇt, ɪ'kwɪvḷ(ə)nt, -s
AM ə'kwɪv(ə)lənt, i'kwɪv(ə)lənt, -s

equivalently
BR ɪ'kwɪvələntli, ɪ'kwɪv(ə)lṇtli, ɪ'kwɪvḷ(ə)ntli
AM ə'kwɪvələn(t)li, i'kwɪvələn(t)li

equivocacy
BR ɪ'kwɪvəkəsi
AM ə'kwɪvəkəsi, i'kwɪvəkəsi

equivocal
BR ɪ'kwɪvəkl
AM ə'kwɪvəkəl, i'kwɪvəkəl

equivocality
BR ɪˌkwɪvə'kalɪti
AM əˌkwɪvə'kælədi, iˌkwɪvə'kælədi

equivocally
BR ɪ'kwɪvəkḷi, ɪ'kwɪvəkəli
AM ə'kwɪvək(ə)li, i'kwɪvək(ə)li

equivocalness
BR ɪ'kwɪvəklnəs
AM ə'kwɪvəkəlnəs, i'kwɪvəkəlnəs

equivocate
BR ɪ'kwɪvəkeɪt, -s, -ɪŋ, -ɪd
AM ə'kwɪvəˌkeɪ|t, i'kwɪvəˌkeɪ|t, -ts, -dɪŋ, -dɪd

equivocation
BR ɪˌkwɪvə'keɪʃn, -z
AM əˌkwɪvə'keɪʃən, i'kwɪvə'keɪʃən, -z

equivocator
BR ɪ'kwɪvəkeɪtə(r), -z
AM ə'kwɪvəˌkeɪdər, i'kwɪvəˌkeɪdər, -z

equivocatory
BR ɪ'kwɪvəkeɪt(ə)ri
AM ə'kwɪvəkəˌtɔri, i'kwɪvəkəˌtɔri

equivoke
BR 'ɛkwɪvəʊk, -s
AM 'ɛkwəˌvoʊk, 'ikwəˌvoʊk, -s

equivoque
BR 'ɛkwɪvəʊk, -s
AM 'ɛkwəˌvoʊk, 'ikwəˌvoʊk, -s

Equuleus
BR ɪ'kwʊlɪəs
AM i'kwʊliəs

equus
BR 'ɛkwəs
AM 'ɛkwəs

er
BR əː(r)
AM ər

era
BR 'ɪərə(*r*), -z
AM 'ɛrə, 'ɪrə, -z

eradicable
BR ɪ'radɪkəbl
AM ə'rædəkəbəl, i'rædəkəbəl

eradicate
BR ɪ'radɪkeɪt, -s, -ɪŋ, -ɪd
AM ə'rædəˌkeɪ|t, i'rædəˌkeɪ|t, -ts, -dɪŋ, -dɪd

eradication
BR ɪˌradɪ'keɪʃn
AM əˌrædə'keɪʃən, iˌrædə'keɪʃən

eradicator
BR ɪ'radɪkeɪtə(r), -z
AM ə'rædəˌkeɪdər, i'rædəˌkeɪdər, -z

erasable
BR ɪ'reɪzəbl
AM ə'reɪsəbəl, i'reɪsəbəl

erase
BR ɪ'reɪz, -ɪz, -ɪŋ, -d
AM ə'reɪs, i'reɪs, -ɪz, -ɪŋ, -t

eraser
BR ɪ'reɪzə(r), -z
AM ə'reɪsər, i'reɪsər, -z

Erasmus
BR ɪ'razməs
AM ə'ræzməs

Erastian
BR ɪ'rastɪən, ɛ'rastɪən, -z
AM ə'ræstiən, i'ræstiən, ə'ræstʃən, i'ræstʃən, -z

Erastianism
BR ɪ'rastɪənɪz(ə)m, ɛ'rastɪənɪz(ə)m
AM ə'ræstiəˌnɪzəm, i'ræstiəˌnɪzəm, ə'ræstʃəˌnɪzəm, i'ræstʃəˌnɪzəm

erasure
BR ɪ'reɪʒə(r), -z
AM ə'reɪʃər, i'reɪʃər, -z

Erato
BR 'ɛrətəʊ
AM 'ɛrədoʊ

Eratosthenes
BR ˌɛrə'tɒsθɪniːz
AM ˌɛrə'tɑsθəˌniz

erbium
BR 'əːbɪəm
AM 'ərbiəm

ere
before
BR ɛː(r)
AM ɛ(ə)r

'ere
here
BR ɪə(r)
AM ɪ(ə)r

Erebus
BR 'ɛrɪbəs
AM 'ɛrəbəs

Erechtheum
BR ˌɛrɛk'θiːəm, ˌɛrɪk'θiːəm
AM ˌɛrɛk'θiəm

Erechtheus
BR ɪ'rɛkθɪəs, ɛ'rɛkθɪəs
AM ə'rɛkθiəs

erect
BR ɪ'rɛkt, -s, -ɪŋ, -ɪd
AM ə'rɛk|(t), i'rɛk|(t), -(t)s, -tɪŋ, -təd

erectable
BR ɪ'rɛktəbl
AM ə'rɛktəbəl, i'rɛktəbəl

erectile
BR ɪ'rɛktʌɪl
AM ə'rɛktl, ə'rɛkˌtaɪl, i'rɛktl, i'rɛkˌtaɪl

erection
BR ɪ'rɛkʃn, -z
AM ə'rɛkʃən, i'rɛkʃən, -z

erectly
BR ɪ'rɛktli
AM ə'rɛk(t)li, i'rɛk(t)li

erectness
BR ɪ'rɛk(t)nəs
AM ə'rɛk(t)nəs, i'rɛk(t)nəs

erector
BR ɪ'rɛktə(r), -z
AM ə'rɛktər, i'rɛktər, -z

eremite
BR 'ɛrɪmʌɪt, -s
AM 'ɛrəˌmaɪt, -s

eremitic
BR ˌɛrɪ'mɪtɪk
AM ˌɛrə'mɪdɪk

eremitical
BR ˌɛrɪ'mɪtɪkl
AM ˌɛrə'mɪdɪkəl

eremitism
BR ˌɛrɪ'mɪtɪz(ə)m
AM ˌɛrə'mɪˌdɪzəm

erethism
BR 'ɛrɪθɪz(ə)m
AM 'ɛrəˌθɪzəm

Erewhon
BR 'ɛrɪwɒn
AM 'ɛrə(h)wɑn

erg
BR əːg, -z
AM ərg, -z

ergative
BR 'əːgətɪv, -z
AM 'ərgədɪv, -z

ergatively
BR 'əːgətɪvli
AM 'ərgədəvli

ergativity
BR ˌəːgə'tɪvɪti
AM ˌərgə'tɪvɪdi

ergo
BR 'əːgəʊ
AM 'ərgoʊ, 'ɛrgoʊ

ergocalciferol
BR ˌəːgə(ʊ)kal'sɪfərɒl, -z
AM ˌərgəˌkæl'sɪfərɑl, -z

ergonomic
BR ˌəːgə'nɒmɪk, -s
AM ˌərgə'nɑmɪk, -s

ergonomically
BR ˌəːgə'nɒmɪkli
AM ˌərgə'nɑmək(ə)li

ergonomist
BR əː'gɒnəmɪst, -s
AM ər'gɑnəməst, -s

ergosterol
BR əː'gɒstərɒl
AM ər'gɑstəˌroʊl, ər'gɑstəˌrɑl

ergot
BR 'əːgət, 'əːgɒt, -s
AM 'ərgət, 'ərˌgɑt, -s

ergotism
BR 'əːgətɪz(ə)m
AM 'ərgəˌtɪzəm

erhu
BR əː'huː, -z
AM ər'hu, -z

Eric
BR 'ɛrɪk
AM 'ɛrɪk

erica
BR 'ɛrɪkə(*r*), -z
AM 'ɛrəkə, -z

ericaceous
BR ˌɛrɪ'keɪʃəs
AM ˌɛrə'keɪʃəs

Erickson
BR 'ɛrɪksn
AM 'ɛrɪksən

Ericsson
BR 'ɛrɪksn
AM 'ɛrɪksən

Eridanus
BR ɪ'rɪdənəs, ɪ'rɪdṇəs
AM ə'rɪdənəs

Erie
BR 'ɪəri
AM 'ɪri

erigeron
BR ɪˈrɪdʒərɒn, ɛˈrɪdʒərɒn
AM əˈrɪdʒərən, əˈrɪdʒəˌrɑn

Erin
BR ˈɛrɪn
AM ˈɛrən

Erinys
BR ˈɛrɪnɪs, -ɪz
AM ˈɛrənəs, -əz

Eris
BR ˈɛrɪs
AM ˈɛrəs

eristic
BR ɛˈrɪstɪk, ɪˈrɪstɪk, -s
AM əˈrɪstɪk, ɛˈrɪstɪk, -s

eristically
BR ɛˈrɪstɨkli, ɪˈrɪstɨkli
AM əˈrɪstək(ə)li, ɛˈrɪstək(ə)li

Eritrea
BR ˌɛrɪˈtreɪə(r), ˌɛrɪˈtriːə(r)
AM ˌɛrəˈtriə, ˌɛrəˈtreɪə

Eritrean
BR ˌɛrɪˈtreɪən, ˌɛrɪˈtriːən, -z
AM ˌɛrəˈtriən, ˌɛrəˈtreɪən, -z

erk
BR əːk, -s
AM ərk, -s

Erlang
BR ˈəːlaŋ
AM ˈərˌlæŋ

Erlanger
BR ˈəːlaŋgə(r)
AM ˈərˌlæŋgər

Erle
BR əːl
AM ərl

erl-king
BR ˈəːlkɪŋ, -z
AM ˈər(ə)lˌkɪŋ, -z

ermine
BR ˈəːmɪn, -z, -d
AM ˈərmən, -z, -d

Ermintrude
BR ˈəːmɪntruːd
AM ˈərmənˌtrud

ern
BR əːn, -z
AM ərn, -z

erne
BR əːn, -z
AM ərn, -z

Ernest
BR ˈəːnɪst
AM ˈərnəst

Ernestine
BR ˈəːnɪstiːn
AM ˈərnəsˌtin

Ernie
BR ˈəːni
AM ˈərni

Ernle
BR ˈəːnli
AM ˈərnli

Ernst
BR ɛːnst, əːnst
AM ərnst

erode
BR ɪˈrəʊd, -z, -ɪŋ, -ɨd
AM əˈroʊd, iˈroʊd, -z, -ɪŋ, -əd

erogenous
BR ɪˈrɒdʒɪnəs, ɪˈrɒdʒn̩əs, ɛˈrɒdʒɪnəs, ɛˈrɒdʒn̩əs
AM əˈrɑdʒənəs, iˈrɑdʒənəs, ɛˈrɑdʒənəs

Eroica
BR ɪˈrəʊɪkə(r), ɛˈrəʊɪkə(r)
AM ɛˈroʊɪkə

Eros
BR ˈɪərɒs
AM ˈɛˌrɑs, ˈiˌrɑs

erosion
BR ɪˈrəʊʒn
AM əˈroʊʒən, iˈroʊʒən

erosional
BR ɪˈrəʊʒn̩(ə)l, ɪˈrəʊʒən(ə)l
AM əˈroʊʒ(ə)nəl, iˈroʊʒ(ə)nəl

erosive
BR ɪˈrəʊsɪv
AM əˈroʊsɪv

erosively
BR ɪˈrəʊsɨvli
AM əˈroʊsəvli

erotic
BR ɪˈrɒtɪk
AM əˈrɑdɪk, iˈrɑdɪk

erotica
BR ɪˈrɒtɨkə(r)
AM əˈrɑdəkə, iˈrɑdəkə

erotically
BR ɪˈrɒtɨkli
AM əˈrɑdək(ə)li, iˈrɑdək(ə)li

eroticise
BR ɪˈrɒtɨsʌɪz, -ɨz, -ɪŋ, -d
AM əˈrɑdəˌsaɪz, iˈrɑdəˌsaɪz, -ɨz, -ɪŋ, -d

eroticism
BR ɪˈrɒtɨsɪz(ə)m
AM əˈrɑdəˌsɪzəm, iˈrɑdəˌsɪzəm

eroticize
BR ɪˈrɒtɨsʌɪz, -ɨz, -ɪŋ, -d
AM əˈrɑdəˌsaɪz, iˈrɑdəˌsaɪz, -ɨz, -ɪŋ, -d

erotism
BR ˈɛrətɪz(ə)m
AM əˈrɑdɪzəm, iˈrɑdɪzəm

erotogenic
BR ɪˌrɒtə(ʊ)ˈdʒɛnɪk
AM əˌrɑdəˈdʒɛnɪk, iˌrɑdəˈdʒɛnɪk

erotogenous
BR ˌɛrəˈtɒdʒɪnəs
AM ˌɛrəˈtɑdʒənəs

erotology
BR ˌɛrəˈtɒlədʒi
AM ˌɛrəˈtɑlədʒi

erotomania
BR ɪˌrɒtə(ʊ)ˈmeɪnɪə(r)
AM əˌrɑdəˈmeɪniə, iˌrɑdəˈmeɪniə

erotomaniac
BR ɪˌrɒtə(ʊ)ˈmeɪnɪak, -s
AM əˌrɑdəˈmeɪniæk, iˌrɑdəˈmeɪniˌæk, -s

err
BR əː(r), -z, -ɪŋ, -d
AM ər, ɛ(ə)r, -z, -ɪŋ, -d

errancy
BR ˈɛrənsi, ˈɛrn̩si
AM ˈɛrənsi

errand
BR ˈɛrənd, ˈɛrn̩d, -z
AM ˈɛrənd, -z

errant
BR ˈɛrənt, ˈɛrn̩t
AM ˈɛrənt

errantly
BR ˈɛrəntli, ˈɛrn̩tli
AM ˈɛrən(t)li

errantry
BR ˈɛrəntri, ˈɛrn̩tri
AM ˈɛrəntri

errata
BR ɛˈrɑːtə(r), ɪˈrɑːtə(r)
AM ɛˈrɑdə

erratic
BR ɪˈratɪk
AM əˈrædɪk, ɛˈrædɪk, iˈrædɪk

erratically
BR ɪˈratɨkli
AM əˈrædək(ə)li, ɛˈrædək(ə)li, iˈrædək(ə)li

erraticism
BR ɪˈratɨsɪz(ə)m
AM əˈrædəˌsɪzəm, ɛˈrædəˌsɪzəm, iˈrædəˌsɪzəm

erratum
BR ɛˈrɑːtəm, ɪˈrɑːtəm
AM ɛˈrɑdəm

Errol
BR ˈɛrəl, ˈɛrl̩
AM ˈɛrəl

Erroll
BR ˈɛrəl, ˈɛrl̩
AM ˈɛrəl

erroneous
BR ɪˈrəʊnɪəs
AM ɛˈroʊniəs, iˈroʊniəs, iˈroʊnjəs, ɛˈroʊnjəs

erroneously
BR ɪˈrəʊnɪəsli
AM ɛˈroʊniəsli, iˈroʊniəsli, iˈroʊnjəsli, ɛˈroʊnjəsli

erroneousness
BR ɪˈrəʊnɪəsnəs
AM ɛˈroʊniəsnəs, iˈroʊniəsnəs, iˈroʊnjəsnəs, ɛˈroʊnjəsnəs

error
BR ˈɛrə(r), -z
AM ˈɛrər, -z

errorless
BR ˈɛrələs
AM ˈɛrərləs

ersatz
BR ˈəːsats, ˈɛːsats, ˈəːzats, ˈɛːzats
AM ˈɛrˌsɑts, ˈɛrˌzæts, ˈɛrˌzɑts

Erse
BR əːs
AM ərs

erst
BR əːst
AM ərst

erstwhile
BR ˈəːstwʌɪl
AM ˈərstˌ(h)waɪl

Ertebølle
BR ˌəːtəˈbəːlə(r)
AM ˌərdəˈbɑlə
DAN ˈʌʌdəˌbœlə

erubescence
BR ˌɛrʉˈbɛsns
AM ˌɛruˈbɛsəns

erubescent
BR ˌɛrʉˈbɛsnt
AM ˌɛruˈbɛsənt

eructation
BR ˌiːrʌkˈteɪʃn, ɪˌrʌkˈteɪʃn, ˌɛrʌkˈteɪʃn, -z
AM əˌrəkˈteɪʃən, iˌrəkˈteɪʃən, -z

erudite
BR ˈɛr(j)ʉdʌɪt
AM ˈɛr(j)əˌdaɪt

eruditely
BR ˈɛr(j)ʉdʌɪtli
AM ˈɛr(j)əˌdaɪtli

erudition
BR ˌɛr(j)ʉˈdɪʃn
AM ˌɛrəˈdɪʃən, ˈɛr(j)ʊˌdɪʃən

erupt
BR ɪˈrʌpt, -s, -ɪŋ, -ɨd
AM əˈrəpt, iˈrəpt, -s, -ɪŋ, -əd

eruption
BR ɪˈrʌpʃn, -z
AM əˈrəpʃən, iˈrəpʃən, -z

eruptive
BR ɪˈrʌptɪv
AM əˈrəptɪv, iˈrəptɪv

eruptively
BR ɪˈrʌptɨvli

AM ə'rəptəvli, i'rəptəvli

eruptivity
BR ɪˌrʌp'tɪvɪti
AM əˌrəp'tɪvɨdi, iˌrəp'tɪvɨdi

Erving
BR 'əːvɪŋ
AM 'ərvɪŋ

eryngo
BR ɪ'rɪŋɡəʊ
AM ə'rɪŋɡoʊ

erysipelas
BR ˌɛrɪ'sɪpɨləs, ˌɛrɪ'sɪpl̩əs
AM ˌɛrə'sɪp(ə)ləs

erythema
BR ˌɛrɪ'θiːmə(r)
AM ˌɛrə'θimə

erythemal
BR ˌɛrɪ'θiːml
AM ˌɛrə'θiməl

erythematic
BR ˌɛrɪθɪ'matɪk
AM ˌɛrəθə'mædɪk

erythroblast
BR ɪ'rɪθrə(ʊ)blɑːst, ɪ'rɪθrə(ʊ)blast, -s
AM ə'rɪθroʊˌblæst, i'rɪθroʊˌblæst, -s

erythrocyte
BR ɪ'rɪθrəsʌɪt, -s
AM ə'rɪθroʊˌsaɪt, i'rɪθroʊˌsaɪt, -s

erythrocytic
BR ɪˌrɪθrə'sʌɪtɪk
AM əˌrɪθrə'sɪdɪk, iˌrɪθrə'sɪdɪk

erythroid
BR ɪ'rɪθrɔɪd
AM ə'rɪθˌrɔɪd, i'rɪθˌrɔɪd

erythromycin
BR ɪˌrɪθrə(ʊ)'mʌɪsɪn
AM əˌrɪθroʊ'maɪsɪn, iˌrɪθroʊ'maɪsɪn

erythropoietic
BR ɪˌrɪθrə(ʊ)pɔɪ'ɛtɪk
AM əˌrɪθrəˌpɔɪ'ɛdɪk, iˌrɪθrəˌpɔɪ'ɛdɪk

Erzgebirge
BR 'əːtsɡəˌbəːɡə(r)
AM 'ɛrtsɡəˌbɪrɡə
GER 'eːɐtsɡəbɪrɡə

Esau
BR 'iːsɔː(r)
AM 'isɔ, 'isɑ

Esbjerg
BR 'ɛsbjəːɡ
AM 'ɛsˌb(j)ər(ɡ)
DAN 'ɛsˌbjaʌ'

escadrille
BR 'ɛskədrɪl, ˌɛskə'drɪl, -z
AM 'ɛskəˌdrɪl, ˌɛskə'drɪl, -z

escalade
BR ˌɛskə'leɪd, -z, -ɪŋ, -ɨd
AM ˌɛskə'leɪd, -z, -ɪŋ, -ɨd

escalate
BR 'ɛskəleɪt, -s, -ɪŋ, -ɨd
AM 'ɛskəˌleɪ|t, -ts, -dɪŋ, -dɨd

escalation
BR ˌɛskə'leɪʃn, -z
AM ˌɛskə'leɪʃən, -z

escalator
BR 'ɛskəleɪtə(r), -z
AM 'ɛskəˌleɪdər, -z

escallonia
BR ˌɛskə'ləʊnɪə(r), -z
AM ˌɛkə'loʊniə, -z

escallop
BR ɪ'skaləp, ɛ'skaləp, 'ɛskəlɒp, ˌɛskə'lɒp, -s
AM ə'skɑləp, ɛ'skɑləp, ə'skæləp, ɛ'skæləp, -s

escalope
BR ɪ'skaləp, ɛ'skaləp, 'ɛskəlɒp, ˌɛskə'lɒp, 'ɛskələʊp, -s
AM ə'skɑləp, ɛ'skɑləp, ə'skæləp, ɛ'skæləp, -s

escapable
BR ɪ'skeɪpəbl
AM ə'skeɪpəbəl, ɛ'skeɪpəbəl

escapade
BR 'ɛskəpeɪd, -z
AM 'ɛskəˌpeɪd, -z

escape
BR ɪ'skeɪp, -s, -ɪŋ, -t
AM ə'skeɪp, ɛ'skeɪp, -s, -ɪŋ, -t

escapee
BR ˌɛskeɪ'piː, -z
AM ˌɛsˌkeɪ'pi, əˌskeɪ'pi, -z

escapement
BR ɪ'skeɪpm(ə)nt, -s
AM ə'skeɪpmənt, ɛ'skeɪpmənt, -s

escaper
BR ɪ'skeɪpə(r), -z
AM ə'skeɪpər, ɛ'skeɪpər, -z

escapism
BR ɪ'skeɪpɪz(ə)m
AM ə'skeɪpˌɪzəm, ɛ'skeɪpˌɪzəm

escapist
BR ɪ'skeɪpɪst, -s
AM ə'skeɪpɪst, ɛ'skeɪpɪst, -s

escapologist
BR ˌɛskə'pɒlədʒɪst, -s
AM əˌskeɪ'pɑlədʒəst, ɛˌskeɪ'pɑlədʒəst, -s

escapology
BR ˌɛskə'pɒlədʒi
AM əˌskeɪ'pɑlədʒi, ɛˌskeɪ'pɑlədʒi

escargot
BR ɪ'skɑːɡəʊ, ɛ'skɑːɡəʊ, -z
AM ˌɛskɑr'ɡoʊ, -z

escarp
BR ɪ'skɑːp, ɛ'skɑːp, -s
AM ə'skɑrp, ɛ'skɑrp, -s

escarpment
BR ɪ'skɑːpm(ə)nt, ɛ'skɑːpm(ə)nt, -s
AM ə'skɑrpmənt, ɛ'skɑrpmənt, -s

eschar
BR 'ɛskɑː(r), -z
AM 'ɛskɑr, 'ɛskər, -z

eschatological
BR ˌɛskətə'lɒdʒɨkl, ˌɛskatə'lɒdʒɨkl
AM ˌɛsˌkædl'ɑdʒəkəl, ˌɛskədl'ɑdʒəkəl

eschatologist
BR ˌɛskə'tɒlədʒɪst, -s
AM ˌɛskə'tɑlədʒəst, -s

eschatology
BR ˌɛskə'tɒlədʒi
AM ˌɛskə'tɑlədʒi

eschaton
BR 'ɛskətɒn
AM 'ɛskəˌtɑn

escheat
BR ɪs'tʃiːt, ɛs'tʃiːt, -s, -ɪŋ, -ɨd
AM əs'tʃi|t, əʃ'tʃi|t, ɛs'tʃi|t, ɛʃ'tʃi|t, -ts, -dɪŋ, -dɨd

eschew
BR ɪs'tʃuː, ɛs'tʃuː, -z, -ɪŋ, -d
AM əs'tʃu, ɛs'tʃu, -z, -ɪŋ, -d

eschewal
BR ɪs'tʃʊəl, ɛs'tʃʊəl
AM əs'tʃʊəl, ɛs'tʃʊəl

eschscholtzia
BR ɪ'ʃɒltsɪə(r), ɛ'ʃɒltsɪə(r), ɪ'skɒltsɪə(r), ɛ'skɒltsɪə(r), ɪ'skɒlʃə(r), ɛ'skɒlʃə(r)
AM ə'ʃɑltsiə

Escoffier
BR ɪ'skɒfɪeɪ, ɛ'skɒfɪeɪ
AM ˌɛskɔf'jeɪ, ˌɛskɑf'jeɪ

Escondido
BR ˌɛskɒn'diːdəʊ, ˌɛsk(ə)n'diːdəʊ
AM ˌɛskən'didoʊ

Escorial
BR ˌɛskɒrɪ'ɑːl, ɛ'skɔːrɪəl, ɛ'skɔːrɪal
AM ˌɛskɔr'jɑl

escort¹
noun
BR 'ɛskɔːt, -s
AM 'ɛsˌkɔ(ə)rt, -s

escort²
verb
BR ɪ'skɔːt, ɛ'skɔːt, -s, -ɪŋ, -ɨd
AM əs'kɔ(ə)rt, ɛs'kɔ(ə)rt, -ts, -'kɔrdɪŋ, -'kɔrdəd

escribe
BR ɪ'skrʌɪb, ɛ'skrʌɪb, -z, -ɪŋ, -d
AM ə'skraɪb, -z, -ɪŋ, -d

escritoire
BR ˌɛskrɪ'twɑː(r), -z
AM 'ɛskrəˌtwɑr, ˌɛskrə'twɑr, -z

escrow
BR 'ɛskrəʊ, ɛ'skrəʊ
AM 'ɛskˌroʊ, ɛ'skroʊ

escudo
BR ɛ'sk(j)uːdəʊ, ɪ'sk(j)uːdəʊ, ɛ'ʃkuːdəʊ, ɪ'ʃkuːdəʊ, -z
AM ə'sk(j)udoʊ, ɛ'sk(j)udoʊ, -z

esculent
BR 'ɛskjʉlənt, 'ɛskjʉlnt
AM 'ɛskjələnt

escutcheon
BR ɪ'skʌtʃ(ə)n, -z
AM ə'skətʃən, ɛ'skətʃən, -z

escutcheoned
BR ɪ'skʌtʃ(ə)nd
AM ə'skətʃənd, ɛ'skətʃənd

Esdras
BR 'ɛzdras, 'ɛzdrəs
AM 'ɛzdrəs

Esfahan
BR ˌɛsfə'hɑːn
AM ˌɛsfə'hɑn

Esher
BR 'iːʃə(r)
AM 'iʃər

Esk
BR ɛsk
AM ɛsk

eskar
BR 'ɛskə(r), -z
AM 'ɛskər, -z

Eskdale
BR 'ɛskdeɪl
AM 'ɛskˌdeɪl

esker
BR 'ɛskə(r), -z
AM 'ɛskər, -z

Eskimo
BR 'ɛskɪməʊ, -z
AM 'ɛskəˌmoʊ, -z

Esky®
BR 'ɛsk|i, -ɪz
AM 'ɛski, -z

Esme
BR 'ɛzmi
AM 'ɛzmi

Esmeralda
BR ˌɛzmə'raldə(r)
AM ˌɛzmə'rɑldə

Esmond
BR 'ɛzmənd

AM 'ɛzmənd

ESOL
BR 'iːsɒl
AM 'iˌsɑl

esophageal
BR ɪˌsɒfə'dʒiːəl, iːˌsɒfə'dʒiːəl
AM əˌsɑfə'dʒiəl, iˌsɑfə'dʒiəl

esophagi
BR ɪ'sɒfəgʌɪ, iː'sɒfəgʌɪ, ɪ'sɒfədʒʌɪ, iː'sɒfədʒʌɪ
AM ə'sɑfəˌgaɪ, i'sɑfəˌgaɪ, ə'sɑfəˌdʒaɪ, i'sɑfəˌdʒaɪ

esophagus
BR ɪ'sɒfəgəs, iː'sɒfəgəs
AM ə'sɑfəgəs, i'sɑfəgəs

esoteric
BR ˌɛsə(ʊ)'tɛrɪk, ˌiːsə(ʊ)'tɛrɪk
AM ˌɛsə'tɛrɪk

esoterical
BR ˌɛsə(ʊ)'tɛrɪkl, ˌiːsə(ʊ)'tɛrɪkl
AM ˌɛsə'tɛrəkəl

esoterically
BR ˌɛsə(ʊ)'tɛrɪkli, ˌiːsə(ʊ)'tɛrɪkli
AM ˌɛsə'tɛrək(ə)li

esotericism
BR ˌɛsə(ʊ)'tɛrɪsɪz(ə)m, ˌiːsə(ʊ)'tɛrɪsɪz(ə)m
AM ˌɛsə'tɛrəˌsɪzəm

esotericist
BR ˌɛsə(ʊ)'tɛrɪsɪst, ˌiːsə(ʊ)'tɛrɪsɪst, -s
AM ˌɛsə'tɛrəsəst, -s

espadrille
BR 'ɛspədrɪl, ˌɛspə'drɪl, -z
AM ˈˌɛspəˌdrɪl, -z

espalier
BR ɪ'spalɪə(r), ɛ'spalɪə(r), ɪ'spalɪeɪ, ɛ'spalɪeɪ, -z
AM əs'pæljər, ɛs'pæljər, əs'pɑljər, ɛs'pɑljər, əs'peɪljər, ɛs'peɪljər, -z

esparto
BR ɪ'spɑːtəʊ, ɛ'spɑːtəʊ, -z
AM ə'spɑrdoʊ, ɛ'spɑrdoʊ, -z

especial
BR ɪ'spɛʃl, ɛ'spɛʃl
AM əs'pɛʃəl, ɛs'pɛʃəl

especially
BR ɪ'spɛʃḷi, ɪ'spɛʃəli, ɛ'spɛʃḷi, ɛ'spɛʃəli
AM əs'pɛʃəli, ɛs'pɛʃəli

Esperantist
BR ˌɛspə'rantɪst, -s
AM ˌɛspə'rɑn(t)əst, -s

Esperanto
BR ˌɛspə'rantəʊ
AM ˌɛspə'rɑn(t)oʊ

espial
BR ɪ'spʌɪəl, ɛ'spʌɪəl
AM əs'paɪ(ə)l, ɛs'paɪ(ə)l

espionage
BR 'ɛspɪənɑː(d)ʒ
AM 'ɛspiəˌnɑʒ

esplanade
BR ˌɛsplə'neɪd, 'ɛspləneɪd, -z
AM ˌɛsplə'nɑd, ˌɛsplə'neɪd, -z

Esposito
BR ˌɛspə'ziːtəʊ
AM ˌɛspə'zidoʊ

espousal
BR ɪ'spaʊzl, ɛ'spaʊzl, -z
AM əs'paʊzəl, ɛs'paʊzəl, -z

espouse
BR ɪ'spaʊz, ɛ'spaʊz, -ɪz, -ɪŋ, -d
AM əs'paʊz, ɛs'paʊz, -əz, -ɪŋ, -t

espouser
BR ɪ'spaʊzə(r), ɛ'spaʊzə(r), -z
AM əs'paʊzər, ɛs'paʊzər, -z

espresso
BR ɛ'sprɛsəʊ, -z
AM ɛs'prɛsoʊ, -z

esprit
BR ɛ'spriː, 'ɛspriː
AM əs'pri, ɛs'pri

esprit de corps
BR ɛˌspriː də 'kɔː(r), ˌɛspriː +
AM ɛsˌpri də 'kɔ(ə)r

esprit de l'escalier
BR ɛˌspriː də lɛ'skalɪeɪ, ˌɛspriː +
AM ɛsˌpri də ˌlɛskəl'jeɪ

espy
BR ɪ'spʌɪ, ɛ'spʌɪ, -z, -ɪŋ, -d
AM əs'paɪ, ɛs'paɪ, -z, -ɪŋ, -d

Esq.
BR ɪ'skwʌɪə(r), ɛ'skwʌɪə(r), -z
AM 'ɛsˌkwaɪ(ə)r , əs'kwaɪ(ə)r, -z

Esquimau
BR 'ɛskɪməʊ, -z
AM 'ɛskəˌmoʊ, -z

Esquimaux
BR 'ɛskəməʊz
AM 'ɛskəˌmoʊz

esquire
BR ɪ'skwʌɪə(r), ɛ'skwʌɪə(r), -z
AM 'ɛsˌkwaɪ(ə)r, əs'kwaɪ(ə)r, -z

essay[1]
noun
BR 'ɛseɪ, -z
AM 'ɛseɪ, -z

essay[2]
verb
BR ɛ'seɪ, -z, -ɪŋ, -d
AM ɛ'seɪ, -z, -ɪŋ, -d

essayist
BR 'ɛseɪɪst, -s
AM 'ɛseɪəst, -s

Essen
BR 'ɛsn
AM 'ɛsən

essence
BR 'ɛsns, -ɪz
AM 'ɛsəns, -əz

Essendon
BR 'ɛsnd(ə)n
AM 'ɛsənd(ə)n

Essene
BR 'ɛsiːn, ɛ'siːn, -z
AM ə'sin, ɛ'sin, 'ɛˌsin, -z

essential
BR ɪ'sɛnʃl
AM ə'sɛn(t)ʃəl

essentialism
BR ɪ'sɛnʃḷɪz(ə)m, ɪ'sɛnʃəlɪz(ə)m
AM ə'sɛn(t)ʃəˌlɪzəm

essentialist
BR ɪ'sɛnʃḷɪst, ɪ'sɛnʃəlɪst, -s
AM ə'sɛn(t)ʃ(ə)ləst, -s

essentiality
BR ɪˌsɛnʃɪ'alɪti
AM əˌsɛn(t)ʃi'ælədi

essentially
BR ɪ'sɛnʃḷi, ɪ'sɛnʃəli
AM ə'sɛn(t)ʃəli

essentialness
BR ɪ'sɛnʃ(ə)lnəs
AM ə'sɛn(t)ʃəlnəs

Essequibo
BR ˌɛsɪ'kwiːbəʊ
AM ˌɛsə'kwiboʊ

Essex
BR 'ɛsɪks
AM 'ɛsəks

essive
BR 'ɛsɪv, -z
AM 'ɛsɪv, -z

Esso®
BR 'ɛsəʊ
AM 'ɛsoʊ

Essoldo
BR ɛ'sɒldəʊ, ɪ'sɒldəʊ
AM ɛ'sɔldoʊ, ɛ'sɑldoʊ

establish
BR ɪ'stabl|ɪʃ, ɛ'stabl|ɪʃ, -ɪʃɪz, -ɪʃɪŋ, -ɪʃt
AM əs'tæblɪʃ, ɛs'tæblɪʃ, -ɪz, -ɪŋ, -t

establisher
BR ɪ'stablɪʃə(r), ɛ'stablɪʃə(r), -z
AM əs'tæblɪʃər, ɛs'tæblɪʃər, -z

establishment
BR ɪ'stablɪʃm(ə)nt, ɛ'stablɪʃm(ə)nt, -s
AM əs'tæblɪʃmənt, ɛs'tæblɪʃmənt, -s

establishmentarian
BR ɪˌstablɪʃm(ə)n'tɛːrɪən, ɛˌstablɪʃm(ə)n'tɛːrɪən, -z
AM əsˌtæblɪʃmən'tɛriən, ɛsˌtæblɪʃmən'tɛriən, -z

establishmentariani
BR ɪˌstablɪʃm(ə)n'tɛːrɪənɪː
ɛstablɪʃm(ə)n'tɛːrɪənɪz(ə)
AM əsˌtæblɪʃmən'tɛriəˌnɪz
ɛsˌtæblɪʃmən'tɛriəˌnɪzəm

estaminet
BR ɛ'stamɪneɪ, -z
AM ɛsˌtæmi'neɪ, -z

estancia
BR ɪ'stansɪə(*r*), ɛ'stansɪə(*r*), -z
AM ɛ'stænsiə, -z

estate
BR ɪ'steɪt, ɛ'steɪt, -s
AM əs'teɪt, ɛs'teɪt, -s

esteem
BR ɪ'stiːm, ɛ'stiːm, -z, -ɪŋ, -d
AM əs'tim, ɛs'tim, -z, -ɪŋ, -d

Estella
BR ɪ'stɛlə(*r*), ɛ'stɛlə(*r*)
AM ɛs'tɛlə

Estelle
BR ɛ'stɛl
AM ə'stɛl

ester
BR 'ɛstə(r), -z
AM 'ɛstər, -z

Esterhazy
BR 'ɛstəhɑːzi
AM 'ɛstərˌ(h)ɑzi

esterify
BR ɪ'stɛrɪfʌɪ, ɛ'stɛrɪfʌɪ, -z, -ɪŋ, -d
AM ə'stɛrəˌfaɪ, -z, -ɪŋ, -d

Estes
BR 'ɛstɪz, 'ɛsteɪz
AM 'ɛstiz

Esther
BR 'ɛstə(r), 'ɛsθə(r)
AM 'ɛstər

esthete
BR 'iːsθiːt, -s
AM 'ɛsˌθit, -s

esthetic
BR iːs'θɛtɪk, ɪs'θɛtɪk, -s
AM ɛs'θɛdɪk, -s

esthetical
BR iːs'θɛtɪkl, ɪs'θɛtɪkl
AM ɛs'θɛdəkəl

esthetically
BR iːs'θɛtɪkli, ɪs'θɛtɪkli
AM ɛs'θɛdək(ə)li

esthetician
BR ˌiːsθəˈtɪʃn
AM ˌɛsθəˈtɪʃən

estheticism
BR iːsˈθɛtɪsɪz(ə)m, ɪsˈθɛtɪsɪz(ə)m
AM ɛsˈθɛdəˌsɪzəm

estimable
BR ˈɛstɪməbl
AM ˈɛstəməbəl

estimableness
BR ˈɛstɪməblnəs
AM ˈɛstəməbəlnəs

estimably
BR ˈɛstɪməbli
AM ˈɛstəməbli

estimate[1]
noun
BR ˈɛstɪmət, -s
AM ˈɛstɪmət, -s

estimate[2]
verb
BR ˈɛstɪmeɪt, -s, -ɪŋ, -ɪd
AM ˈɛstəˌmeɪ|t, -ts, -dɪŋ, -dɪd

estimation
BR ˌɛstɪˈmeɪʃn
AM ˌɛstəˈmeɪʃən

estimative
BR ˈɛstɪmətɪv
AM ˈɛstəˌmeɪdɪv, ˈɛstəmədɪv

estimator
BR ˈɛstɪmeɪtə(r), -z
AM ˈɛstəˌmeɪdər, -z

estival
BR ˈiːstɪvl, ˈɛstɪvl, iːˈstʌɪvl, ɛˈstʌɪvl
AM ˈɛstəvəl

estivate
BR ˈiːstɪveɪt, ˈɛstɪveɪt, -s, -ɪŋ, -ɪd
AM ˈɛstəˌveɪ|t, -ts, -dɪŋ, -dɪd

estivation
BR ˌiːstɪˈveɪʃn, ˌɛstɪˈveɪʃn, -z
AM ˌɛstəˈveɪʃən, -z

estoile
BR ɪˈstɔɪl, ɛˈstɔɪl, -z
AM əˈstɔɪl, ɛˈstɔɪl, -z

Estonia
BR ɛˈstəʊnɪə(r), ɪˈstəʊnɪə(r)
AM ɛˈstoʊniə

Estonian
BR ɛˈstəʊnɪən, ɪˈstəʊnɪən, -z
AM ɛˈstoʊniən, -z

estop
BR ɪˈstɒp, ɛˈstɒp, -s, -ɪŋ, -t
AM əˈstɑp, ɛˈstɑp, -s, -ɪŋ, -t

estoppage
BR ɪˈstɒpɪdʒ, ɛˈstɒpɪdʒ
AM əˈstɑpɪdʒ, ɛˈstɑpɪdʒ

estoppel
BR ɪˈstɒpl, ɛˈstɒpl
AM əˈstɑpəl, ɛˈstɑpəl

Estoril
BR ˌɛstəˈrɪl
AM ˈɛstəˌrɪl
B PORT isˈtoriw
L PORT əʃtuˈril

estovers
BR ɪˈstəʊvəz, ɛˈstəʊvəz
AM əˈstoʊvərz, ɛˈstoʊvərz

estrade
BR ɛˈstrɑːd, ɪˈstrɑːd, -z
AM ɛsˈtrɑd, -z

estragon
BR ˈɛstrəgɒn, ˈɛstrəg(ə)n
AM ˈɛstrəˌgɑn

estrange
BR ɪˈstreɪn(d)ʒ, ɛˈstreɪn(d)ʒ, -ɪz, -ɪŋ, -d
AM əsˈtreɪndʒ, ɛsˈtreɪndʒ, -ɪz, -ɪŋ, -d

estrangement
BR ɪˈstreɪn(d)ʒm(ə)nt, ɪˈstreɪn(d)ʒm(ə)nt, -s
AM əsˈtreɪndʒmənt, ɛsˈtreɪndʒmənt, -s

estreat
BR ɪˈstriːt, ɛˈstriːt
AM əsˈtrit, ɛsˈtrit

Estremadura
BR ˌɛstrəməˈd(j)ʊərə(r), ˌɛstrəməˈdʒʊərə(r)
AM ˌɛstrəməˈd(j)urə

estrogen
BR ˈiːstrədʒ(ə)n, ˈɛstrədʒ(ə)n
AM ˈɛstrədʒən

estrous
BR ˈiːstrəs, ˈɛstrəs
AM ˈɛstrəs

estrus
BR ˈiːstrəs, ˈɛstrəs
AM ˈɛstrəs

estuarine
BR ˈɛstjʊərʌɪn, ˈɛstjʊrʌɪn, ˈɛstʃʊrʌɪn
AM ˈɛstʃəwəˌraɪn, ˈɛstʃəwərən, ˈɛstʃəwəˌrin

estuary
BR ˈɛstjʊr|i, ˈɛstjʊər|i, ˈɛstʃʊr|i, -ɪz
AM ˈɛstʃəˌwɛri, -z

esurience
BR ɪˈsjʊərɪəns, ɛˈsjʊərɪəns, ɪˈsjɔːrɪəns, ɛˈsjɔːrɪəns, ɪˈsʊrɪəns, ɛˈsʊrɪəns
AM əˈsʊriəns, iˈsʊriəns

esuriency
BR ɪˈsjʊərɪənsi, ɛˈsjʊərɪənsi, ɪˈsjɔːrɪənsi, ɛˈsjɔːrɪənsi, ɪˈsʊrɪənsi, ɛˈsʊrɪənsi
AM əˈsʊriənsi, iˈsʊriənsi

esurient
BR ɪˈsjʊərɪənt, ɛˈsjʊərɪənt, ɪˈsjɔːrɪənt, ɛˈsjɔːrɪənt, ɪˈsʊrɪənt, ɛˈsʊrɪənt
AM əˈsʊriənt, iˈsʊriənt

esuriently
BR ɪˈsjʊərɪəntli, ɛˈsjʊərɪəntli, ɪˈsjɔːrɪəntli, ɛˈsjɔːrɪəntli, ɪˈsʊrɪəntli, ɛˈsʊrɪəntli
AM əˈsʊriən(t)li, iˈsʊriən(t)li

ETA
Basque organization
BR ˈɛtə(r)
AM ˈɛdə

eta
Greek letter
BR ˈiːtə(r)
AM ˈeɪdə, ˈidə

etaerio
BR ɛˈtɪərɪəʊ, -z
AM ɛˈtirioʊ, -z

et al.
BR ˌɛt ˈal
AM ˌɛtˈæl, ˌɛtˈɑl

etalon
BR ˈɛtəlɒn, -z
AM ˈeɪdlˌɑn, -z

Etam®
BR ˈiːtam
AM ˈidəm

etc
UNIX directory
BR ˈɛtsi
AM ˈɛtsi

etc.
BR ˌɛt ˈsɛt(ə)rə(r)
AM ɛt ˈsɛdərə

et cetera
BR ˌɛt ˈsɛt(ə)rə(r)
AM ɛt ˈsɛdərə

etch
BR ɛtʃ, -ɪz, -ɪŋ, -t
AM ɛtʃ, -əz, -ɪŋ, -t

etchant
BR ˈɛtʃ(ə)nt, -s
AM ˈɛtʃənt, -s

etcher
BR ˈɛtʃə(r), -z
AM ˈɛtʃər, -z

etching
BR ˈɛtʃɪŋ, -z
AM ˈɛtʃɪŋ, -z

eternal
BR ɪˈtəːnl
AM əˈtərnəl, iˈtərnəl

eternalise
BR ɪˈtəːnəlʌɪz, ɪˈtəːnl̩ʌɪz, -ɪz, -ɪŋ, -d
AM əˈtərnlˌaɪz, iˈtərnlˌaɪz, -ɪz, -ɪŋ, -d

eternality
BR ɪˌtəːˈnalɪti
AM ˌidərˈnælədi

eternalize
BR ɪˈtəːnəlʌɪz, ɪˈtəːnl̩ʌɪz, -ɪz, -ɪŋ, -d
AM əˈtərnlˌaɪz, iˈtərnlˌaɪz, -ɪz, -ɪŋ, -d

eternally
BR ɪˈtəːnl̩i, ɪˈtəːnəli
AM əˈtərnəli, iˈtərnəli

eternalness
BR ɪˈtəːnl̩nəs
AM əˈtərnlnəs, iˈtərnlnəs

eternise
BR ɪˈtəːnʌɪz, -ɪz, -ɪŋ, -d
AM əˈtərˌnaɪz, iˈtərˌnaɪz, -ɪz, -ɪŋ, -d

eternity
BR ɪˈtəːnɪt|i, -ɪz
AM əˈtərnədi, iˈtərnədi, -z

eternize
BR ɪˈtəːnʌɪz, -ɪz, -ɪŋ, -d
AM iˈtərˌnaɪz, əˈtərˌnaɪz, -ɪz, -ɪŋ, -d

Etesian
BR ɪˈtiːzɪən, ɪˈtiːʒɪən, ɪˈtiːʒn
AM əˈtiʒən, iˈtiʒən

eth
BR ɛð, -z
AM ɛð, -z

Ethan
BR ˈiːθn
AM ˈiθən

ethanal
BR ˈɛθənal
AM ˈɛθəˌnɑl

ethane
BR ˈiːθeɪn, ˈɛθeɪn
AM ˈɛθˌeɪn

ethanoate
BR ˈiːθeɪnəʊət, ˈɛθeɪnəʊət, -s
AM ˈɛθənəwət, ɛˈθeɪnəwət, -s

ethanoic
BR ˌɛθəˈnəʊɪk
AM ˌɛθəˈnoʊɪk

ethanol
BR ˈɛθənɒl
AM ˈɛθəˌnɔl, ˈɛθəˌnɑl

Ethel
BR ˈɛθl
AM ˈɛθəl

Ethelbert
BR ˈɛθlbəːt
AM ˈɛθəlˌbərt

Ethelberta
BR ˌɛθlˈbəːtə(r), ˈɛθlbəːtə(r)
AM ˌɛθəlˈbərdə

Ethelburga
BR ˌɛθlˈbəːgə(r), ˈɛθlbəːgə(r)
AM ˌɛθəlˈbərgə

Etheldreda
BR ˌɛθl'dri:də(r), 'ɛθldri:də(r)
AM ˌɛθəl'drɛdə

Ethelred
BR 'ɛθlrɛd
AM 'ɛθəlˌrɛd

ethene
BR 'i:θi:n, 'ɛθi:n
AM 'ɛθin

ether
BR 'i:θə(r)
AM 'iθər

ethereal
BR ɪ'θɪərɪəl
AM ə'θɪriəl, i'θɪriəl, ɛ'θɪriəl

etherealise
BR ɪ'θɪərɪəlʌɪz, -ɪz, -ɪŋ, -d
AM ə'θɪriəˌlaɪz, i'θɪriəˌlaɪz, ɛ'θɪriəˌlaɪz, -ɪz, -ɪŋ, -d

ethereality
BR ɪˌθɪərɪ'alɪti
AM əˌθɪri'ælədi, iˌθɪri'ælədi, ɛˌθɪri'ælədi

etherealize
BR ɪ'θɪərɪəlʌɪz, -ɪz, -ɪŋ, -d
AM ə'θɪriəˌlaɪz, i'θɪriəˌlaɪz, ɛ'θɪriəˌlaɪz, -ɪz, -ɪŋ, -d

ethereally
BR ɪ'θɪərɪəli
AM ə'θɪriəli, i'θɪriəli, ɛ'θɪriəli

Etheredge
BR 'ɛθ(ə)rɪdʒ
AM 'ɛθ(ə)rədʒ

etherial
BR ɪ'θɪərɪəl
AM ə'θɪriəl, i'θɪriəl, ɛ'θɪriəl

etheric
BR i:'θɛrɪk, ɪ'θɛrɪk
AM ə'θɛrɪk, i'θɛrɪk, ɛ'θɛrɪk

Etheridge
BR 'ɛθ(ə)rɪdʒ
AM 'ɛθ(ə)rədʒ

etherisation
BR ˌi:θ(ə)rʌɪ'zeɪʃn
AM ˌiθərə'zeɪʃən, ˌiθəˌraɪ'zeɪʃən

etherise
BR 'i:θərʌɪz, -ɪz, -ɪŋ, -d
AM 'iθəˌraɪz, -ɪz, -ɪŋ, -d

etherization
BR ˌi:θ(ə)rʌɪ'zeɪʃn
AM ˌiθərə'zeɪʃən, ˌiθəˌraɪ'zeɪʃən

etherize
BR 'i:θ(ə)rʌɪz, -ɪz, -ɪŋ, -d
AM 'iθəˌraɪz, -ɪz, -ɪŋ, -d

Ethernet
BR 'i:θənɛt, -s
AM 'iθərˌnɛt, -s

ethic
BR 'ɛθɪk, -s
AM 'ɛθɪk, -s

ethical
BR 'ɛθɨkl
AM 'ɛθəkəl

ethicality
BR ˌɛθɪ'kalɨti
AM ˌɛθə'kælədi

ethically
BR 'ɛθɨkli
AM 'ɛθək(ə)li

ethicise
BR 'ɛθɨsʌɪz, -ɪz, -ɪŋ, -d
AM 'ɛθəˌsaɪz, -ɪz, -ɪŋ, -d

ethicist
BR 'ɛθɨsɪst, -s
AM 'ɛθəsəst, -s

ethicize
BR 'ɛθɨsʌɪz, -ɪz, -ɪŋ, -d
AM 'ɛθəˌsaɪz, -ɪz, -ɪŋ, -d

Ethiopia
BR ˌi:θɪ'əʊpɪə(r)
AM ˌiθi'oʊpiə

Ethiopian
BR ˌi:θɪ'əʊpɪən, -z
AM ˌiθi'oʊpiən, -z

Ethiopic
BR ˌi:θɪ'əʊpɪk, ˌi:θɪ'ɒpɪk
AM ˌiθi'ɑpɪk, ˌiθi'oʊpɪk

ethmoid
BR 'ɛθmɔɪd, -z
AM 'ɛθˌmɔɪd, -z

ethmoidal
BR ɛθ'mɔɪdl
AM ˌɛθ'mɔɪdəl

ethnarch
BR 'ɛθnɑ:k, -s
AM 'ɛθˌnɑrk, -s

ethnarchy
BR 'ɛθnɑ:k|i, -ɪz
AM 'ɛθˌnɑrki, -z

Ethne
BR 'ɛθni
AM 'ɛθni

ethnic
BR 'ɛθnɪk
AM 'ɛθnɪk

ethnical
BR 'ɛθnɨkl
AM 'ɛθnəkəl

ethnically
BR 'ɛθnɨkli
AM 'ɛθnək(ə)li

ethnicity
BR ɛθ'nɪsɨti
AM ɛθ'nɪsɨdi

ethnoarchaeological
BR ˌɛθnəʊˌɑ:kɪə'lɒdʒɨkl
AM ˌɛθnoʊˌɑrkiə'lɑdʒəkəl

ethnoarchaeologist
BR ˌɛθnəʊˌɑ:kɪ'ɒlədʒɪst, -s
AM ˌɛθnoʊˌɑrki'ɑlədʒəst, -s

ethnoarchaeology
BR ˌɛθnəʊˌɑ:kɪ'ɒlədʒi
AM ˌɛθnoʊˌɑrki'ɑlədʒi

ethnocentric
BR ˌɛθnə(ʊ)'sɛntrɪk
AM ˌɛθnoʊ'sɛntrɪk

ethnocentrically
BR ˌɛθnə(ʊ)'sɛntrɪkli
AM ˌɛθnoʊ'sɛntrək(ə)li

ethnocentricity
BR ˌɛθnə(ʊ)sɛn'trɪsɨti
AM ˌɛθnoʊˌsɛn'trɪsɨdi

ethnocentrism
BR ˌɛθnə(ʊ)'sɛntrɪz(ə)m
AM ˌɛθnoʊ'sɛnˌtrɪzəm

ethnographer
BR ɛθ'nɒgrəfə(r), -z
AM ɛθ'nɑgrəfər, -z

ethnographic
BR ˌɛθnə'grafɪk
AM ˌɛθnə'græfɪk

ethnographical
BR ˌɛθnə'grafɨkl
AM ˌɛθnə'græfɨkl

ethnographically
BR ˌɛθnə'grafɨkli
AM ˌɛθnə'græfək(ə)li

ethnography
BR ɛθ'nɒgrəfi
AM ɛθ'nɑgrəfi

ethnohistory
BR ˌɛθnəʊ'hɪst(ə)ri
AM ˌɛθnoʊ'hɪst(ə)ri

ethnologic
BR ˌɛθnə'lɒdʒɪk
AM ˌɛθnə'lɑdʒɪk

ethnological
BR ˌɛθnə'lɒdʒɨkl
AM ˌɛθnə'lɑdʒəkəl

ethnologically
BR ˌɛθnə'lɒdʒɨkli
AM ˌɛθnə'lɑdʒək(ə)li

ethnologist
BR ɛθ'nɒlədʒɪst, -s
AM ɛθ'nɑlədʒəst, -s

ethnology
BR ɛθ'nɒlədʒi
AM ɛθ'nɑlədʒi

ethnomethodological
BR ˌɛθnəʊˌmɛθədə'lɒdʒɨkl
AM ˌɛθnoʊˌmɛθədə'lɑdʒəkəl

ethnomethodologist
BR ˌɛθnəʊˌmɛθə'dɒlədʒɪst, -s
AM ˌɛθnoʊˌmɛθə'dɑlədʒəst, -s

ethnomethodology
BR ˌɛθnəʊˌmɛθə'dɒlədʒi
AM ˌɛθnoʊˌmɛθə'dɑlədʒi

ethnomusicologist
BR ˌɛθnəʊˌmju:zɪ'kɒlədʒɪst, -s
AM ˌɛθnoʊˌmjuzə'kɑlədʒəst, -s

ethnomusicology
BR ˌɛθnəʊˌmju:zɪ'kɒlədʒi
AM ˌɛθnoʊˌmjuzə'kɑlədʒi

ethogram
BR 'i:θəgram, -z
AM 'iθəˌgræm, 'ɛθəˌgræm, -z

ethological
BR ˌi:θə'lɒdʒɨkl
AM ˌiθə'lɑdʒəkəl, ˌɛθə'lɑdʒəkəl

ethologically
BR ˌi:θə'lɒdʒɨkli
AM ˌiθə'lɑdʒək(ə)li, ˌɛθə'lɑdʒək(ə)li

ethologist
BR i:'θɒlədʒɪst, -s
AM i'θɑlədʒəst, ɛ'θɑlədʒəst, -s

ethology
BR i:'θɒlədʒi
AM i'θɑlədʒi, ɛ'θɑlədʒi

ethos
BR 'i:θɒs
AM 'iθɑs

ethoxyethane
BR ɪˌθɒksɪ'i:θeɪn, ɪˌθɒksɪ'ɛθeɪn
AM əˌθɑksi'ɛθˌeɪn

ethyl
BR 'ɛθ(ɪ)l, 'ɛθʌɪl, 'i:θʌɪl
AM 'ɛθəl

ethylene
BR 'ɛθɨli:n, 'ɛθl̩i:n
AM 'ɛθəˌlin

ethylenic
BR ˌɛθɪ'lɛnɪk
AM ˌɛθə'lɛnɪk

Etienne
BR ˌɛtɪ'ɛn
AM ˌeɪdi'ɛn, ˌeɪ'tiɛn

etiolate
BR 'i:tɪə(ʊ)leɪt
AM 'idiəˌleɪt, i'tiəˌleɪt

etiolation
BR ˌi:tɪə(ʊ)'leɪʃn
AM ˌidiə'leɪʃən

etiologic
BR ˌi:tɪə'lɒdʒɪk, ˌɛtɪə'lɒdʒɪk
AM ˌidiə'lɑdʒɪk, ˌɛdiə'lɑdʒɪk

etiological
BR ˌi:tɪə'lɒdʒɨkl, ˌɛtɪə'lɒdʒɨkl
AM ˌidiə'lɑdʒəkəl, ˌɛdiə'lɑdʒəkəl

etiologically
BR ˌi:tɪə'lɒdʒɨkli, ˌɛtɪə'lɒdʒɨkli

AM ˌidiəˈlɑdʒək(ə)li, ˌɛdiəˈlɑdʒək(ə)li

etiology
BR ˌiːtɪˈɒlədʒi, ˌɛtɪˈɒlədʒi
AM ˌidiˈɑlədʒi, ˌɛdiˈɑlədʒi

etiquette
BR ˈɛtɪkɛt, ˈɛtɪkət
AM ˈɛdəkət

Etive
BR ˈɛtɪv
AM ˈɛdɪv

Etna
BR ˈɛtnə(r)
AM ˈɛtnə

Eton
BR ˈiːtn
AM ˈitn

Etonian
BR iːˈtəʊnɪən, -z
AM iˈtoʊniən, -z

étouffée
BR ˌeɪtuːˈfeɪ, -z
AM ˌeɪtuˈfeɪ, -z

Etruria
BR ɪˈtrʊərɪə(r)
AM əˈtrʊriə

Etruscan
BR ɪˈtrʌsk(ə)n, -z
AM əˈtrəskən, -z

Etruscology
BR ɪˌtrʌsˈkɒlədʒi
AM əˌtrəsˈkɑlədʒi

Ettrick
BR ˈɛtrɪk
AM ˈɛtrək

étude
BR eɪˈt(j)uːd, eɪˈtʃuːd, ˈeɪt(j)uːd, ˈeɪtʃuːd, -z
AM eɪˈt(j)ud, -z

etyma
BR ˈɛtɪmə(r)
AM ˈɛdəmə

etymologic
BR ˌɛtɪməˈlɒdʒɪk
AM ˌɛdəməˈlɑdʒɪk

etymological
BR ˌɛtɪməˈlɒdʒɪkl
AM ˌɛdəməˈlɑdʒəkəl

etymologically
BR ˌɛtɪməˈlɒdʒɪkli
AM ˌɛdəməˈlɑdʒək(ə)li

etymologise
BR ˌɛtɪˈmɒlədʒʌɪz, -ɪz, -ɪŋ, -d
AM ˌɛdəˈmɑləˌdʒaɪz, -ɪz, -ɪŋ, -d

etymologist
BR ˌɛtɪˈmɒlədʒɪst, -s
AM ˌɛdəˈmɑlədʒəst, -s

etymologize
BR ˌɛtɪˈmɒlədʒʌɪz, -ɪz, -ɪŋ, -d
AM ˌɛdəˈmɑləˌdʒaɪz, -ɪz, -ɪŋ, -d

etymology
BR ˌɛtɪˈmɒlədʒ|i, -ɪz
AM ˌɛdəˈmɑlədʒi, -z

etymon
BR ˈɛtɪmɒn, ˈɛtɪmən, -z
AM ˈɛdəˌmɑn, -z

Euan
BR ˈjuːən
AM ˈjʊən

eubacteria
BR ˌjuːbakˈtɪərɪə(r)
AM ˌjubækˈtɪriə

eubacterium
BR ˌjuːbakˈtɪərɪəm
AM ˌjubækˈtɪriəm

Euboea
BR juːˈbiːə(r), jʊˈbiːə(r)
AM juˈbiə

eucalypt
BR ˈjuːkəlɪpt, -s
AM ˈjukəˌlɪpt, -s

eucalyptus
BR ˌjuːkəˈlɪptəs, -ɪz
AM ˌjukəˈlɪptəs, -əz

eucaryote
BR juːˈkarɪət, juːˈkarɪɒt
AM juˈkɛriˌoʊt

eucaryotic
BR ˌjuːkarɪˈɒtɪk
AM ˌjukɛriˈɑdɪk

eucharis
BR ˈjuːkərɪs, -ɪz
AM ˈjuk(ə)rəs, -əz

Eucharist
BR ˈjuːkərɪst
AM ˈjuk(ə)rəst

eucharist
BR ˈjuːkərɪst, -s
AM ˈjuk(ə)rəst, -s

eucharistic
BR ˌjuːkəˈrɪstɪk
AM ˌjukəˈrɪstɪk

Eucharistical
BR ˌjuːkəˈrɪstɪkl
AM ˌjukəˈrɪstəkəl

euchre
BR ˈjuːkə(r)
AM ˈjukər

Euclid
BR ˈjuːklɪd
AM ˈjuˌklɪd

Euclidean
BR juːˈklɪdɪən
AM juˈklɪdiən

euclidean
BR juːˈklɪdɪən
AM juˈklɪdiən

euclidian
BR juːˈklɪdɪən
AM juˈklɪdiən

eudaemonic
BR ˌjuːdiːˈmɒnɪk, ˌjuːdɪˈmɒnɪk
AM ˌjudəˈmɑnɪk

eudaemonism
BR juːˈdiːmənɪz(ə)m
AM juˈdiməˌnɪzəm

eudaemonist
BR juːˈdiːmənɪst, -s
AM juˈdimənəst, -s

eudaemonistic
BR juːˌdiːməˈnɪstɪk
AM juˌdiməˈnɪstɪk

eudemonic
BR ˌjuːdiːˈmɒnɪk, ˌjuːdɪˈmɒnɪk
AM ˌjudəˈmɑnɪk

eudemonism
BR juːˈdiːmənɪz(ə)m
AM juˈdiməˌnɪzəm

eudemonist
BR juːˈdiːmənɪst, -s
AM juˈdimənəst, -s

eudemonistic
BR juːˌdiːməˈnɪstɪk
AM juˌdiməˈnɪstɪk

eudiometer
BR ˌjuːdɪˈɒmɪtə(r), -z
AM ˌjudiˈɑmədər, -z

eudiometric
BR ˌjuːdɪə(ʊ)ˈmɛtrɪk
AM ˌjudioʊˈmɛtrɪk

eudiometrical
BR ˌjuːdɪə(ʊ)ˈmɛtrɪkl
AM ˌjudioʊˈmɛtrəkəl

eudiometry
BR ˌjuːdɪˈɒmɪtri
AM ˌjudiˈɑmətri

Eudora
BR jʊˈdɔːrə(r)
AM juˈdɔrə

Euen
BR ˈjuːən
AM ˈjuən

Eugene
BR ˈjuːdʒiːn, juːˈdʒiːn
AM ˈjuˌdʒin

Eugene Onegin
BR ˌjuːdʒiːn ɒˈneɪɡɪn, juːˈdʒiːn
AM ˈjuˌdʒin oʊˈnɛɡɪn

Eugenia
BR juːˈdʒiːnɪə(r)
AM juˈdʒiniə

eugenic
BR juːˈdʒɛnɪk, -s
AM juˈdʒɛnɪk, -s

eugenically
BR juːˈdʒɛnɪkli
AM juˈdʒɛnək(ə)li

eugenicist
BR juːˈdʒɛnɪsɪst, -s
AM juˈdʒɛnəsəst, -s

Eugénie
BR juːˈʒeɪni
AM juˌʒeɪˈni

eugenist
BR juːˈdʒɛnɪst, -s
AM juˈdʒɛnəst, -s

euglena
BR juːˈɡliːnə(r), -z
AM juˈɡlinə, -z

euhemerism
BR juːˈhiːmərɪz(ə)m
AM juˈhiməˌrɪzəm

eukaryote
BR juːˈkarɪət, juːˈkarɪɒt
AM juˈkɛriˌoʊt

eukaryotic
BR ˌjuːkarɪˈɒtɪk
AM ˌjukɛriˈɑdɪk

Eulalia
BR juːˈleɪlɪə(r)
AM uˈleɪljə, uˈleɪliə

Euler
BR ˈɔɪlə(r), ˈjuːlə(r)
AM ˈɔɪlər

eulogia
BR juːˈləʊdʒɪə(r)
AM juˈloʊdʒiə

eulogise
BR ˈjuːlədʒʌɪz, -ɪz, -ɪŋ, -d
AM ˈjuləˌdʒaɪz, -ɪz, -ɪŋ, -d

eulogist
BR ˈjuːlədʒɪst, -s
AM ˈjulədʒəst, -s

eulogistic
BR ˌjuːləˈdʒɪstɪk
AM ˌjuləˈdʒɪstɪk

eulogistically
BR ˌjuːləˈdʒɪstɪkli
AM ˌjuləˈdʒɪstək(ə)li

eulogium
BR juːˈləʊdʒɪəm, -z
AM juˈloʊdʒiəm, -z

eulogize
BR ˈjuːlədʒʌɪz, -ɪz, -ɪŋ, -d
AM ˈjuləˌdʒaɪz, -ɪz, -ɪŋ, -d

eulogy
BR ˈjuːlədʒ|i, -ɪz
AM ˈjulədʒi, -z

Eumenides
BR juːˈmɛnɪdiːz
AM juˈmɛnəˌdiz

Eunice
BR ˈjuːnɪs
AM ˈjunəs

eunuch
BR ˈjuːnək, -s
AM ˈjunək, -s

eunuchoid
BR ˈjuːnəkɔɪd
AM ˈjunəˌkɔɪd

euonymus
BR juːˈɒnɪməs
AM juˈɑnəməs

eupeptic
BR juːˈpɛptɪk
AM juˈpɛptɪk

Euphemia
BR juːˈfiːmɪə(r)
AM juˈfimiə

euphemise
BR ˈjuːfɨmʌɪz, -ɨz, -ɪŋ, -d
AM ˈjufəˌmaɪz, -ɨz, -ɪŋ, -d
euphemism
BR ˈjuːfɨmɪz(ə)m, -z
AM ˈjufəˌmɪzəm, ˈjufm̩ˌɪzəm, -z
euphemist
BR ˈjuːfɨmɪst, -s
AM ˈjufəməst, -s
euphemistic
BR ˌjuːfɪˈmɪstɪk
AM ˌjufəˈmɪstɪk, ˌjufmˈɪstɪk
euphemistically
BR ˌjuːfɪˈmɪstɨkli
AM ˌjufəˈmɪstək(ə)li, ˌjufmˈɪstək(ə)li
euphemize
BR ˈjuːfɨmʌɪz, -ɨz, -ɪŋ, -d
AM ˈjufəˌmaɪz, -ɨz, -ɪŋ, -d
euphonic
BR juːˈfɒnɪk
AM juˈfɑnɪk
euphonious
BR juːˈfəʊnɪəs
AM juˈfoʊniəs, juˈfoʊnjəs
euphoniously
BR juːˈfəʊnɪəsli
AM juˈfoʊniəsli, juˈfoʊnjəsli
euphonise
BR ˈjuːfənʌɪz, ˈjuːfn̩ʌɪz, -ɨz, -ɪŋ, -d
AM ˈjufəˌnaɪz, -ɨz, -ɪŋ, -d
euphonium
BR juːˈfəʊnɪəm, -z
AM juˈfoʊniəm, -z
euphonize
BR ˈjuːfənʌɪz, ˈjuːfn̩ʌɪz, -ɨz, -ɪŋ, -d
AM ˈjufəˌnaɪz, -ɨz, -ɪŋ, -d
euphony
BR ˈjuːfəni, ˈjuːfn̩i
AM ˈjufəni
euphorbia
BR juːˈfɔːbɪə(r), -z
AM juˈfɔrbiə, -z
euphoria
BR juːˈfɔːrɪə(r)
AM juˈfɔriə
euphoriant
BR juːˈfɔːrɪənt, -s
AM juˈfɔriənt, -s
euphoric
BR juːˈfɒrɪk
AM juˈfɔrɪk
euphorically
BR juːˈfɒrɨkli
AM juˈfɔrək(ə)li
euphrasy
BR ˈjuːfrəz|i, -ɪz
AM ˈjufrəsi, -z
Euphrates
BR juːˈfreɪtiːz
AM juˈfreɪdiz
Euphues
BR ˈjuːfjʊiːz
AM ˈjuˌfjuiz
euphuism
BR ˈjuːfjʊɪz(ə)m
AM ˈjufjəˌwɪzəm
euphuist
BR ˈjuːfjʊɪst, -s
AM ˈjufjəˌwəst, -s
euphuistic
BR ˌjuːfjʊˈɪstɪk
AM ˌjufjəˈwɪstɪk
euphuistically
BR ˌjuːfjʊˈɪstɨkli
AM ˌjufjəˈwɪstək(ə)li
euploid
BR ˈjuːplɔɪd, -z
AM ˈjuˌplɔɪd, -z
Eurasian
BR jʊˈreɪʒn, jʊˈreɪʃn, -z
AM jərˈeɪʒən, jurˈeɪʒən, jərˈeɪʃən, jurˈeɪʃən, -z
Euratom
BR jʊrˈatəm
AM jərˈædəm, jurˈædəm
eureka
BR jʊˈriːkə(r)
AM jəˈrikə, juˈrikə
eurhythmic
BR jʊˈrɪðmɪk, -s
AM juˈrɪðmɪk, -s
Euripides
BR jʊˈrɪpɨdiːz
AM jəˈrɪpəˌdiz, juˈrɪpəˌdiz
Euro-
BR ˈjʊərə(ʊ), ˈjɔːrə(ʊ)
AM ˈjəroʊ, ˈjərə, ˈjuroʊ, ˈjurə
euro
BR ˈjʊərə(ʊ), ˈjɔːrəʊ, -z
AM ˈjəroʊ, ˈjuroʊ, -z
Eurobond
BR ˈjʊərə(ʊ)bɒnd, ˈjɔːrə(ʊ)bɒnd, -z
AM ˈjəroʊˌbɑnd, ˈjərəˌbɑnd, ˈjuroʊˌbɑnd, -z
Eurocentric
BR ˌjʊərəʊˈsɛntrɪk, ˌjɔːrəʊˈsɛntrɪk
AM ˌjəroʊˈsɛntrɪk, ˌjuroʊˈsɛntrɪk
Eurocentrism
BR ˌjʊərəʊˈsɛntrɪz(ə)m, ˌjɔːrəʊˈsɛntrɪz(ə)m
AM ˌjəroʊˈsɛnˌtrɪzəm, ˌjuroʊˈsɛnˌtrɪzəm
Eurocheque
BR ˈjʊərəʊtʃɛk, ˈjɔːrəʊtʃɛk, -s
AM ˈjəroʊˌtʃɛk, ˈjərəˌtʃɛk, ˈjuroʊˌtʃɛk, ˈjurəˌtʃɛk, -s
Eurocommunism
BR ˌjʊərəʊˈkɒmjʊnɪz(ə)m, ˌjɔːrəʊˈkɒmjʊnɪz(ə)m
AM ˌjəroʊˈkɑmjəˌnɪzəm, ˌjuroʊˈkɑmjəˌnɪzəm
Eurocommunist
BR ˌjʊərəʊˈkɒmjʊnɪst, ˌjɔːrəʊˈkɒmjʊnɪst, -s
AM ˌjəroʊˈkɑmjənəst, ˌjuroʊˈkɑmjənəst, -s
Eurocrat
BR ˈjʊərə(ʊ)krat, ˈjɔːrə(ʊ)krat, -s
AM ˈjərəˌkræt, ˈjurəˌkræt, -s
Euro-currency
BR ˈjʊərəʊˌkʌrənsi, ˈjʊərəʊˌkʌrn̩si, ˈjɔːrəʊˌkʌrənsi, ˈjɔːrəʊˌkʌrn̩si
AM ˈjəroʊˌkərənsi, ˈjuroʊˌkərənsi
Eurodollar
BR ˈjʊərə(ʊ)ˌdɒlə(r), ˈjɔːrə(ʊ)ˌdɒlə(r), -z
AM ˈjəroʊˌdɑlər, ˈjuroʊˌdɑlər, -z
Euro-election
BR ˈjʊərəʊɪˌlɛkʃn, ˈjɔːrəʊɪˌlɛkʃn, -z
AM ˌjəroʊəˈlɛkʃən, ˌjuroʊəˈlɛkʃən, -z
Euromarket
BR ˈjʊərəʊˌmɑːkɪt, ˈjɔːrəʊˌmɑːkɪt, -s
AM ˈjəroʊˌmɑrkət, ˈjuroʊˌmɑrkət, -s
Europa
BR jʊˈrəʊpə(r)
AM juˈroʊpə
Europarliament
BR ˈjʊərəʊˌpɑːləm(ə)nt, ˈjɔːrəʊˌpɑːləm(ə)nt
AM ˈjəroʊˌpɑrləmənt, ˈjuroʊˌpɑrləmənt
Europarliamentarian
BR ˌjʊərəʊˌpɑːləm(ə)nˈtɛːrɪən, ˌjɔːrəʊˌpɑːləm(ə)nˈtɛːrɪən, -z
AM ˌjəroʊˌpɑrləmənˈtɛriən, ˌjuroʊˌpɑrləmənˈtɛriən, -z
Europarliamentary
BR ˌjʊərəʊˌpɑːləˈmɛnt(ə)ri, ˌjɔːrəʊˌpɑːləˈmɛnt(ə)ri
AM ˌjəroʊˌpɑrləˈmɛn(t)əri, ˌjuroʊˌpɑrləˈmɛn(t)əri
Europe
BR ˈjʊərəp, ˈjɔːrəp
AM ˈjərəp, ˈjurəp
European
BR ˌjʊərəˈpiːən, ˌjɔːrəˈpiːən, -z
AM ˌjərəˈpiən, ˌjurəˈpiən, -z
Europeanisation
BR ˌjʊərəpiːənʌɪˈzeɪʃn, ˌjɔːrəpiːənʌɪˈzeɪʃn
AM ˌjərəˌpiənəˈzeɪʃən, ˌjurəˌpiənəˈzeɪʃən, ˌjərəˌpiəˌnaɪˈzeɪʃən, ˌjurəˌpiəˌnaɪˈzeɪʃən
Europeanise
BR ˌjʊərəˈpiːənʌɪz, ˌjɔːrəˈpiːənʌɪz, -ɨz, -ɪŋ, -d
AM ˌjərəˈpiəˌnaɪz, ˌjurəˈpiəˌnaɪz, -ɨz, -ɪŋ, -d
Europeanism
BR ˌjʊərəˈpiːənɪz(ə)m, ˌjɔːrəˈpiːənɪz(ə)m
AM ˌjərəˈpiəˌnɪzəm, ˌjurəˈpiəˌnɪzəm
Europeanization
BR ˌjʊərəpiːənʌɪˈzeɪʃn, ˌjɔːrəpiːənʌɪˈzeɪʃn
AM ˌjərəˌpiənəˈzeɪʃən, ˌjurəˌpiənəˈzeɪʃən, ˌjərəˌpiəˌnaɪˈzeɪʃən, ˌjurəˌpiəˌnaɪˈzeɪʃən
Europeanize
BR ˌjʊərəˈpiːənʌɪz, ˌjɔːrəˈpiːənʌɪz, -ɨz, -ɪŋ, -d
AM ˌjərəˈpiəˌnaɪz, ˌjurəˈpiəˌnaɪz, -ɨz, -ɪŋ, -d
Europhile
BR ˈjʊərə(ʊ)fʌɪl, ˈjɔːrə(ʊ)fʌɪl, -z
AM ˈjərəˌfaɪl, ˈjurəˌfaɪl, -z
europium
BR jʊˈrəʊpɪəm
AM jəˈroʊpiəm, juˈroʊpiəm
Europort
BR ˈjʊərəʊpɔːt, ˈjɔːrəʊpɔːt
AM ˈjəroʊˌpɔ(ə)rt, ˈjʊroʊˌpɔ(ə)rt
Eurotunnel
BR ˈjʊərəʊˌtʌnl, ˈjɔːrəʊˌtʌnl
AM ˈjəroʊˌtənəl, ˈjuroʊˌtənəl
Eurovision
BR ˈjʊərəvɪʒn, ˈjɔːrəvɪʒn
AM ˈjəroʊˌvɪʒən, ˈjuroʊˌvɪʒən
Eurydice
BR jʊˈrɪdɨsi, jʊˈrɪdɨsiː, ˌjʊərɪˈdiːtʃi, ˌjʊərɪˈdiːtʃeɪ
AM jəˈrɪdəsi, jəˈrɪdətʃi

eurythmic
BR jʊˈrɪðmɪk, -s
AM juˈrɪðmɪk, -s
Eusebius
BR juːˈsiːbɪəs
AM juˈseɪbiəs
Eustace
BR ˈjuːstəs
AM ˈjustəs
eustachian
BR juːˈsteɪʃn
AM juˈsteɪʃ(i)ən
eustacy
BR ˈjuːstəsi
AM ˈjustəsi
eustasy
BR ˈjuːstəsi
AM ˈjustəsi
eustatic
BR juːˈstatɪk
AM juˈstædɪk
Euston
BR ˈjuːst(ə)n
AM ˈjustən
eutectic
BR juːˈtɛktɪk, -s
AM juˈtɛktɪk, -s
Euterpe
BR juːˈtəːpi
AM juˈtərpi
euthanasia
BR ˌjuːθəˈneɪzɪə(r),
ˌjuːθəˈneɪʒə(r)
AM ˌjuθəˈneɪʒ(i)ə,
ˌjuθəˈneɪziə
eutherian
BR juːˈθɪərɪən, -z
AM juˈθɪriən, -z
eutrophic
BR juːˈtrɒfɪk,
juːˈtrəʊfɪk
AM juˈtrɑfɪk
eutrophicate
BR juːˈtrəʊfɪkeɪt,
juːˈtrɒfɪkeɪt, -s, -ɪŋ, -ɨd
AM juˈtrɑfəˌkeɪ|t, -ts,
-dɪŋ, -dɨd
eutrophication
BR ˌjuːtrə(ʊ)fɪˈkeɪʃn
AM juˌtrɑfəˈkeɪʃən
eutrophy
BR ˈjuːtrəfi
AM ˈjutrəfi
Euxine
BR ˈjuːksʌɪn
AM ˈjʊksən, ˈjʊkˌsaɪn
Eva
BR ˈiːvə(r)
AM ˈivə
evacuant
BR ɪˈvakjʊənt, -s
AM əˈvækjəwənt,
iˈvækjəwənt, -s
evacuate
BR ɪˈvakjʊeɪt, -s, -ɪŋ, -ɨd
AM əˈvækjəˌweɪ|t,
iˈvækjəˌweɪ|t, -ts, -dɪŋ,
-dɨd
evacuation
BR ɪˌvakjʊˈeɪʃn, -z
AM əˌvækjəˈweɪʃən,
iˌvækjəˈweɪʃən, -z
evacuative
BR ɪˈvakjʊətɪv
AM əˈvækjəˌweɪdɪv,
iˈvækjəˌweɪdɪv
evacuator
BR ɪˈvakjʊeɪtə(r), -z
AM əˈvækjəˌweɪdər,
iˈvækjəˌweɪdər, -z
evacuee
BR ɪˌvakjʊˈiː, -z
AM əˌvækjəˈwi,
iˌvækjəˈwi, -z
evadable
BR ɪˈveɪdəbl
AM əˈveɪdəbəl,
iˈveɪdəbəl
evade
BR ɪˈveɪd, -z, -ɪŋ, -ɨd
AM əˈveɪd, iˈveɪd, -z, -ɪŋ,
-ɨd
evader
BR ɪˈveɪdə(r), -z
AM əˈveɪdər, iˈveɪdər,
-z
Evadne
BR ɪˈvadni
AM əˈvædni, iˈvædni
evaginate
BR ɪˈvadʒɪneɪt, -s, -ɪŋ,
-ɨd
AM əˈvædʒəˌneɪ|t,
iˈvædʒəˌneɪ|t, -ts, -dɪŋ,
-dɨd
evagination
BR ɪˌvadʒɪˈneɪʃn
AM əˌvædʒəˈneɪʃən,
iˌvædʒəˈneɪʃən
evaluate
BR ɪˈvaljʊeɪt, -s, -ɪŋ, -ɨd
AM əˈvæljəˌweɪ|t,
iˈvæljəˌweɪ|t, -ts, -dɪŋ,
-dɨd
evaluation
BR ɪˌvaljʊˈeɪʃn, -z
AM əˌvæljəˈweɪʃən,
iˌvæljəˈweɪʃən, -z
evaluative
BR ɪˈvaljʊətɪv
AM əˈvæljəˌweɪdɪv,
iˈvæljəˌweɪdɪv
evaluator
BR ɪˈvaljʊeɪtə(r), -z
AM əˈvæljəˌweɪdər,
iˈvæljəˌweɪdər, -z
Evan
BR ˈɛvn
AM ˈɛvən
evanesce
BR ˌɛvəˈnɛs, -ɨz, -ɪŋ, -t
AM ˌɛvəˈnɛs, -əz, -ɪŋ, -t
evanescence
BR ˌɛvəˈnɛsns
AM ˌɛvəˈnɛsəns
evanescent
BR ˌɛvəˈnɛsnt
AM ˌɛvəˈnɛsənt
evanescently
BR ˌɛvəˈnɛsntli
AM ˌɛvəˈnɛsn(t)li
evangel
BR iːˈvan(d)ʒ(ə)l, -z
AM iˈvændʒəl,
ɛˈvændʒəl, -z
evangelic
BR ˌiːvanˈdʒɛlɪk
AM ˌiˌvænˈdʒɛlɪk,
ˌɛvənˈdʒɛlɪk
evangelical
BR ˌiːvanˈdʒɛlɪkl, -z
AM ˌiˌvænˈdʒɛləkəl,
ˌɛvənˈdʒɛləkəl, -z
evangelicalism
BR ˌiːvanˈdʒɛlɪkəl-
ɪz(ə)m,
ˌiːvanˈdʒɛlɪklɪz(ə)m
AM ˌiˌvænˈdʒɛləkə-
ˌlɪzəm,
ˌɛvənˈdʒɛləkəˌlɪzəm
evangelically
BR ˌiːvanˈdʒɛlɪkli
AM ˌiˌvænˈdʒɛlək(ə)li,
ˌɛvənˈdʒɛlək(ə)li
Evangeline
BR ɪˈvan(d)ʒəliːn
AM əˈvændʒəˌlaɪn
evangelisation
BR ɪˌvan(d)ʒəlʌɪˈzeɪʃn,
ɪˌvan(d)ʒl̩ʌɪˈzeɪʃn
AM əˌvændʒələˈzeɪʃən,
iˌvændʒələˈzeɪʃən,
əˌvændʒəˌlaɪˈzeɪʃən,
iˌvændʒəˌlaɪˈzeɪʃən
evangelise
BR ɪˈvan(d)ʒəlʌɪz,
ɪˈvan(d)ʒl̩ʌɪz, -ɨz, -ɪŋ,
-d
AM əˈvændʒəˌlaɪz,
iˈvændʒəˌlaɪz, -ɨz, -ɪŋ,
-d
evangeliser
BR ɪˈvan(d)ʒəlʌɪzə(r),
ɪˈvan(d)ʒl̩ʌɪzə(r), -z
AM əˈvændʒəˌlaɪzər,
iˈvændʒəˌlaɪzər, -z
evangelism
BR ɪˈvan(d)ʒəlɪz(ə)m,
ɪˈvan(d)ʒl̩ɪz(ə)m
AM əˈvændʒəˌlɪzəm,
iˈvændʒəˌlɪzəm
evangelist
BR ɪˈvan(d)ʒəlɪst,
ɪˈvan(d)ʒl̩ɪst, -s
AM əˈvændʒələst,
iˈvændʒələst, -s
evangelistic
BR ɪˌvan(d)ʒəˈlɪstɪk,
ɪˌvan(d)ʒl̩ˈɪstɪk
AM əˌvændʒəˈlɪstɪk,
iˌvændʒəˈlɪstɪk
evangelistically
BR ɪˌvan(d)ʒəˈlɪstɪkli,
ɪˌvan(d)ʒl̩ˈɪstɪkli
AM əˌvændʒəˈlɪstək(ə)li,
iˌvændʒəˈlɪstək(ə)li
evangelization
BR ɪˌvan(d)ʒəlʌɪˈzeɪʃn,
ɪˌvan(d)ʒl̩ʌɪˈzeɪʃn
AM əˌvændʒələˈzeɪʃən,
iˌvændʒələˈzeɪʃən,
əˌvændʒəˌlaɪˈzeɪʃən,
iˌvændʒəˌlaɪˈzeɪʃən
evangelize
BR ɪˈvan(d)ʒəlʌɪz,
ɪˈvan(d)ʒl̩ʌɪz, -ɨz, -ɪŋ,
-d
AM əˈvændʒəˌlaɪz,
iˈvændʒəˌlaɪz, -ɨz, -ɪŋ,
-d
evangelizer
BR ɪˈvan(d)ʒəlʌɪzə(r),
ɪˈvan(d)ʒl̩ʌɪzə(r), -z
AM əˈvændʒəˌlaɪzər,
iˈvændʒəˌlaɪzər, -z
Evans
BR ˈɛvnz
AM ˈɛvənz
evaporable
BR ɪˈvap(ə)rəbl
AM əˈvæpərəbəl,
iˈvæpərəbəl
evaporate
BR ɪˈvapəreɪt, -s, -ɪŋ, -ɨd
AM əˈvæpəˌreɪ|t,
iˈvæpəˌreɪ|t, -ts, -dɪŋ,
-dɨd
evaporation
BR ɪˌvapəˈreɪʃn
AM əˌvæpəˈreɪʃən,
iˌvæpəˈreɪʃən
evaporative
BR ɪˈvap(ə)rətɪv
AM əˈvæpəˌreɪdɪv,
iˈvæpəˌreɪdɪv
evaporator
BR ɪˈvapəreɪtə(r), -z
AM əˈvæpəˌreɪdər,
iˈvæpəˌreɪdər, -z
evasion
BR ɪˈveɪʒn, -z
AM əˈveɪʒən, iˈveɪʒən,
-z
evasive
BR ɪˈveɪsɪv
AM əˈveɪsɪv, iˈveɪsɪv
evasively
BR ɪˈveɪsɨvli
AM əˈveɪsɨvli,
iˈveɪsɨvli
evasiveness
BR ɪˈveɪsɨvnɨs
AM əˈveɪsɪvnɨs,
iˈveɪsɪvnɨs
eve
BR iːv, -z
AM iv, -z
evection
BR ɪˈvɛkʃn

AM ə'vɛkʃən, i'vɛkʃən

Evelyn
BR 'i:vlɪn, 'ɛvlɪn
AM 'ɛv(ə)lən

even
BR 'i:vn, -z
AM 'ivən, -z

evening
BR 'i:vnɪŋ, -z
AM 'iv(ə)nɪŋ, -z

Evenlode
BR 'i:vnləʊd
AM 'ivən,loʊd

evenly
BR 'i:vnli
AM 'ivənli

evenness
BR 'i:vnnəs
AM 'ivə(n)nəs

evensong
BR 'i:vnsɒŋ
AM 'ivən,sɔŋ, 'ivən,sɑŋ

event
BR ɪ'vɛnt, -s, -ɪŋ, -ɪd
AM ə'vɛn|t, i'vɛn|t, -ts, -(t)ɪŋ, -(t)əd

eventer
BR ɪ'vɛntə(r), -z
AM ə'vɛn(t)ər, i'vɛn(t)ər, -z

eventful
BR ɪ'vɛntf(ʊ)l
AM ə'vɛntfəl, i'vɛntfəl

eventfully
BR ɪ'vɛntfʊli, ɪ'vɛntfl̩i
AM ə'vɛntfəli, i'vɛntfəli

eventfulness
BR ɪ'vɛntf(ʊ)lnəs
AM ə'vɛntfəlnəs, i'vɛntfəlnəs

eventide
BR i:vntʌɪd, -z
AM 'ivən,taɪd, -z

eventless
BR ɪ'vɛntləs
AM ə'vɛn(t)ləs, i'vɛn(t)ləs

eventlessly
BR ɪ'vɛntləsli
AM ə'vɛn(t)ləsli, i'vɛn(t)ləsli

eventual
BR ɪ'vɛn(t)ʃʊəl, ɪ'vɛn(t)ʃ(ʊ)l
AM ə'vɛn(t)ʃ(əw)əl, i'vɛn(t)ʃ(əw)əl

eventuality
BR ɪ,vɛn(t)ʃʊ'alɪt|i, -ɪz
AM ə,vɛn(t)ʃə'wælədi, i,vɛn(t)ʃə'wælədi, -z

eventually
BR ɪ'vɛn(t)ʃʊəli, ɪ'vɛn(t)ʃʊli, ɪ'vɛn(t)ʃl̩i
AM ə'vɛn(t)ʃəli, ə'vɛn(t)ʃ(ə)wəli, i'vɛn(t)ʃəli, i'vɛn(t)ʃ(ə)wəli

eventuate
BR ɪ'vɛn(t)ʃʊeɪt, -s, -ɪŋ, -ɪd
AM ə'vɛn(t)ʃə,weɪ|t, i'vɛn(t)ʃə,weɪ|t, -ts, -dɪŋ, -dɪd

eventuation
BR ɪ,vɛn(t)ʃʊ'eɪʃn
AM ə,vɛn(t)ʃə'weɪʃən, i,vɛn(t)ʃə'weɪʃən

ever
BR 'ɛvə(r)
AM 'ɛvər

Everard
BR 'ɛv(ə)rɑ:d
AM 'ɛvə,rɑrd

Everest
BR 'ɛv(ə)rɪst
AM 'ɛv(ə)rəst

Everett
BR 'ɛv(ə)rɪt, 'ɛv(ə)rɛt
AM 'ɛvərət

Everglades
BR 'ɛvəgleɪdz
AM 'ɛvər,gleɪdz

evergreen
BR 'ɛvəgri:n, -z
AM 'ɛvər,grin, -z

everlasting
BR ,ɛvə'lɑ:stɪŋ, ,ɛvə'lastɪŋ
AM ',ɛvər',læstɪŋ

everlastingly
BR ,ɛvə'lɑ:stɪŋli, ,ɛvə'lastɪŋli
AM ',ɛvər',læstɪŋli

everlastingness
BR ,ɛvə'lɑ:stɪŋnɪs, ,ɛvə'lastɪŋnɪs
AM ',ɛvər',læstɪŋnɪs

Everley
BR 'ɛvəli
AM 'ɛvərli

Everly
BR 'ɛvəli
AM 'ɛvərli

evermore
BR ,ɛvə'mɔ:(r)
AM ',ɛvər',mɔ(ə)r

everpresent
BR ,ɛvə'prɛznt
AM ',ɛvər',prɛzənt

Evers
BR 'ɛvəz
AM 'ɛvərz

Evershed
BR 'ɛvəʃɛd
AM 'ɛvər,ʃɛd

Eversholt
BR 'ɛvəʃɒlt, 'ɛvəʃəʊlt
AM 'ɛvər,ʃoʊlt

eversion
BR ɪ'və:ʃn
AM ə'vərʒən, i'vərʒən

Evert
BR 'ɛvət
AM 'ɛvərt

evert
BR ɪ'və:t, -s, -ɪŋ, -ɪd
AM ə'vər|t, i'vər|t, -ts, -dɪŋ, -dəd

Everton
BR 'ɛvət(ə)n
AM 'ɛvərt(ə)n

every
BR 'ɛvri
AM 'ɛv(ə)ri

everybody
BR 'ɛvrɪbɒdi, 'ɛvrɪbədi
AM 'ɛv(ə)ri,bədi, 'ɛv(ə)ri,bɑdi

everyday
BR ,ɛvrɪ'deɪ
AM ',ɛv(ə)ri',deɪ

everyman
BR 'ɛvrɪman
AM 'ɛv(ə)ri,mæn

everyone
BR 'ɛvrɪwʌn
AM 'ɛv(ə)ri,wən

everyplace
BR 'ɛvrɪpleɪs
AM 'ɛv(ə)ri,pleɪs

everything
BR 'ɛvrɪθɪŋ
AM 'ɛv(ə)ri,θɪŋ

everyway
BR ,ɛvrɪ'weɪ
AM 'ɛv(ə)ri,weɪ

everywhere
BR 'ɛvrɪwɛ:(r)
AM 'ɛv(ə)ri,(h)wɛ(ə)r

everywoman
BR 'ɛvrɪ,wʊmən
AM 'ɛv(ə)ri,wʊmən

Evesham
BR 'i:v(ɪ)ʃ(ə)m
AM 'ivʃəm

Évian®
BR 'eɪvɪən, 'eɪvjɒ̃
AM 'ɛviən, 'ɛvi,jɑn

evict
BR ɪ'vɪkt, -s, -ɪŋ, -ɪd
AM ə'vɪk|(t), i'vɪk|(t), -(t)s, -tɪŋ, -tɪd

eviction
BR ɪ'vɪkʃn, -z
AM ə'vɪkʃən, i'vɪkʃən, -z

evictor
BR ɪ'vɪktə(r), -z
AM ə'vɪktər, i'vɪktər, -z

evidence
BR 'ɛvɪd(ə)ns, -ɪz, -ɪŋ, -t
AM 'ɛvədns, 'ɛvə,dɛns, -əz, -ɪŋ, -t

evident
BR 'ɛvɪd(ə)nt
AM 'ɛvəd(ə)nt, 'ɛvə,dɛnt

evidential
BR ,ɛvɪ'dɛnʃl
AM ,ɛvə'dɛn(t)ʃəl

evidentially
BR ,ɛvɪ'dɛnʃl̩i, ,ɛvɪ'dɛnʃəli
AM ,ɛvə'dɛntʃəli

evidentiary
BR ,ɛvɪ'dɛnʃ(ə)ri
AM ,ɛvə'dɛn(t)ʃəri

evidently
BR 'ɛvɪd(ə)ntli
AM 'ɛvə,dɛntli, 'ɛvəd(ə)n(t)li, ,ɛvə'dɛn(t)li

evil
BR 'i:vl, -z
AM 'ivəl, -z

evildoer
BR 'i:vl,du:ə(r), ,i:vl'du:ə(r), -z
AM ',ivəl',duər, -z

evildoing
BR 'i:vl,du:ɪŋ, ,i:vl'du:ɪŋ
AM ',ivəl',duɪŋ

evilly
BR 'i:vl̩(l)i
AM 'ivə(l)li

evilness
BR 'i:vlnəs
AM 'ivəlnəs

evince
BR ɪ'vɪns, -ɪz, -ɪŋ, -t
AM ə'vɪns, i'vɪns, -ɪz, -ɪŋ, -t

evincible
BR ɪ'vɪnsɪbl
AM ə'vɪnsəbəl, i'vɪnsəbəl

evincive
BR ɪ'vɪnsɪv
AM ə'vɪnsɪv, i'vɪnsɪv

eviscerate
BR ɪ'vɪsəreɪt, -s, -ɪŋ, -ɪd
AM ə'vɪsə,reɪ|t, i'vɪsə,reɪ|t, -ts, -dɪŋ, -dɪd

evisceration
BR ɪ,vɪsə'reɪʃn
AM ə,vɪsə'reɪʃən, i,vɪsə'reɪʃən

Evita
BR ɪ'vi:tə(*r*), ɛ'vi:tə(*r*)
AM ə'vidə

evocation
BR ,i:və(ʊ)'keɪʃn, ,ɛvə(ʊ)'keɪʃn, -z
AM ,ivoʊ'keɪʃən, ,ɛvə'keɪʃən, ,ɛvoʊ'keɪʃən, -z

evocative
BR ɪ'vɒkətɪv
AM ə'vɑkədɪv, i'vɑkədɪv

evocatively
BR ɪ'vɒkətɪvli

AM ə'vɑkədəvli, i'vɑkədəvli

evocativeness
BR ɪ'vɒkətɪvnɪs
AM ə'vɑkədɪvnɪs, i'vɑkədɪvnɪs

evocatory
BR ɪ'vɒkət(ə)ri
AM ə'vɑkəˌtɔri

evoke
BR ɪ'vəʊk, -s, -ɪŋ, -t
AM ə'voʊk, i'voʊk, -s, -ɪŋ, -t

evoker
BR ɪ'vəʊkə(r), -z
AM ə'voʊkər, i'voʊkər, -z

evolute
BR 'iːvəl(j)uːt, 'ɛvəl(j)uːt, -s, -ɪŋ, -ɪd
AM 'ɛvəˌl(j)u|t, -ts, -dɪŋ, -dəd

evolution
BR ˌiːvə'l(j)uːʃn, ˌɛvə'l(j)uːʃn, -z
AM ˌɛvə'luʃən, -z

evolutional
BR ˌiːvə'l(j)uːʃn̩(ə)l, ˌiːvə'l(j)uːʃən(ə)l, ˌɛvə'l(j)uːʃn̩(ə)l, ˌɛvə'l(j)uːʃən(ə)l
AM ˌɛvə'luʃ(ə)nəl

evolutionally
BR ˌiːvə'l(j)uːʃn̩əli, ˌiːvə'l(j)uːʃn̩l̩i, ˌiːvə'l(j)uːʃənl̩i, ˌiːvə'l(j)uːʃ(ə)nəli, ˌɛvə'l(j)uːʃn̩əli, ˌɛvə'l(j)uːʃn̩l̩i, ˌɛvə'l(j)uːʃənl̩i, ˌɛvə'l(j)uːʃ(ə)nəli
AM ˌɛvə'luʃ(ə)nəli

evolutionarily
BR ˌiːvə'l(j)uːʃnərɪli, ˌɛvə'l(j)uːʃnərɪli
AM ˌɛvəˌluʃə'nɛrəli

evolutionary
BR ˌiːvə'l(j)uːʃn̩(ə)ri, ˌɛvə'l(j)uːʃn̩(ə)ri
AM ˌɛvə'luʃəˌnɛri

evolutionism
BR ˌiːvə'l(j)uːʃn̩ɪz(ə)m, ˌɛvə'l(j)uːʃn̩ɪz(ə)m
AM ˌɛvə'luʃəˌnɪzəm

evolutionist
BR ˌiːvə'l(j)uːʃn̩ɪst, ˌɛvə'l(j)uːʃn̩ɪst, -s
AM ˌɛvə'luʃənəst, -s

evolutionistic
BR ˌiːvəˌl(j)uːʃə'nɪstɪk, ˌiːvəˌl(j)uːʃn'ɪstɪk, ˌɛvəˌl(j)uːʃə'nɪstɪk, ˌɛvəˌl(j)uːʃn'ɪstɪk
AM ˌɛvəˌluʃə'nɪstɪk

evolutive
BR ˌiːvə'l(j)uːtɪv, ˌɛvə'l(j)uːtɪv
AM ˌɛvə'ludɪv

evolvable
BR ɪ'vɒlvəbl
AM ə'vɔlvəbəl, i'vɔlvəbəl, ə'vɑlvəbəl, i'vɑlvəbəl

evolve
BR ɪ'vɒlv, -z, -ɪŋ, -d
AM ə'vɔlv, i'vɔlv, ə'vɑlv, i'vɑlv, -z, -ɪŋ, -d

evolvement
BR ɪ'vɒlvm(ə)nt
AM ə'vɔlvmənt, i'vɔlvmənt, ə'vɑlvmənt, i'vɑlvmənt

Evonne
BR ɪ'vɒn, ˌiː'vɒn
AM ɪ'vɑn, i'vɑn

Evo-stik®
BR 'iːvəʊstɪk
AM 'ivoʊˌstɪk

evulsion
BR ɪ'vʌlʃn
AM ə'vəlʒən, i'vəlʒən

evzone
BR 'ɛvzəʊn, -z
AM 'ɛvˌzoʊn, -z

Ewan
BR 'juːən
AM 'juən

Ewart
BR 'juːət
AM 'juərt

Ewbank
BR 'juːbaŋk
AM 'juˌbæŋk

Ewe[1]
African language and people
BR 'eɪweɪ, 'ɛweɪ
AM 'eɪweɪ

Ewe[2]
Scottish loch
BR juː
AM ju

ewe
BR juː, -z
AM ju, -z

Ewen
BR 'juːən
AM 'juən

ewer
BR 'juːə(r), -z
AM 'juər, -z

Ewhurst
BR 'juːhəːst
AM 'juˌhərst

Ewing
BR 'juːɪŋ
AM 'juɪŋ

Ewyas
BR 'juːəs
AM 'juəs

ex
BR ɛks, -ɪz
AM ɛks, -əz

exacerbate
BR ɪg'zasəbeɪt, ɛg'zasəbeɪt, -s, -ɪŋ, -ɪd
AM ɪg'zæsərˌbeɪ|t, ɛg'zæsərˌbeɪ|t, -ts, -dɪŋ, -dɪd

exacerbation
BR ɪgˌzasə'beɪʃn, ɛgˌzasə'beɪʃn, -z
AM ɪgˌzæsər'beɪʃən, ɛgˌzæsər'beɪʃən, -z

exact
BR ɪg'zakt, ɛg'zakt, -s, -ɪŋ, -ɪd
AM ɪg'zæk|(t), ɛg'zæk|(t), -(t)s, -tɪŋ, -təd

exacta
BR ɪg'zaktə(r), ɛg'zaktə(r)
AM ɪg'zæktə, ɛg'zæktə

exactable
BR ɪg'zaktəbl, ɛg'zaktəbl
AM ɪg'zæktəbəl, ɛg'zæktəbəl

exacting
BR ɪg'zaktɪŋ, ɛg'zaktɪŋ
AM ɪg'zæktɪŋ, ɛg'zæktɪŋ

exactingly
BR ɪg'zaktɪŋli, ɛg'zaktɪŋli
AM ɪg'zæktɪŋli, ɛg'zæktɪŋli

exactingness
BR ɪg'zaktɪŋnɪs, ɛg'zaktɪŋnɪs
AM ɪg'zæktɪŋnəs, ɛg'zæktɪŋnəs

exaction
BR ɪg'zakʃn, ɛg'zakʃn, -z
AM ɪg'zækʃən, ɛg'zækʃən, -z

exactitude
BR ɪg'zaktɪtjuːd, ɪg'zaktɪtʃuːd, ɛg'zaktɪtjuːd, ɛg'zaktɪtʃuːd
AM ɪg'zæktəˌt(j)ud, ɛg'zæktəˌt(j)ud

exactly
BR ɪg'zak(t)li, ɛg'zak(t)li
AM ɪg'zæk(t)li, ɛg'zæk(t)li

exactness
BR ɪg'zak(t)nəs, ɛg'zak(t)nəs
AM ɪg'zæk(t)nəs, ɛg'zæk(t)nəs

exactor
BR ɪg'zaktə(r), ɛg'zaktə(r), -z
AM ɪg'zæktər, ɛg'zæktər, -z

exaggerate
BR ɪg'zadʒəreɪt, ɛg'zadʒəreɪt, -s, -ɪŋ, -ɪd
AM ɪg'zædʒəˌreɪ|t, ɛg'zædʒəˌreɪ|t, -ts, -dɪŋ, -dɪd

exaggeratedly
BR ɪg'zadʒəreɪtɪdli, ɛg'zadʒəreɪtɪdli
AM ɪg'zædʒəˌreɪdɪdli, ɛg'zædʒəˌreɪdɪdli

exaggeratingly
BR ɪg'zadʒəreɪtɪŋli, ɛg'zadʒəreɪtɪŋli
AM ɪg'zædʒəˌreɪdɪŋli, ɛg'zædʒəˌreɪdɪŋli

exaggeration
BR ɪgˌzadʒə'reɪʃn, ɛgˌzadʒə'reɪʃn, -z
AM ɪgˌzædʒə'reɪʃən, ɛgˌzædʒə'reɪʃən, -z

exaggerative
BR ɪg'zadʒ(ə)rətɪv, ɛg'zadʒ(ə)rətɪv
AM ɪg'zædʒəˌreɪdɪv, ɛg'zædʒəˌreɪdɪv

exaggerator
BR ɪg'zadʒəreɪtə(r), ɛg'zadʒəreɪtə(r), -z
AM ɪg'zædʒəˌreɪdər, ɛg'zædʒəˌreɪdər, -z

exalt
BR ɪg'zɔːlt, ɛg'zɔːlt, ɪg'zɒlt, ɛg'zɒlt, -s, -ɪŋ, -ɪd
AM ɪg'zɔlt, ɛg'zɔlt, ɪg'zɑlt, ɛg'zɑlt, -s, -ɪŋ, -əd

exaltation
BR ˌɛgzɔːl'teɪʃn, ˌɛgzɒl'teɪʃn
AM ˌɛgˌzɔl'teɪʃən, ˌɛgˌzɑl'teɪʃən

exaltedly
BR ɪg'zɔːltɪdli, ɛg'zɔːltɪdli, ɪg'zɒltɪdli, ɛg'zɒltɪdli
AM ɪg'zɔltədli, ɛg'zɔltədli, ɪg'zɑltədli, ɛg'zɑltədli

exaltedness
BR ɪg'zɔːltɪdnɪs, ɛg'zɔːltɪdnɪs, ɪg'zɒltɪdnɪs, ɛg'zɒltɪdnɪs
AM ɪg'zɔltədnəs, ɛg'zɔltədnəs, ɪg'zɑltədnəs, ɛg'zɑltədnəs

exalter
BR ɪg'zɔːltə(r), ɛg'zɔːltə(r), ɪg'zɒltə(r), ɛg'zɒltə(r), -z
AM ɪg'zɔltər, ɛg'zɔltər, ɪg'zɑltər, ɛg'zɑltər, -z

exam
BR ɪg'zam, ɛg'zam, -z
AM ɪg'zæm, ɛg'zæm, -z

examen
BR ɛɡ'zeɪmɛn, -z
AM ɪɡ'zeɪmən, ɛɡ'zeɪmən, -z

examinable
BR ɪɡ'zamɪnəbl, ɛɡ'zamɪnəbl
AM ɪɡ'zæmənəbəl, ɛɡ'zæmənəbəl

examination
BR ɪɡˌzamɪ'neɪʃn, ɛɡˌzamɪ'neɪʃn, -z
AM ɪɡˌzæmə'neɪʃən, ɛɡˌzæmə'neɪʃən, -z

examinational
BR ɪɡˌzamɪ'neɪʃn̩(ə)l, ɪɡˌzamɪ'neɪʃən(ə)l, ɛɡˌzamɪ'neɪʃn̩(ə)l, ɛɡˌzamɪ'neɪʃən(ə)l
AM ɪɡˌzæmə'neɪʃ(ə)nəl, ɛɡˌzæmə'neɪʃ(ə)nəl

examine
BR ɪɡ'zam|ɪn, ɛɡ'zam|ɪn, -ɪnz, -ɪnɪŋ, -ɪnd
AM ɪɡ'zæmən, ɛɡ'zæmən, -z, -ɪŋ, -d

examinee
BR ɪɡˌzamɪ'niː, ɛɡˌzamɪ'niː, -z
AM ɪɡˌzæmə'ni, ɛɡˌzæmə'ni, -z

examiner
BR ɪɡ'zamɪnə(r), ɛɡ'zamɪnə(r), -z
AM ɪɡ'zæmənər, ɛɡ'zæmənər, -z

example
BR ɪɡ'zɑːmpl, ɪɡ'zampl, ɛɡ'zɑːmpl, ɛɡ'zampl, -z
AM ɪɡ'zæmpəl, ɛɡ'zæmpəl, -z

exanthema
BR ˌɛksan'θiːmə(*r*), ɪk'sanθɪmə(*r*)
AM ˌɛɡzæn'θimə, ˌɪɡzæn'θimə

exarch
BR 'ɛksɑːk, -s
AM 'ɛkˌsɑrk, -s

exarchate
BR 'ɛksɑːkeɪt, -s
AM 'ɛksɑrˌkeɪt, -s

ex-army
BR ˌɛks'ɑːmi
AM ˌɛks'ɑrmi

exasperate
BR ɪɡ'zasp(ə)reɪt, ɪɡ'zɑːsp(ə)reɪt, ɛɡ'zasp(ə)reɪt, ɛɡ'zɑːsp(ə)reɪt, -s, -ɪŋ, -ɪd
AM ɪɡ'zæspəˌreɪ|t, ɛɡ'zæspəˌreɪ|t, -ts, -dɪŋ, -dɪd

exasperatedly
BR ɪɡ'zasp(ə)reɪtɪdli, ɪɡ'zɑːsp(ə)reɪtɪdli, ɛɡ'zasp(ə)reɪtɪdli, ɛɡ'zɑːsp(ə)reɪtɪdli
AM ɪɡ'zæspəˌreɪdɪdli, ɛɡ'zæspəˌreɪdɪdli

exasperatingly
BR ɪɡ'zasp(ə)reɪtɪŋli, ɪɡ'zɑːsp(ə)reɪtɪŋli, ɛɡ'zasp(ə)reɪtɪŋli, ɛɡ'zɑːsp(ə)reɪtɪŋli
AM ɪɡ'zæspəˌreɪdɪŋli, ɛɡ'zæspəˌreɪdɪŋli

exasperation
BR ɪɡ'zaspə'reɪʃn, ɪɡˌzɑːspə'reɪʃn, ɛɡˌzaspə'reɪʃn, ɛɡˌzɑːspə'reɪʃn
AM ɪɡˌzæspə'reɪʃən, ɛɡˌzæspə'reɪʃən

Excalibur
BR ɛk'skalɪbə(r)
AM ɛk'skæləbər

ex cathedra
BR ˌɛks kə'θiːdrə(*r*)
AM ˌɛks kə'θidrə

excavate
BR 'ɛkskəveɪt, -s, -ɪŋ, -ɪd
AM 'ɛkskəˌveɪ|t, -ts, -dɪŋ, -dɪd

excavation
BR ˌɛkskə'veɪʃn, -z
AM ˌɛkskə'veɪʃən, -z

excavator
BR 'ɛkskəveɪtə(r), -z
AM 'ɛkskəˌveɪdər, -z

exceed
BR ɪk'siːd, ɛk'siːd, -z, -ɪŋ, -ɪd
AM ɪk'sid, ɛk'sid, -z, -ɪŋ, -ɪd

exceeding
BR ɪk'siːdɪŋ, ɛk'siːdɪŋ
AM ɪk'sidɪŋ, ɛk'sidɪŋ

exceedingly
BR ɪk'siːdɪŋli, ɛk'siːdɪŋli
AM ɪk'sidɪŋli, ɛk'sidɪŋli

excel
BR ɪk'sɛl, ɛk'sɛl, -z, -ɪŋ, -d
AM ɪk'sɛl, ɛk'sɛl, -z, -ɪŋ, -d

excellence
BR 'ɛksələns, 'ɛksəln̩s, 'ɛksl̩(ə)ns
AM 'ɛks(ə)ləns

excellency
BR 'ɛksələns|i, 'ɛksəln̩s|i, 'ɛksl̩(ə)ns|i, -ɪz
AM 'ɛks(ə)lənsi, -z

excellent
BR 'ɛksələnt, 'ɛksəln̩t, 'ɛksl̩(ə)nt
AM 'ɛks(ə)lənt

excellently
BR 'ɛksələntli, 'ɛksəln̩tli, 'ɛksl̩(ə)ntli
AM 'ɛks(ə)lən(t)li

excelsior
BR ɪk'sɛlsɪɔː(r), ɛk'sɛlsɪɔː(r), ɪk'sɛlsɪə(r), ɛk'sɛlsɪə(r)
AM ɪk'sɛlsiər, ɛk'sɛlsiər

excentric
BR ɪk'sɛntrɪk, ɛk'sɛntrɪk, -s
AM ɪk'sɛntrɪk, ɛk'sɛntrɪk, -s

except
BR ɪk'sɛpt, ɛk'sɛpt, -s, -ɪŋ, -ɪd
AM ɪk'sɛpt, ɛk'sɛpt, -s, -ɪŋ, -əd

excepting
BR ɪk'sɛptɪŋ, ɛk'sɛptɪŋ
AM ɪk'sɛptɪŋ, ɛk'sɛptɪŋ

exception
BR ɪk'sɛpʃn, ɛk'sɛpʃn, -z
AM ɪk'sɛpʃən, ɛk'sɛpʃən, -z

exceptionable
BR ɪk'sɛpʃn̩əbl, ɪk'sɛpʃ(ə)nəbl, ɛk'sɛpʃn̩əbl, ɛk'sɛpʃ(ə)nəbl
AM ɪk'sɛpʃ(ə)nəbəl, ɛk'sɛpʃ(ə)nəbəl

exceptionableness
BR ɪk'sɛpʃn̩əblnəs, ɪk'sɛpʃ(ə)nəblnəs, ɛk'sɛpʃn̩əblnəs, ɛk'sɛpʃ(ə)nəblnəs
AM ɪk'sɛpʃ(ə)nəbəlnəs, ɛk'sɛpʃ(ə)nəblnəs

exceptionably
BR ɪk'sɛpʃn̩əbli, ɪk'sɛpʃ(ə)nəbli, ɛk'sɛpʃn̩əbli, ɛk'sɛpʃ(ə)nəbli
AM ɪk'sɛpʃ(ə)nəbli, ɛk'sɛpʃ(ə)nəbli

exceptional
BR ɪk'sɛpʃn̩(ə)l, ɪk'sɛpʃən(ə)l, ɛk'sɛpʃn̩(ə)l, ɛk'sɛpʃən(ə)l
AM ɪk'sɛpʃ(ə)nəl, ɛk'sɛpʃ(ə)nəl

exceptionality
BR ɪkˌsɛpʃə'nalɪti, ɛkˌsɛpʃə'nalɪti
AM ɪkˌsɛpʃə'nælədi, ɛkˌsɛpʃə'nælədi

exceptionally
BR ɪk'sɛpʃn̩əli, ɪk'sɛpʃn̩li, ɪk'sɛpʃənl̩i, ɪk'sɛpʃ(ə)nəli, ɛk'sɛpʃn̩əli, ɛk'sɛpʃn̩li, ɛk'sɛpʃənl̩i, ɛk'sɛpʃ(ə)nəli
AM ɪk'sɛpʃ(ə)nəli, ɛk'sɛpʃ(ə)nəli

excerpt[1]
noun
BR 'ɛksəːpt, 'ɛɡzəːpt, -s
AM 'ɛkˌsərpt, ɛɡ'zərpt, -s

excerpt[2]
verb
BR ɪk'səːpt, ɛk'səːpt, ɪɡ'zəːpt, ɛɡ'zəːpt, -s, -ɪŋ, -ɪd
AM ɛk'sərpt, ɪk'sərpt, ɛɡ'zərpt, ɪɡ'zərpt, -s, -ɪŋ, -əd

excerptible
BR ɪk'səːptəbl, ɛk'səːptəbl, ɪɡ'zəːptəbl, ɛɡ'zəːptəbl
AM ɛk'sərptəbəl, ɪk'sərptəbəl, ɛɡ'zərptəbəl, ɪɡ'zərptəbəl

excerption
BR ɪk'səːpʃn, ɛk'səːpʃn, ɪɡ'zəːpʃn, ɛɡ'zəːpʃn
AM ɛk'sərpʃən, ɪk'sərpʃən, ɛɡ'zərpʃən, ɪɡ'zərpʃən

excess[1]
adjective
BR 'ɛksɛs, ɛk'sɛs, ɪk'sɛs
AM 'ɛkˌsɛs, ɪk'sɛs, ɛk'sɛs

excess[2]
noun
BR ɪk'sɛs, ɛk'sɛs, 'ɛksɛs, -ɪz
AM ɪk'sɛs, ɛk'sɛs, -əz

excessive
BR ɪk'sɛsɪv, ɛk'sɛsɪv
AM ɪk'sɛsɪv, ɛk'sɛsɪv

excessively
BR ɪk'sɛsɪvli, ɛk'sɛsɪvli
AM ɪk'sɛsəvli, ɛk'sɛsəvli

excessiveness
BR ɪk'sɛsɪvnɪs, ɛk'sɛsɪvnɪs
AM ɪk'sɛsɪvnɪs, ɛk'sɛsɪvnɪs

exchange
BR ɪks'tʃeɪn(d)ʒ, ɛks'tʃeɪn(d)ʒ, -ɪz, -ɪŋ, -d
AM ɪks'tʃeɪndʒ, ɛks'tʃeɪndʒ, -ɪz, -ɪŋ, -d

exchangeability
BR ɪksˌtʃeɪn(d)ʒə'bɪlɪti, ɛksˌtʃeɪn(d)ʒə'bɪlɪti

AM ɪks,tʃeɪndʒə'bɪlɨdi, ɛks,tʃeɪndʒə'bɪlɨdi

exchangeable
BR ɨks'tʃeɪn(d)ʒəbl, ɛks'tʃeɪn(d)ʒəbl
AM ɪks'tʃeɪndʒəbəl, ɛks'tʃeɪndʒəbəl

exchanger
BR ɨks'tʃeɪn(d)ʒə(r), ɛks'tʃeɪn(d)ʒə(r), -z
AM ɪks'tʃeɪndʒər, ɛks'tʃeɪndʒər, -z

exchequer
BR ɨks'tʃɛkə(r), ɛks'tʃɛkə(r), -z
AM ɛks'tʃɛkər, ɪks'tʃɛkər, -z

excipient
BR ɨk'sɪpɪənt, ɛk'sɪpɪənt, -s
AM ɪk'sɪpiənt, ɛk'sɪpiənt, -s

excisable
BR ɨk'sʌɪzəbl, ɛk'sʌɪzəbl
AM ɪk'saɪzəbəl, ɛk'saɪzəbəl

excise¹
noun
BR 'ɛksʌɪz
AM 'ɛk,saɪz

excise²
verb
BR ɨk'sʌɪz, ɛk'sʌɪz, -ɨz, -ɪŋ, -d
AM ɪk'saɪz, ɛk'saɪz, -ɨz, -ɪŋ, -d

exciseman
BR 'ɛksʌɪzmən
AM 'ɛk,saɪzmən

excisemen
BR 'ɛksʌɪzmən
AM 'ɛk,saɪzmən

excision
BR ɨk'sɪʒn, ɛk'sɪʒn, -z
AM ɪk'sɪʒən, ɛk'sɪʒən, -z

excitability
BR ɨk,sʌɪtə'bɪlɨti, ɛk,sʌɪtə'bɪlɨti
AM ɪk,saɪdə'bɪlɨdi, ɛk,saɪdə'bɪlɨdi

excitable
BR ɨk'sʌɪtəbl, ɛk'sʌɪtəbl
AM ɪk'saɪdəbəl, ɛk'saɪdəbəl

excitableness
BR ɨk'sʌɪtəblnəs, ɛk'sʌɪtəblnəs
AM ɪk'saɪdəbəlnəs, ɛk'saɪdəbəlnəs

excitably
BR ɨk'sʌɪtəbli, ɛk'sʌɪtəbli
AM ɪk'saɪdəbli, ɛk'saɪdəbli

excitant
BR ɨk'sʌɪtnt, ɛk'sʌɪtnt, -s
AM ɪk'saɪtnt, ɛk'saɪtnt, -s

excitation
BR ,ɛksʌɪ'teɪʃn
AM ,ɛksə'teɪʃən, ɛk,saɪ'teɪʃən

excitative
BR ɨk'sʌɪtətɪv, ɛk'sʌɪtətɪv
AM ɪk'saɪdədɪv, ɛk'saɪdədɪv

excitatory
BR ɨk'sʌɪtət(ə)ri, ɛk'sʌɪtət(ə)ri
AM ɪk'saɪdə,tɔri, ɛk'saɪdə,tɔri

excite
BR ɨk'sʌɪt, ɛk'sʌɪt, -s, -ɪŋ, -ɨd
AM ɪk'saɪ|t, ɛk'saɪ|t, -ts, -dɪŋ, -dɨd

excitedly
BR ɨk'sʌɪtɨdli, ɛk'sʌɪtɨdli
AM ɪk'saɪdɨdli, ɛk'saɪdɨdli

excitedness
BR ɨk'sʌɪtɨdnɨs, ɛk'sʌɪtɨdnɨs
AM ɪk'saɪdɨdnɨs, ɛk'saɪdɨdnɨs

excitement
BR ɨk'sʌɪtm(ə)nt, ɛk'sʌɪtm(ə)nt, -s
AM ɪk'saɪtmənt, ɛk'saɪtmənt, -s

exciter
BR ɨk'sʌɪtə(r), ɛk'sʌɪtə(r), -z
AM ɪk'saɪdər, ɛk'saɪdər, -z

excitingly
BR ɨk'sʌɪtɪŋli, ɛk'sʌɪtɪŋli
AM ɪk'saɪdɪŋli, ɛk'saɪdɪŋli

excitingness
BR ɨk'sʌɪtɪŋnɨs, ɛk'sʌɪtɪŋnɨs
AM ɪk'saɪdɪŋnɨs, ɛk'saɪdɪŋnɨs

exciton
BR 'ɛksɨtɒn, -z
AM 'ɛksə,tɑn, -z

exclaim
BR ɨk'skleɪm, ɛk'skleɪm, -z, -ɪŋ, -d
AM ɪk'skleɪm, ɛk'skleɪm, -z, -ɪŋ, -d

exclamation
BR ,ɛksklə'meɪʃn, -z
AM ,ɛksklə'meɪʃən, -z

exclamatory
BR ɨk'sklamət(ə)ri, ɛk'sklamət(ə)ri
AM ɪk'sklæmə,tɔri, ɛk'sklæmə,tɔri

exclave
BR 'ɛkskleɪv, -z
AM 'ɛk,skleɪv, -z

exclosure
BR ɨk'skləʊʒə(r), ɛk'skləʊʒə(r), -z
AM ɪk'skloʊʒər, ɛk'skloʊʒər, -z

excludable
BR ɨk'sklu:dəbl, ɛk'sklu:dəbl
AM ɪk'skludəbəl, ɛk'skludəbəl

exclude
BR ɨk'sklu:d, ɛk'sklu:d, -z, -ɪŋ, -ɨd
AM ɪk'asklud, ɛk'sklud, -z, -ɪŋ, -əd

excluder
BR ɨk'sklu:də(r), ɛk'sklu:də(r), -z
AM ɪk'skludər, ɛk'skludər, -z

exclusion
BR ɨk'sklu:ʒn, ɛk'sklu:ʒn
AM ɪk'skluʒən, ɛk'skluʒən

exclusionary
BR ɨk'sklu:ʒən(ə)ri, ɨk'sklu:ʒn̩(ə)ri, ɛk'sklu:ʒən(ə)ri, ɛk'sklu:ʒn̩(ə)ri
AM ɪk'skluʒə,nɛri, ɛk'skluʒə,nɛri

exclusionist
BR ɨk'sklu:ʒənɪst, ɨk'sklu:ʒn̩ɪst, ɛk'sklu:ʒənɪst, ɛk'sklu:ʒn̩ɪst, -s
AM ɪk'skluʒənəst, ɛk'skluʒənəst, -s

exclusive
BR ɨk'sklu:sɪv, ɛk'sklu:sɪv
AM ɪk'sklusɪv, ɪk'skluzɪv, ɛk'sklusɪv, ɛk'skluzɪv

exclusively
BR ɨk'sklu:sɨvli, ɛk'sklu:sɨvli
AM ɪk'sklusəvli, ɪk'skluzəvli, ɛk'sklusəvli, ɛk'skluzəvli

exclusiveness
BR ɨk'sklu:sɨvnɨs, ɛk'sklu:sɨvnɨs
AM ɪk'sklusɪvnɨs, ɪk'skluzɪvnɨs, ɛk'sklusɪvnɨs, ɛk'skluzɪvnɨs

exclusivity
BR ,ɛksklu:'sɪvɨti
AM ,ɛksklu'sɪvɨdi

excogitable
BR ɛks'kɒdʒɪtəbl, ɨks'kɒdʒɪtəbl
AM ɛk'skɑdʒədəbəl

excogitate
BR ɛks'kɒdʒɪteɪt, ɨks'kɒdʒɪteɪt, -s, -ɪŋ, -ɨd
AM ɛk'skɑdʒə,teɪ|t, -ts, -dɪŋ, -dɨd

excogitation
BR ,ɛkskɒdʒɪ'teɪʃn, ɛks,kɒdʒɪ'teɪʃn, ,ɨkskɒdʒɪ'teɪʃn, ɨks,kɒdʒɪ'teɪʃn, -z
AM ɛk,skɑdʒə'teɪʃən, -z

excogitative
BR ɛks'kɒdʒɪtətɪv, ɨks'kɒdʒɪtətɪv
AM ɛk'skɑdʒə,teɪdɪv

excommunicate
BR ,ɛkskə'mju:nɪkeɪt, -s, -ɪŋ, -ɨd
AM ,ɛkskə'mjunə,keɪ|t, -ts, -dɪŋ, -dɨd

excommunication
BR ,ɛkskə,mju:nɪ'keɪʃn, -z
AM ,ɛkskə,mjunə'keɪʃən, -z

excommunicative
BR ,ɛkskə'mju:nɪkətɪv
AM ,ɛkskə'mjunə,keɪdɪv

excommunicator
BR ,ɛkskə'mju:nɪkeɪtə(r), -z
AM ,ɛkskə'mjunə,keɪdər, -z

excommunicatory
BR ,ɛkskə'mju:nɪkət(ə)ri
AM ,ɛkskə'mjunəkə,tɔri

excoriate
BR ɛk'skɔ:rɪeɪt, ɨk'skɔ:rɪeɪt, ɛk'skɒrɪeɪt, ɨk'skɒrɪeɪt, -s, -ɪŋ, -ɨd
AM ɪk'skɔri,eɪ|t, ɛk'skɔri,eɪ|t, -ts, -dɪŋ, -dɨd

excoriation
BR ɛk,skɔ:rɪ'eɪʃn, ɨk,skɔ:rɪ'eɪʃn, ɛk,skɒrɪ'eɪʃn, ɨk,skɒrɪ'eɪʃn, -z
AM ɪk,skɔri'eɪʃən, ɛk,skɔri'eɪʃən, -z

excrement
BR 'ɛkskrɨm(ə)nt
AM 'ɛkskrəmənt

excremental
BR ,ɛkskrɪ'mɛntl
AM ,ɛkskrə'mɛn(t)l

excrescence
BR ɨk'skrɛsns, ɛk'skrɛsns, -ɨz
AM ɪk'skrɛsəns, ɛk'skrɛsəns, -əz

excrescent
BR ɪk'skrɛsnt, ɛk'skrɛsnt
AM ɪk'skrɛsnt, ɛk'skrɛsnt

excrescential
BR ˌɛkskrɪ'sɛnʃl
AM ˌɛkskrə'sɛntʃəl

excreta
BR ɪk'skriːtə(*r*), ɛk'skriːtə(*r*)
AM ɛk'skridə, ɪk'skridə

excrete
BR ɪk'skriːt, ɛk'skriːt, -s, -ɪŋ, -ɪd
AM ɪk'skri|t, ɛk'skri|t, -ts, -dɪŋ, -dɪd

excreter
BR ɪk'skriːtə(r), ɛk'skriːtə(r), -z
AM ɪk'skridər, ɛk'skridər, -z

excretion
BR ɪk'skriːʃn, ɛk'skriːʃn, -z
AM ɪk'skriʃən, ɛk'skriʃən, -z

excretive
BR ɪk'skriːtɪv, ɛk'skriːtɪv
AM 'ɛkskrədɪv, ɪk'skridɪv, ɛk'skridɪv

excretory
BR ɪk'skriːt(ə)ri, ɛk'skriːt(ə)ri
AM 'ɛkskrəˌtɔri

excretum
BR ɪk'skriːtəm, ɛk'skriːtəm
AM ɛk'skridəm, ɪk'skridəm

excruciate
BR ɪk'skruːʃɪeɪt, ɛk'skruːʃɪeɪt, -s, -ɪŋ, -ɪd
AM ɪk'skruʃiˌeɪ|t, ɛk'skruʃiˌeɪ|t, -ts, -dɪŋ, -dɪd

excruciatingly
BR ɪk'skruːʃɪeɪtɪŋli, ɛk'skruːʃɪeɪtɪŋli
AM ɪk'skruʃiˌeɪdɪŋli, ɛk'skruʃiˌeɪdɪŋli

excruciation
BR ɪkˌskruːʃɪ'eɪʃn, ɛkˌskruːʃɪ'eɪʃn
AM ɪkˌskruʃi'eɪʃən, ɛkˌskruʃi'eɪʃən

exculpate
BR 'ɛkskʌlpeɪt, -s, -ɪŋ, -ɪd
AM 'ɛkskəlˌpeɪ|t, -ts, -dɪŋ, -dɪd

exculpation
BR ˌɛkskʌl'peɪʃn
AM ˌɛkskəl'peɪʃən

exculpatory
BR ɪks'kʌlpət(ə)ri, ɛks'kʌlpət(ə)ri
AM ˌɛks'kəlpəˌtɔri

excursion
BR ɪk'skəːʃn, ɛk'skəːʃn, -z
AM ɪk'skərʒən, ɛk'skərʒən, -z

excursional
BR ɪk'skəːʃn̩(ə)l, ɪk'skəːʃən(ə)l, ɛk'skəːʃn̩(ə)l, ɛk'skəːʃən(ə)l
AM ɪk'skərʒ(ə)nəl, ɛk'skərʒ(ə)nəl

excursionary
BR ɪk'skəːʃn̩(ə)ri, ɛk'skəːʃn̩(ə)ri
AM ɪk'skərʒəˌnɛri, ɛk'skərʒəˌnɛri

excursionist
BR ɪk'skəːʃn̩ɪst, ɪk'skəːʃənɪst, ɛk'skəːʃn̩ɪst, ɛk'skəːʃənɪst, -s
AM ɪk'skərʒ(ə)nəst, ɛk'skərʒ(ə)nəst, -s

excursive
BR ɪk'skəːsɪv, ɛk'skəːsɪv
AM ɪk'skərsɪv, ɛk'skərsɪv

excursively
BR ɪk'skəːsɪvli, ɛk'skəːsɪvli
AM ɪk'skərsəvli, ɛk'skərsəvli

excursiveness
BR ɪk'skəːsɪvnɪs, ɛk'skəːsɪvnɪs
AM ɪk'skərsɪvnɪs, ɛk'skərsɪvnɪs

excursus
BR ɪk'skəːsəs, ɛk'skəːsəs
AM ɛk'skərsəs

excusable
BR ɪk'skjuːzəbl, ɛk'sjuːzəbl
AM ɪk'skjuzəbəl, ɛk'skjuzəbəl

excusably
BR ɪk'skjuːzəbli, ɛk'sjuːzəbli
AM ɪk'skjuzəbli, ɛk'skjuzəbli

excusatory
BR ɪk'skjuːzət(ə)ri, ɛk'sjuːzət(ə)ri
AM ɪk'skjuzəˌtɔri, ɛk'skjuzəˌtɔri

excuse[1]
noun
BR ɪk'skjuːs, ɛk'skjuːs, -ɪz
AM ɪk'skjus, ɛk'skjus, -əz

excuse[2]
verb
BR ɪk'sjuːz, ɛk'skjuːz, -ɪz, -ɪŋ, -d
AM ɪk'skjuz, ɛk'skjuz, -əz, -ɪŋ, -d

excuse-me
BR ɪk'sjuːzmiː, ɛk'skjuːzmiː, -z
AM ɪk'skjuzˌmi, ɛk'skjuzˌmi, -z

ex-directory
BR ˌɛksdɪ'rɛkt(ə)ri, ˌɛksdʌɪ'rɛkt(ə)ri
AM ˌɛksdə'rɛkt(ə)ri

Exe
BR ɛks
AM ɛks

exeat
BR 'ɛksɪat, -s
AM 'ɛksiˌæt, -s

exec
BR ɪg'zɛk, ɛg'zɛk, -s
AM ɛg'zɛk, -s

execrable
BR 'ɛksɪkrəbl
AM 'ɛksəkrəbəl

execrably
BR 'ɛksɪkrəbli
AM 'ɛksəkrəbli

execrate
BR 'ɛksɪkreɪt, -s, -ɪŋ, -ɪd
AM 'ɛksəˌkreɪ|t, -ts, -dɪŋ, -dɪd

execration
BR ˌɛksɪ'kreɪʃn, -z
AM ˌɛksə'kreɪʃən, -z

execrative
BR 'ɛksɪkreɪtɪv
AM 'ɛksəˌkreɪdɪv

execratory
BR 'ɛksɪkreɪt(ə)ri
AM 'ɛksəkrəˌtɔri

executable
BR 'ɛksɪkjuːtəbl
AM 'ɛksəˌkjudəbəl

executant
BR ɪg'zɛkjʊt(ə)nt, ɛg'zɛkjʊt(ə)nt, -s
AM ɪg'zɛkjədnt, ɛg'zɛkjədnt, -s

execute
BR 'ɛksɪkjuːt, -s, -ɪŋ, -ɪd
AM 'ɛksəˌkju|t, -ts, -dɪŋ, -dəd

execution
BR ˌɛksɪ'kjuːʃn, -z
AM ˌɛksə'kjuʃən, -z

executionary
BR ˌɛksɪ'kjuːʃn̩(ə)ri
AM ˌɛksə'kjuʃəˌnɛri

executioner
BR ˌɛksɪ'kjuːʃn̩ə(r), ˌɛksɪ'kjuːʃənə(r), -z
AM ˌɛksə'kjuʃ(ə)nər, -z

executive
BR ɪg'zɛkjʊtɪv, ɛg'zɛkjʊtɪv, -z
AM ɪg'zɛkjədɪv, ɛg'zɛkjədɪv, -z

executively
BR ɪg'zɛkjʊtɪvli, ɛg'zɛkjʊtɪvli
AM ɪg'zɛkjədəvli, ɛg'zɛkjədəvli

executor
BR ɪg'zɛkjʊtə(r), ɛg'zɛkjʊtə(r), -z
AM ɪg'zɛkjədər, ɛg'zɛkjədər, 'ɛksəˌkjudər, -z

executorial
BR ɪgˌzɛkjʊ'tɔːrɪəl, ɛgˌzɛkjʊ'tɔːrɪəl
AM ɪgˌzɛkjə'tɔriəl, ɛgˌzɛkjə'tɔriəl

executorship
BR ɪg'zɛkjʊtəʃɪp, ɛg'zɛkjʊtəʃɪp, -s
AM ɪg'zɛkjədərˌʃɪp, ɛg'zɛkjədərˌʃɪp, -s

executory
BR ɪg'zɛkjʊt(ə)ri, ɛg'zɛkjʊt(ə)ri
AM ɪg'zɛkjəˌtɔri, ɛg'zɛkjəˌtɔri

executrices
BR ɪg'zɛkjʊtrɪsiːz
AM ɪg'zɛkjəˌtrɪsiz, ɛg'zɛkjəˌtrɪsiz

executrix
BR ɪg'zɛkjʊtrɪks, ɛg'zɛkjʊtrɪks, -ɪz
AM ɪg'zɛkjəˌtrɪks, ɛg'zɛkjəˌtrɪks, -ɪz

exegeses
BR ˌɛksɪ'dʒiːsiːz
AM ˌɛksə'dʒisiz

exegesis
BR ˌɛksɪ'dʒiːsɪs
AM ˌɛksə'dʒisɪs

exegete
BR 'ɛksɪdʒiːt, -s
AM 'ɛksəˌdʒit, -s

exegetic
BR ˌɛksɪ'dʒɛtɪk
AM ˌɛksə'dʒɛdɪk

exegetical
BR ˌɛksɪ'dʒɛtɪkl
AM ˌɛksə'dʒɛdəkəl

exegetist
BR 'ɛksɪdʒiːtɪst, -s
AM 'ɛksəˌdʒɛdəst, -s

exempla
BR ɪg'zɛmplə(*r*), ɛg'zɛmplə(*r*)
AM ɪg'zɛmplə, ɛg'zɛmplə

exemplar
BR ɪg'zɛmplə(r), ɛg'zɛmplə(r), -z
AM ɪg'zɛmplər, ɛg'zɛmplər, -z

exemplarily
BR ɪg'zɛmplərɪli, ɛg'zɛmplərɪli

AM ɪɡ'zɛmplərəli, ɛɡ'zɛmplərəli, ɪɡzɛm'plərəli, ɛɡzəm'plərəli

exemplariness
BR ɪɡ'zɛmplərɪnɪs, ɛɡ'zɛmplərɪnɪs
AM ɪɡ'zɛmplərinɪs, ɛɡ'zɛmplərinɪs

exemplary
BR ɪɡ'zɛmpləri, ɛɡ'zɛmpləri
AM ɪɡ'zɛmpləri, ɛɡ'zɛmpləri

exemplification
BR ɪɡ,zɛmplɪfɪ'keɪʃn, ɛɡ,zɛmplɪfɪ'keɪʃn, -z
AM ɪɡ,zɛmpləfə'keɪʃən, ɛɡ,zɛmpləfə'keɪʃən, -z

exemplify
BR ɪɡ'zɛmplɪfʌɪ, ɛɡ'zɛmplɪfʌɪ, -z, -ɪŋ, -d
AM ɪɡ'zɛmplə,faɪ, ɛɡ'zɛmplə,faɪ, -z, -ɪŋ, -d

exemplum
BR ɪɡ'zɛmpləm, ɛɡ'zɛmpləm
AM ɪɡ'zɛmpləm, ɛɡ'zɛmpləm

exempt
BR ɪɡ'zɛm(p)t, ɛɡ'zɛm(p)t, -s, -ɪŋ, -ɪd
AM ɪɡ'zɛm(p)t, ɛɡ'zɛm(p)t, -s, -ɪŋ, -əd

exemption
BR ɪɡ'zɛm(p)ʃn, ɛɡ'zɛm(p)ʃn, -z
AM ɪɡ'zɛm(p)ʃən, ɛɡ'zɛm(p)ʃən, -z

exequatur
BR ,ɛksɪ'kweɪtə(r), -z
AM ,ɛksə'kweɪdər, -z

exequies
BR 'ɛksɪkwɪz
AM 'ɛksəkwiz

exercisable
BR 'ɛksəsʌɪzəbl
AM 'ɛksər,saɪzəbəl

exercise
BR 'ɛksəsʌɪz, -ɪz, -ɪŋ, -d
AM 'ɛksər,saɪz, -ɪz, -ɪŋ, -d

exerciser
BR 'ɛksəsʌɪzə(r), -z
AM 'ɛksər,saɪzər, -z

exergual
BR ɛk'səːɡl, 'ɛksəːɡl
AM ɛk'sərɡəl, ɛɡ'zərɡəl

exergue
BR ɛk'səːɡ, 'ɛksəːɡ, -z
AM ɛk'sərɡ, ɛɡ'zərɡ, 'ɛksərɡ, 'ɛɡzərɡ, -z

exert
BR ɪɡ'zəːt, ɛɡ'zəːt, -s, -ɪŋ, -ɪd
AM ɪɡ'zər|t, ɛɡ'zər|t, -ts, -dɪŋ, -dəd

exertion
BR ɪɡ'zəːʃn, ɛɡ'zəːʃn, -z
AM ɪɡ'zərʃən, ɛɡ'zərʃən, -z

Exeter
BR 'ɛksɪtə(r)
AM 'ɛksətər, 'ɛɡzətər

exeunt
BR 'ɛksɪʌnt, 'ɛksɪʊnt
AM 'ɛksi,ənt, 'ɛksi,ʊnt

exfiltrate
BR 'ɛksfɪltreɪt, -s, -ɪŋ, -ɪd
AM ɛk'sfɪl,treɪ|t, ɪk'sfɪl,treɪ|t, -ts, -dɪŋ, -dɪd

exfiltration
BR ,ɛksfɪl'treɪʃn
AM ɛk,sfɪl'treɪʃən, ɪk,sfɪl'treɪʃən

exfoliate
BR (,)ɛks'fəʊlɪeɪt, ɪks'fəʊlɪeɪt, -s, -ɪŋ, -ɪd
AM ɛk'sfoʊli,eɪ|t, ɪk'sfoʊli,eɪt, -ts, -dɪŋ, -dɪd

exfoliation
BR ɛks,fəʊlɪ'eɪʃn, ɪks,fəʊlɪ'eɪʃn, -z
AM ɛk,sfoʊli'eɪʃən, ɪk,sfoʊli'eɪʃən, -z

exfoliative
BR ɛks'fəʊlɪətɪv, ɪks'fəʊlɪətɪv
AM ɛk'sfoʊli,eɪdɪv, ɪk'sfoʊli,eɪdɪv

ex gratia
BR ,ɛks 'ɡreɪʃə(r)
AM ɛks 'ɡreɪdiə, + 'ɡreɪʃ(i)ə

exhalable
BR ɛks'heɪləbl, ɪks'heɪləbl
AM ɛks'heɪləbəl, ɪks'heɪləbəl, 'ɛks,heɪləbəl

exhalation
BR ,ɛks(h)ə'leɪʃn, -z
AM ,ɛks(h)ə'leɪʃən, -z

exhale
BR ɛks'heɪl, ɪks'heɪl, -z, -ɪŋ, -d
AM ɛks'heɪl, ɪks'heɪl, 'ɛks,(h)eɪl, -z, -ɪŋ, -d

exhaust
BR ɪɡ'zɔːst, ɛɡ'zɔːst, -s, -ɪŋ, -ɪd
AM ɪɡ'zɔst, ɛɡ'zɔst, ɪɡ'zɑst, ɛɡ'zɑst, -s, -ɪŋ, -əd

exhauster
BR ɪɡ'zɔːstə(r), ɛɡ'zɔːstə(r), -z
AM ɪɡ'zɔstər, ɛɡ'zɔstər, ɪɡ'zɑstər, ɛɡ'zɑstər, -z

exhaustibility
BR ɪɡ,zɔːstɪ'bɪlɪti, ɛɡ,zɔːstɪ'bɪlɪti
AM ɪɡ,zɔstə'bɪlɪdi, ɛɡ,zɔstə'bɪlɪdi, ɪɡ,zɑstə'bɪlɪdi, ɛɡ,zɑstə'bɪlɪdi

exhaustible
BR ɪɡ'zɔːstɪbl, ɛɡ'zɔːstɪbl
AM ɪɡ'zɔstəbəl, ɛɡ'zɔstəbəl, ɪɡ'zɑstəbəl, ɛɡ'zɑstəbəl

exhaustibly
BR ɪɡ'zɔːstɪbli, ɛɡ'zɔːstɪbli
AM ɪɡ'zɔstəbli, ɛɡ'zɔstəbli, ɪɡ'zɑstəbli, ɛɡ'zɑstəbli

exhaustion
BR ɪɡ'zɔːstʃ(ə)n, ɛɡ'zɔːstʃ(ə)n
AM ɪɡ'zɔstʃən, ɛɡ'zɔstʃən, ɪɡ'zɑstʃən, ɛɡ'zɑstʃən

exhaustive
BR ɪɡ'zɔːstɪv, ɛɡ'zɔːstɪv
AM ɪɡ'zɔstɪv, ɛɡ'zɔstɪv, ɪɡ'zɑstɪv, ɛɡ'zɑstɪv

exhaustively
BR ɪɡ'zɔːstɪvli, ɛɡ'zɔːstɪvli
AM ɪɡ'zɔstəvli, ɛɡ'zɔstəvli, ɪɡ'zɑstəvli, ɛɡ'zɑstəvli

exhaustiveness
BR ɪɡ'zɔːstɪvnɪs, ɛɡ'zɔːstɪvnɪs
AM ɪɡ'zɔstɪvnɪs, ɛɡ'zɔstɪvnɪs, ɪɡ'zɑstɪvnɪs, ɛɡ'zɑstɪvnɪs

exhibit
BR ɪɡ'zɪb|ɪt, ɛɡ'zɪb|ɪt, -s, -ɪtɪŋ, -ɪtɪd
AM ɪɡ'zɪbə|t, ɛɡ'zɪbə|t, -ts, -dɪŋ, -dəd

exhibition
BR ,ɛksɪ'bɪʃn, -z
AM ,ɛksə'bɪʃən, -z

exhibitioner
BR ,ɛksɪ'bɪʃn̩ə(r), ,ɛksɪ'bɪʃənə(r), -z
AM ,ɛksə'bɪʃənər, -z

exhibitionism
BR ,ɛksɪ'bɪʃn̩ɪz(ə)m, ,ɛksɪ'bɪʃənɪz(ə)m
AM ,ɛksə'bɪʃə,nɪzəm

exhibitionist
BR ,ɛksɪ'bɪʃn̩ɪst, ,ɛksɪ'bɪʃənɪst, -s
AM ,ɛksə'bɪʃ(ə)nəst, -s

exhibitionistic
BR ,ɛksɪ,bɪʃə'nɪstɪk, ,ɛksɪ,bɪʃn'ɪstɪk
AM ,ɛksə,bɪʃə'nɪstɪk

exhibitionistically
BR ,ɛksɪbɪʃə'nɪstɪkli
AM ,ɛksə,bɪʃə'nɪstɪk(ə)li

exhibitor
BR ɪɡ'zɪbɪtə(r), ɛɡ'zɪbɪtə(r), -z
AM ɪɡ'zɪbədər, ɛɡ'zɪbədər, -z

exhibitory
BR ɪɡ'zɪbɪt(ə)ri, ɛɡ'zɪbɪt(ə)ri
AM ɪɡ'zɪbə,tɔri, ɛɡ'zɪbə,tɔri

exhilarant
BR ɪɡ'zɪlərənt, ɪɡ'zɪlərn̩t, ɛɡ'zɪlərənt, ɛɡ'zɪlərn̩t, -s
AM ɪɡ'zɪlərənt, ɛɡ'zɪlərənt, -s

exhilarate
BR ɪɡ'zɪləreɪt, ɛɡ'zɪləreɪt, -s, -ɪŋ, -ɪd
AM ɪɡ'zɪlə,reɪ|t, ɛɡ'zɪlə,reɪ|t, -ts, -dɪŋ, -dɪd

exhilaratingly
BR ɪɡ'zɪləreɪtɪŋli, ɛɡ'zɪləreɪtɪŋli
AM ɪɡ'zɪlə,reɪdɪŋli, ɛɡ'zɪlə,reɪdɪŋli

exhilaration
BR ɪɡ,zɪlə'reɪʃn, ɛɡ,zɪlə'reɪʃn
AM ɪɡ,zɪlə'reɪʃən, ɛɡ,zɪlə'reɪʃən

exhilarative
BR ɪɡ'zɪl(ə)rətɪv, ɛɡ'zɪl(ə)rətɪv
AM ɪɡ'zɪlə,reɪdɪv, ɛɡ'zɪlə,reɪdɪv

exhort
BR ɪɡ'zɔːt, ɛɡ'zɔːt, -s, -ɪŋ, -ɪd
AM ɪɡ'zɔ(ə)rt, ɛɡ'zɔ(ə)rt, -ts, -'zɔrdɪŋ, -'zɔrdəd

exhortation
BR ,ɛɡzɔː'teɪʃn, ,ɛksɔː'teɪʃn, -z
AM ,ɛɡ,zɔr'teɪʃən, ,ɛk,sɔr'teɪʃən, ,ɛksər'teɪʃən, ,ɛks,(h)ɔr'teɪʃən, -z

exhortative
BR ɪɡ'zɔːtətɪv, ɛɡ'zɔːtətɪv
AM ɪɡ'zɔrdədɪv, ɛɡ'zɔrdədɪv

exhortatory
BR ɪɡ'zɔːtət(ə)ri, ɛɡ'zɔːtət(ə)ri
AM ɪɡ'zɔrdə,tɔri, ɛɡ'zɔrdə,tɔri

exhorter
BR ɪɡ'zɔːtə(r), ɛɡ'zɔːtə(r), -z

AM ɪɡ'zɔrdər, ɛɡ'zɔrdər, -z
exhumation
BR ˌɛks(h)jʊ'meɪʃn, ˌɛɡzjʊ'meɪʃn, -z
AM ˌɛks(h)ju'meɪʃən, ˌɛɡz(j)u'meɪʃən, -z
exhume
BR ɛks'hjuːm, ɪɡ'zjuːm, ɛɡ'zjuːm, -z, -ɪŋ, -d
AM ɪɡ'z(j)um, ɛɡ'z(j)um, -z, -ɪŋ, -d
ex hypothesi
BR ˌɛks hʌɪ'pɒθɪsʌɪ
AM ˌɛks haɪ'pɑθəˌsaɪ
Exide®
BR 'ɛksʌɪd
AM 'ɛksaɪd, 'ɛɡzaɪd
exigence
BR 'ɛksɪdʒ(ə)ns, 'ɛɡzɪdʒ(ə)ns, -ɪz
AM 'ɛksədʒəns, 'ɛɡzədʒəns, -əz
exigency
BR 'ɛksɪdʒ(ə)ns|i, 'ɛɡzɪdʒ(ə)ns|i, ɪɡ'zɪdʒ(ə)ns|i, -ɪz
AM 'ɛɡzədʒənsi, 'ɛksədʒənsi, -z
exigent
BR 'ɛksɪdʒ(ə)nt, 'ɛɡzɪdʒ(ə)nt
AM 'ɛɡzədʒənt, 'ɛksədʒənt
exigently
BR 'ɛksɪdʒ(ə)ntli, 'ɛɡzɪdʒ(ə)ntli
AM 'ɛɡzədʒən(t)li, 'ɛksədʒən(t)li
exigible
BR 'ɛksɪdʒəbl, 'ɛɡzɪdʒəbl
AM 'ɛɡzədʒəbəl, 'ɛksədʒəbəl
exiguity
BR ˌɛksɪ'ɡjuːɪti, ˌɛɡzɪ'ɡjuːɪti
AM ˌɛɡzə'ɡjʊədi, ˌɛksə'ɡjuədi
exiguous
BR ɪɡ'zɪɡjʊəs, ɛɡ'zɪɡjʊəs, ɪk'sɪɡjʊəs, ɛk'sɪɡjʊəs
AM ɛɡ'zɪɡjəwəs, ɛk'sɪɡjəwəs
exiguously
BR ɛɡ'zɪɡjʊəsli, ɪɡ'zɪɡjʊəsli, ɪk'sɪɡjʊəsli, ɛk'sɪɡjʊəsli
AM ɛɡ'zɪɡjəwəsli, ɛk'sɪɡjəwəsli
exiguousness
BR ɛɡ'zɪɡjʊəsnəs, ɪɡ'zɪɡjʊəsnəs, ɪk'sɪɡjʊəsnəs, ɛk'sɪɡjʊəsnəs
AM ɛɡ'zɪɡjəwəsnəs, ɛk'sɪɡjəwəsnəs
exile
BR 'ɛkzʌɪl, 'ɛɡzʌɪl, -z, -ɪŋ, -d
AM 'ɛɡˌzaɪl, 'ɛkˌsaɪl, -z, -ɪŋ, -d
exilic
BR ɛk'sɪlɪk, ɛɡ'zɪlɪk
AM ɛɡ'zɪlɪk, ɛk'sɪlɪk
eximious
BR ɪɡ'zɪmɪəs, ɛɡ'zɪmɪəs, ɛk'sɪmɪəs
AM ɪɡ'zɪmiəs, ɛk'sɪmiəs
exist
BR ɪɡ'zɪst, ɛɡ'zɪst, -s, -ɪŋ, -ɪd
AM ɪɡ'zɪst, ɛɡ'zɪst, -s, -ɪŋ, -ɪd
existence
BR ɪɡ'zɪst(ə)ns, ɛɡ'zɪst(ə)ns
AM ɪɡ'zɪstns, ɛɡ'zɪstns
existent
BR ɪɡ'zɪst(ə)nt, ɛɡ'zɪst(ə)nt
AM ɪɡ'zɪstənt, ɛɡ'zɪstənt
existential
BR ˌɛɡzɪ'stɛnʃl
AM ˌɛɡzə'stɛn(t)ʃəl, ˌɛksə'stɛn(t)ʃəl
existentialism
BR ˌɛɡzɪ'stɛnʃəlɪz(ə)m, ˌɛɡzɪ'stɛnʃl̩ɪz(ə)m
AM ˌɛɡzə'stɛn(t)ʃəˌlɪzəm, ˌɛksə'stɛn(t)ʃəˌlɪzəm
existentialist
BR ˌɛɡzɪ'stɛnʃəlɪst, ˌɛɡzɪ'stɛnʃl̩ɪst, -s
AM ˌɛɡzə'stɛn(t)ʃələst, ˌɛksə'stɛn(t)ʃələst, -s
existentially
BR ˌɛɡzɪ'stɛnʃl̩i, ˌɛɡzɪ'stɛnʃəli
AM ˌɛɡzə'stɛn(t)ʃəli, ˌɛksə'stɛn(t)ʃəli
exit
BR 'ɛks|ɪt, 'ɛɡz|ɪt, -ɪts, -ɪtɪŋ, -ɪtɪd
AM 'ɛɡzə|t, 'ɛksə|t, -ts, -dɪŋ, -dəd
Ex-lax®
BR 'ɛkslaks
AM 'ɛksˌlæks
ex libris
BR ˌɛks 'lɪbrɪs
AM ˌɛks 'librɪs
Exmoor
BR 'ɛksmʊə(r), 'ɛksmɔː(r)
AM 'ɛksˌmɔ(ə)r
Exmouth
BR 'ɛksməθ, 'ɛksmaʊθ
AM 'ɛksməθ
ex nihilo
BR ˌɛks 'nʌɪɪləʊ
AM ˌɛks 'ni(h)əloʊ
exobiologist
BR ˌɛksəʊbʌɪ'ɒlədʒɪst, -s
AM ˌɛksəˌbaɪ'ɑlədʒəst, -s
exobiology
BR ˌɛksəʊbʌɪ'ɒlədʒi
AM ˌɛksəˌbaɪ'ɑlədʒi
exocentric
BR ˌɛksə(ʊ)'sɛntrɪk
AM ˌɛksoʊ'sɛntrɪk
Exocet®
BR 'ɛksəsɛt, -s
AM 'ɛksəˌsɛt, -s
exocrine
BR 'ɛksə(ʊ)krʌɪn, 'ɛksə(ʊ)krɪn
AM 'ɛksəkrən, 'ɛksəˌkraɪn, 'ɛksəˌkrɪn
exoderm
BR 'ɛksə(ʊ)dəːm, -z
AM 'ɛksəˌdərm, -z
exodus
BR 'ɛksədəs, -ɪz
AM 'ɛksədəs, 'ɛɡzədəs, -əz
ex officio
BR ˌɛks ə'fɪʃɪəʊ
AM ˌɛks ə'fɪʃioʊ
exogamous
BR ɛk'sɒɡəməs
AM ɛk'sɑɡəməs
exogamy
BR ɛk'sɒɡəmi
AM ɛk'sɑɡəmi
exogen
BR 'ɛksədʒ(ə)n, -z
AM 'ɛksədʒən, 'ɛɡzədʒən, -z
exogenous
BR ɛk'sɒdʒɪnəs, ɛk'sɒdʒn̩əs, ɪk'sɒdʒɪnəs, ɪk'sɒdʒn̩əs
AM ɪɡ'zɑdʒənəs, ɛɡ'zɑdʒənəs
exogenously
BR ɛk'sɒdʒɪnəsli, ɛk'sɒdʒnəsli, ɪk'sɒdʒɪnəsli, ɪk'sɒdʒn̩əsli
AM ɪɡ'zɑdʒənəsli, ɛɡ'zɑdʒənəsli
exon
BR 'ɛksɒn, -z
AM 'ɛkˌsɑn, -z
exonerate
BR ɪɡ'zɒnəreɪt, ɛɡ'zɒnəreɪt, -s, -ɪŋ, -ɪd
AM ɪɡ'zɑnəˌreɪ|t, ɛɡ'zɑnəˌreɪ|t, -ts, -dɪŋ, -dɪd
exoneration
BR ɪɡˌzɒnə'reɪʃn, ɛɡˌzɒnə'reɪʃn
AM ɪɡˌzɑnə'reɪʃən, ɛɡˌzɑnə'reɪʃən
exonerative
BR ɪɡ'zɒn(ə)rətɪv, ɛɡ'zɒn(ə)rətɪv
AM ɪɡ'zɑnəˌreɪdɪv, ɛɡ'zɑnəˌreɪdɪv
exophera
BR ɛk'sɒf(ə)rə(r), ɪk'sɒf(ə)rə(r)
AM ɛk'sɑf(ə)rə
exophoric
BR ˌɛksə(ʊ)'fɒrɪk
AM ˌɛksoʊ'fɔrɪk
exophthalmia
BR ˌɛksɒf'θalmɪə(r)
AM ˌɛksɑf'θælmiə, ˌɛksɑp'θælmiə
exophthalmic
BR ˌɛksɒf'θalmɪk
AM ˌɛksɑf'θælmɪk, ˌɛksɑp'θælmɪk
exophthalmos
BR ˌɛksɒf'θalmɒs
AM ˌɛksɑf'θælməs, ˌɛksɑp'θælməs
exophthalmus
BR ˌɛksɒf'θalməs
AM ˌɛksɑf'θælməs, ˌɛksɑp'θælməs
exoplasm
BR 'ɛksə(ʊ)plaz(ə)m
AM 'ɛksoʊˌplæz(ə)m
exorbitance
BR ɪɡ'zɔːbɪt(ə)ns, ɛɡ'zɔːbɪt(ə)ns
AM ɪɡ'zɔrbədəns, ɛɡ'zɔrbədəns
exorbitant
BR ɪɡ'zɔːbɪt(ə)nt, ɛɡ'zɔːbɪt(ə)nt
AM ɪɡ'zɔrbədnt, ɛɡ'zɔrbədnt
exorbitantly
BR ɪɡ'zɔːbɪt(ə)ntli, ɛɡ'zɔːbɪt(ə)ntli
AM ɪɡ'zɔrbədən(t)li, ɛɡ'zɔrbədən(t)li, ɪɡ'zɔrbətn(t)li, ɛɡ'zɔrbətn(t)li
exorcisation
BR ˌɛksəsʌɪ'zeɪʃn, ˌɛksɔːsʌɪ'zeɪʃn
AM ˌɛkˌsɔrsə'zeɪʃən, ˌɛksərsə'zeɪʃən, ˌɛkˌsɔrˌsaɪ'zeɪʃən, ˌɛksərˌsaɪ'zeɪʃən
exorcise
BR 'ɛksɔːsʌɪz, 'ɛksəsʌɪz, -ɪz, -ɪŋ, -d
AM 'ɛkˌsɔrˌsaɪz, 'ɛksərˌsaɪz, -ɪz, -ɪŋ, -d
exorcism
BR 'ɛksɔːsɪz(ə)m, 'ɛksəsɪz(ə)m, -z
AM 'ɛkˌsɔrˌsɪzəm, 'ɛksərˌsɪzəm, -z

exorcist
BR 'ɛksɔːsɪst, 'ɛksəsɪst
AM 'ɛkˌsɔrˌsəst, 'ɛksərˌsəst

exorcization
BR ˌɛksɔːsʌɪ'zeɪʃn, ˌɛksəsʌɪ'zeɪʃn
AM ˌɛkˌsɔrsə'zeɪʃən, ˌɛksərsə'zeɪʃən, ˌɛkˌsɔrˌsaɪ'zeɪʃən, ˌɛksərˌsaɪ'zeɪʃən

exorcize
BR 'ɛksɔːsʌɪz, 'ɛksəsʌɪz, -ɨz, -ɪŋ, -d
AM 'ɛkˌsɔrˌsaɪz, 'ɛksərˌsaɪz, -ɨz, -ɪŋ, -d

exordia
BR ɨg'zɔːdɪə(r), ɛg'zɔːdɪə(r)
AM ɪg'zɔrdiə, ɛg'zɔrdiə

exordial
BR ɨg'zɔːdɪəl, ɛg'zɔːdɪəl
AM ɪg'zɔrdiəl, ɛg'zɔrdiəl

exordially
BR ɨg'zɔːdɪəli, ɛg'zɔːdɪəli
AM ɪg'zɔrdiəli, ɛg'zɔrdiəli

exordium
BR ɨg'zɔːdɪəm, ɛg'zɔːdɪəm
AM ɪg'zɔrdiəm, ɛg'zɔrdiəm

exoskeletal
BR ˌɛksə(ʊ)'skɛlɨtl
AM ˌɛksoʊ'skɛlədl

exoskeleton
BR 'ɛksə(ʊ)ˌskɛlɨt(ə)n, -z
AM ˌɛksə'skɛlətn, -z

exosphere
BR ˌɛksə(ʊ)sfɪə(r), -z
AM ˌɛksoʊ'sfɪ(ə)r, -z

exoteric
BR ˌɛksə(ʊ)'tɛrɪk, -s
AM ˌɛksə'tɛrɪk, -s

exoterical
BR ˌɛksə(ʊ)'tɛrɨkl
AM ˌɛksə'tɛrəkəl

exoterically
BR ˌɛksə(ʊ)'tɛrɨkli
AM ˌɛksə'tɛrək(ə)li

exotericism
BR ˌɛksə(ʊ)'tɛrɨsɪz(ə)m
AM ˌɛksə'tɛrəˌsɪzəm

exothermal
BR ˌɛksə(ʊ)'θəːml
AM ˌɛksə'θərməl

exothermally
BR ˌɛksə(ʊ)'θəːml̩i, ˌɛksə(ʊ)'θəːməli
AM ˌɛksə'θərməli

exothermic
BR ˌɛksə(ʊ)'θəːmɪk
AM ˌɛksə'θərmɪk

exothermically
BR ˌɛksə(ʊ)'θəːmɨkli
AM ˌɛksə'θərmək(ə)li

exotic
BR ɨg'zɒtɪk, ɛg'zɒtɪk
AM ɪgˌzɑdɪk, ɛg'zɑdɪk

exotica
BR ɨg'zɒtɨkə(r), ɛg'zɒtɨkə(r)
AM ɪgˌzɑdɪkə, ɛg'zɑdɪkə

exotically
BR ɨg'zɒtɨkli, ɛg'zɒtɨkli
AM ɪgˌzɑdək(ə)li, ɛg'zɑdək(ə)li

exoticism
BR ɨg'zɒtɨsɪz(ə)m, ɛg'zɒtɨsɪz(ə)m
AM ɪgˌzɑdəˌsɪzəm, ɛg'zɑdəˌsɪzəm

expand
BR ɨk'spand, ɛk'spand, -z, -ɪŋ, -ɨd
AM ɪk'spænd, ɛk'spænd, -z, -ɪŋ, -əd

expandable
BR ɨk'spandəbl, ɛk'spandəbl
AM ɪk'spændəbəl, ɛk'spændəbəl

expander
BR ɨk'spandə(r), ɛk'spandə(r), -z
AM ɪk'spændər, ɛk'spændər, -z

expanse
BR ɨk'spans, ɛk'spans, -ɨz
AM ɪk'spæns, ɛk'spæns, -əz

expansibility
BR ɨkˌspansɪ'bɪlɨti, ɛkˌspansɪ'bɪlɨti
AM ɪkˌspænsə'bɪlɨdi, ɛkˌspænsə'bɪlɨdi

expansible
BR ɨk'spansɨbl, ɛk'spansɨbl
AM ɪk'spænsəbəl, ɛk'spænsəbəl

expansile
BR ɨk'spansʌɪl, ɛk'spansʌɪl
AM ɪk'spænsl, ɛk'spænsl, ɪk'spænˌsaɪl, ɛk'spænˌsaɪl

expansion
BR ɨk'spanʃn, ɛk'spanʃn, -z
AM ɪk'spænʃən, ɛk'spænʃən, -z

expansionary
BR ɨk'spanʃn̩(ə)ri, ɛk'spanʃn̩(ə)ri, ɨk'spanʃən(ə)ri, ɛk'spanʃən(ə)ri
AM ɪk'spænʃəˌnɛri, ɛk'spænʃəˌnɛri

expansionism
BR ɨk'spanʃn̩ɪz(ə)m, ɛk'spanʃn̩ɪz(ə)m, ɨk'spanʃənɪz(ə)m, ɛk'spanʃənɪz(ə)m
AM ɪk'spænʃəˌnɪzəm, ɛk'spænʃəˌnɪzəm

expansionist
BR ɨk'spanʃn̩ɪst, ɛk'spanʃn̩ɪst, ɨk'spanʃənɪst, ɛk'spanʃənɪst, -s
AM ɪk'spæn(t)ʃ(ə)nəst, ɛk'spæn(t)ʃ(ə)nəst, -s

expansionistic
BR ɨkˌspanʃə'nɪstɪk, ɛkˌspanʃə'nɪstɪk, ɨkˌspanʃn'ɪstɪk, ɛkˌspanʃn'ɪstɪk
AM ɪkˌspæn(t)ʃə'nɪstɪk, ɛkˌspæn(t)ʃə'nɪstɪk

expansive
BR ɨk'spansɪv, ɛk'spansɪv
AM ɪk'spænsɪv, ɛk'spænsɪv

expansively
BR ɨk'spansɨvli, ɛk'spansɨvli
AM ɪk'spænsəvli, ɛk'spænsəvli

expansiveness
BR ɨk'spansɨvnɨs, ɛk'spansɪvnɨs
AM ɪk'spænsɪvnɨs, ɛk'spænsɪvnɨs

expansivity
BR ɨkˌspan'sɪvɨti, ɛkˌspan'sɪvɨti
AM ɪkˌspæn'sɪvɨdi, ɛkˌspæn'sɪvɨdi

ex parte
BR ˌɛks 'pɑːti
AM ˌɛks 'pɑrdi

expat
BR ˌɛks'pat, -s
AM ˌɛks'pæt, -s

expatiate
BR ɨk'speɪʃɪeɪt, ɛk'speɪʃɪeɪt, -s, -ɪŋ, -ɨd
AM ɪk'speɪʃiˌeɪ|t, ɛk'speɪʃiˌeɪ|t, -ts, -dɪŋ, -dɨd

expatiation
BR ɨkˌspeɪʃɪ'eɪʃn, ɛkˌspeɪʃɪ'eɪʃn
AM ɪkˌspeɪʃi'eɪʃən, ɛkˌspeɪʃi'eɪʃən

expatiatory
BR ɨk'speɪʃɪətri, ɛk'speɪʃɪətri
AM ɪk'speɪʃiəˌtɔri, ɛk'speɪʃiəˌtɔri

expatriate[1]
noun, adjective
BR ɛks'patrɪət, ɨks'patrɪət, ɛks'peɪtrɪət, ɨks'peɪtrɪət, -s
AM ɛk'speɪtriət, -s

expatriate[2]
verb
BR ɛks'patrɪeɪt, ɨks'patrɪeɪt, ɛks'peɪtrɪeɪt, ɨks'peɪtrɪeɪt, -s, -ɪŋ, -ɨd
AM ɛk'speɪtriˌeɪ|t, -ts, -dɪŋ, -dɨd

expatriation
BR ɛksˌpatrɪ'eɪʃn, ɨksˌpatrɪ'eɪʃn, ɛksˌpeɪtrɪ'eɪʃn, ɨksˌpeɪtrɪ'eɪʃn
AM ɛkˌspeɪtri'eɪʃən

expect
BR ɨk'spɛkt, ɛk'spɛkt, -s, -ɪŋ, -ɨd
AM ɪk'spɛk|(t), ɛk'spɛk|(t), -(t)s, -tɪŋ, -təd

expectable
BR ɨk'spɛktəbl, ɛk'spɛktəbl
AM ɪk'spɛktəbəl, ɛk'spɛktəbəl

expectance
BR ɨk'spɛkt(ə)ns, ɛk'spɛkt(ə)ns
AM ɪk'spɛktns, ɛk'spɛktns

expectancy
BR ɨk'spɛkt(ə)nsi, ɛk'spɛkt(ə)nsi
AM ɪk'spɛktənsi, ɛk'spɛktnsi

expectant
BR ɨk'spɛkt(ə)nt, ɛk'spɛkt(ə)nt
AM ɪk'spɛktnt, ɛk'spɛktnt

expectantly
BR ɨk'spɛkt(ə)ntli, ɛk'spɛkt(ə)ntli
AM ɪk'spɛktən(t)li, ɛk'spɛktən(t)li

expectation
BR ˌɛkspɛk'teɪʃn, -z
AM ˌɛkˌspɛk'teɪʃən, ɪkˌspɛk'teɪʃən, -z

expectorant
BR ɨk'spɛkt(ə)rənt, ɛk'spɛkt(ə)rənt, ɨk'spɛkt(ə)rn̩t, ɛk'spɛkt(ə)rn̩t, -s
AM ɪk'spɛktərənt, ɛk'spɛktərənt, -s

expectorate
BR ɨk'spɛktəreɪt, ɛk'spɛktəreɪt, -s, -ɪŋ, -ɨd

AM ɪk'spɛktəˌreɪ|t, ɛk'spɛktəˌreɪ|t, -ts, -dɪŋ, -dɨd

expectoration
BR ɨkˌspɛktə'reɪʃn, ɛkˌspɛktə'reɪʃn
AM ˌɛkˌspɛktə'reɪʃən, ɪkˌspɛktə'reɪʃən

expectorator
BR ɨk'spɛktəreɪtə(r), ɛk'spɛktəreɪtə(r), -z
AM ɪk'spɛktəˌreɪdər, ɛk'spɛktəˌreɪdər, -z

expedience
BR ɨk'spi:dɪəns, ɛk'spi:dɪəns
AM ɪk'spidiəns, ɛk'spidiəns

expediency
BR ɨk'spi:dɪənsi, ɛk'spi:dɪənsi
AM ɪk'spidiənsi, ɛk'spidiənsi

expedient
BR ɨk'spi:dɪənt, ɛk'spi:dɪənt
AM ɪk'spidiənt, ɛk'spidiənt

expediently
BR ɨk'spi:dɪəntli, ɛk'spi:dɪəntli
AM ɪk'spidiən(t)li, ɛk'spidiən(t)li

expedite
BR 'ɛkspɨdʌɪt, -s, -ɪŋ, -ɨd
AM 'ɛkspəˌdaɪ|t, -ts, -dɪŋ, -dɨd

expediter
BR 'ɛkspɨdʌɪtə(r), -z
AM 'ɛkspəˌdaɪdər, -z

expedition
BR ˌɛkspɨ'dɪʃn, -z
AM ˌɛkspə'dɪʃən, -z

expeditionary
BR ˌɛkspɨ'dɪʃn̩(ə)ri
AM ˌɛkspə'dɪʃəˌnɛri

expeditionist
BR ˌɛkspɨ'dɪʃn̩ɪst, ˌɛkspɨ'dɪʃənɪst, -s
AM ˌɛkspə'dɪʃənəst, -s

expeditious
BR ˌɛkspɨ'dɪʃəs
AM ˌɛkspə'dɪʃəs

expeditiously
BR ˌɛkspɨ'dɪʃəsli
AM ˌɛkspə'dɪʃəsli

expeditiousness
BR ˌɛkspɨ'dɪʃəsnəs
AM ˌɛkspə'dɪʃəsnəs

expel
BR ɨk'spɛl, ɛk'spɛl, -z, -ɪŋ, -d
AM ɪk'spɛl, ɛk'spɛl, -z, -ɪŋ, -d

expellable
BR ɨk'spɛləbl, ɛk'spɛləbl
AM ɪk'spɛləbəl, ɛk'spɛləbəl

expellee
BR ɨkˌspɛ'li:, ɛkˌspɛ'li:, ˌɛkspɛ'li:, -z
AM ɪkˌspɛ'li, ɛkˌspɛ'li, -z

expellent
BR ɨk'spɛlənt, ɛk'spɛlənt, ɨk'spɛln̩t, ɛk'spɛln̩t, -s
AM ɪk'spɛlənt, ɛk'spɛlənt, -s

expeller
BR ɨk'spɛlə(r), ɛk'spɛlə(r), -z
AM ɪk'spɛlər, ɛk'spɛlər, -z

expend
BR ɨk'spɛnd, ɛk'spɛnd, -z, -ɪŋ, -ɨd
AM ɪk'spɛnd, ɛk'spɛnd, -z, -ɪŋ, -əd

expendability
BR ɨkˌspɛndə'bɪlɨti, ɛkˌspɛndə'bɪlɨti
AM ɪkˌspɛndə'bɪlɨdi, ɛkˌspɛndə'bɪlɨdi

expendable
BR ɨk'spɛndəbl, ɛk'spɛndəbl, -z
AM ɪk'spɛndəbəl, ɛk'spɛndəbəl, -z

expendably
BR ɨk'spɛndəbli, ɛk'spɛndəbli
AM ɪk'spɛndəbli, ɛk'spɛndəbli

expenditure
BR ɨk'spɛndɪtʃə(r), ɛk'spɛndɪtʃə(r), -z
AM ɪk'spɛndətʃər, ɛk'spɛndətʃər, ɪk'spɛndəˌtʃʊ(ə)r, ɛk'spɛndəˌtʃʊ(ə)r, -z

expense
BR ɨk'spɛns, ɛk'spɛns, -ɨz
AM ɪk'spɛns, ɛk'spɛns, -əz

expensive
BR ɨk'spɛnsɪv, ɛk'spɛnsɪv
AM ɪk'spɛnsɪv, ɛk'spɛnsɪv

expensively
BR ɨk'spɛnsɨvli, ɛk'spɛnsɨvli
AM ɪk'spɛnsəvli, ɛk'spɛnsəvli

expensiveness
BR ɨk'spɛnsɨvnɨs, ɛk'spɛnsɨvnɨs
AM ɪk'spɛnsɪvnɨs, ɛk'spɛnsɪvnɨs

experience
BR ɨk'spɪərɪəns, ɛk'spɪərɪəns, -ɨz, -ɪŋ, -t
AM ɪk'spɪriəns, ɛk'spɪriəns, ɪk'spiriəns, ɛk'spiriəns, -əz, -ɪŋ, -t

experienceable
BR ɨk'spɪərɪənsəbl, ɛk'spɪərɪənsəbl
AM ɪk'spɪriənsəbəl, ɛk'spɪriənsəbəl, ɪk'spiriənsəbəl, ɛk'spiriənsəbəl

experiential
BR ɨkˌspɪərɪ'ɛnʃl, ɛk'spɪərɪ'ɛnʃl
AM ɛkˌspɪri'ɛn(t)ʃəl, ɪkˌspɪri'ɛn(t)ʃəl

experientialism
BR ɨkˌspɪərɪ'ɛnʃl̩ɪz(ə)m, ɛkˌspɪərɪ'ɛnʃl̩ɪz(ə)m, ɨkˌspɪərɪ'ɛnʃəlɪz(ə)m, ɛkˌspɪərɪ'ɛnʃəlɪz(ə)m
AM ɛkˌspɪri'ɛn(t)ʃəˌlɪzəm, ɪkˌspɪri'ɛn(t)ʃəˌlɪzəm

experientialist
BR ɨkˌspɪərɪ'ɛnʃl̩ɪst, ɛkˌspɪərɪ'ɛnʃl̩ɪst, ɨkˌspɪərɪ'ɛnʃəlɪst, ɛkˌspɪərɪ'ɛnʃəlɪst, -s
AM ɛkˌspɪri'ɛn(t)ʃ(ə)ləst, ɪkˌspɪri'ɛn(t)ʃ(ə)ləst, -s

experientially
BR ɨkˌspɪərɪ'ɛnʃl̩i, ɛkˌspɪərɪ'ɛnʃl̩i, ɨkˌspɪərɪ'ɛnʃəli, ɛkˌspɪərɪ'ɛnʃəli
AM ɛkˌspɪri'ɛn(t)ʃəli, ɪkˌspɪri'ɛn(t)ʃəli

experiment[1]
noun
BR ɨk'spɛrɪm(ə)nt, ɛk'spɛrɪm(ə)nt, -s
AM ɪk'spɛrəmənt, ɛk'spɛrəmənt, -s

experiment[2]
verb
BR ɨk'spɛrɪm(ə)nt, ɛk'spɛrɪm(ə)nt, ɨk'spɛrɪmɛnt, ɛk'spɛrɪmɛnt, -s, -ɪŋ, -ɨd
AM ɪk'spɛrəmən|t, ɛk'spɛrəmən|t, -ts, -(t)ɪŋ, -(t)əd

experimental
BR ɨkˌspɛrɪ'mɛntl, ɛkˌspɛrɪ'mɛntl
AM ɪkˌspɛrə'mɛn(t)l, ɛkˌspɛrə'mɛn(t)l

experimentalise
BR ɨkˌspɛrɪ'mɛntl̩ʌɪz, ɛkˌspɛrɪ'mɛntl̩ʌɪz, ɨkˌspɛrɪ'mɛntəlʌɪz, ɛkˌspɛrɪ'mɛntəlʌɪz, -ɨz, -ɪŋ, -d
AM ɪkˌspɛrə'mɛntəˌlaɪz, ɛkˌspɛrə'mɛntəˌlaɪz, -ɨz, -ɪŋ, -d

experimentalism
BR ɨkˌspɛrɪ'mɛntl̩ɪz(ə)m, ɛkˌspɛrɪ'mɛntl̩ɪz(ə)m, ɨkˌspɛrɪ'mɛntəlɪz(ə)m, ɛkˌspɛrɪ'mɛntəlɪz(ə)m
AM ɪkˌspɛrə'mɛn(t)əˌlɪzəm, ɛkˌspɛrə'mɛn(t)əˌlɪzəm

experimentalist
BR ɨkˌspɛrɪ'mɛntl̩ɪst, ɛkˌspɛrɪ'mɛntl̩ɪst, ɨkˌspɛrɪ'mɛntəlɪst, ɛkˌspɛrɪ'mɛntəlɪst, -s
AM ɪkˌspɛrə'mɛn(t)l̩əst, ɛkˌspɛrə'mɛn(t)l̩əst, -s

experimentalize
BR ɨkˌspɛrɪ'mɛntl̩ʌɪz, ɛkˌspɛrɪ'mɛntl̩ʌɪz, ɨkˌspɛrɪ'mɛntəlʌɪz, ɛkˌspɛrɪ'mɛntəlʌɪz, -ɨz, -ɪŋ, -d
AM ɪkˌspɛrə'mɛn(t)əˌlaɪz, ɛkˌspɛrə'mɛn(t)əˌlaɪz, -ɨz, -ɪŋ, -d

experimentally
BR ɨkˌspɛrɪ'mɛntl̩i, ɛkˌspɛrɪ'mɛntl̩i, ɨkˌspɛrɪ'mɛntəli, ɛkˌspɛrɪ'mɛntəli
AM ɪkˌspɛrə'mɛn(t)l̩i, ɛkˌspɛrə'mɛn(t)l̩i

experimentation
BR ɨkˌspɛrɪmɛn'teɪʃn, ɛkˌspɛrɪmɛn'teɪʃn, ɨkˌspɛrɪm(ə)n'teɪʃn, ɛkˌspɛrɪm(ə)n'teɪʃn
AM ɪkˌspɛrəmən'teɪʃən, ɛkˌspɛrəmən'teɪʃən

experimenter
BR ɨk'spɛrɪmɛntə(r), ɛk'spɛrɪmɛntə(r), ɨk'spɛrɪm(ə)ntə(r), ɛk'spɛrɪm(ə)ntə(r), -z
AM ɪk'spɛrəˌmɛn(t)ər, ɛk'spɛrəˌmɛn(t)ər, -z

expert
BR 'ɛkspə:t, -s
AM 'ɛkˌspərt, -s

expertise
noun
BR ˌɛkspə:'ti:z, ˌɛkspə'ti:z
AM ˌɛkˌspər'tiz, ˌɛkˌspər'tis

expertize
verb
BR 'ɛkspətʌɪz, 'ɛkspə:tʌɪz, -ɨz, -ɪŋ, -d
AM 'ɛkspərˌtaɪz, -ɨz, -ɪŋ, -d

expertly
BR 'ɛkspə:tli
AM ˈɛkˈspərtli

expertness
BR 'ɛkspə:tnəs

AM ˌɛkˌspərtnəs
expiable
BR ˈɛkspɪəbl
AM ˈɛkspiəbəl
expiate
BR ˈɛkspɪeɪt, -s, -ɪŋ, -ɪd
AM ˈɛkspiˌeɪ|t, -ts, -dɪŋ, -dɪd
expiation
BR ˌɛkspɪˈeɪʃn
AM ˌɛkspiˈeɪʃən
expiator
BR ˈɛkspɪeɪtə(r), -z
AM ˈɛkspiˌeɪdər, -z
expiatory
BR ˈɛkspɪət(ə)ri
AM ˈɛkspiəˌtɔri
expiration
BR ˌɛkspɪˈreɪʃn
AM ˌɛkspəˈreɪʃən
expiratory
BR ɪkˈspʌɪərət(ə)ri, ɛkˈspʌɪərət(ə)ri
AM ɪkˈspaɪ(ə)rəˌtɔri, ɛkˈspaɪ(ə)rəˌtɔri
expire
BR ɪkˈspʌɪə(r), ɛkˈspʌɪə(r), -z, -ɪŋ, -d
AM ɪkˈspaɪ(ə)r, ɛkˈspaɪ(ə)r, -z, -ɪŋ, -d
expiry
BR ɪkˈspʌɪəri, ɛkˈspʌɪəri
AM ɪkˈspaɪri, ɛkˈspaɪri
explain
BR ɪkˈspleɪn, ɛkˈspleɪn, -z, -ɪŋ, -d
AM ɪkˈspleɪn, ɛkˈspleɪn, -z, -ɪŋ, -d
explainable
BR ɪkˈspleɪnəbl, ɛkˈspleɪnəbl
AM ɪkˈspleɪnəbəl, ɛkˈspleɪnəbəl
explainer
BR ɪkˈspleɪnə(r), ɛkˈspleɪnə(r), -z
AM ɪkˈspleɪnər, ɛkˈspleɪnər, -z
explananda
BR ˌɛkspləˈnandə(r)
AM ˌɛkspləˈnɑndə
explanandum
BR ˌɛkspləˈnandəm
AM ˌɛkspləˈnɑndəm
explanans
BR ˌɛkspləˈnanz
AM ˌɛkspləˈnænz, ˌɛksˈplænənz
explanantia
BR ˌɛkspləˈnantɪə(r)
AM ˌɛkspləˈnæn(t)iə
explanation
BR ˌɛkspləˈneɪʃn, -z
AM ˌɛkspləˈneɪʃən, -z
explanatorily
BR ɪkˈsplanət(ə)rɪli, ɛkˈsplanət(ə)rɪli
AM ɪkˌsplænəˈtɔrəli, ɛkˌsplænəˈtɔrəli
explanatory
BR ɪkˈsplanət(ə)ri, ɛkˈsplanət(ə)ri
AM ɪkˈsplænəˌtɔri, ɛkˈsplænəˌtɔri
explant
BR ɪksˈplɑːnt, ɛksˈplɑːnt, ɪksˈplant, ɛksˈplant, -s, -ɪŋ, -ɪd
AM ɪkˈsplæn|t, ɛkˈsplæn|t, -ts, -(t)ɪŋ, -(t)əd
explantation
BR ɪksˌplɑːnˈteɪʃn, ɛksˌplɑːnˈteɪʃn, ɪksˌplanˈteɪʃn, ɛksˌplanˈteɪʃn
AM ɪkˌsplænˈteɪʃən, ɛkˌsplænˈteɪʃən
expletive
BR ɪkˈspliːtɪv, ɛkˈspliːtɪv, -z
AM ˈɛkspləd̮ɪv, -z
explicable
BR ɪkˈsplɪkəbl, ɛkˈsplɪkəbl, ˈɛksplɪkəbl
AM ɛkˈsplɪkəbəl, ɪkˈsplɪkəbəl, ˈɛkspləkəbəl
explicably
BR ɪkˈsplɪkəbli, ɛkˈsplɪkəbli, ˈɛksplɪkəbli
AM ɛkˈsplɪkɪbli, ɪkˈsplɪkɪbli, ˈɛkspləkɪbli
explicate
BR ˈɛksplɪkeɪt, -s, -ɪŋ, -ɪd
AM ˈɛkspləˌkeɪ|t, -ts, -dɪŋ, -dɪd
explication
BR ˌɛksplɪˈkeɪʃn, -z
AM ˌɛkspləˈkeɪʃən, -z
explicative
BR ɪkˈsplɪkətɪv, ɛkˈsplɪkətɪv, ˈɛksplɪkətɪv
AM ˈɛkspləˌkeɪdɪv
explicator
BR ˈɛksplɪkeɪtə(r), -z
AM ˈɛkspləˌkeɪdər, -z
explicatory
BR ɪkˈsplɪkət(ə)ri, ɛkˈsplɪkət(ə)ri, ˈɛksplɪkət(ə)ri
AM ɪkˈsplɪkəˌtɔri, ɛkˈsplɪkəˌtɔri
explicature
BR ɪkˈsplɪkətʃə(r), ɛkˈsplɪkətʃə(r), ˈɛksplɪkətʃə(r), -z
AM ɪkˈsplɪkətʃər, ɛkˈsplɪkətʃər, -z
explicit
BR ɪkˈsplɪsɪt, ɛkˈsplɪsɪt
AM ɪkˈsplɪsɪt, ɛkˈsplɪsɪt
explicitly
BR ɪkˈsplɪsɪtli, ɛkˈsplɪsɪtli
AM ɪkˈsplɪsɪtli, ɛkˈsplɪsɪtli
explicitness
BR ɪkˈsplɪsɪtnɪs, ɛkˈsplɪsɪtnɪs
AM ɪkˈsplɪsɪtnɪs, ɛkˈsplɪsɪtnɪs
explode
BR ɪkˈspləʊd, ɛkˈspləʊd, -z, -ɪŋ, -ɪd
AM ɪkˈsploʊd, ɛkˈsploʊd, -z, -ɪŋ, -əd
exploder
BR ɪkˈspləʊdə(r), ɛkˈspləʊdə(r), -z
AM ɪkˈsploʊdər, ɛkˈsploʊdər, -z
exploit[1]
noun
BR ˈɛksplɔɪt, -s
AM ˈɛkˌsplɔɪt, -s
exploit[2]
verb
BR ɪkˈsplɔɪt, ɛkˈsplɔɪt, -s, -ɪŋ, -ɪd
AM ɪkˈsplɔɪ|t, ɛkˈsplɔɪ|t, -ts, -dɪŋ, -dɪd
exploitable
BR ɪkˈsplɔɪtəbl, ɛkˈsplɔɪtəbl
AM ɪkˈsplɔɪdəbəl, ɛkˈsplɔɪdəbəl
exploitation
BR ˌɛksplɔɪˈteɪʃn
AM ˌɛkˌsplɔɪˈteɪʃən
exploitative
BR ɪkˈsplɔɪtətɪv, ɛkˈsplɔɪtətɪv
AM ɪkˈsplɔɪdədɪv, ɛkˈsplɔɪdədɪv
exploitatively
BR ɪkˈsplɔɪtətɪvli, ɛkˈsplɔɪtətɪvli
AM ɪkˈsplɔɪdədəvli, ɛkˈsplɔɪdədəvli
exploiter
BR ɪkˈsplɔɪtə(r), ɛkˈsplɔɪtə(r), -z
AM ɪkˈsplɔɪdər, ɛkˈsplɔɪdər, -z
exploitive
BR ɪkˈsplɔɪtɪv, ɛkˈsplɔɪtɪv
AM ɪkˈsplɔɪdɪv, ɛkˈsplɔɪdɪv
exploration
BR ˌɛkspləˈreɪʃn, -z
AM ˌɛkspləˈreɪʃən, -z
explorational
BR ˌɛkspləˈreɪʃn̩(ə)l, ˌɛkspləˈreɪʃən(ə)l
AM ˌɛkspləˈreɪʃ(ə)nəl
explorative
BR ɪkˈsplɒrətɪv, ɛkˈsplɒrətɪv
AM ɪkˈsplɔrədɪv, ɛkˈsplɔrədɪv
exploratory
BR ɪkˈsplɒrət(ə)ri, ɛkˈsplɒrət(ə)ri
AM ɪkˈsplɔrəˌtɔri, ɛkˈsplɔrəˌtɔri
explore
BR ɪkˈsplɔː(r), ɛkˈsplɔː(r), -z, -ɪŋ, -d
AM ɪkˈsplɔ(ə)r, ɛkˈsplɔ(ə)r, -z, -ɪŋ, -d
explorer
BR ɪkˈsplɔːrə(r), ɛkˈsplɔːrə(r), -z
AM ɪkˈsplɔrər, ɛkˈsplɔrər, -z
explosion
BR ɪkˈspləʊʒn, ɛkˈspləʊʒn, -z
AM ɪkˈsploʊʒən, ɛkˈsploʊʒən, -z
explosive
BR ɪkˈspləʊsɪv, ɪkˈspləʊzɪv, ɛkˈspləʊsɪv, ɛkˈspləʊzɪv, -z
AM ɪkˈsploʊsɪv, ɛkˈsploʊsɪv, ɪkˈsploʊzɪv, ɛkˈsploʊzɪv, -z
explosively
BR ɪkˈspləʊsɪvli, ɪkˈspləʊzɪvli, ɛkˈspləʊsɪvli, ɛkˈspləʊzɪvli
AM ɪkˈsploʊsəvli, ɛkˈsploʊsəvli, ɪkˈsploʊzəvli, ɛkˈsploʊzəvli
explosiveness
BR ɪkˈspləʊsɪvnɪs, ɪkˈspləʊzɪvnɪs, ɛkˈspləʊsɪvnɪs, ɛkˈspləʊzɪvnɪs
AM ɪkˈsploʊsɪvnɪs, ɛkˈsploʊsɪvnɪs, ɪkˈsploʊzɪvnɪs, ɛkˈsploʊzɪvnɪs
Expo
BR ˈɛkspəʊ, -z
AM ˈɛkˌspoʊ, -z
exponent
BR ɪkˈspəʊnənt, ɛkˈspəʊnənt, -s
AM ɪkˈspoʊnənt, ɛkˈspoʊnənt, ˈɛksˌpoʊnənt, -s
exponential
BR ˌɛkspə(ʊ)ˈnɛnʃl
AM ˌɛkspəˈnɛn(t)ʃəl, ˌɛkspoʊˈnɛn(t)ʃəl

exponentially
BR ˌɛkspəˈnɛnʃl̩i, ˌɛkspəˈnɛnʃəli
AM ˌɛkspəˈnɛn(t)ʃəli, ˌɛkspoʊˈnɛn(t)ʃəli

export¹
noun
BR ˈɛkspɔːt, -s
AM ˈɛkˌspɔ(ə)rt, -s

export²
verb
BR ɪkˈspɔːt, ɛkˈspɔːt, -s, -ɪŋ, -ɪd
AM ɪkˈspɔ(ə)r|t, ɛkˈspɔ(ə)r|t, -ts, -dɪŋ, -dəd

exportability
BR ɪkˌspɔːtəˈbɪlɪti, ɛkˌspɔːtəˈbɪlɪti
AM ɪkˌspɔrdəˈbɪlɪdi, ɛkˌspɔrdəˈbɪlɪdi

exportable
BR ɪkˈspɔːtəbl, ɛkˈspɔːtəbl
AM ɪkˈspɔrdəbəl, ɛkˈspɔrdəbəl

exportation
BR ˌɛkspɔːˈteɪʃn
AM ˌɛkˌspɔrˈteɪʃən, ˌɛkspərˈteɪʃən

exporter
BR ɪkˈspɔːtə(r), ɛkˈspɔːtə(r), -z
AM ˈɛkspɔrdər, ɪkˈspɔrdər, -z

expose
BR ɪkˈspəʊz, ɛkˈspəʊz, -ɪz, -ɪŋ, -d
AM ɪkˈspoʊz, ɛkˈspoʊz, -əz, -ɪŋ, -d

exposé
BR ɪkˈspəʊzeɪ, ɛkˈspəʊzeɪ, -z
AM ˌɛksˌpoʊˈzeɪ, ˈɛkspəˌzeɪ, -z

exposer
BR ɪkˈspəʊzə(r), ɛkˈspəʊzə(r), -z
AM ɪkˈspoʊzər, ɛkˈspoʊzər, -z

exposition
BR ˌɛkspəˈzɪʃn, -z
AM ˌɛkspəˈzɪʃən, ˌɛkspoʊˈzɪʃən, -z

expositional
BR ˌɛkspəˈzɪʃn̩(ə)l, ˌɛkspəˈzɪʃən(ə)l
AM ˌɛkspəˈzɪʃ(ə)nəl, ˌɛkspoʊˈzɪʃ(ə)nəl

expositive
BR ɪkˈspɒzɪtɪv, ɛkˈspɒzɪtɪv
AM ɪkˈspɑzədɪv, ɛkˈspɑzədɪv

expositor
BR ɪkˈspɒzɪtə(r), ɛkˈspɒzɪtə(r), -z
AM ɪkˈspɑzədər, ɛkˈspɑzədər, -z

expository
BR ɪkˈspɒzɪt(ə)ri, ɛkˈspɒzɪt(ə)ri
AM ɪkˈspɑzəˌtɔri, ɛkˈspɑzəˌtɔri

ex post facto
BR ˌɛks pəʊs(t) ˈfaktəʊ
AM ˌɛkˌspoʊs(t) ˌfæktoʊ

expostulate
BR ɪkˈspɒstjʊleɪt, ɛkˈspɒstjʊleɪt, ɪkˈspɒstʃʊleɪt, ɛkˈspɒstʃʊleɪt, -s, -ɪŋ, -ɪd
AM ɪkˈspɑstʃəˌleɪ|t, ɛkˈspɑstʃəˌleɪ|t, -ts, -dɪŋ, -dɪd

expostulation
BR ɪkˌspɒstjʊˈleɪʃn, ɛkˌspɒstjʊˈleɪʃn, ɪkˌspɒstʃʊˈleɪʃn, ɛkˌspɒstʃʊˈleɪʃn, -z
AM ɪkˌspɑstʃəˈleɪʃən, ɛkˌspɑstʃəˈleɪʃən, -z

expostulatory
BR ɪkˈspɒstjʊlət(ə)ri, ɛkˈspɒstjʊlət(ə)ri, ɪkˈspɒstʃʊlət(ə)ri, ɛkˈspɒstʃʊlət(ə)ri
AM ɪkˈspɑstʃələˌtɔri, ɛkˈspɑstʃələˌtɔri

exposure
BR ɪkˈspəʊʒə(r), ɛkˈspəʊʒə(r), -z
AM ɪkˈspoʊʒər, ɛkˈspoʊʒər, -z

expound
BR ɪkˈspaʊnd, ɛkˈspaʊnd, -z, -ɪŋ, -ɪd
AM ɪkˈspaʊnd, ɛkˈspaʊnd, -z, -ɪŋ, -əd

expounder
BR ɪkˈspaʊndə(r), ɛkˈspaʊndə(r), -z
AM ɪkˈspaʊndər, ɛkˈspaʊndər, -z

ex-president
BR ɛksˈprɛzɪd(ə)nt, -s
AM ɛksˈprɛzədnt, -s

express
BR ɪkˈsprɛs, ɛkˈsprɛs, -ɪz, -ɪŋ, -t
AM ɪkˈsprɛs, ɛkˈsprɛs, -əz, -ɪŋ, -t

expresser
BR ɪkˈsprɛsə(r), ɛkˈsprɛsə(r), -z
AM ɪkˈsprɛsər, ɛkˈsprɛsər, -z

expressible
BR ɪkˈsprɛsɪbl, ɛkˈsprɛsɪbl
AM ɪkˈsprɛsəbəl, ɛkˈsprɛsəbəl

expression
BR ɪkˈsprɛʃn, ɛkˈsprɛʃn, -z
AM ɪkˈsprɛʃən, ɛkˈsprɛʃən, -z

expressional
BR ɪkˈsprɛʃn̩(ə)l, ɛkˈsprɛʃn̩(ə)l, ɪkˈsprɛʃən(ə)l, ɛkˈsprɛʃən(ə)l
AM ɪkˈsprɛʃ(ə)nəl, ɛkˈsprɛʃ(ə)nəl

expressionism
BR ɪkˈsprɛʃn̩ɪz(ə)m, ɛkˈsprɛʃn̩ɪz(ə)m, ɪkˈsprɛʃənɪz(ə)m, ɛkˈsprɛʃənɪz(ə)m
AM ɪkˈsprɛʃəˌnɪzəm, ɛkˈsprɛʃəˌnɪzəm

expressionist
BR ɪkˈsprɛʃn̩ɪst, ɛkˈsprɛʃn̩ɪst, ɪkˈsprɛʃənɪst, ɛkˈsprɛʃənɪst, -s
AM ɪkˈsprɛʃ(ə)nəst, ɛkˈsprɛʃ(ə)nəst, -s

expressionistic
BR ɪkˌsprɛʃəˈnɪstɪk, ɛkˌsprɛʃəˈnɪstɪk, ɪkˌsprɛʃnˈɪstɪk, ɛkˌsprɛʃnˈɪstɪk
AM ɪkˌsprɛʃəˈnɪstɪk, ɛkˌsprɛʃəˈnɪstɪk

expressionistically
BR ɪkˌsprɛʃəˈnɪstɪkli, ɛkˌsprɛʃəˈnɪstɪkli, ɪkˌsprɛʃnˈɪstɪkli, ɛkˌsprɛʃnˈɪstɪkli
AM ɪkˌsprɛʃəˈnɪstək(ə)li, ɛkˌsprɛʃəˈnɪstək(ə)li

expressionless
BR ɪkˈsprɛʃnləs, ɛkˈsprɛʃnləs
AM ɪkˈsprɛʃənləs, ɛkˈsprɛʃənləs

expressionlessly
BR ɪkˈsprɛʃnləsli, ɛkˈsprɛʃnləsli
AM ɪkˈsprɛʃənləsli, ɛkˈsprɛʃənləsli

expressionlessness
BR ɪkˈsprɛʃnləsnəs, ɛkˈsprɛʃnləsnəs
AM ɪkˈsprɛʃənləsnəs, ɛkˈsprɛʃənləsnəs

expressive
BR ɪkˈsprɛsɪv, ɛkˈsprɛsɪv
AM ɪkˈsprɛsɪv, ɛkˈsprɛsɪv

expressively
BR ɪkˈsprɛsɪvli, ɛkˈsprɛsɪvli
AM ɪkˈsprɛsəvli, ɛkˈsprɛsəvli

expressiveness
BR ɪkˈsprɛsɪvnɪs, ɛkˈsprɛsɪvnɪs
AM ɪkˈsprɛsɪvnɪs, ɛkˈsprɛsɪvnɪs

expressivity
BR ˌɛksprɛˈsɪvɪti
AM ˌɛksprɛˈsɪvɪdi

expressly
BR ɪkˈsprɛsli, ɛkˈsprɛsli
AM ɪkˈsprɛsli, ɛkˈsprɛsli

expresso
BR ɪkˈsprɛsəʊ, ɛkˈsprɛsəʊ, -z
AM ɪkˈsprɛsoʊ, ɛkˈsprɛsoʊ, -z

expressway
BR ɪkˈsprɛsweɪ, ɛkˈsprɛsweɪ, -z
AM ɪkˈsprɛsˌweɪ, ɛkˈsprɛsˌweɪ, -z

expropriate
BR ɪkˈsprəʊprɪeɪt, ɛkˈsprəʊprɪeɪt, -s, -ɪŋ, -ɪd
AM ˌɛksˈproʊpriˌeɪ|t, ɪkˈsproʊpriˌeɪ|t, -ts, -dɪŋ, -dɪd

expropriation
BR ɪkˌsprəʊprɪˈeɪʃn, ɛkˌsprəʊprɪˈeɪʃn, -z
AM ˌɛksˌproʊpriˈeɪʃən, ɪkˌsproʊpriˈeɪʃən, -z

expropriator
BR ɪkˈsprəʊprɪeɪtə(r), ɛkˈsprəʊprɪeɪtə(r), -z
AM ˌɛksˈproʊpriˌeɪdər, ɪkˈsproʊpriˌeɪdər, -z

expulsion
BR ɪkˈspʌlʃn, ɛkˈspʌlʃn, -z
AM ɪkˈspəlʃən, ɛkˈspəlʃən, -z

expulsive
BR ɪkˈspʌlsɪv, ɛkˈspʌlsɪv
AM ɪkˈspəlsɪv, ɛkˈspəlsɪv

expunction
BR ɪkˈspʌŋ(k)ʃn, ɛkˈspʌŋ(k)ʃn
AM ɪkˈspəŋkʃən, ɛkˈspəŋkʃən

expunge
BR ɪkˈspʌn(d)ʒ, ɛkˈspʌn(d)ʒ, -ɪz, -ɪŋ, -d
AM ɪkˈspəndʒ, ɛkˈspəndʒ, -əz, -ɪŋ, -t

expunger
BR ɪkˈspʌn(d)ʒə(r), ɛkˈspʌn(d)ʒə(r), -z
AM ɪkˈspəndʒər, ɛkˈspəndʒər, -z

expurgate
BR ˈɛkspəgeɪt, -s, -ɪŋ, -ɪd

AM 'ɛkspər,geɪ|t, -ts, -dɪŋ, -dɨd
expurgation
BR ˌɛkspə'geɪʃn, -z
AM ˌɛkspər'geɪʃən, -z
expurgator
BR 'ɛkspəgeɪtə(r), -z
AM 'ɛkspər,geɪdər, -z
expurgatorial
BR ɪk,spəːgə'tɔːrɪəl, ɛk,spəːgə'tɔːrɪəl
AM ɪk,spərgə'tɔriəl, ɛk,spərgə'tɔriəl
expurgatory
BR ɪk'spəːgət(ə)ri, ɛk'spəːgət(ə)ri
AM ɪk'spərgə,tɔri, ɛk'spərgə,tɔri
exquisite
BR ɪk'skwɪzɪt, ɛk'skwɪzɪt, 'ɛkskwɪzɪt
AM ɛk'skwɪzət, 'ɛk,skwɪzət, 'ɛkskwəzət
exquisitely
BR ɪk'skwɪzɪtli, ɛk'skwɪzɪtli, 'ɛkskwɪzɪtli
AM ɛk'skwɪzətli, 'ɛk,skwɪzətli, 'ɛkskwəzətli
exquisiteness
BR ɪk'skwɪzɪtnɪs, ɛk'skwɪzɪtnɪs, 'ɛkskwɪzɪtnɪs
AM ɛk'skwɪzətnəs, 'ɛk,skwɪzətnəs, 'ɛkskwəzətnəs
exsanguinate
BR ɛk'saŋgwɪneɪt, -s, -ɪŋ, -ɨd
AM ɛk'sæŋgwə,neɪ|t, ɪk'sæŋgwə,neɪ|t, -ts, -dɪŋ, -dɨd
exsanguination
BR ɛk,saŋgwɪ'neɪʃn
AM ɛk,sæŋwə'neɪʃən, ɪk,sæŋwə'neɪʃən
exsanguinity
BR ˌɛksaŋ'gwɪnɪti
AM ɛk,sæŋ'gwɪnɨdi, ɪk,sæŋ'gwɪnɨdi
exscind
BR ɪk'sɪnd, ɛk'sɪnd, -z, -ɪŋ, -ɨd
AM ɛk'sɪnd, ɪk'sɪnd, -z, -ɪŋ, -ɨd
exsert
BR ɪk'səːt, ɛk'səːt, -s, -ɪŋ, -ɨd
AM ɛk'sər|t, ɪk'sər|t, -ts, -dɪŋ, -dəd
exsiccate
BR 'ɛksɪkeɪt, -s, -ɪŋ, -ɨd
AM 'ɛksə,keɪ|t, -ts, -dɪŋ, -dɨd
ex silentio
BR ˌɛks sɪ'lɛn(t)ʃɪəʊ
AM ˌɛk(s) sə'lɛn(t)ʃioʊ
exsolve
BR ɪk'sɒlv, ɛk'sɒlv, -z, -ɪŋ, -d
AM ɪk'sɑlv, ɛk'sɑlv, -z, -ɪŋ, -d
extant
BR ɛk'stant, ɪk'stant, 'ɛkst(ə)nt
AM 'ɛkstənt, ɛk'stænt, 'ɛk,stænt
Extel
BR 'ɛkstɛl
AM 'ɛks,tɛl
extemporaneous
BR ɪk,stɛmpə'reɪnɪəs, ɛk,stɛmpə'reɪnɪəs
AM ɪk,stɛmpə'reɪniəs, ɛk,stɛmpə'reɪniəs
extemporaneously
BR ɪk,stɛmpə'reɪnɪəsli, ɛk,stɛmpə'reɪnɪəsli
AM ɪk,stɛmpə'reɪniəsli, ɛk,stɛmpə'reɪniəsli
extemporaneousness
BR ɪk,stɛmpə'reɪnɪəsnəs, ɛk,stɛmpə'reɪnɪəsnəs
AM ɪk,stɛmpə'reɪniəsnəs, ɛk,stɛmpə'reɪniəsnəs
extemporarily
BR ɪk'stɛmp(ə)rərɪli, ɛk'stɛmp(ə)rərɪli
AM ɪk,stɛmpə'rɛrəli, ɛk,stɛmpə'rɛrəli
extemporariness
BR ɪk'stɛmp(ə)rərɪnɪs, ɛk'stɛmp(ə)rərɪnɪs
AM ɪk'stɛmpə,rɛrinɪs, ɛk'stɛmpə,rɛrinɪs
extemporary
BR ɪk'stɛmp(ə)r(ər)i, ɛk'stɛmp(ə)r(ər)i
AM ɪk'stɛmpə,rɛri, ɛk'stɛmpə,rɛri
extempore
BR ɪk'stɛmp(ə)ri, ɛk'stɛmp(ə)ri
AM ɪk'stɛmpəri, ɛk'stɛmpəri
extemporisation
BR ɪk,stɛmpərʌɪ'zeɪʃn, ɛk,stɛmpərʌɪ'zeɪʃn, ɪk,stɛmpərə'zeɪʃn, ɛk,stɛmpərə'zeɪʃn, -z
AM ɪk,stɛmpərə'zeɪʃən, ɛk,stɛmpərə'zeɪʃən, ɪk,stɛmpə,raɪ'zeɪʃən, ɛk,stɛmpə,raɪ'zeɪʃən, -z
extemporise
BR ɪk'stɛmpərʌɪz, ɛk'stɛmpərʌɪz, -ɪz, -ɪŋ, -d
AM ɪk'stɛmpə,raɪz, ɛk'stɛmpə,raɪz, -ɪz, -ɪŋ, -d
extemporization
BR ɪk,stɛmpərʌɪ'zeɪʃn, ɛk,stɛmpərʌɪ'zeɪʃn, ɪk,stɛmpərə'zeɪʃn, ɛk,stɛmpərə'zeɪʃn, -z
AM ɪk,stɛmpərə'zeɪʃən, ɛk,stɛmpərə'zeɪʃən, ɪk,stɛmpə,raɪ'zeɪʃən, ɛk,stɛmpə,raɪ'zeɪʃən, -z
extemporize
BR ɪk'stɛmpərʌɪz, ɛk'stɛmpərʌɪz, -ɪz, -ɪŋ, -d
AM ɪk'stɛmpə,raɪz, ɛk'stɛmpə,raɪz, -ɪz, -ɪŋ, -d
extend
BR ɪk'stɛnd, ɛk'stɛnd, -z, -ɪŋ, -ɨd
AM ɪk'stɛnd, ɛk'stɛnd, -z, -ɪŋ, -əd
extendability
BR ɪk,stɛndə'bɪlɪti, ɛk,stɛndə'bɪlɪti
AM ɪk,stɛndə'bɪlɨdi, ɛk,stɛndə'bɪlɨdi
extendable
BR ɪk'stɛndəbl, ɛk'stɛndəbl
AM ɪk'stɛndəbəl, ɛk'stɛndəbəl
extender
BR ɪk'stɛndə(r), ɛk'stɛndə(r), -z
AM ɪk'stɛndər, ɛk'stɛndər, -z
extendibility
BR ɪk,stɛndɪ'bɪlɪti, ɛk,stɛndɪ'bɪlɪti
AM ɪk,stɛndə'bɪlɨdi, ɛk,stɛndə'bɪlɨdi
extendible
BR ɪk'stɛndɪbl, ɛk'stɛndɪbl
AM ɪk'stɛndəbəl, ɛk'stɛndəbəl
extensibility
BR ɪk,stɛnsɪ'bɪlɪti, ɛk,stɛnsɪ'bɪlɪti
AM ɪk,stɛnsə'bɪlɨdi, ɛk,stɛnsə'bɪlɨdi
extensible
BR ɪk'stɛnsɪbl, ɛk'stɛnsɪbl
AM ɪk'stɛnsəbəl, ɛk'stɛnsəbəl
extensile
BR ɪk'stɛnsʌɪl, ɛk'stɛnsʌɪl
AM ɪk'stɛnsəl, ɛk'stɛnsəl, ɪk'stɛn,saɪl, ɛk'stɛn,saɪl
extension
BR ɪk'stɛnʃn, ɛk'stɛnʃn, -z
AM ɪk'stɛn(t)ʃən, ɛk'stɛn(t)ʃən, -z
extensional
BR ɪk'stɛnʃn̩(ə)l, ɛk'stɛnʃn̩(ə)l, ɪk'stɛnʃən(ə)l, ɛk'stɛnʃən(ə)l
AM ɪk'stɛn(t)ʃ(ə)nəl, ɛk'stɛn(t)ʃ(ə)nəl
extensionality
BR ɪk,stɛnʃə'nalɪti, ɛk,stɛnʃə'nalɪti
AM ɪk,stɛn(t)ʃə'nælədi, ɛk,stɛn(t)ʃə'nælədi
extensive
BR ɪk'stɛnsɪv, ɛk'stɛnsɪv
AM ɪk'stɛnsɪv, ɛk'stɛnsɪv
extensively
BR ɪk'stɛnsɪvli, ɛk'stɛnsɪvli
AM ɪk'stɛnsəvli, ɛk'stɛnsəvli
extensiveness
BR ɪk'stɛnsɪvnɪs, ɛk'stɛnsɪvnɪs
AM ɪk'stɛnsɪvnɪs, ɛk'stɛnsɪvnɪs
extensometer
BR ˌɛkstɛn'sɒmɪtə(r), -z
AM ɪk,stɛn'sɑmədər, ɛk,stɛn'sɑmədər, -z
extensor
BR ɪk'stɛnsə(r), ɛk'stɛnsə(r), -z
AM ɪk'stɛnsər, ɛk'stɛnsər, -z
extent
BR ɪk'stɛnt, ɛk'stɛnt, -s
AM ɪk'stɛnt, ɛk'stɛnt, -s
extenuate
BR ɪk'stɛnjʊeɪt, ɛk'stɛnjʊeɪt, -s, -ɪŋ, -ɨd
AM ɪk'stɛnjə,weɪ|t, ɛk'stɛnjə,weɪ|t, -ts, -dɪŋ, -dɨd
extenuatingly
BR ɪk'stɛnjʊeɪtɪŋli, ɛk'stɛnjʊeɪtɪŋli
AM ɪk'stɛnjə,weɪdɪŋli, ɛk'stɛnjə,weɪdɪŋli
extenuation
BR ɪk,stɛnjʊ'eɪʃn, ɛk,stɛnjʊ'eɪʃn, -z
AM ɪk,stɛnjə'weɪʃən, ɛk,stɛnjə'weɪʃən, -z
extenuatory
BR ɪk'stɛnjʊət(ə)ri, ɛk'stɛnjʊət(ə)ri
AM ɪk'stɛnjəwə,tɔri, ɛk'stɛnjəwə,tɔri

exterior
BR ɪk'stɪərɪə(r), ɛk'stɪərɪə(r), -z
AM ɪk'stɪriər, ɛk'stɪriər, ɛk'stiriər, ɪk'stiriər, -z

exteriorise
BR ɪk'stɪərɪərʌɪz, ɛk'stɪərɪərʌɪz, -ɪz, -ɪŋ, -d
AM ɪk'stɪriəˌraɪz, ɛk'stɪriəˌraɪz, ɛk'stiriəˌraɪz, ɪk'stiriəˌraɪz, -ɪz, -ɪŋ, -d

exteriority
BR ɪkˌstɪərɪ'ɒrɪti, ɛkˌstɪərɪ'ɒrɪti
AM ɪkˌstɪri'ɔrədi, ɛkˌstɪri'ɔrədi, ɛkˌstiri'ɔrədi, ɪkˌstiri'ɔrədi

exteriorize
BR ɪk'stɪərɪərʌɪz, ɛk'stɪərɪərʌɪz, -ɪz, -ɪŋ, -d
AM ɪk'stɪriəˌraɪz, ɛk'stɪriəˌraɪz, ɛk'stiriəˌraɪz, ɪk'stiriəˌraɪz, -ɪz, -ɪŋ, -d

exteriorly
BR ɪk'stɪərɪəli, ɛk'stɪərɪəli
AM ɪk'stɪriərli, ɛk'stɪriərli, ɛk'stiriərli, ɪk'stiriərli

exterminate
BR ɪk'stəːmɪneɪt, ɛk'stəːmɪneɪt, -s, -ɪŋ, -ɪd
AM ɪk'stərməˌneɪ|t, ɛk'stərməˌneɪ|t, -ts, -dɪŋ, -dɪd

extermination
BR ɪkˌstəːmɪ'neɪʃn, ɛkˌstəːmɪ'neɪʃn, -z
AM ɪkˌstərmə'neɪʃən, ɛkˌstərmə'neɪʃən, -z

exterminator
BR ɪk'stəːmɪneɪtə(r), ɛk'stəːmɪneɪtə(r), -z
AM ɪk'stərməˌneɪdər, ɛk'stərməˌneɪdər, -z

exterminatory
BR ɪk'stəːmɪnət(ə)ri, ɛk'stəːmɪnət(ə)ri
AM ɪk'stərmənəˌtɔri, ɛk'stərmənəˌtɔri

extern
BR 'ɛkstəːn, -z
AM 'ɛksˌtərn, -z

external
BR ɪk'stəːnl, ɛk'stəːnl, -z
AM ɪk'stərnəl, ɛk'stərnəl-z

externalisation
BR ɪkˌstəːnəlʌɪ'zeɪʃn, ɛkˌstəːnəlʌɪ'zeɪʃn, ɪkˌstəːnl̩ʌɪ'zeɪʃn, ɛkˌstəːnl̩ʌɪ'zeɪʃn
AM ɪkˌstərnlə'zeɪʃən, ɛkˌstərnlə'zeɪʃən, ɪkˌstərnəˌlaɪ'zeɪʃən, ɛkˌstərnəˌlaɪ'zeɪʃən

externalise
BR ɪk'stəːnəlʌɪz, ɛk'stəːnəlʌɪz, ɪk'stəːnl̩ʌɪz, ɛk'stəːnl̩ʌɪz, -ɪz, -ɪŋ, -d
AM ɪk'stərnəˌlaɪz, ɛk'stərnəˌlaɪz, -ɪz, -ɪŋ, -d

externality
BR ˌɛkstəː'nalɪt|i, -ɪz
AM ˌɛkˌstər'nælədi, ɪkˌstər'nælədi, -z

externalization
BR ɪkˌstəːnl̩ʌɪ'zeɪʃn, ɛkˌstəːnl̩ʌɪ'zeɪʃn
AM ɪkˌstərnlə'zeɪʃən, ɛkˌstərnlə'zeɪʃən, ɪkˌstərnəˌlaɪ'zeɪʃən, ɛkˌstərnəˌlaɪ'zeɪʃən

externalize
BR ɪk'stəːnəlʌɪz, ɛk'stəːnəlʌɪz, ɪk'stəːnl̩ʌɪz, ɛk'stəːnl̩ʌɪz, -ɪz, -ɪŋ, -d
AM ɪk'stərnəˌlaɪz, ɛk'stərnəˌlaɪz, -ɪz, -ɪŋ, -d

externally
BR ɪk'stəːnl̩i, ɛk'stəːnl̩i, ɪk'stəːnəli, ɛk'stəːnəli
AM ˌɛk'stərnəli, ɪk'stərnəli

exteroceptive
BR ˌɛkstərə(ʊ)'sɛptɪv
AM ˌɛkstəroʊ'sɛptɪv

exterritorial
BR ˌɛkstɛrɪ'tɔːrɪəl
AM ˌɛksˌtɛrə'tɔriəl

exterritoriality
BR ˌɛkstɛrɪˌtɔːrɪ'alɪti
AM ˌɛksˌtɛrəˌtɔri'ælədi

extinct
BR ɪk'stɪŋ(k)t, ɛk'stɪŋ(k)t
AM ɪk'stɪŋ(k)t, ɛk'stɪŋ(k)t, ɪk'stɪŋk(t), ɛk'stɪŋk(t)

extinction
BR ɪk'stɪŋ(k)ʃn, ɛk'stɪŋ(k)ʃn
AM ɪk'stɪŋ(k)ʃən, ɛk'stɪŋ(k)ʃən

extinctive
BR ɪk'stɪŋ(k)tɪv, ɛk'stɪŋ(k)tɪv
AM ɪk'stɪŋ(k)tɪv, ɛk'stɪŋ(k)tɪv

extinguish
BR ɪk'stɪŋgw|ɪʃ, ɛk'stɪŋgw|ɪʃ, -ɪʃɪz, -ɪʃɪŋ, -ɪʃt
AM ɪk'stɪŋgwɪʃ, ɛk'stɪŋgwɪʃ, -ɪz, -ɪŋ, -t

extinguishable
BR ɪk'stɪŋgwɪʃəbl, ɛk'stɪŋgwɪʃəbl
AM ɪk'stɪŋgwɪʃəbəl, ɛk'stɪŋgwɪʃəbəl

extinguisher
BR ɪk'stɪŋgwɪʃə(r), ɛk'stɪŋgwɪʃə(r), -z
AM ɪk'stɪŋgwɪʃər, ɛk'stɪŋgwɪʃər, -z

extinguishment
BR ɪk'stɪŋgwɪʃm(ə)nt, ɛk'stɪŋgwɪʃm(ə)nt
AM ɪk'stɪŋgwɪʃmənt, ɛk'stɪŋgwɪʃmənt

extirpate
BR 'ɛkstəpeɪt, -s, -ɪŋ, -ɪd
AM 'ɛkstərˌpeɪ|t, -ts, -dɪŋ, -dɪd

extirpation
BR ˌɛkstə'peɪʃn, -z
AM ˌɛkstər'peɪʃən, -z

extirpator
BR 'ɛkstəpeɪtə(r), -z
AM 'ɛkstərˌpeɪdər, -z

extol
BR ɪk'stəʊl, ɪk'stɒl, ɛk'stəʊl, ɛk'stɒl, -z, -ɪŋ, -d
AM ɪk'stoʊl, ɛk'stoʊl, -z, -ɪŋ, -d

extoller
BR ɪk'stəʊlə(r), ɪk'stɒlə(r), ɛk'stəʊlə(r), ɛk'stɒlə(r), -z
AM ɪk'stoʊlər, ɛk'stoʊlər, -z

extolment
BR ɪk'stəʊlm(ə)nt, ɪk'stɒlm(ə)nt, ɛk'stəʊlm(ə)nt, ɛk'stɒlm(ə)nt
AM ɪk'stoʊlmənt, ɛk'stoʊlmənt

Exton
BR 'ɛkst(ə)n
AM 'ɛkstən

extort
BR ɪk'stɔːt, ɛk'stɔːt, -s, -ɪŋ, -ɪd
AM ɪk'stɔ(ə)r|t, ɛk'stɔ(ə)r t, -ts, -dɪŋ, -dəd

extorter
BR ɪk'stɔːtə(r), ɛk'stɔːtə(r), -z
AM ɪk'stɔrdər, ɛk'stɔrdər, -z

extortion
BR ɪk'stɔːʃn, ɛk'stɔːʃn, -z
AM ɪk'stɔrʃən, ɛk'stɔrʃən, -z

extortionate
BR ɪk'stɔːʃn̩ət, ɪk'stɔːʃ(ə)nət, ɛk'stɔːʃn̩ət, ɛk'stɔːʃ(ə)nət
AM ɪk'stɔrʃ(ə)nət, ɛk'stɔrʃ(ə)nət

extortionately
BR ɪk'stɔːʃn̩ətli, ɪk'stɔːʃ(ə)nətli, ɛk'stɔːʃn̩ətli, ɛk'stɔːʃ(ə)nətli
AM ɪk'stɔrʃ(ə)nətli, ɛk'stɔrʃ(ə)nətli

extortioner
BR ɪk'stɔːʃn̩ə(r), ɛk'stɔːʃn̩ə(r), -z
AM ɪk'stɔrʃənər, ɛk'stɔrʃənər, -z

extortionist
BR ɪk'stɔːʃn̩ɪst, ɛk'stɔːʃn̩ɪst, -s
AM ɪk'stɔrʃənəst, ɛk'stɔrʃənəst, -s

extortive
BR ɪk'stɔːtɪv, ɛk'stɔːtɪv
AM ɪk'stɔrdɪv, ɛk'stɔrdɪv

extra
BR 'ɛkstrə(*r*), -z
AM 'ɛkstrə, -z

extracellular
BR ˌɛkstrə'sɛljʉlə(r)
AM ˌɛkstrə'sɛljələr

extracranial
BR ˌɛkstrə'kreɪnɪəl
AM ˌɛkstrə'kreɪniəl

extract[1]
noun
BR 'ɛkstrakt, -s
AM 'ɛkˌstræk(t), -s

extract[2]
verb
BR ɪk'strakt, ɛk'strakt, -s, -ɪŋ, -ɪd
AM ɪk'stræk|(t), ɛk'stræk|(t), -(t)s, -tɪŋ, -təd

extractability
BR ɪkˌstraktə'bɪlɪti, ɛkˌstraktə'bɪlɪti
AM ɪkˌstræktə'bɪlɪdi, ɛkˌstræktə'bɪlɪdi

extractable
BR ɪk'straktəbl, ɛk'straktəbl
AM ɪk'stræktəbəl, ɛk'stræktəbəl

extraction
BR ɪk'strakʃn, ɛk'strakʃn
AM ɪk'strækʃən, ɛk'strækʃən

extractive
BR ɪk'straktɪv, ɛk'straktɪv

AM ɪk'stræktɪv, ɛk'stræktɪv

extractor
BR ɪk'straktə(r), ɛk'straktə(r), -z
AM ɪk'stræktər, ɛk'stræktər, -z

extracurricular
BR ˌɛkstrəkə'rɪkjʊlə(r)
AM ¦ɛkstrəkə'rɪkjələr

extraditable
BR 'ɛkstrədʌɪtəbl, ˌɛkstrə'dʌɪtəbl
AM 'ɛkstrəˌdaɪdəbəl, ˌɛkstrə'daɪdəbəl

extradite
BR 'ɛkstrədʌɪt, -s, -ɪŋ, -ɪd
AM 'ɛkstrəˌdaɪ|t, -ts, -dɪŋ, -dɪd

extradition
BR ˌɛkstrə'dɪʃn, -z
AM ˌɛkstrə'dɪʃən, -z

extrados
BR ɛk'streɪdɒs, ɪk'streɪdɒs, -ɪz
AM 'ɛkstrəˌdɑs, ɛk'strɑˌdɑs, -əz

extragalactic
BR ˌɛkstrəgə'laktɪk
AM ¦ɛkstrəgə'læktɪk

extrajudicial
BR ˌɛkstrədʒuː'dɪʃl
AM ¦ɛkstrədʒu'dɪʃəl

extrajudicially
BR ˌɛkstrədʒuː'dɪʃl̩i, ˌɛkstrədʒuː'dɪʃəli
AM ˌɛkstrədʒu'dɪʃ(ə)li

extralinguistic
BR ˌɛkstrəlɪŋ'gwɪstɪk
AM ˌɛkstrəˌlɪŋ'gwɪstɪk

extramarital
BR ˌɛkstrə'marɪtl
AM ˌɛkstrə'mɛrədl

extramaritally
BR ˌɛkstrə'marɪtl̩i
AM ˌɛkstrə'mɛrədəli

extramundane
BR ˌɛkstrəmʌn'deɪn
AM ˌɛkstrəmən'deɪn

extramural
BR ˌɛkstrə'mjʊərəl, ˌɛkstrə'mjʊərl̩, ˌɛkstrə'mjɔːrəl, ˌɛkstrə'mjɔːrl̩
AM ˌɛkstrə'mjʊrəl, ˌɛkstrə'mjurəl

extramurally
BR ˌɛkstrə'mjʊərəli, ˌɛkstrə'mjʊərl̩i, ˌɛkstrə'mjɔːrəli, ˌɛkstrə'mjɔːrl̩i
AM ˌɛkstrə'mjʊrəli, ˌɛkstrə'mjurəli

extraneous
BR ɪk'streɪnɪəs, ɛk'streɪnɪəs
AM ɪk'streɪniəs, ɛk'streɪniəs

extraneously
BR ɪk'streɪnɪəsli, ɛk'streɪnɪəsli
AM ɪk'streɪniəsli, ɛk'streɪniəsli

extraneousness
BR ɪk'streɪnɪəsnəs, ɛk'streɪnɪəsnəs
AM ɪk'streɪniəsnəs, ɛk'streɪniəsnəs

extraordinarily
BR ɪk'strɔːdn̩(ə)rəli, ɛk'strɔːdn̩(ə)rəli, ˌɛkstrə'ɔːdn̩(ə)rəli
AM ɪk¦strɔrdn¦ɛrəli, ɛk¦strɔrdn¦ɛrəli

extraordinariness
BR ɪk'strɔːdn̩(ə)rɪnɪs, ɛk'strɔːdn̩(ə)rɪnɪs, ˌɛkstrə'ɔːdn̩(ə)rɪnɪs
AM ɪk'strɔrdnˌɛrinɪs, ɛk'strɔrdnˌɛrinɪs

extraordinary
BR ɪk'strɔːdn̩(ə)ri, ɛk'strɔːdn̩(ə)ri, ˌɛkstrə'ɔːdn̩(ə)ri
AM ɪk'strɔrdnˌɛri, ɛk'strɔrdnˌɛri

extraphysical
BR ˌɛkstrə'fɪzɪkl
AM ˌɛkstrə'fɪzɪkəl

extrapolate
BR ɪk'strapəleɪt, ɛk'strapəleɪt, -s, -ɪŋ, -ɪd
AM ɪk'stræpəˌleɪ|t, ɛk'stræpəˌleɪ|t, -ts, -dɪŋ, -dɪd

extrapolation
BR ɪkˌstrapə'leɪʃn, ɛkˌstrapə'leɪʃn
AM ɪkˌstræpə'leɪʃən, ɛkˌstræpə'leɪʃən

extrapolative
BR ɪk'strapələtɪv, ɛk'strapələtɪv
AM ɪk'stræpəˌleɪdɪv, ɛk'stræpəˌleɪdɪv

extrapolator
BR ɪk'strapəleɪtə(r), ɛk'strapəleɪtə(r), -z
AM ɪk'stræpəˌleɪdər, ɛk'stræpəˌleɪdər, -z

extrasensory
BR ˌɛkstrə'sɛns(ə)ri
AM ˌɛkstrə'sɛnsəri

extraterrestrial
BR ˌɛkstrətɪ'rɛstrɪəl
AM ˌɛkstrətə'rɛstriəl

extraterritorial
BR ˌɛkstrəˌtɛrɪ'tɔːrɪəl
AM ˌɛkstrəˌtɛrə'tɔriəl

extraterritoriality
BR ˌɛkstrəˌtɛrɪtɔːrɪ'alɪti
AM ˌɛkstrəˌtɛrəˌtɔri'ælədi

extravagance
BR ɪk'stravəg(ə)ns, ɛk'stravəg(ə)ns, -ɪz
AM ɪk'strævəgəns, ɛk'strævəgəns, -əz

extravagancy
BR ɪk'stravəg(ə)ns|i, ɛk'stravəg(ə)ns|i, -ɪz
AM ɪk'strævəgənsi, ɛk'strævəgənsi, -z

extravagant
BR ɪk'stravəg(ə)nt, ɛk'stravəg(ə)nt
AM ɪk'strævəgənt, ɛk'strævəgənt

extravagantly
BR ɪk'stravəg(ə)ntli, ɛk'stravəg(ə)ntli
AM ɪk'strævəgən(t)li, ɛk'strævəgən(t)li

extravaganza
BR ɪkˌstravə'ganzə(*r*), ɛkˌstravə'ganzə(*r*), -z
AM ɪkˌstrævə'gænzə, ɛkˌstrævə'gænzə, -z

extravasate
BR ɪk'stravəseɪt, ɛk'stravəseɪt, -s, -ɪŋ, -ɪd
AM ɪk'strævəˌseɪ|t, ɛk'strævəˌseɪ|t, -ts, -dɪŋ, -dɪd

extravasation
BR ɪkˌstravə'seɪʃn, ɛkˌstravə'seɪʃn
AM ɪkˌstrævə'seɪʃən, ɛkˌstrævə'seɪʃən

extravehicular
BR ˌɛkstrəvɪ'(h)ɪkjʊlə(r)
AM ˌɛkstrəvə'hɪkjələr, ˌɛkstrəvi'hɪkjələr

extraversion
BR ˌɛkstrə'vəːʃn
AM ¦ɛkstrə¦vərʒən

extravert
BR 'ɛkstrəvəːt, -s
AM 'ɛkstrəˌvərt, -s

extrema
BR ɪk'striːmə(*r*), ɛk'striːmə(*r*)
AM ɪk'strimə, ɛk'strimə

extremal
BR ɪk'striːml, ɛk'striːml
AM ɪk'striməl, ɛk'striməl

extreme
BR ɪk'striːm, ɛk'striːm, -z
AM ɪk'strim, ɛk'strim, -z

extremely
BR ɪk'striːmli, ɛk'striːmli
AM ɪk'strimli, ɛk'strimli

extremeness
BR ɪk'striːmnɪs, ɛk'striːmnɪs
AM ɪk'strimnɪs, ɛk'strimnɪs

extremis
BR ɪk'striːmɪs, ɛk'striːmɪs
AM ɪk'strimɪs, ɛk'strimɪs

extremism
BR ɪk'striːmɪz(ə)m, ɛk'striːmɪz(ə)m
AM ɪk'striˌmɪzəm, ɛk'striˌmɪzəm

extremist
BR ɪk'striːmɪst, ɛk'striːmɪst, -s
AM ɪk'strimɪst, ɛk'strimɪst, -s

extremity
BR ɪk'strɛmɪt|i, ɛk'strɛmɪt|i, -ɪz
AM ɪk'strɛmədi, ɛk'strɛmədi, -z

extremum
BR ɪk'striːməm, ɛk'striːməm, -z
AM ɪk'striməm, ɛk'striməm, -z

extricable
BR ɪk'strɪkəbl, ɛkˌstrɪkəbl, 'ɛkstrɪkəbl
AM ɪk'strɪkəbəl, ɛk'strɪkəbəl, 'ɛkstrɪkəbəl

extricate
BR 'ɛkstrɪkeɪt, -s, -ɪŋ, -ɪd
AM 'ɛkstrəˌkeɪ|t, -ts, -dɪŋ, -dɪd

extrication
BR ˌɛkstrɪ'keɪʃn
AM ˌɛkstrə'keɪʃən

extrinsic
BR ɛk'strɪnsɪk, ɪk'strɪnsɪk, ɛk'strɪnzɪk, ɪk'strɪnzɪk
AM ɪk'strɪnzɪk, ɛk'strɪnzɪk, ɛk'strɪnsɪk, ɪk'strɪnsɪk

extrinsically
BR ɛk'strɪnsɪkli, ɪk'strɪnsɪkli, ɛk'strɪnzɪkli, ɪk'strɪnzɪkli
AM ɪk'strɪnzək(ə)li, ɛk'strɪnzək(ə)li, ɛk'strɪnsək(ə)li, ɪk'strɪnsək(ə)li

extroversion
BR ˌɛkstrə'vəːʃn
AM ¦ɛkstrə¦vərʒən, ¦ɛkstroʊ¦vərʒən

extrovert
BR 'ɛkstrəvəːt, -s
AM 'ɛkstrəˌvərt, -s

extroverted
BR 'ɛkstrəvəːtɨd
AM 'ɛkstrəˌvərdəd

extrude
BR ɨk'struːd, ɛk'struːd, -z, -ɪŋ, -ɨd
AM ɪk'strud, ɛk'strud, -z, -ɪŋ, -əd

extrusile
BR ɨk'struːsʌɪl, ɛk'struːsʌɪl
AM ɪk'strusəl, ɛk'strusəl, ɪk'struˌsaɪl, ɛk'struˌsaɪl

extrusion
BR ɨk'struːʒn, ɛk'struːʒn
AM ɪk'struʒn, ɛk'struʒən

extrusive
BR ɨk'struːsɪv, ɛk'struːsɪv
AM ɪk'strusɪv, ɛk'strusɪv

exuberance
BR ɨg'z(j)uːb(ə)rəns, ɛg'z(j)uːb(ə)rəns, ɨg'z(j)uːb(ə)rn̩s, ɛg'z(j)uːb(ə)rn̩s
AM ɪg'zub(ə)rəns, ɛg'zub(ə)rəns

exuberant
BR ɨg'z(j)uːb(ə)rənt, ɛg'z(j)uːb(ə)rənt, ɨg'z(j)uːb(ə)rn̩t, ɛg'z(j)uːb(ə)rn̩t
AM ɪg'zub(ə)rənt, ɛg'zub(ə)rənt

exuberantly
BR ɨg'z(j)uːb(ə)rəntli, ɛg'z(j)uːb(ə)rəntli, ɨg'z(j)uːb(ə)rn̩tli, ɛg'z(j)uːb(ə)rn̩tli
AM ɪg'zub(ə)rən(t)li, ɛg'zub(ə)rən(t)li

exuberate
BR ɨg'z(j)uːbəreɪt, ɛg'z(j)uːbəreɪt, -s, -ɪŋ, -ɨd
AM ɪg'zubəˌreɪ|t, ɛg'zubəˌreɪ|t, -ts, -dɪŋ, -dɨd

exudate
BR 'ɛksjʉdeɪt, 'ɛgzjʉdeɪt, -s, -ɪŋ, -ɨd
AM 'ɛksəˌdeɪ|t, 'ɛksjuˌdeɪ|t, -ts, -dɪŋ, -dɨd

exudation
BR ˌɛksjʉ'deɪʃn, ˌɛgzjʉ'deɪʃn
AM ˌɛksə'deɪʃən, ˌɛksju'deɪʃən

exudative
BR 'ɛksjʉdeɪtɪv, 'ɛgzjʉdeɪtɪv
AM 'ɛksəˌdeɪdɪv, 'ɛksjuˌdeɪdɪv

exude
BR ɨg'zjuːd, ɛg'zjuːd, -z, -ɪŋ, -ɨd
AM ɪg'zud, ɛg'zud, -z, -ɪŋ, -əd

exult
BR ɨg'zʌlt, ɛg'zʌlt, -s, -ɪŋ, -ɨd
AM ɪg'zəlt, ɛg'zəlt, -s, -ɪŋ, -əd

exultancy
BR ɨg'zʌlt(ə)nsi, ɛg'zʌlt(ə)nsi
AM ɪg'zəltnsi, ɛg'zəltnsi

exultant
BR ɨg'zʌlt(ə)nt, ɛg'zʌlt(ə)nt
AM ɪg'zəltnt, ɛg'zəltnt

exultantly
BR ɨg'zʌlt(ə)ntli, ɛg'zʌlt(ə)ntli
AM ɪg'zəltn(t)li, ɛg'zəltn(t)li

exultation
BR ˌɛgz(ʌ)l'teɪʃn, ˌɛks(ʌ)l'teɪʃn
AM ˌɛksəl'teɪʃən, ˌɛgzəl'teɪʃən

exultingly
BR ɨg'zʌltɪŋli, ɛg'zʌltɪŋli
AM ɪg'zəltɪŋli, ɛg'zəltɪŋli

exurb
BR 'ɛksəːb, -z
AM 'ɛksərb, 'ɛgzərb, -z

exurban
BR (ˌ)ɛks'əːb(ə)n
AM ɛk'sərbən, ɛg'zərbən

exurbanite
BR (ˌ)ɛks'əːbənʌɪt, -s
AM ɛk'sərbəˌnaɪt, ɛg'zərbəˌnaɪt, -s

exurbia
BR (ˌ)ɛks'əːbɪə(*r*)
AM ɛk'sərbiə, ɛg'zərbiə

exuviae
BR ɨg'zjuːvɪiː, ɛg'zjuːvɪiː, ɨg'zjuːvɪʌɪ, ɛg'zjuːvɪʌɪ
AM ɪg'zuviˌi, ɛg'zuviˌi, ɪg'zuviˌaɪ, ɛg'zuviˌaɪ

exuvial
BR ɨg'zjuːvɪəl, ɛg'zjuːvɪəl
AM ɪg'zuviəl, ɛg'zuviəl

exuviate
BR ɨg'zjuːvɪeɪt, ɛg'zjuːvɪeɪt, -s, -ɪŋ, -ɨd
AM ɪg'zuviˌeɪ|t, ɛg'zuviˌeɪ|t, -ts, -dɪŋ, -dɨd

exuviation
BR ɨgˌzjuːvɪ'eɪʃn, ɛgˌzjuːvɪ'eɪʃn
AM ɪgˌzuvi'eɪʃən, ɛgˌzuvi'eɪʃən

ex voto
BR ˌɛks 'vəʊtəʊ, -z
AM ˌɛks 'voʊdoʊ, -z

Exxon®
BR 'ɛksɒn
AM 'ɛkˌsɑn

Eyam
BR iːm
AM im

eyas
BR 'ʌɪəs, -ɨz
AM 'aɪəs, -əz

eye
BR ʌɪ, -z, -ɪŋ, -d
AM aɪ, -z, -ɪŋ, -d

eyeball
BR 'ʌɪbɔːl, -z, -ɪŋ, -d
AM 'aɪˌbɔl, 'aɪˌbɑl, -z, -ɪŋ, -d

eyebath
BR 'ʌɪ|bɑːθ, 'ʌɪ|baθ, -bɑːðz\-bɑːθs\-baθs
AM 'aɪˌbæθ, -s, -ðz

eyeblack
BR 'ʌɪblak
AM 'aɪˌblæk

eyebright
BR 'ʌɪbrʌɪt
AM 'aɪˌbraɪt

eyebrow
BR 'ʌɪbraʊ, -z
AM 'aɪˌbraʊ, -z

eyedropper
BR 'ʌɪˌdrɒpə(r), -z
AM 'aɪˌdrɑpər, -z

eyeful
BR 'ʌɪfʊl, -z
AM 'aɪˌfʊl, -z

eyeglass
BR 'ʌɪglɑːs, 'ʌɪglas, -ɨz
AM 'aɪˌglæs, -əz

eyehole
BR 'ʌɪhəʊl, -z
AM 'aɪˌ(h)oʊl, -z

eyelash
BR 'ʌɪlaʃ, -ɨz
AM 'aɪˌlæʃ, -əz

eyeless
BR 'ʌɪlɨs
AM 'aɪlɨs

eyelet
BR 'ʌɪlɨt, -s
AM 'aɪlət, -s

eyelevel
BR 'ʌɪˌlɛvl
AM 'aɪˌlɛvəl

eyelid
BR 'ʌɪlɪd, -z
AM 'aɪˌlɪd, -z

eyeliner
BR 'ʌɪˌlʌɪnə(r), -z
AM 'aɪˌlaɪnər, -z

eyepatch
BR 'ʌɪpatʃ, -ɨz
AM 'aɪˌpætʃ, -əz

eyepiece
BR 'ʌɪpiːs, -ɨz
AM 'aɪˌpis, -ɨz

eyeshade
BR 'ʌɪʃeɪd, -z
AM 'aɪˌʃeɪd, -z

eyeshadow
BR 'ʌɪˌʃadəʊ, -z
AM 'aɪˌʃædoʊ, -z

eyeshot
BR 'ʌɪʃɒt
AM 'aɪˌʃɑt

eyesight
BR 'ʌɪsʌɪt
AM 'aɪˌsaɪt

eyesore
BR 'ʌɪsɔː(r), -z
AM 'aɪˌsɔ(ə)r, -z

eyess
BR 'ʌɪəs, -ɨz
AM 'aɪəs, -əz

eyestrain
BR 'ʌɪstreɪn
AM 'aɪˌstreɪn

eyeteeth
BR 'ʌɪtiːθ, ˌʌɪ'tiːθ
AM 'aɪˌtiθ

Eyetie
BR 'ʌɪtʌɪ, -z
AM 'aɪˌtaɪ, -z

eyetooth
BR 'ʌɪtuːθ, ˌʌɪ'tuːθ
AM 'aɪˌtuθ

eyewash
BR 'ʌɪwɒʃ
AM 'aɪˌwɔʃ, 'aɪˌwɑʃ

eyewitness
BR 'ʌɪˌwɪtnɨs, -ɨz
AM ˌaɪ'wɪtnəs, -əz

Eynon
BR 'ʌɪnən
AM 'aɪnən
WE 'eɪnɒn

Eynsford
BR 'eɪnzfəd
AM 'eɪnzfərd

Eynsham
BR 'eɪnʃ(ə)m
AM 'eɪnʃəm

eyot
BR eɪt, 'eɪət, -s
AM eɪt, 'eɪət, -s

eyra
BR 'eɪrə(*r*), -z
AM 'eɪrə, -z

Eyre
BR ɛː(r)
AM ɛ(ə)r

eyrie
BR 'ɪər|i, 'ʌɪr|i, 'ɛːr|i, -ɪz
AM 'aɪri, 'ɛri, 'iri, 'ɪri, -z

eyry
BR ˈɪər|i, ˈʌɪr|i, ˈɛːr|i, -ɪz
AM ˈaɪri, ˈɛri, ˈiri, ˈɪri, -z

Eysenck
BR ˈʌɪzɛŋk
AM ˈaɪzəŋk

Ezekiel
BR ɪˈziːkɪəl
AM əˈzikiəl, iˈzikiəl

Ezra
BR ˈɛzrə(*r*)
AM ˈɛzrə

Ff

f
BR ɛf, -s
AM ɛf, -s
FA
BR ˌɛf ˈeɪ
AM ˌɛf ˈeɪ
fa
BR fɑː(r)
AM fɑ
fab
BR fab
AM fæb
Fabergé
BR ˈfabəʒeɪ
AM ˌfæbərˈʒeɪ
Fabia
BR ˈfeɪbɪə(r)
AM ˈfeɪbiə
Fabian
BR ˈfeɪbɪən, -z
AM ˈfeɪbiən, -z
Fabianism
BR ˈfeɪbɪənɪz(ə)m
AM ˈfeɪbiəˌnɪzəm
Fabianist
BR ˈfeɪbɪənɪst, -s
AM ˈfeɪbiənəst, -s
Fabius
BR ˈfeɪbɪəs
AM ˈfeɪbiəs
fable
BR ˈfeɪbl, -z, -d
AM ˈfeɪbəl, -z, -d
fabler
BR ˈfeɪblə(r), -z
AM ˈfeɪb(ə)lər, -z
fabliau
BR ˈfablɪəʊ, -z
AM ˈfæblioʊ, -z
Fablon®
BR ˈfablɒn
AM ˈfæblən
fabric
BR ˈfabrɪk, -s
AM ˈfæbrɪk, -s
fabricate
BR ˈfabrɪkeɪt, -s, -ɪŋ, -ɪd
AM ˈfæbrəˌkeɪ|t, -ts, -dɪŋ, -dɪd
fabrication
BR ˌfabrɪˈkeɪʃn, -z
AM ˌfæbrəˈkeɪʃən, -z
fabricator
BR ˈfabrɪkeɪtə(r), -z
AM ˈfæbrəˌkeɪdər, -z
fabulist
BR ˈfabjʊlɪst, -s
AM ˈfæbjələst, -s
fabulosity
BR ˌfabjʊˈlɒsɪti
AM ˌfæbjəˈlɑsədi
fabulous
BR ˈfabjʊləs
AM ˈfæbjələs
fabulously
BR ˈfabjʊləsli
AM ˈfæbjələsli
fabulousness
BR ˈfabjʊləsnəs
AM ˈfæbjələsnəs
facade
BR fəˈsɑːd, -z
AM fəˈsɑd, -z
façade
BR fəˈsɑːd, -z
AM fəˈsɑd, -z
face
BR feɪs, -ɪz, -ɪŋ, -t
AM feɪs, -ɪz, -ɪŋ, -t
facecloth
BR ˈfeɪsklɒ|θ, -θs\-ðz
AM ˈfeɪsˌklɔ|θ, ˈfeɪsˌklɑ|θ, -θs\-ðz
faceless
BR ˈfeɪslɪs
AM ˈfeɪslɪs
facelessly
BR ˈfeɪslɪsli
AM ˈfeɪslɪsli
facelessness
BR ˈfeɪslɪsnɪs
AM ˈfeɪslɪsnɪs
facelift
BR ˈfeɪslɪf|t, -(t)s
AM ˈfeɪsˌlɪft, -s
facemask
BR ˈfeɪsmɑːsk, ˈfeɪsmask, -s
AM ˈfeɪsˌmæsk, -s
faceplate
BR ˈfeɪspleɪt, -s
AM ˈfeɪsˌpleɪt, -s
facer
BR ˈfeɪsə(r), -z
AM ˈfeɪsər, -z
facet
BR ˈfasɪt, ˈfasɛt, -s
AM ˈfæsət, -s
faceted
BR ˈfasɪtɪd
AM ˈfæsədəd
facetiae
BR fəˈsiːʃɪiː
AM fəˈsiʃiˌi, fəˈsiʃiˌaɪ
facetious
BR fəˈsiːʃəs
AM fəˈsiʃəs
facetiously
BR fəˈsiːʃəsli
AM fəˈsiʃəsli
facetiousness
BR fəˈsiːʃəsnəs
AM fəˈsiʃəsnəs
facetted
BR ˈfasɪtɪd
AM ˈfæsədəd
faceworker
BR ˈfeɪsˌwəːkə(r), -z
AM ˈfeɪsˌwərkər, -z
facia
BR ˈfeɪʃə(r), -z
AM ˈfæʃ(i)ə, ˈfeɪʃ(i)ə, -z
facial
BR ˈfeɪʃl
AM ˈfeɪʃəl
facially
BR ˈfeɪʃl̩i, ˈfeɪʃəli
AM ˈfeɪʃəli
facies
BR ˈfeɪʃɪiːz
AM ˈfeɪʃiz, ˈfeɪʃiˌiz
facile
BR ˈfasʌɪl
AM ˈfæsəl
facilely
BR ˈfasʌɪl(l)i
AM ˈfæsə(l)li
facileness
BR ˈfasʌɪlnɪs
AM ˈfæsəlnəs
facilitate
BR fəˈsɪlɪteɪt, -s, -ɪŋ, -ɪd
AM fəˈsɪləˌteɪ|t, -ts, -dɪŋ, -dɪd
facilitation
BR fəˌsɪlɪˈteɪʃn
AM fəˌsɪləˈteɪʃən
facilitative
BR fəˌsɪlɪtətɪv
AM fəˈsɪləˌteɪdɪv
facilitator
BR fəˈsɪlɪteɪtə(r), -z
AM fəˈsɪləˌteɪdər, -z
facility
BR fəˈsɪlɪt|i, -ɪz
AM fəˈsɪlɪdi, -z
facing
BR ˈfeɪsɪŋ, -z
AM ˈfeɪsɪŋ, -z
facsimile
BR fakˈsɪmɪl|i, fakˈsɪml̩|i, -ɪz
AM fækˈsɪməli, -z
fact
BR fakt, -s
AM fæk|(t), -(t)s
facta
BR ˈfaktə(r)
AM ˈfæktə
fact-finding
BR ˈfak(t)ˌfʌɪndɪŋ
AM ˈfæk(t)ˌfaɪndɪŋ
factice
BR ˈfaktɪs
AM ˈfæktəs
faction
BR ˈfakʃn, -z
AM ˈfækʃən, -z
factional
BR ˈfakʃn̩(ə)l, ˈfakʃən(ə)l
AM ˈfækʃ(ə)nəl
factionalise
BR ˈfakʃn̩əlʌɪz, ˈfakʃn̩l̩ʌɪz, ˈfakʃənl̩ʌɪz, ˈfakʃ(ə)nəlʌɪz, -ɪz, -ɪŋ, -d
AM ˈfækʃ(ə)nəˌlaɪz, -ɪz, -ɪŋ, -d
factionalism
BR ˈfakʃn̩əlɪz(ə)m, ˈfakʃn̩l̩ɪz(ə)m, ˈfakʃənl̩ɪz(ə)m, ˈfakʃ(ə)nəlɪz(ə)m
AM ˈfækʃənlˌɪzəm, ˈfækʃnəˌlɪzəm
factionalize
BR ˈfakʃn̩əlʌɪz, ˈfakʃn̩l̩ʌɪz, ˈfakʃənlˌʌɪz, ˈfakʃ(ə)nəlʌɪz, -ɪz, -ɪŋ, -d
AM ˈfækʃ(ə)nəˌlaɪz, -ɪz, -ɪŋ, -d
factionally
BR ˈfakʃn̩əli, ˈfakʃn̩l̩i, ˈfakʃənl̩i, ˈfakʃ(ə)nəli
AM ˈfækʃ(ə)nəli
factious
BR ˈfakʃəs
AM ˈfækʃəs
factiously
BR ˈfakʃəsli
AM ˈfækʃəsli
factiousness
BR ˈfakʃəsnəs
AM ˈfækʃəsnəs
factitious
BR fakˈtɪʃəs
AM fækˈtɪʃəs
factitiously
BR fakˈtɪʃəsli
AM fækˈtɪʃəsli
factitiousness
BR fakˈtɪʃəsnəs
AM fækˈtɪʃəsnəs
factitive
BR ˈfaktɪtɪv
AM ˈfæktəˌtɪv
facto
BR ˈfaktəʊ
AM ˈfæktoʊ
factoid
BR ˈfaktɔɪd, -z
AM ˈfækˌtɔɪd, -z
factor
BR ˈfaktə(r), -z
AM ˈfæktər, ˈfæktɔ(ə)r, -z
factorable
BR ˈfakt(ə)rəbl
AM ˈfæktərəbəl
factorage
BR ˈfakt(ə)r|ɪdʒ, -ɪdʒɪz
AM ˈfæktərɪdʒ, -ɪz
factorial
BR fakˈtɔːrɪəl, -z
AM fækˈtɔriəl, -z
factorially
BR fakˈtɔːrɪəli
AM fækˈtɔriəli

factorisation
BR ˌfakt(ə)rʌɪˈzeɪʃn
AM ˌfæktərəˈzeɪʃən, ˌfæktəˌraɪˈzeɪʃən

factorise
BR ˈfaktərʌɪz, -ɪz, -ɪŋ, -d
AM ˈfæktəˌraɪz, -ɪz, -ɪŋ, -d

factorization
BR ˌfakt(ə)rʌɪˈzeɪʃn
AM ˌfæktərəˈzeɪʃən, ˌfæktəˌraɪˈzeɪʃən

factorize
BR ˈfaktərʌɪz, -ɪz, -ɪŋ, -d
AM ˈfæktəˌraɪz, -ɪz, -ɪŋ, -d

factory
BR ˈfakt(ə)r|i, -ɪz
AM ˈfækt(ə)ri, -z

factotum
BR fakˈtəʊtəm, -z
AM fækˈtoʊdəm, -z

factual
BR ˈfaktʃʊəl, ˈfaktʃ(ʉ)l, ˈfaktjʊəl, ˈfaktjʉl
AM ˈfæk(t)ʃ(əw)əl

factualism
BR ˈfaktʃʊəlɪz(ə)m, ˈfaktʃʉlɪz(ə)m, ˈfaktʃlɪz(ə)m
AM ˈfæk(t)ʃ(əw)əˌlɪzəm

factualist
BR ˈfaktʃʊəlɪst, ˈfaktʃʉlɪst, ˈfaktʃlɪst, -s
AM ˈfæk(t)ʃ(əw)ələst, -s

factuality
BR ˌfaktʃʊˈalɪti, ˌfaktjʊˈalɪti
AM ˌfæk(t)ʃəˈwælədi

factually
BR ˈfaktʃʊəli, ˈfaktʃʉli, ˈfaktʃli
AM ˈfæk(t)ʃ(əw)əli

factualness
BR ˈfaktʃʊəlnəs, ˈfaktʃ(ʉ)lnəs
AM ˈfæk(t)ʃ(əw)əlnəs

factum
BR ˈfaktəm, -z
AM ˈfæktəm, -z

facture
BR ˈfaktʃə(r), -z
AM ˈfæk(t)ʃər, -z

facula
BR ˈfakjʉlə(*r*)
AM ˈfækjələ

facular
BR ˈfakjʉlə(r)
AM ˈfækjələr

faculous
BR ˈfakjʉləs
AM ˈfækjələs

facultative
BR ˈfakltətɪv
AM ˈfækəlˌteɪdɪv

facultatively
BR ˈfakltətɪvli
AM ˈfækəlˌteɪdɪvli

faculty
BR ˈfaklt|i, -ɪz
AM ˈfækəlti, ˈfækəldi, -z

fad
BR fad, -z
AM fæd, -z

faddily
BR ˈfadɪli
AM ˈfædəli

faddiness
BR ˈfadɪnɪs
AM ˈfædinɪs

faddish
BR ˈfadɪʃ
AM ˈfædɪʃ

faddishly
BR ˈfadɪʃli
AM ˈfædɪʃli

faddishness
BR ˈfadɪʃnɪs
AM ˈfædɪʃnɪs

faddism
BR ˈfadɪz(ə)m
AM ˈfæˌdɪzəm

faddist
BR ˈfadɪst, -s
AM ˈfædəst, -s

faddy
BR ˈfadi
AM ˈfædi

fade
BR feɪd, -z, -ɪŋ, -ɪd
AM feɪd, -z, -ɪŋ, -ɪd

fadeaway
BR ˈfeɪdəweɪ
AM ˈfeɪdəˌweɪ

fadeless
BR ˈfeɪdlɪs
AM ˈfeɪdlɪs

fader
BR ˈfeɪdə(r), -z
AM ˈfeɪdər, -z

fadge
BR fadʒ, -ɪz
AM fædʒ, -əz

faecal
BR ˈfiːkl
AM ˈfikəl

faeces
BR ˈfiːsiːz
AM ˈfisiz

Faenza
BR fɑːˈɛntsə(*r*)
AM fɑˈɛn(t)zə

faerie
BR ˈfɛːri
AM ˈfɛri

Faeroe Islands
BR ˈfɛːrəʊ ˌʌɪlən(d)z
AM ˈfɛroʊ ˈaɪlən(d)z

Faeroes
BR ˈfɛːrəʊz
AM ˈfɛroʊz

Faeroese
BR ˌfɛːrəʊˈiːz
AM ˌfɛrəˈwiz

faery
BR ˈfɛːri
AM ˈfɛri

faff
BR faf, -s, -ɪŋ, -t
AM fæf, -s, -ɪŋ, -t

fag
BR fag, -z, -ɪŋ, -d
AM fæg, -z, -ɪŋ, -d

Fagan
BR ˈfeɪg(ə)n
AM ˈfeɪgən

faggot
BR ˈfagət, -s, -ɪŋ, -ɪd
AM ˈfægə|t, -ts, -dɪŋ, -dəd

faggotry
BR ˈfagətri
AM ˈfægətri

faggoty
BR ˈfagəti
AM ˈfægədi

Fagin
BR ˈfeɪgɪn
AM ˈfeɪgɪn

fagot
BR ˈfagət, -s, -ɪŋ, -ɪd
AM ˈfægə|t, -ts, -dɪŋ, -dəd

fah
BR fɑː(*r*)
AM fɑ

Fahd
BR fɑːd
AM fɑd

Fahrenheit
BR ˈfarənhʌɪt, ˈfarn̩hʌɪt
AM ˈfɛrənˌ(h)aɪt

Fahy
BR ˈfɑːhi
AM ˈfeɪˌhi

faience
BR fʌɪˈɑːns, fʌɪˈɒ̃s
AM faɪˈɑns, feɪˈɑns

fail
BR feɪl, -z, -ɪŋ, -d
AM feɪl, -z, -ɪŋ, -d

failing
BR ˈfeɪlɪŋ, -z
AM ˈfeɪlɪŋ, -z

faille
BR feɪl
AM faɪl

failure
BR ˈfeɪljə(r), -z
AM ˈfeɪljər, -z

fain
BR feɪn
AM feɪn

fainéancy
BR ˈfeɪnɪəns|i, ˈfeɪneɪɒ̃s|i, -ɪz
AM ˈfeɪniənsi, -z

fainéant
BR ˈfeɪnɪənt, ˈfeɪneɪɒ̃, -s
AM ˈfeɪniənt, -s

faint
BR feɪnt, -s, -ɪŋ, -ɪd, -ə(r), -ɪst
AM feɪn|t, -ts, -(t)ɪŋ, -(t)ɪd, -(t)ər, -(t)ɪst

faintly
BR ˈfeɪntli
AM ˈfeɪn(t)li

faintness
BR ˈfeɪntnɪs
AM ˈfeɪn(t)nɪs

fair
BR fɛː(r)
AM fɛ(ə)r

Fairbairn
BR ˈfɛːbɛːn
AM ˈfɛrˌbɛrn

Fairbanks
BR ˈfɛːbaŋks
AM ˈfɛrˌbæŋks

Fairbourn
BR ˈfɛːbɔːn
AM ˈfɛrˌbɔ(ə)rn

Fairbourne
BR ˈfɛːbɔːn
AM ˈfɛrˌbɔ(ə)rn

Fairbrother
BR ˈfɛːˌbrʌðə(r)
AM ˈfɛrˌbrəðər

Fairchild
BR ˈfɛːtʃʌɪld
AM ˈfɛrˌtʃaɪld

Fairclough
BR ˈfɛːklʌf
AM ˈfɛrˌkləf

Fairfax
BR ˈfɛːfaks
AM ˈfɛrˌfæks

Fairford
BR ˈfɛːfəd
AM ˈfɛrfərd

fairground
BR ˈfɛːgraʊnd, -z
AM ˈfɛrˌgraʊnd, -z

Fairhaven
BR ˈfɛːˌheɪvn
AM ˈfɛrˌ(h)eɪvən

Fairhurst
BR ˈfɛːhəːst
AM ˈfɛrˌ(h)ərst

fairing
BR ˈfɛːrɪŋ, -z
AM ˈfɛrɪŋ, -z

fairish
BR ˈfɛːrɪʃ
AM ˈfɛrɪʃ

fairlead
BR ˈfɛːliːd, -z
AM ˈfɛrˌlid, -z

Fairley
BR ˈfɛːli
AM ˈfɛrli

Fairlie
BR ˈfɛːli
AM ˈfɛrli

fairly
BR ˈfɛːli
AM ˈfɛrli

fairness
BR ˈfɛːnəs
AM ˈfɛrnəs

Fairport
BR ˈfɛːpɔːt
AM ˈfɛrˌpɔ(ə)rt

fairway
BR ˈfɛːweɪ, -z
AM ˈfɛrˌweɪ, -z

fairy
BR ˈfɛːr|i, -ɪz
AM ˈfɛri, -z

fairyland
BR ˈfɛːrɪland, -z
AM ˈfɛriˌlænd, -z

Faisal
BR ˈfʌɪsl
AM ˈfaɪˈzɑl

Faisalabad
BR ˈfʌɪs(ə)ləbad, ˌfʌɪsl̩ˈəbad, ˈfʌɪs(ə)ləbɑːd, ˌfʌɪsl̩əbɑːd
AM ˌfaɪˈzɑləˌbɑd, ˌfaɪˈzɑləˌbæd

fait accompli
BR ˌfeɪt əˈkɒmpli, ˌfɛt +
AM ˌfɛt əkɑmˈpli, ˌfeɪt +

faith
BR feɪθ, -s
AM feɪθ, -s

faithful
BR ˈfeɪθf(ʊ)l
AM ˈfeɪθfəl

Faithfull
BR ˈfeɪθf(ʊ)l
AM ˈfeɪθfəl

faithfully
BR ˈfeɪθfʊli, ˈfeɪθfl̩i
AM ˈfeɪθfəli

faithfulness
BR ˈfeɪθf(ʊ)lnəs
AM ˈfeɪθfəlnəs

faithless
BR ˈfeɪθlɪs
AM ˈfeɪθlɪs

faithlessly
BR ˈfeɪθlɪsli
AM ˈfeɪθlɪsli

faithlessness
BR ˈfeɪθlɪsnɪs
AM ˈfeɪθlɪsnɪs

fake
BR feɪk, -s, -ɪŋ, -t
AM feɪk, -s, -ɪŋ, -t

Fakenham
BR ˈfeɪkənəm, ˈfeɪkn̩əm
AM ˈfeɪkənəm

faker
BR ˈfeɪkə(r), -z
AM ˈfeɪkər, -z

fakery
BR ˈfeɪk(ə)ri
AM ˈfeɪkəri

fakir
BR ˈfeɪkɪə(r), ˈfakɪə(r), fəˈkɪə(r), -z
AM fəˈkɪ(ə)r, -z

falafel
BR fəˈlɑːfl
AM fəˈlɑfəl

Falange
BR fəˈlan(d)ʒ
AM fəˈlændʒ
SP faˈlaŋxe

Falangism
BR fəˈlan(d)ʒɪz(ə)m
AM fəˈlænˌdʒɪzəm, feɪˈlænˌdʒɪzəm

Falangist
BR fəˈlan(d)ʒɪst, -s
AM fəˈlændʒəst, feɪˈlændʒəst, -s

Falasha
BR fəˈlaʃə(r)
AM fəˈlɑʃə

falbala
BR ˈfalbələ(r)
AM ˈfælbələ

falcate
BR ˈfalkeɪt
AM ˈfælˌkeɪt, ˈfɔlˌkeɪt, ˈfælˌkeɪt, ˈfɑlˌkeɪt

falchion
BR ˈfɔːl(t)ʃ(ə)n, -z
AM ˈfɔl(t)ʃən, ˈfɑl(t)ʃən, -z

falciform
BR ˈfalsɪfɔːm
AM ˈfælsəˌfɔ(ə)rm

falcon
BR ˈfɔː(l)k(ə)n, ˈfɒlk(ə)n, ˈfalk(ə)n, -z
AM ˈfælkən, -z

falconer
BR ˈfɔː(l)kənə(r), ˈfɔː(l)kn̩ə(r), ˈfɒlkənə(r), ˈfɒlkn̩ə(r), ˈfalkənə(r), ˈfalkn̩ə(r), -z
AM ˈfælkənər, -z

falconet
BR ˈfɔː(l)kənɪt, ˈfɔː(l)kn̩ɪt, ˈfɔː(l)kənɪt, ˈfɔː(l)kn̩ɪt, ˈfɒlkənɪt, ˈfɒlkn̩ɪt, ˈfalkənɪt, ˈfalkn̩ɪt, -s
AM ˈfælkənət, -s

falconry
BR ˈfɔː(l)k(ə)nri, ˈfɒlk(ə)nri, ˈfalk(ə)nri
AM ˈfælkənri

falderal
BR ˈfaldəral, -z
AM ˈfɔldəˌrɔl, ˈfældəˌræl, ˈfɑldəˌrɑl, -z

Faldo
BR ˈfaldəʊ
AM ˈfɔldoʊ, ˈfɑldoʊ

faldstool
BR ˈfɔːl(d)stuːl, -z
AM ˈfɔl(d)ˌstul, ˈfɑl(d)ˌstul, -z

Falernian
BR fəˈləːnɪən
AM fəˈlərniən

Falk
BR fɔː(l)k
AM fɔk, fɑk

Falkender
BR ˈfɔːlk(ə)ndə(r)
AM ˈfɔlkəndər, ˈfɑlkəndər

Falkirk
BR ˈfɔːlkəːk, ˈfɒlkəːk
AM ˈfɔlˌkərk, ˈfɑlˌkərk

Falkland Islands
BR ˈfɔː(l)klənd ˌʌɪlən(d)z, ˈfɒlklənd +
AM ˈfɔklən(d) ˈaɪlən(d)z, ˈfɑklən(d) ˈaɪlən(d)z

Falklands
BR ˈfɔː(l)kləndz, ˈfɒlkləndz
AM ˈfɔklən(d)z, ˈfɑklən(d)z

fall
BR fɔːl, -z, -ɪŋ
AM fɔl, fɑl, -z, -ɪŋ

fallacious
BR fəˈleɪʃəs
AM fəˈleɪʃəs

fallaciously
BR fəˈleɪʃəsli
AM fəˈleɪʃəsli

fallaciousness
BR fəˈleɪʃəsnəs
AM fəˈleɪʃəsnəs

fallacy
BR ˈfaləs|i, -ɪz
AM ˈfæləsi, -z

fallback
BR ˈfɔːlbak, -s
AM ˈfɔlˌbæk, ˈfɑlˌbæk, -s

fallen
BR ˈfɔːlən
AM ˈfɔlən, ˈfɑlən

fallenness
BR ˈfɔːlənnəs
AM ˈfɔlə(n)nəs, ˈfɑlə(n)nəs

faller
BR ˈfɔːlə(r), -z
AM ˈfɔlər, ˈfɑlər, -z

fallibility
BR ˌfalɪˈbɪlɪti
AM ˌfæləˈbɪlɪdi

fallible
BR ˈfalɪbl
AM ˈfæləbəl

fallibleness
BR ˈfalɪblnəs
AM ˈfæləbəlnəs

fallibly
BR ˈfalɪbli
AM ˈfæləbli

Fallon
BR ˈfalən
AM ˈfælən

fallopian
BR fəˈləʊpɪən
AM fəˈloʊpiən

fallout
BR ˈfɔːlaʊt
AM ˈfɔlˌaʊt, ˈfɑlˌaʊt

fallow
BR ˈfaləʊ
AM ˈfæloʊ

Fallowfield
BR ˈfalə(ʊ)fiːld
AM ˈfæloʊˌfild

fallowness
BR ˈfaləʊnəs
AM ˈfæloʊnəs

Falmouth
BR ˈfalməθ
AM ˈfælməθ

false
BR fɔːls, fɒls, -ə(r), -ɪst
AM fɔls, fɑls, -ər, -əst

falsehood
BR ˈfɔːlshʊd, ˈfɒlshʊd, -z
AM ˈfɔlsˌ(h)ʊd, ˈfɑlsˌ(h)ʊd, -z

falsely
BR ˈfɔːlsli, ˈfɒlsli
AM ˈfɔlsli, ˈfɑlsli

falseness
BR ˈfɔːlsnəs, ˈfɒlsnəs
AM ˈfɔlsnəs, ˈfɑlsnəs

falsetto
BR ˌfɔːlˈsɛtəʊ, ˌfɒlˈsɛtəʊ, -z
AM fɔlˈsɛdoʊ, fɑlˈsɛdoʊ, -z

falsework
BR ˈfɔːlswəːk, ˈfɒlswəːk
AM ˈfɔlsˌwərk, ˈfɑlsˌwərk

falsies
BR ˈfɔːlsɪz, ˈfɒlsɪz
AM ˈfɔlsiz, ˈfɑlsiz

falsifiability
BR ˌfɔːlsɪfʌɪəˈbɪlɪti, ˌfɒlsɪfʌɪəˈbɪlɪti
AM ˌfɔlsəˌfaɪəˈbɪlɪdi, ˌfɑlsəˌfaɪəˈbɪlɪdi

falsifiable
BR ˈfɔːlsɪfʌɪəbl, ˈfɒlsɪfʌɪəbl
AM ˌfɔlsəˌfaɪəbəl, ˌfɑlsəˌfaɪəbəl

falsification
BR ˌfɔːlsɪfɪˈkeɪʃn, ˌfɒlsɪfɪˈkeɪʃn, -z

AM ˌfɔlsəfəˈkeɪʃən, ˌfɑlsəfəˈkeɪʃən, -z

falsify
BR ˈfɔːlsɪfʌɪ, ˈfɒlsɪfʌɪ, -z, -ɪŋ, -d
AM ˈfɔlsəˌfaɪ, ˈfɑlsəˌfaɪ, -z, -ɪŋ, -d

falsity
BR ˈfɔːlsɪti, ˈfɒlsɪti
AM ˈfɔlsədi, ˈfɑlsədi

Falstaff
BR ˈfɔːlstɑːf, ˈfɔːlstaf, ˈfɒlstɑːf, ˈfɒlstaf
AM ˈfɔlˌstæf, ˈfɑlˌstæf

Falstaffian
BR fɔːlˈstɑːfɪən, fɔːlˈstafɪən, fɒlˈstɑːfɪən, fɒlˈstafɪən
AM fɔlˈstæfiən, fɑlˈstæfiən

Falster
BR ˈfɔːlstə(r), ˈfɒlstə(r)
AM ˈfɔlstər, ˈfɑlstər

falter
BR ˈfɔːl|tə(r), ˈfɒlt|ə(r), -əz, -(ə)rɪŋ, -əd
AM ˈfɔlt|ər, ˈfɑlt|ər, -ərz, -(ə)rɪŋ, -ərd

falterer
BR ˈfɔːlt(ə)rə(r), ˈfɒlt(ə)rə(r), -z
AM ˈfɔltərər, ˈfɑltərər, -z

faltering
BR ˈfɔːlt(ə)rɪŋ, ˈfɒlt(ə)rɪŋ
AM ˈfɔlt(ə)rɪŋ, ˈfɑlt(ə)rɪŋ

falteringly
BR ˈfɔːlt(ə)rɪŋli, ˈfɒlt(ə)rɪŋli
AM ˈfɔlt(ə)rɪŋli, ˈfɑlt(ə)rɪŋli

Falwell
BR ˈfɔːlwɛl, ˈfɒlwɛl
AM ˈfɔlˌwɛl, ˈfɑlˌwɛl

Famagusta
BR ˌfaməˈgʊstə(*r*)
AM ˌfɑməˈgustə

fame
BR feɪm, -d
AM feɪm, -d

familial
BR fəˈmɪlɪəl
AM fəˈmɪljəl, fəˈmɪliəl

familiar
BR fəˈmɪlɪə(r)
AM fəˈmɪljər, fəˈmɪliər

familiarisation
BR fəˌmɪlɪərʌɪˈzeɪʃn
AM fəˌmɪljərəˈzeɪʃən, fəˌmɪljəˌraɪˈzeɪʃən

familiarise
BR fəˈmɪlɪərʌɪz, -ɪz, -ɪŋ, -d
AM fəˈmɪljəˌraɪz, -ɪz, -ɪŋ, -d

familiarity
BR fəˌmɪlɪˈarɪt|i, -ɪz
AM fəˌmɪliˈɛrədi, fəˌmɪlˈjɛrədi, -z

familiarization
BR fəˌmɪlɪərʌɪˈzeɪʃn
AM fəˌmɪljərəˈzeɪʃən, fəˌmɪljəˌraɪˈzeɪʃən

familiarize
BR fəˈmɪlɪərʌɪz, -ɪz, -ɪŋ, -d
AM fəˈmɪljəˌraɪz, -ɪz, -ɪŋ, -d

familiarly
BR fəˈmɪlɪəli
AM fəˈmɪljərli

famille jaune
BR fəˌmiː ˈʒɔːn
AM fəˌmi ˈʒoʊn

famille noire
BR fəˌmiː ˈnwɑː(r)
AM fəˌmi ˈnwɑr

famille rose
BR fəˌmiː ˈrəʊz
AM fəˌmi ˈroʊz

famille verte
BR fəˌmiː ˈvɛːt
AM fəˌmi ˈvɛr(t)

family
BR ˈfam(ɪ)l|i, ˈfamḷ|i, -ɪz
AM ˈfæm(ə)li, -z

famine
BR ˈfamɪn, -z
AM ˈfæmən, -z

famish
BR ˈfam|ɪʃ, -ɪʃɪz, -ɪʃɪŋ, -ɪʃt
AM ˈfæmɪʃ, -ɪz, -ɪŋ, -t

famous
BR ˈfeɪməs
AM ˈfeɪməs

famously
BR ˈfeɪməsli
AM ˈfeɪməsli

famousness
BR ˈfeɪməsnəs
AM ˈfeɪməsnəs

famuli
BR ˈfamjʉlʌɪ, ˈfamjʉliː
AM ˈfæmjəˌlaɪ

famulus
BR ˈfamjʉləs
AM ˈfæmjələs

fan
BR fan, -z, -ɪŋ, -d
AM fæn, -z, -ɪŋ, -d

Fanagalo
BR ˌfanəgəˈləʊ, ˈfanəgələʊ, ˈfanəgḷəʊ
AM ˌfænəgəˈloʊ

fanatic
BR fəˈnatɪk, -s
AM fəˈnædɪk, -s

fanatical
BR fəˈnatɪkl
AM fəˈnædəkəl

fanatically
BR fəˈnatɪkli
AM fəˈnædək(ə)li

fanaticise
BR fəˈnatɪsʌɪz, -ɪz, -ɪŋ, -d
AM fəˈnædəˌsaɪz, -ɪz, -ɪŋ, -d

fanaticism
BR fəˈnatɪsɪz(ə)m, -z
AM fəˈnædəˌsɪzəm, -z

fanaticize
BR fəˈnatɪsʌɪz, -ɪz, -ɪŋ, -d
AM fəˈnædəˌsaɪz, -ɪz, -ɪŋ, -d

fanbelt
BR ˈfanbɛlt, -s
AM ˈfænˌbɛlt, -s

fanciable
BR ˈfansɪəbl
AM ˈfænsiəbl

fancier
BR ˈfansɪə(r), -z
AM ˈfænsiər, -z

fanciful
BR ˈfansɪf(ʊ)l
AM ˈfænsɪfəl

fancifully
BR ˈfansɪfʊli, ˈfansɪfḷi
AM ˈfænsɪf(ə)li

fancifulness
BR ˈfansɪf(ʊ)lnəs
AM ˈfænsɪfəlnəs

fancily
BR ˈfansɪli
AM ˈfænsəli

fanciness
BR ˈfansɪnɪs
AM ˈfænsinɪs

fancy
BR ˈfans|i, -ɪz, -ɪɪŋ, -ɪd
AM ˈfænsi, -z, -ɪŋ, -d

fancywork
BR ˈfansɪwəːk
AM ˈfænsiˌwərk

fandangle
BR fanˈdaŋgl, -z
AM fænˈdæŋgəl, -z

fandango
BR fanˈdaŋgəʊ, -z
AM fænˈdæŋgoʊ, -z

fandom
BR ˈfandəm
AM ˈfændəm

fane
BR feɪn, -z
AM feɪn, -z

fanfare
BR ˈfanfɛː(r), -z
AM ˈfænˌfɛ(ə)r, -z

fanfaronade
BR ˌfanfarəˈneɪd, -z
AM ˌfænˌfɛrəˈneɪd, -z

fanfold
BR ˈfanfəʊld
AM ˈfænˌfoʊld

fang
BR faŋ, -z, -d
AM fæŋ, -z, -d

Fangio
BR ˈfan(d)ʒɪəʊ
AM ˈfɑndʒ(i)oʊ

fangless
BR ˈfaŋləs
AM ˈfæŋləs

fanlight
BR ˈfanlʌɪt, -s
AM ˈfænˌlaɪt, -s

fanlike
BR ˈfanlʌɪk
AM ˈfænˌlaɪk

fanner
BR ˈfanə(r), -z
AM ˈfænər, -z

Fannie
BR ˈfani
AM ˈfæni

fanny
BR ˈfan|i, -ɪz
AM ˈfæni, -z

Fanshawe
BR ˈfanʃɔː(*r*)
AM ˈfænˌsɔ

Fanta®
BR ˈfantə(*r*), -z
AM ˈfæn(t)ə, -z

fantail
BR ˈfanteɪl, -z, -d
AM ˈfænˌteɪl, -z, -d

fan-tan
BR ˈfantan
AM ˈfænˌtæn

fantasia
BR fanˈteɪzɪə(*r*), ˌfantəˈziːə(*r*), -z
AM fænˈteɪʒ(i)ə, fænˈteɪziə , -z

fantasise
BR ˈfantəsʌɪz, -ɪz, -ɪŋ, -d
AM ˈfæn(t)əˌsaɪz, -ɪz, -ɪŋ, -d

fantasist
BR ˈfantəsɪst, -s
AM ˈfæn(t)əsəst, -s

fantasize
BR ˈfantəsʌɪz, -ɪz, -ɪŋ, -d
AM ˈfæn(t)əˌsaɪz, -ɪz, -ɪŋ, -d

fantasmatic
BR ˌfantəzˈmatɪk
AM ˌfæn(t)əzˈmædɪk, ˌfænˌtæzˈmædɪk

fantast
BR ˈfantast, -s
AM ˈfænˌtæst, -s

fantastic
BR fanˈtastɪk
AM fænˈtæstɪk

fantastical
BR fanˈtastɪkl
AM fænˈtæstəkəl

fantasticality
BR fanˌtastɪˈkalɪti

AM fæn,tæstə'kælədi

fantastically
BR fan'tastɪkli
AM fæn'tæstək(ə)li

fantasticate
BR fan'tastɪkeɪt, -s, -ɪŋ, -ɪd
AM fæn'tæstə,keɪ|t, -ts, -dɪŋ, -dɪd

fantastication
BR fan,tastɪ'keɪʃn
AM fæn,tæstə'keɪʃən

fantasticism
BR fan'tastɪsɪz(ə)m
AM fæn'tæstə,sɪzəm

fantasy
BR 'fantəs|i, -ɪz
AM 'fæn(t)əsi, -z

Fante
BR 'fanti, -ɪz
AM 'fɑnti, -z

Fanti
BR 'fanti, -ɪz
AM 'fɑnti, -z

fantod
BR 'fantɒd, -z
AM 'fæn,tɑd, -z

Fanum
BR 'feɪnəm
AM 'feɪnəm

fanzine
BR 'fanziːn, -z
AM 'fæn,zin, -z

faquir
BR 'feɪkɪə(r), 'fakɪə(r), fə'kɪə(r), -z
AM fə'kɪ(ə)r, -z

far
BR fɑː(r)
AM fɑr

Fara
BR 'farə(r)
AM 'fɛrə

farad
BR 'farad, 'farəd, -z
AM 'fɛr,æd, -z

faradaic
BR ,farə'deɪɪk
AM ,fɛrə'deɪɪk

faraday
BR 'farədeɪ, -z
AM 'fɛrə,deɪ, -z

faradic
BR fə'radɪk
AM fə'rædɪk

Farah
BR 'farə(r)
AM 'fɛrə

farandole
BR 'farəndəʊl, 'farn̩dəʊl, -z
AM 'fɛrəndoʊl, -z

faraway
BR ,fɑːrə'weɪ
AM ¦fɑrə¦weɪ

farce
BR fɑːs, -ɪz
AM fɑrs, -əz

farceur
BR ,fɑː'səː(r), -z
AM fɑr'sər, -z

farcical
BR 'fɑːsɪkl
AM 'fɑrsəkəl

farcicality
BR ,fɑːsɪ'kalɪti
AM ,fɑrsə'kælədi

farcically
BR 'fɑːsɪkl̩i, 'fɑːsɪk(ə)li
AM 'fɑrsək(ə)li

farcy
BR 'fɑːsi
AM 'fɑrsi

farded
BR 'fɑːdɪd
AM 'fɑrdəd

fare
BR fɛː(r), -z, -ɪŋ, -d
AM fɛ(ə)r, -z, -ɪŋ, -d

Fareham
BR 'fɛːrəm
AM 'fɛrəm

farewell
BR ,fɛː'wɛl, -z
AM ,fɛr'wɛl, -z

farfalle
BR fɑː'falei, fɑː'fali
AM ,fɑr'fɑlə, 'fɑrfələ

farfetched
BR ,fɑː'fɛtʃt
AM ¦fɑr'fɛtʃt

farfetchedness
BR ,fɑː'fɛtʃtnəs, ,fɑː'fɛtʃɪdnɪs
AM ¦fɑr'fɛtʃ(t)nəs, ¦fɑr'fɛtʃədnəs

Fargo
BR 'fɑːgəʊ
AM 'fɑrgoʊ

Faridabad
BR fə'riːdəbad, fə'riːdəbɑːd
AM fə'ridə,bɑd, fə'ridə,bæd

farina
BR fə'riːnə(r), fə'rʌɪnə(r)
AM fə'rinə

farinaceous
BR ,farɪ'neɪʃəs
AM ,fɛrə'neɪʃəs

Faringdon
BR 'farɪŋd(ə)n
AM 'fɛrɪŋdən

Farjeon
BR 'fɑːdʒ(ə)n
AM 'fɑrdʒən

farl
BR fɑːl, -z
AM 'fɑr(ə)l, -z

Farleigh
BR 'fɑːli
AM 'fɑrli

Farley
BR 'fɑːli
AM 'fɑrli

farm
BR fɑːm, -z, -ɪŋ, -d
AM fɑrm, -z, -ɪŋ, -d

farmable
BR 'fɑːməbl
AM 'fɑrməbəl

farmer
BR 'fɑːmə(r), -z
AM 'fɑrmər, -z

farmhand
BR 'fɑːmhand, -z
AM 'fɑrm,(h)ænd, -z

farmhouse
BR 'fɑːmhaʊ|s, -zɪz
AM 'fɑrm,(h)aʊ|s, -zəz

farmland
BR 'fɑːmland, -z
AM 'fɑrm,lænd, -z

farmstead
BR 'fɑːmstɛd, -z
AM 'fɑrm,stɛd, -z

farmwork
BR 'fɑːmwəːk
AM 'fɑrm,wərk

farmworker
BR 'fɑːm,wəːkə(r), -z
AM 'fɑrm,wərkər, -z

farmyard
BR 'fɑːmjɑːd, -z
AM 'fɑrm,jɑrd, -z

Farnborough
BR 'fɑːnb(ə)rə(r)
AM 'fɑrnb(ə)rə

Farne Islands
BR 'fɑːn ,ʌɪlən(d)z
AM 'fɑrn 'aɪlən(d)z

Farnese
BR fɑː'neɪzi
AM fɑr,neɪzi

farness
BR 'fɑːnəs
AM 'fɑrnəs

Farnham
BR 'fɑːnəm
AM 'fɑrnəm

Farnley
BR 'fɑːnli
AM 'fɑrnli

Farnworth
BR 'fɑːnwəːθ
AM 'fɑrn,wərθ

Faro
place in Portugal
BR 'fɑːrəʊ, 'fɛːrəʊ
AM 'fɛroʊ
PORT 'faru

faro
card-game
BR 'fɛːrəʊ
AM 'fɛroʊ

Faroe
BR 'fɛːrəʊ, -z
AM 'fɛroʊ, -z

Faroese
BR ,fɛːrəʊ'iːz
AM ¦fɛrə'wiz

far-off
BR ,fɑːr'ɒf
AM 'fɑ¦rɔf, 'fɑ¦rɑf

farouche
BR fə'ruːʃ
AM fə'ruʃ

Farouk
BR fə'ruːk
AM fə'ruk

Farquhar
BR 'fɑːk(w)ɑː(r)
AM 'fɑr,kwɑr

Farquharson
BR 'fɑːk(w)əs(ə)n
AM 'fɑrk(w)əsən, 'fɑrk,wɑrsən

Farr
BR fɑː(r)
AM fɑr

farraginous
BR fə'radʒɪnəs
AM fə'rædʒənəs

farrago
BR fə'rɑːgəʊ, -z
AM fə'rɑgoʊ, fə'reɪgoʊ, -z

Farrah
BR 'farə(r)
AM 'fɛrə

Farrar
BR 'farə(r)
AM fə'rɑr, 'fɛrər

Farrell
BR 'farəl, 'farl̩
AM 'fɛrəl

Farrelly
BR 'farəli, 'farl̩i
AM 'fɑr(ə)li

farrier
BR 'farɪə(r), -z
AM 'fɛriər, -z

farriery
BR 'farɪəri
AM 'fɛriəri, 'fɛrjəri

Farringdon
BR 'farɪŋd(ə)n
AM 'fɛrɪŋdən

Farris
BR 'farɪs
AM 'fɛrəs

farrow
BR 'farəʊ, -z, -ɪŋ, -d
AM 'fɛroʊ, -z, -ɪŋ, -d

farruca
BR fə'ruːkə(r), -z
AM fə'rukə, -z

far-seeing
BR ,fɑː'siːɪŋ
AM 'fɑr¦siɪŋ

Farsi
BR 'fɑːsiː, ,fɑː'si
AM 'fɑrsi

fart
BR fɑːt, -s, -ɪŋ, -ɪd

AM ˈfɑr|t, -ts, -dɪŋ, -dəd

farther
BR ˈfɑːðə(r)
AM ˈfɑrðər

farthest
BR ˈfɑːðɪst
AM ˈfɑrðəst

farthing
BR ˈfɑːðɪŋ
AM ˈfɑrðɪŋ

farthingale
BR ˈfɑːðɪŋgeɪl, -z
AM ˈfɑrðɪŋˌgeɪl, -z

fartlek
BR ˈfɑːtlɛk
AM ˈfɑrtlək

fasces
BR ˈfasiːz
AM ˈfæsiz

fascia[1]
BR ˈfeɪʃɪə(r), -z
AM ˈfæʃ(i)ə, ˈfeɪʃ(i)ə, -z

fascia[2]
architectural
BR ˈfeɪsɪə(r), -z
AM ˈfæʃ(i)ə, ˈfeɪʃ(i)ə, -z

fascia[3]
medical
BR ˈfaʃɪə(r), -z
AM ˈfæʃ(i)ə, -z

fascial
BR ˈfeɪʃl
AM ˈfæʃ(i)əl

fasciate
BR ˈfaʃɪeɪt, -s, -ɪŋ, -ɪd
AM ˈfæʃiˌeɪ|t, -ts, -dɪŋ, -dɪd

fasciation
BR ˌfaʃɪˈeɪʃn
AM ˌfæʃiˈeɪʃən

fascicle
BR ˈfasɪkl, -z, -d
AM ˈfæsəkəl, -z, -d

fascicular
BR fəˈsɪkjʊlə(r)
AM fəˈsɪkjələr

fasciculate
BR fəˈsɪkjʊleɪt, fəˈsɪkjʊlət
AM fəˈsɪkjəˌleɪt, fəˈsɪkjələt

fasciculation
BR fəˌsɪkjʊˈleɪʃn
AM fəˌsɪkjəˈleɪʃən

fascicule
BR ˈfasɪkjuːl, -z
AM ˈfæsəˌkjul, -z

fasciculi
BR fəˈsɪkjʊlʌɪ, fəˈsɪkjʊliː
AM fəˈsɪkjəˌlaɪ

fasciculus
BR fəˈsɪkjʊləs
AM fəˈsɪkjələs

fasciitis
BR ˌfasɪˈʌɪtɪs, ˌfaʃɪˈʌɪtɪs
AM ˌfæʃiˈaɪdɪs

fascinate
BR ˈfasɪneɪt, -s, -ɪŋ, -ɪd
AM ˈfæsəˌneɪ|t, -ts, -dɪŋ, -dɪd

fascinatingly
BR ˈfasɪneɪtɪŋli
AM ˈfæsəˌneɪdɪŋli

fascination
BR ˌfasɪˈneɪʃn, -z
AM ˌfæsəˈneɪʃən, -z

fascinator
BR ˈfasɪneɪtə(r), -z
AM ˈfæsəˌneɪdər, -z

fascine
BR faˈsiːn, -z
AM fəˈsin, -z

fascism
BR ˈfaʃɪz(ə)m
AM ˈfæˌʃɪzəm

fascist
BR ˈfaʃɪst, -s
AM ˈfæʃəst, -s

fascistic
BR fəˈʃɪstɪk
AM fæˈʃɪstɪk, fəˈʃɪstɪk

Fashanu
BR ˈfɑːʃənuː
AM ˈfæʃənu

fashion
BR ˈfaʃ|n, -nz, -n̩ɪŋ\-ənɪŋ, -nd
AM ˈfæʃ|ən, -ənz, -(ə)nɪŋ, -ənd

fashionability
BR ˌfaʃ(ə)nəˈbɪlɪti, ˌfaʃn̩əˈbɪlɪti
AM ˌfæʃ(ə)nəˈbɪlɪdi

fashionable
BR ˈfaʃ(ə)nəbl, ˈfaʃn̩əbl
AM ˈfæʃ(ə)nəbəl

fashionableness
BR ˈfaʃ(ə)nəblnəs, ˈfaʃn̩əblnəs
AM ˈfæʃ(ə)nəbəlnəs

fashionably
BR ˈfaʃ(ə)nəbli, ˈfaʃn̩əbli
AM ˈfæʃ(ə)nəbli

fashioner
BR ˈfaʃənə(r), ˈfaʃn̩ə(r), -z
AM ˈfæʃənər, -z

Fashoda
BR fəˈʃəʊdə(r)
AM fəˈʃoʊdə

Faslane
BR fazˈleɪn
AM fæzˈleɪn

Fassbinder
BR ˈfasbʌɪndə(r)
AM ˈfæsˌbaɪndər
GER ˈfasbɪndɐ

fast
BR fɑːst, fast, -s, -ɪŋ, -ɪd, -ə(r), -ɪst
AM fæst, -s, -ɪŋ, -əd, -ər, -əst

fastback
BR ˈfɑːs(t)bak, ˈfas(t)bak, -s
AM ˈfæs(t)ˌbæk, -s

fastball
BR ˈfɑːs(t)bɔːl, ˈfas(t)bɔːl
AM ˈfæs(t)ˌbɔl, ˈfæs(t)ˌbɑl

fasten
BR ˈfɑːs|n, ˈfas|n, -nz, -n̩ɪŋ\-nɪŋ, -nd
AM ˈfæsn, -z, -ɪŋ, -d

fastener
BR ˈfɑːsn̩ə(r), ˈfɑːsnə(r), ˈfasn̩ə(r), ˈfasnə(r), -z
AM ˈfæs(ə)nər, -z

fastening
BR ˈfɑːsn̩ɪŋ, ˈfɑːsnɪŋ, ˈfasn̩ɪŋ, ˈfasnɪŋ, -z
AM ˈfæs(ə)nɪŋ, -z

faster
BR ˈfɑːstə(r), ˈfastə(r), -z
AM ˈfæstər, -z

fastidious
BR faˈstɪdɪəs
AM fæˈstɪdiəs

fastidiously
BR faˈstɪdɪəsli
AM fæˈstɪdiəsli

fastidiousness
BR faˈstɪdɪəsnəs
AM fæˈstɪdiəsnəs

fastigiate
BR faˈstɪdʒɪət, faˈstɪdʒɪeɪt
AM fəˈstɪdʒiət

fasting
BR ˈfɑːstɪŋ, ˈfastɪŋ, -z
AM ˈfæstɪŋ, -z

fastness
BR ˈfɑːs(t)nəs, ˈfas(t)nəs, -ɪz
AM ˈfæs(t)nəs, -əz

Fastnet
BR ˈfɑːs(t)nɛt, ˈfɑːs(t)nɪt, ˈfas(t)nɛt, ˈfas(t)nɪt
AM ˈfæs(t)ˌnɛt

fat
BR fat, -ə(r), -ɪst
AM fæ|t, -dər, -dəst

Fatah, Al
BR ˌal fəˈtɑː(r), ˈfatə(r)
AM ˌɑl fəˈtɑ

fatal
BR ˈfeɪtl
AM ˈfeɪdl

fatalism
BR ˈfeɪtl̩ɪz(ə)m, ˈfeɪtəlɪz(ə)m
AM ˈfeɪdlˌɪzəm

fatalist
BR ˈfeɪtl̩ɪst, ˈfeɪtəlɪst, -s
AM ˈfeɪdlɪst, -s

fatalistic
BR ˌfeɪtlˈɪstɪk, ˌfeɪtəˈlɪstɪk
AM ˌfeɪdlˈɪstɪk

fatalistically
BR ˌfeɪtlˈɪstɪkli, ˌfeɪtəˈlɪstɪkli
AM ¦feɪdlˈɪstək(ə)li

fatality
BR fəˈtalɪt|i, -ɪz
AM feɪˈtælədi, fəˈtælədi, -z

fatally
BR ˈfeɪtl̩i, ˈfeɪtəli
AM ˈfeɪdl̩i

fatalness
BR ˈfeɪtlnəs
AM ˈfeɪdlnəs

Fata Morgana
BR ˌfɑːtə mɔːˈgɑːnə(r), ˌfatə mɔːˈganə(r)
AM ¦fɑdə ˌmɔrˈgɑnə

fatback
BR ˈfatbak, -s
AM ˈfætˌbæk, -s

fatcat
BR ˈfatkat, -s
AM ˈfætˌkæt, -s

fate
BR feɪt, -s, -ɪd
AM feɪ|t, -ts, -dɪd

fateful
BR ˈfeɪtf(ʊ)l
AM ˈfeɪtfəl

fatefully
BR ˈfeɪtfʊli, ˈfeɪtfl̩i
AM ˈfeɪtfəli

fatefulness
BR ˈfeɪtf(ʊ)lnəs
AM ˈfeɪtfəlnəs

Fates
BR feɪts
AM feɪts

fathead
BR ˈfathɛd, -z
AM ˈfætˌ(h)ɛd, -z

fatheaded
BR ˌfatˈhɛdɪd
AM ¦fæt¦hɛdəd

father
BR ˈfɑːð|ə(r), -əz, -(ə)rɪŋ, -əd
AM ˈfɑð|ər, -ərz, -(ə)rɪŋ, -ərd

fatherhood
BR ˈfɑːðəhʊd
AM ˈfɑðərˌ(h)ʊd

fatherland
BR ˈfɑːðəland, -z
AM ˈfæðərˌlænd, -z

fatherless
BR ˈfɑːðələs
AM ˈfɑðərləs

fatherlessness
BR 'fɑːðələsnəs
AM 'fɑðərləsnəs

fatherlike
BR 'fɑːðəlʌɪk
AM 'fɑðər,laɪk

fatherliness
BR 'fɑːðəlɪnɨs
AM 'fɑðərlinɨs

fatherly
BR 'fɑːðəli
AM 'fɑðərli

fathership
BR 'fɑːðəʃɪp
AM 'fɑðər,ʃɪp

fathom
BR 'fað|(ə)m, -(ə)mz, -əmɪŋ\-m̩ɪŋ, -(ə)md
AM 'fæðəm, -z, -ɪŋ, -d

fathomable
BR 'faðəməbl, 'faðm̩əbl
AM 'fæðəməbəl

Fathometer®
BR fa'ðɒmɪtə(r), -z
AM fæ'ðɑmədər, 'fæðə(m),midər, -z

fathomless
BR 'fað(ə)mləs
AM 'fæðəmləs

fatidical
BR feɪ'tɪdɪkl, fə'tɪdɪkl
AM feɪ'tɪdɪkəl, fə'tɪdɪkəl

fatiguability
BR fə,tiːgə'bɪlɨti
AM fə,tigə'bɪlɨdi

fatiguable
BR fə'tiːgəbl
AM fə'tigəbəl

fatigue
BR fə'tiːg, -z, -ɪŋ, -d
AM fə'tig, -z, -ɪŋ, -d

fatigueless
BR fə'tiːglɨs
AM fə'tiglɨs

Fatiha
BR 'fɑːtɪhə(r), 'fatɪhə(r)
AM 'fɑdi,hɑ

Fatihah
BR 'fɑːtɪhə(r), 'fatɪhə(r)
AM 'fɑdi,hɑ

Fatima
BR 'fatɪmə(r)
AM fə'timə, 'fædəmə

Fatimid
BR 'fatɪmɪd, -z
AM 'fædəməd, 'fædə,mɪd, -z

Fatimite
BR 'fatɪmʌɪt, -s
AM 'fædə,maɪt, -s

fatism
BR 'feɪtɪz(ə)m
AM 'feɪdɪzəm

fatist
BR 'feɪtɪst, -s
AM 'feɪdɪst, -s

fatless
BR 'fatləs
AM 'fætləs

fatling
BR 'fatlɪŋ, -z
AM 'fætlɪŋ, -z

fatly
BR 'fatli
AM 'fætli

fatness
BR 'fatnəs
AM 'fætnəs

fatsia
BR 'fatsɪə(r)
AM 'fætsiə

fatso
BR 'fatsəʊ, -z
AM 'fætsoʊ, -z

fatstock
BR 'fatstɒk
AM 'fæt,stɑk

fatted
BR 'fatɨd
AM 'fædəd

fatten
BR 'fat|n, -nz, -nɪŋ\-n̩ɪŋ, -nd
AM 'fætn, -z, -ɪŋ, -d

fattily
BR 'fatɨli
AM 'fædəli

fattiness
BR 'fatɪnɪs
AM 'fædinɨs

fattish
BR 'fatɪʃ
AM 'fædɪʃ

fattism
BR 'fatɪz(ə)m
AM 'fædɪzəm

fattist
BR 'fatɪst, -s
AM 'fædəst, -s

fatty
BR 'fati
AM 'fædi

fatuity
BR fə'tjuːɪti, fə'tʃuːɪti
AM fə'tuədi

fatuous
BR 'fatjʊəs, 'fatʃʊəs
AM 'fætʃ(əw)əs

fatuously
BR 'fatjʊəsli, 'fatʃʊəsli
AM 'fætʃ(əw)əsli

fatuousness
BR 'fatjʊəsnəs, 'fatʃʊəsnəs
AM 'fætʃ(əw)əsnəs

fatwa
BR 'fatwɑː(r), 'fatwə(r), -z
AM 'fætwə, -z

faubourg
BR 'fəʊbʊəg, -z
AM 'foʊbərg, foʊ'bʊ(ə)r, -z

fauces
BR 'fɔːsiːz
AM 'foʊ,siz

faucet
BR 'fɔːsɪt, -s
AM 'fɔsət, 'fɑsət, -s

Faucett
BR 'fɔːsɪt
AM 'fɔsət, 'fɑsət

faucial
BR 'fɔːʃl
AM 'fɔʃəl, 'fɑʃəl

Faucitt
BR 'fɔːsɪt
AM 'fɔsət, 'fɑsət

Faulds
BR fəʊldz, fɔːldz
AM fɔldz, foʊldz

Faulkner
BR 'fɔː(l)knə(r)
AM 'fɔknər, 'fɑknər

fault
BR fɔːlt, fɒlt, -s, -ɪŋ, -ɨd
AM fɔlt, fɑlt, -s, -ɪŋ, -əd

faultfinder
BR 'fɔːlt,fʌɪndə(r), 'fɒlt,fʌɪndə(r), -z
AM 'fɔlt,faɪndər, 'fɑlt,faɪndər, -z

faultfinding
BR 'fɔːlt,fʌɪndɪŋ, 'fɒlt,fʌɪndɪŋ
AM 'fɔlt,faɪndɪŋ, 'fɑlt,faɪndɪŋ

faultily
BR 'fɔːltɨli, 'fɒltɨli
AM 'fɔltəli, 'fɑltəli

faultiness
BR 'fɔːltɪnɪs, 'fɒltɪnɪs
AM 'fɔltinɨs, 'fɑltinɨs

faultless
BR 'fɔːltləs, 'fɒltləs
AM 'fɔltləs, 'fɑltləs

faultlessly
BR 'fɔːltləsli, 'fɒltləsli
AM 'fɔltləsli, 'fɑltləsli

faultlessness
BR 'fɔːltləsnəs, 'fɒltləsnəs
AM 'fɔltləsnəs, 'fɑltləsnəs

faulty
BR 'fɔːlti, 'fɒlti
AM 'fɔlti, 'fɑlti

faun
BR fɔːn, -z
AM fɔn, fɑn, -z

fauna
BR 'fɔːnə(r)
AM 'fɔnə, 'fɑnə

faunal
BR 'fɔːnl
AM 'fɔnəl, 'fɑnəl

faunist
BR 'fɔːnɪst, -s
AM 'fɔnəst, 'fɑnəst, -s

faunistic
BR fɔː'nɪstɪk
AM fɔ'nɪstɪk, fɑ'nɪstɪk

faunistical
BR fɔː'nɪstɪkl
AM fɔ'nɪstəkəl, fɑ'nɪstəkəl

Fauntleroy
BR 'fɒntlərɔɪ, 'fɔːntlərɔɪ
AM 'fɔntlə,rɔɪ, 'fɑntlə,rɔɪ

Faunus
BR 'fɔːnəs
AM 'fɔnəs, 'fɑnəs

Fauré
BR 'fɔːreɪ
AM fɔ'reɪ

Faust
BR faʊst
AM faʊst

Faustian
BR 'faʊstɪən
AM 'faʊstiən

Faustus
BR 'faʊstəs
AM 'faʊstəs

faute de mieux
BR ,fəʊt də 'mjəː(r)
AM ¦foʊt də 'mjə

fauteuil
BR fəʊ'təːɪ, -z
AM foʊ'təɪ, -z

fauve
BR fəʊv, -z
AM foʊv, -z

fauvism
BR 'fəʊvɪz(ə)m
AM 'foʊ,vɪzəm

fauvist
BR 'fəʊvɪst, -s
AM 'foʊvəst, -s

Faux
BR fɔːks, fəʊ
AM foʊ

faux pas
BR ,fəʊ 'pɑː(r), -z
AM ,foʊ 'pɑ, -z

fave
BR feɪv
AM feɪv

favela
BR fə'vɛlə(r), -z
AM fə'vɛlə, -z

Favell
BR 'feɪvl
AM fɑ'vɛl, 'feɪvəl

Faversham
BR 'favəʃ(ə)m
AM 'fævərʃəm

favor
BR 'feɪv|ə(r), -əz, -(ə)rɪŋ, -əd

AM 'feɪv|ər, -ərz, -(ə)rɪŋ, -ərd
favorable
BR 'feɪv(ə)rəbl
AM 'feɪvər(ə)bəl, 'feɪvrəbəl
favorableness
BR 'feɪv(ə)rəblnəs
AM 'feɪvər(ə)bəlnəs, 'feɪvrəbəlnəs
favorably
BR 'feɪv(ə)rəbli
AM 'feɪvər(ə)bli, 'feɪvrəbli
favorer
BR 'feɪv(ə)rə(r), -z
AM 'feɪv(ə)rər, -z
favorite
BR 'feɪv(ə)rɪt, -s
AM 'feɪv(ə)rɪt, -s
favoritism
BR 'feɪv(ə)rɪtɪz(ə)m
AM 'feɪv(ə)rɪˌtɪzəm
favour
BR 'feɪv|ə(r), -əz, -(ə)rɪŋ, -əd
AM 'feɪv|ər, -ərz, -(ə)rɪŋ, -ərd
favourable
BR 'feɪv(ə)rəbl
AM 'feɪv(ə)r(ə)bəl
favourableness
BR 'feɪv(ə)rəblnəs
AM 'feɪvər(ə)bəlnəs, 'feɪvrəbəlnəs
favourably
BR 'feɪv(ə)rəbli
AM 'feɪvər(ə)bli, 'feɪvrəbli
favourer
BR 'feɪv(ə)rə(r), -z
AM 'feɪv(ə)rər, -z
favourite
BR 'feɪv(ə)rɪt, -s
AM 'feɪv(ə)rɪt, -s
favouritism
BR 'feɪv(ə)rɪtɪz(ə)m
AM 'feɪv(ə)rɪˌtɪzəm
Fawcett
BR 'fɔːsɪt
AM 'fɔsət, 'fɑsət
Fawkes
BR fɔːks
AM fɔks, fɑks
Fawley
BR 'fɔːli
AM 'fɔli, 'fɑli
fawn
BR fɔːn, -z, -ɪŋ, -d
AM fɔn, fɑn, -z, -ɪŋ, -d
fawner
BR 'fɔːnə(r), -z
AM 'fɔnər, 'fɑnər, -z
fawningly
BR 'fɔːnɪŋli
AM 'fɔnɪŋli, 'fɑnɪŋli
fawr
BR 'vaʊə(r)
AM 'vaʊər
WE vaʊr
fax
BR faks, -ɪz, -ɪŋ, -t
AM fæks, -əz, -ɪŋ, -t
fay
BR feɪ
AM feɪ
Faye
BR feɪ
AM feɪ
Fayette
BR feɪ'ɛt
AM ˌfeɪ'ɛt
Fayetteville
BR 'feɪɪtvɪl
AM 'feɪɪtˌvɪl
fayre
BR fɛː(r), -z
AM fɛ(ə)r, -z
Fazackerley
BR fə'zakəli
AM fə'zækərli
Fazakerley
BR fə'zakəli
AM fə'zækərli
faze
BR feɪz, -ɪz, -ɪŋ, -d
AM feɪz, -ɪz, -ɪŋ, -d
fazenda
BR fə'zɛndə(r), -z
AM fə'zɛndə, -z
fealty
BR 'fiːəlt|i, -ɪz
AM 'fi(ə)lti, -z
fear
BR fɪə(r), -z, -ɪŋ, -d
AM fɪ(ə)r, -z, -ɪŋ, -d
fearful
BR 'fɪəf(ʊ)l
AM 'fɪrfəl
fearfully
BR 'fɪəfʊli, 'fɪəfl̩i
AM 'fɪrfəli
fearfulness
BR 'fɪəf(ʊ)lnəs
AM 'fɪrfəlnəs
Feargal
BR 'fəːgl
AM 'fərgəl
Feargus
BR 'fəːgəs
AM 'fərgəs
fearless
BR 'fɪələs
AM 'fɪrləs
fearlessly
BR 'fɪələsli
AM 'fɪrləsli
fearlessness
BR 'fɪələsnəs
AM 'fɪrləsnəs
fearsome
BR 'fɪəs(ə)m
AM 'fɪrsəm
fearsomely
BR 'fɪəs(ə)mli
AM 'fɪrsəmli
fearsomeness
BR 'fɪəs(ə)mnəs
AM 'fɪrsəmnəs
feasibility
BR ˌfiːzɪ'bɪlɪti
AM ˌfizə'bɪlɪdi
feasible
BR 'fiːzɪbl
AM 'fizəbəl
feasibly
BR 'fiːzɪbli
AM 'fizəbli
feast
BR fiːst, -s, -ɪŋ, -ɪd
AM fis|t, -s, -ɪŋ, -ɪd
feaster
BR 'fiːstə(r), -z
AM 'fistər, -z
feat
BR fiːt, -s
AM fit, -s
feather
BR 'fɛð|ə(r), -əz, -(ə)rɪŋ, -əd
AM 'fɛð|ər, -ərz, -(ə)rɪŋ, -ərd
featherbed
verb
BR 'fɛðəbɛd, ˌfɛðə'bɛd, -z, -ɪŋ, -ɪd
AM 'fɛðərˌbɛd, -z, -ɪŋ, -əd
featherbrained
BR 'fɛðəbreɪnd
AM 'fɛðərˌbreɪnd
featherhead
BR 'fɛðəhɛd, -z
AM 'fɛðərˌ(h)ɛd, -z
featheriness
BR 'fɛð(ə)rɪnɪs
AM 'fɛð(ə)rinɪs
featherless
BR 'fɛðələs
AM 'fɛðərləs
featherlight
BR 'fɛðəlʌɪt
AM 'fɛðərˌlaɪt
Featherstone
BR 'fɛðəst(ə)n, 'fəːst(ə)n
AM 'fɛðərstən
Featherstone-haugh
BR 'fɛðəst(ə)nhɔː(r), 'fanʃɔː(r), 'fɛst(ə)nhɔː(r), 'fɪəst(ə)nhɔː(r)
AM 'fɛðərstənˌ(h)ɔ
featherweight
BR 'fɛðəweɪt, -s
AM 'fɛðərˌweɪt, -s
feathery
BR 'fɛð(ə)ri
AM 'fɛð(ə)ri
feature
BR 'fiːtʃ|ə(r), -əz, -(ə)rɪŋ, -əd
AM 'fitʃər, -z, -ɪŋ, -d
featureless
BR 'fiːtʃələs
AM 'fitʃərləs
febrifugal
BR fɪ'brɪfjʊgl, 'fɛbrɪˌfjuːgl
AM fə'brɪf(j)ugəl, 'fɛbrəˌf(j)ugəl
febrifuge
BR 'fɛbrɪfjuːdʒ, -ɪz
AM 'fɛbrəˌfjudʒ, -əz
febrile
BR 'fiːbrʌɪl, 'fɛbrʌɪl
AM 'fɛˌbraɪl, 'fiˌbraɪl
febrility
BR fɪ'brɪlɪti
AM fɛ'brɪlɪdi, fi'brɪlɪdi
February
BR 'fɛbr(ər)|i, 'fɛbjʊr|i, 'fɛbjʊər|i, -ɪz
AM 'fɛb(j)əˌwɛri, 'fɛbrəˌwɛri, -z
fecal
BR 'fiːkl
AM 'fikəl
feces
BR 'fiːsiːz
AM 'fisiz
feckless
BR 'fɛkləs
AM 'fɛkləs
fecklessly
BR 'fɛkləsli
AM 'fɛkləsli
fecklessness
BR 'fɛkləsnəs
AM 'fɛkləsnəs
feculence
BR 'fɛkjʊləns, 'fɛkjʊln̩s
AM 'fɛkjələns
feculent
BR 'fɛkjʊlənt, 'fɛkjʊln̩t
AM 'fɛkjələnt
fecund
BR 'fɛk(ə)nd, 'fɛkʌnd, 'fiːk(ə)nd, 'fiːkʌnd
AM 'fɛkənd, 'fikənd
fecundability
BR fɪˌkʌndə'bɪlɪti, fɛˌkʌndə'bɪlɪti
AM fɛˌkəndə'bɪlɪdi, fiˌkəndə'bɪlɪdi
fecundate
BR 'fɛk(ə)ndeɪt, 'fɛkʌndeɪt, 'fiːk(ə)ndeɪt, 'fiːkʌndeɪt, -s, -ɪŋ, -ɪd
AM 'fɛkənˌdeɪ|t, -ts, -dɪŋ, -dɪd
fecundation
BR ˌfɛk(ə)n'deɪʃn, ˌfɛkʌn'deɪʃn,

ˌfi:k(ə)n'deɪʃn, ˌfi:kʌn'deɪʃn
AM ˌfik(ə)n'deɪʃ(ə)n

fecundity
BR fɪ'kʌndɪti, fɛ'kʌndɪti
AM fɛ'kəndədi, fi'kəndədi

fed
BR fɛd, -z
AM fɛd, -z

fedayeen
BR ˌfɛdʌɪ'i:n, fɪ'dɑ:ji:n
AM ˌfɛdeɪ'in

federal
BR 'fɛd(ə)rəl, 'fɛd(ə)rl̩
AM 'fɛd(ə)rəl

federalisation
BR ˌfɛd(ə)rəlʌɪ'zeɪʃn, ˌfɛd(ə)rl̩ʌɪ'zeɪʃn
AM ˌfɛd(ə)rələ'zeɪʃən, ˌfɛd(ə)rəˌlaɪ'zeɪʃən

federalise
BR 'fɛd(ə)rəlʌɪz, 'fɛd(ə)rl̩ʌɪz, -ɪz, -ɪŋ, -d
AM 'fɛd(ə)rəˌlaɪz, -ɪz, -ɪŋ, -d

federalism
BR 'fɛd(ə)rəlɪz(ə)m, 'fɛd(ə)rl̩ɪz(ə)m
AM 'fɛd(ə)rəˌlɪzəm

federalist
BR 'fɛd(ə)rəlɪst, 'fɛd(ə)rl̩ɪst, -s
AM 'fɛd(ə)rələst, -s

federalization
BR ˌfɛd(ə)rəlʌɪ'zeɪʃn, ˌfɛd(ə)rl̩ʌɪ'zeɪʃn
AM ˌfɛd(ə)rələ'zeɪʃən, ˌfɛd(ə)rəˌlaɪ'zeɪʃən

federalize
BR 'fɛd(ə)rəlʌɪz, 'fɛd(ə)rl̩ʌɪz, -ɪz, -ɪŋ, -d
AM 'fɛd(ə)rəˌlaɪz, -ɪz, -ɪŋ, -d

federally
BR 'fɛd(ə)rəli, 'fɛd(ə)rl̩i
AM 'fɛd(ə)rəli

federate
BR 'fɛdəreɪt, -s, -ɪŋ, -ɪd
AM 'fɛdəˌreɪ|t, -ts, -dɪŋ, -dɪd

federation
BR ˌfɛdə'reɪʃn, -z
AM ˌfɛdə'reɪʃən, -z

federationist
BR ˌfɛdə'reɪʃn̩ɪst, -s
AM ˌfɛdə'reɪʃənəst, -s

federative
BR 'fɛd(ə)rətɪv
AM 'fɛdərəˌtɪv, 'fɛdəˌreɪdɪv

fedora
BR fɪ'dɔ:rə(r), -z
AM fə'dɔrə, -z

fed up
BR ˌfɛd 'ʌp
AM ˌfɛd 'əp

fee
BR fi:, -z, -ɪŋ, -d
AM fi, -z, -ɪŋ, -d

feeble
BR 'fi:bl
AM 'fibəl

feebleness
BR 'fi:blnəs
AM 'fibəlnəs

feeblish
BR 'fi:blɪʃ
AM 'fiblɪʃ

feebly
BR 'fi:bli
AM 'fibli

feed
BR fi:d, -z, -ɪŋ
AM fid, -z, -ɪŋ

feedable
BR 'fi:dəbl
AM 'fidəbəl

feedback
BR 'fi:dbak
AM 'fidˌbæk

feedbag
BR 'fi:dbag, -z
AM 'fidˌbæg, -z

feeder
BR 'fi:də(r), -z
AM 'fidər, -z

feedlot
BR 'fi:dlɒt, -s
AM 'fidˌlɑt, -s

feedstock
BR 'fi:dstɒk
AM 'fidˌstɑk

feedstuff
BR 'fi:dstʌf, -s
AM 'fidˌstəf, -s

feel
BR fi:l, -z, -ɪŋ
AM fil, -z, -ɪŋ

feeler
BR 'fi:lə(r), -z
AM 'filər, -z

feeling
BR 'fi:lɪŋ, -z
AM 'filɪŋ, -z

feelingless
BR 'fi:lɪŋlɪs
AM 'filɪŋlɪs

feelingly
BR 'fi:lɪŋli
AM 'filɪŋli

feelings
BR 'fi:lɪŋz
AM 'filɪŋz

Feeney
BR 'fi:ni
AM 'fini

feet
BR fi:t
AM fit

feign
BR feɪn, -z, -ɪŋ, -d
AM feɪn, -z, -ɪŋ, -d

feignedly
BR 'feɪnɪdli
AM 'feɪnɪdli

feijoa
BR feɪ'(d)ʒəʊə(r), fɛ'(d)ʒəʊə(r), fi:'(d)ʒəʊə(r), feɪ'jəʊə(r), fɛ'jəʊə(r), fi:'jəʊə(r), -z
AM feɪ'dʒoʊə, feɪ'hoʊə, -z

feint
BR feɪnt, -s, -ɪŋ, -ɪd
AM feɪn|t, -ts, -(t)ɪŋ, -(t)ɪd

feis
BR fɛʃ, feɪʃ
AM fɛʃ
IR f'esʲ

Feisal
BR 'fʌɪsl
AM 'faɪzɑl

feiseanna
BR 'fɛʃənə(r), 'feɪʃənə(r)
AM 'fɛʃənə
IR 'f'esʲənə

feistiness
BR 'fʌɪstɪnɪs
AM 'faɪstinɪs

feisty
BR 'fʌɪsti
AM 'faɪsti

felafel
BR fɪ'lafl, fɪ'lɑ:fl
AM fə'lɑfəl

felching
BR 'fɛltʃɪŋ
AM 'fɛltʃɪŋ

Feldman
BR 'fɛldmən
AM 'fɛl(d)mən

feldspar
BR 'fɛl(d)spɑ:(r)
AM 'fɛldˌspɑr

feldspathic
BR ˌfɛl(d)'spaθɪk
AM ˌfɛlz'pæθɪk, ˌfɛl(d)'spæθɪk

feldspathoid
BR 'fɛl(d)spəθɔɪd, -z
AM ˌfɛlz'pæˌθɔɪd, ˌfɛl(d)'spæˌθɔɪd, -z

Felicia
BR fɪ'lɪsɪə(r)
AM fə'liʃ(i)ə

felicific
BR ˌfi:lɪ'sɪfɪk, ˌfɛlɪ'sɪfɪk
AM ˌfɛlə'sɪfɪk

felicitate
BR fɪ'lɪsɪteɪt, -s, -ɪŋ, -ɪd
AM fə'lɪsɪˌteɪ|t, -ts, -dɪŋ, -dɪd

felicitation
BR fɪˌlɪsɪ'teɪʃn, -z
AM fəˌlɪsɪ'teɪʃən, -z

felicitous
BR fɪ'lɪsɪtəs
AM fə'lɪsɪdɪs

felicitously
BR fɪ'lɪsɪtəsli
AM fə'lɪsɪdɪsli

felicitousness
BR fɪ'lɪsɪtəsnəs
AM fə'lɪsɪdɪsnɪs

felicity
BR fɪ'lɪsɪt|i, -ɪz
AM fə'lɪsɪdi, -z

Felindre
BR vɪ'lɪndrə(r)
AM fə'lɪndər
WE ve'lɪndre

feline
BR 'fi:lʌɪn
AM 'fiˌlaɪn

felinity
BR fɪ'lɪnɪti
AM fi'lɪnɪdi

Felix
BR 'fi:lɪks
AM 'fiˌlɪks

Felixstowe
BR 'fi:lɪkstəʊ
AM 'filɪkˌstoʊ

fell
BR fɛl, -z
AM fɛl, -z

fellah
BR 'fɛlə(r), -z
AM 'fɛlə, -z

fellate
BR fɛ'leɪt, fɪ'leɪt, -s, -ɪŋ, -ɪd
AM 'fɛlˌeɪ|t, -ts, -dɪŋ, -dɪd

fellatio
BR fɛ'leɪʃɪəʊ, fɪ'leɪʃɪəʊ
AM fə'leɪʃioʊ

fellation
BR fɛ'leɪʃn, fɪ'leɪʃn, -z
AM fə'leɪʃən, -z

fellator
BR fɛ'leɪtə(r), fɪ'leɪtə(r), -z
AM 'fɛlˌeɪdər, -z

feller
BR 'fɛlə(r), -z
AM 'fɛlər, -z

Fellini
BR fɛ'li:ni, fɪ'li:ni
AM fə'lini

fellmonger
BR 'fɛlˌmʌŋgə(r)
AM 'fɛlˌmɑŋgər, 'fɛlˌməŋgər

felloe
BR 'fɛləʊ, -z
AM 'fɛloʊ, -z

fellow
BR 'fɛləʊ, 'fɛlə(r), -z
AM 'fɛloʊ, 'fɛlə, -z

Fellowes
BR 'fɛləʊz
AM 'fɛloʊz

Fellows
BR 'fɛləʊz
AM 'fɛloʊz

fellowship
BR 'fɛlə(ʊ)ʃɪp, -s
AM 'fɛloʊˌʃɪp, 'fɛləˌʃɪp, -s

fellwort
BR 'fɛlwəːt
AM 'fɛlwərt, 'fɛlwɔ(ə)rt

felly
BR 'fɛl|i, -ɪz
AM 'fɛli, -z

felon
BR 'fɛlən, -z
AM 'fɛlən, -z

felonious
BR fɪ'ləʊnɪəs
AM fə'loʊniəs, fɛ'loʊniəs

feloniously
BR fɪ'ləʊnɪəsli
AM fə'loʊniəsli, fɛ'loʊniəsli

feloniousness
BR fɪ'ləʊnɪəsnəs
AM fə'loʊniəsnəs, fɛ'loʊniəsnəs

felonry
BR 'fɛlənri
AM 'fɛlənri

felony
BR 'fɛlən|i, -ɪz
AM 'fɛləni, -z

felspar
BR 'fɛlspɑː(r)
AM 'fɛlˌspɑr

Felstead
BR 'fɛlstɛd
AM 'fɛlˌstɛd

felt
BR fɛlt, -s, -ɪŋ, -ɨd
AM fɛlt, -s, -ɪŋ, -əd

Feltham[1]
place in UK
BR 'fɛltəm
AM 'fɛltəm

Feltham[2]
surname
BR 'fɛltəm, 'fɛlθ(ə)m
AM 'fɛltəm, 'fɛlθəm

Felton
BR 'fɛlt(ə)n
AM 'fɛltən

felty
BR 'fɛlti
AM 'fɛlti

felucca
BR fɛ'lʌkə(r), fɪ'lʌkə(r), -z
AM fə'lukə, -z

felwort
BR 'fɛlwəːt
AM 'fɛlwərt, 'fɛlwɔ(ə)rt

female
BR 'fiːmeɪl, -z
AM 'fiˌmeɪl, -z

femaleness
BR 'fiːmeɪlnɨs
AM 'fiˌmeɪlnɨs

feme
BR fiːm, fɛm, -z
AM fɛm, -z

feme covert
BR ˌfiːm 'kʌvət, ˌfɛm +
AM 'fɛm 'kəvərt

femes covert
BR ˌfiːmz 'kʌvət, ˌfɛmz +
AM 'fɛmz 'kəvərt

feme sole
BR ˌfiːm 'səʊl, ˌfɛm +
AM 'fɛm 'soʊl

femes sole
BR ˌfiːmz 'səʊl, ˌfɛmz +
AM 'fɛmz 'soʊl

feminal
BR 'fɛmɪnl
AM 'fɛmənəl

feminality
BR ˌfɛmɪ'nalɪti
AM ˌfɛmə'nælədi

femineity
BR ˌfɛmɪ'niːɪti
AM ˌfɛmə'niɪdi

feminine
BR 'fɛmɪnɪn
AM 'fɛmənən

femininely
BR 'fɛmɪnɪnli
AM 'fɛmənənli

feminineness
BR 'fɛmɪnɪnnɪs
AM 'fɛmɛnə(n)nəs

femininity
BR ˌfɛmɪ'nɪnɪti
AM ˌfɛmə'nɪnɪdi

feminisation
BR ˌfɛmɪnʌɪ'zeɪʃn
AM ˌfɛmənə'zeɪʃən, ˌfɛmɛˌnaɪ'zeɪʃən

feminise
BR 'fɛmɪnʌɪz, -ɪz, -ɪŋ, -d
AM 'fɛməˌnaɪz, -ɪz, -ɪŋ, -d

feminism
BR 'fɛmɪnɪz(ə)m
AM 'fɛməˌnɪzəm

feminist
BR 'fɛmɪnɪst, -s
AM 'fɛmənəst, -s

feminity
BR fɪ'mɪnɪti
AM fə'mɪnɪdi

feminization
BR ˌfɛmɪnʌɪ'zeɪʃn
AM ˌfɛmənə'zeɪʃən, ˌfɛmɛˌnaɪ'zeɪʃən

feminize
BR 'fɛmɪnʌɪz, -ɪz, -ɪŋ, -d
AM 'fɛməˌnaɪz, -ɪz, -ɪŋ, -d

femme
BR fam, fɛm, -z
AM fɛm, -z

femme fatale
BR ˌfam fə'tɑːl, -z
AM ˌfɛm fə'tæl, + fə'tɑl, -z

femora
BR 'fɛm(ə)rə(r)
AM 'fɛmərə

femoral
BR 'fɛm(ə)rəl, 'fɛm(ə)rḷ
AM 'fɛmərəl

femtometer
BR 'fɛmtəˌmiːtə(r), -z
AM 'fɛmtəˌmidər, -z

femtometre
BR 'fɛmtəˌmiːtə(r), -z
AM 'fɛmtəˌmidər, -z

femur
BR 'fiːmə(r), -z
AM 'fimər, -z

fen
BR fɛn, -z
AM fɛn, -z

fen-berry
BR 'fɛnb(ə)r|i, -ɪz
AM 'fɛnˌbɛri, -z

fence
BR fɛns, -ɪz, -ɪŋ, -t
AM fɛns, -əz, -ɪŋ, -t

fenceless
BR 'fɛnsləs
AM 'fɛnsləs

fencer
BR 'fɛnsə(r), -z
AM 'fɛnsər, -z

Fenchurch
BR 'fɛntʃəːtʃ
AM 'fɛnˌtʃərtʃ

fencible
BR 'fɛnsɪbl, -z
AM 'fɛnsəbəl, -z

fend
BR fɛnd, -z, -ɪŋ, -ɨd
AM fɛnd, -z, -ɪŋ, -əd

fender
BR 'fɛndə(r), -z
AM 'fɛndər, -z

Fenella
BR fɪ'nɛlə(r)
AM fə'nɛlə

fenestella
BR ˌfɛnɪ'stɛlə(r), -z
AM ˌfɛnə'stɛlə, -z

fenestra
BR fɪ'nɛstrə(r)
AM fə'nɛstrə

fenestrae
BR fɪ'nɛstriː
AM fə'nɛstri, fə'nɛˌstraɪ

fenestrate
BR 'fɛnɪstreɪt, -s, -ɪŋ, -ɨd
AM 'fɛnəˌstreɪ|t, -ts, -dɪŋ, -dɨd

fenestration
BR ˌfɛnɪ'streɪʃn
AM ˌfɛnə'streɪʃən

feng shui
BR ˌfɛŋ 'ʃuːi, ˌfʌŋ 'ʃweɪ
AM ˌfɛŋ 'ʃui

Fenian
BR 'fiːnɪən, -z
AM 'finiən, -z

Fenianism
BR 'fiːnɪənɪz(ə)m
AM 'finiəˌnɪzəm

Fenimore
BR 'fɛnɪmɔː(r)
AM 'fɛnəˌmɔ(ə)r

fenland
BR 'fɛnland, 'fɛnlənd, -z
AM 'fɛnˌlænd, -z

fenman
BR 'fɛnman, 'fɛnmən
AM 'fɛnˌmæn

fenmen
BR 'fɛnmɛn, 'fɛnmən
AM 'fɛnˌmɛn

fennec
BR 'fɛnɪk, -s
AM 'fɛnɪk, -s

fennel
BR 'fɛnl
AM 'fɛnəl

Fennimore
BR 'fɛnɪmɔː(r)
AM 'fɛnəˌmɔ(ə)r

Fennoscandia
BR ˌfɛnə(ʊ)'skandɪə(r)
AM ˌfɛnə'skændiə

fenny
BR 'fɛni
AM 'fɛni

Fens
BR fɛnz
AM fɛnz

Fenton
BR 'fɛnt(ə)n
AM 'fɛn(t)ən

fenugreek
BR 'fɛnjʉgriːk
AM 'fɛn(j)əˌgrik

Fenwick
BR 'fɛn(w)ɪk
AM 'fɛnˌwɪk

feoff
BR fiːf, fɛf, -s, -ɪŋ, -t
AM fif, -s, -ɪŋ, -t

feoffee
BR fɛ'fiː, fiː'fiː, -z
AM fɛ'fi, fi'fi, -z

feoffment
BR 'fiːfm(ə)nt, 'fɛfm(ə)nt, -s
AM 'fifmənt, -s

feoffor
BR 'fiːfə(r), 'fɛfə(r), -z
AM 'fifər, -z

feral
BR 'fɛrəl, 'fɛrl̩
AM 'fɛrəl, 'fɪrəl

fer de lance
BR ˌfɛː də 'lɑːns, + 'lans, -ɨz
AM ˌfɛr də ˌlæns, -əz

Ferdinand
BR 'fəːdɪnand, 'fəːdɪnənd
AM 'fərd(ə)ˌnænd

feretory
BR 'fɛrət(ə)r|i, -ɪz
AM 'fɛrəˌtɔri, -z

Fergal
BR 'fəːgl
AM 'fərgəl

Fergie
BR 'fəːgi
AM 'fərgi

Fergus
BR 'fəːgəs
AM 'fərgəs

Ferguson
BR 'fəːgəs(ə)n
AM 'fərgəsən

ferial
BR 'fɪərɪəl, 'fɛrɪəl
AM 'fɛriəl, 'fɪriəl

Fermanagh
BR fə'manə(*r*)
AM fər'mænə

Fermat
BR 'fəːmɑː(*r*), fə'mat, 'fəːmat
AM fər'mɑt

fermata
BR fəː'mɑːtə(*r*), -z
AM fər'mɑdə, -z

ferment¹
noun
BR 'fəːmɛnt, -s
AM 'fərˌmɛnt, -s

ferment²
verb
BR fə(ː)'mɛnt, -s, -ɪŋ, -ɨd
AM fər'mɛn|t, -ts, -(t)ɪŋ, -(t)əd

fermentable
BR fə'mɛntəbl
AM fər'mɛn(t)əbəl

fermentation
BR ˌfəːmɛn'teɪʃn, ˌfəːm(ə)n'teɪʃn, -z
AM ˌfərmən'teɪʃən, -z

fermentative
BR fə'mɛntətɪv
AM fər'mɛn(t)ədɪv

fermenter
BR fə'mɛntə(r), -z
AM fər'mɛn(t)ər, -z

fermi
BR 'fəːm|i, 'fɛːm|i, -ɪz
AM 'fɛrˌmi, -z

fermion
BR 'fəːmɪɒn, 'fəːmɪən
AM 'fɛrmiɑn, 'fərmiɑn

fermium
BR 'fəːmɪəm
AM 'fɛrmiəm, 'fərmiəm

Fermor
BR 'fəːmɔː(r)
AM 'fərˌmɔ(ə)r

Fermoy
BR fə'mɔɪ
AM 'fərˌmɔɪ

fern
BR fəːn, -z
AM fərn, -z

Fernández
BR fə'nandɛz
AM fər'nændɛz

Fernando Póo
BR fəˌnandəʊ 'pəʊ
AM fərˌnændoʊ 'poʊ

fernery
BR 'fəːn(ə)r|i, -ɪz
AM 'fərnəri, -z

Ferneyhough
BR 'fəːnɪhʌf, 'fəːnɪhəʊ
AM 'fərnihəf

Fernihough
BR 'fəːnɪhʌf, 'fəːnɪhəʊ
AM 'fərnihəf

fernless
BR 'fəːnləs
AM 'fərnləs

ferny
BR 'fəːn|i, -ɪə(r), -ɪɪst
AM 'fərni, -ər, -ɨst

Fernyhough
BR 'fəːnɪhʌf, 'fəːnɪhəʊ
AM 'fərnihəf

ferocious
BR fɪ'rəʊʃəs
AM fə'roʊʃəs

ferociously
BR fɪ'rəʊʃəsli
AM fə'roʊʃəsli

ferociousness
BR fɪ'rəʊʃəsnəs
AM fə'roʊʃəsnəs

ferocity
BR fɪ'rɒsɪti
AM fə'rɑsədi

Ferodo
BR fɪ'rəʊdəʊ
AM fə'roʊdoʊ

Ferranti
BR fɪ'ranti
AM fə'rɑn(t)i

Ferrara
BR fə'rɑːrə(*r*)
AM fə'rɑrə

Ferrari®
BR fə'rɑːr|i, -ɪz
AM fə'rɑri, -z

ferrate
BR 'fɛreɪt, -s
AM 'fɛˌreɪt, -s

ferrel
BR 'fɛrəl, 'fɛrl̩, -z
AM 'fɛrəl, -z

Ferrell
BR 'fɛrəl, 'fɛrl̩
AM 'fɛrəl

Ferrer
BR 'fɛrə(r)
AM fə'rɑr, 'fɛrər

ferret
BR 'fɛrɪt, -s, -ɪŋ, -ɨd
AM 'fɛrə|t, -ts, -dɪŋ, -dəd

ferreter
BR 'fɛrɪtə(r), -z
AM 'fɛrədər, -z

ferrety
BR 'fɛrɪti
AM 'fɛrədi

ferriage
BR 'fɛrɪ|ɪdʒ, -ɪdʒɪz
AM 'fɛriɪdʒ, -ɪz

ferric
BR 'fɛrɪk
AM 'fɛrɪk

Ferrier
BR 'fɛrɪə(r)
AM 'fɛriər

ferrimagnetic
BR ˌfɛrɪmag'nɛtɪk
AM ˌfɛriˌmæg'nɛdɪk

ferrimagnetism
BR ˌfɛrɪ'magnɪtɪz(ə)m
AM ˌfɛri'mægnəˌtɪzəm

Ferris
BR 'fɛrɪs
AM 'fɛrəs

ferrite
BR 'fɛrʌɪt
AM 'fɛraɪt

ferritic
BR fɪ'rɪtɪk
AM fə'rɪdɪk

ferroconcrete
BR ˌfɛrə(ʊ)'kɒŋkriːt
AM ˌfɛroʊ'kɑnˌkrit

ferroelectric
BR ˌfɛrəʊɪ'lɛktrɪk
AM ˌfɛroʊə'lɛktrɪk, ˌfɛroʊɪ'lɛktrɪk

ferroelectricity
BR ˌfɛrəʊɪlɛk'trɪsɪti
AM ˌfɛroʊəˌlɛk'trɪsɨdi, ˌfɛroʊɪˌlɛk'trɪsɨdi

Ferrograph®
BR 'fɛrə(ʊ)grɑːf, 'fɛrə(ʊ)graf
AM 'fɛrəˌgræf

ferromagnetic
BR ˌfɛrə(ʊ)mag'nɛtɪk
AM ˌfɛroʊˌmæg'nɛdɪk

ferromagnetism
BR ˌfɛrəʊ'magnɪtɪz(ə)m
AM ˌfɛroʊ'mægnəˌtɪzəm

ferrous
BR 'fɛrəs
AM 'fɛrəs

ferruginous
BR fɪ'ruːdʒɪnəs, fɪ'ruːdʒn̩əs, fɛ'ruːdʒɪnəs, fɛ'ruːdʒn̩əs
AM fə'rudʒənəs

ferrule
BR 'fɛr(j)uːl, 'fɛrəl, 'fɛrl̩, -z
AM 'fɛrəl, 'fɛˌrul, -z

ferry
BR 'fɛr|i, -ɪz, -ɪɪŋ, -ɪd
AM 'fɛri, -z, -ɪŋ, -d

ferryage
BR 'fɛrɪ|ɪdʒ, -ɨdʒɪz
AM 'fɛriɪdʒ, -ɪz

ferryboat
BR 'fɛrɪbəʊt, -s
AM 'fɛriˌboʊt, -s

Ferrybridge
BR 'fɛrɪbrɪdʒ
AM 'fɛriˌbrɪdʒ

ferryman
BR 'fɛrɪmən
AM 'fɛriˌmæn, fɛrimən

ferrymen
BR 'fɛrɪmən
AM 'fɛriˌmɛn

fers de lance
BR ˌfɛː də 'lɑːns, + 'lans
AM ˌfɛ(ə)r(z) də 'læns

fertile
BR 'fəːtʌɪl
AM 'fərdl

fertilisable
BR 'fəːtɪlʌɪzəbl, 'fəːtl̩ʌɪzəbl
AM 'fərdlˌaɪzəbəl

fertilisation
BR ˌfəːtɪlʌɪ'zeɪʃn, ˌfəːtl̩ʌɪ'zeɪʃn
AM ˌfərdl̩ə'zeɪʃən, ˌfərdlˌaɪ'zeɪʃən

fertilise
BR 'fəːtɪlʌɪz, 'fəːtl̩ʌɪz, -ɪz, -ɪŋ, -d
AM 'fərdlˌaɪz, -ɪz, -ɪŋ, -d

fertiliser
BR 'fəːtɪlʌɪzə(r), 'fəːtl̩ʌɪzə(r), -z
AM 'fərdlˌaɪzər, -z

fertility
BR fə(ː)'tɪlɪti
AM fər'tɪlɨdi

fertilizable
BR 'fəːtɪlʌɪzəbl, 'fəːtl̩ʌɪzəbl
AM 'fərdlˌaɪzəbəl

fertilization
BR ˌfəːtɪlʌɪ'zeɪʃn, ˌfəːtl̩ʌɪ'zeɪʃn
AM ˌfərdlə'zeɪʃən, ˌfərdlˌaɪ'zeɪʃən

fertilize
BR 'fəːtɪlʌɪz, 'fəːtl̩ʌɪz, -ɪz, -ɪŋ, -d
AM 'fərdlˌaɪz, -ɪz, -ɪŋ, -d

fertilizer
BR 'fəːtɪlʌɪzə(r), 'fəːtl̩ʌɪzə(r), -z
AM 'fərdl̩ˌaɪzər, -z

Fertö Tó
BR ˌfɛːtəʊ 'təʊ
AM ¦fɛrdoʊ 'toʊ
HU 'fɛrtœ 'toː

ferula
BR 'fɛr(j)ʊlə(r), -z
AM 'fɛrələ, -z

ferule
BR 'fɛr(j)uːl, 'fɛrəl, 'fɛrl̩, -z
AM 'fɛrəl, -z

fervency
BR 'fəːvnsǀi, -ɪz
AM 'fərvənsi, -z

fervent
BR 'fəːv(ə)nt
AM 'fərvənt

fervently
BR 'fəːv(ə)ntli
AM 'fərvən(t)li

ferventness
BR 'fəːv(ə)ntnəs
AM 'fərvən(t)nəs

fervid
BR 'fəːvɪd
AM 'fərvəd

fervidly
BR 'fəːvɪdli
AM 'fərvədli

fervidness
BR 'fəːvɪdnɪs
AM 'fərvədnəs

fervor
BR 'fəːvə(r)
AM 'fərvər

fervour
BR 'fəːvə(r)
AM 'fərvər

Fès
BR fɛz, -ɪz
AM fɛz, -əz

Fescennine
BR 'fɛsɪnʌɪn, 'fɛsn̩ʌɪn
AM 'fɛsn̩ˌin, 'fɛsn̩ˌaɪn

fescue
BR 'fɛskjuː
AM 'fɛskju

fess
BR fɛs, -ɪz
AM fɛs, -əz

fesse
BR fɛs, -ɪz
AM fɛs, -əz

festal
BR 'fɛstl̩
AM 'fɛstl

festally
BR 'fɛstl̩i, 'fɛstəli
AM 'fɛstəli

fester
BR 'fɛstǀə(r), -əz, -(ə)rɪŋ, -əd
AM 'fɛstǀər, -ərz, -(ə)rɪŋ, -ərd

festination
BR ˌfɛstɪ'neɪʃn
AM ˌfɛstə'neɪʃən

festival
BR 'fɛstɪvl, -z
AM 'fɛstəvəl, -z

festive
BR 'fɛstɪv
AM 'fɛstɪv

festively
BR 'fɛstɪvli
AM 'fɛstɪvli

festiveness
BR 'fɛstɪvnɪs
AM 'fɛstɪvnɪs

festivity
BR fɛ'stɪvɪtǀi, -ɪz
AM fɛ'stɪvɪdi, -z

festoon
BR fɛ'stuːn, -z, -ɪŋ, -d
AM fɛ'stun, -z, -ɪŋ, -d

festoonery
BR fɛ'stuːn(ə)ri
AM fɛ'stunəri

Festschrift
BR 'fɛs(t)ʃrɪft, -s
AM 'fɛs(t)ˌʃrɪft, -s

Festschriften
BR 'fɛs(t)ʃrɪftən
AM 'fɛs(t)ˌʃrɪftən

Festus
BR 'fɛstəs
AM 'fɛstəs

feta
BR 'fɛtə(r)
AM 'fɛdə

fetal
BR 'fiːtl
AM 'fidl

fetch
BR fɛtʃ, -ɪz, -ɪŋ, -t
AM fɛtʃ, -əz, -ɪŋ, -t

fetcher
BR 'fɛtʃə(r), -z
AM 'fɛtʃər, -z

fetchingly
BR 'fɛtʃɪŋli
AM 'fɛtʃɪŋli

fête
BR feɪt, -s, -ɪŋ, -ɪd
AM feɪǀt, -ts, -dɪŋ, -dɪd

fête champêtre
BR ˌfeɪt ʃɒ̃'peɪtr(ə), -z
AM ¦feɪt ʃɑm'pɛtr(ə), -z

fête galante
BR ˌfeɪt gə'lɑːnt
AM ¦feɪt gə'lɑnt

fêtes champêtres
BR ˌfeɪt ʃɒ̃'peɪtr(ə)z
AM ¦feɪt ʃɑm'pɛtr(ə)z

fêtes galantes
BR ˌfeɪt gə'lɑːnt
AM ¦feɪt(s) gə'lɑnt

feticide
BR 'fɛtɪsʌɪd
AM 'fɛdəˌsaɪd

fetid
BR 'fɛtɪd
AM 'fɛdɪd

fetidly
BR 'fɛtɪdli
AM 'fɛdɪdli

fetidness
BR 'fɛtɪdnɪs
AM 'fɛdɪdnɪs

fetish
BR 'fɛtǀɪʃ, -ɪʃɪz
AM 'fɛdɪʃ, -ɪz

fetishise
BR 'fɛtɪʃʌɪz, -ɪz, -ɪŋ, -d
AM 'fɛdəˌʃaɪz, -ɪz, -ɪŋ, -d

fetishism
BR 'fɛtɪʃɪz(ə)m
AM 'fɛdɪʃˌɪzəm

fetishist
BR 'fɛtɪʃɪst, -s
AM 'fɛdɪʃɪst, -s

fetishistic
BR ˌfɛtɪ'ʃɪstɪk
AM ˌfɛdə'ʃɪstɪk

fetishize
BR 'fɛtɪʃʌɪz, -ɪz, -ɪŋ, -d
AM 'fɛdəˌʃaɪz, -ɪz, -ɪŋ, -d

Fetlar
BR 'fɛtlə(r)
AM 'fɛtlər

fetlock
BR 'fɛtlɒk, -s
AM 'fɛtˌlɑk, -s

fetor
BR 'fiːtə(r)
AM 'fidər

fetta
BR 'fɛtə(r)
AM 'fɛdə

fetter
BR 'fɛtǀə(r), -əz, -(ə)rɪŋ, -əd
AM 'fɛdər, -z, -ɪŋ, -d

fetterlock
BR 'fɛtəlɒk, -s
AM 'fɛdərˌlɑk, -s

fettle
BR 'fɛtǀl, -lz, -l̩ɪŋ\-lɪŋ, -ld
AM 'fɛdəl, -z, -ɪŋ, -d

fettler
BR 'fɛtl̩ə(r), 'fɛtlə(r), -z
AM 'fɛdl̩ər, -z

fettuccine
BR ˌfɛtʊ'tʃiːni
AM ˌfɛdə'tʃini

fettucine
BR ˌfɛtʊ'tʃiːni
AM ˌfɛdə'tʃini

fettucini
BR ˌfɛtʊ'tʃiːni
AM ˌfɛdə'tʃini

fetus
BR 'fiːtəs, -ɪz
AM 'fidəs, -əz

feu
BR fjuː, -z, -ɪŋ, -d
AM fju, -z, -ɪŋ, -d

feud
BR fjuːd, -z, -ɪŋ, -ɪd
AM fjud, -z, -ɪŋ, -əd

feudal
BR 'fjuːdl
AM 'fjudəl

feudalisation
BR ˌfjuːdl̩ʌɪ'zeɪʃn
AM ˌfjudlə'zeɪʃən, fjudlˌaɪ'zeɪʃən

feudalise
BR 'fjuːdl̩ʌɪz, -ɪz, -ɪŋ, -d
AM 'fjudlˌaɪz, -ɪz, -ɪŋ, -d

feudalism
BR 'fjuːdl̩ɪz(ə)m
AM 'fjudlˌɪzəm

feudalist
BR 'fjuːdl̩ɪst, -s
AM 'fjudl̩əst, -s

feudalistic
BR ˌfjuːdl'ɪstɪk
AM ˌfjudl'ɪstɪk

feudalistically
BR ˌfjuːdl'ɪstɪkli
AM ¦fjudl'ɪstək(ə)li

feudality
BR fjuː'dalɪti
AM fju'dælədi

feudalization
BR ˌfjuːdl̩ʌɪ'zeɪʃn
AM ˌfjudlə'zeɪʃən, fjudlˌaɪ'zeɪʃən

feudalize
BR 'fjuːdl̩ʌɪz, -ɪz, -ɪŋ, -d
AM 'fjudlˌaɪz, -ɪz, -ɪŋ, -d

feudally
BR 'fjuːdl̩i
AM 'fjudl̩i

feudatory
BR 'fjuːdət(ə)ri
AM 'fjudəˌtɔri

feu de joie
BR ˌfəː də 'ʒwɑː(r)
AM ˌfə də 'ʒwɑ

feudist
BR 'fjuːdɪst, -s
AM 'fjudəst, -s

feuilleton
BR 'fəːɪtɒ̃, -z
AM ¦fəɪ¦tɔn, -z

feux de joie
BR ˌfəː də 'ʒwɑː(r)
AM ˌfə(z) də 'ʒwɑ

fever
BR 'fiːvə(r), -z, -d
AM 'fivər, -z, -d

feverfew
BR 'fiːvəfjuː
AM 'fivərˌfju

feverish
BR 'fiːv(ə)rɪʃ
AM 'fiv(ə)rɪʃ

feverishly
BR 'fiːv(ə)rɪʃli
AM 'fiv(ə)rɪʃli
feverishness
BR 'fiːv(ə)rɪʃnɨs
AM 'fiv(ə)rɪʃnɨs
feverous
BR 'fiːv(ə)rəs
AM 'fiv(ə)rəs
few
BR fjuː, -ə(r), -ɨst
AM fju, -ər, -əst
fewness
BR 'fjuːnəs
AM 'fjunəs
fey
BR feɪ
AM feɪ
Feydeau
BR 'feɪdəʊ
AM feɪ'doʊ, 'feɪdoʊ
feyly
BR 'feɪli
AM 'feɪli
feyness
BR 'feɪnɨs
AM 'feɪnɨs
Feynman
BR 'fʌɪnmən
AM 'faɪnmən
fez
BR fɛz, -ɪz, -d
AM fɛz, -əz, -d
Ffestiniog
BR fɛ'stɪnɪɒɡ
AM fə'stɪni,ɔɡ, fɛs'tini,ɑɡ
Ffolkes
BR fəʊks
AM foʊks
Ffoulkes
BR fuːks, fəʊks
AM foʊks, fuks
fiacre
BR fɪ'ɑːkrə(r), fɪ'akrə(r), -z
AM fi'ækrə, -z
fiancé
BR fɪ'ɑːnseɪ, -z
AM ,fi,ɑn'seɪ, ,fi'ɑn,seɪ, -z
fiancée
BR fɪ'ɑːnseɪ, -z
AM ,fi,ɑn'seɪ, ,fi'ɑn,seɪ, -z
fianchetto
BR ,fɪən'tʃɛtəʊ, ,fɪən'kɛtəʊ, -z
AM ,fiən'tʃɛdoʊ, ,fiən'kɛdoʊ, -z
Fianna Fáil
BR fɪ,anə 'fɔɪl
AM fi,ɑnə 'fɔɪl
IR ,fʲiənə 'faːlʲ
fiasco
BR fɪ'askəʊ, -z
AM fi'æskoʊ, -z
fiat
BR 'fiːat, 'fʌɪat, -s
AM 'fiət, 'fi,ɑt, -s
fib
BR fɪb, -z, -ɪŋ, -d
AM fɪb, -z, -ɪŋ, -d
fibber
BR 'fɪbə(r), -z
AM 'fɪbər, -z
fiber
BR 'fʌɪbə(r), -z, -d
AM 'faɪbər, -z, -d
fiberboard
BR 'fʌɪbəbɔːd
AM 'faɪbər,bɔ(ə)rd
fiberfill
BR 'fʌɪbəfɪl
AM 'faɪbər,fɪl
fiberglass
BR 'fʌɪbəɡlɑːs, 'faɪbəɡlas
AM 'faɪbər,ɡlæs
fiberless
BR 'fʌɪbələs
AM 'faɪbərləs
Fibonacci
BR fɪbə'nɑːtʃi
AM fibə'nɑtʃi
fibre
BR 'fʌɪbə(r), -z, -d
AM 'faɪbər, -z, -d
fibreboard
BR 'fʌɪbəbɔːd
AM 'faɪbər,bɔ(ə)rd
fibrefill
BR 'fʌɪbəfɪl
AM 'faɪbər,fɪl
fibreglass
BR 'fʌɪbəɡlɑːs, 'fʌɪbəɡlas
AM 'faɪbər,ɡlæs
fibreless
BR 'fʌɪbələs
AM 'faɪbərləs
fibriform
BR 'fɪbrɨfɔːm, 'fʌɪbrɨfɔːm
AM 'fɪbrə,fɔ(ə)rm
fibril
BR 'fʌɪbr(ɨ)l, -z
AM 'fɪbrəl, -z
fibrillar
BR fɪ'brɪlə(r), fʌɪ'brɪlə(r)
AM 'fɪbrələr
fibrillary
BR fɪ'brɪl(ə)ri, fʌɪ'brɪl(ə)ri
AM 'fɪbrə,lɛri
fibrillate
BR 'fɪbrɪleɪt, 'fʌɪbrɪleɪt, -s, -ɪŋ, -ɨd
AM 'fɪbrə,leɪ|t, -ts, -dɪŋ, -dɨd
fibrillation
BR ,fɪbrɪ'leɪʃn, ,fʌɪbrɪ'leɪʃn
AM ,fɪbrə'leɪʃən
fibrin
BR 'faɪbrɪn, 'fɪbrɪn
AM 'faɪbrɨn
fibrinogen
BR fʌɪ'brɪnədʒ(ə)n, fɪ'brɪnədʒ(ə)n
AM faɪ'brɪnədʒən
fibrinoid
BR 'fʌɪbrɨnɔɪd, 'fɪbrɨnɔɪd
AM 'faɪbrə,nɔɪd
fibro
BR 'fʌɪbrəʊ, -z
AM 'faɪbroʊ, -z
fibroid
BR 'fʌɪbrɔɪd, -z
AM 'faɪ,brɔɪd, -z
fibroin
BR 'fʌɪbrəʊɪn
AM 'faɪbrəwən
fibroma
BR fʌɪ'brəʊmə(r), -z
AM faɪ'broʊmə, -z
fibromata
BR fʌɪ'brəʊmətə(r)
AM faɪ'broʊmədə
fibrosis
BR fʌɪ'brəʊsɪs
AM faɪ'broʊsəs
fibrositic
BR ,fʌɪbrə'sɪtɪk
AM ,faɪbrə'sɪdɪk
fibrositis
BR ,fʌɪbrə'sʌɪtɪs
AM ,faɪbrə'saɪdɨs
fibrotic
BR fʌɪ'brɒtɪk
AM faɪ'brɑdɪk
fibrous
BR 'fʌɪbrəs
AM 'faɪbrəs
fibrously
BR 'fʌɪbrəsli
AM 'faɪbrəsli
fibrousness
BR 'fʌɪbrəsnəs
AM 'faɪbrəsnəs
fibula
BR 'fɪbjʉlə(r), -z
AM 'fɪbjələ, -z
fibular
BR 'fɪbjʉlə(r)
AM 'fɪbjələr
fiche
BR fiːʃ, -ɪz
AM fiʃ, -ɪz
Fichte
BR fɪxt
AM 'fɪktə
GER 'fɪçtə
Fichtean
BR 'fɪxtɪən
AM 'fɪktiən
fichu
BR 'fiːʃuː, 'fɪʃuː, -z
AM 'fɪ,ʃu, -z
fickle
BR 'fɪkl̩, -ə(r), -ɨst
AM 'fɪk|əl, -(ə)lər, -(ə)ləst
fickleness
BR 'fɪklnəs
AM 'fɪkəlnəs
fickly
BR 'fɪkl̩(l)i
AM 'fɪk(ə)li
fictile
BR 'fɪktʌɪl, 'fɪkt(ɨ)l
AM 'fɪktl, 'fɪk,taɪl
fiction
BR 'fɪkʃn, -z
AM 'fɪkʃən, -z
fictional
BR 'fɪkʃn̩(ə)l, 'fɪkʃən(ə)l
AM 'fɪkʃ(ə)nəl
fictionalisation
BR ,fɪkʃn̩əlʌɪ'zeɪʃn, ,fɪkʃn̩l̩ʌɪ'zeɪʃn, ,fɪkʃənl̩ʌɪ'zeɪʃn, ,fɪkʃ(ə)nəlʌɪ'zeɪʃn, -z
AM ,fɪkʃənl̩ə'zeɪʃən, ,fɪkʃnələ'zeɪʃən, ,fɪkʃnə,laɪ'zeɪʃən, -z
fictionalise
BR 'fɪkʃn̩əlʌɪz, 'fɪkʃn̩l̩ʌɪz, 'fɪkʃənl̩ʌɪz, 'fɪkʃ(ə)nəlʌɪz, -ɪz, -ɪŋ, -d
AM 'fɪkʃ(ə)nə,laɪz, -ɪz, -ɪŋ, -d
fictionality
BR ,fɪkʃə'nalɨti
AM ,fɪkʃə'nælədi
fictionalization
BR ,fɪkʃn̩əlʌɪ'zeɪʃn, ,fɪkʃn̩l̩ʌɪ'zeɪʃn, ,fɪkʃənl̩ʌɪ'zeɪʃn, ,fɪkʃ(ə)nəlʌɪ'zeɪʃn, -z
AM ,fɪkʃənl̩ə'zeɪʃən, ,fɪkʃnələ'zeɪʃən, ,fɪkʃnə,laɪ'zeɪʃən, -z
fictionalize
BR 'fɪkʃn̩əlʌɪz, 'fɪkʃn̩l̩ʌɪz, 'fɪkʃənl̩ʌɪz, 'fɪkʃ(ə)nəlʌɪz, -ɪz, -ɪŋ, -d
AM 'fɪkʃ(ə)nə,laɪz, -ɪz, -ɪŋ, -d
fictionally
BR 'fɪkʃn̩əli, 'fɪkʃn̩l̩i, 'fɪkʃənl̩i, 'fɪkʃ(ə)nəli
AM 'fɪkʃ(ə)nəli
fictionist
BR 'fɪkʃn̩ɪst, 'fɪkʃənɪst, -s
AM 'fɪkʃ(ə)nəst, -s
fictitious
BR fɪk'tɪʃəs
AM fɪk'tɪʃəs
fictitiously
BR fɪk'tɪʃəsli

AM fɪk'tɪʃəsli
fictitiousness
BR fɪk'tɪʃəsnəs
AM fɪk'tɪʃəsnəs
fictive
BR 'fɪktɪv
AM 'fɪktɪv
fictively
BR 'fɪktɨvli
AM 'fɪktɨvli
fictiveness
BR 'fɪktɨvnɨs
AM 'fɪktɪvnɨs
fid
BR fɪd, -z
AM fɪd, -z
fiddle
BR 'fɪd|l, -lz, -lɪŋ\-lɪŋ, -ld
AM 'fɪd|əl, -əlz, -(ə)lɪŋ, -əld
fiddle-de-dee
BR ˌfɪdldɪ'diː
AM ˌfɪdəldi'di
fiddler
BR 'fɪdlə(r), -z
AM 'fɪd(ə)lər, -z
fiddlestick
BR 'fɪdlstɪk, -s
AM 'fɪdlˌstɪk, -s
fiddly
BR 'fɪdl̩i, 'fɪdli
AM 'fɪdl̩i
Fidei Defensor
BR ˌfɪdeɪiː dɪ'fɛnsɔː(r), ˌfʌɪdɪʌɪ +
AM ˌfɪdeɪˌi dəˈfɛnˌsɔ(ə)r
fideism
BR 'fiːdeɪɪz(ə)m, 'fʌɪdɪɪz(ə)m
AM 'fideɪˌɪzəm
fideist
BR 'fiːdeɪɪst, 'fʌɪdɪɪst, -s
AM 'fideɪɪst, -s
fideistic
BR ˌfiːdeɪ'ɪstɪk, ˌfʌɪdɪ'ɪstɪk
AM ˌfideɪ'ɪstɪk
Fidel
BR fɪ'dɛl
AM fə'dɛl
Fidelio
BR fɪ'deɪlɪəʊ
AM fɪ'deɪlioʊ
Fidelis
BR fɪ'deɪlɪs
AM fɪ'deɪlɨs
fidelity
BR fɪ'dɛlɪti
AM fɪ'dɛlədi
fidget
BR 'fɪdʒɪt, -s, -ɪŋ, -ɨd
AM 'fɪdʒɪ|t, -ts, -dɪŋ, -dɨd
fidgetiness
BR 'fɪdʒɪtɪnɨs
AM 'fɪdʒɨdinɨs
fidgety
BR 'fɪdʒɪti
AM 'fɪdʒɨdi
Fidler
BR 'fɪdlə(r), 'fiːdlə(r)
AM 'fɪdlər, 'fidlər
Fido
BR 'fʌɪdəʊ
AM 'faɪdoʊ
fiducial
BR fɪ'djuːʃ(ə)l, fɪ'dʒuːʃ(ə)l, fɪ'djuːʃɪəl, fɪ'dʒuːʃɪəl, fɪ'djuːsɪəl, fɪ'dʒuːsɪəl
AM fə'duʃiəl
fiducially
BR fɪ'djuːʃl̩i, fɪ'djuːʃəli, fɪ'dʒuːʃl̩i, fɪ'dʒuːʃəli, fɪ'djuːʃɪəli, fɪ'dʒuːʃɪəli, fɪ'djuːsɪəli, fɪ'dʒuːsɪəli
AM fə'duʃ(i)əli
fiduciary
BR fɪ'djuːʃ(ə)r|i, fɪ'dʒuːʃ(ə)r|i fɪ'djuːs(ə)r|i, fɪ'dʒuːs(ə)ri, fɪ'djuːʃɪər|i, fɪ'dʒuːʃɪəri, fɪ'djuːsɪəri, fɪ'dʒuːsɪəri, -ɪz
AM fə'duʃiˌɛri, fə'dusiˌɛri, -z
fidus Achates
BR ˌfʌɪdəs ə'keɪtiːz
AM 'faɪdəs ə'kɑdiz
fie
BR fʌɪ
AM faɪ
Fiedler
BR 'fiːdlə(r)
AM 'fidlər
fief
BR fiːf, -s
AM fif, -s
fiefdom
BR 'fiːfdəm, -z
AM 'fifdəm, -z
field
BR fiːld, -z, -ɪŋ, -ɨd
AM fild, -z, -ɪŋ, -ɨd
Fielden
BR 'fiːld(ə)n
AM 'fildən
fielder
BR 'fiːldə(r), -z
AM 'fildər, -z
fieldfare
BR 'fiːldfɛː(r), -z
AM 'fil(d),fɛ(ə)r, -z
Fielding
BR 'fiːldɪŋ
AM 'fildɪŋ
fieldmice
BR 'fiːldmʌɪs
AM 'fil(d),maɪs
fieldmouse
BR 'fiːldmaʊs
AM 'fil(d),maʊs
Fields
BR fiːldz
AM fil(d)z
fieldsman
BR 'fiːldzmən
AM 'fil(d)zmən
fieldsmen
BR 'fiːldzmən
AM 'fil(d)zmən
fieldstone
BR 'fiːldstəʊn, -z
AM 'fil(d),stoʊn, -z
fieldwork
BR 'fiːldwəːk
AM 'fil(d),wərk
fieldworker
BR 'fiːldwəːkə(r), -z
AM 'fil(d),wərkər, -z
fiend
BR fiːnd, -z
AM find, -z
fiendish
BR 'fiːndɪʃ
AM 'findɪʃ
fiendishly
BR 'fiːndɪʃli
AM 'findɪʃli
fiendishness
BR 'fiːndɪʃnɨs
AM 'findɪʃnɨs
fiendlike
BR 'fiːndlʌɪk
AM 'fin(d),laɪk
Fiennes
BR fʌɪnz
AM faɪnz
fierce
BR fɪəs, -ə(r), -ɨst
AM fɪ(ə)rs, -ər, -ɨst
fiercely
BR 'fɪəsli
AM 'fɪrsli
fierceness
BR 'fɪəsnəs
AM 'fɪrsnəs
fieri facias
BR ˌfʌɪərʌɪ 'feɪʃɪas
AM ˌfaɪri 'feɪʃ(i)əs
fierily
BR 'fʌɪərɨli
AM 'faɪrəli
fieriness
BR 'fʌɪərɪnɨs
AM 'faɪrinɨs
fiery
BR 'fʌɪər|i, -ɪə(r), -ɪɨst
AM 'faɪri, -ər, -ɨst
fiesta
BR fɪ'ɛstə(*r*)
AM fi'ɛstə
FIFA
BR 'fiːfə(*r*)
AM 'fifə
fife
BR fʌɪf, -s, -ɪŋ, -t
AM faɪf, -s, -ɪŋ, -t
fifer
BR 'fʌɪfə(r), -z
AM 'faɪfər, -z
Fifi
BR 'fiːfiː
AM 'fifi
Fifield
BR 'fʌɪfiːld
AM 'faɪˌfild
FIFO
BR 'fiːfəʊ
AM 'fiˌfoʊ
fifteen
BR ˌfɪf'tiːn
AM ˌfɪf'tin
fifteenth
BR ˌfɪf'tiːnθ
AM ˌfɪf'tinθ
fifth
BR fɪfθ
AM fɪ(f)θ
fifthly
BR 'fɪfθli
AM 'fɪ(f)θli
Fifth Monarchy
BR ˌfɪfθ 'mɒnəki
AM ˌfɪ(f)θ 'mɑnərki
fiftieth
BR 'fɪftɪɨθ
AM 'fɪftiɨθ
fifty
BR 'fɪfti
AM 'fɪfti
fifty-fifty
BR ˌfɪftɪ'fɪfti
AM ˌfɪfti'fɪfti
fiftyfold
BR 'fɪftɪfəʊld
AM 'fɪftiˌfoʊld
fig
BR fɪɡ, -z
AM fɪɡ, -z
Figaro
BR 'fɪɡərəʊ
AM 'fɪɡəroʊ
Figg
BR fɪɡ
AM fɪɡ
Figgis
BR 'fɪɡɪs
AM 'fɪɡɨs
fight
BR fʌɪt, -s, -ɪŋ
AM faɪ|t, -ts, -dɪŋ
fightback
BR 'fʌɪtbak, -s
AM 'faɪtˌbæk, -s
fighter
BR 'fʌɪtə(r), -z
AM 'faɪdər, -z

figleaf
BR ˈfɪɡliːf
AM ˈfɪɡˌlif
figleaves
BR ˈfɪɡliːvz
AM ˈfɪɡˌlivz
figment
BR ˈfɪɡm(ə)nt, -s
AM ˈfɪɡmənt, -s
figtree
BR ˈfɪɡtriː, -z
AM ˈfɪɡˌtri, -z
Figueroa
BR ˌfɪɡəˈrəʊə(r)
AM ˌfɪɡəˈroʊə
figura
BR fɪˈɡjʊərə(r), fɪˈɡjɔːrə(r), -z
AM fɪˈɡjərə, -z
figural
BR ˈfɪɡjʊrəl, ˈfɪɡjʊrḷ
AM fɪˈɡjərəl
figurant
BR ˈfɪɡjʊrənt, ˈfɪɡjʊrn̩t, -s
AM ˈfɪɡ(j)ərənt, ˌfɪɡ(j)əˈrɑnt, -s
figurante
BR ˌfɪɡjʊˈrant|i, -ɪz
AM ˌfɪɡjəˈrɑn(t)i, -z
figuranti
BR ˌfɪɡjʊˈrant|i, -ɪz
AM ˌfɪɡjəˈrɑn(t)i, -z
figuration
BR ˌfɪɡjʊˈreɪʃn, -z
AM ˌfɪɡjəˈreɪʃən, -z
figurative
BR ˈfɪɡ(ə)rətɪv, ˈfɪɡjʊrətɪv
AM ˈfɪɡjərədɪv
figuratively
BR ˈfɪɡ(ə)rətɪvli, ˈfɪɡjʊrətɪvli
AM ˈfɪɡjərədəvli
figurativeness
BR ˈfɪɡ(ə)rətɪvnɪs, ˈfɪɡjʊrətɪvnɪs
AM ˈfɪɡjərədɪvnɪs
figure
BR ˈfɪɡə(r), -z, -ɪŋ, -d
AM ˈfɪɡjər, -z, -ɪŋ, -d
figurehead
BR ˈfɪɡəhɛd, -z
AM ˈfɪɡjərˌ(h)ɛd, -z
figureless
BR ˈfɪɡələs
AM ˈfɪɡjərləs
figurine
BR ˌfɪɡəˈriːn, -z
AM ˌfɪɡjəˈrin, -z
figwort
BR ˈfɪɡwəːt
AM ˈfɪɡˌwərt, ˈfɪɡˌwɔ(ə)rt
Fiji
BR ˈfiːdʒiː, ˌfiːˈdʒiː
AM ˈfiˌdʒi
Fijian
BR fɪˈdʒiːən, fiːˈdʒiːən, -z
AM fiˈdʒiən, fəˈdʒiən, -z
filagree
BR ˈfɪləɡriː, -z
AM ˈfɪləˌɡri, -z
filament
BR ˈfɪləm(ə)nt, -s
AM ˈfɪləmənt, -s
filamentary
BR ˌfɪləˈmɛnt(ə)ri
AM ˌfɪləˈmɛn(t)əri
filamented
BR ˈfɪləmɛntɪd
AM ˈfɪləˌmɛn(t)əd
filamentous
BR ˌfɪləˈmɛntəs
AM ˌfɪləˈmɛn(t)əs
filaria
BR fɪˈlɛːrɪə(r), -z
AM fəˈlɛriə, -z
filariae
BR fɪˈlɛːrɪiː
AM fəˈlɛriˌi, fəˈlɛriˌaɪ
filarial
BR fɪˈlɛːrɪəl
AM fəˈlɛriəl
filariasis
BR ˌfɪləˈrʌɪəsɪs, fɪˌlɛːrɪˈeɪsɪs
AM ˌfɪləˈraɪəsəs
filature
BR ˈfɪlətʃə(r), ˈfɪlətʃʊə(r), -z
AM ˈfɪlətʃər, ˈfɪləˌtʃʊ(ə)r, -z
filbert
BR ˈfɪlbət, -s
AM ˈfɪlbərt, -s
filch
BR fɪltʃ, -ɪz, -ɪŋ, -t
AM fɪltʃ, -ɪz, -ɪŋ, -t
filcher
BR ˈfɪltʃə(r), -z
AM ˈfɪltʃər, -z
file
BR fʌɪl, -z, -ɪŋ, -d
AM faɪl, -z, -ɪŋ, -d
filefish
BR ˈfʌɪlfɪʃ
AM ˈfaɪlˌfɪʃ
filename
BR ˈfʌɪlneɪm, -z
AM ˈfaɪlˌneɪm, -z
filer
BR ˈfʌɪlə(r), -z
AM ˈfaɪlər, -z
filet
BR ˈfɪlɪt, ˈfɪleɪ, -s\-z
AM fɪˈleɪ, ˈfɪleɪ, -z
filet mignon
BR ˌfɪleɪ ˈmiːnjɒ̃, + ˈmɪnjɒ̃, -z
AM fɪˌleɪ mɪnˈjɑn, -z
Filey
BR ˈfʌɪli
AM ˈfaɪli
filial
BR ˈfɪlɪəl
AM ˈfɪljəl, ˈfɪliəl
filially
BR ˈfɪlɪəli
AM ˈfɪljəli, ˈfɪliəli
filialness
BR ˈfɪlɪəlnəs
AM ˈfɪljəlnəs, ˈfɪliəlnəs
filiation
BR ˌfɪlɪˈeɪʃn
AM ˌfɪliˈeɪʃən
filibeg
BR ˈfɪlɪbɛɡ, -z
AM ˈfɪləˌbɛɡ, -z
filibuster
BR ˈfɪlɪbʌst|ə(r), -əz, -(ə)rɪŋ, -əd
AM ˈfɪləˌbəst|ər, -ərz, -(ə)rɪŋ, -ərd
filibusterer
BR ˈfɪlɪbʌst(ə)rə(r), -z
AM ˈfɪləˌbəstərər, -z
filicide
BR ˈfɪlɪsʌɪd, -z
AM ˈfɪləˌsaɪd, -z
filiform
BR ˈfʌɪlɪfɔːm
AM ˈfɪləˌfɔ(ə)rm, ˈfaɪləˌfɔ(ə)rm
filigree
BR ˈfɪlɪɡriː
AM ˈfɪləˌɡri
filigreed
BR ˈfɪlɪɡriːd
AM ˈfɪləˌɡrid
filing
BR ˈfʌɪlɪŋ, -z
AM ˈfaɪlɪŋ, -z
filings
BR ˈfʌɪlɪŋz
AM ˈfaɪlɪŋz
Filioque
BR ˌfiːlɪˈəʊkwi, ˌfɪlɪˈəʊkwi
AM ˌfɪliˈoʊkwə
Filipina
BR ˌfɪlɪˈpiːnə(r), -z
AM ˌfɪləˈpinə, -z
Filipino
BR ˌfɪlɪˈpiːnəʊ, -z
AM ˌfɪləˈpinoʊ, -z
fill
BR fɪl, -z, -ɪŋ, -d
AM fɪl, -z, -ɪŋ, -d
fille de joie
BR ˌfiː də ˌʒwɑː(r)
AM ˌfɪ də ˈʒwɑ
filler
BR ˈfɪlə(r), -z
AM ˈfɪlər, -z
filles de joie
BR ˌfiː də ˌʒwɑː(r)
AM ˌfɪ(z) də ˈʒwɑ
fillet
BR ˈfɪlɪt, -s, -ɪŋ, -ɪd
AM ˈfɪlɪ|t, -ts, -dɪŋ, -dɪd
filleter
BR ˈfɪlɪtə(r), -z
AM ˈfɪlɪdər, -z
fill-in
BR ˈfɪlɪn, -z
AM ˈfɪlˌɪn, -z
filling
BR ˈfɪlɪŋ, -z
AM ˈfɪlɪŋ, -z
fillip
BR ˈfɪlɪp, -s, -ɪŋ, -t
AM ˈfɪlɪp, -s, -ɪŋ, -t
fillis
BR ˈfɪlɪs
AM ˈfɪlɪs
fillister
BR ˈfɪlɪstə(r), -z
AM ˈfɪlɪstər, -z
Fillmore
BR ˈfɪlmɔː(r)
AM ˈfɪlˌmɔ(ə)r
fill-up
BR ˈfɪlʌp, -s
AM ˈfɪləp, -s
filly
BR ˈfɪl|i, -ɪz
AM ˈfɪli, -z
film
BR fɪlm, -z, -ɪŋ, -d
AM fɪlm, -z, -ɪŋ, -d
filmable
BR ˈfɪlməbl
AM ˈfɪlməbəl
filmgoer
BR ˈfɪlmˌɡəʊə(r), -z
AM ˈfɪlmˌɡoʊər, -z
filmic
BR ˈfɪlmɪk
AM ˈfɪlmɪk
filmily
BR ˈfɪlmɪli
AM ˈfɪlmɪli
filminess
BR ˈfɪlmɪnɪs
AM ˈfɪlminɪs
filmmaker
BR ˈfɪlmˌmeɪkə(r), -z
AM ˈfɪlmˌmeɪkər, -z
filmmaking
BR ˈfɪlmˌmeɪkɪŋ
AM ˈfɪlmˌmeɪkɪŋ
film noir
BR ˌfɪlm ˈnwɑː(r)
AM ˌfɪlm ˈnwɑr
filmography
BR fɪlˈmɒɡrəfi
AM fɪlˈmɑɡrəfi
filmset
BR ˈfɪlmsɛt, -s, -ɪŋ
AM ˈfɪlmˌsɛ|t, -ts, -dɪŋ
filmsetter
BR ˈfɪlmˌsɛtə(r), -z
AM ˈfɪlmˌsɛdər, -z
filmstrip
BR ˈfɪlmstrɪp, -s
AM ˈfɪlmˌstrɪp, -s

filmy
BR ˈfɪlm|i, -ɪə(r), -ɪɪst
AM ˈfɪlmi, -ər, -ɪst

filo
BR ˈfiːləʊ
AM ˈfiloʊ

Filofax®
BR ˈfʌɪlə(ʊ)faks, -ɪz
AM ˈfaɪloʊˌfæks

filoplume
BR ˈfʌɪlə(ʊ)pluːm, -z
AM ˈfɪləˌplum, ˈfaɪləˌplum, -z

filoselle
BR ˈfɪləsɛl
AM ˌfɪləˈsɛl

filovirus
BR ˈfiːləʊˌvʌɪrəs
AM ˈfiloʊˌvaɪrəs, ˈfiləˌvaɪrəs

fils
BR fiːs
AM fis

filter
BR ˈfɪlt|ə(r), -əz, -(ə)rɪŋ, -əd
AM ˈfɪlt|ər, -ərz, -(ə)rɪŋ, -ərd

filterable
BR ˈfɪlt(ə)rəbl
AM ˈfɪlt(ə)rəbəl

filth
BR fɪlθ
AM fɪlθ

filthily
BR ˈfɪlθɪli
AM ˈfɪlθɪli

filthiness
BR ˈfɪlθɪnɪs
AM ˈfɪlθinɪs

filthy
BR ˈfɪlθ|i, -ɪə(r), -ɪɪst
AM ˈfɪlθi, -ər, -ɪst

Filton
BR ˈfɪlt(ə)n
AM ˈfɪltən

filtrable
BR ˈfɪltrəbl
AM ˈfɪltrəbəl

filtrate
BR ˈfɪltreɪt, -s, -ɪŋ, -ɪd
AM ˈfɪltˌreɪ|t, -ts, -dɪŋ, -dɪd

filtration
BR fɪlˈtreɪʃn
AM fɪlˈtreɪʃən

fimbria
BR ˈfɪmbrɪə(r)
AM ˈfɪmbriə

fimbriae
BR ˈfɪmbriiː
AM ˈfɪmbrii, ˈfɪmbriaɪ

fimbriate
BR ˈfɪmbrɪeɪt, ˈfɪmbrɪət
AM ˈfɪmbriət

fimbriated
BR ˈfɪmbrɪeɪtɪd
AM ˈfɪmbriˌeɪdɪd

fin
BR fɪn, -z, -d
AM fɪn, -z, -d

finable
BR ˈfʌɪnəbl
AM ˈfaɪnəbəl

finagle
BR fɪˈneɪɡ|l, -lz, -l̩ɪŋ\-lɪŋ, -ld
AM fɪˈneɪɡ|əl, -əlz, -(ə)lɪŋ, -əld

finagler
BR fɪˈneɪɡl̩ə(r), fɪˈneɪɡlə(r), -z
AM fɪˈneɪɡ(ə)lər, -z

final
BR ˈfʌɪnl, -z
AM ˈfaɪnl, -z

finale
BR fɪˈnɑːl|i, -ɪz
AM fɪˈnæli, fɪˈnɑli, -z

finalisation
BR ˌfʌɪnəlʌɪˈzeɪʃn, ˌfʌɪnl̩ʌɪˈzeɪʃn
AM ˌfaɪnələˈzeɪʃən, ˌfaɪnəˌlaɪˈzeɪʃən

finalise
BR ˈfʌɪnəlʌɪz, ˈfʌɪnl̩ʌɪz, -ɪz, -ɪŋ, -d
AM ˈfaɪnlˌaɪz, -ɪz, -ɪŋ, -d

finalism
BR ˈfʌɪnəlɪz(ə)m, ˈfʌɪnl̩ɪz(ə)m
AM ˈfaɪnlˌɪzəm

finalist
BR ˈfʌɪnəlɪst, ˈfʌɪnl̩ɪst, -s
AM ˈfaɪnl̩ɪst, -s

finalistic
BR ˌfʌɪnəˈlɪstɪk, ˌfʌɪnlˈɪstɪk
AM ˌfaɪnlˈɪstɪk

finality
BR fʌɪˈnalɪti
AM faɪˈnælədi, fɪˈnælədi

finalization
BR ˌfʌɪnəlʌɪˈzeɪʃn, ˌfʌɪnl̩ʌɪˈzeɪʃn
AM ˌfaɪnələˈzeɪʃən, ˌfaɪnəˌlaɪˈzeɪʃən

finalize
BR ˈfʌɪnəlʌɪz, ˈfʌɪnl̩ʌɪz, -ɪz, -ɪŋ, -d
AM ˈfaɪnlˌaɪz, -ɪz, -ɪŋ, -d

finally
BR ˈfʌɪnəli, ˈfʌɪnl̩i
AM ˈfaɪn(ə)li

finance
BR fʌɪˈnans, fɪˈnans, ˈfʌɪnans, -ɪz, -ɪŋ, -t
AM ˈfaɪˌnæns, fɪˈnæns, -əz, -ɪŋ, -t

financial
BR fɪˈnanʃl, fʌɪˈnanʃl
AM fɪˈnæn(t)ʃəl, faɪˈnæn(t)ʃəl

financially
BR fɪˈnanʃl̩i, fɪˈnanʃəli, fʌɪˈnanʃl̩i, fʌɪˈnanʃəli
AM fɪˈnæn(t)ʃ(ə)li, faɪˈnæn(t)ʃ(ə)li

financier
BR fɪˈnansɪə(r), -z
AM ˌfɪnənˈsɪ(ə)r, -z

Finbar
BR ˈfɪnbɑː(r)
AM ˈfɪnˌbɑr

finca
BR ˈfɪŋkə(r), -z
AM ˈfɪŋkə, -z

finch
BR fɪn(t)ʃ, -ɪz
AM fɪn(t)ʃ, -ɪz

Finchale
BR ˈfɪŋkl
AM ˈfɪŋkəl

Finchampstead
BR ˈfɪn(t)ʃəm(p)stɛd, ˈfɪn(t)ʃəm(p)stɪd
AM ˈfɪn(t)ʃəm(p)ˌstɛd

Finchley
BR ˈfɪn(t)ʃli
AM ˈfɪn(t)ʃli

find
BR fʌɪnd, -z, -ɪŋ
AM faɪnd, -z, -ɪŋ

findable
BR ˈfʌɪndəbl
AM ˈfaɪndəbəl

finder
BR ˈfʌɪndə(r), -z
AM ˈfaɪndər, -z

fin de siècle
BR ˌfã də ˈsjɛklə(r)
AM ˌfan də sˈjɛkl

Findhorn
BR ˈfɪndhɔːn
AM ˈfaɪndˌ(h)ɔ(ə)rn

finding
BR ˈfʌɪndɪŋ, -z
AM ˈfaɪndɪŋ, -z

Findlater
BR ˈfɪn(d)lətə(r)
AM ˈfɪn(d)lədər

Findlay
BR ˈfɪn(d)li
AM ˈfɪnli

Findon
BR ˈfɪnd(ə)n
AM ˈfɪndən

findspot
BR ˈfʌɪn(d)spɒt, -s
AM ˈfaɪn(d)ˌspɑt, -s

Findus
BR ˈfɪndəs
AM ˈfɪndəs

fine
BR fʌɪn, -z, -ɪŋ, -d, -ə(r), -ɪst
AM faɪn, -z, -ɪŋ, -d, -ər, -ɪst

fineable
BR ˈfʌɪnəbl
AM ˈfaɪnəbəl

Fine Gael
BR ˌfɪnə ˈɡeɪl
AM ˌfɪnə ˈɡeɪl
IR ˌfʲinʲə ˈɡeːl

finely
BR ˈfʌɪnli
AM ˈfaɪnli

fineness
BR ˈfʌɪnnɪs
AM ˈfaɪ(n)nɪs

finery
BR ˈfʌɪnəri
AM ˈfaɪnəri

fines herbes
BR ˌfiːn(z) ˈɛːb
AM ˌfin ˈ(z)ɛrb

fine-spun
BR ˌfʌɪnˈspʌn
AM ˈfaɪnˌspən

finesse
BR fɪˈnɛs
AM fɪˈnɛs

Fingal
BR ˈfɪŋɡl
AM ˈfɪŋɡəl

finger
BR ˈfɪŋɡ|ə(r), -əz, -(ə)rɪŋ, -əd
AM ˈfɪŋɡ|ər, -ərz, -(ə)rɪŋ, -ərd

fingerboard
BR ˈfɪŋɡəbɔːd, -z
AM ˈfɪŋɡərˌbɔ(ə)rd, -z

fingering
BR ˈfɪŋɡ(ə)rɪŋ, -z
AM ˈfɪŋɡərɪŋ, -z

fingerless
BR ˈfɪŋɡələs
AM ˈfɪŋɡərləs

fingerling
BR ˈfɪŋɡəlɪŋ, -z
AM ˈfɪŋɡərlɪŋ, -z

fingernail
BR ˈfɪŋɡəneɪl, -z
AM ˈfɪŋɡərˌneɪl, -z

fingerplate
BR ˈfɪŋɡəpleɪt, -s
AM ˈfɪŋɡərˌpleɪt, -s

fingerpost
BR ˈfɪŋɡəpəʊst, -s
AM ˈfɪŋɡərˌpoʊst, -s

fingerprint
BR ˈfɪŋɡəprɪnt, -s, -ɪŋ, -ɪd
AM ˈfɪŋɡərˌprɪn|t, -ts, -dɪŋ, -dɪd

fingerstall
BR ˈfɪŋɡəstɔːl, -z
AM ˈfɪŋɡərˌstɔl, ˈfɪŋɡərˌstɑl, -z

fingertip
BR ˈfɪŋɡətɪp, -s

AM ˈfɪŋgərˌtɪp, -s

finial
BR ˈfɪnɪəl, ˈfʌɪnɪəl, -z
AM ˈfiniəl, -z

finical
BR ˈfɪnɨkl
AM ˈfɪnɨkəl

finicality
BR ˌfɪnɪˈkalɨti
AM ˌfɪnɪˈkælədi

finically
BR ˈfɪnɨkļi, ˈfɪnɨkəli
AM ˈfɪnɨk(ə)li

finicalness
BR ˈfɪnɨklnəs
AM ˈfɪnɨkəlnəs

finickily
BR ˈfɪnɨkɨli, ˈfɪnɨkļi
AM ˈfɪnɨk(ə)li

finickiness
BR ˈfɪnɨkɪnɨs
AM ˈfɪnɪkinɨs

finicking
BR ˈfɪnɨkɪŋ
AM ˈfɪnɨkɪŋ

finickity
BR fɪˈnɪkɨti
AM fəˈnɪkɨdi

finicky
BR ˈfɪnɨk|i, -ɪə(r), -ɪɪst
AM ˈfɪnɨki, -ər, -ɨst

finis
BR ˈfiːnɪs, ˈfɪnɪs, ˈfʌɪnɪs
AM ˈfɪnɨs, ˈfɪni, fɪˈni

finish
BR ˈfɪn|ɪʃ, -ɨʃɨz, -ɨʃɪŋ, -ɪʃt
AM ˈfɪnɨʃ, -ɨz, -ɪŋ, -t

finisher
BR ˈfɪnɨʃə(r), -z
AM ˈfɪnɪʃər, -z

Finisterre
BR ˌfɪnɪˈstɛː(r)
AM ˌfɪnɨsˈtɛ(ə)r

finite
BR ˈfʌɪnʌɪt
AM ˈfaɪˌnaɪt

finitely
BR ˈfʌɪnʌɪtli
AM ˈfaɪˌnaɪtli

finiteness
BR ˈfʌɪnʌɪtnɨs
AM ˈfaɪˌnaɪtnɨs

finitism
BR ˈfʌɪnʌɪtɪz(ə)m
AM ˈfaɪnəˌtɪzəm

finitist
BR ˈfʌɪnʌɪtɪst, -s
AM ˈfaɪˌnaɪdɪst, -s

finitude
BR ˈfɪnɨtjuːd, ˈfʌɪnɨtjuːd, ˈfɪnɨtʃuːd, ˈfʌɪnɨtʃuːd
AM ˈfɪnəˌt(j)ud, ˈfaɪnəˌt(j)ud

fink
BR fɪŋk, -s
AM fɪŋk, -s

Finkelstein
BR ˈfɪŋklstʌɪn
AM ˈfɪŋkəlˌstin, ˈfɪŋkəlˌstaɪn

Finland
BR ˈfɪnlənd
AM ˈfɪnlənd

Finlandia
BR fɪnˈlandɪə(r)
AM fɪnˈlændiə

Finlay
BR ˈfɪnli, ˈfɪnleɪ
AM ˈfɪnli

Finlayson
BR ˈfɪnlɨs(ə)n
AM ˈfɪnlisən

finless
BR ˈfɪnlɨs
AM ˈfɪnlɨs

Finley
BR ˈfɪnli
AM ˈfɪnli

Finn
BR fɪn, -z
AM fɪn, -z

Finnair
BR ˌfɪnˈɛː(r), ˈfɪnɛː(r)
AM ˈfɪnˈɛ(ə)r

finnan
BR ˈfɪnən, -z
AM ˈfɪnən, -z

finnanhaddie
BR ˌfɪnənˈhadi
AM ˌfɪnənˈhædi

Finnegan
BR ˈfɪnɨg(ə)n
AM ˈfɪnəgən

finner
BR ˈfɪnə(r), -z
AM ˈfɪnər, -z

finnesko
BR ˈfɪn(ɨ)skəʊ, -z
AM ˈfɪnzkoʊ, ˈfɪnəˌskoʊ, -z

finneskoe
BR ˈfɪn(ɨ)skəʊ, -z
AM ˈfɪnzkoʊ, ˈfɪnəˌskoʊ, -z

Finney
BR ˈfɪni
AM ˈfɪni

Finnic
BR ˈfɪnɪk
AM ˈfɪnɪk

Finningley
BR ˈfɪnɪŋli
AM ˈfɪnɪŋli

Finnish
BR ˈfɪnɪʃ
AM ˈfɪnɪʃ

Finno-Ugrian
BR ˌfɪnəʊˈjuːgrɪən
AM ˌfɪnoʊˈugriən

Finno-Ugric
BR ˌfɪnəʊˈjuːgrɪk
AM ˌfɪnoʊˈugrɪk

finny
BR ˈfɪni
AM ˈfɪni

fino
BR ˈfiːnəʊ, -z
AM ˈfinoʊ, -z

Finola
BR fɪˈnəʊlə(r)
AM fəˈnoʊlə

Finsberg
BR ˈfɪnzbəːg
AM ˈfɪnzˌbərg

Finsbury
BR ˈfɪnsb(ə)ri
AM ˈfɪnzˌbɛri

Finucane
BR fɪˈnuːk(ə)n
AM ˈfɪnəˌkeɪn

Fiona
BR fɪˈəʊnə(r)
AM fiˈoʊnə

fiord
BR ˈfiːɔːd, fɪˈɔːd, fjɔːd, -z
AM fiˈɔ(ə)rd, fjɔ(ə)rd, -z

fioritura
BR fɪˌɔːrɪˈtʊərə(r)
AM fiˌɔrəˈtʊrə

fioriture
BR fɪˌɔːrɪˈtʊəri, fɪˌɔːrɪˈtʊəreɪ
AM fiˌɔrəˈtʊˌreɪ

fipple
BR ˈfɪpl, -z
AM ˈfɪpəl, -z

fir
BR fəː(r), -z
AM fər, -z

fire
BR ˈfʌɪə(r), -z, -ɪŋ, -d
AM ˈfaɪ(ə)r, -z, -ɪŋ, -d

firearm
BR ˈfʌɪərɑːm, -z
AM ˈfaɪ(ə)rˌɑrm, -z

fireback
BR ˈfʌɪəbak, -s
AM ˈfaɪ(ə)rˌbæk, -s

fireball
BR ˈfʌɪəbɔːl, -z
AM ˈfaɪ(ə)rˌbɔl, ˈfaɪ(ə)rˌbɑl, -z

firebird
BR ˈfʌɪəbəːd, -z
AM ˈfaɪ(ə)rˌbərd, -z

firebomb
BR ˈfʌɪəbɒm, -z, -ɪŋ, -d
AM ˈfaɪ(ə)rˌbɑm, -z, -ɪŋ, -d

firebox
BR ˈfʌɪəbɒks, -ɨz
AM ˈfaɪ(ə)rˌbɑks, -əz

firebrand
BR ˈfʌɪəbrand, -z
AM ˈfaɪ(ə)rˌbrænd, -z

firebrat
BR ˈfʌɪəbrat, -s
AM ˈfaɪ(ə)rˌbræt, -s

firebreak
BR ˈfʌɪəbreɪk, -s
AM ˈfaɪ(ə)rˌbreɪk, -s

firebrick
BR ˈfʌɪəbrɪk, -s
AM ˈfaɪ(ə)rˌbrɪk, -s

firebug
BR ˈfʌɪəbʌg, -z
AM ˈfaɪ(ə)rˌbəg, -z

firecat
BR ˈfaɪəkat, -s
AM ˈfaɪ(ə)rˌkæt, -s

fireclay
BR ˈfʌɪəkleɪ
AM ˈfaɪ(ə)rˌkleɪ

firecracker
BR ˈfʌɪəˌkrakə(r), -z
AM ˈfaɪ(ə)rˌkrækər, -z

firecrest
BR ˈfʌɪəkrɛst, -s
AM ˈfaɪ(ə)rˌkrɛst, -s

firedamp
BR ˈfʌɪədamp
AM ˈfaɪ(ə)rˌdæmp

firedog
BR ˈfʌɪədɒg, -z
AM ˈfaɪ(ə)rˌdɔg, ˈfaɪ(ə)rˌdɑg, -z

firefly
BR ˈfʌɪəflʌɪ, -z
AM ˈfaɪ(ə)rˌflaɪ, -z

fireguard
BR ˈfʌɪəgɑːd, -z
AM ˈfaɪ(ə)rˌgɑrd, -z

firehouse
BR ˈfʌɪəˌhaʊ|s, -zɪz
AM ˈfaɪ(ə)rˌ(h)aʊ|s, -zəz

fireless
BR ˈfʌɪələs
AM ˈfaɪ(ə)rləs

firelight
BR ˈfʌɪəlʌɪt
AM ˈfaɪ(ə)rˌlaɪt

firelighter
BR ˈfʌɪəlʌɪtə(r), -z
AM ˈfaɪ(ə)rˌlaɪdər, -z

firelock
BR ˈfʌɪəlɒk, -s
AM ˈfaɪ(ə)rˌlɑk, -s

fireman
BR ˈfʌɪəmən
AM ˈfaɪ(ə)rmən

firemen
BR ˈfʌɪəˌmɛn, ˈfʌɪəmən
AM ˈfaɪ(ə)rˌmɛn, ˈfaɪ(ə)rmən

Firenze
BR fɪˈrɛnzi
AM fɪˈrɛn(t)zə
IT fiˈrɛntse

fireplace
BR ˈfʌɪəpleɪs, -ɨz
AM ˈfaɪ(ə)rˌpleɪs, -ɨz

fireplug
BR ˈfʌɪəplʌg, -z
AM ˈfaɪ(ə)rˌpləg, -z

firepower
BR ˈfʌɪəˌpaʊə(r)
AM ˈfaɪ(ə)rˌpaʊər
fireproof
BR ˈfʌɪəpruːf
AM ˈfaɪ(ə)rˌpruf
firer
BR ˈfʌɪərə(r), -z
AM ˈfaɪ(ə)rər, -z
fire sale
BR ˈfʌɪə seɪl, -z
AM ˈfaɪ(ə)r ˌseɪl, -z
fire screen
BR ˈfʌɪə skriːn, -z
AM ˈfaɪ(ə)r ˌskrin, -z
fireship
BR ˈfʌɪəʃɪp, -s
AM ˈfaɪ(ə)rˌʃɪp, -s
fireside
BR ˈfʌɪəsʌɪd, -z
AM ˈfaɪ(ə)rˌsaɪd, -z
firestorm
BR ˈfʌɪəstɔːm, -z
AM ˈfaɪ(ə)rˌstɔ(ə)rm, -z
firetrap
BR ˈfʌɪətrap, -s
AM ˈfaɪ(ə)rˌtræp, -s
firewalker
BR ˈfʌɪəˌwɔːkə(r), -z
AM ˈfaɪ(ə)rˌwɔkər, ˈfaɪ(ə)rˌwɑkər, -z
firewalking
BR ˈfʌɪəˌwɔːkɪŋ
AM ˈfaɪ(ə)rˌwɔkɪŋ, ˈfaɪ(ə)rˌwɑkɪŋ
firewatcher
BR ˈfʌɪəˌwɒtʃə(r), -z
AM ˈfaɪ(ə)rˌwɑtʃər, ˈfaɪ(ə)rˌwɔtʃər, -z
firewatching
BR ˈfʌɪəˌwɒtʃɪŋ
AM ˈfaɪ(ə)rˌwɑtʃɪŋ, ˈfaɪ(ə)rˌwɔtʃɪŋ
firewater
BR ˈfʌɪəˌwɔːtə(r)
AM ˈfaɪ(ə)rˌwɔdər, ˈfaɪ(ə)rˌwɑdər
fireweed
BR ˈfʌɪəwiːd
AM ˈfaɪ(ə)rˌwid
firewoman
BR ˈfʌɪəˌwʊmən
AM ˈfaɪ(ə)rˌwʊmən
firewomen
BR ˈfʌɪəˌwɪmɪn
AM ˈfaɪ(ə)rˌwɪmɪn
firewood
BR ˈfʌɪəwʊd
AM ˈfaɪ(ə)rˌwʊd
firework
BR ˈfʌɪəwəːk, -s
AM ˈfaɪ(ə)rˌwərk, -s
firing
BR ˈfʌɪərɪŋ, -z
AM ˈfaɪ(ə)rɪŋ, -z
firkin
BR ˈfəːkɪn, -z
AM ˈfərkən, -z
firm
BR fəːm, -z, -ɪŋ, -d, -ə(r), -ɪst
AM fərm, -z, -ɪŋ, -d, -ər, -əst
firmament
BR ˈfəːməm(ə)nt
AM ˈfərməmənt
firmamental
BR ˌfəːməˈmɛntl
AM ˌfərməˈmɛn(t)l
firman
BR ˈfəːmən, -z
AM ˈfərmən, -z
firmly
BR ˈfəːmli
AM ˈfərmli
firmness
BR ˈfəːmnəs
AM ˈfərmnəs
firmware
BR ˈfəːmwɛː(r)
AM ˈfərmˌwɛ(ə)r
firry
BR ˈfəːri
AM ˈfəri
first
BR fəːst, -s
AM fərst, -s
firstborn
BR ˈfəːs(t)bɔːn, -z
AM ˈfərs(t)ˌbɔ(ə)rn, -z
firstfruits
BR ˈfəːs(t)fruːts
AM ˈfərs(t)ˈfruts
firsthand
BR ˌfəːstˈhand
AM ˌfərstˈhænd
firstling
BR ˈfəːs(t)lɪŋ, -z
AM ˈfərs(t)lɪŋ, -z
firstly
BR ˈfəːstli
AM ˈfərs(t)li
first-nighter
BR ˌfəːs(t)ˈnʌɪtə(r), -z
AM ˈfərs(t)ˈnaɪdər, -z
firth
BR fəːθ, -s
AM fərθ, -s
firtree
BR ˈfəːtriː, -z
AM ˈfərˌtri, -z
fisc
BR fɪsk, -s
AM fɪsk, -s
fiscal
BR ˈfɪskl, -z
AM ˈfɪskəl, -z
fiscality
BR fɪˈskalɪti
AM fɪˈskælədi
fiscally
BR ˈfɪskl̩i, ˈfɪskəli
AM ˈfɪskəli
Fischer
BR ˈfɪʃə(r)
AM ˈfɪʃər
Fischer-Dieskau
BR ˌfɪʃəˈdɪskaʊ
AM ˈfɪʃərˈdiskaʊ
fish
BR fɪʃ, -ɪz, -ɪŋ, -t
AM fɪʃ, -ɪz, -ɪŋ, -t
fishable
BR ˈfɪʃəbl
AM ˈfɪʃəbəl
fishbowl
BR ˈfɪʃbəʊl, -z
AM ˈfɪʃˌboʊl, -z
fishcake
BR ˈfɪʃkeɪk, -s
AM ˈfɪʃˌkeɪk, -s
fisher
BR ˈfɪʃə(r), -z
AM ˈfɪʃər, -z
fisherfolk
BR ˈfɪʃəfəʊk
AM ˈfɪʃərˌfoʊk
fisherman
BR ˈfɪʃəmən
AM ˈfɪʃərmən
fishermen
BR ˈfɪʃəmən
AM ˈfɪʃərˌmɛn, fɪʃərmən
fisherwoman
BR ˈfɪʃəˌwʊmən
AM ˈfɪʃərˌwʊmən
fisherwomen
BR ˈfɪʃəˌwɪmɪn
AM ˈfɪʃərˌwɪmɪn
fishery
BR ˈfɪʃ(ə)r|i, -ɪz
AM ˈfɪʃəri, -z
Fishguard
BR ˈfɪʃgɑːd
AM ˈfɪʃˌgɑrd
fishhook
BR ˈfɪʃhʊk, -s
AM ˈfɪʃˌ(h)ʊk, -s
fishily
BR ˈfɪʃɪli
AM ˈfɪʃɪli
fishiness
BR ˈfɪʃɪnɪs
AM ˈfɪʃinɪs
fishlike
BR ˈfɪʃlʌɪk
AM ˈfɪʃˌlaɪk
Fishlock
BR ˈfɪʃlɒk
AM ˈfɪʃˌlɑk
fishmeal
BR ˈfɪʃmiːl
AM ˈfɪʃˌmil
fishmonger
BR ˈfɪʃˌmʌŋgə(r), -z
AM ˈfɪʃˌmɑŋgər, ˈfɪʃˌməŋgər, -z
fishnet
BR ˈfɪʃnɛt, -s
AM ˈfɪʃˌnɛt, -s
fishplate
BR ˈfɪʃpleɪt, -s
AM ˈfɪʃˌpleɪt, -s
fishpot
BR ˈfɪʃpɒt, -s
AM ˈfɪʃˌpɑt, -s
fishstick
BR ˈfɪʃstɪk, -s
AM ˈfɪʃˌstɪk, -s
fishtail
BR ˈfɪʃteɪl
AM ˈfɪʃˌteɪl
Fishwick
BR ˈfɪʃwɪk
AM ˈfɪʃˌwɪk
fishwife
BR ˈfɪʃwʌɪf
AM ˈfɪʃˌwaɪf
fishwives
BR ˈfɪʃwʌɪvz
AM ˈfɪʃˌwaɪvz
fishy
BR ˈfɪʃ|i, -ɪə(r), -ɪɪst
AM ˈfɪʃi, -ər, -ɪst
fisk
BR fɪsk, -s
AM fɪsk, -s
Fiske
BR fɪsk
AM fɪsk
Fison
BR ˈfʌɪsn
AM ˈfaɪsən
fissile
BR ˈfɪsʌɪl
AM ˈfɪsəl, ˈfɪˌsaɪl
fissility
BR fɪˈsɪlɪti
AM fɪˈsɪlɪdi
fission
BR ˈfɪʃn
AM ˈfɪʃən
fissionable
BR ˈfɪʃn̩əbl, ˈfɪʃənəbl
AM ˈfɪʃ(ə)nəbəl
fissiparity
BR ˌfɪsɪˈparɪti
AM ˌfɪsəˈpɛrədi
fissiparous
BR fɪˈsɪp(ə)rəs
AM fɪˈsɪp(ə)rəs
fissiparously
BR fɪˈsɪp(ə)rəsli
AM fɪˈsɪp(ə)rəsli
fissiparousness
BR fɪˈsɪp(ə)rəsnəs
AM fɪˈsɪp(ə)rəsnəs
fissure
BR ˈfɪʃə(r), -z
AM ˈfɪʃər, -z
fist
BR fɪst, -s
AM fɪst, -s
fistful
BR ˈfɪs(t)fʊl
AM ˈfɪs(t)ˌfʊl

fistic
BR 'fɪstɪk
AM 'fɪstɪk
fistical
BR 'fɪstɪkl
AM 'fɪstɪkəl
fisticuffs
BR 'fɪstɪkʌfs
AM 'fɪstɪˌkəfs
fistula
BR 'fɪstjʊlə(*r*), 'fɪstʃʊlə(*r*), -z
AM 'fɪstʃələ, 'fɪʃtʃələ, -z
fistular
BR 'fɪstjʊlə(r), 'fɪstʃʊlə(r)
AM 'fɪstʃələr, 'fɪʃtʃələr
fistulous
BR 'fɪstjʊləs, 'fɪstʃʊləs
AM 'fɪstʃələs, 'fɪʃtʃələs
fit
BR fɪt, -s, -ɪŋ, -ɨd, -ə(r), -ɨst
AM fɪ|t, -ts, -dɪŋ, -dɨd, -dər, -dəst
fitch
BR fɪtʃ, -ɨz
AM fɪtʃ, -ɨz
fitchew
BR 'fɪtʃuː, -z
AM 'fɪtʃu, -z
fitful
BR 'fɪtf(ʊ)l
AM 'fɪtfəl
fitfully
BR 'fɪtfʊli, 'fɪtfl̩i
AM 'fɪtfəli
fitfulness
BR 'fɪtf(ʊ)lnəs
AM 'fɪtfəlnəs
fitly
BR 'fɪtli
AM 'fɪtli
fitment
BR 'fɪtm(ə)nt, -s
AM 'fɪtmənt, -s
fitness
BR 'fɪtnɪs
AM 'fɪtnɪs
fitter
BR 'fɪtə(r), -z
AM 'fɪdər, -z
fitting
BR 'fɪtɪŋ, -z
AM 'fɪdɪŋ, -z
fittingly
BR 'fɪtɪŋli
AM 'fɪdɪŋli
fittingness
BR 'fɪtɪŋnɪs
AM 'fɪdɪŋnɪs
Fittipaldi
BR ˌfɪtɪ'paldi
AM ˌfɪdə'pɑldi
Fitz
BR fɪts
AM fɪts
Fitzgerald
BR ˌfɪts'dʒɛrəld, ˌfɪts'dʒɛrl̩d
AM ˌfɪts'dʒɛrəld
Fitzgibbon
BR fɪts'gɪb(ə)n
AM fɪts'gɪbən
Fitzjames
BR fɪts'dʒeɪmz
AM fɪts'dʒeɪmz
Fitzjohn
BR fɪts'dʒɒn
AM fɪts'dʒɑn
Fitzpatrick
BR fɪts'patrɪk
AM fɪts'pætrək
Fitzrovia
BR fɪts'rəʊvɪə(*r*)
AM fɪts'roʊviə
Fitzroy
BR 'fɪtsrɔɪ, fɪts'rɔɪ
AM 'fɪtsˌrɔɪ, ˌfɪts'rɔɪ
Fitzsimmons
BR fɪt(s)'sɪmənz
AM fɪts'sɪmənz
Fitzwalter
BR fɪts'wɔːltə(r)
AM fɪts'wɔltər, fɪts'wɑltər
Fitzwilliam
BR ˌfɪts'wɪlɪəm
AM ˌfɪts'wɪljəm, ˌfɪts'wɪliəm
Fiume
BR 'fjuːmeɪ
AM 'fjuˌmeɪ
five
BR fʌɪv, -z
AM faɪv, -z
five-a-side
BR ˌfʌɪvə'sʌɪd, -z
AM ˈfaɪvə'saɪd, -z
fivefold
BR 'fʌɪvfəʊld
AM ˈfaɪv'foʊld
fivepence
BR 'fʌɪvp(ə)ns, 'fʌɪfp(ə)ns, -ɨz
AM 'faɪvˌpɛns, -əz
fivepenny
BR 'fʌɪvpən|i, 'fʌɪvpn̩|i, -ɪz
AM 'faɪvˌpɛni, -z
fiver
BR 'fʌɪvə(r), -z
AM 'faɪvər, -z
fivestones
BR 'fʌɪvstəʊnz
AM 'faɪvˌstoʊnz
fix
BR fɪks, -ɨz, -ɪŋ, -t
AM fɪks, -ɨz, -ɪŋ, -t
fixable
BR 'fɪksəbl
AM 'fɪksəbəl
fixate
BR fɪk'seɪt, -s, -ɪŋ, -ɨd
AM 'fɪkˌseɪ|t, -ts, -dɪŋ, -dɨd
fixatedly
BR fɪk'seɪtɨdli
AM 'fɪkˌseɪdɨdli
fixation
BR fɪk'seɪʃn, -z
AM fɪk'seɪʃən, -z
fixative
BR 'fɪksətɪv, -z
AM 'fɪksədɪv, -z
fixedly
BR 'fɪksɨdli
AM 'fɪksɨdli
fixedness
BR 'fɪksɨdnɪs
AM 'fɪksɨdnɪs
fixer
BR 'fɪksə(r), -z
AM 'fɪksər, -z
fixings
BR 'fɪksɪŋz
AM 'fɪksɪŋz, 'fɪksɨnz
fixity
BR 'fɪksɨti
AM 'fɪksɨdi
fixture
BR 'fɪkstʃə(r), -z
AM 'fɪkstʃər, -z
fizgig
BR 'fɪzgɪg, -z
AM 'fɪzˌgɪg, -z
fizz
BR fɪz, -ɨz, -ɪŋ, -d
AM fɪz, -ɨz, -ɪŋ, -d
fizzer
BR 'fɪzə(r), -z
AM 'fɪzər, -z
fizzily
BR 'fɪzɨli
AM 'fɪzɨli
fizziness
BR 'fɪzɪnɪs
AM 'fɪzinɪs
fizzle
BR 'fɪz|l, -lz, -l̩ɪŋ\-lɪŋ, -ld
AM 'fɪz|əl, -əlz, -(ə)lɪŋ, -əld
fizzy
BR 'fɪz|i, -ɪə(r), -ɪɪst
AM 'fɪzi, -ər, -ɨst
fjord
BR 'fiːɔːd, fɪ'ɔːd, fjɔːd
AM fi'ɔ(ə)rd, fjɔ(ə)rd
flab
BR flab
AM flæb
flabbergast
BR 'flabəgɑːst, 'flabəgast, -s, -ɪŋ, -ɨd
AM 'flæbərˌgæst, -s, -ɪŋ, -əd
flabbily
BR 'flabɪli
AM 'flæbəli
flabbiness
BR 'flabɪnɪs
AM 'flæbinɪs
flabby
BR 'flab|i, -ɪə(r), -ɪɪst
AM 'flæbi, -ər, -ɨst
flaccid
BR 'fla(k)sɪd
AM 'flæ(k)səd
flaccidity
BR flə'sɪdɨti, fla(k)'sɪdɨti
AM flæ(k)'sɪdɨdi
flaccidly
BR 'fla(k)sɪdli
AM 'flæ(k)sədli
flaccidness
BR 'fla(k)sɪdnɪs
AM 'flæ(k)sədnəs
flack
BR flak
AM flæk
flag
BR flag, -z, -ɪŋ, -d
AM flæg, -z, -ɪŋ, -d
flagella
BR flə'dʒɛlə(*r*)
AM ˌflə'dʒɛlə
flagellant
BR 'fladʒɪlənt, 'fladʒɪln̩t, 'fladʒl̩(ə)nt, flə'dʒɛlənt, flə'dʒɛln̩t, -s
AM 'flædʒələnt, flə'dʒɛlənt, -s
flagellar
BR 'fladʒɪlə(r), 'fladʒl̩ə(r), flə'dʒɛlə(r)
AM 'flædʒələr
flagellate[1]
noun, adjective
BR 'fladʒɪlət, 'fladʒl̩ət, 'fladʒɪleɪt, 'fladʒl̩eɪt, -s
AM 'flædʒələt, 'flædʒəˌleɪt, -s
flagellate[2]
verb
BR 'fladʒɪleɪt, -s, -ɪŋ, -ɨd
AM 'flædʒəˌleɪ|t, -ts, -dɪŋ, -dɨd
flagellation
BR ˌfladʒɪ'leɪʃn, -z
AM ˌflædʒə'leɪʃən, -z
flagellator
BR 'fladʒɪleɪtə(r), -z
AM 'flædʒəˌleɪdər, -z
flagellatory
BR 'fladʒɪleɪt(ə)ri
AM ˌflæ'dʒɛləˌtɔri
flagelliform
BR flə'dʒɛlɪfɔːm
AM ˌflæ'dʒɛləˌfɔ(ə)rm
flagellum
BR flə'dʒɛləm

AM ˌflæˈdʒɛləm
flageolet
BR ˌfladʒəˈlɛt, ˈfladʒəlɨt, -s
AM ˈflædʒəˈlɛt, -s
Flagg
BR flag
AM flæg
flagger
BR ˈflagə(r), -z
AM ˈflægər, -z
flagitious
BR fləˈdʒɪʃəs
AM fləˈdʒɪʃəs
flagitiously
BR fləˈdʒɪʃəsli
AM fləˈdʒɪʃəsli
flagitiousness
BR fləˈdʒɪʃəsnəs
AM fləˈdʒɪʃəsnəs
flagman
BR ˈflagmən
AM ˈflægmæn
flagmen
BR ˈflagmən
AM ˈflægmən
flagon
BR ˈflag(ə)n, -z
AM ˈflægən, -z
flagpole
BR ˈflagpəʊl, -z
AM ˈflægˌpoʊl, -z
flagrancy
BR ˈfleɪgr(ə)nsi
AM ˈfleɪgrənsi
flag-rank
BR ˈflagraŋk, -s
AM ˈflægˌræŋk, -s
flagrant
BR ˈfleɪgr(ə)nt
AM ˈfleɪgrənt
flagrante
BR fləˈgranti
AM fləˈgrɑn(t)i
flagrantly
BR ˈfleɪgr(ə)ntli
AM ˈfleɪgrən(t)li
flagship
BR ˈflagʃɪp, -s
AM ˈflægˌʃɪp, -s
flagstaff
BR ˈflagstɑːf, ˈflagstaf, -s
AM ˈflægˌstæf, -s
flagstick
BR ˈflagstɪk, -s
AM ˈflægˌstɪk, -s
flagstone
BR ˈflagstəʊn, -z, -d
AM ˈflægˌstoʊn, -z, -d
Flaherty
BR ˈflɑː(h)əti
AM ˈflɛrdi
flail
BR fleɪl, -z, -ɪŋ, -d
AM fleɪl, -z, -ɪŋ, -d
flair
BR flɛː(r)
AM flɛ(ə)r
flak
BR flak
AM flæk
flake
BR fleɪk, -s, -ɪŋ, -t
AM fleɪk, -s, -ɪŋ, -t
flakily
BR ˈfleɪkɨli
AM ˈfleɪkɨli
flakiness
BR ˈfleɪkɪnɨs
AM ˈfleɪkinɨs
flaky
BR ˈfleɪk|i, -ɪə(r), -ɪɨst
AM ˈfleɪki, -ər, -ɨst
flam
BR flam, -z
AM flæm, -z
flambé
BR ˈflɒmbeɪ, ˈflambeɪ, ˈflɑːmbeɪ
AM flɑmˈbeɪ
flambeau
BR ˈflambəʊ, -z
AM ˈflæmboʊ, -z
flambeaux
BR ˈflambəʊz
AM ˈflæmboʊ
flambée
BR ˈflɒmbeɪ, ˈflambeɪ, ˈflɑːmbeɪ, -d
AM flɑmˈbeɪ, -d
Flamborough
BR ˈflamb(ə)rə(r)
AM ˈflæmˌbəroʊ, ˈflæmˌbərə
flamboyance
BR flamˈbɔɪəns
AM flæmˈbɔɪ(j)əns
flamboyancy
BR flamˈbɔɪənsi
AM flæmˈbɔɪ(j)ənsi
flamboyant
BR flamˈbɔɪənt
AM flæmˈbɔɪ(j)ənt
flamboyantly
BR flamˈbɔɪəntli
AM flæmˈbɔɪ(j)ən(t)li
flame
BR fleɪm, -z, -ɪŋ, -d
AM fleɪm, -z, -ɪŋ, -d
flameless
BR ˈfleɪmlɨs
AM ˈfleɪmlɨs
flamelike
BR ˈfleɪmlʌɪk
AM ˈfleɪmˌlaɪk
flamen
BR ˈfleɪmɛn, ˈflɑːmɛn, -z
AM ˈfleɪmən, -z
flamenco
BR fləˈmɛŋkəʊ, -z
AM fləˈmɛŋkoʊ, -z
flameproof
BR ˈfleɪmpruːf
AM ˈfleɪmˌprʊf
flamingo
BR fləˈmɪŋgəʊ, -z
AM fləˈmɪŋgoʊ, -z
flammability
BR ˌflaməˈbɪlɨti
AM ˌflæməˈbɪlɨdi
flammable
BR ˈflaməbl
AM ˈflæməbəl
Flamsteed
BR ˈflamstiːd
AM ˈflæmˌstid
flamy
BR ˈfleɪm|i, -ɪə(r), -ɪɨst
AM ˈfleɪmi, -ər, -ɨst
flan
BR flan, -z
AM flæn, -z
Flanagan
BR ˈflanəg(ə)n
AM ˈflænəgən
flanch
BR flɑːn(t)ʃ, flan(t)ʃ, -ɨz, -ɪŋ, -t
AM flæn(t)ʃ, -əz, -ɪŋ, -t
Flanders
BR ˈflɑːndəz, ˈflandəz
AM ˈflændərz
flânerie
BR ˌflɑːnˈriː
AM ˌflɑn(ə)ˈri
flâneur
BR flɑːˈnəː(r), -z
AM flɑˈnər, -z
flange
BR flan(d)ʒ, -ɨz
AM flændʒ, -əz
flangeless
BR ˈflan(d)ʒləs
AM ˈflændʒləs
flank
BR flaŋ|k, -ks, -kɪŋ, -(k)t
AM flæŋ|k, -ks, -kɪŋ, -(k)t
flanker
BR ˈflaŋkə(r), -z
AM ˈflæŋkər, -z
flannel
BR ˈflan|l, -lz, -l̩ɪŋ\-əlɪŋ, -ld
AM ˈflænəl, -z, -ɪŋ, -d
flannelboard
BR ˈflanlbɔːd, -z
AM ˈflænlˌbɔ(ə)rd, -z
flannelette
BR ˌflanəˈlɛt, ˌflanlˈɛt
AM ˈflænlˈɛt
flannelgraph
BR ˈflanlgrɑːf, ˈflanlgraf, -s
AM ˈflænlˌgræf, -s
flannelly
BR ˈflanl̩i
AM ˈflænl̩i
flannely
BR ˈflanl̩i
AM ˈflænl̩i
flap
BR flap, -s, -ɪŋ, -t
AM flæp, -s, -ɪŋ, -t
flapdoodle
BR ˈflapˌduːdl
AM ˈflæpˌdudəl
flapjack
BR ˈflapdʒak, -s
AM ˈflæpˌdʒæk, -s
flapper
BR ˈflapə(r), -z
AM ˈflæpər, -z
flappy
BR ˈflap|i, -ɪə(r), -ɪɨst
AM ˈflæpi, -ər, -ɨst
flare
BR flɛː(r), -z, -ɪŋ, -d
AM flɛ(ə)r, -z, -ɪŋ, -d
flash
BR flaʃ, -ɨz, -ɪŋ, -t
AM flæʃ, -əz, -ɪŋ, -t
flashback
BR ˈflaʃbak, -s
AM ˈflæʃˌbæk, -s
flashbulb
BR ˈflaʃbʌlb, -z
AM ˈflæʃˌbəlb, -z
flashcard
BR ˈflaʃkɑːd, -z
AM ˈflæʃˌkɑrd, -z
flashcube
BR ˈflaʃkjuːb, -z
AM ˈflæʃˌkjub, -z
flasher
BR ˈflaʃə(r), -z
AM ˈflæʃər, -z
flashgun
BR ˈflaʃgʌn, -z
AM ˈflæʃˌgən, -z
flashily
BR ˈflaʃɨli
AM ˈflæʃəli
flashiness
BR ˈflaʃɪnɨs
AM ˈflæʃinɨs
flashing
BR ˈflaʃɪŋ, -z
AM ˈflæʃɪŋ, -z
flash lamp
BR ˈflaʃ lamp, -s
AM ˈflæʃ ˌlæmp, -s
flashlight
BR ˈflaʃlʌɪt, -s
AM ˈflæʃˌlaɪt, -s
Flashman
BR ˈflaʃmən
AM ˈflæʃmən
flashover
BR ˈflaʃˌəʊvə(r), -z
AM ˈflæʃˌoʊvər, -z
flashpoint
BR ˈflaʃpɔɪnt, -s
AM ˈflæʃˌpɔɪnt, -s

flashy
BR 'flaʃ|i, -ɪə(r), -ɪɪst
AM 'flæʃi, -ər, -ɪst
flask
BR flɑːsk, flask, -s
AM flæsk, -s
flat
BR flat, -s, -ə(r), -ɪst
AM flæ|t, -ts, -dər, -dəst
flatbed
BR 'flatbɛd, -z
AM 'flæt,bɛd, -z
flatboat
BR 'flatbəʊt, -s
AM 'flæt,boʊt, -s
flatbread
BR 'flatbrɛd, -z
AM 'flæt,brɛd, -z
flatcar
BR 'flatkɑː(r), -z
AM 'flæt,kɑr, -z
flatfeet
BR 'flatfiːt
AM 'flæt,fit
flatfish
BR 'flatfɪʃ, -ɪz
AM 'flæt,fɪʃ, -ɪz
flatfoot
BR 'flatfʊt
AM 'flæt,fut
Flathead
BR 'flathɛd
AM 'flæt,(h)ɛd
flatiron
BR 'flatʌɪən, -z
AM 'flæt,aɪərn, -z
flatland
BR 'flatland, -z
AM 'flæt,lænd, -z
flatlander
BR 'flat,landə(r), -z
AM 'flæt,lændər, -z
flatlet
BR 'flatlɨt, -s
AM 'flætlət, -s
flatly
BR 'flatli
AM 'flætli
flatmate
BR 'flatmeɪt, -s
AM 'flæt,meɪt, -s
flatness
BR 'flatnəs
AM 'flætnəs
flatshare
BR 'flatʃɛː(r), -z
AM 'flæt,ʃɛ(ə)r, -z
flatsie
BR 'flats|i, -ɪz
AM 'flætsi, -z
flatten
BR 'flat|n, -nz,
-n̩ɪŋ\-nɪŋ, -nd
AM 'flætn, -z, -ɪŋ, -d
flattener
BR 'flatn̩ə(r),
'flatnə(r), -z
AM 'flætn̩ər, -z
flatter
BR 'flat|ə(r), -əz,
-(ə)rɪŋ, -əd
AM 'flædər, -z, -ɪŋ, -d
flatterer
BR 'flat(ə)rə(r), -z
AM 'flædərər, -z
flatteringly
BR 'flat(ə)rɪŋli
AM 'flædərɪŋli
flattery
BR 'flat(ə)r|i, -ɪz
AM 'flædəri, -z
flattie
BR 'flat|i, -ɪz
AM 'flædi, -z
flattish
BR 'flatɪʃ
AM 'flædɪʃ
flattop
BR 'flattɒp, -s
AM 'flæt,tɑp, -s
flatulence
BR 'flatjʊləns,
'flatjʊln̩s, 'flatʃʊləns,
'flatʃʊln̩s
AM 'flætʃələns
flatulency
BR 'flatjʊlənsi,
'flatjʊln̩si,
'flatʃʊlənsi,
'flatʃʊln̩si
AM 'flætʃələnsi
flatulent
BR 'flatjʊlənt,
'flatjʊln̩t, 'flatʃʊlənt,
'flatʃʊln̩t
AM 'flætʃələnt
flatulently
BR 'flatjʊləntli,
'flatjʊln̩tli,
'flatʃʊləntli,
'flatʃʊln̩tli
AM 'flætʃələn(t)li
flatus
BR 'fleɪtəs, -ɪz
AM 'fleɪdəs, -əz
flatware
BR 'flatwɛː(r)
AM 'flæt,wɛ(ə)r
flatworm
BR 'flatwəːm, -z
AM 'flæt,wərm, -z
Flaubert
BR 'fləʊbɛː(r)
AM floʊ'bɛ(ə)r
flaunch
BR flɔːn(t)ʃ, -ɪz, -ɪŋ, -t
AM flɔntʃ, flɑntʃ, -əz,
-ɪŋ, -t
flaunt
BR flɔːnt, -s, -ɪŋ, -ɪd
AM flɔn|t, flɑn|t, -ts,
-(t)ɪŋ, -(t)əd
flaunter
BR 'flɔːntə(r), -z
AM 'flɔn(t)ər,
'flɑn(t)ər, -z
flaunty
BR 'flɔːnti
AM 'flɔn(t)i, 'flɑn(t)i
flautist
BR 'flɔːtɪst, -s
AM 'flɔdəst, 'flaʊdəst,
-s
flavescent
BR flə'vɛsnt
AM flə'vɛsənt
Flavia
BR 'fleɪvɪə(*r*)
AM 'fleɪviə
Flavian
BR 'fleɪvɪən, -z
AM 'fleɪviən, -z
flavin
BR 'fleɪvɪn, -z
AM 'fleɪvɨn, -z
flavine
BR 'fleɪviːn
AM 'fleɪvin
Flavius
BR 'fleɪvɪəs
AM 'fleɪviəs
flavone
BR 'fleɪvəʊn
AM 'fleɪ,voʊn
flavoprotein
BR ,fleɪvə(ʊ)'prəʊtiːn,
-z
AM ,fleɪvə'proʊ,tin, -z
flavor
BR 'fleɪv|ə(r), -əz,
-(ə)rɪŋ, -əd
AM 'fleɪv|ər, -ərz,
-(ə)rɪŋ, -ərd
flavorful
BR 'fleɪvəf(ʊ)l
AM 'fleɪvərfəl
flavorfully
BR 'fleɪvəfʊli,
'fleɪvəfli
AM 'fleɪvərf(ə)li
flavoring
BR 'fleɪv(ə)rɪŋ, -z
AM 'fleɪvərɪŋ, -z
flavorless
BR 'fleɪvələs
AM 'fleɪvərləs
flavorous
BR 'fleɪv(ə)rəs
AM 'fleɪvərəs
flavorously
BR 'fleɪv(ə)rəsli
AM 'fleɪvərəsli
flavorsome
BR 'fleɪvəs(ə)m
AM 'fleɪvərsəm
flavour
BR 'fleɪv|ə(r), -əz,
-(ə)rɪŋ, -əd
AM 'fleɪv|ər, -ərz,
-(ə)rɪŋ, -ərd
flavourful
BR 'fleɪvəf(ʊ)l
AM 'fleɪvərfəl
flavourfully
BR 'fleɪvəfʊli,
'fleɪvəfli
AM 'fleɪvərf(ə)li
flavouring
BR 'fleɪv(ə)rɪŋ, -z
AM 'fleɪvərɪŋ, -z
flavourless
BR 'fleɪvələs
AM 'fleɪvərləs
flavourous
BR 'fleɪv(ə)rəs
AM 'fleɪvərəs
flavourously
BR 'fleɪv(ə)rəsli
AM 'fleɪvərəsli
flavoursome
BR 'fleɪvəs(ə)m
AM 'fleɪvərsəm
flaw
BR flɔː(*r*), -z, -ɪŋ, -d
AM flɔ, flɑ, -z, -ɪŋ, -d
flawless
BR 'flɔːləs
AM 'flɔləs, 'flɑləs
flawlessly
BR 'flɔːləsli
AM 'flɔləsli, 'flɑləsli
flawlessness
BR 'flɔːləsnəs
AM 'flɔləsnəs,
'flɑləsnəs
flax
BR flaks
AM flæks
flaxen
BR 'flaksn
AM 'flæksən
Flaxman
BR 'flaksmən
AM 'flæksmən
flaxseed
BR 'flak(s)siːd
AM 'flæk(s),sid
flay
BR fleɪ, -z, -ɪŋ, -d
AM fleɪ, -z, -ɪŋ, -d
flayer
BR 'fleɪə(r), -z
AM 'fleɪər, -z
flea
BR fliː, -z
AM fli, -z
fleabag
BR 'fliːbag, -z
AM 'fli,bæg, -z
fleabane
BR 'fliːbeɪn
AM 'fli,beɪn
fleabite
BR 'fliːbʌɪt, -s
AM 'fli,baɪt, -s
fleapit
BR 'fliːpɪt, -s

AM 'fli,pɪt, -s

flèche
BR fleɪʃ, flɛʃ, -ɨz
AM fleɪʃ, flɛʃ, -ɨz

fleck
BR flɛk, -s, -ɪŋ, -t
AM flɛk, -s, -ɪŋ, -t

Flecker
BR 'flɛkə(r)
AM 'flɛkər

flection
BR 'flɛkʃn, -z
AM 'flɛkʃən, -z

flectional
BR 'flɛkʃn̩(ə)l, 'flɛkʃən(ə)l
AM 'flɛkʃ(ə)nəl

flectionless
BR 'flɛkʃnləs
AM 'flɛkʃənləs

fled
BR flɛd
AM flɛd

Fledermaus, Die
BR ˌdiː 'fleɪdəmaʊs
AM ˌdi 'fleɪdərˌmaʊs

fledge
BR flɛdʒ, -ɨz, -ɪŋ, -d
AM flɛdʒ, -əz, -ɪŋ, -d

fledgeling
BR 'flɛdʒlɪŋ, -z
AM 'flɛdʒlɪŋ, -z

fledgling
BR 'flɛdʒlɪŋ, -z
AM 'flɛdʒlɪŋ, -z

flee
BR fliː, -z, -ɪŋ
AM fli, -z, -ɪŋ

fleece
BR fliːs, -ɨz, -ɪŋ, -t
AM flis, -ɨz, -ɪŋ, -t

fleeceable
BR 'fliːsəbl
AM 'flisəbəl

fleecily
BR 'fliːsɨli
AM 'flisɨli

fleeciness
BR 'fliːsɪnɨs
AM 'flisinɨs

fleecy
BR 'fliːs|i, -ɪə(r), -ɪɨst
AM 'flisi, -ər, -ɨst

fleer
BR flɪə(r), -z, -rɪŋ, -d
AM 'flɪ|(ə)r, -ərd, -(ə)rɪŋ, -ərd

fleet
BR fliːt, -s, -ɪŋ
AM fli|t, -ts, -dɪŋ

Fleet Air Arm
BR ˌfliːt 'ɛːr ɑːm
AM ˈflid 'ɛr ˌɑrm

fleeting
BR 'fliːtɪŋ
AM 'flidɪŋ

fleetingly
BR 'fliːtɪŋli
AM 'flidɪŋli

fleetly
BR 'fliːtli
AM 'flitli

fleetness
BR 'fliːtnɨs
AM 'flitnɨs

Fleetwood
BR 'fliːtwʊd
AM 'flitˌwʊd

Fleming
BR 'flɛmɪŋ, -z
AM 'flɛmɪŋ, -z

Flemish
BR 'flɛmɪʃ
AM 'flɛmɪʃ

flense
BR flɛns, -ɨz, -ɪŋ, -t
AM flɛns, -əz, -ɪŋ, -t

flesh
BR flɛʃ, -ɨz, -ɪŋ, -t
AM flɛʃ, -əz, -ɪŋ, -t

flesher
BR 'flɛʃə(r), -z
AM 'flɛʃər, -z

fleshiness
BR 'flɛʃɪnɨs
AM 'flɛʃinɨs

fleshings
BR 'flɛʃɪŋz
AM 'flɛʃɪŋz

fleshless
BR 'flɛʃləs
AM 'flɛʃləs

fleshliness
BR 'flɛʃlɪnɨs
AM 'flɛʃlinɨs

fleshly
BR 'flɛʃli
AM 'flɛʃli

fleshpot
BR 'flɛʃpɒt, -s
AM 'flɛʃˌpɑt, -s

fleshy
BR 'flɛʃ|i, -ɪə(r), -ɪɨst
AM 'flɛʃi, -ər, -ɨst

fletcher
BR 'flɛtʃə(r), -z
AM 'flɛtʃər, -z

Fleur
BR fləː(r), -z
AM flər, -z

fleur-de-lis
BR ˌfləː də 'liː, -z
AM ˈflər də ˈli, -z

fleur-de-lys
BR ˌfləːdə'liː, -z
AM ˈflərdəˈli, -z

fleurette
BR ˌflʊə'rɛt, ˌfləː'rɛt, -s
AM ˈfləˈrɛt, flʊ'rɛt, -s

fleuron
BR 'flʊərɒn, 'fləːrɒn, -z
AM 'fləˌrɑn, 'flʊˌrɑn, -z

fleury
BR 'flʊəri
AM 'fləri

flew
BR fluː, -z
AM flu, -z

flex
BR flɛks, -ɨz, -ɪŋ, -t
AM flɛks, -əz, -ɪŋ, -t

flexibility
BR ˌflɛksɪ'bɪlɨti
AM ˌflɛksə'bɪlɨdi

flexible
BR 'flɛksɨbl
AM 'flɛksəbəl

flexibleness
BR 'flɛksɨblnəs
AM 'flɛksəbəlnəs

flexibly
BR 'flɛksɨbli
AM 'flɛksəbli

flexile
BR 'flɛksʌɪl
AM 'flɛksəl

flexility
BR flɛk'sɪlɨt|i, -ɪz
AM flɛk'sɪlɨdi, -z

flexion
BR 'flɛkʃn
AM 'flɛkʃən

flexional
BR 'flɛkʃn̩(ə)l, 'flɛkʃən(ə)l
AM 'flɛkʃ(ə)nəl

flexionless
BR 'flɛkʃnləs
AM 'flɛkʃənləs

flexitime
BR 'flɛksɪtʌɪm
AM 'flɛksiˌtaɪm

Flexner
BR 'flɛksnə(r)
AM 'flɛksnər

flexographic
BR ˌflɛksə'grafɪk
AM ˌflɛksə'græfɪk

flexography
BR flɛk'sɒgrəfi
AM flɛk'sɑgrəfi

flexor
BR 'flɛksə(r), -z
AM 'flɛksər, 'flɛkˌsɔ(ə)r, -z

flextime
BR 'flɛkstʌɪm
AM 'flɛksˌtaɪm

flexuosity
BR ˌflɛksjʊ'ɒsɨti, ˌflɛkʃʊ'ɒsɨti
AM ˌflɛkʃə'wɑsədi

flexuous
BR 'flɛksjʊəs, 'flɛkʃʊəs
AM 'flɛkʃəwəs

flexuously
BR 'flɛksjʊəsli, 'flɛkʃʊəsli
AM 'flɛkʃəwəsli

flexural
BR 'flɛksjʊrəl, 'flɛksjʊrl̩, 'flɛkʃ(ə)rəl, 'flɛkʃ(ə)rl̩
AM 'flɛkʃ(ə)rəl

flexure
BR 'flɛkʃə(r), -z
AM 'flɛkʃər, -z

flibbertigibbet
BR 'flɪbətɪˌdʒɪbɨt, -s
AM ˈflɪbərdiˈdʒɪbɨt, -s

flick
BR flɪk, -s, -ɪŋ, -t
AM flɪk, -s, -ɪŋ, -t

flicker
BR 'flɪk|ə(r), -əz, -(ə)rɪŋ, -əd
AM 'flɪk|ər, -ərz, -(ə)rɪŋ, -ərd

flickering
BR 'flɪk(ə)rɪŋ, -z
AM 'flɪk(ə)rɪŋ, -z

flier
BR 'flʌɪə(r), -z
AM 'flaɪər, -z

flies
BR flʌɪz
AM flaɪz

flight
BR flʌɪt, -s
AM flaɪt, -s

flightily
BR 'flʌɪtɨli
AM 'flaɪdɨli

flightiness
BR 'flʌɪtɪnɨs
AM 'flaɪdinɨs

flightless
BR 'flʌɪtlɨs
AM 'flaɪtlɨs

flighty
BR 'flʌɪt|i, -ɪə(r), -ɪɨst
AM 'flaɪdi, -ər, -ɨst

flimflam
BR 'flɪmflam, -z, -ɪŋ, -d
AM 'flɪmˌflæm, -z, -ɪŋ, -d

flimflammer
BR 'flɪmˌflamə(r), -z
AM 'flɪmˌflæmər, -z

flimflammery
BR 'flɪmˌflam(ə)ri
AM 'flɪmˌflæməri

flimsily
BR 'flɪmzɨli
AM 'flɪmzɨli

flimsiness
BR 'flɪmzɪnɨs
AM 'flɪmzinɨs

flimsy
BR 'flɪmz|i, -ɪə(r), -ɪɨst
AM 'flɪmzi, -ər, -ɨst

flinch
BR flɪn(t)ʃ, -ɨz, -ɪŋ, -t
AM flɪn(t)ʃ, -ɨz, -ɪŋ, -t

flincher
BR 'flɪn(t)ʃə(r), -z
AM 'flɪn(t)ʃər, -z

flinchingly
BR 'flɪn(t)ʃɪŋli
AM 'flɪn(t)ʃɪŋli

flinders
BR 'flɪndəz
AM 'flɪndərz

fling
BR flɪŋ, -z, -ɪŋ
AM flɪŋ, -z, -ɪŋ

flinger
BR 'flɪŋə(r), -z
AM 'flɪŋər, -z

Flinn
BR flɪn
AM flɪn

flint
BR flɪnt, -s
AM flɪnt, -s

flintily
BR 'flɪntɨli
AM 'flɪn(t)ɨli

flintiness
BR 'flɪntɪnɨs
AM 'flɪn(t)inɨs

flintlock
BR 'flɪntlɒk, -s
AM 'flɪnt,lɑk, -s

Flintshire
BR 'flɪntʃ(ɪ)ə(r)
AM 'flɪn(t)ʃɪ(ə)r

Flintstones
BR 'flɪntstəʊnz
AM 'flɪn(t),stoʊnz

flinty
BR 'flɪnt|i, -ɪə(r), -ɪɪst
AM 'flɪn(t)i, -ər, -ɨst

flip
BR flɪp, -s, -ɪŋ, -t
AM flɪp, -s, -ɪŋ, -t

flipflop
BR 'flɪpflɒp, -s, -ɪŋ, -t
AM 'flɪp,flɑp, -s, -ɪŋ, -t

flippancy
BR 'flɪp(ə)nsi
AM 'flɪpənsi

flippant
BR 'flɪp(ə)nt
AM 'flɪpənt

flippantly
BR 'flɪp(ə)ntli
AM 'flɪpən(t)li

flippantness
BR 'flɪp(ə)ntnəs
AM 'flɪpən(t)nəs

flipper
BR 'flɪpə(r), -z
AM 'flɪpər, -z

FLIR
BR flɪə(r)
AM flɪ(ə)r

flirt
BR flə:t, -s, -ɪŋ, -ɨd
AM flər|t, -ts, -dɪŋ, -dəd

flirtation
BR flə:'teɪʃn, -z
AM flər'teɪʃən, -z

flirtatious
BR flə:'teɪʃəs
AM flər'teɪʃəs

flirtatiously
BR flə:'teɪʃəsli
AM flər'teɪʃəsli

flirtatiousness
BR flə:'teɪʃəsnəs
AM flər'teɪʃəsnəs

flirty
BR 'flə:t|i, -ɪə(r), -ɪɪst
AM 'flərdi, -ər, -ɨst

flit
BR flɪt, -s, -ɪŋ, -ɨd
AM flɪ|t, -ts, -dɪŋ, -dɨd

flitch
BR flɪtʃ, -ɨz
AM flɪtʃ, -ɨz

flitter
BR 'flɪt|ə(r), -əz, -(ə)rɪŋ, -əd
AM 'flɪd|ər, -ərd, -(ə)rɪŋ, -ərd

Flitton
BR 'flɪtn
AM 'flɪtn

flivver
BR 'flɪvə(r), -z
AM 'flɪvər, -z

Flixton
BR 'flɪkst(ə)n
AM 'flɪkstən

flixweed
BR 'flɪkswi:d
AM 'flɪks,wid

Flo
BR fləʊ
AM floʊ

float
BR fləʊt, -s, -ɪŋ, -ɨd
AM floʊ|t, -ts, -dɪŋ, -dəd

floatability
BR ,fləʊtə'bɪlɨti
AM ,floʊdə'bɪlɨdi

floatable
BR 'fləʊtəbl
AM 'floʊdəbəl

floatage
BR 'fləʊtɪdʒ
AM 'floʊdɪdʒ

floatation
BR fləʊ'teɪʃn, -z
AM floʊ'teɪʃən, -z

floater
BR 'fləʊtə(r), -z
AM 'floʊdər, -z

floatingly
BR 'fləʊtɪŋli
AM 'floʊdɪŋli

floatplane
BR 'fləʊtpleɪn, -z
AM 'floʊt,pleɪn, -z

floaty
BR 'fləʊt|i, -ɪz
AM 'floʊdi, -z

floc
BR flɒk, -s
AM flɑk, -s

flocci
BR 'flɒksʌɪ
AM 'flɑ,kaɪ, 'flɑk,saɪ

flocculate
BR 'flɒkjʉleɪt, -s, -ɪŋ, -ɨd
AM 'flɑkjə,leɪ|t, -ts, -dɪŋ, -dɨd

flocculation
BR ,flɒkjʉ'leɪʃn
AM ,flɑkjə'leɪʃən

floccule
BR 'flɒkju:l, -z
AM 'flɑ,kjul, -z

flocculence
BR 'flɒkjʉləns, 'flɒkjʉlṇs
AM 'flɑkjələns

flocculent
BR 'flɒkjʉlənt, 'flɒkjʉlṇt
AM 'flɑkjələnt

flocculently
BR 'flɒkjʉləntli, 'flɒkjʉlṇtli
AM 'flɑkjələn(t)li

flocculi
BR 'flɒkjʉlʌɪ
AM 'flɑkjə,laɪ

flocculus
BR 'flɒkjʉləs
AM 'flɑkjələs

floccus
BR 'flɒkəs
AM 'flɑkəs

flock
BR flɒk, -s, -ɪŋ, -t
AM flɑk, -s, -ɪŋ, -t

flocky
BR 'flɒk|i, -ɪə(r), -ɪɪst
AM 'flɑki, -ər, -ɨst

Flodden Field
BR ,flɒdn 'fi:ld
AM ,flɑdən 'fild

floe
BR fləʊ, -z
AM floʊ, -z

Floella
BR fləʊ'ɛlə(r)
AM flə'wɛlə

flog
BR flɒg, -z, -ɪŋ, -d
AM flɑg, -z, -ɪŋ, -d

flogger
BR 'flɒgə(r), -z
AM 'flɑgər, -z

flong
BR flɒŋ
AM flɔŋ, flɑŋ

flood
BR flʌd, -z, -ɪŋ, -ɨd
AM fləd, -z, -ɪŋ, -əd
AM 'floʊdi, -z

floodgate
BR 'flʌdgeɪt, -s
AM 'fləd,geɪt, -s

floodlight
BR 'flʌdlʌɪt, -s, -ɪŋ, -ɨd
AM 'fləd,laɪ|t, -ts, -dɪŋ, -dɨd

floodlit
BR 'flʌdlɪt
AM 'fləd,lɪt

Flook
BR flʊk, flu:k
AM flʊk, fluk

floor
BR flɔ:(r), -z, -ɪŋ, -d
AM flɔ(ə)r, -z, -ɪŋ, -d

floorboard
BR 'flɔ:bɔ:d, -z
AM 'flɔr,bɔ(ə)rd, -z

floorcloth
BR 'flɔ: klɒ|θ, -θs\-ðz
AM 'flɔr ,klɔ|θ, 'flɔr ,klɑ|θ, -θs\-ðz

flooring
BR 'flɔ:rɪŋ, -z
AM 'flɔrɪŋ, -z

floorless
BR 'flɔ:ləs
AM 'flɔrləs

floosie
BR 'flu:z|i, -ɪz
AM 'fluzi, -z

floosy
BR 'flu:z|i, -ɪz
AM 'fluzi, -z

floozie
BR 'flu:z|i, -ɪz
AM 'fluzi, -z

floozy
BR 'flu:z|i, -ɪz
AM 'fluzi, -z

flop
BR flɒp, -s, -ɪŋ, -t
AM flɑp, -s, -ɪŋ, -t

flophouse
BR 'flɒphaʊ|s, -zɨz
AM 'flɑp,(h)aʊ|s, -zəz

floppily
BR 'flɒpɨli
AM 'flɑpəli

floppiness
BR 'flɒpɪnɨs
AM 'flɑpinɨs

floppy
BR 'flɒp|i, -ɪə(r), -ɪɪst
AM 'flɑpi, -ər, -ɨst

flora
BR 'flɔ:rə(*r*)
AM 'flɔrə

floral
BR 'flɔ:rəl, 'flɔ:rḷ
AM 'flɔrəl

florally
BR 'flɔ:rḷi, 'flɔ:rəli
AM 'flɔrəli

floreat
BR 'flɒrɪat, 'flɔ:rɪat

AM 'flɔriˌæt

Florence
BR 'flɒrəns, 'flɒrn̩s
AM 'flɔrəns

Florentine
BR 'flɒrəntʌɪn, 'flɒrn̩tʌɪn, 'flɒrəntiːn, 'flɒrn̩tiːn, -z
AM 'flɔrənˌtin, -z

Flores
BR 'flɔːrɪz, 'flɔːriːz, 'flɔːrɪs
AM 'flɔrəs

florescence
BR flə'rɛsns, flɔː'rɛsns, flɒ'rɛsns
AM flʊ'rɛsəns, flɔ'rɛsəns, flə'rɛsəns

floret
BR 'flɒrɪt, 'flɔːrɪt, -s
AM 'flɔrət, -s

Florey
BR 'flɔːri
AM 'flɔri

floriate
BR 'flɒrɪeɪt, 'flɔːrɪeɪt, -s, -ɪŋ, -ɨd
AM 'flɔriˌeɪ|t, -ts, -dɪŋ, -dɨd

floribunda
BR ˌflɒrɪ'bʌndə(r), ˌflɔːrɪ'bʌndə(r)
AM ˌflɔrə'bəndə

floricultural
BR ˌflɔːrɪ'kʌltʃ(ə)rəl, ˌflɔːrɪ'kʌltʃ(ə)rl̩, ˌflɒrɪ'kʌltʃ(ə)rəl, ˌflɒrɪ'kʌltʃ(ə)rl̩
AM 'flɔrəˌkəltʃ(ə)rəl

floriculture
BR 'flɔːrɪˌkʌltʃə(r), 'flɒrɪˌkʌltʃə(r)
AM 'flɔrəˌkəltʃər

floriculturist
BR ˌflɔːrɪ'kʌltʃ(ə)rɪst, ˌflɒrɪ'kʌltʃ(ə)rɪst, -s
AM ˌflɔrə'kəltʃ(ə)rəst, -s

florid
BR 'flɒr|ɪd, -ɨdɨst
AM 'flɔrɨd, 'flɑrɨd, -ɨst

Florida
BR 'flɒrɪdə(r)
AM 'flɔrɨdə

Floridian
BR flɒ'rɪdɪən, flə'rɪdɪən, -z
AM 'flɔrɨdiən, -z

floridity
BR flɒ'rɪdɨti, flə'rɪdɨti
AM flə'rɪdɨdi

floridly
BR 'flɒrɨdli
AM 'flɔrɨdli, 'flɑrɨdli

floridness
BR 'flɒrɨdnɨs
AM 'flɔrɨdnɨs, 'flɑrɨdnɨs

floriferous
BR flɒ'rɪf(ə)rəs, flə'rɪf(ə)rəs
AM flɔ'rɪfərəs

florilegia
BR ˌflɒrɪ'liːdʒɪə(r), ˌflɔːrɪ'liːdʒɪə(r)
AM ˌflɔri'lidʒiə

florilegium
BR ˌflɒrɪ'liːdʒɪəm, ˌflɔːrɪ'liːdʒɪəm
AM ˌflɔri'lidʒiəm

florin
BR 'flɒrɪn, -z
AM 'flɔrən, 'flɑrən, -z

Florio
BR 'flɒrɪəʊ
AM 'flɔrioʊ

florist
BR 'flɒrɪst, -s
AM 'flɔrəst, -s

floristic
BR flɒ'rɪstɪk, flə'rɪstɪk, -s
AM flə'rɪstɪk, -s

floristically
BR flɒ'rɪstɪkli, flə'rɪstɪkli
AM flə'rɪstɪk(ə)li

floristry
BR 'flɒrɪstri
AM 'flɔrəstri

Florrie
BR 'flɒri
AM 'flɔri

floruit
BR 'flɒrʊɪt, 'flɔːrʊɪt
AM 'flɔrəwət

flory
BR 'flɔːri
AM 'flɔri

floscular
BR 'flɒskjʉlə(r)
AM 'flɑskjələr

flosculous
BR 'flɒskjʉləs
AM 'flɑskjələs

floss
BR flɒs, -ɨz, -ɪŋ, -t
AM flɔs, flɑs, -əz, -ɪŋ, -t

Flossie
BR 'flɒsi
AM 'flɔsi, 'flɑsi

flossy
BR 'flɒs|i, -ɪə(r), -ɪɨst
AM 'flɔsi, 'flɑsi, -ər, -ɨst

flotation
BR flə(ʊ)'teɪʃn, -z
AM floʊ'teɪʃən, -z

flote
BR fləʊt
AM floʊt

flotilla
BR flə'tɪlə(r), -z
AM floʊ'tɪlə, flə'tɪlə, -z

flotsam
BR 'flɒts(ə)m
AM 'flɑtsəm

Flotta
BR 'flɒtə(r)
AM 'flɔdə, 'flɑdə

flounce
BR flaʊns, -ɨz, -ɪŋ, -t
AM flaʊns, -əz, -ɪŋ, -t

flounder
BR 'flaʊnd|ə(r), -əz, -(ə)rɪŋ, -əd
AM 'flaʊnd|ər, -ərz, -(ə)rɪŋ, -ərd

flounderer
BR 'flaʊnd(ə)rə(r), -z
AM 'flaʊndərər, -z

flour
BR 'flaʊə(r), -z, -ɪŋ, -d
AM 'flaʊ(ə)r, -z, -ɪŋ, -d

flouresce
BR flʊə'rɛs, flʉ'rɛs, -ɨz, -ɪŋ, -t
AM flə'rɛs, flɔ'rɛs, -əz, -ɪŋ, -t

flouriness
BR 'flaʊ(ə)rɪnɨs
AM 'flaʊ(ə)rinɨs

flourish
BR 'flʌr|ɪʃ, -ɪʃɨz, -ɪʃɪŋ, -ɪʃt
AM 'flərɪʃ, -ɨz, -ɪŋ, -t

flourisher
BR 'flʌrɪʃə(r)
AM 'flərɪʃər

flourishy
BR 'flʌrɪʃi
AM 'flərɪʃi

flourmill
BR 'flaʊəmɪl, -z
AM 'flaʊ(ə)rˌmɪl, -z

floury
BR 'flaʊ(ə)r|i, -ɪə(r), -ɪɨst
AM 'flaʊ(ə)ri, -ər, -ɨst

flout
BR flaʊt, -s, -ɪŋ, -ɨd
AM flaʊ|t, -ts, -dɪŋ, -dəd

flow
BR fləʊ, -z, -ɪŋ, -d
AM floʊ, -z, -ɪŋ, -d

flowage
BR 'fləʊ|ɪdʒ, -ɨdʒɨz
AM 'floʊɪdʒ, -ɨz

flowchart
BR 'fləʊtʃɑːt, -s
AM 'floʊˌtʃɑrt, -s

flower
BR 'flaʊə(r), -z, -ɪŋ, -d
AM 'fla|ʊər, -ʊərz, -ʊ(ə)rɪŋ, -ʊərd

flowerbed
BR 'flaʊəbɛd, -z
AM 'flaʊərˌbɛd, -z

flowerer
BR 'flaʊərə(r), -z
AM 'flaʊərər, -z

floweret
BR 'flaʊərɪt, -s
AM 'flaʊəˌrɛt, -s

flowerily
BR 'flaʊərɨli
AM 'flaʊ(ə)rɨli

floweriness
BR 'flaʊ(ə)rɪnɨs
AM 'flaʊ(ə)rinɨs

flowerless
BR 'flaʊələs
AM 'flaʊərləs

flowerlike
BR 'flaʊəlʌɪk
AM 'flaʊərˌlaɪk

flowerpot
BR 'flaʊəpɒt, -s
AM 'flaʊərˌpɑt, -s

Flowers
BR 'flaʊəz
AM 'flaʊərz

flowery
BR 'flaʊər|i, -ɪə(r), -ɪɨst
AM 'fla|ʊ(ə)ri, -ʊ(ə)riər, -ʊ(ə)riɨst

flowing
BR 'fləʊɪŋ
AM 'floʊɪŋ

flowingly
BR 'fləʊɪŋli
AM 'floʊɪŋli

flown
BR fləʊn
AM floʊn

flowsheet
BR 'fləʊʃiːt, -s
AM 'floʊˌʃit, -s

flowstone
BR 'fləʊstəʊn
AM 'floʊˌstoʊn

Floyd
BR flɔɪd
AM flɔɪd

flu
BR fluː, -z
AM flu, -z

flub
BR flʌb, -z
AM fləb, -z

Fluck
BR flʌk
AM flək

fluctuate
BR 'flʌktʃʊeɪt, 'flʌktjʊeɪt, -s, -ɪŋ, -ɨd
AM 'fləktʃəˌweɪ|t, -ts, -dɪŋ, -dɨd

fluctuation
BR ˌflʌktʃʊ'eɪʃn, ˌflʌktjʊ'eɪʃn, -z
AM ˌfləktʃə'weɪʃən, -z

flue
BR fluː, -z
AM flu, -z

fluence
BR 'fluːəns
AM 'fluəns

fluency
BR 'fluːənsi

AM 'fluənsi

fluent
BR 'flu:ənt
AM 'fluənt

fluently
BR 'flu:əntli
AM 'fluən(t)li

fluff
BR flʌf, -s, -ɪŋ, -t
AM fləf, -s, -ɪŋ, -t

fluffily
BR 'flʌfɪli
AM 'fləfəli

fluffiness
BR 'flʌfɪnɪs
AM 'fləfinɪs

fluffy
BR 'flʌf|i, -ɪə(r), -ɪɪst
AM 'fləfi, -ər, -ɪst

Flügelhorn
BR 'flu:glhɔ:n, -z
AM 'flugəl,(h)ɔ(ə)rn, -z

fluid
BR 'flu:ɪd, -z
AM 'fluɪd, -z

fluidic
BR flu:'ɪdɪk, -s
AM 'fluɪdɪk, -s

fluidify
BR flu:'ɪdɪfʌɪ, -z, -ɪŋ, -d
AM flu'ɪdə,faɪ, -z, -ɪŋ, -d

fluidisation
BR ,flu:ɪdʌɪ'zeɪʃn
AM ,fluədə'zeɪʃən, ,fluə,daɪ'zeɪʃən

fluidise
BR 'flu:ɪdʌɪz, -ɪz, -ɪŋ, -d
AM 'fluə,daɪz, -ɪz, -ɪŋ, -d

fluidity
BR flu:'ɪdɪti
AM flu'ɪdɪdi

fluidization
BR ,flu:ɪdʌɪ'zeɪʃn
AM ,fluədə'zeɪʃən, ,fluə,daɪ'zeɪʃən

fluidize
BR 'flu:ɪdʌɪz, -ɪz, -ɪŋ, -d
AM 'fluə,daɪz, -ɪz, -ɪŋ, -d

fluidly
BR 'flu:ɪdli
AM 'fluɪdli

fluidness
BR 'flu:ɪdnɪs
AM 'fluɪdnɪs

fluidounce
BR ,flu:ɪd'aʊns, -ɪz
AM ˈfluɪd'aʊns, -əz

fluke
BR flu:k, -s
AM fluk, -s

flukey
BR 'flu:k|i, -ɪə(r), -ɪɪst
AM 'fluki, -ər, -ɪst

flukily
BR 'flu:kɪli
AM 'flukɪli

flukiness
BR 'flu:kɪnɪs
AM 'flukinɪs

fluky
BR 'flu:k|i, -ɪə(r), -ɪɪst
AM 'fluki, -ər, -ɪst

flume
BR flu:m, -z
AM flum, -z

flummery
BR 'flʌm(ə)ri
AM 'fləməri

flummox
BR 'flʌməks, -ɪz, -ɪŋ, -t
AM 'fləməks, -əz, -ɪŋ, -t

flump
BR flʌm|p, -ps, -pɪŋ, -(p)t
AM fləmp, -s, -ɪŋ, -t

flung
BR flʌŋ
AM fləŋ

flunk
BR flʌŋ|k, -ks, -kɪŋ, -(k)t
AM fləŋ|k, -ks, -kɪŋ, -(k)t

flunkey
BR 'flʌŋk|i, -ɪz
AM 'fləŋki, -z

flunkeyism
BR 'flʌŋkɪɪz(ə)m
AM 'fləŋki,ɪzəm

flunky
BR 'flʌŋk|i, -ɪz
AM 'fləŋki, -z

Fluon®
BR 'flu:ɒn
AM 'flu,ɑn

fluoresce
BR flʊə'rɛs, flɔ:'rɛs, flə'rɛs, -ɪz, -ɪŋ, -t
AM flʊ'rɛs, flɔ'rɛs, -əz, -ɪŋ, -t

fluorescence
BR flʊə'rɛsns, flɔ:'rɛsns, flə'rɛsns
AM flʊ'rɛsəns, flɔ'rɛsəns, flə'rɛsəns

fluorescent
BR flʊə'rɛsnt, flɔ:'rɛsnt, flə'rɛsnt
AM ,flʊ'rɛsənt, flɔ'rɛsənt

fluoridate
BR 'flʊərɪdeɪt, 'flɔ:rɪdeɪt
AM 'flʊrə,deɪt, 'flɔrə,deɪt

fluoridation
BR ,flʊərɪ'deɪʃn, ,flɔ:rɪ'deɪʃn
AM ,flʊrə'deɪʃən, ,flɔrə'deɪʃən

fluoride
BR 'flʊərʌɪd, 'flɔ:rʌɪd
AM 'flʊ,raɪd, 'flɔ,raɪd

fluoridisation
BR ,flʊərɪdʌɪ'zeɪʃn, ,flɔ:rɪdʌɪ'zeɪʃn
AM ,flʊrɪdə'zeɪʃən, ,flʊrɪ,daɪ'zeɪʃən

fluoridization
BR ,flʊərɪdʌɪ'zeɪʃn, ,flɔ:rɪdʌɪ'zeɪʃn
AM ,flʊrɪdə'zeɪʃən, ,flʊrɪ,daɪ'zeɪʃən

fluorinate
BR 'flʊərɪneɪt, 'flɔ:rɪneɪt, -s, -ɪŋ, -ɪd
AM 'flʊrə,neɪ|t, 'flɔrə,neɪ|t, -ts, -dɪŋ, -dɪd

fluorination
BR ,flʊərɪ'neɪʃn, ,flɔ:rɪ'neɪʃn
AM ,flʊrə'neɪʃən, ,flɔrə'neɪʃən

fluorine
BR 'flʊəri:n, 'flɔ:ri:n
AM 'flʊ,rin, 'flɔ,rin

fluorite
BR 'flʊərʌɪt, 'flɔ:rʌɪt
AM 'flʊ,raɪt, 'flɔ,raɪt

fluorocarbon
BR 'flʊərə(ʊ),kɑ:b(ə)n, 'flɔ:rə(ʊ),kɑ:b(ə)n, -z
AM 'flʊroʊ,kɑrbən, 'flɔroʊ,kɑrbən, -z

fluoroscope
BR 'flʊərəskəʊp, 'flɔ:rəskəʊp, -s
AM 'flʊrə,skoʊp, 'flɔrə,skoʊp, -s

fluoroscopy
BR flʊə'rɒskəpi, flɔ:'rɒskəpi, flə'rɒskəpi
AM flʊ'rɑskəpi, flɔ'rɑskəpi

fluorosis
BR flʊə'rəʊsɪs, flɔ:'rəʊsɪs, flə'rəʊsɪs
AM flʊ'roʊsəs, flɔ'roʊsəs

fluorspar
BR 'flʊəspɑ:(r), 'flɔ:spɑ:(r)
AM 'flʊr,spɑr, 'flɔr,spɑr

flurry
BR 'flʌr|i, -ɪz, -ɪɪŋ, -ɪd
AM 'fləri, -z, -ɪŋ, -d

flush
BR flʌʃ, -ɪz, -ɪŋ, -t
AM fləʃ, -əz, -ɪŋ, -t

flusher
BR 'flʌʃə(r), -z
AM 'fləʃər, -z

Flushing
BR 'flʌʃɪŋ
AM 'fləʃɪŋ

flushness
BR 'flʌʃnəs
AM 'fləʃnəs

fluster
BR 'flʌst|ə(r), -əz, -(ə)rɪŋ, -əd
AM 'fləst|ər, -ərz, -(ə)rɪŋ, -ərd

flute
BR flu:t, -s, -ɪŋ, -ɪd
AM flu|t, -ts, -dɪŋ, -dəd

flutelike
BR 'flu:tlʌɪk
AM 'flut,laɪk

flutey
BR 'flu:t|i, -ɪə(r), -ɪɪst
AM 'fludi, -ər, -ɪst

flutist
BR 'flu:tɪst, -s
AM 'fludəst, -s

flutter
BR 'flʌt|ə(r), -əz, -(ə)rɪŋ, -əd
AM 'flədər, -z, -ɪŋ, -d

flutterer
BR 'flʌt(ə)rə(r), -z
AM 'flədərər, -z

fluttery
BR 'flʌt(ə)ri
AM 'flədəri

fluty
BR 'flu:t|i, -ɪə(r), -ɪɪst
AM 'fludi, -ər, -ɪst

fluvial
BR 'flu:vɪəl
AM 'fluviəl

fluviatile
BR 'flu:vɪətʌɪl
AM 'fluviə,taɪl

fluvioglacial
BR ,flu:vɪəʊ'gleɪʃl
AM ˈfluvioʊ'gleɪʃəl

fluviometer
BR ,flu:vɪ'ɒmɪtə(r), -z
AM ,fluvi'ɑmədər, -z

flux
BR flʌks, -ɪz
AM fləks, -əz

fluxion
BR 'flʌkʃn, -z
AM 'flәkʃən, -z

fluxional
BR 'flʌkʃn̩(ə)l, 'flʌkʃən(ə)l
AM 'fləkʃ(ə)nəl

fluxionary
BR 'flʌkʃn̩ri
AM 'fləkʃə,nɛri

fly
BR flʌɪ, -z, -ɪŋ
AM flaɪ, -z, -ɪŋ

flyable
BR 'flʌɪəbl
AM 'flaɪəbəl

flyaway
BR 'flʌɪəweɪ
AM 'flaɪə,weɪ

flyback
BR 'flʌɪbak
AM 'flaɪ,bæk

flyblown
BR ˈflʌɪbləʊn
AM ˈflaɪˌbloʊn
flyby
BR ˈflʌɪbʌɪ, -z
AM ˈflaɪˌbaɪ, -z
flycatcher
BR ˈflʌɪˌkatʃə(r), -z
AM ˈflaɪˌkætʃər, -z
flyer
BR ˈflʌɪə(r), -z
AM ˈflaɪər, -z
flyleaf
BR ˈflʌɪliːf
AM ˈflaɪˌlif
flyleaves
BR ˈflʌɪliːvz
AM ˈflaɪˌlivz
Flymo®
BR ˈflʌɪməʊ, -z
AM ˈflaɪmoʊ, -z
flyness
BR ˈflʌɪnɪs
AM ˈflaɪnɨs
Flynn
BR flɪn
AM flɪn
flyover
BR ˈflʌɪ(ˌ)əʊvə(r), -z
AM ˈflaɪˌoʊvər, -z
flypaper
BR ˈflʌɪˌpeɪpə(r), -z
AM ˈflaɪˌpeɪpər, -z
flypast
BR ˈflʌɪpɑːst, ˈflʌɪpast, -s
AM ˈflaɪˌpæst, -s
flysheet
BR ˈflʌɪʃiːt, -s
AM ˈflaɪˌʃit, -s
flyswatter
BR ˈflʌɪˌswɒtə(r), -z
AM ˈflaɪˌswɑdər, -z
flyting
BR ˈflʌɪtɪŋ, -z
AM ˈflaɪdɪŋ, -z
flytrap
BR ˈflʌɪtrap, -s
AM ˈflaɪˌtræp, -s
flyway
BR ˈflʌɪweɪ, -z
AM ˈflaɪˌweɪ, -z
flyweight
BR ˈflʌɪweɪt, -s
AM ˈflaɪˌweɪt, -s
flywheel
BR ˈflʌɪwiːl, -z
AM ˈflaɪˌ(h)wil, -z
flywhisk
BR ˈflʌɪwɪsk, -s
AM ˈflaɪˌ(h)wɪsk, -s
FNMA
BR ˌfanɪˈmeɪ
AM ˌfæniˈmeɪ
foal
BR fəʊl, -z, -ɪŋ, -d
AM foʊl, -z, -ɪŋ, -d
foam
BR fəʊm, -z, -ɪŋ, -d
AM foʊm, -z, -ɪŋ, -d
foaminess
BR ˈfəʊmɪnɪs
AM ˈfoʊminɨs
foamless
BR ˈfəʊmləs
AM ˈfoʊmləs
foamy
BR ˈfəʊmi
AM ˈfoʊmi
fob
BR fɒb, -z, -ɪŋ, -d
AM fɑb, -z, -ɪŋ, -d
fobwatch
BR ˈfɒbwɒtʃ, -ɨz
AM ˈfɑbˌwɑtʃ, ˈfɑbˌwɔtʃ, -əz
focaccia
BR fəˈkatʃə(r)
AM foʊˈkatʃiə
focal
BR ˈfəʊkl
AM ˈfoʊkəl
focalisation
BR ˌfəʊkəlʌɪˈzeɪʃn, ˌfəʊkl̩ʌɪˈzeɪʃn
AM ˌfoʊkələˈzeɪʃən, ˌfoʊkəˌlaɪˈzeɪʃən
focalise
BR ˈfəʊkəlʌɪz, ˈfəʊkl̩ʌɪz, -ɨz, -ɪŋ, -d
AM ˈfoʊkəˌlaɪz, -ɨz, -ɪŋ, -d
focalization
BR ˌfəʊkəlʌɪˈzeɪʃn, ˌfəʊkl̩ʌɪˈzeɪʃn
AM ˌfoʊkələˈzeɪʃən, ˌfoʊkəˌlaɪˈzeɪʃən
focalize
BR ˈfəʊkəlʌɪz, ˈfəʊkl̩ʌɪz, -ɨz, -ɪŋ, -d
AM ˈfoʊkəˌlaɪz, -ɨz, -ɪŋ, -d
Foch
BR fɒʃ
AM fɔʃ, fɑʃ
Fochabers
BR ˈfɒxəbəz, ˈfɒkəbəz
AM ˈfɑkəbərs
foci
BR ˈfəʊkʌɪ, ˈfəʊsʌɪ
AM ˈfoʊˌsaɪ
foc's'le
BR ˈfəʊksl, -z
AM ˈfoʊksəl, -z
fo'c'sle
BR ˈfəʊksl, -z
AM ˈfoʊksəl, -z
fo'c's'le
BR ˈfəʊksl, -z
AM ˈfoʊksəl, -z
focus
BR ˈfəʊkəs, -ɨz, -ɪŋ, -t
AM ˈfoʊkəs, -əz, -ɪŋ, -t
focuser
BR ˈfəʊkəsə(r), -z
AM ˈfoʊkəsər, -z
fodder
BR ˈfɒd|ə(r), -əz, -(ə)rɪŋ, -əd
AM ˈfɑdər, -z, -ɪŋ, -d
Foden
BR ˈfəʊdn
AM ˈfoʊdən
foe
BR fəʊ, -z
AM foʊ, -z
foehn
BR fəːn
AM fən
foeman
BR ˈfəʊmən
AM ˈfoʊmən
foemen
BR ˈfəʊmən, ˈfəʊmɛn
AM ˈfoʊˌmɛn, ˈfoʊmən
foetal
BR ˈfiːtl
AM ˈfidl
foeticide
BR ˈfiːtɪsʌɪd
AM ˈfidəˌsaɪd
foetid
BR ˈfɛtɪd, ˈfiːtɪd
AM ˈfɛdəd
foetus
BR ˈfiːtəs, -ɨz
AM ˈfidəs, -əz
fog
BR fɒg, -z, -ɪŋ, -d
AM fɔg, fɑg, -z, -ɪŋ, -d
Fogarty
BR ˈfɒgəti
AM ˈfoʊgərdi
fogau
BR ˈfəʊguː, ˈfəʊgəʊ, -z
AM ˈfoʊgu, ˈfoʊgoʊ, -z
fogbank
BR ˈfɒgbaŋk, -s
AM ˈfɔgˌbæŋk, ˈfɑgˌbæŋk, -s
fogbound
BR ˈfɒgbaʊnd
AM ˈfɔgˌbaʊnd, ˈfɑgˌbaʊnd
fog-bow
BR ˈfɒgbəʊ, -z
AM ˈfɔgˌboʊ, ˈfɑgˌboʊ, -z
Fogerty
BR ˈfɒgəti
AM ˈfoʊgərdi
fogey
BR ˈfəʊg|i, -ɪz
AM ˈfoʊgi, -z
fogeydom
BR ˈfəʊgɪdəm
AM ˈfoʊgidəm
fogeyish
BR ˈfəʊgɪɪʃ
AM ˈfoʊgiɪʃ
Fogg
BR fɒg
AM fɔg, fɑg
foggily
BR ˈfɒgɨli
AM ˈfɔgəli, ˈfɑgəli
fogginess
BR ˈfɒgɪnɪs
AM ˈfɔginɨs, ˈfɑginɨs
foggy
BR ˈfɒg|i, -ɪə(r), -ɪɨst
AM ˈfɔgi, ˈfɑgi, -ər, -ɨst
foghorn
BR ˈfɒghɔːn, -z
AM ˈfɔgˌ(h)ɔ(ə)rn, ˈfɑgˌ(h)ɔ(ə)rn, -z
fogy
BR ˈfəʊg|i, -ɪz
AM ˈfoʊgi, -z
fogydom
BR ˈfəʊgɪdəm
AM ˈfoʊgidəm
fogyish
BR ˈfəʊgɪɪʃ
AM ˈfoʊgiɪʃ
fohn
BR fəːn
AM fən
föhn
BR fəːn
AM fən
foible
BR ˈfɔɪbl, -z
AM ˈfɔɪbəl, -z
foie gras
BR ˌfwɑː ˈgrɑː(r)
AM ˌfwɑ ˈgrɑ
foil
BR fɔɪl, -z, -ɪŋ, -d
AM fɔɪl, -z, -ɪŋ, -d
foilist
BR ˈfɔɪlɪst, -s
AM ˈfɔɪlɨst, -s
foist
BR fɔɪst, -s, -ɪŋ, -ɨd
AM fɔɪst, -s, -ɪŋ, -ɨd
Fokker®
BR ˈfɒkə(r), -z
AM ˈfɑkər, -z
folacin
BR ˈfəʊləsɪn
AM ˈfɔləsən, ˈfɑləsən
fold
BR fəʊld, -z, -ɪŋ, -ɨd
AM foʊld, -z, -ɪŋ, -əd
foldable
BR ˈfəʊldəbl
AM ˈfoʊldəbəl
foldaway
BR ˈfəʊldəweɪ
AM ˈfoʊldəˌweɪ
foldback
BR ˈfəʊl(d)bak, -s
AM ˈfoʊl(d)ˌbæk, -s
foldboat
BR ˈfəʊl(d)bəʊt, -s
AM ˈfoʊl(d)ˌboʊt, -s
folder
BR ˈfəʊldə(r), -z
AM ˈfoʊldər, -z

folderol
BR 'fɒldərɒl, -z
AM 'fɔldə,rɔl, 'fɑldə,rɑl, -z

foldout
BR 'fəʊldaʊt, -s
AM 'foʊl,daʊt, -s

fold-up
BR 'fəʊldʌp
AM 'foʊldəp

Foley
BR 'fəʊli
AM 'foʊli

Folger
BR 'fəʊldʒə(r), 'fɒldʒə(r)
AM 'foʊldʒər

folia
BR 'fəʊlɪə(r)
AM 'foʊljə, 'foʊliə

foliaceous
BR ,fəʊlɪ'eɪʃəs
AM ,foʊli'eɪʃəs

foliage
BR 'fəʊlɪɪdʒ
AM 'foʊl(i)ɪdʒ

foliar
BR 'fəʊlɪə(r)
AM 'foʊljər, 'foʊliər

foliate[1]
adjective
BR 'fəʊlɪət, 'fəʊlɪeɪt
AM 'foʊliət, 'foʊli,eɪt

foliate[2]
verb
BR 'fəʊlɪeɪt, -s, -ɪŋ, -ɪd
AM 'foʊli,eɪ|t, -ts, -dɪŋ, -dɪd

foliation
BR ,fəʊlɪ'eɪʃn, -z
AM ,foʊli'eɪʃən, -z

folic
BR 'fəʊlɪk, 'fɒlɪk
AM 'foʊlɪk, 'fɑlɪk

Folies-Bergère
BR ,fɒlɪbə'ʒɛː(r), ,fɒlɪbɛː'ʒɛː(r)
AM fɔ,libər'ʒɛ(ə)r

folio
BR 'fəʊlɪəʊ, -z
AM 'foʊlioʊ, -z

foliole
BR 'fəʊlɪəʊl, -z
AM 'foʊli,oʊl, -z

foliot
BR 'fɒlɪət, -s
AM 'foʊliət, -s

folium
BR 'fəʊlɪəm
AM 'foʊliəm

folk
BR fəʊk, -s
AM foʊk, -s

Folkestone
BR 'fəʊkst(ə)n
AM 'foʊk,stoʊn

folkie
BR 'fəʊk|i, -ɪz
AM 'foʊki, -z

folkiness
BR 'fəʊkɪnɨs
AM 'foʊkinɨs

folkish
BR 'fəʊkɪʃ
AM 'foʊkɪʃ

folklore
BR 'fəʊklɔː(r)
AM 'foʊk,lɔ(ə)r

folkloric
BR fəʊk'lɔːrɪk
AM foʊk'lɔrɪk

folklorist
BR 'fəʊklɔːrɪst, -s
AM 'foʊk,lɔrəst, -s

folkloristic
BR ,fəʊklə'rɪstɪk
AM ,foʊklə'rɪstɪk

folksily
BR 'fəʊksɨli
AM 'foʊksəli

folksiness
BR 'fəʊksɪnɨs
AM 'foʊksinɨs

folksong
BR 'fəʊksɒŋ, -z
AM 'foʊk,sɔŋ, 'foʊk,sɑŋ, -z

folksy
BR 'fəʊks|i, -ɪə(r), -ɪɨst
AM 'foʊksi, -ər, -ɨst

folktale
BR 'fəʊkteɪl, -z
AM 'foʊk,teɪl, -z

folkway
BR 'fəʊkweɪ, -z
AM 'foʊk,weɪ, -z

folkweave
BR 'fəʊkwiːv
AM 'foʊk,wiv

folky
BR 'fəʊki
AM 'foʊki

Follick
BR 'fɒlɪk
AM 'fɑlək

follicle
BR 'fɒlɪkl, -z
AM 'fɑləkəl, -z

follicular
BR fɒ'lɪkjʉlə(r), fə'lɪkjʉlə(r)
AM fə'lɪkjələr

folliculate
BR fɒ'lɪkjʉlət, fə'lɪkjʉlət
AM fə'lɪkjələt, fə'lɪkjə,leɪt

folliculated
BR fɒ'lɪkjʉleɪtɪd, fə'lɪkjʉleɪtɪd
AM fə'lɪkjə,leɪdɪd

follow
BR 'fɒləʊ, -z, -ɪŋ, -d
AM 'fɑloʊ, -z, -ɪŋ, -d

follower
BR 'fɒləʊə(r), -z
AM 'fɑloʊər, -z

following
BR 'fɒləʊɪŋ, -z
AM 'fɑloʊɪŋ, -z

follow-my-leader
BR ,fɒlə(ʊ)mə'liːdə(r)
AM ,fɑloʊmaɪ'lidər

folly
BR 'fɒl|i, -ɪz
AM 'fɑli, -z

Folsom[1]
places in US
BR 'fəʊls(ə)m
AM 'foʊlsəm

Folsom[2]
surname
BR 'fəʊls(ə)m, 'fɒls(ə)m
AM 'foʊlsəm

Fomalhaut
BR 'fɒml̩əʊt, 'fɒmələʊt
AM 'foʊməl,(h)ɔt, 'foʊməl,(h)ɑt

foment[1]
noun
BR 'fəʊmɛnt
AM 'foʊ,mɛnt

foment[2]
verb
BR fə'mɛnt, -s, -ɪŋ, -ɨd
AM ,foʊ'mɛn|t, -ts, -(t)ɪŋ, -(t)əd

fomentation
BR ,fəʊmɛn'teɪʃn, ,fəʊm(ə)n'teɪʃn
AM ,foʊmɛn'teɪʃən, ,foʊmən'teɪʃən

fomenter
BR fə'mɛntə(r), -z
AM ,foʊ'mɛn(t)ər, -z

fomites
BR 'fəʊmɪtiːz
AM 'foʊmə,tiz

fond
BR fɒnd, -ə(r), -ɨst
AM fɑnd, -ər, -əst

Fonda
BR 'fɒndə(r)
AM 'fɑndə

fondant
BR 'fɒnd(ə)nt, -s
AM 'fɑndnt, -s

fondle
BR 'fɒnd|l, -lz, -l̩ɪŋ\-lɪŋ, -ld
AM 'fɑn|dəl, -dəlz, -(d)(ə)lɪŋ, -dəld

fondler
BR 'fɒndl̩ə(r), 'fɒndlə(r), -z
AM 'fɑn(də)lər, -z

fondly
BR 'fɒndli
AM 'fɑn(d)li

fondness
BR 'fɒn(d)nəs
AM 'fɑn(d)nəs

fondu
BR 'fɒnd(j)uː, -z
AM ˌfɑnˈd(j)u, -z

fondue
BR 'fɒnd(j)uː, -z
AM ˌfɑnˈd(j)u, -z

font
BR fɒnt, -s
AM fɑnt, -s

Fontainebleau
BR 'fɒntɪnbləʊ
AM 'fɑntn,bloʊ

fontal
BR 'fɒntl
AM 'fɑntl

Fontana
BR fɒn'tɑːnə(r)
AM ,fɑn'tænə

fontanel
BR ,fɒntə'nɛl, -z
AM ˌfɑntnˈɛl, -z

fontanelle
BR ,fɒntə'nɛl, -z
AM ˌfɑntnˈɛl, -z

Fonteyn
BR 'fɒnteɪn
AM ˌfɑnˈteɪn

Fontwell
BR 'fɒntw(ɛ)l
AM 'fɑnt,wɛl

Foochow
BR 'fuː'tʃaʊ
AM ˌfuˈtʃaʊ

food
BR fuːd, -z
AM fud, -z

foodie
BR 'fuːd|i, -ɪz
AM 'fudi, -z

foodism
BR 'fuːdɪz(ə)m
AM 'fudɪzəm

foodstuff
BR 'fuːdstʌf, -s
AM 'fud,stəf, -s

Fookes
BR fuːks
AM fuks

fool
BR fuːl, -z, -ɪŋ, -d
AM ful, -z, -ɪŋ, -d

foolery
BR 'fuːlər|i, -ɪz
AM 'fuləri, -z

foolhardily
BR 'fuːl,hɑːdɨli
AM 'ful,(h)ɑrdəli

foolhardiness
BR 'fuːl,hɑːdɪnɨs
AM 'ful,(h)ɑrdinɨs

foolhardy
BR 'fuːl,hɑːdi
AM 'ful,(h)ɑrdi

foolish
BR 'fu:lɪʃ
AM 'fulɪʃ
foolishly
BR 'fu:lɪʃli
AM 'fulɪʃli
foolishness
BR 'fu:lɪʃnɪs
AM 'fulɪʃnɪs
foolproof
BR 'fu:lpru:f
AM 'ful,pruf
foolscap
BR 'fu:lskap, 'fu:lzkap
AM 'fʊlz,kæp
Foord
BR fɔ:d
AM fɔ(ə)rd
foot
BR fʊt, -s, -ɪŋ, -ɪd
AM fʊ|t, -ts, -dɪŋ, -dəd
footage
BR 'fʊtɪdʒ
AM 'fʊdɪdʒ
football
BR 'fʊtbɔ:l, -z
AM 'fʊt,bɔl, 'fʊt,bɑl, -z
footballer
BR 'fʊtbɔ:lə(r), -z
AM 'fʊt,bɔlər, 'fʊt,bɑlər, -z
footbath
BR 'fʊt|bɑ:θ, 'fʊt|baθ, -bɑ:ðz\-bɑ:θs\-baθs
AM 'fʊt,bæθ, -s, -ðz
footbed
BR 'fʊtbɛd, -z
AM 'fʊt,bɛd, -z
footboard
BR 'fʊtbɔ:d, -z
AM 'fʊt,bɔ(ə)rd, -z
footbrake
BR 'fʊtbreɪk, -s
AM 'fʊt,breɪk, -s
footbridge
BR 'fʊtbrɪdʒ, -ɪz
AM 'fʊt,brɪdʒ, -ɪz
footcandle
BR 'fʊt,kandl, -z
AM 'fʊt,kændəl, -z
Foote
BR fʊt
AM fʊt
footer
BR 'fʊtə(r)
AM 'fʊdər
footfall
BR 'fʊtfɔ:l, -z
AM 'fʊt,fɔl, 'fʊt,fɑl, -z
footgear
BR 'fʊtgɪə(r)
AM 'fʊt,gɪ(ə)r
foothill
BR 'fʊthɪl, -z
AM 'fʊt,(h)ɪl, -z
foothold
BR 'fʊthəʊld, -z
AM 'fʊt,(h)oʊld, -z
footing
BR 'fʊtɪŋ, -z
AM 'fʊdɪŋ, -z
footle
BR 'fu:t|l, -lz, -l̩ɪŋ\-lɪŋ, -ld
AM 'fudəl, -z, -ɪŋ, -d
footless
BR 'fʊtləs
AM 'fʊtləs
footlights
BR 'fʊtlʌɪts
AM 'fʊt,laɪts
footlocker
BR 'fʊt,lɒkə(r), -z
AM 'fʊt,lɑkər, -z
footloose
BR 'fʊtlu:s
AM 'fʊt,lus
footman
BR 'fʊtmən
AM 'fʊtmən
footmark
BR 'fʊtmɑ:k, -s
AM 'fʊt,mɑrk, -s
footmen
BR 'fʊtmən
AM 'fʊt,mɛn, fʊtmən
footnote
BR 'fʊtnəʊt, -s, -ɪŋ, -ɪd
AM 'fʊt,noʊ|t, -ts, -dɪŋ, -dəd
footpad
BR 'fʊtpad, -z
AM 'fʊt,pæd, -z
footpath
BR 'fʊtpɑ:|θ, 'fʊtpa|θ, -ðz
AM 'fʊt,pæ|θ, -ðz
footplate
BR 'fʊtpleɪt, -s
AM 'fʊt,pleɪt, -s
footprint
BR 'fʊtprɪnt, -s
AM 'fʊt,prɪnt, -s
footrest
BR 'fʊtrɛst, -s
AM 'fʊt,rɛst, -s
footsie
BR 'fʊtsi
AM 'fʊtsi
footslog
BR 'fʊtslɒg, -z, -ɪŋ, -d
AM 'fʊt,slɑg, -z, -ɪŋ, -d
footslogger
BR 'fʊt,slɒgə(r), -z
AM 'fʊt,slɑgər, -z
footsore
BR 'fʊtsɔ:(r)
AM 'fʊt,sɔ(ə)r
footstalk
BR 'fʊtstɔ:k, -s
AM 'fʊt,stɔk, 'fʊt,stɑk, -s
footstep
BR 'fʊtstɛp, -s
AM 'fʊt,stɛp, -s
footstool
BR 'fʊtstu:l, -z
AM 'fʊt,stul, -z
footstrap
BR 'fʊtstrap, -s
AM 'fʊt,stræp, -s
footsure
BR 'fʊtʃʊə(r), 'fʊtʃɔ:(r)
AM 'fʊt,ʃʊr
footway
BR 'fʊtweɪ, -z
AM 'fʊt,weɪ, -z
footwear
BR 'fʊtwɛ:(r)
AM 'fʊt,wɛ(ə)r
footwork
BR 'fʊtwə:k
AM 'fʊt,wərk
foozle
BR 'fu:z|l, -lz, -l̩ɪŋ\-lɪŋ, -ld
AM 'fuzəl, -z, -ɪŋ, -d
foozler
BR 'fu:zl̩ə(r), -z
AM 'fuz(ə)lər, -z
fop
BR fɒp
AM fɑp
foppery
BR 'fɒp(ə)ri
AM 'fɑpəri
foppish
BR 'fɒpɪʃ
AM 'fɑpɪʃ
foppishly
BR 'fɒpɪʃli
AM 'fɑpɪʃli
foppishness
BR 'fɒpɪʃnɪs
AM 'fɑpɪʃnɪs
for¹
strong form
BR fɔ:(r)
AM fɔ(ə)r
for²
weak form
BR fə(r)
AM fər
fora
BR 'fɔ:rə(r)
AM 'fɔrə
forage
BR 'fɒr|ɪdʒ, -ɪdʒɪz, -ɪdʒɪŋ, -ɪdʒd
AM 'fɔrɪdʒ, 'fɑrɪdʒ, -ɪz, -ɪŋ, -d
forager
BR 'fɒrɪdʒə(r), -z
AM 'fɔrɪdʒər, 'fɑrɪdʒər, -z
foramen
BR fə'reɪmɛn
AM fə'reɪmən
foramina
BR fə'ramɪnə(r)
AM fə'ræmənə
foraminate
BR fə'ramɪneɪt
AM fə'ræmə,neɪt
foraminated
BR fə'ramɪneɪtɪd
AM fə'ræmə,neɪdɪd
foraminifer
BR ,fɒrə'mɪnɪfə(r), -z
AM ,fɔrə'mɪnəfər, -z
foraminiferan
BR fə,ramɪ'nɪf(ə)rən, fə,ramɪ'nɪf(ə)rn̩, ,fɒrəmɪ'nɪf(ə)rən, ,fɒrəmɪ'nɪf(ə)rn̩, -z
AM fə,ræmə'nɪf(ə)rən, -z
foraminiferous
BR fə,ramɪ'nɪf(ə)rəs, ,fɒrəmɪ'nɪf(ə)rəs
AM fə,ræmə'nɪf(ə)rəs
forasmuch
BR ,f(ə)rəz'mʌtʃ
AM ',fɔrəz',mətʃ, ,fərəz'mətʃ
forastero
BR ,fɒrə'stɛ:rəʊ, -z
AM ,fɔrə'stɛroʊ, -z
foray
BR 'fɒreɪ, -z, -ɪŋ, -d
AM 'fɔ,reɪ, 'fɑ,reɪ, -z, -ɪŋ, -d
forb
BR fɔ:b, -z
AM fɔ(ə)rb, -z
forbad
BR fə'bad
AM fər'bæd, fɔr'bæd
forbade
BR fə'bad, fə'beɪd
AM fər'bæd, fɔr'bæd, fər'beɪd, fɔr'beɪd
forbear¹
noun, ancestor
BR 'fɔ:bɛ:(r), -z
AM 'fɔr,bɛ(ə)r, -z
forbear²
verb
BR fə'bɛ:(r), fɔ:'bɛ:(r), -z, -ɪŋ
AM fər'bɛ(ə)r, fɔr'bɛ(ə)r, -z, -ɪŋ
forbearance
BR fə'bɛ:rəns, fə'bɛ:rn̩s, fɔ:'bɛ:rəns, fɔ:'bɛ:rn̩s
AM fər'bɛrəns, fɔr'bɛrəns
forbearingly
BR fə'bɛ:rɪŋli, fɔ:'bɛ:rɪŋli
AM fər'bɛrɪŋli, fɔr'bɛrɪŋli
Forbes
BR fɔ:bz, 'fɔ:bɪs, fɔ:'bɪs
AM fɔrbz
forbid
BR fə'bɪd, -z, -ɪŋ

AM fər'bɪd, fɔr'bɪd, -z, -ɪŋ

forbiddance
BR fə'bɪdns
AM fər'bɪdns, fɔr'bɪdns

forbidden
BR fə'bɪdn
AM fər'bɪdən, fɔr'bɪdən

forbidding
BR fə'bɪdɪŋ
AM fər'bɪdɪŋ, fɔr'bɪdɪŋ

forbiddingly
BR fə'bɪdɪŋli
AM fər'bɪdɪŋli, fɔr'bɪdɪŋli

forbore
BR fə'bɔː(r), fɔː'bɔː(r)
AM fər'bɔ(ə)r, fɔr'bɔ(ə)r

forborne
BR fə'bɔːn, fɔː'bɔːn
AM fər'bɔ(ə)rn, fɔr'bɔ(ə)rn

forbye
BR fə'bʌɪ, fɔː'bʌɪ
AM fər'baɪ, fɔr'baɪ

force
BR fɔːs, -ɪz, -ɪŋ, -t
AM fɔ(ə)rs, -əz, -ɪŋ, -t

forceable
BR 'fɔːsəbl
AM 'fɔrsəbəl

forceful
BR 'fɔːsf(ʊ)l
AM 'fɔrsfəl

forcefully
BR 'fɔːsfʊli, 'fɔːsfl̩i
AM 'fɔrsfəli

forcefulness
BR 'fɔːsf(ʊ)lnəs
AM 'fɔrsfəlnəs

force majeure
BR ˌfɔːs ma'ʒəː(r)
AM ˌfɔ(ə)rs mɑ'ʒər

forcemeat
BR 'fɔːsmiːt
AM 'fɔrsˌmit

forceps
BR 'fɔːsɛps, 'fɔːsɪps
AM 'fɔrsəps, 'fɔrˌsɛps

forcer
BR 'fɔːsə(r), -z
AM 'fɔrsər, -z

forcible
BR 'fɔːsɪbl
AM 'fɔrsəbəl

forcibleness
BR 'fɔːsɪblnəs
AM 'fɔrsəbəlnəs

forcibly
BR 'fɔːsɪbli
AM 'fɔrsəbli

ford
BR fɔːd, -z, -ɪŋ, -ɪd
AM fɔ(ə)rd, -z, -ɪŋ, -əd

fordable
BR 'fɔːdəbl
AM 'fɔrdəbəl

Forde
BR fɔːd
AM fɔ(ə)rd

Fordham
BR 'fɔːdəm
AM 'fɔrdəm

Fordingbridge
BR 'fɔːdɪŋbrɪdʒ
AM 'fɔrdɪŋˌbrɪdʒ

fordless
BR 'fɔːdləs
AM 'fɔrdləs

Fordyce
BR 'fɔːdʌɪs, fɔː'dʌɪs
AM 'fɔrˌdaɪs

fore
BR fɔː(r)
AM fɔ(ə)r

forearm[1]
noun
BR 'fɔːrɑːm, -z
AM 'fɔrˌɑrm, -z

forearm[2]
verb
BR (ˌ)fɔːr'ɑːm, -z, -ɪŋ, -d
AM ˌfɔr'ɑrm, -z, -ɪŋ, -d

forebad
BR fə'bad, fə'beɪd
AM fər'bæd, fɔr'beɪd

forebade
BR fə'bad, fə'beɪd
AM fər'bæd, fɔr'beɪd

forebear
BR 'fɔːbɛː(r), -z
AM 'fɔrˌbɛ(ə)r, -z

forebode
BR fə'bəʊd, fɔː'bəʊd, -z, -ɪŋ, -ɪd
AM fɔr'boʊd, -z, -ɪŋ, -əd

foreboding
BR fə'bəʊdɪŋ, fɔː'bəʊdɪŋ, -z
AM fɔr'boʊdɪŋ, -z

forebodingly
BR fə'bəʊdɪŋli, fɔː'bəʊdɪŋli
AM fɔr'boʊdɪŋli

forebrain
BR 'fɔːbreɪn, -z
AM 'fɔrˌbreɪn, -z

forecast
BR 'fɔːkɑːst, 'fɔːkast, -s, -ɪŋ, -ɪd
AM 'fɔrˌkæst, -s, -ɪŋ, -əd

forecaster
BR 'fɔːkɑːstə(r), 'fɔːkastə(r), -z
AM 'fɔrˌkæstər, -z

forecastle
BR 'fəʊksl, -z
AM 'foʊksəl, 'fɔrˌkæsəl, -z

foreclose
BR (ˌ)fɔː'kləʊz, -ɪz, -ɪŋ, -d
AM ˌfɔr'kloʊz, -ɪz, -ɪŋ, -d

foreclosure
BR (ˌ)fɔː'kləʊʒə(r), -z
AM ˌfɔr'kloʊʒər, -z

foreconscious
BR 'fɔːˌkɒnʃəs
AM 'fɔrˌkɑnʃəs

forecourt
BR 'fɔːkɔːt, -s
AM 'fɔrˌkɔ(ə)rt, -s

foredeck
BR 'fɔːdɛk, -s
AM 'fɔrˌdɛk, -s

foredge
BR 'fɔːrɛdʒ, -ɪz
AM 'fɔrˌɛdʒ, -əz

foredoom
BR (ˌ)fɔː'duːm, -z, -ɪŋ, -d
AM ˌfɔr'dum, -z, -ɪŋ, -d

forefather
BR 'fɔːˌfɑːðə(r), -z
AM 'fɔrˌfɑðər, -z

forefeel
BR (ˌ)fɔː'fiːl, -z, -ɪŋ
AM ˌfɔr'fil, -z, -ɪŋ

forefeet
BR 'fɔːfiːt
AM 'fɔrˌfit

forefelt
BR (ˌ)fɔː'fɛlt
AM ˌfɔr'fɛlt

forefinger
BR 'fɔːˌfɪŋgə(r), -z
AM 'fɔrˌfɪŋgər, -z

forefoot
BR 'fɔːfʊt
AM 'fɔrˌfʊt

forefront
BR 'fɔːfrʌnt
AM 'fɔrˌfrənt

foregather
BR fə'gað|ə(r), (ˌ)fɔː'gað|ə(r), -əz, -(ə)rɪŋ, -əd
AM fər'gæðər, fɔr'gæðər, -z, -ɪŋ, -d

forego
verb, give up, renounce
BR fə'gəʊ, (ˌ)fɔː'gəʊ, -z, -ɪŋ
AM fər'goʊ, fɔr'goʊ, -z, -ɪŋ

foregoer
BR fə'gəʊə(r), (ˌ)fɔː'gəʊə(r), -z
AM fər'goʊər, fɔr'goʊər, -z

foregoing
adjective, preceding
BR 'fɔːˌgəʊɪŋ
AM 'fɔrˌgoʊɪŋ

foregone
BR (ˌ)fɔː'gɒn
AM ˈfɔrˈgɔn

foreground
BR 'fɔːgraʊnd, -z
AM 'fɔrˌgraʊnd, -z

forehand
BR 'fɔːhand, -z
AM 'fɔrˌ(h)ænd, -z

forehead
BR 'fɒrɪd, 'fɔːhɛd, -z
AM 'fɔrˌ(h)ɛd, -z

forehock
BR 'fɔːhɒk, -s
AM 'fɔrˌ(h)ɑk, -s

forehold
BR 'fɔːhəʊld, -z
AM 'fɔrˌ(h)oʊld, -z

foreign
BR 'fɒrɪn, 'fɒrn̩
AM 'fɔrən

foreigner
BR 'fɒrɪnə(r), 'fɒrn̩ə(r), -z
AM 'fɔrənər, -z

foreignness
BR 'fɒrɪnnɪs, 'fɒrn̩nəs
AM 'fɔrə(n)nəs

forejudge
BR fə'dʒʌdʒ, (ˌ)fɔː'dʒʌdʒ, -ɪz, -ɪŋ, -d
AM fər'dʒədʒ, fɔr'dʒədʒ, -əz, -ɪŋ, -d

foreknew
BR (ˌ)fɔː'njuː
AM fɔr'n(j)u

foreknow
BR (ˌ)fɔː'nəʊ, -z, -ɪŋ
AM fɔr'noʊ, -z, -ɪŋ

foreknowledge
BR (ˌ)fɔː'nɒlɪdʒ
AM ˈfɔrˈnɑlədʒ

foreknown
BR (ˌ)fɔː'nəʊn
AM fɔr'noʊn

forelady
BR 'fɔːˌleɪd|i, -ɪz
AM 'fɔrˌleɪdi, -z

foreland
BR 'fɔːlənd, -z
AM 'fɔrlənd, -z

foreleg
BR 'fɔːlɛg, -z
AM 'fɔrˌlɛg, -z

forelimb
BR 'fɔːlɪm, -z
AM 'fɔrˌlɪm, -z

forelock
BR 'fɔːlɒk, -s
AM 'fɔrˌlɑk, -s

foreman
BR 'fɔːmən
AM 'fɔrmən

foremast
BR 'fɔːmɑːst, 'fɔːmast, 'fɔːməst, -s
AM 'fɔrˌmæst, 'fɔrməst, -s

foremen
BR 'fɔːmən
AM 'fɔrˌmɛn, fɔrmən

foremost
BR 'fɔːməʊst

AM ˈfɔrˌmoʊst

forename
BR ˈfɔːneɪm, -z
AM ˈfɔrˌneɪm, -z

forenoon
BR ˈfɔːnuːn
AM ˈfɔrˌnun

forensic
BR fəˈrɛnzɪk, fəˈrɛnsɪk
AM fəˈrɛnzɪk, fəˈrɛnsɪk

forensically
BR fəˈrɛnzɨkli, fəˈrɛnsɨkli
AM fəˈrɛnzɨkli, fəˈrɛnsək(ə)li

foreordain
BR ˌfɔːrɔːˈdeɪn, -z, -ɪŋ, -d
AM ˌfɔrɔrˈdeɪn, -z, -ɪŋ, -d

foreordination
BR ˌfɔːrɔːdɪˈneɪʃn
AM fɔrˌɔrdəˈneɪʃən

forepart
BR ˈfɔːpɑːt, -s
AM ˈfɔrˌpɑrt, -s

forepaw
BR ˈfɔːpɔː(r), -z
AM ˈfɔrˌpɔ, ˈfɔrˌpɑ, -z

forepeak
BR ˈfɔːpiːk, -s
AM ˈfɔrˌpik, -s

foreplay
BR ˈfɔːpleɪ
AM ˈfɔrˌpleɪ

forequarter
BR ˈfɔːˌkwɔːtə(r), -z
AM ˈfɔrˌkwɔrdər, -z

foreran
BR (ˌ)fɔːˈran
AM fɔ(r)ˈræn

forerun
BR (ˌ)fɔːˈrʌn, -z, -ɪŋ
AM fɔ(r)ˈrən, -z, -ɪŋ

forerunner
BR ˈfɔːˌrʌnə(r), -z
AM ˈfɔrˌrənər, -z

foresail
BR ˈfɔːseɪl, ˈfɔːsl, -z
AM ˈfɔrˌseɪl, ˈfɔrsəl, -z

foresaw
BR fəˈsɔː(r), (ˌ)fɔːˈsɔː(r)
AM fərˈsɔ, fɔrˈsɔ, fərˈsɑ, fɔrˈsɑ

foresee
BR fəˈsiː, (ˌ)fɔːˈsiː, -z, -ɪŋ
AM fərˈsi, fɔrˈsi, -z, -ɪŋ

foreseeability
BR fəˌsiːəˈbɪlɨti, fɔːˌsiːəˈbɪlɨti
AM fərˌsiəˈbɪlɨdi, fɔrˌsiəˈbɪlɨdi

foreseeable
BR fəˈsiːəbl, (ˌ)fɔːˈsiːəbl
AM fərˈsiəbəl, fɔrˈsiəbəl

foreseeably
BR fəˈsiːəbli, (ˌ)fɔːˈsiːəbli
AM fərˈsiəbli, fɔrˈsiəbli

foreseen
BR fəˈsiːn, (ˌ)fɔːˈsiːn
AM fərˈsin, fɔrˈsin

foreseer
BR fəˈsiːə(r), (ˌ)fɔːˈsiːə(r), -z
AM fərˈsiər, fɔrˈsiər, -z

foreshadow
BR fəˈʃadəʊ, (ˌ)fɔːˈʃadəʊ, -z, -ɪŋ, -d
AM fərˈʃædoʊ, fɔrˈʃædoʊ, -z, -ɪŋ, -d

foresheets
BR ˈfɔːʃiːts
AM ˈfɔrˌʃits

foreshore
BR ˈfɔːʃɔː(r), -z
AM ˈfɔrˌʃɔ(ə)r, -z

foreshorten
BR fəˈʃɔːt|n, (ˌ)fɔːˈʃɔːt|n, -nz, -nɪŋ\-n̩ɪŋ, -nd
AM fərˈʃɔrtən, fɔrˈʃɔrtən, -z, -ɪŋ, -d

foreshow
BR fəˈʃəʊ, (ˌ)fɔːˈʃəʊ, -z, -ɪŋ, -d
AM fɔrˈʃoʊ, -z, -ɪŋ, -d

foreshown
BR fəˈʃəʊn, (ˌ)fɔːˈʃəʊn
AM fɔrˈʃoʊn

foresight
BR ˈfɔːsʌɪt, -s
AM ˈfɔrˌsaɪt, -s

foresighted
BR ˈfɔːsʌɪtɨd
AM ˈfɔrˌsaɪdɨd

foresightedly
BR ˈfɔːsʌɪtɨdli
AM ˈfɔrˌsaɪdɨdli

foresightedness
BR ˈfɔːsʌɪtɨdnɨs
AM ˈfɔrˌsaɪdɨdnɨs

foreskin
BR ˈfɔːskɪn, -z
AM ˈfɔrˌskɪn, -z

forest
BR ˈfɒrɪst, -s
AM ˈfɔrəst, -s

forestall
BR (ˌ)fɔːˈstɔːl, -z, -ɪŋ, -d
AM fərˈstɔl, fɔrˈstɔl, fərˈstɑl, fɔrˈstɑl, -z, -ɪŋ, -d

forestaller
BR (ˌ)fɔːˈstɔːlə(r), -z
AM fərˈstɔlər, fɔrˈstɔlər, fərˈstɑlər, fɔrˈstɑlər, -z

forestalment
BR (ˌ)fɔːˈstɔːlm(ə)nt
AM fərˈstɔlmənt, fɔrˈstɔlmənt, fərˈstɑlmənt, fɔrˈstɑlmənt

forestation
BR ˌfɒrɪˈsteɪʃn
AM ˌfɔrəˈsteɪʃən

forestay
BR ˈfɔːsteɪ, -z
AM ˈfɔrˌsteɪ, -z

forester
BR ˈfɒrɪstə(r), -z
AM ˈfɔrəstər, -z

forestry
BR ˈfɒrɪstri
AM ˈfɔrəstri

foreswear
BR fəˈswɛː(r), (ˌ)fɔːˈswɛː(r), -z, -ɪŋ
AM fərˈswɛ(ə)r, fɔrˈswɛ(ə)r, -z, -ɪŋ

foreswore
BR fəˈswɔː(r), (ˌ)fɔːˈswɔː(r)
AM fərˈswɔ(ə)r, fɔrˈswɔ(ə)r

foresworn
BR fəˈswɔːn, (ˌ)fɔːˈswɔːn
AM fərˈswɔ(ə)rn, fɔrˈswɔ(ə)rn

foretaste
BR ˈfɔːteɪst, -s
AM ˈfɔrˌteɪst, -s

foretell
BR fəˈtɛl, (ˌ)fɔːˈtɛl, -z, -ɪŋ
AM fərˈtɛl, fɔrˈtɛl, -z, -ɪŋ

foreteller
BR fəˈtɛlə(r), (ˌ)fɔːˈtɛlə(r), -z
AM fərˈtɛlər, fɔrˈtɛlər, -z

forethought
BR ˈfɔːθɔːt
AM ˈfɔrˌθɔt, ˈfɔrˌθɑt

foretoken
BR (ˌ)fɔːˈtəʊk|(ə)n, -(ə)nz, -ənɪŋ\-n̩ɪŋ, -(ə)nd
AM fɔrˈtoʊkən, -z, -ɪŋ, -d

foretold
BR fəˈtəʊld, (ˌ)fɔːˈtəʊld
AM fərˈtoʊld, fɔrˈtoʊld

foretop
BR ˈfɔːtɒp, -s
AM ˈfɔrˌtɑp, -s

forever
BR fərˈɛvə(r)
AM fəˈrɛvər

forevermore
BR fərˌɛvəˈmɔː(r)
AM fəˌrɛvərˈmɔ(ə)r

forewarn
BR fəˈwɔːn, (ˌ)fɔːˈwɔːn, -z, -ɪŋ, -d
AM fərˈwɔ(ə)rn, fɔrˈwɔ(ə)rn, -z, -ɪŋ, -d

forewarner
BR fəˈwɔːnə(r), (ˌ)fɔːˈwɔːnə(r), -z
AM fərˈwɔrnər, fɔrˈwɔrnər, -z

forewent
BR fəˈwɛnt, (ˌ)fɔːˈwɛnt
AM fɔrˈwɛnt

forewing
BR ˈfɔːwɪŋ, -z
AM ˈfɔrˌwɪŋ, -z

forewoman
BR ˈfɔːˌwʊmən
AM ˈfɔrˌwʊmən

forewomen
BR ˈfɔːˌwɪmɪn
AM ˈfɔrˌwɪmɨn

foreword
BR ˈfɔːwəːd, -z
AM ˈfɔrˌwərd, -z

foreyard
BR ˈfɔːjɑːd, -z
AM ˈfɔrˌjɑrd, -z

Forfar
BR ˈfɔːfə(r)
AM ˈfɔrfər

Forfarshire
BR ˈfɔːfəʃ(ɪ)ə(r)
AM ˈfɔrfərˌʃɪ(ə)r

forfeit
BR ˈfɔːfɪt, -s, -ɪŋ, -ɨd
AM ˈfɔrfə|t, -ts, -dɪŋ, -dəd

forfeitable
BR ˈfɔːfɪtəbl
AM ˈfɔrfədəbəl

forfeiter
BR ˈfɔːfɪtə(r), -z
AM ˈfɔrfədər, -z

forfeiture
BR ˈfɔːfɪtʃə(r)
AM ˈfɔrfətʃʊ(ə)r, ˈfɔrfətʃər

forfend
BR fɔːˈfɛnd, -z, -ɪŋ, -ɨd
AM fɔrˈfɛnd, -z, -ɪŋ, -əd

forgather
BR fəˈgað|ə(r), (ˌ)fɔːˈgað|ə(r), -ə(r)z, -(ə)rɪŋ, -ə(r)d
AM fərˈgæðər, fɔrˈgæðər, -z, -ɪŋ, -d

forgave
BR fəˈgeɪv
AM fərˈgeɪv

forge
BR fɔːdʒ, -ɨz, -ɪŋ, -d
AM fɔrdʒ, -əz, -ɪŋ, -t

forgeable
BR ˈfɔːdʒəbl
AM ˈfɔrdʒəbəl

forger
BR ˈfɔːdʒə(r), -z
AM ˈfɔrdʒər, -z

forgery
BR ˈfɔːdʒ(ə)r|i, -ɪz
AM ˈfɔrdʒəri, -z

forget
BR fə'gɛt, -s, -ɪŋ
AM fər'gɛ|t, -ts, -dɪŋ
forgetful
BR fə'gɛtf(ʊ)l
AM fər'gɛtfəl
forgetfully
BR fə'gɛtfʊli, fə'gɛtfḷi
AM fər'gɛtfəli
forgetfulness
BR fə'gɛtf(ʊ)lnəs
AM fər'gɛtfəlnəs
forget-me-not
BR fə'gɛtmɪnɒt, -s
AM fər'gɛdmɪˌnɑt, -s
forgettable
BR fə'gɛtəbl
AM fər'gɛdəbəl
forgetter
BR fə'gɛtə(r), -z
AM fər'gɛdər, -z
forgivable
BR fə'gɪvəbl
AM fər'gɪvəbəl
forgivably
BR fə'gɪvəbli
AM fər'gɪvəbli
forgive
BR fə'gɪv, -z, -ɪŋ
AM fər'gɪv, -z, -ɪŋ
forgiven
BR fə'gɪvn
AM fər'gɪvən
forgiveness
BR fə'gɪvnɪs
AM fər'gɪvnɪs
forgiver
BR fə'gɪvə(r), -z
AM fər'gɪvər, -z
forgivingly
BR fə'gɪvɪŋli
AM fər'gɪvɪŋli
forgo
BR fə'gəʊ, fɔː'gəʊ, -z, -ɪŋ
AM fər'goʊ, fɔr'goʊ, -z, -ɪŋ
forgot
BR fə'gɒt
AM fər'gɑt
forgotten
BR fə'gɒtn
AM fər'gɑtn
forint
BR 'fɒrɪnt, -s
AM 'fɔrɪnt, -s
fork
BR fɔːk, -s, -ɪŋ, -t
AM fɔ(ə)rk, -s, -ɪŋ, -t
forkful
BR 'fɔːkfʊl, -z
AM 'fɔrkˌfʊl, -z
forklift
BR 'fɔːklɪft, -s
AM 'fɔrkˌlɪft, -s
forlorn
BR fə'lɔːn
AM fər'lɔ(ə)rn
forlornly
BR fə'lɔːnli
AM fər'lɔrnli
forlornness
BR fə'lɔːnnəs
AM fər'lɔr(n)nəs
form
BR fɔːm, -z, -ɪŋ, -d
AM fɔ(ə)rm, -z, -ɪŋ, -d
formal
BR 'fɔːml
AM 'fɔrməl
formaldehyde
BR fɔː'maldɪhʌɪd, fə'maldɪhʌɪd
AM fɔr'mældəˌhaɪd, fər'mældəˌhaɪd
formalin
BR 'fɔːməlɪn
AM 'fɔrməlɪn
formalisation
BR ˌfɔːmḷʌɪ'zeɪʃn
AM ˌfɔrmələ'zeɪʃən, ˌfɔrməˌlaɪ'zeɪʃən
formalise
BR 'fɔːməlʌɪz, 'fɔːmḷʌɪz, -ɪz, -ɪŋ, -d
AM 'fɔrməˌlaɪz, -ɪz, -ɪŋ, -d
formalism
BR 'fɔːməlɪz(ə)m, 'fɔːmḷɪz(ə)m
AM 'fɔrməˌlɪzəm
formalist
BR 'fɔːməlɪst, 'fɔːmḷɪst, -s
AM 'fɔrməlәst, -s
formalistic
BR ˌfɔːmə'lɪstɪk, ˌfɔːmḷ'ɪstɪk
AM ˌfɔrmə'lɪstɪk
formality
BR fə'malɪt|i, fɔː'malɪt|i, -ɪz
AM fɔr'mælədi, -z
formalization
BR ˌfɔːmḷʌɪ'zeɪʃn
AM ˌfɔrmələ'zeɪʃən, ˌfɔrməˌlaɪ'zeɪʃən
formalize
BR 'fɔːməlʌɪz, 'fɔːmḷʌɪz, -ɪz, -ɪŋ, -d
AM 'fɔrməˌlaɪz, -ɪz, -ɪŋ, -d
formally
BR 'fɔːmḷi
AM 'fɔrməli
formalness
BR 'fɔːmlnəs
AM 'fɔrməlnəs
formant
BR 'fɔːm(ə)nt, -s
AM 'fɔrmənt, -s
format
BR 'fɔːmat, -s, -ɪŋ, -ɪd
AM 'fɔrˌmæ|t, -ts, -dɪŋ, -dəd
formate
BR 'fɔːmeɪt
AM 'fɔrˌmeɪt
formation
BR fə'meɪʃn, fɔː'meɪʃn, -z
AM fɔr'meɪʃən, fər'meɪʃən, -z
formational
BR fə'meɪʃṇ(ə)l, fə'meɪʃən(ə)l, fɔː'meɪʃṇ(ə)l, fɔː'meɪʃən(ə)l
AM fɔr'meɪʃ(ə)nəl, fər'meɪʃ(ə)nəl
formative
BR 'fɔːmətɪv
AM 'fɔrmədɪv
formatively
BR 'fɔːmətɪvli
AM 'fɔrmədəvli
formbook
BR 'fɔːmbʊk
AM 'fɔrmˌbʊk
Formby
BR 'fɔːmbi
AM 'fɔrmbi
forme
BR fɔːm, -z
AM fɔ(ə)rm, -z
former
BR 'fɔːmə(r)
AM 'fɔrmər
formerly
BR 'fɔːməli
AM 'fɔrmərli
formic
BR 'fɔːmɪk
AM 'fɔrmɪk
Formica®
BR fɔː'mʌɪkə(r), fə'mʌɪkə(r)
AM fər'maɪkə, fɔr'maɪkə
formication
BR ˌfɔːmɪ'keɪʃn
AM ˌfɔrmə'keɪʃən
formidable
BR 'fɔːmɪdəbl, fə'mɪdəbl
AM 'fɔrmədəbəl, fər'mɪdəbəl, fɔr'mɪdəbəl
formidableness
BR 'fɔːmɪdəblnəs, fə'mɪdəblnəs
AM 'fɔrmədəbəlnəs, fər'mɪdəbəlnəs, fɔr'mɪdəbəlnəs
formidably
BR 'fɔːmɪdəbli, fə'mɪdəbli
AM 'fɔrmədəbli, fər'mɪdəbli, fɔr'mɪdəbli
formless
BR 'fɔːmləs
AM 'fɔrmləs
formlessly
BR 'fɔːmləsli
AM 'fɔrmləsli
formlessness
BR 'fɔːmləsnəs
AM 'fɔrmləsnəs
Formosa
BR fɔː'məʊsə(r), fɔː'məʊzə(r)
AM fɔr'moʊsə
Formosan
BR fɔː'məʊsn, fɔː'məʊzn, -z
AM fɔr'moʊsən, -z
formula
BR 'fɔːmjʊlə(r), -z
AM 'fɔrmjələ, -z
formulae
BR 'fɔːmjʊliː
AM 'fɔrmjəˌli, 'fɔrmjəˌlaɪ
formulaic
BR ˌfɔːmjʊ'leɪɪk
AM ˌfɔrmjə'leɪɪk
formularise
BR 'fɔːmjʊlərʌɪz, -ɪz, -ɪŋ, -d
AM 'fɔrmjələˌraɪz, -ɪz, -ɪŋ, -d
formularize
BR 'fɔːmjʊlərʌɪz, -ɪz, -ɪŋ, -d
AM 'fɔrmjələˌraɪz, -ɪz, -ɪŋ, -d
formulary
BR 'fɔːmjʊlər|i, -ɪz
AM 'fɔrmjəˌlɛri, -z
formulate
BR 'fɔːmjʊleɪt, -s, -ɪŋ, -ɪd
AM 'fɔrmjəˌleɪ|t, -ts, -dɪŋ, -dɪd
formulation
BR ˌfɔːmjʊ'leɪʃn, -z
AM ˌfɔrmjə'leɪʃən, -z
formulator
BR 'fɔːmjʊleɪtə(r), -z
AM 'fɔrmjəˌleɪdər, -z
formulise
BR 'fɔːmjʊlʌɪz, -ɪz, -ɪŋ, -d
AM 'fɔrmjəˌlaɪz, -ɪz, -ɪŋ, -d
formulism
BR 'fɔːmjʊlɪz(ə)m
AM 'fɔrmjəˌlɪzəm
formulist
BR 'fɔːmjʊlɪst, -s
AM 'fɔrmjələst, -s
formulistic
BR ˌfɔːmjʊ'lɪstɪk
AM ˌfɔrmjə'lɪstɪk
formulize
BR 'fɔːmjʊlʌɪz, -ɪz, -ɪŋ, -d
AM 'fɔrmjəˌlaɪz, -ɪz, -ɪŋ, -d

formwork
BR 'fɔːmwəːk
AM 'fɔrm,wərk

fornicate
BR 'fɔːnɪkeɪt, -s, -ɪŋ, -ɨd
AM 'fɔrnə,keɪ|t, -ts, -dɪŋ, -dɨd

fornication
BR ,fɔːnɪ'keɪʃn
AM ,fɔrnə'keɪʃən

fornicator
BR 'fɔːnɪkeɪtə(r), -z
AM 'fɔrnə,keɪdər, -z

fornices
BR 'fɔːnɪsiːz
AM 'fɔrnə,siz

fornix
BR 'fɔːnɪks
AM 'fɔrnɪks

forrader
BR 'fɒrədə(r)
AM 'fɔrədər

Forres
BR 'fɒrɪs
AM 'fɔrəs, 'fɑrəs

Forrest
BR 'fɒrɪst
AM 'fɔrəst

Forrester
BR 'fɒrɪstə(r)
AM 'fɔrəstər, 'fɑrəstər

forsake
BR fə'seɪk, fɔː'seɪk, -s, -ɪŋ
AM fər'seɪk, -s, -ɪŋ

forsaken
BR fə'seɪk(ə)n, fɔː'seɪk(ə)n
AM fər'seɪkən

forsakenness
BR fə'seɪknnəs, fɔː'seɪknnəs
AM fər'seɪkə(n)nəs

forsaker
BR fə'seɪkə(r), fɔː'seɪkə(r), -z
AM fər'seɪkər, -z

Forshaw
BR 'fɔːʃɔː(r)
AM 'fɔr,ʃɔ

forsook
BR fə'sʊk, fɔː'sʊk
AM fər'sʊk

forsooth
BR fə'suːθ, fɔː'suːθ
AM fər'suθ

Forster
BR 'fɔːstə(r)
AM 'fɔrstər

forswear
BR fə'swɛː(r), fɔː'swɛː(r), -z, -ɪŋ
AM fər'swɛ(ə)r, fɔ(ə)r'swɛ(ə)r, -z, -ɪŋ

forswore
BR fə'swɔː(r), fɔː'swɔː(r)
AM fər'swɔ(ə)r, fɔr'swɔ(ə)r

Forsyte
BR 'fɔːsʌɪt
AM 'fɔrsaɪt

Forsyth
BR 'fɔːsʌɪθ, fɔː'sʌɪθ
AM 'fɔr,saɪθ

forsythia
BR fɔː'sʌɪθɪə(r), fə'sʌɪθɪə(r)
AM fər'sɪθiə, fɔr'sɪθiə

fort
BR fɔːt, -s
AM fɔ(ə)rt, -s

fortalice
BR 'fɔːtəlɪs, -ɪz
AM 'fɔrdələs, -əz

Fort-de-France
BR ,fɔː(t)də'frɑːns, ,fɔː(t)də'frans
AM ,fɔrdə'fræns

forte
BR 'fɔːteɪ, -z
AM 'fɔr,teɪ, fɔ(ə)rt, -z

Fortean
BR 'fɔːtɪən
AM 'fɔrdiən

forte-piano
BR ,fɔːtɪpɪ'anəʊ, ,fɔːtɪ'pjɑːnəʊ
AM 'fɔr,teɪ'pjɑnoʊ

Fortescue
BR 'fɔːtɪskjuː
AM 'fɔrdəs,kju

forth
BR fɔːθ
AM fɔ(ə)rθ

forthcoming
BR ,fɔːθ'kʌmɪŋ
AM ',fɔrθ'kəmɪŋ

forthcomingness
BR ,fɔːθ'kʌmɪŋnɪs
AM ',fɔrθ'kəmɪŋnɪs

forthright
BR 'fɔːθrʌɪt
AM 'fɔrθ,raɪt

forthrightly
BR 'fɔːθrʌɪtli
AM 'fɔrθ,raɪtli

forthrightness
BR 'fɔːθrʌɪtnɪs
AM 'fɔrθ,raɪtnɪs

forthwith
BR ,fɔːθ'wɪð, ,fɔːθ'wɪθ
AM ',fɔrθ'wɪθ

fortieth
BR 'fɔːtɪɪθ
AM 'fɔrdiɪθ

fortifiable
BR 'fɔːtɪfʌɪəbl
AM 'fɔrdə,faɪəbəl

fortification
BR ,fɔːtɪfɪ'keɪʃn, -z
AM ,fɔrdəfə'keɪʃən, -z

fortifier
BR 'fɔːtɪfʌɪə(r), -z
AM 'fɔrdə,faɪər, -z

fortify
BR 'fɔːtɪfʌɪ, -z, -ɪŋ, -d
AM 'fɔrdə,faɪ, -z, -ɪŋ, -d

Fortinbras
BR 'fɔːt(ɪ)nbras
AM 'fɔrtn,bræs

fortis
BR 'fɔːtɪs
AM 'fɔrdəs

fortissimo
BR fɔː'tɪsɪməʊ
AM fɔr'tɪsəmoʊ

fortitude
BR 'fɔːtɪtjuːd, fɔːtɪtʃuːd
AM 'fɔrdə,tud

Fort Knox
BR ,fɔːt 'nɒks
AM ,fɔ(ə)rt 'nɑks

fortnight
BR 'fɔːtnʌɪt, -s
AM 'fɔrt,naɪt, -s

fortnightly
BR 'fɔːtnʌɪtl|i, -ɪz
AM 'fɔrt,naɪtli, -z

Fortnum and Mason
BR ,fɔːtnəm (ə)n(d) 'meɪsn
AM 'fɔrtnəm ən 'meɪsən

FORTRAN
BR 'fɔːtran
AM 'fɔr,træn

fortress
BR 'fɔːtrɪs, -ɪz
AM 'fɔrtrəs, -əz

fortuitism
BR fɔː'tjuːɪtɪz(ə)m, fɔː'tʃuːɪtɪz(ə)m
AM fɔr'tuə,tɪzəm

fortuitist
BR fɔː'tjuːɪtɪst, fɔː'tʃuːɪtɪst, -s
AM fɔr'tuədəst, -s

fortuitous
BR fɔː'tjuːɪtəs, fɔː'tʃuːɪtəs
AM fɔr'tuədəs

fortuitously
BR fɔː'tjuːɪtəsli, fɔː'tʃuːɪtəsli
AM fɔr'tuədəsli

fortuitousness
BR fɔː'tjuːɪtəsnəs, fɔː'tʃuːɪtəsnəs
AM fɔr'tuədəsnəs

fortuity
BR fɔː'tjuːɪt|i, fɔː'tʃuːɪt|i, -ɪz
AM fɔr'tuədi, -z

fortunate
BR 'fɔːtʃn̩ət, 'fɔːtʃ(ə)nət, 'fɔːtjʉnət
AM 'fɔrtʃ(ə)nət

fortunately
BR 'fɔːtʃn̩ətli, 'fɔːtʃ(ə)nətli, 'fɔːtjʉnətli
AM 'fɔrtʃ(ə)nətli

fortune
BR 'fɔːtʃuːn, 'fɔːtʃ(ə)n, 'fɔːtjuːn, -z
AM 'fɔrtʃən, -z

forty
BR 'fɔːti
AM 'fɔrdi

fortyfold
BR 'fɔːtɪfəʊld
AM 'fɔrdi,foʊld

forty-niner
BR ,fɔːtɪ'nʌɪnə(r), -z
AM ,fɔrdi'naɪnər, -z

forum
BR 'fɔːrəm, -z
AM 'fɔrəm, -z

forward
BR 'fɔːwəd, -z, -ɪŋ, -ɨd
AM 'fɔrwərd, -z, -ɪŋ, -əd

forwarder
BR 'fɔːwədə(r), -z
AM 'fɔrwərdər, -z

forwardly
BR 'fɔːwədli
AM 'fɔrwərdli

forwardness
BR 'fɔːwədnəs
AM 'fɔrwərdnəs

forwards
BR 'fɔːwədz
AM 'fɔrwərdz

forwent
BR (,)fɔː'wɛnt
AM fɔr'wɛnt

Fosbury
BR 'fɒzb(ə)ri
AM 'fɑs,bɛri

Fosdick
BR 'fɒzdɪk
AM 'fɑzdɪk

Fosdyke
BR 'fɒzdʌɪk
AM 'fɑz,daɪk

foss
BR fɒs, -ɪz
AM fɔs, fɑs, -əz

fossa
BR 'fɒsə(r), -z
AM 'fɔsə, 'fɑsə, -z

fossae
BR 'fɒsiː
AM 'fɔsi, 'fɔ,saɪ, 'fɑsi, 'fɑ,saɪ

fosse
BR fɒs, -ɪz
AM fɑs, -əz

fossick
BR 'fɒs|ɪk, -ɪks, -ɪkɪŋ, -ɪkt
AM 'fɑsɪk, -s, -ɪŋ, -t

fossicker
BR 'fɒsɪkə(r), -z

AM 'fɑsɪkər, -z

fossil
BR 'fɒsl, -z
AM 'fɑsəl, -z

fossil fuel
BR ˌfɒsl 'fjuːəl
AM 'fɑsəl ˌfju(ə)l

fossiliferous
BR ˌfɒsɪ'lɪf(ə)rəs
AM ˌfɑsə'lɪfərəs

fossilisation
BR ˌfɒsl̩ʌɪ'zeɪʃn, ˌfɒsɪlʌɪ'zeɪʃn
AM ˌfɑsələ'zeɪʃən, ˌfɑsəˌlaɪ'zeɪʃən

fossilise
BR 'fɒsl̩ʌɪz, 'fɒsɪlʌɪz, -ɪz, -ɪŋ, -d
AM 'fɑsəˌlaɪz, -ɪz, -ɪŋ, -d

fossilization
BR ˌfɒsl̩ʌɪ'zeɪʃn, ˌfɒsɪlʌɪ'zeɪʃn
AM ˌfɑsələ'zeɪʃən, ˌfɑsəˌlaɪ'zeɪʃən

fossilize
BR 'fɒsl̩ʌɪz, 'fɒsɪlʌɪz, -ɪz, -ɪŋ, -d
AM 'fɑsəˌlaɪz, -ɪz, -ɪŋ, -d

fossorial
BR fɒ'sɔːrɪəl
AM fɑ'sɔriəl

foster
BR 'fɒst|ə(r), -əz, -(ə)rɪŋ, -əd
AM 'fɔst|ər, 'fɑst|ər, -ərz, -(ə)rɪŋ, -ərd

fosterage
BR 'fɒst(ə)rɪdʒ
AM 'fɔstərɪdʒ, 'fɑstərɪdʒ

fosterer
BR 'fɒst(ə)rə(r), -z
AM 'fɔstərər, 'fɑstərər, -z

fosterling
BR 'fɒstəlɪŋ, -z
AM 'fɔstərlɪŋ, 'fɑstərlɪŋ, -z

Fothergill
BR 'fɒðəgɪl
AM 'fɑðərˌgɪl

Fotheringay
BR 'fɒð(ə)rɪŋgeɪ
AM 'fɑðərənˌgeɪ

Fotheringham
BR 'fɒð(ə)rɪŋ(ə)m
AM 'fɑðərɪŋəm

Foucault
BR fuː'kəʊ
AM fu'koʊ

fouetté
BR 'fweteɪ, 'fuːəteɪ, -z
AM ˌfuə'teɪ, -z

fought
BR fɔːt
AM fɔt, fɑt

foul
BR faʊl, -z, -ɪŋ, -d, -ə(r), -ɪst
AM faʊl, -z, -ɪŋ, -d, -ər, -əst

Foula
BR 'fuːlə(r)
AM 'fulə

foulard
BR 'fuːlɑː(r), 'fuːlɑːd, fuː'lɑː(r), fuː'lɑːd, -z
AM fu'lɑrd, fə'lɑrd, -z

Foulds
BR fəʊldz
AM foʊl(d)z

Foulkes
BR fəʊks, faʊks
AM foʊlks

foully
BR 'faʊlli
AM 'faʊ(l)li

foulmart
BR 'fuːmət, 'fuːmɑːt, -s
AM 'fumərt, 'fuˌmɑrt, -s

foulness
BR 'faʊlnəs
AM 'faʊlnəs

foumart
BR 'fuːmət, 'fuːmɑːt, -s
AM 'fumərt, 'fuˌmɑrt, -s

found
BR faʊnd
AM faʊnd

foundation
BR faʊn'deɪʃn, -z
AM faʊn'deɪʃən, -z

foundational
BR faʊn'deɪʃn̩(ə)l, faʊn'deɪʃən(ə)l
AM faʊn'deɪʃ(ə)nəl

foundationer
BR faʊn'deɪʃn̩ə(r), faʊn'deɪʃ(ə)nə(r), -z
AM faʊn'deɪʃ(ə)nər, -z

founder
BR 'faʊnd|ə(r), -əz, -(ə)rɪŋ, -əd
AM 'faʊnd|ər, -ərz, -(ə)rɪŋ, -ərd

foundership
BR 'faʊndəʃɪp
AM 'faʊndərˌʃɪp

foundling
BR 'faʊndlɪŋ, -z
AM 'faʊndlɪŋ, -z

foundress
BR 'faʊndrɪs, -ɪz
AM 'faʊndrəs, -əz

foundry
BR 'faʊndr|i, -ɪz
AM 'faʊndri, -z

fount[1]
in printing
BR fɒnt, faʊnt, -s
AM fɑnt, faʊnt, -s

fount[2]
spring of water, beginning
BR faʊnt, -s
AM faʊnt, -s

fountain
BR 'faʊnt(ɪ)n, -z, -d
AM 'faʊnt(ə)n, -z, -d

fountainhead
BR 'faʊnt(ɪ)nhɛd, -z
AM 'faʊnt(ə)nˌ(h)ɛd, -z

fountainpen
BR 'faʊnt(ɪ)npɛn, -z
AM 'faʊnt(ə)nˌpɛn, -z

four
BR fɔː(r), -z
AM fɔ(ə)r, -z

four-bagger
BR 'fɔːˌbagə(r), -z
AM ˌfɔr'bægər, -z

fourchette
BR ˌfʊə'ʃɛt, ˌfɔː'ʃɛt, -s
AM ˌfʊr'ʃɛt, -s

fourdrinier
BR ˌfʊə'drɪnɪə(r), ˌfʊə'drɪnɪeɪ, ˌfɔː'drɪnɪə(r), ˌfɔː'drɪnɪeɪ, -z
AM ˌfɔrdrə'nɪ(ə)r, -z

fourfold
BR 'fɔːfəʊld
AM 'fɔrˌfoʊld

Fourier
BR 'fʊrɪə(r), 'fʊrɪeɪ
AM ˌfʊri'eɪ

Fourierism
BR 'fʊrɪərɪz(ə)m
AM 'fʊriəˌrɪzəm

fourpence
BR 'fɔːp(ə)ns, -ɪz
AM 'fɔrˌpɛns, -əz

fourpenny
BR 'fɔːpn̩|i, 'fɔːpn|i, -ɪz
AM 'fɔrˌpɛni, -z

fourscore
BR ˌfɔː'skɔː(r)
AM 'fɔr'skɔ(ə)r

foursome
BR 'fɔːs(ə)m, -z
AM 'fɔrsəm, -z

foursquare
BR ˌfɔː'skwɛː(r)
AM ˌfɔr'skwɛ(ə)r

fourteen
BR ˌfɔː'tiːn, -z
AM ˌfɔr'ˌtin, -z

fourteenth
BR ˌfɔː'tiːnθ
AM ˌfɔr'ˌtinθ

fourth
BR fɔːθ, -s
AM fɔ(ə)rθ, -s

fourthly
BR 'fɔːθli
AM 'fɔrθli

fovea
BR 'fəʊvɪə(r)
AM 'foʊviə

foveae
BR 'fəʊviiː
AM 'foʊviˌi, 'foʊviˌaɪ

foveal
BR 'fəʊvɪəl
AM 'foʊviəl

foveate
BR 'fəʊvɪət
AM 'foʊviˌeɪt, 'foʊviət

foveola
BR fə(ʊ)'viːələ(r)
AM foʊ'violə

foveolae
BR fə(ʊ)'viːəliː
AM foʊ'violi, foʊ'vioˌlaɪ

foveolate
BR fə(ʊ)'viːələt
AM foʊ'vioˌleɪt, foʊ'violət

Fowey
BR fɔɪ
AM fɔɪ

Fowkes
BR fəʊks, faʊks
AM foʊks, faʊks

fowl
BR faʊl, -z
AM faʊl, -z

fowler
BR 'faʊlə(r), -z
AM 'faʊlər, -z

Fowles
BR faʊlz
AM faʊls, foʊls

fowling
BR 'faʊlɪŋ
AM 'faʊlɪŋ

Fowlmere
BR 'faʊlmɪə(r)
AM 'faʊlˌmaɪər

fox
BR fɒks, -ɪz
AM fɑks, -əz

Foxcroft
BR 'fɒkskrɒft
AM 'fɑksˌkrɔft, 'fɑksˌkrɑft

Foxe
BR fɒks
AM fɑks

foxfire
BR 'fɒksˌfʌɪə(r)
AM 'fɑksˌfaɪ(ə)r

foxglove
BR 'fɒksglʌv, -z
AM 'fɑksˌgləv, -z

foxhole
BR 'fɒkshəʊl, -z
AM 'fɑksˌ(h)oʊl, -z

foxhound
BR 'fɒkshaʊnd, -z
AM 'fɑksˌ(h)aʊnd, -z

foxhunt
BR 'fɒkshʌnt, -s, -ɪŋ, -ɪd

AM 'fɑks,(h)ən|t, -ts, -(t)ɪŋ, -(t)əd

foxily
BR 'fɒksɨli
AM 'fɑksəli

foxiness
BR 'fɒksɪnɨs
AM 'fɑksinɨs

foxlike
BR 'fɒkslʌɪk
AM 'fɑks,laɪk

foxtail
BR 'fɒksteɪl, -z
AM 'fɑks,teɪl, -z

Foxton
BR 'fɒkst(ə)n
AM 'fɑkstən

foxtrot
BR 'fɒkstrɒt, -s
AM 'fɑks,trɑt, -s

foxy
BR 'fɒks|i, -ɪə(r), -ɪɪst
AM 'fɑksi, -ər, -ɨst

foyer
BR 'fɔɪeɪ, 'fɔɪə(r), -z
AM 'fɔɪər, -z

Foyle
BR fɔɪl
AM fɔɪl

Fra
BR frɑː(r)
AM frɑ

frabjous
BR 'frabdʒəs
AM 'fræbdʒəs

frabjously
BR 'frabdʒəsli
AM 'fræbdʒəsli

fracas¹
singular
BR 'frakɑː(r)
AM 'freɪkəs, 'frækəs

fracas²
plural
BR 'frakɑːz
AM 'freɪkəs, 'frækəs

fracases
BR 'frakəsɪz
AM 'freɪkəsəz, 'frækəsəz

fractal
BR 'fraktl, -z
AM 'fræktəl, -z

fraction
BR 'frakʃn, -z
AM 'frækʃən, -z

fractional
BR 'frakʃn̩(ə)l, 'frakʃən(ə)l
AM 'frækʃ(ə)nəl

fractionalise
BR 'frakʃn̩əlʌɪz, 'frakʃn̩l̩ʌɪz, 'frakʃənl̩ʌɪz, 'frakʃ(ə)nəlʌɪz, -ɪz, -ɪŋ, -d
AM 'frækʃənl,aɪz, 'frækʃnə,laɪz, -ɪz, -ɪŋ, -d

fractionalize
BR 'frakʃn̩əlʌɪz, 'frakʃn̩l̩ʌɪz, 'frakʃənl̩ʌɪz, 'frakʃ(ə)nəlʌɪz, -ɪz, -ɪŋ, -d
AM 'frækʃənl,aɪz, 'frækʃnə,laɪz, -ɪz, -ɪŋ, -d

fractionally
BR 'frakʃn̩əli, 'frakʃn̩l̩i, 'frakʃənl̩i, 'frakʃ(ə)nəli
AM 'frækʃ(ə)nəli

fractionary
BR 'frakʃn̩(ə)ri
AM 'frækʃə,nɛri

fractionate
BR 'frakʃəneɪt, 'frakʃn̩eɪt, -s, -ɪŋ, -ɪd
AM 'frækʃə,neɪ|t, -ts, -dɪŋ, -dɨd

fractionation
BR ,frakʃə'neɪʃn
AM ,frækʃə'neɪʃən

fractionator
BR 'frakʃəneɪtə(r), 'frakʃn̩eɪtə(r), -z
AM 'frækʃə,neɪdər, -z

fractionise
BR 'frakʃənʌɪz, 'frakʃn̩ʌɪz, -ɪz, -ɪŋ, -d
AM 'frækʃə,naɪz, -ɪz, -ɪŋ, -d

fractionize
BR 'frakʃənʌɪz, 'frakʃn̩ʌɪz, -ɪz, -ɪŋ, -d
AM 'frækʃə,naɪz, -ɪz, -ɪŋ, -d

fractious
BR 'frakʃəs
AM 'frækʃəs

fractiously
BR 'frakʃəsli
AM 'frækʃəsli

fractiousness
BR 'frakʃəsnəs
AM 'frækʃəsnəs

fracture
BR 'fraktʃ|ə(r), -əz, -(ə)rɪŋ, -əd
AM 'fræktʃər, -ərz, -ərɪŋ, -ərd

fraena
BR 'friːnə(r)
AM 'frinə

fraenula
BR 'friːnjʉlə(r), 'frɛnjʉlə(r)
AM 'frɛnjələ

fraenulum
BR 'friːnjʉləm, 'frɛnjʉləm
AM 'frɛnjələm

fraenum
BR 'friːnəm
AM 'frɛnəm

fragile
BR 'fradʒʌɪl
AM 'frædʒəl

fragilely
BR 'fradʒʌɪl(l)i
AM 'frædʒə(l)li

fragility
BR frə'dʒɪlɨti
AM frə'dʒɪlɨdi

fragment¹
noun
BR 'fragm(ə)nt, -s
AM 'frægmənt, -s

fragment²
verb
BR frag'mɛnt, -s, -ɪŋ, -ɨd
AM ,fræg'mɛn|t, -ts, -(t)ɪŋ, -(t)əd

fragmental
BR frag'mɛntl
AM fræg'mɛn(t)l

fragmentarily
BR 'fragm(ə)nt(ə)rɨli
AM ,frægmən'tɛrəli

fragmentary
BR 'fragm(ə)ntri
AM 'frægmən,tɛri

fragmentation
BR ,fragm(ə)n'teɪʃn, ,fragmɛn'teɪʃn
AM ,frægmən'teɪʃən

fragmentise
BR 'fragm(ə)ntʌɪz, -ɪz, -ɪŋ, -d
AM 'frægmən,taɪz, -ɪz, -ɪŋ, -d

fragmentize
BR 'fragm(ə)ntʌɪz, -ɪz, -ɪŋ, -d
AM 'frægmən,taɪz, -ɪz, -ɪŋ, -d

Fragonard
BR 'fragənɑː(r)
AM ,frægə'nɑr

fragrance
BR 'freɪgr(ə)ns, -ɪz
AM 'freɪgrəns, -əz

fragranced
BR 'freɪgr(ə)nst
AM 'freɪgrənst

fragrancy
BR 'freɪgr(ə)nsi
AM 'freɪgrənsi

fragrant
BR 'freɪgr(ə)nt
AM 'freɪgrənt

fragrantly
BR 'freɪgr(ə)ntli
AM 'freɪgrən(t)li

fragrantness
BR 'freɪgr(ə)ntnəs
AM 'freɪgrən(t)nəs

frail
BR freɪl, -ə(r), -ɨst
AM freɪ(ə)l, -ər, -ɨst

frailly
BR 'freɪlli
AM 'freɪ(əl)li

frailness
BR 'freɪlnɨs
AM 'freɪ(ə)lnɨs

frailty
BR 'freɪlt|i, -ɪz
AM 'freɪ(ə)lti, -z

fraise
BR frɛz, freɪz
AM frɛz

fraises
BR frɛz, freɪz
AM frɛz

Fraktur
BR 'fraktʊə(r), frak'tʊə(r)
AM fræk'tʊ(ə)r

framable
BR 'freɪməbl
AM 'freɪməbəl

frambesia
BR fram'biːzɪə(r), fram'biːʒə(r)
AM fræm'biʒə

framboesia
BR fram'biːzɪə(r), fram'biːʒə(r)
AM fræm'biʒə

frame
BR freɪm, -z, -ɪŋ, -d
AM freɪm, -z, -ɪŋ, -d

frameless
BR 'freɪmlɨs
AM 'freɪmlɨs

framer
BR 'freɪmə(r), -z
AM 'freɪmər, -z

framework
BR 'freɪmwəːk, -s
AM 'freɪm,wərk, -s

Framlingham
BR 'framlɪŋ(ə)m
AM 'fræmlɪŋəm

Framlington
BR 'framlɪŋt(ə)n
AM 'fræmlɪŋtən

Frampton
BR 'fram(p)t(ə)n
AM 'fræmtən

Fran
BR fran
AM fræn

franc
BR fraŋk, -s
AM fræŋk, -s

France
BR frɑːns, frans
AM fræns

Frances
BR 'frɑːnsɪs, 'fransɪs
AM 'frænsəs

Francesca
BR fran'tʃɛskə(r)
AM fræn'(t)ʃɛskə

Franche-Comté
BR ˌfrɒ̃ʃˈkɒ̃teɪ
AM ˌfrɑnʃˌkɔnˈteɪ

franchise
BR ˈfran(t)ʃʌɪz, -ɪz, -ɪŋ, -d
AM ˈfrænˌ(t)ʃaɪz, -ɪz, -ɪŋ, -d

franchisee
BR ˌfran(t)ʃʌɪˈziː, -z
AM ˌfrænˌ(t)ʃaɪˈzi, -z

franchiser
BR ˈfran(t)ʃʌɪzə(r), -z
AM ˈfrænˌ(t)ʃaɪzər, -z

Francine
BR frɑːnˈsiːn, franˈsiːn
AM ˌfrænˈsin

Francis
BR ˈfrɑːnsɪs, ˈfransɪs
AM ˈfrænsəs

Franciscan
BR franˈsɪsk(ə)n, -z
AM frænˈsɪskən, -z

francium
BR ˈfransɪəm, ˈfrɑːnsɪəm
AM ˈfræn(t)siəm

Franck
BR frɑːŋk
AM frɑŋk

Franco
BR ˈfraŋkəʊ
AM ˈfræŋkoʊ

Franco-
BR ˈfraŋkəʊ
AM ˈfræŋkoʊ

Franco-German
BR ˈfraŋkəʊˈdʒəːmən
AM ˌfræŋkoʊˈdʒərmən

François
BR ˈfrɒnswɑː(r), ˈfrɑːnswɑː(r), ˈfranswɑː(r)
AM ˌfrænˈswɑ

Françoise
BR ˈfrɒnswɑː(r), ˈfrɑːnswɑː(r), ˈfranswɑː(r)
AM ˌfrænˈswɑz

francolin
BR ˈfraŋkəlɪn, -z
AM ˈfræŋkələn, -z

Francomania
BR ˌfraŋkəʊˈmeɪnɪə(r)
AM ˌfræŋkoʊˈmeɪniə

Franconia
BR fraŋˈkəʊnɪə(r)
AM fræŋˈkoʊniə

Francophile
BR ˈfraŋkə(ʊ)fʌɪl, -z
AM ˈfræŋkəˌfaɪl, -z

Francophobe
BR ˈfraŋkə(ʊ)fəʊb, -z
AM ˈfræŋkəˌfoʊb, -z

Francophobia
BR ˌfraŋkə(ʊ)ˈfəʊbɪə(r)
AM ˌfræŋkəˈfoʊbiə

francophone
BR ˈfraŋkə(ʊ)fəʊn
AM ˈfræŋkəˌfoʊn

frangibility
BR ˌfran(d)ʒɪˈbɪlɪti
AM ˌfrændʒəˈbɪlɪdi

frangible
BR ˈfran(d)ʒɪbl
AM ˈfrændʒəbəl

frangibleness
BR ˈfran(d)ʒɪblnəs
AM ˈfrændʒəbəlnəs

frangipane
BR ˈfran(d)ʒɪpeɪn, -z
AM ˈfrændʒəˌpeɪn, -z

frangipani
BR ˌfran(d)ʒɪˈpɑːn|i, -ɪz
AM ˌfrændʒəˈpɑni, ˌfræn(d)ʒəˈpæni, -z

franglais
BR ˈfrɑːŋgleɪ, ˈfrɒŋgleɪ
AM ˌfrɑŋˈgleɪ

frank
BR fraŋ|k, -ks, -kɪŋ, -(k)t, -kə(r), -kɪst
AM fræŋ|k, -ks, -kɪŋ, -(k)t, -kər, -kəst

frankable
BR ˈfraŋkəbl
AM ˈfræŋkəbəl

Frankenstein
BR ˈfraŋk(ɪ)nstʌɪn
AM ˈfræŋkənˌstaɪn

franker
BR ˈfraŋkə(r), -z
AM ˈfræŋkər, -z

Frankfort
BR ˈfraŋkfət
AM ˈfræŋkfərt

Frankfurt
BR ˈfraŋkfə(ː)t
AM ˈfræŋkfərt

frankfurter
BR ˈfraŋkfəːtə(r), -z
AM ˈfræŋkfərdər, -z

Frankie
BR ˈfraŋki
AM ˈfræŋki

frankincense
BR ˈfraŋk(ɪ)nsɛns
AM ˈfræŋkənˌsɛns

Frankish
BR ˈfraŋkɪʃ
AM ˈfræŋkɪʃ

Frankland
BR ˈfraŋklənd
AM ˈfræŋklənd

franklin
BR ˈfraŋklɪn, -z
AM ˈfræŋklən, -z

frankly
BR ˈfraŋkli
AM ˈfræŋkli

Franklyn
BR ˈfraŋklɪn
AM ˈfræŋklən

frankness
BR ˈfraŋknəs
AM ˈfræŋknəs

Franks
BR fraŋks
AM fræŋks

frantic
BR ˈfrantɪk
AM ˈfræn(t)ɪk

frantically
BR ˈfrantɪkli
AM ˈfræn(t)ək(ə)li

franticly
BR ˈfrantɪkli
AM ˈfræn(t)ək(ə)li

franticness
BR ˈfrantɪknɪs
AM ˈfræn(t)ɪknɪs

Franz Joseph Land
BR ˌfran(t)s ˈdʒəʊsɪf ˌland
AM ˌfrɑn(t)s ˈdʒoʊsəf ˌlænd

frap
BR frap, -s, -ɪŋ, -t
AM fræp, -s, -ɪŋ, -t

frappé
BR ˈfrapeɪ
AM fræˈpeɪ, fræp

Frascati
BR fraˈskɑːti
AM fræsˈkɑdi

Fraser
BR ˈfreɪzə(r)
AM ˈfreɪzər, ˈfreɪʒər

Fraserburgh
BR ˈfreɪzəb(ə)rə(r), ˈfreɪzəˌbʌrə(r)
AM ˈfreɪzərˌbərə

frass
BR fras
AM fræs

frat
BR frat
AM fræt

fratchiness
BR ˈfratʃɪnɪs
AM ˈfrætʃinɪs

fratchy
BR ˈfratʃi
AM ˈfrætʃi

fraternal
BR frəˈtəːnl
AM frəˈtərnəl

fraternalism
BR frəˈtəːnlɪz(ə)m, frəˈtəːnəlɪz(ə)m
AM frəˈtərnlˌɪzəm

fraternally
BR frəˈtəːnli, frəˈtəːnəli
AM frəˈtərnəli

fraternisation
BR ˌfratənʌɪˈzeɪʃn
AM ˌfrædərnəˈzeɪʃən, ˈfrædərˌnaɪˈzeɪʃən

fraternise
BR ˈfratənʌɪz, -ɪz, -ɪŋ, -d
AM ˈfrædərˌnaɪz, -ɪz, -ɪŋ, -d

fraternity
BR frəˈtəːnɪt|i, -ɪz
AM frəˈtərnədi, -z

fraternization
BR ˌfratənʌɪˈzeɪʃn
AM ˌfrædərnəˈzeɪʃən, ˈfrædərˌnaɪˈzeɪʃən

fraternize
BR ˈfratənʌɪz, -ɪz, -ɪŋ, -d
AM ˈfrædərˌnaɪz, -ɪz, -ɪŋ, -d

fratricidal
BR ˌfratrɪˈsʌɪdl
AM ˈfrætrəˌsaɪdəl

fratricide
BR ˈfratrɪsʌɪd, -z
AM ˈfrætrəˌsaɪd, -z

Frau
BR fraʊ, -z
AM fraʊ, -z

fraud
BR frɔːd, -z
AM frɔd, frɑd, -z

fraudster
BR ˈfrɔːdstə(r), -z
AM ˈfrɔdˌstər, -z

fraudulence
BR ˈfrɔːdjʊləns, ˈfrɔːdjʊlns, ˈfrɔːdʒʊləns, ˈfrɔːdʒʊlns, ˈfrɔːdʒl(ə)ns
AM ˈfrɔdʒələns, ˈfrɑdʒələns

fraudulent
BR ˈfrɔːdjʊlənt, ˈfrɔːdjʊlnt, ˈfrɔːdʒʊlənt, ˈfrɔːdʒʊlnt, ˈfrɔːdʒl(ə)nt
AM ˈfrɔdʒələnt, ˈfrɑdʒələnt

fraudulently
BR ˈfrɔːdjʊləntli, ˈfrɔːdjʊlntli, ˈfrɔːdʒʊləntli, ˈfrɔːdʒʊlntli, ˈfrɔːdʒlntli
AM ˈfrɔdʒələn(t)li, ˈfrɑdʒələn(t)li

fraught
BR frɔːt
AM frɔt, frɑt

Fräulein
BR ˈfrɔɪlʌɪn, -z
AM ˈfrɔɪˌlaɪn, -z

fraulein
BR ˈfrɔɪlʌɪn, -z
AM ˈfrɔɪˌlaɪn, -z

Fraunhofer
BR ˈfraʊnhəʊfə(r)
AM ˈfraʊnˌ(h)oʊfər

fraxinella
BR ˌfraksɪˈnɛlə(*r*)
AM ˌfræksəˈnɛlə

fray
BR freɪ, -z, -ɪŋ, -d
AM freɪ, -z, -ɪŋ, -d

Fray Bentos
BR ˌfreɪ ˈbɛntɒs
AM ˌfreɪ ˈbɛn(t)əs

Frayn
BR freɪn
AM freɪn

Frayne
BR freɪn
AM freɪn

Frazer
BR ˈfreɪzə(r)
AM ˈfreɪzər, ˈfreɪʒər

Frazier
BR ˈfreɪzɪə(r)
AM ˈfreɪzər, ˈfreɪʒər

frazil
BR ˈfreɪz(ɪ)l, frəˈzɪl
AM ˈfreɪzl, ˈfræzəl

frazzle
BR ˈfraz|l, -lz, -ḷɪŋ\-lɪŋ, -ld
AM ˈfræz|əl, -əlz, -(ə)lɪŋ, -əld

freak
BR friːk, -s, -ɪŋ, -t
AM frik, -s, -ɪŋ, -t

freakily
BR ˈfriːkɨli
AM ˈfrikɨli

freakiness
BR ˈfriːkɪnɨs
AM ˈfrikinɨs

freakish
BR ˈfriːkɪʃ
AM ˈfrikɪʃ

freakishly
BR ˈfriːkɪʃli
AM ˈfrikɪʃli

freakishness
BR ˈfriːkɪʃnɨs
AM ˈfrikɪʃnɨs

freaky
BR ˈfriːk|i, -ɪə(r), -ɪɨst
AM ˈfriki, -ər, -ɨst

freckle
BR ˈfrɛkl, -z, -d
AM ˈfrɛkəl, -z, -d

freckly
BR ˈfrɛkli
AM ˈfrɛkli, ˈfrɛkḷi

Fred
BR frɛd
AM frɛd

Freddie
BR ˈfrɛdi
AM ˈfrɛdi

Freddy
BR ˈfrɛdi
AM ˈfrɛdi

Frederic
BR ˈfrɛd(ə)rɪk
AM ˈfrɛd(ə)rɪk

Frederica
BR ˌfrɛdəˈriːkə(*r*), frɛˈdriːkə(*r*)
AM ˌfrɛd(ə)ˈrikə

Frederick
BR ˈfrɛd(ə)rɪk
AM ˈfrɛdrɪk

Fredericton
BR ˈfrɛd(ə)rɪkt(ə)n
AM ˈfrɛdrɪktən

free
BR friː, -z, -ɪŋ, -d, -ə(r), -ɨst
AM fri, -s, -ɪŋ, -d, -ər, -ɨst

freebase
BR ˈfriːbeɪs, -ɨz, -ɪŋ, -d
AM ˈfriˌbeɪs, -ɨz, -ɪŋ, -d

freebee
BR ˈfriːb|i, -ɪz
AM ˈfribi, -z

freebie
BR ˈfriːb|i, -ɪz
AM ˈfribi, -z

freeboard
BR ˈfriːbɔːd, -z
AM ˈfriˌbɔ(ə)rd, -z

freeboot
BR ˈfriːbuːt, -s, -ɪŋ, -ɨd
AM ˈfriˌbu|t, -ts, -dɪŋ, -dəd

freebooter
BR ˈfriːˌbuːtə(r), -z
AM ˈfriˌbudər, -z

freeborn
BR ˌfriːˈbɔːn
AM ˈfriˌbɔ(ə)rn

freedman
BR ˈfriːdman, ˈfriːdmən
AM ˈfridˌmæn, ˈfridmən

freedmen
BR ˈfriːdmɛn, ˈfriːdmən
AM ˈfridˌmɛn, ˈfridmən

freedom
BR ˈfriːdəm, -z
AM ˈfridəm, -z

freedwoman
BR ˈfriːdˌwʊmən
AM ˈfridˌwʊmən

freedwomen
BR ˈfriːdˌwɪmɪn
AM ˈfridˌwɪmɪn

Freefone®
BR ˈfriːfəʊn
AM ˈfriˌfoʊn

freehand
BR ˈfriːhand
AM ˈfriˌ(h)ænd

freehold
BR ˈfriːhəʊld, -z
AM ˈfriˌ(h)oʊld, -z

freeholder
BR ˈfriːhəʊldə(r), -z
AM ˈfriˌ(h)oʊldər, -z

freelance
BR ˈfriːlɑːns, ˈfriːlans, -ɨz, -ɪŋ, -t
AM ˈfriˌlæns, -əz, -ɪŋ, -t

freeload
BR ˈfriːləʊd, -z, -ɪŋ, -ɨd
AM ˈfriˌloʊd, -z, -ɪŋ, -əd

freeloader
BR ˈfriːləʊdə(r), -z
AM ˈfriˌloʊdər, -z

freely
BR ˈfriːli
AM ˈfrili

Freeman
BR ˈfriːmən
AM ˈfrimən

freeman
BR ˈfriːmən
AM ˈfrimən, friˌmæn

freemartin
BR ˈfriːˌmɑːtɪn, -z
AM ˈfriˌmartn, -z

Freemason
BR ˈfriːˌmeɪsn, -z
AM ˈfriˌmeɪsən, -z

freemasonry
BR ˈfriːˌmeɪsnri
AM ˈfriˌmeɪsnri

freemen
BR ˈfriːmən
AM ˈfrimən, friˌmɛn

freeness
BR ˈfriːnɨs
AM ˈfrinɨs

freephone
BR ˈfriːfəʊn
AM ˈfriˌfoʊn

Freeport
BR ˈfriːpɔːt
AM ˈfriˌpɔ(ə)rt

Freepost
BR ˈfriːpəʊst
AM ˈfriˌpoʊst

Freer
BR frɪə(r)
AM ˈfri(ə)r

freer
BR ˈfriːə(r)
AM ˈfriər

freesheet
BR ˈfriːʃiːt, -s
AM ˈfriˌʃit, -s

freesia
BR ˈfriːzɪə(*r*), ˈfriːʒə(*r*), -z
AM ˈfriʒ(i)ə, ˈfriziə, -z

freest
BR ˈfriːɨst
AM ˈfriɨst

freestanding
BR ˌfriːˈstandɪŋ
AM ˈfriˈstændɪŋ

freestone
BR ˈfriːstəʊn
AM ˈfriˌstoʊn

freestyle
BR ˈfriːstʌɪl
AM ˈfriˌstaɪl

freestyler
BR ˈfriːstʌɪlə(r), -z
AM ˈfriˌstaɪlər, -z

freethinker
BR ˌfriːˈθɪŋkə(r), -z
AM ˈfriˈθɪŋkər, -z

freethinking
BR ˌfriːˈθɪŋkɪŋ
AM ˈfriˈθɪŋkɪŋ

Freetown
BR ˈfriːtaʊn
AM ˈfriˌtaʊn

freeware
BR ˈfriːwɛː(r)
AM ˈfriˌwɛ(ə)r

freeway
BR ˈfriːweɪ, -z
AM ˈfriˌweɪ, -z

freewheel
BR ˌfriːˈwiːl, -z, -ɪŋ, -d
AM ˈfriˈ(h)wil, -z, -ɪŋ, -d

freewheeler
BR ˌfriːˈwiːlə(r), -z
AM ˈfriˈ(h)wilər, -z

freewill
BR ˌfriːˈwɪl
AM ˈfriˈwɪl

freezable
BR ˈfriːzəbl
AM ˈfrizəbəl

freeze
BR friːz, -ɨz, -ɪŋ
AM friz, -ɨz, -ɪŋ

freezer
BR ˈfriːzə(r), -z
AM ˈfrizər, -z

Freiburg
BR ˈfrʌɪbəːg
AM ˈfraɪˌbərg

freight
BR freɪt, -s, -ɪŋ, -ɨd
AM freɪ|t, -ts, -dɪŋ, -dɨd

freightage
BR ˈfreɪtɪdʒ
AM ˈfreɪdɪdʒ

freighter
BR ˈfreɪtə(r), -z
AM ˈfreɪdər, -z

freightliner
BR ˈfreɪtˌlʌɪnə(r), -z
AM ˈfreɪtˌlaɪnər, -z

Freischütz, Der
BR ˌdəː ˈfrʌɪʃuːts
AM ˌdər ˈfraɪˌʃuts

Frelimo
BR frɛˈliːməʊ, frɪˈliːməʊ
AM frɛˈlimoʊ

Fremantle
BR ˈfriːmantl
AM ˈfriˌmæn(t)əl

fremitus
BR ˈfrɛmɪtəs
AM ˈfrɛmədəs

Frémont
BR ˈfriːmɒnt
AM ˈfriˌmɑnt
frena
BR ˈfriːnə(*r*)
AM ˈfrinə
French
BR frɛn(t)ʃ
AM frɛn(t)ʃ
Frenchification
BR ˌfrɛn(t)ʃɪfɪˈkeɪʃn
AM ˌfrɛn(t)ʃəfəˈkeɪʃən
Frenchify[1]
BR ˈfrɛn(t)ʃɪfʌɪ, -z, -ɪŋ, -d
AM ˈfrɛn(t)ʃəˌfaɪ, -z, -ɪŋ, -d
Frenchify[2]
BR ˈfrɛn(t)ʃɪfʌɪ, -z, -ɪŋ, -d
AM ˈfrɛntʃəˌfaɪ, -z, -ɪŋ, -d
Frenchman
BR ˈfrɛn(t)ʃmən
AM ˈfrɛn(t)ʃmən
Frenchmen
BR ˈfrɛn(t)ʃmən
AM ˈfrɛn(t)ʃmən
Frenchness
BR ˈfrɛn(t)ʃnəs
AM ˈfrɛn(t)ʃnəs
Frenchwoman
BR ˈfrɛn(t)ʃˌwʊmən
AM ˈfrɛn(t)ʃˌwʊmən
Frenchwomen
BR ˈfrɛn(t)ʃˌwɪmɪn
AM ˈfrɛn(t)ʃˌwɪmɨn
Frenchy
BR ˈfrɛn(t)ʃ|i, -ɪz
AM ˈfrɛn(t)ʃi, -z
frenetic
BR frɪˈnɛtɪk
AM frəˈnɛdɪk
frenetically
BR frɪˈnɛtɪkli
AM frəˈnɛdək(ə)li
frenula
BR ˈfrɛnjʉlə(*r*)
AM ˈfrɛnjələ
frenulum
BR ˈfrɛnjʉləm
AM ˈfrɛnjələm
frenum
BR ˈfriːnəm
AM ˈfrinəm
frenzied
BR ˈfrɛnzɪd
AM ˈfrɛnzid
frenziedly
BR ˈfrɛnzɪdli
AM ˈfrɛnzidli
frenzy
BR ˈfrɛnz|i, -ɪz
AM ˈfrɛnzi, -z
Freon®
BR ˈfriːɒn, -z
AM ˈfriˌɑn, -z
frequency
BR ˈfriːkw(ə)ns|i, -ɪz
AM ˈfrikwənsi, -z
frequent[1]
adjective
BR ˈfriːkw(ə)nt
AM ˈfrikwənt
frequent[2]
verb
BR frɪˈkwɛnt, -s, -ɪŋ, -ɨd
AM friˈkwɛn|t, -ts, -(t)ɪŋ, -(t)əd
frequentation
BR ˌfriːkw(ə)nˈteɪʃn
AM ˌfrikwənˈteɪʃən
frequentative
BR frɪˈkwɛntətɪv
AM friˈkwən(t)ədɪv
frequenter
BR frɪˈkwɛntə(r), -z
AM friˈkwɛn(t)ər, -z
frequently
BR ˈfriːkw(ə)ntli
AM ˈfrikwən(t)li
Frere
BR frɪə(r), frɛː(r)
AM ˈfrɛr(i)
fresco
BR ˈfrɛskəʊ, -z, -d
AM ˈfrɛskoʊ, -z, -d
fresco secco
BR ˌfrɛskəʊ ˈsɛkəʊ
AM ˌfrɛskoʊ ˈsɛkoʊ
fresh
BR frɛʃ, -ə(r), -ɪst
AM frɛʃ, -ər, -əst
freshen
BR ˈfrɛʃ|n, -nz, -n̩ɪŋ\-(ə)nɪŋ, -nd
AM ˈfrɛʃ|ən, -ənz, -(ə)nɪŋ, -ənd
fresher
BR ˈfrɛʃə(r), -z
AM ˈfrɛʃər, -z
freshet
BR ˈfrɛʃɪt, -s
AM ˈfrɛʃət, -s
freshly
BR ˈfrɛʃli
AM ˈfrɛʃli
freshman
BR ˈfrɛʃmən
AM ˈfrɛʃmən
freshmen
BR ˈfrɛʃmən
AM ˈfrɛʃˌmɛn, ˈfrɛʃmən
freshness
BR ˈfrɛʃnəs
AM ˈfrɛʃnəs
freshwater
BR ˈfrɛʃˌwɔːtə(r)
AM ˈfrɛʃˌwɔdər, ˈfrɛʃˌwɑdər
freshwoman
BR ˈfrɛʃˌwʊmən
AM ˈfrɛʃˌwʊmən
freshwomen
BR ˈfrɛʃˌwɪmɪn
AM ˈfrɛʃˌwɪmɨn
Fresnel
BR ˈfreɪnɛl, frəˈnɛl
AM frəˈnɛl
Fresno
BR ˈfrɛznəʊ
AM ˈfrɛznoʊ
fret
BR frɛt, -s, -ɪŋ, -ɨd
AM frɛ|t, -ts, -dɪŋ, -dəd
fretboard
BR ˈfrɛtbɔːd, -z
AM ˈfrɛtˌbɔ(ə)rd, -z
fretful
BR ˈfrɛtf(ʊ)l
AM ˈfrɛtfəl
fretfully
BR ˈfrɛtfʊli, ˈfrɛtfl̩i
AM ˈfrɛtfəli
fretfulness
BR ˈfrɛtf(ʊ)lnəs
AM ˈfrɛtfəlnəs
fretless
BR ˈfrɛtləs
AM ˈfrɛtləs
fretsaw
BR ˈfrɛtsɔː(*r*), -z
AM ˈfrɛtˌsɔ, ˈfrɛtˌsɑ, -z
fretwork
BR ˈfrɛtwəːk
AM ˈfrɛtˌwərk
Freud
BR frɔɪd
AM frɔɪd
Freudian
BR ˈfrɔɪdɪən
AM ˈfrɔɪdiən
Freudianism
BR ˈfrɔɪdɪənɪz(ə)m
AM ˈfrɔɪdiəˌnɪzəm
Frey
BR freɪ
AM freɪ
Freya
BR ˈfreɪə(*r*)
AM ˈfreɪə
Freyr
BR ˈfreɪə(r)
AM ˈfreɪər
friability
BR ˌfrʌɪəˈbɪlɨti
AM ˌfraɪəˈbɪlɨdi
friable
BR ˈfrʌɪəbl
AM ˈfraɪəbəl
friableness
BR ˈfrʌɪəblnəs
AM ˈfraɪəbəlnəs
friar
BR ˈfrʌɪə(r), -z
AM ˈfraɪər, -z
friarly
BR ˈfrʌɪəli
AM ˈfraɪərli
friary
BR ˈfrʌɪər|i, -ɪz
AM ˈfraɪəri, -z
fribble
BR ˈfrɪbl̩, -z, -ɪŋ, -d
AM ˈfrɪb|əl, -əld, -(ə)lɪŋ, -əld
fricandeau
BR ˈfrɪk(ə)ndəʊ, -z
AM ˈfrɪkənˌdoʊ, ˌfrɪkənˈdoʊ, -z
fricandeaux
BR ˈfrɪk(ə)ndəʊz
AM ˈfrɪkənˌdoʊz ˌfrɪkənˈdoʊ
fricassee
BR ˈfrɪkəsiː, ˌfrɪkəˈsiː, -z, -ɪŋ, -d
AM ˈfrɪkəˌsi, ˌfrɪkəˈsi, -z, -ɪŋ, -d
fricative
BR ˈfrɪkətɪv, -z
AM ˈfrɪkədiv, -z
friction
BR ˈfrɪkʃn
AM ˈfrɪkʃən
frictional
BR ˈfrɪkʃn̩(ə)l, ˈfrɪkʃən(ə)l, -z
AM ˈfrɪkʃ(ə)nəl, -z
frictionally
BR ˈfrɪkʃn̩əli, ˈfrɪkʃn̩l̩i, ˈfrɪkʃənl̩i, ˈfrɪkʃ(ə)nəli
AM ˈfrɪkʃ(ə)nəli
frictionless
BR ˈfrɪkʃnləs
AM ˈfrɪkʃənləs
Friday
BR ˈfrʌɪd|eɪ, ˈfrʌɪd|i, -eɪz\-ɪz
AM ˈfraɪˌdeɪ, ˈfraɪdi, -z
fridge
BR frɪdʒ, -ɪz
AM frɪdʒ, -ɪz
Friedan
BR friːˈdan
AM friˈdæn
Friedman
BR ˈfriːdmən
AM ˈfridmən
Friedrich
BR ˈfriːdrɪk
AM ˈfridrɪk
friend
BR frɛnd, -z
AM frɛnd, -z
friendless
BR ˈfrɛndləs
AM ˈfrɛn(d)ləs
friendlessness
BR ˈfrɛndləsnəs
AM ˈfrɛn(d)ləsnəs
friendlily
BR ˈfrɛndlɨli
AM ˈfrɛn(d)ləli
friendliness
BR ˈfrɛndlɪnɪs

AM 'frɛn(d)linɨs

friendly
BR 'frɛndli
AM 'frɛn(d)li

friendship
BR 'frɛn(d)ʃɪp, -s
AM 'frɛn(d)ˌʃɪp, -s

frier
BR 'frʌɪə(r), -z
AM 'fraɪər, -z

Friern Barnet
BR ˌfrʌɪən 'bɑːnɨt
AM ˌfraɪərn 'bɑrnət

Fries
BR friːz
AM friz

Friesian
BR 'friːʒn, -z
AM 'friʒən, 'friʒən, -z

Friesland
BR 'friːzlənd
AM 'frizlənd

frieze
BR friːz, -ɨz
AM friz, -ɨz

frig¹
noun, refrigerator
BR frɪdʒ, -ɨz
AM frɪdʒ, -ɨz

frig²
verb, copulate, masturbate
BR frɪɡ, -z, -ɪŋ, -d
AM frɪɡ, -z, -ɪŋ, -d

frigate
BR 'frɪɡɨt, -s
AM 'frɪɡɨt, -s

Frigg
BR frɪɡ
AM frɪɡ

Frigga
BR 'frɪɡə(r)
AM 'frɪɡə

fright
BR frʌɪt, -s
AM fraɪt, -s

frighten
BR 'frʌɪt|n, -nz, -n̩ɪŋ\-nɪŋ, -nd
AM 'fraɪtn, -z, -ɪŋ, -d

frightener
BR 'frʌɪtn̩ə(r), 'frʌɪtnə(r), -z
AM 'fraɪtn̩ər, 'fraɪtnər, -z

frighteningly
BR 'frʌɪtn̩ɪŋli, 'frʌɪtnɪŋli
AM 'fraɪtn̩ɪŋli, 'fraɪtnɪŋli

frightful
BR 'frʌɪtf(ʊ)l
AM 'fraɪtfəl

frightfully
BR 'frʌɪtfəli, 'frʌɪtfl̩i
AM 'fraɪtfəli

frightfulness
BR 'frʌɪtf(ʊ)lnəs
AM 'fraɪtfəlnəs

frigid
BR 'frɪdʒɪd
AM 'frɪdʒɨd

Frigidaire®
BR ˌfrɪdʒɪ'dɛː(r), -z
AM ˌfrɪdʒɪ'dɛ(ə)r, -z

frigidaria
BR ˌfrɪdʒɪ'dɛːrɪə(r)
AM ˌfrɪdʒə'dɛriə

frigidarium
BR ˌfrɪdʒɪ'dɛːrɪəm, -z
AM ˌfrɪdʒə'dɛriəm, -z

frigidity
BR frɪ'dʒɪdɪti
AM frə'dʒɪdɨdi

frigidly
BR 'frɪdʒɨdli
AM 'frɪdʒɨdli

frigidness
BR 'frɪdʒɨdnɨs
AM 'frɪdʒɨdnɨs

frijoles
BR frɪ'həʊles
AM fri'hoʊˌleɪs

frill
BR frɪl, -z, -d
AM frɪl, -z, -d

frillery
BR 'frɪlər|i, -ɪz
AM 'frɪləri, -z

frilliness
BR 'frɪlɪnɨs
AM 'frɪlinɨs

frilling
BR 'frɪlɪŋ, -z
AM 'frɪlɪŋ, -z

frilly
BR 'frɪli
AM 'frɪli

fringe
BR frɪn(d)ʒ, -ɨz
AM frɪndʒ, -ɨz

fringeless
BR 'frɪn(d)ʒlɨs
AM 'frɪndʒləs

fringy
BR 'frɪn(d)ʒi
AM 'frɪndʒi

Frink
BR frɪŋk
AM frɪŋk

Frinton
BR 'frɪnt(ə)n
AM 'frɪn(t)ən

frippery
BR 'frɪp(ə)r|i, -ɪz
AM 'frɪp(ə)ri, -z

frippet
BR 'frɪpɨt, -s
AM 'frɪpɨt, -s

frisbee®
BR 'frɪzb|iː, -ɪz
AM 'frɪzˌbi, -z

Frisch
BR frɪʃ
AM frɪʃ

frisé
BR 'friːzeɪ, 'frɪzeɪ
AM fri'zeɪ

frisée
BR 'friːzeɪ, 'frɪzeɪ
AM fri'zeɪ

Frisia
BR 'frɪzɪə(r), 'frɪʒə(r), 'friːzɪə(r), 'friːʒə(r)
AM 'frɪʒə, 'friʒə

Frisian
BR 'frɪzɪən, 'frɪʒn, 'friːzɪən, 'friːʒn, -z
AM 'frɪʒən, 'friʒən, -z

frisk
BR frɪsk, -s, -ɪŋ, -t
AM frɪsk, -s, -ɪŋ, -t

frisker
BR 'frɪskə(r), -z
AM 'frɪskər, -z

frisket
BR 'frɪskɪt, -s
AM 'frɪskɪt, -s

friskily
BR 'frɪskɨli
AM 'frɪskɨli

friskiness
BR 'frɪskɪnɨs
AM 'frɪskinɨs

frisky
BR 'frɪski
AM 'frɪski

frisson
BR 'friːsɒn, 'frɪsɒn, -z
AM fri'sɔn, -z

frit
BR frɪt, -s, -ɪŋ, -ɨd
AM frɪ|t, -ts, -dɪŋ, -dɨd

frites
plural noun
BR friːt
AM frit

frith
BR frɪθ, -s
AM frɪθ, -s

fritillary
BR frɪ'tɪl(ə)r|i, -ɪz
AM 'frɪdlˌɛri, -z

fritter
BR 'frɪt|ə(r), -əz, -(ə)rɪŋ, -əd
AM 'frɪdər, -z, -ɪŋ, -d

fritto misto
BR ˌfrɪtəʊ 'mɪstəʊ
AM ˌfrɪdoʊ 'mɪstoʊ

Fritz
BR frɪts
AM frɪts

Friuli
BR frɪ'uːli
AM fri'uli

Friulian
BR frɪ'uːlɪən
AM fri'uljən, fri'uliən

frivol
BR 'frɪv|l, -lz, -l̩ɪŋ\-lɪŋ, -ld
AM 'frɪv|əl, -əlz, -(ə)lɪŋ, -əld

frivolity
BR frɪ'vɒlɪt|i, -ɪz
AM frɪ'vɑlədi, -z

frivolous
BR 'frɪvələs, 'frɪvl̩əs
AM 'frɪvələs

frivolously
BR 'frɪvələsli, 'frɪvl̩əsli
AM 'frɪvələsli

frivolousness
BR 'frɪvələsnəs, 'frɪvl̩əsnəs
AM 'frɪvələsnəs

friz
BR frɪz, -ɨz, -ɪŋ, -d
AM frɪz, -ɨz, -ɪŋ, -d

frizz
BR frɪz, -ɨz, -ɪŋ, -d
AM frɪz, -ɨz, -ɪŋ, -d

frizzily
BR 'frɪzɨli
AM 'frɪzɨli

frizziness
BR 'frɪzɪnɨs
AM 'frɪzinɨs

frizzle
BR 'frɪz|l, -lz, -l̩ɪŋ\-lɪŋ, -ld
AM 'frɪz|əl, -əlz, -(ə)lɪŋ, -əld

frizzly
BR 'frɪzl̩i, 'frɪzli
AM 'frɪzl̩i, 'frɪzli

frizzy
BR 'frɪz|i, -ɪə(r), -ɪɪst
AM 'frɪzi, -ər, -ɪst

fro
BR frəʊ
AM froʊ

Frobisher
BR 'frəʊbɪʃə(r)
AM 'froʊbɪʃər

frock
BR frɒk, -s
AM frɑk, -s

Frodsham
BR 'frɒdʃ(ə)m
AM 'frɔdʃəm, 'frɑdʃəm

froe
BR frəʊ, -z
AM froʊ, -z

Froebel
BR 'frəʊbl, 'frəːbl
AM 'freɪbəl

Froebelian
BR frə(ʊ)'biːlɪən, frəː'biːlɪən, -z
AM frə'biliən, -z

Froebelism
BR 'frəʊbɪlɪz(ə)m, 'frəʊbl̩ɪz(ə)m,

'frəːbɨlɪz(ə)m, 'frəːbl̩ɪz(ə)m
AM 'freɪbəˌlɪzəm

frog
BR frɒɡ, -z, -d
AM frɔɡ, frɑɡ, -z, -d

frogbit
BR 'frɒɡbɪt, -s
AM 'frɔɡˌbɪt, 'frɑɡˌbɪt, -s

frogfish
BR 'frɒɡfɪʃ, -ɨz
AM 'frɔɡˌfɪʃ, 'frɑɡˌfɪʃ, -ɨz

Froggie
BR 'frɒɡ|i, -ɪz
AM 'frɔɡi, 'frɑɡi, -z

frogging
BR 'frɒɡɪŋ, -z
AM 'frɔɡɪŋ, 'frɑɡɪŋ, -z

froggy
BR 'frɒɡi
AM 'frɔɡi, 'frɑɡi

froghopper
BR 'frɒɡˌhɒpə(r), -z
AM 'frɔɡˌ(h)ɑpər, 'frɑɡˌ(h)ɑpər, -z

frogman
BR 'frɒɡmən
AM 'frɔɡmən, 'frɔɡˌmæn, 'frɑɡmən, 'frɑɡˌmæn

frogmarch
BR 'frɒɡmɑːtʃ, -ɨz, -ɪŋ, -t
AM 'frɔɡˌmɑrtʃ, 'frɑɡˌmɑrtʃ, -əz, -ɪŋ, -t

frogmen
BR 'frɒɡmən
AM 'frɔɡmən, 'frɔɡˌmɛn, 'frɑɡmən, 'frɑɡˌmɛn

Frogmore
BR 'frɒɡmɔː(r)
AM 'frɔɡˌmɔ(ə)r, 'frɑɡˌmɔ(ə)r

frogmouth
BR 'frɒɡmaʊ|θ, -ðz
AM 'frɔɡˌmaʊ|θ, 'frɑɡˌmaʊ|θ, -θz\-ðz

frogspawn
BR 'frɒɡspɔːn
AM 'frɔɡˌspɔn, 'frɑɡˌspɑn

froing
BR 'frəʊɪŋ, -z
AM 'froʊɪŋ, -z

frolic
BR 'frɒl|ɪk, -ɪks, -ɨkɪŋ, -ɪkt
AM 'frɑlɪk, -s, -ɪŋ, -t

frolicker
BR 'frɒlɨkə(r), -z
AM 'frɑlɪkər, -z

frolicsome
BR 'frɒlɨks(ə)m
AM 'frɑlɨksəm

frolicsomely
BR 'frɒlɨks(ə)mli
AM 'frɑlɪksəmli

frolicsomeness
BR 'frɒlɨks(ə)mnəs
AM 'frɑlɪksəmnəs

from[1]
strong form
BR frɒm
AM frəm

from[2]
weak form
BR frəm
AM frəm

fromage blanc
BR ˌfrɒmɑːʒ 'blɒ̃
AM froʊ'mɑʒ 'blɑŋk

fromage frais
BR ˌfrɒmɑːʒ 'freɪ
AM froʊ'mɑʒ 'freɪ

Frome[1]
Australia
BR frəʊm
AM froʊm

Frome[2]
England, West Indies
BR fruːm
AM frum

Fron
in Welsh placenames
BR vrɒn
AM vrɑn

frond
BR frɒnd, -z
AM frɑnd, -z

frondage
BR 'frɒndɪdʒ
AM 'frɑndɪdʒ

Fronde
BR frɒnd
AM frɔnd

Frondes
BR frɒnd
AM frɔnd

frondeur
BR ˌfrɒn'dəː(r)
AM ˌfrɔn'dər

frondeurs
BR ˌfrɒn'dəː(r), ˌfrɒn'dəːz
AM ˌfrɔn'dərz, ˌfrɑn'dərz

frondose
BR frɒn'dəʊs
AM 'frɔnˌdoʊs, 'frɑnˌdoʊs

front
BR frʌnt, -s, -ɪŋ, -ɨd
AM frən|t, -ts, -(t)ɪŋ, -(t)əd

frontage
BR 'frʌnt|ɪdʒ, -ɨdʒɨz
AM 'frən(t)ɪdʒ, -ɨz

frontager
BR 'frʌntɨdʒə(r), -z
AM 'frən(t)ɪdʒər, -z

frontal
BR 'frʌntl, -z
AM 'frən(t)l, -z

frontally
BR 'frʌntl̩i
AM 'frən(t)l̩i

frontbench
adjective
BR ˌfrʌn'tbɛn(t)ʃ
AM ˌfrənt'bɛn(t)ʃ

front bench
noun
BR ˌfrʌnt 'bɛn(t)ʃ, -ɨz
AM ˌfrənt 'bɛn(t)ʃ, -əz

front-bencher
BR ˌfrʌnt'bɛn(t)ʃə(r), -z
AM ˌfrənt'bɛn(t)ʃər, -z

frontier
BR 'frʌntɪə(r), frʌn'tɪə(r), -z
AM frən'tɪ(ə)r, -z

frontierless
BR 'frʌntɪələs, frʌn'tɪələs
AM frən'tɪrləs

frontiersman
BR 'frʌntɪəzmən, frʌn'tɪəzmən
AM frən'tɪrzmən

frontiersmen
BR 'frʌntɪəzmən, frʌn'tɪəzmən
AM frən'tɪrzmən

frontierswoman
BR 'frʌntɪəzˌwʊmən, frʌn'tɪəzˌwʊmən
AM frən'tɪrzˌwʊmən

frontierswomen
BR 'frʌntɪəzˌwɪmɪn, frʌn'tɪəzˌwɪmɪn
AM frən'tɪrzˌwɪmɨn

frontispiece
BR 'frʌntɪspiːs, -ɨz
AM 'frən(t)ɪsˌpis, -ɨz

frontless
BR 'frʌntləs
AM 'frən(t)ləs

frontlet
BR 'frʌntlɨt, -s
AM 'frən(t)lət, -s

frontline
BR ˌfrʌnt'lʌɪn
AM ˌfrən(t)'laɪn

frontman
BR 'frʌntman
AM 'frəntˌmæn

frontmen
BR 'frʌntmɛn
AM 'frəntmɛn

frontogenesis
BR ˌfrʌntə(ʊ)'dʒɛnɨsɪs
AM ˌfrən(t)oʊ'dʒɛnəsəs, ˌfrɑn(t)oʊ'dʒɛnəsəs

frontogenetic
BR ˌfrʌntə(ʊ)dʒɨ'nɛtɪk
AM ˌfrən(t)oʊdʒə'nɛdɪk, ˌfrɑn(t)oʊdʒə'nɛdɪk

fronton
BR 'frʌnt(ə)n, -z
AM 'frɑnˌtɑn, -z

frontpage
BR ˌfrʌnt'peɪdʒ
AM ˌfrənt'peɪdʒ

front-runner
BR ˌfrʌnt'rʌnə(r), 'frʌntˌrʌnə(r), -z
AM 'frəntˌrənər, -z

frontward
BR 'frʌntwəd, -z
AM 'frəntwərd, -z

frore
BR frɔː(r)
AM frɔ(ə)r

frosh
BR frɒʃ, -ɨz
AM frɔʃ, frɑʃ, -əz

frost
BR frɒst, -s, -ɪŋ, -ɨd
AM frɔst, frɑst, -s, -ɪŋ, -əd

frostbite
BR 'frɒs(t)bʌɪt
AM 'frɔs(t)ˌbaɪt, 'frɑs(t)ˌbaɪt

frostbitten
BR 'frɒs(t)ˌbɪtn
AM 'frɔs(t)ˌbɪtn, 'frɑs(t)ˌbɪtn

frostbound
BR 'frɒs(t)baʊnd
AM 'frɔs(t)ˌbaʊnd, 'frɑs(t)ˌbaʊnd

frost-free
BR ˌfrɒs(t)'friː
AM 'frɔs(t)'fri, 'frɑs(t)'fri

frostily
BR 'frɒstɨli
AM 'frɔstəli, 'frɑstəli

frostiness
BR 'frɒstɪnɨs
AM 'frɔstinɨs, 'frɑstinɨs

frosting
BR 'frɒstɪŋ, -z
AM 'frɔstɪŋ, 'frɑstɪŋ, -z

frostless
BR 'frɒs(t)ləs
AM 'frɔs(t)ləs, 'frɑs(t)ləs

frost-work
BR 'frɒstwəːk
AM 'frɔs(t)ˌwərk, 'frɑs(t)ˌwərk

frosty
BR 'frɒst|i, -ɪə(r), -ɪɪst
AM 'frɔsti, 'frɑsti, -ər, -ɨst

froth
BR frɒθ, -s, -ɪŋ, -t
AM frɔθ, frɑθ, -s, -ɪŋ, -t

frothily
BR 'frɒθɨli
AM 'frɔθəli, 'frɑθəli

frothiness
BR 'frɒθɪnɨs
AM 'frɔθinɨs, 'frɑθinɨs

frothy
BR ˈfrɒθ|i, -ɪə(r), -ɪɪst
AM ˈfrɔθi, ˈfrɑθi, -ər, -ɨst
frottage
BR ˈfrɒtɑːʒ, ˈfrɒtɪdʒ, frɒˈtɑːʒ
AM frɔˈtɑʒ
froufrou
BR ˈfruːfruː, -z
AM ˈfruˌfru, -z
frow
BR frəʊ, -z
AM froʊ, -z
froward
BR ˈfrəʊəd
AM ˈfroʊ(w)ərd
frowardly
BR ˈfrəʊədli
AM ˈfroʊ(w)ərdli
frowardness
BR ˈfrəʊədnəs
AM ˈfroʊ(w)ərdnəs
frown
BR fraʊn, -z, -ɪŋ, -d
AM fraʊn, -z, -ɪŋ, -d
frowner
BR ˈfraʊnə(r)
AM ˈfraʊnər
frowningly
BR ˈfraʊnɪŋli
AM ˈfroʊnɪŋli
frowsily
BR ˈfraʊzɨli
AM ˈfraʊzəli
frowst
BR fraʊst, -s, -ɪŋ, -ɨd
AM fraʊst, -s, -ɪŋ, -əd
frowster
BR ˈfraʊstə(r), -z
AM ˈfraʊstər, -z
frowstily
BR ˈfraʊstɨli
AM ˈfraʊstəli
frowstiness
BR ˈfraʊstɪnɨs
AM ˈfraʊstinɨs
frowsty
BR ˈfraʊst|i, -ɪə(r), -ɪɪst
AM ˈfraʊsti, -ər, -ɨst
frowsy
BR ˈfraʊz|i, -ɪə(r), -ɪɪst
AM ˈfraʊzi, -ər, -ɨst
frowzily
BR ˈfraʊzɨli
AM ˈfraʊzəli
frowziness
BR ˈfraʊzɪnɨs
AM ˈfraʊzinɨs
frowzy
BR ˈfraʊz|i, -ɪə(r), -ɪɪst
AM ˈfraʊzi, -ər, -ɨst
froze
BR frəʊz
AM froʊz
frozen
BR ˈfrəʊzn
AM ˈfroʊzən
frozenly
BR ˈfrəʊznli
AM ˈfroʊzənli
fructiferous
BR ˌfrʌkˈtɪf(ə)rəs
AM ˌfrəkˈtɪfərəs
fructification
BR ˌfrʌktɪfɪˈkeɪʃn
AM ˌfrəktəfəˈkeɪʃən
fructify
BR ˈfrʌktɪfʌɪ, -z, -ɪŋ, -d
AM ˈfrəktəˌfaɪ, -z, -ɪŋ, -d
fructose
BR ˈfrʌktəʊz, ˈfrʌktəʊs, ˈfrʊktəʊz, ˈfrʊktəʊs
AM ˈfrʊkˌtoʊs, ˈfrəkˌtoʊs, ˈfrʊkˌtoʊz, ˈfrəkˌtoʊz
fructuous
BR ˈfrʌktjʊəs, ˈfrʌktʃʊəs
AM ˈfrək(t)ʃ(əw)əs
frugal
BR ˈfruːɡl
AM ˈfruɡəl
frugality
BR fruːˈɡalɪti
AM fruˈɡælədi
frugally
BR ˈfruːɡḷi, ˈfruːɡəli
AM ˈfruɡəli
frugalness
BR ˈfruːɡlnəs
AM ˈfruɡəlnəs
frugivorous
BR fruːˈdʒɪv(ə)rəs
AM fruˈdʒɪvərəs
fruit
BR fruːt, -s, -ɪŋ, -ɨd
AM fru|t, -ts, -dɪŋ, -dəd
fruitage
BR ˈfruːtɪdʒ
AM ˈfrudɪdʒ
fruitarian
BR fruːˈtɛːrɪən, -z
AM fruˈtɛriən, -z
fruitbat
BR ˈfruːtbat, -s
AM ˈfrutˌbæt, -s
fruitcake
BR ˈfruːtkeɪk, -s
AM ˈfrutˌkeɪk, -s
fruiter
BR ˈfruːtə(r), -z
AM ˈfrudər, -z
fruiterer
BR ˈfruːt(ə)rə(r), -z
AM ˈfrudərər, -z
fruitful
BR ˈfruːtf(ʊ)l
AM ˈfrutfəl
fruitfully
BR ˈfruːtfəli, ˈfruːtfḷi
AM ˈfrutfəli
fruitfulness
BR ˈfruːtf(ʊ)lnəs
AM ˈfrutfəlnəs
fruitily
BR ˈfruːtɨli
AM ˈfrudəli
fruitiness
BR ˈfruːtɪnɨs
AM ˈfrudinɨs
fruition
BR fruːˈɪʃn
AM fruˈɪʃən
fruitless
BR ˈfruːtləs
AM ˈfrutləs
fruitlessly
BR ˈfruːtləsli
AM ˈfrutləsli
fruitlessness
BR ˈfruːtləsnəs
AM ˈfrutləsnəs
fruitlet
BR ˈfruːtlɨt, -s
AM ˈfrutlət, -s
fruitwood
BR ˈfruːtwʊd, -z
AM ˈfrutˌwʊd, -z
fruity
BR ˈfruːt|i, -ɪə(r), -ɪɪst
AM ˈfrudi, -ər, -ɨst
frumenty
BR ˈfruːm(ə)nti
AM ˈfrumən(t)i
frump
BR frʌmp, -s
AM frəmp, -s
frumpily
BR ˈfrʌmpɨli
AM ˈfrəmpəli
frumpiness
BR ˈfrʌmpɪnɨs
AM ˈfrəmpinɨs
frumpish
BR ˈfrʌmpɪʃ
AM ˈfrəmpɪʃ
frumpishly
BR ˈfrʌmpɪʃli
AM ˈfrəmpɪʃli
frumpy
BR ˈfrʌmp|i, -ɪə(r), -ɪɪst
AM ˈfrəmpi, -ər, -ɨst
frusemide
BR ˈfruːsəmʌɪd
AM ˈfrusəˌmaɪd
frusta
BR ˈfrʌstə(r)
AM ˈfrəstə
frustrate
BR frʌˈstreɪt, -s, -ɪŋ, -ɨd
AM ˈfrəˌstreɪ|t, -ts, -dɪŋ, -dɨd
frustratedly
BR frʌˈstreɪtɨdli
AM ˈfrəˌstreɪdɨdli
frustrater
BR frʌˈstreɪtə(r), -z
AM ˈfrəˌstreɪdər, -z
frustratingly
BR frʌˈstreɪtɪŋli
AM ˈfrəˌstreɪdɪŋli
frustration
BR frʌˈstreɪʃn, -z
AM frəˈstreɪʃən, -z
frustule
BR ˈfrʌstjuːl, ˈfrʌstʃuːl, -z
AM ˈfrəsˌtʃul, -z
frustum
BR ˈfrʌstəm, -z
AM ˈfrəstəm, -z
frutescent
BR fruːˈtɛsnt
AM fruˈtɛsənt
frutex
BR ˈfruːtɛks, -ɪz
AM ˈfruˌdɛks, -əz
frutices
BR ˈfruːtɪsiːz
AM ˈfrudəˌsiz
fruticose
BR ˈfruːtɪkəʊz, ˈfruːtɪkəʊs
AM ˈfrudəˌkoʊs
fry
BR frʌɪ, -z, -ɪŋ, -d
AM fraɪ, -z, -ɪŋ, -d
Frye
BR frʌɪ
AM fraɪ
fryer
BR ˈfrʌɪə(r), -z
AM ˈfraɪər, -z
frypan
BR ˈfrʌɪpan, -z
AM ˈfraɪˌpæn, -z
Fryston
BR ˈfrʌɪst(ə)n
AM ˈfraɪstən
fry-up
BR ˈfrʌɪʌp, -s
AM ˈfraɪˌəp, -s
FT-SE
BR ˈfʊtsi
AM ˈfʊtsi
fubsy
BR ˈfʌbs|i, -ɪə(r), -ɪɪst
AM ˈfəbsi, -ər, -ɨst
Fuchs
BR fuːks, fʊks
AM f(j)uks
fuchsia
BR ˈfjuːʃə(r), -z
AM ˈfjuʃə, -z
fuchsine
BR ˈfuːksiːn
AM ˈfjuksən, ˈfjukˌsin
fuci
BR ˈfjuːsʌɪ
AM ˈfjuˌsaɪ
fuck
BR fʌk, -s, -ɪŋ, -t
AM fək, -s, -ɪŋ, -t
fucker
BR ˈfʌkə(r), -z
AM ˈfəkər, -z

fucoid
BR 'fju:kɔɪd
AM 'fju,kɔɪd

fucous
BR 'fju:kəs
AM 'fjukəs

fucus
BR 'fju:kəs
AM 'fjukəs

fuddle
BR 'fʌd|l, -lz, -l̩ɪŋ\-lɪŋ, -ld
AM 'fəd|əl, -əlz, -(ə)lɪŋ, -əld

fuddy-duddy
BR 'fʌdɪ,dʌd|i, -ɪz
AM 'fədi,dədi, -z

fudge
BR fʌdʒ, -ɪz, -ɪŋ, -d
AM fədʒ, -əz, -ɪŋ, -d

fudgeable
BR 'fʌdʒəbl
AM 'fədʒəbəl

fudgicle
BR 'fʌdʒɪkl, -z
AM 'fədʒəkəl, -z

fuehrer
BR 'fjʊərə(r), -z
AM 'fjʊrər, -z

fuel
BR 'fju:əl, -z, -ɪŋ, -d
AM 'fju(ə)l, -z, -ɪŋ, -d

Fuentes
BR fʊ'ɛnteɪs
AM fʊ'ɛnteɪs, 'fwɛnteɪs

fug
BR fʌg, -z
AM fəg, -z

fugacious
BR fju:'geɪʃəs
AM fju'geɪʃəs

fugaciously
BR fju:'geɪʃəsli
AM fju'geɪʃəsli

fugaciousness
BR fju:'geɪʃəsnəs
AM fju'geɪʃəsnəs

fugacity
BR fju:'gasɪti
AM fju'gæsədi

fugal
BR 'fju:gl
AM 'fjugəl

fugally
BR 'fju:gl̩i, 'fju:gəli
AM 'fjugəli

fugginess
BR 'fʌgɪnɪs
AM 'fəginɪs

fuggy
BR 'fʌg|i, -ɪə(r), -ɪɪst
AM 'fəgi, -ər, -ɪst

fugitive
BR 'fju:dʒɪtɪv, -z
AM 'fjudʒədɪv, 'fjudʒə,tɪv, -z

fugitively
BR 'fju:dʒɪtɪvli
AM 'fjudʒədəvli, 'fjudʒə,tɪvli

fugle
BR 'fju:g|l, -lz, -l̩ɪŋ\-lɪŋ, -ld
AM 'fjug|əl, -əlz, -(ə)lɪŋ, -əld

fugleman
BR 'fju:glmən
AM 'fjugəlmən

fuglemen
BR 'fju:glmən
AM 'fjugəlmən

fugu
BR 'fu:gu:, -z
AM 'f(j)ugu, -z

fugue
BR fju:g, -z
AM fjug, -z

fuguist
BR 'fju:gɪst, -s
AM 'fjugəst, -s

Führer
BR 'fjʊərə(r)
AM 'fjʊrər

Fujairah
BR fʊ'dʒʌɪrə(r)
AM fu'dʒaɪrə

Fuji
BR 'fu:dʒi
AM 'fudʒi

Fujian
BR 'fu:dʒɪən
AM 'fudʒiən

Fujica
BR 'fu:dʒɪkə(r)
AM 'fudʒəkə

Fujitsu
BR fu:'dʒɪtsu:
AM fu'dʒɪtsu

Fujiyama
BR ,fu:dʒɪ'jɑ:mə(r)
AM ,fudʒi'jɑmə

Fulani
BR fʊ'lɑ:ni
AM fə'lɑni

Fulbright
BR 'fʊlbrʌɪt
AM 'fʊl,braɪt

fulcra
BR 'fʊlkrə(r)
AM 'fʊlkrə, 'fəlkrə

fulcrum
BR 'fʊlkrəm, -z
AM 'fʊlkrəm, 'fəlkrəm, -z

fulfil
BR fʊl'fɪl, -z, -ɪŋ, -d
AM fʊl'fɪl, -z, -ɪŋ, -d

fulfill
BR fʊl'fɪl, -z, -ɪŋ, -d
AM fʊl'fɪl, -z, -ɪŋ, -d

fulfillable
BR fʊl'fɪləbl
AM fʊl'fɪləbəl

fulfiller
BR fʊl'fɪlə(r), -z
AM fʊl'fɪlər, -z

fulfillment
BR fʊl'fɪlm(ə)nt, -s
AM fʊl'fɪlmənt, -s

fulfilment
BR fʊl'fɪlm(ə)nt, -s
AM fʊl'fɪlmənt, -s

Fulford
BR 'fʊlfəd
AM 'fʊlfərd

fulgent
BR 'fʌldʒ(ə)nt
AM 'fəldʒənt

fulgid
BR 'fʌldʒɪd
AM 'fʊldʒəd

fulguration
BR ,fʌlgjʊ'reɪʃn
AM ,fʊlg(j)ə'reɪʃən

fulgurite
BR 'fʌlgjʊrʌɪt
AM 'fʊlg(j)ə,raɪt

Fulham
BR 'fʊləm
AM 'fʊləm

fuliginous
BR fju:'lɪdʒɪnəs
AM fju'lɪdʒənəs

fuliginously
BR fju:'lɪdʒɪnəsli
AM fju'lɪdʒənəsli

full
BR fʊl, -z, -ɪŋ, -d, -ə(r), -ɪst
AM fʊl, -z, -ɪŋ, -d, -ər, -əst

fullback
BR 'fʊlbak, -s
AM 'fʊl,bæk, 'fə(l),bæk, -s

fuller
BR 'fʊlə(r), -z
AM 'fʊlər, -z

fullness
BR 'fʊlnəs
AM 'fʊlnəs

fully
BR 'fʊli
AM 'fʊli

fulmar
BR 'fʊlmə(r), 'fʊlmɑ:(r), -z
AM 'fʊlmər, 'fʊl,mɑr, -z

fulminant
BR 'fʊlmɪnənt, 'fʌlmɪnənt
AM 'fʊlmənənt

fulminate
BR 'fʊlmɪneɪt, 'fʌlmɪneɪt, -s, -ɪŋ, -ɪd
AM 'fʊlmə,neɪ|t, -ts, -dɪŋ, -dɪd

fulmination
BR ,fʊlmɪ'neɪʃn, ,fʌlmɪ'neɪʃn, -z
AM ,fəlmə'neɪʃən, -z

fulminatory
BR 'fʊlmɪnət(ə)ri, 'fʌlmɪnət(ə)ri
AM 'fəlmɪnə,tɔri

fulminic acid
BR fʊl,mɪnɪk 'asɪd, fʌl,mɪnɪk +
AM fəl,mɪnɪk 'æsəd

fulness
BR 'fʊlnəs
AM 'fʊlnəs

fulsome
BR 'fʊls(ə)m
AM 'fʊlsəm

fulsomely
BR 'fʊls(ə)mli
AM 'fʊlsəmli

fulsomeness
BR 'fʊls(ə)mnəs
AM 'fʊlsəmnəs

Fulton
BR 'fʊlt(ə)n
AM 'fʊlt(ə)n

fulvescent
BR fʌl'vɛsnt, fʊl'vɛsnt
AM fəl'vɛsənt

fulvous
BR 'fʌlvəs, 'fʊlvəs
AM 'fʊlvəs, 'fəlvəs

Fulwell
BR 'fʊlwɛl
AM 'fʊl,wɛl

Fulwood
BR 'fʊlwʊd
AM 'fʊl,wʊd

Fu Manchu
BR ,fu: man'tʃu:
AM ,fu ,mæn'tʃu

fumaric
BR fjʊ'marɪk, fju:'marɪk
AM fju'mɛrɪk

fumarole
BR 'fju:mərəʊl, -z
AM 'fjumə,roʊl, -z

fumarolic
BR ,fju:mə'rɒlɪk
AM ,fjumə'roʊlɪk, ,fjumə'rɑlɪk

fumble
BR 'fʌmb|l, -lz, -l̩ɪŋ\-lɪŋ, -ld
AM 'fəmb|əl, -əlz, -(ə)lɪŋ, -əld

fumbler
BR 'fʌmbl̩ə(r), 'fʌmblə(r), -z
AM 'fəmb(ə)lər, -z

fumblingly
BR 'fʌmblɪŋli
AM 'fəmb(ə)lɪŋli

fume
BR fju:m, -z, -ɪŋ, -d
AM fjum, -z, -ɪŋ, -d

fumeless
BR 'fju:mləs
AM 'fjumləs

fumigant
BR 'fju:mɪg(ə)nt, -s
AM 'fjuməgənt, -s

fumigate
BR 'fju:mɪgeɪt, -s, -ɪŋ, -ɪd
AM 'fjumə,geɪ|t, -ts, -dɪŋ, -dɨd

fumigation
BR ,fju:mɪ'geɪʃn
AM ,fjumə'geɪʃən

fumigator
BR 'fju:mɪgeɪtə(r), -z
AM 'fjumə,geɪdər, -z

fumingly
BR 'fju:mɪŋli
AM 'fjumɪŋli

fumitory
BR 'fju:mɪt(ə)r|i, -ɪz
AM 'fjumə,tɔri, -z

fumy
BR 'fju:m|i, -ɪə(r), -ɪɪst
AM 'fjumi, -ər, -ɨst

fun
BR fʌn
AM fən

Funafuti
BR ,fu:nə'fu:ti
AM ,f(j)unə'f(j)udi

funambulist
BR fju:'nambjʊlɪst, -s
AM fju'næmbjələst, -s

funboard
BR 'fʌnbɔ:d, -z
AM 'fən,bɔ(ə)rd, -z

Funchal
BR ,fʊn'tʃɑ:l
AM fun'ʃɑl, fən'ʃɑl

function
BR 'fʌŋ(k)ʃ|n, -nz, -n̩ɪŋ\-ənɪŋ, -nd
AM 'fəŋ(k)ʃ|ən, -ənz, -(ə)nɪŋ, -ənd

functional
BR 'fʌŋ(k)ʃn̩(ə)l, 'fʌŋ(k)ʃən(ə)l
AM 'fəŋ(k)ʃ(ə)nəl

functionalism
BR 'fʌŋ(k)ʃn̩əlɪz(ə)m, 'fʌŋ(k)ʃn̩lɪz(ə)m, 'fʌŋ(k)ʃənlɪz(ə)m, 'fʌŋ(k)ʃ(ə)nəlɪz(ə)m
AM 'fəŋ(k)ʃənl,ɪzəm, 'fəŋ(k)ʃnə,lɪzəm

functionalist
BR 'fʌŋ(k)ʃn̩əlɪst, 'fʌŋ(k)ʃn̩lɪst, 'fʌŋ(k)ʃənlɪst, 'fʌŋ(k)ʃ(ə)nəlɪst, -s
AM 'fəŋ(k)ʃənləst, 'fəŋ(k)ʃnələst, -s

functionality
BR ,fʌŋ(k)ʃə'nalɪt|i, -ɪz
AM ,fəŋ(k)ʃə'nælədi, -z

functionally
BR 'fʌŋ(k)ʃn̩əli, 'fʌŋ(k)ʃn̩li, 'fʌŋ(k)ʃənli, 'fʌŋ(k)ʃ(ə)nəli
AM 'fəŋ(k)ʃ(ə)nəli

functionary
BR 'fʌŋ(k)ʃn̩(ə)r|i, -ɪz
AM 'fəŋ(k)ʃə,nɛri, -z

functionate
BR 'fʌŋ(k)ʃəneɪt, 'fʌŋ(k)ʃn̩eɪt, -s, -ɪŋ, -ɪd
AM 'fəŋ(k)ʃə,neɪ|t, -ts, -dɪŋ, -dɨd

functionless
BR 'fʌŋ(k)ʃnləs
AM 'fəŋ(k)ʃənləs

functor
BR 'fʌŋ(k)tə(r), -z
AM 'fəŋ(k)tər, -z

fund
BR fʌnd, -z, -ɪŋ, -ɪd
AM fənd, -z, -ɪŋ, -əd

fundament
BR 'fʌndəm(ə)nt, -s
AM 'fəndəmənt, -s

fundamental
BR ,fʌndə'mɛntl
AM ,fəndə'mɛn(t)l

fundamentalism
BR ,fʌndə'mɛntl̩ɪz(ə)m
AM ,fəndə'mɛn(t)l,ɪzəm

fundamentalist
BR ,fʌndə'mɛntl̩ɪst, -s
AM ,fəndə'mɛn(t)l̩əst, -s

fundamentality
BR ,fʌndəmɛn'talɪti
AM ,fəndəmən'tælədi

fundamentally
BR ,fʌndə'mɛntl̩i
AM ,fəndə'mɛn(t)l̩i

fundholder
BR 'fʌnd,həʊldə(r), -z
AM 'fən(d),(h)oʊldər, -z

fundholding
BR 'fʌnd,həʊldɪŋ
AM 'fən(d),(h)oʊldɪŋ

fundi
BR 'fʌndʌɪ
AM 'fən,daɪ

fundus
BR 'fʌndəs
AM 'fəndəs

Fundy
BR 'fʌndi
AM 'fəndi

funebrial
BR fju:'ni:brɪəl, fju:'nɛbrɪəl
AM fju'nibriəl, fju'nɛbriəl

funeral
BR 'fju:n(ə)rəl, 'fju:n(ə)rl̩, -z
AM 'fjun(ə)rəl, -z

funerary
BR 'fju:n(ə)rəri
AM 'fjunə,rɛri

funereal
BR fjʊ'nɪərɪəl, fju:'nɪərɪəl
AM fjə'nɪriəl

funereally
BR fjʊ'nɪərɪəli, fju:'nɪərɪəli
AM fjə'nɪriəli

funfair
BR 'fʌnfɛ:(r), -z
AM 'fən,fɛ(ə)r, -z

fungal
BR 'fʌŋgl
AM 'fəŋgəl

fungi
BR 'fʌŋgʌɪ, 'fʌn(d)ʒʌɪ
AM 'fən,dʒaɪ, 'fəŋ,gaɪ

fungibility
BR ,fʌn(d)ʒɪ'bɪlɪti
AM ,fəndʒə'bɪlɨdi

fungible
BR 'fʌn(d)ʒɪbl
AM 'fəndʒəbəl

fungicidal
BR ,fʌn(d)ʒɪ'sʌɪdl, ,fʌŋgɪ'sʌɪdl
AM 'fəndʒə,saɪdəl, 'fəŋgə,saɪdəl

fungicide
BR 'fʌn(d)ʒɪsʌɪd, 'fʌŋgɪsʌɪd, -z
AM 'fəndʒə,saɪd, 'fəŋgə,saɪd, -z

fungiform
BR 'fʌn(d)ʒɪfɔ:m, 'fʌŋgɪfɔ:m
AM 'fəndʒə,fɔ(ə)rm, 'fəŋgə,fɔ(ə)rm

fungistatic
BR ,fʌn(d)ʒɪ'statɪk, ,fʌŋgɪ'statɪk
AM ,fəndʒə'stædɪk, ,fəŋgə'stædɪk

fungistatically
BR ,fʌn(d)ʒɪ'statɪkli, ,fʌŋgɪ'statɪkli
AM ,fəndʒə'stædək(ə)li, ,fəŋgə'stædək(ə)li

fungivorous
BR ,fʌn'(d)ʒɪv(ə)rəs
AM ,fən'dʒɪvərəs, ,fən'gɪvərəs

fungo
BR 'fʌŋgəʊ, -z
AM 'fəŋgoʊ, -z

fungoid
BR 'fʌŋgɔɪd
AM 'fəŋ,gɔɪd

fungous
BR 'fʌŋgəs
AM 'fəŋgəs

fungus
BR 'fʌŋgəs, -ɪz
AM 'fəŋgəs, -əz

funhouse
BR 'fʌnhaʊ|s, -zɪz
AM 'fən,(h)aʊ|s, -zəz

funicle
BR 'fju:nɪkl, -z
AM 'fjunəkl, -z

funicular
BR f(j)ʊ'nɪkjʊlə(r), -z
AM fju'nɪkjələr, -z

funiculi
BR fjʊ'nikjʊlʌɪ
AM ,fju'nɪkjə,laɪ

funiculus
BR fjʊ'nɪkjʊləs
AM ,fju'nɪkjələs

funk
BR fʌŋ|k, -ks, -kɪŋ, -(k)t
AM fəŋ|k, -ks, -kɪŋ, -(k)t

funkia
BR 'fʌŋkɪə(r), -z
AM 'fəŋkiə, 'fʊŋkiə, -z

funkily
BR 'fʌŋkɪli
AM 'fəŋkəli

funkiness
BR 'fʌŋkɪnɪs
AM 'fəŋkinɨs

funkster
BR 'fʌŋ(k)stə(r), -z
AM 'fəŋ(k)stər, -z

funky
BR 'fʌŋk|i, -ɪə(r), -ɪɪst
AM 'fəŋki, -ər, -ɨst

fun-lover
BR 'fʌn,lʌvə(r), -z
AM 'fən,ləvər, -z

fun-loving
BR 'fʌn,lʌvɪŋ
AM 'fən,ləvɪŋ

funnel
BR 'fʌn|l, -lz, -l̩ɪŋ\-əlɪŋ, -ld
AM 'fənəl, -z, -ɪŋ, -d

funnily
BR 'fʌnɪli
AM 'fənəli

funniness
BR 'fʌnɪnɪs
AM 'fəninɨs

funniosity
BR ,fʌnɪ'ɒsɪti, -ɪz
AM ,fəni'ɑsədi, -z

funny
BR 'fʌn|i, -ɪz, -ɪə(r), -ɪɪst
AM 'fəni, -z, -ər, -ɨst

funster
BR 'fʌnstə(r), -z
AM 'fənstər, -z

fur
BR fə:(r), -z
AM fər, -z

furbelow
BR 'fə:bɪləʊ, -z
AM 'fərbə,loʊ, -z

furbish
BR 'fə:b|ɪʃ, -ɪʃɪz, -ɪʃɪŋ, -ɪʃt
AM 'fərbɪʃ, -ɨz, -ɪŋ, -t

furbisher
BR 'fə:bɪʃə(r), -z

AM ˈfərbɪʃər, -z

Furby
BR ˈfəːbi
AM ˈfərbi

furcate
BR ˈfəːkeɪt, fəːˈkeɪt, -s, -ɪŋ, -ɨd
AM ˈfərˌkeɪ|t, -ts, -dɪŋ, -dɨd

furcation
BR fəːˈkeɪʃn
AM fərˈkeɪʃən

furfuraceous
BR ˌfəːfəˈreɪʃəs
AM ˌfərf(j)əˈreɪʃəs

Furies
BR ˈfjʊərɪz, ˈfjɔːrɪz
AM ˈfjʊriz

furious
BR ˈfjʊərɪəs, ˈfjɔːrɪəs
AM ˈfjʊriəs

furiously
BR ˈfjʊərɪəsli, ˈfjɔːrɪəsli
AM ˈfjʊriəsli

furiousness
BR ˈfjʊərɪəsnəs, ˈfjɔːrɪəsnəs
AM ˈfjʊriəsnəs

furl
BR fəːl, -z, -ɪŋ, -d
AM fərl, -z, -ɪŋ, -d

furlable
BR ˈfəːləbl
AM ˈfərləbəl

furless
BR ˈfəːləs
AM ˈfərləs

furlong
BR ˈfəːlɒŋ, -z
AM ˈfərˌlɔŋ, ˈfərˌlɑŋ, -z

furlough
BR ˈfəːləʊ, -z
AM ˈfərˌloʊ, -z

furmety
BR ˈfəːmɪti
AM ˈfərmədi

furnace
BR ˈfəːnɪs, -ɨz
AM ˈfərnəs, -əz

Furneaux
BR ˈfəːnəʊ
AM ˈfərnoʊ

Furness
BR ˈfəːnɪs, fəˈnɛs
AM fərˈnɛs

furnish
BR ˈfəːn|ɪʃ, -ɨʃɨz, -ɨʃɪŋ, -ɪʃt
AM ˈfərnɪʃ, -ɨz, -ɪŋ, -t

furnisher
BR ˈfəːnɨʃə(r), -z
AM ˈfərnɪʃər, -z

furnishing
BR ˈfəːnɨʃɪŋ, -z
AM ˈfərnɪʃɪŋ, -z

furnishings
BR fəːnɨʃɪŋz
AM ˈfərnɪʃɪŋz

furniture
BR ˈfərnɨtʃə(r)
AM ˈfərnɪtʃər, ˈfərnɪtʃʊ(ə)r

Furnivall
BR ˈfəːnɪvl
AM ˈfərnəvəl

furor
BR ˈfjʊərɔː(r), ˈfjɔːrɔː(r), -z
AM ˈfjʊˌrɔ(ə)r, ˈfjuˌrɔ(ə)r, -z

furore
BR fjʉˈrɔːri, ˈfjʊərɔː(r), ˈfjɔːrɔː(r)
AM ˈfjʊˌrɔ(ə)r, ˈfjuˌrɔ(ə)r

furores
BR fjʉˈrɔːrɪz, ˈfjʊərɔːz, ˈfjɔːrɔːz
AM ˈfjʊˌrɔ(ə)rz, ˈfjuˌrɔ(ə)rz

furphy
BR ˈfəːf|i, -ɪz
AM ˈfərfi, -z

furrier
BR ˈfʌrɪə(r), -z
AM ˈfəriər, -z

furriery
BR ˈfʌrɪəri
AM ˈfəriəri

furriness
BR ˈfəːrɪnɨs
AM ˈfərinɨs

furring
BR ˈfəːrɪŋ
AM ˈfərɪŋ

furrow
BR ˈfʌrəʊ, -z, -ɪŋ, -d
AM ˈfəroʊ, -z, -ɪŋ, -d

furrowless
BR ˈfʌrəʊləs
AM ˈfəroʊləs

furrowy
BR ˈfʌrəʊi
AM ˈfərəwi

furry
BR ˈfəːr|i, -ɪə(r), -ɪɨst
AM ˈfəri, -ər, -ɨst

further
BR ˈfəːð|ə(r), -əz, -(ə)rɪŋ, -əd
AM ˈfərðər, -z, -ɪŋ, -d

furtherance
BR ˈfəːð(ə)rəns, ˈfəːð(ə)rn̩s
AM ˈfərð(ə)rəns

furtherer
BR ˈfəːð(ə)rə(r), -z
AM ˈfərðərər, -z

furthermore
BR ˌfəːðəˈmɔː(r), ˈfəːðəmɔː(r)
AM ˈfərðərˌmɔ(ə)r, ˌfərðərˈmɔ(ə)r

furthermost
BR ˈfəːðəməʊst
AM ˈfərðərˌmoʊst

furthest
BR ˈfəːðɪst
AM ˈfərðəst

furtive
BR ˈfəːtɪv
AM ˈfərdɪv

furtively
BR ˈfəːtɨvli
AM ˈfərdɨvli

furtiveness
BR ˈfəːtɨvnɨs
AM ˈfərdɪvnɨs

furuncle
BR ˈfjʊərʌŋkl, ˈfjɔːrʌŋkl, -z
AM ˈfjuˌrəŋkəl, -z

furuncular
BR fjʉˈrʌŋkjʉlə(r)
AM fjuˈrəŋkjələr

furunculosis
BR fjʉˌrʌŋkjʉˈləʊsɪs
AM fjuˌrəŋkjəˈloʊsəs

furunculous
BR fjʉˈrʌŋkjʉləs
AM fjuˈrəŋkjələs

fury
BR ˈfjʊəri, ˈfjɔːri
AM ˈfjʊri

furze
BR fəːz
AM fərz

furzy
BR ˈfəːzi
AM ˈfərzi

fusaria
BR fjʉˈzɛːrɪə(r)
AM fjəˈzɛriə

fusarium
BR fjʉˈzɛːrɪəm
AM fjəˈzɛriəm

fuscous
BR ˈfʌskəs
AM ˈfəskəs

fuse
BR fjuːz, -ɨz, -ɪŋ, -d
AM fjuz, -əz, -ɪŋ, -d

fusee
BR fjuːˈziː, -z
AM fjuˈzi, -z

fusel
BR ˈfjuːzl
AM ˈfjuzəl

fuselage
BR ˈfjuːzɨl|ɑːʒ, ˈfjuːzɨl|ɪdʒ, -ɑːʒɪz\-ɨdʒɨz
AM ˈfjusəˌlɑʒ, ˈfjuzəˌlɑʒ, -ɨz

fuseless
BR ˈfjuːzləs
AM ˈfjuzləs

fusibility
BR ˌfjuːzɪˈbɪlɪti

AM ˌfjuzəˈbɪlɨdi

fusible
BR ˈfjuːzɪbl
AM ˈfjuzəbəl

fusiform
BR ˈfjuːzɨfɔːm
AM ˈfjuzəˌfɔ(ə)rm

fusil
BR ˈfjuːz(ɪ)l, -z
AM ˈfjuzəl, -z

fusilier
BR ˌfjuːzɪˈlɪə(r), -z
AM ˌfjuzəˈlɪ(ə)r, -z

fusillade
BR ˌfjuːzɪˈleɪd, ˌfjuːzɪˈlɑːd, -z
AM ˌfjuzəˈleɪd, ˌfjuzəˈlɑd, -z

fusilli
BR f(j)ʉˈziːli
AM ˌfjuˈsɪli

fusion
BR ˈfjuːʒn
AM ˈfjuʒən

fusional
BR ˈfjuːʒn̩(ə)l, ˈfjuːʒən(ə)l
AM ˈfjuʒ(ə)nəl

fusionist
BR ˈfjuːʒn̩ɪst, ˈfjuːʒənɪst, -s
AM ˈfjuʒənəst, -s

fuss
BR fʌs, -ɨz, -ɪŋ, -t
AM fəs, -əz, -ɪŋ, -t

fusser
BR ˈfʌsə(r), -z
AM ˈfəsər, -z

fussily
BR ˈfʌsɨli
AM ˈfəsəli

fussiness
BR ˈfʌsɪnɨs
AM ˈfəsinɨs

fusspot
BR ˈfʌspɒt, -s
AM ˈfəsˌpɑt, -s

fussy
BR ˈfʌs|i, -ɪə(r), -ɪɨst
AM ˈfəsi, -ər, -ɨst

fustanella
BR ˌfʌstəˈnɛlə(r), -z
AM ˌfəstəˈnɛlə, -z

fustian
BR ˈfʌstɪən
AM ˈfəstʃən

fustic
BR ˈfʌstɪk
AM ˈfəstɪk

fustigate
BR ˈfʌstɪgeɪt, -s, -ɪŋ, -ɨd
AM ˈfəstəˌgeɪ|t, -ts, -dɪŋ, -dɨd

fustigation
BR ˌfʌstɪˈgeɪʃn, -z
AM ˌfəstəˈgeɪʃən, -z

fustily
BR ˈfʌstɨli
AM ˈfəstəli

fustiness
BR ˈfʌstɪnɨs
AM ˈfəstinɨs

fusty
BR ˈfʌst|i, -ɪə(r), -ɪɨst
AM ˈfəsti, -ər, -ɪst

futharc
BR ˈfuːθɑːk
AM ˈfuˌθɑrk

futhorc
BR ˈfuːθɔːk
AM ˈfuˌθɔ(ə)rk

futile
BR ˈfjuːtʌɪl
AM ˈfjudl

futilely
BR ˈfjuːtʌɪlli
AM ˈfjud(l)li

futileness
BR ˈfjuːtʌɪlnɨs
AM ˈfjudlnəs

futilitarian
BR ˌfjuːtɪlɪˈtɛːrɪən
AM fjuˌtɪləˈtɛriən

futility
BR fjuːˈtɪlɨti, fjʉˈtɪlɨti
AM ˈfjuˈtɪlɨdi

futon
BR ˈf(j)uːtɒn, ˌfuːˈtɒn, -z
AM ˈf(j)uˌtɑn, -z

futtock
BR ˈfʌtək, -s
AM ˈfədək, -s

future
BR ˈfjuːtʃə(r), -z
AM ˈfjutʃər, -z

futureless
BR ˈfjuːtʃələs
AM ˈfjutʃərləs

futurism
BR ˈfjuːtʃ(ə)rɪz(ə)m
AM ˈfjutʃəˌrɪzəm

futurist
BR ˈfjuːtʃ(ə)rɪst, -s
AM ˈfjutʃəˌrəst, -s

futuristic
BR ˌfjuːtʃəˈrɪstɪk
AM ˌfjutʃəˈrɪstɪk

futuristically
BR ˌfjuːtʃəˈrɪstɨkli
AM ˌfjutʃəˈrɪstək(ə)li

futurity
BR fjʉˈtjʊərɪt|i, fjʉˈtʃʊərɪt|i, fjʉˈtjɔːrɪt|i, fjʉˈtʃɔːrɪt|i-ɪz
AM fjəˈtʊrədi, fjəˈturədi, fjəˈtʃʊrədi, -z

futurologist
BR ˌfjuːtʃəˈrɒlədʒɪst, -s
AM ˌfjutʃəˈrɑlədʒəst, -s

futurology
BR ˌfjuːtʃəˈrɒlədʒi
AM ˌfjutʃəˈrɑlədʒi

futz
BR fʌts, -ɨz, -ɪŋ, -t
AM fəts, -əz, -ɪŋ, -t

fuze
BR fjuːz, -ɨz, -ɪŋ, -d
AM fjuz, -əz, -ɪŋ, -d

fuzee
BR fjuːˈziː, -z
AM fjuˈzi, -z

fuzz
BR fʌz
AM fəz

fuzzily
BR ˈfʌzɨli
AM ˈfəzəli

fuzziness
BR ˈfʌzɪnɨs
AM ˈfəzinɨs

fuzzy
BR ˈfʌz|i, -ɪə(r), -ɪɨst
AM ˈfəzi, -ər, -ɪst

fuzzy-wuzzy
BR ˈfʌzɪˌwʌz|i, -ɪz
AM ˈfəziˈwəzi, -z

Fyfe
BR fʌɪf
AM faɪf

Fyffe
BR fʌɪf
AM faɪf

Fylde
BR fʌɪld
AM faɪld

fylfot
BR ˈfɪlfɒt, -s
AM ˈfɪlˌfɑt, -s

Fylingdales
BR ˈfʌlɪŋdeɪlz
AM ˈfaɪlɪŋˌdeɪlz

Fyne
BR fʌɪn
AM faɪn

fyrd
BR fəːd, fɪəd, -z
AM fərd, fɪ(ə)rd, -z

fytte
BR fɪt
AM fɪt

Gg

g
BR dʒiː, -z
AM dʒi, -z

gab
BR gab, -z, -ɪŋ, -d
AM gæb, -z, -ɪŋ, -d

Gabalfa
BR gəˈbalvə(r), gəˈbalfə(r)
AM gəˈbælfə

gabardine
BR ˈgabədiːn, ˌgabəˈdiːn, -z
AM ˈgæbərˌdin, -z

gabber
BR ˈgabə(r), -z
AM ˈgæbər, -z

Gabbitas
BR ˈgabɪtas
AM ˈgæbədəs

gabble
BR ˈgab|l, -lz, -l̩ɪŋ\-lɪŋ, -ld
AM ˈgæb|əl, -əlz, -(ə)lɪŋ, -əld

gabbler
BR ˈgablə(r), -z
AM ˈgæblər, -z

gabbro
BR ˈgabrəʊ, -z
AM ˈgæbroʊ, -z

gabbroic
BR gaˈbrəʊɪk
AM gəˈbroʊɪk

gabbroid
BR ˈgabrɔɪd
AM ˈgæˌbrɔɪd

gabby
BR ˈgab|i, -ɪə(r), -ɪɪst
AM ˈgæbi, -ər, -ɨst

gabelle
BR gaˈbɛl, gəˈbɛl, -z
AM gəˈbɛl, -z

gaberdine
BR ˈgabədiːn, ˌgabəˈdiːn, -z
AM ˈgæbərˌdin, -z

gabfest
BR ˈgabfɛst, -s
AM ˈgæbˌfɛst, -s

gabion
BR ˈgeɪbɪən, -z
AM ˈgeɪbiən, -z

gabionade
BR ˌgeɪbɪəˈneɪd, -z
AM ˌgeɪbiəˈneɪd, -z

gabionage
BR ˈgeɪbɪənɪdʒ
AM ˈgeɪbiəˌnɑ(d)ʒ

gable
BR ˈgeɪbl, -z, -d
AM ˈgeɪbəl, -z, -d

gablet
BR ˈgeɪblɨt, -s
AM ˈgeɪblət, -s

Gabo
BR ˈgɑːbəʊ
AM ˈgɑboʊ

Gabon
BR gəˈbɒn
AM gəˈbɑn, gəˈboʊn

Gabonese
BR ˌgabəˈniːz
AM ˌgæbəˈniz

Gábor
BR gəˈbɔː(r)
AM gəˈbɔ(ə)r
HU ˈgɑːbɔr

Gaborone
BR ˌgabəˈrəʊni
AM ˌgɑbəˈroʊn

Gabriel
BR ˈgeɪbrɪəl
AM ˈgeɪbriəl

Gabrielle
BR ˌgeɪbrɪˈɛl
AM ˌgæbriˈɛl

gad
BR gad, -z, -ɪŋ, -ɨd
AM gæd, -z, -ɪŋ, -ɨd

gadabout
BR ˈgadəbaʊt, -s
AM ˈgædəˌbaʊt, -s

Gadarene
BR ˈgadəriːn, ˌgadəˈriːn
AM ˈgædəˌrin, ˌgædəˈrin

Gaddafi
BR gəˈdɑːfi, gəˈdafi
AM gəˈdɑfi

gadfly
BR ˈgadflʌɪ, -z
AM ˈgædˌflaɪ, -z

gadget
BR ˈgadʒɨt, -s
AM ˈgædʒət, -s

gadgeteer
BR ˌgadʒɪˈtɪə(r), -z
AM ˌgædʒəˈtɪ(ə)r, -z

gadgetry
BR ˈgadʒɨtri
AM ˈgædʒətri

gadgety
BR ˈgadʒɨti
AM ˈgædʒədi

Gadhelic
BR gəˈdɛlɪk, gaˈdɛlɪk
AM gəˈdɛlɪk, gæˈdɛlɪk

gadid
BR ˈgeɪdɪd, -z
AM ˈgeɪdɪd, -z

gadoid
BR ˈgadɔɪd, -z
AM ˈgeɪˌdɔɪd, ˈgæˌdɔɪd, -z

gadolinite
BR ˈgadəlɪnʌɪt, ˈgadl̩ɪnʌɪt, gəˈdəʊlɪnʌɪt
AM ˈgædl̩əˌnaɪt

gadolinium
BR ˌgadəˈlɪnɪəm, ˌgadl̩ˈɪnɪəm
AM ˌgædlˈɪniəm

gadroon
BR gəˈdruːn, -z
AM gəˈdrun, -z, -d

gadwall
BR ˈgadwɔːl, -z
AM ˈgæˌdwɔl, ˈgæˌdwɑl, -z

gadzooks
BR (ˌ)gadˈzuːks
AM gædˈzuks

Gaea
BR ˈdʒiːə(r)
AM ˈdʒiə

Gael
BR geɪl, -z
AM geɪl, -z

Gaeldom
BR ˈgeɪldəm
AM ˈgeɪldəm

Gaelic
BR ˈgeɪlɪk, ˈgalɪk
AM ˈgeɪlɪk

Gaeltacht
BR ˈgeɪltaxt
AM ˈgeɪlˌtækt
IR ˈgeːltəxt

Gaenor
BR ˈgeɪnə(r)
AM ˈgeɪnər

gaff
BR gaf, -s, -ɪŋ, -t
AM gæf, -s, -ɪŋ, -t

gaffe
BR gaf, -s
AM gæf, -s

gaffer
BR ˈgafə(r), -z
AM ˈgæfər, -z

Gaffney
BR ˈgafni
AM ˈgæfni

Gafsa
BR ˈgafsə(r)
AM ˈgæfsə

gag
BR gag, -z, -ɪŋ, -d
AM gæg, -z, -ɪŋ, -d

gaga
BR ˈgɑːgɑː(r)
AM ˈgɑˌgɑ

Gagarin
BR gəˈgɑːrɪn
AM gəˈgɑrən

gage
BR geɪdʒ, -ɨz, -ɪŋ, -d
AM geɪdʒ, -ɨz, -ɪŋ, -d

gaggle
BR ˈgagl, -z
AM ˈgægəl, -z

gagman
BR ˈgagman
AM ˈgægˌmæn

gagmen
BR ˈgagmɛn
AM ˈgægˌmɛn

gagster
BR ˈgagstə(r), -z
AM ˈgægstər, -z

Gaia
BR ˈgʌɪə(r)
AM ˈgaɪə

Gaian
BR ˈgʌɪən, -z
AM ˈgaɪən, -z

gaiety
BR ˈgeɪɪti
AM ˈgaɪɨdi

gaijin
BR (ˌ)gʌɪˈdʒɪn
AM gaɪˈdʒɪn

Gail
BR geɪl
AM geɪl

gaillardia
BR geɪˈlɑːdɪə(r), gəˈlɑːdɪə(r), -z
AM gəˈlɑrd(i)ə, -z

gaily
BR ˈgeɪli
AM ˈgeɪli

gain
BR geɪn, -z, -ɪŋ, -d
AM geɪn, -z, -ɪŋ, -d

gainable
BR ˈgeɪnəbl
AM ˈgeɪnəbəl

gainer
BR ˈgeɪnə(r), -z
AM ˈgeɪnər, -z

Gaines
BR geɪnz
AM geɪnz

gainful
BR ˈgeɪnf(ʊ)l
AM ˈgeɪnfəl

gainfully
BR ˈgeɪnfʊli, ˈgeɪnfl̩i
AM ˈgeɪnfəli

gainfulness
BR ˈgeɪnf(ʊ)lnəs
AM ˈgeɪnfəlnəs

gainings
BR ˈgeɪnɪŋz
AM ˈgeɪnɪŋz

gainsaid
BR ˌgeɪnˈsɛd
AM ˈgeɪnˌseɪd

gainsay
BR ˌgeɪnˈseɪ, -z, -ɪŋ
AM ˈgeɪnˌseɪ, -z, -ɪŋ

gainsayer
BR ˌgeɪnˈseɪə(r), -z
AM ˈgeɪnˌseɪər, -z

Gainsborough
BR ˈgeɪnzb(ə)rə(r)

AM 'geɪnzbərə

'gainst
BR gɛnst, geɪnst
AM gɛnst, geɪnst

Gairloch
BR 'gɛːlɒx, 'gɛːlɒk
AM 'gɛrlɑk

gait
BR geɪt, -s
AM geɪt, -s

gaiter
BR 'geɪtə(r), -z, -d
AM 'geɪdər, -z, -d

Gaitskell
BR 'geɪtsk(ɪ)l
AM 'geɪtskəl

Gaius
BR 'gʌɪəs
AM 'gaɪəs

gal
BR gal, -z
AM gæl, -z

gala
BR 'gɑːlə(r), 'geɪlə(r), -z
AM 'geɪlə, 'gælə, -z

galactagogue
BR gə'laktəgɒg, -z
AM gə'læktə,gɑg, -z

galactic
BR gə'laktɪk
AM gə'læktɪk

galactogogue
BR gə'laktəgɒg, -z
AM gə'læktə,gɑg, -z

galactose
BR gə'laktəʊz, gə'laktəʊs
AM gə'læk,toʊs, gə'læk,toʊz

galago
BR gə'leɪgəʊ, -z
AM gə'leɪgoʊ, gə'lɑgoʊ, 'gælə,goʊ, -z

galah
BR gə'lɑː(r), -z
AM gə'lɑ, -z

Galahad
BR 'galəhad
AM 'gælə,hæd

galantine
BR 'galəntiːn, 'galn̩tiːn, ,galən'tiːn, ,galn̩'tiːn, -z
AM 'gælən,tin, -z

galanty show
BR gə'lantɪ ʃəʊ, -z
AM gə'læn(t)i ,ʃoʊ, -z

Galapagos
BR gə'lapəgəs
AM gə'lɑpə,goʊs, gə'lɑpəgəs

Galashiels
BR ,galə'ʃiːlz
AM ,gælə'ʃilz

Galatea
BR ,galə'tɪə(r)
AM ,gælə'tiə

Galatia
BR gə'leɪʃ(ɪ)ə(r)
AM gə'leɪʃ(i)ə

Galatian
BR gə'leɪʃ(ə)n, -z
AM gə'leɪʃ(i)ən, -z

galaxy
BR 'galəks|i, -ɪz
AM 'gæləksi, -z

Galba
BR 'galbə(r)
AM 'gælbə

galbanum
BR 'galbənəm
AM 'gælbənəm

Galbraith
BR gal'breɪθ
AM 'gæl,breɪθ

gale
BR geɪl, -z
AM geɪl, -z

galea
BR 'geɪlɪə(r), -z
AM 'geɪliə, -z

galeae
BR 'geɪlɪʌɪ
AM 'geɪli,i, 'geɪli,aɪ

galeate
BR 'geɪlɪət
AM 'geɪliət

galeated
BR 'geɪlɪeɪtɪd
AM 'geɪli,eɪdɪd

Galen
BR 'geɪlɪn
AM 'geɪlən

galena
BR gə'liːnə(r)
AM gə'linə

galenic
BR gə'lɛnɪk
AM geɪ'lɛnɪk, gə'lɛnɪk

galenical
BR gə'lɛnɪkl
AM geɪ'lɛnəkəl, gə'lɛnəkəl

galette
BR gə'lɛt, -s
AM gə'lɛt, -s

Galicia
BR gə'lɪsɪə(r), gə'lɪʃ(ɪ)ə(r)
AM gə'lɪʃə
SP ga'liθja, ga'lisja

Galician
BR gə'lɪsɪən, gə'lɪʃ(ɪ)ən, gə'lɪʃn, -z
AM gə'lɪʃən, -z

Galilean
BR ,galɪ'liːən
AM ,gælə'liən

Galilee
BR 'galɪliː, -z
AM 'gælə,li, -z

Galileo
BR ,galɪ'leɪəʊ
AM ,gælə'leɪoʊ

galimatias
BR ,galɪ'matɪəs, ,galɪ'meɪʃəs
AM ,gælə'meɪʃəs, ,gælə'mædiəs

galingale
BR 'galɪŋgeɪl, -z
AM 'gælən,geɪl, -z

galiot
BR 'galɪət, -s
AM 'gæliət, 'gæli,ɑt, -s

galipot
BR 'galɪpɒt
AM 'gæli,pɑt

gall
BR gɔːl, -z, -ɪŋ, -d
AM gɔl, gɑl, -z, -ɪŋ, -d

Galla
BR 'galə(r), -z
AM 'gælə, 'gɑlə, -z

Gallacher
BR 'galəhə(r), 'galəxə(r)
AM 'gæləkər

Gallagher
BR 'galəhə(r), 'galəxə(r), 'galəgə(r)
AM 'gæləgər

Gallaher
BR 'galəhə(r), 'galəxə(r)
AM 'gælə,hər

gallant[1]
adjective, brave, splendid
BR 'galənt, 'galn̩t
AM 'gælənt

gallant[2]
noun, adjective, courteous
BR 'galənt, 'galn̩t, gə'lant, -s
AM gə'lænt, gə'lɑnt, 'gælənt, -s

gallant[3]
verb
BR gə'lant, -s, -ɪŋ, -ɪd
AM gə'læn|t, gə'lɑn|t, -ts, -(t)ɪŋ, -(t)əd

gallantly
BR 'galəntli, 'galn̩tli
AM 'gælən(t)li

gallantry
BR 'galəntri, 'galn̩tri
AM 'gæləntri

Galle
BR gɔːl
AM gɔl, gɑl

galleon
BR 'galɪən, -z
AM 'gæliən, 'gæljən, -z

galleria
BR ,galə'riːə(r), -z
AM ,gælə'riə, -z

gallery
BR 'gal(ə)r|i, -ɪz, -d
AM 'gæl(ə)ri, -z, -d

galleryite
BR 'galərɪʌɪt, -s
AM 'gæl(ə)ri,aɪt, -s

galley
BR 'gal|i, -ɪz
AM 'gæli, -z

galliambic
BR ,galɪ'ambɪk, -s
AM ,gæli'æmbɪk, -s

galliard
BR 'galɪɑːd, -z
AM 'gæljərd, -z

Gallic
BR 'galɪk
AM 'gælɪk

Gallican
BR 'galɪk(ə)n, -z
AM 'gæləkən, -z

Gallicanism
BR 'galɪkənɪz(ə)m, 'galɪkn̩ɪz(ə)m
AM 'gæləkə,nɪzəm

gallice
BR 'galɪsiː
AM 'gæləs

Gallicise
BR 'galɪsʌɪz, -ɪz, -ɪŋ, -d
AM 'gælə,saɪz, -ɪz, -ɪŋ, -d

Gallicism
BR 'galɪsɪz(ə)m, -z
AM 'gælə,sɪzəm, -z

Gallicize
BR 'galɪsʌɪz, -ɪz, -ɪŋ, -d
AM 'gælə,saɪz, -ɪz, -ɪŋ, -d

galligaskins
BR 'galɪ,gaskɪnz
AM ,gælə'gæskənz, ,gæli'gæskənz

gallimaufry
BR ,galɪ'mɔːfr|i, -ɪz
AM ,gælə'mɔfri, ,gælə'mɑfri, -z

gallinaceous
BR ,galɪ'neɪʃəs
AM ,gælə'neɪʃəs

gallingly
BR 'gɔːlɪŋli
AM 'gɔlɪŋli, 'gɑlɪŋli

gallinule
BR 'galɪnjuːl, -z
AM 'gælə,n(j)ul, -z

galliot
BR 'galɪət, -s
AM 'gæliət, 'gæli,ɑt, -s

Gallipoli
BR gə'lɪpəli, gə'lɪpl̩i
AM gə'lɪp(ə)li

gallipot
BR 'galɪpɒt, -s
AM 'gælə,pɑt, -s

gallium
BR 'galɪəm
AM 'gæliəm

gallivant
BR 'galɪvant, -s, -ɪŋ, -ɪd

AM ˌgæləˈvæn|t, -ts, -(t)ɪŋ, -(t)əd

galliwasp
BR ˈgalɪwɒsp, -s
AM ˈgæləˌwɑsp, -s

gallnut
BR ˈgalnʌt, -s
AM ˈgælˌnət, -s

Gallo
BR ˈgaləʊ
AM ˈgæloʊ

Gallo-
BR ˈgaləʊ
AM ˈgæloʊ

Gallois
BR ˈgalwɑː(r)
AM gɑlˈwɑ

Gallomania
BR ˌgalə(ʊ)ˈmeɪnɪə(r)
AM ˌgæloʊˈmeɪniə

Gallomaniac
BR ˌgalə(ʊ)ˈmeɪnɪak, -s
AM ˌgæloʊˈmeɪniˌæk, -s

gallon
BR ˈgalən, -z
AM ˈgælən, -z

gallonage
BR ˈgalən|ɪdʒ, -ɨdʒɪz
AM ˈgælənɪdʒ, -ɨz

galloon
BR gəˈluːn
AM gəˈlun

gallop
BR ˈgaləp, -s, -ɪŋ, -t
AM ˈgæləp, -s, -ɪŋ, -t

galloper
BR ˈgaləpə(r), -z
AM ˈgæləpər, -z

Gallophile
BR ˈgalə(ʊ)fʌɪl, -z
AM ˈgæləˌfaɪl, -z

Gallophobe
BR ˈgalə(ʊ)fəʊb, -z
AM ˈgæləˌfoʊb, -z

Gallophobia
BR ˌgalə(ʊ)ˈfəʊbɪə(r)
AM ˌgæləˈfoʊbiə

Gallo-Roman
BR ˌgaləʊˈrəʊmən, -z
AM ˌgæloʊˈroʊmən, -z

galloway
BR ˈgaləweɪ, -z
AM ˈgæləˌweɪ, -z

gallowglass
BR ˈgaləʊglɑːs, ˈgaləʊglas, -ɨz
AM ˈgæloʊˌglæs, -əz

gallows
BR ˈgaləʊz
AM ˈgæloʊz

gallstone
BR ˈgɔːlstəʊn, -z
AM ˈgɔlˌstoʊn, ˈgɑlˌstoʊn, -z

Gallup
BR ˈgaləp
AM ˈgæləp

galluses
BR ˈgaləsɪz
AM ˈgæləsəz

gall-wasp
BR ˈgɔːlwɒsp, -s
AM ˈgɔlˌwɑsp, ˈgɑlˌwɑsp, -s

galoot
BR gəˈluːt, -s
AM gəˈlut, -s

galop
BR ˈgaləp, -s, -ɪŋ, -t
AM ˈgæləp, -s, -ɪŋ, -t

galore
BR gəˈlɔː(r)
AM gəˈlɔ(ə)r

galosh
BR gəˈlɒʃ, -ɨz
AM gəˈlɑʃ, -əz

Galsworthy
BR ˈgɔːlzˌwəːði
AM ˈgɔlzˌwərði, ˈgɑlzˌwərði

Galt
BR gɔːlt, gɒlt
AM gɔlt, gɑlt

Galton
BR ˈgɔːlt(ə)n, ˈgɒlt(ə)n
AM ˈgɔltən, ˈgɑltən

galumph
BR gəˈlʌmf, -s, -ɪŋ, -t
AM gəˈləm(p)f, -s, -ɪŋ, -t

Galvani
BR galˈvɑːni
AM gælˈvɑni

galvanic
BR galˈvanɪk
AM gælˈvænɪk

galvanically
BR galˈvanɨkli
AM gælˈvænək(ə)li

galvanise
BR ˈgalvənʌɪz, -ɨz, -ɪŋ, -d
AM ˈgælvəˌnaɪz, -ɨz, -ɪŋ, -d

galvaniser
BR ˈgalvənʌɪzə(r), -z
AM ˈgælvəˌnaɪzər, -z

galvanism
BR ˈgalvənɪz(ə)m
AM ˈgælvəˌnɪzəm

galvanist
BR ˈgalvənɪst, -s
AM ˈgælvənəst, -s

galvanization
BR ˌgalvənʌɪˈzeɪʃn
AM ˌgælvənəˈzeɪʃən, ˌgælvəˌnaɪˈzeɪʃən

galvanize
BR ˈgalvənʌɪz, -ɨz, -ɪŋ, -d
AM ˈgælvəˌnaɪz, -ɨz, -ɪŋ, -d

galvanizer
BR ˈgalvənʌɪzə(r), -z
AM ˈgælvəˌnaɪzər, -z

galvanometer
BR ˌgalvəˈnɒmɨtə(r), -z
AM ˌgælvəˈnɑmədər, -z

galvanometric
BR ˌgalvənəˈmɛtrɪk, ˌgalvn̩əˈmɛtrɪk
AM ˌgælvənəˈmɛtrɪk

Galveston
BR ˈgalvɪst(ə)n
AM ˈgælvəstən

galvo
BR ˈgalvəʊ, -z
AM ˈgælˌvoʊ, -z

Galway
BR ˈgɔːlweɪ
AM ˈgɔlˌweɪ, ˈgɑlˌweɪ

gam
BR gam, -z
AM gæm, -z

Gama, da
BR də ˈgɑːmə(r)
AM də ˈgæmə

Gamage
BR ˈgamɪdʒ
AM ˈgæmɪdʒ

Gamaliel
BR gəˈmeɪlɪəl
AM gəˈmeɪliəl

gamay
BR ˈgameɪ, -z
AM gæˈmeɪ, -z

gamba
BR ˈgambə(r), -z
AM ˈgæmbə, ˈgɑmbə, -z

Gambaccini
BR ˌgambəˈtʃiːni
AM ˌgæmbəˈtʃini

gambade
BR gamˈbeɪd, gamˈbɑːd, -z
AM gæmˈbeɪd, gæmˈbɑd, -z

gambado
BR gamˈbeɪdəʊ, gamˈbɑːdəʊ, -z
AM gæmˈbeɪˌdoʊ, gæmˈbɑˌdoʊ, -z

Gambia
BR ˈgambɪə(r)
AM ˈgæmbiə

Gambian
BR ˈgambɪən, -z
AM ˈgæmbiən, -z

gambier
BR ˈgambɪə(r), -z
AM ˈgæmˌbɪ(ə)r, -z

gambit
BR ˈgambɪt, -s
AM ˈgæmbət, -s

gamble
BR ˈgamb|l, -lz, -l̩ɪŋ\-lɪŋ, -ld
AM ˈgæmb|əl, -əlz, -(ə)lɪŋ, -əld

gambler
BR ˈgamblə(r), -z
AM ˈgæmblər, -z

gamboge
BR gamˈbəʊ(d)ʒ, gamˈbuːʒ
AM gæmˈboʊdʒ, gæmˈbuʒ

gambol
BR ˈgamb|l, -lz, -l̩ɪŋ\-lɪŋ, -ld
AM ˈgæmb|əl, -əlz, -(ə)lɪŋ, -əld

gambrel
BR ˈgambr(ə)l, -z
AM ˈgæmbrəl, -z

game
BR geɪm, -z, -ɪŋ, -d, -ə(r), -ɨst
AM geɪm, -z, -ɪŋ, -d, -ər, -ɨst

gamebook
BR ˈgeɪmbʊk, -s
AM ˈgeɪmˌbʊk, -s

gamecock
BR ˈgeɪmkɒk, -s
AM ˈgeɪmˌkɑk, -s

gamefowl
BR ˈgeɪmfaʊl, -z
AM ˈgeɪmˌfaʊl, -z

gamekeeper
BR ˈgeɪmˌkiːpə(r), -z
AM ˈgeɪmˌkipər, -z

gamekeeping
BR ˈgeɪmˌkiːpɪŋ
AM ˈgeɪmˌkipɪŋ

gamelan
BR ˈgamɨlan
AM ˈgæməˌlæn

gamely
BR ˈgeɪmli
AM ˈgeɪmli

gameness
BR ˈgeɪmnɨs
AM ˈgeɪmnɨs

gamesman
BR ˈgeɪmzmən
AM ˈgeɪmzmən

gamesmanship
BR ˈgeɪmzmənʃɪp
AM ˈgeɪmzmənˌʃɪp

gamesmen
BR ˈgeɪmzmən
AM ˈgeɪmzmən

gamesome
BR ˈgeɪms(ə)m
AM ˈgeɪmsəm

gamesomely
BR ˈgeɪms(ə)mli
AM ˈgeɪmsəmli

gamesomeness
BR ˈgeɪms(ə)mnəs
AM ˈgeɪmsəmnəs

gamesplayer
BR ˈgeɪmzˌpleɪə(r), -z
AM ˈgeɪmzˌpleɪər, -z

gamester
BR 'geɪmstə(r), -z
AM 'geɪmstər, -z
gametangia
BR ˌgamɪ'tan(d)ʒ(ɪ)ə(r)
AM ˌgæmə'tændʒ(i)ə
gametangium
BR ˌgamɪ'tan(d)ʒɪəm
AM ˌgæmə'tændʒiəm
gamete
BR 'gamiːt, gə'miːt
AM 'gæmˌit, gə'mit
gametic
BR gə'mɛtɪk, ga'mɛtɪk
AM gə'mɛdɪk
gametocyte
BR gə'miːtə(ʊ)sʌɪt, 'gamɪtəsʌɪt, -s
AM gə'midəˌsaɪt, -s
gametogenesis
BR gəˌmiːtə(ʊ)'dʒɛnɪsɪs, ˌgamɪtə(ʊ)'dʒɛnɪsɪs
AM gəˌmidə'dʒɛnəsəs, ˌgæmɛdoʊ'dʒɛnəsəs
gametophyte
BR gə'miːtə(ʊ)fʌɪt, 'gamɪtəfʌɪt, -s
AM gə'midəˌfaɪt, -s
gametophytic
BR gəˌmiːtə(ʊ)'fɪtɪk, ˌgamɪtə(ʊ)'fɪtɪk
AM gəˌmidə'fɪdɪk
gamey
BR 'geɪm|i, -ɪə(r), -ɪɪst
AM 'geɪmi, -ər, -ɨst
gamily
BR 'geɪmɨli
AM 'geɪmɨli
gamin
BR 'gamɪn, -z
AM 'gæmən, -z
gamine
BR 'gamiːn, -z
AM 'gæmin, -z
gaminess
BR 'geɪmɪnɨs
AM 'geɪminɨs
gamma
BR 'gamə(r), -z
AM 'gæmə, -z
gammadion
BR gə'meɪdɪən, ga'meɪdɪən, gə'madɪən, ga'madɪən, -z
AM gə'meɪdiˌɑn, gə'mædiˌɑn, gə'meɪdiən, gə'mædiən, gæ'meɪdiˌɑn, gæ'mædiˌɑn, gæ'meɪdiən, gæ'mædiən, -z
gammer
BR 'gamə(r), -z
AM 'gæmər, -z
gamminess
BR 'gamɪnɨs
AM 'gæminɨs
gammon
BR 'gamən, -z
AM 'gæmən, -z
gammy
BR 'gam|i, -ɪə(r), -ɪɪst
AM 'gæmi, -ər, -ɨst
Gamow
BR 'gaməʊ
AM 'gæˌmoʊ
RUS 'gaməf
gamp
BR gamp, -s
AM gæmp, -s
gamut
BR 'gamət, -s
AM 'gæmət, -s
gamy
BR 'geɪm|i, -ɪə(r), -ɪɪst
AM 'geɪmi, -ər, -ɨst
gander
BR 'gandə(r), -z
AM 'gændər, -z
Gandhi
BR 'gandi, 'gɑːndi
AM 'gɑndi
Ganesha
BR gə'neɪʃə(r)
AM gə'neɪʃə
gang
BR gaŋ, -z, -ɪŋ, -d
AM gæŋ, -z, -ɪŋ, -d
gangboard
BR 'gaŋbɔːd, -z
AM 'gæŋˌbɔ(ə)rd, -z
gangbuster
BR 'gaŋˌbʌstə(r), -z
AM 'gæŋˌbəstər, -z
ganger
BR 'gaŋə(r), -z
AM 'gæŋər, -z
Ganges
BR 'gandʒiːz
AM 'gænˌdʒiz
Gangetic
BR gan'dʒɛtɪk
AM gæn'dʒɛdɪk
gangland
BR 'gaŋland
AM 'gæŋˌlænd
gangle
BR 'gaŋg|l, -lz, -l̩ɪŋ\-lɪŋ, -ld
AM 'gæŋg|əl, -əlz, -(ə)lɪŋ, -əld
ganglia
BR 'gaŋglɪə(r)
AM 'gæŋgliə
gangliar
BR 'gaŋglɪə(r)
AM 'gæŋgliər
gangliform
BR 'gaŋglɪfɔːm
AM 'gæŋgləˌfɔ(ə)rm
gangling
BR 'gaŋglɪŋ
AM 'gæŋglɪŋ
ganglion
BR 'gaŋglɪən, -z
AM 'gæŋgliən, -z
ganglionated
BR 'gaŋglɪəneɪtɨd
AM 'gæŋgliəˌneɪdɨd
ganglionic
BR ˌgaŋglɪ'ɒnɪk
AM ˌgæŋgli'ɑnɪk
gangly
BR 'gaŋgl|i, -ɪə(r), -ɪɪst
AM 'gæŋgli, -ər, -ɨst
gangplank
BR 'gaŋplaŋk, -s
AM 'gæŋˌplæŋk, -s
gangrene
BR 'gaŋgriːn
AM 'gæŋgrin
gangrenous
BR 'gaŋgrɪnəs
AM 'gæŋgrənəs
gangster
BR 'gaŋstə(r), -z
AM 'gæŋgstər, -z
gangsterism
BR 'gaŋst(ə)rɪz(ə)m
AM 'gæŋgstəˌrɪzəm
gangue
BR gaŋ
AM gæŋ
gangway
BR 'gaŋweɪ, -z
AM 'gæŋˌweɪ, -z
ganister
BR 'ganɪstə(r)
AM 'gænəstər
ganja
BR 'gandʒə(r)
AM 'gɑndʒə, 'gændʒə
gannet
BR 'ganɪt, -s
AM 'gænət, -s
gannetry
BR 'ganɪtr|i, -ɪz
AM 'gænətri, -z
Gannex
BR 'ganɛks
AM 'gænəks
gannister
BR 'ganɪstə(r)
AM 'gænəstər
Gannon
BR 'ganən
AM 'gænən
ganoid
BR 'ganɔɪd, -z
AM 'gæˌnɔɪd, -z
gantlet
BR 'gantlɨt, 'gɔːntlɨt, -s
AM 'gɔntlət, 'gɑntlət, -s
gantry
BR 'gantr|i, -ɪz
AM 'gæntri, -z
Ganymede
BR 'ganɪmiːd
AM 'gænəˌmid
gaol
BR dʒeɪl, -z, -ɪŋ, -d
AM dʒeɪl, -z, -ɪŋ, -d
gaolbird
BR 'dʒeɪlbəːd, -z
AM 'dʒeɪlˌbərd, -z
gaoler
BR 'dʒeɪlə(r), -z
AM 'dʒeɪlər, -z
gap
BR gap, -s, -ɪŋ, -t
AM gæp, -s, -ɪŋ, -t
gape
BR geɪp, -s, -ɪŋ, -t
AM geɪp, -s, -ɪŋ, -t
gaper
BR 'geɪpə(r), -z
AM 'geɪpər, -z
gapeworm
BR 'geɪpwəːm, -z
AM 'geɪpˌwərm, -z
gapingly
BR 'geɪpɪŋli
AM 'geɪpɪŋli
gappy
BR 'gap|i, -ɪə(r), -ɪɪst
AM 'gæpi, -ər, -ɨst
gar
BR gɑː(r)
AM gɑr
garage
BR 'garɑː(d)ʒ, 'garɪdʒ, gə'rɑː(d)ʒ, 'garɑː(d)ʒɪz\'garɪdʒɪz\gə'rɑː(d)ʒɪz, 'garɑː(d)ʒɪŋ\'garɪdʒɪŋ\gə'rɑː(d)ʒɪŋ, 'garɑː(d)ʒd\'garɪdʒd\gə'rɑː(d)ʒd
AM gə'rɑʒ, -əz, -ɪŋ, -t
garam masala
BR ˌgɑːrəm mə'sɑːlə(r)
AM ˌgɑrəm mə'sɑlə
Garard
BR 'garɑːd
AM 'gɛrɑrd
garb
BR gɑːb, -z, -d
AM gɑrb, -z, -d
garbage
BR 'gɑːbɪdʒ
AM 'gɑrbɪdʒ
garbanzo
BR gɑː'banzəʊ, -z
AM gɑr'bɑnzoʊ, -z
Garbett
BR 'gɑːbɪt
AM 'gɑrbət
garble
BR 'gɑːb|l, -lz, -l̩ɪŋ\-lɪŋ, -ld
AM 'gɑrb|əl, -əlz, -(ə)lɪŋ, -əld
garbler
BR 'gɑːblə(r), -z
AM 'gɑrb(ə)lər, -z

Garbo
BR ˈgɑːbəʊ
AM ˈgɑrˌboʊ

garboard
BR ˈgɑːbɔːd, -z
AM ˈgɑrˌbɔ(ə)rd, -z

García
BR gɑːˈsiːə(r)
AM gɑrˈsiə
SP garˈθia, garˈsia

garçon
BR ˈgɑːsɒn, ˈgɑːsɒ̃, -z
AM gɑrˈsɔn, -z

Garda
BR ˈgɑːdə(r)
AM ˈgɑrdə

Gardaí
BR (ˌ)gɑːˈdiː
AM gɑrˈdi

garden
BR ˈgɑːd|n, -nz, -n̩ɪŋ\-nɪŋ, -nd
AM ˈgɑrdən, -z, -ɪŋ, -d

gardener
BR ˈgɑːdn̩ə(r), ˈgɑːdnə(r), -z
AM ˈgɑrdn̩ər, -z

gardenesque
BR ˌgɑːdnˈɛsk
AM ˌgɑrdnˈɛsk

gardenia
BR gɑːˈdiːnɪə(r), -z
AM gɑrˈdinjə, -z

Gardiner
BR ˈgɑːdnə(r)
AM ˈgɑrd(ə)nər

Gardner
BR ˈgɑːdnə(r)
AM ˈgɑrdnər

Gardyne
BR gɑːˈdʌɪn, ˈgɑːdʌɪn
AM ˈgɑrdaɪn

Gareloch
BR ˈgɛːlɒx, ˈgɛːlɒk
AM ˈgɛrlɑk

Gareth
BR ˈgarəθ
AM ˈgɛrəθ

Garfield
BR ˈgɑːfiːld
AM ˈgɑrˌfild

garfish
BR ˈgɑːfɪʃ
AM ˈgɑrˌfɪʃ

Garforth
BR ˈgɑːfɔːθ, ˈgɑːfəθ
AM ˈgɑrˌfɔ(ə)rθ

Garfunkel
BR gɑːˈfʌŋkl, ˈgɑːˌfʌŋkl
AM ˈgɑrˌfəŋkəl

garganey
BR ˈgɑːgən|i, ˈgɑːgn̩|i, -ɪz
AM ˈgɑrgəni, -z

Gargantua
BR gɑːˈgantjʊə(r), gɑːˈgantʃʊə(r)
AM ˌgɑrˈgæn(t)ʃuə

gargantuan
BR gɑːˈgantjʊən, gɑːˈgantʃʊən
AM gɑrˈgæn(t)ʃ(əw)ən

garget
BR ˈgɑːgɪt
AM ˈgɑrgət

gargle
BR ˈgɑːg|l, -lz, -l̩ɪŋ\-lɪŋ, -ld
AM ˈgɑrg|əl, -əlz, -(ə)lɪŋ, -əld

gargoyle
BR ˈgɑːgɔɪl, -z
AM ˈgɑrˌgɔɪl, -z

gargoylism
BR ˈgɑːgɔɪlɪz(ə)m
AM ˈgɑrˌgɔɪˌlɪzəm

Garibaldi
BR ˌgarɪˈbɔːldi, ˌgarɪˈbɒldi, ˌgarɪˈbaldi
AM ˌgɛrəˈbɔldi, ˌgɛrəˈbɑldi

garish
BR ˈgɛːrɪʃ, ˈgarɪʃ
AM ˈgɛrɪʃ

garishly
BR ˈgɛːrɪʃli, ˈgarɪʃli
AM ˈgɛrəʃli

garishness
BR ˈgɛːrɪʃnɪs, ˈgarɪʃnɪs
AM ˈgɛrɪʃnɪs

garland
BR ˈgɑːlənd, -z, -ɪŋ, -ɪd
AM ˈgɑrlən(d), -z, -ɪŋ, -əd

garlic
BR ˈgɑːlɪk
AM ˈgɑrlɪk

garlicky
BR ˈgɑːlɪki
AM ˈgɑrlɪki

Garman
BR ˈgɑːmən
AM ˈgɑrmən

garment
BR ˈgɑːm(ə)nt, -s, -ɪd
AM ˈgɑrmən|t, -ts, -(t)əd

Garmondsway
BR ˈgɑːmən(d)zweɪ
AM ˈgɑrmənzˌweɪ

Garmonsway
BR ˈgɑːmənzweɪ
AM ˈgɑrmənzˌweɪ

garner
BR ˈgɑːn|ə(r), -əz, -(ə)rɪŋ, -əd
AM ˈgɑrnər, -z, -ɪŋ, -d

garnet
BR ˈgɑːnɪt, -s
AM ˈgɑrnət, -s

Garnett
BR ˈgɑːnɪt
AM ˈgɑrnət

garnish
BR ˈgɑːn|ɪʃ, -ɪʃɪz, -ɪʃɪŋ, -ɪʃt
AM ˈgɑrnɪʃ, -ɪz, -ɪŋ, -t

garnishee
BR ˌgɑːnɪˈʃiː, -z
AM ˌgɑrnɪˈʃi, -z

garnishing
BR ˈgɑːnɪʃɪŋ, -z
AM ˈgɑrnɪʃɪŋ, -z

garnishment
BR ˈgɑːnɪʃm(ə)nt
AM ˈgɑrnɪʃmənt

garniture
BR ˈgɑːnɪtʃə(r)
AM ˈgɑrnətʃʊ(ə)r, ˈgɑrnətʃər

Garonne
BR gəˈrɒn
AM gəˈrɑn, gəˈrɔn

garotte
BR gəˈrɒt, -s, -ɪŋ, -ɪd
AM gəˈrɑ|t, -ts, -dɪŋ, -dəd

garpike
BR ˈgɑːpʌɪk
AM ˈgærˌpaɪk

Garrard
BR ˈgarɑːd, ˈgarəd
AM gəˈrɑrd

Garratt
BR ˈgarət
AM ˈgɛrət

garret
BR ˈgarət, -s
AM ˈgɛrət, -s

garreteer
BR ˌgarɪˈtiːə(r), -z
AM ˌgɛrəˈtɪ(ə)r, -z

Garrick
BR ˈgarɪk
AM ˈgɛrɪk

garrison
BR ˈgarɪs(ə)n, -z, -ɪŋ, -d
AM ˈgɛrəsən, -z, -ɪŋ, -d

garrote
BR gəˈrɒt, -s, -ɪŋ, -ɪd
AM gəˈrɑ|t, -ts, -dɪŋ, -dəd

garrotte
BR gəˈrɒt, -s, -ɪŋ, -ɪd
AM gəˈrɑ|t, -ts, -dɪŋ, -dəd

garrotter
BR gəˈrɒtə(r), -z
AM gəˈrɑdər, -z

garrulity
BR gəˈr(j)uːlɪti, gaˈr(j)uːlɪti
AM gəˈrulədi

garrulous
BR ˈgar(j)ʊləs
AM ˈgɛrələs

garrulously
BR ˈgar(j)ʊləsli
AM ˈgɛrələsli

garrulousness
BR ˈgar(j)ʊləsnəs
AM ˈgɛrələsnəs

Garry
BR ˈgari
AM ˈgɛri

garrya
BR ˈgarɪə(r), -z
AM ˈgɛriə, -z

garter
BR ˈgɑːt|ə(r), -əz, -(ə)rɪŋ, -əd
AM ˈgɑrdər, -z, -ɪŋ, -d

garth
BR gɑːθ, -s
AM gɑrθ, -s

garuda
BR ˈgarʊdə(r), -z
AM gəˈrudə, -z

Garvey
BR ˈgɑːvi
AM ˈgɑrvi

Gary
BR ˈgari
AM ˈgɛri

Garza
BR ˈgɑːzə(r)
AM ˈgɑrzə

gas
BR gas, -ɪz, -ɪŋ, -t
AM gæs, -əz, -ɪŋ, -t

gasbag
BR ˈgasbag, -z
AM ˈgæsˌbæg, -z

gas chamber
BR ˈgas ˌtʃeɪmbə(r), -z
AM ˈgæs ˌtʃeɪmbər, -z

Gascogne
BR ˈgaskɔɪn
AM gæsˈkɔɪn
FR gaskɔɲ

Gascoigne
BR ˈgaskɔɪn
AM gæsˈkɔɪn

Gascoin
BR ˈgaskɔɪn
AM gæsˈkɔɪn

Gascoine
BR ˈgaskɔɪn
AM gæsˈkɔɪn

Gascon
BR ˈgaskən, -z
AM ˈgæskən, -z

gasconade
BR ˌgaskəˈneɪd, -z, -ɪŋ, -ɪd
AM ˌgæskəˈneɪd, -z, -ɪŋ, -ɪd

Gascony
BR ˈgaskəni
AM ˈgæskəni

gaseous
BR ˈgasɪəs, ˈgeɪsɪəs
AM ˈgæʃ(j)əs, ˈgæsiəs

gaseousness
BR 'gasɪəsnəs, 'geɪsɪəsnəs
AM 'gæʃ(j)əsnəs, 'gæsiəsnəs

gasfield
BR 'gasfiːld, -z
AM 'gæsˌfild, -z

gash
BR gaʃ, -ɪz, -ɪŋ, -t
AM gæʃ, -əz, -ɪŋ, -t

gasholder
BR 'gasˌhəʊldə(r), -z
AM 'gæsˌ(h)oʊldər, -z

gashouse
BR 'gashaʊ|s, -zɪz
AM 'gæsˌ(h)aʊ|s, -zəz

gasification
BR ˌgasɪfɪ'keɪʃn
AM ˌgæsəfə'keɪʃən

gasify
BR 'gasɪfʌɪ, -z, -ɪŋ, -d
AM 'gæsəˌfaɪ, -z, -ɪŋ, -d

Gaskell
BR 'gaskl
AM 'gæskəl

gasket
BR 'gaskɪt, -s
AM 'gæskət, -s

gaskin
BR 'gaskɪn, -z
AM 'gæskən, -z

gaslamp
BR 'gaslamp, -s
AM 'gæsˌlæmp, -s

gaslight
BR 'gaslʌɪt
AM 'gæsˌlaɪt

gasman
BR 'gasman
AM 'gæsmən

gasmen
BR 'gasmɛn
AM 'gæsmən

gasohol
BR 'gasəhɒl
AM 'gæsəˌhɔl, 'gæsəˌhɑl

gasolene
BR 'gasəliːn, ˌgasə'liːn
AM 'gæsəlin, ˌgæsə'lin

gasoline
BR 'gasəliːn, ˌgasə'liːn
AM 'gæsəlin, ˌgæsə'lin

gasometer
BR ga'sɒmɪtə(r), gə'sɒmɪtə(r), -z
AM gæ'sɑmədər, -z

gasp
BR gɑːsp, gasp, -s, -ɪŋ, -t
AM gæsp, -s, -ɪŋ, -t

gasper
BR 'gɑːspə(r), 'gaspə(r), -z
AM 'gæspər, -z

gaspereau
BR 'gaspərəʊ, -z
AM 'gæspəroʊ, -z

gaspereaux
BR 'gaspərəʊz
AM 'gæspəroʊ

gasproof
BR 'gaspruːf
AM 'gæsˌpruf

Gassendi
BR gə'sɛndi
AM gə'sɛndi

gasser
BR 'gasə(r), -z
AM 'gæsər, -z

gassiness
BR 'gasɪnɪs
AM 'gæsinɪs

gassy
BR 'gas|i, -ɪə(r), -ɪɪst
AM 'gæsi, -ər, -ɪst

gasteropod
BR 'gast(ə)rəpɒd, -z
AM 'gæst(ə)rəˌpɑd, -z

Gasthaus
BR 'gasthaʊ|s, -zɪz
AM 'gɑstˌ(h)aʊ|s, -zəz

Gasthäuser
BR 'gasthɔɪzə(r)
AM 'gɑstˌ(h)ɔɪzər

Gasthof
BR 'gasthɒf, -s
AM 'gɑstˌ(h)ɔf, 'gɑstˌ(h)ɑf, -s

Gasthöfe
BR 'gastˌhɒfə(r)
AM 'gɑs(t)ˌ(h)ɔfə, 'gɑs(t)ˌ(h)ɑfə

gastrectomy
BR ga'strɛktəm|i, -ɪz
AM gæ'strɛktəmi, -z

gastric
BR 'gastrɪk
AM 'gæstrɪk

gastritis
BR ga'strʌɪtɪs
AM gæ'straɪdɪs

gastroenteric
BR ˌgastrəʊɛn'tɛrɪk
AM ˌgæstroʊˌɛn'tɛrɪk

gastroenteritis
BR ˌgastrəʊˌɛntə'rʌɪtɪs
AM ˌgæstroʊˌɛn(t)ə'raɪdɪs

gastroenterology
BR ˌgastrəʊˌɛntə'rɒlədʒi
AM ˌgæstroʊˌɛn(t)ə'rɑlədʒi

gastrointestinal
BR ˌgastrəʊɪn'tɛstɪnl, ˌgastrəʊˌɪntɛ'stʌɪnl
AM ˌgæstroʊɪn'tɛstənəl

gastronome
BR 'gastrənəʊm, -z
AM 'gæstrəˌnoʊm, -z

gastronomic
BR ˌgastrə'nɒmɪk
AM ˌgæstrə'nɑmɪk

gastronomical
BR ˌgastrə'nɒmɪkl
AM ˌgæstrə'nɑməkəl

gastronomically
BR ˌgastrə'nɒmɪkli
AM ˌgæstrə'nɑmək(ə)li

gastronomy
BR ga'strɒnəmi
AM gæ'strɑnəmi

gastropod
BR 'gastrəpɒd, -z
AM 'gæstrəˌpɑd, -z

gastropodous
BR ga'strɒpədəs
AM gæ'strɑpədəs

gastroscope
BR 'gastrəskəʊp, -s
AM 'gæstrəˌskoʊp, -s

gastrula
BR 'gastrʊlə(r), -z
AM 'gæstrələ, -z

gastrulae
BR 'gastrʊliː
AM 'gæstrəˌli, 'gæstrəˌlaɪ

gasworks
BR 'gaswəːks
AM 'gæsˌwərks

gat
BR gat, -s
AM gæt, -s

gate
BR geɪt, -s, -ɪŋ, -ɪd
AM geɪ|t, -ts, -dɪŋ, -dɪd

gateau
BR 'gatəʊ, -z
AM gɑ'toʊ, gæ'toʊ, -z

gateaux
BR 'gatəʊz
AM gɑ'toʊ, gæ'toʊ

gatecrash
BR 'geɪtkraʃ, -ɪz, -ɪŋ, -t
AM 'geɪtˌkræʃ, -əz, -ɪŋ, -t

gatecrasher
BR 'geɪtkraʃə(r), -z
AM 'geɪtˌkræʃər, -z

gatefold
BR 'geɪtfəʊld, -z
AM 'geɪtˌfoʊld, -z

gatehouse
BR 'geɪthaʊ|s, -zɪz
AM 'geɪtˌ(h)aʊ|s, -zɪz

gatekeeper
BR 'geɪtˌkiːpə(r), -z
AM 'geɪtˌkipər, -z

gateleg
BR 'geɪtlɛg, -z
AM 'geɪtˌlɛg, -z

gatelegged
BR ˌgeɪt'lɛgd
AM 'geɪtˌlɛgəd

gateman
BR 'geɪtman
AM 'geɪtmən

gatemen
BR 'geɪtmɛn
AM 'geɪtmən

gatepost
BR 'geɪtpəʊst, -s
AM 'geɪtˌpoʊst, -s

Gates
BR geɪts
AM geɪts

Gateshead
BR 'geɪtshɛd, ˌgeɪts'hɛd
AM 'geɪtsˌ(h)ɛd

gateway
BR 'geɪtweɪ, -z
AM 'geɪtˌweɪ, -z

gather
BR 'gað|ə(r), -əz, -(ə)rɪŋ, -əd
AM 'gæð|ər, -ərz, -(ə)rɪŋ, -ərd

gatherer
BR 'gað(ə)rə(r), -z
AM 'gæðərər, -z

gathering
BR 'gað(ə)rɪŋ, -z
AM 'gæð(ə)rɪŋ, -z

Gatling
BR 'gatlɪŋ, -z
AM 'gætˌlɪŋ, -z

'gator
BR 'geɪtə(r), -z
AM 'geɪdər, -z

GATT
BR gat
AM gæt

Gatting
BR 'gatɪŋ
AM 'gædɪŋ

Gatwick
BR 'gatwɪk
AM 'gætˌwɪk

gauche
BR gəʊʃ
AM goʊʃ

gauchely
BR 'gəʊʃli
AM 'goʊʃli

gaucheness
BR 'gəʊʃnəs
AM 'goʊʃnəs

gaucherie
BR 'gəʊʃ(ə)r|i, -ɪz
AM 'goʊʃəri, -z

gaucho
BR 'gaʊtʃəʊ, -z
AM 'gaʊtʃoʊ, -z

gaud
BR gɔːd, -z
AM gɔd, gɑd, -z

gaudeamus
BR ˌgaʊdɪ'ɑːməs
AM ˌgaʊdi'ɑməs

Gaudí
BR 'gaʊdi
AM 'gaʊdi

gaudily
BR 'gɔːdɪli
AM 'gɔdəli, 'gɑdəli

gaudiness
BR ˈɡɔːdɪnɨs
AM ˈɡɔdinɨs, ˈɡɑdinɨs

gaudy
BR ˈɡɔːd|i, -ɪə(r), -ɪɨst
AM ˈɡɔdi, ˈɡɑdi, -ər, -ɨst

gauge
BR ɡeɪdʒ, -ɨz, -ɪŋ, -d
AM ɡeɪdʒ, -ɨz, -ɪŋ, -d

gaugeable
BR ˈɡeɪdʒəbl
AM ˈɡeɪdʒəbəl

gauger
BR ˈɡeɪdʒə(r), -z
AM ˈɡeɪdʒər, -z

Gauguin
BR ˈɡəʊɡã, ˈɡəʊɡan
AM ɡɔˈɡɛn, ɡɑˈɡɛn

Gaul
BR ɡɔːl, -z
AM ɡɔl, ɡɑl, -z

gauleiter
BR ˈɡaʊlʌɪtə(r), -z
AM ˈɡaʊˌlaɪdər, -z

Gaulish
BR ˈɡɔːlɪʃ
AM ˈɡɔlɪʃ, ˈɡɑlɪʃ

Gaullism
BR ˈɡəʊlɪz(ə)m
AM ˈɡɔˌlɪzəm, ˈɡɑˌlɪzəm

Gaullist
BR ˈɡəʊlɪst, -s
AM ˈɡɔləst, ˈɡɑləst, -s

Gauloise
BR ˈɡəʊlwɑːz, ˈɡɔːlwɑːz, -ɨz
AM ˈɡɔlˌwɑz, ˈɡɑlˌwɑz, -əz

gault
BR ɡɔːlt, ɡɒlt
AM ɡɔlt, ɡɑlt

gaultheria
BR ɡɔːlˈθɪrɪə(r), -z
AM ɡɔlˈθɪriə, ɡɑlˈθɪriə, -z

gaunt
BR ɡɔːnt, -ə(r), -ɨst
AM ɡɔnt, ɡɑnt, -ər, -əst

gauntlet
BR ˈɡɔːntlɨt, -s
AM ˈɡɔn(t)lət, ˈɡɑn(t)lət, -s

gauntly
BR ˈɡɔːntli
AM ˈɡɔn(t)li, ˈɡɑn(t)li

gauntness
BR ˈɡɔːntnəs
AM ˈɡɔn(t)nəs, ˈɡɑn(t)nəs

gauntry
BR ˈɡɔːntr|i, -ɪz
AM ˈɡɔntri, ˈɡɑntri, -z

gaur
BR ˈɡaʊə(r), -z
AM ˈɡaʊ(ə)r, -z

Gauss
BR ɡaʊs, -ɨz, -ɪŋ, -t
AM ɡaʊs, -əz, -ɪŋ, -t

Gaussian
BR ˈɡaʊsɪən
AM ˈɡaʊsɪən

Gautama
BR ˈɡaʊtəmə(r), ˈɡəʊtəmə(r)
AM ˈɡɔdəmə, ˈɡaʊdəmə

gauze
BR ɡɔːz
AM ɡɔz, ɡɑz

gauzily
BR ˈɡɔːzɨli
AM ˈɡɔzəli, ˈɡɑzəli

gauziness
BR ˈɡɔːzɪnɨs
AM ˈɡɔzinɨs, ˈɡɑzinɨs

gauzy
BR ˈɡɔːz|i, -ɪə(r), -ɪɨst
AM ˈɡɔzi, ˈɡɑzi, -ər, -ɨst

gave
BR ɡeɪv
AM ɡeɪv

gavel
BR ˈɡavl, -z
AM ˈɡævəl, -z

gavial
BR ˈɡeɪvɪəl, ˈɡavɪəl, -z
AM ˈɡeɪviəl, -z

Gavin
BR ˈɡavɪn
AM ˈɡævən

gavotte
BR ɡəˈvɒt, -s
AM ɡəˈvɑt, -s

Gawain
BR ˈɡɑːweɪn, ˈɡaweɪn, ɡəˈweɪn
AM ɡəˈweɪn, ˈɡɑweɪn

Gawd
God in exclamations
BR ɡɔːd
AM ɡɔd, ɡɑd

gawk
BR ɡɔːk, -s, -ɪŋ, -t
AM ɡɔk, ɡɑk, -s, -ɪŋ, -t

gawkily
BR ˈɡɔːkɨli
AM ˈɡɔkəli, ˈɡɑkəli

gawkiness
BR ˈɡɔːkɪnɨs
AM ˈɡɔkinɨs, ˈɡɑkinɨs

gawkish
BR ˈɡɔːkɪʃ
AM ˈɡɔkɪʃ, ˈɡɑkɪʃ

gawky
BR ˈɡɔːk|i, -ɪə(r), -ɪɨst
AM ˈɡɔki, ˈɡɑki, -ər, -ɨst

gawp
BR ɡɔːp, -s, -ɪŋ, -t
AM ɡɔp, ɡɑp, -s, -ɪŋ, -t

gawper
BR ˈɡɔːpə(r), -z
AM ˈɡɔpər, ˈɡɑpər, -z

gay
BR ɡeɪ, -ə(r), -ɨst
AM ɡeɪ, -ər, -ɨst

gayal
BR ɡʌɪˈjɑːl, ɡʌɪˈjal, -z
AM ɡəˈjɑl, -z

Gaydon
BR ˈɡeɪdn
AM ˈɡeɪdən

Gaye
BR ɡeɪ
AM ɡeɪ

gayety
BR ˈɡeɪɨti
AM ˈɡeɪɨdi

Gayle
BR ɡeɪl
AM ɡeɪl

Gay-Lussac
BR ˌɡeɪˈluːsak
AM ˈɡeɪləˈsæk

gayness
BR ˈɡeɪnɨs
AM ˈɡeɪnɨs

Gaynor
BR ˈɡeɪnə(r)
AM ˈɡeɪnər

Gaza
BR ˈɡɑːzə(r)
AM ˈɡɑzə

gazania
BR ɡəˈzeɪnɪə(r), -z
AM ɡəˈzeɪniə, -z

gaze
BR ɡeɪz, -ɨz, -ɪŋ, -d
AM ɡeɪz, -ɨz, -ɪŋ, -d

gazebo
BR ɡəˈziːbəʊ, -z
AM ɡəˈziboʊ, -z

gazelle
BR ɡəˈzɛl, -z
AM ɡəˈzɛl, -z

gazer
BR ˈɡeɪzə(r), -z
AM ˈɡeɪzər, -z

gazette
BR ɡəˈzɛt, -s, -ɪŋ, -ɨd
AM ɡəˈzɛ|t, -ts, -dɪŋ, -dəd

gazetteer
BR ˌɡazɪˈtɪə(r), -z
AM ˌɡæzəˈtɪ(ə)r, -z

gazpacho
BR ɡazˈpatʃəʊ, ɡaˈspatʃəʊ, ɡəˈspatʃəʊ, ɡaˈspɑːtʃəʊ, ɡəˈspɑːtʃəʊ, -z
AM ɡɑzˈpɑtʃoʊ, -z

gazump
BR ɡəˈzʌm|p, -ps, -pɪŋ, -(p)t
AM ɡəˈzəmp, -s, -ɪŋ, -t

gazumper
BR ɡəˈzʌmpə(r), -z
AM ɡəˈzəmpər, -z

gazunder
BR ɡəˈzʌnd|ə(r), -əz, -(ə)rɪŋ, -əd
AM ɡəˈzənd|ər, -ərz, -(ə)rɪŋ, -ərd

Gdansk
BR ɡəˈdansk
AM ɡəˈdɑnsk

Gdańsk
BR ɡəˈdansk
AM ɡəˈdɑnsk

GDP
BR ˌdʒiːdiːˈpiː
AM ˌdʒiˌdiˈpi

Gdynia
BR ɡəˈdɪnɪə(r)
AM ɡəˈdɪniə

gean
BR ɡiːn, -z
AM ɡin, -z

gear
BR ɡɪə(r), -z, -ɪŋ, -d
AM ɡɪ(ə)r, -z, -ɪŋ, -d

gearbox
BR ˈɡɪəbɒks, -ɨz
AM ˈɡɪrˌbɑks, -əz

gearing
BR ˈɡɪərɪŋ
AM ˈɡɪrɪŋ

gearstick
BR ˈɡɪəstɪk, -s
AM ˈɡɪrˌstɪk, -s

gearwheel
BR ˈɡɪəwiːl, -z
AM ˈɡɪrˌ(h)wil, -z

Geary
BR ˈɡɪəri
AM ˈɡɪri

Geber
BR ˈdʒiːbə(r)
AM ˈdʒibər

gecko
BR ˈɡɛkəʊ, -z
AM ˈɡɛkoʊ, -z

Geddes
BR ˈɡɛdɪs
AM ˈɡɛdiz

gee
BR dʒiː, -z, -ɪŋ, -d
AM dʒi, -z, -ɪŋ, -d

Geechee
BR ˈɡiːtʃiː
AM ˈɡiˌtʃi

gee-gee
BR ˈdʒiːdʒiː, -z
AM ˈdʒiˌdʒi, -z

geek
BR ɡiːk, -s
AM ɡik, -s

Geelong
BR dʒiːˈlɒŋ, dʒɪˈlɒŋ
AM dʒiˈlɔŋ, dʒiˈlɑŋ

geese
BR ɡiːs
AM ɡis

gee-string
BR ˈdʒiːstrɪŋ, -z
AM ˈdʒiˌstrɪŋ, -z

gee-whiz
BR ˌdʒiːˈwɪz
AM ˈdʒiˈ(h)wɪz

gee-whizz
BR ˌdʒiːˈwɪz
AM ˈdʒiˈ(h)wɪz

Ge'ez
BR ˈgiːɛz
AM giˈɛz, geɪˈɛz

geezer
BR ˈgiːzə(r), -z
AM ˈgizər, -z

gefilte fish
BR gɪˈfɪltə fɪʃ
AM gəˈfɪltə ˌfɪʃ

Gehenna
BR gɪˈhɛnə(r)
AM gəˈhɛnə

Gehrig
BR ˈgɛrɪg
AM ˈgɛrɪg

Geiger counter
BR ˈgʌɪgə ˌkaʊntə(r), -z
AM ˈgaɪgər ˌkaʊn(t)ər, -z

Geikie
BR ˈgiːki
AM ˈgiki

Geisel
BR ˈgʌɪsl
AM ˈgaɪsəl

geisha
BR ˈgeɪʃə(r), -z
AM ˈgeɪʃə, ˈgiʃə, -z

Geissler
BR ˈgʌɪslə(r)
AM ˈgeɪslər

gel
BR dʒɛl, -z, -ɪŋ, -d
AM dʒɛl, -z, -ɪŋ, -d

gelada
BR dʒɪˈlɑːdə(r), -z
AM ˈdʒɛlədə, ˈgɛlədə, dʒəˈlɑdə, gəˈlɑdə, -z

gelatin
BR ˈdʒɛlətɪn
AM ˈdʒɛlətn, ˈdʒɛlədən

gelatine
BR ˈdʒɛlətiːn
AM ˈdʒɛlətn, ˈdʒɛlədən

gelatinisation
BR dʒɪˌlatɪnʌɪˈzeɪʃn
AM dʒɛˌlætnˌaɪˈzeɪʃən, ˌdʒɛlədəˌnaɪˈzeɪʃən, dʒɛˌlætn̩əˈzeɪʃən, ˌdʒɛlədənəˈzeɪʃən

gelatinise
BR dʒɪˈlatɪnʌɪz, -ɪz, -ɪŋ, -d
AM dʒəˈlætnˌaɪz, ˈdʒɛlədəˌnaɪz, -ɪz, -ɪŋ, -d

gelatinization
BR dʒɪˌlatɪnʌɪˈzeɪʃn
AM dʒɛˌlætnˌaɪˈzeɪʃən, ˌdʒɛlədəˌnaɪˈzeɪʃən, dʒɛˌlætn̩əˈzeɪʃən, ˌdʒɛlədənəˈzeɪʃən

gelatinize
BR dʒɪˈlatɪnʌɪz, -ɪz, -ɪŋ, -d
AM dʒəˈlætnˌaɪz, ˈdʒɛlədəˌnaɪz, -ɪz, -ɪŋ, -d

gelatinous
BR dʒɪˈlatɪnəs
AM dʒəˈlætn̩əs

gelatinously
BR dʒɪˈlatɪnəsli
AM dʒəˈlætn̩əsli

gelation
BR dʒɪˈleɪʃn, dʒɛˈleɪʃn
AM dʒəˈleɪʃən, dʒɛˈleɪʃən

gelato
BR dʒɪˈlatəʊ
AM dʒəˈlædoʊ

gelcoat
BR ˈdʒɛlkəʊt, -s
AM ˈdʒɛlˌkoʊt, -s

geld
BR gɛld, -z, -ɪŋ, -ɪd
AM gɛld, -z, -ɪŋ, -əd

Geldart
BR ˈgɛldɑːt
AM ˈgɛldɑrt

Gelderland
BR ˈgɛldəland
AM ˈgɛldərˌlænd
DU ˈxɛldərˌlɑnt

gelding
BR ˈgɛldɪŋ, -z
AM ˈgɛldɪŋ, -z

Geldof
BR ˈgɛldɒf
AM ˈgɛldɔf, ˈgɛldɑf

gelid
BR ˈdʒɛlɪd
AM ˈdʒɛlid

gelignite
BR ˈdʒɛlɪgnʌɪt
AM ˈdʒɛləgˌnaɪt

Gell
BR dʒɛl, gɛl
AM gɛl

Gelligaer
BR ˌgɛlɪˈgʌɪə(r), ˌgɛθlɪˈgʌɪə(r), ˌgɛlɪˈgɛː(r), ˌgɛθlɪˈgɛː(r)
AM ˌgɛləˈgɛ(ə)r

Gell-Mann
BR ˌgɛlˈman
AM ˈgɛlˈmæn

gelly
BR ˈdʒɛli
AM ˈdʒɛli

gelsemium
BR dʒɛlˈsiːmɪəm
AM dʒɛlˈsimiəm

gelt
BR gɛlt
AM gɛlt

gem
BR dʒɛm, -z
AM dʒɛm, -z

Gemara
BR gəˈmɑːrə(r), gɛˈmɑːrə(r)
AM gəˈmɑrə

gematria
BR gɪˈmeɪtrɪə(r)
AM gəˈmeɪtriə

geminal
BR ˈdʒɛmɪnl
AM ˈdʒɛmənəl

geminally
BR ˈdʒɛmɪnəli, ˈdʒɛmɪnl̩i
AM ˈdʒɛmənəli

geminate¹
adjective
BR ˈdʒɛmɪnət
AM ˈdʒɛmənət

geminate²
verb
BR ˈdʒɛmɪneɪt, -s, -ɪŋ, -ɪd
AM ˈdʒɛməˌneɪ|t, -ts, -dɪŋ, -dɪd

gemination
BR ˌdʒɛmɪˈneɪʃn
AM ˌdʒɛməˈneɪʃən

Gemini¹
constellation
BR ˈdʒɛmɪnʌɪ, ˈdʒɛmɪniː
AM ˈdʒɛməˌnaɪ, ˈdʒɛməˌni

Gemini²
spacecraft
BR ˈdʒɛmɪniː
AM ˈdʒɛməˌnaɪ

Geminian
BR ˌdʒɛmɪˈnʌɪən, ˌdʒɛmɪˈniːən, -z
AM ˌdʒɛməˈnaɪən, ˌdʒɛməˈniən, -z

Geminids
BR ˈdʒɛmɪnɪdz
AM ˈdʒɛmənɪdz

gemlike
BR ˈdʒɛmlʌɪk
AM ˈdʒɛmˌlaɪk

gemma
BR ˈdʒɛmə(r), -z
AM ˈdʒɛmə, -z

gemmae
BR ˈdʒɛmiː
AM ˈdʒɛmi, ˈdʒɛmaɪ

gemmation
BR dʒɛˈmeɪʃn
AM dʒɛˈmeɪʃən

Gemmell
BR ˈgɛml
AM ˈgɛml

gemmiferous
BR dʒɛˈmɪf(ə)rəs
AM dʒɛˈmɪf(ə)rəs

Gemmill
BR ˈgɛml
AM ˈgɛml

gemmiparous
BR dʒɛˈmɪp(ə)rəs
AM dʒɛˈmɪpərəs

gemmologist
BR dʒɛˈmɒlədʒɪst, -s
AM dʒɛˈmɑlədʒəst, -s

gemmology
BR dʒɛˈmɒlədʒi
AM dʒɛˈmɑlədʒi

gemmule
BR ˈdʒɛmjuːl, -z
AM ˈdʒɛˌm(j)ul, -z

gemmy
BR ˈdʒɛmi
AM ˈdʒɛmi

gemologist
BR dʒɛˈmɒlədʒɪst, -s
AM dʒɛˈmɑlədʒəst, -s

gemology
BR dʒɛˈmɒlədʒi
AM dʒɛˈmɑlədʒi

gemsbok
BR ˈgɛmzbɒk, -s
AM ˈgɛmzˌbɑk, -s

gemstone
BR ˈdʒɛmstəʊn, -z
AM ˈdʒɛmˌstoʊn, -z

gemütlich
BR gəˈmuːtlɪk, gəˈmuːtlɪʃ, gəˈmuːtlɪx
AM gəˈmʊtlɪk

gen
BR dʒɛn, -z, -ɪŋ, -d
AM dʒɛn, -z, -ɪŋ, -d

gendarme
BR ˈʒɒndɑːm, ˈʒɒ̃dɑːm, -z
AM ˌʒɑnˈdɑrm, -z

gendarmerie
BR ʒɒnˈdɑːm(ə)r|i, ʒɒ̃ˈdɑːm(ə)r|i, -ɪz
AM ˌʒɑnˈdɑrməri, -z

gender
BR ˈdʒɛndə(r), -z
AM ˈdʒɛndər, -z

gene
BR dʒiːn, -z
AM dʒin, -z

genealogical
BR ˌdʒiːnɪəˈlɒdʒɪkl
AM ˌdʒiniəˈlɑdʒəkəl

genealogically
BR ˌdʒiːnɪəˈlɒdʒɪkli
AM ˌdʒiniəˈlɑdʒək(ə)li

genealogise
BR ˌdʒiːnɪˈalədʒʌɪz, -ɪz, -ɪŋ, -d
AM ˌdʒiniˈɑləˌdʒaɪz, -ɪz, -ɪŋ, -d

genealogist
BR ˌdʒiːnɪˈalədʒɪst, -s
AM ˌdʒiniˈɑlədʒəst, ˌdʒiniˈælədʒəst, -s

genealogize
BR ˌdʒiːnɪˈalədʒʌɪz, -ɪz, -ɪŋ, -d
AM ˌdʒiniˈɑləˌdʒaɪz, -ɪz, -ɪŋ, -d

genealogy
BR ˌdʒiːnɪˈalədʒ|i, -ɪz
AM ˌdʒiniˈɑlədʒi, ˌdʒiniˈælədʒi, -z

genera
BR ˈdʒɛn(ə)rə(r)
AM ˈdʒɛnərə

generable
BR ˈdʒɛn(ə)rəbl
AM ˈdʒɛnərəbəl

general
BR ˈdʒɛn(ə)rəl, ˈdʒɛn(ə)rl̩, -z
AM ˈdʒɛn(ə)rəl, -z

generalisability
BR ˌdʒɛn(ə)rəlʌɪzəˈbɪlɪti, ˌdʒɛn(ə)rl̩ʌɪzəˈbɪlɪti
AM ˌdʒɛn(ə)rəˌlaɪzəˈbɪlɪdi

generalisable
BR ˈdʒɛn(ə)rəlʌɪzəbl, ˈdʒɛn(ə)rl̩ʌɪzəbl
AM ˌdʒɛn(ə)rəˌlaɪzəbəl

generalisation
BR ˌdʒɛn(ə)rəlʌɪˈzeɪʃn, ˌdʒɛn(ə)rl̩ʌɪˈzeɪʃn, -z
AM ˌdʒɛn(ə)rələˈzeɪʃən, ˌdʒɛn(ə)rəˌlaɪˈzeɪʃən, -z

generalise
BR ˈdʒɛn(ə)rəlʌɪz, ˈdʒɛn(ə)rl̩ʌɪz, -ɪz, -ɪŋ, -d
AM ˈdʒɛn(ə)rəˌlaɪz, -ɪz, -ɪŋ, -d

generaliser
BR ˈdʒɛn(ə)rəlʌɪzə(r), ˈdʒɛn(ə)rl̩ʌɪzə(r), -z
AM ˈdʒɛn(ə)rəˌlaɪzər, -z

generalissimo
BR ˌdʒɛn(ə)rəˈlɪsɪməʊ, -z
AM ˌdʒɛn(ə)rəˈlɪsəˌmoʊ, -z

generalist
BR ˈdʒɛn(ə)rəlɪst, ˈdʒɛn(ə)rl̩ɪst, -s
AM ˈdʒɛn(ə)rələst, -s

generality
BR ˌdʒɛnəˈralɪt|i, -ɪz
AM ˌdʒɛnəˈrælədi, -z

generalizability
BR ˌdʒɛn(ə)rəlʌɪzəˈbɪlɪti, ˌdʒɛn(ə)rl̩ʌɪzəˈbɪlɪti
AM ˌdʒɛn(ə)rəˌlaɪzəˈbɪlɪdi

generalizable
BR ˈdʒɛn(ə)rəlʌɪzəbl, ˈdʒɛn(ə)rl̩ʌɪzəbl
AM ˌdʒɛn(ə)rəˌlaɪzəbəl

generalization
BR ˌdʒɛn(ə)rəlʌɪˈzeɪʃn, ˌdʒɛn(ə)rl̩ʌɪˈzeɪʃn, -z
AM ˌdʒɛn(ə)rələˈzeɪʃən, ˌdʒɛn(ə)rəˌlaɪˈzeɪʃən, -z

generalize
BR ˈdʒɛn(ə)rəlʌɪz, ˈdʒɛn(ə)rl̩ʌɪz, -ɪz, -ɪŋ, -d
AM ˈdʒɛn(ə)rəˌlaɪz, -ɪz, -ɪŋ, -d

generalizer
BR ˈdʒɛn(ə)rəlʌɪzə(r), ˈdʒɛn(ə)rl̩ʌɪzə(r), -z
AM ˈdʒɛn(ə)rəˌlaɪzər, -z

generally
BR ˈdʒɛn(ə)rəli, ˈdʒɛn(ə)rl̩i
AM ˈdʒɛn(ə)rəli

generalness
BR ˈdʒɛn(ə)rəlnəs, ˈdʒɛn(ə)rl̩nəs
AM ˈdʒɛn(ə)rəlnəs

generalship
BR ˈdʒɛn(ə)rəlʃɪp, ˈdʒɛn(ə)rl̩ʃɪp, -s
AM ˈdʒɛn(ə)rəlˌʃɪp, -s

generate
BR ˈdʒɛnəreɪt, -s, -ɪŋ, -ɪd
AM ˈdʒɛnəˌreɪ|t, -ts, -dɪŋ, -dɪd

generation
BR ˌdʒɛnəˈreɪʃn, -z
AM ˌdʒɛnəˈreɪʃən, -z

generational
BR ˌdʒɛnəˈreɪʃn̩(ə)l, ˌdʒɛnəˈreɪʃən(ə)l
AM ˌdʒɛnəˈreɪʃ(ə)nəl

generative
BR ˈdʒɛn(ə)rətɪv
AM ˈdʒɛn(ə)rədɪv, ˈdʒɛnəˌreɪdɪv

generatively
BR ˈdʒɛn(ə)rətɪvli
AM ˈdʒɛn(ə)rədɪvli, ˈdʒɛnəˌreɪdɪvli

generativeness
BR ˈdʒɛn(ə)rətɪvnɪs
AM ˈdʒɛn(ə)rədɪvnɪs, ˈdʒɛnəˌreɪdɪvnɪs

generator
BR ˈdʒɛnəreɪtə(r), -z
AM ˈdʒɛnəˌreɪdər, -z

generic
BR dʒɪˈnɛrɪk
AM dʒəˈnɛrɪk

generically
BR dʒɪˈnɛrɪkli
AM dʒəˈnɛrək(ə)li

generosity
BR ˌdʒɛnəˈrɒsɪti
AM ˌdʒɛnəˈrɑsədi

generous
BR ˈdʒɛn(ə)rəs
AM ˈdʒɛn(ə)rəs

generously
BR ˈdʒɛn(ə)rəsli
AM ˈdʒɛn(ə)rəsli

generousness
BR ˈdʒɛn(ə)rəsnəs
AM ˈdʒɛn(ə)rəsnəs

genesis
BR ˈdʒɛnɪsɪs, -ɪz
AM ˈdʒɛnəsəs, -əz

Genet
BR ʒəˈneɪ
AM dʒəˈneɪ

genet
BR ˈdʒɛnɪt, -s
AM ˈdʒɛnət, -s

genetic
BR dʒɪˈnɛtɪk, -s
AM dʒəˈnɛdɪk, -s

genetically
BR dʒɪˈnɛtɪkli
AM dʒəˈnɛdək(ə)li

geneticist
BR dʒɪˈnɛtɪsɪst, -s
AM dʒəˈnɛdəsəst, -s

genette
BR dʒɪˈnɛt, -s
AM ˈdʒɛnət, -s

Geneva
BR dʒɪˈniːvə(r)
AM dʒəˈnivə

Genevan
BR dʒɪˈniːvn, -z
AM dʒəˈnivən, -z

genever
BR dʒɪˈniːvə(r)
AM dʒəˈnivər

Genevieve
BR ˈdʒɛnɪviːv
AM ˈdʒɛnəviv

Genghis Khan
BR ˌgɛŋgɪs ˈkɑːn
AM ˈgɛŋgɪs ˈkɑn

genial[1]
jovial, kindly
BR ˈdʒiːnɪəl
AM ˈdʒinjəl, ˈdʒiniəl

genial[2]
of the chin
BR dʒɪˈniːəl, dʒɪˈnʌɪəl
AM dʒəˈniəl

geniality
BR ˌdʒiːnɪˈalɪt|i, -ɪz
AM ˌdʒiniˈælədi, ˌdʒinˈjælədi, -z

genially
BR ˈdʒiːnɪəli
AM ˈdʒinjəli, ˈdʒiniəli

genic
BR ˈdʒɛnɪk
AM ˈdʒɛnɪk

genie
BR ˈdʒiːn|i, -ɪz
AM ˈdʒini, -z

genii
BR ˈdʒiːnɪʌɪ
AM ˈdʒiniˌaɪ

genipapo
BR ˌdʒɛnɪˈpapəʊ, -z
AM ˌdʒɛnəˈpɑpoʊ, -z

genital
BR ˈdʒɛnɪtl, -z
AM ˈdʒɛnədl, -z

genitalia
BR ˌdʒɛnɪˈteɪlɪə(r)
AM dʒɛnəˈteɪljə, ˌdʒɛnəˈteɪliə

genitally
BR ˈdʒɛnɪtl̩i
AM ˈdʒɛnədl̩i

genitival
BR ˌdʒɛnɪˈtʌɪvl
AM ˌdʒɛnəˈtaɪvəl

genitivally
BR ˌdʒɛnɪˈtʌɪvl̩i
AM ˌdʒɛnəˈtaɪvəli

genitive
BR ˈdʒɛnɪtɪv, -z
AM ˈdʒɛnədɪv, -z

genito-urinary
BR ˌdʒɛnɪtəʊˈjʊərɪn(ə)ri, ˌdʒɛnɪtəʊˈjɔːrɪn(ə)ri
AM ˌdʒɛnətoʊˈjʊrəˌnɛri

genius
BR ˈdʒiːnɪəs, -ɪz
AM ˈdʒinjəs, -ɪz

genizah
BR dʒɛˈniːzə(r), gɛˈniːzə(r), -z
AM dʒəˈniˌzɑ, -z

genlock
BR ˈdʒɛnlɒk, -s
AM ˈdʒɛnˌlɑk, -s

Gennesaret
BR gɪˈnɛz(ə)rɪt
AM gɛˈnɛzərət

Gennesareth
BR gɪˈnɛz(ə)rɪt
AM gɛˈnɛzərət

genoa
BR ˈdʒɛnəʊə(r), dʒɪˈnəʊə(r), -z
AM dʒəˈnoʊə, -z

genocidal
BR ˌdʒɛnəˈsʌɪdl
AM ˌdʒɛnəˈsaɪdəl

genocide
BR ˈdʒɛnəsʌɪd
AM ˈdʒɛnəˌsaɪd

Genoese
BR ˌdʒɛnəʊˈiːz
AM ˌdʒɛnoʊˈiz

genome
BR ˈdʒiːnəʊm, -z
AM ˈdʒiˌnoʊm, -z

genotype
BR ˈdʒɛnətʌɪp, -s
AM ˈdʒinəˌtaɪp, ˈdʒɛnəˌtaɪp

genotypic
BR ˌdʒɛnəˈtɪpɪk
AM ˌdʒɛnəˈtɪpɪk

Genova
BR ˈdʒɛnəvə(r)
AM ˈdʒɛnəvə

genre
BR 'ʒɒ̃rə(r), 'ʒɒnrə(r), 'ʒɑːnrə(r), -z
AM 'ʒɑnrə, -z

gens
BR dʒɛnz, -ɪz
AM dʒɛnz, -əz

gent
BR dʒɛnt, -s
AM dʒɛnt, -s

genteel
BR dʒɛn'tiːl
AM dʒɛn'til

genteelism
BR dʒɛn'tiːlɪz(ə)m
AM dʒɛn'ti,lɪzəm

genteelly
BR dʒɛn'tiːlli
AM dʒɛn'ti(l)li

genteelness
BR dʒɛn'tiːlnɪs
AM dʒɛn'tilnɪs

gentes
BR 'dʒɛntiːz
AM 'dʒɛn,tiz

gentian
BR 'dʒɛnʃn, 'dʒɛnʃɪən, -z
AM 'dʒɛn(t)ʃən, -z

gentile
BR 'dʒɛntʌɪl, -z
AM 'dʒɛn,taɪl, -z

gentility
BR dʒɛn'tɪlɪti
AM dʒɛn'tɪlɨdi

gentle
BR 'dʒɛntl, -ə(r), -ɨst
AM 'dʒɛn(t)əl, -ər, -əst

gentlefolk
BR 'dʒɛntlfəʊk, -s
AM 'dʒɛn(t)l,foʊk, -s

gentleman
BR 'dʒɛntlmən
AM 'dʒɛn(t)lmən

gentlemanliness
BR 'dʒɛntlmənlɪnɪs
AM 'dʒɛn(t)lmənlinɪs

gentlemanly
BR 'dʒɛntlmənli
AM 'dʒɛn(t)lmənli

gentlemen
BR 'dʒɛntlmən
AM 'dʒɛn(t)lmən

gentleness
BR 'dʒɛntlnəs
AM 'dʒɛn(t)lnəs

gentlewoman
BR 'dʒɛntl,wʊmən
AM 'dʒɛn(t)l,wʊmən

gentlewomen
BR 'dʒɛntl,wɪmɪn
AM 'dʒɛn(t)l,wɪmɪn

gently
BR 'dʒɛntli
AM 'dʒɛn(t)li

gentoo
BR 'dʒɛntuː, -z
AM 'dʒɛn,tu, -z

gentrification
BR ,dʒɛntrɪfɪ'keɪʃn
AM ,dʒɛntrəfə'keɪʃən

gentrifier
BR 'dʒɛntrɪfʌɪə(r), -z
AM 'dʒɛntrə,faɪər, -z

gentrify
BR 'dʒɛntrɪfʌɪ, -z, -ɪŋ, -d
AM 'dʒɛntrə,faɪ, -z, -ɪŋ, -d

gentry
BR 'dʒɛntri
AM 'dʒɛntri

genuflect
BR 'dʒɛnjʉflɛkt, -s, -ɪŋ, -ɨd
AM 'dʒɛnjə,flɛk|(t), -(t)s, -tɪŋ, -təd

genuflection
BR ,dʒɛnjʉ'flɛkʃn, -z
AM ,dʒɛnjə'flɛkʃən, -z

genuflector
BR 'dʒɛnjʉflɛktə(r), -z
AM 'dʒɛnjə,flɛktər, -z

genuflectory
BR ,dʒɛnjʉ'flɛkt(ə)ri
AM ,dʒɛnjə'flɛk,tɔri

genuflexion
BR ,dʒɛnjʉ'flɛkʃn, -z
AM ,dʒɛnjə'flɛkʃən, -z

genuine
BR 'dʒɛnjʊɪn
AM 'dʒɛnjəwən

genuinely
BR 'dʒɛnjʊɪnli
AM 'dʒɛnjəwənli

genuineness
BR 'dʒɛnjʊɪnnəs
AM 'dʒɛnjəwə(n)nəs

genus
BR 'dʒiːnəs
AM 'dʒinəs

geobotanist
BR ,dʒiːəʊ'bɒtənɪst, ,dʒiːəʊ'bɒtn̩ɪst, -s
AM ¦dʒioʊ'batn̩əst, -s

geobotany
BR ,dʒiːəʊ'bɒtəni, ,dʒiːə'bɒtn̩i
AM ¦dʒioʊ'batn̩i

geocentric
BR ,dʒiːə(ʊ)'sɛntrɪk, dʒɪə'sɛntrɪk
AM ¦dʒioʊ'sɛntrɪk

geocentrically
BR ,dʒiːə(ʊ)'sɛntrɪkli, dʒɪə'sɛntrɪkli
AM ¦dʒioʊ'sɛntrək(ə)li

geochemical
BR ,dʒiːəʊ'kɛmɪkl
AM ¦dʒioʊ'kɛməkəl

geochemist
BR ,dʒiːəʊ'kɛmɪst, -s
AM ¦dʒioʊ'kɛməst, -s

geochemistry
BR ,dʒiːəʊ'kɛmɪstri
AM ¦dʒioʊ'kɛməstri

geochronological
BR ,dʒiːəʊ,krɒnə'lɒdʒɪkl
AM ¦dʒioʊ,krɑnə'lɑdʒəkəl

geochronologist
BR ,dʒiːəʊkrə'nɒlədʒɪst, -s
AM ¦dʒioʊkrə'nɑlədʒəst, -s

geochronology
BR ,dʒiːəʊkrə'nɒlədʒi
AM ¦dʒioʊkrə'nɑlədʒi

geode
BR 'dʒiːəʊd, -z
AM 'dʒi,oʊd, -z

geodesic
BR ,dʒiːə(ʊ)'dɛsɪk, ,dʒiːə(ʊ)'diːsɪk, ,dʒiːə(ʊ)'diːzɪk, dʒɪə'dɛsɪk, dʒɪə'diːsɪk, dʒɪə'diːzɪk
AM ¦dʒioʊ'dɛsɪk

geodesist
BR dʒɪ'ɒdɪsɪst, -s
AM dʒi'ɑdəsəst, -s

geodesy
BR dʒɪ'ɒdɪsi
AM dʒi'ɑdəsi

geodetic
BR ,dʒiːə(ʊ)'dɛtɪk, dʒɪə'dɛtɪk
AM ¦dʒiə'dɛdɪk

geodic
BR dʒɪ'ɒdɪk
AM dʒi'ɑdɪk

Geoff
BR dʒɛf
AM dʒɛf

Geoffrey
BR 'dʒɛfri
AM 'dʒɛfri

geographer
BR dʒɪ'ɒgrəfə(r), 'dʒɒgrəfə(r), -z
AM dʒɪ'ɑgrəfər, -z

geographic
BR ,dʒiːə'grafɪk, dʒɪə'grafɪk
AM ,dʒiə'græfɪk

geographical
BR ,dʒiːə'grafɪkl, dʒɪə'grafɪkl
AM ,dʒiə'græfəkəl

geographically
BR ,dʒiːə'grafɪkli, dʒɪə'grafɪkli
AM ,dʒiə'græfək(ə)li

geography
BR dʒɪ'ɒgrəfi, 'dʒɒgrəfi
AM dʒɪ'ɑgrəfi

geoid
BR 'dʒiːɔɪd, -z
AM 'dʒi,ɔɪd, -z

geologic
BR ,dʒiːə'lɒdʒɪk, dʒɪə'lɒdʒɪk
AM ,dʒiə'lɑdʒɪk

geological
BR ,dʒiːə'lɒdʒɪkl, dʒɪə'lɒdʒɪkl
AM ,dʒiə'lɑdʒəkəl

geologically
BR ,dʒiːə'lɒdʒɪkli, dʒɪə'lɒdʒɪkli
AM ,dʒiə'lɑdʒək(ə)li

geologise
BR dʒɪ'ɒlədʒʌɪz, -ɨz, -ɪŋ, -d
AM dʒi'ɑlə,dʒaɪz, -ɨz, -ɪŋ, -d

geologist
BR dʒɪ'ɒlədʒɪst, -s
AM dʒi'ɑlədʒəst, -s

geologize
BR dʒɪ'ɒlədʒʌɪz, -ɨz, -ɪŋ, -d
AM dʒi'ɑlə,dʒaɪz, -ɨz, -ɪŋ, -d

geology
BR dʒɪ'ɒlədʒi
AM dʒi'ɑlədʒi

geomagnetic
BR ,dʒiːə(ʊ)mag'nɛtɪk
AM ¦dʒiə,mæg'nɛdɪk

geomagnetically
BR ,dʒiːə(ʊ)mag'nɛtɪkli
AM ¦dʒiə,mæg'nɛdək(ə)li

geomagnetism
BR ,dʒiːəʊ'magnɪtɪz(ə)m
AM ,dʒiə'mægnə,tɪzəm

geomancy
BR 'dʒiːəmansi
AM 'dʒiə,mænsi

geomantic
BR ,dʒiːə(ʊ)'mantɪk
AM ¦dʒiə¦mæn(t)ɪk

geometer
BR dʒɪ'ɒmɪtə(r), -z
AM dʒi'ɑmədər, -z

geometric
BR ,dʒiːə'mɛtrɪk, dʒɪə'mɛtrɪk
AM ,dʒiə'mɛtrɪk

geometrical
BR ,dʒiːə'mɛtrɪkl, dʒɪə'mɛtrɪkl
AM ,dʒiə'mɛtrəkəl

geometrically
BR ,dʒiːə'mɛtrɪkli, dʒɪə'mɛtrɪkli
AM ,dʒiə'mɛtrək(ə)li

geometrician
BR ,dʒiːə(ʊ)mɪ'trɪʃn, -z
AM dʒi,ɑmə'trɪʃən, -z

geometrise
BR dʒɪ'ɒmɪtrʌɪz, 'dʒɒmɪtrʌɪz, -ɨz, -ɪŋ, -d
AM dʒi'ɑmə,traɪz, -ɨz, -ɪŋ, -d

geometrize
BR dʒɪˈɒmɨtrʌɪz, ˈdʒɒmɨtrʌɪz, -ɨz, -ɪŋ, -d
AM dʒiˈɑməˌtraɪz, -ɨz, -ɪŋ, -d

geometry
BR dʒɪˈɒmɨtri, ˈdʒɒmɨtri
AM dʒiˈɑmətri

geomorphological
BR ˌdʒɪəʊˌmɔːfəˈlɒdʒɨkl
AM ˈdʒioʊˌmɔrfəˈlɑdʒəkəl

geomorphologist
BR ˌdʒɪə(ʊ)mɔːˈfɒlədʒɪst, -s
AM ˈdʒioʊˌmɔrˈfɑlədʒəst, -s

geomorphology
BR ˌdʒɪə(ʊ)mɔːˈfɒlədʒi
AM ˈdʒioʊˌmɔrˈfɑlədʒi

geophagy
BR dʒɪˈɒfədʒi
AM dʒiˈɑfədʒi

geophone
BR ˈdʒiːə(ʊ)fəʊn, -z
AM ˈdʒiəˌfoʊn, -z

geophysical
BR ˌdʒiːə(ʊ)ˈfɪzɨkl
AM ˌdʒiəˈfɪzɨkəl

geophysically
BR ˌdʒiːə(ʊ)ˈfɪzɨkli
AM ˌdʒiəˈfɪzɨk(ə)li

geophysicist
BR ˌdʒiːə(ʊ)ˈfɪzɨsɪst, -s
AM ˌdʒiəˈfɪzɨsɪst, -s

geophysics
BR ˌdʒiːə(ʊ)ˈfɪzɪks
AM ˌdʒiəˈfɪzɪks

geopolitical
BR ˌdʒiːəʊpəˈlɪtɨkl
AM ˌdʒioʊpəˈlɪdɪkəl

geopolitically
BR ˌdʒiːəʊpəˈlɪtɨkli
AM ˌdʒioʊpəˈlɪdɪk(ə)li

geopolitician
BR ˌdʒiːəʊˌpɒlɪˈtɪʃn, -z
AM ˈdʒioʊˌpɑləˈtɪʃən, -z

geopolitics
BR ˌdʒiːə(ʊ)ˈpɒlɪtɪks
AM ˌdʒioʊˈpɑlədɪks

Geordie
BR ˈdʒɔːd|i, -ɪz
AM ˈdʒɔrdi, -z

George
BR dʒɔːdʒ
AM dʒɔrdʒ

Georgetown
BR ˈdʒɔːdʒtaʊn
AM ˈdʒɔrdʒˌtaʊn

Georgette
BR dʒɔːˈdʒɛt
AM dʒɔrˈdʒɛt

Georgia
BR ˈdʒɔːdʒə(r)
AM ˈdʒɔrdʒə

Georgian
BR ˈdʒɔːdʒ(ə)n, -z
AM ˈdʒɔrdʒən, -z

Georgiana
BR ˌdʒɔːdʒɪˈɑːnə(r)
AM ˌdʒɔrdʒiˈænə

georgic
BR ˈdʒɔːdʒɪk, -s
AM ˈdʒɔrdʒɪk, -s

Georgie
BR ˈdʒɔːdʒi
AM ˈdʒɔrdʒi

Georgina
BR dʒɔːˈdʒiːnə(r)
AM dʒɔrˈdʒinə

geoscience
BR ˌdʒiːəʊˈsʌɪəns, -ɨz
AM ˈdʒioʊˌsaɪəns, -əz

geoscientist
BR ˌdʒiːəʊˈsʌɪəntɪst, -s
AM ˌdʒioʊˈsaɪən(t)əst, -s

geosphere
BR ˈdʒiːə(ʊ)sfɪə(r), -z
AM ˈdʒioʊˌsfɪ(ə)r, -z

geostationary
BR ˌdʒiːə(ʊ)ˈsteɪʃn(ə)ri
AM ˌdʒioʊˈsteɪʃənɛri

geostrophic
BR ˌdʒiːəˈstrɒfɪk, ˌdʒiːəˈstrəʊfɪk
AM ˌdʒiəˈstrɑfɪk

geosynchronous
BR ˌdʒiːə(ʊ)ˈsɪŋkrənəs
AM ˌdʒioʊˈsɪŋkrənəs

geotechnical
BR ˌdʒiːə(ʊ)ˈtɛknɨkl
AM ˌdʒiəˈtɛknəkəl

geothermal
BR ˌdʒiːə(ʊ)ˈθəːml
AM ˌdʒioʊˈθərməl

geothermally
BR ˌdʒiːə(ʊ)ˈθəːml̩i
AM ˌdʒioʊˈθərməli

geotropic
BR ˌdʒiːəˈtrɒpɪk, ˌdʒiːəˈtrəʊpɪk
AM ˌdʒiəˈtrɑpɪk

geotropism
BR ˌdʒiːəʊˈtrəʊpɪz(ə)m
AM ˌdʒiəˈtrɑˌpɪzəm

Geraint
BR ˈgɛrʌɪnt
AM ˈdʒɛraɪnt

Gerald
BR ˈdʒɛrəld, ˈdʒɛrl̩d
AM ˈdʒɛrəl(d)

Geraldine
BR ˈdʒɛrəldiːn, ˈdʒɛrl̩diːn
AM ˈdʒɛrəlˌdin

Geraldton
BR ˈdʒɛrəl(d)t(ə)n, ˈdʒɛrl̩(d)t(ə)n
AM ˈdʒɛrəl(d)tən

geranium
BR dʒɪˈreɪnɪəm, -z
AM dʒəˈreɪniəm, dʒəˈreɪnjəm, -z

Gerard
BR ˈdʒɛrɑːd, dʒəˈrɑːd
AM dʒəˈrɑrd

gerbera
BR ˈdʒəːb(ə)rə(r), ˈgəːb(ə)rə(r), -z
AM ˈgərbərə, ˈdʒərbərə, dʒərˈbɛrə, -z

gerbil
BR ˈdʒəːb(ɪ)l, -z
AM ˈdʒərbəl, -z

Gerda
BR ˈgəːdə(r)
AM ˈgərdə

gerenuk
BR ˈgɛrənʊk, ˈdʒɛrənʊk, -s
AM ˈgɛrəˌnʊk, gəˈrɛnək, -s

gerfalcon
BR ˈdʒəːˌfɔːlk(ə)n, ˈdʒəːˌfalk(ə)n, -z
AM ˈdʒərˌfælkən, -z

geriatric
BR ˌdʒɛrɪˈatrɪk, -s
AM ˌdʒɛriˈætrɪk, -s

geriatrician
BR ˌdʒɛrɪəˈtrɪʃn, -z
AM ˌdʒɛriəˈtrɪʃən, -z

geriatrist
BR ˌdʒɛrɪˈatrɪst, -s
AM ˌdʒɛriˈætrəst, -s

gerkin
BR ˈgəːkɪn, -z
AM ˈgərkən, -z

germ
BR dʒəːm, -z
AM dʒərm, -z

Germaine
BR ʒəːˈmeɪn
AM ʒərˈmeɪn

German
BR ˈdʒəːmən, -z
AM ˈdʒərmən, -z

germander
BR dʒəːˈmandə(r), dʒəˈmandə(r), -z
AM dʒərˈmændər, -z

germane
BR dʒəːˈmeɪn, dʒəˈmeɪn
AM dʒərˈmeɪn

germanely
BR dʒəːˈmeɪnli, dʒəˈmeɪnli
AM dʒərˈmeɪnli

germaneness
BR dʒəːˈmeɪnnɨs, dʒəˈmeɪnnɨs
AM dʒərˈmeɪ(n)nɨs

Germanic
BR dʒəˈmanɪk
AM dʒərˈmænɪk

Germanicism
BR dʒəˈmanɨsɪz(ə)m, -z
AM dʒərˈmænəˌsɪzəm, -z

Germanicus
BR dʒəˈmanɨkəs
AM ˌdʒərˈmænəkəs

Germanisation
BR ˌdʒəːmənʌɪˈzeɪʃn
AM ˌdʒərmənəˈzeɪʃən, ˌdʒərməˌnaɪˈzeɪʃən

Germanise
BR ˈdʒəːmənʌɪz, -ɨz, -ɪŋ, -d
AM ˈdʒərməˌnaɪz, -ɨz, -ɪŋ, -d

Germaniser
BR ˈdʒəːmənʌɪzə(r), -z
AM ˈdʒərməˌnaɪzər, -z

Germanism
BR ˈdʒəːmənɪz(ə)m, -z
AM ˈdʒərməˌnɪzəm, -z

Germanist
BR ˈdʒəːmənɪst, -s
AM ˈdʒərmənəst, -s

germanium
BR dʒəːˈmeɪnɪəm, dʒəˈmeɪnɪəm
AM dʒɛrˈmeɪniəm

Germanization
BR ˌdʒəːmənʌɪˈzeɪʃən
AM ˌdʒərmənəˈzeɪʃən, ˌdʒərməˌnaɪˈzeɪʃən

Germanize
BR ˈdʒəːmənʌɪz, -ɨz, -ɪŋ, -d
AM ˈdʒərməˌnaɪz, -ɨz, -ɪŋ, -d

Germanizer
BR ˈdʒəːmənʌɪzə(r), -z
AM ˈdʒərməˌnaɪzər, -z

germanous
BR ˈdʒəːmənəs
AM ˈdʒərmənəs

Germany
BR ˈdʒəːmən|i, -ɪz
AM ˈdʒərməni, -z

germen
BR ˈdʒəːmən, -z
AM ˈdʒərmən, -z

germicidal
BR ˌdʒəːmɪˈsʌɪdl
AM ˈdʒərməˈsaɪdəl

germicide
BR ˈdʒəːmɪsʌɪd, -z, -əl
AM ˈdʒərməˌsaɪd, -z, -əl

germinal
BR ˈdʒəːmɪnl
AM ˈdʒərmənəl

germinally
BR ˈdʒəːmɪnl̩i
AM ˈdʒərmənəli

germinant
BR ˈdʒəːmɪnənt
AM ˈdʒərmənənt

germinate
BR 'dʒəːmɪneɪt, -s, -ɪŋ, -ɨd
AM 'dʒərmə,neɪ|t, -ts, -dɪŋ, -dɨd

germination
BR ,dʒəːmɪ'neɪʃn
AM ,dʒərmə'neɪʃən

germinative
BR 'dʒəːmɪnətɪv
AM 'dʒərmə,neɪdɪv

germinator
BR 'dʒəːmɪneɪtə(r), -z
AM 'dʒərmə,neɪdər, -z

Germiston
BR 'dʒəːmɪst(ə)n
AM 'dʒərməstən

Germolene
BR 'dʒəːməliːn
AM 'dʒərmə,lin

germon
BR 'dʒəːmən, -z
AM ʒər'mɔn, ʒər'mɑn, -z

germy
BR 'dʒəːm|i, -ɪə(r), -ɪɪst
AM 'dʒərmi, -ər, -ɨst

Geronimo
BR dʒɪ'rɒnɪməʊ
AM dʒə'rɑnə,moʊ

gerontocracy
BR ,dʒɛrən'tɒkrəs|i, ,dʒɛrn̩'tɒkrəsi, -ɪz
AM ,dʒɛrən'tɑkrəsi, -z

gerontological
BR dʒə,rɒntə'lɒdʒɪkl, ,dʒɛrn̩tə'lɒdʒɪkl
AM dʒə,rɑn(t)ə'lɑdʒəkəl

gerontologist
BR ,dʒɛrən'tɒlədʒɪst, ,dʒɛrn̩'tɒlədʒɪst, -s
AM ,dʒɛrən'tɑlədʒəst, -s

gerontology
BR ,dʒɛrən'tɒlədʒi, ,dʒɛrn̩'tɒlədʒi
AM ,dʒɛrən'tɑlədʒi

Gerrard
BR 'dʒɛrɑːd, dʒə'rɑːd
AM dʒə'rɑrd

Gerry
BR 'dʒɛri
AM 'dʒɛri

gerrymander
BR 'dʒɛrɪmand|ə(r), -əz, -(ə)rɪŋ, -əd
AM 'dʒɛri,mændər, -ərz, -(ə)rɪŋ, -ərd

gerrymanderer
BR 'dʒɛrɪmand(ə)rə(r), -z
AM 'dʒɛri,mænd(ə)rər, -z

Gershwin
BR 'gəːʃwɪn
AM 'gərʃwɪn

Gertie
BR 'gəːti
AM 'gərdi

Gertrude
BR 'gəːtruːd
AM 'gər,trud

gerund
BR 'dʒɛrənd, 'dʒɛrn̩d, 'dʒɛrʌnd, -z
AM 'dʒɛrənd, -z

gerundial
BR dʒɪ'rʌndɪəl, dʒɛ'rʌndɪəl
AM dʒə'rəndiəl

gerundival
BR ,dʒɛrən'dʌɪvl, ,dʒɛrn̩'dʌɪvl, ,dʒɛrʌn'dʌɪvl
AM ,dʒɛrən'daɪvəl

gerundive
BR dʒɪ'rʌndɪv, dʒɛ'rʌndɪv, -z
AM dʒə'rəndɪv, -z

Gervaise
BR 'dʒəːveɪz, dʒəː'veɪz, 'dʒəːveɪs, dʒəː'veɪs
AM ʒər'veɪ(z)

Gervase
BR 'dʒəːveɪz, dʒəː'veɪz, 'dʒəːveɪs, dʒəː'veɪs
AM ʒər'veɪ(z)

gesnieriad
BR gɛs'nɪərɪad, dʒɛs'nɪərɪad, -z
AM gɛs'nɪriæd, dʒɛs'nɪriæd, -z

gesso
BR 'dʒɛsəʊ
AM 'dʒɛsoʊ

gest
BR dʒɛst, -s
AM dʒɛst, -s

gestagen
BR 'dʒɛstədʒ(ə)n, -z
AM 'dʒɛstədʒən, 'dʒɛstə,dʒɛn, -z

gestagenic
BR ,dʒɛstə'dʒɛnɪk
AM ,dʒɛstə'dʒɛnɪk

gestalt
BR gə'ʃtalt, gə'ʃtɑːlt
AM gə'ʃtɑlt, gə'stɑlt

gestaltism
BR gə'ʃtaltɪz(ə)m, gə'ʃtɑːltɪz(ə)m
AM gə'ʃtɑl,tɪzəm, gə'stɑl,tɪzəm

gestaltist
BR gə'ʃtaltɪst, gə'ʃtɑːltɪst, -s
AM gə'ʃtɑltəst, gə'stɑltəst, -s

Gestapo
BR gɛ'stɑːpəʊ, gə'stɑːpəʊ
AM gə'stɑpoʊ

gestate
BR dʒɛ'steɪt, 'dʒɛsteɪt, -s, -ɪŋ, -ɨd
AM 'dʒɛ,steɪ|t, -ts, -dɪŋ, -dɨd

gestation
BR dʒɛ'steɪʃn
AM dʒɛ'steɪʃən

gestatorial
BR ,dʒɛstə'tɔːrɪəl
AM ,dʒɛstə'tɔriəl

gestatory
BR dʒɛ'steɪt(ə)ri, 'dʒɛstət(ə)ri
AM 'dʒɛstə,tɔri

Gestetner
BR gɛ'stɛtnə(r), gɪ'stɛtnə(r)
AM gə'stɛtnər

gesticulate
BR dʒɛ'stɪkjʉleɪt, dʒə'stɪkjʉleɪt, -s, -ɪŋ, -ɨd
AM dʒɛ'stɪkjə,leɪ|t, -ts, -dɪŋ, -dɨd

gesticulation
BR dʒɛ,stɪkjʉ'leɪʃn, dʒə,stɪkjʉ'leɪʃn, -z
AM dʒɛ,stɪkjə'leɪʃən, -z

gesticulative
BR dʒɛ'stɪkjʉlətɪv, dʒə'stɪkjʉlətɪv
AM dʒɛ'stɪkjə,leɪdɪv, dʒɛ'stɪkjələdɪv

gesticulator
BR dʒɛ'stɪkjʉleɪtə(r), dʒə'stɪkjʉleɪtə(r), -z
AM dʒɛ'stɪkjə,leɪdər, -z

gesticulatory
BR dʒɛ'stɪkjʉlət(ə)ri, dʒə'stɪkjʉlət(ə)ri
AM ,dʒɛstə'kjulə,tɔri

gestural
BR 'dʒɛstʃ(ə)rəl, 'dʒɛstʃ(ə)rl̩
AM 'dʒɛstʃ(ə)rəl, 'dʒɛʃtʃ(ə)rəl

gesture
BR 'dʒɛstʃ|ə(r), -əz, -(ə)rɪŋ, -əd
AM 'dʒɛstʃər, 'dʒɛʃtʃər, -z, -ɪŋ, -d

gesturer
BR 'dʒɛstʃ(ə)rə(r), -z
AM 'dʒɛstʃərər, 'dʒɛʃtʃərər, -z

gesundheit
BR gə'zʊndhʌɪt, gə'zʊnthʌɪt
AM gə'zʊn(d),(h)aɪt

get
BR gɛt, -s, -ɪŋ
AM gɛ|t, -ts, -dɪŋ

geta
BR 'geɪtə(r)
AM 'gɛ,tɑ

get-at-able
BR ,gɛt'atəbl
AM gɛd'ædəbəl

getaway
BR 'gɛtəweɪ, -z
AM 'gɛdə,weɪ, -z

Gethin
BR 'gɛθɪn
AM 'gɛθən

Gethsemane
BR gɛθ'sɛməni
AM ,gɛθ'sɛməni

gettable
BR 'gɛtəbl
AM 'gɛdəbəl

getter
BR 'gɛtə(r), -z
AM 'gɛdər, -z

Getty
BR 'gɛti
AM 'gɛdi

Gettysburg
BR 'gɛtɪzbəːg
AM 'gɛdiz,bərg

geum
BR 'dʒiːəm, -z
AM 'dʒiəm, -z

gewgaw
BR 'gjuːgɔː(r), -z
AM 'gju,gɔ, 'gju,gɑ, -z

Gewürztraminer
BR gə'vʊətstrə,miːnə(r), -z
AM gə'wərts,trɑmənər, -z

geyser
BR 'giːzə(r), 'gʌɪzə(r), -z
AM 'gaɪzər, -z

Ghana
BR 'gɑːnə(r)
AM 'gɑnə

Ghanaian
BR gɑː'neɪən, -z
AM 'gɑniən, -z

gharial
BR 'garɪəl, 'garɪɑːl, 'gɛːrɪəl, ,gʌrɪ'ɑːl, -z
AM 'gɛriəl, -z

gharry
BR 'gar|i, -ɪz
AM 'gɛri, -z

ghastlily
BR 'gɑːs(t)lɨli, 'gas(t)lɨli
AM 'gæs(t)ləli

ghastliness
BR 'gɑːs(t)lɪnɨs, 'gas(t)lɪnɨs
AM 'gæs(t)linɨs

ghastly
BR 'gɑːs(t)l|i, 'gas(t)l|i, -ɪə(r), -ɪɪst
AM 'gæs(t)li, -ər, -ɨst

ghat
BR gɑːt, gɔːt, gʌt, -s
AM gɔt, gɑt, -s

ghaut
BR gɑːt, gɔːt, gʌt, -s
AM gɔt, gɑt, -s

Ghazi
BR 'gɑːz|i, -ɪz

AM 'gɑzi, -z
ghee
BR giː
AM gi
Gheg
BR gɛg, -z
AM gɛg, -z
Ghent
BR gɛnt
AM gɛnt
gherao
BR gɛ'raʊ, -z, -ɪŋ, -d
AM gə'raʊ, -z, -ɪŋ, -d
gherkin
BR 'gəːkɪn, -z
AM 'gərkən, -z
ghetto
BR 'gɛtəʊ, -z
AM 'gɛdoʊ, -z
ghettoise
BR 'gɛtəʊʌɪz, -ɪz, -ɪŋ, -d
AM 'gɛdoʊ,aɪz, -ɪz, -ɪŋ, -d
ghettoize
BR 'gɛtəʊʌɪz, -ɪz, -ɪŋ, -d
AM 'gɛdoʊ,aɪz, -ɪz, -ɪŋ, -d
ghi
BR giː
AM gi
Ghibelline
BR 'gɪbɪliːn, 'gɪbɪlʌɪn, -z
AM 'gɪbə,lin, 'gɪbə,laɪn, 'gɪbələn, -z
Ghibellinism
BR 'gɪbɪlɪnɪz(ə)m
AM 'gɪbələ,nɪzəm, 'gɪbə,laɪ,nɪzəm
Ghiberti
BR gɪ'bɛːti
AM gi'bɛrdi
ghillie
BR 'gɪl|i, -ɪz
AM 'gɪli, -z
ghost
BR gəʊst, -s, -ɪŋ, -ɪd
AM goʊst, -s, -ɪŋ, -əd
ghostbuster
BR 'gəʊs(t),bʌstə(r), -z
AM 'goʊs(t),bəstər, -z
ghostbusting
BR 'gəʊs(t),bʌstɪŋ
AM 'goʊs(t),bəstɪŋ
ghostlike
BR 'gəʊs(t)lʌɪk
AM 'goʊs(t),laɪk
ghostliness
BR 'gəʊs(t)lɪnɪs
AM 'goʊs(t)linɪs
ghostly
BR 'gəʊs(t)l|i, -ɪə(r), -ɪɪst
AM 'goʊs(t)li, -ər, -ɪst
ghostwriter
BR 'gəʊs(t),rʌɪtə(r), -z
AM 'goʊs(t),raɪdər, -z
ghoul
BR guːl, -z
AM gul, -z
ghoulish
BR 'guːlɪʃ
AM 'gulɪʃ
ghoulishly
BR 'guːlɪʃli
AM 'gulɪʃli
ghoulishness
BR 'guːlɪʃnɪs
AM 'gulɪʃnɪs
ghyll
BR gɪl, -z
AM gɪl, -z
Giacometti
BR ,dʒakə'mɛti
AM ,dʒækə'mɛdi
giant
BR 'dʒʌɪənt, -s
AM 'dʒaɪənt, -s
giantess
BR 'dʒʌɪəntɪs, 'dʒʌɪəntɛs, ,dʒʌɪən'tɛs, -ɪz
AM 'dʒaɪən(t)əs, -əz
giantism
BR 'dʒʌɪəntɪz(ə)m
AM 'dʒaɪən(t),ɪzəm
giaour
BR 'dʒaʊə(r), -z
AM 'dʒaʊ(ə)r, -z
giardiasis
BR ,dʒɪɑː'dʌɪəsɪs
AM ,dʒ(i)ɑr'daɪəsɪs
gib
BR dʒɪb, -z, -ɪŋ, -d
AM dʒɪb, -z, -ɪŋ, -d
Gibb
BR gɪb
AM gɪb
gibber
BR 'dʒɪb|ə(r), -əz, -(ə)rɪŋ, -əd
AM 'dʒɪb|ər, -ərz, -(ə)rɪŋ, -ərd
gibberellin
BR ,dʒɪbə'rɛlɪn
AM ,dʒɪbə'rɛlən
gibberish
BR 'dʒɪb(ə)rɪʃ
AM 'dʒɪb(ə)rɪʃ
gibbet
BR 'dʒɪbɪt, -s
AM 'dʒɪbɪt, -s
gibbon
BR 'gɪbən, -z
AM 'gɪbən, -z
Gibbons
BR 'gɪbənz
AM 'gɪbənz
gibbosity
BR gɪ'bɒsɪti
AM gɪ'bɑsədi
gibbous
BR 'gɪbəs
AM 'gɪbəs
gibbously
BR 'gɪbəsli
AM 'gɪbəsli
gibbousness
BR 'gɪbəsnəs
AM 'gɪbəsnəs
Gibbs
BR gɪbz
AM gɪbz
gibe
BR dʒʌɪb, -z, -ɪŋ, -d
AM dʒaɪb, -z, -ɪŋ, -d
Gibeon
BR 'gɪbɪən
AM 'gɪbiən
Gibeonite
BR 'gɪbɪənʌɪt
AM 'gɪbiə,naɪt
giber
BR 'dʒʌɪbə(r), -z
AM 'dʒaɪbər, -z
giblets
BR 'dʒɪblɪts
AM 'dʒɪbləts
Gibraltar
BR dʒɪ'brɔːltə(r), dʒɪ'brɒltə(r)
AM dʒə'brɔltər, dʒə'brɑltər
Gibraltarian
BR ,dʒɪbrɔːl'tɛːrɪən, ,dʒɪbrɒl'tɛːrɪən, -z
AM ,dʒɪbrɔl'tɛriən, ,dʒɪbrɑl'tɛriən, -z
Gibson
BR 'gɪbsn
AM 'gɪbsən
gid
BR gɪd
AM gɪd
giddily
BR 'gɪdɪli
AM 'gɪdɪli
giddiness
BR 'gɪdɪnɪs
AM 'gɪdinɪs
giddy
BR 'gɪd|i, -ɪə(r), -ɪɪst
AM 'gɪdi, -ər, -ɪst
Gide
BR ʒiːd
AM ʒid
Gideon
BR 'gɪdɪən
AM 'gɪdiən
gie
BR giː, -z, -ɪŋ, -d
AM gi, -z, -ɪŋ, -d
Gielgud
BR 'giːlgʊd
AM 'gil,gʊd
gift
BR gɪft, -s, -ɪd
AM gɪft, -s, -ɪd
giftedly
BR 'gɪftɪdli
AM 'gɪftɪdli
giftedness
BR 'gɪftɪdnɪs
AM 'gɪftɪdnɪs
giftware
BR 'gɪftwɛː(r)
AM 'gɪf(t),wɛ(ə)r
giftwrap
BR ,gɪft'rap, 'gɪftrap, -s, -ɪŋ, -t
AM 'gɪf(t),ræp, -s, -ɪŋ, -t
gig
BR gɪg, -z
AM gɪg, -z
gigabit
BR 'gɪgəbɪt, -s
AM 'gɪgə,bɪt, -s
gigabyte
BR 'gɪgəbʌɪt, -s
AM 'gɪgə,baɪt, -s
gigaflop
BR 'gɪgəflɒp, -s
AM 'gɪgə,flɑp, -s
gigametre
BR 'gɪgə,miːtə(r), -z
AM 'gɪgə,midər, -z
gigantesque
BR ,dʒʌɪgan'tɛsk
AM ,dʒaɪgən'tɛsk
gigantic
BR dʒʌɪ'gantɪk
AM dʒaɪ'gæn(t)ɪk
gigantically
BR dʒʌɪ'gantɪkli
AM dʒaɪ'gæn(t)ək(ə)li
gigantism
BR dʒʌɪ'gantɪz(ə)m
AM dʒaɪ'gæn,tɪzəm
Gigantopithecus
BR dʒʌɪ,gantəʊ'pɪθɪkəs, ,dʒʌɪgantəʊ'pɪθɪkəs
AM dʒaɪ,gæn(t)oʊ'pɪθɪkəs
gigawatt
BR 'gɪgəwɒt, -s
AM 'gɪgə,wɑt, -s
giggle
BR 'gɪg|l, -lz, -l̩ɪŋ\-lɪŋ, -ld
AM 'gɪg|əl, -əlz, -(ə)lɪŋ, -əld
giggler
BR 'gɪgl̩ə(r), 'gɪglə(r), -z
AM 'gɪg(ə)lər, -z
Giggleswick
BR 'gɪglzwɪk
AM 'gɪgəlzwɪk
giggliness
BR 'gɪgl̩ɪnɪs, 'gɪglɪnɪs
AM 'gɪg(ə)linɪs
giggly
BR 'gɪgl|i, -ɪə(r), -ɪɪst
AM 'gɪgli, 'gɪgl̩i, -ər, -ɪst
Gigli
BR 'dʒiːli
AM 'dʒili
IT 'dʒiʎʎi

GIGO
BR ˈɡɪɡəʊ
AM ˈɡɪˌɡoʊ

gigolo
BR ˈ(d)ʒɪɡələʊ, -z
AM ˈdʒɪɡəˌloʊ, -z

gigot
BR ˈdʒɪɡət, -s
AM ˈdʒɪɡət, -s

gigue
BR ʒiːɡ, -z
AM ʒiɡ, -z

Gila monster
BR ˈhiːlə ˌmɒnstə(r), -z
AM ˈhilə ˌmɑnstər, -z

Gilbert
BR ˈɡɪlbət
AM ˈɡɪlbərt

Gilbertian
BR ɡɪlˈbəːtɪən
AM ɡɪlˈbərdiən

gild
BR ɡɪld, -z, -ɪŋ, -ɨd
AM ɡɪld, -z, -ɪŋ, -ɨd

gilder
BR ˈɡɪldə(r), -z
AM ˈɡɪldər, -z

Gilead
BR ˈɡɪlɪad
AM ˈɡɪliˌæd

Giles
BR dʒʌɪlz
AM dʒaɪlz

gilet
BR (d)ʒɪˈleɪ, -z
AM ʒəˈleɪ, -z

gilgai
BR ˈɡɪlɡʌɪ, -z
AM ˈɡɪlˌɡaɪ, -z

Gilgamesh
BR ˈɡɪlɡəmɛʃ
AM ˈɡɪlɡəˌmɛʃ

Gilgit
BR ˈɡɪlɡɪt
AM ˈɡɪlɡɨt

Gill¹
surname
BR ɡɪl
AM ɡɪl

Gill²
woman's forename
BR dʒɪl
AM dʒɪl

gill¹
liquid measure
BR dʒɪl, -z
AM dʒɪl, -z

gill²
of fish
BR ɡɪl, -z
AM ɡɪl, -z

gill³
verb
BR ɡɪl, -z, -ɪŋ, -d
AM ɡɪl, -z, -ɪŋ, -d

Gillard
BR ˈɡɪlɑːd
AM ˈɡɪlərd

gillaroo
BR ˌɡɪləˈruː, -z
AM ˌɡɪləˈru, -z

gill cover
BR ˈɡɪl ˌkʌvə(r), -z
AM ˈɡɪl ˌkəvər, -z

Gillespie
BR ɡɪˈlɛspi
AM ɡəˈlɛspi

Gillette
BR dʒɪˈlɛt
AM dʒəˈlɛt

Gillian
BR ˈdʒɪlɪən
AM ˈdʒɪljən, ˈdʒɪliən

gillie
BR ˈɡɪl|i, -ɪz
AM ˈɡɪli, -z

Gillies
BR ˈɡɪlɪz
AM ˈɡɪliz

Gilligan
BR ˈɡɪlɪɡ(ə)n
AM ˈɡɪlɨɡən

Gillingham¹
place in Kent, UK
BR ˈdʒɪlɪŋəm
AM ˈdʒɪlɪŋəm

Gillingham²
places in Dorset and Norfolk, UK
BR ˈɡɪlɪŋəm
AM ˈɡɪlɪŋəm

gillion
BR ˈɡɪljən, -z
AM ˈɡɪljən, -z

gill-net
BR ˈɡɪlnɛt, -s
AM ˈɡɪlˌnɛt, -s

Gillow
BR ˈɡɪləʊ
AM ˈɡɪloʊ

Gilly
BR ˈdʒɪli
AM ˈdʒɪli

gilly
BR ˈɡɪl|i, -ɪz
AM ˈɡɪli, -z

gillyflower
BR ˈdʒɪlɪˌflaʊə(r), -z
AM ˈdʒɪliˌflaʊər, -z

Gilman
BR ˈɡɪlmən
AM ˈɡɪlmən

Gilmore
BR ˈɡɪlmɔː(r)
AM ˈɡɪlˌmɔ(ə)r

Gilmour
BR ˈɡɪlmɔː(r)
AM ˈɡɪlˌmɔ(ə)r

Gilpin
BR ˈɡɪlpɪn
AM ˈɡɪlpɨn

Gilroy
BR ˈɡɪlrɔɪ
AM ˈɡɪlˌrɔɪ

gilt
BR ɡɪlt, -s
AM ɡɪlt, -s

gilt-edged
BR ˌɡɪltˈɛdʒd
AM ˈɡɪltˈɛdʒd

giltwood
BR ˈɡɪltwʊd
AM ˈɡɪltˌwʊd

gimbal
BR ˈdʒɪmbl, ˈɡɪmbl, -z
AM ˈɡɪmbəl, ˈdʒɪmbəl, -z

gimcrack
BR ˈdʒɪmkrak
AM ˈdʒɪmˌkræk

gimcrackery
BR ˈdʒɪmkrak(ə)ri
AM ˈdʒɪmˌkrækəri

gimcracky
BR ˈdʒɪmkraki
AM ˈdʒɪmˌkræki

gimlet
BR ˈɡɪmlɪt, -s
AM ˈɡɪmlət, -s

gimme
BR ˈɡɪmi
AM ˈɡɪmi

gimmick
BR ˈɡɪmɪk, -s
AM ˈɡɪmɪk, -s

gimmickry
BR ˈɡɪmɨkri
AM ˈɡɪmɨkri

gimmicky
BR ˈɡɪmɨki
AM ˈɡɪmɨki

gimp
BR ɡɪm|p, -ps, -pɪŋ, -(p)t
AM ɡɪm|p, -(p)s, -pɪŋ, -(p)t

gimpy
BR ˈɡɪmpi
AM ˈɡɪmpi

Gimson
BR ˈɡɪmsn, ˈdʒɪmsn
AM ˈɡɪmsən, ˈdʒɪmsən

gin
BR dʒɪn, -z
AM dʒɪn, -z

Gina
BR ˈdʒiːnə(r)
AM ˈdʒɪnə

ging
BR ɡɪŋ, -z, -ɪŋ, -d
AM ɡɪŋ, -z, -ɪŋ, -d

ginger
BR ˈdʒɪn(d)ʒ|ə(r), -əz, -(ə)rɪŋ, -əd
AM ˈdʒɪndʒ|ər, -ərz, -(ə)rɪŋ, -ərd

ginger ale
BR ˌdʒɪn(d)ʒər ˈeɪl
AM ˈdʒɪndʒər ˌeɪl, ˌdʒɪndʒər ˈeɪl

gingerbread
BR ˈdʒɪn(d)ʒəbrɛd
AM ˈdʒɪndʒərˌbrɛd

gingerliness
BR ˈdʒɪn(d)ʒəlɪnɪs
AM ˈdʒɪndʒərlinɨs

gingerly
BR ˈdʒɪn(d)ʒəli
AM ˈdʒɪndʒərli

gingery
BR ˈdʒɪn(d)ʒ(ə)ri
AM ˈdʒɪndʒəri

gingham
BR ˈɡɪŋəm
AM ˈɡɪŋəm

gingili
BR ˈdʒɪn(d)ʒɪli
AM ˈdʒɪndʒəli

gingiva
BR dʒɪnˈdʒʌɪvə(*r*), ˈdʒɪn(d)ʒɨvə(*r*)
AM dʒənˈdʒaɪvə

gingivae
BR dʒɪnˈdʒʌɪviː, ˈdʒɪn(d)ʒɨviː
AM dʒənˈdʒaɪvi, ˈdʒɪndʒəˌvaɪ

gingival
BR dʒɪnˈdʒʌɪvl, ˈdʒɪn(d)ʒɨvl
AM dʒənˈdʒaɪvəl, ˈdʒɪndʒəvəl

gingivitis
BR ˌdʒɪn(d)ʒɨˈvʌɪtɨs
AM ˌdʒɪndʒəˈvaɪdɨs

gingko
BR ˈɡɪŋkəʊ, -z
AM ˈɡɪŋkoʊ, -z

ginglymi
BR ˈɡɪŋɡlɨmʌɪ, ˈɡɪŋɡlɨmiː, ˈdʒɪŋɡlɨmʌɪ, ˈdʒɪŋɡlɨmiː
AM ˈdʒɪŋɡləˌmaɪ, ˈɡɪŋɡləˌmaɪ, ˈdʒɪŋɡləmi, ˈɡɪŋɡləmi

ginglymus
BR ˈɡɪŋɡlɨməs, ˈdʒɪŋɡlɨməs
AM ˈdʒɪŋɡləməs, ˈɡɪŋɡləməs

Gingold
BR ˈɡɪŋɡəʊld
AM ˈɡɪŋˌɡoʊld

gink
BR ˈɡɪŋk, -s
AM ˈɡɪŋk, -s

ginkgo
BR ˈɡɪŋkəʊ, -z
AM ˈɡɪŋkoʊ, -z

Ginn
BR ɡɪn
AM ɡɪn, dʒɪn

ginner
BR ˈdʒɪnə(r), -z
AM ˈdʒɪnər, -z

Ginny
BR ˈdʒɪni
AM ˈdʒɪni

Gino
BR 'dʒiːnəʊ
AM 'dʒinoʊ

ginormous
BR dʒʌɪ'nɔːməs
AM dʒaɪ'nɔrməs

Ginsberg
BR 'gɪnzbəːg
AM 'gɪnz,bərg

ginseng
BR 'dʒɪnsɛŋ
AM 'dʒɪn¦sɛŋ

Ginsu
BR 'gɪnsuː
AM 'gɪnsu

Gioconda, La
BR la ,dʒɪə'kɒndə(r)
AM ,la dʒɔ'kɑndə, ,la dʒa'kandə

Giorgione
BR ,dʒɔːdʒɪ'əʊni
AM dʒɔr'dʒ(i)oʊni

Giotto
BR 'dʒɒtəʊ, dʒɪ'ɒtəʊ
AM 'dʒɔdoʊ, 'dʒadoʊ

Giovanni
BR dʒə(ʊ)'vɑːni, ,dʒiːə'vɑːni, dʒə(ʊ)'vani, ,dʒiːə'vani
AM dʒə'vɑni, ,dʒiə'vɑni

gip
BR dʒɪp, -s, -ɪŋ, -t
AM dʒɪp, -s, -ɪŋ, -t

gippo
BR 'dʒɪpəʊ, -z
AM 'dʒɪpoʊ, -z

gippy
BR 'dʒɪpi
AM 'dʒɪpi

Gipsy
BR 'dʒɪps|i, -ɪz
AM 'dʒɪpsi, -z

giraffe
BR dʒɪ'rɑːf, dʒɪ'raf, -s
AM dʒə'ræf, -s

Giraldus Cambrensis
BR dʒɪ,raldəs kam'brɛnsɪs
AM dʒə,rɔldəs kæm'brɛnsəs, dʒə,rɑldəs kæm'brɛnsəs

girandole
BR 'dʒɪrəndəʊl, 'dʒɪrn̩dəʊl, -z
AM 'dʒɪrən,doʊl, -z

Girard
BR 'dʒɛrɑːd, dʒə'rɑːd
AM dʒə'rɑrd

girasol
BR 'dʒɪrəsɒl, -z
AM 'dʒɪrə,sɑl, -z

girasole
BR 'dʒɪrəsəʊl, -z
AM 'dʒɪrə,soʊl, -z

gird
BR gəːd, -z, -ɪŋ, -ɪd
AM gərd, -z, -ɪŋ, -əd

girder
BR 'gəːdə(r), -z
AM 'gərdər, -z

girdle
BR 'gəːd|l, -lz, -l̩ɪŋ\-lɪŋ, -ld
AM 'gərd|əl, -əlz, -(ə)lɪŋ, -əld

girl
BR gəːl, -z
AM gərl, -z

girlfriend
BR 'gəːlfrɛnd, -z
AM 'gərl,frɛnd, -z

girlhood
BR 'gəːlhʊd
AM 'gərl,(h)ʊd

girlie
BR 'gəːli
AM 'gərli

girlish
BR 'gəːlɪʃ
AM 'gərlɪʃ

girlishly
BR 'gəːlɪʃli
AM 'gərlɪʃli

girlishness
BR 'gəːlɪʃnɪs
AM 'gərlɪʃnɪs

girly
BR 'gəːli
AM 'gərli

giro[1]
banking
BR 'dʒʌɪrəʊ, -z
AM 'dʒɪroʊ, -z

giro[2]
gyroscope
BR 'dʒʌɪrəʊ, -z
AM 'dʒaɪroʊ, -z

giro[3]
verb
BR 'dʒʌɪrəʊ, -z, -ɪŋ, -d
AM 'dʒɪroʊ, -z, -ɪŋ, -d

Gironde
BR (d)ʒɪ'rɒnd
AM dʒə'rɑnd

Girondin
BR (d)ʒɪ'rɒndɪn, -z
AM dʒə'rɑndən, -z
FR ʒiʀɔ̃dɛ̃

Girondist
BR (d)ʒɪ'rɒndɪst, -s
AM dʒə'rɑndəst, -s

girt
BR gəːt
AM gərt

girth
BR gəːθ, -s
AM gərθ, -s

Girton
BR 'gəːtn
AM 'gərtən

Gisborne
BR 'gɪzbɔːn
AM 'gɪzbərn

Giselle
BR (d)ʒɪ'zɛl
AM ʒə'zɛl

Gish
BR gɪʃ
AM gɪʃ

gismo
BR 'gɪzməʊ, -z
AM 'gɪzmoʊ, -z

Gissing
BR 'gɪsɪŋ
AM 'gɪsɪŋ

gist
BR dʒɪst
AM dʒɪst

git
BR gɪt, -s
AM gɪt, -s

gîte
BR ʒiːt, -s
AM ʒit, -s

gittern
BR 'gɪtəːn, -z
AM 'gɪdərn, -z

Gittins
BR 'gɪtɪnz
AM 'gɪtnz

Giuseppe
BR dʒʊ'zɛpi, dʒʊ'sɛpi
AM dʒə'sɛpi

givable
BR 'gɪvəbl
AM 'gɪvəbəl

give
BR gɪv, -z, -ɪŋ
AM gɪv, -z, -ɪŋ

giveable
BR 'gɪvəbl
AM 'gɪvəbəl

giveaway
BR 'gɪvəweɪ, -z
AM 'gɪvə,weɪ, -z

given
BR 'gɪvn
AM 'gɪvən

Givenchy
BR ʒɪ'vɒ̃ʃi, ʒiː'vɒ̃ʃi, ʒɪ'vɒnʃi, ʒiː'vɒnʃi
AM ʒə'vɑnʃi

giver
BR 'gɪvə(r), -z
AM 'gɪvər, -z

gizmo
BR 'gɪzməʊ, -z
AM 'gɪzmoʊ, -z

gizzard
BR 'gɪzəd, -z
AM 'gɪzərd, -z

glabella
BR glə'bɛlə(r)
AM glə'bɛlə

glabellae
BR glə'bɛliː
AM glə'bɛli, glə'bɛ,laɪ

glabellar
BR glə'bɛlə(r)
AM glə'bɛlər

glabrous
BR 'gleɪbrəs
AM 'gleɪbrəs

glacé
BR 'glaseɪ
AM glæ'seɪ, glɑ'seɪ

glacial
BR 'gleɪʃl, 'gleɪsɪəl
AM 'gleɪʃəl

glacially
BR 'gleɪʃli, 'gleɪʃəli, 'gleɪsɪəli
AM 'gleɪʃəli

glaciate
BR 'gleɪsɪeɪt, 'gleɪʃɪeɪt, -s, -ɪŋ, -ɪd
AM 'gleɪʃi,eɪ|t, -ts, -dɪŋ, -dɪd

glaciated
BR 'gleɪsɪeɪtɪd, 'gleɪʃɪeɪtɪd
AM 'gleɪʃi,eɪdɪd

glaciation
BR ,gleɪsɪ'eɪʃn, ,gleɪʃɪ'eɪʃn, -z
AM ,gleɪʃi'eɪʃən, -z

glacier
BR 'glasɪə(r), 'gleɪsɪə(r), -z
AM 'gleɪʃər, -z

glaciological
BR ,gleɪsɪə'lɒdʒɪkl, ,gleɪʃɪə'lɒdʒɪkl
AM ,gleɪʃiə'lɑdʒəkəl

glaciologist
BR ,gleɪsɪ'ɒlədʒɪst, ,gleɪʃɪ'ɒlədʒɪst, -s
AM ,gleɪʃi'ɑlədʒəst, -s

glaciology
BR ,gleɪsɪ'ɒlədʒi, ,gleɪʃɪ'ɒlədʒi
AM ,gleɪʃi'ɑlədʒi

glacis[1]
singular
BR 'glas|ɪs, 'glas|i, -ɪsɪz
AM 'glæsiz, 'glæsəs, 'gleɪsɪz, -ɪsɪz

glacis[2]
plural
BR 'glasɪz
AM 'gleɪsiz

glad
BR glad, -ə(r), -ɪst
AM glæd, -ər, -əst

gladden
BR 'gladn, -z, -ɪŋ, -d
AM 'glæd(ə)n, -z, -ɪŋ, -d

gladdener
BR 'gladn̩ə(r), -z
AM 'glædn̩ər, -z

gladdie
BR 'glad|i, -ɪz
AM 'glædi, -z

gladdon
BR 'gladn, -z

AM 'glæd(ə)n, -z
glade
BR gleɪd, -z
AM gleɪd, -z
gladiator
BR 'gladɪeɪtə(r), -z
AM 'glædi,eɪdər, -z
gladiatorial
BR ,gladɪə'tɔːrɪəl
AM ,glædiə'tɔriəl
gladioli
BR ,gladɪ'əʊlʌɪ
AM ,glædi'oʊ,laɪ
gladiolus
BR ,gladɪ'əʊləs, -ɪz
AM ,glædi'oʊləs, -ɪz
gladly
BR 'gladli
AM 'glædli
gladness
BR 'gladnəs
AM 'glædnəs
gladsome
BR 'glads(ə)m
AM 'glædsəm
gladsomely
BR 'glads(ə)mli
AM 'glædsəmli
gladsomeness
BR 'glads(ə)mnəs
AM 'glædsəmnəs
Gladstone
BR 'gladst(ə)n
AM 'glædz,toʊn
Gladwin
BR 'gladwɪn
AM 'glædwɪn
Gladys
BR 'gladɪs
AM 'glædəs
Glagolitic
BR ,glagə'lɪtɪk
AM ,glægə'lɪdɪk
glair
BR glɛː(r)
AM glɛ(ə)r
glaire
BR glɛː(r)
AM glɛ(ə)r
glaireous
BR 'glɛːrəs
AM 'glɛrəs
glairiness
BR 'glɛːrɪnɪs
AM 'glɛrinɪs
glairy
BR 'glɛːri
AM 'glɛri
glaive
BR gleɪv, -z
AM gleɪv, -z
glam
BR glam, -z, -ɪŋ, -d
AM glæm, -z, -ɪŋ, -d
Glamis
BR glɑːmz
AM glɑmz
glamor
BR 'glamə(r)
AM 'glæmər
Glamorgan
BR glə'mɔːg(ə)n
AM glə'mɔrgən
glamorisation
BR ,glam(ə)rʌɪ'zeɪʃn
AM ,glæm(ə)rə'zeɪʃən, ,glæmə,raɪ'zeɪʃən
glamorise
BR 'glamərʌɪz, -ɪz, -ɪŋ, -d
AM 'glæmə,raɪz, -ɪz, -ɪŋ, -d
glamorization
BR ,glam(ə)rʌɪ'zeɪʃn
AM ,glæm(ə)rə'zeɪʃən, ,glæmə,raɪ'zeɪʃən
glamorize
BR 'glamərʌɪz, -ɪz, -ɪŋ, -d
AM 'glæmə,raɪz, -ɪz, -ɪŋ, -d
glamorous
BR 'glam(ə)rəs
AM 'glæm(ə)rəs
glamorously
BR 'glam(ə)rəsli
AM 'glæm(ə)rəsli
glamour
BR 'glamə(r)
AM 'glæmər
glamourisation
BR ,glam(ə)rʌɪ'zeɪʃn
AM ,glæm(ə)rə'zeɪʃən, ,glæmə,raɪ'zeɪʃən
glamourise
BR 'glamərʌɪz, -ɪz, -ɪŋ, -d
AM 'glæmə,raɪz, -ɪz, -ɪŋ, -d
glamourization
BR ,glam(ə)rʌɪ'zeɪʃn
AM ,glæm(ə)rə'zeɪʃən, ,glæmə,raɪ'zeɪʃən
glamourize
BR 'glamərʌɪz, -ɪz, -ɪŋ, -d
AM 'glæmə,raɪz, -ɪz, -ɪŋ, -d
glamourous
BR 'glam(ə)rəs
AM 'glæm(ə)rəs
glamourously
BR 'glam(ə)rəsli
AM 'glæm(ə)rəsli
glance
BR glɑːns, glans, -ɪz, -ɪŋ, -t
AM glæns, -əz, -ɪŋ, -t
glancingly
BR 'glɑːnsɪŋli, 'glansɪŋli
AM 'glænsɪŋli
gland
BR gland, -z
AM glænd, -z
glandered
BR 'glandəd
AM 'glændərd
glanderous
BR 'gland(ə)rəs
AM 'glændərəs
glanders
BR 'glandəz
AM 'glændərz
glandes
BR 'glandiːz
AM 'glændiz
glandular
BR 'glandjʉlə(r), 'glandʒʉlə(r)
AM 'glændʒələr, 'glændjələr
glandule
BR 'glandjuːl, 'glandʒuːl, -z
AM 'glændʒul, 'glændjul, -z
glans
BR glanz
AM glænz
Glanville
BR 'glanvɪl
AM 'glæn,vɪl
Glanyrafon
BR ,glanər'avn
AM ,glænər'ævən
Glaramara
BR ,glarə'mɑːrə(r)
AM ,glɛrə'mɑrə
glare
BR glɛː(r), -z, -ɪŋ, -d
AM glɛ(ə)r, -z, -ɪŋ, -d
glaringly
BR 'glɛːrɪŋli
AM 'glɛrɪŋli
glaringness
BR 'glɛːrɪŋnɪs
AM 'glɛrɪŋnɪs
glary
BR 'glɛːri
AM 'glɛri
Glaser
BR 'gleɪzə(r)
AM 'gleɪzər
Glasgow
BR 'glazgəʊ, 'glɑːzgəʊ
AM 'glæz,goʊ, 'glæs,goʊ
Glaslyn
BR 'glaslɪn
AM 'glæslən
glasnost
BR 'glaznɒst
AM 'glɑz,noʊst, 'glɑz,nɔst, 'glɑz,nɑst
glass
BR glɑːs, glas, -ɪz
AM glæs, -əz
glassful
BR 'glɑːsfʊl, 'glasfʊl, -z
AM 'glæs,fʊl, -z
glassfull
BR 'glɑːsfʊl, 'glasfʊl, -z
AM 'glæs,fʊl, -z
glasshouse
BR 'glɑːshaʊ|s, 'glashaʊ|s, -zɪz
AM 'glæs,(h)aʊ|s, -zəz
glassie
BR 'glɑːs|i, 'glas|i, -ɪz
AM 'glæsi, -z
glassily
BR 'glɑːsɪli, 'glasɪli
AM 'glæsəli
glassine
BR 'glɑːsiːn, 'glasiːn
AM 'glæ,sin
glassiness
BR 'glɑːsɪnɪs, 'glasɪnɪs
AM 'glæsinɪs
glassless
BR 'glɑːsləs, 'glasləs
AM 'glæsləs
glasslike
BR 'glɑːslʌɪk, 'glaslʌɪk
AM 'glæs,laɪk
glassmaker
BR 'glɑːs,meɪkə(r), 'glas,meɪkə(r), -z
AM 'glæs,meɪkər, -z
glasspaper
BR 'glɑːs,peɪpə(r), 'glas,peɪpə(r)
AM 'glæs,peɪpər
glassware
BR 'glɑːswɛː(r), 'glaswɛː(r)
AM 'glæs,wɛ(ə)r
glasswork
BR 'glɑːswəːk, 'glaswəːk, -s
AM 'glæs,wərk, -s
glasswort
BR 'glɑːswəːt, 'glaswəːt, -s
AM 'glæs,wərt, 'glæs,wɔ(ə)rt, -s
glassy
BR 'glɑːs|i, 'glas|i, -ɪə(r), -ɪɪst
AM 'glæsi, -ər, -ɪst
Glastonbury
BR 'glast(ə)nb(ə)ri, 'glɑːst(ə)nb(ə)ri
AM 'glæstən,bɛri
Glaswegian
BR glaz'wiːdʒ(ə)n, glɑːz'wiːdʒ(ə)n, -z
AM glæz'widʒiən, glæs'widʒiən, -z
glaucoma
BR glɔː'kəʊmə(r), glaʊ'kəʊmə(r)
AM glɔ'koʊmə, glɑ'koʊmə
glaucomatous
BR glɔː'kəʊmətəs, glaʊ'kəʊmətəs

AM glɔˈkoʊmədəs, glɔˈkɑmədəs, glɑˈkoʊmədəs, glɑˈkɑmədəs

glaucous
BR ˈglɔːkəs
AM ˈglɔkəs, ˈglɑkəs

Glaxo
BR ˈglaksəʊ
AM ˈglæksoʊ

glaze
BR gleɪz, -ɪz, -ɪŋ, -d
AM gleɪz, -ɪz, -ɪŋ, -d

glazer
BR ˈgleɪzə(r), -z
AM ˈgleɪzər, -z

glazier
BR ˈgleɪzɪə(r), -z
AM ˈgleɪʒər, ˈgleɪzɪər, -z

glaziery
BR ˈgleɪzɪəri
AM ˈgleɪʒəri, ˈgleɪzɪˌɛri

glazy
BR ˈgleɪzi
AM ˈgleɪzi

gleam
BR gliːm, -z, -ɪŋ, -d
AM glim, -z, -ɪŋ, -d

gleamingly
BR ˈgliːmɪŋli
AM ˈglimɪŋli

gleamy
BR ˈgliːmi
AM ˈglimi

glean
BR gliːn, -z, -ɪŋ, -d
AM glin, -z, -ɪŋ, -d

gleaner
BR ˈgliːnə(r), -z
AM ˈglinər, -z

gleanings
BR ˈgliːnɪŋz
AM ˈglinɪŋz

Gleason
BR ˈgliːs(ə)n
AM ˈglisən

Gleave
BR gliːv
AM gliv

glebe
BR gliːb, -z
AM glib, -z

glee
BR gliː
AM gli

gleeful
BR ˈgliːf(ʊ)l
AM ˈglifəl

gleefully
BR ˈgliːfʊli, ˈgliːfl̩i
AM ˈglifəli

gleefulness
BR ˈgliːf(ʊ)lnəs
AM ˈglifəlnəs

gleesome
BR ˈgliːs(ə)m
AM ˈglisəm

Gleeson
BR ˈgliːs(ə)n
AM ˈglisən

Gleichschaltung
BR ˈglʌɪkˌʃaltʊŋ
AM ˈglaɪkˌʃæltʊŋ

glen
BR glɛn, -z
AM glɛn, -z

Glencoe
BR ˌglɛnˈkəʊ
AM ˈglɛnˌkoʊ

Glenda
BR ˈglɛndə(*r*)
AM ˈglɛndə

Glendale
BR ˈglɛndeɪl
AM ˈglɛnˌdeɪl

Glendenning
BR glɛnˈdɛnɪŋ
AM glɛnˈdɛnɪŋ

Glendinning
BR glɛnˈdɪnɪŋ
AM glɛnˈdɪnɪŋ

Glendower
BR glɛnˈdaʊə(r)
AM ˈglɛndaʊər

Gleneagles
BR glɛnˈiːglz
AM glɛnˈigəlz

Glenfiddich
BR glɛnˈfɪdɪk, glɛnˈfɪdɪx
AM glɛnˈfɪdɪk, glɛnˈfɪdɪtʃ

glengarry
BR glɛnˈgar|i, -ɪz
AM glɛnˈgɛri, -z

Glenlivet
BR glɛnˈlɪvɪt
AM glɛnˈlɪvɪt

Glenn
BR glɛn
AM glɛn

glenoid cavity
BR ˌgliːnɔɪd ˈkavɪt|i, -ɪz
AM ˈglɛˌnɔɪd ˈkævədi, -z

Glenrothes
BR glɛnˈrɒθɪs
AM glɛnˈrɑθəs

Glenys
BR ˈglɛnɪs
AM ˈglɛnəs

gley
BR gleɪ, -z
AM gleɪ, -z

glia
BR ˈglʌɪə(*r*), ˈgliːə(*r*), -z
AM ˈgliə, ˈglaɪə, -z

glial
BR ˈglʌɪəl, ˈgliːəl
AM ˈgliəl, ˈglaɪəl

glib
BR glɪb, -ə(r), -ɪst
AM glɪb, -ər, -ɪst

glibly
BR ˈglɪbli
AM ˈglɪbli

glibness
BR ˈglɪbnɪs
AM ˈglɪbnɪs

glide
BR glʌɪd, -z, -ɪŋ, -ɪd
AM glaɪd, -z, -ɪŋ, -ɪd

glider
BR ˈglʌɪdə(r), -z
AM ˈglaɪdər, -z

glidingly
BR ˈglʌɪdɪŋli
AM ˈglaɪdɪŋli

glim
BR glɪm, -z
AM glɪm, -z

glimmer
BR ˈglɪm|ə(r), -əz, -(ə)rɪŋ, -əd
AM ˈglɪmər, -z, -ɪŋ, -d

glimmering
BR ˈglɪm(ə)rɪŋ, -z
AM ˈglɪmərɪŋ, -z

glimmeringly
BR ˈglɪm(ə)rɪŋli
AM ˈglɪmərɪŋli

glimpse
BR glɪm(p)s, -ɪz, -ɪŋ, -t
AM glɪm(p)s, -ɪz, -ɪŋ, -t

Glinka
BR ˈglɪŋkə(*r*)
AM ˈglɪŋkə

glint
BR glɪnt, -s, -ɪŋ, -ɪd
AM glɪn|t, -ts, -(t)ɪŋ, -(t)ɪd

glioma
BR glʌɪˈəʊmə(*r*), -z
AM glaɪˈoʊmə, -z

glissade
BR glɪˈsɑːd, glɪˈseɪd, -z, -ɪŋ, -ɪd
AM gləˈsɑd, -z, -ɪŋ, -əd

glissandi
BR glɪˈsandiː
AM gləˈsɑnˌdaɪ

glissando
BR glɪˈsandəʊ, -z
AM gləˈsɑndoʊ, -z

glissé
BR glɪˈseɪ, -z
AM gləˈseɪ, gliˈseɪ, -z

glisten
BR ˈglɪs|n, -nz, -n̩ɪŋ\-nɪŋ, -nd
AM ˈglɪsn, -z, -ɪŋ, -d

glister
BR ˈglɪst|ə(r), -əz, -(ə)rɪŋ, -əd
AM ˈglɪst|ər, -ərz, -(ə)rɪŋ, -ərd

glitch
BR glɪtʃ, -ɪz
AM glɪtʃ, -ɪz

glitter
BR ˈglɪt|ə(r), -əz, -(ə)rɪŋ, -əd
AM ˈglɪdər, -z, -ɪŋ, -d

glitterati
BR ˌglɪtəˈrɑːti
AM ˌglɪdəˈrɑdi

glitteringly
BR ˈglɪt(ə)rɪŋli
AM ˈglɪdərɪŋli

glittery
BR ˈglɪt(ə)ri
AM ˈglɪdəri

glitz
BR glɪts
AM glɪts

glitzily
BR ˈglɪtsɪli
AM ˈglɪtsɪli

glitziness
BR ˈglɪtsɪnɪs
AM ˈglɪtsinɪs

glitzy
BR ˈglɪts|i, -ɪə(r), -ɪɪst
AM ˈglɪtsi, -ər, -ɪst

gloaming
BR ˈgləʊmɪŋ
AM ˈgloʊmɪŋ

gloat
BR gləʊt, -s, -ɪŋ, -ɪd
AM gloʊ|t, -ts, -dɪŋ, -dəd

gloater
BR ˈgləʊtə(r), -z
AM ˈgloʊdər, -z

gloatingly
BR ˈgləʊtɪŋli
AM ˈgloʊdɪŋli

glob
BR glɒb, -z
AM glɑb, -z

global
BR ˈgləʊbl
AM ˈgloʊbəl

globalisation
BR ˌgləʊbl̩ʌɪˈzeɪʃn, ˌgləʊbəlʌɪˈzeɪʃn
AM ˌgloʊbələˈzeɪʃən, ˌgloʊbəˌlaɪˈzeɪʃən

globalise
BR ˈgləʊbl̩ʌɪz, ˈgləʊbəlʌɪz, -ɪz, -ɪŋ, -d
AM ˈgloʊbəˌlaɪz, -ɪz, -ɪŋ, -d

globalization
BR ˌgləʊbl̩ʌɪˈzeɪʃn, ˌgləʊbəlʌɪˈzeɪʃn
AM ˌgloʊbələˈzeɪʃən, ˌgloʊbəˌlaɪˈzeɪʃən

globalize
BR ˈgləʊbl̩ʌɪz, ˈgləʊbəlʌɪz, -ɪz, -ɪŋ, -d
AM ˈgloʊbəˌlaɪz, -ɪz, -ɪŋ, -d

globally
BR ˈgləʊbl̩i, ˈgləʊbəli
AM ˈgloʊbəli

globe
BR gləʊb, -z

AM ˈgloʊb, -z

globefish
BR ˈgləʊbfɪʃ, -ɪz
AM ˈgloʊbˌfɪʃ, -ɪz

globelike
BR ˈgləʊblʌɪk
AM ˈgloʊbˌlaɪk

globetrotter
BR ˈgləʊbˌtrɒtə(r), -z
AM ˈgloʊbˌtrɑdər, -z

globigerina
BR ˌgləʊbɪdʒəˈrʌɪnə(r), -z
AM gloʊˌbɪdʒəˈraɪnə, gloʊˌbɪdʒəˈrinə, -z

globigerinae
BR ˌgləʊbɪdʒəˈrʌɪniː
AM gloʊˌbɪdʒəˈraɪni, gloʊˌbɪdʒəˈriˌnaɪ

globoid
BR ˈgləʊbɔɪd, -z
AM ˈgloʊˌbɔɪd, -z

globose
BR ˈgləʊbəʊs, gləʊˈbəʊs
AM ˈgloʊˌboʊs

globosely
BR ˈgləʊbəʊsli, gləʊˈbəʊsli
AM ˈgloʊˌboʊsli

globoseness
BR ˈgləʊbəʊsnəs, gləʊˈbəʊsnəs
AM ˈgloʊˌboʊsnəs

globular
BR ˈglɒbjʉlə(r)
AM ˈglɑbjələr

globularity
BR ˌglɒbjʉˈlarɪti
AM ˌglɑbjəˈlɛrədi

globularly
BR ˈglɒbjʉləli
AM ˈglɑbjələrli

globule
BR ˈglɒbjuːl, -z
AM ˈglɑbˌjul, -z

globulin
BR ˈglɒbjʉlɪn
AM ˈglɑbjələn

globulous
BR ˈglɒbjʉləs
AM ˈglɑbjələs

Glockenspiel
BR ˈglɒk(ə)nspiːl, ˈglɒk(ə)nʃpiːl, -z
AM ˈglɑkənˌspil, ˈglɑkənˌʃpil, -z

glom
BR glɒm, -z, -ɪŋ, -d
AM glɑm, -z, -ɪŋ, -d

glomata
BR glʌɪˈəʊmətə(r)
AM glaɪˈoʊmədə

glomerate¹
adjective
BR ˈglɒm(ə)rət
AM ˈglɑməˌreɪt, ˈglɑmərət

glomerate²
verb
BR ˈglɒməreɪt, -s, -ɪŋ, -ɪd
AM ˈglɑməˌreɪ|t, -ts, -dɪŋ, -dɪd

glomerular
BR glɒˈmɛr(j)ʉlə(r)
AM gləˈmɛr(j)ələr

glomerule
BR ˈglɒməruːl, -z
AM ˈglɑməˌrul, -z

glomeruli
BR glɒˈmɛr(j)ʉlʌɪ, glɒˈmɛr(j)ʉliː
AM gləˈmɛrjəˌlaɪ

glomerulus
BR glɒˈmɛr(j)ʉləs
AM gləˈmɛrjələs

gloom
BR gluːm
AM glum

gloomily
BR ˈgluːmɪli
AM ˈgluməli

gloominess
BR ˈgluːmɪnɪs
AM ˈgluminɪs

gloomy
BR ˈgluːm|i, -ɪə(r), -ɪɪst
AM ˈglumi, -ər, -ɪst

glop
BR glɒp, -s
AM glɑp, -s

Gloria
BR ˈglɔːrɪə(r)
AM ˈglɔriə

Gloriana
BR ˌglɔːrɪˈɑːnə(r)
AM ˌglɔriˈænə

glorification
BR ˌglɔːrɪfɪˈkeɪʃn
AM ˌglɔrəfəˈkeɪʃən

glorifier
BR ˈglɔːrɪfʌɪə(r), -z
AM ˈglɔrəˌfaɪ(ə)r, -z

glorify
BR ˈglɔːrɪfʌɪ, -z, -ɪŋ, -d
AM ˈglɔrəˌfaɪ, -z, -ɪŋ, -d

gloriole
BR ˈglɔːrɪəʊl, -z
AM ˈglɔriˌoʊl, -z

glorious
BR ˈglɔːrɪəs
AM ˈglɔriəs

gloriously
BR ˈglɔːrɪəsli
AM ˈglɔriəsli

gloriousness
BR ˈglɔːrɪəsnəs
AM ˈglɔriəsnəs

glory
BR ˈglɔːr|i, -ɪz
AM ˈglɔri, -z

gloss
BR glɒs, -ɪz, -ɪŋ, -t
AM glɔs, glɑs, -əz, -ɪŋ, -t

glossal
BR ˈglɒsl
AM ˈglɑsəl

glossarial
BR glɒˈsɛːrɪəl
AM glɔˈsɛriəl, glɑˈsɛriəl

glossarist
BR ˈglɒsərɪst, -s
AM ˈglɔsərəst, ˈglɑsərəst, -s

glossary
BR ˈglɒs(ə)r|i, -ɪz
AM ˈglɔsəri, ˈglɑsəri, -z

glossator
BR ˈglɒseɪtə(r), glɒˈseɪtə(r), -z
AM ˈglɔˌseɪdər, ˈglɑˌseɪdər, -z

glosseme
BR ˈglɒsiːm, -z
AM ˈglɔˌsim, ˈglɑˌsim, -z

glosser
BR ˈglɒsə(r), -z
AM ˈglɔsər, ˈglɑsər, -z

glossily
BR ˈglɒsɪli
AM ˈglɔsəli, ˈglɑsəli

glossiness
BR ˈglɒsɪnɪs
AM ˈglɔsinɪs, ˈglɑsinɪs

glossitis
BR glɒˈsʌɪtɪs
AM glɔˈsaɪdɪs, glɑˈsaɪdɪs

glossographer
BR glɒˈsɒgrəfə(r), -z
AM glɔˈsɑgrəfər, glɑˈsɑgrəfər, -z

glossolalia
BR ˌglɒsəˈleɪlɪə(r)
AM ˌglɑsəˈleɪljə, ˌglɔsəˈleɪljə, ˌglɑsəˈleɪliə, ˌglɔsəˈleɪliə

glosso-laryngeal
BR ˌglɒsəʊləˈrɪndʒɪəl, ˌglɒsəʊˌlarɪnˈdʒiːəl, ˌglɒsəʊˌlarn̩ˈdʒiːəl
AM ˈglɔsoʊləˈrɪndʒəl, ˈglɑsoʊləˈrɪndʒəl

glossology
BR glɒˈsɒlədʒi
AM glɔˈsɑlədʒi, glɑˈsɑlədʒi

Glossop
BR ˈglɒsəp
AM ˈglɔsəp, ˈglɑsəp

glossy
BR ˈglɒs|i, -ɪz, -ɪə(r), -ɪɪst
AM ˈglɔsi, ˈglɑsi, -z, -ər, -ɪst

Gloster
BR ˈglɒstə(r)
AM ˈglɔstər, ˈglɑstər

glottal
BR ˈglɒtl, -z
AM ˈglɑdl, -z

glottalisation
BR ˌglɒtl̩ʌɪˈzeɪʃn
AM ˌglɑdl̩əˈzeɪʃən, ˌglɑdlˌaɪˈzeɪʃən

glottalise
BR ˈglɒtl̩ʌɪz, -ɪz, -ɪŋ, -d
AM ˈglɑdlˌaɪz, -ɪz, -ɪŋ, -d

glottalization
BR ˌglɒtl̩ʌɪˈzeɪʃn
AM ˌglɑdl̩əˈzeɪʃən, ˌglɑdlˌaɪˈzeɪʃən

glottalize
BR ˈglɒtl̩ʌɪz, -ɪz, -ɪŋ, -d
AM ˈglɑdlˌaɪz, -ɪz, -ɪŋ, -d

glottis
BR ˈglɒtɪs, -ɪz
AM ˈglɑdəs, -ɪz

glottochronology
BR ˌglɒtəʊkrəˈnɒlədʒi
AM ˌglɑdoʊkrəˈnɑlədʒi

Gloucester
BR ˈglɒstə(r)
AM ˈglɔstər, ˈglɑstər

glove
BR glʌv, -z
AM gləv, -z

Glover
BR ˈglʌvə(r)
AM ˈgləvər

glow
BR gləʊ, -z, -ɪŋ, -d
AM gloʊ, -z, -ɪŋ, -d

glower
BR ˈglaʊə(r), -z, -ɪŋ, -d
AM ˈglaʊər, ˈgloʊər, -z, -(ə)rɪŋ, -d

gloxinia
BR glɒkˈsɪnɪə(r)
AM glɑkˈsɪniə

Gloy
BR glɔɪ
AM glɔɪ

Gluck
BR glʊk
AM glʊk

glucose
BR ˈgluːkəʊz, ˈgluːkəʊs
AM ˈgluˌkoʊs

glucoside
BR ˈgluːkəsʌɪd
AM ˈglukəˌsaɪd

glucosidic
BR ˌgluːkəˈsɪdɪk
AM ˌglukəˈsɪdɪk

glue
BR gluː, -z, -ɪŋ, -d
AM glu, -z, -ɪŋ, -d

gluer
BR ˈgluːə(r), -z
AM ˈgluər, -z

gluey
BR ˈgluː|i, -ɪə(r), -ɪɪst
AM ˈglui, -ər, -ɪst

glueyly
BR ˈgluːɨli
AM ˈgluəli

glueyness
BR ˈgluːɪnɨs
AM ˈgluinɨs

glug
BR glʌg, -z, -ɪŋ, -d
AM gləg, -z, -ɪŋ, -d

Glühwein
BR ˈgluːvʌɪn, -z
AM ˈgluˌvaɪn, ˈgluˌwaɪn, -z

glum
BR glʌm, -ə(r), -ɨst
AM gləm, -ər, -əst

glumaceous
BR gluːˈmeɪʃəs
AM gluˈmeɪʃəs

glume
BR gluːm, -z
AM glum, -z

glumly
BR ˈglʌmli
AM ˈgləmli

glumness
BR ˈglʌmnəs
AM ˈgləmnəs

glumose
BR ˈglʌməʊs
AM ˈgləmoʊs, ˈgləmoʊz

gluon
BR ˈgluːɒn
AM ˈgluˌɑn

glut
BR glʌt, -s, -ɪŋ, -ɨd
AM glə|t, -ts, -dɪŋ, -dəd

glutamate
BR ˈgluːtəmeɪt
AM ˈgludəˌmeɪt

glutamic
BR gluːˈtamɪk
AM gluˈtæmɪk

gluteal
BR ˈgluːtɪəl
AM ˈgludiəl

gluten
BR ˈgluːt(ɪ)n
AM ˈglutn

gluteus
BR ˈgluːtɪəs
AM ˈgludiəs

glutinous
BR ˈgluːtɪnəs, ˈgluːtn̩əs
AM ˈglutn̩əs, ˈgludənəs

glutinously
BR ˈgluːtɪnəsli, ˈgluːtn̩əsli
AM ˈglutn̩əsli, ˈgludənəsli

glutinousness
BR ˈgluːtɪnəsnəs, ˈgluːtn̩əsnəs
AM ˈglutn̩əsnəs, ˈgludənəsnəs

glutton
BR ˈglʌtn, -z
AM ˈglətn, -z

gluttonise
BR ˈglʌtənʌɪz, ˈglʌtn̩ʌɪz, -ɨz, -ɪŋ, -d
AM ˈglətnˌaɪz, ˈglədəˌnaɪz, -ɨz, -ɪŋ, -d

gluttonize
BR ˈglʌtənʌɪz, ˈglʌtn̩ʌɪz, -ɨz, -ɪŋ, -d
AM ˈglətnˌaɪz, ˈglədəˌnaɪz, -ɨz, -ɪŋ, -d

gluttonous
BR ˈglʌtənəs, ˈglʌtn̩əs
AM ˈglətnəs, ˈglədənəs

gluttonously
BR ˈglʌtənəsli, ˈglʌtn̩əsli
AM ˈglətnəsli, ˈglədənəs

gluttony
BR ˈglʌtəni, ˈglʌtn̩i
AM ˈglətni, ˈglədəni

glyceride
BR ˈglɪsərʌɪd, -z
AM ˈglɪsəˌraɪd, -z

glycerin
BR ˈglɪs(ə)rɪn
AM ˈglɪsərən, ˈglɪsrɨn

glycerine
BR ˈglɪs(ə)riːn, ˈglɪs(ə)rɪn
AM ˈglɪsərən, ˈglɪsrɨn

glycerol
BR ˈglɪsərɒl
AM ˈglɪsərɔl, ˈglɪsəˌrɑl

glycin
BR ˈglʌɪsɪn
AM ˈglaɪsən

glycine
BR ˈglʌɪsiːn
AM ˈglaɪˌsin

glycogen
BR ˈglʌɪkədʒ(ə)n
AM ˈglaɪkədʒən, ˈglaɪkəˌdʒɛn

glycogenesis
BR ˌglʌɪkəˈdʒɛnɪsɪs
AM ˌglaɪkəˈdʒɛnəsəs

glycogenic
BR ˌglʌɪkəˈdʒɛnɪk
AM ˌglaɪkəˈdʒɛnɪk

glycol
BR ˈglʌɪkɒl
AM ˈglaɪkɔl, ˈglaɪˌkɑl

glycolic
BR glʌɪˈkɒlɪk
AM glaɪˈkɔlɪk, glaɪˈkɑlɪk

glycollic
BR glʌɪˈkɒlɪk
AM glaɪˈkɔlɪk, ˌglaɪˈkɑlɪk

glycolyses
BR glʌɪˈkɒlɪsiːz
AM glaɪˈkɔləˌsiz, ˌglaɪˈkɑləˌsiz

glycolysis
BR glʌɪˈkɒlɪsɪs
AM ˌglaɪˈkɔləsəs, ˌglaɪˈkɑləsəs

glycoprotein
BR ˌglʌɪkəʊˈprəʊtiːn, -z
AM ˈglaɪkoʊˈproʊˌtin, -z

glycoside
BR ˈglʌɪkəsʌɪd, -z
AM ˈglaɪkəˌsaɪd, -z

glycosidic
BR ˌglʌɪkə(ʊ)ˈsɪdɪk
AM ˈglaɪkoʊˈsɪdɪk

glycosuria
BR ˌglʌɪkəˈsjʊərɪə(r), ˌglʌɪkəˈʃʊərɪə(r), ˌglʌɪkəˈsjɔːrɪə(r), ˌglʌɪkəˈʃɔːrɪə(r)
AM ˈglaɪkoʊˈsʊriə, ˈglaɪkoʊˈʃʊriə

glycosuric
BR ˌglʌɪkəˈsjʊərɪk, ˌglʌɪkəˈʃʊərɪk, ˌglʌɪkəˈsjɔːrɪk, ˌglʌɪkəˈʃɔːrɪk
AM ˈglaɪkoʊˈsʊrɪk, ˈglaɪkoʊˈʃʊrɪk

Glyn
BR glɪn
AM glɪn

Glyndebourne
BR ˈglʌɪn(d)bɔːn
AM ˈglaɪn(d)ˌbɔ(ə)rn

Glynis
BR ˈglɪnɪs
AM ˈglɪnɨs

Glynn
BR glɪn
AM glɪn

glyph
BR glɪf, -s
AM glɪf, -s

glyphic
BR ˈglɪfɪk
AM ˈglɪfɪk

glyptal
BR ˈglɪptl, -z
AM ˈglɪptl, -z

glyptic
BR ˈglɪptɪk
AM ˈglɪptɪk

glyptodon
BR ˈglɪptədɒn, -z
AM ˈglɪptəˌdɑn, -z

glyptodont
BR ˈglɪptədɒnt, -s
AM ˈglɪptəˌdɑnt, -s

glyptography
BR glɪpˈtɒgrəfi
AM glɪpˈtɑgrəfi

gnamma
BR ˈnamə(r), -z
AM (gə)ˈnæmə, -z

gnarl
BR nɑːl, -z
AM nɑrl, -z, -d

gnarly
BR ˈnɑːl|i, -ɪə(r), -ɪɨst
AM ˈnɑrli, -ər, -ɨst

gnash
BR naʃ, -ɨz, -ɪŋ, -t
AM næʃ, -əz, -ɪŋ, -t

gnasher
BR ˈnaʃə(r), -z
AM ˈnæʃər, -z

gnat
BR nat, -s
AM næt, -s

gnathic
BR ˈnaθɪk
AM ˈnæθɪk

gnaw
BR nɔː(r), -z, -ɪŋ, -d
AM nɔ, nɑ, -z, -ɪŋ, -d

gnawingly
BR ˈnɔː(r)ɪŋli
AM ˈnɔɪŋli

gneiss
BR nʌɪs
AM naɪs

gneissic
BR ˈnʌɪsɪk
AM ˈnaɪsɪk

gneissoid
BR ˈnʌɪsɔɪd
AM ˈnaɪˌsɔɪd

gneissose
BR ˈnʌɪsəʊs
AM ˈnaɪˌsoʊs

gnocchi
BR ˈnɒki
AM ˈnɑki

gnome
BR nəʊm, -z
AM noʊm, -z

gnomic
BR ˈnəʊmɪk
AM ˈnoʊmɪk

gnomically
BR ˈnəʊmɪkli
AM ˈnoʊmək(ə)li

gnomish
BR ˈnəʊmɪʃ
AM ˈnoʊmɪʃ

gnomon
BR ˈnəʊmɒn, -z
AM ˈnoʊˌmɑn, ˈnoʊmən, -z

gnomonic
BR nəʊˈmɒnɪk
AM noʊˈmɑnɪk

gnoses
BR ˈnəʊsiːz
AM ˈnoʊsiz

gnosis
BR ˈnəʊsɪs
AM ˈnoʊsəs

gnostic
BR ˈnɒstɪk, -s
AM ˈnɑstɪk, -s

gnosticism
BR ˈnɒstɪsɪz(ə)m
AM ˈnɑstəˌsɪzəm

gnosticize
BR ˈnɒstɪsʌɪz, -ɨz, -ɪŋ, -d

AM 'nɑstəˌsaɪz, -ɨz, -ɪŋ, -d

gnotobiotic
BR ˌnəʊtə(ʊ)bʌɪ'ɒtɪk
AM ˌnoʊdəˌbaɪ'ɑdɪk

gnu
BR n(j)uː, -z
AM n(j)u, -z

go
BR gəʊ, -z, -ɪŋ
AM goʊ, -z, -ɪŋ

goa
BR 'gəʊə(r), -z
AM 'goʊə, -z

goad
BR gəʊd, -z, -ɪŋ, -ɨd
AM goʊd, -z, -ɪŋ, -əd

go-ahead
BR 'gəʊəhɛd
AM 'goʊəˌhɛd

goal
BR gəʊl, -z
AM goʊl, -z

goalball
BR 'gəʊlˌbɔːl
AM 'goʊlˌbɔl, 'goʊlˌbɑl

goalie
BR 'gəʊl|i, -ɪz
AM 'goʊli, -z

goalkeeper
BR 'gəʊlˌkiːpə(r), -z
AM 'goʊlˌkipər, -z

goalkeeping
BR 'gəʊlˌkiːpɪŋ
AM 'goʊlˌkipɪŋ

goalless
BR 'gəʊlləs
AM 'goʊ(l)ləs

goalminder
BR 'gəʊlˌmʌɪndə(r), -z
AM 'goʊlˌmaɪndər, -z

goalmouth
BR 'gəʊlmaʊ|θ, -ðs
AM 'goʊlˌmaʊθ, -s

goalpost
BR 'gəʊlpəʊst, -s
AM 'goʊlˌpoʊst, -s

goalscorer
BR 'gəʊlˌskɔːrə(r), -z
AM 'goʊlˌskɔrər, -z

goalscoring
BR 'gəʊlˌskɔːrɪŋ
AM 'goʊlˌskɔrɪŋ

goaltender
BR 'gəʊlˌtɛndə(r), -z
AM 'goʊlˌtɛndər, -z

goaltending
BR 'gəʊlˌtɛndɪŋ
AM 'goʊlˌtɛndɪŋ

Goan
BR 'gəʊən
AM 'goʊən

Goanese
BR ˌgəʊə'niːz
AM goʊə'niz

goanna
BR gəʊ'anə(r), -z
AM goʊ'ænə, -z

goat
BR gəʊt, -s
AM goʊt, -s

goatee
BR ˌgəʊ'tiː, -z
AM goʊ'ti, -z

goatherd
BR 'gəʊthəːd, -z
AM 'goʊtˌ(h)ərd, -z

Goathland
BR 'gəʊθlənd
AM 'goʊθˌlænd

goatish
BR 'gəʊtɪʃ
AM 'goʊdɪʃ

goatling
BR 'gəʊtlɪŋ, -z
AM 'goʊtlɪŋ, -z

goatsbeard
BR 'gəʊtsbɪəd, -z
AM 'goʊtsˌbɪ(ə)rd, -z

goatskin
BR 'gəʊtskɪn, -z
AM 'goʊtˌskɪn, -z

goatsucker
BR 'gəʊtˌsʌkə(r), -z
AM 'goʊtˌsəkər, -z

goaty
BR 'gəʊt|i, -ɪə(r), -ɪɪst
AM 'goʊdi, -ər, -ɨst

gob
BR gɒb, -z
AM gɑb, -z

gobang
BR ˌgəʊ'baŋ
AM goʊ'baŋ

gobbet
BR 'gɒbɪt, -s
AM 'gɑbət, -s

Gobbi
BR 'gɒbi
AM 'gɑbi

gobble
BR 'gɒb|l, -lz, -l̩ɪŋ\-lɪŋ, -ld
AM 'gɑb|əl, -əlz, -(ə)lɪŋ, -əld

gobbledegook
BR 'gɒbldɪguːk
AM 'gɑbəldiˌgʊk

gobbledygook
BR 'gɒbldɪguːk
AM 'gɑbəldiˌgʊk

gobbler
BR 'gɒblə(r), -z
AM 'gɑb(ə)lər, -z

gobby
BR 'gɒb|i, -ɪz
AM 'gɑbi, -z

Gobelins
BR 'gəʊbəlɪnz, 'gəʊbl̩ɪnz
AM 'goʊbələnz
FR gɔblɛ̃

gobemouche
BR 'gɒbmuːʃ, -ɨz
AM goʊb'muʃ, -əz

go-between
BR 'gəʊbɪtwiːn, -z
AM 'goʊbəˌtwin, -z

Gobi Desert
BR ˌgəʊbɪ 'dɛzət
AM ˌgoʊbi 'dɛzərt

Gobineau
BR 'gɒbɪnəʊ
AM 'gɑbəˌnoʊ

goblet
BR 'gɒblɪt, -s
AM 'gɑblət, -s

goblin
BR 'gɒblɪn, -z
AM 'gɑblən, -z

gobsmack
BR 'gɒbsmak, -s, -ɪŋ, -t
AM 'gɑbˌsmæk, -s, -ɪŋ, -t

goby
fish
BR 'gəʊb|i, -ɪz
AM 'goʊbi, -z

go-by
BR 'gəʊbʌɪ
AM 'goʊˌbaɪ

go-cart
BR 'gəʊkɑːt, -s
AM 'goʊˌkɑrt, -s

god
BR gɒd, -z
AM gɑd, -z

Godalming
BR 'gɒdlmɪŋ
AM 'gɑdəlmɪŋ

Godard
BR 'gɒdɑː(d)
AM 'goʊˌdɑrd, 'gɑdərd

godchild
BR 'gɒdtʃʌɪld
AM 'gɑdˌtʃaɪld

godchildren
BR 'gɒdˌtʃɪldr(ə)n
AM 'gɑdˌtʃɪldrən

Godd
BR gɒd
AM gɒd

goddam
BR 'gɒdam, -d
AM 'gɑd'dæm, -d

goddamn
BR 'gɒdam, -d
AM 'gɑd'dæm, -d

Goddard
BR 'gɒdɑːd, 'gɒdəd
AM 'gɑdərd

goddess
BR 'gɒdɪs, 'gɒdɛs, -ɨz
AM 'gɑdəs, -əz

Gödel
BR 'gəʊdl
AM 'goʊdəl

godet
BR ˌgəʊ'dɛt, 'gəʊdeɪ
AM goʊ'dɛt

godetia
BR gə(ʊ)'diːʃ(ɪ)ə(r), -z
AM gə'diʃə, -z

godets
BR ˌgəʊ'dɛts, 'gəʊdeɪz
AM goʊ'dɛts

go-devil
BR 'gəʊˌdɛvl, -z
AM 'goʊˌdɛvəl, -z

godfather
BR 'gɒdˌfɑːðə(r), -z
AM 'gɑdˌfɑðər, -z

godfearing
BR 'gɒdˌfɪərɪŋ
AM 'gɑdˌfɪrɪŋ

godforsaken
BR 'gɒdfəˌseɪk(ə)n
AM 'gɑdfər'seɪkən

Godfrey
BR 'gɒdfri
AM 'gɑdfri

Godgiven
BR 'gɒdˌgɪvn
AM ˌgɑd'gɪvən

godhead
BR 'gɒdhɛd, -z
AM 'gɑdˌ(h)ɛd, -z

godhood
BR 'gɒdhʊd, -z
AM 'gɑdˌ(h)ʊd, -z

Godiva
BR gə'dʌɪvə(r)
AM gə'daɪvə

godless
BR 'gɒdləs
AM 'gɑdləs

godlessly
BR 'gɒdləsli
AM 'gɑdləsli

godlessness
BR 'gɒdləsnəs
AM 'gɑdləsnəs

godlike
BR 'gɒdlʌɪk
AM 'gɑdˌlaɪk

godliness
BR 'gɒdlɪnɪs
AM 'gɑdlinɨs

godly
BR 'gɒdl|i, -ɪə(r), -ɪɪst
AM 'gɑdli, -ər, -ɨst

Godman
BR 'gɒdmən
AM 'gɑdmən

godmother
BR 'gɒdˌmʌðə(r), -z
AM 'gɑdˌməðər, -z

Godolphin
BR gə'dɒlfɪn
AM gə'dɔlfən, gə'dɑlfən

godown
BR 'gəʊdaʊn, -z
AM 'goʊˌdaʊn, -z

godparent
BR 'gɒdˌpɛːrənt, 'gɒdˌpɛːrn̩t, -s
AM 'gɑdˌpɛrənt, -s

godsend
BR ˈɡɒdsɛnd, -z
AM ˈɡɑdˌsɛnd, -z

godship
BR ˈɡɒdʃɪp, -s
AM ˈɡɑdˌʃɪp, -s

godson
BR ˈɡɒdsʌn, -z
AM ˈɡɑdˌsən, -z

god-speed
BR ˌɡɒdˈspiːd
AM ˌɡɑdzˈpid, ˌɡɑdˈspid

Godunov
BR ˈɡɒdʉnɒf
AM ˈɡɔdəˌnɔv, ˈɡɔdəˌnɔf, ˈɡɑdəˌnɑv, ˈɡɑdəˌnɑf
RUS ɡəduˈnof

godward
BR ˈɡɒdwəd, -z
AM ˈɡɑdwərd, -z

Godwin
BR ˈɡɒdwɪn
AM ˈɡɑdwən

godwit
BR ˈɡɒdwɪt, -s
AM ˈɡɑdˌwɪt, -s

Godwottery
BR ˌɡɒdˈwɒt(ə)ri
AM ˈɡɑdˌwɑdəri

Godzilla
BR ɡɒdˈzɪlə(r)
AM ɡɑdˈzɪlə

Goebbels
BR ˈɡəːblz
AM ˈɡʊbəlz

goer
BR ˈɡəʊə(r), -z
AM ˈɡoʊ(ə)r, -z

Goering
BR ˈɡəːrɪŋ
AM ˈɡʊrɪŋ

goest
BR ˈɡəʊɪst
AM ˈɡoʊ(ə)st

goeth
BR ˈɡəʊɪθ
AM ˈɡoʊ(ə)θ

Goethe
BR ˈɡəːtə(r)
AM ˈɡʊdə

Goethean
BR ˈɡəːtiən, -z
AM ˈɡʊdiən, -z

Goethian
BR ˈɡəːtiən, -z
AM ˈɡʊdiən, -z

gofer
BR ˈɡəʊfə(r), -z
AM ˈɡoʊfər, -z

Goff
BR ɡɒf
AM ɡɔf, ɡɑf

goffer
BR ˈɡəʊf|ə(r), ˈɡɒf|ə(r), -əz, -(ə)rɪŋ, -əd
AM ˈɡɔfər, ˈɡɑfər, -z, -ɪŋ, -d

Gog
BR ɡɒɡ
AM ɡɔɡ, ɡɑɡ

go-getter
BR ˌɡəʊˈɡɛtə(r), ˈɡəʊˌɡɛtə(r), -z
AM ˌɡoʊˈɡɛdər, -z

goggle
BR ˈɡɒɡ|l, -lz, -l̩ɪŋ\-lɪŋ, -ld
AM ˈɡɑɡ|əl, -əlz, -(ə)lɪŋ, -əld

goglet
BR ˈɡɒɡlɨt, -s
AM ˈɡɑɡlət, -s

Gogmagog
BR ˌɡɒɡməˈɡɒɡ
AM ˌɡɔɡməˈɡɔɡ, ˌɡɑɡməˈɡɑɡ

go-go
BR ˈɡəʊɡəʊ
AM ˈɡoʊˌɡoʊ

Gogol
BR ˈɡəʊɡɒl
AM ˈɡoʊˌɡɔl, ˈɡoʊɡəl
RUS ˈɡoɡəlʲ

Goiânia
BR ɡɔɪˈanɪə(r)
AM ɡɔɪˈæniə

Goidel
BR ˈɡɔɪdl, -z
AM ˈɡɔɪdəl, -z

Goidelic
BR ɡɔɪˈdɛlɪk
AM ɡɔɪˈdɛlɪk

going
BR ˈɡəʊɪŋ, -z
AM ˈɡoʊɪŋ, -z

goiter
BR ˈɡɔɪtə(r), -z, -d
AM ˈɡɔɪdər, -z, -d

goitre
BR ˈɡɔɪtə(r), -z, -d
AM ˈɡɔɪdər, -z, -d

goitrous
BR ˈɡɔɪtrəs
AM ˈɡɔɪtrəs

go-kart
BR ˈɡəʊkɑːt, -s
AM ˈɡoʊˌkɑrt, -s

Golan Heights
BR ˌɡəʊlan ˈhʌɪts, ˌɡəʊlɑːn +, ɡəʊˈlɑːn +
AM ˌɡoʊlɑn ˈhaɪts

Golborne
BR ˈɡəʊlbɔːn
AM ˈɡoʊlˌbɔ(ə)rn

Golconda
BR ɡɒlˈkɒndə(r), -z
AM ɡɑlˈkɑndə, -z

gold
BR ɡəʊld
AM ɡoʊld

Golda
BR ˈɡəʊldə(r)
AM ˈɡoʊldə

Goldberg
BR ˈɡəʊl(d)bəːɡ
AM ˈɡoʊl(d)ˌbərɡ

golden
BR ˈɡəʊld(ə)n
AM ˈɡoʊldən

golden-ager
BR ˌɡəʊld(ə)nˈeɪdʒə(r), -z
AM ˌɡoʊldənˈeɪdʒər, -z

goldeneye
BR ˈɡəʊldənʌɪ, ˈɡəʊldn̩ʌɪ, -z
AM ˈɡoʊldənˌaɪ, -z

goldenly
BR ˈɡəʊld(ə)nli
AM ˈɡoʊldənli

goldenness
BR ˈɡəʊld(ə)nnəs
AM ˈɡoʊldə(n)nəs

goldenrod
BR ˈɡəʊld(ə)nrɒd, ˌɡəʊld(ə)nˈrɒd
AM ˈɡoʊldənˌrɑd

goldfield
BR ˈɡəʊl(d)fiːld, -z
AM ˈɡoʊl(d)ˌfild, -z

goldfinch
BR ˈɡəʊl(d)fɪn(t)ʃ, -ɪz
AM ˈɡoʊl(d)ˌfɪn(t)ʃ, -ɪz

goldfish
BR ˈɡəʊl(d)fɪʃ
AM ˈɡoʊl(d)ˌfɪʃ

Goldie
BR ˈɡəʊldi
AM ˈɡoʊldi

Goldilocks
BR ˈɡəʊldɪlɒks
AM ˈɡoʊldiˌlɑks

Golding
BR ˈɡəʊldɪŋ
AM ˈɡoʊldɪŋ

Goldman
BR ˈɡəʊl(d)mən
AM ˈɡoʊl(d)mən

Goldmark
BR ˈɡəʊl(d)mɑːk
AM ˈɡoʊl(d)ˌmɑrk

goldmine
BR ˈɡəʊl(d)mʌɪn, -z
AM ˈɡoʊl(d)ˌmaɪn, -z

Goldschmidt
BR ˈɡəʊl(d)ʃmɪt
AM ˈɡoʊl(d)ˌʃmɪt

goldsmith
BR ˈɡəʊl(d)smɪθ, -s
AM ˈɡoʊl(d)ˌsmɪθ, -s

Goldstein
BR ˈɡəʊl(d)stiːn, ˈɡəʊl(d)stʌɪn
AM ˈɡoʊl(d)ˌstaɪn, ˈɡoʊl(d)ˌstin

Goldwater
BR ˈɡəʊldˌwɔːtə(r)
AM ˈɡoʊl(d)ˌwɔdər, ˈɡoʊl(d)ˌwɑdər

Goldwyn
BR ˈɡəʊldwɪn
AM ˈɡoʊl(d)wən

golem
BR ˈɡəʊləm, ˈɡɔɪləm, -z
AM ˈɡoʊləm, -z

golf
BR ɡɒlf, -ɪŋ
AM ɡɔlf, ɡɑlf, -ɪŋ

golfer
BR ˈɡɒlfə(r), -z
AM ˈɡɔlfər, ˈɡɑlfər, -z

Golgi
BR ˈɡɒldʒi
AM ˈɡɔldʒi, ˈɡoʊldʒi

Golgotha
BR ˈɡɒlɡəθə(r), ɡɒlˈɡɒðə(r)
AM ˈɡɑlɡəθə, ˈɡɔlɡəθə, ˌɡɑlˈɡɑθə, ˌɡɔlˈɡɔθə

Goliath
BR ɡəˈlʌɪəθ, -s
AM ɡəˈlaɪəθ, -s

Golightly
BR ɡə(ʊ)ˈlʌɪtli
AM ɡoʊˈlaɪtli

Gollancz
BR ˈɡɒlaŋks, ɡəˈlaŋks
AM ˈɡɑlæŋks, ɡəˈlæŋkʃ

golliwog
BR ˈɡɒlɪwɒɡ, -z
AM ˈɡɑliˌwɑɡ, -z

gollop
BR ˈɡɒləp, -s, -ɪŋ, -t
AM ˈɡɑləp, -s, -ɪŋ, -t

golly
BR ˈɡɒli
AM ˈɡɑli

gollywog
BR ˈɡɒlɪwɒɡ, -z
AM ˈɡɑliˌwɑɡ, -z

golosh
BR ɡəˈlɒʃ, -ɪz
AM ɡəˈlɑʃ, -əz

gombeen
BR ɡɒmˈbiːn, -z
AM ɡɑmˈbin, -z

Gomer
BR ˈɡəʊmə(r)
AM ˈɡoʊmər

Gomes
BR ˈɡəʊmɛz
AM ˈɡoʊmɛz

Gómez
BR ˈɡəʊmɛz
AM ˈɡoʊmɛz

Gomorrah
BR ɡəˈmɒrə(r)
AM ɡəˈmɔrə

Gompers
BR ˈɡɒmpəz
AM ˈɡɑmpərz

gonad
BR ˈɡəʊnad, ˈɡɒnad, -z
AM ˈɡoʊˌnæd, -z

gonadal
BR gə(ʊ)'neɪdl
AM goʊ'nædəl

gonadotrophic
BR ˌgəʊnədə'trɒfɪk, ˌgəʊnədə'trəʊfɪk, ˌgɒnədə'trɒfɪk, ˌgɒnədə'trəʊfɪk
AM ˌgoʊˌnædə'trɑfɪk, ˌgoʊˌnædə'troʊfɪk

gonadotrophin
BR ˌgəʊnədə'trəʊfɪn, ˌgəʊnədə'trɒfɪn, ˌgɒnədə'trəʊfɪn, ˌgɒnədə'trɒfɪn
AM ˌgoʊˌnædə'troʊfən

gonadotropic
BR ˌgəʊnədə'trɒpɪk, ˌgəʊnədə'trəʊpɪk, ˌgɒnədə'trɒpɪk, ˌgɒnədə'trəʊpɪk
AM ˌgoʊˌnædə'trɑpɪk

Goncourt
BR 'gɒŋkʊə(r), 'gɒŋkɔː(r)
AM 'gɔnˌkʊ(ə)r, 'gɑnˌkʊ(ə)r

gondola
BR 'gɒndələ(r), 'gɒndl̩ə(r), -z
AM 'gɑndələ, -z

gondolier
BR ˌgɒndə'lɪə(r), -z
AM ˌgɑndə'lɪ(ə)r, -z

Gondwana
BR gɒn'dwɑːnə(r)
AM gɑn'dwɑnə

Gondwanaland
BR gɒn'dwɑːnəland
AM gɑn'dwɑnəˌlænd

gone
BR gɒn
AM gɔn, gɑn

goner
BR 'gɒnə(r), -z
AM 'gɔnər, 'gɑnər, -z

Goneril
BR 'gɒn(ə)rɪl, 'gɒn(ə)rl̩
AM 'gɑnərəl

gonfalon
BR 'gɒnfələn, 'gɒnfl̩ən, -z
AM 'gɑnfələn, -z

gonfalonier
BR ˌgɒnfələ'nɪə(r), ˌgɒnfl̩ə'nɪə(r), -z
AM ˌgɑnfələ'nɪ(ə)r, -z

gong
BR gɒŋ, -z
AM gɔŋ, gɑŋ, -z

goniometer
BR ˌgəʊnɪ'ɒmɪtə(r), -z
AM ˌgoʊni'ɑmədər, -z

goniometric
BR ˌgəʊnɪə'mɛtrɪk
AM ˌgoʊniə'mɛtrɪk

goniometrical
BR ˌgəʊnɪə'mɛtrɪkl
AM ˌgoʊniə'mɛtrəkəl

goniometrically
BR ˌgəʊnɪə'mɛtrɪkli
AM ˌgoʊniə'mɛtrək(ə)li

goniometry
BR ˌgəʊnɪ'ɒmɪtri
AM ˌgoʊni'ɑmətri

gonk
BR gɒŋk, -s
AM gɔŋk, gɑŋk, -s

gonna[1]
strong form
BR 'gɒnə(r)
AM 'gənə, 'gɔnə, 'gɑnə

gonna[2]
weak form
BR 'gənə(r), 'gn̩ə(r)
AM 'gənə

gonococcal
BR ˌgɒnə'kɒkl
AM ˌgɑnə'kɑkəl

gonococci
BR ˌgɒnə'kɒk(s)ʌɪ, ˌgɒnə'kɒk(s)iː
AM ˌgɑnə'kɑ(k)ˌsaɪ

gonococcus
BR ˌgɒnə'kɒkəs
AM ˌgɑnə'kɑkəs

gonorrhea
BR ˌgɒnə'rɪə(r)
AM ˌgɑnə'riə

gonorrheal
BR ˌgɒnə'rɪəl
AM ˌgɑnə'riəl

gonorrhoea
BR ˌgɒnə'rɪə(r)
AM ˌgɑnə'riə

gonorrhoeal
BR ˌgɒnə'rɪəl
AM ˌgɑnə'riəl

Gonville
BR 'gɒnvɪl
AM 'gɑnˌvɪl

Gonzales
BR gɒn'zɑːlɪz, gɒn'zɑːlɛz, gən'zɑːlɪz, gən'zɑːlɛz
AM gɑn'zɑləs, gɑn'zɑləz

González
BR gɒn'zɑːlɪz, gɒn'zɑːlɛz, gən'zɑːlɪz, gən'zɑːlɛz
AM gɑn'zɑləs, gɑn'zɑləz
SP gon'θaleθ, gon'sales

gonzo
BR 'gɒnzəʊ, -z
AM 'gɑnzoʊ, -z

goo
BR guː, -z
AM gu, -z

goober
BR 'guːbə(r), -z
AM 'gubər, -z

Gooch
BR guːtʃ
AM gutʃ

good
BR gʊd, -z
AM gʊd, -z

Goodall
BR 'gʊdɔːl
AM 'gʊdˌɔl, 'gʊdˌɑl

Goodbody
BR 'gʊdˌbɒdi
AM 'gʊdˌbɑdi

goodby
BR (ˌ)gʊd'bʌɪ, -z
AM gʊd'baɪ, -z

goodbye
BR (ˌ)gʊd'bʌɪ, -z
AM gʊd'baɪ, -z

Goodchild
BR 'gʊdtʃʌɪld
AM 'gʊdˌtʃaɪld

Goode
BR gʊd
AM gʊd

Goodenough
BR 'gʊdɪnʌf, 'gʊdn̩ʌf
AM 'gʊdənəf

Goodfellow
BR 'gʊdˌfɛləʊ
AM 'gʊdˌfɛloʊ

Goodge
BR guːdʒ
AM gʊdʒ

Goodhart
BR 'gʊdhɑːt
AM 'gʊdˌ(h)ɑrt

good-hearted
BR ˌgʊd'hɑːtɪd
AM ¦gʊd¦(h)ɑrdəd

good-heartedness
BR ˌgʊd'hɑːtɪdnɪs
AM ¦gʊd¦(h)ɑrdədnəs

goodie
BR 'gʊd|i, -ɪz
AM 'gʊdi, -z

goodish
BR 'gʊdɪʃ
AM 'gʊdɪʃ

Goodison
BR 'gʊdɪs(ə)n
AM 'gʊdəsən

goodliness
BR 'gʊdlɪnɪs
AM 'gʊdlinɪs

goodly
BR 'gʊdl|i, -ɪə(r), -ɪɪst
AM 'gʊdli, -ər, -ɪst

goodman
BR 'gʊdmən
AM 'gʊdmən

goodmen
BR 'gʊdmən
AM 'gʊdmən

good-natured
BR ˌgʊd'neɪtʃəd
AM ¦gʊd¦neɪtʃərd

good-naturedly
BR ˌgʊd'neɪtʃədli
AM ¦gʊd¦neɪtʃərdli

goodness
BR 'gʊdnəs
AM 'gʊdnəs

goodnight
BR (ˌ)gʊd'nʌɪt, -s
AM gʊd'naɪt, -s

goodo
BR ˌgʊd'əʊ
AM ˌgʊd'oʊ

good-oh
BR ˌgʊd'əʊ
AM ˌgʊd'oʊ

Goodrich
BR 'gʊdrɪtʃ
AM 'gʊdrɪtʃ

goods
BR gʊdz
AM gʊdz

goodwife
BR 'gʊdwʌɪf
AM 'gʊdˌwaɪf

goodwill
BR ˌgʊd'wɪl
AM ˌgʊd'wɪl

Goodwin
BR 'gʊdwɪn
AM 'gʊdwɪn

goodwives
BR 'gʊdwʌɪvz
AM 'gʊdˌwaɪvz

Goodwood
BR 'gʊdwʊd
AM 'gʊdˌwʊd

Goodwright
BR 'gʊdrʌɪt
AM 'gʊdˌraɪt

goody
BR 'gʊd|i, -ɪz
AM 'gʊdi, -z

Goodyear
BR 'gʊdjɪə(r), 'gʊdjəː(r)
AM 'gʊdˌjɪ(ə)r

gooey
BR 'guː|i, -ɪə(r), -ɪɪst
AM 'gui, -ər, -ɪst

gooeyly
BR 'guːɪli
AM 'guəli

gooeyness
BR 'guːɪnɪs
AM 'guinɪs

goof
BR guːf, -s, -ɪŋ, -t
AM guf, -s, -ɪŋ, -t

goofball
BR 'guːfbɔːl, -z
AM 'gufˌbɔl, 'gufˌbɑl, -z

goofily
BR 'guːfɪli
AM 'gufəli

goofiness
BR 'guːfɪnɪs
AM 'gufinɪs

goofy
BR 'gu:f|i, -ɪə(r), -ɪɪst
AM 'gufi, -ər, -ɨst

goog
BR gu:g, -z
AM gug, -z

Googie
BR 'gu:gi
AM 'gʊgi

googly
BR 'gu:gl|i, -ɪz
AM 'gugli, -z

googol
BR 'gu:gɒl
AM 'gugəl, 'gu,gɔl, 'gu,gɑl

gook
BR gu:k, -s
AM gʊk, -s

Goole
BR gu:l
AM gul

goolie
BR 'gu:l|i, -ɪz
AM 'guli, -z

goon
BR gu:n, -z
AM gun, -z

goonery
BR 'gu:n(ə)ri
AM 'gunəri

gooney
BR 'gu:ni
AM 'guni

Goonhilly
BR gʊn'hɪli, ,gu:n'hɪli
AM gʊn'hɪli

goop
BR gu:p, -s
AM gup, -s

goopiness
BR 'gu:pɪnɪs
AM 'gupinɨs

goopy
BR 'gu:p|i, -ɪə(r), -ɪɪst
AM 'gupi, -ər, -ɨst

goosander
BR gu:'sandə(r), -z
AM gu'sændər, -z

goose
BR gu:s, -ɪz, -ɪŋ, -t
AM gus, -əz, -ɪŋ, -t

gooseberry
BR 'gʊzb(ə)r|i, -ɪz
AM 'gus,bɛri, -z

goosebumps
BR 'gu:sbʌmps
AM 'gus,bəm(p)s

gooseflesh
BR 'gu:sflɛʃ
AM 'gus,flɛʃ

goosefoot
BR 'gu:sfʊt, -s
AM 'gus,fʊt, -s

goosegog
BR 'gʊzgɒg, -z
AM 'gʊz,gɑg, -z

goosegrass
BR 'gu:sgrɑ:s, 'gu:sgras, -ɪz
AM 'gus,græs, -əz

gooseherd
BR 'gu:shə:d, -z
AM 'gus,(h)ərd, -z

goosestep
BR 'gu:sstɛp, -s, -ɪŋ, -t
AM 'gu(s),stɛp, -s, -ɪŋ, -t

goosey
BR 'gu:si
AM 'gusi

Goossens
BR 'gu:snz
AM 'gusəns

gopher
BR 'gəʊfə(r), -z
AM 'goʊfər, -z

goral
BR 'gɔ:rəl, 'gɔ:rl̩, -z
AM 'goʊrəl, -z

Gorbachev
BR 'gɔ:bətʃɒf
AM 'gɔrbə,tʃɔv, 'gɔrbə,tʃɔf, 'gɔrbə,tʃɑv, 'gɔrbə,tʃɑf

Gorbals
BR 'gɔ:blz
AM 'gɔrbəlz

gorblimey
BR (,)gɔ:'blʌɪm|i, -ɪz
AM gɔr'blaɪmi, -z

gorcock
BR 'gɔ:kɒk, -s
AM 'gɔr,kɑk, -s

Gordian
BR 'gɔ:dɪən
AM 'gɔrdiən

Gordimer
BR 'gɔ:dɪmə(r)
AM 'gɔrdəmər

Gordium
BR 'gɔ:dɪəm
AM 'gɔrdiəm

gordo
BR 'gɔ:dəʊ, -z
AM 'gɔr,doʊ, -z

Gordon
BR 'gɔ:dn
AM 'gɔrdən

Gordonstoun
BR 'gɔ:dnst(ə)n, 'gɔ:dnzt(ə)n
AM 'gɔrdən,stoʊn

gore
BR gɔ:(r), -z, -ɪŋ, -d
AM gɔ(ə)r, -z, -ɪŋ, -d

Górecki
BR gʉ'rɛtski
AM gʊ'rɛtski

Gore-tex®
BR 'gɔ:tɛks
AM 'gɔr,tɛks

gorge
BR gɔ:dʒ, -ɪz, -ɪŋ, -d
AM gɔrdʒ, -əz, -ɪŋ, -t

gorgeous
BR 'gɔ:dʒəs
AM 'gɔrdʒəs

gorgeously
BR 'gɔ:dʒəsli
AM 'gɔrdʒəsli

gorgeousness
BR 'gɔ:dʒəsnəs
AM 'gɔrdʒəsnəs

gorger
BR 'gɔ:dʒə(r), -z
AM 'gɔrdʒər, -z

gorget
BR 'gɔ:dʒɪt, -s
AM 'gɔrdʒət, -s

Gorgio
BR 'gɔ:dʒəʊ, -z
AM 'gɔr,dʒoʊ, -z

gorgon
BR 'gɔ:g(ə)n, -z
AM 'gɔrgən, -z

gorgonia
BR gɔ:'gəʊnɪə(*r*), -z
AM gɔr'goʊniə, -z

gorgoniae
BR gɔ:'gəʊnɪi:
AM gɔr'goʊni,i, gɔr'goʊni,aɪ

gorgonian
BR gɔ:'gəʊnɪən, -z
AM gɔr'goʊniən, -z

gorgonise
BR 'gɔ:gənʌɪz, 'gɔ:gn̩ʌɪz, -ɪz, -ɪŋ, -d
AM 'gɔrgə,naɪz, -ɨz, -ɪŋ, -d

gorgonize
BR 'gɔ:gənʌɪz, 'gɔ:gn̩ʌɪz, -ɪz, -ɪŋ, -d
AM 'gɔrgə,naɪz, -ɨz, -ɪŋ, -d

Gorgonzola
BR ,gɔ:g(ə)n'zəʊlə(*r*)
AM ,gɔrgən'zoʊlə

gorilla
BR gə'rɪlə(*r*), -z
AM gə'rɪlə, -z

gorily
BR 'gɔ:rɨli
AM 'gɔrəli

goriness
BR 'gɔ:rɪnɪs
AM 'gɔrinɨs

Goring
BR 'gɔ:rɪŋ
AM 'gɔrɪŋ

Gorki
BR 'gɔ:ki
AM 'gɔrki

Gorky
BR 'gɔ:ki
AM 'gɔrki

Gorman
BR 'gɔ:mən
AM 'gɔrmən

gormandise
BR 'gɔ:m(ə)ndʌɪz, -ɪz, -ɪŋ, -d
AM 'gɔrmən,daɪz, -ɨz, -ɪŋ, -d

gormandiser
BR 'gɔ:m(ə)ndʌɪzə(r), -z
AM 'gɔrmən,daɪzər, -z

gormandize
BR 'gɔ:m(ə)ndʌɪz, -ɪz, -ɪŋ, -d
AM 'gɔrmən,daɪz, -ɨz, -ɪŋ, -d

gormandizer
BR 'gɔ:m(ə)ndʌɪzə(r), -z
AM 'gɔrmən,daɪzər, -z

gormless
BR 'gɔ:mləs
AM 'gɔrmləs

gormlessly
BR 'gɔ:mləsli
AM 'gɔrmləsli

gormlessness
BR 'gɔ:mləsnəs
AM 'gɔrmləsnəs

Gormley
BR 'gɔ:mli
AM 'gɔrmli

Goronwy
BR gə'rɒnwi
AM gə'rɑnwi

go-round
BR 'gəʊraʊnd
AM 'goʊ,raʊnd

Gor-Ray
BR 'gɔ:reɪ
AM 'gɔ(r),reɪ

gorse
BR gɔ:s
AM gɔ(ə)rs

Gorsedd
BR 'gɔ:sɛð
AM 'gɔrsɛð

Gorseinon
BR gɔ:'sʌɪnən
AM gɔr'saɪnən

gorsy
BR 'gɔ:s|i, -ɪə(r), -ɪɪst
AM 'gɔrsi, -ər, -ɨst

Gorton
BR 'gɔ:tn
AM 'gɔrt(ə)n

gory
BR 'gɔ:r|i, -ɪə(r), -ɪɪst
AM 'gɔri, -ər, -ɨst

Gosforth
BR 'gɒsfəθ, 'gɒsfɔ:θ
AM 'gɑsfərθ

gosh
BR gɒʃ
AM gɑʃ

goshawk
BR 'gɒshɔ:k, -s
AM 'gɑs,(h)ɔk, 'gɑs,(h)ɑk, -s

Goshen
BR ˈɡəʊʃn
AM ˈɡoʊʃən

gosling
BR ˈɡɒzlɪŋ, -z
AM ˈɡɑzlɪŋ, -z

go-slow
BR ˌɡəʊˈsləʊ, -z
AM ˌɡoʊˈsloʊ, -z

gospel
BR ˈɡɒspl, -z
AM ˈɡɑspəl, -z

gospeler
BR ˈɡɒspələ(r), ˈɡɒspl̩ə(r), -z
AM ˈɡɑspələr, -z

gospeller
BR ˈɡɒspələ(r), ˈɡɒspl̩ə(r), -z
AM ˈɡɑspələr, -z

Gosport
BR ˈɡɒspɔːt
AM ˈɡɑsˌpɔ(ə)rt

Goss
BR ɡɒs
AM ɡɔs, ɡɑs

gossamer
BR ˈɡɒsəmə(r), -d
AM ˈɡɑsəmər, -d

gossamery
BR ˈɡɒsəm(ə)ri
AM ˈɡɑsəˌmɛri

gossan
BR ˈɡɒzn
AM ˈɡɑsən

Gosse
BR ɡɒs
AM ɡɔs, ɡɑs

gossip
BR ˈɡɒs|ɪp, -ɪps, -ɪpɪŋ, -ɪpt
AM ˈɡɑsəp, -s, -ɪŋ, -t

gossiper
BR ˈɡɒsɪpə(r), -z
AM ˈɡɑsəpər, -z

gossipmonger
BR ˈɡɒsɪpˌmʌŋɡə(r), -z
AM ˈɡɑsəpˌmɑŋɡər, ˈɡɑsəpˌməŋɡər, -z

gossipy
BR ˈɡɒsɪpi
AM ˈɡɑsəpi

gossoon
BR ɡɒˈsuːn, -z
AM ɡɑˈsun, -z

got
BR ɡɒt
AM ɡɑt

gotcha
BR ˈɡɒtʃə(r), -z
AM ˈɡɑtʃə, -z

Goth
BR ɡɒθ, -s
AM ɡɔθ, ɡɑθ, -s

Gotha
BR ˈɡəʊθə(r), ˈɡəʊtə(r)
AM ˈɡoʊθə

Gotham[1]
New York
BR ˈɡɒθ(ə)m
AM ˈɡɑθəm

Gotham[2]
place in UK
BR ˈɡəʊtəm, ˈɡɒtəm
AM ˈɡoʊdəm

Gothamite
BR ˈɡɒθəmʌɪt, ˈɡɒθm̩ʌɪt, -s
AM ˈɡɑθəˌmaɪt, -s

Gothard
BR ˈɡɒθɑːd
AM ˈɡɑθərd

Gothenburg
BR ˈɡɒθnbəːɡ
AM ˈɡɑθənˌbərɡ

Gothic
BR ˈɡɒθɪk
AM ˈɡɑθɪk

Gothically
BR ˈɡɒθɨkli
AM ˈɡɑθək(ə)li

Gothicise
BR ˈɡɒθɪsʌɪz, -ɪz, -ɪŋ, -d
AM ˈɡɑθəˌsaɪz, -ɨz, -ɪŋ, -d

Gothicism
BR ˈɡɒθɪsɪz(ə)m
AM ˈɡɑθəˌsɪzəm

Gothicize
BR ˈɡɒθɪsʌɪz, -ɨz, -ɪŋ, -d
AM ˈɡɑθəˌsaɪz, -ɨz, -ɪŋ, -d

Gotland
BR ˈɡɒtland
AM ˈɡɑtˌlænd

gotta
BR ˈɡɒtə(r)
AM ˈɡɑdə

gotten
BR ˈɡɒtn
AM ˈɡɑtn

Götterdämmerung
BR ˌɡɒtəˈdamərʊŋ, ˌɡəːtəˈdamərʊŋ, ˌɡɒtəˈdamərʌŋ, ˌɡəːtəˈdamərʌŋ
AM ˌɡɑdərˈdæmərʊŋ
GER ˈɡœtɐdɛmərʊŋ

gouache
BR ɡʊˈɑːʃ, ɡwɑːʃ, -ɨz
AM ɡwɑʃ, ɡuˈɑʃ, -əz

Gouda
BR ˈɡaʊdə(r), ˈɡuːdə(r)
AM ˈɡudə
DU ˈxɔʊdɑ

Goudge
BR ɡuːdʒ
AM ɡudʒ

Goudy
BR ˈɡaʊdi
AM ˈɡaʊdi

gouge
BR ɡaʊdʒ, -ɨz, -ɪŋ, -d
AM ɡaʊdʒ, -əz, -ɪŋ, -t

gouger
BR ˈɡaʊdʒə(r), -z
AM ˈɡaʊdʒər, -z

Gough
BR ɡɒf
AM ɡɔf, ɡɑf

goujons
BR ˈɡuː(d)ʒ(ə)nz, ˈɡuː(d)ʒɒnz, ˈɡuːʒɒ̃
AM ˈɡudʒənz

goulash
BR ˈɡuːlaʃ, -ɨz
AM ˈɡuˌlɑʃ, -əz

Gould
BR ɡuːld
AM ɡuld

Gounod
BR ˈɡuːnəʊ
AM ɡuˈnoʊ

gourami
BR ɡʊˈrɑːm|i, ˈɡʊərəm|i, -ɪz
AM ɡəˈrɑmi, -z

gouramy
BR ɡʊˈrɑːm|i, ˈɡʊərəm|i, -ɪz
AM ɡəˈrɑmi, -z

gourd
BR ɡʊəd, ɡɔːd, -z
AM ɡɔ(ə)rd, -z

gourdful
BR ˈɡʊədfʊl, ˈɡɔːdfʊl, -z
AM ˈɡɔrdˌfʊl, -z

Gourlay
BR ˈɡʊəli
AM ˈɡərli

Gourley
BR ˈɡʊəli
AM ˈɡərli

gourmand
BR ˈɡʊəmənd, ˈɡɔːmənd, -z
AM ˌɡʊrˈmɑnd, -z

gourmandise
BR ˈɡʊəm(ə)ndʌɪz, ˈɡɔːm(ə)ndʌɪz, -ɨz, -ɪŋ, -d
AM ˈɡʊrmənˌdaɪz, -ɨz, -ɪŋ, -d

gourmandism
BR ˈɡʊəm(ə)ndɪz(ə)m, ˈɡɔːm(ə)ndɪz(ə)m
AM ˈɡʊrmənˌdɪzəm

gourmandize
BR ˈɡʊəm(ə)ndʌɪz, ˈɡɔːm(ə)ndʌɪz, -ɨz, -ɪŋ, -d
AM ˈɡʊrmənˌdaɪz, -ɨz, -ɪŋ, -d

gourmet
BR ˈɡʊəmeɪ, ˈɡɔːmeɪ, -z
AM ˌɡʊrˈmeɪ, ˌɡɔrˈmeɪ, -z

gout
BR ɡaʊt
AM ɡaʊt

goutily
BR ˈɡaʊtɨli
AM ˈɡaʊdəli

goutiness
BR ˈɡaʊtɪnɨs
AM ˈɡaʊdinɨs

goutweed
BR ˈɡaʊtwiːd
AM ˈɡaʊtˌwid

gouty
BR ˈɡaʊt|i, -ɪə(r), -ɪɨst
AM ˈɡaʊdi, -ər, -ɨst

Govan
BR ˈɡʌvn
AM ˈɡəvən

govern
BR ˈɡʌv|n, -nz, -n̩ɪŋ\-ənɪŋ, -nd
AM ˈɡəvərn, -z, -ɪŋ, -d

governability
BR ˌɡʌvn̩əˈbɪlɪti, ˌɡʌvənəˈbɪlɪti
AM ˌɡəvərnəˈbɪlɨdi

governable
BR ˈɡʌvn̩əbl, ˈɡʌvənəbl
AM ˈɡəvərnəbəl

governableness
BR ˈɡʌvn̩əblnəs, ˈɡʌv(ə)nəblnəs
AM ˈɡəvərnəbəlnəs

governance
BR ˈɡʌvn̩əns, ˈɡʌvənəns
AM ˈɡəvərnəns

governess
BR ˈɡʌvn̩ɪs, ˈɡʌvn̩ɛs, -ɨz
AM ˈɡəvərnəs, -əz

governessy
BR ˈɡʌvn̩ɪsi
AM ˈɡəvərnəsi

government
BR ˈɡʌvnm(ə)nt, ˈɡʌvəm(ə)nt, -s
AM ˈɡəvər(n)mənt, ˈɡəvə(r)mənt, -s

governmental
BR ˌɡʌvnˈmɛntl, ˌɡʌvəˈmɛntl
AM ˌɡəvər(n)ˈmɛn(t)l

governmentally
BR ˌɡʌvnˈmɛntl̩i, ˌɡʌvəˈmɛntl̩i, ˌɡʌvnˈmɛntəli, ˌɡʌvəˈmɛntəli
AM ˌɡəvər(n)ˈmɛn(t)l̩i

governor
BR ˈɡʌvn̩ə(r), ˈɡʌvənə(r), -z
AM ˈɡəv(ə)nər, -z

governorate
BR ˈɡʌvn̩ərət, ˈɡʌvənərət, -s
AM ˈɡəv(ə)nərət, ˈɡəv(ə)nəˌreɪt, -s

governorship
BR ˈɡʌvn̩əʃɪp, ˈɡʌvənəʃɪp, -s
AM ˈɡəv(ə)nərˌʃɪp, -s

Gow
BR ɡaʊ

AM gaʊ

gowan
BR ˈgaʊən, -z
AM ˈgoʊən, -z

Gower
BR ˈgaʊə(r)
AM ˈgaʊər

Gowing
BR ˈgaʊɪŋ
AM ˈgaʊɪŋ

gowk
BR gaʊk, -s
AM gaʊk, -s

gown
BR gaʊn, -z
AM gaʊn, -z

gownsman
BR ˈgaʊnzmən
AM ˈgaʊnzmən

gownsmen
BR ˈgaʊnzmən
AM ˈgaʊnzmən

Gowrie
BR ˈgaʊri
AM ˈgaʊri

goy
BR gɔɪ, -z
AM gɔɪ, -z

Goya
BR ˈgɔɪə(r)
AM ˈgɔɪə

goyim
BR ˈgɔɪ(j)ɪm
AM ˈgɔɪ(j)ɨm

goyisch
BR gɔɪˈ(j)ɪʃ
AM ˈgɔɪɪʃ

goyish
BR gɔɪˈ(j)ɪʃ
AM ˈgɔɪɪʃ

Gozo
BR ˈgəʊzəʊ
AM ˈgoʊˌzoʊ

Graafian
BR ˈgrɑːfɪən, ˈgrafɪən
AM ˈgrɑfiən, ˈgræfiən

grab
BR grab, -z, -ɪŋ, -d
AM græb, -z, -ɪŋ, -d

grabber
BR ˈgrabə(r), -z
AM ˈgræbər, -z

grabble
BR ˈgrab|l, -lz, -lɪŋ\-lɪŋ, -ld
AM ˈgræb|əl, -əlz, -(ə)lɪŋ, -əld

grabby
BR ˈgrab|i, -ɪə(r), -ɪɪst
AM ˈgræbi, -ər, -ɨst

graben
BR ˈgrɑːb(ə)n, -z
AM ˈgrɑbən, -z

Gracchus
BR ˈgrakəs
AM ˈgrækəs

grace
BR greɪs, -ɨz, -ɪŋ, -t
AM greɪs, -ɨz, -ɪŋ, -t

graceful
BR ˈgreɪsf(ʊ)l
AM ˈgreɪsfəl

gracefully
BR ˈgreɪsfʊli, ˈgreɪsfḷi
AM ˈgreɪsfəli

gracefulness
BR ˈgreɪsf(ʊ)lnəs
AM ˈgreɪsfəlnəs

graceless
BR ˈgreɪslɨs
AM ˈgreɪslɨs

gracelessly
BR ˈgreɪslɨsli
AM ˈgreɪslɨsli

gracelessness
BR ˈgreɪslɨsnɨs
AM ˈgreɪslɨsnɨs

Gracie
BR ˈgreɪsi
AM ˈgreɪsi

gracile
BR ˈgrasɪl, ˈgrasʌɪl
AM ˈgræsəl, ˈgræˌsaɪl

gracility
BR graˈsɪlɨti, grəˈsɪlɨti
AM græˈsɪlɨdi, grəˈsɪlɨdi

graciosity
BR ˌgreɪʃɪˈɒsɨti, ˌgreɪsɪˈɒsɨti
AM ˌgreɪʃiˈɑsədi, ˌgreɪsiˈɑsədi

gracious
BR ˈgreɪʃəs
AM ˈgreɪʃəs

graciously
BR ˈgreɪʃəsli
AM ˈgreɪʃəsli

graciousness
BR ˈgreɪʃəsnəs
AM ˈgreɪʃəsnəs

grackle
BR ˈgrakl, -z
AM ˈgrækəl, -z

grad
BR grad, -z
AM græd, -z

gradability
BR ˌgreɪdəˈbɪlɨti
AM ˌgreɪdəˈbɪlɨdi

gradable
BR ˈgreɪdəbl
AM ˈgreɪdəbəl

gradate
BR grəˈdeɪt, -s, -ɪŋ, -ɨd
AM ˈgreɪˌdeɪ|t, -ts, -dɪŋ, -dɨd

gradation
BR grəˈdeɪʃn, -z
AM greɪˈdeɪʃən, -z

gradational
BR grəˈdeɪʃṇ(ə)l, grəˈdeɪʃən(ə)l
AM greɪˈdeɪʃ(ə)nəl

gradationally
BR grəˈdeɪʃṇəli, grəˈdeɪʃṇḷi, grəˈdeɪʃənḷi, grəˈdeɪʃ(ə)nəli
AM greɪˈdeɪʃ(ə)nəli

grade
BR greɪd, -z, -ɪŋ, -ɨd
AM greɪd, -z, -ɪŋ, -ɨd

grader
BR ˈgreɪdə(r), -z
AM ˈgreɪdər, -z

Gradgrind
BR ˈgradgrʌɪnd
AM ˈgrædˌgraɪnd

gradience
BR ˈgreɪdɪəns
AM ˈgreɪdiəns

gradient
BR ˈgreɪdɪənt, -s
AM ˈgreɪdiənt, -s

gradin
BR ˈgreɪdɪn, -z
AM ˈgreɪdn, -z

gradine
BR ˈgreɪdiːn, -z
AM ˈgreɪˌdin, grəˈdin, -z

grading
BR ˈgreɪdɪŋ, -z
AM ˈgreɪdɪŋ, -z

gradual
BR ˈgradʒʊəl, ˈgradjʊəl, ˈgradʒ(ʊ)l
AM ˈgrædʒ(ə)wəl, ˈgrædʒəl

gradualism
BR ˈgradʒʊəlɪz(ə)m, ˈgradjʊəlɪz(ə)m, ˈgradʒʊlɪz(ə)m, ˈgradʒḷɪz(ə)m
AM ˈgrædʒ(ə)wəˌlɪzəm, ˈgrædʒəˌlɪzəm

gradualist
BR ˈgradʒʊəlɪst, ˈgradjʊəlɪst, ˈgradʒʊlɪst, ˈgradʒḷɪst, -s
AM ˈgrædʒ(ə)wələst, ˈgrædʒələst, -s

gradualistic
BR ˌgradʒʊəˈlɪstɪk, ˌgradjʊəˈlɪstɪk, ˌgradʒ(ʊ)lˈɪstɪk
AM ˌgrædʒ(ə)wəˈlɪstɪk, ˌgrædʒəˈlɪstɪk

gradually
BR ˈgradʒʊli, ˈgradjʊəli
AM ˈgrædʒ(ə)wəli, ˈgrædʒəli

gradualness
BR ˈgradʒʊəlnəs, ˈgradʒʊlnəs, ˈgradjʊəlnəs
AM ˈgrædʒ(ə)wəlnəs, ˈgrædʒəlnəs

graduand
BR ˈgradʒʊand, ˈgradjʊand, -z
AM ˈgrædʒ(ə)wənd, -z

graduate[1]
noun
BR ˈgradʒʊət, ˈgradjʊət, -s
AM ˈgrædʒ(ə)wət, -s

graduate[2]
verb
BR ˈgradʒʊeɪt, ˈgradjʊeɪt, -s, -ɪŋ, -ɨd
AM ˈgrædʒəˌweɪ|t, -ts, -dɪŋ, -dɨd

graduation
BR ˌgradʒʊˈeɪʃn, ˌgradjʊˈeɪʃn, -z
AM ˌgrædʒəˈweɪʃən, -z

graduator
BR ˈgradʒʊeɪtə(r), ˈgradjʊeɪtə(r), -z
AM ˈgrædʒəˌweɪdər, -z

Grady
BR ˈgreɪdi
AM ˈgreɪdi

Graecise
BR ˈgriːsʌɪz, ˈgrʌɪsʌɪz, -ɨz, -ɪŋ, -d
AM ˈgriˌsaɪz, -ɨz, -ɪŋ, -d

Graecism
BR ˈgriːsɪz(ə)m, ˈgrʌɪsɪz(ə)m, -z
AM ˈgriˌsɪzəm, -z

Graecize
BR ˈgriːsʌɪz, ˈgrʌɪsʌɪz, -ɨz, -ɪŋ, -d
AM ˈgriˌsaɪz, -ɨz, -ɪŋ, -d

Graeco-
BR ˈgriːkəʊ, ˈgrʌɪkəʊ, ˈgrɛkəʊ
AM ˈgrɛkoʊ

Graecomania
BR ˌgriːkəʊˈmeɪnɪə(r), ˌgrʌɪkəʊˈmeɪnɪə(r), ˌgrɛkəʊˈmeɪnɪə(r)
AM ˌgrɛkoʊˈmeɪniə

Graecomaniac
BR ˌgriːkəʊˈmeɪnɪak, ˌgrʌɪkəʊˈmeɪnɪak, ˌgrɛkəʊˈmeɪnɪak, -s
AM ˌgrɛkoʊˈmeɪniˌæk, -s

Graecophile
BR ˈgriːkəʊfʌɪl, ˈgrʌɪkəʊfʌɪl, ˈgrɛkəʊfʌɪl, -z
AM ˈgrɛkoʊˌfaɪl, -z

Graeco-Roman
BR ˌgriːkəʊˈrəʊmən, ˌgrʌɪkəʊˈrəʊmən, ˌgrɛkəʊˈrəʊmən
AM ˌgrɛkoʊˈroʊmən

Graeme
BR ˈgreɪəm
AM ˈgreɪəm

Graf
BR grɑːf, graf

AM grɑf, græf
graffiti
BR grəˈfiːt|i, -ɪd
AM grəˈfidi, -d
graffitist
BR grəˈfiːtɪst, -s
AM grəˈfidɨst, -s
graffito
BR grəˈfiːtəʊ
AM grəˈfidoʊ
graft
BR grɑːft, graft, -s, -ɪŋ, -ɪd
AM græft, -s, -ɪŋ, -əd
grafter
BR ˈgrɑːftə(r), ˈgraftə(r), -z
AM ˈgræftər, -z
Grafton
BR ˈgrɑːft(ə)n, ˈgraft(ə)n
AM ˈgræftən
graham
BR ˈgreɪəm, -z
AM græm, ˈgreɪəm, -z
Grahame
BR ˈgreɪəm
AM ˈgreɪəm
Grahamstown
BR ˈgreɪəmztaʊn
AM ˈgreɪəmzˌtaʊn
Graig
BR grʌɪg
AM graɪg, greɪg
Grail
BR greɪl
AM greɪl
grail
BR greɪl, -z
AM greɪl, -z
grain
BR greɪn, -z
AM greɪn, -z
grainer
BR ˈgreɪnə(r), -z
AM ˈgreɪnər, -z
grainfield
BR ˈgreɪnfiːld, -z
AM ˈgreɪnˌfild, -z
Grainger
BR ˈgreɪn(d)ʒə(r)
AM ˈgreɪndʒər
grainily
BR ˈgreɪnɨli
AM ˈgreɪnɨli
graininess
BR ˈgreɪnɪnɨs
AM ˈgreɪninɨs
grainless
BR ˈgreɪnlɨs
AM ˈgreɪnlɨs
grainy
BR ˈgreɪn|i, -ɪə(r), -ɪɪst
AM ˈgreɪni, -ər, -ɨst
grallatorial
BR ˌgraləˈtɔːrɪəl
AM ˌgræləˈtɔriəl
gram
BR gram, -z
AM græm, -z
graminaceous
BR ˌgramɪˈneɪʃəs
AM ˌgræməˈneɪʃəs
gramineous
BR grəˈmɪnɪəs
AM grəˈmɪniəs
graminivorous
BR ˌgramɪˈnɪv(ə)rəs
AM ˌgræməˈnɪvərəs
grammalogue
BR ˈgraməlɒg, -z
AM ˈgræməˌlɑg, ˈgræməˌlɔg, -z
grammar
BR ˈgramə(r), -z
AM ˈgræmər, -z
grammarian
BR grəˈmɛːrɪən, -z
AM grəˈmɛriən, -z
grammarless
BR ˈgraməlәs
AM ˈgræmərləs
grammatical
BR grəˈmatɪkl
AM grəˈmædəkəl
grammaticality
BR grəˌmatɪˈkalɪti
AM grəˌmædəˈkælədi
grammatically
BR grəˈmatɪkli
AM grəˈmædək(ə)li
grammaticalness
BR grəˈmatɪklnəs
AM grəˈmædəkəlnəs
grammaticise
BR grəˈmatɪsʌɪz, -ɪz, -ɪŋ, -d
AM grəˈmædəˌsaɪz, -ɪz, -ɪŋ, -d
grammaticize
BR grəˈmatɪsʌɪz, -ɪz, -ɪŋ, -d
AM grəˈmædəˌsaɪz, -ɪz, -ɪŋ, -d
gramme
BR gram, -z
AM græm, -z
Grammy
BR ˈgram|i, -ɪz
AM ˈgræmi, -z
gramophone
BR ˈgraməfəʊn, -z
AM ˈgræməˌfoʊn, -z
gramophonic
BR ˌgraməˈfɒnɪk
AM ˌgræməˈfɑnɪk
Grampian
BR ˈgrampɪən, -z
AM ˈgræmpiən, -z
grampus
BR ˈgrampəs, -ɪz
AM ˈgræmpəs, -əz
Gramsci
BR ˈgramʃi
AM ˈgræmʃi
gran
BR gran, -z
AM græn, -z
Granada
BR grəˈnɑːdə(r)
AM grəˈnɑdə
granadilla
BR ˌgranəˈdɪlə(r), -z
AM ˌgrænəˈdɪlə, -z
Granados
BR grəˈnɑːdɒs
AM grəˈnɑdəs
granary
BR ˈgran(ə)r|i, -ɪz
AM ˈgreɪn(ə)ri, ˈgræn(ə)ri, -z
Gran Canaria
BR ˌgran kəˈnɛːrɪə(r)
AM ˌgræn kəˈnɛriə
Gran Chaco
BR ˌgran ˈtʃɑːkəʊ, + ˈtʃakəʊ
AM ˌgrɑn ˈtʃɑkoʊ
grand
BR grand, -ə(r), -ɨst
AM grænd, -ər, -əst
grandad
BR ˈgrandad, -z
AM ˈgrænˌdæd, -z
grandam
BR ˈgrandam, -z
AM ˈgrænˌdæm, ˈgrændəm, -z
grandame
BR ˈgrandeɪm, -z
AM ˈgrænˌdeɪm, ˈgrændəm, -z
grandchild
BR ˈgran(d)tʃʌɪld
AM ˈgræn(d)ˌtʃaɪld
grandchildren
BR ˈgran(d)ˌtʃɪldr(ə)n
AM ˈgræn(d)ˌtʃɪldrən
Grand Coulee
BR ˌgran(d) ˈkuːli
AM ˌgræn(d) ˈkuli
granddad
BR ˈgrandad, -z
AM ˈgrænˌdæd, -z
granddaddy
BR ˈgranˌdad|i, -ɪz
AM ˈgrænˌdædi, -z
granddaughter
BR ˈgranˌdɔːtə(r), -z
AM ˈgrænˌdɔdər, ˈgrænˌdɑdər, -z
grandee
BR granˈdiː, -z
AM grænˈdi, -z
grandeur
BR ˈgran(d)ʒə(r), ˈgrandjʊə(r)
AM ˈgrændʒər, ˈgrænd(j)ʊr
grandfather
BR ˈgran(d)ˌfɑːðə(r), -z
AM ˈgræn(d)ˌfɑðər, -z
grandfatherly
BR ˈgran(d)ˌfɑːðəli
AM ˈgræn(d)ˌfɑðərli
Grand Guignol
BR ˌgrɒn ˈgiːnjɒl, ˌgrɒ̃ +
AM ˌgræn(d) ˈginjɔl
grandiflora
BR ˌgrandɪˈflɔːrə(r)
AM ˌgrændəˌflɔrə
grandiloquence
BR granˈdɪləkw(ə)ns
AM grænˈdɪləkwəns
grandiloquent
BR granˈdɪləkw(ə)nt
AM grænˈdɪləkwənt
grandiloquently
BR granˈdɪləkw(ə)ntli
AM grænˈdɪləkwən(t)li
grandiose
BR ˈgrandɪəʊs, ˈgrandɪəʊz
AM ˈgrændiˌoʊs, ˌgrændiˈoʊs, ˈgrændiˌoʊz, ˌgrændiˈoʊz
grandiosely
BR ˈgrandɪəʊsli, ˈgrandɪəʊzli
AM ˈgrændiˌoʊsli, ˌgrændiˈoʊsli, ˈgrændiˌoʊzli, ˌgrændiˈoʊzli
grandiosity
BR ˌgrandɪˈɒsɪti
AM ˌgrændiˈɑsədi
Grandison
BR ˈgrandɪs(ə)n
AM ˈgrændəsən
Grandisonian
BR ˌgrandɪˈsəʊnɪən
AM ˌgrændəˈsoʊniən
grandly
BR ˈgrandli
AM ˈgræn(d)li
grandma
BR ˈgran(d)mɑː(r), -z
AM ˈgræn(d)ˌmɑ, ˈgræ(m)ˌmɑ, -z
grand mal
BR ˌgrɒn ˈmal, ˌgrɒ̃ +
AM ˌgræn(d) ˈmɑl
grandmama
BR ˈgran(d)məˌmɑː(r), -z
AM ˈgræn(d)ˌmɑmə, ˈgræn(d)məˌmɑ, -z
grandmamma
BR ˈgran(d)məˌmɑː(r), -z
AM ˈgræn(d)ˌmɑmə, ˈgræn(d)məˌmɑ, -z
grandmaster
BR ˌgran(d)ˈmɑːstə(r), ˌgran(d)ˈmastə(r), -z
AM -z ˌgræn(d)ˈmæstər, -z

grandmother
BR 'gran(d),mʌðə(r), -z
AM 'græn(d),məðər, -z

grandmotherly
BR 'gran(d),mʌðəli
AM 'græn(d),məðərli

grandness
BR 'gran(d)nəs
AM 'græn(d)nəs

grandpa
BR 'gran(d)pɑː(r), 'grampɑː(r), -z
AM 'græn(d),pɑ, 'græm,pɑ, -z

grandpapa
BR 'gran(d)pə,pɑː(r), -z
AM 'græn(d),pɑpə, 'græn(d)pə,pɑ, -z

grandparent
BR 'gran(d),pɛːrənt, 'gran(d),pɛːrn̩t, -s
AM 'græn(d),pɛrənt, -s

Grand Prix
BR ,grɒ̃ 'priː
AM ,grɑn 'pri, ,græn(d) +

grandsire
BR 'gran(d)sʌɪə(r), -z
AM 'græn(d),saɪ(ə)r, -z

grandson
BR 'gran(d)sʌn, -z
AM 'græn(d),sən, -z

Grands Prix
BR ,grɒ̃ 'priː(z)
AM ,grɑn 'pri, ,græn(d) +

grandstand
BR 'gran(d)stand, -z
AM 'græn(d),stænd, -z

granduncle
BR 'grand,ʌŋkl
AM 'grænd,əŋkəl

grange
BR greɪn(d)ʒ, -ɨz
AM greɪndʒ, -ɨz

Grangemouth
BR 'greɪn(d)ʒmaʊθ
AM 'greɪndʒ,maʊθ

graniferous
BR grə'nɪf(ə)rəs, gra'nɪf(ə)rəs
AM grə'nɪf(ə)rəs

graniform
BR 'granɨfɔːm
AM 'grænə,fɔ(ə)rm

granita
BR grə'niːtə(r), gra'niːtə(r)
AM grə'nidə

granite[1]
BR 'granɨt
AM 'grænət

granite[2]
plural of granita
BR grə'niːti, gra'niːti
AM grə'nidi

graniteware
BR 'granɨtwɛː(r)
AM 'grænət,wɛ(ə)r

granitic
BR grə'nɪtɪk, gra'nɪtɪk
AM grə'nɪdɪk

granitoid
BR 'granɨtɔɪd
AM 'grænə,tɔɪd

granivore
BR 'granɨvɔː(r), -z
AM 'grænə,vɔ(ə)r, -z

granivorous
BR grə'nɪv(ə)rəs, gra'nɪv(ə)rəs
AM grə'nɪv(ə)rəs

granma
BR 'granmɑː(r), -z
AM 'græn,mɑ, 'græ(m),mɑ, -z

grannie
BR 'gran|i, -ɪz
AM 'græni, -z

granny
BR 'gran|i, -ɪz
AM 'græni, -z

granola
BR grə'nəʊlə(r), gra'nəʊlə(r)
AM grə'noʊlə

granolithic
BR ,granə'lɪθɪk
AM ,grænə'lɪθɪk

granophyre
BR 'granə(ʊ)fʌɪə(r)
AM 'grænə,faɪ(ə)r

granpa
BR 'granpɑː(r), 'grampɑː(r), -z
AM 'græn,pɑ, 'græm,pɑ, -z

grant
BR grɑːnt, grant, -s, -ɪŋ, -ɨd
AM græn|t, -ts, -(t)ɪŋ, -(t)əd

Granta
BR 'grɑːntə(r), 'grantə(r)
AM 'græn(t)ə

grantable
BR 'grɑːntəbl, 'grantəbl
AM 'græn(t)əbəl

Grantchester
BR 'grɑːntʃɪstə(r), 'grantʃɪstə(r)
AM 'græn,(t)ʃɛstər

grantee
BR (,)grɑːn'tiː, (,)gran'tiː, -z
AM græn'ti, -z

granter
BR 'grɑːntə(r), 'grantə(r), -z
AM 'græn(t)ər, -z

Granth
BR grʌnt
AM grənt

Grantha
BR 'grʌntə(r)
AM 'grən(t)ə

Grantham
BR 'granθəm
AM 'grænθəm

Grantley
BR 'grɑːntli, 'grantli
AM 'græn(t)li

grantor
BR (,)grɑːn'tɔː(r), (,)gran'tɔː(r), 'grɑːntə(r), 'grantə(r), -z
AM græn'tɔ(ə)r, -z

grantsmanship
BR 'grɑːntsmənʃɪp, 'grantsmənʃɪp
AM 'græn(t)smən,ʃɪp

gran turismo
BR ,gran tʊə'rɪzməʊ, + tᵿ'rɪzməʊ, + tɔː'rɪzməʊ, -z
AM ,græn tʊ'rɪzmoʊ, -z

granular
BR 'granjᵿlə(r)
AM 'grænjələr

granularity
BR ,granjᵿ'larɪti
AM ,grænjə'lɛrədi

granularly
BR 'granjᵿləli
AM 'grænjələrli

granulate
BR 'granjᵿleɪt, -s, -ɪŋ, -ɨd
AM 'grænjə,leɪ|t, -ts, -dɪŋ, -dɨd

granulation
BR ,granjᵿ'leɪʃn
AM ,grænjə'leɪʃən

granulator
BR 'granjᵿleɪtə(r), -z
AM 'grænjə,leɪdər, -z

granule
BR 'granjuːl, -z
AM 'græn,jul, -z

granulocyte
BR 'granjᵿləsʌɪt, -s
AM 'grænjələ,saɪt, -s

granulocytic
BR ,granjᵿlə'sɪtɪk
AM ,grænjələ'sɪdɪk

granulometric
BR ,granjᵿlə'mɛtrɪk
AM ,grænjələ'mɛtrɪk

Granville
BR 'granv(ɪ)l
AM 'græn,vɪl

grape
BR greɪp, -s
AM greɪp, -s

grapefruit
BR 'greɪpfruːt, -s
AM 'greɪp,frut, -s

grapery
BR 'greɪp(ə)r|i, -ɪz
AM 'greɪpəri, -z

grapeseed
BR 'greɪpsiːd
AM 'greɪp,sid

grapeshot
BR 'greɪpʃɒt
AM 'greɪp,ʃɑt

grapevine
BR 'greɪpvʌɪn, -z
AM 'greɪp,vaɪn, -z

grapey
BR 'greɪp|i, -ɪə(r), -ɪɪst
AM 'greɪpi, -ər, -ɨst

graph
BR grɑːf, graf, -s
AM græf, -s

graphematic
BR ,grafə'matɪk
AM ,græfə'mædɪk

grapheme
BR 'grafiːm, -z
AM 'græfim, -z

graphemic
BR gra'fiːmɪk, grə'fiːmɪk, -s
AM grə'fimɪk, -s

graphemically
BR gra'fiːmɪkli, grə'fiːmɪkli
AM grə'fimək(ə)li

graphic
BR 'grafɪk, -s
AM 'græfɪk, -s

graphicacy
BR 'grafɪkəsi
AM 'græfəkəsi

graphical
BR 'grafɪkl
AM 'græfəkəl

graphically
BR 'grafɪkli
AM 'græfək(ə)li

graphicness
BR 'grafɪknɨs
AM 'græfɪknɨs

graphite
BR 'grafʌɪt
AM 'græ,faɪt

graphitic
BR grə'fɪtɪk, gra'fɪtɪk
AM grə'fɪdɪk

graphitise
BR 'grafɪtʌɪz, -ɨz, -ɪŋ, -d
AM 'græfə,taɪz, -ɨz, -ɪŋ, -d

graphitize
BR 'grafɪtʌɪz, -ɨz, -ɪŋ, -d
AM 'græfə,taɪz, -ɨz, -ɪŋ, -d

graphological
BR ,grafə'lɒdʒɪkl
AM ,græfə'lɑdʒəkəl

graphologist
BR grə'fɒlədʒɪst, gra'fɒlədʒɪst, -s

AM grə'fɑlədʒəst, -s
graphology
BR grə'fɒlədʒi,
gra'fɒlədʒi
AM grə'fɑlədʒi
grapnel
BR 'grapnl, -z
AM 'græpnəl, -z
grappa
BR 'grapə(r)
AM 'grɑpə
Grappelli
BR grə'pɛli
AM grə'pɛli
grapple
BR 'grap|l, -lz,
-l̩ɪŋ\-lɪŋ, -ld
AM 'græp|əl, -əlz,
-(ə)lɪŋ, -əld
grappler
BR 'grapl̩ə(r),
'graplə(r), -z
AM 'græp(ə)lər, -z
graptolite
BR 'graptəlʌɪt, -s
AM 'græptəˌlaɪt, -s
grapy
BR 'greɪp|i, -ɪə(r), -ɪɪst
AM 'greɪpi, -ər, -ɪst
Grasmere
BR 'grasmɪə(r),
'grɑːsmɪə(r)
AM 'græsˌmɪ(ə)r
grasp
BR grɑːsp, grasp, -s, -ɪŋ,
-t
AM græsp, -s, -ɪŋ, -t
graspable
BR 'grɑːspəbl,
'graspəbl
AM 'græspəbəl
grasper
BR 'grɑːspə(r),
'graspə(r), -z
AM 'græspər, -z
graspingly
BR 'grɑːspɪŋli,
'graspɪŋli
AM 'græspɪŋli
graspingness
BR 'grɑːspɪŋnɪs,
'graspɪŋnɪs
AM 'græspɪŋnɪs
grass
BR grɑːs, gras, -ɪz
AM græs, -əz
grasscloth
BR 'grɑːsklɒ|θ,
'grasklɒ|θ, -θs\-ðz
AM 'græsˌklɔ|θ,
'græsˌklɑ|θ, -θs\-ðz
Grasse
BR grɑːs
AM grɑs
grasshopper
BR 'grɑːsˌhɒpə(r),
'grasˌhɒpə(r), -z
AM 'græsˌ(h)ɑpər, -z
grassiness
BR 'grɑːsɪnɪs,
'grasɪnɪs
AM 'græsinɪs
Grassington
BR 'grasɪŋt(ə)n,
'grɑːsɪŋt(ə)n
AM 'græsɪŋt(ə)n
grassland
BR 'grɑːsland,
'grasland, -z
AM 'græsˌlænd, -z
grassless
BR 'grɑːsləs, 'grasləs
AM 'græsləs
grasslike
BR 'grɑːslʌɪk,
'graslʌɪk
AM 'græsˌlaɪk
grassy
BR 'grɑːs|i, 'gras|i,
-ɪə(r), -ɪɪst
AM 'græsi, -ər, -ɪst
grate
BR greɪt, -s, -ɪŋ, -ɪd
AM greɪ|t, -ts, -dɪŋ, -dɪd
grateful
BR 'greɪtf(ʊ)l
AM 'greɪtfəl
gratefully
BR 'greɪtfʊli, 'greɪtfl̩i
AM 'greɪtfəli
gratefulness
BR 'greɪtf(ʊ)lnəs
AM 'greɪtfəlnəs
grater
BR 'greɪtə(r), -z
AM 'greɪdər, -z
graticule
BR 'gratɪkjuːl, -z
AM 'grædəˌkjul, -z
gratification
BR ˌgratɪfɪ'keɪʃn
AM ˌgrædəfə'keɪʃən
gratifier
BR 'gratɪfʌɪə(r), -z
AM 'grædəˌfaɪ(ə)r, -z
gratify
BR 'gratɪfʌɪ, -z, -ɪŋ, -d
AM 'grædəˌfaɪ, -z, -ɪŋ, -d
gratifyingly
BR 'gratɪfʌɪɪŋli
AM 'grædəˌfaɪɪŋli
gratin
BR 'gratã, 'grataŋ, -z
AM 'grɑtn, 'grætn,
grə'tɑn, -z
gratiné
BR 'gratɪneɪ, -z
AM ˌgrætn'eɪ, -z
gratinée
BR 'gratɪneɪ, -z
AM ˌgrætn'eɪ, -z
grating
BR 'greɪtɪŋ, -z
AM 'greɪdɪŋ, -z
gratingly
BR 'greɪtɪŋli
AM 'greɪdɪŋli
gratis
BR 'gratɪs, 'grɑːtɪs,
'greɪtɪs
AM 'grædəs
gratitude
BR 'gratɪtjuːd,
'gratɪtʃuːd
AM 'grædəˌt(j)ud
Grattan
BR 'gratn
AM 'grætn
Gratton
BR 'gratn
AM 'grætn
gratuitous
BR grə'tjuːɪtəs,
grə'tʃuːɪtəs
AM grə't(j)uədəs
gratuitously
BR grə'tjuːɪtəsli,
grə'tʃuːɪtəsli
AM grə't(j)uədəsli
gratuitousness
BR grə'tjuːɪtəsnəs,
grə'tʃuːɪtəsnəs
AM grə't(j)uədəsnəs
gratuity
BR grə'tjuːɪt|i,
grə'tʃuːɪt|i, -ɪz
AM grə't(j)uədi, -z
gratulatory
BR 'gratjʊlət(ə)ri,
'gratʃʊlət(ə)ri
AM 'grætʃələˌtɔri
graunch
BR grɔːn(t)ʃ, -ɪz, -ɪŋ, -t
AM grɔntʃ, grɑntʃ, -əz,
-ɪŋ, -t
gravadlax
BR 'gravɛdlaks
AM 'grɑvədˌlɑks
gravamen
BR grə'veɪmɛn,
grə'veɪmən,
grə'vɑːmɛn,
grə'vɑːmən,
'gravəmɛn,
'gravəmən, -z
AM grə'veɪmən,
grə'vɑmən,
'grɑvəmən,
'grævəmən, -z
gravamina
BR grə'veɪmɪnə(r),
grə'vɑːmɪnə(r)
AM grə'vɑmənə,
grə'væmənə
grave[1]
accent
BR grɑːv, -z
AM grɑv, greɪv, -z
grave[2]
burial place
BR greɪv, -z
AM greɪv, -z
grave[3]
adjective
BR greɪv, -ə(r), -ɪst
AM greɪv, -ər, -əst
gravedigger
BR 'greɪvˌdɪgə(r), -z
AM 'greɪvˌdɪgər, -z
gravel
BR 'gravl, -d
AM 'grævəl, -d
graveless
BR 'greɪvlɪs
AM 'greɪvlɪs
gravelly
BR 'gravl̩i
AM 'grævəli
gravely
BR 'greɪvli
AM 'greɪvli
graven
BR 'greɪvn
AM 'greɪvən
graveness
BR 'greɪvnɪs
AM 'greɪvnɪs
Graveney
BR 'greɪvni
AM 'greɪvni
graver
BR 'greɪvə(r), -z
AM 'greɪvər, -z
Graves[1]
surname
BR greɪvz
AM greɪvz
Graves[2]
wine
BR grɑːv
AM grɑv
Gravesend
BR ˌgreɪvz'ɛnd
AM ˌgreɪvz'ɛnd
graveside
BR 'greɪvsʌɪd
AM 'greɪvˌsaɪd
gravestone
BR 'greɪvstəʊn, -z
AM 'greɪvˌstoʊn, -z
Gravettian
BR grə'vɛtɪən
AM grə'vɛdiən
graveward
BR 'greɪvwəd
AM 'greɪvwərd
graveyard
BR 'greɪvjɑːd, -z
AM 'greɪvˌjɑrd, -z
gravid
BR 'gravɪd
AM 'grævəd
gravimeter
BR grə'vɪmɪtə(r), -z
AM grə'vɪmədər,
græ'vɪmədər, -z
gravimetric
BR ˌgravɪ'mɛtrɪk
AM ˌgrævə'mɛtrɪk

gravimetry
BR grəˈvɪmɨtri
AM grəˈvɪmətri, græˈvɪmətri

gravitas
BR ˈgravɨtas, ˈgravɨtɑːs
AM ˈgrævəˌtɑs

gravitate
BR ˈgravɨteɪt, -s, -ɪŋ, -ɨd
AM ˈgrævəˌteɪ|t, -ts, -dɪŋ, -dɨd

gravitation
BR ˌgravɨˈteɪʃn
AM ˌgrævəˈteɪʃən

gravitational
BR ˌgravɨˈteɪʃn̩(ə)l, ˌgravɨˈteɪʃən(ə)l
AM ˌgrævəˈteɪʃ(ə)nəl

gravitationally
BR ˌgravɨˈteɪʃn̩əli, ˌgravɨˈteɪʃn̩li, ˌgravɨˈteɪʃənl̩i, ˌgravɨˈteɪʃ(ə)nəli
AM ˌgrævəˈteɪʃ(ə)nəli

graviton
BR ˈgravɨtɒn, -z
AM ˈgrævəˌtɑn, -z

gravity
BR ˈgravɨti
AM ˈgrævədi

gravlax
BR ˈgravlaks
AM ˈgrɑvˌlɑks

gravure
BR grəˈvjʊə(r), grəˈvjɔː(r)
AM grəˈvjʊ(ə)r

gravy
BR ˈgreɪvi
AM ˈgreɪvi

gray
BR greɪ, -z, -ɪŋ, -d, -ə(r), -ɨst
AM greɪ, -z, -ɪŋ, -d, -ər, -ɨst

graybeard
BR ˈgreɪbɪəd, -z
AM ˈgreɪˌbɪ(ə)rd, -z

grayish
BR ˈgreɪɪʃ
AM ˈgreɪɪʃ

grayling
BR ˈgreɪlɪŋ, -z
AM ˈgreɪlɪŋ, -z

Grayson
BR ˈgreɪsn
AM ˈgreɪsən

graywacke
BR ˈgreɪˌwakə(r)
AM ˈgreɪˌwækə

Graz
BR grɑːts
AM grɑts

graze
BR greɪz, -ɨz, -ɪŋ, -d
AM greɪz, -ɨz, -ɪŋ, -d

grazer
BR ˈgreɪzə(r), -z
AM ˈgreɪzər, -z

grazier
BR ˈgreɪzɪə(r), -z
AM ˈgreɪziər, ˈgreɪʒər, -z

graziery
BR ˈgreɪzɪər|i, -ɪz
AM ˈgreɪziəri, ˈgreɪʒəri, -z

grease¹
noun
BR griːs, -ɨz
AM gris, -ɨz

grease²
verb
BR griː|s, griː|z, -sɪz\-zɪz, -sɪŋ\-zɪŋ, -st\-zd
AM gri|s, gri|z, -sɪz\-zɪz, -sɪŋ\-zɪŋ, -st\-zd

greaseless
BR ˈgriːslɨs
AM ˈgrislɨs

greasepaint
BR ˈgriːspeɪnt
AM ˈgrisˌpeɪnt

greaseproof
BR ˈgriːspruːf
AM ˈgrisˌpruf

greaser
BR ˈgriːsə(r), ˈgriːzə(r), -z
AM ˈgrisər, ˈgrizər, -z

greasily
BR ˈgriːsɨli, ˈgriːzɨli
AM ˈgrisɨli, ˈgrizɨli

greasiness
BR ˈgriːsɪnɨs, ˈgriːzɪnɨs
AM ˈgrisinɨs, ˈgrizinɨs

greasy
BR ˈgriːs|i, ˈgriːz|i, -ɪə(r), -ɪɨst
AM ˈgrisi, ˈgrizi, -ər, -ɨst

great
BR greɪt, -ə(r), -ɨst
AM greɪ|t, -dər, -dɨst

greatcoat
BR ˈgreɪtkəʊt, -s
AM ˈgreɪtˌkoʊt, -s

greatness
BR ˈgreɪtnɨs
AM ˈgreɪtnɨs

greave
BR griːv, -z, -ɪŋ, -d
AM griv, -z, -ɪŋ, -d

Greaves
BR griːvz
AM grivz

grebe
BR griːb, -z
AM grib, -z

grebo
BR ˈgriːbəʊ, -z
AM ˈgreɪˌboʊ, -z

Grecian
BR ˈgriːʃn
AM ˈgriʃən

Grecise
BR ˈgriːsʌɪz, -ɨz, -ɪŋ, -d
AM ˈgriˌsaɪz, -ɨz, -ɪŋ, -d

Grecism
BR ˈgriːsɪz(ə)m, -z
AM ˈgriˌsɪzəm, -z

Grecize
BR ˈgriːsʌɪz, -ɨz, -ɪŋ, -d
AM ˈgriˌsaɪz, -ɨz, -ɪŋ, -d

Greco-
BR ˈgriːkəʊ, ˈgrɛkəʊ
AM ˈgrɛkoʊ

Grecomania
BR ˈgriːkəʊˌmeɪnɪə(*r*), ˈgrɛkəʊˌmeɪnɪə(*r*)
AM ˌgrɛkoʊˈmeɪniə

Grecomaniac
BR ˌgriːkəʊˈmeɪnɪak, ˌgrɛkəʊˈmeɪnɪak, -s
AM ˌgrɛkoʊˈmeɪniˌæk, -s

Grecophile
BR ˈgriːkəʊfʌɪl, ˈgrɛkəʊfʌɪl, -z
AM ˈgrɛkoʊˌfaɪl, -z

Greece
BR griːs
AM gris

greed
BR griːd
AM grid

greedily
BR ˈgriːdɨli
AM ˈgridɨli

greediness
BR ˈgriːdɪnɨs
AM ˈgridinɨs

greedy
BR ˈgriːd|i, -ɪə(r), -ɪɨst
AM ˈgridi, -ər, -ɨst

greegree
BR ˈgriːgriː, -z
AM ˈgriˌgri, -z

Greek
BR griːk, -s
AM grik, -s

Greekness
BR ˈgriːknɨs
AM ˈgriknɨs

Greeley
BR ˈgriːli
AM ˈgrili

Greely
BR ˈgriːli
AM ˈgrili

green
BR griːn, -z, -ɪŋ, -ə(r), -ɨst
AM grin, -z, -ɪŋ, -ər, -ɨst

Greenaway
BR ˈgriːnəweɪ
AM ˈgrinəˌweɪ

greenback
BR ˈgriːnbak, -s
AM ˈgrinˌbæk, -s

Greenbaum
BR ˈgriːnbaʊm
AM ˈgrinˌbɑm

Green Beret
BR ˌgriːn ˈbɛreɪ, -z
AM ˌgrin bəˈreɪ, -z

greenbottle
BR ˈgriːnˌbɒtl, -z
AM ˈgrinˌbɑdəl, -z

greenbrier
BR ˈgriːnˌbrʌɪə(r)
AM ˈgrinˌbraɪ(ə)r

Greene
BR griːn
AM grin

greenery
BR ˈgriːn(ə)ri
AM ˈgrinəri

greenfeed
BR ˈgriːnfiːd
AM ˈgrinˌfid

Greenfield
BR ˈgriːnfiːld
AM ˈgrinˌfild

greenfinch
BR ˈgriːnfɪn(t)ʃ, -ɨz
AM ˈgrinˌfɪn(t)ʃ, -ɨz

greenfly
BR ˈgriːnflʌɪ, -z
AM ˈgrinˌflaɪ, -z

greengage
BR ˈgriːngeɪdʒ, -ɨz
AM ˈgrinˌgeɪdʒ, -ɨz

greengrocer
BR ˈgriːnˌgrəʊsə(r), -z
AM ˈgrinˌgroʊsər, -z

greengrocery
BR ˈgriːnˌgrəʊs(ə)r|i, -ɪz
AM ˈgrinˌgroʊs(ə)ri, -z

Greengross
BR ˈgriːngrɒs
AM ˈgrinˌgrɔs, ˈgrinˌgrɑs

Greenhalgh
BR ˈgriːnhalʃ, ˈgriːnhɔːlʃ, ˈgriːnhɒlʃ, ˈgriːnhaldʒ
AM ˈgrinˌ(h)ælʃ

Greenham
BR ˈgriːnəm
AM ˈgrinəm

greenhead
BR ˈgriːnhɛd, -z
AM ˈgrinˌ(h)ɛd, -z

greenheart
BR ˈgriːnhɑːt, -s
AM ˈgrinˌ(h)ɑrt, -s

greenhide
BR ˈgriːnhʌɪd, -z
AM ˈgrinˌ(h)aɪd, -z

greenhorn
BR ˈgriːnhɔːn, -z
AM ˈgrinˌ(h)ɔ(ə)rn, -z

Greenhough
BR 'gri:n(h)ɒf, 'gri:n(h)ʌf, 'gri:nhəʊ, 'gri:nhaʊ
AM 'grin(h)əf

greenhouse
BR 'gri:nhaʊ|s, -zɪz
AM 'grin,(h)aʊ|s, -zəz

greening
BR 'gri:nɪŋ, -z
AM 'grinɪŋ, -z

greenish
BR 'gri:nɪʃ
AM 'grinɪʃ

greenishness
BR 'gri:nɪʃnɪs
AM 'grinɪʃnɪs

greenkeeper
BR 'gri:n,ki:pə(r), -z
AM 'grin,kipər, -z

greenkeeping
BR 'gri:n,ki:pɪŋ
AM 'grin,kipɪŋ

Greenland
BR 'gri:nlənd
AM 'grinlənd

Greenlander
BR 'gri:nləndə(r), -z
AM 'grinləndər, -z

greenlet
BR 'gri:nlɨt, -s
AM 'grinlət, -s

greenly
BR 'gri:nli
AM 'grinli

greenmail
BR 'gri:nmeɪl
AM 'grin,meɪl

greenmailer
BR 'gri:n,meɪlə(r), -z
AM 'grin,meɪlər, -z

greenness
BR 'gri:nnɪs
AM 'gri(n)nɪs

Greenock
BR 'gri:nək
AM 'grinək

Greenough
BR 'gri:nəʊ
AM 'grinoʊ

Greenpeace
BR 'gri:npi:s
AM 'grin,pis

greenroom
BR 'gri:nru:m, 'gri:nrʊm, -z
AM 'grin,rum, 'grin,rʊm, -z

greensand
BR 'gri:nsand, -z
AM 'grin,sænd, -z

greenshank
BR 'gri:nʃaŋk, -s
AM 'grin,ʃæŋk, -s

greensick
BR 'gri:nsɪk
AM 'grin,sɪk

greensickness
BR 'gri:n,sɪknɪs
AM 'grin,sɪknɪs

greenskeeper
BR 'gri:nz,ki:pə(r), -z
AM 'grinz,kipər, -z

Greenslade
BR 'gri:nsleɪd
AM 'grin,sleɪd

Greensleeves
BR 'gri:nsli:vz
AM 'grin,slivz

greenstick
BR 'gri:nstɪk
AM 'grin,stɪk

greenstone
BR 'gri:nstəʊn
AM 'grin,stoʊn

Greenstreet
BR 'gri:nstri:t
AM 'grin,strit

greenstuff
BR 'gri:nstʌf
AM 'grin,stəf

greensward
BR 'gri:nswɔ:d
AM 'grin,swɔ(ə)rd, 'grin,swɑrd

greenweed
BR 'gri:nwi:d, -z
AM 'grin,wid, -z

Greenwell
BR 'gri:nw(ɛ)l
AM 'grin,wɛl

Greenwich
BR 'grɛnɪtʃ, 'grɪnɪtʃ, 'grɛnɪdʒ, 'grɪnɪdʒ
AM 'grɛnɪtʃ

greenwood
BR 'gri:nwʊd, -z
AM 'grin,wʊd, -z

greeny
BR 'gri:ni
AM 'grini

greenyard
BR 'gri:njɑ:d, -z
AM 'grin,jɑrd, -z

Greer
BR grɪə(r)
AM grɪ(ə)r

greet
BR gri:t, -s, -ɪŋ, -ɨd
AM gri|t, -ts, -dɪŋ, -dɨd

greeter
BR 'gri:tə(r), -z
AM 'gridər, -z

greeting
BR 'gri:tɪŋ, -z
AM 'gridɪŋ, -z

greffier
BR 'grɛfɪə(r), -z
AM 'grɛfi,eɪ, -z

Greg
BR grɛg
AM grɛg

gregarious
BR grɪ'gɛ:rɪəs
AM grə'gɛriəs

gregariously
BR grɪ'gɛ:rɪəsli
AM grə'gɛriəsli

gregariousness
BR grɪ'gɛ:rɪəsnəs
AM grə'gɛriəsnəs

Gregg
BR grɛg
AM grɛg

Gregor
BR 'grɛgə(r)
AM 'grɛgər

Gregorian
BR grɪ'gɔ:rɪən
AM grə'gɔriən

Gregory
BR 'grɛg(ə)ri
AM 'grɛg(ə)ri

Gregson
BR 'grɛgsn
AM 'grɛgsən

Greig
BR grɛg
AM grɛg

greisen
BR 'grʌɪzn
AM 'graɪzn

gremial
BR 'gri:mɪəl, -z
AM 'grimiəl, -z

gremlin
BR 'grɛmlɪn, -z
AM 'grɛmlən, -z

Grenada
BR grɪ'neɪdə(r)
AM grə'neɪdə

grenade
BR grɪ'neɪd, -z
AM grə'neɪd, -z

Grenadian
BR grɪ'neɪdɪən, -z
AM grə'neɪdiən, -z

grenadier
BR ,grɛnə'dɪə(r), -z
AM ,grɛnə'dɪ(ə)r, -z

grenadilla
BR ,grɛnə'dɪlə(r), -z
AM ,grɛnə'dɪlə, -z

grenadine
BR 'grɛnədi:n, ,grɛnə'di:n, -z
AM ,grɛnə,din, -z

Grendel
BR 'grɛndl
AM 'grɛndəl

Grendon
BR 'grɛnd(ə)n
AM 'grɛnd(ə)n

Grenfell
BR 'grɛnf(ɛ)l
AM 'grɛn,fɛl

Grenoble
BR grɪ'nəʊbl
AM grə'noʊbəl
FR ɡʀənɔbl

Grenville
BR 'grɛnv(ɪ)l
AM 'grɛnvəl

Grepo
BR 'grɛpəʊ, -z
AM 'grɛ,poʊ, -z

Gresham
BR 'grɛʃəm
AM 'grɛʃəm

gressorial
BR grɛ'sɔ:rɪəl
AM grɛ'sɔriəl

Greta
BR 'grɛtə(r), 'gri:tə(r)
AM 'grɛdə

Gretel
BR 'grɛtl
AM 'grɛdəl

Gretna Green
BR ,grɛtnə 'gri:n
AM ,grɛtnə 'grin

Gretzky
BR 'grɛtski
AM 'grɛtski

Greville
BR 'grɛv(ɪ)l
AM 'grɛvɨl

grew
BR gru:
AM gru

grey
BR greɪ, -z, -ɪŋ, -d, -ə(r), -ɪst
AM greɪ, -z, -ɪŋ, -d, -ər, -ɪst

greybeard
BR 'greɪbɪəd, -z
AM 'greɪ,bɪ(ə)rd, -z

Greyfriars
BR 'greɪ,frʌɪəz
AM 'greɪ,fraɪ(ə)rz

greyhen
BR 'greɪhɛn, -z
AM 'greɪ,(h)ɛn, -z

greyhound
BR 'greɪhaʊnd, -z
AM 'greɪ,(h)aʊnd, -z

greyish
BR 'greɪɪʃ
AM 'greɪɪʃ

greylag
BR 'greɪlag, -z
AM 'greɪ,læg, -z

greyly
BR 'greɪli
AM 'greɪli

greyness
BR 'greɪnɪs
AM 'greɪnɪs

Greystoke
BR 'greɪstəʊk
AM 'greɪ,stoʊk

greywacke
BR 'greɪ,wakə(r)
AM 'greɪ,wækə

Gribble
BR 'grɪbl

AM 'grɪbəl
gricer
BR 'grʌɪsə(r), -z
AM 'graɪsər, -z
grid
BR grɪd, -z, -ɨd
AM grɪd, -z, -ɨd
griddle
BR 'grɪdl, -z
AM 'grɪdəl, -z
griddlecake
BR 'grɪdlkeɪk, -s
AM 'grɪdl,keɪk, -s
gridiron
BR 'grɪd,ʌɪən, -z
AM 'grɪd,aɪ(ə)rn, -z
gridlock
BR 'grɪdlɒk, -s, -t
AM 'grɪd,lɑk, -s, -t
grief
BR gri:f, -s
AM grif, -s
Grieg
BR gri:g
AM grig
Grier
BR grɪə(r)
AM grɪ(ə)r
Grierson
BR 'grɪəsn
AM 'grɪrsən
grievance
BR 'gri:vns, -ɪz
AM 'grivəns, -əz
grieve
BR gri:v, -z, -ɪŋ, -d
AM griv, -z, -ɪŋ, -d
griever
BR 'gri:və(r), -z
AM 'grivər, -z
grievous
BR 'gri:vəs
AM 'grivəs
grievously
BR 'gri:vəsli
AM 'grivəsli
grievousness
BR 'gri:vəsnəs
AM 'grivəsnəs
griff
BR grɪf, -s
AM grɪf, -s
griffe
BR grɪf, -s
AM grɪf, -s
griffin
BR 'grɪf(ɪ)n, -z
AM 'grɪfən, -z
Griffith
BR 'grɪfɪθ
AM 'grɪfɪθ
Griffiths
BR 'grɪfɪθs
AM 'grɪfɪθs
griffon
BR 'grɪfn, -z
AM 'grɪfən, -z
grift
BR grɪft
AM grɪft
grifter
BR 'grɪftə(r), -z
AM 'grɪftər, -z
grig
BR grɪg, -z
AM grɪg, -z
Griggs
BR grɪgz
AM grɪgz
Grignard
BR 'gri:njɑ:(*r*)
AM 'grin,jɑrd
Grigson
BR 'grɪgsn
AM 'grɪgsən
grike
BR grʌɪk, -s
AM graɪk, -s
grill
BR grɪl, -z, -ɪŋ, -d
AM grɪl, -z, -ɪŋ, -d
grillade
BR grɪ'leɪd, grɪ'jɑ:d, 'gri:ɑ:d, -z
AM grə'lɑd, gri'jɑd, -z
grillage
BR 'grɪl|ɪdʒ, -ɪdʒɪz
AM 'grɪlɪdʒ, grə'lɑʒ, -əz
grille
BR grɪl, -z
AM grɪl, -z
griller
BR 'grɪlə(r), -z
AM 'grɪlər, -z
grilling
BR 'grɪlɪŋ, -z
AM 'grɪlɪŋ, -z
grillroom
BR 'grɪlru:m, 'grɪlrʊm, -z
AM 'grɪl,rum, 'grɪl,rʊm, -z
grillwork
BR 'grɪlwə:k
AM 'grɪl,wərk
grilse
BR grɪls
AM grɪls
grim
BR grɪm, -ə(r), -ɪst
AM grɪm, -ər, -ɪst
grimace
BR 'grɪməs, grɪ'meɪs, -ɪz, -ɪŋ, -t
AM 'grɪməs, grə'meɪs, -ɪz, -ɪŋ, -t
grimacer
BR 'grɪməsə(r), grɪ'meɪsə(r), -z
AM 'grɪməsər, grə'meɪsər, -z
Grimaldi
BR grɪ'mɔ:ldi, grɪ'mɒldi
AM grə'mɔldi, grə'mɑldi
grimalkin
BR grɪ'malkɪn, grɪ'mɔ:lkɪn, -z
AM grə'mɑlkən, -z
grime
BR grʌɪm, -z, -ɪŋ, -d
AM graɪm, -z, -ɪŋ, -d
Grimes
BR grʌɪmz
AM graɪmz
Grimethorpe
BR 'grʌɪmθɔ:p
AM 'graɪm,θɔ(ə)rp
grimily
BR 'grʌɪmɨli
AM 'graɪmɨli
griminess
BR 'grʌɪmɪnɪs
AM 'graɪmɪnɪs
grimly
BR 'grɪmli
AM 'grɪmli
Grimm
BR grɪm
AM grɪm
grimness
BR 'grɪmnɪs
AM 'grɪmnɪs
Grimond
BR 'grɪmənd
AM 'grɪmənd
Grimsby
BR 'grɪmzbi
AM 'grɪmzbi
Grimshaw
BR 'grɪmʃɔ:(*r*)
AM 'grɪm,ʃɔ
grimy
BR 'grʌɪm|i, -ɪə(r), -ɪɪst
AM 'graɪmi, -ər, -ɪst
grin
BR grɪn, -z, -ɪŋ, -d
AM grɪn, -z, -ɪŋ, -d
grind
BR grʌɪnd, -z, -ɪŋ
AM graɪnd, -z, -ɪŋ
grinder
BR 'grʌɪndə(r), -z
AM 'graɪndər, -z
grindingly
BR 'grʌɪndɪŋli
AM 'graɪndɪŋli
grindstone
BR 'grʌɪn(d)stəʊn, -z
AM 'graɪn(d),stoʊn, -z
gringo
BR 'grɪŋgəʊ, -z
AM 'grɪŋgoʊ, -z
grinner
BR 'grɪnə(r), -z
AM 'grɪnər, -z
grinningly
BR 'grɪnɪŋli
AM 'grɪnɪŋli
Grinstead
BR 'grɪnstɛd, 'grɪnstɪd
AM 'grɪn,stɛd
grip
BR grɪp, -s, -ɪŋ, -t
AM grɪp, -s, -ɪŋ, -t
gripe
BR grʌɪp, -s, -ɪŋ, -t
AM graɪp, -s, -ɪŋ, -t
griper
BR 'grʌɪpə(r), -z
AM 'graɪpər, -z
gripingly
BR 'grʌɪpɪŋli
AM 'graɪpɪŋli
grippe
BR grɪp, gri:p
AM grɪp
gripper
BR 'grɪpə(r), -z
AM 'grɪpər, -z
grippingly
BR 'grɪpɪŋli
AM 'grɪpɪŋli
grippy
BR 'grɪp|i, -ɪə(r), -ɪɪst
AM 'grɪpi, -ər, -ɪst
Griqua
BR 'gri:k(w)ə(*r*)
AM 'grikwə
Griqualand
BR 'gri:k(w)əland
AM 'grikwə,lænd
grisaille
BR grɪ'zeɪl, grɪ'zʌɪ(l)
AM grə'zaɪ, grə'zeɪl
Griselda
BR grɪ'zɛldə(*r*)
AM grə'zɛldə
griseofulvin
BR ,grɪzɪə(ʊ)'fʊlvɪn
AM ,grɪzioʊ'fʊlvən
grisette
BR grɪ'zɛt, -s
AM grə'zɛt, -s
Grisewood
BR 'grʌɪzwʊd
AM 'graɪz,wʊd
griskin
BR 'grɪskɪn, -z
AM 'grɪskɪn, -z
grisliness
BR 'grɪzlɪnɪs
AM 'grɪzlɪnɪs
grisly
BR 'grɪzl|i, -ɪə(r), -ɪɪst
AM 'grɪzli, -ər, -ɪst
grison
BR 'grɪzn, 'grʌɪsn
AM 'grɪzn
grissini
BR grɪ'si:ni
AM grə'sini
grist
BR grɪst
AM grɪst

gristle
BR ˈgrɪsl
AM ˈgrɪsəl

gristly
BR ˈgrɪsl|i, ˈgrɪsḷ|i, -ɪə(r), -ɪɪst
AM ˈgrɪs(ə)li, -ər, -ɪst

gristmill
BR ˈgrɪs(t)mɪl, -z
AM ˈgrɪs(t),mɪl, -z

Griswold
BR ˈgrɪzwld, ˈgrɪzwəʊld
AM ˈgrɪz,wɔld, ˈgrɪz,wɑld

grit
BR grɪt, -s
AM grɪt, -s

gritstone
BR ˈgrɪtstəʊn, -z
AM ˈgrɪt,stoʊn, -z

gritter
BR ˈgrɪtə(r), -z
AM ˈgrɪdər, -z

grittily
BR ˈgrɪtɨli
AM ˈgrɪdɨli

grittiness
BR ˈgrɪtɪnɨs
AM ˈgrɪdinɨs

gritty
BR ˈgrɪt|i, -ɪə(r), -ɪɪst
AM ˈgrɪdi, -ər, -ɪst

Grizedale
BR ˈgrʌɪzdeɪl
AM ˈgraɪz,deɪl

grizzle
BR ˈgrɪz|l, -lz, -ḷɪŋ\-lɪŋ, -ld
AM ˈgrɪz|əl, -əlz, -(ə)lɪŋ, -əld

grizzler
BR ˈgrɪzlə(r), -z
AM ˈgrɪz(ə)lər, -z

grizzly
BR ˈgrɪzl|i, -ɪz, -ɪə(r), -ɪɪst
AM ˈgrɪzli, -z, -ər, -ɪst

groan
BR grəʊn, -z, -ɪŋ, -d
AM groʊn, -z, -ɪŋ, -d

groaner
BR ˈgrəʊnə(r), -z
AM ˈgroʊnər, -z

groaningly
BR ˈgrəʊnɪŋli
AM ˈgroʊnɪŋli

groat
BR grəʊt, -s
AM groʊt, -s

Gro-bag®
BR ˈgrəʊbag, -z
AM ˈgroʊ,bæg, -z

Grobian
BR ˈgrəʊbɪən
AM ˈgroʊbiən

grocer
BR ˈgrəʊsə(r), -z
AM ˈgroʊsər, -z

grocery
BR ˈgrəʊs(ə)r|i, -ɪz
AM ˈgroʊs(ə)ri, -z

grockle
BR ˈgrɒkl, -z
AM ˈgrɑkəl, -z

Grocott
BR ˈgrəʊkɒt
AM ˈgroʊ,kɑt

Grodno
BR ˈgrɒdnəʊ
AM ˈgrɑd,noʊ

grog
BR grɒg
AM grɑg

Grogan
BR ˈgrəʊg(ə)n
AM ˈgroʊgən

groggily
BR ˈgrɒgɨli
AM ˈgrɑgəli

grogginess
BR ˈgrɒgɪnɨs
AM ˈgrɑginɨs

groggy
BR ˈgrɒg|i, -ɪə(r), -ɪɪst
AM ˈgrɑgi, -ər, -ɪst

grogram
BR ˈgrɒgrəm
AM ˈgrɑgrəm

groin
BR grɔɪn, -z
AM grɔɪn, -z

Grolier
BR ˈgrəʊlɪə(r)
AM ˈgroʊliər

grommet
BR ˈgrɒmɪt, ˈgrʌmɪt, -s
AM ˈgrɑmət, -s

gromwell
BR ˈgrɒmw(ɛ)l, -z
AM ˈgrɑmwəl, -z

Gromyko
BR grəˈmiːkəʊ
AM grəˈmikoʊ
RUS graˈmɪkə

Groningen
BR ˈgrəʊnɪŋən, ˈgrɒnɪŋən
AM ˈgroʊnɪŋən
DU ˈxronɪŋə(n)

groom
BR gruːm, -z, -ɪŋ, -d
AM grum, -z, -ɪŋ, -d

groomsman
BR ˈgruːmzmən
AM ˈgrumzmən

groomsmen
BR ˈgruːmzmən
AM ˈgrumzmən

groove
BR gruːv, -z, -ɪŋ, -d
AM gruv, -z, -ɪŋ, -d

groover
BR ˈgruːvə(r), -z
AM ˈgruvər, -z

groovily
BR ˈgruːvɨli
AM ˈgruvəli

grooviness
BR ˈgruːvɪnɨs
AM ˈgruvinɨs

groovy
BR ˈgruːv|i, -ɪə(r), -ɪɪst
AM ˈgruvi, -ər, -ɪst

grope
BR grəʊp, -s, -ɪŋ, -t
AM groʊp, -s, -ɪŋ, -t

groper
BR ˈgrəʊpə(r), -z
AM ˈgroʊpər, -z

gropingly
BR ˈgrəʊpɪŋli
AM ˈgroʊpɪŋli

Gropius
BR ˈgrəʊpɪəs
AM ˈgroʊpiəs

grosbeak
BR ˈgrəʊsbiːk, ˈgrɒsbiːk, -s
AM ˈgroʊs,bik, -s

groschen
BR ˈgrəʊʃn, ˈgrɒʃn
AM ˈgroʊʃən

grosgrain
BR ˈgrəʊgreɪn
AM ˈgroʊ,greɪn

Grosmont¹
in Monmouthshire, UK
BR ˈgrɒsm(ə)nt, ˈgrəʊsm(ə)nt, ˈgrɒsmɒnt, ˈgrəʊsmɒnt
AM ˈgroʊs,mɑnt

Grosmont²
in Yorkshire, UK
BR ˈgrəʊ(s)m(ə)nt, ˈgrəʊ(s)mɒnt
AM ˈgroʊs,mɑnt

gros point
BR ˌgrəʊ ˈpɔɪnt
AM ˈgroʊ ˌpɔɪnt

gross
BR grəʊs, -ɪz, -ɪŋ, -t, -ə(r), -ɪst
AM groʊs, -əz, -ɪŋ, -t, -ər, -əst

Grosseteste
BR ˈgrəʊstɛst, ˈgrəʊsteɪt
AM ˈgroʊs,tɛst

grossly
BR ˈgrəʊsli
AM ˈgroʊsli

Grossmith
BR ˈgrəʊsmɪθ
AM ˈgroʊ,smɪθ

grossness
BR ˈgrəʊsnəs
AM ˈgroʊsnəs

Grosvenor
BR ˈgrəʊvnə(r), ˈgrəʊvṇə(r)
AM ˈgroʊvnər

Grosz
BR grəʊs
AM groʊs

grot
BR grɒt, -s
AM grɑt, -s

grotesque
BR grə(ʊ)ˈtɛsk
AM groʊˈtɛsk, grəˈtɛsk

grotesquely
BR grə(ʊ)ˈtɛskli
AM groʊˈtɛskli, grəˈtɛskli

grotesqueness
BR grə(ʊ)ˈtɛsknəs
AM groʊˈtɛsknəs, grəˈtɛsknəs

grotesquerie
BR grə(ʊ)ˈtɛsk(ə)r|i, -ɪz
AM groʊˈtɛskəri, -z

grotesquery
BR grə(ʊ)ˈtɛsk(ə)r|i, -ɪz
AM groʊˈtɛskəri, -z

Grotius
BR ˈgrəʊtɪəs
AM ˈgroʊʃ(i)əs

grottily
BR ˈgrɒtɨli
AM ˈgrɑdəli

grottiness
BR ˈgrɒtɪnɨs
AM ˈgrɑdinɨs

grotto
BR ˈgrɒtəʊ, -z
AM ˈgrɑdoʊ, -z

grotty
BR ˈgrɒt|i, -ɪə(r), -ɪɪst
AM ˈgrɑdi, -ər, -ɪst

grouch
BR graʊtʃ, -ɪz, -ɪŋ, -t
AM graʊtʃ, -əz, -ɪŋ, -t

grouchily
BR ˈgraʊtʃɨli
AM ˈgraʊtʃəli

grouchiness
BR ˈgraʊtʃɪnɨs
AM ˈgraʊtʃinɨs

Groucho
BR ˈgraʊtʃəʊ
AM ˈgraʊtʃoʊ

grouchy
BR ˈgraʊtʃ|i, -ɪə(r), -ɪɪst
AM ˈgraʊtʃi, -ər, -ɪst

ground
BR graʊnd, -z, -ɪŋ, -ɪd
AM graʊnd, -z, -ɪŋ, -əd

groundage
BR ˈgraʊndɪdʒ
AM ˈgraʊndɪdʒ

groundbait
BR 'graʊn(d)beɪt, -s
AM 'graʊn(d),beɪt, -s

grounder
BR 'graʊndə(r), -z
AM 'graʊndər, -z

groundhog
BR 'graʊndhɒg, -z
AM 'graʊn(d),(h)ɔg, 'graʊn(d),(h)ɑg, -z

grounding
BR 'graʊndɪŋ, -z
AM 'graʊndɪŋ, -z

groundless
BR 'graʊndləs
AM 'graʊn(d)ləs

groundlessly
BR 'graʊndləsli
AM 'graʊn(d)ləsli

groundlessness
BR 'graʊndləsnəs
AM 'graʊn(d)ləsnəs

groundling
BR 'graʊndlɪŋ, -z
AM 'graʊn(d)lɪŋ, -z

groundnut
BR 'graʊn(d)nʌt, -s
AM 'graʊn(d),nət, -s

groundout
BR 'graʊndaʊt, -s
AM 'graʊn,daʊt, -s

grounds
BR graʊn(d)z
AM graʊn(d)z

groundsel
BR 'graʊn(d)sl
AM 'graʊn(d)səl

groundsheet
BR 'graʊn(d)ʃiːt, -s
AM 'graʊn(d),ʃit, -s

groundsman
BR 'graʊn(d)zmən
AM 'graʊn(d)zmən

groundsmen
BR 'graʊn(d)zmən
AM 'graʊn(d)zmən, 'graʊn(d)z,mɛn

groundswell
BR 'graʊn(d)swɛl
AM 'graʊn(d),swɛl

groundwater
BR 'graʊnd,wɔːtə(r), -z
AM 'graʊn(d),wɔdər, 'graʊn(d),wɑdər, -z

groundwork
BR 'graʊndwəːk
AM 'graʊn(d),wərk

group
BR gruːp, -s, -ɪŋ, -t
AM grup, -s, -ɪŋ, -t

groupage
BR 'gruːpɪdʒ
AM 'grupɪdʒ

grouper
BR 'gruːpə(r), -z
AM 'grupər, -z

groupie
BR 'gruːp|i, -ɪz
AM 'grupi, -z

grouping
BR 'gruːpɪŋ, -z
AM 'grupɪŋ, -z

groupware
BR 'gruːpwɛː(r)
AM 'grup,wɛ(ə)r

grouse
BR graʊs, -ɪz, -ɪŋ, -t
AM graʊs, -əz, -ɪŋ, -t

grouser
BR 'graʊsə(r), -z
AM 'graʊsər, -z

grout
BR graʊt, -s, -ɪŋ, -ɨd
AM graʊ|t, -ts, -dɪŋ, -dəd

grouter
BR 'graʊtə(r), -z
AM 'graʊdər, -z

grove
BR grəʊv, -z
AM groʊv, -z

grovel
BR 'grɒv|l, -lz, -l̩ɪŋ\-lɪŋ, -ld
AM 'grɑv|əl, 'grəv|əl, -əlz, -(ə)lɪŋ, -əld

groveler
BR 'grɒvl̩ə(r), 'grɒvlə(r), -z
AM 'grɑv(ə)lər, 'grəv(ə)lər, -z

grovelingly
BR 'grɒvl̩ɪŋli, 'grɒvlɪŋli
AM 'grɑv(ə)lɪŋli

groveller
BR 'grɒvl̩ə(r), 'grɒvlə(r), -z
AM 'grɑv(ə)lər, 'grəv(ə)lər, -z

grovellingly
BR 'grɒvl̩ɪŋli, 'grɒvlɪŋli
AM 'grɑv(ə)lɪŋli

Grover
BR 'grəʊvə(r)
AM 'groʊvər

Groves
BR grəʊvz
AM groʊvz

grovy
BR 'grəʊvi
AM 'groʊvi

grow
BR grəʊ, -z, -ɪŋ
AM groʊ, -z, -ɪŋ

growable
BR 'grəʊəbl
AM 'groʊəbəl

growbag
BR 'grəʊbag, -z
AM 'groʊ,bæg, -z

grower
BR 'grəʊə(r), -z
AM 'groʊər, -z

growl
BR graʊl, -z, -ɪŋ, -d
AM graʊl, -z, -ɪŋ, -d

growler
BR 'graʊlə(r), -z
AM 'graʊlər, -z

growlingly
BR 'graʊlɪŋli
AM 'graʊlɪŋli

Growmore
BR 'grəʊmɔː(r)
AM 'groʊ,mɔ(ə)r

grown
BR grəʊn
AM groʊn

grownup
noun
BR 'grəʊnʌp, -s
AM 'groʊ,nəp, -s

grown-up
adjective
BR ,grəʊn'ʌp
AM 'groʊ,nəp

growth
BR grəʊθ, -s
AM groʊθ, -s

groyne
BR grɔɪn, -z
AM grɔɪn, -z

Grozny
BR 'grɒzni
AM 'grɔzni, 'grɑzni

grub
BR grʌb, -z, -ɪŋ, -d
AM grəb, -z, -ɪŋ, -d

grubber
BR 'grʌbə(r), -z
AM 'grəbər, -z

grubbily
BR 'grʌbɨli
AM 'grəbəli

grubbiness
BR 'grʌbɪnɪs
AM 'grəbinɪs

grubby
BR 'grʌb|i, -ɪə(r), -ɪɪst
AM 'grəbi, -ər, -ɪst

grubstake
BR 'grʌbsteɪk, -s
AM 'grəb,steɪk, -s

grubstaker
BR 'grʌbsteɪkə(r), -z
AM 'grəb,steɪkər, -z

grudge
BR grʌdʒ, -ɪz, -ɪŋ, -d
AM grədʒ, -əz, -ɪŋ, -d

grudger
BR 'grʌdʒə(r), -z
AM 'grədʒər, -z

grudgingly
BR 'grʌdʒɪŋli
AM 'grədʒɪŋli

grudgingness
BR 'grʌdʒɪŋnɪs
AM 'grədʒɪŋnɪs

gruel
BR 'gruːəl
AM 'gru(ə)l

grueling
BR 'gruːəlɪŋ
AM 'gru(ə)lɪŋ

gruelingly
BR 'gruːəlɪŋli
AM 'gru(ə)lɪŋli

gruelling
BR 'gruːəlɪŋ
AM 'gru(ə)lɪŋ

gruellingly
BR 'gruːəlɪŋli
AM 'gru(ə)lɪŋli

gruesome
BR 'gruːs(ə)m
AM 'grusəm

gruesomely
BR 'gruːs(ə)mli
AM 'grusəmli

gruesomeness
BR 'gruːs(ə)mnəs
AM 'grusəmnəs

gruff
BR grʌf, -ə(r), -ɪst
AM grəf, -ər, -əst

gruffly
BR 'grʌfli
AM 'grəfli

gruffness
BR 'grʌfnəs
AM 'grəfnəs

Gruffydd
BR 'grɪfɪð
AM 'grɪfɪθ

grumble
BR 'grʌmbl, -z, -ɪŋ, -d
AM 'grəmb|əl, -əlz, -(ə)lɪŋ, -əld

grumbler
BR 'grʌmblə(r), -z
AM 'grəmb(ə)lər, -z

grumbling
BR 'grʌmblɪŋ, -z
AM 'grəmb(ə)lɪŋ, -z

grumblingly
BR 'grʌmblɪŋli
AM 'grəmb(ə)lɪŋli

grumbly
BR 'grʌmbli
AM 'grəmb(ə)li

grummet
BR 'grʌmɪt, -s
AM 'grəmət, -s

grumous
BR 'gruːməs
AM 'grəməs

grump
BR grʌm|p, -(p)s
AM grəm|p, -(p)s

grumpily
BR 'grʌmpɨli
AM 'grəmpəli

grumpiness
BR 'grʌmpɪnɪs
AM 'grəmpinɪs

grumpish
BR 'grʌmpɪʃ
AM 'grəmpɪʃ
grumpishly
BR 'grʌmpɪ̵ʃli
AM 'grəmpɪʃli
grumpy
BR 'grʌmp|i, -ɪə(r), -ɪɪst
AM 'grəmpi, -ər, -ɪ̵st
Grundig
BR 'grʌndɪg, 'grʊndɪg
AM 'grəndɪg
Grundy
BR 'grʌnd|i, -ɪz
AM 'grəndi, -z
Grundyism
BR 'grʌndiɪz(ə)m
AM 'grəndi,ɪzəm
grunge
BR grʌn(d)ʒ
AM grəndʒ
grungy
BR 'grʌn(d)ʒi
AM 'grəndʒi
grunion
BR 'grʌnjən
AM 'grənjən
grunt
BR grʌnt, -s, -ɪŋ, -ɪ̵d
AM grən|t, -ts, -(t)ɪŋ, -(t)əd
grunter
BR 'grʌntə(r), -z
AM 'grən(t)ər, -z
Grunth
BR grʌnt
AM grənθ
Gruyère
BR 'gru:jɛ:(r), grʊ'jɛ:(r)
AM gru'jɛ(ə)r
Gruyères
BR 'gru:jɛ:(r), grʊ'jɛ:(r)
AM gru'jɛ(ə)r(z)
gryphon
BR 'grɪfn, -z
AM 'grɪfən, -z
grysbok
BR 'grʌɪsbɒk, 'xreɪsbɒk, -s
AM 'greɪs,bak, 'graɪs,bak, -s
guacamole
BR ,gwa:kə'məʊli
AM ,gwakə'moʊli
guacharo
BR 'gwa:tʃərəʊ, -z
AM 'gwatʃə,roʊ, -z
Guadalajara
BR ,gwa:dələ'ha:rə(r)
AM ,gwadələ'harə
Guadalcanál
BR ,gwa:dlkə'nal
AM ,gwadəlkə'næl
Guadaloupe
BR ,gwa:də'lu:p
AM ,gwadə'lup
Guadaloupian
BR ,gwa:də'lu:pɪən, -z
AM ,gwadə'lupiən, -z
Guadalquivír
BR ,gwa:dlkwɪ'vɪə(r), ,gwa:dl'kwɪvə(r)
AM ,gwadl'k(w)ɪvər
Guadeloupe
BR ,gwa:də'lu:p
AM ,gwadə'lup
Guadeloupian
BR ,gwa:də'lu:pɪən, -z
AM ,gwadə'lupiən, -z
guaiac
BR 'g(w)ʌɪak, 'g(w)ʌɪək, -s
AM 'g(w)aɪ,æk, 'g(w)aɪək, -s
guaiacum
BR 'g(w)ʌɪəkəm, -z
AM 'g(w)aɪəkəm, -z
Guam
BR gwa:m
AM gwam
guan
BR gwa:n, -z
AM gwan, -z
guanaco
BR 'gwa:nəkəʊ, -z
AM gwə'nakoʊ, -z
Guangdong
BR 'gwaŋ'dɒŋ
AM 'gwaŋ'dɔŋ, 'gwaŋ'daŋ
guanine
BR 'gwa:ni:n, 'gu:əni:n
AM 'gwa,nin, 'gwanən
guano
BR 'gwa:nəʊ
AM 'gwanoʊ
Guantánamo
BR gwan'tanəməʊ, gwa:n'tanəməʊ
AM gwan'tanəmoʊ
guar
BR gwa:(r), 'gu:a:(r)
AM gwar
Guarani
BR ,gwa:rə'ni:, 'gwa:rəni, 'gwa:rn̩i, -z
AM ¦gwarə¦ni, -z
guarantee
BR ,garən'ti:, ,garn̩'ti:, -z, -ɪŋ, -d
AM ,gɛrən'ti, -z, -ɪŋ, -d
guarantor
BR ,garən'tɔ:(r), ,garn̩'tɔ:(r), -z
AM ¦gɛ(ə)rən¦tɔ(ə)r, -z
guaranty
BR 'garənt|i, 'garn̩t|i, -ɪz
AM 'gɛrənti, -z
guard
BR ga:d, -z, -ɪŋ, -ɪ̵d
AM gard, -z, -ɪŋ, -əd
guardant
BR 'ga:dnt
AM 'gardənt
guardedly
BR 'ga:dɪ̵dli
AM 'gardədli
guardedness
BR 'ga:dɪ̵dnɪ̵s
AM 'gardədnəs
guardee
BR ,ga:'di:, -z
AM ,gar'di, -z
guarder
BR 'ga:də(r), -z
AM 'gardər, -z
guardhouse
BR 'ga:dhaʊ|s, -zɪz
AM 'gard,(h)aʊ|s, -zəz
Guardi
BR 'gwa:di
AM 'gardi
guardian
BR 'ga:dɪən, -z
AM 'gardiən, -z
guardianship
BR 'ga:dɪənʃɪp, -s
AM 'gardiənʃɪp, -s
guardless
BR 'ga:dləs
AM 'gardləs
guardrail
BR 'ga:dreɪl, -z
AM 'gard,reɪl, -z
guardroom
BR 'ga:dru:m, 'ga:drʊm, -z
AM 'gard,rum, 'gard,rʊm, -z
guardsman
BR 'ga:dzmən
AM 'gardzmən
guardsmen
BR 'ga:dzmən
AM 'gardzmən, 'gardz,mɛn
Guarneri
BR gwa:'nɛ:ri
AM ,gwar'nɛri
Guarnerius
BR gwa:'nɪərɪəs, gwa:'nɛ:rɪəs
AM gwar'nɛriəs
Guatemala
BR ,gwa:tə'ma:lə(r), ,gwatə'ma:lə(r)
AM ,gwadə'malə
Guatemalan
BR ,gwa:tə'ma:lən, ,gwatə'ma:lən, -z
AM ,gwadə'malən, -z
guava
BR 'gwa:və(r), -z
AM 'gwavə, -z
Guayaquil
BR ,gwʌɪə'ki:l
AM ,gaɪə'ki(ə)l
guayule
BR (g)wa:'(j)u:l|i, -ɪz
AM (g)wa'juli, -z
gubbins
BR 'gʌbɪnz
AM 'gəbənz
gubernatorial
BR ,gu:bənə'tɔ:rɪəl
AM ¦gubə(r)nə'tɔriəl
Gucci
BR 'gu:tʃi
AM 'gutʃi
gudgeon
BR 'gʌdʒ(ə)n, -z
AM 'gədʒən, -z
Gudrun
BR 'gʊdrʊn, 'gʊdru:n
AM 'gʊdrən, 'gudrən
guelder-rose
BR 'gɛldərəʊz, ,gɛldə'rəʊz, -ɪz
AM 'gɛldər,roʊz, -ɪz
Guelph
BR gwɛlf, -s
AM gwɛlf, -s
Guelphic
BR 'gwɛlfɪk
AM 'gwɛlfɪk
Guelphism
BR 'gwɛlfɪz(ə)m
AM 'gwɛl,fɪzəm
guenon
BR gə'nɒn, 'gweɪnɒn, -z
AM gə'nan, -z
guerdon
BR 'gə:dn, -z
AM 'gərdən, -z
guerilla
BR gə'rɪlə(r), gɛ'rɪlə(r), -z
AM gə'rɪlə, -z
Guernica
BR 'gə:nɪ̵kə(r), gə:'ni:kə(r)
AM 'gɛr,nikə, gɛr'nikə
Guernsey
BR 'gə:nz|i, -ɪz
AM 'gərnzi, -z
Guerrero
BR gɛ'rɛ:rəʊ, gə'rɛ:rəʊ
AM gə'rɛroʊ
guerrilla
BR gə'rɪlə(r), gɛ'rɪlə(r), -z
AM gə'rɪlə, -z
guess
BR gɛs, -ɪz, -ɪŋ, -t
AM gɛs, -əz, -ɪŋ, -t
guessable
BR 'gɛsəbl
AM 'gɛsəbəl
guesser
BR 'gɛsə(r), -z

AM ˈɡɛsər, -z

guesstimate¹
noun
BR ˈɡɛstɨmət, -s
AM ˈɡɛstəmət, -s

guesstimate²
verb
BR ˈɡɛstɨmeɪt, -s, -ɪŋ, -ɨd
AM ˈɡɛstəˌmeɪ|t, -ts, -dɪŋ, -dɨd

guesswork
BR ˈɡɛswəːk
AM ˈɡɛsˌwərk

guest
BR ɡɛst, -s, -ɪŋ, -ɨd
AM ɡɛst, -s, -ɪŋ, -əd

guesthouse
BR ˈɡɛsthaʊ|s, -zɨz
AM ˈɡɛstˌ(h)aʊ|s, -zəz

guestimate¹
noun
BR ˈɡɛstɨmət, -s
AM ˈɡɛstəmət, -s

guestimate²
verb
BR ˈɡɛstɨmeɪt, -s, -ɪŋ, -ɨd
AM ˈɡɛstəˌmeɪ|t, -ts, -dɪŋ, -dɨd

guestroom
BR ˈɡɛstruːm, ˈɡɛstrʊm, -z
AM ˈɡɛstˌrum, ˈɡɛstˌrʊm, -z

guestship
BR ˈɡɛstʃɪp
AM ˈɡɛs(t)ˌʃɪp

Guevara
BR ɡɨˈvɑːrə(*r*), ɡɛˈvɑːrə(*r*)
AM ɡəˈvɑrə

guff
BR ɡʌf
AM ɡəf

guffaw
BR ɡəˈfɔː(*r*), -z, -ɪŋ, -d
AM ɡəˈfɔ, ɡəˈfɑ, -z, -ɪŋ, -d

Guggenheim
BR ˈɡʊɡ(ə)nhʌɪm
AM ˈɡʊɡənˌ(h)aɪm

guggle
BR ˈɡʌɡ|l, -lz, -l̩ɪŋ\-lɪŋ, -ld
AM ˈɡəɡ|əl, -əlz, -(ə)lɪŋ, -əld

Guiana
BR ɡʌɪˈɑːnə(*r*), ɡɪˈɑːnə(*r*), ɡʌɪˈanə(*r*)
AM ɡiˈɑnə

Guianese
BR ˌɡʌɪəˈniːz
AM ˌɡiəˈniz

guidable
BR ˈɡʌɪdəbl
AM ˈɡaɪdəbəl

guidance
BR ˈɡʌɪdns
AM ˈɡaɪdns

guide
BR ɡʌɪd, -z, -ɪŋ, -ɨd
AM ɡaɪd, -z, -ɪŋ, -ɨd

guidebook
BR ˈɡʌɪdbʊk, -s
AM ˈɡaɪdˌbʊk, -s

guideline
BR ˈɡʌɪdlʌɪn, -z
AM ˈɡaɪdˌlaɪn, -z

guidepost
BR ˈɡʌɪdpəʊst, -s
AM ˈɡaɪdˌpoʊst, -s

Guider
BR ˈɡʌɪdə(r), -z
AM ˈɡaɪdər, -z

guideway
BR ˈɡʌɪdweɪ, -z
AM ˈɡaɪdˌweɪ, -z

Guido
BR ˈɡ(w)iːdəʊ
AM ˈɡ(w)idoʊ

guidon
BR ˈɡʌɪdn, -z
AM ˈɡaɪˌdɑn, ˈɡaɪdən, -z

Guignol
BR ɡiːnˈjɒl
AM ɡinˈjɔl, ɡinˈjɑl

Guignolesque
BR ˌɡiːnjəˈlɛsk
AM ˌɡinjəˈlɛsk

guild
BR ɡɪld, -z
AM ɡɪld, -z

guilder
BR ˈɡɪldə(r), -z
AM ˈɡɪldər, -z

Guildford
BR ˈɡɪl(d)fəd
AM ˈɡɪl(d)fərd

guildhall
BR ˈɡɪldhɔːl, -z
AM ˈɡɪl(d)ˌ(h)ɔl, ˈɡɪl(d)ˌ(h)ɑl, -z

guildsman
BR ˈɡɪldzmən
AM ˈɡɪl(d)zmən

guildsmen
BR ˈɡɪldzmən
AM ˈɡɪl(d)zmən

guildswoman
BR ˈɡɪldzˌwʊmən
AM ˈɡɪl(d)zˌwʊmən

guildswomen
BR ˈɡɪldzˌwɪmɪn
AM ˈɡɪl(d)zˌwɪmɨn

guile
BR ɡʌɪl
AM ɡaɪl

guileful
BR ˈɡʌɪlf(ʊ)l
AM ˈɡaɪlfəl

guilefully
BR ˈɡʌɪlfʊli, ˈɡʌɪlfl̩i
AM ˈɡaɪlfəli

guilefulness
BR ˈɡʌɪlf(ʊ)lnəs
AM ˈɡaɪlfəlnəs

guileless
BR ˈɡʌɪllɨs
AM ˈɡaɪ(l)lɨs

guilelessly
BR ˈɡʌɪllɨsli
AM ˈɡaɪ(l)lɨsli

guilelessness
BR ˈɡʌɪllɨsnɨs
AM ˈɡaɪ(l)lɨsnɨs

Guillaume
BR ˈɡiːəʊm
AM ɡiˈoʊm

guillemot
BR ˈɡɪlɨmɒt, -s
AM ˈɡɪləˌmɑt, -s

guilloche
BR ɡɪˈləʊʃ, ɡɪˈlɒʃ, -ɨz
AM ɡəˈloʊʃ, ɡiˈjoʊʃ, -əz

guillotine
BR ˈɡɪlətiːn, ˌɡɪləˈtiːn, ˌɡiːjəˈtiːn, -z, -ɪŋ, -d
AM ˈɡɪləˌtin, ˈɡi(j)əˌtin, -z, -ɪŋ, -d

guillotiner
BR ˈɡɪlətiːnə(r), ˌɡɪləˈtiːnə(r), ˌɡiːjəˈtiːnə(r), -z
AM ˈɡɪləˌtinər, ˈɡi(j)əˌtinər, -z

guilt
BR ɡɪlt
AM ɡɪlt

guiltily
BR ˈɡɪltɨli
AM ˈɡɪltɨli

guiltiness
BR ˈɡɪltɪnɨs
AM ˈɡɪltinɨs

guiltless
BR ˈɡɪltlɨs
AM ˈɡɪltlɨs

guiltlessly
BR ˈɡɪltlɨsli
AM ˈɡɪltlɨsli

guiltlessness
BR ˈɡɪltlɨsnɨs
AM ˈɡɪltlɨsnɨs

guilty
BR ˈɡɪlt|i, -ɪə(r), -ɪɪst
AM ˈɡɪlti, -ər, -ɨst

guimp
BR ɡɪmp, -s
AM ɡɪmp, -s

guimpe
BR ɡɪmp, -s
AM ɡɪmp, -s

guinea
BR ˈɡɪn|i, -ɪz
AM ˈɡɪni, -z

Guinea-Bissau
BR ˌɡɪnɪbɪˈsaʊ
AM ˈɡɪnibɪˈsaʊ

Guinean
BR ˈɡɪnɪən, -z
AM ˈɡɪniən, -z

Guinevere
BR ˈɡwɪnɪvɪə(r)
AM ˈɡwɪnɨˌvɪ(ə)r

Guinness
BR ˈɡɪnɪs, -ɨz
AM ˈɡɪnɪs, -ɨz

guipure
BR ɡɪˈpjʊə(r)
AM ɡɪˈp(j)u(ə)r

guise
BR ɡʌɪz, -ɨz
AM ɡaɪz, -ɨz

Guiseley
BR ˈɡʌɪzli
AM ˈɡaɪzli

guitar
BR ɡɪˈtɑː(r), -z
AM ɡəˈtɑr, -z

guitarist
BR ɡɪˈtɑːrɪst, -s
AM ɡəˈtɑrəst, -s

guiver
BR ˈɡʌɪvə(r)
AM ˈɡaɪvər

Gujarat
BR ˌɡʊdʒəˈrɑːt, ˌɡuːdʒəˈrɑːt
AM ˌɡʊdʒəˈrɑt

Gujarati
BR ˌɡʊdʒəˈrɑːt|i, ˌɡuːdʒəˈrɑːti, -ɪz
AM ˌɡʊdʒəˈrɑd|i, -z

Gujerat
BR ˌɡʊdʒəˈrɑːt, ˌɡuːdʒəˈrɑːt
AM ˌɡʊdʒəˈrɑt

Gujerati
BR ˌɡʊdʒəˈrɑːt|i, ˌɡuːdʒəˈrɑːt|i, -ɪz
AM ˌɡʊdʒəˈrɑdi, -z

Gujranwala
BR ˌɡʊdʒrənˈwɑːlə(*r*)
AM ˈɡʊdʒrənˈwɑlə

Gujrat
BR ˌɡʊdʒ(ə)ˈrɑːt, ˌɡuːdʒəˈrɑːt
AM ˌɡʊdʒ(ə)ˈrɑt

gulag
BR ˈɡuːlaɡ, -z
AM ˈɡuˌlɑɡ, -z

gular
BR ˈɡjuːlə(r)
AM ˈɡ(j)ulər

Gulbenkian
BR ɡʊlˈbɛŋkɪən
AM ɡʊlˈbɛŋkiən

gulch
BR ɡʌltʃ, -ɨz
AM ɡəltʃ, -əz

gulden
BR ˈɡʊld(ə)n, -z
AM ˈɡuldən, ˈɡʊldən, -z
DU ˈxəldə(n)

gules
BR ɡjuːlz
AM ɡjulz

gulf
BR gʌlf, -s
AM gəlf, -s

gulfweed
BR 'gʌlfwiːd
AM 'gəlf,wid

gull
BR gʌl, -z, -ɪŋ, -d
AM gəl, -z, -ɪŋ, -d

Gullah
BR 'gʌlə(r)
AM 'gələ

gullery
BR 'gʌl(ə)r|i, -ɪz
AM 'gələri, -z

gullet
BR 'gʌlɨt, -s
AM 'gələt, -s

gulley
BR 'gʌl|i, -ɪz, -ɪd
AM 'gəli, -z, -d

gullibility
BR ˌgʌlə'bɪlɨti
AM ˌgələ'bɪlɨdi

gullible
BR 'gʌlɨbl
AM 'gələbəl

gullibly
BR 'gʌlɨbli
AM 'gələbli

Gulliver
BR 'gʌlɨvə(r)
AM 'gələvər

gully
BR 'gʌl|i, -ɪz, -ɪd
AM 'gəli, -z, -d

gulp
BR gʌlp, -s, -ɪŋ, -t
AM gəlp, -s, -ɪŋ, -t

gulper
BR 'gʌlpə(r), -z
AM 'gəlpər, -z

gulpingly
BR 'gʌlpɪŋli
AM 'gəlpɪŋli

gulpy
BR 'gʌlpi
AM 'gəlpi

gum
BR gʌm, -z, -ɪŋ, -d
AM gəm, -z, -ɪŋ, -d

gumbo
BR 'gʌmbəʊ, -z
AM 'gəm,boʊ, -z

gumboil
BR 'gʌmbɔɪl, -z
AM 'gəm,bɔɪl, -z

gumboot
BR 'gʌmbuːt, -s
AM 'gəm,but, -s

gumdrop
BR 'gʌmdrɒp, -s
AM 'gəm,drɑp, -s

gumma
BR 'gʌmə(r), -z
AM 'gəmə, -z

gummatous
BR 'gʌmətəs
AM 'gəmə,toʊs

Gummer
BR 'gʌmə(r)
AM 'gəmər

Gummidge
BR 'gʌmɪdʒ
AM 'gəmɪdʒ

gummily
BR 'gʌmɨli
AM 'gəməli

gumminess
BR 'gʌmɪnɨs
AM 'gəminɨs

gummy
BR 'gʌmi
AM 'gəmi

gumption
BR 'gʌm(p)ʃn
AM 'gəm(p)ʃən

gumshield
BR 'gʌmʃiːld, -z
AM 'gəm,ʃild, -z

gumshoe
BR 'gʌmʃuː, -z
AM 'gəm,ʃu, -z

gun
BR gʌn, -z, -ɪŋ, -d
AM gən, -z, -ɪŋ, -d

gunboat
BR 'gʌnbəʊt, -s
AM 'gən,boʊt, -s

gundi
BR 'gʌnd|i, -ɪz
AM 'gʊndi, 'gəndi, -z

gundog
BR 'gʌndɒg, -z
AM 'gən,dɔg, 'gən,dɑg, -z

gundy
BR 'gʌndi
AM 'gəndi

gunfight
BR 'gʌnfʌɪt, -s
AM 'gən,faɪt, -s

gunfighter
BR 'gʌn,fʌɪtə(r), -z
AM 'gən,faɪdər, -z

gunfire
BR 'gʌn,fʌɪə(r)
AM 'gən,faɪ(ə)r

Gunga Din
BR ˌgʌŋgə 'dɪn
AM ˌgəŋgə 'dɪn

gunge
BR gʌn(d)ʒ
AM gəndʒ

gung-ho
BR ˌgʌŋ'həʊ
AM 'gəŋ'hoʊ

gungy
BR 'gʌn(d)ʒi
AM 'gəndʒi

gunk
BR gʌŋk
AM gəŋk

gunless
BR 'gʌnləs
AM 'gənləs

gunlock
BR 'gʌnlɒk, -s
AM 'gən,lɑk, -s

gunmaker
BR 'gʌn,meɪkə(r), -z
AM 'gən,meɪkər, -z

gunman
BR 'gʌnmən, 'gʌnman
AM 'gənmən

gunmen
BR 'gʌnmən, 'gʌnmɛn
AM 'gənmən, 'gən,mɛn

gunmetal
BR 'gʌn,mɛtl
AM 'gən,mɛdl

Gunn
BR gʌn
AM gən

gunnel
BR 'gʌnl, -z
AM 'gənəl, -z

gunner
BR 'gʌnə(r), -z
AM 'gənər, -z

gunnera
BR 'gʌn(ə)rə(r), -z
AM 'gən(ə)rə, -z

gunnery
BR 'gʌn(ə)ri
AM 'gən(ə)ri

gunny
BR 'gʌn|i, -ɪz
AM 'gəni, -z

gunnysack
BR 'gʌnɪsak, -s
AM 'gəni,sæk, -s

gunplay
BR 'gʌnpleɪ, -z
AM 'gən,pleɪ, -z

gunpoint
BR 'gʌnpɔɪnt
AM 'gən,pɔɪnt

gunpowder
BR 'gʌn,paʊdə(r)
AM 'gən,paʊdər

gunpower
BR 'gʌnpaʊə(r)
AM 'gən,paʊər

gunroom
BR 'gʌnruːm, 'gʌnrʊm, -z
AM 'gən,rum, 'gən,rʊm, -z

gunrunner
BR 'gʌn,rʌnə(r), -z
AM 'gən,rənər, -z

gunrunning
BR 'gʌn,rʌnɪŋ
AM 'gən,rənɪŋ

gunsel
BR 'gʌnsl, -z
AM 'gən(t)səl, -z

gunship
BR 'gʌnʃɪp, -s
AM 'gən,ʃɪp, -s

gunshot
BR 'gʌnʃɒt, -s
AM 'gən,ʃɑt, -s

gunshy
BR 'gʌnʃʌɪ
AM 'gən,ʃaɪ

gunsight
BR 'gʌnsʌɪt, -s
AM 'gən,saɪt, -s

gunslinger
BR 'gʌn,slɪŋə(r), -z
AM 'gən,slɪŋər, -z

gunslinging
BR 'gʌn,slɪŋɪŋ
AM 'gən,slɪŋɪŋ

gunsmith
BR 'gʌnsmɪθ, -s
AM 'gən,smɪθ, -s

gunstock
BR 'gʌnstɒk, -s
AM 'gən,stɑk, -s

Gunter
BR 'gʌntə(r), 'gʊntə(r)
AM 'gən(t)ər

Gunther
BR 'gʌnθə(r), 'gʊntə(r)
AM 'gənθər, 'gʊn(t)ər

gunwale
BR 'gʌnl, -z
AM 'gənl, -z

gunyah
BR 'gʌnjə(r), -z
AM 'gənjə, -z

Guomindang
BR ˌgwəʊmɪn'daŋ
AM 'gwɔ,mɪn'dæŋ

guppy
BR 'gʌp|i, -ɪz
AM 'gəpi, -z

Gupta
BR 'gʊptə(r)
AM 'guptə

gurdwara
BR 'gəːdwɑːrə(r), gəd'wɑːrə(r), -z
AM ˌgərd'wɑrə, -z

gurgitation
BR ˌgəːdʒɪ'teɪʃn
AM ˌgərdʒə'teɪʃən

gurgle
BR 'gəːg|l, -lz, -l̩ɪŋ\-lɪŋ, -ld
AM 'gərg|əl, -əlz, -(ə)lɪŋ, -əld

gurgler
BR 'gəːgl̩ə(r), 'gəːglə(r), -z
AM 'gərg(ə)lər, -z

gurjun
BR 'gəːdʒ(ə)n, -z
AM 'gərjən, -z

Gurkha
BR 'gəːkə(r), 'gʊəkə(r), -z
AM 'gʊrkə, 'gərkə, -z

Gurkhali
BR ˌgəːˈkɑːli
AM ˌgərˈkɑli

gurnard
BR ˈgəːnəd, -z
AM ˈgərnərd, -z

gurnet
BR ˈgəːnɪt, -s
AM ˈgərnət, -s

gurney
BR ˈgəːn|i, -ɪz
AM ˈgərni, -z

guru
BR ˈgʊruː, -z
AM ˈgʊˌru, gəˈru, -z

Gus
BR gʌs
AM gəs

gush
BR gʌʃ, -ɨz, -ɪŋ, -t
AM gəʃ, -əz, -ɪŋ, -t

gusher
BR ˈgʌʃə(r), -z
AM ˈgəʃər, -z

gushily
BR ˈgʌʃɨli
AM ˈgəʃəli

gushiness
BR ˈgʌʃɪnɨs
AM ˈgəʃinɨs

gushing
BR ˈgʌʃɪŋ
AM ˈgəʃɪŋ

gushingly
BR ˈgʌʃɪŋli
AM ˈgəʃɪŋli

gushy
BR ˈgʌʃ|i, -ɪə(r), -ɪɨst
AM ˈgəʃi, -ər, -ɨst

gusset
BR ˈgʌs|ɪt, -ɪts, -ɨtɨd
AM ˈgəsə|t, -ts, -dəd

gust
BR gʌst, -s, -ɪŋ, -ɨd
AM gəst, -s, -ɪŋ, -əd

Gustafson
BR ˈgʊstɑːfs(ə)n, ˈgʌstɑːfs(ə)n, ˈgʊstafs(ə)n, ˈgʌstafs(ə)n
AM ˈgəstəfsən

gustation
BR gʌˈsteɪʃn
AM gəˈsteɪʃən

gustative
BR ˈgʌstətɪv, gʌˈsteɪtɪv
AM ˈgəstədɪv

gustatory
BR ˈgʌstət(ə)ri, gʌˈsteɪt(ə)ri
AM ˈgəstəˌtɔri

Gustave
BR ˈgʊstɑːv, ˈgʌstɑːv
AM ˈgʊsˌtɑv

Gustavus
BR gʊˈstɑːvəs, gʌˈstɑːvəs
AM gʊˈstɑvəs

gustily
BR ˈgʌstɨli
AM ˈgəstəli

gustiness
BR ˈgʌstɪnɨs
AM ˈgəstinɨs

gusto
BR ˈgʌstəʊ
AM ˈgəstoʊ

gusty
BR ˈgʌst|i, -ɪə(r), -ɪɨst
AM ˈgəsti, -ər, -ɨst

gut
BR gʌt, -s, -ɪŋ, -ɨd
AM gə|t, -ts, -dɪŋ, -dəd

Gutenberg
BR ˈguːtnbəːg, ˈgʊtnbəːg
AM ˈgʊtnˌbərg

Guthrie
BR ˈgʌθri
AM ˈgəθri

Gutiérrez
BR ˌgʊtɪˈɛːrɛz
AM ˌgudiˈɛrəs, ˌgudiˈɛrəz
SP guˈtjerreθ, guˈtjerres

gutless
BR ˈgʌtləs
AM ˈgətləs

gutlessly
BR ˈgʌtləsli
AM ˈgətləsli

gutlessness
BR ˈgʌtləsnəs
AM ˈgətləsnəs

gutrot
BR ˈgʌtrɒt
AM ˈgətˌrɑt

gutser
BR ˈgʌtsə(r), -z
AM ˈgətsər, -z

gutsily
BR ˈgʌtsɨli
AM ˈgətsəli

gutsiness
BR ˈgʌtsɪnɨs
AM ˈgətsinɨs

gutsy
BR ˈgʌts|i, -ɪə(r), -ɪɨst
AM ˈgətsi, -ər, -ɨst

guttapercha
BR ˌgʌtəˈpəːtʃə(*r*)
AM ˌgədəˈpərtʃə

guttate
BR ˈgʌteɪt
AM ˈgədˌeɪt

gutter
BR ˈgʌt|ə(r), -əz, -(ə)rɪŋ, -əd
AM ˈgədər, -z, -ɪŋ, -d

guttersnipe
BR ˈgʌtəsnʌɪp, -s
AM ˈgədərˌsnaɪp, -s

guttle
BR ˈgʌt|l, -lz, -l̩ɪŋ\-lɪŋ, -ld
AM ˈgədəl, -z, -ɪŋ, -d

guttural
BR ˈgʌt(ə)rəl, ˈgʌt(ə)rl̩, -z
AM ˈgədərəl, -z

gutturalise
BR ˈgʌt(ə)rəlʌɪz, ˈgʌt(ə)rl̩ʌɪz, -ɨz, -ɪŋ, -d
AM ˈgədərəˌlaɪz, -ɨz, -ɪŋ, -d

gutturalism
BR ˈgʌt(ə)rəlɪz(ə)m, ˈgʌt(ə)rl̩ɪz(ə)m
AM ˈgədərəˌlɪzəm

gutturality
BR ˌgʌtəˈralɪti
AM ˌgədəˈrælədi

gutturalize
BR ˈgʌt(ə)rəlʌɪz, ˈgʌt(ə)rl̩ʌɪz, -ɨz, -ɪŋ, -d
AM ˈgədərəˌlaɪz, -ɨz, -ɪŋ, -d

gutturally
BR ˈgʌt(ə)rəli, ˈgʌt(ə)rl̩i
AM ˈgədərəli

gutty
BR ˈgʌti
AM ˈgədi

gutzer
BR ˈgətsə(r), -z
AM ˈgətsər, -z

guv
BR gʌv
AM gəv

guvnor
BR ˈgʌvnə(r), -z
AM ˈgəvnər, -z

guv'nor
BR ˈgʌvnə(r), -z
AM ˈgəvnər, -z

guy
BR gʌɪ, -z, -ɪŋ, -d
AM gaɪ, -z, -ɪŋ, -d

Guyana
BR gʌɪˈanə(*r*)
AM gaɪˈɑnə

Guyanese
BR ˌgʌɪəˈniːz
AM ˌgiəˈniz

Guyenne
BR g(w)ɪˈjɛn
AM g(w)iˈ(j)ɛn
FR gɥijɛn

Guy Fawkes
BR ˌgʌɪ ˈfɔːks
AM ˌgaɪ ˈfɔks, ˌgaɪ ˈfɑks

Guzmán
BR ˈgʊθmən
AM ˈgusmən
SP guθˈman, gusˈman

guzzle
BR ˈgʌz|l, -lz, -l̩ɪŋ\-lɪŋ, -ld
AM ˈgəz|əl, -əlz, -(ə)lɪŋ, -əld

guzzler
BR ˈgʌzl̩ə(r), ˈgʌzlə(r), -z
AM ˈgəz(ə)lər, -z

Gwalia
BR ˈgwɑːlɪə(*r*)
AM ˈgwɑljə, ˈgwɑliə

Gwalior
BR ˈgwɑːlɪɔː(r)
AM ˈgwɑliˌɔ(ə)r

Gwen
BR gwɛn
AM gwɛn

Gwenda
BR ˈgwɛndə(*r*)
AM ˈgwɛndə

Gwendolen
BR ˈgwɛndəlɪn, ˈgwɛndl̩ɪn
AM ˈgwɛndələn

Gwendoline
BR ˈgwɛndəlɪn, ˈgwɛndl̩ɪn
AM ˈgwɛndələn

Gwendraeth
BR ˈgwɛndrʌɪθ
AM ˈgwɛnˌdraɪθ

Gwenllian
BR ˈgwɛnɬɪən
AM ˈgwɛnljən

Gwent
BR gwɛnt
AM gwɛnt

Gwenyth
BR ˈgwɛnɪθ
AM ˈgwɛnɪθ

Gwyn
BR gwɪn
AM gwɪn

Gwynedd
BR ˈgwɪnəð
AM ˈgwɪnəð

Gwyneth
BR ˈgwɪnɪθ
AM ˈgwɪnɪθ

Gwynfor
BR ˈgwɪnvɔː(r), ˈgwɪnvə(r)
AM ˈgwɪnvɔ(ə)r

Gwynn
BR gwɪn
AM gwɪn

gybe
BR dʒʌɪb, -z, -ɪŋ, -d
AM dʒaɪb, -z, -ɪŋ, -d

Gyles
BR dʒʌɪlz
AM dʒaɪlz

gym
BR dʒɪm, -z
AM dʒɪm, -z

gymkhana
BR dʒɪmˈkɑːnə(*r*), -z
AM dʒɪmˈkɑnə, dʒɪmˈkænə, -z

gymnasia
BR dʒɪm'neɪzɪə(r)
AM dʒɪm'neɪziə, dʒɪm'neɪʒə

gymnasial
BR dʒɪm'neɪzɪəl
AM dʒɪm'neɪziəl

gymnasium
BR dʒɪm'neɪzɪəm, -z
AM dʒɪm'neɪziəm, -z

gymnast
BR 'dʒɪmnast, -s
AM 'dʒɪmnəst, 'dʒɪm,næst, -s

gymnastic
BR dʒɪm'nastɪk, -s
AM dʒɪm'næstɪk, -s

gymnastically
BR dʒɪm'nastɪkli
AM dʒɪm'næstək(ə)li

gymnosophist
BR dʒɪm'nɒsəfɪst, -s
AM dʒɪm'nɑsəfəst, -s

gymnosophy
BR dʒɪm'nɒsəfi
AM dʒɪm'nɑsəfi

gymnosperm
BR 'dʒɪmnə(ʊ)spəːm, -z
AM 'dʒɪmnə,spərm, -z

gymnospermous
BR ,dʒɪmnə(ʊ)'spəːməs
AM ,dʒɪmnə'spərməs

gymp
BR gɪm|p, -ps, -pɪŋ, -(p)t
AM gɪm|p, -ps, -pɪŋ, -(p)t

gymslip
BR 'dʒɪmslɪp, -s
AM 'dʒɪm,slɪp, -s

gynaecea
BR ,dʒʌɪnɪ'siːə(r), ,gʌɪnɪ'siːə(r)
AM ,dʒɪnə'siə

gynaeceum
BR ,dʒʌɪnɪ'siːəm, ,gʌɪnɪ'siːəm, -z
AM ,dʒɪnə'siəm, -z

gynaecocracy
BR ,gʌɪnə'kɒkrəs|i, ,dʒʌɪnə'kɒkrəs|i, -ɪz
AM ,gaɪnə'kɑkrəsi, -z

gynaecologic
BR ,gʌɪnəkə'lɒdʒɪk
AM ,gaɪnəkə'lɑdʒɪk

gynaecological
BR ,gʌɪnəkə'lɒdʒɪkl
AM ,gaɪnəkə'lɑdʒəkəl

gynaecologically
BR ,gʌɪnəkə'lɒdʒɪkli
AM ,gaɪnəkə'lɑdʒək(ə)li

gynaecologist
BR ,gʌɪnə'kɒlədʒɪst, -s
AM ,gaɪnə'kɑlədʒəst, -s

gynaecology
BR ,gʌɪnə'kɒlədʒi
AM ,gaɪnə'kɑlədʒi

gynaecomastia
BR ,gʌɪnəkə(ʊ)'mastɪə(r)
AM ,gaɪnəkoʊ'mæstiə

gynandromorph
BR dʒɪ'nandrəmɔːf, -s
AM dʒɪ'nændrə,mɔ(ə)rf, -s

gynandromorphic
BR dʒɪ,nandrə'mɔːfɪk
AM dʒɪ,nændrə'mɔrfɪk

gynandromorphism
BR dʒɪ,nandrə'mɔːfɪz(ə)m
AM dʒɪ,nændrə'mɔrfɪzəm

gynandrous
BR dʒɪ'nandrəs
AM dʒɪ'nændrəs

gynecia
BR gʌɪ'niːsɪə(r), dʒʌɪ'niːsɪə(r)
AM gaɪ'niʃiə

gynecium
BR gʌɪ'niːsɪəm, dʒʌɪ'niːsɪəm, -z
AM gaɪ'niʃiəm, -z

gynecocracy
BR ,gʌɪnə'kɒkrəs|i, ,dʒʌɪnə'kɒkrəsi, -ɪz
AM ,gaɪnə'kɑkrəsi, -z

gynecologic
BR ,gʌɪnəkə'lɒdʒɪk
AM ,gaɪnəkə'lɑdʒɪk

gynecological
BR ,gʌɪnəkə'lɒdʒɪkl
AM ,gaɪnəkə'lɑdʒəkəl

gynecologically
BR ,gʌɪnəkə'lɒdʒɪkli
AM ,gaɪnəkə'lɑdʒək(ə)li

gynecologist
BR ,gʌɪnə'kɒlədʒɪst, -s
AM ,gaɪnə'kɑlədʒəst, -s

gynecology
BR ,gʌɪnə'kɒlədʒi
AM ,gaɪnə'kɑlədʒi

gynecomastia
BR ,gʌɪnəkə'mastɪə(r)
AM ,gaɪnəkoʊ'mæstiə

gynobase
BR 'gʌɪnə(ʊ)beɪs, -ɪz
AM 'gaɪnoʊ,beɪs, -ɪz

gynocracy
BR gʌɪ'nɒkrəs|i, dʒʌɪ'nɒkrəsi, -ɪz
AM gaɪ'nɑkrəsi, -z

gynoecia
BR gʌɪ'niːsɪə(r), dʒʌɪ'niːsɪə(r)
AM gaɪ'niʃiə

gynoecium
BR gʌɪ'niːsɪəm
AM gaɪ'niʃiəm

gynophobia
BR ,gʌɪnə'fəʊbɪə(r), ,dʒʌɪnə'fəʊbɪə(r)
AM ,gaɪnə'foʊbiə

gyp
BR dʒɪp, -s
AM dʒɪp, -s

gyppy tummy
BR ,dʒɪpɪ 'tʌmi
AM 'dʒɪpi 'təmi

gypseous
BR 'dʒɪpsɪəs
AM 'dʒɪpsiəs

gypsiferous
BR dʒɪp'sɪf(ə)rəs
AM dʒɪp'sɪf(ə)rəs

gypsophila
BR dʒɪp'sɒfɪlə(r), -z
AM dʒɪp'sɑfələ, -z

gypsum
BR 'dʒɪps(ə)m
AM 'dʒɪpsəm

Gypsy
BR 'dʒɪps|i, -ɪz
AM 'dʒɪpsi, -z

Gypsydom
BR 'dʒɪpsɪdəm
AM 'dʒɪpsidəm

Gypsyfied
BR 'dzɪpsɪfʌɪd
AM 'dʒɪpsə,faɪd

Gypsyhood
BR 'dʒɪpsɪhʊd
AM 'dʒɪpsi,hʊd

Gypsyish
BR 'dʒɪpsɪɪʃ
AM 'dʒɪpsiɪʃ

gyrate
BR dʒʌɪ'reɪt, -s, -ɪŋ, -ɪd
AM 'dʒaɪ,reɪ|t, -ts, -dɪŋ, -dɪd

gyration
BR dʒʌɪ'reɪʃn, -z
AM dʒaɪ'reɪʃən, -z

gyrator
BR dʒʌɪ'reɪtə(r), -z
AM 'dʒaɪ,reɪdər, -z

gyratory
BR dʒʌɪ'reɪt(ə)ri, 'dʒʌɪrət(ə)ri
AM 'dʒaɪrə,tɔri

gyre
BR 'dʒʌɪə(r), -z
AM 'dʒaɪ(ə)r, -z

gyrfalcon
BR 'dʒəː,fɔːlk(ə)n, 'dʒəː,falk(ə)n, -z
AM 'dʒər,fælkən, -z

gyri
BR 'dʒʌɪrʌɪ
AM 'dʒaɪ,raɪ

gyro[1]
gyroscope
BR 'dʒʌɪrəʊ
AM 'dʒaɪroʊ

gyro[2]
sandwich
BR 'jɪərəʊ, 'dʒɪərəʊ, 'dʒʌɪrəʊ, -z
AM 'dʒiroʊ, 'jɪroʊ, -z

gyrocompass
BR 'dʒʌɪrə(ʊ),kʌmpəs, -ɪz
AM 'dʒaɪroʊ,kəmpəs, -əz

gyrograph
BR 'dʒʌɪrəgrɑːf, 'dʒʌɪrəgraf, -s
AM 'dʒaɪrə,græf, -s

gyromagnetic
BR ,dʒʌɪrə(ʊ)mag'nɛtɪk
AM ¦dʒaɪroʊ,mæg'nɛdɪk

gyronny
BR dʒʌɪ'rɒni
AM dʒaɪ'rɑni

gyropilot
BR 'dʒʌɪrə(ʊ),pʌɪlət, -s
AM 'dʒaɪrə,paɪlət, -s

gyroplane
BR 'dʒʌɪrəpleɪn, -z
AM 'dʒaɪrə,pleɪn, -z

gyroscope
BR 'dʒʌɪrəskəʊp, -s
AM 'dʒaɪrə,skoʊp, -s

gyroscopic
BR ,dʒʌɪrə'skɒpɪk
AM ¦dʒaɪrə'skɑpɪk

gyrostabiliser
BR 'dʒʌɪrəʊ,steɪbɪlʌɪzə(r) 'dʒʌɪrəʊ,steɪbl̩ʌɪzə(r), -z
AM ¦dʒaɪroʊ'steɪbə,laɪzər, -z

gyrostabilizer
BR 'dʒʌɪrəʊ,stabɪlʌɪzə(r), 'dʒʌɪrəʊ,stabl̩ʌɪzə(r), 'dʒʌɪrəʊ,steɪbl̩ʌɪzə(r), -z
AM ¦dʒaɪroʊ'steɪbə,laɪzər, -z

gyrostatic
BR ,dʒʌɪrə'statɪk
AM ¦dʒaɪrə'stædɪk

gyrus
BR 'dʒʌɪrəs
AM 'dʒaɪrəs

gyttja
BR 'jɪtʃə(r)
AM 'jɪ,tʃɑ

gyve
BR dʒʌɪv, -z, -ɪŋ, -d
AM dʒaɪv, -z, -ɪŋ, -d

gyver
BR 'gʌɪvə(r)
AM 'gaɪvər

Hh

h
BR eɪtʃ, -ɪz
AM eɪtʃ, -ɪz

ha
BR hɑː(r)
AM hɑ

haar
BR hɑː(r), -z
AM (h)ɑr, -z

Haarlem
BR 'hɑːləm
AM 'hɑrləm

Haas
BR hɑːs, has
AM hɑs

Habakkuk
BR 'habəkʌk
AM 'hæbəˌkʊk, hə'bækək

habanera
BR ˌhabə'nɛːrə(r), ˌ(h)ɑːbə'nɛːrə(r), -z
AM (h)ɑbə'nɛrə, -z

habeas corpus
BR ˌheɪbɪəs 'kɔːpəs
AM 'heɪbiə 'skɔrpəs

Haber-Bosch
BR ˌheɪbə'bɒʃ
AM 'heɪbər'bɔʃ, 'heɪbər'bɑʃ

haberdasher
BR 'habədaʃə(r), -z
AM 'habərˌdæʃər, -z

haberdashery
BR 'habədaʃ(ə)r|i, -ɪz
AM 'habərˌdæʃəri, -z

habergeon
BR 'habədʒ(ə)n, -z
AM 'hæbərdʒən, hə'bərdʒ(i)ən, -z

Habgood
BR 'habgʊd
AM 'hæbˌgʊd

habile
BR 'habɪl
AM 'hæbəl

habiliment
BR hə'bɪlɪm(ə)nt, -s
AM hə'bɪləmənt, -s

habilitate
BR hə'bɪlɪteɪt, -s, -ɪŋ, -ɪd
AM hə'bɪləˌteɪ|t, -ts, -dɪŋ, -dɪd

habilitation
BR həˌbɪlɪ'teɪʃn
AM həˌbɪlə'teɪʃən

habit
BR 'habɪt, -s
AM 'hæbət, -s

habitability
BR ˌhabɪtə'bɪlɪti
AM ˌhæbədə'bɪlɪdi

habitable
BR 'habɪtəbl
AM 'hæbədəbəl

habitableness
BR 'habɪtəblnəs
AM 'hæbədəbəlnəs

habitably
BR 'habɪtəbli
AM 'hæbədəbli

habitant
BR 'habɪt(ə)nt, -s
AM 'hæbədənt, 'hæbətnt, -s

habitat
BR 'habɪtat, -s
AM 'hæbəˌtæt, -s

habitation
BR ˌhabɪ'teɪʃn, -z
AM ˌhæbə'teɪʃən, -z

habited
BR 'habɪtɪd
AM 'hæbədəd

habitual
BR hə'bɪtʃʊəl, hə'bɪtʃ(ʉ)l, hə'bɪtjʊəl, hə'bɪtjʉl
AM hə'bɪtʃ(əw)əl

habitually
BR hə'bɪtʃʊəli, hə'bɪtʃʉli, hə'bɪtʃl̩i, hə'bɪtjʊəli, hə'bɪtjʉli
AM hə'bɪtʃ(əw)əli

habitualness
BR hə'bɪtʃʊəlnəs, hə'bɪtʃ(ʉ)lnəs, hə'bɪtjʊəlnəs, hə'bɪtjʉlnəs
AM hə'bɪtʃ(əw)əlnəs

habituate
BR hə'bɪtʃʊeɪt, hə'bɪtjʊeɪt, -s, -ɪŋ, -ɪd
AM hə'bɪtʃəˌweɪ|t, -ts, -dɪŋ, -dɪd

habituation
BR həˌbɪtʃʊ'eɪʃn, həˌbɪtjʊ'eɪʃn
AM həˌbɪtʃə'weɪʃən

habitude
BR 'habɪtʃuːd, 'habɪtjuːd, -z
AM 'hæbəˌt(j)ud, -z

habitué
BR hə'bɪtʃʊeɪ, hə'bɪtjʊeɪ, -z
AM hə'bɪtʃəˌweɪ, həˌbɪtʃə'weɪ, -z

Habsburg
BR 'hapsbəːg, 'habzbəːg, -z
AM 'hæpsˌbərg, 'hɑbsˌbərg, -z

habutai
BR 'hɑːbʉtʌɪ
AM 'hɑbəˌtaɪ

haček
BR 'hatʃɛk, 'hɑːtʃɛk, -s
AM 'hæˌtʃɛk, 'hɑˌtʃɛk, -s

hachure
BR 'haʃə(r), ha'ʃʊə(r), 'haʃəz\ha'ʃʊəz, 'haʃ(ə)rɪŋ\ha'ʃʊərɪŋ, 'haʃəd\ha'ʃʊəd
AM hæ'ʃʊ(ə)r, 'hæʃər, -z, -ɪŋ, -d

hacienda
BR ˌhasɪ'ɛndə(r), -z
AM ˌhɑsi'ɛndə, -z

hack
BR hak, -s, -ɪŋ, -t
AM hæk, -s, -ɪŋ, -t

hackamore
BR 'hakəmɔː(r), -z
AM 'hækəˌmɔ(ə)r, -z

hackberry
BR 'hakb(ə)r|i, -ɪz
AM 'hækˌbɛri, -z

hacker
BR 'hakə(r), -z
AM 'hækər, -z

hackery
BR 'hak(ə)r|i, -ɪz
AM 'hækəri, -z

Hackett
BR 'hakɪt
AM 'hækət

hackette
BR ha'kɛt, -s
AM hæ'kɛt, -s

hackle
BR 'hakl, -lz, -l̩ɪŋ\-lɪŋ, -ld
AM 'hæk|əl, -əlz, -(ə)lɪŋ, -əld

hackly
BR 'hakli
AM 'hækli

hackmatack
BR 'hakmətak, -s
AM 'hækməˌtæk, -s

hackney
BR 'hakn|i, -ɪz, -ɪd
AM 'hækni, -z, -d

hacksaw
BR 'haksɔː(r), -z
AM 'hækˌsɔ, 'hækˌsɑ, -z

hackwork
BR 'hakwəːk
AM 'hækˌwərk

had[1]
strong form
BR had
AM hæd

had[2]
weak form
BR həd, əd, d
AM həd, əd, d

haddie
BR 'had|i, -ɪz
AM 'hædi, -z

Haddington
BR 'hadɪŋt(ə)n
AM 'hædɪŋtən

haddock
BR 'hadək, -s
AM 'hædək, -s

Haddon
BR 'hadn
AM 'hædən

hade
BR heɪd, -z, -ɪŋ, -ɪd
AM heɪd, -z, -ɪŋ, -ɪd

Hadean
BR 'heɪdɪən
AM 'heɪdiən

Hades
BR 'heɪdiːz
AM 'heɪdiz

Hadfield
BR 'hadfiːld
AM 'hædˌfild

Hadith
BR hə'diːθ
AM hə'diθ

hadj
BR hadʒ, hɑːdʒ, -ɪz
AM hɑdʒ, hædʒ, -əz

hadji
BR 'hadʒiː, 'hɑːdʒiː, -ɪz\-iːz
AM 'hɑdʒi, 'hædʒi, -z

Hadlee
BR 'hadli
AM 'hædli

Hadley
BR 'hadli
AM 'hædli

hadn't
BR 'hadnt
AM 'hædnt

Hadrian
BR 'heɪdrɪən
AM 'heɪdriən

hadron
BR 'hadrɒn, 'hadrən, -z
AM 'hædrən, 'hædˌrɑn, -z

hadronic
BR ha'drɒnɪk
AM hæd'rɑnɪk

hadrosaur
BR 'hadrəsɔː(r), -z
AM 'hædrəˌsɔ(ə)r, -z

hadst[1]
strong form
BR hadst
AM hædst

hadst[2]
weak form
BR hədst
AM hədst

haecceity
BR hɛk'siːɪt|i, hiːk'siːɪti, -ɪz
AM hæk'siɪdi, -z

haem
BR hiːm
AM him

haemal
BR ˈhiːml
AM ˈhiməl
haematic
BR hiːˈmatɪk
AM hiˈmædɪk
haematin
BR ˈhiːmətɪn
AM ˈhiməˌtin
haematite
BR ˈhiːmətʌɪt
AM ˈhiməˌtaɪt
haematocele
BR hɪˈmatəsiːl
AM hiˈmædoʊˌsil
haematocrit
BR hɪˈmatəkrɪt
AM hiˈmædəˌkrɪt
haematologic
BR ˌhiːmətəˈlɒdʒɪk
AM ˈhimədoʊˈlɑdʒɪk
haematological
BR ˌhiːmətəˈlɒdʒɪkl
AM ˈhimədoʊˈlɑdʒəkəl
haematologist
BR ˌhiːməˈtɒlədʒɪst, -s
AM ˌhiməˈtɑlədʒəst, -s
haematology
BR ˌhiːməˈtɒlədʒi
AM ˌhiməˈtɑlədʒi
haematoma
BR ˌhiːməˈtəʊmə(*r*), -z
AM ˌhiməˈtoʊmə, -z
haematuria
BR ˌhiːməˈtjʊərɪə(*r*)
AM ˌhiməˈtʊriə
haemocyanin
BR ˌhiːmə(ʊ)ˈsʌɪənɪn
AM ˌhiməˈsaɪənən
haemodialysis
BR ˌhiːmə(ʊ)dʌɪˈalɪsɪs
AM ˌhimoʊdaɪˈæləsəs
haemodynamic
BR ˌhiːmə(ʊ)dʌɪˈnamɪk
AM ˌhimoʊdaɪˈnæmɪk
haemoglobin
BR ˌhiːməˈgləʊbɪn
AM ˈhiməˌgloʊbən
haemolysis
BR hiːˈmɒlɪsɪs
AM hiˈmɑləsəs
haemolytic
BR ˌhiːməˈlɪtɪk
AM ˌhiməˈlɪdɪk
haemophilia
BR ˌhiːməˈfɪlɪə(*r*)
AM ˌhiməˈfɪljə, ˌhiməˈfɪliə
haemophiliac
BR ˌhiːməˈfɪlɪak, -s
AM ˌhiməˈfɪliˌæk, -s
haemophilic
BR ˌhiːməˈfɪlɪk
AM ˌhiməˈfɪlɪk
haemorrhage
BR ˈhɛm(ə)r|ɪdʒ, -ɪdʒɪz, -ɪdʒɪŋ, -ɪdʒd
AM ˈhɛm(ə)rɪdʒ, -ɪz, -ɪŋ, -d
haemorrhagic
BR ˌhɛməˈradʒɪk
AM ˌhɛməˈrædʒɪk
haemorrhoid
BR ˈhɛmərɔɪd, -z
AM ˈhɛm(ə)ˌrɔɪd, -z
haemorrhoidal
BR ˌhɛməˈrɔɪdl
AM ˌhɛm(ə)ˈrɔɪdəl
haemostasis
BR ˌhiːmə(ʊ)ˈsteɪsɪs
AM ˌhiməˈsteɪsəs
haemostatic
BR ˌhiːməˈstatɪk
AM ˌhiməˈstædɪk
haere mai
BR ˈhʌɪrə ˈmʌɪ
AM ˈhirə ˈmaɪ
hafiz
BR ˈhɑːfɪz, -ɪz
AM ˈhɑfəz, -əz
hafnium
BR ˈhafnɪəm
AM ˈhæfniəm
Hafod
BR ˈhavɒd
AM ˈhævəd
haft
BR hɑːft, haft, -s, -ɪŋ, -ɪd
AM hæft, -s, -ɪŋ, -əd
haftara
BR ˌhɑːftəˈrɑː(*r*), ˌhaftəˈrɑː(*r*)
AM ˌhɑftəˈrɑ
haftarah
BR ˌhɑːftəˈrɑː(*r*), ˌhaftəˈrɑː(*r*)
AM ˌhɑftəˈrɑ
hag
BR hag, -z
AM hæg, -z
Hagan
BR ˈheɪg(ə)n
AM ˈheɪgən
Hagar
BR ˈheɪgɑː(r), ˈheɪgə(r)
AM ˈheɪgər
hagfish
BR ˈhagfɪʃ, -ɪz
AM ˈhægˌfɪʃ, -ɪz
Haggada
BR həˈgɑːdə(*r*), ˌhagəˈdɑː(*r*)
AM həˈgɑdə
Haggadah
BR həˈgɑːdə(*r*), ˌhagəˈdɑː(*r*)
AM həˈgɑdə
Haggadic
BR həˈgɑːdɪk, həˈgadɪk
AM həˈgɑdɪk
Haggadoth
BR həˈgɑːdəʊt, ˌhagəˈdəʊt
AM həˈgɑˌdoʊθ
Haggai
BR ˈhagʌɪ, ˈhagɪʌɪ, ˈhageɪʌɪ
AM ˈhægaɪ
haggard
BR ˈhagəd
AM ˈhægərd
haggardly
BR ˈhagədli
AM ˈhægərdli
haggardness
BR ˈhagədnəs
AM ˈhægərdnəs
haggis
BR ˈhag|ɪs, -ɪsɪz
AM ˈhɑgəs, -əz
haggish
BR ˈhagɪʃ
AM ˈhægɪʃ
haggle
BR ˈhag|l, -lz, -l̩ɪŋ\-lɪŋ, -ld
AM ˈhæg|əl, -əlz, -(ə)lɪŋ, -əld
haggler
BR ˈhagl̩ə(r), ˈhaglə(r), -z
AM ˈhæg(ə)lər, -z
hagiocracy
BR ˌhagɪˈɒkrəs|i, -ɪz
AM ˌhægiˈɑkrəsi, ˌheɪgiˈɑkrəsi, ˌhɑgiˈɑkrəsi, -z
Hagiographa
BR ˌhagɪˈɒgrəfə(*r*)
AM ˌhægiˈɑgrəfə, ˌheɪgiˈɑgrəfə, ˌhɑgiˈɑgrəfə
hagiographer
BR ˌhagɪˈɒgrəfə(r), -z
AM ˌhægiˈɑgrəfər, ˌheɪgiˈɑgrəfər, ˌhɑgiˈɑgrəfər, -z
hagiographic
BR ˌhagɪəˈgrafɪk
AM ˌhægiəˈgræfɪk, ˌheɪgiəˈgræfɪk, ˌhɑgiəˈgræfɪk
hagiographical
BR ˌhagɪəˈgrafɪkl
AM ˌhægiəˈgræfəkəl, ˌheɪgiəˈgræfəkəl, ˌhɑgiəˈgræfɪkəl
hagiography
BR ˌhagɪˈɒgrəfi
AM ˌhægiˈɑgrəfi, ˌheɪgiˈɑgrəfi, ˌhɑgiˈɑgrəfi
hagiolater
BR ˌhagɪˈɒlətə(r), -z
AM ˌhagiˈɑlədər, ˌheɪgiˈɑlədər, ˌhɑgiˈɑlədər, -z
hagiolatry
BR ˌhagɪˈɒlətri
AM ˌhagiˈɑlətri, ˌheɪgiˈɑlətri, ˌhagiˈɑlətri
hagiological
BR ˌhagɪəˈlɒdʒɪkl
AM ˌhagiəˈlɑdʒəkəl, ˌheɪgiəˈlɑdʒəkəl, ˌhɑgiəˈlɑdʒəkəl
hagiologist
BR ˌhagɪˈɒlədʒɪst, -s
AM ˌhægiˈɑlədʒəst, ˌheɪgiˈɑlədʒəst, ˌhɑgiˈɑlədʒəst, -s
hagiology
BR ˌhagɪˈɒlədʒi
AM ˌhægiˈɑlədʒi, ˌheɪgiˈɑlədʒi, ˌhɑgiˈɑlədʒi
hagioscope
BR ˈhagɪəskəʊp, -s
AM ˈhægiəˌskoʊp, ˈheɪgiəˌskoʊp, ˈhɑgiəˌskoʊp, -s
hagioscopic
BR ˌhagɪəˈskɒpɪk
AM ˌhægiəˈskɑpɪk, ˌheɪgiəˈskɑpɪk, ˌhɑgiəˈskɑpɪk
hagridden
BR ˈhagˌrɪdn
AM ˈhægˌrɪdən
Hague
BR heɪg
AM heɪg
hah
interjection
BR hɑː(*r*)
AM hɑ
ha-ha¹
ditch
BR ˈhɑːhɑː(*r*), -z
AM ˈhɑˌhɑ, -z
ha-ha²
interjection, laughter
BR (ˌ)hɑːˈhɑː(r), -z
AM ˈhɑˈhɑ, -z
Hahn
BR hɑːn
AM hɑn
hahnium
BR ˈhɑːnɪəm
AM ˈhɑniəm
haick
BR hʌɪk, ˈhɑːɪk, heɪk, -s
AM haɪk, -s
Haida
BR ˈhʌɪdə(*r*), -z
AM ˈhaɪdə, -z
Haifa
BR ˈhʌɪfə(*r*)
AM ˈhaɪfə
Haig
BR heɪg
AM heɪg
Haigh¹
placename
BR heɪ
AM heɪ
Haigh²
surname
BR heɪg

AM heɪɡ

Haight
BR hʌɪt, heɪt
AM heɪt

Haight-Ashbury
BR ˌhʌɪt'aʃb(ə)ri
AM ˌheɪt'aʃbɛri

haik
BR hʌɪk, 'hɑːɪk, heɪk, -s
AM haɪk, -s

haiku
BR 'hʌɪkuː, -z
AM 'haɪˌku, -z

hail
BR heɪl, -z, -ɪŋ, -d
AM heɪl, -z, -ɪŋ, -d

hailer
BR 'heɪlə(r), -z
AM 'heɪlər, -z

Haile Selassie
BR ˌhʌɪlɪ sɪ'lasi
AM ˌhaɪli sə'læsi

Hailey
BR 'heɪli
AM 'heɪli

Haileybury
BR 'heɪlɪb(ə)ri
AM 'heɪliˌbɛri

Hailsham
BR 'heɪlʃ(ə)m
AM 'heɪlʃəm

hailstone
BR 'heɪlstəʊn, -z
AM 'heɪlˌstoʊn, -z

hailstorm
BR 'heɪlstɔːm, -z
AM 'heɪlˌstɔ(ə)rm, -z

Hailwood
BR 'heɪlwʊd
AM 'heɪlˌwʊd

haily
BR 'heɪli
AM 'heɪli

Hain
BR heɪn
AM heɪn

Hainault
BR 'heɪnɔː(l)t, 'heɪnɒlt
AM (h)eɪ'noʊ

Haines
BR heɪnz
AM heɪnz

Hainsworth
BR 'heɪnzwəːθ, 'heɪnzwəθ
AM 'heɪnzˌwərθ

Haiphong
BR ˌhʌɪ'fɒŋ
AM 'haɪ'fɔŋ, 'haɪ'fɑŋ

hair
BR hɛː(r), -z, -d
AM hɛ(ə)r, -z, -d

hairbreadth
BR 'hɛːbrɛdθ, 'hɛːbrɛtθ
AM 'hɛrˌbrɛ(d)θ

hairbrush
BR 'hɛːbrʌʃ, -ɪz
AM 'hɛrˌbrəʃ, -əz

haircare
BR 'hɛːkɛː(r)
AM 'hɛrˌkɛ(ə)r

haircloth
BR 'hɛːklɒ|θ, -θs\-ðz
AM 'hɛrˌklɔθ, 'hɛrˌklɑθ, -θs\-ðz

haircut
BR 'hɛːkʌt, -s, -ɪŋ
AM 'hɛrˌkət, -s, -ɪŋ

hairdo
BR 'hɛːduː, -z
AM 'hɛrˌdu, -z

hairdresser
BR 'hɛːˌdrɛsə(r), -z
AM 'hɛrˌdrɛsər, -z

hairdressing
BR 'hɛːˌdrɛsɪŋ
AM 'hɛrˌdrɛsɪŋ

hairdrier
BR 'hɛːˌdrʌɪə(r), -z
AM 'hɛrˌdraɪər, -z

hairdryer
BR 'hɛːˌdrʌɪə(r), -z
AM 'hɛrˌdraɪər, -z

hairgrip
BR 'hɛːɡrɪp, -s
AM 'hɛrˌɡrɪp, -s

hairily
BR 'hɛːrɪli
AM 'hɛrəli

hairiness
BR 'hɛːrɪnɪs
AM 'hɛrinɪs

hairless
BR 'hɛːləs
AM 'hɛrləs

hairlessness
BR 'hɛːləsnəs
AM 'hɛrləsnəs

hairlike
BR 'hɛːlʌɪk
AM 'hɛrˌlaɪk

hairline
BR 'hɛːlʌɪn, -z
AM 'hɛrˌlaɪn, -z

hairnet
BR 'hɛːnɛt, -s
AM 'hɛrˌnɛt, -s

hairpiece
BR 'hɛːpiːs, -ɪz
AM 'hɛrˌpis, -ɪz

hairpin
BR 'hɛːpɪn, -z
AM 'hɛrˌpɪn, -z

hairsbreadth
BR 'hɛːzbrɛdθ, 'hɛːzbrɛtθ
AM 'hɛrzˌbrɛ(d)θ

hairspray
BR 'hɛːspreɪ, -z
AM 'hɛrˌspreɪ, -z

hairspring
BR 'hɛːsprɪŋ, -z
AM 'hɛrˌsprɪŋ, -z

hairstreak
BR 'hɛːstriːk, -s
AM 'hɛrˌstrik, -s

hairstyle
BR 'hɛːstʌɪl, -z
AM 'hɛrˌstaɪl, -z

hairstyling
BR 'hɛːˌstʌɪlɪŋ
AM 'hɛrˌstaɪlɪŋ

hairstylist
BR 'hɛːˌstʌɪlɪst, -s
AM 'hɛrˌstaɪlɪst, -s

hairy
BR 'hɛːr|i, -ɪə(r), -ɪɪst
AM 'hɛri, -ər, -ɪst

Haiti
BR 'heɪti, 'hʌɪti, heɪ'iːti, hʌɪ'iːti, hɑː'iːti
AM 'heɪdi

Haitian
BR 'heɪʃn, 'heɪʃɪən, 'heɪtɪən, 'hʌɪʃn, heɪ'iːʃn, hʌɪ'iːʃn, hɑː'iːʃn, -z
AM 'heɪʃən, -z

haj
BR hadʒ, hɑːdʒ, -ɪz
AM hadʒ, hædʒ, -ɪz

haji
BR 'hadʒ|i, 'hadʒ|iː, 'hɑːdʒ|i, 'hɑːdʒ|iː, -ɪz\-iːz
AM 'hɑdʒi, 'hædʒi, -z

hajj
BR hadʒ, hɑːdʒ, -ɪz
AM hɑdʒ, hædʒ, -ɪz

hajji
BR 'hadʒ|i, 'hadʒ|iː, 'hɑːdʒ|i, 'hɑːdʒ|iː, -ɪz\-iːz
AM 'hɑdʒi, 'hædʒi, -z

haka
BR 'hɑːkə(r), -z
AM 'hɑkə, -z

hake
BR heɪk, -s
AM heɪk, -s

Hakenkreuz
BR 'hɑːk(ə)nkrɔɪts
AM 'hɑkənˌkrɔɪts

Hakenkreuze
BR 'hɑːk(ə)nˌkrɔɪtsə(r)
AM 'hɑkənˌkrɔɪtsə

hakim
BR ha'kiːm, -z
AM hə'kim, -z

Hakka
BR 'hakə(r), -z
AM 'hɑkə, 'hækə, -z

Hakluyt
BR 'hakluːt
AM 'hæˌklut

Hal
BR hal
AM hæl

Halacha
BR ˌhalɑː'xɑː(r), hə'lɑːxə(r), hə'lɑːkɑː(r)
AM hɑ'lɑkɑ

Halachic
BR hə'lɑːkɪk
AM hə'lɑkɪk

Halafian
BR hə'lɑːfɪən
AM hə'lɑfiən

Halakah
BR ˌhalɑː'xɑː(r), hə'lɑːxə(r), hə'lɑːkɑː(r)
AM hɑ'lɑkɑ

halal
BR hə'lɑːl, hə'lal, 'halal
AM hə'lɑl, hə'læl

halation
BR hə'leɪʃn
AM hə'leɪʃən

halberd
BR 'halbəd, -z
AM 'hælbərd, 'hɔlbərd, 'hɑlbərd, -z

halberdier
BR ˌhalbə'dɪə(r), -z
AM ˌhælbər'dɪ(ə)r, ˌhɔlbər'dɪ(ə)r, ˌhɑlbər'dɪ(ə)r, -z

halcyon
BR 'halsɪən
AM 'hælsiən, 'hælsiˌɑn

Haldane
BR 'hɔːldeɪn, 'hɒldeɪn, 'haldeɪn
AM 'hælˌdeɪn, 'hɔlˌdeɪn, 'hɑlˌdeɪn

hale
BR heɪl, -z, -ɪŋ, -d
AM heɪl, -z, -ɪŋ, -d

haleness
BR 'heɪlnəs
AM 'heɪlnɪs

háleř
currency
BR 'hɑːlə(r)
AM 'hɑlər
CZ 'hʌleː(r)ʒ

haleru
BR 'hɑːləruː
AM 'hɑləru

Hales
BR heɪlz
AM heɪlz

Halesowen
BR (ˌ)heɪlz'əʊɪn
AM ˌheɪlz'oʊən

Halesworth
BR 'heɪlzwəːθ, 'heɪlzwəθ
AM 'heɪlzˌwərθ

Halewood
BR 'heɪlwʊd
AM 'heɪlˌwʊd

Halex®
BR 'heɪlɛks
AM 'heɪlɛks

Haley
BR 'heɪli
AM 'heɪli

half
BR hɑːf
AM hæf

halfback
BR 'hɑːfbak, -s
AM 'hæf,bæk, -s

halfpence
BR 'heɪp(ə)ns
AM 'hæf,pɛns, 'heɪpəns

halfpenny
BR 'heɪpn|i, -ɪz
AM 'hæf,pɛni, 'heɪp(ə)ni, -z

halfpennyworth
BR 'heɪpnɪwəːθ, ,hɑːf'pɛnəθ, -s
AM ¦hæf'pɛni,wərθ, 'heɪpnɪ,wərθ, -s

halftime
BR ,hɑːf'tʌɪm
AM 'hæf,taɪm

halftone
BR ,hɑːf'təʊn, 'hɑːftəʊn, -z
AM 'hæf,toʊn, -z

halftrack
noun
BR 'hɑːftrak, -s
AM 'hæf,træk, -s

half-track
adjective
BR ,hɑːf'trak, -t
AM ¦hæf¦træk, -t

halfway
BR ,hɑːf'weɪ
AM ¦hæf¦weɪ

halfwit
BR 'hɑːfwɪt, -s
AM 'hæf,wɪt, -s

half-witted
BR ,hɑːf'wɪtɪd
AM ¦hæf'wɪdɪd

half-wittedly
BR ,hɑːf'wɪtɪdli
AM ¦hæf'wɪdɪdli

half-wittedness
BR ,hɑːf'wɪtɪdnɪs
AM ¦hæf'wɪdɪdnɪs

halibut
BR 'halɪbət, -s
AM 'hæləbət, -s

Halicarnassus
BR ,halɪkɑː'nasəs
AM ,hælə,kɑr'næsəs

halide
BR 'heɪlʌɪd, 'halʌɪd, -z
AM 'heɪ,laɪd, 'hæ,laɪd, -z

halieutic
BR ,halɪ'juːtɪk, -s
AM ,hæli'(j)udɪk, -s

Halifax
BR 'halɪfaks
AM 'hælə,fæks

haliotis
BR ,halɪ'əʊtɪs
AM ,hæli'oʊdəs

halite
BR 'halʌɪt, -s
AM 'hæ,laɪt, 'heɪ,laɪt, -s

halitosis
BR ,halɪ'təʊsɪs
AM ,hælə'toʊsəs

hall
BR hɔːl, -z
AM hɔl, hɑl, -z

hallal
BR hə'lɑːl, hə'lal, 'halal
AM hə'lɑl, hə'læl

Hallam
BR 'haləm
AM 'hæləm

Halle
BR 'haleɪ, 'hali
AM 'hɑlə

Hallé
BR 'haleɪ, 'hali
AM 'hɑleɪ

halleluja
BR ,halɪ'luːjə(r), -z
AM ,hælə'lujə, -z

hallelujah
BR ,halɪ'luːjə(r), -z
AM ,hælə'lujə, -z

Haller
BR 'halə(r)
AM 'hælər

Halley
BR 'hali
AM 'hæli

halliard
BR 'haljəd, -z
AM 'hæljərd, -z

Halliday
BR 'halɪdeɪ
AM 'hælə,deɪ

Halliwell
BR 'halɪwɛl
AM 'hælə,wɛl

hallmark
BR 'hɔːlmɑːk, -s, -ɪŋ, -t
AM 'hɔl,mark, 'hɑl,mark, -s, -ɪŋ, -t

hallo
BR hə'ləʊ, -z
AM hə'loʊ, -z

halloo
BR hə'luː, -z, -ɪŋ, -d
AM hə'lu, -z, -ɪŋ, -d

hallow
BR 'haləʊ, -z, -ɪŋ, -d
AM 'hæloʊ, -z, -ɪŋ, -d

Halloween
BR ,haləʊ'iːn
AM ,hælə'win, ,hɑlə'win

Hallowe'en
BR ,haləʊ'iːn
AM ,hælə'win, ,hɑlə'win

Hallowes
BR 'haləʊz
AM 'hæloʊz

hallstand
BR 'hɔːlstand, -z
AM 'hɔl,stænd, 'hɑl,stænd, -z

Hallstatt
BR 'hɑːlʃtɑːt, 'hɑːlʃtat
AM 'hɑl,ʃtat, 'hɑl,stɑt

halluces
BR 'haljʊsiːz
AM 'hælə,siz

hallucinant
BR hə'l(j)uːsɪnənt, -s
AM hə'lusənənt, -s

hallucinate
BR hə'l(j)uːsɪneɪt, -s, -ɪŋ, -ɪd
AM hə'lusn,eɪ|t, -ts, -dɪŋ, -dɪd

hallucination
BR hə,l(j)uːsɪ'neɪʃn, -z
AM hə,lusn'eɪʃn, -z

hallucinator
BR hə'l(j)uːsɪneɪtə(r), -z
AM hə'lusn,eɪdər, -z

hallucinatory
BR hə'l(j)uːsɪnət(ə)ri, hə'l(j)uːsn̩ət(ə)ri, hə,l(j)uːsɪ'neɪt(ə)ri
AM hə'lusn̩ə,tɔri

hallucinogen
BR hə'l(j)uːs(ɪ)nədʒ(ə)n, hə'l(j)uːsn̩ədʒ(ə)n, -z
AM hə'lusənə,dʒɛn, -z

hallucinogenic
BR hə,l(j)uːs(ɪ)nə'dʒɛnɪk, hə,l(j)uːsn̩ə'dʒɛnɪk
AM hə,lusn̩ə'dʒɛnɪk

hallux
BR 'haləks, -ɪz
AM 'hæləks, -əz

hallway
BR 'hɔːlweɪ, -z
AM 'hɔl,weɪ, 'hɑl,weɪ, -z

halm
BR hɔːm, -z
AM hɔm, hɑ(l)m, -z

halma
BR 'halmə(r)
AM 'hælmə

Halmahera
BR ,halmə'hɛːrə(r)
AM ,hælmə'hɛrə

halo
BR 'heɪləʊ, -z, -d
AM 'heɪloʊ, -z, -d

halocarbon
BR 'halə(ʊ),kɑːbn, -z
AM 'hælə,kɑrbən, -z

halogen
BR 'halədʒ(ə)n, -z
AM 'hælədʒən, -z

halogenation
BR ,halədʒə'neɪʃn
AM ,hælədʒə'neɪʃən, hə,lɑdʒə'neɪʃən

halogenic
BR ,halə'dʒɛnɪk
AM ,hælə'dʒɛnɪk

halon
BR 'heɪlɒn
AM 'heɪlɑn

halophyte
BR 'haləfʌɪt, -s
AM 'hælə,faɪt, -s

Halpern
BR 'halp(ə)n
AM 'hælpərn

Halpin
BR 'halpɪn
AM 'hælpən

Hals
BR hals, halz
AM hɑls

Halstead
BR 'halstɛd, 'halstɪd, 'hɔːlstɛd, 'hɔːlstɪd, 'hɒlstɛd, 'hɒlstɪd
AM 'hɔl,stɛd, 'hɑl,stɛd

halt
BR hɔːlt, hɒlt, -s, -ɪŋ, -ɪd
AM hɔlt, hɑlt, -s, -ɪŋ, -əd

Haltemprice
BR 'hɔːltəmprʌɪs, 'hɒltəmprʌɪs
AM 'hɔltəm,praɪs, 'hɑltəm,praɪs

halter
BR 'hɔːltə(r), 'hɒltə(r), -z
AM 'hɔltər, 'hɑltər, -z

halteres
BR 'haltɪəz, 'hɔːltɪəz, 'hɒltɪəz, hal'tɪəz
AM 'hæl,tɪ(ə)rz, 'hɔl,tɪ(ə)rz, 'hɑl,tɪ(ə)rz

halterneck
BR 'hɔːltənɛk, 'hɒltənɛk, -s
AM 'hɔltər,nɛk, 'hɑltər,nɛk, -s

haltingly
BR 'hɔːltɪŋli, 'hɒltɪŋli
AM 'hɔltɪŋli, 'hɑltɪŋli

Halton
BR 'hɔːlt(ə)n, 'hɒlt(ə)n
AM 'hɔltən, 'hɑltən

halva
BR 'halvə(r), 'halvɑː(r), -z
AM ¦hɑl¦vɑ, -z

halvah
BR 'halvə(r), 'halvɑː(r), -z
AM ¦hɑl¦vɑ, -z

halve
BR hɑːv, -z, -ɪŋ, -d
AM hæv, -z, -ɪŋ, -d
halyard
BR 'haljəd, -z
AM 'hæljərd, -z
ham
BR ham, -z, -ɪŋ, -d
AM hæm, -z, -ɪŋ, -d
Hamada
BR hə'mɑːdə(r)
AM hə'mɑdə
hamadryad
BR ˌhamə'drʌɪəd, ˌhamə'drʌɪad, -z
AM ˌhæmə'draɪəd, ˌhæmə'draɪˌæd, -z
hamadryas
BR ˌhamə'drʌɪəs, ˌhamə'drʌɪas, -ɨz
AM ˌhæmə'draɪəs, -ɨz
hamamelis
BR ˌhamə'miːl|ɪs, -ɪsɪz
AM ˌhæmə'milɨs, -ɨz
hamartia
BR hə'mɑːtɪə(r)
AM hə'mɑrdiə
Hamas
BR ha'mas
AM hɑ'mɑs
Hambly
BR 'hambli
AM 'hæmbli
hambone
BR 'hambəʊn, -z
AM 'hæmˌboʊn, -z
Hambro
BR 'hambrəʊ
AM 'hæmbroʊ
Hamburg
BR 'hambəːg
AM 'hæmˌbərg
hamburger
BR 'hamˌbəːgə(r), -z
AM 'hæmˌbərgər, -z
Hamelin
BR 'ham(ɨ)lɪn
AM 'hæm(ə)lən
Hamer
BR 'heɪmə(r)
AM 'heɪmər
hames
BR heɪmz
AM heɪmz
Hamilcar
BR 'ham(ɨ)lkɑː(r), hə'mɪlkɑː(r)
AM hə'mɪlˌkɑr, 'hæməlˌkɑr
Hamill
BR 'ham(ɪ)l
AM 'hæməl
Hamilton
BR 'ham(ɨ)lt(ə)n
AM 'hæməltən
Hamish
BR 'heɪmɪʃ
AM 'heɪmɪʃ
Hamite
BR 'hamʌɪt, -s
AM 'hæˌmaɪt, -s
Hamitic
BR ha'mɪtɪk, hə'mɪtɪk
AM hə'mɪdɪk
Hamito-Semitic
BR ˌhamɨtəʊsɪ'mɪtɪk
AM ˌhæməˌtoʊsə'mɪdɪk
hamlet
BR 'hamlɨt, -s
AM 'hæmlət, -s
Hamley
BR 'hamli
AM 'hæmli
Hamlin
BR 'hamlɪn
AM 'hæmlən
Hamlyn
BR 'hamlɪn
AM 'hæmlən
hammam
BR 'hamam, hə'mɑːm, 'hʌmʌm, -z
AM hə'mɑm, -z
hammer
BR 'ham|ə(r), -əz, -(ə)rɪŋ, -əd
AM 'hæmər, -z, -ɪŋ, -d
hammerbeam
BR 'haməbiːm, -z
AM 'hæmərˌbim, -z
hammerer
BR 'ham(ə)rə(r), -z
AM 'hæmərər, -z
Hammerfest
BR 'haməfɛst
AM 'hæmərˌfɛst
hammerhead
BR 'haməhɛd, -z
AM 'hæmərˌ(h)ɛd, -z
hammering
BR 'ham(ə)rɪŋ, -z
AM 'hæmərɪŋ, -z
hammerless
BR 'haməlǝs
AM 'hæmərləs
hammerlock
BR 'haməlɒk, -s
AM 'hæmərˌlɑk, -s
hammerman
BR 'hamǝman
AM 'hæmərˌmæn
hammermen
BR 'haməmɛn
AM 'hæmərˌmɛn
Hammersmith
BR 'haməsmɪθ
AM 'hæmərˌsmɪθ
Hammerstein
BR 'haməstʌɪn
AM 'hæmərˌstin, 'hæmərˌstaɪn
Hammett
BR 'hamɨt
AM 'hæmət
hammock
BR 'hamək, -s
AM 'hæmək, -s
Hammond
BR 'hamənd
AM 'hæmənd
Hammurabi
BR ˌhamʉ'rɑːbi
AM ˌhæmə'rɑbi
hammy
BR 'ham|i, -ɪə(r), -ɪɪst
AM 'hæmi, -ər, -ɨst
Hamnett
BR 'hamnɨt
AM 'hæmnət
hamper
BR 'hamp|ə(r), -əz, -(ə)rɪŋ, -əd
AM 'hæmp|ər, -ərz, -(ə)rɪŋ, -ərd
Hampshire
BR 'ham(p)ʃ(ɪ)ə(r)
AM 'hæm(p)ʃɪ(ə)r
Hampson
BR 'ham(p)s(ə)n
AM 'hæm(p)sən
Hampstead
BR 'ham(p)stɪd, 'ham(p)stɛd
AM 'hæm(p)ˌstɛd
Hampton
BR 'ham(p)t(ə)n
AM 'hæm(p)tən
Hampton Court
BR ˌham(p)t(ə)n 'kɔːt
AM ¦hæm(p)tən 'kɔ(ə)rt
Hampton Roads
BR ˌham(p)t(ə)n 'rəʊdz
AM ¦hæm(p)tən 'roʊdz
hamsin
BR 'hamsɪn
AM 'hæmsɪn
hamster
BR 'hamstə(r), -z
AM 'hæmstər, -z
hamstring
BR 'hamstrɪŋ, -z, -ɪŋ
AM 'hæmˌstrɪŋ, -z, -ɪŋ
hamstrung
BR 'hamstrʌŋ
AM 'hæmˌstrəŋ
hamuli
BR 'hamjʉlʌɪ, 'hamjʉliː
AM 'hæmjəˌlaɪ
hamulus
BR 'hamjʉləs
AM 'hæmjələs
hamza
BR 'hamzə(r), -z
AM 'hæmzə, -z
hamzah
BR 'hamzə(r), -z
AM 'hæmzə, -z
Han
BR han
AM hæn
Hancock
BR 'hankɒk, 'haŋkɒk
AM 'hænˌkɑk, 'hæŋˌkɑk
Hancox
BR 'hankɒks, 'haŋkɒks
AM 'hænkɑks, 'hæŋkɑks
hand
BR hand, -z, -ɪŋ, -ɨd
AM hænd, -z, -ɪŋ, -əd
hand-axe
BR 'handaks, -ɨz
AM 'hændˌæks, -əz
handbag
BR 'han(d)bag, -z
AM 'hæn(d)ˌbæg, -z
handball
BR 'han(d)bɔːl, -z
AM 'hæn(d)ˌbɔl, 'hæn(d)ˌbɑl, -z
handbasin
BR 'han(d)ˌbeɪsn, -z
AM 'hæn(d)ˌbeɪsn, -z
handbell
BR 'han(d)bɛl, -z
AM 'hæn(d)ˌbɛl, -z
handbill
BR 'han(d)bɪl, -z
AM 'hæn(d)ˌbɪl, -z
handbook
BR 'han(d)bʊk, -s
AM 'hæn(d)ˌbʊk, -s
handbrake
BR 'han(d)breɪk, -s
AM 'hæn(d)ˌbreɪk, -s
handbreadth
BR 'han(d)brɛdθ, 'han(d)brɛtθ, -s
AM 'hæn(d)ˌbrɛ(d)θ, -s
handcar
BR 'han(d)kɑː(r), -z
AM 'hæn(d)ˌkɑr, -z
handcart
BR 'han(d)kɑːt, -s
AM 'hæn(d)ˌkɑrt, -s
handclap
BR 'han(d)klap, -s
AM 'hæn(d)ˌklæp, -s
handclapping
BR 'han(d)ˌklapɪŋ
AM 'hæn(d)ˌklæpɪŋ
handcraft
BR 'han(d)krɑːft, 'han(d)kraft, -s, -ɪŋ, -ɨd
AM 'hæn(d)ˌkræft, -s, -ɪŋ, -d
handcuff
BR 'han(d)kʌf, -s, -ɪŋ, -t
AM 'hæn(d)ˌkəf, -s, -ɪŋ, -t
handedness
BR 'handɪdnɪs

AM 'hændədnəs

Handel
BR 'handl
AM 'hɑndəl

Handelian
BR han'di:lɪən
AM hæn'dɛliən

handful
BR 'han(d)fʊl, -z
AM 'hæn(d),fʊl, -z

handglass
BR 'han(d)glɑ:s, 'han(d)glas, -ɪz
AM 'hæn(d),glæs, -əz

handgrip
BR 'han(d)grɪp, -s
AM 'hæn(d),grɪp, -s

handgun
BR 'han(d)gʌn, -z
AM hæn(d),gən, -z

handhold
BR 'handhəʊld, -z
AM 'hæn(d),(h)oʊld, -z

hand-holding
BR 'hand,həʊldɪŋ
AM 'hæn(d),(h)oʊldɪŋ

handicap
BR 'handɪkap, -s, -ɪŋ, -t
AM 'handi,kæp, -s, -ɪŋ, -t

handicapper
BR 'handɪ,kapə(r), -z
AM 'handi,kæpər, -z

handicraft
BR 'handɪkrɑ:ft, 'handɪkraft, -s
AM 'hændi,kræft, -s

handily
BR 'hændɪli
AM 'hændəli

handiness
BR 'handɪnɪs
AM 'hændinɪs

handiwork
BR 'handɪwə:k
AM 'hændi,wərk

handkerchief
BR 'haŋkətʃɪf, 'haŋkətʃi:f
AM 'hæŋkərtʃəf, 'hæŋkər,tʃif

handkerchiefs
BR 'haŋkətʃɪfs, 'haŋkətʃi:fs, 'haŋkətʃi:vz
AM 'hæŋkərtʃəfs, 'hæŋkər,tʃivz, 'hæŋkər,tʃifs

handle
BR 'hand|l, -lz, -l̩ɪŋ\-lɪŋ, -ld
AM 'hæn|dəl, -dəlz, -(d)(ə)lɪŋ, -dəld

handleability
BR ,handlə'bɪlɪti, ,handl̩ə'bɪlɪti
AM ,hændl̩ə'bɪlɪdi

handleable
BR 'handləbl, 'handl̩əbl
AM 'hændl̩əbəl

handlebar
BR 'handlbɑ:(r), -z
AM 'hændl,bɑr, -z

handler
BR 'handlə(r), 'handl̩ə(r), -z
AM 'hæn(də)lər, -z

handless
BR 'handləs
AM 'hæn(d)ləs

Handley
BR 'handli
AM 'hæn(d)li

handline
BR 'han(d)lʌɪn, -z, -ɪŋ, -d
AM 'hæn(d),laɪn, -z, -ɪŋ, -d

handlist
BR 'han(d)lɪst, -s
AM 'hæn(d),lɪst, -s

handloom
BR 'han(d)lu:m, -z
AM 'hæn(d),lum, -z

handmade
BR ,han(d)'meɪd
AM ¦hæn(d)¦meɪd

handmaid
BR 'han(d)meɪd, -z
AM 'hæn(d),meɪd, -z

handmaiden
BR 'han(d),meɪdn, -z
AM 'hæn(d),meɪdən, -z

handout
BR 'handaʊt, -s
AM 'hænd,aʊt, -s

handover
BR 'hand,əʊvə(r), -z
AM 'hænd,oʊvər, -z

hand-painted
BR ,han(d)'peɪntɪd
AM ¦hæn(d)¦peɪn(t)ɪd

hand-pick
BR ,han(d)'pɪk, -s, -ɪŋ, -t
AM ¦hæn(d)¦pɪk, -s, -ɪŋ, -t

handpicked
BR ,han(d)'pɪkt
AM ,hæn(d)¦pɪkt

handpump
BR 'han(d)pʌmp, -s
AM 'hæn(d),pəmp, -s

handrail
BR 'handreɪl, -z
AM 'hæn(d),reɪl, -z

handsaw
BR 'han(d)sɔ:(r), -z
AM 'hæn(d),sɔ, 'hæn(d),sɑ, -z

handsbreadth
BR 'han(d)zbrɛdθ, 'han(d)zbrɛtθ, -s
AM 'hæn(d)z,brɛ(d)θ, -s

handsel
BR 'han(d)s|l, -lz, -əlɪŋ\-l̩ɪŋ, -ld
AM 'hæn(t)s|əl, -əlz, -(ə)lɪŋ, -əld

handset
BR 'han(d)sɛt, -s
AM 'hæn(d),sɛt, -s

handshake
BR 'han(d)ʃeɪk, -s
AM 'hæn(d),ʃeɪk, -s

handsome
BR 'hans(ə)m, -əmə(r)\-m̩ə(r), -əmɪst\-m̩ɪst
AM 'hæn(t)səm, -ər, -əst

handsomely
BR 'hans(ə)mli
AM 'hæn(t)səmli

handsomeness
BR 'hans(ə)mnəs
AM 'hæn(t)səmnəs

handspike
BR 'han(d)spʌɪk, -s
AM 'hæn(d),spaɪk, -s

handspring
BR 'han(d)sprɪŋ, -z
AM 'hæn(d),sprɪŋ, -z

handstand
BR 'han(d)stand, -z
AM 'hæn(d),stænd, -z

handwork
BR 'handwə:k
AM 'hæn(d),wərk

handworked
BR ,hand'wə:kt
AM ¦hæn(d)¦wərkt

handwriting
BR 'hand,rʌɪtɪŋ
AM 'hæn(d),raɪdɪŋ

handwritten
BR ,hand'rɪtn
AM ¦hæn(d)¦rɪtn

handy
BR 'hand|i, -ɪə(r), -ɪɪst
AM 'hændi, -ər, -ɪst

handyman
BR 'handɪman
AM 'hændi,mæn

handymen
BR 'handɪmɛn
AM 'hændi,mɛn

Haney
BR 'heɪni
AM 'heɪni

hang
BR haŋ, -z, -ɪŋ, -d
AM hæŋ, -z, -ɪŋ, -d

hangar
BR 'haŋ(g)ə(r), -z
AM 'hæŋər, -z

hangarage
BR 'haŋ(g)(ə)rɪdʒ
AM 'hæŋərɪdʒ

Hangchow
BR ,haŋ'tʃaʊ
AM 'hæŋ'tʃaʊ

hangdog
BR 'haŋdɒg
AM 'hæŋ,dɔg, 'hæŋ,dɑg

hanger
BR 'haŋə(r), -z
AM 'hæŋər, -z

hangi
BR 'haŋ|i, 'hɑ:ŋ|i, -ɪz
AM 'hæŋi, -z

hanging
BR 'haŋɪŋ, -z
AM 'hæŋɪŋ, -z

hangman
BR 'haŋmən, 'haŋman
AM 'hæŋmən, 'hæŋ,mæn

hangmen
BR 'haŋmən, 'haŋmɛn
AM 'hæŋmən, 'hæŋ,mɛn

hangnail
BR 'haŋneɪl, -z
AM 'hæŋ,neɪl, -z

hangout
BR 'haŋaʊt, -s
AM 'hæŋ,aʊt, -s

hangover
BR 'haŋ,əʊvə(r), -z
AM 'hæŋ,oʊvər, -z

Hang Seng
BR ,haŋ 'sɛŋ
AM 'hæŋ 'sɛŋ

hangup
BR 'haŋʌp, -s
AM 'hæŋ,əp, -s

Hangzhou
BR ,haŋ'(d)ʒaʊ
AM 'hæŋ'(d)ʒaʊ

Hanif
BR ha'ni:f
AM hə'nif

hank
BR haŋk, -s
AM hæŋk, -s

hanker
BR 'haŋk|ə(r), -əz, -(ə)rɪŋ, -əd
AM 'hæŋk|ər, -ərz, -(ə)rɪŋ, -ərd

hankerer
BR 'haŋk(ə)rə(r), -z
AM 'hæŋk(ə)rər, -z

hankering
BR 'haŋk(ə)rɪŋ, -z
AM 'hæŋk(ə)rɪŋ, -z

hankie
BR 'haŋk|i, -ɪz
AM 'hæŋki, -z

Hanks
BR haŋks
AM hæŋks

hanky
BR 'haŋk|i, -ɪz

AM ˈhæŋki, -z

hanky-panky
BR ˌhaŋkɪˈpaŋki
AM ¦hæŋkiˈpæŋki

Hanley
BR ˈhanli
AM ˈhænli

Hanna
BR ˈhanə(*r*)
AM ˈhænə

Hannah
BR ˈhanə(*r*)
AM ˈhænə

Hannibal
BR ˈhanɪbl
AM ˈhænəbəl

Hannon
BR ˈhanən
AM ˈhænən

Hannover
BR ˈhanə(ʊ)və(r)
AM ˈhænˌoʊvər
GER haˈnoːfɐ

Hanoi
BR haˈnɔɪ
AM hæˈnɔɪ

Hanover
BR ˈhanə(ʊ)və(r)
AM ˈhænˌoʊvər

Hanoverian
BR ˌhanə(ʊ)ˈvɛːrɪən, ˌhanə(ʊ)ˈvɪərɪən, -z
AM ˌhænəˈvɛriən, -z

Hanrahan
BR ˈhanrəhən, ˈhanrəhan
AM ˈhænrəˌhæn

Hanratty
BR hanˈrati
AM ˈhænˌrædi

Hans
BR hans, hanz
AM hɑns

Hansa
BR ˈhansə(*r*)
AM ˈhænsə

Hansard
BR ˈhansɑːd
AM ˈhænsɑrd

Hanse
BR hans, -ɪz
AM hænz, hɑns, -əz

Hanseatic
BR ˌhansɪˈatɪk
AM ˌhænsiˈædɪk

Hänsel
BR ˈhansl
AM ˈhɑn(t)səl, ˈhæn(t)səl
GER ˈhɛnzl

hansel
BR ˈhans|l, -lz, -lɪŋ\-əlɪŋ, -ld
AM ˈhæn(t)s|əl, -əlz, -(ə)lɪŋ, -əld

Hansen
BR ˈhansn
AM ˈhænsən

hansom
BR ˈhans(ə)m, -z
AM ˈhænsəm, -z

Hanson
BR ˈhansn
AM ˈhænsən

Hants
Hampshire
BR hants
AM hænts

Hanukkah
BR ˈhanʉkə(*r*), ˈxanʉkə(*r*), ˈhɑːnʉkə(*r*), ˈxɑːnʉkə(*r*), -z
AM ˈhɑnəkə, -z

Hanuman
BR ˌhʌnʊˈmɑːn
AM ¦hɑnəˌmɑn

hanuman
BR ˌhʌnʊˈmɑːn, -z
AM ˈhænəˌmɑn, həˈnʊmən, -z

hap
BR hap, -s, -ɪŋ, -t
AM hæp, -s, -ɪŋ, -t

hapax
BR ˈhapaks
AM ˈhæˌpæks

hapax legomena
BR ˌhapaks lɪˈɡɒmɪnə(*r*)
AM ˌhæpæks ləˈɡɑmənə

hapax legomenon
BR ˌhapaks lɪˈɡɒmɪnən, + lɪˈɡɒmɪnɒn
AM ˌhæpæks ləˈɡɑməˌnɑn

ha'penny
BR ˈheɪpn|i, -ɪz
AM ˈheɪp(ə)ni, -z

haphazard
BR ˌhapˈhazəd
AM ¦hæpˈhæzərd

haphazardly
BR ˌhapˈhazədli
AM ¦hæpˈhæzərdli

haphazardness
BR ˌhapˈhazədnəs
AM ¦hæpˈhæzərdnəs

haphtarah
BR ˌhɑːftɑːˈrɑː(*r*)
AM ˌhɑftəˈrɑ

haphtaroth
BR ˌhɑːftɑːˈrəʊt
AM ˌhɑftəˈrɑθ

haphtorah
BR ˌhɑːfˈtɔːrɑː(*r*), ˌhɑːfˈtɔːrə(*r*)
AM ˌhɑftəˈrɑ

hapless
BR ˈhapləs
AM ˈhæpləs

haplessly
BR ˈhapləsli
AM ˈhæpləsli

haplessness
BR ˈhapləsnəs
AM ˈhæpləsnəs

haplography
BR hapˈlɒɡrəfi
AM hæpˈlɑɡrəfi

haploid
BR ˈhaplɔɪd
AM ˈhæpˌlɔɪd

haplology
BR hapˈlɒlədʒ|i, -ɪz
AM hæpˈlɑlədʒi, -z

haply
BR ˈhapli
AM ˈhæpli

hap'orth
BR ˈheɪpəθ, -s
AM ˈheɪpərθ, -s

ha'p'orth
BR ˈheɪpəθ
AM ˈheɪpərθ

happen
BR ˈhap|(ə)n, -(ə)nz, -(ə)nɪŋ\-n̩ɪŋ, -(ə)nd
AM ˈhæp|ən, -ənz\m̩z, -(ə)nɪŋ, -ənd\n̩d

happening
BR ˈhap(ə)nɪŋ, ˈhapn̩ɪŋ, -z
AM ˈhæp(ə)nɪŋ, -z

happenstance
BR ˈhap(ə)nstans, ˈhap(ə)nstɑːns
AM ˈhæpənˌstæns

happi
BR ˈhap|i, -ɪz
AM ˈhæpi, -z

happi-coat
BR ˈhapɪkəʊt, -s
AM ˈhæpiˌkoʊt, -s

happily
BR ˈhapɪli
AM ˈhæp(ə)li

happiness
BR ˈhapɪnɪs, -ɪz
AM ˈhæpinɪs, -ɪz

Happisburgh
BR ˈheɪzb(ə)rə(*r*)
AM ˈheɪzbərə

happy
BR ˈhap|i, -ɪə(r), -ɪɪst
AM ˈhæpi, -ər, -ɪst

happy-go-lucky
BR ˌhapɪɡə(ʊ)ˈlʌki
AM ¦hæpiˌɡoʊˈləki

Hapsburg
BR ˈhapsbəːɡ, ˈhabzbəːɡ, -z
AM ˈhæpsˌbərɡ, ˈhɑbsˌbərɡ, -z

haptic
BR ˈhaptɪk
AM ˈhæptɪk

hara-kiri
BR ˌharəˈkɪri
AM ˌhɛrəˈkɪri, ˌhɛrəˈkɛri

harangue
BR həˈraŋ, -z, -ɪŋ, -d
AM həˈræŋ, -z, -ɪŋ, -d

haranguer
BR həˈraŋə(r), -z
AM həˈræŋər, -z

Harappa
BR həˈrapə(*r*)
AM həˈræpə

Harare
BR həˈrɑːri
AM həˈrɑri

harass
BR ˈharəs, həˈras, -ɪz, -ɪŋ, -t
AM həˈræs, ˈhɛrəs, -əz, -ɪŋ, -t

harasser
BR ˈharəsə(r), həˈrasə(r), -z
AM həˈræsər, ˈhɛrəsər, -z

harassingly
BR ˈharəsɪŋli, həˈrasɪŋli
AM həˈræsɪŋli, ˈhɛrəsɪŋli

harassment
BR ˈharəsm(ə)nt, həˈrasm(ə)nt
AM həˈræsmənt, ˈhɛrəsmənt

Harben
BR ˈhɑːb(ə)n
AM ˈhɑrbən

harbinger
BR ˈhɑːbɪn(d)ʒə(r), -z
AM ˈhɑrbəndʒər, -z

harbor
BR ˈhɑːb|ə(r), -əz, -(ə)rɪŋ, -əd
AM ˈhɑrbər, -z, -ɪŋ, -d

harborage
BR ˈhɑːb(ə)rɪdʒ
AM ˈhɑrbərɪdʒ

harborless
BR ˈhɑːbələs
AM ˈhɑrbərləs

harbormaster
BR ˈhɑːbəˌmɑːstə(r), ˈhɑːbəˌmastə(r), -z
AM ˈhɑrbərˌmæstər, -z

harbour
BR ˈhɑːb|ə(r), -əz, -(ə)rɪŋ, -əd
AM ˈhɑrbər, -z, -ɪŋ, -d

harbourage
BR ˈhɑːb(ə)rɪdʒ
AM ˈhɑrbərɪdʒ

harbourless
BR ˈhɑːbələs
AM ˈhɑrbərləs

harbourmaster
BR ˈhɑːbəˌmɑːstə(r), ˈhɑːbəˌmastə(r), -z
AM ˈhɑrbərˌmæstər, -z

Harcourt
BR ˈhɑːkɔːt
AM ˈhɑrˌkɔ(ə)rt

hard
BR hɑːd, -ə(r), -ɨst
AM hɑrd, -ər, -əst

hardback
BR ˈhɑːdbak, -s
AM ˈhɑrdˌbæk, -s

hardbake
BR ˈhɑːdbeɪk
AM ˈhɑrdˌbeɪk

hardball
BR ˈhɑːdbɔːl
AM ˈhɑrdˌbɔl, ˈhɑrdˌbɑl

hardbitten
BR ˌhɑːdˈbɪtn
AM ˈhɑrdˈbɪtn

hardboard
BR ˈhɑːdbɔːd
AM ˈhɑrdˌbɔ(ə)rd

hardbound
BR ˈhɑːdbaʊnd
AM ˈhɑrdˌbaʊnd

Hardcastle
BR ˈhɑːdˌkɑːsl, ˈhɑːdˌkasln
AM ˈhɑrdˌkæsəl

hardcore
noun
BR ˈhɑːdkɔː(r)
AM ˈhærdˌkɔ(ə)r

hard-core
adjective
BR ˌhɑːdˈkɔː(r)
AM ˈhɑrdˈkɔ(ə)r

hardcover
BR ˌhɑːdˈkʌvə(r)
AM ˈhɑrdˌkəvər

harden
BR ˈhɑːd|n, -nz, -n̩ɪŋ\-nɪŋ, -nd
AM ˈhɑrdən, -z, -ɪŋ, -d

hardener
BR ˈhɑːdn̩ə(r), ˈhɑːdnə(r), -z
AM ˈhɑrdn̩ər, -z

hardhat
BR ˈhɑːdhat, -s
AM ˈhɑrdˌ(h)æt, -s

hardheaded
BR ˌhɑːdˈhɛdɪd
AM ˈhɑrdˈhɛdəd

hard-headedly
BR ˌhɑːdˈhɛdɪdli
AM ˈhɑrdˈhɛdədli

hard-headedness
BR ˌhɑːdˈhɛdɪdnɨs
AM ˈhɑrdˈhɛdədnəs

hard-hearted
BR ˌhɑːdˈhɑːtɪd
AM ˈhɑrdˈhɑrdəd

hard-heartedly
BR ˌhɑːdˈhɑːtɨdli
AM ˈhɑrdˈhɑrdədli

hard-heartedness
BR ˌhɑːdˈhɑːtɨdnɨs
AM ˈhɑrdˈhɑrdədnəs

Hardicanute
BR ˈhɑːdɨkəˌnjuːt
AM ˈhɑrdəkəˌnut

Hardie
BR ˈhɑːdi
AM ˈhɑrdi

hardihood
BR ˈhɑːdɪhʊd
AM ˈhɑrdiˌ(h)ʊd

hardily
BR ˈhɑːdɪli
AM ˈhɑrdəli

Hardin
BR ˈhɑːdɪn
AM ˈhɑrdən

hardiness
BR ˈhɑːdɪnɨs
AM ˈhɑrdinɨs

Harding
BR ˈhɑːdɪŋ
AM ˈhɑrdɪŋ

hardish
BR ˈhɑːdɪʃ
AM ˈhɑrdɪʃ

hardline
adjective
BR ˌhɑːdˈlʌɪn
AM ˈhɑrdˈlaɪn

hardliner
BR ˌhɑːdˈlʌɪnə(r), -z
AM ˈhɑrdˈlaɪnər, -z

hardly
BR ˈhɑːdli
AM ˈhɑrdli

Hardman
BR ˈhɑːdmənn
AM ˈhɑrdmən

hardness
BR ˈhɑːdnəs
AM ˈhɑrdnəs

hardpan
BR ˈhɑːdpan, -z
AM ˈhɑrdˌpæn, -z

hardshell
BR ˈhɑːdʃɛl, -z
AM ˈhɑrdˌʃɛl, -z

hardship
BR ˈhɑːdʃɪp, -s
AM ˈhɑrdˌʃɪp, -s

hardstanding
BR ˌhɑːdˈstandɪŋ
AM ˈhɑrdˈstændɪŋ

hardtack
BR ˈhɑːdtak
AM ˈhɑrdˌtæk

hardtop
BR ˈhɑːdtɒp, -s
AM ˈhɑrdˌtɑp, -s

Hardwar
BR ˈhɑːdwɑː(r)
AM ˈhɑrˌdwɑr

hardware
BR ˈhɑːdwɛː(r)
AM ˈhɑrdˌwɛ(ə)r

hardwearing
BR ˌhɑːdˈwɛːrɪŋ
AM ˈhɑrdˈwɛrɪŋ

Hardwick
BR ˈhɑːdwɪk
AM ˈhɑrdˌwɪk

Hardwicke
BR ˈhɑːdwɪk
AM ˈhɑrdˌwɪk

hardwood
BR ˈhɑːdwʊd, -z
AM ˈhɑrdˌwʊd, -z

hardworking
BR ˌhɑːdˈwəːkɪŋ
AM ˈhɑrdˈwərkɪŋ

hardy
BR ˈhɑːd|i, -ɪə(r), -ɪɪst
AM ˈhɑrdi, -ər, -ɨst

hare
BR hɛː(r), -z, -ɪŋ, -d
AM hɛ(ə)r, -z, -ɪŋ, -d

harebell
BR ˈhɛːbɛl, -z
AM ˈhɛrˌbɛl, -z

harebrained
BR ˈhɛːbreɪnd
AM ˈhɛrˌbreɪn(d)

Hare Krishna
BR ˌharɪ ˈkrɪʃnə(*r*)
AM ˌhɑri ˈkriʃnə, ˌhɛri +

harelip
BR ˌhɛːˈlɪp, -s
AM ˈhɛrˌlɪp, -s

harelipped
BR ˌhɛːˈlɪpt
AM ˈhɛrˈlɪpt

harem
BR ˈhɛːrəm, ˈhɑːriːm, (ˌ)hɑːˈriːm, -z
AM ˈhɛrəm, -z

Harewood[1]
name of Earl and House in UK
BR ˈhɑːwʊd
AM ˈhɑrˌwʊd

Harewood[2]
place in UK
BR ˈhɛːwʊd
AM ˈhɛrˌwʊd

harewood
BR ˈhɛːwʊd
AM ˈhɛrˌwʊd

Hargraves
BR ˈhɑːgreɪvz
AM ˈhɑrˌgreɪvz

Hargreaves
BR ˈhɑːgriːvz, ˈhɑːgreɪvz
AM ˈhɑrˌgreɪvz

haricot
BR ˈharɨkəʊ, -z
AM ˈhɛrəˌkoʊ, -z

Harijan
BR ˈhʌrɪdʒ(ə)n, ˈharɪdʒ(ə)n, ˈharɪdʒan, -z
AM ˈhɛrəˌdʒæn, -z

hark
BR hɑːk, -s, -ɪŋ, -t
AM hɑrk, -s, -ɪŋ, -t

harken
BR ˈhɑːk|n, -nz, -n̩ɪŋ\-(ə)nɪŋ, -nd
AM ˈhɑrk|ən, -ənz, -(ə)nɪŋ, -ənd

Harkness
BR ˈhɑːknɨs
AM ˈhɑrknəs

harl
BR hɑːl, -z
AM hɑrl, -z

Harland
BR ˈhɑːlənd
AM ˈhɑrlən(d)

harle
BR hɑːl
AM hɑrl

Harlech
BR ˈhɑːləx, ˈhɑːlək
AM ˈhɑrlɛk

Harlem
BR ˈhɑːləm
AM ˈhɑrləm

harlequin
BR ˈhɑːlɨkwɪn, -z
AM ˈhɑrlək(w)ən, -z

harlequinade
BR ˌhɑːlɨkwɪˈneɪd, -z
AM ˌhɑrlək(w)əˈneɪd, -z

Harlesden
BR ˈhɑːlzd(ə)n
AM ˈhɑrlzdən

Harley Street
BR ˈhɑːlɪ striːt
AM ˈhɑrli ˌstrit

harlot
BR ˈhɑːlət, -s
AM ˈhɑrlət, -s

harlotry
BR ˈhɑːlətri
AM ˈhɑrlətri

Harlow
BR ˈhɑːləʊ
AM ˈhɑrloʊ

Harlowe
BR ˈhɑːləʊ
AM ˈhɑrloʊ

harm
BR hɑːm, -z, -ɪŋ, -d
AM hɑrm, -z, -ɪŋ, -d

Harman
BR ˈhɑːmən
AM ˈhɑrmən

harmattan
BR hɑːˈmatn, -z
AM ˌhɑrməˈtɑn, -z

Harmer
BR ˈhɑːmə(r)

AM 'hɑrmər

harmful
BR 'hɑːmf(ʊ)l
AM 'hɑrmfəl

harmfully
BR 'hɑːmfʊli, 'hɑːmfl̩i
AM 'hɑrmfəli

harmfulness
BR 'hɑːmf(ʊ)lnəs
AM 'hɑrmfəlnəs

harmless
BR 'hɑːmləs
AM 'hɑrmləs

harmlessly
BR 'hɑːmləsli
AM 'hɑrmləsli

harmlessness
BR 'hɑːmləsnəs
AM 'hɑrmləsnəs

Harmon
BR 'hɑːmən
AM 'hɑrmən

Harmondsworth
BR 'hɑːmən(d)zwəːθ
AM 'hɑrmən(d)zˌwərθ

harmonic
BR hɑː'mɒnɪk
AM hɑr'mɑnɪk

harmonica
BR hɑː'mɒnᵻkə(r), -z
AM hɑr'mɑnəkə, -z

harmonically
BR hɑː'mɒnᵻkli
AM hɑr'mɑnək(ə)li

harmonious
BR hɑː'məʊnɪəs
AM hɑr'moʊniəs

harmoniously
BR hɑː'məʊnɪəsli
AM hɑr'moʊniəsli

harmoniousness
BR hɑː'məʊnɪəsnəs
AM hɑr'moʊniəsnəs

harmonisation
BR ˌhɑːmənʌɪ'zeɪʃn, -z
AM ˌhɑrmənə'zeɪʃən, ˌhɑrməˌnaɪ'zeɪʃən, -z

harmonise
BR 'hɑːmənʌɪz, -ᵻz, -ɪŋ, -d
AM 'hɑrməˌnaɪz, -ᵻz, -ɪŋ, -d

harmonist
BR 'hɑːmənɪst, -s
AM 'hɑrmənəst, -s

harmonistic
BR ˌhɑːmə'nɪstɪk
AM ˌhɑrmə'nɪstɪk

harmonium
BR hɑː'məʊnɪəm, -z
AM hɑr'moʊniəm, -z

harmonization
BR ˌhɑːmənʌɪ'zeɪʃn, -z
AM ˌhɑrmənə'zeɪʃən, ˌhɑrməˌnaɪ'zeɪʃən, -z

harmonize
BR 'hɑːmənʌɪz, -ᵻz, -ɪŋ, -d
AM 'hɑrməˌnaɪz, -ᵻz, -ɪŋ, -d

harmony
BR 'hɑːmən|i, -ɪz
AM 'hɑrməni, -z

Harmsworth
BR 'hɑːmzwəːθ
AM 'hɑrmzˌwərθ

harness
BR 'hɑːnɪs, -ᵻz, -ɪŋ, -t
AM 'hɑrnəs, -əz, -ɪŋ, -t

harnesser
BR 'hɑːnᵻsə(r), -z
AM 'hɑrnəsər, -z

Harold
BR 'harl̩d
AM 'hɛrəld

harp
BR hɑːp, -s, -ɪŋ, -t
AM hɑrp, -s, -ɪŋ, -t

Harpenden
BR 'hɑːp(ə)ndən
AM 'hɑrpəndən

harper
BR 'hɑːpə(r), -z
AM 'hɑrpər, -z

Harpic®
BR 'hɑːpɪk
AM 'hɑrpək

harpie
BR 'hɑːp|i, -ɪz
AM 'hɑrpi, -z

harpist
BR 'hɑːpɪst, -s
AM 'hɑrpəst, -s

Harpocrates
BR hɑː'pɒkrətiːz
AM hɑr'pɑkrəˌtiz

harpoon
BR hɑː'puːn, -z, -ɪŋ, -d
AM ˌhɑr'pun, -z, -ɪŋ, -d

harpooner
BR hɑː'puːnə(r), -z
AM ˌhɑr'punər, -z

harpsichord
BR 'hɑːpsɪkɔːd, -z
AM 'hɑrpsəˌkɔ(ə)rd, -z

harpsichordist
BR 'hɑːpsɪkɔːdɪst, -s
AM 'hɑrpsəˌkɔrdəst, -s

harpy
BR 'hɑːp|i, -ɪz
AM 'hɑrpi, -z

harquebus
BR '(h)ɑːkwɪbəs, -ᵻz
AM '(h)ɑrk(w)əbəs, -əz

harquebusier
BR ˌ(h)ɑːkwɪbə'sɪə(r), -z
AM ˌ(h)ɑrk(w)əbə'sɪ(ə)r, -z

Harrap
BR 'harəp
AM 'hɛrəp

Harrell
BR 'harəl, 'harl̩
AM 'hɛrəl

harridan
BR 'harɪd(ə)n, -z
AM 'hɛrədən, -z

harrier
BR 'harɪə(r), -z
AM 'hɛriər, -z

Harries
BR 'harɪs, 'harɪz
AM 'hɛriz

Harriet
BR 'harɪət
AM 'hɛriət

Harriman
BR 'harɪmən
AM 'hɛrəmən

Harrington
BR 'harɪŋt(ə)n
AM 'hɛrɪŋtən

Harris
BR 'harɪs
AM 'hɛrəs

Harrisburg
BR 'harɪsbəːg
AM 'hɛrəsˌbərg

Harrison
BR 'harɪs(ə)n
AM 'hɛrəsən

Harrod
BR 'harəd, -z
AM 'hɛrəd, -z

Harrogate
BR 'harəgət, 'harəgeɪt
AM 'hɛrəˌgeɪt

Harrovian
BR hə'rəʊvɪən, ha'rəʊvɪən, -z
AM hə'roʊviən, -z

harrow
BR 'harəʊ, -z, -ɪŋ, -d
AM 'hɛr|oʊ, -oʊz, -əwɪŋ, -oʊd

harrower
BR 'harəʊə(r), -z
AM 'hɛrəwər, -z

harrowingly
BR 'harəʊɪŋli
AM 'hɛrəwɪŋli

harrumph
BR hə'rʌmf, -s, -ɪŋ, -t
AM hə'rəm(p)f, -s, -ɪŋ, -t

harry
BR 'har|i, -ɪz, -ɪɪŋ, -ɪd
AM 'hɛri, -z, -ɪŋ, -d

harsh
BR hɑːʃ, -ə(r), -ɪst
AM hɑrʃ, -ər, -əst

harshen
BR 'hɑːʃ|n, -nz, -n̩ɪŋ\-ənɪŋ, -nd
AM 'hɑrʃ|ən, -ənz, -(ə)nɪŋ, -ənd

harshly
BR 'hɑːʃli
AM 'hɑrʃli

harshness
BR 'hɑːʃnəs
AM 'hɑrʃnəs

harslet
BR 'hɑːslɪt
AM 'hɑrslət

hart
BR hɑːt, -s
AM hɑrt, -s

hartal
BR 'hɑːtɑːl, 'həːtɑːl, hɑː'tɑːl, həː'tɑːl
AM hɑr'tɑl

Harte
BR hɑːt
AM hɑrt

hartebeest
BR 'hɑːtɪbiːst, -s
AM 'hɑrdəˌbist, -s

Hartford
BR 'hɑːtfəd
AM 'hɑrtfərd

Hartland
BR 'hɑːtlənd
AM 'hɑrtlənd

Hartlepool
BR 'hɑːtlɪpuːl
AM 'hɑrtliˌpul

Hartley
BR 'hɑːtli
AM 'hɑrtli

Hartman
BR 'hɑːtmən
AM 'hɑrtmən

Hartnell
BR 'hɑːtnl
AM 'hɑrtnəl

hartshorn
BR 'hɑːtshɔːn
AM 'hɑrtsˌ(h)ɔ(ə)rn

Hartshorne
BR 'hɑːtshɔːn
AM 'hɑrtˌʃɔ(ə)rn

harum-scarum
BR ˌhɛːrəm'skɛːrəm
AM ˌhɛrəm'skɛrəm

haruspex
BR hə'rʌspɛks, ha'rʌspɛks, 'harəspɛks
AM hə'rəˌspɛks, 'hɛrəˌspɛks

haruspices
BR hə'rʌspɪsiːz, ha'rʌspɪsiːz
AM hə'rəspəˌsiz

haruspicy
BR hə'rʌspɪsi, ha'rʌspɪsi
AM hə'rəspəsi

Harvard
BR 'hɑːvəd
AM 'hɑrvərd

harvest
BR 'hɑːvɪst, -s, -ɪŋ, -ɪd
AM 'hɑrvəst, -s, -ɪŋ, -əd

harvestable
BR 'hɑːvɪstəbl
AM 'hɑrvəstəbəl
harvester
BR 'hɑːvɪstə(r), -z
AM 'hɑrvəstər, -z
harvestman
BR 'hɑːvɪs(t)mən
AM 'hɑrvəs(t)mən
harvestmen
BR 'hɑːvɪs(t)mən
AM 'hɑrvəs(t)mən
Harvey
BR 'hɑːvi
AM 'hɑrvi
Harwich
BR 'harɪdʒ, 'harɪtʃ
AM 'hɛrɪdʒ
Harwood
BR hɑːwʊd
AM 'hɑr,wʊd
Haryana
BR ,harɪ'ɑːnə(r)
AM ,hɑri'ɑnə
Harz
BR hɑːts
AM hɑrts
has[1]
strong
BR haz
AM hæz
has[2]
weak
BR (h)əz, z, s
AM (h)əz, z, s
Hasdrubal
BR 'hazdrʊbl, 'hazdruːbl, 'hazdrʉbal
AM 'hæzdrubəl
Hašek
BR 'haʃɛk
AM 'hæʃɛk
CZ 'hʌʃɛk
Haseldine
BR 'heɪzldʌɪn
AM 'heɪzəl,daɪn
hash
BR haʃ, -ɪz, -ɪŋ, -t
AM hæʃ, -əz, -ɪŋ, -t
hash-browns
BR ,haʃ'braʊnz
AM 'hæʃ,braʊnz
hasheesh
BR 'haʃiːʃ, 'haʃɪʃ, ha'ʃiːʃ
AM 'hæ,ʃiʃ, hɑ'ʃiʃ
Hashemite
BR 'haʃɪmʌɪt, -s
AM 'hæʃə,maɪt, -s
hashish
BR 'haʃiːʃ, 'haʃɪʃ, ha'ʃiːʃ
AM hæ'ʃiʃ, hɑ'ʃiʃ
Hasid
BR 'hasɪd
AM 'hæsɪd
hasidic
BR ha'sɪdɪk
AM hə'sɪdɪk
Hasidim
BR 'hasɪdɪm
AM hə'sidɪm
Hasidism
BR 'hasɪdɪz(ə)m
AM 'hæsə,dɪzəm
Haslam
BR 'hazləm
AM 'hæzləm
Haslemere
BR 'heɪzlmɪə(r)
AM 'heɪzəl,mɪ(ə)r
haslet
BR 'hazlɨt, 'heɪzlɨt
AM 'hæslət, 'heɪzlət
Haslett
BR 'heɪzlɨt, 'hazlɨt
AM 'hæzlət
Hasmonean
BR ,hazmə'niːən
AM ,hæzmə'niən
hasn't
BR 'haznt
AM 'hæznt
hasp
BR hɑːsp, hasp, -s
AM hæsp, -s
Hassall
BR 'hasl
AM 'hæsəl
Hassan
BR hə'sɑːn, ha'sɑːn, 'hasn
AM hɑ'sɑn
Hasselt
BR 'haslt
AM 'hæsəlt
hassle
BR 'has|l, -lz, -l̩ɪŋ\-lɪŋ, -ld
AM 'hæs|əl, -əlz, -(ə)lɪŋ, -əld
hassock
BR 'hasək, -s
AM 'hæsək, -s
hast
BR hast
AM hæst
hastate
BR 'hasteɪt
AM 'hæ,steɪt
haste
BR heɪst
AM heɪst
hasten
BR 'heɪs|n, -nz, -n̩ɪŋ\-nɪŋ, -nd
AM 'heɪs|n, -nz, -n̩ɪŋ, -nd
Hastie
BR 'heɪsti
AM 'heɪsti
hastily
BR 'heɪstɨli
AM 'heɪstɨli
hastiness
BR 'heɪstɪnɨs
AM 'heɪstinɨs
Hastings
BR 'heɪstɪŋz
AM 'heɪstɪŋz
hasty
BR 'heɪst|i, -ɪə(r), -ɪɨst
AM 'heɪsti, -ər, -ɨst
hat
BR hat, -s
AM hæt, -s
hatable
BR 'heɪtəbl
AM 'heɪdəbəl
hatband
BR 'hatband, -z
AM 'hæt,bænd, -z
hatbox
BR 'hatbɒks, -ɨz
AM 'hæt,bɑks, -əz
hatch
BR hatʃ, -ɨz, -ɪŋ, -t
AM hætʃ, -ɨz, -ɪŋ, -t
hatchback
BR 'hatʃbak, -s
AM 'hætʃ,bæk, -s
Hatcher
BR 'hatʃə(r)
AM 'hætʃər
hatchery
BR 'hatʃ(ə)r|i, -ɪz
AM 'hætʃəri, -z
hatchet
BR 'hatʃɪt, -s
AM 'hætʃət, -s
hatching
BR 'hatʃɪŋ, -z
AM 'hætʃɪŋ, -z
hatchling
BR 'hatʃlɪŋ, -z
AM 'hætʃlɪŋ, -z
hatchment
BR 'hatʃm(ə)nt, -s
AM 'hætʃmənt, -s
hatchway
BR 'hatʃweɪ, -z
AM 'hætʃ,weɪ, -z
hate
BR heɪt, -s, -ɪŋ, -ɨd
AM heɪ|t, -ts, -dɪŋ, -dɨd
hateful
BR 'heɪtf(ʊ)l
AM 'heɪtfəl
hatefully
BR 'heɪtfʊli, 'heɪtfl̩i
AM 'heɪtfəli
hatefulness
BR 'heɪtf(ʊ)lnəs
AM 'heɪtfəlnəs
hater
BR 'heɪtə(r), -z
AM 'heɪdər, -z
Hatfield
BR 'hatfiːld
AM 'hæt,fild
hatful
BR 'hatfʊl, -z
AM 'hæt,fʊl, -z
hath
BR haθ
AM hæθ
Hathaway
BR 'haθəweɪ
AM 'hæθə,weɪ
hatha-yoga
BR ,hʌtə'jəʊgə(r), ,haθə'jəʊgə(r)
AM 'hɑθə'joʊgə, 'hɑdə'joʊgə
Hatherley
BR 'haðəli
AM 'hæðərli
Hathern
BR 'haðn
AM 'hæðərn
Hathersage
BR 'haðəseɪdʒ, 'haðəsɪdʒ
AM 'hæðər,seɪdʒ, 'hæðərsɪdʒ
Hathor
BR 'haθɔː(r)
AM 'hæθɔr
hatless
BR 'hatləs
AM 'hætləs
hatpeg
BR 'hatpɛg, -z
AM 'hæt,pɛg, -z
hatpin
BR 'hatpɪn, -z
AM 'hæt,pɪn, -z
hatred
BR 'heɪtrɪd
AM 'heɪtrəd
Hatshepsut
BR hat'ʃɛpsuːt
AM hæt'ʃɛp,sut
hatstand
BR 'hatstand, -z
AM 'hæt,stænd, -z
hatter
BR 'hatə(r), -z
AM 'hædər, -z
Hatteras
BR 'hat(ə)rəs
AM 'hædərəs
Hattersley
BR 'hatəzli
AM 'hædərzli
Hattie
BR 'hati
AM 'hædi
Hatton
BR 'hatn
AM 'hætn
Hattusas
BR hat'tuːsəs
AM hæ(t)'tusəs
hauberk
BR 'hɔːbəːk, -s
AM 'hɔbərk, 'hɑbərk, -s

Haugh
BR hɔː(r), hɔːf
AM haʊ, hɔf, hɑf

Haughey
BR 'hɒxi, 'hɔːhi
AM 'haʊi, 'hɔi

haughtily
BR 'hɔːtɨli
AM 'hɔdəli, 'hɑdəli

haughtiness
BR 'hɔːtɪnɨs
AM 'hɔdinɨs, 'hɑdinɨs

Haughton
BR 'hɔːtn
AM 'hɔtn, 'hɑtn

haughty
BR 'hɔːt|i, -ɪə(r), -ɪɪst
AM 'hɔdi, 'hɑdi, -ər, -ɨst

haul
BR hɔːl, -z, -ɪŋ, -d
AM hɔl, hɑl, -z, -ɪŋ, -d

haulage
BR 'hɔːlɪdʒ
AM 'hɔlɪdʒ, 'hɑlɪdʒ

hauler
BR 'hɔːlə(r), -z
AM 'hɔlər, 'hɑlər, -z

haulier
BR 'hɔːlɪə(r), -z
AM 'hɔljər, 'hɑljər, -z

haulm
BR hɔːm, -z
AM hɔm, hɑ(l)m, -z

haulyard
BR 'hɔːljəd, -z
AM 'hɔljərd, 'hɑljərd, -z

haunch
BR hɔːn(t)ʃ, -ɪz
AM hɔn(t)ʃ, hɑn(t)ʃ, -əz

haunt
BR hɔːnt, -s, -ɪŋ, -ɨd
AM hɔn|t, hɑn|t, -ts, -(t)ɪŋ, -(t)əd

haunter
BR 'hɔːntə(r), -z
AM 'hɔn(t)ər, 'hɑn(t)ər, -z

hauntingly
BR 'hɔːntɪŋli
AM 'hɔn(t)ɪŋli, 'hɑn(t)ɪŋli

Hauptmann
BR 'haʊp(t)mən
AM 'haʊp(t)mɑn

Hausa
BR 'haʊsə(r), 'haʊzə(r), -z
AM 'haʊsə, 'haʊzə, -z

Hausfrau
BR 'haʊsfraʊ, -z
AM 'haʊs,fraʊ, -z

hautbois
BR '(h)əʊbɔɪ, -z
AM '(h)oʊ(t),bɔɪ, -z

hautboy
BR '(h)əʊbɔɪ, -z
AM '(h)oʊ(t),bɔɪ, -z

haute couture
BR ,əʊt kʊ'tjʊə(r), + kʊ'tʃʊə(r)
AM ,(h)oʊt ,ku'tʊ(ə)r

haute cuisine
BR ,əʊt kwɪ'ziːn
AM ,(h)oʊt ,kwə'zin

haute école
BR ,əʊt eɪ'kɒl
AM ,(h)oʊ 'tɛkɔl
FR 'ot ekɔl

hauteur
BR əʊ'təː(r), hɔː'təː(r)
AM (h)oʊ'tər

haut monde
BR ,əʊ 'mɒnd
AM ,(h)oʊ 'mɔnd, + 'mɑnd

Havana
BR hə'vanə(r), -z
AM hə'vænə, hə'vɑnə, -z

Havant
BR 'havnt
AM 'hævənt

have¹
strong
BR hav, -z, -ɪŋ
AM hæv, -z, -ɪŋ

have²
weak
BR həv, (ə)v
AM həv, (ə)v

have-a-go
BR ,havə'gəʊ
AM ,hævə'goʊ

Havel
BR 'hɑːv(ə)l
AM 'hɑvəl

Havelock
BR 'havlɒk
AM 'hævə,lɑk, 'hæv(ə),lɑk, 'hæv,lɑk

havelock
BR 'havlɒk, 'havlək, -s
AM 'hævə,lɑk, 'hæv(ə),lɑk, 'hæv,lɑk, -s

haven
BR 'heɪvn, -z
AM 'heɪvən, -z

have-not
BR ,hav'nɒt, 'havnɒt, -s
AM 'hæv,nɑt, -s

haven't
BR 'havnt
AM 'hævənt

haver
BR 'heɪv|ə(r), -əz, -(ə)rɪŋ, -əd
AM 'heɪvər, -z, -ɪŋ, -d

Haverfordwest
BR ,havəfəd'wɛst
AM ,hævərfərd'wɛst

Haverhill
BR 'heɪv(ə)rɪl, 'heɪv(ə)rl̩, 'heɪvəhɪl
AM 'hævər,hɪl

Havering
BR 'heɪv(ə)rɪŋ
AM 'hævərɪŋ

Havers
BR 'heɪvəz
AM 'heɪvərs

haversack
BR 'havəsak, -s
AM 'hævər,sæk, -s

haversine
BR 'havəsʌɪn, -z
AM 'hævər,saɪn, -z

haves
BR havz
AM hævz

Haviland
BR 'havɪlənd
AM 'hævələnd

havildar
BR 'hav(ɪ)ldɑː(r), -z
AM 'hævəl,dɑr, -z

havoc
BR 'havək
AM 'hævək

haw
BR hɔː(r), -z, -ɪŋ, -d
AM hɔ, hɑ, -z, -ɪŋ, -d

Hawaii
BR hə'wʌɪiː
AM hə'waɪ(j)i

Hawaiian
BR hə'wʌɪən, -z
AM hə'waɪ(j)ən, -z

Hawes
BR hɔːz
AM hɔz, hɑz

hawfinch
BR 'hɔːfɪn(t)ʃ, -ɪz
AM 'hɔ,fɪntʃ, 'hɑ,fɪntʃ, -ɪz

haw-haw¹
interjection
BR ,hɔː'hɔː(r)
AM ,hɔ'hɔ, ,hɑ'hɑ

haw-haw²
noun
BR 'hɔːhɔː(r)
AM ,hɔ'hɔ, ,hɑ'hɑ

Hawick
BR 'hɔːɪk, hɔɪk
AM 'hɔwɨk, 'hɑwɨk

hawk
BR hɔːk, -s, -ɪŋ, -t
AM hɔk, hɑk, -s, -ɪŋ, -t

hawkbit
BR 'hɔːkbɪt, -s
AM 'hɔk,bɪt, 'hɑk,bɪt, -s

Hawke
BR hɔːk
AM hɔk, hɑk

Hawke Bay
BR ,hɔːk 'beɪ
AM 'hɔk 'beɪ, 'hɑk 'beɪ

hawker
BR 'hɔːkə(r), -z
AM 'hɔkər, 'hɑkər, -z

Hawkes
BR hɔːks
AM hɔks, hɑks

Hawke's Bay
BR ,hɔːks 'beɪ
AM 'hɔks 'beɪ, 'hɑks 'beɪ

Hawking
BR 'hɔːkɪŋ
AM 'hɔkɪŋ, 'hɑkɪŋ

Hawkins
BR 'hɔːkɪnz
AM 'hɔkɪŋz, 'hɑkɪŋz

hawkish
BR 'hɔːkɪʃ
AM 'hɔkɪʃ, 'hɑkɪʃ

hawkishness
BR 'hɔːkɪʃnɪs
AM 'hɔkɪʃnɪs, 'hɑkɪʃnɪs

hawklike
BR 'hɔːklʌɪk
AM 'hɔk,laɪk, 'hɑk,laɪk

hawkmoth
BR 'hɔːkmɒθ, -s
AM 'hɔk,mɔθ, 'hɑk,mɑθ, -s

hawksbill
BR 'hɔːksbɪl, -z
AM 'hɔks,bɪl, 'hɑks,bɪl, -z

Hawksmoor
BR 'hɔːksmʊə(r), 'hɔːksmɔː(r)
AM 'hɔks,mɔ(ə)r, 'hɑks,mɔ(ə)r

hawkweed
BR 'hɔːkwiːd, -z
AM 'hɔk,wid, 'hɑk,wid, -z

Hawley
BR 'hɔːli
AM 'hɔli, 'hɑli

Haworth
BR 'haʊəθ, 'hɔːwəθ
AM 'hɔ,wərθ, 'hɑ,wərθ

hawse
BR hɔːz, -ɪz
AM hɔz, hɑz, -əz

hawser
BR 'hɔːzə(r), -z
AM 'hɔzər, 'hɑzər, -z

hawthorn
BR 'hɔːθɔːn, -z
AM 'hɔ,θɔ(ə)rn, 'hɑ,θɔ(ə)rn, -z

Hawtrey
BR 'hɔːtri
AM 'hɔtri, 'hɑtri

Haxey
BR 'haksi
AM 'hæksi

hay
BR heɪ
AM heɪ

Hayakawa
BR ˌhʌɪəˈkɑːwə(r)
AM ˌhaɪəˈkɑwə
haybox
BR ˈheɪbɒks, -ɪz
AM ˈheɪˌbɑks, -əz
haycock
BR ˈheɪkɒk, -s
AM ˈheɪˌkɑk, -s
Hayden
BR ˈheɪdn
AM ˈheɪd(ə)n
Haydn[1]
composer
BR ˈhʌɪdn
AM ˈhaɪdn
Haydn[2]
forename
BR ˈheɪdn
AM ˈheɪd(ə)n
Hayek
BR ˈhʌɪɛk, ˈhɑːjɛk
AM ˈhaɪɛk
Hayes
BR heɪz
AM heɪz
hayfield
BR ˈheɪfiːld, -z
AM ˈheɪˌfild, -z
hayfork
BR ˈheɪfɔːk, -s
AM ˈheɪˌfɔ(ə)rk, -s
haylage
BR ˈheɪlɨdʒ
AM ˈheɪlɨdʒ
Hayle
BR heɪl
AM heɪl
Hayley
BR ˈheɪli
AM ˈheɪli
Hayling
BR ˈheɪlɪŋ
AM ˈheɪlɪŋ
hayloft
BR ˈheɪlɒft, -s
AM ˈheɪˌlɔft, ˈheɪˌlɑft, -s
haymaker
BR ˈheɪˌmeɪkə(r), -z
AM ˈheɪˌmeɪkər, -z
haymaking
BR ˈheɪˌmeɪkɪŋ
AM ˈheɪˌmeɪkɪŋ
Hayman
BR ˈheɪmən
AM ˈheɪmən
Haymarket
BR ˈheɪˌmɑːkɪt
AM ˈheɪˌmɑrkət
haymow
BR ˈheɪməʊ
AM ˈheɪˌmoʊ
Haynes
BR heɪnz
AM heɪnz
hayrack
BR ˈheɪrak, -s
AM ˈheɪˌræk, -s
hayrick
BR ˈheɪrɪk, -s
AM ˈheɪˌrɪk, -s
hayride
BR ˈheɪrʌɪd, -z
AM ˈheɪˌraɪd, -z
Hays
BR heɪz
AM heɪz
hayseed
BR ˈheɪsiːd, -z
AM ˈheɪˌsid, -z
haystack
BR ˈheɪstak, -s
AM ˈheɪˌstæk, -s
Hayter
BR ˈheɪtə(r)
AM ˈheɪdər
haywain
BR ˈheɪweɪn, -z
AM ˈheɪˌweɪn, -z
Hayward
BR ˈheɪwəd
AM ˈheɪwərd
haywire
BR ˈheɪˌwʌɪə(r)
AM ˈheɪˌwaɪ(ə)r
Haywood
BR ˈheɪwʊd, ˈheɪwəd
AM ˈheɪˌwʊd
Hayworth
BR ˈheɪwəθ, ˈheɪwəːθ
AM ˈheɪˌwərθ
Hazan
BR həˈzan
AM həˈzɑn
hazard
BR ˈhazəd, -z, -ɪŋ, -ɨd
AM ˈhæzərd, -z, -ɪŋ, -əd
hazardous
BR ˈhazədəs
AM ˈhæzərdəs
hazardously
BR ˈhazədəsli
AM ˈhæzərdəsli
hazardousness
BR ˈhazədəsnəs
AM ˈhæzərdəsnəs
haze
BR heɪz, -ɨz
AM heɪz, -ɨz
hazel
BR ˈheɪzl, -z
AM ˈheɪzəl, -z
hazelnut
BR ˈheɪzlnʌt, -s
AM ˈheɪzəlˌnət, -s
hazily
BR ˈheɪzɨli
AM ˈheɪzɨli
haziness
BR ˈheɪzɪnɨs
AM ˈheɪzinɨs
Hazlitt
BR ˈhazlɪt, ˈheɪzlɪt
AM ˈhæzlət
hazy
BR ˈheɪz|i, -ɪə(r), -ɪɨst
AM ˈheɪzi, -ər, -ɨst
Hazzard
BR ˈhazəd
AM ˈhæzərd
he[1]
noun
BR hiː, -z
AM hi, -z
he[2]
strong form pronoun
BR hiː
AM hi
he[3]
weak form pronoun
BR (h)iː
AM (h)i
head
BR hɛd, -z, -ɪŋ, -ɨd
AM hɛd, -z, -ɪŋ, -əd
headache
BR ˈhɛdeɪk, -s
AM ˈhɛdˌeɪk, -s
headachy
BR ˈhɛdeɪki
AM ˈhɛdˌeɪki
headage
BR ˈhɛdɪdʒ
AM ˈhɛdɪdʒ
headband
BR ˈhɛdband, -z
AM ˈhɛdˌbænd, -z
headbanger
BR ˈhɛdˌbaŋə(r), -z
AM ˈhɛdˌbæŋər, -z
headbanging
BR ˈhɛdˌbaŋɪŋ
AM ˈhɛdˌbæŋɪŋ
headboard
BR ˈhɛdbɔːd, -z
AM ˈhɛdˌbɔ(ə)rd, -z
headcheese
BR ˈhɛdtʃiːz
AM ˈhɛdˌtʃiz
headcount
BR ˈhɛdkaʊnt, -s
AM ˈhɛdˌkaʊnt, -s
headdress
BR ˈhɛddrɛs, -ɨz
AM ˈhɛ(d)ˌdrɛs, -əz
header
BR ˈhɛdə(r), -z
AM ˈhɛdər, -z
headfast
BR ˈhɛdfɑːst, ˈhɛdfast, -s
AM ˈhɛdˌfæst, -s
headfirst
BR ˌhɛdˈfəːst
AM ˈhɛdˈfərst
headgear
BR ˈhɛdgɪə(r)
AM ˈhɛdˌgɪ(ə)r
headhunt
BR ˈhɛdhʌnt, -s, -ɪŋ, -ɨd
AM ˈhɛd,(h)ən|t, -ts, -(t)ɪŋ, -(t)əd
headhunter
BR ˈhɛdˌhʌntə(r), -z
AM ˈhɛdˌ(h)ən(t)ər, -z
headily
BR ˈhɛdɨli
AM ˈhɛdəli
headiness
BR ˈhɛdɪnɨs
AM ˈhɛdinɨs
heading
BR ˈhɛdɪŋ, -z
AM ˈhɛdɪŋ, -z
headlamp
BR ˈhɛdlamp, -s
AM ˈhɛdˌlæmp, -s
headland
BR ˈhɛdlənd, -z
AM ˈhɛdlənd, ˈhɛdˌlænd, -z
headless
BR ˈhɛdləs
AM ˈhɛdləs
headlight
BR ˈhɛdlʌɪt, -s
AM ˈhɛdˌlaɪt, -s
headline
BR ˈhɛdlʌɪn, -z, -ɪŋ, -d
AM ˈhɛdˌlaɪn, -z, -ɪŋ, -d
headliner
BR ˈhɛdˌlʌɪnə(r), -z
AM ˈhɛdˌlaɪnər, -z
headlock
BR ˈhɛdlɒk, -s
AM ˈhɛdˌlɑk, -s
headlong
BR ˈhɛdlɒŋ
AM ˈhɛdˌlɔŋ, ˈhɛdˌlɑŋ
headman[1]
chief
BR ˈhɛdmən, ˈhɛdman
AM ˌhɛdˈmæn
headman[2]
executioner
BR ˈhɛdmən, ˈhɛdman
AM ˈhɛdmən
headmaster
BR ˌhɛdˈmɑːstə(r), ˌhɛdˈmastə(r), -z
AM ˌhɛdˈmæstər, -z
headmasterly
BR ˌhɛdˈmɑːstəli, ˌhɛdˈmastəli
AM ˌhɛdˈmæstərli
headmen[1]
chiefs
BR ˈhɛdmən, ˈhɛdmɛn
AM ˈhɛdˈmɛn
headmen[2]
executioners
BR ˈhɛdmən, ˈhɛdmɛn
AM ˈhɛdmən
headmistress
BR ˌhɛdˈmɪstrɪs, -ɨz
AM ˌhɛdˈmɪstrɪs, -ɨz

headmost
BR ˈhɛdməʊst
AM ˈhɛdˌmoʊst
headnote
BR ˈhɛdnəʊt, -s
AM ˈhɛdˌnoʊt, -s
headphone
BR ˈhɛdfəʊn, -z
AM ˈhɛdˌfoʊn, -z
headpiece
BR ˈhɛdpiːs, -ɨz
AM ˈhɛdˌpis, -ɨz
headpin
BR ˈhɛdpɪn, -z
AM ˈhɛdˌpɪn, -z
headquarter
verb
BR ˈhɛdˌkwɔːt|ə(r), -əz, -(ə)rɪŋ, -əd
AM ˈhɛdˌkwɔrdər, -ərz, -(ə)rɪŋ, -ərd
headquarters
noun
BR ˌhɛdˈkwɔːtəz, ˈhɛdˌkwɔːtəz
AM ˈhɛdˌkwɔrdərz
headrest
BR ˈhɛdrɛst, -s
AM ˈhɛdˌrɛst, -s
headroom
BR ˈhɛdruːm, ˈhɛdrʊm
AM ˈhɛdˌrum, ˈhɛdˌrʊm
headsail
BR ˈhɛdseɪl, -z
AM ˈhɛdˌseɪl, -z
headscarf
BR ˈhɛdskɑːf
AM ˈhɛdˌskɑrf
headscarves
BR ˈhɛdskɑːvz
AM ˈhɛdˌskɑrvz
headset
BR ˈhɛdsɛt, -s
AM ˈhɛdˌsɛt, -s
headship
BR ˈhɛdʃɪp, -s
AM ˈhɛdˌʃɪp, -s
headshrinker
BR ˈhɛdˌʃrɪŋkə(r), -z
AM ˈhɛdˌʃrɪŋkər, -z
headsman
BR ˈhɛdzmən
AM ˈhɛdzmən
headsmen
BR ˈhɛdzmən
AM ˈhɛdzmən
headspace
BR ˈhɛdspeɪs
AM ˈhɛdˌspeɪs
headspring
BR ˈhɛdsprɪŋ, -z
AM ˈhɛdˌsprɪŋ, -z
headsquare
BR ˈhɛdskwɛː(r), -z
AM ˈhɛdˌskwɛ(ə)r, -z
headstall
BR ˈhɛdstɔːl, -z
AM ˈhɛdˌstɔl, ˈhɛdˌstɑl, -z
headstock
BR ˈhɛdstɒk, -s
AM ˈhɛdˌstɑk, -s
headstone
BR ˈhɛdstəʊn, -z
AM ˈhɛdˌstoʊn, -z
headstrong
BR ˈhɛdstrɒŋ
AM ˈhɛdˌstrɔŋ, ˈhɛdˌstrɑŋ
headstrongly
BR ˈhɛdstrɒŋli
AM ˈhɛdˌstrɔŋli, ˈhɛdˌstrɑŋli
headstrongness
BR ˈhɛdstrɒŋnəs
AM ˈhɛdˌstrɔŋnəs, ˈhɛdˌstrɑŋnəs
headteacher
BR ˌhɛdˈtiːtʃə(r), -z
AM ˈhɛdˈtitʃər, -z
headward
BR ˈhɛdwəd
AM ˈhɛdwərd
headwater
BR ˈhɛdˌwɔːtə(r), -z
AM ˈhɛdˌwɔdər, ˈhɛdˌwɑdər, -z
headway
BR ˈhɛdweɪ
AM ˈhɛdˌweɪ
headwind
BR ˈhɛdwɪnd, -z
AM ˈhɛdˌwɪnd, -z
headword
BR ˈhɛdwəːd, -z
AM ˈhɛdˌwərd, -z
headwork
BR ˈhɛdwəːk
AM ˈhɛdˌwərk
heady
BR ˈhɛd|i, -ɪə(r), -ɪɪst
AM ˈhɛdi, -ər, -ɨst
heal
BR hiːl, -z, -ɪŋ, -d
AM hil, -z, -ɪŋ, -d
healable
BR ˈhiːləbl
AM ˈhiləbəl
heald
BR hiːld, -z
AM hild, -z
healer
BR ˈhiːlə(r), -z
AM ˈhilər, -z
Healey
BR ˈhiːli
AM ˈhili
health
BR hɛlθ
AM hɛlθ
healthful
BR ˈhɛlθf(ʊ)l
AM ˈhɛlθfəl
healthfully
BR ˈhɛlθfʊli, ˈhɛlθfl̩i
AM ˈhɛlθfəli
healthfulness
BR ˈhɛlθf(ʊ)lnəs
AM ˈhɛlθfəlnəs
healthily
BR ˈhɛlθɨli
AM ˈhɛlθəli
healthiness
BR ˈhɛlθɪnɨs
AM ˈhɛlθinɨs
healthy
BR ˈhɛlθ|i, -ɪə(r), -ɪɪst
AM ˈhɛlθi, -ər, -ɨst
Healy
BR ˈhiːli
AM ˈhili
Heaney
BR ˈhiːni
AM ˈhini
Heanor
BR ˈhiːnə(r)
AM ˈhinər
heap
BR hiːp, -s, -ɪŋ, -t
AM hip, -s, -ɪŋ, -t
hear
BR hɪə(r), -z, -ɪŋ
AM hɪ|(ə)r, -(ə)rz, -rɪŋ
hearable
BR ˈhɪərəbl
AM ˈhɪrəbəl
Heard
BR həːd
AM hərd
hearer
BR ˈhɪərə(r), -z
AM ˈhɪrər, -z
hearken
BR ˈhɑːk|(ə)n, -(ə)nz, -n̩ɪŋ\-(ə)nɪŋ, -(ə)nd
AM ˈhɑrkən, -z, -ɪŋ, -d
Hearn
BR həːn
AM hərn
Hearne
BR həːn
AM hərn
hearsay
BR ˈhɪəseɪ
AM ˈhɪrˌseɪ
hearse
BR həːs, -ɨz
AM hərs, -əz
Hearst
BR həːst
AM hərst
heart
BR hɑːt, -s
AM hɑrt, -s
heartache
BR ˈhɑːteɪk, -s
AM ˈhɑrˌdeɪk, -s
heartbeat
BR ˈhɑːtbiːt, -s
AM ˈhɑrtˌbit, -s
heartbreak
BR ˈhɑːtbreɪk, -s, -ɪŋ
AM ˈhɑrtˌbreɪk, -s, -ɪŋ
heartbreaker
BR ˈhɑːtˌbreɪkə(r), -z
AM ˈhɑrtˌbreɪkər, -z
heartbreaking
BR ˈhɑːtˌbreɪkɪŋ
AM ˈhɑrtˌbreɪkɪŋ
heartbroken
BR ˈhɑːtˌbrəʊk(ə)n
AM ˈhɑrtˌbroʊkən
heartburn
BR ˈhɑːtbəːn
AM ˈhɑrtˌbərn
hearten
BR ˈhɑːt|n, -nz, -n̩ɪŋ\-nɪŋ, -nd
AM ˈhɑrtən, -z, -ɪŋ, -d
hearteningly
BR ˈhɑːtn̩ɪŋli, ˈhɑːtnɪŋli
AM ˈhɑrtn̩ɪŋli
heartfelt
BR ˈhɑːtfɛlt
AM ˈhɑrtˌfɛlt
hearth
BR hɑːθ, -s
AM hɑrθ, -s
hearthrug
BR ˈhɑːθrʌg, -z
AM ˈhɑrθˌrəg, -z
hearthstone
BR ˈhɑːθstəʊn, -z
AM ˈhɑrθˌstoʊn, -z
heartily
BR ˈhɑːtɨli
AM ˈhɑrdəli
heartiness
BR ˈhɑːtɪnɨs
AM ˈhɑrdinɨs
heartland
BR ˈhɑːtlənd, ˈhɑːtland, -z
AM ˈhɑrtˌlænd, -z
heartless
BR ˈhɑːtləs
AM ˈhɑrtləs
heartlessly
BR ˈhɑːtləsli
AM ˈhɑrtləsli
heartlessness
BR ˈhɑːtləsnəs
AM ˈhɑrtləsnəs
heartrending
BR ˈhɑːtˌrɛndɪŋ
AM ˈhɑrtˌrɛndɪŋ
heartsearching
BR ˈhɑːtˌsəːtʃɪŋ
AM ˈhɑrtˌsərtʃɪŋ
heartsease
BR ˈhɑːtsiːz
AM ˈhɑrtˌsiz
heartsick
BR ˈhɑːtsɪk
AM ˈhɑrtˌsɪk

heartsickness
BR ˈhɑːtˌsɪknɨs
AM ˈhɑrtˌsɪknɨs
heartsore
BR ˈhɑːtsɔː(r)
AM ˈhɑrtˌsɔ(ə)r
heartstrings
BR ˈhɑːtstrɪŋz
AM ˈhɑrtˌstrɪŋz
heartthrob
BR ˈhɑːtθrɒb, -z
AM ˈhɑrtˌθrɑb, -z
heart-to-heart
BR ˌhɑːttəˈhɑːt, -s
AM ˈ¦hɑr(t)təˈhɑrt, -s
heartwarming
BR ˈhɑːtˌwɔːmɪŋ
AM ˈhɑrtˌwɔrmɪŋ
heartwarmingly
BR ˈhɑːtˌwɔːmɪŋli
AM ˈhɑrtˌwɔrmɪŋli
heartwood
BR ˈhɑːtwʊd
AM ˈhɑrtˌwʊd
hearty
BR ˈhɑːt|i, -ɪə(r), -ɪɨst
AM ˈhɑrdi, -ər, -ɨst
heat
BR hiːt, -s, -ɪŋ, -ɨd
AM hi|t, -ts, -dɪŋ, -dɨd
heatedly
BR ˈhiːtɨdli
AM ˈhidɨdli
heater
BR ˈhiːtə(r), -z
AM ˈhidər, -z
heath
BR hiːθ, -s
AM hiθ, -s
Heathcliff
BR ˈhiːθklɪf
AM ˈhiθˌklɪf
Heathcliffe
BR ˈhiːθklɪf
AM ˈhiθˌklɪf
Heathcote
BR ˈhiːθkət, ˈhɛθkət
AM ˈhiθˌkoʊt
heathen
BR ˈhiːðn, -z
AM ˈhiðən, -z
heathendom
BR ˈhiːðndəm
AM ˈhiðəndəm
heathenish
BR ˈhiːðn̩ɪʃ, ˈhiːðənɪʃ
AM ˈhiðənɪʃ
heathenishly
BR ˈhiːðn̩ɨʃli, ˈhiːðənɨʃli
AM ˈhiðənɨʃli
heathenishness
BR ˈhiːðn̩ɨʃnɨs, ˈhiːðənɨʃnɨs
AM ˈhiðənɪʃnɨs
heathenism
BR ˈhiːðn̩ɪz(ə)m
AM ˈhiðəˌnɪzəm
heathenry
BR ˈhiːðnri
AM ˈhiðənri
heather
BR ˈhɛðə(r), -z
AM ˈhɛðər, -z
heathery
BR ˈhɛð(ə)ri
AM ˈhɛðəri
Heathfield
BR ˈhiːθfiːld
AM ˈhiθˌfild
heathland
BR ˈhiːθlənd, ˈhiːθland, -z
AM ˈhiθˌlænd, -z
heathless
BR ˈhiːθlɨs
AM ˈhiθlɨs
heathlike
BR ˈhiːθlʌɪk
AM ˈhiθˌlaɪk
Heathrow
BR ˌhiːθˈrəʊ
AM ˈhiθˌroʊ
heathy
BR ˈhiːθi
AM ˈhiθi
Heaton
BR ˈhiːtn
AM ˈhitn
heatproof
BR ˈhiːtpruːf
AM ˈhitˌpruf
heatstroke
BR ˈhiːtstrəʊk
AM ˈhitˌstroʊk
heatwave
BR ˈhiːtweɪv, -z
AM ˈhitˌweɪv, -z
heave
BR hiːv, -z, -ɪŋ, -d
AM hiv, -z, -ɪŋ, -d
heave-ho
BR ˌhiːvˈhəʊ
AM ˈ¦hivˈhoʊ
heaven
BR ˈhɛvn, -z
AM ˈhɛvən, -z
heavenliness
BR ˈhɛvnlɪnɨs
AM ˈhɛvənlinɨs
heavenly
BR ˈhɛvnli
AM ˈhɛvənli
heavenward
BR ˈhɛvnwəd, -z
AM ˈhɛvənwərd, -z
heaver
BR ˈhiːvə(r), -z
AM ˈhivər, -z
heavily
BR ˈhɛvɨli
AM ˈhɛvəli
heaviness
BR ˈhɛvɪnɨs
AM ˈhɛvinɨs
Heaviside
BR ˈhɛvɪsʌɪd
AM ˈhɛviˌsaɪd
heavy
BR ˈhɛv|i, -ɪə(r), -ɪɨst
AM ˈhɛvi, -ər, -ɨst
heavy-footed
BR ˌhɛvɪˈfʊtɨd
AM ˈhɛviˈfʊdəd
heavy-handed
BR ˌhɛvɪˈhandɨd
AM ˈ¦hɛviˈ¦hændəd
heavy-handedly
BR ˌhɛvɪˈhandɨdli
AM ˈ¦hɛviˈ¦hændədli
heavy-handedness
BR ˌhɛvɪˈhandɨdnɨs
AM ˈ¦hɛviˈ¦hændədnəs
heavy-hearted
BR ˌhɛvɪˈhɑːtɨd
AM ˈ¦hɛviˈhɑrdəd
heavyish
BR ˈhɛvɪɪʃ
AM ˈhɛviɪʃ
heavyset
BR ˌhɛvɪˈsɛt
AM ˈ¦hɛviˈ¦sɛt
heavyweight
BR ˈhɛvɪweɪt, -s
AM ˈhɛviˌweɪt, -s
Hebburn
BR ˈhɛb(əː)n
AM ˈhɛbərn
Hebden
BR ˈhɛbd(ə)n
AM ˈhɛbdən
hebdomadal
BR hɛbˈdɒmədl
AM hɛbˈdɑmədəl
hebdomadally
BR hɛbˈdɒmədl̩i
AM hɛbˈdɑmədl̩i
Hebe
BR ˈhiːbi
AM ˈhibi
Hebert
BR ˈhiːbət, ˈhɛbət
AM ˈhɛbərt, ˈeɪˌbɛ(ə)r
hebetude
BR ˈhɛbɨtjuːd, ˈhɛbɨtʃuːd
AM ˈhɛbəˌt(j)ud
Hebraic
BR hɪˈbreɪɪk, hiːˈbreɪɪk
AM hiˈbreɪɪk
Hebraically
BR hɪˈbreɪɪkli, hiːˈbreɪɪkli
AM hiˈbreɪɪk(ə)li
Hebraise
BR ˈhiːbreɪʌɪz, -ɨz, -ɪŋ, -d
AM ˈhiˌbreɪˌaɪz, -ɨz, -ɪŋ, -d
Hebraism
BR ˈhiːbreɪɪz(ə)m, -z
AM ˈhiˌbreɪˌɪzəm, -z
Hebraist
BR ˈhiːbreɪɪst, -s
AM ˈhiˌbreɪɨst, -s
Hebraistic
BR ˌhiːbreɪˈɪstɪk
AM ˌhibreɪˈɪstɪk
Hebraize
BR ˈhiːbreɪʌɪz, -ɨz, -ɪŋ, -d
AM ˈhiˌbreɪˌaɪz, -ɨz, -ɪŋ, -d
Hebrew
BR ˈhiːbruː, -z
AM ˈhiˌbru, -z
Hebridean
BR ˌhɛbrɪˈdiːən, -z
AM ˈ¦hɛbrəˈdiən, -z
Hebrides
BR ˈhɛbrɪdiːz
AM ˈhɛbrədiz
Hebron
BR ˈhiːbrɒn, ˈhɛbrɒn
AM ˈhibrən, ˈhiˌbrɑn
Hecate[1]
Shakespearean
BR ˈhɛkəti, ˈhɛkət
AM ˈhɛkədi
Hecate[2]
BR ˈhɛkəti
AM ˈhɛkədi
hecatomb
BR ˈhɛkətuːm, -z
AM ˈhɛkəˌtoʊm, -z
heck
BR hɛk
AM hɛk
heckelphone
BR ˈhɛklfəʊn, -z
AM ˈhɛkəlˌfoʊn, -z
heckle
BR ˈhɛk|l, -lz, -l̩ɪŋ\-lɪŋ, -ld
AM ˈhɛk|əl, -əlz, -(ə)lɪŋ, -əld
heckler
BR ˈhɛkl̩ə(r), ˈhɛklə(r), -z
AM ˈhɛk(ə)lər, -z
Heckmondwike
BR ˈhɛkmən(d)wʌɪk
AM ˈhɛkmən(d)ˌwaɪk
hectarage
BR ˈhɛkt(ə)rɪdʒ
AM ˈhɛktərɪdʒ
hectare
BR ˈhɛktɛː(r), -z
AM ˈhɛkˌtɛ(ə)r, -z
hectic
BR ˈhɛktɪk
AM ˈhɛktɪk
hectically
BR ˈhɛktɨkli
AM ˈhɛktək(ə)li

hectogram
BR ˈhɛktəgram, -z
AM ˈhɛktəˌgræm, -z

hectograph
BR ˈhɛktəgrɑːf, ˈhɛktəgraf, -s
AM ˈhɛktəˌgræf, -s

hectoliter
BR ˈhɛktəˌliːtə(r), -z
AM ˈhɛktəˌlidər, -z

hectolitre
BR ˈhɛktəˌliːtə(r), -z
AM ˈhɛktəˌlidər, -z

hectometer
BR ˈhɛktəˌmiːtə(r), -z
AM ˈhɛktəˌmidər, -z

hectometre
BR ˈhɛktəˌmiːtə(r), -z
AM ˈhɛktəˌmidər, -z

hector
BR ˈhɛkt|ə(r), -əz, -(ə)rɪŋ, -əd
AM ˈhɛkt|ər, -ərz, -(ə)rɪŋ, -ərd

hectoringly
BR ˈhɛkt(ə)rɪŋli
AM ˈhɛkt(ə)rɪŋli

Hecuba
BR ˈhɛkjʊbə(r)
AM ˈhɛkjəbə

he'd[1]
strong form
BR hiːd
AM hid

he'd[2]
weak form
BR (h)ɪd
AM (h)ɪd

heddle
BR ˈhɛdl, -z
AM ˈhɛdəl, -z

Hedex®
BR ˈhɛdɛks
AM ˈhɛdɛks

hedge
BR hɛdʒ, -ɪz, -ɪŋ, -d
AM hɛdʒ, -əz, -ɪŋ, -d

hedgehog
BR ˈhɛdʒ(h)ɒg, -z
AM ˈhɛdʒˌ(h)ɔg, ˈhɛdʒˌ(h)ɑg, -z

hedgehop
BR ˈhɛdʒhɒp, -s, -ɪŋ, -t
AM ˈhɛdʒˌ(h)ɑp, -s, -ɪŋ, -t

hedgehopper
BR ˈhɛdʒˌhɒpə(r), -z
AM ˈhɛdʒˌ(h)ɑpər, -z

hedger
BR ˈhɛdʒə(r), -z
AM ˈhɛdʒər, -z

hedgerow
BR ˈhɛdʒrəʊ, -z
AM ˈhɛdʒˌroʊ, -z

Hedges
BR ˈhɛdʒɪz
AM ˈhɛdʒəs

Hedley
BR ˈhɛdli
AM ˈhɛdli

hedonic
BR hiːˈdɒnɪk, hɪˈdɒnɪk
AM hiˈdɑnɪk

hedonism
BR ˈhiːdn̩ɪz(ə)m, ˈhiːdənɪz(ə)m, ˈhɛdn̩ɪz(ə)m, ˈhɛdənɪz(ə)m
AM ˈhidnˌɪzəm, ˈhidəˌnɪzəm

hedonist
BR ˈhiːdn̩ɪst, ˈhiːdənɪst, ˈhɛdn̩ɪst, ˈhɛdənɪst, -s
AM ˈhidn̩əst, ˈhidənəst, -s

hedonistic
BR ˌhiːdəˈnɪstɪk, ˌhɛdəˈnɪstɪk
AM ˌhidnˈɪstɪk

hedonistically
BR ˌhiːdəˈnɪstɪkli, ˌhɛdəˈnɪstɪkli
AM ˌhidnˈɪstək(ə)li, ˌhidəˈnɪstək(ə)li

heebie-jeebies
BR ˌhiːbɪˈdʒiːbɪz
AM ˈhibiˈdʒibiz

heed
BR hiːd, -z, -ɪŋ, -ɪd
AM hid, -z, -ɪŋ, -ɪd

heedful
BR ˈhiːdf(ʊ)l
AM ˈhidfəl

heedfully
BR ˈhiːdfʊli, ˈhiːdfl̩i
AM ˈhidfəli

heedfulness
BR ˈhiːdf(ʊ)lnəs
AM ˈhidfəlnəs

heedless
BR ˈhiːdlɪs
AM ˈhidlɪs

heedlessly
BR ˈhiːdlɪsli
AM ˈhidlɪsli

heedlessness
BR ˈhiːdlɪsnɪs
AM ˈhidlɪsnɪs

hee-haw
BR ˈhiːhɔː(r), ˌhiːˈhɔː(r), -z, -ɪŋ, -d
AM ˈhiˌhɔ, ˈhiˌhɑ, -z, -ɪŋ, -d

heel
BR hiːl, -z, -ɪŋ, -d
AM hil, -z, -ɪŋ, -d

heelball
BR ˈhiːlbɔːl
AM ˈhilˌbɔl, ˈhilˌbɑl

heelbar
BR ˈhiːlbɑː(r), -z
AM ˈhilˌbɑr, -z

heelless
BR ˈhiː(l)lɪs
AM ˈhi(l)lɪs

heeltap
BR ˈhiːltap, -s
AM ˈhilˌtæp, -s

Heep
BR hiːp
AM hip

Heffernan
BR ˈhɛfənən
AM ˈhɛfərnən

heft
BR hɛft, -s, -ɪŋ, -ɪd
AM hɛft, -s, -ɪŋ, -əd

heftily
BR ˈhɛftɪli
AM ˈhɛftəli

heftiness
BR ˈhɛftɪnɪs
AM ˈhɛftinɪs

hefty
BR ˈhɛft|i, -ɪə(r), -ɪɪst
AM ˈhɛfti, -ər, -ɪst

Hegarty
BR ˈhɛgəti
AM ˈhɛgərdi

Hegel
BR ˈheɪgl
AM ˈheɪgəl

Hegelian
BR hɪˈgeɪlɪən, heɪˈgeɪlɪən, -z
AM həˈgeɪliən, -z

Hegelianism
BR hɪˈgeɪlɪənɪz(ə)m, heɪˈgeɪlɪənɪz(ə)m
AM həˈgeɪliəˌnɪzəm

hegemonic
BR ˌhɛgɪˈmɒnɪk, ˌhɛdʒɪˈmɒnɪk
AM ˌhɛgəˈmɑnɪk

hegemony
BR hɪˈgɛməni, hɪˈdʒɛməni, ˈhɛgɪməni, ˈhɛdʒɪməni
AM həˈdʒɛməni, ˈhɛdʒəˌmoʊni

Hegira
BR hɪˈdʒʌɪrə(r)
AM həˈdʒaɪrə, ˈhɛdʒərə

Heidegger
BR ˈhʌɪdɛgə(r), ˈhʌɪdɪgə(r)
AM ˈhaɪdəgər

Heidelberg
BR ˈhʌɪdlbəːg
AM ˈhaɪdlˌbərg

Heidi
BR ˈhʌɪdi
AM ˈhaɪdi

heifer
BR ˈhɛfə(r), -z
AM ˈhɛfər, -z

heigh
BR heɪ
AM haɪ, heɪ

heigh-ho
BR ˌheɪˈhəʊ, ˈheɪhəʊ
AM ˈheɪˈhoʊ

height
BR hʌɪt, -s
AM haɪt, -s

heighten
BR ˈhʌɪtn̩, -z, -ɪŋ, -d
AM ˈhaɪtn, -z, -ɪŋ, -d

Heilbronn
BR ˈhʌɪlbrɒn
AM ˈhaɪlˌbrɑn
GER haɪlˈbrɔn

Heilong
BR ˌhʌɪˈlɒŋ
AM ˈhaɪˈlɔŋ, ˈhaɪˈlɑŋ

Heimlich
BR ˈhʌɪmlɪç
AM ˈhaɪmlɪk

Heine
BR ˈhʌɪni, ˈhʌɪnə(r)
AM ˈhaɪnə, ˈhaɪni

Heineken®
BR ˈhʌɪnɪk(ə)n
AM ˈhaɪnəkən

Heinemann
BR ˈhʌɪnɪmən
AM ˈhaɪnəmən

Heiney
BR ˈhʌɪni
AM ˈhaɪni

Heinkel
BR ˈhʌɪŋkl
AM ˈhaɪŋkəl

Heinlein
BR ˈhʌɪnlʌɪn
AM ˈhaɪnˌlaɪn

heinous
BR ˈheɪnəs, ˈhiːnəs
AM ˈheɪnəs

heinously
BR ˈheɪnəsli, ˈhiːnəsli
AM ˈheɪnəsli

heinousness
BR ˈheɪnəsnəs, ˈhiːnəsnəs
AM ˈheɪnəsnəs

Heinz
BR hʌɪnz, hʌɪns
AM haɪn(t)s

heir
BR ɛː(r), -z
AM ɛ(ə)r, -z

heirdom
BR ˈɛːdəm
AM ˈɛrdəm

heiress
BR ˈɛːrɪs, ˈɛːrɛs, ˌɛːˈrɛs, -ɪz
AM ˈɛrəs, -əz

heirless
BR ˈɛːləs
AM ˈɛrləs

heirloom
BR ˈɛːluːm, -z
AM ˈɛrˌlum, -z

heirship
BR ˈɛːʃɪp
AM ˈɛrˌʃɪp

Heisenberg
BR ˈhʌɪznbəːg
AM ˈhaɪzən,bərg
heist
BR hʌɪst, -s, -ɪŋ, -ɨd
AM haɪst, -s, -ɪŋ, -ɨd
hei-tiki
BR ˌheɪˈtɪk|i, -ɪz
AM ˌheɪˈti,ki, -z
Hejira
BR hɪˈdʒʌɪrə(r)
AM həˈdʒaɪrə, ˈhɛdʒərə
Hekla
BR ˈhɛklə(r)
AM ˈhɛklə
HeLa
BR ˈhiːlə(r)
AM ˈhɛlə
held
BR hɛld
AM hɛld
Heldentenor
BR ˌhɛldnˈtɛnə(r), -z
AM ˈhɛldən,tɛnər, -z
hele
BR hiːl, -z, -ɪŋ, -d
AM hil, -z, -ɪŋ, -d
Helen
BR ˈhɛlɪn
AM ˈhɛlən
Helena
BR ˈhɛlɪnə(r)
AM ˈhɛlənə
helenium
BR hɪˈliːnɪəm
AM həˈliniəm
Helga
BR ˈhɛlgə(r)
AM ˈhɛlgə
Helgoland
BR ˈhɛlgəland
AM ˈhɛlgə,lænd
heliacal
BR hɪˈlʌɪəkl, hɛˈlʌɪəkl
AM həˈlaɪəkəl, hiˈlaɪəkəl
helianthemum
BR ˌhiːlɪˈanθɨməm, -z
AM ˌhiliˈænθəməm, -z
helianthus
BR ˌhiːlɪˈanθəs, -ɪz
AM ˌhiliˈænθəs, -əz
helical
BR ˈhɛlɨkl
AM ˈhilɨkəl, ˈhɛləkəl
helically
BR ˈhɛlɨkli
AM ˈhilɨk(ə)li, ˈhɛlək(ə)li
helices
BR ˈhɛlɨsiːz
AM ˈhilə,siz, ˈhɛlə,siz
helichrysum
BR ˌhɛlɪˈkrʌɪsəm, -z
AM ˌhɛləˈkraɪsəm, -z
helicity
BR hiːˈlɪsɪti
AM ˌhiˈlɪsɨdi
helicoid
BR ˈhɛlɨkɔɪd, -z
AM ˈhɛlə,kɔɪd, -z
Helicon
BR ˈhɛlɨk(ə)n, ˈhɛlɨkɒn, -z
AM ˈhɛlə,kɑn, ˈhɛləkən, -z
helicopter
BR ˈhɛlɨkɒptə(r), -z
AM ˈhɛlə,kɑptər, -z
helideck
BR ˈhɛlɪdɛk, -s
AM ˈhɛlə,dɛk, -s
Heligoland
BR ˈhɛlɨgə(ʊ)land
AM ˈhɛləgoʊ,lænd
heliocentric
BR ˌhiːlɪə(ʊ)ˈsɛntrɪk
AM ˌhiliəˈsɛntrɪk
heliocentrically
BR ˌhiːlɪə(ʊ)ˈsɛntrɪkli
AM ˌhiliəˈsɛntrək(ə)li
Heliogabalus
BR ˌhiːlɪə(ʊ)ˈgabələs, ˌhiːlɪə(ʊ)ˈgabl̩əs
AM ˌhiliəˈgæbələs
heliogram
BR ˈhiːlɪəgram, -z
AM ˈhilioʊ,græm, -z
heliograph
BR ˈhiːlɪəgrɑːf, ˈhiːlɪəgraf, -s, -ɪŋ, -t
AM ˈhilioʊ,græf, -s, -ɪŋ, -t
heliography
BR ˌhiːlɪˈɒgrəfi
AM ˌhiliˈɑgrəfi
heliogravure
BR ˌhiːlɪəʊgrəˈvjʊə(r)
AM ˌhilioʊgrəˈvjʊ(ə)r
heliolithic
BR ˌhiːlɪəˈlɪθɪk
AM ˌhiliəˈlɪθɪk
heliometer
BR ˌhiːlɪˈɒmɪtə(r), -z
AM ˌhiliˈɑmədər, -z
Heliopolis
BR ˌhiːlɪˈɒpəlɪs, ˌhiːlɪˈɒplɪs
AM ˌhiliˈɑpələs
Helios
BR ˈhiːlɪɒs
AM ˈhili,ɑs, ˈhiliəs
heliostat
BR ˈhiːlɪəstat, -s
AM ˈhiliə,stæt, ˈhiljə,stæt, -s
heliostatic
BR ˌhiːlɪəˈstatɪk
AM ˌhiliəˈstædɪk
heliotherapy
BR ˌhiːlɪəʊˈθɛrəpi
AM ˌhiliəˈθɛrəpi, ˌhiljəˈθɛrəpi
heliotrope
BR ˈhiːlɪətrəʊp, -s
AM ˈhiliə,troʊp, ˈhiljə,troʊp, -s
heliotropic
BR ˌhiːlɪə(ʊ)ˈtrɒpɪk, ˌhiːlɪəˈtrəʊpɪk
AM ˌhiliəˈtrɑpɪk
heliotropically
BR ˌhiːlɪə(ʊ)ˈtrəʊpɨkli, ˌhiːlɪəˈtrɒpɨkli
AM ˌhiliəˈtrɑpək(ə)li
heliotropism
BR ˌhiːlɪə(ʊ)ˈtrəʊpɪz(ə)m, ˌhiːlɪˈɒtrəpɪz(ə)m
AM ˌhiliəˈtrɑ,pɪzəm
heliotype
BR ˈhiːlɪətʌɪp, -s
AM ˈhiliə,taɪp, ˈhiljə,taɪp, -s
helipad
BR ˈhɛlɪpad, -z
AM ˈhɛlə,pæd, -z
heliport
BR ˈhɛlɪpɔːt, -s
AM ˈhɛlə,pɔ(ə)rt, -s
heli-skiing
BR ˈhɛlɪ,skiːɪŋ
AM ˈhɛli,skiɪŋ
helium
BR ˈhiːlɪəm
AM ˈhiliəm
helix
BR ˈhiːlɪks, -ɪz
AM ˈhilɪks, -ɪz
hell
BR hɛl
AM hɛl
he'll
BR hiːl
AM hil
hellacious
BR hɛˈleɪʃəs
AM hɛˈleɪʃəs
hellaciously
BR hɛˈleɪʃəsli
AM hɛˈleɪʃəsli
Helladic
BR hɛˈladɪk, -s
AM hɛˈlædɪk, -s
Hellas
BR ˈhɛlas
AM ˈhɛləs
hellcat
BR ˈhɛlkat, -s
AM ˈhɛl,kæt, -s
hellebore
BR ˈhɛlɪbɔː(r)
AM ˈhɛlə,bɔ(ə)r
helleborine
BR ˈhɛlɪbəriːn, ˈhɛlɪbərʌɪn, -z
AM ˈhɛləbə,raɪn, ˈhɛləbə,rin, -z
Hellene
BR ˈhɛliːn, -z
AM ˈhɛ,lin, -z
Hellenic
BR hɪˈlɛnɪk, hɛˈlɛnɪk
AM hɛˈlɛnɪk
Hellenisation
BR ˌhɛlɪnʌɪˈzeɪʃn
AM ˌhɛlənəˈzeɪʃən, ˌhɛlə,naɪˈzeɪʃən
Hellenise
BR ˈhɛlɪnʌɪz, -ɪz, -ɪŋ, -d
AM ˈhɛlə,naɪz, -ɪz, -ɪŋ, -d
Hellenism
BR ˈhɛlɪnɪz(ə)m, -z
AM ˈhɛlə,nɪzəm, -z
Hellenist
BR ˈhɛlɪnɪst, -s
AM ˈhɛlənəst, -s
Hellenistic
BR ˌhɛlɪˈnɪstɪk
AM ˌhɛləˈnɪstɪk
Hellenization
BR ˌhɛlɪnʌɪˈzeɪʃn
AM ˌhɛlənəˈzeɪʃən, ˌhɛlə,naɪˈzeɪʃən
Hellenize
BR ˈhɛlɪnʌɪz, -ɪz, -ɪŋ, -d
AM ˈhɛlə,naɪz, -ɪz, -ɪŋ, -d
Heller
BR ˈhɛlə(r)
AM ˈhɛlər
Hellespont
BR ˈhɛlɪspɒnt
AM ˈhɛlə,spɑnt
hellfire
BR ˌhɛlˈfʌɪə(r), ˈhɛlfʌɪə(r)
AM ˈhɛlˈfaɪ(ə)r
hell-for-leather
BR ˌhɛlfəˈlɛðə(r)
AM ˈhɛlfərˈlɛðər
hellgrammite
BR ˈhɛlgrəmʌɪt, -s
AM ˈhɛlgrə,maɪt, -s
hellhole
BR ˈhɛlhəʊl, -z
AM ˈhɛl,(h)oʊl, -z
hellhound
BR ˈhɛlhaʊnd, -z
AM ˈhɛl,(h)aʊnd, -z
hellion
BR ˈhɛljən, -z
AM ˈhɛljən, -z
hellish
BR ˈhɛlɪʃ
AM ˈhɛlɪʃ
hellishly
BR ˈhɛlɪʃli
AM ˈhɛlɪʃli
hellishness
BR ˈhɛlɪʃnɪs
AM ˈhɛlɪʃnɪs
hell-like
BR ˈhɛllʌɪk
AM ˈhɛl,laɪk
Hellman
BR ˈhɛlmən
AM ˈhɛlmən

hello
BR həˈləʊ, hɛˈləʊ, -z
AM həˈloʊ, hɛˈloʊ, -z

hellraiser
BR ˈhɛlˌreɪzə(r), -z
AM ˈhɛlˌreɪzər, -z

hellraising
BR ˈhɛlˌreɪzɪŋ
AM ˈhɛlˌreɪzɪŋ

helluva
BR ˈhɛləvə(*r*)
AM ˈhɛləvə

hellward
BR ˈhɛlwəd
AM ˈhɛlwərd

helm
BR hɛlm, -z
AM hɛlm, -z

helmet
BR ˈhɛlmɪt, -s, -ɪd
AM ˈhɛlmə|t, -ts, -dəd

Helmholtz
BR ˈhɛlmhɒlts, ˈhɛlmhəʊlts
AM ˈhɛlmˌ(h)oʊlts

helminth
BR ˈhɛlmɪnθ, -s
AM ˈhɛlmənθ, -s

helminthiasis
BR ˌhɛlmɪnˈθʌɪəsɪs
AM ˌhɛlmənˈθaɪəsəs

helminthic
BR hɛlˈmɪnθɪk
AM hɛlˈmɪnθɪk

helminthoid
BR ˈhɛlmɪnθɔɪd
AM hɛlˈmɪnˌθɔɪd, ˈhɛlmənˌθɔɪd

helminthologist
BR ˌhɛlmɪnˈθɒlədʒɪst, -s
AM ˌhɛlmənˈθɑlədʒəst, -s

helminthology
BR ˌhɛlmɪnˈθɒlədʒi
AM ˌhɛlmənˈθɑlədʒi

Helms
BR hɛlmz
AM hɛlmz

helmsman
BR ˈhɛlmzmən
AM ˈhɛlmzmən

helmsmen
BR ˈhɛlmzmən
AM ˈhɛlmzmən

Héloïse
BR ˈɛləʊiːz, ˌɛləʊˈiːz
AM ˈ(h)ɛləˌwiz

Helot
BR ˈhɛlət, -s
AM ˈhɛlət, -s

helotism
BR ˈhɛlətɪz(ə)m
AM ˈhɛləˌtɪzəm

helotry
BR ˈhɛlətri
AM ˈhɛlətri

help
BR hɛlp, -s, -ɪŋ, -t
AM hɛlp, -s, -ɪŋ, -t

helper
BR ˈhɛlpə(r), -z
AM ˈhɛlpər, -z

helpful
BR ˈhɛlpf(ʊ)l
AM ˈhɛlpfəl

helpfully
BR ˈhɛlpfʊli, ˈhɛlpfl̩i
AM ˈhɛlpfəli

helpfulness
BR ˈhɛlpf(ʊl)nəs
AM ˈhɛlpfəlnəs

helping
BR ˈhɛlpɪŋ, -z
AM ˈhɛlpɪŋ, -z

helpless
BR ˈhɛlpləs
AM ˈhɛlpləs

helplessly
BR ˈhɛlpləsli
AM ˈhɛlpləsli

helplessness
BR ˈhɛlpləsnəs
AM ˈhɛlpləsnəs

helpline
BR ˈhɛlplʌɪn, -z
AM ˈhɛlpˌlaɪn, -z

Helpmann
BR ˈhɛlpmən
AM ˈhɛlpmən

helpmate
BR ˈhɛlpmeɪt, -s
AM ˈhɛlpˌmeɪt, -s

helpmeet
BR ˈhɛlpmiːt, -s
AM ˈhɛlpˌmit, -s

Helsingborg
BR ˈhɛlsɪŋbɔːɡ
AM ˈhɛlsɪŋˌbɔ(ə)rɡ

Helsingfors
BR ˈhɛlsɪŋfɔːz
AM ˈhɛlsɪŋˌfɔ(ə)rz

Helsingør
BR ˈhɛlsɪŋə(r)
AM ˈhɛlsɪŋər
DAN ˌhɛlseŋˈœːˀʌ

Helsinki
BR hɛlˈsɪŋki, ˈhɛlsɪŋki
AM hɛlˈsɪŋki, ˈhɛlsɪŋki

helter-skelter
BR ˌhɛltəˈskɛltə(r), -z
AM ¦hɛltərˈskɛltər, -z

helve
BR hɛlv, -z
AM hɛlv, -z

Helvellyn
BR hɛlˈvɛlɪn
AM hɛlˈvɛlən

Helvetia
BR hɛlˈviːʃ(ɪ)ə(*r*)
AM hɛlˈviʃə

Helvetian
BR hɛlˈviːʃ(ə)n, -z
AM hɛlˈviʃən, -z

Helvetic
BR hɛlˈvɛtɪk
AM hɛlˈvɛdɪk

hem
BR hɛm, -z, -ɪŋ, -d
AM hɛm, -z, -ɪŋ, -d

hemal
BR ˈhiːml
AM ˈhiməl

he-man
BR ˈhiːman
AM ˈhiˌmæn

hematic
BR hiːˈmatɪk
AM hiˈmædɪk

hematin
BR ˈhiːmətɪn
AM ˈhiməˌtin

hematite
BR ˈhiːmətʌɪt
AM ˈhiməˌtaɪt

hematocele
BR hɪˈmatəsiːl
AM hiˈmædoʊˌsil

hematocrit
BR hɪˈmatəkrɪt, ˈhiːmətə(ʊ)krɪt, -s
AM hiˈmædəˌkrɪt, -s

hematologic
BR ˌhiːmətəˈlɒdʒɪk
AM ˌhimədoʊˈlɑdʒɪk

hematological
BR ˌhiːmətəˈlɒdʒɪkl
AM ˌhimədoʊˈlɑdʒəkəl

hematologist
BR ˌhiːməˈtɒlədʒɪst, -s
AM ˌhiməˈtɑlədʒəst, -s

hematology
BR ˌhiːməˈtɒlədʒi
AM ˌhiməˈtɑlədʒi

hematoma
BR ˌhiːməˈtəʊmə(*r*), -z
AM ˌhiməˈtoʊmə, -z

hematuria
BR ˌhiːməˈtjʊərɪə(*r*), ˌhiːməˈtʃʊərɪə(*r*)
AM ˌhiməˈtʊriə

heme
BR hiːm
AM him

Hemel Hempstead
BR ˌhɛml ˈhɛm(p)stɛd
AM ¦hɛməl ˈhɛm(p)ˌstɛd

he-men
BR ˈhiːmɛn
AM ˈhiˌmɛn

hemerocallis
BR ˌhɛm(ə)rəʊˈkalɪs
AM ˌhɛməroʊˈkæləs

hemianopia
BR ˌhɛmɪəˈnəʊpɪə(*r*)
AM ˌhimiəˈnoʊpiə

hemianopsia
BR ˌhɛmɪəˈnɒpsɪə(*r*)
AM ˌhimiəˈnɑpsiə

hemicellulose
BR ˌhɛmɪˈsɛljʊləʊs, ˌhɛmɪˈsɛljʊləʊz, -ɪz
AM ¦hɛməˈsɛl(j)əloʊs, ¦hɛməˈsɛl(j)əloʊz, -əz

hemicycle
BR ˈhɛmɪˌsʌɪkl, -z
AM ˈhɛməˌsaɪkəl, -z

hemidemisemiquav
BR ˌhɛmɪˌdɛmɪˈsɛmɪˌkweɪ
-z
AM ˈhɛmiˌdɛmiˌsɛməɪˈkw
-z

hemihedral
BR ˌhɛmɪˈhiːdr(ə)l
AM ¦hɛməˈhidrəl

Hemingway
BR ˈhɛmɪŋweɪ
AM ˈhɛmɪŋɡweɪ

hemiplegia
BR ˌhɛmɪˈpliːdʒ(ɪ)ə(*r*)
AM ˌhɛməˈpli(d)ʒə

hemiplegic
BR ˌhɛmɪˈpliːdʒɪk, -s
AM ¦hɛməˈplidʒɪk, -s

Hemiptera
BR hɪˈmɪpt(ə)rə(*r*)
AM həˈmɪptərə

hemipteran
BR hɪˈmɪpt(ə)rən, hɪˈmɪpt(ə)rn̩, -z
AM həˈmɪptərən, -z

hemipterous
BR hɪˈmɪpt(ə)rəs
AM həˈmɪptərəs

hemisphere
BR ˈhɛmɪsfɪə(r), -z
AM ˈhɛməˌsfɪ(ə)r, -z

hemispheric
BR ˌhɛmɪˈsfɛrɪk
AM ¦hɛməˈsfɪrɪk, ¦hɛməˈsfɛrɪk

hemispherical
BR ˌhɛmɪˈsfɛrɪkl
AM ¦hɛməˈsfɪrɪkəl, ¦hɛməˈsfɛrəkəl

hemispherically
BR ˌhɛmɪˈsfɛrɪkli
AM ¦hɛməˈsfɪrɪk(ə)li, ¦hɛməˈsfɛrək(ə)li

hemistich
BR ˈhɛmɪstɪk, -s
AM ˈhɛməstɪk, -s

hemline
BR ˈhɛmlʌɪn, -z
AM ˈhɛmˌlaɪn, -z

hemlock
BR ˈhɛmlɒk
AM ˈhɛmˌlɑk

hemocyanin
BR ˌhiːmə(ʊ)ˈsʌɪənɪn, -z
AM ˌhiməˈsaɪənən, -z

hemodialysis
BR ˌhiːmə(ʊ)dʌɪˈalɪsɪs, -ɪz
AM ˌhimoʊˌdaɪˈæləsəs, -əs

hemodynamic
BR ˌhiːmə(ʊ)dʌɪˈnamɪk
AM ˌhimoʊdaɪˈnæmɪk
hemoglobin
BR ˌhiːməˈgləʊbɪn
AM ˈhiməˌgloʊbən
hemolysis
BR hiːˈmɒlɨsɪs
AM hiˈmɑləsəs
hemolytic
BR ˌhiːməˈlɪtɪk
AM ˌhiməˈlɪdɪk
hemophilia
BR ˌhiːməˈfɪlɪə(r)
AM ˌhiməˈfɪljə, ˌhiməˈfɪliə
hemophiliac
BR ˌhiːməˈfɪlɪak, -s
AM ˌhiməˈfɪliˌæk, -s
hemophilic
BR ˌhiːməˈfɪlɪk, -s
AM ˌhiməˈfɪlɪk, -s
hemophyliac
BR ˌhiːməˈfɪlɪak, -s
AM ˌhiməˈfɪliˌæk, -s
hemorrhage
BR ˈhɛm(ə)r|ɪdʒ, -ɪdʒɪz, -ɪdʒɪŋ, -ɪdʒd
AM ˈhɛm(ə)rɪdʒ, -ɪz, -ɪŋ, -d
hemorrhagic
BR ˌhɛməˈradʒɪk
AM ˌhɛməˈrædʒɪk
hemorrhoid
BR ˈhɛmərɔɪd, -z
AM ˈhɛm(ə)ˌrɔɪd, -z
hemorrhoidal
BR ˌhɛməˈrɔɪdl
AM ˌhɛm(ə)ˈrɔɪdəl
hemostasis
BR ˌhiːmə(ʊ)ˈsteɪsɪs
AM ˌhiməˈsteɪsəs
hemostat
BR ˈhiːməstat, -s
AM ˈhiməˌstæt, -s
hemostatic
BR ˌhiːməˈstatɪk
AM ˌhiməˈstædɪk
hemp
BR hɛmp
AM hɛmp
hempen
BR ˈhɛmpən
AM ˈhɛmpən
hemp-nettle
BR ˈhɛmpˌnɛtl, -z
AM ˈhɛmpˌnɛdəl, -z
hemstitch
BR ˈhɛmstɪtʃ
AM ˈhɛmˌstɪtʃ
hen
BR hɛn, -z
AM hɛn, -z
Henan
BR ˈhiːnən
AM ˈhinən
henbane
BR ˈhɛnbeɪn
AM ˈhɛnˌbeɪn
hence
BR hɛns
AM hɛns
henceforth
BR ˌhɛnsˈfɔːθ, ˈhɛnsfɔːθ
AM ˌhɛnsˈfɔ(ə)rθ
henceforward
BR ˌhɛnsˈfɔːwəd
AM ˌhɛnsˈfɔrwərd
henchman
BR ˈhɛn(t)ʃmən
AM ˈhɛn(t)ʃmən
henchmen
BR ˈhɛn(t)ʃmən
AM ˈhɛn(t)ʃmən
hencoop
BR ˈhɛnkuːp, -s
AM ˈhɛnˌkup, -s
hendecagon
BR hɛnˈdɛkəg(ə)n, hɛnˈdɛkəgɒn, -z
AM hɛnˈdɛkəˌgɑn, -z
hendecasyllabic
BR ˌhɛndɛkəsɪˈlabɪk, -s
AM hɛnˌdɛkəsəˈlæbɪk, -s
hendecasyllable
BR ˌhɛndɛkəˈsɪləbl, hɛnˌdɛkəˈsɪləbl, -z
AM hɛnˈdɛkəˌsɪləbəl, hɛnˌdɛkəˈsɪləbəl, -z
Henderson
BR ˈhɛndəs(ə)n
AM ˈhɛndərsən
hendiadys
BR hɛnˈdʌɪədɪs
AM hɛnˈdaɪədəs
Hendon
BR ˈhɛnd(ə)n
AM ˈhɛndən
Hendricks
BR ˈhɛndrɪks
AM ˈhɛndrɪks
Hendrickson
BR ˈhɛndrɪks(ə)n
AM ˈhɛndrɪksən
Hendrix
BR ˈhɛndrɪks
AM ˈhɛndrɪks
Hendry
BR ˈhɛndri
AM ˈhɛndri
Hendy
BR ˈhɛndi
AM ˈhɛndi
henequen
BR ˈhɛnɪkɛn
AM ˈhɛnəkən
henge
BR hɛn(d)ʒ, -ɪz
AM hɛndʒ, -əz
Hengist
BR ˈhɛŋgɪst
AM ˈhɛŋgəst
henhouse
BR ˈhɛnhaʊ|s, -zɪz
AM ˈhɛnˌ(h)aʊ|s, -zəz
Henley
BR ˈhɛnli
AM ˈhɛnli
henna
BR ˈhɛnə(r), -d
AM ˈhɛnə, -d
Hennessey
BR ˈhɛnɪsi
AM ˈhɛnəsi
Hennessy
BR ˈhɛnɪsi
AM ˈhɛnəsi
henotheism
BR ˈhɛnəʊˌθiːɪz(ə)m, ˌhɛnəʊˈθiːɪz(ə)m
AM ˈhɛnoʊθiˌɪzəm, ˌhɛnoʊˈθiˌɪzəm
henpeck
BR ˈhɛnpɛk, -s, -ɪŋ, -t
AM ˈhɛnˌpɛk, -s, -ɪŋ, -t
Henri
English surname
BR ˈhɛnri
AM ˈhɛnri
Henrietta
BR ˌhɛnrɪˈɛtə(r)
AM ˌhɛnriˈɛdə
Henriques
BR hɛnˈriːkɪz
AM hɛnˈrikɪz
henry
BR ˈhɛnr|i, -ɪz
AM ˈhɛnri, -z
Henshaw
BR ˈhɛnʃɔː(r)
AM ˈhɛnˌʃɔ
Hensley
BR ˈhɛnzli
AM ˈhɛnzli
Henson
BR ˈhɛnsn
AM ˈhɛnsən
Henty
BR ˈhɛnti
AM ˈhɛn(t)i
Henze
BR ˈhɛntsə(r)
AM ˈhɛn(t)sə
heortologist
BR ˌhɪɔːˈtɒlədʒɪst, -s
AM hiˌɔrˈtɑlədʒəst, -s
heortology
BR ˌhɪɔːˈtɒlədʒi
AM hiˌɔrˈtɑlədʒi
hep
BR hɛp
AM hɛp, həp
heparin
BR ˈhɛpərɪn
AM ˈhɛpərən
heparinise
BR ˈhɛp(ə)rɪnʌɪz, -ɪz, -ɪŋ, -d
AM ˈhɛpərəˌnaɪz, -ɪz, -ɪŋ, -d
heparinize
BR ˈhɛp(ə)rɪnʌɪz, -ɪz, -ɪŋ, -d
AM ˈhɛpərəˌnaɪz, -ɪz, -ɪŋ, -d
hepatic
BR hɪˈpatɪk, hɛˈpatɪk
AM həˈpædɪk
hepatica
BR hɪˈpatɪkə(r), hɛˈpatɪkə(r)
AM həˈpædɪkə
hepatitis
BR ˌhɛpəˈtʌɪtɪs
AM ˌhɛpəˈtaɪdɪs
hepatocyte
BR ˈhɛpətə(ʊ)sʌɪt, hɪˈpatə(ʊ)sʌɪt, hɛˈpatəʊsʌɪt, -s
AM həˈpædəˌsaɪt, -s
hepatomegaly
BR ˌhɛpətəʊˈmɛgəli, ˌhɛpətəʊˈmɛgḷi
AM həˌpædəˈmɛgəli, ˌhɛpədoʊˈmɛgəli
hepatotoxic
BR ˌhɛpətəʊˈtɒksɪk, hɪˌpatəʊˈtɒksɪk, hɛˌpatəʊˈtɒksɪk
AM həˌpædəˈtɑksɪk
Hepburn
BR ˈhɛ(p)bəːn, ˈhɛb(ə)n
AM ˈhɛpbərn
Hephaestus
BR hɪˈfiːstəs
AM hɪˈfɛstəs
Hephzibah
BR ˈhɛfzɪbɑː(r), ˈhɛpsɪbɑː(r)
AM ˈhɛpzəˌbɑ
Hepplewhite
BR ˈhɛplwʌɪt
AM ˈhɛpəlˌ(h)waɪt
heptachord
BR ˈhɛptəkɔːd, -z
AM ˈhɛptəˌkɔ(ə)rd, -z
heptad
BR ˈhɛptad, -z
AM ˈhɛpˌtæd, -z
heptaglot
BR ˈhɛptəglɒt, -s
AM ˈhɛptəˌglɑt, -s
heptagon
BR ˈhɛptəg(ə)n, ˈhɛptəgɒn, -z
AM ˈhɛptəˌgɑn, -z
heptagonal
BR hɛpˈtagənl, hɛpˈtagṇl
AM hɛpˈtægənəl
heptahedra
BR ˈhɛptəˌhiːdrə(r)
AM ˌhɛptəˈhidrə
heptahedral
BR ˌhɛptəˈhiːdr(ə)l

AM ˌhɛptəˈhidrəl

heptahedron
BR ˈhɛptəˌhiːdr(ə)n, -z
AM ˌhɛptəˈhidˌrɑn, ˌhɛptəˈhidrən, -z

heptameter
BR hɛpˈtamɪtə(r), -z
AM hɛpˈtæmədər, -z

heptane
BR ˈhɛpteɪn, -z
AM ˈhɛpˌteɪn, -z

heptarchic
BR hɛpˈtɑːkɪk
AM hɛpˈtɑrkɪk

heptarchical
BR hɛpˈtɑːkɪkl
AM hɛpˈtɑrkəkəl

heptarchy
BR ˈhɛptɑːk|i, -ɪz
AM ˈhɛpˌtɑrki, -z

heptasyllabic
BR ˌhɛptəsɪˈlabɪk
AM ˌhɛptəsəˈlæbɪk

Heptateuch
BR ˈhɛptətjuːk
AM ˈhɛptəˌt(j)uk

heptathlete
BR hɛpˈtaθliːt, -s
AM hɛpˈtæθlit, -s

heptathlon
BR hɛpˈtaθlən, hɛpˈtaθlɒn, -z
AM hɛpˈtæθˌlɑn, -z

heptavalent
BR ˌhɛptəˈveɪlənt, ˌhɛptəˈveɪln̩t
AM ˌhɛptəˈveɪlənt

Hepworth
BR ˈhɛpwəːθ, ˈhɛpwəθ
AM ˈhɛpˌwərθ

her[1]
strong form
BR həː(r)
AM hər

her[2]
weak form
BR (h)ə(r)
AM (h)ər

Hera
BR ˈhɪərə(r)
AM ˈhɛrə

Heracles
BR ˈhɛrəkliːz
AM ˈhɛrəkliz

Heraclitus
BR ˌhɛrəˈklʌɪtəs
AM ˌhɛrəˈklaɪdəs

Heraklion
BR hɛˈraklɪən
AM hɛˈrækliən

herald
BR ˈhɛrəld, ˈhɛrl̩d, -z, -ɪŋ, -ɪd
AM ˈhɛrəld, -z, -ɪŋ, -əd

heraldic
BR hɪˈraldɪk, hɛˈraldɪk
AM hɛˈrældɪk, həˈrældɪk

heraldically
BR hɪˈraldɪkli, hɛˈraldɪkli
AM hɛˈrældək(ə)li, həˈrældək(ə)li

heraldist
BR ˈhɛrəldɪst, ˈhɛrl̩dɪst, -s
AM ˈhɛrəldəst, -s

heraldry
BR ˈhɛrəldri, ˈhɛrl̩dri
AM ˈhɛrəldri

herb
BR həːb, -z
AM (h)ərb, -z

herbaceous
BR hə(ː)ˈbeɪʃəs
AM (h)ərˈbeɪʃəs

herbage
BR ˈhəːbɪdʒ
AM ˈ(h)ərbɪdʒ

herbal
BR ˈhəːbl
AM ˈ(h)ərbəl

herbalism
BR ˈhəːbəlɪz(ə)m, ˈhəːbl̩ɪz(ə)m
AM ˈ(h)ərbəˌlɪzəm

herbalist
BR ˈhəːbəlɪst, ˈhəːbl̩ɪst, -s
AM ˈ(h)ərbələst, -s

herbaria
BR həːˈbɛːrɪə(r)
AM (h)ərˈbɛriə

herbarium
BR həːˈbɛːrɪəm, -z
AM (h)ərˈbɛriəm, -z

Herbert
BR ˈhəːbət
AM ˈhərbərt

herbicidal
BR ˌhəːbɪˈsʌɪdl
AM ˈ(h)ərbəˌsaɪdəl

herbicide
BR ˈhəːbɪsʌɪd, -z
AM ˈ(h)ərbəˌsaɪd, -z

Herbie
BR ˈhəːbi
AM ˈhərbi

herbiferous
BR həːˈbɪf(ə)rəs, həˈbɪf(ə)rəs
AM (h)ərˈbɪfərəs

herbivore
BR ˈhəːbɪvɔː(r), -z
AM ˈ(h)ərbəˌvɔ(ə)r, -z

herbivorous
BR həːˈbɪv(ə)rəs, həˈbɪv(ə)rəs
AM (h)ərˈbɪvərəs

herbless
BR ˈhəːbləs
AM ˈ(h)ərbləs

herblike
BR ˈhəːblʌɪk
AM ˈ(h)ərbˌlaɪk

herb Paris
BR ˌhəːb ˈparɪs
AM ¦(h)ərb ˈpɛrəs

herb Robert
BR ˌhəːb ˈrɒbət
AM ¦(h)ərb ˈrɑbərt

herb tea
BR ˌhəːb ˈtiː, -z
AM ¦(h)ərb ˈti, -z

herb tobacco
BR ˌhəːb təˈbakəʊ
AM ¦(h)ərb təˈbækoʊ

herby
BR ˈhəːb|i, -ɪə(r), -ɪɪst
AM ˈ(h)ərbi, -ər, -ɪst

Hercegovina
BR ˌhəːtsəˈgɒvɪnə(r), ˌhəːtsəgəˈviːnə(r)
AM ˌhərtsəˈgoʊvinə

Herculaneum
BR ˌhəːkjʊˈleɪnɪəm
AM ˌhərkjəˈleɪniəm

Herculean
BR ˌhəːkjʊˈliːən
AM ˌhərkjəˈliən, hərˈkjuliən

Hercules
BR ˈhəːkjʊliːz, -ɪz
AM ˈhərkjəˌliz, -ɪz

Hercynian
BR həːˈsɪnɪən
AM hərˈsɪniən

herd
BR həːd, -z, -ɪŋ, -ɪd
AM hərd, -z, -ɪŋ, -əd

herder
BR ˈhəːdə(r), -z
AM ˈhərdər, -z

herdsman
BR ˈhəːdzmən
AM ˈhərdzmən

herdsmen
BR ˈhəːdzmən
AM ˈhərdzmən

Herdwick
BR ˈhəːdwɪk, -s
AM ˈhərdˌwɪk, -s

here
BR hɪə(r)
AM hɪ(ə)r

hereabout
BR ˈhɪərəbaʊt, ˌhɪərəˈbaʊt, -s
AM ˌhɪrəˈbaʊt, -s

hereafter
BR ˌhɪərˈɑːftə(r), ˌhɪərˈaftə(r)
AM hɪrˈæftər

hereat
BR ˌhɪərˈat
AM ˈhɪrˈæt

hereby
BR ˌhɪəˈbʌɪ, ˈhɪəbʌɪ
AM ˈhɪrˌbaɪ

hereditable
BR hɪˈrɛdɪtəbl
AM həˈrɛdədəbəl

hereditament
BR ˌhɛrɪˈdɪtəm(ə)nt, -s
AM ˌhɛrəˈdɪdəmənt, -s

hereditarily
BR hɪˈrɛdɪt(ə)rəli, hɪˈrɛdɪt(ə)rl̩i
AM həˌrɛdəˈtɛrəli

hereditariness
BR hɪˈrɛdɪt(ə)rɪnɪs
AM həˈrɛdəˌtɛrinəs

hereditary
BR hɪˈrɛdɪt(ə)ri
AM həˈrɛdəˌtɛri

heredity
BR hɪˈrɛdɪti
AM həˈrɛdədi

Hereford
English town
BR ˈhɛrɪfəd
AM ˈhɛrəfərd

Herefordshire
BR ˈhɛrɪfədʃ(ɪ)ə(r)
AM ˈhɛrəfərdˌʃɪ(ə)r

herein
BR ˌhɪərˈɪn
AM ¦hɪrˈɪn

hereinafter
BR ˌhɪərɪnˈɑːftə(r), ˌhɪərɪnˈaftə(r)
AM ¦hɪrɪn¦æftər

hereinbefore
BR ˌhɪərɪnbɪˈfɔː(r)
AM ¦hɪrɪnbəˌfɔ(ə)r

hereof
BR ˌhɪərˈɒv
AM ¦hɪrˈəv

Herero
BR hɛˈrɛːrəʊ, həˈrɛːrəʊ, həˈrɪərəʊ, -z
AM həˈrɛroʊ, -z

heresiarch
BR hɪˈriːzɪɑːk, hɛˈriːzɪɑːk, -s
AM həˈriziˌɑrk, hɛˈriziˌɑrk, -s

heresiology
BR hɪˌriːzɪˈɒlədʒi, hɛˌriːzɪˈɒlədʒi
AM həˌriziˈɑlədʒi, hɛˌriziˈɑlədʒi

heresy
BR ˈhɛrɪs|i, -ɪz
AM ˈhɛrəsi, -z

heretic
BR ˈhɛrɪtɪk, -s
AM ˈhɛrəˌtɪk, -s

heretical
BR hɪˈrɛtɪkl, hɛˈrɛtɪkl
AM həˈrɛdəkəl, hɛˈrɛdəkəl

heretically
BR hɪˈrɛtɪkli, hɛˈrɛtɪkli

AM hə'rɛdək(ə)li, hɛ'rɛdək(ə)li
hereto
BR ˌhɪə'tuː
AM ˈhɪrˈtu
heretofore
BR ˌhɪətʊ'fɔː(r)
AM ˌhɪrdə'fɔ(ə)r
hereunder
BR ˌhɪər'ʌndə(r)
AM ˌhɪr'əndər
hereunto
BR ˌhɪər'ʌntuː
AM ˈhɪrˈənˈtʊ
hereupon
BR ˌhɪərə'pɒn
AM ˈhɪrə'pɑn
Hereward
BR 'hɛrɪwəd
AM 'hɛrəˌwərd
herewith
BR ˌhɪə'wɪð
AM ˌhɪr'wɪθ, ˌhɪr'wɪð
Herford
BR 'həːfəd
AM 'hərfərd
heriot
BR 'hɛrɪət, -s
AM 'hɛriət, -s
Heriott
BR 'hɛrɪət
AM 'hɛriət
heritability
BR ˌhɛrɪtə'bɪlɪti
AM ˌhɛrədə'bɪlɨdi
heritable
BR 'hɛrɪtəbl
AM 'hɛrədəbəl
heritably
BR 'hɛrɪtəbli
AM 'hɛrədəbli
heritage
BR 'hɛrɪt|ɪdʒ, -ɪdʒɪz
AM 'hɛrədɪdʒ, -ɨz
heritor
BR 'hɛrɪtə(r), -z
AM 'hɛrədər, -z
herky-jerky
BR ˌhəːkɪ'dʒəːki
AM 'hərki'dʒərki
herl
BR həːl
AM hərl
herm
BR həːm, -z
AM hərm, -z
Herman
BR 'həːmən
AM 'hərmən
hermaphrodite
BR hə(ː)'mafrədʌɪt, -s
AM hər'mæfrədaɪt, -s
hermaphroditic
BR hə(ː)ˌmafrə'dɪtɪk
AM hərˌmæfrə'dɪdɪk
hermaphroditical
BR hə(ː)ˌmafrə'dɪtɪkl
AM hərˌmæfrə'dɪdəkəl
hermaphroditism
BR hə(ː)'mafrədɪtɪz(ə)m
AM hər'mæfrədɪˌtɪzəm
hermeneutic
adjective
BR ˌhəːmə'njuːtɪk, -s
AM ˌhərmə'n(j)udɪk, -s
hermeneutical
BR ˌhəːmə'njuːtɪkl
AM ˌhərmə'n(j)udəkəl
hermeneutically
BR ˌhəːmə'njuːtɪkli
AM ˌhərmə'n(j)udək(ə)li
Hermes
BR 'həːmiːz
AM 'hərmiz
hermetic
BR hə(ː)'mɛtɪk
AM hər'mɛdɪk
hermetically
BR hə(ː)'mɛtɪkli
AM hər'mɛdək(ə)li
hermetism
BR 'həːmɪtɪz(ə)m
AM 'hərməˌtɪzəm
Hermia
BR 'həːmɪə(*r*)
AM 'hərmiə
Hermione
BR həː'mʌɪəni, hə'mʌɪəni
AM hər'maɪəni
hermit
BR 'həːmɪt, -s
AM 'hərmət, -s
hermitage
BR 'həːmɪt|ɪdʒ, -ɪdʒɪz
AM 'hərmədɪdʒ, -ɨz
Hermitian
BR hə(ː)'mɪʃn
AM hər'mɪʃən
hermitic
BR hə(ː)'mɪtɪk
AM hər'mɪdɪk
Hermon
BR 'həːmən
AM 'hərmən
Hern
BR həːn
AM hərn
Hernández
BR hə'nandɛz
AM hər'nænˌdɛz
Herne
BR həːn
AM hərn
hernia
BR 'həːnɪə(*r*), -z
AM 'hərniə, -z
hernial
BR 'həːnɪəl
AM 'hərniəl
herniary
BR 'həːnɪəri
AM 'hərniɛri
herniated
BR 'həːnɪeɪtɪd
AM 'hərniˌeɪdɨd
Herning
BR 'həːnɪŋ
AM 'hərnɪŋ
hero
BR 'hɪərəʊ, -z
AM 'hiroʊ, -z
Herod
BR 'hɛrəd
AM 'hɛrəd
Herodias
BR hɪ'rəʊdɪas, hɪ'rəʊdɪəs, hɛ'rəʊdɪas, hɛ'rəʊdɪəs
AM hə'roʊdiəs
Herodotus
BR hɪ'rɒdətəs, hɛ'rɒdətəs
AM hɛ'rɑdədəs
heroic
BR hɪ'rəʊɪk, -s
AM hə'roʊɪk, -s
heroically
BR hɪ'rəʊɪkli
AM hə'roʊək(ə)li
heroi-comic
BR hɪˌrəʊɪ'kɒmɪk
AM həˌroʊə'kɑmɪk, hɛˌroʊə'kɑmɪk
heroi-comical
BR hɪˌrəʊɪ'kɒmɪkl
AM həˌroʊə'kɑməkəl, hɛˌroʊə'kɑməkəl
heroin
BR 'hɛrəʊɪn
AM 'hɛrəwən
heroine
BR 'hɛrəʊɪn, -z
AM 'hɛrəwən, -z
heroise
BR 'hɪərəʊʌɪz, -ɪz, -ɪŋ, -d
AM 'hirəˌwaɪz, -ɨz, -ɪŋ, -d
heroism
BR 'hɛrəʊɪz(ə)m
AM 'hɛrəˌwɪzəm
heroize
BR 'hɪərəʊʌɪz, -ɪz, -ɪŋ, -d
AM 'hirəˌwaɪz, -ɨz, -ɪŋ, -d
heron
BR 'hɛrən, 'hɛrn̩, -z
AM 'hɛrən, -z
heronry
BR 'hɛrənr|i, 'hɛrn̩r|i, -ɪz
AM 'hɛrənri, -z
herpes
BR 'həːpiːz
AM 'hərpiz
herpes simplex
BR ˌhəːpiːz 'sɪmplɛks
AM ˈhərpiz 'sɪmˌplɛks
herpes zoster
BR ˌhəːpiːz 'zɒstə(r)
AM ˈhərpiz 'zɑstər
herpetic
BR həː'pɛtɪk
AM hər'pɛdɪk
herpetological
BR ˌhəːpɪtə'lɒdʒɪkl
AM ˈhərpədə'lɑdʒəkəl
herpetologically
BR ˌhəːpɪtə'lɒdʒɪkli
AM ˈhərpədə'lɑdʒək(ə)li
herpetologist
BR ˌhəːpɪ'tɒlədʒɪst, -s
AM ˌhərpə'tɑlədʒəst, -s
herpetology
BR ˌhəːpɪ'tɒlədʒi
AM ˌhərpə'tɑlədʒi
Herr
BR hɛː(r)
AM hɛ(ə)r
Herrera
BR hɪ'rɛːrə(*r*)
AM hə'rɛrə
Herrick
BR 'hɛrɪk
AM 'hɛrɪk
herring
BR 'hɛrɪŋ, -z
AM 'hɛrɪŋ, -z
herringbone
BR 'hɛrɪŋbəʊn
AM 'hɛrɪŋˌboʊn
Herriot
BR 'hɛrɪət
AM 'hɛriət
Herrnhuter
BR 'həːnˌhuːtə(r), 'hɛːnˌhuːtə(r), 'hɛrənˌhuːtə(r), 'hɛrn̩ˌhuːtə(r), -z
AM 'hərnˌ(h)udər, -z
hers
BR həːz
AM hərz
Herschel
BR 'həːʃl
AM 'hərʃəl
herself¹
strong form
BR həː'sɛlf
AM hər'sɛlf
herself²
weak form
BR (h)ə'sɛlf
AM (h)ər'sɛlf
Hersey
BR 'həːsi
AM 'hərsi
Hershey
BR 'həːʃi
AM 'hərʃi
Herstmonceaux
BR ˌhəːs(t)mən's(j)uː
AM ˌhərs(t)mən'su
Hertford
BR 'hɑːtfəd

AM ˈhɑrtfərd
Hertfordshire
BR ˈhɑːtfədʃ(ɪ)ə(r)
AM ˈhɑrtfərd,ʃɪ(ə)r
Herts.
Hertfordshire
BR hɑːts
AM hɑrts
Hertz
BR həːts
AM hərts
hertz
BR həːts
AM hərts
Hertzog
BR ˈhəːtsɒg, ˈhəːzɒg
AM ˈhərt,sɔg, ˈhər,zɔg, ˈhərt,sɑg, ˈhər,zɑg
Herzegovina
BR ,həːtsəˈgɒvɪnə(r), ,həːtsəgəˈviːnə(r)
AM ,hərtsəˈgoʊvinə
Herzl
BR ˈhəːtsl
AM ˈhərtsəl
Herzog
BR ˈhəːzɒg, ˈhəːtsɒg
AM ˈhər,zɔg, ˈhər,zɑg
he's[1]
strong form
BR hiːz
AM hiz
he's[2]
weak form
BR (h)ɪz
AM (h)ɪz
Heseltine
BR ˈhɛsltʌɪn, ˈhɛzltʌɪn
AM ˈhɛsəl,taɪn
Heshvan
BR ˈhɛʃvən
AM ˈhɛʃvən
Hesiod
BR ˈhɛsjəd
AM ˈhɛsiəd, ˈhɛsjəd
hesitance
BR ˈhɛzɪt(ə)ns
AM ˈhɛzədns
hesitancy
BR ˈhɛzɪt(ə)nsi
AM ˈhɛzədnsi
hesitant
BR ˈhɛzɪt(ə)nt
AM ˈhɛzədənt
hesitantly
BR ˈhɛzɪt(ə)ntli
AM ˈhɛzədən(t)li
hesitate
BR ˈhɛzɪteɪt, -s, -ɪŋ, -ɪd
AM ˈhɛzə,teɪ|t, -ts, -dɪŋ, -dɪd
hesitater
BR ˈhɛzɪteɪtə(r), -z
AM ˈhɛzə,teɪdər, -z
hesitatingly
BR ˈhɛzɪteɪtɪŋli
AM ˈhɛzə,teɪdɪŋli
hesitation
BR ,hɛzɪˈteɪʃn, -z
AM ,hɛzəˈteɪʃən, -z
hesitative
BR ˈhɛzɪtətɪv, ˈhɛzɪteɪtɪv
AM ˈhɛzə,teɪdɪv
Hesketh
BR ˈhɛskɪθ
AM ˈhɛskəθ
Hesperian
BR hɛˈspɪərɪən
AM hɛˈspɪriən
Hesperides
BR hɛˈspɛrɪdiːz
AM hɛˈspɛrədiz
hesperidia
BR ,hɛspɪˈrɪdɪə(r)
AM ,hɛspəˈrɪdiə
hesperidium
BR ,hɛspɪˈrɪdɪəm
AM ,hɛspəˈrɪdiəm
Hesperus
BR ˈhɛsp(ə)rəs
AM ˈhɛspərəs
Hess
BR hɛs
AM hɛs
Hesse
BR hɛs, ˈhɛsə(r)
AM hɛs
Hessen
BR ˈhɛsn
AM ˈhɛsən
Hessian
BR ˈhɛsɪən, -z
AM ˈhɛʃən, -z
Hessle
BR ˈhɛzl
AM ˈhɛsəl
hest
BR hɛst
AM hɛst
Hester
BR ˈhɛstə(r)
AM ˈhɛstər
Heston
BR ˈhɛst(ə)n
AM ˈhɛstən
Hesvan
BR ˈhɛsvən
AM ˈhɛsvən
het
BR hɛt, -s
AM hɛt, -s
hetaera
BR hɪˈtɪərə(r), -z
AM həˈtɪrə, -z
hetaerae
BR hɪˈtɪəriː, hɪˈtɪərʌɪ
AM həˈtɪri, həˈtɛ,raɪ
hetaerism
BR hɪˈtɪərɪz(ə)m
AM həˈtɪ,rɪzəm
hetaira
BR hɪˈtʌɪrə(r), -z
AM həˈtaɪrə, -z
hetairai
BR hɪˈtʌɪrʌɪ
AM həˈtaɪ,raɪ
hetairism
BR hɪˈtʌɪrɪz(ə)m
AM həˈtaɪ,rɪzəm
hetero
BR ˈhɛt(ə)rəʊ, -z
AM ˈhɛdəroʊ, -z
heterochromatic
BR ,hɛt(ə)rəʊkrəˈmatɪk
AM ¦hɛdərəkrəˈmædɪk
heteroclite
BR ˈhɛt(ə)rəklʌɪt, -s
AM ˈhɛdərə,klaɪt, -s
heterocyclic
BR ,hɛt(ə)rə(ʊ)ˈsʌɪklɪk
AM ¦hɛdərəˈsaɪklɪk
heterodox
BR ˈhɛt(ə)rədɒks
AM ˈhɛdərə,dɑks, ˈhɛtrə,dɑks
heterodoxy
BR ˈhɛt(ə)rədɒksi
AM ˈhɛdərə,dɑksi, ˈhɛtrə,dɑksi
heterodyne
BR ˈhɛt(ə)rədʌɪn, -z, -ɪŋ, -d
AM ˈhɛdərə,daɪn, -z, -ɪŋ, -d
heterogamous
BR ,hɛtəˈrɒgəməs
AM ,hɛdəˈrɑgəməs
heterogamy
BR ,hɛtəˈrɒgəmi
AM ,hɛdəˈrɑgəmi
heterogeneity
BR ,hɛt(ə)rə(ʊ)dʒɪˈniːɪti, ,hɛt(ə)rə(ʊ)dʒɪˈneɪɪti
AM ,hɛdərədʒəˈniɪdi, ,hɛdərədʒəˈneɪɪdi
heterogeneous
BR ,hɛt(ə)rəˈdʒiːnɪəs
AM ¦hɛdərəˈdʒiniəs, ¦hɛdərəˈdʒinjəs
heterogeneously
BR ,hɛt(ə)rəˈdʒiːnɪəsli
AM ¦hɛdərəˈdʒiniəsli, ¦hɛdərəˈdʒinjəsli
heterogeneousness
BR ,hɛt(ə)rəˈdʒiːnɪəsnəs
AM ¦hɛdərəˈdʒiniəsnəs, ¦hɛdərəˈdʒinjəsnəs
heterogeneses
BR ,hɛt(ə)rə(ʊ)ˈdʒɛnɪsiːz
AM ¦hɛdərəˈdʒɛnə,siz
heterogenesis
BR ,hɛt(ə)rə(ʊ)ˈdʒɛnɪsɪs
AM ¦hɛdərəˈdʒɛnəsəs
heterogenetic
BR ,hɛt(ə)rədʒɪˈnɛtɪk
AM ¦hɛdərədʒəˈnɛdɪk
heterogeny
BR ,hɛtəˈrɒdʒɪni
AM ,hɛdəˈrɑdʒəni
heterogonous
BR ,hɛtəˈrɒgənəs
AM ,hɛdəˈrɑgənəs
heterogony
BR ,hɛtəˈrɒgəni
AM ,hɛdəˈrɑgəni
heterograft
BR ˈhɛt(ə)rəgrɑːft, ˈhɛt(ə)rəgraft, -s
AM ˈhɛdəroʊ,græft, -s
heterologous
BR ,hɛtəˈrɒləgəs
AM ,hɛdəˈrɑləgəs
heterology
BR ,hɛtəˈrɒlədʒi
AM ,hɛdəˈrɑlədʒi
heteromerous
BR ,hɛtəˈrɒm(ə)rəs
AM ,hɛdəˈrɑm(ə)rəs
heteromorphic
BR ,hɛt(ə)rəˈmɔːfɪk
AM ¦hɛdərəˈmɔrfɪk
heteromorphism
BR ,hɛt(ə)rəˈmɔːfɪz(ə)m
AM ¦hɛdərəˈmɔr,fɪzəm
heteronomous
BR ,hɛtəˈrɒnəməs
AM ,hɛdəˈrɑnəməs
heteronomy
BR ,hɛtəˈrɒnəmi
AM ,hɛdəˈrɑnəmi
heteropathic
BR ,hɛt(ə)rəˈpaθɪk
AM ¦hɛdərəˈpæθɪk
heterophony
BR ,hɛtəˈrɒfən|i, ,hɛtəˈrɒfn̩i, -ɪz
AM ,hɛdəˈrɑfəni, -z
heterophyllous
BR ,hɛtəˈrɒfɪləs
AM ,hɛdəˈrɑfələs
heterophylly
BR ,hɛtəˈrɒfɪli
AM ,hɛdəˈrɑfəli
heteroplastic
BR ,hɛt(ə)rəˈplastɪk
AM ¦hɛdərəˈplæstɪk
heteroploid
BR ˈhɛt(ə)rəplɔɪd
AM ˈhɛdərə,plɔɪd
heteropolar
BR ,hɛt(ə)rə(ʊ)ˈpəʊlə(r)
AM ¦hɛdərəˈpoʊlər
Heteroptera
BR ,hɛtəˈrɒpt(ə)rə(r)
AM ,hɛdəˈrɑptərə
heteropteran
BR ,hɛtəˈrɒpt(ə)rən, ,hɛtəˈrɒpt(ə)rn̩, -z
AM ,hɛdəˈrɑptərən, -z
heteropterous
BR ,hɛtəˈrɒpt(ə)rəs
AM ,hɛdəˈrɑptərəs
heterosexism
BR ,hɛt(ə)rəʊˈsɛksɪz(ə)m
AM ,hɛdərəˈsɛk,sɪzəm

heterosexist
BR ˌhɛt(ə)rəʊˈsɛksɪst
AM ˌhɛdərəˈsɛksəst

heterosexual
BR ˌhɛt(ə)rə(ʊ)ˈsɛkʃʊəl, ˌhɛt(ə)rə(ʊ)ˈsɛkʃ(ʉ)l, ˌhɛt(ə)rə(ʊ)ˈsɛksjʊ(ə)l
AM ¦hɛdərəˈsɛkʃ(əw)əl

heterosexuality
BR ˌhɛt(ə)rə(ʊ)ˌsɛkʃʊˈalɪti, ˌhɛt(ə)rə(ʊ)ˌsɛksjʊˈalɪti
AM ¦hɛdəroʊˌsɛkʃəˈwælədi

heterosexually
BR ˌhɛt(ə)rə(ʊ)ˈsɛkʃʊəli, ˌhɛt(ə)rə(ʊ)ˈsɛkʃʉli, ˌhɛt(ə)rə(ʊ)ˈsɛkʃl̩i, ˌhɛt(ə)rə(ʊ)ˈsɛksjʊ(ə)li
AM ¦hɛdərəˈsɛkʃ(əw)əli

heterosis
BR ˌhɛtəˈrəʊsɪs, -ɪz
AM ˌhɛdəˈroʊsəs, -əz

heterotaxy
BR ˈhɛt(ə)rə(ʊ)ˌtaksi
AM ˈhɛdəroʊˌtæksi

heterotransplant
BR ˌhɛt(ə)rəʊˈtransplɑːnt, ˌhɛt(ə)rəʊˈtrɑːnsplɑːnt, ˌhɛt(ə)rəʊˈtransplant, -s
AM ¦hɛdəroʊˈtrænsˌplænt, -s

heterotrophic
BR ˌhɛt(ə)rə(ʊ)ˈtrɒfɪk, ˌhɛt(ə)rə(ʊ)ˈtrəʊfɪk
AM ˌhɛdərəˈtrɑfɪk

heterozygote
BR ˌhɛt(ə)rə(ʊ)ˈzʌɪgəʊt, -s
AM ¦hɛdəroʊˈzaɪgoʊt, -s

heterozygotic
BR ˌhɛt(ə)rəzʌɪˈgɒtɪk
AM ¦hɛdəroʊˌzaɪˈgɑdɪk

heterozygous
BR ˌhɛt(ə)rə(ʊ)ˈzʌɪgəs
AM ¦hɛdəroʊˈzaɪgəs

Hetherington
BR ˈhɛð(ə)rɪŋt(ə)n
AM ˈhɛðərɪŋtən

hetman
BR ˈhɛtmən
AM ˈhɛtmən

hetmen
BR ˈhɛtmən
AM ˈhɛtmən

Hettie
BR ˈhɛti
AM ˈhɛdi

Hetton-le-Hole
BR ˌhɛtnlɪˈhəʊl
AM ˌhɛdənləˈhoʊl

het up
BR ˌhɛt ˈʌp
AM ˌhɛt ˈəp

heuchera
BR ˈhjuːk(ə)rə(r), ˈhɔɪk(ə)rə(r), -z
AM ˈhjukərə, -z

Heugh[1]
place in UK
BR hjuːf
AM hjuf

Heugh[2]
surname
BR hjuː
AM hju

heuristic
BR hjʊəˈrɪstɪk, -s
AM hjuˈrɪstɪk, -s

heuristically
BR hjʊəˈrɪstɪkli
AM hjuˈrɪstək(ə)li

hevea
BR ˈhiːvɪə(r), -z
AM ˈhiviə, -z

hew
BR hjuː, -z, -ɪŋ, -d
AM hju, -z, -ɪŋ, -d

hewer
BR ˈhjuːə(r), -z
AM ˈhjuər, -z

Hewett
BR ˈhjuːɪt
AM ˈhjuɨt

Hewitt
BR ˈhjuːɪt
AM ˈhjuɨt

Hewlett
BR ˈhjuːlɪt
AM ˈhjulɨt

hex
BR hɛks, -ɪz, -ɪŋ, -t
AM hɛks, -əz, -ɪŋ, -t

hexachord
BR ˈhɛksəkɔːd, -z
AM ˈhɛksəˌkɔ(ə)rd, -z

hexad
BR ˈhɛksad, -z
AM ˈhɛkˌsæd, -z

hexadecimal
BR ˌhɛksəˈdɛsɪml
AM ˌhɛksəˈdɛs(ə)məl

hexadecimally
BR ˌhɛksəˈdɛsɪməli, ˌhɛksəˈdɛsɪml̩i
AM ˌhɛksəˈdɛs(ə)məli

hexagon
BR ˈhɛksəg(ə)n, -z
AM ˈhɛksəˌgɑn, -z

hexagonal
BR hɛkˈsagənl, hɛkˈsagn̩l
AM hɛkˈsægənəl

hexagonally
BR hɛkˈsagənəli, hɛkˈsagənl̩i, hɛkˈsagn̩əli, hɛkˈsagn̩l̩i
AM hɛkˈsægənəli

hexagram
BR ˈhɛksəgram, -z
AM ˈhɛksəˌgræm, -z

hexahedra
BR ˌhɛksəˈhiːdrə(r)
AM ˌhɛksəˈhidrə

hexahedral
BR ˌhɛksəˈhiːdr(ə)l
AM ˌhɛksəˈhidrəl

hexahedron
BR ˌhɛksəˈhiːdr(ə)n, -z
AM ˌhɛksəˈhidrən, -z

hexameron
BR hɛkˈsam(ə)rən, hɛkˈsam(ə)rn̩
AM hɛkˈsæmərən

hexameter
BR hɛkˈsamɪtə(r), -z
AM hɛkˈsæmədər, -z

hexametric
BR ˌhɛksəˈmɛtrɪk
AM ˌhɛksəˈmɛtrɪk

hexametrist
BR hɛkˈsamɪtrɪst, -s
AM ˌhɛksəˈmɛtrəst, -s

hexane
BR ˈhɛkseɪn
AM ˈhɛkˌseɪn

hexapla
BR ˈhɛksəplə(r)
AM ˈhɛksəplə

hexapod
BR ˈhɛksəpɒd, -z
AM ˈhɛksəˌpɑd, -z

Hexapoda
BR ˌhɛksəˈpəʊdə(r)
AM ˌhɛksəˈpoʊdə

hexapody
BR hɛkˈsapəd|i, -ɪz
AM hɛkˈsæpədi, -z

hexastyle
BR ˈhɛksəstʌɪl, -z
AM ˈhɛksəˌstaɪl, -z

hexasyllabic
BR ˌhɛksəsɪˈlabɪk
AM ˌhɛksəsəˈlæbɪk

Hexateuch
BR ˈhɛksətjuːk, ˈhɛksətʃuːk
AM ˈhɛksəˌtɔɪk

hexavalent
BR ˌhɛksəˈveɪlənt, ˌhɛksəˈveɪln̩t
AM ¦hɛksəˈveɪlənt

hexode
BR ˈhɛksəʊd, -z
AM ˈhɛkˌsoʊd, -z

hexose
BR ˈhɛksəʊz, ˈhɛksəʊs, -ɪz
AM ˈhɛkˌsoʊs, -əz

hey
BR heɪ
AM heɪ

heyday
BR ˈheɪdeɪ
AM ˈheɪˌdeɪ

Heyerdahl
BR ˈhʌɪədɑːl
AM ˈhaɪərˌdɑl

Heyes
BR heɪz
AM heɪz

Heyford
BR ˈheɪfəd
AM ˈheɪfərd

Heyhoe
BR ˈheɪhəʊ
AM ˈheɪˌ(h)oʊ

hey presto
BR ˌheɪ ˈprɛstəʊ
AM ¦heɪ ˈprɛstoʊ

Heysham
BR ˈhiːʃ(ə)m
AM ˈhiʃəm

Heythrop
BR ˈhiːθrɒp
AM ˈhiθrəp

Heywood
BR ˈheɪwʊd
AM ˈheɪˌwʊd

Hezbollah
BR ˌhɛzˈbɒlə(r), ˌhɛzbəˈlɑː(r)
AM ˌhɛzbəˈlɑ, hɛzˈbɑlə

Hezekiah
BR ˌhɛzɪˈkʌɪə(r)
AM ˌhɛzəˈkaɪə

hi
BR hʌɪ
AM haɪ

Hialeah
BR ˌhʌɪəˈliːə(r)
AM ˌhaɪəˈliə

hiatal
BR hʌɪˈeɪtl
AM haɪˈeɪdəl

hiatus
BR hʌɪˈeɪtəs, -ɪz
AM haɪˈeɪdəs, -əz

Hiawatha
BR ˌhʌɪəˈwɒθə(r)
AM ˌhaɪəˈwɑθə

hibachi
BR hɪˈbɑːtʃ|i, -ɪz
AM həˈbɑtʃi, -z

hibernal
BR hʌɪˈbəːnl
AM haɪˈbɛrnəl

hibernate
BR ˈhʌɪbəneɪt, -s, -ɪŋ, -ɪd
AM ˈhaɪbərˌneɪ|t, -ts, -dɪŋ, -dɨd

hibernation
BR ˌhʌɪbəˈneɪʃn
AM ˌhaɪbərˈneɪʃən

hibernator
BR ˈhʌɪbəneɪtə(r), -z
AM ˈhaɪbərˌneɪdər, -z

Hibernia
BR hʌɪˈbəːnɪə(r), hɪˈbəːnɪə(r)
AM haɪˈbərnɪə

Hibernian
BR hʌɪˈbəːnɪən, hɪˈbəːnɪən, -z

AM haɪˈbərniən, -z
Hibernicism
BR hʌɪˈbəːnɪsɪz(ə)m, hɪˈbəːnɪsɪz(ə)m, -z
AM haɪˈbərnəˌsɪzəm, -z
hibiscus
BR hɪˈbɪskəs
AM haɪˈbɪskəs
Hibs
BR hɪbz
AM hɪbz
hic
BR hɪk
AM hɪk
hiccough
BR ˈhɪkʌp, -s, -ɪŋ, -t
AM ˈhɪkəp, -s, -ɪŋ, -t
hiccoughy
BR ˈhɪkʌpi
AM ˈhɪkəpi
hiccup
BR ˈhɪkʌp, -s, -ɪŋ, -t
AM ˈhɪkəp, -s, -ɪŋ, -t
hiccupy
BR ˈhɪkʌpi
AM ˈhɪkəpi
hic jacet
BR ˌhɪk ˈdʒeɪsɛt, + ˈjakɛt, -s
AM ˌhɪk ˈdʒeɪsət, -s
hick
BR hɪk, -s
AM hɪk, -s
hickey
BR ˈhɪk|i, -ɪz
AM ˈhɪki, -z
Hickling
BR ˈhɪklɪŋ
AM ˈhɪklɪŋ
Hickman
BR ˈhɪkmən
AM ˈhɪkmən
Hickok
BR ˈhɪkɒk
AM ˈhɪkɑk
hickory
BR ˈhɪk(ə)r|i, -ɪz
AM ˈhɪk(ə)ri, -z
Hicks
BR hɪks
AM hɪks
Hickson
BR ˈhɪks(ə)n
AM ˈhɪksən
hid
BR hɪd
AM hɪd
Hidalgo
BR hɪˈdalgəʊ
AM həˈdɑlgoʊ
Hidcote
BR ˈhɪdkət
AM ˈhɪdkət
hidden
BR ˈhɪdn
AM ˈhɪd(ə)n
hiddenness
BR ˈhɪdnnəs
AM ˈhɪd(ᵻn)nɪs
hide
BR hʌɪd, -z, -ɪŋ
AM haɪd, -z, -ɪŋ
hide-and-seek
BR ˌhʌɪd(ə)n(d)ˈsiːk
AM ˌhaɪdənˈsik
hideaway
BR ˈhʌɪdəweɪ, -z
AM ˈhaɪdˌəweɪ, -z
hidebound
BR ˈhʌɪdbaʊnd
AM ˈhaɪdˌbaʊnd
hi-de-hi
BR ˌhʌɪdɪˈhʌɪ
AM ˌhaɪdiˈhaɪ
hideosity
BR ˌhɪdɪˈɒsɪt|i, -ɪz
AM ˌhɪdiˈɑsədi, -z
hideous
BR ˈhɪdɪəs
AM ˈhɪdiəs
hideously
BR ˈhɪdɪəsli
AM ˈhɪdiəsli
hideousness
BR ˈhɪdɪəsnəs
AM ˈhɪdiəsnəs
hideout
BR ˈhʌɪdaʊt, -s
AM ˈhaɪdˌaʊt, -s
hider
BR ˈhʌɪdə(r), -z
AM ˈhaɪdər, -z
hidey-hole
BR ˈhʌɪdɪhəʊl, -z
AM ˈhaɪdiˌ(h)oʊl, -z
hiding
BR ˈhʌɪdɪŋ, -z
AM ˈhaɪdɪŋ, -z
hidrosis
BR hʌɪˈdrəʊsɪs
AM hɪˈdroʊsəs, haɪˈdroʊsəs
hidrotic
BR hʌɪˈdrɒtɪk
AM hɪˈdrɑtɪk, haɪˈdrɑtɪk
hie
BR hʌɪ, -z, -ɪŋ, -d
AM haɪ, -z, -ɪŋ, -d
hierarch
BR ˈhʌɪ(ə)rɑːk, -s
AM ˈhaɪ(ə)ˌrɑrk, -s
hierarchal
BR ˌhʌɪ(ə)ˈrɑːkl
AM ˌhaɪ(ə)ˈrɑrkəl
hierarchic
BR ˌhʌɪ(ə)ˈrɑːkɪk
AM ˌhaɪ(ə)ˈrɑrkɪk
hierarchical
BR ˌhʌɪ(ə)ˈrɑːkɪkl
AM ˌhaɪ(ə)ˈrɑrkəkəl
hierarchically
BR ˌhʌɪ(ə)ˈrɑːkɪkli
AM ˌhaɪ(ə)ˈrɑrkək(ə)li
hierarchise
BR ˈhʌɪ(ə)rɑːkʌɪz, -ɪz, -ɪŋ, -d
AM ˈhaɪ(ə)ˌrɑrˌkaɪz, -ɪz, -ɪŋ, -d
hierarchism
BR ˈhʌɪ(ə)rɑːkɪz(ə)m
AM ˈhaɪ(ə)ˌrɑrˌkɪzəm
hierarchize
BR ˈhʌɪ(ə)rɑːkʌɪz, -ɪz, -ɪŋ, -d
AM ˈhaɪ(ə)ˌrɑrˌkaɪz, -ɪz, -ɪŋ, -d
hierarchy
BR ˈhʌɪ(ə)rɑːk|i, -ɪz
AM ˈhaɪ(ə)ˌrɑrki, -z
hieratic
BR hʌɪ(ə)ˈratɪk
AM ˌhaɪ(ə)ˈrædɪk
hieratically
BR hʌɪ(ə)ˈratɪkli
AM ˌhaɪ(ə)ˈrædək(ə)li
hierocracy
BR hʌɪ(ə)ˈrɒkrəs|i, -ɪz
AM ˌhaɪ(ə)ˈrɑkrəsi, -z
hieroglyph
BR ˈhʌɪ(ə)rəglɪf, -s
AM ˈhaɪrəˌglɪf, ˈhaɪroʊˌglɪf, -s
hieroglyphic
BR ˌhʌɪ(ə)rəˈglɪfɪk, -s
AM ˌhaɪrəˈglɪfɪk, ˌhaɪroʊˈglɪfɪk, -s
hieroglyphical
BR ˌhʌɪ(ə)rəˈglɪfɪkl
AM ˌhaɪrəˈglɪfəkəl, ˌhaɪroʊˈglɪfəkəl
hieroglyphically
BR ˌhʌɪ(ə)rəˈglɪfɪkli
AM ˌhaɪrəˈglɪfək(ə)li, ˌhaɪ(ə)roʊˈglɪfək(ə)li
hierogram
BR ˈhʌɪ(ə)rəgram, -z
AM ˈhaɪrəˌgræm, ˈhaɪroʊˌgræm, -z
hierograph
BR ˈhʌɪ(ə)rəgrɑːf, ˈhʌɪ(ə)rəgraf, -s
AM ˈhaɪrəˌgræf, ˈhaɪroʊˌgræf, -s
hierolatry
BR hʌɪ(ə)ˈrɒlətri
AM ˌhaɪ(ə)ˈrɑlətri
hierology
BR hʌɪ(ə)ˈrɒlədʒi
AM ˌhaɪ(ə)ˈrɑlədʒi
Hieronymus
BR hʌɪˈrɒnɪməs, hɪˈrɒnɪməs
AM h(ɪ)əˈrɑnəməs
hierophant
BR ˈhʌɪ(ə)rəfant, -s
AM ˈhaɪrəˌfænt, -s
hierophantic
BR ˌhʌɪ(ə)rəˈfantɪk
AM ˌhaɪrəˈfæn(t)ɪk
hifalutin
BR ˌhʌɪfəˈluːt(ɪ)n
AM ˌhaɪfəˈlutn
hifalutin'
BR ˌhʌɪfəˈluːt(ɪ)n
AM ˌhaɪfəˈlutn
hi-fi
BR ˈhʌɪfʌɪ, -z
AM ˈhaɪˈfaɪ, -z
Higginbotham
BR ˈhɪg(ɪ)nˌbɒtəm
AM ˈhɪgɪnˌbɑθəm, ˈhɪgɪnˌbɑdəm
Higginbottom
BR ˈhɪg(ɪ)nˌbɒtəm
AM ˈhɪgɪnˌbɑdəm
Higgins
BR ˈhɪgɪnz
AM ˈhɪgɪnz
higgle
BR ˈhɪg|l, -lz, -l̩ɪŋ\-lɪŋ, -ld
AM ˈhɪg|əl, -əlz, -(ə)lɪŋ, -əld
higgledy-piggledy
BR ˌhɪgldɪˈpɪgldi
AM ˌhɪgəldiˈpɪgəldi
Higgs
BR hɪgz
AM hɪgz
high
BR hʌɪ, -z, -ə(r), -ɪst
AM haɪ, -z, -ər, -ɪst
Higham
BR ˈhʌɪəm
AM ˈhaɪəm
high-and-dry
BR ˌhʌɪənˈdrʌɪ, ˌhʌɪn̩ˈdrʌɪ
AM ˌhaɪənˈdraɪ
high-and-mighty
BR ˌhʌɪən(d)ˈmʌɪti, ˌhʌɪn̩(d)ˈmʌɪti
AM ˌhaɪənˈmaɪdi
highball
BR ˈhʌɪbɔːl, -z
AM ˈhaɪˌbɔl, ˈhaɪˌbɑl, -z
highbinder
BR ˈhʌɪˌbʌɪndə(r), -z
AM ˈhaɪˌbaɪndər, -z
highborn
BR ˈhʌɪbɔːn, ˌhʌɪˈbɔːn
AM ˈhaɪˌbɔ(ə)rn
highboy
BR ˈhʌɪbɔɪ, -z
AM ˈhaɪˌbɔɪ, -z
highbrow
BR ˈhʌɪbraʊ
AM ˈhaɪˌbraʊ
Highclere
BR ˈhʌɪklɪə(r)
AM ˈhaɪˌklɪ(ə)r
Highcliffe
BR ˈhʌɪklɪf
AM ˈhaɪˌklɪf

highfalutin
BR ˌhʌɪfəˈluːt(ɪ)n
AM ¦haɪfəˈlutn

highfalutin'
BR ˌhʌɪfəˈluːt(ɪ)n
AM ¦haɪfəˈlutn

highfaluting
BR ˌhʌɪfəˈluːtɪŋ
AM ¦haɪfəˈlutn

Highgate
BR ˈhʌɪɡeɪt, ˈhʌɪɡət
AM ˈhaɪˌɡeɪt

high-handed
BR ˌhʌɪˈhandɨd
AM ¦haɪˈhæn(d)əd

high-handedly
BR ˌhʌɪˈhandɨdli
AM ¦haɪˈhæn(d)ədli

high-handedness
BR ˌhʌɪˈhandɨdnɨs
AM ¦haɪˈhæn(d)ədnəs

high-hat
BR ˌhʌɪˈhat, -s, -ɪŋ, -ɨd
AM ¦haɪ¦hæ|t, -ts, -dɪŋ, -dəd

highland
BR ˈhʌɪlənd, -z
AM ˈhaɪlənd, -z

Highlander
BR ˈhʌɪləndə(r), -z
AM ˈhaɪləndər, -z

Highlandman
BR ˈhʌɪləndmən
AM ˈhaɪlən(d)ˌmæn

Highlandmen
BR ˈhʌɪləndmən
AM ˈhaɪlən(d)ˌmɛn

highlight
BR ˈhʌɪlʌɪt, -s, -ɪŋ, -ɨd
AM ˈhaɪˌlaɪ|t, -ts, -dɪŋ, -dɨd

highlighter
BR ˈhʌɪlʌɪtə(r), -z
AM ˈhaɪˌlaɪdər, -z

highly
BR ˈhʌɪli
AM ˈhaɪli

high-muck-a-muck
BR ˈhʌɪmʌkəˌmʌk, -s
AM ¦haɪˈməkəˌmək, ˈˌhaɪˈməkiˌmək, -s

highness
BR ˈhʌɪnɨs, -ɨz
AM ˈhaɪnɨs, -ɨz

highrise
BR ˈhʌɪrʌɪz, ˌhʌɪˈrʌɪz, -ɨz
AM ˈhaɪˌraɪz, -ɨz

highroad
BR ˈhʌɪrəʊd, -z
AM ˈhaɪˌroʊd, -z

high-stepper
BR ˌhʌɪˈstɛpə(r), -z
AM ¦haɪˈstɛpər, -z

hight
BR hʌɪt
AM haɪt

hightail
BR ˈhʌɪteɪl, -z, -ɪŋ, -d
AM ˈhaɪˌteɪl, -z, -ɪŋ, -d

highway
BR ˈhʌɪweɪ, -z
AM ˈhaɪˌweɪ, -z

highwayman
BR ˈhʌɪweɪmən
AM ˈhaɪˌweɪmən

highwaymen
BR ˈhʌɪweɪmən
AM ˈhaɪweɪmən, ˈhaɪweɪˌmɛn

hijack
BR ˈhʌɪdʒak, -s, -ɪŋ, -t
AM ˈhaɪˌdʒæk, -s, -ɪŋ, -t

hijacker
BR ˈhʌɪdʒakə(r), -z
AM ˈhaɪˌdʒækər, -z

hijinks
BR ˈhʌɪdʒɪŋks
AM ˈhaɪˌdʒɪŋks

Hijra
BR ˈhɪdʒrə(r)
AM ˈhɪdʒrə

hike
BR hʌɪk, -s, -ɪŋ, -t
AM haɪk, -s, -ɪŋ, -t

hiker
BR ˈhʌɪkə(r), -z
AM ˈhaɪkər, -z

hila
BR ˈhʌɪlə(r)
AM ˈhaɪlə

hilarious
BR hɪˈlɛːrɪəs
AM həˈlɛriəs

hilariously
BR hɪˈlɛːrɪəsli
AM həˈlɛriəsli

hilariousness
BR hɪˈlɛːrɪəsnəs
AM həˈlɛriəsnəs

hilarity
BR hɪˈlarɪti
AM həˈlɛrədi

Hilary
BR ˈhɪləri
AM ˈhɪləri

Hilbert
BR ˈhɪlbət
AM ˈhɪlbərt

Hilda
BR ˈhɪldə(r)
AM ˈhɪldə

Hildesheim
BR ˈhɪldəshʌɪm
AM ˈhɪldəsˌhaɪm

hill
BR hɪl, -z
AM hɪl, -z

Hillary
BR ˈhɪləri
AM ˈhɪləri

hillbilly
BR ˈhɪlˌbɪl|i, -ɪz
AM ˈhɪlˌbɪli, -z

hillcrest
BR ˈhɪlkrɛst, -s
AM ˈhɪlˌkrɛst, -s

Hillel
BR ˈhɪlɛl, ˈhɪləl
AM ˌhɪlˈɛl

Hiller
BR ˈhɪlə(r)
AM ˈhɪlər

Hillhead
BR ˌhɪlˈhɛd
AM ˌhɪlˈhɛd

Hilliard
BR ˈhɪlɪɑːd, ˈhɪlɪəd
AM ˈhɪljərd, ˈhɪliərd

Hillier
BR ˈhɪlɪə(r)
AM ˈhɪliər

hilliness
BR ˈhɪlɪnɪs
AM ˈhɪlinɪs

Hillingdon
BR ˈhɪlɪŋdən
AM ˈhɪlɪŋdən

Hillman
BR ˈhɪlmən
AM ˈhɪlmən

hillmen
BR ˈhɪlmən
AM ˈhɪlmən

hillock
BR ˈhɪlək, -s
AM ˈhɪlək, -s

hillocky
BR ˈhɪləki
AM ˈhɪləki

Hills
BR hɪlz
AM hɪlz

Hillsboro
BR ˈhɪlzb(ə)rə(r)
AM ˈhɪlzˌbərə

Hillsborough
BR ˈhɪlzb(ə)rə(r)
AM ˈhɪlzˌbərə

hillside
BR ˈhɪlsʌɪd, -z
AM ˈhɪlˌsaɪd, -z

hilltop
BR ˈhɪltɒp, -s
AM ˈhɪlˌtɑp, -s

hillwalker
BR ˈhɪlˌwɔːkə(r), -z
AM ˈhɪlˌwɔkər, ˈhɪlˌwɑkər, -z

hillwalking
BR ˈhɪlˌwɔːkɪŋ
AM ˈhɪlˌwɔkɪŋ, ˈhɪlˌwɑkɪŋ

hilly
BR ˈhɪl|i, -ɪə(r), -ɪɪst
AM ˈhɪli, -ər, -ɨst

Hilo
BR ˈhiːləʊ, ˈhʌɪləʊ
AM ˈhaɪloʊ, ˈhiloʊ

hilt
BR hɪlt, -s
AM hɪlt, -s

Hilton
BR ˈhɪlt(ə)n
AM ˈhɪlt(ə)n

hilum
BR ˈhʌɪləm
AM ˈhaɪləm

Hilversum
BR ˈhɪlvəs(ə)m
AM ˈhɪlvərsəm

him[1]
strong form
BR hɪm
AM hɪm

him[2]
weak form
BR ɪm
AM ɪm

Himalaya
BR ˌhɪməˈleɪə(r), hɪˈmɑːlɪə(r), -z
AM ˌhɪməˈleɪə, -z

Himalayan
BR ˌhɪməˈleɪən, hɪˈmɑːlɪən
AM ˌhɪməˈleɪən

himation
BR hɪˈmatɪən, hɪˈmatɪɒn
AM həˈmædiən, həˈmædiˌɑn

Himmler
BR ˈhɪmlə(r)
AM ˈhɪmlər

himself[1]
strong form
BR hɪmˈsɛlf
AM hɪmˈsɛlf

himself[2]
weak form
BR ɪmˈsɛlf
AM ɪmˈsɛlf

Hinayana
BR ˌhiːnəˈjɑːnə(r)
AM ˌhinəˈjɑnə

Hinchcliffe
BR ˈhɪn(t)ʃklɪf
AM ˈhɪn(t)ʃˌklɪf

Hinchingbrooke
BR ˈhɪn(t)ʃɪŋbrʊk
AM ˈhɪn(t)ʃɪŋˌbrʊk

Hinchliffe
BR ˈhɪn(t)ʃlɪf
AM ˈhɪn(t)ʃlɪf

Hinckley
BR ˈhɪŋkli
AM ˈhɪŋkli

hind
BR hʌɪnd, -z
AM haɪnd, -z

hindbrain
BR ˈhʌɪn(d)breɪn, -z
AM ˈhaɪn(d)ˌbreɪn, -z

Hinde
BR hʌɪnd
AM haɪnd

Hindemith
BR ˈhɪndəmɪt, ˈhɪndəmɪθ
AM ˈhɪndəˌmɪθ

Hindenburg
BR ˈhɪndənbəːg
AM ˈhɪndənˌbərg

hinder¹
adjective
BR ˈhʌɪndə(r)
AM ˈhaɪndər

hinder²
verb, delay
BR ˈhɪnd|ə(r), -əz, -(ə)rɪŋ, -əd
AM ˈhɪnd|ər, -ərz, -(ə)rɪŋ, -ərd

Hindhead
BR ˈhʌɪndhɛd
AM ˈhaɪn(d)ˌ(h)ɛd

Hindi
BR ˈhɪndi, ˈhɪndiː
AM ˈhɪndi

Hindle
BR ˈhɪndl
AM ˈhɪndəl

Hindley
BR ˈhɪndli, ˈhʌɪndli
AM ˈhɪn(d)li

Hindmarsh
BR ˈhʌɪn(d)mɑːʃ
AM ˈhaɪn(d)ˌmɑrʃ

hindmost
BR ˈhʌɪn(d)məʊst
AM ˈhaɪn(d)ˌmoʊst

Hindoo
BR ˌhɪnˈduː, ˈhɪnduː, -z
AM ˈhɪndu, -z

hindquarters
BR ˌhʌɪn(d)ˈkwɔːtəz, ˈhʌɪn(d)ˌkwɔːtəz
AM ˈhaɪn(d)ˌkwɔrdərz

hindrance
BR ˈhɪndr(ə)ns, -ɨz
AM ˈhɪndrəns, -əz

hindsight
BR ˈhʌɪn(d)sʌɪt
AM ˈhaɪn(d)ˌsaɪt

Hindu
BR ˌhɪnˈduː, ˈhɪnduː, -z
AM ˈhɪndu, -z

Hinduise
BR ˈhɪnduːʌɪz, -ɨz, -ɪŋ, -d
AM ˈhɪnduˌaɪz, -ɨz, -ɪŋ, -d

Hinduism
BR ˈhɪnduːɪz(ə)m
AM ˈhɪnduˌɪzəm

Hinduize
BR ˈhɪnduːʌɪz, -ɨz, -ɪŋ, -d
AM ˈhɪnduˌaɪz, -ɨz, -ɪŋ, -d

Hindu Kush
BR ˌhɪnduː ˈkʊʃ
AM ˌhɪndu ˈkʊʃ

Hindustan
BR ˌhɪndʊˈstɑːn, ˌhɪndʊˈstan
AM ˈhɪnduˌstæn

Hindustani
BR ˌhɪndʊˈstɑːni
AM ˌhɪnduˈstɑni

hindwing
BR ˈhʌɪndwɪŋ, -z
AM ˈhaɪn(d)ˌwɪŋ, -z

Hines
BR hʌɪnz
AM haɪnz

hinge
BR hɪn(d)ʒ, -ɨz, -ɪŋ, -d
AM hɪndʒ, -ɨz, -ɪŋ, -d

hingeless
BR ˈhɪn(d)ʒlɨs
AM ˈhɪndʒlɨs

hingewise
BR ˈhɪn(d)ʒwʌɪz
AM ˈhɪndʒˌwaɪz

hinny
BR ˈhɪn|i, -ɪz
AM ˈhɪni, -z

Hinshelwood
BR ˈhɪnʃlwʊd
AM ˈhɪnʃəlˌwʊd

hint
BR hɪnt, -s, -ɪŋ, -ɨd
AM hɪn|t, -ts, -(t)ɪŋ, -(t)ɨd

hinterland
BR ˈhɪntəland, -z
AM ˈhɪn(t)ərˌlænd, -z

Hinton
BR ˈhɪnt(ə)n
AM ˈhɪn(t)ən

hip
BR hɪp, -s, -t
AM hɪp, -s, -t

hipbath
BR ˈhɪp|bɑːθ, ˈhɪp|baθ, -bɑːðz\-bɑːθs\-baθs
AM ˈhɪpˌbæ|θ, -θs\-ðz

hipbone
BR ˈhɪpbəʊn, -z
AM ˈhɪpˌboʊn, -z

hip-hip-hooray
BR ˌhɪpˌhɪphʊˈreɪ
AM ˌhɪpˌ(h)ɪphəˈreɪ

hiphop
noun
BR ˈhɪphɒp
AM ˈhɪpˌ(h)ɑp

hipless
BR ˈhɪplɨs
AM ˈhɪpləs

hipline
BR ˈhɪplʌɪn, -z
AM ˈhɪpˌlaɪn, -z

hipness
BR ˈhɪpnɨs
AM ˈhɪpnɨs

Hipparchus
BR hɪˈpɑːkəs
AM ˈhɪˌpɑrkəs

hippeastrum
BR ˌhɪpɪˈastrəm, -z
AM ˌhɪpəˈæstrəm, -z

hipped
BR hɪpt
AM hɪpt

hipper
BR ˈhɪpə(r), -z
AM ˈhɪpər, -z

hippety-hop
BR ˌhɪpɪtɪˈhɒp
AM ˌhɪpədiˌhɑp

hippie
BR ˈhɪp|i, -ɪz
AM ˈhɪpi, -z

hippo
BR ˈhɪpəʊ, -z
AM ˈhɪpoʊ, -z

hippocampi
BR ˌhɪpə(ʊ)ˈkampʌɪ
AM ˌhɪpəˈkæmˌpaɪ

hippocampus
BR ˌhɪpə(ʊ)ˈkampəs
AM ˌhɪpəˈkæmpəs

hippocentaur
BR ˌhɪpə(ʊ)ˈsɛntɔː(r), -z
AM ˌhɪpəˈsɛnˌtɔ(ə)r, -z

hippocras
BR ˈhɪpəkras
AM ˈhɪpəˌkræs

Hippocrates
BR hɪˈpɒkrətiːz
AM hɪˈpɑkrədiz

Hippocratic
BR ˌhɪpəˈkratɪk
AM ˌhɪpəˈkrædɪk

Hippocrene
BR ˈhɪpəkriːn
AM ˈhɪpəˌkrin

hippodrome
BR ˈhɪpədrəʊm, -z
AM ˈhɪpəˌdroʊm, -z

hippogriff
BR ˈhɪpə(ʊ)grɪf, -s
AM ˈhɪpəˌgrɪf, -s

hippogryph
BR ˈhɪpə(ʊ)grɪf, -s
AM ˈhɪpəˌgrɪf, -s

Hippolyta
BR hɪˈpɒlɨtə(*r*)
AM həˈpɑlədə

Hippolytus
BR hɪˈpɒlɨtəs
AM hɪˈpɑlədəs

hippophagy
BR hɪˈpɒfədʒi
AM hɪˈpɑfədʒi

hippophile
BR ˈhɪpəfʌɪl, -z
AM ˈhɪpəˌfaɪl, -z

hippophobia
BR ˌhɪpə(ʊ)ˈfəʊbɪə(*r*)
AM ˈhɪpəˌfoʊbiə

hippopotamus
BR ˌhɪpəˈpɒtəməs, -ɨz
AM ˌhɪpəˈpɑdəməs, -əz

Hippo Regius
BR ˌhɪpəʊ ˈriːdʒɪəs
AM ˌhɪpoʊ ˈridʒ(i)əs

hippy
BR ˈhɪp|i, -ɪz
AM ˈhɪpi, -z

hipster
BR ˈhɪpstə(r), -z
AM ˈhɪpstər, -z

hipsterism
BR ˈhɪpstərɪz(ə)m
AM ˈhɪpstəˌrɪzəm

hiragana
BR ˌhɪrəˈgɑːnə(*r*), ˌhɪərəˈgɑːnə(*r*)
AM ˌhɪrəˈgɑnə

Hiram
BR ˈhʌɪrəm
AM ˈhaɪrəm

hircine
BR ˈhəːsʌɪn, ˈhəːsɪn
AM ˈhərˌsaɪn, ˈhərsən

hire
BR ˈhʌɪə(r), -z, -ɪŋ, -d
AM ˈhaɪ(ə)r, -z, -ɪŋ, -d

hireable
BR ˈhʌɪərəbl
AM ˈhaɪrəbəl

hireling
BR ˈhʌɪəlɪŋ, -z
AM ˈhaɪrlɪŋ, -z

hirer
BR ˈhʌɪərə(r), -z
AM ˈhaɪrər, -z

Hirohito
BR ˌhɪrəˈhiːtəʊ
AM ˌhɪroʊˈhɪdoʊ

Hiroshima
BR hɪˈrɒʃɪmə(*r*), ˌhɪrəˈʃiːmə(*r*)
AM ˌhɪroʊˈʃimə, hɪˈroʊʃəmə

Hirst
BR həːst
AM hərst

hirsute
BR ˈhəːsjuːt, həːˈsjuːt
AM ˈhərˌsut, hərˈsut, ˈhɪrˌsut, hɪrˈsut

hirsuteness
BR ˈhəːsjuːtnəs, həːˈsjuːtnəs
AM ˈhərˌsutnəs, hərˈsutnəs, ˈhɪrˌsutnəs, hɪrˈsutnəs

hirsutism
BR ˈhəːsjuːtɪz(ə)m, həːˈsjuːtɪz(ə)m
AM ˈhərˌsuˌtɪzəm, hərˈsuˌtɪzəm, ˈhɪrˌsuˌtɪzəm, hɪrˈsuˌtɪzəm

hirundine
BR ˈhɪrʌndʌɪn, hɪˈrʌndʌɪn, -z
AM hɪˈrəndən, hɪˈrənˌdaɪn, -z

Hirwaun
BR ˈhɪrʊʌɪn
AM ˈhɪrʊaɪn
WE ˈhɪrwaɪn

his¹
strong form
BR hɪz
AM hɪz

his²
weak form
BR ɪz
AM ɪz

Hislop
BR ˈhɪzlɒp, ˈhɪzləp
AM ˈhɪzləp

Hispanic
BR hɪˈspanɪk, -s
AM hɪˈspænɪk, -s

Hispanicise
BR hɪˈspanɪsʌɪz, -ɪz, -ɪŋ, -d
AM hɪˈspænəˌsaɪz, -ɪz, -ɪŋ, -d

Hispanicist
BR hɪˈspanɪsɪst, -s
AM hɪˈspænəsəst, -s

Hispanicize
BR hɪˈspanɪsʌɪz, -ɪz, -ɪŋ, -d
AM hɪˈspænəˌsaɪz, -ɪz, -ɪŋ, -d

Hispaniola
BR ˌhɪspanɪˈəʊlə(r), hɪˌspanɪˈəʊlə(r), ˌhɪspanˈjəʊlə(r)
AM ˌhɪspənˈjoʊlə

Hispanist
BR hɪˈspanɪst, -s
AM ˈhɪspənəst, -s

Hispano-Suiza
BR hɪˌspanəʊˈswiːzə(r)
AM hɪˌspænoʊˈswizə

hispid
BR ˈhɪspɪd
AM ˈhɪspɪd

hiss
BR hɪs, -ɪz, -ɪŋ, -t
AM hɪs, -ɪz, -ɪŋ, -t

hist
BR hɪst
AM hɪst

histamine
BR ˈhɪstəmiːn, ˈhɪstəmɪn
AM ˈhɪstəˌmin

histaminic
BR ˌhɪstəˈmɪnɪk
AM ˌhɪstəˈmɪnɪk

histidine
BR ˈhɪstədiːn
AM ˈhɪstəˌdin

histiocyte
BR ˈhɪstɪəsʌɪt, -s
AM ˈhɪstiəˌsaɪt, -s

histochemical
BR ˌhɪstəʊˈkɛmɪkl
AM ˌhɪstəˈkɛməkəl

histochemistry
BR ˌhɪstəʊˈkɛmɪstri
AM ˌhɪstəˈkɛməstri

histogenesis
BR ˌhɪstə(ʊ)ˈdʒɛnɪsɪs
AM ˌhɪstəˈdʒɛnəsəs

histogenetic
BR ˌhɪstəʊdʒɪˈnɛtɪk
AM ˌhɪstədʒəˈnɛdɪk

histogenic
BR ˌhɪstəˈdʒɛnɪk
AM ˌhɪstəˈdʒɛnɪk

histogeny
BR hɪˈstɒdʒɪni
AM hɪˈstɑdʒəni

histogram
BR ˈhɪstəgram, -z
AM ˈhɪstəˌgræm, -z

histological
BR ˌhɪstəˈlɒdʒɪkl
AM ˌhɪstəˈlɑdʒəkəl

histologist
BR hɪˈstɒlədʒɪst, -s
AM hɪˈstɑlədʒəst, -s

histology
BR hɪˈstɒlədʒi
AM hɪˈstɑlədʒi

histolysis
BR hɪˈstɒlɪsɪs
AM hɪˈstɑləsəs

histolytic
BR ˌhɪstəˈlɪtɪk
AM ˌhɪstəˈlɪdɪk

histone
BR ˈhɪstəʊn, -z
AM ˈhɪˌstoʊn, -z

histopathology
BR ˌhɪstəʊpəˈθɒlədʒi
AM ˌhɪstəpəˈθɑlədʒi

historian
BR hɪˈstɔːrɪən, -z
AM hɪˈstɔriən, -z

historiated
BR hɪˈstɔːrɪeɪtɪd
AM hɪˈstɔriˌeɪdɪd

historic
BR hɪˈstɒrɪk
AM hɪˈstɔrɪk

historical
BR hɪˈstɒrɪkl
AM hɪˈstɔrəkəl

historically
BR hɪˈstɒrɪkli
AM hɪˈstɔrək(ə)li

historicism
BR hɪˈstɒrɪsɪz(ə)m
AM hɪˈstɔrəˌsɪzəm

historicist
BR hɪˈstɒrɪsɪst, -s
AM hɪˈstɔrəsəst, -s

historicity
BR ˌhɪstəˈrɪsɪti
AM ˌhɪstəˈrɪsɪdi

historiographer
BR hɪˌstɒrɪˈɒgrəfə(r), hɪˌstɔːrɪˈɒgrəfə(r), ˌhɪstɒrɪˈɒgrəfə(r), ˌhɪstɔːrɪˈɒgrəfə(r), -z
AM hɪˌstɔriˈɑgrəfər, -z

historiographic
BR hɪˌstɒrɪəˈgrafɪk, hɪˌstɔːrɪəˈgrafɪk
AM hɪˌstɔriəˈgræfɪk

historiographical
BR hɪˌstɒrɪəˈgrafɪkl, hɪˌstɔːrɪəˈgrafɪkl
AM hɪˌstɔriəˈgræfəkəl

historiography
BR hɪˌstɒrɪˈɒgrəfi, hɪˌstɔːrɪˈɒgrəfi, ˌhɪstɒrɪˈɒgrəfi, ˌhɪstɔːrɪˈɒgrəfi
AM hɪˌstɔriˈɑgrəfi

history
BR ˈhɪst(ə)r|i, -ɪz
AM ˈhɪst(ə)ri, -z

histrionic
BR ˌhɪstrɪˈɒnɪk, -s
AM ˌhɪstriˈɑnɪk, -s

histrionically
BR ˌhɪstrɪˈɒnɪkli
AM ˌhɪstriˈɑnək(ə)li

histrionicism
BR ˌhɪstrɪˈɒnɪsɪz(ə)m
AM ˌhɪstriˈɑnəˌsɪzəm

histrionism
BR ˈhɪstrɪənɪz(ə)m
AM ˈhɪstriəˌnɪzəm

hit
BR hɪt, -s, -ɪŋ
AM hɪ|t, -ts, -dɪŋ

hit-and-miss
BR ˌhɪt(ə)n(d)ˈmɪs
AM ˈhɪtnˈmɪs

hit-and-run
BR ˌhɪt(ə)n(d)ˈrʌn
AM ˈhɪtnˈrən

hitch
BR hɪtʃ, -ɪz, -ɪŋ, -t
AM hɪtʃ, -ɪz, -ɪŋ, -t

Hitchcock
BR ˈhɪtʃkɒk
AM ˈhɪtʃˌkɑk

Hitchen
BR ˈhɪtʃɪn
AM ˈhɪtʃɪn

Hitchens
BR ˈhɪtʃ(ɪ)nz
AM ˈhɪtʃənz

hitcher
BR ˈhɪtʃə(r), -z
AM ˈhɪtʃər, -z

hitchhike
BR ˈhɪtʃhʌɪk, -s, -ɪŋ, -t
AM ˈhɪtʃˌhaɪk, -s, -ɪŋ, -t

Hitchin
BR ˈhɪtʃɪn
AM ˈhɪtʃɪn

hitech
BR ˌhʌɪˈtɛk
AM ˈhaɪˈtɛk

hither
BR ˈhɪðə(r)
AM ˈhɪðər

hitherto
BR ˌhɪðəˈtuː, ˈhɪðətuː
AM ˈhɪðərˌtu, ˌhɪðərˈtu

hitherward
BR ˈhɪðəwəd, -z
AM ˈhɪðərwərd, -z

Hitler
BR ˈhɪtlə(r)
AM ˈhɪtlər

Hitlerian
BR hɪtˈlɪərɪən
AM hɪtˈlɛriən

Hitlerism
BR ˈhɪtlərɪz(ə)m
AM ˈhɪtləˌrɪzəm

Hitlerite
BR ˈhɪtlərʌɪt, -s
AM ˈhɪtləˌraɪt, -s

hitman
BR ˈhɪtman
AM ˈhɪtˌmæn

hitmen
BR ˈhɪtmɛn
AM ˈhɪtˌmɛn

hitter
BR ˈhɪtə(r), -z
AM ˈhɪdər, -z

Hittite
BR ˈhɪtʌɪt, -s
AM ˈhɪˌtaɪt, -s

hive
BR hʌɪv, -z, -ɪŋ, -d
AM haɪv, -z, -ɪŋ, -d

hiya!
BR ˈhʌɪə(r)
AM ˈhaɪə

Hizbollah
BR ˌhɛzbəˈlɑː(r), ˌhɪzbəˈlɑː(r)
AM ˌhɛzbəˈlɑ

h'm
BR (h)m
AM (h)m

hmm
BR (h)m, -z
AM (h)m, -z

ho
BR həʊ
AM hoʊ

hoagie
BR ˈhəʊg|i, -ɪz
AM ˈhoʊgi, -z

hoar
BR hɔː(r)
AM hɔ(ə)r

hoard
BR hɔːd, -z, -ɪŋ, -ɪd
AM hɔ(ə)rd, -z, -ɪŋ, -əd

hoarder
BR ˈhɔːdə(r), -z
AM ˈhɔrdər, -z

hoarding
BR ˈhɔːdɪŋ, -z
AM ˈhɔrdɪŋ, -z

Hoare
BR hɔː(r)

AM hɔ(ə)r

hoarfrost
BR 'hɔːfrɒst
AM 'hɔrˌfrɔst, 'hɔrˌfrɑst

hoarhound
BR 'hɔːhaʊnd
AM 'hɔrˌ(h)aʊnd

hoarily
BR 'hɔːrɨli
AM 'hɔrəli

hoariness
BR 'hɔːrɪnɨs
AM 'hɔrinɨs

hoarse
BR hɔːs, -ə(r), -ɨst
AM hɔ(ə)rs, -ər, -əst

hoarsely
BR 'hɔːsli
AM 'hɔrsli

hoarsen
BR 'hɔːs|n, -nz, -n̩ɪŋ\-nɪŋ, -nd
AM 'hɔrsən, -z, -ɪŋ, -d

hoarseness
BR 'hɔːsnəs
AM 'hɔrsnəs

hoarstone
BR 'hɔːstəʊn, -z
AM 'hɔrˌstoʊn, -z

hoary
BR 'hɔːr|i, -ɪə(r), -ɪɨst
AM 'hɔri, -ər, -ɨst

hoatzin
BR həʊ'atsɪn, ˌwɑːt'siːn, -z
AM ˌwɑt'sin, -z

hoax
BR həʊks, -ɨz, -ɪŋ, -t
AM hoʊks, -əz, -ɪŋ, -t

hoaxer
BR 'həʊksə(r), -z
AM 'hoʊksər, -z

hob
BR hɒb, -z
AM hɑb, -z

Hobart
BR 'həʊbɑːt
AM 'hoʊbərt

Hobbes
BR hɒbz
AM hɑbz

hobbit
BR 'hɒbɪt, -s
AM 'hɑbət, -s

hobbitry
BR 'hɒbɨtri
AM 'hɑbətri

hobble
BR 'hɒb|l, -lz, -l̩ɪŋ\-lɪŋ, -ld
AM 'hɑb|əl, -əlz, -(ə)lɪŋ, -əld

hobbledehoy
BR 'hɒbldɪˌhɔɪ, -z
AM ˈhɑbəldiˈhɔɪ, -z

hobbler
BR 'hɒbl̩ə(r), 'hɒblə(r), -z
AM 'hɑb(ə)lər, -z

Hobbs
BR hɒbz
AM hɑbz

hobby
BR 'hɒb|i, -ɪz
AM 'hɑbi, -z

hobbyhorse
BR 'hɒbɪhɔːs
AM 'hɑbiˌhɔ(ə)rs

hobbyist
BR 'hɒbɪɪst, -s
AM 'hɑbiɨst, -s

Hobday
BR 'hɒbdeɪ
AM 'hɑbˌdeɪ

hobday
BR 'hɒbdeɪ, -z, -ɪŋ, -d
AM 'hɑbˌdeɪ, -z, -ɪŋ, -d

hobgoblin
BR ˌhɒb'gɒblɪn, 'hɒbˌgɒblɪn, -z
AM 'hɑbˌgɑblən, -z

Hobley
BR 'həʊbli
AM 'hoʊbli

hobnail
BR 'hɒbneɪl, -z, -d
AM 'hɑbˌneɪl, -z, -d

hobnob
BR 'hɒbnɒb, -z, -ɪŋ, -d
AM 'hɑbˌnɑb, -z, -ɪŋ, -d

hobo
BR 'həʊbəʊ, -z
AM 'hoʊˌboʊ, -z

Hoboken
BR 'həʊbəʊk(ə)n
AM 'hoʊˌboʊkən

Hobsbawm
BR 'hɒbzbɔːm
AM 'hɑbzˌbɔm, 'hɑbzˌbɑm

Hobson
BR 'hɒbsn
AM 'hɑbsən

Hobson-Jobson
BR ˌhɒbsn'dʒɒbsn
AM ˌhɑbsən'dʒɑbsən

Ho Chi Minh
BR ˌhəʊ ˌ(t)ʃiː 'mɪn
AM ˌhoʊ ˌ(t)ʃi 'mɪn

hock
BR hɒk, -s, -ɪŋ, -t
AM hɑk, -s, -ɪŋ, -t

hockey
BR 'hɒki
AM 'hɑki

hockeyist
BR 'hɒkɪɪst, -s
AM 'hɑkiɨst, -s

hockney
BR 'hɒkni
AM 'hɑkni

hockshop
BR 'hɒkʃɒp, -s
AM 'hɑkˌʃɑp, -s

Hocktide
BR 'hɒktʌɪd
AM 'hɑkˌtaɪd

hocus
BR 'həʊkəs, -ɨz, -ɪŋ, -t
AM 'hoʊkəs, -əz, -ɪŋ, -t

hocus-pocus
BR ˌhəʊkəs'pəʊkəs
AM ˈhoʊkəs'poʊkəs

hod
BR hɒd, -z
AM hɑd, -z

hodden
BR 'hɒdn
AM 'hɑdən

Hodder
BR 'hɒdə(r)
AM 'hɑdər

Hoddesdon
BR 'hɒdzd(ə)n
AM 'hɑdzdən

hoddie
BR 'hɒd|i, -ɪz
AM 'hɑdi, -z

Hoddinott
BR 'hɒdɪnɒt
AM 'hɑdənɑt

Hoddle
BR 'hɒdl
AM 'hɑdəl

Hodeida
BR hə(ʊ)'deɪdə(*r*)
AM hoʊ'deɪdə

Hodge
BR hɒdʒ, -ɨz
AM hɑdʒ, -əz

hodgepodge
BR 'hɒdʒpɒdʒ
AM 'hɑdʒˌpɑdʒ

Hodges
BR 'hɒdʒɪz
AM 'hɑdʒəz

Hodgetts
BR 'hɒdʒɪts
AM 'hɑdʒəts

Hodgkin
BR 'hɒdʒkɪn
AM 'hɑdʒkən

Hodgkinson
BR 'hɒdʒkɪns(ə)n
AM 'hɑdʒkənsən

Hodgson
BR 'hɒdʒsn
AM 'hɑdʒsən

hodiernal
BR ˌhɒdɪ'əːnl, ˌhəʊdɪ'əːnl
AM ˌhoʊdi'ərnəl, ˌhɑdi'ərnəl

hodman
BR 'hɒdmən
AM 'hɑdmən

hodmen
BR 'hɒdmən
AM 'hɑdmən

hodograph
BR 'hɒdəgrɑːf, 'hɒdəgraf, -s
AM 'hɑdəˌgræf, 'hoʊdəˌgræf, -s

hodometer
BR hɒ'dɒmɪtə(r)
AM hɑ'dɑmədər, hoʊ'dɑmədər

Hodson
BR 'hɒdsn
AM 'hɑdsən

hoe
BR həʊ, -z, -ɪŋ, -d
AM hoʊ, -z, -ɪŋ, -d

hoedown
BR 'həʊdaʊn, -z
AM 'hoʊˌdaʊn, -z

hoer
BR 'həʊə(r), -z
AM 'hoʊər, -z

Hoey
BR 'həʊi
AM 'hoʊi

Hoffman
BR 'hɒfmən
AM 'hɔfmən, 'hɑfmən

Hoffnung
BR 'hɒfnʊŋ, 'hɒfnʌŋ
AM 'hɔfnəŋ, 'hɑfnəŋ

Hofmannsthal
BR 'hɒfmənʃtɑːl
AM 'hɔfmənˌstɔl, 'hɑfmənˌstɑl

Hofmeister
BR 'hɒfˌmʌɪstə(r)
AM 'hɔfˌmaɪstər, 'hɑfˌmaɪstər

hog
BR hɒg, -z, -ɪŋ, -d
AM hɔg, hɑg, -z, -ɪŋ, -d

hogan
BR 'həʊg(ə)n, -z
AM 'hoʊgən, 'hoʊˌgɑn, -z

Hogarth
BR 'həʊgɑːθ
AM 'hoʊˌgɑrθ

Hogarthian
BR həʊ'gɑːθɪən
AM hoʊ'gɑrθiən

hogback
BR 'hɒgbak, -s
AM 'hɔgˌbæk, 'hɑgˌbæk, -s

Hogben
BR 'hɒgbən
AM 'hɔgbən, 'hɑgbən

Hogg
BR hɒg
AM hɑg

Hoggar Mountains
BR ˌhɒgə 'maʊntɪnz
AM ˌhɑgər 'maʊntnz

Hoggart
BR 'hɒgət
AM 'hɔgərt, 'hɑgərt

hogger
BR 'hɒgə(r), -z
AM 'hɔgər, 'hɑgər, -z

hoggery
BR 'hɒg(ə)r|i, -ɪz
AM 'hɔgəri, 'hɑgəri, -z

hogget
BR 'hɒgɪt, -s
AM 'hɔgət, 'hɑgət, -s

hoggin
BR 'hɒgɪn
AM 'hɔgən, 'hɑgən

hoggish
BR 'hɒgɪʃ
AM 'hɔgɪʃ, 'hɑgɪʃ

hoggishly
BR 'hɒgɨʃli
AM 'hɔgɨʃli, 'hɑgɨʃli

hoggishness
BR 'hɒgɨʃnɨs
AM 'hɔgɪʃnɨs, 'hɑgɪʃnɨs

hoglike
BR 'hɒglʌɪk
AM 'hɔg,laɪk, 'hɑg,laɪk

Hogmanay
BR 'hɒgməneɪ, ,hɒgmə'neɪ, -z
AM ¦hɑgmə¦neɪ, -z

hogshead
BR 'hɒgzhɛd, -z
AM 'hɔgz,(h)ɛd, 'hɑgz,(h)ɛd, -z

hogtie
BR 'hɒgtʌɪ, -z, -ɪŋ, -d
AM 'hɔg,taɪ, 'hɑg,taɪ, -z, -ɪŋ, -d

hogwash
BR 'hɒgwɒʃ
AM 'hɔg,wɔʃ, 'hɑg,wɑʃ

hogweed
BR 'hɒgwiːd
AM 'hɔg,wid, 'hɑg,wid

Hohenstaufen
BR 'həʊən,staʊfn, 'həʊən,ʃtaʊfn
AM 'hoʊən,staʊfən, 'hoʊən,ʃtaʊfən

Hohenzollern
BR ,həʊən'zɒlən
AM ¦hoʊən¦zɑlərn

ho-ho
BR ,həʊ'həʊ
AM ¦hoʊ¦hoʊ

ho-hum
BR ,həʊ'hʌm
AM 'hoʊ¦həm

hoick
BR hɔɪk, -s, -ɪŋ, -t
AM hɔɪk, -s, -ɪŋ, -t

hoi polloi
BR ,hɔɪ pə'lɔɪ
AM ¦hɔɪ pə'lɔɪ

hoisin
BR 'hɔɪzɪn
AM 'hɔɪzɨn

hoist
BR hɔɪst, -s, -ɪŋ, -ɨd
AM hɔɪst, -s, -ɪŋ, -ɨd

hoister
BR 'hɔɪstə(r), -z
AM 'hɔɪstər, -z

hoity-toity
BR ,hɔɪtɪ'tɔɪti
AM ¦hɔɪdi'tɔɪdi

hokey
BR 'həʊki
AM 'hoʊki

hokey-cokey
BR ,həʊkɪ'kəʊki
AM 'hoʊki'koʊki

hokeyness
BR 'həʊkɪnɨs
AM 'hoʊkinɨs

hokey-pokey
BR ,həʊkɪ'pəʊki
AM 'hoʊki'poʊki

hoki
BR 'həʊki
AM 'hoʊki

hokily
BR 'həʊkɨli
AM 'hoʊkəli

Hokkaido
BR hɒ'kʌɪdəʊ
AM hɑ'kaɪ,doʊ

hokku
BR 'hɒkuː, -z
AM 'hɔ,ku, 'hɑ,ku, -z

hokonui
BR 'hɒkənʊɪ
AM 'hɑkənui

hokum
BR 'həʊkəm
AM 'hoʊkəm

hoky
BR 'həʊk|i, -ɪə(r), -ɪɪst
AM 'hoʊki, -ər, -ɨst

Holarctic
BR hɒl'ɑːktɪk
AM ¦hɑl'ɑrktɪk, ¦hɔl'ɑrktɪk, ¦hoʊl'ɑrktɪk, ¦hɑl'ɑrdɪk, ¦hɔl'ɑrdɪk, ¦hoʊl'ɑrdɪk

Holbeach
BR 'hɒlbiːtʃ
AM 'hɔl,bitʃ, 'hɑl,bitʃ

Holbech
BR 'hɒlbiːtʃ
AM 'hɔl,bɛk, 'hɑl,bɛk

Holbeche
BR 'hɒlbiːtʃ
AM 'hɔl,bɛk, 'hɑl,bɛk

Holbein
BR 'hɒlbʌɪn
AM 'hoʊl,baɪn

Holborn
BR 'həʊbn
AM 'hoʊ(l),bɔ(ə)rn

Holborne
BR 'həʊ(l)bn
AM 'hoʊ(l),bɔ(ə)rn

Holbrook
BR 'həʊlbrʊk
AM 'hoʊl,brʊk

Holbrooke
BR 'həʊlbrʊk
AM 'hoʊl,brʊk

Holcomb
BR 'həʊ(l)kəm
AM 'hoʊ(l)kəm

Holcombe
BR 'həʊ(l)kəm
AM 'hoʊ(l)kəm

hold
BR həʊld, -z, -ɪŋ
AM hoʊld, -z, -ɪŋ

holdable
BR 'həʊldəbl
AM 'hoʊldəbəl

holdall
BR 'həʊldɔːl, -z
AM 'hoʊld,ɔl, 'hoʊld,ɑl, -z

holdback
BR 'həʊl(d)bak, -s
AM 'hoʊl(d),bæk, -s

hold-down
BR 'həʊl(d)daʊn, -z
AM 'hoʊl,daʊn, -z

Holden
BR 'həʊld(ə)n
AM 'hoʊldən

holder
BR 'həʊldə(r), -z
AM 'hoʊldər, -z

Hölderlin
BR 'həːldəliːn
AM 'həldərlin

Holderness
BR 'həʊldənɨs
AM 'hoʊldərnəs

holdfast
BR 'həʊl(d)fɑːst, 'həʊl(d)fast, -s
AM 'hoʊl(d),fæst, -s

holding
BR 'həʊldɪŋ, -z
AM 'hoʊldɪŋ, -z

holdout
BR 'həʊldaʊt, -s
AM 'hoʊl,daʊt, -s

holdover
BR 'həʊld,əʊvə(r), -z
AM 'hoʊl,doʊvər, -z

Holdsworth
BR 'həʊl(d)zwəːθ, 'həʊl(d)zwəθ
AM 'hoʊl(d)z,wərθ

holdup
BR 'həʊldʌp, -s
AM 'hoʊl,dəp, -s

hole
BR həʊl, -z, -ɪŋ, -d
AM hoʊl, -z, -ɪŋ, -d

holey
BR 'həʊli
AM 'hoʊli

Holford
BR 'həʊlfəd, 'hɒlfəd
AM 'hoʊ(l)fərd

Holi
BR 'həʊliː
AM 'hoʊli

holibut
BR 'hɒlɨbʌt, -s
AM 'hɑləbət, -s

holiday
BR 'hɒlɨd|eɪ, 'hɒlɨd|i, -eɪz\-ɪz
AM 'hɑlə,deɪ, -z

holidaymaker
BR 'hɒlɨdɪ,meɪkə(r), -z
AM 'hɑlədeɪ,meɪkər, -z

holily
BR 'həʊlɨli
AM 'hoʊləli

holiness
BR 'həʊlɪnɨs
AM 'hoʊlinɨs

Holinshed
BR 'hɒlɪnʃɛd, 'hɒlɪnzhɛd
AM 'hɑlənz,(h)ɛd, 'hɑlənʃɛd

holism
BR 'həʊlɪz(ə)m
AM 'hoʊl,ɪzəm

holist
BR 'həʊlɪst, -s
AM 'hoʊləst, -s

holistic
BR hə(ʊ)'lɪstɪk, hɒ'lɪstɪk
AM hoʊ'lɪstɪk

holistically
BR hə(ʊ)'lɪstɨkli, hɒ'lɪstɨkli
AM hoʊ'lɪstək(ə)li

holla
BR 'hɒlə(r), -z, -ɪŋ, -d
AM 'hɑlə, -z, -ɪŋ, -d

Holland
BR 'hɒlənd, -z
AM 'hɑlən(d), -z

hollandaise
BR ,hɒlən'deɪz
AM ¦hɑlən¦deɪz

Hollander
BR 'hɒləndə(r), -z
AM 'hɑləndər, -z

Hollands
BR 'hɒlən(d)z
AM 'hɑlən(d)z

holler
BR 'hɒl|ə(r), -əz, -(ə)rɪŋ, -əd
AM 'hɑlər, -z, -ɪŋ, -əd

Hollerith
BR 'hɒlərɪθ
AM 'hɑlərɪθ

Holley
BR ˈhɒli
AM ˈhɑli

Holliday
BR ˈhɒlɨdeɪ
AM ˈhɑləˌdeɪ

Hollingsworth
BR ˈhɒlɪŋzwəːθ, ˈhɒlɪŋzwəθ
AM ˈhɑlɪŋzˌwərθ

Hollins
BR ˈhɒlɪnz
AM ˈhɑlənz

Hollis
BR ˈhɒlɪs
AM ˈhɑləs

hollo
BR ˈhɒləʊ, -z, -ɪŋ, -d
AM ˈhɑl|oʊ, -oʊz, -əwɪŋ, -oʊd

hollow
BR ˈhɒləʊ, -z, -ɪŋ, -d
AM ˈhɑl|oʊ, -oʊz, -əwɪŋ, -oʊd

holloware
BR ˈhɒlə(ʊ)wɛː(r)
AM ˈhɑləˌwɛ(ə)r

Holloway
BR ˈhɒləweɪ
AM ˈhɑləˌweɪ

hollow-cheeked
BR ˌhɒlə(ʊ)ˈtʃiːkt
AM ˈhɑloʊˌtʃikt

hollow-eyed
BR ˌhɒləʊˈʌɪd
AM ˈhɑloʊˌaɪd

hollow-hearted
BR ˌhɒləʊˈhɑːtɨd
AM ˈhɑloʊˌhɑrdəd

hollowly
BR ˈhɒləʊli
AM ˈhɑloʊli

hollowness
BR ˈhɒləʊnəs
AM ˈhɑloʊnəs

hollowware
BR ˈhɒlə(ʊ)wɛː(r)
AM ˈhɑloʊˌwɛ(ə)r

holly
BR ˈhɒli
AM ˈhɑli

hollyhock
BR ˈhɒlɪhɒk, -s
AM ˈhɑliˌhɑk, -s

Hollywood
BR ˈhɒlɪwʊd
AM ˈhɑliˌwʊd

holm
BR həʊm, -z
AM hoʊm, -z

Holman
BR ˈhəʊlmən
AM ˈhoʊ(l)mən

Holme
BR həʊm
AM hoʊm

Holmes
BR həʊmz
AM hoʊmz

Holmesian
BR ˈhəʊmzɪən
AM ˈhoʊmziən

Holmfirth
BR ˈhəʊmfəːθ, ˌhəʊmˈfəːθ
AM ˈhoʊ(l)mˌfərθ

holmium
BR ˈhəʊlmɪəm, ˈhɒlmɪəm
AM ˈhoʊ(l)miəm

holmoak
BR ˈhəʊməʊk, -s
AM ˈhoʊmˌoʊk, -s

Holmwood
BR ˈhəʊmwʊd
AM ˈhoʊ(l)mˌwʊd

holocaust
BR ˈhɒləkɔːst, -s
AM ˈhɑləˌkɔst, ˈhoʊləˌkɔst, ˈhɑləˌkɑst, ˈhoʊləˌkɑst, -s

Holocene
BR ˈhɒləsiːn
AM ˈhɑləˌsin, ˈhoʊləˌsin

holoenzyme
BR ˌhɒləʊˈɛnzʌɪm, -z
AM ˈhɑloʊˈɛnˌzaɪm, ˈhoʊloʊˈɛnˌzaɪm, -z

Holofernes
BR ˌhɒləˈfəːniːz, həˈlɒfəniːz
AM ˌhɑləˈfərniz

hologram
BR ˈhɒləgram, -z
AM ˈhɑləˌgræm, ˈhoʊləˌgræm, -z

holograph
BR ˈhɒləgrɑːf, ˈhɒləgraf, -s
AM ˈhɑləˌgræf, ˈhoʊləˌgræf, -s

holographic
BR ˌhɒləˈgrafɪk
AM ˌhɑləˈgræfɪk, ˌhoʊləˈgræfɪk

holographically
BR ˌhɒləˈgrafɪkli
AM ˌhɑləˈgræfək(ə)li, ˌhoʊləˈgræfək(ə)li

holography
BR hɒˈlɒgrəfi
AM hoʊˈlɑgrəfi

holohedral
BR ˌhɒləˈhiːdr(ə)l
AM ˌhɑləˈhidrəl, ˌhoʊləˈhidrəl

holometabolous
BR ˌhɒlə(ʊ)mɪˈtabələs
AM ˈhɑloʊməˈtæbələs, ˈhoʊloʊməˈtæbələs

holophote
BR ˈhɒləfəʊt, -s
AM ˈhɑləˌfoʊt, ˈhoʊləˌfoʊt, -s

holophyte
BR ˈhɒləfʌɪt, -s
AM ˈhɑləˌfaɪt, ˈhoʊləˌfaɪt, -s

holophytic
BR ˌhɒləˈfɪtɪk
AM ˌhɑləˈfɪdɪk, ˌhoʊləˈfɪdɪk

holothurian
BR ˌhɒləˈθ(j)ʊərɪən, ˌhɒləˈθjɔːrɪən, -z
AM ˈhɑləˈθʊriən, ˈhoʊləˈθʊriən, -z

holotype
BR ˈhɒlətʌɪp, -s
AM ˈhɑləˌtaɪp, ˈhoʊləˌtaɪp, -s

Holroyd
BR ˈhɒlrɔɪd, ˈhəʊlrɔɪd
AM ˈhɔlrɔɪd, ˈhoʊlrɔɪd

hols
holidays
BR hɒlz
AM hɑlz

Holst
BR həʊlst
AM hoʊlst

Holstein
BR ˈhɒlsteɪn, -z
AM ˈhoʊlˌsteɪn, ˈhoʊlˌstin, -z
GER ˈhɔlʃtaɪn

holster
BR ˈhəʊlstə(r), ˈhɒlstə(r), -z
AM ˈhoʊlstər, -z

holt
BR həʊlt, -s
AM hoʊlt, -s

holus-bolus
BR ˌhəʊləsˈbəʊləs
AM ˈhoʊləsˈboʊləs

holy
BR ˈhəʊl|i, -ɪə(r), -ɪɪst
AM ˈhoʊli, -ər, -ɨst

Holyhead
BR ˈhɒlɪhɛd
AM ˈhɑliˌhɛd, ˈhoʊliˌ(h)ɛd

Holyoake
BR ˈhəʊlɪəʊk
AM ˈhoʊliˌoʊk

Holyrood
BR ˈhɒlɪruːd
AM ˈhɑliˌrud, ˈhoʊliˌrud

holystone
BR ˈhəʊlɪstəʊn, -z, -ɪŋ, -d
AM ˈhoʊliˌstoʊn, -z, -ɪŋ, -d

Holywell
BR ˈhɒlɪwɛl
AM ˈhɑliˌwɛl, ˈhoʊliˌwɛl

hom
BR həʊm
AM hoʊm

homa
BR ˈhəʊmə(r)
AM ˈhoʊmə

homage
BR ˈhɒmɪdʒ
AM ˈ(h)ɑmɪdʒ

hombre
BR ˈɒmbr|eɪ, ˈɒmbr|i, -eɪz\-ɪz
AM ˈɑmbreɪ, ˈɑmbri, -z

homburg
BR ˈhɒmbəːg, -z
AM ˈhɑmˌbərg, -z

home
BR həʊm, -z, -ɪŋ, -d
AM hoʊm, -z, -ɪŋ, -d

homebody
BR ˈhəʊmˌbɒd|i, -ɪz
AM ˈhoʊmˌbɑdi, -z

homebound
BR ˈhəʊmbaʊnd
AM ˈhoʊmˌbaʊnd

homeboy
BR ˈhəʊmbɔɪ, -z
AM ˈhoʊmˌbɔɪ, -z

homebuyer
BR ˈhəʊmˌbʌɪə(r), -z
AM ˈhoʊmˌbaɪər, -z

homecoming
BR ˈhəʊmˌkʌmɪŋ, -z
AM ˈhoʊmˈkəmɪŋ, -z

homegrown
BR ˌhəʊmˈgrəʊn
AM ˈhoʊmˈgroʊn

homeland
BR ˈhəʊmland, -z
AM ˈhoʊmˌlænd, -z

homeless
BR ˈhəʊmləs
AM ˈhoʊmləs

homelessness
BR ˈhəʊmləsnəs
AM ˈhoʊmləsnəs

homelike
BR ˈhəʊmlʌɪk
AM ˈhoʊmˌlaɪk

homeliness
BR ˈhəʊmlɪnɨs
AM ˈhoʊmlinɨs

homely
BR ˈhəʊml|i, -ɪə(r), -ɪɪst
AM ˈhoʊmli, -ər, -ɨst

homemade
BR ˌhəʊmˈmeɪd
AM ˈhoʊ(m)ˈmeɪd

homemaker
BR ˈhəʊmˌmeɪkə(r), -z
AM ˈhoʊ(m)ˌmeɪkər, -z

home-making
BR ˈhəʊmˌmeɪkɪŋ
AM ˈhoʊ(m)ˌmeɪkɪŋ

homeomorphism
BR ˌhɒmɪə(ʊ)ˈmɔːfɪz(ə)m,

ˌhəʊmɪə(ʊ)'mɔːfɪz(ə)m
AM ˌhoʊmioʊ'mɔrfɪzəm

homeopath
BR 'həʊmɪəpaθ, 'hɒmɪəpaθ, -s
AM 'hoʊmiəˌpæθ, -s

homeopathic
BR ˌhəʊmɪə'paθɪk, ˌhɒmɪə'paθɪk
AM ¦hoʊmiə'pæθɪk

homeopathically
BR ˌhəʊmɪə'paθɨkli, ˌhɒmɪə'paθɨkli
AM ¦hoʊmiə'pæθək(ə)li

homeopathist
BR ˌhəʊmɪ'ɒpəθɪst, ˌhɒmɪ'ɒpəθɪst, -s
AM ¦hoʊmi'ɑpəθəst, -s

homeopathy
BR ˌhəʊmɪ'ɒpəθi, ˌhɒmɪ'ɒpəθi
AM ˌhoʊmi'ɑpəθi

homeostasis
BR ˌhəʊmɪə(ʊ)'steɪsɪs, ˌhɒmɪə(ʊ)'steɪsɪs
AM ¦hoʊmiə'steɪsɪs, ¦hoʊmiə'stæsəs

homeostatic
BR ˌhəʊmɪə(ʊ)'statɪk, ˌhɒmɪə(ʊ)'statɪk
AM ¦hoʊmiə'stædɪk

homeostatically
BR ˌhəʊmɪə(ʊ)'statɨkli, ˌhɒmɪə(ʊ)'statɨkli
AM ¦hoʊmiə'stædək(ə)li

homeotherm
BR 'həʊmɪə(ʊ)θəːm, -z
AM 'hoʊmiəˌθərm, -z

homeothermal
BR ˌhəʊmɪə(ʊ)'θəːml
AM ˌhoʊmiə'θərməl

homeothermic
BR ˌhəʊmɪə(ʊ)'θəːmɪk, ˌhɒmɪə(ʊ)'θəːmɪk
AM ˌhoʊmiə'θərmɪk

homeothermy
BR 'həʊmɪə(ʊ)ˌθəːmi
AM 'hoʊmiəˌθərmi

homeowner
BR 'həʊmˌəʊnə(r), -z
AM 'hoʊmˌoʊnər, -z

Homer
BR 'həʊmə(r), -z
AM 'hoʊmər, -z

Homeric
BR hə(ʊ)'mɛrɪk
AM hoʊ'mɛrɪk

homeroom
BR 'həʊmruːm, 'həʊmrʊm, -z
AM 'hoʊmˌrum, 'hoʊmˌrʊm, -z

Homerton
BR 'hɒmət(ə)n
AM 'hɑmərtən, 'hoʊmərtən

homesick
BR 'həʊmsɪk
AM 'hoʊmˌsɪk

homesickness
BR 'həʊmˌsɪknɪs
AM 'hoʊmˌsɪknɪs

homespun
BR 'həʊmspʌn
AM 'hoʊmˌspən

homestead
BR 'həʊmstɛd, -z, -ɪŋ
AM 'hoʊmˌstɛd, -z, -ɪŋ

homesteader
BR 'həʊmstɛdə(r), -z
AM 'hoʊmˌstɛdər, -z

homestyle
BR 'həʊmstʌɪl
AM 'hoʊmˌstaɪl

hometown
BR 'həʊmtaʊn, ˌhəʊm'taʊn
AM ¦hoʊm¦taʊn

homeward
BR 'həʊmwəd, -z
AM 'hoʊmwərd, -z

homework
BR 'həʊmwəːk
AM 'hoʊmˌwərk

homeworker
BR 'həʊmˌwəːkə(r), -z
AM 'hoʊmˌwərkər, -z

homey
BR 'həʊm|i, -ɪə(r), -ɪɪst
AM 'hoʊmi, -ər, -ɪst

homeyly
BR 'həʊmɨli
AM 'hoʊməli

homeyness
BR 'həʊmɪnɪs
AM 'hoʊminɪs

homicidal
BR ˌhɒmɪ'sʌɪdl
AM ¦hɑmə'saɪdəl

homicidally
BR ˌhɒmɪ'sʌɪdl̩i
AM ¦hɑmə'saɪdl̩i

homicide
BR 'hɒmɪsʌɪd, -z
AM 'hɑməˌsaɪd, -z

homiletic
BR ˌhɒmɪ'lɛtɪk, -s
AM ˌhɑmə'lɛdɪk, -s

homiliary
BR hɒ'mɪlɪər|i, -ɪz
AM hɑ'mɪliˌɛri, -z

homilist
BR 'hɒmɪlɪst, 'hɒml̩ɪst, -s
AM 'hɑmələst, -s

homily
BR 'hɒmɪl|i, 'hɒml̩|i, -ɪz
AM 'hɑməli, -z

homing
BR 'həʊmɪŋ
AM 'hoʊmɪŋ

hominid
BR 'hɒmɪnɪd, -z
AM 'hɑmənəd, 'hɑməˌnɪd, -z

hominoid
BR 'hɒmɪnɔɪd, -z
AM 'hɑməˌnɔɪd, -z

hominy
BR 'hɒmɪni
AM 'hɑməni

Homo
BR 'həʊməʊ, 'hɒməʊ
AM 'hoʊˌmoʊ

homo
BR 'həʊməʊ, -z
AM 'hoʊˌmoʊ, -z

homocentric
BR ˌhəʊmə(ʊ)'sɛntrɪk, ˌhɒmə(ʊ)'sɛntrɪk
AM ˌhoʊmoʊ'sɛntrɪk

homoeopath
BR 'həʊmɪəpaθ, 'hɒmɪəpaθ, -s
AM 'hoʊmiəˌpæθ, -s

homoeopathic
BR ˌhəʊmɪə'paθɪk, ˌhɒmɪə'paθɪk
AM ¦hoʊmiə'pæθɪk

homoeopathically
BR ˌhəʊmɪə'paθɨkli, ˌhɒmɪə'paθɨkli
AM ¦hoʊmiə'pæθək(ə)li

homoeopathist
BR ˌhəʊmɪ'ɒpəθɪst, ˌhɒmɪ'ɒpəθɪst, -s
AM ¦hoʊmi'ɑpəθəst, -s

homoeopathy
BR ˌhəʊmɪ'ɒpəθi, ˌhɒmɪ'ɒpəθi
AM ˌhoʊmi'ɑpəθi

homoeostasis
BR ˌhəʊmɪə(ʊ)'steɪsɪs, ˌhɒmɪə(ʊ)'steɪsɪs
AM ¦hoʊmiə'steɪsɪs, ¦hoʊmiə'stæsəs

homoeostatic
BR ˌhəʊmɪə(ʊ)'statɪk, ˌhɒmɪə(ʊ)'statɪk
AM ¦hoʊmiə'stædɪk

homoeostatically
BR ˌhəʊmɪə(ʊ)'statɨkli, ˌhɒmɪə(ʊ)'statɨkli
AM ¦hoʊmiə'stædək(ə)li

homoeotherm
BR 'həʊmɪə(ʊ)θəːm, 'hɒmɪə(ʊ)θəːm, -z
AM 'hoʊmiəˌθərm, -z

homoeothermal
BR ˌhəʊmɪə(ʊ)'θəːml, ˌhɒmɪə(ʊ)'θəːml
AM ˌhoʊmiə'θərməl

homoeothermic
BR ˌhəʊmɪə(ʊ)'θəːmɪk, ˌhɒmɪə(ʊ)'θəːmɪk
AM ˌhoʊmiə'θərmɪk

homoeothermy
BR 'həʊmɪə(ʊ)ˌθəːmi, 'hɒmɪə(ʊ)ˌθəːmi
AM 'hoʊmiəˌθərmi

homoerotic
BR ˌhəʊməʊɪ'rɒtɪk, ˌhɒməʊɪ'rɒtɪk
AM ˌhoʊmoʊə'rɑdɪk

homogametic
BR ˌhəʊməʊgə'mɛtɪk, ˌhɒməʊgə'mɛtɪk
AM ˌhoʊmoʊgə'mɛdɪk

homogamous
BR hə(ʊ)'mɒgəməs, hɒ'mɒgəməs
AM hoʊ'mɑgəməs, hɑ'mɑgəməs

homogamy
BR hə(ʊ)'mɒgəmi, hɒ'mɒgəmi
AM hoʊ'mɑgəmi, hɑ'mɑgəmi

homogenate
BR hə(ʊ)'mɒdʒɪneɪt, hɒ'mɒdʒɪneɪt, -s
AM hoʊ'mɑdʒəˌneɪt, hə'mɑdʒəˌneɪt, hoʊ'mɑdʒənət, hə'mɑdʒənət, -s

homogeneity
BR ˌhəʊmə(ʊ)dʒɪ'niːɪti, ˌhɒmə(ʊ)dʒɪ'niːɪti, ˌhəʊmə(ʊ)dʒɪ'neɪɪti, ˌhɒmə(ʊ)dʒɪ'neɪɪti
AM ˌhoʊmədʒə'niɪdi, ˌhoʊmoʊdʒə'niɪdi, ˌhoʊmədʒə'neɪɪdi, ˌhoʊmoʊdʒə'neɪɪdi

homogeneous
BR ˌhəʊmə(ʊ)'dʒiːnɪəs, ˌhɒmə(ʊ)'dʒiːnɪəs
AM ˌhoʊmə'dʒiniəs, ˌhoʊmoʊ'dʒiniəs

homogeneously
BR ˌhəʊmə(ʊ)'dʒiːnɪəsli, ˌhɒmə(ʊ)'dʒiːnɪəsli
AM ˌhoʊmə'dʒiniəsli, ˌhoʊmoʊ'dʒiniəsli

homogeneousness
BR ˌhəʊmə(ʊ)'dʒiːnɪəsnəs, ˌhɒmə(ʊ)'dʒiːnɪəsnəs
AM ˌhoʊmə'dʒiniəsnəs, ˌhoʊmoʊ'dʒiniəsnəs

homogenetic
BR ˌhəʊmə(ʊ)dʒɪ'nɛtɪk, ˌhɒmə(ʊ)dʒɪ'nɛtɪk
AM ˌhoʊmədʒə'nɛdɪk, ˌhoʊmoʊdʒə'nɛdɪk

homogenisation
BR həˌmɒdʒɪnʌɪ'zeɪʃn, həˌmɒdʒn̩ʌɪ'zeɪʃn, hɒˌmɒdʒɪnʌɪ'zeɪʃn, hɒˌmɒdʒn̩ʌɪ'zeɪʃn
AM həˌmɑdʒənə'zeɪʃən, həˌmɑdʒəˌnaɪ'zeɪʃən

homogenise
BR hə'mɒdʒɪnʌɪz, hə'mɒdʒn̩ʌɪz, hɒ'mɒdʒɪnʌɪz, hɒ'mɒdʒn̩ʌɪz, -ɪz, -ɪŋ, -d
AM hə'mɑdʒəˌnaɪz, -ɪz, -ɪŋ, -d

homogeniser
BR hə'mɒdʒɪnʌɪzə(r), hə'mɒdʒn̩ʌɪzə(r), hɒ'mɒdʒɪnʌɪzə(r), hɒ'mɒdʒn̩ʌɪzə(r), -z
AM hə'mɑdʒə,naɪzər, -z

homogenization
BR hə,mɒdʒɪnʌɪ'zeɪʃn, hə,mɒdʒn̩ʌɪ'zeɪʃn, hɒ,mɒdʒɪnʌɪ'zeɪʃn, hɒ,mɒdʒn̩ʌɪ'zeɪʃn
AM hə,mɑdʒənə'zeɪʃən, hə,mɑdʒə,naɪ'zeɪʃən

homogenize
BR hə'mɒdʒɪnʌɪz, hə'mɒdʒn̩ʌɪz, hɒ'mɒdʒɪnʌɪz, hɒ'mɒdʒn̩ʌɪz, -ɪz, -ɪŋ, -d
AM hə'mɑdʒə,naɪz, -ɪz, -ɪŋ, -d

homogenizer
BR hə'mɒdʒɪnʌɪzə(r), hə'mɒdʒn̩ʌɪzə(r), hɒ'mɒdʒɪnʌɪzə(r), hɒ'mɒdʒn̩ʌɪzə(r), -z
AM hə'mɑdʒə,naɪzər, -z

homogenous
BR hə'mɒdʒɪnəs, hə'mɒdʒn̩əs, hɒ'mɒdʒɪnəs, hɒ'mɒdʒn̩əs
AM hə'mɑdʒənəs

homogeny
BR hə'mɒdʒɪni, hə'mɒdʒn̩i, hɒ'mɒdʒɪni, hɒ'mɒdʒn̩i
AM hə'mɑdʒəni

homograft
BR 'hɒməgrɑːft, 'hɒməgraft, 'həʊməgrɑːft, 'həʊməgraft, -s
AM 'hɑmə,græft, 'hoʊmə,græft, -s

homograph
BR 'hɒməgrɑːf, 'hɒməgraf, 'həʊməgrɑːf, 'həʊməgraf, -s
AM 'hɑmə,græf, 'hoʊmə,græf, -s

homographic
BR ,hɒmə'grafɪk, ,həʊmə'grafɪk
AM ¦hɑmə'græfɪk, ¦hoʊmə'græfɪk

homoiotherm
BR 'həʊmɔɪə(ʊ)θəːm, 'hɒmɔɪə(ʊ)θəːm, -z
AM ¦hoʊ'mɔɪə,θərm, -z

homoiothermal
BR ,həʊmɔɪə(ʊ)'θəːml, ,hɒmɔɪə(ʊ)'θəːml
AM ¦hoʊ,mɔɪə'θərməl

homoiothermic
BR ,həʊmɔɪə(ʊ)'θəːmɪk, ,hɒmɔɪə(ʊ)'θəːmɪk
AM ¦hoʊ,mɔɪə'θərmɪk

homoiothermy
BR 'həʊmɔɪə(ʊ),θəːmi, 'hɒmɔɪə(ʊ),θəːmi
AM ¦hoʊ'mɔɪə,θərmi

homoiousian
BR ,hɒmɔɪ'uːsɪən, ,həʊmɔɪ'uːsɪən, ,hɒmɔɪ'aʊsɪən, ,həʊmɔɪ'aʊsɪən, ,hɒmɔɪ'uːzɪən, ,həʊmɔɪ'uːzɪən, ,hɒmɔɪ'aʊzɪən, ,həʊmɔɪ'aʊzɪən, -z
AM ¦hoʊ,mɔɪ'usiən, ¦hoʊ,mɔɪ'uziən, -z

homolog
BR 'hɒməlɒg, -z
AM 'hɑmə,lɑg, 'hoʊmə,lɑg, 'hoʊmə,lɔg, -z

homologate
BR hɒ'mɒləgeɪt, hə'mɒləgeɪt, -s, -ɪŋ, -ɪd
AM hoʊ'mɑlə,geɪ|t, hə'mɑlə,geɪ|t, -ts, -dɪŋ, -dɪd

homologation
BR hɒ,mɒlə'geɪʃn, hə,mɒlə'geɪʃn, ,hɒmə(ʊ)lə'geɪʃn
AM hoʊ,mɑlə'geɪʃən, hə,mɑlə'geɪʃən

homological
BR ,hɒmə'lɒdʒɪkl
AM ,hɑmə'lɑdʒəkəl, ,hoʊmə'lɑdʒəkəl

homologise
BR hə'mɒlədʒʌɪz, hɒ'mɒlədʒʌɪz, -ɪz, -ɪŋ, -d
AM hoʊ'mɑlə,dʒaɪz, hə'mɑlə,dʒaɪz, -ɪz, -ɪŋ, -d

homologize
BR hə'mɒlədʒʌɪz, hɒ'mɒlədʒʌɪz, -ɪz, -ɪŋ, -d
AM hoʊ'mɑlə,dʒaɪz, hə'mɑlə,dʒaɪz, -ɪz, -ɪŋ, -d

homologous
BR hə'mɒləgəs, hɒ'mɒləgəs
AM hoʊ'mɑləgəs, hə'mɑləgəs

homologue
BR 'hɒməlɒg, -z
AM 'hɑmə,lɑg, 'hoʊmə,lɑg, 'hoʊmə,lɔg, -z

homology
BR hə'mɒlədʒ|i, hɒ'mɒlədʒ|i, -ɪz
AM hə'mɑlədʒi, hoʊ'mɑlədʒi, -z

homomorph
BR 'həʊmə(ʊ)mɔːf, 'hɒmə(ʊ)mɔːf, -s
AM 'hoʊmə,mɔ(ə)rf, 'hɑmə,mɔ(ə)rf, -s

homomorphic
BR ,həʊmə(ʊ)'mɔːfɪk, ,hɒmə(ʊ)'mɔːfɪk
AM ,hoʊmə'mɔrfɪk, ,hɑmə'mɔrfɪk

homomorphically
BR ,həʊmə(ʊ)'mɔːfɪkli, ,hɒmə(ʊ)'mɔːfɪkli
AM ,hoʊmə'mɔrfək(ə)li, ,hɑmə'mɔrfək(ə)li

homomorphism
BR ,həʊmə(ʊ)'mɔːfɪz(ə)m, ,hɒmə(ʊ)'mɔːfɪz(ə)m, -z
AM ,hoʊmə'mɔr,fɪzəm, ,hɑmə'mɔr,fɪzəm, -z

homomorphous
BR ,həʊmə(ʊ)'mɔːfəs, ,hɒmə(ʊ)'mɔːfəs
AM ¦hoʊmə'mɔrfəs, ¦hɑmə'mɔrfəs

homomorphy
BR 'həʊmə(ʊ),mɔːfi, 'hɒmə(ʊ),mɔːfi
AM 'hoʊmə,mɔrfi, 'hɑmə,mɔrfi

homonym
BR 'hɒmənɪm, -z
AM 'hɑmə,nɪm, -z

homonymic
BR ,hɒmə'nɪmɪk
AM ,hɑmə'nɪmɪk, ,hoʊmə'nɪmɪk

homonymous
BR hə'mɒnɪməs, hɒ'mɒnɪməs
AM hə'mɑnəməs, hoʊ'mɑnəməs

homonymously
BR hə'mɒnɪməsli, hɒ'mɒnɪməsli
AM hə'mɑnəməsli, hoʊ'mɑnəməsli

homonymy
BR hə'mɒnɪmi, hɒ'mɒnɪmi
AM hə'mɑnəmi, hoʊ'mɑnəmi

homoousian
BR ,hɒməʊ'uːsɪən, ,həʊməʊ'uːsɪən, ,hɒməʊ'aʊsɪən, ,həʊməʊ'aʊsɪən, ,hɒməʊ'uːzɪən, ,həʊməʊ'uːzɪən, ,hɒməʊ'aʊzɪən, ,həʊməʊ'aʊzɪən, -z
AM ¦hoʊmoʊ¦usiən, ¦hoʊmoʊ¦uziən, -z

homophile
BR 'həʊməfʌɪl, 'hɒməfʌɪl, -z
AM 'hoʊmə,faɪl, -z

homophobe
BR 'həʊməfəʊb, 'hɒməfəʊb, -z
AM 'hoʊmə,foʊb, -z

homophobia
BR ,həʊmə'fəʊbɪə(r), ,hɒmə'fəʊbɪə(r)
AM ,hoʊmə'foʊbiə

homophobic
BR ,həʊmə'fəʊbɪk, ,hɒmə'fəʊbɪk
AM ¦hoʊmə'foʊbɪk

homophone
BR 'hɒməfəʊn, -z
AM 'hɑmə,foʊn, 'hoʊmə,foʊn, -z

homophonic
BR ,hɒmə'fɒnɪk, ,həʊmə'fɒnɪk
AM ¦hɑmə'fɑnɪk, ¦hoʊmə'fɑnɪk

homophonically
BR ,hɒmə'fɒnɪkli
AM ¦hɑmə'fɑnək(ə)li, ¦hoʊmə'fɑnək(ə)li

homophonous
BR hə'mɒfənəs, hə'mɒfn̩əs, hɒ'mɒfənəs, hɒ'mɒfn̩əs
AM hoʊ'mɑfənəs, hə'mɑfənəs

homophony
BR hə'mɒfəni, hə'mɒfn̩i, hɒ'mɒfəni, hɒ'mɒfn̩i
AM hoʊ'mɑfəni, hə'mɑfəni

homoplastic
BR ,həʊmə(ʊ)'plastɪk, ,hɒmə(ʊ)'plastɪk
AM ¦hɑmə'plæstɪk, ¦hoʊmə'plæstɪk

homopolar
BR ,həʊmə(ʊ)'pəʊlə(r), ,hɒmə(ʊ)'pəʊlə(r)
AM ¦hɑmə'poʊlər, ¦hoʊmə'poʊlər

Homoptera
BR hə'mɒpt(ə)rə(r), hɒ'mɒpt(ə)rə(r)
AM hoʊ'mɑptərə

homopteran
BR hə'mɒpt(ə)rən, hə'mɒpt(ə)rn̩, hɒ'mɒpt(ə)rən, hɒ'mɒpt(ə)rn̩, -z
AM hoʊ'mɑptərən, -z

homopterous
BR hə'mɒpt(ə)rəs, hɒ'mɒpt(ə)rəs
AM hoʊ'mɑptərəs

Homo sapiens
BR ,həʊməʊ 'sapɪɛnz, ,hɒməʊ +, + 'sapɪənz, + 'seɪpɪɛnz, + 'seɪpɪənz

AM ˌhoʊmoʊ ˈseɪpiənz, + ˈsæpiənz

homosexual
BR ˌhəʊmə(ʊ)ˈsɛkʃʊəl, ˌhəʊmə(ʊ)ˈsɛkʃ(ʉ)l, ˌhəʊmə(ʊ)ˈsɛksjʊ(ə)l, ˌhɒmə(ʊ)ˈsɛkʃʊəl, ˌhɒmə(ʊ)ˈsɛkʃ(ʉ)l, ˌhɒmə(ʊ)ˈsɛksjʊ(ə)l, -z
AM ¦hoʊməˈsɛkʃ(əw)əl, ¦hoʊmoʊˈsɛkʃ(əw)əl, -z

homosexuality
BR ˌhəʊmə(ʊ)ˌsɛkʃʊˈalɨti, ˌhəʊmə(ʊ)ˌsɛksjʊˈalɨti, ˌhɒmə(ʊ)ˌsɛkʃʊˈalɨti, ˌhɒmə(ʊ)ˌsɛksjʊˈalɨti
AM ˌhoʊməˌsɛkʃəˈwælədi, ˌhoʊmoʊˌsɛkʃəˈwælədi

homosexually
BR ˌhəʊmə(ʊ)ˈsɛkʃʊəli, ˌhəʊmə(ʊ)ˈsɛkʃʉli, ˌhəʊmə(ʊ)ˈsɛkʃl̩i, ˌhəʊmə(ʊ)ˈsɛksjʊ(ə)li, ˌhɒmə(ʊ)ˈsɛkʃʊəli, ˌhɒmə(ʊ)ˈsɛkʃʉli, ˌhɒmə(ʊ)ˈsɛkʃl̩i, ˌhɒmə(ʊ)ˈsɛksjʊ(ə)li
AM ¦hoʊməˈsɛkʃ(əw)əli, ¦hoʊmoʊˈsɛkʃ(əw)əli

homotransplant
BR ˌhəʊməʊˈtranspla:nt, ˌhəʊməʊˈtra:nspla:nt, ˌhəʊməʊˈtransplant, ˌhɒməʊˈtranspla:nt, ˌhɒməʊˈtra:nspla:nt, ˌhɒməʊˈtransplant, -s
AM ¦hoʊmoʊˈtrænsˌplænt, -s

homousian
BR hɒˈmu:sɪən, hɒˈmaʊsɪən, hɒˈmu:zɪən, hɒˈmaʊzɪən, -z
AM ¦hoʊmoʊ¦usiən, ¦hoʊmoʊˈuziən, -z

homozygote
BR ˌhəʊməʊˈzʌɪgəʊt, ˌhɒməʊˈzʌɪgəʊt, -s
AM ¦hoʊmoʊˈzaɪgoʊt, -s

homozygous
BR ˌhəʊməʊˈzʌɪgəs, ˌhɒməʊˈzʌɪgəs
AM ¦hoʊmoʊˈzaɪgəs

homuncule
BR hɒˈmʌŋkju:l, həˈmʌŋkju:l, -z
AM həˈməŋkjul, -z

homunculus
BR hɒˈmʌŋkjʉləs, həˈmʌŋkjʉləs, -ɨz
AM hoʊˈməŋkjələs, -əz

homy
BR ˈhəʊmi
AM ˈhoʊmi

Hon.
Honorary, Honourable
BR ɒn
AM ɑn

hon
honey
BR hʌn
AM hən

Honan
BR ˈhəʊˈnan
AM ˈhoʊˈnæn

honcho
BR ˈhɒntʃəʊ, -z
AM ˈhɑn(t)ʃoʊ, -z

Honda®
BR ˈhɒndə(*r*), -z
AM ˈhɑndə, -z

Honddu
BR ˈhɒnði
AM ˈhɔnði, ˈhɑnði

Honduran
BR hɒnˈdjʊərən, hɒnˈdjʊərn̩, hɒnˈdʒʊərən, hɒnˈdʒʊərn̩, -z
AM hɑnˈd(j)ʊrən, -z

Honduras
BR hɒnˈdjʊərəs, hɒnˈdʒʊərəs
AM hɑnˈd(j)ʊrəs

hone
BR həʊn, -z, -ɪŋ, -d
AM hoʊn, -z, -ɪŋ, -d

Honecker
BR ˈhɒnɨkə(r)
AM ˈhɑnəkər

Honegger
BR ˈhɒnɨgə(r)
AM ˈhɑnəgər

honest
BR ˈɒnɪst
AM ˈɑnəst

honestly
BR ˈɒnɪstli
AM ˈɑnəs(t)li

honesty
BR ˈɒnɪsti
AM ˈɑnəsti

honey
BR ˈhʌn|i, -ɪz, -d
AM ˈhəni, -z, -d

honeybee
BR ˈhʌnɪbi:, -z
AM ˈhəniˌbi, -z

honeybun
BR ˈhʌnɪbʌn, -z
AM ˈhəniˌbən, -z

honeybunch
BR ˈhʌnɪbʌn(t)ʃ, -ɨz
AM ˈhəniˌbən(t)ʃ, -ɨz

honeycomb
BR ˈhʌnɪkəʊm, -z, -d
AM ˈhəniˌkoʊm, -z, -d

honeydew
BR ˈhʌnɪdju:, ˈhʌnɪdʒu:
AM ˈhəniˌd(j)u

honeyguide
BR ˈhʌnɪgʌɪd, -z
AM ˈhəniˌgaɪd, -z

honeymoon
BR ˈhʌnɪmu:n, -z
AM ˈhəniˌmun, -z

honeymooner
BR ˈhʌnɪmu:nə(r), -z
AM ˈhəniˌmunər, -z

honeysuckle
BR ˈhʌnɪˌsʌkl
AM ˈhəniˌsəkəl

Hong Kong
BR ˌhɒŋ ˈkɒŋ
AM ¦hɔŋ¦kɔŋ, ¦hɑŋ¦kɑŋ

Honiara
BR ˌhɒnɪˈɑ:rə(r)
AM ˌhoʊniˈɑrə

honied
BR ˈhʌnɪd
AM ˈhənid

Honiton
BR ˈhʌnɪt(ə)n, ˈhɒnɪt(ə)n
AM ˈhɑnətn, ˈhənətn

honk
BR hɒŋ|k, -ks, -kɪŋ, -(k)t
AM hɔŋ|k, hɑŋ|k, -ks, -kɪŋ, -(k)t

honkie
BR ˈhɒŋk|i, -ɪz
AM ˈhɔŋki, ˈhɑŋki, -z

honky
BR ˈhɒŋk|i, -ɪz
AM ˈhɔŋki, ˈhɑŋki, -z

honky-tonk
BR ˈhɒŋkɪtɒŋk, -s
AM ˈhɔŋkiˌtɔŋk, ˈhɑŋkiˌtɑŋk, -s

honnête homme
BR ɒˌnɛt ˈɒm, -z
AM ɔ¦nɛt ˈɔm, ɑ¦nɛt ˈɑm, -z

Honolulu
BR ˌhɒnəˈlu:lu:
AM ˌhɑnəˈlulu

honor
BR ˈɒn|ə(r), -əz, -(ə)rɪŋ, -əd
AM ˈɑnər, -z, -ɪŋ, -d

honorable
BR ˈɒn(ə)rəbl
AM ˈɑnər(ə)bəl, ˈɑnrəbəl

honorableness
BR ˈɒn(ə)rəblnəs
AM ˈɑnər(ə)bəlnəs, ˈɑnrəbəlnəs

honorably
BR ˈɒn(ə)rəbli
AM ˈɑnər(ə)bli, ˈɑnrəbli

honorand
BR ˈɒnərand, -z
AM ˈɑnərənd, -z

honoraria
BR ˌɒnəˈrɛ:rɪə(*r*)
AM ˌɑnəˈrɛriə

honorarium
BR ˌɒnəˈrɛ:rɪəm, -z
AM ˌɑnəˈrɛriəm, -z

honorary
BR ˈɒn(ə)rəri
AM ˈɑnəˌrɛri

honorific
BR ˌɒnəˈrɪfɪk
AM ˌɑnəˈrɪfɪk

honorifically
BR ˌɒnəˈrɪfɪkli
AM ˌɑnəˈrɪfək(ə)li

honoris causa
BR (h)ɒˌnɔ:rɪs ˈkaʊzə(*r*)
AM (h)ə¦nɔrəs ˈkɔzə, + ˈkɑzə

honour
BR ˈɒn|ə(r), -əz, -(ə)rɪŋ, -əd
AM ˈɑnər, -z, -ɪŋ, -d

honourable
BR ˈɒn(ə)rəbl
AM ˈɑn(ə)r(ə)bəl

honourableness
BR ˈɒn(ə)rəblnəs
AM ˈɑnər(ə)bəlnəs, ˈɑnrəbəlnəs

honourably
BR ˈɒn(ə)rəbli
AM ˈɑnər(ə)bli, ˈɑnrəbli

Hon. Sec.
Honorary Secretary
BR ˌɒn ˈsɛk, -s
AM ˌɑn ˈsɛk, -s

Honshu
BR ˈhɒnʃu:
AM ˈhɑnˌʃu

hooch
BR hu:tʃ
AM hutʃ

hood
BR hʊd, -z, -ɪŋ, -ɨd
AM hʊd, -z, -ɪŋ, -əd

hoodie
BR ˈhʊd|i, -ɪz
AM ˈhʊdi, -z

hoodless
BR ˈhʊdləs
AM ˈhʊdləs

hoodlike
BR ˈhʊdlʌɪk
AM ˈhʊdˌlaɪk

hoodlum
BR ˈhu:dləm, -z
AM ˈhudləm, ˈhʊdləm, -z

hoodoo
BR ˈhu:du:, -z
AM ˈhuˌdu, -z

hoodwink
BR ˈhʊdwɪŋ|k, -ks, -kɪŋ, -(k)t
AM ˈhʊˌdwɪŋ|k, -ks, -kɪŋ, -(k)t

hooey
BR ˈhuːi
AM ˈhui

hoof
BR huːf, hʊf, -s, -ɪŋ, -t
AM hʊf, huf, -s, -ɪŋ, -t

hoofbeat
BR ˈhuːfbiːt, ˈhʊfbiːt, -s
AM ˈhʊfˌbit, ˈhufˌbit, -s

hoofer
BR ˈhuːfə(r), ˈhʊfə(r), -z
AM ˈhʊfər, ˈhufər, -z

hoofmark
BR ˈhuːfmɑːk, ˈhʊfmɑːk, -s
AM ˈhʊfˌmɑrk, ˈhufˌmɑrk, -s

Hooghly
BR ˈhuːgli
AM ˈhugli

hoo-ha
BR ˈhuːhɑː(r), -z
AM ˈhuˌhɑ, -z

hoo-hah
BR ˈhuːhɑː(r), -z
AM ˈhuˌhɑ, -z

hook
BR hʊk, -s, -ɪŋ, -t
AM hʊk, -s, -ɪŋ, -t

hooka
BR ˈhʊkə(r), ˈhuːkɑː(r), -z
AM ˈhʊkə, ˈhukə, -z

hookah
BR ˈhʊkə(r), ˈhuːkɑː(r), -z
AM ˈhʊkə, ˈhukə, -z

Hooke
BR hʊk
AM hʊk

hooker
BR ˈhʊkə(r), -z
AM ˈhʊkər, -z

hookey
BR ˈhʊki
AM ˈhʊki

hookless
BR ˈhʊkləs
AM ˈhʊkləs

hooklet
BR ˈhʊklɪt, -s
AM ˈhʊklət, -s

hooklike
BR ˈhʊklʌɪk
AM ˈhʊkˌlaɪk

hookup
BR ˈhʊkʌp, -s
AM ˈhʊˌkəp, -s

hookworm
BR ˈhʊkwəːm, -z
AM ˈhʊkˌwərm, -z

hooky
BR ˈhʊki
AM ˈhʊki

Hooley
BR ˈhuːli
AM ˈhuli

hooligan
BR ˈhuːlɪg(ə)n, -z
AM ˈhuləgən, -z

hooliganism
BR ˈhuːlɪgənɪz(ə)m, ˈhuːlɪgn̩ɪz(ə)m
AM ˈhuləgəˌnɪzəm

hoon
BR huːn, -z, -ɪŋ, -d
AM hun, -z, -ɪŋ, -d

hoop
BR huːp, -s
AM hup, -s

Hooper
BR ˈhuːpə(r)
AM ˈhupər

hoopla
BR ˈhuːplɑː(r), ˈhʊplɑː(r), -z
AM ˈhuˌplɑ, ˈhʊˌplɑ, -z

hoopoe
BR ˈhuːpuː, ˈhuːpəʊ, -z
AM ˈhuˌpoʊ, ˈhuˌpu, -z

hooray
BR hʉˈreɪ
AM həˈreɪ, huˈreɪ

hooroo
BR hʉˈruː, -z
AM ˌhuˈru, -z

hoosegow
BR ˈhuːsgaʊ, -z
AM ˈhusˌgaʊ, -z

Hoosier
BR ˈhuːʒə(r), ˈhuːzɪə(r), -z
AM ˈhuʒər, -z

Hooson
BR ˈhuːsn
AM ˈhusən

hoot
BR huːt, -s, -ɪŋ, -ɪd
AM hu|t, -ts, -dɪŋ, -dəd

hootch
BR huːtʃ
AM hutʃ

hootenanny
BR ˈhuːtn̩an|i, ˌhuːtnˈan|i, -ɪz
AM ˈhutnˌæni, -z

hooter
BR ˈhuːtə(r), -z
AM ˈhudər, -z

hoover
BR ˈhuːv|ə(r), -əz, -(ə)rɪŋ, -əd
AM ˈhuvər, -z, -ɪŋ, -d

Hooverville
BR ˈhuːvəvɪl
AM ˈhuvərˌvɪl, ˈhuvərvəl

hooves
BR huːvz
AM hʊvz, huvz

hop
BR hɒp, -s, -ɪŋ, -t
AM hɑp, -s, ɪŋ, -t

hop-bine
BR ˈhɒpbʌɪn, -z
AM ˈhɑ(p)ˌbaɪn, -z

Hopcraft
BR ˈhɒpkrɑːft, ˈhɒpkraft
AM ˈhɑpˌkræft

Hopcroft
BR ˈhɒpkrɒft
AM ˈhɑpˌkrɔft, ˈhɑpˌkrɑft

hope
BR həʊp, -s, -ɪŋ, -t
AM hoʊp, -s, -ɪŋ, -t

hopeful
BR ˈhəʊpf(ʊ)l
AM ˈhoʊpfəl

hopefully
BR ˈhəʊpfʊli, ˈhəʊpfl̩i
AM ˈhoʊpfəli

hopefulness
BR ˈhəʊpf(ʊ)lnəs
AM ˈhoʊpfəlnəs

hopeless
BR ˈhəʊpləs
AM ˈhoʊpləs

hopelessly
BR ˈhəʊpləsli
AM ˈhoʊpləsli

hopelessness
BR ˈhəʊpləsnəs
AM ˈhoʊpləsnəs

hoper
BR ˈhəʊpə(r), -z
AM ˈhoʊpər, -z

hophead
BR ˈhɒphɛd, -z
AM ˈhɑpˌ(h)ɛd, -z

Hopi
BR ˈhəʊp|i, -ɪz
AM ˈhoʊpi, -z

Hopkin
BR ˈhɒpkɪn
AM ˈhɑpkən

Hopkins
BR ˈhɒpkɪnz
AM ˈhɑpkənz

Hopkinson
BR ˈhɒpkɪns(ə)n
AM ˈhɑpkənsən

hoplite
BR ˈhɒplʌɪt, -s
AM ˈhɑˌplaɪt, -s

hop-o'-my-thumb
BR ˌhɒpəməˈθʌm, -z
AM ˈhɑpəməˈθəm, ˈhɑpəˌmaɪˈθəm, -z

hopper
BR ˈhɒpə(r), -z
AM ˈhɑpər, -z

hopple
BR ˈhɒp|l, -lz, -l̩ɪŋ\-lɪŋ, -ld
AM ˈhɑp|əl, -əlz, -(ə)lɪŋ, -əld

hopsack
BR ˈhɒpsak
AM ˈhɑpˌsæk

hopsacking
BR ˈhɒpˌsakɪŋ
AM ˈhɑpˌsækɪŋ

hopscotch
BR ˈhɒpskɒtʃ
AM ˈhɑpˌskɑtʃ

Hopwood
BR ˈhɒpwʊd
AM ˈhɑpˌwʊd

Horabin
BR ˈhɒrəbɪn
AM ˈhɔrəbən

Horace
BR ˈhɒrɪs
AM ˈhɔrəs

Horan
BR ˈhɔːrən, ˈhɔːrn̩
AM ˈhɔrən

horary
BR ˈhɔːrər|i, -ɪz
AM ˈhɔrəri, -z

Horatia
BR həˈreɪʃ(ɪ)ə(r)
AM həˈreɪʃə

Horatian
BR həˈreɪʃn
AM həˈreɪʃən

Horatio
BR həˈreɪʃ(ɪ)əʊ
AM həˈreɪʃ(i)oʊ

Horbury
BR ˈhɔːb(ə)ri
AM ˈhɔrˌbɛri

horde
BR hɔːd, -z
AM hɔ(ə)rd, -z

Hordern
BR ˈhɔːdn
AM ˈhɔrdərn

Horeb
BR ˈhɔːrɛb
AM ˈhɔrəb

horehound
BR ˈhɔːhaʊnd, -z
AM ˈhɔrˌ(h)aʊnd, -z

Horgan
BR ˈhɔːg(ə)n
AM ˈhɔrgən

horizon
BR həˈrʌɪzn, -z
AM həˈraɪzn, -z

horizontal
BR ˌhɒrɪˈzɒntl
AM ˌhɔrəˈzɑn(t)l

horizontality
BR ˌhɒrɪzɒnˈtalɪti
AM ˌhɔrəˌzɑnˈtælədi

horizontally
BR ˌˌhɒrɪˈzɒntḷi, hɒrɪˈzɒntəli
AM ˌhɔrəˈzɑn(t)ḷi
horizontalness
BR ˌhɒrɪˈzɒntlnəs
AM ˌhɔrəˈzɑn(t)lnəs
Horkheimer
BR ˈhɔːkˌhʌɪmə(r)
AM ˈhɔrkˌ(h)aɪmər
Horlicks®
BR ˈhɔːlɪks
AM ˈhɔrˌlɪks
hormonal
BR hɔːˈməʊnl
AM hɔrˈmoʊnəl
hormonally
BR hɔːˈməʊnḷi
AM hɔrˈmoʊnəli
hormone
BR ˈhɔːməʊn, -z
AM ˈhɔrˌmoʊn, -z
Hormuz
BR ˌhɔːˈmʊz, ˌhɔːˈmuːz
AM ˌhɔrˈmuz
horn
BR hɔːn, -z, -d
AM hɔ(ə)rn, -z, -d
hornbeam
BR ˈhɔːnbiːm, -z
AM ˈhɔrnˌbim, -z
hornbill
BR ˈhɔːnbɪl, -z
AM ˈhɔrnˌbɪl, -z
hornblende
BR ˈhɔːnblɛnd, -z
AM ˈhɔrnˌblɛnd, -z
Hornblower
BR ˈhɔːnˌbləʊə(r)
AM ˈhɔrnˌbloʊər
hornbook
BR ˈhɔːnbʊk, -s
AM ˈhɔrnˌbʊk, -s
Hornby
BR ˈhɔːnbi
AM ˈhɔrnbi
Horncastle
BR ˈhɔːnˌkɑːsl, ˈhɔːnˌkasl
AM ˈhɔrnˌkæsəl
Hornchurch
BR ˈhɔːntʃəːtʃ
AM ˈhɔrnˌtʃərtʃ
Horne
BR hɔːn
AM hɔ(ə)rn
Horner
BR ˈhɔːnə(r)
AM ˈhɔrnər
horner
BR ˈhɔːnə(r), -z
AM ˈhɔrnər, -z
hornet
BR ˈhɔːnɪt, -s
AM ˈhɔrnət, -s
horniness
BR ˈhɔːnɪnɪs
AM ˈhɔrninɨs
hornist
BR ˈhɔːnɪst, -s
AM ˈhɔrnəst, -s
hornless
BR ˈhɔːnləs
AM ˈhɔrnləs
hornlike
BR ˈhɔːnlʌɪk
AM ˈhɔrnˌlaɪk
hornpipe
BR ˈhɔːnpʌɪp, -s
AM ˈhɔrnˌpaɪp, -s
Hornsby
BR ˈhɔːnzbi
AM ˈhɔrnzbi
hornstone
BR ˈhɔːnstəʊn
AM ˈhɔrnˌstoʊn
hornswoggle
BR ˈhɔːnˌswɒg|l, -lz, -ḷɪŋ\-lɪŋ, -ld
AM ˈhɔrnˌswɑg|əl, -əlz, -(ə)lɪŋ, -əld
Hornung
BR ˈhɔːnʊŋ
AM ˈhɔrnɪŋ, ˈhɔrnʊŋ
hornwort
BR ˈhɔːnwəːt, -s
AM ˈhɔrnˌwərt, ˈhɔrnˌwɔ(ə)rt, -s
horny
BR ˈhɔːn|i, -ɪə(r), -ɪɪst
AM ˈhɔrni, -ər, -ɪst
horologe
BR ˈhɒrəlɒdʒ, -ɪz
AM ˈhɔrəˌlɑdʒ, -əz
horologer
BR həˈrɒlədʒə(r), hɒˈrɒlədʒə(r), -z
AM həˈrɑlədʒər, -z
horologic
BR ˌhɒrəˈlɒdʒɪk
AM ˌhɔrəˈlɑdʒɪk
horological
BR ˌhɒrəˈlɒdʒɪkl
AM ˌhɔrəˈlɑdʒəkəl
horologist
BR həˈrɒlədʒɪst, hɒˈrɒlədʒɪst, -s
AM həˈrɑlədʒəst, -s
horology
BR həˈrɒlədʒi, hɒˈrɒlədʒi
AM həˈrɑlədʒi
horoscope
BR ˈhɒrəskəʊp, -s
AM ˈhɔrəˌskoʊp, -s
horoscopic
BR ˌhɒrəˈskɒpɪk
AM ˌhɔrəˈskɑpɪk
horoscopical
BR ˌhɒrəˈskɒpɪkl
AM ˌhɔrəˈskɑpəkəl
horoscopy
BR həˈrɒskəpi, hɒˈrɒskəpi
AM həˈrɑskəpi
Horowitz
BR ˈhɒrəwɪts, ˈhɒrəvɪts
AM ˈhɔrəˌwɪts
RUS ˈgorəvʲits
horrendous
BR həˈrɛndəs, hɒˈrɛndəs
AM həˈrɛndəs, hɔˈrɛndəs
horrendously
BR həˈrɛndəsli, hɒˈrɛndəsli
AM həˈrɛndəsli, hɔˈrɛndəsli
horrendousness
BR həˈrɛndəsnəs, hɒˈrɛndəsnəs
AM həˈrɛndəsnəs, hɔˈrɛndəsnəs
horrent
BR ˈhɒrənt, ˈhɒrn̩t
AM ˈhɔrənt
horrible
BR ˈhɒrɪbl
AM ˈhɔrəbəl
horribleness
BR ˈhɒrɪblnəs
AM ˈhɔrəbəlnəs
horribly
BR ˈhɒrɪbli
AM ˈhɔrəbli
horrid
BR ˈhɒrɪd
AM ˈhɔrəd
horridly
BR ˈhɒrɪdli
AM ˈhɔrədli
horridness
BR ˈhɒrɪdnɪs
AM ˈhɔrədnəs
horrific
BR həˈrɪfɪk
AM hɔˈrɪfɪk, həˈrɪfɪk
horrifically
BR həˈrɪfɪkli
AM hɔˈrɪfək(ə)li, həˈrɪfək(ə)li
horrification
BR ˌhɒrɪfɪˈkeɪʃn
AM hɔˌrɪfəˈkeɪʃən
horrifiedly
BR ˈhɒrɪfʌɪdli
AM ˈhɔrəˌfaɪdli
horrify
BR ˈhɒrɪfʌɪ, -z, -ɪŋ, -d
AM ˈhɔrəˌfaɪ, -z, -ɪŋ, -d
horrifyingly
BR ˈhɒrɪfʌɪɪŋli
AM ˈhɔrəˌfaɪɪŋli
horripilation
BR həˌrɪpɪˈleɪʃn, hɒˌrɪpɪˈleɪʃn
AM hɔˌrɪpəˈleɪʃən
horror
BR ˈhɒrə(r), -z
AM ˈhɔrər, -z
Horsa
BR ˈhɔːsə(r)
AM ˈhɔrsə
hors concours
BR ˌɔː ˈkõkʊə(r)
AM ˌɔ(ə)r kɔnˈkʊ(ə)r
hors de combat
BR ˌɔː də ˈkɒmbɑː(r)
AM ˌɔr də ˌkɑmˈbɑ
hors-d'œuvre
BR ˌɔːˈdəːv, -z
AM ˌɔrˈdərv, -z
horse
BR hɔːs, -ɪz, -ɪŋ, -t
AM hɔ(ə)rs, -ɪz, -ɪŋ, -t
horseback
BR ˈhɔːsbak
AM ˈhɔrsˌbæk
horsebean
BR ˈhɔːsbiːn, -z
AM ˈhɔrsˌbin, -z
horsebox
BR ˈhɔːsbɒks, -ɪz
AM ˈhɔrsˌbɑks, -əz
horsebreaker
BR ˈhɔːsˌbreɪkə(r), -z
AM ˈhɔrsˌbreɪkər, -z
horse-coper
BR ˈhɔːsˌkəʊpə(r), -z
AM ˈhɔrsˌkoʊpər, -z
Horseferry
BR ˈhɔːsˌfɛri
AM ˈhɔrsˌfɛri
horseflesh
BR ˈhɔːsflɛʃ
AM ˈhɔrsˌflɛʃ
horsefly
BR ˈhɔːsflʌɪ, -z
AM ˈhɔrsˌflaɪ, -z
Horseforth
BR ˈhɔːsfəθ
AM ˈhɔrsˌfɔ(ə)rθ
Horseguard
BR ˈhɔːsgɑːd, -z
AM ˈhɔrsˌgɑrd, -z
horsehair
BR ˈhɔːshɛː(r)
AM ˈhɔrsˌ(h)ɛ(ə)r
horsehide
BR ˈhɔːshʌɪd
AM ˈhɔrsˌ(h)aɪd
horseleech
BR ˈhɔːsliːtʃ, -ɪz
AM ˈhɔrsˌlitʃ, -ɪz
horseless
BR ˈhɔːsləs
AM ˈhɔrsləs
horselike
BR ˈhɔːslʌɪk
AM ˈhɔrsˌlaɪk
horseman
BR ˈhɔːsmən
AM ˈhɔrsmən
horsemanship
BR ˈhɔːsmənʃɪp
AM ˈhɔrsmənˌʃɪp

horsemeat
BR 'hɔːsmiːt
AM 'hɔrs,mit

horseplay
BR 'hɔːspleɪ
AM 'hɔrs,pleɪ

horsepower
BR 'hɔːs,paʊə(r)
AM 'hɔrs,paʊər

horseradish
BR 'hɔːs,rad|ɪʃ, -ɪʃɪz
AM 'hɔrs,rædɪʃ, -ɪz

horseshit
BR 'hɔː(s)ʃɪt
AM 'hɔr(s),ʃɪt

horseshoe
BR 'hɔː(s)ʃuː, 'hɔːʃʃuː, -z
AM 'hɔr(s),ʃu, -z

horsetail
BR 'hɔːsteɪl, -z
AM 'hɔrs,teɪl, -z

horsewhip
BR 'hɔːswɪp, -s, -ɪŋ, -t
AM 'hɔrs,(h)wɪp, -s, -ɪŋ, -t

horsewoman
BR 'hɔːs,wʊmən
AM 'hɔrs,wʊmən

horsewomen
BR 'hɔːs,wɪmɪn
AM 'hɔrs,wɪmɪn

horsey
BR 'hɔːsi
AM 'hɔrsi

Horsham
BR 'hɔːʃɛm
AM 'hɔrʃəm

horsily
BR 'hɔːsɪli
AM 'hɔrsəli

horsiness
BR 'hɔːsɪnɪs
AM 'hɔrsinɪs

horst
BR hɔːst, -s
AM hɔ(ə)rst, -s

horsy
BR 'hɔːs|i, -ɪə(r), -ɪɪst
AM 'hɔrsi, -ər, -ɪst

Horta
BR 'hɔːtə(r)
AM 'hɔrdə

hortation
BR hɔː'teɪʃn, -z
AM ,hɔr'teɪʃən, -z

hortative
BR 'hɔːtətɪv
AM 'hɔrdədɪv

hortatory
BR 'hɔːtət(ə)ri, hɔː'teɪt(ə)ri
AM 'hɔdə,tɔri

Hortense
BR hɔː'tɛns
AM 'hɔr,tɛns

hortensia
BR hɔː'tɛnsɪə(r)
AM hɔr'tɛnsiə

horticultural
BR ,hɔːtɪ'kʌltʃ(ə)rəl, ,hɔːtɪ'kʌltʃ(ə)rl̩
AM ˌhɔrdə'kəltʃ(ə)rəl

horticulturalist
BR ,hɔːtɪ'kʌltʃ(ə)rəlɪst, ,hɔːtɪ'kʌltʃ(ə)rl̩ɪst, -s
AM ˌhɔrdə'kəltʃ(ə)rələst, -s

horticulturally
BR ,hɔːtɪ'kʌltʃ(ə)rəli, ,hɔːtɪ'kʌtʃ(ə)rl̩i
AM ˌhɔrdə'kəltʃ(ə)rəli

horticulture
BR 'hɔːtɪ,kʌltʃə(r)
AM 'hɔrdə,kəltʃər

horticulturist
BR ,hɔːtɪ'kʌltʃ(ə)rɪst, -s
AM ˌhɔrdə'kəltʃərə()st, -s

horti sicci
BR ,hɔːtʌɪ 'sɪkʌɪ, ,hɔːtiː 'sɪkiː
AM ˌhɔrdaɪ 'sɪ,kaɪ

Horton
BR 'hɔːtn
AM 'hɔrt(ə)n

hortus siccus
BR ,hɔːtəs 'sɪkəs
AM ˌhɔrdəs 'sɪkəs

Horus
BR 'hɔːrəs
AM 'hɔrəs

hosanna
BR hə(ʊ)'zanə(r), -z
AM hoʊ'zænə, -z

hose
BR həʊz, -ɪz, -ɪŋ, -d
AM hoʊz, -ɪz, -ɪŋ, -d

Hosea
BR hə(ʊ)'zɪə(r)
AM hoʊ'zeɪə

Hoseason
BR həʊ'siːzn
AM hoʊ'sizn

hosepipe
BR 'həʊzpʌɪp, -s
AM 'hoʊz,paɪp, -s

hosier
BR 'həʊzɪə(r), -z
AM 'hoʊʒər, -z

hosiery
BR 'həʊz(ɪ)əri
AM 'hoʊʒ(ə)ri

hospice
BR 'hɒsp|ɪs, -ɪsɪz
AM 'hɑspəs, -əz

hospitable
BR hɒ'spɪtəbl, hə'spɪtəbl, 'hɒspɪtəbl
AM hɑ'spɪdəbəl, 'hɑspɪdəbəl

hospitably
BR hɒ'spɪtəbli, hə'spɪtəbli, 'hɒspɪtəbli
AM hɑ'spɪdɪbli, 'hɑspɪdɪbli

hospital
BR 'hɒspɪtl, -z
AM 'hɑ,spɪdl, -z

hospitaler
BR 'hɒspɪtl̩ə(r)
AM 'hɑ,spɪdl̩ər

hospitalisation
BR ,hɒspɪtl̩ʌɪ'zeɪʃn
AM ,hɑ,spɪdələ'zeɪʃən, ,hɑ,spɪdəl,aɪ'zeɪʃən

hospitalise
BR 'hɒspɪtl̩ʌɪz, 'hɒspɪtəlʌɪz, -ɪz, -ɪŋ, -d
AM 'hɑ,spədə,laɪz, -ɪz, -ɪŋ, -d

hospitalism
BR 'hɒspɪtl̩ɪz(ə)m, 'hɒspɪtəlɪz(ə)m
AM 'hɑ,spədə,lɪzəm

hospitality
BR ,hɒspɪ'talɪti
AM ,hɑspə'tælədi

hospitalization
BR ,hɒspɪtl̩ʌɪ'zeɪʃn
AM ,hɑ,spɪdələ'zeɪʃən, ,hɑ,spɪdəl,aɪ'zeɪʃən

hospitalize
BR 'hɒspɪtl̩ʌɪz, 'hɒspɪtəlʌɪz, -ɪz, -ɪŋ, -d
AM 'hɑ,spədə,laɪz, -ɪz, -ɪŋ, -d

hospitaller
BR 'hɒspɪtl̩ə(r)
AM 'hɑ,spɪdl̩ər

host
BR həʊst, -s, -ɪŋ, -ɪd
AM hoʊst, -s, -ɪŋ, -əd

hosta
BR 'hɒstə(r), -z
AM 'hɑstə, -z

hostage
BR 'hɒst|ɪdʒ, -ɪdʒɪz
AM 'hɑstɪdʒ, -ɪz

hostageship
BR 'hɒstɪdʒʃɪp
AM 'hɑstɪdʒ,ʃɪp

hostel
BR 'hɒstl̩, -z, -ɪŋ
AM 'hɑst|l, -lz, -l̩ɪŋ

hosteller
BR 'hɒstl̩ə(r), 'hɒstələ(r), -z
AM 'hɑstələr, -z

hostelry
BR 'hɒstlr|i, -ɪz
AM 'hɑstlri, -z

hostess
BR 'həʊstəs, həʊ'stɛs, -ɪz
AM 'hoʊstəs, -əz

hostile
BR 'hɒstʌɪl
AM 'hɑstl, 'hɑ,staɪl

hostilely
BR 'hɒstʌɪlli
AM 'hɑst(l)li, 'hɑ,staɪ(l)li

hostility
BR hɒ'stɪlɪt|i, -ɪz
AM hɑ'stɪlɪdi, -z

hostler
BR '(h)ɒslə(r), -z
AM '(h)ɑslər, -z

hot
BR hɒt, -ə(r), -ɪst
AM hɑt, -dər, -dəst

hotbed
BR 'hɒtbɛd, -z
AM 'hɑt,bɛd, -z

hot-blooded
BR ,hɒt'blʌdɪd
AM 'hɑt'blədəd

hot-bloodedly
BR ,hɒt'blʌdɪdli
AM 'hɑt'blədədli

hot cake
BR ,hɒt 'keɪk, -s
AM 'hɑt ,keɪk, -s

Hotchkiss
BR 'hɒtʃkɪs, -z
AM 'hɑtʃ,kɪs, -z

hotchpot
BR 'hɒtʃpɒt
AM 'hɑtʃ,pɑt

hotchpotch
BR 'hɒtʃpɒtʃ
AM 'hɑtʃ,pɑtʃ

hotdog
BR ,hɒt'dɒg, -z, -ɪŋ
AM 'hɑt,dɔg, 'hɑt,dɑg, -z, -ɪŋ

hotel
BR ,həʊ'tɛl, hə(ʊ)'tɛl, -z
AM hoʊ'tɛl, -z

hotelier
BR hə(ʊ)'tɛlɪə(r), hə(ʊ)'tɛlɪeɪ, -z
AM hoʊ'tɛljər, ˌɔtɛl'jeɪ, -z

hotelkeeper
BR hə(ʊ)'tɛl,kiːpə(r), -z
AM hoʊ'tɛl,kipər, -z

hotfoot[1]
adverb
BR ,hɒt'fʊt
AM 'hɑt,fʊt

hotfoot[2]
verb
BR 'hɒtfʊt, ,hɒt'fʊt, -s, -ɪŋ, -ɪd
AM 'hɑt,fʊ|t, -ts, -dɪŋ, -dəd

hot gospeler
BR ,hɒt 'gɒspl̩ə(r), + 'gɒspələ(r), -z
AM ,hɑt 'gɑspələr, -z

hot gospeller
BR ,hɒt 'gɒspl̩ə(r), + 'gɒsp(ə)lə(r), -z

AM ˌhɑt ˈɡɑspələr, -z

hothead
BR ˈhɒthɛd, -z
AM ˈhɑtˌ(h)ɛd, -z

hotheaded
BR ˌhɒtˈhɛdɪd
AM ˌhɑtˌhɛdəd

hotheadedly
BR ˌhɒtˈhɛdɪdli
AM ˌhɑtˌhɛdədli

hotheadedness
BR ˌhɒtˈhɛdɪdnɨs
AM ˌhɑtˌhɛdədnəs

hothouse
BR ˈhɒthaʊ|s, -zɨz
AM ˈhɑtˌ(h)aʊ|s, -zəz

hotline
BR ˈhɒtlʌɪn, -z
AM ˈhɑtˌlaɪn, -z

hotly
BR ˈhɒtli
AM ˈhɑtli

hotness
BR ˈhɒtnəs
AM ˈhɑtnəs

hotplate
BR ˈhɒtpleɪt, -s
AM ˈhɑtˌpleɪt, -s

hotpot
BR ˈhɒtpɒt, -s
AM ˈhɑtˌpɑt, -s

hotrod
BR ˈhɒtrɒd, -z
AM ˈhɑtˌrɑd, -z

hot-rodder
BR ˈhɒtˌrɒdə(r), -z
AM ˈhɑtˌrɑdər, -z

hot-rodding
BR ˈhɒtˌrɒdɪŋ
AM ˈhɑtˌrɑdɪŋ

hotshot
BR ˈhɒtʃɒt, -s
AM ˈhɑtˌʃɑt, -s

hotspot
BR ˈhɒtspɒt, -s
AM ˈhɑtˌspɑt, -s

hotspur
BR ˈhɒtspəː(r), -z
AM ˈhɑtˌspər, -z

Hottentot
BR ˈhɒtntɒt, -s
AM ˈhɑtnˌtɑt, -s

hotter
BR ˈhɒtə(r), -z
AM ˈhɑdər, -z

hottie
BR ˈhɒt|i, -ɪz
AM ˈhɑdi, -z

hottish
BR ˈhɒtɪʃ
AM ˈhɑdɪʃ

hotty
BR ˈhɒt|i, -ɪz
AM ˈhɑdi, -z

Houdini
BR huːˈdiːni, hʊˈdiːni
AM huˈdini

Hough
BR haʊ, hʌf, hɒf
AM haʊ, həf

hough
BR hɒk, -s, -ɪŋ, -t
AM hɑk, -s, -ɪŋ, -t

hougher
BR ˈhɒkə(r), -z
AM ˈhɑkər, -z

Houghton
BR ˈhaʊtn, ˈhəʊtn, ˈhɔːtn
AM ˈhoʊtn

Houghton-le-Spring
BR ˌhəʊtnlɪˈsprɪŋ
AM ˌhoʊtnləˈsprɪŋ

Houlihan
BR ˈhuːlɪhən
AM ˈhuləˌhæn

hoummos
BR ˈhʊmʊs, ˈhuːmʊs
AM ˈ(h)juməs

hound
BR haʊnd, -z, -ɪŋ, -ɨd
AM haʊnd, -z, -ɪŋ, -əd

hounder
BR ˈhaʊndə(r), -z
AM ˈhaʊndər, -z

houndish
BR ˈhaʊndɪʃ
AM ˈhaʊndɪʃ

Houndsditch
BR ˈhaʊn(d)zdɪtʃ
AM ˈhaʊn(d)zˌdɪtʃ

houndstooth
BR ˈhaʊn(d)ztuːθ
AM ˈhaʊn(d)zˌtuθ

hour
BR ˈaʊə(r), -z
AM ˈaʊ(ə)r, -z

hourglass
BR ˈaʊəɡlɑːs, ˈaʊəɡlas, -ɨz
AM ˈaʊ(ə)rˌɡlæs, -əz

houri
BR ˈhʊər|i, -ɪz
AM ˈhuri, -z

hourly
BR ˈaʊəli
AM ˈaʊ(ə)rli

house[1]
BR haʊs, -zɨz
AM haʊs, -zəz

house[2]
verb
BR haʊz, -ɨz, -ɪŋ, -d
AM haʊz, -əz, -ɪŋ, -t

houseboat
BR ˈhaʊsbəʊt, -s
AM ˈhaʊsˌboʊt, -s

housebound
BR ˈhaʊsbaʊnd
AM ˈhaʊsˌbaʊnd

houseboy
BR ˈhaʊsbɔɪ, -z
AM ˈhaʊsˌbɔɪ, -z

housebreaker
BR ˈhaʊsˌbreɪkə(r), -z
AM ˈhaʊsˌbreɪkər, -z

housebreaking
BR ˈhaʊsˌbreɪkɪŋ
AM ˈhaʊsˌbreɪkɪŋ

housebuilder
BR ˈhaʊsˌbɪldə(r), -z
AM ˈhaʊsˌbɪldər, -z

housebuilding
BR ˈhaʊsˌbɪldɪŋ
AM ˈhaʊsˌbɪldɪŋ

housebuyer
BR ˈhaʊsˌbʌɪə(r), -z
AM ˈhaʊsˌbaɪər, -z

housebuying
BR ˈhaʊsˌbʌɪɪŋ
AM ˈhaʊsˌbaɪɪŋ

housecarl
BR ˈhaʊskɑːl, -z
AM ˈhaʊsˌkɑrl, -z

housecarle
BR ˈhaʊskɑːl, -z
AM ˈhaʊsˌkɑrl, -z

housecoat
BR ˈhaʊskəʊt, -s
AM ˈhaʊsˌkoʊt, -s

housecraft
BR ˈhaʊskrɑːft, ˈhaʊskraft
AM ˈhaʊsˌkræft

housedog
BR ˈhaʊsdɒɡ, -z
AM ˈhaʊsˌdɔɡ, ˈhaʊsˌdɑɡ, -z

housedress
BR ˈhaʊsdrɛs, -ɨz
AM ˈhaʊsˌdrɛs, -əz

housefly
BR ˈhaʊsflʌɪ, -z
AM ˈhaʊsˌflaɪ, -z

houseful
BR ˈhaʊsfʊl, -z
AM ˈhaʊsˌfʊl, -z

Housego
BR ˈhaʊsɡəʊ
AM ˈhaʊsɡoʊ

housegroup
BR ˈhaʊsɡruːp, -s
AM ˈhaʊsˌɡrup, -s

houseguest
BR ˈhaʊsɡɛst, -s
AM ˈhaʊsˌɡɛst, -s

household
BR ˈhaʊs(h)əʊld, -z
AM ˈhaʊsˌ(h)oʊld, -z

householder
BR ˈhaʊs(h)əʊldə(r), -z
AM ˈhaʊsˌ(h)oʊldər, -z

househusband
BR ˈhaʊsˌhʌzbənd, -z
AM ˈhaʊsˌ(h)əzbənd, -z

housekeep
BR ˈhaʊskiːp, -s
AM ˈhaʊsˌkip, -s

housekeeper
BR ˈhaʊsˌkiːpə(r), -z
AM ˈhaʊsˌkipər, -z

housekeeping
BR ˈhaʊsˌkiːpɪŋ
AM ˈhaʊsˌkipɪŋ

housekept
BR ˈhaʊskɛpt
AM ˈhaʊsˌkɛpt

houseleek
BR ˈhaʊsliːk, -s
AM ˈhaʊsˌlik, -s

houseless
BR ˈhaʊsləs
AM ˈhaʊsləs

houselights
BR ˈhaʊslʌɪts
AM ˈhaʊsˌlaɪts

housemaid
BR ˈhaʊsmeɪd, -z
AM ˈhaʊsˌmeɪd, -z

houseman
BR ˈhaʊsmən
AM ˈhaʊsmən

housemaster
BR ˈhaʊsˌmɑːstə(r), ˈhaʊsˌmastə(r), -z
AM ˈhaʊsˌmæstər, -z

housemate
BR ˈhaʊsmeɪt, -s
AM ˈhaʊsˌmeɪt, -s

housemistress
BR ˈhaʊsˌmɪstrɪs, -ɨz
AM ˈhaʊsˌmɪstrɪs, -ɨz

housemother
BR ˈhaʊsˌmʌðə(r), -z
AM ˈhaʊsˌməðər, -z

housepainter
BR ˈhaʊsˌpeɪntə(r), -z
AM ˈhaʊsˌpeɪn(t)ər, -z

houseparent
BR ˈhaʊsˌpɛːrənt, ˈhaʊsˌpɛːrn̩t, -s
AM ˈhaʊsˌpɛrənt, -s

houseplant
BR ˈhaʊsplɑːnt, ˈhaʊsplant, -s
AM ˈhaʊsˌplænt, -s

houseroom
BR ˈhaʊsruːm, ˈhaʊsrʊm
AM ˈhaʊsˌrum, ˈhaʊsˌrʊm

housesitter
BR ˈhaʊsˌsɪtə(r), -z
AM ˈhaʊ(s)ˌsɪdər, -z

housetop
BR ˈhaʊstɒp, -s
AM ˈhaʊsˌtɑp, -s

housewares
BR ˈhaʊswɛːz
AM ˈhaʊsˌwɛrz

housewarming
BR ˈhaʊsˌwɔːmɪŋ, -z
AM ˈhaʊsˌwɔrmɪŋ, -z

housewife
BR ˈhaʊswʌɪf

AM 'haʊs,waɪf
housewifeliness
BR 'haʊswʌɪflɪnɪs
AM 'haʊs,waɪflinɪs
housewifely
BR 'haʊswʌɪfli
AM 'haʊs,waɪfli
housewifery
BR 'haʊswɪf(ə)ri
AM 'haʊs,waɪfəri
housewives
BR 'haʊswʌɪvz
AM 'haʊs,waɪvz
housework
BR 'haʊswəːk
AM 'haʊs,wərk
housey-housey
BR ,haʊzɪ'haʊzi
AM ¦haʊzi'haʊzi
housing
BR 'haʊzɪŋ
AM 'haʊzɪŋ
Housman
BR 'haʊsmən
AM 'haʊsmən
Houston
BR 'h(j)uːst(ə)n
AM '(h)justən, 'hʊstən
Houyhnhnm
BR 'wɪnɪm, hʊ'ɪnɪm, -z
AM 'wɪnɪm, 'hʊɪn(ɪ)m, -z
hove
BR həʊv
AM hoʊv
hovel
BR 'hɒvl, -z
AM 'həvəl, -z
hover
BR 'hɒv|ə(r), -əz, -(ə)rɪŋ, -əd
AM 'həv|ər, -ərz, -(ə)rɪŋ, -ərd
hovercraft
BR 'hɒvəkrɑːft, 'hɒvəkraft, -s
AM 'həvər,kræft, -s
hoverer
BR 'hɒv(ə)rə(r), -z
AM 'həvərər, -z
hoverfly
BR 'hɒvəflʌɪ, -z
AM 'həvər,flaɪ, -z
hoverport
BR 'hɒvəpɔːt, -s
AM 'həvər,pɔ(ə)rt, -s
hovertrain
BR 'hɒvətreɪn, -z
AM 'həvər,treɪn, -z
Hovis®
BR 'həʊvɪs
AM 'hoʊvəs
how
BR haʊ
AM haʊ
Howard
BR 'haʊəd
AM 'haʊərd
Howarth
BR 'haʊəθ
AM 'haʊərθ
howbeit
BR haʊ'biːɪt
AM haʊ'biɪt
howdah
BR 'haʊdə(r), -z
AM 'haʊdə, -z
Howden
BR 'haʊdn
AM 'haʊdən
how-do-you-do
BR ,haʊdʒə'duː, ,haʊd(ə)jə'duː, -z
AM ,haʊdəjə'du, ,haʊdi'du, -z
howdy
BR 'haʊdi
AM 'haʊdi
how-d'ye-do
BR ,haʊdjə'duː, ,haʊdʒə'duː, -z
AM ,haʊdəjə'du, ,haʊdi'du, -z
Howe
BR haʊ
AM haʊ
Howell
BR 'haʊ(ə)l
AM 'haʊəl
Howells
BR 'haʊəlz
AM 'haʊəlz
Howerd
BR 'haʊəd
AM 'haʊərd
Howes
BR haʊz
AM haʊz
however
BR haʊ'ɛvə(r)
AM haʊ'ɛvər
Howie
BR 'haʊi
AM 'haʊi
howitzer
BR 'haʊɪtsə(r), -z
AM 'haʊətsər, -z
howl
BR haʊl, -z, -ɪŋ, -d
AM haʊl, -z, -ɪŋ, -d
howler
BR 'haʊlə(r), -z
AM 'haʊlər, -z
Howlett
BR 'haʊlɪt
AM 'haʊlət
howsoever
BR ,haʊsəʊ'ɛvə(r)
AM ¦haʊsə'wɛvər, ¦haʊsoʊ'ɛvər
howzat
BR (,)haʊ'zat
AM haʊ'zæt
Hoxton
BR 'hɒkst(ə)n
AM 'hɑkstən
hoy
BR hɔɪ, -z, -ɪŋ, -d
AM hɔɪ, -z, -ɪŋ, -d
hoya
BR 'hɔɪə(r), -z
AM 'hɔɪə, -z
hoyden
BR 'hɔɪdn, -z
AM 'hɔɪdn, -z
hoydenish
BR 'hɔɪdənɪʃ, 'hɔɪdn̩ɪʃ
AM 'hɔɪdn̩ɪʃ
Hoylake
BR 'hɔɪleɪk
AM 'hɔɪ,leɪk
Hoyle
BR hɔɪl
AM hɔɪl
Hsing-king
BR 'ʃɪn'dʒɪŋ
AM 'ʃɪn'dʒɪŋ
Huascarán
BR ,wɑːskə'rɑːn
AM ,wɑskə'rɑn
hub
BR hʌb, -z
AM həb, -z
Hubbard
BR 'hʌbəd
AM 'həbərd
Hubble
BR 'hʌbl
AM 'həbəl
hubbub
BR 'hʌbʌb
AM 'həbəb
hubby
BR 'hʌb|i, -ɪz
AM 'həbi, -z
hubcap
BR 'hʌbkap, -s
AM 'həb,kæp, -s
Hubei
BR 'huː'beɪ
AM 'hu'beɪ
Huber
BR 'hjuːbə(r)
AM 'hjubər
Hubert
BR 'hjuːbət
AM '(h)jubərt
hubris
BR 'h(j)uːbrɪs
AM '(h)jubrəs
hubristic
BR h(j)uː'brɪstɪk
AM (h)ju'brɪstɪk
Huck
BR hʌk
AM hək
huckaback
BR 'hʌkəbak
AM 'həkə,bæk
huckle
BR 'hʌkl, -z
AM 'həkəl, -z
huckle-back
BR 'hʌklbak, -s
AM 'həkəl,bæk, -s
huckleberry
BR 'hʌklb(ə)r|i, -ɪz
AM 'həkəl,bɛri, -z
huckster
BR 'hʌkstə(r), -z
AM 'həkstər, -z
huckstery
BR 'hʌkstəri
AM 'həkstəri
hucksterism
BR 'hʌkstərɪz(ə)m
AM 'həkstə,rɪzəm
Huddersfield
BR 'hʌdəzfiːld
AM 'hədərs,fild
huddle
BR 'hʌdl̩, -əlz, -(ə)lɪŋ, -əld
AM 'həd|əl, -əlz, -(ə)lɪŋ, -əld
Huddleston
BR 'hʌdlst(ə)n
AM 'hədlstən
Hudibras
BR 'hjuːdɪbras
AM 'hjudə,bræs
Hudibrastic
BR ,hjuːdɪ'brastɪk
AM ,hjudə'bræstɪk
Hudson
BR 'hʌdsn
AM 'hədsən
Hué
BR '(h)weɪ
AM '(h)weɪ
hue
BR hjuː, -z
AM (h)ju, -z
hueless
BR 'hjuːləs
AM 'hjuləs
Huey
BR 'hjuːi
AM 'hjui
huff
BR hʌf, -s, -ɪŋ, -t
AM həf, -s, -ɪŋ, -t
huffily
BR 'hʌfɪli
AM 'həfəli
huffiness
BR 'hʌfɪnɪs
AM 'həfinɪs
huffish
BR 'hʌfɪʃ
AM 'həfɪʃ
huffishly
BR 'hʌfɪʃli
AM 'həfɪʃli
huffishness
BR 'hʌfɪʃnɪs

AM 'həfɪʃnɪs

Huffman
BR 'hʌfmən
AM 'həfmən

huffy
BR 'hʌf|i, -ɪə(r), -ɪɪst
AM 'həfi, -ər, -ɪst

hug
BR hʌg, -z, -ɪŋ, -d
AM həg, -z, -ɪŋ, -d

huge
BR hjuːdʒ, -ə(r), -ɪst
AM (h)judʒ, -ər, -əst

hugely
BR 'hjuːdʒli
AM '(h)judʒli

hugeness
BR 'hjuːdʒnəs
AM '(h)judʒnəs

huggable
BR 'hʌgəbl
AM 'həgəbəl

hugger
BR 'hʌgə(r), -z
AM 'həgər, -z

hugger-mugger
BR 'hʌgə,mʌgə(r)
AM 'həgər'məgər

Huggins
BR 'hʌgɪnz
AM 'həgənz

Hugh
BR hjuː
AM (h)ju

Hughenden
BR 'hjuːənd(ə)n
AM 'hjuəndən

Hughes
BR hjuːz
AM (h)juz

Hughey
BR 'hjuːi
AM '(h)jui

Hughie
BR 'hjuːi
AM '(h)jui

Hugo
BR 'hjuːgəʊ
AM '(h)jugoʊ

Huguenot
BR 'hjuːgənəʊ, -z
AM 'hjugə,nɑt, -s

huh
BR hʌ(r)
AM hə

hula
BR 'huːlə(r), -z, -ɪŋ, -d
AM 'hulə, -z, -ɪŋ, -d

hula-hoop
BR 'huːləhuːp, -s
AM 'hulə,hup, -s

hula-hula
BR ,huːlə'huːlə(r), -z, -ɪŋ, -d
AM ¦hulə'hulə, -z, -ɪŋ, -d

hulk
BR hʌlk, -s, -ɪŋ
AM həlk, -s, -ɪŋ

hull
BR hʌl, -z, -ɪŋ, -d
AM həl, -z, -ɪŋ, -d

hullabaloo
BR ,hʌləbə'luː, -z
AM ,hələbə'lu, -z

hullo
BR hə'ləʊ, -z
AM hə'loʊ, -z

Hulme
BR hjuːm, hʌlm
AM hjum

Hulot
BR 'uːləʊ
AM 'uloʊ, 'hjulət

Hulse
BR hʌls
AM həls

hum
BR hʌm, -z, -ɪŋ, -d
AM həm, -z, -ɪŋ, -d

human
BR 'hjuːmən, -z
AM '(h)jumən, -z

humane
BR hjʊ'meɪn, ,hjuː'meɪn, -ə(r), -ɪst
AM hju'meɪn, -ər, -ɪst

humanely
BR hjʊ'meɪnli, ,hjuː'meɪnli
AM hju'meɪnli

humaneness
BR hjʊ'meɪnnɪs, hjuː'meɪnnɪs
AM hju'meɪ(n)nɪs

humanisation
BR ,hjuːmənʌɪ'zeɪʃn
AM ,hjumənə,zeɪʃən, ,(h)jumə,naɪ'zeɪʃən

humanise
BR 'hjuːmənʌɪz, -ɪz, -ɪŋ, -d
AM 'hjumə,naɪz, -ɪz, -ɪŋ, -d

humanism
BR 'hjuːmənɪz(ə)m
AM 'hjumə,nɪzəm

humanist
BR 'hjuːmənɪst, -s
AM 'hjumənəst, -s

humanistic
BR ,hjuːmə'nɪstɪk
AM ,hjumə'nɪstɪk

humanistically
BR ,hjuːmə'nɪstɪkli
AM ¦hjumə'nɪstək(ə)li

humanitarian
BR hjʊ,manɪ'tɛːrɪən, ,hjuːmanɪ'tɛːrɪən, -z
AM hju,mænə'tɛriən, -z

humanitarianism
BR hjʊ,manɪ'tɛːrɪənɪz(ə)m, ,hjuːmanɪ'tɛːrɪənɪz(ə)m
AM hju,mænə'tɛriə,nɪzəm

humanity
BR hjʊ'manɪt|i, -ɪz
AM hju'mænədi, -z

humanization
BR ,hjuːmənʌɪ'zeɪʃn
AM ,hjumənə,zeɪʃən, ,(h)jumə,naɪ'zeɪʃən

humanize
BR 'hjuːmənʌɪz, -ɪz, -ɪŋ, -d
AM '(h)jumə,naɪz, -ɪz, -ɪŋ, -d

humankind
BR ,hjuːmən'kʌɪnd, 'hjuːmənkʌɪnd
AM ,(h)jumən'kaɪnd

humanly
BR 'hjuːmənli
AM 'hjumənli

humanness
BR 'hjuːmənnəs
AM 'hjumə(n)nəs

humanoid
BR 'hjuːmənɔɪd, -z
AM 'hjumə,nɔɪd, -z

Humber
BR 'hʌmbə(r)
AM 'həmbər

Humberside
BR 'hʌmbəsʌɪd
AM 'həmbər,saɪd

Humbert
BR 'hʌmbət
AM 'həmbərt

humble
BR 'hʌmb|l, -lz, -lɪŋ\-lɪŋ, -ld, -lə(r), -lɪst
AM 'həmb|əl, -əlz, -(ə)lɪŋ, -əld, -lər, -ləst

humbleness
BR 'hʌmblnəs
AM 'həmbəlnəs

humbly
BR 'hʌmbli
AM 'həmbli

Humboldt
BR 'hʌmbəʊlt
AM 'həm,boʊlt

humbug
BR 'hʌmbʌg, -z, -ɪŋ, -d
AM 'həm,bəg, -z, -ɪŋ, -d

humbuggery
BR 'hʌmbʌg(ə)ri
AM 'həm,bəgəri

humdinger
BR ,hʌm'dɪŋə(r), -z
AM ¦həm'dɪŋgər, -z

humdrum
BR 'hʌmdrʌm
AM 'həm,drəm

Hume
BR hjuːm
AM hjum

humectant
BR hjʊ'mɛkt(ə)nt, -s
AM hju'mɛktnt, -s

humeral
BR 'hjuːm(ə)rəl, 'hjuːm(ə)rl
AM 'hjumərəl

humerus
BR 'hjuːm(ə)rəs, -ɪz
AM 'hjumərəs, -əz

humic
BR 'hjuːmɪk
AM 'hjumɪk

humid
BR 'hjuːmɪd
AM '(h)jumэd

humidification
BR hjʊ,mɪdɪfɪ'keɪʃn
AM hju,mɪdəfə'keɪʃən

humidifier
BR hjʊ'mɪdɪfʌɪə(r), -z
AM hju'mɪdə,faɪər, -z

humidify
BR hjʊ'mɪdɪfʌɪ, -z, -ɪŋ, -d
AM hju'mɪdə,faɪ, -z, -ɪŋ, -d

humidity
BR hjʊ'mɪdɪti
AM (h)ju'mɪdɪdi

humidly
BR 'hjuːmɪdli
AM 'hjumədli

humidness
BR 'hjuːmɪdnəs
AM 'hjumədnəs

humidor
BR 'hjuːmɪdɔː(r), -z
AM 'hjumə,dɔ(ə)r, -z

humification
BR ,hjuːmɪfɪ'keɪʃn
AM hju,mɪfə'keɪʃən

humify
BR 'hjuːmɪfʌɪ, -z, -ɪŋ, -d
AM 'hjumə,faɪ, -z, -ɪŋ, -d

humiliate
BR hjʊ'mɪlɪeɪt, -s, -ɪŋ, -ɪd
AM (h)ju'mɪli,eɪ|t, -ts, -dɪŋ, -dɪd

humiliatingly
BR hjʊ'mɪlɪeɪtɪŋli
AM hju'mɪli,eɪdɪŋli

humiliation
BR hjʊ,mɪlɪ'eɪʃn, ,hjuːmɪlɪ'eɪʃn, -z
AM hju,mɪli'eɪʃən, -z

humiliator
BR hjʊ'mɪlɪeɪtə(r), -z
AM hju'mɪli,eɪdər, -z

humility
BR hjʊ'mɪlɪti
AM hju'mɪlɪdi

hummable
BR 'hʌməbl
AM 'həməbəl

hummer
BR 'hʌmə(r), -z
AM 'həmər, -z

hummingbird
BR 'hʌmɪŋbəːd, -z
AM 'həmɪŋ,bərd, -z

hummock
BR 'hʌmək, -s
AM 'həmək, -s

hummocky
BR 'hʌməki
AM 'həməki

hummus
BR 'hjuːməs
AM 'həməs, 'hʊməs

humongous
BR hjuː'mʌŋgəs
AM hju'mɑŋgəs

humor
BR 'hjuːm|ə(r), -əz, -(ə)rɪŋ, -əd
AM '(h)jumər, -z, -ɪŋ, -d

humoral
BR 'hjuːm(ə)rəl, 'hjuːm(ə)rl̩
AM 'hjumərəl

humoresque
BR ˌhjuːmə'rɛsk, -s
AM ˌhjumə'rɛsk, -s

humorist
BR 'hjuːmərɪst, -s
AM 'hjumərəst, -s

humoristic
BR ˌhjuːmə'rɪstɪk
AM ˌhjumə'rɪstɪk

humorless
BR 'hjuːmələs
AM 'hjumərləs

humorlessly
BR 'hjuːmələsli
AM 'hjumərləsli

humorlessness
BR 'hjuːmələsnəs
AM 'hjumərləsnəs

humorous
BR 'hjuːm(ə)rəs
AM 'hjumərəs

humorously
BR 'hjuːm(ə)rəsli
AM 'hjumərəsli

humorousness
BR 'hjuːm(ə)rəsnəs
AM 'hjumərəsnəs

humorsome
BR 'hjuːməs(ə)m
AM 'hjumərsəm

humorsomely
BR 'hjuːməs(ə)mli
AM 'hjumərsəmli

humorsomeness
BR 'hjuːməs(ə)mnəs
AM 'hjumərsəmnəs

humour
BR 'hjuːm|ə(r), -əz, -(ə)rɪŋ, -əd
AM '(h)jumər, -z, -ɪŋ, -d

humourist
BR 'hjuːm(ə)rɪst, -s
AM 'hjumərəst, -s

humourless
BR 'hjuːmələs
AM 'hjumərləs

humourlessly
BR 'hjuːmələsli
AM 'hjumərləsli

humourlessness
BR 'hjuːmələsnəs
AM 'hjumərləsnəs

humoursome
BR 'hjuːməs(ə)m
AM 'hjumərsəm

humous
BR 'hjuːməs
AM 'hjuməs

hump
BR hʌm|p, -ps, -pɪŋ, -(p)t
AM həmp, -s, -ɪŋ, -t

humpback
BR 'hʌmpbak, -s
AM 'həmp,bæk, -s

humpbacked
BR ˌhʌmp'bakt
AM 'həmp,bækt

humper
BR 'hʌmpə(r), -z
AM 'həmpər, -z

Humperdinck
BR 'hʊmpədɪŋk, 'hʌmpədɪŋk
AM 'həmpər,dɪŋk

humph
BR hʌmf, hə̃h
AM həm(p)f

Humphrey
BR 'hʌmfri
AM 'həm(p)fri

Humphreys
BR 'hʌmfrɪz
AM 'həm(p)friz

Humphries
BR 'hʌmfrɪz
AM 'həm(p)friz

humpiness
BR 'hʌmpɪnɪs
AM 'həmpinɪs

humpless
BR 'hʌmpləs
AM 'həmpləs

humpty
BR 'hʌm(p)t|i, -ɪz
AM 'həmti, -z

humpty-dumpty
BR ˌhʌm(p)tɪ'dʌm(p)t|i, -ɪz
AM 'həmti'dəmti, -z

humpy
BR 'hʌmp|i, -ɪə(r), -ɪɪst
AM 'həmpi, -ər, -ɪst

humus
BR 'hjuːməs
AM 'hjuməs

humusify
BR 'hjuːməsɪfʌɪ, -z, -ɪŋ, -d
AM 'hjuməsə,faɪ, -z, -ɪŋ, -d

Hun
BR hʌn, -z
AM hən, -z

Hunan
BR ˌhuː'nan
AM 'hu'nɑn

hunch
BR hʌn(t)ʃ, -ɪz, -ɪŋ, -t
AM hən(t)ʃ, -əz, -ɪŋ, -t

hunchback
BR 'hʌn(t)ʃbak, -s
AM 'hən(t)ʃ,bæk, -s

hunchbacked
BR ˌhʌn(t)ʃ'bakt
AM 'hən(t)ʃ,bækt

hundred
BR 'hʌndrəd, -z
AM 'həndrəd, -z

hundredfold
BR 'hʌndrədfəʊld
AM 'həndrəd,foʊld

hundredth
BR 'hʌndrədθ, 'hʌndrətθ
AM 'həndrədθ, 'həndrətθ

hundredweight
BR 'hʌndrədweɪt, -s
AM 'həndrəd,weɪt, -s

hung
BR hʌŋ
AM həŋ

Hungarian
BR hʌŋ'gɛːrɪən, -z
AM həŋ'gɛriən, -z

Hungary
BR 'hʌŋg(ə)ri
AM 'həŋgəri

hunger
BR 'hʌŋg|ə(r), -əz, -(ə)rɪŋ, -əd
AM 'həŋgər, -z, -ɪŋ, -d

Hungerford
BR 'hʌŋgəfəd
AM 'həŋgərfərd

hungrily
BR 'hʌŋgrɪli
AM 'həŋgrəli

hungriness
BR 'hʌŋgrɪnɪs
AM 'həŋgrinɪs

hungry
BR 'hʌŋgr|i, -ɪə(r), -ɪɪst
AM 'həŋgri, -ər, -ɪst

hunk
BR hʌŋk, -s
AM həŋk, -s

hunker
BR 'hʌŋk|ə(r), -əz, -(ə)rɪŋ, -əd
AM 'həŋkər, -z, -ɪŋ, -d

Hunkpapa
BR 'hʌŋk,pɑːpə(r), -z
AM 'həŋk,pɑpə, -z

hunky
BR 'hʌŋk|i, -ɪz
AM 'həŋki, -z

hunky-dory
BR ˌhʌŋkɪ'dɔːri
AM 'həŋki'dɔri

Hunniford
BR 'hʌnɪfəd
AM 'hənəfərd

Hunnish
BR 'hʌnɪʃ
AM 'hənɪʃ

Hunslet
BR 'hʌnzlɪt
AM 'hənzlət

Hunstanton
BR hʌn'stant(ə)n, 'hʌnst(ə)n
AM 'hənstən(t)ən

hunt
BR hʌnt, -s, -ɪŋ, -ɪd
AM hən|t, -ts, -(t)ɪŋ, -(t)əd

huntaway
BR 'hʌntəweɪ, -z
AM 'hən(t)ə,weɪ, -z

hunter
BR 'hʌntə(r), -z
AM 'hən(t)ər, -z

Huntingdon
BR 'hʌntɪŋd(ə)n
AM 'hən(t)ɪŋdən

Huntingdonshire
BR 'hʌntɪŋd(ə)nʃ(ɪ)ə(r)
AM 'hən(t)ɪŋdən,ʃɪ(ə)r

Huntington
BR 'hʌntɪŋt(ə)n
AM 'hən(t)ɪŋtən

Huntley
BR 'hʌntli
AM 'hən(t)li

huntress
BR 'hʌntrɪs, -ɪz
AM 'həntrəs, -əz

huntsman
BR 'hʌn(t)smən
AM 'hən(t)smən

huntsmen
BR 'hʌn(t)smən
AM 'hən(t)smən

Huntsville
BR 'hʌn(t)svɪl
AM 'hən(t)s,vɪl

hup
BR hʌp, -s
AM həp, -s

Hupeh
BR ˌhuː'peɪ
AM 'hu'peɪ

hurdle
BR 'həːd|l, -lz, -l̩ɪŋ\-lɪŋ, -ld
AM 'hərd|əl, -əlz, -(ə)lɪŋ, -əld

hurdler
BR 'həːdḷə(r), 'həːdlə(r), -z
AM 'hərd(ə)lər, -z
hurdy-gurdy
BR ˌhəːdɪ'gəːd|i, 'həːdɪˌgəːd|i, -ɪz
AM ˈhərdiˈgərdi, -z
Hurford
BR 'həːfəd
AM 'hərfərd
hurl
BR həːl, -z, -ɪŋ, -d
AM hərl, -z, -ɪŋ, -d
hurley
BR 'həːli
AM 'hərli
Hurlingham
BR 'həːlɪŋəm
AM 'hərlɪŋəm
hurly-burly
BR ˌhəːlɪ'bəːli, 'həːlɪˌbəːli
AM ˈhərliˈbərli
Hurn
BR həːn
AM hərn
Huron
BR 'hjʊərɒn
AM 'hjʊˌrɑn
hurrah
BR hʉ'rɑː(r), -z
AM hə'rɑ, -z
hurray
BR hʉ'reɪ, -z
AM hə'reɪ, hu'reɪ, -z
Hurri
BR 'hʊr|i, -ɪz
AM 'hʊri, -z
hurricane
BR 'hʌrɪk(ə)n, -z
AM 'hərəˌkeɪn, -z
hurried
BR 'hʌrɪd
AM 'hərid
hurriedly
BR 'hʌrɪdli
AM 'həridli, 'hərədli
hurriedness
BR 'hʌrɪdnɪs
AM 'həridnɪs
hurroo
BR hʉ'ruː, -z
AM ˌhə'ru, -z
hurry
BR 'hʌr|i, -ɪz, -ɪɪŋ, -ɪd
AM 'həri, -z, -ɪŋ, -d
hurry-scurry
BR ˌhʌrɪ'skʌri
AM 'həri'skəri
Hurst
BR həːst
AM hərst
hurst
BR həːst, -s
AM hərst, -s
Hurstmonceux
BR ˌhəːs(t)mən's(j)uː
AM ˌhərs(t)mən'su
Hurston
BR 'həːst(ə)n
AM 'hərstən
Hurstpierpoint
BR ˌhəːs(t)pɪə'pɔɪnt
AM ˌhərs(t)pɪr'pɔɪnt
hurt
BR həːt, -s, -ɪŋ
AM hər|t, -ts, -dɪŋ
hurtful
BR 'həːtf(ʉ)l
AM 'hərtfəl
hurtfully
BR 'həːtfʉli, 'həːtfḷi
AM 'hərtfəli
hurtfulness
BR 'həːtf(ʉ)lnəs
AM 'hərtfəlnəs
hurtle
BR 'həːt|l, -lz, -ḷɪŋ\-lɪŋ, -ld
AM 'hərdəl, -z, -ɪŋ, -d
hurtless
BR 'həːtləs
AM 'hərtləs
Husain
BR hʊ'seɪn
AM hʊ'seɪn
Husák
BR 'huːsak
AM 'husæk
husband
BR 'hʌzbənd, -z, -ɪŋ, -ɪd
AM 'həzbən(d), -z, -ɪŋ, -əd
husbander
BR 'hʌzbəndə(r), -z
AM 'həzbəndər, -z
husbandhood
BR 'hʌzbəndhʊd
AM 'həzbən(dh)ʊd
husbandless
BR 'hʌzbəndləs
AM 'həzbən(d)ləs
husbandlike
BR 'hʌzbəndlʌɪk
AM 'həzbəndˌlaɪk
husbandly
BR 'hʌzbəndli
AM 'həzbən(d)li
husbandman
BR 'hʌzbən(d)mən
AM 'həzbən(d)mən
husbandmen
BR 'hʌzbən(d)mən
AM 'həzbən(d)mən
husbandry
BR 'hʌzbəndri
AM 'həzbəndri
husbandship
BR 'hʌzbən(d)ʃɪp
AM 'həzbən(d)ˌʃɪp
hush
BR hʌʃ, -ɪz, -ɪŋ, -t
AM həʃ, -əz, -ɪŋ, -t
hushaby
BR 'hʌʃəbʌɪ
AM 'həʃəˌbaɪ
hushabye
BR 'hʌʃəbʌɪ
AM 'həʃəˌbaɪ
hush-hush
BR ˌhʌʃ'hʌʃ
AM ˌhəʃ'həʃ
hush money
BR 'hʌʃ ˌmʌni
AM 'həʃ ˌməni
hush-up
BR 'hʌʃʌp
AM 'həʃəp
husk
BR hʌsk, -s, -ɪŋ, -t
AM həsk, -s, -ɪŋ, -t
huskily
BR 'hʌskɨli
AM 'həskəli
huskiness
BR 'hʌskɪnɪs
AM 'həskinɪs
Huskisson
BR 'hʌskɪs(ə)n
AM 'həskənsən
husky
BR 'hʌsk|i, -ɪz, -ɪə(r), -ɪɪst
AM 'həski, -z, -ər, -ɪst
huss
BR hʌs, -ɪz
AM həs, -əz
Hussain
BR hʊ'seɪn
AM hə'seɪn
hussar
BR hʉ'zɑː(r), -z
AM hə'zɑr, -z
Hussein
BR hʊ'seɪn
AM hʊ'seɪn
Husserl
BR 'hʊsəːl
AM 'hʊsərl
Hussey
BR 'hʌsi
AM 'həsi
Hussite
BR 'hʌsʌɪt, 'hʊsʌɪt, -s
AM 'həˌsaɪt, 'hʊˌsaɪt, -s
Hussitism
BR 'hʌsʌɪtɪz(ə)m, 'hʊsʌɪtɪz(ə)m
AM 'həˌsaɪˌtɪzəm, 'hʊˌsaɪˌtɪzəm
hussy
BR 'hʌs|i, 'hʌz|i, -ɪz
AM 'həzi, 'həsi, -z
hustings
BR 'hʌstɪŋz
AM 'həstɪŋz
hustle
BR 'hʌs|l, -lz, -ḷɪŋ\-lɪŋ, -ld
AM 'həs|əl, -əlz, -(ə)lɪŋ, -əld
hustler
BR 'hʌslə(r), -z
AM 'həs(ə)lər, -z
Huston
BR 'hjuːst(ə)n
AM 'hjustən
hut
BR hʌt, -s
AM hət, -s
hutch
BR hʌtʃ, -ɪz
AM hətʃ, -əz
Hutcheson
BR 'hʌtʃɪs(ə)n
AM 'hətʃəsən
Hutchings
BR 'hʌtʃɪŋz
AM 'hətʃɪŋz
Hutchins
BR 'hʌtʃɪnz
AM 'hətʃənz
Hutchinson
BR 'hʌtʃ(ɪ)ns(ə)n
AM 'hətʃənsən
Hutchison
BR 'hʌtʃɪs(ə)n
AM 'hətʃəsən
hutia
BR hʌ'tiː(r), -z
AM hə'tiə, -z
hutlike
BR 'hʌtlʌɪk
AM 'hətˌlaɪk
hutment
BR 'hʌtm(ə)nt, -s
AM 'hətmənt, -s
Hutterite
BR 'hʌtərʌɪt, 'hʊtərʌɪt
AM 'hədəˌraɪt
Hutton
BR 'hʌtn
AM 'hətn
Hutu
BR 'huːtuː, -z
AM 'huˌtu, -z
Huw
BR hjuː
AM hju
WE hɪʊ
Huxley
BR 'hʌksli
AM 'həksli
Huxtable
BR 'hʌkstəbl
AM 'həkstəbəl
Huygens
BR 'hɔɪgənz
AM 'hɔɪgənz
DU 'hœyxəns
Huyton
BR 'hʌɪtn
AM 'haɪtn
huzza
BR hʉ'zɑː(r)
AM hə'zɑ

huzzah
BR hʊˈzɑː(*r*)
AM həˈzɑ
huzzy
BR ˈhʌz|i, -ɪz
AM ˈhəzi, -z
Hwange
BR ˈhwaŋgi, ˈhwaŋgeɪ
AM ˈ(h)wɑŋi
Hwang-Ho
BR ˈhwaŋˈhəʊ
AM ˈ(h)wɑŋˈhoʊ
hwyl
BR ˈhuːɪl, hwiːl
AM ˈhuɪl, (h)wil
WE hwɪl
hyacinth
BR ˈhʌɪəsɪnθ, -s
AM ˈhaɪəˌsɪnθ, -s
hyacinthine
BR ˌhʌɪəˈsɪnθʌɪn
AM ˌhaɪəˌsɪnθən, ˌhaɪəˌsɪnˌθaɪn
Hyacinthus
BR ˌhʌɪəˈsɪnθəs
AM ˌhaɪəˈsɪnθəs
Hyades
BR ˈhʌɪədiːz
AM ˈhaɪˌdiz
hyaena
BR hʌɪˈiːnə(*r*), -z
AM haɪˈinə, -z
hyalin
BR ˈhʌɪəlɪn
AM ˈhaɪələn, ˈhaɪəˌlaɪn
hyaline
BR ˈhʌɪəlɪn, ˈhʌɪəliːn, ˈhʌɪəlʌɪn
AM ˈhaɪələn, ˈhaɪəˌlaɪn
hyalite
BR ˈhʌɪəlʌɪt
AM ˈhaɪəˌlaɪt
hyaloid
BR ˈhʌɪəlɔɪd
AM ˈhaɪəˌlɔɪd
Hyatt
BR ˈhʌɪət
AM ˈhaɪət
hybrid
BR ˈhʌɪbrɪd, -z
AM ˈhaɪˌbrɪd, -z
hybridisable
BR ˈhʌɪbrɪdʌɪzəbl
AM ˈhaɪbrəˌdaɪzəbəl, ˌhaɪbrəˈdaɪzəbəl
hybridisation
BR ˌhʌɪbrɪdʌɪˈzeɪʃn
AM ˌhaɪbrədəˈzeɪʃən, ˌhaɪbrəˌdaɪˈzeɪʃən
hybridise
BR ˈhʌɪbrɪdʌɪz, -ɪz, -ɪŋ, -d
AM ˈhaɪbrəˌdaɪz, -ɪz, -ɪŋ, -d
hybridism
BR ˈhʌɪbrɪdɪz(ə)m
AM ˈhaɪbrəˌdɪzəm
hybridity
BR hʌɪˈbrɪdɪti
AM haɪˈbrɪdɪdi
hybridizable
BR ˈhʌɪbrɪdʌɪzəbl
AM ˈhaɪbrəˌdaɪzəbəl, ˌhaɪbrəˈdaɪzəbəl
hybridization
BR ˌhʌɪbrɪdʌɪˈzeɪʃn
AM ˌhaɪbrədəˈzeɪʃən, ˌhaɪbrəˌdaɪˈzeɪʃən
hybridize
BR ˈhʌɪbrɪdʌɪz, -ɪz, -ɪŋ, -d
AM ˈhaɪbrəˌdaɪz, -ɪz, -ɪŋ, -d
hydantoin
BR hʌɪˈdantəʊɪn
AM haɪˈdænˌtoʊən, haɪˈdæn(t)oʊən
hydathode
BR ˈhʌɪdəθəʊd, -z
AM ˈhaɪdəˌθoʊd, -z
hydatid
BR ˈhʌɪdətɪd, hʌɪˈdatɪd, -z
AM ˈhaɪdədəd, -z
hydatidiform
BR ˌhʌɪdəˈtɪdɪfɔːm
AM ˌhaɪdəˈtɪdəˌfɔ(ə)rm
Hyde
BR hʌɪd
AM haɪd
Hyderabad
BR ˈhʌɪd(ə)rəbad, ˈhʌɪd(ə)rəbɑːd
AM ˈhaɪd(ə)rəˌbɑd, ˈhaɪd(ə)rəˌbæd
Hydra
BR ˈhʌɪdrə(*r*)
AM ˈhaɪdrə
hydra
BR ˈhʌɪdrə(*r*), -z
AM ˈhaɪdrə, -z
hydrangea
BR hʌɪˈdreɪn(d)ʒə(*r*), -z
AM haɪˈdrændʒə, -z
hydrant
BR ˈhʌɪdr(ə)nt, -s
AM ˈhaɪdrənt, -s
hydratable
BR hʌɪˈdreɪtəbl
AM ˈhaɪˌdreɪdəbəl
hydrate[1]
noun
BR ˈhʌɪdreɪt, -s
AM ˈhaɪˌdreɪt, -s
hydrate[2]
verb
BR hʌɪˈdreɪt, -s, -ɪŋ, -ɪd
AM ˈhaɪˌdreɪ|t, -ts, -dɪŋ, -dɪd
hydration
BR hʌɪˈdreɪʃn
AM haɪˈdreɪʃən
hydrator
BR hʌɪˈdreɪtə(r), -z
AM ˈhaɪˌdreɪdər, -z
hydraulic
BR hʌɪˈdrɒlɪk, -s
AM haɪˈdrɔlɪk, haɪˈdrɑlɪk, -s
hydraulically
BR hʌɪˈdrɒlɪkli
AM haɪˈdrɔlək(ə)li, haɪˈdrɑlək(ə)li
hydraulicity
BR ˌhʌɪdrəˈlɪsɪti
AM ˌhaɪdrəˈlɪsɪdi
hydrazine
BR ˈhʌɪdrəziːn
AM ˈhaɪdərəzən, ˈhaɪdrəˌzin
hydric
BR ˈhʌɪdrɪk
AM ˈhaɪdrɪk
hydride
BR ˈhʌɪdrʌɪd, -z
AM ˈhaɪˌdraɪd, -z
hydriodic acid
BR ˌhʌɪdrɪɒdɪk ˈasɪd
AM ˈhaɪdriˌɑdɪk ˈæsəd
hydro
BR ˈhʌɪdrəʊ, -z
AM ˈhaɪdroʊ, -z
hydrobromic acid
BR ˌhʌɪdrəbrəʊmɪk ˈasɪd
AM ˈhaɪdroʊˌbrɑmɪk ˈæsəd
hydrocarbon
BR ˌhʌɪdrə(ʊ)ˈkɑːb(ə)n, -z
AM ˈhaɪdroʊˌkɑrbən, -z
hydrocele
BR ˈhʌɪdrə(ʊ)siːl, -z
AM ˈhaɪdroʊˌsil, -z
hydrocephalic
BR ˌhʌɪdrə(ʊ)sɪˈfalɪk, ˌhʌɪdrəʊkɛˈfalɪk
AM ˌhaɪdroʊsəˈfælɪk
hydrocephalus
BR ˌhʌɪdrə(ʊ)ˈsɛfələs, ˌhʌɪdrə(ʊ)ˈsɛfl̩əs, ˌhʌɪdrə(ʊ)ˈkɛfələs, ˌhʌɪdrə(ʊ)ˈkɛfl̩əs
AM ˌhaɪdroʊˈsɛfələs
hydrochloric acid
BR ˌhʌɪdrəklɒrɪk ˈasɪd
AM ˈhaɪdroʊˌklɔrɪk ˈæsəd
hydrochloride
BR ˌhʌɪdrə(ʊ)ˈklɔːrʌɪd, -z
AM ˈhaɪdroʊˈklɔˌraɪd, -z
hydrocortisone
BR ˌhʌɪdrəʊˈkɔːtɪzəʊn
AM ˈhaɪdroʊˈkɔrdəˌzoʊn
hydrocyanic acid
BR ˌhʌɪdrə(ʊ)sʌɪˌanɪk ˈasɪd
AM ˈhaɪdroʊˌsaɪˌænɪk ˈæsəd
hydrodynamic
BR ˌhʌɪdrə(ʊ)dʌɪˈnamɪk, -s
AM ˈhaɪdroʊˌdaɪˈnæmɪk, -s
hydrodynamical
BR ˌhʌɪdrə(ʊ)dʌɪˈnamɪkl
AM ˈhaɪdroʊˌdaɪˈnæməkəl
hydrodynamicist
BR ˌhʌɪdrə(ʊ)dʌɪˈnamɪsɪst, -s
AM ˈhaɪdroʊˌdaɪˈnæməsəst, -s
hydroelectric
BR ˌhʌɪdrəʊɪˈlɛktrɪk
AM ˈhaɪdroʊəˈlɛktrɪk, ˈhaɪdroʊiˈlɛktrɪk
hydroelectrically
BR ˌhʌɪdrəʊɪˈlɛktrɪkli
AM ˈhaɪdroʊəˈlɛktrək(ə)li, ˈhaɪdroʊiˈlɛktrək(ə)li
hydroelectricity
BR ˌhʌɪdrəʊɪlɛkˈtrɪsɪti
AM ˈhaɪdroʊəˌlɛkˈtrɪsɪdi, ˈhaɪdroʊiˌlɛkˈtrɪsɪdi
hydrofined
BR ˈhʌɪdrəfʌɪnd
AM ˈhaɪdroʊˌfaɪnd, ˈhaɪdrəˌfaɪnd
hydrofining
BR ˈhʌɪdrəˌfʌɪnɪŋ
AM ˈhaɪdroʊˌfaɪnɪŋ, ˈhaɪdrəˌfaɪnɪŋ
hydrofluoric acid
BR ˌhʌɪdrəflʊərɪk ˈasɪd, ˌhʌɪdrəflɔːrɪk +
AM ˈhaɪdroʊˌflʊrɪk ˈæsəd
hydrofoil
BR ˈhʌɪdrəfɔɪl, -z
AM ˈhaɪdroʊˌfɔɪl, ˈhaɪdrəˌfɔɪl, -z
hydrogen
BR ˈhʌɪdrədʒ(ə)n
AM ˈhaɪdrədʒən
hydrogenase
BR hʌɪˈdrɒdʒɪneɪz, hʌɪˈdrɒdʒɪneɪs, -ɪz
AM ˈhaɪdrədʒəˌneɪz, haɪˈdrɑdʒəˌneɪz, ˈhaɪdrədʒəˌneɪs, haɪˈdrɑdʒəˌneɪs, -ɪz
hydrogenate
BR ˈhʌɪdrədʒɪneɪt, hʌɪˈdrɒdʒɪneɪt, -s, -ɪŋ, -ɪd
AM ˈhaɪdrədʒəˌneɪ|t, haɪˈdrɑdʒəneɪ|t, -ts, -dɪŋ, -dɪd
hydrogenation
BR ˌhʌɪdrədʒɪˈneɪʃn, hʌɪˌdrɒdʒɪˈneɪʃn
AM ˌhaɪdrədʒəˈneɪʃən, haɪˌdrɑdʒəˈneɪʃən
hydrogenous
BR hʌɪˈdrɒdʒɪnəs

AM haɪˈdrɑdʒənəs

hydrogeological
BR ˌhʌɪdrəʊˌdʒɪəˈlɒdʒɪkl
AM ˈhaɪdrəˌdʒiəˈlɑdʒəkəl

hydrogeologist
BR ˌhʌɪdrəʊdʒɪˈɒlədʒɪst, -s
AM ˌhaɪdrədʒiˈɑlədʒəst, -s

hydrogeology
BR ˌhʌɪdrəʊdʒɪˈɒlədʒi
AM ˌhaɪdrədʒiˈɑlədʒi

hydrographer
BR hʌɪˈdrɒgrəfə(r), -z
AM haɪˈdrɑgrəfər, -z

hydrographic
BR ˌhʌɪdrəˈgrafɪk
AM ˈhaɪdrəˈgræfɪk

hydrographical
BR ˌhʌɪdrəˈgrafɪkl
AM ˈhaɪdrəˈgræfəkəl

hydrographically
BR ˌhʌɪdrəˈgrafɪkli
AM ˈhaɪdrəˈgræfək(ə)li

hydrography
BR hʌɪˈdrɒgrəfi
AM haɪˈdrɑgrəfi

hydroid
BR ˈhʌɪdrɔɪd, -z
AM ˈhaɪˌdrɔɪd, -z

hydrolase
BR ˈhʌɪdrəleɪz, -ɪz
AM ˈhaɪd(ə)rəˌleɪs, ˈhaɪd(ə)rəˌleɪz, -ɪz

hydrologic
BR ˌhʌɪdrəˈlɒdʒɪk
AM ˈhaɪdrəˈlɑdʒɪk

hydrological
BR ˌhʌɪdrəˈlɒdʒɪkl
AM ˈhaɪdrəˈlɑdʒəkəl

hydrologically
BR ˌhʌɪdrəˈlɒdʒɪkli
AM ˈhaɪdrəˈlɑdʒək(ə)li

hydrologist
BR hʌɪˈdrɒlədʒɪst, -s
AM haɪˈdrɑlədʒəst, -s

hydrology
BR hʌɪˈdrɒlədʒi
AM haɪˈdrɑlədʒi

hydrolyse
BR ˈhʌɪdrəlʌɪz, -ɪz, -ɪŋ, -d
AM ˈhaɪdrəˌlaɪz, -ɪz, -ɪŋ, -d

hydrolysis
BR hʌɪˈdrɒlɪsɪs
AM haɪˈdrɑləsəs

hydrolytic
BR ˌhʌɪdrəˈlɪtɪk
AM ˈhaɪdrəˈlɪdɪk

hydrolytically
BR ˌhʌɪdrəˈlɪtɪkli
AM ˈhaɪdrəˈlɪdək(ə)li

hydrolyze
BR ˈhʌɪdrəlʌɪz, -ɪz, -ɪŋ, -d
AM ˈhaɪdrəˌlaɪz, -ɪz, -ɪŋ, -d

hydromagnetic
BR ˌhʌɪdrəʊmagˈnɛtɪk, -s
AM ˈhaɪdrəmægˈnɛdɪk, -s

hydromania
BR ˈhʌɪdrəˌmeɪnɪə(r)
AM ˌhaɪdrəˈmeɪniə

hydromechanics
BR ˌhʌɪdrəʊmɪˈkanɪks
AM ˈhaɪdrəməˈkænɪks

hydromel
BR ˈhʌɪdrəmɛl
AM ˈhaɪdrəˌmɛl

hydrometer
BR hʌɪˈdrɒmɪtə(r), -z
AM haɪˈdrɑmədər, -z

hydrometric
BR ˌhʌɪdrəˈmɛtrɪk
AM ˌhaɪdrəˈmɛtrɪk

hydrometrical
BR ˌhʌɪdrəˈmɛtrɪkl
AM ˌhaɪdrəˈmɛtrəkəl

hydrometrically
BR ˌhʌɪdrəˈmɛtrɪkli
AM ˌhaɪdrəˈmɛtrək(ə)li

hydrometry
BR hʌɪˈdrɒmɪtri
AM haɪˈdrɑmətri

hydronium ion
BR hʌɪˈdrəʊnɪəm ˌʌɪən, -z
AM haɪˈdroʊniəm ˈaɪɑn, -z

hydropathic
BR ˌhʌɪdrəˈpaθɪk, -s
AM ˌhaɪdrəˈpæθɪk, -s

hydropathically
BR ˌhʌɪdrəˈpaθɪkli
AM ˌhaɪdrəˈpæθək(ə)li

hydropathist
BR hʌɪˈdrɒpəθɪst, -s
AM haɪˈdrɑpəθəst, -s

hydropathy
BR hʌɪˈdrɒpəθi
AM haɪˈdrɑpəθi

hydrophane
BR ˈhʌɪdrəfeɪn
AM ˈhaɪdrəˌfeɪn

hydrophil
BR ˈhʌɪdrəfɪl
AM ˈhaɪdrəˌfɪl

hydrophile
BR ˈhʌɪdrəfʌɪl
AM ˈhaɪdrəˌfaɪl

hydrophilic
BR ˌhʌɪdrəˈfɪlɪk
AM ˌhaɪdrəˈfɪlɪk

hydrophobia
BR ˌhʌɪdrəˈfəʊbɪə(r)
AM ˌhaɪdrəˈfoʊbiə

hydrophobic
BR ˌhʌɪdrəˈfəʊbɪk
AM ˌhaɪdrəˈfoʊbɪk

hydrophone
BR ˈhʌɪdrəfəʊn, -z
AM ˈhaɪdrəˌfoʊn, -z

hydrophyte
BR ˈhʌɪdrəfʌɪt, -s
AM ˈhaɪdrəˌfaɪt, -s

hydropic
BR hʌɪˈdrɒpɪk
AM haɪˈdrɑpɪk

hydroplane
BR ˈhʌɪdrəpleɪn, -z
AM ˈhaɪdrəˌpleɪn, -z

hydropneumatic
BR ˌhʌɪdrəʊnjuːˈmatɪk, ˌhʌɪdrəʊnjʊˈmatɪk
AM ˈhaɪdrəˌnjʊˈmædɪk

hydroponic
BR ˌhʌɪdrəˈpɒnɪk, -s
AM ˌhaɪdrəˈpɑnɪk, -s

hydroponically
BR ˌhʌɪdrəˈpɒnɪkli
AM ˌhaɪdrəˈpɑnək(ə)li

hydroquinone
BR ˌhʌɪdrəʊˈkwɪnəʊn
AM ˈhaɪdrəˈkwɪˌnoʊn

hydrosphere
BR ˈhʌɪdrə(ʊ)sfɪə(r)
AM ˈhaɪdrəˌsfɪ(ə)r

hydrostatic
BR ˌhʌɪdrəˈstatɪk, -s
AM ˌhaɪdrəˈstædɪk, -s

hydrostatical
BR ˌhʌɪdrəˈstatɪkl
AM ˌhaɪdrəˈstædəkəl

hydrostatically
BR ˌhʌɪdrəˈstatɪkli
AM ˌhaɪdrəˈstædək(ə)li

hydrotherapist
BR ˌhʌɪdrə(ʊ)ˈθɛrəpɪst, -s
AM ˈhaɪdroʊˈθɛrəpəst, -s

hydrotherapy
BR ˌhʌɪdrə(ʊ)ˈθɛrəpi
AM ˈhaɪdroʊˈθɛrəpi

hydrothermal
BR ˌhʌɪdrə(ʊ)ˈθəːml
AM ˈhaɪdroʊˈθərməl

hydrothermally
BR ˌhʌɪdrə(ʊ)ˈθəːml̩i, ˌhʌɪdrə(ʊ)ˈθəːməli
AM ˈhaɪdroʊˈθərməli

hydrothorax
BR ˌhʌɪdrəʊˈθɔːraks
AM ˈhaɪdroʊˈθɔˌræks

hydrotropism
BR ˌhʌɪdrəʊˈtrəʊpɪz(ə)m
AM ˈhaɪdroʊˈtrɑˌpɪzəm

hydrous
BR ˈhʌɪdrəs
AM ˈhaɪdrəs

hydroxide
BR hʌɪˈdrɒksʌɪd, -z
AM haɪˈdrɑkˌsaɪd, -z

hydroxonium ion
BR ˌhʌɪdrɒkˈsəʊnɪəm ˌʌɪən, -z
AM haɪˌdrɑkˈsoʊniəm ˌaɪɑn, -z

hydroxy
BR hʌɪˈdrɒksi
AM haɪˈdrɑksi

hydroxyl
BR hʌɪˈdrɒksɪl, hʌɪˈdrɒksʌɪl, -z
AM haɪˈdrɑksəl, -z

hydrozoan
BR ˌhʌɪdrəˈzəʊən, -z
AM ˌhaɪdrəˈzoʊən, -z

hyena
BR hʌɪˈiːnə(r), -z
AM haɪˈinə, -z

Hygeia
BR hʌɪˈdʒiːə(r)
AM haɪˈdʒiə

hygeian
BR hʌɪˈdʒiːən
AM haɪˈdʒiən

Hygena
BR hʌɪˈdʒiːnə(r)
AM haɪˈdʒinə

hygiene
BR ˈhʌɪdʒiːn
AM ˈhaɪˌdʒin

hygienic
BR hʌɪˈdʒiːnɪk, -s
AM ˌhaɪˈdʒɛnɪk, ˌhaɪˈdʒinɪk, -s

hygienically
BR hʌɪˈdʒiːnɪkli
AM ˌhaɪˈdʒɛnək(ə)li, ˌhaɪˈdʒinək(ə)li

hygienist
BR ˈhʌɪdʒiːnɪst, hʌɪˈdʒiːnɪst, -s
AM ˈhaɪˌdʒinɪst, ˈhaɪˌdʒɛnəst, -s

hygrology
BR hʌɪˈgrɒlədʒi
AM haɪˈgrɑlədʒi

hygrometer
BR hʌɪˈgrɒmɪtə(r), -z
AM haɪˈgrɑmədər, -z

hygrometric
BR ˌhʌɪgrəˈmɛtrɪk
AM ˌhaɪgrəˈmɛtrɪk

hygrometrically
BR ˌhʌɪgrəˈmɛtrɪkli
AM ˌhaɪgrəˈmɛtrək(ə)li

hygrometry
BR hʌɪˈgrɒmɪtri
AM haɪˈgrɑmətri

hygrophilous
BR hʌɪˈgrɒfɪləs, hʌɪˈgrɒfl̩əs
AM haɪˈgrɑfələs

hygrophyte
BR ˈhʌɪgrəfʌɪt, -s
AM ˈhaɪgrəˌfaɪt, -s

hygrophytic
BR ˌhʌɪgrəˈfɪtɪk
AM ˌhaɪgrəˈfɪdɪk

hygroscope
BR 'hʌɪgrəskəʊp, -s
AM 'haɪgrəˌskoʊp, -s
hygroscopic
BR ˌhʌɪgrə'skɒpɪk
AM ˌhaɪgrə'skɑpɪk
hygroscopically
BR ˌhʌɪgrə'skɒpɨkli
AM ˌhaɪgrə'skɑpək(ə)li
hying
BR 'hʌɪɪŋ
AM 'haɪɪŋ
Hyksos
BR 'hɪksɒs
AM 'hɪkˌsɔs, 'hɪkˌsɑs
Hyland
BR 'hʌɪlənd
AM 'haɪlənd
Hylda
BR 'hɪldə(r)
AM 'hɪldə
hylic
BR 'hʌɪlɪk
AM 'haɪlɪk
hylomorphism
BR ˌhʌɪlə(ʊ)'mɔːfɪz(ə)m
AM ˌhaɪlə'mɔrˌfɪzəm
hylotheism
BR ˌhʌɪlə(ʊ)'θiːɪz(ə)m
AM ˌhaɪlə'θiˌɪzəm
hylozoism
BR ˌhʌɪlə(ʊ)'zəʊɪz(ə)m
AM ˌhaɪlə'zoʊˌɪzəm
hylozoist
BR ˌhʌɪlə(ʊ)'zəʊɪst, -s
AM ˌhaɪlə'zoʊəst, -s
Hylton
BR 'hɪlt(ə)n
AM 'hɪlt(ə)n
Hyman
BR 'hʌɪmən
AM 'haɪmən
hymen
BR 'hʌɪmɛn, 'hʌɪmən, -z
AM 'haɪmən, -z
hymenal
BR 'hʌɪmənl
AM 'haɪmənəl
hymeneal
BR ˌhʌɪmɨ'niːəl, ˌhʌɪmɛ'niːəl
AM ˌhaɪmə'niəl
hymenia
BR hʌɪ'miːnɪə(r)
AM haɪ'miniə
hymenium
BR hʌɪ'miːnɪəm
AM haɪ'miniəm
Hymenoptera
BR ˌhʌɪmɨ'nɒpt(ə)rə(r), ˌhʌɪmɛ'nɒpt(ə)rə(r)
AM ˌhaɪmə'nɑptərə
hymenopteran
BR ˌhʌɪmɨ'nɒpt(ə)rən, ˌhʌɪmɨ'nɒpt(ə)rn̩, ˌhʌɪmɛ'nɒpt(ə)rən, ˌhʌɪmɛ'nɒpt(ə)rn̩, -z
AM ˌhaɪmə'nɑptərən, -z
hymenopterous
BR ˌhʌɪmɨ'nɒpt(ə)rəs, ˌhʌɪmɛ'nɒpt(ə)rəs
AM ˌhaɪmə'nɑptərəs
hymn
BR hɪm, -z, -ɪŋ, -d
AM hɪm, -z, -ɪŋ, -d
hymnal
BR 'hɪmn(ə)l, -z
AM 'hɪmnəl, -z
hymnary
BR 'hɪmnər|i, -ɪz
AM 'hɪmnəri, -z
hymnbook
BR 'hɪmbʊk, -s
AM 'hɪmˌbʊk, -s
hymnic
BR 'hɪmnɪk
AM 'hɪmnɪk
hymnist
BR 'hɪmnɪst, -s
AM 'hɪmnɨst, -s
hymnodist
BR 'hɪmnədɪst, -s
AM 'hɪmnədəst, -s
hymnody
BR 'hɪmnəd|i, -ɪz
AM 'hɪmnədi, -z
hymnographer
BR hɪm'nɒgrəfə(r), -z
AM hɪm'nɑgrəfər, -z
hymnography
BR hɪm'nɒgrəfi
AM hɪm'nɑgrəfi
hymnologist
BR hɪm'nɒlədʒɪst, -s
AM hɪm'nɑlədʒəst, -s
hymnology
BR hɪm'nɒlədʒi
AM hɪm'nɑlədʒi
Hynes
BR hʌɪnz
AM haɪnz
hyoid
BR 'hʌɪɔɪd
AM 'haɪˌɔɪd
hyoscine
BR 'hʌɪəsiːn
AM 'haɪəˌsin
hyoscyamine
BR ˌhʌɪə(ʊ)'sʌɪəmiːn, ˌhʌɪə(ʊ)'sʌɪəmɪn
AM ˌhaɪə'saɪəmən, ˌhaɪə'saɪəˌmin
hypaesthesia
BR ˌhʌɪpɨs'θiːzɪə(r), ˌhʌɪpɨs'θiːʒə(r)
AM ˌhɪpəs'θiʒ(i)ə, ˌhaɪpəs'θiʒ(i)ə, ˌhɪpəs'θiziə, ˌhaɪpəs'θiziə
hypaesthetic
BR ˌhʌɪpɨs'θɛtɪk
AM ˌhɪpəs'θɛdɪk, ˌhaɪpəs'θɛdɪk
hypaethral
BR hʌɪ'piːθr(ə)l
AM haɪ'piθrəl, hə'piθrəl
hypallage
BR hʌɪ'palədʒ|i, -ɪz
AM haɪ'pælədʒi, hɪ'pælədʒi, -z
Hypatia
BR hʌɪ'peɪʃ(ɪ)ə(r)
AM ˌhaɪ'peɪʃə, ˌhaɪ'peɪdiə
hype
BR hʌɪp, -s, -ɪŋ, -t
AM haɪp, -s, -ɪŋ, -t
hyperactive
BR ˌhʌɪpər'aktɪv
AM ¦haɪpər'æktɪv
hyperactivity
BR ˌhʌɪpərak'tɪvɨti
AM ¦haɪpərˌæk'tɪvɨdi
hyperaemia
BR ˌhʌɪpə'riːmɪə(r)
AM ˌhaɪpə'rimiə
hyperaemic
BR ˌhʌɪpə'riːmɪk
AM ˌhaɪpə'rimɪk
hyperaesthesia
BR ˌhʌɪp(ə)rɪs'θiːzɪə(r), ˌhʌɪp(ə)rɪs'θiːʒə(r)
AM ˌhaɪpərəs'θiʒ(i)ə, ˌhaɪpərəs'θiziə
hyperaesthetic
BR ˌhʌɪp(ə)rɪs'θɛtɪk
AM ˌhaɪpərəs'θɛdɪk
hyperbaric
BR ˌhʌɪpə'barɪk
AM ˌhaɪpər'bɛrɪk
hyperbaton
BR hʌɪ'pəːbət(ə)n, hʌɪ'pəːbətɒn
AM haɪ'pərbəˌtɑn
hyperbola
BR hʌɪ'pəːbələ(r), hʌɪ'pəːbl̩ə(r), -z
AM haɪ'pərbələ, -z
hyperbole
BR hʌɪ'pəːbəl|i, hʌɪ'pəːbl̩|i, -ɪz
AM haɪ'pərbəli, -z
hyperbolic
BR ˌhʌɪpə'bɒlɪk
AM ¦haɪpər'bɑlɪk
hyperbolical
BR ˌhʌɪpə'bɒlɪkl
AM ¦haɪpər'bɑləkəl
hyperbolically
BR ˌhʌɪpə'bɒlɪkli
AM ¦haɪpər'bɑlək(ə)li
hyperbolism
BR hʌɪ'pəːbəlɪz(ə)m, hʌɪ'pəːbl̩ɪz(ə)m
AM haɪ'pərbəˌlɪzəm
hyperbolist
BR hʌɪ'pəːbəlɪst, hʌɪ'pəːbl̩ɪst, -s
AM haɪ'pərbələst, -s
hyperboloid
BR hʌɪ'pəːbəlɔɪd, hʌɪ'pəːbl̩ɔɪd, -z
AM haɪ'pərbəˌlɔɪd, -z
hyperboloidal
BR hʌɪˌpəːbə'lɔɪdl
AM haɪ¦pərbə¦lɔɪdəl
Hyperborean
BR ˌhʌɪpə'bɔːrɪən, ˌhʌɪpəbə'riːən, -z
AM ˌhaɪpə(r)'bɔriən, ¦haɪpərbə'riən, -z
hypercatalectic
BR ˌhʌɪpəˌkatə'lɛktɪk, ˌhʌɪpəˌkatl̩'ɛktɪk
AM ¦haɪpərˌkædə'lɛktɪk
hyperconscious
BR ˌhʌɪpə'kɒnʃəs
AM ¦haɪpər'kɑnʃəs
hypercorrect
BR ˌhʌɪpəkə'rɛkt
AM ˌhaɪpərkə'rɛk(t)
hypercorrection
BR ˌhʌɪpəkə'rɛkʃn
AM ˌhaɪpərkə'rɛkʃən
hypercritical
BR ˌhʌɪpə'krɪtɪkl
AM ¦haɪpər'krɪdəkəl
hypercritically
BR ˌhʌɪpə'krɪtɪkli
AM ¦haɪpər'krɪdək(ə)li
hypercriticism
BR ˌhʌɪpə'krɪtɪsɪz(ə)m
AM ¦haɪpər'krɪdəˌsɪzəm
hypercube
BR 'hʌɪpəkjuːb, -z
AM 'haɪpərˌkjub, -z
hyperdulia
BR ˌhʌɪpədjʉ'lʌɪə(r), ˌhʌɪpədʒʉ'lʌɪə(r)
AM ¦haɪpərˌd(j)u'laɪə
hyperemia
BR ˌhʌɪpə'riːmɪə(r)
AM ˌhaɪpə'rimiə
hyperemic
BR ˌhʌɪpə'riːmɪk
AM ˌhaɪpə'rimɪk
hyperesthesia
BR ˌhʌɪp(ə)rɪs'θiːzɪə(r), ˌhʌɪp(ə)rɪs'θiːʒə(r)
AM ˌhaɪpərəs'θiʒ(i)ə, ˌhaɪpərəs'θiziə
hyperesthetic
BR ˌhʌɪp(ə)rɪs'θɛtɪk
AM ˌhaɪpərəs'θɛdɪk
hyperfocal
BR ˌhʌɪpə'fəʊkl
AM ˌhaɪpər'foʊkəl
hypergamy
BR hʌɪ'pəːgəmi
AM haɪ'pərgəmi
hyperglycaemia
BR ˌhʌɪpəglʌɪ'siːmɪə(r)
AM ˌhaɪpərglaɪ'simiə
hyperglycaemic
BR ˌhʌɪpəglʌɪ'siːmɪk

AM 'haɪpərglaɪ'simɪk

hyperglycemia
BR ˌhʌɪpəglʌɪ'siːmɪə(r)
AM ˌhaɪpərglaɪ'simiə

hyperglycemic
BR ˌhʌɪpəglʌɪ'siːmɪk
AM 'haɪpərglaɪ'simɪk

hypergolic
BR ˌhʌɪpə'gɒlɪk
AM ˌhaɪpər'gɑlɪk

hypericum
BR hʌɪ'pɛrɪkəm, -z
AM haɪ'pɛrəkəm, -z

Hyperion
BR hʌɪ'pɪərɪən
AM haɪ'piriən

hyperkinetic
BR ˌhʌɪpəkʌɪ'nɛtɪk, ˌhʌɪpəkɪ'nɛtɪk
AM ˌhaɪpərkə'nɛdɪk

hyperlipidaemia
BR ˌhʌɪpəˌlɪpɪ'diːmɪə(r)
AM ¦haɪpəˌlɪpə'dimiə

hyperlipidaemic
BR ˌhʌɪpəˌlɪpɪ'diːmɪk
AM ¦haɪpəˌlɪpə'dimɪk

hyperlipidemia
BR ˌhʌɪpəˌlɪpɪ'diːmɪə(r)
AM ¦haɪpəˌlɪpə'dimiə

hyperlipidemic
BR ˌhʌɪpəˌlɪpɪ'diːmɪk
AM ¦haɪpəˌlɪpə'dimɪk

hypermarket
BR 'hʌɪpəˌmɑːkɪt, -s
AM 'haɪpərˌmɑrkət, -s

hypermetric
BR ˌhʌɪpə'mɛtrɪk
AM ¦haɪpər'mɛtrɪk

hypermetrical
BR ˌhʌɪpə'mɛtrɪkl
AM ¦haɪpər'mɛtrəkəl

hypermetropia
BR ˌhʌɪpəmɪ'trəʊpɪə(r)
AM ˌhaɪpərmə'troʊpiə

hypermetropic
BR ˌhʌɪpəmɪ'trɒpɪk, ˌhʌɪpəmɪ'trəʊpɪk
AM ˌhaɪpərmə'trɑpɪk

hypernym
BR 'hʌɪpənɪm, -z
AM 'haɪpərˌnɪm, -z

hyperon
BR 'hʌɪpərɒn, -z
AM 'haɪpəˌrɑn, -z

hyperonic
BR ˌhʌɪpə'rɒnɪk
AM ˌhaɪpə'rɑnɪk

hyperopia
BR ˌhʌɪpə'rəʊpɪə(r)
AM ˌhaɪpə'roʊpiə

hyperopic
BR ˌhʌɪpə'rɒpɪk
AM ˌhaɪpə'rɑpɪk

hyperphysical
BR ˌhʌɪpə'fɪzɪkl
AM ˌhaɪpər'fɪzɪkəl

hyperphysically
BR ˌhʌɪpə'fɪzɪkli
AM ˌhaɪpər'fɪzɪk(ə)li

hyperplasia
BR ˌhʌɪpə'pleɪzɪə(r), ˌhʌɪpə'pleɪʒə(r)
AM ˌhaɪpər'pleɪʒ(i)ə, ˌhaɪpər'pleɪziə

hypersensitive
BR ˌhʌɪpə'sɛnsɪtɪv
AM ˌhaɪpər'sɛnsədɪv

hypersensitiveness
BR ˌhʌɪpə'sɛnsɪtɪvnɪs
AM ˌhaɪpər'sɛnsədɪvnɪs

hypersensitivity
BR ˌhʌɪpəˌsɛnsɪ'tɪvɪti
AM ¦haɪpərˌsɛnsə'tɪvɪdi

hypersonic
BR ˌhʌɪpə'sɒnɪk
AM ˌhaɪpər'sɑnɪk

hypersonically
BR ˌhʌɪpə'sɒnɪkli
AM ˌhaɪpər'sɑnək(ə)li

hyperspace
BR 'hʌɪpəspeɪs
AM 'haɪpərˌspeɪs

hypersthene
BR 'hʌɪpəsθiːn
AM 'haɪpərˌsθin

hypertension
BR ˌhʌɪpə'tɛnʃn
AM ˌhaɪpər'tɛnʃən

hypertensive
BR ˌhʌɪpə'tɛnsɪv
AM ˌhaɪpər'tɛnsɪv

hypertext
BR 'hʌɪpətɛkst, -s
AM 'haɪpərˌtɛkst, -s

hyperthermia
BR ˌhʌɪpə'θəːmɪə(r)
AM ¦haɪpər'θərmiə

hyperthermic
BR ˌhʌɪpə'θəːmɪk
AM ¦haɪpər'θərmɪk

hyperthyroid
BR ˌhʌɪpə'θʌɪrɔɪd
AM ¦haɪpər'θaɪˌrɔɪd

hyperthyroidic
BR ˌhʌɪpəθʌɪ'rɔɪdɪk
AM ¦haɪpərˌθaɪ'rɔɪdɪk

hyperthyroidism
BR ˌhʌɪpə'θʌɪrɔɪdɪz(ə)m
AM ¦haɪpər'θaɪˌrɔɪˌdɪzəm

hypertonia
BR ˌhʌɪpə'təʊnɪə(r)
AM ˌhaɪpər'toʊniə

hypertonic
BR ˌhʌɪpə'tɒnɪk
AM ˌhaɪpər'tɑnɪk

hypertonicity
BR ˌhʌɪpətə(ʊ)'nɪsɪti
AM ˌhaɪpərtə'nɪsɪdi

hypertrophic
BR ˌhʌɪpə'trɒfɪk, ˌhʌɪpə'trəʊfɪk
AM ˌhaɪpər'trɑfɪk

hypertrophied
BR hʌɪ'pəːtrəfɪd
AM haɪ'pərtrəfid

hypertrophy
BR hʌɪ'pəːtrəfi
AM haɪ'pərtrəfi

hyperventilate
BR ˌhʌɪpə'vɛntɪleɪt, -s, -ɪŋ, -ɪd
AM ˌhaɪpər'vɛn(t)əˌleɪ|t, -ts, -dɪŋ, -dɪd

hyperventilation
BR ˌhʌɪpəˌvɛntɪ'leɪʃn
AM ˌhaɪpərˌvɛn(t)ə'leɪʃən

hypesthesia
BR ˌhʌɪpɪs'θiːzɪə(r), ˌhʌɪpɪs'θiːʒə(r)
AM ˌhɪpəs'θiʒ(i)ə, ˌhaɪpəs'θiʒ(i)ə, ˌhɪpəs'θiziə, ˌhaɪpəs'θiziə

hypesthetic
BR ˌhʌɪpɪs'θɛtɪk
AM ˌhɪpəs'θɛdɪk, ˌhaɪpəs'θɛdɪk

hypethral
BR hʌɪ'piːθr(ə)l
AM haɪ'piθrəl, hə'piθrəl

hypha
BR 'hʌɪfə(r)
AM 'haɪfə

hyphae
BR 'hʌɪfiː
AM 'haɪfi, 'haɪˌfaɪ

hyphal
BR 'hʌɪfl
AM 'haɪfəl

hyphen
BR 'hʌɪfn, -z
AM 'haɪfən, -z

hyphenate
BR 'hʌɪfəneɪt, 'hʌɪfn̩eɪt, -s, -ɪŋ, -ɪd
AM 'haɪfəˌneɪ|t, -ts, -dɪŋ, -dɪd

hyphenation
BR ˌhʌɪfə'neɪʃn
AM ˌhaɪfə'neɪʃən

hypnogenesis
BR ˌhɪpnə(ʊ)'dʒɛnɪsɪs
AM ˌhɪpnoʊ'dʒɛnəsəs

hypnologist
BR hɪp'nɒlədʒɪst, -s
AM hɪp'nɑlədʒəst, -s

hypnology
BR hɪp'nɒlədʒi
AM hɪp'nɑlədʒi

hypnopaedia
BR ˌhɪpnə(ʊ)'piːdɪə(r)
AM ˌhɪpnoʊ'pidiə

hypnopedia
BR ˌhɪpnə(ʊ)'piːdɪə(r)
AM ˌhɪpnoʊ'pidiə

Hypnos
BR 'hɪpnɒs
AM 'hɪpnɔs, 'hɪpˌnɑs

hypnoses
BR hɪp'nəʊsiːz
AM hɪp'noʊsiz

hypnosis
BR hɪp'nəʊsɪs
AM hɪp'noʊsəs

hypnotherapist
BR ˌhɪpnə(ʊ)'θɛrəpɪst, -s
AM ˌhɪpnoʊ'θɛrəpəst, -s

hypnotherapy
BR ˌhɪpnə(ʊ)'θɛrəpi
AM ˌhɪpnoʊ'θɛrəpi

hypnotic
BR hɪp'nɒtɪk
AM hɪp'nɑdɪk

hypnotically
BR hɪp'nɒtɪkli
AM hɪp'nɑdək(ə)li

hypnotisable
BR 'hɪpnətʌɪzəbl
AM 'hɪpnəˌtaɪzəbəl

hypnotise
BR 'hɪpnətʌɪz, -ɪz, -ɪŋ, -d
AM 'hɪpnəˌtaɪz, -ɪz, -ɪŋ, -d

hypnotism
BR 'hɪpnətɪz(ə)m
AM 'hɪpnəˌtɪzəm

hypnotist
BR 'hɪpnətɪst, -s
AM 'hɪpnədəst, -s

hypnotizable
BR 'hɪpnətʌɪzəbl
AM 'hɪpnəˌtaɪzəbəl

hypnotize
BR 'hɪpnətʌɪz, -ɪz, -ɪŋ, -d
AM 'hɪpnəˌtaɪz, -ɪz, -ɪŋ, -d

hypo
BR 'hʌɪpəʊ
AM 'haɪpoʊ

hypoaesthesia
BR ˌhʌɪpəʊɪs'θiːzɪə(r), ˌhʌɪpəʊɪs'θiːʒə(r)
AM ˌhaɪp(oʊ)ə'sθiʒ(i)ə, ˌhaɪp(oʊ)ə'sθiziə

hypo-allergenic
BR ˌhʌɪpəʊˌalə'dʒɛnɪk
AM ¦haɪpoʊˌælər'dʒɛnɪk

hypoblast
BR 'hʌɪpə(ʊ)blɑːst, 'hʌɪpə(ʊ)blast
AM 'haɪpəˌblæst

hypocaust
BR 'hʌɪpə(ʊ)kɔːst, -s
AM 'haɪpəˌkɔst, 'haɪpəˌkɑst, -s

hypochlorite
BR ˌhʌɪpə(ʊ)'klɔːrʌɪt, -s
AM ˌhaɪpə'klɔˌraɪt, -s

hypochlorous acid
BR ˌhʌɪpəklɔːrəs ˈasɪd
AM ˌhaɪpəˌklɔrəs ˈæsəd

hypochondria
BR ˌhʌɪpəˈkɒndrɪə(r)
AM ˌhaɪpəˈkɑndriə

hypochondriac
BR ˌhʌɪpəˈkɒndrɪak, -s
AM ˌhaɪpəˈkɑndriˌæk, -s

hypocoristic
BR ˌhʌɪpə(ʊ)kəˈrɪstɪk
AM ˌhaɪpəkəˈrɪstɪk

hypocotyl
BR ˈhʌɪpə(ʊ)ˌkɒtl, -z
AM ˈhaɪpəˌkɑdl, ˌhaɪpəˈkɑdl, -z

hypocrisy
BR hɪˈpɒkrəs|i, -ɪz
AM həˈpɑkrəsi, -z

hypocrite
BR ˈhɪpəkrɪt, -s
AM ˈhɪpəˌkrɪt, -s

hypocritical
BR ˌhɪpəˈkrɪtɨkl
AM ¦hɪpəˈkrɪdəkəl

hypocritically
BR ˌhɪpəˈkrɪtɨkli
AM ¦hɪpəˈkrɪdək(ə)li

hypocycloid
BR ˌhʌɪpə(ʊ)ˈsʌɪklɔɪd, -z
AM ¦haɪpəˈsaɪˌklɔɪd, -z

hypocycloidal
BR ˌhʌɪpə(ʊ)sʌɪˈklɔɪdl
AM ˌhaɪpəˌsaɪˈklɔɪdəl

hypoderma
BR ˌhʌɪpəˈdəːmə(r)
AM ˌhaɪpəˈdərmə

hypodermal
BR ˌhʌɪpəˈdəːml
AM ˌhaɪpəˈdərməl

hypodermata
BR ˌhʌɪpə(ʊ)ˈdəːmətə(r)
AM ˌhaɪpəˈdərmədə

hypodermic
BR ˌhʌɪpəˈdəːmɪk, -s
AM ˌhaɪpəˈdərmɪk, -s

hypodermically
BR ˌhʌɪpəˈdəːmɨkli
AM ˌhaɪpəˈdərmək(ə)li

hypodermis
BR ˌhʌɪpə(ʊ)ˈdəːmɪs
AM ˌhaɪpəˈdərməs

hypoesthesia
BR ˌhʌɪpəʊɪsˈθiːzɪə(r), ˌhʌɪpəʊɪsˈθiːʒə(r)
AM ˌhaɪp(oʊ)əˈsθiʒ(i)ə, ˌhaɪp(oʊ)əˈsθiziə

hypogastria
BR ˌhʌɪpə(ʊ)ˈgastrɪə(r)
AM ˌhaɪpəˈgæstriə

hypogastric
BR ˌhʌɪpə(ʊ)ˈgastrɪk
AM ˌhaɪpəˈgæstrɪk

hypogastrium
BR ˌhʌɪpə(ʊ)ˈgastrɪəm
AM ˌhaɪpəˈgæstriəm

hypogea
BR ˌhʌɪpə(ʊ)ˈdʒiːə(r)
AM ˌhaɪpəˈdʒiə

hypogeal
BR ˌhʌɪpə(ʊ)ˈdʒiːəl
AM ˌhaɪpəˈdʒiəl

hypogean
BR ˌhʌɪpə(ʊ)ˈdʒiːən
AM ˌhaɪpəˈdʒiən

hypogene
BR ˈhʌɪpə(ʊ)dʒiːn
AM ˈhaɪpəˌdʒin

hypogeum
BR ˌhʌɪpə(ʊ)ˈdʒiːəm
AM ˌhaɪpəˈdʒiəm

hypoglycaemia
BR ˌhʌɪpə(ʊ)glʌɪˈsiːmɪə(r)
AM ˌhaɪpoʊglaɪˈsimiə

hypoglycaemic
BR ˌhʌɪpə(ʊ)glʌɪˈsiːmɪk
AM ˈhaɪpoʊglaɪˈsimɪk

hypoglycemia
BR ˌhʌɪpə(ʊ)glʌɪˈsiːmɪə(r)
AM ˌhaɪpoʊglaɪˈsimiə

hypoglycemic
BR ˌhʌɪpə(ʊ)glʌɪˈsiːmɪk
AM ˈhaɪpoʊglaɪˈsimɪk

hypoid
BR ˈhʌɪpɔɪd, -z
AM ˈhaɪˌpɔɪd, -z

hypolimnia
BR ˌhʌɪpəˈlɪmnɪə(r)
AM ˌhaɪpəˈlɪmniə

hypolimnion
BR ˌhʌɪpəˈlɪmnɪən
AM ˌhaɪpəˈlɪmniˌɑn, ˌhaɪpəˈlɪmniən

hypomania
BR ˌhʌɪpə(ʊ)ˈmeɪnɪə(r)
AM ˌhaɪpəˈmeɪniə

hypomaniac
BR ˌhʌɪpə(ʊ)ˈmeɪnɪak
AM ˌhaɪpəˈmeɪniˌæk, -s

hypomanic
BR ˌhʌɪpə(ʊ)ˈmanɪk, -s
AM ˌhaɪpəˈmænɪk, -s

hyponastic
BR ˌhʌɪpəˈnastɪk
AM ˌhaɪpəˈnæstɪk

hyponasty
BR ˈhʌɪpə(ʊ)ˌnasti
AM ˈhaɪpəˌnasti

hyponym
BR ˈhʌɪpənɪm, -z
AM ˈhaɪpəˌnɪm, -z

hyponymous
BR hʌɪˈpɒnɨməs
AM haɪˈpɑnəməs, həˈpɑnəməs

hyponymy
BR hʌɪˈpɒnɨmi
AM haɪˈpɑnəmi, həˈpɑnəmi

hypophyseal
BR ˌhʌɪpə(ʊ)ˈfɪzɪəl
AM ¦haɪpəˈfɪziəl

hypophysial
BR ˌhʌɪpə(ʊ)ˈfɪzɪəl
AM ¦haɪpəˈfɪziəl

hypophysis
BR hʌɪˈpɒfɨsɪs, -ɨz
AM haɪˈpɑfəsəs, -əz

hypostases
BR hʌɪˈpɒstəsɪs
AM haɪˈpɑstəsiz

hypostasis
BR hʌɪˈpɒstəsɪs
AM haɪˈpɑstəsəs

hypostasise
BR hʌɪˈpɒstəsʌɪz, -ɨz, -ɪŋ, -d
AM haɪˈpɑstəˌsaɪz, -ɨz, -ɪŋ, -d

hypostasize
BR hʌɪˈpɒstəsʌɪz, -ɨz, -ɪŋ, -d
AM haɪˈpɑstəˌsaɪz, -ɨz, -ɪŋ, -d

hypostatic
BR ˌhʌɪpə(ʊ)ˈstatɪk
AM ¦haɪpəˈstædɪk

hypostatical
BR ˌhʌɪpə(ʊ)ˈstatɨkl
AM ¦haɪpəˈstædəkəl

hypostatically
BR ˌhʌɪpə(ʊ)ˈstatɨkli
AM ¦haɪpəˈstædək(ə)li

hypostatise
BR hʌɪˈpɒstətʌɪz, -ɨz, -ɪŋ, -d
AM haɪˈpɑstəˌtaɪz, -ɨz, -ɪŋ, -d

hypostatize
BR hʌɪˈpɒstətʌɪz, -ɨz, -ɪŋ, -d
AM haɪˈpɑstəˌtaɪz, -ɨz, -ɪŋ, -d

hypostyle
BR ˈhʌɪpəstʌɪl
AM ˈhaɪpəˌstaɪl

hyposulfite
BR ˌhʌɪpə(ʊ)ˈsʌlfʌɪt, -s
AM ¦haɪpəˈsəlˌfaɪt, -s

hyposulphite
BR ˌhʌɪpə(ʊ)ˈsʌlfʌɪt, -s
AM ¦haɪpəˈsəlˌfaɪt, -s

hypotactic
BR ˌhʌɪpə(ʊ)ˈtaktɪk
AM ˌhaɪpoʊˈtæktɪk

hypotaxes
BR ˌhʌɪpə(ʊ)ˈtaksiːz
AM ˌhaɪpəˈtæksiz

hypotaxis
BR ˌhʌɪpə(ʊ)ˈtaksɪs
AM ˌhaɪpəˈtæksəs

hypotension
BR ˌhʌɪpə(ʊ)ˈtɛnʃn
AM ¦haɪpəˈtɛn(t)ʃən

hypotensive
BR ˌhʌɪpə(ʊ)ˈtɛnsɪv
AM ˌhaɪpoʊˈtɛnsɪv

hypotenuse
BR hʌɪˈpɒtɨnjuːs, hʌɪˈpɒtɨnjuːz, -ɨz
AM haɪˈpɑtnˌ(j)us, -əz

hypothalami
BR ˌhʌɪpə(ʊ)ˈθaləmʌɪ, ˌhʌɪpə(ʊ)ˈθaləmiː
AM ¦haɪpəˈθælˌmaɪ

hypothalamic
BR ˌhʌɪpə(ʊ)ˈθaləmɪk
AM ¦haɪpəˈθælmɪk

hypothalamus
BR ˌhʌɪpə(ʊ)ˈθaləməs
AM ¦haɪpəˈθælməs

hypothec
BR hʌɪˈpɒθɪk
AM həˈpɑθək, haɪˈpɑθək

hypothecary
BR hʌɪˈpɒθɨk(ə)r|i, -ɪz
AM həˈpɑθəˌkɛri, haɪˈpɑθəˌkɛri, -z

hypothecate
BR hʌɪˈpɒθɨkeɪt, -s, -ɪŋ, -ɨd
AM həˈpɑθəˌkeɪ|t, haɪˈpɑθəˌkeɪ|t, -ts, -dɪŋ, -dɨd

hypothecation
BR hʌɪˌpɒθɨˈkeɪʃn
AM həˌpɑθəˈkeɪʃən, haɪˌpɑθəˈkeɪʃən

hypothecator
BR hʌɪˈpɒθɨkeɪtə(r), -z
AM həˈpɑθəˌkeɪdər, haɪˈpɑθəˌkeɪdər, -z

hypothermia
BR ˌhʌɪpə(ʊ)ˈθəːmɪə(r)
AM ˌhaɪpəˈθərmiə

hypotheses
BR hʌɪˈpɒθɨsiːz
AM haɪˈpɑθəˌsiz

hypothesis
BR hʌɪˈpɒθɨsɪs
AM haɪˈpɑθəsəs

hypothesise
BR hʌɪˈpɒθɨsʌɪz, -ɨz, -ɪŋ, -d
AM haɪˈpɑθəˌsaɪz, -ɨz, -ɪŋ, -d

hypothesiser
BR hʌɪˈpɒθɨsʌɪzə(r), -z
AM haɪˈpɑθəˌsaɪzər, -z

hypothesist
BR hʌɪˈpɒθɨsɪst, -s
AM haɪˈpɑθəsəst, -s

hypothesize
BR hʌɪˈpɒθɨsʌɪz, -ɨz, -ɪŋ, -d
AM haɪˈpɑθəˌsaɪz, -ɨz, -ɪŋ, -d

hypothesizer
BR hʌɪˈpɒθɨsʌɪzə(r), -z
AM haɪˈpɑθəˌsaɪzər, -z

hypothetical
BR ˌhʌɪpəˈθɛtɨkl
AM ˈhaɪpəˈθɛdəkəl

hypothetically
BR ˌhʌɪpəˈθɛtɨkli
AM ˈhaɪpəˈθɛdək(ə)li

hypothyroid
BR ˌhʌɪpə(ʊ)ˈθʌɪrɔɪd
AM ˌhaɪpoʊˈθaɪˌrɔɪd

hypothyroidic
BR ˌhʌɪpə(ʊ)θʌɪˈrɔɪdɪk
AM ˈhaɪpərˌθaɪˈrɔɪdɪk

hypothyroidism
BR ˌhʌɪpə(ʊ)ˈθʌɪrɔɪd-ɪz(ə)m
AM ˈhaɪpoʊˈθaɪˌrɔɪˌd-ɪzəm

hypoventilation
BR ˌhʌɪpə(ʊ)ˌvɛntɨˈleɪʃn
AM ˌhaɪpoʊˌvɛn(t)əˈleɪ-ʃən

hypoxaemia
BR ˌhʌɪpɒkˈsiːmɪə(r)
AM haɪˌpɑkˈsimiə

hypoxemia
BR ˌhʌɪpɒkˈsiːmɪə(r)
AM haɪˌpɑkˈsimiə

hypoxia
BR hʌɪˈpɒksɪə(r)
AM haɪˈpɔksiə, haɪˈpɑksiə

hypoxic
BR hʌɪˈpɒksɪk
AM haɪˈpɔksɪk, haɪˈpɑksɪk

hypsilophodont
BR ˌhɪpsɪˈlɒfədɒnt, -s
AM ˌhɪpsəˈlɑfəˌdɑnt, -s

hypsographic
BR ˌhɪpsə(ʊ)ˈgrafɪk
AM ˌhɪpsoʊˈgræfɪk

hypsographical
BR ˌhɪpsə(ʊ)ˈgrafɪkl
AM ˌhɪpsoʊˈgræfəkəl

hypsography
BR hɪpˈsɒgrəfi
AM hɪpˈsɑgrəfi

hypsometer
BR hɪpˈsɒmɨtə(r), -z
AM hɪpˈsɑmədər, -z

hypsometric
BR ˌhɪpsə(ʊ)ˈmɛtrɪk
AM ˌhɪpsoʊˈmɛtrɪk

hypsometry
BR hɪpˈsɒmɨtri
AM hɪpˈsɑmətri

hyracotherium
BR ˌhʌɪrakəˈθɪərɪəm, -z
AM ˌhaɪrəkəˈθɛriəm, ˌhaɪrəkəˈθɪriəm, -z

hyrax
BR ˈhʌɪraks, -ɪz
AM ˈhaɪˌræks, -əz

Hyrcania
BR həːˈkeɪnɪə(r)
AM hərˈkeɪniə

hyson
BR ˈhʌɪsn
AM ˈhaɪsən

hyssop
BR ˈhɪsəp
AM ˈhɪsəp

hysterectomise
BR ˌhɪstəˈrɛktəmʌɪz, -ɨz, -ɪŋ, -d
AM ˌhɪstəˈrɛktəˌmaɪz, -ɨz, -ɪŋ, -d

hysterectomize
BR ˌhɪstəˈrɛktəmʌɪz, -ɨz, -ɪŋ, -d
AM ˌhɪstəˈrɛktəˌmaɪz, -ɨz, -ɪŋ, -d

hysterectomy
BR ˌhɪstəˈrɛktəm|i, -ɪz
AM ˌhɪstəˈrɛktəmi, -z

hysteresis
BR ˌhɪstəˈriːsɪs
AM ˌhɪstəˈrisɪs

hysteria
BR hɪˈstɪərɪə(r)
AM həˈstɛriə, həˈstɪriə

hysteric
BR hɪˈstɛrɪk, -s
AM həˈstɛrɪk, -s

hysterical
BR hɪˈstɛrɨkl
AM həˈstɛrəkəl

hysterically
BR hɪˈstɛrɨkli
AM həˈstɛrək(ə)li

hysteron proteron
BR ˌhɪstərɒn ˈprəʊtərɒn
AM ˈhɪstəˌrɑn ˈproʊdəˌrɑn

Hythe
BR hʌɪð
AM haɪð

Hyundai®
BR ˈhʌɪəndʌɪ, hʌɪˈʌndʌɪ
AM ˈhaɪənˌdaɪ

Hywel
BR ˈhəwəl, ˈhaʊəl
AM ˈhəwəl
WE ˈhʌwel

Ii

i
BR ʌɪ, -z
AM aɪ, -z

Iain
BR 'iːən
AM 'iən

iamb
BR 'ʌɪam(b), -z
AM 'aɪ,æm(b), -z

iambic
BR ʌɪ'ambɪk
AM aɪ'æmbɪk

iambus
BR ʌɪ'ambəs, -ɪz
AM aɪ'æmbəs, -əz

Ian
BR 'iːən
AM 'iən

Iapetus
BR ʌɪ'apɪtəs
AM aɪə'pɛdəs

Iasi
BR 'jɑːsi
AM 'jɑʃi, 'jɑsi

IATA
BR ɪ'ɑːtə(r), ʌɪ'ɑːtə(r)
AM aɪ'ɑdə

iatrogenic
BR ʌɪ,atrə'dʒɛnɪk
AM aɪ,ætrə'dʒɛnɪk

Ibadan
BR ɪ'badn
AM i'badɑn

Iban
BR ɪ'bɑːn
AM i'bɑn, ɪ'bɑn

Ibbotson
BR 'ɪbəts(ə)n
AM 'ɪbɪtsən

Ibcol
BR 'ɪbkɒl
AM 'ɪb,kɔl, 'ɪb,kɑl

I-beam
BR 'ʌɪbiːm, -z
AM 'aɪ,bim, -z

Iberia
BR ʌɪ'bɪərɪə(r)
AM aɪ'bɪriə
SP i'βerja

Iberian
BR ʌɪ'bɪərɪən, -z
AM aɪ'bɪriən, -z

Ibero-American
BR ʌɪ,bɪərəʊə'mɛrɪk(ə)n, -z
AM aɪ,bɪroʊə'mɛrəkən, -z

ibex
BR 'ʌɪbɛks, -ɪz
AM 'aɪ,bɛks, -əz

ibid
BR 'ɪbɪd
AM 'ɪbɪd

ibidem
BR 'ɪbɪdɛm
AM 'ɪbə,dɛm

ibis
BR 'ʌɪb|ɪs, -ɪsɪz
AM 'aɪbɪs, -ɪz

Ibiza
BR ɪ'biːθə(r)
AM ə'biθə
SP i'βiθa, i'βisa

IBM®
BR ,ʌɪbiː'ɛm
AM ,aɪbi'ɛm

Ibo
BR 'iːbəʊ, -z
AM 'i,boʊ, -z

ibogaine
BR ɪ'bəʊgeɪːn
AM ə'boʊ,geɪn

Ibrahim
BR 'ɪbrəhɪm, 'ɪbrəhiːm
AM 'ibrə,him

Ibrox
BR 'ʌɪbrɒks
AM 'aɪbrɑks

Ibsen
BR 'ɪbs(ə)n
AM 'ɪbsən

ibuprofen
BR ,ʌɪbjuː'prəʊf(ə)n
AM ,aɪbju,proʊfən

Icarus
BR 'ɪk(ə)rəs
AM 'ɪkərəs

ICBM
BR ,ʌɪsiːbiː'ɛm, -z
AM ,aɪ,si,bi'ɛm, -z

ice
BR ʌɪs, -ɪz, -ɪŋ, -t
AM aɪs, -ɪz, -ɪŋ, -t

iceberg
BR 'ʌɪsbəːg, -z
AM 'aɪs,bərg, -z

iceblink
BR 'ʌɪsblɪŋk, -s
AM 'aɪs,blɪnk, -s

iceboat
BR 'ʌɪsbəʊt, -s
AM 'aɪs,boʊt, -s

icebound
BR 'ʌɪsbaʊnd
AM 'aɪs,baʊnd

icebox
BR 'ʌɪsbɒks, -ɪz
AM 'aɪs,bɑks, -əz

icebreaker
BR 'ʌɪs,breɪkə(r), -z
AM 'aɪs,breɪkər, -z

ice cream
BR ,ʌɪs 'kriːm, 'ʌɪs kriːm, -z
AM 'aɪs ,krim, ,aɪs 'krim, -z

icefall
BR 'ʌɪsfɔːl, -z
AM 'aɪs,fɔl, 'aɪs,fɑl, -z

icehouse
BR 'ʌɪshaʊ|s, -zɪz
AM 'aɪs,(h)aʊ|s, -zəz

Iceland
BR 'ʌɪslənd
AM 'aɪslənd

Icelander
BR 'ʌɪsləndə(r), -z
AM 'aɪsləndər, -z

Icelandic
BR ʌɪs'landɪk
AM aɪs'lændɪk

iceman
BR 'ʌɪsman
AM 'aɪsmən

icemen
BR 'ʌɪsmɛn
AM 'aɪsmən

Iceni
BR ʌɪ'siːnʌɪ
AM aɪ'si,naɪ

Ichabod
BR 'ɪkəbɒd, 'ɪxəbɒd
AM 'ɪkə,bɑd

I Ching
BR 'ʌɪ 'tʃɪŋ
AM 'i 'tʃɪŋ

ichneumon
BR ɪk'njuːmən
AM ɪk'n(j)umən

ichnography
BR ɪk'nɒgrəfi
AM ɪk'nɑgrəfi

ichor
BR 'ʌɪkɔː(r)
AM 'aɪ,kɔ(ə)r

ichorous
BR 'ʌɪk(ə)rəs
AM 'aɪkərəs

ichthyographer
BR ,ɪkθɪ'ɒgrəfə(r), -z
AM ,ɪkθi'ɑgrəfər, -z

ichthyography
BR ,ɪkθɪ'ɒgrəfi
AM ,ɪkθi'ɑgrəfi

ichthyoid
BR 'ɪkθɪɔɪd, -z
AM 'ɪkθi,ɔɪd, -z

ichthyolatry
BR ,ɪkθɪ'ɒlətri
AM ,ɪkθi'ɑlətri

ichthyolite
BR 'ɪkθɪəlʌɪt, -s
AM 'ɪkθiə,laɪt, -s

ichthyological
BR ,ɪkθɪə'lɒdʒɪkl
AM ,ɪkθiə'lɑdʒəkəl

ichthyologist
BR ,ɪkθɪ'ɒlədʒɪst, -s
AM ,ɪkθi'ɑlədʒəst, -s

ichthyology
BR ,ɪkθɪ'ɒlədʒi
AM ,ɪkθi'ɑlədʒi

ichthyophagous
BR ,ɪkθɪ'ɒfəgəs
AM ,ɪkθi'ɑfəgəs

ichthyophagy
BR ,ɪkθɪ'ɒfədʒi
AM ,ɪkθi'ɑfədʒi

ichthyosaur
BR 'ɪkθɪəsɔː(r), -z
AM 'ɪkθiə,sɔ(ə)r, -z

ichthyosauri
BR ,ɪkθɪə'sɔːrʌɪ
AM ,ɪkθiə'sɔ,raɪ

ichthyosaurus
BR ,ɪkθɪə'sɔːrəs, -ɪz
AM ,ɪkθiə'sɔrəs, -əz

ichthyosis
BR ,ɪkθɪ'əʊsɪs
AM ,ɪkθi'oʊsəs

ichthyotic
BR ,ɪkθɪ'ɒtɪk
AM ,ɪkθi'ɑdɪk

icicle
BR 'ʌɪsɪkl, -z
AM 'aɪ,sɪkəl, 'aɪskəl, -z

icily
BR 'ʌɪsɪli
AM 'aɪsɪli

iciness
BR 'ʌɪsɪnɪs
AM 'aɪsinɪs

icing
BR 'ʌɪsɪŋ
AM 'aɪsɪŋ

Icknield Way
BR ,ɪkniːld 'weɪ
AM ,ɪknild 'weɪ

icky
BR 'ɪki
AM 'ɪki

icon
BR 'ʌɪkɒn, -z
AM 'aɪ,kɑn, -z

iconic
BR ʌɪ'kɒnɪk
AM aɪ'kɑnɪk

iconicity
BR ,ʌɪkə'nɪsɪti
AM ,aɪkə'nɪsɪdi

iconium
BR ʌɪ'kəʊnɪəm
AM aɪ'koʊniəm

iconoclasm
BR ʌɪ'kɒnəklaz(ə)m
AM aɪ'kɑnə,klæzəm

iconoclast
BR ʌɪ'kɒnəklast, ʌɪ'kɒnəklɑːst, -s
AM aɪ'kɑnə,klæst, -s

iconoclastic
BR ʌɪ,kɒnə'klastɪk, ,ʌɪkɒnə'klastɪk
AM aɪ,kɑnə'klæstɪk

iconoclastically
BR ʌɪ,kɒnə'klastɪkli, ,ʌɪkɒnə'klastɪkli
AM aɪ,kɑnə'klæstək(ə)li

iconographer
BR ˌʌɪkəˈnɒɡrəfə(r), -z
AM ˌaɪkəˈnɑɡrəfər, -z

iconographic
BR ˌʌɪkənəˈɡrafɪk, ˌʌɪkn̩əˈɡrafɪk
AM ˌaɪkənəˈɡræfɪk

iconographical
BR ˌʌɪkənəˈɡrafɪkl, ˌʌɪkn̩əˈɡrafɪkl
AM ˌaɪkənəˈɡræfəkəl

iconographically
BR ˌʌɪkənəˈɡrafɪkli, ˌʌɪkn̩əˈɡrafɪkli
AM ˌaɪkənəˈɡræfək(ə)li

iconography
BR ˌʌɪkəˈnɒɡrəfi
AM ˌaɪkəˈnɑɡrəfi

iconolater
BR ˌʌɪkəˈnɒlətə(r), -z
AM ˌaɪkəˈnɑlədər, -z

iconolatry
BR ˌʌɪkəˈnɒlətri
AM ˌaɪkəˈnɑlətri

iconology
BR ˌʌɪkəˈnɒlədʒi
AM ˌaɪkəˈnɑlədʒi

iconometer
BR ˌʌɪkəˈnɒmɨtə(r), -z
AM ˌaɪkəˈnɑmədər, -z

iconometry
BR ˌʌɪkəˈnɒmɨtri
AM ˌaɪkəˈnɑmətri

iconostases
BR ˌʌɪkəˈnɒstəsiːz
AM ˌaɪkəˈnɑstəsiz

iconostasis
BR ˌʌɪkəˈnɒstəsɪs
AM ˌaɪkəˈnɑstəsəs

icosahedral
BR ˌʌɪkɒsəˈhiːdr(ə)l, ʌɪˌkɒsəˈhiːdr(ə)l
AM aɪˌkoʊsəˈhidrəl

icosahedron
BR ˌʌɪkɒsəˈhiːdr(ə)n, ʌɪˌkɒsəˈhiːdr(ə)n, -z
AM aɪˌkoʊsəˈhidrən, -z

icosidodecahedra
BR ˌʌɪkɒsɪˌdəʊdɛkəˈhiːdrə(r)
AM aɪˌkoʊsəˌdoʊˌdɛkəˈhidrə

icosidodecahedron
BR ˌʌɪkɒsɪˌdəʊdɛkəˈhiːdr(ə)n
AM aɪˌkoʊsəˌdoʊˌdɛkəˈhidrən

ictal
BR ˈɪktl
AM ˈɪktl

icteric
BR ɪkˈtɛrɪk
AM ɪkˈtɛrɪk

icterus
BR ˈɪkt(ə)rəs
AM ˈɪktərəs

ictus
BR ˈɪktəs, -ɪz
AM ˈɪktəs, -əz

icy
BR ˈʌɪs|i, -ɪə(r), -ɪɪst
AM ˈaɪsi, -ər, -ɪst

ID
BR ˌʌɪ ˈdiː
AM ˌaɪ ˈdi

I'd
BR ʌɪd
AM aɪd

id
BR ɪd
AM ɪd

Ida
BR ˈʌɪdə(*r*)
AM ˈaɪdə

Idaho
BR ˈʌɪdəhəʊ
AM ˈaɪdəˌhoʊ

Idahoan
BR ˈʌɪdəhəʊən, -z
AM ˈaɪdəˌhoʊən, -z

ide
BR ʌɪd, -z
AM aɪd, -z

idea
BR ʌɪˈdɪə(*r*), -z, -d
AM aɪˈdiə, -z, -d

ideal
BR ʌɪˈdɪəl, ʌɪˈdiː(ə)l, -z
AM aɪˈdi(ə)l, -z

idealess
BR ʌɪˈdɪələs
AM aɪˈdiələs

idealisation
BR ʌɪˌdɪəlʌɪˈzeɪʃn, ʌɪˌdiːəlʌɪˈzeɪʃn, ˌʌɪdɪəlʌɪˈzeɪʃn
AM aɪˌdi(ə)ləˈzeɪʃən, aɪˌdi(ə)ˌlaɪˈzeɪʃən

idealise
BR ʌɪˈdɪəlʌɪz, ʌɪˈdiːəlʌɪz, -ɪz, -ɪŋ, -d
AM aɪˈdi(ə)ˌlaɪz, -ɪz, -ɪŋ, -d

idealiser
BR ʌɪˈdɪəlʌɪzə(r), ʌɪˈdiːəlʌɪzə(r), -z
AM aɪˈdi(ə)ˌlaɪzər, -z

idealism
BR ʌɪˈdɪəlɪz(ə)m, ʌɪˈdiːəlɪz(ə)m
AM ˌaɪˈdi(ə)ˌlɪzəm

idealist
BR ʌɪˈdɪəlɪst, ʌɪˈdiːəlɪst, -s
AM aɪˈdi(ə)ləst, -s

idealistic
BR ʌɪˌdɪəˈlɪstɪk, ʌɪˌdiːəˈlɪstɪk, ˌʌɪdɪəˈlɪstɪk
AM ˌaɪˌdi(ə)ˈlɪstɪk

idealistically
BR ʌɪˌdɪəˈlɪstɪkli, ʌɪˌdiːəˈlɪstɪkli, ˌʌɪdɪ(ə)ˈlɪstɪkli
AM ˌaɪˌdi(ə)ˈlɪstək(ə)li

ideality
BR ˌʌɪdɪˈalɪt|i, -ɪz
AM ˌaɪdiˈælədi, -z

idealization
BR ʌɪˌdɪəlʌɪˈzeɪʃn, ʌɪˌdiːəlʌɪˈzeɪʃn, ˌʌɪdɪəlʌɪˈzeɪʃn
AM aɪˌdi(ə)ləˈzeɪʃən, aɪˌdi(ə)ˌlaɪˈzeɪʃən

idealize
BR ʌɪˈdɪəlʌɪz, ʌɪˈdiːəlʌɪz, -ɪz, -ɪŋ, -d
AM aɪˈdi(ə)ˌlaɪz, -ɪz, -ɪŋ, -d

idealizer
BR ʌɪˈdɪəlʌɪzə(r), ʌɪˈdiːəlʌɪzə(r), -z
AM aɪˈdi(ə)ˌlaɪzər, -z

ideally
BR ʌɪˈdɪəl(l)i, ʌɪˈdiːəl(l)i
AM aɪˈdi(ə)li

ideate
BR ˈʌɪdɪeɪt, -s, -ɪŋ, -ɪd
AM ˈaɪdiˌeɪ|t, -ts, -dɪŋ, -dɪd

ideation
BR ˌʌɪdɪˈeɪʃn, -z
AM ˌaɪdiˈeɪʃən, -z

ideational
BR ˌʌɪdɪˈeɪʃn̩(ə)l, ˌʌɪdɪˈeɪʃən(ə)l
AM ˌaɪdiˈeɪʃ(ə)nəl

ideationally
BR ˌʌɪdɪˈeɪʃn̩əli, ˌʌɪdɪˈeɪʃn̩li, ˌʌɪdɪˈeɪʃənli, ˌʌɪdɪˈeɪʃ(ə)nəli
AM ˌaɪdiˈeɪʃ(ə)nəli

idée fixe
BR ˌiːdeɪ ˈfiːks
AM iˌdeɪ ˈfiks

idée reçue
BR ˌiːdeɪ rəˈsjuː, -z
AM iˌdeɪ rəˈsu, -z

idées fixes
BR ˌiːdeɪ ˈfiːks
AM iˌdeɪ ˈfiks

idem
BR ˈɪdɛm, ˈʌɪdɛm
AM ˈaɪˌdɛm, ˈiˌdɛm

identic
BR ʌɪˈdɛntɪk
AM aɪˈdɛn(t)ɪk, əˈdɛn(t)ɪk

identical
BR ʌɪˈdɛntɪkl
AM aɪˈdɛn(t)əkəl, əˈdɛn(t)əkəl

identically
BR ʌɪˈdɛntɪkli
AM aɪˈdɛn(t)ək(ə)li, əˈdɛn(t)ək(ə)li

identicalness
BR ʌɪˈdɛntɪklnəs
AM aɪˈdɛn(t)əkəlnəs, əˈdɛn(t)əkəlnəs

identifiable
BR ʌɪˈdɛntɪfʌɪəbl
AM aɪˌdɛn(t)əˌfaɪəbəl, əˌdɛn(t)əˌfaɪəbəl

identifiably
BR ʌɪˈdɛntɪfʌɪəbli
AM aɪˌdɛn(t)əˌfaɪəbli, əˌdɛn(t)əˌfaɪəbli

identification
BR ʌɪˌdɛntɪfɪˈkeɪʃn
AM aɪˌdɛn(t)əfəˈkeɪʃən

identifier
BR ʌɪˈdɛntɪfʌɪə(r), -z
AM aɪˈdɛn(t)əˌfaɪər, əˈdɛn(t)əˌfaɪər, -z

identify
BR ʌɪˈdɛntɪfʌɪ, -z, -ɪŋ, -d
AM aɪˈdɛn(t)əˌfaɪ, əˈdɛn(t)əˌfaɪ, -z, -ɪŋ, -d

identikit®
BR ʌɪˈdɛntɪkɪt, -s
AM aɪˈdɛn(t)əˌkɪt, -s

identity
BR ʌɪˈdɛntɪt|i, -ɪz
AM aɪˈdɛn(t)ədi, -z

ideogram
BR ˈɪdɪəɡram, ˈʌɪdɪəɡram, -z
AM ˈɪdiəˌɡræm, ˈaɪdiəˌɡræm, -z

ideograph
BR ˈɪdɪəɡrɑːf, ˈɪdɪəɡraf, ˈʌɪdɪəɡrɑːf, ˈʌɪdɪəɡraf, -s
AM ˈɪdiəˌɡræf, ˈaɪdiəˌɡræf, -s

ideographic
BR ˌɪdɪəˈɡrafɪk, ˌʌɪdɪəˈɡrafɪk
AM ˌɪdiəˈɡræfɪk, ˌaɪdiəˈɡræfɪk

ideographical
BR ˌɪdɪəˈɡrafɪkl, ˌʌɪdɪəˈɡrafɪkl
AM ˌɪdiəˈɡræfəkəl, ˌaɪdiəˈɡræfəkəl

ideological
BR ˌʌɪdɪəˈlɒdʒɪkl, ˌɪdɪəˈlɒdʒɪkl
AM ˌɪdiəˈlɑdʒəkəl, ˌaɪdiəˈlɑdʒəkəl

ideologically
BR ˌʌɪdɪəˈlɒdʒɪkli, ˌɪdɪəˈlɒdʒɪkli
AM ˌɪdiəˈlɑdʒək(ə)li, ˌaɪdiəˈlɑdʒək(ə)li

ideologist
BR ˌʌɪdɪˈɒlədʒɪst, ˌɪdɪˈɒlədʒɪst, -s
AM ˌɪdiˈɑlədʒəst, ˌaɪdiˈɑlədʒəst, -s

ideologue
BR ˈʌɪdɪəlɒɡ, ˈɪdɪəlɒɡ, -z
AM ˈɪdiəˌlɔɡ, ˈaɪdiəˌlɔɡ, ˈɪdiəˌlɑɡ, ˈaɪdiəˌlɑɡ, -z

ideology
BR ˌʌɪdɪˈɒlədʒ|i, ˌɪdɪˈɒlədʒ|i, -ɪz
AM ˌɪdiˈɑlədʒi, ˌaɪdiˈɑlədʒi, -z

ides
BR ʌɪdz
AM aɪdz

idiocy
BR ˈɪdɪəs|i, -ɪz
AM ˈɪdiəsi, -z

idiolect
BR ˈɪdɪəlɛkt, -s
AM ˈɪdiəˌlɛk|(t), -(t)s

idiom
BR ˈɪdɪəm, -z
AM ˈɪdiəm, -z

idiomatic
BR ˌɪdɪəˈmatɪk
AM ˌ¦ɪdiəˈmædɪk

idiomatically
BR ˌɪdɪəˈmatɪkli
AM ˌ¦ɪdiəˈmædək(ə)li

idiopathic
BR ˌɪdɪəˈpaθɪk
AM ˌɪdiəˈpæθɪk

idiopathy
BR ˌɪdɪˈɒpəθ|i, -ɪz
AM ˌɪdiˈɑpəθi, -z

idiosyncrasy
BR ˌɪdɪə(ʊ)ˈsɪŋkrəs|i, -ɪz
AM ˌɪdiəˈsɪŋkrəsi, -z

idiosyncratic
BR ˌɪdɪə(ʊ)sɪŋˈkratɪk
AM ˌɪdiəsɪŋˈkrædɪk

idiosyncratically
BR ˌɪdɪə(ʊ)sɪŋˈkratɪkli
AM ˌɪdiəsɪŋˈkrædək(ə)li

idiot
BR ˈɪdɪət, -s
AM ˈɪdiət, -s

idiotic
BR ˌɪdɪˈɒtɪk
AM ˌ¦ɪdiˈɑdɪk

idiotically
BR ˌɪdɪˈɒtɪkli
AM ˌ¦ɪdiˈɑdək(ə)li

Iditarod
BR ʌɪˈdɪtərɒd
AM aɪˈdɪdəˌrɑd

idle
BR ˈʌɪd|l, -lz, -l̩ɪŋ\-lɪŋ, -ld
AM ˈaɪd|əl, -əlz, -(ə)lɪŋ, -əld

idleness
BR ˈʌɪdlnəs
AM ˈaɪdlnəs

idler
BR ˈʌɪdlə(r), ˈʌɪdl̩ə(r), -z
AM ˈaɪd(ə)lər, -z

idly
BR ˈʌɪdli
AM ˈaɪdli, ˈaɪdl̩i

Ido
BR ˈiːdəʊ
AM ˈiˌdoʊ

idol
BR ˈʌɪdl, -z
AM ˈaɪdəl, -z

idola
BR ʌɪˈdəʊlə(*r*)
AM aɪˈdoʊlə

idolater
BR ʌɪˈdɒlətə(r), -z
AM aɪˈdɑlədər, -z

idolatress
BR ʌɪˈdɒlətrəs, -ɪz
AM aɪˈdɑlətrəs, -əz

idolatrous
BR ʌɪˈdɒlətrəs
AM aɪˈdɑlətrəs

idolatrously
BR ʌɪˈdɒlətrəsli
AM aɪˈdɑlətrəsli

idolatry
BR ʌɪˈdɒlətri
AM aɪˈdɑlətri

idolisation
BR ˌʌɪdəlʌɪˈzeɪʃn, ˌʌɪdl̩ʌɪˈzeɪʃn
AM ˌaɪdləˈzeɪʃən, ˌaɪdlaɪˈzeɪʃən

idolise
BR ˈʌɪdəlʌɪz, ˈʌɪdl̩ʌɪz, -ɪz, -ɪŋ, -d
AM ˈaɪdlˌaɪz, -ɪz, -ɪŋ, -d

idoliser
BR ˈʌɪdəlʌɪzə(r), ˈʌɪdl̩ʌɪzə(r), -z
AM ˈaɪdlˌaɪzər, -z

idolization
BR ˌʌɪdəlʌɪˈzeɪʃn, ˌʌɪdl̩ʌɪˈzeɪʃn
AM ˌaɪdləˈzeɪʃən, ˌaɪdlaɪˈzeɪʃən

idolize
BR ˈʌɪdəlʌɪz, ˈʌɪdl̩ʌɪz, -ɪz, -ɪŋ, -d
AM ˈaɪdlˌaɪz, -ɪz, -ɪŋ, -d

idolizer
BR ˈʌɪdəlʌɪzə(r), ˈʌɪdl̩ʌɪzə(r), -z
AM ˈaɪdlˌaɪzər, -z

idolum
BR ʌɪˈdəʊləm
AM aɪˈdoʊləm

Idomeneus
BR ʌɪˈdɒmɪnjuːs, ɪˈdɒmɪnjuːs
AM ˌaɪˈdɑmən(j)us

idyl
BR ˈɪd(ɪ)l, ˈʌɪd(ɪ)l, -z
AM ˈaɪdl, -z

idyll
BR ˈɪd(ɪ)l, ˈʌɪd(ɪ)l, -z
AM ˈaɪdl, -z

idyllic
BR ɪˈdɪlɪk, ʌɪˈdɪlɪk
AM aɪˈdɪlɪk

idyllically
BR ɪˈdɪlɪkli, ʌɪˈdɪlɪkli
AM aɪˈdɪlək(ə)li

idyllise
BR ˈɪdl̩ʌɪz, ˈɪdɪlʌɪz, ˈʌɪdl̩ʌɪz, ˈʌɪdɪlʌɪz, -ɪz, -ɪŋ, -d
AM ˈaɪdlˌaɪz, -ɪz, -ɪŋ, -d

idyllist
BR ˈɪdl̩ɪst, ˈɪdɪlɪst, ˈʌɪdl̩ɪst, ˈʌɪdɪlɪst, -s
AM ˈaɪdl̩əst, -s

idyllize
BR ˈɪdl̩ʌɪz, ˈɪdɪlʌɪz, ˈʌɪdl̩ʌɪz, ˈʌɪdɪlʌɪz, -ɪz, -ɪŋ, -d
AM ˈaɪdlˌaɪz, -ɪz, -ɪŋ, -d

i.e.
BR ˌʌɪ ˈiː
AM ˌaɪ ˈi

Iestyn
BR ˈjɛstɪn
AM ˈjɛstən

Ieuan
BR ˈjʌɪən
AM ˈjaɪən

if
BR ɪf, -s
AM ɪf, -s

iff
BR ɪf
AM ɪf

iffy
BR ˈɪfi
AM ˈɪfi

Ifni
BR ˈɪfni
AM ˈɪfni

Ifor
BR ˈiːvɔː(r), ˈʌɪvɔː(r), ˈʌɪvə(r)
AM ˈivɔ(ə)r, ˈaɪvɔ(ə)r
WE ˈɪvɒr

Igbo
BR ˈɪgbəʊ, -z
AM ˈɪgˌboʊ, -z

Ightham
BR ˈʌɪtəm
AM ˈaɪdəm

igloo
BR ˈɪgluː, -z
AM ˈɪglu, -z

Ignatius
BR ɪgˈneɪʃəs
AM ɪgˈneɪʃəs

igneous
BR ˈɪgnɪəs
AM ˈɪgniəs

ignis fatuus
BR ˌɪgnɪs ˈfatjʊəs, + ˈfatʃʊəs
AM ˌ¦ɪgnəs ˈfætʃ(əw)əs

ignitability
BR ɪgˌnʌɪtəˈbɪlɪti
AM ɪgˌnaɪdəˈbɪlɪdi

ignitable
BR ɪgˈnʌɪtəbl
AM ɪgˈnaɪdəbəl

ignite
BR ɪgˈnʌɪt, -s, -ɪŋ, -ɪd
AM ɪgˈnaɪ|t, -ts, -dɪŋ, -dɪd

igniter
BR ɪgˈnʌɪtə(r), -z
AM ɪgˈnaɪdər, -z

ignitibility
BR ɪgˌnʌɪtɪˈbɪlɪti
AM ɪgˌnaɪdəˈbɪlɪdi

ignitible
BR ɪgˈnʌɪtɪbl
AM ɪgˈnaɪdəbəl

ignition
BR ɪgˈnɪʃn
AM ɪgˈnɪʃən

ignitron
BR ɪgˈnʌɪtrɒn, ˈɪgnɪtrɒn, -z
AM ˈɪgnəˌtrɑn, -z

ignobility
BR ˌɪgnə(ʊ)ˈbɪlɪti
AM ɪgˌnoʊˈbɪlɪdi

ignoble
BR ɪgˈnəʊbl
AM ɪgˈnoʊbəl

ignobly
BR ɪgˈnəʊbli
AM ɪgˈnoʊbli

ignominious
BR ˌɪgnəˈmɪnɪəs
AM ˌ¦ɪgnəˈmɪniəs

ignominiously
BR ˌɪgnəˈmɪnɪəsli
AM ˌ¦ɪgnəˈmɪniəsli

ignominiousness
BR ˌɪgnəˈmɪnɪəsnəs
AM ˌ¦ɪgnəˈmɪniəsnəs

ignominy
BR ˈɪgnəmɪni
AM ˈɪgnəˌmɪni, ˌɪgˈnɑmɪni

ignoramus
BR ˌɪgnəˈreɪməs, -ɪz
AM ˌɪgnəˈreɪməs, ˌɪgnəˈræməs, -əz

ignorance
BR ˈɪgn(ə)rəns, ˈɪgn(ə)rn̩s
AM ˈɪgnərəns

ignorant
BR ˈɪgn(ə)rənt, ˈɪgn(ə)rn̩t
AM ˈɪgnərənt

ignorantly
BR ˈɪgn(ə)rəntli, ˈɪgn(ə)rn̩tli
AM ˈɪgnərən(t)li

ignore
BR ɪgˈnɔː(r), -z, -ɪŋ, -d
AM ɪgˈnɔ(ə)r, -z, -ɪŋ, -d

ignorer
BR ɪgˈnɔːrə(r), -z
AM ɪgˈnɔrər, -z

ignotum per ignotius
BR ɪɡˌnəʊtəm pər ɪɡˈnəʊtɪəs, + ɪɡˈnəʊʃəs
AM ɪɡˈnoʊdəm pər ɪɡˈnoʊʃəs

Igor
BR ˈiːɡɔː(r)
AM ˈiɡɔ(ə)r

Iguaçu
BR ɪˈɡwɑːsuː
AM ɪˈɡwɑˌsu

iguana
BR ˌɪɡjʊˈɑːnə(r), ɪˈɡwɑːnə(r), -z
AM əˈɡwɑnə, iˈɡwɑnə, -z

iguanodon
BR ˌɪɡjʊˈɑːnədɒn, ɪˈɡwɑːnədɒn, -z
AM əˈɡwɑnəˌdɑn, iˈɡwɑnəˌdɑn, -z

IKEA®
BR ʌɪˈkiːə(r)
AM aɪˈkiə

ikebana
BR ˌɪkɪˈbɑːnə(r), ˌiːkeɪˈbɑːnə(r)
AM ˌɪkəˈbɑnə

Ikhnaton
BR ɪkˈnɑːtɒn, ɪkˈnɑːt(ə)n
AM ɪkˈnɑtn

ikky
BR ˈɪki
AM ˈɪki

ikon
BR ˈʌɪkɒn, -z
AM ˈaɪˌkɑn, -z

ilang-ilang
BR ˈiːlaŋˈiːlaŋ
AM ˈilæŋˈilæŋ

Ilchester
BR ˈɪltʃɪstə(r)
AM ˈɪltʃɪstər

ILEA
BR ˈɪlɪə(r), ˌʌɪɛlɪˈeɪ
AM ˌaɪˌɛlˌiˈeɪ

ileac
BR ˈɪlɪak
AM ˈɪliˌæk

ileal
BR ˈɪlɪəl
AM ˈɪliəl

Île-de-France
BR ˌiːldəˈfrɑːns, ˌiːldəˈfrans
AM ˌildəˈfrɑns

ileitis
BR ˌɪlɪˈʌɪtɪs
AM ˌɪliˈaɪdɪs

ileostomy
BR ˌɪlɪˈɒstəm|i, -ɪz
AM ˌɪliˈɑstəmi, -z

Iles
BR ʌɪlz
AM aɪlz

ileum
BR ˈɪlɪəm, -z
AM ˈɪliəm, -z

ileus
BR ˈɪlɪəs, -ɪz
AM ˈɪliəs, -ɪz

ilex
BR ˈʌɪlɛks, -ɪz
AM ˈaɪˌlɛks, -əz

ilia
BR ˈɪlɪə(r)
AM ˈɪljə, ˈɪliə

iliac
BR ˈɪlɪak
AM ˈɪliˌæk

Iliad
BR ˈɪlɪəd, ˈɪlɪad
AM ˈɪliəd

ilium
BR ˈɪlɪəm
AM ˈɪliəm

ilk
BR ɪlk
AM ɪlk

I'll
BR ʌɪl
AM aɪl

ill
BR ɪl
AM ɪl

illation
BR ɪˈleɪʃn, -z
AM əˈleɪʃən, -z

illative
BR ɪˈleɪtɪv, ˈɪlətɪv
AM ˈɪlədɪv, əˈleɪdɪv

illatively
BR ɪˈleɪtɪvli, ˈɪlətɪvli
AM ˈɪlədɪvli, əˈleɪdɪvli

illegal
BR ɪˈliːɡl
AM ɪ(l)ˈliɡəl, əˈliɡəl

illegality
BR ˌɪlɪˈɡalɪt|i, -ɪz
AM ˌɪ(l)ləˈɡælədi, -z

illegally
BR ɪˈliːɡl̩i, ɪˈliːɡəli
AM ɪ(l)ˈliɡ(ə)li, əˈliɡ(ə)li

illegibility
BR ɪˌlɛdʒɪˈbɪlɪti
AM ˌɪ(l)ˌlɛdʒəˈbɪlɪdi, əˌlɛdʒəˈbɪlɪdi

illegible
BR ɪˈlɛdʒɪbl
AM ɪ(l)ˈlɛdʒəbəl, əˈlɛdʒəbəl

illegibly
BR ɪˈlɛdʒɪbli
AM ɪ(l)ˈlɛdʒəbli, əˈlɛdʒəbli

illegitimacy
BR ˌɪlɪˈdʒɪtɪməsi
AM ˌɪ(l)ləˈdʒɪdəməsi

illegitimate
BR ˌɪlɪˈdʒɪtɪmət
AM ˌɪ(l)ləˈdʒɪdəmət

illegitimately
BR ˌɪlɪˈdʒɪtɪmətli
AM ˌɪ(l)ləˈdʒɪdəmətli

illegitimation
BR ˌɪlɪˌdʒɪtɪˈmeɪʃn
AM ˌɪ(l)ləˌdʒɪdəˈmeɪʃən

illegitimise
BR ˌɪlɪˈdʒɪtɪmʌɪz, -ɪz, -ɪŋ, -d
AM ˌɪ(l)ləˈdʒɪdəˌmaɪz, -ɪz, -ɪŋ, -d

illegitimize
BR ˌɪlɪˈdʒɪtɪmʌɪz, -ɪz, -ɪŋ, -d
AM ˌɪ(l)ləˈdʒɪdəˌmaɪz, -ɪz, -ɪŋ, -d

ill-gotten
BR ˌɪlˈɡɒtn
AM ˈɪlˌɡɑtn

ill-humored
BR ˌɪlˈhjuːməd
AM ˈɪlˌ(h)jumərd

ill-humoured
BR ˌɪlˈhjuːməd
AM ˈɪlˌ(h)jumərd

illiberal
BR ɪˈlɪb(ə)rəl, ɪˈlɪb(ə)rl̩
AM ɪ(l)ˈlɪb(ə)rəl

illiberality
BR ɪˌlɪbəˈralɪti
AM ˌɪ(l)ˌlɪbəˈrælədi

illiberally
BR ɪˈlɪb(ə)rəli, ɪˈlɪb(ə)rl̩i
AM ɪ(l)ˈlɪb(ə)rəli

illicit
BR ɪˈlɪsɪt
AM ɪ(l)ˈlɪsɪt

illicitly
BR ɪˈlɪsɪtli
AM ɪ(l)ˈlɪsɪtli

illicitness
BR ɪˈlɪsɪtnɪs
AM ɪ(l)ˈlɪsɪtnɪs

illimitability
BR ɪˌlɪmɪtəˈbɪlɪti
AM ɪ(l)ˌlɪmədəˈbɪlɪdi

illimitable
BR ɪˈlɪmɪtəbl
AM ɪ(l)ˈlɪmədəbəl

illimitableness
BR ɪˈlɪmɪtəblnəs
AM ɪ(l)ˈlɪmədəbəlnəs

illimitably
BR ɪˈlɪmɪtəbli
AM ɪ(l)ˈlɪmədəbli

Illingworth
BR ˈɪlɪŋwəːθ, ˈɪlɪŋwəθ
AM ˈɪlɪŋˌwərθ

Illinois
BR ˌɪlɪˈnɔɪ
AM ˌɪləˈnɔɪ

Illinoisan
BR ˌɪlɪˈnɔɪən, -z
AM ˌɪləˈnɔɪən, -z

illiquid
BR ɪˈlɪkwɪd
AM ɪ(l)ˈlɪkwɪd

illiquidity
BR ˌɪlɪˈkwɪdɪti
AM ɪ(l)ˌləˈkwɪdɪdi

illiteracy
BR ɪˈlɪt(ə)rəsi
AM ɪ(l)ˈlɪtrəsi, ɪ(l)ˈlɪdərəsi

illiterate
BR ɪˈlɪt(ə)rət
AM ɪ(l)ˈlɪdərət

illiterately
BR ɪˈlɪt(ə)rətli
AM ɪ(l)ˈlɪdərətli

illiterateness
BR ɪˈlɪt(ə)rətnəs
AM ɪ(l)ˈlɪdərətnəs

ill-natured
BR ˌɪlˈneɪtʃəd
AM ˈɪlˌneɪtʃərd

ill-naturedly
BR ˌɪlˈneɪtʃədli
AM ˈɪlˌneɪtʃərdli

illness
BR ˈɪlnɪs, -ɪz
AM ˈɪlnəs, -əz

illogical
BR ɪˈlɒdʒɪkl
AM ɪ(l)ˈlɑdʒəkəl

illogicality
BR ɪˌlɒdʒɪˈkalɪti
AM ɪ(l)ˌlɑdʒəˈkælədi

illogically
BR ɪˈlɒdʒɪkli
AM ɪ(l)ˈlɑdʒək(ə)li

ill-omened
BR ˌɪlˈəʊmɛnd, ˌɪlˈəʊmənd
AM ˈɪlˌoʊmənd

ill-starred
BR ˌɪlˈstɑːd
AM ˈɪlˌstɑrd

illude
BR ɪˈl(j)uːd, -z, -ɪŋ, -ɪd
AM ɪˈlud, -z, -ɪŋ, -əd

illume
BR ɪˈl(j)uːm, -z, -ɪŋ, -d
AM ɪˈlum, -z, -ɪŋ, -d

illuminance
BR ɪˈl(j)uːmɪnəns, -ɪz
AM ɪˈlumənəns, -əz

illuminant
BR ɪˈl(j)uːmɪnənt, -s
AM ɪˈlumənənt, -s

illuminate
BR ɪˈl(j)uːmɪneɪt, -s, -ɪŋ, -ɪd
AM ɪˈluməˌneɪ|t, -ts, -dɪŋ, -dɪd

illuminati
BR ɪˌl(j)uːmɪˈnɑːtiː
AM ɪˌluməˈnɑdi

illuminatingly
BR ɪˈl(j)uːmɪneɪtɪŋli
AM ɪˈluməˌneɪdɪŋli

illumination
BR ɪˌl(j)uːmɪˈneɪʃn, -z
AM ɪˌluməˈneɪʃən, -z
illuminative
BR ɪˈl(j)uːmɪnətɪv
AM ɪˈluməˌneɪdɪv
illuminator
BR ɪˈl(j)uːmɪneɪtə(r), -z
AM ɪˈluməˌneɪdər, -z
illumine
BR ɪˈl(j)uːm|ɪn, -ɪnz, -ɪnɪŋ, -ɪnd
AM ɪˈlumən, -z, -ɪŋ, -d
illuminism
BR ɪˈl(j)uːmɪnɪz(ə)m
AM ɪˈluməˌnɪzəm
illuminist
BR ɪˈl(j)uːmɪnɪst, -s
AM ɪˈlumənəst, -s
ill-use
BR ˌɪlˈjuːz, -ɪz, -ɪŋ, -d
AM ˈɪlˌjuz, -əz, -ɪŋ, -d
illusion
BR ɪˈl(j)uːʒn, -z
AM ɪˈluʒən, -z
illusional
BR ɪˈl(j)uːʒn̩(ə)l, ɪˈl(j)uːʒən(ə)l
AM ɪˈluʒ(ə)nəl
illusionism
BR ɪˈl(j)uːʒn̩ɪz(ə)m, ɪˈl(j)uːʒənɪz(ə)m
AM ɪˈluʒəˌnɪzəm
illusionist
BR ɪˈl(j)uːʒn̩ɪst, ɪˈl(j)uːʒənɪst, -s
AM ɪˈluʒənəst, -s
illusionistic
BR ɪˌl(j)uːʒəˈnɪstɪk, ɪˌl(j)uːʒnˈɪstɪk
AM ɪˌluʒəˈnɪstɪk
illusive
BR ɪˈl(j)uːsɪv
AM ɪˈlusɪv
illusively
BR ɪˈl(j)uːsɪvli
AM ɪˈlusɪvli
illusiveness
BR ɪˈl(j)uːsɪvnɪs
AM ɪˈlusɪvnɪs
illusorily
BR ɪˈl(j)uːs(ə)rɪli, ɪˈl(j)uːz(ə)rɪli
AM ɪˈlus(ə)rəli, ɪˈluz(ə)rəli
illusoriness
BR ɪˈl(j)uːs(ə)rɪnɪs, ɪˈl(j)uːz(ə)rɪnɪs
AM ɪˈlus(ə)rinɪs, ɪˈluz(ə)rinɪs
illusory
BR ɪˈl(j)uːs(ə)ri, ɪˈl(j)uːz(ə)ri
AM ɪˈlus(ə)ri, ɪˈluz(ə)ri
illustrate
BR ˈɪləstreɪt, -s, -ɪŋ, -ɪd
AM ˈɪləˌstreɪ|t, -ts, -dɪŋ, -dɪd
illustration
BR ˌɪləˈstreɪʃn, -z
AM ˌɪləˈstreɪʃən, -z
illustrational
BR ˌɪləˈstreɪʃn̩(ə)l, ˌɪləˈstreɪʃən(ə)l
AM ˌɪləˈstreɪʃ(ə)nəl
illustrative
BR ˈɪləstrətɪv, ˈɪləstreɪtɪv, ɪˈlʌstrətɪv
AM ɪˈləstrədɪv, ˈɪləˌstreɪdɪv
illustratively
BR ˈɪləstrətɪvli, ˈɪləstreɪtɪvli, ɪˈlʌstrətɪvli
AM ɪˈləstrədɪvli, ˈɪləˌstreɪdɪvli
illustrator
BR ˈɪləstreɪtə(r), -z
AM ˈɪləˌstreɪdər, -z
illustrious
BR ɪˈlʌstriəs
AM ɪˈləstriəs
illustriously
BR ɪˈlʌstriəsli
AM ɪˈləstriəsli
illustriousness
BR ɪˈlʌstriəsnəs
AM ɪˈləstriəsnəs
Illyria
BR ɪˈlɪrɪə(*r*)
AM ɪˈlɪriə
Illyrian
BR ɪˈlɪrɪən, -z
AM ɪˈlɪriən, -z
Illyricum
BR ɪˈlɪrɪkəm
AM ɪˈlɪrɪkəm
illywhacker
BR ˈɪlɪˌwakə(r), -z
AM ˈɪliˌ(h)wækər, -z
ilmenite
BR ˈɪlmɪnʌɪt, -s
AM ˈɪlməˌnaɪt, -s
Ilminster
BR ˈɪlmɪnstə(r)
AM ˈɪlˌmɪnstər
Ilona
BR ɪˈləʊnə(*r*)
AM ɪˈloʊnə
Ilson
BR ˈɪls(ə)n
AM ˈɪlsən
Ilyushin
BR ɪlˈjuːʃ(ɪ)n
AM ɪlˈjuʃɪn
I'm
BR ʌɪm
AM aɪm
image
BR ˈɪm|ɪdʒ, -ɪdʒɪz, -ɪdʒɪŋ, -ɪdʒd
AM ˈɪmɪdʒ, -ɪz, -ɪŋ, -d
imageable
BR ˈɪmɪdʒəbl
AM ˈɪmɪdʒəbəl
imageless
BR ˈɪmɪdʒlɪs
AM ˈɪmɪdʒlɪs
imagery
BR ˈɪmɪdʒ(ə)ri
AM ˈɪmɪdʒ(ə)ri
imaginable
BR ɪˈmadʒɪnəbl, ɪˈmadʒn̩əbl
AM ɪˈmædʒ(ə)nəbəl
imaginably
BR ɪˈmadʒɪnəbli, ɪˈmadʒn̩əbli
AM ɪˈmædʒ(ə)nəbli
imaginal
BR ɪˈmadʒɪnl, ɪˈmadʒn̩l
AM ɪˈmædʒ(ə)nəl
imaginarily
BR ɪˈmadʒɪn(ə)rɪli, ɪˈmadʒɪn(ə)rl̩i, ɪˈmadʒn̩(ə)rɪli, ɪˈmadʒn̩(ə)rl̩i
AM ɪˌmædʒəˈnɛrəli
imaginary
BR ɪˈmadʒɪn(ə)ri, ɪˈmadʒn̩(ə)ri
AM ɪˈmædʒəˌnɛri
imagination
BR ɪˌmadʒɪˈneɪʃn
AM ɪˌmædʒəˈneɪʃən
imaginative
BR ɪˈmadʒɪnətɪv, ɪˈmadʒn̩ətɪv
AM ɪˈmædʒ(ə)nədɪv
imaginatively
BR ɪˈmadʒɪnətɪvli, ɪˈmadʒn̩ətɪvli
AM ɪˈmædʒ(ə)nədɪvli
imaginativeness
BR ɪˈmadʒɪnətɪvnɪs, ɪˈmadʒn̩ətɪvnɪs
AM ɪˈmædʒ(ə)nədɪvnɪs
imagine
verb
BR ɪˈmadʒɪn, ɪˈmadʒn̩, -z, -ɪŋ, -d
AM ɪˈmædʒən, -z, -ɪŋ, -d
imaginer
BR ɪˈmadʒɪnə(r), ɪˈmadʒn̩ə(r), -z
AM ɪˈmædʒənər, -z
imagines[1]
from imagine
BR ɪˈmadʒɪnz, ɪˈmadʒn̩z
AM ɪˈmædʒənz
imagines[2]
plural of imago
BR ɪˈmeɪdʒɪniːz, ɪˈmɑːdʒɪniːz
AM ɪˈmeɪgəˌniz, ɪˈmɑgəˌniz, ɪˈmeɪdʒəˌniz, ɪˈmædʒəˌniz
imaginings
BR ɪˈmadʒɪnɪŋz, ɪˈmadʒn̩ɪŋz
AM ɪˈmædʒənɪŋz
imagism
BR ˈɪmɪdʒɪz(ə)m
AM ˈɪməˌdʒɪzəm
imagist
BR ˈɪmɪdʒɪst, -s
AM ˈɪmədʒəst, -s
imagistic
BR ˌɪmɪˈdʒɪstɪk
AM ˌɪməˈdʒɪstɪk
imago
BR ɪˈmeɪgəʊ, ɪˈmɑːgəʊ, -z
AM ɪˈmeɪgoʊ, ɪˈmɑgoʊ, -z
imam
BR ɪˈmɑːm, ɪˈmam, -z
AM ɪˈmɑm, ɪˈmæm, -z
imamate
BR ɪˈmɑːmət, ɪˈmamət, -s
AM ɪˈmɑˌmeɪt, ɪˈmæˌmeɪt, -s
IMAX®
BR ˈʌɪmaks
AM ˈaɪˌmæks
imbalance
BR (ˌ)ɪmˈbaləns, (ˌ)ɪmˈbalns
AM ɪmˈbæləns
imbecile
BR ˈɪmbɪsiːl, -z
AM ˈɪmbəsəl, ˈɪmbəˌsaɪl, -z
imbecilely
BR ˈɪmbɪsiːlli
AM ˈɪmbəsə(l)li, ˈɪmbəˌsaɪ(l)li
imbecilic
BR ˌɪmbɪˈsɪlɪk
AM ˌɪmbəˈsɪlɪk
imbecility
BR ˌɪmbɪˈsɪlɪti
AM ˌɪmbəˈsɪlɪdi
imbed
BR ɪmˈbɛd, -z, -ɪŋ, -ɪd
AM ɪmˈbɛd, -z, -ɪŋ, -əd
Imbert
BR ˈɪmbət
AM ˈɪmbərt
imbibe
BR ɪmˈbʌɪb, -z, -ɪŋ, -d
AM ɪmˈbaɪb, -z, -ɪŋ, -d
imbiber
BR ɪmˈbʌɪbə(r), -z
AM ɪmˈbaɪbər, -z
imbibition
BR ˌɪmbɪˈbɪʃn, -z
AM ɪmˌbaɪˈbɪʃən, -z
imbricate
BR ˈɪmbrɪkeɪt, -s, -ɪŋ, -ɪd
AM ˈɪmbrəˌkeɪ|t, -ts, -dɪŋ, -dɪd

imbrication
BR ˌɪmbrɪˈkeɪʃn
AM ˌɪmbrəˈkeɪʃən
imbroglio
BR ɪmˈbrəʊlɪəʊ, -z
AM ɪmˈbroʊljoʊ, ɪmˈbrɔljoʊ, -z
Imbros
BR ˈɪmbrɒs
AM ˈɪmˌbrɔs, ˈɪmˌbrɑs
imbrue
BR ɪmˈbruː, -z, -ɪŋ, -d
AM ɪmˈbru, -z, -ɪŋ, -d
imbrute
BR ɪmˈbruːt, -s, -ɪŋ, -ɪd
AM ɪmˈbru|t, -ts, -dɪŋ, -dəd
imbue
BR ɪmˈbjuː, -z, -ɪŋ, -d
AM ɪmˈbju, -z, -ɪŋ, -d
Imhotep
BR ˈɪmhəʊtɛp
AM ɪmˈhoʊˌtɛp
imide
BR ˈɪmʌɪd, -z
AM ˈɪˌmaɪd, -z
imidozole
BR ˌɪmɪˈdeɪzəʊl, ɪˈmɪdəzəʊl
AM əˈmɪdəˌzoʊl
imine
BR ˈɪmiːn, ɪˈmiːn, -z
AM ˈɪˌmin, ˈɪmɪn, -z
imitability
BR ˌɪmɪtəˈbɪlɪti
AM ˌɪmədəˈbɪlɪdi
imitable
BR ˈɪmɪtəbl
AM ˈɪmədəbəl
imitate
BR ˈɪmɪteɪt, -s, -ɪŋ, -ɪd
AM ˈɪməˌteɪ|t, -ts, -dɪŋ, -dɪd
imitation
BR ˌɪmɪˈteɪʃn, -z
AM ˌɪməˈteɪʃən, -z
imitative
BR ˈɪmɪtətɪv
AM ˈɪməˌteɪdɪv, ˈɪmədədɪv
imitatively
BR ˈɪmɪtətɪvli
AM ˈɪməˌteɪdɪvli, ˈɪmədədəvli
imitativeness
BR ˈɪmɪtətɪvnɪs
AM ˈɪməˌteɪdɪvnɪs, ˈɪmədədɪvnɪs
imitator
BR ˈɪmɪteɪtə(r), -z
AM ˈɪməˌteɪdər, -z
immaculacy
BR ɪˈmakjʉləsi
AM ɪˈmækjələsi
immaculate
BR ɪˈmakjʉlət
AM ɪˈmækjələt
immaculately
BR ɪˈmakjʉlətli
AM ɪˈmækjələtli
immaculateness
BR ɪˈmakjʉlətnəs
AM ɪˈmækjələtnəs
immanence
BR ˈɪmənəns
AM ˈɪmənəns
immanency
BR ˈɪmənənsi
AM ˈɪmənənsi
immanent
BR ˈɪmənənt
AM ˈɪmənənt
immanentism
BR ˈɪmənəntɪz(ə)m
AM ˈɪmənənˌtɪzəm
immanentist
BR ˈɪmənəntɪst, -s
AM ˈɪmənən(t)əst, -s
Immanuel
BR ɪˈmanjʊəl, ɪˈmanjʉl
AM ɪˈmænjəwəl
immaterial
BR ˌɪməˈtɪərɪəl
AM ˌɪ(m)məˈtɪriəl
immaterialise
BR ˌɪməˈtɪərɪəlʌɪz, -ɪz, -ɪŋ, -d
AM ˌɪ(m)məˈtɪriəˌlaɪz, -ɪz, -ɪŋ, -d
immaterialism
BR ˌɪməˈtɪərɪəlɪz(ə)m
AM ˌɪ(m)məˈtɪriəˌlɪzəm
immaterialist
BR ˌɪməˈtɪərɪəlɪst, -s
AM ˌɪ(m)məˈtɪriələst, -s
immateriality
BR ˌɪməˌtɪərɪˈalɪti
AM ˌɪ(m)məˌtɪriˈælədi
immaterialize
BR ˌɪməˈtɪərɪəlʌɪz, -ɪz, -ɪŋ, -d
AM ˌɪ(m)məˈtɪriəˌlaɪz, -ɪz, -ɪŋ, -d
immaterially
BR ˌɪməˈtɪərɪəli
AM ˌɪ(m)məˈtɪriəli
immature
BR ˌɪməˈtjʊə(r), ˌɪməˈtʃʊə(r), ˌɪməˈtjɔː(r), ˌɪməˈtʃɔː(r)
AM ˌɪ(m)məˈtʊ(ə)r, ˌɪ(m)məˈtʃʊ(ə)r, ˌɪ(m)məˈtʃər
immaturely
BR ˌɪməˈtjʊəli, ˌɪməˈtʃʊəli, ˌɪməˈtjɔːli, ˌɪməˈtʃɔːli
AM ˌɪ(m)məˈtʊrli, ˌɪ(m)məˈtʃʊrli, ˌɪ(m)məˈtʃərli
immaturity
BR ˌɪməˈtjʊərɪti, ˌɪməˈtʃʊərɪti, ˌɪməˈtjɔːrɪti, ˌɪməˈtʃɔːrɪti
AM ˌɪ(m)məˈtʊrədi, ˌɪ(m)məˈtʃʊrədi, ˌɪ(m)məˈtʃərədi
immeasurability
BR ɪˌmɛʒ(ə)rəˈbɪlɪti
AM ɪ(m)ˌmɛʒ(ə)rəˈbɪlɪdi
immeasurable
BR (ˌ)ɪˈmɛʒ(ə)rəbl
AM ɪ(m)ˈmɛʒ(ə)r(ə)bəl
immeasurableness
BR (ˌ)ɪˈmɛʒ(ə)rəblnəs
AM ɪ(m)ˈmɛʒ(ə)rəbəlnəs
immeasurably
BR (ˌ)ɪˈmɛʒ(ə)rəbli
AM ɪ(m)ˈmɛʒ(ə)rəbli
immediacy
BR ɪˈmiːdɪəsi
AM ɪˈmidiəsi
immediate
BR ɪˈmiːdɪət
AM ɪˈmidiət
immediately
BR ɪˈmiːdɪətli
AM ɪˈmidiətli
immediateness
BR ɪˈmiːdɪətnəs
AM ɪˈmidiətnəs
immedicable
BR ɪˈmɛdɪkəbl
AM ɪˈmɛdəkəbəl
immedicably
BR ɪˈmɛdɪkəbli
AM ɪˈmɛdəkəbli
immemorial
BR ˌɪməˈmɔːrɪəl
AM ˌɪ(m)məˈmɔriəl
immemorially
BR ˌɪmɪˈmɔːrɪəli
AM ˌɪ(m)məˈmɔriəli
immense
BR ɪˈmɛns
AM ɪˈmɛns
immensely
BR ɪˈmɛnsli
AM ɪˈmɛnsli
immenseness
BR ɪˈmɛnsnəs
AM ɪˈmɛnsnəs
immensity
BR ɪˈmɛnsɪti
AM ɪˈmɛnsədi
immerse
BR ɪˈməːs, -ɪz, -ɪŋ, -t
AM ɪˈmərs, -əz, -ɪŋ, -t
immersion
BR ɪˈməːʃn, ɪˈməːʒn
AM ɪˈmərʒən, ɪˈmərʃən
immigrant
BR ˈɪmɪgr(ə)nt, -s
AM ˈɪməgrənt, -s
immigrate
BR ˈɪmɪgreɪt, -s, -ɪŋ, -ɪd
AM ˈɪməˌgreɪ|t, -ts, -dɪŋ, -dɪd
immigration
BR ˌɪmɪˈgreɪʃn
AM ˌɪməˈgreɪʃən
immigratory
BR ˈɪmɪgrət(ə)ri
AM ˈɪməgrəˌtɔri
imminence
BR ˈɪmɪnəns
AM ˈɪmənəns
imminent
BR ˈɪmɪnənt
AM ˈɪmənənt
imminently
BR ˈɪmɪnəntli
AM ˈɪmənən(t)li
immiscibility
BR ɪˌmɪsɪˈbɪlɪti
AM ɪ(m)ˌmɪsəˈbɪlɪdi
immiscible
BR (ˌ)ɪˈmɪsɪbl
AM ɪ(m)ˈmɪsɪbəl
immiscibly
BR (ˌ)ɪˈmɪsɪbli
AM ɪ(m)ˈmɪsɪbli
immitigable
BR (ˌ)ɪˈmɪtɪgəbl
AM ɪ(m)ˈmɪdəgəbəl
immitigably
BR (ˌ)ɪˈmɪtɪgəbli
AM ɪ(m)ˈmɪdəgəbli
immittance
BR ɪˈmɪt(ə)ns, -ɪz
AM ɪ(m)ˈmɪtns, -ɪz
immixture
BR ɪˈmɪkstʃə(r), -z
AM ɪ(m)ˈmɪkstʃər, -z
immobile
BR ɪˈməʊbʌɪl
AM ɪ(m)ˈmoʊbəl, ɪ(m)ˌmoʊbail
immobilisation
BR ɪˌməʊbɪlʌɪˈzeɪʃn, ɪˌməʊbl̩ʌɪˈzeɪʃn
AM ˌɪ(m)ˌmoʊbələˈzeɪʃən, ˌɪ(m)ˌmoʊbəˌlaɪˈzeɪʃən, əmoʊbələˈzeɪʃən, əˌmoʊbəˌlaɪˈzeɪʃən
immobilise
BR ɪˈməʊbɪlʌɪz, ɪˈməʊbl̩ʌɪz, -ɪz, -ɪŋ, -d
AM ɪ(m)ˈmoʊbəˌlaɪz, əˈmoʊbəˌlaɪz, -ɪz, -ɪŋ, -d
immobiliser
BR ɪˈməʊbɪlʌɪzə(r), ɪˈməʊbl̩ʌɪzə(r), -z
AM ɪ(m)ˈmoʊbəˌlaɪzər, əˈmoʊbəˌlaɪzər, -z
immobilism
BR ɪˈməʊbɪlɪz(ə)m, ɪˈməʊbl̩ɪz(ə)m
AM ɪ(m)ˈmoʊbəˌlɪzəm, əˈmoʊbəˌlɪzəm

immobility
BR ˌɪmə(ʊ)ˈbɪlɨti
AM ˈɪ(m)moʊˈbɪlɨdi

immobilization
BR ɪˌməʊbɨlʌɪˈzeɪʃn, ɪˌməʊbl̩ʌɪˈzeɪʃn
AM ˈɪ(m)ˌmoʊbələˈzeɪʃən, ˈɪ(m)ˌmoʊbəˌlaɪˈzeɪʃən, əmoʊbələˈzeɪʃən, əˌmoʊbəˌlaɪˈzeɪʃən

immobilize
BR ɪˈməʊbɨlʌɪz, ɪˈməʊbl̩ʌɪz, -ɨz, -ɪŋ, -d
AM ɪ(m)ˈmoʊbəˌlaɪz, əˈmoʊbəˌlaɪz, -ɨz, -ɪŋ, -d

immobilizer
BR ɪˈməʊbɨlʌɪzə(r), ɪˈməʊbl̩ʌɪzə(r), -z
AM ɪ(m)ˈmoʊbəˌlaɪzər, əˈmoʊbəˌlaɪzər, -z

immoderacy
BR (ˌ)ɪˈmɒd(ə)rəsi
AM ɪ(m)ˈmɑd(ə)rəsi, əˈmɑd(ə)rəsi

immoderate
BR (ˌ)ɪˈmɒd(ə)rət
AM ɪ(m)ˈmɑd(ə)rət, əˈmɑd(ə)rət

immoderately
BR ɪˈmɒd(ə)rətli
AM ɪ(m)ˈmɑd(ə)rətli, əˈmɑd(ə)rətli

immoderateness
BR (ˌ)ɪˈmɒd(ə)rətnəs
AM ɪ(m)ˈmɑd(ə)rətnəs, əˈmɑd(ə)rətnəs

immoderation
BR ɪˌmɒd(ə)ˈreɪʃn
AM ɪ(m)ˌmɑd(ə)ˈreɪʃən, əˌmɑd(ə)ˈreɪʃən

immodest
BR (ˌ)ɪˈmɒdɪst
AM ɪ(m)ˈmɑdəst, əˈmɑdəst

immodestly
BR (ˌ)ɪˈmɒdɪstli
AM ɪ(m)ˈmɑdəs(t)li, əˈmɑdəs(t)li

immodesty
BR (ˌ)ɪˈmɒdɪsti
AM ɪ(m)ˈmɑdəsti, əˈmɑdəsti

immolate
BR ˈɪməleɪt, -s, -ɪŋ, -ɨd
AM ˈɪməˌleɪ|t, -ts, -dɪŋ, -dɨd

immolation
BR ˌɪməˈleɪʃn
AM ˌɪməˈleɪʃən

immolator
BR ˈɪməleɪtə(r), -z
AM ˈɪməˌleɪdər, -z

immoral
BR (ˌ)ɪˈmɒrəl, (ˌ)ɪˈmɒrl̩
AM ɪ(m)ˈmɔrəl, əˈmɔrəl

immorality
BR ˌɪməˈralɨti
AM ˌɪməˈrælədi, ˌɪmɔˈrælədi

immorally
BR (ˌ)ɪˈmɒrəli, (ˌ)ɪˈmɒrl̩i
AM ɪ(m)ˈmɔrəli, əˈmɔrəli

immortal
BR (ˌ)ɪˈmɔːtl, -z
AM ɪ(m)ˈmɔrdl, əˈmɔrdl, -z

immortalisation
BR ɪˌmɔːtl̩ʌɪˈzeɪʃn, ɪˌmɔːtəlʌɪˈzeɪʃn, -z
AM ɪ(m)ˌmɔrdlˌaɪˈzeɪʃən, ɪ(m)ˌmɔrdləˈzeɪʃən, -z

immortalise
BR ɪˈmɔːtl̩ʌɪz, ɪˈmɔːtəlʌɪz, -ɨz, -ɪŋ, -d
AM ɪ(m)ˈmɔrdlˌaɪz, -ɨz, -ɪŋ, -d

immortality
BR ˌɪmɔːˈtalɨti
AM ˈɪ(m)ˌmɔrˈtælədi

immortalization
BR ɪˈmɔːtl̩ʌɪˈzeɪʃn, ɨˌmɔːtəlʌɪˈzeɪʃn, -z
AM ɪ(m)ˌmɔrdlˌaɪˈzeɪʃən, ɪ(m)ˌmɔrdləˈzeɪʃən, -z

immortalize
BR ɪˈmɔːtl̩ʌɪz, ɪˈmɔːtəlʌɪz, -ɨz, -ɪŋ, -d
AM ɪ(m)ˈmɔrdlˌaɪz, -ɨz, -ɪŋ, -d

immortally
BR ɪˈmɔːtl̩i
AM ɪ(m)ˈmɔrdl̩i, əˈmɔrdl̩i

immortelle
BR ˌɪmɔːˈtɛl, -z
AM ˈɪˌmɔrˈtɛl, əˌmɔrˈtɛl, -z

immovability
BR ɪˌmuːvəˈbɪlɨti
AM ɪ(m)ˌmuvəˈbɪlɨdi, əˌmuvəˈbɪlɨdi

immovable
BR (ˌ)ɪˈmuːvəbl, -z
AM ɪ(m)ˈmuvəbəl, əˈmuvəbəl, -z

immovableness
BR (ˌ)ɪˈmuːvəblnəs
AM ɪ(m)ˈmuvəbəlnəs, əˈmuvəbəlnəs

immovably
BR (ˌ)ɪˈmuːvəbli
AM ɪ(m)ˈmuvəbli, əˈmuvəbli

immoveable
BR (ˌ)ɪˈmuːvəbl, -z
AM ɪ(m)ˈmuvəbəl, əˈmuvəbəl, -z

immoveableness
BR (ˌ)ɪˈmuːvəblnəs
AM ɪ(m)ˈmuvəbəlnəs, əˈmuvəbəlnəs

immoveably
BR (ˌ)ɪˈmuːvəbli
AM ɪ(m)ˈmuvəbli, əˈmuvəbli

immune
BR ɨˈmjuːn
AM ɨˈmjun

immunisation
BR ˌɪmjʉnʌɪˈzeɪʃn
AM ˌɪmjənəˈzeɪʃən, ˌɪmjəˌnaɪˈzeɪʃən

immunise
BR ˈɪmjʉnʌɪz, -ɨz, -ɪŋ, -d
AM ˈɪmjəˌnaɪz, -ɨz, -ɪŋ, -d

immuniser
BR ˈɪmjʉnʌɪzə(r), -z
AM ˈɪmjəˌnaɪzər, -z

immunity
BR ɨˈmjuːnɨti
AM ɨˈmjunədi, -z

immunization
BR ˌɪmjʉnʌɪˈzeɪʃn
AM ˌɪmjənəˈzeɪʃən, ˌɪmjəˌnaɪˈzeɪʃən

immunize
BR ˈɪmjʉnʌɪz, -ɨz, -ɪŋ, -d
AM ˈɪmjəˌnaɪz, -ɨz, -ɪŋ, -d

immunizer
BR ˈɪmjʉnʌɪzə(r), -z
AM ˈɪmjəˌnaɪzər, -z

immunoassay
BR ˌɪmjʉnəʊəˈseɪ, ˌɪmjʉnəʊˈaseɪ, -z
AM ˌɪmjənoʊˈæˌseɪ, -z

immunochemistry
BR ˌɪmjʉnəʊˈkɛmɪstri
AM ˌɪmjənoʊˈkɛməstri

immunocompetence
BR ˌɪmjʉnəʊˈkɒmpɪt(ə)ns
AM ˌɪmjənoʊˈkɑmpədns

immunocompetent
BR ˌɪmjʉnəʊˈkɒmpɪt(ə)nt
AM ˌɪmjənoʊˈkɑmpədnt

immunocompromised
BR ˌɪmjʉnəʊˈkɒmprəmʌɪzd
AM ˌɪmjənoʊˈkɑmprəˌmaɪzd

immunodeficiency
BR ˌɪmjʉnəʊdɪˈfɪʃnsi
AM ˌɪmjənoʊdəˈfɪʃənsi

immunodeficient
BR ˌɪmjʉnəʊdɪˈfɪʃnt
AM ˌɪmjənoʊdəˈfɪʃənt

immunodepressed
BR ˌɪmjʉnəʊdɪˈprɛst
AM ˌɪmjənoʊdəˈprɛst

immunodepression
BR ˌɪmjʉnəʊdɪˈprɛʃn
AM ˌɪmjənoʊdəˈprɛʃən

immunogenic
BR ˌɪmjʉnəʊˈdʒɛnɪk
AM ˌɪmjənoʊˈdʒɛnɪk

immunoglobulin
BR ˌɪmjʉnəʊˈglɒbjʉlɪn, -z
AM ˌɪmjənoʊˈglɑbjələn, -z

immunologic
BR ˌɪmjʉnəˈlɒdʒɪk
AM ˈɪmjənəˈlɑdʒɪk

immunological
BR ˌɪmjʉnəˈlɒdʒɪkl
AM ˈɪmjənəˈlɑdʒəkəl

immunologically
BR ˌɪmjʉnəˈlɒdʒɪkli
AM ˈɪmjənəˈlɑdʒək(ə)li

immunologist
BR ˌɪmjʉˈnɒlədʒɪst, -s
AM ˌɪmjəˈnɑlədʒəst, -s

immunology
BR ˌɪmjʉˈnɒlədʒi
AM ˌɪmjəˈnɑlədʒi

immunosuppressant
BR ˌɪmjʉnəʊsəˈprɛsnt, -s
AM ˌɪmjənoʊsəˈprɛsənt, -s

immunosuppressed
BR ˌɪmjʉnəʊsəˈprɛst
AM ˌɪmjənoʊsəˈprɛst

immunosuppression
BR ˌɪmjʉnəʊsəˈprɛʃn
AM ˌɪmjənoʊsəˈprɛʃən

immunosuppressive
BR ˌɪmjʉnəʊsəˈprɛsɪv, -z
AM ˌɪmjənoʊsəˈprɛsɪv, -z

immunotherapy
BR ɪˌmjuːnə(ʊ)ˈθɛrəpi, ˌɪmjʉnəʊˈθɛrəpi
AM ˈɪmjənoʊˈθɛrəpi, əˌmjunoʊˈθɛrəpi

immure
BR ɪˈmjʊə(r), ɪˈmjɔː(r), -z, -ɪŋ, -d
AM ɨˈmjʊ(ə)r, -z, -ɪŋ, -d

immurement
BR ɪˈmjʊəm(ə)nt, ɪˈmjɔːm(ə)nt, -s
AM ɨˈmjʊrmənt, -s

immutability
BR ɪˌmjuːtəˈbɪlɨti
AM ɪ(m)ˌmjudəˈbɪlɨdi, əˌmjudəˈbɪlɨdi

immutable
BR (ˌ)ɪˈmjuːtəbl
AM ɪ(m)ˈmjudəbəl, əˈmjudəbəl

immutably
BR (ˌ)ɪˈmjuːtəbli

AM ɪ(m)ˈmjudəbli, əˈmjudəbli

Imogen
BR ˈɪmədʒ(ə)n
AM ˈɪmədʒən

imp
BR ɪmp, -s
AM ɪmp, -s

impact[1]
noun
BR ˈɪmpakt, -s
AM ˈɪmˌpæk(t), -s

impact[2]
verb
BR ɪmˈpakt, -s, -ɪŋ, -ɨd
AM ɪmˈpæk|(t), -(t)s, -tɪŋ, -təd

impaction
BR ɪmˈpakʃn, -z
AM ɪmˈpækʃən, -z

impair
BR ɪmˈpɛː(r), -z, -ɪŋ, -d
AM ɪmˈpɛ(ə)r, -z, -ɪŋ, -d

impairment
BR ɪmˈpɛːm(ə)nt
AM ɪmˈpɛrmənt

impala
BR ɪmˈpɑːlə(r), -z
AM ɪmˈpælə, ɪmˈpɑlə, -z

impale
BR ɪmˈpeɪl, -z, -ɪŋ, -d
AM ɪmˈpeɪl, -z, -ɪŋ, -d

impalement
BR ɪmˈpeɪlm(ə)nt
AM ɪmˈpeɪlmənt

impalpability
BR ɪmˌpalpəˈbɪlɨti
AM ɪmˌpælpəˈbɪlɨdi

impalpable
BR (ˌ)ɪmˈpalpəbl
AM ɪmˈpælpəbəl

impalpably
BR (ˌ)ɪmˈpalpəbli
AM ɪmˈpælpəbli

impanel
BR ɪmˈpanl, -z, -ɪŋ, -d
AM ɪmˈpænəl, -z, -ɪŋ, -d

imparisyllabic
BR ɪmˌparɪsɪˈlabɪk
AM ˌɪmˌpɛrəsəˈlæbɪk

impark
BR ɪmˈpɑːk, -s, -ɪŋ, -t
AM ɪmˈpɑrk, -s, -ɪŋ, -t

impart
BR ɪmˈpɑːt, -s, -ɪŋ, -ɨd
AM ɪmˈpɑr|t, -ts, -dɪŋ, -dəd

impartable
BR ɪmˈpɑːtəbl
AM ɪmˈpɑrdəbəl

impartation
BR ˌɪmpɑːˈteɪʃn, -z
AM ɪmˌpɑrˈteɪʃən, -z

impartial
BR (ˌ)ɪmˈpɑːʃl
AM ɪmˈpɑrʃəl

impartiality
BR ˌɪmpɑːʃɪˈalɨti, ɪmˌpɑːʃɪˈalɨti
AM ɪmˌpɑrʃiˈælədi

impartially
BR ɪmˈpɑːʃli, ɪmˈpɑːʃəli
AM ɪmˈpɑrʃəli

impartialness
BR ɪmˈpɑːʃlnəs
AM ɪmˈpɑrʃəlnəs

impartible
BR ɪmˈpɑːtɪbl
AM ɪmˈpɑrdəbəl

impartment
BR ɪmˈpɑːtm(ə)nt, -s
AM ɪmˈpɑrtmənt, -s

impassability
BR ɪmˌpɑːsəˈbɪlɨti, ɪmˌpasəˈbɪlɨti
AM ɪmˌpæsəˈbɪlɨdi

impassable
BR (ˌ)ɪmˈpɑːsəbl, (ˌ)ɪmˈpasəbl
AM ɪmˈpæsəbəl

impassableness
BR (ˌ)ɪmˈpɑːsəblnəs, (ˌ)ɪmˈpasəblnəs
AM ɪmˈpæsəbəlnəs

impassably
BR (ˌ)ɪmˈpɑːsəbli, (ˌ)ɪmˈpasəbli
AM ɪmˈpæsəbli

impasse
BR amˈpɑːs, ɪmˈpɑːs, ɒmˈpɑːs, amˈpas, ɪmˈpas, ɒmˈpas, ˈampɑːs, ˈɪmpɑːs, ˈɒmpɑːs, ˈampas, ˈɪmpas, ˈɒmpas, -ɨz
AM ˈɪmˌpæs, ɪmˈpæs, -əz

impassibility
BR ɪmˌpɑːsɪˈbɪlɨti, ɪmˌpasɪˈbɪlɨti
AM ɪmˌpæsəˈbɪlɨdi

impassible
BR (ˌ)ɪmˈpɑːsɪbl, (ˌ)ɪmˈpasɪbl
AM ɪmˈpæsəbəl

impassibleness
BR (ˌ)ɪmˈpɑːsɪblnəs, (ˌ)ɪmˈpasɪblnəs
AM ɪmˈpæsəbəlnəs

impassibly
BR (ˌ)ɪmˈpɑːsɪbli, (ˌ)ɪmˈpasɪbli
AM ɪmˈpæsəbli

impassion
BR ɪmˈpaʃ|n, -nz, -n̩ɪŋ\-nɪŋ, -nd
AM ɪmˈpæʃən, -z, -ɪŋ, -d

impassive
BR ɪmˈpasɪv
AM ɪmˈpæsɪv

impassively
BR ɪmˈpasɪvli
AM ɪmˈpæsəvli

impassiveness
BR ɪmˈpasɪvnɪs
AM ɪmˈpæsɪvnɪs

impassivity
BR ˌɪmpaˈsɪvɨti, ˌɪmpəˈsɪvɨti
AM ˌɪmpəˈsɪvɨdi

impasto
BR ɪmˈpastəʊ, ɪmˈpɑːstəʊ, -z
AM ɪmˈpæstoʊ, ɪmˈpɑstoʊ, -z

impatience
BR ɪmˈpeɪʃns
AM ɪmˈpeɪʃəns

impatiens
BR ɪmˈpeɪʃɪɛnz, ɪmˈpatɪɛnz
AM ɪmˈpeɪʃəns

impatient
BR ɪmˈpeɪʃnt
AM ɪmˈpeɪʃənt

impatiently
BR ɪmˈpeɪʃntli
AM ɪmˈpeɪʃən(t)li

impeach
BR ɪmˈpiːtʃ, -ɨz, -ɪŋ, -t
AM ɪmˈpitʃ, -ɨz, -ɪŋ, -t

impeachable
BR ɪmˈpiːtʃəbl
AM ɪmˈpitʃəbəl

impeachment
BR ɪmˈpiːtʃm(ə)nt, -s
AM ɪmˈpitʃmənt, -s

impeccability
BR ɪmˌpɛkəˈbɪlɨti
AM ɪmˌpɛkəˈbɪlɨdi

impeccable
BR ɪmˈpɛkəbl
AM ɪmˈpɛkəbəl

impeccably
BR ɪmˈpɛkəbli
AM ɪmˈpɛkəbli

impeccancy
BR ɪmˈpɛk(ə)nsi
AM ɪmˈpɛkənsi

impeccant
BR ɪmˈpɛk(ə)nt
AM ɪmˈpɛkənt

impecuniosity
BR ˌɪmpɪˌkjuːnɪˈɒsɨti
AM ˌɪmpəˌkjuniˈɑsədi, ˌɪmpiˌkjuniˈɑsədi

impecunious
BR ˌɪmpɪˈkjuːnɪəs
AM ˌɪmpəˈkjuniəs

impecuniously
BR ˌɪmpɪˈkjuːnɪəsli
AM ˌɪmpəˈkjuniəsli

impecuniousness
BR ˌɪmpɪˈkjuːnɪəsnəs
AM ˌɪmpəˈkjuniəsnəs

impedance
BR ɪmˈpiːdns
AM ɪmˈpidns

impede
BR ɪmˈpiːd, -z, -ɪŋ, -ɨd
AM ɪmˈpid, -z, -ɪŋ, -ɨd

impediment
BR ɪmˈpɛdɨm(ə)nt, -s
AM ɪmˈpɛdəmənt, -s

impedimenta
BR ɪmˌpɛdɪˈmɛntə(r)
AM əmˌpɛdəˈmɛn(t)ə, ˌɪmˌpɛdəˈmɛn(t)ə

impedimental
BR ɪmˌpɛdɪˈmɛntl
AM əmˌpɛdəˈmɛn(t)l, ˌɪmˌpɛdəˈmɛn(t)l

impel
BR ɪmˈpɛl, -z, -ɪŋ, -d
AM ɪmˈpɛl, -z, -ɪŋ, -d

impellent
BR ɪmˈpɛlənt, ɪmˈpɛln̩t, -s
AM ɪmˈpɛlənt, -s

impeller
BR ɪmˈpɛlə(r), -z
AM ɪmˈpɛlər, -z

impend
BR ɪmˈpɛnd, -z, -ɪŋ, -ɨd
AM ɪmˈpɛnd, -z, -ɪŋ, -əd

impendence
BR ɪmˈpɛnd(ə)ns
AM ɪmˈpɛndns

impendency
BR ɪmˈpɛnd(ə)nsi
AM ɪmˈpɛndnsi

impendent
BR ɪmˈpɛnd(ə)nt, -s
AM ɪmˈpɛndnt, -s

impending
BR ɪmˈpɛndɪŋ
AM ɪmˈpɛndɪŋ

impenetrability
BR ɪmˌpɛnɪtrəˈbɪlɨti
AM ɪmˌpɛnətrəˈbɪlɨdi

impenetrable
BR (ˌ)ɪmˈpɛnɪtrəbl
AM ɪmˈpɛnətrəbəl

impenetrablness
BR (ˌ)ɪmˈpɛnɪtrəblnəs
AM ɪmˈpɛnətrəbəlnəs

impenetrably
BR (ˌ)ɪmˈpɛnɪtrəbli
AM ɪmˈpɛnətrəbli

impenetrate
BR (ˌ)ɪmˈpɛnɪtreɪt, -s, -ɪŋ, -ɨd
AM ɪmˈpɛnəˌtreɪ|t, -ts, -dɪŋ, -dɨd

impenitence
BR (ˌ)ɪmˈpɛnɪt(ə)ns
AM ɪmˈpɛnədəns, ɪmˈpɛnətns

impenitency
BR (ˌ)ɪmˈpɛnɪt(ə)nsi
AM ɪmˈpɛnədənsi, ɪmˈpɛnətnsi

impenitent
BR (ˌ)ɪmˈpɛnɪt(ə)nt
AM ɪmˈpɛnədnt

impenitently
BR (ˌ)ɪmˈpɛnɪt(ə)ntli

AM ɪm'pɛnədən(t)li, ɪm'pɛnətn(t)li

imperatival
BR ɪm,pɛrə'tʌɪvl
AM ɪm,pɛrə'taɪvəl

imperative
BR ɪm'pɛrətɪv, -z
AM əm'pɛrədɪv, -z

imperatively
BR ɪm'pɛrətɪvli
AM əm'pɛrədəvli

imperativeness
BR ɪm'pɛrətɪvnɪs
AM əm'pɛrədɪvnɪs

imperator
BR ,ɪmpə'rɑːtɔː(r), -z
AM ,ɪmpə'reɪdər, ,ɪmpə'rɑ,tɔ(ə)r, -z

imperatorial
BR ɪm,pɛrə'tɔːrɪəl, ,ɪmpɛrə,tɔːrɪəl
AM ɪm,pɛrə'tɔriəl

imperceptibility
BR ,ɪmpə,sɛptɪ'bɪlɪti
AM ',ɪmpər,sɛptə'bɪlɪdi

imperceptible
BR ,ɪmpə'sɛptɪbl
AM ',ɪmpər'sɛptəbəl

imperceptibly
BR ,ɪmpə'sɛptɪbli
AM ',ɪmpər'sɛptəbli

impercipience
BR ,ɪmpə'sɪpɪəns
AM ',ɪmpər'sɪpiəns

impercipient
BR ,ɪmpə'sɪpɪənt
AM ',ɪmpər'sɪpiənt

imperfect
BR (,)ɪm'pəːfɪkt, -s
AM ɪm'pərfək|(t), -(t)s

imperfection
BR ,ɪmpə'fɛkʃn, -z
AM ',ɪmpər'fɛkʃən, -z

imperfective
BR ,ɪmpə'fɛktɪv, -z
AM ',ɪmpər'fɛktɪv, -z

imperfectly
BR (,)ɪm'pəːfɪktli
AM ɪm'pərfək(t)li

imperfectness
BR (,)ɪm'pəːfɪk(t)nəs
AM ɪm'pərfək(t)nəs

imperforate
BR (,)ɪm'pəːf(ə)rət
AM ɪm'pərfərət

imperia
BR ɪm'pɪərɪə(r)
AM ɪm'pɪriə

imperial
BR ɪm'pɪərɪəl
AM ɪm'pɪriəl

imperialise
BR ɪm'pɪərɪəlʌɪz, -ɪz, -ɪŋ, -d
AM ɪm'pɪriə,laɪz, -ɪz, -ɪŋ, -d

imperialism
BR ɪm'pɪərɪəlɪz(ə)m
AM ɪm'pɪriə,lɪzəm

imperialist
BR ɪm'pɪərɪəlɪst, -s
AM ɪm'pɪriələst, -s

imperialistic
BR ɪm,pɪərɪə'lɪstɪk
AM ɪm,pɪriə'lɪstɪk

imperialistically
BR ɪm,pɪərɪə'lɪstɪkli
AM ɪm,pɪriə'lɪstək(ə)li

imperialize
BR ɪm'pɪərɪəlʌɪz, -ɪz, -ɪŋ, -d
AM ɪm'pɪriə,laɪz, -ɪz, -ɪŋ, -d

imperially
BR ɪm'pɪərɪəli
AM ɪm'pɪriəli

imperil
BR ɪm'pɛrɪl, ɪm'pɛrl̩, -z, -ɪŋ, -d
AM ɪm'pɛrəl, -z, -ɪŋ, -d

imperious
BR ɪm'pɪərɪəs
AM ɪm'pɪriəs

imperiously
BR ɪm'pɪərɪəsli
AM ɪm'pɪriəsli

imperiousness
BR ɪm'pɪərɪəsnəs
AM ɪm'pɪriəsnəs

imperishability
BR ɪm,pɛrɪʃə'bɪlɪti, ,ɪmpɛrɪʃə'bɪlɪti
AM ɪm,pɛrəʃə'bɪlɪdi

imperishable
BR ɪm'pɛrɪʃəbl
AM ɪm'pɛrəʃəbəl

imperishableness
BR ɪm'pɛrɪʃəbli
AM ɪm'pɛrəʃəbli

imperishably
BR ɪm'pɛrɪʃəblnəs
AM ɪm'pɛrəʃəbəlnəs

imperium
BR ɪm'pɪərɪəm
AM ɪm'pɪriəm

impermanence
BR (,)ɪm'pəːmənəns
AM ɪm'pərmənəns

impermanency
BR (,)ɪm'pəːmənəns|i, -ɪz
AM ɪm'pərmənənsi, -z

impermanent
BR (,)ɪm'pəːmənənt
AM ɪm'pərmənənt

impermanently
BR (,)ɪm'pəːmənəntli
AM ɪm'pərmənən(t)li

impermeability
BR ɪm,pəːmɪə'bɪlɪti, ,ɪmpəːmɪə'bɪlɪti
AM ɪm,pərmiə'bɪlɪdi

impermeable
BR (,)ɪm'pəːmɪəbl
AM ɪm'pərmiəbəl

impermeableness
BR (,)ɪm'pəːmɪəblnəs
AM ɪm'pərmiəbəlnəs

impermeably
BR (,)ɪm'pəːmɪəbli
AM ɪm'pərmiəbli

impermissibility
BR ,ɪmpə,mɪsɪ'bɪlɪti
AM ɪm,pərmɪsə'bɪlɪdi

impermissible
BR ,ɪmpə'mɪsɪbl
AM ɪm,pər'mɪsɪbəl

imperscriptible
BR ,ɪmpə'skrɪptɪbl
AM ɪm,pər'skrɪptɪbəl

impersonal
BR (,)ɪm'pəːs(ə)nl, (,)ɪm'pəːsn̩l
AM ɪm'pərs(ə)nəl

impersonality
BR ɪm,pəːsə'nalɪti
AM ɪm,pərsn'ælədi

impersonally
BR (,)ɪm'pəːs(ə)nəli, (,)ɪm'pəːsn̩əli
AM ɪm'pərs(ə)nəli

impersonate
BR ɪm'pəːsəneɪt, ɪm'pəːsn̩eɪt, -s, -ɪŋ, -ɪd
AM ɪm'pərsn,eɪ|t, -ts, -dɪŋ, -dɪd

impersonation
BR ɪm,pəːsə'neɪʃn, ɪm,pəːsn'eɪʃn, -z
AM əm,pərsn̩'eɪʃən, ,ɪm,pərsə'neɪʃən, -z

impersonator
BR ɪm'pəːsəneɪtə(r), ɪm'pəːsn̩eɪtə(r), -z
AM ɪm'pərsn,eɪdər, -z

impertinence
BR ɪm'pəːtɪnəns, ɪm'pəːtn̩əns
AM ɪm'pərtn̩əns

impertinent
BR ɪm'pəːtɪnənt, ɪm'pəːtn̩ənt
AM ɪm'pərtn̩ənt

impertinently
BR ɪm'pəːtɪnəntli, ɪm'pəːtn̩əntli
AM ɪm'pərtn̩ən(t)li

imperturbability
BR ,ɪmpə,təːbə'bɪlɪti
AM ',ɪmpərtərbə'bɪlɪdi

imperturbable
BR ,ɪmpə'təːbəbl
AM ',ɪmpər'tərbəbəl

imperturbableness
BR ,ɪmpə'təːbəblnəs
AM ',ɪmpər'tərbəbəlnəs

imperturbably
BR ,ɪmpə'təːbəbli
AM ',ɪmpər'tərbəbli

impervious
BR ɪm'pəːvɪəs
AM ɪm'pərviəs

imperviously
BR ɪm'pəːvɪəsli
AM ɪm'pərviəsli

imperviousness
BR ɪm'pəːvɪəsnəs
AM ɪm'pərviəsnəs

impetiginous
BR ,ɪmpɪ'tɪdʒɪnəs
AM ',ɪmpə'tɪdʒɪnəs

impetigo
BR ,ɪmpɪ'tʌɪgəʊ
AM ,ɪmpə'tigoʊ, ,ɪmpə'taɪgoʊ

impetrate
BR 'ɪmpɪtreɪt, -s, -ɪŋ, -ɪd
AM 'ɪmpə,treɪ|t, -ts, -dɪŋ, -dɪd

impetration
BR ,ɪmpɪ'treɪʃn, -z
AM ,ɪmpə'treɪʃən, -z

impetratory
BR 'ɪmpɪtrət(ə)ri
AM 'ɪmpətrə,tɔri

impetuosity
BR ɪm,pɛtjʊ'ɒsɪti, ɪm,pɛtʃʊ'ɒsɪti
AM ɪm,pɛtʃə'wɑsədi

impetuous
BR ɪm'pɛtjʊəs, ɪm'pɛtʃʊəs
AM ɪm'pɛtʃ(əw)əs

impetuously
BR ɪm'pɛtjʊəsl, ɪm'pɛtʃʊəsli
AM ɪm'pɛtʃ(əw)əsli

impetuousness
BR ɪm'pɛtjʊəsnəs, ɪm'pɛtʃʊəsnəs
AM ɪm'pɛtʃ(əw)əsnəs

impetus
BR 'ɪmpɪtəs
AM 'ɪmpədəs

impi
BR 'ɪmp|i, -ɪz
AM 'ɪmpi, -z

impiety
BR (,)ɪm'pʌɪɪt|i, -ɪz
AM ɪm'paɪədi, -z

impinge
BR ɪm'pɪn(d)ʒ, -ɪz, -ɪŋ, -d
AM ɪm'pɪndʒ, -ɪz, -ɪŋ, -d

impingement
BR ɪm'pɪn(d)ʒm(ə)nt, -s
AM ɪm'pɪndʒmənt, -s

impinger
BR ɪm'pɪn(d)ʒə(r), -z
AM ɪm'pɪndʒər, -z

impious
BR 'ɪmpɪəs, (,)ɪm'pʌɪəs
AM 'ɪmpiəs, ɪm'paɪəs

impiously
BR 'ɪmpɪəsli, (,)ɪm'pʌɪəsli

AM ˈɪmpiəsli, ɪmˈpaɪəsli
impiousness
BR ˈɪmpɪəsnəs, (ˌ)ɪmˈpʌɪəsnəs
AM ˈɪmpiəsnəs, ɪmˈpaɪəsnəs
impish
BR ˈɪmpɪʃ
AM ˈɪmpɪʃ
impishly
BR ˈɪmpɨʃli
AM ˈɪmpɨʃli
impishness
BR ˈɪmpɨʃnɨs
AM ˈɪmpɪʃnɨs
implacability
BR ɪmˌplakəˈbɪlɨti
AM ɪmˌplækəˈbɪlɨdi
implacable
BR ɪmˈplakəbl
AM ɪmˈplækəbəl
implacableness
BR ɪmˈplakəblnəs
AM ɪmˈplækəbəlnəs
implacably
BR ɪmˈplakəbli
AM ɪmˈplækəbli
implant[1]
noun
BR ˈɪmplɑːnt, ˈɪmplant, -s
AM ˈɪmˌplænt, -s
implant[2]
verb
BR ɪmˈplɑːnt, ɪmˈplant, -s, -ɪŋ, -ɨd
AM ɪmˈplæn|t, -ts, -(t)ɪŋ, -(t)əd
implantation
BR ˌɪmplɑːnˈteɪʃn, ˌɪmplanˈteɪʃn, -z
AM ˌɪmplənˈteɪʃən, ɪmˌplænˈteɪʃən, -z
implausibility
BR ɪmˌplɔːzɪˈbɪlɨti
AM ɪmˌplɔzəˈbɪlɨdi, ɪmˌplɑzəˈbɪlɨdi
implausible
BR (ˌ)ɪmˈplɔːzɪbl
AM ɪmˈplɔzəbəl, ɪmˈplɑzəbəl
implausibly
BR (ˌ)ɪmˈplɔːzɪbli
AM ɪmˈplɔzəbli, ɪmˈplɑzəbli
implead
BR ɪmˈpliːd, -z, -ɪŋ, -ɨd
AM ɪmˈplid, -z, -ɪŋ, -ɨd
implement[1]
noun
BR ˈɪmplɪm(ə)nt, -s
AM ˈɪmpləmənt, -s
implement[2]
verb
BR ˈɪmplɪmɛnt, -s, -ɪŋ, -ɨd
AM ˈɪmpləˌmɛn|t, -ts, -(t)ɪŋ, -(t)əd
implementation
BR ˌɪmplɪmɛnˈteɪʃn, ˌɪmplɪm(ə)nˈteɪʃn, -z
AM ˌɪmpləmənˈteɪʃən, -z
implementer
BR ˈɪmplɪmɛntə(r), -z
AM ˈɪmpləˌmɛn(t)ər, -z
implicate
BR ˈɪmplɪkeɪt, -s, -ɪŋ, -ɨd
AM ˈɪmpləˌkeɪ|t, -ts, -dɪŋ, -dɨd
implication
BR ˌɪmplɪˈkeɪʃn, -z
AM ˌɪmpləˈkeɪʃən, -z
implicative
BR ɪmˈplɪkətɪv, ˈɪmplɪkeɪtɪv
AM ˈɪmpləˌkeɪdɪv, ɪmˈplɪkədɪv
implicatively
BR ɪmˈplɪkətɪvli, ˈɪmplɪkeɪtɪvli
AM ˈɪmpləˌkeɪdɪvli, ɪmˈplɪkədəvli
implicature
BR ˈɪmplɪkətʃə(r), -z
AM ˈɪmplɪkəˌtʃər, -z
implicit
BR ɪmˈplɪsɪt
AM ɪmˈplɪsɨt
implicitly
BR ɪmˈplɪsɪtli
AM ɪmˈplɪsɨtli
implicitness
BR ɪmˈplɪsɪtnɨs
AM ɪmˈplɪsɨtnɨs
implied
BR ɪmˈplʌɪd
AM ɪmˈplaɪd
impliedly
BR ɪmˈplʌɪ(ɨ)dli
AM ɪmˈplaɪ(ə)dli
implode
BR ɪmˈpləʊd, -z, -ɪŋ, -ɨd
AM ɪmˈploʊd, -z, -ɪŋ, -ɨd
implore
BR ɪmˈplɔː(r), -z, -ɪŋ, -d
AM ɪmˈplɔ(ə)r, -z, -ɪŋ, -d
imploringly
BR ɪmˈplɔːrɪŋli
AM ɪmˈplɔrɪŋli
implosion
BR ɪmˈpləʊʒn, -z
AM ɪmˈploʊʒən, -z
implosive
BR ɪmˈpləʊsɪv, ɪmˈpləʊzɪv, -z
AM ɪmˈploʊzɪv, -z
imply
BR ɪmˈplʌɪ, -z, -ɪŋ, -d
AM ɪmˈplaɪ, -z, -ɪŋ, -d
impolder
BR ɪmˈpəʊld|ə(r), -əz, -(ə)rɪŋ, -əd
AM ɪmˈpoʊldər, -d, -ɪŋ, -d
impolicy
BR ɪmˈpɒlɪs|i, -ɪz
AM ɪmˈpɑləsi, -z
impolite
BR ˌɪmpəˈlʌɪt
AM ˌɪmpəˈlaɪt
impolitely
BR ˌɪmpəˈlʌɪtli
AM ˌɪmpəˈlaɪtli
impoliteness
BR ˌɪmpəˈlʌɪtnɨs
AM ˌɪmpəˈlaɪtnəs
impolitic
BR (ˌ)ɪmˈpɒlɪtɪk
AM ɪmˈpɑləˌtɪk
imponderability
BR ɪmˌpɒnd(ə)rəˈbɪlɪt|i, ˌɪmpɒnd(ə)rəˈbɪlɨti, -ɪz
AM ɪmˌpɑndərəˈbɪlɨdi, -z
imponderable
BR (ˌ)ɪmˈpɒnd(ə)rəbl, -z
AM ɪmˈpɑndərəbəl, -z
imponderably
BR (ˌ)ɪmˈpɒnd(ə)rəbli
AM ɪmˈpɑndərəbli
imponent
BR ɪmˈpəʊnənt, -s
AM ˈɪmˌpoʊnənt, ɪmˈpoʊnənt, -s
import[1]
noun
BR ˈɪmpɔːt, -s
AM ˈɪmˌpɔ(ə)rt, -s
import[2]
verb
BR ɪmˈpɔːt, -s, -ɪŋ, -ɨd
AM ɪmˈpɔ(ə)rt, -ts, -ˈpɔrdɪŋ, -ˈpɔrdɨd
importable
BR ɪmˈpɔːtəbl
AM ɪmˈpɔrdəbəl
importance
BR ɪmˈpɔːtns
AM ɪmˈpɔrtns
important
BR ɪmˈpɔːtnt
AM ɪmˈpɔrtnt
importantly
BR ɪmˈpɔːtntli
AM ɪmˈpɔrtn(t)li
importation
BR ˌɪmpɔːˈteɪʃn, -z
AM ˌɪmpɔrˈteɪʃən, -z
importer
BR ɪmˈpɔːtə(r), -z
AM ɪmˈpɔrdər, -z
importunate
BR ɪmˈpɔːtjʊnət, ɪmˈpɔːtʃʊnət, ɪmˈpɔːtʃn̩ət
AM əmˈpɔrtʃənət
importunately
BR ɪmˈpɔːtʃn̩ətli, ɪmˈpɔːtʃ(ə)nətli, ɪmˈpɔːtjʊnətli
AM əmˈpɔrtʃənətli
importune
BR ˌɪmpəˈtjuːn, ˌɪmpɔːˈtjuːn, ˌɪmpəˈtʃuːn, ˌɪmpɔːˈtʃuːn, -z, -ɪŋ, -d
AM ˌɪmpərˈt(j)un, ˌɪmpɔrˈt(j)un, -z, -ɪŋ, -d
importunity
BR ˌɪmpəˈtjuːnɨti, ˌɪmpɔːˈtjuːnɨti, ˌɪmpəˈtʃuːnɨti, ˌɪmpɔːˈtʃuːnɨti
AM ˌɪmpərˈt(j)unədi, ˌɪmpɔrˈt(j)unədi
impose
BR ɪmˈpəʊz, -ɪz, -ɪŋ, -d
AM ɪmˈpoʊz, -əz, -ɪŋ, -t
imposingly
BR ɪmˈpəʊzɪŋli
AM ɪmˈpoʊzɪŋli
imposingness
BR ɪmˈpəʊzɪŋnɨs
AM ɪmˈpoʊzɪŋnɨs
imposition
BR ˌɪmpəˈzɪʃn, -z
AM ˌɪmpəˈzɪʃən, -z
impossibility
BR ɪmˌpɒsɪˈbɪlɪt|i, ˌɪmpɒsɪˈbɪlɨti, -ɪz
AM ˌɪmˌpɑsəˈbɪlɨdi, əmˌpɑsəˈbɪlɨdi, -z
impossible
BR ɪmˈpɒsɪbl
AM ɪmˈpɑsəbəl
impossibly
BR ɪmˈpɒsɪbli
AM ɪmˈpɑsəbli
impost
BR ˈɪmpəʊst, ˈɪmpɒst, -s
AM ˈɪmˌpoʊst, -s
imposter
BR ɪmˈpɒstə(r), -z
AM ɪmˈpɑstər, -z
impostor
BR ɪmˈpɒstə(r), -z
AM ɪmˈpɑstər, -z
impostorous
BR ɪmˈpɒst(ə)rəs
AM ɪmˈpɑst(ə)rəs
impostrous
BR ɪmˈpɒstrəs
AM ɪmˈpɑstrəs
imposture
BR ɪmˈpɒstʃə(r), -z
AM ɪmˈpɑstʃər, -z
impotence
BR ˈɪmpət(ə)ns
AM ˈɪmpədəns, ˈɪmpətns
impotency
BR ˈɪmpət(ə)nsi

AM ˈɪmpədənsi, ˈɪmpətnsi
impotent
BR ˈɪmpət(ə)nt
AM ˈɪmpədənt, ˈɪmpədnt
impotently
BR ˈɪmpət(ə)ntli
AM ˈɪmpədən(t)li, ˈɪmpətn(t)li
impound
BR ɪmˈpaʊnd, -z, -ɪŋ, -ɪd
AM ɪmˈpaʊnd, -z, -ɪŋ, -əd
impoundable
BR ɪmˈpaʊndəbl
AM ɪmˈpaʊndəbəl
impounder
BR ɪmˈpaʊndə(r), -z
AM ɪmˈpaʊndər, -z
impoundment
BR ɪmˈpaʊndm(ə)nt, -s
AM ɪmˈpaʊndmənt, -s
impoverish
BR ɪmˈpɒv(ə)r|ɪʃ, -ɪʃɪz, -ɪʃɪŋ, -ɪʃt
AM ɪmˈpɑv(ə)rɪʃ, -ɪz, -ɪŋ, -t
impoverishment
BR ɪmˈpɒv(ə)rɪʃm(ə)nt, -s
AM ɪmˈpɑv(ə)rɪʃmənt, -s
impracticability
BR ɪmˌpraktɪkəˈbɪlɪti, ˌɪmpraktɪkəˈbɪlɪti
AM ˌɪmˌpræktəkəˈbɪlɪdi, əmˌpræktəkəˈbɪlɪdi
impracticable
BR (ˌ)ɪmˈpraktɪkəbl
AM ɪmˈpræktəkəbəl
impracticableness
BR (ˌ)ɪmˈpraktɪkəblnəs
AM ɪmˈpræktəkəbəlnəs
impracticably
BR (ˌ)ɪmˈpraktɪkəbli
AM ɪmˈpræktəkəbli
impractical
BR (ˌ)ɪmˈpraktɪkl
AM ɪmˈpræktəkəl
impracticality
BR ɪmˌpraktɪˈkalɪti, ˌɪmpraktɪˈkalɪti
AM ˌɪmˌpræktəˈkælədi, əmˌpræktəˈkælədi
impractically
BR (ˌ)ɪmˈpraktɪk(ə)li, (ˌ)ɪmˈpraktɪkl̩i
AM ɪmˈpræktək(ə)li
imprecate
BR ˈɪmprɪkeɪt, -s, -ɪŋ, -ɪd
AM ˈɪmprəˌkeɪ|t, -ts, -dɪŋ, -dɪd
imprecation
BR ˌɪmprɪˈkeɪʃn, -z
AM ˌɪmprəˈkeɪʃən, -z
imprecatory
BR ˈɪmprɪkeɪt(ə)ri, ɪmˈprɛkət(ə)ri
AM ˈɪmpərəkəˌtɔri
imprecise
BR ˌɪmprɪˈsʌɪs
AM ˌɪmprəˈsaɪs
imprecisely
BR ˌɪmprɪˈsʌɪsli
AM ˌɪmprəˈsaɪsli
impreciseness
BR ˌɪmprɪˈsʌɪsnɪs
AM ˌɪmprəˈsaɪsnɪs
imprecision
BR ˌɪmprɪˈsɪʒn, -z
AM ˌɪmprəˈsɪʒən, -z
impregnability
BR ɪmˌprɛgnəˈbɪlɪti
AM əmˌprɛgnəˈbɪlɪdi, ɪmˌprɛgnəˈbɪlɪdi
impregnable
BR (ˌ)ɪmˈprɛgnəbl
AM əmˈprɛgnəbəl, ɪmˈprɛgnəbəl
impregnably
BR (ˌ)ɪmˈprɛgnəbli
AM əmˈprɛgnəbli, ɪmˈprɛgnəbli
impregnatable
BR ˈɪmprɛgneɪtəbl, ˌɪmprɛgˈneɪtəbl
AM ɪmˌprɛgˈneɪdəbəl
impregnate[1]
adjective
BR (ˌ)ɪmˈprɛgnət
AM ɪmˈprɛgnət
impregnate[2]
verb
BR ˈɪmprɛgneɪt, -s, -ɪŋ, -ɪd
AM ɪmˈprɛgˌneɪ|t, -ts, -dɪŋ, -dɪd
impregnation
BR ˌɪmprɛgˈneɪʃn, -z
AM ˌɪmˌprɛgˈneɪʃən, -z
impresario
BR ˌɪmprɪˈsɑːrɪəʊ, -z
AM ˌɪmprəˈsɑrioʊ, ˌɪmprəˈsɛrioʊ, -z
imprescriptible
BR ˌɪmprɪˈskrɪptɪbl
AM ˌɪmprəˈskrɪptəbəl
impress[1]
noun
BR ˈɪmprɛs, -ɪz
AM ˈɪmˌprɛs, -əz
impress[2]
verb
BR ɪmˈprɛs, -ɪz, -ɪŋ, -t
AM ɪmˈprɛs, -əz, -ɪŋ, -t
impressible
BR ɪmˈprɛsɪbl
AM ˈɪmˌprɛsəbəl
impression
BR ɪmˈprɛʃn, -z
AM ɪmˈprɛʃən, -z
impressionability
BR ɪmˌprɛʃ(ə)nəˈbɪlɪti, ɪmˌprɛʃn̩əˈbɪlɪti
AM ɪmprəʃ(ə)nəˈbɪlɪdi
impressionable
BR ɪmˈprɛʃ(ə)nəbl, ɪmˈprɛʃn̩əbl
AM ɪmˈprɛʃ(ə)nəbəl
impressionably
BR ɪmˈprɛʃ(ə)nəbli, ɪmˈprɛʃn̩əbli
AM ɪmˈprɛʃ(ə)nəbli
impressional
BR ɪmˈprɛʃn̩(ə)l, ɪmˈprɛʃən(ə)l
AM ɪmˈprɛʃ(ə)nəl
impressionism
BR ɪmˈprɛʃn̩ɪz(ə)m, ɪmˈprɛʃənɪz(ə)m
AM ɪmˈprɛʃəˌnɪzəm
impressionist
BR ɪmˈprɛʃn̩ɪst, ɪmˈprɛʃənɪst, -s
AM ɪmˈprɛʃ(ə)nəst, -s
impressionistic
BR ɪmˌprɛʃəˈnɪstɪk, ɪmˌprɛʃn̩ˈɪstɪk
AM ɪmˌprɛʃəˈnɪstɪk, əmˌprɛʃəˈnɪstɪk
impressionistically
BR ɪmˌprɛʃəˈnɪstɪkli
AM (ˌ)ɪmˌprɛʃəˌnɪstək(ə)li, əmˌprɛʃəˌnɪstək(ə)li
impressive
BR ɪmˈprɛsɪv
AM əmˈprɛsɪv, ˈɪmˌprɛsɪv
impressively
BR ɪmˈprɛsɪvli
AM əmˈprɛsəvli, ˈɪmˌprɛsəvli
impressiveness
BR ɪmˈprɛsɪvnɪs
AM əmˈprɛsɪvnɪs
impressment
BR ɪmˈprɛsm(ə)nt
AM ɪmˈprɛsmənt
imprest
BR ˈɪmprɛst, -s
AM ˈɪmˌprɛst, -s
imprimatur
BR ˌɪmprɪˈmɑːtə(r), ˌɪmprɪˈmeɪtə(r), -z
AM ˌɪmprəˈmɑdər, ɪmˈprɪməˌt(j)ʊ(ə)r, -z
imprimatura
BR ˌɪmpriːməˈtʊərə(r), -z
AM ɪmˌpriməˈtʊrə, -z
imprint[1]
noun
BR ˈɪmprɪnt, -s
AM ˈɪmˌprɪnt, -s
imprint[2]
verb
BR ɪmˈprɪnt, -s, -ɪŋ, -ɪd
AM ɪmˈprɪn|t, -ts, -(t)ɪŋ, -(t)əd
imprison
BR ɪmˈprɪzn̩, -z, -ɪŋ, -d
AM ɪmˈprɪzn̩, -z, -ɪŋ, -d
imprisonment
BR ɪmˈprɪznm(ə)nt, -s
AM ɪmˈprɪznmənt, -s
impro
BR ˈɪmprəʊ, -z
AM ˈɪmˌproʊ, -z
improbability
BR ɪmˌprɒbəˈbɪlɪt|i, -ɪz
AM ˌɪmˌprɑbəˈbɪlɪdi, əmˌprɑbəˈbɪlɪdi, -z
improbable
BR (ˌ)ɪmˈprɒbəbl
AM ɪmˈprɑbəbəl
improbably
BR (ˌ)ɪmˈprɒbəbli
AM ɪmˈprɑbəbli
improbity
BR (ˌ)ɪmˈprəʊbɪti
AM ɪmˈproʊbədi, ɪmˈprɑbədi
impromptu
BR ɪmˈprɒm(p)tjuː, ɪmˈprɒm(p)tʃuː, -z
AM ɪmˈprɑm(p)ˌt(j)u, -z
improper
BR (ˌ)ɪmˈprɒpə(r)
AM ɪmˈprɑpər
improperly
BR (ˌ)ɪmˈprɒpəli
AM ɪmˈprɑpərli
impropriate
BR (ˌ)ɪmˈprəʊprɪeɪt, -s, -ɪŋ, -ɪd
AM ɪmˈproʊpriˌeɪ|t, -ts, -dɪŋ, -dɪd
impropriation
BR ɪmˌprəʊprɪˈeɪʃn, -z
AM ɪmˌproʊpriˈeɪʃən, -z
impropriator
BR (ˌ)ɪmˈprəʊprɪeɪtə(r), -z
AM ɪmˈproʊpriˌeɪdər, -z
impropriety
BR ˌɪmprəˈprʌɪɪt|i, -ɪz
AM ˌɪmprəˈpraɪədi, ˌɪmproʊˈpraɪədi, -z
improv
BR ˈɪmprɒv, -z
AM ˈɪmˌprɑv, -z
improvability
BR ɪmˌpruːvəˈbɪlɪt|i, -ɪz
AM ɪmˌpruvəˈbɪlɪdi, -z
improvable
BR ɪmˈpruːvəbl
AM ɪmˈpruvəbəl
improve
BR ɪmˈpruːv, -z, -ɪŋ, -d
AM ɪmˈpruv, -z, -ɪŋ, -d

improvement
BR ɪm'pru:vm(ə)nt, -s
AM ɪm'pruvmənt, -s
improver
BR ɪm'pru:və(r), -z
AM ɪm'pruvər, -z
improvidence
BR (ˌ)ɪm'prɒvɪd(ə)ns
AM ɪm'prɑvədns
improvident
BR (ˌ)ɪm'prɒvɪd(ə)nt
AM ɪm'prɑvədnt
improvidently
BR (ˌ)ɪm'prɒvɪd(ə)ntli
AM ɪm'prɑvəd(ə)n(t)li
improvisation
BR ˌɪmprəvʌɪ'zeɪʃn, -z
AM ɪmˌprɑvə'zeɪʃən, ˌɪmprəvə'zeɪʃən, -z
improvisational
BR ˌɪmprəvʌɪ'zeɪʃn̩(ə)l, ˌɪmprəvʌɪ'zeɪʃən(ə)l
AM ɪmˌprɑvə'zeɪʃ(ə)nəl, ˌɪmprəvə'zeɪʃ(ə)nəl
improvisatorial
BR ˌɪmprəvʌɪzə'tɔ:rɪəl, ɪmˌprɒvɪzə'tɔ:rɪəl
AM ɪmˌprɑvəzə'tɔriəl
improvisatory
BR ˌɪmprə'vʌɪzət(ə)ri
AM ɪm'prɑvəzəˌtɔri, ˌɪmprə'vaɪzəˌtɔri
improvise
BR 'ɪmprəvʌɪz, -ɪz, -ɪŋ, -d
AM 'ɪmprəˌvaɪz, -ɪz, -ɪŋ, -d
improviser
BR 'ɪmprəvʌɪzə(r), -z
AM 'ɪmprəˌvaɪzər, -z
imprudence
BR (ˌ)ɪm'pru:d(ə)ns
AM ɪm'prudns
imprudent
BR (ˌ)ɪm'pru:d(ə)nt
AM ɪm'prudnt
imprudently
BR (ˌ)ɪm'pru:d(ə)ntli
AM ɪm'prudn(t)li
impudence
BR 'ɪmpjʊd(ə)ns
AM 'ɪmpjədns
impudent
BR 'ɪmpjʊd(ə)nt
AM 'ɪmpjədnt
impudently
BR 'ɪmpjʊd(ə)ntli
AM 'ɪmpjəd(ə)n(t)li
impudicity
BR ˌɪmpjʊ'dɪsɪti
AM ˌɪmpjə'dɪsɪdi, ˌɪmpjʊ'dɪsɪdi
impugn
BR ɪm'pju:n, -z, -ɪŋ, -d
AM ɪm'pjun, -z, -ɪŋ, -d
impugnable
BR ɪm'pju:nəbl
AM ɪm'pjunəbəl
impugnment
BR ɪm'pju:nm(ə)nt, -s
AM ɪm'pjunmənt, -s
impuissance
BR (ˌ)ɪm'pwɪsns, (ˌ)ɪm'pju:ɪsns
AM ɪm'pjusəns, ɪm'pwɪsəns
impuissant
BR (ˌ)ɪm'pwɪsnt, (ˌ)ɪm'pju:ɪsnt
AM ɪm'pjusənt, ɪm'pwɪsənt
impulse
BR 'ɪmpʌls, -ɪz
AM 'ɪmˌpəls, -əz
impulsion
BR ɪm'pʌlʃn, -z
AM ɪm'pəlʃən, -z
impulsive
BR ɪm'pʌlsɪv
AM ɪm'pəlsɪv
impulsively
BR ɪm'pʌlsɪvli
AM ɪm'pəlsəvli
impulsiveness
BR ɪm'pʌlsɪvnɪs
AM ɪm'pəlsɪvnɪs
impunity
BR ɪm'pju:nɪti
AM ɪm'pjunədi
impure
BR (ˌ)ɪm'pjʊə(r), (ˌ)ɪm'pjɔ:(r)
AM ɪm'pjʊ(ə)r
impurely
BR (ˌ)ɪm'pjʊəli, (ˌ)ɪm'pjɔ:li
AM ɪm'pjʊrli
impureness
BR (ˌ)ɪm'pjʊənəs, (ˌ)ɪm'pjɔ:nəs
AM ɪm'pjʊrnəs
impurity
BR (ˌ)ɪm'pjʊərɪt|i, ˌɪm'pjɔ:rɪt|i, -ɪz
AM ɪm'pjʊrədi, -z
imputable
BR ɪm'pju:təbl
AM ɪm'pjʊdəbəl
imputation
BR ˌɪmpjʊ'teɪʃn, -z
AM ˌɪmpjə'teɪʃən, -z
imputative
BR ɪm'pju:tətɪv
AM ɪm'pjʊdədɪv
impute
BR ɪm'pju:t, -s, -ɪŋ, -ɪd
AM ɪm'pju|t, -ts, -dɪŋ, -dəd
imshi
BR 'ɪmʃi
AM 'ɪmˌʃi
in
BR ɪn
AM ɪn
Ina
BR 'i:nə(r), 'ʌɪnə(r)
AM 'aɪnə, 'inə
inability
BR ˌɪnə'bɪlɪti
AM ˌɪnə'bɪlɪdi
in absentia
BR ˌɪn əb'sɛntɪə(r), + əb'sɛnʃ(ɪ)ə(r)
AM ˌɪn əb'sɛnʃə, ˌɪn ˌæb'sɛnʃə
inaccessibility
BR ˌɪnəkˌsɛsɪ'bɪlɪti, ˌɪnakˌsɛsɪ'bɪlɪti
AM ˌɪnækˌsɛsə'bɪlɪdi, ˌɪnəkˌsɛsə'bɪlɪdi
inaccessible
BR ˌɪnək'sɛsɪbl, ˌɪnak'sɛsɪbl
AM ˌɪnæk'sɛsəbəl, ˌɪnək'sɛsəbəl
inaccessibleness
BR ˌɪnək'sɛsɪblnəs, ˌɪnak'sɛsɪblnəs
AM ˌɪnæk'sɛsəbəlnəs, ˌɪnək'sɛsəbəlnəs
inaccessibly
BR ˌɪnək'sɛsɪbli, ˌɪnak'sɛsɪbli
AM ˌɪnæk'sɛsəbli, ˌɪnək'sɛsəbli
inaccuracy
BR (ˌ)ɪn'akjʊrəs|i, -ɪz
AM ɪn'ækjərəsi, -z
inaccurate
BR (ˌ)ɪn'akjʊrət
AM ɪn'ækjərət
inaccurately
BR (ˌ)ɪn'akjʊrətli
AM ɪn'ækjərətli
inaction
BR ɪn'akʃn
AM ɪn'ækʃən
inactivate
BR ɪn'aktɪveɪt, -s, -ɪŋ, -ɪd
AM ɪn'æktəˌveɪ|t, -ts, -dɪŋ, -dɪd
inactivation
BR ɪnˌaktɪ'veɪʃn, ˌɪnaktɪ'veɪʃn, -z
AM ɪnˌæktə'veɪʃən, -z
inactive
BR (ˌ)ɪn'aktɪv
AM ɪn'æktɪv
inactively
BR (ˌ)ɪn'aktɪvli
AM ɪn'æktəvli
inactivity
BR ˌɪnak'tɪvɪti
AM ˌɪnæk'tɪvɪdi
inadequacy
BR (ˌ)ɪn'adɪkwəs|i, -ɪz
AM ɪn'ædəkwəsi, -z
inadequate
BR (ˌ)ɪn'adɪkwət
AM ɪn'ædəkwət
inadequately
BR (ˌ)ɪn'adɪkwətli
AM ɪn'ædəkwətli
inadmissibility
BR ˌɪnədˌmɪsɪ'bɪlɪti
AM ˌɪnədˌmɪsə'bɪlɪdi
inadmissible
BR ˌɪnəd'mɪsɪbl
AM ˌɪnəd'mɪsəbəl
inadmissibly
BR ˌɪnəd'mɪsɪbli
AM ˌɪnəd'mɪsɪbli
inadvertence
BR ˌɪnəd'və:t(ə)ns
AM ˌɪnəd'vərtns, ˌɪˌnæd'vərtns
inadvertency
BR ˌɪnəd'və:t(ə)nsi
AM ˌɪnəd'vərtnsi, ˌɪˌnæd'vərtnsi
inadvertent
BR ˌɪnəd'və:t(ə)nt
AM ˌɪnəd'vərtnt
inadvertently
BR ˌɪnəd'və:t(ə)ntli
AM ˌɪnəd'vərtn(t)li
inadvisability
BR ˌɪnədˌvʌɪzə'bɪlɪti
AM ˌɪnədˌvaɪzə'bɪlɪdi
inadvisable
BR ˌɪnəd'vʌɪzəbl
AM ˌɪnəd'vaɪzəbəl
inalienability
BR ɪnˌeɪlɪənə'bɪlɪti
AM ɪnˌeɪliənə'bɪlɪdi
inalienable
BR (ˌ)ɪn'eɪlɪənəbl
AM ɪn'eɪliənəbəl
inalienableness
BR (ˌ)ɪn'eɪlɪənəblnəs
AM ɪn'eɪliənəbəlnəs
inalienably
BR (ˌ)ɪn'eɪlɪənəbli
AM ɪn'eɪliənəbli
inalterability
BR ɪnˌɔ:lt(ə)rə'bɪlɪti, ˌɪnɔ:lt(ə)rə'bɪlɪti, ɪnˌɒlt(ə)rə'bɪlɪti, ˌɪnɒlt(ə)rə'bɪlɪti
AM ɪnˌɔlt(ə)rə'bɪlɪdi, ɪnˌɑlt(ə)rə'bɪlɪdi
inalterable
BR (ˌ)ɪn'ɔ:lt(ə)rəbl, (ˌ)ɪn'ɒlt(ə)rəbl
AM ɪn'ɔlt(ə)rəbəl, ɪn'ɑlt(ə)rəbəl
inalterably
BR (ˌ)ɪn'ɔ:lt(ə)rəbli, (ˌ)ɪn'ɒlt(ə)rəbli
AM ɪn'ɔlt(ə)rəbli, ɪn'ɑlt(ə)rəbli
inamorata
BR ɪnˌamə'rɑ:tə(r), ˌɪnamə'rɑ:tə(r), -z
AM ɪˌnæmə'rɑdə, -z
inamorato
BR ɪnˌamə'rɑ:təʊ, ˌɪnamə'rɑ:təʊ, -z
AM ɪˌnæmə'rɑdoʊ, -z
inane
BR ɪ'neɪn

AM ɪ'neɪn

inanely
BR ɪ'neɪnli
AM ɪ'neɪnli

inaneness
BR ɪ'neɪnnɪs
AM ɪ'neɪ(n)nɪs

inanga
BR 'iːnaŋgə(r), -z
AM 'iˌnɑŋgə, -z

inanimate
BR ɪn'anɪmət
AM ɪn'ænəmət

inanimately
BR ɪn'anɪmətli
AM ɪn'ænəmətli

inanimation
BR ɪnˌanɪ'meɪʃn
AM ɪnˌænə'meɪʃən

inanition
BR ˌɪnə'nɪʃn
AM ˌɪnə'nɪʃən

inanity
BR ɪ'nanɪt|i, -ɪz
AM ɪ'nænədi, -z

inappeasable
BR ˌɪnə'piːzəbl
AM ¦ɪnə'pizəbəl

inappellable
BR ˌɪnə'pɛləbl
AM ¦ɪnə'pɛləbəl

inappetence
BR (ˌ)ɪn'apɪt(ə)ns
AM ɪn'æpədəns, ɪn'æpətns

inappetency
BR (ˌ)ɪn'apɪt(ə)nsi
AM ɪn'æpədənsi, ɪn'æpətnsi

inappetent
BR (ˌ)ɪn'apɪt(ə)nt
AM ɪn'æpədənt, ɪn'æpədnt

inapplicability
BR ˌɪnəˌplɪkə'bɪlɪti, ɪnˌaplɪkə'bɪlɪti
AM ¦ɪnˌæpləkə'bɪlɪdi, ənˌæpləkə'bɪlɪdi

inapplicable
BR ˌɪnə'plɪkəbl, (ˌ)ɪn'aplɪkəbl
AM ¦ɪn'æpləkəbəl, ən'æpləkəbəl

inapplicably
BR ˌɪnə'plɪkəbli, (ˌ)ɪn'aplɪkəbli
AM ¦ɪn'æpləkəbli, ən'æpləkəbli

inapposite
BR (ˌ)ɪn'apəzɪt
AM ɪn'æpəzət

inappositely
BR (ˌ)ɪn'apəzɪtli
AM ɪn'æpəzətli

inappositeness
BR (ˌ)ɪn'apəzɪtnɪs
AM ɪn'æpəzətnəs

inappreciable
BR ˌɪnə'priːʃ(ɪ)əbl
AM ¦ɪnə'priʃəbəl

inappreciably
BR ˌɪnə'priːʃ(ɪ)əbli
AM ¦ɪnə'priʃəbli

inappreciation
BR ˌɪnəˌpriːʃɪ'eɪʃn, ˌɪnəˌpriːsɪ'eɪʃn
AM ¦ɪnəpriʃi'eɪʃən

inappreciative
BR ˌɪnə'priːʃ(ɪ)ətɪv, ˌɪnə'priːsɪətɪv
AM ¦ɪnə'priʃədɪv

inapprehensible
BR ɪnˌaprɪ'hɛnsɪbl, ˌɪnaprɪ'hɛnsɪbl
AM ɪn¦æprə'hɛnsəbəl

inappropriate
BR ˌɪnə'prəʊprɪət
AM ¦ɪnə'proʊpriət

inappropriately
BR ˌɪnə'prəʊprɪətli
AM ¦ɪnə'proʊpriətli

inappropriateness
BR ˌɪnə'prəʊprɪətnəs
AM ¦ɪnə'proʊpriətnəs

inapt
BR (ˌ)ɪn'apt
AM ɪn'æpt

inaptitude
BR (ˌ)ɪn'aptɪtjuːd, (ˌ)ɪn'aptɪtʃuːd
AM ɪn'æptəˌt(j)ud

inaptly
BR (ˌ)ɪn'aptli
AM ɪn'æp(t)li

inaptness
BR (ˌ)ɪn'ap(t)nəs
AM ɪn'æp(t)nəs

inarch
BR ɪn'ɑːtʃ, -ɪz, -ɪŋ, -t
AM ɪn'ɑrtʃ, -əz, -ɪŋ, -t

inarguable
BR (ˌ)ɪn'ɑːgjʊəbl
AM ¦ɪn'ɑrgjə(wə)bəl

inarguably
BR (ˌ)ɪn'ɑːgjʊəbli
AM ¦ɪn'ɑrgjə(wə)bli

inarticulacy
BR ˌɪnɑː'tɪkjʊləsi
AM ¦ɪnɑr'tɪkjələsi

inarticulate
BR ˌɪnɑː'tɪkjʊlət
AM ¦ɪnɑr'tɪkjələt

inarticulately
BR ˌɪnɑː'tɪkjʊlətli
AM ¦ɪnɑr'tɪkjələtli

inarticulateness
BR ˌɪnɑː'tɪkjʊlətnəs
AM ¦ɪnɑr'tɪkjələtnəs

inartistic
BR ˌɪnɑː'tɪstɪk
AM ˌɪnɑr'tɪstɪk

inartistically
BR ˌɪnɑː'tɪstɪkli
AM ¦ɪnɑr'tɪstək(ə)li

inasmuch
BR ˌɪnəz'mʌtʃ
AM ¦ɪnəzˌmətʃ

inattention
BR ˌɪnə'tɛnʃn
AM ¦ɪnə'tɛn(t)ʃən

inattentive
BR ˌɪnə'tɛntɪv
AM ¦ɪnə'tɛn(t)ɪv

inattentively
BR ˌɪnə'tɛntɪvli
AM ¦ɪnə'tɛn(t)əvli

inattentiveness
BR ˌɪnə'tɛntɪvnɪs
AM ¦ɪnə'tɛn(t)ɪvnɪs

inaudibility
BR ɪnˌɔːdɪ'bɪlɪti, ˌɪnɔːdɪ'bɪlɪti
AM ¦ɪnɔdə'bɪlɪdi, ɪˌnɔdə'bɪlɪdi, ¦ɪnɑdə'bɪlɪdi, ɪˌnɑdə'bɪlɪdi

inaudible
BR (ˌ)ɪn'ɔːdɪbl
AM ɪn'ɔdəbəl, ɪn'ɑdəbəl

inaudibly
BR (ˌ)ɪn'ɔːdɪbli
AM ɪn'ɔdəbli, ɪn'ɑdəbli

inaugural
BR ɪ'nɔːgjʊrəl, ɪ'nɔːgjʊrl̩, -z
AM ɪ'nɔgjərəl, ɪ'nɔg(ə)rəl, ɪ'nɑgjərəl, ɪ'nɑg(ə)rəl, -z

inaugurate
BR ɪ'nɔːgjʊreɪt, -s, -ɪŋ, -ɪd
AM ɪ'nɔg(j)əˌreɪ|t, ɪ'nɑg(j)əˌreɪ|t, -ts, -dɪŋ, -dɪd

inauguration
BR ɪˌnɔːgjʊ'reɪʃn, -z
AM ɪˌnɔg(j)ə'reɪʃən, ɪˌnɑg(j)ə'reɪʃən, -z

inaugurator
BR ɪ'nɔːgjʊreɪtə(r), -z
AM ɪ'nɔg(j)əˌreɪdər, ɪ'nɑg(j)əˌreɪdər, -z

inauguratory
BR ɪ'nɔːgjʊrət(ə)ri
AM ɪ'nɔg(j)ərəˌtɔri, ɪ'nɑg(j)ərəˌtɔri

inauspicious
BR ˌɪnɔː'spɪʃəs
AM ¦ɪnɔ'spɪʃəs, ¦ɪnɑ'spɪʃəs

inauspiciously
BR ˌɪnɔː'spɪʃəsli
AM ¦ɪnɔ'spɪʃəsli, ¦ɪnɑ'spɪʃəsli

inauspiciousness
BR ˌɪnɔː'spɪʃəsnəs
AM ¦ɪnɔ'spɪʃəsnəs, ¦ɪnɑ'spɪʃəsnəs

inauthentic
BR ˌɪnɔː'θɛntɪk
AM ¦ɪnɔ'θɛn(t)ɪk, ¦ɪnɑ'θɛn(t)ɪk

inauthenticity
BR ˌɪnɔːθɛn'tɪsɪti
AM ¦ɪnɔθən'tɪsɪdi, ¦ɪnɑθən'tɪsɪdi

in-between
BR ˌɪnbɪ'twiːn
AM ¦ɪnbəˌtwin

inboard
BR 'ɪnbɔːd
AM 'ɪnˌbɔ(ə)rd

inborn
BR ˌɪn'bɔːn
AM ¦ɪnˌbɔ(ə)rn

inbound
BR 'ɪnbaʊnd
AM 'ɪnˌbaʊnd

inbreathe
BR ˌɪn'briːð, -z, -ɪŋ, -d
AM ɪn'brið, -z, -ɪŋ, -d

inbred
BR ˌɪn'brɛd
AM 'ɪnˌbrɛd

inbreed
BR ˌɪn'briːd, -z, -ɪŋ
AM 'ɪnˌbrid, -z, -ɪŋ

inbreeding
BR 'ɪnˌbriːdɪŋ, ˌɪn'briːdɪŋ
AM 'ɪnˌbridɪŋ

inbuilt
BR ˌɪn'bɪlt
AM 'ɪnˌbɪlt

Inc.
BR ɪŋk
AM ɪŋk

Inca
BR 'ɪŋkə(r), -z
AM 'ɪŋkə, -z

Incaic
BR ɪŋ'keɪɪk
AM ɪn'keɪɪk, ɪŋ'keɪɪk

incalculability
BR ɪnˌkalkjʊlə'bɪlɪti, ɪŋˌkalkjʊlə'bɪlɪti
AM 'ɪŋˌkælkjələ'bɪlɪdi, ɪnˌkælkjələ'bɪlɪdi, 'ɪnˌkælkjələ'bɪlɪdi

incalculable
BR (ˌ)ɪn'kalkjʊləbl, (ˌ)ɪŋ'kalkjʊləbl
AM ɪn'kælkjələbəl, ɪŋ'kælkjələbəl

incalculably
BR (ˌ)ɪn'kalkjʊləbli, (ˌ)ɪŋ'kalkjʊləbli
AM ɪn'kælkjələbli, ɪŋ'kælkjələbli

in camera
BR ˌɪn 'kam(ə)rə(r)
AM ˌɪn 'kæm(ə)rə

Incan
BR 'ɪŋkən
AM 'ɪŋkən

incandesce
BR ˌɪnkan'dɛs, ˌɪnkən'dɛs,

ˌɪŋkanˈdɛs,
ˌɪŋkənˈdɛs, -ɨz, -ɪŋ, -t
AM ˌɪnkənˈdɛs,
ˌɪŋkənˈdɛs, -əz, -ɪŋ, -t

incandescence
BR ˌɪnkanˈdɛsns,
ˌɪnkənˈdɛsns,
ˌɪŋkanˈdɛsns,
ˌɪŋkənˈdɛsns
AM ˌɪnkənˈdɛsəns,
ˌɪŋkənˈdɛsəns

incandescent
BR ˌɪnkanˈdɛsnt,
ˌɪnkənˈdɛsnt,
ˌɪŋkanˈdɛsnt,
ˌɪŋkənˈdɛsnt
AM ˌɪnkənˈdɛsənt,
ˌɪŋkənˈdɛsənt

incandescently
BR ˌɪnkanˈdɛsntli,
ˌɪnkənˈdɛsntli,
ˌɪŋkanˈdɛsntli,
ˌɪŋkənˈdɛsntli
AM ˌɪnkənˈdɛsn(t)li,
ˌɪŋkənˈdɛsn(t)li

incantation
BR ˌɪnkanˈteɪʃn,
ˌɪŋkanˈteɪʃn, -z
AM ˌɪnˌkænˈteɪʃən,
ˌɪŋˌkænˈteɪʃən, -z

incantational
BR ˌɪnkanˈteɪʃn̩(ə)l,
ˌɪnkanˈteɪʃən(ə)l,
ˌɪŋkanˈteɪʃn̩(ə)l,
ˌɪŋkanˈteɪʃən(ə)l
AM ˌɪnˌkænˈteɪʃ(ə)nəl,
ˌɪŋˌkænˈteɪʃ(ə)nəl

incantatory
BR ˌɪnkanˈteɪt(ə)ri,
ɪnˈkantət(ə)ri,
ˌɪŋkanˈteɪt(ə)ri,
ɪŋˈkantət(ə)ri
AM ˌɪnˈkæn(t)əˌtɔri,
ˌɪŋˈkæn(t)əˌtɔri

incapability
BR ɪnˌkeɪpəˈbɪlɨti,
ˌɪnkeɪpəˈbɪlɨti,
ɪŋˌkeɪpəˈbɪlɨti,
ˌɪŋkeɪpəˈbɪlɨti
AM ˌɪnˌkeɪpəˈbɪlɨdi,
ɨnˌkeɪpəˈbɪlɨdi,
ˌɪŋˌkeɪpəˈbɪlɨdi

incapable
BR ɪnˈkeɪpəbl,
ɪŋˈkeɪpəbl
AM ɨnˈkeɪpəbəl,
ɪŋˈkeɪpəbəl

incapably
BR ɪnˈkeɪpəbli,
ɪŋˈkeɪpəbli
AM ɪnˈkeɪpəbli,
ɪŋˈkeɪpəbli

incapacitant
BR ˌɪnkəˈpasɨtnt,
ˌɪŋkəˈpasɨtnt, -s
AM ˌɪnkəˈpæsətnt,
ˌɪŋkəˈpæsətnt, -s

incapacitate
BR ˌɪnkəˈpasɨteɪt,
ˌɪŋkəˈpasɨteɪt, -s, -ɪŋ,
-ɨd
AM ˌɪnkəˈpæsəˌteɪ|t,
ˌɪŋkəˈpæsəˌteɪ|t, -ts,
-dɪŋ, -dɨd

incapacitation
BR ˌɪnkəˌpasɪˈteɪʃn,
ˌɪŋkəˌpasɪˈteɪʃn
AM ˌɪnkəˌpæsəˈteɪʃən,
ˌɪŋkəˌpæsəˈteɪʃən

incapacity
BR ˌɪnkəˈpasɨti,
ˌɪŋkəˈpasɨti
AM ˌɪnkəˈpæsədi,
ˌɪŋkəˈpæsədi

in-car
BR ˌɪnˈkɑː(r), ˌɪŋˈkɑː(r)
AM ˌɪnˈkɑr

incarcerate
BR ɪnˈkɑːsəreɪt,
ɪŋˈkɑːsəreɪt, -s, -ɪŋ, -ɨd
AM ɨnˈkɑrsəˌreɪ|t,
ɪŋˈkɑrsəˌreɪ|t, -ts,
-dɪŋ, -dɨd

incarceration
BR ɪnˌkɑːsəˈreɪʃn,
ɪŋˌkɑːsəˈreɪʃn
AM ɨnˌkɑrsəˈreɪʃən,
ɪŋˌkɑrsəˈreɪʃən

incarcerator
BR ɪnˈkɑːsəreɪtə(r),
ɪŋˈkɑːsəreɪtə(r), -z
AM ɨnˈkɑrsəˌreɪdər,
ɪŋˈkɑrsəˌreɪdər, -z

incarnadine
BR ɪnˈkɑːnədʌɪn,
ɪŋˈkɑːnədʌɪn, -z, -ɪŋ,
-d
AM ɨnˈkɑrnəˌdaɪn,
ɪŋˈkɑrnəˌdaɪn, -z, -ɪŋ,
-d

incarnate[1]
adjective
BR ɪnˈkɑːnət,
ɪŋˈkɑːnət
AM ənˈkɑrnət,
ɪnˈkɑrnət, ɪŋˈkɑrnət

incarnate[2]
verb
BR ɪnˈkɑːneɪt,
ɪŋˈkɑːneɪt, -s, -ɪŋ, -ɨd
AM ənˈkɑrˌneɪ|t,
ˈɪnˌkɑrnˌeɪ|t,
ˈɪŋˌkɑrnˌeɪ|t, -ts, -dɪŋ,
-dɨd

incarnation
BR ˌɪnkɑːˈneɪʃn,
ˌɪŋkɑːˈneɪʃn, -z
AM ˌɪnˌkɑrˈneɪʃən,
ˌɪŋˌkɑrˈneɪʃən, -z

incase
BR ɪnˈkeɪs, ɪŋˈkeɪs, -ɨz,
-ɪŋ, -t
AM ɪnˈkeɪs, ɪŋˈkeɪs, -ɨz,
-ɪŋ, -t

incaution
BR ɪnˈkɔːʃn, ɪŋˈkɔːʃn,
-z
AM ɨnˈkɔʃən, ɪŋˈkɔʃən,
ɨnˈkɑʃən, ɪŋˈkɑʃən, -z

incautious
BR (ˌ)ɪnˈkɔːʃəs,
(ˌ)ɪŋˈkɔːʃəs
AM ɨnˈkɔʃəs, ɪŋˈkɔʃəs,
ɨnˈkɑʃəs, ɪŋˈkɑʃəs

incautiously
BR (ˌ)ɪnˈkɔːʃəsli,
(ˌ)ɪŋˈkɔːʃəsli
AM ɨnˈkɔʃəsli,
ɪŋˈkɔʃəsli, ɨnˈkɑʃəsli,
ɪŋˈkɑʃəsli

incautiousness
BR (ˌ)ɪnˈkɔːʃəsnəs,
(ˌ)ɪŋˈkɔːʃəsnəs
AM ɪnˈkɔʃəsnəs,
ɪŋˈkɔʃəsnəs,
ɨnˈkɑʃəsnəs,
ɪŋˈkɑʃəsnəs

incendiarism
BR ɪnˈsɛndɪərɪz(ə)m,
ɪnˈsɛndʒərɪz(ə)m
AM ɨnˈsɛndiəˌrɪzəm

incendiary
BR ɪnˈsɛndɪər|i,
ɪnˈsɛndʒ(ə)r|i, -ɪz
AM ɨnˈsɛndiˌɛri, -z

incensation
BR ˌɪnsɛnˈseɪʃn, -z
AM ɪnˌsɛnˈseɪʃən, -z

incense[1]
noun
BR ˈɪnsɛns
AM ˈɪnˌsɛns

incense[2]
verb
BR ɪnˈsɛns, -ɨz, -ɪŋ, -t
AM ɪnˈsɛns, -əz, -ɪŋ, -t

incensory
BR ɪnˈsɛns(ə)r|i, -ɪz
AM ɨnˈsɛns(ə)ri, -z

incentive
BR ɪnˈsɛntɪv, -z
AM ɨnˈsɛn(t)ɪv, -z

incept
BR ɪnˈsɛpt, -s, -ɪŋ, -ɨd
AM ɨnˈsɛpt, -s, -ɪŋ, -əd

inception
BR ɪnˈsɛpʃn
AM ɨnˈsɛpʃən

inceptive
BR ɪnˈsɛptɪv
AM ɨnˈsɛptɪv

inceptor
BR ɪnˈsɛptə(r), -z
AM ɨnˈsɛptər, -z

incertitude
BR (ˌ)ɪnˈsəːtɨtjuːd,
(ˌ)ɪnˈsəːtɨtʃuːd
AM ɨnˈsərdəˌt(j)ud

incessancy
BR ɪnˈsɛsnsi
AM ɨnˈsɛsənsi

incessant
BR ɪnˈsɛsnt
AM ɨnˈsɛsnt

incessantly
BR ɪnˈsɛsntli
AM ɨnˈsɛsn(t)li

incessantness
BR ɪnˈsɛsntnəs
AM ɨnˈsɛsn(t)nəs

incest
BR ˈɪnsɛst
AM ˈɪnˌsɛst

incestuous
BR ɪnˈsɛstjʊəs,
ɪnˈsɛstʃʊəs
AM ɨnˈsɛstʃ(əw)əs

incestuously
BR ɪnˈsɛstjʊəsli,
ɪnˈsɛstʃʊəsli
AM ɨnˈsɛstʃ(əw)əsli

incestuousness
BR ɪnˈsɛstjʊəsnəs,
ɪnˈsɛstʃʊəsnəs
AM ɨnˈsɛstʃ(əw)əsnəs

inch
BR ɪn(t)ʃ, -ɨz, -ɪŋ, -t
AM ɪn(t)ʃ, -ɨz, -ɪŋ, -t

Inchcape
BR ˈɪn(t)ʃkeɪp
AM ˈɪn(t)ʃˌkeɪp

inchmeal
BR ˈɪn(t)ʃmiːl
AM ˈɪn(t)ʃˌmil

inchoate[1]
adjective
BR ɪnˈkəʊət, ɪnˈkəʊeɪt,
ˈɪnkəʊət, ˈɪnkəʊeɪt,
ɪŋˈkəʊət, ɪŋˈkəʊeɪt,
ˈɪŋkəʊət, ˈɪŋkəʊeɪt
AM ɨnˈkoʊət,
ˈɪnkəˌweɪt, ɪŋˈkoʊət,
ˈɪŋkəˌweɪt

inchoate[2]
verb
BR ˈɪnkəʊeɪt,
ˈɪŋkəʊeɪt, -s, -ɪŋ, -ɨd
AM ˈɪnkəˌweɪ|t,
ˈɪŋkəˌweɪ|t, -ts, -dɪŋ,
-dɨd

inchoately
BR ɪnˈkəʊətli,
ɪnˈkəʊeɪtli,
ˈɪnkəʊətli, ˈɪnkəʊeɪtli,
ɪŋˈkəʊətli,
ɪŋˈkəʊeɪtli, ˈɪŋkəʊətli,
ˈɪŋkəʊeɪtli
AM ɨnˈkoʊətli,
ˈɪnkəˌweɪtli,
ɪŋˈkoʊətli,
ˈɪŋkəˌweɪtli

inchoateness
BR ɪnˈkəʊətnəs,
ɪnˈkəʊeɪtnɨs,
ˈɪnkəʊətnəs,
ˈɪnkəʊeɪtnɨs,
ɪŋˈkəʊətnəs,
ɪŋˈkəʊeɪtnɨs,

'ɪŋkəʊətnəs, 'ɪŋkəʊeɪtnɨs
AM ɨn'koʊətnəs, 'ɪnkəˌweɪtnɨs, ɪŋ'koʊətnəs, 'ɪŋkəˌweɪtnɨs

inchoation
BR ˌɪnkəʊ'eɪʃn, ˌɪŋkəʊ'eɪʃn, -z
AM ˌɪnkə'weɪʃən, ˌɪŋkə'weɪʃən, -z

inchoative
BR 'ɪnkəʊeɪtɪv, 'ɪŋkəʊeɪtɪv
AM 'ɪnkəˌweɪdɪv, 'ɪŋkəˌweɪdɪv

Inchon
BR 'ɪn'tʃɒn
AM 'ɪn'tʃɑn

inchworm
BR 'ɪn(t)ʃwəːm, -z
AM 'ɪn(t)ʃˌwərm, -z

incidence
BR 'ɪnsɨd(ə)ns
AM 'ɪnsədns

incident
BR 'ɪnsɨd(ə)nt, -s
AM 'ɪnsədnt, -s

incidental
BR ˌɪnsɪ'dɛntl, -z
AM ˌɪnsə'dɛn(t)l, -z

incidentally
BR ˌɪnsɪ'dɛntḷi, ˌɪnsɪ'dɛntli
AM ˌɪnsə'dɛn(t)li

incidentalness
BR ˌɪnsɪ'dɛntlnəs
AM ˌɪnsə'dɛn(t)lnəs

incinerate
BR ɪn'sɪnəreɪt, -s, -ɪŋ, -ɨd
AM ɨn'sɪnəˌreɪ|t, -ts, -dɪŋ, -dɨd

incineration
BR ɪnˌsɪnə'reɪʃn
AM ɨnˌsɪnə'reɪʃən

incinerator
BR ɪn'sɪnəreɪtə(r), -z
AM ɨn'sɪnəˌreɪdər, -z

incipience
BR ɪn'sɪpɪəns
AM ɨn'sɪpiəns

incipiency
BR ɪn'sɪpɪəns|i, -ɪz
AM ɨn'sɪpiənsi, -z

incipient
BR ɪn'sɪpɪənt
AM ɨn'sɪpiənt

incipiently
BR ɪn'sɪpɪəntli
AM ɨn'sɪpiən(t)li

incipit
BR 'ɪnsɪpɪt, -s
AM ɨn'sɪpɨt, -s

incise
BR ɪn'sʌɪz, -ɨz, -ɪŋ, -d
AM ɨn'saɪz, -ɨz, -ɪŋ, -d

incision
BR ɪn'sɪʒn, -z
AM ɨn'sɪʒən, -z

incisive
BR ɪn'sʌɪsɪv
AM ɨn'saɪsɪv

incisively
BR ɪn'sʌɪsɨvli
AM ɨn'saɪsɨvli

incisiveness
BR ɪn'sʌɪsɪvnɨs
AM ɨn'saɪsɪvnɨs

incisor
BR ɪn'sʌɪzə(r), -z
AM ɨn'saɪzər, ˌɪn'saɪzər, -z

incitation
BR ˌɪnsʌɪ'teɪʃn, ˌɪnsɪ'teɪʃn, -z
AM ɪnˌsaɪ'teɪʃən, ˌɪnsə'teɪʃən, -z

incite
BR ɪn'sʌɪt, -s, -ɪŋ, -ɨd
AM ɨn'saɪ|t, -ts, -dɪŋ, -dɨd

incitement
BR ɪn'sʌɪtm(ə)nt, -s
AM ɨn'saɪtmənt, -s

inciter
BR ɪn'sʌɪtə(r), -z
AM ɨn'saɪdər, -z

incivility
BR ˌɪnsɪ'vɪlɪt|i, -ɪz
AM ˌɪnsə'vɪlɨdi, -z

incivism
BR 'ɪnsɪvɪz(ə)m
AM ɨn'sɪˌvɪzəm

inclemency
BR (ˌ)ɪn'klɛm(ə)nsi, (ˌ)ɪŋ'klɛm(ə)nsi
AM ɨn'klɛmənsi, ɪŋ'klɛmənsi

inclement
BR (ˌ)ɪn'klɛm(ə)nt, (ˌ)ɪŋ'klɛm(ə)nt
AM ɨn'klɛmənt, ɪŋ'klɛmənt

inclemently
BR (ˌ)ɪn'klɛm(ə)ntli, (ˌ)ɪŋ'klɛm(ə)ntli
AM ɨn'klɛmən(t)li, ɪŋ'klɛmən(t)li

inclinable
BR ɪn'klʌɪnəbl, ɪŋ'klʌɪnəbl
AM ɨn'klaɪnəbəl, ɪŋ'klaɪnəbəl

inclination
BR ˌɪnklɪ'neɪʃn, ˌɪŋklɪ'neɪʃn, -z
AM ˌɪnklə'neɪʃən, ˌɪŋklə'neɪʃən, -z

incline¹
noun
BR 'ɪnklʌɪn, 'ɪŋklʌɪn, -z
AM 'ɪnˌklaɪn, 'ɪŋˌklaɪn, -z

incline²
verb
BR ɪn'klʌɪn, ɪŋ'klʌɪn, -z, -ɪŋ, -d
AM ɨn'klaɪn, ɪŋ'klaɪn, -z, -ɪŋ, -d

incliner
BR ɪn'klʌɪnə(r), ɪŋ'klʌɪnə(r), -z
AM ɨn'klaɪnər, ɪŋ'klaɪnər, -z

inclinometer
BR ˌɪnklɪ'nɒmɨtə(r), ˌɪŋklɪ'nɒmɨtə(r), -z
AM ɨnˌklaɪ'nɑmədər, ɪŋˌklaɪ'nɑmədər, -z

inclose
BR ɪn'kləʊz, ɪŋ'kləʊz, -ɨz, -ɪŋ, -d
AM ɨn'kloʊz, ɨŋ'kloʊz, -əz, -ɪŋ, -t

inclosure
BR ɪn'kləʊʒə(r), ɪŋ'kləʊʒə(r), -z
AM ɨn'kloʊʒər, ɪŋ'kloʊʒər, -z

includable
BR ɪn'kluːdəbl, ɪŋ'kluːdəbl
AM ɨn'kludəbəl, ɪŋ'kludəbəl

include
BR ɪn'kluːd, ɪŋ'kluːd, -z, -ɪŋ, -ɨd
AM ɨn'klud, ɪŋ'klud, -z, -ɪŋ, -əd

includible
BR ɪn'kluːdɨbl, ɪŋ'kluːdɨbl
AM ɨn'kludəbəl, ɪŋ'kludəbəl

inclusion
BR ɪn'kluːʒn, ɪŋ'kluːʒn, -z
AM ɨn'kluʒən, ɪŋ'kluʒən, -z

inclusive
BR ɪn'kluːsɪv, ɪŋ'kluːsɪv
AM ɨn'klusɪv, ɪŋ'klusɪv

inclusively
BR ɪn'kluːsɨvli, ɪŋ'kluːsɨvli
AM ɨn'klusəvli, ɪŋ'klusəvli

inclusiveness
BR ɪn'kluːsɪvnɨs, ɪŋ'kluːsɪvnɨs
AM ɨn'klusɪvnɨs, ɪŋ'klusɪvnɨs

incog
incognito
BR ɪn'kɒg, ɪŋ'kɒg
AM ɨn'kɑg, ɪŋ'kɑg

incognisance
BR ɪn'kɒgnɪz(ə)ns, ɪŋ'kɒgnɪz(ə)ns
AM ɨn'kɑgnəzns, ɪŋ'kɑgnəzns

incognisant
BR ɪn'kɒgnɪz(ə)nt, ɪŋ'kɒgnɪz(ə)nt
AM ɨn'kɑgnəznt, ɪŋ'kɑgnəznt

incognito
BR ˌɪnkɒg'niːtəʊ, ˌɪŋkɒg'niːtəʊ
AM ˌɪnˌkɑg'nidoʊ, ˌɪŋˌkɑg'nidoʊ

incognizance
BR ɪn'kɒgnɪz(ə)ns, ɪŋ'kɒgnɪz(ə)ns
AM ɨn'kɑgnəzns, ɪŋ'kɑgnəzns

incognizant
BR ɪn'kɒgnɪz(ə)nt, ɪŋ'kɒgnɪz(ə)nt
AM ɨn'kɑgnəznt, ɪŋ'kɑgnəznt

incoherence
BR ˌɪnkə(ʊ)'hɪərəns, ˌɪnkə(ʊ)'hɪərn̩s, ˌɪŋkə(ʊ)'hɪərəns, ˌɪŋkə(ʊ)'hɪərn̩s
AM ¦ɪnkoʊ'hɪrəns, ¦ɪnkoʊ'hɛrəns, ¦ɪŋkoʊ'hɪrəns, ¦ɪŋkoʊ'hɛrəns

incoherency
BR ˌɪnkə(ʊ)'hɪərəns|i, ˌɪnkə(ʊ)'hɪərn̩s|i, ˌɪŋkə(ʊ)'hɪərəns|i, ˌɪŋkə(ʊ)'hɪərn̩s|i, -ɪz
AM ¦ɪnkoʊ'hɪrənsi, ¦ɪnkoʊ'hɛrənsi, ¦ɪŋkoʊ'hɪrənsi, ¦ɪŋkoʊ'hɛrənsi, -z

incoherent
BR ˌɪnkə(ʊ)'hɪərənt, ˌɪnkə(ʊ)'hɪərn̩t, ˌɪŋkə(ʊ)'hɪərənt, ˌɪŋkə(ʊ)'hɪərn̩t
AM ¦ɪnkoʊ'hɪrənt, ¦ɪnkoʊ'hɛrənt, ¦ɪŋkoʊ'hɪrənt, ¦ɪŋkoʊ'hɛrənt

incoherently
BR ˌɪnkə(ʊ)'hɪərəntli, ˌɪnkə(ʊ)'hɪərn̩tli, ˌɪŋkə(ʊ)'hɪərəntli, ˌɪŋkə(ʊ)'hɪərn̩tli
AM ¦ɪnkoʊ'hɪrən(t)li, ¦ɪnkoʊ'hɛrən(t)li, ¦ɪŋkoʊ'hɪrən(t)li, ¦ɪŋkoʊ'hɛrən(t)li

incombustibility
BR ˌɪnkəmˌbʌstɪ'bɪlɨti, ˌɪŋkəmˌbʌstɪ'bɪlɨti
AM ¦ɪnkəmˌbəstə'bɪlɨdi, ¦ɪŋkəmˌbəstə'bɪlɨdi

incombustible
BR ˌɪnkəm'bʌstɨbl, ˌɪŋkəm'bʌstɨbl
AM ¦ɪnkəm'bəstəbəl, ¦ɪŋkəm'bəstəbəl

incombustibleness
BR ˌɪnkəmˈbʌstɨblnəs, ˌɪŋkəmˈbʌstɨblnəs
AM ¦ɪnkəmˈbəstəbəlnəs, ¦ɪŋkəmˈbəstəbəlnəs

income
BR ˈɪŋkʌm, ˈɪnkʌm, ˈɪŋkəm, ˈɪnkəm, -z
AM ˈɪnˌkəm, ˈɪŋˌkəm, -z

incomer
BR ˈɪnˌkʌmə(r), ˈɪŋˌkʌmə(r), -z
AM ˈɪnˌkəmər, ˈɪŋˌkəmər, -z

incoming
BR ˈɪnˌkʌmɪŋ, ˈɪŋˌkʌmɪŋ
AM ˈɪnˌkəmɪŋ, ˈɪŋˌkəmɪŋ

incommensurability
BR ˌɪnkəˌmɛnʃ(ə)rəˈbɪlɨti, ˌɪnkəˌmɛns(ə)rəˈbɪlɨti, ˌɪnkəˌmɛnsjərəˈbɪlɨti, ˌɪŋkəˌmɛns(ə)rəˈbɪlɨti, ˌɪŋkəˌmɛns(ə)rəˈbɪlɨti, ˌɪŋkəˌmɛnsjərəˈbɪlɨti
AM ¦ɪnkəˌmɛns(ə)rəˈbɪlɨdi, ¦ɪŋkəˌmɛns(ə)rəˈbɪlɨdi, ¦ɪnkəˌmɛnʃ(ə)rəˈbɪlɨdi, ¦ɪŋkəˌmɛnʃ(ə)rəˈbɪlɨdi

incommensurable
BR ˌɪnkəˈmɛnʃ(ə)rəbl, ˌɪnkəˈmɛns(ə)rəbl, ˌɪnkəˈmɛnsjərəbl, ˌɪŋkəˈmɛnʃ(ə)rəbl, ˌɪŋkəˈmɛns(ə)rəbl, ˌɪŋkəˈmɛnsjərəbl
AM ¦ɪnkəˈmɛns(ə)rəbəl, ¦ɪŋkəˈmɛns(ə)rəbəl, ¦ɪnkəˈmɛn(t)ʃ(ə)rəbəl, ¦ɪŋkəˈmɛn(t)ʃ(ə)rəbəl

incommensurably
BR ˌɪnkəˈmɛnʃ(ə)rəbli, ˌɪnkəˈmɛns(ə)rəbli, ˌɪnkəˈmɛnsjərəbli, ˌɪŋkəˈmɛnʃ(ə)rəbli, ˌɪŋkəˈmɛns(ə)rəbli, ˌɪŋkəˈmɛnsjərəbli
AM ¦ɪnkəˈmɛns(ə)rəbli, ¦ɪŋkəˈmɛns(ə)rəbli, ¦ɪnkəˈmɛnʃ(ə)rəbli, ¦ɪŋkəˈmɛnʃ(ə)rəbli

incommensurate
BR ˌɪnkəˈmɛnʃ(ə)rət, ˌɪnkəˈmɛns(ə)rət, ˌɪnkəˈmɛnsjərət, ˌɪŋkəˈmɛnʃ(ə)rət, ˌɪŋkəˈmɛns(ə)rət, ˌɪŋkəˈmɛnsjərət
AM ¦ɪnkəˈmɛns(ə)rət, ¦ɪŋkəˈmɛns(ə)rət, ¦ɪnkəˈmɛnʃ(ə)rət, ¦ɪŋkəˈmɛnʃ(ə)rət

incommensurately
BR ˌɪnkəˈmɛnʃ(ə)rətli, ˌɪnkəˈmɛns(ə)rətli, ˌɪnkəˈmɛnsjərətli, ˌɪŋkəˈmɛnʃ(ə)rətli, ˌɪŋkəˈmɛns(ə)rətli, ˌɪŋkəˈmɛnsjərətli
AM ¦ɪnkəˈmɛns(ə)rətli, ¦ɪŋkəˈmɛns(ə)rətli, ¦ɪnkəˈmɛnʃ(ə)rətli, ¦ɪŋkəˈmɛnʃ(ə)rətli

incommensurateness
BR ˌɪnkəˈmɛnʃ(ə)rətnəs, ˌɪnkəˈmɛns(ə)rətnəs, ˌɪnkəˈmɛnsjərətnəs, ˌɪŋkəˈmɛnʃ(ə)rətnəs, ˌɪŋkəˈmɛns(ə)rətnəs, ˌɪŋkəˈmɛnsjərətnəs
AM ¦ɪnkəˈmɛns(ə)rətnəs, ¦ɪŋkəˈmɛns(ə)rətnəs, ¦ɪnkəˈmɛnʃ(ə)rətnəs, ¦ɪŋkəˈmɛnʃ(ə)rətnəs

incommode
BR ˌɪnkəˈməʊd, ˌɪŋkəˈməʊd, -z, -ɪŋ, -ɨd
AM ¦ɪnkəˈmoʊd, ¦ɪŋkəˈmoʊd, -z, -ɪŋ, -əd

incommodious
BR ˌɪnkəˈməʊdɪəs, ˌɪŋkəˈməʊdɪəs
AM ¦ɪnkəˈmoʊdiəs, ¦ɪŋkəˈmoʊdiəs

incommodiously
BR ˌɪnkəˈməʊdɪəsli, ˌɪŋkəˈməʊdɪəsli
AM ¦ɪnkəˈmoʊdiəsli, ¦ɪŋkəˈmoʊdiəsli

incommodiousness
BR ˌɪnkəˈməʊdɪəsnəs, ˌɪŋkəˈməʊdɪəsnəs
AM ¦ɪnkəˈmoʊdiəsnəs, ¦ɪŋkəˈmoʊdiəsnəs

incommunicability
BR ˌɪnkəˌmjuːnɨkəˈbɪlɨti, ˌɪŋkəˌmjuːnɨkəˈbɪlɨti
AM ¦ɪnkəˌmjunəkəˈbɪlɨdi, ¦ɪŋkəˌmjunəkəˈbɪlɨdi

incommunicable
BR ˌɪnkəˈmjuːnɨkəbl, ˌɪŋkəˈmjuːnɨkəbl
AM ¦ɪnkəˈmjunəkəbəl, ¦ɪŋkəˈmjunəkəbəl

incommunicableness
BR ˌɪnkəˈmjuːnɨkəblnəs, ˌɪŋkəˈmjuːnɨkəblnəs
AM ¦ɪnkəˈmjunəkəbəlnəs, ¦ɪŋkəˈmjunəkəbəlnəs

incommunicably
BR ˌɪnkəˈmjuːnɨkəbli, ˌɪŋkəˈmjuːnɨkəbli
AM ¦ɪnkəˈmjunəkəbli, ¦ɪŋkəˈmjunəkəbli

incommunicado
BR ˌɪnkəˌmjuːnɪˈkɑːdəʊ, ˌɪŋkəˌmjuːnɪˈkɑːdəʊ
AM ˌɪnkəˌmjunəˈkɑdoʊ, ¦ɪŋkəˌmjunəˈkɑdoʊ

incommunicative
BR ˌɪnkəˈmjuːnɨkətɪv, ˌɪŋkəˈmjuːnɨkətɪv
AM ¦ɪnkəˈmjunəˌkeɪdɪv, ¦ɪnkəˈmjunəkədɪv, ¦ɪŋkəˈmjunəˌkeɪdɪv, ¦ɪŋkəˈmjunəkədɪv

incommunicatively
BR ˌɪnkəˈmjuːnɨkətɨvli, ˌɪŋkəˈmjuːnɨkətɨvli
AM ¦ɪnkəˈmjunəˌkeɪdɨvli, ¦ɪnkəˈmjunəkədəvli, ¦ɪŋkəˈmjunəˌkeɪdɪvli, ¦ɪŋkəˈmjunəkədəvli

incommunicativeness
BR ˌɪnkəˈmjuːnɨkətɪvnɪs, ˌɪŋkəˈmjuːnɨkətɪvnɪs
AM ¦ɪnkəˈmjunəˌkeɪdɪvnɪs, ¦ɪnkəˈmjunəkədɪvnɪs, ¦ɪŋkəˈmjunəˌkeɪdɪvnɪs, ¦ɪŋkəˈmjunəkədɪvnɪs

incommutable
BR ˌɪnkəˈmjuːtəbl, ˌɪŋkəˈmjuːtəbl
AM ˌɪnkəˈmjudəbəl, ˌɪŋkəˈmjudəbəl

incommutably
BR ˌɪnkəˈmjuːtəbli, ˌɪŋkəˈmjuːtəbli
AM ˌɪnkəˈmjudəbli, ˌɪŋkəˈmjudəbli

incomparability
BR ɪnˌkɒmp(ə)rəˈbɪlɨti, ˌɪnkəmˌparəˈbɪlɨti, ɪŋˌkɒmp(ə)rəˈbɪlɨti, ˌɪŋkəmˌparəˈbɪlɨti
AM ¦ɪnˌkɑmp(ə)rəˈbɪlɨdi, ɨnˌkɑmp(ə)rəˈbɪlɨdi, ¦ɪŋˌkɑmp(ə)rəˈbɪlɨdi

incomparable
BR ɪnˈkɒmp(ə)rəbl, ˌɪnkəmˈparəbl, ɪŋˈkɒmp(ə)rəbl, ˌɪŋkəmˈparəbl
AM ¦ɪnˈkɑmp(ə)rəbəl, ɨnˈkɑmp(ə)rəbəl, ¦ɪŋˈkɑmp(ə)rəbəl

incomparableness
BR ɪnˈkɒmp(ə)rəblnəs, ˌɪnkəmˈparəblnəs, ɪŋˈkɒmp(ə)rəblnəs, ˌɪŋkəmˈparəblnəs
AM ¦ɪnˈkɑmp(ə)rəbəlnəs, ɨnˈkɑmp(ə)rəbəlnəs, ¦ɪŋˈkɑmp(ə)rəbəlnəs

incomparably
BR ɪnˈkɒmp(ə)rəbli, ˌɪnkəmˈparəbli, ɪŋˈkɒmp(ə)rəbli, ˌɪŋkəmˈparəbli
AM ¦ɪnˈkɑmp(ə)rəbli, ɨnˈkɑmp(ə)rəbli, ¦ɪŋˈkɑmp(ə)rəbli

incompatibility
BR ˌɪnkəmˌpatɪˈbɪlɨti, ˌɪŋkəmpatɪˈbɪlɨti
AM ¦ɪnkəmˌpædəˈbɪlɨdi, ¦ɪŋkəmˌpædəˈbɪlɨdi

incompatible
BR ˌɪnkəmˈpatɨbl, ˌɪŋkəmˈpatɨbl
AM ¦ɪnkəmˈpædəbəl, ¦ɪŋkəmˈpædəbəl

incompatibleness
BR ˌɪnkəmˈpatɨblnəs, ˌɪŋkəmˈpatɨblnəs
AM ¦ɪnkəmˈpædəbəlnəs, ¦ɪŋkəmˈpædəbəlnəs

incompatibly
BR ˌɪnkəmˈpatɨbli, ˌɪŋkəmˈpatɨbli
AM ¦ɪnkəmˈpædəbli, ¦ɪŋkəmˈpædəbli

incompetence
BR ɪnˈkɒmpɪt(ə)ns, ɪŋˈkɒmpɪt(ə)ns
AM ɨnˈkɑmpədns, ɪŋˈkɑmpədns

incompetency
BR ɪnˈkɒmpɪt(ə)nsi, ɪŋˈkɒmpɪt(ə)nsi
AM ɨnˈkɑmpədənsi, ɪŋˈkɑmpədənsi

incompetent
BR ɪnˈkɒmpɪt(ə)nt, ɪŋˈkɒmpɪt(ə)nt
AM ɪnˈkɑmpədnt, ɪŋˈkɑmpədnt

incompetently
BR ɪnˈkɒmpɪt(ə)ntli, ɪŋˈkɒmpɪt(ə)ntli
AM ɨnˈkɑmpədən(t)li, ɪŋˈkɑmpədən(t)li

incomplete
BR ˌɪnkəmˈpliːt, ˌɪŋkəmˈpliːt
AM ¦ɪnkəmˈplit, ¦ɪŋkəmˈplit

incompletely
BR ˌɪnkəmˈpliːtli, ˌɪŋkəmˈpliːtli
AM ¦ɪnkəmˈplitli, ¦ɪŋkəmˈplitli

incompleteness
BR ˌɪnkəmˈpliːtnɪs, ˌɪŋkəmˈpliːtnɪs
AM ¦ɪnkəmˈplitnɪs, ¦ɪŋkəmˈplitnɪs

incomprehensibility
BR ɪnˌkɒmprɪˌhɛnsɪˈbɪlɨti, ˌɪnkɒmprɪˌhɛnsɪˈbɪlɨti, ɪŋˌkɒmprɪˌhɛnsɪˈbɪlɨti, ˌɪŋkɒmprɪˌhɛnsɪˈbɪlɨti
AM ¦ɪnˌkɑmprəˌhɛnsəˈbɪlɨdi, ɨnˌkɑmprəˌhɛnsəˈbɪlɨdi, ¦ɪŋˌkɑmprəˌhɛnsəˈbɪlɨdi

incomprehensible
BR ɪn,kɒmprɪ'hɛnsɪbl, ,ɪnkɒmprɪ'hɛnsɪbl, ɪŋ,kɒmprɪ'hɛnsɪbl, ,ɪŋkɒmprɪ'hɛnsɪbl
AM ˌɪn,kamprə'hɛn-səbəl, ˌɪŋ,kamprə'hɛnsəbəl

incomprehensibleness
BR ɪn,kɒmprɪ'hɛnsɪbl-nəs, ,ɪnkɒmprɪ'hɛnsɪblnəs, ɪŋ,kɒmprɪ'hɛnsɪblnəs, ,ɪŋkɒmprɪ'hɛnsɪblnəs
AM ˌɪn,kamprə'hɛns-əbəlnəs, ˌɪŋ,kamprə'hɛnsəbəl-nəs

incomprehensibly
BR ɪn,kɒmprɪ'hɛnsɪbli, ,ɪnkɒmprɪ'hɛnsɪbli, ɪŋ,kɒmprɪ'hɛnsɪbli, ,ɪŋkɒmprɪ'hɛnsɪbli
AM ˌɪn,kamprə'hɛns-əbli, ˌɪŋ,kamprə'hɛnsəbli

incomprehension
BR ɪn,kɒmprɪ'hɛnʃn, ,ɪnkɒmprɪ'hɛnʃn, ɪŋ,kɒmprɪ'hɛnʃn, ,ɪŋkɒmprɪ'hɛnʃn
AM ˌɪn,kamprə'hɛn-(t)ʃən, ɪn,kamprə'hɛn(t)ʃən, ˌɪŋ,kamprə'hɛn(t)ʃən

incompressibility
BR ,ɪnkəm,prɛsɪ'bɪlɪti, ,ɪŋkəm,prɛsɪ'bɪlɪti
AM ˌɪnkəm,prɛsə'bɪlɪdi, ˌɪŋkəm,prɛsə'bɪlɪdi

incompressible
BR ,ɪnkəm'prɛsɪbl, ,ɪŋkəm'prɛsɪbl
AM ,ɪnkəm'prɛsəbəl, ,ɪŋkəm'prɛsəbəl

inconceivability
BR ,ɪnkən,si:və'bɪlɪti, ,ɪŋkən,si:və'bɪlɪti
AM ˌɪnkən,sivə'bɪlɪdi, ˌɪŋkən,sivə'bɪlɪdi

inconceivable
BR ,ɪnkən'si:vəbl, ,ɪŋkən'si:vəbl
AM ˌɪnkən'sivəbəl, ˌɪŋkən'sivəbəl

inconceivableness
BR ,ɪnkən'si:vəblnəs, ,ɪŋkən'si:vəblnəs
AM ˌɪnkən'sivəbəlnəs, ˌɪŋkən'sivəbəlnəs

inconceivably
BR ,ɪnkən'si:vəbli, ,ɪŋkən'si:vəbli
AM ˌɪnkən'sivəbli, ˌɪŋkən'sivəbli

inconclusive
BR ,ɪnkən'klu:sɪv, ,ɪŋkən'klu:sɪv
AM ˌɪnkən'klusɪv, ˌɪŋkən'klusɪv

inconclusively
BR ,ɪnkən'klu:sɪvli, ,ɪŋkən'klu:sɪvli
AM ˌɪnkən'klusəvli, ˌɪŋkən'klusəvli

inconclusiveness
BR ,ɪnkən'klu:sɪvnɪs, ,ɪŋkən'klu:sɪvnɪs
AM ˌɪnkən'klusɪvnɪs, ˌɪŋkən'klusɪvnɪs

incondensable
BR ,ɪnkən'dɛnsəbl, ,ɪŋkən'dɛnsəbl
AM ˌɪnkən'dɛnsəbəl, ˌɪŋkən'dɛnsəbəl

incondite
BR ɪn'kɒndɪt, ɪn'kɒndʌɪt, ɪŋ'kɒndɪt, ɪŋ'kɒndʌɪt
AM ɪn'kan,daɪt, ɪŋ'kan,daɪt, ɪn'kandət, ɪŋ'kandət

incongruity
BR ,ɪnkən'gru:ɪti, ,ɪŋkən'gru:ɪti, ,ɪŋkəŋ'gru:ɪti
AM ˌɪnkən'gruədi, ˌɪŋkaŋ'gruədi, ˌɪnkən'gruədi, ˌɪŋkaŋ'gruədi

incongruous
BR ɪn'kɒŋgrʊəs, ɪŋ'kɒŋgrʊəs
AM ɪn'kaŋgrʊəs, ɪŋ'kaŋgrʊəs

incongruously
BR ɪn'kɒŋgrʊəsli, ɪŋ'kɒŋgrʊəsli
AM ɪn'kaŋgrʊəsli, ɪŋ'kaŋgrʊəsli

incongruousness
BR ɪn'kɒŋgrʊəsnəs, ɪŋ'kɒŋgrʊəsnəs
AM ɪn'kaŋgrʊəsnəs, ɪŋ'kaŋgrʊəsnəs

inconsecutive
BR ,ɪnkən'sɛkjʊtɪv, ,ɪŋkən'sɛkjʊtɪv
AM ˌɪnkən'sɛkjədɪv, ˌɪŋkən'sɛkjədɪv

inconsecutively
BR ,ɪnkən'sɛkjʊtɪvli, ,ɪŋkən'sɛkjʊtɪvli
AM ˌɪnkən'sɛkjədəvli, ˌɪŋkən'sɛkjədəvli

inconsecutiveness
BR ,ɪnkən'sɛkjʊtɪvnɪs, ,ɪŋkən'sɛkjʊtɪvnɪs
AM ˌɪnkən'sɛkjədɪvnɪs, ˌɪŋkən'sɛkjədɪvnɪs

inconsequence
BR ɪn'kɒnsɪkw(ə)ns, ɪŋ'kɒnsɪkw(ə)ns
AM ɪn'kansə,kwɛns, ɪŋ'kansə,kwɛns

inconsequent
BR ɪn'kɒnsɪkw(ə)nt, ɪŋ'kɒnsɪkw(ə)nt
AM ɪn'kansə(,)kwɛnt, ɪŋ'kansə(,)kwɛnt

inconsequential
BR ɪn,kɒnsɪ'kwɛnʃl, ,ɪnkɒnsɪ'kwɛnʃl, ɪŋ,kɒnsɪ'kwɛnʃl, ,ɪŋkɒnsɪ'kwɛnʃl
AM ˌɪn,kansə'kwɛn-(t)ʃəl, ˌɪŋ,kansə'kwɛn(t)ʃəl

inconsequentiality
BR ɪn,kɒnsɪ,kwɛnʃɪ-'alɪt|i, ,ɪnkɒnsɪ,kwɛnʃɪ'alɪt|i, ɪŋ,kɒnsɪ,kwɛnʃɪ'alɪt|i, ,ɪŋkɒnsɪ,kwɛnʃɪ'alɪt|i, -ɪz
AM ˌɪn,kansə,kwɛn(t)ʃi-'ælədi, ˌɪŋ,kansə,kwɛn(t)ʃi'æl-ədi, -z

inconsequentially
BR ɪn,kɒnsɪ'kwɛnʃl̩i, ɪn,kɒnsɪ'kwɛnʃəli, ,ɪnkɒnsɪ'kwɛnʃl̩i, ,ɪnkɒnsɪ'kwɛnʃəli, ɪŋ,kɒnsɪ'kwɛnʃl̩i, ɪŋ,kɒnsɪ'kwɛnʃəli, ,ɪŋkɒnsɪ'kwɛnʃl̩i, ,ɪŋkɒnsɪ'kwɛnʃəli
AM ˌɪn,kansə'kwɛn-(t)ʃəli, ˌɪŋ,kansə'kwɛn(t)ʃəli

inconsequentialness
BR ɪn,kɒnsɪ'kwɛnʃlnəs, ,ɪnkɒnsɪ'kwɛnʃlnəs, ɪŋ,kɒnsɪ'kwɛnʃlnəs, ,ɪŋkɒnsɪ'kwɛnʃlnəs
AM ˌɪn,kansə'kwɛn-(t)ʃəlnəs, ˌɪŋ,kansə'kwɛn(t)ʃəl-nəs

inconsequently
BR ɪn'kɒnsɪkw(ə)ntli, ɪŋ'kɒnsɪkw(ə)ntli
AM ɪn'kansə(,)kwɛn-(t)li, ɪŋ'kansə(,)kwɛn(t)li

inconsiderable
BR ,ɪnkən'sɪd(ə)rəbl, ,ɪŋkən'sɪd(ə)rəbl
AM ˌɪnkən'sɪdər(ə)bəl, ˌɪnkən'sɪdrəbəl, ˌɪŋkən'sɪdər(ə)bəl, ˌɪŋkən'sɪdrəbəl

inconsiderableness
BR ,ɪnkən'sɪd(ə)rəbl-nəs, ,ɪŋkən'sɪd(ə)rəblnəs
AM ˌɪnkən'sɪdər(ə)bəl-nəs, ˌɪnkən'sɪdrəbəlnəs, ˌɪŋkən'sɪdər(ə)bəlnəs, ˌɪŋkən'sɪdrəbəlnəs

inconsiderably
BR ,ɪnkən'sɪd(ə)rəbli, ,ɪŋkən'sɪd(ə)rəbli
AM ˌɪnkən'sɪdər(ə)bli, ˌɪnkən'sɪdrəbli, ˌɪŋkən'sɪdər(ə)bli, ˌɪŋkən'sɪdrəbli

inconsiderate
BR ,ɪnkən'sɪd(ə)rət, ,ɪŋkən'sɪd(ə)rət
AM ˌɪnkən'sɪd(ə)rət, ˌɪŋkən'sɪd(ə)rət

inconsiderately
BR ,ɪnkən'sɪd(ə)rətli, ,ɪŋkən'sɪd(ə)rətli
AM ˌɪnkən'sɪd(ə)rətli, ˌɪŋkən'sɪd(ə)rətli

inconsiderateness
BR ,ɪnkən'sɪd(ə)rətnəs, ,ɪŋkən'sɪd(ə)rətnəs
AM ˌɪnkən'sɪd(ə)rətnəs, ˌɪŋkən'sɪd(ə)rətnəs

inconsideration
BR ,ɪnkən,sɪdə'reɪʃn, ,ɪŋkən,sɪdə'reɪʃn, -z
AM ˌɪnkən,sɪd(ə)'reɪʃən, ˌɪŋkən,sɪd(ə)'reɪʃən, -z

inconsistency
BR ,ɪnkən'sɪst(ə)ns|i, ,ɪŋkən'sɪst(ə)ns|i, -ɪz
AM ˌɪnkən'sɪstnsi, ˌɪŋkən'sɪstnsi, -z

inconsistent
BR ,ɪnkən'sɪst(ə)nt, ,ɪŋkən'sɪst(ə)nt
AM ˌɪnkən'sɪstənt, ˌɪŋkən'sɪstənt

inconsistently
BR ,ɪnkən'sɪst(ə)ntli, ,ɪŋkən'sɪst(ə)ntli
AM ˌɪnkən'sɪstən(t)li, ˌɪŋkən'sɪstən(t)li

inconsolability
BR ,ɪnkən,səʊlə'bɪlɪti, ,ɪŋkən,səʊlə'bɪlɪti
AM ˌɪnkən,soʊlə'bɪlɪdi, ˌɪŋkən,soʊlə'bɪlɪdi

inconsolable
BR ,ɪnkən'səʊləbl, ,ɪŋkən'səʊləbl
AM ˌɪnkən'soʊləbəl, ˌɪŋkən'soʊləbəl

inconsolableness
BR ,ɪnkən'səʊləblnəs, ,ɪŋkən'səʊləblnəs
AM ˌɪnkən'soʊləbəlnəs, ˌɪŋkən'soʊləbəlnəs

inconsolably
BR ,ɪnkən'səʊləbli, ,ɪŋkən'səʊləbli
AM ˌɪnkən'soʊləbli, ˌɪŋkən'soʊləbəli

inconsonance
BR ɪn'kɒnsənəns, ɪn'kɒnsn̩əns, ɪŋ'kɒnsənəns, ɪŋ'kɒnsn̩əns, -ɪz

AM ɪn'kɑnsənəns, ɪŋ'kɑnsənəns, -əz

inconsonant
BR ɪn'kɒnsənənt, ɪn'kɒnsn̩ənt, ɪŋ'kɒnsənənt, ɪŋ'kɒnsn̩ənt
AM ɪn'kɑnsənənt, ɪŋ'kɑnsənənt

inconsonantly
BR ɪn'kɒnsənəntli, ɪn'kɒnsn̩əntli, ɪŋ'kɒnsənəntli, ɪŋ'kɒnsn̩əntli
AM ɪn'kɑnsənən(t)li, ɪŋ'kɑnsənən(t)li

inconspicuous
BR ˌɪnkən'spɪkjʊəs, ˌɪŋkən'spɪkjʊəs
AM ¦ɪnkənz'pɪkjəwəs, ¦ɪnkən'spɪkjəwəs, ¦ɪŋkənz'pɪkjəwəs, ¦ɪŋkən'spɪkjəwəs

inconspicuously
BR ˌɪnkən'spɪkjʊəsli, ˌɪŋkən'spɪkjʊəsli
AM ¦ɪnkənz'pɪkjəwəsli, ¦ɪnkən'spɪkjəwəsli, ¦ɪŋkənz'pɪkjəwəsli, ¦ɪŋkən'spɪkjəwəsli

inconspicuousness
BR ˌɪnkən'spɪkjʊəsnəs, ˌɪŋkən'spɪkjʊəsnəs
AM ¦ɪnkənz'pɪkjəwəsnəs, ¦ɪnkən'spɪkjəwəsnəs, ¦ɪŋkənz'pɪkjəwəsnəs, ¦ɪŋkən'spɪkjəwəsnəs

inconstancy
BR ɪn'kɒnst(ə)nsi, ɪŋ'kɒnst(ə)nsi
AM ɪn'kɑnztnsi, ɪn'kɑnstnsi, ɪŋ'kɑnztnsi, ɪŋ'kɑnstnsi

inconstant
BR ɪn'kɒnst(ə)nt, ɪŋ'kɒnst(ə)nt
AM ɪn'kɑnztənt, ɪn'kɑnstənt, ɪŋ'kɑnztənt, ɪŋ'kɑnstənt

inconstantly
BR ɪn'kɒnst(ə)ntli, ɪŋ'kɒnst(ə)ntli
AM ɪn'kɑnztən(t)li, ɪn'kɑnstən(t)li, ɪŋ'kɑnztən(t)li, ɪŋ'kɑnstən(t)li

incontestability
BR ˌɪnkənˌtɛstə'bɪlɪti, ˌɪŋkənˌtɛstə'bɪlɪti
AM ˌɪnkənˌtɛstə'bɪlɪdi, ˌɪŋkənˌtɛstə'bɪlɪdi

incontestable
BR ˌɪnkən'tɛstəbl, ˌɪŋkən'tɛstəbl
AM ¦ɪnkən'tɛstəbəl, ¦ɪŋkən'tɛstəbəl

incontestably
BR ˌɪnkən'tɛstəbli, ˌɪŋkən'tɛstəbli
AM ¦ɪnkən'tɛstəbli, ¦ɪŋkən'tɛstəbli

incontinence
BR ɪn'kɒntɪnəns, ɪŋ'kɒntɪnəns
AM ɪn'kɑnt(ə)nəns, ɪŋ'kɑnt(ə)nəns

incontinent
BR ɪn'kɒntɪnənt, ɪŋ'kɒntɪnənt
AM ɪn'kɑnt(ə)nənt, ɪŋ'kɑnt(ə)nənt

incontinently
BR ɪn'kɒntɪnəntli, ɪŋ'kɒntɪnəntli
AM ɪn'kɑnt(ə)nən(t)li, ɪŋ'kɑnt(ə)nən(t)li

incontrovertibility
BR ɪnˌkɒntrəˌvəːtə'bɪlɪti, ˌɪnkɒntrəˌvəːtə'bɪlɪti, ɪŋˌkɒntrəˌvəːtə'bɪlɪti, ˌɪŋkɒntrəˌvəːtə'bɪlɪti
AM ¦ɪnˌkɑntrəˌvərdə'bɪlɪdi, ɪnˌkɑntrəˌvərdə'bɪlɪdi, ¦ɪŋˌkɑntrəˌvərdə'bɪlɪdi

incontrovertible
BR ɪnˌkɒntrə'vəːtəbl, ˌɪnkɒntrə'vəːtəbl, ɪŋˌkɒntrə'vəːtəbl, ˌɪŋkɒntrə'vəːtəbl
AM ¦ɪnˌkɑntrə'vərdəbəl, ɪnˌkɑntrə'vərdəbəl, ¦ɪŋˌkɑntrə'vərdəbəl

incontrovertibly
BR ɪnˌkɒntrə'vəːtəbli, ˌɪnkɒntrə'vəːtəbli, ɪŋˌkɒntrə'vəːtəbli, ˌɪŋkɒntrə'vəːtəbli
AM ¦ɪnˌkɑntrə¦vərdəbli, ənˌkɑntrə¦vərdəbli, ¦ɪŋˌkɑntrə¦vərdəbli

inconvenience
BR ˌɪnkən'viːnɪəns, ˌɪŋkən'viːnɪəns, -ɪz
AM ¦ɪnkən'vinjəns, ¦ɪŋkən'vinjəns, -əz

inconvenient
BR ˌɪnkən'viːnɪənt, ˌɪŋkən'viːnɪənt
AM ¦ɪnkən'vinjənt, ¦ɪŋkən'vinjənt

inconveniently
BR ˌɪnkən'viːnɪəntli, ˌɪŋkən'viːnɪəntli
AM ¦ɪnkən'vinjən(t)li, ¦ɪŋkən'vinjən(t)li

inconvertibility
BR ˌɪnkənˌvəːtɪ'bɪlɪti, ˌɪŋkənˌvəːtɪ'bɪlɪti
AM ¦ɪnˌkɑnˌvərdə'bɪlɪdi, ɪnˌkɑnˌvərdə'bɪlɪdi, ¦ɪŋˌkɑnˌvərdə'bɪlɪdi

inconvertible
BR ˌɪnkən'vəːtɪbl, ˌɪŋkən'vəːtɪbl
AM ¦ɪnˌkɑn¦vərdəbəl, ɪnˌkɑn¦vərdəbəl, ¦ɪŋˌkɑn¦vərdəbəl

inconvertibly
BR ˌɪnkən'vəːtɪbli, ˌɪŋkən'vəːtɪbli
AM ¦ɪnˌkɑn¦vərdəbli, ɪnˌkɑn¦vərdəbli, ¦ɪŋˌkɑn¦vərdəbli

incoordination
BR ˌɪnkəʊˌɔːdɪ'neɪʃn, ˌɪŋkəʊˌɔːdɪ'neɪʃn
AM ¦ɪnkoʊˌɔrdə'neɪʃən, ¦ɪŋkoʊˌɔrdə'neɪʃən

incorporate[1]
adjective
BR ɪn'kɔːp(ə)rət, ɪŋ'kɔːp(ə)rət
AM ɪn'kɔrp(ə)rət, ɪŋ'kɔrp(ə)rət

incorporate[2]
verb
BR ɪn'kɔːpəreɪt, ɪŋ'kɔːpəreɪt, -s, -ɪŋ, -ɪd
AM ɪn'kɔrpəˌreɪ|t, ɪŋ'kɔrpəˌreɪ|t, -ts, -dɪŋ, -dɪd

incorporation
BR ɪnˌkɔːpə'reɪʃn, ɪŋˌkɔːpə'reɪʃn, -z
AM ɪnˌkɔrpə'reɪʃən, ɪŋˌkɔrpə'reɪʃən, -z

incorporator
BR ɪn'kɔːpəreɪtə(r), ɪŋ'kɔːpəreɪtə(r), -z
AM ɪn'kɔrpəˌreɪdər, ɪŋ'kɔrpəˌreɪdər, -z

incorporeal
BR ˌɪnkɔː'pɔːrɪəl, ˌɪŋkɔː'pɔːrɪəl
AM ¦ɪnˌkɔr'pɔriəl, ¦ɪŋˌkɔr'pɔriəl

incorporeality
BR ˌɪnkɔːˌpɔːrɪ'alɪti, ˌɪŋkɔːˌpɔːrɪ'alɪti
AM ¦ɪnˌkɔrˌpɔri'ælədi, ¦ɪŋˌkɔrˌpɔri'ælədi

incorporeally
BR ˌɪnkɔː'pɔːrɪəli, ˌɪŋkɔː'pɔːrɪəli
AM ¦ɪnˌkɔr'pɔriəli, ¦ɪŋˌkɔr'pɔriəli

incorporeity
BR ˌɪnkɔːpə'riːɪti, ˌɪnkɔːpə'reɪɪti, ˌɪŋkɔːpə'riːɪti, ˌɪŋkɔːpə'reɪɪti
AM ¦ɪnˌkɔrpə'riɪdi, ¦ɪŋˌkɔrpə'riɪdi, ¦ɪnˌkɔrpə'reɪɪdi, ¦ɪŋˌkɔrpə'reɪɪdi

incorporial
BR ˌɪnkɔː'pɔːrɪəl, ˌɪŋkɔː'pɔːrɪəl
AM ¦ɪnˌkɔr'pɔriəl, ¦ɪŋˌkɔr'pɔriəl

incorrect
BR ˌɪnkə'rɛkt, ˌɪŋkə'rɛkt
AM ¦ɪnkə'rɛk(t), ¦ɪŋkə'rɛk(t)

incorrectly
BR ˌɪnkə'rɛktli, ˌɪŋkə'rɛktli
AM ¦ɪnkə'rɛk(t)li, ¦ɪŋkə'rɛk(t)li

incorrectness
BR ˌɪnkə'rɛk(t)nəs, ˌɪŋkə'rɛk(t)nəs
AM ¦ɪnkə'rɛk(t)nəs, ¦ɪŋkə'rɛk(t)nəs

incorrigibility
BR ɪnˌkɒrɪdʒə'bɪlɪti, ˌɪnkɒrɪdʒə'bɪlɪti, ɪŋˌkɒrɪdʒə'bɪlɪti, ˌɪŋkɒrɪdʒə'bɪlɪti
AM ¦ɪnˌkɔrədʒə'bɪlɪdi, ɪnˌkɔrədʒə'bɪlɪdi, ɪŋˌkɔrədʒə'bɪlɪdi

incorrigible
BR ɪn'kɒrɪdʒəbl, ɪŋ'kɒrɪdʒəbl
AM ¦ɪn'kɔrədʒəbəl, ɪn'kɔrədʒəbəl, ɪŋ'kɔrədʒəbəl

incorrigibleness
BR ɪn'kɒrɪdʒəblnəs, ɪŋ'kɒrɪdʒəblnəs
AM ¦ɪn'kɔrədʒəbəlnəs, ɪn'kɔrədʒəbəlnəs, ɪŋ'kɔrədʒəbəlnəs

incorrigibly
BR ɪn'kɒrɪdʒəbli, ɪŋ'kɒrɪdʒəbli
AM ¦ɪn'kɔrədʒəbli, ɪn'kɔrədʒəbli, ɪŋ'kɔrədʒəbli

incorruptibility
BR ˌɪnkəˌrʌptə'bɪlɪti, ˌɪŋkəˌrʌptə'bɪlɪti
AM ¦ɪnkəˌrəptə'bɪlɪdi, ¦ɪŋkəˌrəptə'bɪlɪdi

incorruptible
BR ˌɪnkə'rʌptɪbl, ˌɪŋkə'rʌptɪbl
AM ¦ɪnkə'rəptəbəl, ¦ɪŋkə'rəptəbəl

incorruptibly
BR ˌɪnkə'rʌptɪbli, ˌɪŋkə'rʌptɪbli
AM ¦ɪnkə'rəptəbli, ¦ɪŋkə'rəptəbli

incorruption
BR ˌɪnkə'rʌpʃn, ˌɪŋkə'rʌpʃn
AM ¦ɪnkə'rəpʃən, ¦ɪŋkə'rəpʃən

incrassate
BR ɪn'kraseɪt, ɪŋ'kraseɪt, -s, -ɪŋ, -ɪd
AM ɪn'kræˌseɪ|t, ɪŋ'kræˌseɪ|t, -ts, -dɪŋ, -dɪd

increasable
BR ɪn'kri:səbl, ɪŋ'kri:səbl
AM ɪn'krisəbəl, ɪŋ'krisəbəl

increase¹
noun
BR 'ɪnkri:s, 'ɪŋkri:s, -ɪz
AM 'ɪn,kris, 'ɪŋ,kris, -ɪz

increase²
verb
BR ɪn'kri:s, ɪŋ'kri:s, -ɪz, -ɪŋ, -t
AM ɪn'kris, ɪŋ'kris, -ɪz, -ɪŋ, -t

increaser
BR ɪn'kri:sə(r), ɪŋ'kri:sə(r), -z
AM ɪn'krisər, ɪŋ'krisər, -z

increasingly
BR ɪn'kri:sɪŋli, ɪŋ'kri:sɪŋli
AM ɪn'krisɪŋli, ɪŋ'krisɪŋli

incredibility
BR ɪn,krɛdɪ'bɪlɪti, ɪŋ,krɛdɪ'bɪlɪti
AM ¦ɪn,krɛdə'bɪlɪdi, ɪn,krɛdə'bɪlɪdi, ¦ɪŋ,krɛdə'bɪlɪdi

incredible
BR ɪn'krɛdɪbl, ɪŋ'krɛdɪbl
AM ɪn'krɛdəbəl, ɪŋ'krɛdəbəl

incredibleness
BR ɪn'krɛdɪblnəs, ɪŋ'krɛdɪblnəs
AM ɪn'krɛdəbəlnəs, ɪŋ'krɛdəbəlnəs

incredibly
BR ɪn'krɛdɪbli, ɪŋ'krɛdɪbli
AM ɪn'krɛdəbli, ɪŋ'krɛdəbli

incredulity
BR ,ɪnkrɪ'dju:lɪti, ,ɪnkrɪ'dʒu:lɪti, ,ɪŋkrɪ'dju:lɪti, ,ɪŋkrɪ'dʒu:lɪti
AM ¦ɪnkrə'd(j)ulədi, ¦ɪŋkrə'd(j)ulədi

incredulous
BR ɪn'krɛdjʊləs, ɪn'krɛdʒʊləs, ɪŋ'krɛdjʊləs, ɪŋ'krɛdʒʊləs
AM ɪn'krɛdʒələs, ɪŋ'krɛdʒələs

incredulously
BR ɪn'krɛdjʊləsli, ɪn'krɛdʒʊləsli, ɪŋ'krɛdjʊləsli, ɪŋ'krɛdʒʊləsli
AM ɪn'krɛdʒələsli, ɪŋ'krɛdʒələsli

incredulousness
BR ɪn'krɛdjʊləsnəs, ɪn'krɛdʒʊləsnəs, ɪŋ'krɛdjʊləsnəs, ɪŋ'krɛdʒʊləsnəs
AM ɪn'krɛdʒələsnəs, ɪŋ'krɛdʒələsnəs

increment
BR 'ɪnkrɪm(ə)nt, 'ɪŋkrɪm(ə)nt, -s
AM 'ɪŋkrəmənt, 'ɪnkrəmənt, -s

incremental
BR ,ɪnkrɪ'mɛntl, ,ɪŋkrɪ'mɛntl
AM ¦ɪŋkrə¦mɛn(t)l, ¦ɪnkrə¦mɛn(t)l

incrementally
BR ,ɪnkrɪ'mɛntļi, ,ɪŋkrɪ'mɛntļi
AM ¦ɪŋkrə¦mɛn(t)ļi, ¦ɪnkrə¦mɛn(t)ļi

incriminate
BR ɪn'krɪmɪneɪt, ɪŋ'krɪmɪneɪt, -s, -ɪŋ, -ɪd
AM ɪn'krɪmə,neɪ|t, ɪŋ'krɪmə,neɪ|t, -ts, -dɪŋ, -dɪd

incriminatingly
BR ɪn'krɪmɪneɪtɪŋli, ɪŋ'krɪmɪneɪtɪŋli
AM ɪn'krɪmə,neɪdɪŋli, ɪŋ'krɪmə,neɪdɪŋli

incrimination
BR ɪn,krɪmɪ'neɪʃn, ɪŋ,krɪmɪ'neɪʃn
AM ɪn,krɪmə'neɪʃən, ɪŋ,krɪmə'neɪʃən

incriminatory
BR ɪn'krɪmɪnət(ə)ri, ɪŋ'krɪmɪnət(ə)ri
AM ɪn'krɪmənə,tɔri, ɪŋ'krɪmənə,tɔri

in-crowd
BR 'ɪnkraʊd, 'ɪŋkraʊd, -z
AM 'ɪn,kraʊd, -z

incrust
BR ɪn'krʌst, ɪŋ'krʌst, -s, -ɪŋ, -ɪd
AM ɪn'krəst, ɪŋ'krəst, -s, -ɪŋ, -əd

incrustation
BR ,ɪnkrʌ'steɪʃn, ,ɪŋkrʌ'steɪʃn, -z
AM ,ɪn,krə'steɪʃən, ,ɪŋ,krə'steɪʃən, -z

incubate
BR 'ɪŋkjʊbeɪt, 'ɪnkjʊbeɪt, -s, -ɪŋ, -ɪd
AM 'ɪnkjə,beɪ|t, 'ɪŋkjə,beɪ|t, -ts, -dɪŋ, -dɪd

incubation
BR ,ɪŋkjʊ'beɪʃn, ,ɪnkjʊ'beɪʃn
AM ,ɪnkjə'beɪʃən, ,ɪŋkjə'beɪʃən

incubational
BR ,ɪŋkjʊ'beɪʃn̩(ə)l, ,ɪŋkjʊ'beɪʃən(ə)l, ,ɪnkjʊ'beɪʃn̩(ə)l, ,ɪnkjʊ'beɪʃən(ə)l
AM ,ɪnkjə'beɪʃ(ə)nəl, ,ɪŋkjə'beɪʃ(ə)nəl

incubative
BR 'ɪŋkjʊbeɪtɪv, 'ɪnkjʊbeɪtɪv
AM 'ɪnkjə,beɪdɪv, 'ɪŋkjə,beɪdɪv

incubator
BR 'ɪŋkjʊbeɪtə(r), 'ɪnkjʊbeɪtə(r), -z
AM 'ɪnkjə,beɪdər, 'ɪŋkjə,beɪdər, -z

incubatory
BR ,ɪŋkjʊ'beɪt(ə)ri, ,ɪnkjʊ'beɪt(ə)ri
AM ɪn'kjubə,tɔri, ɪŋ'kjubətri

incubi
BR 'ɪŋkjʊbʌɪ, 'ɪnkjʊbʌɪ
AM 'ɪŋkjə,baɪ, 'ɪnkjə,baɪ

incubus
BR 'ɪŋkjʊbəs, 'ɪnkjʊbəs, -ɪz
AM 'ɪŋkjəbəs, 'ɪnkjəbəs, -əz

incudes
BR 'ɪŋkjʊdi:z, ɪŋ'kju:di:z, ɪn'kju:di:z
AM ɪn'k(j)u,diz

inculcate
BR 'ɪnk(ʌ)lkeɪt, 'ɪŋk(ʌ)lkeɪt, -s, -ɪŋ, -ɪd
AM ɪn'kəl,keɪ|t, 'ɪnkəl,keɪ|t 'ɪŋkəl,keɪ|t, -ts, -dɪŋ, -dɪd

inculcation
BR ,ɪnk(ʌ)l'keɪʃn, ,ɪŋk(ʌ)l'keɪʃn
AM ,ɪnkəl'keɪʃən, ,ɪŋkəl'keɪʃən

inculcator
BR 'ɪnk(ʌ)lkeɪtə(r), 'ɪŋk(ʌ)lkeɪtə(r), -z
AM ɪn'kəl,keɪdər, 'ɪnkəl,keɪdər 'ɪŋkəl,keɪdər, -z

inculpate
BR 'ɪnkʌlpeɪt, 'ɪŋkʌlpeɪt, -s, -ɪŋ, -ɪd
AM ɪn'kəl,peɪ|t, 'ɪnkəl,peɪ|t, 'ɪŋkəl,peɪ|t, -ts, -dɪŋ, -dɪd

inculpation
BR ,ɪnkʌl'peɪʃn, ,ɪŋkʌl'peɪʃn
AM ,ɪnkəl'peɪʃən, ,ɪŋkəl'peɪʃən

inculpative
BR ɪn'kʌlpətɪv, ɪŋ'kʌlpətɪv
AM ɪn'kəl,peɪdɪv, 'ɪnkəl,peɪdɪv, 'ɪŋkəl,peɪdɪv

inculpatory
BR ɪn'kʌlpət(ə)ri, ɪŋ'kʌlpət(ə)ri
AM ɪn'kəlpə,tɔri, ɪŋ'kəlpə,tɔri

incult
BR ɪn'kʌlt, ɪŋ'kʌlt
AM ɪn'kəlt, ɪŋ'kəlt

inculturation
BR ɪn,kʌltʃə'reɪʃn
AM ɪn,kəltʃə'reɪʃ(ə)n

incumbency
BR ɪn'kʌmbəns|i, ɪŋ'kʌmbəns|i, -ɪz
AM ɪn'kəmbənsi, ɪŋ'kəmbənsi, -z

incumbent
BR ɪn'kʌmbənt, ɪŋ'kʌmbənt, -s
AM ɪn'kəmbənt, ɪŋ'kəmbənt, -s

incunable
BR ɪn'kju:nəbl, ɪŋ'kju:nəbl
AM ɪn'kjunəbəl, ɪŋ'kjunəbəl

incunabula
BR ,ɪnkjʊ'nabjʊlə(*r*), ,ɪŋkjʊ'nabjʊlə(*r*)
AM ,ɪnkjə'næbjələ, ,ɪŋkjə'næbjələ

incunabular
BR ,ɪnkjʊ'nabjʊlə(r), ,ɪŋkjʊ'nabjʊlə(r)
AM ,ɪnkjə'næbjələr, ,ɪŋkjə'næbjələr

incunabulum
BR ,ɪnkjʊ'nabjʊləm, ,ɪŋkjʊ'nabjʊləm
AM ,ɪnkjə'næbjələm, ,ɪŋkjə'næbjələm

incur
BR ɪn'kə:(r), ɪŋ'kə:(r), -z, -ɪŋ, -d
AM ɪn'kər, ɪŋ'kər, -z, -ɪŋ, -d

incurability
BR ɪn,kjʊərə'bɪlɪti, ɪn,kjɔ:rə'bɪlɪti, ɪŋ,kjʊərə'bɪlɪti, ɪŋ,kjɔ:rə'bɪlɪti
AM ¦ɪn,kjʊrə'bɪlɪdi, ən,kjʊrə'bɪlɪdi, ¦ɪŋ,kjʊrə'bɪlɪdi

incurable
BR ɪn'kjʊərəbl, ɪn'kjɔ:rəbl, ɪŋ'kjʊərəbl, ɪŋ'kjɔ:rəbl

AM ɪnˈkjʊrəbəl, ɪŋˈkjʊrəbəl

incurableness
BR ɪnˈkjʊərəblnəs, ɪnˈkjɔːrəblnəs, ɪŋˈkjʊərəblnəs, ɪŋˈkjɔːrəblnəs
AM ɪnˈkjʊrəbəlnəs, ɪŋˈkjʊrəbəlnəs

incurably
BR ɪnˈkjʊərəbli, ɪnˈkjɔːrəbli, ɪŋˈkjʊərəbli, ɪŋˈkjɔːrəbli
AM ɪnˈkjʊrəbli, ɪŋˈkjʊrəbli

incuriosity
BR ɪnˌkjʊərɪˈɒsɪti, ɪnˌkjɔːrɪˈɒsɪti, ɪŋˌkjʊərɪˈɒsɪti, ɪŋˌkjɔːrɪˈɒsɪti, ˌɪnkjʊərɪˈɒsɪti, ˌɪnkjɔːrɪˈɒsɪti, ˌɪŋkjʊərɪˈɒsɪti, ˌɪŋkjɔːrɪˈɒsɪti
AM ¦ɪnˌkjʊriˈɑsədi, ɪnˌkjʊriˈɑsədi, ¦ɪŋˌkjʊriˈɑsədi

incurious
BR ɪnˈkjʊərɪəs, ɪnˈkjɔːrɪəs, ɪŋˈkjʊərɪəs, ɪŋˈkjɔːrɪəs
AM ɪnˈkjʊriəs, ɪnˈkjʊriəs, ɪŋˈkjʊriəs

incuriously
BR ɪnˈkjʊərɪəsli, ɪnˈkjɔːrɪəsli, ɪŋˈkjʊərɪəsli, ɪŋˈkjɔːrɪəsli
AM ɪnˈkjʊriəsli, ɪnˈkjʊriəsli, ɪŋˈkjʊriəsli

incuriousness
BR ɪnˈkjʊərɪəsnəs, ɪnˈkjɔːrɪəsnəs, ɪŋˈkjʊərɪəsnəs, ɪŋˈkjɔːrɪəsnəs
AM ɪnˈkjʊriəsnəs, ɪnˈkjʊriəsnəs, ɪŋˈkjʊriəsnəs

incurrable
BR ɪnˈkəːrəbl, ɪŋˈkəːrəbl
AM ɪnˈkərəbəl, ɪŋˈkərəbəl

incursion
BR ɪnˈkəːʃn, ɪnˈkəːʒn, ɪŋˈkəːʃn, ɪŋˈkəːʒn, -z
AM ɪnˈkərʒən, ɪŋˈkərʒən, -z

incursive
BR ɪnˈkəːsɪv, ɪŋˈkəːsɪv
AM ɪnˈkərsɪv, ɪŋˈkərsɪv

incurvation
BR ˌɪnkəːˈveɪʃn, ˌɪŋkəːˈveɪʃn, -z
AM ˌɪnkərˈveɪʃən, ˌɪŋkərˈveɪʃən, -z

incurve
BR ɪnˈkəːv, ɪŋˈkəːv, -z, -ɪŋ, -d
AM ɪnˈkərv, ɪŋˈkərv, -z, -ɪŋ, -d

incus
BR ˈɪŋkəs
AM ˈɪŋkəs

incuse
BR ɪnˈkjuːz, ɪŋˈkjuːz, -ɪz, -ɪŋ, -d
AM ɪnˈkjuz, ɪŋˈkjuz, -əz, -ɪŋ, -d

indaba
BR ɪnˈdɑːbə(r), -z
AM ɪnˈdɑbə, -z

Indebele
BR ˌɪndəˈbiːli, ˌɪndəˈbeɪli
AM ˌɪndəˈbili

indebted
BR ɪnˈdɛtɪd
AM ɪnˈdɛdəd

indebtedness
BR ɪnˈdɛtɪdnɪs
AM ɪnˈdɛdədnəs

indecency
BR ɪnˈdiːsns|i, -ɪz
AM ɪnˈdisənsi, -z

indecent
BR ɪnˈdiːsnt
AM ɪnˈdisənt

indecently
BR ɪnˈdiːsntli
AM ɪnˈdisn(t)li

indecipherability
BR ˌɪndɪˌsʌɪf(ə)rəˈbɪlɪti
AM ¦ɪndəˌsaɪf(ə)rəˈbɪlɪdi

indecipherable
BR ˌɪndɪˈsʌɪf(ə)rəbl
AM ¦ɪndəˈsaɪf(ə)rəbəl

indecipherably
BR ˌɪndɪˈsʌɪf(ə)rəbli
AM ¦ɪndəˈsaɪf(ə)rəbli

indecision
BR ˌɪndɪˈsɪʒn
AM ˌɪndəˈsɪʒən

indecisive
BR ˌɪndɪˈsʌɪsɪv
AM ˌɪndəˈsaɪsɪv

indecisively
BR ˌɪndɪˈsʌɪsɪvli
AM ˌɪndəˈsaɪsɪvli

indecisiveness
BR ˌɪndɪˈsʌɪsɪvnɪs
AM ˌɪndəˈsaɪsɪvnɪs

indeclinable
BR ˌɪndɪˈklʌɪnəbl
AM ˌɪndəˈklaɪnəbəl

indecorous
BR (ˌ)ɪnˈdɛk(ə)rəs
AM ɪnˈdɛkərəs

indecorously
BR (ˌ)ɪnˈdɛk(ə)rəsli
AM ɪnˈdɛkərəsli

indecorousness
BR (ˌ)ɪnˈdɛk(ə)rəsnəs
AM ɪnˈdɛkərəsnəs

indecorum
BR ˌɪndɪˈkɔːrəm
AM ¦ɪndəˈkɔrəm

indeed
BR ɪnˈdiːd
AM ɪnˈdid

indefatigability
BR ˌɪndɪˌfatɪgəˈbɪlɪti
AM ¦ɪndəˌfædəgəˈbɪlɪdi

indefatigable
BR ˌɪndɪˈfatɪgəbl
AM ¦ɪndəˈfædəgəbəl

indefatigableness
BR ˌɪndɪˈfatɪgəblnəs
AM ¦ɪndəˈfædəgəbəlnəs

indefatigably
BR ˌɪndɪˈfatɪgəbli
AM ¦ɪndəˈfædəgəbli

indefeasibility
BR ˌɪndɪˌfiːzɪˈbɪlɪti
AM ¦ɪndəˌfizəˈbɪlɪdi

indefeasible
BR ˌɪndɪˈfiːzɪbl
AM ¦ɪndəˈfizəbəl

indefeasibly
BR ˌɪndɪˈfiːzɪbli
AM ¦ɪndəˈfizəbli

indefectible
BR ˌɪndɪˈfɛktɪbl
AM ¦ɪndəˈfɛktəbəl

indefensibility
BR ˌɪndɪˌfɛnsɪˈbɪlɪti
AM ¦ɪndəˌfɛnsəˈbɪlɪdi

indefensible
BR ˌɪndɪˈfɛnsɪbl
AM ¦ɪndəˈfɛnsəbəl

indefensibly
BR ˌɪndɪˈfɛnsɪbli
AM ¦ɪndəˈfɛnsəbli

indefinable
BR ˌɪndɪˈfʌɪnəbl
AM ¦ɪndəˈfaɪnəbəl

indefinably
BR ˌɪndɪˈfʌɪnəbli
AM ¦ɪndəˈfaɪnəbli

indefinite
BR (ˌ)ɪnˈdɛf(ɪ)nɪt, (ˌ)ɪnˈdɛfn̩ɪt
AM ɪnˈdɛf(ə)nət

indefinitely
BR (ˌ)ɪnˌdɛf(ɪ)nɪtli, (ˌ)ɪnˈdɛfn̩ɪtli
AM ɪnˈdɛf(ə)nətli

indefiniteness
BR (ˌ)ɪnˈdɛf(ɪ)nɪtnəs, (ˌ)ɪnˈdɛfn̩ɪtnɪs
AM ɪnˈdɛf(ə)nətnəs

indehiscence
BR ˌɪndɪˈhɪsns
AM ¦ɪndəˈhɪsəns, ¦ɪndiˈhɪsəns

indehiscent
BR ˌɪndɪˈhɪsnt
AM ¦ɪndəˈhɪsənt, ¦ɪndiˈhɪsənt

indelibility
BR ɪnˌdɛlɪˈbɪlɪti
AM ɪnˌdɛləˈbɪlɪdi

indelible
BR (ˌ)ɪnˈdɛlɪbl
AM ɪnˈdɛləbəl

indelibly
BR (ˌ)ɪnˈdɛlɪbli
AM ɪnˈdɛləbli

indelicacy
BR (ˌ)ɪnˈdɛlɪkəs|i, -ɪz
AM ɪnˈdɛləkəsi, -z

indelicate
BR (ˌ)ɪnˈdɛlɪkət
AM ɪnˈdɛləkət

indelicately
BR (ˌ)ɪnˈdɛlɪkətli
AM ɪnˈdɛləkətli

indelicateness
BR (ˌ)ɪnˈdɛlɪkətnəs
AM ɪnˈdɛləkətnəs

indeminify
BR ɪnˈdɛmnɪfʌɪ, -z, -ɪŋ, -d
AM ɪnˈdɛmnəˌfaɪ, -z, -ɪŋ, -d

indemnification
BR ɪnˌdɛmnɪfɪˈkeɪʃn
AM ɪnˌdɛmnəfəˈkeɪʃən

indemnifier
BR ɪnˈdɛmnɪfʌɪə(r), -z
AM ɪnˈdɛmnəˌfaɪər, -z

indemnity
BR ɪnˈdɛmnɪti
AM ɪnˈdɛmnədi, -z

indemonstrable
BR ˌɪndɪˈmɒnstrəbl, ɪnˈdɛmənstrəbl
AM ɪndəˈmɑnstrəbəl, ɪnˈdɛmənstrəbəl

indene
BR ˈɪndiːn, -z
AM ˈɪnˌdin, -z

indent¹
noun
BR ˈɪndɛnt, -s
AM ˈɪnˌdɛnt, -s

indent²
verb
BR ɪnˈdɛnt, -s, -ɪŋ, -ɪd
AM ɪnˈdɛn|t, -ts, -(t)ɪŋ, -(t)əd

indentation
BR ˌɪndɛnˈteɪʃn, -z
AM ˌɪnˌdɛnˈteɪʃən, -z

indenter
BR ɪnˈdɛntə(r), -z
AM ɪnˈdɛn(t)ər, -z

indentor
BR ɪnˈdɛntə(r), -z
AM ɪnˈdɛn(t)ər, -z

indenture
BR ɪnˈdɛntʃ|ə(r), -əz, -(ə)rɪŋ, -əd
AM ɪnˈdɛn(t)ʃər, -z, -ɪŋ, -d

indentureship
BR ɪn'dɛntʃəʃɪp, -s
AM ɨn'dɛn(t)ʃərˌʃɪp, -s

independence
BR ˌɪndɪ'pɛnd(ə)ns
AM ˌɪndə'pɛndəns

independency
BR ˌɪndɪ'pɛnd(ə)ns|i, -ɪz
AM ˌɪndə'pɛndnsi, -z

independent
BR ˌɪndɪ'pɛnd(ə)nt, -s
AM ˌɪndə'pɛndənt, -s

independently
BR ˌɪndɪ'pɛnd(ə)ntli
AM ˌɪndə'pɛndən(t)li

in-depth
BR ˌɪn'dɛpθ
AM ¦ɪn'dɛpθ

indescribability
BR ˌɪndɪˌskrʌɪbə'bɪlɨti
AM ¦ɪndəˌskraɪbə'bɪlɨdi

indescribable
BR ˌɪndɪ'skrʌɪbəbl
AM ¦ɪndə'skraɪbəbəl

indescribably
BR ˌɪndɪ'skrʌɪbəbli
AM ¦ɪndə'skraɪbəbli

indestructibility
BR ˌɪndɪˌstrʌktɪ'bɪlɨti
AM ¦ɪndəˌstrəktə'bɪlɨdi

indestructible
BR ˌɪndɪ'strʌktɨbl
AM ¦ɪndə'strəktəbəl

indestructibly
BR ˌɪndɪ'strʌktɨbli
AM ¦ɪndə'strəktəbli

indeterminable
BR ˌɪndɪ'tə:mɨnəbl
AM ¦ɪndə'tərmənəbəl

indeterminably
BR ˌɪndɪ'tə:mənɨbli
AM ¦ɪndə'tərmənəbli

indeterminacy
BR ˌɪndɪ'tə:mɨnəsi
AM ¦ɪndə'tərmənəsi

indeterminate
BR ˌɪndɪ'tə:mɨnət
AM ¦ɪndə'tərmənət

indeterminately
BR ˌɪndɪ'tə:mɨnətli
AM ¦ɪndə'tərmənətli

indeterminateness
BR ˌɪndɪ'tə:mɨnətnəs
AM ¦ɪndə'tərmənətnəs

indetermination
BR ˌɪndɪˌtə:mɪ'neɪʃn
AM ¦ɪndəˌtərmə'neɪʃən

indeterminism
BR ˌɪndɪ'tə:mɨnɪz(ə)m
AM ¦ɪndə'tərməˌnɪzəm

indeterminist
BR ˌɪndɪ'tə:mɨnɪst, -s
AM ¦ɪndə'tərmənəst, -s

indeterministic
BR ˌɪndɪˌtə:mɪ'nɪstɪk
AM ˌɪndəˌtərmə'nɪstɪk

index
BR 'ɪndɛks, -ɨz, -ɪŋ, -t
AM 'ɪnˌdɛks, -əz, -ɪŋ, -t

indexation
BR ˌɪndɛk'seɪʃn
AM ˌɪnˌdɛk'seɪʃən

indexer
BR 'ɪndɛksə(r), -z
AM 'ɪnˌdɛksər, -z

indexible
BR 'ɪndɛksɨbl, ɪn'dɛksɨbl
AM 'ɪnˌdɛksəbəl

indexical
BR ɪn'dɛksɪkl
AM 'ɪnˌdɛksəkəl

indexless
BR 'ɪndɛksləs
AM 'ɪnˌdɛksləs

India
BR 'ɪndɪə(r)
AM 'ɪndiə

Indiaman
BR 'ɪndɪəman
AM 'ɪndiəˌmæn

Indiamen
BR 'ɪndɪəmɛn
AM 'ɪndiəˌmɛn

Indian
BR 'ɪndɪən, -z
AM 'ɪndiən, -z

Indiana
BR ˌɪndɪ'anə(r)
AM ˌɪndi'ænə

Indianapolis
BR ˌɪndɪə'napəlɪs, ˌɪndɪə'naplɪs
AM ˌɪndiə'næp(ə)ləs

Indic
BR 'ɪndɪk, -s
AM 'ɪndɪk, -s

indicate
BR 'ɪndɨkeɪt, -s, -ɪŋ, -ɨd
AM 'ɪndəˌkeɪ|t, -ts, -dɪŋ, -dɨd

indication
BR ˌɪndɪ'keɪʃn, -z
AM ˌɪndə'keɪʃən, -z

indicative
BR ɪn'dɪkətɪv, -z
AM ɨn'dɪkədɪv, -z

indicatively
BR ɪn'dɪkətɪvli
AM ɨn'dɪkədəvli

indicator
BR 'ɪndɨkeɪtə(r), -z
AM 'ɪndəˌkeɪdər, -z

indicatory
BR ɪn'dɪkət(ə)ri, 'ɪndɨkeɪt(ə)ri
AM ɨn'dɪkəˌtɔri

indices
BR 'ɪndɨsi:z
AM 'ɪndəˌsiz

indicia
BR ɪn'dɪsɪə(r), ɪn'dɪʃɪə(r)
AM ɨn'dɪʃ(i)ə

indicial
BR ɪn'dɪʃ(ə)l
AM ɨn'dɪʃ(i)əl

indicium
BR ɪn'dɪsɪəm, ɪn'dɪʃɪəm
AM ɨn'dɪʃ(i)əm

indict
BR ɪn'dʌɪt, -s, -ɪŋ, -ɨd
AM ɨn'daɪ|t, -ts, -dɪŋ, -dɨd

indictable
BR ɪn'dʌɪtəbl
AM ɨn'daɪdəbəl

indictee
BR ˌɪndʌɪ'ti:, -z
AM ɨnˌdaɪ'ti, -z

indicter
BR ɪn'dʌɪtə(r), -z
AM ɨn'daɪdər, -z

indiction
BR ɪn'dɪkʃn, -z
AM ɨn'dɪkʃən, -z

indictment
BR ɪn'dʌɪtm(ə)nt, -s
AM ɨn'daɪtmənt, -s

indie
BR 'ɪnd|i, -ɪz
AM 'ɪndi, -z

Indies
BR 'ɪndɪz
AM 'ɪndiz

indifference
BR ɪn'dɪf(ə)rəns, ɪn'dɪf(ə)rn̩s
AM ɨn'dɪf(ə)rəns

indifferent
BR ɪn'dɪf(ə)rənt, ɪn'dɪf(ə)rn̩t
AM ɨn'dɪf(ə)rənt, ɨn'dɪfərnt

indifferentism
BR ɪn'dɪf(ə)rəntɪz(ə)m, ɪn'dɪf(ə)rn̩tɪz(ə)m
AM ɨn'dɪfərn̩ˌtɪzəm, ɨn'dɪf(ə)rənˌtɪzəm

indifferentist
BR ɪn'dɪf(ə)rəntɪst, ɪn'dɪf(ə)rn̩tɪst, -s
AM ɨn'dɪfərn̩təst, ɨn'dɪf(ə)rən(t)əst, -s

indifferently
BR ɪn'dɪf(ə)rəntli, ɪn'dɪf(ə)rn̩tli
AM ɨn'dɪfərn̩tli, ɨn'dɪf(ə)rən(t)li

indigence
BR 'ɪndɪdʒ(ə)ns
AM 'ɪndədʒəns

indigene
BR 'ɪndɪdʒi:n, -z
AM 'ɪndəˌdʒin, -z

indigenisation
BR ɪnˌdɪdʒɨnʌɪ'zeɪʃn, ɪnˌdɪdʒn̩ʌɪ'zeɪʃn
AM ɨnˌdɪdʒənə'zeɪʃən, ɨnˌdɪdʒəˌnaɪ'zeɪʃən

indigenise
BR ɪn'dɪdʒɨnʌɪz, ɪn'dɪdʒn̩ʌɪz, -ɨz, -ɪŋ, -d
AM ɨn'dɪdʒəˌnaɪz, -ɨz, -ɪŋ, -d

indigenization
BR ɪnˌdɪdʒɨnʌɪ'zeɪʃn, ɪnˌdɪdʒn̩ʌɪ'zeɪʃn
AM ɨnˌdɪdʒənə'zeɪʃən, ɨnˌdɪdʒəˌnaɪ'zeɪʃən

indigenize
BR ɪn'dɪdʒɨnʌɪz, ɪn'dɪdʒn̩ʌɪz, -ɨz, -ɪŋ, -d
AM ɨn'dɪdʒəˌnaɪz, -ɨz, -ɪŋ, -d

indigenous
BR ɪn'dɪdʒɨnəs, ɪn'dɪdʒn̩əs
AM ɨn'dɪdʒənəs

indigenously
BR ɪn'dɪdʒɨnəsli, ɪn'dɪdʒn̩əsli
AM ɨn'dɪdʒənəsli

indigenousness
BR ɪn'dɪdʒɨnəsnəs, ɪn'dɪdʒn̩əsnəs
AM ɨn'dɪdʒənəsnəs

indigent
BR 'ɪndɪdʒ(ə)nt
AM 'ɪndədʒənt

indigently
BR 'ɪndɪdʒ(ə)ntli
AM 'ɪndədʒən(t)li

indigested
BR ˌɪndɪ'dʒɛstɨd, ˌɪndʌɪ'dʒɛstɨd
AM ¦ɪndə'dʒɛstəd

indigestibility
BR ˌɪndɪˌdʒɛstɪ'bɪlɨti, ˌɪndʌɪˌdʒɛstɪ'bɪlɨti
AM ¦ɪndəˌdʒɛstə'bɪlɨdi

indigestible
BR ˌɪndɪ'dʒɛstɨbl, ˌɪndʌɪ'dʒɛstɨbl
AM ¦ɪndə'dʒɛstəbəl

indigestibly
BR ˌɪndɪ'dʒɛstɨbli, ˌɪndʌɪ'dʒɛstɨbli
AM ¦ɪndə'dʒɛstəbli

indigestion
BR ˌɪndɪ'dʒɛstʃ(ə)n
AM ¦ɪndə'dʒɛstʃən, ¦ɪnˌdaɪ'dʒɛstʃən

indigestive
BR ˌɪndɪ'dʒɛstɪv
AM ¦ɪndə'dʒɛstɪv

indignant
BR ɪn'dɪgnənt
AM ɨn'dɪgnənt

indignantly
BR ɪn'dɪgnəntli
AM ɨn'dɪgnən(t)li

indignation
BR ˌɪndɪg'neɪʃn
AM ˌɪndɪg'neɪʃən

indignity
BR ɪn'dɪgnɪt|i, -ɪz
AM ɨn'dɪgnɨdi, -z

indigo
BR ˈɪndᵻɡəʊ
AM ˈɪndəˌɡoʊ

indigotic
BR ˌɪndᵻˈɡɒtɪk
AM ˌɪndəˈɡɑdɪk

Indira
BR ˈɪndɪrə(r), ɪnˈdɪərə(r)
AM ɪnˈdirə

indirect
BR ˌɪndᵻˈrɛkt, ˌɪndʌɪˈrɛkt
AM ˌɪndəˈrɛk(t)

indirection
BR ˌɪndᵻˈrɛkʃn, ˌɪndʌɪˈrɛkʃn
AM ˌɪndəˈrɛkʃən

indirectly
BR ˌɪndᵻˈrɛktli, ˌɪndʌɪˈrɛktli
AM ˌɪndəˈrɛk(t)li

indirectness
BR ˌɪndᵻˈrɛk(t)nəs, ˌɪndʌɪˈrɛk(t)nəs
AM ˌɪndəˈrɛktnəs

indiscernibility
BR ˌɪndᵻˌsəːnᵻˈbɪlᵻti
AM ˈɪndəˌsərnəˈbɪlᵻdi

indiscernible
BR ˌɪndᵻˈsəːnᵻbl
AM ˈɪndəˈsərnəbəl

indiscernibly
BR ˌɪndᵻˈsəːnᵻbli
AM ˈɪndəˈsərnəbli

indiscipline
BR (ˌ)ɪnˈdɪsɪplɪn
AM ᵻnˈdɪsəplən

indiscreet
BR ˌɪndᵻˈskriːt
AM ˈɪndəˈskrit

indiscreetly
BR ˌɪndᵻˈskriːtli
AM ˈɪndəˈskritli

indiscreetness
BR ˌɪndᵻˈskriːtnᵻs
AM ˈɪndəˈskritnᵻs

indiscrete
BR ˌɪndᵻˈskriːt
AM ˈɪndəˈskrit

indiscretion
BR ˌɪndᵻˈskrɛʃn, -z
AM ˈɪndəˌskrɛʃən, -z

indiscriminate
BR ˌɪndᵻˈskrɪmᵻnət
AM ˈɪndəˈskrɪm(ə)nət

indiscriminately
BR ˌɪndᵻˈskrɪmᵻnətli
AM ˈɪndəˈskrɪm(ə)nətli

indiscriminateness
BR ˌɪndᵻˈskrɪmᵻnətnəs
AM ˈɪndəˈskrɪm(ə)nətnəs

indiscrimination
BR ˌɪndᵻˌskrɪmᵻˈneɪʃn, -z
AM ˈɪndəˌskrɪməˈneɪʃən, -z

indiscriminative
BR ˌɪndᵻˈskrɪmᵻnətɪv
AM ˈɪndəˈskrɪməˌneɪdɪv

indispensability
BR ˌɪndᵻˌspɛnsəˈbɪlᵻti
AM ˈɪndəˌspɛnsəˈbɪlᵻdi

indispensable
BR ˌɪndᵻˈspɛnsəbl
AM ˈɪndəˈspɛnsəbəl

indispensableness
BR ˌɪndᵻˈspɛnsəblnəs
AM ˈɪndəˈspɛnsəbəlnəs

indispensably
BR ˌɪndᵻˈspɛnsəbli
AM ˈɪndəˈspɛnsəbli

indispose
BR ˌɪndᵻˈspəʊz, -ᵻz, -ɪŋ, -d
AM ˈɪndəˈspoʊz, -əz, -ɪŋ, -d

indisposition
BR ˌɪndɪspəˈzɪʃn, ɪnˌdɪspəˈzɪʃn, -z
AM ˈɪnˌdɪspəˈzɪʃən, ᵻnˌdɪspəˈzɪʃən, -z

indisputability
BR ˌɪndᵻˌspjuːtəˈbɪlᵻti
AM ˈɪndəˌspjudəˈbɪlᵻdi, ᵻndəˌspjudəˈbɪlᵻdi

indisputable
BR ˌɪndᵻˈspjuːtəbl
AM ˈɪndəˈspjudəbəl, ᵻndəˈspjudəbəl

indisputableness
BR ˌɪndᵻˈspjuːtəblnəs
AM ˈɪndəˈspjudəbəlnəs, ᵻndəˈspjudəbəlnəs

indisputably
BR ˌɪndᵻˈspjuːtəbli
AM ˈɪndəˈspjudəbli, ᵻndəˈspjudəbli

indissolubilist
BR ˌɪndᵻˈsɒljᵿbᵻlɪst, ˌɪndᵻˈsɒljᵿblɪst, -s
AM ˈɪndəˈsɑljəˌbɪlɪst, ˈᵻndəˈsɑljəˌbɪlɪst, -s

indissolubility
BR ˌɪndᵻˌsɒljᵿˈbɪlᵻti
AM ˈɪndəˌsɑljəˈbɪlᵻdi, ᵻndəˌsɑljəˈbɪlᵻdi

indissoluble
BR ˌɪndᵻˈsɒljᵿbl
AM ˈɪndəˈsɑljəbəl, ᵻndəˈsɑljəbəl

indissolubly
BR ˌɪndᵻˈsɒljᵿbli
AM ˈɪndəˈsɑljəbli, ᵻndəˈsɑljəbli

indistinct
BR ˌɪndᵻˈstɪŋ(k)t
AM ˈɪndəˈstɪŋ(k)t, ˈɪndəˈstɪŋk(t)

indistinctive
BR ˌɪndᵻˈstɪŋ(k)tɪv
AM ˈɪndəˈstɪŋ(k)tɪv

indistinctively
BR ˌɪndᵻˈstɪŋ(k)tᵻvli
AM ˈɪndəˈstɪŋ(k)tᵻvli

indistinctiveness
BR ˌɪndᵻˈstɪŋ(k)tᵻvnᵻs
AM ˈɪndəˈstɪŋ(k)tɪvnəs

indistinctly
BR ˌɪndᵻˈstɪŋ(k)tli
AM ˈɪndəˈstɪŋ(k)tli, ˈˌɪndəˈstɪŋkli

indistinctness
BR ˌɪndᵻˈstɪŋ(k)tnᵻs, ˌɪndᵻˈstɪŋk(t)nᵻs
AM ˈɪndəˈstɪŋ(k)tnəs, ˈɪndəˈstɪŋk(t)nəs

indistinguishable
BR ˌɪndᵻˈstɪŋɡwᵻʃəbl
AM ˈɪndəˈstɪŋɡwəʃəbəl

indistinguishableness
BR ˌɪndᵻˈstɪŋɡwᵻʃəblnəs
AM ˈɪndəˈstɪŋɡwəʃəbəlnəs

indistinguishably
BR ˌɪndᵻˈstɪŋɡwᵻʃəbli
AM ˈɪndəˈstɪŋɡwəʃəbli

indite
BR ɪnˈdʌɪt, -s, -ɪŋ, -ᵻd
AM ᵻnˈdaɪ|t, -ts, -dɪŋ, -dᵻd

indium
BR ˈɪndɪəm
AM ˈɪndiəm

indivertible
BR ˌɪndʌɪˈvəːtᵻbl, ˌɪndᵻˈvəːtᵻbl
AM ˈɪndəˈvərdəbəl, ˈɪnˌdaɪˈvərdəbəl

indivertibly
BR ˌɪndʌɪˈvəːtᵻbli, ˌɪndᵻˈvəːtᵻbli
AM ˈɪndəˈvərdəbli, ˈɪnˌdaɪˈvərdəbli

individual
BR ˌɪndᵻˈvɪdʒʊəl, ˌɪndᵻˈvɪdʒ(ᵿ)l, ˌɪndᵻˈvɪdjʊəl, ˌɪndᵻˈvɪdjᵿl, -z
AM ˈɪndəˈvɪdʒ(ə)wəl, ˈɪndəˈvɪdʒəl, -z

individualisation
BR ˌɪndᵻˌvɪdʒʊəlʌɪˈzeɪʃn, ˌɪndᵻˌvɪdʒᵿlʌɪˈzeɪʃn, ˌɪndᵻˌvɪdʒḷʌɪˈzeɪʃn, ˌɪndᵻˌvɪdjʊəlʌɪˈzeɪʃn, ˌɪndᵻˌvɪdjᵿlʌɪˈzeɪʃn, -z
AM ˈɪndəˌvɪdʒ(ə)wəˌlaɪˈzeɪʃən, ˈɪndəˌvɪdʒəˌlaɪˈzeɪʃən, ˈɪndəˌvɪdʒ(ə)wələˈzeɪʃən, ˈɪndəˌvɪdʒələˈzeɪʃən, -z

individualise
BR ˌɪndᵻˈvɪdʒʊəlʌɪz, ɪndᵻˈvɪdʒᵿlʌɪz, ɪndᵻˈvɪdʒḷʌɪz, ˌɪndᵻˈvɪdjʊəlʌɪz, ɪndᵻˈvɪdjᵿlʌɪz, -ᵻz, -ɪŋ, -d
AM ˌɪndəˈvɪdʒ(ə)wəˌlaɪz, ˌɪndəˈvɪdʒəˌlaɪz, -ᵻz, -ɪŋ, -d

individualism
BR ˌɪndᵻˈvɪdʒʊəlɪz(ə)m, ˌɪndᵻˈvɪdʒᵿlɪz(ə)m, ˌɪndᵻˈvɪdʒḷɪz(ə)m, ˌɪndᵻˈvɪdjʊəlɪz(ə)m, ˌɪndᵻˈvɪdjᵿlɪz(ə)m
AM ˌɪndəˈvɪdʒ(ə)wəˌlɪzəm, ˌɪndəˈvɪdʒəˌlɪzəm

individualist
BR ˌɪndᵻˈvɪdʒʊəlɪst, ˌɪndᵻˈvɪdʒᵿlɪst, ˌɪndᵻˈvɪdʒḷɪst, ˌɪndᵻˈvɪdjʊəlɪst, ˌɪndᵻˈvɪdjᵿlɪst, -s
AM ˌɪndəˈvɪdʒ(ə)wələst, ˌɪndəˈvɪdʒələst, -s

individualistic
BR ˌɪndᵻˌvɪdʒʊəˈlɪstɪk, ˌɪndᵻˌvɪdʒᵿˈlɪstɪk, ˌɪndᵻˌvɪdʒḷˈɪstɪk, ˌɪndᵻˌvɪdjʊəˈlɪstɪk, ˌɪndᵻˌvɪdjᵿˈlɪstɪk
AM ˌɪndəˌvɪdʒ(ə)wəˈlɪstɪk, ˌɪndəˌvɪdʒəˈlɪstɪk

individualistically
BR ˌɪndᵻˌvɪdʒʊəˈlɪstɪkli, ˌɪndᵻˌvɪdʒᵿˈlɪstɪkli, ˌɪndᵻˌvɪdʒḷˈɪstɪkli, ˌɪndᵻˌvɪdjʊəˈlɪstɪkli, ˌɪndᵻˌvɪdjᵿˈlɪstɪkli
AM ˈɪndəˌvɪdʒ(ə)wəˈlɪstək(ə)li, ˈɪndəˌvɪdʒəˈlɪstək(ə)li

individuality
BR ˌɪndᵻˌvɪdʒʊˈalᵻti, ˌɪndᵻˌvɪdjʊˈalᵻti
AM ˌɪndəˌvɪdʒəˈwælədi

individualization
BR ˌɪndᵻˌvɪdʒʊəlʌɪˈzeɪʃn, ˌɪndᵻˌvɪdʒᵿlʌɪˈzeɪʃn, ˌɪndᵻˌvɪdʒḷʌɪˈzeɪʃn, ˌɪndᵻˌvɪdjʊəlʌɪˈzeɪʃn, ˌɪndᵻˌvɪdjᵿlʌɪˈzeɪʃn, -z
AM ˈɪndəˌvɪdʒ(ə)wəˌlaɪˈzeɪʃən, ˈɪndəˌvɪdʒəˌlaɪˈzeɪʃən, ˈɪndəˌvɪdʒ(ə)wələˈzeɪʃən, ˈɪndəˌvɪdʒələˈzeɪʃən, -z

individualize
BR ˌɪndᵻˈvɪdʒʊəlʌɪz, ɪndᵻˈvɪdʒᵿlʌɪz, ɪndᵻˈvɪdʒḷʌɪz, ˌɪndᵻˈvɪdjʊəlʌɪz, ɪndᵻˈvɪdjᵿlʌɪz, -ᵻz, -ɪŋ, -d
AM ˌɪndəˈvɪdʒ(ə)wəˌlaɪz, ˌɪndəˈvɪdʒəˌlaɪz, -ᵻz, -ɪŋ, -d

individually
BR ˌɪndɪˈvɪdʒʊəli, ˌɪndɪˈvɪdʒᵾli, ˌɪndɪˈvɪdʒl̩i, ˌɪndɪˈvɪdjʊəli, ˌɪndɪˈvɪdjᵾli
AM ¦ɪndəˈvɪdʒ(ə)wəli, ¦ɪndəˈvɪdʒəli

individuate
BR ˌɪndɪˈvɪdʒʊeɪt, ˌɪndɪˈvɪdjʊeɪt, -s, -ɪŋ, -ɨd
AM ¦ɪndəˈvɪdʒəˌweɪ|t, -ts, -dɪŋ, -dɨd

individuation
BR ˌɪndɪˌvɪdʒʊˈeɪʃn, ˌɪndɪˌvɪdjʊˈeɪʃn, -z
AM ¦ɪndəˌvɪdʒəˈweɪʃən, -z

indivisibility
BR ˌɪndɪˌvɪzɪˈbɪlɨti
AM ¦ɪndəˌvɪzəˈbɪlɨdi

indivisible
BR ˌɪndɪˈvɪzɪbl
AM ¦ɪndəˈvɪzəbəl

indivisibly
BR ˌɪndɪˈvɪzɪbli
AM ¦ɪndəˈvɪzəbli

Indo-Aryan
BR ˌɪndəʊˈɛːrɪən, ˌɪndəʊˈɑːrɪən, ˌɪndəʊˈarɪən, -z
AM ˌɪndoʊˈɛriən, -z

Indo-China
BR ˌɪndəʊˈtʃʌɪnə(r)
AM ˌɪndoʊˈtʃaɪnə

Indo-Chinese
BR ˌɪndəʊˌtʃʌɪˈniːz
AM ˌɪndoʊˌtʃaɪˈniz

indocile
BR (ˌ)ɪnˈdəʊsʌɪl
AM ɪnˈdɑsəl

indocility
BR ˌɪndəˈsɪlɨti
AM ¦ɪnˌdɑˈsɪlɨdi, ¦ɪndəˈsɪlɨdi

indoctrinate
BR ɪnˈdɒktrɪneɪt, -s, -ɪŋ, -ɨd
AM ɪnˈdɑktrəˌneɪ|t, -ts, -dɪŋ, -dɨd

indoctrination
BR ɪnˌdɒktrɪˈneɪʃn
AM ɪnˌdɑktrəˈneɪʃən

indoctrinator
BR ɪnˈdɒktrɪneɪtə(r), -z
AM ɪnˈdɑktrəˌneɪdər, -z

Indo-European
BR ˌɪndəʊˌjʊərəˈpiːən, ˌɪndəʊˌjɔːrəˈpiːən, -z
AM ˌɪndoˌjurəˈpiən, ˌɪndoʊˌjʊrəˈpiən, -z

Indo-Germanic
BR ˌɪndəʊˌdʒəːˈmanɪk, ˌɪndəʊdʒəˈmanɪk, -s
AM ˌɪndoʊdʒərˈmænɪk, -s

Indo-Iranian
BR ˌɪndəʊɪˌreɪnɪən, -z
AM ˌɪndoʊəˈreɪniən, -z

indole
BR ˈɪndəʊl, -z
AM ˈɪnˌdoʊl, -z

indoleacetic acid
BR ˌɪndəʊləˌsiːtɪk ˈasɪd, ˌɪndəʊləˌsɛtɪk +, -z
AM ɪnˌdoʊliəˌsɛdɪk ˈæsəd, -z

indolence
BR ˈɪndələns, ˈɪndəl̩ns, ˈɪndl̩(ə)ns
AM ˈɪndələns

indolent
BR ˈɪndələnt, ˈɪndəl̩nt, ˈɪndl̩(ə)nt
AM ˈɪndələnt

indolently
BR ˈɪndələntli, ˈɪndəl̩ntli, ˈɪndl̩(ə)ntli
AM ˈɪndələn(t)li

Indologist
BR ɪnˈdɒlədʒɪst, -s
AM ɪnˈdɑlədʒəst, -s

Indology
BR ɪnˈdɒlədʒi
AM ɪnˈdɑlədʒi

indomitability
BR ɪnˌdɒmɪtəˈbɪlɨti
AM ɪnˌdɑmədəˈbɪlɨdi

indomitable
BR ɪnˈdɒmɪtəbl
AM ɪnˈdɑmədəbəl

indomitableness
BR ɪnˈdɒmɪtəblnəs
AM ɪnˈdɑmədəbəlnəs

indomitably
BR ɪnˈdɒmɪtəbli
AM ɪnˈdɑmədəbəli

Indonesia
BR ˌɪndəˈniːzɪə(r), ˌɪndəˈniːʒə(r)
AM ˌɪndəˈniʒə, ˌɪndəˈniʃə, ˌɪndoʊˈniʒə, ˌɪndoʊˈniʃə

Indonesian
BR ˌɪndəˈniːzɪən, ˌɪndəˈniːʒn, -z
AM ˌɪndəˈniʒən, ˌɪndəˈniʃən, ˌɪndəˈniziən, ˌɪndoʊˈniʒən, ˌɪndoʊˈniʃən, ˌɪndoʊˈniziən, -z

indoor
BR ˌɪnˈdɔː(r)
AM ˈɪnˌdɔ(ə)r

indoors
BR ˌɪnˈdɔːz
AM ˌɪnˈdɔ(ə)rz, ɪnˈdɔ(ə)rz

Indo-Pacific
BR ˌɪndəʊpəˈsɪfɪk
AM ˌɪndoʊpəˈsɪfɪk

Indore
BR (ˌ)ɪnˈdɔː(r)
AM ɪnˈdɔ(ə)r

indorse
BR ɪnˈdɔːs, -ɪz, -ɪŋ, -t
AM ɪnˈdɔ(ə)rs, -əz, -ɪŋ, -t

indorsement
BR ɪnˈdɔːsm(ə)nt, -s
AM ɪnˈdɔrsmənt, -s

Indra
BR ˈɪndrə(*r*)
AM ˈɪndrə

indraft
BR ˈɪndrɑːft, ˈɪndraft, -s
AM ˈɪnˌdræft, -s

indraught
BR ˈɪndrɑːft, ˈɪndraft, -s
AM ˈɪnˌdræft, -s

indrawn
BR ˌɪnˈdrɔːn
AM ˈɪnˌdrɔn, ˈɪnˌdrɑn

indri
BR ˈɪndr|i, -ɪz
AM ˈɪndri, -z

indubitable
BR ɪnˈdjuːbɪtəbl, ɪnˈdʒuːbɪtəbl
AM ɪnˈd(j)ubədəbəl

indubitably
BR ɪnˈdjuːbɪtəbli, ɪnˈdʒuːbɪtəbli
AM ɪnˈd(j)ubədəbli

induce
BR ɪnˈdjuːs, ɪnˈdʒuːs, -ɪz, -ɪŋ, -t
AM ənˈd(j)us, ɪnˈd(j)us, -əz, -ɪŋ, -t

inducement
BR ɪnˈdjuːsm(ə)nt, ɪnˈdʒuːsm(ə)nt, -s
AM ɪnˈd(j)usmənt, ɪnˈd(j)usmənt, -s

inducer
BR ɪnˈdjuːsə(r), ɪnˈdʒuːsə(r), -z
AM ɪnˈd(j)usər, ɪnˈd(j)usər, -z

inducible
BR ɪnˈdjuːsɪbl, ɪnˈdʒuːsɪbl
AM ɪnˈd(j)usəbəl, ɪnˈd(j)usəbəl

induct
BR ɪnˈdʌkt, -s, -ɪŋ, -ɨd
AM ɪnˈdək|(t), -(t)s, -tɪŋ, -təd

inductance
BR ɪnˈdʌkt(ə)ns, -ɪz
AM ɪnˈdəktns, -əz

inductee
BR ˌɪndʌkˈtiː, -z
AM ɪnˌdəkˈti, -z

induction
BR ɪnˈdʌkʃn, -z
AM ɪnˈdəkʃən, -z

inductive
BR ɪnˈdʌktɪv
AM ɪnˈdəktɪv

inductively
BR ɪnˈdʌktɪvli
AM ɪnˈdəktəvli

inductiveness
BR ɪnˈdʌktɪvnɪs
AM ɪnˈdəktɪvnɪs

inductor
BR ɪnˈdʌktə(r), -z
AM ɪnˈdəktər, -z

indue
BR ɪnˈdjuː, ɪnˈdʒuː, -z, -ɪŋ, -d
AM ɪnˈd(j)u, -z, -ɪŋ, -d

indulge
BR ɪnˈdʌldʒ, -ɪz, -ɪŋ, -d
AM ɪnˈdəldʒ, -əz, -ɪŋ, -t

indulgence
BR ɪnˈdʌldʒ(ə)ns, -ɪz, -t
AM ɪnˈdəldʒəns, -əz, -t

indulgent
BR ɪnˈdʌldʒ(ə)nt
AM ɪnˈdəldʒənt

indulgently
BR ɪnˈdʌldʒ(ə)ntli
AM ɪnˈdəldʒən(t)li

indulger
BR ɪnˈdʌldʒə(r), -z
AM ɪnˈdəldʒər, -z

indult
BR ɪnˈdʌlt, -s
AM ɪnˈdəlt, -s

indumenta
BR ˌɪndjᵾˈmɛntə(*r*), ˌɪndʒᵾˈmɛntə(*r*)
AM ˌɪnd(j)əˈmɛn(t)ə

indumentum
BR ˌɪndjᵾˈmɛntəm, ˌɪndʒᵾˈmɛntəm
AM ˌɪnd(j)əˈmɛn(t)əm

induna
BR ɪnˈduːnə(r), -z
AM ɪnˈdunə, -z

indurate¹
adjective
BR ˈɪndjᵾrət, ˈɪndʒᵾrət
AM ˈɪnd(j)ərət

indurate²
verb
BR ˈɪndjᵾreɪt, ˈɪndʒᵾreɪt, -s, -ɪŋ, -ɨd
AM ˈɪnd(j)əˌreɪ|t, -ts, -dɪŋ, -dɨd

induration
BR ˌɪndjᵾˈreɪʃn, ˌɪndʒᵾˈreɪʃn, -z
AM ˌɪnd(j)əˈreɪʃən, -z

indurative
BR ˈɪndjᵾrətɪv, ˈɪndʒᵾrətɪv
AM ˈɪnd(j)əˌreɪdɪv

Indus
BR ˈɪndəs
AM ˈɪndəs

indusia
BR ɪnˈdjuːzɪə(*r*), ɪnˈdʒuːzɪə(*r*)
AM ɪnˈd(j)uʒ(i)ə, ɪnˈd(j)uziə

indusial
BR ɪnˈdjuːzɪəl, ɪnˈdʒuːzɪəl
AM ɪnˈd(j)uʒ(i)əl, ɪnˈd(j)uziəl

indusium
BR ɪnˈdjuːzɪəm, ɪnˈdʒuːzɪəm
AM ɪnˈd(j)uʒ(i)əm, ɪnˈd(j)uziəm

industrial
BR ɪnˈdʌstrɪəl, -z
AM ɪnˈdəstriəl, -z

industrialisation
BR ɪnˌdʌstrɪəlʌɪˈzeɪʃn
AM ɪnˌdəstriələˈzeɪʃən, ɪnˌdəstriəˌlaɪˈzeɪʃən

industrialise
BR ɪnˈdʌstrɪəlʌɪz, -ɪz, -ɪŋ, -d
AM ɪnˈdəstriəˌlaɪz, -ɪz, -ɪŋ, -d

industrialism
BR ɪnˈdʌstrɪəlɪz(ə)m
AM ɪnˈdəstriəˌlɪzəm

industrialist
BR ɪnˈdʌstrɪəlɪst, -s
AM ɪnˈdəstriələst, -s

industrialization
BR ɪnˌdʌstrɪəlʌɪˈzeɪʃn
AM ɪnˌdəstriələˈzeɪʃən, ɪnˌdəstriəˌlaɪˈzeɪʃən

industrialize
BR ɪnˈdʌstrɪəlʌɪz, -ɪz, -ɪŋ, -d
AM ɪnˈdəstriəˌlaɪz, -ɪz, -ɪŋ, -d

industrially
BR ɪnˈdʌstrɪəli
AM ɪnˈdəstriəli

industrious
BR ɪnˈdʌstrɪəs
AM ɪnˈdəstriəs

industriously
BR ɪnˈdʌstrɪəsli
AM ɪnˈdəstriəsli

industriousness
BR ɪnˈdʌstrɪəsnəs
AM ɪnˈdəstriəsnəs

industry
BR ˈɪndəstr|i, -ɪz
AM ˈɪndəstri, -z

indwell
BR (ˌ)ɪnˈdwɛl, -z, -ɪŋ, -d
AM ɪnˈdwɛl, -z, -ɪŋ, -d

indweller
BR (ˌ)ɪnˈdwɛlə(r), -z
AM ɪnˈdwɛlər, -z

Indy
Indianapolis
BR ˈɪndi
AM ˈɪndi

Indycar
BR ˈɪndɪkɑː(r), -z
AM ˈɪndiˌkɑr, -z

inebriate[1]
noun
BR ɪˈniːbrɪət, -s
AM ɪˈnibriət, ɪˈnibriˌeɪt, ɪˈnibriət, ɪˈnibriˌeɪt, -s

inebriate[2]
verb
BR ɪˈniːbrɪeɪt, -s, -ɪŋ, -ɪd
AM ɪˈnibriˌeɪ|t, ɪˈnibriˌeɪ|t, -ts, -dɪŋ, -dɪd

inebriation
BR ɪˌniːbrɪˈeɪʃn
AM ɪˌnibriˈeɪʃən

inebriety
BR ˌɪnɪˈbrʌɪɪti
AM ˌɪnəˈbraɪədi

inedibility
BR ɪnˌɛdɪˈbɪlɪti
AM ˌɪnˌɛdəˈbɪlɪdi, ɪnˌɛdəˈbɪlɪdi

inedible
BR (ˌ)ɪnˈɛdɪbl
AM ɪnˈɛdəbəl

inedibly
BR (ˌ)ɪnˈɛdɪbli
AM ɪnˈɛdəbli

ineducability
BR ɪnˌɛdjʊkəˈbɪlɪti, ɪnˌɛdʒʊkəˈbɪlɪti
AM ˌɪnˌɛdʒəkəˈbɪlɪdi

ineducable
BR (ˌ)ɪnˈɛdjʊkəbl, (ˌ)ɪnˈɛdʒʊkəbl
AM ɪnˈɛdʒəkəbəl

ineducably
BR (ˌ)ɪnˈɛdjʊkəbli, (ˌ)ɪnˈɛdʒʊkəbli
AM ɪnˈɛdʒəkəbli

ineffability
BR ɪnˌɛfəˈbɪlɪti
AM ɪˌnɛfəˈbɪlɪdi

ineffable
BR ɪnˈɛfəbl
AM ɪnˈɛfəbəl

ineffably
BR ɪnˈɛfəbli
AM ɪnˈɛfəbli

ineffaceability
BR ˌɪnɪˌfeɪsəˈbɪlɪti
AM ˌɪnəˌfeɪsəˈbɪlɪdi, ˌɪniˌfeɪsəˈbɪlɪdi

ineffaceable
BR ˌɪnɪˈfeɪsəbl
AM ˌɪnəˈfeɪsəbəl, ˌɪniˈfeɪsəbəl

ineffaceably
BR ˌɪnɪˈfeɪsəbli
AM ˌɪnəˈfeɪsəbli, ˌɪniˈfeɪsəbli

ineffective
BR ˌɪnɪˈfɛktɪv
AM ˌɪnəˈfɛktɪv, ˌɪniˈfɛktɪv

ineffectively
BR ˌɪnɪˈfɛktɪvli
AM ˌɪnəˈfɛktəvli, ˌɪniˈfɛktəvli

ineffectiveness
BR ˌɪnɪˈfɛktɪvnɪs
AM ˌɪnəˈfɛktɪvnɪs, ˌɪniˈfɛktɪvnɪs

ineffectual
BR ˌɪnɪˈfɛktʃʊəl, ˌɪnɪˈfɛktʃ(ʊ)l, ˌɪnɪˈfɛktjʊəl, ˌɪnɪˈfɛktjʊl
AM ˌɪnəˈfɛk(t)ʃ(əw)əl

ineffectuality
BR ˌɪnɪˌfɛktʃʊˈalɪt|i, ˌɪnɪˌfɛktjʊˈalɪt|i, -ɪz
AM ˌɪnəˈfɛk(t)ʃəˈwælədi, -z

ineffectually
BR ˌɪnɪˈfɛktʃʊəli, ˌɪnɪˈfɛktʃʊli, ˌɪnɪˈfɛktʃli, ˌɪnɪˈfɛktjʊəli, ˌɪnɪˈfɛktjʊli
AM ˌɪnəˈfɛk(t)ʃ(əw)əli

ineffectualness
BR ˌɪnɪˈfɛktʃʊəlnəs, ˌɪnɪˈfɛktʃ(ʊ)lnəs, ˌɪnɪˈfɛktjʊəlnəs, ˌɪnɪˈfɛktjʊlnəs
AM ˌɪnəˈfɛk(t)ʃ(əw)əlnəs

inefficacious
BR ˌɪnɛfɪˈkeɪʃəs, ɪnˌɛfɪˈkeɪʃəs
AM ˌɪnɛfəˈkeɪʃəs

inefficaciously
BR ˌɪnɛfɪˈkeɪʃəsli, ɪnˌɛfɪˈkeɪʃəsli
AM ˌɪnɛfəˈkeɪʃəsli

inefficaciousness
BR ˌɪnɛfɪˈkeɪʃəsnəs, ɪnˌɛfɪˈkeɪʃəsnəs
AM ˌɪnɛfəˈkeɪʃəsnəs

inefficacy
BR ɪnˈɛfɪkəs|i, -ɪz
AM ɪnˈɛfəkəsi, -z

inefficiency
BR ˌɪnɪˈfɪʃnsi
AM ˌɪnəˈfɪʃənsi, ˌɪniˈfɪʃənsi

inefficient
BR ˌɪnɪˈfɪʃnt
AM ˌɪnəˈfɪʃənt, ˌɪniˈfɪʃənt

inefficiently
BR ˌɪnɪˈfɪʃntli
AM ˌɪnəˈfɪʃən(t)li, ˌɪniˈfɪʃən(t)li

inegalitarian
BR ˌɪnɪˌgalɪˈtɛːrɪən, -z
AM ˌɪniˌgæləˈtɛriən, ˌɪnəˌgæləˈtɛriən, -z

inelastic
BR ˌɪnɪˈlastɪk
AM ˌɪnəˈlæstɪk

inelastically
BR ˌɪnɪˈlastɪkli
AM ˌɪnəˈlæstək(ə)li

inelasticity
BR ˌɪnɪlaˈstɪsɪti, ˌɪniːlaˈstɪsɪti
AM ˌɪnəˌlæˈstɪsɪdi, ˌɪniˌlæˈstɪsɪdi

inelegance
BR (ˌ)ɪnˈɛlɪg(ə)ns
AM ɪnˈɛləgəns

inelegant
BR (ˌ)ɪnˈɛlɪg(ə)nt
AM ɪnˈɛləgənt

inelegantly
BR (ˌ)ɪnˈɛlɪg(ə)ntli
AM ɪnˈɛləgən(t)li

ineligibility
BR ɪnˌɛlɪdʒɪˈbɪlɪti
AM ˌɪnˌɛlədʒəˈbɪlɪdi, ɪnˌɛlədʒəˈbɪlɪdi

ineligible
BR (ˌ)ɪnˈɛlɪdʒɪbl
AM ɪnˈɛlədʒəbəl

ineligibly
BR (ˌ)ɪnˈɛlɪdʒɪbli
AM ɪnˈɛlədʒəbli

ineluctability
BR ˌɪnɪˌlʌktəˈbɪlɪti
AM ˌɪnəˌləktəˈbɪlɪdi

ineluctable
BR ˌɪnɪˈlʌktəbl
AM ˌɪnəˈləktəbəl

ineluctably
BR ˌɪnɪˈlʌktəbli
AM ˌɪnəˈləktəbli

inept
BR ɪˈnɛpt, ˌɪnˈɛpt
AM ɪˈnɛpt

ineptitude
BR ɪˈnɛptɪtjuːd, ɪˈnɛptɪtʃuːd
AM ɪˈnɛptəˌt(j)ud

ineptly
BR ɪˈnɛptli
AM ɪˈnɛp(t)li

ineptness
BR ɪˈnɛp(t)nəs
AM ɪˈnɛp(t)nəs

inequable
BR (ˌ)ɪnˈɛkwəbl
AM ɪnˈɛkwəbəl

inequality
BR ˌɪnɪˈkwɒlɪt|i, -ɪz
AM ˌɪnəˈkwɑlədi, ˌɪnəˈkwɔlədi, ˌɪniˈkwɑlədi, ˌɪniˈkwɔlədi, -z

inequitable
BR (ˌ)ɪnˈɛkwɪtəbl
AM ɪnˈɛkwədəbəl

inequitably
BR (ˌ)ɪnˈɛkwɪtəbli
AM ɪnˈɛkwədəbli

inequity
BR (ˌ)ɪnˈɛkwɪt|i, -ɪz
AM ɪnˈɛkwədi, -z

ineradicable
BR ˌɪnɪˈradɪkəbl
AM ˌɪnəˈrædəkəbəl

ineradicably
BR ˌɪnɪˈradɪkəbli
AM ˌɪnəˈrædəkəbli

inerrability
BR ɪnˌəːrəˈbɪlɪti
AM ˌɪnˌɛrəˈbɪlɪdi

inerrable
BR (ˌ)ɪnˈəːrəbl
AM ɪˈnɛrəbəl

inerrably
BR (ˌ)ɪnˈəːrəbli
AM ɪˈnɛrəbli

inerrancy
BR (ˌ)ɪnˈɛrənsi, (ˌ)ɪnˈɛrn̩si
AM ɪˈnɛrənsi

inerrant
BR (ˌ)ɪnˈɛrənt, (ˌ)ɪnˈɛrn̩t
AM ɪˈnɛrənt

inert
BR ɪˈnəːt
AM ɪˈnərt

inertia
BR ɪˈnəːʃə(r)
AM ɪˈnərʃə

inertial
BR ɪˈnəːʃl, ɪˈnəːʃɪəl
AM ɪˈnərʃəl

inertialess
BR ɪˈnəːʃələs
AM ɪˈnərʃələs

inertly
BR ɪˈnəːtli
AM ɪˈnərtli

inertness
BR ɪˈnəːtnəs
AM ɪˈnərtnəs

inescapability
BR ˌɪnɪˌskeɪpəˈbɪlɪti
AM ˌɪnəˌskeɪpəˈbɪlɪdi

inescapable
BR ˌɪnɪˈskeɪpəbl
AM ˌɪnəˈskeɪpəbəl

inescapably
BR ˌɪnɪˈskeɪpəbli
AM ˌɪnəˈskeɪpəbli

inescutcheon
BR ˌɪnɪˈskʌtʃ(ə)n
AM ˌɪnəˈskətʃən, ˌɪnɛˈskətʃən

in essence
BR ɪn ˈɛsns
AM ɪ ˈnɛsəns

inessential
BR ˌɪnɪˈsɛnʃl, -z
AM ˌɪnəˈsɛn(t)ʃəl, ˌɪniˈsɛn(t)ʃəl, -z

inestimable
BR ˌɪnˈɛstɪməbl
AM ɪnˈɛstəməbəl, ɪnˈɛstəməbəl

inestimably
BR ˌɪnˈɛstɪməbli
AM ɪnˈɛstəməbli, ɪnˈɛstəməbli

inevitability
BR ɪnˌɛvɪtəˈbɪlɪti, ɪˌnɛvɪtəˈbɪlɪti
AM ɪˌnɛvədəˈbɪlɪdi, ɪˌnɛvtəˈbɪlɪdi

inevitable
BR ɪnˈɛvɪtəbl, ɪˈnɛvɪtəbl
AM ɪˈnɛvədəbəl, ɪˈnɛvtəbəl

inevitableness
BR ɪnˈɛvɪtəblnəs, ɪˈnɛvɪtəblnəs
AM ɪˈnɛvədəbəlnəs, ɪˈnɛvtəbəlnəs

inevitably
BR ɪnˈɛvɪtəbli, ɪˈnɛvɪtəbli
AM ɪˈnɛvədəbli, ɪˈnɛvtəbli

inexact
BR ˌɪnɪɡˈzakt, ˌɪnɛɡˈzakt
AM ˌɪnɪɡˈzæk(t), ˌɪnɛɡˈzæk(t)

inexactitude
BR ˌɪnɪɡˈzaktɪtjuːd, ˌɪnɛɡˈzaktɪtjuːd, ˌɪnɪɡˈzaktɪtʃuːd, ˌɪnɛɡˈzaktɪtʃuːd, -z
AM ˌɪnɪɡˈzæktəˌt(j)ud, ˌɪnɛɡˈzæktət(j)ud, -z

inexactly
BR ˌɪnɪɡˈzak(t)li, ˌɪnɛɡˈzak(t)li
AM ˌɪnɪɡˈzæk(t)li, ˌɪnɛɡˈzæk(t)li

inexactness
BR ˌɪnɪɡˈzak(t)nəs, ˌɪnɛɡˈzak(t)nəs
AM ˌɪnɪɡˈzæk(t)nəs, ˌɪnɛɡˈzæk(t)nəs

inexcusable
BR ˌɪnɪkˈskjuːzəbl, ˌɪnɛkˈskjuːzəbl
AM ˌɪnɪkˈskjuzəbəl, ˌɪnɛkˈskjuzəbəl

inexcusably
BR ˌɪnɪkˈskjuːzəbli, ˌɪnɛkˈskjuːzəbli
AM ˌɪnɪkˈskjuzəbli, ˌɪnɛkˈskjuzəbli

inexhaustibility
BR ˌɪnɪɡˌzɔːstɪˈbɪlɪti, ˌɪnɛɡˌzɔːstɪˈbɪlɪti
AM ˌɪnɪɡˌzɔstəˈbɪlɪdi, ˌɪnɛɡˌzɔstəˈbɪlɪdi, ˌɪnɪɡˌzɑstəˈbɪlɪdi, ˌɪnɛɡˌzɑstəˈbɪlɪdi

inexhaustible
BR ˌɪnɪɡˈzɔːstɪbl, ˌɪnɛɡˈzɔːstɪbl
AM ˌɪnɪɡˈzɔstəbəl, ˌɪnɛɡˈzɔstəbəl, ˌɪnɪɡˈzɑstəbəl, ˌɪnɛɡˈzɑstəbəl

inexhaustibly
BR ˌɪnɪɡˈzɔːstɪbli, ˌɪnɛɡˈzɔːstɪbli
AM ˌɪnɪɡˈzɔstəbli, ˌɪnɛɡˈzɔstəbli, ˌɪnɪɡˈzɑstəbli, ˌɪnɛɡˈzɑstəbli

inexorability
BR ɪnˌɛks(ə)rəˈbɪlɪti
AM ɪˌnɛks(ə)rəˈbɪlɪdi

inexorable
BR ɪnˈɛks(ə)rəbl
AM ɪˈnɛks(ə)rəbəl

inexorably
BR ɪnˈɛks(ə)rəbli
AM ɪˈnɛks(ə)rəbli

inexpedience
BR ˌɪnɪkˈspiːdɪəns, ˌɪnɛkˈspiːdɪəns
AM ˌɪnɪkˈspidiəns, ˌɪnɛkˈspidiəns

inexpediency
BR ˌɪnɪkˈspiːdɪənsi, ˌɪnɛkˈspiːdɪənsi
AM ˌɪnɪkˈspidiənsi, ˌɪnɛkˈspidiənsi

inexpedient
BR ˌɪnɪkˈspiːdɪənt, ˌɪnɛkˈspiːdɪənt
AM ˌɪnɪkˈspidiənt, ˌɪnɛkˈspidiənt

inexpensive
BR ˌɪnɪkˈspɛnsɪv, ˌɪnɛkˈspɛnsɪv
AM ˌɪnɪkˈspɛnsɪv, ˌɪŋɛkˈspɛnsɪv

inexpensively
BR ˌɪnɪkˈspɛnsɪvli, ˌɪnɛkˈspɛnsɪvli
AM ˌɪnɪkˈspɛnsəvli, ˌɪŋɛkˈspɛnsəvli

inexpensiveness
BR ˌɪnɪkˈspɛnsɪvnɪs, ˌɪnɛkˈspɛnsɪvnɪs
AM ˌɪnɪkˈspɛnsɪvnɪs, ˌɪŋɛkˈspɛnsɪvnɪs

inexperience
BR ˌɪnɪkˈspɪərɪəns, ˌɪnɛkˈspɪərɪəns, -t
AM ˌɪnɪkˈspiriəns, ˌɪnɛkˈspiriəns, -t

inexpert
BR (ˌ)ɪnˈɛkspəːt
AM ɪnˈɛkspərt, ˌɪnəkˈspərt

inexpertly
BR (ˌ)ɪnˈɛkspəːtli
AM ɪnˈɛkspərtli, ˌɪnəkˈspərtli

inexpertness
BR (ˌ)ɪnˈɛkspəːtnəs
AM ɪnˈɛkspərtnəs, ˌɪnəkˈspərtnəs

inexpiable
BR (ˌ)ɪnˈɛkspɪəbl
AM ɪnˈɛkspiəbəl

inexpiably
BR (ˌ)ɪnˈɛkspɪəbli
AM ɪnˈɛkspiəbli

inexplicability
BR ˌɪnɪkˌsplɪkəˈbɪlɪti, ˌɪnɛkˌsplɪkəˈbɪlɪti, ɪnˌɛksplɪkəˈbɪlɪti
AM ˌɪnɛkˌsplɪkəˈbɪlɪdi, ɪnˌɛkˌsplɪkəˈbɪlɪdi

inexplicable
BR ˌɪnɪkˈsplɪkəbl, ˌɪnɛkˈsplɪkəbl, ɪnˈɛksplɪkəbl
AM ˌɪnɛkˈsplɪkəbəl, ɪnˌɛkˈsplɪkəbəl, ˌɪnˈɛkspləkəbəl, ɪnˈɛkspləkəbəl

inexplicably
BR ˌɪnɪkˈsplɪkəbli, ˌɪnɛkˈsplɪkəbli, ɪnˈɛksplɪkəbli
AM ˌɪnɛkˈsplɪkəbli, ɪnˌɛkˈsplɪkəbli, ˌɪnˈɛkspləkəbli, ɪnˈɛkspləkəbli

inexplicit
BR ˌɪnɪkˈsplɪsɪt, ˌɪnɛkˈsplɪsɪt
AM ˌɪnɪkˈsplɪsɪt, ˌɪnɛkˈsplɪsɪt

inexplicitly
BR ˌɪnɪkˈsplɪsɪtli, ˌɪnɛkˈsplɪsɪtli
AM ˌɪnɪkˈsplɪsɪtli, ˌɪnɛkˈsplɪsɪtli

inexplicitness
BR ˌɪnɪkˈsplɪsɪtnɪs, ˌɪnɛkˈsplɪsɪtnɪs
AM ˌɪnɪkˈsplɪsɪtnɪs, ˌɪnɛkˈsplɪsɪtnɪs

inexpressible
BR ˌɪnɪkˈsprɛsɪbl, ˌɪnɛkˈsprɛsɪbl
AM ˌɪnɪkˈsprɛsəbəl, ˌɪnəkˈsprɛsəbəl, ɪnɪkˈsprɛsəbəl, ɪnɛkˈsprɛsəbəl

inexpressibly
BR ˌɪnɪkˈsprɛsɪbli, ˌɪnɛkˈsprɛsɪbli
AM ˌɪnɪkˈsprɛsəbli, ˌɪnəkˈsprɛsəbli, ɪnɪkˈsprɛsəbli, ɪnɛkˈsprɛsəbli

inexpressive
BR ˌɪnɪkˈsprɛsɪv, ˌɪnɛkˈsprɛsɪv
AM ˌɪnɪkˈsprɛsɪv, ˌɪnɛkˈsprɛsɪv

inexpressively
BR ˌɪnɪkˈsprɛsɪvli, ˌɪnɛkˈsprɛsɪvli
AM ˌɪnɪkˈsprɛsəvli, ˌɪnɛkˈsprɛsəvli

inexpressiveness
BR ˌɪnɪk'sprɛsɪvnɨs, ˌɪnɛk'sprɛsɪvnɨs
AM ¦ɪnɪk'sprɛsɪvnɨs, ¦ɪnɛk'sprɛsɪvnɨs

inexpugnable
BR ˌɪnɨk'spʌgnəbl, ˌɪnɛk'spʌgnəbl
AM ¦ɪnɛk'spjunəbəl, ¦ɪnɛk'spənəbəl

inexpungible
BR ˌɪnɨk'spʌn(d)ʒɨbl, ˌɪnɛk'spʌn(d)ʒɨbl
AM ¦ɪnɪk'spəndʒəbəl, ¦ɪnɛk'spəndʒəbəl

in extenso
BR ˌɪn ɨk'stɛnsəʊ, + ɛk'stɛnsəʊ
AM ˌɪ nək'stɛnˌsoʊ

inextinguishable
BR ˌɪnɨk'stɪŋgwɪʃəbl, ˌɪnɛk'stɪŋgwɪʃəbl
AM ¦ɪnɪk'stɪŋgwɪʃəbəl

inextinguishably
BR ˌɪnɨk'stɪŋgwɪʃəbli, ˌɪnɛk'stɪŋgwɪʃəbli
AM ¦ɪnɪk'stɪŋgwɪʃəbli

in extremis
BR ˌɪn ɨk'striːmɪs, + ɛk'striːmɪs
AM ˌɪn ɪk'streɪməs, + ɛk'streɪməs, + ɪk'striməs, + ɛk'striməs

inextricability
BR ˌɪnɨkˌstrɪkə'bɪlɨti, ˌɪnɛkˌstrɪkə'bɪlɨti, ɪnˌɛkstrɪkə'bɪlɨti
AM ¦ɪnɛk'strɪkə'bɪlɨdi, ¦ɪnɪk'strɪkə'bɪlɨdi, ¦ɪn'ɛkstrəkə'bɪlɨdi, ɨnɪk'strɪkə'bɪlɨdi, ɨnˌɛk'strɪkə'bɪlɨdi, ɨn'ɛkstrəkə'bɪlɨdi

inextricable
BR ˌɪnɨk'strɪkəbl, ˌɪnɛk'strɪkəbl, ɪn'ɛkstrɪkəbl
AM ¦ɪnɛk'strɪkəbəl, ¦ɪnɪk'strɪkəbəl, ¦ɪn'ɛkstrəkəbəl, ɨnɪk'strɪkəbəl, ɨnˌɛk'strɪkəbəl, ɨn'ɛkstrəkəbəl

inextricably
BR ˌɪnɨk'strɪkəbli, ˌɪnɛk'strɪkəbli, ɪn'ɛkstrɪkəbli
AM ¦ɪnɛk'strɪkəbli, ¦ɪnɪk'strɪkəbli, ¦ɪn'ɛkstrəkəbli, ɨnɪk'strɪkəbli, ɨnˌɛk'strɪkəbli, ɨn'ɛkstrəkəbli

Inez
BR 'iːnɛz, 'ʌɪnɛz
AM aɪ'nɛz

infallibility
BR ɪnˌfalɪ'bɪlɨti, ˌɪnfalɪ'bɪlɨti
AM ¦ɪnˌfælə'bɪlɨdi

infallible
BR ɪn'falɨbl
AM ɨn'fæləbəl

infallibly
BR ɪn'falɨbli
AM ɨn'fæləbli

infamous
BR 'ɪnfəməs
AM 'ɪnfəməs

infamously
BR 'ɪnfəməsli
AM 'ɪnfəməsli

infamy
BR 'ɪnfəmi
AM 'ɪnfəmi

infancy
BR 'ɪnf(ə)nsi
AM 'ɪnfənsi

infant
BR 'ɪnf(ə)nt, -s
AM 'ɪnfənt, -s

infanta
BR ɪn'fantə(r), -z
AM ɨn'fæn(t)ə, -z

infante
BR ɪn'fant|i, -ɪz
AM ɨn'fænˌteɪ, -z

infanticidal
BR ɪnˌfantɪ'sʌɪdl
AM ɨnˌfæn(t)əˌsaɪdəl

infanticide
BR ɪn'fantɪsʌɪd, -z
AM ɪn'fæn(t)əˌsaɪd, -z

infantile
BR 'ɪnf(ə)ntʌɪl
AM 'ɪnfənˌtaɪl, 'ɪnfəntl

infantilism
BR ɪn'fantɨlɪz(ə)m
AM 'ɪnfən(t)lˌɪzəm, ɪn'fæn(t)lˌɪzəm

infantility
BR ˌɪnf(ə)n'tɪlɨti, -ɪz
AM ˌɪnfən'tɪlɨdi, -z

infantine
BR 'ɪnf(ə)ntʌɪn
AM 'ɪnfənˌtaɪn, 'ɪnfənˌtin

infantry
BR 'ɪnf(ə)ntri
AM 'ɪnfəntri

infantryman
BR 'ɪnf(ə)ntrɪmən
AM 'ɪnfəntrimən

infantrymen
BR 'ɪnf(ə)ntrɪmən
AM 'ɪnfəntrimən

infarct
BR 'ɪnfɑːkt, ɪn'fɑːkt, -s
AM 'ɪnˌfɑrk|(t), -(t)s

infarction
BR ɪn'fɑːkʃn
AM ɨn'fɑrkʃən

infatuate
BR ɪn'fatjʊeɪt, ɪn'fatʃʊeɪt, -s, -ɪŋ, -ɨd
AM ɨn'fætʃəˌweɪ|t, -ts, -dɪŋ, -dɨd

infatuation
BR ɪnˌfatjʊ'eɪʃn, ɪnˌfatʃʊ'eɪʃn, -z
AM ɨnˌfætʃə'weɪʃən, -z

infauna
BR 'ɪnˌfɔːnə(r)
AM ɨn'fɔnə, ɨn'fɑnə

infeasibility
BR ˌɪnfiːzɪ'bɪlɨti, ɪnˌfiːzɪ'bɪlɨti
AM ¦ɪnfizə'bɪlɨdi

infeasible
BR ɪn'fiːzɨbl
AM ɨn'fizɨbəl

infect
BR ɪn'fɛkt, -s, -ɪŋ, -ɨd
AM ɨn'fɛk|(t), -(t)s, -tɪŋ, -təd

infection
BR ɪn'fɛkʃn, -z
AM ɨn'fɛkʃən, -z

infectious
BR ɪn'fɛkʃəs
AM ɨn'fɛkʃəs

infectiously
BR ɪn'fɛkʃəsli
AM ɨn'fɛkʃəsli

infectiousness
BR ɪn'fɛkʃəsnəs
AM ɨn'fɛkʃəsnəs

infective
BR ɪn'fɛktɪv
AM ɨn'fɛktɪv

infectiveness
BR ɪn'fɛktɪvnɨs
AM ɨn'fɛktɪvnɨs

infector
BR ɪn'fɛktə(r), -z
AM ɨn'fɛktər, -z

infelicitous
BR ˌɪnfɪ'lɪsɪtəs
AM ¦ɪnfə'lɪsədəs

infelicitously
BR ˌɪnfɪ'lɪsɪtəsli
AM ¦ɪnfə'lɪsədəsli

infelicity
BR ˌɪnfɪ'lɪsɪt|i, -ɪz
AM ¦ɪnfə'lɪsɨdi, -z

infer
BR ɪn'fəː(r), -z, -ɪŋ, -d
AM ɨn'fər, -z, -ɪŋ, -d

inferable
BR ɪn'fəːrəbl
AM ɨn'fərəbəl

inference
BR 'ɪnf(ə)rəns, 'ɪnf(ə)rn̩s, -ɨz
AM 'ɪnf(ə)rəns, -əz

inferential
BR ˌɪnfə'rɛnʃl
AM ¦ɪnfə'rɛn(t)ʃəl

inferentially
BR ˌɪnfə'rɛnʃl̩i, ˌɪnfə'rɛnʃəli
AM ¦ɪnfə'rɛn(t)ʃəli

inferior
BR ɪn'fɪərɪə(r), -z
AM ɨn'fɪriər, -z

inferiority
BR ɪnˌfɪərɪ'ɒrɪti
AM ɨnˌfɪri'ɔrədi, ɨnˌfɪri'ɑrədi

inferiorly
BR ɪn'fɪərɪəli
AM ɨn'fɪriərli

infernal
BR ɪn'fəːnl
AM ɨn'fərnəl

infernally
BR ɪn'fəːnl̩i, ɪn'fəːnəli
AM ɨn'fərnəli

inferno
BR ɪn'fəːnəʊ, -z
AM ɨn'fərnoʊ, -z

infertile
BR ɪn'fəːtʌɪl
AM ɨn'fərdl

infertility
BR ˌɪnfə'tɪlɨti
AM ˌɪnfər'tɪlɨdi

infest
BR ɪn'fɛst, -s, -ɪŋ, -ɨd
AM ɨn'fɛst, -s, -ɪŋ, -əd

infestation
BR ˌɪnfɛ'steɪʃn, -z
AM ˌɪnfə'steɪʃən, -z

infeudation
BR ˌɪnfjuː'deɪʃn
AM ˌɪnfju'deɪʃ(ə)n

infibulate
BR ɪn'fɪbjʊleɪt, -s, -ɪŋ, -ɨd
AM ɪn'fɪbjəˌleɪ|t, -ts, -dɪŋ, -dɨd

infibulation
BR ɪnˌfɪbjʊ'leɪʃn
AM ɨnˌfɪbjə'leɪʃən

infidel
BR 'ɪnfɨd(ɛ)l, -z
AM 'ɪnfədəl, 'ɪnfəˌdɛl, -z

infidelity
BR ˌɪnfɪ'dɛlɪt|i, -ɪz
AM ˌɪnfə'dɛlədi, -z

infield
BR 'ɪnfiːld, -z
AM 'ɪnˌfild, -z

infielder
BR 'ɪnˌfiːldə(r), -z
AM 'ɪnˌfildər, -z

infighter
BR 'ɪnˌfʌɪtə(r), -z
AM 'ɪnˌfaɪdər, -z

infighting
BR 'ɪnˌfʌɪtɪŋ
AM 'ɪnˌfaɪdɪŋ

infill
BR 'ɪnfɪl, -z, -ɪŋ, -d
AM 'ɪnˌfɪl, -z, -ɪŋ, -d

infiltrate
BR 'ɪnf(ɪ)ltreɪt, -s, -ɪŋ, -ɪd
AM ɪn'fɪl,treɪ|t, 'ɪnfɪl,treɪ|t, -ts, -dɪŋ, -dɪd
infiltration
BR ,ɪnf(ɪ)l'treɪʃn
AM ,ɪnfɪl'treɪʃən
infiltrator
BR 'ɪnf(ɪ)ltreɪtə(r), -z
AM ən'fɪl,treɪdər, 'ɪnfɪl,treɪdər, -z
infinite
BR 'ɪnfɪnət
AM 'ɪnfənət
infinitely
BR 'ɪnfɪnətli
AM 'ɪnfənətli
infiniteness
BR 'ɪnfɪnətnəs
AM 'ɪnfənətnəs
infinitesimal
BR ,ɪnfɪnɪ'tɛsɪml
AM ¦ɪn,fɪnə¦tɛs(ə)məl, ¦ɪn,fɪnə¦tɛz(ə)məl
infinitesimally
BR ,ɪnfɪnɪ'tɛsɪmḷi, ,ɪnfɪnɪ'tɛsɪməli
AM ¦ɪn,fɪnə¦tɛs(ə)məli, ¦ɪn,fɪnə¦tɛz(ə)məli
infinitival
BR ,ɪnfɪnɪ'tʌɪvl, ɪn,fɪnɪ'tʌɪvl
AM ¦ɪn,fɪnə¦taɪvəl
infinitivally
BR ,ɪnfɪnɪ'tʌɪvḷi, ,ɪnfɪnɪ'tʌɪvəli, ɪn,fɪnɪ'tʌɪvḷi, ɪn,fɪnɪ'tʌɪvəli
AM ¦ɪn,fɪnə¦taɪvəli
infinitive
BR ɪn'fɪnɪtɪv, -z
AM ɪn'fɪnədɪv, -z
infinitude
BR ɪn'fɪnɪtjuːd, ɪn'fɪnɪtʃuːd, -z
AM ɪn'fɪnə,t(j)ud, -z
infinity
BR ɪn'fɪnɪt|i, -ɪz
AM ɪn'fɪnɪdi, -z
infirm
BR ɪn'fəːm
AM ɪn'fərm
infirmary
BR ɪn'fəːm(ə)r|i, -ɪz
AM ɪn'fərm(ə)ri, -z
infirmity
BR ɪn'fəːmɪt|i, -ɪz
AM ɪn'fərmədi, -z
infirmly
BR ɪn'fəːmli
AM ɪn'fərmli
infix[1]
noun
BR 'ɪnfɪks, -ɪz
AM 'ɪn,fɪks, -ɪz

infix[2]
verb
BR (,)ɪn'fɪks, -ɪz, -ɪŋ, -t
AM ɪn'fɪks, -ɪz, -ɪŋ, -t
infixation
BR ,ɪnfɪk'seɪʃn, -z
AM ¦ɪn,fɪk'seɪʃən, -z
in flagrante delicto
BR ,ɪn flə,grantɪ dɪ'lɪktəʊ
AM ,ɪn flə¦gran,teɪ də'lɪk,toʊ
inflame
BR ɪn'fleɪm, -z, -ɪŋ, -d
AM ɪn'fleɪm, -z, -ɪŋ, -d
inflamer
BR ɪn'fleɪmə(r), -z
AM ɪn'fleɪmər, -z
inflammability
BR ɪn,flamə'bɪlɪti
AM ɪn,flæmə'bɪlɪdi
inflammable
BR ɪn'flaməbl
AM ɪn'flæməbəl
inflammableness
BR ɪn'flaməblnəs
AM ɪn'flæməbəlnəs
inflammably
BR ɪn'flaməbli
AM ɪn'flæməbli
inflammation
BR ,ɪnflə'meɪʃn, -z
AM ,ɪnflə'meɪʃən, -z
inflammatory
BR ɪn'flamət(ə)ri
AM ɪn'flæmə,tɔri
inflatable
BR ɪn'fleɪtəbl, -z
AM ɪn'fleɪdəbəl, -z
inflate
BR ɪn'fleɪt, -s, -ɪŋ, -ɪd
AM ɪn'fleɪ|t, -ts, -dɪŋ, -dɪd
inflatedly
BR ɪn'fleɪtɪdli
AM ɪn'fleɪdɪdli
inflatedness
BR ɪn'fleɪtɪdnɪs
AM ɪn'fleɪdɪdnɪs
inflater
BR ɪn'fleɪtə(r), -z
AM ɪn'fleɪdər, -z
inflation
BR ɪn'fleɪʃn
AM ɪn'fleɪʃən
inflationary
BR ɪn'fleɪʃn̩(ə)ri
AM ɪn'fleɪʃə,nɛri
inflationism
BR ɪn'fleɪʃn̩ɪz(ə)m, ɪn'fleɪʃənɪz(ə)m
AM ɪn'fleɪʃə,nɪzəm
inflationist
BR ɪn'fleɪʃn̩ɪst, ɪn'fleɪʃənɪst, -s
AM ɪn'fleɪʃənəst, -s

inflator
BR ɪn'fleɪtə(r), -z
AM ɪn'fleɪdər, -z
inflect
BR ɪn'flɛkt, -s, -ɪŋ, -ɪd
AM ɪn'flɛk|(t), -(t)s, -tɪŋ, -təd
inflection
BR ɪn'flɛkʃn, -z
AM ɪn'flɛkʃən, -z
inflectional
BR ɪn'flɛkʃn̩(ə)l, ɪn'flɛkʃən(ə)l
AM ɪn'flɛkʃ(ə)nəl
inflectionally
BR ɪn'flɛkʃn̩əli, ɪn'flɛkʃn̩ḷi, ɪn'flɛkʃənḷi, ɪn'flɛkʃ(ə)nəli
AM ɪn'flɛkʃ(ə)nəli
inflectionless
BR ɪn'flɛkʃnləs
AM ɪn'flɛkʃənləs
inflective
BR ɪn'flɛktɪv
AM ɪn'flɛktɪv
inflexibility
BR ɪn,flɛksɪ'bɪlɪti
AM ¦ɪn,flɛksə'bɪlɪdi, ɪn,flɛksə'bɪlɪdi
inflexible
BR ɪn'flɛksɪbl
AM ɪn'flɛksəbəl
inflexibly
BR ɪn'flɛksɪbli
AM ɪn'flɛksəbli
inflexion
BR ɪn'flɛkʃn, -z
AM ɪn'flɛkʃən, -z
inflexional
BR ɪn'flɛkʃn̩(ə)l, ɪn'flɛkʃən(ə)l
AM ɪn'flɛkʃ(ə)nəl
inflexionally
BR ɪn'flɛkʃn̩əli, ɪn'flɛkʃn̩ḷi, ɪn'flɛkʃənḷi, ɪn'flɛkʃ(ə)nəli
AM ɪn'flɛkʃ(ə)nəli
inflexionless
BR ɪn'flɛkʃnləs
AM ɪn'flɛkʃənləs
inflict
BR ɪn'flɪkt, -s, -ɪŋ, -ɪd
AM ɪn'flɪk|(t), -(t)s, -tɪŋ, -tɪd
inflictable
BR ɪn'flɪktəbl
AM ɪn'flɪktɪbəl
inflicter
BR ɪn'flɪktə(r), -z
AM ɪn'flɪktər, -z
infliction
BR ɪn'flɪkʃn, -z
AM ɪn'flɪkʃən, -z
inflictor
BR ɪn'flɪktə(r), -z
AM ɪn'flɪktər, -z

in-flight
BR ,ɪn'flʌɪt
AM 'ɪn¦flaɪt
inflorescence
BR ,ɪnflə'rɛsns
AM ,ɪnfloʊ'rɛsəns, ,ɪnflə'rɛsəns
inflow
BR 'ɪnfləʊ, -z
AM 'ɪn,floʊ, -z
inflowing
BR 'ɪn,fləʊɪŋ, -z
AM 'ɪn,floʊɪŋ, -z
influence
BR 'ɪnflʊəns, -ɪz, -ɪŋ, -t
AM 'ɪnflʊəns, -əz, -ɪŋ, -t
influenceable
BR 'ɪnflʊənsəbl
AM 'ɪnflʊənsəbəl
influencer
BR 'ɪnflʊənsə(r), -z
AM 'ɪnflʊənsər, -z
influent
BR 'ɪnflʊənt, -s
AM 'ɪnflʊənt, -s
influential
BR ,ɪnflʊ'ɛnʃl
AM ¦ɪn,flu'ɛn(t)ʃəl
influentially
BR ,ɪnflʊ'ɛnʃḷi, ,ɪnflʊ'ɛnʃəli
AM ¦ɪn,flu'ɛn(t)ʃəli
influenza
BR ,ɪnflʊ'ɛnzə(*r*)
AM ,ɪn,flu'ɛnzə
influenzal
BR ,ɪnflʊ'ɛnzl
AM ,ɪn,flu'ɛnzəl
influx
BR 'ɪnflʌks, -ɪz
AM 'ɪn,fləks, -əz
info
BR 'ɪnfəʊ
AM 'ɪnfoʊ
infobit
BR 'ɪnfəʊbɪt, -s
AM 'ɪnfoʊ,bɪt, -s
infold
BR (,)ɪn'fəʊld, -z, -ɪŋ, -ɪd
AM ɪn'foʊld, -z, -ɪŋ, -ɪd
in folio
BR ,ɪn 'fəʊlɪəʊ
AM ,ɪn 'foʊlioʊ
infomania
BR ,ɪnfə(ʊ)'meɪnɪə(*r*), -z
AM ¦ɪnfoʊ'meɪniə, -z
infomercial
BR ,ɪnfə(ʊ)'məːʃl, -z
AM 'ɪnfoʊ,mərʃəl, -z
infopreneur
BR ,ɪnfə(ʊ)prə'nəː(r), -z
AM ,ɪnfoʊprə'nər, ,ɪnfoʊprə'nʊ(ə)r, -z

inform
BR ɪn'fɔːm, -z, -ɪŋ, -d
AM ɪn'fɔ(ə)rm, -z, -ɪŋ, -d

informal
BR ɪn'fɔːml
AM ɪn'fɔrməl

informality
BR ˌɪnfɔː'malɪti
AM ˌɪnfɔr'mælədi

informally
BR ɪn'fɔːmḷi, ɪn'fɔːməli
AM ɪn'fɔrməli

informant
BR ɪn'fɔːm(ə)nt, -s
AM ɪn'fɔrmənt, -s

informatics
BR ˌɪnfə'matɪks
AM ˌɪnfər'mædɪks

information
BR ˌɪnfə'meɪʃn
AM ˌɪnfər'meɪʃən

informational
BR ˌɪnfə'meɪʃn̩(ə)l, ˌɪnfə'meɪʃən(ə)l
AM ˌɪnfər'meɪʃ(ə)nəl

informationally
BR ˌɪnfə'meɪʃn̩əli, ˌɪnfə'meɪʃn̩ḷi, ˌɪnfə'meɪʃənḷi, ˌɪnfə'meɪʃ(ə)nəli
AM ˌɪnfər'meɪʃ(ə)nəli

informative
BR ɪn'fɔːmətɪv
AM ɪn'fɔrmədɪv

informatively
BR ɪn'fɔːmətɪvli
AM ɪn'fɔrmədəvli

informativeness
BR ɪn'fɔːmətɪvnɪs
AM ɪn'fɔrmədɪvnɪs

informatory
BR ɪn'fɔːmət(ə)ri
AM ɪn'fɔrməˌtɔri

informedly
BR ɪn'fɔːmɪdli
AM ɪn'fɔrm(ə)dli

informedness
BR ɪn'fɔːmɪdnɪs
AM ɪn'fɔrm(əd)nəs

informer
BR ɪn'fɔːmə(r), -z
AM ɪn'fɔrmər, -z

infosphere
BR 'ɪnfə(ʊ)sfɪə(r), -z
AM 'ɪnfoʊˌsfɪ(ə)r, -z

infotainment
BR ˌɪnfə(ʊ)'teɪnm(ə)nt
AM ¦ɪnfoʊ¦teɪ(n)mənt

infotech
BR 'ɪnfəʊtɛk
AM 'ɪnfoʊˌtɛk

infra
BR 'ɪnfrə(r)
AM 'ɪnfrə

infraclass
BR 'ɪnfrəklɑːs, 'ɪnfrəklas, -ɪz
AM 'ɪnfrəˌklæs, -əz

infract
BR ɪn'frakt, -s, -ɪŋ, -ɪd
AM ɪn'fræk|(t), -(t)s, -tɪŋ, -təd

infraction
BR ɪn'frakʃn, -z
AM ɪn'frækʃən, -z

infractor
BR ɪn'fraktə(r), -z
AM ɪn'fræktər, -z

infradian
BR ɪn'freɪdɪən
AM ɪn'freɪdiən

infra dig
BR ˌɪnfrə 'dɪg
AM ¦ɪnfrə ¦dɪg

infralapsarian
BR ˌɪnfrəlap'sɛːrɪən, -z
AM ¦ɪnfrəˌlæp'sɛriən, -z

infrangibility
BR ɪnˌfran(d)ʒɪ'bɪlɪti
AM ¦ɪnˌfrændʒə'bɪlɪdi

infrangible
BR ɪn'fran(d)ʒɪbl
AM ɪn'frændʒəbəl

infrangibleness
BR ɪn'fran(d)ʒɪblnəs
AM ɪn'frændʒəbəlnəs

infrangibly
BR ɪn'fran(d)ʒɪbli
AM ɪn'frændʒəbli

infrared
BR ˌɪnfrə'rɛd
AM ¦ɪnfrə'rɛd

infrarenal
BR ˌɪnfrə'riːnl
AM ¦ɪnfrə'rinəl

infrasonic
BR ˌɪnfrə'sɒnɪk
AM ¦ɪnfrə'sɑnɪk

infrasonically
BR ˌɪnfrə'sɒnɪkli
AM ¦ɪnfrə'sɑnək(ə)li

infrasound
BR 'ɪnfrəsaʊnd
AM ¦ɪnfrə'saʊnd

infrastructural
BR ˌɪnfrə'strʌktʃ(ə)rəl, ˌɪnfrə'strʌktʃ(ə)rḷ
AM ¦ɪnfrə'strək(t)ʃ(ə)rəl

infrastructure
BR 'ɪnfrəˌstrʌktʃə(r), -z
AM 'ɪnfrəˌstrək(t)ʃər, -z

infrequency
BR ɪn'friːkw(ə)nsi
AM ɪn'frikwənsi

infrequent
BR ɪn'friːkw(ə)nt
AM ɪn'frikwənt

infrequently
BR ɪn'friːkw(ə)ntli
AM ɪn'frikwən(t)li

infringe
BR ɪn'frɪn(d)ʒ, -ɪz, -ɪŋ, -d
AM ɪn'frɪndʒ, -ɪz, -ɪŋ, -d

infringement
BR ɪn'frɪn(d)ʒm(ə)nt, -s
AM ɪn'frɪndʒmənt, -s

infringer
BR ɪn'frɪn(d)ʒə(r), -z
AM ɪn'frɪndʒər, -z

infructescence
BR ˌɪnfrʌk'tɛsns, -ɪz
AM ɪnˌfrək'tɛsəns, -əz

infula
BR 'ɪnfjʊlə(r)
AM 'ɪnfjələ

infulae
BR 'ɪnfjʊliː
AM 'ɪnfjəli, 'ɪnf(j)əˌlaɪ

infundibular
BR ˌɪnfʌn'dɪbjʊlə(r)
AM ¦ɪnfən'dɪbjələr

infuriate
BR ɪn'fjʊərɪeɪt, ɪn'fjɔːrɪeɪt, -s, -ɪŋ, -ɪd
AM ɪn'fjuriˌeɪ|t, -ts, -dɪŋ, -dɪd

infuriatingly
BR ɪn'fjʊərɪeɪtɪŋli, ɪn'fjɔːrɪeɪtɪŋli
AM ɪn'fjuriˌeɪdɪŋli

infuriation
BR ɪnˌfjʊərɪ'eɪʃn, ɪnˌfjɔːrɪ'eɪʃn, -z
AM ɪnˌfjuri'eɪʃən, -z

infusable
BR ɪn'fjuːzəbl
AM ɪn'fjuzəbəl

infuse
BR ɪn'fjuːz, -ɪz, -ɪŋ, -d
AM ɪn'fjuz, -ɪz, -ɪŋ, -d

infuser
BR ɪn'fjuːzə(r), -z
AM ɪn'fjuzər, -z

infusibility
BR ɪnˌfjuːzɪ'bɪlɪti
AM ɪnˌfjuzə'bɪlɪdi

infusible
BR ɪn'fjuːzɪbl
AM ɪn'fjuzəbəl

infusion
BR ɪn'fjuːʒn, -z
AM ɪn'fjuʒən, -z

infusive
BR ɪn'fjuːzɪv
AM ɪn'fjuzɪv

infusorial earth
BR ˌɪnfjʊˌzɔːrɪəl 'əːθ, ˌɪnfjʊˌsɔːrɪəl +, -s
AM ¦ɪnfjə¦zɔriəl 'ərθ, -s

Inga
BR 'ɪŋə(r)
AM 'ɪŋ(g)ə

Ingatestone
BR 'ɪŋgətstəʊn, 'ɪŋgeɪtstəʊn
AM 'ɪŋgeɪtsˌtoʊn

ingather
BR ˌɪn'gað|ə(r), -əz, -(ə)rɪŋ, -əd
AM 'ɪn¦gæð|ər, -ərz, -(ə)rɪŋ, -ərd

ingathering
noun
BR 'ɪnˌgað(ə)rɪŋ, -z
AM 'ɪn¦gæð(ə)rɪŋ, -z

ingeminate
BR ɪn'dʒɛmɪneɪt, -s, -ɪŋ, -ɪd
AM ɪn'dʒɛməˌneɪ|t, -ts, -dɪŋ, -dɪd

ingenious
BR ɪn'dʒiːnɪəs
AM ɪn'dʒinjəs, ɪn'dʒiniəs

ingeniously
BR ɪn'dʒiːnɪəsli
AM ɪn'dʒinjəsli, ɪn'dʒiniəsli

ingeniousness
BR ɪn'dʒiːnɪəsnəs
AM ɪn'dʒinjəsnəs, ɪn'dʒiniəsnəs

ingénue
BR 'anʒən(j)uː, 'anʒeɪn(j)uː, ˌanʒə'n(j)uː, ˌanʒeɪ'n(j)uː, -z
AM 'ændʒəˌnu, 'ɑndʒəˌnu, -z

ingenuity
BR ˌɪndʒɪ'njuːɪti
AM ˌɪndʒə'n(j)uədi

ingenuous
BR ɪn'dʒɛnjʊəs
AM ɪn'dʒɛnjəwəs

ingenuously
BR ɪn'dʒɛnjʊəsli
AM ɪn'dʒɛnjəwəsli

ingenuousness
BR ɪn'dʒɛnjʊəsnəs
AM ɪn'dʒɛnjəwəsnəs

Ingersoll®
BR 'ɪŋgəsɒl
AM 'ɪŋgərˌsɔl, 'ɪŋgərˌsɑl

ingest
BR ɪn'dʒɛst, -s, -ɪŋ, -ɪd
AM ɪn'dʒɛst, -s, -ɪŋ, -əd

ingestion
BR ɪn'dʒɛstʃn
AM ɪn'dʒɛstʃən

ingestive
BR ɪn'dʒɛstɪv
AM ɪn'dʒɛstɪv

Ingham
BR 'ɪŋəm
AM 'ɪŋəm

inglenook
BR 'ɪŋglnʊk, -s
AM 'ɪŋgəlˌnʊk, -s

Ingleton
BR 'ɪŋglt(ə)n
AM 'ɪŋgəltən

Inglewood
BR 'ɪŋglwʊd
AM 'ɪŋgəl,wʊd

Inglis
BR 'ɪŋglɪs
AM 'ɪŋglɪs

inglorious
BR (,)ɪn'glɔːrɪəs, (,)ɪŋ'glɔːrɪəs
AM ɪn'glɔriəs, ɪŋ'glɔriəs

ingloriously
BR (,)ɪn'glɔːrɪəsli, (,)ɪŋ'glɔːrɪəsli
AM ɪn'glɔriəsli, ɪŋ'glɔriəsli

ingloriousness
BR (,)ɪn'glɔːrɪəsnəs, (,)ɪŋ'glɔːrɪəsnəs
AM ɪn'glɔriəsnəs, ɪŋ'glɔriəsnəs

Ingmar
BR 'ɪŋmɑː(r)
AM 'ɪŋgmɑr

ingoing
BR 'ɪn,gəʊɪŋ, 'ɪŋ,gəʊɪŋ
AM 'ɪn,goʊɪŋ, ,ɪn'goʊɪŋ, 'ɪŋ,goʊɪŋ, ,ɪŋ'goʊɪŋ

Ingoldsby
BR 'ɪŋgl(d)zbi
AM 'ɪŋgəl(d)zbi

ingot
BR 'ɪŋgət, -s
AM 'ɪŋgət, -s

ingraft
BR ɪn'grɑːft, ɪn'graft, ɪŋ'grɑːft, ɪŋ'graft, -s, -ɪŋ, -ɪd
AM ɪn'græft, ɪŋ'græft, -s, -ɪŋ, -əd

ingrain
adjective
BR 'ɪngreɪn, (,)ɪn'greɪn, 'ɪŋgreɪn, (,)ɪŋ'greɪn
AM ɪn'greɪn, 'ɪn,greɪn, 'ɪŋ,greɪn

ingrained
BR (,)ɪn'greɪnd, (,)ɪŋ'greɪnd
AM ɪn'greɪnd, 'ɪn,greɪnd, 'ɪŋ,greɪnd

ingrainedly
BR (,)ɪn'greɪnɪdli, (,)ɪŋ'greɪnɪdli
AM ɪn'greɪnɪdli, 'ɪn,greɪnɪdli, 'ɪŋ,greɪnɪdli

Ingram
BR 'ɪŋgrəm
AM 'ɪŋgrəm

Ingrams
BR 'ɪŋgrəmz
AM 'ɪŋgrəmz

ingrate
BR 'ɪngreɪt, ɪn'greɪt, 'ɪŋgreɪt, ɪŋ'greɪt, -s, -ɪŋ, -ɪd
AM 'ɪn,greɪ|t, 'ɪŋ,greɪ|t, ɪn'greɪ|t, ɪŋ'greɪ|t, -ts, -dɪŋ, -dɪd

ingratiate
BR ɪn'greɪʃɪeɪt, ɪŋ'greɪʃɪeɪt, -s, -ɪŋ, -ɪd
AM ɪn'greɪʃi,eɪ|t, ɪŋ'greɪʃi,eɪ|t, -ts, -dɪŋ, -dɪd

ingratiatingly
BR ɪn'greɪʃɪeɪtɪŋli, ɪŋ'greɪʃɪeɪtɪŋli
AM ɪn'greɪʃi,eɪdɪŋli, ɪŋ'greɪʃi,eɪdɪŋli

ingratiation
BR ɪn,greɪʃɪ'eɪʃn, ɪŋ,greɪʃɪ'eɪʃn, -z
AM ɪn,greɪʃi'eɪʃən, ɪŋ,greɪʃi'eɪʃən, -z

ingratitude
BR ɪn'gratɪtjuːd, ɪn'gratɪtʃuːd, ɪŋ'gratɪtjuːd, ɪŋ'gratɪtʃuːd
AM ɪn'grædə,t(j)ud, ɪŋ'grædə,t(j)ud

ingravescence
BR ,ɪngrə,vɛsns, ,ɪŋgrə'vɛsns, -ɪz
AM ,ɪngrə'vɛsəns, ,ɪŋgrə'vɛsəns, -əz

ingravescent
BR ,ɪngrə,vɛsnt, ,ɪŋgrə'vɛsnt
AM ,ɪngrə'vɛsənt, ,ɪŋgrə'vɛsənt

ingredient
BR ɪn'griːdɪənt, ɪŋ'griːdɪənt, -s
AM ɪn'gridiənt, ɪŋ'gridiənt, -s

Ingres
BR 'aŋgr(ər)
AM 'æŋgr(əs)

ingress
BR 'ɪngrɛs, 'ɪŋgrɛs
AM 'ɪn,grɛs, 'ɪŋ,grɛs

ingression
BR (,)ɪn'grɛʃn, (,)ɪŋ'grɛʃn, -z
AM ɪn'grɛsən, ɪŋ'grɛʃən, -z

ingressive
BR (,)ɪn'grɛsɪv, (,)ɪŋ'grɛsɪv
AM ɪn'grɛsɪv, ɪŋ'grɛsɪv

ingressively
BR (,)ɪn'grɛsɪvli, (,)ɪŋ'grɛsɪvli
AM ɪn'grɛsɪvli, ɪŋ'grɛsɪvli

ingressiveness
BR (,)ɪn'grɛsɪvnɪs, (,)ɪŋ'grɛsɪvnɪs
AM ɪn'grɛsɪvli, ɪŋ'grɛsɪvnɪs

Ingrid
BR 'ɪŋgrɪd
AM 'ɪŋgrɪd

in-group
BR 'ɪngruːp, 'ɪŋgruːp, -s
AM 'ɪn,grup, -s

ingrowing
BR ,ɪn'grəʊɪŋ, ,ɪŋ'grəʊɪŋ
AM 'ɪn,groʊɪŋ

ingrown
BR ,ɪn'grəʊn, ,ɪŋ'grəʊn
AM 'ɪn,groʊn

ingrowth
BR 'ɪngrəʊθ, 'ɪŋgrəʊθ, -s
AM 'ɪn,groʊθ, -s

inguinal
BR 'ɪŋgwɪnl
AM 'ɪŋgwənəl

inguinally
BR 'ɪŋgwɪnl̩i, 'ɪŋgwɪnəli
AM 'ɪŋgwənəli

ingulf
BR ɪn'gʌlf, ɪŋ'gʌlf
AM ɪn'gəlf, ɪŋ'gəlf

ingurgitate
BR (,)ɪn'gəːdʒɪteɪt, (,)ɪŋ'gəːdʒɪteɪt, -s, -ɪŋ, -ɪd
AM ɪŋ'gərdʒə,teɪ|t, -ts, -dɪŋ, -dɪd

ingurgitation
BR ɪn,gəːdʒɪ'teɪʃn, ɪŋ,gəːdʒɪ'teɪʃn, -z
AM ɪŋ,gərdʒə,teɪʃən, -z

inhabit
BR ɪn'hab|ɪt, -ɪts, -ɪtɪŋ, -ɪtɪd
AM ɪn'hæbə|t, -ts, -dɪŋ, -dəd

inhabitability
BR ɪn,habɪtə'bɪlɪti
AM ɪn,(h)æbədə'bɪlɪdi

inhabitable
BR ɪn'habɪtəbl
AM ɪn'hæbədəbəl

inhabitance
BR ɪn'habɪt(ə)ns, -ɪz
AM ɪn'hæbədəns, ɪn'hæbətns, -əz

inhabitancy
BR ɪn'habɪt(ə)ns|i, -ɪz
AM ɪn'hæbədnsi, ɪn'hæbətnsi, -z

inhabitant
BR ɪn'habɪt(ə)nt, -s
AM ɪn'hæbədnt, -s

inhabitation
BR ɪn,habɪ'teɪʃn, -z
AM ɪn,(h)æbə'teɪʃən, -z

inhalant
BR ɪn'heɪlənt, ɪn'heɪlnt, -s
AM ɪn'heɪlənt, -s

inhalation
BR ,ɪnhə'leɪʃn, -z
AM ,ɪnhə'leɪʃən, -z

inhale
BR ɪn'heɪl, -z, -ɪŋ, -d
AM ɪn'heɪl, -z, -ɪŋ, -d

inhaler
BR ɪn'heɪlə(r), -z
AM ɪn'heɪlər, -z

inharmonic
BR ,ɪnhɑː'mɒnɪk
AM ',ɪnhɑr'mɑnɪk

inharmonious
BR ,ɪnhɑː'məʊnɪəs
AM ',ɪnhɑr'moʊniəs

inharmoniously
BR ,ɪnhɑː'məʊnɪəsli
AM ',ɪnhɑr'moʊniəsli

inharmoniousness
BR ,ɪnhɑː'məʊnɪəsnəs
AM ',ɪnhɑr'moʊniəsnəs

inhere
BR ɪn'hɪə(r), -z, -ɪŋ, -d
AM ɪn'hɪ(ə)r, -z, -ɪŋ, -d

inherence
BR ɪn'hɛrəns, ɪn'hɛrn̩s, ɪn'hɪərəns, ɪn'hɪərn̩s
AM ɪn'hɪrəns, ɪn'hɛrəns

inherent
BR ɪn'hɛrənt, ɪn'hɛrn̩t, ɪn'hɪərənt, ɪn'hɪərn̩t
AM ɪn'hɪrənt, ɪn'hɛrənt

inherently
BR ɪn'hɛrəntli, ɪn'hɛrn̩tli, ɪn'hɪərəntli, ɪn'hɪərn̩tli
AM ɪn'hɪrən(t)li, ɪn'hɛrən(t)li

inherit
BR ɪn'hɛr|ɪt, -ɪts, -ɪtɪŋ, -ɪtɪd
AM ɪn'hɛrə|t, -ts, -dɪŋ, -dəd

inheritability
BR ɪn,hɛrɪtə'bɪlɪti
AM ɪn,(h)ɛrədə'bɪlɪdi

inheritable
BR ɪn'hɛrɪtəbl
AM ɪn'hɛrədəbəl

inheritance
BR ɪn'hɛrɪt(ə)ns, -ɪz
AM ɪn'hɛrədəns, ɪn'hɛrətns, -əz

inheritor
BR ɪn'hɛrɪtə(r), -z
AM ɪn'hɛrədər, -z

inheritress
BR ɪn'hɛrɪtrɪs, -ɪz
AM ɪn'hɛrətrəs, -əz

inheritrices
BR ɪn'hɛrɪtrɪsiːz

AM ɪn'hɛrətrəsiz

inheritrix
BR ɪn'hɛrɪtrɪks, -ɪz
AM ɪn'hɛrə,trɪks, -ɪz

inhesion
BR ɪn'hiːʒn, -z
AM ɪn'hiʒən, -z

inhibit
BR ɪn'hɪb|ɪt, -ɪts, -ɪtɪŋ, -ɪtɪd
AM ɪn'hɪbɪ|t, -ts, -dɪŋ, -dɪd

inhibition
BR ,ɪn(h)ɪ'bɪʃn, -z
AM ,ɪnə'bɪʃən, ,ɪnhə'bɪʃən, ,ɪn(h)ɪ'bɪʃən, -z

inhibitive
BR ɪn'hɪbɪtɪv
AM ɪn'hɪbɪdɪv

inhibitor
BR ɪn'hɪbɪtə(r), -z
AM ɪn'hɪbədər, -z

inhibitory
BR ɪn'hɪbɪt(ə)ri
AM ɪn'hɪbə,tɔri

inhomogeneity
BR ɪn,həʊmə(ʊ)dʒɪ'niːɪti, ɪn,hɒmə(ʊ)dʒɪ'niːɪti, ɪn,həʊmə(ʊ)dʒɪ'neɪɪti, ɪn,hɒmə(ʊ)dʒɪ'neɪɪti
AM ɪn,(h)oʊmədʒə'niɪdi, ɪn,(h)oʊmoʊdʒə'niɪdi, ɪn,(h)oʊmədʒə'neɪɪdi, ɪn,(h)oʊmoʊdʒə'neɪɪdi

inhomogeneous
BR ɪn,həʊmə(ʊ)'dʒiːnɪəs, ɪn,hɒmə(ʊ)'dʒiːnɪəs
AM ɪn,(h)oʊmə'dʒiniəs, ɪn,(h)oʊmoʊ'dʒiniəs

inhospitable
BR ,ɪnhɒ'spɪtəbl, ɪn'hɒspɪtəbl
AM ¦ɪnhɑ'spɪdəbəl, ¦ɪn'hɑspɪdəbəl, ɪnhɑ'spɪdəbəl, ɪn'hɑspɪdəbəl

inhospitableness
BR ,ɪnhɒ'spɪtəblnəs, (,)ɪn'hɒspɪtəblnəs
AM ¦ɪnhɑ'spɪdəbəlnəs, ¦ɪn'hɑspɪdəbəlnəs, ɪnhɑ'spɪdəbəlnəs, ɪn'hɑspɪdəbəlnəs

inhospitably
BR ,ɪnhɒ'spɪtəbli, (,)ɪn'hɒspɪtəbli
AM ¦ɪnhɑ'spɪdəbli, ¦ɪn'hɑspɪdəbli, ɪnhɑ'spɪdəbli, ɪn'hɑspɪdəbli

inhospitality
BR ,ɪnhɒspɪ'talɪti, ɪn,hɒspɪ'talɪti
AM ɪn,(h)ɑspə'tælədi

in-house
BR ,ɪn'haʊs
AM 'ɪn'haʊs

inhuman
BR (,)ɪn'hjuːmən
AM ɪn'(h)jumən

inhumane
BR ,ɪnhjʊ'meɪn
AM ¦ɪn(h)ju'meɪn, ɪn(h)ju'meɪn

inhumanely
BR ,ɪnhjʊ'meɪnli
AM ¦ɪn(h)ju'meɪnli, ɪn(h)ju'meɪnli

inhumanity
BR ,ɪnhjʊ'manɪti
AM ¦ɪn(h)ju'mænədi, -z

inhumanly
BR ɪn'hjuːmənli
AM ɪn'(h)jumənli

inhumanness
BR ɪn'hjuːmənnəs
AM ɪn'(h)jumənnəs

inhumation
BR ,ɪnhjʊ'meɪʃn, -z
AM ¦ɪn(h)ju'meɪʃən, -z

inhume
BR (,)ɪn'hjuːm, -z, -ɪŋ, -d
AM ɪn'(h)jum, -z, -ɪŋ, -d

Inigo
BR 'ɪnɪgəʊ
AM 'ɪnɪgoʊ

inimical
BR ɪ'nɪmɪkl
AM ɪ'nɪməkəl

inimically
BR ɪ'nɪmɪkli
AM ɪ'nɪmək(ə)li

inimitability
BR ɪ,nɪmɪtə'bɪlɪti
AM ɪ,nɪmədə'bɪlɪdi

inimitable
BR ɪ'nɪmɪtəbl
AM ɪ'nɪmədəbəl

inimitableness
BR ɪ'nɪmɪtəblnəs
AM ɪ'nɪmədəbəlnəs

inimitably
BR ɪ'nɪmɪtəbli
AM ɪ'nɪmədəbli

iniquitous
BR ɪ'nɪkwɪtəs
AM ɪ'nɪkwədəs

iniquitously
BR ɪ'nɪkwɪtəsli
AM ɪ'nɪkwədəsli

iniquitousness
BR ɪ'nɪkwɪtəsnəs
AM ɪ'nɪkwədəsnəs

iniquity
BR ɪ'nɪkwɪt|i, -ɪz
AM ɪ'nɪkwɪdi, -z

initial
BR ɪ'nɪʃl, -lz, -l̩ɪŋ\-əlɪŋ, -ld
AM ɪ'nɪʃəl, -əlz, -(ə)lɪŋ, -əld

initialisation
BR ɪ,nɪʃəlʌɪ'zeɪʃn, ɪ,nɪʃl̩ʌɪ'zeɪʃn, -z
AM ɪ,nɪʃələ'zeɪʃən, ɪ,nɪʃə,laɪ'zeɪʃən, -z

initialise
BR ɪ'nɪʃəlʌɪz, ɪ'nɪʃl̩ʌɪz, -ɪz, -ɪŋ, -d
AM ɪ'nɪʃə,laɪz, -ɪz, -ɪŋ, -d

initialism
BR ɪ'nɪʃəlɪz(ə)m, ɪ'nɪʃl̩ɪz(ə)m, -z
AM ɪ'nɪʃə,lɪzəm, -z

initialization
BR ɪ,nɪʃəlʌɪ'zeɪʃn, ɪ,nɪʃl̩ʌɪ'zeɪʃn, -z
AM ɪ,nɪʃələ'zeɪʃən, ɪ,nɪʃə,laɪ'zeɪʃən|, -z

initialize
BR ɪ'nɪʃəlʌɪz, ɪ'nɪʃl̩ʌɪz, -ɪz, -ɪŋ, -d
AM ɪ'nɪʃə,laɪz, -ɪz, -ɪŋ, -d

initially
BR ɪ'nɪʃl̩i, ɪ'nɪʃəli
AM ɪ'nɪʃ(ə)li

initiate[1]
noun
BR ɪ'nɪʃɪət, -s
AM ɪ'nɪʃiət, -s

initiate[2]
verb
BR ɪ'nɪʃɪeɪt, -s, -ɪŋ, -ɪd
AM ɪ'nɪʃi,eɪ|t, -ts, -dɪŋ, -dɪd

initiation
BR ɪ,nɪʃɪ'eɪʃn, -z
AM ɪ'nɪʃi,eɪʃən, -z

initiative
BR ɪ'nɪʃətɪv, -z
AM ɪ'nɪʃədɪv, -z

initiator
BR ɪ'nɪʃɪeɪtə(r), -z
AM ɪ'nɪʃi,eɪdər, -z

initiatory
BR ɪ'nɪʃ(ɪ)ət(ə)ri
AM ɪ'nɪʃ(i)ə,tɔri

inject
BR ɪn'dʒɛkt, -s, -ɪŋ, -ɪd
AM ɪn'dʒɛk|(t), -(t)s, -tɪŋ, -təd

injectable
BR ɪn'dʒɛktəbl, -z
AM ɪn'dʒɛktəbəl, -z

injection
BR ɪn'dʒɛkʃn, -z
AM ɪn'dʒɛkʃən, -z

injector
BR ɪn'dʒɛktə(r), -z
AM ɪn'dʒɛktər, -z

in-joke
BR 'ɪndʒəʊk, -s
AM 'ɪn,dʒoʊk, -s

injudicious
BR ,ɪndʒʊ'dɪʃəs
AM ¦ɪndʒu'dɪʃəs

injudiciously
BR ,ɪndʒʊ'dɪʃəsli
AM ¦ɪndʒu'dɪʃəsli

injudiciousness
BR ,ɪndʒʊ'dɪʃəsnəs
AM ¦ɪndʒu'dɪʃəsnəs

Injun
BR 'ɪndʒ(ə)n, -z
AM 'ɪndʒən, -z

injunct
BR ɪn'dʒʌŋ(k)t
AM ɪn'dʒəŋ(k)t, ɪn'dʒəŋk(t)

injunction
BR ɪn'dʒʌŋ(k)ʃn, -z
AM ɪn'dʒəŋ(k)ʃən, -z

injunctive
BR ɪn'dʒʌŋ(k)tɪv
AM ɪn'dʒəŋ(k)tɪv

injure
BR 'ɪn(d)ʒ|ə(r), -əz, -(ə)rɪŋ, -əd
AM 'ɪndʒ|ər, -ərz, -(ə)rɪŋ, -ərd

injurer
BR 'ɪn(d)ʒ(ə)rə(r), -z
AM 'ɪndʒərər, -z

injuria
BR ɪn'dʒʊərɪə(r)
AM ɪn'dʒʊriə

injuriae
BR ɪn'dʒʊərɪiː, ɪn'dʒʊərɪʌɪ
AM ɪn'dʒʊri,i, ɪn'dʒʊri,aɪ

injurious
BR ɪn'dʒʊərɪəs
AM ɪn'dʒʊriəs

injuriously
BR ɪn'dʒʊərɪəsli
AM ɪn'dʒʊriəsli

injuriousness
BR ɪn'dʒʊərɪəsnəs
AM ɪn'dʒʊriəsnəs

injury
BR 'ɪn(d)ʒ(ə)r|i, -ɪz
AM 'ɪndʒ(ə)ri, -z

injustice
BR ɪn'dʒʌst|ɪs, -ɪsɪz
AM ɪn'dʒəstəs, -əz

ink
BR ɪŋ|k, -ks, -kɪŋ, -(k)t
AM ɪŋ|k, -ks, -kɪŋ, -(k)t

Inkatha
BR ɪn'kɑːtə(r), ɪŋ'kɑːtə(r)
AM ɪn'kɑdə, ɪŋ'kɑdə

inkblot
BR 'ɪŋkblɒt, -s
AM 'ɪŋk,blɑt, -s

inkbottle
BR 'ɪŋk,bɒtl, -z
AM 'ɪŋk,bɑdəl, -z

inker
BR 'ɪŋkə(r), -z
AM 'ɪŋkər, -z

inkhorn
BR ˈɪŋkhɔːn, -z
AM ˈɪŋk,(h)ɔ(ə)rn, -z
inkily
BR ˈɪŋkɨli
AM ˈɪŋkɨli
inkiness
BR ˈɪŋkɪnɨs
AM ˈɪŋkinɨs
inkling
BR ˈɪŋklɪŋ, -z
AM ˈɪŋklɪŋ, -z
inkpad
BR ˈɪŋkpad, -z
AM ˈɪŋk,pæd, -z
Inkpen
BR ˈɪŋkpɛn
AM ˈɪŋk,pɛn
inkpot
BR ˈɪŋkpɒt, -s
AM ˈɪŋk,pɑt, -s
inkstand
BR ˈɪŋkstand, -z
AM ˈɪŋk,stænd, -z
inkwell
BR ˈɪŋkwɛl, -z
AM ˈɪŋk,wɛl, -z
inky
BR ˈɪŋk|i, -ɪə(r), -ɪɪst
AM ˈɪŋki, -ər, -ɨst
INLA
BR ,ʌɪɛnɛlˈeɪ
AM ,aɪ,ɛn,ɛlˈeɪ
inlaid
BR ,ɪnˈleɪd
AM ˌɪnˈleɪd
inland[1]
adjective
BR ˈɪnland, ˈɪnlənd
AM ˈɪn,lænd, ˈɪnlənd
inland[2]
adverb
BR ɪnˈland, ˈɪnland
AM ˈɪn,lænd, ˈɪnlənd
inlander
BR ˈɪnlandə(r),
ˈɪnləndə(r), -z
AM ˈɪn,lændər,
ˈɪnləndər, -z
inlandish
BR ˈɪnlandɪʃ, ˈɪnləndɪʃ
AM ˈɪn,lændɪʃ,
ˈɪnləndɪʃ
in-law
BR ˈɪnlɔː(*r*), -z
AM ˈɪn,lɔ, ˈɪn,lɑ, -z
inlay[1]
noun
BR ˈɪnleɪ, -z
AM ˈɪn,leɪ, -z
inlay[2]
verb
BR ,ɪnˈleɪ, -z, -ɪŋ, -d
AM ,ɪnˈleɪ, -z, -ɪŋ, -d
inlayer
BR ɪnˈleɪə(r),
ˈɪnleɪə(r), -z
AM ,ɪnˈleɪər, ˈɪn,leɪər, -z

inlet
BR ˈɪnlɪt, ˈɪnlɛt, -s
AM ˈɪn,lɛt, ˈɪnlət, -s
inlier
BR ˈɪn,lʌɪə(r), -z
AM ˈɪn,laɪər, -z
in loco parentis
BR ɪn ,ləʊkəʊ
pəˈrɛntɪs
AM ˌɪn ,loʊkoʊ
pəˈrɛn(t)əs
inly
BR ˈɪnli
AM ˈɪnli
inlying
BR ˈɪn,lʌɪɪŋ
AM ˈɪn,laɪɪŋ
Inmarsat
BR ˈɪnmɑːsat
AM ˈɪnmɑr,sæt
inmate
BR ˈɪnmeɪt, -s
AM ˈɪn,meɪt, -s
in medias res
BR ɪn ,miːdɪas ˈreɪz,
+ ,miːdɪɑːs +,
+ ,mɛdɪas +,
+ ,mɛdɪɑːs +,
+ ˈreɪs
AM ,ɪn ˌmeɪdi,ɑs ˈreɪs,
,ɪn ˌmidi,ɑs ˈreɪs
in memoriam
BR ,ɪn mɨˈmɔːrɪam,
+ mɨˈmɔːrɪəm
AM ,ɪn məˈmɔriəm,
,ɪn məˈmɔri,æm
inmost
BR ˈɪnməʊst
AM ˈɪn,moʊst
inn
BR ɪn, -z
AM ɪn, -z
innards
BR ˈɪnədz
AM ˈɪnərdz
innate
BR ɪˈneɪt
AM ɨˈneɪt
innately
BR ɪˈneɪtli
AM ɨˈneɪtli
innateness
BR ɪˈneɪtnɨs
AM ɨˈneɪtnɨs
inner
BR ˈɪnə(r)
AM ˈɪnər
innerly
BR ˈɪnəli
AM ˈɪnərli
innermost
BR ˈɪnəməʊst
AM ˈɪnər,moʊst
innerness
BR ˈɪnənəs
AM ˈɪnərnəs

innervate
BR ˈɪnəːveɪt, ˈɪnəveɪt,
ɪˈnəːveɪt, -s, -ɪŋ, -ɨd
AM ɨˈnər,veɪ|t,
ˈɪnər,veɪ|t, -ts, -dɪŋ,
-dɨd
innervation
BR ,ɪnəːˈveɪʃn,
,ɪnəˈveɪʃn
AM ,ɪnərˈveɪʃən
Innes
BR ˈɪnɪs, ˈɪnɪz
AM ˈɪnɨs
inning
BR ˈɪnɪŋ, -z
AM ˈɪnɪŋ, -z
Innisfail
BR ,ɪnɪsˈfeɪl
AM ,ɪnɨsˈfeɪl
innkeeper
BR ˈɪn,kiːpə(r), -z
AM ˈɪn,kipər, -z
innocence
BR ˈɪnəs(ə)ns
AM ˈɪnəsəns
innocency
BR ˈɪnəs(ə)nsi
AM ˈɪnəsənsi
innocent
BR ˈɪnəs(ə)nt, -s
AM ˈɪnəsənt, -s
innocently
BR ˈɪnəs(ə)ntli
AM ˈɪnəsən(t)li
innocuity
BR ,ɪnɒˈkjuːɪti
AM ɪ,nɑˈkjuədi
innocuous
BR ɪˈnɒkjʊəs
AM ɨˈnɑkjəwəs
innocuously
BR ɪˈnɒkjʊəsli
AM ɨˈnɑkjəwəsli
innocuousness
BR ɪˈnɒkjʊəsnəs
AM ɨˈnɑkjəwəsnəs
innominate
BR ɪˈnɒmɨnət
AM ɨˈnɑmənət
innovate
BR ˈɪnəveɪt, -s, -ɪŋ, -ɨd
AM ˈɪnə,veɪ|t,
ˈɪnoʊ,veɪ|t, -ts, -dɪŋ,
-dɨd
innovation
BR ,ɪnəˈveɪʃn, -z
AM ,ɪnəˈveɪʃən,
,ɪnoʊˈveɪʃən, -z
innovational
BR ,ɪnəˈveɪʃn̩(ə)l,
,ɪnəˈveɪʃən(ə)l
AM ,ɪnəˈveɪʃ(ə)nəl,
,ɪnoʊˈveɪʃ(ə)nəl
innovative
BR ˈɪnəveɪtɪv,
ˈɪnəvətɪv
AM ˈɪnə,veɪdɪv

innovatively
BR ˈɪnəveɪtɨvli,
ˈɪnəvətɨvli
AM ˈɪnə,veɪdɨvli
innovativeness
BR ˈɪnəveɪtɨvnɨs,
ˈɪnəvətɨvnɨs
AM ˈɪnə,veɪdɪvnɨs
innovator
BR ˈɪnəveɪtə(r), -z
AM ˈɪnə,veɪdər,
ˈɪnoʊ,veɪdər, -z
innovatory
BR ˈɪnəveɪt(ə)ri,
ˈɪnəvət(ə)ri
AM ˈɪnəvə,tɔri,
ˈɪnoʊvə,tɔri
innoxious
BR ɪˈnɒkʃəs
AM ɪ(n)ˈnɑkʃəs,
ɨˈnɑkʃəs
innoxiously
BR ɪˈnɒkʃəsli
AM ɪ(n)ˈnɑkʃəsli,
ɨˈnɑkʃəsli
innoxiousness
BR ɪˈnɒkʃəsnəs
AM ɪ(n)ˈnɑkʃəsnəs,
ɨˈnɑkʃəsnəs
Innsbruck
BR ˈɪnzbrʊk
AM ˈɪnz,brʊk
Inns of Court
BR ,ɪnz əv ˈkɔːt
AM ˌɪnz əv ˈkɔ(ə)rt
innuendo
BR ,ɪnjʊˈɛndəʊ, -z
AM ,ɪnjəˈwɛndoʊ, -z
Innuit
BR ˈɪn(j)ʊɪt
AM ˈɪn(j)ʊɪt
innumerability
BR ɪ,njuːm(ə)rəˈbɪlɨti
AM ɨ,n(j)um(ə)rəˈbɪlɨdi
innumerable
BR ɪˈnjuːm(ə)rəbl
AM ɨˈn(j)um(ə)rəbəl
innumerably
BR ɪˈnjuːm(ə)rəbli
AM ɨˈn(j)um(ə)rəbli
innumeracy
BR ɪˈnjuːm(ə)rəsi
AM ɨˈn(j)um(ə)rəsi
innumerate
BR ɪˈnjuːm(ə)rət
AM ɨˈn(j)umərət
innutrition
BR ,ɪnjʊˈtrɪʃn
AM ɨ,n(j)uˈtrɪʃən,
ɪ(n),n(j)uˈtrɪʃən
innutritious
BR ,ɪnjʊˈtrɪʃəs
AM ɨˈn(j)utrɪʃəs,
ɪ(n)ˈn(j)utrɪʃəs
inobservance
BR ,ɪnəbˈzəːvns
AM ˌɪnəbˈzərvəns

inobservant
BR ˌɪnəbˈzəːvnt
AM ˌɪnəbˈzərvənt
inocula
BR ɪˈnɒkjʊlə(r)
AM ɪˈnɑkjələ
inoculable
BR ɪˈnɒkjʊləbl
AM ɪˈnɑkjələbəl
inoculate
BR ɪˈnɒkjʊleɪt, -s, -ɪŋ, -ɪd
AM ɪˈnɑkjəˌleɪ|t, -ts, -dɪŋ, -dɪd
inoculation
BR ɪˌnɒkjʊˈleɪʃn, -z
AM ɪˌnɑkjəˈleɪʃən, -z
inoculative
BR ɪˈnɒkjʊlətɪv
AM ɪˈnɑkjəˌleɪdɪv
inoculator
BR ɪˈnɒkjʊleɪtə(r), -z
AM ɪˈnɑkjəˌleɪdər, -z
inoculum
BR ɪˈnɒkjʊləm
AM ɪˈnɑkjələm
inodorous
BR ɪnˈəʊd(ə)rəs
AM ɪnˈoʊdərəs
in-off
BR ˌɪnˈɒf, -s
AM ˈɪnˌɑf, -s
inoffensive
BR ˌɪnəˈfɛnsɪv
AM ¦ɪnəˈfɛnsɪv
inoffensively
BR ˌɪnəˈfɛnsɪvli
AM ¦ɪnəˈfɛnsəvli
inoffensiveness
BR ˌɪnəˈfɛnsɪvnɪs
AM ¦ɪnəˈfɛnsɪvnɪs
inofficious
BR ˌɪnəˈfɪʃəs
AM ¦ɪnəˈfɪʃəs
inoperability
BR ɪnˌɒp(ə)rəˈbɪlɪti
AM ɪnˌɑp(ə)rəˈbɪlɪdi
inoperable
BR (ˌ)ɪnˈɒp(ə)rəbl
AM ɪnˈɑp(ə)rəbəl
inoperably
BR (ˌ)ɪnˈɒp(ə)rəbli
AM ɪnˈɑp(ə)rəbli
inoperative
BR (ˌ)ɪnˈɒp(ə)rətɪv
AM ɪnˈɑp(ə)rədɪv
inoperativeness
BR (ˌ)ɪnˈɒp(ə)rətɪvnɪs
AM ɪnˈɑp(ə)rədɪvnɪs
inopportune
BR (ˌ)ɪnˈɒpətjuːn, ˌɪnɒpəˈtjuːn, (ˌ)ɪnˈɒpətʃuːn, ˌɪnɒpəˈtʃuːn
AM ¦ɪnˌɑpərˈt(j)un, ɪnˌɑpərˈt(j)un
inopportunely
BR (ˌ)ɪnˈɒpətjuːnli, ˌɪnɒpəˈtjuːnli, (ˌ)ɪnˈɒpətʃuːnli, ˌɪnɒpəˈtʃuːnli
AM ¦ɪnˌɑpərˈt(j)unli, ɪnˌɑpərˈt(j)unli
inopportuneness
BR (ˌ)ɪnˈɒpətjuːnnəs, ˌɪnɒpəˈtjuːnnəs, (ˌ)ɪnˈɒpətʃuːnnəs, ˌɪnɒpəˈtʃuːnnəs
AM ¦ɪnˌɑpərˈt(j)u(n)nəs, ɪnˌɑpərˈt(j)u(n)nəs
inordinate
BR ɪnˈɔːdɪnət, ɪnˈɔːdn̩ət
AM ɪˈnɔrdn̩ət
inordinately
BR ɪnˈɔːdɪnətli, ɪnˈɔːdn̩ətli
AM ɪˈnɔrdn̩ətli
inordinateness
BR ɪnˈɔːdɪnətnəs, ɪnˈɔːdn̩ətnəs
AM ɪˈnɔrdn̩ətnəs
inorganic
BR ˌɪnɔːˈganɪk
AM ¦ɪnɔrˈgænɪk
inorganically
BR ˌɪnɔːˈganɪkli
AM ¦ɪnɔrˈgænək(ə)li
inosculate
BR ɪnˈɒskjʊleɪt, -s, -ɪŋ, -ɪd
AM ɪnˈɑskjəˌleɪ|t, -ts, -dɪŋ, -dɪd
inosculation
BR ɪnˌɒskjʊˈleɪʃn, -z
AM ɪnˌɑskjəˈleɪʃən, -z
inositol
BR ʌɪˈnəʊsɪtɒl
AM aɪˈnoʊsədɔl, aɪˈnoʊsədɑl
in-patient
BR ˈɪnˌpeɪʃnt, -s
AM ˈɪnˌpeɪʃənt, -s
in propria persona
BR ɪn ˌprəʊprɪə pəˈsəʊnə(r), + pəːˈsəʊnə(r)
AM ˌɪn ¦proʊpriə pərˈsoʊnə
input
BR ˈɪnpʊt, -s, -ɪŋ, -ɪd
AM ˈɪnˌpʊ|t, -ts, -dɪŋ, -dəd
inputter
BR ˈɪnpʊtə(r), -z
AM ˈɪnˌpʊdər, -z
inquest
BR ˈɪŋkwɛst, ˈɪnkwɛst, -s
AM ˈɪnˌkwɛst, ˈɪŋˌkwɛst, -s
inquietude
BR ɪnˈkwʌɪɪtjuːd, ɪŋˈkwʌɪɪtjuːd, ɪnˈkwʌɪɪtʃuːd, ɪŋˈkwʌɪɪtʃuːd
AM ɪnˈkwaɪəˌt(j)ud, ɪŋˈkwaɪəˌt(j)ud
inquiline
BR ˈɪnkwɪlʌɪn, ˈɪŋkwɪlʌɪn, -z
AM ˈɪŋkwəˌlaɪn, ˈɪŋkwələn, -z
inquire
BR ɪnˈkwʌɪə(r), ɪŋˈkwʌɪə(r), -z, -ɪŋ, -d
AM ɪnˈkwaɪ(ə)r, ɪŋˈkwaɪ(ə)r, -z, -ɪŋ, -d
inquirer
BR ɪnˈkwʌɪərə(r), ɪŋˈkwʌɪərə(r), -z
AM ɪnˈkwaɪ(ə)rər, ɪŋˈkwaɪ(ə)rər, -z
inquiry
BR ɪnˈkwʌɪ(ə)r|i, ɪŋˈkwʌɪ(ə)r|i, -ɪz
AM ˈɪnˌkwaɪri, ɪnˈkwaɪri, ˈɪnkwəri, ˈɪŋˌkwaɪri, ˈɪŋkwəri, -z
inquisition
BR ˌɪnkwɪˈzɪʃn, ˌɪŋkwɪˈzɪʃn, -z
AM ˌɪnkwəˈzɪʃən, ˌɪŋkwəˈzɪʃən, -z
inquisitional
BR ˌɪnkwɪˈzɪʃn(ə)l, ˌɪŋkwɪˈzɪʃən(ə)l
AM ˌɪnkwəˈzɪʃ(ə)nəl, ˌɪŋkwəˈzɪʃ(ə)nəl
inquisitive
BR ɪnˈkwɪzɪtɪv, ɪŋˈkwɪzɪtɪv
AM ɪnˈkwɪzədɪv, ɪŋˈkwɪzədɪv
inquisitively
BR ɪnˈkwɪzɪtɪvli, ɪŋˈkwɪzɪtɪvli
AM ɪnˈkwɪzədəvli, ɪŋˈkwɪzədəvli
inquisitiveness
BR ɪnˈkwɪzɪtɪvnɪs, ɪŋˈkwɪzɪtɪvnɪs
AM ɪnˈkwɪzədɪvnɪs, ɪŋˈkwɪzədɪvnɪs
inquisitor
BR ɪnˈkwɪzɪtə(r), ɪŋˈkwɪzɪtə(r), -z
AM ɪnˈkwɪzədər, ɪŋˈkwɪzədər, -z
inquisitorial
BR ɪnˌkwɪzɪˈtɔːrɪəl, ɪŋˌkwɪzɪˈtɔːrɪəl, ˌɪnkwɪzɪˈtɔːrɪəl, ˌɪŋkwɪzɪˈtɔːrɪəl
AM ɪnˌkwɪzəˈtɔriəl, ɪŋˌkwɪzəˈtɔriəl
inquisitorially
BR ɪnˌkwɪzɪˈtɔːrɪəli, ɪŋˌkwɪzɪˈtɔːrɪəli, ˌɪnkwɪzɪˈtɔːrɪəli, ˌɪŋkwɪzɪˈtɔːrɪəli
AM ɪnˌkwɪzəˈtɔriəli, ɪŋˌkwɪzəˈtɔriəli
inquorate
BR ˌɪnˈkwɔːreɪt, ˌɪŋˈkwɔːreɪt
AM ɪnˈkwɔˌreɪt, ɪŋˈkwɔˌreɪt
in re
BR ˌɪn ˈreɪ, + ˈriː
AM ˌɪn ˈreɪ
in rem
BR ɪn ˈrɛm
AM ɪn ˈrɛm
inroad
BR ˈɪnrəʊd, -z
AM ˈɪnˌroʊd, -z
inrush
BR ˈɪnrʌʃ, -ɪz
AM ˈɪnˌrəʃ, -əz
inrushing
BR ˈɪnˌrʌʃɪŋ, -z
AM ˈɪnˌrəʃɪŋ, -z
insalubrious
BR ˌɪnsəˈl(j)uːbrɪəs
AM ¦ɪnsəˈlubriəs
insalubrity
BR ˌɪnsəˈl(j)uːbrɪti
AM ¦ɪnsəˈlubrədi
insane
BR ɪnˈseɪn
AM ɪnˈseɪn
insanely
BR ɪnˈseɪnli
AM ɪnˈseɪnli
insaneness
BR ɪnˈseɪnnɪs
AM ɪnˈseɪ(n)nɪs
insanitarily
BR ɪnˈsanɪt(ə)rɪli
AM ɪnˌsænəˈtɛrəli
insanitariness
BR ɪnˈsanɪt(ə)rɪnɪs
AM ɪnˈsænəˌtɛrinɪs
insanitary
BR ɪnˈsanɪt(ə)ri
AM ɪnˈsænəˌtɛri
insanity
BR ɪnˈsanɪti
AM ɪnˈsænədi
insatiability
BR ɪnˌseɪʃəˈbɪlɪti
AM ¦ɪnˌseɪʃəˈbɪlɪdi, ənˌseɪʃəˈbɪlɪdi
insatiable
BR ɪnˈseɪʃ(ɪ)əbl
AM ɪnˈseɪʃəbəl
insatiably
BR ɪnˈseɪʃ(ɪ)əbli
AM ɪnˈseɪʃəbli
insatiate
BR ɪnˈseɪʃɪət
AM ɪnˈseɪʃ(i)ɪt
inscape
BR ˈɪnskeɪp, -s
AM ˈɪnzˌkeɪp, ˈɪnˌskeɪp, -s

inscribable
BR ɪn'skrʌɪbəbl
AM ɪnz'kraɪbəbəl, ɪn'skraɪbəbəl
inscribe
BR ɪn'skrʌɪb, -z, -ɪŋ, -d
AM ɪnz'kraɪb, ɪn'skraɪb, -z, -ɪŋ, -d
inscriber
BR ɪn'skrʌɪbə(r), -z
AM ɪnz'kraɪbər, ɪn'skraɪbər, -z
inscription
BR ɪn'skrɪpʃn, -z
AM ɪnz'krɪpʃən, ɪn'skrɪpʃən, -z
inscriptional
BR ɪn'skrɪpʃn̩(ə)l, ɪn'skrɪpʃən(ə)l
AM ɪnz'krɪpʃ(ə)nəl, ɪn'skrɪpʃ(ə)nəl
inscriptive
BR ɪn'skrɪptɪv
AM ɪnz'krɪptɪv, ɪn'skrɪptɪv
inscrutability
BR ɪn,skru:tə'bɪlɪti
AM ɪnz,krudə'bɪlɪdi, ən,skrudə'bɪlɪdi
inscrutable
BR ɪn'skru:təbl
AM ɪnz'krudəbəl, ən'skrudəbəl
inscrutableness
BR ɪn'skru:təblnəs
AM ɪnz'krudəbəlnəs, ən'skrudəbəlnəs
inscrutably
BR ɪn'skru:təbli
AM ɪnz'krudəbli, ən'skrudəbli
inscrutibility
BR ɪn,skru:tə'bɪlɪti
AM ɪnz,krudə'bɪlɪdi, ən,skrudə'bɪlɪdi
inseam
BR 'ɪnsi:m, -z
AM 'ɪn,sim, -z
insect
BR 'ɪnsɛkt, -s
AM 'ɪn,sɛk|(t), -(t)s
insectaria
BR ,ɪnsɛk'tɛ:rɪə(r)
AM ɪn,sɛk'tɛriə
insectarium
BR ,ɪnsɛk'tɛ:rɪəm, -z
AM ɪn,sɛk'tɛriəm, -z
insectary
BR ɪn'sɛkt(ə)r|i, -ɪz
AM 'ɪn,sɛk,tɛri, -z
insecticidal
BR ɪn,sɛktɪ'sʌɪdl
AM ɪn'sɛktə,saɪdəl
insecticide
BR ɪn'sɛktɪsʌɪd, -z
AM ɪn'sɛktə,saɪd, -z
insectile
BR ɪn'sɛktʌɪl
AM ɪn'sɛktl, ɪn'sɛk,taɪl
insectivore
BR ɪn'sɛktɪvɔ:(r), -z
AM ɪn'sɛktə,vɔ(ə)r, -z
insectivorous
BR ,ɪnsɛk'tɪv(ə)rəs
AM ¦ɪn,sɛk'tɪv(ə)rəs
insectology
BR ,ɪnsɛk'tɒlədʒi
AM ,ɪn,sɛk'tɑlədʒi
insecure
BR ,ɪnsɪ'kjʊə(r), ,ɪnsɪ'kjɔ:(r)
AM ¦ɪnsə'kjʊ(ə)r
insecurely
BR ,ɪnsɪ'kjʊəli, ,ɪnsɪ'kjɔ:li
AM ¦ɪnsə'kjʊrli
insecurity
BR ,ɪnsɪ'kjʊərɪti, ,ɪnsɪ'kjɔ:rɪti
AM ¦ɪnsə'kjʊrədi
Inselberg
BR 'ɪnslbə:g, -z
AM 'ɪnsəl,bərg, -z
inseminate
BR ɪn'sɛmɪneɪt, -s, -ɪŋ, -ɪd
AM ɪn'sɛmə,neɪ|t, -ts, -dɪŋ, -dɪd
insemination
BR ɪn,sɛmɪ'neɪʃn
AM ɪn,sɛmə'neɪʃən
inseminator
BR ɪn'sɛmɪneɪtə(r), -z
AM ɪn'sɛmə,neɪdər, -z
insensate
BR ɪn'sɛnseɪt, ɪn'sɛnsət
AM ɪn'sɛn,seɪt, 'ɪn,sɛn,seɪt
insensately
BR ɪn'sɛnseɪtli, ɪn'sɛnsətli
AM ɪn'sɛn,seɪtli, 'ɪn,sɛn,seɪtli
insensibility
BR ɪn,sɛnsɪ'bɪlɪti
AM ¦ɪn,sɛnsə'bɪlɪdi, ən,sɛnsə'bɪlɪdi
insensible
BR ɪn'sɛnsɪbl
AM ɪn'sɛnsəbəl
insensibleness
BR ɪn'sɛnsɪblnəs
AM ɪn'sɛnsəbəlnəs
insensibly
BR ɪn'sɛnsɪbli
AM ɪn'sɛnsəbli
insensitive
BR ɪn'sɛnsɪtɪv
AM ɪn'sɛnsədɪv
insensitively
BR ɪn'sɛnsɪtɪvli
AM ɪn'sɛnsədəvli
insensitiveness
BR ɪn'sɛnsɪtɪvnɪs
AM ɪn'sɛnsədɪvnɪs
insensitivity
BR ,ɪnsɛnsɪ'tɪvɪti, ɪn,sɛnsɪ'tɪvɪti
AM ¦ɪn,sɛnsə'tɪvɪdi, ən,sɛnsə'tɪvɪdi
insentience
BR ɪn'sɛnʃns, ɪn'sɛnʃɪəns, ɪn'sɛntɪəns
AM ɪn'sɛnʃ(i)əns
insentient
BR ɪn'sɛnʃnt, ɪn'sɛnʃɪənt, ɪn'sɛntɪənt
AM ɪn'sɛnʃ(i)ənt
inseparability
BR ɪn,sɛp(ə)rə'bɪlɪti, ,ɪnsɛp(ə)rə'bɪlɪti
AM ¦ɪn,sɛp(ə)rə'bɪlɪdi, ɪn,sɛp(ə)rə'bɪlɪdi
inseparable
BR ɪn'sɛp(ə)rəbl
AM ɪn'sɛpərəbəl
inseparably
BR ɪn'sɛp(ə)rəbli
AM ɪn'sɛpərəbli
insert[1]
noun
BR 'ɪnsə:t, -s
AM 'ɪn,sərt, -s
insert[2]
verb
BR ɪn'sə:t, -s, -ɪŋ, -ɪd
AM ɪn'sər|t, -ts, -dɪŋ, -dəd
insertable
BR ɪn'sə:təbl
AM ɪn'sərdəbəl
inserter
BR ɪn'sə:tə(r), -z
AM ɪn'sərdər, -z
insertion
BR ɪn'sə:ʃn, -z
AM ɪn'sərʃən, -z
inset[1]
noun
BR 'ɪnsɛt, -s
AM 'ɪn,sɛt, -s
inset[2]
verb
BR ɪn'sɛt, 'ɪnsɛt, -s, -ɪŋ
AM ɪn'sɛ|t, -ts, -dɪŋ
insetter
BR 'ɪn,sɛtə(r), -z
AM 'ɪn,sɛdər, -z
inshallah
BR ɪn'ʃalə(r)
AM ɪn'ʃɑlə
inshore
BR ,ɪn'ʃɔ:(r)
AM ¦ɪn¦ʃɔ(ə)r, ɪn'ʃɔ(ə)r
inside
BR ,ɪn'sʌɪd, -z
AM ɪn'saɪd, -z
insider
BR (,)ɪn'sʌɪdə(r), -z
AM ɪn'saɪdər, -z
insidious
BR ɪn'sɪdɪəs
AM ɪn'sɪdiəs
insidiously
BR ɪn'sɪdɪəsli
AM ɪn'sɪdiəsli
insidiousness
BR ɪn'sɪdɪəsnəs
AM ɪn'sɪdiəsnəs
insight
BR 'ɪnsʌɪt, -s
AM 'ɪn,saɪt, -s
insightful
BR 'ɪnsʌɪtf(ʊ)l
AM ɪn'saɪtfəl
insightfully
BR 'ɪnsʌɪtfʊli, 'ɪnsʌɪtfli
AM ɪn'saɪtfəli
insignia
BR ɪn'sɪgnɪə(r)
AM ɪn'sɪgniə
insignificance
BR ,ɪnsɪg'nɪfɪk(ə)ns
AM ¦ɪnsɪg'nɪfəkəns
insignificancy
BR ,ɪnsɪg'nɪfɪk(ə)nsi
AM ¦ɪnsɪg'nɪfəkənsi
insignificant
BR ,ɪnsɪg'nɪfɪk(ə)nt
AM ¦ɪnsɪg'nɪfəkənt
insignificantly
BR ,ɪnsɪg'nɪfɪk(ə)ntli
AM ¦ɪnsɪg'nɪfəkən(t)li
insincere
BR ,ɪns(ɪ)n'sɪə(r)
AM ¦ɪnsɪn'sɪ(ə)r
insincerely
BR ,ɪns(ɪ)n'sɪəli
AM ¦ɪnsɪn'sɪrli
insincerity
BR ,ɪns(ɪ)n'sɛrɪti
AM ¦ɪnsɪn'sɛrədi
insinuate
BR ɪn'sɪnjʊeɪt, -s, -ɪŋ, -ɪd
AM ɪn'sɪnjə,weɪ|t, -ts, -dɪŋ, -dɪd
insinuatingly
BR ɪn'sɪnjʊeɪtɪŋli
AM ɪn'sɪnjə,weɪdɪŋli
insinuation
BR ɪn,sɪnjʊ'eɪʃn, -z
AM ɪn,sɪnjə'weɪʃən, -z
insinuative
BR ɪn'sɪnjʊətɪv, ɪn'sɪnjʊeɪtɪv
AM ɪn'sɪnjə,weɪdɪv
insinuator
BR ɪn'sɪnjʊeɪtə(r), -z
AM ɪn'sɪnjə,weɪdər, -z
insinuatory
BR ɪn'sɪnjʊət(ə)ri
AM ɪn'sɪnjəwə,tɔri
insipid
BR ɪn'sɪpɪd
AM ɪn'sɪpɪd

insipidity
BR ˌɪnsɨˈpɪdɨti, -ɪz
AM ˌɪnsəˈpɪdɨdi, -z

insipidly
BR ɨnˈsɪpɨdli
AM ɨnˈsɪpɨdli

insipidness
BR ɨnˈsɪpɨdnɨs
AM ɨnˈsɪpɨdnɨs

insist
BR ɪnˈsɪst, -s, -ɪŋ, -ɨd
AM ɨnˈsɪst, -s, -ɪŋ, -ɨd

insistence
BR ɪnˈsɪst(ə)ns
AM ɨnˈsɪstns

insistency
BR ɪnˈsɪst(ə)nsi
AM ɨnˈsɪstənsi

insistent
BR ɪnˈsɪst(ə)nt
AM ɨnˈsɪstənt

insistently
BR ɪnˈsɪst(ə)ntli
AM ɨnˈsɪstən(t)li

insister
BR ɪnˈsɪstə(r), -z
AM ɨnˈsɪstər, -z

insistingly
BR ɪnˈsɪstɪŋli
AM ɨnˈsɪstɪŋli

in situ
BR ˌɪn ˈsɪtjuː, + ˈsɪtʃuː
AM ˌɪn ˈsaɪtu, + ˈsɪtu

insobriety
BR ˌɪnsə(ʊ)ˈbrʌɪɨti
AM ¦ɪnsəˈbraɪədi, ¦ɪnsoʊˈbraɪədi

insofar
BR ˌɪnsə(ʊ)ˈfɑː(r)
AM ¦ɪnsoʊ¦fɑr

insolation
BR ˌɪnsə(ʊ)ˈleɪʃn
AM ˌɪnsəˈleɪʃən, ˌɪnˌsoʊˈleɪʃən

insole
BR ˈɪnsəʊl, -z
AM ˈɪnˌsoʊl, -z

insolence
BR ˈɪnsələns, ˈɪnsəl̩ns, ˈɪnsl̩(ə)ns
AM ˈɪnsələns

insolent
BR ˈɪnsələnt, ˈɪnsəl̩nt, ˈɪnsl̩(ə)nt
AM ˈɪnsələnt

insolently
BR ˈɪnsələntli, ˈɪnsəl̩ntli, ˈɪnsl̩(ə)ntli
AM ˈɪnsələn(t)li

insolubilise
BR ɪnˈsɒljʉbl̩ʌɪz, ɪnˈsɒljʉbɨlʌɪz, -ɨz, -ɪŋ, -d
AM ¦ɪnˈsɑljəbəˌlaɪz, ɨnˈsɑljəbəˌlaɪz, -ɨz, -ɪŋ, -d

insolubility
BR ɪnˌsɒljʉˈbɪlɨti, ˌɪnsɒljʉˈbɪlɨti
AM ¦ɪnˌsɑljəˈbɪlɨdi, ɨnˌsɑljəˈbɪlɨdi

insolubilize
BR ɪnˈsɒljʉbl̩ʌɪz, ɪnˈsɒljʉbɨlʌɪz, -ɨz, -ɪŋ, -d
AM ¦ɪnˈsɑljəbəˌlaɪz, ɨnˈsɑljəbəˌlaɪz, -ɨz, -ɪŋ, -d

insoluble
BR (ˌ)ɪnˈsɒljʉbl
AM ¦ɪnˈsɑljəbəl, ɨnˈsɑljəbəl

insolubleness
BR (ˌ)ɪnˈsɒljʉblnəs
AM ¦ɪnˈsɑljəbəlnəs, ɨnˈsɑljəbəlnəs

insolubly
BR (ˌ)ɪnˈsɒljʉbli
AM ¦ɪnˈsɑljəbli, ɨnˈsɑljəbli

insolvable
BR (ˌ)ɪnˈsɒlvəbl
AM ɨnˈsɑlvəbəl

insolvency
BR (ˌ)ɪnˈsɒlv(ə)nsi
AM ɨnˈsɑlvənsi

insolvent
BR (ˌ)ɪnˈsɒlv(ə)nt
AM ɨnˈsɑlvənt

insomnia
BR ɪnˈsɒmnɪə(*r*)
AM ɨnˈsɑmniə

insomniac
BR ɪnˈsɒmnɪak, -s
AM ɨnˈsɑmniˌæk, -s

insomuch
BR ˌɪnsə(ʊ)ˈmʌtʃ
AM ¦ɪnsoʊ¦mətʃ

insouciance
BR ɪnˈsuːsɪəns, ɪnˈsuːsɪɒ̃s
AM ɨnˈsusiəns, ɨnˈsuʃəns

insouciant
BR ɪnˈsuːsɪənt, ɪnˈsuːsɪɒ̃
AM ɨnˈsusiənt, ɨnˈsuʃənt

insouciantly
BR ɪnˈsuːsɪəntli
AM ɨnˈsusiən(t)li, ɨnˈsuʃən(t)li

insousiant
BR ɪnˈsuːsɪənt, ɪnˈsuːsɪɒ̃
AM ɨnˈsusiənt, ɨnˈsuʃənt

inspan
BR ˈɪnspan, ɪnˈspan, -z, -ɪŋ, -d
AM ɪnzˈpæn, ɪnˈspæn, -z, -ɪŋ, -d

inspect
BR ɪnˈspɛkt, -s, -ɪŋ, -ɨd
AM ɨnzˈpɛk|(t), ɨnˈspɛk|(t), -(t)s, -tɪŋ, -təd

inspection
BR ɪnˈspɛkʃn, -z
AM ɨnzˈpɛkʃən, ɨnˈspɛkʃən, -z

inspector
BR ɪnˈspɛktə(r), -z
AM ɨnzˈpɛktər, ɨnˈspɛktər, -z

inspectorate
BR ɪnˈspɛkt(ə)rət, -s
AM ɨnzˈpɛktərət, ɨnˈspɛktərət, -s

inspectorial
BR ˌɪnspɛkˈtɔːrɪəl
AM ɨnzˌpɛkˈtɔriəl, ɨnˌspɛkˈtɔriəl

inspectorship
BR ɪnˈspɛktəʃɪp, -s
AM ɨnzˈpɛktərˌʃɪp, ɨnˈspɛktərˌʃɪp, -s

inspiration
BR ˌɪnspɨˈreɪʃn, -z
AM ˌɪnspəˈreɪʃən, -z

inspirational
BR ˌɪnspɨˈreɪʃn̩(ə)l, ˌɪnspɨˈreɪʃən(ə)l
AM ˌɪnspəˈreɪʃ(ə)nəl

inspirationally
BR ˌɪnspɨˈreɪʃn̩əli, ˌɪnspɨˈreɪʃn̩l̩i, ˌɪnspɨˈreɪʃənl̩i, ˌɪnspɨˈreɪʃ(ə)nəli
AM ˌɪnspəˈreɪʃ(ə)nəli

inspirationism
BR ˌɪnspɨˈreɪʃn̩ɪz(ə)m, ˌɪnspɨˈreɪʃənɪz(ə)m
AM ˌɪnspəˈreɪʃəˌnɪzəm, ˌɪnspəˈreɪʃn̩ˌɪzəm

inspirationist
BR ˌɪnspɨˈreɪʃn̩ɪst, ˌɪnspɨˈreɪʃənɪst, -s
AM ˌɪnspəˈreɪʃənəst, ˌɪnspəˈreɪʃn̩ɪst, -s

inspirator
BR ˈɪnspɨreɪtə(r), -z
AM ˈɪnspəˌreɪdər, -z

inspiratory
BR ɪnˈspɪrət(ə)ri, ɪnˈspʌɪ(ə)rət(ə)ri
AM ˈɪnspərəˌtɔri

inspire
BR ɪnˈspʌɪə(r), -z, -ɪŋ, -d
AM ɨnzˈpaɪ(ə)r, ɨnˈspaɪ(ə)r, -z, -ɪŋ, -d

inspiredly
BR ɪnˈspʌɪədli
AM ɨnzˈpaɪ(ə)rdli, ɨnˈspaɪ(ə)rdli

inspirer
BR ɪnˈspʌɪərə(r), -z
AM ɨnzˈpaɪ(ə)rər, ɨnˈspaɪ(ə)rər, -z

inspiringly
BR ɪnˈspʌɪərɪŋli
AM ɨnzˈpaɪ(ə)rɪŋli, ɨnˈspaɪ(ə)rɪŋli

inspirit
BR ɪnˈspɪr|ɪt, -ɪts, -ɨtɪŋ, -ɨtɨd
AM ɨnzˈpɪrɨ|t, ɨnˈspɪrɨ|t, -ts, -dɪŋ, -dɨd

inspiritingly
BR ɪnˈspɪrɨtɪŋli
AM ɨnzˈpɪrɨdɪŋli, ɨnˈspɪrɨdɪŋli

inspissate
BR ɪnˈspɪseɪt, ˈɪnspɨseɪt, -s, -ɪŋ, -ɨd
AM ˈɪnspəˌseɪ|t, ɨnzˈpɪˌseɪ|t, ɨnˈspɪˌseɪ|t, -ts, -dɪŋ, -dɨd

inspissation
BR ˌɪnspɨˈseɪʃn, -z
AM ˌɪnspəˈseɪʃən, ɨnzˌpɪˈseɪʃən, ɨnˌspɪˈseɪʃən, -z

inspissator
BR ˈɪnspɨseɪtə(r), -z
AM ˈɪnspəˌseɪdər, ɨnzˈpɪˌseɪdər, ɨnˈspɪˌseɪdər, -z

inst.
BR ɪnst
AM ɪnst

instability
BR ˌɪnstəˈbɪlɨti
AM ¦ɪnztə¦bɪlɨdi, ¦ɪnstə¦bɪlɨdi

instal
BR ɪnˈstɔːl, -z, -ɪŋ, -d
AM ɨnzˈtɔl, ɨnˈstɔl, ɨnzˈtɑl, ɨnˈstɑl, -z, -ɪŋ, -d

install
BR ɪnˈstɔːl, -z, -ɪŋ, -d
AM ɨnzˈtɔl, ɨnˈstɔl, ɨnzˈtɑl, ɨnˈstɑl, -z, -ɪŋ, -d

installant
BR ɪnˈstɔːlənt, ɪnˈstɔːl̩nt, -s
AM ɨnzˈtɔlənt, ɨnˈstɔlənt, ɨnzˈtɑlənt, ɨnˈstɑlənt, -s

installation
BR ˌɪnstəˈleɪʃn, -z
AM ˌɪnztəˈleɪʃən, ˌɪnstəˈleɪʃən, -z

installer
BR ɪnˈstɔːlə(r), -z
AM ɨnzˈtɔlər, ɨnˈstɔlər, ɨnzˈtɑlər, ɨnˈstɑlər, -z

installment
BR ɪnˈstɔːlm(ə)nt, -s
AM ɨnzˈtɔlmənt, ɨnˈstɔlmənt, ɨnzˈtɑlmənt, ɨnˈstɑlmənt, -s

instalment
BR ɪnˈstɔːlm(ə)nt, -s

AM ɪnzˈtɔlmənt, ɪnˈstɔlmənt, ɪnzˈtɑlmənt, ɪnˈstɑlmənt, -s

instance
BR ˈɪnst(ə)ns, -ɪz, -ɪŋ, -t
AM ˈɪnztəns, ˈɪnstəns, -əz, -ɪŋ, -t

instancy
BR ˈɪnst(ə)ns|i, -ɪz
AM ˈɪnztənsi, ˈɪnstənsi, -z

instant
BR ˈɪnst(ə)nt, -s
AM ˈɪnztənt, ˈɪnstənt, -s

instantaneity
BR ɪnˌstantəˈniːɪti, ɪnˌstantəˈneɪɪti
AM ɪnzˌtæntn̩ˈiɪdi, ɪnˌstæntn̩ˈiɪdi, ɪnzˌtæntn̩ˈeɪɪdi, ɪnˌstæntn̩ˈeɪɪdi

instantaneous
BR ˌɪnst(ə)nˈteɪnɪəs
AM ˌɪnztənˈteɪniəs, ˌɪnstənˈteɪniəs, ˌɪnztənˈteɪnjəs, ˌɪnstənˈteɪnjəs

instantaneously
BR ˌɪnst(ə)nˈteɪnɪəsli
AM ˌɪnztənˈteɪniəsli, ˌɪnstənˈteɪniəsli, ˌɪnztənˈteɪnjəsli, ˌɪnstənˈteɪnjəsli

instantaneousness
BR ˌɪnst(ə)nˈteɪnɪəsnəs
AM ˌɪnztənˈteɪniəsnəs, ˌɪnstənˈteɪniəsnəs, ˌɪnztənˈteɪnjəsnəs, ˌɪnstənˈteɪnjəsnəs

instanter
adverb
BR ɪnˈstantə(r)
AM ɪnzˈtæn(t)ər, ɪnˈstæn(t)ər

instantiate
BR ɪnˈstanʃɪeɪt, -s, -ɪŋ, -ɪd
AM ɪnzˈtæn(t)ʃiˌeɪ|t, ɪnˈstæn(t)ʃiˌeɪ|t, -ts, -dɪŋ, -dɪd

instantiation
BR ɪnˌstanʃɪˈeɪʃn, -z
AM ɪnzˌtæn(t)ʃiˈeɪʃən, ɪnˌstæn(t)ʃiˈeɪʃən, -z

instantly
BR ˈɪnst(ə)ntli
AM ˈɪnztən(t)li, ˈɪnstən(t)li

instar
BR ˈɪnstɑː(r), -z
AM ˈɪnzˌtɑr, ˈɪnˌstɑr, -z

instate
BR ɪnˈsteɪt, -s, -ɪŋ, -ɪd
AM ɪnzˈteɪ|t, ɪnˈsteɪ|t, -ts, -dɪŋ, -dɪd

in statu pupillari
BR ɪn ˌstatjuː ˌpjuːpɪˈlɑːri
AM ˌɪn ˈsteɪˌtu ˈpjupəˌlɛri, ˌɪn ˈstɑˌtu ˈpjupəˌlɛri, ˌɪn ˈstædu ˈpjupəˌlɛri

instauration
BR ˌɪnstɔːˈreɪʃn, -z
AM ˌɪnzˌtɔˈreɪʃən, ˌɪnˌstɔˈreɪʃən, -z

instaurator
BR ˈɪnstɔːreɪtə(r), -z
AM ˈɪnztəˌreɪdər, ˈɪnstəˌreɪdər, -z

instead
BR ɪnˈstɛd
AM ɪnzˈtɛd, ɪnˈstɛd

instep
BR ˈɪnstɛp, -s
AM ˈɪnzˌtɛp, ˈɪnˌstɛp, -s

instigate
BR ˈɪnstɪɡeɪt, -s, -ɪŋ, -ɪd
AM ˈɪnztəˌɡeɪ|t, ˈɪnstəˌɡeɪ|t, -ts, -dɪŋ, -dɪd

instigation
BR ˌɪnstɪˈɡeɪʃn
AM ˌɪnztəˈɡeɪʃən, ˌɪnstəˈɡeɪʃən

instigative
BR ˈɪnstɪɡətɪv
AM ˈɪnztəˌɡeɪdɪv, ˈɪnstəˌɡeɪdɪv

instigator
BR ˈɪnstɪɡeɪtə(r), -z
AM ˈɪnztəˌɡeɪdər, ˈɪnstəˌɡeɪdər, -z

instil
BR ɪnˈstɪl, -z, -ɪŋ, -d
AM ɪnzˈtɪl, ɪnˈstɪl, -z, -ɪŋ, -d

instill
BR ɪnˈstɪl, -z, -ɪŋ, -d
AM ɪnzˈtɪl, ɪnˈstɪl, -z, -ɪŋ, -d

instillation
BR ˌɪnstɪˈleɪʃn, -z
AM ˌɪnztəˈleɪʃən, ˌɪnstəˈleɪʃən, -z

instiller
BR ɪnˈstɪlə(r), -z
AM ɪnzˈtɪlər, ɪnˈstɪlər, -z

instillment
BR ɪnˈstɪlm(ə)nt, -s
AM ɪnzˈtɪlmənt, ɪnˈstɪlmənt, -s

instilment
BR ɪnˈstɪlm(ə)nt, -s
AM ɪnzˈtɪlmənt, ɪnˈstɪlmənt, -s

instinct
BR ˈɪnstɪŋ(k)t, -s
AM ˈɪnztɪŋ(k)t, ˈɪnstɪŋ(k)t, ˈɪnztɪŋk(t), ˈɪnstɪŋk(t), -(t)s

instinctive
BR ɪnˈstɪŋ(k)tɪv
AM ɪnzˈtɪŋ(k)tɪv, ɪnˈstɪŋ(k)tɪv

instinctively
BR ɪnˈstɪŋ(k)tɪvli
AM ɪnzˈtɪŋ(k)tɪvli, ɪnˈstɪŋ(k)tɪvli

instinctual
BR ɪnˈstɪŋ(k)tʃʊəl, ɪnˈstɪŋ(k)tʃ(ʊ)l, ɪnˈstɪŋ(k)tjʊəl, ɪnˈstɪŋ(k)tjʊl
AM ɪnzˈtɪŋ(k)(t)ʃə(wə)l, ɪnˈstɪŋ(k)(t)ʃə(wə)l

instinctually
BR ɪnˈstɪŋ(k)tʃʊəli, ɪnˈstɪŋ(k)tʃʊli, ɪnˈstɪŋ(k)tʃl̩i, ɪnˈstɪŋ(k)tjʊəli, ɪnˈstɪŋktjʊli
AM ɪnzˈtɪŋ(k)(t)ʃə(wə)li, ɪnˈstɪŋ(k)(t)ʃə(wə)li

institute
BR ˈɪnstɪtjuːt, ˈɪnstɪtʃuːt, -s
AM ˈɪnztəˌt(j)ut, ˈɪnstəˌt(j)ut, -s

institution
BR ˌɪnstɪˈtjuːʃn, ˌɪnstɪˈtʃuːʃn, -z
AM ˌɪnztəˈt(j)uʃən, ˌɪnstəˈt(j)uʃən, -z

institutional
BR ˌɪnstɪˈtjuːʃn̩(ə)l, ˌɪnstɪˈtjuːʃən(ə)l, ˌɪnstɪˈtʃuːʃn̩(ə)l, ˌɪnstɪˈtʃuːʃən(ə)l
AM ˌɪnztəˈt(j)uʃ(ə)nəl, ˌɪnstəˈt(j)uʃ(ə)nəl

institutionalisation
BR ˌɪnstɪˌtjuːʃn̩əlʌɪˈzeɪʃn, ˌɪnstɪˌtjuːʃn̩l̩ʌɪˈzeɪʃn, ˌɪnstɪˌtjuːʃənl̩ʌɪˈzeɪʃn, ˌɪnstɪˌtjuːʃ(ə)nəlʌɪˈzeɪʃn, ˌɪnstɪˌtʃuːʃn̩əlʌɪˈzeɪʃn, ˌɪnstɪˌtʃuːʃn̩l̩ʌɪˈzeɪʃn, ˌɪnstɪˌtʃuːʃənl̩ʌɪˈzeɪʃn, ˌɪnstɪˌtʃuːʃ(ə)nəlʌɪˈzeɪʃn
AM ˌɪnztəˈt(j)uʃənl̩əˈzeɪʃən, ˌɪnztəˈt(j)uʃnələˈzeɪʃən, ˌɪnstəˈt(j)uʃənl̩əˈzeɪʃən, ˌɪnstəˈt(j)uʃnələˈzeɪʃən, ˌɪnztəˈt(j)uʃənlˌaɪˈzeɪʃən, ˌɪnztəˈt(j)uʃnəˌlaɪˈzeɪʃən, ˌɪnstəˈt(j)uʃənlˌaɪˈzeɪʃən, ˌɪnstəˈt(j)uʃnəˌlaɪˈzeɪʃən

institutionalise
BR ˌɪnstɪˈtjuːʃn̩əlʌɪz, ˌɪnstɪˈtjuːʃn̩l̩ʌɪz, ˌɪnstɪˈtjuːʃənl̩ʌɪz, ˌɪnstɪˈtjuːʃ(ə)nəlʌɪz, ˌɪnstɪˈtʃuːʃn̩əlʌɪz, ˌɪnstɪˈtʃuːʃn̩l̩ʌɪz, ˌɪnstɪˈtʃuːʃənl̩ʌɪz, ˌɪnstɪˈtʃuːʃ(ə)nəlʌɪz, -ɪz, -ɪŋ, -d
AM ˌɪnztəˈt(j)uʃənlˌaɪz, ˌɪnztəˈtuʃnəˌlaɪz, ˌɪnstəˈt(j)uʃənlˌaɪz, ˌɪnstəˈtuʃnəˌlaɪz, -ɪz, -ɪŋ, -d

institutionalism
BR ˌɪnstɪˈtjuːʃn̩əlɪz(ə)m, ˌɪnstɪˈtjuːʃn̩l̩ɪz(ə)m, ˌɪnstɪˈtjuːʃənl̩ɪz(ə)m, ˌɪnstɪˈtjuːʃ(ə)nəlɪz(ə)m, ˌɪnstɪˈtʃuːʃn̩əlɪz(ə)m, ˌɪnstɪˈtʃuːʃn̩l̩ɪz(ə)m, ˌɪnstɪˈtʃuːʃənl̩ɪz(ə)m, ˌɪnstɪˈtʃuːʃ(ə)nəlɪz(ə)m
AM ˌɪnztəˈt(j)uʃənlˌɪzəm, ˌɪnztəˈt(j)uʃnəˌlɪzəm, ˌɪnstəˈt(j)uʃənlˌɪzəm, ˌɪnstəˈt(j)uʃnəˌlɪzəm

institutionalization
BR ˌɪnstɪˌtjuːʃn̩əlʌɪˈzeɪʃn, ˌɪnstɪˌtjuːʃn̩l̩ʌɪˈzeɪʃn, ˌɪnstɪˌtjuːʃənl̩ʌɪˈzeɪʃn, ˌɪnstɪˌtjuːʃ(ə)nəlʌɪˈzeɪʃn, ˌɪnstɪˌtʃuːʃn̩əlʌɪˈzeɪʃn, ˌɪnstɪˌtʃuːʃn̩l̩ʌɪˈzeɪʃn, ˌɪnstɪˌtʃuːʃənl̩ʌɪˈzeɪʃn, ˌɪnstɪˌtʃuːʃ(ə)nəlʌɪˈzeɪʃn
AM ˌɪnztəˈt(j)uʃənl̩əˈzeɪʃən, ˌɪnztəˈt(j)uʃnələˈzeɪʃən, ˌɪnstəˈt(j)uʃənl̩əˈzeɪʃən, ˌɪnstəˈt(j)uʃnələˈzeɪʃən, ˌɪnztəˈt(j)uʃənlˌaɪˈzeɪʃən, ˌɪnztəˈt(j)uʃnəˌlaɪˈzeɪʃən, ˌɪnstəˈt(j)uʃənlˌaɪˈzeɪʃən, ˌɪnstəˈt(j)uʃnəˌlaɪˈzeɪʃən

institutionalize
BR ˌɪnstɪˈtjuːʃn̩əlʌɪz, ˌɪnstɪˈtjuːʃn̩l̩ʌɪz, ˌɪnstɪˈtjuːʃənl̩ʌɪz, ˌɪnstɪˈtjuːʃ(ə)nəlʌɪz, ˌɪnstɪˈtʃuːʃn̩əlʌɪz, ˌɪnstɪˈtʃuːʃn̩l̩ʌɪz, ˌɪnstɪˈtʃuːʃənl̩ʌɪz, ˌɪnstɪˈtʃuːʃ(ə)nəlʌɪz, -ɪz, -ɪŋ, -d
AM ˌɪnztəˈt(j)uʃənlˌaɪz, ˌɪnztəˈtuʃnəˌlaɪz, ˌɪnstəˈt(j)uʃənlˌaɪz, ˌɪnstəˈtuʃnəˌlaɪz, -ɪz, -ɪŋ, -d

institutionally
BR ˌɪnstɪˈtjuːʃn̩əli, ˌɪnstɪˈtjuːʃn̩l̩i, ˌɪnstɪˈtjuːʃənl̩i,

ˌɪnstɪˈtjuːʃ(ə)nəli,
ˌɪnstɪˈtʃuːʃn̩əli,
ˌɪnstɪˈtʃuːʃn̩li,
ˌɪnstɪˈtʃuːʃənl̩i,
ˌɪnstɪˈtʃuːʃ(ə)nəli
AM ˌɪnztəˈt(j)uʃ(ə)nəli,
ˌɪnstəˈt(j)uʃ(ə)nəli

in-store
BR ˌɪnˈstɔː(r)
AM ˈˌɪnˈstɔ(ə)r

INSTRAW
BR ˈɪnstrɔː(*r*)
AM ˈɪnzˌtrɔ, ˈɪnˌstrɔ,
ˈɪnzˌtrɑ, ˈɪnˌstrɑ

instruct
BR ɪnˈstrʌkt, -s, -ɪŋ, -ɪd
AM ɪnzˈtrək|(t),
ɪnˈstrək|(t), -(t)s, -tɪŋ,
-təd

instruction
BR ɪnˈstrʌkʃn, -z
AM ɪnzˈtrəkʃən,
ɪnˈstrəkʃən, -z

instructional
BR ɪnˈstrʌkʃn̩(ə)l,
ɪnˈstrʌkʃən(ə)l
AM ɪnˈstrəkʃ(ə)nəl

instructive
BR ɪnˈstrʌktɪv
AM ɪnˈstrəktɪv

instructively
BR ɪnˈstrʌktɨvli
AM ɪnˈstrəktəvli

instructiveness
BR ɪnˈstrʌktɨvnɨs
AM ɪnˈstrəktɪvnɪs

instructor
BR ɪnˈstrʌktə(r), -z
AM ɪnˈstrəktər, -z

instructorship
BR ɪnˈstrʌktəʃɪp
AM ɪnˈstrəktərˌʃɪp

instructress
BR ɪnˈstrʌktrɪs, -ɪz
AM ɪnˈstrəktrəs, -əz

instrument
BR ˈɪnstrʉm(ə)nt, -s
AM ˈɪnztrəmənt,
ˈɪnstrəmənt, -s

instrumental
BR ˌɪnstrʉˈmɛntl
AM ˈˌɪnztrəˈˌmɛn(t)l,
ˈˌɪnstrəˈˌmɛn(t)l

instrumentalist
BR ˌɪnstrʉˈmɛntl̩ɪst, -s
AM ˈˌɪnztrəˈmɛn(t)ləst,
ˈˌɪnstrəˈmɛn(t)ləst, -s

instrumentality
BR ˌɪnstrʉmɛnˈtalɪti
AM ˌɪnztrəmənˈtælədi,
ˌɪnztrəˌmɛnˈtælədi,
ˌɪnstrəmənˈtælədi,
ˌɪnstrəˌmɛnˈtælədi

instrumentally
BR ˌɪnstrʉˈmɛntl̩i
AM ˈˌɪnztrəˈˌmɛn(t)l̩i,
ˈˌɪnstrəˈˌmɛn(t)l̩i

instrumentation
BR ˌɪnstrʉmɛnˈteɪʃn,
ˌɪnstrʉm(ə)nˈteɪʃn
AM ˌɪnztrəmənˈteɪʃən,
ˌɪnztrəˌmɛnˈteɪʃən,
ˌɪnstrəmənˈteɪʃən,
ˌɪnstrəˌmɛnˈteɪʃən

insubordinate
BR ˌɪnsəˈbɔːdɪnət,
ˌɪnsəˈbɔːdn̩ət
AM ˈˌɪnsəˈbɔrdn̩ət

insubordinately
BR ˌɪnsəˈbɔːdɪnətli,
ˌɪnsəˈbɔːdn̩ətli
AM ˈˌɪnsəˈbɔrdn̩ətli

insubordination
BR ˌɪnsəˌbɔːdɪˈneɪʃn
AM ˈˌɪnsəˌbɔrdəˈneɪʃən

insubstantial
BR ˌɪnsəbˈstanʃl
AM ˈˌɪnsəbˈstæn(t)ʃəl

insubstantiality
BR ˌɪnsəbˌstanʃɪˈalɪt|i,
-ɪz
AM ˈˌɪnsəbˌstæn(t)ʃi-
ˈælədi, -z

insubstantially
BR ˌɪnsəbˈstanʃl̩i,
ˌɪnsəbˈstanʃəli
AM ˈˌɪnsəbˈstæn(t)ʃəli

insufferable
BR ɪnˈsʌf(ə)rəbl
AM ɪnˈsəf(ə)rəbəl

insufferableness
BR ɪnˈsʌf(ə)rəblnəs
AM ɪnˈsəf(ə)rəbəlnəs

insufferably
BR ɪnˈsʌf(ə)rəbli
AM ɪnˈsəf(ə)rəbli

insufficiency
BR ˌɪnsəˈfɪʃns|i, -ɪz
AM ˈˌɪnsəˈfɪʃənsi, -z

insufficient
BR ˌɪnsəˈfɪʃnt
AM ˈˌɪnsəˈfɪʃənt

insufficiently
BR ˌɪnsəˈfɪʃntli
AM ˈˌɪnsəˈfɪʃən(t)li

insufflate
BR ˈɪnsəfleɪt,
ɪnˈsʌfleɪt, -s, -ɪŋ, -ɪd
AM ˈɪnsəˌfleɪ|t, -ts, -dɪŋ,
-dɪd

insufflation
BR ˌɪnsəˈfleɪʃn, -z
AM ˌɪnsəˈfleɪʃən, -z

insufflator
BR ˈɪnsəˌfleɪtə(r), -z
AM ˈɪnsəˌfleɪdər, -z

insular
BR ˈɪnsjʉlə(r)
AM ˈɪns(j)ələr

insularism
BR ˈɪnsjʉlərɪz(ə)m
AM ˈɪns(j)ələˌrɪzəm

insularity
BR ˌɪnsjʉˈlarɪti
AM ˌɪns(j)əˈlɛrədi

insularly
BR ˈɪnsjʉləli
AM ˈɪns(j)ələrli

insulate
BR ˈɪnsjʉleɪt, -s, -ɪŋ, -ɪd
AM ˈɪnsəˌleɪ|t, -ts, -dɪŋ,
-dɪd

insulation
BR ˌɪnsjʉˈleɪʃn
AM ˌɪnsəˈleɪʃən

insulator
BR ˈɪnsjʉleɪtə(r), -z
AM ˈɪnsəˌleɪdər, -z

insulin
BR ˈɪnsjʉlɪn
AM ˈɪnsələn

insult[1]
noun
BR ˈɪnsʌlt, -s
AM ˈɪnˌsəlt, -s

insult[2]
verb
BR ɪnˈsʌlt, -s, -ɪŋ, -ɪd
AM ɪnˈsəlt, -s, -ɪŋ, -əd

insulter
BR ɪnˈsʌltə(r), -z
AM ɪnˈsəltər, -z

insultingly
BR ɪnˈsʌltɪŋli
AM ɪnˈsəltɪŋli

insuperability
BR ɪnˌs(j)uːp(ə)rəˈbɪlɪti
AM ˈˌɪnˌsup(ə)rəˈbɪlɪdi,
ənˌsup(ə)rəˈbɪlɪdi

insuperable
BR ɪnˈs(j)uːp(ə)rəbl
AM ɪnˈsup(ə)rəbəl

insuperably
BR ɪnˈs(j)uːp(ə)rəbli
AM ɪnˈsup(ə)rəbli

insupportable
BR ˌɪnsəˈpɔːtəbl
AM ˈˌɪnsəˈpɔrdəbəl

insupportableness
BR ˌɪnsəˈpɔːtəblnəs
AM ˈˌɪnsəˈpɔrdəbəlnəs

insupportably
BR ˌɪnsəˈpɔːtəbli
AM ˈˌɪnsəˈpɔrdəbli

insurability
BR ɪnˌʃʊərəˈbɪlɪti,
ɪnˌʃɔːrəˈbɪlɪti
AM ɪnˌʃʊrəˈbɪlɪdi

insurable
BR ɪnˈʃʊərəbl,
ɪnˈʃɔːrəbl
AM ɪnˈʃʊrəbəl

insurance
BR ɪnˈʃʊərəns,
ɪnˈʃʊərn̩s, ɪnˈʃɔːrəns,
ɪnˈʃɔːrn̩s, -ɪz
AM ɪnˈʃʊrəns, -əz

insurant
BR ɪnˈʃʊərənt,
ɪnˈʃʊərn̩t, ɪnˈʃɔːrənt,
ɪnˈʃɔːrn̩t, -s
AM ɪnˈʃʊrənt, -s

insure
BR ɪnˈʃʊə(r), ɪnˈʃɔː(r),
-z, -ɪŋ, -d
AM ɪnˈʃʊ(ə)r, -z, -ɪŋ, -d

insurer
BR ɪnˈʃʊərə(r),
ɪnˈʃɔːrə(r), -z
AM ɪnˈʃʊrər, -z

insurgence
BR ɪnˈsəːdʒ(ə)ns, -ɪz
AM ɪnˈsərdʒəns, -əz

insurgency
BR ɪnˈsəːdʒ(ə)ns|i, -ɪz
AM ɪnˈsərdʒənsi, -z

insurgent
BR ɪnˈsəːdʒ(ə)nt, -s
AM ɪnˈsərdʒənt, -s

insurmountability
BR ˌɪnsəˌmaʊntəˈbɪlɪti
AM ˈˌɪnsərˌmaʊn(t)əˈbɪl-
ɪdi

insurmountable
BR ˌɪnsəˈmaʊntəbl
AM ˈˌɪnsərˈmaʊn(t)əbəl

insurmountably
BR ˌɪnsəˈmaʊntəbli
AM ˈˌɪnsərˈmaʊn(t)əbli

insurrection
BR ˌɪnsəˈrɛkʃn, -z
AM ˌɪnsəˈrɛkʃən, -z

insurrectional
BR ˌɪnsəˈrɛkʃn̩(ə)l,
ˌɪnsəˈrɛkʃən(ə)l
AM ˌɪnsəˈrɛkʃ(ə)nəl

insurrectionary
BR ˌɪnsəˈrɛkʃn̩(ə)r|i,
-ɪz
AM ˌɪnsəˈrɛkʃəˌnɛri, -z

insurrectionism
BR ˌɪnsəˈrɛkʃn̩ɪz(ə)m,
ˌɪnsəˈrɛkʃənɪz(ə)m
AM ˌɪnsəˈrɛkʃəˌnɪzəm

insurrectionist
BR ˌɪnsəˈrɛkʃn̩ɪst,
ˌɪnsəˈrɛkʃənɪst, -s
AM ˌɪnsəˈrɛkʃənəst, -s

insusceptibility
BR ˌɪnsəˌsɛptɪˈbɪlɪti
AM ˈˌɪnsəˌsɛptəˈbɪlɪdi

insusceptible
BR ˌɪnsəˈsɛptɪbl
AM ˌɪnsəˈsɛptəbəl

inswing
BR ˈɪnswɪŋ, -z
AM ˈɪnˌswɪŋ, -z

inswinger
BR ˈɪnˌswɪŋə(r), -z
AM ˈɪnˌswɪŋər, -z

intact
BR (ˌ)ɪnˈtakt
AM ɪnˈtæk(t)

intactness
BR (ˌ)ɪnˈtak(t)nəs
AM ɪnˈtæk(t)nəs

intaglio
BR ɪnˈtalɪəʊ, ɪnˈtɑːlɪəʊ
AM ɪnˈtæljoʊ,
ɪnˈtɑljoʊ, ɪnˈtæglioʊ

intake
BR ˈɪnteɪk, -s
AM ˈɪnˌteɪk, -s

intangibility
BR ɪnˌtan(d)ʒᵻˈbɪlᵻti
AM ˌɪnˌtændʒəˈbɪlᵻdi, ᵻnˌtændʒəˈbɪlᵻdi

intangible
BR ɪnˈtan(d)ʒᵻbl
AM ᵻnˈtændʒəbəl

intangibly
BR ɪnˈtan(d)ʒᵻbli
AM ᵻnˈtændʒəbli

intarsia
BR ɪnˈtɑːsɪə(r)
AM ᵻnˈtɑrsiə

Intasun
BR ˈɪntəsʌn
AM ˈɪn(t)əˌsən

integer
BR ˈɪntᵻdʒə(r), -z
AM ˈɪn(t)ədʒər, -z

integrability
BR ˌɪntᵻgrəˈbɪlᵻti
AM ˌɪn(t)əgrəˈbɪlᵻdi

integrable
BR ˈɪntᵻgrəbl, ɪnˈtɛgrəbl
AM ˈɪn(t)əgrəbəl

integral¹
general use
BR ˈɪntᵻgr(ə)l, ɪnˈtɛgr(ə)l
AM ˈɪn(t)əgrəl

integral²
mathematical
BR ˈɪntᵻgr(ə)l, -z
AM ˈɪn(t)əgrəl, -z

integrality
BR ˌɪntᵻˈgralᵻt|i, -ɪz
AM ˌɪn(t)əˈgrælədi, -z

integrally
BR ˈɪntᵻgrəli, ˈɪntᵻgrl̩i, ɪnˈtɛgrəli, ɪnˈtɛgrl̩i
AM ˈɪn(t)əgrəli, ɪnˈtɛgrəli

integrand
BR ˈɪntᵻgrand, -z
AM ˈɪn(t)əgrənd, -z

integrant
BR ˈɪntᵻgr(ə)nt, -s
AM ˈɪn(t)əgrənt, -s

integrate
BR ˈɪntᵻgreɪt, -s, -ɪŋ, -ᵻd
AM ˈɪn(t)əˌgreɪ|t, -ts, -dɪŋ, -dᵻd

integration
BR ˌɪntᵻˈgreɪʃn
AM ˌɪn(t)əˈgreɪʃən

integrationist
BR ˌɪntᵻˈgreɪʃn̩ɪst, ˌɪntᵻˈgreɪʃənɪst, -s
AM ˌɪn(t)əˈgreɪʃənəst, -s

integrative
BR ˈɪntᵻgrətɪv
AM ˈɪn(t)əˌgreɪdɪv

integrator
BR ˈɪntᵻgreɪtə(r), -z
AM ˈɪn(t)əˌgreɪdər, -z

integrity
BR ɪnˈtɛgrᵻti
AM ᵻnˈtɛgrədi

integument
BR ɪnˈtɛgjʉm(ə)nt, -s
AM ᵻnˈtɛgjəmənt, -s

integumental
BR ɪnˌtɛgjʉˈmɛntl
AM ᵻnˌtɛgjəˌmɛn(t)l

integumentary
BR ɪnˌtɛgjʉˈmɛnt(ə)ri
AM ᵻnˌtɛgjəˈmɛn(t)əri

intellect
BR ˈɪntᵻlɛkt, -s
AM ˈɪn(t)lˌɛk|(t), -(t)s

intellection
BR ˌɪntᵻˈlɛkʃn, -z
AM ˌɪn(t)lˈɛkʃən, -z

intellective
BR ˌɪntᵻˈlɛktɪv
AM ˈɪn(t)lˌɛktɪv

intellectual
BR ˌɪntᵻˈlɛktʃʊəl, ˌɪntᵻˈlɛktʃ(ʉ)l, ˌɪntᵻˈlɛktjʊəl, ˌɪntᵻˈlɛktjʉl, -z
AM ˌɪn(t)əˈlɛk(t)ʃ(əw)əl, -z

intellectualise
BR ˌɪntᵻˈlɛktʃʊəlʌɪz, ˌɪntᵻˈlɛktʃʉlʌɪz, ˌɪntᵻˈlɛktʃl̩ʌɪz, ˌɪntᵻˈlɛktjʊəlʌɪz, ˌɪntᵻˈlɛktjʉlʌɪz, -ᵻz, -ɪŋ, -d
AM ˌɪn(t)əˈlɛk(t)ʃ(əw)əˌlaɪz, -ᵻz, -ɪŋ, -d

intellectualism
BR ˌɪntᵻˈlɛktʃʊəlɪz(ə)m, ˌɪntᵻˈlɛktʃʉlɪz(ə)m, ˌɪntᵻˈlɛktʃl̩ɪz(ə)m, ˌɪntᵻˈlɛktjʊəlɪz(ə)m, ˌɪntᵻˈlɛktjʉlɪz(ə)m
AM ˌɪn(t)əˈlɛk(t)ʃ(əw)əˌlɪzəm

intellectualist
BR ˌɪntᵻˈlɛktʃʊəlɪst, ˌɪntᵻˈlɛktʃʉlɪst, ˌɪntᵻˈlɛktʃl̩ɪst, ˌɪntᵻˈlɛktjʊəlɪst, ˌɪntᵻˈlɛktjʉlɪst, -s
AM ˌɪn(t)əˈlɛk(t)ʃ(əw)ələst, -s

intellectuality
BR ˌɪntᵻˌlɛktʃʊˈalᵻti, ˌɪntᵻˌlɛktjʊˈalᵻti
AM ˌɪn(t)əˌlɛk(t)ʃəˈwælədi

intellectualize
BR ˌɪntᵻˈlɛktʃʊəlʌɪz, ˌɪntᵻˈlɛktʃʉlʌɪz, ˌɪntᵻˈlɛktʃl̩ʌɪz, ˌɪntᵻˈlɛktjʊəlʌɪz, ˌɪntᵻˈlɛktjʉlʌɪz, -ᵻz, -ɪŋ, -d
AM ˌɪn(t)əˈlɛk(t)ʃ(əw)əˌlaɪz, -ᵻz, -ɪŋ, -d

intellectually
BR ˌɪntᵻˈlɛktʃʊəli, ˌɪntᵻˈlɛktʃʉli, ˌɪntᵻˈlɛktʃl̩i, ˌɪntᵻˈlɛktjʊəli, ˌɪntᵻˈlɛktjʉli
AM ˌɪn(t)əˈlɛk(t)ʃ(əw)əli

intelligence
BR ɪnˈtɛlᵻdʒ(ə)ns, -ᵻz
AM ᵻnˈtɛlədʒəns, -əz

intelligent
BR ɪnˈtɛlᵻdʒ(ə)nt
AM ᵻnˈtɛlədʒənt

intelligential
BR ɪnˌtɛlᵻˈdʒɛnʃl
AM ᵻnˌtɛləˈdʒɛnʃəl

intelligently
BR ɪnˈtɛlᵻdʒ(ə)ntli
AM ᵻnˈtɛlədʒən(t)li

intelligentsia
BR ɪnˌtɛlᵻˈdʒɛnsɪə(r), ˌɪntɛlᵻˈdʒɛnsɪə(r)
AM ᵻnˌtɛləˈdʒɛn(t)siə

intelligibility
BR ɪnˌtɛlᵻdʒᵻˈbɪlᵻti
AM ɪnˌtɛlədʒəˈbɪlᵻdi

intelligible
BR ɪnˈtɛlᵻdʒᵻbl
AM ᵻnˈtɛlədʒəbəl

intelligibly
BR ɪnˈtɛlᵻdʒᵻbli
AM ᵻnˈtɛlədʒəbli

Intelpost
BR ˈɪntɛlpəʊst
AM ˈɪnˌtɛlˈpoʊst

Intelsat
BR ˈɪntɛlsat
AM ˈɪnˌtɛlˌsæt

intemperance
BR ɪnˈtɛmp(ə)rəns, ɪnˈtɛmp(ə)rn̩s
AM ᵻnˈtɛmp(ə)rəns

intemperate
BR ɪnˈtɛmp(ə)rət
AM ᵻnˈtɛmp(ə)rət

intemperately
BR ɪnˈtɛmp(ə)rətli
AM ᵻnˈtɛmp(ə)rətli

intemperateness
BR ɪnˈtɛmp(ə)rətnəs
AM ᵻnˈtɛmp(ə)rətnəs

intend
BR ɪnˈtɛnd, -z, -ɪŋ, -ᵻd
AM ᵻnˈtɛnd, -z, -ɪŋ, -əd

intendancy
BR ɪnˈtɛnd(ə)ns|i, -ɪz
AM ᵻnˈtɛndnsi, -z

intendant
BR ɪnˈtɛnd(ə)nt, -s
AM ᵻnˈtɛndnt, -s

intended
BR ɪnˈtɛndᵻd, -z
AM ᵻnˈtɛndəd, -z

intendedly
BR ɪnˈtɛndᵻdli
AM ᵻnˈtɛndədli

intendment
BR ɪnˈtɛn(d)m(ə)nt, -s
AM ᵻnˈtɛn(d)mənt, -s

intense
BR ɪnˈtɛns, -ə(r), -ɪst
AM ᵻnˈtɛns, -ər, -əst

intensely
BR ɪnˈtɛnsli
AM ᵻnˈtɛnsli

intenseness
BR ɪnˈtɛnsnəs
AM ᵻnˈtɛnsnəs

intensification
BR ɪnˌtɛnsᵻfᵻˈkeɪʃn
AM ᵻnˌtɛnsəfəˈkeɪʃən

intensifier
BR ɪnˈtɛnsᵻfʌɪə(r), -z
AM ᵻnˈtɛnsəˌfaɪər, -z

intensify
BR ɪnˈtɛnsᵻfʌɪ, -z, -ɪŋ, -d
AM ᵻnˈtɛnsəˌfaɪ, -z, -ɪŋ, -d

intension
BR ɪnˈtɛnʃn, -z
AM ᵻnˈtɛnʃən, -z

intensional
BR ɪnˈtɛnʃn̩(ə)l, ɪnˈtɛnʃən(ə)l
AM ᵻnˈtɛn(t)ʃ(ə)nəl

intensionally
BR ɪnˈtɛnʃn̩əli, ɪnˈtɛnʃn̩l̩i, ɪnˈtɛnʃənl̩i, ɪnˈtɛnʃ(ə)nəli
AM ᵻnˈtɛn(t)ʃ(ə)nəli

intensity
BR ɪnˈtɛnsᵻti
AM ᵻnˈtɛnsədi

intensive
BR ɪnˈtɛnsɪv
AM ᵻnˈtɛnsɪv

intensively
BR ɪnˈtɛnsᵻvli
AM ᵻnˈtɛnsəvli

intensiveness
BR ɪnˈtɛnsɪvnᵻs
AM ᵻnˈtɛnsɪvnᵻs

intent
BR ɪnˈtɛnt, -s
AM ᵻnˈtɛnt, -s

intention
BR ɪnˈtɛnʃn, -z, -d
AM ᵻnˈtɛn(t)ʃən, -z, -d

intentional
BR ɪnˈtɛnʃn̩(ə)l, ɪnˈtɛnʃən(ə)l
AM ᵻnˈtɛn(t)ʃ(ə)nəl

intentionality
BR ɪnˌtɛnʃəˈnalᵻt|i, -ɪz
AM ᵻnˌtɛn(t)ʃəˈnælədi, -z

intentionally
BR ɪnˈtɛnʃn̩əli, ɪnˈtɛnʃn̩l̩i,

ɪn'tɛnʃənl̩i, ɪn'tɛnʃ(ə)nəli
AM ɪn'tɛn(t)ʃ(ə)nəli

intentioned
BR ɪn'tɛnʃ(ə)nd
AM ɪn'tɛn(t)ʃənd

intently
BR ɪn'tɛntli
AM ɪn'tɛn(t)li

intentness
BR ɪn'tɛntnəs
AM ɪn'tɛntnəs

inter
verb
BR ɪn'təː(r), -z, -ɪŋ, -d
AM ɪn'tər, -z, -ɪŋ, -d

interact
BR ˌɪntər'akt, -s, -ɪŋ, -ɪd
AM ˈɪn(t)ər'æk|(t), -(t)s, -tɪŋ, -təd

interactant
BR ˌɪntər'aktnt, -s
AM ˈɪn(t)ər'æktnt, -s

interaction
BR ˌɪntər'akʃn
AM ˈɪn(t)ər'ækʃən

interactional
BR ˌɪntər'akʃn̩(ə)l, ˌɪntər'akʃən(ə)l
AM ˈɪn(t)ər'ækʃ(ə)nəl

interactive
BR ˌɪntər'aktɪv
AM ˈɪn(t)ər'æktɪv

interactively
BR ˌɪntər'aktɨvli
AM ˈɪn(t)ər'æktəvli

inter alia
BR ˌɪntər 'eɪlɪə(*r*), + 'ɑːlɪə(*r*), + 'alɪə(*r*)
AM ˈɪntə'rɑljə, ˈɪntə'reɪljə, ˈɪntə'rɑliə, ˈɪntə'reɪliə

interAmerican
BR ˌɪnt(ə)rə'mɛrɪk(ə)n
AM ˌɪn(t)ərə'mɛrəkən

interarticular
BR ˌɪnt(ə)rɑː'tɪkjʉlə(r)
AM ˈɪn(t)ərˌɑr'tɪkjələr

interatomic
BR ˌɪnt(ə)rə'tɒmɪk
AM ˈɪn(t)ərə'tɑmɪk

interbank
BR ˌɪntə'baŋk
AM 'ɪn(t)ərˌbæŋk

interbed
BR ˌɪntə'bɛd, -z, -ɪŋ, -ɪd
AM 'ɪn(t)ərˌbɛd, -z, -ɪŋ, -əd

interblend
BR ˌɪntə'blɛnd, -z, -ɪŋ, -ɪd
AM 'ɪn(t)ərˌblɛnd, -z, -ɪŋ, -əd

interbred
BR ˌɪntə'brɛd
AM ˈɪn(t)ər'brɛd

interbreed
BR ˌɪntə'briːd, -z, -ɪŋ
AM ˈɪn(t)ər'brid, -z, -ɪŋ

intercalary
BR ɪn'təːkəl(ə)ri, ɪn'təːkl̩(ə)ri, ˌɪntə'kal(ə)ri
AM ɪn'tərkəˌlɛri, ˈɪn(t)ərˈkæləri

intercalate
BR ɪn'təːkəleɪt, ɪn'təːkl̩eɪt, ˌɪntəkə'leɪt, -s, -ɪŋ, -ɪd
AM ɪn'tərkəˌleɪ|t, -ts, -dɪŋ, -dɪd

intercalation
BR ɪnˌtəːkə'leɪʃn, ˌɪntəkə'leɪʃn, -z
AM ɪnˌtərkə'leɪʃən, -z

intercede
BR ˌɪntə'siːd, -z, -ɪŋ, -ɪd
AM ˌɪn(t)ər'sid, -z, -ɪŋ, -ɪd

interceder
BR ˌɪntə'siːdə(r), -z
AM ˌɪn(t)ər'sidər, -z

intercellular
BR ˌɪntə'sɛljʉlə(r)
AM ˌɪn(t)ər'sɛljələr

intercensal
BR ˌɪntə'sɛnsl
AM ˌɪn(t)ər'sɛnsəl

intercept
BR ˌɪntə'sɛpt, -s, -ɪŋ, -ɪd
AM ˌɪn(t)ər'sɛpt, -s, -ɪŋ, -əd

interception
BR ˌɪntə'sɛpʃn, -z
AM ˌɪn(t)ər'sɛpʃən, -z

interceptive
BR ˌɪntə'sɛptɪv
AM ˌɪn(t)ər'sɛptɪv

interceptor
BR 'ɪntəˌsɛptə(r), ˌɪntə'sɛptə(r), -z
AM ˌɪn(t)ər'sɛptər, -z

intercession
BR ˌɪntə'sɛʃn, -z
AM ˌɪn(t)ər'sɛʃən, -z

intercessional
BR ˌɪntə'sɛʃn̩(ə)l, ˌɪntə'sɛʃən(ə)l
AM ˌɪn(t)ər'sɛʃ(ə)nəl

intercessor
BR ˌɪntə'sɛsə(r), 'ɪntəˌsɛsə(r), -z
AM 'ɪn(t)ərˌsɛsər, -z

intercessorial
BR ˌɪntəsɪ'sɔːrɪəl, ˌɪntəsɛ'sɔːrɪəl
AM ˈɪn(t)ərsə'sɔriəl

intercessory
BR ˌɪntə'sɛs(ə)ri
AM ˈɪn(t)ər'sɛsəri

interchange¹
noun
BR 'ɪntətʃeɪn(d)ʒ, -ɪz
AM 'ɪn(t)ərˌtʃeɪndʒ, -ɪz

interchange²
verb
BR ˌɪntə'tʃeɪn(d)ʒ, -ɪz, -ɪŋ, -d
AM ˌɪn(t)ər'tʃeɪndʒ, -ɪz, -ɪŋ, -d

interchangeability
BR ˌɪntəˌtʃeɪn(d)ʒə'bɪlɨti
AM ˌɪn(t)ərˌtʃeɪndʒə'bɪlɨdi

interchangeable
BR ˌɪntə'tʃeɪn(d)ʒəbl
AM ˌɪn(t)ər'tʃeɪndʒəbəl

interchangeableness
BR ˌɪntə'tʃeɪn(d)ʒəblnəs
AM ˌɪn(t)ər'tʃeɪndʒəbəlnəs

interchangeably
BR ˌɪntə'tʃeɪn(d)ʒəbli
AM ˌɪn(t)ər'tʃeɪndʒəbli

inter-city
BR ˌɪntə'sɪti
AM ˈɪn(t)ər'sɪdi

inter-class
BR ˌɪntə'klɑːs, ˌɪntə'klas
AM ˈɪn(t)ər'klæs

intercollegiate
BR ˌɪntəkə'liːdʒɪət
AM ˌɪn(t)ərkə'lidʒ(i)ət

intercolonial
BR ˌɪntəkə'ləʊnɪəl
AM ˌɪn(t)ərkə'loʊniəl

intercom
BR 'ɪntəkɒm, -z
AM 'ɪn(t)ərˌkɑm, -z

intercommunicate
BR ˌɪntəkə'mjuːnɪkeɪt, -s, -ɪŋ, -ɪd
AM ˈɪn(t)ərkə'mjunəˌkeɪ|t, -ts, -dɪŋ, -dɪd

intercommunication
BR ˌɪntəkəˌmjuːnɪ'keɪʃn
AM ˈɪn(t)ərkəˌmjunə'keɪʃən

intercommunicative
BR ˌɪntəkə'mjuːnɪkətɪv
AM ˈɪn(t)ərkə'mjunəˌkeɪdɪv, ˈɪn(t)ərkə'mjunəkədɪv

intercommunion
BR ˌɪntəkə'mjuːnɪən
AM ˌɪn(t)ərkə'mjunjən

intercommunity
BR ˌɪntəkə'mjuːnɪti
AM ˈɪn(t)ərkə'mjunədi

interconnect
BR ˌɪntəkə'nɛkt, -s, -ɪŋ, -ɪd
AM ˈɪn(t)ərkə'nɛk|(t), -(t)s, -tɪŋ, -təd

interconnection
BR ˌɪntəkə'nɛkʃn, -z
AM ˈɪn(t)ərkə'nɛkʃən, -z

intercontinental
BR ˌɪntəˌkɒntɪ'nɛntl
AM ˈɪn(t)ərˌkɑntn'ɛn(t)l, ˈɪn(t)ərˌkɑn(t)ə'nɛn(t)l

intercontinentally
BR ˌɪntəˌkɒntɪ'nɛntl̩i
AM ˈɪn(t)ərˌkɑntn'ɛn(t)l̩i, ˈɪn(t)ərˌkɑn(t)ə'nɛn(t)l̩i

interconversion
BR ˌɪntəkən'vəːʃn, -z
AM ˈɪn(t)ərkən'vərʒən, -z

interconvert
BR ˌɪntəkən'vəːt, -s, -ɪŋ, -ɪd
AM ˈɪn(t)ərkən'vər|t, -ts, -dɪŋ, -dəd

interconvertible
BR ˌɪntəkən'vəːtɪbl
AM ˈɪn(t)ərkən'vərdəbəl

intercool
BR 'ɪntəkuːl, -z, -ɪŋ, -d
AM ˈɪn(t)ər'kul, -z, -ɪŋ, -d

intercooler
BR 'ɪntəˌkuːlə(r), -z
AM 'ɪn(t)ərˌkulər, -z

intercooling
BR 'ɪntəˌkuːlɪŋ, -z
AM 'ɪn(t)ərˌkulɪŋ, -z

intercorrelate
BR ˌɪntə'kɒrɪleɪt, -s, -ɪŋ, -ɪd
AM ˈɪn(t)ər'kɔrəˌleɪ|t, -ts, -dɪŋ, -dɪd

intercorrelation
BR ˌɪntəˌkɒrɪ'leɪʃn, -z
AM ˈɪn(t)ərˌkɔrə'leɪʃən, -z

intercostal
BR ˌɪntə'kɒstl
AM ˌɪn(t)ər'kɑstəl

intercostally
BR ˌɪntə'kɒstl̩i, ˌɪntə'kɒstəli
AM ˌɪn(t)ər'kɑstəli

intercounty
BR ˌɪntə'kaʊnti
AM ˈɪn(t)ər'kaʊn(t)i

intercourse
BR 'ɪntəkɔːs
AM 'ɪn(t)ərˌkɔ(ə)rs

intercrop
BR ˌɪntə'krɒp, -s, -ɪŋ, -t
AM ˈɪn(t)ər'krɑp, -s, -ɪŋ, -t

intercross
BR ˌɪntə'krɒs, -ɪz, -ɪŋ, -t
AM ˈɪn(t)ər'krɔs, ˈɪn(t)ər'krɑs, -əz, -ɪŋ, -t

intercrural
BR ˌɪntəˈkrʊərəl, ˌɪntəˈkrʊərl̩
AM ˈɪn(t)ərˈkrʊrəl

intercurrence
BR ˌɪntəˈkʌrəns, ˌɪntəˈkʌrn̩s, -ɪz
AM ˈɪn(t)ərˈkərəns, -əz

intercurrent
BR ˌɪntəˈkʌrənt, ˌɪntəˈkʌrn̩t
AM ˈɪn(t)ərˈkərənt

intercut
BR ˌɪntəˈkʌt, -s, -ɪŋ
AM ˈɪn(t)ərˈkə|t, -ts, -dɪŋ

interdenominational
BR ˌɪntədɪˌnɒmɪˈneɪʃn̩(ə)l, ˌɪntədɪˌnɒmɪˈneɪʃən(ə)l
AM ˈɪn(t)ərdəˌnɑməˈneɪʃ(ə)nəl

interdenominationally
BR ˌɪntədɪˌnɒmɪˈneɪʃn̩əli, ˌɪntədɪˌnɒmɪˈneɪʃn̩l̩i, ˌɪntədɪˌnɒmɪˈneɪʃənl̩i, ˌɪntədɪˌnɒmɪˈneɪʃ(ə)nəli
AM ˈɪn(t)ərdəˌnɑməˈneɪʃ(ə)nəli

interdepartmental
BR ˌɪntəˌdiːpɑːtˈmɛntl, ˌɪntədɪˌpɑːtˈmɛntl
AM ˈɪn(t)ərdəˌpɑrtˈmɛn(t)l, ˈɪn(t)ərdiˌpɑrtˈmɛn(t)l

interdepartmentally
BR ˌɪntəˌdiːpɑːtˈmɛntl̩i, ˌɪntədɪˌpɑːtˈmɛntl̩i
AM ˈɪn(t)ərdəˌpɑrtˈmɛn(t)li, ˈɪn(t)ərdiˌpɑrtˈmɛn(t)li

interdepend
BR ˌɪntədɪˈpɛnd, -z, -ɪŋ, -ɪd
AM ˈɪn(t)ərdəˈpɛnd, -z, -ɪŋ, -əd

interdependence
BR ˌɪntədɪˈpɛnd(ə)ns
AM ˈɪn(t)ərdəˈpɛndns

interdependency
BR ˌɪntədɪˈpɛnd(ə)ns|i, -ɪz
AM ˈɪn(t)ərdəˈpɛndnsi, -z

interdependent
BR ˌɪntədɪˈpɛnd(ə)nt
AM ˈɪn(t)ərdəˈpɛndənt

interdependently
BR ˌɪntədɪˈpɛnd(ə)ntli
AM ˈɪn(t)ərdəˈpɛndən(t)li

interdict[1]
noun
BR ˈɪntədɪkt, -s
AM ˈɪn(t)ərˌdɪk(t), -s

interdict[2]
verb
BR ˌɪntəˈdɪkt, -s, -ɪŋ, -ɪd
AM ˈɪn(t)ərˈdɪk|(t), -(t)s, -tɪŋ, -tɪd

interdiction
BR ˌɪntəˈdɪkʃn, -z
AM ˈɪn(t)ərˈdɪkʃən, -z

interdictory
BR ˌɪntəˈdɪkt(ə)ri
AM ˈɪn(t)ərˈdɪkˌtɔri

interdigital
BR ˌɪntəˈdɪdʒɪtl
AM ˈɪn(t)ərˈdɪdʒɪdl

interdigitally
BR ˌɪntəˈdɪdʒɪtl̩i
AM ˈɪn(t)ərˈdɪdʒɪdl̩i

interdigitate
BR ˌɪntəˈdɪdʒɪteɪt, -s, -ɪŋ, -ɪd
AM ˈɪn(t)ərˈdɪdʒɪˌteɪ|t, -ts, -dɪŋ, -dɪd

interdisciplinary
BR ˌɪntəˌdɪsɪˈplɪn(ə)ri, ˌɪntəˈdɪsɪplɪn(ə)ri
AM ˈɪn(t)ərˈdɪs(ə)pləˌnɛri

interest
BR ˈɪntrɪst, ˈɪnt(ə)rɛst, -s, -ɪŋ, -ɪd
AM ˈɪnt(ə)rəst, -s, -ɪŋ, -əd

interestedly
BR ˈɪntrɪstɪdli, ˈɪnt(ə)rɛstɪdli
AM ˈɪnt(ə)rəstəd

interestedness
BR ˈɪntrɪstɪdnɪs, ˈɪnt(ə)rɛstɪdnɪs
AM ˈɪnt(ə)rəstədnəs, ˈɪn(t)əˌrɛstədnəs

interestingly
BR ˈɪntrɪstɪŋli, ˈɪnt(ə)rɛstɪŋli
AM ˈɪnt(ə)rəstɪŋli

interestingness
BR ˈɪntrɪstɪŋnɪs, ˈɪnt(ə)rɛstɪŋnɪs
AM ˈɪnt(ə)rəstɪŋnɪs

interface
BR ˈɪntəfeɪs, -ɪz, -ɪŋ, -t
AM ˈɪn(t)ərˌfeɪs, -ɪz, -ɪŋ, -t

interfacial
BR ˌɪntəˈfeɪʃl
AM ˈɪn(t)ərˈfeɪʃəl

interfacially
BR ˌɪntəˈfeɪʃl̩i, ˌɪntəˈfeɪʃəli
AM ˈɪn(t)ərˈfeɪʃəli

interfacing
BR ˈɪntəˌfeɪsɪŋ, -z
AM ˈɪn(t)ərˌfeɪsɪŋ, -z

inter-faith
BR ˌɪntəˈfeɪθ
AM ˈɪn(t)ərˈfeɪθ

interfemoral
BR ˌɪntəˈfɛm(ə)rəl, ˌɪntəˈfɛm(ə)rl̩
AM ˈɪn(t)ərˈfɛm(ə)rəl

interfere
BR ˌɪntəˈfɪə(r), -z, -ɪŋ, -d
AM ˈɪn(t)ərˈfɪ(ə)r, -z, -ɪŋ, -d

interference
BR ˌɪntəˈfɪərəns, ˌɪntəˈfɪərn̩s
AM ˌɪn(t)ərˈfɪrəns

interferential
BR ˌɪntəfəˈrɛnʃl
AM ˈɪn(t)ərfəˈrɛn(t)ʃəl

interferer
BR ˌɪntəˈfɪərə(r), -z
AM ˈɪn(t)ərˈfɪrər, -z

interferingly
BR ˌɪntəˈfɪərɪŋli
AM ˈɪn(t)ərˈfɪrɪŋli

interferometer
BR ˌɪntəfəˈrɒmɪtə(r), -z
AM ˌɪn(t)ərfəˈrɑmədər, -z

interferometric
BR ˌɪntəˌfɛrə(ʊ)ˈmɛtrɪk, ˌɪntəˌfɪərə(ʊ)ˈmɛtrɪk
AM ˌɪn(t)ərˌfɪrəˈmɛtrɪk

interferometrically
BR ˌɪntəˌfɛrəˈmɛtrɪkli, ˌɪntəˌfɪərəˈmɛtrɪkli
AM ˌɪn(t)ərˌfɪrəˈmɛtrək(ə)li

interferometry
BR ˌɪntəfɪˈrɒmɪtri
AM ˌɪn(t)ərfəˈrɑmətri

interferon
BR ˌɪntəˈfɪərɒn
AM ˌɪntərˈfɪrˌɑn

interfile
BR ˌɪntəˈfʌɪl, -z, -ɪŋ, -d
AM ˈɪn(t)ərˈfaɪl, -z, -ɪŋ, -d

interflow
BR ˌɪntəˈfləʊ, -z, -ɪŋ, -d
AM ˈɪn(t)ərˈfloʊ, -z, -ɪŋ, -d

interfluent
BR ˌɪntəˈflʊənt
AM ˈɪn(t)ərˈflʊənt

interfluve
BR ˈɪntəfluːv, -z
AM ˈɪn(t)ərˌfluv, -z

interfuse
BR ˌɪntəˈfjuːz, -ɪz, -ɪŋ, -d
AM ˈɪn(t)ərˈfjuz, -əz, -ɪŋ, -d

interfusion
BR ˌɪntəˈfjuːʒn, -z
AM ˈɪn(t)ərˈfjuʒən, -z

intergalactic
BR ˌɪntəgəˈlaktɪk
AM ˈɪn(t)ərgəˈlæktɪk

intergalactically
BR ˌɪntəgəˈlaktɪkli
AM ˈɪn(t)ərgəˈlæktək(ə)li

interglacial
BR ˌɪntəˈgleɪʃl, ˌɪntəˈgleɪsɪəl, -z
AM ˈɪn(t)ərˈgleɪʃəl, -z

intergovernmental
BR ˌɪntəˌgʌvnˈmɛntl, ˌɪntəˌgʌvəˈmɛntl
AM ˈɪn(t)ərˌgəvər(n)ˈmɛn(t)l

intergovernmentally
BR ˌɪntəˌgʌvnˈmɛntl̩i, ˌɪntəˌgʌvəˈmɛntl̩i, ˌɪntəˌgʌvnˈmɛntəli, ˌɪntəˌgʌvəˈmɛntəli
AM ˈɪn(t)ərˌgəvər(n)ˈmɛn(t)li

intergradation
BR ˌɪntəgrəˈdeɪʃn, -z
AM ˈɪn(t)ərgrəˈdeɪʃən, -z

intergrade
BR ˌɪntəˈgreɪd, -z, -ɪŋ, -ɪd
AM ˈɪn(t)ərˈgreɪd, -z, -ɪŋ, -ɪd

intergrowth
BR ˈɪntəgrəʊθ, -s
AM ˈɪn(t)ərˌgroʊθ, -s

interim
BR ˈɪnt(ə)rɪm
AM ˈɪn(t)ərəm

interior
BR ɪnˈtɪərɪə(r), -z
AM ɪnˈtɪriər, -z

interiorise
BR ɪnˈtɪərɪərʌɪz, -ɪz, -ɪŋ, -d
AM ɪnˈtɪriəˌraɪz, -ɪz, -ɪŋ, -d

interiorize
BR ɪnˈtɪərɪərʌɪz, -ɪz, -ɪŋ, -d
AM ɪnˈtɪriəˌraɪz, -ɪz, -ɪŋ, -d

interiorly
BR ɪnˈtɪərɪəli
AM ɪnˈtɪriərli

interject
BR ˌɪntəˈdʒɛkt, -s, -ɪŋ, -ɪd
AM ˌɪn(t)ərˈdʒɛk|(t), -(t)s, -tɪŋ, -təd

interjection
BR ˌɪntəˈdʒɛkʃn, -z
AM ˌɪn(t)ərˈdʒɛkʃən, -z

interjectional
BR ˌɪntəˈdʒɛkʃn̩(ə)l, ˌɪntəˈdʒɛkʃən(ə)l
AM ˌɪn(t)ərˈdʒɛkʃ(ə)nəl

interjectionary
BR ˌɪntəˈdʒɛkʃn̩(ə)ri
AM ˌɪn(t)ərˈdʒɛkʃəˌnɛri

interjectory
BR ˌɪntəˈdʒɛkt(ə)ri
AM ˌɪn(t)ərˈdʒɛkt(ə)ri

interknit
BR ˌɪntəˈnɪt, -s, -ɪŋ, -ɨd
AM ˈɪn(t)ərˈnɪ|t, -ts, -dɪŋ, -dəd

interlace
BR ˌɪntəˈleɪs, -ɨz, -ɪŋ, -t
AM ˈɪn(t)ərˈleɪs, -ɨz, -ɪŋ, -t

interlacement
BR ˌɪntəˈleɪsm(ə)nt, -s
AM ˈɪn(t)ərˈleɪsmənt, -s

Interlaken
BR ˈɪntəˌlɑːk(ə)n
AM ˈɪn(t)ərˌlɑkən

interlanguage
BR ˈɪntəˌlaŋ(g)w|ɪdʒ, -ɪdʒɨz
AM ˈɪn(t)ərˈlæŋ(g)wədʒ, -z

interlap
BR ˌɪntəˈlap, -s, -ɪŋ, -t
AM ˌɪn(t)ərˈlæp, -s, -ɪŋ, -t

interlard
BR ˌɪntəˈlɑːd, -z, -ɪŋ, -ɨd
AM ˌɪn(t)ərˈlɑrd, -z, -ɪŋ, -ɨd

interleaf
BR ˌɪntəˈliːf, -s, -ɪŋ, -t
AM ˈɪn(t)ərˈlif, -s, -ɪŋ, -t

interleave
BR ˌɪntəˈliːv, -z, -ɪŋ, -d
AM ˌɪn(t)ərˈliv, -z, -ɪŋ, -d

interleukin
BR ˌɪntəˈluːkɪn, -z
AM ˈɪn(t)ərˈlukən, -z

interlibrary
BR ˌɪntəˈlʌɪbr(ər)i
AM ˈɪn(t)ərˈlaɪb(r)əri

interline
BR ˌɪntəˈlʌɪn, -z, -ɪŋ, -d
AM ˈɪn(t)ərˈlaɪn, -z, -ɪŋ, -d

interlinear
BR ˌɪntəˈlɪnɪə(r)
AM ˈɪn(t)ərˈlɪniər

interlineation
BR ˌɪntəˌlɪnɪˈeɪʃn, -z
AM ˈɪn(t)ərˌlɪniˈeɪʃən, -z

Interlingua
BR ˌɪntəˈlɪŋgwə(r)
AM ˌɪn(t)ərˈlɪŋgwə

interlining[1]
interlineation
BR ˌɪntəˈlʌɪnɪŋ, -z
AM ˈɪn(t)ərˈlaɪnɪŋ, -z

interlining[2]
layer between two others
BR ˈɪntəˌlʌɪnɪŋ, -z
AM ˈɪn(t)ərˌlaɪnɪŋ, -z

interlink
BR ˌɪntəˈlɪŋ|k, -ks, -kɪŋ, -(k)t
AM ˈɪn(t)ərˈlɪŋ|k, -ks, -kɪŋ, -(k)t

interlobular
BR ˌɪntəˈlɒbjʉlə(r)
AM ˈɪn(t)ərˈlɑbjələr

interlock[1]
noun
BR ˈɪntəlɒk, -s
AM ˈɪn(t)ərˌlɑk, -s

interlock[2]
verb
BR ˌɪntəˈlɒk, -s, -ɪŋ, -t
AM ˈɪn(t)ərˈlɑk, -s, -ɪŋ, -t

interlocker
BR ˌɪntəˈlɒkə(r), -z
AM ˈɪn(t)ərˈlɑkər, -z

interlocution
BR ˌɪntələˈkjuːʃn, -z
AM ˌɪn(t)ərˌloʊˈkjuʃən, -z

interlocutor
BR ˌɪntəˈlɒkjʉtə(r), -z
AM ˌɪn(t)ərˈlɑkjədər, -z

interlocutory
BR ˌɪntəˈlɒkjʉt(ə)r|i, -ɪz
AM ˈɪn(t)ərˈlɑkjəˌtɔri, -z

interlocutrix
BR ˌɪntəˈlɒkjʉtrɪks, -ɨz
AM ˌɪn(t)ərˈlɑkjəˌtrɪks, -ɨz

interlope
BR ˌɪntəˈləʊp, -s, -ɪŋ, -t
AM ˈɪn(t)ərˌloʊp, ˌɪn(t)ərˈloʊp, -s, -ɪŋ, -t

interloper
BR ˈɪntəˌləʊpə(r), -z
AM ˈɪn(t)ərˌloʊpər, ˌɪn(t)ərˈloʊpər, -z

interlude
BR ˈɪntəl(j)uːd, -z
AM ˈɪn(t)ərˌlud, -z

intermarriage
BR ˌɪntəˈmarɪdʒ
AM ˈɪn(t)ərˈmɛrɪdʒ

intermarry
BR ˌɪntəˈmar|i, -ɪz, -ɪɪŋ, -ɪd
AM ˈɪn(t)ərˈmɛri, -z, -ɪŋ, -d

intermedia
BR ˌɪntəˈmiːdɪə(r)
AM ˈɪn(t)ərˈmidiə

intermediacy
BR ˌɪntəˈmiːdɪəs|i, -ɪz
AM ˈɪn(t)ərˈmidiəsi, -z

intermediary
BR ˌɪntəˈmiːdɪər|i, -ɪz
AM ˈɪn(t)ərˈmidiˌɛri, -z

intermediate
BR ˌɪntəˈmiːdɪət, -s
AM ˈɪn(t)ərˈmidiət, -s

intermediately
BR ˌɪntəˈmiːdɪətli
AM ˈɪn(t)ərˈmidiətli

intermediateness
BR ˌɪntəˈmiːdɪətnəs
AM ˈɪn(t)ərˈmidiətnəs

intermediation
BR ˌɪntəˌmiːdɪˈeɪʃn, -z
AM ˈɪn(t)ərˌmidiˈeɪʃən, -z

intermediator
BR ˌɪntəˈmiːdɪeɪtə(r), -z
AM ˈɪn(t)ərˈmidiˌeɪdər, -z

intermedium
BR ˌɪntəˈmiːdɪəm
AM ˈɪn(t)ərˈmidiəm

interment
BR ɪnˈtəːm(ə)nt, -s
AM ɨnˈtərmənt, -s

intermesh
BR ˌɪntəˈmɛʃ, -ɨz, -ɪŋ, -t
AM ˌɪn(t)ərˈmɛʃ, -əz, -ɪŋ, -t

intermezzo
BR ˌɪntəˈmɛtsəʊ, -z
AM ˌɪn(t)ərˈmɛtsoʊ, -z

interminable
BR ɪnˈtəːmɨnəbl
AM ɨnˈtərmənəbəl

interminableness
BR ɪnˈtəːmɨnəblnəs
AM ɨnˈtərmənəbəlnəs

interminably
BR ɪnˈtəːmɨnəbli
AM ɨnˈtərmənəbli

intermingle
BR ˌɪntəˈmɪŋgl, -z, -ɪŋ, -d
AM ˈɪn(t)ərˈmɪŋgəl, -əlz, -(ə)lɪŋ, -əld

intermission
BR ˌɪntəˈmɪʃn, -z
AM ˌɪn(t)ərˈmɪʃən, -z

intermit
BR ˌɪntəˈmɪt, -s, -ɪŋ, -ɨd
AM ˌɪn(t)ərˈmɪ|t, -ts, -dɪŋ, -dɨd

intermittence
BR ˌɪntəˈmɪt(ə)ns, -ɨz
AM ˈɪn(t)ərˈmɪtns, -əz

intermittency
BR ˌɪntəˈmɪt(ə)nsi
AM ˈɪn(t)ərˈmɪtnsi

intermittent
BR ˌɪntəˈmɪt(ə)nt
AM ˈɪn(t)ərˈmɪtnt

intermittently
BR ˌɪntəˈmɪt(ə)ntli
AM ˈɪn(t)ərˈmɪtn(t)li

intermix
BR ˌɪntəˈmɪks, -ɨz, -ɪŋ, -t
AM ˈɪn(t)ərˈmɪks, -ɨz, -ɪŋ, -t

intermixable
BR ˌɪntəˈmɪksəbl
AM ˈɪn(t)ərˈmɪksəbəl

intermixture
BR ˌɪntəˈmɪkstʃə(r), -z
AM ˈɪn(t)ərˈmɪkstʃər, -z

intermolecular
BR ˌɪntəməˈlɛkjʉlə(r)
AM ˈɪn(t)ərməˈlɛkjələr

intern[1]
noun
BR ˈɪntəːn, -z
AM ˈɪnˌtərn, -z

intern[2]
verb
BR ɪnˈtəːn, -z, -ɪŋ, -d
AM ɨnˈtərn, -z, -ɪŋ, -d

internal
BR ɪnˈtəːnl
AM ɨnˈtərnəl

internalisation
BR ɪnˌtəːnl̩ʌɪˈzeɪʃn, ɪnˌtəːnəlʌɪˈzeɪʃn
AM ɨnˌtərnl̩əˈzeɪʃən, ɪnˌtərnlˌaɪˈzeɪʃən

internalise
BR ɪnˈtəːnl̩ʌɪz, ɪnˈtəːnəlʌɪz, -ɨz, -ɪŋ, -d
AM ɨnˈtərnlˌaɪz, -ɨz, -ɪŋ, -d

internality
BR ˌɪntəːˈnalɨti
AM ˌɪntərˈnælədi

internalization
BR ɪnˌtəːnl̩ʌɪˈzeɪʃn, ɪnˌtəːnəlʌɪˈzeɪʃn
AM ɨnˌtərnl̩əˈzeɪʃən, ɨnˌtərnlˌaɪˈzeɪʃən

internalize
BR ɪnˈtəːnl̩ʌɪz, ɪnˈtəːnəlʌɪz, -ɨz, -ɪŋ, -d
AM ɨnˈtərnlˌaɪz, -ɨz, -ɪŋ, -d

internally
BR ɪnˈtəːnl̩i, ɪnˈtəːnəli
AM ɨnˈtərnəli

international
BR ˌɪntəˈnaʃn̩(ə)l, ˌɪntəˈnaʃən(ə)l, -z
AM ˌɪn(t)ərˈnæʃ(ə)nəl, -z

Internationale
BR ˌɪntəˌnaʃ(ɪ)əˈnɑːl, ˌɪntəˌnaʃ(ɪ)əˈnal
AM ˌɪn(t)ərˌnæʃəˈnæl, ˌɪn(t)ərˌnæʃəˈnɑl
FR ɛ̃tɛʀnasjɔnal

internationalisation
BR ˌɪntəˌnaʃn̩əlʌɪˈzeɪʃn, ˌɪntəˌnaʃn̩l̩ʌɪˈzeɪʃn, ˌɪntəˌnaʃənl̩ʌɪˈzeɪʃn, ˌɪntəˌnaʃ(ə)nəlʌɪˈzeɪʃn
AM ˌɪn(t)ərˌnæʃənl̩əˈzeɪʃən, ˌɪn(t)ərˌnæʃnələˈzeɪʃən, ˌɪn(t)ərˌnæʃənlˌaɪˈzeɪʃən,

ˌɪn(t)ərˌnæʃnəlˌaɪ-ˈzeɪʃən

internationalise
BR ˌɪntəˈnaʃn̩əlʌɪz, ˌɪntəˈnaʃn̩l̩ʌɪz, ˌɪntəˈnaʃənl̩ʌɪz, ˌɪntəˈnaʃ(ə)nəlʌɪz, -ɪz, -ɪŋ, -d
AM ˌɪn(t)ərˈnæʃənlˌaɪz, ˌɪn(t)ərˈnæʃnəlˌaɪz, -ɪz, -ɪŋ, -d

internationalism
BR ˌɪntəˈnaʃn̩əlɪz(ə)m, ˌɪntəˈnaʃn̩l̩ɪz(ə)m, ˌɪntəˈnaʃənl̩ɪz(ə)m, ˌɪntəˈnaʃ(ə)nəlɪz(ə)m
AM ˌɪn(t)ərˈnæʃənlˌɪzəm, ˌɪn(t)ərˈnæʃnəlˌɪzəm

internationalist
BR ˌɪntəˈnaʃn̩əlɪst, ˌɪntəˈnaʃn̩l̩ɪst, ˌɪntəˈnaʃənl̩ɪst, ˌɪntəˈnaʃ(ə)nəlɪst, -s
AM ˌɪn(t)ərˈnæʃənl̩əst, ˌɪn(t)ərˈnæʃnələst, -s

internationality
BR ˌɪntəˌnaʃəˈnalɪti
AM ˈˌɪn(t)ərˌnæʃ(ə)ˈnæl-ədi

internationalization
BR ˌɪntəˌnaʃn̩əlʌɪˈzeɪʃn, ˌɪntəˌnaʃn̩l̩ʌɪˈzeɪʃn, ˌɪntəˌnaʃənl̩ʌɪˈzeɪʃn, ˌɪntəˌnaʃ(ə)nəlʌɪˈzeɪʃn
AM ˌɪn(t)ərˌnæʃənlə-ˈzeɪʃən, ˌɪn(t)ərˌnæʃnələˈzeɪʃən, ˌɪn(t)ərˌnæʃənlˌaɪ-ˈzeɪʃən, ˌɪn(t)ərˌnæʃnəlˌaɪ-ˈzeɪʃən

internationalize
BR ˌɪntəˈnaʃn̩əlʌɪz, ˌɪntəˈnaʃn̩l̩ʌɪz, ˌɪntəˈnaʃənl̩ʌɪz, ˌɪntəˈnaʃ(ə)nəlʌɪz, -ɪz, -ɪŋ, -d
AM ˌɪn(t)ərˈnæʃənlˌaɪz, ˌɪn(t)ərˈnæʃnəlˌaɪz, -ɪz, -ɪŋ, -d

internationally
BR ˌɪntəˈnaʃn̩əli, ˌɪntəˈnaʃn̩l̩i, ˌɪntəˈnaʃənl̩i, ˌɪntəˈnaʃ(ə)nəli
AM ˈˌɪn(t)ərˈˌnæʃ(ə)nəli

interne
BR ˈɪntəːn, -z
AM ˈɪnˌtərn, -z

internecine
BR ˌɪntəˈniːsʌɪn
AM ˈˌɪn(t)ərˈˌnɛˌsin, ˈˌɪn(t)ərˈˌnisɪn

internee
BR ˌɪntəːˈniː, -z
AM ˈˌɪnˌtərˈni, -z

internist
BR ɪnˈtəːnɪst, -s
AM ˈɪnˌtərnəst, -s

internment
BR ɪnˈtəːnm(ə)nt, -s
AM ɪnˈtərnmənt, -s

internode
BR ˈɪntənəʊd, -z
AM ˈɪn(t)ərˌnoʊd, -z

internship
BR ˈɪntəːnʃɪp, -s
AM ˈɪnˌtərnˌʃɪp, -s

internuclear
BR ˌɪntəˈnjuːklɪə(r)
AM ˈˌɪn(t)ərˈn(j)ʊkliər

internuncial
BR ˌɪntəˈnʌnsɪəl
AM ˈˌɪn(t)ərˈnənsiəl

internuncio
BR ˌɪntəˈnʌnsɪəʊ, -z
AM ˈˌɪn(t)ərˈnənsioʊ, -z

interoceanic
BR ˌɪntərˌəʊʃɪˈanɪk, ˌɪntərˌəʊsɪˈanɪk
AM ˈˌɪn(t)ərˌoʊʃiˈænɪk

interoceptive
BR ˌɪnt(ə)rəˈsɛptɪv
AM ˈˌɪn(t)ərə-ˈsɛptɪv

interoperability
BR ˌɪntərˌɒp(ə)rəˈbɪlɪti
AM ˈˌɪn(t)ərˌɑp(ə)rəˈbɪl-ɪdi

interoperable
BR ˌɪntərˈɒp(ə)rəbl
AM ˈˌɪn(t)ərˈɑp(ə)rəbəl

interosculate
BR ˌɪntərˈɒskjʉleɪt, -s, -ɪŋ, -ɪd
AM ˈˌɪn(t)ərˈɑskjəˌleɪ|t, -ts, -dɪŋ, -dɪd

interosseous
BR ˌɪntərˈɒsɪəs
AM ˈˌɪn(t)ərˈɑsiəs

interpage
BR ˌɪntəˈpeɪdʒ, -ɪz, -ɪŋ, -d
AM ˌɪn(t)ərˈpeɪdʒ, -ɪz, -ɪŋ, -d

interparietal
BR ˌɪntəpəˈrʌɪɪtl
AM ˈˌɪn(t)ərpəˈraɪɪdl

interparietally
BR ˌɪntəpəˈrʌɪɪtl̩i
AM ˈˌɪn(t)ərpəˈraɪɪdl̩i

interpellate
BR ɪnˈtəːpəleɪt, ˌɪntəˈpɛleɪt, -s, -ɪŋ, -ɪd
AM ˌɪn(t)ərˈpɛˌleɪ|t, ɪnˈtərpəˌleɪ|t, -ts, -dɪŋ, -dɪd

interpellation
BR ɪnˌtəːpəˈleɪʃn, ˌɪntəpəˈleɪʃn, -z
AM ɪnˌtərpəˈleɪʃən, ˌɪn(t)ərpəˈleɪʃən, -z

interpellator
BR ɪnˈtəːpəleɪtə(r), -z
AM ˌɪn(t)ərˈpɛˌleɪdər, ɪnˈtərpəˌleɪdər, -z

interpenetrate
BR ˌɪntəˈpɛnɪtreɪt, -s, -ɪŋ, -ɪd
AM ˈˌɪn(t)ərˈpɛnəˌtreɪ|t, -ts, -dɪŋ, -dɪd

interpenetration
BR ˌɪntəˌpɛnɪˈtreɪʃn
AM ˈˌɪn(t)ərˌpɛnəˈtreɪʃən

interpenetrative
BR ˌɪntəˈpɛnɪtrətɪv
AM ˈˌɪn(t)ərˈpɛnəˌtreɪdɪv, ˈˌɪn(t)ərˈpɛnətrədɪv

interpersonal
BR ˌɪntəˈpəːsn̩(ə)l, ˌɪntəˈpəːsən(ə)l
AM ˈˌɪn(t)ərˈpərs(ə)nəl

interpersonally
BR ˌɪntəˈpəːsn̩əli, ˌɪntəˈpəːsn̩l̩i, ˌɪntəˈpəːsənl̩i, ˌɪntəˈpəːs(ə)nəli
AM ˈˌɪn(t)ərˈpərs(ə)nəli

interplait
BR ˌɪntəˈplat, -s, -ɪŋ, -ɪd
AM ˌɪn(t)ərˈpl|eɪt, ˌɪn(t)ərˈl|æt, -eɪts\-æts, -eɪdɪŋ\-ædɪŋ, -eɪdɪd\-ædəd

interplanetary
BR ˌɪntəˈplanɪt(ə)ri
AM ˈˌɪn(t)ərˈplænəˌtɛri

interplay
BR ˈɪntəpleɪ
AM ˈɪn(t)ərˌpleɪ

interplead
BR ˌɪntəˈpliːd, -z, -ɪŋ, -ɪd
AM ˌɪn(t)ərˈplid, -z, -ɪŋ, -ɪd

interpleader
BR ˌɪntəˈpliːdə(r), -z
AM ˌɪn(t)ərˈplidər, -z

Interpol
BR ˈɪntəpɒl
AM ˈɪn(t)ərˌpoʊl

interpolate
BR ɪnˈtəːpəleɪt, -s, -ɪŋ, -ɪd
AM ɪnˈtərpəˌleɪ|t, -ts, -dɪŋ, -dɪd

interpolation
BR ɪnˌtəːpəˈleɪʃn, -z
AM ɪnˌtərpəˈleɪʃən, -z

interpolative
BR ɪnˈtəːpələtɪv
AM ɪnˈtərpəˌleɪdɪv, ɪnˈtərpələdɪv

interpolator
BR ɪnˈtəːpəleɪtə(r), -z
AM ɪnˈtərpəˌleɪdər, -z

interposal
BR ˌɪntəˈpəʊzl, -z
AM ˌɪn(t)ərˈpoʊzəl, -z

interpose
BR ˌɪntəˈpəʊz, -ɪz, -ɪŋ, -d
AM ˌɪn(t)ərˈpoʊz, -əz, -ɪŋ, -t

interposition
BR ˌɪntəpəˈzɪʃn
AM ˌɪn(t)ərpəˈzɪʃən

interpret
BR ɪnˈtəːprɪt, -s, -ɪŋ, -ɪd
AM ɪnˈtərprə|t, -ts, -dɪŋ, -dəd

interpretability
BR ɪnˌtəːprɪtəˈbɪlɪti
AM ɪnˌtərprədəˈbɪlɪdi

interpretable
BR ɪnˈtəːprɪtəbl
AM ɪnˈtərprədəbəl

interpretation
BR ɪnˌtəːprɪˈteɪʃn, -z
AM ɪnˌtərprəˈteɪʃən, -z

interpretational
BR ɪnˌtəːprɪˈteɪʃn̩(ə)l, ɪnˌtəːprɪˈteɪʃən(ə)l
AM ɪnˌtərprəˈteɪʃ(ə)nəl

interpretative
BR ɪnˈtəːprɪtətɪv
AM ɪnˈtərprəˌteɪdɪv, ɪnˈtərprədədɪv

interpreter
BR ɪnˈtəːprɪtə(r), -z
AM ɪnˈtərprədər, -z

interpretive
BR ɪnˈtəːprɪtɪv
AM ɪnˈtərprədɪv

interpretively
BR ɪnˈtəːprɪtɪvli
AM ɪnˈtərprədɪvli

interprovincial
BR ˌɪntəprəˈvɪnʃl
AM ˈˌɪn(t)ərprəˈvɪnʃəl

interracial
BR ˌɪntəˈreɪʃl
AM ˈˌɪn(t)ərˈreɪʃəl

interracially
BR ˌɪntəˈreɪʃl̩i, ˌɪntəˈreɪʃəli
AM ˈˌɪn(t)ərˈreɪʃəli

interregna
BR ˌɪntəˈrɛgnə(*r*)
AM ˈˌɪn(t)ərˈrɛgnə

interregnum
BR ˌɪntəˈrɛgnəm, -z
AM ˈˌɪn(t)ərˈrɛgnəm, -z

interrelate
BR ˌɪntərɪˈleɪt, -s, -ɪŋ, -ɪd
AM ˈˌɪn(t)ərəˈleɪ|t, -ts, -dɪŋ, -dɪd

interrelation
BR ˌɪntərɪˈleɪʃn, -z
AM ˈˌɪn(t)ərəˈleɪʃən, -z

interrelationship
BR ˌɪntərɪˈleɪʃnʃɪp, -s
AM ˈˌɪn(t)ərəˈleɪʃənˌʃɪp, -s

interrogate
BR ɪnˈtɛrəgeɪt, -s, -ɪŋ, -ɪd
AM ɪnˈtɛrəˌgeɪ|t, -ts, -dɪŋ, -dɪd

interrogation
BR ɪnˌtɛrəˈgeɪʃn, -z

AM ɪnˌtɛrəˈɡeɪʃən, -z

interrogational
BR ɪnˌtɛrəˈɡeɪʃn̩(ə)l, ɪnˌtɛrəˈɡeɪʃən(ə)l
AM ɪnˌtɛrəˈɡeɪʃ(ə)nəl

interrogative
BR ˌɪntəˈrɒɡətɪv, -z
AM ˌɪn(t)əˈrɑɡədɪv, -z

interrogatively
BR ˌɪntəˈrɒɡətɪvli
AM ˌɪn(t)əˈrɑɡədəvli

interrogator
BR ɪnˈtɛrəɡeɪtə(r), -z
AM ɪnˈtɛrəˌɡeɪdər, -z

interrogatory
BR ˌɪntəˈrɒɡət(ə)ri
AM ˌɪn(t)əˈrɑɡəˌtɔri

interrupt
BR ˌɪntəˈrʌpt, -s, -ɪŋ, -ɪd
AM ˌɪn(t)əˈrəpt, -s, -ɪŋ, -əd

interrupter
BR ˌɪntəˈrʌptə(r), -z
AM ˌɪn(t)əˈrəptər, -z

interruptible
BR ˌɪntəˈrʌptɪbl
AM ˌɪn(t)əˈrəptəbəl

interruption
BR ˌɪntəˈrʌpʃn, -z
AM ˌɪn(t)əˈrəpʃən, -z

interruptive
BR ˌɪntəˈrʌptɪv
AM ˌɪn(t)əˈrəptɪv

interruptor
BR ˌɪntəˈrʌptə(r), -z
AM ˌɪn(t)əˈrəptər, -z

interruptory
BR ˌɪntəˈrʌpt(ə)ri
AM ˌɪn(t)əˈrəpt(ə)ri

intersect
BR ˌɪntəˈsɛkt, -s, -ɪŋ, -ɪd
AM ˌɪn(t)ərˈsɛk|(t), -(t)s, -tɪŋ, -təd

intersection[1]
dividing
BR ˌɪntəˈsɛkʃn, -z
AM ˌɪn(t)ərˈsɛkʃən, -z

intersection[2]
road
BR ˈɪntəˌsɛkʃn, -z
AM ˈɪn(t)ərˌsɛkʃən, -z

intersectional
BR ˌɪntəˈsɛkʃn̩(ə)l, ˌɪntəˈsɛkʃən(ə)l
AM ˌɪn(t)ərˈsɛkʃ(ə)nəl

interseptal
BR ˌɪntəˈsɛptl
AM ˌɪn(t)ərˈsɛptl

intersex
BR ˈɪntəsɛks, -ɪz
AM ˈɪn(t)ərˌsɛks, -əz

intersexual
BR ˌɪntəˈsɛkʃʊəl, ˌɪntəˈsɛkʃ(ʉ)l, ˌɪntəˈsɛksjʊ(ə)l
AM ˈɪn(t)ərˈsɛkʃ(əw)əl

intersexuality
BR ˌɪntəˌsɛkʃʊˈalɪt|i, ˌɪntəˌsɛksjʊˈalɪt|i, -ɪz
AM ˈɪn(t)ərˌsɛkʃəˈwælədi, -z

intersexually
BR ˌɪntəˈsɛkʃʊəli, ˌɪntəˈsɛkʃʉli, ˌɪntəˈsɛkʃli, ˌɪntəˈsɛksjʊ(ə)li
AM ˈɪn(t)ərˈsɛkʃ(əw)əli

interspace[1]
noun
BR ˈɪntəspeɪs, -ɪz
AM ˈɪn(t)ərˌspeɪs, -ɪz

interspace[2]
verb
BR ˌɪntəˈspeɪs, -ɪz, -ɪŋ, -t
AM ˌɪn(t)ərˈspeɪs, -ɪz, -ɪŋ, -t

interspecific
BR ˌɪntəspɪˈsɪfɪk
AM ˈɪn(t)ərspəˈsɪfɪk

intersperse
BR ˌɪntəˈspəːs, -ɪz, -ɪŋ, -t
AM ˌɪn(t)ərˈspərs, -ɪz, -ɪŋ, -t

interspersion
BR ˌɪntəˈspəːʃn
AM ˌɪn(t)ərˈspərʒən

interspinal
BR ˌɪntəˈspʌɪnl
AM ˈɪn(t)ərˈspaɪnəl

interspinous
BR ˌɪntəˈsɛptl
AM ˈɪn(t)ərˈspaɪnəs

interstate
BR ˌɪntəˈsteɪt
AM ˈɪn(t)ərˈsteɪt

interstellar
BR ˌɪntəˈstɛlə(r)
AM ˈɪn(t)ərˈstɛlər

interstice
BR ɪnˈtəːstɪs, -ɪz
AM ɪnˈtərstəs, -əz

interstitial
BR ˌɪntəˈstɪʃl
AM ˈɪn(t)ərˈstɪʃəl

interstitially
BR ˌɪntəˈstɪʃl̩i, ˌɪntəˈstɪʃəli
AM ˈɪn(t)ərˈstɪʃəli

intertextuality
BR ˌɪntəˌtɛkstjʊˈalɪti, ˌɪntəˌtɛkstʃʊˈalɪt|i, -ɪz
AM ˈɪn(t)ərˌtɛk(st)ʃəˈwælədi, -z

intertidal
BR ˌɪntəˈtʌɪdl
AM ˈɪn(t)ərˈtaɪdəl

intertribal
BR ˌɪntəˈtrʌɪbl
AM ˈɪn(t)ərˈtraɪbəl

intertrigo
BR ˌɪntəˈtrʌɪɡəʊ, -z
AM ˈɪn(t)ərˈtraɪˌɡoʊ, -z

intertwine
BR ˌɪntəˈtwʌɪn, -z, -ɪŋ, -d
AM ˈɪn(t)ərˈtwaɪn, -z, -ɪŋ, -d

intertwinement
BR ˌɪntəˈtwʌɪnm(ə)nt, -s
AM ˈɪn(t)ərˈtwaɪnmənt, -s

intertwist
BR ˌɪntəˈtwɪst, -s, -ɪŋ, -ɪd
AM ˈɪn(t)ərˈtwɪst, -s, -ɪŋ, -əd

interval
BR ˈɪntəvl, -z
AM ˈɪn(t)ərvəl, -z

intervallic
BR ˌɪntəˈvalɪk
AM ˈɪn(t)ərˈvælɪk

intervene
BR ˌɪntəˈviːn, -z, -ɪŋ, -d
AM ˌɪn(t)ərˈvin, -z, -ɪŋ, -d

intervener
BR ˌɪntəˈviːnə(r), -z
AM ˌɪn(t)ərˈvinər, -z

intervenient
BR ˌɪntəˈviːnɪənt
AM ˌɪn(t)ərˈviniənt

intervenor
BR ˌɪntəˈviːnə(r), -z
AM ˌɪn(t)ərˈvinər, -z

intervention
BR ˌɪntəˈvɛnʃn, -z
AM ˌɪn(t)ərˈvɛn(t)ʃən, -z

interventionism
BR ˌɪntəˈvɛnʃn̩ɪz(ə)m
AM ˌɪn(t)ərˈvɛn(t)ʃəˌnɪzəm

interventionist
BR ˌɪntəˈvɛnʃn̩ɪst, -s
AM ˌɪn(t)ərˈvɛn(t)ʃənəst, -s

intervertebral
BR ˌɪntəˈvəːtɪbr(ə)l
AM ˌɪn(t)ərˈvərdəbrəl

interview
BR ˈɪntəvjuː, -z, -ɪŋ, -d
AM ˈɪn(t)ərˌvju, -z, -ɪŋ, -d

interviewee
BR ˌɪntəvjuːˈiː, -z
AM ˈɪn(t)ərˌvjuˈi, -z

interviewer
BR ˈɪntəvjuːə(r), -z
AM ˈɪn(t)ərˌvjuər, -z

inter vivos
BR ˌɪntə ˈviːvəʊs
AM ˈɪn(t)ər ˈviˌvoʊs, + ˈvaɪˌvoʊs

interwar
BR ˌɪntəˈwɔː(r)
AM ˈɪn(t)ərˈwɔ(ə)r

interweave
BR ˌɪntəˈwiːv, -z, -ɪŋ
AM ˈɪn(t)ərˈwiv, -z, -ɪŋ

interwind
BR ˌɪntəˈwʌɪnd, -z, -ɪŋ
AM ˈɪn(t)ərˈwaɪnd, -z, -ɪŋ

interwork
BR ˌɪntəˈwəːk, -s, -ɪŋ, -t
AM ˈɪn(t)ərˈwərk, -s, -ɪŋ, -t

interwound
BR ˌɪntəˈwaʊnd
AM ˌɪn(t)ərˈwaʊnd

interwove
BR ˌɪntəˈwəʊv
AM ˈɪn(t)ərˈwoʊv

interwoven
BR ˌɪntəˈwəʊvn
AM ˌɪn(t)ərˈwoʊvən

intestacy
BR ɪnˈtɛstəsi
AM ɪnˈtɛstəsi

intestate
BR ɪnˈtɛsteɪt, ɪnˈtɛstət
AM ɪnˈtɛˌsteɪt, ɪnˈtɛstət

intestinal
BR ɪnˈtɛstɪnl, ˌɪntɛˈstʌɪnl
AM ɪnˈtɛstənəl

intestine
BR ɪnˈtɛst(ɪ)n, -z
AM ɪnˈtɛstən, -z

inthrall
BR ɪnˈθrɔːl
AM ɪnˈθrɔl, ɪnˈθrɑl

intifada
BR ˌɪntɪˈfɑːdə(*r*), -z
AM ˌɪn(t)əˈfɑdə, -z

intimacy
BR ˈɪntɪməs|i, -ɪz
AM ˈɪn(t)əməsi, -z

intimate[1]
noun, adjective
BR ˈɪntɪmət, -s
AM ˈɪn(t)əmət, -s

intimate[2]
verb
BR ˈɪntɪmeɪt, -s, -ɪŋ, -ɪd
AM ˈɪn(t)əˌmeɪ|t, -ts, -dɪŋ, -dɪd

intimately
BR ˈɪntɪmətli
AM ˈɪn(t)əmətli

intimater
BR ˈɪntɪmeɪtə(r), -z
AM ˈɪn(t)əˌmeɪdər, -z

intimation
BR ˌɪntɪˈmeɪʃn, -z
AM ˌɪn(t)əˈmeɪʃən, -z

intimidate
BR ɪnˈtɪmɪdeɪt, -s, -ɪŋ, -ɪd
AM ɪnˈtɪməˌdeɪ|t, -ts, -dɪŋ, -dɪd

intimidatingly
BR ɪnˈtɪmɪdeɪtɪŋli
AM ɪnˈtɪməˌdeɪdɪŋli

intimidation
BR ɪnˌtɪmɪˈdeɪʃn
AM ɪnˌtɪməˈdeɪʃən

intimidator
BR ɪnˈtɪmɪdeɪtə(r), -z
AM ɪnˈtɪməˌdeɪdər, -z

intimidatory
BR ɪnˌtɪmɪˈdeɪt(ə)ri
AM ɪnˈtɪmədəˌtɔri

intinction
BR ɪnˈtɪŋ(k)ʃn, -z
AM ɪnˈstɪŋ(k)ʃən, -z

intitule
BR ɪnˈtɪtjuːl, ɪnˈtɪtʃuːl, -z, -ɪŋ, -d
AM ɪnˈtɪˌtʃʊl, ɪnˈtɪtʃəl, -z, -ɪŋ, -d

into¹
strong form
BR ˈɪntuː
AM ˈɪntu

into²
weak form, before consonants
BR ˈɪntə
AM ˈɪn(t)ə

into³
weak form, before vowels
BR ˈɪntʊ
AM ˈɪn(t)ʊ

intolerable
BR ɪnˈtɒl(ə)rəbl
AM ɪnˈtɑl(ə)rəbəl, ɪnˈtɑlərbəl

intolerableness
BR ɪnˈtɒl(ə)rəblnəs
AM ɪnˈtɑl(ə)rəbəlnəs, ɪnˈtɑlərbəlnəs

intolerably
BR ɪnˈtɒl(ə)rəbli
AM ɪnˈtɑl(ə)rəbli, ɪnˈtɑlərbli

intolerance
BR ɪnˈtɒl(ə)rəns, ɪnˈtɒl(ə)rn̩s
AM ɪnˈtɑl(ə)rəns

intolerant
BR ɪnˈtɒl(ə)rənt, ɪnˈtɒl(ə)rn̩t
AM ɪnˈtɑl(ə)rənt

intolerantly
BR ɪnˈtɒl(ə)rəntli, ɪnˈtɒl(ə)rn̩tli
AM ɪnˈtɑl(ə)rən(t)li

intonate
BR ˈɪntəneɪt, -s, -ɪŋ, -ɪd
AM ˈɪn(t)əˌneɪ|t, -ts, -dɪŋ, -dɪd

intonation
BR ˌɪntəˈneɪʃn, -z
AM ˌɪn(t)əˈneɪʃən, ˌɪntoʊˈneɪʃən, -z

intonational
BR ˌɪntəˈneɪʃn̩(ə)l, ˌɪntəˈneɪʃən(ə)l
AM ˌɪn(t)əˈneɪʃ(ə)nəl, ˌɪntoʊˈneɪʃ(ə)nəl

intone
BR ɪnˈtəʊn, -z, -ɪŋ, -d
AM ɪnˈtoʊn, -z, -ɪŋ, -d

intoner
BR ɪnˈtəʊnə(r), -z
AM ɪnˈtoʊnər, -z

in toto
BR ˌɪn ˈtəʊtəʊ
AM ˌɪn ˈtoʊdoʊ

intoxicant
BR ɪnˈtɒksɪk(ə)nt, -s
AM ɪnˈtɑksəkənt, -s

intoxicate
BR ɪnˈtɒksɪkeɪt, -s, -ɪŋ, -ɪd
AM ɪnˈtɑksəkeɪ|t, -ts, -dɪŋ, -dɪd

intoxicatingly
BR ɪnˈtɒksɪkeɪtɪŋli
AM ɪnˈtɑksəkeɪdɪŋli

intoxication
BR ɪnˌtɒksɪˈkeɪʃn
AM ɪnˌtɑksəˈkeɪʃən

intracellular
BR ˌɪntrəˈsɛljʊlə(r)
AM ¦ɪntrəˈsɛljələr

intracranial
BR ˌɪntrəˈkreɪnɪəl
AM ¦ɪntrəˈkreɪniəl

intracranially
BR ˌɪntrəˈkreɪnɪəli
AM ¦ɪntrəˈkreɪniəli

intractability
BR ɪnˌtraktəˈbɪlɪti
AM ¦ɪnˌtræktəˈbɪlɪdi, ɪnˌtræktəˈbɪlɪdi

intractable
BR ɪnˈtraktəbl
AM ¦ɪnˈtræktəbəl, ɪnˈtræktəbəl

intractableness
BR ɪnˈtraktəblnəs
AM ¦ɪnˈtræktəbəlnəs, ɪnˈtræktəbəlnəs

intractably
BR ɪnˈtraktəbli
AM ¦ɪnˈtræktəbli, ɪnˈtræktəbli

intrados
BR ˈɪntrədɒs, -ɪz
AM ˈɪntrəˌdɑs, ˈɪntrəˌdoʊs, -əz

intramolecular
BR ˌɪntrəməˈlɛkjʊlə(r)
AM ¦ɪntrəməˈlɛkjələr

intramural
BR ˌɪntrəˈmjʊərəl, ˌɪntrəˈmjʊərl̩, ˌɪntrəˈmjɔːrəl, ˌɪntrəˈmjɔːrl̩
AM ¦ɪntrəˈmjʊr(ə)l

intramurally
BR ˌɪntrəˈmjʊərəli, ˌɪntrəˈmjʊərl̩i, ˌɪntrəˈmjɔːrəli, ˌɪntrəˈmjɔːrl̩i
AM ¦ɪntrəˈmjʊr(ə)li

intramuscular
BR ˌɪntrəˈmʌskjʊlə(r)
AM ¦ɪntrəˈməskjələr

intranational
BR ˌɪntrəˈnaʃn̩(ə)l, ˌɪntrəˈnaʃən(ə)l
AM ¦ɪntrəˈnæʃ(ə)nəl

Intranet
BR ˈɪntrənɛt
AM ˈɪntrəˌnɛt

intransigence
BR ɪnˈtransɪdʒ(ə)ns, ɪnˈtranzɪdʒ(ə)ns, ɪnˈtrɑːnsɪdʒ(ə)ns, ɪnˈtrɑːnzɪdʒ(ə)ns
AM ɪnˈtrænsədʒəns, ɪnˈtrænzədʒəns

intransigency
BR ɪnˈtransɪdʒ(ə)ns|i, ɪnˈtranzɪdʒ(ə)ns|i, ɪnˈtrɑːnsɪdʒ(ə)ns|i, ɪnˈtrɑːnzɪdʒ(ə)ns|i, -ɪz
AM ɪnˈtrænsədʒənsi, ɪnˈtrænzədʒənsi, -z

intransigent
BR ɪnˈtransɪdʒ(ə)nt, ɪnˈtranzɪdʒ(ə)nt, ɪnˈtrɑːnsɪdʒ(ə)nt, ɪnˈtrɑːnzɪdʒ(ə)nt
AM ɪnˈtrænsədʒənt, ɪnˈtrænzədʒənt

intransigently
BR ɪnˈtransɪdʒ(ə)ntli, ɪnˈtranzɪdʒ(ə)ntli, ɪnˈtrɑːnsɪdʒ(ə)ntli, ɪnˈtrɑːnzɪdʒ(ə)ntli
AM ɪnˈtrænsədʒən(t)li, ɪnˈtrænzədʒən(t)li

intransitive
BR ɪnˈtransɪtɪv, ɪnˈtranzɪtɪv, ɪnˈtrɑːnsɪtɪv, ɪnˈtrɑːnzɪtɪv
AM ɪnˈtrænzədɪv

intransitively
BR ɪnˈtransɪtɪvli, ɪnˈtranzɪtɪvli, ɪnˈtrɑːnsɪtɪvli, ɪnˈtrɑːnzɪtɪvli
AM ɪnˈtrænzədəvli

intransitivity
BR ɪnˌtransɪˈtɪvɪti, ɪnˌtranzɪˈtɪvɪti, ɪnˌtrɑːnsɪˈtɪvɪti, ɪnˌtrɑːnzɪˈtɪvɪti
AM ɪnˌtrænzəˈtɪvɪdi

intrapreneur
BR ˌɪntrəprəˈnəː(r)
AM ˌɪntrəprəˈnər, ˌɪntrəprəˈnʊ(ə)r

intrauterine
BR ˌɪntrəˈjuːtərʌɪn
AM ¦ɪntrəˈjudərən, ¦ɪntrəˈjudəraɪn

intravasate
BR ɪnˈtravəseɪt, -s, -ɪŋ, -ɪd
AM ɪnˈtrævəˌseɪ|t, -ts, -dɪŋ, -dɪd

intravasation
BR ɪnˌtravəˈseɪʃn, -z
AM ɪnˌtrævəˈseɪʃən, -z

intravenous
BR ˌɪntrəˈviːnəs
AM ¦ɪntrəˈvinəs

intravenously
BR ˌɪntrəˈviːnəsli
AM ¦ɪntrəˈvinəsli

in-tray
BR ˈɪntreɪ, -z
AM ˈɪnˌtreɪ, -z

intrench
BR ɪnˈtrɛn(t)ʃ, -ɪz, -ɪŋ, -t
AM ɪnˈtrɛn(t)ʃ, -əz, -ɪŋ, -t

intrenchment
BR ɪnˈtrɛn(t)ʃm(ə)nt, -s
AM ɪnˈtrɛn(t)ʃmənt, -s

intrepid
BR ɪnˈtrɛpɪd
AM ɪnˈtrɛpəd

intrepidity
BR ˌɪntrɪˈpɪdɪti, ˌɪntrɛˈpɪdɪti
AM ˌɪntrəˈpɪdɪdi, ˌɪntrɛˈpɪdɪdi

intrepidly
BR ɪnˈtrɛpɪdli
AM ɪnˈtrɛpədli

intricacy
BR ˈɪntrɪkəs|i, -ɪz
AM ˈɪntrəkəsi, -z

intricate
BR ˈɪntrɪkət
AM ˈɪntrəkət

intricately
BR ˈɪntrɪkətli
AM ˈɪntrəkətli

intrigant
BR ˈɪntrɪg(ə)nt, -s
AM ˈɪntrəˌgɑnt, -s

intrigante
BR ˈɪntrɪg(ə)nt, -s
AM ˈɪntrəˌgɑnt, -s

intrigue¹
noun
BR ˈɪntriːg, -z
AM ˈɪnˌtrig, ɪnˈtrig, -z

intrigue²
verb
BR ɪnˈtriːg, -z, -ɪŋ, -d
AM ɪnˈtrig, -z, -ɪŋ, -d

intriguer
BR ɪnˈtriːgə(r), -z
AM ɪnˈtrigər, -z

intriguingly
BR ɪnˈtriːgɪŋli
AM ɪnˈtrigɪŋli

intrinsic
BR ɪnˈtrɪnsɪk, ɪnˈtrɪnzɪk
AM ɪnˈtrɪnzɪk, ɪnˈtrɪnsɪk

intrinsically
BR ɪn'trɪnsɪkli, ɪn'trɪnzɪkli
AM ɨn'trɪnzək(ə)li, ɨn'trɪnsək(ə)li

intro
BR 'ɪntrəʊ, -z
AM 'ɪntroʊ, -z

introduce
BR ˌɪntrə'djuːs, ˌɪntrə'dʒuːs, -ɨz, -ɪŋ, -t
AM ˌ¦ɪntrə'd(j)us, ¦ɪntroʊ'd(j)us, -əz, -ɪŋ, -t

introducer
BR ˌɪntrə'djuːsə(r), ˌɪntrə'dʒuːsə(r), -z
AM ¦ɪntrə'd(j)usər, ¦ɪntroʊ'd(j)usər, -z

introducible
BR ˌɪntrə'djuːsɨbl, ˌɪntrə'dʒuːsɨbl
AM ¦ɪntrə'd(j)usəbəl, ¦ɪntroʊ'd(j)usəbəl

introduction
BR ˌɪntrə'dʌkʃn, -z
AM ˌɪntrə'dəkʃən, ˌɪntroʊ'dəkʃən, -z

introductory
BR ˌɪntrə'dʌkt(ə)ri
AM ¦ɪntrə'dəkt(ə)ri, ¦ɪntroʊ'dəkt(ə)ri

introflexion
BR ˌɪntrə(ʊ)'flɛkʃn, -z
AM ˌɪntrə'flɛkʃən, ˌɪntroʊ'flɛkʃən, -z

introgression
BR ˌɪntrə(ʊ)'ɡrɛʃn, -z
AM ˌɪntrə'ɡrɛʃən, ˌɪntroʊ'ɡrɛʃən, -z

introit
BR 'ɪntrɔɪt, -s
AM 'ɪnˌtrɔɪt, ɨn'trɔɪt, -s

introjection
BR ˌɪntrə(ʊ)'dʒɛkʃn, -z
AM ˌɪntrə'dʒɛkʃən, ˌɪntroʊ'dʒɛkʃən, -z

intromission
BR ˌɪntrə(ʊ)'mɪʃn, -z
AM ˌɪntrə'mɪʃən, ˌɪntroʊ'mɪʃən, -z

intromit
BR ˌɪntrə(ʊ)'mɪt, -s, -ɪŋ, -ɨd
AM ¦ɪntrə'mɪ|t, ¦ɪntroʊ'mɪ|t, -ts, -dɪŋ, -dɨd

intromittent
BR ˌɪntrə(ʊ)'mɪtnt
AM ¦ɪntrə'mɪtnt, ¦ɪntroʊ'mɪtnt

introrse
BR ɪn'trɔːs
AM ɪn'trɔ(ə)rs

introspect
BR ˌɪntrə(ʊ)'spɛkt, -s, -ɪŋ, -ɨd
AM ¦ɪntrə'spɛk|(t), ¦ɪntroʊ'spɛk|(t), -(t)s, -tɪŋ, -təd

introspection
BR ˌɪntrə(ʊ)'spɛkʃn
AM ¦ɪntrə'spɛkʃən, ¦ɪntroʊ'spɛkʃən

introspective
BR ˌɪntrə(ʊ)'spɛktɪv
AM ¦ɪntrə'spɛktɪv, ¦ɪntroʊ'spɛktɪv

introspectively
BR ˌɪntrə(ʊ)'spɛktɨvli
AM ¦ɪntrə'spɛktəvli, ¦ɪntroʊ'spɛktəvli

introspectiveness
BR ˌɪntrə(ʊ)'spɛktɨvnɨs
AM ¦ɪntrə'spɛktɪvnɨs, ¦ɪntroʊ'spɛktɪvnɨs

introsusception
BR ˌɪntrə(ʊ)sə'sɛpʃn, -z
AM ˌɪntrəsə'sɛpʃən, -z

introversible
BR ˌɪntrə(ʊ)'vəːsɨbl
AM 'ɪntrəˌvərsəbəl, 'ɪntroʊˌvərsəbəl

introversion
BR ˌɪntrə(ʊ)'vəːʃn
AM ¦ɪntrə¦vərʒən, ¦ɪntroʊ¦vərʒən

introversive
BR ˌɪntrə(ʊ)'vəːsɪv
AM ¦ɪntrə¦vərsɪv, ¦ɪntroʊ¦vərsɪv

introvert[1]
noun
BR 'ɪntrəvəːt, -s
AM 'ɪntrəˌvərt, 'ɪntroʊˌvərt, -s

introvert[2]
verb
BR ˌɪntrə(ʊ)'vəːt, -s, -ɪŋ, -ɨd
AM 'ɪntrəˌvər|t, 'ɪntroʊˌvər|t, -ts, -dɪŋ, -dəd

introverted
adjective
BR 'ɪntrəvəːtɨd
AM 'ɪntrəˌvərdəd, 'ɪntroʊˌvərdəd

introvertive
BR ˌɪntrə(ʊ)'vəːtɪv
AM 'ɪntrəˌvərdɪv, 'ɪntroʊˌvərdɪv

intrude
BR ɪn'truːd, -z, -ɪŋ, -ɨd
AM ɨn'trud, -z, -ɪŋ, -əd

intruder
BR ɪn'truːdə(r), -z
AM ɨn'trudər, -z

intrudingly
BR ɪn'truːdɪŋli
AM ɨn'trudɪŋli

intrusion
BR ɪn'truːʒn, -z
AM ɨn'truʒən, -z

intrusionist
BR ɪn'truːʒn̩ɪst, -s
AM ɨn'truʒənəst, -s

intrusive
BR ɪn'truːsɪv
AM ɨn'trusɪv

intrusively
BR ɪn'truːsɨvli
AM ɨn'trusəvli

intrusiveness
BR ɪn'truːsɨvnɨs
AM ɨn'trusɪvnɨs

intrust
BR ɪn'trʌst, -s, -ɪŋ, -ɨd
AM ɨn'trəst, -s, -ɪŋ, -əd

intubate
BR 'ɪntjʉbeɪt, 'ɪntʃʉbeɪt, -s, -ɪŋ, -ɨd
AM 'ɪntjəˌbeɪ|t, -ts, -dɪŋ, -dɨd

intubation
BR ˌɪntjʉ'beɪʃn, ˌɪntʃʉ'beɪʃn, -z
AM ˌɪntjə'beɪʃən, -z

intuit
BR ɪn'tjuː|ɪt, ɪn'tʃuː|ɪt, -ɪts, -ɨtɪŋ, -ɨtɨd
AM ɨn't(j)uə|t, -ts, -dɪŋ, -dɨd

intuitable
BR ɪn'tjuːɨtəbl, ɪn'tʃuːɨtəbl
AM ɨn't(j)uədəbəl

intuition
BR ˌɪntjʊ'ɪʃn, ˌɪntʃʊ'ɪʃn, -z
AM ˌɪnt(j)u'ɪʃən, ˌɪntə'wɪʃən, -z

intuitional
BR ˌɪntjʊ'ɪʃn̩(ə)l, ˌɪntjʊ'ɪʃən(ə)l, ˌɪntʃʊ'ɪʃn̩(ə)l, ˌɪntʃʊ'ɪʃən(ə)l
AM ˌɪnt(j)u'ɪʃ(ə)nəl, ˌɪntə'wɪʃ(ə)nəl

intuitionalism
BR ˌɪntjʊ'ɪʃn̩əlɪz(ə)m, ˌɪntjʊ'ɪʃn̩lɪz(ə)m, ˌɪntjʊ'ɪʃənl̩ɪz(ə)m, ˌɪntjʊ'ɪʃ(ə)nəlɪz(ə)m, ˌɪntʃʊ'ɪʃn̩əlɪz(ə)m, ˌɪntʃʊ'ɪʃn̩lɪz(ə)m, ˌɪntʃʊ'ɪʃənl̩ɪz(ə)m, ˌɪntʃʊ'ɪʃ(ə)nəlɪz(ə)m
AM ˌɪnt(j)u'ɪʃənlˌɪzəm, ˌɪntə'wɪʃənlˌɪzəm, ˌɪnt(j)u'ɪʃnəˌlɪzəm, ˌɪntə'wɪʃnəˌlɪzəm

intuitionalist
BR ˌɪntjʊ'ɪʃn̩əlɪst, ˌɪntjʊ'ɪʃn̩lɪst, ˌɪntjʊ'ɪʃənl̩ɪst, ˌɪntjʊ'ɪʃ(ə)nəlɪst, ˌɪntʃʊ'ɪʃn̩əlɪst, ˌɪntʃʊ'ɪʃn̩lɪst, ˌɪntʃʊ'ɪʃənl̩ɪst, ˌɪntʃʊ'ɪʃ(ə)nəlɪst, -s
AM ˌɪnt(j)u'ɪʃənl̩əst, ˌɪntə'wɪʃənl̩əst, ˌɪnt(j)u'ɪʃnələst, ˌɪntə'wɪʃnələst, -s

intuitionism
BR ˌɪntjʊ'ɪʃn̩ɪz(ə)m, ˌɪntjʊ'ɪʃənɪz(ə)m, ˌɪntʃʊ'ɪʃn̩ɪz(ə)m, ˌɪntʃʊ'ɪʃənɪz(ə)m
AM ˌɪnt(j)u'ɪʃəˌnɪzəm, ˌɪntə'wɪʃəˌnɪzəm

intuitionist
BR ˌɪntjʊ'ɪʃn̩ɪst, ˌɪntjʊ'ɪʃənɪst, ˌɪntʃʊ'ɪʃn̩ɪst, ˌɪntʃʊ'ɪʃənɪst, -s
AM ˌɪnt(j)u'ɪʃənəst, ˌɪntə'wɪʃənəst, -s

intuitive
BR ɪn'tjuːɨtɪv, ɪn'tʃuːɨtɪv
AM ɨn't(j)uədɪv

intuitively
BR ɪn'tjuːɨtɨvli, ɪn'tʃuːɨtɨvli
AM ɨn't(j)uədəvli

intuitiveness
BR ɪn'tjuːɨtɨvnɨs, ɪn'tʃuːɨtɨvnɨs
AM ɨn't(j)uədɪvnɨs

intuitivism
BR ɪn'tjuːɨtɨvɪz(ə)m, ɪn'tʃuːɨtɨvɪz(ə)m
AM ɨn't(j)uədɪˌvɪzəm

intuitivist
BR ɪn'tjuːɨtɨvɪst, ɪn'tʃuːɨtɨvɪst, -s
AM ɨn't(j)uədɪvɪst, -s

intumesce
BR ˌɪntjʉ'mɛs, ˌɪntʃʉ'mɛs, -ɨz, -ɪŋ, -t
AM ˌɪnt(j)u'mɛs, -əz, -ɪŋ, -t

intumescence
BR ˌɪntjʉ'mɛsns, ˌɪntʃʉ'mɛsns
AM ˌɪnt(j)u'mɛsəns

intumescent
BR ˌɪntjʉ'mɛsnt, ˌɪntʃʉ'mɛsnt
AM ˌɪnt(j)u'mɛsənt

intumescently
BR ˌɪntjʉ'mɛsntli, ˌɪntʃʉ'mɛsntli
AM ˌɪnt(j)u'mɛsn(t)li

intussusception
BR ˌɪntəsə'sɛpʃn, -z
AM ˌɪn(t)əsə'sɛpʃən, -z

intwine
BR ɪn'twʌɪn, -z, -ɪŋ, -d
AM ɨn'twaɪn, -z, -ɪŋ, -d

Inuit
BR 'ɪn(j)ʊɪt, -s
AM 'ɪn(j)əwɪt, -s

Inuk
BR 'ɪnʊk, -s
AM 'iˌnək, -s

Inuktitut
BR ɪˈnʊktɪtʊt
AM ɪˈnʊktəˌtʊt

inunction
BR ɪˈnʌŋ(k)ʃn, -z
AM ɪˈnəŋkʃən, -z

inundate
BR ˈɪnʌndeɪt, -s, -ɪŋ, -ɪd
AM ˈɪnənˌdeɪ|t, -ts, -dɪŋ, -dɪd

inundation
BR ˌɪnʌnˈdeɪʃn, -z
AM ˌɪnənˈdeɪʃən, -z

Inupik
BR ɪˈnuːpɪk, -s
AM ɪˈnuˌpɪk, -s

inure
BR ɪˈnjʊə(r), ɪˈnjɔː(r), -z, -ɪŋ, -d
AM ɪˈn(j)ʊ(ə)r, -z, -ɪŋ, -d

inurement
BR ɪˈnjʊəm(ə)nt, ɪˈnjɔːm(ə)nt, -s
AM ɪˈn(j)ʊrmənt, -s

in utero
BR ɪn ˈjuːt(ə)rəʊ
AM ɪn ˈjudəroʊ

in vacuo
BR ɪn ˈvakjʊəʊ
AM ɪn ˈvækjəˌwoʊ

invade
BR ɪnˈveɪd, -z, -ɪŋ, -ɪd
AM ɪnˈveɪd, -z, -ɪŋ, -ɪd

invader
BR ɪnˈveɪdə(r), -z
AM ɪnˈveɪdər, -z

invaginate
BR ɪnˈvadʒɪneɪt, ɪnˈvadʒn̩eɪt, -s, -ɪŋ, -ɪd
AM ɪnˈvædʒəˌneɪ|t, -ts, -dɪŋ, -dɪd

invagination
BR ɪnˌvadʒɪˈneɪʃn, -z
AM ɪnˌvædʒəˈneɪʃən, -z

invalid¹
adjective, not valid
BR (ˌ)ɪnˈvalɪd
AM ɪnˈvæləd

invalid²
noun
BR ˈɪnvəlɪd, ˈɪnvəliːd, -z
AM ˈɪnvələd, -z

invalid³
verb
BR ˈɪnvəliːd, ˈɪnvəlɪd, -z, -ɪŋ, -ɪd
AM ˈɪnvələd, -z, -ɪŋ, -əd

invalidate
BR ɪnˈvalɪdeɪt, -s, -ɪŋ, -ɪd
AM ɪnˈvæləˌdeɪ|t, -ts, -dɪŋ, -dɪd

invalidation
BR ɪnˌvalɪˈdeɪʃn
AM ɪnˌvæləˈdeɪʃən

invalidism
BR ˌɪnvəˈliːdɪz(ə)m
AM ˈɪnvələˌdɪzəm

invalidity
BR ˌɪnvəˈlɪdɪti
AM ˌɪnvəˈlɪdɪdi, ˌɪnvæˈlɪdɪdi

invalidly
BR (ˌ)ɪnˈvalɪdli
AM ɪnˈvælədli

invaluable
BR ɪnˈvaljʊəbl, ɪnˈvaljʉbl
AM ɪnˈvæljəbəl

invaluableness
BR ɪnˈvaljʊəblnəs, ɪnˈvaljʉblnəs
AM ɪnˈvæljəbəlnəs

invaluably
BR ɪnˈvaljʊəbli, ɪnˈvaljʉbli
AM ɪnˈvæljəbli

Invar®
BR ɪnˈvɑː(r), ˈɪnvɑː(r)
AM ˈɪnˌvɑr

invariability
BR ɪnˌvɛːrɪəˈbɪlɪti
AM ˌɪnˌvɛriəˈbɪlɪdi, ɪnˌvɛriəˈbɪlɪdi

invariable
BR (ˌ)ɪnˈvɛːrɪəbl
AM ˌɪnˈvɛriəbəl, ɪnˈvɛriəbəl

invariableness
BR (ˌ)ɪnˈvɛːrɪəblnəs
AM ˌɪnˈvɛriəbəlnəs, ɪnˈvɛriəbəlnəs

invariably
BR (ˌ)ɪnˈvɛːrɪəbli
AM ˌɪnˈvɛriəbli, ɪnˈvɛriəbli

invariance
BR (ˌ)ɪnˈvɛːrɪəns, -ɪz
AM ˌɪnˈvɛriəns, ɪnˈvɛriəns, -əz

invariant
BR (ˌ)ɪnˈvɛːrɪənt, -s
AM ˌɪnˈvɛriənt, ɪnˈvɛriənt, -s

invasion
BR ɪnˈveɪʒn, -z
AM ɪnˈveɪʒən, -z

invasive
BR ɪnˈveɪsɪv, ɪnˈveɪzɪv
AM ɪnˈveɪsɪv, ɪnˈveɪzɪv

invasively
BR ɪnˈveɪsɪvli, ɪnˈveɪzɪvli
AM ɪnˈveɪsɪvli, ɪnˈveɪzɪvli

invasiveness
BR ɪnˈveɪsɪvnɪs, ɪnˈveɪzɪvnɪs
AM ɪnˈveɪsɪvnɪs, ɪnˈveɪzɪvnɪs

invected
BR ɪnˈvɛktɪd
AM ɪnˈvɛktəd

invective
BR ɪnˈvɛktɪv
AM ɪnˈvɛktɪv

invectively
BR ɪnˈvɛktɪvli
AM ɪnˈvɛktəvli

invectiveness
BR ɪnˈvɛktɪvnɪs
AM ɪnˈvɛktɪvnɪs

inveigh
BR ɪnˈveɪ, -z, -ɪŋ, -d
AM ɪnˈveɪ, -z, -ɪŋ, -d

inveigle
BR ɪnˈveɪɡ|l, ɪnˈviːɡ|l, -lz, -l̩ɪŋ\-lɪŋ, -ld
AM ɪnˈveɪɡ|əl, -əlz, -(ə)lɪŋ, -əld

inveiglement
BR ɪnˈveɪɡlm(ə)nt, ɪnˈviːɡlm(ə)nt, -s
AM ɪnˈveɪɡəlmənt, -s

invent
BR ɪnˈvɛnt, -s, -ɪŋ, -ɪd
AM ɪnˈvɛn|t, -ts, -(t)ɪŋ, -(t)əd

inventable
BR ɪnˈvɛntəbl
AM ɪnˈvɛn(t)əbəl

invention
BR ɪnˈvɛnʃn, -z
AM ɪnˈvɛnʃən, -z

inventive
BR ɪnˈvɛntɪv
AM ɪnˈvɛn(t)ɪv

inventively
BR ɪnˈvɛntɪvli
AM ɪnˈvɛn(t)əvli

inventiveness
BR ɪnˈvɛntɪvnɪs
AM ɪnˈvɛn(t)ɪvnɪs

inventor
BR ɪnˈvɛntə(r), -z
AM ɪnˈvɛn(t)ər, -z

inventory
BR ˈɪnv(ə)nt(ə)r|i, -ɪz
AM ˈɪnvənˌtɔri, -z

inventress
BR ɪnˈvɛntrɪs, -ɪz
AM ɪnˈvɛntrəs, -əz

Inveraray
BR ˌɪnvəˈrɛːri
AM ˌɪnvəˌrɛri

Invercargill
BR ˌɪnvəˈkɑːɡ(ɪ)l
AM ˌɪnvərˈkɑrɡəl

Invergordon
BR ˌɪnvəˈɡɔːdn
AM ˌɪnvərˈɡɔrdən

Inverness
BR ˌɪnvəˈnɛs
AM ˌɪnvərˈnɛs

Inverness-shire
BR ˌɪnvəˈnɛsʃ(ɪ)ə(r)
AM ˌɪnvərˈnɛsˌʃɪ(ə)r

inverse
BR ˈɪnvəːs, ɪnˈvəːs, -ɪz
AM ˈɪnvərs, ɪnˈvərs, -əz

inversely
BR ˈɪnvəːsli, ɪnˈvəːsli
AM ˈɪnvərsli, ɪnˈvərsli

inversion
BR ɪnˈvəːʃn, -z
AM ɪnˈvərʒən, -z

inversive
BR ɪnˈvəːsɪv
AM ɪnˈvərsɪv

invert¹
noun
BR ˈɪnvəːt, -s
AM ˈɪnvərt, -s

invert²
verb
BR ɪnˈvəːt, -s, -ɪŋ, -ɪd
AM ɪnˈvər|t, -ts, -dɪŋ, -dəd

invertase
BR ˈɪnvəteɪz, ɪnˈvəːteɪz
AM ˈɪnvərˌteɪz, ɪnˈvərˌteɪz

invertebrate
BR ɪnˈvəːtɪbrət, ɪnˈvəːtɪbreɪt, -s
AM ɪnˈvərdəbrət, ɪnˈvərdəˌbreɪt, -s

inverter
BR ɪnˈvəːtə(r), -z
AM ɪnˈvərdər, -z

invertibility
BR ɪnˌvəːtɪˈbɪlɪti
AM ɪnˌvərdəˈbɪlɪdi

invertible
BR ɪnˈvəːtɪbl
AM ɪnˈvərdəbəl

Inverurie
BR ˌɪnvəˈrʊəri
AM ˌɪnvəˌrʊri

invest
BR ɪnˈvɛst, -s, -ɪŋ, -ɪd
AM ɪnˈvɛst, -s, -ɪŋ, -əd

investable
BR ɪnˈvɛstəbl
AM ɪnˈvɛstəbəl

investible
BR ɪnˈvɛstɪbl
AM ɪnˈvɛstəbəl

investigate
BR ɪnˈvɛstɪɡeɪt, -s, -ɪŋ, -ɪd
AM ɪnˈvɛstəˌɡeɪ|t, -ts, -dɪŋ, -dɪd

investigation
BR ɪnˌvɛstɪˈɡeɪʃn, -z
AM ɪnˌvɛstəˈɡeɪʃən, -z

investigational
BR ɪnˌvɛstɪˈɡeɪʃn̩(ə)l, ɪnˌvɛstɪˈɡeɪʃən(ə)l
AM ɪnˌvɛstəˈɡeɪʃ(ə)nəl

investigative
BR ɪnˈvɛstɪɡətɪv
AM ɪnˈvɛstəˌɡeɪdɪv

investigator
BR ɪnˈvɛstɪɡeɪtə(r), -z
AM ɪnˈvɛstəˌɡeɪdər, -z

investigatory
BR ɪnˈvɛstɪɡet(ə)ri

AM ɪn'vɛstəɡəˌtɔri

investiture
BR ɪn'vɛstɪtʃə(r), ɪn'vɛstɪtjʊə(r), -z
AM ɪn'vɛstətʃʊ(ə)r, ɪn'vɛstətʃər, -z

investment
BR ɪn'vɛs(t)m(ə)nt, -s
AM ɪn'vɛs(t)mənt, -s

investor
BR ɪn'vɛstə(r), -z
AM ɪn'vɛstər, -z

inveteracy
BR ɪn'vɛt(ə)rəs|i, -ɪz
AM ɪn'vɛdərəsi, -z

inveterate
BR ɪn'vɛt(ə)rət
AM ɪn'vɛdərət

inveterately
BR ɪn'vɛt(ə)rətli
AM ɪn'vɛdərətli

inveterateness
BR ɪn'vɛt(ə)rətnəs
AM ɪn'vɛdərətnəs

invidious
BR ɪn'vɪdɪəs
AM ɪn'vɪdiəs

invidiously
BR ɪn'vɪdɪəsli
AM ɪn'vɪdiəsli

invidiousness
BR ɪn'vɪdɪəsnəs
AM ɪn'vɪdiəsnəs

invigilate
BR ɪn'vɪdʒɪleɪt, -s, -ɪŋ, -ɪd
AM ɪn'vɪdʒəˌleɪ|t, -ts, -dɪŋ, -dɪd

invigilation
BR ɪnˌvɪdʒɪ'leɪʃn
AM ɪnˌvɪdʒə'leɪʃən

invigilator
BR ɪn'vɪdʒɪleɪtə(r), -z
AM ɪn'vɪdʒəˌleɪdər, -z

invigorate
BR ɪn'vɪɡəreɪt, -s, -ɪŋ, -ɪd
AM ɪn'vɪɡəˌreɪ|t, -ts, -dɪŋ, -dɪd

invigoratingly
BR ɪn'vɪɡəreɪtɪŋli
AM ɪn'vɪɡəˌreɪdɪŋli

invigoration
BR ɪnˌvɪɡə'reɪʃn
AM ɪnˌvɪɡə'reɪʃən

invigorative
BR ɪn'vɪɡ(ə)rətɪv
AM ɪn'vɪɡəˌreɪdɪv

invigorator
BR ɪn'vɪɡəreɪtə(r), -z
AM ɪn'vɪɡəˌreɪdər, -z

invincibility
BR ɪnˌvɪnsɪ'bɪlɪti, ˌɪnvɪnsɪ'bɪlɪti
AM ɪnˌvɪnsə'bɪlɪdi

invincible
BR ɪn'vɪnsɪbl
AM ɪn'vɪnsəbəl

invincibleness
BR ɪn'vɪnsɪblnəs
AM ɪn'vɪnsəbəlnəs

invincibly
BR ɪn'vɪnsɪbli
AM ɪn'vɪnsəbli

inviolability
BR ɪnˌvʌɪələ'bɪlɪti, ˌɪnvʌɪələ'bɪlɪti
AM ˈɪnˌvaɪələ'bɪlɪdi, ɪnˌvaɪələ'bɪlɪdi

inviolable
BR (ˌ)ɪn'vʌɪələbl
AM ɪn'vaɪələbəl

inviolableness
BR (ˌ)ɪn'vʌɪələblnəs
AM ɪn'vaɪələbəlnəs

inviolably
BR (ˌ)ɪn'vʌɪələbli
AM ɪn'vaɪələbli

inviolacy
BR (ˌ)ɪn'vʌɪələsi
AM ɪn'vaɪələsi

inviolate
BR (ˌ)ɪn'vʌɪələt
AM ɪn'vaɪələt

inviolately
BR (ˌ)ɪn'vʌɪələtli
AM ɪn'vaɪələtli

inviolateness
BR (ˌ)ɪn'vʌɪələtnəs
AM ɪn'vaɪələtnəs

inviscid
BR ɪn'vɪsɪd
AM ɪn'vɪsɪd

invisibility
BR ɪnˌvɪzɪ'bɪlɪti, ˌɪnvɪzɪ'bɪlɪti
AM ˈɪnˌvɪzə'bɪlɪdi, ɪnˌvɪzə'bɪlɪdi

invisible
BR (ˌ)ɪn'vɪzɪbl
AM ɪn'vɪzəbəl

invisibleness
BR (ˌ)ɪn'vɪzɪblnəs
AM ɪn'vɪzəbəlnəs

invisibly
BR (ˌ)ɪn'vɪzɪbli
AM ɪn'vɪzəbli

invitation
BR ˌɪnvɪ'teɪʃn, -z
AM ˌɪnvə'teɪʃən, -z

invitatory
BR ɪn'vʌɪtət(ə)ri
AM ɪn'vaɪdəˌtɔri

invite
BR ɪn'vʌɪt, -s, -ɪŋ, -ɪd
AM ɪn'vaɪ|t, -ts, -dɪŋ, -dɪd

invitee
BR ˌɪnvʌɪ'tiː, ɪnˌvʌɪ'tiː, -z
AM ɪnˌvaɪ'ti, -z

inviter
BR ɪn'vʌɪtə(r), -z
AM ɪn'vaɪdər, -z

invitingly
BR ɪn'vʌɪtɪŋli
AM ɪn'vaɪdɪŋli

invitingness
BR ɪn'vʌɪtɪŋnɪs
AM ɪn'vaɪdɪŋnɪs

in vitro
BR ɪn 'viːtrəʊ, + 'vɪtrəʊ
AM ɪn 'viˌtroʊ

in vivo
BR ɪn 'viːvəʊ, + 'vʌɪvəʊ
AM ɪn 'viˌvoʊ

invocable
BR 'ɪnvəkəbl, ɪn'vəʊkəbl
AM ɪn'voʊkəbəl, 'ɪnvəkəbəl

invocation
BR ˌɪnvə(ʊ)'keɪʃn, -z
AM ˌɪnvə'keɪʃən, ˌɪnvoʊ'keɪʃən, -z

invocatory
BR ɪn'vɒkət(ə)ri
AM ɪn'vɑkəˌtɔri

invoice
BR 'ɪnvɔɪs, -ɪz, -ɪŋ, -t
AM 'ɪnˌvɔɪs, -ɪz, -ɪŋ, -t

invoke
BR ɪn'vəʊk, -s, -ɪŋ, -t
AM ɪn'voʊk, -s, -ɪŋ, -t

invoker
BR ɪn'vəʊkə(r), -z
AM ɪn'voʊkər, -z

involucral
BR ˌɪnvə'l(j)uːkr(ə)l
AM ˈɪnvə'lukrəl

involucre
BR 'ɪnvəˌl(j)uːkə(r), -z
AM 'ɪnvəˌlukər, -z

involuntarily
BR (ˌ)ɪn'vɒlənt(ə)rɪli, (ˌ)ɪn'vɒlṇtrɪli
AM ɪn'vɑlənˌtɛrəli

involuntariness
BR (ˌ)ɪn'vɒlənt(ə)rɪnɪs, (ˌ)ɪn'vɒlṇtrɪnɪs
AM ɪn'vɑlənˌtɛrinɪs

involuntary
BR (ˌ)ɪn'vɒlənt(ə)ri, (ˌ)ɪn'vɒlṇt(ə)ri
AM ɪn'vɑlənˌtɛri

involute
BR 'ɪnvəl(j)uːt, -s, -ɪd
AM 'ɪnvəˌl(j)u|t, -ts, -dəd

involution
BR ˌɪnvə'l(j)uːʃn, -z
AM ˌɪnvə'l(j)uʃən, -z

involutional
BR ˌɪnvə'l(j)uːʃṇ(ə)l, ˌɪnvə'l(j)uːʃən(ə)l
AM ˌɪnvə'l(j)uʃ(ə)nəl

involve
BR ɪn'vɒlv, -z, -ɪŋ, -d
AM ɪn'vɑ(l)v, ɪn'vɔ(l)v, -z, -ɪŋ, -d

involvement
BR ɪn'vɒlvm(ə)nt, -s
AM ɪn'vɑ(l)vmənt, ɪn'vɔ(l)vmənt, -s

invulnerability
BR ɪnˌvʌln(ə)rə'bɪlɪti, ˌɪnvʌln(ə)rə'bɪlɪti
AM ˈɪnˌvəln(ə)rə'bɪlɪdi, ɪnˌvəln(ə)rə'bɪlɪdi

invulnerable
BR (ˌ)ɪn'vʌln(ə)rəbl
AM ɪn'vəlnər(ə)bəl

invulnerably
BR (ˌ)ɪn'vʌln(ə)rəbli
AM ɪn'vəlnər(ə)bli

inward
BR 'ɪnwəd, -z
AM 'ɪnwərd, -z

inwardly
BR 'ɪnwədli
AM 'ɪnwərdli

inwardness
BR 'ɪnwədnəs
AM 'ɪnwərdnəs

inweave
BR ˌɪn'wiːv, -z, -ɪŋ
AM ˌɪn'wiv, ɪn'wiv, -z, -ɪŋ

inwove
BR ˌɪn'wəʊv
AM ˌɪn'woʊv, ɪn'woʊv

inwoven
BR ˌɪn'wəʊvn
AM ˌɪn'woʊvən, ɪn'woʊvən

inwrap
BR ˌɪn'rap, -s, -ɪŋ, -t
AM ˌɪn'ræp, ɪn'ræp, -s, -ɪŋ, -t

inwreathe
BR ˌɪn'riːð, -z, -ɪŋ, -d
AM ˌɪn'rið, ɪn'rið, -z, -ɪŋ, -d

inwrought
BR ˌɪn'rɔːt
AM ˌɪn'rɔt, ɪn'rɔt, ˌɪn'rɑt, ɪn'rɑt

inyala
BR ɪn'jɑːlə(r), -z
AM ɪn'jɑlə, -z

in-your-face
adjective
BR ˌɪnjə'feɪs
AM ˈɪnjər'feɪs

Io
BR 'ʌɪəʊ
AM 'aɪˌoʊ

iodate
BR 'ʌɪədeɪt, -s
AM 'aɪəˌdeɪt, -s

iodic
BR ʌɪ'ɒdɪk
AM aɪ'ɑdɪk

iodide
BR 'ʌɪədʌɪd, -z
AM 'aɪəˌdaɪd, -z

iodin
BR 'ʌɪədɪn, -z

AM 'aɪəˌdaɪn, -z
iodinate
BR 'ʌɪədɨneɪt, ʌɪ'ɒdɨneɪt, -s, -ɪŋ, -ɨd
AM 'aɪədəˌneɪ|t, -ts, -dɪŋ, -dɨd
iodination
BR ˌʌɪədɪ'neɪʃn, ʌɪˌɒdɪ'neɪʃn, -z
AM ˌaɪədə'neɪʃən, -z
iodine
BR 'ʌɪədiːn, -z
AM 'aɪəˌdaɪn, -z
iodinise
BR 'ʌɪədɨnʌɪz, -ɨz, -ɪŋ, -d
AM 'aɪədəˌnaɪz, -ɨz, -ɪŋ, -d
iodinize
BR 'ʌɪədɨnʌɪz, -ɨz, -ɪŋ, -d
AM 'aɪədəˌnaɪz, -ɨz, -ɪŋ, -d
iodisation
BR ˌʌɪədʌɪ'zeɪʃn
AM ˌaɪədə'zeɪʃən, ˌaɪəˌdaɪ'zeɪʃən
iodise
BR 'ʌɪədʌɪz, -ɨz, -ɪŋ, -d
AM 'aɪəˌdaɪz, -ɨz, -ɪŋ, -d
iodism
BR 'ʌɪədɪz(ə)m
AM 'aɪəˌdɪzəm
iodization
BR ˌʌɪədʌɪ'zeɪʃn
AM ˌaɪədə'zeɪʃən, ˌaɪəˌdaɪ'zeɪʃən
iodize
BR 'ʌɪədʌɪz, -ɨz, -ɪŋ, -d
AM 'aɪəˌdaɪz, -ɨz, -ɪŋ, -d
iodoform
BR ʌɪ'ɒdə(ʊ)fɔːm, ʌɪ'əʊdə(ʊ)fɔːm, 'ʌɪədəfɔːm, -z
AM aɪ'oʊdəˌfɔ(ə)rm, aɪ'ɑdəˌfɔ(ə)rm, -z
Iolanthe
BR ˌʌɪə'lanθi
AM ˌaɪə'lænθi
Iolo
BR 'jəʊləʊ
AM 'joʊloʊ
WE 'jɒlɒ
ion
BR 'ʌɪən, 'ʌɪɒn, -z
AM 'aɪən, 'aɪˌɑn, -z
Iona
BR ʌɪ'əʊnə(r)
AM aɪ'oʊnə
Ionesco
BR ˌiːə'nɛskəʊ, jɒ'nɛskəʊ
AM jə'nɛskoʊ
Ionia
BR ʌɪ'əʊnɪə(r)
AM aɪ'oʊniə
Ionian
BR ʌɪ'əʊnɪən, -z
AM aɪ'oʊniən, -z
ionic
BR ʌɪ'ɒnɪk
AM aɪ'ɑnɪk
ionically
BR ʌɪ'ɒnɨkli
AM aɪ'ɑnək(ə)li
ionisable
BR 'ʌɪənʌɪzəbl
AM 'aɪəˌnaɪzəbəl
ionisation
BR ˌʌɪənʌɪ'zeɪʃn
AM ˌaɪənə'zeɪʃən, ˌaɪəˌnaɪ'zeɪʃən
ionise
BR 'ʌɪənʌɪz, -ɨz, -ɪŋ, -d
AM 'aɪəˌnaɪz, -ɨz, -ɪŋ, -d
ioniser
BR 'ʌɪənʌɪzə(r), -z
AM 'aɪəˌnaɪzər, -z
ionium
BR ʌɪ'əʊnɪəm, -z
AM aɪ'oʊniəm, -z
ionizable
BR 'ʌɪənʌɪzəbl
AM 'aɪəˌnaɪzəbəl
ionization
BR ˌʌɪənʌɪ'zeɪʃn
AM ˌaɪənə'zeɪʃən, ˌaɪəˌnaɪ'zeɪʃən
ionize
BR 'ʌɪənʌɪz, -ɨz, -ɪŋ, -d
AM 'aɪəˌnaɪz, -ɨz, -ɪŋ, -d
ionizer
BR 'ʌɪənʌɪzə(r), -z
AM 'aɪəˌnaɪzər, -z
ionophore
BR ʌɪ'ɒnə(ʊ)fɔː(r), -z
AM aɪ'ɑnəˌfɔ(ə)r, -z
ionosphere
BR ʌɪ'ɒnəsfɪə(r)
AM aɪ'ɑnəˌsfɪ(ə)r
ionospheric
BR ʌɪˌɒnə(ʊ)'sfɛrɪk
AM aɪˌɑnə'sfɪrɪk
iontophoresis
BR ʌɪˌɒntə(ʊ)fə'riːsɪs
AM aɪ'ɑn(t)əfə'risis
Iorwerth
BR 'jɔːwəːθ, 'jɔːwəθ
AM 'jɔrˌwərθ
WE 'jɒrwerθ
iota
BR ʌɪ'əʊtə(r), -z
AM aɪ'oʊdə, -z
IOU
BR ˌʌɪəʊ'juː, -z
AM ˌaɪˌoʊ'ju, -z
Iowa
BR 'ʌɪəwə(r)
AM 'aɪəwə
Iowan
BR 'ʌɪəwən, -z
AM 'aɪəwən, -z
Ipatieff
BR ɪ'patɪɛf
AM ɨ'pætˌjɛf
ipecac
BR 'ɪpɨkak
AM 'ɪpəkæk
ipecacuanha
BR ˌɪpɨkakjʊ'anə(r), ˌɪpɨkakjʊ'ɑːnə(r)
AM ˌɪpəˌkækjə'wɑn(j)ə, iˌpeɪkə'kwɑnjə
Iphigenia
BR ɪˌfɪdʒɪ'niːə(r), ˌʌɪfɪdʒɪ'nʌɪə(r)
AM ˌɪfədʒə'niə
Ipoh
BR 'iːpəʊ
AM 'iˌpoʊ
ipomoea
BR ˌɪpə'miːə(r), -z
AM ˌɪpə'miə, -z
ipse dixit
BR ˌɪpsɪ 'dɪksɪt, ˌɪpseɪ +
AM ˌɪpsi 'dɪksɪt
ipsilateral
BR ˌɪpsɪ'lat(ə)rəl, ˌɪpsɪ'lat(ə)rl
AM ˌɪpsi'læd(ə)rəl
ipsissima verba
BR ɪpˌsɪsɨmə 'vəːbə(r)
AM ɨpˌsɪsəmə 'vərbə
ipso facto
BR ˌɪpsəʊ 'faktəʊ
AM ˌɪpsoʊ 'fæktoʊ
Ipswich
BR 'ɪpswɪtʃ
AM 'ɪpswɪtʃ
Iqbal
BR 'ɪkbal, 'ɪkbɑːl
AM 'ɪkˌbɑl
IRA[1]
banking
BR 'ʌɪrə(r)
AM 'aɪrə, ˌaɪˌɑr'eɪ
IRA[2]
Irish Republican Army
BR ˌʌɪɑːr'eɪ
AM ˌaɪˌɑr'eɪ
Ira
BR 'ʌɪrə(r)
AM 'aɪrə
irade
BR ɪ'rɑːd|i, -ɪz
AM ɪ'rɑdi, -z
Iran
BR ɪ'rɑːn, ɪ'ran
AM ɪ'rɑn, ɪ'ræn
Iran-Contra
BR ɪˌrɑːn'kɒntrə(r), ɪˌran'kɒntrə(r)
AM ɪˌrɑn'kɑntrə, ɪˌræn'kɑntrə
Irangate
BR ɪ'rɑːngeɪt, ɪ'rangeɪt
AM ɪ'rɑnˌgeɪt, ɪ'rænˌgeɪt
Iranian
BR ɪ'reɪnɪən, -z
AM ɪ'reɪniən, ɪ'rɑniən, -z
Iraq
BR ɪ'rɑːk, ɪ'rak
AM ɪ'rɑk, ɪ'ræk
Iraqi
BR ɪ'rɑːk|i, ɪ'rak|i, -ɪz
AM ɪ'rɑki, ɪ'ræki, -z
IRAS
BR 'ʌɪras
AM 'aɪˌræs
irascibility
BR ɪˌrasɪ'bɪlɨti
AM ɨˌræsə'bɪlɨdi
irascible
BR ɪ'rasɨbl
AM ɨ'ræsəbəl
irascibleness
BR ɪ'rasɨblnəs
AM ɨ'ræsəbəlnəs
irascibly
BR ɪ'rasɨbli
AM ɨ'ræsəbli
irate
BR ʌɪ'reɪt
AM aɪ'reɪt
irately
BR ʌɪ'reɪtli
AM aɪ'reɪtli
irateness
BR ʌɪ'reɪtnɨs
AM aɪ'reɪtnɨs
ire
BR 'ʌɪə(r)
AM 'aɪ(ə)r
ireful
BR 'ʌɪəf(ʊ)l
AM 'aɪrfəl
irefully
BR 'ʌɪəfʊli, 'ʌɪəfli
AM 'aɪrfəli
irefulness
BR 'ʌɪəf(ʊ)lnəs
AM 'aɪrfəlnəs
Ireland
BR 'ʌɪələnd
AM 'aɪrlən(d)
Irenaeus
BR ʌɪ'riːnɪəs
AM aɪ'riniəs
Irene
BR 'ʌɪriːn, ʌɪ'riːn
AM aɪ'rin, 'aɪˌrin
irenic
BR ʌɪ'riːnɪk, ʌɪ'rɛnɪk
AM aɪ'rɛnɪk, aɪ'rinɪk
irenical
BR ʌɪ'riːnɨkl, ʌɪ'rɛnɨkl
AM aɪ'rɛnəkəl, aɪ'rinɨkəl
irenicon
BR ʌɪ'riːnɨkɒn, ʌɪ'rɛnɨkɒn, -z
AM aɪ'rɛnəˌkɑn, aɪ'rinəˌkɑn, -z
Ireton
BR 'ʌɪət(ə)n

AM ˈaɪ(ə)rtən
Irgun
BR əːˈguːn
AM ərˈgun
Irian
BR ˈɪrɪən
AM ˈɪriən
Irian Jaya
BR ˌɪrɪən ˈdʒʌɪə(r)
AM ˌiriən ˈdʒaɪə
iridaceous
BR ˌɪrɪˈdeɪʃəs
AM ˌɪrəˈdeɪʃəs
iridescence
BR ˌɪrɪˈdɛsns
AM ˌɪrəˈdɛsəns
iridescent
BR ˌɪrɪˈdɛsnt
AM ˌɪrəˈdɛsənt
iridescently
BR ˌɪrɪˈdɛsntli
AM ˌɪrəˈdɛsn(t)li
iridium
BR ɪˈrɪdɪəm
AM ɪˈrɪdiəm
iridologist
BR ˌɪrɪˈdɒlədʒɪst, -s
AM ˌɪrəˈdɑlədʒəst, -s
iridology
BR ˌɪrɪˈdɒlədʒi
AM ˌɪrəˈdɑlədʒi
iris
BR ˈʌɪr|ɪs, -ɪsɪz
AM ˈaɪrɪs, -ɪz
Irish
BR ˈʌɪrɪʃ
AM ˈaɪrɪʃ
Irishman
BR ˈʌɪrɪʃmən
AM ˈaɪrɪʃmən
Irishmen
BR ˈʌɪrɪʃmən
AM ˈaɪrɪʃmən
Irishness
BR ˈʌɪrɪʃnɪs
AM ˈaɪrɪʃnɪs
Irishwoman
BR ˈʌɪrɪʃˌwʊmən
AM ˈaɪrɪʃˌwʊmən
Irishwomen
BR ˈʌɪrɪʃˌwɪmɪn
AM ˈaɪrɪʃˌwɪmɪn
iritis
BR ʌɪˈrʌɪtɪs
AM aɪˈraɪdɪs
irk
BR əːk, -s, -ɪŋ, -t
AM ərk, -s, -ɪŋ, -t
irksome
BR ˈəːks(ə)m
AM ˈərksəm
irksomely
BR ˈəːks(ə)mli
AM ˈərksəmli
irksomeness
BR ˈəːks(ə)mnəs
AM ˈərksəmnəs
Irkutsk
BR əːˈkʊtsk, ɪəˈkʊtsk
AM ˈɪrˌkʊ(t)sk
Irlam
BR ˈəːləm
AM ˈərləm
Irma
BR ˈəːmə(r)
AM ˈərmə
Irnbru
BR ˈʌɪənbruː
AM ˈaɪ(ə)rnˌbru
iroko
BR ɪˈrəʊkəʊ, iːˈrəʊkəʊ, -z
AM ɪˈroʊˌkoʊ, -z
iron
BR ˈʌɪən, -z, -ɪŋ, -d
AM ˈaɪ(ə)rn, -z, -ɪŋ, -d
Iron Age
BR ˈʌɪən eɪdʒ
AM ˈaɪ(ə)rn ˌeɪdʒ
ironbark
BR ˈʌɪənbɑːk, -s
AM ˈaɪ(ə)rnˌbɑrk, -s
ironclad
BR ˈʌɪənklad, -z
AM ˈaɪ(ə)rnˌklæd, -z
ironer
BR ˈʌɪənə(r), -z
AM ˈaɪ(ə)rnər, -z
ironic
BR ʌɪˈrɒnɪk
AM aɪˈrɑnɪk
ironical
BR ʌɪˈrɒnɪkl
AM aɪˈrɑnəkəl
ironically
BR ʌɪˈrɒnɪkli
AM aɪˈrɑnək(ə)li
ironise
BR ˈʌɪrənʌɪz, -ɪz, -ɪŋ, -d
AM ˈaɪrəˌnaɪz, -ɪz, -ɪŋ, -d
ironist
BR ˈʌɪrənɪst, -s
AM ˈaɪrənəst, -s
ironize
BR ˈʌɪrənʌɪz, -ɪz, -ɪŋ, -d
AM ˈaɪrəˌnaɪz, -ɪz, -ɪŋ, -d
ironless
BR ˈʌɪənləs
AM ˈaɪ(ə)rnləs
ironmaster
BR ˈʌɪənˌmɑːstə(r), ˈʌɪənˌmastə(r), -z
AM ˈaɪ(ə)rnˌmæstər, -z
ironmonger
BR ˈʌɪənˌmʌŋgə(r), -z
AM ˈaɪ(ə)rnˌmɑŋgər, ˈaɪ(ə)rnˌməŋgər, -z
ironmongery
BR ˈʌɪənˌmʌŋg(ə)ri
AM ˈaɪ(ə)rnˌməŋg(ə)ri, ˈaɪ(ə)rnˌmɑŋg(ə)ri
Ironside
BR ˈʌɪənsʌɪd, -z
AM ˈaɪ(ə)rnˌsaɪd, -z
ironstone
BR ˈʌɪənstəʊn
AM ˈaɪ(ə)rnˌstoʊn
ironware
BR ˈʌɪənwɛː(r)
AM ˈaɪ(ə)rnˌwɛ(ə)r
ironwood
BR ˈʌɪənwʊd
AM ˈaɪ(ə)rnˌwʊd
ironwork
BR ˈʌɪənwəːk, -s
AM ˈaɪ(ə)rnˌwərk, -s
irony
BR ˈʌɪrən|i, -ɪz
AM ˈaɪrəni, ˈaɪərni, -z
Iroquoian
BR ˌɪrəˈkwɔɪən, -z
AM ˈɪrəˌk(w)ɔɪən, -z
Iroquois
BR ˈɪrəkwɔɪ, -z
AM ˈɪrəˌk(w)ɔɪ, -z
irradiance
BR ɪˈreɪdɪəns, -ɪz
AM ɪˈreɪdiəns, -əz
irradiant
BR ɪˈreɪdɪənt
AM ɪˈreɪdiənt
irradiate
BR ɪˈreɪdɪeɪt, -s, -ɪŋ, -ɪd
AM ɪˈreɪdiˌeɪ|t, -ts, -dɪŋ, -dɪd
irradiation
BR ɪˌreɪdɪˈeɪʃn
AM ɪˌreɪdiˈeɪʃən
irradiative
BR ɪˈreɪdɪətɪv
AM ɪˌreɪdiˌeɪdɪv
irrational
BR (ˌ)ɪˈraʃn̩(ə)l, (ˌ)ɪˈraʃən(ə)l
AM ɪ(r)ˈræʃ(ə)nəl
irrationalise
BR (ˌ)ɪˈraʃn̩əlʌɪz, (ˌ)ɪˈraʃn̩lʌɪz, (ˌ)ɪˈraʃənl̩ʌɪz, (ˌ)ɪˈraʃ(ə)nəlʌɪz, -ɪz, -ɪŋ, -d
AM ɪ(r)ˈræʃənlˌaɪz, ɪ(r)ˈræʃnəˌlaɪz, -ɪz, -ɪŋ, -d
irrationality
BR ɪˌraʃəˈnalɪti
AM ˌɪ(r)ˌræʃəˈnælədi, əˌræʃəˈnælədi
irrationalize
BR (ˌ)ɪˈraʃn̩əlʌɪz, (ˌ)ɪˈraʃn̩lʌɪz, (ˌ)ɪˈraʃənl̩ʌɪz, (ˌ)ɪˈraʃ(ə)nəlʌɪz, -ɪz, -ɪŋ, -d
AM ɪ(r)ˈræʃənlˌaɪz, ɪ(r)ˈræʃnəˌlaɪz, -ɪz, -ɪŋ, -d
irrationally
BR (ˌ)ɪˈraʃn̩əli, (ˌ)ɪˈraʃn̩li, (ˌ)ɪˈraʃənl̩i, (ˌ)ɪˈraʃ(ə)nəli
AM ɪ(r)ˈræʃ(ə)nəli
Irrawaddy
BR ˌɪrəˈwɒdi
AM ˌɪrəˈwɑdi
Irrawady
BR ˌɪrəˈwɒdi
AM ˌɪrəˈwɑdi
irreclaimable
BR ˌɪrɪˈkleɪməbl
AM ˌɪ(r)rəˈkleɪməbəl
irreclaimably
BR ˌɪrɪˈkleɪməbli
AM ˌɪ(r)rəˈkleɪməbli
irreconcilability
BR ɪˌrɛk(ə)nˌsʌɪləˈbɪlɪti, ˌɪrɛk(ə)nˌsʌɪləˈbɪlɪti
AM ˌɪ(r)ˌrɛkənˌsaɪləˈbɪlɪdi, ɪˌrɛkənˌsaɪləˈbɪlɪdi
irreconcilable
BR ˌɪrɛk(ə)nˈsʌɪləbl, ɪˌrɛk(ə)nˈsʌɪləbl, ɪˈrɛk(ə)nsʌɪləbl
AM ˌɪ(r)ˌrɛkənˈsaɪləbəl, ɪˌrɛkənˈsaɪləbəl
irreconcilableness
BR ˌɪrɛk(ə)nˈsʌɪləblnəs, ɪˌrɛk(ə)nˈsʌɪləblnəs, ɪˈrɛk(ə)nsʌɪləblnəs
AM ˌɪ(r)ˌrɛkənˈsaɪləbəlnəs, ɪˌrɛkənˈsaɪləbəlnəs
irreconcilably
BR ˌɪrɛk(ə)nˈsʌɪləbli, ɪˌrɛk(ə)nˈsʌɪləbli, ɪˈrɛk(ə)nsʌɪləbli
AM ˌɪ(r)ˌrɛkənˈsaɪləbli, ɪˌrɛkənˈsaɪləbli
irrecoverable
BR ˌɪrɪˈkʌv(ə)rəbl
AM ˌɪ(r)rəˈkəv(ə)rəbəl
irrecoverably
BR ˌɪrɪˈkʌv(ə)rəbli
AM ˌɪ(r)rəˈkəv(ə)rəbli
irrecusable
BR ˌɪrɪˈkjuːzəbl
AM ˌɪ(r)rəˈkjuzəbəl
irredeemability
BR ˌɪrɪˌdiːməˈbɪlɪti
AM ˌɪ(r)rəˌdiməˈbɪlɪdi
irredeemable
BR ˌɪrɪˈdiːməbl
AM ˌɪ(r)rəˈdiməbəl
irredeemably
BR ˌɪrɪˈdiːməbli
AM ˌɪ(r)rəˈdiməbli
irredentism
BR ˌɪrɪˈdɛntɪz(ə)m
AM ˌɪ(r)rəˈdɛnˌtɪzəm
irredentist
BR ˌɪrɪˈdɛntɪst, -s
AM ˌɪ(r)rəˈdɛn(t)əst, -s
irreducibility
BR ˌɪrɪˌdjuːsɪˈbɪlɪti, ˌɪrɪˌdʒuːsɪˈbɪlɪti
AM ˌɪ(r)rəˌd(j)usəˈbɪlɪdi

irreducible
BR ˌɪrɨˈdjuːsɨbl, ˌɪrɨˈdʒuːsɨbl
AM ¦ɪ(r)rəˈd(j)usəbəl

irreducibly
BR ˌɪrɨˈdjuːsɨbli, ˌɪrɨˈdʒuːsɨbli
AM ¦ɪ(r)rəˈd(j)usəbli

irrefragability
BR ɪˌrɛfrəgəˈbɪlɨti
AM ¦i(r)ˌrɛfrəgəˈbɪlɨdi

irrefragable
BR (ˌ)ɪˈrɛfrəgəbl
AM ɪ(r)ˈrɛfrəgəbəl, ɨˈrɛfrəgəbəl

irrefragableness
BR (ˌ)ɪˈrɛfrəgəblnəs
AM ɪ(r)ˈrɛfrəgəbəlnəs, ɨˈrɛfrəgəbəlnəs

irrefragably
BR (ˌ)ɪˈrɛfrəgəbli
AM ɪ(r)ˈrɛfrəgəbli, ɨˈrɛfrəgəbli

irrefrangible
BR ˌɪrɨˈfran(d)ʒɨbl
AM ¦ɪ(r)rəˈfrændʒəbəl

irrefutability
BR ˌɪrɨˌfjuːtəˈbɪlɨti, ɪˌrɛfjʉtəˈbɪlɨti
AM ¦ɪ(r)rəˌfjudəˈbɪlɨdi, ¦ɪ(r)ˌrɛfjədəˈbɪlɨdi, ɨˌrɛfjədəˈbɪlɨdi

irrefutable
BR ˌɪrɨˈfjuːtəbl, ɪˈrɛfjʉtəbl
AM ¦ɪ(r)rəˈfjudəbəl, ¦ɪ(r)ˈrɛfjədəbəl, ɨˈrɛfjədəbəl

irrefutably
BR ˌɪrɨˈfjuːtəbli, ɪˈrɛfjʉtəbli
AM ¦ɪ(r)rəˈfjudəbli, ¦ɪ(r)ˈrɛfjədəbli, ɨˈrɛfjədəbli

irregardless
BR ˌɪrɨˈgɑːdləs
AM ¦ɪ(r)rəˈgɑrdləs

irregular
BR (ˌ)ɪˈrɛgjʉlə(r)
AM ɪ(r)ˈrɛgjələr

irregularity
BR ɪˌrɛgjʉˈlarɪt|i, -ɪz
AM ¦ɪ(r)ˌrɛgjəˈlɛrədi, ɨˌrɛgjəˈlɛrədi, -z

irregularly
BR (ˌ)ɪˈrɛgjʉləli
AM ɪ(r)ˈrɛgjələrli

irrelative
BR (ˌ)ɪˈrɛlətɪv
AM ¦ɪ(r)ˈrɛlədɪv, ɨˈrɛlədɪv

irrelatively
BR (ˌ)ɪˈrɛlətɨvli
AM ¦ɪ(r)ˈrɛlədəvli, ɨˈrɛlədəvli

irrelevance
BR (ˌ)ɪˈrɛlɨv(ə)ns, -ɨz
AM ¦ɪ(r)ˈrɛləvəns, ɨˈrɛləvəns, -əz

irrelevancy
BR (ˌ)ɪˈrɛlɨv(ə)ns|i, -ɪz
AM ¦ɪ(r)ˈrɛləvənsi, ɨˈrɛləvənsi, -z

irrelevant
BR (ˌ)ɪˈrɛlɨv(ə)nt
AM ¦ɪ(r)ˈrɛləvənt, ɨˈrɛləvənt

irrelevantly
BR (ˌ)ɪˈrɛlɨv(ə)ntli
AM ¦ɪ(r)ˈrɛləvən(t)li, ɨˈrɛləvən(t)li

irreligion
BR ˌɪrɨˈlɪdʒ(ə)n
AM ¦ɪ(r)rəˈlɪdʒən

irreligionist
BR ˌɪrɨˈlɪdʒənɪst, ˌɪrɨˈlɪdʒn̩ɪst, -s
AM ¦ɪ(r)rəˈlɪdʒənəst, -s

irreligious
BR ˌɪrɨˈlɪdʒəs
AM ¦ɪ(r)rəˈlɪdʒəs

irreligiously
BR ˌɪrɨˈlɪdʒəsli
AM ¦ɪ(r)rəˈlɪdʒəsli

irreligiousness
BR ˌɪrɨˈlɪdʒəsnəs
AM ¦ɪ(r)rəˈlɪdʒəsnəs

irremediable
BR ˌɪrɨˈmiːdɪəbl
AM ¦ɪ(r)rəˈmidiəbəl

irremediably
BR ˌɪrɨˈmiːdɪəbli
AM ¦ɪ(r)rəˈmidiəbli

irremissible
BR ˌɪrɨˈmɪsɨbl
AM ¦ɪ(r)rəˈmɪsɨbəl

irremissibly
BR ˌɪrɨˈmɪsɨbli
AM ¦ɪ(r)rəˈmɪsɨbli

irremovability
BR ˌɪrɨˌmuːvəˈbɪlɪt|i, -ɪz
AM ¦ɪ(r)rəˌmuvəˈbɪlɨdi, -z

irremovable
BR ˌɪrɨˈmuːvəbl
AM ¦ɪ(r)rəˈmuvəbəl

irremovably
BR ˌɪrɨˈmuːvəbli
AM ¦ɪ(r)rəˈmuvəbli

irremoveability
BR ˌɪrɨˌmuːvəˈbɪlɨti
AM ¦ɪ(r)rəˌmuvəˈbɪlɨdi

irremoveable
BR ˌɪrɨˈmuːvəbl
AM ¦ɪ(r)rəˈmuvəbəl

irreparability
BR ɪˌrɛp(ə)rəˈbɪlɨti
AM ¦ɪ(r)ˌrɛp(ə)rəˈbɪlɨdi

irreparable
BR (ˌ)ɪˈrɛp(ə)rəbl
AM ¦ɪrˈrɛp(ə)rəbəl, ɨˈrɛp(ə)rəbəl

irreparableness
BR (ˌ)ɪˈrɛp(ə)rəblnəs
AM ¦ɪrˈrɛp(ə)rəbəlnəs, ɨˈrɛp(ə)rəbəlnəs

irreparably
BR (ˌ)ɪˈrɛp(ə)rəbli
AM ¦ɪrˈrɛp(ə)rəbli, ɨˈrɛp(ə)rəbli

irreplaceable
BR ˌɪrɨˈpleɪsəbl
AM ¦ɪ(r)rəˈpleɪsəbəl

irreplaceably
BR ˌɪrɨˈpleɪsəbli
AM ¦ɪ(r)rəˈpleɪsəbli

irrepressibility
BR ˌɪrɨˌprɛsɨˈbɪlɨti
AM ¦ɪ(r)rəˌprɛsəˈbɪlɨdi

irrepressible
BR ˌɪrɨˈprɛsɨbl
AM ¦ɪ(r)rəˈprɛsəbəl

irrepressibleness
BR ˌɪrɨˈprɛsɨblnəs
AM ¦ɪ(r)rəˈprɛsəbəlnəs

irrepressibly
BR ˌɪrɨˈprɛsɨbli
AM ¦ɪ(r)rəˈprɛsəbli

irreproachability
BR ˌɪrɨˌprəʊtʃəˈbɪlɨti
AM ¦ɪ(r)rəˌproʊtʃəˈbɪlɨdi

irreproachable
BR ˌɪrɨˈprəʊtʃəbl
AM ¦ɪ(r)rəˈproʊtʃəbəl

irreproachableness
BR ˌɪrɨˈprəʊtʃəblnəs
AM ¦ɪ(r)rəˈproʊtʃəbəlnəs

irreproachably
BR ˌɪrɨˈprəʊtʃəbli
AM ¦ɪ(r)rəˈproʊtʃəbli

irresistibility
BR ˌɪrɨˌzɪstɨˈbɪlɨti
AM ¦ɪ(r)rəˌzɪstəˈbɪlɨdi

irresistible
BR ˌɪrɨˈzɪstɨbl
AM ¦ɪ(r)rəˈzɪstəbəl

irresistibleness
BR ˌɪrɨˈzɪstɨblnəs
AM ¦ɪ(r)rəˈzɪstəbəlnəs

irresistibly
BR ˌɪrɨˈzɪstɨbli
AM ¦ɪ(r)rəˈzɪstəbli

irresolute
BR (ˌ)ɪˈrɛzəl(j)uːt
AM ɪ(r)ˈrɛzəˌlut

irresolutely
BR (ˌ)ɪˈrɛzəl(j)uːtli
AM ɪ(r)ˈrɛzəˌlutli

irresoluteness
BR (ˌ)ɪˈrɛzəl(j)uːtnəs
AM ɪ(r)ˈrɛzəˌlutnəs

irresolution
BR ɪˌrɛzəˈl(j)uːʃn, ˌɪrɛzəˈl(j)uːʃn
AM ¦ɨ(r)ˌrɛzəˈluʃən

irresolvability
BR ˌɪrɨˌzɒlvəˈbɪlɨti
AM ¦ɪ(r)rəˌzɑlvəˈbɪlɨdi

irresolvable
BR ˌɪrɨˈzɒlvəbl
AM ¦ɪ(r)rəˈzɑlvəbəl

irrespective
BR ˌɪrɨˈspɛktɪv
AM ¦ɪ(r)rəˈspɛktɪv

irrespectively
BR ˌɪrɨˈspɛktɨvli
AM ¦ɪ(r)rəˈspɛktəvli

irresponsibility
BR ˌɪrɨˌspɒnsɨˈbɪlɨti
AM ¦ɪ(r)rəˌspɑnsəˈbɪlɨdi

irresponsible
BR ˌɪrɨˈspɒnsɨbl
AM ¦ɪ(r)rəˈspɑnsəbəl

irresponsibly
BR ˌɪrɨˈspɒnsɨbli
AM ¦ɪ(r)rəˈspɑnsəbli

irresponsive
BR ˌɪrɨˈspɒnsɪv
AM ¦ɪ(r)rəˈspɑnsɪv

irresponsively
BR ˌɪrɨˈspɒnsɨvli
AM ¦ɪ(r)rəˈspɑnsəvli

irresponsiveness
BR ˌɪrɨˈspɒnsɪvnɪs
AM ¦ɪ(r)rəˈspɑnsɪvnɪs

irretentive
BR ˌɪrɨˈtɛntɪv
AM ¦ɪ(r)rəˈtɛn(t)ɪv

irretrievability
BR ˌɪrɨˌtriːvəˈbɪlɨti
AM ¦ɪ(r)rəˌtrivəˈbɪlɨdi

irretrievable
BR ˌɪrɨˈtriːvəbl
AM ¦ɪ(r)rəˈtrivəbəl

irretrievably
BR ˌɪrɨˈtriːvəbli
AM ¦ɪ(r)rəˈtrivəbli

irreverence
BR ɪˈrɛv(ə)rəns, ɪˈrɛv(ə)rn̩s
AM ɪ(r)ˈrɛv(ə)rəns

irreverent
BR ɪˈrɛv(ə)rənt, ɪˈrɛv(ə)rn̩t
AM ɪ(r)ˈrɛv(ə)rənt

irreverential
BR ɪˌrɛvəˈrɛnʃl, ˌɪrɛvəˈrɛnʃl
AM ɪ(r)ˌrɛvəˈrɛn(t)ʃəl

irreverently
BR ɪˈrɛv(ə)rəntli, ɪˈrɛv(ə)rn̩tli
AM ɪ(r)ˈrɛv(ə)rən(t)li

irreversibility
BR ˌɪrɨˌvəːsɨˈbɪlɨti
AM ¦ɪ(r)rəˌvərsəˈbɪlɨdi

irreversible
BR ˌɪrɨˈvəːsɨbl
AM ¦ɪ(r)rəˈvərsəbəl

irreversibly
BR ˌɪrɨˈvəːsɨbli
AM ¦ɪ(r)rəˈvərsəbli

irrevocability
BR ɪˌrɛvəkəˈbɪlɨti

AM ˌɪ(r)ˌrɛvəkəˈbɪlɨdi, ɪˌrɛvəkəˈbɪlɨdi
irrevocable
BR ɪˈrɛvəkəbl
AM ˌɪ(r)ˈrɛvəkəbəl, ɪˈrɛvəkəbəl, ˌɪ(r)rəˈvoʊkəbəl
irrevocably
BR ɪˈrɛvəkəbli
AM ˌɪ(r)ˈrɛvəkəbli, ɪˈrɛvəkəbli, ˌɪ(r)rəˈvoʊkəbli
irrigable
BR ˈɪrɨgəbl
AM ˈɪrəgəbəl
irrigate
BR ˈɪrɨgeɪt, -s, -ɪŋ, -ɨd
AM ˈɪrəgeɪ|t, -ts, -dɪŋ, -dɨd
irrigation
BR ˌɪrɨˈgeɪʃn
AM ˌɪrəˈgeɪʃən
irrigative
BR ˈɪrɨgətɪv
AM ˈɪrəˌgeɪdɪv
irrigator
BR ˈɪrɨgeɪtə(r), -z
AM ˈɪrəˌgeɪdər, -z
irritability
BR ˌɪrɪtəˈbɪlɨti
AM ˌɪrədəˈbɪlɨdi
irritable
BR ˈɪrɪtəbl
AM ˈɪrədəbəl
irritably
BR ˈɪrɪtəbli
AM ˈɪrədəbli
irritancy
BR ˈɪrɪt(ə)nsi
AM ˈɪrədnsi
irritant
BR ˈɪrɪt(ə)nt, -s
AM ˈɪrədnt, -s
irritate
BR ˈɪrɪteɪt, -s, -ɪŋ, -ɨd
AM ˈɪrəˌteɪ|t, -ts, -dɪŋ, -dɨd
irritatedly
BR ˈɪrɪteɪtɨdli
AM ˈɪrəˌteɪdɨdli
irritatingly
BR ˈɪrɪteɪtɪŋli
AM ˈɪrəˌteɪdɪŋli
irritation
BR ˌɪrɪˈteɪʃn, -z
AM ˌɪrəˈteɪʃən, -z
irritative
BR ˈɪrɪtətɪv
AM ˈɪrəˌteɪdɪv
irritator
BR ˈɪrɪteɪtə(r), -z
AM ˈɪrəˌteɪdər, -z
irrupt
BR ɪˈrʌpt, -s, -ɪŋ, -ɨd
AM ɪˈrəpt, -s, -ɪŋ, -əd
irruption
BR ɪˈrʌpʃn, -z
AM ɪˈrəpʃən, -z
irruptive
BR ɪˈrʌptɪv
AM ɪˈrəptɪv
Irvine[1]
placename in UK
BR ˈəːvɪn
AM ˈərvən
Irvine[2]
placename in USA
BR ˈəːvʌɪn
AM ˈərˌvaɪn
Irvine[3]
surname
BR ˈəːvɪn
AM ˈərvən
Irving
BR ˈəːvɪŋ
AM ˈərvɪŋ
Irvingite
BR ˈəːvɪŋʌɪt, -s
AM ˈərvɪŋˌgaɪt, -s
Irwell
BR ˈəːwɛl
AM ˈərˌwɛl
Irwin
BR ˈəːwɪn
AM ˈərwən
is[1]
strong
BR ɪz
AM ɪz
is[2]
weak
BR s, z
AM s, z
Isaac
BR ˈʌɪzək
AM ˈaɪzək
Isaacs
BR ˈʌɪzəks
AM ˈaɪzəks
Isabel
BR ˈɪzəbɛl
AM ˈɪzəˌbɛl
Isabella
BR ˌɪzəˈbɛlə(r)
AM ˌɪzəˈbɛlə
Isabelle
BR ˈɪzəbɛl, ˌɪzəˈbɛl
AM ˈɪzəˌbɛl, ˌɪzəˈbɛl
isabelline
BR ˌɪzəˈbɛliːn, ˌɪzəˈbɛlɪn, ˌɪzəˈbɛlʌɪn
AM ˌɪzəˌbɛlən, ˌɪzəˌbɛˌlaɪn, ˌɪzəˌbɛˌlin
Isadora
BR ˌɪzəˈdɔːrə(r)
AM ˌɪzəˈdɔrə
Isadore
BR ˈɪzədɔː(r)
AM ˈɪzəˌdɔ(ə)r
isagogic
BR ˌʌɪsəˈgɒdʒɪk, -s
AM ˌaɪsəˈgɑdʒɪk, -s
Isaiah
BR ʌɪˈzʌɪə(r)
AM aɪˈzeɪə
Isambard
BR ˈɪz(ə)mbɑːd
AM ˈɪzəmˌbɑrd
isatin
BR ˈʌɪsətɪn
AM ˈaɪsədən, ˈaɪsətn
Iscariot
BR ɪˈskarɪət
AM ɨsˈkɛriət
ischaemia
BR ɪˈskiːmɪə(r)
AM ɪsˈkimiə
ischaemic
BR ɪˈskiːmɪk
AM ɪsˈkimɪk
ischemia
BR ɪˈskiːmɪə(r)
AM ɪsˈkimiə
ischemic
BR ɪˈskiːmɪk
AM ɪsˈkimɪk
Ischia
BR ˈɪskɪə(r)
AM ˈɪskiə
ischiadic
BR ˌɪskɪˈadɪk
AM ˌɪskiˈædɪk
ischial
BR ˈɪskɪəl
AM ˈɪskiəl
ischiatic
BR ˌɪskɪˈatɪk
AM ˌɪskiˈædɪk
ischium
BR ˈɪskɪəm
AM ˈɪskiə
isentropic
BR ˌʌɪsɛnˈtrɒpɪk, ˌʌɪzɛnˈtrɒpɪk, ˌʌɪs(ɨ)nˈtrɒpɪk, ˌʌɪz(ɨ)nˈtrɒpɪk, ˌʌɪsɛnˈtrəʊpɪk, ˌʌɪzɛnˈtrəʊpɪk, ˌʌɪs(ɨ)nˈtrəʊpɪk, ˌʌɪz(ɨ)nˈtrəʊpɪk
AM ˌaɪsənˈtrɑpɪk, ˌaɪzənˈtrɑpɪk
Iseult
BR ɪˈzuːlt, ɪˈsuːlt
AM ˌɪˈsolt, ˌɪˈzolt
Isfahan
BR ˌɪsfəˈhɑːn, ˈɪsfəhɑːn
AM ˌɪsfəˈhɑn
Isherwood
BR ˈɪʃəwʊd
AM ˈɪʃərˌwʊd
Ishiguro
BR ˌɪʃɪˈgʊərəʊ
AM ˌɪʃiˈguˌroʊ
Ishmael
BR ˈɪʃmeɪl, ˈɪʃmɪəl
AM ˈɪʃˌmeɪl, ˈɪʃmiəl
Ishmaelite
BR ˈɪʃməlʌɪt, ˈɪʃmeɪlʌɪt, ˈɪʃmɪəlʌɪt, -s
AM ˈɪʃˌmeɪˌlaɪt, ˈɪʃmiəˌlaɪt, -s
Ishtar
BR ˈɪʃtɑː(r)
AM ˈɪʃˌtɑr
Isidore
BR ˈɪzɨdɔː(r)
AM ˈɪzəˌdɔ(ə)r
isinglass
BR ˈʌɪzɪŋglɑːs, ˈʌɪzɪŋglas
AM ˈaɪznˌglæs, ˈaɪzɪŋˌglæs
Isis
BR ˈʌɪsɪs
AM ˈaɪsɪs
Isla
BR ˈʌɪlə(r)
AM ˈaɪlə
Islam
BR ˈɪzlɑːm, ˈɪslɑːm, ˈɪzlam, ˈɪslam, ɪzˈlɑːm, ɪsˈlɑːm, ɪzˈlam, ɪsˈlam
AM ɪˈslɑm, ɪzˈlɑm, ˈɪsˌlɑm, ˈɪzˌlɑm
Islamabad
BR ɪzˈlɑːməbad, ɪsˈlɑːməbad, ɪzˈlaməbad, ɪsˈlaməbad, ɪzˈlɑːməbɑːd, ɪsˈlɑːməbɑːd, ɪzˈlaməbɑːd, ɪsˈlaməbɑːd
AM ɪˌslɑməˈbɑd, ɪˌzlɑməˈbɑd, ɪˌslæməˈbæd, ɪˌzlæməˈbæd
Islamic
BR ɪzˈlamɪk, ɪsˈlamɪk
AM ɪˈslɑmɪk, ɪzˈlɑmɪk
Islamisation
BR ɪzˌlɑːmʌɪˈzeɪʃn, ɪsˌlɑːmʌɪˈzeɪʃn, ɪzˌlamʌɪˈzeɪʃn, ɪsˌlamʌɪˈzeɪʃn
AM ɪˌslɑməˈzeɪʃən, ɪˌzlɑməˈzeɪʃən, ɪˌslɑmˌaɪˈzeɪʃən, ɪˌzlɑmˌaɪˈzeɪʃən
Islamise
BR ˈɪzləmʌɪz, ˈɪsləmʌɪz, -ɨz, -ɪŋ, -d
AM ˈɪsləˌmaɪz, ˈɪzləˌmaɪz, -ɨz, -ɪŋ, -d
Islamism
BR ˈɪzləmɪz(ə)m, ˈɪsləmɪz(ə)m
AM ˈɪsləˌmɪzəm, ˈɪzləˌmɪzəm
Islamist
BR ˈɪzləmɪst, ˈɪsləmɪst, -s
AM ˈɪsləməst, ˈɪzləməst, -s
Islamite
BR ˈɪzləmʌɪt, ˈɪsləmʌɪt, -s

AM ˈɪsləˌmaɪt, ˈɪzləˌmaɪt, -s

Islamitic
BR ˌɪzləˈmɪtɪk, ˌɪsləˈmɪtɪk
AM ˌɪsləˈmɪdɪk, ˌɪzləˈmɪdɪk

Islamization
BR ɪzˌlɑːmʌɪˈzeɪʃn, ɪsˌlɑːmʌɪˈzeɪʃn, ɪzˌlamʌɪˈzeɪʃn, ɪsˌlamʌɪˈzeɪʃn
AM ɪˌslɑməˈzeɪʃən, ɪˌzlɑməˈzeɪʃən, ɪˌslɑmˌaɪˈzeɪʃən, ɪˌzlɑmˌaɪˈzeɪʃən

Islamize
BR ˈɪzləmʌɪz, ˈɪsləmʌɪz, -ɪz, -ɪŋ, -d
AM ˈɪsləˌmaɪz, ˈɪzləˌmaɪz, -ɪz, -ɪŋ, -d

island
BR ˈʌɪlən|d, -(d)z
AM ˈaɪlən|d, -(d)z

islander
BR ˈʌɪləndə(r), -z
AM ˈaɪləndər, -z

isle
BR ʌɪl, -z
AM aɪl, -z

Isle of Man
BR ˌʌɪl əv ˈman
AM ˌaɪl əv ˈmæn

Isle of Wight
BR ˌʌɪl əv ˈwʌɪt
AM ˌaɪl əv ˈwaɪt

islet
BR ˈʌɪlɨt, -s
AM ˈaɪlət, -s

Isleworth
BR ˈʌɪzlwəːθ, ˈʌɪzlwəθ
AM ˈaɪlˌwərθ

Islington
BR ˈɪzlɪŋt(ə)n
AM ˈaɪlɪŋtən

Islwyn
BR ˈɪslʊɪn
AM ˈɪslʊɪn
WE ˈɪslwɪn

ism
BR ˈɪz(ə)m, -z
AM ˈɪzəm, -z

Ismaili
BR ˌɪzməˈiːl|i, ˌɪzmɑːˈiːl|i, -ɪz
AM ˌɪzməˈili, ˌɪzmɑˈili, -z

Ismailia
BR ˌɪzmʌɪˈliːə(r), ˌɪsmʌɪˈliːə(r)
AM ˌɪzmaɪˈliə, ˌɪsmaɪˈliə

Ismay
BR ˈɪzmeɪ
AM ˈɪzmaɪ

isn't
BR ˈɪznt
AM ˈɪznt

isobar
BR ˈʌɪsə(ʊ)bɑː(r), -z
AM ˈaɪsəˌbɑr, ˈaɪsoʊˌbɑr, -z

isobaric
BR ˌʌɪsə(ʊ)ˈbarɪk
AM ˌaɪsəˈbɛrɪk, ˌaɪsoʊˈbɛrɪk

Isobel
BR ˈɪzəbɛl
AM ˈɪzəˌbɛl

isocheim
BR ˈʌɪsə(ʊ)kʌɪm, -z
AM ˈaɪsəˌkaɪm, ˈaɪsoʊˌkaɪm, -z

isochromatic
BR ˌʌɪsə(ʊ)krəˈmatɪk
AM ˌaɪsəkrəˈmædɪk

isochronal
BR ʌɪˈsɒkrənl, ʌɪˈsɒkrn̩l
AM aɪˈsɑkrənəl

isochronally
BR ʌɪˈsɒkrənl̩i, ʌɪˈsɒkrn̩l̩i
AM aɪˈsɑkrənəli

isochronicity
BR ʌɪˌsɒkrəˈnɪsɪt|i, -ɪz
AM aɪˌsɑkrəˈnɪsɪdi, -z

isochronize
BR ʌɪˈsɒkrənʌɪz, -ɪz, -ɪŋ, -d
AM aɪˈsɑkrəˌnaɪz, -ɪz, -ɪŋ, -d

isochronous
BR ʌɪˈsɒkrənəs
AM aɪˈsɑkrənəs

isochronously
BR ʌɪˈsɒkrənəsli
AM aɪˈsɑkrənəsli

isochrony
BR ʌɪˈsɒkrəni
AM aɪˈsɑkrəni

isoclinal
BR ˌʌɪsə(ʊ)ˈklʌɪnl
AM ˌaɪsəˈklaɪnəl, ˌaɪsoʊˈklaɪnl

isoclinic
BR ˌʌɪsə(ʊ)ˈklɪnɪk
AM ˌaɪsəˈklɪnɪk, ˌaɪsoʊˈklɪnɪk

isocracy
BR ʌɪˈsɒkrəs|i, -ɪz
AM aɪˈsɑkrəsi, -z

Isocrates
BR ʌɪˈsɒkrətiːz
AM aɪˈsɑkrəˌtiz

isocratic
BR ˌʌɪsə(ʊ)ˈkratɪk
AM ˌaɪsəˈkrædɪk, ˌaɪsoʊˈkrædɪk

isocyclic
BR ˌʌɪsə(ʊ)ˈsʌɪklɪk
AM ˌaɪsəˈsaɪklɪk, ˌaɪsoʊˈsaɪklɪk

isodynamic
BR ˌʌɪsə(ʊ)dʌɪˈnamɪk
AM ˌaɪsəˌdaɪˈnæmɪk, ˌaɪsoʊˌdaɪˈnæmɪk

isoenzyme
BR ˈʌɪsəʊˌɛnzʌɪm, -z
AM ˌaɪsəˈɛnˌzaɪm, ˌaɪsoʊˈɛnˌzaɪm, -z

isogeotherm
BR ˌʌɪsə(ʊ)ˈdʒɪə(ʊ)θəːm, -z
AM ˌaɪsəˈdʒiəˌθərm, ˌaɪsoʊˈdʒiəˌθərm, -z

isogeothermal
BR ˌʌɪsəʊˌdʒiːə(ʊ)ˈθəːml
AM ˌaɪsəˌdʒiəˈθərməl, ˌaɪsoʊˌdʒiəˈθərməl

isogloss
BR ˈʌɪsəglɒs, -ɪz
AM ˈaɪsəˌglɔs, ˈaɪsəˌglɑs, ˈaɪsoʊˌglɔs, ˈaɪsoʊˌglɑs, -əz

isogonic
BR ˌʌɪsə(ʊ)ˈgɒnɪk
AM ˌaɪsəˈgɑnɪk

isohel
BR ˈʌɪsə(ʊ)hɛl, -z
AM ˈaɪsəˌhɛl, ˈaɪsoʊˌhɛl, -z

isohyet
BR ˌʌɪsə(ʊ)ˈhʌɪɨt, -s
AM ˌaɪsəˈhaɪət, ˌaɪsoʊˈhaɪət, -s

isolable
BR ˈʌɪs(ə)ləbl
AM ˈaɪsələbəl

isolatable
BR ˈʌɪsəleɪtəbl
AM ˈaɪsəˌleɪdəbəl

isolate[1]
noun, adjective
BR ˈʌɪs(ə)lət, -s
AM ˈaɪsələt, -s

isolate[2]
verb
BR ˈʌɪsəleɪt, -s, -ɪŋ, -ɨd
AM ˈaɪsəˌleɪ|t, -ts, -dɪŋ, -dɨd

isolation
BR ˌʌɪsəˈleɪʃn
AM ˌaɪsəˈleɪʃən

isolationism
BR ˌʌɪsəˈleɪʃn̩ɪz(ə)m, ˌʌɪsəˈleɪʃənɪz(ə)m
AM ˌaɪsəˈleɪʃəˌnɪzəm

isolationist
BR ˌʌɪsəˈleɪʃn̩ɪst, ˌʌɪsəˈleɪʃənɪst, -s
AM ˌaɪsəˈleɪʃənəst, -s

isolative
BR ˈʌɪs(ə)lətɪv
AM ˈaɪsəˌleɪdɪv

isolatively
BR ˈʌɪs(ə)lətɪvli
AM ˈaɪsəˌleɪdɪvli

isolator
BR ˈʌɪsəleɪtə(r), -z
AM ˈaɪsəˌleɪdər, -z

Isolde
BR ɪˈzɒldə(r)
AM ɪˈsɔld, ɪˈzɔld

isolette
BR ˌʌɪsəˈlɛt
AM ˌaɪsəˈlɛt

isoleucine
BR ˌʌɪsə(ʊ)ˈluːsiːn
AM ˌaɪsəˈlusən, ˌaɪsoʊˈlusən

isomer
BR ˈʌɪsəmə(r), -z
AM ˈaɪsəmər, -z

isomerase
BR ʌɪˈsɒməreɪz
AM aɪˈsɑməˌreɪz

isomeric
BR ˌʌɪsəˈmɛrɪk
AM ˌaɪsoʊˈmɛrɪk, ˌaɪzəˈmɛrɪk

isomerise
BR ʌɪˈsɒmərʌɪz, -ɪz, -ɪŋ, -d
AM aɪˈsɑməˌraɪz, -ɪz, -ɪŋ, -d

isomerism
BR ʌɪˈsɒmərɪz(ə)m
AM aɪˈsɑməˌrɪzəm

isomerize
BR ʌɪˈsɒmərʌɪz, -ɪz, -ɪŋ, -d
AM aɪˈsɑməˌraɪz, -ɪz, -ɪŋ, -d

isomerous
BR ʌɪˈsɒm(ə)rəs
AM aɪˈsɑmərəs

isometric
BR ˌʌɪsə(ʊ)ˈmɛtrɪk, -s
AM ˌaɪsoʊˈmɛtrɪk, ˌaɪzəˈmɛtrɪk, -s

isometrically
BR ˌʌɪsə(ʊ)ˈmɛtrɪkli
AM ˌaɪsoʊˈmɛtrək(ə)li, ˌaɪzəˈmɛtrək(ə)li

isometry
BR ʌɪˈsɒmɪtri
AM aɪˈsɑmətri

isomorph
BR ˈʌɪsə(ʊ)mɔːf, -s
AM ˈaɪsəˌmɔ(ə)rf, ˈaɪsoʊˌmɔ(ə)rf, -s

isomorphic
BR ˌʌɪsə(ʊ)ˈmɔːfɪk
AM ˌaɪsoʊˈmɔrfɪk

isomorphically
BR ˌʌɪsə(ʊ)ˈmɔːfɪkli
AM ˌaɪsoʊˈmɔrfək(ə)li

isomorphism
BR ˌʌɪsə(ʊ)ˈmɔːfɪz(ə)m
AM ˌaɪsoʊˈmɔrˌfɪzəm

isomorphous
BR ˌʌɪsə(ʊ)ˈmɔːfəs
AM ˌaɪsoʊˈmɔrfəs

isonomy
BR ʌɪˈsɒnəmi
AM aɪˈsɑnəmi

isooctane
BR ˌʌɪsəʊˈɒkteɪn
AM ˌaɪsoʊˈɑkteɪn

isophote
BR ˈʌɪsə(ʊ)fəʊt, -s
AM ˈaɪsəˌfoʊt, -s

isopleth
BR ˈʌɪsə(ʊ)plɛθ, -s
AM ˈaɪsəˌplɛθ, ˈaɪsoʊˌplɛθ, -s

isopod
BR ˈʌɪsə(ʊ)pɒd, -z
AM ˈaɪsəˌpɑd, -z

isopropyl
BR ˌʌɪsəʊˈprəʊpʌɪl, ˌʌɪsəʊˈprəʊpɪl
AM ˌaɪsəˈproʊpəl, ˌaɪsoʊˌproʊpəl

isoproterenol
BR ˌʌɪsə(ʊ)ˌprəʊtəˈriːnɒl
AM ˌaɪsəˌproʊdəˈrinɑl, ˌaɪsoʊˌproʊdəˈrinal, ˌaɪsəˌproʊdəˈrinɔl, ˌaɪsoʊˌproʊdəˈrinɔl

isosceles
BR ʌɪˈsɒsɨliːz, ʌɪˈsɒsl̩iːz
AM aɪˈsɑsəˌliz

isoseismal
BR ˌʌɪsə(ʊ)ˈsʌɪzml
AM ˌaɪsəˈsaɪzməl, ˌaɪsoʊˈsaɪzməl

isoseismic
BR ˌʌɪsə(ʊ)ˈsʌɪzmɪk
AM ˌaɪsəˈsaɪzmɪk, ˌaɪsoʊˈsaɪzmɪk

isospin
BR ˈʌɪsə(ʊ)spɪn
AM ˈaɪsəˌspɪn, ˈaɪsəʊˌspɪn

isostasy
BR ʌɪˈsɒstəs|i, -ɪz
AM aɪˈsɑstəsi, -z

isostatic
BR ˌʌɪsə(ʊ)ˈstatɪk
AM ˌaɪsəˈstædɪk, ˌaɪsoʊˈstædɪk

isothere
BR ˈʌɪsə(ʊ)θɪə(r), -z
AM ˈaɪsəˌθɪ(ə)r, -z

isotherm
BR ˈʌɪsə(ʊ)θəːm, -z
AM ˈaɪsəˌθərm, ˈaɪsoʊˌθərm, -z

isothermal
BR ˌʌɪsə(ʊ)ˈθəːml
AM ˌaɪsəˈθərməl, ˌaɪsoʊˈθərməl

isothermally
BR ˌʌɪsə(ʊ)ˈθəːml̩i, ˌʌɪsə(ʊ)ˈθəːməli
AM ˌaɪsəˈθərməli, ˌaɪsoʊˈθərməli

isotonic
BR ˌʌɪsə(ʊ)ˈtɒnɪk
AM ˌaɪsəˈtɑnɪk, ˌaɪsoʊˈtɑnɪk

isotonically
BR ˌʌɪsə(ʊ)ˈtɒnɨkli
AM ˌaɪsəˈtɑnək(ə)li, ˌaɪsoʊˈtɑnək(ə)li

isotonicity
BR ˌʌɪsə(ʊ)təˈnɪsɨti
AM ˌaɪsətəˈnɪsɨdi, ˌaɪsoʊtəˈnɪsɨdi

isotope
BR ˈʌɪsətəʊp, -s
AM ˈaɪsəˌtoʊp, ˈaɪsoʊˌtoʊp, -s

isotopic
BR ˌʌɪsə(ʊ)ˈtɒpɪk
AM ˌaɪsəˈtɑpɪk, ˌaɪsoʊˈtɑpɪk

isotopically
BR ˌʌɪsə(ʊ)ˈtɒpɨkli
AM ˌaɪsəˈtɑpək(ə)li, ˌaɪsoʊˈtɑpək(ə)li

isotopy
BR ʌɪˈsɒtəpi
AM ˈaɪsəˌtɑpi, ˈaɪsəˌtoʊpi, aɪˈsɑdəpi

isotropic
BR ˌʌɪsə(ʊ)ˈtrɒpɪk, ˌʌɪsə(ʊ)ˈtrəʊpɪk
AM ˌaɪsəˈtrɑpɪk, ˌaɪsoʊˈtrɑpɪk

isotropically
BR ˌʌɪsə(ʊ)ˈtrɒpɨkli, ˌʌɪsə(ʊ)ˈtrəʊpɨkli
AM ˌaɪsəˈtrɑpək(ə)li, ˌaɪsoʊˈtrɑpək(ə)li

isotropy
BR ʌɪˈsɒtrəpi
AM aɪˈsɑtrəpi

Ispahan
BR ˌɪspəˈhɑːn, ˈɪspəhɑːn
AM ˌɪspəˈhɑn

I-spy
BR ˌʌɪˈspʌɪ
AM ˌaɪˈspaɪ

Israel
BR ˈɪzreɪl
AM ˈɪzriəl, ˈɪzˌreɪl

Israeli
BR ɪzˈreɪl|i, -ɪz
AM ɪzˈreɪli, -z

Israelite
BR ˈɪzrəlʌɪt, -s
AM ˈɪzriəˌlaɪt, -s

Issachar
BR ˈɪsəkɑː(r)
AM ˈɪsəˌkɑr

Issigonis
BR ˌɪsɨˈɡəʊnɪs, ˌɪzɨˈɡəʊnɪs
AM ˌɪsɨˈɡoʊnəs

issuable
BR ˈɪʃ(j)ʊəbl, ˈɪsjʊəbl
AM ˈɪʃ(j)u(w)əbəl

issuance
BR ˈɪʃ(j)ʊəns, ˈɪsjʊəns, -ɪz
AM ˈɪʃ(j)u(w)əns, -əz

issuant
BR ˈɪʃ(j)ʊənt, ˈɪsjʊənt
AM ˈɪʃ(j)u(w)ənt

issue
BR ˈɪʃ(j)uː, ˈɪsjuː, -z, -ɪŋ, -d
AM ˈɪʃ(j)u, -z, -ɪŋ, -d

issueless
BR ˈɪʃ(j)uːləs, ˈɪsjuːləs
AM ˈɪʃ(j)uləs

issuer
BR ˈɪʃ(j)uːə(r), ˈɪsjuːə(r), -z
AM ˈɪʃ(j)u(w)ər, -z

Istanbul
BR ˌɪstanˈbʊl
AM ˌɪstænˌbʊl, ˌɪstæmˌbʊl

isthmian
BR ˈɪs(θ)mɪən
AM ˈɪsmiən

isthmus
BR ˈɪs(θ)məs, -ɪz
AM ˈɪsməs, -əz

istle
BR ˈɪstli
AM ˈɪs(t)li

Istria
BR ˈɪstrɪə(r)
AM ˈɪstriə

Istrian
BR ˈɪstrɪən, -z
AM ˈɪstriən, -z

it
BR ɪt
AM ɪt

Italian
BR ɨˈtaljən, -z
AM ɨˈtæljən, -z

Italianate
BR ɨˈtaljəneɪt
AM ɨˈtæljəˌneɪt

italic
BR ɨˈtalɪk, -s
AM ɨˈtælɪk, aɪˈtælɪk, -s

italicisation
BR ɨˌtalɨsʌɪˈzeɪʃn
AM ɨˌtæləsəˈzeɪʃən, aɪˌtæləsəˈzeɪʃən, ɨˌtæləˌsaɪˈzeɪʃən, aɪˌtæləˌsaɪˈzeɪʃən

italicise
BR ɨˈtalɨsʌɪz, -ɪz, -ɪŋ, -d
AM ɨˈtæləˌsaɪz, aɪˈtæləˌsaɪz, -ɪz, -ɪŋ, -d

italicization
BR ɨˌtalɨsʌɪˈzeɪʃn
AM əˌtæləsəˈzeɪʃən, aɪˌtæləsəˈzeɪʃən, ɨˌtæləˌsaɪˈzeɪʃən, aɪˌtæləˌsaɪˈzeɪʃən

italicize
BR ɨˈtalɨsʌɪz, -ɪz, -ɪŋ, -d
AM ɨˈtæləˌsaɪz, aɪˈtæləˌsaɪz, -ɪz, -ɪŋ, -d

Italiot
BR ɨˈtalɪət, -s
AM ɨˈtæliˌɑt, ɨˈtæliət, -s

Italy
BR ˈɪtəli, ˈɪtl̩i
AM ˈɪdəli

itch
BR ɪtʃ, -ɪz, -ɪŋ, -t
AM ɪtʃ, -ɪz, -ɪŋ, -t

Itchen
BR ˈɪtʃ(ɨ)n
AM ˈɪtʃɨn

itchiness
BR ˈɪtʃɪnɨs
AM ˈɪtʃinɨs

itchy
BR ˈɪtʃ|i, -ɪə(r), -ɪɨst
AM ˈɪtʃi, -ər, -ɨst

it'd
BR ˈɪtəd
AM ˈɪdɨd

item
BR ˈʌɪtɨm, -z
AM ˈaɪdəm, -z

itemisation
BR ˌʌɪtɨmʌɪˈzeɪʃn
AM ˌaɪdəməˈzeɪʃən, ˌaɪdəˌmaɪˈzeɪʃən

itemise
BR ˈʌɪtɨmʌɪz, -ɪz, -ɪŋ, -d
AM ˈaɪdəˌmaɪz, -ɪz, -ɪŋ, -d

itemiser
BR ˈʌɪtɨmʌɪzə(r), -z
AM ˈaɪdəˌmaɪzər, -z

itemization
BR ˌʌɪtɨmʌɪˈzeɪʃn
AM ˌaɪdəməˈzeɪʃən, ˌaɪdəˌmaɪˈzeɪʃən

itemize
BR ˈʌɪtɨmʌɪz, -ɪz, -ɪŋ, -d
AM ˈaɪdəˌmaɪz, -ɪz, -ɪŋ, -d

itemizer
BR ˈʌɪtɨmʌɪzə(r), -z
AM ˈaɪdəˌmaɪzər, -z

iterance
BR ˈɪt(ə)rəns, ˈɪt(ə)rn̩s, -ɪz
AM ˈɪdərəns, -əz

iterancy
BR ˈɪt(ə)rənsi, ˈɪt(ə)rn̩si
AM ˈɪdərənsi

iterate
BR ˈɪtəreɪt, -s, -ɪŋ, -ɨd
AM ˈɪdəˌreɪ|t, -ts, -dɪŋ, -dɨd

iteration
BR ˌɪtəˈreɪʃn, -z
AM ˌɪdəˈreɪʃən, -z

iterative
BR ˈɪt(ə)rətɪv
AM ˈɪdəˌreɪdɪv, ˈɪdərədɪv

iteratively
BR ˈɪt(ə)rətɨvli
AM ˈɪdəˌreɪdɨvli, ˈɪdərədɨvli

iterativeness
BR ˈɪt(ə)rətɨvnɨs
AM ˈɪdəˌreɪdɨvnɨs, ˈɪdərədɨvnɨs

iterativity
BR ˌɪt(ə)rəˈtɪvɪti
AM ˌɪd(ə)rəˈtɪvɨdi
Ithaca
BR ˈɪθəkə(r)
AM ˈɪθəkə
ithyphallic
BR ˌɪθɪˈfalɪk
AM ˌɪθəˈfælɪk
itineracy
BR ʌɪˈtɪn(ə)rəsi
AM aɪˈtɪn(ə)rəsi, ɨˈtɪn(ə)rəsi
itinerancy
BR ʌɪˈtɪn(ə)rənsi, ʌɪˈtɪn(ə)rn̩si
AM aɪˈtɪn(ə)rənsi, ɨˈtɪn(ə)rənsi
itinerant
BR ʌɪˈtɪn(ə)rənt, ʌɪˈtɪn(ə)rn̩t, -s
AM aɪˈtɪn(ə)rənt, ɨˈtɪn(ə)rənt, -s
itinerary
BR ʌɪˈtɪn(ə)rər|i, -ɪz
AM aɪˈtɪnəˌrɛri, ɨˈtɪnəˌrɛri, -z
itinerate
BR ʌɪˈtɪn(ə)reɪt, -s, -ɪŋ, -ɪd
AM aɪˈtɪnəˌreɪ|t, ɨˈtɪnəˌreɪ|t, -ts, -dɪŋ, -dɨd
itineration
BR ʌɪˌtɪnəˈreɪʃn, -z
AM aɪˌtɪnəˈreɪʃən, ɨˌtɪnəˈreɪʃən, -z
it'll
BR ˈɪtl
AM ˈɪdl
Ito
BR ˈiːtəʊ
AM ˈiˌdoʊ
its
BR ɪts
AM ɪts
it's
BR ɪts
AM ɪts
itself
BR ɪtˈsɛlf
AM ɨtˈsɛlf
itsy-bitsy
BR ˌɪtsɪˈbɪtsi
AM ˈˌɪtsiˈbɪtsi
itty-bitty
BR ˌɪtɪˈbɪti
AM ˈˌɪdiˈˌbɪdi
Ivan[1]
BR ˈʌɪvn
AM ˈaɪvən
Ivan[2]
foreign
BR ɪˈvan, ɪˈvɑːn
AM ˈaɪvən
Ivanhoe
BR ˈʌɪvnhəʊ
AM ˈaɪvənˌ(h)oʊ
I've
BR ʌɪv
AM aɪv
Iveagh
BR ˈʌɪvi, ˈʌɪveɪ
AM ˈaɪvi, ˈaɪveɪ
Iveco®
BR ɪˈveɪkəʊ
AM ɨˈveɪkoʊ
Ivens
BR ˈʌɪvnz
AM ˈaɪvənz
Iver
BR ˈʌɪvə(r)
AM ˈaɪvər
Ives
BR ʌɪvz
AM aɪvz
ivied
BR ˈʌɪvɪd
AM ˈaɪvid
Ivor
BR ˈʌɪvə(r)
AM ˈaɪvər
ivoried
BR ˈʌɪv(ə)rɪd
AM ˈaɪv(ə)rid
ivory
BR ˈʌɪv(ə)r|i, -ɪz
AM ˈaɪv(ə)ri, -z
ivy
BR ˈʌɪv|i, -ɪz, -ɪd
AM ˈaɪvi, -z, -d
Iwo Jima
BR ˌɪwə(ʊ) ˈdʒiːmə(r)
AM ˈˌɪwoʊ ˈdʒimə
ixia
BR ˈɪksɪə(r), -z
AM ˈɪksiə, -z
Ixion
BR ɪkˈsʌɪən
AM ˈɪksiˌɑn, ˈɪksiən
Iyar
BR ˈiːjɑː(r)
AM ˈiˌjɑr, ˈijər
Iyyar
BR ˈiːjɑː(r)
AM ˈiˌjɑr, ˈijər
izard
BR ˈɪzəd, -z
AM iˈzɑrd, -z
Izmir
BR ɪzˈmɪə(r)
AM ɪzˈmɪ(ə)r
Iznik
BR ˈɪznɪk
AM ˈɪznɪk
TU ɪzˈnɪk
Izvestia
BR ɪzˈvɛstɪə(r)
AM ɪzˈvɛstiə
RUS izˈvʲestʲijə
Izzard
BR ˈɪzɑːd, ˈɪzəd
AM ˈɪzərd
Izzy
BR ˈɪzi
AM ˈɪzi

Jj

j
BR dʒeɪ, -z
AM dʒeɪ, -z

jab
BR dʒab, -z, -ɪŋ, -d
AM dʒæb, -z, -ɪŋ, -d

Jabalpur
BR 'dʒablpʊə(r), 'dʒablpɔː(r)
AM 'dʒɑbəl,pʊ(ə)r

jabber
BR 'dʒab|ə(r), -əz, -(ə)rɪŋ, -əd
AM 'dʒæbər, -z, -ɪŋ, -d

jabberer
BR 'dʒab(ə)rə(r), -z
AM 'dʒæbərər, -z

jabberwock
BR 'dʒabəwɒk
AM 'dʒæbər,wɔk, 'dʒæbər,wɑk

jabberwocky
BR 'dʒabə,wɒki
AM 'dʒæbər,wɔki, 'dʒæbər,wɑki

Jabez
BR 'dʒeɪbɛz, 'dʒeɪbɪz
AM 'dʒeɪbɛz

jabiru
BR 'dʒabɪruː, ,dʒabɪ'ruː, -z
AM ',dʒæbə'ru, -z

jaborandi
BR ,dʒabə'rand|i, -ɪz
AM ,dʒæbə'rændi, -z

jabot
BR 'ʒabəʊ, -z
AM ʒæ'boʊ, 'ʒæ,boʊ, -z

jacana
BR 'dʒakənə(r), ,dʒasə'nɑː(r), -z
AM 'dʒækənə, -z

jacaranda
BR ,dʒakə'randə(r), -z
AM ,dʒækə'rændə, -z

Jacinta
BR dʒə'sɪntə(r)
AM dʒə'sɪn(t)ə

jacinth
BR 'dʒasɪnθ, 'dʒeɪsɪnθ, -s
AM 'dʒeɪsənθ, 'dʒæsənθ, -s

Jacintha
BR dʒə'sɪnθə(r)
AM dʒə'sɪnθə

jack
BR dʒak, -s, -ɪŋ, -t
AM dʒæk, -s, -ɪŋ, -t

jackal
BR 'dʒakl, -z
AM 'dʒækəl, -z

jackanapes
BR 'dʒakəneɪps
AM 'dʒækə,neɪps

jackaroo
BR ,dʒakə'ruː, -z
AM ,dʒækə'ru, -z

jackass
BR 'dʒakas, -ɪz
AM 'dʒæ,kæs, -əz

jackboot
BR 'dʒakbuːt, -s, -ɪd
AM 'dʒæk,bu|t, -ts, -dəd

jackdaw
BR 'dʒakdɔː(r), -z
AM 'dʒæk,dɔ, 'dʒæk,dɑ, -z

jackeroo
BR ,dʒakə'ruː, -z
AM ,dʒækə'ru, -z

jacket
BR 'dʒak|ɪt, -ɪts, -ɪtɪd
AM 'dʒækə|t, -ts, -dəd

jackfish
BR 'dʒakfɪʃ
AM 'dʒæk,fɪʃ

Jack Frost
BR ,dʒak 'frɒst
AM ',dʒæk 'frɔst, ',dʒæk 'frɑst

jackfruit
BR 'dʒakfruːt
AM 'dʒæk,frut

jackhammer
BR 'dʒak,hamə(r), -z
AM 'dʒæk,(h)æmər, -z

Jackie
BR 'dʒaki
AM 'dʒæki

jackknife
noun
BR 'dʒaknʌɪf
AM 'dʒæk,naɪf

jack-knife
verb
BR 'dʒaknʌɪf, -s, -ɪŋ, -t
AM 'dʒæk,naɪf, -s, -ɪŋ, -t

jackknives
noun
BR 'dʒaknʌɪvz
AM 'dʒæk,naɪvz

jackleg
BR 'dʒaklɛg, -z
AM 'dʒæk,lɛg, -z

jacklight
BR 'dʒaklʌɪt, -s
AM 'dʒæk,laɪt, -s

Jacklin
BR 'dʒaklɪn
AM 'dʒæklɪn

jack-o'-lantern
BR ,dʒakə'lantən, -z
AM 'dʒækə,læn(t)ərn, -z

jackpot
BR 'dʒakpɒt, -s
AM 'dʒæk,pɑt, -s

jackrabbit
BR 'dʒak,rabɪt, -s
AM 'dʒæk,ræbət, -s

Jack Russell
BR ,dʒak 'rʌsl, -z
AM ,dʒæk 'rəsəl, -z

jackscrew
BR 'dʒakskruː, -z
AM 'dʒæk,skru, -z

jackshaft
BR 'dʒakʃɑːft, 'dʒakʃaft, -s
AM 'dʒæk,ʃæf|t, -(t)s

jacksnipe
BR 'dʒaksnʌɪp, -s
AM 'dʒæk,snaɪp, -s

Jackson
BR 'dʒaksn
AM 'dʒæksən

Jacksonville
BR 'dʒaksnvɪl
AM 'dʒæksən,vɪl, 'dʒæksənvəl

jackstaff
BR 'dʒakstɑːf, 'dʒakstaf, -s
AM 'dʒæk,stæf, -s

jackstaves
BR 'dʒaksteɪvz
AM 'dʒæk,steɪvz

jackstone
BR 'dʒakstəʊn, -z
AM 'dʒæk,stoʊn, -z

jackstraw
BR 'dʒakstrɔː(r), -z
AM 'dʒæk,strɔ, 'dʒæk,strɑ, -z

Jacky
BR 'dʒaki
AM 'dʒæki

Jacob
BR 'dʒeɪkəb
AM 'dʒeɪkəb

Jacobean
BR ,dʒakə'biːən, -z
AM ',dʒækə'biən, ,dʒeɪkə'biən, -z

Jacobi
BR 'dʒakəbi, dʒə'kəʊbi
AM dʒə'koʊbi

Jacobin
BR 'dʒakəbɪn, -z
AM 'dʒækəbən, 'dʒeɪkəbən, -z

Jacobinic
BR ,dʒakə'bɪnɪk
AM ',dʒækə'bɪnɪk

Jacobinical
BR ,dʒakə'bɪnɪkl
AM ',dʒækə'bɪnɪkəl

Jacobinism
BR 'dʒakəbɪnɪz(ə)m
AM 'dʒækəbə,nɪzəm

Jacobite
BR 'dʒakəbʌɪt, -s
AM 'dʒækə,baɪt, 'dʒeɪkə,baɪt, -s

Jacobitical
BR ,dʒakə'bɪtɪkl
AM ',dʒækə'bɪdɪkəl

Jacobitism
BR 'dʒakəbɪtɪz(ə)m
AM 'dʒækə,baɪt,ɪzəm

Jacobs
BR 'dʒeɪkəbz
AM 'dʒeɪkəbz

Jacobson
BR 'dʒeɪkəbs(ə)n, 'jɑːkəbs(ə)n
AM 'dʒeɪkəbsən

jaconet
BR 'dʒakənɛt, -s
AM 'dʒækə,nɛt, ,dʒækə'nɛt, -s

Jacquard
BR 'dʒakɑːd, -z
AM 'dʒæ,kɑrd, dʒə'kɑrd, -z

Jacqueline
BR 'dʒak(ə)liːn, 'dʒakl̩iːn, 'dʒak(ə)lɪn, 'dʒakl̩ɪn
AM 'dʒæk(ə)lən, 'dʒækwələn

Jacquelyn
BR 'dʒak(ə)lɪn, 'dʒakl̩ɪn
AM 'dʒæk(ə)lən, 'dʒækwələn

jacquerie
BR 'dʒeɪk(ə)r|i, -ɪz
AM ,(d)ʒɑkə'ri, -z

Jacques
BR dʒeɪks, dʒaks, ʒak
AM ʒɑk, dʒæk

Jacqui
BR 'dʒaki
AM 'dʒæki, 'dʒeɪ,kwi

jactation
BR dʒak'teɪʃn
AM dʒæk'teɪʃən

jactitation
BR ,dʒaktɪ'teɪʃn
AM ,dʒæktə'teɪʃən

jacuzzi
BR dʒə'kuːz|i, -ɪz
AM dʒə'kuzi, -z

jade
BR dʒeɪd, -z, -ɪd
AM dʒeɪd, -z, -ɪd

jadedly
BR 'dʒeɪdɪdli
AM 'dʒeɪdɪdli

jadedness
BR 'dʒeɪdɪdnɪs
AM 'dʒeɪdɪdnɪs

jadeite
BR 'dʒeɪdʌɪt, -s
AM 'dʒeɪd,aɪt, -s

j'adoube
BR ʒa'duːb, ʒə'duːb
AM ʒɑ'dub

Jaeger®
BR 'jeɪgə(r)
AM 'jeɪgər, 'dʒægər

Jaffa
BR 'dʒafə(r), -z
AM 'dʒæfə, -z

Jaffna
BR 'dʒafnə(r)
AM 'dʒæfnə

jag
BR dʒag, -z, -ɪŋ, -d
AM dʒæg, -z, -ɪŋ, -d

jagged[1]
adjective
BR 'dʒagɨd
AM 'dʒægəd

jagged[2]
verb
BR dʒagd
AM dʒægd

jaggedly
BR 'dʒagɨdli
AM 'dʒægədli

jaggedness
BR 'dʒagɨdnɨs
AM 'dʒægədnəs

Jagger
BR 'dʒagə(r)
AM 'dʒægər

jagger
BR 'dʒagə(r), -z
AM 'dʒægər, -z

jagginess
BR 'dʒagɪnɨs
AM 'dʒæginɨs

jaggy
BR 'dʒag|i, -ɪə(r), -ɪɨst
AM 'dʒægi, -ər, -ɨst

Jago
BR 'dʒeɪgəʊ, 'jeɪgəʊ
AM 'dʒeɪˌgoʊ

jaguar
BR 'dʒagjʊə(r), -z
AM 'dʒægˌwɑr, -z

jaguarundi
BR ˌdʒagwə'rʌnd|i, ˌdʒagwɑː'rʌnd|i, -ɪz
AM ˌdʒægwə'rəndi, -z

jail
BR dʒeɪl, -z, -ɪŋ, -d
AM dʒeɪl, -z, -ɪŋ, -d

jailbait
BR 'dʒeɪlbeɪt
AM 'dʒeɪlˌbeɪt

jailbird
BR 'dʒeɪlbəːd, -z
AM 'dʒeɪlˌbərd, -z

jailbreak
BR 'dʒeɪlbreɪk, -s
AM 'dʒeɪlˌbreɪk, -s

jailer
BR 'dʒeɪlə(r), -z
AM 'dʒeɪlər, -z

jailhouse
BR 'dʒeɪlhaʊ|s, -zɪz
AM 'dʒeɪlˌ(h)aʊ|s, -zəz

Jain
BR dʒeɪn, -z
AM dʒeɪn, -z

Jainism
BR 'dʒeɪnɪz(ə)m
AM 'dʒeɪˌnɪzəm

Jainist
BR 'dʒeɪnɪst, -s
AM 'dʒeɪnɨst, -s

Jaipur
BR ˌdʒʌɪ'pʊə(r), ˌdʒʌɪ'pɔː(r)
AM 'dʒaɪˌpʊ(ə)r

Jakarta
BR dʒə'kɑːtə(r)
AM dʒə'kɑrdə

Jake
BR dʒeɪk
AM dʒeɪk

jake
BR dʒeɪk, -s
AM dʒeɪk, -s

Jalalabad
BR dʒə'lɑːləbad, dʒə'laləbad, dʒə'lɑːləbɑːd, dʒə'laləbɑːd
AM dʒə'lɑləˌbɑd, dʒə'læləˌbæd

jalap
BR 'dʒaləp, 'dʒɒləp
AM 'dʒɑləp

jalapeño
BR ˌhalə'peɪnjəʊ, ˌhalə'piːnjəʊ, -z
AM ˌhɑlə'peɪnjoʊ, ˌhɑlə'pinjoʊ, -z

jalopy
BR dʒə'lɒp|i, -ɪz
AM dʒə'lɑpi, -z

jalousie
BR 'ʒalʊziː, -z
AM 'dʒæləˌsi, -z

jam
BR dʒam, -z, -ɪŋ, -d
AM dʒæm, -z, -ɪŋ, -d

Jamaica
BR dʒə'meɪkə(r)
AM dʒə'meɪkə

Jamaican
BR dʒə'meɪk(ə)n, -z
AM dʒə'meɪkən, -z

Jamal
BR dʒə'mɑːl
AM dʒə'mɑl

jamb
BR dʒam, -z
AM dʒæm, -z

jambalaya
BR ˌdʒambə'lʌɪə(r), -z
AM ˌdʒæmbə'laɪə, -z

jamberoo
BR ˌdʒambə'ruː, -z
AM ˌdʒæmbə'ru, -z

jamboree
BR ˌdʒambə'riː, -z
AM ˌdʒæmbə'ri, -z

James
BR dʒeɪmz
AM dʒeɪmz

Jameson
BR 'dʒeɪms(ə)n
AM ˌ'dʒeɪm(ə)sən

Jamestown
BR 'dʒeɪmztaʊn
AM 'dʒeɪmˌstaʊn

Jamie
BR 'dʒeɪmi
AM 'dʒeɪmi

Jamieson
BR 'dʒeɪmɨs(ə)n
AM 'dʒeɪməsən

jammer
BR 'dʒamə(r), -z
AM 'dʒæmər, -z

jammies
BR 'dʒamɪz
AM 'dʒæmiz

jamminess
BR 'dʒamɪnɨs
AM 'dʒæminɨs

Jammu
BR 'dʒamuː, 'dʒʌmuː
AM 'dʒəmu

jammy
BR 'dʒam|i, -ɪə(r), -ɪɨst
AM 'dʒæmi, -ər, -ɨst

Jamshid
BR ˌdʒam'ʃiːd, 'dʒamʃiːd, ˌdʒam'ʃɪd, 'dʒamʃɪd
AM ˌ'dʒæmˌʃɪd

Jan[1]
English female forename
BR dʒan
AM dʒæn

Jan[2]
non-English male forename
BR jan
AM jɑn

Janáček
BR 'janətʃɛk, 'jɑːnətʃɛk
AM 'jɑnəˌtʃɛk, 'jænəˌtʃɛk
CZ 'jʌnɑːtʃɛk

Jancis
BR 'dʒansɪs
AM 'dʒænsəs

Jane
BR dʒeɪn
AM dʒeɪn

jane
BR dʒeɪn, -z
AM dʒeɪn, -z

Janet
BR 'dʒanɪt
AM 'dʒænət

Janette
BR dʒə'nɛt
AM dʒə'nɛt

Janey
BR 'dʒeɪni
AM 'dʒeɪni

jangle
BR 'dʒaŋg|l, -lz, -l̩ɪŋ\-lɪŋ, -ld
AM 'dʒæŋg|əl, -əlz, -(ə)lɪŋ, -əld

Janglish
BR 'dʒaŋglɪʃ
AM 'dʒæŋglɪʃ

Janice
BR 'dʒanɨs
AM 'dʒænəs

Janine
BR dʒə'niːn
AM dʒə'nin

Janis
BR 'dʒanɨs
AM 'dʒænəs

janissary
BR 'dʒanɨs(ə)r|i, -ɪz
AM 'dʒænəˌsɛri, -z

janitor
BR 'dʒanɨtə(r), -z
AM 'dʒænədər, -z

janitorial
BR ˌdʒanɪ'tɔːrɪəl
AM ˌ'dʒænə'tɔriəl

janizary
BR 'dʒanɨz(ə)r|i, -ɪz
AM 'dʒænəˌzɛri, -z

jankers
BR 'dʒaŋkəz
AM 'dʒæŋkərz

Jansen
BR 'dʒans(ə)n
AM 'dʒænsən

Jansenism
BR 'dʒansənɪz(ə)m, 'dʒansn̩ɪz(ə)m
AM 'dʒænsəˌnɪzəm

Jansenist
BR 'dʒansənɪst, 'dʒansn̩ɪst, -s
AM 'dʒænsənəst, -s

January
BR 'dʒanjʊər|i, 'dʒanjʊr|i, -ɪz
AM 'dʒænjəˌwɛri, -z

Janus
BR 'dʒeɪnəs
AM 'dʒeɪnəs

Jap
BR dʒap, -s
AM dʒæp, -s

Japan
BR dʒə'pan, -z, -ɪŋ, -d
AM dʒə'pæn, -z, -ɪŋ, -d

Japanese
BR ˌdʒapə'niːz
AM ˌdʒæpə'niz

jape
BR dʒeɪp, -s
AM dʒeɪp, -s

japery
BR 'dʒeɪp(ə)ri
AM 'dʒeɪp(ə)ri

Japheth
BR 'dʒeɪfɛθ, 'dʒeɪfɪθ

AM 'dʒeɪˌfɛθ

Japhetic
BR dʒə'fɛtɪk
AM dʒə'fɛdɪk

japonica
BR dʒə'pɒnɪkə(*r*), -z
AM dʒə'pɑnəkə, -z

Jaques[1]
general name
BR dʒeɪks
AM dʒeɪks

Jaques[2]
Shakespearian name
BR 'dʒeɪkwɪz
AM 'dʒeɪkwɪz

Jaques-Dalcroze
BR dʒeɪks ˌdal'krəʊz
AM dʒeɪks ˌdæl'kroʊz
FR ʒak dalkʀoz

jar
BR dʒɑː(r), -z, -ɪŋ, -d
AM dʒɑr, -z, -ɪŋ, -d

Jardine
BR 'dʒɑːdiːn, 'dʒɑːdʌɪn
AM dʒɑr'din

jardinière
BR ˌʒɑːdɪ'njɛː(r), -z
AM ˌdʒɑrdn'ɪ(ə)r, -z

jarful
BR 'dʒɑːfʊl, -z
AM 'dʒɑrˌfʊl, -z

jargon
BR 'dʒɑːg(ə)n
AM 'dʒɑrgən

jargonelle
BR ˌdʒɑːgə'nɛl, -z
AM ˌdʒɑrgə'nɛl, -z

jargonise
BR 'dʒɑːgənʌɪz, 'dʒɑːgn̩ʌɪz, -ɨz, -ɪŋ, -d
AM 'dʒɑrgəˌnaɪz, -ɨz, -ɪŋ, -d

jargonistic
BR ˌdʒɑːgə'nɪstɪk
AM ˌdʒɑrgə'nɪstɪk

jargonize
BR 'dʒɑːgənʌɪz, 'dʒɑːgn̩ʌɪz, -ɨz, -ɪŋ, -d
AM 'dʒɑrgəˌnaɪz, -ɨz, -ɪŋ, -d

jargoon
BR dʒɑː'guːn, -z
AM dʒɑr'gun, -z

Jarman
BR 'dʒɑːmən
AM 'dʒɑrmən

Jarndyce
BR 'dʒɑːndʌɪs
AM 'dʒɑrndəs, 'dʒɑrnˌdaɪs

jarrah
BR 'dʒarə(*r*), -z
AM 'dʒɛrə, -z

Jarratt
BR 'dʒarət
AM 'dʒɛrət

Jarrett
BR 'dʒarət
AM 'dʒɛrət

Jarrold
BR 'dʒarəld, 'dʒarl̩d
AM 'dʒɛrəld

Jarrow
BR 'dʒarəʊ
AM 'dʒɛroʊ

Jarvis
BR 'dʒɑːvɪs
AM 'dʒɑrvəs

jasmin
BR 'dʒasmɪn, 'dʒazmɪn, -z
AM 'dʒæzmən, -z

jasmine
BR 'dʒasmɪn, 'dʒazmɪn, -z
AM 'dʒæzmən, -z

Jason
BR 'dʒeɪsn
AM 'dʒeɪsən

jaspé
BR '(d)ʒaspeɪ
AM ʒæ'speɪ

jasper
BR 'dʒaspə(r)
AM 'dʒæspər

Jat
BR dʒɑːt, -s
AM dʒɑt, -s

Jataka
BR 'dʒɑːtəkə(*r*)
AM 'dʒɑdəkə

jati
BR 'dʒɑːt|i, -ɪz
AM 'dʒɑdi, -z

JATO
BR 'dʒeɪtəʊ
AM 'dʒeɪdoʊ, 'dzeɪˌtoʊ

jaundice
BR 'dʒɔːndɪs, -t
AM 'dʒɔndəs, 'dʒɑndəs, -t

jaunt
BR dʒɔːnt, -s, -ɪŋ, -ɨd
AM dʒɔn|t, dʒɑn|t, -ts, -(t)ɪŋ, -(t)əd

jauntily
BR 'dʒɔːntɨli
AM 'dʒɔn(t)əli, 'dʒɑn(t)əli

jauntiness
BR 'dʒɔːntɪnɨs
AM 'dʒɔn(t)inɨs, 'dʒɑn(t)inɨs

jaunty
BR 'dʒɔːnt|i, -ɪə(r), -ɪɨst
AM 'dʒɔn(t)i, 'dʒɑn(t)i, -ər, -ɨst

Java
BR 'dʒɑːvə(*r*)
AM 'dʒɑvə

Javan
BR 'dʒɑːvn, -z
AM 'dʒɑvən, -z

Javanese
BR ˌdʒɑːvə'niːz
AM ˌdʒɑvə'niz

javelin
BR 'dʒav(ə)lɪn, -z
AM 'dʒæv(ə)lən, -z

Javelle water
BR dʒə'vɛl ˌwɔːtə(r)
AM dʒə'vɛl ˌwɔdər, + ˌwɑdər

jaw
BR dʒɔː(*r*), -z, -ɪŋ, -d
AM dʒɔ, dʒɑ, -z, -ɪŋ, -d

jawbone
BR 'dʒɔːbəʊn, -z
AM 'dʒɔˌboʊn, 'dʒɑˌboʊn, -z

jawbreaker
BR 'dʒɔːˌbreɪkə(r), -z
AM 'dʒɔˌbreɪkər, 'dʒɑˌbreɪkər, -z

jawline
BR 'dʒɔːlʌɪn, -z
AM 'dʒɔˌlaɪn, 'dʒɑˌlaɪn, -z

jay
BR dʒeɪ, -z
AM dʒeɪ, -z

jaybird
BR 'dʒeɪbəːd, -z
AM 'dʒeɪˌbərd, -z

Jaycee
BR ˌdʒeɪ'siː, -z
AM ˌdʒeɪ'si, -z

Jayne
BR dʒeɪn
AM dʒeɪn

jaywalk
BR 'dʒeɪwɔːk, -s, -ɪŋ, -d
AM 'dʒeɪˌwɔk, 'dʒeɪˌwɑk, -s, -ɪŋ, -d

jaywalker
BR 'dʒeɪˌwɔːkə(r), -z
AM 'dʒeɪˌwɔkər, 'dʒeɪˌwɑkər, -z

jazz
BR dʒaz, -ɨz, -ɪŋ, -d
AM dʒæz, -əz, -ɪŋ, -t

jazzband
BR 'dʒazband, -z
AM 'dʒæzˌbænd, -z

jazzer
BR 'dʒazə(r), -z
AM 'dʒæzər, -z

jazzily
BR 'dʒazɨli
AM 'dʒæzəli

jazziness
BR 'dʒazɪnɨs
AM 'dʒæzinɨs

jazzman
BR 'dʒazman
AM 'dʒæzmən, 'dʒæzˌmæn

jazzmen
BR 'dʒazmɛn
AM 'dʒæzmən, 'dʒæzˌmɛn

jazzy
BR 'dʒaz|i, -ɪə(r), -ɪɨst
AM 'dʒæzi, -ər, -ɨst

J-cloth®
BR 'dʒeɪ klɒ|θ, -θs\-ðz
AM 'dʒeɪ ˌklɔ|θ, 'dʒeɪ ˌklɑ|θ, -θs\-ðz

jealous
BR 'dʒɛləs
AM 'dʒɛləs

jealously
BR 'dʒɛləsli
AM 'dʒɛləsli

jealousness
BR 'dʒɛləsnəs
AM 'dʒɛləsnəs

jealousy
BR 'dʒɛləs|i, -ɪz
AM 'dʒɛləsi, -z

Jean[1]
female forename
BR dʒiːn
AM dʒin

Jean[2]
male forename
BR ʒɒ̃
AM dʒin, ʒɔn, ʒɑn

jean
BR dʒiːn, -z
AM dʒin, -z

Jeanette
BR dʒɪ'nɛt
AM dʒə'nɛt

Jeanie
BR 'dʒiːni
AM 'dʒini

Jeanne d'Arc
BR (d)ʒan 'dɑːk
AM (d)ʒɑn 'dɑrk

Jeannette
BR dʒɪ'nɛt
AM dʒə'nɛt

Jeannie
BR 'dʒiːni
AM 'dʒini

Jeannine
BR dʒɪ'niːn
AM dʒə'nin

Jeans
BR dʒiːnz
AM dʒinz

Jeavons
BR 'dʒɛvnz
AM 'dʒɛvəns

Jedah
BR 'dʒɛdə(*r*)
AM 'dʒɛdə

Jedburgh
BR 'dʒɛdb(ə)rə(*r*)
AM 'dʒɛdbərə

Jeddah
BR 'dʒɛdə(*r*)
AM 'dʒɛdə

Jeep®
BR dʒiːp, -s
AM dʒip, -s

jeepers
BR 'dʒiːpəz
AM 'dʒipərz

jeer
BR dʒɪə(r), -z, -ɪŋ, -d
AM dʒɪ(ə)r, -z, -ɪŋ, -d

jeeringly
BR 'dʒɪərɪŋli
AM 'dʒɪrɪŋli

Jeeves
BR dʒiːvz
AM dʒivz

jeez
BR dʒiːz
AM dʒiz

Jeff
BR dʒɛf
AM dʒɛf

Jefferies
BR 'dʒɛfrɪz
AM 'dʒɛfriz

Jefferson
BR 'dʒɛfəs(ə)n
AM 'dʒɛfərsən

Jeffery
BR 'dʒɛfri
AM 'dʒɛfri

Jeffrey
BR 'dʒɛfri
AM 'dʒɛfri

Jeffreys
BR 'dʒɛfrɪz
AM 'dʒɛfriz

jehad
BR dʒɪ'had, dʒɪ'hɑːd, -z
AM dʒə'hæd, dʒə'hɑd, -z

Jehoshaphat
BR dʒɪ'hɒʃəfat, dʒɪ'hɒsəfat
AM dʒə'hɑsəˌfæt

Jehovah
BR dʒɪ'həʊvə(r)
AM dʒə'hoʊvə

Jehovist
BR dʒɪ'həʊvɪst, -s
AM dʒə'hoʊvəst, -s

Jehu
BR 'dʒiːhjuː
AM 'dʒiˌh(j)u

jejune
BR dʒɪ'dʒuːn
AM dʒə'dʒun

jejunely
BR dʒɪ'dʒuːnli
AM dʒə'dʒunli

jejuneness
BR dʒɪ'dʒuːnnəs
AM dʒə'dʒu(n)nəs

jejunum
BR dʒɪ'dʒuːnəm
AM dʒə'dʒunəm

Jekyll
BR 'dʒɛkl, 'dʒiːk(ɪ)l
AM 'dʒɛkəl

jell
BR dʒɛl, -z, -ɪŋ, -d
AM dʒɛl, -z, -ɪŋ, -d

jellaba
BR 'dʒɛləbə(r), dʒɪ'lɑːbə(r), -z
AM 'dʒɛləbə, -z

jellabah
BR 'dʒɛləbə(r), dʒɪ'lɑːbə(r), -z
AM 'dʒɛləbə, -z

Jellicoe
BR 'dʒɛlɪkəʊ
AM 'dʒɛləkoʊ

jellification
BR ˌdʒɛlɪfɪ'keɪʃn
AM ˌdʒɛləfə'keɪʃən

jellify
BR 'dʒɛlɪfʌɪ, -z, -ɪŋ, -d
AM 'dʒɛləˌfaɪ, -z, -ɪŋ, -d

jello
BR 'dʒɛləʊ
AM 'dʒɛloʊ

jelly
BR 'dʒɛl|i, -ɪz, -ɪɪŋ, -ɪd
AM 'dʒɛli, -z, -ɪŋ, -d

jellyfish
BR 'dʒɛlɪfɪʃ, -ɪz
AM 'dʒɛliˌfɪʃ, -ɪz

Jem
BR dʒɛm
AM dʒɛm

Jemima
BR dʒɪ'mʌɪmə(r)
AM dʒə'maɪmə

Jemma
BR 'dʒɛmə(r)
AM 'dʒɛmə

jemmy
BR 'dʒɛm|i, -ɪz, -ɪɪŋ, -ɪd
AM 'dʒɛmi, -z, -ɪŋ, -d

Jena
BR 'jeɪnə(r)
AM 'jeɪnə

je ne sais quoi
BR ˌʒə nə seɪ 'kwɑː(r)
AM ˌʒə nə seɪ 'kwɑ

Jenifer
BR 'dʒɛnɪfə(r)
AM 'dʒɛnəfər

Jenkin
BR 'dʒɛŋkɪn
AM 'dʒɛŋkən

Jenkins
BR 'dʒɛŋkɪnz
AM 'dʒɛŋkənz

Jenkinson
BR 'dʒɛŋkɪns(ə)n
AM 'dʒɛŋkənsən

Jenna
BR 'dʒɛnə(r)
AM 'dʒɛnə

Jenner
BR 'dʒɛnə(r)
AM 'dʒɛnər

jennet
BR 'dʒɛnɪt, -s
AM 'dʒɛnət, -s

Jennifer
BR 'dʒɛnɪfə(r)
AM 'dʒɛnəfər

Jennings
BR 'dʒɛnɪŋz
AM 'dʒɛnɪŋz

jenny
BR 'dʒɛn|i, -ɪz
AM 'dʒɛni, -z

Jensen[1]
foreign name
BR 'jɛnsn
AM 'jɛnsən

Jensen[2]
BR 'dʒɛnsn
AM 'dʒɛnsən

jeon
BR 'dʒiːɒn
AM 'dʒiˌɑn

jeopardise
BR 'dʒɛpədʌɪz, -ɪz, -ɪŋ, -d
AM 'dʒɛpərˌdaɪz, -ɪz, -ɪŋ, -d

jeopardize
BR 'dʒɛpədʌɪz, -ɪz, -ɪŋ, -d
AM 'dʒɛpərˌdaɪz, -ɪz, -ɪŋ, -d

jeopardy
BR 'dʒɛpədi
AM 'dʒɛpərdi

Jephthah
BR 'dʒɛfθə(r)
AM 'dʒɛfˌtɑ

jequirity
BR dʒɪ'kwɪrɪti, -ɪz
AM dʒə'kwɪrɪdi, -z

Jerba
BR 'dʒəːbə(r)
AM 'dʒərbə

jerbil
BR 'dʒəːb(ɪ)l, -z
AM 'dʒərbəl, -z

jerboa
BR dʒəː'bəʊə(r), dʒə'bəʊə(r), -z
AM dʒər'boʊə, -z

jeremiad
BR ˌdʒɛrɪ'mʌɪəd, ˌdʒɛrɪ'mʌɪad, -z
AM ˌdʒɛrə'maɪəd, ˌdʒɛrə'maɪˌæd, -z

Jeremiah
BR ˌdʒɛrɪ'mʌɪə(r), -z
AM ˌdʒɛrə'maɪə, -z

Jeremy
BR 'dʒɛrɪmi
AM 'dʒɛrəmi

Jerez
BR hɛ'rɛθ
AM hɛ'rɛs, hɛ'rɛθ
SP xe'reθ, xe'res

Jericho
BR 'dʒɛrɪkəʊ
AM 'dʒɛrəˌkoʊ

jerk
BR dʒəːk, -s, -ɪŋ, -t
AM dʒərk, -s, -ɪŋ, -t

jerker
BR 'dʒəːkə(r), -z
AM 'dʒərkər, -z

jerkily
BR 'dʒəːkɪli
AM 'dʒərkəli

jerkin
BR 'dʒəːkɪn, -z
AM 'dʒərkən, -z

jerkiness
BR 'dʒəːkɪnɪs
AM 'dʒərkinɪs

jerky
BR 'dʒəːk|i, -ɪə(r), -ɪɪst
AM 'dʒərki, -ər, -ɪst

Jermaine
BR dʒə'meɪn
AM dʒər'meɪn

Jermyn
BR 'dʒəːmɪn
AM 'dʒərmən

jeroboam
BR ˌdʒɛrə'bəʊəm, -z
AM ˌdʒɛrə'boʊəm, -z

Jerome
BR dʒɪ'rəʊm, dʒɛ'rəʊm
AM dʒə'roʊm

jerry
BR 'dʒɛr|i, -ɪz
AM 'dʒɛri, -z

jerrycan
BR 'dʒɛrɪkan, -z
AM 'dʒɛriˌkæn, -z

jerrymander
BR 'dʒɛrɪmand|ə(r), ˌdʒɛrɪ'mand|ə(r), -əz, -(ə)rɪŋ, -əd
AM 'dʒɛriˌmænd|ər, -ərz, -(ə)rɪŋ, -ərd

jersey
BR 'dʒəːz|i, -ɪz
AM 'dʒərzi, -z

Jerusalem
BR dʒɪ'ruːs(ə)ləm
AM dʒə'rus(ə)ləm

Jervaulx[1]
placename
BR 'dʒəːvəʊ
AM 'dʒərvoʊ

Jervaulx[2]
surname
BR 'dʒəːvɪs
AM 'dʒərvəs

Jervis
BR 'dʒəːvɪs
AM 'dʒərvəs

Jespersen
BR 'jɛspəs(ə)n, 'dʒɛspəs(ə)n
AM 'dzɛspərsən, 'jɛspərsən

jess
BR dʒɛs, -ɪz, -ɪŋ, -t
AM dʒɛs, -əz, -ɪŋ, -t

jessamin
BR 'dʒɛsəmɪn, -z
AM 'dʒɛz(ə)mən, -z

jesse
BR 'dʒɛs|i, -ɪz
AM 'dʒɛs, -z

Jessel
BR 'dʒɛsl
AM 'dʒɛsəl

Jessica
BR 'dʒɛsɨkə(r)
AM 'dʒɛsəkə

Jessie
BR 'dʒɛsi
AM 'dʒɛsi

Jessop
BR 'dʒɛsəp
AM 'dʒɛsəp

jest
BR dʒɛst, -s, -ɪŋ, -ɨd
AM dʒɛst, -s, -ɪŋ, -əd

jester
BR 'dʒɛstə(r), -z
AM 'dʒɛstər, -z

jestful
BR 'dʒɛs(t)fʊl
AM 'dʒɛs(t)fəl

Jesu[1]
when singing
BR 'dʒiːzjuː, 'jeɪzuː, 'jeɪsuː
AM 'dʒeɪzu

Jesu[2]
BR 'dʒiːzjuː
AM 'dʒizu

Jesuit
BR 'dʒɛzjʊɪt, 'dʒɛʒʊɪt, -s
AM 'dʒɛʒəwət, 'dʒɛzəwət, -s

jesuitic
BR ˌdʒɛzjʊ'ɪtɪk, ˌdʒɛʒʊ'ɪtɪk
AM ¦dʒɛʒə'wɪdɪk

Jesuitical
BR ˌdʒɛzjʊ'ɪtɨkl, ˌdʒɛʒʊ'ɪtɨkl
AM ¦dʒɛʒə'wɪdɨkəl

Jesuitically
BR ˌdʒɛzjʊ'ɪtɨkli, ˌdʒɛʒʊ'ɪtɨkli
AM ¦dʒɛʒə'wɪdɨk(ə)li

Jesus
BR 'dʒiːzəs
AM 'dʒizəs

jet
BR dʒɛt, -s, -ɪŋ, -ɨd
AM dʒɛ|t, -ts, -dɪŋ, -dəd

jeté
BR 'ʒɛteɪ, -z
AM ʒə'teɪ, -z

jetfoil
BR 'dʒɛtfɔɪl, -z
AM 'dʒɛtˌfɔɪl, -z

Jethro
BR 'dʒɛθrəʊ
AM 'dʒɛθroʊ

jetlag
BR 'dʒɛtlag, -d
AM 'dʒɛtˌlæg, -d

jetliner
BR 'dʒɛtˌlʌɪnə(r), -z
AM 'dʒɛtˌlaɪnə(r), -z

jeton
BR 'dʒɛt(ə)n, -z
AM 'dʒɛtn, ʒə'tɑn, -z

jetsam
BR 'dʒɛts(ə)m
AM 'dʒɛtsəm

jetstream
BR 'dʒɛtstriːm
AM 'dʒɛtˌstrim

jettison
BR 'dʒɛtɨs|(ə)n, 'dʒɛtɨz|(ə)n, -(ə)nz, -n̩ɪŋ\-ənɪŋ, -(ə)nd
AM 'dʒɛdəsən, 'dʒɛdəzən, -z, -ɪŋ, -d

jetton
BR 'dʒɛt(ə)n, -z
AM 'dʒɛtn, ʒə'tɑn, -z

jetty
BR 'dʒɛt|i, -ɪz
AM 'dʒɛdi, -z

jeu
BR ʒəː(r), -z
AM ʒə, -z

jeu d'esprit
BR ˌʒəː dɛ'spriː
AM ˌʒə də'spri

jeunesse dorée
BR ʒəːˌnɛs dɔː'reɪ, ˌʒəːnɛs 'dɔːreɪ
AM ʒəˌnɛs də'reɪ, + dɔ'reɪ

jeux d'esprit
BR ˌʒəː dɛ'spriː
AM ˌʒə(z) də'spri

Jevons
BR 'dʒɛvnz
AM 'dʒɛvənz

Jew
BR dʒuː, -z
AM dʒu, -z

jewel
BR 'dʒuː(ə)l, -z, -d
AM 'dʒu(ə)l, -z, -d

jeweler
BR 'dʒuː(ə)lə(r), -z
AM 'dʒu(ə)lər, -z

Jewell
BR 'dʒuː(ə)l
AM 'dʒu(ə)l

jeweller
BR 'dʒuː(ə)lə(r), -z
AM 'dʒu(ə)lər, -z

jewellery
BR 'dʒuː(ə)lri
AM 'dʒu(ə)lri

jewelly
BR 'dʒuːəli
AM 'dʒu(ə)li

jewelry
BR 'dʒuː(ə)lri
AM 'dʒu(ə)lri

Jewess
BR 'dʒuːɛs, 'dʒuːɪs, dʒuː'ɛs, -ɨz
AM 'dʒuəs, -əz

jewfish
BR 'dʒuːfɪʃ, -ɨz
AM 'dʒuˌfɪʃ, -ɨz

Jewish
BR 'dʒuːɪʃ
AM 'dʒuɪʃ

Jewishly
BR 'dʒuːɨʃli
AM 'dʒuəʃli

Jewishness
BR 'dʒuːɨʃnɨs
AM 'dʒuɪʃnɨs

Jewry
BR 'dʒʊəri
AM 'dʒuri

Jewson
BR 'dʒuːsn
AM 'dʒusən

Jeyes
BR dʒeɪz
AM dʒeɪz

jezail
BR dʒɨ'zʌɪl, dʒɨ'zeɪl, -z
AM dʒə'zaɪ(ə)l, dʒə'zeɪl, -z

Jezebel
BR 'dʒɛzəbɛl, -z
AM 'dʒɛzəˌbɛl, 'dʒɛzəbəl, -z

Jezreel
BR 'dʒɛzrɪəl, dʒɛz'riːl
AM ¦dʒɛz'ril

jib
BR dʒɪb, -z, -ɪŋ, -d
AM dʒɪb, -z, -ɪŋ, -d

jibba
BR 'dʒɪbə(r), -z
AM 'dʒɪbə, -z

jibbah
BR 'dʒɪbə(r), -z
AM 'dʒɪbə, -z

jibber
BR 'dʒɪb|ə(r), -əz, -(ə)rɪŋ, -əd
AM 'dʒɪb|ər, -ərz, -(ə)rɪŋ, -ərd

jibe
BR dʒʌɪb, -z, -ɪŋ, -d
AM dʒaɪb, -z, -ɪŋ, -d

Jibuti
BR dʒɨ'buːti
AM dʒɪ'budi

JICTAR
BR 'dʒɪktɑː(r)
AM 'dʒɪkˌtɑr

Jiddah
BR 'dʒɪdə(r)
AM 'dʒɪdə

Jif®
BR dʒɪf
AM dʒɪf

jiff
BR dʒɪf, -s
AM dʒɪf, -s

jiffy
BR 'dʒɪf|i, -ɪz
AM 'dʒɪfi, -z

jig
BR dʒɪg, -z, -ɪŋ, -d
AM dʒɪg, -z, -ɪŋ, -d

jigaboo
BR 'dʒɪgəbuː, -z
AM 'dʒɪgəˌbu, -z

jigger
BR 'dʒɪgə(r), -z, -d
AM 'dʒɪgər, -z, -d

jiggery-pokery
BR ˌdʒɪg(ə)rɪ'pəʊk(ə)ri
AM ¦dʒɪgərɪ¦poʊkərɪ

jiggle
BR 'dʒɪg|l, -lz, -lɪŋ\-lɪŋ, -ld
AM 'dʒɪg|əl, -əlz, -(ə)lɪŋ, -əld

jiggly
BR 'dʒɪgl̩i, 'dʒɪgli
AM 'dʒɪg(ə)li

jigot
BR 'dʒɪgət, -s
AM 'dʒɪgət, -s

jigsaw
BR 'dʒɪgsɔː(r), -z
AM 'dʒɪgˌsɔ, 'dʒɪgˌsɑ, -z

jihad
BR dʒɨ'had, dʒɨ'hɑːd, -z
AM dʒə'hæd, dʒə'hɑd, -z

jill
BR dʒɪl, -z
AM dʒɪl, -z

jillaroo
BR ˌdʒɪlə'ruː, -z
AM ˌdʒɪlə'ru, -z

jilleroo
BR ˌdʒɪlə'ruː, -z
AM ˌdʒɪlə'ru, -z

Jillian
BR 'dʒɪlɪən
AM 'dʒɪliən, 'dʒɪljən

jillion
BR 'dʒɪljən, -z
AM 'dʒɪljən, -z

jilt
BR dʒɪlt, -s, -ɪŋ, -ɨd
AM dʒɪlt, -s, -ɪŋ, -ɨd

Jim
BR dʒɪm
AM dʒɪm

Jim Crowism
BR ˌdʒɪm 'krəʊɪz(ə)m
AM 'dʒɪm 'kroʊˌɪzəm

jim-dandy
BR ˌdʒɪm'dandi
AM ¦dʒɪm'dændi

Jiménez
BR 'hɪmɪnɛz, hɪ'mɛnɛz
AM hɨ'mænɛz, 'hɪmənɛz

SP xi'meneθ, xi'menes

jiminy
BR 'dʒɪmɨni
AM 'dʒɪməni

jimjams
BR 'dʒɪmdʒamz
AM 'dʒɪm,dʒæmz

Jimmi
BR 'dʒɪmi
AM 'dʒɪmi

Jimmie
BR 'dʒɪmi
AM 'dʒɪmi

jimmy
BR 'dʒɪm|i, -ɪz, -ɪɪŋ, -ɪd
AM 'dʒɪmi, -z, -ɪŋ, -d

jimmygrant
BR 'dʒɪmɪgrɑːnt, 'dʒɪmɪgrant, -s
AM 'dʒɪmi,grænt, -s

jimpson
BR 'dʒɪm(p)s(ə)n, -z
AM 'dʒɪmsən, -z

jimson
BR 'dʒɪms(ə)n, -z
AM 'dʒɪmsən, -z

Jin
BR dʒɪn
AM dʒɪn

Jinan
BR ,dʒɪ'nan
AM ˌdʒɪ'næn

jingle
BR 'dʒɪŋg|l, -lz, -l̩ɪŋ\-lɪŋ, -ld
AM 'dʒɪŋg|əl, -əlz, -(ə)lɪŋ, -əld

jingly
BR 'dʒɪŋgl|i, -ɪə(r), -ɪɪst
AM 'dʒɪŋli, -ər, -ɪst

jingo
BR 'dʒɪŋgəʊ
AM 'dʒɪŋgoʊ

jingoism
BR 'dʒɪŋgəʊɪz(ə)m
AM 'dʒɪŋgoʊ,ɪzəm

jingoist
BR 'dʒɪŋgəʊɪst, -s
AM 'dʒɪŋgoʊəst, -s

jingoistic
BR ,dʒɪŋgəʊ'ɪstɪk
AM ,dʒɪŋgoʊ'ɪstɪk

jink
BR dʒɪŋ|k, -ks, -kɪŋ, -(k)t
AM dʒɪŋ|k, -ks, -kɪŋ, -(k)t

jinker
BR 'dʒɪŋkə(r), -z
AM 'dʒɪŋkər, -z

jinks
BR dʒɪŋks
AM dʒɪŋks

jinn
BR dʒɪn, -z
AM dʒɪn, -z

Jinnah
BR 'dʒɪnə(*r*)
AM 'dʒɪnə

jinnee
BR 'dʒɪn|i, -ɪz
AM 'dʒɪni, -z

jinni
BR 'dʒɪn|i, -ɪz
AM 'dʒɪni, -z

Jinnie
BR 'dʒɪni
AM 'dʒɪni

Jinny
BR 'dʒɪni
AM 'dʒɪni

jinricksha
BR dʒɪn'rɪkʃə(*r*), dʒɪn'rɪkʃɔː(*r*), -z
AM ,dʒɪn'rɪkʃɔ, ,dʒɪn'rɪkʃɑ, -z

jinrickshaw
BR dʒɪn'rɪkʃɔː(*r*), -z
AM ,dʒɪn'rɪkʃɔ, ,dʒɪn'rɪkʃɑ, -z

jinx
BR dʒɪŋks, -ɨz, -ɪŋ, -t
AM dʒɪŋks, -ɨz, -ɪŋ, -t

jipijapa
BR ,hiːpɪ'hɑːpə(*r*), -z
AM ˌhipi'hɑpə, -z

jitney
BR 'dʒɪtn|i, -ɪz
AM 'dʒɪtni, -z

jitter
BR 'dʒɪt|ə(r), -əz, -(ə)rɪŋ, -əd
AM 'dʒɪdər, -z, -ɪŋ, -d

jitterbug
BR 'dʒɪtəbʌg, -z, -ɪŋ, -d
AM 'dʒɪdər,bəg, -z, -ɪŋ, -d

jitteriness
BR 'dʒɪt(ə)rɪnɨs
AM 'dʒɪdərinɨs

jittery
BR 'dʒɪt(ə)ri
AM 'dʒɪdəri

jiujitsu
BR ,dʒuː'dʒɪtsuː
AM ,dʒu'dʒɪtsu

Jivaro
BR 'hiːvərəʊ, -z
AM 'jivəroʊ, -z

jive
BR dʒʌɪv, -z, -ɪŋ, -d
AM dʒaɪv, -z, -ɪŋ, -d

jiver
BR 'dʒʌɪvə(r), -z
AM 'dʒaɪvər, -z

jizz
BR dʒɪz
AM dʒɪz

Jnr
BR 'dʒuːnɪə(r)
AM 'dʒunjər

jo
BR dʒəʊ, -z
AM dʒoʊ, -z

Joachim
BR 'dʒəʊəkɪm
AM wɑ'kim, 'dʒoʊə,kɪm

Joan
BR dʒəʊn
AM dʒoʊn

Joanna
BR dʒəʊ'anə(*r*)
AM dʒoʊ'ænə, dʒə'wænə

Joanne
BR dʒəʊ'an
AM dʒoʊ'æn, dʒə'wæn

Joan of Arc
BR ,dʒəʊn əv 'ɑːk
AM 'dʒoʊn əv 'ɑrk

Job
name
BR dʒəʊb
AM dʒoʊb

job
BR dʒɒb, -z, -ɪŋ
AM dʒɑb, -z, -ɪŋ

jobber
BR 'dʒɒbə(r), -z
AM 'dʒɑbər, -z

jobbery
BR 'dʒɒb(ə)ri
AM 'dʒɑbəri

jobcentre
BR 'dʒɒb,sɛntə(r), -z
AM 'dʒɑb,sɛn(t)ər, -z

jobholder
BR 'dʒɒb,həʊldə(r), -z
AM 'dʒɑb,(h)oʊldər, -z

jobless
BR 'dʒɒbləs
AM 'dʒɑbləs

joblessness
BR 'dʒɒbləsnəs
AM 'dʒɑbləsnəs

Jobling
BR 'dʒɒblɪŋ
AM 'dʒɑblɪŋ

Job's comforter
BR ,dʒəʊbz 'kʌmfətə(r), -z
AM ,dʒoʊbz 'kəmfərdər, -z

jobsheet
BR 'dʒɒbʃiːt, -s
AM 'dʒɑb,ʃit, -s

jobsworth
BR 'dʒɒbzwəːθ, 'dʒɒbzwəθ, -s
AM 'dʒɑbz,wər|θ, -θs\-ðz

Jo'burg
BR 'dʒəʊbəːg
AM 'dʒoʊ,bərg

jobwork
BR 'dʒɒbwəːk
AM 'dʒɑb,wərk

Jocasta
BR dʒə(ʊ)'kastə(*r*)
AM dʒoʊ'kæstə

Jocelyn
BR 'dʒɒs(ə)lɪn, 'dʒɒsl̩ɪn
AM 'dʒɑs(ə)lən

jock
BR dʒɒk, -s
AM dʒɑk, -s

jockey
BR 'dʒɒk|i, -ɪz, -ɪɪŋ, -ɪd
AM 'dʒɑki, -z, -ɪŋ, -d

jockeydom
BR 'dʒɒkɪdəm
AM 'dʒɑkidəm

jockeyship
BR 'dʒɒkɪʃɪp
AM 'dʒɑki,ʃɪp

jockstrap
BR 'dʒɒkstrap, -s
AM 'dʒɑk,stræp, -s

jocose
BR dʒə(ʊ)'kəʊs
AM dʒoʊ'koʊs

jocosely
BR dʒə(ʊ)'kəʊsli
AM dʒoʊ'koʊsli

jocoseness
BR dʒə(ʊ)'kəʊsnəs
AM dʒoʊ'koʊsnəs

jocosity
BR dʒə(ʊ)'kɒsɨti
AM dʒoʊ'kɑsədi

jocular
BR 'dʒɒkjʉlə(r)
AM 'dʒɑkjələr

jocularity
BR ,dʒɒkjʉ'larɪt|i, -ɪz
AM ,dʒɑkjə'lɛrədi, -z

jocularly
BR 'dʒɒkjʉləli
AM 'dʒɑkjələrli

jocund
BR 'dʒɒk(ə)nd, 'dʒɒkʌnd, 'dʒəʊk(ə)nd, 'dʒəʊkʌnd
AM 'dʒɑkənd, 'dʒoʊkənd

jocundity
BR dʒə'kʌndɨti, dʒɒ'kʌndɨti, dʒəʊ'kʌndɨti
AM dʒɑ'kəndədi, dʒoʊ'kəndədi

jocundly
BR 'dʒɒk(ə)ndli, 'dʒɒkʌndli, 'dʒəʊk(ə)ndli, 'dʒəʊkʌndli
AM 'dʒɑkən(d)li, 'dʒoʊkən(d)li

jocundness
BR 'dʒɒk(ə)n(d)nəs, 'dʒɒkʌn(d)nəs, 'dʒəʊk(ə)n(d)nəs, 'dʒəʊkʌn(d)nəs
AM 'dʒɑkən(d)nəs, 'dʒoʊkən(d)nəs

jodel
BR ˈjəʊd|l, -lz, -l̩ɪŋ\-lɪŋ, -ld
AM ˈjoʊd|əl, -əlz, -(ə)lɪŋ, -əld

Jodhpur
BR ˈdʒɒdpʊə(r), ˈdʒɒdpɔː(r)
AM ˈdʒɑdpər

jodhpurs
BR ˈdʒɒdpəz
AM ˈdʒɑdpərz

Jodie
BR ˈdʒəʊdi
AM ˈdʒoʊdi

Jodrell Bank
BR ˌdʒɒdr(ə)l ˈbaŋk
AM ˌdʒɑdrəl ˈbæŋk

Jody
BR ˈdʒəʊdi
AM ˈdʒoʊdi

Joe
BR dʒəʊ
AM dʒoʊ

Joe Bloggs
BR ˌdʒəʊ ˈblɒgz
AM ˌdʒoʊ ˈblɑgz

Joe Blow
BR ˌdʒəʊ ˈbləʊ
AM ˌdʒoʊ ˈbloʊ

Joel
BR dʒəʊl
AM dʒoʊ(ə)l

joey
BR ˈdʒəʊ|i, -ɪz
AM ˈdʒoʊi, -z

jog
BR dʒɒg, -z, -ɪŋ, -d
AM dʒɑg, -z, -ɪŋ, -d

jogger
BR ˈdʒɒgə(r), -z
AM ˈdʒɑgər, -z

joggle
BR ˈdʒɒg|l, -lz, -l̩ɪŋ\-lɪŋ, -ld
AM ˈdʒɑg|əl, -əlz, -(ə)lɪŋ, -əld

Jogjakarta
BR ˌdʒɒgdʒəˈkɑːtə(r)
AM ˌdʒɑgdʒəˌkɑrdə

jogtrot
BR ˈdʒɒgtrɒt, -s, -ɪŋ, -ɨd
AM ˈdʒɑgˌtrɑ|t, -ts, -dɪŋ, -dəd

Johanna
BR dʒəʊˈanə(r)
AM dʒoʊˈænə

Johannesburg
BR dʒə(ʊ)ˈhanɪzbəːg, dʒə(ʊ)ˈhanɪsbəːg
AM dʒoʊˈhɑnəsˌbərg

john
BR dʒɒn, -z
AM dʒɑn, -z

Johnnie
BR ˈdʒɒni
AM ˈdʒɑni

johnny
BR ˈdʒɒn|i, -ɪz
AM ˈdʒɑni, -z

johnnycake
BR ˈdʒɒnɪkeɪk, -s
AM ˈdʒɑniˌkeɪk, -s

John o'Groats
BR ˌdʒɒn əˈgrəʊts
AM ˌdʒɑn əˈgroʊts

Johns
BR dʒɒnz
AM dʒɑnz

Johnson
BR ˈdʒɒnsn
AM ˈdʒɑnsən

Johnsonian
BR ˌdʒɒnˈsəʊnɪən
AM ˌdʒɑnˈsoʊniən

Johnston
BR ˈdʒɒnst(ə)n, ˈdʒɒnsn
AM ˈdʒɑnstən

Johnstone
BR ˈdʒɒnst(ə)n, ˈdʒɒnsn, ˈdʒɒnstəʊn
AM ˈdʒɑnstən, ˈdʒɑnˌstoʊn

Johor
BR dʒəˈhɔː(r)
AM dʒəˈhɔ(ə)r

Johore
BR dʒəˈhɔː(r)
AM dʒəˈhɔ(ə)r

joie de vivre
BR ˌʒwɑː də ˈviːvr(ər)
AM ˌʒwɑ də ˈvivrə

join
BR dʒɔɪn, -z, -ɪŋ, -d
AM dʒɔɪn, -z, -ɪŋ, -d

joinable
BR ˈdʒɔɪnəbl
AM ˈdʒɔɪnəbəl

joinder
BR ˈdʒɔɪndə(r)
AM ˈdʒɔɪndər

joiner
BR ˈdʒɔɪnə(r), -z
AM ˈdʒɔɪnər, -z

joinery
BR ˈdʒɔɪn(ə)ri
AM ˈdʒɔɪnəri

joint
BR dʒɔɪnt, -s, -ɪŋ, -ɨd
AM dʒɔɪn|t, -ts, -(t)ɪŋ, -(t)ɨd

jointedly
BR ˈdʒɔɪntɨdli
AM ˈdʒɔɪn(t)ɨdli

jointedness
BR ˈdʒɔɪntɨdnɨs
AM ˈdʒɔɪn(t)ɨdnɨs

jointer
BR ˈdʒɔɪntə(r), -z
AM ˈdʒɔɪn(t)ər, -z

jointless
BR ˈdʒɔɪntlɨs
AM ˈdʒɔɪntləs

jointly
BR ˈdʒɔɪntli
AM ˈdʒɔɪn(t)li

jointress
BR ˈdʒɔɪntrɨs, -ɪz
AM ˈdʒɔɪntrəs, -əz

jointure
BR ˈdʒɔɪntʃə(r), -z
AM ˈdʒɔɪn(t)ʃər, -z

joist
BR dʒɔɪst, -s
AM dʒɔɪst, -s

jojoba
BR hə(ʊ)ˈhəʊbə(r)
AM hoʊˈhoʊbə

joke
BR dʒəʊk, -s, -ɪŋ, -t
AM dʒoʊk, -s, -ɪŋ, -t

joker
BR ˈdʒəʊkə(r), -z
AM ˈdʒoʊkər, -z

jokesmith
BR ˈdʒəʊksmɪθ, -s
AM ˈdʒoʊkˌsmɪ|θ, -θs\-ðz

jokey
BR ˈdʒəʊki
AM ˈdʒoʊki

jokily
BR ˈdʒəʊkɨli
AM ˈdʒoʊkəli

jokiness
BR ˈdʒəʊkɪnɨs
AM ˈdʒoʊkinɨs

jokingly
BR ˈdʒəʊkɪŋli
AM ˈdʒoʊkɪŋli

joky
BR ˈdʒəʊki
AM ˈdʒoʊki

Jolene
BR dʒəʊˈliːn
AM dʒoʊˈlin

Jolley
BR ˈdʒɒli
AM ˈdʒɑli

Jollie
BR ˈdʒɒli
AM ˈdʒɑli

jollification
BR ˌdʒɒlɨfɨˈkeɪʃn, -z
AM ˌdʒɑləfəˈkeɪʃən, -z

jollify
BR ˈdʒɒlɨfʌɪ, -z, -ɪŋ, -d
AM ˈdʒɑləˌfaɪ, -z, -ɪŋ, -d

jollily
BR ˈdʒɒlɨli
AM ˈdʒɑləli

jolliness
BR ˈdʒɒlɪnɨs
AM ˈdʒɑlinɨs

jollity
BR ˈdʒɒlɨti
AM ˈdʒɑlədi

jollo
BR ˈdʒɒləʊ, -z
AM ˈdʒɑˌloʊ, -z

jolly
BR ˈdʒɒl|i, -ɪz, -ɪɪŋ, -ɪd, -ɪə(r), -ɪɪst
AM ˈdʒɑli, -z, -ɪŋ, -d, -ər, -ɨst

jollyboat
BR ˈdʒɒlɪbəʊt, -s
AM ˈdʒɑliˌboʊt, -s

Jolson
BR ˈdʒəʊls(ə)n
AM ˈdʒoʊlsən

jolt
BR dʒəʊlt, -s, -ɪŋ, -ɨd
AM dʒoʊlt, -s, -ɪŋ, -ɨd

joltily
BR ˈdʒəʊltɨli
AM ˈdʒoʊltəli

joltiness
BR ˈdʒəʊltɪnɪs
AM ˈdʒoʊltinɨs

jolty
BR ˈdʒəʊlt|i, -ɪə(r), -ɪɪst
AM ˈdʒoʊlti, -ər, -ɨst

Jolyon
BR ˈdʒəʊlɪən, ˈdʒɒlɪən
AM ˈdʒɑliən

Jomon
BR ˈdʒəʊmɒn
AM ˈdʒoʊmɑn

Jon
BR dʒɒn
AM dʒɑn

Jonah
BR ˈdʒəʊnə(r), -z
AM ˈdʒoʊnə, -z

Jonas
BR ˈdʒəʊnəs
AM ˈdʒoʊnəs

Jonathan
BR ˈdʒɒnəθ(ə)n
AM ˈdʒɑnəθən

Jones
BR dʒəʊnz
AM dʒoʊnz

Joneses
BR ˈdʒəʊnzɪz
AM ˈdʒoʊnzəz

Jong
BR jɒŋ
AM jɔŋ, jɑŋ

jongleur
BR ʒɒ̃ˈgləː(r), ʒɒŋˈgləː(r), -z
AM ʒɔnˈglər, ˈdʒɑŋglər, -z

jonquil
BR ˈdʒɒŋkw(ɪ)l, -z
AM ˈdʒɑnkwəl, -z

Jonson
BR ˈdʒɒns(ə)n
AM ˈdʒɑnsən

Jools
BR dʒuːlz
AM dʒulz

Joplin
BR ˈdʒɒplɪn
AM ˈdʒɑplən

Jopling
BR ˈdʒɒplɪŋ
AM ˈdʒɑplɪŋ

Joppa
BR ˈdʒɒpə(r)
AM ˈdʒɑpə

Jordan
BR ˈdʒɔːdn
AM ˈdʒɔrdən

Jordanhill
BR ˌdʒɔːdnˈhɪl
AM ˌdʒɔrdənˈhɪl

Jordanian
BR dʒɔːˈdeɪnɪən, -z
AM dʒɔrˈdeɪniən, -z

jorum
BR ˈdʒɔːrəm, -z
AM ˈdʒɔrəm, -z

Jorvik
BR ˈjɔːvɪk
AM ˈjɔrˌvɪk

Josceline
BR ˈdʒɒs(ə)lɪn
AM ˈdʒɑslən

José
BR həʊˈzeɪ, həʊˈseɪ
AM hoʊˈzeɪ, hoʊˈseɪ

Joseph
BR ˈdʒəʊzɪf
AM ˈdʒoʊzəf, ˈdʒoʊsəf

Josephine
BR ˈdʒəʊzɪfiːn
AM ˈdʒoʊzəfin

Josephus
BR dʒə(ʊ)ˈsiːfəs
AM ˌdʒoʊˈsifəs

josh
BR dʒɒʃ, -ɪz, -ɪŋ, -t
AM dʒɑʃ, -əz, -ɪŋ, -t

josher
BR ˈdʒɒʃə(r), -z
AM ˈdʒɑʃər, -z

Joshua
BR ˈdʒɒʃ(j)ʊə(r)
AM ˈdʒɑʃ(ə)wə

Josiah
BR dʒə(ʊ)ˈzʌɪə(r), dʒə(ʊ)ˈsʌɪə(r)
AM ˌdʒoʊˈsaɪə, ˌdʒoʊˈzaɪə

Josie
BR ˈdʒəʊzi, ˈdʒəʊsi
AM ˈdʒoʊzi

joss
BR dʒɒs
AM dʒɔs, dʒɑs

josser
BR ˈdʒɒsə(r), -z
AM ˈdʒɔsər, ˈdʒɑsər, -z

jostle
BR ˈdʒɒs|l, -lz, -l̩ɪŋ\-lɪŋ, -ld
AM ˈdʒɑs|əl, -əlz, -(ə)lɪŋ, -əld

jot
BR dʒɒt, -s, -ɪŋ, -ɪd
AM dʒɑ|t, -ts, -dɪŋ, -dəd

jota
BR ˈxəʊtə(r), -z
AM ˈhoʊdə, -z

jotter
BR ˈdʒɒtə(r), -z
AM ˈdʒɑdər, -z

jougs
BR dʒuːgz
AM dʒugz

Joule
BR dʒuːl
AM dʒul

joule
BR dʒuːl, -z
AM dʒul, -z

jounce
BR dʒaʊns, -ɪz, -ɪŋ, -t
AM dʒaʊns, -əz, -ɪŋ, -t

journal
BR ˈdʒəːnl, -z
AM ˈdʒərnəl, -z

journalese
BR ˌdʒəːnəˈliːz, ˌdʒəːnlˈiːz
AM ˌdʒərnlˌiz

journalise
BR ˈdʒəːnəlʌɪz, ˈdʒəːnl̩ʌɪz, -ɪz, -ɪŋ, -d
AM ˈdʒərnlˌaɪz, -ɪz, -ɪŋ, -d

journalism
BR ˈdʒəːnəlɪz(ə)m, ˈdʒəːnl̩ɪz(ə)m
AM ˈdʒərnlˌɪzəm

journalist
BR ˈdʒəːnəlɪst, ˈdʒəːnl̩ɪst, -s
AM ˈdʒərnl̩əst, -s

journalistic
BR ˌdʒəːnəˈlɪstɪk, ˌdʒəːnlˈɪstɪk
AM ˌdʒərnlˈɪstɪk

journalistically
BR ˌdʒəːnəˈlɪstɪkli, ˌdʒəːnlˈɪstɪkli
AM ˌdʒərnlˈɪstək(ə)li

journalize
BR ˈdʒəːnəlʌɪz, ˈdʒəːnl̩ʌɪz, -ɪz, -ɪŋ, -d
AM ˈdʒərnlˌaɪz, -ɪz, -ɪŋ, -d

journey
BR ˈdʒəːn|i, -ɪz, -ɪɪŋ, -ɪd
AM ˈdʒərni, -z, -ɪŋ, -d

journeyer
BR ˈdʒəːnɪə(r), -z
AM ˈdʒərniər, -z

journeyman
BR ˈdʒəːnɪmən
AM ˈdʒərnimən

journeymen
BR ˈdʒəːnɪmən
AM ˈdʒərnimən

journo
BR ˈdʒəːnəʊ, -z
AM ˈdʒərnoʊ, -z

joust
BR dʒaʊst, -s, -ɪŋ, -ɪd
AM dʒaʊst, -s, -ɪŋ, -ɪd

jouster
BR ˈdʒaʊstə(r), -z
AM ˈdʒaʊstər, -z

Jove
BR dʒəʊv
AM dʒoʊv

jovial
BR ˈdʒəʊvɪəl
AM ˈdʒoʊviəl

joviality
BR ˌdʒəʊvɪˈalɪti
AM ˌdʒoʊviˈælədi

jovially
BR ˈdʒəʊvɪəli
AM ˈdʒoʊviəli

Jovian
BR ˈdʒəʊvɪən
AM ˈdʒoʊviən

jowar
BR dʒaʊˈwɑː(r)
AM dʒəˈwɑr

Jowett
BR ˈdʒaʊɪt, ˈdʒəʊɪt, -s
AM ˈdʒaʊət, ˈdʒoʊət, -s

Jowitt
BR ˈdʒaʊɪt, ˈdʒəʊɪt
AM ˈdʒaʊət, ˈdʒoʊət

jowl
BR dʒaʊl, -z, -d
AM dʒaʊl, -z, -d

jowly
BR ˈdʒaʊli
AM ˈdʒaʊli, ˈdʒaʊəli

joy
BR dʒɔɪ, -z
AM dʒɔɪ, -z

Joyce
BR dʒɔɪs
AM dʒɔɪs

Joycean
BR ˈdʒɔɪsɪən
AM ˈdʒɔɪsiən

joyful
BR ˈdʒɔɪf(ʊ)l
AM ˈdʒɔɪfəl

joyfully
BR ˈdʒɔɪfʊli, ˈdʒɔɪfl̩i
AM ˈdʒɔɪfəli

joyfulness
BR ˈdʒɔɪf(ʊ)lnəs
AM ˈdʒɔɪfəlnəs

joyless
BR ˈdʒɔɪlɪs
AM ˈdʒɔɪlɪs

joylessly
BR ˈdʒɔɪlɪsli
AM ˈdʒɔɪlɪsli

joylessness
BR ˈdʒɔɪlɪsnɪs
AM ˈdʒɔɪlɪsnɪs

joyous
BR ˈdʒɔɪəs
AM ˈdʒɔɪəs

joyously
BR ˈdʒɔɪəsli
AM ˈdʒɔɪəsli

joyousness
BR ˈdʒɔɪəsnəs
AM ˈdʒɔɪəsnəs

joyride
BR ˈdʒɔɪrʌɪd, -z, -ɪŋ
AM ˈdʒɔɪˌraɪd, -z, -ɪŋ

joyrider
BR ˈdʒɔɪrʌɪdə(r), -z
AM ˈdʒɔɪˌraɪdər, -z

joystick
BR ˈdʒɔɪstɪk, -s
AM ˈdʒɔɪˌstɪk, -s

JPEG
BR ˈdʒeɪpɛg
AM ˈdʒeɪˌpɛg

Jr
BR ˈdʒuniə(r)
AM ˈdʒunjər

Juan
BR hwɑːn
AM (h)wɑn

Juanita
BR (h)wəˈniːtə(r)
AM (h)wəˈnidə

Juárez
BR ˈhwɑːrɛz
AM ˌ(h)wɑˌrɛz

Juba
BR ˈdʒuːbə(r)
AM ˈdʒubə

jube[1]
in a church
BR ˈdʒuːb|i, -ɪz
AM ˈjuˌbeɪ, -z

jube[2]
watercourse
BR dʒuːb, -z
AM dʒub, -z

jubilance
BR ˈdʒuːbɪləns, ˈdʒuːbɪl̩ns, ˈdʒuːbl̩(ə)ns
AM ˈdʒubələns

jubilant
BR ˈdʒuːbɪlənt, ˈdʒuːbɪl̩nt, ˈdʒuːbl̩(ə)nt
AM ˈdʒubələnt

jubilantly
BR ˈdʒuːbɪləntli, ˈdʒuːbɪl̩ntli, ˈdʒuːbl̩(ə)ntli
AM ˈdʒubələn(t)li

Jubilate
noun
BR ˌdʒuːbɪˈlɑːteɪ
AM ˌdʒubəˈlɑdeɪ

jubilate
verb
BR ˈdʒuːbɪleɪt, -s, -ɪŋ, -ɪd
AM ˈdʒubəˌleɪ|t, -ts, -dɪŋ, -dɪd

jubilation
BR ˌdʒuːbɪˈleɪʃn
AM ˌdʒubəˈleɪʃən

jubilee
BR 'dʒuːbɨliː, -z
AM 'dʒubəˌli, ˌdʒubə'li, -z
Judaea
BR dʒuː'dɪə(r), dʒʉ'dɪə(r)
AM dʒu'diə
Judaean
BR dʒuː'dɪən, dʒʉ'dɪən
AM dʒu'diən
Judaeo-Christian
BR dʒʉˌdeɪəʊ'krɪstʃ(ə)n
AM dʒuˌdeɪoʊ'krɪstʃən
Judah
BR 'dʒuːdə(r)
AM 'dʒudə
Judaic
BR dʒuː'deɪɪk, dʒʉ'deɪɪk
AM dʒu'deɪɪk
Judaism
BR 'dʒuːdeɪɪz(ə)m
AM 'dʒudəˌɪzəm, 'dʒudiˌɪzəm
Judaization
BR ˌdʒuːdə(r)ʌɪ'zeɪʃn
AM ˌdʒudeɪɪ'zəɪʃən, ˌdʒudiɪ'zeɪʃən
Judaize
BR 'dʒuːdə(r)ʌɪz, -ɨz, -ɪŋ, -d
AM 'dʒudəˌaɪz, 'dʒudiˌaɪz, -ɨz, -ɪŋ, -d
Judas
BR 'dʒuːdəs, -ɨz
AM 'dʒudəs, -əz
Judas Iscariot
BR ˌdʒuːdəs ɪ'skarɪət
AM ˌdʒudəs ɪs'kɛriət
Judas Maccabaeus
BR ˌdʒuːdəs ˌmakə'biːəs
AM ˌdʒudəs ˌmækə'biəs
Judd
BR dʒʌd
AM dʒəd
judder
BR 'dʒʌd|ə(r), -əz, -(ə)rɪŋ, -əd
AM 'dʒədər, -z, -ɪŋ, -d
Jude
BR dʒuːd
AM dʒud
Judea
BR dʒuː'dɪə(r), dʒʉ'dɪə(r)
AM dʒu'diə
Judean
BR dʒuː'dɪən, dʒʉ'dɪən
AM dʒu'diən
Judeo-Christian
BR dʒʉˌdeɪəʊ'krɪstʃ(ə)n
AM dʒuˌdeɪoʊ'krɪstʃən
judge
BR dʒʌdʒ, -ɨz, -ɪŋ, -d
AM dʒədʒ, -əz, -ɪŋ, -d
judgelike
BR 'dʒʌdʒlʌɪk
AM 'dʒədʒˌlaɪk
judgematic
BR dʒʌdʒ'matɪk
AM dʒədʒ'mædɪk
judgematical
BR dʒʌdʒ'matɨkl
AM dʒədʒ'mædəkəl
judgematically
BR dʒʌdʒ'matɨkli
AM dʒədʒ'mædək(ə)li
judgement
BR 'dʒʌdʒm(ə)nt, -s
AM 'dʒədʒmənt, -s
judgemental
BR dʒʌdʒ'mɛntl
AM dʒədʒ'mɛn(t)l
judgementally
BR dʒʌdʒ'mɛntl̩i, dʒʌdʒ'mɛntəli
AM dʒədʒ'mɛn(t)l̩i
Judges
BR 'dʒʌdʒɪz
AM 'dʒədʒəz
judgeship
BR 'dʒʌdʒʃɪp, -s
AM 'dʒədʒˌʃɪp, -s
judgment
BR 'dʒʌdʒm(ə)nt, -s
AM 'dʒədʒmənt, -s
judgmental
BR dʒʌdʒ'mɛntl
AM dʒədʒ'mɛn(t)l
judgmentally
BR dʒʌdʒ'mɛntl̩i, dʒʌdʒ'mɛntəli
AM dʒədʒ'mɛn(t)l̩i
Judi
BR 'dʒuːd|i, -ɪz
AM 'dʒudi, -z
judicative
BR 'dʒuːdɨkətɪv
AM 'dʒudəˌkeɪdɪv
judicatory
BR 'dʒuːdɨkət(ə)r|i, dʒʉ'dɪkət(ə)r|i, -ɪz
AM 'dʒudəkəˌtɔri, -z
judicature
BR 'dʒuːdɨkətʃə(r), dʒʉ'dɪkətʃə(r)
AM 'dʒudəkəˌtʃʊ(ə)r, dʒudəkətʃər, 'dʒudəˌkeɪtʃər
judicial
BR dʒʉ'dɪʃl
AM dʒu'dɪʃəl
judicially
BR dʒʉ'dɪʃl̩i, dʒʉ'dɪʃəli
AM dʒu'dɪʃ(ə)li
judiciary
BR dʒʉ'dɪʃ(ə)ri
AM dʒu'dɪʃiˌɛri, dʒu'dɪʃəri
judicious
BR dʒʉ'dɪʃəs
AM dʒu'dɪʃəs
judiciously
BR dʒʉ'dɪʃəsli
AM dʒu'dɪʃəsli
judiciousness
BR dʒʉ'dɪʃəsnəs
AM dʒu'dɪʃəsnəs
Judith
BR 'dʒuːdɪθ
AM 'dʒudəθ
judo
BR 'dʒuːdəʊ
AM 'dʒudoʊ
judoist
BR 'dʒuːdəʊɪst, -s
AM 'dʒudoʊəst, -s
judoka
BR 'dʒuːdəʊkə(r), -z
AM 'dʒudoʊˌkɑ, ˌdʒudoʊ'kɑ, -z
Judy
BR 'dʒuːd|i, -ɪz
AM 'dʒudi, -z
jug
BR dʒʌg, -z, -ɪŋ, -d
AM dʒəg, -z, -ɪŋ, -d
Jugendstil
BR 'juːgənt-ʃtiːl
AM 'jugəntˌstil
jugful
BR 'dʒʌgfʊl, -z
AM 'dʒəgˌfʊl, -z
juggernaut
BR 'dʒʌgənɔːt, -s
AM 'dʒəgərˌnɔt, 'dʒəgərˌnɑt, -s
juggins
BR 'dʒʌgɪnz, -ɨz
AM 'dʒəgənz, -əz
juggle
BR 'dʒʌg|l, -lz, -l̩ɪŋ\-lɪŋ, -ld
AM 'dʒəg|əl, -əlz, -(ə)lɪŋ, -əld
juggler
BR 'dʒʌglə(r), -z
AM 'dʒəg(ə)lər, -z
jugglery
BR 'dʒʌglər|i, -ɪz
AM 'dʒəgləri, -z
Jugoslav
BR 'juːgə(ʊ)slɑːv, -z
AM 'jugoʊˌslɑv, 'jugəˌslɑv, -z
Jugoslavia
BR ˌjuːgə(ʊ)'slɑːvɪə(r)
AM ˌjugoʊ'slɑviə, ˌjugə'slɑviə
Jugoslavian
BR ˌjuːgə(ʊ)'slɑːvɪən, -z
AM ˌjugoʊ'slɑviən, ˌjugə'slɑviən, -z
jugular
BR 'dʒʌgjʉlə(r), -z
AM 'dʒəgjələr, -z
jugulate
BR 'dʒʌgjʉleɪt, -s, -ɪŋ, -ɨd
AM 'dʒəgjəˌleɪ|t, -ts, -dɪŋ, -dɨd
Jugurtha
BR dʒʊ'gəːθə(r)
AM dʒu'gərθə
Jugurthine
BR dʒʊ'gəːθʌɪn
AM dʒu'gərθən, dʒu'gərˌθin
juice
BR dʒuːs, -ɨz
AM dʒus, -əz
juiceless
BR 'dʒuːsləs
AM 'dʒusləs
juicer
BR 'dʒuːsə(r), -z
AM 'dʒusər, -z
juicily
BR 'dʒuːsɨli
AM 'dʒusəli
juiciness
BR 'dʒuːsɪnɨs
AM 'dʒusinɨs
juicy
BR 'dʒuːs|i, -ɪə(r), -ɪɪst
AM 'dʒusi, -ər, -ɨst
jujitsu
BR ˌdʒuː'dʒɪtsuː
AM ˌdʒu'dʒɪtsu
juju
BR 'dʒuːdʒuː, -z
AM 'dʒudʒu, -z
jujube
BR 'dʒuːdʒuːb, -z
AM 'dʒuˌdʒub, 'dʒudʒəbi, -z
jujutsu
BR ˌdʒuː'dʒʌtsuː
AM ˌdʒu'dʒɪtsu
jukebox
BR 'dʒuːkbɒks, -ɨz
AM 'dʒukˌbɑks, -əz
Jukes
BR dʒuːks
AM dʒuks
juku
BR 'dʒʊkuː, -z
AM 'dʒʊku, -z
julep
BR 'dʒuːlɪp, 'dʒuːlɛp, -s
AM 'dʒuləp, -s
Jules
BR dʒuːlz
AM dʒulz
Julia
BR 'dʒuːlɪə(r)
AM 'dʒuljə, 'dʒuliə
Julian
BR 'dʒuːlɪən
AM 'dʒuliən
Julie
BR 'dʒuːli
AM 'dʒuli

Julien
BR 'dʒuːlɪən
AM 'dʒuliən

julienne
BR ˌdʒuːlɪ'ɛn
AM ˈ(d)ʒuli'ɛn, (d)ʒul'jɛn

Juliet
BR 'dʒuːlɪət, ˌdʒuːlɪ'ɛt
AM ˌdʒuli'ɛt, 'dʒuljət

Julius
BR 'dʒuːlɪəs
AM 'dʒuliəs

July
BR dʒʊ'lʌɪ, -z
AM dʒə'laɪ, dʒu'laɪ, -z

jumble
BR 'dʒʌmb|l, -lz, -l̩ɪŋ\-lɪŋ, -ld
AM 'dʒəmb|əl, -əlz, -(ə)lɪŋ, -əld

jumbly
BR 'dʒʌmbl|i, -ɪə(r), -ɪɪst
AM 'dʒəmbli, 'dʒəmbəli, -ər, -ɪst

jumbo
BR 'dʒʌmbəʊ, -z
AM 'dʒəmboʊ, -z

jumboise
BR 'dʒʌmbəʊʌɪz, -ɪz, -ɪŋ, -d
AM 'dʒəmboʊˌaɪz, -ɪz, -ɪŋ, -d

jumboize
BR 'dʒʌmbəʊʌɪz, -ɪz, -ɪŋ, -d
AM 'dʒəmboʊˌaɪz, -ɪz, -ɪŋ, -d

jumbuck
BR 'dʒʌmbʌk, -s
AM 'dʒəmbək, -s

jump
BR dʒʌm|p, -ps, -pɪŋ, -(p)t
AM dʒəmp, -s, -ɪŋ, -t

jumpable
BR 'dʒʌmpəbl
AM 'dʒəmpəbəl

jumper
BR 'dʒʌmpə(r), -z
AM 'dʒəmpər, -z

jumpily
BR 'dʒʌmpɪli
AM 'dʒəmpəli

jumpiness
BR 'dʒʌmpɪnɪs
AM 'dʒəmpinɪs

jumpsuit
BR 'dʒʌmps(j)uːt, -s
AM 'dʒəm(p)ˌsut, -s

jumpy
BR 'dʒʌmp|i, -ɪə(r), -ɪɪst
AM 'dʒəmpi, -ər, -ɪst

Jun.
BR 'dʒuːnɪə(r)
AM 'dʒunjər

junco
BR 'dʒʌŋkəʊ, -z
AM 'dʒəŋkoʊ, -z

junction
BR 'dʒʌŋ(k)ʃn, -z
AM 'dʒəŋ(k)ʃən, -z

juncture
BR 'dʒʌŋ(k)tʃə(r), -z
AM 'dʒəŋ(k)(t)ʃər, -z

June
BR dʒuːn, -z
AM dʒun, -z

Juneau
BR 'dʒuːnəʊ
AM 'dʒuˌnoʊ

Jung
BR jʊŋ
AM jʊŋ

Jungfrau
BR 'jʊŋfraʊ
AM 'jʊŋˌfraʊ

Jungian
BR 'jʊŋɡɪən
AM 'jʊŋɡiən

jungle
BR 'dʒʌŋɡl, -z, -d
AM 'dʒəŋɡəl, -z, -d

jungly
BR 'dʒʌŋɡl|i, -ɪə(r), -ɪɪst
AM 'dʒəŋɡli, 'dʒəŋɡəli, -ər, -ɪst

junior
BR 'dʒuːnɪə(r), -z
AM 'dʒunjər, -z

juniorate
BR 'dʒuːnɪərət, -s
AM 'dʒunjərət, 'dʒunjəˌreɪt, -s

juniority
BR dʒuːnɪ'ɒrɪti
AM dʒun'jɔrədi

juniper
BR 'dʒuːnɪpə(r), -z
AM 'dʒunəpər, -z

junk
BR dʒʌŋ|k, -ks, -kɪŋ, -(k)t
AM dʒəŋ|k, -ks, -kɪŋ, -(k)t

Junker
BR 'jʊŋkə(r), -z
AM 'dʒəŋkər, -z

junkerdom
BR 'jʊŋkədəm
AM 'jʊŋkərdəm

junket
BR 'dʒʌŋk|ɪt, -ɪts, -ɪtɪŋ, -ɪtɪd
AM 'dʒəŋkə|t, -ts, -dɪŋ, -dəd

junkie
BR 'dʒʌŋk|i, -ɪz
AM 'dʒəŋki, -z

Junkin
BR 'dʒʌŋkɪn
AM 'dʒəŋkən

junk mail
BR 'dʒʌŋk meɪl, ˌdʒʌŋk 'meɪl
AM 'dʒəŋk ˌmeɪl

junky
BR 'dʒʌŋk|i, -ɪz
AM 'dʒəŋki, -z

junkyard
BR 'dʒʌŋkjɑːd, -z
AM 'dʒəŋkˌjɑrd, -z

Juno
BR 'dʒuːnəʊ
AM 'dʒunoʊ

Junoesque
BR ˌdʒuːnəʊ'ɛsk
AM ˈdʒunoʊ'ɛsk

Junor
BR 'dʒuːnə(r)
AM 'dʒunər

junta
BR 'dʒʌntə(*r*), 'hʊntə(*r*), -z
AM 'hʊntə, 'huntə, 'dʒəntə, -z

Jupiter
BR 'dʒuːpɪtə(r)
AM 'dʒupədər

Jura
BR 'dʒʊərə(*r*)
AM 'dʒurə

jural
BR 'dʒʊərəl, 'dʒʊərl̩
AM 'dʒurəl

Jurassic
BR dʒʊ'rasɪk
AM dʒə'ræsɪk

jurat
BR 'dʒʊərat, -s
AM 'dʒʊræt, -s

juridical
BR dʒʊ'rɪdɪkl
AM dʒə'rɪdəkəl, dʒu'rɪdəkəl

juridically
BR dʒʊ'rɪdɪkli
AM dʒə'rɪdək(ə)li, dʒu'rɪdək(ə)li

jurisconsult
BR ˌdʒʊərɪskən'sʌlt, -s
AM ˌdʒʊrə'skənsəlt, ˌdʒʊrəskən'səlt, -s

jurisdiction
BR ˌdʒʊərɪz'dɪkʃn, ˌdʒʊərɪs'dɪkʃn, -z
AM ˌdʒʊrəs'dɪkʃən, ˌdʒʊrəz'dɪkʃən, -z

jurisdictional
BR ˌdʒʊərɪz'dɪkʃn̩(ə)l, ˌdʒʊərɪz'dɪkʃən(ə)l, ˌdʒʊərɪs'dɪkʃn̩(ə)l, ˌdʒʊərɪs'dɪkʃən(ə)l
AM ˌdʒʊrəs'dɪkʃ(ə)nəl, ˌdʒʊrəz'dɪkʃ(ə)nəl

jurisprudence
BR ˌdʒʊərɪs'pruːd(ə)ns
AM ˌdʒʊrə'sprudns, 'dʒʊrəˌsprudns, ˌdʒurə'sprudns, 'dʒurəˌsprudns

jurisprudent
BR ˌdʒʊərɪs'pruːd(ə)nt
AM ˌdʒʊrə'sprudnt, 'dʒʊrəˌsprudnt, ˌdʒurə'sprudnt, 'dʒurəˌsprudnt

jurisprudential
BR ˌdʒʊərɪsprʊ'dɛnʃl
AM ˌdʒʊrəˌspru'dɛn(t)ʃəl, ˌdʒurəˌspru'dɛn(t)ʃəl

jurist
BR 'dʒʊərɪst, -s
AM 'dʒʊrəst, 'dʒurəst, -s

juristic
BR dʒʊ'rɪstɪk
AM dʒʊ'rɪstɪk, dʒu'rɪstɪk

juristical
BR dʒʊ'rɪstɪkl
AM dʒʊ'rɪstɪkəl, dʒu'rɪstɪkəl

juror
BR 'dʒʊərə(r), -z
AM 'dʒʊrər, 'dʒurər, 'dʒʊˌrɔ(ə)r, 'dʒuˌrɔ(ə)r, -z

jury
BR 'dʒʊər|i, -ɪz
AM 'dʒʊri, 'dʒuri, -z

juryman
BR 'dʒʊərɪmən
AM 'dʒʊrimən, 'dʒurimən

jurymen
BR 'dʒʊərɪmən
AM 'dʒʊrimən, 'dʒurimən

jurywoman
BR 'dʒʊərɪˌwʊmən
AM 'dʒʊriˌwʊmən, 'dʒuriˌwʊmən

jurywomen
BR 'dʒʊərɪˌwɪmɪn
AM 'dʒʊriˌwɪmɪn, 'dʒuriˌwɪmɪn

jussive
BR 'dʒʌsɪv, -z
AM 'dʒəsɪv, -z

just[1]
adjective, adverb strong form
BR dʒʌst
AM dʒəst

just[2]
adverb weak form
BR dʒəst
AM dʒəst

juste milieu
BR ʒuːst 'miːljəː(*r*), + mɪl'jəː(*r*)
AM 'ʒust mɪl'ju, 'ʒəst mɪl'jə

justice
BR 'dʒʌst|ɪs, -ɪsɪz
AM 'dʒəstəs, -əz

justiceship
BR 'dʒʌstɪsʃɪp
AM 'dʒəstə(s),ʃɪp

justiciable
BR dʒʌ'stɪʃ(ɪ)əbl, dʒə'stɪʃ(ɪ)əbl
AM ,dʒə'stɪʃ(i)əbəl

justiciar
BR dʒʌ'stɪʃə(r), dʒə'stɪʃə(r)
AM ,dʒə'stɪʃ(i)ər

justiciary
BR dʒʌ'stɪʃɪər|i, dʒə'stɪʃɪər|i, dʒʌ'stɪʃ(ə)r|i, dʒə'stɪʃ(ə)r|i, -ɪz
AM ,dʒə'stɪʃi,ɛri, -z

justifiability
BR ,dʒʌstɪfʌɪə'bɪlɪti
AM ,dʒəstə,faɪə'bɪlɪdi

justifiable
BR 'dʒʌstɪfʌɪəbl, ,dʒʌstɪ'fʌɪəbl
AM 'dʒəstə,faɪəbəl, ,dʒəstə'faɪəbəl

justifiableness
BR 'dʒʌstɪfʌɪəblnəs, ,dʒʌstɪ'fʌɪəblnəs
AM 'dʒəstə,faɪəbəlnəs, ,dʒəstə'faɪəbəlnəs

justifiably
BR 'dʒʌstɪfʌɪəbli, ,dʒʌstɪ'fʌɪəbli
AM 'dʒəstə,faɪəbli, ,dʒəstə'faɪəbli

justification
BR ,dʒʌstɪfɪ'keɪʃn, -z
AM ,dʒəstəfə'keɪʃən, -z

justificatory
BR 'dʒʌstɪfɪkeɪt(ə)ri, 'dʒʌstɪfɪkət(ə)ri, ,dʒʌstɪfɪ'keɪt(ə)ri
AM dʒə'stɪfəkə,tɔri, ,dʒəstə'fɪkə,tɔri

justifier
BR 'dʒʌstɪfʌɪə(r)
AM 'dʒəstə,faɪər

justify
BR 'dʒʌstɪfʌɪ, -z, -ɪŋ, -d
AM 'dʒəstə,faɪ, -z, -ɪŋ, -d

Justin
BR 'dʒʌstɪn
AM 'dʒəstən

Justine
BR 'dʒʌsti:n, dʒʌ'sti:n
AM 'dʒəstin

Justinian
BR dʒʌs'tɪnɪən, dʒəs'tɪnɪən
AM dʒəs'tɪniən

justly
BR 'dʒʌs(t)li
AM 'dʒəs(t)li

justness
BR 'dʒʌs(t)nəs
AM 'dʒəs(t)nəs

jut
BR dʒʌt, -s, -ɪŋ, -ɪd
AM dʒə|t, -ts, -dɪŋ, -dəd

jute
BR dʒu:t, -s
AM dʒut, -s

Jutish
BR 'dʒu:tɪʃ
AM 'dʒudɪʃ

Jutland
BR 'dʒʌtlənd
AM 'dʒətlənd

Juvenal
BR 'dʒu:vɪnl, 'dʒu:vn̩l
AM 'dʒuvənəl

juvenescence
BR ,dʒu:vɪ'nɛsns
AM ,dʒuvə'nɛsəns

juvenescent
BR ,dʒu:vɪ'nɛsnt
AM ,dʒuvə'nɛsənt

juvenile
BR 'dʒu:vɪnʌɪl, -z
AM 'dʒuvə,naɪl, 'dʒuvənl, -z

juvenilely
BR 'dʒu:vɪnʌɪlli
AM 'dʒuvə,naɪ(l)li, 'dʒuvənl̩i

juvenilia
BR ,dʒu:vɪ'nɪlɪə(*r*)
AM ,dʒuvə'nɪljə, ,dʒuvə'nɪliə

juvenility
BR ,dʒu:vɪ'nɪlɪti
AM ,dʒuvə'nɪlɪdi

juxtapose
BR ,dʒʌkstə'pəʊz, 'dʒʌkstəpəʊz, -ɪz, -ɪŋ, -d
AM 'dʒəkstə,poʊz, ,dʒəkstə'poʊz, -əz, -ɪŋ, -t

juxtaposition
BR ,dʒʌkstəpə'zɪʃn
AM ,dʒəkstəpə'zɪʃən

juxtapositional
BR ,dʒʌkstəpə'zɪʃn̩(ə)l, ,dʒʌkstəpə'zɪʃən(ə)l
AM ,dʒəkstəpə'zɪʃ(ə)nəl

Kk

k
BR keɪ, -z
AM keɪ, -z

ka
BR kɑː(r)
AM kɑ

Kaaba
BR 'kɑːbə(r)
AM 'kɑbə, 'kæbə

kabaddi
BR kə'badi
AM kə'bɑdi

Kabaka
BR kə'bɑːkə(r)
AM kə'bɑkə

kabala
BR kə'bɑːlə(r),
ka'bɑːlə(r)
AM kə'bɑlə, 'kɑbələ

Kabalega
BR ˌkabə'leɪgə(r)
AM ˌkæbə'lɛgə

kabbala
BR kə'bɑːlə(r),
ka'bɑːlə(r)
AM kə'bɑlə, 'kæbələ

kabbalism
BR 'kabəlɪz(ə)m,
'kabl̩ɪz(ə)m
AM 'kæbəˌlɪzm,
kə'bɑˌlɪzəm

kabbalist
BR 'kabəlɪst, 'kabl̩ɪst,
-s
AM 'kæbələst,
kə'bɑləst, -s

kabob
BR kə'bɑːb, -z
AM kə'bɑb, -z

kabuki
BR kə'buːki
AM kə'buki

Kabul
BR 'kɑːb(ʊ)l, kə'bʊl
AM 'kɑbʊl, kə'bʊl

Kabwe
BR 'kabweɪ, 'kabwi
AM 'kɑbweɪ

Kabyle
BR kə'bʌɪl, -z
AM kə'baɪ(ə)l, -z

kachina
BR kə'tʃiːnə(r), -z
AM kə'tʃinə, -z

Kádáar
BR 'kɑːdɑː(r)
AM 'kɑˌdɑr
HU 'kɑːdɑːr

Kaddafi
BR kə'dafi, kə'dɑːfi
AM kə'dɑfi

kaddish
BR 'kad|ɪʃ, -ɪʃɪz
AM 'kɑdɪʃ, -ɪz

kadi
BR 'kɑːd|i, -ɪz
AM 'kɑdi, -z

kaffir
BR 'kafə(r), -z
AM 'kæfər, -z

kaffiyeh
BR kə'fiː(j)ə(r),
ka'fiː(j)ə(r), -z
AM kə'fi(j)ə, -z

kafir
BR 'kafə(r), -z
AM 'kæfər, -z

Kafka
BR 'kafkə(r)
AM 'kɑfkə

Kafkaesque
BR ˌkafkə(r)'ɛsk
AM ˌkɑfkə'ɛsk

kaftan
BR 'kaftan, -z
AM 'kæftən, 'kæfˌtæn,
-z

Kagan
BR 'keɪg(ə)n
AM 'keɪgən

Kagoshima
BR 'kagə'ʃiːmə(r)
AM 'kɑgə'ʃimə

kagoul
BR kə'guːl, -z
AM kə'gul, -z

kagoule
BR kə'guːl, -z
AM kə'gul, -z

Kahlua®
BR kə'luːə(r)
AM kə'luə

Kahn
BR kɑːn
AM kɑn

kahuna
BR kə'huːnə(r)
AM kə'hunə

kai
BR kʌɪ
AM kaɪ

Kaifeng
BR ˌkʌɪ'fɛŋ
AM ˌkaɪ'fɛŋ

kail
BR keɪl, -z
AM keɪl, -z

kailyard
BR 'keɪljɑːd
AM 'keɪlˌjɑrd

kainite
BR 'kʌɪnʌɪt, 'keɪnʌɪt
AM 'kaɪnaɪt, 'keɪnaɪt

Kaiser
BR 'kʌɪzə(r), -z
AM 'kaɪzər, -z

kaisership
BR kʌɪzəʃɪp, -s
AM 'kaɪzərʃɪp, -s

Kai Tak
BR ˌkʌɪ 'tak
AM ˌkaɪ 'tɑk

kaizen
BR 'kʌɪzn
AM 'kaɪzən

kaka
BR 'kɑːkɑː(r),
'kɑːkə(r), -z
AM 'kɑkɑ, -z

kakapo
BR 'kɑːkəpəʊ, -z
AM 'kɑkəˌpoʊ, -z

kakemono
BR ˌkɑːkɪ'məʊnəʊ, -z
AM ˌkɑkə'moʊnoʊ,
ˌkækə'moʊnoʊ, -z

kala-azar
BR ˌkɑːlə(r)ə'zɑː(r)
AM ˌkɑlə'zɑr

Kalahari
BR ˌkalə'hɑːri
AM ˌkɑlə'hɑri

Kalamazoo
BR ˌkaləmə'zuː
AM ˌkæləmə'zu

Kalashnikov
BR kə'laʃnɪkɒf, -s
AM kə'læʃnəˌkɑf, -s

kale
BR keɪl, -z
AM keɪl, -z

kaleidoscope
BR kə'lʌɪdəskəʊp, -s
AM kə'laɪdəˌskoʊp, -s

kaleidoscopic
BR kəˌlʌɪdə'skɒpɪk
AM kəˌlaɪdə'skɑpɪk

kaleidoscopical
BR kəˌlʌɪdə'skɒpɪkl
AM kəˌlaɪdə'skɑpəkəl

kaleidoscopically
BR kəˌlʌɪdə'skɒpɪkli
AM kəˌlaɪdə'skɑpək(ə)li

kalenchoe
BR ˌkalən'kəʊi,
ˌkaləŋ'kəʊi
AM ˌkælən'koʊi

kalends
BR 'kalɛndz, 'kalɪndz
AM 'kælən(d)z

kaleyard
BR 'keɪljɑːd, -z
AM 'keɪlˌjɑrd, -z

Kalgoorlie
BR kal'gʊəli
AM kal'gʊrli

Kali
BR 'kɑːli
AM 'kɑli

kali
BR 'kali, 'keɪli, 'keɪlʌɪ
AM 'keɪli

Kalinin
BR kə'liːnɪn
AM kə'linɪn
RUS ka'lʲinʲin

Kaliningrad
BR kə'liːnɪngrad
AM kə'linɪnˌgræd
RUS kəlʲinʲin'grat

Kalmar
BR 'kalmɑː(r),
'kɑːlmə(r)
AM 'kɑlmɑr

kalmia
BR 'kalmɪə(r), -z
AM 'kɑlmiə, -z

Kalmuck
BR 'kalmʌk, -s
AM 'kɑlmək, -s

Kalmuk
BR 'kalmʌk, -s
AM 'kɑlmək, -s

Kalmyk
BR 'kalmɪk, -s
AM 'kælmɪk, -s

kalong
BR 'kalɒŋ, 'kɑːlɒŋ, -z
AM 'kɑlɔŋ, 'kɑlɑŋ, -z

kalpa
BR 'kʌlpə(r), 'kalpə(r),
-z
AM 'kɑlpə, -z

Kaluga
BR kə'luːgə(r)
AM kə'lugə

Kama
BR 'kɑːmə(r)
AM 'kɑmə

Kama Sutra
BR ˌkɑːmə 'suːtrə(r)
AM ˌkɑmə 'sutrə

Kamchatka
BR kam'tʃatkə(r)
AM kɑm'tʃatkə

kame
BR keɪm, -z
AM keɪm, -z

Kamenskoye
BR kə'mɛnskɔɪə(r)
AM kə'mɛnˌskɔɪə
RUS 'kamʲinskəji

Kamensk-Uralski
BR ˌkamɛnsk
jʊ'ralski
AM ˌkɑmɛnsk
jʊ'rɑlski

kamikaze
BR ˌkamɪ'kɑːzi
AM ˌkɑmə'kɑzi

Kampala
BR kam'pɑːlə(r)
AM kɑm'pɑlə

kampong
BR 'kampɒn,
'kampɒŋ, -z
AM 'kɑmˌpɔŋ,
'kɑmˌpɑŋ, -z

Kampuchea
BR ˌkampʉ'tʃiːə(r)
AM ˌkɑmpə'tʃiə

Kampuchean
BR ˌkampʊˈtʃiːən, -z
AM ˌkɑmpəˈtʃiən, -z
kana
BR ˈkɑːnə(r)
AM ˈkɑnə
kanaka
BR kəˈnakə(r), -z
AM kəˈnɑkə, -z
Kanarese
BR ˌkanəˈriːz
AM ˌkɑnəˈriz
Kanawa
BR ˈkanəwə(r), kəˈnɑːwə(r)
AM kəˈnɑwə, ˈkɑnəwə
kanban
BR ˈkanban, -z
AM ˈkɑnˌbɑn, -z
Kanchenjunga
BR ˌkantʃ(ə)nˈdʒʊŋgə(r)
AM ˌkɑn(t)ʃənˈdʒʊŋgə
Kandahar
BR ˌkandəˈhɑː(r)
AM ˌkɑndəˈhɑr
Kandinsky
BR kanˈdɪnski
AM kænˈdɪnski
Kandy
BR ˈkandi
AM ˈkændi
Kandyan
BR ˈkandɪən, -z
AM ˈkændiən, -z
Kane
BR keɪn
AM keɪn
kanga
BR ˈkaŋgə(r), -z
AM ˈkæŋgə, -z
kangaroo
BR ˌkaŋgəˈruː, -z
AM ˌkæŋgəˈru, -z
Kangchenjunga
BR ˌkaŋtʃ(ə)nˈdʒʊŋgə(r)
AM ˌkɑŋtʃənˈdʒʊŋgə
kanji
BR ˈkandʒi
AM ˈkɑndʒi
Kannada
BR ˈkɑːnədə(r), ˈkanədə(r)
AM ˈkɑnədə, ˈkænədə
Kano
BR ˈkɑːnəʊ
AM ˈkɑnoʊ
kanoon
BR kəˈnuːn, -z
AM kɑˈnun, -z
Kansan
BR ˈkanz(ə)n, -z
AM ˈkænzn, -z
Kansas
BR ˈkanzəs
AM ˈkænzəs
Kant
BR kant
AM kɑnt
Kantian
BR ˈkantɪən, -z
AM ˈkɑn(t)iən, -z
KANU
BR ˈkɑːnuː
AM ˈkɑnu
kaolin
BR ˈkeɪəlɪn
AM ˈkeɪələn
kaolinic
BR ˌkeɪəˈlɪnɪk
AM ˌkeɪəˈlɪnɪk
kaolinise
BR ˈkeɪəlɨnʌɪz, -ɨz, -ɪŋ, -d
AM ˈkeɪələˌnaɪz, -ɨz, -ɪŋ, -d
kaolinite
BR ˈkeɪəlɪnʌɪt
AM ˈkeɪələˌnaɪt
kaolinize
BR ˈkeɪəlɨnʌɪz, -ɨz, -ɪŋ, -d
AM ˈkeɪələˌnaɪz, -ɨz, -ɪŋ, -d
kaon
BR ˈkeɪɒn, -z
AM ˈkeɪˌɑn, ˈkeɪən, -z
Kapellmeister
BR kəˈpɛlmʌɪstə(r), -z
AM kəˈpɛlˌmaɪstər, -z
Kap Farvel
BR ˌkap fɑːˈvɛl
AM ˌkæp fɑrˈvɛl
Kaplan
BR ˈkaplən
AM ˈkæplən
kapok
BR ˈkeɪpɒk
AM ˈkeɪˌpɑk
kappa
BR ˈkapə(r)
AM ˈkæpə
kaput
BR kəˈpʊt
AM kəˈpʊt, kɑˈpʊt
Karabiner
BR ˌkarəˈbiːnə(r), -z
AM ˌkɛrəˈbinər, -z
Karachi
BR kəˈrɑːtʃi
AM kəˈrɑtʃi
Karaite
BR ˈkɛːrəʌɪt, -s
AM ˈkɛrəˌaɪt, -s
Karajan
BR ˈkarəjɑːn
AM ˈkɛrəˌjɑn
Karakoram
BR ˌkarəˈkɔːrəm
AM ˌkɛrəˈkɔrəm
Karakorum
BR ˌkarəˈkɔːrəm
AM ˌkɛrəˈkɔrəm
karakul
BR ˈkarək(ʊ)l, -z
AM ˈkɛrəkəl, -z
Kara Kum
BR ˌkarə ˈkʌm
AM ˈkɛrə ˈkəm
karaoke
BR ˌkarɪˈəʊki
AM ˌkɛriˈoʊki
karat
BR ˈkarət, -s
AM ˈkɛrət, -s
karate
BR kəˈrɑːti
AM kəˈrɑdi
Kardomah
BR kɑːˈdəʊmə(r)
AM kɑrˈdoʊmə
karela
BR kəˈrɛlə(r), kəˈreɪlə(r), -z
AM kəˈrɛlə, -z
Karelia
BR kəˈriːlɪə(r)
AM kəˈriljə, kəˈriliə
Karelian
BR kəˈriːlɪən, -z
AM kəˈriliən, -z
Karen[1]
Burmese people
BR kəˈrɛn, kaˈrɛn, -z
AM kəˈrɛn, -z
Karen[2]
forename
BR ˈkarən, ˈkarn̩
AM ˈkɛrən
Kariba
BR kəˈriːbə(r)
AM kəˈribə
Karin
BR ˈkarɪn, ˈkarn̩
AM ˈkɛrən, ˈkɑrən
Karl
BR kɑːl
AM kɑrl
Karloff
BR ˈkɑːlɒf
AM ˈkɑrˌlɔf, ˈkɑrˌlɑf
Karlsbad
BR ˈkɑːlzbad
AM ˈkɑrlzˌbɑd, ˈkɑrlzˌbæd
Karlsruhe
BR ˈkɑːlzrʊə(r)
AM ˈkɑrlzˌrʊə
karma
BR ˈkɑːmə(r)
AM ˈkɑrmə
karmic
BR ˈkɑːmɪk
AM ˈkɑrmɪk
Karnak
BR ˈkɑːnak
AM ˈkɑrˌnæk
Karnataka
BR kəˈnɑːtəkə(r)
AM kɑrˈnɑdəkə
Karno
BR ˈkɑːnəʊ
AM ˈkɑrnoʊ
karoo
BR kəˈruː, -z
AM kəˈru, -z
Karpov
BR ˈkɑːpɒv
AM ˈkɑrˌpɔv, ˈkɑrˌpɑv
karri
BR ˈkar|i, -ɪz
AM ˈkɛri, -z
Karroo
BR kəˈruː
AM kəˈru
Kars
BR kɑːs
AM kɑrs
karst
BR kɑːst
AM kɑrst
kart
BR kɑːt, -s, -ɪŋ, -ɨd
AM kɑr|t, -ts, -dɪŋ, -dɨd
karyokinesis
BR ˌkarɪəʊkɪˈniːsɪs
AM ˌkɛriəkəˈnisɨs
karyotype
BR ˈkarɪə(ʊ)tʌɪp, -s
AM ˈkɛrioʊˌtaɪp, ˈkɛriəˌtaɪp, -s
kasbah
BR ˈkazbɑː(r), -z
AM ˈkæzˌbɑ, ˈkæsˌbɑ, -z
Kashmir
BR ˌkaʃˈmɪə(r)
AM ˈkæʃˌmɪ(ə)r, ˈkæʒˌmɪ(ə)r
Kashmiri
BR ˌkaʃˈmɪər|i, -ɪz
AM ˌkæʃˈmɪri, ˌkæʒˈmɪri, -z
Kasparov
BR ˈkaspərɒv, kaˈspɑːrɒv
AM ˈkæspəˌrɔv, ˈkæspəˌrɑv, kæsˈpɛrɔv, kæsˈpɛrɑv
Kassel
BR ˈkasl
AM ˈkæsəl
Kassite
BR ˈkasʌɪt, -s
AM ˈkæˌsaɪt, -s
katabatic
BR ˌkatəˈbatɪk, -s
AM ˌkædəˈbædɪk, -s
katabolism
BR kəˈtabəlɪz(ə)m
AM kəˈtæbəˌlɪzm
katakana
BR ˌkatəˈkɑːnə(r), -z
AM ˌkɑdəˈkɑnə, -z
Katanga
BR kəˈtaŋgə(r)
AM kəˈtæŋ(g)ə

katathermometer
BR ˌkatəθəˈmɒmɪtə(r), -z
AM ˌkædəθərˈmɑmədər, -z

Kate
BR keɪt
AM keɪt

Kath
BR kaθ
AM kæθ

katharevousa
BR ˌkaθəˈrɛvuːsə(r)
AM ˌkɑθəˈrɛvəsə

Katharine
BR ˈkaθ(ə)rɪn, ˈkaθ(ə)rn̩
AM ˈkæθ(ə)rən

Katherine
BR ˈkaθ(ə)rɪn, ˈkaθ(ə)rn̩
AM ˈkæθ(ə)rən

Kathie
BR ˈkaθi
AM ˈkæθi

Kathleen
BR ˈkaθliːn
AM kæθˈlin

Kathmandu
BR ˌkatmanˈduː
AM ˌkɑtmɑnˈdu, ˌkætmænˈdu

kathode
BR ˈkaθəʊd, -z
AM ˈkæθoʊd, -z

Kathryn
BR ˈkaθr(ɪ)n
AM ˈkæθrən

Kathy
BR ˈkaθi
AM ˈkæθi

Katia
BR ˈkatɪə(r)
AM ˈkɑdiə, ˈkɑtjə

Katie
BR ˈkeɪti
AM ˈkeɪdi

Katmandu
BR ˌkatmanˈduː
AM ˌkɑtmɑnˈdu, ˌkætmænˈdu

Katowice
BR ˌkatəˈviːtʃə(r), ˌkatəˈviːtsə(r)
AM ˌkɑdəˈvɪtsə

Katrina
BR kəˈtriːnə(r)
AM kəˈtrinə

Katrine
BR ˈkatrɪn
AM ˈkætrɪn, kəˈtrin(ə)

Kattegat
BR ˈkatɪgat
AM ˈkædəˌgæt

Katy
BR ˈkeɪti
AM ˈkeɪdi

Katya
BR ˈkatjə(r)
AM ˈkɑdiə, ˈkɑtjə

katydid
BR ˈkeɪtɪdɪd, -z
AM ˈkeɪdiˌdɪd, -z

Katz
BR kats
AM kætz

Kauffmann
BR ˈkɔːfmən, ˈkaʊfmən
AM ˈkɔfmən, ˈkɑfmən

Kaufman
BR ˈkɔːfmən, ˈkaʊfmən
AM ˈkɔfmən, ˈkɑfmən

Kaunas
BR ˈkaʊnəs
AM ˈkaʊnəs

Kaunda
BR kaʊˈʊndə(r)
AM kəˈwʊndə

kauri
BR ˈkaʊr|i, -ɪz
AM ˈkaʊri, -z

kava
BR ˈkɑːvə(r)
AM ˈkɑvə

Kavanagh
BR ˈkavənə(r), ˈkavn̩ə(r), kəˈvanə(r)
AM ˈkævəˌnɔ

kawakawa
BR ˈkɑːwəˌkɑːwə(r), -z
AM ˈkɑwəˈkɑwə, -z

Kawasaki
BR ˌkawəˈsɑːk|i, ˌkɑːwəˈsɑːk|i, ˌkawəˈsak|i, -ɪz
AM ˌkɑwəˈsɑki, -z

Kawthulei
BR kɔːˈθuːleɪ
AM kɔˈθuləɪ, kɑˈθuləɪ

Kay
BR keɪ
AM keɪ

kayak
BR ˈkʌɪak, -s
AM ˈkaɪˌæk, -s

Kaye
BR keɪ
AM keɪ

kayo
BR ˌkeɪˈəʊ, -z, -ɪŋ, -d
AM ˈkeɪˌoʊ, -z, -ɪŋ, -d

Kazakh
BR kəˈzak, ˈkazak, -s
AM kəˈzɑk, -s

Kazakhstan
BR ˌkazəkˈstɑːn, ˌkazəkˈstan
AM ˌkɑzɑkˈstɑn, ˈkɑzəkˌstɑn

Kazan
BR kəˈzan
AM kəˈzæn

kazoo
BR kəˈzuː, -z
AM kəˈzu, -z

kea
BR ˈkiːə(r), ˈkeɪə(r), -z
AM kiə, -z

Kean
BR kiːn
AM kin

Keane
BR kiːn
AM kin

Kearney
BR ˈkɑːni, ˈkəːni
AM ˈkərni

Kearns
BR kəːnz
AM kərnz

Kearny
BR ˈkɑːni, ˈkəːni
AM ˈkərni

Keating
BR ˈkiːtɪŋ
AM ˈkidɪŋ

Keaton
BR ˈkiːtn
AM ˈkitn

Keats
BR kiːts
AM kits

Keatsian
BR ˈkiːtsɪən, -z
AM ˈkitsiən, -z

Keays
BR kiːz
AM kiz

kebab
BR kɪˈbab, -z
AM kəˈbɑb, -z

Keble
BR ˈkiːbl
AM ˈkibəl

keck
BR kɛk, -s, -ɪŋ, -t
AM kɛk, -s, -ɪŋ, -t

ked
BR kɛd, -z
AM kɛd, -z

Kedah
BR ˈkɛdə(r)
AM ˈkɛdə, kəˈdɑ

kedge
BR kɛdʒ, -ɪz, -ɪŋ, -d
AM kɛdʒ, -əz, -ɪŋ, -d

kedgeree
BR ˈkɛdʒəriː, ˌkɛdʒəˈriː
AM ˈkɛdʒəˌri, ˌkɛdʒəˈri

Keeble
BR ˈkiːbl
AM ˈkibəl

Keefe
BR kiːf
AM kif

Keegan
BR ˈkiːg(ə)n
AM ˈkigən

keek
BR kiːk, -s, -ɪŋ, -t
AM kik, -s, -ɪŋ, -t

keel
BR kiːl, -z, -ɪŋ, -d
AM kil, -z, -ɪŋ, -d

keelboat
BR ˈkiːlbəʊt, -s
AM ˈkilˌboʊt, -s

Keele
BR kiːl
AM kil

Keeler
BR ˈkiːlə(r)
AM ˈkilər

Keeley
BR ˈkiːli
AM ˈkili

keelhaul
BR ˈkiːlhɔːl, -z, -ɪŋ, -d
AM ˈkilˌ(h)ɔl, ˈkilˌ(h)ɑl, -z, -ɪŋ, -d

Keeling
BR ˈkiːlɪŋ
AM ˈkilɪŋ

keelless
BR ˈkiːllɪs
AM ˈki(l)lɪs

keelson
BR ˈkɛlsn, ˈkiːlsn, -z
AM ˈkilsən, -z

keen
BR kiːn, -z, -ɪŋ, -d, -ə(r), -ɪst
AM kin, -z, -ɪŋ, -d, -ər, -ɪst

Keenan
BR ˈkiːnən
AM ˈkinən

Keene
BR kiːn
AM kin

keenly
BR ˈkiːnli
AM ˈkinli

keenness
BR ˈkiːnnɪs
AM ˈki(n)nɪs

keep
BR kiːp, -s, -ɪŋ
AM kip, -s, -ɪŋ

keepable
BR ˈkiːpəbl
AM ˈkipəbəl

keeper
BR ˈkiːpə(r), -z
AM ˈkipər, -z

keepnet
BR ˈkiːpnɛt, -s
AM ˈkipˌnɛt, -s

keepsake
BR ˈkiːpseɪk, -s
AM ˈkipˌseɪk, -s

keeshond
BR ˈkeɪshɒnd, -z
AM ˈkeɪsˌ(h)ɑnd, -z

kef
BR kɛf
AM kɛf
keffiyeh
BR kəˈfiː(j)ə(*r*), -z
AM kəˈfi(j)ə, -z
Keflavik
BR ˈkɛfləvɪk
AM ˈkɛfləvɪk
keg
BR kɛg, -z
AM kɛg, -z
kegler
BR ˈkɛglə(r), -z
AM ˈkɛglər, -z
Kehoe
BR ˈkiːəʊ
AM ˈki,(h)oʊ
Keighley[1]
place in UK
BR ˈkiːθli
AM ˈkiθli
Keighley[2]
surname
BR ˈkiːθli, ˈkiːli
AM ˈkili
Keillor
BR ˈkiːlə(r)
AM ˈkilər
Keir
BR kɪə(r)
AM kɛ(ə)r
keiretsu
BR keɪˈrɛtsuː, -z
AM keɪˈrɛtsu, -z
keister
BR ˈkiːstə(r), -z
AM ˈkistər, -z
Keith
BR kiːθ
AM kiθ
kelim
BR kɛˈliːm, -z
AM kəˈlim, -z
Kelleher
BR ˈkɛləhə(r)
AM ˈkɛləhər
Keller
BR ˈkɛlə(r)
AM ˈkɛlər
Kellet
BR ˈkɛlɨt
AM ˈkɛlət
Kellett
BR ˈkɛlɨt
AM ˈkɛlət
Kelley
BR ˈkɛli
AM ˈkɛli
Kellogg
BR ˈkɛlɒg
AM ˈkɛlɔg, ˈkɛlɑg
Kells
BR kɛlz
AM kɛlz
kelly
BR ˈkɛl|i, -ɪz
AM ˈkɛli, -z
keloid
BR ˈkiːlɔɪd, -z
AM ˈki,lɔɪd, -z
kelp
BR kɛlp
AM kɛlp
kelpie
BR ˈkɛlp|i, -ɪz
AM ˈkɛlpi, -z
kelpy
BR ˈkɛlp|i, -ɪz
AM ˈkɛlpi, -z
Kelso
BR ˈkɛlsəʊ
AM ˈkɛl,soʊ
kelson
BR ˈkɛlsn, -z
AM ˈkɛlsən, -z
kelt
BR kɛlt, -s
AM kɛlt, -s
kelter
BR ˈkɛltə(r)
AM ˈkɛltər
kelvin
BR ˈkɛlvɪn, -z
AM ˈkɛlvən, -z
Kelvinator
BR ˈkɛlvɨneɪtə(r)
AM ˈkɛlvə,neɪdər
Kelvinside
BR ,kɛlv(ɪ)nˈsʌɪd
AM ˈkɛlvən,saɪd
Kemble
BR ˈkɛmbl
AM ˈkɛmbəl
kemp
BR kɛmp
AM kɛmp
Kempis
BR ˈkɛmpɪs
AM ˈkɛmpəs
kempt
BR kɛm(p)t
AM kɛm(p)t
kempy
BR ˈkɛmpi
AM ˈkɛmpi
ken
BR kɛn, -z, -ɪŋ, -d
AM kɛn, -z, -ɪŋ, -d
Kenco
BR ˈkɛnkəʊ, ˈkɛŋkəʊ
AM ˈkɛŋkoʊ
Kendall
BR ˈkɛndl
AM ˈkɛndl
kendo
BR ˈkɛndəʊ
AM ˈkɛndoʊ
Kendrick
BR ˈkɛndrɪk
AM ˈkɛndrɪk
Keneally
BR kɪˈniːli
AM kəˈnili
Kenelm
BR ˈkɛnɛlm
AM ˈkɛnɛlm
Kenilworth
BR ˈkɛn(ɪ)lwəːθ, ˈkɛn(ɪ)lwəθ
AM ˈkɛnəl,wərθ
Kennebunkport
BR ,kɛnɪˈbʌŋkpɔːt
AM ,kɛnəˈbəŋk,pɔ(ə)rt
Kennedy
BR ˈkɛnɨdi
AM ˈkɛnədi
kennel
BR ˈkɛnl, -z
AM ˈkɛnəl, -z
Kennelly
BR ˈkɛnəli, ˈkɛnl̩i
AM ˈkɛnəli
Kennet
BR ˈkɛnɨt
AM ˈkɛnət
Kenneth
BR ˈkɛnɨθ
AM ˈkɛnəθ
Kenney
BR ˈkɛni
AM ˈkɛni
kenning
BR ˈkɛnɪŋ, -z
AM ˈkɛnɪŋ, -z
Kennington
BR ˈkɛnɪŋt(ə)n
AM ˈkɛnɪŋtən
Kenny
BR ˈkɛni
AM ˈkɛni
keno
BR ˈkiːnəʊ
AM ˈkinoʊ
kenosis
BR kɪˈnəʊsɪs
AM kəˈnoʊsəs, kiˈnoʊsəs
kenotic
BR kɪˈnɒtɪk
AM kəˈnɑdɪk, kiˈnɑdɪk
kenotron
BR ˈkɛnətrɒn
AM ˈkɛnə,trɑn
Kenrick
BR ˈkɛnrɪk
AM ˈkɛnrɪk
Kensal
BR ˈkɛnsl
AM ˈkɛnsəl
Kensington
BR ˈkɛnzɪŋt(ə)n
AM ˈkɛnsɪŋtən
Kensitas
BR ˈkɛnzɪtas, ˈkɛnzɪtəs
AM ˈkɛnzədəs
kent
BR kɛnt, -s, -ɪŋ, -ɨd
AM kɛn|t, -ts, -(t)ɪŋ, -(t)ɨd
Kentigern
BR ˈkɛntɪgəːn, ˈkɛntɪg(ə)n
AM ˈkɛn(t)ə,gərn
Kentish
BR ˈkɛntɪʃ
AM ˈkɛn(t)ɪʃ
kentledge
BR ˈkɛntlɪdʒ
AM ˈkɛnt,lɛdʒ
Kenton
BR ˈkɛntən
AM ˈkɛn(t)ən
Kentuckian
BR kɛnˈtʌkɪən, -z
AM kənˈtəkiən, -z
Kentucky
BR kɛnˈtʌki, kənˈtʌki
AM kənˈtəki
Kenwood®
BR ˈkɛnwʊd
AM ˈkɛn,wʊd
Kenya[1]
before independence
BR ˈkiːnjə(*r*)
AM ˈkinjə, ˈkɛnjə
Kenya[2]
BR ˈkɛnjə(*r*)
AM ˈkinjə, ˈkɛnjə
Kenyan[1]
before independence
BR ˈkiːnjən, -z
AM ˈkinjən, ˈkɛnjən, -z
Kenyan[2]
BR ˈkɛnjən, -z
AM ˈkinjən, ˈkɛnjən, -z
Kenyatta
BR kɛnˈjatə(*r*)
AM kɛˈnjɑdə
Kenyon
BR ˈkɛnjən
AM ˈkɛnjən
Keogh
BR ˈkiːəʊ
AM ˈkioʊ
Keough
BR ˈkiːəʊ
AM ˈkioʊ
kepi
BR ˈkeɪp|i, ˈkɛp|i, -ɪz
AM ˈkeɪpi, ˈkɛpi, -z
Kepler
BR ˈkɛplə(r)
AM ˈkɛplər
Keplerian
BR kɛˈplɪərɪən
AM kɛˈplɛriən
Keppel
BR ˈkɛpl
AM ˈkɛpəl
kept
BR kɛpt
AM kɛp(t)
Kerala
BR ˈkɛrələ(*r*)
AM ˈkɛrələ

Keralite
BR 'kɛrəlʌɪt, -s
AM 'kɛrəˌlaɪt, -s

keratin
BR 'kɛrətɪn
AM 'kɛrətən

keratinisation
BR ˌkɛrətɪnʌɪ'zeɪʃn, ˌkɛrətn̩ʌɪ'zeɪʃn
AM ˌkɛrəˌtɪnɪ'zeɪʃən, ˌkɛrətnˌaɪ'zeɪʃən

keratinise
BR 'kɛrətɪnʌɪz, 'kɛrətn̩ʌɪz, -ɪz, -ɪŋ, -d
AM 'kɛrətnˌaɪz, -ɪz, -ɪŋ, -d

keratinization
BR ˌkɛrətɪnʌɪ'zeɪʃn, ˌkɛrətn̩ʌɪ'zeɪʃn
AM ˌkɛrəˌtɪnɪ'zeɪʃən, ˌkɛrətnˌaɪ'zeɪʃən

keratinize
BR 'kɛrətɪnʌɪz, 'kɛrətn̩ʌɪz, -ɪz, -ɪŋ, -d
AM 'kɛrətnˌaɪz, -ɪz, -ɪŋ, -d

keratose
BR 'kɛrətəʊs, 'kɛrətəʊz
AM 'kɛrəˌtoʊs, 'kɛrəˌtoʊz

keratosis
BR ˌkɛrə'təʊsɪs
AM ˌkɛrə'toʊsəs

kerb
BR kəːb, -z
AM kərb, -z

kerbside
BR 'kəːbsʌɪd
AM 'kərbˌsaɪd

kerbstone
BR 'kəːbstəʊn, -z
AM 'kərbˌstoʊn, -z

kerchief
BR 'kəːtʃɪf, 'kəːtʃiːf, -s
AM 'kərtʃəf, 'kərˌtʃif, -s, -t

Kerensky
BR kə'rɛnski
AM kə'rɛnski

kerf
BR kəːf, -s
AM kərf, -s

kerfuffle
BR kə'fʌfl, -z
AM kər'fəfəl, -z

Kerguelen
BR 'kəːgɪlɪn, 'kəːglɪn
AM kər'gjulən

kermes
BR 'kəːmɪz, 'kəːmiːz
AM 'kərmiz, 'kərməs

kermess
BR 'kəːmɛs, kə'mɛs, -ɪz
AM 'kərməs, -əz

kermesse
BR 'kəːmɛs, kə'mɛs, -ɪz
AM 'kərməs, -əz

kermis
BR 'kəːm|ɪs, -ɪsɪz
AM 'kərməs, -əz

Kermit
BR 'kəːmɪt
AM 'kərmɨt

Kermode
BR kə'məʊd, 'kəːməʊd
AM ˌkər'ˌmoʊd, 'kərmədi

kern
BR kəːn, -z, -ɪŋ, -d
AM kərn, -z, -ɪŋ, -d

kernel
BR 'kəːnl, -z
AM 'kərnəl, -z

kero
kerosene
BR 'kɛrəʊ
AM 'kɛˌroʊ

kerosene
BR 'kɛrəsiːn
AM ˌkɛrə'ˌsin

kerosine
BR 'kɛrəsiːn
AM ˌkɛrə'ˌsin

Kerouac
BR 'kɛrʊak
AM 'kɛrəˌwæk

kerplunk
BR kə'plʌŋk
AM kər'pləŋk

Kerr
BR kəː(r), kɛː(r), kɑː(r)
AM kər, kɑr

Kerrigan
BR 'kɛrɪg(ə)n
AM 'kɛrəgən

Kerry
BR 'kɛr|i, -ɪz
AM 'kɛri, -z

kersey
BR 'kəːzi
AM 'kərzi

kerseymere
BR 'kəːzɪmɪə(r), -z
AM 'kərziˌmɪ(ə)r, -z

Kershaw
BR 'kəːʃɔː(*r*)
AM 'kərˌʃɔ

kerygma
BR kə'rɪgmə(*r*)
AM kə'rɪgmə

kerygmata
BR kə'rɪgmətə(*r*)
AM kə'rɪgmədə

kerygmatic
BR ˌkɛrɪg'matɪk
AM ˌkɛrɪg'mædɪk

Kes
BR kɛz, kɛs
AM kɛs, kɛz

Kesey
BR 'kiːzi
AM 'kizi

Kesh
BR kɛʃ
AM kɛʃ

kesh
BR keɪʃ
AM keɪʃ

keskidee
BR 'kɛskɪdiː, -z
AM 'kɛskəˌdi, -z

Kessler
BR 'kɛslə(r)
AM 'kɛslər

Kesteven
BR kɪ'stiːvn, kɛ'stiːvn, 'kɛstɪvn
AM kə'stivn, 'kɛstəvn

Keston
BR 'kɛst(ə)n
AM 'kɛstən

kestrel
BR 'kɛstr(ə)l, -z
AM 'kɛstrəl, -z

Keswick
BR 'kɛzɪk
AM 'kɛsˌwɪk

ketch
BR kɛtʃ, -ɪz
AM kɛtʃ, -əz

ketchup
BR 'kɛtʃəp, 'kɛtʃʌp, -s
AM 'kɛtʃəp, -s

ketoacidosis
BR ˌkiːtəʊˌasɪ'dəʊsɪs
AM ˌkidoʊˌæsə'doʊsəs

ketone
BR 'kiːtəʊn, -z
AM 'kiˌtoʊn, -z

ketonic
BR kiː'tɒnɪk
AM ki'tɑnɪk

ketonuria
BR ˌkiːtə'njʊərɪə(*r*)
AM ˌkidə'n(j)uriə

ketosis
BR kiː'təʊsɪs
AM ki'toʊsəs

ketotic
BR kiː'tɒtɪk
AM ki'tɑdɪk

Kettering
BR 'kɛt(ə)rɪŋ
AM 'kɛdərɪŋ

kettle
BR 'kɛtl, -z
AM 'kɛdəl, -z

kettledrum
BR 'kɛtldrʌm, -z
AM 'kɛdlˌdrəm, -z

kettledrummer
BR 'kɛtlˌdrʌmə(r), -z
AM 'kɛdlˌdrəmər, -z

kettleful
BR 'kɛtlfʊl, -z
AM 'kɛdlˌfʊl, -z

keuper
BR 'kɔɪpə(r)
AM 'kɔɪpər

kevel
BR 'kɛvl, -z
AM 'kɛvəl, -z

Kevin
BR 'kɛvɪn
AM 'kɛvən

kevlar
BR 'kɛvlɑː(r)
AM 'kɛvˌlɑr

Kew
BR kjuː
AM kju

Kewpie®
BR 'kjuːp|i, -ɪz
AM 'kjupi, -z

kex
BR kɛks
AM kɛks

key
BR kiː, -z, -ɪŋ, -d
AM ki, -z, -ɪŋ, -d

keyboard
BR 'kiːbɔːd, -z, -ɪŋ, -ɪd
AM 'kiˌbɔ(ə)rd, -z, -ɪŋ, -əd

keyboarder
BR 'kiːbɔːdə(r), -z
AM 'kiˌbɔrdər, -z

keyboardist
BR 'kiːbɔːdɪst, -s
AM 'kiˌbɔrdəst, -s

keyer
BR 'kiːə(r), -z
AM 'kiər, -z

Keyes
BR kiːz
AM kiz

keyholder
BR 'kiːˌhəʊldə(r), -z
AM 'kiˌ(h)oʊldər, -z

keyhole
BR 'kiːhəʊl, -z
AM 'kiˌ(h)oʊl, -z

Key Largo
BR ˌkiː 'lɑːgəʊ
AM ˌki 'lɑrˌgoʊ

keyless
BR 'kiːlɨs
AM 'kilɨs

Keynes
BR keɪnz, kiːnz
AM kinz, keɪnz

Keynesian
BR 'keɪnzɪən, -z
AM 'keɪnziən, -z

Keynesianism
BR 'keɪnzɪənɪz(ə)m
AM 'keɪnziəˌnɪzəm

keynote
BR 'kiːnəʊt, -s, -ɪŋ, -ɪd
AM 'kiˌnoʊ|t, -ts, -dɪŋ, -dəd

Keynsham
BR 'keɪnʃ(ə)m
AM 'keɪnʃəm

keypad
BR 'kiːpad, -z
AM 'kiˌpæd, -z

keypunch
BR 'ki:pʌn(t)ʃ, -ɨz
AM 'ki,pən(t)ʃ, -əz

keypuncher
BR 'ki:,pʌn(t)ʃə(r), -z
AM 'ki,pən(t)ʃər, -z

keyring
BR 'ki:rɪŋ, -z
AM 'ki,rɪŋ, -z

Keys
BR ki:z
AM kiz

Keyser
BR 'kʌɪzə(r), 'ki:zə(r)
AM 'kaɪzər

keystone
BR 'ki:stəʊn, -z
AM 'ki,stoʊn, -z

Keystone Kops
BR ,ki:stəʊn 'kɒps
AM 'ki,stoʊn 'kɑps

keystroke
BR 'ki:strəʊk, -s
AM 'ki,stroʊk, -s

keyway
BR 'ki:weɪ, -z
AM 'ki,weɪ, -z

Key West
BR ,ki: 'wɛst
AM ,ki 'wɛst

keyword
BR 'ki:wə:d, -z
AM 'ki,wərd, -z

KGB
BR ,keɪdʒi:'bi:
AM ,keɪ,dʒi'bi

Khabarovsk
BR 'kɑ:bərɒfsk,
,kɑ:bə'rɒfsk
AM 'kɑbə,rɑfsk
RUS xa'barəfsk

Khachaturian
BR ,katʃə'tjʊərɪən,
,katʃə'tʃʊərɪən
AM ,katʃə'tʊriən
RUS xətʃətu'rjan

khaddar
BR 'kadə(r)
AM 'kadər

khaki
BR 'kɑ:ki
AM 'kæki

khalif
BR 'keɪlɪf, -s
AM 'keɪlɪf, -s

khalifate
BR 'keɪlɪfeɪt, -s
AM 'keɪlə,feɪt,
'keɪləfət, -s

Khalki
BR 'kalki
AM 'kɑlki

khamsin
BR 'kamsɪn, -z
AM ,kɑm'sin, -z

khan
BR kɑ:n, -z
AM kɑn, -z

khanate
BR 'kɑ:neɪt, -s
AM 'kɑneɪt, -s

Kharg
BR kɑ:g
AM kɑrg

Kharkov
BR 'kɑ:kɒv
AM 'kɑr,kɔv, 'kɑr,kɑv

Khartoum
BR kɑ:'tu:m
AM kɑr'tum

Khayyam
BR kʌɪ'am, kʌɪ'ɑ:m
AM kaɪ'æm

khazi
BR 'kɑ:z|i, -ɪz
AM 'kɑzi, -z

Khedival
BR kɪ'di:vl, kɛ'di:vl
AM kə'divəl, kɛ'divəl

khedive
BR kɪ'di:v, kɛ'di:v, -z
AM kə'div, kɛ'div, -z

Khedivial
BR kɪ'di:vɪəl,
kɛ'di:vɪəl
AM kə'diviəl, kɛ'diviəl

Khíos
BR 'kʌɪɒs
AM 'kaɪɔs, 'kaɪɑs
GR 'hi:ɔs

Khitai
BR ,ki:'tʌɪ
AM ,ki'taɪ

Khmer
BR kmɛ:(r), kə'mɛ:(r)
AM k(ə)'mɛ(ə)r

Khmer Rouge
BR ,kmɛ: 'ru:ʒ,
kə,mɛ: +
AM k(ə),mɛ(ə)r 'ruʒ

Khoikhoi
BR 'kɔɪkɔɪ
AM 'kɔɪ'kɔɪ

Khoisan
BR 'kɔɪsɑ:n
AM 'kɔɪ,sɑn

Khomeini
BR kə'meɪni, kɒ'meɪni
AM koʊ'meɪni,
hoʊ'meɪni

Khorramshahr
BR ,kɒrəm'ʃɑ:(r)
AM ,kɔrəm'ʃɑr

khoum
BR ku:m, -z
AM kum, -z

Khrushchev
BR 'krʊstʃɒf, 'krʊʃtʃɒf
AM 'krʊʃ,(t)ʃɛv,
'krʊʃ,(t)ʃɔf,
'krʊʃ,(t)ʃɛv,
'krʊʃ,(t)ʃɑf
RUS xruʃ'tʃʲof

Khufu
BR 'ku:fu:
AM 'ku,fu

Khyber Pass
BR ,kʌɪbə 'pɑ:s,
,xʌɪbə +, + 'pas
AM ,kaɪbər 'pæs

kHz
BR 'kɪləhə:ts
AM 'kɪlə,hərts

kiang
BR kɪ'aŋ, -z
AM ki'(j)æŋ, -z

Kiangsu
BR kɪ,aŋ'su:
AM ki,(j)æŋ'su

Kia-Ora®
BR ,ki:ə'ɔ:rə(r)
AM ,kiə'ɔrə

kibble
BR 'kɪb|l, -lz, -l̩ɪŋ\-lɪŋ,
-ld
AM 'kɪb|əl, -əlz, -(ə)lɪŋ,
-əld

kibbutz
BR kɪ'bʊts, -ɪz
AM kɪ'bʊts, -əz

kibbutzim
BR kɪ'bʊtsɪm
AM kɪ,bʊt'sim

kibbutznik
BR kɪ'bʊtsnɪk, -s
AM kɪ'bʊtsnɪk, -s

kibe
BR kʌɪb, -z
AM kaɪb, -z

kibitka
BR kɪ'bɪtkə(r), -z
AM kə'bɪ(t)kə, -z

kibitz
BR 'kɪb|ɪts, -ɪtsɪz,
-ɪtsɪŋ, -ɪtst
AM 'kɪbəts, -əz, -ɪŋ, -t

kibitzer
BR 'kɪbɪtsə(r), -z
AM 'kɪbətsər, -z

kiblah
BR 'kɪblə(r)
AM 'kɪblə

kibosh
BR 'kʌɪbɒʃ
AM kə'bɑʃ, 'kaɪ,bɑʃ

kick
BR kɪk, -s, -ɪŋ, -t
AM kɪk, -s, -ɪŋ, -t

kickable
BR 'kɪkəbl
AM 'kɪkəbəl

kick-ass
BR ,kɪk'ɑ:s, ,kɪk'as
AM 'kɪk,æs

kickback
BR 'kɪkbak, -s
AM 'kɪk,bæk, -s

kick-boxer
BR 'kɪk,bɒksə(r), -z
AM 'kɪk,bɑksər, -z

kick-boxing
BR 'kɪk,bɒksɪŋ
AM 'kɪk,bɑksɪŋ

kickdown
BR 'kɪkdaʊn
AM 'kɪk,daʊn

kicker
BR 'kɪkə(r), -z
AM 'kɪkər, -z

kickoff
BR 'kɪkɒf, -s
AM 'kɪk,ɔf, 'kɪk,ɑf, -s

kick-pleat
BR 'kɪkpli:t, -s
AM 'kɪk,plit, -s

kickshaw
BR 'kɪkʃɔ:(r), -z
AM 'kɪk,ʃɔ, 'kɪk,ʃɑ, -z

kicksorter
BR 'kɪk,sɔ:tə(r), -z
AM 'kɪk,sɔrdər, -z

kickstand
BR 'kɪkstand, -z
AM 'kɪk,stænd, -z

kickstart
BR 'kɪkstɑ:t, ,kɪk'stɑ:t,
-s, -ɪŋ, -ɪd
AM 'kɪk,stɑr|t, -ts, -dɪŋ,
-dəd

kid
BR kɪd, -z, -ɪŋ, -ɪd
AM kɪd, -z, -ɪŋ, -ɪd

Kidd
BR kɪd
AM kɪd

kidder
BR 'kɪdə(r), -z
AM 'kɪdər, -z

Kidderminster
BR 'kɪdə,mɪnstə(r)
AM 'kɪdər,mɪnstər

kiddie
BR 'kɪd|i, -ɪz
AM 'kɪdi, -z

kiddiewink
BR 'kɪdɪwɪŋk, -s
AM 'kɪdi,wɪŋk, -s

kiddingly
BR 'kɪdɪŋli
AM 'kɪdɪŋli

kiddle
BR 'kɪdl, -z
AM 'kɪdəl, -z

kiddo
BR 'kɪdəʊ
AM 'kɪdoʊ

kiddush
BR 'kɪdʊʃ
AM 'kɪdəʃ

kiddy
BR 'kɪd|i, -ɪz
AM 'kɪdi, -z

kidnap
BR 'kɪdnap, -s, -ɪŋ, -t
AM 'kɪd,næp, -s, -ɪŋ, -t

kidnaper
BR 'kɪdnapə(r), -z

AM 'kɪd,næpər, -z

kidnaping
BR 'kɪdnapɪŋ, -z
AM 'kɪd,næpɪŋ, -z

kidnapper
BR 'kɪdnapə(r), -z
AM 'kɪd,næpər, -z

kidnapping
BR 'kɪdnapɪŋ, -z
AM 'kɪd,næpɪŋ, -z

kidney
BR 'kɪdn|i, -ɪz
AM 'kɪdni, -z

kidology
BR kɪ'dɒlədʒi
AM kɪ'dɑlədʒi

kidskin
BR 'kɪdskɪn
AM 'kɪd,skɪn

Kidwelly
BR kɪd'wɛli
AM kɪd'wɛli

Kiel
BR kiːl
AM kil

Kielce
BR 'kjɛl(t)sə(*r*)
AM 'kjɛl(t)sə

Kielder
BR 'kiːldə(r)
AM 'kildər

Kiely
BR 'kiːli
AM 'kili

kier
BR kɪə(r), -z
AM kɪ(ə)r, -z

Kieran
BR 'kɪərən, 'kɪərn̩
AM 'kɪrɑn

Kierkegaard
BR 'kɪəkəgɑːd
AM 'kɪrkɛ,gɑrd
DAN 'kiʌgə,gɒː'

Kieron
BR 'kɪərən, 'kɪərn̩
AM 'kɪrən

kieselguhr
BR 'kiːzlgʊə(r)
AM 'kizɛlgər

Kiev
BR ˌkiː'ɛf, ˌkiː'ɛv, 'kiːɛf, 'kiːɛv
AM ˌki'ɛv, 'kiɛv

kif
BR kɪf, -s
AM kɪf, -s

Kigali
BR kɪ'gɑːli
AM kɪ'gɑli

kike
BR kʌɪk, -s
AM kaɪk, -s

Kikuyu
BR kɪ'kuːyuː, -z
AM kɪ'kuyu, -z

Kilbracken
BR kɪl'brak(ə)n
AM kɪl'brækən

Kilbride
BR kɪl'brʌɪd
AM kɪl'braɪd

Kilburn
BR 'kɪlb(ə)n, 'kɪlbəːn
AM 'kɪlbərn

Kildare
BR kɪl'dɛː(r)
AM ˌkɪl'dɛ(ə)r

kilderkin
BR 'kɪldəkɪn, -z
AM 'kɪldərkən, -z

Kilfedder
BR kɪl'fɛdə(r)
AM kɪl'fɛdər

kilim
BR kɪ'liːm, -z
AM kə'lim, -z

Kilimanjaro
BR ˌkɪlɪmən'dʒɑːrəʊ, ˌkɪlɪman'dʒɑːrəʊ
AM ˌkɪləmən'dʒɑroʊ

Kilkenny
BR kɪl'kɛni
AM kɪl'kɛnni

kill
BR kɪl, -z, -ɪŋ, -d
AM kɪl, -z, -ɪŋ, -d

Killamarsh
BR 'kɪləmɑːʃ
AM 'kɪlə,mɑrʃ

Killanin
BR kɪ'lanɪn
AM kɪ'lænən

Killarney
BR kɪ'lɑːni
AM kɪ'lɑrni

killdeer
BR 'kɪldɪə(r), -z
AM 'kɪldɪ(ə)r, -z

killer
BR 'kɪlə(r), -z
AM 'kɪlər, -z

killick
BR 'kɪlɪk, -s
AM 'kɪlɪk, -s

Killiecranckie
BR ˌkɪlɪ'kraŋki
AM ˌkɪli'kræŋki

killifish
BR 'kɪlɪfɪʃ, -ɪz
AM 'kɪli,fɪʃ, -ɪz

killing
BR 'kɪlɪŋ, -z
AM 'kɪlɪŋ, -z

killingly
BR 'kɪlɪŋli
AM 'kɪlɪŋli

killjoy
BR 'kɪldʒɔɪ, -z
AM 'kɪl,dʒɔɪ, -z

Kilmarnock
BR kɪl'mɑːnək, kɪl'mɑːnɒk
AM kɪl'mɑrnək

Kilmuir
BR kɪl'mjʊə(r)
AM kɪl'mjʊ(ə)r

kiln
BR kɪln, -z
AM kɪln, -z

Kilner®
BR 'kɪlnə(r)
AM 'kɪlnər

kilo
BR 'kiːləʊ, -z
AM 'kiloʊ, -z

kilobyte
BR 'kɪlə(ʊ)bʌɪt, -s
AM 'kɪlə,baɪt, -s

kilocalorie
BR 'kɪlə(ʊ),kal(ə)r|i, -ɪz
AM 'kɪlə,kæl(ə)ri, -z

kilocycle
BR 'kɪlə(ʊ),sʌɪkl, -z
AM 'kɪlə,saɪkəl, -z

kilogram
BR 'kɪləgram, -z
AM 'kɪlə,græm, -z

kilogramme
BR 'kɪləgram, -z
AM 'kɪlə,græm, -z

kilohertz
BR 'kɪlə(ʊ)həːts
AM 'kɪlə,hərts

kilojoule
BR 'kɪlə(ʊ)dʒuːl, -z
AM 'kɪlə,dʒul, -z

kiloliter
BR 'kɪlə(ʊ),liːtə(r)
AM 'kɪlə,lidər

kilolitre
BR 'kɪlə(ʊ),liːtə(r)
AM 'kɪlə,lidər

kilometer
BR 'kɪlə,miːtə(r), kɪ'lɒmɪtə(r), -z
AM kə'lɑmədər, 'kɪlə,midər, -z

kilometre
BR 'kɪlə,miːtə(r), kɪ'lɒmɪtə(r), -z
AM kə'lɑmədər, 'kɪlə,midər, -z

kilometric
BR ˌkɪlə'mɛtrɪk
AM ˌkɪlə'mɛtrɪk

kiloton
BR 'kɪlə(ʊ)tʌn, -z
AM 'kɪlə,tən, 'kɪlə,tɑn, -z

kilotonne
BR 'kɪlə(ʊ)tʌn, -z
AM 'kɪlə,tən, -z

kilovolt
BR 'kɪlə(ʊ)vəʊlt, -s
AM 'kɪlə,voʊlt, -s

kilowatt
BR 'kɪləwɒt, -s
AM 'kɪlə,wɑt, -s

Kilpatrick
BR kɪl'patrɪk
AM kɪl'pætrɪk

Kilroy
BR 'kɪlrɔɪ, ˌkɪl'rɔɪ
AM 'kɪl,rɔɪ

kilt
BR kɪlt, -s, -ɪd
AM kɪlt, -s, -ɪd

kilter
BR 'kɪltə(r)
AM 'kɪltər

kiltie
BR 'kɪlt|i, -ɪz
AM 'kɪlti, -z

Kim
BR kɪm
AM kɪm

Kimber
BR 'kɪmbə(r)
AM 'kɪmbər

Kimberley
BR 'kɪmbəli
AM 'kɪmbərli

kimberlite
BR 'kɪmbəlʌɪt
AM 'kɪmbər,laɪt

Kimberly
BR 'kɪmbəli
AM 'kɪmbərli

Kimbolton
BR kɪm'bəʊlt(ə)n
AM kɪm'boʊltən

kimchi
BR 'kɪmtʃi
AM kɪm'tʃi

kimono
BR kɪ'məʊnəʊ, -z, -d
AM kə'moʊnoʊ, kə'moʊnə, -z, -d

kin
BR kɪn
AM kɪn

kina
BR 'kiːnə(*r*), -z
AM 'kinə, -z

Kinabalu
BR ˌkiːnə'bɑːluː
AM ˌkinə'bɑ,lu

kinaesthesia
BR ˌkɪnɪs'θiːzɪə(*r*), ˌkɪnɪs'θiːʒə(*r*), ˌkʌɪnɪs'θiːzɪə(*r*), ˌkʌɪnɪs'θiːʒə(*r*)
AM ˌkɪnəs'θiʒ(i)ə, ˌkɪnəs'θiziə

kinaesthetic
BR ˌkɪnɪs'θɛtɪk, ˌkʌɪnɪs'θɛtɪk
AM ˌkɪnəs'θɛdɪk

kinaesthetically
BR ˌkɪnɪs'θɛtɪkli, ˌkʌɪnɪs'θɛtɪkli
AM ˌkɪnəs'θɛdək(ə)li

Kincaid
BR kɪn'keɪd
AM kɪn'keɪd

Kincardine
BR kɪn'kɑːd(ɪ)n
AM kɪn'kɑrdən

Kinchinjunga
BR ˌkɪntʃ(ɪ)n'dʒʊŋɡə(r)
AM ˌkɪn(t)ʃən'dʒʊŋɡə

kincob
BR 'kɪŋkəb
AM 'kɪnˌkɑb, 'kɪŋˌkɑb

kind
BR kʌɪnd, -ə(r), -ɪst
AM kaɪnd, -ər, -ɪst

kinda
kind of
BR 'kʌɪndə(r)
AM 'kaɪndə

Kinder
BR 'kɪndə(r)
AM 'kɪndər

kindergarten
BR 'kɪndəˌɡɑːtn, -z
AM 'kɪndərˌɡɑrtən, 'kɪndərˌɡɑrdən, -z

kind-hearted
BR ˌkʌɪnd'hɑːtɪd
AM ˈkaɪn(d)ˈhɑrdəd

kind-heartedly
BR ˌkʌɪnd'hɑːtɪdli
AM ˈkaɪn(d)ˈhɑrdədli

kind-heartedness
BR ˌkʌɪnd'hɑːtɪdnɪs
AM ˈkaɪn(d)ˈhɑrdədnəs

kindle
BR 'kɪnd|l, -lz, -ḷɪŋ\-lɪŋ, -ld
AM 'kɪn|dəl, -dəlz, -(d)(ə)lɪŋ, -dəld

kindler
BR 'kɪndlə(r), 'kɪndḷə(r), -z
AM 'kɪn(də)lər, -z

kindlily
BR 'kʌɪndlɪli
AM 'kaɪn(d)lɪli

kindliness
BR 'kʌɪndlɪnɪs
AM 'kaɪn(d)linɪs

kindling
BR 'kɪndlɪŋ
AM 'kɪn(d)lɪŋ

kindly
BR 'kʌɪndl|i, -ɪə(r), -ɪɪst
AM 'kaɪn(d)li, -ər, -ɪst

kindness
BR 'kʌɪn(d)nɪs, -ɪz
AM 'kaɪn(d)nɪs, -ɪz

kindred
BR 'kɪndrɪd
AM 'kɪndrɪd

kine
BR kʌɪn
AM kaɪn

kinematic
BR ˌkɪnɪ'matɪk, ˌkʌɪnɪ'matɪk, -s
AM ˌkɪnə'mædɪk, -s

kinematical
BR ˌkɪnɪ'matɪkl, ˌkʌɪnɪ'matɪkl
AM ˌkɪnə'mædəkəl

kinematically
BR ˌkɪnɪ'matɪkli, ˌkʌɪnɪ'matɪkli
AM ˌkɪnə'mædək(ə)li

kinematograph
BR ˌkɪnɪ'matəɡrɑːf, ˌkɪnɪ'matəɡraf, -s
AM ˌkɪnə'mædəˌɡræf, -s

kinescope
BR 'kɪnɪskəʊp, -s
AM 'kɪnəˌskoʊp, -s

kinesics
BR kɪ'niːsɪks, kʌɪ'niːsɪks
AM kə'nisɪks

kinesiology
BR kɪˌniːsɪ'ɒlədʒi, kɪˌniːzɪ'ɒlədʒi, kʌɪˌniːsɪ'ɒlədʒi, kʌɪˌniːzɪ'ɒlədʒi
AM kəˌnisi'ɑlədʒi, kəˌnizi'ɑlədʒi

kinesthesia
BR ˌkɪnɪs'θiːzɪə(r), ˌkɪnɪs'θiːʒə(r), ˌkʌɪnɪs'θiːzɪə(r), ˌkʌɪnɪs'θiːʒə(r)
AM ˌkɪnəs'θiʒ(i)ə, ˌkɪnəs'θiziə

kinesthetic
BR ˌkɪnɪs'θɛtɪk, ˌkʌɪnɪs'θɛtɪk
AM ˈkɪnəs'θɛdɪk

kinesthetically
BR ˌkɪnɪs'θɛtɪkli, ˌkʌɪnɪs'θɛtɪkli
AM ˈkɪnəs'θɛdək(ə)li

kinetic
BR kɪ'nɛtɪk, kʌɪ'nɛtɪk, -s
AM kə'nɛdɪk, -s

kinetically
BR kɪ'nɛtɪkli, kʌɪ'nɛtɪkli
AM kə'nɛdək(ə)li

kinetin
BR 'kʌɪnɪtɪn, -z
AM 'kɪnətn, -z

kinfolk
BR 'kɪnfəʊk
AM 'kɪnˌfoʊk

king
BR kɪŋ, -z
AM kɪŋ, -z

kingbird
BR 'kɪŋbəːd, -z
AM 'kɪŋˌbərd, -z

kingbolt
BR 'kɪŋbəʊlt
AM 'kɪŋˌboʊlt

kingcraft
BR 'kɪŋkrɑːft, 'kɪŋkraft
AM 'kɪŋˌkræft

kingcup
BR 'kɪŋkʌp, -s
AM 'kɪŋˌkəp, -s

kingdom
BR 'kɪŋdəm, -z, -d
AM 'kɪŋdəm, -z, -d

kingfish
BR 'kɪŋfɪʃ, -ɪz
AM 'kɪŋˌfɪʃ, -ɪz

kingfisher
BR 'kɪŋˌfɪʃə(r), -z
AM 'kɪŋˌfɪʃər, -z

kinghood
BR 'kɪŋhʊd, -z
AM 'kɪŋˌ(h)ʊd, -z

King Kong
BR ˌkɪŋ 'kɒŋ
AM ˈkɪŋ 'kɔŋ, ˈkɪŋ 'kɑŋ

kingless
BR 'kɪŋlɪs
AM 'kɪŋlɪs

kinglet
BR 'kɪŋlɪt, -s
AM 'kɪŋlɪt, -s

kinglike
BR 'kɪŋlʌɪk
AM 'kɪŋˌlaɪk

kingliness
BR 'kɪŋlɪnɪs
AM 'kɪŋlinɪs

kingling
BR 'kɪŋlɪŋ, -z
AM 'kɪŋlɪŋ, -z

kingly
BR 'kɪŋl|i, -ɪə(r), -ɪɪst
AM 'kɪŋli, -ər, -ɪst

kingmaker
BR 'kɪŋˌmeɪkə(r), -z
AM 'kɪŋˌmeɪkər, -z

kingpin
BR 'kɪŋpɪn, -z
AM 'kɪŋˌpɪn, -z

Kingsbridge
BR 'kɪŋzbrɪdʒ
AM 'kɪŋzˌbrɪdʒ

Kingsbury
BR 'kɪŋzb(ə)ri
AM 'kɪŋzˌbɛri

kingship
BR 'kɪŋʃɪp
AM 'kɪŋˌʃɪp

Kingsley
BR 'kɪŋzli
AM 'kɪŋzli

Kingston
BR 'kɪŋst(ə)n
AM 'kɪŋstən

Kingstown
BR 'kɪŋstaʊn
AM 'kɪŋˌstoʊn

Kingsway
BR 'kɪŋzweɪ
AM 'kɪŋzˌweɪ

Kingswear
BR 'kɪŋzwɪə(r)
AM 'kɪŋzˌwɪ(ə)r

Kingswinford
BR kɪŋ'swɪnfəd, kɪŋz'wɪnfəd
AM kɪŋz'wɪnfərd

Kingswood
BR 'kɪŋzwʊd
AM 'kɪŋzˌwʊd

kinin
BR 'kʌɪnɪn, -z
AM 'kaɪnɪn, -z

kink
BR kɪŋ|k, -ks, -kɪŋ, -(k)t
AM kɪŋ|k, -ks, -kɪŋ, -(k)t

kinkajou
BR 'kɪŋkədʒuː, -z
AM 'kɪŋkəˌdʒu, -z

Kinki
BR 'kɪŋki
AM 'kɪŋki

kinkily
BR 'kɪŋkɪli
AM 'kɪŋkɪli

kinkiness
BR 'kɪŋkɪnɪs
AM 'kɪŋkinɪs

kinky
BR 'kɪŋk|i, -ɪə(r), -ɪɪst
AM 'kɪŋki, -ər, -ɪst

kinless
BR 'kɪnlɪs
AM 'kɪnlɪs

Kinloch
BR kɪn'lɒx, kɪn'lɒk
AM 'kɪnlɑk, kɪn'lɑk

Kinloss
BR kɪn'lɒs
AM kɪn'lɔs, kɪn'lɑs

Kinnear
BR kɪ'nɪə(r)
AM kɪ'nɪ(ə)r

Kinney
BR 'kɪni
AM 'kɪni

Kinnock
BR 'kɪnək
AM 'kɪnək

kino
BR 'kiːnəʊ, -z
AM 'kinoʊ, -z

Kinross
BR kɪn'rɒs
AM 'kɪnˌrɑs, 'kɪnˌrɔs, ˌkɪn'rɑs, ˌkɪn'rɑs

Kinsale
BR kɪn'seɪl
AM kɪn'seɪl

Kinsella
BR kɪn'sɛlə(r), 'kɪns(ə)lə(r)
AM kɪn'sɛlə

Kinsey
BR 'kɪnzi
AM 'kɪnzi

kinsfolk
BR 'kɪnzfəʊk
AM 'kɪnzˌfoʊk

Kinshasa
BR kɪnˈʃɑːsə(*r*), kɪnˈʃasə(*r*)
AM kənˈʃɑsə

kinship
BR ˈkɪnʃɪp
AM ˈkɪnˌʃɪp

kinsman
BR ˈkɪnzmən
AM ˈkɪnzmən

kinsmen
BR ˈkɪnzmən
AM ˈkɪnzmən

kinswoman
BR ˈkɪnzˌwʊmən
AM ˈkɪnzˌwʊmən

kinswomen
BR ˈkɪnzˌwɪmɪn
AM ˈkɪnzˌwɪmɨn

Kintyre
BR kɪnˈtʌɪə(r)
AM kɪnˈtaɪ(ə)r

kiosk
BR ˈkiːɒsk, -s
AM ˈkiɑsk, -s

Kiowa
BR ˈkʌɪəwə(*r*), -z
AM ˈkaɪəwə, -z

kip
BR kɪp, -s, -ɪŋ, -t
AM kɪp, -s, -ɪŋ, -t

Kipling
BR ˈkɪplɪŋ
AM ˈkɪplɪŋ

Kippax
BR ˈkɪpaks
AM ˈkɪpæks

kipper
BR ˈkɪp|ə(r), -əz, -(ə)rɪŋ, -əd
AM ˈkɪpər, -z, -ɪŋ, -d

kipsie
BR ˈkɪps|i, -ɪz
AM ˈkɪpsi, -z

kipsy
BR ˈkɪps|i, -ɪz
AM ˈkɪpsi, -z

kir
BR kɪə(r)
AM kɪ(ə)r

Kirbigrip®
BR ˈkəːbɪɡrɪp, -s
AM ˈkərbiˌɡrɪp, -s

Kirby
BR ˈkəːbi
AM ˈkərbi

kirby-grip
BR ˈkəːbɪɡrɪp, -s
AM ˈkərbiˌɡrɪp, -s

Kirchhoff
BR ˈkəːkɒf
AM ˈkərkˌ(h)ɔf, ˈkərkˌ(h)ɑf, ˈkərˌtʃɔf, ˈkərˌtʃɑf
GER ˈkɪrçhɔf

Kirghiz
BR ˈkəːɡɪz, ˈkɪəɡɪz, kɪəˈɡɪz
AM kɪrˈɡiz

Kirghizia
BR kəːˈɡɪzɪə(*r*), kɪəˈɡɪzɪə(*r*)
AM kərˈɡɪziə

Kirgiz
BR ˈkəːɡɪz, ˈkɪəɡɪz, kɪəˈɡɪz
AM kɪrˈɡiz

Kirgizia
BR kəːˈɡɪzɪə(*r*), kɪəˈɡɪzɪə(*r*)
AM kərˈɡɪziə

Kiribati
BR ˌkɪrɪˈbɑːti, ˌkɪrɪˈbas
AM ˌkɪrəˈbɑdi, ˌkɪrəˈbɑs

Kirin
BR ˈkɪərɪn
AM ˈkɪrɪn

kirk
BR kəːk, -s
AM kərk, -s

Kirkbride
BR kəːkˈbrʌɪd
AM ˌkərkˈbraɪd

Kirkby
BR ˈkəː(k)bi
AM ˈkərkbi

Kirkcaldy
BR kəˈkɒdi, kəːˈkɒdi, kəˈkɔːdi, kəːˈkɔːdi
AM kərˈkɔ(l)di, kərˈkɑ(l)di

Kirkcudbright
BR kəˈkuːbri, kəːˈkuːbri
AM kərˈkubri

Kirkgate
BR ˈkəːɡət
AM ˈkər(k)ˌɡeɪt

Kirkham
BR ˈkəːkəm
AM ˈkərkəm

Kirkland
BR ˈkəːklənd
AM ˈkərklən(d)

Kirklees
BR kəːkˈliːz
AM kərkˈliz

kirkman
BR ˈkəːkmən
AM ˈkərkmən

kirkmen
BR ˈkəːkmən
AM ˈkərkmən

Kirkpatrick
BR kəːkˈpatrɪk
AM ˌkərkˈpætrɪk

Kirkstall
BR ˈkəːkst(ə)l, ˈkəːkstɔːl
AM ˈkərkˌstɔl, ˈkərkˌstɑl

Kirkstone
BR ˈkəːkst(ə)n
AM ˈkərkˌstoʊn

Kirkwall
BR ˈkəːkwɔːl
AM kərˈkwɔl, kərˈkwɑl

Kirkwood
BR kəːkwʊd
AM ˈkərkˌwʊd

Kirov
BR ˈkɪərɒv, ˈkɪərɒf
AM ˈkɪˌrɔv, ˈkɪˌrɑv
RUS ˈkʲirəf

Kirriemuir
BR ˌkɪrɪˈmjʊə(r)
AM ˌkɪriˈmjʊ(ə)r

kirsch
BR kɪəʃ, kəːʃ
AM kɪrʃ

kirschwasser
BR ˈkɪəʃˌvasə(r), ˈkəːʃˌvasə(r), -z
AM ˈkɪrʃˌvɑsər, -z

Kirsten
BR ˈkəːst(ɨ)n
AM ˈkərstən

Kirstie
BR ˈkəːsti
AM ˈkərsti

kirtle
BR ˈkəːtl, -z
AM ˈkərdəl, -z

Kirundi
BR kɪˈrʊndi
AM kiˈrʊndi

Kirwan
BR ˈkəːw(ə)n
AM ˈkərwən

kishke
BR ˈkɪʃkə(*r*), -z
AM ˈkɪʃkə, -z

kiskadee
BR ˌkɪskəˈdiː, -z
AM ˈkɪskəˌdi, -z

Kislev
BR ˈkɪslɛf
AM ˈkɪsləv, ˈkɪsləf

Kislew
BR ˈkɪslɛf
AM ˈkɪsləv, ˈkɪsləf

kismet
BR ˈkɪzmɪt, ˈkɪzmɛt
AM ˈkɪzmət, ˈkɪzˌmɛt, ˌkɪzˈmɛt

kiss
BR kɪs, -ɪz, -ɪŋ, -t
AM kɪs, -ɪz, -ɪŋ, -t

kissable
BR ˈkɪsəbl
AM ˈkɪsəbəl

kissagram
BR ˈkɪsəɡram, -z
AM ˈkɪsəˌɡræm, -z

kisser
BR ˈkɪsə(r), -z
AM ˈkɪsər, -z

Kissinger
BR ˈkɪs(ɪ)ndʒə(r)
AM ˈkɪsəndʒər

kissogram
BR ˈkɪsəɡram, -z
AM ˈkɪsəˌɡræm, -z

kissy
BR ˈkɪsi
AM ˈkɪsi

kist
BR kɪst, -s
AM kɪst, -s

Kiswahili
BR ˌkiːswɑːˈhiːli, ˌkiːswəˈhiːli
AM ˌkiswɑˈhili

kit
BR kɪt, -s, -ɪŋ, -ɪd
AM kɪ|t, -ts, -dɪŋ, -dɨd

kitbag
BR ˈkɪtbaɡ, -z
AM ˈkɪtˌbæɡ, -z

kitchen
BR ˈkɪtʃ(ɪ)n, -z
AM ˈkɪtʃən, -z

Kitchener
BR ˈkɪtʃɪnə(r)
AM ˈkɪtʃ(ə)nər

kitchenette
BR ˌkɪtʃɪˈnɛt, -s
AM ˌkɪtʃəˈnɛt, -s

kitchenware
BR ˈkɪtʃ(ɪ)nwɛː(r)
AM ˈkɪtʃənˌwɛ(ə)r

kite
BR kʌɪt, -s
AM kaɪt, -s

Kitemark®
BR ˈkʌɪtmɑːk, -s
AM ˈkaɪtˌmɑrk, -s

kith
BR kɪθ
AM kɪθ

Kit-Kat
BR ˈkɪtkat, -s
AM ˈkɪ(t)ˌkæt, -s

kitsch
BR kɪtʃ
AM kɪtʃ

kitschiness
BR ˈkɪtʃɪnɪs
AM ˈkɪtʃinɨs

kitschy
BR ˈkɪtʃ|i, -ɪə(r), -ɪɪst
AM ˈkɪtʃi, -ər, -ɨst

Kitson
BR ˈkɪts(ə)n
AM ˈkɪtsən

kitten
BR ˈkɪtn̩, -z, -ɪŋ, -d
AM ˈkɪtn, -z, -ɪŋ, -d

kittenish
BR ˈkɪtn̩ɪʃ
AM ˈkɪtn̩ɪʃ

kittenishly
BR ˈkɪtn̩ɪʃli
AM ˈkɪtn̩ɪʃli

kittenishness
BR 'kɪtn̩ɪʃnɪs
AM 'kɪtn̩ɪʃnɪs

kittiwake
BR 'kɪtɪweɪk, -s
AM 'kɪdi,weɪk, -s

kittle
BR 'kɪtl
AM 'kɪdəl

kitty
BR 'kɪt|i, -ɪz
AM 'kɪdi, -z

Kitwe
BR 'kɪtweɪ
AM 'kɪt,weɪ

Kivu
BR 'kiːvuː
AM 'ki,vu

Kiwanis
BR kɪ'wɑːnɪs
AM kə'wɑnəs

kiwi
BR 'kiːwiː, -z
AM 'kiwi, -z

Klan
BR klan
AM klæn

Klansman
BR 'klanzmən
AM 'klænzmən

Klansmen
BR 'klanzmən
AM 'klænzmən

Klaus
BR klaʊs
AM klaʊs

klavier
BR klə'vɪə(r), kla'vɪə(r), -z
AM klə'vɪ(ə)r, -z

klaxon
BR 'klaksn, -z
AM 'klæksən, -z

klebsiella
BR ,klɛbzɪ'ɛlə(r)
AM ,klɛbsi'ɛlə, ,klɛbzi'ɛlə

Klee
BR kleɪ
AM kleɪ

Kleenex®
BR 'kliːnɛks, -ɪz
AM 'kli,nɛks, -əz

Klein
BR klʌɪn
AM klaɪn

Kleinwort
BR 'klʌɪnwɔːt
AM 'klaɪnwərt, 'klaɪn,wɔ(ə)rt

Kleist
BR klʌɪst
AM klaɪst

Klemperer
BR 'klɛmp(ə)rə(r)
AM 'klɛmpərər

klepht
BR klɛft, -s
AM klɛft, -s

kleptomania
BR ,klɛptə(ʊ)'meɪnɪə(r)
AM ,klɛptə'meɪniə

kleptomaniac
BR ,klɛptə(ʊ)'meɪnɪak, -s
AM ,klɛptə'meɪni,æk, -s

Klerksdorp
BR 'kləːksdɔːp
AM 'klərks,dɔ(ə)rp

klieg
BR kliːg, -z
AM klig, -z

Klimt
BR klɪmt
AM klɪmt

Kline
BR klʌɪn
AM klaɪn

klipspringer
BR 'klɪp,sprɪŋə(r), -z
AM 'klɪp,sprɪŋər, -z

Klondike
BR 'klɒndʌɪk
AM 'klɑn,daɪk

kloof
BR kluːf, -s
AM kluf, -s

Klosters
BR 'kləʊstəz, 'klɒstəz
AM 'klɔstərz, 'klɑstərz

kludge
BR kluːdʒ
AM klʊdʒ, kludʒ

klutz
BR klʌts, -ɪz
AM kləts, -əz

klutzy
BR 'klʌtz|i, -ɪə(r), -ɪɪst
AM 'klətzi, -ər, -ɪst

klystron
BR 'klʌɪstrɒn, -z
AM 'klaɪ,strɑn, -z

K-meson
BR ,keɪ'mɛzɒn, ,keɪ'miːzɒn
AM 'keɪ¦meɪ,zɑn, 'keɪ,mɛzn

knack
BR nak, -s
AM næk, -s

knacker
BR 'nakə(r), -z, -d
AM 'nækər, -z, -d

knackery
BR 'nak(ə)r|i, -ɪz
AM 'næk(ə)ri, -z

knackwurst
BR 'nakwəːst, 'nakvʊəst
AM 'nɑk,wərst, 'nɑk,wʊrst

knag
BR nag, -z
AM næg, -z

knaggy
BR 'nag|i, -ɪə(r), -ɪɪst
AM 'nægi, -ər, -ɪst

knap
BR nap, -s, -ɪŋ, -t
AM næp, -s, -ɪŋ, -t

Knapp
BR nap
AM næp

knapper
BR 'napə(r), -z
AM 'næpər, -z

knapsack
BR 'napsak, -s
AM 'næp,sæk, -s

knapweed
BR 'napwiːd, -z
AM 'næp,wid, -z

knar
BR nɑː(r), -z
AM nɑr, -z

Knaresborough
BR 'nɛːzb(ə)rə(r)
AM 'nɛrz,bərə

Knatchbull
BR 'natʃbʊl
AM 'nætʃ,bʊl

knave
BR neɪv, -z
AM neɪv, -z

knavery
BR 'neɪv(ə)ri
AM 'neɪvəri

knavish
BR 'neɪvɪʃ
AM 'neɪvɪʃ

knavishly
BR 'neɪvɪʃli
AM 'neɪvɪʃli

knavishness
BR 'neɪvɪʃnɪs
AM 'neɪvɪʃnɪs

knawel
BR nɔː(ə)l
AM nɔl, nɑl

knead
BR niːd, -z, -ɪŋ, -ɪd
AM nid, -z, -ɪŋ, -ɪd

kneadable
BR 'niːdəbl
AM 'nidəbəl

kneader
BR 'niːdə(r), -z
AM 'nidər, -z

Knebworth
BR 'nɛbwəːθ
AM 'nɛb,wərθ

knee
BR niː, -z, -ɪŋ, -d
AM ni, -z, -ɪŋ, -d

kneecap
BR 'niːkap, -s, -ɪŋ, -t
AM 'ni,kæp, -s, -ɪŋ, -t

kneecapping
BR 'niː,kapɪŋ, -z
AM 'ni,kæpɪŋ, -z

kneehole
BR 'niːhəʊl, -z
AM 'ni,hoʊl, -z

kneel
BR niːl, -z, -ɪŋ
AM nil, -z, -ɪŋ

kneeler
BR 'niːlə(r), -z
AM 'nilər, -z

knee-trembler
BR 'niː,trɛmblə(r), -z
AM 'ni,trɛmb(ə)lər, -z

knell
BR nɛl, -z, -ɪŋ, -d
AM nɛl, -z, -ɪŋ, -d

Kneller
BR 'nɛlə(r)
AM 'nɛlər

knelt
BR nɛlt
AM nɛlt

Knesset
BR (kə)'nɛsɪt
AM (kə)'nɛsət

knew
BR njuː
AM n(j)u

knicker
BR 'nɪkə(r), -z
AM 'nɪkər, -z

Knickerbocker
BR 'nɪkə,bɒkə(r), -z
AM 'nɪkər,bɑkər, -z

knick-knack
BR 'nɪknak, -s
AM 'nɪk,næk, -s

knick-knackery
BR 'nɪk,nak(ə)ri
AM 'nɪk,nækəri

knick-knackish
BR 'nɪk,nakɪʃ
AM 'nɪk,nækɪʃ

knife
BR nʌɪf
AM naɪf

knifelike
BR 'nʌɪflʌɪk
AM 'naɪf,laɪk

knifepoint
BR 'nʌɪfpɔɪnt
AM 'naɪf,pɔɪnt

knifer
BR 'nʌɪfə(r), -z
AM 'naɪfər, -z

knight
BR nʌɪt, -s, -ɪŋ, -ɪd
AM naɪ|t, -ts, -dɪŋ, -dɪd

knightage
BR 'nʌɪt|ɪdʒ, -ɪdʒɪz
AM 'naɪdɪdʒ, -ɪz

knight-errant
BR ,nʌɪt'ɛrənt, ,nʌɪt'ɛrn̩t
AM ¦naɪt'ɛrənt

knight-errantry
BR ˌnʌɪt'ɛrəntri, ˌnʌɪt'ɛrn̩tri
AM ¦naɪt'ɛrəntri

knighthood
BR 'nʌɪthʊd, -z
AM 'naɪt,(h)ʊd, -z

Knight Hospitaller
BR ˌnʌɪt 'hɒspɪtl̩ə(r)
AM ¦naɪt 'hɑˌspɪtl̩ər

knightlike
BR 'nʌɪtlʌɪk
AM 'naɪtˌlaɪk

knightliness
BR 'nʌɪtlɪnɪs
AM 'naɪtlinɪs

knightly
BR 'nʌɪtl|i, -ɪə(r), -ɪɪst
AM 'naɪtli, -ər, -ɪst

Knighton
BR 'nʌɪt(ə)n
AM 'naɪtn

Knights
BR nʌɪts
AM naɪts

Knightsbridge
BR 'nʌɪtsbrɪdʒ
AM 'naɪtsˌbrɪdʒ

knights-errant
BR ˌnʌɪts'ɛrənt, ˌnʌɪts'ɛrn̩t
AM ¦naɪts'ɛrənt

Knights Hospitaller
BR ˌnʌɪts 'hɒspɪtl̩ə(r)
AM ¦naɪts 'hɑˌspɪtl̩ər

Knights Templar
BR ˌnʌɪts 'tɛmplə(r)
AM ¦naɪts 'tɛmplər

Knight Templar
BR ˌnʌɪt 'tɛmplə(r)
AM ¦naɪt 'tɛmplər

kniphofia
BR nɪ'fəʊfɪə(*r*), nʌɪ'fəʊfɪə(*r*), nɪp'həʊfɪə(*r*)
AM nə'foʊfiə

knish
BR kə'nɪʃ, knɪʃ, -ɪz
AM kə'nɪʃ, -ɪz

knit
BR nɪt, -s, -ɪŋ, -ɪd
AM nɪ|t, -ts, -dɪŋ, -dɪd

knitter
BR 'nɪtə(r), -z
AM 'nɪdər, -z

knitwear
BR 'nɪtwɛː(r)
AM 'nɪtˌwɛ(ə)r

knives
BR nʌɪvz
AM naɪvz

knob
BR nɒb, -z
AM nɑb, -z

knobbiness
BR 'nɒbɪnɪs
AM 'nɑbinɪs

knobble
BR 'nɒbl, -z
AM 'nɑbəl, -z

knobbliness
BR 'nɒblɪnɪs
AM 'nɑb(ə)linɪs

knobbly
BR 'nɒbl|i, 'nɒbl̩|i, -ɪə(r), -ɪɪst
AM 'nɑb(ə)li, -ər, -ɪst

knobby
BR 'nɒb|i, -ɪə(r), -ɪɪst
AM 'nɑbi, -ər, -ɪst

knobkerrie
BR 'nɒbˌkɛr|i, -ɪz
AM 'nɑbˌkɛri, -z

knoblike
BR 'nɒblʌɪk
AM 'nɑbˌlaɪk

knobstick
BR 'nɒbstɪk, -s
AM 'nɑbˌstɪk, -s

knock
BR nɒk, -s, -ɪŋ, -t
AM nɑk, -s, -ɪŋ, -t

knockabout
BR 'nɒkəbaʊt
AM 'nɑkəˌbaʊt

knocker
BR 'nɒkə(r), -z
AM 'nɑkər, -z

knockout
BR 'nɒkaʊt, -s
AM 'nɑˌkaʊt, -s

knockwurst
BR 'nɒkwəːst, 'nɒkvʊəst
AM 'nɑkˌwərst, 'nɑkˌwʊrst

knoll
BR nəʊl, nɒl, -z
AM noʊl, -z

Knollys
BR nəʊlz
AM noʊlz

knop
BR nɒp, -s
AM nɑp, -s

knopkierie
BR 'knɒpˌkɪər|i, -ɪz
AM '(k)nɑpˌkiri, -z

Knossos
BR '(k)nɒsɒs
AM '(k)nɑsɔs, '(k)nɑsɑs

knot
BR nɒt, -s, -ɪŋ, -ɪd
AM nɑ|t, -ts, -dɪŋ, -dəd

knotgrass
BR 'nɒtgrɑːs, 'nɒtgras
AM 'nɑtˌgræs

knothole
BR 'nɒthəʊl, -z
AM 'nɑtˌ(h)oʊl, -z

knotless
BR 'nɒtləs
AM 'nɑtlɛs

Knott
BR nɒt
AM nɑt

knotter
BR 'nɒtə(r), -z
AM 'nɑdər, -z

knottily
BR 'nɒtɪli
AM 'nɑdəli

knottiness
BR 'nɒtɪnɪs
AM 'nɑdinɪs

knotting
BR 'nɒtɪŋ, -z
AM 'nɑdɪŋ, -z

knotty
BR 'nɒt|i, -ɪə(r), -ɪɪst
AM 'nɑdi, -ər, -ɪst

knotweed
BR 'nɒtwiːd
AM 'nɑtˌwid

knotwork
BR 'nɒtwəːk
AM 'nɑtˌwərk

knout
BR naʊt, nuːt, -s, -ɪŋ, -ɪd
AM naʊ|t, -ts, -dɪŋ, -dəd

know
BR nəʊ, -z, -ɪŋ
AM noʊ, -z, -ɪŋ

knowable
BR 'nəʊəbl
AM 'noʊəbəl

knower
BR 'nəʊə(r), -z
AM 'noʊər, -z

know-how
BR 'nəʊhaʊ
AM 'noʊˌhaʊ

knowing
BR 'nəʊɪŋ
AM 'noʊɪŋ

knowingly
BR 'nəʊɪŋli
AM 'noʊɪŋli

knowingness
BR 'nəʊɪŋnɪs
AM 'noʊɪŋnɪs

Knowle
BR nəʊl
AM noʊl

knowledgability
BR ˌnɒlɪdʒə'bɪlɪti
AM ˌnɑlədʒə'bɪlɪdi

knowledgable
BR 'nɒlɪdʒəbl
AM 'nɑlədʒəbəl

knowledgableness
BR 'nɒlɪdʒəblnəs
AM 'nɑlədʒəbəlnəs

knowledgably
BR 'nɒlɪdʒəbli
AM 'nɑlədʒəbli

knowledge
BR 'nɒlɪdʒ
AM 'nɑlədʒ

knowledgeability
BR ˌnɒlɪdʒə'bɪlɪti
AM ˌnɑlədʒə'bɪlɪdi

knowledgeable
BR 'nɒlɪdʒəbl
AM 'nɑlədʒəbəl

knowledgeableness
BR 'nɒlɪdʒəblnəs
AM 'nɑlədʒəbəlnəs

knowledgeably
BR 'nɒlɪdʒəbli
AM 'nɑlədʒəbli

Knowles
BR nəʊlz
AM noʊlz

known
BR nəʊn
AM noʊn

Knox
BR nɒks
AM nɑks

Knoxville
BR 'nɒksvɪl
AM 'nɑksˌvɪl, 'nɑksvəl

knuckle
BR 'nʌk|l, -lz, -l̩ɪŋ\-lɪŋ, -ld
AM 'nək|əl, -əlz, -(ə)lɪŋ, -əld

knuckleball
BR 'nʌklbɔːl, -z
AM 'nəkəlˌbɔl, 'nəkəlˌbɑl, -z

knucklebone
BR 'nʌklbəʊn, -z
AM 'nəkəlˌboʊn, -z

knucklehead
BR 'nʌklhɛd, -z
AM 'nəkəlˌ(h)ɛd, -z

knuckly
BR 'nʌkl̩i, 'nʌkli
AM 'nəkli

knur
BR nəː(r), -z
AM nər, -z

knurl
BR nəːl, -d
AM nərl, -d

knurr
BR nəː(r), -z
AM nər, -z

Knut
BR knʌt, kə'nuːt
AM kə'nut

Knutsford
BR 'nʌtsfəd
AM 'nətsfərd

KO
BR ˌkeɪ'əʊ, -z, -ɪŋ, -d
AM ˌkeɪ'oʊ, -z, -ɪŋ, -d

koa
BR 'kəʊə(*r*), -z
AM 'koʊə, -z

koala
BR kəʊˈɑːlə(r), -z
AM koʊˈɑlə, kəˈwɑlə, -z
koan
BR ˈkəʊan, -z
AM ˈkoʊˌɑn, -z
Kobe
BR ˈkəʊbi, ˈkəʊbeɪ
AM ˈkoʊbi
kobold
BR ˈkəʊb(ə)ld
AM ˈkoʊˌbɔld, ˈkoʊˌbɑld
Koch
BR kəʊk, kɒtʃ, kɒk, kɒx
AM kɔk, kʊk, kɑk
Köchel
BR ˈkəːkl, ˈkəːxl
AM ˈkoʊkəl
Kodachrome
BR ˈkəʊdəkrəʊm
AM ˈkoʊdəˌkroʊm
Kodak®
BR ˈkəʊdak, -s
AM ˈkoʊˌdæk, -s
Kodály
BR ˈkəʊdʌɪ
AM ˌkoʊˈdaɪ(i)
HU ˈkodaːj
Kodiak
BR ˈkəʊdɪak, -s
AM ˈkoʊdiˌæk, -s
koel
BR ˈkəʊəl, -z
AM ˈkoʊəl, -z
Koestler
BR ˈkəːs(t)lə(r)
AM ˈkɛs(t)lər
Koh-i-noor
BR ˌkəʊɪˈnʊə(r), ˌkəʊɪˈnɔː(r)
AM ˈkoʊəˌnʊ(ə)r
kohl
BR kəʊl
AM koʊl
kohlrabi
BR ˌkəʊlˈrɑːb|i, -ɪz
AM ˌkoʊlˈrɑbi, -z
koi
BR kɔɪ
AM kɔɪ
Koil
BR kɔɪl
AM kɔɪl
koiné
BR ˈkɔɪneɪ, ˈkɔɪniː, ˈkɔɪni
AM kɔɪˈneɪ
Kojak
BR ˈkəʊdʒak
AM ˈkoʊˌdʒæk
Kokoschka
BR kəˈkɒʃkə(r)
AM kəˈkɔʃkə, kəˈkɑʃkə
kola
BR ˈkəʊlə(r)
AM ˈkoʊlə
Kolhapur
BR ˈkɒləpʊə(r)
AM ˈkɔləˌpʊ(ə)r, ˈkɑləˌpʊ(ə)r
kolinsky
BR kəˈlɪnsk|i, -ɪz
AM kəˈlɪnski, -z
kolkhoz
BR ˌkɒlˈkɒz, ˌkɒlˈkɔːz, ˌkʌlkˈhɔːz
AM kəlˈkɔz, kəlˈkɑz
Köln
BR kəːln, kəʊln
AM kəln
Koluma
BR kəˈluːmə(r)
AM kəˈlumə
RUS kəlɪˈma
komitadji
BR ˌkɒmɪˈtadʒ|i, -ɪz
AM ˌkɑməˈtɑdʒi, ˌkoʊməˈtɑdʒi, -z
Komodo
BR kəˈməʊdəʊ
AM kəˈmoʊˌdoʊ
Kompong Cham
BR ˌkɒmpɒŋ ˈtʃam
AM ˈkɑmˈpɔŋ ˈtʃɑm, ˈkɑmˈpɑŋ ˈtʃɑm
Kompong Som
BR ˌkɒmpɒŋ ˈsɒm
AM ˈkɑmˈpɔŋ ˈsɑm, ˈkɑmˈpɑŋ ˈsɑm
Komsomol
BR ˈkɒmsəmɒl
AM ˈkɑmsəˈmɔl, ˈkɑmsəˈmɑl
RUS kəmsaˈmol
Komsomolsk
BR ˈkɒmsəmɒlsk
AM ˈkɑmsəˌmɑlsk
RUS kəmsaˈmolsk
Kongo
BR ˈkɒŋgəʊ
AM ˈkɑŋgoʊ
Königsberg
BR ˈkəːnɪgzbəːg
AM ˈkənɪgzˌbərg
GER ˈkœːnɪçsbɛrk
Konika
BR ˈkɒnɪkə(r), ˈkəʊnɪkə(r)
AM ˈkɑnəkə
Konopka
BR kəˈnɒpkə(r)
AM kəˈnɑpkə
Konrad
BR ˈkɒnrad
AM ˈkɑnˌræd
Kon-Tiki
BR ˌkɒnˈtiːki
AM ˈkɑnˈtiki
koodoo
BR ˈkuːduː, -z
AM ˈkuˌdu, -z
kook
BR kuːk, -s
AM kuk, -s
kookaburra
BR ˈkʊkəˌbʌrə(r), -z
AM ˈkʊkəˌbərə, -z
kookily
BR ˈkuːkɪli
AM ˈkukəli
kookiness
BR ˈkuːkɪnɪs
AM ˈkukinɪs
kooky
BR ˈkuːk|i, ˈkʊk|i, -ɪə(r), -ɪɪst
AM ˈkuki, -ər, -ɪst
kop
BR kɒp, -s
AM kɑp, -s
kopeck
BR ˈkəʊpɛk, -s
AM ˈkoʊˌpɛk, -s
kopek
BR ˈkəʊpɛk, -s
AM ˈkoʊˌpɛk, -s
kopi
BR ˈkəʊpi
AM ˈkoʊpi
kopje
BR ˈkɒp|i, -ɪz
AM ˈkɑpi, -z
koppa
BR ˈkɒpə(r), -z
AM ˈkɑpə, -z
koppie
BR ˈkɒp|i, -ɪz
AM ˈkɑpi, -z
koradji
BR ˈkɒrədʒ|i, kəˈradʒ|i, -ɪz
AM kəˈrɑdʒi, -z
Koran
BR kəˈrɑːn, kɔːˈrɑːn
AM kəˈrɑn, kɔˈrɑn
Koranic
BR kəˈranɪk
AM kəˈrɑnɪk, kɔˈrɑnɪk
Korda
BR ˈkɔːdə(r)
AM ˈkɔrdə
Kordofan
BR ˌkɔːdə(ʊ)ˈfan, ˌkɔːdə(ʊ)ˈfɑːn
AM ˌkɔrdoʊˈfɑn
Korea
BR kəˈrɪə(r)
AM kəˈriə
Korean
BR kəˈrɪən, -z
AM kəˈriən, -z
korfball
BR ˈkɔːfbɔːl
AM ˈkɔrfˌbɔl, ˈkɔrfˌbɑl
Kórinthos
BR kəˈrɪnθɒs
AM kəˈrɪnθɔs, kɔˈrɪnθɔs, kəˈrɪnθɑs, kɔˈrɪnθɑs
GR ˈkoriːnθɔs
korma
BR ˈkɔːmə(r), -z
AM ˈkɔrmə, -z
Korsakoff
BR ˈkɔːsəkɒf
AM ˈkɔrsəˌkɔf, ˈkɔrsəˌkɑf
koruna
BR ˈkɒrʉnə(r), -z
AM ˈkɔrənə, -z
CZ ˈkorunʌ
Kos
BR kɒs
AM kɔs, kɑs
Kościuszko
BR ˌkɒsɪˈʌskəʊ, ˌkɒsɪˈʊskəʊ
AM ˌkɑsiˈəsˌkoʊ
POL kɒʃjˈtʃʊʃkɒ
kosher
BR ˈkəʊʃə(r)
AM ˈkoʊʃər
Kosovo
BR ˈkɒsəvəʊ
AM ˈkɔsəˌvə, ˈkɑsəˌvə
Kostroma
BR ˈkɒstrəmɑː(r)
AM ˈkɑstrəˌmɑ
RUS kəstraˈma
Kosygin
BR kəˈsiːgɪn
AM kəˈsigɪn, kəˈsidʒɪn
Kota
BR ˈkəʊtə(r)
AM ˈkoʊdə
Kota Baharu
BR ˌkəʊtə bəˈhɑːruː, + ˈbɑːruː
AM ˈkoʊdə bəˈhɑˌru
Kota Kinabalu
BR ˌkəʊtə ˌkɪnəˈbɑːluː
AM ˈkoʊdə ˌkɪnəˈbɑˌlu
Kotka
BR ˈkɒtkə(r)
AM ˈkɑtkə
koto
BR ˈkəʊtəʊ, -z
AM ˈkoʊdoʊ, -z
kotow
BR ˌkəʊˈtaʊ, ˌkaʊˈtaʊ, -z, -ɪŋ, -d
AM ˈkaʊˈtaʊ, -z, -ɪŋ, -d
koulan
BR ˈkuːlən, -z
AM ˈkuˌlɑn, -z
koumis
BR ˈkuːmɪs
AM kuˈmɪs, ˈkuməs
koumiss
BR ˈkuːmɪs
AM kuˈmɪs, ˈkuməs
kouprey
BR ˈkuːpreɪ, -z
AM ˈkuˌpreɪ, -z
kourbash
BR ˈkʊəbaʃ, -ɪz
AM ˈkʊrˌbaʃ, ˌkʊrˈbaʃ, -əz

kowhai
BR ˈkəʊwʌɪ, ˈkɔːfʌɪ, -z
AM ˈkoʊˌwaɪ, -z

Kowloon
BR ˌkaʊˈluːn
AM ˌkaʊˈlun

kowtow
BR ˌkaʊˈtaʊ, -z, -ɪŋ, -d
AM ˈkaʊˌtaʊ, -z, -ɪŋ, -d

Kra
BR krɑː(r)
AM krɑ

kraal
BR krɑːl, -z
AM krɑl, -z

kraft
BR krɑːft, kraft
AM kræft

krait
BR krʌɪt, -s
AM kraɪt, -s

Krakatoa
BR ˌkrakəˈtəʊə(r)
AM ˌkrækəˈtoʊə

kraken
BR ˈkrɑːk(ə)n, -z
AM ˈkrɑkən, -z

Kraków
BR ˈkrakaʊ, ˈkrakɒf
AM ˈkrɑˌkaʊ, ˈkrɑkɔf, ˈkrɑkɑf
POL ˈkrakʊf

Kramer
BR ˈkreɪmə(r)
AM ˈkreɪmər

krans
BR krɑːns, krans
AM kræns

krantz
BR krɑːns, krans
AM kræn(t)s

Krasnodar
BR ˌkraznə(ʊ)ˈdɑː(r)
AM ˈkrɑsnəˌdɑr

Krasnoyarsk
BR ˌkrasnəˈjɑːsk
AM ˈkrɑsnəˌjɑrsk

krater
BR ˈkreɪtə(r), -z, -d
AM ˈkreɪdər, -z, -d

K-ration
BR ˈkeɪˌraʃn, -z
AM ˈkeɪˌræʃən, ˈkeɪˌreɪʃən, -z

Kraus
BR kraʊs
AM kraʊs

Krause
BR kraʊs
AM kraʊs
GER ˈkraʊzə

Krauss
BR kraʊs
AM kraʊs

Kraut
BR kraʊt, -s
AM kraʊt, -s

Kray
BR kreɪ
AM kreɪ

Krebs
BR krɛbz
AM krɛbz

Krefeld
BR ˈkreɪfɛld
AM ˈkreɪˌfɛld

Kreisler
BR ˈkrʌɪzlə(r)
AM ˈkraɪslər

Kremlin
BR ˈkrɛmlɪn
AM ˈkrɛmlən

Kremlinologist
BR ˌkrɛmlɪˈnɒlədʒɪst, -s
AM ˌkrɛmləˈnɑlədʒəst, -s

Kremlinology
BR ˌkrɛmlɪˈnɒlədʒi
AM ˌkrɛmləˈnɑlədʒi

Kretzschmar
BR ˈkrɛtʃmɑː(r)
AM ˈkrɛtʃˌmɑr

kriegspiel
BR ˈkriːgspiːl
AM ˈkrigˌʃpil, ˈkrigzˌpil

krill
BR krɪl
AM krɪl

krimmer
BR ˈkrɪmə(r)
AM ˈkrɪmər

Krio
BR ˈkriːəʊ, -z
AM ˈkrioʊ, -z

kris
BR kriːs, -ɪz
AM krɪs, kris, -ɪz

Krishna
BR ˈkrɪʃnə(r)
AM ˈkrɪʃnə

Krishnaism
BR ˈkrɪʃnə(r)ɪz(ə)m
AM ˈkrɪʃnəˌɪzəm

Krishnamurti
BR ˌkrɪʃnəˈmʊəti, ˌkrɪʃnəˈməːti
AM ˈkrɪʃnəˈmərdi

Krista
BR ˈkrɪstə(r)
AM ˈkrɪstə

Kristallnacht
BR ˈkrɪstlnaxt
AM ˈkrɪstlˌnɑkt
GER krɪsˈtalnaxt

Kroeber
BR ˈkrəʊbə(r)
AM ˈkroʊbər

kromesky
BR krə(ʊ)ˈmɛsk|i, ˈkrɒmɛsk|i, -ɪz
AM kroʊˈmɛski, -z

krona
BR ˈkrəʊnə(r)
AM ˈkroʊnə
SW ˈkroːna

krone
BR ˈkrəʊnə(r)
AM ˈkroʊnə
DAN ˈkʀoːnə
NO ˈkruːne

kroner
BR ˈkrəʊnə(r)
AM ˈkroʊnər
DAN ˈkʀoːnʌ
NO ˈkruːner

kronor
BR ˈkrəʊnə(r)
AM ˈkroʊnər
SW ˈkroːnɒr

Kronos
BR ˈkrɒnɒs
AM ˈkroʊˌnɔs, ˈkroʊˌnɑs

Kronstadt
BR ˈkrɒnstat
AM ˈkrɑnˌstɑd

kronur
BR ˈkrəʊnə(r)
AM ˈkroʊnər

Kroo
BR kruː
AM kru

Kropotkin
BR krəˈpɒtkɪn
AM krəˈpɑtkən

Kru
BR kruː
AM kru

Krueger
BR ˈkruːgə(r)
AM ˈkrugər

Kruger
BR ˈkruːgə(r)
AM ˈkrugər
AFK ˈkryər

Krugerrand
BR ˈkruːgərand, -z
AM ˈkrugərænd, -(d)z
AFK ˈkryəˌrant

krumhorn
BR ˈkrʌmhɔːn, -z
AM ˈkrʊmˌ(h)ɔ(ə)rn, -z

krummholz
BR ˈkrʌmhɒlts
AM ˈkrəmˌ(h)ɔlts, ˈkrəmˌ(h)ɑlts

krummhorn
BR ˈkrʌmhɔːn, -z
AM ˈkrʊmˌ(h)ɔ(ə)rn, -z

Krupp
BR krʊp, krʌp
AM krʊp

krypton
BR ˈkrɪptɒn
AM ˈkrɪpˌtɑn

Kshatriya
BR ˈkʃatrɪə(r), -z
AM (kə)ˈʃɑtri(j)ə, -z

K2
BR ˌkeɪˈtuː
AM ˌkeɪˈtu

Kuala Lumpur
BR ˌkwɑːlə ˈlʊmpʊə(r), + ˈlʌmpə(r)
AM ˌkwɑlə lʊmˈpʊ(ə)r

Kublai Khan
BR ˌkuːblə ˈkɑːn, ˌkuːblʌɪ +
AM ˈkʊblə ˈkɑn

Kubrick
BR ˈk(j)uːbrɪk
AM ˈkʊbrɪk

kuccha
BR ˈkʌtʃə(r)
AM ˈkətʃə

kudos
BR ˈkjuːdɒs
AM ˈkuˌdoʊs

kudu
BR ˈkuːduː, -z
AM ˈkudu, -z

kudzu
BR ˈkʊdzuː
AM ˈkədˌzu

Kufic
BR ˈk(j)uːfɪk
AM ˈk(j)ufɪk

Kuhn
BR kuːn
AM k(j)un

Ku Klux Klan
BR ˌkuː klʌks ˈklan
AM ˈku ˌkləks ˈklæn

Ku Klux Klansman
BR ˌkuː klʌks ˈklanzmən
AM ˈku ˌkləks ˈklænzmən

Ku Klux Klansmen
BR ˌkuː klʌks ˈklanzmən
AM ˈku ˌkləks ˈklænzmən

kukri
BR ˈkʊkr|i, -ɪz
AM ˈkʊkri, -z

kulak
BR ˈkuːlak, -s
AM ˈkulæk, kuˈlɑk, -s
RUS kuˈlak

kulan
BR ˈkuːlən, -z
AM ˈkulɑn, -z

Kultur
BR kʊlˈtʊə(r)
AM kʊlˈtʊ(ə)r

Kulturkampf
BR kʊlˈtʊəkam(p)f
AM kʊlˈtʊrˌkɑm(p)f

Kumamoto
BR ˌkuːməˈməʊtəʊ
AM ˈkuməˈmoʊdoʊ

kumara
BR ˈkuːmərə(r), -z

AM ˈkumərə, -z

kumis
BR ˈkuːmɪs
AM kuˈmɪs, ˈkuməs

kumiss
BR ˈkuːmɪs
AM kuˈmɪs, ˈkuməs

Kümmel
BR ˈkʊml
AM ˈkɪməl

kumquat
BR ˈkʌmkwɒt, -s
AM ˈkəmˌkwɑt, -s

Kundera
BR ˈkʊndərə(r)
AM ˈkʊndərə

Kung
BR kʊŋ
AM kʊŋ

kung fu
BR ˌkʊŋ ˈfuː, ˌkʌŋ +
AM ˈkʊŋ ˈfu

Kunlun Shan
BR ˌkʊnlʊn ˈʃan
AM ˈkʊnˈlʊn ˈʃɑn

Kunming
BR ˌkʊnˈmɪŋ
AM ˈkʊnˈmɪŋ

Kuomintang
BR ˌkwəʊmɪnˈtaŋ
AM ˈkwoˌmɪnˈtæŋ

Kuoni
BR kʊˈəʊni
AM kʊˈoʊni

kurbash
BR ˈkʊəbaʃ, -ɪz
AM ˈkʊrˌbɑʃ, ˌkʊrˈbɑʃ, -əz

kurchatovium
BR ˌkəːtʃəˈtəʊvɪəm
AM ˌkərtʃəˈtoʊvɪəm

Kurd
BR kəːd, -z
AM kərd, -z

kurdaitcha
BR kəˈdʌɪtʃə(r), -z
AM kərˈdaɪtʃə, -z

Kurdish
BR ˈkəːdɪʃ
AM ˈkərdɪʃ

Kurdistan
BR ˌkəːdɪˈstɑːn, ˌkəːdɪˈstan
AM ˈkərdəˌstæn

Kurgan
BR kʊəˈɡɑːn
AM kʊrˈɡɑn

Kurile
BR kjʊˈriːl
AM ˈkurəl

Kurosawa
BR ˌkʊrəˈsɑːwə(r)
AM ˌkʊrəˈsɑwə

kurrajong
BR ˈkʌrədʒɒŋ, -z
AM ˈkərəˌdʒɔŋ, ˈkərəˌdʒɑŋ, -z

Kursaal
BR ˈkʊəzɑːl, ˈkʊəsɑːl, ˈkəːzl, ˈkəːsl, -z
AM ˈkʊrˌzɑl, -z

Kurt
BR kəːt
AM kərt

kurta
BR ˈkəːtə(r), -z
AM ˈkərdə, -z

kurtosis
BR kəːˈtəʊsɪs
AM kərˈtoʊsəs

kurus
BR kʊˈrʊʃ, kʊˈruːʃ
AM kəˈruʃ

Kurzweil
BR ˈkəːtswʌɪl, ˈkəːtsvʌɪl
AM ˈkərtsˌwaɪl

Kush
BR kʊʃ
AM kʊʃ

Kuwait
BR k(j)ʊˈweɪt, -i
AM ˌkuˈweɪ|t, kəˈweɪ|t, -di

Kuwaiti
BR k(j)ʊˈweɪt|i, -ɪz
AM kəˈweɪdi, -z

Kuznetz Basin
BR kʊzˌnɛts ˈbeɪsn
AM ˈkʊzˌnɛts ˈbeɪsən

kvas
BR kvɑːs
AM kəˈvɑs, kvɑs

kvass
BR kvɑːs
AM kəˈvɑs, kvɑs

kvetch
BR kvɛtʃ, -ɪz, -ɪŋ, -t
AM kəˈvɛtʃ, kvɛtʃ, -əz, -ɪŋ, -t

kvetcher
BR ˈkvɛtʃə(r), -z
AM ˈkvɛtʃər, -z

Kwa
BR kwɑː(r)
AM kwɑ

KWAC
BR kwak
AM kwæk

kwacha
BR ˈkwɑːtʃə(r), ˈkwatʃə(r), -z
AM ˈkwɑtʃə, -z

KwaNdebele
BR ˌkwɑːn̩dɪˈbiːli, ˌkwɑːn̩dɪˈbeɪli
AM ˈkwɑndəˈbiˌli

kwanza
BR ˈkwanzə(r), -z
AM ˈkwɑnˌzɑ, -z

kwashiorkor
BR ˈkwɒʃɪəkɔː(r), ˌkwɒʃɪˈɔːkɔː(r)
AM ˈkwɑʃiˌɔrˈkɔ(ə)r

KwaZulu
BR ˌkwɑːˈzuːluː
AM ˌkwɑˈzulu

Kweilin
BR ˌkweɪˈlɪn
AM ˈkweɪˈlɪn

Kweiyang
BR ˌkweɪˈjaŋ
AM ˈkweɪˈjæŋ

kwela
BR ˈkweɪlə(r)
AM ˈkweɪlə

Kwells
BR kwɛlz
AM kwɛlz

KWIC
BR kwɪk
AM kwɪk

Kwik-Fit
BR ˈkwɪkfɪt
AM ˈkwɪkˌfɪt

KWOC
BR kwɒk
AM kwɑk

kyanise
BR ˈkʌɪənʌɪz, -ɪz, -ɪŋ, -d
AM ˈkaɪəˌnaɪz, -ɪz, -ɪŋ, -d

kyanite
BR ˈkʌɪənʌɪt
AM ˈkaɪəˌnaɪt

kyanitic
BR ˌkʌɪəˈnɪtɪk
AM ˌkaɪəˈnɪdɪk

kyanize
BR ˈkʌɪənʌɪz, -ɪz, -ɪŋ, -d
AM ˈkaɪəˌnaɪz, -ɪz, -ɪŋ, -d

kyat
BR kiːˈɑːt, -s
AM kiˈ(j)ɑt, -s

kybosh
BR ˈkʌɪbɒʃ
AM ˈkaɪˌbɑʃ, kəˈbɑʃ

Kyd
BR kɪd
AM kɪd

kyle
BR kʌɪl, -z
AM kaɪl, -z

kylie
BR ˈkʌɪl|i, -ɪz
AM ˈkaɪli, -z

kylin
BR ˈkiːlɪn, -z
AM ˈkilɪn, -z

kylix
BR ˈkʌɪlɪks
AM ˈkaɪlɨks

kyloe
BR ˈkʌɪləʊ, -z
AM ˈkaɪloʊ, -z

kymogram
BR ˈkʌɪmə(ʊ)ɡram, -z
AM ˈkaɪməˌɡræm, -z

kymograph
BR ˈkʌɪmə(ʊ)ɡrɑːf, ˈkʌɪmə(ʊ)ɡraf, -s
AM ˈkaɪməˌɡræf, -s

kymographic
BR ˌkʌɪmə(ʊ)ˈɡrafɪk
AM ˈkaɪməˈɡræfɪk

kymographically
BR ˌkʌɪmə(ʊ)ˈɡrafɨkli
AM ˈkaɪməˈɡræfək(ə)li

Kyoto
BR kɪˈəʊtəʊ
AM kiˈ(j)oʊdoʊ, kiˈ(j)oʊˌtoʊ

kyphosis
BR kʌɪˈfəʊsɪs
AM kaɪˈfoʊsəs

kyphotic
BR kʌɪˈfɒtɪk
AM kaɪˈfɑdɪk

Kyrenia
BR kʌɪˈriːnɪə(r)
AM kəˈriniə

Kyrgyz
BR ˈkəːɡɪz, ˈkɪəɡɪz, kɪəˈɡɪz
AM kɪrˈɡɪz
RUS kʲirˈɡʲis

Kyrgyzstan
BR ˌkəːɡɪˈstɑːn, ˈkɪəɡɪˈstɑːn, ˌkəːɡɪˈstan, ˌkɪəɡɪˈstan
AM ˈkɪrɡəˌstæn
RUS kʲirɡʲiˈstan

kyrie
BR ˈkɪrɪeɪ, -z
AM ˈkɪriˌeɪ, -z

Kyushu
BR kɪˈuːʃuː, ˈkjuːʃuː
AM kiˈjuʃu

Ll

l
BR ɛl, -z
AM ɛl, -z

la
BR lɑː(*r*)
AM lɑ

laager
BR ˈlɑːɡə(r), -z
AM ˈlɑɡər, -z

lab
BR lab, -z
AM læb, -z

Laban¹
dancer/choreographer
BR ˈlɑːb(ə)n
AM ˈlɑbən

Laban²
in Bible
BR ˈleɪb(ə)n, ˈleɪban
AM ˈleɪbən

labara
BR ˈlab(ə)rə(*r*), ˈleɪb(ə)rə(*r*)
AM ˈlæbərə

labarum
BR ˈlab(ə)rəm, ˈleɪb(ə)rəm, -z
AM ˈlæbərəm, -z

labdanum
BR ˈlabdənəm, -z
AM ˈlæbdənəm, -z

labefaction
BR ˌlabɪˈfakʃn, -z
AM ˌlæbəˈfækʃən, -z

label
BR ˈleɪbl, -lz, -l̩ɪŋ\-lɪŋ, -ld
AM ˈleɪbəl, -əlz, -(ə)lɪŋ, -əld

labeler
BR ˈleɪbl̩ə(r), ˈleɪblə(r), -z
AM ˈleɪb(ə)lər, -z

labeller
BR ˈleɪbl̩ə(r), ˈleɪblə(r), -z
AM ˈleɪb(ə)lər, -z

labia
BR ˈleɪbɪə(*r*)
AM ˈleɪbiə

labial
BR ˈleɪbɪəl, -z
AM ˈleɪbiəl, -z

labialisation
BR ˌleɪbɪəlʌɪˈzeɪʃn, -z
AM ˌleɪbiələˈzeɪʃən, ˌleɪbiəˌlaɪˈzeɪʃən, -z

labialise
BR ˈleɪbɪəlʌɪz, -ɪz, -ɪŋ, -d
AM ˈleɪbiəˌlaɪz, -ɪz, -ɪŋ, -d

labialism
BR ˈleɪbɪəlɪz(ə)m, -z
AM ˈleɪbiəˌlɪzəm, -z

labiality
BR ˌleɪbɪˈalɪti
AM ˌleɪbiˈælədi

labialization
BR ˌleɪbɪəlʌɪˈzeɪʃn, -z
AM ˌleɪbiələˈzeɪʃən, ˌleɪbiəˌlaɪˈzeɪʃən, -z

labialize
BR ˈleɪbɪəlʌɪz, -ɪz, -ɪŋ, -d
AM ˈleɪbiəˌlaɪz, -ɪz, -ɪŋ, -d

labially
BR ˈleɪbɪəli
AM ˈleɪbiəli

labia majora
BR ˌleɪbɪə məˈdʒɔːrə(*r*)
AM ˈleɪbiə məˈdʒɔrə

labia minora
BR ˌleɪbɪə mɪˈnɔːrə(*r*)
AM ˈleɪbiə məˈnɔrə

labiate
BR ˈleɪbɪeɪt, ˈleɪbɪət, -s
AM ˈleɪbiɪt, ˈleɪbiˌeɪt, -s

labile
BR ˈleɪbʌɪl
AM ˈleɪbəl, ˈleɪˌbaɪl

lability
BR leɪˈbɪlɪti, ləˈbɪlɪti
AM leɪˈbɪlɪdi, ləˈbɪlɪdi

labiodental
BR ˌleɪbɪə(ʊ)ˈdɛntl
AM ˌleɪbioʊˈdɛn(t)l

labiovelar
BR ˌleɪbɪə(ʊ)ˈviːlə(r)
AM ˌleɪbioʊˈvilər

labium
BR ˈleɪbɪəm
AM ˈleɪbiəm

La Bohème
BR ˌlɑː bəʊˈɛm, ˌla +
AM ˌlɑ boʊˈɛm

labor
BR ˈleɪb|ə(r), -əz, -(ə)rɪŋ, -əd
AM ˈleɪb|ər, -ərz, -(ə)rɪŋ, -ərd

laboratory
BR ləˈbɒrət(ə)r|i, -ɪz
AM ˈlæbrəˌtɔri, -z

laborer
BR ˈlab(ə)rə(r), -z
AM ˈleɪb(ə)rər, -z

laborious
BR ləˈbɔːrɪəs
AM ləˈbɔriəs

laboriously
BR ləˈbɔːrɪəsli
AM ləˈbɔriəsli

laboriousness
BR ləˈbɔːrɪəsnəs
AM ləˈbɔriəsnəs

laborism
BR ˈleɪbərɪz(ə)m
AM ˈleɪbəˌrɪzəm

Laborite
BR ˈleɪbərʌɪt, -s
AM ˈleɪbəˌraɪt, -s

Labouchere
BR ˌlabuːˈʃɛː(r)
AM ˌlɑbuˈʃɛ(ə)r

labour
BR ˈleɪb|ə(r), -əz, -(ə)rɪŋ, -əd
AM ˈleɪb|ər, -ərz, -(ə)rɪŋ, -ərd

labourer
BR ˈlab(ə)rə(r), -z
AM ˈleɪb(ə)rər, -z

labourism
BR ˈleɪbərɪz(ə)m
AM ˈleɪbəˌrɪzəm

Labourite
BR ˈleɪbərʌɪt, -s
AM ˈleɪbəˌraɪt, -s

Labov
BR ləˈbɒv, ləˈbəʊv
AM ləˈbɔv, ləˈboʊv, ləˈbɑv

Labovian
BR ləˈbɒvɪən, ləˈbəʊvɪən
AM ləˈbɔviən, ləˈboʊviən, ləˈbɑviən

labra
BR ˈleɪbrə(*r*), ˈlabrə(*r*)
AM ˈleɪbrə, ˈlæbrə

Labrador
BR ˈlabrədɔː(r), -z
AM ˈlæbrəˌdɔ(ə)r, -z

labret
BR ˈleɪbrɪt, -s
AM ˈleɪˌbrɛt, -s

labrum
BR ˈleɪbrəm, ˈlabrəm
AM ˈleɪbrəm, ˈlæbrəm

La Bruyère
BR ˌla brʊˈjɛː(r)
AM ˌlɑ brʊˈjɛ(ə)r

Labuan
BR ləˈbuːən
AM ˈlɑbjəwən

laburnum
BR ləˈbəːnəm, -z
AM ləˈbərnəm, -z

labyrinth
BR ˈlab(ə)rɪnθ, -s
AM ˈlæb(ə)ˌrɪnθ, -s

labyrinthian
BR ˌlabəˈrɪnθɪən
AM ˌlæb(ə)ˈrɪnθiən

labyrinthine
BR ˌlabəˈrɪnθʌɪn
AM ˌlæb(ə)ˈrɪnˌθin, ˌlæb(ə)ˈrɪnθən, ˌlæb(ə)ˈrɪnˌθaɪn

lac
BR lak, -s
AM læk, -s

Lacan
BR laˈkan
AM lɑˈkɑn

Laccadive
BR ˈlakədɪv, ˈlakədiːv
AM ˈlɑkədɪv

laccolith
BR ˈlakəlɪθ, -s
AM ˈlækəˌlɪθ, -s

lace
BR leɪs, -ɪz, -ɪŋ, -t
AM leɪs, -ɪz, -ɪŋ, -t

lacemaker
BR ˈleɪsˌmeɪkə(r), -z
AM ˈleɪsˌmeɪkər, -z

lacemaking
BR ˈleɪsˌmeɪkɪŋ
AM ˈleɪsˌmeɪkɪŋ

lacerable
BR ˈlas(ə)rəbl
AM ˈlæsərəbəl

lacerate
BR ˈlasəreɪt, -s, -ɪŋ, -ɪd
AM ˈlæsəˌreɪ|t, -ts, -dɪŋ, -dɪd

laceration
BR ˌlasəˈreɪʃn, -z
AM ˌlæsəˈreɪʃən, -z

lacertian
BR ləˈsəːtɪən, ləˈsəːʃn, -z
AM ləˈsərʃ(i)ən, -z

lacertilian
BR ˌlasəˈtɪlɪən, -z
AM ˌlæsərˈtɪljən, ˌlæsərˈtɪliən, -z

lacertine
BR ləˈsəːtʌɪn
AM ˈlæsərˌtaɪn

lacewing
BR ˈleɪswɪŋ, -z
AM ˈleɪsˌwɪŋ, -z

lacewood
BR ˈleɪswʊd
AM ˈleɪsˌwʊd

lacework
BR ˈleɪswəːk
AM ˈleɪswərk

lacey
BR ˈleɪsi
AM ˈleɪsi

laches
BR ˈlatʃɪz, ˈleɪtʃɪz
AM ˈlætʃəz

Lachesis
BR ˈlakɪsɪs
AM ˈlɑkəsəs

Lachlan
BR ˈlɒklən, ˈlaklən
AM ˈlɑklən

lachryma Christi
BR ˈlakrɪmə ˈkrɪsti
AM ˈlɑkrəmə ˈkrɪsti

lachrymal
BR ˈlakrɪml
AM ˈlækrəməl

lachrymation
BR ˌlakrɪˈmeɪʃn, -z
AM ˌlækrəˈmeɪʃən, -z

lachrymator
BR ˈlakrɪmeɪtə(r), -z
AM ˈlækrəˌmeɪdər, -z

lachrymatory
BR ˈlakrɪmət(ə)r|i, -ɪz
AM ˈlækrəməˌtɔri, -z

lachrymose
BR ˈlakrɪməʊs, ˈlakrɪməʊz
AM ˈlækrəˌmoʊs, ˈlækrəˌmoʊz

lachrymosely
BR ˈlakrɪməʊsli, ˈlakrɪməʊzli
AM ˈlækrəˌmoʊsli, ˈlækrəˌmoʊzli

lacily
BR ˈleɪsɨli
AM ˈleɪsɨli

laciness
BR ˈleɪsɪnɨs
AM ˈleɪsinɨs

lacing
BR ˈleɪsɪŋ, -z
AM ˈleɪsɪŋ, -z

laciniate
BR ləˈsɪnɪət
AM ləˈsɪniˌeɪt

laciniated
BR ləˈsɪnɪeɪtɨd
AM ləˈsɪniˌeɪdɨd

laciniation
BR ləˌsɪnɪˈeɪʃn, -z
AM ləˌsɪniˈeɪʃən, -z

lack
BR lak, -s, -ɪŋ, -t
AM læk, -s, -ɪŋ, -t

lackadaisical
BR ˌlakəˈdeɪzɪkl
AM ˌlækəˈdeɪzɪkəl

lackadaisically
BR ˌlakəˈdeɪzɪkli
AM ˌlækəˈdeɪzɪk(ə)li

lackadaisicalness
BR ˌlakəˈdeɪzɪklnəs
AM ˌlækəˈdeɪzɪkəlnəs

lacker
BR ˈlak|ə(r), -əz, -(ə)rɪŋ, -əd
AM ˈlækər, -z, -ɪŋ, -d

lackey
BR ˈlak|i, -ɪz
AM ˈlæki, -z

lackland
BR ˈlakˌland, ˈlaklənd, -z
AM ˈlæklənd, ˈlækˌlænd, -z

lackluster
BR ˈlakˌlʌstə(r)
AM ˈlækˌləstər

lacklustre
BR ˈlakˌlʌstə(r)
AM ˈlækˌləstər

Lacock
BR ˈleɪkɒk
AM ˈleɪˌkɑk

Laconia
BR ləˈkəʊnɪə(r)
AM ləˈkoʊniə

Laconian
BR ləˈkəʊnɪən, -z
AM ləˈkoʊniən, -z

laconic
BR ləˈkɒnɪk
AM ləˈkɑnɪk

laconically
BR ləˈkɒnɪkli
AM ləˈkɑnək(ə)li

laconicism
BR ləˈkɒnɪsɪz(ə)m, -z
AM ləˈkɑnəˌsɪzəm, -z

laconism
BR ˈlakənɪz(ə)m
AM ˈlɑkəˌnɪzəm

La Coruña
BR ˌlɑː kəˈruːnjə(r), ˌla +
AM ˌlɑ kəˈrunə

lacquer
BR ˈlak|ə(r), -əz, -(ə)rɪŋ, -əd
AM ˈlækər, -z, -ɪŋ, -d

lacquerer
BR ˈlak(ə)rə(r), -z
AM ˈlækərər, -z

lacquerware
BR ˈlakəwɛː(r)
AM ˈlækərˌwɛ(ə)r

lacquey
BR ˈlak|i, -ɪz
AM ˈlæki, -z

lacrimal
BR ˈlakrɪml, -z
AM ˈlækrəməl, -z

lacrimation
BR ˌlakrɪˈmeɪʃn
AM ˌlækrəˈmeɪʃən

lacrosse
BR ləˈkrɒs
AM ləˈkrɔs, ləˈkrɑs

lacrymal
BR ˈlakrɪml, -z
AM ˈlækrəməl, -z

lacrymation
BR ˌlakrɪˈmeɪʃn
AM ˌlækrəˈmeɪʃən

lactase
BR ˈlakteɪz, -ɨz
AM ˈlækˌteɪs, ˈlækˌteɪz, -ɨz

lactate[1]
noun
BR ˈlakteɪt, -s
AM ˈlækˌteɪt, -s

lactate[2]
verb
BR lakˈteɪt, -s, -ɪŋ, -ɨd
AM lækˈteɪ|t, -ts, -dɪŋ, -dɨd

lactation
BR lakˈteɪʃn
AM lækˈteɪʃən

lacteal
BR ˈlaktɪəl, -z
AM ˈlæktiəl, -z

lactescence
BR lakˈtɛsns, -ɨz
AM lækˈtɛsəns, -əz

lactescent
BR lakˈtɛsnt
AM lækˈtɛsənt

lactic
BR ˈlaktɪk
AM ˈlæktɪk

lactiferous
BR lakˈtɪf(ə)rəs
AM lækˈtɪf(ə)rəs

lactobacilli
BR ˌlaktəʊbəˈsɪlʌɪ
AM ˌlæktoʊbəˈsɪˌlaɪ

lactobacillus
BR ˌlaktəʊbəˈsɪləs
AM ˌlæktoʊbəˈsɪləs

lactometer
BR lakˈtɒmɨtə(r), -z
AM lækˈtɑmədər, -z

lactone
BR ˈlaktəʊn, -z
AM ˈlækˌtoʊn, -z

lactoprotein
BR ˌlaktə(ʊ)ˈprəʊtiːn, -z
AM ˌlæktoʊˈproʊˌtin, -z

lactose
BR ˈlaktəʊs, ˈlaktəʊz
AM ˈlækˌtoʊs, ˈlækˌtoʊz

lacuna
BR ləˈkjuːnə(r), -z
AM ləˈk(j)unə, -z

lacunae
BR ləˈkjuːniː, ləˈkjuːnʌɪ
AM ləˈk(j)uˌnaɪ, ləˈk(j)uni

lacunal
BR ləˈkjuːnl
AM ləˈk(j)unəl

lacunar
BR ləˈkjuːnə(r)
AM ˈlæk(j)ənər

lacunary
BR ˈlakjʊn(ə)ri, ləˈkjuːn(ə)ri
AM ˈlækjəˌnɛri, ləˈk(j)unəri

lacunose
BR ləˈkjuːnəʊs
AM ˈlækjəˌnoʊs, ˈlakjəˌnoʊz

lacustrine
BR ləˈkʌstrʌɪn, ləˈkʌstrɪn
AM ləˈkəstrən

lacy
BR ˈleɪsi
AM ˈleɪsi

lad
BR lad, -z
AM læd, -z

Lada®
BR ˈlɑːdə(r), -z
AM ˈlɑdə, -z

Ladakh
BR ləˈdɑːk, ləˈdak
AM ləˈdɑk

ladanum
BR ˈladənəm, ˈladn̩əm
AM ˈlɑdənəm

Ladbroke
BR ˈladbrʊk, -s
AM ˈlædˌbrʊk, -s

ladder
BR ˈlad|ə(r), -əz, -(ə)rɪŋ, -əd
AM ˈlædər, -z, -ɪŋ, -d

laddie
BR ˈlad|i, -ɪz
AM ˈlædi, -z

laddish
BR ˈladɪʃ
AM ˈlædɪʃ

laddishness
BR ˈladɪʃnɪs
AM ˈlædɪʃnɪs

laddy
BR ˈlad|i, -ɪz
AM ˈlædi, -z

lade
BR leɪd, -z, -ɪŋ, -ɨd
AM leɪd, -z, -ɪŋ, -ɨd

Ladefoged
BR ˈladɪfəʊgɪd
AM ˈlædəˌfoʊgəd

laden
BR ˈleɪdn
AM ˈleɪdən

la-di-da
BR ˌlɑːdɪˈdɑː(r, -z
AM ˌlɑdiˌdɑ, -z

ladify
BR ˈleɪdɪfʌɪ, -z, -ɪŋ, -d
AM ˈleɪdiˌfaɪ, -z, -ɪŋ, -d

Ladin
BR laˈdiːn, ləˈdiːn
AM ləˈdin

lading
BR ˈleɪdɪŋ
AM ˈleɪdɪŋ

Ladino
BR laˈdiːnəʊ, ləˈdiːnəʊ, -z
AM ləˈdinoʊ, -z

ladle
BR ˈleɪd|l, -lz, -l̩ɪŋ\-lɪŋ, -ld
AM ˈleɪd|əl, -əlz, -(ə)lɪŋ, -əld

ladleful
BR ˈleɪdlfʊl, -z
AM ˈleɪdəlˌfʊl, -z

ladler
BR 'leɪdl̩ə(r), 'leɪdlə(r), -z
AM 'leɪd(ə)lər, -z

Ladoga
BR lə'dəʊgə(r), la'dəʊgə(r)
AM lɑ'doʊgə, lɑ'dɔgə

lady
BR 'leɪd|i, -ɪz
AM 'leɪdi, -z

ladybird
BR 'leɪdɪbəːd, -z
AM 'leɪdi,bərd, -z

ladybug
BR 'leɪdɪbʌg, -z
AM 'leɪdi,bəg, -z

lady-fern
BR 'leɪdɪfəːn, -z
AM 'leɪdi,fərn, -z

ladyfinger
BR 'leɪdɪ,fɪŋgə(r)
AM 'leɪdi,fɪŋgər

ladyfy
BR 'leɪdɪfʌɪ, -z, -ɪŋ, -d
AM 'leɪdi,faɪ, -z, -ɪŋ, -d

ladyhood
BR 'leɪdɪhʊd
AM 'leɪdi,(h)ʊd

ladykiller
BR 'leɪdɪ,kɪlə(r), -z
AM 'leɪdi,kɪlər, -z

ladylike
BR 'leɪdɪlʌɪk
AM 'leɪdi,laɪk

ladyship
BR 'leɪdɪʃɪp, -s
AM 'leɪdi,ʃɪp, -s

Ladysmith
BR 'leɪdɪsmɪθ
AM 'leɪdɪ,smɪθ

Lae
BR leɪ
AM leɪ

Laertes
BR leɪ'əːtiːz
AM leɪ'ɛrtiz

Laetitia
BR lɪ'tɪʃə(r)
AM lə'tɪʃə

laetrile
BR 'leɪtrʌɪl, 'leɪtr(ɪ)l
AM 'leɪə,trɪl

laevodopa
BR 'liːvə,dəʊpə(r)
AM 'livoʊ,doʊpə

laevorotatory
BR ,liːvəʊ'rəʊtət(ə)ri
AM ˌlivə'roʊdə,tɔri

laevotartaric
BR ,liːvəʊtɑː'tarɪk
AM ˌlivoʊ,tɑr'tɛrɪk

laevulose
BR 'liːvjʊləʊs, 'liːvjʊləʊz, 'lɛvjʊləʊs, 'lɛvjʊləʊz
AM 'lɛvjəloʊs, 'lɛvjəloʊz

La Fayette
BR ,lɑː fʌɪ'jɛt, ,la +, + feɪ'jɛt
AM lɑ fə'jɛt, lɑ,faɪ'jɛt, lɑ,feɪ'jɛt

La Fontaine
BR ,lɑː fɒn'teɪn, ,la +
AM lɑ fɑn'teɪn

lag
BR lag, -z, -ɪŋ, -d
AM læg, -z, -ɪŋ, -d

lagan
BR 'lag(ə)n, -z
AM 'lægən, -z

lager
BR 'lɑːgə(r), -z
AM 'lɑgər, -z

Lagerkvist
BR 'lɑːgəkfɪst
AM 'lɑgər,kvɪst

Lagerlöf
BR 'lɑːgələʊf
AM 'lɑgər,loʊf
SW 'lɑːgər,ləːv

lagerphone
BR 'lɑːgəfəʊn, -z
AM 'lɑgər,foʊn, -z

laggard
BR 'lagəd, -z
AM 'lægərd, -z

laggardly
BR 'lagədli
AM 'lægərdli

laggardness
BR 'lagədnəs
AM 'lægərdnəs

lagger
BR 'lagə(r), -z
AM 'lægər, -z

lagging
BR 'lagɪŋ, -z
AM 'lægɪŋ, -z

lagniappe
BR 'lanjap, ,lan'jap, -s
AM ,læn'jæp, -s

lagomorph
BR 'lagəmɔːf, -s
AM 'lægə,mɔ(ə)rf, -s

Lagonda
BR lə'gɒndə(r)
AM lə'gɑndə

lagoon
BR lə'guːn, -z
AM lə'gun, -z

lagoonal
BR lə'guːnl
AM lə'gunəl

Lagos
BR 'leɪgɒs
AM 'lɑgoʊs

Lagrange
BR lə'greɪn(d)ʒ
AM lə'greɪndʒ

La Guardia
BR lə 'gwɑːdɪə(r)
AM lə 'gwɑrdiə

lah
BR lɑː(r)
AM lɑ

lahar
BR 'lɑːhɑː(r), -z
AM lə'hɑr, 'lɑhɑr, -z

lah-di-dah
BR ,lɑːdɪ'dɑː(r)
AM ˌlɑdiˌdɑ

Lahnda
BR 'lɑːndə(r)
AM 'lɑndə

Lahore
BR lə'hɔː(r)
AM lə'hɔ(ə)r

Lahu
BR lɑː'huː, -z
AM lɑ'hu, -z

laic
BR 'leɪɪk
AM 'leɪɪk

laical
BR 'leɪɪkl
AM 'leɪɪkəl

laically
BR 'leɪɪkli
AM 'leɪɪk(ə)li

laicisation
BR ,leɪɪsʌɪ'zeɪʃn, -z
AM ,leɪəsə'zeɪʃən, ,leɪə,saɪ'zeɪʃən, -z

laicise
BR 'leɪɪsʌɪz, -ɪz, -ɪŋ, -d
AM 'leɪə,saɪz, -ɪz, -ɪŋ, -d

laicity
BR leɪ'ɪsɪti
AM leɪ'ɪsɪdi

laicization
BR ,leɪɪsʌɪ'zeɪʃn, -z
AM ,leɪəsə'zeɪʃən, ,leɪə,saɪ'zeɪʃən, -z

laicize
BR 'leɪɪsʌɪz, -ɪz, -ɪŋ, -d
AM 'leɪə,saɪz, -ɪz, -ɪŋ, -d

laid
BR leɪd
AM leɪd

Laidlaw
BR 'leɪdlɔː(r)
AM 'leɪd,lɔ

lain
BR leɪn
AM leɪn

Laing
BR laŋ
AM læŋ

lair
BR lɛː(r), -z
AM lɛ(ə)r, -z

lairage
BR 'lɛːr|ɪdʒ, -ɪdʒɪz
AM 'lɛrɪdʒ, -ɪz

laird
BR lɛːd, -z
AM lɛ(ə)rd, -z

lairdship
BR 'lɛːdʃɪp, -s
AM 'lɛrd,ʃɪp, -s

lairy
BR 'lɛːri
AM 'lɛri

laisser-aller
BR ,leɪseɪ'aleɪ
AM ˌlɛseɪə'leɪ, ˌlɛzeɪə'leɪ

laisser-faire
BR ,leɪseɪ'fɛː(r)
AM ,lɛseɪ'fɛ(ə)r, ,lɛzeɪ'fɛ(ə)r

laissez-faire
BR ,leɪseɪ'fɛː(r)
AM ,lɛseɪ'fɛ(ə)r, ,lɛzeɪ'fɛ(ə)r

laissez-passer
BR ,leɪseɪ'paseɪ
AM ,lɛseɪpə'seɪ, ,lɛzeɪpə'seɪ

laity
BR 'leɪɪti
AM 'leɪɪdi

Laius
BR 'leɪəs
AM 'leɪəs

La Jolla
BR lə 'hɔɪə(r)
AM lə 'hɔɪə

lake
BR leɪk, -s
AM leɪk, -s

lakefront
BR 'leɪkfrʌnt
AM 'leɪk,frənt

Lakeland
BR 'leɪklənd
AM 'leɪklənd

lakeless
BR 'leɪklɪs
AM 'leɪklɪs

lakelet
BR 'leɪklɪt, -s
AM 'leɪklət, -s

Lakenheath
BR 'leɪk(ə)nhiːθ
AM 'leɪkən,(h)iθ

Laker
BR 'leɪkə(r)
AM 'leɪkər

lakeshore
BR 'leɪkʃɔː(r)
AM 'leɪk,ʃɔ(ə)r

lakeside
BR 'leɪksʌɪd
AM 'leɪk,saɪd

lakh
BR lak, -s
AM lɑk, -s

Lakshmi
BR 'lakʃmi
AM 'lɑkʃmi

Lalage
BR 'laləgi, 'lalədʒi
AM 'læləgi, 'lælədʒi

lalapalooza
BR ˌlaləpəˈluːzə(r)
AM ˌlɑləpəˈluzə

Lalique®
BR laˈliːk, ləˈliːk
AM lɑˈlik

Lallan
BR ˈlalən, -z
AM ˈlɑlən, -z

lallation
BR laˈleɪʃn
AM ləˈleɪʃən

lalling
BR ˈlalɪŋ
AM ˈlɑlɪŋ

lallygag
BR ˈlalɪgag, -z, -ɪŋ, -d
AM ˈlɑliˌgæg, -z, -ɪŋ, -d

Lalo
BR ˈlɑːləʊ
AM ˈlɑˌloʊ

lam
BR lam, -z, -ɪŋ, -d
AM læm, -z, -ɪŋ, -d

lama
BR ˈlɑːmə(r), -z
AM ˈlɑmə, -z

Lamaism
BR ˈlɑːmə(r)ɪz(ə)m
AM ˈlɑməˌɪzəm

Lamaist
BR ˈlɑːmə(r)ɪst
AM ˈlɑmə(j)əst

Lamarck
BR ləˈmɑːk, laˈmɑːk
AM lɑˈmɑrk

Lamarckian
BR ləˈmɑːkɪən, laˈmɑːkɪən, -z
AM ləˈmɑrkiən, -z

Lamarckism
BR ləˈmɑːkɪz(ə)m, laˈmɑːkɪz(ə)m
AM ləˈmɑrˌkɪzəm

lamasery
BR ˈlɑːməs(ə)r|i, -ɪz
AM ˈlɑməˌsɛri, -z

Lamaze
BR ləˈmɑːz, ləˈmeɪz
AM ləˈmɑz

lamb
BR lam, -z, -ɪŋ, -d
AM læm, -z, -ɪŋ, -d

lambada
BR lamˈbɑːdə(r), -z
AM læmˈbɑdə, -z

lambast
BR lamˈbast, -s, -ɪŋ, -ɪd
AM ˌlæmˈbæst, -s, -ɪŋ, -əd

lambaste
BR lamˈbeɪst, -s, -ɪŋ, -ɪd
AM læmˈbeɪst, -s, -ɪŋ, -ɪd

lambda
BR ˈlamdə(r), -z
AM ˈlæmdə, -z

lambdacism
BR ˈlamdəsɪz(ə)m
AM ˈlæmdəˌsɪzəm

lambency
BR ˈlamb(ə)nsi
AM ˈlæmbənsi

lambent
BR ˈlambənt
AM ˈlæmbənt

lambently
BR ˈlambəntli
AM ˈlæmbən(t)li

lamber
BR ˈlamə(r), -z
AM ˈlæmər, -z

lambert
BR ˈlambət, -s
AM ˈlæmbərt, -s

Lambeth
BR ˈlambəθ
AM ˈlæmbəθ

lambhood
BR ˈlamhʊd
AM ˈlæmˌ(h)ʊd

lambkin
BR ˈlamkɪn, -z
AM ˈlæmkən, -z

lamblike
BR ˈlamlʌɪk
AM ˈlæmˌlaɪk

Lamborghini®
BR ˌlambəˈgiːn|i, -ɪz
AM ˌlɑmbərˈgini, -z

lambrequin
BR ˈlamb(r)əkɪn, -z
AM ˈlæmbərkən, ˈlæmbrəkən, -z

Lambretta®
BR lamˈbrɛtə(r)
AM læmˈbrɛdə

Lambrusco
BR lamˈbrʊskəʊ
AM lɑmˈbrʊskoʊ

lambskin
BR ˈlamskɪn, -z
AM ˈlæmˌskɪn, -z

lambswool
BR ˈlamzwʊl, -z
AM ˈlæmzˌwul, -z

Lambton
BR ˈlamtən
AM ˈlæmtən

LAMDA
BR ˈlamdə(r)
AM ˈlæmdə

lame
BR leɪm
AM leɪm

lamé
BR ˈlɑːmeɪ
AM lɑˈmeɪ

lamebrain
BR ˈleɪmbreɪn, -z
AM ˈleɪmˌbreɪn, -z

lamella
BR ləˈmɛlə(r)
AM ləˈmɛlə

lamellae
BR ləˈmɛliː
AM ləˈmɛli, ləˈmɛˌlaɪ

lamellar
BR ləˈmɛlə(r)
AM ləˈmɛlər

lamellate
BR ˈlamələt, ˈlamḷət
AM ˈlæmələt, ləˈmɛlət, ˈlæməˌleɪt

lamellibranch
BR ləˈmɛlɪbraŋk, -s
AM ləˈmɛləˌbræŋk, -s

lamellicorn
BR ləˈmɛlɪkɔːn, -z
AM ləˈmɛləˌkɔ(ə)rn, -z

lamelliform
BR ləˈmɛlɪfɔːm
AM ləˈmɛləˌfɔ(ə)rm

lamellose
BR ləˈmɛləʊs
AM ləˈmɛˌloʊs, ˈlæməˌloʊs, ləˈmɛˌloʊz, ˈlæməˌloʊz

lamely
BR ˈleɪmli
AM ˈleɪmli

lameness
BR ˈleɪmnɨs
AM ˈleɪmnɨs

lament
BR ləˈmɛnt, -s, -ɪŋ, -ɪd
AM ləˈmɛn|t, -ts, -(t)ɪŋ, -(t)əd

lamentable
BR ˈlam(ɪ)ntəbl, ləˈmɛntəbl
AM ˈlæmən(t)əbəl, ləˈmɛn(t)əbəl

lamentably
BR ˈlam(ɪ)ntəbli, ləˈmɛntəbli
AM ˈlæmən(t)əbli, ləˈmɛn(t)əbli

lamentation
BR ˌlam(ɪ)nˈteɪʃn, -z
AM ˌlæmənˈteɪʃən, -z

Lamentations
BR ˌlam(ɪ)nˈteɪʃnz
AM ˌlæmənˈteɪʃənz

lamenter
BR ləˈmɛntə(r), -z
AM ləˈmɛn(t)ər, -z

lamentingly
BR ləˈmɛntɪŋli
AM ləˈmɛn(t)ɪŋli

lamina
BR ˈlamɪnə(r), ˈlamṇə(r), -z
AM ˈlæmənə, -z

laminae
BR ˈlamɪniː, ˈlamṇiː, ˈlamɪnʌɪ, ˈlamṇʌɪ
AM ˈlæməˌni, ˈlæməˌnaɪ

laminar
BR ˈlamɪnə(r), ˈlamṇə(r)
AM ˈlæmənər

laminate¹
noun
BR ˈlamɪnət, ˈlamṇət, -s
AM ˈlæmənət, ˈlæməˌneɪt, -s

laminate²
verb
BR ˈlamɪneɪt, ˈlamṇeɪt, -s, -ɪŋ, -ɪd
AM ˈlæməˌneɪ|t, -ts, -dɪŋ, -dɪd

lamination
BR ˌlamɪˈneɪʃn, -z
AM ˌlæməˈneɪʃən, -z

laminator
BR ˈlamɪneɪtə(r), ˈlamṇeɪtə(r), -z
AM ˈlæməˌneɪdər, -z

lamington
BR ˈlamɪŋt(ə)n, -z
AM ˈlæmɪŋtən, -z

laminose
BR ˈlamɪnəʊs, ˈlamṇəʊs
AM ˈlæməˌnoʊs, ˈlæməˌnoʊz

lamish
BR ˈleɪmɪʃ
AM ˈleɪmɪʃ

Lammas
BR ˈlaməs
AM ˈlæməs

lammergeier
BR ˈlaməˌgʌɪə(r), -z
AM ˈlɑmərˌgaɪ(ə)r, -z

lammergeyer
BR ˈlaməˌgʌɪə(r), -z
AM ˈlɑmərˌgaɪ(ə)r, -z

Lammermuir
BR ˈlaməmjʊə(r), ˈlaməmjɔː(r)
AM ˈlæmərˌmjʊ(ə)r

Lamont
BR ləˈmɒnt, ˈlam(ə)nt
AM ləˈmɑnt

lamp
BR lamp, -s
AM læmp, -s

lampblack
BR ˈlampblak
AM ˈlæm(p)ˌblæk

lampern
BR ˈlampən, -z
AM ˈlæmpərn, -z

Lampeter
BR ˈlampɪtə(r)
AM ˈlæmpədər

lampless
BR ˈlampləs
AM ˈlæmpləs

lamplight
BR ˈlamplʌɪt
AM ˈlæmpˌlaɪt

lamplighter
BR 'lamp,lʌɪtə(r), -z
AM 'læmp,laɪdər, -z

lamplit
BR 'lamplɪt
AM 'læmp,lɪt

Lamplugh
BR 'lamplu:
AM 'læmplu

lampoon
BR lam'pu:n, -z, -ɪŋ, -d
AM læm'pun, -z, -ɪŋ, -d

lampooner
BR lam'pu:nə(r), -z
AM læm'punər, -z

lampoonery
BR lam'pu:n(ə)ri
AM læm'pun(ə)ri

lampoonist
BR lam'pu:nɪst, -s
AM læm'punəst, -s

lamp-post
BR 'lam(p)pəʊst, -s
AM 'læm(p),poʊst, -s

lamprey
BR 'lampr|i, -ɪz
AM 'læmpri, -z

lampshade
BR 'lampʃeɪd, -z
AM 'læm(p),ʃeɪd, -z

Lana
BR 'lɑ:nə(*r*)
AM 'lɑnə

Lanark
BR 'lanək
AM 'lænərk

Lanarkshire
BR 'lanəkʃ(ɪ)ə(r)
AM 'lænərkʃ(ɪ)ər

Lancashire
BR 'laŋkəʃ(ɪ)ə(r)
AM 'læŋkəʃɪ(ə)r

Lancaster
BR 'laŋkəstə(r), 'laŋkastə(r), 'laŋkɑ:stə(r)
AM 'læŋ,kæstər, 'læŋkəstər

Lancastrian
BR laŋ'kastrɪən, -z
AM læŋ'kæstriən, -z

lance
BR lɑ:ns, lans, -ɪz, -ɪŋ, -t
AM læns, -əz, -ɪŋ, -t

lancelet
BR 'lɑ:nslɪt, 'lanslɪt, -s
AM 'lænslət, -s

Lancelot
BR 'lɑ:nsəlɒt, 'lɑ:ns(ə)lət, 'lansəlɒt, 'lans(ə)lət
AM 'lænsə,lɑt

lanceolate
BR 'lɑ:nsɪəleɪt, 'lɑ:nsɪələt, 'lansɪəleɪt, 'lansɪələt
AM 'lænsiələt, 'lænsiə,leɪt

lancer
BR 'lɑ:nsə(r), 'lansə(r), -z
AM 'lænsər, -z

lancet
BR 'lɑ:nsɪt, 'lansɪt, -s, -ɪd
AM 'lænsə|t, -ts, -dəd

lancewood
BR 'lɑ:nswʊd, 'lanswʊd, -z
AM 'læns,wʊd, -z

Lanchester
BR 'lɑ:ntʃɪstə(r), 'lantʃɪstə(r)
AM 'læn(t)ʃɪstər

Lanchow
BR ,lan'tʃaʊ
AM 'lɑn'tʃaʊ

Lancia®
BR 'lɑ:nsɪə(*r*), 'lansɪə(*r*), -z
AM 'lɑnsiə, -z

lancinate
BR 'lɑ:nsɪneɪt, 'lansɪneɪt, -s, -ɪŋ, -ɪd
AM 'lænsə,neɪ|t, -ts, -dɪŋ, -dɪd

Lancing
BR 'lɑ:nsɪŋ, 'lansɪŋ
AM 'lænsɪŋ

Lancôme®
BR 'lɒŋkəʊm
AM ',lɑŋ'koʊm

Lancs.
Lancashire
BR laŋks
AM læŋks

Land
German province
BR land, lant
AM lɑnd, lɑnt

land
BR land, -z, -ɪŋ, -ɪd
AM lænd, -z, -ɪŋ, -ɪd

landau
BR 'landɔ:(*r*), 'landaʊ, -z
AM 'læn,daʊ, -z

landaulet
BR ,landɔ:'lɛt, -s
AM ,lændɔ'lɛt, ,lændɑ'lɛt, -s

landaulette
BR ,landɔ:'lɛt, -s
AM ,lændɔ'lɛt, ,lændɑ'lɛt, -s

Länder
BR 'lɛndə(r)
AM 'lɛndər

Landers
BR 'landəz
AM 'lændərz

Landes
BR lɒ̃d
AM læn(d)z

landfall
BR 'lan(d)fɔ:l
AM 'læn(d),fɔl, 'læn(d),fɑl

landfill
BR 'lan(d)fɪl, -z
AM 'læn(d),fɪl, -z

landform
BR 'lan(d)fɔ:m, -z
AM 'læn(d),fɔ(ə)rm, -z

landgrave
BR 'lan(d)greɪv, -z
AM 'læn(d),greɪv, -z

landgraviate
BR lan(d)'greɪvɪət, -s
AM læn(d)'greɪvi,eɪt, -s

landgravine
BR 'lan(d)grəvi:n, -z
AM 'læn(d)grə,vin, -z

landholder
BR 'land,həʊldə(r), -z
AM 'læn(d),(h)oʊldər, -z

landholding
BR 'land,həʊldɪŋ, -z
AM 'læn(d),(h)oʊldɪŋ, -z

landing
BR 'landɪŋ, -z
AM 'lændɪŋ, -z

Landis
BR 'landɪs
AM 'lændəs

landlady
BR 'lan(d),leɪd|i, -ɪz
AM 'læn(d),leɪdi, -z

Ländler
BR 'lɛndlə(r), -z
AM 'lɛn(d)lər, -z

landless
BR 'lan(d)ləs
AM 'læn(d)ləs

landline
BR 'lan(d)lʌɪn, -z
AM 'læn(d),laɪn, -z

landlocked
BR 'lan(d)lɒkt
AM 'læn(d),lɑkt

landloper
BR 'lan(d),ləʊpə(r), -z
AM 'læn(d),loʊpər, -z

landlord
BR 'lan(d)lɔ:d, -z
AM 'læn(d),lɔ(ə)rd, -z

landlubber
BR 'lan(d),lʌbə(r), -z
AM 'læn(d),ləbər, -z

landmark
BR 'lan(d)mɑ:k, -s
AM 'læn(d),mɑrk, -s

landmass
BR 'lan(d)mas, -ɪz
AM 'læn(d),mæs, -əz

landmine
BR 'lan(d)mʌɪn, -z
AM 'læn(d),maɪn, -z

landocracy
BR lan'dɒkrəs|i, -ɪz
AM læn'dɑkræsi, -z

landocrat
BR 'landə(ʊ)krat, -s
AM 'lændə,kræt, -s

Landon
BR 'landən
AM 'lændən

Landor
BR 'landɔ:(r), 'landə(r)
AM 'lændər

landowner
BR 'landəʊnə(r), -z
AM 'læn,doʊnər, -z

landownership
BR 'land,əʊnəʃɪp
AM 'læn,doʊnər,ʃɪp

landowning
BR 'landəʊnɪŋ
AM 'læn,doʊnɪŋ

landrail
BR 'landreɪl, -z
AM 'læn(d),reɪl, -z

Land-Rover®
BR 'land,rəʊvə(r), -z
AM 'læn(d),roʊvər, -z

Landry
BR 'landri
AM 'lændri

landscape
BR 'lan(d)skeɪp, -s, -ɪŋ, -t
AM 'lænz,keɪp, 'læn(d),skeɪp, -s, -ɪŋ, -t

landscapist
BR 'lan(d)skeɪpɪst, -s
AM 'læn(d),skeɪpɪst, -s

Landseer
BR 'lan(d)sɪə(r)
AM 'læn(d),sɪ(ə)r

Landshut
BR 'landzhʊt
AM 'lɑndz,(h)ʊt

landslide
BR 'lan(d)slʌɪd, -z
AM 'læn(d),slaɪd, -z

landslip
BR 'lan(d)slɪp, -s
AM 'læn(d),slɪp, -s

Landsmål
BR 'lan(d)zmɔ:l
AM 'lɑndz,mɔl, 'lɑndz,mɑl

landsman
BR 'lan(d)zmən
AM 'læn(d)zmən

landsmen
BR 'lan(d)zmən
AM 'læn(d)zmən

Landsteiner
BR 'lan(d),ʃtʌɪnə(r)
AM 'lɑn(d),staɪnər

landward
BR 'landwəd, -z
AM 'læn(d)wərd, 'lændərd, -z

lane
BR leɪn, -z
AM leɪn, -z

Lang
BR laŋ
AM læŋ

Langbaurgh
BR ˈlaŋbɑːf
AM ˈlæŋbæf

Langdale
BR ˈlandeɪl
AM ˈlæŋˌdeɪl

Lange[1]
New Zealand politician
BR ˈlɒŋi
AM ˈlæŋi, læŋ

Lange[2]
BR laŋ
AM ˈlæŋi, læŋ

Langerhans
BR ˈlaŋəhanz
AM ˈlæŋərˌhænz

Langford
BR ˈlaŋfəd
AM ˈlæŋfərd

Langland
BR ˈlaŋlənd
AM ˈlæŋlənd

langlauf
BR ˈlaŋlaʊf, -s
AM ˈlɑŋˌlaʊf, -s

Langley
BR ˈlaŋli
AM ˈlæŋli

Langmuir
BR ˈlaŋmjʊə(r)
AM ˈlæŋˌmjuər

Lango
BR ˈlaŋgəʊ
AM ˈlæŋgoʊ

Langobardic
BR ˌlaŋgə(ʊ)ˈbɑːdɪk
AM ˌlæŋgoʊˈbardək

langouste
BR ˌlɒŋˈguːst, ˈlɒŋguːst, -s
AM lɑŋˈgust, -s

langoustine
BR ˌlɒŋgʊˈstiːn, ˈlɒŋgʊstiːn, -z
AM ˈlæŋgəˌstin, -z

Langton
BR ˈlaŋt(ə)n
AM ˈlæŋtən

Langtry
BR ˈlaŋtri
AM ˈlæŋtri

language
BR ˈlaŋgw|ɪdʒ, -ɪdʒɪz
AM ˈlæŋgwɪdʒ, -ɪz

langue
BR lɒŋ(g), lɒ̃g, lɑːŋ(g)
AM lɑŋ(g)

langue de chat
BR ˌlɒŋ də ˈʃɑː(*r*), ˌlɒ̃g +, ˌlɑːŋ +
AM ˈlɑŋ də ˈʃɑ

Languedoc
BR ˈlɒŋgədɒk, ˈlɑːŋgədɒk
AM ˈlɑŋ(gə)ˈdɔk, ˈlɑŋ(gə)ˈdɑk

langue d'oc
BR ˌlɒŋ ˈdɒk, ˌlɒ̃g +, ˌlɑːŋ +
AM ˈlɑŋ(gə) ˈdɔk, ˈlɑŋ(gə) ˈdɑk

langue d'oïl
BR ˌlɒŋ ˈdɔɪ(l), ˌlɒ̃g +, ˌlɑːŋ +
AM ˈlɑŋ(gə) ˈdɔɪl

langues de chat
BR ˌlɒŋ də ˈʃɑː(*r*), ˌlɒ̃g +, ˌlɑːŋ +
AM ˈlɑŋ də ˈʃɑ

languid
BR ˈlaŋgwɪd
AM ˈlæŋgwəd

languidly
BR ˈlaŋgwɪdli
AM ˈlæŋgwədli

languidness
BR ˈlaŋgwɪdnɪs
AM ˈlæŋgwədnəs

languish
BR ˈlaŋgw|ɪʃ, -ɪʃɪz, -ɪʃɪŋ, -ɪʃt
AM ˈlæŋgwɪʃ, -ɪz, -ɪŋ, -t

languisher
BR ˈlaŋgwɪʃə(r), -z
AM ˈlæŋgwɪʃər, -z

languishingly
BR ˈlaŋgwɪʃɪŋli
AM ˈlæŋgwɪʃɪŋli

languishment
BR ˈlaŋgwɪʃm(ə)nt
AM ˈlæŋgwɪʃmənt

languor
BR ˈlaŋgə(r)
AM ˈlæŋ(g)ər

languorous
BR ˈlaŋg(ə)rəs
AM ˈlæŋ(g)(ə)rəs

languorously
BR ˈlaŋg(ə)rəsli
AM ˈlæŋ(g)(ə)rəsli

langur
BR ˈlaŋgəː(r), laŋˈgʊə(r), lʌŋˈgʊə(r), -z
AM lʊŋˈgʊr, -z

laniary
BR ˈlanɪər|i, -ɪz
AM ˈleɪniˌɛri, -z

laniferous
BR laˈnɪf(ə)rəs, ləˈnɪf(ə)rəs
AM ləˈnɪfərəs

lanigerous
BR laˈnɪdʒ(ə)rəs, ləˈnɪdʒ(ə)rəs
AM ləˈnɪdʒ(ə)rəs

lank
BR laŋk, -ə(r), -ɪst
AM læŋk, -ər, -əst

Lankester
BR ˈlaŋkɪstə(r)
AM ˈlæŋkəstər

lankily
BR ˈlaŋkɪli
AM ˈlæŋkəli

lankiness
BR ˈlaŋkɪnɪs
AM ˈlæŋkinɪs

lankly
BR ˈlaŋkli
AM ˈlæŋkli

lankness
BR ˈlaŋknəs
AM ˈlæŋknəs

lanky
BR ˈlaŋk|i, -ɪə(r), -ɪɪst
AM ˈlæŋki, -ər, -ɪst

lanner
BR ˈlanə(r), -z
AM ˈlænər, -z

lanneret
BR ˈlanərɪt, -s
AM ˈlænəˌrɛt, ˌlænəˈrɛt, -s

lanolin
BR ˈlanəlɪn, ˈlanl̩ɪn
AM ˈlænl̩ən

lanoline
BR ˈlanəliːn, ˈlanl̩iːn
AM ˈlænəˌlin

Lansbury
BR ˈlanzb(ə)ri
AM ˈlænzˌbɛri

Lansdown
BR ˈlanzdaʊn
AM ˈlænzˌdaʊn

Lansdowne
BR ˈlanzdaʊn
AM ˈlænzˌdaʊn

Lansing
BR ˈlɑːnsɪŋ, ˈlansɪŋ
AM ˈlænsɪŋ

lansker
BR ˈlanskə(r)
AM ˈlænskər

lansquenet
BR ˈlɑːnskənɛt, ˌlanskənɛt, -s
AM ˈlænskəˈnɛt, -s

lantana
BR lanˈtɑːnə(*r*), lanˈteɪnə(*r*), -z
AM lænˈtænə, -z

lantern
BR ˈlantən, -z
AM ˈlæn(t)ərn, -z

lanthanide
BR ˈlanθənʌɪd, -z
AM ˈlænθəˌnaɪd, -z

lanthanum
BR ˈlanθənʌm
AM ˈlænθənəm

lanugo
BR ləˈnjuːgəʊ
AM ləˈn(j)ugoʊ

lanyard
BR ˈlanjəd, ˈlanjɑːd, -z
AM ˈlænjərd, -z

Lanza
BR ˈlanzə(*r*)
AM ˈlænzə, ˈlɑnzə

Lanzarote
BR ˌlanzəˈrɒti
AM ˌlɑnsəˈroʊdi
SP ˌlanθaˈrote, ˌlansaˈrote

Lanzhou
BR ˌlanˈʒuː
AM ˈlænˈʒu

Lao
BR laʊ
AM laʊ

Laocoon
BR leɪˈɒkəʊɒn, leɪˈɒkəʊən
AM leɪˈɑkəˌwɑn

Laodicean
BR ˌleɪə(ʊ)dɪˈsiːən, -z
AM leɪˌɑdiˈsiən, -z

Laois
BR liːʃ
AM liʃ

Laos
BR ˈlɑːɒs, laʊs
AM ˈlɑoʊs

Laotian
BR leɪˈəʊʃn, -z
AM leɪˈoʊʃən, -z

Lao-tzu
BR ˌlaʊˈtsuː
AM ˈlɑoʊˈtsu

lap
BR lap, -s, -ɪŋ, -t
AM læp, -s, -ɪŋ, -t

laparoscope
BR ˈlap(ə)rəskəʊp, -s
AM ˈlæpərəˌskoʊp, -s

laparoscopy
BR ˌlapəˈrɒskəp|i, -ɪz
AM ˌlæpəˈrɑskəpi, -z

laparotomy
BR ˌlapəˈrɒtəm|i, -ɪz
AM ˌlæpəˈrɑdəmi, -z

La Paz
BR la ˈpaz
AM lə ˈpɑz

lapdog
BR ˈlapdɒg, -z
AM ˈlæpˌdɔg, ˈlæpˌdɑg, -z

lapel
BR ləˈpɛl, -z
AM ləˈpɛl, -z, -d

lapful
BR ˈlapfʊl, -z
AM ˈlæpˌfʊl, -z

lapicide
BR ˈlapɪsʌɪd, -z
AM ˈlæpəˌsaɪd, -z

lapidary
BR ˈlapɪd(ə)r|i, -ɪz
AM ˈlæpəˌdɛri, -z

lapidate
BR 'lapɪdeɪt, -s, -ɪŋ, -ɪd
AM 'læpəˌdeɪ|t, -ts, -dɪŋ, -dɪd

lapidation
BR ˌlapɪ'deɪʃn
AM ˌlæpə'deɪʃən

lapilli
BR lə'pɪlʌɪ
AM lə'pɪˌlaɪ

lapis lazuli
BR ˌlapɪs 'lazjʉlʌɪ, + 'lazjʉli:
AM ˌlæpəs 'læzjəlaɪ, + 'læʒəlaɪ, + 'læzjəli

Lapith
BR 'lapɪθ, -s
AM 'læpəθ, -s

Laplace
BR lə'plɑ:s, lə'plas, la'plɑ:s, la'plas
AM lɑ'plɑs

Lapland
BR 'lapland
AM 'læpˌlænd

Laplander
BR 'lapˌlandə(r), -z
AM 'læpˌlændər, -z

Lapotaire
BR ˌlapə'tɛ:(r), ˌlapɒ'tɛ:(r)
AM ˌlɑpə'tɛ(ə)r

Lapp
BR lap, -s
AM læp, -s

Lappard
BR 'lɛpɑ:d
AM 'lɛˌpɑrd, 'læpərd

lappet
BR 'lap|ɪt, -s, -ɪtɪŋ, -ɪtɪd
AM 'læpə|t, -ts, -dəd

Lappish
BR 'lapɪʃ
AM 'læpɪʃ

Lapsang Souchong
BR ˌlapsaŋ 'su:ʃɒŋ, + su:'ʃɒŋ
AM ˌlɑpsɑŋ su'tʃɑŋ

lapse
BR laps, -ɪz, -ɪŋ, -t
AM læps, -əz, -ɪŋ, -t

lapser
BR 'lapsə(r), -z
AM 'læpsər, -z

lapstone
BR 'lapstəʊn, -z
AM 'læpˌstoʊn, -z

lapsus calami
BR ˌlapsəs 'kaləmʌɪ
AM ˌlæpsəs 'kɑləˌmaɪ, + 'kɑləmi

lapsus linguae
BR ˌlapsəs 'lɪŋgwʌɪ
AM ˌlɑpsəs 'lɪŋgwaɪ

Laptev
BR 'laptɛv
AM 'lɑpˌtɛv
RUS 'laptʲif

laptop
BR 'laptɒp, -s
AM 'læpˌtɑp, -s

Laputa
BR lə'pju:tə(r)
AM lə'p(j)udə

Laputan
BR lə'pju:tn, -z
AM lə'pjutn, -z

lapwing
BR 'lapwɪŋ, -z
AM 'læpˌwɪŋ, -z

Lara
BR 'lɑ:rə(*r*)
AM 'lɑrə

Laramie
BR 'larəmi
AM 'lɛrəˌmi

larboard
BR 'lɑ:bɔ:d, 'labəd
AM 'lɑrˌbɔ(ə)rd, 'læbərd

larcener
BR 'lɑ:sɪnə(r), 'lɑ:sn̩ə(r), -z
AM 'lɑrsənər, 'lɑrsn̩ər, -z

larcenist
BR 'lɑ:sɪnɪst, 'lɑ:sn̩ɪst, -s
AM 'lɑrsənəst, 'lɑrsn̩əst, -s

larcenous
BR 'lɑ:sɪnəs, 'lɑ:sn̩əs
AM 'lɑrsənəs, 'lɑrsn̩əs

larcenously
BR 'lɑ:sɪnəsli, 'lɑ:sn̩əsli
AM 'lɑrsənəsli, 'lɑrsn̩əsli

larceny
BR 'lɑ:sɪn|i, 'lɑ:sn̩|i, -ɪz
AM 'lɑrsəni, 'lɑrsn̩i, -z

larch
BR lɑ:tʃ, -ɪz
AM lɑrtʃ, -əz

larchwood
BR 'lɑ:tʃwʊd, -z
AM 'lɑrtʃˌwʊd, -z

lard
BR lɑ:d, -z, -ɪŋ, -ɪd
AM lɑrd, -z, -ɪŋ, -əd

lardass
BR 'lɑ:dɑ:s, 'lɑ:das, -ɪz
AM 'lɑrdæs, -əz

larder
BR 'lɑ:də(r), -z
AM 'lɑrdər, -z

Lardner
BR 'lɑ:dnə(r)
AM 'lɑrdnər

lardon
BR 'lɑ:dn
AM 'lɑrdən

lardoon
BR lɑ:'du:n, -z
AM lɑr'dun, -z

lardy
BR 'lɑ:di
AM 'lɑrdi

lardy-dardy
BR ˌlɑ:dɪ'dɑ:di
AM 'lɑrdi'dɑrdi

Laredo
BR lə'reɪdəʊ
AM lə'reɪdoʊ

lares
BR 'lɑ:ri:z, 'lɑ:reɪz, 'lɛ:ri:z
AM 'leɪˌriz, 'lɛriz

Largactil®
BR lɑ:'gaktɪl
AM lɑr'gæktəl

large
BR lɑ:dʒ, -ə(r), -ɪst
AM lɑrdʒ, -ər, -əst

largely
BR 'lɑ:dʒli
AM 'lɑrdʒli

largen
BR 'lɑ:dʒ|(ə)n, -(ə)nz, -n̩ɪŋ\-(ə)nɪŋ, -(ə)nd
AM 'lɑrdʒən, -z, -ɪŋ, -d

largeness
BR 'lɑ:dʒnəs
AM 'lɑrdʒnəs

largess
BR lɑ:'(d)ʒɛs
AM lɑr'(d)ʒɛs

largesse
BR lɑ:'(d)ʒɛs
AM lɑr'(d)ʒɛs

larghetto
BR lɑ:'gɛtəʊ, -z
AM lɑr'gɛdoʊ, -z

largish
BR 'lɑ:dʒɪʃ
AM 'lɑrdʒɪʃ

largo
BR 'lɑ:gəʊ, -z
AM 'lɑrgoʊ, -z

Largs
BR lɑ:gz
AM lɑrgz

lariat
BR 'larɪət, -s
AM 'lɛriət, -s

Larissa
BR lə'rɪsə(*r*)
AM lə'rɪsə

lark
BR lɑ:k, -s, -ɪŋ, -t
AM lɑrk, -s, -ɪŋ, -t

Larkin
BR 'lɑ:kɪn
AM 'lɑrkən

larkiness
BR 'lɑ:kɪnɪs
AM 'lɑrkinɪs

larkspur
BR 'lɑ:kspə:(r), -z
AM 'lɑrkˌspər, -z

larky
BR 'lɑ:ki
AM 'lɑrki

larn
BR lɑ:n, -z, -ɪŋ, -d
AM lɑrn, -z, -ɪŋ, -d

La Rochelle
BR ˌlɑ: rɒ'ʃɛl, ˌla +
AM lɑ rə'ʃɛl

Larousse
BR lə'ru:s, la'ru:s
AM lə'rus

larrikin
BR 'larɪkɪn, -z
AM 'lɛrəkən, -z

larrup
BR 'larəp, -s, -ɪŋ, -t
AM 'lɛrəp, -s, -ɪŋ, -t

Larry
BR 'lari
AM 'lɛri

Lars
BR lɑ:z
AM lɑrz

Larsen
BR 'lɑ:sn
AM 'lɑrsən
DAN 'lɑ:sən
SW 'lɑ:ʃɛn

Larson
BR 'lɑ:sn
AM 'lɑrsən

larva
BR 'lɑ:və(*r*), -z
AM 'lɑrvə, -z

larvae
BR 'lɑ:vi:
AM 'lɑrvi, 'lɑrˌvaɪ, 'lɑrveɪ

larval
BR 'lɑ:vl
AM 'lɑrvəl

larvicide
BR 'lɑ:vɪsʌɪd, -z
AM 'lɑrvəˌsaɪd, -z

Larwood
BR 'lɑ:wʊd
AM 'lɑrˌwʊd

laryngeal
BR lə'rɪn(d)ʒɪəl, ˌlarɪn'dʒi:əl, ˌlarn̩'dʒi:əl
AM lə'rɪndʒ(i)əl, ˌlɛrən'dʒiəl

larynges
BR lə'rɪn(d)ʒi:z, la'rɪn(d)ʒi:z
AM lə'rɪnˌdʒiz

laryngic
BR lə'rɪndʒɪk, la'rɪndʒɪk
AM lə'rɪndʒɪk

laryngitic
BR ˌlarɪn'dʒɪtɪk, ˌlarn̩'dʒɪtɪk
AM ˌlɛrən'dʒɪdɪk

laryngitis
BR ˌlarɪnˈdʒʌɪtɪs, ˌlarn̩ˈdʒʌɪtɪs
AM ˌlɛrənˈdʒaɪdɪs

laryngology
BR ˈlarɪŋˈɡɒlədʒi
AM ˌlɛrənˈɡɑlədʒi

laryngoscope
BR ləˈrɪŋɡəskəʊp, laˈrɪŋɡəskəʊp, -s
AM ləˈrɪŋɡəˌskoʊp, ləˈrɪndʒəˌskoʊp, -s

laryngoscopic
BR ləˌrɪŋɡəˈskɒpɪk, laˌrɪŋɡəˈskɒpɪk
AM ləˌrɪŋɡəˈskɑpɪk, ləˌrɪndʒəˈskɑpɪk

laryngoscopically
BR ləˌrɪŋɡəˈskɒpɪkli, laˌrɪŋɡəˈskɒpɪkli
AM ləˌrɪŋɡəˈskɑpək(ə)li, ləˌrɪndʒəˈskɑpək(ə)li

laryngoscopy
BR ˌlarɪŋˈɡɒskəp|i, -ɪz
AM ˌlɛrənˈɡɑskəpi, -z

laryngotomy
BR ˌlarɪŋˈɡɒtəm|i, -ɪz
AM ˌlɛrənˈɡɑdəmi, -z

larynx
BR ˈlarɪŋks, -ɪz
AM ˈlɛrɪŋks, -ɪz

lasagna
BR ləˈzanjə(r)
AM ləˈzɑnjə

lasagne
BR ləˈzanjə(r)
AM ləˈzɑnjə

La Salle
BR la ˈsal
AM lə ˈsɑl

La Scala
BR la ˈskɑːlə(r)
AM lɑ ˈskɑlə

lascar
BR ˈlaskə(r), -z
AM ˈlæskər, -z

lascivious
BR ləˈsɪvɪəs
AM ləˈsɪviəs

lasciviously
BR ləˈsɪvɪəsli
AM ləˈsɪviəsli

lasciviousness
BR ləˈsɪvɪəsnəs
AM ləˈsɪviəsnəs

laser
BR ˈleɪzə(r), -z
AM ˈleɪzər, -z

laserdisc
BR ˈleɪzədɪsk, -s
AM ˈleɪzərˌdɪsk, -s

LaserVision®
BR ˈleɪzəˌvɪʒn
AM ˈleɪzərˌvɪʒən

lash
BR laʃ, -ɪz, -ɪŋ, -t
AM læʃ, -əz, -ɪŋ, -t

lasher
BR ˈlaʃə(r), -z
AM ˈlæʃər, -z

lashing
BR ˈlaʃɪŋ, -z
AM ˈlæʃɪŋ, -z

lashingly
BR ˈlaʃɪŋli
AM ˈlæʃɪŋli

lashkar
BR ˈlaʃkɑː(r), ˈlaʃkə(r), -z
AM ˈlæʃkər, -z

lashless
BR ˈlaʃləs
AM ˈlæʃləs

Lasker
BR ˈlaskə(r), -z
AM ˈlæskər, -z

Laski
BR ˈlaski
AM ˈlæski

Las Palmas
BR las ˈpalməs, + ˈpɑː(l)məs
AM ˌlɑs ˈpɑlməs

lasque
BR lɑːsk, lask, -s
AM læsk, -s

lass
BR las, -ɪz
AM læs, -əz

Lassa fever
BR ˈlasə ˌfiːvə(r)
AM ˈlɑsə ˈfivər

lassie
BR ˈlas|i, -ɪz
AM ˈlæsi, -z

lassitude
BR ˈlasɪtjuːd, ˈlasɪtʃuːd
AM ˈlæsəˌt(j)ud

lasso
BR ləˈsuː, laˈsuː, ˈlasəʊ, -z, -ɪŋ, -d
AM ˈlæsoʊ, ˈlæsu, læˈsu, -z, -ɪŋ, -d

lassoer
BR ləˈsuːə(r), laˈsuːə(r), ˈlasəʊə(r), -z
AM ˈlæsəwər, -z

Lassus
BR ˈlasəs
AM ˈlɑsəs

last
BR lɑːst, last, -s, -ɪŋ, -ɪd
AM læst, -s, -ɪŋ, -əd

lasting
BR ˈlɑːstɪŋ, ˈlastɪŋ
AM ˈlæstɪŋ

lastingly
BR ˈlɑːstɪŋli, ˈlastɪŋli
AM ˈlæstɪŋli

lastingness
BR ˈlɑːstɪŋnɪs, ˈlastɪŋnɪs
AM ˈlæstɪŋnɪs

lastly
BR ˈlɑːstli, ˈlastli
AM ˈlæs(t)li

Las Vegas
BR las ˈveɪɡəs
AM lɑs ˈveɪɡəs

lat
BR lat, -s
AM læt, -s

Latakia
BR ˌlatəˈkiːə(r)
AM ˌlɑdəˈkiə

latch
BR latʃ, -ɪz, -ɪŋ, -t
AM lætʃ, -əz, -ɪŋ, -t

latchet
BR ˈlatʃɪt, -s
AM ˈlætʃət, -s

latchkey
BR ˈlatʃkiː, -z
AM ˈlætʃˌki, -z

late
BR leɪt, -ə(r), -ɪst
AM leɪ|t, -dər, -dɪst

latecomer
BR ˈleɪtˌkʌmə(r), -z
AM ˈleɪtˌkəmər, -z

lateen
BR ləˈtiːn, laˈtiːn
AM ləˈtin, læˈtin

lateish
BR ˈleɪtɪʃ
AM ˈleɪdɪʃ

lately
BR ˈleɪtli
AM ˈleɪtli

laten
BR ˈleɪt|n, -nz, -n̩ɪŋ\-ənɪŋ, -nd
AM ˈleɪtn, -z, -ɪŋ, -d

latency
BR ˈleɪt(ə)nsi
AM ˈleɪtnsi

La Tène
BR lə ˈtɛn
AM lə ˈtɛn

lateness
BR ˈleɪtnɪs
AM ˈleɪtnɪs

latent
BR ˈleɪt(ə)nt
AM ˈleɪtnt

latently
BR ˈleɪt(ə)ntli
AM ˈleɪtn(t)li

later
BR ˈleɪtə(r)
AM ˈleɪdər

lateral
BR ˈlat(ə)rəl, ˈlat(ə)rl̩, -z
AM ˈlædərəl, ˈlætrəl, -z

laterally
BR ˈlat(ə)rəli, ˈlat(ə)rl̩i
AM ˈlædərəli, ˈlætrəli

Lateran
BR ˈlat(ə)rən, ˈlat(ə)rn̩
AM ˈlæd(ə)rən

laterite
BR ˈlatərʌɪt
AM ˈlædəˌraɪt

lateritic
BR ˌlatəˈrɪtɪk
AM ˌlædəˈrɪdɪk

latex
BR ˈleɪtɛks
AM ˈleɪˌtɛks

lath
BR lɑː|θ, la|θ, lɑːðz\lɑːθs\laθs
AM læ|θ, -ðz\-θs

Latham
BR ˈleɪθ(ə)m, ˈleɪð(ə)m
AM ˈleɪθəm

lathe
BR leɪð, -z
AM leɪð, -z

lather
BR ˈlɑːð|ə(r), ˈlað|ə(r), -əz, -(ə)rɪŋ, -əd
AM ˈlæð|ər, -ərz, -(ə)rɪŋ, -ərd

lathery
BR ˈlɑːð(ə)ri, ˈlað(ə)ri
AM ˈlæðəri

lathi
BR ˈlɑːt|i, -ɪz
AM ˈlɑdi, -z

lathy
BR ˈleɪði
AM ˈleɪði

latices
BR ˈlatɪsiːz
AM ˈlædəˌsiz

latifundia
BR ˌlatɪˈfʌndɪə(r)
AM ˌlædəˈfəndiə

latifundium
BR ˌlatɪˈfʌndɪəm
AM ˌlædəˈfəndiəm

Latimer
BR ˈlatɪmə(r)
AM ˈlædəmər

Latin
BR ˈlatɪn, -z
AM ˈlætn, -z

Latinate
BR ˈlatɪneɪt
AM ˈlætnˌeɪt

Latinisation
BR ˌlatɪnʌɪˈzeɪʃn
AM ˌlætn̩əˈzeɪʃən, ˌlætnˌaɪˈzeɪʃən

Latinise
BR ˈlatɪnʌɪz, -ɪz, -ɪŋ, -d
AM ˈlætnˌaɪz, -ɪz, -ɪŋ, -d

Latiniser
BR ˈlatɪnʌɪzə(r), -z
AM ˈlætnˌaɪzər, -z

Latinism
BR ˈlatɪnɪz(ə)m, -z
AM ˈlætnˌɪzəm, -z

Latinist
BR ˈlatɪnɪst, -s
AM ˈlætnəst, -s

Latinization
BR ˌlatɪnʌɪˈzeɪʃn
AM ˌlætn̩əˈzeɪʃən, ˌlætnˌaɪˈzeɪʃən

Latinize
BR ˈlatɪnʌɪz, -ɪz, -ɪŋ, -d
AM ˈlætnˌaɪz, -ɪz, -ɪŋ, -d

Latinizer
BR ˈlatɪnʌɪzə(r), -z
AM ˈlætnˌaɪzər, -z

Latino
BR laˈtiːnəʊ, ləˈtiːnəʊ, -z
AM ləˈtiˌnoʊ, -z

latish
BR ˈleɪtɪʃ
AM ˈleɪdɪʃ

latitude
BR ˈlatɪtjuːd, ˈlatɪtʃuːd, -z
AM ˈlædəˌt(j)ud, -z

latitudinal
BR ˌlatɪˈtjuːdɪnl, ˌlatɪˈtʃuːdɪnl
AM ˌlædəˈt(j)udn̩əl

latitudinally
BR ˌlatɪˈtjuːdɪnl̩i, ˌlatɪˈtjuːdɪnəli, ˌlatɪˈtʃuːdɪnl̩i, ˌlatɪˈtʃuːdɪnəli
AM ˌlædəˈt(j)udn̩əli

latitudinarian
BR ˌlatɪˌtjuːdɪˈnɛːrɪən, ˌlatɪˌtʃuːdɪˈnɛːrɪən, -z
AM ˌlædəˌt(j)udnˈɛriən, -z

latitudinarianism
BR ˌlatɪˌtjuːdɪˈnɛːrɪənɪz(ə)m, ˌlatɪˌtʃuːdɪˈnɛːrɪənɪz(ə)m
AM ˌlædəˌt(j)udnˈɛriəˌnɪzəm

Latium
BR ˈleɪʃ(ɪ)əm, ˈlɑːtɪəm
AM ˈleɪʃ(i)əm

latke
BR ˈlʌtkə(r), -z
AM ˈlɑtkə, -z

Latona
BR ləˈtəʊnə(r)
AM ləˈtoʊnə

Latoya
BR ləˈtɔɪə(r)
AM ləˈtɔɪə

latria
BR ləˈtrʌɪə(r)
AM ləˈtraɪə

latrine
BR ləˈtriːn, -z
AM ləˈtrin, -z

Latrobe
BR ləˈtrəʊb
AM ləˈtroʊb

latten
BR ˈlatn, -z
AM ˈlætn, -z

latter
BR ˈlatə(r)
AM ˈlædər

latterly
BR ˈlatəli
AM ˈlædərli

lattice
BR ˈlatɪs, -ɪz, -t
AM ˈlædəs, -əz, -t

latticing
BR ˈlatɪsɪŋ
AM ˈlædəsɪŋ

Latvia
BR ˈlatvɪə(r)
AM ˈlætviə

Latvian
BR ˈlatvɪən, -z
AM ˈlætviən, -z

laud
BR lɔːd, -z, -ɪŋ, -ɪd
AM lɔd, lɑd, -z, -ɪŋ, -əd

Lauda
BR ˈlaʊdə(r)
AM ˈlaʊdə

laudability
BR ˌlɔːdəˈbɪlɪti
AM ˌlɔdəˈbɪlɪdi, ˌlɑdəˈbɪlɪdi

laudable
BR ˈlɔːdəbl
AM ˈlɔdəbəl, ˈlɑdəbəl

laudably
BR ˈlɔːdəbli
AM ˈlɔdəbli, ˈlɑdəbli

laudanum
BR ˈlɔːd(ə)nəm, ˈlɔːdn̩əm
AM ˈlɔdn̩əm, ˈlɑdn̩əm

laudation
BR lɔːˈdeɪʃn, -z
AM lɔˈdeɪʃən, lɑˈdeɪʃən, -z

laudative
BR ˈlɔːdətɪv
AM ˈlɔdədɪv, ˈlɑdədɪv

laudatory
BR ˈlɔːdət(ə)ri
AM ˈlɔdəˌtɔri, ˈlɑdəˌtɔri

Lauderdale
BR ˈlɔːdədeɪl
AM ˈlɔdərˌdeɪl, ˈlɑdərˌdeɪl

laugh
BR lɑːf, laf, -s, -ɪŋ, -t
AM læf, -s, -ɪŋ, -t

laughable
BR ˈlɑːfəbl, ˈlafəbl
AM ˈlæfəbəl

laughably
BR ˈlɑːfəbli, ˈlafəbli
AM ˈlæfəbli

Laugharne
BR lɑːn
AM lɑrn

laugher
BR ˈlɑːfə(r), ˈlafə(r), -z
AM ˈlæfər, -z

laughingly
BR ˈlɑːfɪŋli, ˈlafɪŋli
AM ˈlæfɪŋli

laughingstock
BR ˈlɑːfɪŋstɒk, ˈlafɪŋstɒk, -s
AM ˈlæfɪŋˌstɑk, -s

laughter
BR ˈlɑːftə(r), ˈlaftə(r)
AM ˈlæftər

Laughton
BR ˈlɔːtn
AM ˈlɔtn, ˈlɑtn

launce
BR lɔːns, -ɪz
AM lɔns, lɑns, -əz

Launceston
BR ˈlɔːnst(ə)n, ˈlɑːnst(ə)n
AM ˈlɔnstən, ˈlɑnstən

launch
BR lɔːn(t)ʃ, -ɪz, -ɪŋ, -t
AM lɔn(t)ʃ, lɑn(t)ʃ, -əz, -ɪŋ, -t

launcher
BR ˈlɔːn(t)ʃə(r), -z
AM ˈlɔn(t)ʃər, ˈlɑn(t)ʃər, -z

launchpad
BR ˈlɔːn(t)ʃpad, -z
AM ˈlɔn(t)ʃˌpæd, ˈlɑn(t)ʃˌpæd, -z

launder
BR ˈlɔːnd|ə(r), -əz, -(ə)rɪŋ, -əd
AM ˈlɔnd|ər, ˈlɑnd|ər, -ərz, -(ə)rɪŋ, -ərd

launderer
BR ˈlɔːnd(ə)rə(r), -z
AM ˈlɔndərər, ˈlɑndərər, -z

launderette
BR lɔːnˈdrɛt, ˌlɔːndəˈrɛt, -s
AM ˌlɔndəˈrɛt, ˌlɑndəˈrɛt, -s

laundress
BR ˈlɔːndrɪs, lɔːnˈdrɛs, -ɪz
AM ˈlɔndrəs, ˈlɑndrəs, -əz

laundromat
BR ˈlɔːndrəmat, -s
AM ˈlɔndrəˌmæt, ˈlɑndrəˌmæt, -s

laundry
BR ˈlɔːndr|i, -ɪz
AM ˈlɔndri, ˈlɑndri, -z

Laura
BR ˈlɔːrə(r)
AM ˈlɔrə

Laurasia
BR lɔːˈreɪʃə(r), lɔːˈreɪʒə(r)
AM lɔˈreɪʒə, lɔˈreɪʃə

laureate
BR ˈlɔːrɪət, ˈlɒrɪət, -s
AM ˈlɔriɪt, -s

laureateship
BR ˈlɔːrɪətʃɪp, ˈlɒrɪətʃɪp, -s
AM ˈlɔriɪtˌʃɪp, -s

laurel
BR ˈlɒrəl, ˈlɒrl̩, -z
AM ˈlɔrəl, -z

Lauren
BR ˈlɔːrən, ˈlɔːrn̩, ˈlɒrən, ˈlɒrn̩
AM ˈlɔrən

Laurence
BR ˈlɒrəns, ˈlɒrn̩s
AM ˈlɔrəns

Laurentian
adjective
BR lɒˈrɛnʃn, lɔːˈrɛnʃn, ləˈrɛnʃn
AM lɔˈrɛn(t)ʃən

Laurie
BR ˈlɒri
AM ˈlɔri

Laurier
BR ˈlɒrɪə(r), ˈlɒrɪeɪ
AM ˈlɔriər

Lauriston
BR ˈlɒrɪst(ə)n
AM ˈlɔrəstən

laurustinus
BR ˌlɒrəˈstʌɪnəs, -ɪz
AM lɔˈrəstənəs, -əz

Lausanne
BR ləʊˈzan
AM lɔˈzɑn, lɑˈzɑn

LAUTRO
BR ˈlaʊtrəʊ
AM ˈlɔˌtroʊ, ˈlɑˌtroʊ

lav
BR lav, -z
AM læv, -z

lava
BR ˈlɑːvə(r)
AM ˈlɑvə

lavabo
BR ləˈvɑːbəʊ, ləˈveɪbəʊ, -z
AM ləˈvɑboʊ, ləˈveɪboʊ, -z

lavage
BR ˈlavɪdʒ
AM ləˈvɑʒ, ˈlævɪdʒ

Laval
BR ləˈval, laˈval
AM lɑˈvɑl

lavaliere
BR ləˌvalɪˈɛː(r), ləˈvaljɛː(r)
AM ˌlɑvəˈlɪ(ə)r, ˌlævəˈlɪ(ə)r

lavation
BR ləˈveɪʃn
AM ləˈveɪʃən

lavatorial
BR ˌlavəˈtɔːrɪəl
AM ˌlævəˈtɔriəl

lavatory
BR ˈlavət(ə)r|i, -ɪz
AM ˈlævəˌtɔri, -z

lave
BR leɪv, -z, -ɪŋ, -d
AM leɪv, -z, -ɪŋ, -d

lavender
BR ˈlav(ɪ)ndə(r)
AM ˈlævəndər

laver
BR ˈleɪvə(r), -z
AM ˈleɪvər, -z

Laverick
BR ˈlav(ə)rɪk
AM ˈlæv(ə)rək

laverock
BR ˈlav(ə)rək, -s
AM ˈlæv(ə)rək, -s

Lavery
BR ˈleɪv(ə)ri
AM ˈleɪvəri

Lavinia
BR ləˈvɪnɪə(r)
AM ləˈvɪniə, ləˈvɪnjə

lavish
BR ˈlavɪʃ
AM ˈlævɪʃ

lavishly
BR ˈlavɪʃli
AM ˈlævɪʃli

lavishness
BR ˈlavɪʃnɪs
AM ˈlævɪʃnɪs

Lavoisier
BR ləˈvwɑːzɪeɪ, laˈvwɑːzɪeɪ, ləˈvwazɪeɪ, laˈvwazɪeɪ
AM ləˌvwɑˈzieɪ

lavvy
BR ˈlav|i, -ɪz
AM ˈlævi, -z

law
BR lɔː(r), -z
AM lɔ, lɑ, -z

Lawes
BR lɔːz
AM lɔz, lɑz

Lawford
BR ˈlɔːfəd
AM ˈlɔfərd, ˈlɑfərd

lawful
BR ˈlɔːf(ʊ)l
AM ˈlɔfəl, ˈlɑfəl

lawfully
BR ˈlɔːfʊli, ˈlɔːfl̩i
AM ˈlɔf(ə)li, ˈlɑf(ə)li

lawfulness
BR ˈlɔːf(ʊ)lnəs
AM ˈlɔfəlnəs, ˈlɑfəlnəs

lawgiver
BR ˈlɔːˌɡɪvə(r), -z
AM ˈlɔˌɡɪvər, ˈlɑˌɡɪvər, -z

Lawler
BR ˈlɔːlə(r)
AM ˈlɔlər, ˈlɑlər

lawless
BR ˈlɔːləs
AM ˈlɔləs, ˈlɑləs

lawlessly
BR ˈlɔːləsli
AM ˈlɔləsli, ˈlɑləsli

lawlessness
BR ˈlɔːləsnəs
AM ˈlɔləsnəs, ˈlɑləsnəs

Lawley
BR ˈlɔːli
AM ˈlɔli, ˈlɑli

Lawlor
BR ˈlɔːlə(r)
AM ˈlɔlər, ˈlɑlər

lawmaker
BR ˈlɔːˌmeɪkə(r), -z
AM ˈlɔˌmeɪkər, ˈlɑˌmeɪkər, -z

lawman
BR ˈlɔːman, ˈlɔːmən
AM ˈlɔˌmæn, ˈlɔmən, ˈlɑˌmæn, ˈlɑmən

lawmen
BR ˈlɔːmɛn, ˈlɔːmən
AM ˈlɔˌmɛn, ˈlɔmən, ˈlɑˌmɛn, ˈlɑmən

lawn
BR lɔːn, -z
AM lɔn, lɑn, -z, -d

lawnmower
BR ˈlɔːnˌməʊə(r), -z
AM ˈlɔnˌmoʊ(ə)r, ˈlɑnˌmoʊ(ə)r, -z

lawny
BR ˈlɔːni
AM ˈlɔni, ˈlɑni

Lawrence
BR ˈlɒrəns, ˈlɒrn̩s
AM ˈlɔrəns

lawrencium
BR ləˈrɛnsɪəm
AM lɔˈrɛn(t)siəm, lɑˈrɛn(t)siəm

Lawrey
BR ˈlɒri
AM ˈlaʊri

Lawrie
BR ˈlɒri
AM ˈlaʊri, ˈlɔri

Laws
BR lɔːz
AM lɔz, lɑz

Lawson
BR ˈlɔːsn
AM ˈlɔsən, ˈlɑsən

lawsuit
BR ˈlɔːs(j)uːt, -s
AM ˈlɔˌsut, ˈlɑˌsut, -s

Lawton
BR ˈlɔːtn
AM ˈlɔtn, ˈlɑtn

lawyer
BR ˈlɔɪə(r), ˈlɔːjə(r), -z
AM ˈlɔɪər, ˈlɔjər, ˈlɑjər, -z

lawyerly
BR ˈlɔːɪəli, ˈlɔːjəli
AM ˈlɔɪərli, ˈlɔjərli, ˈlɑjərli

lax
BR laks, -ə(r), -ɪst
AM læks, -ər, -əst

laxative
BR ˈlaksətɪv, -z
AM ˈlæksədɪv, -z

Laxey
BR ˈlaksi
AM ˈlæksi

laxity
BR ˈlaksɪti
AM ˈlæksədi

laxly
BR ˈlaksli
AM ˈlæksli

laxness
BR ˈlaksnəs
AM ˈlæksnəs

lay
BR leɪ, -z, -ɪŋ, -d
AM leɪ, -z, -ɪŋ, -d

layabout
BR ˈleɪəbaʊt, -s
AM ˈleɪəˌbaʊt, -s

Layamon
BR ˈleɪəmən
AM ˈleɪəˌmɑn, ˈleɪəmən

lay-by
BR ˈleɪbʌɪ, -z
AM ˈleɪˌbaɪ, -z

Laycock
BR ˈleɪkɒk
AM ˈleɪkɑk

layer
BR ˈleɪə(r), -z, -ɪŋ, -d
AM ˈleɪər, ˈlɛ(ə)r, -z, -ɪŋ, -d

layette
BR leɪˈɛt, -s
AM leɪˈɛt, -s

layman
BR ˈleɪmən
AM ˈleɪmən

laymen
BR ˈleɪmən
AM ˈleɪmən

lay-off
noun
BR ˈleɪɒf, -s
AM ˈleɪˌɔf, ˈleɪˌɑf, -s

layout
BR ˈleɪaʊt, -s
AM ˈleɪˌaʊt, -s

layover
BR ˈleɪˌəʊvə(r), -z
AM ˈleɪˌoʊvər, -z

layperson
BR ˈleɪˌpəːsn, -z
AM ˈleɪˌpərsən, -z

layshaft
BR ˈleɪʃɑːft, ˈleɪʃaft, -s
AM ˈleɪˌʃæft, -s

laystall
BR ˈleɪstɔːl, -z
AM ˈleɪˌstɔl, ˈleɪˌstɑl, -z

Layton
BR ˈleɪtn
AM ˈleɪtn

laywoman
BR ˈleɪˌwʊmən
AM ˈleɪˌwʊmən

laywomen
BR ˈleɪˌwɪmɪn
AM ˈleɪˌwɪmɨn

lazar
BR ˈlazə(r), -z
AM ˈlæzər, ˈleɪzər, -z

lazaret
BR ˌlazəˈrɛt, -s
AM ˌlæzəˈrɛt, -s

lazaretto
BR ˌlazəˈrɛtəʊ, -z
AM ˌlæzəˈrɛdoʊ, -z

Lazarist
BR ˈlaz(ə)rɪst, -s
AM ˈlæzərəst, -s

Lazarus
BR ˈlaz(ə)rəs
AM ˈlæzərəs

laze
BR leɪz, -ɪz, -ɪŋ, -d
AM leɪz, -ɨz, -ɪŋ, -d

lazily
BR ˈleɪzɨli
AM ˈleɪzɨli

laziness
BR ˈleɪzɪnɨs
AM ˈleɪzinɨs

Lazio
BR ˈlatsɪəʊ
AM ˈlɑtsioʊ

Lazonby
BR leɪznbi
AM ˈleɪzənbi

lazuli
BR ˈlazjʊlʌɪ, ˈlazjʊliː
AM ˈlæzjəlaɪ, ˈlɑʒəlaɪ, ˈlæzjəli

lazy
BR ˈleɪz|i, -ɪə(r), -ɪɪst
AM ˈleɪzi, -ər, -ɨst

lazybones
BR ˈleɪzɪbəʊnz
AM ˈleɪziˌboʊnz

L-dopa
BR ˌɛlˈdəʊpə(r)
AM ˌɛlˈdoʊpə

LEA
BR ˌɛliːˈeɪ, -z
AM ˌɛlˌiˈeɪ, -z

Lea
BR liː
AM ˈli(ə), ˈleɪə

lea
BR liː, -z
AM li, -z

leach
BR liːtʃ, -ɪz, -ɪŋ, -t
AM litʃ, -ɪz, -ɪŋ, -t

leacher
BR ˈliːtʃə(r), -z
AM ˈlitʃər, -z

Leacock
BR ˈliːkɒk
AM ˈliˌkɑk, ˈleɪˌkɑk

lead[1]
noun, verb present, guide etc
BR liːd, -z, -ɪŋ
AM lid, -z, -ɪŋ

lead[2]
noun, verb past, metal
BR lɛd, -z, -ɪŋ, -ɪd
AM lɛd, -z, -ɪŋ, -ɪd

leadable
BR ˈliːdəbl
AM ˈlidəbəl

Leadbelly
BR ˈlɛdˌbɛli
AM ˈlɛdˌbɛli

Leadbetter
BR ˈlɛdˌbɛtə(r)
AM ˈlɛdˌbɛdər

leaden
BR ˈlɛdn
AM ˈlɛdən

Leadenhall
BR ˈlɛdnhɔːl
AM ˈlɛdənˌ(h)ɔl, ˈlɛdənˌ(h)ɑl

leadenly
BR ˈlɛdnli
AM ˈlɛdnli

leadenness
BR ˈlɛdnnəs
AM ˈlɛd(n)nəs

leader
BR ˈliːdə(r), -z
AM ˈlidər, -z

leaderene
BR ˌliːdəˈriːn, -z
AM ˈlidəˌrin, -z

leaderless
BR ˈliːdələs
AM ˈlidərləs

leadership
BR ˈliːdəʃɪp
AM ˈlidərˌʃɪp

lead-free
BR ˌlɛdˈfriː
AM ˌlɛdˈfri

lead-in
BR ˈliːdɪn, -z
AM ˈliˌdɪn, -z

leading
BR ˈliːdɪŋ, -z
AM ˈlidɪŋ, -z

leadless
BR ˈliːdlɪs
AM ˈlidlɪs

leadwort
BR ˈlɛdwəːt
AM ˈlɛdwərt, ˈlɛdwɔ(ə)rt

leaf[1]
noun
BR liːf
AM lif

leaf[2]
verb
BR liːf, -s, -ɪŋ, -t
AM lif, -s, -ɪŋ, -t

leafage
BR ˈliːfɪdʒ
AM ˈlifɪdʒ

leafcutter
BR ˈliːfˌkʌtə(r), -z
AM ˈlifˌkədər, -z

leafhopper
BR ˈliːfˌhɒpə(r), -z
AM ˈlifˌ(h)ɑpər, -z

leafiness
BR ˈliːfɪnɪs
AM ˈlifinɪs

leafless
BR ˈliːflɪs
AM ˈliflɪs

leaflessness
BR ˈliːflɪsnɪs
AM ˈliflɪsnɪs

leaflet
BR ˈliːflɪt, -s, -ɪŋ, -ɪd
AM ˈliflɪ|t, -ts, -dɪŋ, -dɪd

leaflike
BR ˈliːflʌɪk
AM ˈlifˌlaɪk

leafy
BR ˈliːf|i, -ɪə(r), -ɪɪst
AM ˈlifi, -ər, -ɪst

league
BR liːg, -z, -ɪŋ, -d
AM lig, -z, -ɪŋ, -d

leaguer
BR ˈliːgə(r), -z
AM ˈligər, -z

Leah
BR ˈliːə(r)
AM ˈliə, ˈleɪə

Leahy
BR ˈliːhi, ˈleɪhi
AM ˈleɪ(h)i, ˈlihi

leak
BR liːk, -s, -ɪŋ, -t
AM lik, -s, -ɪŋ, -t

leakage
BR ˈliːk|ɪdʒ, -ɪdʒɪz
AM ˈlikɪdʒ, -ɪz

leaker
BR ˈliːkə(r), -z
AM ˈlikər, -z

Leakey
BR ˈliːki
AM ˈliki

leakiness
BR ˈliːkɪnɪs
AM ˈlikinɪs

leakproof
BR ˈliːkpruːf
AM ˈlikˌpruf

leaky
BR ˈliːk|i, -ɪə(r), -ɪɪst
AM ˈliki, -ər, -ɪst

leal
BR liːl
AM lil

Leamington Spa
BR ˌlɛmɪŋt(ə)n ˈspɑː(r)
AM ˌlɛmɪŋtən ˈspɑ

lean
BR liːn, -z, -ɪŋ, -d, -ə(r), -ɪst
AM lin, -z, -ɪŋ, -d, -ər, -ɪst

lean-burn
BR ˌliːnˈbəːn
AM ˈlinˌbərn

Leander
BR lɪˈandə(r)
AM liˈændər

leaning
BR ˈliːnɪŋ, -z
AM ˈlinɪŋ, -z

leanly
BR ˈliːnli
AM ˈlinli

Leanne
BR liːˈan
AM liˈæn

leanness
BR ˈliːnnɪs
AM ˈli(n)nɪs

leant
BR lɛnt
AM lɛnt

lean-to
BR ˈliːntuː, -z
AM ˈlinˌtu, -z

leap
BR liːp, -s, -ɪŋ, -t
AM lip, -s, -ɪŋ, -t

leaper
BR ˈliːpə(r), -z
AM ˈlipər, -z

leapfrog
BR ˈliːpfrɒg
AM ˈlipˌfrɔg, ˈlipˌfrɑg

leapt
BR lɛpt
AM lɛpt

Lear
BR lɪə(r)
AM lɪ(ə)r

learn
BR ləːn, -z, -ɪŋ
AM lərn, -z, -ɪŋ

learnability
BR ˌləːnəˈbɪlɪti
AM ˌlərnəˈbɪlɪdi

learnable
BR ˈləːnəbl
AM ˈlərnəbəl

learned[1]
adjective
BR ˈləːnɪd
AM ˈlərnəd

learned[2]
verb
BR ləːnd, ləːnt
AM lərnd, lərnt

learnedly
BR ˈləːnɪdli
AM ˈlərnədli

learnedness
BR ˈləːnɪdnɪs
AM ˈlərnədnəs

learner
BR ˈləːnə(r), -z
AM ˈlərnər, -z

learnt
BR ləːnt
AM lərnt

leasable
BR ˈliːsəbl
AM ˈlisəbəl

lease
BR liːs, -ɪz, -ɪŋ, -t
AM lis, -ɪz, -ɪŋ, -t

leaseback
BR ˈliːsbak, -s
AM ˈlisˌbæk, -s

leasehold
BR ˈliːshəʊld, -z
AM ˈlisˌ(h)oʊld, -z

leaseholder
BR ˈliːsˌhəʊldə(r), -z
AM ˈlisˌ(h)oʊldər, -z

leaser
BR ˈliːsə(r), -z
AM ˈlisər, -z

leash
BR liːʃ, -ɪz
AM liʃ, -ɪz

least
BR liːst
AM list

leastways
BR ˈliːstweɪz
AM ˈlistˌweɪz

leastwise
BR ˈliːstwʌɪz
AM ˈlistˌwaɪz

leat
BR liːt, -s
AM lit, -s

leather
BR ˈlɛð|ə(r), -əz, -(ə)rɪŋ, -əd
AM ˈlɛðər, -z, -ɪŋ, -d

leatherback
BR ˈlɛðəbak, -s
AM ˈlɛðərˌbæk, -s

leathercloth
BR ˈlɛðəklɒθ, -θs\-ðz
AM ˈlɛðərˌklɔ|θ, ˈlɛðərˌklɑ|θ, -θs\-ðz

leatherette
BR ˌlɛðəˈrɛt
AM ˌlɛðərˈɛt

Leatherhead
BR ˈlɛðəhɛd
AM ˈlɛðərˌ(h)ɛd

leatheriness
BR ˈlɛð(ə)rɪnɪs
AM ˈlɛð(ə)rinɪs

leatherjacket
BR ˈlɛðəˌdʒakɪt, -s
AM ˌlɛðərˈdʒækət, -s

leathern
BR ˈlɛðn̩
AM ˈlɛðərn

leatherneck
BR ˈlɛðənɛk, -s
AM ˈlɛðərˌnɛk, -s

leatheroid
BR ˈlɛðərɔɪd
AM ˈlɛðəˌrɔɪd

leatherwear
BR ˈlɛðəwɛː(r)
AM ˈlɛðərˌwɛ(ə)r

leathery
BR ˈlɛð(ə)ri
AM ˈlɛð(ə)ri

leave
BR liːv, -z, -ɪŋ
AM liv, -z, -ɪŋ

leaven
BR ˈlɛvn̩, -z, -ɪŋ, -d
AM ˈlɛv|ən, -ənz, -(ə)nɪŋ, -ənd

leaver
BR ˈliːvə(r), -z
AM ˈlivər, -z

leaves
BR liːvz
AM livz

leavings
BR ˈliːvɪŋz
AM ˈlivɪŋz

Leavis
BR ˈliːvɪs
AM ˈlivɪs

Lebanese
BR ˌlɛbəˈniːz
AM ˌlɛbəˈniz

Lebanon
BR ˈlɛbənən
AM ˈlɛbəˌnɑn, ˈlɛbənən

Le Bardo
BR lə ˈbɑːdəʊ
AM lə ˈbardoʊ

Lebensraum
BR ˈleɪb(ə)nzraʊm, ˈleɪb(ə)nsraʊm
AM ˈleɪbənˌsraʊm, ˈleɪbənzˌraʊm

Leblanc
BR ləˈblɒŋk, ləˈblɑːŋk, ləˈblɒ̃
AM ləˈblɑŋk

Lebowa
BR ləˈbəʊə(r)
AM ləˈboʊə

Lec®
BR lɛk
AM lɛk

Le Carré
BR lə ˈkareɪ
AM lə kəˈreɪ

lech
BR lɛtʃ, -ɪz, -ɪŋ, -t
AM lɛtʃ, -əz, -ɪŋ, -t

lecher
BR ˈlɛtʃə(r), -z
AM ˈlɛtʃər, -z

lecherous
BR ˈlɛtʃ(ə)rəs
AM ˈlɛtʃ(ə)rəs

lecherously
BR ˈlɛtʃ(ə)rəsli
AM ˈlɛtʃ(ə)rəsli

lecherousness
BR ˈlɛtʃ(ə)rəsnəs
AM ˈlɛtʃ(ə)rəsnəs

lechery
BR ˈlɛtʃ(ə)r|i, -ɪz
AM ˈlɛtʃ(ə)ri, -z

Lechlade
BR ˈlɛtʃleɪd
AM ˈlɛtʃˌleɪd

lecithin
BR ˈlɛsɪθ(ɪ)n
AM ˈlɛsəθən

Leclanché
BR ləˈklɑːnʃeɪ, ləˈklɒ̃ʃeɪ
AM ləˈklɑnʃ

Leconfield
BR ˈlɛk(ə)nfiːld
AM ˈlɛkənˌfild

Le Corbusier
BR lə ˌkɔːˈb(j)uːzɪeɪ
AM lə ˌkɔrbəˈzjeɪ
FR lə kɔʀbyzje

lectern
BR ˈlɛkt(ə)n, ˈlɛktəːn, -z
AM ˈlɛktərn, -z

lection
BR ˈlɛkʃn, -z
AM ˈlɛkʃən, -z

lectionary
BR ˈlɛkʃn̩(ə)ri, -ɪz
AM ˈlɛkʃəˌnɛri, -z

lector
BR ˈlɛktɔː(r), -z
AM ˈlɛktər, ˈlɛkˌtɔ(ə)r, -z

lectrice
BR lɛkˈtriːs, ˈlɛktriːs, -ɪz
AM ˈlɛktrəs, -əz

lecture
BR ˈlɛktʃ|ə(r), -əz, -(ə)rɪŋ, -əd
AM ˈlɛk|(t)ʃər, -(t)ʃərz, -tʃərɪŋ\-ʃ(ə)rɪŋ, -(t)ʃərd

lecturer
BR ˈlɛktʃ(ə)rə(r), -z
AM ˈlɛk(t)ʃərər, -z

lecturership
BR ˈlɛktʃ(ə)rəʃɪp, -s
AM ˈlɛk(t)ʃərərˌʃɪp, -s

lectureship
BR ˈlɛktʃəʃɪp, -s
AM ˈlɛk(t)ʃərˌʃɪp, -s

lecythi
BR ˈlɛsɪθʌɪ
AM ˈlɛsəθaɪ

lecythus
BR ˈlɛsɪθəs
AM ˈlɛsəθəs

LED
BR ˌɛliːˈdiː
AM ˌɛlˌiˈdi

led
BR lɛd
AM lɛd

Leda
BR ˈliːdə(r)
AM ˈlidə

Ledbetter
BR ˈlɛdbɛtə(r)
AM ˈlɛdˌbɛdər

Ledbury
BR ˈlɛdb(ə)ri
AM ˈlɛdˌbɛri

Lederhosen
BR ˈleɪdəˌhəʊzn
AM ˈleɪdərˌ(h)oʊzn

ledge
BR lɛdʒ, -ɪz
AM lɛdʒ, -əz, -d

ledger
BR ˈlɛdʒə(r), -z
AM ˈlɛdʒər, -z

ledgy
BR ˈlɛdʒ|i, -ɪə(r), -ɪɪst
AM ˈlɛdʒi, -ər, -ɪst

Led Zeppelin
BR ˌlɛd ˈzɛpəlɪn, + ˈzɛpl̩ɪn
AM ˌlɛd ˈzɛp(ə)lən

lee
BR liː, -z
AM li, -z

leech
BR liːtʃ, -ɪz
AM litʃ, -ɪz

leechcraft
BR ˈliːtʃkrɑːft, ˈliːtʃkraft
AM ˈlitʃˌkræft

Leeds
BR liːdz
AM lidz

Lee-Enfield
BR ˈliːˈɛnfiːld, -z
AM ˈliˈɛnˌfild, -z

leek
BR liːk, -s
AM lik, -s

leer
BR lɪə(r), -z, -ɪŋ, -d
AM lɪ(ə)r, -z, -ɪŋ, -d

leeriness
BR ˈlɪərɪnɪs
AM ˈlɪrinɪs

leeringly
BR ˈlɪərɪŋli
AM ˈlɪrɪŋli

leery
BR ˈlɪəri
AM ˈlɪri

lees
BR liːz
AM liz

leet
BR liːt, -s
AM lit, -s

leeward[1]
non-technical
BR ˈliːwəd
AM ˈliwərd

leeward[2]
technical, shipping
BR ˈluːəd
AM ˈluərd

Leeward Islands
BR ˈliːwəd ˌʌɪlən(d)z
AM ˈliwərd ˈaɪlən(d)z

leewardly[1]
non-technical
BR ˈliːwədli
AM ˈliwərdli

leewardly[2]
technical, shipping
BR ˈluːədli
AM ˈluərdli

leeway
BR ˈliːweɪ
AM ˈliˌweɪ

left
BR lɛft, -s
AM lɛft, -s

leftie
BR ˈlɛft|i, -ɪz
AM ˈlɛfti, -z

leftish
BR ˈlɛftɪʃ
AM ˈlɛftɪʃ

leftism
BR ˈlɛftɪz(ə)m
AM ˈlɛfˌtɪzəm

leftist
BR ˈlɛftɪst, -s
AM ˈlɛftəst, -s

leftmost
BR ˈlɛf(t)məʊst
AM ˈlɛf(t)ˌmoʊst

leftover
noun
BR ˈlɛftəʊvə(r), -z
AM ˈlɛftˌoʊvər, -z

left-over
adjective
BR ˌlɛftˈəʊvə(r)
AM ˈlɛftˈoʊvər

leftward
BR ˈlɛftwəd, -z
AM ˈlɛf(t)wərd, -z

lefty
BR ˈlɛft|i, -ɪz
AM ˈlɛfti, -z

leg
BR lɛg, -z, -ɪŋ, -d
AM lɛg, -z, -ɪŋ, -d

legacy
BR ˈlɛgəs|i, -ɪz
AM ˈlɛgəsi, -z

legal
BR 'li:gl
AM 'ligəl
legalese
BR ˌli:gə'li:z, ˌli:gl'i:z
AM ˌligə'liz
legalisation
BR ˌli:gəlʌɪ'zeɪʃn, ˌli:gl̩ʌɪ'zeɪʃn
AM ˌligələ'zeɪʃən, ˌligəˌlaɪ'zeɪʃən
legalise
BR 'li:gəlʌɪz, 'li:gl̩ʌɪz, -ɨz, -ɪŋ, -d
AM 'ligəˌlaɪz, -ɨz, -ɪŋ, -d
legalism
BR 'li:gəlɪz(ə)m, 'li:gl̩ɪz(ə)m
AM 'ligəˌlɪzəm
legalist
BR 'li:gəlɪst, 'li:gl̩ɪst, -s
AM 'ligələst, -s
legalistic
BR ˌli:gə'lɪstɪk, ˌlɪgl'ɪstɪk
AM ˌligə'lɪstɪk
legalistically
BR ˌli:gə'lɪstɨkli, ˌli:gl'ɪstɨkli
AM ˌligə'lɪstək(ə)li
legality
BR li:'galɨt|i, lɪ'galɨt|i, -ɪz
AM lə'gælədi, li'gælədi, -z
legalization
BR ˌli:gəlʌɪ'zeɪʃn, ˌli:gl̩ʌɪ'zeɪʃn
AM ˌligələ'zeɪʃən, ˌligəˌlaɪ'zeɪʃən
legalize
BR 'li:gəlʌɪz, 'li:gl̩ʌɪz, -ɨz, -ɪŋ, -d
AM 'ligəˌlaɪz, -ɨz, -ɪŋ, -d
legally
BR 'li:gl̩i, 'li:gəli
AM 'ligəli
legate
BR 'lɛgət, -s
AM 'lɛgət, -s
legatee
BR ˌlɛgə'ti:, -z
AM ˌlɛgə'ti, -z
legateship
BR 'lɛgətʃɪp, -s
AM 'lɛgətˌʃɪp, -s
legatine
BR 'lɛgətɪn
AM 'lɛgəˌtin
legation
BR lɪ'geɪʃn, -z
AM lə'geɪʃən, -z
legato
BR lɪ'gɑ:təʊ
AM lə'gɑdoʊ
legator
BR lɪ'geɪtə(r), -z
AM lə'geɪdər, -z
legend
BR 'lɛdʒ(ə)nd, -z
AM 'lɛdʒənd, -z
legendarily
BR 'lɛdʒ(ə)ndrɨli
AM 'lɛdʒənˌdɛrəli
legendary
BR 'lɛdʒ(ə)nd(ə)ri
AM 'lɛdʒənˌdɛri
legendry
BR 'lɛdʒ(ə)ndri
AM 'lɛdʒəndri
leger
BR 'lɛdʒə(r), -z
AM 'lɛdʒər, -z
legerdemain
BR ˌlɛdʒədə'meɪn
AM ˌlɛdʒərdəˌmeɪn
leger line
BR 'lɛdʒə lʌɪn, -z
AM 'lɛdʒər ˌlaɪn, -z
Legg
BR lɛg
AM lɛg
Leggatt
BR 'lɛgət
AM 'lɛgət
Legge
BR lɛg
AM 'lɛg(gi)
legged
BR 'lɛg(ɪ)d
AM 'lɛg(ə)d
legger
BR 'lɛgə(r), -z
AM 'lɛgər, -z
legginess
BR 'lɛgɪnɨs
AM 'lɛginɨs
legging
BR 'lɛgɪŋ, -z
AM 'lɛgɪŋ, -z
leggy
BR 'lɛgi
AM 'lɛgi
leghorn
BR 'lɛghɔ:n, -z
AM 'lɛgˌ(h)ɔ(ə)rn, -z
legibility
BR ˌlɛdʒɪ'bɪlɨti
AM ˌlɛdʒə'bɪlɨdi
legible
BR 'lɛdʒɪbl
AM 'lɛdʒəbəl
legibly
BR 'lɛdʒɪbli
AM 'lɛdʒəbli
legion
BR 'li:dʒ(ə)n, -z
AM 'lidʒən, -z, -d
legionary
BR 'li:dʒən(ə)r|i, 'li:dʒn̩(ə)ri, -ɪz
AM 'lidʒəˌnɛri, -z
legionella
BR ˌli:dʒə'nɛlə(r), -z
AM ˌlidʒə'nɛlə, -z
legionellae
BR ˌli:dʒə'nɛli:
AM ˌlidʒə'nɛli
legionnaire
BR ˌli:dʒə'nɛ:(r), -z
AM ˌlidʒə'nɛ(ə)r, -z
legislate
BR 'lɛdʒɨsleɪt, -s, -ɪŋ, -ɨd
AM 'lɛdʒəˌsleɪ|t, -ts, -dɪŋ, -dɨd
legislation
BR ˌlɛdʒɪ'sleɪʃn
AM ˌlɛdʒə'sleɪʃən
legislative
BR 'lɛdʒɨslətɪv
AM 'lɛdʒəˌsleɪdɪv
legislatively
BR 'lɛdʒɨslətɨvli
AM ˌlɛdʒəˌsleɪdɨvli
legislator
BR 'lɛdʒɨsleɪtə(r), -z
AM 'lɛdʒəˌsleɪdər, -z
legislature
BR 'lɛdʒɨslətʃə(r), -z
AM 'lɛdʒəˌsleɪtʃər, -z
legit
BR lɪ'dʒɪt
AM lə'dʒɪt
legitimacy
BR lɪ'dʒɪtɨməsi
AM lə'dʒɪdəməsi
legitimate
BR lɪ'dʒɪtɨmət
AM lə'dʒɪdəmət
legitimately
BR lə'dʒɪtɨmətli
AM lə'dʒɪdəmətli
legitimation
BR lɪˌdʒɪtɪ'meɪʃn
AM ləˌdʒɪtɪ'meɪʃən
legitimatisation
BR lɪˌdʒɪtɨmətʌɪ'zeɪʃn
AM ləˌdʒɪdəmədə'zeɪʃən, ləˌdʒɪdəməˌtaɪ'zeɪʃən
legitimatise
BR lɪ'dʒɪtɨmətʌɪz, -ɨz, -ɪŋ, -d
AM lə'dʒɪdəməˌtaɪz, -ɨz, -ɪŋ, -d
legitimatization
BR lɪˌdʒɪtɨmətʌɪ'zeɪʃn
AM ləˌdʒɪdəmədə'zeɪʃən, ləˌdʒɪdəməˌtaɪ'zeɪʃən
legitimatize
BR lɪ'dʒɪtɨmətʌɪz, -ɨz, -ɪŋ, -d
AM lə'dʒɪdəməˌtaɪz, -ɨz, -ɪŋ, -d
legitimisation
BR lɪˌdʒɪtɨmʌɪ'zeɪʃn
AM ləˌdʒɪdəmə'zeɪʃən, ləˌdʒɪdəˌmaɪ'zeɪʃən
legitimise
BR lɪ'dʒɪtɨmʌɪz, -ɨz, -ɪŋ, -d
AM lə'dʒɪdəˌmaɪz, -ɨz, -ɪŋ, -d
legitimism
BR lə'dʒɪtɨmɪz(ə)m
AM lə'dʒɪdəˌmɪzəm
legitimist
BR lə'dʒɪtɨmɪst, -s
AM lə'dʒɪdəmɪst, -s
legitimization
BR lɪˌdʒɪtɨmʌɪ'zeɪʃn
AM ləˌdʒɪdəmə'zeɪʃən, ləˌdʒɪdəˌmaɪ'zeɪʃən
legitimize
BR lɪ'dʒɪtɨmʌɪz, -ɨz, -ɪŋ, -d
AM lə'dʒɪdəˌmaɪz, -ɨz, -ɪŋ, -d
legless
BR 'lɛgləs
AM 'lɛgləs
legman
BR 'lɛgman
AM 'lɛgˌmæn
legmen
BR 'lɛgmɛn
AM 'lɛgˌmɛn
Lego®
BR 'lɛgəʊ
AM 'lɛgoʊ
legroom
BR 'lɛgru:m, 'lɛgrʊm
AM 'lɛgˌrum, 'lɛgˌrʊm
legume
BR 'lɛgju:m, -z
AM 'lɛg(j)um, -z
leguminous
BR lɪ'gju:mɨnəs
AM lə'g(j)umənəs
legwork
BR 'lɛgwə:k
AM 'lɛgˌwərk
Lehár
BR leɪ'hɑ:(r), lə'hɑ:(r), 'leɪhɑ:(r)
AM 'leɪˌhɑr
Le Havre
BR lə 'ɑ:vrə(r)
AM lə 'hɑvrə
Lehman
BR 'leɪmən, 'li:mən
AM 'leɪmən, 'limən
Lehmann
BR 'leɪmən, 'li:mən
AM 'leɪmən, 'limən
lehr
BR lɪə(r), lɛ:(r), -z
AM lɛ(ə)r, -z
Lehrer
BR 'lɛ:rə(r), 'lɪərə(r)
AM 'lɛrər
lei
BR leɪ, -z
AM leɪ, -z
Leibniz
BR 'lʌɪbnɪts, 'li:bnɪts
AM 'laɪbˌnɪts
Leibnizian
BR lʌɪb'nɪtsɪən, li:b'nɪtsɪən, -z

AM laɪb'nɪtsiən, -z

Leica®
BR 'lʌɪkə(r)
AM 'laɪkə

Leicester
BR 'lɛstə(r)
AM 'lɛstər

Leicestershire
BR 'lɛstəʃ(ɪ)ə(r)
AM 'lɛstərʃɪ(ə)r

Leichhardt
BR 'lʌɪkhɑːt
AM 'laɪk,(h)ɑrd

Leiden
BR 'lʌɪdn, 'leɪdn
AM 'laɪdən, 'leɪdn

Leif
BR liːf
AM lif

Leigh
BR liː
AM li

Leighton
BR 'leɪtn
AM 'leɪtn

Leila
BR 'liːlə(r), 'leɪlə(r)
AM 'lilə

Leinster
BR 'lɛnstə(r)
AM 'lɛnstər

Leipzig
BR 'lʌɪpsɪɡ
AM 'laɪpsɪɡ, 'laɪpzɪɡ
GER 'laɪptsɪç

Leishman
BR 'liːʃmən, 'lɪʃmən
AM 'liʃmən

leishmaniasis
BR ˌliːʃmə'nʌɪəsɪs
AM ˌliʃmə'naɪəsəs

Leister
BR 'lɛstə(r)
AM 'lɛstər, 'lɪstər

leister
BR 'liːstə(r), -z
AM 'listər, -z

leisure
BR 'lɛʒə(r), -d
AM 'liʒər, 'lɛʒər, -d

leisureless
BR 'lɛʒələs
AM 'liʒərləs, 'lɛʒərləs

leisureliness
BR 'lɛʒəlɪnɨs
AM 'liʒərlinɨs, 'lɛʒərlinɨs

leisurely
BR 'lɛʒəli
AM 'liʒərli, 'lɛʒərli

leisurewear
BR 'lɛʒəwɛː(r)
AM 'liʒər,wɛ(ə)r, 'lɛʒər,wɛ(ə)r

Leitch
BR liːtʃ
AM litʃ

Leith
BR liːθ
AM liθ

leitmotif
BR 'lʌɪtməʊˌtiːf, -s
AM ˌlaɪtmoʊˌtif, -s

leitmotiv
BR 'lʌɪtməʊˌtiːf, -s
AM ˌlaɪtmoʊˌtif, -s

leitmotive
BR 'lʌɪt|məʊˌtiːf, 'lʌɪt|ˌməʊtɪv, -məʊˌtiːfs\-ˌməʊtɪvz
AM ˌlaɪtmoʊˌtif, -s

Leitrim
BR 'liːtrɪm
AM 'litrəm

Leix
BR liːʃ, leɪʃ
AM leɪʃ, liʃ

lek
BR lɛk, -s, -ɪŋ, -t
AM lɛk, -s, -ɪŋ, -t

Leland
BR 'liːlənd
AM 'lilənd

Lely
BR 'liːli
AM 'lili

LEM
BR lɛm, -z
AM lɛm, -z

leman
BR 'lɛmən, 'liːmən, -z
AM 'lɛmən, -z

Le Mans
BR lə 'mɒ̃
AM lə 'mɑn(z)

Lemesurier
BR lə'mɛʒ(ə)rə(r)
AM ləˌmɛʒəri'eɪ

lemma
BR 'lɛmə(r), -z
AM 'lɛmə, -z

lemmatisation
BR ˌlɛmətʌɪ'zeɪʃn, -z
AM ˌlɛmədə'zeɪʃən, ˌlɛməˌtaɪ'zeɪʃən, -z

lemmatise
BR 'lɛmətʌɪz, -ɨz, -ɪŋ, -d
AM 'lɛməˌtaɪz, -ɨz, -ɪŋ, -d

lemmatization
BR ˌlɛmətʌɪ'zeɪʃn, -z
AM ˌlɛmədə'zeɪʃən, ˌlɛməˌtaɪ'zeɪʃən, -z

lemmatize
BR 'lɛmətʌɪz, -ɨz, -ɪŋ, -d
AM 'lɛməˌtaɪz, -ɨz, -ɪŋ, -d

lemme
BR 'lɛmi
AM 'lɛmi

lemming
BR 'lɛmɪŋ, -z
AM 'lɛmɪŋ, -z

Lemmon
BR 'lɛmən
AM 'lɛmən

Lemnos
BR 'lɛmnɒs
AM 'lɛmnoʊs, 'lɛmˌnɑs

lemon
BR 'lɛmən, -z
AM 'lɛmən, -z

lemonade
BR ˌlɛmə'neɪd, -z
AM ˌlɛməˌneɪd, -z

lemony
BR 'lɛməni
AM 'lɛməni

lempira
BR lɛm'pɪərə(r), -z
AM lɛm'pɪrə, -z

Lemuel
BR 'lɛmjʊəl, 'lɛmjʉl
AM 'lɛmjəwəl

lemur
BR 'liːmə(r), -z
AM 'limər, -z

lemurine
BR 'liːmjʉrʌɪn, 'lɛmjʉrʌɪn
AM 'lim(j)əˌraɪn, 'lɛm(j)əˌraɪn,

lemuroid
BR 'liːmjʉrɔɪd, 'lɛmjʉrɔɪd
AM 'limjəˌrɔɪd, 'lɛmjəˌrɔɪd

Len
BR lɛn
AM lɛn

Lena[1]
forename
BR 'liːnə(r)
AM 'linə

Lena[2]
river
BR 'leɪnə(r), 'liːnə(r)
AM 'leɪnə

lend
BR lɛnd, -z, -ɪŋ
AM lɛnd, -z, -ɪŋ

lendable
BR 'lɛndəbl
AM 'lɛndəbəl

lender
BR 'lɛndə(r), -z
AM 'lɛndər, -z

Lendl
BR 'lɛndl
AM 'lɛndl

length
BR lɛŋ(k)θ, -s
AM lɛŋθ, -s

lengthen
BR 'lɛŋ(k)θ|(ə)n, -(ə)nz, -(ə)nɪŋ\-n̩ɪŋ, -(ə)nd
AM 'lɛŋθ|ən, -ənz, -(ə)nɪŋ, -ənd

lengthener
BR 'lɛŋ(k)θ(ə)nə(r), 'lɛŋ(k)θn̩ə(r), -z
AM 'lɛŋθ(ə)nər, -z

lengthily
BR 'lɛŋ(k)θɨli
AM 'lɛŋθəli

lengthiness
BR 'lɛŋ(k)θɪnɨs
AM 'lɛŋθinɨs

lengthman
BR 'lɛŋ(k)θmən
AM 'lɛŋθˌmæn, 'lɛŋθmən

lengthmen
BR 'lɛŋ(k)θmən
AM 'lɛŋθˌmɛn, 'lɛŋθmən

lengthways
BR 'lɛŋ(k)θweɪz
AM 'lɛŋθˌweɪz

lengthwise
BR 'lɛŋ(k)θwʌɪz
AM 'lɛŋθˌwaɪz

lengthy
BR 'lɛŋ(k)θ|i, -ɪə(r), -ɪɪst
AM 'lɛŋθi, -ər, -ɨst

lenience
BR 'liːnɪəns
AM 'liniəns, 'linjəns

leniency
BR 'liːnɪənsi
AM 'liniənsi, 'linjənsi

lenient
BR 'liːnɪənt
AM 'liniənt, 'linjənt

leniently
BR 'liːnɪəntli
AM 'liniən(t)li, 'linjən(t)li

Lenihan
BR 'lɛnəhən
AM 'lɛnəˌhæn

Lenin
BR 'lɛnɪn
AM 'lɛnən
RUS 'lʲenʲin

Leninakan
BR lə'nɪnəkan
AM ˌlɛnənə'kɑn
RUS lʲinʲina'kan

Leningrad
BR 'lɛnɪngrad
AM 'lɛnənˌɡræd
RUS lʲinʲin'ɡrat

Leninism
BR 'lɛnɨnɪz(ə)m
AM 'lɛnənˌɪzəm

Leninist
BR 'lɛnɨnɪst, -s
AM 'lɛnənəst, -s

Leninite
BR 'lɛnɨnʌɪt, -s
AM 'lɛnəˌnaɪt, -s

lenis
BR 'liːnɪs
AM 'linɨs, 'leɪnɨs

lenite
BR lɪˈnʌɪt, -s, -ɪŋ, -ɨd
AM ˈliˌnaɪ|t, -ts, -dɪŋ, -dɨd

lenition
BR lɪˈnɪʃn, -z
AM ləˈnɪʃən, -z

lenitive
BR ˈlɛnɨtɪv, -z
AM ˈlɛnədɪv, -z

lenity
BR ˈlɛnɨti
AM ˈlɛnədi

Lennie
BR ˈlɛni
AM ˈlɛni

Lennon
BR ˈlɛnən
AM ˈlɛnən

Lennox
BR ˈlɛnəks
AM ˈlɛnəks

Lenny
BR ˈlɛni
AM ˈlɛni

Leno
BR ˈliːnəʊ
AM ˈlɛnoʊ

leno
BR ˈliːnəʊ, -z
AM ˈlinoʊ, ˈleɪnoʊ, -z

Lenor®
BR lɪˈnɔː(r)
AM ləˈnɔ(ə)r

Lenora
BR lɪˈnɔːrə(r)
AM ləˈnɔrə

Lenore
BR lɪˈnɔː(r)
AM ləˈnɔ(ə)r

Le Nôtre
BR lə ˈnɒtrə(r)
AM lə ˈnotrə

Lenox
BR ˈlɛnəks
AM ˈlɛnəks

lens
BR lɛnz, -ɨz, -d
AM lɛnz, -əz, -d

lensless
BR ˈlɛnzləs
AM ˈlɛnzləs

lensman
BR ˈlɛnzmən
AM ˈlɛnzmən

lensmen
BR ˈlɛnzmən
AM ˈlɛnzmən

lent
BR lɛnt
AM lɛnt

Lenten
BR ˈlɛnt(ə)n
AM ˈlɛn(t)ən

lenticel
BR ˈlɛntɪsɛl, -z
AM ˈlɛn(t)əˌsɛl, -z

lenticular
BR lɛnˈtɪkjʉlə(r)
AM lɛnˈtɪkjələr

lentigo
BR lɛnˈtʌɪgəʊ
AM lɛnˈtaɪgoʊ

lentil
BR ˈlɛnt(ɪ)l, -z
AM ˈlɛn(t)l, -z

lentisc
BR lɛnˈtɪsk, -s
AM ˈlɛnˌtɪsk, -s

lentisk
BR lɛnˈtɪsk, -s
AM ˈlɛnˌtɪsk, -s

lento
BR ˈlɛntəʊ
AM ˈlɛn(t)oʊ

lentoid
BR ˈlɛntɔɪd
AM ˈlɛnˌtɔɪd

Leo
BR ˈliːəʊ
AM ˈlioʊ

Leofric
BR ˈleɪəfrɪk, ˈliːəfrɪk, ˈlɛfrɪk
AM ˈleɪəfrɪk, ˈliəfrɪk, ˈlɛfrɪk

Leominster
BR ˈlɛmstə(r)
AM ˈlɛmstər

Leon
forename
BR ˈliːɒn, ˈliːən, ˈleɪɒn, ˈleɪən
AM ˈliˌɑn

León
place in Spain
BR leɪˈɒn
AM leɪˈoʊn

Leona
BR lɪˈəʊnə(r)
AM liˈoʊnə

Leonard
BR ˈlɛnəd
AM ˈlɛnərd

Leonardo
BR ˌliːəˈnɑːdəʊ, ˌleɪəˈnɑːdəʊ
AM liəˈnɑrdoʊ

leone
BR liːˈəʊn, -z
AM liˈoʊn, -z

Leonid
BR ˈliːənɪd, ˈleɪənɪd
AM ˈliəˌnɪd, ˈleɪəˌnɪd
RUS lʲiaˈnʲit

Léonie
BR ˈliːəni, lɪˈəʊni
AM ˈleɪəni

leonine
BR ˈliːənʌɪn
AM ˈliəˌnaɪn

Leonora
BR ˌliːəˈnɔːrə(r)
AM l(i)əˈnɔrə

leopard
BR ˈlɛpəd, -z
AM ˈlɛpərd, -z

leopardess
BR ˈlɛpədɛs, ˌlɛpəˈdɛs, -ɨz
AM ˈlɛpərdəs, -əz

Leopold
BR ˈliːəpəʊld
AM ˈliəˌpoʊld

Léopoldville
BR ˈliːəpəʊldˌvɪl
AM ˈliəˌpoʊl(d)ˌvɪl

leotard
BR ˈliːə(ʊ)tɑːd, -z
AM ˈliəˌtɑrd, -z

leper
BR ˈlɛpə(r), -z
AM ˈlɛpər, -z

lepidolite
BR ˈlɛpɨdəlʌɪt, lɪˈpɪdəlʌɪt
AM ləˈpɪdəˌlaɪt, ˈlɛpədəˌlaɪt

Lepidoptera
BR ˌlɛpɨˈdɒpt(ə)rə(r)
AM ˌlɛpəˈdɑptərə

lepidopteran
BR ˌlɛpɨˈdɒpt(ə)rən, ˌlɛpɨˈdɒpt(ə)rn̩, -z
AM ˌlɛpəˈdɑptərən, -z

lepidopterist
BR ˌlɛpɨˈdɒpt(ə)rɪst, -s
AM ˌlɛpəˈdɑpt(ə)rəst, -s

lepidopterous
BR ˌlɛpɨˈdɒpt(ə)rəs
AM ˌlɛpəˈdɑptərəs

Lepidus
BR ˈlɛpɨdəs
AM ˈlɛpədəs

leporine
BR ˈlɛpərʌɪn
AM ˈlɛpəˌraɪn, ˈlɛpərən

leprechaun
BR ˈlɛprɪkɔːn, -z
AM ˈlɛprəˌkɑn, ˈlɛprəˌkɔn, -z

leprosaria
BR ˌlɛprəˈsɛːrɪə(r)
AM ˌlɛprəˈsɛriə

leprosarium
BR ˌlɛprəˈsɛːrɪəm
AM ˌlɛprəˈsɛriəm

leprosy
BR ˈlɛprəsi
AM ˈlɛprəsi

leprous
BR ˈlɛprəs
AM ˈlɛprəs

lepta
BR ˈlɛptə(r)
AM ˈlɛptə

Leptis Magna
BR ˌlɛptɪs ˈmagnə(r)
AM ˌlɛptəs ˈmɑgnə

leptocephalic
BR ˌlɛptəʊsɪˈfalɪk, ˌlɛptəʊkɛˈfalɪk
AM ˌlɛptəsəˈfælɪk

leptocephalous
BR ˌlɛptəʊˈsɛf(ə)ləs, ˌlɛptəʊˈsɛfl̩əs, ˌlɛptəʊˈkɛf(ə)ləs, ˌlɛptəʊˈkɛfl̩əs
AM ˌlɛptəˈsɛfələs

leptodactyl
BR ˌlɛptəʊˈdakt(ɪ)l, -z
AM ˌlɛptəˈdæktl, -z

lepton
BR ˈlɛptɒn
AM ˈlɛpˌtɑn, ˈlɛptən

leptonic
BR lɛpˈtɒnɪk
AM lɛpˈtɑnɪk

leptospirosis
BR ˌlɛptə(ʊ)spʌɪˈrəʊsɪs, ˌlɛptə(ʊ)spɪˈrəʊsɪs
AM ˌlɛptəˌspaɪˈroʊsəs

leptotene
BR ˈlɛptə(ʊ)tiːn, -z
AM ˈlɛptəˌtin, -z

Lepus
BR ˈliːpəs, ˈlɛpəs
AM ˈlɛpəs, ˈlipəs

Lermontov
BR ˈləːm(ə)ntɒv
AM lərˈmɑnˌtɔv, ˈlərmɑnˌtɔv, lərˈmɑnˌtɑv, ˈlərmɑnˌtɑv

Leroy
BR ˈliːrɔɪ, ləˈrɔɪ
AM ˈliˌrɔɪ

Lerwick
BR ˈləːwɪk
AM ˈlər(w)ɪk

Les
BR lɛz
AM lɛs

Lesage
BR ləˈsɑːʒ
AM ləˈsɑʒ

lesbian
BR ˈlɛzbɪən, -z
AM ˈlɛzbiən, -z

lesbianism
BR ˈlɛzbɪənɪz(ə)m
AM ˈlɛzbiəˌnɪzəm

Lesbos
BR ˈlɛzbɒs
AM ˈlɛzbɔs, ˈlɛzˌboʊs

lèse-majesté
BR ˌliːzˈmadʒɪsti
AM ˌlɛzˌmɑdʒəsˈteɪ

lesion
BR ˈliːʒn, -z
AM ˈliʒən, -z

Lesley
BR ˈlɛzli
AM ˈlɛzli, ˈlɛsli

Leslie
BR ˈlɛzli

AM 'lɛzli, 'lɛsli

Lesney
BR 'lɛzni
AM 'lɛzni

Lesotho
BR lɪ'suːtuː, lɪ'səʊtəʊ
AM lə'sutˌ(h)u, lə'soʊˌðoʊ

less
BR lɛs, -ə(r)
AM lɛs, -ər

lessee
BR lɛ'siː, -z
AM lɛ'si, -z

lesseeship
BR lɛ'siːʃɪp, -s
AM lɛ'siˌʃɪp, -s

lessen
BR 'lɛs|n, -nz, -n̩ɪŋ\-nɪŋ, -nd
AM 'lɛsən, -z, -ɪŋ, -d

Lesseps
BR 'lɛsɛps, 'lɛsəps
AM lə'sɛps

lesser
BR 'lɛsə(r)
AM 'lɛsər

Lessing
BR 'lɛsɪŋ
AM 'lɛsɪŋ

lesson
BR 'lɛsn, -z
AM 'lɛsən, -z

lessor
BR lɛ'sɔː(r), 'lɛsɔː(r), -z
AM 'lɛˌsɔ(ə)r, -z

lest
BR lɛst
AM lɛst

Lester
BR 'lɛstə(r)
AM 'lɛstər

let
BR lɛt, -s, -ɪŋ
AM lɛ|t, -ts, -dɪŋ

letch
BR lɛtʃ, -ɪz, -ɪŋ, -t
AM lɛtʃ, -əz, -ɪŋ, -t

Letchworth
BR 'lɛtʃwəθ
AM 'lɛtʃˌwərθ

letdown
BR 'lɛtdaʊn, -z
AM 'lɛtˌdaʊn, -z

lethal
BR 'liːθl
AM 'liθəl

lethality
BR liː'θalɪti
AM li'θælədi

lethally
BR 'liːθl̩i, 'liːθəli
AM 'liθəli

lethargic
BR lɪ'θɑːdʒɪk
AM lə'θɑrdʒɪk

lethargically
BR lɪ'θɑːdʒɪkli
AM lə'θɑrdʒək(ə)li

lethargy
BR 'lɛθədʒi
AM 'lɛθərdʒi

Lethbridge
BR 'lɛθbrɪdʒ
AM 'lɛθˌbrɪdʒ

Lethe
BR 'liːθi
AM 'liθi

Lethean
BR 'liːθɪən
AM 'liθiən

Leticia
BR lɪ'tɪʃ(ɪ)ə(r)
AM lə'tɪʃə

Letitia
BR lɪ'tɪʃ(ɪ)ə(r)
AM lə'tɪʃə

Letraset®
BR 'lɛtrəsɛt
AM 'lɛtrəˌsɛt

Lett
BR lɛt, -s
AM lɛt, -s

letter
BR 'lɛt|ə(r), -əz, -(ə)rɪŋ, -əd
AM 'lɛdər, -z, -ɪŋ, -d

letterbox
BR 'lɛtəbɒks, -ɪz
AM 'lɛdərˌbɑks, -əz

letterer
BR 'lɛt(ə)rə(r), -z
AM 'lɛdərər, -z

letterhead
BR 'lɛtəhɛd, -z
AM 'lɛdərˌ(h)ɛd, -z

letterless
BR 'lɛtələs
AM 'lɛdərləs

Letterman
BR 'lɛtəmən
AM 'lɛdərmən

letterpress
BR 'lɛtəprɛs, -ɪz
AM 'lɛdərˌprɛs, -əz

Lettic
BR 'lɛtɪk, -s
AM 'lɛdɪk, -s

Lettice
BR 'lɛtɪs
AM 'lɛdɪs

letting
BR 'lɛtɪŋ, -z
AM 'lɛdɪŋ, -z

Lettish
BR 'lɛtɪʃ
AM 'lɛdɪʃ

lettuce
BR 'lɛtɪs, -ɪz
AM 'lɛdəs, -ɪz

letup
BR 'lɛtʌp, -s
AM 'lɛdˌəp, -s

leu
BR 'leɪuː
AM 'lɛʊ

Leuchars[1]
place in UK
BR 'luːxəz, 'luːkəz
AM 'lukərz

Leuchars[2]
surname
BR 'luːkəz
AM 'lukərz

leucine
BR 'l(j)uːsiːn, -z
AM 'lusən, 'luˌsin, -z

leucoblast
BR 'l(j)uːkə(ʊ)blɑːst, 'l(j)uːkə(ʊ)blast, -s
AM 'lukəˌblæst, -s

leucocyte
BR 'l(j)uːkə(ʊ)sʌɪt, -s
AM 'lukəˌsaɪt, -s

leucocytic
BR ˌl(j)uːkə(ʊ)'sɪtɪk
AM ˌlukə'sɪtɪk

leucoderma
BR ˌluːkə'dəːmə(r)
AM ˌlukə'dərmə

leucoma
BR l(j)uː'kəʊmə(r), -z
AM lu'koʊmə, -z

leucopathy
BR l(j)uː'kɒpəθi
AM lu'kɑpəθi

leucopenia
BR ˌluːkə'piːnɪə(r)
AM ˌlukə'piniə

leucoplast
BR 'luːkəplast, 'luːkəplɑːst
AM 'lukəˌplæst

leucorrhoea
BR ˌl(j)uːkə'rɪːə(r)
AM ˌlukə'rɪə

leucotome
BR 'l(j)uːkətəʊm, -z
AM 'lukəˌtoʊm, -z

leucotomize
BR l(j)uː'kɒtəmʌɪz, -ɪz, -ɪŋ, -d
AM lu'kɑdəˌmaɪz, -ɪz, -ɪŋ, -d

leucotomy
BR l(j)uː'kɒtəm|i, -ɪz
AM lu'kɑdəmi, -z

leukaemia
BR l(j)uː'kiːmɪə(r)
AM lu'kimiə

leukaemic
BR l(j)uː'kiːmɪk
AM lu'kimɪk

leukaemogen
BR luː'ki'mədʒ(ə)n, -z
AM lu'kimədʒən, lu'kiməˌdʒɛn, -z

leukaemogenic
BR luːˌkiːmə'dʒɛnɪk
AM luˌkimə'dʒɛnɪk

leukemia
BR l(j)uː'kiːmɪə(r)
AM lu'kimiə

leukemic
BR l(j)uː'kiːmɪk
AM lu'kimɪk

leukemogen
BR luː'kiːmədʒ(ə)n, -z
AM lu'kimədʒən, lu'kiməˌdʒɛn, -z

leukemogenic
BR luːˌkiːmə'dʒɛnɪk
AM luˌkimə'dʒɛnɪk

leukocyte
BR 'l(j)uːkəsʌɪt, -s
AM 'lukəˌsaɪt, -s

leukotriene
BR ˌluːkə(ʊ)'trʌɪiːn, -z
AM ˌlukə'traɪin, -z

Leuven
BR 'luːvɛn
AM 'lʊˌvɛn
FL 'løvə(n)

lev
BR lɛv, -z
AM lɛv, -z

leva
BR 'lɛvə(r), -z
AM 'lɛvə, 'lɛˌvɑ, -z

Levalloisean
BR ˌləva'lwɑːzɪən
AM ˌlɛvə'lɔɪziən

levant
BR lɪ'vant, -s, -ɪŋ, -ɪd
AM lə'vænt, lə'vɑnt, -s, -ɪŋ, -ɪd

levanter
BR lə'vantə(r), -z
AM lə'væn(t)ər, lə'vɑn(t)ər, -z

Levantine
BR 'lɛvntʌɪn
AM lə'væn(t)ən, 'lɛvənˌtaɪn

levator
BR lɪ'veɪtə(r), -z
AM lə'veɪdər, -z

levee
BR 'lɛv|i, 'lɛv|eɪ, -ɪz\-eɪz
AM 'lɛvi, -z

level
BR 'lɛv|l, -lz, -l̩ɪŋ\-(ə)lɪŋ, -ld
AM 'lɛv|əl, -əlz, -(ə)lɪŋ, -əld

leveller
BR 'lɛvl̩ə(r), 'lɛv(ə)lə(r), -z
AM 'lɛv(ə)lər, -z

levelly
BR 'lɛvl̩i
AM 'lɛvəli

levelness
BR 'lɛvlnəs
AM 'lɛvəlnəs

lever
BR ˈliːv|ə(r), -əz, -(ə)rɪŋ, -əd
AM ˈlɛv|ər, ˈliv|ər, -ərz, -(ə)rɪŋ, -ərd

leverage
BR ˈliːv(ə)rɪdʒ, ˈlɛv(ə)rɪdʒ
AM ˈlɛv(ə)rɪdʒ

leveret
BR ˈlɛv(ə)rɪt, -s
AM ˈlɛv(ə)rət, -s

Leverhulme
BR ˈliːvəhjuːm
AM ˈlɛvərˌhjum

Le Verrier
BR lə ˈvɛrɪeɪ
AM lə vɛrˈjeɪ

Levi[1]
Biblical name
BR ˈliːvʌɪ
AM ˈliˌvaɪ

Levi[2]
surname
BR ˈlɛvi, ˈliːvi
AM ˈlɛvi

leviable
BR ˈlɛvɪəbl
AM ˈlɛviəbəl

leviathan
BR lɪˈvʌɪəθn, -z
AM ləˈvaɪəθən, -z

levigate
BR ˈlɛvɪɡeɪt, -s, -ɪŋ, -ɪd
AM ˈlɛvəˌɡeɪ|t, -ts, -dɪŋ, -dɪd

levigation
BR ˌlɛvɪˈɡeɪʃn, -z
AM ˌlɛvəˈɡeɪʃən, -z

levin
BR ˈlɛvɪn, -z
AM ˈlɛvən, -z

Levine
BR ləˈviːn
AM ləˈvin, ləˈvaɪn

levirate
BR ˈliːvɪrət, ˈlɛvɪrət, -s
AM ˈlɛvərət, ˈlɛvəˌreɪt, -s

leviratic
BR ˌliːvɪˈratɪk, ˌlɛvɪˈratɪk
AM ˌlɛvəˈrædɪk

leviratical
BR ˌliːvɪˈratɪkl, ˌlɛvɪˈratɪkl
AM ˌlɛvəˈrædəkəl

Levi's®
BR ˈliːvʌɪz
AM ˈliˌvaɪz

levitate
BR ˈlɛvɪteɪt, -s, -ɪŋ, -ɪd
AM ˈlɛvəˌteɪ|t, -ts, -dɪŋ, -dɪd

levitation
BR ˌlɛvɪˈteɪʃn
AM ˌlɛvəˈteɪʃən

levitator
BR ˈlɛvɪteɪtə(r), -z
AM ˈlɛvɪˌteɪdər, -z

Levite
BR ˈliːvʌɪt, -s
AM ˈliˌvaɪt, -s

Levitical
BR lɪˈvɪtɪkl
AM ləˈvɪdəkəl

Leviticus
BR lɪˈvɪtɪkəs
AM ləˈvɪdəkəs

Levittown
BR ˈlɛvɪttaʊn
AM ˈlɛvə(t)ˌtaʊn

levity
BR ˈlɛvɪti
AM ˈlɛvədi

levodopa
BR ˌliːvəˈdəʊpə(r), ˌlɛvəˈdəʊpə(r)
AM ˌlɛvəˈdoʊpə

levorotatory
BR ˌliːvəʊˈrəʊtət(ə)ri
AM ˌlivoʊˈroʊdəˌtɔri

levulose
BR ˈliːvjʊləʊs, ˈliːvjʊləʊz, ˈlɛvjʊləʊs, ˈlɛvjʊləʊz
AM ˈlɛvjəloʊs, ˈlɛvjəloʊz

levy
BR ˈlɛv|i, -ɪz, -ɪɪŋ, -ɪd
AM ˈlɛvi, -z, -ɪŋ, -d

lewd
BR l(j)uːd, -ə(r), -ɪst
AM lud, -ər, -əst

lewdly
BR ˈl(j)uːdli
AM ˈludli

lewdness
BR ˈl(j)uːdnəs
AM ˈludnəs

Lewes
BR ˈluːɪs
AM ˈluwəs

lewis
BR ˈluːɪs, -ɪz
AM ˈluwəs, -ɪz

Lewisham
BR ˈluːɪʃ(ə)m
AM ˈluwəʃəm

lewisite
BR ˈluːɪsʌɪt
AM ˈluəˌsaɪt

lex
BR lɛks
AM lɛks

lex domicilii
BR ˌlɛks dɒmɪˈsɪlɪʌɪ
AM ˌlɛks ˌdaməˈsɪliˌi

lexeme
BR ˈlɛksiːm, -z
AM ˈlɛkˌsim, -z

lexemic
BR lɛkˈsiːmɪk
AM lɛkˈsimɪk

lex fori
BR ˌlɛks ˈfɔːrʌɪ
AM ˌlɛks ˈfɔri

lexical
BR ˈlɛksɪkl
AM ˈlɛksəkəl

lexically
BR ˈlɛksɪkli
AM ˈlɛksək(ə)li

lexicographer
BR ˌlɛksɪˈkɒɡrəfə(r), -z
AM ˌlɛksəˈkɑɡrəfər, -z

lexicographic
BR ˌlɛksɪkəˈɡrafɪk
AM ˌlɛksəkəˈɡræfɪk

lexicographical
BR ˌlɛksɪkəˈɡrafɪkl
AM ˌlɛksəkəˈɡræfəkəl

lexicographically
BR ˌlɛksɪkəˈɡrafɪkli
AM ˌlɛksəkəˈɡræfək(ə)li

lexicography
BR ˌlɛksɪˈkɒɡrəfi
AM ˌlɛksəˈkɑɡrəfi

lexicological
BR ˌlɛksɪkəˈlɒdʒɪkl
AM ˌlɛksəkəˈlɑdʒəkəl

lexicologically
BR ˌlɛksɪkəˈlɒdʒɪkli
AM ˌlɛksəkəˈlɑdʒək(ə)li

lexicologist
BR ˌlɛksɪˈkɒlədʒɪst, -s
AM ˌlɛksəˈkɑlədʒəst, -s

lexicology
BR ˌlɛksɪˈkɒlədʒi
AM ˌlɛksəˈkɑlədʒi

lexicon
BR ˈlɛksɪk(ə)n, -z
AM ˈlɛksəˌkɑn, ˈlɛksəkən, -z

lexicostatistics
BR ˌlɛksɪkəʊstəˈtɪstɪks
AM ˌlɛksəkoʊstəˈtɪstɪks

lexigraphy
BR lɛkˈsɪɡrəfi
AM lɛkˈsɪɡrəfi

Lexington
BR ˈlɛksɪŋt(ə)n
AM ˈlɛksɪŋtən

lexis
BR ˈlɛksɪs
AM ˈlɛksəs

lex loci
BR ˌlɛks ˈləʊsʌɪ
AM ˌlɛks ˈloʊsi

lex talionis
BR ˌlɛks talɪˈəʊnɪs
AM ˈlɛks ˌtaliˈoʊnəs

Ley
BR liː, leɪ
AM leɪ, li

ley
BR liː, leɪ, -z
AM leɪ, -z

Leyburn
BR ˈleɪbəːn
AM ˈleɪbərn

Leyden
BR ˈlʌɪdn
AM ˈlaɪdən

Leyland
BR ˈleɪlənd
AM ˈleɪlənd, ˈlilənd

leylandii
BR leɪˈlandɪʌɪ
AM leɪˈlændiaɪ

Leyte
BR ˈleɪti
AM ˈleɪˌti

Leyton
BR ˈleɪtn
AM ˈleɪtn

Leytonstone
BR ˈleɪtnstəʊn
AM ˈleɪtnˌstoʊn

Lhasa
BR ˈlɑːsə(r), ˈlasə(r)
AM ˈlɑsə

lhasa apso
BR ˌlɑːsə(r) ˈapsəʊ, ˌlasə(r) +, -z
AM ˌlɑsə ˈɑpsoʊ, -z

liability
BR ˌlʌɪəˈbɪlɪt|i, -ɪz
AM ˌlaɪəˈbɪlɪdi, -z

liable
BR ˈlʌɪəbl
AM ˈlaɪəbəl

liaise
BR lɪˈeɪz, -ɪz, -ɪŋ, -d
AM liˈeɪz, -ɪz, -ɪŋ, -d

liaison
BR lɪˈeɪzn, lɪˈeɪzɒn, lɪˈeɪzɔ̃
AM ˈliəˌzɑn, liˈeɪˌzɑn

Liam
BR ˈliːəm
AM ˈlaɪəm, ˈliəm

liana
BR lɪˈɑːnə(r), -z
AM liˈɑnə, liˈænə, -z

liane
BR lɪˈɑːn, lɪˈan, -z
AM liˈɑn, liˈæn, -z

Lianne
BR lɪˈan
AM liˈæn

Liao
BR lɪˈaʊ
AM lɪˈaʊ

liar
BR ˈlʌɪə(r), -z
AM ˈlaɪ(ə)r, -z

Lias
BR ˈlʌɪəs
AM ˈlaɪəs

liassic
BR lʌɪˈasɪk
AM laɪˈæsɪk

lib
BR lɪb
AM lɪb

libation
BR lʌɪˈbeɪʃn, -z

AM laɪˈbeɪʃən, -z

libber
BR ˈlɪbə(r), -z
AM ˈlɪbər, -z

Libby
BR ˈlɪbi
AM ˈlɪbi

LibDem
BR ˌlɪbˈdɛm, -z
AM ˈlɪbˈdɛm, -z

libel
BR ˈlʌɪbl, -lz, -l̩ɪŋ\-əlɪŋ, -ld
AM ˈlaɪbəl, -əlz, -(ə)lɪŋ, -əld

libelant
BR ˈlʌɪbələnt, ˈlʌɪbəln̩t, ˈlʌɪbl̩(ə)nt, -s
AM ˈlaɪbələnt, -s

libelee
BR ˌlʌɪbəˈliː, -z
AM ˌlaɪbəˈli, -z

libeler
BR ˈlʌɪbl̩ə(r), ˈlʌɪbələ(r), -z
AM ˈlaɪbələr, -z

libelist
BR ˈlʌɪbl̩ɪst, ˈlʌɪbəlɪst, -s
AM ˈlaɪbələst, -s

libellant
BR ˈlʌɪbələnt, ˈlʌɪbəln̩t, ˈlʌɪbl̩(ə)nt, -s
AM ˈlaɪbələnt, -s

libellee
BR ˌlʌɪbəˈliː, -z
AM ˌlaɪbəˈli, -z

libeller
BR ˈlʌɪbl̩ə(r), ˈlʌɪbələ(r), -z
AM ˈlaɪbələr, -z

libellist
BR ˈlʌɪbl̩ɪst, ˈlʌɪbəlɪst, -s
AM ˈlaɪbələst, -s

libellous
BR ˈlʌɪbl̩əs, ˈlʌɪbələs
AM ˈlaɪbələs

libellously
BR ˈlʌɪbl̩əsli, ˈlʌɪbələsli
AM ˈlaɪbələsli

libelous
BR ˈlʌɪbl̩əs, ˈlʌɪbələs
AM ˈlaɪbələs

libelously
BR ˈlʌɪbl̩əsli, ˈlʌɪbələsli
AM ˈlaɪbələsli

liber
BR ˈlʌɪbə(r)
AM ˈlaɪbər, ˈlibər

Liberace
BR ˌlɪbəˈrɑːtʃi
AM ˌlɪbəˈrɑtʃi

liberal
BR ˈlɪb(ə)rəl, ˈlɪb(ə)rl̩, -z
AM ˈlɪb(ə)rəl, -z

liberalisation
BR ˌlɪb(ə)rəlʌɪˈzeɪʃn, ˌlɪb(ə)rl̩ʌɪˈzeɪʃn
AM ˌlɪb(ə)rələˈzeɪʃən, ˌlɪb(ə)rəˌlaɪˈzeɪʃən

liberalise
BR ˈlɪb(ə)rəlʌɪz, ˈlɪb(ə)rl̩ʌɪz, -ɪz, -ɪŋ, -d
AM ˈlɪb(ə)rəˌlaɪz, -ɪz, -ɪŋ, -d

liberaliser
BR ˈlɪb(ə)rəlʌɪzə(r), ˈlɪb(ə)rl̩ʌɪzə(r), -z
AM ˈlɪb(ə)rəˌlaɪzər, -z

liberalism
BR ˈlɪb(ə)rəlɪz(ə)m, ˈlɪb(ə)rl̩ɪz(ə)m
AM ˈlɪb(ə)rəˌlɪzəm

liberalist
BR ˈlɪb(ə)rəlɪst, ˈlɪb(ə)rl̩ɪst, -s
AM ˈlɪb(ə)rələst, -s

liberalistic
BR ˌlɪb(ə)rəˈlɪstɪk, ˌlɪb(ə)rl̩ˈɪstɪk
AM ˌlɪb(ə)rəˈlɪstɪk

liberality
BR ˌlɪbəˈralɪti
AM ˌlɪbəˈrælədi

liberalization
BR ˌlɪb(ə)rəlʌɪˈzeɪʃn, ˌlɪb(ə)rl̩ʌɪˈzeɪʃn
AM ˌlɪb(ə)rələˈzeɪʃən, ˌlɪb(ə)rəˌlaɪˈzeɪʃən

liberalize
BR ˈlɪb(ə)rəlʌɪz, ˈlɪb(ə)rl̩ʌɪz, -ɪz, -ɪŋ, -d
AM ˈlɪb(ə)rəˌlaɪz, -ɪz, -ɪŋ, -d

liberalizer
BR ˈlɪb(ə)rəlʌɪzə(r), ˈlɪb(ə)rl̩ʌɪzə(r), -z
AM ˈlɪb(ə)rəˌlaɪzər, -z

liberally
BR ˈlɪb(ə)rəli, ˈlɪb(ə)rl̩i
AM ˈlɪb(ə)rəli

liberalness
BR ˈlɪb(ə)rəlnəs, ˈlɪb(ə)rl̩nəs
AM ˈlɪb(ə)rəlnəs

liberate
BR ˈlɪbəreɪt, -s, -ɪŋ, -ɪd
AM ˈlɪbəˌreɪ|t, -ts, -dɪŋ, -dɪd

liberation
BR ˌlɪbəˈreɪʃn
AM ˌlɪbəˈreɪʃən

liberationist
BR ˌlɪbəˈreɪʃnɪst, ˌlɪbəˈreɪʃənɪst, -s
AM ˌlɪbəˈreɪʃənəst, -s

liberator
BR ˈlɪbəreɪtə(r), -z
AM ˈlɪbəˌreɪdər, -z

Liberia
BR lʌɪˈbɪərɪə(r)
AM laɪˈbɪriə

Liberian
BR lʌɪˈbɪərɪən, -z
AM laɪˈbɪriən, -z

libertarian
BR ˌlɪbəˈtɛːrɪən, -z
AM ˌlɪbərˈtɛriən, -z

libertarianism
BR ˌlɪbəˈtɛːrɪənɪz(ə)m
AM ˌlɪbərˈtɛriəˌnɪzəm

libertinage
BR ˈlɪbətɪnɪdʒ
AM ˈlɪbərˌtinɪdʒ

libertine
BR ˈlɪbətiːn, -z
AM ˈlɪbərˌtin, -z

libertinism
BR ˈlɪbətɪnɪz(ə)m
AM ˈlɪbərˌtiˌnɪzəm

liberty
BR ˈlɪbət|i, -ɪz
AM ˈlɪbərdi, -z

libidinal
BR lɪˈbɪdɪn(ə)l, lɪˈbɪdn̩(ə)l
AM ləˈbɪdn̩əl

libidinally
BR lɪˈbɪdɪnəli, lɪˈbɪdɪnl̩i, lɪˈbɪdn̩əli, lɪˈbɪdn̩l̩i
AM ləˈbɪd(ə)nəli

libidinous
BR lɪˈbɪdɪnəs, lɪˈbɪdn̩əs
AM ləˈbɪdn̩əs

libidinously
BR lɪˈbɪdɪnəsli, lɪˈbɪdn̩əsli
AM ləˈbɪdn̩əsli

libidinousness
BR lɪˈbɪdɪnəsnəs, lɪˈbɪdn̩əsnəs
AM ləˈbɪdn̩əsnəs

libido
BR lɪˈbiːdəʊ, -z
AM ləˈbidoʊ, -z

libitum
BR ˈlɪbɪtəm
AM ˈlɪbɪdəm

Lib-Lab
BR ˌlɪbˈlab
AM ˈlɪbˌlæb

Li Bo
BR ˌliː ˈbəʊ
AM ˈli ˈboʊ

LIBOR
BR ˈlʌɪbɔː(r)
AM ˈlaɪbɔ(ə)r

Libra
BR ˈliːbrə(r), -z
AM ˈlibrə, -z

Libran
BR ˈliːbrən, ˈlɪbrən, -z
AM ˈlaɪbrən, -z

librarian
BR lʌɪˈbrɛːrɪən, -z
AM laɪˈbrɛriən, -z

librarianship
BR lʌɪˈbrɛːrɪənʃɪp, -s
AM laɪˈbrɛriənˌʃɪp, -s

library
BR ˈlʌɪb(rə)r|i, -ɪz
AM ˈlaɪˌbrɛri, -z

librate
BR lʌɪˈbreɪt, ˈlʌɪbreɪt, -s, -ɪŋ, -ɪd
AM ˈlaɪˌbreɪ|t, -ts, -dɪŋ, -dɪd

libration
BR lʌɪˈbreɪʃn, -z
AM laɪˈbreɪʃən, -z

libratory
BR ˈlʌɪbrət(ə)ri
AM ˈlaɪbrəˌtɔri

librettist
BR lɪˈbrɛtɪst, -s
AM ləˈbrɛdəst, -s

libretto
BR lɪˈbrɛtəʊ, -z
AM ləˈbrɛdoʊ, -z

Libreville
BR ˈliːbrəvɪl
AM ˈlibrəˌvɪl

Librium®
BR ˈlɪbrɪəm
AM ˈlɪbrɪəm

Libya
BR ˈlɪbɪə(r), ˈlɪbjə(r)
AM ˈlɪbiə

Libyan
BR ˈlɪbɪən, ˈlɪbjən, -z
AM ˈlɪbiən, -z

lice
BR lʌɪs
AM laɪs

licence
BR ˈlʌɪs(ə)ns, -ɪz, -ɪŋ, -t
AM ˈlaɪsns, -ɪz, -ɪŋ, -t

licensable
BR ˈlʌɪs(ə)nsəbl
AM ˈlaɪsnsəbəl

license
BR ˈlʌɪs(ə)ns, -ɪz, -ɪŋ, -t
AM ˈlaɪsns, -ɪz, -ɪŋ, -t

licensee
BR ˌlʌɪs(ə)nˈsiː, -z
AM ˌlaɪsnˈsi, -z

licenser
BR ˈlʌɪs(ə)nsə(r), -z
AM ˈlaɪsnsər, -z

licensor
BR ˈlʌɪs(ə)nsə(r), -z
AM ˈlaɪsnsər, -z

licentiate
BR lʌɪˈsɛnʃɪət, -s
AM laɪˈsɛnʃ(i)ɪt, -s

licentious
BR lʌɪˈsɛnʃəs
AM laɪˈsɛnʃəs

licentiously
BR lʌɪˈsɛnʃəsli

AM laɪˈsɛnʃəsli

licentiousness
BR lʌɪˈsɛnʃəsnəs
AM laɪˈsɛnʃəsnəs

lichee
BR lʌɪˈtʃiː, ˈlʌɪtʃiː, ˈliːtʃiː, ˈlɪtʃiː, -z
AM ˈlitʃi, -z

lichen
BR ˈlɪtʃ(ɪ)n, ˈlʌɪk(ə)n, -z, -d
AM ˈlaɪkən, -z, -d

lichenology
BR ˌlɪtʃɪˈnɒlədʒi, ˌlʌɪkəˈnɒlədʒi
AM ˌlaɪkəˈnɑlədʒi

lichenous
BR ˈlɪtʃɪnəs, ˈlʌɪkənəs
AM ˈlaɪkənəs

Lichfield
BR ˈlɪtʃfiːld
AM ˈlɪtʃˌfild

lich-gate
BR ˈlɪtʃgeɪt, -s
AM ˈlɪtʃˌgeɪt, -s

Lichtenstein
BR ˈlɪkt(ə)nstʌɪn, ˈlɪxt(ə)nstʌɪn
AM ˈlɪktənˌstaɪn

licit
BR ˈlɪsɪt
AM ˈlɪsɪt

licitly
BR ˈlɪsɪtli
AM ˈlɪsɪtli

lick
BR lɪk, -s, -ɪŋ, -t
AM lɪk, -s, -ɪŋ, -t

licker
BR ˈlɪkə(r), -z
AM ˈlɪkər, -z

lickerish
BR ˈlɪk(ə)rɪʃ
AM ˈlɪk(ə)rɪʃ

lickety-split
BR ˌlɪkɪtɪˈsplɪt
AM ˌlɪkədiˈsplɪt

licking
BR ˈlɪkɪŋ, -z
AM ˈlɪkɪŋ, -z

lickspittle
BR ˈlɪkˌspɪtl, -z
AM ˈlɪkˌspɪdəl, -z

licorice
BR ˈlɪk(ə)rɪʃ, ˈlɪk(ə)rɪs
AM ˈlɪk(ə)rɪʃ

lictor
BR ˈlɪktə(r), ˈlɪktɔː(r), -z
AM ˈlɪktər, -z

lid
BR lɪd, -z, -ɪd
AM lɪd, -z, -ɪd

lidar
BR ˈlʌɪdɑː(r)
AM ˈlaɪˌdɑr

Liddell
BR ˈlɪdl
AM ˈlɪdəl, lɪˈdɛl

lidless
BR ˈlɪdlɪs
AM ˈlɪdləs

lido
BR ˈliːdəʊ, ˈlʌɪdəʊ, -z
AM ˈlidoʊ, -z

lidocaine
BR ˈlʌɪdəkeɪn
AM ˈlaɪdəˌkeɪn

lie
BR lʌɪ, -z, -ɪŋ, -d
AM laɪ, -z, -ɪŋ, -d

Liebfraumilch
BR ˈliːbfraʊmɪlk, ˈliːbfraʊmɪlʃ, ˈliːbfraʊmɪlx
AM ˈlibˌfraʊˌmɪltʃ

Liebig
BR ˈliːbɪg
AM ˈlibɪg

Liechtenstein
BR ˈlɪkt(ə)nstʌɪn, ˈlɪxt(ə)nstʌɪn
AM ˈlɪktənˌstaɪn

Liechtensteiner
BR ˈlɪkt(ə)nstʌɪnə(r), ˈlɪxt(ə)nstʌɪnə(r), -z
AM ˈlɪktənˌstaɪnər, -z

Lied
song
BR liːd
AM lid

lied
past tense
BR lʌɪd
AM laɪd

Lieder
BR ˈliːdə(r)
AM ˈlidər

Liederkrantz
BR ˈliːdəkranz, ˈliːdəkrants
AM ˈlidərˌkrænz, ˈlidərˌkræn(t)s

lief
BR liːf
AM lif

Liège
BR lɪˈeɪʒ
AM liˈɛʒ

liege
BR liːdʒ, -ɪz
AM li(d)ʒ, -ɪz

liegeman
BR ˈliːdʒmən
AM ˈli(d)ʒˌmæn, ˈli(d)ʒmən

liegemen
BR ˈliːdʒmən
AM ˈli(d)ʒˌmɛn, ˈli(d)ʒmən

lie-in
BR ˈlʌɪɪn, ˌlʌɪˈɪn, -z
AM ˈlaɪˌɪn, -z

lien
BR ˈliː(ə)n, -z
AM ˈli(ə)n, -z

lierne
BR lɪˈəːn, -z
AM liˈərn, -z

lieu
BR l(j)uː
AM l(j)u

lieutenancy
BR lɛfˈtɛnəns|i, ləfˈtɛnəns|i, -ɪz
AM luˈtɛnənsi, -z

lieutenant
BR lɛfˈtɛnənt, ləfˈtɛnənt, -s
AM luˈtɛnənt, -s

lieux
BR l(j)uː
AM l(j)u

life
BR lʌɪf
AM laɪf

lifebelt
BR ˈlʌɪfbɛlt, -s
AM ˈlaɪfˌbɛlt, -s

lifeblood
BR ˈlʌɪfblʌd
AM ˈlaɪfˌbləd

lifeboat
BR ˈlʌɪfbəʊt, -s
AM ˈlaɪfˌboʊt, -s

lifeboatman
BR ˈlʌɪfbəʊtmən
AM ˈlaɪfˌboʊtmən

lifeboatmen
BR ˈlʌɪfbəʊtmən
AM ˈlaɪfˌboʊtmən

lifebuoy
BR ˈlʌɪfbɔɪ, -z
AM ˈlaɪfˌbɔɪ, ˈlaɪfˌbui, -z

lifeguard
BR ˈlʌɪfgɑːd, -z
AM ˈlaɪfˌgɑrd, -z

lifejacket
BR ˈlʌɪfˌdʒakɪt, -s
AM ˈlaɪfˌdʒækət, -s

lifeless
BR ˈlʌɪflɪs
AM ˈlaɪflɪs

lifelessly
BR ˈlʌɪflɪsli
AM ˈlʌɪflɪsli

lifelessness
BR ˈlʌɪflɪsnɪs
AM ˈlaɪflɪsnɪs

lifelike
BR ˈlʌɪflʌɪk
AM ˈlaɪfˌlaɪk

lifelikeness
BR ˈlʌɪflʌɪknɪs
AM ˈlaɪfˌlaɪknɪs

lifeline
BR ˈlʌɪflʌɪn, -z
AM ˈlaɪfˌlaɪn, -z

lifelong
BR ˈlʌɪflɒŋ, ˌlʌɪfˈlɒŋ
AM ˈlaɪfˌlɔŋ, ˈlaɪfˌlɑŋ

lifer
BR ˈlʌɪfə(r), -z
AM ˈlaɪfər, -z

lifesaver
BR ˈlʌɪfˌseɪvə(r), -z
AM ˈlaɪfˌseɪvər, -z

lifespan
BR ˈlʌɪfspan, -z
AM ˈlaɪfˌspæn, -z

lifestyle
BR ˈlʌɪfstʌɪl, -z
AM ˈlaɪfˌstaɪl, -z

lifetime
BR ˈlʌɪftʌɪm, -z
AM ˈlaɪfˌtaɪm, -z

Liffey
BR ˈlɪfi
AM ˈlɪfi

Lifford
BR ˈlɪfəd
AM ˈlɪfərd

LIFO
last in, first out
BR ˈliːfəʊ
AM ˈlifoʊ

lift
BR lɪft, -s, -ɪŋ, -ɪd
AM lɪft, -s, -ɪŋ, -ɪd

liftable
BR ˈlɪftəbl
AM ˈlɪftəbəl

liftboy
BR ˈlɪf(t)bɔɪ, -z
AM ˈlɪf(t)ˌbɔɪ, -z

lifter
BR ˈlɪftə(r), -z
AM ˈlɪftər, -z

liftgate
BR ˈlɪf(t)geɪt, -s
AM ˈlɪf(t)ˌgeɪt, -s

liftman
BR ˈlɪf(t)man
AM ˈlɪf(t)ˌmæn

liftmen
BR ˈlɪf(t)mɛn
AM ˈlɪf(t)ˌmɛn

lig
BR lɪg, -z, -ɪŋ, -d
AM lɪg, -z, -ɪŋ, -d

ligament
BR ˈlɪgəm(ə)nt, -s
AM ˈlɪgəmənt, -s

ligamental
BR ˌlɪgəˈmɛntl
AM ˌlɪgəˈmɛn(t)l

ligamentary
BR ˌlɪgəˈmɛnt(ə)ri
AM ˌlɪgəˈmɛn(t)əri

ligamentous
BR ˌlɪgəˈmɛntəs
AM ˌlɪgəˈmɛn(t)əs

ligand
BR ˈlɪg(ə)nd, -z
AM ˈlɪgənd, ˈlaɪgənd, -z

ligate
BR ˈlʌɪɡeɪt, lɪˈɡeɪt, -s, -ɪŋ, -d
AM ˈlaɪˌɡeɪ|t, -ts, -dɪŋ, -dɨd

ligation
BR lʌɪˈɡeɪʃn, lɪˈɡeɪʃn, -z
AM laɪˈɡeɪʃən, -z

ligature
BR ˈlɪɡətʃə(r), ˈlɪɡətʃʊə(r), ˈlɪɡətjʊə(r), -z
AM ˈlɪɡətʃər, ˈlɪɡəˌtʃʊ(ə)r, -z

liger
BR ˈlʌɪɡə(r), -z
AM ˈlaɪɡər, -z

ligger
BR ˈlɪɡə(r), -z
AM ˈlɪɡər, -z

light
BR lʌɪt, -s, -ɪŋ, -ə(r), -ɨst
AM laɪ|t, -ts, -dɪŋ, -dər, -dɨst

lighten
BR ˈlʌɪt|n, -nz, -n̩ɪŋ\-nɪŋ, -nd
AM ˈlaɪtn, -z, -ɪŋ, -d

lightening
BR ˈlʌɪtn̩ɪŋ, ˈlʌɪtnɪŋ, -z
AM ˈlaɪtn̩ɪŋ, ˈlaɪtnɪŋ, -z

lighter
BR ˈlʌɪtə(r), -z
AM ˈlaɪdər, -z

lighterage
BR ˈlʌɪt(ə)rɪdʒ
AM ˈlaɪdərɪdʒ

lighterman
BR ˈlʌɪtəmən
AM ˈlaɪdərmən

lightermen
BR ˈlʌɪtəmən
AM ˈlaɪdərmən

lightfast
BR ˈlʌɪtfɑːst, ˈlʌɪtfast
AM ˈlaɪtˌfæst

lightfoot
BR ˈlʌɪtfʊt, -s
AM ˈlaɪtˌfʊt, -s

light-footed
BR ˌlʌɪtˈfʊtɨd
AM ˌlaɪtˌfʊdəd

light-footedly
BR ˌlʌɪtˈfʊtɨdli
AM ˌlaɪtˌfʊdədli

light-footedness
BR ˌlʌɪtˈfʊtɨdnɨs
AM ˌlaɪtˌfʊdədnəs

light-handed
BR ˌlʌɪtˈhandɨd
AM ˌlaɪtˌhæn(d)əd

light-handedly
BR ˌlʌɪtˈhandɨdli
AM ˌlaɪtˌhæn(d)ədli

light-handedness
BR ˌlʌɪtˈhandɨdnɨs
AM ˌlaɪtˌhæn(d)ədnəs

light-headed
BR ˌlʌɪtˈhɛdɨd
AM ˌlaɪtˌhɛdəd

light-headedly
BR ˌlʌɪtˈhɛdɨdli
AM ˌlaɪtˌhɛdədli

light-headedness
BR ˌlʌɪtˈhɛdɨdnɨs
AM ˌlaɪtˌhɛdədnəs

light-hearted
BR ˌlʌɪtˈhɑːtɨd
AM ˌlaɪtˌhɑrdəd

light-heartedly
BR ˌlʌɪtˈhɑːtɨdli
AM ˌlaɪtˌhɑrdədli

light-heartedness
BR ˌlʌɪtˈhɑːtɨdnɨs
AM ˌlaɪtˌhɑrdədnəs

lighthouse
BR ˈlʌɪthaʊ|s, -zɪz
AM ˈlaɪtˌ(h)aʊ|s, -zəz

lighting
BR ˈlʌɪtɪŋ
AM ˈlaɪdɪŋ

lightish
BR ˈlʌɪtɪʃ
AM ˈlaɪdɪʃ

lightless
BR ˈlʌɪtlɨs
AM ˈlaɪtlɨs

lightly
BR ˈlʌɪtli
AM ˈlaɪtli

lightness
BR ˈlʌɪtnɨs
AM ˈlaɪtnɨs

lightning
BR ˈlʌɪtnɪŋ
AM ˈlaɪtnɪŋ

light of day
BR ˌlʌɪt əv ˈdeɪ
AM ˌlaɪt əv ˈdeɪ

light-o'-love
BR ˌlʌɪtəˈlʌv
AM ˌlaɪdəˈləv

lightproof
BR ˈlʌɪtpruːf
AM ˈlaɪtˌpruf

lightship
BR ˈlʌɪtʃɪp, -s
AM ˈlaɪtˌʃɪp, -s

lightsome
BR ˈlʌɪts(ə)m
AM ˈlaɪtsəm

lightsomely
BR ˈlʌɪts(ə)mli
AM ˈlaɪtsəmli

lightsomeness
BR ˈlʌɪts(ə)mnəs
AM ˈlaɪtsəmnəs

lightweight
BR ˈlʌɪtweɪt, -s
AM ˈlaɪtˌweɪt, -s

lightwood
BR ˈlʌɪtwʊd, -z
AM ˈlaɪtˌwʊd, -z

lign-aloe
BR ˈlʌɪnˌaləʊ, -z
AM ˈlaɪnˌæloʊ, -z

ligneous
BR ˈlɪɡnɪəs
AM ˈlɪɡniəs

ligniferous
BR lɪɡˈnɪf(ə)rəs
AM lɪɡˈnɪfərəs

lignification
BR ˌlɪɡnɨfɨˈkeɪʃn
AM ˌlɪɡnəfəˈkeɪʃən

ligniform
BR ˈlɪɡnɨfɔːm
AM ˈlɪɡnəˌfɔ(ə)rm

lignify
BR ˈlɪɡnɨfʌɪ, -z, -ɪŋ, -d
AM ˈlɪɡnəˌfaɪ, -z, -ɪŋ, -d

lignin
BR ˈlɪɡnɪn
AM ˈlɪɡnən

lignite
BR ˈlɪɡnʌɪt
AM ˈlɪɡˌnaɪt

lignitic
BR lɪɡˈnɪtɪk
AM lɪɡˈnɪdɪk

lignocaine
BR ˈlɪɡnə(ʊ)keɪn
AM ˈlɪɡnəˌkeɪn

lignum
BR ˈlɪɡnəm
AM ˈlɪɡnəm

lignum vitae
BR ˌlɪɡnəm ˈvʌɪtiː, + ˈviːtʌɪ
AM ˌlɪɡnəm ˈvaɪˌdi, + ˈviˌtaɪ

ligroin
BR ˈlɪɡrəʊɪn
AM ˈlɪɡroʊwən

ligroine
BR ˈlɪɡrəʊiːn
AM ˈlɪɡroʊwən

ligulate
BR ˈlɪɡjʊlət
AM ˈlɪɡjəˌleɪt

ligule
BR ˈlɪɡjuːl, -z
AM ˈlɪˌɡjul, -z

Liguria
BR lɪˈɡjʊərɪə(r)
AM ləˈɡuriə

Ligurian
BR lɪˈɡjʊərɪən, -z
AM ləˈɡuriən, -z

ligustrum
BR lɪˈɡʌstrəm, -z
AM ləˈɡəstrəm, -z

likability
BR ˌlʌɪkəˈbɪlɨti
AM ˌlaɪkəˈbɪlɨdi

likable
BR ˈlʌɪkəbl
AM ˈlaɪkəbəl

likableness
BR ˈlʌɪkəblnəs
AM ˈlaɪkəbəlnəs

like
BR lʌɪk, -s, -ɪŋ, -t
AM laɪk, -s, -ɪŋ, -t

likeability
BR ˌlʌɪkəˈbɪlɨti
AM ˌlɪkəˈbɪlɨdi

likeable
BR ˈlʌɪkəbl
AM ˈlaɪkəbəl

likeableness
BR ˈlʌɪkəblnəs
AM ˈlaɪkəbəlnəs

likeably
BR ˈlʌɪkəbli
AM ˈlaɪkəbli

likelihood
BR ˈlʌɪklɪhʊd
AM ˈlaɪkliˌ(h)ʊd

likeliness
BR ˈlʌɪklɪnɨs
AM ˈlaɪklinɨs

likely
BR ˈlʌɪkl|i, -ɪə(r), -ɪɪst
AM ˈlaɪkli, -ər, -ɨst

like-minded
BR ˌlʌɪkˈmʌɪndɨd
AM ˌlaɪkˌmaɪndɨd

like-mindedly
BR ˌlʌɪkˈmʌɪndɨdli
AM ˌlaɪkˌmaɪndɨdli

like-mindedness
BR ˌlʌɪkˈmʌɪndɨdnɨs
AM ˌlaɪkˌmaɪndɨdnɨs

liken
BR ˈlʌɪk|(ə)n, -(ə)nz, -n̩ɪŋ\-(ə)nɪŋ, -(ə)nd
AM ˈlaɪk|ən, -ənz, -(ə)nɪŋ, -ənd

likeness
BR ˈlʌɪknɪs, -ɪz
AM ˈlaɪknɨs, -ɨz

likewise
BR ˈlʌɪkwʌɪz
AM ˈlaɪkˌwaɪz

liking
BR ˈlʌɪkɪŋ, -z
AM ˈlaɪkɪŋ, -z

Likud
BR lɪˈkʊd
AM lɪˈkʊd

likuta
BR lɪˈkuːtə(*r*)
AM lɪˈkudə

lilac
BR ˈlʌɪlək, -s
AM ˈlaɪˌlɑk, ˈlaɪlək, -s

lilangeni
BR ˌliːlaŋˈɡeɪni
AM ˌlɪləŋˈɡeɪni

liliaceous
BR ˌlɪlɪˈeɪʃəs
AM ˌlɪliˈeɪʃəs

Lilian
BR ˈlɪlɪən
AM ˈlɪliən

Lilienthal
BR ˈlɪlɪəntɑːl
AM ˈlɪliənˌtɑl

Lilith
BR ˈlɪlɨθ
AM ˈlɪlɨθ

Lille
BR liːl
AM lɪl

Lillee
BR ˈlɪli
AM ˈlɪli

Lil-lets®
BR lɪˈlɛts
AM lɪˈlɛts

Lilley
BR ˈlɪli
AM ˈlɪli

Lillian
BR ˈlɪlɪən
AM ˈlɪljən, ˈlɪliən

Lilliburlero
BR ˌlɪlɪbəˈlɛːrəʊ
AM ˌlɪlibərˈlɛroʊ

Lillie
BR ˈlɪli
AM ˈlɪli

Lilliput
BR ˈlɪlɨpʌt, ˈlɪlɨpʊt
AM ˈlɪlipʊt, ˈlɪlipət

Lilliputian
BR ˌlɪlɪˈpjuːʃn
AM ˌlɪləˈpjuʃən

Lilly
BR ˈlɪli
AM ˈlɪli

lillywhite
BR ˌlɪlɪˈwʌɪt
AM ˈlɪliˌ(h)waɪt

lilo
BR ˈlʌɪləʊ, -z
AM ˈlaɪloʊ, -z

Lilongwe
BR lɪˈlɒŋwi, lɪˈlɒŋweɪ
AM ləˈlɑŋwi, ləˈlɑŋweɪ

lilt
BR lɪlt, -s, -ɪŋ, -ɨd
AM lɪlt, -s, -ɪŋ, -ɨd

lily
BR ˈlɪl|i, -ɪz, -ɪd
AM ˈlɪli, -z, -d

lily-livered
BR ˌlɪlɪˈlɪvəd
AM ˈlɪliˌlɪvərd

Lima
Peru
BR ˈliːmə(*r*)
AM ˈlimə

lima bean
BR ˈliːmə ˌbiːn, ˈlaɪmə +, -z
AM ˈlaɪmə ˌbin, -z

Limassol
BR ˈlɪməsɒl
AM ˈlɪməˌsɔl, ˈlɪməˌsɑl

limb
BR lɪm, -z, -d
AM lɪm, -z, -(b)d

limber¹
limb cutter
BR ˈlɪmə(r), -z
AM ˈlɪmər, -z

limber²
verb, adjective, noun 'gun carriage'
BR ˈlɪmb|ə(r), -əz, -(ə)rɪŋ, -əd
AM ˈlɪmb|ər, -ərz, -(ə)rɪŋ, -ərd

limberness
BR ˈlɪmbənəs
AM ˈlɪmbərnəs

limbi
BR ˈlɪmbʌɪ
AM ˈlɪmˌbaɪ

limbic
BR ˈlɪmbɪk
AM ˈlɪmbɪk

limbless
BR ˈlɪmlɨs
AM ˈlɪmlɨs

limbo
BR ˈlɪmbəʊ, -z
AM ˈlɪmboʊ, -z

Limburg
BR ˈlɪmbəːg
AM ˈlɪmˌbərg

Limburger
BR ˈlɪmbəːgə(r), -z
AM ˈlɪmˌbərgər, -z

limbus
BR ˈlɪmbəs
AM ˈlɪmbəs

lime
BR lʌɪm, -z, -ɪŋ, -d
AM laɪm, -z, -ɪŋ, -d

limeade
BR ˌlʌɪmˈeɪd, -z
AM ˈlaɪmˌeɪd, -z

Limehouse
BR ˈlʌɪmhaʊs
AM ˈlaɪmˌ(h)aʊs

limejuice
BR ˈlʌɪmdʒuːs, -ɨz
AM ˈlaɪmˌdʒus, -əz

limekiln
BR ˈlʌɪmkɪln, -z
AM ˈlaɪmˌkɪl(n), -z

limeless
BR ˈlʌɪmlɨs
AM ˈlaɪmlɨs

limelight
BR ˈlʌɪmlʌɪt, -s
AM ˈlaɪmˌlaɪt, -s

limen
BR ˈlʌɪmɛn, ˈlʌɪmən
AM ˈlaɪmən

limepit
BR ˈlʌɪmpɪt, -s
AM ˈlaɪmˌpɪt, -s

limerick
BR ˈlɪm(ə)rɪk, -s
AM ˈlɪm(ə)rɪk, -s

limestone
BR ˈlʌɪmstəʊn
AM ˈlaɪmˌstoʊn

limewash
BR ˈlʌɪmwɒʃ, -ɨz
AM ˈlaɪmˌwɔʃ, ˈlaɪmˌwɑʃ, -əz

lime-wort
BR ˈlʌɪmwəːt, -s
AM ˈlaɪmˌwərt, ˈlaɪmˌwɔ(ə)rt, -s

limey
BR ˈlʌɪm|i, -ɪz
AM ˈlaɪmi, -z

limina
BR ˈlɪmɨnə(*r*)
AM ˈlɪmɨnə

liminal
BR ˈlɪmɨnl
AM ˈlɪmɨnəl

liminality
BR ˌlɪmɪˈnalɨti
AM ˌlɪməˈnælədi

limit
BR ˈlɪm|ɪt, -ɪts, -ɨtɪŋ, -ɨtɨd
AM ˈlɪmɨ|t, -ts, -dɪŋ, -dɨd

limitable
BR ˈlɪmɨtəbl
AM ˈlɪmɨdəbəl

limitary
BR ˈlɪmɨt(ə)ri
AM ˈlɪməˌtɛri

limitation
BR ˌlɪmɪˈteɪʃn, -z
AM ˌlɪməˈteɪʃən, -z

limitative
BR ˈlɪmɨtətɪv
AM ˈlɪməˌteɪdɪv

limitedly
BR ˈlɪmɨtɨdli
AM ˈlɪmɨdɨdli

limitedness
BR ˈlɪmɨtɨdnɪs
AM ˈlɪmɨdɨdnɪs

limiter
BR ˈlɪmɪtə(r), -z
AM ˈlɪmɨdər, -z

limitless
BR ˈlɪmɨtlɨs
AM ˈlɪmɨtlɨs

limitlessly
BR ˈlɪmɨtlɨsli
AM ˈlɪmɨtlɨsli

limitlessness
BR ˈlɪmɨtlɨsnɪs
AM ˈlɪmɨtlɨsnɪs

limn
BR lɪm, -z, -ɪŋ, -d
AM lɪm, -z, -ɪŋ, -d

limner
BR ˈlɪm(n)ə(r), -z
AM ˈlɪm(n)ər, -z

limnological
BR ˌlɪmnəˈlɒdʒɨkl
AM ˌlɪmnəˈlɑdʒəkəl

limnologist
BR lɪmˈnɒlədʒɪst, -s
AM lɪmˈnɑlədʒəst, -s

limnology
BR lɪmˈnɒlədʒi
AM lɪmˈnɑlədʒi

limo
BR ˈlɪməʊ, -z
AM ˈlɪmoʊ, -z

Limoges
BR lɪˈməʊʒ
AM ləˈmoʊʒ

Limousin
BR ˌlɪmʉˈzã, -z
AM ˈlɪməˌzin, ˌlɪməˈzin, -z

limousine
BR ˌlɪməˈziːn, ˈlɪməziːn, -z
AM ˈlɪməˌzin, ˌlɪməˈzin, -z

limp
BR lɪm|p, -ps, -pɪŋ, -(p)t
AM lɪmp, -s, -ɪŋ, -t

limpet
BR ˈlɪmpɪt, -s
AM ˈlɪmpɨt, -s

limpid
BR ˈlɪmpɪd
AM ˈlɪmpɨd

limpidity
BR lɪmˈpɪdɨti
AM lɪmˈpɪdɨdi

limpidly
BR ˈlɪmpɨdli
AM ˈlɪmpɨdli

limpidness
BR ˈlɪmpɨdnɪs
AM ˈlɪmpɨdnɪs

limpingly
BR ˈlɪmpɪŋli
AM ˈlɪmpɪŋli

limpkin
BR ˈlɪm(p)kɪn
AM ˈlɪm(p)kɪn

limply
BR ˈlɪmpli
AM ˈlɪmpli

limpness
BR ˈlɪmpnɪs
AM ˈlɪmpnɪs

Limpopo
BR lɪmˈpəʊpəʊ
AM lɪmˈpoʊpoʊ

limpwort
BR ˈlɪmpwəːt, -s
AM ˈlɪmpwərt, ˈlɪmpwɔ(ə)rt, -s

limp-wristed
BR ˌlɪmpˈrɪstɪd
AM ˈlɪmpˌrɪstɪd

limuli
BR ˈlɪmjʉlʌɪ
AM ˈlɪmjəˌlaɪ

limulus
BR ˈlɪmjʉləs
AM ˈlɪmjələs

limy
BR 'lʌɪm|i, -ɪə(r), -ɪɪst
AM 'laɪmi, -ər, -ɪst

Linacre
BR 'lɪnəkə(r)
AM 'lɪnəkər

linage
BR 'lʌɪn|ɪdʒ, -ɨdʒɪz
AM 'laɪnɪdʒ, -ɨz

Linch
BR lɪn(t)ʃ
AM lɪn(t)ʃ

linchpin
BR 'lɪn(t)ʃpɪn, -z
AM 'lɪn(t)ʃˌpɪn, -z

Lincoln
BR 'lɪŋk(ə)n
AM 'lɪŋkən

Lincolnshire
BR 'lɪŋk(ə)nʃ(ɪ)ə(r)
AM 'lɪŋkənʃɪ(ə)r

Lincrusta®
BR ˌlɪŋ'krʌstə(r)
AM ˌlɪn'krəstə, ˌlɪŋ'krəstə

Lincs.
Lincolnshire
BR lɪŋks
AM lɪŋks

linctus
BR 'lɪŋ(k)təs
AM 'lɪŋktəs

Lind
BR lɪnd
AM lɪnd

Linda
BR 'lɪndə(r)
AM 'lɪndə

lindane
BR 'lɪndeɪn
AM 'lɪnˌdeɪn

Lindbergh
BR 'lɪn(d)bəːg
AM 'lɪn(d)ˌbərg

Lindemann
BR 'lɪndɪmən
AM 'lɪndəmən

linden
BR 'lɪndən, -z
AM 'lɪndən, -z

Lindisfarne
BR 'lɪndɪsfɑːn
AM 'lɪndɪsˌfɑrn

Lindley
BR 'lɪn(d)li
AM 'lɪn(d)li

Lindon
BR 'lɪndən
AM 'lɪndən

Lindsay
BR 'lɪn(d)zi
AM 'lɪnzi

Lindsey
BR 'lɪn(d)zi
AM 'lɪnzi

Lindwall
BR 'lɪndwɔːl
AM 'lɪn(d)ˌwɔl, 'lɪn(d)ˌwɑl

Lindy
BR 'lɪndi
AM 'lɪndi

line
BR lʌɪn, -z, -ɪŋ, -d
AM laɪn, -z, -ɪŋ, -d

lineage
BR 'lɪnɪ|ɪdʒ, -ɨdʒɪz
AM 'laɪnɪdʒ, -ɨz

lineal
BR 'lɪnɪəl
AM 'lɪniəl

lineally
BR 'lɪnɪəli
AM 'lɪniəli

lineament
BR 'lɪnɪəm(ə)nt, -s
AM 'lɪn(i)əmənt, -s

linear
BR 'lɪnɪə(r)
AM 'lɪniər

linearise
BR 'lɪnɪərʌɪz, -ɨz, -ɪŋ, -d
AM 'lɪniəˌraɪz, -ɨz, -ɪŋ, -d

linearity
BR ˌlɪnɪ'arɪt|i, -ɪz
AM ˌlɪni'ɛrədi, -z

linearize
BR 'lɪnɪərʌɪz, -ɨz, -ɪŋ, -d
AM 'lɪniəˌraɪz, -ɨz, -ɪŋ, -d

linearly
BR 'lɪnɪəli
AM 'lɪniərli

lineation
BR ˌlɪnɪ'eɪʃn, -z
AM ˌlɪni'eɪʃən, -z

linebacker
BR 'lʌɪnˌbakə(r), -z
AM 'laɪnˌbækər, -z

linefeed
BR 'lʌɪnfiːd
AM 'laɪnˌfid

Linehan
BR 'lɪnɨhən
AM 'lɪnəhæn

Lineker
BR 'lɪnɨkə(r)
AM 'lɪnəkər

lineman
BR 'lʌɪnmən
AM 'laɪnmən

linemen
BR 'lʌɪnmən
AM 'laɪnmən

linen
BR 'lɪnɪn
AM 'lɪnɨn

linenfold
BR 'lɪnɪnfəʊld
AM 'lɪnənˌfoʊld

lineout
BR 'lʌɪnaʊt, -s
AM 'laɪnˌaʊt, -s

liner
BR 'lʌɪnə(r), -z
AM 'laɪnər, -z

linertrain
BR 'lʌɪnətreɪn, -z
AM 'laɪnərˌtreɪn, -z

lineshooter
BR 'lʌɪnˌʃuːtə(r), -z
AM 'laɪnˌʃudər, -z

lineside
BR 'lʌɪnsʌɪd
AM 'laɪnˌsaɪd

linesman
BR 'lʌɪnzmən
AM 'laɪnzmən

linesmen
BR 'lʌɪnzmən
AM 'laɪnzmən

lineup
BR 'lʌɪnʌp, -s
AM 'laɪnˌəp, -s

Linford
BR 'lɪnfəd
AM 'lɪnfərd

ling
BR lɪŋ, -z
AM lɪŋ, -z

linga
BR 'lɪŋgə(r), -z
AM 'lɪŋgə, -z

Lingala
BR lɪŋ'gɑːlə(r)
AM lɪŋ'gɑlə

lingam
BR 'lɪŋgəm, -z
AM 'lɪŋgəm, -z

linger
BR 'lɪŋg|ə(r), -əz, -(ə)rɪŋ, -əd
AM 'lɪŋg|ər, -ərz, -(ə)rɪŋ, -ərd

lingerer
BR 'lɪŋg(ə)rə(r), -z
AM 'lɪŋgərər, -z

lingerie
BR 'lãʒ(ə)ri, 'lɒ̃ʒ(ə)ri, 'lɒn(d)ʒ(ə)ri, 'lɑːn(d)ʒ(ə)ri
AM ˌlɑn(d)ʒə'reɪ

lingeringly
BR 'lɪŋg(ə)rɪŋli
AM 'lɪŋg(ə)rɪŋli

Lingfield
BR 'lɪŋfiːld
AM 'lɪŋˌfild

lingo
BR 'lɪŋgəʊ, -z
AM 'lɪŋgoʊ, -z

lingua franca
BR ˌlɪŋgwə 'fraŋkə(r), -z
AM 'lɪŋgwə 'fræŋkə, -z

lingual
BR 'lɪŋgw(ə)l
AM 'lɪŋgwəl

lingualise
BR 'lɪŋgwəlʌɪz, 'lɪŋgwl̩ʌɪz, -ɨz, -ɪŋ, -d
AM 'lɪŋgwəˌlaɪz, -ɨz, -ɪŋ, -d

lingualize
BR 'lɪŋgwəlʌɪz, 'lɪŋgwl̩ʌɪz, -ɨz, -ɪŋ, -d
AM 'lɪŋgwəˌlaɪz, -ɨz, -ɪŋ, -d

lingually
BR 'lɪŋgwəli, 'lɪŋgwl̩i
AM 'lɪŋgwəli

Linguaphone®
BR 'lɪŋgwəfəʊn
AM 'lɪŋgwəˌfoʊn

linguiform
BR 'lɪŋgwɪfɔːm
AM 'lɪŋgwəˌfɔ(ə)rm

linguine
BR lɪŋ'gwiːni
AM lɪŋ'gwini

linguist
BR 'lɪŋgwɪst, -s
AM 'lɪŋgwɨst, -s

linguistic
BR lɪŋ'gwɪstɪk, -s
AM lɪŋ'gwɪstɪk, -s

linguistically
BR lɪŋ'gwɪstɨkli
AM lɪŋ'gwɪstək(ə)li

linguistician
BR ˌlɪŋgwɪ'stɪʃn, -z
AM ˌlɪŋgwə'stɪʃən, -z

linguodental
BR ˌlɪŋgwəʊ'dɛntl
AM ˌlɪŋgwoʊ'dɛn(t)l

lingy
BR 'lɪŋi
AM 'lɪŋgi

liniment
BR 'lɪnɨm(ə)nt, -s
AM 'lɪnəmənt, -s

lining
BR 'lʌɪnɪŋ, -z
AM 'laɪnɪŋ, -z

link
BR lɪŋ|k, -ks, -kɪŋ, -(k)t
AM lɪŋ|k, -ks, -kɪŋ, -(k)t

linkage
BR 'lɪŋk|ɪdʒ, -ɨdʒɪz
AM 'lɪŋkɪdʒ, -ɨz

Linklater
BR 'lɪŋkˌleɪtə(r), 'lɪŋklətə(r)
AM 'lɪŋkˌlɛdər

linkman
BR 'lɪŋkman
AM 'lɪŋkmən

linkmen
BR 'lɪŋkmɛn
AM 'lɪŋkmən

linkup
BR 'lɪŋkʌp, -s
AM 'lɪŋkˌəp, -s

Linley
BR 'lɪnli

AM ˈlɪnli

Linlithgow
BR lɪnˈlɪθɡəʊ
AM lɪnˈlɪθ,ɡoʊ

linn
BR lɪn, -z
AM lɪn, -z

Linnaean
BR lɪˈniːən, lɪˈneɪən, -z
AM lɪˈniən, lɪˈneɪən, -z

Linnaeus
BR lɪˈniːəs, lɪˈneɪəs
AM lɪˈniəs

linnet
BR ˈlɪnɪt, -s
AM ˈlɪnɪt, -s

Linnhe
BR ˈlɪni
AM ˈlɪni

lino
BR ˈlʌɪnəʊ
AM ˈlaɪnoʊ

linocut
BR ˈlʌɪnəʊkʌt, -s
AM ˈlaɪnoʊ,kət, -s

linocutting
BR ˈlʌɪnəʊ,kʌtɪŋ, -z
AM ˈlaɪnoʊ,kədɪŋ, -z

linoleic acid
BR ,lɪnəliːɪk ˈasɪd, ,lɪnəleɪɪk +
AM ,lɪnəˈliɪk ˈæsəd, ləˈnoʊliɪk +

linolenic acid
BR ,lɪnəlɛnɪk ˈasɪd
AM ,lɪnəˈlinɪk ˈæsəd, ,lɪnəˈlɛnɪk +

linoleum
BR lɪˈnəʊlɪəm, -d
AM ləˈnoʊliəm, -d

linotype
BR ˈlʌɪnə(ʊ)tʌɪp
AM ˈlaɪnə,taɪp

linsang
BR ˈlɪnsaŋ, -z
AM ˈlɪn,sæŋ, -z

linseed
BR ˈlɪnsiːd
AM ˈlɪn,sid

linsey-woolsey
BR ,lɪnzɪˈwʊlzi
AM ˈlɪnziˈwʊlzi

linstock
BR ˈlɪnstɒk, -s
AM ˈlɪnz,tɑk, ˈlɪn,stɑk, -s

lint
BR lɪnt
AM lɪnt

lintel
BR ˈlɪntl, -z
AM ˈlɪn(t)l, -z, -d

linter
BR ˈlɪntə(r), -z
AM ˈlɪn(t)ər, -z

Linton
BR ˈlɪntən
AM ˈlɪn(t)ən

linty
BR ˈlɪnti
AM ˈlɪn(t)i

Linus
BR ˈlʌɪnəs
AM ˈlaɪnəs

Linwood
BR ˈlɪnwʊd
AM ˈlɪn,wʊd

liny
BR ˈlʌɪn|i, -ɪə(r), -ɪɪst
AM ˈlaɪni, -ər, -ɪst

Linz
BR lɪn(t)s
AM lɪn(t)s

lion
BR ˈlʌɪən, -z
AM ˈlaɪən, -z

Lionel
BR ˈlʌɪənl
AM ˈlaɪ(ə)nl, ,laɪəˈnɛl

lioness
BR ˈlʌɪənɛs, ˈlʌɪənɪs, ,lʌɪəˈnɛs, -ɪz
AM ˈlaɪənɪs, -ɪz

lionet
BR ˈlʌɪənɪt, -s
AM ˈlaɪənət, -s

lion-hearted
BR ,lʌɪənˈhɑːtɪd
AM ˈlaɪənˌ(h)ɑrdəd

lionhood
BR ˈlʌɪənhʊd
AM ˈlɪən,(h)ʊd

lionisation
BR ,lʌɪənʌɪˈzeɪʃn
AM ,lɪənəˈzeɪʃən, ,lɪən,aɪˈzeɪʃən

lionise
BR ˈlʌɪənʌɪz, -ɪz, -ɪŋ, -d
AM ˈlaɪə,naɪz, -ɪz, -ɪŋ, -d

lioniser
BR ˈlʌɪənʌɪzə(r), -z
AM ˈlaɪə,naɪzər, -z

lionization
BR ,lʌɪənʌɪˈzeɪʃn
AM ,laɪənəˈzeɪʃən, ,lɪən,aɪˈzeɪʃən

lionize
BR ˈlʌɪənʌɪz, -ɪz, -ɪŋ, -d
AM ˈlaɪə,naɪz, -ɪz, -ɪŋ, -d

lionizer
BR ˈlʌɪənʌɪzə(r), -z
AM ˈlaɪə,naɪzər, -z

lion-like
BR ˈlʌɪənlʌɪk
AM ˈlaɪən,laɪk

Lions
BR ˈlʌɪənz
AM ˈlaɪənz

lion-tamer
BR ˈlʌɪən,teɪmə(r), -z
AM ˈlaɪən,teɪmər, -z

lip
BR lɪp, -s, -t
AM lɪp, -s, -t

lipase
BR ˈlʌɪpeɪz, ˈlʌɪpeɪs, ˈlɪpeɪz, ˈlɪpeɪs
AM ˈlɪ,peɪs, ˈlaɪ,peɪs

lipid
BR ˈlɪpɪd, -z
AM ˈlɪpɨd, -z

lipidoses
BR ,lɪpɪˈdəʊsiːz
AM ,lɪpəˈdoʊsiz

lipidosis
BR ,lɪpɪˈdəʊsɪs, -ɪz
AM ,lɪpəˈdoʊsəs, -əz

Lipizzaner
BR ,lɪpɪtˈsɑːnə(r), -z
AM ˈlɪpə,zɑnər, ,lɪpəˈtsɑnər, -z

lipless
BR ˈlɪplɪs
AM ˈlɪpləs

liplike
BR ˈlɪplʌɪk
AM ˈlɪp,laɪk

Li Po
BR ,liː ˈpəʊ
AM ˈli ˈpoʊ

lipography
BR lɪˈpɒɡrəfi
AM ləˈpɑɡrəfi

lipoid
BR ˈlɪpɔɪd, ˈlʌɪpɔɪd, -z
AM ˈlɪ,pɔɪd, ˈlaɪ,pɔɪd, -z

lipoma
BR lɪˈpəʊmə(r), lʌɪˈpəʊmə(r), -z
AM laɪˈpoʊmə, -z

lipomata
BR lɪˈpəʊmətə(r), lʌɪˈpəʊmətə(r)
AM laɪˈpoʊmədə

lipoprotein
BR ,lɪpəʊˈprəʊtiːn, -z
AM ,lɪpəˈproʊ,tin, -z

liposome
BR ˈlɪpə(ʊ)səʊm, -z
AM ˈlɪpə,soʊm, -z

liposuction
BR ˈlɪpəʊ,sʌkʃn, ˈlʌɪpəʊ,sʌkʃn
AM ˈlaɪpoʊ,səkʃən, ˈlɪpoʊ,səkʃən

Lippi
BR ˈlɪpi
AM ˈlɪpi

Lippizaner
BR ,lɪpɪtˈsɑːnə(r), -z
AM ˈlɪpə,zɑnər, ,lɪpəˈtsɑnər, -z

Lippmann
BR ˈlɪpmən
AM ˈlɪpmən

lippy
BR ˈlɪp|i, -ɪə(r), -ɪɪst
AM ˈlɪpi, -ər, -ɪst

lipsalve
BR ˈlɪpsalv, -z
AM ˈlɪp,sæ(l)v, -z

lipstick
BR ˈlɪpstɪck, -s
AM ˈlɪp,stɪk, -s

lip-sync
BR ˈlɪpsɪŋ|k, -ks, -kɪŋ, -(k)t
AM ˈlɪp,sɪŋk, -s, -ɪŋ, -t

lip-syncer
BR ˈlɪp,sɪŋkə(r), -z
AM ˈlɪp,sɪŋkər, -z

lip-synch
BR ˈlɪpsɪŋ|k, -ks, -kɪŋ, -(k)t
AM ˈlɪp,sɪŋk, -s, -ɪŋ, -t

lip-syncher
BR ˈlɪp,sɪŋkə(r), -z
AM ˈlɪp,sɪŋkər, -z

Lipton
BR ˈlɪpt(ə)n
AM ˈlɪptən

liquate
BR lɪˈkweɪt, -s, -ɪŋ, -ɪd
AM ˈlaɪ,kweɪ|t, ˈlɪ,kweɪ|t, -ts, -dɪŋ, -dɨd

liquation
BR lɪˈkweɪʃn
AM laɪˈkweɪʃən, ləˈkweɪʃən

liquefacient
BR ,lɪkwɪˈfeɪʃnt
AM ˈlɪkwə,feɪʃənt

liquefaction
BR ,lɪkwɪˈfakʃn
AM ,lɪkwəˈfækʃən

liquefactive
BR ,lɪkwɪˈfaktɪv
AM ,lɪkwəˈfæktɪv

liquefiable
BR ˈlɪkwɪfʌɪəbl
AM ˈlɪkwə,faɪəbəl

liquefier
BR ˈlɪkwɪfʌɪə(r), -z
AM ˈlɪkwə,faɪər, -z

liquefy
BR ˈlɪkwɪfʌɪ, -z, -ɪŋ, -d
AM ˈlɪkwə,faɪ, -z, -ɪŋ, -d

liquescent
BR lɪˈkwɛsnt
AM lɪˈkwɛsənt

liqueur
BR lɪˈkjʊə(r), lɪˈkjɔː(r), lɪˈkjəː(r), -z
AM lɪˈkər, -z

liquid
BR ˈlɪkwɪd, -z
AM ˈlɪkwɨd, -z

liquidambar
BR ˈlɪkwɪdˈambə(r), -z
AM ˈlɪkwəˈdæmbər, -z

liquidate
BR ˈlɪkwɪdeɪt, -s, -ɪŋ, -ɪd
AM ˈlɪkwə,deɪ|t, -ts, -dɪŋ, -dɨd

liquidation
BR ,lɪkwɪˈdeɪʃn
AM ,lɪkwəˈdeɪʃən

liquidator
BR ˈlɪkwɨdeɪtə(r), -z
AM ˈlɪkwəˌdeɪdər, -z
liquidise
BR ˈlɪkwɨdʌɪz, -ɨz, -ɪŋ, -d
AM ˈlɪkwəˌdaɪz, -ɨz, -ɪŋ, -d
liquidiser
BR ˈlɪkwɨdʌɪzə(r), -z
AM ˈlɪkwəˌdaɪzər, -z
liquidity
BR lɪˈkwɪdɨti
AM lɪˈkwɪdɨdi
liquidize
BR ˈlɪkwɨdʌɪz, -ɨz, -ɪŋ, -d
AM ˈlɪkwəˌdaɪz, -ɨz, -ɪŋ, -d
liquidizer
BR ˈlɪkwɨdʌɪzə(r), -z
AM ˈlɪkwəˌdaɪzər, -z
liquidly
BR ˈlɪkwɨdli
AM ˈlɪkwɨdli
liquidness
BR ˈlɪkwɨdnɨs
AM ˈlɪkwɨdnɨs
liquidus
BR ˈlɪkwɨdəs, -ɨz
AM ˈlɪkwɨdəs, -əz
liquify
BR ˈlɪkwɨfʌɪ, -z, -ɪŋ, -d
AM ˈlɪkwəˌfaɪ, -z, -ɪŋ, -d
liquor
BR ˈlɪkə(r), -z
AM ˈlɪkər, -z
liquorice
BR ˈlɪk(ə)rɪʃ, ˈlɪk(ə)rɪs
AM ˈlɪk(ə)rɪʃ
liquorish
BR ˈlɪk(ə)rɪʃ
AM ˈlɪk(ə)rɪʃ
liquorishly
BR ˈlɪk(ə)rɨʃli
AM ˈlɪk(ə)rɨʃli
liquorishness
BR ˈlɪk(ə)rɨʃnɨs
AM ˈlɪk(ə)rɪʃnɨs
lira
BR ˈlɪərə(r), -z
AM ˈlɪrə, -z
lire
BR ˈlɪərə(r), -z
AM ˈlɪrə, -z
liripipe
BR ˈlɪrɨpʌɪp, -s
AM ˈlɪrəˌpaɪp, -s
Lisa
BR ˈliːsə(r), ˈliːzə(r), ˈlʌɪzə(r)
AM ˈlisə, ˈlaɪzə
Lisbeth
BR ˈlɪzbəθ, ˈlɪzbɛθ
AM ˈlɪzbəθ, ˈlɪzbɛθ
Lisbon
BR ˈlɪzbən
AM ˈlɪzbən
Lisburn
BR ˈlɪzbəːn
AM ˈlɪzbərn
lisente
BR lɪˈsɛnti
AM ləˈsɛn(t)i
Liskeard
BR lɪˈskɑːd
AM lɪˈskɑrd
lisle
BR lʌɪl
AM laɪl
lisp
BR lɪsp, -s, -ɪŋ, -t
AM lɪsp, -s, -ɪŋ, -t
lisper
BR ˈlɪspə(r), -z
AM ˈlɪspər, -z
lispingly
BR ˈlɪspɪŋli
AM ˈlɪspɪŋli
lissom
BR ˈlɪs(ə)m
AM ˈlɪsəm
lissome
BR ˈlɪs(ə)m
AM ˈlɪsəm
lissomly
BR ˈlɪs(ə)mli
AM ˈlɪsəmli
lissomness
BR ˈlɪs(ə)mnəs
AM ˈlɪsəmnəs
list
BR lɪst, -s, -ɪŋ, -ɨd
AM lɪst, -s, -ɪŋ, -ɨd
listable
BR ˈlɪstəbl
AM ˈlɪstəbəl
listel
BR ˈlɪstl, -z
AM ˈlɪstəl, -z
listen
BR ˈlɪs|n, -nz, -n̩ɪŋ\-nɪŋ, -nd
AM ˈlɪs|n, -nz, -nɪŋ, -nd
listenability
BR ˌlɪsn̩əˈbɪlɨti, ˌlɪsnəˈbɪlɨti
AM ˌlɪsn̩əˈbɪlɨdi, ˌlɪsnəˈbɪlɨdi
listenable
BR ˈlɪsn̩əbl, ˈlɪsnəbl
AM ˈlɪsn̩əbəl, ˈlɪsnəbəl
listener
BR ˈlɪsn̩ə(r), ˈlɪsnə(r), -z
AM ˈlɪsn̩ər, ˈlɪsnər, -z
lister
BR ˈlɪstə(r), -z
AM ˈlɪstər, -z
listeria
BR lɪˈstɪərɪə(r)
AM ləˈstɪriə
Listerine®
BR ˈlɪstəriːn
AM ˌlɪstərˈin
listeriosis
BR lɪˌstɪərɪˈəʊsɪs
AM ləˌstɪriˈoʊsəs
listing
BR ˈlɪstɪŋ, -z
AM ˈlɪstɪŋ, -z
listless
BR ˈlɪs(t)lɨs
AM ˈlɪs(t)lɨs
listlessly
BR ˈlɪs(t)lɨsli
AM ˈlɪs(t)lɨsli
listlessness
BR ˈlɪs(t)lɨsnɨs
AM ˈlɪs(t)lɨsnɨs
Liston
BR ˈlɪst(ə)n
AM ˈlɪstən
Liszt
BR lɪst
AM lɪst
lit
BR lɪt
AM lɪt
Li T'ai Po
BR ˌliː tʌɪ ˈpəʊ
AM ˈli ˈtaɪ ˈpoʊ
litany
BR ˈlɪtən|i, ˈlɪtn̩|i, -ɪz
AM ˈlɪtn̩i, -z
Litchfield
BR ˈlɪtʃfiːld
AM ˈlɪtʃˌfild
litchi
BR lʌɪˈtʃiː, ˈlʌɪtʃiː, ˈliːtʃiː, ˈlɪtʃiː, -z
AM ˈlitʃi, -z
lite
BR lʌɪt
AM laɪt
liter
BR ˈliːtə(r), -z
AM ˈlidər, -z
literacy
BR ˈlɪt(ə)rəsi
AM ˈlɪdərəsi, ˈlɪtrəsi
literae humaniores
BR ˌlɪtərʌɪ hjuːˌmanɪˈɔːriːz
AM ˌlɪdəreɪ ˌ(h)juˌmæniˈoʊˌreɪs
literal
BR ˈlɪt(ə)rəl, ˈlɪt(ə)rl̩
AM ˈlɪdərəl, ˈlɪtrəl
literalise
BR ˈlɪt(ə)rəlʌɪz, ˈlɪt(ə)rl̩ʌɪz, -ɨz, -ɪŋ, -d
AM ˈlɪdərəˌlaɪz, ˈlɪtrəˌlaɪz, -ɨz, -ɪŋ, -d
literalism
BR ˈlɪt(ə)rəlɪz(ə)m, ˈlɪt(ə)rl̩ɪz(ə)m
AM ˈlɪdərəˌlɪzəm, ˈlɪtrəˌlɪzəm
literalist
BR ˈlɪt(ə)rəlɪst, ˈlɪt(ə)rl̩ɪst, -s
AM ˈlɪdərələst, ˈlɪtrələst, -s
literalistic
BR ˌlɪt(ə)rəˈlɪstɪk, ˌlɪt(ə)rl̩ˈɪstɪk
AM ˌlɪdərəˈlɪstɪk, ˌlɪtrəˈlɪstɪk
literality
BR ˌlɪtəˈralɨti
AM ˌlɪtəˈrælədi
literalize
BR ˈlɪt(ə)rəlʌɪz, ˈlɪt(ə)rl̩ʌɪz, -ɨz, -ɪŋ, -d
AM ˈlɪdərəˌlaɪz, ˈlɪtrəˌlaɪz, -ɨz, -ɪŋ, -d
literally
BR ˈlɪt(ə)rəli, ˈlɪt(ə)rl̩i
AM ˈlɪdərəli, ˈlɪtrəli
literal-minded
BR ˌlɪt(ə)rəlˈmʌɪndɨd, ˌlɪt(ə)rl̩ˈmʌɪndɨd
AM ˈlɪdərəlˌmaɪnɨd, ˈlɪtrəlˌmaɪndɨd
literalness
BR ˈlɪt(ə)rəlnəs, ˈlɪt(ə)rl̩nəs
AM ˈlɪdərəlnəs, ˈlɪtrəlnəs
literarily
BR ˈlɪt(ə)rərɨli
AM ˌlɪdəˈrɛrəli
literariness
BR ˈlɪt(ə)rərɪnɨs
AM ˈlɪdəˌrɛrinɨs
literary
BR ˈlɪt(ə)rəri
AM ˈlɪdəˌrɛri
literate
BR ˈlɪt(ə)rət
AM ˈlɪdərət
literately
BR ˈlɪt(ə)rətli
AM ˈlɪdərətli
literateness
BR ˈlɪt(ə)rətnəs
AM ˈlɪdərətnəs
literati
BR ˌlɪtəˈrɑːti
AM ˌlɪdəˈrɑdi
literatim
BR ˌlɪtəˈrɑːtɪm
AM ˌlɪdəˈrɑdɨm
literation
BR ˌlɪtəˈreɪʃn
AM ˌlɪdəˈreɪʃən
literator
BR ˈlɪtəreɪtə(r), -z
AM ˈlɪdəˌreɪtər, -z
literature
BR ˈlɪt(ə)rɪtʃə(r)
AM ˈlɪdər(ə)tʃər, ˈlɪdərəˌtʃʊ(ə)r, ˈlɪtrəˌtʃʊ(ə)r, ˈlɪdərəˌt(j)ʊ(ə)r

litharge
BR ˈlɪθɑːdʒ, -ɪz
AM ˈlɪˌθɑrdʒ, lɪˈθɑrdʒ, -əz

lithe
BR lʌɪð, -ə(r), -ɪst
AM laɪð, -ər, -ɪst

lithely
BR ˈlʌɪðli
AM ˈlaɪðli

litheness
BR ˈlʌɪðnɨs
AM ˈlaɪðnɨs

lithesome
BR ˈlʌɪðs(ə)m
AM ˈlaɪθsəm

Lithgow
BR ˈlɪθɡəʊ
AM ˈlɪθɡaʊ, ˈlɪθɡoʊ

lithia
BR ˈlɪθɪə(*r*)
AM ˈlɪθiə

lithic
BR ˈlɪθɪk
AM ˈlɪθɪk

lithium
BR ˈlɪθɪəm
AM ˈlɪθiəm

litho
BR ˈlʌɪθəʊ, -z
AM ˈlɪθoʊ, -z

lithograph
BR ˈlɪθə(ʊ)ɡrɑːf, ˈlɪθə(ʊ)ɡraf, -s, -ɪŋ, -t
AM ˈlɪθəˌɡræf, -s, -ɪŋ, -t

lithographer
BR lɪˈθɒɡrəfə(r), -z
AM ləˈθɑɡrəfər, -z

lithographic
BR ˌlɪθə(ʊ)ˈɡrafɪk
AM ˌlɪθəˈɡræfɪk

lithographically
BR ˌlɪθə(ʊ)ˈɡrafɨkli
AM ˌlɪθəˈɡræfək(ə)li

lithography
BR lɪˈθɒɡrəfi
AM ləˈθɑɡrəfi

lithological
BR ˌlɪθəˈlɒdʒɨkl
AM ˌlɪθəˈlɑdʒəkəl

lithologist
BR lɪˈθɒlədʒɪst, -s
AM ləˈθɑlədʒəst, -s

lithology
BR lɪˈθɒlədʒi
AM ləˈθɑlədʒi

lithophyte
BR ˈlɪθə(ʊ)fʌɪt, -s
AM ˈlɪθəˌfaɪt, -s

lithopone
BR ˈlɪθə(ʊ)pəʊn, -z
AM ˈlɪθəˌpoʊn, -z

lithosphere
BR ˈlɪθə(ʊ)sfɪə(r), -z
AM ˈlɪθəˌsfɪ(ə)r, -z

lithospheric
BR ˌlɪθə(ʊ)ˈsfɛrɪk
AM ˌlɪθəˈsfɛrɪk

lithotomise
BR lɪˈθɒtəmʌɪz, -ɨz, -ɪŋ, -d
AM ləˈθɑdəˌmaɪz, -ɨz, -ɪŋ, -d

lithotomist
BR lɪˈθɒtəmɪst, -s
AM ləˈθɑdəməst, -s

lithotomize
BR lɪˈθɒtəmʌɪz, -ɨz, -ɪŋ, -d
AM ləˈθɑdəˌmaɪz, -ɨz, -ɪŋ, -d

lithotomy
BR lɪˈθɒtəm|i, -ɪz
AM ləˈθɑdəmi, -z

lithotripsy
BR ˈlɪθə(ʊ)ˌtrɪps|i, -ɪz
AM ˈlɪθəˌtrɪpsi, -z

lithotripter
BR ˈlɪθə(ʊ)ˌtrɪptə(r), -z
AM ˈlɪθəˌtrɪptər, -z

lithotriptic
BR ˌlɪθə(ʊ)ˈtrɪptɪk
AM ˌlɪθəˈtrɪptɪk

lithotrity
BR lɪˈθɒtrɨti
AM ləˈθɑˌtrədi

Lithuania
BR ˌlɪθjʊˈeɪnɪə(*r*)
AM ˌlɪθəˈweɪniə

Lithuanian
BR ˌlɪθjʊˈeɪnɪən, -z
AM ˌlɪθəˈweɪniən, -z

litigable
BR ˈlɪtɨɡəbl
AM ˈlɪdəɡəbəl

litigant
BR ˈlɪtɨɡ(ə)nt, -s
AM ˈlɪdəɡənt, -s

litigate
BR ˈlɪtɨɡeɪt, -s, -ɪŋ, -ɨd
AM ˈlɪdəˌɡeɪ|t, -ts, -dɪŋ, -dɨd

litigation
BR ˌlɪtɨˈɡeɪʃn, -z
AM ˌlɪdəˈɡeɪʃən, -z

litigator
BR ˈlɪtɨɡeɪtə(r), -z
AM ˈlɪdəˌɡeɪdər, -z

litigious
BR lɪˈtɪdʒəs
AM ləˈtɪdʒəs

litigiously
BR lɪˈtɪdʒəsli
AM ləˈtɪdʒəsli

litigiousness
BR lɪˈtɪdʒəsnəs
AM ləˈtɪdʒəsnəs

litmus
BR ˈlɪtməs
AM ˈlɪtməs

litotes
BR ˈlʌɪtətiːz, lʌɪˈtəʊtiːz
AM ˈlaɪdəˌtiz, ˈlɪdəˌtiz, laɪˈtoʊdiz

litre
BR ˈliːtə(r), -z
AM ˈlidər, -z

litreage
BR ˈliːt(ə)r|ɪdʒ, -ɨdʒɪz
AM ˈlidərɪdʒ, ˈlitrɪdʒ, -ɪz

Litt.D.
Doctor of Letters
BR ˌlɪtˈdiː
AM ˈlɪt ˈdi

litter
BR ˈlɪt|ə(r), -əz, -(ə)rɪŋ, -əd
AM ˈlɪdər, -z, -ɪŋ, -d

littérateur
BR ˌlɪt(ə)rəˈtəː(r), -z
AM ˌlɪdərəˈtər, -z

litterbag
BR ˈlɪtəbaɡ, -z
AM ˈlɪdərˌbæɡ, -z

litterbin
BR ˈlɪtəbɪn, -z
AM ˈlɪdərˌbɪn, -z

litterbug
BR ˈlɪtəbʌɡ, -z
AM ˈlɪdərˌbəɡ, -z

litterlout
BR ˈlɪtəlaʊt, -s
AM ˈlɪdərˌlaʊt, -s

littery
adjective
BR ˈlɪt(ə)ri
AM ˈlɪdəri

little
BR ˈlɪt|l, -l̩ə(r)\-lə(r), -l̩ɪst\-lɪst
AM ˈlɪdəl, -ər, -ɪst

Little Bighorn
BR ˌlɪtl ˈbɪɡhɔːn
AM ˌlɪdəl ˈbɪɡˌ(h)ɔ(ə)rn

Little Englander
BR ˌlɪtl ˈɪŋɡləndə(r), -z
AM ˌlɪdəl ˈɪŋ(ɡ)ləndər, -z

Littlehampton
BR ˌlɪtlˈham(p)t(ə)n, ˈlɪtlˌham(p)t(ə)n
AM ˈlɪdlˈhæm(p)tən

Littlejohn
BR ˈlɪtldʒɒn
AM ˈlɪdlˌdʒɑn

littleness
BR ˈlɪtlnəs
AM ˈlɪdlnɨs

Littler
BR ˈlɪtlə(r)
AM ˈlɪtlər, ˈlɪdələr

Littleton
BR ˈlɪtlt(ə)n
AM ˈlɪdltən

Littlewood
BR ˈlɪtlwʊd, -z
AM ˈlɪdlˌwʊd, -z

Litton
BR ˈlɪtn
AM ˈlɪtn

littoral
BR ˈlɪt(ə)rəl, ˈlɪt(ə)rl̩, -z
AM ˈlɪdərəl, -z

Littré
BR lɪˈtreɪ
AM ləˈtreɪ

liturgic
BR lɪˈtəːdʒɪk, -s
AM ləˈtərdʒɪk, -s

liturgical
BR lɪˈtəːdʒɨkl
AM ləˈtərdʒəkəl

liturgically
BR lɪˈtəːdʒɨkli
AM ləˈtərdʒək(ə)li

liturgiology
BR lɪˌtəːdʒɪˈɒlədʒi
AM ləˌtərdʒiˈɑlədʒi

liturgist
BR ˈlɪtədʒɪst, -s
AM ˈlɪdərdʒəst, -s

liturgy
BR ˈlɪtədʒ|i, -ɪz
AM ˈlɪdərdʒi, -z

livable
BR ˈlɪvəbl
AM ˈlɪvəbəl

live¹
adjective
BR lʌɪv
AM laɪv

live²
verb
BR lɪv, -z, -ɪŋ, -d
AM lɪv, -z, -ɪŋ, -d

liveability
BR ˌlɪvəˈbɪlɨti
AM ˌlɪvəˈbɪlɨdi

liveable
BR ˈlɪvəbl
AM ˈlɪvəbəl

liveableness
BR ˈlɪvəblnəs
AM ˈlɪvəbəlnəs

livelihood
BR ˈlʌɪvlɪhʊd, -z
AM ˈlaɪvliˌ(h)ʊd, -z

livelily
BR ˈlʌɪvlɨli
AM ˈlaɪvlɨli

liveliness
BR ˈlʌɪvlɪnɨs
AM ˈlaɪvlinɨs

livelong
BR ˈlɪvlɒŋ
AM ˈlɪvˌlɔŋ, ˈlɪvˌlɑŋ

lively
BR ˈlʌɪvl|i, -ɪə(r), -ɪɪst
AM ˈlaɪvli, -ər, -ɪst

liven
BR ˈlʌɪv|n, -nz, -n̩ɪŋ\-nɪŋ, -nd
AM ˈlaɪv|ən, -ənz, -(ə)nɪŋ, -ənd

Liver
connected with Liverpool
BR 'lʌɪvə(r)
AM 'laɪvər
liver
BR 'lɪvə(r), -z
AM 'lɪvər, -z
liveried
BR 'lɪv(ə)rɪd
AM lɪv(ə)rid
liverish
BR 'lɪv(ə)rɪʃ
AM 'lɪv(ə)rɪʃ
liverishly
BR 'lɪv(ə)rɪʃli
AM 'lɪv(ə)rɪʃli
liverishness
BR 'lɪv(ə)rɪʃnɨs
AM 'lɪv(ə)rɪʃnɨs
liverless
BR 'lɪvələs
AM 'lɪvərləs
Liverpool
BR 'lɪvəpu:l
AM 'lɪvər,pul
Liverpudlian
BR ,lɪvə'pʌdlɪən, -z
AM ,lɪvər'pədliən, -z
liverwort
BR 'lɪvəwə:t
AM 'lɪvər,wərt, 'lɪvər,wɔ(ə)rt
liverwurst
BR 'lɪvəwə:st
AM 'lɪvər,wərst
livery
BR 'lɪv(ə)r|i, -ɪz
AM 'lɪv(ə)ri, -z
liveryman
BR 'lɪv(ə)rɪmən
AM 'lɪv(ə)rimən
liverymen
BR 'lɪv(ə)rɪmən
AM 'lɪv(ə)rimən
lives[1]
from verb live
BR lɪvz
AM lɪvz
lives[2]
plural of life
BR lʌɪvz
AM laɪvz
Livesey
BR 'lɪvzi, 'lɪvsi
AM 'lɪvzi, 'lɪvsi
livestock
BR 'lʌɪvstɒk
AM 'laɪv,stɑk
Livia
BR 'lɪvɪə(r)
AM 'lɪviə
livid
BR 'lɪvɪd
AM 'lɪvɨd
lividity
BR lɪ'vɪdɪti
AM lə'vɪdɨdi
lividly
BR 'lɪvɨdli
AM 'lɪvɨdli
lividness
BR 'lɪvɨdnɨs
AM 'lɪvɨdnɨs
living
BR 'lɪvɪŋ, -z
AM 'lɪvɪŋ, -z
Livings
BR 'lɪvɪŋz
AM 'lɪvɪŋz
Livingston
BR 'lɪvɪŋst(ə)n
AM 'lɪvɪŋstən
Livingstone
BR 'lɪvɪŋstən
AM 'lɪvɪŋstən
Livonia
BR lɪ'vəʊnɪə(r)
AM lə'voʊniə
Livorno
BR lɪ'vɔ:nəʊ
AM lə'vɔr,noʊ
Livy
BR 'lɪvi
AM 'lɪvi
lixiviate
BR lɪk'sɪvɪeɪt, -s, -ɪŋ, -ɨd
AM lɪk'sɪvi,eɪ|t, -ts, -dɪŋ, -dɨd
lixiviation
BR lɪk,sɪvɪ'eɪʃn
AM lɪk,sɪvi'eɪʃən
Liz
BR lɪz
AM lɪz
Liza
BR 'lʌɪzə(r), 'li:zə(r)
AM 'laɪzə, 'lizə
lizard
BR 'lɪzəd, -z
AM 'lɪzərd, -z
Lizzie
BR 'lɪzi
AM 'lɪzi
Lizzy
BR 'lɪzi
AM 'lɪzi
Ljubljana
BR ,l(j)u:blɪ'ɑ:nə(r)
AM ,l(j)ʊbli'ɑnə
llama
BR 'lɑ:mə(r), -z
AM 'lɑmə, -z
Llan
BR ɬan, lan
AM læn
WE ɬan
Llanberis
BR ɬan'bɛrɪs, lan'bɛrɪs
AM læn'bɛrəs
Llandaff
BR 'ɬandaf, ɬan'daf, 'landaf, lan'daf
AM 'læn,dæf
Llandeilo
BR ɬan'dʌɪləʊ, lan'dʌɪləʊ
AM læn'daɪloʊ
Llandovery
BR ɬan'dʌv(ə)ri, lan'dʌv(ə)ri
AM læn'dəvəri
Llandrindod Wells
BR ɬan,drɪndɒd 'wɛlz, lan,drɪndɒd +
AM læn,drɪndɑd 'wɛlz
Llandudno
BR ɬan'dɪdnəʊ, lan'dɪdnəʊ, lan'dʌdnəʊ
AM læn'dədnoʊ
Llanelli
BR ɬa'nɛɬi, ɬə'nɛɬi, lə'nɛθli, la'nɛθli
AM lə'nɛθli
llanero
BR l(j)ɑ:'nɛ:rəʊ, -z
AM lɑ'nɛroʊ, -z
Llangollen
BR ɬan'gɒɬən, lan'gɒθlən
AM læŋ'goʊlən
llano
BR 'l(j)ɑ:nəʊ, -z
AM 'lɑ,noʊ, -z
Llanwrtyd
BR ɬan'ʊətɪd, ɬan'ə:tɪd, lan'ə:tɪd
AM læn'ərdəd
WE ɬan'wrtɪd
Llewellyn
BR ɬʊ'ɛlɪn, lʊ'ɛlɪn, lʊ'wɛlɪn
AM lʊ'wɛlɪn
Llewelyn
BR ɬʊ'ɛlɪn, lʊ'ɛlɪn, lʊ'wɛlɪn
AM lʊ'(w)ɛlən
WE ɬe'wɛlɪn
Lleyn
BR ɬi:n, li:n
AM lin
Lloyd
BR lɔɪd
AM lɔɪd
Lloyd's
BR lɔɪdz
AM lɔɪdz
llyn
BR ɬɪn, lɪn, -z
AM lɪn, -z
Llywelyn
BR ɬʊ'ɛlɪn, lʊ'ɛlɪn, lʊ'wɛlɪn
AM lʊ'wɛlən
WE ɬʌ'wɛlɪn
lo
BR ləʊ
AM loʊ
loa
BR 'ləʊə(r), -z
AM lə'wɑ, -z
loach
BR ləʊtʃ, -ɨz
AM loʊ(t)ʃ, -əz
load
BR ləʊd, -z, -ɪŋ, -ɨd
AM loʊd, -z, -ɪŋ, -əd
loader
BR 'ləʊdə(r), -z
AM 'loʊdər, -z
loading
BR 'ləʊdɪŋ, -z
AM 'loʊdɪŋ, -z
loadsamoney
BR 'ləʊdzə,mʌni, ,ləʊdzə'mʌni
AM 'loʊdzə,məni
loadstar
BR 'ləʊdstɑ:(r), -z
AM 'loʊd,stɑr, -z
loadstone
BR 'ləʊdstəʊn, -z
AM 'loʊd,stoʊn, -z
loaf
BR ləʊf, -s, -ɪŋ, -t
AM loʊf, -s, -ɪŋ, -t
loafer
BR 'ləʊfə(r), -z
AM 'loʊfər, -z
loam
BR ləʊm
AM loʊm
loaminess
BR 'ləʊmɪnɨs
AM 'loʊminɨs
loamy
BR 'ləʊmi
AM 'loʊmi
loan
BR ləʊn, -z, -ɪŋ, -d
AM loʊn, -z, -ɪŋ, -d
loanable
BR 'ləʊnəbl
AM 'loʊnəbəl
lo and behold
BR ,ləʊ ən(d) bɪ'həʊld, + n̩(d) +
AM ,loʊ (ə)n bə'hoʊld
loanee
BR ,ləʊn'i:, -z
AM ,loʊ'ni, -z
loaner
BR 'ləʊnə(r), -z
AM 'loʊnər, -z
loanholder
BR 'ləʊn,həʊldə(r), -z
AM 'loʊn,(h)oʊldər, -z
loanshark
BR 'ləʊnʃɑ:k, -s
AM 'loʊn,ʃɑrk, -s
loanword
BR 'ləʊnwə:d, -z
AM 'loʊn,wərd, -z
loath
BR ləʊθ
AM loʊθ

loathe
BR ləʊð, -z, -ɪŋ, -d
AM loʊð, -z, -ɪŋ, -d
loather
BR 'ləʊðə(r), -z
AM 'loʊðər, -z
loathsome
BR 'ləʊðs(ə)m, 'ləʊθs(ə)m
AM 'loʊθsəm, 'loʊðsəm
loathsomely
BR 'ləʊðs(ə)mli, 'ləʊθs(ə)mli
AM 'loʊθsəmli, 'loʊðsəmli
loathsomeness
BR 'ləʊðs(ə)mnəs, 'ləʊθs(ə)mnəs
AM 'loʊθsəmnəs, 'loʊðsəmnəs
loaves
BR ləʊvz
AM loʊvz
lob
BR lɒb, -z, -ɪŋ, -d
AM lɑb, -z, -ɪŋ, -d
lobar
BR 'ləʊbə(r), -z
AM 'loʊˌbɑr, -z
lobate
BR 'ləʊbeɪt
AM 'loʊˌbeɪt
lobation
BR lə(ʊ)'beɪʃn, -z
AM loʊ'beɪʃən, -z
lobby
BR 'lɒb|i, -ɪz, -ɪɪŋ, -ɪd
AM 'lɑbi, -z, -ɪŋ, -d
lobbyer
BR 'lɒbɪə(r), -z
AM 'lɑbiər, -z
lobbyism
BR 'lɒbɪɪz(ə)m
AM 'lɑbiˌɪzəm
lobbyist
BR 'lɒbɪɪst, -s
AM 'lɑbiɪst, -s
lobe
BR ləʊb, -z, -d
AM loʊb, -z, -d
lobectomy
BR ləʊ'bɛktəm|i, -ɪz
AM loʊ'bɛktəmi, -z
lobeless
BR 'ləʊbləs
AM 'loʊbləs
lobelia
BR lə'biːlɪə(r)
AM loʊ'biljə, loʊ'biliə
lobeline
BR 'ləʊbəliːn
AM 'loʊbəˌlin
Lobito
BR lə'biːtəʊ
AM lə'bidoʊ
loblolly
BR 'lɒbˌlɒl|i, -ɪz
AM 'lɑbˌlɑli, -z
lobo
BR 'ləʊbəʊ, -z
AM 'loʊboʊ, -z
lobotomise
BR lə'bɒtəmʌɪz, -ɪz, -ɪŋ, -d
AM lə'bɑdəˌmaɪz, -ɪz, -ɪŋ, -d
lobotomize
BR lə'bɒtəmʌɪz, -ɪz, -ɪŋ, -d
AM lə'bɑdəˌmaɪz, -ɪz, -ɪŋ, -d
lobotomy
BR lə'bɒtəm|i, -ɪz
AM lə'bɑdəmi, -z
lobscouse
BR 'lɒbskaʊs
AM 'lɑbˌskaʊs
lobster
BR 'lɒbstə(r), -z
AM 'lɑbstər, -z
lobsterman
BR 'lɒbstəmən
AM 'lɑbstərmən
lobstermen
BR 'lɒbstəmən
AM 'lɑbstərmən
lobsterpot
BR 'lɒbstəpɒt, -s
AM 'lɑbstərˌpɑt, -s
lobster thermidor
BR ˌlɒbstə 'θəːmɪdɔː(r)
AM ˌlɑbstər 'θərməˌdɔ(ə)r
lobular
BR 'lɒbjʉlə(r)
AM 'lɑbjələr
lobulate
BR 'lɒbjʉlət
AM 'lɑbjəˌleɪt
lobule
BR 'lɒbjuːl, -z
AM 'lɑbjul, -z
lobworm
BR 'lɒbwəːm, -z
AM 'lɑbwərm, -z
local
BR 'ləʊkl, -z
AM 'loʊkəl, -z
locale
BR lə(ʊ)'kɑːl, -z
AM loʊ'kæl, -z
localisable
BR 'ləʊkəlʌɪzəbl, 'ləʊkl̩ʌɪzəbl
AM 'loʊkəˌlaɪzəbəl
localisation
BR ˌləʊkəlʌɪ'zeɪʃn, ˌləʊkl̩ʌɪ'zeɪʃn
AM ˌloʊkələ'zeɪʃən, ˌloʊkəˌlaɪ'zeɪʃən
localise
BR 'ləʊkəlʌɪz, 'ləʊkl̩ʌɪz, -ɪz, -ɪŋ, -d
AM 'loʊkəˌlaɪz, -ɪz, -ɪŋ, -d
localism
BR 'ləʊkəlɪz(ə)m, 'ləʊkl̩ɪz(ə)m, -z
AM 'loʊkəˌlɪzəm, -z
locality
BR lə(ʊ)'kalɪt|i, -ɪz
AM loʊ'kælədi, -z
localizable
BR 'ləʊkəlʌɪzəbl, 'ləʊkl̩ʌɪzəbl
AM 'loʊkəˌlaɪzəbəl
localization
BR ˌləʊkəlʌɪ'zeɪʃn, ˌləʊkl̩ʌɪ'zeɪʃn
AM ˌloʊkələ'zeɪʃən, ˌloʊkəˌlaɪ'zeɪʃən
localize
BR 'ləʊkəlʌɪz, 'ləʊkl̩ʌɪz, -ɪz, -ɪŋ, -d
AM 'loʊkəˌlaɪz, -ɪz, -ɪŋ, -d
locally
BR 'ləʊkl̩i, 'ləʊkəli
AM 'loʊkəli
localness
BR 'ləʊklnəs
AM 'loʊkəlnəs
Locarno
BR lə(ʊ)'kɑːnəʊ
AM loʊ'kɑrˌnoʊ
locatable
BR lə(ʊ)'keɪtəbl
AM ˈloʊˌkeɪdəbəl
locate
BR lə(ʊ)'keɪt, -s, -ɪŋ, -ɪd
AM 'loʊˌkeɪt, loʊ'keɪ|t, -ts, -dɪŋ, -dɪd
location
BR lə(ʊ)'keɪʃn, -z
AM loʊ'keɪʃən, -z
locational
BR lə(ʊ)'keɪʃn̩(ə)l, lə(ʊ)'keɪʃən(ə)l
AM loʊ'keɪʃ(ə)nəl
locative
BR 'lɒkətɪv, -z
AM 'lɑkədɪv, -z
locator
BR lə(ʊ)'keɪtə(r), -z
AM 'loʊˌkeɪdər, -z
loc. cit.
loco citato
BR ˌlɒk 'sɪt
AM 'lɑk 'sɪt
loch
BR lɒx, lɒk, -s
AM lɑk, -s
lochan
BR 'lɒx(ə)n, 'lɒk(ə)n, -z
AM 'lɑkən, -z
Lochgilphead
BR lɒx'gɪlphɛd, lɒk'gɪlphɛd
AM lɑk'gɪlfɛd
lochia
BR 'lɒkɪə(*r*), 'ləʊkɪə(*r*), -z
AM 'loʊkiə, 'lɑkiə, -z
lochial
BR 'lɒkɪəl, 'ləʊkɪəl
AM 'loʊkiəl, 'lɑkiəl
Lochinvar
BR ˌlɒxɪn'vɑː(r), ˌlɒkɪn'vɑː(r)
AM ˌlɑkən'vɑr
lochside
BR 'lɒxsʌɪd, 'lɒksʌɪd
AM 'lɑkˌsaɪd
loci
BR 'ləʊsʌɪ, 'ləʊkʌɪ, 'lɒkʌɪ, 'ləʊsiː, 'ləʊkiː, 'lɒkiː
AM 'loʊˌsaɪ, 'loʊˌsi, 'loʊˌki
loci classici
BR ˌləʊsʌɪ 'klasɪsʌɪ, ˌləʊkʌɪ +, ˌlɒkʌɪ +, ˌləʊsiː 'klasɪsiː, ˌləʊkiː +, ˌlɒkiː +
AM ˈloʊˌsaɪ 'klæsəˌsaɪ, ˈloʊˌsi 'klæsəˌsi, ˈloʊˌki 'klæsəˌki
lock
BR lɒk, -s, -ɪŋ, -t
AM lɑk, -s, -ɪŋ, -t
lockable
BR 'lɒkəbl
AM 'lɑkəbəl
lockage
BR 'lɒkɪdʒ
AM 'lɑkɪdʒ
lockbox
BR 'lɒkbɒks, -ɪz
AM 'lɑkˌbɑks, -əz
Locke
BR lɒk
AM lɑk
locker
BR 'lɒkə(r), -z
AM 'lɑkər, -z
Lockerbie
BR 'lɒkəbi
AM 'lɑkərbi
locket
BR 'lɒkɪt, -s
AM 'lɑkət, -s
lockfast
BR 'lɒkfɑːst, 'lɒkfast
AM 'lɑkˌfæst
lockgate
BR ˌlɒk'geɪt, 'lɒkgeɪt, -s
AM 'lɑkˌgeɪt, -s
Lockhart
BR 'lɒkhɑːt, 'lɒkət
AM 'lɑkˌ(h)ɑrt
Lockheed
BR 'lɒkhiːd
AM 'lɑkˌ(h)id
lockjaw
BR 'lɒkdʒɔː(*r*)
AM 'lɑkˌdʒɔ

lockless
BR 'lɒkləs
AM 'lɑkləs
locknut
BR 'lɒknʌt, -s
AM 'lɑk,nət, -s
lockout
BR 'lɒkaʊt, -s
AM 'lɑk,aʊt, 'lɑkaʊt, -s
Locksley
BR 'lɒksli
AM 'lɑksli
locksman
BR 'lɒksmən
AM 'lɑksmən
locksmen
BR 'lɒksmən
AM 'lɑksmən
locksmith
BR 'lɒksmɪθ, -s
AM 'lɑk,smɪθ, -s
lockstitch
BR 'lɒkstɪtʃ
AM 'lɑk,stɪtʃ
lockup
BR 'lɒkʌp, -s
AM 'lɑkəp, -s
Lockwood
BR 'lɒkwʊd
AM 'lɑk,wʊd
Lockyer
BR 'lɒkjə(r)
AM 'lɑkjər
loco
BR 'ləʊkəʊ, -z
AM 'loʊkoʊ, -z
locomotion
BR ˌləʊkə'məʊʃn
AM ˌloʊkə'moʊʃən
locomotive
BR ˌləʊkə'məʊtɪv, -z
AM ˌloʊkə'moʊdɪv, -z
locomotor
BR ˌləʊkə(ʊ)'məʊtə(r), -z
AM ˌloʊkə'moʊdər, -z
locomotory
BR ˌləʊkə(ʊ)'məʊt(ə)ri
AM ˌloʊkə'moʊdəri
locoweed
BR 'ləʊkəʊwiːd
AM 'loʊkoʊ,wid
locular
BR 'lɒkjʉlə(r)
AM 'lɑkjələr
loculi
BR 'lɒkjʉlʌɪ, 'lɒkjʉliː
AM 'lɑkjə,laɪ
loculus
BR 'lɒkjʉləs
AM 'lɑkjələs
locum
BR 'ləʊkəm, -z
AM 'loʊkəm, -z
locum tenency
BR ˌləʊkəm 'tɛnənsǀi, -ɪz
AM 'loʊkəm 'tɛnənsi, -z
locum tenens
BR ˌləʊkəm 'tɛnɛnz
AM 'loʊkəm 'tɛnɛnz
locus
BR 'ləʊkəs, 'lɒkəs
AM 'loʊkəs
locus classicus
BR ˌləʊkəs 'klasɪkəs, ˌlɒkəs +
AM 'loʊkəs 'klæsəkəs
locus standi
BR ˌləʊkəs 'standʌɪ, ˌlɒkəs +, + 'standiː
AM 'loʊkəs 'stɑn,daɪ, + 'stɑndi
locust
BR 'ləʊkəst, -s
AM 'loʊkəst, -s
locution
BR lə'kjuːʃn, -z
AM lə'kjuʃən, -z
locutory
BR 'lɒkjʉt(ə)rǀi, -ɪz
AM 'lɑkjə,tɔri, -z
lode
BR ləʊd, -z
AM loʊd, -z
loden
BR 'ləʊdn, -z
AM 'loʊdən, -z
lodestar
BR 'ləʊdstɑː(r), -z
AM 'loʊd,stɑr, -z
lodestone
BR 'ləʊdstəʊn, -z
AM 'loʊd,stoʊn, -z
lodge
BR lɒdʒ, -ɪz, -ɪŋ, -d
AM lɑdʒ, -əz, -ɪŋ, -d
lodgement
BR 'lɒdʒm(ə)nt, -s
AM 'lɑdʒmənt, -s
lodger
BR 'lɒdʒə(r), -z
AM 'lɑdʒər, -z
lodging
BR 'lɒdʒɪŋ, -z
AM 'lɑdʒɪŋ, -z
lodgment
BR 'lɒdʒm(ə)nt, -s
AM 'lɑdʒmənt, -s
lodicule
BR 'lɒdɪkjuːl, -z
AM 'lɑdə,kjul, -z
Łódź
BR wʊtʃ
AM lɑdz
POL wutç
Loeb
BR ləʊb, ləːb
AM loʊb
loess
BR 'ləʊɪs, 'ləʊɛs, ləːs
AM lɛs, ləs, 'loʊ,ɛs
loessial
BR ləʊ'ɛsɪəl, 'ləːsɪəl
AM 'lɛsiəl, 'ləsiəl, loʊ'ɛsiəl
Loew
BR ləʊ
AM loʊ
Loewe
BR ləʊ
AM loʊ
Lofoten
BR lə'fəʊtn
AM lo'futn
NO 'luːfuːtən
loft
BR lɒft, -s, -ɪŋ, -ɪd
AM lɔft, lɑft, -s, -ɪŋ, -əd
lofter
BR 'lɒftə(r), -z
AM 'lɔfdər, 'lɑfdər, -z
Lofthouse
BR 'lɒfthaʊs, 'lɒftəs
AM 'lɔft,(h)aʊs, 'lɑft,(h)aʊs
loftily
BR 'lɒftɪli
AM 'lɔfdəli, 'lɑfdəli
loftiness
BR 'lɔːftɪnɪs
AM 'lɔfdinɪs, 'lɑfdinɪs
Loftus
BR 'lɒftəs
AM 'lɔfdəs, 'lɑfdəs
lofty
BR 'lɒftǀi, -ɪə(r), -ɪɪst
AM 'lɔfdi, 'lɑfdi, -ər, -ɪst
log
BR lɒg, -z, -ɪŋ, -d
AM lɔg, lɑg, -z, -ɪŋ, -d
Logan
BR 'ləʊg(ə)n
AM 'loʊgən
logan[1]
BR 'lɒg(ə)n, -z
AM 'lɔgən, -z
logan[2]
BR 'lɒg(ə)n, -z
AM 'lɔgən, 'lɑgən, -z
loganberry
BR 'ləʊg(ə)nb(ə)rǀi, 'ləʊg(ə)n,bɛrǀi, -ɪz
AM 'loʊgən,bɛri, -z
logaoedic
BR ˌlɒgə(r)'iːdɪk
AM ˌlɑgə'idɪk
logarithm
BR 'lɒgərɪð(ə)m, -z
AM 'lɔgə,rɪðəm, 'lɑgə,rɪðəm, -z
logarithmic
BR ˌlɒgə'rɪðmɪk
AM ˌlɔgə'rɪðmɪk, ˌlɑgə'rɪðmɪk
logarithmically
BR ˌlɒgə'rɪðmɪkli
AM ˌlɔgə'rɪθmɪk(ə)li, ˌlɑgə'rɪθmɪk(ə)li
logbook
BR 'lɒgbʊk, -s
AM 'lɔg,bʊk, 'lɑg,bʊk, -s
loge
BR ləʊʒ, -ɪz
AM loʊʒ, -əz
logger
BR 'lɒgə(r), -z
AM 'lɔgər, 'lɑgər, -z
loggerhead
BR 'lɒgəhɛd, -z
AM 'lɔgər,(h)ɛd, 'lɑgər,(h)ɛd, -z
loggia
BR 'lɒdʒ(ɪ)ə(r), 'ləʊdʒ(ɪ)ə(r), -z
AM 'lɔdʒ(i)ə, 'loʊdʒ(i)ə, -z
logia
BR 'ləʊgɪə(r), 'lɒgɪə(r), -z
AM 'loʊdʒ(i)ə, -z
logic
BR 'lɒdʒɪk
AM 'lɑdʒɪk
logical
BR 'lɒdʒɪkl
AM 'lɑdʒəkəl
logicality
BR ˌlɒdʒɪ'kalɪti
AM ˌlɑdʒə'kælədi
logically
BR 'lɒdʒɪkli
AM 'lɑdʒək(ə)li
logical positivism
BR ˌlɒdʒɪkl 'pɒzɪtɪvɪz(ə)m
AM ˌlɑdʒəkəl 'pɑzədə,vɪzəm
logical positivist
BR ˌlɒdʒɪkl 'pɒzɪtɪvɪst, -s
AM ˌlɑdʒəkəl 'pɑzədəvəst, -s
logician
BR lə(ʊ)'dʒɪʃn, lɒ'dʒɪʃn, -z
AM lə'dʒɪʃən, loʊ'dʒɪʃən, -z
logion
BR 'ləʊgɪən, 'lɒgɪən, 'lɒgɪɒn
AM 'loʊdʒɪən
logistic
BR lə'dʒɪstɪk, lɒ'dʒɪstɪk, -s
AM lə'dʒɪstɪk, loʊ'dʒɪstɪk, -s
logistical
BR lə'dʒɪstɪkl, lɒ'dʒɪstɪkl
AM lə'dʒɪstɪkəl
logistically
BR lə'dʒɪstɪkli, lɒ'dʒɪstɪkli
AM ˌlə'dʒɪstɪk(ə)li

logjam
BR ˈlɒɡdʒam, -z
AM ˈlɔɡˌdʒæm, ˈlɑɡˌdʒæm, -z

logo
BR ˈlɒɡəʊ, ˈləʊɡəʊ, -z
AM ˈloʊɡoʊ, -z

logogram
BR ˈlɒɡəɡram, -z
AM ˈloʊɡəˌɡræm, -z

logographer
BR lɒˈɡɒɡrəfə(r), ləˈɡɒɡrəfə(r), -z
AM loʊˈɡɑɡrəfər, -z

logomachy
BR lə(ʊ)ˈɡɒmək|i, -ɪz
AM loʊˈɡɑməki, -z

logon
BR ˈlɒɡɒn, ˌlɒɡˈɒn, -z
AM ˈlɔɡˌɑn, ˈlɑɡˌɑn, -z

logopaedic
BR ˌlɒɡəˈpiːdɪk, -s
AM ˌlɔɡəˈpidɪk, ˌloʊɡəˈpidɪk, -s

logopedic
BR ˌlɒɡəˈpiːdɪk, -s
AM ˌlɔɡəˈpidɪk, ˌloʊɡəˈpidɪk, -s

logorrhea
BR ˌlɒɡəˈriːə(r)
AM ˌlɔɡəˈriə, ˌloʊɡəˈriə

logorrheic
BR ˌlɒɡəˈriːɪk
AM ˌlɔɡəˈriɪk, ˌloʊɡəˈriɪk

logorrhoea
BR ˌlɒɡəˈriːə(r)
AM ˌlɔɡəˈriə, ˌloʊɡəˈriə

logorrhoeic
BR ˌlɒɡəˈriːɪk
AM ˌlɔɡəˈriɪk, ˌloʊɡəˈriɪk

logos
BR ˈlɒɡɒs
AM ˈloʊˌɡoʊs

logotype
BR ˈlɒɡə(ʊ)tʌɪp, -s
AM ˈlɔɡəˌtaɪp, ˈloʊɡəˌtaɪp, -s

logroll
BR ˈlɒɡrəʊl, -z, -ɪŋ, -d
AM ˈlɔɡˌroʊl, ˈlɑɡˌroʊl, -z, -ɪŋ, -d

logroller
BR ˈlɒɡˌrəʊlə(r), -z
AM ˈlɔɡˌroʊlər, ˈlɑɡˌroʊlər, -z

Logue
BR ləʊɡ
AM loʊɡ

logwood
BR ˈlɒɡwʊd
AM ˈlɔɡˌwʊd, ˈlɑɡˌwʊd

Lohengrin
BR ˈləʊəŋɡrɪn
AM ˈloʊənˌɡrɪn

loin
BR lɔɪn, -z
AM lɔɪn, -z

loincloth
BR ˈlɔɪnklɒ|θ, -θs\-ðz
AM ˈlɔɪnˌklɔ|θ, ˈlɔɪnˌklɑ|θ, -θs\-ðz

loir
BR ˈlɔɪə(r), lwɑː(r)
AM ˈlɔɪ(ə)r, l(ə)ˈwɑr

Loire
BR lwɑː(r)
AM l(ə)ˈwɑr

Lois
BR ˈləʊɪs
AM ˈloʊwəs

loiter
BR ˈlɔɪt|ə(r), -əz, -(ə)rɪŋ, -əd
AM ˈlɔɪdər, -z, -ɪŋ, -d

loiterer
BR ˈlɔɪt(ə)rə(r), -z
AM ˈlɔɪdərər, -z

Loki
BR ˈləʊki
AM ˈloʊˌki

Lola
BR ˈləʊlə(r)
AM ˈloʊlə

Lolita
BR lɒˈliːtə(r), lə(ʊ)ˈliːtə(r)
AM loʊˈlidə

loll
BR lɒl, -z, -ɪŋ, -d
AM lɑl, -z, -ɪŋ, -d

Lolland
BR ˈlɒlənd
AM ˈlɑlənd

lollapalooza
BR ˌlɒləpəˈluːzə(r)
AM ˌlɑləpəˈluzə

Lollard
BR ˈlɒləd, ˈlɒlɑːd, -z
AM ˈlɑlərd, -z

Lollardism
BR ˈlɒlədɪz(ə)m, ˈlɒlɑːdɪz(ə)m
AM ˈlɑlərˌdɪzəm

Lollardy
BR ˈlɒlədi, ˈlɒlɑːdi
AM ˈlɑlərdi

loller
BR ˈlɒlə(r), -z
AM ˈlɑlər, -z

lollipop
BR ˈlɒlɪpɒp, -s
AM ˈlɑliˌpɑp, -s

lollop
BR ˈlɒləp, -s, -ɪŋ, -t
AM ˈlɑləp, -s, -ɪŋ, -t

lolly
BR ˈlɒl|i, -ɪz
AM ˈlɑli, -z

Lomas
BR ˈləʊmas, ˈləʊməs
AM ˈloʊməs

Lomax
BR ˈləʊmaks
AM ˈloʊmæks

Lombard
BR ˈlɒmbɑːd, -z
AM ˈlɑmˌbɑrd, -z

Lombardi
BR ləmˈbɑːdi
AM ləmˈbɑrdi

Lombardic
BR (ˌ)lɒmˈbɑːdɪk
AM ˌlɑmˈbɑrdɪk

Lombardy
BR ˈlɒmbədi
AM ˈlɑmˌbɑrdi, ˈlɑmbərdi

Lombok
BR ˈlɒmbɒk
AM ˈlɑmˌbɑk

Lomé
BR ˈləʊmeɪ
AM loʊˈmeɪ

loment
BR ˈləʊmɛnt, ˈləʊm(ə)nt, -s
AM ˈloʊmənt, -s

lomentaceous
BR ˌləʊm(ə)nˈteɪʃəs
AM ˌloʊmənˈteɪʃəs

London
BR ˈlʌndən
AM ˈləndən

Londonderry
BR ˈlʌndʌnˌdɛri, ˌlʌndʌnˈdɛri
AM ˈləndənˌdɛri, ˌləndənˈdɛri

Londoner
BR ˈlʌndənə(r), -z
AM ˈləndənər, -z

lone
BR ləʊn
AM loʊn

loneliness
BR ˈləʊnlɪnɪs
AM ˈloʊnlinɨs

lonely
BR ˈləʊnl|i, -ɪə(r), -ɪɪst
AM ˈloʊnli, -ər, -ɨst

loner
BR ˈləʊnə(r), -z
AM ˈloʊnər, -z

lonesome
BR ˈləʊns(ə)m
AM ˈloʊnsəm

lonesomely
BR ˈləʊns(ə)mli
AM ˈloʊnsəmli

lonesomeness
BR ˈləʊns(ə)mnəs
AM ˈloʊnsəmnəs

long
BR lɒ|ŋ, -ŋz, -ŋɪŋ, -ŋd, -ŋɡə(r), -ŋɡɪst
AM lɔ|ŋ, -ŋz, -ŋɪŋ, -ŋd, -ŋɡər, -ŋɡəst

longanimity
BR ˌlɒŋɡəˈnɪmɪti
AM ˌlɔŋɡəˈnɪmɨdi, ˌlɑŋɡəˈnɪmɨdi

long-awaited
BR ˈlɒŋəˌweɪtɪd
AM ˈlɔŋəˌweɪdɨd, ˈlɑŋəˌweɪdɨd

Long Beach
BR ˈlɒŋ biːtʃ
AM ˈlɔŋ ˌbitʃ, ˈlɑŋ +

longboard
BR ˈlɒŋbɔːd, -z
AM ˈlɔŋˌbɔ(ə)rd, ˈlɑŋˌbɔ(ə)rd, -z

longboat
BR ˈlɒŋbəʊt, -s
AM ˈlɔŋˌboʊt, ˈlɑŋˌboʊt, -s

Longbottom
BR ˈlɒŋˌbɒtəm
AM ˈlɔŋˌbɑdəm, ˈlɑŋˌbɑdəm

longbow
BR ˈlɒŋbəʊ, -z
AM ˈlɔŋˌboʊ, ˈlɑŋˌboʊ, -z

Longbridge
BR ˈlɒŋbrɪdʒ
AM ˈlɔŋˌbrɪdʒ, ˈlɑŋˌbrɪdʒ

Longden
BR ˈlɒŋdən
AM ˈlɔŋdən, ˈlɑŋdən

longe
BR lʌn(d)ʒ, lɒn(d)ʒ, -ɨz, -ɪŋ, -d
AM ləndʒ, -əz, -ɪŋ, -d

longeron
BR ˈlɒn(d)ʒ(ə)rən, ˈlɒn(d)ʒ(ə)rn̩, ˈlɒn(d)ʒ(ə)rɒn, -z
AM ˈlɑndʒərən, ˈlɑndʒəˌrɑn, -z

longevity
BR lɒnˈdʒɛvɪti
AM lɔnˈdʒɛvədi, lɑnˈdʒɛvədi

Longfellow
BR ˈlɒŋˌfɛləʊ
AM ˈlɔŋˌfɛloʊ, ˈlɑŋˌfɛloʊ

Longford
BR ˈlɒŋfəd
AM ˈlɔŋfərd, ˈlɑŋfərd

longhair
BR ˈlɒŋhɛː(r), -z
AM ˈlɔŋˌ(h)ɛ(ə)r, ˈlɑŋˌ(h)ɛ(ə)r, -z

longhand
BR ˈlɒŋhand
AM ˈlɔŋˌ(h)ænd, ˈlɑŋˌ(h)ænd

longhop
BR ˈlɒŋhɒp, -s
AM ˈlɔŋˌ(h)ɑp, ˈlɑŋˌ(h)ɑp, -s

longhorn
BR ˈlɒŋhɔːn, -z

AM 'lɔŋ,(h)ɔ(ə)rn, 'lɑŋ,(h)ɔ(ə)rn, -z

longhouse
BR 'lɒŋhaʊ|s, -zɪz
AM 'lɔŋ,(h)aʊ|s, 'lɑŋ,(h)aʊ|s, -zəz

longicorn
BR 'lɒn(d)ʒɪkɔːn, -z
AM 'lɑndʒə,kɔ(ə)rn, -z

longing
BR 'lɒŋɪŋ, -z
AM 'lɔŋɪŋ, 'lɑŋɪŋ, -z

longingly
BR 'lɒŋɪŋli
AM 'lɔŋɪŋli, 'lɑŋɪŋli

Longinus
BR lɒn'dʒʌɪnəs, lɒŋ'giːnəs
AM lɑn'dʒaɪnəs

longish
BR 'lɒŋɪʃ
AM 'lɔŋɪʃ, 'lɑŋɪʃ

longitude
BR 'lɒŋgɪtjuːd, 'lɒŋgɪtʃuːd, 'lɒn(d)ʒɪtjuːd, 'lɒn(d)ʒɪtʃuːd, -z
AM 'lɑndʒɪ,t(j)ud, 'lɑndʒɪ,t(j)ud, -z

longitudinal
BR ,lɒŋgɪ'tjuːdɪnl, ,lɒŋgɪ'tʃuːdɪnl, ,lɒn(d)ʒɪ'tjuːdɪnl, ,lɒn(d)ʒɪ'tʃuːdɪnl
AM ',lɑndʒə't(j)udn̩əl, ',lɑndʒə't(j)udn̩əl

longitudinally
BR ,lɒŋgɪ'tjuːdɪnl̩i, ,lɒŋgɪ'tʃuːdɪnl̩i, ,lɒn(d)ʒɪ'tjuːdɪnl̩i, ,lɒn(d)ʒɪ'tʃuːdɪnl̩i, ,lɒŋgɪ'tjuːdɪnəli, ,lɒŋgɪ'tʃuːdɪnəli, ,lɒn(d)ʒɪ'tjuːdɪnəli, ,lɒn(d)ʒɪ'tʃuːdɪnəli
AM ',lɑndʒə't(j)udn̩əli, ',lɑndʒə't(j)udn̩əli

long jump
BR 'lɒŋ dʒʌmp
AM 'lɔŋ ,dʒəmp, 'lɑŋ ,dʒəmp

Longleat
BR 'lɒŋliːt
AM 'lɔŋlit, 'lɑŋlit

Longman
BR 'lɒŋmən
AM 'lɔŋmən, 'lɑŋmən

longship
BR 'lɒŋʃɪp, -s
AM 'lɔŋ,ʃɪp, 'lɑŋ,ʃɪp, -s

longshore
BR 'lɒŋʃɔː(r)
AM 'lɔŋ,ʃɔ(ə)r, 'lɑŋ,ʃɔ(ə)r

longshoreman
BR 'lɒŋʃɔːmən
AM ,lɔŋ'ʃɔrmən, ,lɑŋ'ʃɔrmən

longshoremen
BR 'lɒŋʃɔːmən
AM ,lɔŋ'ʃɔrmən, ,lɑŋ'ʃɔrmən

longstop
BR 'lɒŋstɒp, -s
AM 'lɔŋ,stɑp, 'lɑŋ,stɑp, -s

Longton
BR 'lɒŋt(ə)n
AM 'lɔŋtən, 'lɑŋtən

Longtown
BR 'lɒŋtaʊn
AM 'lɔŋ,taʊn, 'lɑŋ,taʊn

longueur
BR (,)lɒŋ'gəː(r), -z
AM lɔŋ'(g)ər, lɑŋ'(g)ər, -z

longways
BR 'lɒŋweɪz
AM 'lɔŋ,weɪz, 'lɑŋ,weɪz

longwise
BR 'lɒŋwʌɪz
AM 'lɔŋ,waɪz, 'lɑŋ,waɪz

lonicera
BR lə'nɪs(ə)rə(*r*), lɒ'nɪs(ə)rə(*r*)
AM loʊ'nɪsərə

Lonnie
BR 'lɒni
AM 'lɑni

Lonrho®
BR 'lɒnrəʊ
AM 'lɑnroʊ

Lonsdale
BR 'lɒnzdeɪl
AM 'lɑnz,deɪl

loo
BR luː, -z
AM lu, -z

Looe
BR luː
AM lu

loof
BR luːf, -s, -ɪŋ, -d
AM luf, -s, -ɪŋ, -d

loofa
BR 'luːfə(*r*), -z
AM 'lufə, -z

loofah
BR 'luːfə(*r*), -z
AM 'lufə, -z

look
BR lʊk, -s, -ɪŋ, -t
AM lʊk, -s, -ɪŋ, -t

lookalike
BR 'lʊkəlʌɪk, -s
AM 'lʊkə,laɪk, -s

looker
BR 'lʊkə(r), -z
AM 'lʊkər, -z

lookout
BR 'lʊkaʊt, -s
AM 'lʊk,aʊt, 'lʊkaʊt, -s

look-see
BR 'lʊksiː
AM 'lʊk,si

lookup
BR 'lʊkʌp, -s
AM 'lʊk,əp, -s

loom
BR luːm, -z, -ɪŋ, -d
AM lum, -z, -ɪŋ, -d

loon
BR luːn, -z
AM lun, -z

looniness
BR 'luːnɪnɪs
AM 'luninɪs

loony
BR 'luːn|i, -ɪz
AM 'luni, -z

loop
BR luːp, -s, -ɪŋ, -t
AM lup, -s, -ɪŋ, -t

looper
BR 'luːpə(r), -z
AM 'lupər, -z

loophole
BR 'luːphəʊl, -z
AM 'lup,(h)oʊl, -z

loopiness
BR 'luːpɪnɪs
AM 'lupinɪs

loopy
BR 'luːp|i, -ɪə(r), -ɪɪst
AM 'lupi, -ər, -ɪst

loose
BR luːs, -ɪz, -ɪŋ, -t, -ə(r), -ɪst
AM lus, -əz, -ɪŋ, -t, -ər, -əst

loosebox
BR 'luːsbɒks, -ɪz
AM 'lus,bɑks, -əz

loosely
BR 'luːsli
AM 'lusli

loosen
BR 'luːs|n, -nz, -n̩ɪŋ\-nɪŋ, -nd
AM 'lusən, -z, -ɪŋ, -d

loosener
BR 'luːsn̩ə(r), 'luːsnə(r), -z
AM 'lusn̩ər, -z

looseness
BR 'luːsnəs
AM 'lusnəs

loosestrife
BR 'luːsstrʌɪf, -s
AM 'lu(s),straɪf, -s

loosish
BR 'luːsɪʃ
AM 'lusɪʃ

loot
BR luːt, -s, -ɪŋ, -ɪd
AM lu|t, -ts, -dɪŋ, -dəd

looter
BR 'luːtə(r), -z
AM 'ludər, -z

lop
BR lɒp, -s, -ɪŋ, -t
AM lɑp, -s, -ɪŋ, -t

lope
BR ləʊp, -s, -ɪŋ, -t
AM loʊp, -s, -ɪŋ, -t

López
BR 'ləʊpɛz
AM 'loʊpɛz
SP 'lopeθ, 'lopes

lophobranch
BR 'ləʊfə(ʊ)braŋk, 'lɒfə(ʊ)braŋk, -s
AM 'lɑfə,bræŋk, 'loʊfə,bræŋk, -s

lophodont
BR 'ləʊfə(ʊ)dɒnt, 'lɒfə(ʊ)dɒnt, -s
AM 'lɑfə,dɑnt, 'loʊfə,dɑnt, -s

lophophore
BR 'ləʊfə(ʊ)fɔː(r), 'lɒfə(ʊ)fɔː(r), -z
AM 'lɑfə,fɔ(ə)r, 'loʊfə,fɔ(ə)r, -z

lopolith
BR 'lɒpəlɪθ, 'lɒpl̩ɪθ, -s
AM 'lɑpə,lɪθ, -s

lopper
BR 'lɒpə(r), -z
AM 'lɑpər, -z

loppy
BR 'lɒp|i, -ɪə(r), -ɪɪst
AM 'lɑpi, -ər, -ɪst

lopsided
BR ,lɒp'sʌɪdɪd
AM 'lɑp',saɪdɪd

lopsidedly
BR ,lɒp'sʌɪdɪdli
AM 'lɑp',saɪdɪdli

lopsidedness
BR ,lɒp'sʌɪdɪdnɪs
AM 'lɑp',saɪdɪdnɪs

loquacious
BR lə'kweɪʃəs
AM loʊ'kweɪʃəs

loquaciously
BR lə'kweɪʃəsli
AM loʊ'kweɪʃəsli

loquaciousness
BR lə'kweɪʃəsnəs
AM loʊ'kweɪʃəsnəs

loquacity
BR lə(ʊ)'kwasɪti
AM loʊ'kwæsədi

loquat
BR 'ləʊkwɒt, 'ləʊkwət, -s
AM 'loʊ,kwɑt, loʊ'kwɑt, -s

loquitur
BR 'lɒkwɪtə(r)
AM 'lɑkwədər, 'loʊkwədər

lor
BR lɔː(r)
AM lɔ(ə)r

loral
BR 'lɔːrəl, 'lɔːrl̩, -z
AM 'lɔrəl, -z

loran
BR 'lɔːrən, 'lɔːrn̩, -z
AM 'lɔrən, -z

Lorca
BR 'lɔːkə(r)
AM 'lɔrkə

Lorcan
BR 'lɔːk(ə)n
AM 'lɔrkən

lorch
BR lɔːtʃ, -ɪz
AM lɔrtʃ, -əz

lorcha
BR 'lɔːtʃə(r), -z
AM 'lɔr(t)ʃə, -z

lord
BR lɔːd, -z, -ɪŋ, -ɪd
AM lɔ(ə)rd, -z, -ɪŋ, -əd

lordless
BR 'lɔːdləs
AM 'lɔrdləs

lordlike
BR 'lɔːdlʌɪk
AM 'lɔrd,laɪk

lordliness
BR 'lɔːdlɪnɪs
AM 'lɔrdlinɪs

lordling
BR 'lɔːdlɪŋ, -z
AM 'lɔrdlɪŋ, -z

lordly
BR 'lɔːdl|i, -ɪə(r), -ɪɪst
AM 'lɔrdli, -ər, -ɪst

lordosis
BR lɔː'dəʊsɪs
AM lɔr'doʊsəs

lordotic
BR lɔː'dɒtɪk
AM lɔr'dɑdɪk

lordship
BR 'lɔːdʃɪp, -s
AM 'lɔrd,ʃɪp, -s

Lordy
BR 'lɔːdi
AM 'lɔrdi

lore
BR lɔː(r)
AM lɔ(ə)r

L'Oréal®
BR 'lɒrɪal
AM ,lɔri'æl

Lorelei
BR 'lɒrəlʌɪ, 'lɔːrəlʌɪ, -z
AM 'lɔrə,laɪ, -z

Loren
BR lə'rɛn, 'lɔːrən, 'lɔːrn̩
AM lə'rɛn

Lorentz
BR 'lɒrən(t)s, 'lɒrn̩(t)s
AM lɔ'rənz

Lorenz
BR 'lɒrənz, 'lɒrn̩z
AM lɔ'rənz

Lorenzo
BR lə'rɛnzəʊ
AM lə'rɛn,zoʊ

Loreto
BR lə'rɛtəʊ
AM lə'rɛdoʊ

Loretta
BR lə'rɛtə(r)
AM lə'rɛdə

lorgnette
BR lɔː'njɛt, -s
AM lɔrn'jɛt, -s

lorgnon
BR 'lɔːnj(ə)n, -z
AM lɔrn'jɔn, -z

loricate
BR 'lɒrɪkeɪt, -s
AM 'lɔrə,keɪt, -s

lorikeet
BR 'lɒrɪkiːt, ,lɒrɪ'kiːt, -s
AM 'lɔrə,kit, -s

lorimer
BR 'lɒrɪmə(r), -z
AM 'lɔrəmər, -z

loris
BR 'lɔːrɪs, -ɪz
AM 'lɔrəs, -əz

lorn
BR lɔːn
AM lɔ(ə)rn

Lorna
BR 'lɔːnə(r)
AM 'lɔrnə

Lorraine
BR lə'reɪn
AM lə'reɪn

lorry
BR 'lɒr|i, -ɪz
AM 'lɔri, -z

lorryload
BR 'lɒrɪləʊd, -z
AM 'lɔri,loʊd, -z

lory
BR 'lɔːr|i, -ɪz
AM 'lɔri, -z

losable
BR 'luːzəbl
AM 'luzəbəl

Los Alamos
BR lɒs 'aləmɒs
AM lɔ 'sæləmoʊs, lɑ 'sæləmoʊs

Los Angeles
BR lɒs 'an(d)ʒɪliːz
AM lɔ 'sændʒələs, lɑ 'sændʒələs

lose
BR luːz, -ɪz, -ɪŋ
AM luz, -əz, -ɪŋ

loser
BR 'luːzə(r), -z
AM 'luzər, -z

Losey
BR 'ləʊzi
AM 'loʊzi

loss
BR lɒs, -ɪz
AM lɔs, lɑs, -əz

löss
BR 'ləʊɪs, 'ləʊɛs, lɜːs
AM lɛs, ləs, 'loʊ,ɛs

Lossiemouth
BR 'lɒsɪmaʊθ, ,lɒsɪ'maʊθ
AM ,lɔsi'maʊθ, ,lɑsi'maʊθ

lost
BR lɒst
AM lɔst, lɑst

Lostwithiel
BR lɒs(t)'wɪθɪəl
AM ,lɔst'wɪθiəl, ,lɑst'wɪθiəl

lot
BR lɒt, -s
AM lɑt, -s

loth
BR ləʊθ
AM loʊθ

Lothario
BR lə'θɑːrɪəʊ, lə'θɛːrɪəʊ, -z
AM loʊ'θɛrioʊ, loʊ'θɑrioʊ, -z

Lothian
BR 'ləʊðɪən
AM 'loʊðiən

loti
BR 'ləʊt|i, 'luːt|i, -ɪz
AM 'loʊdi, -z

lotic
BR 'ləʊtɪk
AM 'loʊdɪk

lotion
BR 'ləʊʃn, -z
AM 'loʊʃən, -z

lotsa
lots of
BR 'lɒtsə(r)
AM 'lɑtsə

lotta
lot of
BR 'lɒtə(r)
AM 'lɑdə

lottery
BR 'lɒt(ə)r|i, -ɪz
AM 'lɑdəri, -z

Lottie
BR 'lɒti
AM 'lɑdi

lotto
BR 'lɒtəʊ
AM 'lɑdoʊ

lotus
BR 'ləʊtəs, -ɪz
AM 'loʊdəs, -əz

Lou
BR luː
AM lu

louche
BR luːʃ
AM luʃ

loud
BR laʊd, -ə(r), -ɪst
AM laʊd, -ər, -əst

louden
BR 'laʊd|n, -nz, -n̩ɪŋ\-nɪŋ, -nd
AM 'laʊdən, -z, -ɪŋ, -d

loudhailer
BR ,laʊd'heɪlə(r), -z
AM 'laʊd,heɪlər, -z

loudish
BR 'laʊdɪʃ
AM 'laʊdɪʃ

loudly
BR 'laʊdli
AM 'laʊdli

loudmouth
BR 'laʊdmaʊ|θ, -ðz\-θs
AM 'laʊd,maʊ|θ, -ðz

loudmouthed
BR ,laʊd'maʊðd
AM 'laʊd,maʊðd

loudness
BR 'laʊdnəs
AM 'laʊdnəs

loudspeaker
BR ,laʊd'spiːkə(r), -z
AM 'laʊd,spikər, -z

Louella
BR lʊ'ɛlə(r)
AM lʊ'ɛlə

lough
BR lɒx, lɒk, -s
AM lɑk, -s

Loughborough
BR 'lʌfb(ə)rə(r)
AM 'ləfbərə

Loughlin
BR 'lɒxlɪn, 'lɒklɪn
AM 'lɑklən

Lough Neagh
BR ,lɒx 'neɪ, ,lɒk +
AM ,lɑk 'neɪ

Loughor
BR 'lʌxə(r), 'lʌkə(r)
AM 'lɑkər

Louie
BR 'luːi
AM 'luwi

Louis
BR 'luːiː, 'luːɪs
AM 'luwəs, 'luwi

louis[1]
coin
BR 'luːi
AM 'luwəs, 'luwi

louis[2]
coins
BR 'luːɪz
AM 'luwiz

Louisa
BR lʊ'iːzə(r)
AM lə'wizə

Louisburg
BR 'luːɪsbəːg
AM 'ləwəs,bərg

Louise
BR lʊ'iːz
AM lə'wiz

Louisiana
BR lʊˌiːzɪˈanə(r)
AM ˌluwiziˈænə

Louisianan
BR lʊˌiːzɪˈanən, -z
AM ˌluwiziˈænən, -z

Louisville
BR ˈluːɪvɪl
AM ˈluwiˌvɪl, ˈlu(wə)vəl

lounge
BR laʊn(d)ʒ, -ɪz, -ɪŋ, -d
AM laʊndʒ, -əz, -ɪŋ, -d

lounger
BR ˈlaʊn(d)ʒə(r), -z
AM ˈlaʊndʒər, -z

Lounsbury
BR ˈlaʊnzb(ə)ri
AM ˈlaʊnzˌbɛri

loupe
BR luːp, -s
AM lup, -s

lour
BR ˈlaʊə(r), -z, -ɪŋ, -d
AM ˈlaʊ(ə)r, -z, -ɪŋ, -d

Lourdes
BR lʊəd(z), lɔːdz
AM lʊ(ə)rd
FR luʀd

Lourenço Marques
BR ləˌrɛnsəʊ ˈmɑːks
AM ləˌrɛn(t)soʊ mɑrˈkɛs
B PORT loˌrẽsu ˈmarkis
L PORT loˌrẽsu ˈmarkəʃ

louringly
BR ˈlaʊərɪŋli
AM ˈlaʊrɪŋli

loury
BR ˈlaʊəri
AM ˈlaʊri

louse
BR laʊs, -ɪz, -ɪŋ, -t
AM laʊs, -əz, -ɪŋ, -t

lousewort
BR ˈlaʊswəːt, -s
AM ˈlaʊswərt, ˈlaʊswɔ(ə)rt, -s

lousily
BR ˈlaʊzɪli
AM ˈlaʊzəli

lousiness
BR ˈlaʊzɪnɪs
AM ˈlaʊzinɪs

lousy
BR ˈlaʊz|i, -ɪə(r), -ɪɪst
AM ˈlaʊzi, -ər, -ɪst

lout
BR laʊt, -s
AM laʊt, -s

Louth
BR laʊθ
AM laʊθ

loutish
BR ˈlaʊtɪʃ
AM ˈlaʊdɪʃ

loutishly
BR ˈlaʊtɪʃli
AM ˈlaʊdɪʃli

loutishness
BR ˈlaʊtɪʃnɪs
AM ˈlaʊdɪʃnɪs

Louvain
BR lʊˈvã, lʊˈvan
AM luˈvæn

louver
BR ˈluːvə(r), -z
AM ˈluvər, -z, -d

Louvre
BR ˈluːvrə(r), luːv
AM ˈluv(rə)

louvre
BR ˈluːvə(r), -z, -d
AM ˈluvər, -z, -d

lovability
BR ˌlʌvəˈbɪlɪti
AM ˌləvəˈbɪlɪdi

lovable
BR ˈlʌvəbl
AM ˈləvəbəl

lovableness
BR ˈlʌvəblnəs
AM ˈləvəbəlnəs

lovably
BR ˈlʌvəbli
AM ˈləvəbli

lovage
BR ˈlʌvɪdʒ
AM ˈləvɪdʒ

lovat
BR ˈlʌvət
AM ˈləvət

love
BR lʌv, -z, -ɪŋ, -d
AM ləv, -z, -ɪŋ, -d

loveable
BR ˈlʌvəbl
AM ˈləvəbəl

loveably
BR ˈlʌvəbli
AM ˈləvəbli

lovebird
BR ˈlʌvbəːd, -z
AM ˈləvˌbərd, -z

lovebite
BR ˈlʌvbʌɪt, -s
AM ˈləvˌbaɪt, -s

lovechild
BR ˈlʌvtʃʌɪld
AM ˈləvˌtʃaɪld

lovechildren
BR ˈlʌvˌtʃɪldr(ə)n
AM ˈləvˌtʃɪldrən

Loveday
BR ˈlʌvdeɪ
AM ˈləvˌdeɪ

Lovejoy
BR ˈlʌvdʒɔɪ
AM ˈləvˌdʒɔɪ

Lovelace
BR ˈlʌvleɪs
AM ˈləvləs

loveless
BR ˈlʌvləs
AM ˈləvləs

lovelessly
BR ˈlʌvləsli
AM ˈləvləsli

lovelessness
BR ˈlʌvləsnəs
AM ˈləvləsnəs

lovelily
BR ˈlʌvlɪli
AM ˈləvləli

loveliness
BR ˈlʌvlɪnɪs
AM ˈləvlinɪs

Lovell
BR ˈlʌvl
AM ləˈvɛl

lovelock
BR ˈlʌvlɒk, -s
AM ˈləvˌlɑk, -s

lovelorn
BR ˈlʌvlɔːn
AM ˈləvˌlɔ(ə)rn

lovely
BR ˈlʌvl|i, -ɪz, -ɪə(r), -ɪɪst
AM ˈləvli, -z, -ər, -ɪst

lovemaking
BR ˈlʌvˌmeɪkɪŋ
AM ˈləvˌmeɪkɪŋ

lover
BR ˈlʌvə(r), -z
AM ˈləvər, -z

Loveridge
BR ˈlʌv(ə)rɪdʒ
AM ˈləvˌrɪdʒ

loverless
BR ˈlʌvələs
AM ˈləvərləs

loverlike
BR ˈlʌvəlʌɪk
AM ˈləvərˌlaɪk

lovesick
BR ˈlʌvsɪk
AM ˈləvˌsɪk

lovesickness
BR ˈlʌvˌsɪknɪs
AM ˈləvˌsɪknɪs

lovesome
BR ˈlʌvs(ə)m
AM ˈləvsəm

loveworthy
BR ˈlʌvˌwəːði
AM ˈləvˌwərði

lovey
BR ˈlʌv|i, -ɪz
AM ˈləvi, -z

lovey-dovey
BR ˌlʌvɪˈdʌvi
AM ˈləviˈdəvi

lovingly
BR ˈlʌvɪŋli
AM ˈləvɪŋli

lovingness
BR ˈlʌvɪŋnɪs
AM ˈləvɪŋnɪs

low
BR ləʊ, -z, -ɪŋ, -d, -ə(r), -ɪst
AM loʊ, -z, -ɪŋ, -d, -(ə)r, -əst

lowball
BR ˈləʊbɔːl, -z
AM ˈloʊˌbɔl, ˈloʊˌbɑl, -z

lowboy
BR ˈləʊbɔɪ, -z
AM ˈloʊˌbɔɪ, -z

lowbrow
BR ˈləʊbraʊ, -z
AM ˈloʊˌbraʊ, -z

lowbrowed
BR ˌləʊˈbraʊd
AM ˈloʊbraʊd

low-cal
BR ˌləʊˈkal
AM ˈloʊˌkæl

low-calorie
BR ˌləʊˈkaləri
AM ˈloʊˌkæl(ə)ri

low-down[1]
adjective
BR ˌləʊˈdaʊn
AM ˈloʊˌdaʊn

low-down[2]
noun
BR ˈləʊdaʊn
AM ˈloʊˌdaʊn

Lowell
BR ˈləʊəl
AM ˈloʊəl

Löwenbräu
BR ˈləʊənbraʊ
AM ˈloʊənˌbraʊ
GER ˈlœːvn̩brɔʏ

lower[1]
lour
BR ˈlaʊə(r), -z, -ɪŋ, -d
AM ˈloʊər, ˈlaʊər, -z, -(ə)rɪŋ, -d

lower[2]
position
BR ˈləʊə(r), -z, -ɪŋ, -d
AM ˈloʊ(ə)r, -z, -ɪŋ, -d

lowermost
BR ˈləʊəməʊst
AM ˈloʊ(ə)rˌmoʊst

Lowery
BR ˈlaʊ(ə)ri
AM ˈlaʊri

Lowestoft
BR ˈləʊ(ɪ)stɒft
AM ˈloʊ(ə)ˌstɔft, ˈloʊ(ə)ˌstɑft

lowish
BR ˈləʊɪʃ
AM ˈloʊɪʃ

lowland
BR ˈləʊlənd, -z
AM ˈloʊlənd, ˈloʊˌlænd, -z

lowlander
BR ˈləʊləndə(r), -z
AM ˈloʊləndər, ˈloʊˌlændər, -z

lowlife
BR ˈləʊlʌɪf
AM ˈloʊˌlaɪf

lowlight
BR ˈləʊlʌɪt, -s
AM ˈloʊˌlaɪt, -s

lowlily
BR ˈləʊlɨli
AM ˈloʊlɨli

lowliness
BR ˈləʊlɪnɨs
AM ˈloʊlinɨs

lowly
BR ˈləʊl|i, -ɪə(r), -ɪɨst
AM ˈloʊli, -ər, -ɨst

Lowman
BR ˈləʊmən
AM ˈloʊmən

Lowndes
BR laʊn(d)z
AM ˈlaʊndəs

lowness
BR ˈləʊnəs, -ɪz
AM ˈloʊnəs, -əz

Lowrie
BR ˈlaʊri
AM ˈlaʊri

low-rise[1]
adjective
BR ˌləʊˈrʌɪz
AM ˈloʊˌraɪz

low-rise[2]
noun
BR ˈləʊrʌɪz, -ɨz
AM ˈloʊˌraɪz, -ɨz

Lowry
BR ˈlaʊri
AM ˈlaʊri

low season[1]
adjective
BR ˌləʊ ˈsiːzn
AM ˈloʊ ˌsizn

low season[2]
noun
BR ˈləʊ ˌsiːzn, -z
AM ˈloʊ ˌsizn, -z

lox
BR lɒks
AM lɑks

Loxene
BR ˈlɒksiːn
AM ˈlɑkˌsin

Loxley
BR ˈlɒksli
AM ˈlɑksli

loxodrome
BR ˈlɒksədrəʊm, -z
AM ˈlɑksəˌdroʊm, -z

loxodromic
BR ˌlɒksəˈdrɒmɪk
AM ˌlɑksəˈdrɑmɪk

loyal
BR ˈlɔɪəl
AM ˈlɔɪ(ə)l

loyalism
BR ˈlɔɪəlɪz(ə)m
AM ˈlɔɪ(ə)lˌɪzəm

loyalist
BR ˈlɔɪəlɪst, -s
AM ˈlɔɪ(ə)ləst, -s

loyally
BR ˈlɔɪəli
AM ˈlɔɪ(ə)li

loyalty
BR ˈlɔɪəlt|i, -ɪz
AM ˈlɔɪ(ə)lti, -z

lozenge
BR ˈlɒz(ɨ)n(d)ʒ, -ɨz, -d
AM ˈlɑzəndʒ, -əz, -d

lozengy
BR ˈlɒz(ɨ)ndʒi
AM ˈlɑzəndʒi

Ltd
BR ˈlɪmɪtɨd
AM ˈlɪmɨdɨd

Lualaba
BR ˌluːəˈlɑːbə(r)
AM ˌluəˈlɑbə

Luanda
BR lʊˈandə(r)
AM ləˈwɑndə

Luandan
BR lʊˈandən, -z
AM ləˈwɑndən, -z

Luang Prabang
BR lʊˌaŋ prəˈbaŋ
AM luˈæŋ prəˈbæŋ

luau
BR ˈluːaʊ, -z
AM ˈluˌaʊ, -z

lubber
BR ˈlʌbə(r), -z
AM ˈləbər, -z

lubberlike
BR ˈlʌbəlʌɪk
AM ˈləbərˌlaɪk

lubberly
BR ˈlʌbəli
AM ˈləbərli

Lubbock
BR ˈlʌbək
AM ˈləbək

lube
BR luːb, -z, -ɪŋ, -d
AM lub, -z, -ɪŋ, -d

Lübeck
BR ˈluːbɛk
AM ˈluˌbɛk

Lublin
BR ˈluːblɪn
AM ˈluˌblɪn

lubra
BR ˈl(j)uːbrə(r), -z
AM ˈlubrə, -z

lubricant
BR ˈl(j)uːbrɪk(ə)nt, -s
AM ˈlubrəkənt, -s

lubricate
BR ˈl(j)uːbrɪkeɪt, -s, -ɪŋ, -ɨd
AM ˈlubrəˌkeɪ|t, -ts, -dɪŋ, -dɨd

lubrication
BR ˌl(j)uːbrɪˈkeɪʃn
AM ˌlubrəˈkeɪʃən

lubricative
BR ˈl(j)uːbrɪkətɪv
AM ˈlubrəˌkeɪdɪv

lubricator
BR ˈl(j)uːbrɪkeɪtə(r), -z
AM ˈlubrəˌkeɪdər, -z

lubricious
BR l(j)uːˈbrɪʃəs
AM luˈbrɪʃəs

lubricity
BR l(j)uːˈbrɪsɨti
AM luˈbrɪsɨdi

Lubumbashi
BR ˌlʊbʊmˈbaʃi
AM ˌlubumˈbɑʃi

Lubyanka
BR ˌlʊbɪˈaŋkə(r)
AM lʊˈbjɑŋkə
RUS lʲuˈbʲankə

Lucan
BR ˈluːk(ə)n
AM ˈlukən

Lucania
BR luːˈkeɪnɪə(r)
AM luˈkeɪnɪə

lucarne
BR ˈl(j)uːkɑːn, -z
AM luˈkɑrn, -z

Lucas
BR ˈluːkəs
AM ˈlukəs

luce
BR luːs
AM lus

lucency
BR ˈluːsnsi
AM ˈlusənsi

lucent
BR ˈluːsnt
AM ˈlusənt

lucently
BR ˈluːsntli
AM ˈlusn(t)li

Lucerne
BR luːˈsəːn
AM luˈsərn

Lucey
BR ˈluːsi
AM ˈlusi

Lucia[1]
Italian
BR lʊˈtʃiːə(r)
AM lʊˈtʃiə

Lucia[2]
BR ˈluːsɪə(r), ˈluːʃ(ɪ)ə(r)
AM ˈluʃə

Lucian
BR ˈluːʃɪən, ˈluːsɪən, ˈluːʃ(ə)n
AM ˈluʃən

lucid
BR ˈl(j)uːsɪd
AM ˈlusəd

lucidity
BR l(j)uːˈsɪdɨti
AM luˈsɪdɨdi

lucidly
BR ˈl(j)uːsɪdli
AM ˈlusədli

lucidness
BR ˈl(j)uːsɪdnɨs
AM ˈlusədnəs

Lucie
BR ˈluːsi
AM ˈlusi

Lucifer
BR ˈl(j)uːsɪfə(r), -z
AM ˈlusəfər, -z

lucifer
BR ˈl(j)uːsɪfə(r), -z
AM ˈlusəfər, -z

luciferin
BR l(j)uːˈsɪf(ə)rɪn
AM luˈsɪf(ə)rən

Lucille
BR luːˈsiːl
AM luˈsil

Lucinda
BR luːˈsɪndə(r)
AM luˈsɪndə

Lucite®
BR ˈluːsʌɪt
AM ˈluˌsaɪt

Lucius
BR ˈluːsɪəs, ˈluːʃəs
AM ˈluʃəs

luck
BR lʌk
AM lək

luckily
BR ˈlʌkɨli
AM ˈləkəli

luckiness
BR ˈlʌkɪnɨs
AM ˈləkinɨs

luckless
BR ˈlʌkləs
AM ˈləkləs

lucklessly
BR ˈlʌkləsli
AM ˈləkləsli

lucklessness
BR ˈlʌkləsnəs
AM ˈləkləsənəs

Lucknow
BR ˈlʌknaʊ
AM ˈləknaʊ

lucky
BR ˈlʌk|i, -ɪə(r), -ɪɨst
AM ˈləki, -ər, -ɨst

Lucozade®
BR ˈluːkəzeɪd
AM ˈlukəˌzeɪd

lucrative
BR ˈl(j)uːkrətɪv
AM ˈlukrədɪv

lucratively
BR ˈl(j)uːkrətɪvli
AM ˈlukrədəvli

lucrativeness
BR ˈl(j)uːkrətɪvnɪs
AM ˈlukrədɪvnɨs

lucre
BR 'l(j)uːkə(r)
AM 'lukər
Lucrece
BR l(j)uː'kriːs
AM lu'kris
Lucretia
BR l(j)uː'kriːʃə(r)
AM lu'kriʃə
Lucretius
BR l(j)uː'kriːʃəs
AM lu'kriʃəs
lucubrate
BR 'l(j)uːkjʉbreɪt, -s, -ɪŋ, -ɨd
AM 'luk(j)əˌbreɪ|t, -ts, -dɪŋ, -dɨd
lucubration
BR ˌl(j)uːkjʉ'breɪʃn
AM ˌluk(j)ə'breɪʃən
lucubrator
BR 'l(j)uːkjʉbreɪtə(r), -z
AM 'luk(j)əˌbreɪdər, -z
luculent
BR 'luːkjʉl(ə)nt
AM 'lukjələnt
luculently
BR 'luːkjʉl(ə)ntli
AM 'lukjələn(t)li
Lucullan
adjective
BR l(j)uː'kʌlən
AM lu'kələn
Lucy
BR 'luːsi
AM 'lusi
Lūda
BR 'luːdə(*r*)
AM 'lʊdə
Luddism
BR 'lʌdɪz(ə)m
AM 'ləˌdɪzəm
Luddite
BR 'lʌdʌɪt, -s
AM 'ləˌdaɪt, -s
Ludditism
BR 'lʌdʌɪtɪz(ə)m
AM 'lədəˌtɪzəm
lude
BR luːd, -z
AM lud, -z
Ludendorff
BR 'luːndɔːf
AM 'ludnˌdɔ(ə)rf
Ludgate
BR 'lʌdgət, 'lʌdgeɪt
AM 'lədgət, 'ləd,geɪt
ludic
BR 'l(j)uːdɪk
AM 'l(j)udɪk
ludicrous
BR 'l(j)uːdɪkrəs
AM 'ludəkrəs
ludicrously
BR 'l(j)uːdɪkrəsli
AM 'ludəkrəsli
ludicrousness
BR 'l(j)uːdɪkrəsnəs
AM 'ludəkrəsnəs
Ludlow
BR 'lʌdləʊ
AM 'ləd,loʊ
Ludlum
BR 'lʌdləm
AM 'lədləm
ludo
BR 'l(j)uːdəʊ
AM 'luˌdoʊ
Ludovic
BR 'luːdəvɪk
AM 'ludəˌvɪk
Ludwig
BR 'lʊdwɪg, 'lʊdvɪg
AM 'lʊdˌwɪg
lues
lues venerea
BR 'l(j)uːiːz
AM 'luiz
luetic
BR l(j)uː'iːtɪk, l(j)uː'ɛtɪk
AM lu'idɪk
luff
BR lʌf, -s, -ɪŋ, -t
AM ləf, -s, -ɪŋ, -t
luffa
BR 'lʌfə(*r*), -z
AM 'ləfə, -z
Luftwaffe
BR 'lʊftˌwafə(*r*), 'lʊftˌvafə(*r*), 'lʊftˌwɑːfə(*r*), 'lʊftˌvɑːfə(*r*)
AM 'lʊf(t)ˌwɑfə
lug
BR lʌg, -z, -ɪŋ, -d
AM ləg, -z, -ɪŋ, -d
Lugano
BR luː'gɑːnəʊ
AM lu'gɑnoʊ
Lugard
BR 'luːgɑːd
AM 'luˌgɑrd
luge
BR luː(d)ʒ, -ɨz, -ɪŋ, -d
AM luʒ, -əz, -ɪŋ, -d
Luger®
BR 'luːgə(r), -z
AM 'lugər, -z
luggable
BR 'lʌgəbl
AM 'ləgəbəl
luggage
BR 'lʌgɪdʒ
AM 'ləgɪdʒ
lugger
BR 'lʌgə(r), -z
AM 'ləgər, -z
lughole
BR 'lʌghəʊl, -z
AM 'ləg,(h)oʊl, -z
lugsail
BR 'lʌgseɪl, 'lʌgsl, -z
AM 'ləgsəl, 'ləgˌseɪl, -z
lugubrious
BR lʉ'g(j)uːbrɪəs
AM lu'gubriəs, lə'gubriəs
lugubriously
BR lʉ'g(j)uːbrɪəsli
AM lu'gubriəsli
lugubriousness
BR lʉ'g(j)uːbrɪəsnəs
AM lu'gubriəsnəs
lugworm
BR 'lʌgwəːm, -z
AM 'ləgˌwərm, -z
Luick
BR 'luːɪk
AM 'luwɪk
Lukács
BR 'luːkatʃ
AM 'luˌkɑtʃ
Luke
BR luːk
AM luk
lukewarm
BR ˌluːk'wɔːm
AM 'luk'wɔ(ə)rm
lukewarmly
BR ˌluːk'wɔːmli
AM 'luk'wɔrmli
lukewarmness
BR ˌluːk'wɔːmnəs
AM 'luk'wɔrmnəs
lull
BR lʌl, -z, -ɪŋ, -d
AM ləl, -z, -ɪŋ, -d
lullaby
BR 'lʌləbʌɪ, -z
AM 'lələˌbaɪ, -z
Lully
BR 'lʊli
AM lʊ'li
lulu
BR 'luːluː, -z
AM 'luˌlu, -z
Lulworth
BR 'lʌlwəθ, 'lʌlwəːθ
AM 'ləlˌwərθ
lum
BR lʌm, -z
AM ləm, -z
Lumb
BR lʌm
AM ləm
lumbago
BR lʌm'beɪgəʊ
AM ˌləm'beɪˌgoʊ
lumbar
BR 'lʌmbə(r)
AM 'ləmˌbɑr, 'ləmbər
lumber
BR 'lʌmb|ə(r), -əz, -(ə)rɪŋ, -əd
AM 'ləmb|ər, -ərz, -(ə)rɪŋ, -ərd
lumberer
BR 'lʌmb(ə)rə(r), -z
AM 'ləmbərər, -z
lumberjack
BR 'lʌmbədʒak, -s
AM 'ləmbərˌdʒæk, -s
lumberman
BR 'lʌmbəmən, 'lʌmbəman
AM 'ləmbərmən
lumbermen
BR 'lʌmbəmən, 'lʌmbəmɛn
AM 'ləmbərmən
lumbersome
BR 'lʌmbəs(ə)m
AM 'ləmbərsəm
lumberyard
BR 'lʌmbəjɑːd, -z
AM 'ləmbərˌjɑrd, -z
lumbrical
BR 'lʌmbrɪkl
AM 'ləmbrəkəl
lumen
BR 'l(j)uːmɪn, 'l(j)uːmɛn, -z
AM 'lumən, -z
lumière
BR 'luːmɪɛː(r), ˌluːmɪ'ɛː(r)
AM ˌlumi'ɛ(ə)r
luminaire
BR ˌl(j)uːmɪ'nɛː(r), -z
AM ˌlumə'nɛ(ə)r, -z
luminal
BR 'l(j)uːmɪnl
AM 'lumənəl
luminance
BR 'l(j)uːmɪnəns
AM 'lumənəns
luminary
BR 'l(j)uːmɪn(ə)r|i, -ɪz
AM 'luməˌnɛri, -z
luminesce
BR ˌl(j)uːmɪ'nɛs, -ɨz, -ɪŋ, -t
AM ˌlumə'nɛs, -əz, -ɪŋ, -t
luminescence
BR ˌl(j)uːmɪ'nɛsns
AM ˌlumə'nɛsəns
luminescent
BR ˌl(j)uːmɪ'nɛsnt
AM ˌlumə'nɛsənt
luminiferous
BR ˌl(j)uːmɪ'nɪf(ə)rəs
AM ˌlumə'nɪf(ə)rəs
luminosity
BR ˌl(j)uːmɪ'nɒsɪti
AM ˌlumə'nɑsədi
luminous
BR 'l(j)uːmɪnəs
AM 'lumənəs
luminously
BR 'l(j)uːmɪnəsli
AM 'lumənəsli
luminousness
BR 'l(j)uːmɪnəsnəs
AM 'lumənəsnəs
Lumley
BR 'lʌmli

AM 'ləmli
lumme
BR 'lʌmi
AM 'ləmi
lummox
BR 'lʌməks, -ɪz
AM 'ləməks, -əz
lummy
BR 'lʌmi
AM 'ləmi
lump
BR lʌm|p, -ps, -pɪŋ, -(p)t
AM ləmp, -s, -ɪŋ, -t
lumpectomy
BR ˌlʌm'pɛktəm|i, -ɪz
AM ˌləm'pɛktəmi, -z
lumpen
BR 'lʌmpən
AM 'ləmpən
lumpenproletariat
BR ˌlʌmpənˌprəʊlɪ'tɛːrɪət
AM ˌləmpənˌproʊlə'tɛriət
lumper
BR 'lʌmpə(r), -z
AM 'ləmpər, -z
lumpfish
BR 'lʌmpfɪʃ, -ɪz
AM 'ləm(p)ˌfɪʃ, -ɪz
lumpily
BR 'lʌmpɨli
AM 'ləmpəli
lumpiness
BR 'lʌmpɪnɨs
AM 'ləmpinɨs
lumpish
BR 'lʌmpɪʃ
AM 'ləmpɪʃ
lumpishly
BR 'lʌmpɨʃli
AM 'ləmpɨʃli
lumpishness
BR 'lʌmpɨʃnɨs
AM 'ləmpɪʃnɨs
lumpsucker
BR 'lʌmpˌsʌkə(r), -z
AM 'ləm(p)ˌsəkər, -z
lumpy
BR 'lʌmp|i, -ɪə(r), -ɪɪst
AM 'ləmpi, -ər, -ɨst
Lumsden
BR 'lʌmzd(ə)n
AM 'ləmzdən
Luna
BR 'luːnə(*r*)
AM 'lunə
lunacy
BR 'luːnəs|i, -ɪz
AM 'lunəsi, -z
lunar
BR 'luːnə(r)
AM 'lunər
lunate
BR 'luːneɪt, 'luːnət
AM 'luˌneɪt
lunatic
BR 'luːnətɪk, -s
AM 'lunəˌtɪk, -s
lunation
BR luː'neɪʃn, -z
AM lu'neɪʃən, -z
lunch
BR lʌn(t)ʃ, -ɪz, -ɪŋ, -t
AM lən(t)ʃ, -əz, -ɪŋ, -t
luncheon
BR 'lʌn(t)ʃ(ə)n, -z
AM 'lən(t)ʃən, -z
luncheonette
BR ˌlʌn(t)ʃə'nɛt, ˌlʌn(t)ʃn'ɛt, -s
AM ˌlən(t)ʃə'nɛt, -s
luncher
BR 'lʌn(t)ʃə(r), -z
AM 'lən(t)ʃər, -z
lunchroom
BR 'lʌn(t)ʃruːm, 'lʌn(t)ʃrʊm, -z
AM 'lən(t)ʃˌrum, 'lən(t)ʃˌrʊm, -z
lunchtime
BR 'lʌn(t)ʃtʌɪm, -z
AM 'lən(t)ʃˌtaɪm, -z
Lund[1]
place in Sweden
BR lʊnd
AM lʊnd
Lund[2]
surname
BR lʌnd
AM lənd
Lundy
BR 'lʌndi
AM 'ləndi
lune
BR luːn, -z
AM lun, -z
lunette
BR luː'nɛt, -s
AM lu'nɛt, -s
lung
BR lʌŋ, -z, -d
AM ləŋ, -z, -d
lunge
BR lʌn(d)ʒ, -ɪz, -ɪŋ, -d
AM ləndʒ, -əz, -ɪŋ, -d
lungfish
BR 'lʌŋfɪʃ, -ɪz
AM 'ləŋˌfɪʃ, -ɪz
lungful
BR 'lʌŋfʊl, -z
AM 'ləŋˌfʊl, -z
lungi
BR 'lʌŋg|i, 'lʊŋg|i, -ɪz
AM 'ləŋgi, -z
lungless
BR 'lʌŋləs
AM 'ləŋləs
lungworm
BR 'lʌŋwəːm, -z
AM 'ləŋwərm, -z
lungwort
BR 'lʌŋwəːt, -s
AM 'ləŋwərt, 'ləŋwɔ(ə)rt, -s
lunisolar
BR ˌluːnɪ'səʊlə(r)
AM 'luni'soʊlər
lunker
BR 'lʌŋkə(r), -z
AM 'ləŋkər, -z
lunkhead
BR 'lʌŋkhɛd, -z
AM 'ləŋkˌ(h)ɛd, -z
Lunn
BR lʌn
AM lən
Lunt
BR lʌnt
AM lənt
lunula
BR 'luːnjʉlə(*r*)
AM 'lunjələ
lunulae
BR 'luːnjʉliː
AM 'lunjəˌli, 'lunjəˌlaɪ
Luo
BR 'luːəʊ
AM 'luˌoʊ
Lupercalia
BR ˌluːpə'keɪlɪə(*r*)
AM ˌlupər'keɪljə, ˌlupər'keɪliə
lupiform
BR 'luːpɨfɔːm
AM 'lupəˌfɔ(ə)rm
lupin
BR 'luːpɪn, -z
AM 'lupən, -z
lupine[1]
flower
BR 'luːpɪn, -z
AM 'lupən, -z
lupine[2]
wolf-like
BR 'l(j)uːpʌɪn
AM 'luˌpaɪn
lupoid
BR 'l(j)uːpɔɪd
AM 'luˌpɔɪd
lupous
BR 'l(j)uːpəs
AM 'lupəs
lupus
BR 'l(j)uːpəs
AM 'lupəs
lupus vulgaris
BR ˌl(j)uːpəs vʌl'gɑːrɪs, + vʌl'gɛːrɪs
AM ˌlupəs vəl'gɛrəs
lur
BR lʊə(r), ləː(r), -z
AM lʊ(ə)r, -z
lurch
BR ləːtʃ, -ɪz, -ɪŋ, -t
AM lərtʃ, -əz, -ɪŋ, -t
lurcher
BR 'ləːtʃə(r), -z
AM 'lərtʃər, -z
lure
BR l(j)ʊə(r), ljɔː(r), -z, -ɪŋ, -d
AM lʊ(ə)r, -z, -ɪŋ, -d
Lurex®
BR 'l(j)ʊərɛks, 'ljɔːrɛks
AM 'lʊˌrɛks
lurgy
BR 'ləːg|i, -ɪz
AM 'lərgi, -z
lurid
BR 'l(j)ʊərɪd, 'ljɔːrɪd
AM 'lʊrəd
luridly
BR 'l(j)ʊərɪdli, 'ljɔːrɪdli
AM 'lʊrədli
luridness
BR 'l(j)ʊərɪdnɪs, 'ljɔːrɪdnɪs
AM 'lʊrədnəs
luringly
BR 'l(j)ʊərɪŋli, 'ljɔːrɪŋli
AM 'lʊrɪŋli
lurk
BR ləːk, -s, -ɪŋ, -t
AM lərk, -s, -ɪŋ, -t
lurker
BR 'ləːkə(r), -z
AM 'lərkər, -z
Lurpak®
BR 'ləːpak
AM 'lərˌpæk
Lusaka
BR lʉ'sɑːkə(*r*)
AM lʊ'sɑkə
luscious
BR 'lʌʃəs
AM 'ləʃəs
lusciously
BR 'lʌʃəsli
AM 'ləʃəsli
lusciousness
BR 'lʌʃəsnəs
AM 'ləʃəsnəs
lush
BR lʌʃ, -ɪz
AM ləʃ, -əz
lushly
BR 'lʌʃli
AM 'ləʃli
lushness
BR 'lʌʃnəs
AM 'ləʃnəs
Lusiad
BR 'l(j)uːsɪad
AM 'luziˌæd
Lusitania
BR ˌluːsɪ'teɪnɪə(*r*)
AM ˌlusə'teɪniə, ˌluzə'teɪniə
lust
BR lʌst, -s, -ɪŋ, -ɪd
AM ləst, -s, -ɪŋ, -əd

luster
BR 'lʌstə(r), -z
AM 'ləstər, -z

lustful
BR 'lʌs(t)f(ʊ)l
AM 'ləs(t)fəl

lustfully
BR 'lʌs(t)fʊli, 'lʌs(t)fl̩i
AM 'ləs(t)fəli

lustfulness
BR 'lʌs(t)f(ʊ)lnəs
AM 'ləs(t)fəlnəs

lustily
BR 'lʌstɨli
AM 'ləstəli

lustiness
BR 'lʌstɪnɪs
AM 'ləstinɪs

lustra
BR 'lʌstrə(r)
AM 'ləstrə

lustral
BR 'lʌstr(ə)l
AM 'ləstrəl

lustrate
BR lʌ'streɪt, 'lʌstreɪt, -s, -ɪŋ, -ɨd
AM 'ləˌstreɪ|t, -ts, -dɪŋ, -dɨd

lustration
BR lʌ'streɪʃn, -z
AM lə'streɪʃən, -z

lustre
BR 'lʌstə(r), -z
AM 'ləstər, -z

lustreless
BR 'lʌstələs
AM 'ləstərləs

lustreware
BR 'lʌstəwɛː(r), -z
AM 'ləstərˌwɛ(ə)r, -z

lustrous
BR 'lʌstrəs
AM 'ləstrəs

lustrously
BR 'lʌstrəsli
AM 'ləstrəsli

lustrousness
BR 'lʌstrəsnəs
AM 'ləstrəsnəs

lustrum
BR 'lʌstrəm, -z
AM 'ləstrəm, -z

lusty
BR 'lʌst|i, -ɪə(r), -ɪɪst
AM 'ləsti, -ər, -ɨst

lusus
BR 'l(j)uːsəs
AM 'lusəs

lutanist
BR 'l(j)uːtənɪst, 'l(j)uːtn̩ɪst, -s
AM 'lutn̩əst, -s

lute
BR l(j)uːt, -s
AM lut, -s

luteal
BR 'l(j)uːtɪəl
AM 'ludiəl

lutecium
BR l(j)uː'tɛʃ(ɪ)əm, l(j)uː'tiːsɪəm
AM lu'tiʃ(i)əm, lu'tisiəm

lutein
BR 'l(j)uːtɪɪn, -z
AM 'ludiən, -z

luteinize
BR 'l(j)uːtɪɨnʌɪz, -ɨz, -ɪŋ, -d
AM 'ludiəˌnaɪz, -ɨz, -ɪŋ, -d

lutenist
BR 'l(j)uːtɨnɪst, 'l(j)uːtn̩ɪst, -s
AM 'lutn̩əst, -s

luteofulvous
BR ˌl(j)uːtɪəʊ'fʌlvəs
AM ˌludioʊ'fəlvəs

luteous
BR 'l(j)uːtɪəs
AM 'ludiəs

lutestring
BR 'l(j)uːtstrɪŋ, -z
AM 'lutˌstrɪŋ, -z

lutetium
BR l(j)uː'tiːʃɪəm, l(j)uː'tiːsɪəm
AM lu'tiʃ(i)əm, lu'tisiəm

Luther
BR 'luːθə(r)
AM 'luθər

Lutheran
BR 'luːθ(ə)rən, 'luːθ(ə)rn̩, -z
AM 'luθ(ə)rən, 'luθərn, -z

Lutheranise
BR 'luːθ(ə)rənʌɪz, 'luːθ(ə)rn̩ʌɪz, -ɨz, -ɪŋ, -d
AM 'luθ(ə)rəˌnaɪz, -ɨz, -ɪŋ, -d

Lutheranism
BR 'luːθ(ə)rənɪz(ə)m, 'luːθ(ə)rn̩ɪz(ə)m
AM 'ləθ(ə)rəˌnɪzəm

Lutheranize
BR 'luːθ(ə)rənʌɪz, 'luːθ(ə)rn̩ʌɪz, -ɨz, -ɪŋ, -d
AM 'luθ(ə)rəˌnaɪz, -ɨz, -ɪŋ, -d

Lutine Bell
BR ˌluːtiːn 'bɛl
AM 'luˌtin 'bɛl

luting
BR 'l(j)uːtɪŋ, -z
AM 'ludɪŋ, -z

Luton
BR 'luːtn
AM 'lutn

Lutterworth
BR 'lʌtəwəθ, 'lʌtəwəːθ
AM 'lədərˌwərθ

Lutyens
BR 'lʌtjənz
AM 'lətjɛnz

Lutz
BR lʊts, luːts, -ɨz
AM lʊts, -əz

luv
BR lʌv, -z
AM ləv, -z

luvvie
BR 'lʌv|i, -ɪz
AM 'ləvi, -z

luvvy
BR 'lʌv|i, -ɪz
AM 'ləvi, -z

lux
BR lʌks
AM ləks

luxate
BR lʌk'seɪt, 'lʌkseɪt, -s, -ɪŋ, -ɨd
AM 'ləkˌseɪ|t, -ts, -dɪŋ, -dɨd

luxation
BR lʌk'seɪʃn
AM lək'seɪʃən

luxe
BR lʌks, lʊks
AM ləks

Luxembourg
BR 'lʌks(ə)mbəːg
AM 'ləksəmˌbərg

Luxembourger
BR 'lʌks(ə)mbəːgə(r), -z
AM 'ləksəmˌbərgər, -z

Luxemburg
BR 'lʌks(ə)mbəːg
AM 'ləksəmˌbərg

Luxemburger
BR 'lʌks(ə)mbəːgə(r), -z
AM 'ləksəmˌbərgər, -z

Luxemburgish
BR 'luːks(ə)mbəːgɪʃ
AM 'ləksəmˌbərgɪʃ

Luxor
BR 'lʌksɔː(r)
AM 'ləkˌsɔ(ə)r

luxuriance
BR lʌg'ʒʊərɪəns, ləg'ʒʊərɪəns, lʌg'zjʊərɪəns, ləg'zjʊərɪəns, lʌk'sjʊərɪəns, lək'sjʊərɪəns
AM ləg'ʒʊriəns, lək'ʃʊriəns

luxuriant
BR lʌg'ʒʊərɪənt, ləg'ʒʊərɪənt, lʌg'zjʊərɪənt, ləg'zjʊərɪənt, lʌk'sjʊərɪənt, lək'sjʊərɪənt
AM ləg'ʒʊriənt, lək'ʃʊriənt

luxuriantly
BR lʌg'ʒʊərɪəntli, ləg'ʒʊərɪəntli, lʌg'zjʊərɪəntli, ləg'zjʊərɪəntli, lʌk'sjʊərɪəntli, lək'sjʊərɪəntli
AM ləg'ʒʊriən(t)li, lək'ʃʊriən(t)li

luxuriate
BR lʌg'ʒʊərɪeɪt, ləg'ʒʊərɪeɪt, lʌg'zjʊərɪeɪt, ləg'zjʊərɪeɪt, lʌk'sjʊərɪeɪt, lək'sjʊərɪeɪt, -s, -ɪŋ, -ɨd
AM ləg'ʒʊriˌeɪ|t, lək'ʃʊriˌeɪ|t, -ts, -dɪŋ, -dɨd

luxurious
BR lʌg'ʒʊərɪəs, ləg'ʒʊərɪəs, lʌg'zjʊərɪəs, ləg'zjʊərɪəs, lʌk'sjʊərɪəs, lək'sjʊərɪəs
AM ləg'ʒʊriəs, lək'ʃʊriəs

luxuriously
BR lʌg'ʒʊərɪəsli, ləg'ʒʊərɪəsli, lʌg'zjʊərɪəsli, ləg'zjʊərɪəsli, lʌk'sjʊərɪəsli, lək'sjʊərɪəsli
AM ləg'ʒʊriəsli, lək'ʃʊriəsli

luxuriousness
BR lʌg'ʒʊərɪəsnəs, ləg'ʒʊərɪəsnəs, lʌg'zjʊərɪəsnəs, ləg'zjʊərɪəsnəs, lʌk'sjʊərɪəsnəs, lək'sjʊərɪəsnəs
AM ləg'ʒʊriəsnəs, lək'ʃʊriəsnəs

luxury
BR 'lʌkʃ(ə)r|i, -ɪz
AM 'ləkʃ(ə)ri, 'ləgʒ(ə)ri, -z

Luzon
BR ˌluː'zɒn
AM ˌlu'zɑn

Lvov
BR lvɒv
AM 'l(ə)vɔv, 'l(ə)vɑv

lwei
BR lweɪ, lə'weɪ, -z
AM lə'weɪ, -z

Lyall
BR 'lʌɪ(ə)l
AM 'laɪəl

lycanthrope
BR 'lʌɪk(ə)nθrəʊp, -s
AM 'laɪkənˌθroʊp, -s

lycanthropy
BR lʌɪ'kanθrəpi
AM laɪ'kænθrəpi

lycée
BR ˈliːseɪ, -z
AM liˈseɪ, -z

lyceum
BR lʌɪˈsiːəm, -z
AM ˈlaɪˌsiəm, -z

lychee
BR lʌɪˈtʃiː, ˈlʌɪtʃiː, ˈliːtʃiː, ˈlɪtʃiː, -z
AM ˈlitʃi, -z

lychgate
BR ˈlɪtʃɡeɪt, -s
AM ˈlɪtʃˌɡeɪt, -s

lychnis
BR ˈlɪknɪs
AM ˈlɪknɨs

Lycia
BR ˈlɪsɪə(*r*)
AM ˈlɪʃə, ˈlɪʃiə

Lycian
BR ˈlɪsɪən, -z
AM ˈlɪʃən, ˈlɪʃiən, -z

Lycidas
BR ˈlɪsɪdas
AM ˈlɪsɨdəs

lycopene
BR ˈlʌɪkə(ʊ)piːn
AM ˈlaɪkəˌpin

lycopod
BR ˈlʌɪkəpɒd, -z
AM ˈlaɪkəˌpɑd, -z

lycopodium
BR ˌlʌɪkə(ʊ)ˈpəʊdɪəm
AM ˌlaɪkəˈpoʊdiəm

Lycra®
BR ˈlʌɪkrə(*r*)
AM ˈlaɪkrə

Lycurgus
BR lʌɪˈkəːɡəs
AM laɪˈkərɡəs

Lydd
BR lɪd
AM lɪd

lyddite
BR ˈlɪdʌɪt
AM ˈlɪˌdaɪt

Lydgate
BR ˈlɪdɡeɪt
AM ˈlɪdˌɡeɪt, ˈlɪdɡət

Lydia
BR ˈlɪdɪə(*r*)
AM ˈlɪdiə

Lydian
BR ˈlɪdɪən, -z
AM ˈlɪdiən, -z

lye
BR lʌɪ
AM laɪ

Lyell
BR ˈlʌɪ(ə)l
AM ˈlaɪ(ə)l

Lygon
BR ˈlɪɡ(ə)n
AM ˈlɪɡən

lying
BR ˈlʌɪɪŋ
AM ˈlaɪɪŋ

lyingly
BR ˈlʌɪɪŋli
AM ˈlaɪɪŋli

lyke wake
BR ˈlʌɪk weɪk, -s
AM ˈlaɪk ˌweɪk, -s

Lyle
BR lʌɪl
AM laɪl

Lyly
BR ˈlɪli
AM ˈlɪli

Lyme disease
BR ˈlʌɪm dɪˌziːz
AM ˈlaɪm dəˌziz

lyme-grass
BR ˈlʌɪmɡrɑːs, ˈlʌɪmɡras
AM ˈlaɪmˌɡræs

Lyme Regis
BR ˌlʌɪm ˈriːdʒɪs
AM ˌlaɪm ˈridʒɪs

Lymington
BR ˈlɪmɪŋt(ə)n
AM ˈlɪmɪŋtən

Lymm
BR lɪm
AM lɪm

lymph
BR lɪmf
AM lɪmf

lymphadenitis
BR ˌlɪmfadɪˈnʌɪtɪs
AM ˌlɪmfædn̩ˈaɪdɪs

lymphadenopathy syndrome
BR ˌlɪmfadɪˈnɒpəθɪ ˌsɪndrəʊm
AM ˌlɪmˌfædn̩ˈɑpəθi ˌsɪnˌdroʊm

lymphangitis
BR ˌlɪmfanˈdʒʌɪtɪs
AM ˌlɪmfændʒaɪdɪs

lymphatic
BR lɪmˈfatɪk
AM lɪmˈfædɪk

lymphocyte
BR ˈlɪmfə(ʊ)sʌɪt, -s
AM ˈlɪmfəˌsaɪt, -s

lymphocytic
BR ˌlɪmfə(ʊ)ˈsɪtɪk
AM ˌlɪmfəˈsɪdɪk

lymphoid
BR ˈlɪmfɔɪd
AM ˈlɪmˌfɔɪd

lymphoma
BR lɪmˈfəʊmə(*r*), -z
AM lɪmˈfoʊmə, -z

lymphomata
BR lɪmˈfəʊmətə(*r*)
AM lɪmˈfoʊmədə

lymphopathy
BR lɪmˈfɒpəθ|i, -ɪz
AM lɪmˈfɑpəθi, -z

lymphous
BR ˈlɪmfəs
AM ˈlɪmfəs

Lympne
BR lɪm
AM lɪm

Lyn
BR lɪn
AM lɪn

Lynam
BR ˈlʌɪnəm
AM ˈlaɪnəm

lyncean
BR lɪnˈsiːən
AM lɪnˈsiən, ˈlɪnsiən

lynch
BR lɪn(t)ʃ, -ɨz, -ɪŋ, -t
AM lɪn(t)ʃ, -ɨz, -ɪŋ, -t

lyncher
BR ˈlɪn(t)ʃə(r), -z
AM ˈlɪn(t)ʃər, -z

lynchet
BR ˈlɪn(t)ʃɪt, -s
AM ˈlɪn(t)ʃɨt, -s

lynching
BR ˈlɪn(t)ʃɪŋ, -z
AM ˈlɪn(t)ʃɪŋ, -z

lynchpin
BR ˈlɪn(t)ʃpɪn, -z
AM ˈlɪn(t)ʃˌpɪn, -z

Lynda
BR ˈlɪndə(*r*)
AM ˈlɪndə

Lynette
BR lɪˈnɛt
AM lɪˈnɛt

Lynmouth
BR ˈlɪnməθ
AM ˈlɪnməθ

Lynn
BR lɪn
AM lɪn

Lynne
BR lɪn
AM lɪn

Lynsey
BR ˈlɪnzi
AM ˈlɪnzi

Lynton
BR ˈlɪntən
AM ˈlɪn(t)ən

lynx
BR lɪŋks, -ɨz
AM lɪŋks, -ɨz

lynxlike
BR ˈlɪŋkslʌɪk
AM ˈlɪŋksˌlaɪk

Lyon
BR ˈlʌɪən
AM ˈlaɪən

Lyonnais
BR ˌliːəˈneɪz, ˌlʌɪəˈneɪz
AM ˌlaɪəˈneɪz, ˌliəˈneɪz

lyonnaise
BR ˌliːəˈneɪz, ˌlʌɪəˈneɪz
AM ˌlaɪəˈneɪz, ˌliəˈneɪz

Lyonnesse
BR ˌlʌɪəˈnɛs
AM ˌlaɪəˈnɛs

Lyons¹
place in France
BR ˈliːɒ̃
AM liˈɔn, liˈɑn

Lyons²
surname
BR ˈlʌɪənz
AM ˈlaɪənz

lyophilic
BR ˌlʌɪə(ʊ)ˈfɪlɪk
AM ˌlaɪəˈfɪlɪk

lyophilise
BR lʌɪˈɒfɨlʌɪz, -ɨz, -ɪŋ, -d
AM laɪˈɑfɪlaɪz, -z, -ɪŋ, -d

lyophilize
BR lʌɪˈɒfɨlʌɪz, -ɨz, -ɪŋ, -d
AM laɪˈɑfɪlaɪz, -z, -ɪŋ, -d

lyophobic
BR ˌlʌɪə(ʊ)ˈfəʊbɪk
AM ˌlaɪəˈfoʊbɪk

Lyra
BR ˈlʌɪrə(*r*)
AM ˈlaɪrə

lyrate
BR ˈlʌɪreɪt, ˈlʌɪrət
AM ˈlaɪˌreɪt, ˈlaɪrət

lyre
BR ˈlʌɪə(r), -z
AM ˈlaɪ(ə)r, -z

lyrebird
BR ˈlʌɪəbəːd, -z
AM ˈlaɪrˌbərd, -z

lyric
BR ˈlɪrɪk, -s
AM ˈlɪrɪk, -s

lyrical
BR ˈlɪrɨkl
AM ˈlɪrɨkəl

lyrically
BR ˈlɪrɨkli
AM ˈlɪrɨk(ə)li

lyricism
BR ˈlɪrɨsɪz(ə)m
AM ˈlɪrəˌsɪzəm

lyricist
BR ˈlɪrɨsɪst, -s
AM ˈlɪrəsəst, -s

lyrist¹
lyre player
BR ˈlʌɪ(ə)rɪst, -s
AM ˈlaɪ(ə)rɨst, -s

lyrist²
lyricist
BR ˈlɪrɪst, -s
AM ˈlɪrɨst, -s

Lysander
BR lʌɪˈsandə(r)
AM laɪˈsændər

lyse
BR lʌɪz, -ɨz, -ɪŋ, -d
AM laɪs, laɪz, -ɨz, -ɪŋ, -d

Lysenko
BR lɪˈsɛŋkəʊ, lʌɪˈsɛŋkəʊ
AM laɪˈsɛnkoʊ

lysergic
BR lʌɪˈsəːdʒɪk
AM laɪˈsərdʒɪk

Lysias
BR ˈlɪsɪas
AM ˈlɪsiəs

lysin
BR ˈlʌɪsɪn
AM ˈlaɪsn

lysine
BR ˈlʌɪsiːn
AM ˈlaɪˌsin

Lysippus
BR lʌɪˈsɪpəs
AM ˈlaɪˈsɪpəs

lysis
BR ˈlʌɪsɪs
AM ˈlaɪsɪs

Lysistrata
BR lʌɪˈsɪstrətə(*r*)
AM ˌlɪsɪˈstrɑdə

Lysol®
BR ˈlʌɪsɒl
AM ˈlaɪˌsɔl, ˈlaɪˌsɑl

lysosome
BR ˈlʌɪsə(ʊ)səʊm, -z
AM ˈlaɪsəˌsoʊm, -z

lysozyme
BR ˈlʌɪsə(ʊ)zʌɪm
AM ˈlaɪzəˌzaɪm

Lytham
BR ˈlɪð(ə)m
AM ˈlɪθəm

lytic
BR ˈlɪtɪk
AM ˈlɪdɪk

lytta
BR ˈlɪtə(*r*)
AM ˈlɪdə

lyttae
BR ˈlɪtiː
AM ˈlɪdi, ˈliˌtaɪ

Lyttleton
BR ˈlɪtlt(ə)n
AM ˈlɪdltən

Lytton
BR ˈlɪtn
AM ˈlɪtn

Mm

m
BR ɛm, -z
AM ɛm, -z
M.A.
BR ˌɛm'eɪ, -z
AM ɛ'meɪ, -z
ma
BR mɑː(r), -z
AM mɑ, -z
ma'am
BR mɑːm, mam, məm
AM mæm
maar
BR mɑː(r), -z
AM mɑr, -z
Maas
BR mɑːs
AM mɑs
Maastricht
BR 'mɑːstrɪxt, 'mɑːstrɪkt
AM 'mɑstrɪk(t)
Maat
BR mɑːt
AM mɑt
Mabel
BR 'meɪbl
AM 'meɪbəl
Mabinogion
BR ˌmabɪ'nɒɡɪɒn
AM ˌmæbə'noʊɡiən
mac
BR mak, -s
AM mæk, -s
macabre
BR mə'kɑːbrə(r)
AM mə'kɑbrə, mə'kɑbr
macaco
BR mə'keɪkəʊ, -z
AM mə'kɑˌkoʊ, -z
macadam
BR mə'kadəm
AM mə'kædəm
macadamia
BR ˌmakə'deɪmɪə(r)
AM ˌmækə'deɪmiə
macadamise
BR mə'kadəmʌɪz, -ɪz, -ɪŋ, -d
AM mə'kædəˌmaɪz, -ɪz, -ɪŋ, -d
macadamization
BR məˌkadəmʌɪ'zeɪʃn
AM məˌkædəmə'zeɪʃən, məˌkædəˌmaɪ'zeɪʃən
macadamize
BR mə'kadəmʌɪz, -ɪz, -ɪŋ, -d
AM mə'kædəˌmaɪz, -ɪz, -ɪŋ, -d
Macanese
BR ˌmakə'niːz
AM ˌmækə'niz
Macao
BR mə'kaʊ
AM mə'kaʊ
macaque
BR mə'kɑːk, mə'kak, -s
AM mə'kɑk, mə'kæk, -s
macaroni
BR ˌmakə'rəʊni
AM ˌmækə'roʊni
macaronic
BR ˌmakə'rɒnɪk, -s
AM ˌmækə'rɑnɪk, -s
macaroon
BR ˌmakə'ruːn, -z
AM ˈmækəˈrun, -z
MacArthur
BR mə'kɑːθə(r)
AM mə'kɑrθər
macassar
BR mə'kasə(r)
AM mə'kæsər
Macau
BR mə'kaʊ
AM mə'kaʊ
Macaulay
BR mə'kɔːli
AM mə'kɔli, mə'kɑli
macaw
BR mə'kɔː(r), -z
AM mə'kɔ, mə'kɑ, -z
Macbeth
BR mək'bɛθ, mak'bɛθ
AM mək'bɛθ, ˌmæk'bɛθ
Maccabean
BR ˌmakə'biːən
AM ˈmækəˈbiən
Maccabees
BR 'makəbiːz
AM 'mækəbiz
MacDiarmid
BR mək'dəːmɪd
AM mək'dɛrməd
Macdonald
BR mək'dɒnld
AM mək'dɑnəl(d)
MacDonnell
BR mək'dɒnl
AM mək'dɑnl
mace
BR meɪs, -ɪz
AM meɪs, -ɪz
mace-bearer
BR 'meɪsˌbɛːrə(r), -z
AM 'meɪsˌbɛrər, -z
macédoine
BR ˌmasɪ'dwɑːn, 'masɪdwɑːn, -z
AM ˈmɑsəˈdwɑn, -z
Macedon
BR 'masɪd(ə)n
AM 'mæsədn, 'mæsəˌdɑn
Macedonia
BR ˌmasɪ'dəʊnɪə(r)
AM ˌmæsə'doʊniə
Macedonian
BR ˌmasɪ'dəʊnɪən, -z
AM ˌmæsə'doʊniən, -z
macer
BR 'meɪsə(r), -z
AM 'meɪsər, -z
macerate
BR 'masəreɪt, -s, -ɪŋ, -ɪd
AM 'mæsəˌreɪ|t, -ts, -dɪŋ, -dɪd
maceration
BR ˌmasə'reɪʃn, -z
AM ˌmæsə'reɪʃən, -z
macerator
BR 'masəreɪtə(r), -z
AM 'mæsəˌreɪdər, -z
Macgillicuddy's Reeks
BR məˌɡɪlɪkʌdɪz 'riːks
AM mə'ɡɪləkədiz ˈriks
mach
BR mak, mɑːk
AM mɑk
machete
BR mə'(t)ʃɛt|i, -ɪz
AM mə'(t)ʃɛdi, -z
Machiavelli
BR ˌmakjə'vɛli
AM ˌmɑkiə'vɛli
Machiavellian
BR ˌmakjə'vɛlɪən
AM ˈmɑkiə'vɛljən, ˈmɑkiə'vɛliən
Machiavellianism
BR 'makjə'vɛlɪənɪz(ə)m
AM ˌmɑkiə'vɛljəˌnɪzəm, ˌmɑkiə'vɛliəˌnɪzəm
machicolate
BR mə'tʃɪkəleɪt, -s, -ɪŋ, -ɪd
AM mə'tʃɪkəˌleɪ|t, -ts, -dɪŋ, -dɪd
machicolation
BR məˌtʃɪkə'leɪʃn, -z
AM məˌtʃɪkə'leɪʃən, -z
Machin
BR 'meɪtʃɪn
AM 'meɪtʃ(ɪ)n
machinability
BR məˌʃiːnə'bɪlɪti
AM məˌʃinə'bɪlɪdi
machinable
BR mə'ʃiːnəbl
AM mə'ʃinəbəl
machinate
BR 'makɪneɪt, 'maʃɪneɪt, -s, -ɪŋ, -ɪd
AM 'mækəˌneɪ|t, 'mæʃəˌneɪ|t, -ts, -dɪŋ, -dɪd
machination
BR ˌmakɪ'neɪʃn, ˌmaʃɪ'neɪʃn, -z
AM ˌmækə'neɪʃən, ˌmæʃə'neɪʃən, -z
machinator
BR 'makɪneɪtə(r), 'maʃɪneɪtə(r), -z
AM 'mækəˌneɪdər, 'mæʃəˌneɪdər, -z
machine
BR mə'ʃiːn, -z, -ɪŋ, -d
AM mə'ʃin, -z, -ɪŋ, -d
machinelike
BR mə'ʃiːnlʌɪk
AM mə'ʃinˌlaɪk
machinery
BR mə'ʃiːn(ə)ri
AM mə'ʃin(ə)ri
machinist
BR mə'ʃiːnɪst, -s
AM mə'ʃinɪst, -s
machismo
BR mə'kɪzməʊ, mə'tʃɪzməʊ
AM mə'kɪzmoʊ, mə'tʃɪzmoʊ
Machmeter
BR 'makˌmiːtə(r), 'mɑːkˌmiːtə(r), -z
AM 'mɑkˌmidər, -z
macho
BR 'matʃəʊ
AM 'mɑtʃoʊ
Machu Picchu
BR ˌmatʃuː 'pɪtʃuː
AM ˈmɑtʃu 'pɪ(k)tʃu
Machynlleth
BR mə'xʌnɬəθ, mə'kʌnɬəθ
AM mə'kənləθ
macintosh
BR 'makɪntɒʃ, -ɪz
AM 'mækənˌtɑʃ, -əz
mack
BR mak
AM mæk
Mackay
BR mə'kʌɪ
AM mə'keɪ
Mackenzie
BR mə'kɛnzi
AM mə'kɛnzi
mackerel
BR 'mak(ə)rəl, 'mk(ə)rl̩, -z
AM 'mæk(ə)rəl, -z
Mackeson
BR 'makɪs(ə)n
AM 'mækəsən
Mackey
BR 'maki
AM 'mæki
Mackie
BR 'maki
AM 'mæki
Mackin
BR 'mak(ɪ)n
AM 'mækən
Mackinac
BR 'makɪnɔː(r), -z
AM 'makəˌnɔ, 'makəˌnɑ, -z

mackinaw
BR 'makɪnɔː(r)
AM 'mækəˌnɔ, 'mækəˌnɑ

mackintosh
BR 'makɪntɒʃ, -ɪz
AM 'mækənˌtɑʃ, -əz

mackle
BR 'makl, -z
AM 'mækəl, -z

Maclaren
BR mə'klarən, mə'klarn̩
AM mə'klɛrən

macle
BR 'makl, -z
AM 'mækəl, -z

Maclean
BR mə'kliːn, mə'kleɪn
AM mə'klin

Macleans®
BR mə'kliːnz
AM mə'klinz

MacLehose
BR 'maklhəʊz
AM 'mækl,(h)oʊz

Macleod
BR mə'klaʊd
AM mə'klaʊd

Macmillan
BR mək'mɪlən
AM mək'mɪlən

MacNeice
BR mək'niːs
AM mək'nis

Macon
city in Georgia, US
BR 'meɪk(ə)n
AM 'meɪkən

Mâcon
BR 'makɒ̃, 'mɑːkɒ̃
AM mɑ'kɔn

Maconachie
BR mə'kɒnəki, mə'kɒnəxi
AM mə'kɑnəki

Maconochie
BR mə'kɒnəki, mə'kɒnəxi
AM mə'kɑnəki

Macquarie
BR mə'kwɒri
AM mə'kwɛri, mə'kwɔri

macrame
BR mə'krɑːmi, mə'krɑːmeɪ
AM ˌmækrə'meɪ

macramé
BR mə'krɑːmi, mə'krɑːmeɪ
AM ˌmækrə'meɪ

Macready
BR mə'kriːdi
AM mə'kridi, mək'ridi

macro
BR 'makrəʊ, -z
AM 'mækroʊ, -z

macrobiotic
BR ˌmakrə(ʊ)bʌɪ'ɒtɪk
AM ˌmækroʊbaɪ'ɑdɪk

macrobiotically
BR ˌmakrə(ʊ)bʌɪ'ɒtɪkli
AM ˌmækroʊbaɪ'ɑdək(ə)li

macrocarpa
BR 'makrə(ʊ)ˌkɑːpə(r), -z
AM 'mækrəˌkɑrpə, -z

macrocephalic
BR ˌmakrə(ʊ)sɪ'falɪk, ˌmakrə(ʊ)kɛ'falɪk
AM ˌmækroʊsə'fælɪk

macrocephalous
BR ˌmakrə(ʊ)'sɛfələs, ˌmakrə(ʊ)'sɛfl̩əs, ˌmakrə(ʊ)'kɛfələs, ˌmakrə(ʊ)'kɛfl̩əs
AM ˌmækroʊ'sɛfələs

macrocephaly
BR ˌmakrə(ʊ)'sɛfəli, ˌmakrə(ʊ)'sɛfl̩i, ˌmakrə(ʊ)'kɛfəli, ˌmakrə(ʊ)'kɛfl̩i
AM ˌmækroʊ'sɛfəli

macrocosm
BR 'makrə(ʊ)kɒz(ə)m, -z
AM 'mækrəˌkɑzəm, 'mækroʊˌkɑzəm, -z

macrocosmic
BR ˌmakrə(ʊ)'kɒzmɪk
AM ˌmækrə'kɑzmɪk

macrocosmically
BR ˌmakrə(ʊ)'kɒzmɪkli
AM ˌmækrə'kɑzmək(ə)li

macroeconomic
BR ˌmakrəʊˌiːkə'nɒmɪk, ˌmakrəʊˌɛkə'nɒmɪk, -s
AM 'mækroʊˌɛkə'nɑmɪk, 'mækroʊˌikə'nɑmɪk, -s

macro-instruction
BR ˌmakrəʊɪn'strʌkʃn, -z
AM ˌmækroʊˌɪn'strəkʃən, -z

macromolecular
BR ˌmakrəʊmə'lɛkjʊlə(r)
AM ˌmækroʊmə'lɛkjələr

macromolecule
BR ˌmakrəʊ'mɒlɪkjuːl, -z
AM ˌmækroʊ'mɑləˌkjul, -z

macron
BR 'makrɒn, 'makr(ə)n, 'meɪkrɒn, 'meɪkr(ə)n, -z
AM 'meɪˌkrɑn, 'mæˌkrɑn, 'meɪkrən, -z

macrophage
BR 'makrə(ʊ)feɪdʒ, -ɪz
AM 'mækrəˌfeɪdʒ, -ɪz

macrophotography
BR ˌmakrəʊfə'tɒgrəfi
AM ˌmækroʊfə'tɑgrəfi

macropod
BR 'makrəpɒd, -z
AM 'mækrəˌpɑd, -z

macroscopic
BR ˌmakrə(ʊ)'skɒpɪk
AM ˌmækrə'skɑpɪk

macroscopically
BR ˌmakrə(ʊ)'skɒpɪkli
AM ˌmækrə'skɑpək(ə)li

macula
BR 'makjʊlə(r), -z
AM 'mækjələ, -z

maculae
BR 'makjʊliː
AM 'mækjəˌli, 'mækjəˌlaɪ

maculae luteae
BR ˌmakjʊliː 'l(j)uːtɪiː
AM ˌmækjəli 'ludiˌi, ˌmækjəˌlaɪ 'ludiˌaɪ

macula lutea
BR ˌmakjʊlə 'l(j)uːtɪə(r)
AM ˌmækjələ 'ludiə

macular
BR 'makjʊlə(r)
AM 'mækjələr

maculation
BR ˌmakjʊ'leɪʃn, -z
AM ˌmækjə'leɪʃən, -z

mad
BR mad, -ə(r), -ɪst
AM mæd, -ər, -əst

Madagascan
BR ˌmadə'gask(ə)n, -z
AM ˌmædə'gæskən, -z

Madagascar
BR ˌmadə'gaskə(r)
AM ˌmædə'gæskər

madam
BR 'madəm, -z
AM 'mædəm, -z

Madame
BR 'madəm, -z
AM 'mædəm, mə'dɑm, -z

Madang
BR mə'daŋ
AM mə'dæŋ

madcap
BR 'madkap, -s
AM 'mædˌkæp, -s

madden
BR 'madn, -z, -ɪŋ, -d
AM 'mædn, -z, -ɪŋ, -d

maddeningly
BR 'madn̩ɪŋli
AM 'mædn̩ɪŋli

madder
BR 'madə(r), -z
AM 'mædər, -z

Maddie
BR 'madi
AM 'mædi

Maddison
BR 'madɪsn
AM 'mædəsən

Maddock
BR 'madək
AM 'mædək

Maddocks
BR 'madəks
AM 'mædəks

Maddox
BR 'madəks
AM 'mædəks

Maddy
BR 'madi
AM 'mædi

made
BR meɪd
AM meɪd

Madeira
BR mə'dɪərə(r)
AM mə'dɛrə, mə'dɪrə

Madeiran
BR mə'dɪərən, -z
AM mə'dɛrən, mə'dɪrən, -z

Madelaine
BR 'madl̩ɪn, 'mad(ə)lɪn, 'madl̩eɪn, 'mad(ə)leɪn
AM 'mædl̩ən, ˌmædl̩'eɪn

madeleine
BR 'madl̩ɪn, 'mad(ə)lɪn, 'madl̩eɪn, 'mad(ə)leɪn, -z
AM 'mædl̩ən, ˌmædl̩'eɪn, -z

Madeley
BR 'meɪdli
AM 'meɪdli

Madeline
BR 'madl̩ɪn, 'mad(ə)lɪn
AM 'mædl̩ən

mademoiselle
BR ˌmadəm(w)ə'zɛl, ˌmam(wə)'zɛl, -z
AM ˌmæd(ə)m(w)əˈzɛl, -z

made-to-measure
BR ˌmeɪdtə'mɛʒə(r)
AM ˌmeɪdtə'mɛʒər

Madge
BR madʒ
AM mædʒ

madhouse
BR 'madhaʊ|s, -zɪz
AM 'mædˌ(h)aʊ|s, -zəz

Madhya Pradesh
BR ˌmadɪə prə'dɛʃ

AM ˌmɑdiə prəˈdɛʃ
Madison
BR ˈmadɪs(ə)n
AM ˈmædəsən
madly
BR ˈmadli
AM ˈmædli
madman
BR ˈmadmən
AM ˈmædˌmæn, ˈmædmən
madmen
BR ˈmadmən
AM ˈmædˌmɛn, ˈmædmən
madness
BR ˈmadnəs, -ɪz
AM ˈmædnəs, -əz
madonna
BR məˈdɒnə(r), -z
AM məˈdɑnə, -z
Madras
BR məˈdrɑːs, məˈdras
AM ˈmædrəs, məˈdræs, məˈdrɑs
madrasa
BR məˈdrasə(r), -z
AM məˈdrɑsə, -z
madrepore
BR ˈmadrɪpɔː(r), -z
AM ˈmædrəˌpɔ(ə)r, -z
madreporic
BR ˌmadrɪˈpɒrɪk
AM ˌmædrəˈpɔrɪk
Madrid
BR məˈdrɪd
AM məˈdrɪd
madrigal
BR ˈmadrɪɡl, -z
AM ˈmædrəɡəl, -z
madrigalesque
BR ˌmadrɪɡəˈlɛsk, ˌmadrɪɡlˈɛsk
AM ˌmædrəɡəˈlɛsk
madrigalian
BR ˌmadrɪˈɡeɪlɪən
AM ˌmædrəˈɡeɪljən, ˌmædrəˈɡeɪliən
madrigalist
BR ˈmadrɪɡəlɪst, ˈmadrɪɡlɪst, -s
AM ˈmædrəɡələst, -s
madrona
BR məˈdrəʊnə(r), -z
AM məˈdroʊnə, -z
madrone
BR məˈdrəʊnə(r), -z
AM məˈdroʊnə, -z
Madura
BR məˈd(j)ʊərə(r)
AM ˈmædʒərə
Madurese
BR ˌmadjʊˈriːz, ˌmadʒʊˈriːz
AM ˌmædəˈriz
madwoman
BR ˈmadˌwʊmən
AM ˈmædˌwʊmən
madwomen
BR ˈmadˌwɪmɪn
AM ˈmædˌwɪmɨn
Mae
BR meɪ
AM meɪ
Maecenas
BR mʌɪˈsiːnəs
AM maɪˈsinəs
maelstrom
BR ˈmeɪlstrəm, ˈmeɪlstrɒm, -z
AM ˈmeɪlˌstrɑm, ˈmeɪlztrəm, -z
maenad
BR ˈmiːnad, ˈmʌɪnad, -z
AM ˈmiˌnæd, -z
maenadic
BR miːˈnadɪk, mʌɪˈnadɪk
AM miˈnædɪk
Maendy
BR ˈmeɪndi
AM ˈmeɪndi
Maerdy
BR ˈmɑːdi
AM ˈmɑrdi, ˈmɛrdi
Maesteg
BR ˌmʌɪˈsteɪɡ
AM ˈmaɪˌsteɪɡ
maestoso
BR mʌɪˈstəʊsəʊ, mʌɪˈstəʊzəʊ, -z
AM maɪˈstoʊˌsoʊ, maɪˈstoʊzoʊ, -z
maestro
BR ˈmʌɪstrəʊ, -z
AM ˈmaɪstroʊ, -z
Maeterlinck
BR ˈmɛtəlɪŋk
AM ˈmɛdərˌlɪŋk
Maeve
BR meɪv
AM meɪv
Mae West
BR ˌmeɪ ˈwɛst, -s
AM ˈmeɪ ˈwɛst, -s
Mafeking
BR ˈmafɨkɪŋ
AM ˈmæfəˌkɪŋ
MAFF
BR maf
AM mæf
maffick
BR ˈmaf|ɪk, -ɪks, -ɨkɪŋ, -ɪkt
AM ˈmæfɪk, -s, -ɪŋ, -t
Mafia
BR ˈmafɪə(r)
AM ˈmɑfiə
mafiosi
BR ˌmafɪˈəʊziː, ˌmafɪˈəʊsiː
AM ˌmɑfiˈoʊzi, ˌmɑfiˈoʊsi
mafioso
BR ˌmafɪˈəʊzəʊ, ˌmafɪˈəʊsəʊ
AM ˌmɑfiˈoʊzoʊ, mɑfiˈoʊsoʊ
mag
BR maɡ, -z
AM mæɡ, -z
magalogue
BR ˈmaɡəlɒɡ, -z
AM ˈmæɡəˌlɔɡ, ˈmæɡəˌlɑɡ, -z
magazine
BR ˌmaɡəˈziːn, -z
AM ˈmæɡəˌzin, -z
Magda
BR ˈmaɡdə(r)
AM ˈmæɡdə
Magdala
BR ˈmaɡdələ(r)
AM ˈmæɡdələ
Magdalen
Oxford college
BR ˈmɔːdlɪn
AM ˈmɔdlən, ˈmæɡdələn
Magdalena
BR ˌmaɡdəˈliːnə(r)
AM ˌmæɡdəˈlinə
Magdalene[1]
biblical name
BR ˌmaɡdəˈliːni, ˈmaɡdəlɪn
AM ˈmæɡdələn, ˈmæɡdəˌlin
Magdalene[2]
Cambridge college
BR ˈmɔːdlɪn
AM ˈmɔdlən, ˈmæɡdələn
Magdalenian
BR ˌmaɡdəˈliːnɪən, -z
AM ˌmæɡdəˈliniən, -z
Magdeburg
BR ˈmaɡdəbəːɡ
AM ˈmæɡdəˌbərɡ
magdelen
BR ˈmaɡdəlɪn, -z
AM ˈmæɡdələn, -z
mage
BR meɪdʒ, -ɪz
AM meɪdʒ, -ɨz
Magee
BR məˈɡiː
AM məˈɡi
Magellan
BR məˈɡɛlən, məˈdʒɛlən
AM məˈdʒɛlən
Magellanic clouds
BR ˌmadʒɪlanɪk ˈklaʊdz
AM ˌmædʒəˌlænɪk ˈklaʊdz
magenta
BR məˈdʒɛntə(r), -z
AM məˈdʒɛn(t)ə, -z
Maggie
BR ˈmaɡi
AM ˈmæɡi
Maggiore
BR ˌmadʒɪˈɔːri
AM məˈdʒɔri
IT madˈdʒore
maggot
BR ˈmaɡət, -s
AM ˈmæɡət, -s
maggoty
BR ˈmaɡəti
AM ˈmæɡədi
Magherafelt
BR ˌmak(ə)rəˈfɛlt
AM ˌmɑk(ə)rəˈfɛlt
Maghrib
BR maˈɡriːb
AM ˈmæˌɡrɪb
magi
BR ˈmeɪdʒʌɪ
AM ˈmeɪˌdʒaɪ, ˈmæˌdʒaɪ
magian
BR ˈmeɪdʒɪən
AM ˈmeɪdʒ(i)ən
magianism
BR ˈmeɪdʒɪənɪz(ə)m
AM ˈmeɪdʒəˌnɪzəm
magic
BR ˈmadʒɪk
AM ˈmædʒɪk
magical
BR ˈmadʒɪkl
AM ˈmædʒəkəl
magically
BR ˈmadʒɪkli
AM ˈmædʒək(ə)li
magician
BR məˈdʒɪʃn, -z
AM məˈdʒɪʃən, -z
Maginnis
BR məˈɡɪnɪs
AM məˈɡɪnɨs
Magilligan
BR məˈɡɪlɪɡ(ə)n
AM məˈɡɪlɨɡ(ɨ)n
magilp
BR məˈɡɪlp
AM məˈɡɪlp
Maginot Line
BR ˈma(d)ʒɪnəʊ lʌɪn
AM ˈmɑ(d)ʒənoʊ ˌlaɪn
magisterial
BR ˌmadʒɪˈstɪərɪəl
AM ˌmædʒəˈstɪriəl, ˌmædʒəˈstɛriəl
magisterially
BR ˌmadʒɪˈstɪərɪəli
AM ˌmædʒəˈstɪriəli, ˌmædʒəˈstɛriəli
magisterium
BR ˌmadʒɪˈstɪərɪəm
AM ˌmædʒəˈstɪriəm, ˌmædʒəˈstɛriəm
magistracy
BR ˈmadʒɪstrəs|i, -ɪz

AM 'mædʒəstrəsi, -z
magistral
BR 'madʒɪstr(ə)l
AM 'mædʒəstrəl
magistrand
BR 'madʒɪstrand, -z
AM 'mædʒəˌstrænd, -z
magistrate
BR 'madʒɪstreɪt, 'madʒɪstrət, -s
AM 'mædʒəˌstreɪt, -s
magistrateship
BR 'madʒɪstreɪtʃɪp, 'madʒɪstrətʃɪp, -s
AM 'mædʒəˌstreɪtˌʃɪp, -s
magistrature
BR 'madʒɪstreɪtʃə(r), 'madʒɪstrətʃə(r), -z
AM 'mædʒəˌstreɪtʃər, 'mædʒəstrəˌtʃʊ(ə)r, -z
Maglemosian
BR ˌmaglə'məʊsɪən, ˌmaglə'məʊzɪən, -z
AM ˌmɑgləˌmoʊsiən, ˌmɑləˌmoʊʒən, -z
maglev
BR 'maglɛv, -z
AM 'mægˌlɛv, -z
magma
BR 'magmə(r)
AM 'mægmə
magmatic
BR mag'matɪk
AM mæg'mædɪk
Magna Carta
BR ˌmagnə 'kɑːtə(r)
AM ˌmægnə 'kɑrdə
magna cum laude
BR ˌmagnə kʊm 'laʊdeɪ, + 'lɔːdi
AM ˌmægnə kəm 'laʊdə, + 'laʊdi
Magna Graecia
BR ˌmagnə 'griːsɪə(r)
AM ˌmægnə 'greɪʃ(i)ə
magnanimity
BR ˌmagnə'nɪmɪti
AM ˌmægnə'nɪmɪdi
magnanimous
BR mag'nanɪməs
AM mæg'nænəməs
magnanimously
BR mag'nanɪməsli
AM mæg'nænəməsli
magnate
BR 'magneɪt, 'magnət, -s
AM 'mægˌneɪt, 'mægnət, -s
magnesia
BR mag'niːʃə(r), mag'niːʒə(r), mag'niːzɪə(r)
AM mæg'niʒə, mæg'niʃə
magnesian
BR mag'niːʃn, mag'niːʒn, mag'niːzɪən
AM mæg'niʒən, mæg'niʃən
magnesite
BR 'magnɪsʌɪt
AM 'mægnəˌsaɪt
magnesium
BR mag'niːzɪəm
AM mæg'niziəm
magnet
BR 'magnɪt, -s
AM 'mægnət, -s
magnetic
BR mag'nɛtɪk, -s
AM mæg'nɛdɪk, -s
magnetically
BR mag'nɛtɪkli
AM mæg'nɛdək(ə)li
magnetisable
BR 'magnɪtʌɪzəbl
AM 'mægnəˌtaɪzəbəl
magnetisation
BR ˌmagnɪtʌɪ'zeɪʃn, -z
AM ˌmægnədə'zeɪʃən, ˌmægnəˌtaɪ'zeɪʃən, -z
magnetise
BR 'magnɪtʌɪz, -ɪz, -ɪŋ, -d
AM 'mægnəˌtaɪz, -ɪz, -ɪŋ, -d
magnetiser
BR 'magnɪtʌɪzə(r), -z
AM 'mægnəˌtaɪzər, -z
magnetism
BR 'magnɪtɪz(ə)m
AM 'mægnəˌtɪzəm
magnetite
BR 'magnɪtʌɪt
AM 'mægnəˌtaɪt
magnetizable
BR 'magnɪtʌɪzəbl
AM 'mægnəˌtaɪzəbəl
magnetization
BR ˌmagnɪtʌɪ'zeɪʃn, -z
AM ˌmægnədə'zeɪʃən, ˌmægnəˌtaɪ'zeɪʃən, -z
magnetize
BR 'magnɪtʌɪz, -ɪz, -ɪŋ, -d
AM 'mægnəˌtaɪz, -ɪz, -ɪŋ, -d
magnetizer
BR 'magnɪtʌɪzə(r), -z
AM 'mægnəˌtaɪzər, -z
magneto
BR mag'niːtəʊ, -z
AM mæg'nidoʊ, -z
magnetograph
BR mag'niːtə(ʊ)grɑːf, mag'niːtə(ʊ)graf, -s
AM mæg'nɛdəˌgræf, -s
magnetohydrodynamic
BR magˌniːtəʊˌhʌɪdrə(ʊ)dʌɪ'namɪk
AM mægˌnɛdoʊˌhaɪdroʊˌdaɪ'næmɪk
magnetometer
BR ˌmagnɪ'tɒmɪtə(r), -z
AM ˌmægnə'tɑmədər, -z
magnetometry
BR ˌmagnɪ'tɒmɪtri
AM ˌmægnə'tɑmətri
magnetomotive
BR magˌniːtə(ʊ)'məʊtɪv
AM mægˌnɛdoʊ'moʊdɪv
magneton
BR 'magnɪtɒn, -z
AM 'mægnətən, 'mægnəˌtɑn, -z
magnetosphere
BR mag'niːtə(ʊ)sfɪə(r)
AM ˌmæg'nɛdəˌsfɪ(ə)r, ˌmæg'nidɪˌsfɪ(ə)r
magnetostriction
BR magˌniːtə(ʊ)'strɪkʃn, -z
AM mægˌnɛdoʊ'strɪkʃən, -z
magnetron
BR 'magnɪtrɒn, -z
AM 'mægnəˌtrɑn, -z
magnifiable
BR 'magnɪfʌɪəbl
AM 'mægnəfaɪəbəl
Magnificat
BR mag'nɪfɪkat, məg'nɪfɪkat, -s
AM mæg'nɪfəˌkɑt, -s
magnification
BR ˌmagnɪfɪ'keɪʃn, -z
AM ˌmægnəfə'keɪʃən, -z
magnificence
BR mag'nɪfɪs(ə)ns, məg'nɪfɪs(ə)ns
AM mæg'nɪfəsəns
magnificent
BR mag'nɪfɪs(ə)nt, məg'nɪfɪs(ə)nt
AM mæg'nɪfəsənt
magnificently
BR mag'nɪfɪs(ə)ntli, məg'nɪfɪs(ə)ntli
AM mæg'nɪfəsən(t)li
magnifico
BR mag'nɪfɪkəʊ, məg'nɪfɪkəʊ, -z
AM mæg'nɪfəˌkoʊ, -z
magnifier
BR 'magnɪfʌɪə(r), -z
AM 'mægnəˌfaɪər, -z
magnify
BR 'magnɪfʌɪ, -z, -ɪŋ, -d
AM 'mægnəˌfaɪ, -z, -ɪŋ, -d
magniloquence
BR mag'nɪləkw(ə)ns
AM mæg'nɪləkwəns
magniloquent
BR mag'nɪləkw(ə)nt
AM mæg'nɪləkwənt
magniloquently
BR mag'nɪlɒkw(ə)ntli
AM mæg'nɪləkwən(t)li
magnitude
BR 'magnɪtʃuːd, 'magnɪtjuːd
AM 'mægnəˌt(j)ud
magnolia
BR mag'nəʊlɪə(r), məg'nəʊlɪə(r), -z
AM mæg'noʊljə, mæg'noʊliə, -z
Magnox
BR 'magnɒks
AM 'mægˌnɑks
magnum
BR 'magnəm, -z
AM 'mægnəm, -z
magnum opus
BR ˌmagnəm 'əʊpəs
AM ˌmægnəm 'oʊpəs
Magnus
BR 'magnəs
AM 'mægnəs
Magog
BR 'meɪgɒg
AM mə'gɑg
Magoo
BR mə'guː
AM mə'gu
Magowan
BR mə'gaʊən
AM mə'gaʊən
magpie
BR 'magpʌɪ, -z
AM 'mægˌpaɪ, -z
Magrath
BR mə'grɑːθ, mə'graθ
AM mə'græθ
Magraw
BR mə'grɔː(r)
AM mə'grɔ, mə'grɑ
Magritte
BR ma'griːt, mə'griːt
AM mə'grit
Magruder
BR mə'gruːdə(r)
AM mə'grudər
magsman
BR 'magzmən
AM 'mægzmən
magsmen
BR 'magzmən
AM 'mægzmən
maguey
BR mə'geɪ, 'magweɪ, -z
AM mə'geɪ, -z
Maguire
BR mə'gwʌɪə(r)
AM mə'gwaɪər
magus
BR 'meɪgəs
AM 'meɪgəs
Magwitch
BR 'magwɪtʃ
AM 'mægˌwɪtʃ

Magyar
BR ˈmagjɑː(r), -z
AM ˈmæɡˌjɑr, -z
HU ˈmɔɟɒr

Mahabharata
BR məˌhɑːˈbɑːrətə(r)
AM ˌmɑhəˈbɑrədə, məˌhɑˈbɑrədə

mahaleb
BR ˈmɑːhəlɛb, -z
AM ˈmɑ(h)əˌlɛb, -z

Mahalia
BR məˈheɪlɪə(r)
AM məˈheɪljə, məˈheɪliə

mahant
BR məˈhʌnt, -s
AM məˈhənt, -s

maharaja
BR ˌmɑː(h)əˈrɑːdʒə(r), -z
AM ˌmɑ(h)əˈrɑ(d)ʒə, -z

maharajah
BR ˌmɑː(h)əˈrɑːdʒə(r), -z
AM ˌmɑ(h)əˈrɑ(d)ʒə, -z

maharanee
BR ˌmɑː(h)əˈrɑːn|i, -ɪz
AM ˌmɑ(h)əˈrɑni, -z

maharani
BR ˌmɑː(h)əˈrɑːn|i, -ɪz
AM ˌmɑ(h)əˈrɑni, -z

Maharashtra
BR ˌmɑː(h)əˈrɑːʃtrə(r)
AM ˌmɑ(h)əˈrɑʃtrə

Maharashtrian
BR ˌmɑː(h)əˈrɑːʃtrɪən, -z
AM ˌmɑ(h)əˈrɑʃtriən, -z

maharishi
BR ˌmɑː(h)əˈrɪʃ|i, -ɪz
AM ˌmɑ(h)əˈrɪʃi, -z

mahatma
BR məˈhatmə(r), məˈhɑːtmə(r), -z
AM məˈhɑtmə, məˈhætmə, -z

Mahaweli
BR ˌmɑːhəˈwɛli
AM ˌmɑ(h)əˈwɛli

Mahayana
BR ˌmɑːhəˈjɑːnə(r)
AM ˌmɑ(h)əˈjɑnə

Mahdi
BR ˈmɑːd|i, -ɪz
AM ˈmɑdi, -z

Mahdism
BR ˈmɑːdɪz(ə)m
AM ˈmɑˌdɪzəm

Mahdist
BR ˈmɑːdɪst, -s
AM ˈmɑdəst, -s

Maher
BR mɑː(r), ˈmeɪə(r)
AM ˈmeɪər

Mahfouz
BR mɑːˈfuːz
AM mɑˈfuz

mah-jong
BR ˌmɑːˈdʒɒŋ
AM ˌmɑˈ(d)ʒɔŋ, ˌmɑˈ(d)ʒɑŋ

mah-jongg
BR ˌmɑːˈdʒɒŋ
AM ˌmɑˈ(d)ʒɔŋ, ˌmɑˈ(d)ʒɑŋ

Mahler
BR ˈmɑːlə(r)
AM ˈmɑlər

mahlstick
BR ˈmɔːlstɪk, -s
AM ˈmɑlˌstɪk, ˈmɔlˌstɪk, -s

mahogany
BR məˈhɒɡəni
AM məˈhɑɡəni

Mahomet
BR məˈhɒmɪt
AM məˈhɑmət

Mahometan
BR məˈhɒmɪt(ə)n, -z
AM məˈhɑmədən, -z

Mahommed
BR məˈhɒmɪd
AM məˈhɑməd

Mahommedan
BR məˈhɒmɨd(ə)n, -z
AM məˈhɑmədən, -z

Mahon
BR mɑːn
AM mæn, ˈmeɪən

Mahoney
BR ˈmɑːni, məˈhəʊni
AM məˈhoʊni

mahonia
BR məˈhəʊnɪə(r), -z
AM məˈhoʊniə, -z

Mahony
BR ˈmɑːni, məˈhəʊni
AM məˈhoʊni

mahout
BR məˈhaʊt, məˈhuːt, -s
AM məˈhaʊt, -s

Mahratta
BR məˈrɑːtə(r), məˈratə(r), -z
AM məˈrɑdə, -z

Mahratti
BR məˈrɑːti, məˈrati
AM məˈrɑdi

mahseer
BR ˈmɑːsɪə(r), -z
AM ˈmɑˌsɪ(ə)r, -z

Maia
BR ˈmʌɪə(r), ˈmeɪə(r)
AM ˈmaɪə, ˈmeɪ(j)ə

maid
BR meɪd, -z
AM meɪd, -z

maidan
BR mʌɪˈdɑːn, ˈmʌɪdɑːn, -z
AM maɪˈdɑn, -z

Maida Vale
BR ˌmeɪdə ˈveɪl
AM ˌmeɪdə ˈveɪl

maiden
BR ˈmeɪdn, -z
AM ˈmeɪdən, -z

maidenhair
BR ˈmeɪdnhɛː(r), -z
AM ˈmeɪdnˌ(h)ɛ(ə)r, -z

maidenhead
BR ˈmeɪdnhɛd, -z
AM ˈmeɪdnˌ(h)ɛd, -z

maidenhood
BR ˈmeɪdnhʊd
AM ˈmeɪdnˌ(h)ʊd

maidenish
BR ˈmeɪdn̩ɪʃ
AM ˈmeɪdn̩ɪʃ

maidenlike
BR ˈmeɪdnlʌɪk
AM ˈmeɪdnˌlaɪk

maidenly
BR ˈmeɪdnli
AM ˈmeɪdnli

maidish
BR ˈmeɪdɪʃ
AM ˈmeɪdɪʃ

maidservant
BR ˈmeɪdˌsəːv(ə)nt, -s
AM ˈmeɪdˌsərvənt, -s

Maidstone
BR ˈmeɪdstən
AM ˈmeɪdˌstoʊn

maieutic
BR meɪˈjuːtɪk, mʌɪˈjuːtɪk
AM meɪˈjudək

maigre
BR ˈmeɪɡə(r)
AM ˈmeɪɡər

Maigret
BR ˈmeɪɡreɪ
AM meɪˈɡreɪ

maihem
BR ˈmeɪhɛm
AM ˈmeɪˌ(h)ɛm

mail
BR meɪl, -z, -ɪŋ, -d
AM meɪl, -z, -ɪŋ, -d

mailable
BR ˈmeɪləbl
AM ˈmeɪləbəl

mailbag
BR ˈmeɪlbaɡ, -z
AM ˈmeɪlˌbæɡ, -z

mailboat
BR ˈmeɪlbəʊt, -s
AM ˈmeɪlˌboʊt, -s

mailbox
BR ˈmeɪlbɒks, -ɪz
AM ˈmeɪlˌbɑks, -əz

mailer
BR ˈmeɪlə(r), -z
AM ˈmeɪlər, -z

mailing
BR ˈmeɪlɪŋ, -z
AM ˈmeɪlɪŋ, -z

maillot
BR mʌɪˈəʊ, -z
AM maɪˈ(j)oʊ, -z

mailman
BR ˈmeɪlman
AM ˈmeɪlˌmæn

mailmen
BR ˈmeɪlmɛn
AM ˈmeɪlˌmɛn

mail order
BR ˌmeɪl ˈɔːdə(r)
AM ˈmeɪl ˌɔrdər

mailshot
BR ˈmeɪlʃɒt, -s
AM ˈmeɪlˌʃɑt, -s

maim
BR meɪm, -z, -ɪŋ, -d
AM meɪm, -z, -ɪŋ, -d

Maimonides
BR mʌɪˈmɒnɪdiːz
AM maɪˈmɑnədiz

Main
German river
BR mʌɪn
AM maɪn

main
BR meɪn, -z
AM meɪn, -z

maincrop
BR ˈmeɪnkrɒp
AM ˈmeɪnˌkrɑp

Maine
BR meɪn
AM meɪn

mainframe
BR ˈmeɪnfreɪm, -z
AM ˈmeɪnˌfreɪm, -z

mainland
BR ˈmeɪnlənd, ˈmeɪnland
AM ˈmeɪnˌlænd, ˈmeɪnlənd

mainlander
BR ˈmeɪnləndə(r), ˈmeɪnlandə(r), -z
AM ˈmeɪnˌlændər, ˈmeɪnləndər, -z

mainline
BR ˈmeɪnlʌɪn, -z, -ɪŋ, -d
AM ˈmeɪnˌlaɪn, -z, -ɪŋ, -d

mainliner
BR ˈmeɪnlʌɪnə(r), -z
AM ˈmeɪnˌlaɪnər, -z

mainly
BR ˈmeɪnli
AM ˈmeɪnli

mainmast
BR ˈmeɪnmɑːst, ˈmeɪnmast, -s
AM ˈmeɪnˌmæst, -s

mainplane
BR ˈmeɪnpleɪn, -z
AM ˈmeɪnˌpleɪn, -z

mainsail
BR ˈmeɪnsl, ˈmeɪnseɪl, -z
AM ˈmeɪnsəl, ˈmeɪnˌseɪl, -z

mainsheet
BR 'meɪnʃiːt, -s
AM 'meɪn,ʃit, -s

mainspring
BR 'meɪnsprɪŋ, -z
AM 'meɪn,sprɪŋ, -z

mainstay
BR 'meɪnsteɪ, -z
AM 'meɪn,steɪ, -z

mainstream
BR 'meɪnstriːm
AM 'meɪn,strim

maintain
BR meɪn'teɪn, mən'teɪn, -z, -ɪŋ, -d
AM meɪn'teɪn, -z, -ɪŋ, -d

maintainability
BR ,meɪnteɪnə'bɪlɪti, mən,teɪnə'bɪlɪti
AM ,meɪnteɪnə'bɪlɪdi

maintainable
BR meɪn'teɪnəbl, mən'teɪnəbl
AM meɪn'teɪnəbəl

maintainer
BR meɪn'teɪnə(r), mən'teɪnə(r), -z
AM meɪn'teɪnər, -z

maintainor
BR meɪn'teɪnə(r), mən'teɪnə(r), -z
AM meɪn'teɪnər, -z

maintenance
BR 'meɪnt(ɪ)nəns, 'meɪntn̩əns
AM 'meɪnt(ə)nəns, 'meɪntn̩əns

Maintenon
BR 'mantənɒn
AM ,mænt(ə)'nɔn
FR mɛ̃tnɔ̃

maintop
BR 'meɪntɒp, -s
AM 'meɪn,tɑp, -s

maintopmast
BR ,meɪn'tɒpmɑːst, ,meɪn'tɒpmast, -s
AM ˌmeɪn'tɑp,mæst, -s

Mainwaring
BR 'manərɪŋ, 'meɪn,wɛːrɪŋ
AM 'meɪn,wɛrɪŋ

Mainz
BR mʌɪnts
AM maɪn(t)s

maiolica
BR mə'jɒlɪkə(*r*)
AM mə'jɑləkə

Mair
BR 'mʌɪə(r)
AM 'maɪər

Mairead
BR mə'reɪd
AM 'meɪ,rid

Maisie
BR 'meɪzi
AM 'meɪzi

maisonette
BR ,meɪzə'nɛt, -s
AM ,meɪzə'nɛt, -s

maisonnette
BR ,meɪzə'nɛt, -s
AM ,meɪzə'nɛt, -s

Maithili
BR 'mʌɪtɪli
AM 'maɪdəli

Maitland
BR 'meɪtlənd
AM 'meɪtlən(d)

maître d'
BR ,meɪtrə 'diː, ,mɛtrə +, -z
AM ,meɪdər 'di, ,meɪtrə +, -z

maître d'hôtel
BR ,meɪtrə dəʊ'tɛl, ,mɛtrə +
AM ,meɪtrə ,doʊ'tɛl

maîtres d'
BR ,meɪtrə 'diː, ,mɛtrə +
AM ,meɪdər 'diz, ,meɪtrə +

maîtres d'hôtel
BR ,meɪtrə dəʊ'tɛl, ,mɛtrə +
AM ,meɪtrə ,doʊ'tɛl

maize
BR meɪz
AM meɪz

majestic
BR mə'dʒɛstɪk
AM mə'dʒɛstɪk

majestically
BR mə'dʒɛstɪkli
AM mə'dʒɛstək(ə)li

majesty
BR 'madʒɪst|i, -ɪz
AM 'mædʒəsti, -z

Maj.-Gen.
BR ,meɪdʒə 'dʒɛn(ə)rəl, + 'dʒɛn(ə)rl̩
AM ˌmeɪdʒər 'dʒɛn(ə)rəl

Majlis
BR madʒ'lɪs, 'madʒlɪs
AM mædʒ'lɪs

majolica
BR mə'dʒɒlɪkə(*r*)
AM mə'dʒɑləkə

major
BR 'meɪdʒə(r), -z, -ɪŋ, -d
AM 'meɪdʒər, -z, -ɪŋ, -d

Majorca
BR mə'jɔːkə(*r*), mə'dʒɔːkə(*r*)
AM mə'jɔrkə

Majorcan
BR mə'jɔːkən, mə'dʒɔːkən
AM mə'jɔrkən

majordomo
BR ,meɪdʒə'dəʊməʊ, -z
AM ,meɪdʒər'doʊmoʊ, -z

majorette
BR ,meɪdʒə'rɛt, -s
AM ,meɪdʒə'rɛt, -s

major general
BR ,meɪdʒə 'dʒɛn(ə)rəl, + 'dʒɛn(ə)rl̩, -z
AM ˌmeɪdʒər 'dʒɛn(ə)rəl, -z

Majorism
BR 'meɪdʒərɪz(ə)m
AM 'meɪdʒə,rɪzəm

majoritarian
BR mə,dʒɒrɪ'tɛːrɪən, -z
AM mə,dʒɔrə'tɛriən, -z

majority
BR mə'dʒɒrɪt|i, -ɪz
AM mə'dʒɔrədi, -z

majorship
BR 'meɪdʒəʃɪp, -s
AM 'meɪdʒər,ʃɪp, -s

majuscular
BR mə'dʒʌskjʊlə(r)
AM mə'dʒəskjələr

majuscule
BR 'madʒəskjuːl
AM 'mædʒəs,kju(ə)l

makable
BR 'meɪkəbl
AM 'meɪkəbəl

Makarios
BR mə'karɪɒs, mə'kɑːrɪɒs
AM mə'kɛriəs

Makassar
BR mə'kasə(r)
AM mə'kɑsər

make
BR meɪk, -s, -ɪŋ
AM meɪk, -s, -ɪŋ

make-believe
BR 'meɪkbɪliːv
AM 'meɪkbə,liv

make-or-break
BR ,meɪkɔː'breɪk
AM 'meɪkər'breɪk

Makepeace
BR 'meɪkpiːs
AM 'meɪk,pis

maker
BR 'meɪkə(r), -z
AM 'meɪkər, -z

makeready
BR 'meɪk,rɛd|i, -ɪz
AM 'meɪk,rɛdi, -z

Makerere
BR mə'kɛrəri
AM mə'kɛrəri

makeshift
BR 'meɪkʃɪft
AM 'meɪk,ʃɪft

makeup
BR 'meɪkʌp, -s
AM 'meɪ,kəp, -s

makeweight
BR 'meɪkweɪt, -s
AM 'meɪk,weɪt, -s

Makgadikgadi
BR mə(k)'gadɪ(k),gɑːdi
AM mə'gædi,gædi

making
BR 'meɪkɪŋ, -z
AM 'meɪkɪŋ, -z

mako[1]
shark
BR 'mɑːkəʊ, 'meɪkəʊ, -z
AM 'meɪkoʊ, -z

mako[2]
tree
BR 'mɑːkəʊ, 'makəʊ, 'meɪkəʊ, -z
AM 'meɪkoʊ, 'mɑkoʊ, -z

Maksutov
BR 'maksʊtɒv, mak'suːtɒv, -z
AM ˌmɑksə,tɔv, mɑk'sudɔv, ˌmɑksə,tɑv, mɑk'sudɑv, -z

Malabar
BR 'maləbɑː(r)
AM 'mæləbɑr

Malabo
BR 'maləbəʊ
AM 'mælə,boʊ

malabsorption
BR ,maləb'sɔːpʃn, -z
AM ,mæləb'sɔrpʃən, ,mæləb'zɔrpʃən, -z

malacca
BR mə'lakə(*r*), -z
AM mə'lɑkə, -z

Malachi
BR 'maləkʌɪ
AM 'mælə,kaɪ

malachite
BR 'maləkʌɪt
AM 'mælə,kaɪt

Malachy
BR 'maləki
AM 'mæləki

malacoderm
BR 'malәkə(ʊ)dəːm, -z
AM 'mæləkoʊ,dərm, -z

malacology
BR ,malə'kɒlədʒi
AM ,mælə'kɑlədʒi

malacostracan
BR ,malə'kɒstrək(ə)n, -z
AM ,mælə'kɑstrəkən, -z

maladaptation
BR ,maladəp'teɪʃn, -z
AM ˌmæl,ædəp'teɪʃən, -z

maladaptive
BR ,malə'daptɪv
AM ˌmælə'dæptɪv

maladjusted
BR ˌmaləˈdʒʌstɪd
AM ˌmæləˈdʒəstəd
maladjustment
BR ˌmaləˈdʒʌs(t)m(ə)nt, -s
AM ˌmæləˈdʒəstmənt, -s
maladminister
BR ˌmaladˈmɪnɪst|ə(r), -əz, -(ə)rɪŋ, -əd
AM ˌmælˌædˈmɪnɪstər, -z, -ɪŋ, -d
maladministration
BR ˌmalədˌmɪnɪˈstreɪʃn
AM ˌmælədˌmɪnəˈstreɪʃən
maladroit
BR ˌmaləˈdrɔɪt
AM ˌmæləˈdrɔɪt
maladroitly
BR ˌmaləˈdrɔɪtli
AM ˌmæləˈdrɔɪtli
maladroitness
BR ˌmaləˈdrɔɪtnɪs
AM ˌmæləˈdrɔɪtnɪs
malady
BR ˈmalәd|i, -ɪz
AM ˈmælədi, -z
mala fide
BR ˌmalə ˈfʌɪdi, ˌmeɪlə +, + ˈfiːdeɪ
AM ˌmɑlə ˈfaɪdi
Málaga
BR ˈmaləgə(r)
AM ˈmɑləgə
Malagasy
BR ˌmaləˈgasi
AM ˌmæləˈgæsi
malagueña
BR ˌmaləˈgeɪnjə(r), -z
AM ˌmɑləˈg(w)eɪnjə, -z
malaise
BR məˈleɪz, maˈleɪz
AM məˈleɪz, mɑˈleɪz, məˈlɛz, mɑˈlɛz
Malamud
BR ˈmaləmʊd
AM ˈmæləməd
malamute
BR ˈmaləmjuːt, -s
AM ˈmæləˌmjut, -s
malanders
BR ˈmaləndəz, ˈmaln̩dəz
AM ˈmæləndərz
malapert
BR ˌmaləˈpəːt, ˈmaləpəːt, -s
AM ˌmæləˌpərt, -s
malaprop
BR ˈmaləprɒp, -s
AM ˈmæləˌprɑp, -s
malapropism
BR ˈmaləprəpɪz(ə)m, -z
AM ˈmæləˌprɑˌpɪzəm, -z
malapropos
BR ˌmalaprəˈpəʊ
AM ˌmæˌlɑprəˈpoʊ, ˌmæˈlɑprəˌpoʊ
malar
BR ˈmeɪlə(r), -z
AM ˈmeɪlər, -z
malaria
BR məˈlɛːrɪə(r)
AM məˈlɛriə
malarial
BR məˈlɛːrɪəl
AM məˈlɛriəl
malarian
BR məˈlɛːrɪən
AM məˈlɛriən
malarious
BR məˈlɛːrɪəs
AM məˈlɛriəs
malarkey
BR məˈlɑːki
AM məˈlɑrki
malarky
BR məˈlɑːki
AM məˈlɑrki
malathion
BR ˌmaləˈθʌɪən
AM ˌmæləˈθaɪɑn
Malawi
BR məˈlɑːwi
AM məˈlɑwi
Malawian
BR məˈlɑːwɪən, -z
AM məˈlɑwiən, -z
Malay
BR məˈleɪ
AM ˈmeɪˌleɪ, məˈleɪ
Malaya
BR məˈleɪə(r)
AM məˈleɪə
Malayalam
BR ˌmaləˈjɑːləm
AM ˌmæləˈjɑləm
Malayan
BR məˈleɪən, -z
AM məˈleɪən, -z
Malayo-Chinese
BR məˌleɪəʊtʃʌɪˈniːz
AM məˈleɪoʊˌtʃaɪˈniz
Malayo-Polynesian
BR məˌleɪəʊˌpɒlɪˈniːzj(ə)n, məˌleɪəʊˌpɒlɪˈniːʒn, -z
AM meˈleɪoʊˌpɑləˈniʒən, meˈleɪoʊˌpɑləˈniʃən, -z
Malaysia
BR məˈleɪzɪə(r), məˈleɪʒə(r)
AM məˈleɪʒə
Malaysian
BR məˈleɪzɪən, məˈleɪʒ(ə)n, -z
AM məˈleɪʒən, -z
Malcolm
BR ˈmalkəm
AM ˈmælkəm
malcontent
BR ˈmalkəntɛnt, -s
AM ˌmælkənˈtɛnt, ˈmælkənˌtɛnt, -s
malcontented
BR ˌmalkənˈtɛntɪd
AM ˌmælkənˈtɛn(t)əd
mal de mer
BR ˌmal də ˈmɛː(r)
AM ˌmɑl də ˈmɛ(ə)r
Malden
BR ˈmɔːld(ə)n, ˈmɒld(ə)n
AM ˈmɔldən, ˈmɑldən
maldistributed
BR ˌmaldɪˈstrɪbjʊtɪd, ˌmalˈdɪstrɪbjuːtɪd
AM ˌmældəˈstrɪbjʊdəd
maldistribution
BR ˌmaldɪstrɪˈbjuːʃn
AM ˌmælˌdɪstrəˈbjuʃən
Maldive
BR ˈmɔːldiːv, ˈmɒldiːv, -z
AM ˈmɑldaɪv, ˈmɑldiv, -z
Maldivian
BR mɔːlˈdɪvɪən, mɒlˈdɪvɪən, -z
AM mɑlˈdɪviən, -z
Maldon
BR ˈmɔːld(ə)n, ˈmɒld(ə)n
AM ˈmɔldən, ˈmɑldən
male
BR meɪl, -z
AM meɪl, -z
malediction
BR ˌmalɪˈdɪkʃn, -z
AM ˌmæləˈdɪkʃən, -z
maledictive
BR ˌmalɪˈdɪktɪv
AM ˌmæləˈdɪktɪv
maledictory
BR ˌmalɪˈdɪkt(ə)ri
AM ˌmæləˈdɪkt(ə)ri
malefaction
BR ˌmalɪˈfakʃn, -z
AM ˌmæləˈfækʃən, -z
malefactor
BR ˈmalɪfaktə(r), -z
AM ˈmæləˌfæktər, -z
malefic
BR məˈlɛfɪk
AM məˈlɛfɪk
maleficence
BR məˈlɛfɪs(ə)ns
AM məˈlɛfəsəns
maleficent
BR məˈlɛfɪs(ə)nt
AM məˈlɛfəsənt
maleic
BR məˈliːɪk
AM məˈliɪk, məˈleɪɪk
malemute
BR ˈmaləmjuːt, -s
AM ˈmæləˌmjut, -s
maleness
BR ˈmeɪlnɪs
AM ˈmeɪlnɪs
Malet
BR ˈmalɪt
AM ˈmælət
malevolence
BR məˈlɛvələns, məˈlɛvəln̩s, məˈlɛvl̩(ə)ns
AM məˈlɛvələns
malevolent
BR məˈlɛvələnt, məˈlɛvəln̩t, məˈlɛvl̩(ə)nt
AM məˈlɛvələnt
malevolently
BR məˈlɛvələntli, məˈlɛvəln̩tli, məˈlɛvl̩(ə)ntli
AM məˈlɛvələn(t)li
malfeasance
BR malˈfiːzns
AM mælˈfizns
malfeasant
BR malˈfiːznt, -s
AM mælˈfiznt, -s
Malfi
BR ˈmalfi
AM ˈmælfi
malformation
BR ˌmalfɔːˈmeɪʃn, ˌmalfəˈmeɪʃn, -z
AM ˌmælfɔrˈmeɪʃən, ˌmælfərˈmeɪʃən, -z
malformed
BR ˌmalˈfɔːmd
AM ˌmælˈfɔrmd
malfunction
BR ˌmalˈfʌŋ(k)ʃn, -z, -ɪŋ, -d
AM ˈmælˌfəŋ(k)ʃən, -z, -ɪŋ, -d
Malham
BR ˈmaləm
AM ˈmæləm
Malherbe
BR malˈɛːb
AM ˌmɑˈlɛrb
Mali
BR ˈmɑːli
AM ˈmɑli
Malian
BR ˈmɑːlɪən, -z
AM ˈmɑljən, ˈmɑliən, -z
Malibu
BR ˈmalɪbuː
AM ˈmæləˌbu
malic
BR ˈmalɪk, ˈmeɪlɪk
AM ˈmælɪk
malice
BR ˈmalɪs
AM ˈmæləs
malice aforethought
BR ˌmalɪs əˈfɔːθɔːt

AM ˌmæləs əˌfɔr'θɔt, ˌmæləs əˌfɔr'θɑt
malicious
BR mə'lɪʃəs
AM mə'lɪʃəs
maliciously
BR mə'lɪʃəsli
AM mə'lɪʃəsli
maliciousness
BR mə'lɪʃəsnəs
AM mə'lɪʃəsnəs
malign
BR mə'lʌɪn, -z, -ɪŋ, -d
AM mə'laɪn, -z, -ɪŋ, -d
malignancy
BR mə'lɪgnəns|i, -ɪz
AM mə'lɪgnənsi, -z
malignant
BR mə'lɪgnənt
AM mə'lɪgnənt
malignantly
BR mə'lɪgnəntli
AM mə'lɪgnən(t)li
maligner
BR mə'lʌɪnə(r), -z
AM mə'laɪnər, -z
malignity
BR mə'lɪgnɪt|i, -ɪz
AM mə'lɪgnɪdi, -z
malignly
BR mə'lʌɪnli
AM mə'laɪnli
Malin
BR 'malɪn
AM 'mælən
Malines
BR ma'li:n, mə'li:n
AM mə'lin
malinger
BR mə'lɪŋg|ə(r), -əz, -(ə)rɪŋ, -əd
AM mə'lɪŋg|ər, -ərz, -(ə)rɪŋ, -ərd
malingerer
BR mə'lɪŋg(ə)rə(r), -z
AM 'mə'lɪŋgərər, -z
Malinowski
BR ˌmalɪ'nɒfski
AM ˌmɑlə'nɑfski
malism
BR 'meɪlɪz(ə)m
AM 'meɪˌlɪzəm
malison
BR 'malɪz(ə)n, 'malɪs(ə)n, -z
AM 'mæləzən, 'mæləsən, -z
mall
BR mal, mɔ:l, -z
AM mɔl, mɑl, -z
Mallaig
BR 'maleɪg, ma'leɪg
AM 'mæˌleɪg
Mallalieu
BR 'maləlju:
AM 'mæləˌlju
mallam
BR 'maləm, -z
AM 'mæləm, -z
mallard
BR 'malɑ:d, 'maləd, -z
AM 'mælərd, -z
Mallarmé
BR ˌmalɑ:'meɪ
AM 'mɑˌlɑrˌmeɪ
malleability
BR ˌmalɪə'bɪlɪti
AM ˌmæl(j)ə'bɪlɪdi, ˌmæliə'bɪlɪdi
malleable
BR 'malɪəbl
AM 'mæl(j)əbəl, 'mæliəbəl
malleableness
BR 'malɪəblnəs
AM 'mæl(j)əbəlnəs, 'mæliəbəlnəs
malleably
BR 'malɪəbli
AM 'mæl(j)əbli, 'mæliəbli
mallee
BR 'mali
AM 'mæli
mallei
BR 'malɪʌɪ
AM 'mæliˌaɪ
mallemuck
BR 'malɪmʌk, -s
AM 'mæləˌmək, -s
mallenders
BR 'maləndəz, 'malndəz
AM 'mæləndərz
malleoli
BR mə'li:əlʌɪ
AM mə'liəˌlaɪ
malleolus
BR mə'li:ələs
AM mə'liələs
mallet
BR 'malɪt, -s
AM 'mælət, -s
malleus
BR 'malɪəs
AM 'mæliəs
Mallorca
BR mə'jɔ:kə(r)
AM mə'jɔrkə
Mallorcan
BR mə'jɔ:k(ə)n, -z
AM mə'jɔrkən, -z
mallow
BR 'maləʊ, -z
AM 'mæloʊ, -z
malm
BR mɑ:m, -z
AM mɑm, -z
Malmesbury
BR 'mɑ:mzb(ə)ri
AM 'mɑmzˌbɛri, 'mæmzˌbɛri
Malmö
BR 'mɑ:lməʊ, 'malməʊ
AM 'mɑlˌmoʊ
SW 'malmø:
malmsey
BR 'mɑ:mzi
AM 'mɑmzi
malnourished
BR ˌmal'nʌrɪʃt
AM ˌmæl'nərɪʃt
malnourishment
BR ˌmal'nʌrɪʃm(ə)nt
AM ˌmæl'nərɪʃmənt
malnutrition
BR ˌmalnjʊ'trɪʃn
AM ˌmæln(j)u'trɪʃən
malodorous
BR mal'əʊd(ə)rəs
AM mæl'oʊdərəs
malodorously
BR mal'əʊd(ə)rəsli
AM mæl'oʊdərəsli
malodorousness
BR mal'əʊd(ə)rəsnəs
AM mæl'oʊdərəsnəs
Malone
BR mə'ləʊn
AM mə'loʊn
Maloney
BR mə'ləʊni
AM mə'loʊni
malope
BR 'maləp|i, -ɪz
AM 'mæləpi, -z
Malory
BR 'maləri
AM 'mæləri
maloti
BR mə'ləʊti, mə'lu:ti
AM mə'lɑdi
Malpas[1]
place in Cheshire, UK
BR 'mɔ:(l)pəs, 'malpəs
AM 'mɑlˌpɑs
Malpas[2]
place in Cornwall, UK
BR 'məʊpəs
AM 'mɑlˌpɑs
Malpas[3]
place in Gwent, UK
BR 'malpas, 'malpəs
AM 'mɑlˌpɑs
Malpighi
BR mal'pi:gi
AM ˌmæl'pɪgi
Malpighian layer
BR mal'pɪgɪən ˌleɪə(r), -z
AM ˌmæl'pɪgiən ˌleɪ(ə)r, -z
Malplaquet
BR 'malpləkeɪ
AM 'mælpləˌkɛt
malpractice
BR ˌmal'prakt|ɪs, -ɪsɪz
AM mæl'præktəs, -əz
malt
BR mɔ:lt, mɒlt, -s, -ɪŋ, -ɪd
AM mɔlt, mɑlt, -s, -ɪŋ, -əd
Malta
BR 'mɔ:ltə(r), 'mɒltə(r)
AM 'mɔltə, 'mɑltə
Maltese
BR mɔ:l'ti:z, mɒl'ti:z
AM mɔl'tiz, mɑl'tiz
Malteser
BR mɔ:l'ti:zə(r), mɒl'ti:zə(r)
AM ˌmɔl'tizər, ˌmɑl'tizər
maltha
BR 'malθə(r), -z
AM 'mɔlθə, 'mɑlθə, -z
malthouse
BR 'mɔ:lthaʊ|s, 'mɒlthaʊ|s, -zɪz
AM 'mɔltˌ(h)aʊ|s, 'mɑltˌ(h)aʊ|s, -zəz
Malthus
BR 'malθəs
AM 'mɔlθəs, 'mɑlθəs
Malthusian
BR mal'θju:zɪən
AM mɔl'θuziən, mɔl'θuʒən
maltiness
BR 'mɔ:ltɪnɪs, ˌmɒltɪnɪs
AM 'mɔltinɪs, 'mɑltinɪs
malting
BR 'mɔ:ltɪŋ, 'mɒltɪŋ, -z
AM 'mɔltɪŋ, 'mɑltɪŋ, -z
maltose
BR 'mɔ:ltəʊz, ˌmɔ:ltəʊs, ˌmɒltəʊz, 'mɒltəʊs
AM 'mɔlˌtoʊs, 'mɔlˌtoʊz, 'mɑlˌtoʊs, 'mɑlˌtoʊz
maltreat
BR mal'tri:t, -s, -ɪŋ, -ɪd
AM mæl'tri|t, -ts, -dɪŋ, -dɪd
maltreater
BR mal'tri:tə(r), -z
AM mæl'tridər, -z
maltreatment
BR mal'tri:tm(ə)nt
AM mæl'tritmənt
maltster
BR 'mɔ:ltstə(r), 'mɒltstə(r), -z
AM 'mɔltstər, 'mɑltstər, -z
malty
BR 'mɔ:lt|i, -ɪə(r), -ɪɪst
AM 'mɔlti, 'mɑlti, -ər, -ɪst
malvaceous
BR mal'veɪʃəs

AM mæl'veɪʃəs

Malvern
BR 'mɔːlv(ə)n, 'mɒlv(ə)n
AM 'mɔlvərn, 'mɑlvərn

malversation
BR ˌmalvə'seɪʃn
AM ˌmælvər'seɪʃən

Malvinas
BR mal'viːnəs
AM mɑl'vinəs

malvoisie
BR 'malvɔɪzi, ˌmalvɔɪ'ziː
AM ˌmɑlˌvwɑ'zi, 'mælvəzi

Malvolio
BR mal'vəʊlɪəʊ
AM mæl'voʊlioʊ

mam
BR mam, -z
AM mæm, -z

mama
BR mə'mɑː(r), 'mamə(r), -z
AM 'mɑmɑ, -z

mamaguy
BR 'mamәgʌɪ, -z, -ɪŋ, -d
AM 'mɑməgaɪ, -z, -ɪŋ, -d

mamba
BR 'mambə(r), -z
AM 'mɑmbə, -z

mambo
BR 'mambəʊ, -z
AM 'mɑmboʊ, -z

mamelon
BR 'mamɨlən, -z
AM 'mæmələn, -z

Mameluke
BR 'mamɨl(j)uːk, -s
AM 'mæməˌluk, -s

Mamet
BR 'mamɪt
AM 'mæmət

Mamie
BR 'meɪmi
AM 'meɪmi

mamilla
BR ma'mɪlə(r), mə'mɪlə(r)
AM mə'mɪlə

mamillae
BR ma'mɪliː, mə'mɪliː
AM mə'mɪli, mə'mɪˌlaɪ

mamillary
BR 'mamɨləri
AM 'mæməˌlɛri

mamillate
BR 'mamɨleɪt
AM 'mæməˌleɪt

mamma¹
gland
BR 'mamə(r)
AM 'mæmə

mamma²
mother
BR mə'mɑː(r), 'mamə(r), -z
AM 'mɑmə, mə'mɑ, -z

mammae
BR 'mamiː
AM 'mæmi, 'mæˌmaɪ

mammal
BR 'maml, -z
AM 'mæməl, -z

mammalian
BR mə'meɪlɪən, ma'meɪlɪən, -z
AM mə'meɪljən, mə'meɪliən, -z

mammaliferous
BR ˌmamə'lɪf(ə)rəs
AM ˌmæmə'lɪfərəs

mammalogy
BR mə'malədʒi, ma'malədʒi
AM mə'mælədʒi

mammary
BR 'mam(ə)ri
AM 'mæm(ə)ri

mammee
BR 'mam|i, -ɪz
AM 'mæmi, -z

mammiform
BR 'mamɪfɔːm
AM 'mæməˌfɔ(ə)rm

mammilla
BR ma'mɪlə(r), mə'mɪlə(r)
AM mə'mɪlə

mammillae
BR ma'mɪliː, mə'mɪliː
AM mə'mɪli, mə'mɪˌlaɪ

mammogram
BR 'mamə(ʊ)gram, -z
AM 'mæməˌgræm, -z

mammography
BR ma'mɒgrəfi, mə'mɒgrəfi
AM mæ'mɑgrəfi

Mammon
BR 'mamən
AM 'mæmən

Mammonish
BR 'mamənɪʃ
AM 'mæmənɪʃ

Mammonism
BR 'mamənɪz(ə)m
AM 'mæməˌnɪzəm

Mammonist
BR 'mamənɪst, -s
AM 'mæmənəst, -s

Mammonite
BR 'mamənʌɪt, -s
AM 'mæməˌnaɪt, -s

mammoth
BR 'maməθ, -s
AM 'mæməθ, -s

mammy
BR 'mam|i, -ɪz
AM 'mæmi, -z

man
BR man, -z, -ɪŋ, -d
AM mæn, -z, -ɪŋ, -d

mana
BR 'mɑːnə(r), -z
AM 'mɑnə, -z

manacle
BR 'manək|l, -lz, -l̩ɪŋ\-lɪŋ, -ld
AM 'mænək|əl, -əlz, -(ə)lɪŋ, -əld

manage
BR 'man|ɪdʒ, -ɨdʒɨz, -ɨdʒɪŋ, -ɪdʒd
AM 'mænɪdʒ, -ɨz, -ɪŋ, -d

manageability
BR ˌmanɨdʒə'bɪlɨti
AM ˌmænɪdʒə'bɪlɨdi

manageable
BR 'manɨdʒəbl
AM 'mænɪdʒəbəl

manageableness
BR 'manɨdʒəblnəs
AM 'mænɪdʒəbəlnəs

manageably
BR 'manɨdʒəbli
AM 'mænɪdʒəbli

management
BR 'manɨdʒm(ə)nt, -s
AM 'mænɪdʒmənt, -s

manager
BR 'manɨdʒə(r), -z
AM 'mænɪdʒər, -z

manageress
BR ˌmanɨdʒə'rɛs, -ɨz
AM 'mænɪdʒ(ə)rəs, -əz

managerial
BR ˌmanɪ'dʒɪərɪəl
AM ˌmænəˌdʒɛriəl, ˌmænəˌdʒɪriəl

managerially
BR ˌmanɪ'dʒɪərɪəli
AM ˌmænəˌdʒɛriəli, ˌmænəˌdʒɪriəli

managership
BR 'manɨdʒəʃɪp, -s
AM 'mænɪdʒərˌʃɪp, -s

managing
BR 'manɨdʒɪŋ
AM 'mænɪdʒɪŋ

Managua
BR mə'nagjʊə(r), mə'nagwə(r)
AM mə'nɑgwə

manakin
BR 'manəkɪn, -z
AM 'mænəˌkɪn, -z

mañana
BR ma'njɑːnə(r), mə'njɑːnə(r)
AM mə'njɑnə

Manasseh
BR mə'nasi, mə'nasə(r)
AM mə'næsə

man-at-arms
BR ˌmanət'ɑːmz
AM 'mænəd'ɑrmz

manatee
BR ˌmanə'tiː, 'manətiː, -z
AM 'mænəˌti, -z

Manaus
BR ma'naʊs
AM mɑ'naʊs

Manawatu
BR ˌmanə'wɑːtuː
AM 'mɑnə'wɑˌtu

Manchester
BR 'mantʃɪstə(r), 'mantʃɛstə(r)
AM 'mæn(t)ʃəstər

manchineel
BR ˌman(t)ʃɪ'niːl, -z
AM ˌmæn(t)ʃə'ni(ə)l, -z

Manchu
BR man'tʃuː, -z
AM mæn'tʃu, -z

Manchuria
BR man'tʃʊərɪə(r)
AM mæn'tʃuriə

Manchurian
BR man'tʃʊərɪən, -z
AM mæn'tʃuriən, -z

manciple
BR 'mansɪpl, -z
AM 'mænsəpəl, -z

Mancunian
BR man'kjuːnɪən, maŋ'kjuːnɪən, -z
AM mæn'kjuniən, -z

Mandaean
BR man'diːən, -z
AM mæn'diən, -z

mandala
BR 'mandələ(r), 'mʌndələ(r), -z
AM 'mændələ, -z

Mandalay
BR ˌmandə'leɪ, 'mandəleɪ
AM 'mændəleɪ

mandamus
BR man'deɪməs, -ɨz
AM mæn'deɪməs, -ɨz

mandarin
BR 'mand(ə)rɪn, -z
AM 'mændərən, -z

mandarinate
BR 'mand(ə)rɨneɪt, -s
AM 'mændərəˌneɪt, -s

mandatary
BR 'mandət(ə)r|i, -ɪz
AM 'mændəˌtɛri, -z

mandate¹
noun
BR 'mandeɪt, -s
AM 'mænˌdeɪt, -s

mandate²
verb
BR ˌman'deɪt, 'mandeɪt, -s, -ɪŋ, -ɨd
AM 'mænˌdeɪ|t, -ts, -dɪŋ, -dɨd

mandator
BR ˌmanˈdeɪtə(r), ˈmandeɪtə(r), -z
AM ˈmænˌdeɪdər, -z

mandatorily
BR ˈmandət(ə)rɪli
AM ˈmændəˌtɔrəli

mandatory
BR ˈmandət(ə)ri
AM ˈmændəˌtɔri

man-day
BR ˈmandeɪ, -z
AM ˈmænˌdeɪ, -z

Mandela
BR manˈdɛlə(r)
AM mænˈdɛlə

Mandelbaum
BR ˈmandlbaʊm
AM ˈmændlbɑm

Mandelstam
BR ˈmandlstam
AM ˈmɑndlˌstɑm
RUS mənˈdʲɪlʲˈstam

Mandeville
BR ˈmandɪvɪl
AM ˈmændəvəl, ˈmændəˌvɪl

mandible
BR ˈmandɪbl, -z
AM ˈmændəbəl, -z

mandibular
BR manˈdɪbjʊlə(r)
AM mænˈdɪbjələr

mandibulate
BR manˈdɪbjʊleɪt
AM mænˈdɪbjəˌleɪt

Mandingo
BR manˈdɪŋɡəʊ
AM mænˈdɪŋɡoʊ

mandola
BR manˈdəʊlə(r), -z
AM mænˈdoʊlə, -z

mandolin
BR ˌmandəˈlɪn, ˈmandəlɪn, ˈmandl̩ɪn, -z
AM ˌmændəˈlɪn, -z

mandoline
BR ˌmandəˈlɪn, ˈmandəlɪn, ˈmandl̩ɪn, -z
AM ˌmændəˈlɪn, -z

mandolinist
BR ˌmandəˈlɪnɪst, ˈmandəlɪnɪst, ˈmandl̩ɪnɪst, -s
AM ˌmændəˈlɪnɪst, -s

mandorla
BR manˈdɔːlə(r), -z
AM ˈmɑndɔrˌlɑ, -z

mandragora
BR manˈdraɡ(ə)rə(r), -z
AM mænˈdræɡərə, -z

mandrake
BR ˈmandreɪk, -s
AM ˈmænˌdreɪk, -s

mandrel
BR ˈmandr(ɪ)l, -z
AM ˈmændrəl, -z

mandril
BR ˈmandr(ɪ)l, -z
AM ˈmændrəl, -z

mandrill
BR ˈmandr(ɪ)l, -z
AM ˈmændrəl, -z

manducate
BR ˈmandjʊkeɪt, ˈmandʒʊkeɪt, -s, -ɪŋ, -ɪd
AM ˈmændʒəˌkeɪ|t, -ts, -dɪŋ, -dɪd

manducation
BR ˌmandjʊˈkeɪʃn, ˌmandʒʊˈkeɪʃn
AM ˌmændʒəˈkeɪʃən

manducatory
BR ˈmandjʊkət(ə)ri, ˈmandʒʊkət(ə)ri
AM ˈmændʒəkəˌtɔri

Mandy
BR ˈmandi
AM ˈmændi

mane
BR meɪn, -z
AM meɪn, -z

maned
BR meɪnd
AM meɪnd

manège
BR maˈneɪʒ, maˈnɛʒ, -ɪz
AM məˈnɛʒ, -əz

maneless
BR ˈmeɪnlɪs
AM ˈmeɪnlɪs

manes
spirit, spirits
BR ˈmɑːneɪz, ˈmeɪniːz
AM ˈmɑˌneɪz, ˈmeɪˌniz

Manet
BR ˈmaneɪ
AM mɑˈneɪ

maneuver
BR məˈnuːv|ə(r), -əz, -(ə)rɪŋ, -əd
AM məˈn(j)uv|ər, -ərz, -(ə)rɪŋ, -ərd

maneuverability
BR məˌnuːv(ə)rəˈbɪlɪti
AM məˌn(j)uv(ə)rəˈbɪlɪdi

maneuverable
BR məˈnuːv(ə)rəbl
AM məˈn(j)uv(ə)rəbəl

maneuverer
BR məˈnuːv(ə)rə(r), -z
AM məˈn(j)uv(ə)rər, -z

maneuvering
BR məˈnuːv(ə)rɪŋ, -z
AM məˈn(j)uv(ə)rɪŋ, -z

Manfred
BR ˈmanfrɪd
AM ˈmænfrəd, ˈmænˌfrɛd

manful
BR ˈmanf(ʊ)l
AM ˈmænfəl

manfully
BR ˈmanfʊli, ˈmanfl̩i
AM ˈmænfəli

manfulness
BR ˈmanf(ʊ)lnəs
AM ˈmænfəlnəs

mangabey
BR ˈmaŋɡəbeɪ, -z
AM ˈmæŋɡəˌbeɪ, -z

Mangan
BR ˈmaŋɡən
AM ˈmæŋɡən

manganese
BR ˈmaŋɡəniːz, ˌmaŋɡəˈniːz
AM ˈmæŋɡəˌniz, ˈmæŋɡəˌniz

manganic
BR manˈɡanɪk, maŋˈɡanɪk
AM mænˈɡænɪk, mæŋˈɡænɪk

manganite
BR ˈmaŋɡənʌɪt
AM ˈmæŋɡənaɪt

manganous
BR ˈmaŋɡənəs
AM ˈmæŋɡənəs

mange
BR meɪn(d)ʒ
AM meɪndʒ

mangel
BR ˈmaŋɡl, -z
AM ˈmæŋɡəl, -z

mangel-wurzel
BR ˈmaŋɡlˌwəːzl, -z
AM ˌmæŋɡəlˈwərzəl, -z

manger
BR ˈmeɪn(d)ʒə(r), -z
AM ˈmeɪndʒər, -z

mangetout
BR ˌmɒn(d)ʒˈtuː, ˌmɒ̃ʒˈtuː, -z
AM ˌmɑnʒˈtu, -z

mangey
BR ˈmeɪn(d)ʒ|i, -ɪə(r), -ɪɪst
AM ˈmeɪndʒi, -ər, -ɪst

mangily
BR ˈmeɪn(d)ʒɪli
AM ˈmeɪndʒɪli

manginess
BR ˈmeɪn(d)ʒɪnɪs
AM ˈmeɪndʒinɪs

mangle
BR ˈmaŋɡ|l, -lz, -l̩ɪŋ\-lɪŋ, -ld
AM ˈmæŋɡ|əl, -əlz, -(ə)lɪŋ, -əld

mangler
BR ˈmaŋɡl̩ə(r), ˈmaŋɡlə(r), -z
AM ˈmæŋɡ(ə)lər, -z

mango
BR ˈmaŋɡəʊ, -z
AM ˈmæŋɡoʊ, -z

mangold
BR ˈmaŋɡəʊld, -z
AM ˈmæŋɡoʊld, -z

mangonel
BR ˈmaŋɡən(ɛ)l, -z
AM ˈmæŋɡəˌnɛl, -z

mangosteen
BR ˈmaŋɡəstiːn, -z
AM ˈmæŋɡəˌstin, -z

mangrove
BR ˈmaŋɡrəʊv, -z
AM ˈmæŋɡroʊv, -z

mangy
BR ˈmeɪn(d)ʒ|i, -ɪə(r), -ɪɪst
AM ˈmeɪndʒi, -ər, -ɪst

manhandle
BR ˈmanhand|l, ˌmanˈhand|l, -lz, -l̩ɪŋ\-lɪŋ, -ld
AM ˈmænˌ(h)æn|dəl, -dəlz, -(d)(ə)lɪŋ, -dəld

Manhattan
BR manˈhatn
AM mænˈhætn, mənˈhætn

manhole
BR ˈmanhəʊl, -z
AM ˈmænˌ(h)oʊl, -z

manhood
BR ˈmanhʊd
AM ˈmænˌ(h)ʊd

man-hour
BR ˈmanˌaʊə(r), -z
AM ˈmænˌaʊ(ə)r, -z

manhunt
BR ˈmanhʌnt, -s
AM ˈmænˌ(h)ənt, -s

mania
BR ˈmeɪnɪə(r), ˈmeɪnjə(r), -z
AM ˈmeɪniə, -z

maniac
BR ˈmeɪnɪak, -s
AM ˈmeɪniˌæk, -s

maniacal
BR məˈnʌɪəkl
AM məˈnaɪəkəl

maniacally
BR məˈnʌɪəkli
AM məˈnaɪək(ə)li

manic
BR ˈmanɪk
AM ˈmænɪk

Manicaland
BR məˈniːkəland
AM məˈnikəˌlænd

manically
BR ˈmanɪkli
AM ˈmænək(ə)li

Manichaean
BR ˌmanɪˈkiːən, -z
AM ˌmænəˈkiən, -z

Manichaeism
BR ˌmanɪˈkiːɪz(ə)m
AM ˌmænəˈkiɪzəm

Manichean
BR ˌmanɪˈkiːən, -z
AM ˌmænəˈkiən, -z

Manichee
BR ˌmanɪˈkiː, -z
AM ˈmænəˌki, -z

Manicheism
BR ˌmanɪˈkiːɪz(ə)m
AM ˌmænəˈkiɪzəm

manicotti
BR ˌmanɪˈkɒti
AM ˌmænəˈkɑdi

manicure
BR ˈmanɪkjʊə(r), ˈmanɪkjɔː(r), -z, -ɪŋ, -d
AM ˈmænəˌkjʊ(ə)r, -z, -ɪŋ, -d

manicurist
BR ˈmanɪkjʊərɪst, ˈmanɪkjɔːrɪst, -s
AM ˈmænəˌkjʊrəst, -s

manifest
BR ˈmanɪfɛst, -s, -ɪŋ, -ɪd
AM ˈmænəˌfɛst, -s, -ɪŋ, -ɪd

manifestation
BR ˌmanɪfɛˈsteɪʃn, ˌmanɪfəˈsteɪʃn, -z
AM ˌmænəfəˈsteɪʃən, ˌmænəˌfɛˈsteɪʃən, -z

manifestative
BR ˌmanɪˈfɛstətɪv
AM ˌmænəˈfɛstədɪv

manifestly
BR ˈmanɪfɛstli, ˈmanɪfəstli
AM ˈmænəˌfɛs(t)li

manifesto
BR ˌmanɪˈfɛstəʊ, -z
AM ˌmænəˈfɛstoʊ, -z

manifold
BR ˈmanɪfəʊld, -z
AM ˈmænəˌfoʊld, -z

manifoldly
BR ˈmanɪfəʊldli
AM ˈmænəˌfoʊl(dl)i

manifoldness
BR ˈmanɪfəʊldnəs
AM ˈmænəˌfoʊl(d)nəs

manikin
BR ˈmanɪkɪn, -z
AM ˈmænəkən, -z

manila
BR məˈnɪlə(*r*)
AM məˈnɪlə

manilla
BR məˈnɪlə(*r*)
AM məˈnɪlə

manille
BR məˈnɪl, -z
AM məˈnil, -z

Manilow
BR ˈmanɪləʊ
AM ˈmænəˌloʊ

manioc
BR ˈmanɪɒk
AM ˈmæniˌɑk

maniple
BR ˈmanɪpl, -z
AM ˈmænəpəl, -z

manipulability
BR məˌnɪpjʊləˈbɪlɪti
AM məˌnɪpjələˈbɪlɪdi

manipulable
BR məˈnɪpjʊləbl
AM məˈnɪpjələbəl

manipulatable
BR məˈnɪpjʊleɪtəbl
AM məˈnɪpjəˌleɪdəbəl

manipulate
BR məˈnɪpjʊleɪt, -s, -ɪŋ, -ɪd
AM məˈnɪpjəˌleɪ|t, -ts, -dɪŋ, -dɪd

manipulation
BR məˌnɪpjʊˈleɪʃn
AM məˌnɪpjəˈleɪʃən

manipulative
BR məˈnɪpjʊlətɪv
AM məˈnɪpjələdɪv, məˈnɪpjəˌleɪdɪv

manipulatively
BR məˈnɪpjʊlətɪvli
AM məˈnɪpjəˌleɪdɪvli

manipulativeness
BR məˈnɪpjʊlətɪvnɪs
AM məˈnɪpjəˌleɪdɪvnɪs

manipulator
BR məˈnɪpjʊleɪtə(r), -z
AM məˈnɪpjəˌleɪdər, -z

manipulatory
BR məˈnɪpjʊlət(ə)ri
AM məˈnɪpjələˌtɔri

Manipur
BR ˈmanɪpʊə(r), ˈmʌnɪpʊə(r), ˈmanɪpɔː(r), ˈmʌnɪpɔː(r)
AM ˈmænəˌpʊ(ə)r

Manipuri
BR ˌmanɪˈpʊəri, ˌmʌnɪˈpʊəri, ˌmanɪˈpɔːri, ˌmʌnɪˈpɔːri, -ɪz
AM ˌmænəˈpʊri, -z

Manitoba
BR ˌmanɪˈtəʊbə(*r*)
AM ˌmænəˈtoʊbə

Manitoban
BR ˌmanɪˈtəʊbən, -z
AM ˌmænəˈtoʊbən, -z

manitou
BR ˈmanɪtuː
AM ˈmænəˌtu

mankind
BR ˌmanˈkʌɪnd
AM ˌmænˈkaɪnd, ˈmænˌkaɪnd

manky
BR ˈmaŋk|i, -ɪə(r), -ɪɪst
AM ˈmæŋki, -ər, -ɪst

manless
BR ˈmanləs
AM ˈmænləs

Manley
BR ˈmanli
AM ˈmænli

manlike
BR ˈmanlʌɪk
AM ˈmænˌlaɪk

manliness
BR ˈmanlɪnɪs
AM ˈmænlinɪs

manly
BR ˈmanl|i, -ɪə(r), -ɪɪst
AM ˈmænli, -ər, -ɪst

man-made
BR ˌmanˈmeɪd
AM ˈmænˈmeɪd

Mann
BR man
AM mæn, mɑn

manna
BR ˈmanə(*r*)
AM ˈmænə

manna-ash
BR ˈmanə(*r*)aʃ, -ɪz
AM ˈmænəˌæʃ, -əz

manned
BR mand
AM mænd

mannequin
BR ˈmanɪkɪn, -z
AM ˈmænəkən, -z

manner
BR ˈmanə(r), -z, -d
AM ˈmænər, -z, -d

mannerism
BR ˈmanərɪz(ə)m, -z
AM ˈmænəˌrɪzəm, -z

mannerist
BR ˈmanərɪst, -s
AM ˈmænərəst, -s

manneristic
BR ˌmanəˈrɪstɪk
AM ˌmænəˈrɪstɪk

manneristical
BR ˌmanəˈrɪstɪkl
AM ˌmænəˈrɪstəkəl

manneristically
BR ˌmanəˈrɪstɪkli
AM ˌmænəˈrɪstək(ə)li

mannerless
BR ˈmanələs
AM ˈmænərləs

mannerliness
BR ˈmanəlɪnɪs
AM ˈmænərlinɪs

mannerly
BR ˈmanəli
AM ˈmænərli

Mannheim
BR ˈmanhʌɪm
AM ˈmænˌ(h)aɪm

mannikin
BR ˈmanɪkɪn, -z
AM ˈmænəkən, -z

Manning
BR ˈmanɪŋ
AM ˈmænɪŋ

Mannion
BR ˈmanɪən, ˈmanjən
AM ˈmænjən, ˈmæniən

mannish
BR ˈmanɪʃ
AM ˈmænɪʃ

mannishly
BR ˈmanɪʃli
AM ˈmænɪʃli

mannishness
BR ˈmanɪʃnɪs
AM ˈmænɪʃnɪs

Mano
BR ˈmanəʊ
AM ˈmæˌnoʊ

manoeuvrability
BR məˌnuːv(ə)rəˈbɪlɪti
AM məˌn(j)uv(ə)rəˈbɪlɪdi

manoeuvrable
BR məˈnuːv(ə)rəbl
AM məˈn(j)uv(ə)rəbəl

manoeuvre
BR məˈnuːv|ə(r), -əz, -(ə)rɪŋ, -əd
AM məˈn(j)uv|ər, -ərz, -(ə)rɪŋ, -ərd

manoeuvrer
BR məˈnuːv(ə)rə(r)
AM məˈn(j)uv(ə)rər

manoeuvring
BR məˈnuːv(ə)rɪŋ, -z
AM məˈn(j)uv(ə)rɪŋ, -z

manometer
BR məˈnɒmɪtə(r), -z
AM məˈnɑmədər, -z

manometric
BR ˌmanə(ʊ)ˈmɛtrɪk
AM ˈmænəˈmɛtrɪk

manometrical
BR ˌmanə(ʊ)ˈmɛtrɪkl
AM ˈmænəˈmɛtrəkəl

manometrically
BR ˌmanə(ʊ)ˈmɛtrɪkli
AM ˈmænəˈmɛtrək(ə)li

ma non troppo
BR ˌmɑː nɒn ˈtrɒpəʊ
AM ˈmɑ nɑn ˈtrɔpoʊ

manor
BR ˈmanə(r), -z
AM ˈmænər, -z

Manorbier
BR ˌmanəˈbɪə(r)
AM ˌmænəˈbɪ(ə)r

manorial
BR məˈnɔːrɪəl
AM məˈnɔriəl

man-o'-war
BR ˌmanəˈwɔː(r)
AM ˈmænəˈwɔ(ə)r

manpower
BR ˈmanpaʊə(r)
AM ˈmænˌpaʊ(ə)r

manqué
BR ˈmɒŋkeɪ
AM mɑŋˈkeɪ

Man Ray
BR ˌman ˈreɪ

AM 'mæn 'reɪ
mansard
BR 'mansɑːd, -z
AM 'mænˌsɑrd, -z
Mansart
BR ˌmɒ̃'sɑːt, ˌmɒn'sɑːt
AM mɑn'sɑr(t)
manse
BR mans, -ɪz
AM mæns, -əz
Mansell
BR 'mansl
AM 'mænsəl
manservant
BR 'manˌsəːv(ə)nt, -s
AM 'mænˌsərvənt, -s
Mansfield
BR 'mansfiːld
AM 'mænsˌfild
mansion
BR 'manʃn, -z
AM 'mæn(t)ʃən, -z
manslaughter
BR 'manˌslɔːtə(r)
AM 'mænˌslɔdər, 'mænˌslɑdər
Manson
BR 'mansn
AM 'mænsən
mansuetude
BR 'manswɨtjuːd, 'manswɨtʃuːd
AM mæn'suəˌt(j)ud
manta
BR 'mantə(*r*), -z
AM 'mæn(t)ə, -z
manteau
BR 'mantəʊ, -z
AM mæn'toʊ, -z
manteaux
BR 'mantəʊz
AM mæn'toʊ
Mantegna
BR man'tɛnjə(*r*), man'teɪnjə(*r*)
AM ˌmɑn'teɪnjə
mantel
BR 'mantl, -z
AM 'mæn(t)l, -z
mantelet
BR 'mantlɪt, 'matlɪt, -s
AM 'mæn(t)lət, -s
mantelletta
BR ˌmantɪ'lɛtə(*r*), -z
AM ˌmæn(t)ə'lɛdə, -z
mantellette
BR ˌmantɪ'lɛteɪ
AM ˌmæn(t)ə'lɛdeɪ
mantelpiece
BR 'mantlpiːs, -ɪz
AM 'mæn(t)lˌpis, -ɪz
mantelshelf
BR 'mantlʃɛlf
AM 'mæn(t)lˌʃɛlf
mantelshelves
BR 'mantlʃɛlvz
AM 'mæn(t)lˌʃɛlvz
mantic
BR 'mantɪk
AM 'mæn(t)ɪk
manticore
BR 'mantɨkɔː(r), -z
AM 'mæn(t)əˌkɔ(ə)r, -z
mantid
BR 'mantɪd, -z
AM 'mæn(t)əd, -z
mantilla
BR man'tɪlə(*r*), -z
AM mæn'ti(j)ə, mæn'tɪlə, -z
mantis
BR 'mantɪs, -ɪz
AM 'mæn(t)əs, -əz
mantissa
BR man'tɪsə(*r*), -z
AM mæn'tɪsə, -z
mantle
BR 'mant|l, -lz, -l̩ɪŋ\-lɪŋ, -ld
AM 'mæn(t)əl, -z, -ɪŋ, -d
mantlet
BR 'mantlɪt
AM 'mæn(t)lɛt
mantling
BR 'mantlɪŋ, -z
AM 'mæn(t)lɪŋ, -z
man-to-man
BR ˌmantə'man
AM 'mæn(t)əˌmæn
Mantovani
BR ˌmantə'vɑːni
AM ˌmɑn(t)ə'vɑni
mantra
BR 'mantrə(*r*), -z
AM 'mæntrə, -z
mantrap
BR 'mantrap, -s
AM 'mænˌtræp, -s
mantua
BR 'mantjʊə(*r*), 'mantʃʊə(*r*), -z
AM 'mæn(t)ʃəwə, -z
Manu
BR 'manuː
AM 'mɑˌnu
manual
BR 'manjʊəl, 'manjʉl, -z
AM 'mænjə(wə)l, -z
manually
BR 'manjʊəli, 'manjʉli
AM 'mænjə(wə)li
Manuel
BR man'wɛl
AM mæn'wɛl
manufactory
BR ˌmanjʉ'fakt(ə)r|i, -ɪz
AM ˌmæn(j)ə'fækt(ə)ri, -z
manufacturability
BR ˌmanjʉˌfaktʃ(ə)rə'bɪlɨti
AM ˌmænjəˌfæktʃərə'bɪlɨdi, ˌmanjəˌfækʃ(ə)rə'bɪlɨdi
manufacturable
BR ˌmanjʉ'faktʃ(ə)rəbl
AM ˌmænjə'fæktʃərəbəl, ˌmænjə'fækʃ(ə)rəbəl
manufacture
BR ˌmanjʉ'faktʃ|ə(r), -əz, -(ə)rɪŋ, -əd
AM ˌmæn(j)ə'fæk|(t)ʃər, -(t)ʃərz, -tʃərɪŋ\-ʃ(ə)rɪŋ, -(t)ʃərd
manufacturer
BR ˌmanjʉ'faktʃ(ə)rə(r), -z
AM ˌmænjə'fæktʃərər, ˌmænjə'fækʃ(ə)rər, -z
manuka
BR 'mɑːnʉkə(*r*), 'manʉkə(*r*), ma'nuːkə(*r*), -z
AM 'mɑnəkə, -z
manumission
BR ˌmanjʉ'mɪʃn
AM ˌmænjə'mɪʃən
manumit
BR ˌmanjʉ'mɪt, -s, -ɪŋ, -ɨd
AM ˌmænjə'mɪ|t, -ts, -dɪŋ, -dɨd
manure
BR mə'njʊə(r), mə'njɔː(r), -z, -ɪŋ, -d
AM mə'n(j)ʊ(ə)r, -z, -ɪŋ, -d
manurial
BR mə'njʊərɪəl, mə'njɔːrɪəl
AM mə'n(j)ʊriəl
manuscript
BR 'manjʉskrɪpt, -s
AM 'mænjəˌskrɪp(t), -s
Manx
BR maŋks
AM mæŋks
Manxman
BR 'maŋksmən
AM 'mæŋksmən
Manxmen
BR 'maŋksmən
AM 'mæŋksmən
Manxwoman
BR 'maŋksˌwʊmən
AM 'mæŋksˌwʊmən
Manxwomen
BR 'maŋksˌwɪmɪn
AM 'mæŋksˌwɪmɨn
many
BR 'mɛni
AM 'mɛni
manyfold
BR 'mɛnɪfəʊld
AM 'mɛniˌfoʊld
manyplies
BR 'mɛnɪplʌɪz
AM 'mɛniˌplaɪz
manzanilla
BR ˌmanzə'nɪlə(*r*), ˌmanzə'niːljə(*r*), -z
AM ˌmænzə'ni(j)ə, -z
manzanita
BR ˌmanzə'niːtə(*r*), -z
AM ˌmænzə'nidə, -z
Manzoni
BR man'zəʊni
AM mɑn'zoʊni
Maoism
BR 'maʊɪz(ə)m
AM 'maʊˌɪzəm
Maoist
BR 'maʊɪst, -s
AM 'maʊəst, -s
Maori
BR 'maʊr|i, -ɪz
AM 'maʊri, -z
Maoriland
BR 'maʊrɪland
AM 'maʊriˌlænd
Mao Tse-tung
BR ˌmaʊ tseɪ'tʊŋ
AM 'maʊ ˌ(t)seɪ'tʊŋ
Mao Zedong
BR ˌmaʊ zeɪ'dɒŋ
AM 'maʊ ˌzeɪ'dɔŋ, 'maʊ ˌzeɪ'dɑŋ
map
BR map, -s, -ɪŋ, -t
AM mæp, -s, -ɪŋ, -t
maple
BR 'meɪpl, -z
AM 'meɪpəl, -z
mapless
BR 'mapləs
AM 'mæpləs
mappable
BR 'mapəbl
AM 'mæpəbəl
Mappa Mundi
BR ˌmapə 'mʊndi
AM ˌmɑpə 'mʊndi
mapper
BR 'mapə(r), -z
AM 'mæpər, -z
Maputo
BR mə'puːtəʊ
AM mə'pudoʊ
maquette
BR ma'kɛt, -s
AM mæ'kɛt, -s
maquilladora
BR məˌkɪlə'dɔːrə(*r*)
AM məˌkilə'dɔrə
maquillage
BR ˌmakɪ'(j)ɑːʒ
AM ˌmɑki'jɑʒ
maquis
BR ma'kiː, 'makiː, 'mɑːkiː
AM mɑ'ki
maquisard
BR ˌmakɪ'zɑː(r), -z
AM ˌmɑkə'zɑr, -z

mar
BR mɑː(r), -z, -ɪŋ, -d
AM mɑr, -z, -ɪŋ, -d
marabou
BR 'marəbuː, -z
AM 'mɛrəˌbu, -z
marabout[1]
stork, silk
BR 'marəbuː, -z
AM 'mɛrəˌbu, -z
marabout[2]
holy man, shrine
BR 'marəbuːt, -s
AM 'mɛrəˌbut, -z
maraca
BR mə'rakə(r), -z
AM mə'rɑkə, -z
Maracaibo
BR ˌmarə'kʌɪbəʊ
AM ˌmɛrə'kaɪboʊ
Maradona
BR ˌmarə'dɒnə(r)
AM ˌmɛrə'dɔnə, ˌmɛrə'dɑnə
Maramba
BR mə'rambə(r)
AM mə'rɑmbə
maranta
BR mə'rantə(r), -z
AM mə'ræn(t)ə, -z
maraschino
BR ˌmarə'skiːnəʊ, ˌmarə'ʃiːnəʊ, -z
AM ˌmɛrə'ʃiˌnoʊ, ˌmɛrə'skiˌnoʊ, -z
marasmic
BR mə'razmɪk
AM mə'ræzmɪk
marasmus
BR mə'razməs
AM mə'ræzməs
Marat
BR 'marɑː(r)
AM mə'rɑ(t)
Maratha
BR mə'rɑːtə(r), mə'ratə(r), -z
AM mə'rɑdə, -z
Marathi
BR mə'rɑːti, mə'rati
AM mə'rɑdi
marathon
BR 'marəθ(ə)n, -z
AM 'mɛrəˌθɑn, -z
marathoner
BR 'marəθənə(r), 'marəθn̩ə(r), -z
AM 'mɛrəˌθɑnər, -z
maraud
BR mə'rɔːd, -z, -ɪŋ, -ɪd
AM mə'rɔd, mə'rɑd, -z, -ɪŋ, -əd
marauder
BR mə'rɔːdə(r), -z
AM mə'rɔdər, mə'rɑdər, -z
maravedi
BR ˌmarə'veɪd|i, -ɪz
AM ˌmɛrə'veɪdi, -z
Marazion
BR ˌmarə'zʌɪən
AM ˌmɛrə'zaɪən
Marbella
BR mɑː'beɪə(r)
AM mɑr'beɪə
marble
BR 'mɑːb|l, -lz, -l̩ɪŋ\-lɪŋ, -ld
AM 'mɑrb|əl, -əlz, -(ə)lɪŋ, -əld
marbling
BR 'mɑːbl̩ɪŋ, 'mɑːblɪŋ, -z
AM 'mɑrb(ə)lɪŋ, -z
marbly
BR 'mɑːbl̩i
AM 'mɑrb(ə)li
marc
BR mɑːk
AM mɑrk
Marcan
BR 'mɑːk(ə)n
AM 'mɑrkən
marcasite
BR 'mɑːkəsʌɪt, 'mɑːkəziːt
AM 'mɑrkəˌsaɪt
marcato
BR mɑː'kɑːtəʊ
AM mɑr'kɑdoʊ
Marceau
BR mɑː'səʊ
AM mɑr'soʊ
marcel
BR mɑː'sɛl, -z, -ɪŋ, -d
AM mɑr'sɛl, -z, -ɪŋ, -d
Marcella
BR mɑː'sɛlə(r)
AM mɑr'sɛlə
Marcellus
BR mɑː'sɛləs
AM mɑr'sɛləs
marcescence
BR mɑː'sɛsns, -ɪz
AM mɑr'sɛsəns, -əz
marcescent
BR mɑː'sɛsnt
AM mɑr'sɛsənt
march
BR mɑːtʃ, -ɪz, -ɪŋ, -t
AM mɑrtʃ, -əz, -ɪŋ, -t
Marchant
BR 'mɑːtʃ(ə)nt
AM 'mɑrtʃənt
Marche
BR mɑːtʃ
AM mɑrtʃ
marcher
BR 'mɑːtʃə(r), -z
AM 'mɑrtʃər, -z
Marches
BR 'mɑːtʃɪz
AM 'mɑrtʃəz
marchioness
BR ˌmɑːʃə'nɛs, -ɪz
AM 'mɑrʃ(ə)nəs, -əz
marchpane
BR 'mɑːtʃpeɪn
AM 'mɑrtʃˌpeɪn
Marcia
BR 'mɑːsɪə(r), 'mɑːʃə(r)
AM 'mɑrʃə
Marciano
BR ˌmɑːsɪ'ɑːnəʊ
AM mɑr'siɑnoʊ
Marconi
BR mɑː'kəʊni
AM mɑr'koʊni
Marco Polo
BR ˌmɑːkəʊ 'pəʊləʊ
AM ˌmɑrkoʊ 'poʊˌloʊ
Marcos
BR 'mɑːkɒs
AM 'mɑrkoʊs
marcottage
BR ˌmɑːkɒ'tɑːʒ, mɑː'kɒtɪdʒ
AM ˌmɑrkə'tɑʒ, ˌmɑr'kɑdɪdʒ
Marcus
BR 'mɑːkəs
AM 'mɑrkəs
Marcus Aurelius
BR ˌmɑːkəs ɔː'riːlɪəs
AM ˌmɑrkəs ɔ'reɪliəs, + ɔ'riliəs
Marcuse
BR ˌmɑː'kuːzə(r)
AM mɑr'kuzə
Mar del Plata
BR ˌmɑː dɛl 'platə(r)
AM ˌmɑr dəl 'plɑdə
Mardi Gras
BR ˌmɑːdɪ 'grɑː(r), -z
AM ˈmɑrdiˌgrɑ, -z
Marduk
BR 'mɑːdʊk
AM 'mɑrdək
mardy
BR 'mɑːdi
AM 'mɑrdi
mare[1]
horse
BR mɛː(r), -z
AM mɛ(ə)r, -z
mare[2]
on moon
BR 'mɑːr|eɪ, 'mɑːr|i, -eɪz\-ɪz
AM 'mɑreɪ, 'mɑri, -z
maremma
BR mə'rɛmə(r)
AM mə'rɛmə
maremme
BR mə'rɛmi
AM mə'rɛmi
Marengo
BR mə'rɛŋgəʊ
AM mə'rɛŋgoʊ
marg
BR mɑːdʒ
AM mɑrdʒ
Margam
BR 'mɑːgəm
AM 'mɑrgəm
Margaret
BR 'mɑːg(ə)rɪt
AM 'mɑrg(ə)rət
margarine
BR ˌmɑːdʒə'riːn, ˌmɑːgə'riːn
AM 'mɑrdʒ(ə)rən
margarita
BR ˌmɑːgə'riːtə(r), -z
AM ˌmɑrgə'ridə, -z
margarite
BR 'mɑːgərʌɪt
AM 'mɑrgəˌraɪt
Margate
BR 'mɑːgeɪt
AM 'mɑrˌgeɪt
margate
fish
BR 'mɑːgɪt, -s
AM 'mɑrgət, -s
margay
BR 'mɑːgeɪ, -z
AM 'mɑrˌgeɪ, -z
marge
BR mɑːdʒ
AM mɑrdʒ
Margerison
BR mə'dʒɛrɪs(ə)n, 'mɑːdʒ(ə)rɪs(ə)n
AM ˌmɑr'dʒɛrəsən
Margery
BR 'mɑːdʒ(ə)ri
AM 'mɑrdʒ(ə)ri
Margeurite
BR ˌmɑːgə'riːt
AM ˌmɑrg(j)ə'rit
margin
BR 'mɑːdʒɪn, -z
AM 'mɑrdʒən, -z
marginal
BR 'mɑːdʒɪnl, 'mɑːdʒn̩l
AM 'mɑrdʒənəl
marginalia
BR ˌmɑːdʒɪ'neɪlɪə(r)
AM ˌmɑrdʒə'neɪljə, ˌmɑrdʒə'neɪliə
marginalisation
BR ˌmɑːdʒɪnəlʌɪ'zeɪʃn, ˌmɑːdʒɪnl̩ʌɪ'zeɪʃn, ˌmɑːdʒn̩əlʌɪ'zeɪʃn, ˌmɑːdʒn̩l̩ʌɪ'zeɪʃn
AM ˌmɑrdʒənələ'zeɪʃən, ˌmɑrdʒənəˌlaɪ'zeɪʃən
marginalise
BR 'mɑːdʒɪnəlʌɪz, 'mɑːdʒɪnl̩ʌɪz, 'mɑːdʒn̩əlʌɪz, 'mɑːdʒn̩l̩ʌɪz, -ɪz, -ɪŋ, -d
AM 'mɑrdʒənəˌlaɪz, -ɪz, -ɪŋ, -d
marginality
BR ˌmɑːdʒɪ'nalɪti
AM ˌmɑrdʒə'nælədi

marginalization
BR ˌmɑːdʒɪnəlʌɪˈzeɪʃn, ˌmɑːdʒɪnl̩ʌɪˈzeɪʃn, ˌmɑːdʒn̩əlʌɪˈzeɪʃn, ˌmɑːdʒn̩l̩ʌɪˈzeɪʃn
AM ˌmɑrdʒənələˈzeɪʃən, ˌmɑrdʒənəˌlaɪˈzeɪʃən

marginalize
BR ˈmɑːdʒɪnəlʌɪz, ˈmɑːdʒɪnl̩ʌɪz, ˈmɑːdʒn̩əlʌɪz, ˈmɑːdʒn̩l̩ʌɪz, -ɪz, -ɪŋ, -d
AM ˈmɑrdʒənəˌlaɪz, -ɪz, -ɪŋ, -d

marginally
BR ˈmɑːdʒɪnəli, ˈmɑːdʒɪnl̩i, ˈmɑːdʒn̩əli, ˈmɑːdʒn̩l̩i
AM ˈmɑrdʒənl̩i

marginate
BR ˈmɑːdʒɪneɪt, -s, -ɪŋ, -ɪd
AM ˈmɑrdʒɪˌneɪ|t, -ts, -dɪŋ, -dɪd

margination
BR ˌmɑːdʒɪˈneɪʃn, -z
AM ˌmɑrdʒəˈneɪʃən, -z

Margo
BR ˈmɑːɡəʊ
AM ˈmɑrɡoʊ

Margolis
BR mɑːˈɡəʊlɪs
AM mɑrˈɡoʊlɪs

Margot
BR ˈmɑːɡəʊ
AM ˈmɑrɡoʊ

margravate
BR ˈmɑːɡrəveɪt, -s
AM ˈmɑrɡrəˌveɪt, -s

margrave
BR ˈmɑːɡreɪv, -z
AM ˈmɑrˌɡreɪv, -z

margravine
BR ˈmɑːɡrəviːn, -z
AM ˈmɑrɡrəˌvin, -z

marguerite
BR ˌmɑːɡəˈriːt, -s
AM ˌmɑrɡ(j)əˈrit, -s

Mari
BR ˈmɑːri
AM ˈmɑri

Maria
BR məˈrɪə(r), məˈrʌɪə(r)
AM məˈriə

maria
plural of mare
BR ˈmɑːrɪə(r)
AM ˈmɑriə

mariage de convenance
BR marɪˌɑːʒ də ˌkɒ̃vəˈnɒ̃s
AM ˌmɑriˈɑʒ də ˌkɔnvəˈnɑns

mariages de convenance
BR marɪˌɑːʒ də ˌkɒ̃vəˈnɒ̃s
AM ˌmɑriˈɑʒ də ˌkɔnvəˈnɑns

Marian[1]
adjective
BR ˈmɛːrɪən
AM ˈmɛriən

Marian[2]
forename
BR ˈmarɪən
AM ˈmɛriən

Mariana
BR ˌmarɪˈɑːnə(r)
AM ˌmɛriˈɑnə

Marianas
BR ˌmarɪˈɑːnəz
AM ˌmɛriˈɑnəz

Marianne
BR ˌmarɪˈan
AM ˌmɛrɪˈæn

Maria Theresa
BR məˌrɪə təˈreɪzə(r)
AM məˈriə təˈreɪsə

Marie
BR məˈriː
AM məˈri

Marie-Antoinette
BR məˌriː antwəˈnɛt
AM məˌri ˌɑntwəˈnɛt

Marienbad
BR ˈmarɪənbad
AM ˈmɛriənˌbɑd, ˈmɛriənˌbæd

marigold
BR ˈmarɪɡəʊld, -z
AM ˈmɛrəˌɡoʊld, -z

marihuana
BR ˌmarɪˈ(h)wɑːnə(r)
AM ˌmɛrəˈ(h)wɑnə

marijuana
BR ˌmarɪˈ(h)wɑːnə(r)
AM ˌmɛrəˈ(h)wɑnə

Marilyn
BR ˈmarɪlɪn, ˈmarl̩ɪn
AM ˈmɛrələn

marimba
BR məˈrɪmbə(r), -z
AM məˈrɪmbə, -z

marina
BR məˈriːnə(r), -z
AM məˈrinə, -z

marinade
BR ˌmarɪˈneɪd, -z
AM ˌmɛrəˌneɪd, -z

marinara
BR ˌmarɪˈnɑːrə(r)
AM ˌmɛrəˈnɛrə

marinate
BR ˈmarɪneɪt, -s, -ɪŋ, -ɪd
AM ˈmɛrəˌneɪ|t, -ts, -dɪŋ, -dɪd

marination
BR ˌmarɪˈneɪʃn, -z
AM ˌmɛrəˈneɪʃən, -z

marine
BR məˈriːn, -z
AM məˈrin, -z

mariner
BR ˈmarɪnə(r), -z
AM ˈmɛrənər, -z

Marinetti
BR ˌmarɪˈnɛtiː
AM ˌmɛrəˈnɛdi

Marino
BR məˈriːnəʊ
AM məˈrinoʊ

Mario
BR ˈmarɪəʊ
AM ˈmɑrioʊ, ˈmɛrioʊ

mariolatry
BR ˌmɛːrɪˈɒlətri, ˌmarɪˈɒlətri
AM ˌmɛriˈɑlətri

Mariology
BR ˌmɛːrɪˈɒlədʒi, ˌmarɪˈɒlədʒi
AM ˌmɛriˈɑlədʒi

Marion
BR ˈmarɪən
AM ˈmɛriən

marionette
BR ˌmarɪəˈnɛt, -s
AM ˌmɛriəˈnɛt, -s

Marisa
BR məˈrɪsə(r)
AM məˈrisə, məˈrɪsə

Marischal
BR ˈmɑːʃl
AM ˈmɛrəˌʃæl

Marist
BR ˈmɛːrɪst, ˈmarɪst, -s
AM ˈmɛrəst, -s

marital
BR ˈmarɪtl
AM ˈmɛrədl

maritally
BR ˈmarɪtl̩i
AM ˈmɛrədl̩i

maritime
BR ˈmarɪtʌɪm
AM ˈmɛrəˌtaɪm

Maritimes
BR ˈmarɪtʌɪmz
AM ˈmɛrəˌtaɪmz

Maritsa
BR məˈrɪtsə(r)
AM məˈrɪtsə

Marius
BR ˈmarɪəs
AM ˈmɛriəs, ˈmɑriəs

marjoram
BR ˈmɑːdʒ(ə)rəm
AM ˈmɑrdʒərəm

Marjoribanks
BR ˈmɑːtʃbaŋks
AM ˈmɑrtʃˌbaŋks

Marjorie
BR ˈmɑːdʒ(ə)ri
AM ˈmɑrdʒ(ə)ri

mark
BR mɑːk, -s, -ɪŋ, -t
AM mɑrk, -s, -ɪŋ, -t

markdown
BR ˈmɑːkdaʊn, -z
AM ˈmɑrkˌdaʊn, -z

marked
adjective
BR mɑːkt, ˈmɑːkɪd
AM ˈmɑrkəd

markedly
BR ˈmɑːkɪdli
AM ˈmɑrkədli

markedness
BR ˈmɑːkɪdnɪs
AM ˈmɑrkədnəs

marker
BR ˈmɑːkə(r), -z
AM ˈmɑrkər, -z

market
BR ˈmɑːk|ɪt, -ɪts, -ɪtɪŋ, -ɪtɪd
AM ˈmɑrkə|t, -ts, -dɪŋ, -dɪd

marketability
BR ˌmɑːkɪtəˈbɪlɪti
AM ˌmɑrkədəˈbɪlɪdi

marketable
BR ˈmɑːkɪtəbl
AM ˈmɑrkədəbəl

marketeer
BR ˌmɑːkɪˈtɪə(r), -z
AM ˌmɑrkəˈtɪ(ə)r, -z

marketer
BR ˈmɑːkɪtə(r), -z
AM ˈmɑrkədər, -z

marketing
BR ˈmɑːkɪtɪŋ, -z
AM ˈmɑrkədɪŋ, -z

marketplace
BR ˈmɑːkɪtpleɪs, -ɪz
AM ˈmɑrkətˌpleɪs, -ɪz

markhor
BR ˈmɑːkɔː(r), -z
AM ˈmɑrˌkɔ(ə)r, -z

marking
BR ˈmɑːkɪŋ, -z
AM ˈmɑrkɪŋ, -z

markka
BR ˈmɑːkɑː(r), ˈmɑːkə(r), -z
AM ˈmɑrkə, -z

Markova
BR mɑːˈkəʊvə(r)
AM mɑrˈkoʊvə

Marks
BR mɑːks
AM mɑrks

marksman
BR ˈmɑːksmən
AM ˈmɑrksmən

marksmanship
BR ˈmɑːksmənʃɪp
AM ˈmɑrksmənˌʃɪp

marksmen
BR ˈmɑːksmən
AM ˈmɑrksmən

markup
BR ˈmɑːkʌp, -s

AM ˈmɑrˌkəp, -s
marl
BR mɑːl
AM mɑrl
Marlboro
BR ˈmɑːlb(ə)rə(r)
AM ˈmɑr(l)ˌb(ə)roʊ
Marlborough
BR ˈmɑːlb(ə)rə(r)
AM ˈmɑr(l)b(ə)roʊ
Marlburian
BR ˌmɑːlˈbjʊərɪən, -z
AM ˌmɑrlˈbɛriən, -z
Marlene[1]
English name
BR ˈmɑːliːn
AM mɑrˈlin
Marlene[2]
German name
BR mɑːˈleɪnə(r)
AM mɑrˈleɪnə
Marley
BR ˈmɑːli
AM ˈmɑrli
marlin
BR ˈmɑːlɪn, -z
AM ˈmɑrlən, -z
marline
BR ˈmɑːlɪn, -z
AM ˈmɑrlən, -z
marlinespike
BR ˈmɑːlɪnspʌɪk, -s
AM ˈmɑrlənˌspaɪk, -s
marlinspike
BR ˈmɑːlɪnspʌɪk, -s
AM ˈmɑrlənˌspaɪk, -s
marlite
BR ˈmɑːlʌɪt, -s
AM ˈmɑrˌlaɪt, -s
Marlon
BR ˈmɑːlən, ˈmɑːlɒn
AM ˈmɑrlən
Marlow
BR ˈmɑːləʊ
AM ˈmɑrloʊ
Marlowe
BR ˈmɑːləʊ
AM ˈmɑrloʊ
marly
BR ˈmɑːl|i, -ɪə(r), -ɪɪst
AM ˈmɑrli, -ər, -ɨst
Marmaduke
BR ˈmɑːmədjuːk, ˈmɑːmədʒuːk
AM ˈmɑrməˌd(j)uk
marmalade
BR ˈmɑːməleɪd
AM ˈmɑrməˌleɪd
Marmara
BR ˈmɑːm(ə)rə(r)
AM ˈmɑrmərə
Marmion
BR ˈmɑːmɪən
AM ˈmɑrmiən
marmite
BR ˈmɑːmʌɪt, -s
AM ˈmɑrˌmaɪt, -s
marmolite
BR ˈmɑːməlʌɪt, -s
AM ˈmɑrməˌlaɪt, -s
Marmora
BR ˈmɑːm(ə)rə(r)
AM ˈmɑrmərə
marmoreal
BR mɑːˈmɔːrɪəl
AM mɑrˈmɔriəl
marmoreally
BR mɑːˈmɔːrɪəli
AM mɑrˈmɔriəli
marmoset
BR ˈmɑːməzɛt, ˌmɑːməˈzɛt, -s
AM ˈmɑrməˌsɛt, ˈmɑrməˌzɛt, -s
marmot
BR ˈmɑːmət, -s
AM ˈmɑrmət, -s
Marne
BR mɑːn
AM mɑrn
Marner
BR ˈmɑːnə(r)
AM ˈmɑrnər
marocain
BR ˈmarəkeɪn, ˌmarəˈkeɪn
AM ˈmɑrəˌkeɪn
Maronite
BR ˈmarənʌɪt, -s
AM ˈmɛrəˌnaɪt, -s
maroon
BR məˈruːn, -z, -ɪŋ, -d
AM məˈrun, -z, -ɪŋ, -d
Marple
BR ˈmɑːpl
AM ˈmɑrpl
marplot
BR ˈmɑːplɒt, -s
AM ˈmɑrˌplɑt, -s
marque
BR mɑːk, -s
AM mɑrk, -s
marquee
BR mɑːˈkiː, -z
AM mɑrˈki, -z
Marquesas
BR mɑːˈkeɪzəz, mɑːˈkeɪsəs
AM ˌmɑrˈkeɪzəz
marquess
BR ˈmɑːkwɪs, -ɪz
AM ˈmɑrkwəs, -əz
marquessate
BR ˈmɑːkwɪsət, -s
AM ˈmɑrkwəseɪt, ˈmɑrkwəsət, -s
marquetry
BR ˈmɑːkɪtri
AM ˈmɑrkətri
Marquette
BR mɑːˈkɛt
AM mɑrˈkɛt
marquis
BR ˈmɑːkwɪs, mɑːˈkiː
AM mɑrˈki, ˈmɑrkwəs
marquisate
BR ˈmɑːkwɪsət, -s
AM ˈmɑrkwəseɪt, ˈmɑrkwəsət, -s
marquise
BR mɑːˈkiːz, -ɪz
AM mɑrˈkiz, -ɪz
marquises
plural
BR ˈmɑːkwɪsɪz, mɑːˈkiːz
AM mɑrˈkiz, ˈmɑrkwəsəz
marquisette
BR ˌmɑːkɪˈzɛt, -s
AM ˌmɑrkwəˈzɛt, ˌmɑrkiˈzɛt, -s
Marr
BR mɑː(r)
AM mɑr
Marrakesh
BR ˌmarəˈkɛʃ
AM ˈmɛrəˌkɛʃ
marram
BR ˈmarəm
AM ˈmɛrəm
Marrano
BR məˈrɑːnəʊ, -z
AM məˈrɑnoʊ, -z
marriage
BR ˈmar|ɪdʒ, -ɪdʒɪz
AM ˈmɛrɪdʒ, -ɪz
marriageability
BR ˌmarɪdʒəˈbɪlɪti
AM ˌmɛrɪdʒəˈbɪlɨdi
marriageable
BR ˈmarɪdʒəbl
AM ˈmɛrɪdʒəbəl
married
BR ˈmarɪd, -z
AM ˈmɛrid, -z
Marriott
BR ˈmarɪət
AM ˈmɛrɪˌɑt
marron glacé
BR ˌmarɒn ˈglaseɪ, -z
AM məˈrɑn glɑˈseɪ, -z
marrow
BR ˈmarəʊ, -z
AM ˈmɛroʊ, -z
marrowbone
BR ˈmarə(ʊ)bəʊn, -z
AM ˈmɛroʊˌboʊn, -z
marrowfat
BR ˈmarə(ʊ)fat
AM ˈmɛroʊˌfæt
marry
BR ˈmar|i, -ɪz, -ɪɪŋ, -ɪd
AM ˈmɛri, -z, -ɪŋ, -d
Marryat
BR ˈmarɪət
AM ˈmɛrɪət
Mars
BR mɑːz
AM mɑrz
Marsala
BR mɑːˈsɑːlə(r)
AM mɑrˈsɑlə
Marsden
BR ˈmɑːzd(ə)n
AM ˈmɑrzdən
Marseillaise
BR ˌmɑːseɪˈjeɪz, ˌmɑːsəˈleɪz, ˌmɑːslˈeɪz
AM ˌmɑrsəˈjeɪ(z), ˌmɑrsəˈjɛz
Marseille
BR mɑːˈseɪ
AM mɑrˈseɪ
Marseilles
BR mɑːˈseɪ
AM mɑrˈseɪ
marsh
BR mɑːʃ, -ɪz
AM mɑrʃ, -ɪz
Marsha
BR ˈmɑːʃə(r)
AM ˈmɑrʃə
marshal
BR ˈmɑːʃ|l, -lz, -lɪŋ\-əlɪŋ, -ld
AM ˈmɑrʃ|əl, -əlz, -(ə)lɪŋ, -əld
marshalship
BR ˈmɑːʃlʃɪp, -s
AM ˈmɑrʃəlˌʃɪp, -s
marshiness
BR ˈmɑːʃɪnɪs
AM ˈmɑrʃinɪs
marshland
BR ˈmɑːʃland, ˈmɑːʃlənd, -z
AM ˈmɑrʃˌlænd, -z
marshmallow
BR ˌmɑːʃˈmaləʊ, -z
AM ˈmɑrʃˌmɛloʊ, -z
marshy
BR ˈmɑːʃ|i, -ɪə(r), -ɪɪst
AM ˈmɑrʃi, -ər, -ɨst
Marston Moor
BR ˌmɑːst(ə)n ˈmʊə(r), + ˈmɔː(r)
AM ˌmɑrstən ˈmɔ(ə)r
marsupial
BR mɑːˈs(j)uːpɪəl, -z
AM mɑrˈsupiəl, -z
mart
BR mɑːt, -s
AM mɑrt, -s
Martaban
BR ˈmɑːtəban
AM ˈmɑrdəˌbæn
martagon
BR ˈmɑːtəg(ə)n, -z
AM ˈmɑrdəgən, -z
martello
BR mɑːˈtɛləʊ, -z
AM mɑrˈtɛloʊ, -z
marten
BR ˈmɑːt(ɪ)n, -z
AM ˈmɑrtən, -z

Martens
BR 'mɑːt(ɪ)nz
AM 'mɑrtənz

martensite
BR 'mɑːtɪnzʌɪt
AM 'mɑrtn,saɪt

Martha
BR 'mɑːθə(r)
AM 'mɑrθə

martial
BR 'mɑːʃl
AM 'mɑrʃəl

martialise
BR 'mɑːʃl̩ʌɪz, 'mɑːʃəlʌɪz, -ɪz, -ɪŋ, -d
AM 'mɑrʃə,laɪz, -ɪz, -ɪŋ, -d

martialize
BR 'mɑːʃl̩ʌɪz, 'mɑːʃəlʌɪz, -ɪz, -ɪŋ, -d
AM 'mɑrʃə,laɪz, -ɪz, -ɪŋ, -d

martially
BR 'mɑːʃl̩i
AM 'mɑrʃəli

Martian
BR 'mɑːʃn, -z
AM 'mɑrʃən, -z

martin
BR 'mɑːtɪn, -z
AM 'mɑrtn, -z

Martina
BR mɑː'tiːnə(r)
AM mɑr'tinə

Martine
BR mɑː'tiːn
AM mɑr'tin

Martineau
BR 'mɑːtɪnəʊ
AM 'mɑrtə,noʊ, 'mɑrtn,oʊ

martinet
BR ,mɑːtɪ'nɛt, -s
AM ,mɑrtn'ɛt, -s

Martínez
BR mɑː'tiːnɛz
AM mɑr'tinəz, 'mɑrtə,nɛz

martingale
BR 'mɑːtɪŋgeɪl, -z
AM 'mɑrtn,geɪl, -z

martini
BR mɑː'tiːn|i, -ɪz
AM mɑr'tini, -z

Martinique
BR ,mɑːtɪ'niːk
AM ,mɑrtn'ik

Martinmas
BR 'mɑːtɪnmas, 'mɑːtɪnməs
AM 'mɑrtnməs

Martinmass
BR 'mɑːtɪnmas, 'mɑːtɪnməs
AM 'mɑrtnməs

martlet
BR 'mɑːtlɪt, -s
AM 'mɑrtlət, -s

Martyn
BR 'mɑːtɪn
AM 'mɑrtn

martyr
BR 'mɑːt|ə(r), -əz, -(ə)rɪŋ, -əd
AM 'mɑrdər, -z, -ɪŋ, -d

martyrdom
BR 'mɑːtədəm, -z
AM 'mɑrdərdəm, -z

martyrisation
BR ,mɑːt(ə)rʌɪ'zeɪʃn
AM ,mɑrdərə'zeɪʃən, ,mɑrdə,raɪ'zeɪʃən

martyrise
BR 'mɑːtərʌɪz, -ɪz, -ɪŋ, -d
AM 'mɑrdə,raɪz, -ɪz, -ɪŋ, -d

martyrization
BR ,mɑːt(ə)rʌɪ'zeɪʃn
AM ,mɑrdərə'zeɪʃən, ,mɑrdə,raɪ'zeɪʃən

martyrize
BR 'mɑːtərʌɪz, -ɪz, -ɪŋ, -d
AM 'mɑrdə,raɪz, -ɪz, -ɪŋ, -d

martyrological
BR ,mɑːt(ə)rə'lɒdʒɪkl
AM ,mɑrdərə'lɑdʒəkəl

martyrologist
BR ,mɑːtə'rɒlədʒɪst, -s
AM ,mɑrdə'rɑlədʒəst, -s

martyrology
BR ,mɑːtə'rɒlədʒ|i, -ɪz
AM ,mɑrdə'rɑlədʒi, -z

martyry
BR 'mɑːtər|i, -ɪz
AM 'mɑrdəri, -z

marvel
BR 'mɑːv|l, -lz, -l̩ɪŋ\-əlɪŋ, -ld
AM 'mɑrv|əl, -əlz, -(ə)lɪŋ, -əld

marveler
BR 'mɑːvl̩ə(r), 'mɑːvələ(r), -z
AM 'mɑrv(ə)lər, -z

Marvell
BR 'mɑːvl
AM 'mɑrvəl

marveller
BR 'mɑːvl̩ə(r), 'mɑːvələ(r), -z
AM 'mɑrv(ə)lər, -z

marvellous
BR 'mɑːv(ə)ləs, 'mɑːvl̩əs
AM 'mɑrv(ə)ləs

marvellously
BR 'mɑːv(ə)ləsli, 'mɑːvl̩əsli
AM 'mɑrv(ə)ləsli

marvellousness
BR 'mɑːv(ə)ləsnəs, 'mɑːvl̩əsnəs
AM 'mɑrv(ə)ləsnəs

marvelous
BR 'mɑːv(ə)ləs, 'mɑːvl̩əs
AM 'mɑrv(ə)ləs

marvelously
BR 'mɑːv(ə)ləsli, 'mɑːvl̩əsli
AM 'mɑrv(ə)ləsli

marvelousness
BR 'mɑːv(ə)ləsnəs, 'mɑːvl̩əsnəs
AM 'mɑrv(ə)ləsnəs

Marvin
BR 'mɑːvɪn
AM 'mɑrv(ə)n

Marx
BR mɑːks
AM mɑrks

Marxian
BR 'mɑːksɪən
AM 'mɑrksiən

Marxism
BR 'mɑːksɪz(ə)m
AM 'mɑrk,sɪzəm

Marxism-Leninism
BR ,mɑːksɪz(ə)m'lɛnɪnɪz(ə)m
AM 'mɑrk,sɪzəm'lɛnə,nɪzəm

Marxist
BR 'mɑːksɪst, -s
AM 'mɑrksəst, -s

Marxist-Leninist
BR ,mɑːksɪst'lɛnɪnɪst, -s
AM 'mɑrksəst'lɛnənəst, -s

Mary
BR 'mɛːri
AM 'mɛri

Mary Celeste
BR ,mɛːrɪ sɪ'lɛst
AM 'mɛri sə'lɛst

Maryland
BR 'mɛːrɪlənd
AM 'mɛrələn(d)

Marylebone
BR 'marɪlɪb(ə)n, 'marl̩ɪb(ə)n, 'marɪlɪbəʊn, 'marl̩ɪbəʊn
AM 'mɛrilə,boʊn

Mary Magdalene
BR ,mɛːrɪ 'magdəlɪn
AM 'mɛri 'mægdələn

Maryport
BR 'mɛːrɪpɔːt
AM 'mɛri,pɔ(ə)rt

marzipan
BR 'mɑːzɪpan
AM 'mɑrtsə,pɑn, 'mɑrtsə,pæn, 'mɑrzə,pæn

Masada
BR mə'sɑːdə(r)
AM mə'sɑdə

Masai
BR 'mɑːsʌɪ, ,mɑː'sʌɪ, 'masʌɪ, ,ma'sʌɪ, mə'sʌɪ
AM 'mɑsaɪ, mɑ'saɪ

masala
BR mə'sɑːlə(r), -z
AM mə'sɑlə, -z

Masaryk
BR 'mazərɪk
AM 'mɑsə,rɪk

Mascagni
BR ma'skanji
AM mə'skɑn(j)i

Mascall
BR 'maskl
AM 'mæskl

mascara
BR ma'skɑːrə(r), mə'skɑːrə(r)
AM mæ'skɛrə, mə'skɛrə

Mascarene Islands
BR ,maskə'riːn ,ʌɪlən(d)z, 'maskəriːn +
AM ,mæskə'rin ,aɪlən(d)z

mascaron
BR 'maskərən, 'maskərn̩, -z
AM 'mɑskə,rɑn, -z

mascarpone
BR ,maskə'pəʊn|i, -ɪz
AM ,mɑskɑr'poʊn(i), -z

mascle
BR 'maskl, 'mɑːskl, -z
AM 'mæskəl, -z

mascon
BR 'maskɒn, -z
AM 'mæskɑn, -z

mascot
BR 'maskɒt, 'maskət, -s
AM 'mæ,skɑt, 'mæskət, -s

masculine
BR 'maskjʉlɪn
AM 'mæskjələn

masculinely
BR 'maskjʉlɪnli
AM 'mæskjələnli

masculineness
BR 'maskjʉlɪnnɪs
AM 'mæskjələ(n)nəs

masculinisation
BR ,maskjʉlɪnʌɪ'zeɪʃn
AM ,mæskjələnə'zeɪʃən, ,mæskjələ,naɪ'zeɪʃən

masculinise
BR 'maskjʉlɪnʌɪz, -ɪz, -ɪŋ, -d
AM 'mæskjələ,naɪz, -ɪz, -ɪŋ, -d

masculinity
BR ,maskjʉ'lɪnɪti

AM ˌmæskjəˈlɪnɨdi
masculinization
BR ˌmaskjʉlɨnʌɪˈzeɪʃn
AM ˌmæskjələnəˈzeɪʃən, ˌmæskjələˌnaɪˈzeɪʃən
masculinize
BR ˈmaskjʉlɨnʌɪz, -ɨz, -ɪŋ, -d
AM ˈmæskjələˌnaɪz, -ɨz, -ɪŋ, -d
masculist
BR ˈmaskjʉlɪst, -s
AM ˈmæskjələst, -s
Masefield
BR ˈmeɪsfiːld
AM ˈmeɪsˌfild
maser
BR ˈmeɪzə(r), -z
AM ˈmeɪzər, -z
Maserati®
BR ˌmazəˈrɑːt|i, -ɪz
AM ˌmɑzəˈrɑdi, ˌmæzəˈrɑdi, -z
Maseru
BR məˈsɛːruː, məˈsɪəruː
AM ˈmæzəˌru, ˈmɑsəˌru
MASH
BR maʃ
AM mæʃ
mash
BR maʃ, -ɨz, -ɪŋ, -t
AM mæʃ, -əz, -ɪŋ, -t
Masham¹
place in Yorkshire
BR ˈmas(ə)m
AM ˈmæʃəm
Masham²
surname, sheep
BR ˈmaʃ(ə)m
AM ˈmæʃəm
masher
BR ˈmaʃə(r), -z
AM ˈmæʃər, -z
mashie
BR ˈmaʃ|i, -ɪz
AM ˈmæʃi, -z
Mashona
BR məˈʃɒnə(r), məˈʃəʊnə(r)
AM məˈʃoʊnə, məˈʃɑnə
Mashonaland
BR məˈʃɒnəland, məˈʃəʊnəland
AM məˈʃoʊnəlænd, məˈʃɑnəlænd
mask
BR mɑːsk, mask, -s, -ɪŋ, -t
AM mæsk, -s, -ɪŋ, -t
Maskall
BR ˈmaskl
AM ˈmæskl
Maskell
BR ˈmaskl
AM ˈmæskl
masker
BR ˈmɑːskə(r), ˈmaskə(r), -z
AM ˈmæskər, -z
maskinonge
BR ˈmaskɪnɒn(d)ʒ, -ɨz
AM ˈmæskəˌnɑndʒ, -əz
masochism
BR ˈmasəkɪz(ə)m, ˈmazəkɪz(ə)m
AM ˈmæzəˌkɪzəm, ˈmæsəˌkɪzəm
masochist
BR ˈmasəkɪst, ˈmazəkɪst, -s
AM ˈmæzəkəst, ˈmæsəkəst, -s
masochistic
BR ˌmasəˈkɪstɪk, ˌmazəˈkɪstɪk
AM ˌmæzəˈkɪstɪk, ˌmæsəˈkɪstɪk
masochistically
BR ˌmasəˈkɪstɨkli, ˌmazəˈkɪstɨkli
AM ¦mæzəˈkɪstək(ə)li, ¦mæsəˈkɪstək(ə)li
mason
BR ˈmeɪsn, -z
AM ˈmeɪs(ə)n, -z
Mason-Dixon Line
BR ˌmeɪsnˈdɪksn lʌɪn
AM ˈmeɪsnˈdɪksənˌlaɪn
Masonic
BR məˈsɒnɪk
AM məˈsɑnɪk
masonry
BR ˈmeɪsnri
AM ˈmeɪsnri
Masorah
BR məˈsɔːrə(r)
AM məˈsɔrə
Masorete
BR ˈmasəriːt, -s
AM ˈmæsəˌrit, -s
Masoretic
BR ˌmasəˈrɛtɪk
AM ˌmæsəˈrɛdɪk
masque
BR mɑːsk, mask, -s
AM mæsk, -s
masquer
BR ˈmɑːskə(r), ˈmaskə(r), -z
AM ˈmæskər, -z
masquerade
BR ˌmɑːskəˈreɪd, ˌmaskəˈreɪd, -z, -ɪŋ, -ɨd
AM ¦mæskəˌreɪd, -z, -ɪŋ, -ɨd
masquerader
BR ˌmɑːskəˈreɪdə(r), ˌmaskəˈreɪdə(r), -z
AM ¦mæskəˌreɪdər, -z
mass
BR mas, -ɨz, -ɪŋ, -t
AM mæs, -əz, -ɪŋ, -t
Massachusetts
BR ˌmasəˈtʃuːsɪts
AM ˌmæsəˈtʃusəts
massacre
BR ˈmasək|ə(r), -əz, -(ə)rɪŋ, -əd
AM ˈmæsəkər, -ərz, -(ə)rɪŋ, -ərd
massage
BR ˈmasɑː(d)ʒ, -ɨz, -ɪŋ, -d
AM məˈsɑ(d)ʒ, -əz, -ɪŋ, -d
massager
BR ˈmasə(d)ʒə(r), -z
AM məˈsɑ(d)ʒər, -z
massasauga
BR ˌmasəˈsɔːɡə(r), -z
AM ˌmæsəˈsɔɡə, ˌmæsəˈsɑɡə, -z
Massawa
BR məˈsɑːwə(r)
AM məˈsɑwə
massé
BR ˈmas|i, -ɪz
AM mæˈseɪ, -z
Massenet
BR ˈmasəneɪ
AM ˌmasəˈneɪ
masseter
BR maˈsiːtə(r), məˈsiːtə(r), ˈmasɨtə(r), -z
AM məˈsidər, -z
masseur
BR maˈsəː(r), məˈsəː(r), -z
AM mæˈsər, məˈsər, -z
masseuse
BR maˈsəːz, məˈsəːz, -ɨz
AM mæˈsus, məˈsus, -əz
Massey
BR ˈmasi
AM ˈmæsi
massicot
BR ˈmasɨkɒt
AM ˈmæsəˌkɑt
massif
BR ˈmasiːf, maˈsiːf, -s
AM mæˈsif, -s
Massif Central
BR ˌmasiːf sɒnˈtrɑːl, maˌsiːf +
AM mɑˌsif ˌsɑnˈtrɑl
Massine
BR maˈsiːn
AM mɑˈsin
massiness
BR ˈmasɪnɨs
AM ˈmæsinɨs
Massinger
BR ˈmasɪn(d)ʒə(r)
AM ˈmæsɪndʒər
massive
BR ˈmasɪv
AM ˈmæsɪv
massively
BR ˈmasɨvli
AM ˈmæsɪvli
massiveness
BR ˈmasɨvnɨs
AM ˈmæsɪvnɨs
massless
BR ˈmasləs
AM ˈmæsləs
Masson
BR ˈmasn
AM məˈsɑn
Massorah
BR məˈsɔːrə(r)
AM məˈsɔrə
Massorete
BR ˈmasəriːt, -s
AM ˈmæsəˌrit, -s
Massoretic
BR ˌmasəˈrɛtɪk
AM ˌmæsəˈrɛdɪk
massy
BR ˈmasi
AM ˈmæsi
mast
BR mɑːst, mast, -s, -ɨd
AM mæst, -s, -əd
mastaba
BR ˈmastəbə(r), -z
AM ˈmæstəbə, -z
mastectomy
BR maˈstɛktəm|i, məˈstɛktəm|i, -ɪz
AM mæˈstɛktəmi, -z
master
BR ˈmɑːst|ə(r), ˈmast|ə(r), -əz, -(ə)rɪŋ, -əd
AM ˈmæst|ər, -ərz, -(ə)rɪŋ, -ərd
masterclass
BR ˈmɑːstəklɑːs, ˈmastəklas, -ɨz
AM ˈmæstərˌklæs, -əz
masterdom
BR ˈmɑːstədəm, ˈmastədəm, -z
AM ˈmæstərdəm, -z
masterful
BR ˈmɑːstəf(ʊ)l, ˈmastəf(ʊ)l
AM ˈmæstərfəl
masterfully
BR ˈmɑːstəfʊli, ˈmɑːstəfl̩i, ˈmastəfʊli, ˈmastəfl̩i
AM ˈmæstərf(ə)li
masterfulness
BR ˈmɑːstəf(ʊ)lnəs, ˈmastəf(ʊ)lnəs
AM ˈmæstərfəlnəs
masterhood
BR ˈmɑːstəhʊd, ˈmastəhʊd, -z
AM ˈmæstərˌ(h)ʊd, -z
masterless
BR ˈmɑːstələs, ˈmastələs

AM 'mæstərləs

masterliness
BR 'mɑːstəlɪnɨs, 'mastəlɪnɨs
AM 'mæstərlinɨs

masterly
BR 'mɑːstəli, 'mastəli
AM 'mæstərli

mastermind
BR 'mɑːstəmʌɪnd, 'mastəmʌɪnd, -z, -ɪŋ, -ɨd
AM 'mæstərˌmaɪnd, -z, -ɪŋ, -ɨd

masterpiece
BR 'mɑːstəpiːs, 'mastəpiːs, -ɨz
AM 'mæstərˌpis, -ɨz

Masters
BR 'mɑːstəz, 'mastəz
AM 'mæstərz

mastership
BR 'mɑːstəʃɪp, 'mastəʃɪp, -s
AM 'mæstərˌʃɪp, -s

mastersinger
BR 'mɑːstəˌsɪŋə(r), 'mastəˌsɪŋə(r), -z
AM 'mæstərˌsɪŋər, -z

masterstroke
BR 'mɑːstəstrəʊk, 'mastəstrəʊk, -s
AM 'mæstərˌstroʊk, -s

masterwork
BR 'mɑːstəwəːk, 'mastəwəːk, -s
AM 'mæstərˌwərk, -s

mastery
BR 'mɑːst(ə)ri, 'mast(ə)ri
AM 'mæst(ə)ri

masthead
BR 'mɑːsthɛd, 'masthɛd, -z
AM 'mæstˌ(h)ɛd, -z

mastic
BR 'mastɪk
AM 'mæstɪk

masticate
BR 'mastɨkeɪt, -s, -ɪŋ, -ɨd
AM 'mæstəˌkeɪ|t, -ts, -dɪŋ, -dɨd

mastication
BR ˌmastɨ'keɪʃn
AM ˌmæstə'keɪʃən

masticator
BR 'mastɨkeɪtə(r), -z
AM 'mæstəˌkeɪdər, -z

masticatory
BR 'mastɨkət(ə)ri, ˌmastɨ'keɪt(ə)ri
AM 'mæstəkəˌtɔri

mastiff
BR 'mastɪf, -s
AM 'mæstəf, -s

mastitis
BR ma'stʌɪtɨs, mə'stʌɪtɨs
AM mæ'staɪdɨs

mastodon
BR 'mastədɒn, 'mastəd(ə)n, -z
AM 'mæstəˌdɑn, -z

mastodontic
BR ˌmastə'dɒntɪk
AM ˌmæstə'dɑn(t)ɪk

mastoid
BR 'mastɔɪd, -z
AM 'mæˌstɔɪd, -z

mastoiditis
BR ˌmastɔɪ'dʌɪtɨs
AM ˌmæstɔɪ'daɪdɨs

masturbate
BR 'mastəbeɪt, -s, -ɪŋ, -ɨd
AM 'mæstərˌbeɪ|t, -ts, -dɪŋ, -dɨd

masturbation
BR ˌmastə'beɪʃn
AM ˌmæstər'beɪʃən

masturbator
BR 'mastəbeɪtə(r), -z
AM 'mæstərˌbeɪdər, -z

masturbatory
BR 'mastəbeɪtri
AM 'mæstərbəˌtɔri

mat
BR mat, -s, -ɪŋ, -ɨd
AM mæ|t, -ts, -dɪŋ, -dəd

Matabele
BR ˌmatə'biːli
AM ˌmædə'bili

Matabeleland
BR ˌmatə'biːlɪland
AM ˌmædə'biliˌlænd

matador
BR 'matədɔː(r), -z
AM 'mædəˌdɔ(ə)r, -z

Mata Hari
BR ˌmɑːtə 'hɑːri
AM ˌmɑdə 'hɑri

matamata
BR ˌmatə'matə(r), -z
AM ˌmædə'mædə, -z

Matapan
BR 'matəpan, ˌmatə'pan
AM 'mædəˌpæn

match
BR matʃ, -ɨz, -ɪŋ, -t
AM mætʃ, -ɨz, -ɪŋ, -t

matchable
BR 'matʃəbl
AM 'mætʃəbəl

matchboard
BR 'matʃbɔːd
AM 'mætʃˌbɔ(ə)rd

matchbook
BR 'matʃbʊk, -s
AM 'mætʃˌbʊk, -s

matchbox
BR 'matʃbɒks, -ɨz
AM 'mætʃˌbɑks, -ɨz

matchet
BR 'matʃɪt, -s
AM 'mætʃət, -s

matchless
BR 'matʃləs
AM 'mætʃləs

matchlessly
BR 'matʃləsli
AM 'mætʃləsli

matchlock
BR 'matʃlɒk, -s
AM 'mætʃˌlɑk, -s

matchmaker
BR 'matʃˌmeɪkə(r), -z
AM 'mætʃˌmeɪkər, -z

matchmaking
BR 'matʃˌmeɪkɪŋ
AM 'mætʃˌmeɪkɪŋ

matchplay
BR 'matʃpleɪ
AM 'mætʃˌpleɪ

matchstick
BR 'matʃstɪk, -s
AM 'mætʃˌstɪk, -s

matchup
BR 'matʃʌp, -s
AM 'mætʃˌəp, -s

matchwood
BR 'matʃwʊd
AM 'mætʃˌwʊd

mate
BR meɪt, -s, -ɪŋ, -ɨd
AM meɪ|t, -ts, -dɪŋ, -dɨd

maté
BR 'mateɪ, 'mɑːteɪ
AM 'mɑˌteɪ

mateless
BR 'meɪtlɨs
AM 'meɪtlɨs

matelot
BR 'matləʊ, 'matl̩əʊ, 'matələʊ, -z
AM 'mætˌloʊ, 'mædlˌoʊ, -z

matelote
BR 'matələʊt, 'matl̩əʊt, 'matələʊt
AM 'mædlˌoʊt, 'mætˌloʊt

mater
BR 'meɪtə(r)
AM 'meɪdər, 'mɑˌtər

materfamilias
BR ˌmeɪtəfə'mɪlɪas
AM ˌmeɪdərfə'mɪliəs, ˌmɑˌtərfə'mɪliəs

material
BR mə'tɪərɪəl, -z
AM mə'tɪriəl, -z

materialisation
BR məˌtɪərɪəlʌɪ'zeɪʃn
AM məˌtɪriələ'zeɪʃən, məˌtɪriəˌlaɪ'zeɪʃən

materialise
BR mə'tɪərɪəlʌɪz, -ɨz, -ɪŋ, -d
AM mə'tɪriəˌlaɪz, -ɨz, -ɪŋ, -d

materialism
BR mə'tɪərɪəlɪz(ə)m
AM mə'tɪriəˌlɪzəm

materialist
BR mə'tɪərɪəlɪst
AM mə'tɪriələst

materialistic
BR məˌtɪərɪə'lɪstɪk
AM məˌtɪriə'lɪstɪk

materialistically
BR məˌtɪərɪə'lɪstɨkli
AM məˌtɪriə'lɪstək(ə)li

materiality
BR məˌtɪərɪ'alɨti
AM məˌtɪri'ælədi

materialization
BR məˌtɪərɪəlʌɪ'zeɪʃn
AM məˌtɪriələ'zeɪʃən, məˌtɪriəˌlaɪ'zeɪʃən

materialize
BR mə'tɪərɪəlʌɪz, -ɨz, -ɪŋ, -d
AM mə'tɪriəˌlaɪz, -ɨz, -ɪŋ, -d

materially
BR mə'tɪərɪəli
AM mə'tɪriəli

materia medica
BR məˌtɪərɪə 'mɛdɪkə(r)
AM mə'tɪriə 'mɛdəkə

matériel
BR məˌtɪərɪ'ɛl
AM məˌtɪri'ɛl

maternal
BR mə'təːnl
AM mə'tərnəl

maternalism
BR mə'təːnəlɪz(ə)m, mə'təːnl̩ɪz(ə)m
AM mə'tərnlˌɪzəm

maternalistic
BR məˌtəːnə'lɪstɪk, məˌtəːnl'ɪstɪk
AM məˌtərnl'ɪstɪk

maternally
BR mə'təːnəli, mə'təːnl̩i
AM mə'tərnl̩i

maternity
BR mə'təːnɨti
AM mə'tərnədi

mateship
BR 'meɪtʃɪp, -s
AM 'meɪtˌʃɪp, -s

matey
BR 'meɪt|i, -ɪə(r), -ɪɪst
AM 'meɪdi, -ər, -ɨst

mateyness
BR 'meɪtɪnɨs
AM 'meɪdinɨs

math
BR maθ, -s

AM mæθ, -s

mathematical
BR ˌmaθ(ə)ˈmatɪkl
AM ˌmæθ(ə)ˈmædəkəl

mathematically
BR maθ(ə)ˈmatɪkli
AM ˌmæθ(ə)ˈmædək(ə)li

mathematician
BR ˌmaθ(ə)məˈtɪʃn, -z
AM ˌmæθ(ə)məˈtɪʃən, -z

mathematics
BR ˌmaθ(ə)ˈmatɪks
AM ˌmæθ(ə)ˈmædɪks

Mather
BR ˈmeɪðə(r), ˈmaðə(r)
AM ˈmæðər

Matheson
BR ˈmaθɪs(ə)n
AM ˈmaθəsən

Mathew
BR ˈmaθjuː
AM ˈmæθju

Mathews
BR ˈmaθjuːz
AM ˈmæθjuz

Mathias
BR məˈθʌɪəs
AM məˈθaɪəs

Mathieson
BR ˈmaθɪs(ə)n
AM ˈmaθəsən

Mathilda
BR məˈtɪldə(*r*)
AM məˈtɪldə

Mathis
BR ˈmaθɪs
AM ˈmæθəs

maths
BR maθs
AM mæθs

matico
BR məˈtiːkəʊ, -z
AM məˈtiˌkoʊ, -z

Matilda
BR məˈtɪldə(*r*), -z
AM məˈtɪldə, -z

matily
BR ˈmeɪtɨli
AM ˈmeɪdɨli

matinée
BR ˈmatɪneɪ, -z
AM ˌmætnˈeɪ, -z

matiness
BR ˈmeɪtɪnɪs
AM ˈmeɪdinɪs

matins
BR ˈmatɪnz
AM ˈmætnz

Matisse
BR maˈtiːs
AM məˈtis

matlo
BR ˈmatləʊ, -z
AM ˈmætˌloʊ, -z

Matlock
BR ˈmatlɒk
AM ˈmætˌlɑk

matlow
BR ˈmatləʊ, -z
AM ˈmætˌloʊ, -z

Matmata
BR matˈmatə(*r*)
AM mɑtˈmɑdə

Mato Grosso
BR ˌmatəʊ ˈgrɒsəʊ
AM ˌmɑdə ˈgroʊsoʊ
PORT ˌmɑtu ˈgrosu

matrass
BR ˈmatrəs, -ɪz
AM ˈmætrəs, -əz

matriarch
BR ˈmeɪtrɪɑːk, -s
AM ˈmeɪtriˌɑrk, -s

matriarchal
BR ˌmeɪtrɪˈɑːkl
AM ˌmeɪtriˈɑrkəl

matriarchy
BR ˈmeɪtrɪɑːk|i, -ɪz
AM ˈmeɪtriˌɑrki, -z

matric
BR məˈtrɪk
AM məˈtrɪk

matrices
BR ˈmeɪtrɪsiːz
AM ˈmeɪtrəˌsiz

matricidal
BR ˌmatrɪˈsʌɪdl
AM ˌmætrəˈsaɪdəl

matricide
BR ˈmatrɪsʌɪd, -z
AM ˈmætrəˌsaɪd, -z

matriculant
BR məˈtrɪkjʉlənt, məˈtrɪkjʉlnt, -s
AM məˈtrɪkjələnt, -s

matriculate
BR məˈtrɪkjʉleɪt, -s, -ɪŋ, -ɨd
AM məˈtrɪkjəˌleɪ|t, -ts, -dɪŋ, -dɨd

matriculation
BR məˌtrɪkjʉˈleɪʃn
AM məˌtrɪkjəˈleɪʃən

matriculatory
BR məˈtrɪkjʉlət(ə)ri
AM ˈməˈtrɪkjələˌtɔri

matrilineal
BR ˌmatrɪˈlɪnɪəl
AM ˌmætrəˈlɪniəl

matrilineally
BR ˌmatrɪˈlɪnɪəli
AM ˌmætrəˈlɪniəli

matrilocal
BR ˌmatrɪˈləʊkl
AM ˌmætrəˈloʊkəl

matrimonial
BR ˌmatrɪˈməʊnɪəl
AM ˌmætrəˈmoʊniəl

matrimonially
BR ˌmatrɪˈməʊnɪəli
AM ˌmætrəˈmoʊniəli

matrimony
BR ˈmatrɪməni
AM ˈmætrəˌmoʊni

matrix
BR ˈmeɪtrɪks, -ɪz
AM ˈmeɪtrɪks, -ɪz

matron
BR ˈmeɪtr(ə)n, -z
AM ˈmeɪtrən, -z

matronal
BR ˈmeɪtr(ə)nl
AM ˈmeɪtrənəl

matronhood
BR ˈmeɪtr(ə)nhʊd, -z
AM ˈmeɪtrənˌ(h)ʊd, -z

matronly
BR ˈmeɪtr(ə)nli
AM ˈmeɪtr(ə)nli

Matsui®
BR matˈsuːi
AM mætˈsui

matsuri
BR matˈsuːr|i, -ɪz
AM ˌmætˈsuri, -z

Matsushita®
BR ˌmatsʊˈʃiːtə(*r*)
AM ˌmætˈsʊʃidə

Matsuyama
BR ˌmatsʉˈjɑːmə(*r*)
AM ˌmɑtsəˈjɑmə

matt
BR mat, -s, -ɪŋ, -ɨd
AM mæ|t, -ts, -dɪŋ, -dəd

mattamore
BR ˈmatəmɔː(r), -z
AM ˌmædəˌmɔ(ə)r, -z

matte
BR mat, -s
AM mæt, -s

matted
BR ˈmatɪd
AM ˈmædəd

mattedly
BR ˈmatɪdli
AM ˈmædədli

mattedness
BR ˈmatɪdnɪs
AM ˈmædədnəs

matter
BR ˈmat|ə(r), -əz, -(ə)rɪŋ, -əd
AM ˈmædər, -z, -ɪŋ, -d

Matterhorn
BR ˈmatəhɔːn
AM ˈmædərˌ(h)ɔ(ə)rn

matter-of-fact
BR ˌmat(ə)rəvˈfakt
AM ˌmædərə(v)ˌfæk(t)

matter-of-factly
BR ˌmat(ə)rəvˈfaktli
AM ˌmædərə(v)ˌfæk(t)li

matter-of-factness
BR ˌmat(ə)rəvˈfak(t)nəs
AM ˌmædərə(v)ˌfæk(t)nəs

mattery
BR ˈmat(ə)ri
AM ˈmædəri

Matthew
BR ˈmaθjuː
AM ˈmæθju

Matthews
BR ˈmaθjuːz
AM ˈmæθjuz

Matthias
BR məˈθʌɪəs
AM məˌθaɪəs

matting
BR ˈmatɪŋ
AM ˈmædɪŋ

mattins
BR ˈmatɪnz
AM ˈmætnz

mattock
BR ˈmatək, -s
AM ˈmædək, -s

mattoid
BR ˈmatɔɪd, -z
AM ˈmædˌɔɪd, -z

mattress
BR ˈmatrɪs, -ɪz
AM ˈmætrəs, -əz

maturate
BR ˈmatʃʉreɪt, ˈmatjʉreɪt, -s, -ɪŋ, -ɨd
AM ˈmætʃəˌreɪ|t, -ts, -dɪŋ, -dɨd

maturation
BR ˌmatʃʉˈreɪʃn, ˌmatjʉˈreɪʃn
AM ˌmætʃəˈreɪʃən

maturational
BR ˌmatʃəˈreɪʃn̩(ə)l, ˌmatʃʉˈreɪʃən(ə)l, matjʉˈreɪʃn̩(ə)l, ˌmatjʉˈreɪʃən(ə)l
AM ˌmætʃəˈreɪʃ(ə)nəl

maturative
BR məˈtʃʊərətɪv, məˈtjʊərətɪv, məˈtʃɔːrətɪv, məˈtjɔːrətɪv
AM ˈmætʃəˌreɪdɪv, məˈtʃərədɪv, məˈtʃʊrədɪv

mature
BR məˈtʃʊə(r), məˈtjʊə(r), məˈtʃɔː(r), məˈtjɔː(r), -z, -ɪŋ, -d
AM məˈtʃər, məˈtʃʊ(ə)r, məˈt(j)ʊ(ə)r, -z, -ɪŋ, -d

maturely
BR məˈtʃʊəli, məˈtjʊəli, məˈtʃɔːli, məˈtjɔːli
AM məˈtʃərli, məˈtʃʊrli, məˈt(j)ʊrli

matureness
BR məˈtʃʊənəs, məˈtjʊənəs, məˈtʃɔːnəs, məˈtjɔːnəs
AM məˈtʃərnəs, məˈtʃʊrnəs, məˈt(j)ʊrnəs

maturity
BR mə'tʃʊərɪti, mə'tjʊərɪti, mə'tʃɔːrɪti, mə'tjɔːrɪti
AM mə'tʃərədi, mə'tʃʊrədi, mə't(j)ʊrədi

matutinal
BR ˌmatjʉ'tʌɪnl, ˌmatʃʉ'tʌɪnl, mə'tjuːtɪnl, mə'tʃuːtɪnl
AM mə't(j)utn̩əl, ˈmætʃəˌtaɪnəl

maty
BR 'meɪti
AM 'meɪdi

matza
BR 'mɒtsə(r), 'matsə(r), 'mʌtsə(r), -z
AM 'mɑtzə, 'mɑtsə, -z

matzah
BR 'mɒtsə(r), 'matsə(r), 'mʌtsə(r), -z
AM 'mɑtzə, 'mɑtsə, -z

matzo
BR 'mɒtsə(r), 'matsə(r), 'mʌtsə(r), 'matsəʊ, -z
AM 'mɑtzə, 'mɑtsə, -z

matzoh
BR 'mɒtsə(r), 'matsə(r), 'mʌtsə(r), 'matsəʊ, -z
AM 'mɑtzə, 'mɑtsə, -z

mauby
BR 'məʊbi, 'mɔːbi
AM 'mɔbi, 'mɑbi

maud
BR mɔːd, -z
AM mɔd, mɑd, -z

Maude
BR mɔːd
AM mɔd, mɑd

maudlin
BR 'mɔːdlɪn
AM 'mɔdlən, 'mɑdlən

Maudling
BR 'mɔːdlɪŋ
AM 'mɔdlɪŋ, 'mɑdlɪŋ

Maudsley
BR 'mɔːdzli
AM 'mɔdzli, 'mɑdzli

Maugham
BR mɔːm
AM mɔm, mɑm

Maughan
BR mɔːn
AM mɔ(ə)n

maul
BR mɔːl, -z, -ɪŋ, -d
AM mɔl, mɑl, -z, -ɪŋ, -d

mauler
BR 'mɔːlə(r), -z
AM 'mɔlər, 'mɑlər, -z

Mauleverer
BR mə'lɛv(ə)rə(r)
AM mɔ'lɛvərər, mɑ'lɛvərər

maulstick
BR 'mɔːlstɪk, -s
AM 'mɔlˌstɪk, 'mɑlˌstɪk, -s

Mau Mau
BR 'maʊ maʊ
AM 'maʊ 'maʊ

Mauna Kea
BR ˌmaʊnə 'keɪə(r)
AM ˌmaʊnə 'keɪə

Mauna Loa
BR ˌmaʊnə 'ləʊə(r)
AM ˌmaʊnə 'loʊə

maunder
BR 'mɔːnd|ə(r), -əz, -(ə)rɪŋ, -əd
AM 'mɔndər, 'mɑndər, -z, -ɪŋ, -d

maundering
BR 'mɔːnd(ə)rɪŋ, -z
AM 'mɔnd(ə)rɪŋ, 'mɑnd(ə)rɪŋ, -z

Maundy
BR 'mɔːndi
AM 'mɔndi, 'mɑndi

Maupassant
BR 'məʊpasɒ̃
AM ˌmɔpə'sɑn

Maura
BR 'mɔːrə(r)
AM 'mɔrə

Maureen
BR 'mɔːriːn
AM mɔ'rin

Mauretania
BR ˌmɒrɪ'teɪnɪə(r), ˌmɔːrɪ'teɪnɪə(r)
AM ˌmɔrə'teɪniə

Mauretanian
BR ˌmɒrɪ'teɪnɪən, ˌmɔːrɪ'teɪnɪən, -z
AM ˌmɔrə'teɪniən, -z

Mauriac
BR 'mɔːrɪak
AM ˌmɔri'(j)ɑk

Maurice
BR 'mɒrɪs
AM mɔ'ris

Maurist
BR 'mɔːrɪst, -s
AM 'mɔrəst, -s

Mauritania
BR ˌmɒrɪ'teɪnɪə(r), ˌmɔːrɪ'teɪnɪə(r)
AM ˌmɔrə'teɪniə

Mauritanian
BR ˌmɒrɪ'teɪnɪən, ˌmɔːrɪ'teɪnɪən, -z
AM ˌmɔrə'teɪniən, -z

Mauritian
BR mə'rɪʃn, -z
AM mɔ'rɪʃən, -z

Mauritius
BR mə'rɪʃəs
AM mɔ'rɪʃəs

Maury
BR 'mɔːri
AM 'mɔri

Maurya
BR 'maʊrɪə(r)
AM 'maʊriə

Mauser®
BR 'maʊzə(r), -z
AM 'maʊzər, -z

mausolea
BR ˌmɔːsə'liːə(r), ˌmɔːzə'liːə(r)
AM ˌmɔzə'liə, ˌmɔsə'liə, ˌmɑzə'liə, ˌmɑsə'liə

mausoleum
BR ˌmɔːsə'liːəm, ˌmɔːzə'liːəm, -z
AM ˌmɔzə'liəm, ˌmɔsə'liəm, ˌmɑzə'liəm, ˌmɑsə'liəm, -z

mauve
BR məʊv
AM mɔv, moʊv, mɑv

mauvish
BR 'məʊvɪʃ
AM 'mɔvɪʃ, 'moʊvɪʃ, 'mɑvɪʃ

maven
BR 'meɪvn, -z
AM 'meɪvən, -z

maverick
BR 'mav(ə)rɪk, -s
AM 'mæv(ə)rɪk, -s

mavis
BR 'meɪv|ɪs, -ɪsɪz
AM 'meɪvɪs, -ɪz

maw
BR mɔː(r), -z
AM mɔ, mɑ, -z

Mawddach
BR 'maʊðax, 'mɔːðak
AM 'mɔðɑk, 'mɑðɑk

Mawdesley
BR 'mɔːdzli
AM 'mɔdzli, 'mɑdzli

Mawer
BR mɔː(r), 'mɔːə(r)
AM 'mɑwər

Mawgan
BR 'mɔːg(ə)n
AM 'mɔgən, 'mɑgən

Mawhinny
BR mə'wɪni
AM mɑ'wɪni

mawkish
BR 'mɔːkɪʃ
AM 'mɔkɪʃ, 'mɑkɪʃ

mawkishly
BR 'mɔːkɪʃli
AM 'mɔkɪʃli, 'mɑkɪʃli

mawkishness
BR 'mɔːkɪʃnɪs
AM 'mɔkɪʃnɪs, 'mɑkɪʃnɪs

Mawson
BR 'mɔːsn
AM 'mɔsən, 'mɑsən

mawworm
BR 'mɔːwəːm, -z
AM 'mɔˌwərm, 'mɑˌwərm, -z

max
BR maks
AM mæks

maxi
BR 'maksi
AM 'mæksi

maxilla
BR mak'sɪlə(r), -z
AM mæk'sɪlə, -z

maxillae
BR mak'sɪliː
AM mæk'sɪli, mæk'sɪlaɪ

maxillary
BR mak'sɪl(ə)ri
AM 'mæksəˌlɛri

maxim
BR 'maksɪm, -z
AM 'mæksəm, -z

maxima
BR 'maksɪmə(r)
AM 'mæksəmə

maximal
BR 'maksɪml
AM 'mæksəməl

maximalist
BR 'maksɪml̩ɪst, 'maksɪməlɪst, -s
AM 'mæksəmələst, -s

maximally
BR 'maksɪml̩i, 'maksɪməli
AM 'mæksəməli

Maximilian
BR ˌmaksɪ'mɪlɪən
AM ˌmæksə'mɪliən

maximin
BR 'maksɪmɪn, ˌmaksɪ'mɪn
AM ˈmæksiˌmɪn

maximisation
BR ˌmaksɪmʌɪ'zeɪʃn
AM ˌmæksəmə'zeɪʃən, ˌmæksəˌmaɪ'zeɪʃən

maximise
BR 'maksɪmʌɪz, -ɪz, -ɪŋ, -d
AM 'mæksəˌmaɪz, -ɪz, -ɪŋ, -d

maximiser
BR 'maksɪmʌɪzə(r), -z
AM 'mæksəˌmaɪzər, -z

maximization
BR ˌmaksɪmʌɪ'zeɪʃn
AM ˌmæksəmə'zeɪʃən, ˌmæksəˌmaɪ'zeɪʃən

maximize
BR 'maksɪmʌɪz, -ɪz, -ɪŋ, -d
AM 'mæksəˌmaɪz, -ɪz, -ɪŋ, -d

maximizer
BR 'maksɪmʌɪzə(r), -z
AM 'mæksəˌmaɪzər, -z

maximum
BR 'maksɪməm, -z
AM 'mæksəməm, -z

maximus
BR 'maksɪməs
AM 'mæksəməs

Maxine
BR mak'siːn
AM mək'sin

maxixe
BR mak'siːks, mə'ʃiːʃə(r), mak'siːksɪz\mə'siːʃəz
AM mæk'siks, mə'ʃiʃə, mæk'siksẓ\mə'ʃiʃɪz

Maxwell
BR 'maksw(ɛ)l
AM 'mæksˌwɛl

may
BR meɪ
AM meɪ

Maya[1]
American people
BR 'mʌɪə(r)
AM 'maɪə

Maya[2]
forename
BR 'meɪə(r), 'mʌɪə(r)
AM 'maɪə

Mayall
BR 'meɪəl, 'meɪɔːl
AM 'mɛɪˌɔl, 'mɛɪˌɑl

Mayan
BR 'mʌɪən, -z
AM 'maɪən, -z

maybe
BR 'meɪbiː
AM 'meɪbi

maybeetle
BR 'meɪˌbiːtl, -z
AM 'meɪˌbidəl, -z

mayday
BR 'meɪdeɪ, -z
AM 'meɪˌdeɪ, -z

Mayer[1]
German
BR 'mʌɪə(r)
AM 'maɪər

Mayer[2]
BR 'meɪə(r)
AM 'meɪər

mayest
BR 'meɪɪst
AM 'meɪɪst

Mayfair
BR 'meɪfɛː(r), -z
AM 'meɪˌfɛ(ə)r, -z

Mayfield
BR 'meɪfiːld
AM 'meɪˌfild

mayflower
BR 'meɪˌflaʊə(r), -z
AM 'meɪˌflaʊər, -z

mayfly
BR 'meɪflʌɪ, -z
AM 'meɪˌflaɪ, -z

mayhap
BR 'meɪhap
AM 'meɪˌhæp

mayhem
BR 'meɪhɛm
AM 'meɪˌhɛm

Mayhew
BR 'meɪhjuː
AM 'meɪˌhju

maying
BR 'meɪɪŋ, -z
AM 'meɪɪŋ, -z

Maynard
BR 'meɪnɑːd
AM 'meɪnərd

Mayne
BR meɪn
AM meɪn

Maynooth
BR mə'nuːθ, meɪ'nuːθ
AM meɪ'nuθ

mayn't
BR 'meɪ(ə)nt, meɪn̩t
AM 'meɪ(ə)nt

Mayo
BR 'meɪəʊ
AM 'meɪoʊ

mayonnaise
BR ˌmeɪə'neɪz
AM 'meɪəˌneɪz, ˌmeɪə'neɪz

mayor
BR mɛː(r), -z
AM 'meɪ(ə)r, -z

mayoral
BR 'mɛːrəl, 'mɛːrl̩
AM meɪ'ɔrəl, 'meɪərəl

mayoralty
BR 'mɛːrəlt|i, 'mɛːrl̩t|i, -ɪz
AM 'meɪərəlti, -z

mayoress
BR 'mɛːrəs, ˌmɛː'rɛs, -ɪz
AM 'meɪərəs, -əz

mayorship
BR 'mɛːʃɪp, -s
AM 'meɪərˌʃɪp, -s

Mayotte
BR ma'jɒt
AM mɑ'jɔt, mɑ'jɑt

maypole
BR 'meɪpəʊl, -z
AM 'meɪˌpoʊl, -z

Mays
BR meɪz
AM meɪz

mayst
BR meɪst
AM meɪst

mayweed
BR 'meɪwiːd, -z
AM 'meɪˌwid, -z

mazard
BR 'mazəd, -z
AM 'mæzərd, -z

Mazar-e-Sharif
BR məˌzɑːrəʃa'riːf, məˌzɑːrəʃə'riːf
AM mə'ˌzɑrəʃə'rif

Mazarin
BR 'mazərɪn, 'mazəran
AM 'mæzərən

mazarine
BR ˌmazə'riːn, 'mazəriːn, -z
AM ˌmæzəˌriːn, 'mæzərən, -z

Mazda®
BR 'mazdə(r), -z
AM 'mɑzdə, -z

Mazdaism
BR 'mazdə(r)ɪz(ə)m
AM 'mɑzdəˌɪzəm

maze
BR meɪz, -ɪz, -d
AM meɪz, -ɪz, -d

mazer
BR 'meɪzə(r), -z
AM 'meɪzər, -z

mazily
BR 'meɪzɨli
AM 'meɪzɨli

maziness
BR 'meɪzɪnɨs
AM 'meɪzinɨs

mazurka
BR mə'zəːkə(r), mə'zʊəkə(r), -z
AM mə'zərkə, mə'zʊrkə, -z

mazy
BR 'meɪz|i, -ɪə(r), -ɪɪst
AM 'meɪzi, -ər, -ɨst

mazzard
BR 'mazəd, -z
AM 'mæzərd, -z

Mazzini
BR mat'siːni
AM mə'zini

Mb
BR 'mɛgəbʌɪt, -s
AM 'mɛgəˌbaɪt, -s

Mbabane
BR m̩ba'bɑːni
AM m̩bɑ'bɑni

McAfee
BR ˌmakə'fiː, mə'kafiː
AM 'mækəˌfi, mə'kæfi

McAleese
BR ˌmakə'liːs
AM ˌmækə'lis

McAlister
BR mə'kalɪstə(r)
AM mə'kæləstər

McAllister
BR mək'alɪstə(r)
AM mə'kæləstər

McAlpine
BR mə'kalpʌɪn
AM mə'kælˌpaɪn

McAnally
BR ˌmakə'nali
AM 'mækəˌnæli

McArdle
BR mə'kɑːdl
AM mə'kɑrdəl

McArthur
BR mək'ɑːθə(r)
AM mə'kɑrθər

McAteer
BR ˌmakə'tɪə(r)
AM 'mækəˌtɪər

McAuliffe
BR mə'kɔːlɪf
AM mə'kɔlɪf, mə'kɑlɪf

McAvoy
BR 'makəvɔɪ
AM 'mækəˌvɔɪ

McBain
BR mək'beɪn
AM mək'beɪn

McBrain
BR mək'breɪn
AM mək'breɪn

McBride
BR mək'brʌɪd
AM mək'braɪd

McCabe
BR mə'keɪb
AM mə'keɪb

McCain
BR mə'keɪn
AM mə'keɪn

McCall
BR mə'kɔːl
AM mə'kɔl, mə'kɑl

McCallum
BR mə'kaləm
AM mə'kæləm

McCann
BR mə'kan
AM mə'kæn

McCarthy
BR mə'kɑːθi
AM mə'kɑrθi

McCarthyism
BR mə'kɑːθɪɪz(ə)m
AM mə'kɑrθiˌɪzəm

McCarthyite
BR mə'kɑːθɪʌɪt
AM mə'kɑrθɪˌaɪt

McCartney
BR mə'kɑːtni
AM mə'kɑrtni

McCarty
BR mə'kɑːti
AM mə'kɑrdi

McCaskill
BR mə'kask(ɪ)l
AM mə'kæskəl

McClain
BR mə'kleɪn
AM mə'kleɪn

McClellan
BR mə'klɛlən
AM mə'klɛlən

McClelland
BR məˈklɛlənd
AM məˈklɛlən(d)

McClintock
BR məˈklɪntɒk
AM məˈklɪnˌtɑk, məˈklɪn(t)ək

McClure
BR məˈklʊə(r)
AM məˈklʊ(ə)r

McCluskie
BR məˈklʌski
AM məˈkləski

McColl
BR məˈkɒl
AM məˈkɔl, məˈkɑl

McConachie
BR məˈkɒnəki
AM məˈkɑnəki

McConachy
BR məˈkɒnəki
AM məˈkɑnəki

McConnell
BR məˈkɒn(ə)l
AM məˈkɑnəl

McCormack
BR məˈkɔːmak
AM məˈkɔrmək

McCormick
BR məˈkɔːmɪk
AM məˈkɔrmək

McCorquodale
BR məˈkɔːkədeɪl
AM məˈkɔrkəˌdeɪl

McCowan
BR məˈkaʊən
AM məˈkaʊən

McCoy
BR məˈkɔɪ, -z
AM məˈkɔɪ, -z

McCracken
BR məˈkrak(ə)n
AM məˈkrækən

McCrae
BR məˈkreɪ
AM məˈkreɪ

McCrea
BR məˈkreɪ
AM məˈkreɪ

McCready
BR məˈkriːdi
AM məˈkridi

McCrindle
BR məˈkrɪndl
AM məˈkrɪndəl

McCrum
BR məˈkrʌm
AM məˈkrəm

McCulloch
BR məˈkʌlək, məˈkʌləx
AM məˈkələ(k)

McCullogh
BR məˈkʌlək, məˈkʌləx
AM məˈkələ(k)

McCullough
BR məˈkʌlək, məˈkʌləx
AM məˈkələ(k)

McCusker
BR məˈkʌskə(r)
AM məˈkəskər

McDade
BR məkˈdeɪd
AM məkˈdeɪd

McDaniel
BR məkˈdanjəl
AM məkˈdænjəl

McDermot
BR məkˈdəːmət
AM məkˈdərmət

McDermott
BR məkˈdəːmət
AM məkˈdərmət

McDonagh
BR məkˈdɒnə(*r*)
AM məkˈdɑnə

McDonald
BR məkˌdɒnld
AM məkˈdɑnəld

McDonnell
BR məkˈdɒnl
AM məkˈdɑnəl

McDougal
BR məkˈduːgl
AM məkˈdugl

McDougall
BR məkˈduːgl
AM məkˈdugl

McDowall
BR məkˈdaʊəl
AM məkˈdaʊəl

McDowell
BR məkˈdaʊəl
AM məkˈdaʊəl

McDuff
BR məkˈdʌf
AM məkˈdəf

McElroy
BR ˈmaklrɔɪ
AM ˈmæklˌrɔɪ

McElwain
BR ˈmaklweɪn, məˈkɛlweɪn
AM ˈmæklˌweɪn, məˈkɛlˌweɪn

McElwie
BR məkˈɛlwi
AM məkˈɛlwi

McEnroe
BR ˈmak(ɪ)nrəʊ
AM ˈmækənˌroʊ

McEvoy
BR ˈmakɪvɔɪ
AM ˈmækəˌvɔɪ

McEwan
BR məˈkjuːən
AM məkˈjuwən

McFadden
BR məkˈfadn
AM məkˈfædən

McFadyean
BR məkˈfadɪən, məkˈfadjən
AM məkˈfædɪən, məkˈfædjən

McFadyen
BR məkˈfadɪən, məkˈfadjən
AM məkˈfædɪən, məkˈfædjən

McFadzean
BR məkˈfadɪən, məkˈfadjən
AM məkˈfædɪən, məkˈfædjən

McFarland
BR məkˈfɑːlənd
AM məkˈfɑrlən(d)

McFarlane
BR məkˈfɑːlən
AM məkˈfɑrlən

McFee
BR məkˈfiː
AM məkˈfi

McGahey
BR məˈgɑːhi, məˈgaxi, məˈgahi
AM məˈgɑhi

McGee
BR məˈgiː
AM məˈgi

McGhee
BR məˈgiː
AM məˈgi

McGill
BR məˈgɪl
AM məˈgɪl

McGilligan
BR məˈgɪlɪg(ə)n
AM məˈgɪlɪgən

McGillivray
BR məˈgɪlɪvreɪ, məˈgɪlɪvri
AM məˈgɪlɪvreɪ

McGinn
BR məˈgɪn
AM məˈgɪn

McGinnis
BR məˈgɪnɪs
AM məˈgɪnɪs

McGinty
BR məˈgɪnti
AM məˈgɪn(t)i

McGoldrick
BR məˈgəʊldrɪk
AM məˈgoʊldrɪk

McGonagall
BR məˈgɒnəgl
AM məˈgɑnəgəl

McGoohan
BR məˈguːən
AM məˈguən

McGough
BR məˈgɒf
AM məˈgɔf, məˈgəf, məˈgɑf

McGovern
BR məˈgʌvn
AM məˈgəvərn

McGowan
BR məˈgaʊən
AM məˈgaʊən

McGrath[1]
BR məˈgrɑːθ, məˈgraθ
AM məˈgræθ

McGrath[2]
in Ireland
BR məˈgrah
AM məˈgræθ

McGraw
BR məˈgrɔː(*r*)
AM məˈgrɔ, məˈgrɑ

McGregor
BR məˈgrɛgə(r)
AM məˈgrɛgər

McGuigan
BR məˈgwɪg(ə)n
AM məˈgwɪgn

McGuinness
BR məˈgɪnɪs
AM məˈgɪnəs

McGuire
BR məˈgwʌɪə(r)
AM məˈgwaɪər

McGurk
BR məˈgəːk
AM məˈgərk

McHenry
BR məkˈhɛnri
AM məkˈhɛnri

McHugh
BR məkˈhjuː
AM məkˈ(h)ju

McIlroy
BR ˈmak(ɪ)lrɔɪ
AM ˈmæklˌrɔɪ

McIlvaney
BR ˌmaklˈveɪni
AM ˈmæklˌveɪni

McIlvenny
BR ˌmaklˈvɛni
AM ˈmæklˌvɛni

McIlwain
BR ˈmaklweɪn
AM ˈmæklˌweɪn

McInerney
BR ˌmakɪˈnəːni
AM ˈmækəˌnərni

McInnes
BR məkˈɪnɪs
AM məkˈɪnɪs

McInnis
BR məkˈɪnɪs
AM məkˈɪnɪs

McIntosh
BR ˈmak(ɪ)ntɒʃ
AM ˈmækənˌtɑʃ

McIntyre
BR ˈmakɪntʌɪə(r)
AM ˈmækənˌtaɪər

McIver
BR məkˈʌɪvə(r)
AM məˈkaɪvər

McKay
BR məˈkeɪ

AM mə'keɪ

McKechnie
BR mə'kɛkni, mə'kɛxni
AM mə'kɛkni

McKee
BR mə'ki:
AM mə'ki

McKellar
BR mə'kɛlə(r)
AM mə'kɛlər

McKellen
BR mə'kɛlən
AM mə'kɛlən

McKendrick
BR mə'kɛndrɪk
AM mə'kɛndrɪk

McKenna
BR mə'kɛnə(*r*)
AM mə'kɛnə

McKenzie
BR mə'kɛnzi
AM mə'kɛnzi

McKeon
BR mə'kjəʊn
AM mə'kiən

McKeown
BR mə'kjəʊn
AM mə'kiən

McKie
BR mə'kʌɪ, mə'ki:
AM mə'ki

McKinlay
BR mə'kɪnli
AM mə'kɪnli

McKinley
BR mə'kɪnli
AM mə'kɪnli

McKinney
BR mə'kɪni
AM mə'kɪni

McKinnon
BR mə'kɪnən
AM mə'kɪnɪn

McKittrick
BR mə'kɪtrɪk
AM mə'kɪtrɪk

McKnight
BR mək'nʌɪt
AM mək'naɪt

McLachlan
BR mə'klɒxlən, mə'klɒklən
AM mə'klɑklən

McLaughlin
BR mə'klɒxlɪn, mə'klɒklɪn
AM mə'klɑklən, mə'klɑflən, mə'klɔklən, mə'klɔflən

McLean
BR mə'kleɪn, mə'kli:n
AM mə'klin

McLeish
BR mə'kli:ʃ
AM mə'kliʃ

McLellan
BR mə'klɛlən
AM mə'klɛlən

McLennan
BR mə'klɛnən
AM mə'klɛnən

McLeod
BR mə'klaʊd
AM mə'klaʊd

McLoughlin
BR mə'klɒxlɪn, mə'klɒklɪn
AM mə'klɑklən, mə'klɑflən, mə'klɔklən, mə'klɔflən

McLuhan
BR mə'klu:ən
AM mə'kluwən

McMahon
BR mək'mɑ:n
AM mək'mæn

McManus
BR mək'manəs
AM mək'mænəs

McMaster
BR mək'mɑ:stə(r), mək'mastə(r)
AM mək'mæstər

McMenemey
BR mək'mɛnəmi
AM mək'mɛnəmi

McMenemy
BR mək'mɛnəmi
AM mək'mɛnəmi

McMillan
BR mək'mɪlən
AM mək'mɪlən

McMurdo
BR mək'mə:dəʊ
AM mək'mərdoʊ

McMurtry
BR mək'mə:tri
AM mək'mərtri

McNab
BR mək'nab
AM mək'næb

McNaghten
BR mək'nɔ:t(ə)n
AM mək'nɔtn, mək'nɑtn

McNaghten rules
BR mək'nɔ:tn ru:lz
AM mək'nɔtn ˌrulz, mək'nɑtn ˌrulz

McNaghton
BR mək'nɔ:t(ə)n
AM mək'nɔtn, mək'nɑtn

McNair
BR mək'nɛ:(r)
AM mək'nɛ(ə)r

McNally
BR mək'nali
AM mək'næli

McNamara
BR ˌmaknə'mɑ:rə(*r*)
AM 'mæknəˌmɛrə

McNamee
BR ˌmaknə'mi:
AM 'mæknəˌmi

McNaughten
BR mək'nɔ:t(ə)n
AM mək'nɔtn, mək'nɑtn

McNaughton
BR mək'nɔ:t(ə)n
AM mək'nɔtn, mək'nɑtn

McNeil
BR mək'ni:l
AM mək'nil

McNeill
BR mək'ni:l
AM mək'nil

McNestry
BR mək'nɛstri
AM mək'nɛstri

McNulty
BR mək'nʌlti
AM mək'nəlti

McPhail
BR mək'feɪl
AM mək'feɪl

McPhee
BR mək'fi:
AM mək'fi

McPherson
BR mək'fə:sn
AM mək'fərsən, mək'fɪrsən

McQueen
BR mə'kwi:n
AM mə'kwin

McRae
BR mə'kreɪ
AM mə'kreɪ

McReady
BR mə'kri:di
AM mə'kridi, mək'ridi

McShane
BR mək'ʃeɪn
AM mək'ʃeɪn

McShea
BR mək'ʃeɪ
AM mək'ʃeɪ

McSweeney
BR mək'swi:ni
AM mək'swini

McTaggart
BR mək'tagət
AM mək'tægərt

McTavish
BR mək'tavɪʃ
AM mək'tævɪʃ

McTeer
BR mək'tɪə(r)
AM mək'tɪ(ə)r

McVay
BR mək'veɪ
AM mək'veɪ

McVey
BR mək'veɪ
AM mək'veɪ

McVicar
BR mək'vɪkə(r)
AM mək'vɪkər

McVitie
BR mək'vɪti
AM mək'vɪdi

McWhirter
BR mək'wə:tə(r)
AM mək'wərdər

McWhorter
BR mək'wɔ:tə(r)
AM mək'wərdər

McWilliam
BR mək'wɪljəm
AM mək'wɪljəm, mək'wɪliəm

McWilliams
BR mək'wɪljəmz
AM mək'wɪljəmz, mək'wɪliəmz

me¹
strong pronoun, musical note
BR mi:
AM mi

me²
weak pronoun
BR mɪ
AM mɪ

Meacham
BR 'mi:tʃ(ə)m
AM 'mitʃəm

Meacher
BR 'mi:tʃə(r)
AM 'mitʃər

mea culpa
BR ˌmeɪə 'kʊlpə(*r*), ˌmi:ə +, + 'kʌlpə(*r*)
AM ˌmeɪə 'kʊlpə

mead
BR mi:d
AM mid

meadow
BR 'mɛdəʊ, -z
AM 'mɛdoʊ, -z

meadowland
BR 'mɛdəʊland, -z
AM 'mɛdoʊˌlænd, -z

meadowlark
BR 'mɛdəʊlɑ:k, -s
AM 'mɛdoʊˌlɑrk, -s

meadowsweet
BR 'mɛdəʊswi:t
AM 'mɛdoʊˌswit

meadowy
BR 'mɛdəʊi
AM 'mɛdoʊi

meager
BR 'mi:gə(r)
AM 'migər

meagerly
BR 'mi:gəli
AM 'migərli

meagerness
BR 'mi:gənəs
AM 'migərnəs

meagre
BR ˈmiːgə(r)
AM ˈmigər
meagrely
BR ˈmiːgəli
AM ˈmigərli
meagreness
BR ˈmiːgənəs
AM ˈmigərnəs
Meakin
BR ˈmiːkɪn
AM ˈmikɪn
meal
BR miːl, -z
AM mil, -z
mealie
BR ˈmiːl|i, -ɪz
AM ˈmili, -z
mealiness
BR ˈmiːlɪnɨs
AM ˈmilinɨs
mealtime
BR ˈmiːltʌɪm, -z
AM ˈmilˌtaɪm, -z
mealworm
BR ˈmiːlwəːm, -z
AM ˈmilˌwərm, -z
mealy
BR ˈmiːl|i, -ɪə(r), -ɪɨst
AM ˈmili, -ər, -ɨst
mealybug
BR ˈmiːlɪbʌg, -z
AM ˈmiliˌbəg, -z
mealy-mouthed
BR ˌmiːlɪˈmaʊðd
AM ˈmiliˌmaʊðd, ˈmiliˌmaʊθt
mean
BR miːn, -z, -ɪŋ, -ə(r), -ɨst
AM min, -z, -ɪŋ, -ə(r), -ɨst
meander
BR mɪˈand|ə(r), -əz, -(ə)rɪŋ, -əd
AM miˈænd|ər, -ərz, -(ə)rɪŋ, -ərd
meandering
BR mɪˈand(ə)rɪŋ, -z
AM miˈænd(ə)rɪŋ, -z
meandrine
BR mɪˈandrʌɪn, mɪˈandrɪn
AM miˈændrin, miˈænˌdraɪn, miˈændrən
meanie
BR ˈmiːn|i, -ɪz
AM ˈmini, -z
meaning
BR ˈmiːnɪŋ, -z
AM ˈminɪŋ, -z
meaningful
BR ˈmiːnɪŋf(ʊ)l
AM ˈminɪŋfəl
meaningfully
BR ˈmiːnɪŋfʊli, ˈmiːnɪŋfl̩i
AM ˈminɪŋf(ə)li
meaningfulness
BR ˈmiːnɪŋf(ʊ)lnəs
AM ˈminɪŋfəlnəs
meaningless
BR ˈmiːnɪŋlɨs
AM ˈminɪŋlɨs
meaninglessly
BR ˈmiːnɪŋlɨsli
AM ˈminɪŋglɨsli
meaninglessness
BR ˈmiːnɪŋlɨsnɨs
AM ˈminɪŋglɨsnɨs
meaningly
BR ˈmiːnɪŋli
AM ˈminɪŋli
meanly
BR ˈmiːnli
AM ˈminli
meanness
BR ˈmiːnnɨs
AM ˈmi(n)nɨs
means
BR miːnz
AM minz
meant
BR mɛnt
AM mɛnt
meantime
BR ˈmiːntʌɪm
AM ˈminˌtaɪm
meanwhile
BR ˈmiːnwʌɪl
AM ˈminˌ(h)waɪl
meany
BR ˈmiːn|i, -ɪz
AM ˈmini, -z
Mearns
BR mɛːnz
AM mərnz
Measham
BR ˈmiːʃ(ə)m
AM ˈmiʃəm
measles
BR ˈmiːzlz
AM ˈmizəlz
measliness
BR ˈmiːzlɪnɨs
AM ˈmizlinɨs
measly
BR ˈmiːzli
AM ˈmizli
measurability
BR ˌmɛʒ(ə)rəˈbɪlɨti
AM ˌmɛʒ(ə)rəˈbɪlɨdi, ˌmɛʒərˈbɪlɨdi
measurable
BR ˈmɛʒ(ə)rəbl
AM ˈmɛʒ(ə)r(ə)bəl
measurableness
BR ˈmɛʒ(ə)rəblnəs
AM ˈmɛʒ(ə)rəbəlnəs, ˈmɛʒərbəlnəs
measurably
BR ˈmɛʒ(ə)rəbli
AM ˈmɛʒ(ə)rəbli, ˈmɛʒərbli
measure
BR ˈmɛʒ|ə(r), -əz, -(ə)rɪŋ, -əd
AM ˈmɛʒ|ər, -ərz, -(ə)rɪŋ, -ərd
measuredly
BR ˈmɛʒədli
AM ˈmɛʒərdli
measureless
BR ˈmɛʒələs
AM ˈmɛʒərləs
measurelessly
BR ˈmɛʒələsli
AM ˈmɛʒərləsli
measurement
BR ˈmɛʒəm(ə)nt, -s
AM ˈmɛʒərmənt, -s
meat
BR miːt, -s
AM mit, -s
meatball
BR ˈmiːtbɔːl, -z
AM ˈmitˌbɔl, ˈmitˌbɑl, -z
Meath
BR miːð, miːθ
AM miθ
meathead
BR ˈmiːthɛd, -z
AM ˈmitˌ(h)ɛd, ˈmidɛd, -z
meatily
BR ˈmiːtɨli
AM ˈmidɨli
meatiness
BR ˈmiːtɪnɨs
AM ˈmidinɨs
meatless
BR ˈmiːtlɨs
AM ˈmitlɨs
meatus
BR mɪˈeɪtəs, -ɪz
AM mɪˈeɪdəs, -əz
meaty
BR ˈmiːt|i, -ɪə(r), -ɪɨst
AM ˈmidi, -ər, -ɨst
Mebyon Kernow
BR ˌmɛbɪən ˈkəːnəʊ
AM ˈmɛbɪən ˈkərˌnoʊ
mecca
BR ˈmɛkə(*r*)
AM ˈmɛkə
meccano
BR mɪˈkɑːnəʊ
AM məˈkænoʊ, məˈkɑnoʊ
mechanic
BR mɪˈkanɪk, -s
AM məˈkænɪk, -s
mechanical
BR mɪˈkanɨkl
AM məˈkænəkəl
mechanicalism
BR mɪˈkanɨkl̩ɪz(ə)m, mɪˈkanɨkəlɪz(ə)m
AM məˈkænəkəˌlɪzəm
mechanically
BR mɪˈkanɨkli
AM məˈkænək(ə)li
mechanicalness
BR mɪˈkanɨklnəs
AM məˈkænɨklnəs
mechanician
BR ˌmɛkəˈnɪʃn, -z
AM ˌmɛkəˈnɪʃən, -z
mechanisation
BR ˌmɛkənʌɪˈzeɪʃn, ˌmɛkn̩ʌɪˈzeɪʃn
AM ˌmɛkənəˈzeɪʃən, ˌmɛkəˌnaɪˈzeɪʃən
mechanise
BR ˈmɛkənʌɪz, ˈmɛkn̩ʌɪz, -ɪz, -ɪŋ, -d
AM ˈmɛkəˌnaɪz, -ɪz, -ɪŋ, -d
mechaniser
BR ˈmɛkənʌɪzə(r), ˈmɛkn̩ʌɪzə(r), -z
AM ˈmɛkəˌnaɪzər, -z
mechanism
BR ˈmɛkənɪz(ə)m, ˈmɛkn̩ɪz(ə)m
AM ˈmɛkəˌnɪzəm
mechanist
BR ˈmɛkənɪst, ˈmɛkn̩ɪst, -s
AM ˈmɛkənəst, -s
mechanistic
BR ˌmɛkəˈnɪstɪk, ˌmɛknˈɪstɪk
AM ˌmɛkəˈnɪstɪk
mechanistically
BR ˌmɛkəˈnɪstɨkli, ˌmɛknˈɪstɨkli
AM ˌmɛkəˈnɪstək(ə)li
mechanization
BR ˌmɛkənʌɪˈzeɪʃn, ˌmɛkn̩ʌɪˈzeɪʃn
AM ˌmɛkənəˈzeɪʃən, ˌmɛkəˌnaɪˈzeɪʃən
mechanize
BR ˈmɛkənʌɪz, ˈmɛkn̩ʌɪz, -ɪz, -ɪŋ, -d
AM ˈmɛkəˌnaɪz, -ɪz, -ɪŋ, -d
mechanizer
BR ˈmɛkanʌɪzə(r), ˈmɛkn̩ʌɪzə(r), -z
AM ˈmɛkəˌnaɪzər, -z
mechanoreceptor
BR ˌmɛkənəʊrɪˈsɛptə(r), ˌmɛkn̩əʊrɪˈsɛptə(r), -z
AM ˈmɛkənoʊrəˈsɛptər, ˈmɛkənoʊriˈsɛptər, -z
mechatronics
BR ˈmɛkəˌtrɒnɪks
AM ˈmɛkəˈtrɑnɪks
Mechlin
BR ˈmɛklɪn, -z
AM ˈmɛklən, -z
Mecklenburg
BR ˈmɛklənbəːg
AM ˈmɛklənˌbərg
meconium
BR mɪˈkəʊnɪəm
AM məˈkoʊniəm

Med
BR mɛd
AM mɛd

medal
BR 'mɛdl, -z, -d
AM 'mɛdəl, -əlz, -(ə)lɪŋ, -əld

medalist
BR 'mɛdl̩ɪst, -s
AM 'mɛdl̩əst, -s

medallic
BR mɪ'dalɪk
AM mə'dælɪk

medallion
BR mɪ'dalɪən, mɪ'daljən, -z
AM mə'dæljən, mɛ'dæljən, -z

medallist
BR 'mɛdl̩ɪst, -s
AM 'mɛdl̩əst, -s

Medawar
BR 'mɛdəwə(r)
AM 'mɛdəwər

meddle
BR 'mɛd|l, -lz, -l̩ɪŋ\-lɪŋ, -ld
AM 'mɛd|əl, -əlz, -(ə)lɪŋ, -əld

meddler
BR 'mɛdl̩ə(r), 'mɛdlə(r), -z
AM 'mɛd(ə)lər, -z

meddlesome
BR 'mɛdls(ə)m
AM 'mɛdlsəm

meddlesomely
BR 'mɛdls(ə)mli
AM 'mɛdlsəmli

meddlesomeness
BR 'mɛdls(ə)mnəs
AM 'mɛdlsəmnəs

Mede
BR mi:d, -z
AM mid, -z

Medea
BR mɪ'dɪə(r)
AM mɪ'diə

Medellín
BR ˌmɛdɪ'ji:n
AM ˌmɛdəˌjin

Medevac
BR 'mɛdɪvak
AM 'mɛdəˌvæk

media
BR 'mi:dɪə(r)
AM 'midiə

mediaeval
BR ˌmɛdɪ'i:vl
AM ˌmɛd(i)'ivəl, mə'divəl

mediaevalist
BR ˌmɛdɪ'i:vl̩ɪst, ˌmɛdɪ'i:vəlɪst, -s
AM ˌmɛd(i)'ivələst, mə'dɪvələst, -s

mediagenic
BR ˌmi:dɪə'dʒɛnɪk
AM ˌmidiə'dʒɛnɪk

medial
BR 'mi:dɪəl
AM 'midiəl

medially
BR 'mi:dɪəli
AM 'midiəli

median
BR 'mi:dɪən, -z
AM 'midiən, -z

medianly
BR 'mi:dɪənli
AM 'midɪənli

mediant
BR 'mi:dɪənt, -s
AM 'midiənt, -s

mediastina
BR ˌmi:dɪə'stʌɪnə(r)
AM ˌmidiə'staɪnə

mediastinal
BR ˌmi:dɪə'stʌɪnl
AM ˌmidiəˌstaɪnəl

mediastinum
BR ˌmi:dɪə'stʌɪnəm
AM ˌmidiə'staɪnəm

mediate
BR 'mi:dɪeɪt, -s, -ɪŋ, -ɪd
AM 'midiˌeɪ|t, -ts, -dɪŋ, -dɪd

mediately
BR 'mi:dɪətli
AM 'midiɪtli

mediation
BR ˌmi:dɪ'eɪʃn
AM ˌmidi'eɪʃən

mediatisation
BR ˌmi:dɪətʌɪ'zeɪʃn, -z
AM ˌmidiədə'zeɪʃən, ˌmidiəˌtaɪ'zeɪʃən, -z

mediatise
BR 'mi:dɪətʌɪz, -ɪz, -ɪŋ, -d
AM 'midiəˌtaɪz, -ɪz, -ɪŋ, -d

mediatization
BR ˌmi:dɪətʌɪ'zeɪʃn, -z
AM ˌmidiədə'zeɪʃən, ˌmidiəˌtaɪ'zeɪʃən, -z

mediatize
BR 'mi:dɪətʌɪz, -ɪz, -ɪŋ, -d
AM 'midɪəˌtaɪz, -ɪz, -ɪŋ, -d

mediator
BR 'mi:dɪeɪtə(r), -z
AM 'midiˌeɪdər, -z

mediatorial
BR ˌmi:dɪə'tɔ:rɪəl
AM ˌmidiəˌtɔriəl

mediatory
BR 'mi:dɪət(ə)ri
AM 'midiəˌtɔri

mediatrices
BR ˌmi:dɪ'eɪtrɪsi:z
AM ˌmidi'eɪtɪsiz

mediatrix
BR 'mi:dɪətrɪks, -ɪz
AM 'midiəˌtrɪks, -ɪz

medic
BR 'mɛdɪk, -s
AM 'mɛdɪk, -s

medicable
BR 'mɛdɪkəbl
AM 'mɛdəkəbəl

Medicaid
BR 'mɛdɪkeɪd
AM 'mɛdəˌkeɪd

medical
BR 'mɛdɪkl
AM 'mɛdəkəl

medically
BR 'mɛdɪkli
AM 'mɛdək(ə)li

medicament
BR mɪ'dɪkəm(ə)nt, -s
AM mə'dɪkəmənt, 'mɛdəkəˌmɛnt, -s

Medicare
BR 'mɛdɪkɛ:(r)
AM 'mɛdəˌkɛ(ə)r

medicate
BR 'mɛdɪkeɪt, -s, -ɪŋ, -ɪd
AM 'mɛdəˌkeɪ|t, -ts, -dɪŋ, -dɪd

medication
BR ˌmɛdɪ'keɪʃn, -z
AM ˌmɛdə'keɪʃən, -z

medicative
BR 'mɛdɪkətɪv
AM 'mɛdəˌkeɪdɪv

Medicean
BR ˌmɛdɪ'tʃi:ən
AM ˌmɛdəˌtʃiən, ˌmɛdəˌsiən

Medici
BR 'mɛdɪtʃi:, mɪ'di:tʃi:
AM 'mɛdətʃi

medicinal
BR mɪ'dɪsn̩(ə)l, mɪ'dɪsɪn(ə)l
AM mə'dɪsn̩l, mɛ'dɪsnəl

medicinally
BR mɪ'dɪsn̩l̩i, mɪ'dɪsn̩əli, mɪ'dɪsɪnl̩i, mɪ'dɪsɪnəli
AM mɛ'dɪsn̩əli, mə'dɪsnəli

medicine
BR 'mɛd(ɪ)s(ɪ)n, -z
AM 'mɛd(ə)s(ə)n, -z

medick
plant
BR 'mi:dɪk, -s
AM 'midɪk, -s

medico
BR 'mɛdɪkəʊ, -z
AM 'mɛdəˌkoʊ, -z

medieval
BR ˌmɛdɪ'i:vl
AM ˌmɛd(i)'ivəl, mə'divəl

medievalise
BR ˌmɛdɪ'i:vl̩ʌɪz, ˌmɛdɪ'i:vəlʌɪz, -ɪz, -ɪŋ, -d
AM ˌmɛd(i)'ivəˌlaɪz, mə'divəˌlaɪz, -ɪz, -ɪŋ, -d

medievalism
BR ˌmɛdɪ'i:vl̩ɪz(ə)m, ˌmɛdɪ'i:vəlɪz(ə)m
AM ˌmɛd(i)'ivəˌlɪzəm, , mə'divəˌlɪzəm

medievalist
BR ˌmɛdɪ'i:vl̩ɪst, ˌmɛdɪ'i:vəlɪst, -s
AM ˌmɛd(i)'ivələst, mə'divələst, -s

medievalize
BR ˌmɛdɪ'i:vl̩ʌɪz, ˌmɛdɪ'i:vəlʌɪz, -ɪz, -ɪŋ, -d
AM ˌmɛd(i)'ivəˌlaɪz, mə'divəˌlaɪz, -ɪz, -ɪŋ, -d

medievally
BR ˌmɛdɪ'i:vl̩i, ˌmɛdɪ'i:vəli
AM ˌmɛd(i)'ivəli, mə'divəli

Medina[1]
place in Saudi Arabia
BR mɛ'di:nə(r), mɪ'di:nə(r)
AM mə'dinə

Medina[2]
place in US
BR mɪ'dʌɪnə(r)
AM mə'daɪnə

mediocre
BR ˌmi:dɪ'əʊkə(r)
AM ˌmidi'oʊkər

mediocrity
BR ˌmi:dɪ'ɒkrɪt|i, -ɪz
AM ˌmidi'ɑkrədi, -z

meditate
BR 'mɛdɪteɪt, -s, -ɪŋ, -ɪd
AM 'mɛdəˌteɪ|t, -ts, -dɪŋ, -dɪd

meditation
BR ˌmɛdɪ'teɪʃn, -z
AM ˌmɛdə'teɪʃən, -z

meditative
BR 'mɛdɪtətɪv
AM 'mɛdəˌteɪdɪv

meditatively
BR 'mɛdɪtətɪvli
AM 'mɛdəˌteɪdɪvli

meditativeness
BR 'mɛdɪtətɪvnɪs
AM 'mɛdəˌteɪdɪvnɪs

meditator
BR 'mɛdɪteɪtə(r), -z
AM 'mɛdəˌteɪdər, -z

Mediterranean
BR ˌmɛdɪtə'reɪnɪən
AM ˌmɛdətəˌreɪniən, ˌmɛdətəˌreɪnjən

medium
BR 'mi:dɪəm, -z
AM 'midiəm, -z
mediumism
BR 'mi:dɪəmɪz(ə)m
AM 'midiə,mɪzəm
mediumistic
BR ,mi:dɪə'mɪstɪk
AM ,midiə'mɪstɪk
mediumship
BR 'mi:dɪəmʃɪp, -s
AM 'midiəm,ʃɪp, -s
medlar
BR 'mɛdlə(r), -z
AM 'mɛdlər, -z
medley
BR 'mɛdl|i, -ɪz
AM 'mɛdli, -z
Médoc
BR ,meɪ'dɒk
AM ,meɪ'dɑk, ,meɪ'dɔk
medrese
BR mɛ'drɛseɪ, -z
AM mɛ'drɛseɪ, -z
medulla
BR mɛ'dʌlə(*r*), mɪ'dʌlə(*r*), -z
AM mə'dələ, -z
medulla oblongata
BR mɛ,dʌlə ,ɒblɒŋ'gɑ:tə(*r*), mɪ,dʌlə +
AM mə,dələ ɑ,bləŋ'gɑdə, + ɔ,bləŋ'gɑdə
medullary
BR mɛ'dʌl(ə)ri, mɪ'dʌl(ə)ri
AM mə'dəl(ə)ri, 'mɛdʒələri
medusa
BR mɪ'dju:zə(*r*), mɪ'dju:sə(*r*), mɪ'dʒu:zə(*r*), mɪ'dʒu:sə(*r*), -z
AM mə'd(j)uzə, mə'd(j)usə, -z
medusae
BR mɪ'dju:zi:, mɪ'dju:si:, mɪ'dʒu:zi:, mɪ'dʒu:si:
AM mə'd(j)uzi, mə'd(j)usi, mə'd(j)uzaɪ, mə'd(j)u,saɪ
medusan
BR mɪ'dju:z(ə)n, mɪ'dju:s(ə)n, mɪ'dʒu:z(ə)n, mɪ'dʒu:s(ə)n
AM mə'd(j)uzən, mə'd(j)usən
Medway
BR 'mɛdweɪ
AM 'mɛdweɪ
Medwin
BR 'mɛdwɪn
AM 'mɛdwɪn
Mee
BR mi:
AM mi
meed
BR mi:d
AM mid
Meehan
BR 'mi:ən
AM 'miən, 'mi,hæn
meek
BR mi:k
AM mik
meekly
BR 'mi:kli
AM 'mikli
meekness
BR 'mi:knɨs
AM 'miknɨs
meerkat
BR 'mɪəkat, -s
AM 'mɪr,kæt, -s
meerschaum
BR 'mɪəʃ(ə)m, 'mɪəʃɔ:m, -z
AM 'mɪr,ʃɔm, 'mɪrʃəm, 'mɪr,ʃɑm, -z
Meerut
BR 'mɪərət
AM 'meɪrət, 'mɪrət
meet
BR mi:t, -s, -ɪŋ
AM mi|t, -ts, -dɪŋ
meeter
BR 'mi:tə(r), -z
AM 'midər, -z
meeting
BR 'mi:tɪŋ, -z
AM 'midɪŋ, -z
meetinghouse
BR 'mi:tɪŋhaʊ|s, -zɪz
AM 'midɪŋ,(h)aʊ|s, -zəz
meetly
BR 'mi:tli
AM 'mitli
meetness
BR 'mi:tnɨs
AM 'mitnɨs
Meg
BR mɛg
AM mɛg
mega
BR 'mɛgə(*r*)
AM 'mɛgə
megabuck
BR 'mɛgəbʌk, -s
AM 'mɛgə,bək, -s
megabyte
BR 'mɛgəbʌɪt, -s
AM 'mɛgə,baɪt, -s
megacephalic
BR ,mɛgəsɪ'falɪk, ,mɛgəkɛ'falɪk
AM ¦mɛgəsə'fælɪk
megacycle
BR 'mɛgə,sʌɪkl, -z
AM 'mɛgə,saɪkəl, -z
megadeath
BR 'mɛgədɛθ, -s
AM 'mɛgə,dɛθ, -s
Megaera
BR mɪ'dʒɪərə(*r*)
AM mə'dʒirə
megaflop
BR 'mɛgəflɒp, -s
AM 'mɛgə,flɑp, -s
megahertz
BR 'mɛgəhə:ts
AM 'mɛgə,hərts
megalith
BR 'mɛgəlɪθ, -s
AM 'mɛgə,lɪθ, -s
megalithic
BR ,mɛgə'lɪθɪk
AM ,mɛgə'lɪθɪk
megalomania
BR ,mɛg(ə)lə(ʊ)'meɪnɪə(*r*), ,mɛgl̩ə(ʊ)'meɪnɪə(*r*)
AM ,mɛg(ə)loʊ'meɪniə, ,mɛg(ə)lə'meɪniə
megalomaniac
BR ,mɛg(ə)lə(ʊ)'meɪnɪak, ,mɛgl̩ə(ʊ)'meɪnɪak, -s
AM ¦mɛg(ə)loʊ'meɪni,æk, ,mɛg(ə)lə'meɪni,æk, -s
megalomaniacal
BR ,mɛgləmə'nʌɪəkl
AM ¦mɛg(ə)ləmə'naɪəkəl
megalopolis
BR ,mɛgə'lɒpəlɪs, -ɪz
AM ,mɛgə'lɑpələs, -əz
megalopolitan
BR ,mɛg(ə)lə'pɒlɪt(ə)n, 'mɛgl̩ə'pɒlɪt(ə)n
AM ,mɛgələ'pɑlədən, ,mɛgələ'pɑlətn
megalosaur
BR 'mɛg(ə)ləsɔ:(r), 'mɛgl̩əsɔ:(r), -z
AM 'mɛgələ,sɔ(ə)r, -z
megalosaurus
BR ,mɛg(ə)lə'sɔ:rəs, ,mɛgl̩ə'sɔ:rəs, -ɪz
AM ,mɛgələ'sɔrəs, -əz
Megan
BR 'mɛg(ə)n
AM 'mɛgən, 'meɪgən
megaphone
BR 'mɛgəfəʊn, -z
AM 'mɛgə,foʊn, -z
megapod
BR 'mɛgəpɒd, -z
AM 'mɛgə,pɑd, -z
megapode
BR 'mɛgəpəʊd, -z
AM 'mɛgə,poʊd, -z
megaron
BR 'mɛgərɒn, 'mɛgərən, 'mɛgərn̩, -z
AM 'mɛgə,rɑn, -z
megascopic
BR ,mɛgə'skɒpɪk
AM ,mɛgə'skɑpɪk
megaspore
BR 'mɛgəspɔ:(r), -z
AM 'mɛgə,spɔ(ə)r, -z
megastar
BR 'mɛgəstɑ:(r), -z
AM 'mɛgə,stɑr, -z
megastore
BR 'mɛgəstɔ:(r), -z
AM 'mɛgə,stɔ(ə)r, -z
megatheria
BR ,mɛgə'θɪərɪə(*r*)
AM ,mɛgə'θɪriə
megatherium
BR ,mɛgə'θɪərɪəm
AM ,mɛgə'θɪriəm
megaton
BR 'mɛgətʌn, -z
AM 'mɛgə,tən, 'mɛgə,tɑn, -z
megatonne
BR 'mɛgətʌn, -z
AM 'mɛgə,tən, 'mɛgə,tɑn, -z
megavolt
BR 'mɛgəvəʊlt, 'mɛgəvɒlt, -s
AM 'mɛgə,voʊlt, -s
megawatt
BR 'mɛgəwɒt, -s
AM 'mɛgə,wɑt, -s
Megger®
BR 'mɛgə(r), -z
AM 'mɛgər, -z
megillah
BR mɪ'gɪlə(*r*), -z
AM mə'gɪlə, -z
megilp
BR mə'gɪlp
AM mə'gɪlp
megohm
BR 'mɛgəʊm, -z
AM 'mɛg,oʊm, -z
megrim
BR 'mi:grɪm, -z
AM 'migrɪm, -z
Mehmet
BR 'mɛmɛt
AM 'mɛmɛt
Meier
BR 'mʌɪə(r)
AM 'maɪər
Meiji Tenno
BR ,meɪdʒɪ 'tɛnəʊ
AM meɪ¦idʒi 'tɛ,noʊ
Meikle
BR 'mi:kl
AM 'mikl
Meiklejohn
BR 'mi:kldʒɒn
AM 'mikl,dʒɑn, 'mɪkl,dʒɑn
meioses
BR mʌɪ'əʊsi:z
AM maɪ'oʊsiz

meiosis
BR mʌɪ'əʊsɪs
AM maɪ'oʊsəs
meiotic
BR mʌɪ'ɒtɪk
AM meɪ'ɑdɪk
meiotically
BR mʌɪ'ɒtɨkli
AM maɪ'ɑdək(ə)li
Meir
BR meɪ'ɪə(r)
AM meɪ'ɪ(ə)r
Meissen
BR 'mʌɪsn
AM 'maɪsən
Meistersinger
BR 'mʌɪstə,sɪŋə(r), 'mʌɪstə,zɪŋə(r), -z
AM 'maɪstər,sɪŋər, -z
Mekong
BR ,miː'kɒŋ
AM ˌmeɪ'kɔŋ, ˌmi'kɔŋ, ˌmeɪ'kɑŋ, ˌmi'kɑŋ
mel
BR mɛl, -z
AM mɛl, -z
melamine
BR 'mɛləmʌɪn, 'mɛləmiːn
AM 'mɛlə,min
melancholia
BR ,mɛlən'kəʊlɪə(r), ,mɛləŋ'kəʊlɪə(r)
AM ,mɛlən'koʊljə, ,mɛlən'kɑljə, ,mɛlən'koʊliə, ,mɛlən'kɑliə
melancholic
BR ,mɛlən'kɒlɪk, ,mɛləŋ'kɒlɪk
AM ˌmɛlən'kɑlɪk
melancholically
BR ,mɛlən'kɒlɨkli, ,mɛləŋ'kɒlɨkli
AM ,mɛlən'kɑlək(ə)li
melancholy
BR 'mɛlənk(ə)li, 'mɛləŋk(ə)li
AM 'mɛlən,kɑli
Melanchthon
BR mɨ'laŋkθən
AM mə'læŋk,θɑn
Melanesia
BR ,mɛlə'niːzjə(r), ,mɛlə'niːʒə(r)
AM ,mɛlə'niʒə, ,mɛlə'niʃə
Melanesian
BR ,mɛlə'niːzj(ə)n, ,mɛlə'niːʒn, -z
AM ,mɛlə'niʒən, ,mɛlə'niʃən, -z
mélange
BR meɪ'lɒ̃ʒ, meɪ'lɑːnʒ, -ɨz
AM meɪ'lɑn(d)ʒ, -əz
Melanie
BR 'mɛləni
AM 'mɛləni
melanin
BR 'mɛlənɪn
AM 'mɛlənən
melanism
BR 'mɛlənɪz(ə)m
AM 'mɛlə,nɪzəm
melanoma
BR ,mɛlə'nəʊmə(r), -z
AM ,mɛlə'noʊmə, -z
melanoses
BR ,mɛlə'nəʊsiːz
AM ,mɛlə'noʊsiz
melanosis
BR ,mɛlə'nəʊsɪs
AM ,mɛlə'noʊsəs
melanotic
BR ,mɛlə'nɒtɪk
AM ,mɛlə'nɑdɪk
melba
BR 'mɛlbə(r)
AM 'mɛlbə
Melbourne
BR 'mɛlbən, 'mɛlbɔːn
AM 'mɛlbərn
Melchett
BR 'mɛltʃɨt
AM 'mɛltʃət
Melchior
BR 'mɛlkɪɔː(r)
AM 'mɛlki,ɔ(ə)r
Melchite
BR 'mɛlkʌɪt, -s
AM 'mɛl,kaɪt, -s
Melchizedek
BR mɛl'kɪzədɛk
AM mɛl'kɪzə,dɛk
meld
BR mɛld, -z, -ɪŋ, -ɨd
AM mɛld, -z, -ɪŋ, -əd
Meldrum
BR 'mɛldrəm
AM 'mɛldrəm
Meleager
BR ,mɛlɪ'eɪgə(r)
AM ,mɛli'eɪgər
melee
BR 'mɛleɪ, mɛ'leɪ, -z
AM 'meɪleɪ, -z
Melhuish
BR mɛl'hjuːɪʃ, 'mɛlhjʊɪʃ, 'mɛlɪʃ
AM mɛl'hjuɪʃ
Melia
BR 'miːlɪə(r)
AM 'miljə, 'miliə
melic
BR 'mɛlɪk
AM 'mɛlɪk
melick
BR 'mɛlɪk
AM 'mɛlɪk
Melilla
BR mɨ'lɪə(r)
AM mə'lijə
melilot
BR 'mɛlɪlɒt, -s
AM 'mɛlə,lɑt, -s
Melina
BR 'mɨ'liːnə(r)
AM mə'linə
Melinda
BR mɨ'lɪndə(r)
AM mə'lɪndə
meliorate
BR 'miːlɪəreɪt, -s, -ɪŋ, -ɨd
AM 'miljə,reɪ|t, 'miliə,reɪ|t, -ts, -dɪŋ, -dɨd
melioration
BR ,miːlɪə'reɪʃn
AM ,miljə'reɪʃən, ,miliə'reɪʃən
meliorative
BR 'miːlɪərətɪv
AM 'miljə,reɪdɪv, 'miliə,reɪdɪv
meliorism
BR 'miːlɪərɪz(ə)m
AM 'miljə,rɪzəm, 'miliə,rɪzəm
meliorist
BR 'miːlɪərɪst, -s
AM 'miljərəst, 'miliərəst, -s
melisma
BR mɨ'lɪzmə(r), -z
AM mə'lɪzmə, -z
melismata
BR mɨ'lɪzmətə(r)
AM mə'lɪzmədə
melismatic
BR ,mɛlɪz'matɪk
AM ˌmɛləz'mædɪk
Melissa
BR mɨ'lɪsə(r)
AM mə'lɪsə
Melksham
BR 'mɛlkʃ(ə)m
AM 'mɛlkʃəm
melliferous
BR mɨ'lɪf(ə)rəs
AM mə'lɪf(ə)rəs
mellifluence
BR mɨ'lɪflʊəns
AM mə'lɪfluəns
mellifluent
BR mɨ'lɪflʊənt
AM mə'lɪfluənt
mellifluous
BR mɨ'lɪflʊəs
AM mə'lɪfləwəs
mellifluously
BR mɨ'lɪflʊəsli
AM mə'lɪfləwəsli
mellifluousness
BR mə'lɪflʊəsnəs
AM mə'lɪfləwəsnəs
Mellish
BR 'mɛlɪʃ
AM 'mɛlɪʃ
Mellon
BR 'mɛlən
AM 'mɛlən
Mellor
BR 'mɛlə(r)
AM 'mɛlər
Mellors
BR 'mɛləz
AM 'mɛlərz
mellotron
BR 'mɛlətrɒn, -z
AM 'mɛlə,trɑn, -z
mellow
BR 'mɛləʊ, -z, -ɪŋ, -d, -ə(r), -ɪst
AM 'mɛloʊ, -z, -ɪŋ, -d, -ər, -əst
mellowly
BR 'mɛləʊli
AM 'mɛloʊli
mellowness
BR 'mɛləʊnəs
AM 'mɛloʊnəs
Melly
BR 'mɛli
AM 'mɛli
melodeon
BR mɨ'ləʊdɪən, -z
AM mə'loʊdiən, -z
melodic
BR mɨ'lɒdɪk
AM mə'lɑdɪk
melodica
BR mɨ'lɒdɨkə(r), -z
AM mə'lɑdəkə, -z
melodically
BR mɨ'lɒdɨkli
AM mə'lɑdək(ə)li
melodious
BR mɨ'ləʊdɪəs
AM mə'loʊdiəs
melodiously
BR mɨ'ləʊdɪəsli
AM mə'loʊdiəsli
melodiousness
BR mɨ'ləʊdɪəsnəs
AM mə'loʊdiəsnəs
melodise
BR 'mɛlədʌɪz, -ɨz, -ɪŋ, -d
AM 'mɛlə,daɪz, -ɨz, -ɪŋ, -d
melodiser
BR 'mɛlədʌɪzə(r), -z
AM 'mɛlə,daɪzər, -z
melodist
BR 'mɛlədɪst, -s
AM 'mɛlədəst, -s
melodize
BR 'mɛlədʌɪz, -ɨz, -ɪŋ, -d
AM 'mɛlə,daɪz, -ɨz, -ɪŋ, -d
melodizer
BR 'mɛlədʌɪzə(r), -z
AM 'mɛlə,daɪzər, -z
melodrama
BR 'mɛlə,drɑːmə(r), -z
AM 'mɛlə,drɑmə, -z
melodramatic
BR ,mɛlədrə'matɪk, -s

AM ˌmɛlədrəˈmædɪk, -s

melodramatically
BR ˌmɛlədrəˈmatɪkli
AM ˌmɛlədrəˈmædək(ə)li

melodramatise
BR ˌmɛlə(ʊ)ˈdramətʌɪz, -ɪz, -ɪŋ, -d
AM ˌmɛləˈdrɑməˌtaɪz, -ɪz, -ɪŋ, -d

melodramatist
BR ˌmɛlə(ʊ)ˈdramətɪst, -s
AM ˌmɛləˈdrɑmədəst, -s

melodramatize
BR ˌmɛlə(ʊ)ˈdramətʌɪz, -ɪz, -ɪŋ, -d
AM ˌmɛləˈdrɑməˌtaɪz, -ɪz, -ɪŋ, -d

melody
BR ˈmɛləd|i, -ɪz
AM ˈmɛlədi, -z

melon
BR ˈmɛlən, -z
AM ˈmɛlən, -z

Melos
BR ˈmiːlɒs, ˈmɛlɒs
AM ˈmilɑs

Melpomene
BR mɛlˈpɒmɨni
AM mɛlˈpɑməni

Melrose
BR ˈmɛlrəʊz
AM ˈmɛlˌroʊz

melt
BR mɛlt, -s, -ɪŋ, -ɨd
AM mɛlt, -s, -ɪŋ, -əd

meltable
BR ˈmɛltəbl
AM ˈmɛltəbəl

meltage
BR ˈmɛlt|ɪdʒ, -ɪdʒɪz
AM ˈmɛltɪdʒ, -ɪz

meltdown
BR ˈmɛltdaʊn, -z
AM ˈmɛltˌdaʊn, -z

melter
BR ˈmɛltə(r), -z
AM ˈmɛltər, -z

meltingly
BR ˈmɛltɪŋli
AM ˈmɛltɪŋli

melton
BR ˈmɛltn, -z
AM ˈmɛltən, -z

Meltonian®
BR mɛlˈtəʊnɪən
AM mɛlˈtoʊnɪən

Melton Mowbray
BR ˌmɛlt(ə)n ˈməʊbri, + ˈməʊbreɪ
AM ˌmɛltn ˈmoʊbri

meltwater
BR ˈmɛltˌwɔːtə(r), -z
AM ˈmɛltˌwɔdər, ˈmɛltˌwɑdər, -z

Melville
BR ˈmɛlvɪl
AM ˈmɛlvəl, ˈmɛlˌvɪl

Melvin
BR ˈmɛlvɪn
AM ˈmɛlvən

member
BR ˈmɛmbə(r), -z, -d
AM ˈmɛmbər, -z, -d

memberless
BR ˈmɛmbələs
AM ˈmɛmbərləs

membership
BR ˈmɛmbəʃɪp, -s
AM ˈmɛmbərˌʃɪp, -s

member state
BR ˌmɛmbə ˈsteɪt, -s
AM ˈmɛmbər ˌsteɪt, -s

membranaceous
BR ˌmɛmbrəˈneɪʃəs
AM ˌmɛmbrəˈneɪʃəs

membrane
BR ˈmɛmbreɪn, -z
AM ˈmɛmˌbreɪn, -z

membraneous
BR mɛmˈbreɪnɪəs
AM mɛmˈbreɪnɪəs

membranous
BR ˈmɛmbrənəs
AM ˈmɛmbrənəs, mɛmˈbreɪnəs

membrum virile
BR ˌmɛmbrəm vɪˈrʌɪli, + vɪˈriːli, -z
AM ˌmɛmbrəm ˈvɪrɪl, -z

memento
BR mɨˈmɛntəʊ, -z
AM məˈmɛnˌtoʊ, məˈmɛnoʊ, -z

memento mori
BR mɨˌmɛntəʊ ˈmɔːrʌɪ, + ˈmɔːri
AM məˌmɛnˌtoʊ ˈmɔri, məˌmɛnoʊ +

Memnon
BR ˈmɛmnɒn, ˈmɛmnən
AM ˈmɛmnən, ˈmɛmnɑn

memo
BR ˈmɛməʊ, -z
AM ˈmɛmoʊ, -z

memoir
BR ˈmɛmwɑː(r), -z
AM ˈmɛmˌwɑr, -z

memoirist
BR ˈmɛmwɑːrɪst, -s
AM ˈmɛmwɑrəst, -s

memorabilia
BR ˌmɛm(ə)rəˈbɪlɪə(r)
AM ˌmɛm(ə)rəˈbɪljə, ˌmɛm(ə)rəˈbɪliə

memorability
BR ˌmɛm(ə)rˈbɪlɨti
AM ˌmɛm(ə)rəˈbɪlɨdi

memorable
BR ˈmɛm(ə)rəbl
AM ˈmɛm(ə)rəbəl, ˈmɛmərbəl

memorableness
BR ˈmɛm(ə)rəblnəs
AM ˈmɛm(ə)rəbəlnəs, ˈmɛmərbəlnəs

memorably
BR ˈmɛm(ə)rəbli
AM ˈmɛm(ə)rəbli, ˈmɛmərbli

memoranda
BR ˌmɛməˈrandə(r)
AM ˌmɛməˈrændə

memorandum
BR ˌmɛməˈrandəm, -z
AM ˌmɛməˈrændəm, -z

memorial
BR mɨˈmɔːrɪəl, -z
AM məˈmɔriəl, -z

memorialise
BR mɨˈmɔːrɪəlʌɪz, -ɪz, -ɪŋ, -d
AM məˈmɔriəˌlaɪz, -ɪz, -ɪŋ, -d

memorialist
BR mɨˈmɔːrɪəlɪst, -s
AM məˈmɔriələst, -s

memorialize
BR mɨˈmɔːrɪəlʌɪz, -ɪz, -ɪŋ, -d
AM məˈmɔriəˌlaɪz, -ɪz, -ɪŋ, -d

memoria technica
BR mɨˌmɔːrɪə ˈtɛknɪkə(r), -z
AM məˌmɔriə ˈtɛknəkə, -z

memorisable
BR ˈmɛmərʌɪzəbl
AM ˈmɛməˌraɪzəbəl

memorisation
BR ˌmɛmərʌɪˈzeɪʃn
AM ˌmɛmərəˈzeɪʃən, ˌmɛməˌraɪˈzeɪʃən

memorise
BR ˈmɛmərʌɪz, -ɪz, -ɪŋ, -d
AM ˈmɛməˌraɪz, -ɪz, -ɪŋ, -d

memoriser
BR ˈmɛmərʌɪzə(r), -z
AM ˈmɛməˌraɪzər, -z

memorizable
BR ˈmɛmərʌɪzəbl
AM ˈmɛməˌraɪzəbəl

memorization
BR ˌmɛmərʌɪˈzeɪʃn
AM ˌmɛmərəˈzeɪʃən, ˌmɛməˌraɪˈzeɪʃən

memorize
BR ˈmɛmərʌɪz, -ɪz, -ɪŋ, -d
AM ˈmɛməˌraɪz, -ɪz, -ɪŋ, -d

memorizer
BR ˈmɛmərʌɪzə(r), -z
AM ˈmɛməˌraɪzər, -z

memory
BR ˈmɛm(ə)r|i, -ɪz
AM ˈmɛm(ə)ri, -z

Memphis
BR ˈmɛmfɪs
AM ˈmɛm(p)fəs

memsahib
BR ˈmɛmsɑː(ɪ)b, -z
AM ˈmɛmˌsɑ(h)ɪb, ˈmɛmˌsɑb, -z

men
BR mɛn
AM mɛn

menace
BR ˈmɛnɪs, -ɪz, -ɪŋ, -t
AM ˈmɛnəs, -əz, -ɪŋ, -t

menacer
BR ˈmɛnɪsə(r), -z
AM ˈmɛnəsər, -z

menacingly
BR ˈmɛnɪsɪŋli
AM ˈmɛnəsɪŋli

ménage
BR meɪˌnɑːʒ, mɛˈnɑːʒ, məˈnɑːʒ, -ɪz
AM meɪˈnɑʒ, məˈnɑʒ, -əz

ménage à trois
BR ˌmeɪnɑːʒ ɑː ˈtrwɑː(r), ˌmɛnɑːʒ +, məˌnɑːʒ +, -z
AM meɪˈnɑʒ ə ˈt(r)wɑ, məˈnɑʒ +, -z

menagerie
BR mɨˈnadʒ(ə)r|i, -ɪz
AM məˈnæ(d)ʒəri, -z

Menai Strait
BR ˌmɛnʌɪ ˈstreɪt
AM ˈmɛˌnaɪ ˈstreɪt

Menander
BR mɨˈnandə(r)
AM məˈnændər

menaquinone
BR ˌmɛnəˈkwɪnəʊn, -z
AM ˌmɛnəˈkwɪnoʊn, -z

menarche
BR mɛˈnɑːki, mɨˈnɑːki
AM məˈnɑrki, ˈmɛnɑrki

Mencken
BR ˈmɛŋk(ə)n
AM ˈmɛŋkən

mend
BR mɛnd, -z, -ɪŋ, -ɨd
AM mɛnd, -z, -ɪŋ, -əd

mendable
BR ˈmɛndəbl
AM ˈmɛndəbəl

mendacious
BR mɛnˈdeɪʃəs
AM mɛnˈdeɪʃəs

mendaciously
BR mɛnˈdeɪʃəsli
AM mɛnˈdeɪʃəsli

mendaciousness
BR mɛnˈdeɪʃəsnəs
AM mɛnˈdeɪʃəsnəs

mendacity
BR mɛn'dasɪti
AM mɛn'dæsədi

Mendel
BR 'mɛndl
AM 'mɛnd(ə)l

Mendeleev
BR ˌmɛndə'leɪɛv
AM ˌmɛndə'leɪɛv

mendelevium
BR ˌmɛndə'li:vɪəm, ˌmɛndə'leɪvɪəm
AM ˌmɛndə'liviəm, ˌmɛndə'leɪviəm

Mendelian
BR mɛn'di:lɪən
AM mɛn'diliən

Mendelism
BR 'mɛndl̩ɪz(ə)m
AM 'mɛndlˌɪzəm

Mendelssohn
BR 'mɛndls(ə)n
AM 'mɛndlsən

mender
BR 'mɛndə(r), -z
AM 'mɛndər, -z

Méndez
BR 'mɛndɛz
AM 'mɛnˌdɛz
SP 'mendeθ, 'mendes

mendicancy
BR 'mɛndɨk(ə)nsi
AM 'mɛndəkənsi

mendicant
BR 'mɛndɨk(ə)nt, -s
AM 'mɛndəkənt, -s

mendicity
BR mɛn'dɪsɨti
AM mɛn'dɪsɨdi

Mendip
BR 'mɛndɪp, -s
AM 'mɛndɪp, -s

Mendoza
BR mɛn'dəʊzə(r)
AM mɛn'doʊzə
SP men'doθa, men'dosa

Menelaus
BR ˌmɛnɪ'leɪəs
AM ˌmɛnə'leɪəs

Menes
BR 'mi:ni:z
AM 'miˌniz

menfolk
BR 'mɛnfəʊk
AM 'mɛnˌfoʊk

Meng-tzu
BR ˌmɛŋ'tsu:
AM 'mɛŋ'tsu

menhaden
BR mɛn'heɪdn, -z
AM mɛn'heɪdən, -z

menhir
BR 'mɛnhɪə(r), -z
AM 'mɛnˌ(h)ɪ(ə)r, -z

menial
BR 'mi:nɪəl, -z
AM 'miniəl, -z

menially
BR 'mi:nɪəli
AM 'miniəli

Meniere
BR 'mɛnɪɛ:(r), ˌmɛnɪ'ɛ:(r)
AM ˌmeɪn'jɛ(ə)r

meningeal
BR mɪ'nɪn(d)ʒɪəl
AM mə'nɪndʒiəl

meninges
BR mɪ'nɪn(d)ʒi:z
AM mə'nɪndʒiz

meningitic
BR ˌmɛnɪn'dʒɪtɪk
AM ˌmɛnən'dʒɪdɪk

meningitis
BR ˌmɛnɪn'dʒʌɪtɪs
AM ˌmɛnən'dʒaɪdɪs

meningocele
BR mɪ'nɪŋgə(ʊ)si:l, -z
AM mə'nɪŋgoʊˌsil, -z

meningococcal
BR məˌnɪŋgə(ʊ)'kɒkl
AM məˌnɪŋgoʊ'kakəl

meningococcus
BR məˌnɪŋgə(ʊ)'kɒkəs
AM məˌnɪŋgoʊ'kakəs

meninx
BR 'mi:nɪŋks, -ɪz
AM 'minɪŋ(k)s, -ɪz

meniscoid
BR mɪ'nɪskɔɪd
AM mə'nɪsˌkɔɪd

meniscus
BR mɪ'nɪskəs, -ɪz
AM mə'nɪskəs, -əz

Menlo Park
BR ˌmɛnləʊ 'pɑ:k
AM ˌmɛnloʊ 'pɑrk

Mennonite
BR 'mɛnənʌɪt, -s
AM 'mɛnəˌnaɪt, -s

menologia
BR ˌmɛnə(ʊ)'ləʊdʒɪə(r)
AM ˌmɛnə'loʊdʒə

menologist
BR mɪ'nɒlədʒɪst, -s
AM mə'nɑlədʒəst, -s

menologium
BR ˌmɛnə(ʊ)'ləʊdʒɪəm, -z
AM ˌmɛnə'loʊgiəm, -z

menology
BR mɪ'nɒlədʒ|i, -ɪz
AM mə'nɑlədʒi, -z

menopausal
BR ˌmɛnə(ʊ)'pɔ:zl
AM ˌmɛnə'pɔzəl, ˌmɛnə'pɑzəl

menopause
BR 'mɛnə(ʊ)pɔ:z, -ɪz
AM 'mɛnəˌpɔz, 'mɛnəˌpɑz, -ɪz

menorah
BR mɪ'nɔ:rə(r), -z
AM mə'nɔrə, -z

Menorca
BR mɪ'nɔ:kə(r)
AM mə'nɔrkə

Menorcan
BR mɪ'nɔ:k(ə)n, -z
AM mə'nɔrkən, -z

menorrhagia
BR ˌmɛnə'reɪdʒɪə(r)
AM ˌmɛnə'reɪdʒ(i)ə

menorrhoea
BR ˌmɛnə'ri:ə(r)
AM ˌmɛnə'riə

Menotti
BR mɪ'nɒti
AM mə'nɑdi

mens
BR mɛnz
AM mɛnz

Mensa
BR 'mɛnsə(r)
AM 'mɛnsə

menses
BR 'mɛnsi:z
AM 'mɛnsiz

Menshevik
BR 'mɛnʃəvɪk, -s
AM 'mɛn(t)ʃəˌvɪk, -s
RUS mʲinʃɪ'vʲik

mens rea
BR ˌmɛnz 'ri:ə(r), + 'reɪə(r)
AM ˌmɛnz 'riə

Menston
BR 'mɛnst(ə)n
AM 'mɛnstən

menstrua
BR 'mɛnstrʊə(r)
AM 'mɛnstr(əw)ə, 'mɛnztr(əw)ə

menstrual
BR 'mɛnstrʊəl, 'mɛnstrʊl
AM 'mɛnstr(əw)əl, 'mɛnztr(əw)əl

menstrual cycle
BR ˌmɛnstrʊl 'sʌɪkl, -z
AM 'mɛnstr(əw)əl ˌsaɪkəl, 'mɛnztr(əw)əl +, -z

menstruate
BR 'mɛnstrʊeɪt, -s, -ɪŋ, -ɪd
AM 'mɛnsˌtreɪ|t, 'mɛnzˌtreɪ|t, 'mɛnstrəˌweɪ|t, 'mɛnztrəˌweɪ|t, -ts, -dɪŋ, -dɪd

menstruation
BR ˌmɛnstrʊ'eɪʃn
AM ˌmɛns'treɪʃən, ˌmɛnz'treɪʃən, ˌmɛnztrə'weɪʃən, ˌmɛnstrə'weɪʃən

menstruous
BR 'mɛnstrʊəs
AM 'mɛnstr(əw)əs, 'mɛnztr(əw)əs

menstruum
BR 'mɛnstrʊəm
AM 'mɛnstr(əw)əm, 'mɛnztr(əw)əm

mensurability
BR ˌmɛnʃ(ʊ)rə'bɪlɨti, ˌmɛnsjʊrə'bɪlɨti, ˌmɛns(ə)rə'bɪlɨti
AM ˌmɛnʃərə'bɪlɨdi, ˌmɛnsərə'bɪlɨdi

mensurable
BR 'mɛnʃ(ʊ)rəbl, 'mɛnsjʊrəbl, 'mɛns(ə)rəbl
AM 'mɛn(t)ʃ(ə)rəbəl, 'mɛns(ə)rəbəl

mensural
BR 'mɛnʃ(ʊ)rəl, 'mɛnʃ(ʊ)rl̩, 'mɛnsjʊrəl, 'mɛnsjʊrl̩, 'mɛns(ə)rəl, 'mɛns(ə)rl̩
AM 'mɛn(t)ʃ(ə)rəl, 'mɛnsərəl

mensuration
BR ˌmɛnʃʊ'reɪʃn, ˌmɛnsjʊ'reɪʃn, ˌmɛnsə'reɪʃn
AM ˌmɛn(t)ʃə'reɪʃən, ˌmɛnsə'reɪʃən

menswear
BR 'mɛnzwɛ:(r)
AM 'mɛnzˌwɛ(ə)r

Mentadent®
BR 'mɛntədɛnt
AM 'mɛn(t)əˌdɛnt

mental
BR 'mɛntl
AM 'mɛn(t)l

mentalism
BR 'mɛntl̩ɪz(ə)m
AM 'mɛn(t)lˌɪzəm

mentalist
BR 'mɛntl̩ɪst, -s
AM 'mɛn(t)l̩əst, -s

mentalistic
BR ˌmɛntə'lɪstɪk, ˌmɛntl'ɪstɪk
AM ˌmɛn(t)l'ɪstɪk

mentalistically
BR ˌmɛntə'lɪstɪkli, ˌmɛntl'ɪstɪkli
AM ˌmɛn(t)l'ɪstɪk(ə)li

mentality
BR mɛn'talɨt|i, -ɪz
AM mɛn'tælədi, -z

mentally
BR 'mɛntl̩i, 'mɛntəli
AM 'mɛn(t)l̩i

mentation
BR mɛn'teɪʃn, -z
AM mɛn'teɪʃən, -z

menthol
BR 'mɛnθɒl
AM 'mɛnˌθɔl, 'mɛnˌθɑl

mentholated
BR 'mɛnθəleɪtɪd

AM ˈmɛnθəˌleɪdɨd

mention
BR ˈmɛnʃ|n, -nz, -n̩ɪŋ\-ənɪŋ, -nd
AM ˈmɛn(t)ʃ|ən, -ənz, -(ə)nɪŋ, -ənd

mentionable
BR ˈmɛnʃn̩əbl, ˈmɛnʃ(ə)nəbl
AM ˈmɛn(t)ʃənəbəl, ˈmɛnʃnəbəl

mentor
BR ˈmɛntɔː(r), -z
AM ˈmɛnˌtɔ(ə)r, ˈmɛn(t)ər, -z

menu
BR ˈmɛnjuː, -z
AM ˈmɛnju, -z

Menuhin
BR ˈmɛnjʊɪn
AM ˈmɛnuɪn

Menzies
BR ˈmɛnzɪz, ˈmɪŋɡɪz, ˈmɪŋɡɪs
AM ˈmɛnziz

Meon
BR ˈmiːən
AM ˈmiˌɑn

Meopham
BR ˈmɛp(ə)m
AM ˈmiəpəm

meow
BR mɪˈaʊ, -z, -ɪŋ, -d
AM miˈaʊ, -z, -ɪŋ, -d

mepacrine
BR ˈmɛpəkrɪn
AM ˈmɛpəˌkrɪn

Mephistophelean
BR ˌmɛfɪstəˈfiːlɪən, mɪˌfɪstəˈfiːlɪən
AM məˌfɪstəˈfiliən, ˌmɛfəˌstɑfəˈliən

Mephistopheles
BR ˌmɛfɪˈstɒfɪliːz
AM ˌmɛfəˈstɑfəliz

Mephistophelian
BR ˌmɛfɪstəˈfiːlɪən, mɪˌfɪstəˈfiːlɪən
AM məˌfɪstəˈfiliən, ˌmɛfəˌstɑfəˈliən

mephitic
BR mɪˈfɪtɪk
AM məˈfɪdɪk

mephitis
BR mɪˈfʌɪtɪs, -ɪz
AM məˈfaɪdɪs, -ɪz

meranti
BR məˈrant|i, -ɪz
AM məˈræn(t)i, -z

mercantile
BR ˈməːk(ə)ntʌɪl
AM ˈmərkənˌtil, ˈmərkənˌtaɪl

mercantilism
BR ˈməːk(ə)ntɪlɪz(ə)m, ˈməːk(ə)ntʌɪlɪz(ə)m
AM ˈmərkən(t)əˌlɪz(ə)m

mercantilist
BR ˈməːk(ə)ntɪlɪst, ˈməːk(ə)ntʌɪlɪst, məːˈkantɪlɪst, -s
AM ˈmərkən(t)ələst, -s

mercaptan
BR məːˈkapt(ə)n, məːˈkaptan
AM mərˈkæpˌtæn

Mercator
BR məːˈkeɪtə(r), məˈkeɪtə(r)
AM mərˈkeɪdər

Mercedes
BR məˈseɪdiːz
AM mərˈseɪdiz

mercenariness
BR ˈməːs(ɪ)n(ə)rɪnɪs, ˈməːsn̩rɪnɪs
AM ˈmərsnˌɛrinɪs

mercenary
BR ˈməːs(ɪ)n(ə)r|i, ˈməːsn̩r|i, -ɪz
AM ˈmərsnˌɛri, -z

mercer
BR ˈməːsə(r), -z
AM ˈmərsər, -z

mercerise
BR ˈməːsərʌɪz, -ɪz, -ɪŋ, -d
AM ˈmərsəˌraɪz, -ɪz, -ɪŋ, -d

mercerize
BR ˈməːsərʌɪz, -z, -ɪŋ, -d
AM ˈmərsərˌaɪz, -z, -ɪŋ, -d

mercery
BR ˈməːs(ə)r|i, -ɪz
AM ˈmərsəri, -z

merchandisable
BR ˈməːtʃ(ə)ndʌɪzəbl
AM ˈmərtʃənˌdaɪzəbəl

merchandise¹
noun
BR ˈməːtʃ(ə)ndʌɪs, ˈməːtʃ(ə)ndʌɪz
AM ˈmərtʃənˌdaɪz, ˈmərtʃənˌdaɪs

merchandise²
verb
BR ˈməːtʃ(ə)ndʌɪz, -ɪz, -ɪŋ, -d
AM ˈmərtʃənˌdaɪz, -ɪz, -ɪŋ, -d

merchandiser
BR ˈməːtʃ(ə)ndʌɪzə(r), -z
AM ˈmərtʃənˌdaɪzər, -z

merchandizable
BR ˈməːtʃ(ə)ndʌɪzəbl
AM ˈmərtʃənˌdaɪzəbəl

merchandize¹
noun
BR ˈməːtʃ(ə)ndʌɪs, ˈməːtʃ(ə)ndʌɪz
AM ˈmərtʃənˌdaɪz

merchandize²
verb
BR ˈməːtʃ(ə)ndʌɪz, -ɪz, -ɪŋ, -d
AM ˈmərtʃənˌdaɪz, -ɪz, -ɪŋ, -d

merchandizer
BR ˈməːtʃ(ə)ndʌɪzə(r), -z
AM ˈmərtʃənˌdaɪzər, -z

merchant
BR ˈməːtʃ(ə)nt, -s
AM ˈmərtʃənt, -s

merchantable
BR ˈməːtʃ(ə)ntəbl
AM ˈmərtʃən(t)əbəl

merchantman
BR ˈməːtʃ(ə)ntmən
AM ˈmərtʃən(t)mən

merchantmen
BR ˈməːtʃ(ə)ntmən
AM ˈmərtʃəntmən

Mercia
BR ˈməːsɪə(*r*), ˈməːʃ(ɪ)ə(*r*)
AM ˈmɛrʃ(i)ə

Mercian
BR ˈməːsɪən, ˈməːʃ(ɪə)n, -z
AM ˈmərʃ(i)ən, -z

merciful
BR ˈməːsɪf(ʊ)l
AM ˈmərsəfəl

mercifully
BR ˈməːsɪfʊli, ˈməːsɪfl̩i
AM ˈmərsəf(ə)li

mercifulness
BR ˈməːsɪf(ʊ)lnəs
AM ˈmərsəfəlnəs

merciless
BR ˈməːsɪlɪs
AM ˈmərsələs

mercilessly
BR ˈməːsɪlɪsli
AM ˈmərsələsli

mercilessness
BR ˈməːsɪlɪnɪs
AM ˈmərsələsnəs

Merck
BR məːk
AM mərk

Merckx
BR məːks
AM mərks

mercurial
BR məːˈkjʊərɪəl
AM ˌmərˈkjʊriəl

mercurialism
BR məːˈkjʊərɪəlɪz(ə)m
AM ˌmərˈkjʊriəˌlɪzəm

mercuriality
BR məːˌkjʊərɪˈalɪti
AM ˌmərˌkjʊriˈælədi

mercurially
BR məːˈkjʊərɪəli
AM ˌmərˈkjʊriəli

mercuric
BR məːˈkjʊərɪk
AM ˌmərˈkjʊrɪk

Mercurochrome®
BR məːˈkjʊərəkrəʊm
AM mə(r)ˈkjʊrəˌkroʊm

mercurous
BR ˈməːkjʊrəs
AM ˈmərkjərəs

mercury
BR ˈməːkjʊri
AM ˈmərkjəri

Mercutio
BR mə(ː)ˈkjuːʃɪəʊ
AM mərˈkjuʃioʊ

mercy
BR ˈməːs|i, -ɪz
AM ˈmərsi, -z

mere
BR mɪə(r)
AM mɪ(ə)r

Meredith
BR ˈmɛrədɪθ, mɛˈrɛdɪθ, mɪˈrɛdɪθ
AM ˈmɛrədəθ

Meredydd
BR məˈrɛdɪð
AM ˈmɛrəˌdɪd
WE meˈredɪð

merely
BR ˈmɪəli
AM ˈmɪrli

meretricious
BR ˌmɛrɪˈtrɪʃəs
AM ˌmɛrəˈtrɪʃəs

meretriciously
BR ˌmɛrɪˈtrɪʃəsli
AM ˌmɛrəˈtrɪʃəsli

meretriciousness
BR ˌmɛrɪˈtrɪʃəsnəs
AM ˌmɛrəˈtrɪʃəsnəs

Merfyn
BR ˈməːvɪn
AM ˈmərfən

merganser
BR məːˈɡansə(r), məːˈɡanzə(r), -z
AM mərˈɡænsər, -z

merge
BR məːdʒ, -ɪz, -ɪŋ, -d
AM mərdʒ, -əz, -ɪŋ, -d

mergence
BR ˈməːdʒns, -ɪz
AM ˈmərdʒəns, -əz

Mergenthaler
BR ˈməːɡ(ə)nˌtɑːlə(r)
AM ˈmərɡənˌtɑlər

merger
BR ˈməːdʒə(r), -z
AM ˈmərdʒər, -z

Mérida
BR ˈmɛrɪdə(*r*)
AM ˈmɛridə

Meriden
BR ˈmɛrɪd(ə)n
AM ˈmɛrədən

meridian
BR mɪˈrɪdɪən, -z
AM məˈrɪdiən, -z

meridional
BR mɪ'rɪdɪənl
AM mə'rɪdiənəl
Meriel
BR 'mɛrɪəl
AM 'mɛriəl
meringue
BR mə'raŋ, -z
AM mə'ræŋ, -z
merino
BR mə'ri:nəʊ, -z
AM mə'rinoʊ, -z
Merioneth
BR ˌmɛrɪ'ɒnɪθ
AM ˌmɛrɪ'ɑnəθ
meristem
BR 'mɛrɪstɛm, -z
AM 'mɛri,stɛm, -z
meristematic
BR ˌmɛrɪstə'matɪk
AM ˌmɛrəstə'mædɪk
merit
BR 'mɛr|ɪt, -ɪts, -ɪtɪŋ, -ɪtɪd
AM 'mɛrə|t, -ts, -dɪŋ, -dəd
meritocracy
BR ˌmɛrɪ'tɒkrəs|i, -ɪz
AM ˌmɛrə'tɑkrəsi, -z
meritocratic
BR ˌmɛrɪtə'kratɪk
AM ˌmɛrədə'krædɪk
meritorious
BR ˌmɛrɪ'tɔ:rɪəs
AM ˌmɛrə'tɔriəs
meritoriously
BR ˌmɛrɪ'tɔ:rɪəsli
AM ˌmɛrə'tɔriəsli
meritoriousness
BR ˌmɛrɪ'tɔ:rɪəsnəs
AM ˌmɛrə'tɔriəsnəs
merkin
BR 'mə:kɪn, -z
AM 'mərkən, -z
merle
BR mə:l, -z
AM 'mər(ə)l, -z
merlin
BR 'mə:lɪn, -z
AM 'mərlən, -z
merlon
BR 'mə:lən, -z
AM 'mərlən, -z
Merlot
BR 'mə:lət, -s
AM mər'loʊ, -s
Merlyn
BR 'mə:lɪn
AM 'mərlən
mermaid
BR 'mə:meɪd, -z
AM 'mər,meɪd, -z
merman
BR 'mə:man
AM 'mər,mæn
mermen
BR 'mə:mɛn
AM 'mər,mɛn
meroblast
BR 'mɛrə(ʊ)blɑ:st, 'mɛrə(ʊ)blast, -s
AM 'mɛrə,blæst, -s
Meroe
BR 'mɛrəʊ
AM 'mɛroʊ
merohedral
BR ˌmɛrə(ʊ)'hi:dr(ə)l
AM ˌmɛroʊ'hidrəl
meronymy
BR mɪ'rɒnɪmi
AM mə'rɑnəmi
Merovingian
BR ˌmɛrə(ʊ)'vɪn(d)ʒɪən, -z
AM ˌmɛrə'vɪndʒ(i)ən, -z
Merrick
BR 'mɛrɪk
AM 'mɛrɪk
Merrill
BR 'mɛrɪl, 'mɛrl̩
AM 'mɛrəl
merrily
BR 'mɛrɪli
AM 'mɛrəli
Merrimac
BR 'mɛrɪmak
AM 'mɛrə,mæk
Merrimack
BR 'mɛrɪmak
AM 'mɛrə,mæk
merriment
BR 'mɛrɪm(ə)nt
AM 'mɛrɪmənt
merriness
BR 'mɛrɪnɪs
AM 'mɛrinɪs
Merrion
BR 'mɛrɪən
AM 'mɛriən
Merritt
BR 'mɛrɪt
AM 'mɛrət
merry
BR 'mɛr|i, -ɪə(r), -ɪɪst
AM 'mɛri, -ər, -ɪst
merry-go-round
BR 'mɛrɪgə(ʊ),raʊnd, -z
AM 'mɛrigoʊ,raʊnd, -z
merrymaker
BR 'mɛrɪ,meɪkə(r), -z
AM 'mɛri,meɪkər, -z
merrymaking
BR 'mɛrɪ,meɪkɪŋ
AM 'mɛri,meɪkɪŋ
Merryweather
BR 'mɛrɪ,wɛðə(r)
AM 'mɛrɪ,wɛðər
Mersa Matruh
BR ˌmə:sə mə'tru:
AM ˌmərsə mə'tru
Mersey
BR 'mə:zi
AM 'mərzi
Merseyside
BR 'mə:zɪsʌɪd
AM 'mərzi,saɪd
Merthiolate®
BR mə:'θʌɪəleɪt
AM mə(r)'θaɪə,leɪt
Merthyr Tydfil
BR ˌmə:θə 'tɪdv(ɪ)l
AM ˌmərθər 'tɪdvɪl
WE ˌmɛrθɪr 'tɪdvɪl
Merton
BR 'mə:tn
AM 'mərt(ə)n
Mervin
BR 'mə:vɪn
AM 'mərvən
Mervyn
BR 'mə:vɪn
AM 'mərvən
Meryl
BR 'mɛrɪl, 'mɛrl̩
AM 'mərəl
mesa
BR 'meɪsə(*r*), -z
AM 'meɪsə, -z
mésalliance
BR mɛ'zalɪəns
AM ˌmeɪzə'laɪəns
Mesa Verde
BR ˌmeɪsə 'vɛ:di, + 'və:di
AM ˌmeɪsə 'vɛrdi
mescal
BR 'mɛskal, mɛ'skal, mə'skal
AM mɛ'skæl, mə'skæl
mescalin
BR 'mɛskəlɪn
AM 'mɛskələn, 'mɛskə,lin
mescaline
BR 'mɛskəlɪn, 'mɛskəli:n
AM 'mɛskə,lin, 'mɛskələn
mesdames
BR meɪ'dam
AM meɪ'dɑm
mesdemoiselles
BR ˌmeɪd(ə)mwə'zɛl
AM ˌmeɪdəm(w)ə'zɛl, ˌmeɪd,mwɑ'zɛl
meseemed
BR mɪ'si:md
AM mi'simd, mə'simd
meseems
BR mɪ'si:mz
AM mi'simz, mə'simz
mesembryanthemum
BR mɪˌzɛmbrɪ'anθɪməm, -z
AM məˌzɛmbri'ænθəməm, -z
mesencephalon
BR ˌmɛsɛn'sɛfəlɒn, ˌmɛsɛn'sɛfl̩ɒn, ˌmɛzɛn'sɛfəlɒn, ˌmɛzɛn'sɛfl̩ɒn, ˌmɛsɛn'kɛfəlɒn, ˌmɛsɛn'kɛfl̩ɒn, ˌmɛzɛn'kɛfəlɒn, ˌmɛzɛn'kɛfl̩ɒn
AM ˌmɛzən'sɛfələn, ˌmɛzən'sɛfələn
mesenterial
BR ˌmɛs(ə)n'tɪərɪəl, ˌmɛz(ə)n'tɪərɪəl
AM ˌmɛzən'tɛriəl, ˌmɛsən'tɛriəl
mesenteric
BR ˌmɛs(ə)n'tɛrɪk, ˌmɛz(ə)n'tɛrɪk
AM ˌmɛzən'tɛrɪk, ˌmɛsən'tɛrɪk
mesenteritis
BR ˌmɛs(ə)ntə'rʌɪtɪs, ˌmɛz(ə)ntə'rʌɪtɪs, mɪˌsɛntə'rʌɪtɪs, mɪˌzɛntə'rʌɪtɪs
AM ˌmɛzən(t)ə'raɪdɪs, ˌmɛsən(t)ə'raɪdɪs
mesentery
BR 'mɛs(ə)nt(ə)ri, 'mɛz(ə)nt(ə)r|i, -ɪz
AM 'mɛzən,tɛri, -z
mesh
BR mɛʃ, -ɪz, -ɪŋ, -t
AM mɛʃ, -əz, -ɪŋ, -t
Meshach
BR 'mi:ʃak
AM 'miʃæk
mesial
BR 'mi:zɪəl, 'mi:sɪəl, 'mɛsɪəl
AM 'mɛziəl, 'mɛsiəl, 'miziəl, 'misiəl
mesially
BR 'mi:zɪəli, 'mi:sɪəli, 'mɛsɪəli
AM 'mɛziəli, 'mɛsiəli, 'miziəli, 'misiəli
mesic
BR 'mi:zɪk, 'mɛzɪk
AM 'mɛzɪk, 'mɛsɪk, 'mizɪk, 'mɪsɪk
Mesmer
BR 'mɛzmə(r)
AM 'mɛsmər, 'mɛzmər
mesmeric
BR mɛz'mɛrɪk
AM mɛz'mɛrɪk, mɛs'mɛrɪk
mesmerically
BR mɛz'mɛrɪkli
AM mɛz'mɛrək(ə)li, mɛs'mɛrək(ə)li
mesmerisation
BR ˌmɛzmərʌɪ'zeɪʃn
AM ˌmɛzmərə'zeɪʃən, ˌmɛsmərə'zeɪʃən, ˌmɛzmə,raɪ'zeɪʃən, ˌmɛsmə,raɪ'zeɪʃən

mesmerise
BR 'mɛzmərʌɪz, -ɨz, -ɪŋ, -d
AM 'mɛzmə,raɪz, 'mɛsmə,raɪz, -ɨz, -ɪŋ, -d

mesmeriser
BR 'mɛzmərʌɪzə(r), -z
AM 'mɛzmə,raɪzər, 'mɛsmə,raɪzər, -z

mesmerisingly
BR 'mɛzmərʌɪzɪŋli
AM 'mɛzmə,raɪzɪŋli, 'mɛsmə,raɪzɪŋli

mesmerism
BR 'mɛzmərɪz(ə)m
AM 'mɛzmə,rɪzəm, 'mɛsmə,rɪzəm

mesmerist
BR 'mɛzm(ə)rɪst, -s
AM 'mɛzmərəst, 'mɛsmərəst, -s

mesmerization
BR ,mɛzmərʌɪ'zeɪʃn
AM ,mɛzmərə'zeɪʃən, ,mɛsmərə'zeɪʃən, ,mɛzmə,raɪ'zeɪʃən, ,mɛsmə,raɪ'zeɪʃən

mesmerize
BR 'mɛzmərʌɪz, -ɨz, -ɪŋ, -d
AM 'mɛzmə,raɪz, 'mɛsmə,raɪz, -ɨz, -ɪŋ, -d

mesmerizer
BR 'mɛzmərʌɪzə(r), -z
AM 'mɛzmə,raɪzər, 'mɛsmə,raɪzər, -z

mesmerizingly
BR 'mɛzmərʌɪzɪŋli
AM 'mɛzmə,raɪzɪŋli, 'mɛsmə,raɪzɪŋli

mesne
BR miːn
AM min

Meso-America
BR ,mɛsəʊə'mɛrɨkə(r), ,mɛzəʊə'mɛrɨkə(r), ,miːsəʊə'mɛrɨkə(r), ,miːzəʊə'mɛrɨkə(r)
AM ¦mɛzoʊə'mɛrəkə, ¦mɛsoʊə'mɛrəkə

Meso-American
BR ,mɛsəʊə'mɛrɨk(ə)n, ,mɛzəʊə'mɛrɨk(ə)n, ,miːsəʊə'mɛrɨk(ə)n, ,miːzəʊə'mɛrɨk(ə)n, -z
AM ¦mɛzoʊə'mɛrəkən, ¦mɛsoʊə'mɛrəkən, -z

mesoblast
BR 'mɛsə(ʊ)blɑːst, 'mɛsə(ʊ)blast, 'mɛzə(ʊ)blɑːst, 'mɛzə(ʊ)blast, 'miːsə(ʊ)blɑːst, 'miːsəʊblast, 'miːzə(ʊ)blɑːst, 'miːzə(ʊ)blast
AM 'mɛzoʊ,blæst, 'mɛsoʊ,blæst

mesocarp
BR 'mɛsə(ʊ)kɑːp, 'mɛzə(ʊ)kɑːp, 'miːsə(ʊ)kɑːp, 'miːzə(ʊ)kɑːp
AM 'mɛzə,kɑrp, 'mɛsə,kɑrp

mesocephalic
BR ,mɛsəʊsɪ'falɪk, ,mɛsəʊkɛ'falɪk, ,mɛzəʊsɪ'falɪk, ,mɛzəʊkɛ'falɪk, ,miːsəʊsɪ'falɪk, ,miːsəʊkɛ'falɪk, ,miːzəʊsɪ'falɪk, ,miːzəʊkɛ'falɪk
AM ¦mɛzoʊsə'fælɪk, ¦mɛsoʊsə'fælɪk

mesoderm
BR 'mɛsə(ʊ)dəːm, 'mɛzə(ʊ)dəːm, 'miːsə(ʊ)dəːm, 'miːzə(ʊ)dəːm
AM 'mɛzə,dərm, 'mɛsə,dərm

mesogaster
BR 'mɛsə(ʊ),gastə(r), 'mɛzə(ʊ),gastə(r), 'miːsə(ʊ),gastə(r), 'miːzə(ʊ),gastə(r), -z
AM 'mɛzoʊ,gæstər, 'mɛsoʊ,gæstər, -z

mesolect
BR 'mɛsə(ʊ)lɛkt, 'mɛzə(ʊ)lɛkt, 'miːsə(ʊ)lɛkt, 'miːzə(ʊ)lɛkt, -s
AM 'mɛzə,lɛk|(t), 'mɛsə,lɛk|(t), -(t)s

mesolectal
BR ,mɛsə(ʊ)'lɛktl, ,mɛzə(ʊ)'lɛktl, ,miːsə(ʊ)'lɛktl, ,miːzə(ʊ)'lɛktl
AM ¦mɛzə'lɛktəl, ¦mɛsə'lɛktəl

Mesolithic
BR ,mɛsə(ʊ)'lɪθɪk, ,mɛzə(ʊ)'lɪθɪk, ,miːsə(ʊ)'lɪθɪk, ,miːzə(ʊ)'lɪθɪk
AM ¦mɛzə'lɪθɪk, ¦mɛsə'lɪθɪk

mesomorph
BR 'mɛsə(ʊ)mɔːf, 'mɛzə(ʊ)mɔːf, 'miːsə(ʊ)mɔːf, 'miːzə(ʊ)mɔːf, -s
AM 'mɛzə,mɔ(ə)rf, 'mɛsə,mɔ(ə)rf, -s

mesomorphic
BR ,mɛsə(ʊ)'mɔːfɪk, ,mɛzə(ʊ)'mɔːfɪk, ,miːsə(ʊ)'mɔːfɪk, ,miːzə(ʊ)'mɔːfɪk
AM ¦mɛzə'mɔrfɪk, ¦mɛsə'mɔrfɪk

mesomorphy
BR 'mɛsə(ʊ),mɔːfi, 'mɛzə(ʊ),mɔːfi, 'miːsə(ʊ),mɔːfi, 'miːzə(ʊ),mɔːfi
AM 'mɛzə,mɔrfi, 'mɛsə,mɔrfi

meson
BR 'miːzɒn, 'miːsɒn, 'mɛzɒn, 'mɛsɒn, 'meɪzɒn, -z
AM 'mi,zɑn, 'meɪ,zɑn, 'mi,sɑn, 'meɪ,sɑn, -z

mesonic
BR mɨ'zɒnɪk, mɨ'sɒnɪk
AM mi'zɑnɪk, mə'zɑnɪk, meɪ'zɑnɪk, mi'sɑnɪk, mə'sɑnɪk, meɪ'sɑnɪk

mesopause
BR 'mɛsə(ʊ)pɔːz, 'mɛzə(ʊ)pɔːz, 'miːsə(ʊ)pɔːz, 'miːzə(ʊ)pɔːz, -z
AM 'mɛzə,pɔz, 'mɛsə,pɔz, 'mɛzə,pɑz, 'mɛsə,pɑz, -z

mesophyll
BR 'mɛsə(ʊ)fɪl, 'mɛzə(ʊ)fɪl, 'miːsə(ʊ)fɪl, 'miːzə(ʊ)fɪl, -z
AM 'mɛzə,fɪl, 'mɛsə,fɪl, -z

mesophyte
BR 'mɛsə(ʊ)fʌɪt, 'mɛzə(ʊ)fʌɪt, 'miːsə(ʊ)fʌɪt, 'miːzə(ʊ)fʌɪt, -s
AM 'mɛzə,faɪt, 'mɛzə,faɪt, -s

Mesopotamia
BR ,mɛsəpə'teɪmɪə(r)
AM ,mɛsəpə'teɪmiə

Mesopotamian
BR ,mɛsəpə'teɪmɪən, -z
AM ,mɛsəpə'teɪmiən, -z

mesosphere
BR 'mɛsə(ʊ)sfɪə(r), 'mɛzə(ʊ)sfɪə(r), 'miːsə(ʊ)sfɪə(r), 'miːzə(ʊ)sfɪə(r), -z
AM 'mɛzə,sfɪ(ə)r, 'mɛsə,sfɪ(ə)r, -z

mesothelium
BR ,mɛsə(ʊ)'θiːˈɪəm, ,mɛzə(ʊ)'θiːlɪəm, ,miːsəʊ'θiːliəm, ,miːzə(ʊ)'θiːlɪəm
AM ,mɛzə'θiliəm, ,mɛsə'θiliəm, ,mizə'θiliəm, ,misə'θiliəm

mesotron
BR 'mɛsətrɒn, 'mɛzətrɒn, 'miːsətrɒn, 'miːzətrɒn, -z
AM 'mɛzə,trɑn, 'mizə,trɑn, 'mɛsə,trɑn, 'misə,trɑn, -z

Mesozoic
BR ,mɛsə(ʊ)'zəʊɪk, ,mɛzə(ʊ)'zəʊɪk, ,miːsə(ʊ)'zəʊɪk, ,miːzə(ʊ)'zəʊɪk, -s
AM ¦mɛzə'zoʊɪk, ¦mizə'zoʊɪk, ¦mɛsə'zoʊɪk, ¦misə'zoʊɪk, -s

mesquit
BR mɛ'skiːt, -s
AM mɛ'skit, -s

mesquite
BR mɛ'skiːt
AM mɛ'skit

mess
BR mɛs, -ɨz, -ɪŋ, -t
AM mɛs, -əz, -ɪŋ, -t

message
BR 'mɛs|ɪdʒ, -ɨdʒɨz
AM 'mɛsɪdʒ, -ɨz

Messalina
BR ,mɛsə'liːnə(r)
AM ,mɛsə'linə

messenger
BR 'mɛs(ɨ)ndʒə(r), -z
AM 'mɛsndʒər, -z

Messerschmitt
BR 'mɛsəʃmɪt, -s
AM 'mɛsər,ʃmɪt, -s

Messiaen
BR 'mɛsjɒ̃
AM mə'saɪən

messiah
BR mɨ'sʌɪə(r), -z
AM mə'saɪə, -z

Messiahship
BR mɨ'sʌɪəʃɪp, -s
AM mə'saɪə,ʃɪp, -s

messianic
BR ,mɛsɪ'anɪk, ,mɛsʌɪ'anɪk
AM ¦mɛsi'ænɪk, ¦mɛsi'ɑnɪk

messianically
BR ,mɛsɪ'anɨkli, ,mɛsʌɪ'anɨkli
AM ¦mɛsi'ænək(ə)li, ¦mɛsi'ɑnək(ə)li

Messianism
BR mɨ'sʌɪənɪz(ə)m
AM mə'saɪə,nɪzəm

messieurs
BR meɪ'sjəːz, mə'sjəːz, 'mɛsəz
AM meɪ'sjərz

messily
BR 'mɛsɨli
AM 'mɛsəli

Messina
BR mɛ'siːnə(r), mɨ'siːnə(r)

AM mə'sinə

messiness
BR 'mɛsɪnɨs
AM 'mɛsinɨs

messmate
BR 'mɛsmeɪt, -s
AM 'mɛsˌmeɪt, -s

Messrs
BR 'mɛsəz
AM 'mɛsərz

messuage
BR 'mɛsw|ɪdʒ, -ɨdʒɨz
AM 'mɛswɪdʒ, -ɨz

messy
BR 'mɛs|i, -ɪə(r), -ɪɨst
AM 'mɛsi, -ər, -ɨst

mestiza
BR mɛ'sti:zə(r), mɪ'sti:zə(r), -z
AM mə'stizə, mə'stisə, -z

mestizo
BR mɛ'sti:zəʊ, mɪ'sti:zəʊ, -z
AM mɛ'stizoʊ, mə'stizoʊ, -z

met
BR mɛt
AM mɛt

metabisulfite
BR ˌmɛtəbʌɪ'sʌlfʌɪt, -s
AM ˌmɛdəˌbaɪ'səlˌfaɪt, -s

metabisulphite
BR ˌmɛtəbʌɪ'sʌlfʌɪt, -s
AM ˌmɛdəˌbaɪ'səlˌfaɪt, -s

metabolic
BR ˌmɛtə'bɒlɪk
AM ˌmɛdə'bɑlɪk

metabolically
BR ˌmɛtə'bɒlɨkli
AM ˌmɛdə'bɑlək(ə)li

metabolisable
BR mɪ'tabəlʌɪzəbl, mɛ'tabəlʌɪzəbl
AM mə'tæbəˌlaɪzəbəl

metabolise
BR mɪ'tabəlʌɪz, mɛ'tabəlʌɪz, -ɨz, -ɪŋ, -d
AM mə'tæbəˌlaɪz, -ɨz, -ɪŋ, -d

metabolism
BR mɪ'tabəlɪz(ə)m, mɛ'tabəlɪz(ə)m
AM mə'tæbəˌlɪzəm

metabolite
BR mɪ'tabəlʌɪt, mɛ'tabəlʌɪt
AM mə'tæbəˌlaɪt

metabolizable
BR mɪ'tabəlʌɪzəbl, mɛ'tabəlʌɪzəbl
AM mə'tæbəˌlaɪzəbəl

metabolize
BR mɪ'tabəlʌɪz, mɛ'tabəlʌɪz, -ɨz, -ɪŋ, -d
AM mə'tæbəˌlaɪz, -ɨz, -ɪŋ, -d

metacarpal
BR ˌmɛtə'kɑ:pl, 'mɛtəˌkɑ:pl, -z
AM ˌmɛdə'kɑrpəl, -z

metacarpus
BR ˌmɛtə'kɑ:pəs, 'mɛtəˌkɑ:pəs
AM ˌmɛdə'kɑrpəs

metacenter
BR 'mɛtəˌsɛntə(r), -z
AM 'mɛdəˌsɛn(t)ər, -z

metacentre
BR 'mɛtəˌsɛntə(r), -z
AM 'mɛdəˌsɛn(t)ər, -z

metacentric
BR ˌmɛtə'sɛntrɪk
AM ˌmɛdə'sɛntrɪk

metage
BR 'mi:t|ɪdʒ, 'mɛt|ɪdʒ, -ɨdʒɨz
AM 'mɛdɪdʒ, -ɨz

metageneses
BR ˌmɛtə'dʒɛnɨsi:z
AM ˌmɛdə'dʒɛnəsiz

metagenesis
BR ˌmɛtə'dʒɛnɨsɪs
AM ˌmɛdə'dʒɛnəsəs

metagenetic
BR ˌmɛtədʒɪ'nɛtɪk
AM ˌmɛdədʒə'nɛdɪk

metal
BR 'mɛtl̩, -z, -ɪŋ, -d
AM 'mɛdl, -z, -ɪŋ, -d

metalanguage
BR 'mɛtəˌlaŋgw|ɪdʒ, -ɨdʒɨz
AM 'mɛdəˌlæŋgwɪdʒ, -ɨz

metalinguistic
BR ˌmɛtəlɪŋ'gwɪstɪk
AM ˌmɛdəˌlɪŋ'gwɪstɪk

metalize
BR 'mɛtl̩ʌɪz, -ɨz, -ɪŋ, -d
AM 'mɛdlˌaɪz, -ɨz, -ɪŋ, -d

metallic
BR mɪ'talɪk
AM mə'tælɪk

metallically
BR mɪ'talɨkli
AM mə'tælək(ə)li

metalliferous
BR ˌmɛtə'lɪf(ə)rəs, ˌmɛtl'ɪf(ə)rəs
AM ˌmɛdl'ɪf(ə)rəs

metalline
BR 'mɛtəlʌɪn, 'mɛtl̩ʌɪn
AM 'mɛdl̩ən, 'mɛdl̩in

metallisation
BR ˌmɛtl̩ʌɪ'zeɪʃn
AM ˌmɛdl̩ə'zeɪʃən, ˌmɛdəˌlaɪ'zeɪʃən

metallise
BR 'mɛtl̩ʌɪz, -ɨz, -ɪŋ, -d
AM 'mɛdlˌaɪz, -ɨz, -ɪŋ, -d

metallization
BR ˌmɛtl̩ʌɪ'zeɪʃn
AM ˌmɛdl̩ə'zeɪʃən, ˌmɛdəˌlaɪ'zeɪʃən

metallize
BR 'mɛtl̩ʌɪz, -ɨz, -ɪŋ, -d
AM 'mɛdlˌaɪz, -ɨz, -ɪŋ, -d

metallographic
BR ˌmɛtl̩ə'grafɪk
AM ˌmɛdl̩ə'græfɪk

metallographical
BR ˌmɛtl̩ə'grafɪkl
AM ˌmɛdl̩ə'græfəkəl

metallographically
BR ˌmɛtl̩ə'grafɨkli
AM ˌmɛdl̩ə'græfək(ə)li

metallography
BR ˌmɛtə'lɒgrəfi, ˌmɛtl'ɒgrəfi
AM ˌmɛdə'lɑgrəfi

metalloid
BR 'mɛtəlɔɪd, 'mɛtl̩ɔɪd, -z
AM 'mɛdlˌɔɪd, -z

metallophone
BR 'mɛtl̩əfəʊn, -z
AM 'mɛdl̩əˌfoʊn, -z

metallurgic
BR ˌmɛtə'lə:dʒɪk
AM ˌmɛdl'ərdʒɪk

metallurgical
BR ˌmɛtə'lə:dʒɨkl
AM ˌmɛdl'ərdʒəkəl

metallurgically
BR ˌmɛtə'lə:dʒɨkli
AM ˌmɛdl'ərdʒək(ə)li

metallurgist
BR mɪ'talədʒɪst, 'mɛtələ:dʒɪst, -s
AM 'mɛdlˌərdʒəst, -s

metallurgy
BR mɪ'talədʒi, 'mɛtələ:dʒi
AM 'mɛdlˌərdʒi

metalwork
BR 'mɛtlwə:k
AM 'mɛdlˌwərk

metalworker
BR 'mɛtlˌwə:kə(r), -z
AM 'mɛdlˌwərkər, -z

metalworking
BR 'mɛtlˌwə:kɪŋ
AM 'mɛdlˌwərkɪŋ

metamer
BR 'mɛtəmə(r), -z
AM 'mɛdəmər, -z

metamere
BR 'mɛtəmɪə(r), -z
AM 'mɛdəmɪ(ə)r, -z

metameric
BR ˌmɛtə'mɛrɪk
AM ˌmɛdə'mɛrɪk

metamerism
BR mɪ'tamərɪz(ə)m
AM mə'tæməˌrɪzəm

metamorphic
BR ˌmɛtə'mɔ:fɪk
AM ˌmɛdə'mɔrfɪk

metamorphism
BR ˌmɛtə'mɔ:fɪz(ə)m
AM ˌmɛdə'mɔrˌfɪzəm

metamorphose
BR ˌmɛtə'mɔ:fəʊz, -ɨz, -ɪŋ, -d
AM ˌmɛdə'mɔrˌfoʊz, -əz, -ɪŋ, -d

metamorphoses
plural of metamorphosis
BR ˌmɛtə'mɔ:fəsi:z
AM ˌmɛdə'mɔrfəsiz

metamorphosis
BR ˌmɛtə'mɔ:fəsɪs
AM ˌmɛdə'mɔrfəsəs

metaphase
BR 'mɛtəfeɪz, -ɨz
AM 'mɛdəˌfeɪz, -ɨz

metaphor
BR 'mɛtəfə(r), 'mɛtəfɔ:(r), -z
AM 'mɛdəˌfɔ(ə)r, -z

metaphoric
BR ˌmɛtə'fɒrɪk
AM ˌmɛdə'fɔrɪk

metaphorical
BR ˌmɛtə'fɒrɪkl
AM ˌmɛdə'fɔrəkəl

metaphorically
BR ˌmɛtə'fɒrɨkli
AM ˌmɛdə'fɔrək(ə)li

metaphrase
BR 'mɛtəfreɪz, -ɨz, -ɪŋ, -d
AM 'mɛdəˌfreɪz, -ɨz, -ɪŋ, -d

metaphrastic
BR ˌmɛtə'frastɪk
AM ˌmɛdə'fræstɪk

metaphysic
BR ˌmɛtə'fɪzɪk, -s
AM ˌmɛdə'fɪzɪk, -s

metaphysical
BR ˌmɛtə'fɪzɪkl
AM ˌmɛdə'fɪzɪkəl

metaphysically
BR ˌmɛtə'fɪzɨkli
AM ˌmɛdə'fɪzɪk(ə)li

metaphysician
BR ˌmɛtəfɪ'zɪʃn, -z
AM ˌmɛdəfə'zɪʃən, -z

metaphysicise
BR ˌmɛtə'fɪzɨsʌɪz, -ɨz, -ɪŋ, -d
AM ˌmɛdə'fɪzəˌsaɪz, -ɨz, -ɪŋ, -d

metaphysicize
BR ˌmɛtə'fɪzɨsʌɪz, -ɨz, -ɪŋ, -d
AM ˌmɛdə'fɪzəˌsaɪz, -ɨz, -ɪŋ, -d

metaplasia
BR ˌmɛtə'pleɪzɪə(r), ˌmɛtə'pleɪʒə(r), -z

AM ˌmɛdəˈpleɪʒ(i)ə, ˌmɛdəˈpleɪziə, -z

metaplasm
BR ˈmɛtəplaz(ə)m, -z
AM ˈmɛdəˌplæzəm, -z

metaplastic
BR ˌmɛtəˈplastɪk
AM ¦mɛdəˈplæstɪk

metapolitics
BR ˌmɛtəˈpɒlɨtɪks
AM ¦mɛdəˈpɑləˌtɪks

metapsychological
BR ˌmɛtəˌsʌɪkəˈlɒdʒɨkl
AM ¦mɛdəˌsaɪkəˈlɑdʒək-əl

metapsychology
BR ˌmɛtəsʌɪˈkɒlədʒi
AM ¦mɛdəˌsaɪˈkɑlədʒi

metastability
BR ˌmɛtəstəˈbɪlɨti
AM ˌmɛdəstəˈbɪlɨdi

metastable
BR ˌmɛtəˈsteɪbl
AM ¦mɛdəˈsteɪbəl

metastases
BR mɪˈtastəsiːz
AM məˈtæstəsiz

metastasis
BR mɪˈtastəsɪs
AM məˈtæstəsəs

metastasise
BR mɪˈtastəsʌɪz, -ɨz, -ɪŋ, -d
AM məˈtæstəˌsaɪz, -ɨz, -ɪŋ, -d

metastasize
BR mɪˈtastəsʌɪz, -ɨz, -ɪŋ, -d
AM məˈtæstəˌsaɪz, -ɨz, -ɪŋ, -d

metastatic
BR ˌmɛtəˈstatɪk
AM ¦mɛdəˈstædɪk

metatarsal
BR ˌmɛtəˈtɑːsl, ˈmɛtəˌtɑːsl, -z
AM ¦mɛdəˈtɑrsəl, -z

metatarsus
BR ˌmɛtəˈtɑːsəs, ˈmɛtəˌtɑːsəs
AM ¦mɛdəˈtɑrsəs

metatherian
BR ˌmɛtəˈθɪərɪən, -z
AM ¦mɛdəˈθɪriən, -z

metathesis
BR mɪˈtaθɨsɪs
AM məˈtæθəsəs

metathetic
BR ˌmɛtəˈθɛtɪk
AM ¦mɛdəˈθɛdɪk

metathetical
BR ˌmɛtəˈθɛtɨkl
AM ¦mɛdəˈθɛdəkəl

metazoan
BR ˌmɛtəˈzəʊən, -z
AM ¦mɛdəˈzoʊən, -z

Metcalf
BR ˈmɛtkɑːf
AM ˈmɛtkæf

Metcalfe
BR ˈmɛtkɑːf
AM ˈmɛtkæf

mete
BR miːt, -s, -ɪŋ, -ɨd
AM mi|t, -ts, -dɪŋ, -dɨd

metempsychosis
BR ˌmɛtəmsʌɪˈkəʊsɪs
AM ˌmɛdəmˌsaɪˈkoʊsəs, məˌtɛmsəˈkoʊsəs

metempsychosist
BR ˌmɛtəmsʌɪˈkəʊsɪst, -s
AM ˌmɛdəmˌsaɪˈkoʊsəst, məˌtɛmsəˈkoʊsəst, -s

meteor
BR ˈmiːtɪə(r), -z
AM ˈmidiər, -z

meteoric
BR ˌmiːtɪˈɒrɪk
AM ¦midiˈɔrɪk

meteorically
BR ˌmiːtɪˈɒrɪkli
AM ¦midiˈɔrək(ə)li

meteorite
BR ˈmiːtɪərʌɪt, -s
AM ˈmidiəˌraɪt, -s

meteoritic
BR ˌmiːtɪəˈrɪtɪk
AM ¦midiəˈrɪdɪk

meteorograph
BR ˈmiːtɪərəˌgrɑːf, ˈmiːtɪərəˌgraf, -s
AM ¦midiˈɔrəgræf, -s

meteoroid
BR ˈmiːtɪərɔɪd, -z
AM ˈmidiəˌrɔɪd, -z

meteoroidal
BR ˌmiːtɪəˈrɔɪdl
AM ¦midiəˈrɔɪdəl

meteorological
BR ˌmiːtɪərəˈlɒdʒɨkl
AM ¦midiər(ə)ˈlɑdʒəkəl

meteorologically
BR ˌmiːtɪərəˈlɒdʒɨkli
AM ¦midiər(ə)ˈlɑdʒə-k(ə)li

meteorologist
BR ˌmiːtɪəˈrɒlədʒɪst, -s
AM ˌmidiəˈrɑlədʒəst, -s

meteorology
BR ˌmiːtɪəˈrɒlədʒi
AM ˌmidiəˈrɑlədʒi

meter
BR ˈmiːt|ə(r), -əz, -(ə)rɪŋ, -əd
AM ˈmi|dər, -dərz, -dərɪŋ\-trɪŋ, -dərd

metermaid
BR ˈmiːtəmeɪd, -z
AM ˈmidərˌmeɪd, -z

mete-wand
BR ˈmiːtwɒnd, -z
AM ˈmitˌwɔnd, ˈmitˌwɑnd, -z

methadone
BR ˈmɛθədəʊn
AM ˈmɛθəˌdoʊn

methamphetamine
BR ˌmɛθəmˈfɛtəmiːn, ˌmɛθəmˈfɛtəmɪn, -z
AM ˌmɛθəmˈfɛdəmin, ˌmɛθəmˈfɛdəmən, -z

methanal
BR ˈmɛθənal
AM ˈmɛθəˌnæl

methane
BR ˈmiːθeɪn
AM ˈmɛˌθeɪn

methanoic acid
BR mɛθəˌnəʊɪk ˈasɨd
AM ˌmɛθəˌnoʊɪk ˈæsəd

methanol
BR ˈmɛθənɒl
AM ˈmɛθəˌnɔl, ˈmɛθəˌnɑl

Methedrine®
BR ˈmɛθədriːn, ˈmɛθədrɪn
AM ˈmɛθəˌdrin, ˈmɛθədrən

metheglin
BR mɪˈθɛglɪn, mɛˈθɛglɪn
AM məˈθɛglən

methinks
BR mɪˈθɪŋks
AM miˈθɪŋks, məˈθɪŋks

methionine
BR mɪˈθʌɪəniːn, mɪˈθʌɪənɪn
AM məˈθaɪəˌnin, məˈθaɪənən

metho
BR ˈmɛθəʊ, -z
AM ˈmɛθoʊ, -z

method
BR ˈmɛθəd, -z
AM ˈmɛθəd, -z

methodic
BR mɪˈθɒdɪk
AM məˈθɑdɪk

methodical
BR mɪˈθɒdɨkl
AM məˈθɑdəkəl

methodically
BR mɪˈθɒdɨkli
AM məˈθɑdək(ə)li

methodise
BR ˈmɛθədʌɪz, -ɨz, -ɪŋ, -d
AM ˈmɛθəˌdaɪz, -ɨz, -ɪŋ, -d

methodiser
BR ˈmɛθədʌɪzə(r)
AM ˈmɛθəˌdaɪzər

Methodism
BR ˈmɛθədɪz(ə)m
AM ˈmɛθəˌdɪzəm

Methodist
BR ˈmɛθədɪst, -s
AM ˈmɛθədəst, -s

Methodistic
BR ˌmɛθəˈdɪstɪk
AM ˌmɛθəˈdɪstɪk

Methodistical
BR ˌmɛθəˈdɪstɨkl
AM ˌmɛθəˈdɪstəkəl

Methodius
BR mɪˈθəʊdɪəs
AM məˈθoʊdiəs

methodize
BR ˈmɛθədʌɪz, -ɨz, -ɪŋ, -d
AM ˈmɛθəˌdaɪz, -ɨz, -ɪŋ, -d

methodizer
BR ˈmɛθədʌɪzə(r), -z
AM ˈmɛθəˌdaɪzər, -z

methodological
BR ˌmɛθədəˈlɒdʒɨkl
AM ¦mɛθədəˈlɑdʒəkəl

methodologically
BR ˌmɛθədəˈlɒdʒɨkli
AM ¦mɛθədəˈlɑdʒək(ə)li

methodologist
BR ˌmɛθəˈdɒlədʒɪst, -s
AM ˌmɛθəˈdɑlədʒəst, -s

methodology
BR ˌmɛθəˈdɒlədʒ|i, -ɪz
AM ˌmɛθəˈdɑlədʒi, -z

methotrexate
BR ˌmɪθə(ʊ)ˈtrɛkseɪt, ˌmiːθə(ʊ)ˈtrɛkseɪt
AM ˌmɛθəˈtrɛkseɪt

methought
BR mɪˈθɔːt
AM miˈθɔt, məˈθɔt, miˈθɑt, məˈθɑt

meths
BR mɛθs
AM mɛθs

Methuen[1]
place in US
BR mɪˈθjuːən
AM məˈθ(j)uən

Methuen[2]
surname
BR ˈmɛθjʊɪn
AM ˈmɛθ(j)ʊən

methuselah
BR mɪˈθjuːzələ(*r*), -z
AM məˈθ(j)uz(ə)lə, məˈθ(j)us(ə)lə, -z

methyl[1]
non-technical
BR ˈmɛθ(ɪ)l
AM ˈmɛθəl

methyl[2]
technical
BR ˈmiːθʌɪl, ˈmɛθʌɪl, ˈmɛθ(ɪ)l
AM ˈmɛθəl

methylate
BR ˈmɛθɨleɪt, -s, -ɪŋ, -ɨd
AM ˈmɛθəˌleɪ|t, -ts, -dɪŋ, -dɨd

methylated spirit
BR ˌmɛθɨleɪtɨd ˈspɪrɪt, -s

AM ˈmɛθəˌleɪdɪd ˌspɪrɪt, -s
methylation
BR ˌmɛθɪˈleɪʃn, -z
AM ˌmɛθəˈleɪʃən, -z
methylene
BR ˈmɛθɪliːn
AM ˈmɛθəˌlin
methylic
BR mɪˈθɪlɪk
AM məˈθɪlɪk
metic
BR ˈmɛtɪk, -s
AM ˈmɛdɪk, -s
metical
BR ˈmɛtɨkl, -z
AM ˈmɛdəkəl, -z
meticulous
BR mɪˈtɪkjʊləs
AM məˈtɪkjələs
meticulously
BR mɪˈtɪkjʊləsli
AM məˈtɪkjələsli
meticulousness
BR mɪˈtɪkjʊləsnəs
AM məˈtɪkjələsnəs
métier
BR ˈmeɪtɪeɪ, ˈmɛtɪeɪ, -z
AM meɪˈtjeɪ, mɛˈtjeɪ, ˈmeɪˌtjeɪ, ˈmɛˌtjeɪ, ˈmeɪdieɪ, -z
metif
BR meɪˈtiːf, -s
AM meɪˈtif, -s
metis
BR meɪˈtiː(s), ˈmeɪtiː, meɪˈtiː(s)\ˈmeɪtiː\ ˈmeɪtɪz
AM meɪˈti|(s), -z\-s
metisse
BR meɪˈtiːs, ˈmeɪtiːs, -ɨz
AM meɪˈtis, -ɨz
metol
BR ˈmɛtɒl, -z
AM ˈmiˌtɔl, ˈmiˌtɑl, -z
Metonic
BR mɛˈtɒnɪk, mɪˈtɒnɪk
AM mɛˈtɑnɪk
metonym
BR ˈmɛtənɪm, -z
AM ˈmɛdəˌnɪm, -z
metonymic
BR ˌmɛtəˈnɪmɪk
AM ˌmɛdəˈnɪmɪk
metonymical
BR ˌmɛtəˈnɪmɨkl
AM ˌmɛdəˈnɪmɨkəl
metonymically
BR ˌmɛtəˈnɪmɨkli
AM ˌmɛdəˈnɪmɨk(ə)li
metonymy
BR mɪˈtɒnəmi
AM məˈtɑnəmi
metope
BR ˈmɛt|əʊp, ˈmɛt|əpi, -əʊps\-əpɪz
AM ˈmɛdoʊpi, -z
metoposcopy
BR ˌmɛtəˈpɒskəp|i, -ɪz
AM ˌmɛdəˈpɑskəpi, -z
metre
BR ˈmiːtə(r), -z
AM ˈmidər, -z
metreage
BR ˈmiːtərɪdʒ, ˈmiːtrɪdʒ
AM ˈmidərɪdʒ
metric
BR ˈmɛtrɪk
AM ˈmɛtrɪk
metrical
BR ˈmɛtrɨkl
AM ˈmɛtrəkəl
metrically
BR ˈmɛtrɨkli
AM ˈmɛtrək(ə)li
metricate
BR ˈmɛtrɨkeɪt, -s, -ɪŋ, -ɨd
AM ˈmɛtrəˌkeɪ|t, -ts, -dɪŋ, -dɨd
metrication
BR ˌmɛtrɪˈkeɪʃn
AM ˌmɛtrəˈkeɪʃən
metrician
BR mɛˈtrɪʃn, mɪˈtrɪʃn, -z
AM mɛˈtrɪʃən, məˈtrɪʃən, -z
metricise
BR ˈmɛtrɪsʌɪz, -ɨz, -ɪŋ, -d
AM ˈmɛtrəˌsaɪz, -ɨz, -ɪŋ, -d
metricize
BR ˈmɛtrɪsʌɪz, -ɨz, -ɪŋ, -d
AM ˈmɛtrəˌsaɪz, -ɨz, -ɪŋ, -d
metrist
BR ˈmɛtrɪst, -s
AM ˈmɛtrəst, -s
metritis
BR mɪˈtrʌɪtɪs
AM məˈtraɪdɪs
metro
BR ˈmɛtrəʊ, -z
AM ˈmɛtroʊ, -z
metrologic
BR ˌmɛtrəˈlɒdʒɪk
AM ˌmɛtrəˈlɑdʒɪk
metrological
BR ˌmɛtrəˈlɒdʒɨkl
AM ˌmɛtrəˈlɑdʒəkəl
metrology
BR mɪˈtrɒlədʒi, mɛˈtrɒlədʒi
AM məˈtrɑlədʒi
metronidazole
BR ˌmɛtrəˈnʌɪdəzəʊl
AM ˌmɛtrəˈnaɪdəzoʊl
metronome
BR ˈmɛtrənəʊm, -z
AM ˈmɛtrəˌnoʊm, -z
metronomic
BR ˌmɛtrəˈnɒmɪk
AM ˌmɛtrəˈnɑmɪk
metronymic
BR ˌmɛtrəˈnɪmɪk, -s
AM ˌmɛtrəˈnɪmɪk, -s
Metropole
BR ˈmɛtrəpəʊl
AM ˈmɛtrəˌpoʊl
metropolis
BR mɪˈtrɒpəlɪs, mɪˈtrɒpl̩ɪs, -ɨz
AM məˈtrɑp(ə)ləs, mɛˈtrɑp(ə)ləs, -əz
metropolitan
BR ˌmɛtrəˈpɒlɪt(ə)n, -z
AM ¦mɛtrəˈpɑlətn, ¦mɛtrəˈpɑlədən, -z
metropolitanate
BR ˌmɛtrəˈpɒlɪtəneɪt, ˌmɛtrəˈpɒlɪtn̩eɪt, -s
AM ¦mɛtrəˈpɑlətn̩eɪt, ¦mɛtrəˈpɑlədəˌneɪt, -s
metropolitanism
BR ˌmɛtrəˈpɒlɪtənɪz(ə)m, ˌmɛtrəˈpɒlɪtn̩ɪz(ə)m, -z
AM ¦mɛtrəˈpɑlətn̩ˌɪzəm, ¦mɛtrəˈpɑlədəˌnɪzəm, -z
metrorrhagia
BR ˌmiːtrəˈreɪdʒɪə(r), ˌmɛtrəˈreɪdʒɪə(r)
AM ˌmitrəˈreɪdʒ(i)ə, ˌmɛtrəˈreɪdʒ(i)ə
Metternich
BR ˈmɛtənɪk, ˈmɛtənɪx
AM ˈmɛdərˌnɪk
mettle
BR ˈmɛtl, -d
AM ˈmɛdəl, -d
mettlesome
BR ˈmɛtls(ə)m
AM ˈmɛdlsəm
Mettoy®
BR ˈmɛtɔɪ
AM ˈmɛdɔɪ
Metz
BR mɛts
AM mɛts
meu
BR mjuː, -z
AM mju, -z
meunière
BR ˌməːˈnjɛː(r)
AM mənˈjɛ(ə)r
Meurig
BR ˈmʌɪrɪɡ
AM ˈmɔɪrɪɡ
Meuse
BR məːz
AM mjuz
mew
BR mjuː, -z, -ɪŋ, -d
AM mju, -z, -ɪŋ, -d
mewl
BR mjuːl, -z, -ɪŋ, -d
AM mjul, -z, -ɪŋ, -d
mews
BR mjuːz
AM mjuz
Mexborough
BR ˈmɛksb(ə)rə(r)
AM ˈmɛksˌbərə, ˈmɛksˌbəroʊ
Mexicali
BR ˌmɛksɪˈkali, ˌmɛksɪˈkɑːli
AM ˌmɛksəˈkæli
Mexican
BR ˈmɛksɨk(ə)n, -z
AM ˈmɛksəkən, -z
Mexico
BR ˈmɛksɪkəʊ
AM ˈmɛksəkoʊ
Meyer
BR ˈmʌɪə(r), ˈmeɪə(r)
AM ˈmaɪər, ˈmeɪər
Meyerbeer
BR ˈmʌɪəˌbɪə(r)
AM ˈmeɪərbɪ(ə)r
Meyerhof
BR ˈmʌɪəhɒf
AM ˈmeɪərhɔf, ˈmeɪərhɑf
Meyers
BR ˈmʌɪəz, ˈmeɪəz
AM ˈmaɪərz, ˈmeɪərz
Meynell
BR ˈmeɪnl, ˈmɛnl
AM ˈmeɪnl
Meyrick
BR ˈmɛrɪk
AM ˈmeɪrɪk
mezereon
BR mɪˈzɪərɪən, -z
AM məˈzɪriən, məˈziriən, -z
mezuzah
BR məˈzuːzə(r), məˈzʊzə(r), -z
AM məˈzʊzə, -z
mezuzoth
BR məˈzuːzəʊt
AM məˈzʊzoʊθ
mezzanine
BR ˈmɛzəniːn, ˈmɛtsəniːn, -z
AM ¦mɛzn̩ˈin, -z
mezza voce
BR ˌmɛtsə ˈvəʊtʃeɪ
AM ¦mɛtsə ˈvoʊˌtʃeɪ
mezzo
BR ˈmɛtsəʊ, -z
AM ˈmɛtsoʊ, -z
mezzo forte
BR ˌmɛtsəʊ ˈfɔːteɪ
AM ¦mɛtsoʊ ˈfɔrteɪ
Mezzogiorno
BR ˌmɛtsəʊˈdʒ(ɪ)ɔːnəʊ
AM ¦mɛtsoʊˈdʒ(i)ɔrnoʊ
mezzo piano
BR ˌmɛtsəʊ ˈpjɑːnəʊ, + ˈpjanəʊ

AM ˈmɛtsoʊ ˈpjɑnoʊ
mezzorilievo
BR ˌmɛtsəʊrɪˈliːvəʊ, -z
AM ˈmɛtsoʊrəˈlivoʊ, -z
mezzo soprano
BR ˌmɛtsəʊ səˈprɑːnəʊ, -z
AM ˈmɛtsoʊ səˈprɑnoʊ, ˈmɛtsoʊ səˈprænoʊ, -z
mezzotint
BR ˈmɛtsəʊtɪnt, ˈmɛzəʊtɪnt, -s
AM ˈmɛtsoʊˌtɪnt, -s
mezzotinter
BR ˈmɛtsəʊˌtɪntə(r), ˈmɛzəʊˌtɪntə(r), -z
AM ˈmɛtsoʊˌtɪn(t)ər, -z
mho
BR məʊ, -z
AM moʊ, -z
Mhz
BR ˈmɛɡəhəːts
AM ˈmɛɡəˌhərts
mi
BR miː
AM mi
Mia
BR ˈmɪə(r)
AM ˈmɪə
Miami
BR mʌɪˈami
AM maɪˈæmi
miaow
BR mɪˈaʊ, -z, -ɪŋ, -d
AM miˈaʊ, -z, -ɪŋ, -d
miasma
BR mɪˈazmə(r), mʌɪˈazmə(r), -z
AM maɪˈæzmə, miˈæzmə, -z
miasmal
BR mɪˈazml, mʌɪˈazml
AM maɪˈæzməl, miˈæzməl
miasmatic
BR ˌmɪəzˈmatɪk, ˌmʌɪəzˈmatɪk
AM ˌmiəzˈmædɪk, ˌmaɪəzˈmædɪk
miasmic
BR mɪˈazmɪk, mʌɪˈazmɪk
AM maɪˈæzmɪk, mɪˈæzmɪk
miasmically
BR mɪˈazmɪkli, mʌɪˈazmɪkli
AM maɪˈæzmək(ə)li
miaul
BR mɪˈɔːl, -z, -ɪŋ, -d
AM miˈaʊl, -z, -ɪŋ, -d
mica
BR ˈmʌɪkə(r)
AM ˈmaɪkə
micaceous
BR mʌɪˈkeɪʃəs
AM maɪˈkeɪʃəs
mica-schist
BR ˈmʌɪkəʃɪst, -s
AM ˈmaɪkəˌʃɪst, -s
Micawber
BR mɪˈkɔːbə(r), -z
AM məˈkɔbər, məˈkɑbər, -z
Micawberish
BR mɪˈkɔːb(ə)rɪʃ
AM məˈkɔbərɪʃ, məˈkɑbərɪʃ
Micawberism
BR mɪˈkɔːbərɪz(ə)m
AM məˈkɔbəˌrɪzəm, məˈkɑbəˌrɪzəm
mice
BR mʌɪs
AM maɪs
micelle
BR mɪˈsɛl, mʌɪˈsɛl, -z
AM məˈsɛl, maɪˈsɛl, -z
Michael
BR ˈmʌɪkl
AM ˈmaɪkəl
Michaela
BR mɪˈkeɪlə(r)
AM məˈkeɪlə
Michaelmas
BR ˈmɪklməs
AM ˈmɪkəlməs
Michel
BR mɪˈʃɛl
AM məˈʃɛl
Michelangelo
BR ˌmʌɪklˈan(d)ʒələʊ
AM ˈmɪkəlˈændʒəloʊ, ˈmaɪkəlˈændʒəloʊ
Micheldever
BR ˈmɪtʃlˌdɛvə(r)
AM ˈmɪtʃlˌdɛvər
Michèle
BR mɪˈʃɛl
AM məˈʃɛl
Michelin®
BR ˈmɪtʃəlɪn, ˈmɪtʃl̩ɪn
AM ˈmɪʃələn
Michelle
BR mɪˈʃɛl
AM məˈʃɛl
Michelmore
BR ˈmɪtʃlmɔː(r)
AM ˈmɪtʃlˌmɔ(ə)r
Michelson
BR ˈmʌɪkls(ə)n
AM ˈmaɪkəlsən
Michener
BR ˈmɪtʃənə(r), ˈmɪtʃn̩ə(r), ˈmɪʃnə(r)
AM mɪtʃ(ə)nər, ˈmɪʃnər
Michigan
BR ˈmɪʃɪɡ(ə)n
AM ˈmɪʃɪɡən
Michoacán
BR ˌmɪtʃəʊəˈkɑːn
AM ˌmɪtʃoʊəˈkɑn
mick
BR mɪk, -s
AM mɪk, -s
mickerie
BR ˈmɪk(ə)r|i, -ɪz
AM ˈmɪk(ə)ri, -z
mickery
BR ˈmɪk(ə)r|i, -ɪz
AM ˈmɪk(ə)ri, -z
mickey
BR ˈmɪk|i, -ɪz
AM ˈmɪki, -z
mickey finn
BR ˌmɪkɪ ˈfɪn, -z
AM ˈmɪki ˈfɪn, -z
Mickiewicz
BR ˌmɪ(t)sˈkjɛvɪtʃ
AM ˈmɪkiˌwɪtʃ
mickle
BR ˈmɪkl
AM ˈmɪkəl
Mickleover
BR ˈmɪklˌəʊvə(r)
AM ˈmɪkəlˌoʊvər
Micklethwaite
BR ˈmɪklθweɪt
AM ˈmɪkəlˌθweɪt
Micklewhite
BR ˈmɪklwʌɪt
AM ˈmɪkəlˌwaɪt
micky
BR ˈmɪki
AM ˈmɪki
micro
BR ˈmʌɪkrəʊ, -z
AM ˈmaɪˌkroʊ, -z
microanalyses
plural noun
BR ˌmʌɪkrəʊəˈnalɪsiːz
AM ˈmaɪkroʊəˈnæləsiz
microanalysis
BR ˌmʌɪkrəʊəˈnalɪsɪs
AM ˈmaɪkroʊəˈnæləsəs
microbe
BR ˈmʌɪkrəʊb, -z
AM ˈmaɪˌkroʊb, -z
microbial
BR mʌɪˈkrəʊbɪəl
AM maɪˈkroʊbiəl
microbic
BR mʌɪˈkrəʊbɪk
AM maɪˈkroʊbɪk
microbiological
BR ˌmʌɪkrə(ʊ)ˌbʌɪəˈlɒdʒɪkl
AM ˈmaɪkroʊˌbaɪəˈlɑdʒəkəl
microbiologically
BR ˌmʌɪkrə(ʊ)ˌbʌɪəˈlɒdʒɪkli
AM ˈmaɪkroʊˌbaɪəˈlɑdʒək(ə)li
microbiologist
BR ˌmʌɪkrə(ʊ)bʌɪˈɒlədʒɪst, -s
AM ˈmaɪkroʊˌbaɪˈɑlədʒəst, -s
microbiology
BR ˌmʌɪkrə(ʊ)bʌɪˈɒlədʒi
AM ˈmaɪkroʊˌbaɪˈɑlədʒi
microburst
BR ˈmʌɪkrə(ʊ)bəːst, -s
AM ˈmaɪkroʊˌbərst, -s
Microcard®
BR ˈmʌɪkrə(ʊ)kɑːd
AM ˈmaɪkroʊˌkɑrd
microcephalic
BR ˌmʌɪkrə(ʊ)sɪˈfalɪk, ˌmʌɪkrə(ʊ)kɛˈfalɪk
AM ˈmaɪkroʊsəˈfælɪk
microcephalous
BR ˌmʌɪkrə(ʊ)ˈsɛfələs, ˌmʌɪkrə(ʊ)ˈsɛfl̩əs, ˌmʌɪkrə(ʊ)ˈkɛfələs, ˌmʌɪkrə(ʊ)ˈkɛfl̩əs
AM ˈmaɪkroʊˈsɛfələs
microcephaly
BR ˌmʌɪkrə(ʊ)ˈsɛfəli, ˌmʌɪkrə(ʊ)ˈsɛfl̩i, ˌmʌɪkrə(ʊ)ˈkɛfəli, ˌmʌɪkrə(ʊ)ˈkɛfl̩i
AM ˈmaɪkroʊˈsɛfəli
microchip
BR ˈmʌɪkrə(ʊ)tʃɪp, -s
AM ˈmaɪkroʊˌtʃɪp, -s
microcircuit
BR ˈmʌɪkrə(ʊ)ˌsəːkɪt, -s
AM ˈmaɪkroʊˌsərkət, -s
microcircuitry
BR ˈmʌɪkrə(ʊ)ˌsəːkɪtri
AM ˈmaɪkroʊˈsərkətri
microclimate
BR ˈmʌɪkrə(ʊ)ˌklʌɪmɪt, -s
AM ˈmaɪkroʊˌklaɪmɪt, -s
microclimatic
BR ˌmʌɪkrə(ʊ)klʌɪˈmatɪk
AM ˈmaɪkroʊˌklaɪˈmædɪk
microclimatically
BR ˌmʌɪkrə(ʊ)klʌɪˈmatɪkli
AM ˈmaɪkroʊˌklaɪˈmædək(ə)li
microcline
BR ˈmʌɪkrə(ʊ)klʌɪn, -z
AM ˈmaɪkroʊˌklaɪn, -z
microcode
BR ˈmʌɪkrə(ʊ)kəʊd, -z
AM ˈmaɪkrəˌkoʊd, -z
microcomputer
BR ˈmʌɪkrə(ʊ)kəmˌpjuːtə(r), -z
AM ˈmaɪkroʊkəmˈpjudər, -z
microcopy
BR ˈmʌɪkrə(ʊ)ˌkɒp|i, -ɪz, -ɪɪŋ, -ɪd
AM ˈmaɪkrəˌkɑpi, -z, -ɪŋ, -d

microcosm
BR 'mʌɪkrə(ʊ),kɒz(ə)m, -z
AM 'maɪkrə,kɑzəm, -z

microcosmic
BR ,mʌɪkrə(ʊ)'kɒzmɪk
AM ¦maɪkrə'kɑzmɪk

microcosmically
BR ,mʌɪkrə(ʊ)'kɒzmɨkli
AM ¦maɪkrə'kɑzmək(ə)li

microcrystalline
BR ,mʌɪkrə(ʊ)'krɪstəlʌɪn, ,mʌɪkrə(ʊ)'krɪstḷʌɪn
AM ¦maɪkroʊ'krɪstələn, ¦maɪkroʊ'krɪstə,laɪn

microdot
BR 'mʌɪkrə(ʊ)dɒt, -s
AM 'maɪkrə,dɑt, -s

microeconomic
BR ,mʌɪkrəʊ,iːkə'nɒmɪk, ,mʌɪkrəʊ,ɛkə'nɒmɪk, -s
AM ¦maɪkroʊ,ɛkə'nɑmɪk, ¦maɪkroʊ,ikə'nɑmɪk, -s

microelectronic
BR ,mʌɪkrəʊɪ,lɛk'trɒnɪk, ,mʌɪkrəʊ,ɛlɛk'trɒnɪk, ,mʌɪkrəʊ,ɛlɪk'trɒnɪk, ,mʌɪkrəʊ,ɪlɛk'trɒnɪk, ,mʌɪkrəʊ,iːlɛk'trɒnɪk, -s
AM ¦maɪkroʊə¦lɛk'trɑnɪk, ¦maɪkroʊi¦lɛk'trɑnɪk, -s

microelectronics
BR ,mʌɪkrəʊɪ,lɛk'trɒnɪks, ,mʌɪkrəʊ,ɛlɛk'trɒnɪks, ,mʌɪkrəʊ,ɛlɪk'trɒnɪks, ,mʌɪkrəʊ,ɪlɛk'trɒnɪks, ,mʌɪkrəʊ,iːlɛk'trɒnɪks
AM ¦maɪkroʊə¦lɛk'trɑnɪks, ¦maɪkroʊi¦lɛk'trɑnɪks

microfiche
BR 'mʌɪkrə(ʊ)fiːʃ, -ɪz
AM 'maɪkrə,fiʃ, -ɪz

microfilm
BR 'mʌɪkrə(ʊ)fɪlm, -z
AM 'maɪkrə,fɪlm, -z

microfloppy
BR 'mʌɪkrə(ʊ),flɒp|i, -ɪz
AM 'maɪkrə,flɑpi, -z

microform
BR 'mʌɪkrə(ʊ)fɔːm, -z
AM 'maɪkrə,fɔ(ə)rm, -z

microgram
BR 'mʌɪkrə(ʊ)gram, -z
AM 'maɪkrə,græm, -z

micrograph
BR 'mʌɪkrə(ʊ)grɑːf, 'mʌɪkrə(ʊ)graf, -s
AM 'maɪkrə,græf, -s

microgroove
BR 'mʌɪkrə(ʊ)gruːv, -z
AM 'maɪkrə,gruv, -z

microinstruction
BR ,mʌɪkrəʊɪn'strʌkʃn, -z
AM ¦maɪkroʊɪnz'trəkʃən, ¦maɪkroʊɪn'strəkʃən, -z

microlight
BR 'mʌɪkrə(ʊ)lʌɪt, -s
AM 'maɪkrə,laɪt, -s

microlith
BR 'mʌɪkrə(ʊ)lɪθ, -s
AM 'mʌɪkrə,lɪθ, -s

microlithic
BR ,mʌɪkrə(ʊ)'lɪθɪk
AM ,mɪkrə'lɪθɪk

micromesh
BR 'mʌɪkrə(ʊ)mɛʃ
AM 'maɪkrə,mɛʃ

micrometer[1]
measurement
BR 'mʌɪkrəʊ,miːtə(r), -z
AM 'maɪkroʊ,midər, -z

micrometer[2]
measuring instrument
BR mʌɪ'krɒmɪtə(r), -z
AM maɪ'krɑmədər, -z

micrometre
measurement
BR 'mʌɪkrəʊ,miːtə(r), -z
AM 'maɪkroʊ,midər, -z

micrometry
BR mʌɪ'krɒmɪtri
AM maɪ'krɑmətri

microminiaturisation
BR ,mʌɪkrəʊ,mɪnɪtʃ(ə)rʌɪ'zeɪʃn, -z
AM ¦maɪkroʊ,mɪnɪtʃərə'zeɪʃən, ¦maɪkroʊ,mɪnɪtʃə,raɪ'zeɪʃən, -z

microminiaturization
BR ,mʌɪkrəʊ,mɪnɪtʃ(ə)rʌɪ'zeɪʃn, -z
AM ¦maɪkroʊ,mɪnɪtʃərə'zeɪʃən, ¦maɪkroʊ,mɪnɪtʃə,raɪ'zeɪʃən, -z

micron
BR 'mʌɪkrɒn, -z
AM 'maɪ,krɑn, -z

Micronesia
BR ,mʌɪkrə(ʊ)'niːzjə(r), ,mʌɪkrə'niːʒə(r)
AM ,maɪkrə'niʒə, ,maɪkrə'nɪʃə

Micronesian
BR ,mʌɪkrə(ʊ)'niːzj(ə)n, ,mʌɪkrə(ʊ)'niːʒn, -z
AM ,maɪkrə'niʒən, ,maɪkrə'nɪʃən, -z

microorganism
BR ,mʌɪkrəʊ'ɔːgənɪz(ə)m, ,mʌɪkrəʊ'ɔːgṇɪz(ə)m, -z
AM ¦maɪkroʊ'ɔrgə,nɪzəm, -z

micro-organism
BR ,mʌɪkrəʊ'ɔːgənɪz(ə)m, ,mʌɪkrəʊ'ɔːgṇɪz(ə)m, -z
AM ¦maɪkroʊ'ɔrgə,nɪzəm, -z

microphone
BR 'mʌɪkrəfəʊn, -z
AM 'maɪkrə,foʊn, -z

microphonic
BR ,mʌɪkrə'fɒnɪk
AM ,maɪkrə'fɑnɪk

microphotograph
BR ,mʌɪkrəʊ'fəʊtəgrɑːf, ,mʌɪkrəʊ'fəʊtəgraf, -s
AM ¦maɪkrə'foʊdə,græf, -s

microphyte
BR 'mʌɪkrə(ʊ)fʌɪt, -s
AM 'maɪkrə,faɪt, -s

microprocessor
BR ,mʌɪkrəʊ'prəʊsɛsə(r), -z
AM ¦maɪkrə'prɑsəsər, -z

microprogram
BR 'mʌɪkrə(ʊ),prəʊgram, -z
AM 'maɪkrə,proʊgrəm, -z

micropyle
BR 'mʌɪkrə(ʊ)pʌɪl, -z
AM 'maɪkrə,paɪl, -z

microscope
BR 'mʌɪkrəskəʊp, -s
AM 'maɪkrə,skoʊp, -s

microscopic
BR ,mʌɪkrə'skɒpɪk
AM ¦maɪkrə'skɑpɪk

microscopical
BR ,mʌɪkrə'skɒpɪkl
AM ¦maɪkrə'skɑpəkəl

microscopically
BR ,mʌɪkrə'skɒpɪkli
AM ¦maɪkrə'skɑpək(ə)li

microscopist
BR mʌɪ'krɒskəpɪst, -s
AM maɪ'krɑskəpəst, -s

microscopy
BR mʌɪ'krɒskəpi
AM maɪ'krɑskəpi

microsecond
BR 'mʌɪkrə(ʊ),sɛknd, -z
AM ¦maɪkroʊ,sɛkənd, -z

microseism
BR 'mʌɪkrə(ʊ),sʌɪz(ə)m, -z
AM 'maɪkroʊ,saɪzəm, -z

Microsoft®
BR 'mʌɪkrəsɒft
AM 'maɪkrə,sɔft, 'maɪkrə,sɑft

microsome
BR 'mʌɪkrəsəʊm, -z
AM 'maɪkrə,soʊm, -z

microspore
BR 'mʌɪkrə(ʊ)spɔː(r), -z
AM 'maɪkrə,spɔ(ə)r, -z

microstructure
BR 'mʌɪkrə(ʊ),strʌktʃə(r), -z
AM ¦maɪkrə'strək(t)ʃər, -z

microsurgery
BR 'mʌɪkrə(ʊ),səːdʒ(ə)ri, ,mʌɪkrə(ʊ)'səːdʒ(ə)ri
AM ¦maɪkrə'sərdʒ(ə)ri

microsurgical
BR ,mʌɪkrə(ʊ)'səːdʒɪkl
AM ¦maɪkrə'sərdʒəkəl

microswitch
BR 'mʌɪkrə(ʊ)swɪtʃ, -ɪz
AM 'maɪkrə,swɪtʃ, -ɪz

microtechnique
BR 'mʌɪkrə(ʊ)tɛk,niːk, -s
AM ¦maɪkroʊ,tɛk'nik, -s

microtome
BR 'mʌɪkrə(ʊ)təʊm, -z
AM 'maɪkrə,toʊm, -z

microtone
BR 'mʌɪkrə(ʊ)təʊn, -z
AM 'maɪkrə,toʊn, -z

microtubule
BR 'mʌɪkrəʊ,tjuːbjuːl, 'mʌɪkrəʊ,tʃuːbjuːl, -z
AM 'maɪkrə,t(j)ubjul, -z

microwave
BR 'mʌɪkrə(ʊ)weɪv, -z, -ɪŋ, -d
AM 'maɪkrə,weɪv, -z, -ɪŋ, -d

micrurgy
BR 'mʌɪkrəːdʒi
AM maɪ'krərdʒi

micturition
BR ,mɪktjʊ'rɪʃn, ,mɪktʃʊ'rɪʃn
AM ,mɪktʃə'rɪʃən

mid
BR mɪd
AM mɪd

midair
BR ˌmɪdˈɛː(r)
AM ˈmɪdˈɛ(ə)r

Midas
BR ˈmʌɪdəs
AM ˈmaɪdəs

midbrain
BR ˈmɪdbreɪn, -z
AM ˈmɪdˌbreɪn, -z

midcourse
BR ˌmɪdˈkɔːs
AM ˈmɪdˈkɔ(ə)rs

midday
BR ˌmɪdˈdeɪ
AM ˈmɪdˌdeɪ

midden
BR ˈmɪdn, -z
AM ˈmɪdən, -z

middle
BR ˈmɪdl, -z
AM ˈmɪd(ə)l, -z

middlebrow
BR ˈmɪdlbraʊ, -z
AM ˈmɪdlˌbraʊ, -z

middleman
BR ˈmɪdlman
AM ˈmɪdlˌmæn

middlemen
BR ˈmɪdlmɛn
AM ˈmɪdlˌmɛn

middle-of-the-road
BR ˌmɪdl̩ə(v)ðəˈrəʊd
AM ˌmɪdələ(v)ðəˈroʊd

Middlesboro
BR ˈmɪdlzb(ə)rə(r)
AM ˈmɪdlzˌbərə,
ˈmɪdlzˌbəroʊ

Middlesborough
BR ˈmɪdlzb(ə)rə(r)
AM ˈmɪdlzˌbərə,
ˈmɪdlzˌbəroʊ

Middlesbrough
BR ˈmɪdlzbrə(r)
AM ˈmɪdlzb(ə)rə

Middlesex
BR ˈmɪdlsɛks
AM ˈmɪdlˌsɛks

Middleton
BR ˈmɪdlt(ə)n
AM ˈmɪdltən

middleweight
BR ˈmɪdlweɪt, -s
AM ˈmɪdlˌweɪt, -s

Middlewich
BR ˈmɪdlwɪtʃ
AM ˈmɪdlˌwɪtʃ

middling
BR ˈmɪdl̩ɪŋ, ˈmɪdlɪŋ
AM ˈmɪdlɪŋ, ˈmɪdl̩ɪŋ

middlingly
BR ˈmɪdl̩ɪŋli, ˈmɪdlɪŋli
AM ˈmɪdlɪŋli,
ˈmɪdl̩ɪŋli

middy
BR ˈmɪd|i, -ɪz
AM ˈmɪdi, -z

Mideast
BR ˌmɪdˈiːst
AM ˌmɪdˈist

midfield
BR ˌmɪdˈfiːld, ˈmɪdfiːld
AM ˌmɪdˈfild

midfielder
BR ˌmɪdˈfiːldə(r), -z
AM ˌmɪdˈfildər, -z

Midgard
BR ˈmɪdgɑːd
AM ˈmɪdˌgɑrd

midge
BR mɪdʒ, -ɪz
AM mɪdʒ, -ɪz

midget
BR ˈmɪdʒɪt, -s
AM ˈmɪdʒɪt, -s

Midgley
BR ˈmɪdʒli
AM ˈmɪdʒli

midgut
BR ˈmɪdgʌt, -s
AM ˈmɪdˌgət, -s

Midhurst
BR ˈmɪdhəːst
AM ˈmɪd(h)ərst

MIDI
BR ˈmɪd|i, -ɪz
AM ˈmɪdi, -z

Midi
south of France
BR mɪˈdiː
AM miˈdi

midi
BR ˈmɪd|i, -ɪz
AM ˈmɪdi, -z

Midian
BR ˈmɪdɪən
AM ˈmɪdiən

Midianite
BR ˈmɪdɪənʌɪt, -s
AM ˈmɪdiəˌnaɪt, -s

midibus
BR ˈmɪdɪbʌs, -ɪz
AM ˈmɪdiˌbəs, -əz

midinette
BR ˌmɪdɪˈnɛt, -s
AM ˌmɪdnˈɛt, ˌmɪdiˈnɛt,
-s

midiron
BR ˈmɪdˌʌɪən, -z
AM ˈmɪdˌaɪ(ə)rn, -z

midland
BR ˈmɪdlənd, -z
AM ˈmɪdlənd,
ˈmidˌlænd, -z

midlander
BR ˈmɪdləndə(r), -z
AM ˈmɪdləndər,
ˈmidˌlændər, -z

midline
BR ˈmɪdlʌɪn, -z
AM ˈmɪdˌlaɪn, -z

Midlothian
BR mɪdˈləʊðɪən
AM mɪdˈloʊðiən

midmost
BR ˈmɪdməʊst
AM ˈmɪdˌmoʊst

midnight
BR ˈmɪdnʌɪt
AM ˈmɪdˌnaɪt

midpoint
BR ˈmɪdpɔɪnt, -s
AM ˈmɪdˌpɔɪnt, -s

Midrash
BR ˈmɪdraʃ, ˈmɪdrʌʃ
AM ˈmɪˌdrɑʃ

Midrashim
BR mɪˈdraʃɪm,
ˌmɪdraˈʃɪm,
ˌmɪdrʌˈʃɪm
AM mɪˌdrɑˈʃim

midrib
BR ˈmɪdrɪb, -z
AM ˈmɪdˌrɪb, -z

midriff
BR ˈmɪdrɪf, -s
AM ˈmɪˌdrɪf(t), -s

midsection
BR ˈmɪdˌsɛkʃn, -z
AM ˈmɪdˌsɛkʃən, -z

midship
BR ˈmɪdʃɪp, -s
AM ˈmɪdˌʃɪp, -s

midshipman
BR ˈmɪdʃɪpmən
AM ˈmɪdˌʃɪpmən,
ˌmɪdˈʃɪpmən

midshipmen
BR ˈmɪdʃɪpmən
AM ˈmɪdˌʃɪpmən,
ˌmɪdˈʃɪpmən

midships
BR ˈmɪdʃɪps
AM ˈmɪdˌʃɪps

midst
BR mɪdst
AM mɪdst

midstream
BR ˌmɪdˈstriːm
AM ˌmɪdˈstrim

midsummer
BR ˌmɪdˈsʌmə(r)
AM ˌmɪdˈsəmər

midterm
BR ˌmɪdˈtəːm, -z
AM ˌmɪdˈtərm, -z

midtown
BR ˈmɪdtaʊn
AM ˈmɪdˌtaʊn

Midway
BR ˈmɪdweɪ
AM ˈmɪdˌweɪ

midway
BR ˌmɪdˈweɪ
AM ˌmɪdˈweɪ

midweek
BR ˌmɪdˈwiːk
AM ˌmɪdˈwik

Midwest
BR ˌmɪdˈwɛst
AM ˌmɪdˈwɛst

Midwestern
BR ˌmɪdˈwɛst(ə)n
AM ˌmɪdˈwɛstərn

Midwesterner
BR ˌmɪdˈwɛstənə(r),
ˌmɪdˈwɛstn̩ə(r), -z
AM ˌmɪdˈwɛstərnər, -z

midwicket
BR ˌmɪdˈwɪkɪt, -s
AM ˌmɪdˈwɪkɪt, -s

midwife
BR ˈmɪdwʌɪf
AM ˈmɪdˌwaɪf

midwifery
BR ˌmɪdˈwɪf(ə)ri,
ˈmɪdwɪf(ə)ri
AM ˌmɪdˈwaɪf(ə)ri

midwinter
BR ˌmɪdˈwɪntə(r)
AM ˌmɪdˈwɪn(t)ər

midwives
BR ˈmɪdwʌɪvz
AM ˈmɪdˌwaɪvz

Miele
BR ˈmiːlə(r)
AM ˈmilə

mielie
BR ˈmiːl|i, -ɪz
AM ˈmili, -z

mien
BR miːn, -z
AM min, -z

Miesian
BR ˈmiːzɪən
AM ˈmisiən, ˈmiziən

Mies van der Rohe
BR ˌmiːz van də
ˈrəʊə(r)
AM ˌmiz væn dər
ˈroʊə, ˌmis +

miff
BR mɪf, -s, -ɪŋ, -t
AM mɪf, -s, -ɪŋ, -t

MI5
BR ˌɛmʌɪˈfʌɪv
AM ˌɛmˌaɪˈfaɪv

MiG
BR mɪg, -z
AM mɪg, -z

might
BR mʌɪt
AM maɪt

mightest
BR ˈmʌɪtɪst
AM ˈmaɪdɪst

might-have-been
BR ˈmʌɪtəvbiːn, -z
AM ˈmaɪdə(v)ˌbɪn, -z

mightily
BR ˈmʌɪtɪli
AM ˈmaɪdɪli

mightiness
BR ˈmʌɪtɪnɪs
AM ˈmaɪdinɪs

mightn't
BR ˈmʌɪtnt

AM ˈmaɪtn(t)

mighty
BR ˈmʌɪt|i, -ɪə(r), -ɪɪst
AM ˈmaɪdi, -ər, -ɪst

migmatite
BR ˈmɪɡmətʌɪt
AM ˈmɪɡməˌtaɪt

mignon
BR ˈmiːnjɒn, ˈmɪnjɒn, ˌmɪnˈjɒn
AM mɪnˈjɔn, mɪnˈjɑn

mignonette
BR ˌmɪnjəˈnɛt, -s
AM ˈmɪnjəˈnɛt, -s

migraine
BR ˈmiːɡreɪn, ˈmʌɪɡreɪn, -z
AM ˈmaɪˌɡreɪn, -z

migrainous
BR miːˈɡreɪnəs, mʌɪˈɡreɪnəs
AM maɪˈɡreɪnəs

migrant
BR ˈmʌɪɡr(ə)nt, -s
AM ˈmaɪɡrənt, -s

migrate
BR mʌɪˈɡreɪt, -s, -ɪŋ, -ɪd
AM ˈmaɪˌɡreɪ|t, -ts, -dɪŋ, -dɪd

migration
BR mʌɪˈɡreɪʃn, -z
AM maɪˈɡreɪʃən, -z

migrational
BR mʌɪˈɡreɪʃn̩(ə)l, mʌɪˈɡreɪʃən(ə)l
AM maɪˈɡreɪʃ(ə)nəl

migrator
BR ˈmʌɪɡreɪtə(r), mʌɪˈɡreɪtə(r), -z
AM ˈmaɪˌɡreɪdər, -z

migratory
BR ˈmʌɪɡrət(ə)ri, mʌɪˈɡreɪt(ə)ri
AM ˈmaɪɡrəˌtɔri

Miguel
BR mɪˈɡɛl
AM məˈɡ(w)ɛl

mihrab
BR ˈmiːrɑːb, -z
AM ˈmirəb, -z

Mikado
BR mɪˈkɑːdəʊ, -z
AM məˈkɑdoʊ, -z

mike
BR mʌɪk, -s
AM maɪk, -s

Mikhail
BR mɪˈkʌɪl, mɪˈxʌɪl
AM məˈkaɪl
RUS mʲixaˈil

Míkonos
BR ˈmɪkənɒs
AM ˈmɪkəˌnɔs, ˈmɪkəˌnɑs

mil
BR mɪl, -z
AM mɪl, -z

milady
BR mɪˈleɪd|i, -ɪz
AM məˈleɪdi, maɪˈleɪdi, -z

milage
BR ˈmʌɪl|ɪdʒ, -ɪdʒɪz
AM ˈmaɪlɪdʒ, -ɪz

Milan
BR mɪˈlan
AM məˈlɑn, məˈlæn

Milanese
BR ˌmɪləˈniːz
AM ˈmɪləˈniz

Milburn
BR ˈmɪlbəːn
AM ˈmɪlbərn

milch
BR mɪl(t)ʃ
AM mɪltʃ, mɪlk

mild
BR mʌɪld, -ə(r), -ɪst
AM maɪld, -ər, -ɪst

milden
BR ˈmʌɪld|n, -nz, -n̩ɪŋ\-nɪŋ, -nd
AM ˈmaɪldən, -z, -ɪŋ, -d

Mildenhall
BR ˈmɪld(ə)nhɔːl
AM ˈmɪldənˌ(h)ɔl, ˈmɪldənˌ(h)ɑl

mildew
BR ˈmɪldjuː, ˈmɪldʒuː, -d
AM ˈmɪlˌd(j)u, -d

mildewy
BR ˈmɪldjuːi, ˈmɪldʒuːi
AM ˈmɪlˌd(j)ui

mildish
BR ˈmʌɪldɪʃ
AM ˈmaɪldɪʃ

mildly
BR ˈmʌɪldli
AM ˈmaɪl(d)li

mildness
BR ˈmʌɪldnɪs
AM ˈmaɪl(d)nɪs

Mildred
BR ˈmɪldrɪd
AM ˈmɪldrɪd

mile
BR mʌɪl, -z
AM maɪl, -z

mileage
BR ˈmʌɪl|ɪdʒ, -ɪdʒɪz
AM ˈmaɪlɪdʒ, -ɪz

mileometer
BR mʌɪˈlɒmɪtə(r), -z
AM maɪˈlɑmədər, -z

milepost
BR ˈmʌɪlpəʊst, -s
AM ˈmaɪlˌpoʊst, -s

miler
BR ˈmʌɪlə(r), -z
AM ˈmaɪlər, -z

Miles
BR mʌɪlz
AM maɪlz

Milesian
BR mʌɪˈliːzɪən, mʌɪˈliːʒn, mɪˈliːzɪən, mɪˈliːʒn, -z
AM məˈliʒən, maɪˈliʒən, -z

milestone
BR ˈmʌɪlstəʊn, -z
AM ˈmaɪlˌstoʊn, -z

Miletus
BR mʌɪˈliːtəs
AM maɪˈlidəs

milfoil
BR ˈmɪlfɔɪl, -z
AM ˈmɪlˌfɔɪl, -z

Milford Haven
BR ˌmɪlfəd ˈheɪvn
AM ˌmɪlfərd ˈheɪvən

Milhaud
BR ˈmiː(j)əʊ
AM miˈ(j)oʊ
FR milo

miliaria
BR ˌmɪlɪˈɛːrɪə(*r*)
AM ˌmɪliˈɛriə

miliary
BR ˈmɪlɪəri
AM ˈmɪliˌɛri

milieu
BR ˈmiːljəː(*r*), mɪlˈjəː(*r*), -z
AM mɪlˈju, mɪlˈjə, -z

milieux
BR ˈmiːljəː(*r*), ˈmiːljəːz, mɪlˈjəː(*r*), mɪlˈjəːz
AM mɪlˈju, mɪlˈjə

militancy
BR ˈmɪlɪt(ə)nsi
AM ˈmɪlədənsi, ˈmɪlətnsi

militant
BR ˈmɪlɪt(ə)nt, -s
AM ˈmɪlədənt, ˈmɪlətnt, -s

militantly
BR ˈmɪlɪt(ə)ntli
AM ˈmɪlədəntli, ˈmɪlətn(t)li

militaria
BR ˌmɪlɪˈtɛːrɪə(*r*)
AM ˌmɪləˈtɛriə

militarily
BR ˈmɪlɪt(ə)rɪli, ˌmɪlɪˈtɛrɪli
AM ˌmɪləˈtɛrəli

militariness
BR ˈmɪlɪt(ə)rɪnɪs
AM ˈmɪləˌtɛrinɪs

militarisation
BR ˌmɪlɪt(ə)rʌɪˈzeɪʃn
AM ˌmɪlədərəˈzeɪʃən, ˌmɪlədəˌraɪˈzeɪʃən

militarise
BR ˈmɪlɪtərʌɪz, -ɪz, -ɪŋ, -d
AM ˈmɪlədəˌraɪz, -ɪz, -ɪŋ, -d

militarism
BR ˈmɪlɪtərɪz(ə)m
AM ˈmɪlədəˌrɪzəm

militarist
BR ˈmɪlɪt(ə)rɪst, -s
AM ˈmɪlədərəst, -s

militaristic
BR ˌmɪlɪtəˈrɪstɪk
AM ˌmɪlədəˈrɪstɪk

militaristically
BR ˌmɪlɪtəˈrɪstɪkli
AM ˈmɪlədəˈrɪstək(ə)li

militarization
BR ˌmɪlɪt(ə)rʌɪˈzeɪʃn
AM ˌmɪlədərəˈzeɪʃən, ˌmɪlədəˌraɪˈzeɪʃən

militarize
BR ˈmɪlɪtərʌɪz, -ɪz, -ɪŋ, -d
AM ˈmɪlədəˌraɪz, -ɪz, -ɪŋ, -d

military
BR ˈmɪlɪt(ə)ri
AM ˈmɪləˌtɛri

militate
BR ˈmɪlɪteɪt, -s, -ɪŋ, -ɪd
AM ˈmɪləˌteɪ|t, -ts, -dɪŋ, -dɪd

militerist
BR ˈmɪlɪt(ə)rɪst, -s
AM ˈmɪlədərəst, -s

militeristically
BR ˌmɪlɪtəˈrɪstɪkli
AM ˈmɪlədəˈrɪstək(ə)li

militerization
BR ˌmɪlɪt(ə)rʌɪˈzeɪʃn
AM ˌmɪlədərəˈzeɪʃən, ˌmɪlədəraɪˈzeɪʃən

militerize
BR ˈmɪlɪtərʌɪz, -ɪz, -ɪŋ, -d
AM ˈmɪlədəˌraɪz, -ɪz, -ɪŋ, -d

militia
BR mɪˈlɪʃə(*r*), -z
AM məˈlɪʃə, -z

militiaman
BR mɪˈlɪʃəmən
AM məˈlɪʃəmən

militiamen
BR mɪˈlɪʃəmən
AM məˈlɪʃəmən

milk
BR mɪlk, -s, -ɪŋ, -t
AM mɪlk, -s, -ɪŋ, -t

milker
BR ˈmɪlkə(r), -z
AM ˈmɪlkər, -z

milkily
BR ˈmɪlkɪli
AM ˈmɪlkɪli

milkiness
BR ˈmɪlkɪnɪs
AM ˈmɪlkinɪs

milkmaid
BR ˈmɪlkmeɪd, -z
AM ˈmɪlkˌmeɪd, -z

milkman
BR ˈmɪlkmən
AM ˈmɪlkˌmæn, ˈmɪlkmən

milkmen
BR ˈmɪlkmɛn, ˈmɪlkmən
AM ˈmɪlkˌmɛn, ˈmɪlkmən

Milk of Magnesia®
BR ˌmɪlk əv magˈniːʃə(r), + magˈniːʒə(r), + magˈniːzɪə(r)
AM ˈmɪlk ə(v) mægˈniʒə, + mægˈniʃə

milksop
BR ˈmɪlksɒp, -s
AM ˈmɪlkˌsɑp, -s

milkwort
BR ˈmɪlkwəːt, -s
AM ˈmɪlkwərt, ˈmɪlkwɔ(ə)rt, -s

milky
BR ˈmɪlk|i, -ɪə(r), -ɪɪst
AM ˈmɪlki, -ər, -ɨst

mill
BR mɪl, -z, -ɪŋ, -d
AM mɪl, -z, -ɪŋ, -d

millable
BR ˈmɪləbl
AM ˈmɪləbəl

millage
BR ˈmɪlɪdʒ
AM ˈmɪlɪdʒ

Millais
BR ˈmɪleɪ
AM məˈleɪ

Millar
BR ˈmɪlə(r)
AM ˈmɪlər

Millard
BR ˈmɪlɑːd
AM ˈmɪlərd

Millay
BR ˈmɪleɪ
AM məˈleɪ

Millbank
BR ˈmɪlbaŋk
AM ˈmɪlˌbæŋk

millboard
BR ˈmɪlbɔːd, -z
AM ˈmɪlˌbɔ(ə)rd, -z

milldam
BR ˈmɪldam, -z
AM ˈmɪlˌdæm, -z

millefeuille
BR ˌmiːlˈfəːj, -z
AM ˌmilˈfəɪ, -z

millenarian
BR ˌmɪlɨˈnɛːrɪən, -z
AM ˌmɪləˈnɛriən, -z

millenarianism
BR ˌmɪlɨˈnɛːrɪənɪz(ə)m
AM ˌmɪləˈnɛriəˌnɪzəm

millenarianist
BR ˌmɪlɨˈnɛːrɪənɪst, -s
AM ˌmɪləˈnɛriənəst, -s

millenary
BR mɪˈlɛnər|i, ˈmɪlɪn(ə)r|i, -ɪz
AM ˈmɪləˌnɛri, -z

millenia
BR mɪˈlɛnɪə(r)
AM məˈlɛniə

millenium
BR mɪˈlɛnɪəm, -z
AM məˈlɛniəm, -z

millennial
BR mɪˈlɛnɪəl
AM məˈlɛniəl

millennialist
BR mɪˈlɛnɪəlɪst, -s
AM məˈlɛniələst, -s

millennium
BR mɪˈlɛnɪəm, -z
AM məˈlɛniəm, -z

millepede
BR ˈmɪlɨpiːd, -z
AM ˈmɪləˌpid, -z

millepore
BR ˈmɪlɨpɔː(r), -z
AM ˈmɪləˌpɔ(ə)r, -z

miller
BR ˈmɪlə(r), -z
AM ˈmɪlər, -z

millesimal
BR mɪˈlɛsɪml
AM məˈlɛsəməl

millesimally
BR mɪˈlɛsɪmli, mɪˈlɛsɪməli
AM məˈlɛsəməli

millet
BR ˈmɪlɪt
AM ˈmɪlɨt

millhand
BR ˈmɪlhand, -z
AM ˈmɪlˌ(h)ænd, -z

milliammeter
BR ˌmɪlɪˈamɪtə(r), -z
AM ˈmɪliˈæ(m)ˌmidər, -z

milliampere
BR ˌmɪlɪˈampɛː(r), -z
AM ˈmɪliˌæmpɪ(ə)r, -z

milliard
BR ˈmɪlɪɑːd, -z
AM ˈmɪlˌjɑrd, ˈmɪliˌɑrd, -z

millibar
BR ˈmɪlɪbɑː(r), -z
AM ˈmɪləˌbɑr, -z

Millicent
BR ˈmɪlɪs(ə)nt
AM ˈmɪləsənt

Millie
BR ˈmɪli
AM ˈmɪli

Milligan
BR ˈmɪlɪg(ə)n
AM ˈmɪləgən

milligram
BR ˈmɪlɪgram, -z
AM ˈmɪləˌgræm, -z

milligramme
BR ˈmɪlɪgram, -z
AM ˈmɪləˌgræm, -z

Millikan
BR ˈmɪlɪk(ə)n
AM ˈmɪləkən

milliliter
BR ˈmɪlɪˌliːtə(r), -z
AM ˈmɪləˌlidər, -z

millilitre
BR ˈmɪlɪˌliːtə(r), -z
AM ˈmɪləˌlidər, -z

millimeter
BR ˈmɪlɨˌmiːtə(r), -z
AM ˈmɪləˌmidər, -z

millimetre
BR ˈmɪlɨˌmiːtə(r), -z
AM ˈmɪləˌmidər, -z

millimicron
BR ˈmɪlɪˌmʌɪkrɒn, -z
AM ˌmɪləˈmaɪˌkrɑn, -z

milliner
BR ˈmɪlɪnə(r), -z
AM ˈmɪlənər, -z

millinery
BR ˈmɪlɪn(ə)ri
AM ˈmɪləˌnɛri

million
BR ˈmɪljən, -z
AM ˈmɪljən, -z

millionaire
BR ˌmɪljəˈnɛː(r), -z
AM ˌmɪljəˈnɛ(ə)r, ˈmɪljəˌnɛ(ə)r, -z

millionairess
BR ˌmɪljəˈnɛːrɪs, ˌmɪljəˈnɛːrɛs, -ɪz
AM ˌmɪljəˈnɛrəs, -əz

millionfold
BR ˈmɪljənfəʊld
AM ˈmɪljənˌfoʊld

millionth
BR ˈmɪljənθ, -s
AM ˈmɪljənθ, -s

millipede
BR ˈmɪlɨpiːd, -z
AM ˈmɪləˌpid, -z

millisecond
BR ˈmɪlɪˌsɛk(ə)nd, -z
AM ˈmɪləˌsɛkənd, -z

millivolt
BR ˈmɪlɪvəʊlt, ˈmɪlɪvɒlt, -s
AM ˈmɪləˌvoʊlt, -s

milliwatt
BR ˈmɪlɪwɒt, -s
AM ˈmɪliˌwɑt, -s

millpond
BR ˈmɪlpɒnd, -z
AM ˈmɪlˌpɑnd, -z

millrace
BR ˈmɪlreɪs, -ɪz
AM ˈmɪlˌreɪs, -ɪz

Mills
BR mɪlz
AM mɪlz

millstone
BR ˈmɪlstəʊn, -z
AM ˈmɪlˌstoʊn, -z

millstream
BR ˈmɪlstriːm, -z
AM ˈmɪlˌstrim, -z

Millwall
BR ˈmɪlwɔːl, ˈmɪlw(ə)l
AM ˈmɪlˌwɔl, ˈmɪlˌwɑl

millwheel
BR ˈmɪlwiːl, -z
AM ˈmɪlˌ(h)wil, -z

millworker
BR ˈmɪlˌwəːkə(r), -z
AM ˈmɪlˌwərkər, -z

millwright
BR ˈmɪlrʌɪt, -s
AM ˈmɪlˌraɪt, -s

Milne
BR mɪln
AM mɪln

Milner
BR ˈmɪlnə(r)
AM ˈmɪlnər

Milngavie
BR mɪlˈgʌɪ
AM mɪlˈgaɪ

milo
BR ˈmʌɪləʊ
AM ˈmaɪloʊ

milometer
BR mʌɪˈlɒmɪtə(r), -z
AM maɪˈlɑmədər, -z

milord
BR mɪˈlɔːd, -z
AM məˈlɔ(ə)rd, maɪˈlɔ(ə)rd, -z

Milosz
BR ˈmiːlɒʃ
AM ˈmiloʃ, ˈmilɑʃ

milquetoast
BR ˈmɪlktəʊst, -s
AM ˈmɪlkˌtoʊst, -s

milt
BR mɪlt, -s, -ɪŋ, -ɨd
AM mɪlt, -s, -ɪŋ, -ɨd

milter
BR ˈmɪltə(r), -z
AM ˈmɪltər, -z

Milton
BR ˈmɪlt(ə)n
AM ˈmɪltən

Miltonian
BR mɪlˈtəʊnɪən, -z
AM mɪlˈtoʊniən, -z

Miltonic
BR mɪlˈtɒnɪk
AM mɪlˈtɑnɪk

Milwaukee
BR mɪlˈwɔːki
AM mɪlˈwɑki, mɪlˈwɔki

Mimas
BR ˈmʌɪməs, ˈmʌɪmas

AM 'maɪməs, 'mimǝs
mimbar
BR 'mɪmbɑː(r), -z
AM 'mɪm,bɑr, -z
mime
BR mʌɪm, -z, -ɪŋ, -d
AM maɪm, -z, -ɪŋ, -d
mimeo
BR 'mɪmɪəʊ, -z, -ɪŋ, -d
AM 'mɪmioʊ, -z, -ɪŋ, -d
mimeograph
BR 'mɪmɪəgrɑːf, 'mɪmɪəgraf, -s, -ɪŋ, -t
AM 'mɪmiə,græf, -s, -ɪŋ, -t
mimer
BR 'mʌɪmə(r), -z
AM 'maɪmər, -z
mimesis
BR mᵻ'miːsɪs, mʌɪ'miːsɪs
AM mə'misᵻs
mimetic
BR mᵻ'mɛtɪk, mʌɪ'mɛtɪk
AM mə'mɛdɪk
mimetically
BR mᵻ'mɛtᵻkli, mʌɪ'mɛtᵻkli
AM mə'mɛdək(ə)li
Mimi
BR 'miːmi
AM 'mimi
mimic
BR 'mɪmɪk, -s, -ɪŋ, -t
AM 'mɪmɪk, -s, -ɪŋ, -t
mimicker
BR 'mɪmᵻkə(r), -z
AM 'mɪmᵻkər, -z
mimicry
BR 'mɪmᵻkri
AM 'mɪmᵻkri
miminy-piminy
BR ,mɪmᵻnɪ'pɪmᵻni
AM 'mɪmᵻni'pɪmᵻni
mimosa
BR mᵻ'məʊzə(r), mᵻ'məʊsə(r)
AM mə'moʊsə, mə'moʊzə
mimulus
BR 'mɪmjʉləs
AM 'mɪmjələs
Min
BR mɪn
AM mɪn
mina
BR 'mʌɪnə(r), -z
AM 'maɪnə, -z
minacious
BR mᵻ'neɪʃəs
AM mə'neɪʃəs
minacity
BR mᵻ'nasᵻt|i, -ɪz
AM mə'næsədi, -z
minae
BR 'mʌɪniː
AM 'maɪni
Minaean
BR mᵻ'niːən, -z
AM mə'niən, -z
minaret
BR ,mɪnə'rɛt, -s
AM ',mɪnə,rɛt, -s
minareted
BR ,mɪnə'rɛtᵻd
AM ',mɪnə,rɛdəd
minatory
BR 'mɪnət(ə)ri
AM 'mɪnə,tɔri, 'maɪnə,tɔri
minbar
BR 'mɪnbɑː(r), -z
AM 'mɪn,bɑr, -z
mince
BR mɪns, -ᵻz, -ɪŋ, -t
AM mɪns, -ᵻz, -ɪŋ, -t
mincemeat
BR 'mɪnsmiːt
AM 'mɪns,mit
mincer
BR 'mɪnsə(r), -z
AM 'mɪnsər, -z
Minch
BR mɪn(t)ʃ
AM mɪn(t)ʃ
mincingly
BR 'mɪnsɪŋli
AM 'mɪnsɪŋli
mind
BR mʌɪnd, -z, -ɪŋ, -ᵻd
AM maɪnd, -z, -ɪŋ, -ᵻd
Mindanao
BR ,mɪndə'naʊ
AM ,mɪndə'nɑoʊ
minder
BR 'mʌɪndə(r), -z
AM 'maɪndər, -z
mindful
BR 'mʌɪn(d)f(ʉ)l
AM 'maɪn(d)fəl
mindfully
BR 'mʌɪn(d)fʉli, 'mʌɪn(d)fl̩i
AM 'maɪn(d)fəli
mindfulness
BR 'mʌɪn(d)f(ʉ)lnəs
AM 'maɪn(d)fəlnəs
mindless
BR 'mʌɪndlᵻs
AM 'maɪn(d)lᵻs
mindlessly
BR 'mʌɪn(d)lᵻsli
AM 'maɪn(d)lᵻsli
mindlessness
BR 'mʌɪndlᵻsnᵻs
AM 'maɪn(d)lᵻnᵻs
mind-numbing
BR 'mʌɪn(d),nʌmɪŋ
AM 'maɪn(d),nəmɪŋ
Mindoro
BR 'mɪndɔːrəʊ
AM mɪn'dɔroʊ
mind-read¹
present tense
BR 'mʌɪndriːd, -z, -ɪŋ
AM 'maɪn(d),rid, -z, -ɪŋ
mind-read²
past tense
BR 'mʌɪndrɛd
AM 'maɪn(d),rɛd
mind-reader
BR 'mʌɪnd,riːdə(r), -z
AM 'maɪn(d),ridər, -z
mindset
BR 'mʌɪn(d)sɛt, -s
AM 'maɪn(d)sɛt, -s
Mindy
BR 'mɪndi
AM 'mɪndi
mine
BR mʌɪn, -z, -ɪŋ, -d
AM maɪn, -z, -ɪŋ, -d
minefield
BR 'mʌɪnfiːld, -z
AM 'maɪn,fild, -z
Minehead
BR 'mʌɪnhɛd
AM 'maɪn,(h)ɛd
minelayer
BR 'mʌɪn,leɪə(r), -z
AM 'maɪn,leɪ(ə)r, -z
minelaying
BR 'mʌɪn,leɪɪŋ
AM 'maɪn,leɪɪŋ
Minelli
BR mᵻ'nɛli
AM mə'nɛli
miner
BR 'mʌɪnə(r), -z
AM 'maɪnər, -z
mineral
BR 'mɪn(ə)rəl, 'mɪn(ə)rl̩, -z
AM 'mɪn(ə)rəl, -z
mineralisation
BR ,mɪn(ə)rəlʌɪ'zeɪʃn, ,mɪn(ə)rl̩ʌɪ'zeɪʃn
AM ,mɪn(ə)rələ'zeɪʃən, ,mɪn(ə)rə,laɪ'zeɪʃən
mineralise
BR 'mɪn(ə)rəlʌɪz, 'mɪn(ə)rl̩ʌɪz, -ᵻz, -ɪŋ, -d
AM 'mɪn(ə)rə,laɪz, -ᵻz, -ɪŋ, -d
mineralization
BR ,mɪn(ə)rəlʌɪ'zeɪʃn, ,mɪn(ə)rl̩ʌɪ'zeɪʃn
AM ,mɪn(ə)rələ'zeɪʃən, ,mɪn(ə)rə,laɪ'zeɪʃən
mineralize
BR 'mɪn(ə)rəlʌɪz, 'mɪn(ə)rl̩ʌɪz, -ᵻz, -ɪŋ, -d
AM 'mɪn(ə)rə,laɪz, -ᵻz, -ɪŋ, -d
mineralogical
BR ,mɪn(ə)rə'lɒdʒᵻkl
AM ',mɪn(ə)rə,lɑdʒəkəl
mineralogist
BR ,mɪnə'ralədʒɪst, -s
AM ,mɪnə'rɑlədʒəst, -s
mineralogy
BR ,mɪnə'ralədʒi
AM ,mɪnə'rɑlədʒi
Minerva
BR mᵻ'nəːvə(r)
AM mə'nərvə
minestrone
BR ,mɪnᵻ'strəʊni
AM ,mɪnə'stroʊni
minesweeper
BR 'mʌɪn,swiːpə(r), -z
AM 'maɪn,swipər, -z
minesweeping
BR 'mʌɪn,swiːpɪŋ
AM 'maɪn,swipɪŋ
minever
BR 'mɪnᵻvə(r), -z
AM 'mɪnəvər, -z
mineworker
BR 'mʌɪn,wəːkə(r), -z
AM 'maɪn,wərkər, -z
Ming
BR mɪŋ
AM mɪŋ
mingily
BR 'mɪn(d)ʒᵻli
AM 'mɪndʒᵻli
mingle
BR 'mɪŋg|l, -lz, -l̩ɪŋ\-lɪŋ, -ld
AM 'mɪŋgəl, -əlz, -(ə)lɪŋ, -əld
mingler
BR 'mɪŋglə(r), 'mɪŋgl̩ə(r), -z
AM 'mɪŋg(ə)lər, -z
Mingulay
BR 'mɪŋgʉleɪ
AM 'mɪŋgə,leɪ
Mingus
BR 'mɪŋgəs
AM 'mɪŋgəs
mingy
BR 'mɪn(d)ʒ|i, -ɪə(r), -ɪɪst
AM 'mɪndʒi, -ər, -ᵻst
mini
BR 'mɪn|i, -ɪz
AM 'mɪni, -z
miniate
BR 'mɪnɪeɪt, -s, -ɪŋ, -ᵻd
AM 'mɪni,eɪ|t, -ts, -dɪŋ, -dᵻd
miniature
BR 'mɪnᵻtʃə(r), -z
AM 'mɪn(i)ə,tʃʊ(ə)r, 'mɪn(i)ətʃər, -z
miniaturisation
BR ,mɪnᵻtʃ(ə)rʌɪ'zeɪʃn
AM ,mɪn(i)ə,tʃʊrə'zeɪʃən, ,mɪn(i)ətʃərə'zeɪʃən, ,mɪn(i)ətʃə,raɪ'zeɪʃən

miniaturise
BR ˈmɪnɨtʃərʌɪz, -ɨz, -ɪŋ, -d
AM ˈmɪn(i)əˌtʃʊˌraɪz, ˈmɪn(i)ətʃəˌraɪz, -ɨz, -ɪŋ, -d
miniaturist
BR ˈmɪnɨtʃ(ə)rɪst, -s
AM ˈmɪn(i)əˌtʃʊrəst, ˈmɪn(i)ətʃərəst, -s
miniaturization
BR ˌmɪnɨtʃ(ə)rʌɪˈzeɪʃn
AM ˌmɪn(i)əˌtʃʊrəˈzeɪʃən, ˌmɪn(i)ətʃərəˈzeɪʃən, ˌmɪn(i)ətʃəˌraɪˈzeɪʃən
miniaturize
BR ˈmɪnɨtʃərʌɪz, -ɨz, -ɪŋ, -d
AM ˈmɪn(i)əˌtʃʊˌraɪz, ˈmɪn(i)ətʃəˌraɪz, -ɨz, -ɪŋ, -d
minibar
BR ˈmɪnɪbɑː(r), -z
AM ˈmɪniˌbɑr, -z
minibike
BR ˈmɪnɪbʌɪk, -s
AM ˈmɪniˌbaɪk, -s
minibus
BR ˈmɪnɪbʌs, -ɨz
AM ˈmɪniˌbəs, -əz
minicab
BR ˈmɪnɪkab, -z
AM ˈmɪniˌkæb, -z
minicam
BR ˈmɪnɪkam, -z
AM ˈmɪniˌkæm, -z
Minicom
BR ˈmɪnɪkɒm, -z
AM ˈmɪniˌkɑm, -z
minicomputer
BR ˈmɪnɪkəmˌpjuːtə(r), -z
AM ˈmɪnikəmˌpjudər, -z
minicourse
BR ˈmɪnɪkɔːs, -ɨz
AM ˈmɪniˌkɔ(ə)rs, -ɨz
minidress
BR ˈmɪnɪdrɛs, -ɨz
AM ˈmɪniˌdrɛs, -əz
minify
BR ˈmɪnɨfʌɪ, -z, -ɪŋ, -d
AM ˈmɪnəˌfaɪ, -z, -ɪŋ, -d
minikin
BR ˈmɪnɨkɪn, -z
AM ˈmɪnɨkɨn, -z
minim
BR ˈmɪnɪm, -z
AM ˈmɪnɨm, -z
minima
BR ˈmɪnɨmə(r)
AM ˈmɪnəmə
minimal
BR ˈmɪnɨml
AM ˈmɪnəməl
minimalism
BR ˈmɪnɨml̩ɪz(ə)m
AM ˈmɪnəməlˌɪzəm
minimalist
BR ˈmɪnɨnəml̩ɪst, -s
AM ˈmɪnəmələst, -s
minimally
BR ˈmɪnɨməli, ˈmɪnɨml̩i
AM ˈmɪnəməli
minimax
BR ˈmɪnɪmaks
AM ˈmɪniˌmæks
minimisation
BR ˌmɪnɨmʌɪˈzeɪʃn
AM ˌmɪnəməˈzeɪʃən, ˌmɪnəˌmaɪˈzeɪʃən
minimise
BR ˈmɪnɨmʌɪz, -ɨz, -ɪŋ, -d
AM ˈmɪnəˌmaɪz, -ɨz, -ɪŋ, -d
minimiser
BR ˈmɪnɨmʌɪzə(r), -z
AM ˈmɪnəˌmaɪzər, -z
minimization
BR ˌmɪnɨmʌɪˈzeɪʃn
AM ˌmɪnəməˈzeɪʃən, ˌmɪnəˌmaɪˈzeɪʃən
minimize
BR ˈmɪnɨmʌɪz, -ɨz, -ɪŋ, -d
AM ˈmɪnəˌmaɪz, -ɨz, -ɪŋ, -d
minimizer
BR ˈmɪnɨmʌɪzə(r), -z
AM ˈmɪnəˌmaɪzər, -z
minimum
BR ˈmɪnɨməm, -z
AM ˈmɪnəməm, -z
minion
BR ˈmɪnjən, ˈmɪnɪən, -z
AM ˈmɪnjən, -z
minipill
BR ˈmɪnɪpɪl, -z
AM ˈmɪniˌpɪl, -z
miniscule
BR ˈmɪnɪskjuːl
AM ˈmɪnəˌskjul
miniseries
BR ˈmɪnɪˌsɪərɪz
AM ˈmɪniˌsɪriz
miniskirt
BR ˈmɪnɪskəːt, -s
AM ˈmɪniˌskərt, -s
minister
BR ˈmɪnɨst|ə(r), -əz, -(ə)rɪŋ, -əd
AM ˈmɪnəst|ər, -ərz, -(ə)rɪŋ, -ərd
ministerial
BR ˌmɪnɨˈstɪərɪəl
AM ¦mɪnəˌstɪriəl, ¦mɪnəˌstɛriəl
ministerialist
BR ˌmɪnɨˈstɪərɪəlɪst, -s
AM ¦mɪnəˈstɪriələst, -s
ministerially
BR ˌmɪnɨˈstɪərɪəli
AM ¦mɪnəˈstɪriəli
ministership
BR ˈmɪnɨstəʃɪp, -s
AM ˈmɪnəstərˌʃɪp, -s
ministrable
BR ˈmɪnɨstrəbl
AM ˈmɪnəstrəbəl
ministrant
BR ˈmɪnɨstr(ə)nt, -s
AM ˈmɪnəstrənt, -s
ministration
BR ˌmɪnɨˈstreɪʃn
AM ˌmɪnəˈstreɪʃən
ministrative
BR ˈmɪnɨstrətɪv
AM ˈmɪnəˌstreɪdɪv
ministry
BR ˈmɪnɨstr|i, -ɪz
AM ˈmɪnəstri, -z
minium
BR ˈmɪnɪəm
AM ˈmɪniəm
minivan
BR ˈmɪnɪvan
AM ˈmɪniˌvæn
miniver
BR ˈmɪnɨvə(r)
AM ˈmɪnəvər
mink
BR mɪŋk, -s
AM mɪŋk, -s
minke
BR ˈmɪŋk|i, ˈmɪŋk|ə(*r*), -ɪz\-əz
AM ˈmɪŋki, -z
Minkowski
BR mɪŋˈkɒfski
AM ˈmɪŋkaʊski
RUS mʲinˈkofskʲij
Minna
BR ˈmɪnə(*r*)
AM ˈmɪnə
Minneapolis
BR ˌmɪnɪˈapəlɪs
AM ˌmɪniˈæpələs
Minnehaha
BR ˌmɪnɪˈhɑːhɑː(*r*)
AM ˌmɪnɪˈhɑhɑ
Minnelli
BR mɪˈnɛli
AM məˈnɛli
Minnesinger
BR ˈmɪnɪˌsɪŋə(r), -z
AM ˈmɪnɪˌsɪŋər, ˈmɪnɪˌzɪŋər, -z
Minnesota
BR ˌmɪnɨˈsəʊtə(*r*)
AM ˌmɪnəˈsoʊdə
Minnesotan
BR ˌmɪnɨˈsəʊt(ə)n, -z
AM ¦mɪnəˈsoʊtn, -z
Minnie
BR ˈmɪni
AM ˈmɪni
minnow
BR ˈmɪnəʊ, -z
AM ˈmɪnoʊ, -z
Minoan
BR mɪˈnəʊən, mʌɪˈnəʊən, -z
AM məˈnoʊn, maɪˈnoʊən, -z
Minogue
BR mɪˈnəʊg
AM məˈnoʊg
Minolta®
BR mɪˈnɒltə(*r*)
AM məˈnoʊltə
minor
BR ˈmʌɪnə(r), -z
AM ˈmaɪnər, -z
Minorca
BR mɪˈnɔːkə(*r*)
AM məˈnɔrkə
Minorcan
BR mɪˈnɔːk(ə)n, -z
AM məˈnɔrkən, -z
Minories
BR ˈmɪn(ə)rɪz
AM ˈmɪnərɪz
Minorite
BR ˈmʌɪnərʌɪt, -s
AM ˈmaɪnəˌraɪt, -s
minority
BR mʌɪˈnɒrɪt|i, mɪˈnɒrɪt|i, -ɪz
AM məˈnɔrədi, -z
Minos
BR ˈmʌɪnɒs
AM ˈmaɪnəs, ˈmaɪnɑs, ˈmaɪnɔs
Minotaur
BR ˈmʌɪnətɔː(r)
AM ˈmɪnəˌtɔ(ə)r
minoxidil
BR mɪˈnɒksɪdɪl
AM məˈnɑksəˌdɪl
Minsk
BR mɪnsk
AM mɪnsk
minster
BR ˈmɪnstə(r), -z
AM ˈmɪnstər, -z
minstrel
BR ˈmɪnstr(ə)l, -z
AM ˈmɪnstrəl, -z
minstrelsy
BR ˈmɪnstr(ə)lsi
AM ˈmɪnstrəlsi
mint
BR mɪnt, -s, -ɪŋ, -ɨd
AM mɪnt, -s, -ɪŋ, -ɨd
mintage
BR ˈmɪnt|ɪdʒ, -ɪdʒɨz
AM ˈmɪn(t)ɪdʒ, -ɨz
Minter
BR ˈmɪntə(r)
AM ˈmɪn(t)ər
mintiness
BR ˈmɪntɪnɨs
AM ˈmɪn(t)inɨs
Minto®
BR ˈmɪntəʊ
AM ˈmɪn(t)oʊ

Minton
BR 'mɪnt(ə)n
AM 'mɪn(t)ən, 'mɪntn

minty
BR 'mɪnt|i, -ɪə(r), -ɪɨst
AM 'mɪn(t)i, -ər, -ɨst

minuend
BR 'mɪnjʊɛnd, -z
AM 'mɪnjəˌwɛnd, -z

minuet
BR ˌmɪnjʊ'ɛt, -s
AM ˌmɪnjə'wɛt, -s

minus
BR 'mʌɪnəs, -ɪz
AM 'maɪnəs, -ɪz

minuscular
BR mɪ'nʌskjʊlə(r)
AM mə'nəskjələr

minuscule
BR 'mɪnɪskjuːl
AM 'mɪnəˌskjul

minute[1]
adjective
BR mʌɪ'njuːt
AM maɪ'n(j)ut

minute[2]
noun, verb
BR 'mɪn|ɪt, -ɪts, -ɪtɪŋ, -ɪtɪd
AM 'mɪnɨ|t, -ts, -dɪŋ, -dɨd

minutely
BR mʌɪ'njuːtli
AM maɪ'n(j)utli, mə'n(j)utli

Minuteman
BR 'mɪnɪtman
AM 'mɪnɨtˌmæn

Minutemen
BR 'mɪnɪtmɛn
AM 'mɪnɨtˌmɛn

minuteness
BR mʌɪ'njuːtnəs
AM maɪ'n(j)utnəs, mə'n(j)utnəs

minutia
BR mʌɪ'njuːʃ(ɪ)ə(r), mɪ'njuːʃ(ɪ)ə(r)
AM mə'n(j)uʃ(i)ə

minutiae
BR mʌɪ'njuːʃɪʌɪ, mɪ'njuːʃɪʌɪ, mʌɪ'njuːʃɪiː, mɪ'njuːʃɪiː
AM mə'n(j)uʃiˌi, mə'n(j)uʃiˌaɪ

minx
BR mɪŋks, -ɪz
AM mɪŋks, -ɪz

minxish
BR 'mɪŋksɪʃ
AM 'mɪŋksɪʃ

minxishly
BR 'mɪŋksɪʃli
AM 'mɪŋksɪʃli

Minya Konka
BR ˌmɪnjə 'kʌŋkə(r)
AM ˈmɪnjə 'kəŋkə

Miocene
BR 'mʌɪəsiːn
AM 'maɪəˌsin

mioses
BR mʌɪ'əʊsiːz
AM maɪ'oʊsiz

miosis
BR mʌɪ'əʊsɪs
AM maɪ'oʊsəs

miotic
BR mʌɪ'ɒtɪk
AM maɪ'ɑdɪk

Miquelon
BR 'miːkəlɒn
AM 'mikəˌlɑn

Mir
BR mɪə(r)
AM mɪ(ə)r

Mira
BR 'mʌɪrə(r)
AM 'maɪrə

Mirabeau
BR 'mɪrəbəʊ
AM ˌmɪrə'boʊ

Mirabel
BR 'mɪrəbɛl
AM 'mɪrəˌbɛl

mirabelle
BR 'mɪrəbɛl, -z
AM 'mɪrəˌbɛl, -z

miracle
BR 'mɪrɨkl, -z
AM 'mɪrɨkəl, -z

miraculous
BR mɪ'rakjʊləs
AM mə'rækjələs

miraculously
BR mɪ'rakjʊləsli
AM mə'rækjələsli

miraculousness
BR mɪ'rakjʊləsnəs
AM mə'rækjələsnəs

mirador
BR ˌmɪrə'dɔː(r), 'mɪrədɔː(r), -z
AM ˈmɪrəˌdɔ(ə)r, -z

mirage
BR 'mɪrɑːʒ, -ɪz
AM mə'rɑʒ, -əz

Miranda
BR mɪ'randə(r)
AM mə'rændə

MIRAS
BR 'mʌɪrəs
AM 'maɪrəs

mire
BR 'mʌɪ|ə(r), -əz, -(ə)rɪŋ, -əd
AM 'maɪ(ə)r, -z, -ɪŋ, -d

mirepoix
BR ˌmɪə'pwɑː(r)
AM mɪr'pwɑ

Mirfield
BR 'məːfiːld
AM 'mərˌfild

Miriam
BR 'mɪrɪəm
AM 'mɪriəm

mirid
BR 'mɪrɪd, 'mʌɪrɪd, -z
AM 'maɪrɨd, 'mɪrɨd, -z

miriness
BR 'mʌɪərɪnɨs
AM 'maɪrinɨs

mirk
BR məːk
AM mərk

mirkily
BR 'məːkɨli
AM 'mərkəli

mirkiness
BR 'məːkɪnɨs
AM 'mərkinɨs

mirky
BR 'məːk|i, -ɪə(r), -ɪɨst
AM 'mərki, -ər, -ɨst

Miró
BR mɪ'rəʊ
AM mɪ'roʊ

Mirren
BR 'mɪrən, 'mɪrn̩
AM 'mɪrən, 'mərən

mirror
BR 'mɪrə(r), -z, -ɪŋ, -d
AM 'mɪrər, -z, -ɪŋ, -d

mirth
BR məːθ
AM mərθ

mirthful
BR 'məːθf(ʊ)l
AM 'mərθfəl

mirthfully
BR 'məːθfʊli, 'məːθfl̩i
AM 'mərθfəli

mirthfulness
BR 'məːθf(ʊ)lnəs
AM 'mərθfəlnəs

mirthless
BR 'məːθləs
AM 'mərθləs

mirthlessly
BR 'məːθləsli
AM 'mərθləsli

mirthlessness
BR 'məːθləsnəs
AM 'mərθləsnəs

MIRV
BR məːv, -z, -ɪŋ, -d
AM mərv, -z, -ɪŋ, -d

miry
BR 'mʌɪ(ə)ri
AM 'maɪri

misaddress
BR ˌmɪsə'drɛs, -ɪz, -ɪŋ, -t
AM ˈmɪsə'drɛs, -əz, -ɪŋ, -t

misadventure
BR ˌmɪsəd'vɛntʃə(r), -z
AM ˈmɪsəd'vɛn(t)ʃər, -z

misadvise
BR ˌmɪsəd'vʌɪz, -ɪz, -ɪŋ, -d
AM ˈmɪsəd'vaɪz, -ɪz, -ɪŋ, -d

misalign
BR ˌmɪsə'lʌɪn, -z, -ɪŋ, -d
AM ˈmɪsə'laɪn, -z, -ɪŋ, -d

misalignment
BR ˌmɪsə'lʌɪnm(ə)nt, -s
AM ˈmɪsə'laɪnmənt, -s

misalliance
BR ˌmɪsə'lʌɪəns, -ɪz
AM ˈmɪsə'laɪəns, -əz

misally
BR ˌmɪsə'lʌɪ, -z, -ɪŋ, -d
AM ˌmɪsə'laɪ, -z, -ɪŋ, -d

misanthrope
BR 'mɪs(ə)nθrəʊp, 'mɪz(ə)nθrəʊp, -s
AM 'mɪsnˌθroʊp, -s

misanthropic
BR ˌmɪs(ə)n'θrɒpɪk, ˌmɪz(ə)n'θrɒpɪk
AM ˈmɪsn'θrɑpɪk

misanthropical
BR ˌmɪs(ə)n'θrɒpɨkl, ˌmɪz(ə)n'θrɒpɨkl
AM ˈmɪsn'θrɑpəkəl

misanthropically
BR ˌmɪs(ə)n'θrɒpɨkli, ˌmɪz(ə)n'θrɒpɨkli
AM ˈmɪsn'θrɑpək(ə)li

misanthropise
BR mɪ'sanθrəpʌɪz, mɪ'zanθrəpʌɪz, -ɪz, -ɪŋ, -d
AM mə'sænθrəˌpaɪz, -ɪz, -ɪŋ, -d

misanthropist
BR mɪ'sanθrəpɪst, mɪ'zanθrəpɪst, -s
AM mə'sænθrəpəst, -s

misanthropize
BR mɪ'sanθrəpʌɪz, mɪ'zanθrəpʌɪz, -ɪz, -ɪŋ, -d
AM mə'sænθrəˌpaɪz, -ɪz, -ɪŋ, -d

misanthropy
BR mɪ'sanθrəpi, mɪ'zanθrəpi
AM mə'sænθrəpi

misapplication
BR ˌmɪsaplɪ'keɪʃn, -z
AM ˈmɪsˌæplə'keɪʃən, -z

misapply
BR ˌmɪsə'plʌɪ, -z, -ɪŋ, -d
AM ˈmɪsə'plaɪ, -z, -ɪŋ, -d

misapprehend
BR ˌmɪsaprɪ'hɛnd, -z, -ɪŋ, -ɪd
AM ˈmɪsˌæprə'hɛnd, -z, -ɪŋ, -ɨd

misapprehension
BR ˌmɪsaprɪ'hɛnʃn, -z
AM ˈmɪsˌæprə'hɛnʃən, -z

misapprehensive
BR ˌmɪsaprɪˈhɛnsɪv
AM ˌmɪsˌæprəˈhɛnsɪv

misappropriate
BR ˌmɪsəˈprəʊprɪeɪt, -s, -ɪŋ, -ɨd
AM ˌmɪsəˈproʊpriˌeɪ|t, -ts, -dɪŋ, -dɨd

misappropriation
BR ˌmɪsəˌprəʊprɪˈeɪʃn
AM ˌmɪsəˌproʊpriˈeɪʃən

misbecame
BR ˌmɪsbɪˈkeɪm
AM ˌmɪsbəˈkeɪm, ˌmɪsbiˈkeɪm

misbecome
BR ˌmɪsbɪˈkʌm, -z, -ɪŋ
AM ˌmɪsbəˈkəm, ˌmɪsbiˈkəm, -z, -ɪŋ

misbegotten
BR ˌmɪsbɪˈgɒtn
AM ˌmɪsbəˈgɑtn

misbehave
BR ˌmɪsbɪˈheɪv, -z, -ɪŋ, -d
AM ˌmɪsbəˈheɪv, ˌmɪsbiˈheɪv, -z, -ɪŋ, -d

misbehaver
BR ˌmɪsbɪˈheɪvə(r), -z
AM ˌmɪsbəˈheɪvər, ˌmɪsbiˈheɪvər, -z

misbehavior
BR ˌmɪsbɪˈheɪvjə(r)
AM ˌmɪsbəˈheɪvjər, ˌmɪsbiˈheɪvjər

misbehaviour
BR ˌmɪsbɪˈheɪvjə(r)
AM ˌmɪsbəˈheɪvjər, ˌmɪsbiˈheɪvjər

misbelief
BR ˌmɪsbɪˈliːf
AM ˌmɪsbəˈlif, ˌmɪsbiˈlif

miscalculate
BR ˌmɪsˈkalkjʊleɪt, -s, -ɪŋ, -ɨd
AM ˌmɪsˈkælkjəˌleɪ|t, -ts, -dɪŋ, -dɨd

miscalculation
BR ˌmɪskalkjʊˈleɪʃn, mɪsˌkalkjʊˈleɪʃn, -z
AM ˌmɪsˌkælkjəˈleɪʃən, -z

miscall
BR ˌmɪsˈkɔːl, -z, -ɪŋ, -d
AM mɪsˈkɔl, mɪsˈkɑl, -z, -ɪŋ, -d

miscarriage
of f(o)etus
BR ˈmɪskar|ɪdʒ, -ɨdʒɪz
AM ˈmɪsˌkɛrɪdʒ, -ɨz

miscarriage¹
of foetus/fetus
BR ˈmɪskar|ɪdʒ, -ɨdʒɪz
AM ˈmɪsˌkɛrɪdʒ, -ɨz

miscarriage²
of justice
BR (ˌ)mɪsˈkar|ɪdʒ, -ɨdʒɪz
AM məsˈkɛrɪdʒ, ˈmɪsˌkɛrɪdʒ, -ɨz

miscarry
BR (ˌ)mɪsˈkar|i, -ɪz, -ɪɪŋ, -ɪd
AM ˌmɪsˈkɛri, -z, -ɪŋ, -d

miscast
BR ˌmɪsˈkɑːst, ˌmɪsˈkast, -s, -ɪŋ
AM mɪsˈkæst, -s, -ɪŋ

miscegenation
BR ˌmɪsɨdʒɪˈneɪʃn, mɪˌsɛdʒɪˈneɪʃn
AM məˌsɛdʒəˈneɪʃən, ˌmɪsədʒəˈneɪʃən

miscellanea
BR ˌmɪsəˈleɪnɪə(r)
AM ˌmɪsəˈleɪniə, ˌmɪsəˈleɪnjə

miscellaneous
BR ˌmɪsəˈleɪnɪəs
AM ˌmɪsəˈleɪniəs, ˌmɪsəˈleɪnjəs

miscellaneously
BR ˌmɪsəˈleɪnɪəsli
AM ˌmɪsəˈleɪniəsli, ˌmɪsəˈleɪnjəsli

miscellaneousness
BR ˌmɪsəˈleɪnɪəsnəs
AM ˌmɪsəˈleɪniəsnəs, ˌmɪsəˈleɪnjəsnəs

miscellanist
BR mɪˈsɛlənɪst, -s
AM ˌmɪsəˈleɪnɪst, ˌmɪsəˈleɪnɪst, -s

miscellany
BR mɪˈsɛlən|i, -ɪz
AM ˈmɪsəˌleɪni, məˈsɛləni, -z

mischance
BR ˌmɪsˈtʃɑːns, ˌmɪsˈtʃans, -ɨz
AM mɪsˈtʃæns, mɪʃˈtʃæns, -əz

mischief
BR ˈmɪstʃɪf
AM ˈmɪstʃɪf

mischiefmaker
BR ˈmɪstʃɪfˌmeɪkə(r), -z
AM ˈmɪstʃɪfˌmeɪkər, -z

mischievous
BR ˈmɪstʃɪvəs
AM ˈmɪstʃɪvəs, ˈmɪʃtʃɪvəs

mischievously
BR ˈmɪstʃɪvəsli
AM ˈmɪstʃɪvəsli

mischievousness
BR ˈmɪstʃɪvəsnəs
AM ˈmɪstʃɪvəsnəs

misch metal
BR ˈmɪʃ ˌmɛtl, -z
AM ˈmɪʃ ˌmɛdl, -z

miscibility
BR ˌmɪsɪˈbɪlɪti
AM ˌmɪsəˈbɪlɨdi

miscible
BR ˈmɪsɨbl
AM ˈmɪsəbəl

miscommunication
BR ˌmɪskəˌmjuːnɪˈkeɪʃn
AM ˌmɪskəˌmjunəˈkeɪʃən

misconceive
BR ˌmɪskənˈsiːv, -z, -ɪŋ, -d
AM ˌmɪskənˈsiv, -z, -ɪŋ, -d

misconceiver
BR ˌmɪskənˈsiːvə(r), -z
AM ˌmɪskənˈsivər, -z

misconception
BR ˌmɪskənˈsɛpʃn, -z
AM ˌmɪskənˈsɛpʃən, -z

misconduct¹
noun
BR ˌmɪsˈkɒndʌkt
AM mɪsˈkɑndək(t)

misconduct²
verb
BR ˌmɪskənˈdʌkt, -s, -ɪŋ, -ɨd
AM ˌmɪskənˈdək|(t), -(t)s, -tɪŋ, -təd

misconstruction
BR ˌmɪskənˈstrʌkʃn, -z
AM ˌmɪskənˈstrəkʃən, -z

misconstrue
BR ˌmɪskənˈstruː, -z, -ɪŋ, -d
AM ˌmɪskənˈstru, -z, -ɪŋ, -d

miscopy
BR ˌmɪsˈkɒp|i, -ɪz, -ɪɪŋ, -ɪd
AM ˌmɪsˈkɑpi, -z, -ɪŋ, -d

miscount¹
noun
BR ˈmɪskaʊnt, -s
AM ˈmɪsˌkaʊnt, -s

miscount²
verb
BR ˌmɪsˈkaʊnt, -s, -ɪŋ, -ɨd
AM ˌmɪsˈkaʊn|t, -ts, -(t)ɪŋ, -(t)əd

miscreant
BR ˈmɪskrɪənt, -s
AM ˈmɪskriənt, -s

miscue¹
noun
BR ˈmɪsˌkjuː, -z
AM ˈmɪsˌkju, -z

miscue²
verb
BR ˌmɪsˈkjuː, -z, -ɪŋ, -d
AM ˌmɪsˈkju, -z, -ɪŋ, -d

misdate
BR ˌmɪsˈdeɪt, -s, -ɪŋ, -ɨd
AM ˌmɪsˈdeɪ|t, -ts, -dɪŋ, -dɨd

misdeal¹
noun
BR ˈmɪsdiːl, -z
AM ˈmɪsˌdil, -z

misdeal²
verb
BR ˌmɪsˈdiːl, -z, -ɪŋ
AM ˌmɪsˈdil, -z, -ɪŋ

misdealt
BR ˌmɪsˈdɛlt
AM ˌmɪsˈdɛlt

misdeclaration
BR ˌmɪsdɛkləˈreɪʃn, -z
AM ˌmɪsˌdɛkləˈreɪʃən, -z

misdeed
BR ˌmɪsˈdiːd, -z
AM ˌmɪsˈdid, -z

misdemeanant
BR ˌmɪsdɪˈmiːnənt, -s
AM ˌmɪsdəˌminənt, -s

misdemeanor
BR ˌmɪsdɪˈmiːnə(r), -z
AM ˌmɪsdəˌminər, -z

misdemeanour
BR ˌmɪsdɪˈmiːnə(r), -z
AM ˌmɪsdəˌminər, -z

misdescribe
BR ˌmɪsdɪˈskrʌɪb, -z, -ɪŋ, -d
AM ˌmɪsdəˈskraɪb, ˌmɪsdiˈskraɪb, -z, -ɪŋ, -d

misdescription
BR ˌmɪsdɪˈskrɪpʃn, -z
AM ˌmɪsdəˈskrɪpʃən, ˌmɪsdiˈskrɪpʃən, -z

misdiagnose
BR ˌmɪsˈdʌɪəgnəʊz, ˌmɪsdʌɪəgˈnəʊz, -ɨz, -ɪŋ, -d
AM ˌmɪsˌdaɪəgˌnoʊz, -əz, -ɪŋ, -d

misdiagnoses
BR ˌmɪsdʌɪəgˈnəʊsiːz
AM ˌmɪsˌdaɪəgˈnoʊsiz

misdiagnosis
BR ˌmɪsdʌɪəgˈnəʊsɪs
AM ˌmɪsˌdaɪəgˈnoʊsəs

misdial
BR ˌmɪsˈdʌɪəl, -z, -ɪŋ, -d
AM ˌmɪsˈdaɪəl, -z, -ɪŋ, -d

misdirect
BR ˌmɪsdʌɪˈrɛkt, ˌmɪsdɪˈrɛkt, -s, -ɪŋ, -ɨd
AM ˌmɪsdəˈrɛk|(t), -(t)s, -tɪŋ, -təd

misdirection
BR ˌmɪsdʌɪˈrɛkʃn, ˌmɪsdɪˈrɛkʃn
AM ˌmɪsdəˈrɛkʃən

misdoing
BR ˌmɪsˈduːɪŋ, -z
AM ˌmɪsˈduɪŋ, -z

misdoubt
BR ˌmɪsˈdaʊt, -s, -ɪŋ, -ɨd

AM ˌmɪsˈdaʊ|t, -ts, -dɪŋ, -dəd

mise au point
BR ˌmiːz əʊ ˈpwã
AM ˈmiˌz oʊ ˈpwɑnt

miseducate
BR ˌmɪsˈɛdjʊkeɪt, ˌmɪsˈɛdʒʊkeɪt, -s, -ɪŋ, -ɪd
AM ˌmɪsˈɛdʒəˌkeɪ|t, -ts, -dɪŋ, -dɪd

miseducation
BR ˌmɪsɛdjʊˈkeɪʃn, ˌmɪsɛdʒʊˈkeɪʃn
AM ˈmɪsˌɛdʒəˈkeɪʃən

mise en scène
BR ˌmiːz ɒn ˈseɪn, ˌmiːz ɒn ˈsɛn
AM ˈmiˌz ɑn ˈsɛn

misemploy
BR ˌmɪsɪmˈplɔɪ, ˌmɪsɛmˈplɔɪ, -z, -ɪŋ, -d
AM ˈmɪsˌɛmˈplɔɪ, -z, -ɪŋ, -d

misemployment
BR ˌmɪsɪmˈplɔɪm(ə)nt, ˌmɪsɛmˈplɔɪm(ə)nt, -s
AM ˈmɪsɛmˈplɔɪmənt, -s

miser
BR ˈmʌɪzə(r), -z
AM ˈmaɪzər, -z

miserable
BR ˈmɪz(ə)rəbl
AM ˈmɪzərbəl, ˈmɪz(ə)r(ə)bəl

miserableness
BR ˈmɪz(ə)rəblnəs
AM ˈmɪzərbəlnəs, ˈmɪz(ə)r(ə)bəlnəs

miserably
BR ˈmɪz(ə)rəbli
AM ˈmɪzərbli, ˈmɪz(ə)rəbli

misère
BR mɪˈzɛː(r), -z
AM məˈzɛ(ə)r, -z

miserere
BR ˌmɪzɪˈrɛːr|i, ˌmɪzəˈrɪər|i, -ɪz
AM ˌmɪzəˈrɛri, ˌmɪzəˈrɪri, -z

misericord
BR mɪˈzɛ(ə)rɪkɔːd, -z
AM ˈmɪzərəˌkɔ(ə)rd, məˈzɛ(ə)rəˌkɔ(ə)rd, -z

miserliness
BR ˈmʌɪzəlɪnɪs
AM ˈmaɪzərlinɪs

miserly
BR ˈmʌɪzəli
AM ˈmaɪzərli

misery
BR ˈmɪz(ə)ri, -ɪz
AM ˈmɪz(ə)ri, -z

misfeasance
BR ˌmɪsˈfiːz(ə)ns
AM ˌmɪsˈfizns

misfield
BR ˌmɪsˈfiːld, -z, -ɪŋ, -ɪd
AM ˌmɪsˈfild, -z, -ɪŋ, -ɪd

misfire[1]
noun
BR ˈmɪsfʌɪə(r), -z
AM ˈmɪsˌfaɪər, -z

misfire[2]
verb
BR ˌmɪsˈfʌɪə(r), -z, -ɪŋ, -d
AM ˌmɪsˈfaɪər, -z, -ɪŋ, -d

misfit
BR ˈmɪsfɪt, -s
AM ˈmɪsˌfɪt, -s

misfortune
BR ˌmɪsˈfɔːtʃuːn, ˌmɪsˈfɔːtʃ(ə)n, ˌmɪsˈfɔːtjuːn, -z
AM ˌmɪsˈfɔrtʃən, -z

misgave
BR ˌmɪsˈgeɪv, -z
AM ˌmɪsˈgeɪv, -z

misgive
BR ˌmɪsˈgɪv, -z
AM ˌmɪsˈgɪv, -z

misgiven
BR ˌmɪsˈgɪvn, -z
AM ˌmɪsˈgɪvən, -z

misgiving
BR (ˌ)mɪsˈgɪvɪŋ, -z
AM ˌmɪsˈgɪvɪŋ, -z

misgovern
BR ˌmɪsˈgʌvn, -z, -ɪŋ, -d
AM ˌmɪsˈgəvərn, -z, -ɪŋ, -d

misgovernment
BR ˌmɪsˈgʌvnm(ə)nt, ˌmɪsˈgʌvəm(ə)nt
AM ˌmɪsˈgəvər(n)mənt, ˌmɪsˈgəvə(r)mənt

misguidance
BR ˌmɪsˈgʌɪdns
AM ˌmɪsgaɪdns

misguide
BR ˌmɪsˈgʌɪd, -z, -ɪŋ, -ɪd
AM ˌmɪsˈgaɪd, -z, -ɪŋ, -ɪd

misguided
BR (ˌ)mɪsˈgʌɪdɪd
AM ˌmɪsˈgaɪdɪd

misguidedly
BR (ˌ)mɪsˈgʌɪdɪdli
AM ˌmɪsˈgaɪdɪdli

misguidedness
BR (ˌ)mɪsˈgʌɪdɪdnɪs
AM ˌmɪsˈgaɪdɪdnɪs

mishandle
BR ˌmɪsˈhand|l, -lz, -lɪŋ\-lɪŋ, -ld
AM ˌmɪsˈhæn|dəl, -dəlz, -(d)(ə)lɪŋ, -dəld

mishap
BR ˈmɪshap, -s
AM ˈmɪsˌ(h)æp, -s

mishear
BR ˌmɪsˈhɪə(r), -z, -ɪŋ
AM ˌmɪsˈhɪ|(ə)r, -(ə)rz, -rɪŋ

misheard
BR ˌmɪsˈhəːd
AM ˌmɪsˈhərd

mishit
BR ˌmɪsˈhɪt, -s, -ɪŋ
AM ˌmɪsˈhɪ|t, -ts, -dɪŋ

mishmash
BR ˈmɪʃmaʃ
AM ˈmɪʃˌmæʃ, ˈmɪʃˌmɑʃ

Mishna
BR ˈmɪʃnə(*r*)
AM ˈmɪʃnə

Mishnah
BR ˈmɪʃnə(*r*)
AM ˈmɪʃnə

Mishnaic
BR mɪʃˈneɪɪk
AM mɪʃˈneɪɪk

misidentification
BR ˌmɪsʌɪˌdɛntɪfɪˈkeɪʃn, -z
AM ˈmɪsaɪˌdɛn(t)əfəˈkeɪʃən, -z

misidentify
BR ˌmɪsʌɪˈdɛntɪfʌɪ, -z, -ɪŋ, -d
AM ˈmɪsaɪˈdɛn(t)əˌfaɪ, -z, -ɪŋ, -d

misinform
BR ˌmɪsɪnˈfɔːm, -z, -ɪŋ, -d
AM ˈmɪsɪnˈfɔ(ə)rm, -z, -ɪŋ, -d

misinformation
BR ˌmɪsɪnfəˈmeɪʃn
AM ˈmɪsɪnfərˈmeɪʃən

misinterpret
BR ˌmɪsɪnˈtəːprɪt, -s, -ɪŋ, -ɪd
AM ˈmɪsɪnˈtərprə|t, -ts, -dɪŋ, -dəd

misinterpretation
BR ˌmɪsɪnˌtəːprɪˈteɪʃn, -z
AM ˈmɪsɪnˌtərprəˈteɪʃən, -z

misinterpreter
BR ˌmɪsɪnˈtəːprɪtə(r), -z
AM ˈmɪsɪnˈtərprədər, -z

MI6
BR ˌɛmʌɪˈsɪks
AM ˌɛmˌaɪˈsɪks

misjudge
BR ˌmɪsˈdʒʌdʒ, -ɪz, -ɪŋ, -d
AM ˌmɪsˈdʒədʒ, -əz, -ɪŋ, -d

misjudgement
BR (ˌ)mɪsˈdʒʌdʒm(ə)nt, -s
AM ˈmɪsˈdʒədʒmənt, -s

misjudgment
BR (ˌ)mɪsˈdʒʌdʒm(ə)nt, -s
AM ˈmɪsˈdʒədʒmənt, -s

miskey
BR ˌmɪsˈkiː, -z, -ɪŋ, -d
AM ˌmɪsˈki, -z, -ɪŋ, -d

miskick
BR ˌmɪsˈkɪk, -s, -ɪŋ, -d
AM ˌmɪsˈkɪk, -s, -ɪŋ, -d

Miskin
BR ˈmɪskɪn
AM ˈmɪskɪn

Miskito
BR mɪˈskiːtəʊ, -z
AM məˈskidoʊ, məˈskiˌtoʊ, -z

mislay
BR (ˌ)mɪsˈleɪ, -z, -ɪŋ, -d
AM ˌmɪsˈleɪ, -z, -ɪŋ, -d

mislead
BR (ˌ)mɪsˈliːd, -z, -ɪŋ
AM ˌmɪsˈlid, -z, -ɪŋ

misleader
BR (ˌ)mɪsˈliːdə(r), -z
AM ˌmɪsˈlidər, -z

misleading
BR (ˌ)mɪsˈliːdɪŋ
AM ˌmɪsˈlidɪŋ

misleadingly
BR (ˌ)mɪsliːdɪŋli
AM ˌmɪsˈlidɪŋli

misleadingness
BR (ˌ)mɪsˈliːdɪŋnɪs
AM ˌmɪsˈlidɪŋnɪs

misled
BR (ˌ)mɪsˈlɛd
AM ˌmɪsˈlɛd

mislike
BR (ˌ)mɪsˈlʌɪk, -s, -ɪŋ, -d
AM ˌmɪsˈlaɪk, -s, -ɪŋ, -d

mismanage
BR ˌmɪsˈman|ɪdʒ, -ɪdʒɪz, -ɪdʒɪŋ, -ɪdʒd
AM ˌmɪsˈmænɪdʒ, -ɪz, -ɪŋ, -d

mismanagement
BR ˌmɪsˈmanɪdʒm(ə)nt
AM ˈmɪsˈmænədʒmənt

mismarriage
BR ˌmɪsˈmar|ɪdʒ, -ɪdʒɪz
AM ˌmɪsˈmɛrɪdʒ, -ɪz

mismatch[1]
noun
BR ˈmɪsmatʃ, -ɪz
AM ˈmɪsˌmætʃ, -əz

mismatch[2]
verb
BR ˌmɪsˈmatʃ, -ɪz, -ɪŋ, -t
AM ˈmɪsˈmætʃ, -əz, -ɪŋ, -t

mismated
BR ˌmɪsˈmeɪtɪd
AM ˌmɪsˈmeɪdɪd

mismeasure
BR ˌmɪsˈmɛʒ|ə(r), -əz, -(ə)rɪŋ, -əd
AM ˌmɪsˈmɛʒ|ər, -ərz, -(ə)rɪŋ, -ərd

mismeasurement
BR ˌmɪsˈmɛʒəm(ə)nt, -s

AM ˌmɪsˈmɛʒərmənt, -s

misname
BR ˌmɪsˈneɪm, -z, -ɪŋ, -d
AM ˌmɪsˈneɪm, -z, -ɪŋ, -d

misnomer
BR ˌmɪsˈnəʊmə(r), -z
AM mɪsˈnoʊmər, -z

misogamist
BR mɨˈsɒgəmɪst, mʌɪˈsɒgəmɪst, -s
AM məˈsɑgəməst, -s

misogamy
BR mɨˈsɒgəmi, mʌɪˈsɒgəmi
AM məˈsɑgəmi

misogynist
BR mɨˈsɒdʒɨnɪst, mʌɪˈsɒdʒɨnɪst, -s
AM məˈsɑdʒənəst, -s

misogynistic
BR mɨˌsɒdʒɪˈnɪstɪk, mʌɪˌsɒdʒɪˈnɪstɪk
AM məˌsɑdʒəˈnɪstɪk

misogynous
BR mɨˈsɒdʒɨnəs, mʌɪˈsɒdʒɨnəs
AM məˈsɑdʒənəs

misogyny
BR mɨˈsɒdʒɨni, mʌɪˈsɒdʒɨni
AM məˈsɑdʒəni

misologist
BR mɨˈsɒlədʒɪst, mʌɪˈsɒlədʒɪst, -s
AM məˈsɑlədʒəst, -s

misology
BR mɨˈsɒlədʒi, mʌɪˈsɒlədʒi
AM məˈsɑlədʒi

misoneism
BR ˌmɪsə(ʊ)ˈniːɪz(ə)m, -z
AM ˌmɪsəˈniˌɪzəm, -z

misoneist
BR ˌmɪsə(ʊ)ˈniːɪst, -s
AM ˌmɪsəˈniɨst, -s

mispickel
BR ˈmɪsˌpɪkl, -z
AM ˈmɪsˌpɪkəl, -z

misplace
BR ˌmɪsˈpleɪs, -ɨz, -ɪŋ, -t
AM ˌmɪsˈpleɪs, -ɨz, -ɪŋ, -t

misplacement
BR ˌmɪsˈpleɪsm(ə)nt
AM ˈmɪsˈpleɪsmənt

misplay[1]
noun
BR ˈmɪspleɪ, -z, -ɪŋ, -d
AM ˈmɪsˌpleɪ, -z, -ɪŋ, -d

misplay[2]
verb
BR ˌmɪsˈpleɪ, -z, -ɪŋ, -d
AM ˌmɪsˈpleɪ, -z, -ɪŋ, -d

misprint[1]
noun
BR ˈmɪsprɪnt, -s
AM ˈmɪsˌprɪnt, -s

misprint[2]
verb
BR ˌmɪsˈprɪnt, -s, -ɪŋ, -ɨd
AM ˈmɪsˈprɪn|t, -ts, -(t)ɪŋ, -(t)ɨd

misprision
BR ˌmɪsˈprɪʒn
AM ˌmɪsˈprɪʒən

misprize
BR ˌmɪsˈprʌɪz, -ɨz, -ɪŋ, -d
AM ˌmɪsˈpraɪz, -ɨz, -ɪŋ, -d

mispronounce
BR ˌmɪsprəˈnaʊns, -ɨz, -ɪŋ, -t
AM ˈmɪsprəˈnaʊns, -əz, -ɪŋ, -t

mispronunciation
BR ˌmɪsprəˌnʌnsɪˈeɪʃn, -z
AM ˈmɪsprəˌnənsiˈeɪʃən, -z

misquotation
BR ˌmɪskwə(ʊ)ˈteɪʃn, -z
AM ˈmɪskwoʊˈteɪʃən, -z

misquote
BR ˌmɪsˈkwəʊt, -s, -ɪŋ, -ɨd
AM ˌmɪsˈkwoʊ|t, -ts, -dɪŋ, -dəd

misread[1]
present tense
BR ˌmɪsˈriːd, -z, -ɪŋ
AM ˌmɪsˈrid, -z, -ɪŋ

misread[2]
past tense
BR ˌmɪsˈrɛd
AM ˌmɪsˈrɛd

misremember
BR ˌmɪsrɪˈmɛmb|ə(r), -əz, -(ə)rɪŋ, -əd
AM ˈmɪsrəˈmɛmb|ər, ˈmɪsriˈmɛmb|ər, -ərz, -(ə)rɪŋ, -ərd

misreport
BR ˌmɪsrɪˈpɔːt, -s, -ɪŋ, -ɨd
AM ˈmɪsrəˈpɔ(ə)rt, -ts, -ˈpɔrdɪŋ, -ˈpɔrdəd

misrepresent
BR ˌmɪsrɛprɪˈzɛnt, -s, -ɪŋ, -ɨd
AM ˈmɪsˌrɛprəˈzɛn|t, -ts, -(t)ɪŋ, -(t)əd

misrepresentation
BR ˌmɪsˌrɛprɪzɛnˈteɪʃn, mɪsˌrɛprɪzɛnˈteɪʃn, -z
AM ˈmɪsˌrɛprəˌzɛnˈteɪʃən, -z

misrepresentative
BR ˌmɪsrɛprɪˈzɛntətɪv
AM ˈmɪsˌrɛprəˈzɛn(t)ədɪv

misrule
BR ˌmɪsˈruːl, -z, -ɪŋ, -d
AM ˌmɪsˈrul, -z, -ɪŋ, -d

miss
BR mɪs, -ɨz, -ɪŋ, -t
AM mɪs, -ɨz, -ɪŋ, -t

missable
BR ˈmɪsəbl
AM ˈmɪsəbəl

missal
BR ˈmɪsl, -z
AM ˈmɪsəl, -z

missel thrush
BR ˈmɪsl θrʌʃ, ˈmɪzl +, -ɨz
AM ˈmɪsəl ˌθrəʃ, -əz

Missenden
BR ˈmɪsndən
AM ˈmɪsəndən

misshape[1]
noun
BR ˈmɪsʃeɪp, ˈmɪʃʃeɪp, -s
AM ˈmɪsˌʃeɪp, ˈmɪʃˌʃeɪp, -s

misshape[2]
verb
BR ˌmɪsˈʃeɪp, ˌmɪʃˈʃeɪp, -s, -ɪŋ, -t
AM ˌmɪsˈʃeɪp, ˌmɪʃˈʃeɪp, -s, -ɪŋ, -t

misshapen
BR ˌmɪsˈʃeɪp(ə)n, ˌmɪʃˈʃeɪp(ə)n
AM ˈmɪsˈʃeɪpən, ˈmɪʃˈʃeɪpən

misshapenly
BR ˌmɪsˈʃeɪp(ə)nli, ˌmɪʃˈʃeɪp(ə)nli
AM ˈmɪsˈʃeɪpənli, ˈmɪʃˈʃeɪpənli

misshapenness
BR ˌmɪsˈʃeɪp(ə)nnəs, ˌmɪʃˈʃeɪp(ə)nnəs
AM ˈmɪsˈʃeɪpə(n)nəs, ˈmɪʃˈʃeɪpə(n)nəs

missile
BR ˈmɪsʌɪl, -z
AM ˈmɪsəl, -z

missilery
BR ˈmɪsʌɪlri
AM ˈmɪsəlri

mission
BR ˈmɪʃn, -z
AM ˈmɪʃən, -z

missionary
BR ˈmɪʃn(ə)r|i, -ɪz
AM ˈmɪʃəˌnɛri, -z

missioner
BR ˈmɪʃ(ə)nə(r), ˈmɪʃn̩ə(r), -z
AM ˈmɪʃənər, -z

missis
BR ˈmɪsɪz
AM ˈmɪsɨz

missish
BR ˈmɪsɪʃ
AM ˈmɪsɪʃ

Mississauga
BR ˌmɪsɪˈsɔːgə(r)
AM ˌmɪsɨˈsɔgə, ˌmɪsɨˈsɑgə

Mississippi
BR ˌmɪsɨˈsɪpi
AM ˌmɪsɨˈsɪpi

Mississippian
BR ˌmɪsɨˈsɪpɪən, -z
AM mɪsɨˈsɪpiən, -z

missive
BR ˈmɪsɪv, -z
AM ˈmɪsɪv, -z

Missolonghi
BR ˌmɪsəˈlɒŋi
AM ˌmɪsəˈlɔŋi, ˌmɪsəˈlɑŋi

Missouri
BR mɨˈzʊəri
AM məˈzʊri, məˈzʊrə

Missourian
BR mɨˈzʊərɪən, -z
AM məˈzʊriən, -z

misspell
BR ˌmɪsˈspɛl, -z, -ɪŋ, -t
AM ˌmɪ(s)ˈspɛl, -z, -ɪŋ, -t

misspelling
BR ˌmɪsˈspɛlɪŋ, -z
AM ˌmɪ(s)ˈspɛlɪŋ, -z

misspend
BR ˌmɪsˈspɛnd, -z, -ɪŋ
AM ˌmɪ(s)ˈspɛnd, -z, -ɪŋ

misspent
BR ˌmɪsˈspɛnt
AM ˌmɪ(s)ˈspɛnt

misstate
BR ˌmɪsˈsteɪt, -s, -ɪŋ, -ɨd
AM ˌmɪ(s)ˈsteɪ|t, -ts, -dɪŋ, -dɨd

misstatement
BR ˌmɪ(s)ˈsteɪtm(ə)nt, -s
AM ˈmɪ(s)ˈsteɪtmənt, -s

misstep
BR ˌmɪsˈstɛp, -s, -ɪŋ, -t
AM ˌmɪ(s)ˈstɛp, -s, -ɪŋ, -t

missus
BR ˈmɪsɪz
AM ˈmɪsɪz

missy
BR ˈmɪs|i, -ɪz
AM ˈmɪsi, -z

mist
BR mɪst, -s, -ɪŋ, -ɨd
AM mɪst, -s, -ɪŋ, -ɨd

mistakable
BR mɨˈsteɪkəbl
AM məˈsteɪkəbəl

mistakably
BR mɨˈsteɪkəbli
AM məˈsteɪkəbli

mistake
BR mɨˈsteɪk, -s, -ɪŋ
AM məˈsteɪk, -s, -ɪŋ

mistaken
BR mɨˈsteɪk(ə)n
AM məˈsteɪkən

mistakenly
BR mɪˈsteɪk(ə)nli
AM məˈsteɪkənli
mistakenness
BR mɪˈsteɪk(ə)nnəs
AM məˈsteɪkə(n)nəs
mistaught
BR ˌmɪsˈtɔːt
AM ˌmɪsˈtɔt, ˌmɪsˈtɑt
misteach
BR ˌmɪsˈtiːtʃ, -ᵻz
AM ˌmɪsˈtitʃ, -ᵻz
misteaching
BR ˌmɪsˈtiːtʃɪŋ, -z
AM ˌmɪsˈtitʃɪŋ, -z
mister
BR ˈmɪstə(r), -z
AM ˈmɪstər, -z
mistful
BR ˈmɪstf(ʊ)l
AM ˈmɪs(t)fəl
mistigris
BR ˈmɪstɪɡrɪs
AM ˈmɪstɪˌɡrɪs
mistily
BR ˈmɪstɨli
AM ˈmɪstɨli
mistime
BR ˌmɪsˈtʌɪm, -z, -ɪŋ, -d
AM ˌmɪsˈtaɪm, -z, -ɪŋ, -d
mistiness
BR ˈmɪstɪnɨs
AM ˈmɪstinɨs
mistitle
BR ˌmɪsˈtʌɪt|l, -lz, -l̩ɪŋ\-lɪŋ, -ld
AM ˌmɪsˈtaɪdəl, -z, -ɪŋ, -d
mistle thrush
BR ˈmɪsl θrʌʃ, ˈmɪzl +, -ᵻz
AM ˈmɪsəl ˌθrəʃ, -əz
mistletoe
BR ˈmɪsltəʊ, ˈmɪzltəʊ
AM ˈmɪsəlˌtoʊ
mistlike
BR ˈmɪstlʌɪk
AM ˈmɪs(t)ˌlaɪk
mistook
BR mɪˈstʊk
AM məˈstʊk
mistral
BR ˈmɪstr(ə)l, mɪˈstrɑːl
AM ˈmɪstrəl, məˈstrɑl
mistranslate
BR ˌmɪstransˈleɪt, ˌmɪstrɑːnsˈleɪt, ˌmɪstranzˈleɪt, ˌmɪstrɑːnzˈleɪt, -s, -ɪŋ, -ᵻd
AM ˌmɪsˌtrænzˌleɪ|t, ˌmɪsˌtrænsˌleɪ|t, -ts, -dɪŋ, -dᵻd
mistranslation
BR ˌmɪstransˈleɪʃn, ˌmɪstrɑːnsˈleɪʃn, ˌmɪstranzˈleɪʃn, ˌmɪstrɑːnzˈleɪʃn, -z
AM ˌmɪsˌtrænzˈleɪʃən, ˌmɪsˌtrænsˈleɪʃən, -z
mistreat
BR ˌmɪsˈtriːt, -s, -ɪŋ, -ᵻd
AM ˌmɪsˈtri|t, -ts, -dɪŋ, -dᵻd
mistreatment
BR ˌmɪsˈtriːtm(ə)nt
AM ˌmɪsˈtritmənt
mistress
BR ˈmɪstrɪs, -ᵻz
AM ˈmɪstrɪs, -ᵻz
mistrial
BR ˌmɪsˈtrʌɪəl, ˈmɪsˌtrʌɪəl, -z
AM ˈmɪsˌtraɪəl, -z
mistrust
BR ˌmɪsˈtrʌst, -s, -ɪŋ, -ᵻd
AM ˌmɪsˈtrəst, -s, -ɪŋ, -ᵻd
mistrustful
BR ˌmɪsˈtrʌs(t)f(ʊ)l
AM ˌmɪsˈtrəs(t)fəl
mistrustfully
BR ˌmɪsˈtrʌs(t)fʊli, ˌmɪsˈtrʌs(t)fl̩i
AM ˌmɪsˈtrəs(t)fəli
mistrustfulness
BR ˌmɪsˈtrʌstf(ʊ)lnəs
AM ˌmɪsˈtrəs(t)fəlnəs
misty
BR ˈmɪst|i, -ɪə(r), -ɪɪst
AM ˈmɪsti, -ər, -ɪst
mistype
BR ˌmɪsˈtʌɪp, -s, -ɪŋ, -t
AM ˌmɪsˈtaɪp, -s, -ɪŋ, -t
misunderstand
BR ˌmɪsʌndəˈstand, -z, -ɪŋ
AM ˌmɪsˌəndərˈstænd, -z, -ɪŋ
misunderstanding
BR ˌmɪsʌndəˈstandɪŋ, -z
AM ˌmɪsˌəndərˈstændɪŋ, -z
misunderstood
BR ˌmɪsʌndəˈstʊd
AM ˌmɪsˌəndərˈstʊd
misusage
BR ˌmɪsˈjuːs|ɪdʒ, -ɪdʒᵻz
AM ˌmɪsˈjusɪdʒ, -ᵻz
misuse¹
noun
BR ˌmɪsˈjuːs
AM ˌmɪsˈjus
misuse²
verb
BR ˌmɪsˈjuːz, -ᵻz, -ɪŋ, -d
AM ˌmɪsˈjuz, -əz, -ɪŋ, -d
misuser
BR ˌmɪsˈjuːzə(r), -z
AM ˌmɪsˈjuzər, -z
Mitanni
BR mɪˈtani
AM məˈtæni
Mitannian
BR mɪˈtanɪən, -z
AM məˈtæniən, məˈtænjən, -z
Mitch
BR mɪtʃ
AM mɪtʃ
Mitcham
BR ˈmɪtʃ(ə)m
AM ˈmɪtʃəm
Mitchell
BR ˈmɪtʃ(ə)l
AM ˈmɪtʃəl
Mitchum
BR ˈmɪtʃ(ə)m
AM ˈmɪtʃəm
mite
BR mʌɪt, -s
AM maɪt, -s
miter
BR ˈmʌɪtə(r), -z
AM ˈmaɪdər, -z
Mitford
BR ˈmɪtfəd
AM ˈmɪtfərd
Mithraic
BR mɪˈθreɪɪk
AM məˈθreɪɪk
Mithraism
BR ˈmɪθreɪɪz(ə)m, ˈmɪθrə-ɪz(ə)m
AM ˈmɪθreɪˌɪzəm
Mithraist
BR ˈmɪθreɪɪst, ˈmɪθrə-ɪst, -s
AM ˈmɪθreɪɪst, -s
Mithras
BR ˈmɪθras
AM ˈmɪθrɑs
Mithridates
BR ˌmɪθrɪˈdeɪtiːz
AM ˌmɪθrəˈdeɪdiz
mithridatic
BR ˌmɪθrɪˈdatɪk
AM ˌmɪθrəˈdeɪdɪk
mithridatise
BR ˈmɪθrɪdeɪtʌɪz, mɪˈθrɪdətʌɪz, -ᵻz, -ɪŋ, -d
AM ˌmɪθrəˈdeɪdaɪz, -ᵻz, -ɪŋ, -d
mithridatism
BR ˈmɪθrɪdeɪtɪz(ə)m, mɪˈθrɪdətɪz(ə)m
AM ˌmɪθrəˈdeɪˌtɪzəm
mithridatize
BR ˈmɪθrɪdeɪtʌɪz, mɪˈθrɪdətʌɪz, -ᵻz, -ɪŋ, -d
AM ˌmɪθrəˈdeɪdaɪz, -ᵻz, -ɪŋ, -d
mitigable
BR ˈmɪtɪɡəbl
AM ˈmɪdəɡəbəl
mitigate
BR ˈmɪtɪɡeɪt, -s, -ɪŋ, -ᵻd
AM ˈmɪdəˌɡeɪ|t, -ts, -dɪŋ, -dᵻd
mitigation
BR ˌmɪtɪˈɡeɪʃn
AM ˌmɪdəˈɡeɪʃən
mitigator
BR ˈmɪtɪɡeɪtə(r), -z
AM ˈmɪdəˌɡeɪdər, -z
mitigatory
BR ˈmɪtɪɡeɪt(ə)ri
AM ˈmɪdəɡəˌtɔri
Mitilíni
BR ˌmiːtɪˈliːni
AM ˌmidɪˈlini
Mitla
BR ˈmɪtlə(*r*)
AM ˈmɪtlə
mitochondria
BR ˌmʌɪtə(ʊ)ˈkɒndrɪə(*r*)
AM ˌmaɪdəˈkɑndriə
mitochondrion
BR ˌmʌɪtə(ʊ)ˈkɒndrɪən
AM ˌmaɪdəˈkɑndriən
mitosis
BR mʌɪˈtəʊsɪs
AM maɪˈtoʊsəs
mitotic
BR mʌɪˈtɒtɪk
AM maɪˈtɑdɪk
mitrailleuse
BR ˌmɪtrʌɪˈəːz, -ᵻz
AM ˌmitrəˈjəz, -əz
mitral
BR ˈmʌɪtr(ə)l
AM ˈmaɪtrəl
mitre
BR ˈmʌɪtə(r), -z, -d
AM ˈmaɪdər, -z, -d
Mitsubishi®
BR ˌmɪtsʊˈbɪʃi
AM ˌmɪtsʊˈbiʃi
mitt
BR mɪt, -s
AM mɪt, -s
mitten
BR mɪtn, -z, -d
AM mɪtn, -z, -d
Mitterrand
BR ˈmɪtərɒ̃
AM ˈmɪtərɑn(d)
mittimus
BR ˈmɪtɪməs, -ᵻz
AM ˈmɪdəməs, -əz
Mitty
BR ˈmɪt|i, -ɪz
AM ˈmɪdi, -z
mity
BR ˈmʌɪti
AM ˈmaɪdi
Mitylene
BR ˌmɪtɪˈliːni, ˌmɪtlˈiːni
AM ˌmɪdɪˈlini
Mitzi
BR ˈmɪtsi
AM ˈmɪtsi
mitzvah
BR ˈmɪtsvə(*r*)
AM ˈmɪtsvə

mitzvoth
BR 'mɪtsvəʊt
AM ˌmɪts'voʊt

mix
BR mɪks, -ɪz, -ɪŋ, -t
AM mɪks, -ɪz, -ɪŋ, -t

mixable
BR 'mɪksəbl
AM 'mɪksəbəl

mixedness
BR 'mɪksɪdnɪs
AM 'mɪksɪdnɪs

mixer
BR 'mɪksə(r), -z
AM 'mɪksər, -z

Mixtec
BR 'miːstɛk, -s
AM 'miˌstɛk, -s

mixture
BR 'mɪkstʃə(r), -z
AM 'mɪk(st)ʃər, -z

mizen
BR 'mɪzn, -z
AM 'mɪzən, -z

mizenmast
BR 'mɪznmɑːst, 'mɪznmast, 'mɪznməst, -s
AM 'mɪzənˌmæst, 'mɪzənməst, -s

mizen-sail
BR 'mɪznseɪl, 'mɪznsl, -z
AM 'mɪzənˌseɪl, 'mɪzənsəl, -z

Mizoram
BR mɪ'zɔːrəm
AM mə'zɔrəm

mizuna
BR mɪ'zuːnə(r)
AM mə'zunə

mizzen
BR 'mɪzn, -z
AM 'mɪzən, -z

mizzenmast
BR 'mɪznmɑːst, 'mɪznmast, 'mɪznməst, -s
AM 'mɪzənˌmæst, 'mɪzənməst, -s

mizzle
BR 'mɪz|l, -lz, -l̩ɪŋ\-lɪŋ, -ld
AM 'mɪz|əl, -əlz, -(ə)lɪŋ, -əld

mizzly
BR 'mɪzli
AM 'mɪzli

M.Litt.
BR ˌɛm 'lɪt, -s
AM ˌɛm 'lɪt, -s

Mlle
Mademoiselle
BR ˌmadəm(w)ə'zɛl, ˌmam(wə)'zɛl, -z
AM ˌmæd(ə)m(w)ə'zɛl, -z

m'lud
BR mə'lʌd, 'mlʌd
AM 'mləd

Mme
Madame
BR mə'dɑːm, 'madəm, -z
AM mə'dɑm, 'mædəm, -z

M.Mus.
Master of Music
BR ˌɛm 'mʌz, -ɪz
AM ˌɛm 'mjuz, -əz

mnemonic
BR nɪ'mɒnɪk, niː'mɒnɪk, -s
AM nə'mɑnɪk, -s

mnemonically
BR nɪ'mɒnɪkli, niː'mɒnɪkli
AM nə'mɑnək(ə)li

mnemonist
BR nɪ'mɒnɪst, 'niːmɒnɪst, -s
AM nə'mɑnəst, -s

Mnemosyne
BR nɪ'mɒzɪni, niː'mɒzɪni, nɪ'mɒsɪni, niː'mɒsɪni
AM nə'mɑsəni, nə'mɑzəni

MO
BR ˌɛm'əʊ, -z
AM ˌɛm'oʊ, -z

mo
BR məʊ
AM moʊ

moa
BR 'məʊə(r), -z
AM 'moʊə, -z

Moab
BR 'məʊab
AM 'moʊæb

Moabite
BR 'məʊəbʌɪt, -s
AM 'moʊəˌbaɪt, -s

moan
BR məʊn, -z, -ɪŋ, -d
AM moʊn, -z, -ɪŋ, -d

moaner
BR 'məʊnə(r), -z
AM 'moʊnər, -z

moanful
BR 'məʊnf(ʊ)l
AM 'moʊnfəl

moaningly
BR 'məʊnɪŋli
AM 'moʊnɪŋli

moat
BR məʊt, -s, -ɪd
AM moʊ|t, -ts, -dəd

mob
BR mɒb, -z, -ɪŋ, -d
AM mɑb, -z, -ɪŋ, -d

mobber
BR 'mɒbə(r), -z
AM 'mɑbər, -z

Mobberley
BR 'mɒbəli
AM 'mɑbərli

mobbish
BR 'mɒbɪʃ
AM 'mɑbɪʃ

Moberly
BR 'məʊbəli
AM 'moʊbərli

Mobil®
BR 'məʊb(ɪ)l
AM 'moʊbəl

Mobile
place in US
BR məʊ'biːl
AM moʊ'bil

mobile
noun
BR 'məʊbʌɪl, -z
AM 'moʊˌbil, -z

mobiliary
BR məʊ'bɪlɪəri
AM moʊ'bɪliˌɛri, moʊ'bɪljəri

mobilisable
BR 'məʊbɪlʌɪzəbl, 'məʊbl̩ʌɪzəbl
AM 'moʊbəˌlaɪzəbəl

mobilisation
BR ˌməʊbɪlʌɪ'zeɪʃn, ˌməʊbl̩ʌɪ'zeɪʃn, -z
AM ˌmoʊbələ'zeɪʃən, ˌmoubəˌlaɪ'zeɪʃən, -z

mobilise
BR 'məʊbɪlʌɪz, 'məʊbl̩ʌɪz, -ɪz, -ɪŋ, -d
AM 'moʊbəˌlaɪz, -ɪz, -ɪŋ, -d

mobiliser
BR 'məʊbɪlʌɪzə(r), 'məʊbl̩ʌɪzə(r), -z
AM 'moʊbəˌlaɪzər, -z

mobility
BR mə(ʊ)'bɪlɪti
AM moʊ'bɪlɪdi

mobilizable
BR 'məʊbɪlʌɪzəbl, 'məʊbl̩ʌɪzəbl
AM 'moʊbəˌlaɪzəbəl

mobilization
BR ˌməʊbɪlʌɪ'zeɪʃn, ˌməʊbl̩ʌɪ'zeɪʃn, -z
AM ˌmoʊbələ'zeɪʃən, ˌmoubəˌlaɪ'zeɪʃən, -z

mobilize
BR 'məʊbɪlʌɪz, 'məʊbl̩ʌɪz, -ɪz, -ɪŋ, -d
AM 'moʊbəˌlaɪz, -ɪz, -ɪŋ, -d

mobilizer
BR 'məʊbɪlʌɪzə(r), 'məʊbl̩ʌɪzə(r), -z
AM 'moʊbəˌlaɪzər, -z

Möbius strip
BR 'məːbɪəs ˌstrɪp, 'məʊbɪəs +
AM 'moʊbiəs ˌstrɪp, 'mibiəs +

mobocracy
BR mɒb'ɒkrəs|i, -ɪz
AM mɑ'bɑkrəsi, -z

mobster
BR 'mɒbstə(r), -z
AM 'mɑbstər, -z

Mobutu
BR mə'buːtuː
AM mə'budu

Moby Dick
BR ˌməʊbɪ 'dɪk
AM ˌmoʊbi 'dɪk

Mocatta
BR mə(ʊ)'katə(r)
AM moʊ'kɑdə

moccasin
BR 'mɒkəsɪn, -z
AM 'mɑkəsən, -z

mocha
BR 'mɒkə(r)
AM 'moʊkə

Mochica
BR mə(ʊ)'tʃiːkə(r)
AM moʊ'tʃikə

mock
BR mɒk, -s, -ɪŋ, -t
AM mɑk, -s, -ɪŋ, -t

mockable
BR 'mɒkəbl
AM 'mɑkəbəl

mocker
BR 'mɒkə(r), -z
AM 'mɑkər, -z

mockery
BR 'mɒk(ə)r|i, -ɪz
AM 'mɑk(ə)ri, -z

mockingbird
BR 'mɒkɪŋbəːd, -z
AM 'mɑkɪŋˌbərd, -z

mockingly
BR 'mɒkɪŋli
AM 'mɑkɪŋli

mod
BR mɒd, -z
AM mɑd, -z

modal
BR 'məʊdl
AM 'moʊdəl

modality
BR mə(ʊ)'dalɪti
AM moʊ'dælədi

modally
BR 'məʊdl̩i, 'məʊdəli
AM 'moʊdli

mod cons
modern conveniences
BR ˌmɒd 'kɒnz
AM ˌmɑd 'kɑnz

mode
BR məʊd, -z
AM moʊd, -z

model
BR 'mɒd|l, -lz, -l̩ɪŋ\-lɪŋ, -ld
AM 'mɑdəl, -əlz, -(ə)lɪŋ, -əld

modeler
BR 'mɒdl̩ə(r), -z
AM 'mad(ə)lər, -z
modeller
BR 'mɒdl̩ə(r), -z
AM 'mad(ə)lər, -z
modem
BR 'məʊdɛm, -z
AM 'moʊdəm, 'moʊ,dɛm, -z
Modena
BR 'mɒdɪnə(r), 'mɒdn̩ə(r)
AM 'moʊdənə
moderate¹
noun, adjective
BR 'mɒd(ə)rət, -s
AM 'mad(ə)rət, -s
moderate²
verb
BR 'mɒdəreɪt, -s, -ɪŋ, -ɪd
AM 'madə,reɪ|t, -ts, -dɪŋ, -dɪd
moderately
BR 'mɒd(ə)rətli
AM 'mad(ə)rətli
moderateness
BR 'mɒd(ə)rətnəs
AM 'mad(ə)rətnəs
moderation
BR ,mɒdə'reɪʃn, -z
AM ,madə'reɪʃən, -z
moderatism
BR 'mɒd(ə)rətɪz(ə)m
AM 'mad(ə)rə,tɪzəm
moderato
BR ,mɒdə'rɑːtəʊ, -z
AM ,madə'radoʊ, -z
moderator
BR 'mɒdəreɪtə(r), -z
AM 'madə,reɪdər, -z
moderatorship
BR 'mɒdəreɪtəʃɪp, -s
AM 'madə,reɪdər,ʃɪp, -s
modern
BR 'mɒdn, -z
AM 'madərn, -z
modernisation
BR ,mɒdənʌɪ'zeɪʃn, ,mɒdn̩ʌɪ'zeɪʃn, -z
AM ,madərnə'zeɪʃən, ,madər,naɪ'zeɪʃən, -z
modernise
BR 'mɒdənʌɪz, 'mɒdn̩ʌɪz, -ɪz, -ɪŋ, -d
AM 'madər,naɪz, -ɪz, -ɪŋ, -d
moderniser
BR 'mɒdənʌɪzə(r), 'mɒdn̩ʌɪzə(r), -z
AM 'madər,naɪzər, -z
modernism
BR 'mɒdn̩ɪz(ə)m, 'mɒdənɪz(ə)m
AM 'madərn,ɪzəm
modernist
BR 'mɒdənɪst, 'mɒdn̩ɪst, -s
AM 'madərnəst, -s
modernistic
BR ,mɒdə'nɪstɪk, ,mɒdn'ɪstɪk
AM ,madər'nɪstɪk
modernistically
BR ,mɒdə'nɪstɪkli, ,mɒdn̩'ɪstɪkli
AM ,madər'nɪstək(ə)li
modernity
BR mə'dəːnɪti
AM ma'dərnədi, mə'dərnədi, ma'dɛrnədi, mə'dɛrnədi
modernization
BR ,mɒdənʌɪ'zeɪʃn, ,mɒdn̩ʌɪ'zeɪʃn, -z
AM ,madərnə'zeɪʃən, ,madər,naɪ'zeɪʃən, -z
modernize
BR 'mɒdənʌɪz, 'mɒdn̩ʌɪz, -ɪz, -ɪŋ, -d
AM 'madər,naɪz, -ɪz, -ɪŋ, -d
modernizer
BR 'mɒdənʌɪzə(r), 'mɒdn̩ʌɪzə(r), -z
AM 'madər,naɪzər, -z
modernly
BR 'mɒdnli
AM 'madərnli
modernness
BR 'mɒdn̩nəs
AM 'madər(n)nəs
modest
BR 'mɒdɪst
AM 'madəst
Modestine
BR 'mɒdɪstiːn, ,mɒdɪ'stiːn
AM 'madə,stin
modestly
BR 'mɒdɪstli
AM 'madəs(t)li
Modesto
BR mɒ'dɛstəʊ
AM mə'dɛstoʊ
modesty
BR 'mɒdɪsti
AM 'madəsti
modicum
BR 'mɒdɪkəm, -z
AM 'madəkəm, -z
modifiable
BR 'mɒdɪfʌɪəbl
AM ,madə'faɪəbəl
modification
BR ,mɒdɪfɪ'keɪʃn, -z
AM ,madəfə'keɪʃən, -z
modificatory
BR ,mɒdɪfɪ'keɪt(ə)ri
AM 'madəfəkə,tɔri, ,madə'fɪkə,tɔri
modifier
BR 'mɒdɪfʌɪə(r), -z
AM 'madə,faɪər, -z
modify
BR 'mɒdɪfʌɪ, -z, -ɪŋ, -d
AM 'madə,faɪ, -z, -ɪŋ, -d
Modigliani
BR ,mɒdɪl'jɑːni
AM ,mɔdil'jani, ,madil'jani
modillion
BR mə(ʊ)'dɪljən, -z
AM moʊ'dɪljən, -z
modi operandi
BR ,məʊdiː ,ɒpə'randiː, ,məʊdʌɪ ,ɒpə'randʌɪ
AM 'moʊ,di ,apə'rændi, 'moʊ,daɪ ,apəræn,daɪ
modish
BR 'məʊdɪʃ
AM 'moʊdɪʃ, 'madɪʃ
modishly
BR 'məʊdɪʃli
AM 'moʊdɪʃli, 'madɪʃli
modishness
BR 'məʊdɪʃnɪs
AM 'moʊdɪʃnɪs, 'madɪʃnɪs
modiste
BR məʊ'diːst, -s
AM moʊ'dist, -s
modi vivendi
BR ,məʊdiː vɪ'vɛndiː, ,məʊdʌɪ vɪ'vɛndʌɪ
AM 'moʊ,di və'vɛndi, 'moʊ,daɪ və'vɛn,daɪ
Mods
BR mɒdz
AM madz
modular
BR 'mɒdjʉlə(r), 'mɒdʒʉlə(r)
AM 'madʒələr
modularisation
BR ,mɒdjʉlərʌɪ'zeɪʃn, ,mɒdʒʉlərʌɪ'zeɪʃn
AM ,madʒələrə'zeɪʃən, ,madʒələ,raɪ'zeɪʃən
modularise
BR 'mɒdjʉlərʌɪz, 'mɒdʒʉlərʌɪz, -ɪz, -ɪŋ, -d
AM 'madʒələ,raɪz, -ɪz, -ɪŋ, -d
modularity
BR ,mɒdjʉ'larɪti, ,mɒdʒʉ'larɪti
AM ,madʒə'lɛrədi
modularization
BR ,mɒdjʉlərʌɪ'zeɪʃn, ,mɒdʒʉlərʌɪ'zeɪʃn
AM ,madʒələrə'zeɪʃən, ,madʒələ,raɪ'zeɪʃən
modularize
BR 'mɒdjʉlərʌɪz, 'mɒdʒʉlərʌɪz, -ɪz, -ɪŋ, -d
AM 'madʒələ,raɪz, -ɪz, -ɪŋ, -d
modulate
BR 'mɒdjʉleɪt, 'mɒdʒʉleɪt, -s, -ɪŋ, -ɪd
AM 'madʒə,leɪ|t, -ts, -dɪŋ, -dɪd
modulation
BR ,mɒdjʉ'leɪʃn, ,mɒdʒʉ'leɪʃn, -z
AM ,madʒə'leɪʃən, -z
modulator
BR 'mɒdjʉleɪtə(r), 'mɒdʒʉleɪtə(r), -z
AM 'madʒə,leɪdər, -z
module
BR 'mɒdjuːl, 'mɒdʒuːl, -z
AM 'madʒul, -z
moduli
BR 'mɒdjʉlʌɪ, 'mɒdʒʉlʌɪ, 'mɒdjʉliː, 'mɒdʒʉliː
AM 'madʒə,laɪ
modulo
BR 'mɒdjʉləʊ, 'mɒdʒʉləʊ
AM 'madʒə,loʊ
modulus
BR 'mɒdjʉləs, 'mɒdʒʉləs
AM 'madʒələs
modus operandi
BR ,məʊdəs ,ɒpə'randiː, + ,ɒpə'randʌɪ
AM 'moʊdəs ,apə'rændi, + ,apəræn,daɪ
modus vivendi
BR ,məʊdəs vɪ'vɛndiː, + vɪ'vɛndʌɪ
AM 'moʊdəs və'vɛndi, + və'vɛn,daɪ
Moesia
BR 'miːsɪə(r), 'miːzɪə(r)
AM 'miziə, 'miʃiə
mofette
BR mɒ'fɛt, -s
AM moʊ'fɛt, -s
Moffat
BR 'mɒfət
AM 'mafət
Moffatt
BR 'mɒfət
AM 'mafət
mog
BR mɒɡ, -z
AM maɡ, -z
Mogadishu
BR ,mɒɡə'dɪʃuː
AM ,moʊɡə'diʃu, ,maɡə'diʃu

Mogadon®
BR ˈmɒɡədɒn, -z
AM ˈmɑɡədn, ˈmɑɡəˌdɑn, -z
Mogen David
BR ˌməʊɡ(ə)n ˈdeɪvɪd
AM ˌmoʊɡən ˈdeɪvɨd
Mogford
BR ˈmɒɡfəd
AM ˈmɑɡfərd
Mogg
BR mɒɡ
AM mɑɡ
moggie
BR ˈmɒɡ|i, -ɪz
AM ˈmɑɡi, -z
moggy
BR ˈmɒɡ|i, -ɪz
AM ˈmɑɡi, -z
mogul
BR ˈməʊɡl, -z
AM ˈmoʊɡəl, -z
mohair
BR ˈməʊhɛː(r)
AM ˈmoʊˌhɛ(ə)r
Mohammed
BR mə(ʊ)ˈhamɪd
AM moʊˈhɑməd
Mohammedan
BR mə(ʊ)ˈhamɪd(ə)n, -z
AM moʊˈhɑmədən, -z
Mohammedanism
BR mə(ʊ)ˈhamɪdən-ɪz(ə)m, mə(ʊ)ˈhamɪdn̩ɪz(ə)m
AM moʊˈhɑmədnˌɪzəm, moʊˈhɑmədəˌnɪzəm
Mohave
BR məˈhɑːv|i, -ɪz
AM moʊˈhɑvi, məˈhɑvi, -z
mohawk
BR ˈməʊhɔːk, -s
AM ˈmoʊˌhɔk, ˈmoʊˌhɑk, -s
Mohican
BR mə(ʊ)ˈhiːk(ə)n, -z
AM moʊˈhikən, -z
Moho
BR ˈməʊhəʊ
AM ˈmoʊˌhoʊ
Mohock
BR ˈməʊhɒk, -s
AM ˈmoʊˌhɑk, -s
Mohole
BR ˈməʊhəʊl
AM ˈmoʊˌhoʊl
Mohs
BR məʊ(z)
AM moʊ(s)
moidore
BR ˈmɔɪdɔː(r), ˌmɔɪˈdɔː(r), -z
AM ˈmɔɪdɔ(ə)r, -z
moiety
BR ˈmɔɪɪt|i, -ɪz
AM ˈmɔɪədi, -z
moil
BR mɔɪl, -z, -ɪŋ, -d
AM mɔɪl, -z, -ɪŋ, -d
Moir
BR ˈmɔɪə(r)
AM ˈmɔɪər
Moira
BR ˈmɔɪrə(r)
AM ˈmɔɪrə
moire
BR mwɑː(r)
AM mwɑr
moiré
BR ˈmwɑːreɪ
AM mɔˈreɪ, mwɑˈreɪ, mɑˈreɪ
moist
BR mɔɪst, -ə(r), -ɨst
AM mɔɪst, -ər, -ɨst
moisten
BR ˈmɔɪs|n, -nz, -n̩ɪŋ\-nɪŋ, -nd
AM ˈmɔɪs|n, -nz, -(ə)nɪŋ, -nd
moistly
BR ˈmɔɪstli
AM ˈmɔɪs(t)li
moistness
BR ˈmɔɪs(t)nɨs
AM ˈmɔɪs(t)nɨs
moisture
BR ˈmɔɪstʃə(r)
AM ˈmɔɪstʃər
moistureless
BR ˈmɔɪstʃələs
AM ˈmɔɪstʃərləs
moisturise
BR ˈmɔɪstʃərʌɪz, -ɪz, -ɪŋ, -d
AM ˈmɔɪstʃəˌraɪz, -ɨz, -ɪŋ, -d
moisturiser
BR ˈmɔɪstʃərʌɪzə(r), -z
AM ˈmɔɪstʃəˌraɪzər, -z
moisturize
BR ˈmɔɪstʃərʌɪz, -ɪz, -ɪŋ, -d
AM ˈmɔɪstʃəˌraɪz, -ɨz, -ɪŋ, -d
moisturizer
BR ˈmɔɪstʃərʌɪzə(r), -z
AM ˈmɔɪstʃəˌraɪzər, -z
Mojave
BR mə(ʊ)ˈhɑːvi
AM moʊˈhɑvi, məˈhɑvi
moke
BR məʊk, -s
AM moʊk, -s
moko
BR ˈməʊkəʊ, -z
AM ˈmoʊˌkoʊ, -z
moksha
BR ˈmɒkʃə(r)
AM ˈmɑkʃə
mol
BR məʊl
AM moʊl
molal
BR ˈməʊləl
AM ˈmoʊləl
molality
BR mə(ʊ)ˈlalɪt|i, -ɪz
AM moʊˈlælədi, -z
molar
BR ˈməʊlə(r), -z
AM ˈmoʊlər, -z
molarity
BR mə(ʊ)ˈlarɪt|i, -ɪz
AM moʊˈlɛrədi, -z
molasses
BR mə(ʊ)ˈlasɪz
AM məˈlæsəz
mold
BR məʊld, -z
AM moʊld, -z
Moldau
BR ˈmɒldaʊ
AM ˈmɔlˌdaʊ, ˈmoʊlˌdaʊ
Moldavia
BR mɒlˈdeɪvɪə(r)
AM mɑlˈdeɪviə, mɔlˈdeɪviə, moʊlˈdeɪviə
Moldavian
BR mɒlˈdeɪvɪən, -z
AM mɑlˈdeɪviən, mɔlˈdeɪviən, moʊlˈdeɪviən, -z
moldboard
BR ˈməʊl(d)bɔːd, -z
AM ˈmoʊl(d)ˌbɔ(ə)rd, -z
molder
BR ˈməʊld|ə(r), -əz, -(ə)rɪŋ, -əd
AM ˈmoʊldər, -z, -ɪŋ, -d
moldiness
BR ˈməʊldɪnɪs
AM ˈmoʊldinɨs
molding
BR ˈməʊldɪŋ, -z
AM ˈmoʊldɪŋ, -z
Moldova
BR mɒlˈdəʊvə(r)
AM mɑlˈdoʊvə, mɔlˈdoʊvə, moʊlˈdoʊvə
moldy
BR ˈməʊld|i, -ɪə(r), -ɪɪst
AM ˈmoʊldi, -ər, -ɨst
mole
BR məʊl, -z
AM moʊl, -z
molecular
BR məˈlɛkjʉlə(r)
AM məˈlɛkjələr
molecularity
BR məˌlɛkjʉˈlarɪti
AM məˌlɛkjəˈlɛrədi
molecularly
BR məˈlɛkjʉləli
AM məˈlɛkjələrli
molecule
BR ˈmɒlɪkjuːl, -z
AM ˈmɑləˌkjul, -z
molehill
BR ˈməʊlhɪl, -z
AM ˈmoʊlˌ(h)ɪl, -z
Molesey
BR ˈməʊlzi
AM ˈmoʊlzi
moleskin
BR ˈməʊlskɪn
AM ˈmoʊlˌskɪn
molest
BR məˈlɛst, -s, -ɪŋ, -ɨd
AM məˈlɛst, -s, -ɪŋ, -əd
molestation
BR ˌməʊlɛˈsteɪʃn, məʊlɪˈsteɪʃn, mɒlɛˈsteɪʃn, mɒlɪˈsteɪʃn
AM ˌmoʊˌlɛˈsteɪʃən, ˌmoʊləˈsteɪʃən
molester
BR məˈlɛstə(r), -z
AM məˈlɛstər, -z
Molesworth
BR ˈməʊlzwəːθ
AM ˈmoʊlzˌwərθ
Molière
BR ˈmɒlɪɛː(r)
AM mɔlˈjɛ(ə)r
Moline
BR məʊˈliːn
AM moʊˈlin
moline
BR məˈlʌɪn
AM ˈmoʊlən, moʊˈlaɪn
moll
BR mɒl, -z
AM mɑl, -z
Mollie
BR ˈmɒli
AM ˈmɑli
mollification
BR ˌmɒlɪfɪˈkeɪʃn
AM ˌmɑləfəˈkeɪʃən
mollifier
BR ˈmɒlɪfʌɪə(r), -z
AM ˈmɑləˌfaɪər, -z
mollify
BR ˈmɒlɪfʌɪ, -z, -ɪŋ, -d
AM ˈmɑləˌfaɪ, -z, -ɪŋ, -d
Molloy
BR məˈlɔɪ
AM məˈlɔɪ
mollusc
BR ˈmɒləsk, -s
AM ˈmɑləsk, -s
molluscan
BR məˈlʌsk(ə)n
AM məˈləskən
molluscoid
BR məˈlʌskɔɪd
AM məˈləsˌkɔɪd
molluscous
BR məˈlʌskəs
AM məˈləskəs
mollusk
BR ˈmɒləsk, -s

AM ˈmɑləsk, -s

molly
BR ˈmɒl|i, -ɪz
AM ˈmɑli, -z

mollycoddle
BR ˈmɒlɪˌkɒd|l, -lz, -l̩ɪŋ\-lɪŋ, -ld
AM ˈmɑliˌkɑd|əl, -əlz, -(ə)lɪŋ, -əld

mollymawk
BR ˈmɒlɪmɔːk, -s
AM ˈmɑliˌmɔk, ˈmɑliˌmɑk, -s

moloch
BR ˈməʊlɒk, -s
AM ˈmɑlək, -s

Moloney
BR məˈləʊni
AM məˈloʊni

Molony
BR məˈləʊni
AM məˈloʊni

molossi
BR məˈlɒsʌɪ
AM məˈlɑˌsaɪ

molossus
BR məˈlɒsəs
AM məˈlɑsəs

Molotov
BR ˈmɒlətɒf, ˈmɒlətɒv
AM ˈmɑləˌtɔf, ˈmoʊləˌtɔv, ˈmɑləˌtɑf, ˈmoʊləˌtɑv

molt
BR məʊlt, -s, -ɪŋ, -ɪd
AM moʊlt, -s, -ɪŋ, -əd

molten
BR ˈməʊlt(ə)n
AM ˈmoʊlt(ə)n

molto
BR ˈmɒltəʊ
AM ˈmoʊlˌtoʊ, ˈmɔlˌtoʊ

Molton
BR ˈməʊlt(ə)n
AM ˈmoʊlt(ə)n

Moluccas
BR məˈlʌkəz
AM məˈləkəz

moly
BR ˈməʊl|i, -ɪz
AM ˈmoʊli, -z

molybdate
BR məˈlɪbdeɪt
AM məˈlɪbdeɪt

molybdenite
BR məˈlɪbdənʌɪt, -s
AM məˈlɪbdəˌnaɪt, -s

molybdenum
BR məˈlɪbdənəm
AM məˈlɪbdənəm

molybdic
BR məˈlɪbdɪk
AM məˈlɪbdɪk

Molyneaux
BR ˈmɒlɪnəʊ
AM ˈmɑlənoʊ

Molyneux
BR ˈmɒlɪnjuː
AM ˈmɑlənju

mom
BR mɒm, -z
AM mɑm, -z

mom-and-pop
BR ˌmɒm(ə)n(d)ˈpɒp
AM ˈ¦mɑmənˈpɑp

Mombasa
BR mɒmˈbasə(r)
AM mɑmˈbɑsə

moment
BR ˈməʊm(ə)nt, -s
AM ˈmoʊmənt, -s

momenta
BR mə(ʊ)ˈmɛntə(r)
AM moʊˈmɛn(t)ə

momentarily
BR ˈməʊm(ə)nt(ə)rɪli, ˌməʊm(ə)nˈtɛrɪli
AM ˌmoʊmənˈtɛrəli

momentariness
BR ˈməʊm(ə)nt(ə)rɪnɪs
AM ˈmoʊmənˌtɛrinɪs

momentary
BR ˈməʊm(ə)nt(ə)ri
AM ˈmoʊmənˌtɛri

momently
BR ˈməʊm(ə)ntli
AM ˈmoʊmən(t)li

momentous
BR məˈmɛntəs
AM moʊˈmɛn(t)əs, məˈmɛn(t)əs

momentously
BR məˈmɛntəsli
AM moʊˈmɛn(t)əsli, məˈmɛn(t)əsli

momentousness
BR məˈmɛntəsnəs
AM moʊˈmɛn(t)əsnəs, məˈmɛn(t)əsnəs

momentum
BR mə(ʊ)ˈmɛntəm
AM moʊˈmɛn(t)əm, məˈmɛn(t)əm

Momi
BR ˈməʊmʌɪ
AM ˈmoʊˌmaɪ

momma
BR ˈmɒmə(r), -z
AM ˈmɑmə, -z

Mommsen
BR ˈmɒms(ə)n
AM ˈmɑmsən

mommy
BR ˈmɒm|i, -ɪz
AM ˈmɑmi, -z

Momus
BR ˈməʊməs, -ɪz
AM ˈmoʊməs, -əz

Mon
BR məʊn, mɒn
AM moʊn

Mona
BR ˈməʊnə(r
AM ˈmoʊnə

monacal
BR ˈmɒnəkl
AM ˈmɑnəkəl

Monacan
BR ˈmɒnək(ə)n, məˈnɑːk(ə)n, -z
AM ˈmɑnəkən, -z

monachal
BR ˈmɒnəkl
AM ˈmɑnəkəl

monachism
BR ˈmɒnəkɪz(ə)m
AM ˈmɑnəˌkɪzəm

Monaco
BR ˈmɒnəkəʊ, məˈnɑːkəʊ
AM ˈmɑnəkoʊ

monad
BR ˈmɒnad, ˈməʊnad, -z
AM ˈmoʊˌnæd, -z

monadelphous
BR ˌmɒnəˈdɛlfəs
AM ˈ¦mɑnəˈ¦dɛlfəs

monadic
BR mɒˈnadɪk, mə(ʊ)ˈnadɪk
AM moʊˈnædɪk

monadism
BR ˈmɒnədɪz(ə)m, ˈməʊnədɪz(ə)m
AM ˈmoʊnædˌɪzəm

monadnock
BR məˈnadnɒk, -s
AM məˈnædˌnɑk, -s

Monaghan
BR ˈmɒnəhən
AM ˈmɑnəˌhæn, ˈmɑnəgən

Monahan
BR ˈmɒnəhən
AM ˈmɑnəˌhæn

monandrous
BR mɒˈnandrəs, məˈnandrəs
AM məˈnændrəs

monandry
BR mɒˈnandri, məˈnandri
AM məˈnændri

monarch
BR ˈmɒnək, -s
AM ˈmɑnərk, ˈmɑˌnɑrk, -s

monarchal
BR məˈnɑːkl
AM məˈnɑrkəl

monarchial
BR məˈnɑːkɪəl
AM məˈnɑrkiəl

monarchic
BR məˈnɑːkɪk
AM məˈnɑrkɪk

monarchical
BR məˈnɑːkɪkl
AM məˈnɑrkəkəl

monarchically
BR məˈnɑːkɪkli
AM məˈnɑrkək(ə)li

monarchism
BR ˈmɒnəkɪz(ə)m
AM ˈmɑnərˌkɪzəm

monarchist
BR ˈmɒnəkɪst, -s
AM ˈmɑnərkəst, -s

monarchy
BR ˈmɒnək|i, -ɪz
AM ˈmɑnərki, -z

Monash
BR ˈmɒnaʃ
AM ˈmoʊˌnæʃ

monastery
BR ˈmɒnəst(ə)r|i, -ɪz
AM ˈmɑnəˌstɛri, -z

monastic
BR məˈnastɪk
AM məˈnæstɪk

monastically
BR məˈnastɪkli
AM məˈnæstək(ə)li

monasticise
BR məˈnastɪsʌɪz, -ɪz, -ɪŋ, -d
AM məˈnæstəˌsaɪz, -ɪz, -ɪŋ, -d

monasticism
BR məˈnastɪsɪz(ə)m
AM məˈnæstəˌsɪzəm

monasticize
BR məˈnastɪsʌɪz, -ɪz, -ɪŋ, -d
AM məˈnæstəˌsaɪz, -ɪz, -ɪŋ, -d

Monastir
BR ˌmɒnəˈstɪə(r)
AM ˈmɔnəˌstɪ(ə)r, ˈmɑnəˌstɪ(ə)r

monatomic
BR ˌmɒnəˈtɒmɪk
AM ˌmɑnəˈtɑmɪk

monaural
BR ˌmɒnˈɔːrəl, ˌmɒnˈɔːrl̩
AM ˌmɑnˈɔrəl

monaurally
BR ˌmɒnˈɔːrəli, ˌmɒnˈɔːrl̩i
AM ˌmɑnˈɔrəli

monazite
BR ˈmɒnəzʌɪt, -s
AM ˈmɑnəˌzaɪt, -s

Monck
BR mʌŋk
AM məŋk

Monckton
BR ˈmʌŋ(k)t(ə)n
AM ˈməŋ(k)tən

Moncreiff
BR mɒnˈkriːf, mənˈkriːf
AM ˈmɑnˌkrif

Moncrieff
BR mɒnˈkriːf, mənˈkriːf

AM 'mɑn,krif

Moncton
BR 'mʌŋ(k)t(ə)n
AM 'məŋ(k)tən

mondaine
BR 'mɒndeɪn, -z
AM ,mɑn'deɪn, -z

Mondale
BR 'mɒndeɪl
AM 'mɑn,deɪl

Monday
BR 'mʌnd|eɪ, 'mʌnd|i, -eɪz\-ɪz
AM 'mən,deɪ, 'məndi, -z

mondial
BR 'mɒndɪəl
AM 'mɑndiəl

Mondriaan
BR 'mɒndrɪən
AM 'mɔndri,ɑn, 'mɔndriən, 'mɑndri,ɑn, 'mɑndriən

monecious
BR mɒ'niːʃəs, mə'niːʃəs
AM mə'niʃəs

Monégasque
BR ,mɒnɪ'gask, -s
AM ,mɑnə'gɑsk, -s

Monel®
BR 'məʊn(ə)l, -z
AM moʊ'nɛl, -z

moneme
BR 'mɒniːm, 'məʊniːm, -z
AM 'moʊ,nim, -z

Monet
BR 'mɒneɪ
AM ,moʊ'neɪ

monetarily
BR 'mʌnɪt(ə)rɪli
AM ¦mɑnə¦tɛrəli

monetarism
BR 'mʌnɪt(ə)rɪz(ə)m
AM 'mɑnədə,rɪzəm

monetarist
BR 'mʌnɪt(ə)rɪst, -s
AM 'mɑnədərəst, -s

monetary
BR 'mʌnɪt(ə)ri
AM 'mɑnə,tɛri

monetisation
BR ,mʌnɪtʌɪ'zeɪʃn
AM ,mɑnədə'zeɪʃən, ,mɑnə,taɪ'zeɪʃən

monetise
BR 'mʌnɪtʌɪz, -ɪz, -ɪŋ, -d
AM 'mɑnə,taɪz, -ɪz, -ɪŋ, -d

monetization
BR ,mʌnɪtʌɪ'zeɪʃn
AM ,mɑnədə'zeɪʃən, ,mɑnə,taɪ'zeɪʃən

monetize
BR 'mʌnɪtʌɪz, -ɪz, -ɪŋ, -d
AM 'mɑnə,taɪz, -ɪz, -ɪŋ, -d

money
BR 'mʌn|i, -ɪz, -d
AM 'məni, -z, -d

moneybags
BR 'mʌnɪbagz
AM 'məni,bægz

moneybox
BR 'mʌnɪbɒks, -ɪz
AM 'məni,bɑks, -əz

moneychanger
BR 'mʌnɪ,tʃeɪn(d)ʒə(r), -z
AM 'məni,tʃeɪndʒər, -z

moneyer
BR 'mʌnɪə(r), -z
AM 'məniər, -z

moneylender
BR 'mʌnɪ,lɛndə(r), -z
AM 'məni,lɛndər, -z

moneylending
BR 'mʌnɪ,lɛndɪŋ
AM 'məni,lɛndɪŋ

moneyless
BR 'mʌnɪlɪs
AM 'mənilɪs

moneymaker
BR 'mʌnɪ,meɪkə(r), -z
AM 'məni,meɪkər, -z

moneymaking
BR 'mʌnɪ,meɪkɪŋ
AM 'məni,meɪkɪŋ

moneywort
BR 'mʌnɪwəːt
AM 'məniwərt, 'məniwɔ(ə)rt

monger
BR 'mʌŋg|ə(r), -əz, -(ə)rɪŋ
AM 'mɑŋg|ər, 'məŋg|ər, -ərz, -(ə)rɪŋ

mongo
BR 'mɒŋgəʊ, -z
AM 'mɑŋgoʊ, -z

Mongol
BR 'mɒŋgl, -z
AM 'mɑŋgəl, 'mɑŋ,goʊl, -z

Mongolia
BR mɒŋ'gəʊlɪə(r)
AM mɑŋ'goʊljə, mɑŋ'goʊliə

Mongolian
BR mɒŋ'gəʊlɪən, -z
AM mɑŋ'goʊljən, mɑŋ'goʊliən, -z

mongolism
BR 'mɒŋgəlɪz(ə)m
AM 'mɑŋgə,lɪzəm

mongoloid
BR 'mɒŋgəlɔɪd, -z
AM 'mɑŋgə,lɔɪd, -z

mongoose
BR 'mɒŋguːs, -ɪz
AM 'mɑŋ,gus, -əz

mongrel
BR 'mʌŋgr(ə)l, -z
AM 'mɑŋgrəl, 'məŋgrəl, -z

mongrelisation
BR ,mʌŋgrəlʌɪ'zeɪʃn, ,mʌŋgr̩lʌɪ'zeɪʃn, -z
AM ,mɑŋgrələ'zeɪʃən, ,məŋgrələ'zeɪʃən, ,məŋgrə,laɪ'zeɪʃən, ,mɑŋgrə,laɪ'zeɪʃən, -z

mongrelise
BR 'mʌŋgrəlʌɪz, 'mʌŋgr̩lʌɪz, -ɪz, -ɪŋ, -d
AM 'mɑŋgrə,laɪz, 'məŋgrə,laɪz, -ɪz, -ɪŋ, -d

mongrelism
BR 'mʌŋgrəlɪz(ə)m, 'mʌŋgr̩lɪz(ə)m
AM 'mɑŋgrə,lɪzəm, 'məŋgrə,lɪzəm

mongrelization
BR ,mʌŋgrəlʌɪ'zeɪʃn, ,mʌŋgr̩lʌɪ'zeɪʃn, -z
AM ,mɑŋgrələ'zeɪʃən, ,məŋgrələ'zeɪʃən, ,məŋgrə,laɪ'zeɪʃən, ,mɑŋgrə,laɪ'zeɪʃən, -z

mongrelize
BR 'mʌŋgrəlʌɪz, 'mʌŋgr̩lʌɪz, -ɪz, -ɪŋ, -d
AM 'mɑŋgrə,laɪz, 'məŋgrə,laɪz, -ɪz, -ɪŋ, -d

mongrelly
BR 'mʌŋgrəli, 'mʌŋgr̩li
AM 'mɑŋgrəli, 'məŋgrəli

'mongst
BR mʌŋst
AM məŋst

monial
BR 'məʊnɪəl, -z
AM 'moʊniəl, -z

Monica
BR 'mɒnɪkə(r)
AM 'mɑnɪkə

monicker
BR 'mɒnɪkə(r), -z
AM 'mɑnəkər, -z

monies
BR 'mʌnɪz
AM 'məniz

moniker
BR 'mɒnɪkə(r), -z
AM 'mɑnəkər, -z

moniliform
BR mə'nɪlɪfɔːm
AM mə'nɪlə,fɔ(ə)rm

Monique
BR mɒ'niːk
AM mə'nik, moʊ'nik

monism
BR 'mɒnɪz(ə)m
AM 'mɑ,nɪzəm, 'moʊ,nɪzəm

monist
BR 'mɒnɪst, -s
AM 'mɑnəst, 'moʊnəst, -s

monistic
BR mɒ'nɪstɪk, mə'nɪstɪk
AM mə'nɪstɪk, moʊ'nɪstɪk

monition
BR mɒ'nɪʃn, mə'nɪʃn, -z
AM mə'nɪʃən, -z

monitor
BR 'mɒnɪt|ə(r), -əz, -(ə)rɪŋ, -əd
AM 'mɑnə|dər, -dərz, -dərɪŋ\-trɪŋ, -dərd

monitorial
BR ,mɒnɪ'tɔːrɪəl
AM ¦mɑnə'tɔriəl

monitorship
BR 'mɒnɪtəʃɪp, -s
AM 'mɑnədər,ʃɪp, -s

monitory
BR 'mɒnɪt(ə)r|i, -ɪz
AM 'mɑnə,tɔri, -z

monk
BR mʌŋk, -s
AM məŋk, -s

monkery
BR 'mʌŋk(ə)ri
AM 'məŋkəri

monkey
BR 'mʌŋk|i, -ɪz, -ɪɪŋ, -ɪd
AM 'məŋki, -z, -ɪŋ, -d

monkeyish
BR 'mʌŋkɪɪʃ
AM 'məŋkiɪʃ

monkeyshine
BR 'mʌŋkɪʃʌɪn, -z
AM 'məŋki,ʃaɪn, -z

monkfish
BR 'mʌŋkfɪʃ
AM 'məŋk,fɪʃ

Mon-Khmer
BR ,məʊn'kmɛː(r), ,mɒn'kmɛː(r), ,məʊnkə'mɛː(r), ,mɒnkə'mɛː(r)
AM 'moʊnkə'mɛ(ə)r

monkhood
BR 'mʌŋkhʊd
AM 'məŋk,(h)ʊd

Monkhouse
BR 'mʌŋkhaʊs
AM 'məŋk,(h)aʊs

monkish
BR 'mʌŋkɪʃ
AM 'məŋkɪʃ

monkishly
BR 'mʌŋkɪʃli
AM 'məŋkɪʃli

monkishness
BR 'mʌŋkɪʃnɪs
AM 'məŋkɪʃnɪs

Monks
BR mʌŋks
AM məŋks

monkshood
BR 'mʌŋkshʊd
AM 'məŋks,(h)ʊd

Monkton
BR ˈmʌŋ(k)t(ə)n
AM ˈməŋ(k)tən
Monmouth
BR ˈmɒnməθ, ˈmʌnməθ
AM ˈmɑnməθ
Monmouthshire
BR ˈmɒnməθʃ(ɪ)ə(r), ˈmʌnməθʃ(ɪ)ə(r)
AM ˈmɑnməθʃɪ(ə)r
monniker
BR ˈmɒnɨkə(r), -z
AM ˈmɑnəkər, -z
Mono
lake in US
BR ˈməʊnəʊ
AM ˈmoʊnoʊ
mono
BR ˈmɒnəʊ
AM ˈmɑnoʊ
monoacid
BR ˈmɒnəʊˌasɨd
AM ¦mɑnoʊˈæsəd
monobasic
BR ˌmɒnə(ʊ)ˈbeɪsɪk
AM ¦mɑnoʊˈbeɪsɪk
monocarpic
BR ˌmɒnə(ʊ)ˈkɑːpɪk
AM ¦mɑnoʊˈkɑrpɪk
monocarpous
BR ˌmɒnə(ʊ)ˈkɑːpəs
AM ¦mɑnoʊˈkɑrpəs
monocausal
BR ˌmɒnə(ʊ)ˈkɔːzl
AM ¦mɑnoʊˈkɔzəl, ¦mɑnoʊˈkɑzəl
monocephalous
BR ˌmɒnə(ʊ)ˈsɛfələs, ˌmɒnə(ʊ)ˈsɛfl̩əs, ˌmɒnə(ʊ)ˈkɛfələs, ˌmɒnə(ʊ)ˈkɛfl̩əs
AM ¦mɑnoʊˈsɛfələs
Monoceros
BR məˈnɒs(ə)rəs
AM məˈnɑsərəs
monochasia
BR ˌmɒnəˈkeɪzɪə(*r*)
AM ˌmɑnəˈkeɪziə, ˌmɑnəˈkeɪʒə
monochasium
BR ˌmɒnəˈkeɪzɪəm
AM ˌmɑnəˈkeɪziəm
monochord
BR ˈmɒnə(ʊ)kɔːd, -z
AM ˈmɑnoʊˌkɔ(ə)rd, -z
monochromatic
BR ˌmɒnə(ʊ)krəˈmatɪk
AM ¦mɑnoʊkrəˈmædɪk
monochromatic-ally
BR ˌmɒnə(ʊ)krəˈmat-ɨkli
AM ¦mɑnoʊkrəˈmæd-ək(ə)li
monochromatism
BR ˌmɒnə(ʊ)ˈkrəʊmət-ɪz(ə)m
AM ¦mɑnəˈkroʊməˌtɪz-əm
monochromator
BR ˈmɒnə(ʊ)krəmeɪ-tə(r), ˌmɒnə(ʊ)ˈkrɒmɨtə(r), -z
AM ˌmɑnəˈkroʊmeɪ-də(r), ˈmɑnəˌkroʊmeɪdər, -z
monochrome
BR ˈmɒnə(ʊ)krəʊm, ˌmɒnə(ʊ)ˈkrəʊm
AM ¦mɑnəˌkroʊm
monochromic
BR ˌmɒnə(ʊ)ˈkrəʊmɪk
AM ˌmɑnəˈkroʊmɪk
monocle
BR ˈmɒnəkl, -z, -d
AM ˈmɑnəkəl, -z, -d
monoclinal
BR ˌmɒnə(ʊ)ˈklʌɪnl
AM ¦mɑnəˈklaɪnəl
monocline
BR ˈmɒnə(ʊ)klʌɪn, -z
AM ˈmɑnəˌklaɪn, -z
monoclinic
BR ˌmɒnə(ʊ)ˈklɪnɪk
AM ¦mɑnəˈklɪnɪk
monoclonal
BR ˌmɒnə(ʊ)ˈkləʊnl
AM ¦mɑnəˈkloʊnəl
monocoque
BR ˈmɒnə(ʊ)kɒk, -s
AM ˈmɑnəˌkɑk, -s
FR mɔnɔcɔk
monocot
BR ˈmɒnə(ʊ)kɒt, -s
AM ˈmɑnəˌkɑt, -s
monocotyledon
BR ˌmɒnə(ʊ)ˌkɒtɪˈliːdn, -z
AM ¦mɑnəˌkɑdlˈidn, -z
monocotyledon-ous
BR ˌmɒnə(ʊ)ˌkɒtɪˈliːdə-nəs
AM ¦mɑnə¦kɑdlˈid(ə)nəs
monocracy
BR mɒˈnɒkrəsi, məˈnɒkrəs|i, -ɪz
AM məˈnɑkrəsi, -z
monocratic
BR ˌmɒnə(ʊ)ˈkratɪk
AM ¦mɑnəˈkrædɪk
monocrotic
BR ˌmɒnə(ʊ)ˈkrɒtɪk
AM ¦mɑnəˈkrɑdɪk
monocular
BR mɒˈnɒkjʉlə(r), məˈnɒkjʉlə(r)
AM məˈnɑkjələr
monocularly
BR mɒˈnɒkjʉləli, məˈnɒkjʉləli
AM məˈnɑkjələrli
monoculture
BR ˈmɒnə(ʊ)ˌkʌltʃə(r)
AM ˈmɑnəˌkəltʃər
monocycle
BR ˈmɒnə(ʊ)ˌsʌɪkl, -z
AM ˈmɑnəˌsaɪkəl, -z
monocyte
BR ˈmɒnə(ʊ)sʌɪt, -s
AM ˈmɑnəˌsaɪt, -s
monodactylous
BR ˌmɒnə(ʊ)ˈdaktɨləs, ˌmɒnə(ʊ)ˈdaktl̩əs
AM ¦mɑnəˈdæktl̩əs
monodic
BR mɒˈnɒdɪk, məˈnɒdɪk
AM məˈnɑdɪk
monodisperse
BR ˌmɒnə(ʊ)ˈdɪspəːs
AM ˌmɑnədɪsˈpərs
monodist
BR ˈmɒnədɪst, -s
AM ˈmɑnədəst, -s
monodrama
BR ˈmɒnə(ʊ)ˌdrɑːmə(*r*), ˌmɒnə(ʊ)ˈdrɑːmə(*r*), -z
AM ¦mɑnoʊˈdrɑmə, -z
monody
BR ˈmɒnəd|i, -ɪz
AM ˈmɑnədi, -z
monoecious
BR mɒˈniːʃəs, məˈniːʃəs
AM məˈniʃəs
monofil
BR ˈmɒnə(ʊ)fɪl
AM ˈmɑnəˌfɪl
monofilament
BR ˈmɒnə(ʊ)ˌfɪləm(ə)nt
AM ˌmɑnəˈfɪləmənt
monogamist
BR məˈnɒgəmɪst, mɒˈnɒgəmɪst, -s
AM məˈnɑgəˌməst, -s
monogamous
BR məˈnɒgəməs, mɒˈnɒgəməs
AM məˈnɑgəməs
monogamously
BR məˈnɒgəməsli, mɒˈnɒgəməsli
AM məˈnɑgəməsli
monogamy
BR məˈnɒgəmi, mɒˈnɒgəmi
AM məˈnɑgəmi
monogenean
BR ˌmɒnə(ʊ)dʒɪˈniːən, ˌmɒnə(ʊ)ˈdʒɛnɪən
AM ˌmɑnədʒəˈniən, ˌmɑnəˈdʒɛniən
monogenesis
BR ˌmɒnə(ʊ)ˈdʒɛnɨsɪs
AM ¦mɑnoʊˈdʒɛnəsəs
monogenetic
BR ˌmɒnə(ʊ)dʒɪˈnɛtɪk
AM ¦mɑnədʒəˈnɛdɪk
monogeny
BR məˈnɒdʒɨni, mɒˈnɒdʒɨni
AM məˈnɑdʒəni
monoglot
BR ˈmɒnə(ʊ)glɒt, -s
AM ˈmɑnəˌglɑt, -s
monogram
BR ˈmɒnəgram, -z, -d
AM ˈmɑnəˌgræm, -z, -d
monogrammatic
BR ˌmɒnə(ʊ)grəˈmatɪk
AM ¦mɑnəgrəˈmædɪk
monograph
BR ˈmɒnəgrɑːf, ˈmɒnəgraf, -s
AM ˈmɑnəˌgræf, -s
monographer
BR məˈnɒgrəfə(r), mɒˈnɒgrəfə(r), -z
AM məˈnɑgrəfər, -z
monographic
BR ˌmɒnə(ʊ)ˈgrafɪk
AM ¦mɑnəˈgræfɪk
monographist
BR məˈnɒgrəfɪst, mɒˈnɒgrəfɪst, -s
AM məˈnɑgrəfəst, -s
monogynous
BR məˈnɒdʒɨnəs, mɒˈnɒdʒɨnəs
AM məˈnɑdʒənəs
monogyny
BR məˈnɒdʒɨni, mɒˈnɒdʒɨni
AM məˈnɑdʒəni
monohull
BR ˈmɒnəʊhʌl, -z
AM ˈmɑnoʊˌhəl, -z
monohybrid
BR ˌmɒnə(ʊ)ˈhʌɪbrɪd, -z
AM ¦mɑnəˈhaɪbrɪd, -z
monohydric
BR ˌmɒnə(ʊ)ˈhʌɪdrɪk
AM ¦mɑnoʊˈhaɪdrɪk
monokini
BR ˈmɒnə(ʊ)ˌkiːn|i, ˌmɒnə(ʊ)ˈkiːn|i, -ɪz
AM ˈmɑnoʊˌkɪni, -z
monolatry
BR məˈnɒlətri, mɒˈnɒlətri
AM məˈnɑlətri
monolayer
BR ˈmɒnə(ʊ)ˌleɪə(r), -z
AM ¦mɑnəˈleɪər, ¦mɑnəˈlɛ(ə)r, -z
monolingual
BR ˌmɒnə(ʊ)ˈlɪŋgw(ə)l
AM ˌmɑnəˈlɪŋgwəl
monolith
BR mɒnəlɪθ, mɒnl̩ɪθ, -s
AM ˈmɑnəˌlɪθ, -s
monolithic
BR ˌmɒnəˈlɪθɪk
AM ¦mɑnəˈlɪθɪk

monolithically
BR ˌmɒnəˈlɪθɨkli
AM ¦manəˈlɪθək(ə)li

monolog
BR ˈmɒnəlɒɡ, -z
AM ˈmanəlɔɡ, ˈmanəlaɡ, -z

monologic
BR ˌmɒnəˈlɒdʒɪk
AM ¦manəˈladʒɪk

monological
BR ˌmɒnəˈlɒdʒɨkl
AM ¦manəˈladʒəkəl

monologise
BR ˈmɒnələdʒʌɪz, məˈnɒlədʒʌɪz, -ɨz, -ɪŋ, -d
AM məˈnaləˌdʒaɪz, -ɨz, -ɪŋ, -d

monologist
BR məˈnɒlədʒɪst, -s
AM məˈnalədʒəst, -s

monologize
BR ˈmɒnələdʒʌɪz, məˈnɒlədʒʌɪz, -ɨz, -ɪŋ, -d
AM məˈnaləˌdʒaɪz, -ɨz, -ɪŋ, -d

monologue
BR ˈmɒnəlɒɡ, -z
AM ˈmanəlɔɡ, ˈmanəlaɡ, -z

monomania
BR ˌmɒnə(ʊ)ˈmeɪnɪə(*r*)
AM ˌmanoʊˈmɛɪniə

monomaniac
BR ˌmɒnə(ʊ)ˈmeɪnɪak, -s
AM ¦manoʊˈmeɪniæk, -s

monomaniacal
BR ˌmɒnə(ʊ)məˈnʌɪəkl
AM ¦manoʊməˈnaɪəkəl

monomark
BR ˈmɒnə(ʊ)mɑːk, -s
AM ˈmanoʊˌmark, -s

monomer
BR ˈmɒnəmə(r), -z
AM ˈmanəmər, -z

monomeric
BR ˌmɒnəˈmɛrɪk
AM ˌmanəˈmɛrɪk

monometallism
BR ˌmɒnə(ʊ)ˈmɛtl̩ɪz(ə)m
AM ¦manoʊˈmɛdlˌɪzəm

monomial
BR mɒˈnəʊmɪəl, məˈnəʊmɪəl, -z
AM məˈnoʊmiəl, -z

monomolecular
BR ˌmɒnə(ʊ)məˈlɛkjʉlə(r)
AM ¦manoʊməˈlɛkjələr

monomorphic
BR ˌmɒnə(ʊ)ˈmɔːfɪk
AM ¦manəˈmɔrfɪk

monomorphism
BR ˌmɒnə(ʊ)ˈmɔːfɪz(ə)m, -z
AM ¦manəˈmɔrˌfɪzəm, -z

monomorphous
BR ˌmɒnə(ʊ)ˈmɔːfəs
AM ˌmanəˈmɔrfəs

Monongahela
BR məˌnɒŋɡəˈhiːlə(*r*)
AM məˌnaŋɡəˈhilə

mononucleosis
BR ˌmɒnəʊˌnjuːklɪˈəʊsɪs
AM ˌmanoʊˌn(j)ukliˈoʊsəs

monopetalous
BR ˌmɒnə(ʊ)ˈpɛtl̩əs
AM ¦manəˈpɛdl̩əs

monophagous
BR məˈnɒfəɡəs
AM məˈnafəɡəs

monophonic
BR ˌmɒnə(ʊ)ˈfɒnɪk
AM ¦manəˈfanɪk

monophonically
BR ˌmɒnə(ʊ)ˈfɒnɨkli
AM ¦manəˈfanək(ə)li

monophthong
BR ˈmɒnə(f)θɒŋ, -z
AM ˈmanə(f)ˌθɔŋ, məˈnapˌθɔŋ, ˈmanə(f)ˌθaŋ, məˈnapˌθaŋ, -z

monophthongal
BR ˌmɒnə(f)ˈθɒŋɡl
AM ¦manə(f)ˈθaŋ(ɡ)əl, ¦manəpˈθaŋ(ɡ)əl

monophthongally
BR ˌmɒnə(f)ˈθɒŋɡl̩i, ˌmɒnə(f)ˈθɒŋɡəli
AM ¦manə(f)ˈθaŋ(ɡ)əli, ¦manəpˈθaŋ(ɡ)əli

Monophysite
BR məˈnɒfɪsʌɪt, -s
AM məˈnafəˌsaɪt, -s

monoplane
BR ˈmɒnəpleɪn, -z
AM ˈmanəˌpleɪn, -z

monopod
BR ˈmɒnəpɒd, -z
AM ˈmanəˌpad, -z

Monopole
BR ˈmɒnə(ʊ)pəʊl
AM ˈmanəˌpoʊl

monopolisation
BR məˌnɒpəlʌɪˈzeɪʃn
AM məˌnapələˈzeɪʃən, məˌnapəˌlaɪˈzeɪʃən

monopolise
BR məˈnɒpəlʌɪz, -ɨz, -ɪŋ, -d
AM məˈnapəˌlaɪz, -ɨz, -ɪŋ, -d

monopoliser
BR məˈnɒpəlʌɪzə(r), -z
AM məˈnapəˌlaɪzər, -z

monopolist
BR məˈnɒpəlɪst, -s
AM məˈnapələst, -s

monopolistic
BR məˌnɒpəˈlɪstɪk
AM məˌnapəˈlɪstɪk

monopolization
BR məˌnɒpəlʌɪˈzeɪʃn
AM məˌnapələˈzeɪʃən, məˌnapəˌlaɪˈzeɪʃən

monopolize
BR məˈnɒpəlʌɪz, -ɨz, -ɪŋ, -d
AM məˈnapəˌlaɪz, -ɨz, -ɪŋ, -d

monopolizer
BR məˈnɒpəlʌɪzə(r), -z
AM məˈnapəˌlaɪzər, -z

monopoly
BR məˈnɒpəl|i, məˈnɒpl̩|i, -ɪz
AM məˈnapəli, -z

monopsony
BR məˈnɒpsən|i, məˈnɒpsn̩i, -ɪz
AM məˈnapsəni, -z

monopsychism
BR ˌmɒnə(ʊ)ˈsʌɪkɪz(ə)m
AM ¦manəˈsaɪˌkɪzəm

monopteros
BR məˈnɒptərɒs, -ɨz
AM məˈnaptərəs, -əz

monorail
BR ˈmɒnəreɪl, -z
AM ˈmanəˌreɪl, -z

monorhyme
BR ˈmɒnə(ʊ)rʌɪm, -z
AM ˈmanəˌraɪm, -z

monosaccharide
BR ˌmɒnə(ʊ)ˈsakərʌɪd, -z
AM ¦manəˈsækəˌraɪd, -z

monosodium glutamate
BR ˌmɒnə(ʊ)səʊdɪəm ˈɡluːtəmeɪt
AM ¦manəˌsoʊdiəm ˈɡludəˌmeɪt

monospermous
BR ˌmɒnə(ʊ)ˈspəːməs
AM ¦manəˈspərməs

monostichous
BR məˈnɒstɪkəs, ˌmɒnə(ʊ)ˈstʌɪkəs
AM ¦manəˈstɪkəs

monostrophic
BR ˌmɒnə(ʊ)ˈstrɒfɪk, ˌmɒnə(ʊ)ˈstrəʊfɪk
AM ¦manəˈstrafɪk

monosyllabic
BR ˌmɒnə(ʊ)sɪˈlabɪk
AM ¦manəsəˈlæbɪk

monosyllabically
BR ˌmɒnə(ʊ)sɪˈlabɨkli
AM ¦manəsəˈlæbək(ə)li

monosyllable
BR ˈmɒnə(ʊ)ˌsɪləbl, -z
AM ¦manəˈsɪləbəl, -z

monotheism
BR ˈmɒnə(ʊ)θɪɪz(ə)m, ˈmɒnə(ʊ)ˌθiːɪz(ə)m
AM ˈmanəθiˌɪzəm, ˌmanəˈθiˌɪzəm

monotheist
BR ˈmɒnə(ʊ)θɪɪst, ˈmɒnə(ʊ)ˌθiːɪst, -s
AM ¦manəˈθiɪst, -s

monotheistic
BR ˌmɒnə(ʊ)θɪˈɪstɪk
AM ˌmanəθiˈɪstɪk

monotheistically
BR ˌmɒnə(ʊ)θɪˈɪstɨkli
AM ¦manəθiˈɪstɪk(ə)li

Monothelite
BR məˈnɒθɪlʌɪt, -s
AM məˈnaθəˌlaɪt, -s

monotint
BR ˈmɒnə(ʊ)tɪnt, -s
AM ˈmanəˌtɪnt, -s

monotone
BR ˈmɒnətəʊn, -z
AM ˈmanəˌtoʊn, -z

monotonic
BR ˌmɒnəˈtɒnɪk
AM ¦manəˈtanɪk

monotonically
BR ˌmɒnəˈtɒnɨkli
AM ¦manəˈtanək(ə)li

monotonise
BR məˈnɒtənʌɪz, məˈnɒtn̩ʌɪz, -ɨz, -ɪŋ, -d
AM məˈnatn̩ˌaɪz, məˈnadəˌnaɪz, -ɨz, -ɪŋ, -d

monotonize
BR məˈnɒtənʌɪz, məˈnɒtn̩ʌɪz, -ɨz, -ɪŋ, -d
AM məˈnatn̩ˌaɪz, məˈnadəˌnaɪz, -ɨz, -ɪŋ, -d

monotonous
BR məˈnɒtənəs, məˈnɒtn̩əs
AM məˈnatn̩əs, məˈnadənəs

monotonously
BR məˈnɒtənəsli, məˈnɒtn̩əsli
AM məˈnatn̩əsli, məˈnadənəsli

monotonousness
BR məˈnɒtənəsnəs, məˈnɒtn̩əsnəs
AM məˈnatn̩əsnəs, məˈnadənəsnəs

monotony
BR məˈnɒt(ə)ni, məˈnɒtn̩i
AM məˈnatn̩i, məˈnadəni

monotreme
BR ˈmɒnətriːm, -z
AM ˈmanəˌtrim, -z

Monotype®
BR ˈmɒnə(ʊ)tʌɪp, -s
AM ˈmanəˌtaɪp, -s

monotypic
BR ˌmɒnə(ʊ)ˈtɪpɪk
AM ¦mɑnəˈtɪpɪk

monounsaturate
BR ˌmɒnəʊʌnˈsatʃʊrət, ˌmɒnəʊʌnˈstjʊrət, -s
AM ¦mɑnoʊənˈsætʃərət, -s

monounsaturated
BR ˌmɒnəʊʌnˈsatʃʊreɪtɪd, ˌmɒnəʊʌnˈsatjʊreɪtɪd
AM ¦mɑnoʊənˈsætʃəˌreɪdɪd

monovalence
BR ˌmɒnə(ʊ)ˈveɪləns, ˌmɒnə(ʊ)ˈveɪln̩s, -ɪz
AM ¦mɑnəˈveɪləns, -əz

monovalency
BR ˌmɒnə(ʊ)ˈveɪləns|i, ˌmɒnə(ʊ)ˈveɪln̩s|i, -ɪz
AM ¦mɑnəˈveɪlənsi, -z

monovalent
BR ˌmɒnə(ʊ)ˈveɪlənt, ˌmɒnə(ʊ)ˈveɪln̩t
AM ¦mɑnəˈveɪlənt

monoxide
BR məˈnɒksʌɪd, -z
AM məˈnɑkˌsaɪd, -z

Monroe
BR mənˈrəʊ, mʌnˈrəʊ
AM mənˈroʊ

Monroe doctrine
BR ˌmənrəʊ ˈdɒktr(ɪ)n, ˌmʌnrəʊ +
AM mənˈroʊ ˈdɑktrən

Monrovia
BR mənˈrəʊvɪə(r), mɒnˈrəʊvɪə(r)
AM mənˈroʊviə, mɑnˈroʊviə

Monrovian
BR mənˈrəʊvɪən, mɒnˈrəʊvɪən, -z
AM mənˈroʊviən, mɑnˈroʊviən, -z

Mons
BR mɒnz
AM mɔnz

Monsarrat
BR ˈmɒnsərat, ˌmɒnsəˈrat
AM ˌmɑnsəˈrɑt

Monseigneur
BR ˌmɒnsɛˈnjəː(r)
AM ¦mɑnˌseɪˈnjər

monsieur
BR məˈsjəː(r)
AM məˈsjər, məˈʃər

Monsignor
BR mɒnˈsiːnjə(r), ˌmɒnsiːˈnjɔː(r), -z
AM mɑnˈsinjər, -z

monsignore
BR ˌmɒnsiːˈnjɔːri
AM ¦mɑnˌsinˈjɔri

monsignori
BR ˌmɒnsiːˈnjɔːriː
AM ¦mɑnˌsinˈjɔri

monsoon
BR mɒnˈsuːn, -z
AM mɑnˈsun, -z

monsoonal
BR mɒnˈsuːnl
AM mɑnˈsunəl

mons pubis
BR ˌmɒnz ˈpjuːbɪs, -ɪz
AM ˈmɑnz ˈpjubəs, -əz

monster
BR ˈmɒnstə(r), -z
AM ˈmɑnstər, -z

monstera
BR mɒnˈstɪərə(r), ˈmɒnst(ə)rə(r), -z
AM ˈmɑnstərə, -z

monstrance
BR ˈmɒnstr(ə)ns, -ɪz
AM ˈmɑnztrəns, ˈmɑnstrəns, -əz

monstrosity
BR mɒnˈstrɒsɪt|i, -ɪz
AM mɑnzˈtrɑsədi, mɑnˈstrɑsədi, -z

monstrous
BR ˈmɒnstrəs
AM ˈmɑnztrəs, ˈmɑnstrəs

monstrously
BR ˈmɒnstrəsli
AM ˈmɑnztrəsli, ˈmɑnstrəsli

monstrousness
BR ˈmɒnstrəsnəs
AM ˈmɑnztrəsnəs, ˈmɑnstrəsnəs

mons veneris
BR ˌmɒnz ˈvɛnər|ɪs, -ɪsɪz
AM ˈmɑnz ˈvɛnərəs, -əz

montage
BR ˈmɒntɑːʒ, -ɪz
AM mɑnˈtɑʒ, -əz

Montagna
BR mɒnˈteɪnjə(r)
AM mɔnˈteɪnjə

Montagnard
BR ˌmɒntəˈnjɑːd, -z
AM ˌmɑntəˈnjɑrd, -z
FR mɔ̃taɲaʀ

Montague
BR ˈmɒntəgjuː
AM ˈmɑn(t)əgju

Montaigne
BR mɒnˈteɪn
AM mɑnˈteɪn

Montana
BR mɒnˈtanə(r)
AM mɑnˈtænə

Montanan
BR mɒnˈtanən, -z
AM mɑnˈtænən, -z

montane
BR ˈmɒnteɪn
AM mɑnˈteɪn

Montanism
BR ˈmɒntənɪz(ə)m
AM ˈmɑn(t)əˌnɪzəm

Montanist
BR ˈmɒntənɪst, -s
AM ˈmən(t)ənəst, -s

Mont Blanc
BR ˌmɒ̃ ˈblɒ̃
AM ˌmɑn ˈblɑŋk

montbretia
BR ˌmɒn(t)ˈbriːʃə(r), -z
AM ˌmɑntˈbriʃ(i)ə, -z

Montcalm
BR ˌmɒntˈkɑːm
AM ˌmɑn(t)ˈkɑm

Monte
BR ˈmɒnti
AM ˈmɑn(t)i

Monte Carlo
BR ˌmɒntɪ ˈkɑːləʊ
AM ˌmɑn(t)ə ˈkɑrˌloʊ, ˌmɑn(t)i +

Monte Cassino
BR ˌmɒntɪ kəˈsiːnəʊ
AM ˌmɑn(t)ə kəˈsiˌnoʊ, ˌmɑn(t)i +

Montefiore
BR ˌmɒntɪfrˈɔːri, ˌmɒntɪˈfjɔːri
AM ˌmɑn(t)əfiˈɔri

Montego Bay
BR mɒnˌtiːgəʊ ˈbeɪ
AM mənˈtigoʊ ˈbeɪ

Monteith
BR mɒnˈtiːθ
AM mɑnˈtiθ

Montenegrin
BR ˌmɒntɪˈniːgrɪn, ˌmɒntɪˈneɪgrɪn, -z
AM ¦mɑn(t)əˈ¦neɪgrɪn, -z

Montenegro
BR ˌmɒntɪˈniːgrəʊ, ˌmɒntɪˈneɪgrəʊ
AM ¦mɑn(t)əˈneɪˌgroʊ

Monterrey
BR ˌmɒntəˈreɪ
AM ˌmɑn(t)əˈreɪ

Montesquieu
BR ˌmɒntɛˈskjəː(r), ˌmɒntɛˈskjuː, ˈmɒntɛskjuː
AM ˈmɑntəˌskju

Montessori
BR ˌmɒntɪˈsɔːri
AM ˌmən(t)əˈsɔri

Monteverdi
BR ˌmɒntɪˈvɛːdi, ˌmɒntɪˈvəːdi
AM ˌmɑn(t)əˈvɛrdi

Montevideo
BR ˌmɒntɪvɪˈdeɪəʊ
AM ˌmɑn(t)əvəˈdeɪoʊ

Montez
BR mɒnˈtɛz
AM mɑnˈtɛz

Montezuma
BR ˌmɒntɪˈz(j)uːmə(r)
AM ˌmɑn(t)əˈzumə

Montfort
BR ˈmɒntfət
AM ˈmɑn(t)fərt

Montgolfier
BR ˌmɒntˈgɒlfɪə(r), ˌmɒntˈgɒlfɪeɪ
AM ˌmɑnˈgɔlfiər, ˌmɑnˈgɔlfieɪ

Montgomery
BR m(ə)ntˈgʌm(ə)ri
AM mɑn(t)ˈgəm(ə)ri

month
BR mʌnθ, -s
AM mənθ, -s

monthly
BR ˈmʌnθl|i, -ɪz
AM ˈmənθli, -z

Monticello
BR ˌmɒntɪˈtʃɛləʊ, ˌmɒntɪˈsɛləʊ
AM ˌmɑn(t)əˈtʃɛloʊ, ˌmɑn(t)əˈsɛloʊ

monticule
BR ˈmɒntɪkjuːl, -z
AM ˈmɑn(t)əˌkjul, -z

Montmartre
BR ˌmɒ̃ˈmɑːtr(ər)
AM ˌmɑnˈmɑrtrə

Montmorency
BR ˌmɒntməˈrɛnsi
AM ˌmɑntməˈrɛnsi

montmorillonite
BR ˌmɒntməˈrɪlənʌɪt
AM ˌmɑntməˈrɪlənaɪt

Mont Pelée
BR ˌmɒnt ˈpɛleɪ
AM ˌmɑn(t) pɛˈleɪ

Montpelier
BR ˌmɒntˈpiːlɪə(r)
AM ˌmɑn(t)ˈpiliər

Montpellier
BR ˌmɒntˈpɛlɪə(r), ˌmɒntˈpɛlɪeɪ
AM ˌmɑnpəlˈjeɪ
FR mɔ̃pəlje

Montreal
BR ˌmɒntrɪˈɔːl
AM ˌmɑntriˈɔl

Montreux
BR mɒnˈtrəː(r)
AM mənˈtrʊ
FR mɔ̃trø

Montrose
BR mɒnˈtrəʊz
AM ˈmɑnˌtroʊz, mɑnˈtroʊz

Mont-Saint-Michel
BR ˌmɒntsanmɪˈʃɛl, ˌmɒ̃sanmɪˈʃɛl
AM ˌmɑnsanməˈʃɛl

Montserrat
BR ˌmɒn(t)səˈrat
AM ˌmɑn(t)səˈrɑt

Montserratian
BR ˌmɒn(t)səˈratɪən, -z
AM ˌmɑn(t)səˈrɑdiən, -z

Monty
BR ˈmɒnti
AM ˈmɑn(t)i

monument
BR ˈmɒnjʊm(ə)nt, -s
AM ˈmɑnjəmənt, -s

monumental
BR ˌmɒnjʊˈmɛntl
AM ˌmɑnjəˈmɛn(t)l

monumentalise
BR ˌmɒnjʊˈmɛntl̩ʌɪz, -ɪz, -ɪŋ, -d
AM ˌmɑnjəˈmɛn(t)l,aɪz, -ɪz, -ɪŋ, -d

monumentalism
BR ˌmɒnjʊˈmɛntl̩ɪz(ə)m
AM ˌmənjəˈmɛn(t)l,ɪzəm

monumentality
BR ˌmʌnjʊmɛnˈtalɪti
AM ˌmɑnjə,mɛnˈtælədi

monumentalize
BR ˌmɒnjʊˈmɛntl̩ʌɪz, -ɪz, -ɪŋ, -d
AM ˌmɑnjəˈmɛn(t)l,aɪz, -ɪz, -ɪŋ, -d

monumentally
BR ˌmɒnjʊˈmɛntl̩i
AM ˌmɑnjəˈmɛn(t)l̩i

Monza
BR ˈmɒnzə(r)
AM ˈmɑnzə, ˈmɔn(t)sə

moo
BR muː, -z, -ɪŋ, -d
AM mu, -z, -ɪŋ, -d

mooch
BR muːtʃ, -ɨz, -ɪŋ, -t
AM mutʃ, -əz, -ɪŋ, -t

moocher
BR ˈmuːtʃə(r), -z
AM ˈmutʃər, -z

moocow
BR ˈmuːkaʊ, -z
AM ˈmu,kaʊ, -z

mood
BR muːd, -z
AM mud, -z

Moodie
BR ˈmuːdi
AM ˈmudi

moodily
BR ˈmuːdɪli
AM ˈmudəli

moodiness
BR ˈmuːdɪnɨs
AM ˈmudinɨs

moody
BR ˈmuːd|i, -ɪə(r), -ɪɪst
AM ˈmudi, -ər, -ɨst

Moog
BR muːg, -z
AM mug, -z

moola
BR ˈmuːlə(r)
AM ˈmu,lɑ

moolah
BR ˈmuːlə(r)
AM ˈmu,lɑ

mooli
BR ˈmuːl|i, -ɪz
AM ˈmuli, -z

moolvi
BR ˈmuːlv|i, -ɪz
AM ˈmulvi, -z

moolvie
BR ˈmuːlv|i, -ɪz
AM ˈmulvi, -z

moon
BR muːn, -z, -ɪŋ, -d
AM mun, -z, -ɪŋ, -d

moonbeam
BR ˈmuːnbiːm, -z
AM ˈmun,bim, -z

mooncalf
BR ˈmuːnkɑːf
AM ˈmun,kæf

mooncalves
BR ˈmuːnkɑːvz
AM ˈmun,kævz

Mooney
BR ˈmuːni
AM ˈmuni

moonfish
BR ˈmuːnfɪʃ
AM ˈmun,fɪʃ

Moonie
BR ˈmuːn|i, -ɪz
AM ˈmuni, -z

moonily
BR muːnɪli
AM ˈmunəli

moonless
BR ˈmuːnləs
AM ˈmunləs

moonlight
BR ˈmuːnlʌɪt, -s, -ɪŋ, -ɨd
AM ˈmun,laɪ|t, -ts, -dɪŋ, -dɨd

moonlighter
BR ˈmuːnlʌɪtə(r), -z
AM ˈmun,laɪdər, -z

moonlit
BR ˈmuːnlɪt
AM ˈmun,lɪt

moonquake
BR ˈmuːnkweɪk, -s
AM ˈmun,kweɪk, -s

moonrise
BR ˈmuːnrʌɪz, -ɨz
AM ˈmun,raɪz, -ɨz

moonscape
BR ˈmuːnskeɪp, -s
AM ˈmun,skeɪp, -s

moonset
BR ˈmuːnsɛt, -s
AM ˈmun,sɛt, -s

moonshee
BR ˈmuːnʃiː, -z
AM ˈmun,ʃi, -z

moonshine
BR ˈmuːnʃʌɪn
AM ˈmun,ʃaɪn

moonshiner
BR ˈmuːnʃʌɪnə(r), -z
AM ˈmun,ʃaɪnər, -z

moonshot
BR ˈmuːnʃɒt, -s
AM ˈmun,ʃɑt, -s

moonstone
BR ˈmuːnstəʊn, -z
AM ˈmun,stoʊn, -z

moonstruck
BR ˈmuːnstrʌk
AM ˈmun,strək

moony
BR ˈmuːn|i, -ɪz, -ɪə(r), -ɪɪst
AM ˈmuni, -z, -ər, -ɨst

moor
BR mʊə(r), mɔː(r), -z, -ɪŋ, -d
AM mʊ|(ə)r, -(ə)rz, -rɪŋ, -(ə)rd

moorage
BR ˈmʊər|ɪdʒ, ˈmɔːr|ɪdʒ, -ɪdʒɪz
AM ˈmʊrɪdʒ, -ɨz

moorcock
BR ˈmʊəkɒk, ˈmɔːkɒk, -s
AM ˈmʊr,kɑk, -s

Moorcroft
BR ˈmʊəkrɒft, ˈmɔːkrɒft
AM ˈmʊr,krɔft, ˈmɔr,krɔft

Moore
BR mʊə(r), mɔː(r)
AM mʊ(ə)r, mɔ(ə)r

moorfowl
BR ˈmʊəfaʊl, ˈmɔːfaʊl
AM ˈmʊr,faʊl

Moorhead
BR ˈmʊəhɛd, ˈmɔːhɛd
AM ˈmʊr,(h)ɛd, ˈmɔr,(h)ɛd

moorhen
BR ˈmʊəhɛn, ˈmɔːhɛn, -z
AM ˈmʊr,(h)ɛn, -z

Moorhouse
BR ˈmʊəhaʊs, ˈmɔːhaʊs
AM ˈmʊr,(h)aʊs, ˈmɔr,(h)aʊs

mooring
BR ˈmʊərɪŋ, ˈmɔːrɪŋ, -z
AM ˈmʊrɪŋ, -z

Moorish
BR ˈmʊərɪʃ, ˈmɔːrɪʃ
AM ˈmʊrɪʃ

Moorish idol
BR ˌmʊərɪʃ ˈʌɪdl, ˌmɔːrɪʃ +, -z
AM ˌmʊrɪʃ ˈaɪdəl, -z

moorland
BR ˈmʊələnd, ˈmɔːlənd
AM ˈmʊr,lænd, ˈmʊrlənd

Moorman
BR ˈmʊəmən, ˈmɔːmən
AM ˈmʊrmən

moory
BR ˈmʊəri, ˈmɔːri
AM ˈmʊri

moose
BR muːs, -ɨz
AM mus, -əz

moot
BR muːt, -s, -ɪŋ, -ɨd
AM mu|t, -ts, -dɪŋ, -dəd

mop
BR mɒp, -s, -ɪŋ, -t
AM mɑp, -s, -ɪŋ, -t

mope
BR məʊp, -s, -ɪŋ, -t
AM moʊp, -s, -ɪŋ, -t

moped
BR ˈməʊpɛd, -z
AM ˈmoʊ,pɛd, -z

moper
BR ˈməʊpə(r), -z
AM ˈmoʊpər, -z

mophead
BR ˈmɒphɛd, -z
AM ˈmɑp,(h)ɛd, -z

mopily
BR ˈməʊpɪli
AM ˈmoʊpəli

mopiness
BR ˈməʊpɪnɪs
AM ˈmoʊpinɨs

mopish
BR ˈməʊpɪʃ
AM ˈmoʊpɪʃ

mopoke
BR ˈməʊpəʊk, -s
AM ˈmoʊ,poʊk, -s

moppet
BR ˈmɒpɪt, -s
AM ˈmɑpət, -s

moppy
BR ˈmɒp|i, -ɪə(r), -ɪɪst
AM ˈmɑpi, -ər, -əst

Mopti
BR ˈmɒpti
AM ˈmɑpti

mopy
BR ˈməʊp|i, -ɪə(r), -ɪɪst
AM ˈmoʊpi, -ər, -əst

moquette
BR mɒˈkɛt, mə(ʊ)ˈkɛt
AM moʊˈkɛt

mor
BR mɔː(r)
AM mɔ(ə)r

Morag
BR ˈmɔːrag
AM ˈmɔræg

morainal
BR məˈreɪnl
AM məˈreɪnəl

moraine
BR məˈreɪn, -z
AM məˈreɪn, -z

morainic
BR məˈreɪnɪk
AM məˈreɪnɪk

moral
BR ˈmɒrəl, ˈmɒrl̩, -z
AM ˈmɔrəl, -z
morale
BR məˈrɑːl
AM məˈræl, mɔˈræl
Morales
BR məˈrɑːlɪz
AM məˈræləs
moralisation
BR ˌmɒrəlʌɪˈzeɪʃn, ˌmɒrl̩ʌɪˈzeɪʃn, -z
AM ˌmɔrələˈzeɪʃən, ˌmɔrəlaɪˈzeɪʃən, -z
moralise
BR ˈmɒrəlʌɪz, mɒrl̩ʌɪz, -ɪz, -ɪŋ, -d
AM ˈmɔrəˌlaɪz, -ɪz, -ɪŋ, -d
moraliser
BR ˈmɒrəlʌɪzə(r), mɒrl̩ʌɪzə(r), -z
AM ˈmɔrəˌlaɪzər, -z
moralisingly
BR ˈmɒrəlʌɪzɪŋli, mɒrl̩ʌɪzɪŋli
AM ˈmɔrəˌlaɪzɪŋli
moralism
BR ˈmɒrəlɪz(ə)m, ˈmɒrl̩ɪz(ə)m
AM ˈmɔrəˌlɪzəm
moralist
BR ˈmɒrəlɪst, ˈmɒrl̩ɪst, -s
AM ˈmɔrələst, -s
moralistic
BR ˌmɒrəˈlɪstɪk, ˌmɒrl̩ˈɪstɪk
AM ˌmɔrəˈlɪstɪk
moralistically
BR ˌmɒrəˈlɪstɪkli, ˌmɒrl̩ˈɪstɪkli
AM ˌmɔrəˈlɪstək(ə)li
morality
BR məˈralɪti
AM məˈrælədi, mɔˈrælədi
moralization
BR ˌmɒrəlʌɪˈzeɪʃn, ˌmɒrl̩ʌɪˈzeɪʃn, -z
AM ˌmɔrələˈzeɪʃən, ˌmɔrəlaɪˈzeɪʃən, -z
moralize
BR ˈmɒrəlʌɪz, mɒrl̩ʌɪz, -ɪz, -ɪŋ, -d
AM ˈmɔrəˌlaɪz, -ɪz, -ɪŋ, -d
moralizer
BR ˈmɒrəlʌɪzə(r), mɒrl̩ʌɪzə(r), -z
AM ˈmɔrəˌlaɪzər, -z
moralizingly
BR ˈmɒrəlʌɪzɪŋli, mɒrl̩ʌɪzɪŋli
AM ˈmɔrəˌlaɪzɪŋli
morally
BR ˈmɒrəli, ˈmɒrl̩i
AM ˈmɔrəli
Moran
BR məˈran, ˈmɔːrən, ˈmɔːrn̩
AM məˈræn
Morant
BR məˈrant
AM məˈrænt
morass
BR məˈras, -ɪz
AM məˈræs, mɔˈræs, -əz
moratoria
BR ˌmɒrəˈtɔːrɪə(r)
AM ˌmɔrəˈtɔriə
moratorium
BR ˌmɒrəˈtɔːrɪəm, -z
AM ˌmɔrəˈtɔriəm, -z
Moravia
BR məˈreɪvɪə(r)
AM məˈreɪviə
Moravian
BR məˈreɪvɪən, -z
AM məˈreɪviən, -z
moray
BR ˈmɒreɪ, ˈmɔːreɪ, mɒˈreɪ, məˈreɪ, -z
AM ˈmɔˌreɪ, məˈreɪ, -z
Moray Firth
BR ˌmʌrɪ ˈfəːθ
AM ˈmɔˌreɪ ˈfərθ, məˈreɪ +
morbid
BR ˈmɔːbɪd
AM ˈmɔrbəd
morbidity
BR mɔːˈbɪdɪti
AM mɔrˈbɪdɪdi
morbidly
BR ˈmɔːbɪdli
AM ˈmɔrbədli
morbidness
BR ˈmɔːbɪdnɪs
AM ˈmɔrbədnəs
morbific
BR mɔːˈbɪfɪk
AM mɔrˈbɪfɪk
morbilli
BR mɔːˈbɪlʌɪ, mɔːˈbɪliː
AM mɔrˈbɪˌlaɪ
morbillivirus
BR mɔːˈbɪlɪvʌɪrəs, -ɪz
AM mɔrˈbɪləˌvaɪrəs, -əz
mordacious
BR mɔːˈdeɪʃəs
AM mɔrˈdeɪʃəs
mordacity
BR mɔːˈdasɪti
AM mɔrˈdæsədi
mordancy
BR ˈmɔːdnsi
AM ˈmɔrdnsi
mordant
BR ˈmɔːdnt, -s
AM ˈmɔrdnt, -s
mordantly
BR ˈmɔːdntli
AM ˈmɔrdn(t)li
Mordecai
BR ˈmɔːdɪkʌɪ
AM ˈmɔrdəˌkaɪ
mordent
BR ˈmɔːdnt, -s
AM ˈmɔrdnt, -s
Mordred
BR ˈmɔːdrɪd
AM ˈmɔrdrəd
Mordvin
BR ˈmɔːdvɪn
AM ˈmɔrdvən
more
BR mɔː(r)
AM mɔ(ə)r
moreen
BR mɒˈriːn
AM mɔˈrin
moreish
BR ˈmɔːrɪʃ
AM ˈmɔrɪʃ
morel
BR məˈrɛl, mɒˈrɛl
AM məˈrɛl, mɔˈrɛl
morello
BR məˈrɛləʊ, mɒˈrɛləʊ, -z
AM məˈrɛloʊ, -z
Moreno
BR məˈriːnəʊ, məˈreɪnəʊ
AM məˈrinoʊ, məˈreɪnoʊ
moreover
BR mɔːrˈəʊvə(r)
AM mɔˈroʊvər
morepork
BR ˈmɔːpɔːk, -s
AM ˈmɔrˌpɔ(ə)rk, -s
mores
BR ˈmɔːreɪz
AM ˈmɔreɪz
Moresby[1]
place in UK
BR ˈmɒrɪsbi
AM ˈmɔrzbi
Moresby[2]
Port Moresby
BR ˈmɔːzbi
AM ˈmɔrzbi
Moresco
BR məˈrɛskəʊ
AM məˈrɛskoʊ
Moresque
BR məˈrɛsk, mɔːˈrɛsk
AM məˈrɛsk
Moretonhampstead
BR ˌmɔːtnˈham(p)stɪd, ˌmɔːtnˈham(p)stɛd
AM ˌmɔr(ə)tənˈhæm(p)stɛd
Morfa
BR ˈmɔːvə(r)
AM ˈmɔrfə
WE ˈmɒrva
Morgan
BR ˈmɔːg(ə)n
AM ˈmɔrgən
morganatic
BR ˌmɔːgəˈnatɪk
AM ˌmɔrgəˈnædɪk
morganatically
BR ˌmɔːgəˈnatɪkli
AM ˌmɔrgəˈnædək(ə)li
Morgan le Fay
BR ˌmɔːg(ə)n lə ˈfeɪ
AM ˌmɔrgən lə ˈfeɪ
morgen
BR ˈmɔːg(ə)n, -z
AM ˈmɔrgən, -z
morgue
BR mɔːg, -z
AM mɔ(ə)rg, -z
Moriarty
BR ˌmɒrɪˈɑːti
AM ˌmɔriˈɑrdi
moribund
BR ˈmɒrɪbʌnd
AM ˈmɔrəˌbənd
moribundity
BR ˌmɒrɪˈbʌndɪti
AM ˌmɔrəˈbəndədi
morion
BR ˈmɒrɪən, -z
AM ˈmɔriən, -z
Morisco
BR məˈrɪskəʊ, -z
AM məˈrɪskoʊ, -z
morish
BR ˈmɔːrɪʃ
AM ˈmɔrɪʃ
Morison
BR ˈmɒrɪs(ə)n
AM ˈmɔrəsən
Morland
BR ˈmɔːlənd
AM ˈmɔrlənd
Morley
BR ˈmɔːli
AM ˈmɔrli
Mormon
BR ˈmɔːmən, -z
AM ˈmɔrmən, -z
Mormonism
BR ˈmɔːmənɪz(ə)m
AM ˈmɔrməˌnɪzəm
morn
BR mɔːn, -z
AM mɔ(ə)rn, -z
Morna
BR ˈmɔːnə(r)
AM ˈmɔrnə
Mornay
BR ˈmɔːneɪ, -z
AM mɔrˈneɪ, -z
morning
BR ˈmɔːnɪŋ, -z
AM ˈmɔrnɪŋ, -z
Mornington
BR ˈmɔːnɪŋt(ə)n
AM ˈmɔrnɪŋtən

Moro
BR 'mɔːrəʊ, -z
AM 'mɔˌroʊ, -z

Moroccan
BR mə'rɒk(ə)n, -z
AM mə'rɑkən, -z

Morocco
BR mə'rɒkəʊ
AM mə'rɑkoʊ

moron
BR 'mɔːrɒn, -z
AM 'mɔˌrɑn, 'moʊˌrɑn, -z

Moroni
BR mə'rəʊni
AM mə'rɑni, mɔ'rɑni

moronic
BR mə'rɒnɪk
AM mə'rɑnɪk, mɔ'rɑnɪk

moronically
BR mə'rɒnɪkli
AM mə'rɑnək(ə)li, mɔ'rɑnək(ə)li

moronism
BR 'mɔːrɒnɪz(ə)m
AM 'mɔrəˌnɪzəm, 'mɔrɑnˌɪzəm

morose
BR mə'rəʊs
AM mɔ'roʊs, mə'roʊs

morosely
BR mə'rəʊsli
AM mə'roʊsli, mɔ'roʊsli

moroseness
BR mə'rəʊsnəs
AM mə'roʊsnəs, mɔ'roʊsnəs

Morpeth
BR 'mɔːpəθ
AM 'mɔrpəθ

morph
BR mɔːf, -s
AM mɔ(ə)rf, -s

morpheme
BR 'mɔːfiːm, -z
AM 'mɔrˌfim, -z

morphemic
BR mɔː'fiːmɪk, -s
AM mɔr'fimɪk, -s

morphemically
BR mɔː'fiːmɪkli
AM mɔr'fimɪk(ə)li

Morpheus
BR 'mɔːfɪəs
AM 'mɔrfiəs, 'mɔrˌfjus

morphia
BR 'mɔːfɪə(r)
AM 'mɔrfiə

morphine
BR 'mɔːfiːn
AM 'mɔrˌfin

morphing
BR 'mɔːfɪŋ, -z
AM 'mɔrfɪŋ, -z

morphinism
BR 'mɔːfɪnɪz(ə)m
AM 'mɔrfəˌnɪzəm

morphogenesis
BR ˌmɔːfə(ʊ)'dʒɛnɪsɪs
AM ˌmɔrfə'dʒɛnəsəs

morphogenetic
BR ˌmɔːfə(ʊ)dʒɪ'nɛtɪk
AM ˌmɔrfədʒə'nɛdɪk

morphogenic
BR ˌmɔːfə(ʊ)'dʒɛnɪk
AM ˌmɔrfə'dʒɛnɪk

morphological
BR ˌmɔːfə'lɒdʒɪkl
AM ˌmɔrfə'lɑdʒəkəl

morphologically
BR ˌmɔːfə'lɒdʒɪkli
AM ˌmɔrfə'lɑdʒək(ə)li

morphologist
BR mɔː'fɒlədʒɪst, -s
AM mɔr'fɑlədʒəst, -s

morphology
BR mɔː'fɒlədʒi
AM mɔr'fɑlədʒi

morphometrics
BR ˌmɔːfə'mɛtrɪks
AM ˌmɔrfə'mɛtrɪks

morphometry
BR mɔː'fɒmɪtri
AM mɔr'fɑmətri

morphophonemic
BR ˌmɔːfəʊfə'niːmɪk
AM ˌmɔrfoʊfə'nimɪk

morphophonemically
BR ˌmɔːfəʊfə'niːmɪkli
AM ˌmɔrfoʊfə'nimək(ə)li

Morphy
BR 'mɔːfi
AM 'mɔrfi

morris
BR 'mɒr|ɪs, -ɪsɪz
AM 'mɔrəs, 'mɑrəs, -əz

Morrison
BR 'mɒrɪs(ə)n
AM 'mɔrəsən, 'mɑrəsən

Morrissey
BR 'mɒrɪsi
AM 'mɔrəsi

morrow
BR 'mɒrəʊ, -z
AM 'mɔroʊ, 'mɑroʊ, -z

morse
BR mɔːs, -ɪz, -ɪŋ, -t
AM mɔ(ə)rs, -əz, -ɪŋ, -t

Morse code
BR ˌmɔːs 'kəʊd
AM ˌmɔrs 'koʊd

morsel
BR 'mɔːsl, -z
AM 'mɔrsəl, -z

mort
BR mɔːt, -s
AM mɔ(ə)rt, -s

mortadella
BR ˌmɔːtə'dɛlə(r)
AM ˌmɔrdə'dɛlə

mortal
BR 'mɔːtl, -z
AM 'mɔrdl, -z

mortality
BR mɔː'talɪti
AM mɔr'tælədi

mortally
BR 'mɔːtl̩i, 'mɔːtəli
AM 'mɔrdl̩i

mortar
BR 'mɔːtə(r), -z
AM 'mɔrdər, -z

mortarboard
BR 'mɔːtəbɔːd, -z
AM 'mɔrdərˌbɔ(ə)rd, -z

mortarless
BR 'mɔːtələs
AM 'mɔrdərləs

mortary
BR 'mɔːtəri
AM 'mɔrdəri

mortgage
BR 'mɔːg|ɪdʒ, -ɪdʒɪz, -ɪdʒɪŋ, -ɪdʒd
AM 'mɔrgɪdʒ, -ɪz, -ɪŋ, -d

mortgageable
BR 'mɔːgɪdʒəbl
AM 'mɔrgədʒəbəl

mortgagee
BR ˌmɔːgɪ'dʒiː, -z
AM ˌmɔrgə'dʒi, -z

mortgager
BR 'mɔːgɪdʒə(r), -z
AM 'mɔrgədʒər, -z

mortgagor
BR ˌmɔːgɪ'dʒɔː(r), 'mɔːgɪdʒə(r), -z
AM ˌmɔrgə'dʒɔ(ə)r, 'mɔrgədʒər, -z

mortice
BR 'mɔːt|ɪs, -ɪsɪz, -ɪsɪŋ, -ɪst
AM 'mɔrdəs, -əz, -ɪŋ, -t

mortician
BR mɔː'tɪʃn, -z
AM mɔr'tɪʃən, -z

mortification
BR ˌmɔːtɪfɪ'keɪʃn
AM ˌmɔrdəfə'keɪʃən

mortify
BR 'mɔːtɪfʌɪ, -z, -ɪŋ, -d
AM 'mɔrdəˌfaɪ, -z, -ɪŋ, -d

mortifyingly
BR 'mɔːtɪfʌɪɪŋli
AM 'mɔrdəˌfaɪɪŋli

Mortimer
BR 'mɔːtɪmə(r)
AM 'mɔrdəmər

mortise
BR 'mɔːt|ɪs, -ɪsɪz, -ɪsɪŋ, -ɪst
AM 'mɔrdəs, -əz, -ɪŋ, -t

Mortlake
BR 'mɔːtleɪk
AM 'mɔrtˌleɪk

mortmain
BR 'mɔːtmeɪn
AM 'mɔrtˌmeɪn

Morton
BR 'mɔːtn
AM 'mɔrt(ə)n

mortuary
BR 'mɔːtjʊər|i, 'mɔːtjər|i, 'mɔːtʃʊər|i, 'mɔːtʃ(ʉ)r|i, -ɪz
AM 'mɔrtʃəˌwɛri, -z

morula
BR 'mɔːr(j)ʉlə(r), 'mɒr(j)ʉlə(r)
AM 'mɔrələ, 'mɑrələ

morulae
BR 'mɔːr(j)ʉliː, 'mɒr(j)ʉliː
AM 'mɔrəli, 'mɑrəli, 'mɑrəˌlaɪ, 'mɔrəlaɪ

Morwenna
BR mɔː'wɛnə(r)
AM ˌmɔr'wɛnə

morwong
BR 'mɔːwɒŋ, -z
AM 'mɔrˌwɔŋ, 'mɑrˌwɑŋ, -z

mosaic
BR mə(ʊ)'zeɪɪk, -s
AM moʊ'zeɪɪk, -s

mosaic gold
BR mə(ʊ)ˌzeɪɪk 'gəʊld
AM moʊˌzeɪɪk 'goʊld

mosaicist
BR mə(ʊ)'zeɪɪsɪst, -s
AM moʊ'zeɪəsəst, -s

Mosaic Law
BR mə(ʊ)ˌzeɪɪk 'lɔː(r)
AM moʊˌzeɪɪk 'lɔ

mosasaur
BR 'məʊsəsɔː(r), -z
AM 'moʊsəˌsɔ(ə)r, -z

mosasauri
BR ˌməʊsə'sɔːrʌɪ
AM ˌmoʊsə'sɔraɪ

mosasaurus
BR ˌməʊsə'sɔːrəs, -ɪz
AM ˌmoʊsə'sɔrəs, -əz

moschatel
BR ˌmɒskə'tɛl
AM ˌmɔskə'tɛl, ˌmɑskə'tɛl

Moscow
BR 'mɒskəʊ
AM 'mɑsˌkaʊ, 'mɑsˌkoʊ

Moseley
BR 'məʊzli
AM 'moʊzli

Moselle
BR mə(ʊ)'zɛl, -z
AM moʊ'zɛl, -z

Moser
BR 'məʊzə(r)
AM 'moʊzər

Moses
BR ˈməʊzɪz
AM ˈmoʊzəs

mosey
BR ˈməʊz|i, -ɪz, -ɪɪŋ, -ɪd
AM ˈmoʊzi, -z, -ɪŋ, -d

moshav
BR ˈməʊʃɑːv, məʊˈʃɑːv
AM moʊˈʃɑv

moshavim
BR mə(ʊ)ˈʃɑːvɪm, ˌməʊʃəˈvɪm
AM ˌmoʊʃəˈvim

Moskva
BR ˈmɒskvə(r)
AM ˈmɑskvə
RUS maˈskva

Moslem
BR ˈmɒzlɪm, ˈmʊzlɪm, -z
AM ˈmɑzləm, -z

Mosley
BR ˈməʊzli, ˈmɒzli
AM ˈmoʊzli

mosque
BR mɒsk, -s
AM mɑsk, -s

mosquito
BR məˈskiːtəʊ, mɒˈskiːtəʊ, -z
AM məˈskidoʊ, -z

moss
BR mɒs, -ɪz
AM mɔs, mɑs, -əz

Mossad
BR ˈmɒsad
AM ˌmɔˈsɑd, ˌmɑˈsɑd

mossback
BR ˈmɒsbak, -s
AM ˈmɔsˌbæk, ˈmɑsˌbæk, -s

Mossel Bay
BR ˌmɒsl ˈbeɪ
AM ˌmɔsəl ˈbeɪ, ˌmɑsəl ˈbeɪ

mossgrown
BR ˌmɒsˈgrəʊn
AM ˈmɔsˌgroʊn, ˈmɑsˌgroʊn

mossie
BR ˈmɒz|i, ˈmɒs|i, -ɪz
AM ˈmɔsi, ˈmɑsi, -z

mossiness
BR ˈmɒsɪnɪs
AM ˈmɔsinɨs, ˈmɑsinɨs

mosslike
BR ˈmɒslʌɪk
AM ˈmɔsˌlaɪk, ˈmɑsˌlaɪk

mosso
BR ˈmɒsəʊ
AM ˈmoʊˌsoʊ

Mossop
BR ˈmɒsəp
AM ˈmɑsəp

mosstrooper
BR ˈmɒsˌtruːpə(r), -z
AM ˈmɔsˌtrupər, ˈmɑsˌtrupər, -z

mossy
BR ˈmɒs|i, -ɪə(r), -ɪɪst
AM ˈmɔsi, ˈmɑsi, -ər, -ɪst

most
BR məʊst
AM moʊst

mostly
BR ˈməʊs(t)li
AM ˈmoʊs(t)li

Mostyn
BR ˈmɒstɪn
AM ˈmɑstən

Mosul
BR ˈməʊs(ə)l
AM məˈsul

MOT
BR ˌɛməʊˈtiː, -z, -ɪŋ, -d
AM ˌɛmˌoʊˈti, -z, -ɪŋ, -d

mot
BR məʊ, -z
AM moʊ, -z

mote
BR məʊt, -s
AM moʊt, -s

motel
BR məʊˈtɛl, -z
AM moʊˈtɛl, -z

motet
BR məʊˈtɛt, -s
AM moʊˈtɛt, -s

moth
BR mɒθ, -s
AM mɔ|θ, mɑ|θ, -ðz

mothball
BR ˈmɒθbɔːl, -z, -ɪŋ, -d
AM ˈmɔθˌbɔl, ˈmɑθˌbɑl, -z, -ɪŋ, -d

mother
BR ˈmʌð|ə(r), -əz, -(ə)rɪŋ, -əd
AM ˈməð|ər, -ərz, -(ə)rɪŋ, -ərd

motherboard
BR ˈmʌðəbɔːd, -z
AM ˈməðərˌbɔ(ə)rd, -z

mothercraft
BR ˈmʌðəkrɑːft, ˈmʌðəkraft
AM ˈməðərˌkræft

motherfucker
BR ˈmʌðəˌfʌkə(r), -z
AM ˈməðərˌfəkər, -z

motherfucking
BR ˈmʌðəˌfʌkɪŋ
AM ˈməðərˌfəkɪŋ

motherhood
BR ˈmʌðəhʊd
AM ˈməðərˌ(h)ʊd

motherland
BR ˈmʌðəland, -z
AM ˈməðərˌlænd, -z

motherless
BR ˈmʌðələs
AM ˈməðərləs

motherlessness
BR ˈmʌðələsnəs
AM ˈməðərləsnəs

motherlike
BR ˈmʌðəlʌɪk
AM ˈməðərˌlaɪk

motherliness
BR ˈmʌðəlɪnɪs
AM ˈməðərlinɨs

motherly
BR ˈmʌðəli
AM ˈməðərli

Motherwell
BR ˈmʌðəwɛl, ˈmʌðəw(ə)l
AM ˈməðərˌwɛl

mothproof
BR ˈmɒθpruːf, -s, -ɪŋ, -t
AM ˈmɔθˌpruf, ˈmɑθˌpruf, -s, -ɪŋ, -t

mothy
BR ˈmɒθ|i, -ɪə(r), -ɪɪst
AM ˈmɑθi, -ər, -ɪst

motif
BR məʊˈtiːf, -s
AM moʊˈtif, -s

motile
BR ˈməʊtʌɪl
AM ˈmoʊtl, ˈmoʊˌtaɪl

motility
BR məʊˈtɪlɪti
AM moʊˈtɪlɨdi

motion
BR ˈməʊʃ|n, -nz, -n̩ɪŋ\-ənɪŋ, -nd
AM ˈmoʊʃ|ən, -ənz, -(ə)nɪŋ, -ənd

motional
BR ˈməʊʃnl
AM ˈmoʊʃənl, ˈmoʊʃnəl

motionless
BR ˈməʊʃnləs
AM ˈmoʊʃənləs

motionlessly
BR ˈməʊʃnləsli
AM ˈmoʊʃənləsli

motionlessness
BR ˈməʊʃnləsnəs
AM ˈmoʊʃənləsnəs

motivate
BR ˈməʊtɪveɪt, -s, -ɪŋ, -ɪd
AM ˈmoʊdəˌveɪ|t, -ts, -dɪŋ, -dɪd

motivation
BR ˌməʊtɪˈveɪʃn
AM ˌmoʊdəˈveɪʃən

motivational
BR ˌməʊtɪˈveɪʃn̩(ə)l, ˌməʊtɪˈveɪʃən(ə)l
AM ˌmoʊdəˈveɪʃ(ə)nəl

motivationally
BR ˌməʊtɪˈveɪʃn̩əli, ˌməʊtɪˈveɪʃn̩l̩i, ˌməʊtɪˈveɪʃənl̩i, ˌməʊtɪˈveɪʃ(ə)nəli
AM ˌmoʊdəˈveɪʃ(ə)nəli

motivator
BR ˈməʊtɪveɪtə(r), -z
AM ˈmoʊdəˌveɪdər, -z

motive
BR ˈməʊtɪv, -z
AM ˈmoʊdɪv, -z

motiveless
BR ˈməʊtɪvlɨs
AM ˈmoʊdɪvlɨs

motivelessly
BR ˈməʊtɪvlɨsli
AM ˈmoʊdɪvlɨsli

motivelessness
BR ˈməʊtɪvlɨsnɨs
AM ˈmoʊdɪvlɨsnɨs

motivity
BR məʊˈtɪvɪti
AM moʊˈtɪvɨdi

mot juste
BR ˌməʊ ˈʒuːst
AM ˌmoʊ ˈʒust

motley
BR ˈmɒtli
AM ˈmɑtli

motmot
BR ˈmɒtmɒt, -s
AM ˈmɑtˌmɑt, -s

motocross
BR ˈməʊtə(ʊ)krɒs
AM ˈmoʊdoʊˌkrɔs, ˈmoʊdoʊˌkrɑs

moto perpetuo
BR ˌməʊtəʊ pəˈpɛtjʊəʊ, + pəˈpɛtʃʊəʊ
AM ˈmoʊˌdoʊ pərˈpɛdəˌwoʊ

motor
BR ˈməʊt|ə(r), -əz, -(ə)rɪŋ, -əd
AM ˈmoʊdər, -z, -ɪŋ, -d

motorable
BR ˈməʊt(ə)rəbl
AM ˈmoʊdərəbəl

motorbike
BR ˈməʊtəbʌɪk, -s
AM ˈmoʊdərˌbaɪk, -s

motorboat
BR ˈməʊtəbəʊt, -s
AM ˈmoʊdərˌboʊt, -s

motorcade
BR ˈməʊtəkeɪd, -z
AM ˈmoʊdərˌkeɪd, -z

motorcar
BR ˈməʊtəkɑː(r), -z
AM ˈmoʊdərˌkɑr, -z

motorcoach
BR ˈməʊtəkəʊtʃ, -ɪz
AM ˈmoʊdərˌkoʊtʃ, -ɪz

motorcycle
BR ˈməʊtəˌsʌɪk|l, -lz, -l̩ɪŋ\-lɪŋ, -ld
AM ˈmoʊdərˌsaɪk|əl, -əlz, -(ə)lɪŋ, -əld

motorcycling
BR ˈməʊtəˌsʌɪklɪŋ
AM ˈmoʊdərˌsaɪk(ə)lɪŋ

motorcyclist
BR ˈməʊtəˌsʌɪklɪst, -s
AM ˈmoʊdərˌsaɪklɪst, -s

motorhome
BR ˈməʊtəhəʊm, -z
AM ˈmoʊdərˌ(h)oʊm, -z

motorial
BR məʊˈtɔːrɪəl
AM moʊˈtɔriəl

motorisation
BR ˌməʊt(ə)rʌɪˈzeɪʃn
AM ˌmoʊdərəˈzeɪʃən, ˌmoʊdəˌraɪˈzeɪʃən

motorise
BR ˈməʊtərʌɪz, -ɪz, -ɪŋ, -d
AM ˈmoʊdərˌraɪz, -ɪz, -ɪŋ, -d

motorist
BR ˈməʊt(ə)rɪst, -s
AM ˈmoʊdərəst, -s

motorization
BR ˌməʊt(ə)rʌɪˈzeɪʃn
AM ˌmoʊdərəˈzeɪʃən, ˌmoʊdəˌraɪˈzeɪʃən

motorize
BR ˈməʊtərʌɪz, -ɪz, -ɪŋ, -d
AM ˈmoʊdərˌraɪz, -ɪz, -ɪŋ, -d

motorman
BR ˈməʊtəman
AM ˈmoʊdərˌmæn

motormen
BR ˈməʊtəmɛn
AM ˈmoʊdərˌmɛn

motormouth
BR ˈməʊtəmaʊ|θ, -ðz
AM ˈmoʊdərˌmaʊ|θ, -ðz

motorway
BR ˈməʊtəweɪ, -z
AM ˈmoʊdərˌweɪ, -z

motory
BR ˈməʊt(ə)ri
AM ˈmoʊdəri

Motown®
BR ˈməʊtaʊn
AM ˈmoʊˌtaʊn

mots justes
BR ˌməʊ ˈʒuːst
AM ˌmoʊ ˈʒust

Mott
BR mɒt
AM mɑt

motte
BR mɒt, -s
AM mɑt, -s

mottle
BR ˈmɒtl̩, -z, -ɪŋ, -d
AM ˈmɑdəl, -z, -ɪŋ, -d

motto
BR ˈmɒtəʊ, -z
AM ˈmɑdoʊ, -z

Mottram
BR ˈmɒtrəm
AM ˈmɑtrəm

Motu
BR ˈməʊtuː
AM ˈmoʊdu

moue
BR muː, -z
AM mu, -z

moufflon
BR ˈmuːflɒn, -z
AM ˈmuflɑn, -z

mouflon
BR ˈmuːflɒn, -z
AM ˈmuflɑn, -z

mouillé
BR ˈmuːjeɪ, ˈmwiːeɪ
AM muˈjeɪ

moujik
BR ˌmuːˈʒɪk, -s
AM muˈʒɪk, -s

mould
BR məʊld, -z, -ɪŋ, -ɪd
AM moʊld, -z, -ɪŋ, -əd

mouldable
BR ˈməʊldəbl
AM ˈmoʊldəbəl

mouldboard
BR ˈməʊl(d)bɔːd, -z
AM ˈmoʊl(d)ˌbɔ(ə)rd, -z

moulder
BR ˈməʊld|ə(r), -əz, -(ə)rɪŋ, -əd
AM ˈmoʊldər, -z, -ɪŋ, -d

mouldiness
BR ˈməʊldɪnɪs
AM ˈmoʊldinɪs

moulding
BR ˈməʊldɪŋ, -z
AM ˈmoʊldɪŋ, -z

mouldy
BR ˈməʊld|i, -ɪə(r), -ɪɪst
AM ˈmoʊldi, -ər, -ɪst

moulin
BR ˈmuːlɪn, -z
AM muˈlɛn, -z

Moulinex®
BR ˈmuːlɪnɛks
AM ˈmulənɛks

Moulin Rouge
BR ˌmuːlã ˈruːʒ
AM muˌlɛn ˈru(d)ʒ

Moulmein
BR ˈmuːlmeɪn
AM ˈmulˌmeɪn

moult
BR məʊlt, -s, -ɪŋ, -ɪd
AM moʊlt, -s, -ɪŋ, -əd

moulter
BR ˈməʊltə(r), -z
AM ˈmoʊltər, -z

Moulton
BR ˈməʊlt(ə)n
AM ˈmoʊltən, ˈmʊltən

mound
BR maʊnd, -z
AM maʊnd, -z

mount
BR maʊnt, -s, -ɪŋ, -ɪd
AM maʊn|t, -ts, -(t)ɪŋ, -(t)əd

mountable
BR ˈmaʊntəbl
AM ˈmaʊn(t)əbəl

mountain
BR ˈmaʊntɪn, -z
AM ˈmaʊnt(ə)n, -z

mountaineer
BR ˌmaʊntɪˈnɪə(r), -z, -ɪŋ
AM ˌmaʊnt(ə)nˈɪ(ə)r, -z, -ɪŋ

mountainous
BR ˈmaʊntɪnəs
AM ˈmaʊntn̩əs, ˈmaʊn(t)ənəs

mountainside
BR ˈmaʊntɪnsʌɪd, -z
AM ˈmaʊntnˌsaɪd, ˈmaʊn(t)ənˌsaɪd, -z

mountaintop
BR ˈmaʊntɪntɒp, -s
AM ˈmaʊntnˌtɑp, ˈmaʊn(t)ənˌtɑp, -s

mountainy
BR ˈmaʊntɪni
AM ˈmaʊntn̩i, ˈmaʊn(t)əni

Mountbatten
BR ˌmaʊntˈbatn
AM ˌmaʊn(t)ˈbætn

mountebank
BR ˈmaʊntɪbaŋk, -s
AM ˈmaʊn(t)əˌbæŋk, -s

mountebankery
BR ˈmaʊntɪˌbaŋk(ə)ri
AM ˈmaʊn(t)əˌbæŋkəri

mounter
BR ˈmaʊntə(r), -z
AM ˈmaʊn(t)ər, -z

Mountie
BR ˈmaʊnt|i, -ɪz
AM ˈmaʊn(t)i, -z

mounting
BR ˈmaʊntɪŋ, -z
AM ˈmaʊn(t)ɪŋ, -z

Mount Isa
BR ˌmaʊnt ˈʌɪzə(r)
AM ˌmaʊn(t) ˈaɪzə

Mountjoy
BR ˈmaʊntdʒɔɪ, ˌmaʊntˈdʒɔɪ
AM ˈmaʊn(t)ˈdʒɔɪ

Mounty
BR ˈmaʊnt|i, -ɪz
AM ˈmaʊn(t)i, -z

mourn
BR mɔːn, -z, -ɪŋ, -d
AM mɔ(ə)rn, -z, -ɪŋ, -d

Mourne
BR mɔːn
AM mɔ(ə)rn

mourner
BR ˈmɔːnə(r), -z
AM ˈmɔrnər, -z

mournful
BR ˈmɔːnf(ʊ)l
AM ˈmɔrnfəl

mournfully
BR ˈmɔːnfəli, ˈmɔːnfl̩i
AM ˈmɔrnfəli

mournfulness
BR ˈmɔːnf(ʊ)lnəs
AM ˈmɔrnfəlnəs

mourning
BR ˈmɔːnɪŋ
AM ˈmɔrnɪŋ

mousaka
BR mʊˈsɑːkə(r), muːˈsɑːkə(r), -z
AM muˈsɑkə, ˌmusəˈkɑ, -z

mouse
BR maʊs
AM maʊs

mousehole
BR ˈmaʊshəʊl, -z
AM ˈmaʊsˌ(h)oʊl, -z

Mousehoule
BR ˈmaʊzl
AM ˈmaʊsˌ(h)oʊl

mouselike
BR ˈmaʊslʌɪk
AM ˈmaʊsˌlaɪk

mouser
BR ˈmaʊsə(r), -z
AM ˈmaʊsər, -z

mousetrap
BR ˈmaʊstrap, -s
AM ˈmaʊsˌtræp, -s

mousey
BR ˈmaʊs|i, -ɪə(r), -ɪɪst
AM ˈmaʊsi, -ər, -ɪst

mousily
BR ˈmaʊsɪli
AM ˈmaʊsəli

mousiness
BR ˈmaʊsɪnɪs
AM ˈmaʊsinɪs

moussaka
BR mʊˈsɑːkə(r), muːˈsɑːkə(r), -z
AM muˈsɑkə, ˌmusɑˈkɑ, -z

mousse
BR muːs, -ɪz
AM mus, -əz

mousseline
BR ˈmuːsliːn, muːˈsliːn
AM ˌmusəˈlin, muˈslin

moustache
BR məˈstɑːʃ, -ɪz, -t
AM ˈməˌstæʃ, məˈstæʃ, -əz, -t

moustachio
BR məˈstɑːʃ(ɪ)əʊ, məˈstaʃ(ɪ)əʊ, -z, -d
AM məˈstæʃioʊ, -z, -d

Mousterian
BR muːˈstɪərɪən, -z
AM muˈstɪriən, -z

mousy
BR ˈmaʊs|i, -ɪə(r), -ɪɪst
AM ˈmaʊsi, -ər, -ɨst

mouth¹
noun
BR maʊ|θ, -ðz
AM maʊ|θ, -ðz

mouth²
verb
BR maʊð, -z, -ɪŋ, -d
AM maʊð, -z, -ɪŋ, -d

mouthbrooder
BR ˈmaʊθˌbruːdə(r), -z
AM ˈmaʊθˌbrudər, -z

mouther
BR ˈmaʊðə(r), -z
AM ˈmaʊðər, -z

mouthful
BR ˈmaʊθfʊl, -z
AM ˈmaʊθˌfʊl, -z

mouthless
BR ˈmaʊθləs
AM ˈmaʊθləs

mouthpart
BR ˈmaʊθpɑːt, -s
AM ˈmaʊθˌpɑrt, -s

mouthpiece
BR ˈmaʊθpiːs, -ɪz
AM ˈmaʊθˌpis, -ɪz

mouth-to-mouth
BR ˌmaʊθtəˈmaʊθ
AM ˈmaʊθtəˈmaʊθ

mouthwash
BR ˈmaʊθwɒʃ, -ɪz
AM ˈmaʊʃˌwɔʃ,
ˈmaʊʃˌwɑʃ, -əz

mouthy
BR ˈmaʊð|i, -ɪə(r), -ɪɪst
AM ˈmaʊði, ˈmaʊθi, -ər,
-əst

movability
BR ˌmuːvəˈbɪlɨti
AM ˌmuvəˈbɪlɨdi

movable
BR ˈmuːvəbl, -z
AM ˈmuvəbəl, -z

movableness
BR ˈmuːvəblnəs
AM ˈmuvəbəlnəs

movably
BR ˈmuːvəbli
AM ˈmuvəbli

move
BR muːv, -z, -ɪŋ, -d
AM muv, -z, -ɪŋ, -d

moveable
BR ˈmuːvəbl, -z
AM ˈmuvəbəl, -z

movement
BR ˈmuːvm(ə)nt, -s
AM ˈmuvmənt, -s

mover
BR ˈmuːvə(r), -z
AM ˈmuvər, -z

movie
BR ˈmuːv|i, -ɪz
AM ˈmuvi, -z

moviegoer
BR ˈmuːvɪˌɡəʊə(r), -z
AM ˈmuviˌɡoʊər, -z

movie house
BR ˈmuːvɪ haʊ|s, -zɪz
AM ˈmuvi ˌhaʊ|s, -zəz

moviemaker
BR ˈmuːvɪˌmeɪkə(r), -z
AM ˈmuviˌmeɪkər, -z

Movietone®
BR ˈmuːvɪtəʊn
AM ˈmuviˌtoʊn

movingly
BR ˈmuːvɪŋli
AM ˈmuvɪŋli

mow¹
noun, in barley mow
BR maʊ, -z
AM moʊ, -z

mow²
noun, verb, stack
BR maʊ, -z, -ɪŋ, -d
AM maʊ, -z, -ɪŋ, -d

mow³
verb, to cut
BR məʊ, -z, -ɪŋ, -d
AM moʊ, -z, -ɪŋ, -d

mowable
BR ˈməʊəbl
AM ˈmoʊəbəl

Mowbray
BR ˈməʊbri, ˈməʊbreɪ
AM ˈmoʊbri, ˈmoʊˌbreɪ

mowburnt
BR ˈməʊbəːnt
AM ˈmoʊˌbərnt

mower
BR ˈməʊə(r), -z
AM ˈmoʊər, -z

Mowgli
BR ˈmaʊɡli
AM ˈmoʊɡli

mowing
BR ˈməʊɪŋ, -z
AM ˈmoʊɪŋ, -z

mowlem
BR ˈməʊləm, -z
AM ˈmoʊləm, -z

mown
BR məʊn
AM moʊn

moxa
BR ˈmɒksə(r)
AM ˈmɑksə

moxibustion
BR ˌmɒksɪˈbʌstʃ(ə)n
AM ˌmɑksəˈbəstʃən

moxie
BR ˈmɒksi
AM ˈmɑksi

Moy
BR mɔɪ
AM mɔɪ

Moya
BR ˈmɔɪə(r)
AM ˈmɔɪə

Moyer
BR ˈmɔɪə(r)
AM ˈmɔɪər

Moyers
BR ˈmɔɪəz
AM ˈmɔɪərz

Moynahan
BR ˈmɔɪnəhən,
ˈmɔɪnəhan
AM ˈmɔɪnəˌhæn

Moyne
BR mɔɪn
AM mɔɪn

Moynihan
BR ˈmɔɪnɪən,
ˈmɔɪnɨhən,
ˈmɔɪnɨhan
AM ˈmɔɪnəˌhæn

Moyra
BR ˈmɔɪrə(r)
AM ˈmɔɪrə

Mozambican
BR ˌməʊz(ə)mˈbiːk(ə)n,
ˌməʊzamˈbiːk(ə)n, -z
AM ˈmoʊzæmˈbikən, -z

Mozambiquan
BR ˌməʊz(ə)mˈbiːk(ə)n,
ˌməʊzamˈbiːk(ə)n, -z
AM ˈmoʊzæmˈbikən, -z

Mozambique
BR ˌməʊz(ə)mˈbiːk,
ˌməʊzamˈbiːk
AM ˌmoʊzæmˈbik

Mozarab
BR məʊˈzarəb, -z
AM moʊˈzɛrəb, -z

Mozarabic
BR məʊˈzarəbɪk
AM moʊˈzɛrəbɪk

Mozart
BR ˈməʊtsɑːt
AM ˈmoʊˌtsɑrt

Mozartian
BR məʊtˈsɑːtɪən, -z
AM moʊˈtsɑrdiən, -z

mozz
BR mɒz
AM mɑz

mozzarella
BR ˌmɒtsəˈrɛlə(r)
AM ˌmɑtsəˈrɛlə

mozzle
BR ˈmɒzl, -z
AM ˈmɑzəl, -z

MP
BR ˌɛmˈpiː, -z
AM ˌɛmˈpi, -z

mph
BR ˌɛmpɪˈeɪtʃ
AM ˌɛmˌpiˈeɪtʃ

M.Phil.
BR ˌɛmˈfɪl, -z
AM ˌɛmˈfɪl, -z

Mr
BR ˈmɪstə(r)
AM ˈmɪstər

Mrs
BR ˈmɪsɪz
AM ˈmɪsɨz, ˈmɪsɨs

Ms
BR mɪz
AM mɪz

MSc
BR ˌɛmɛsˈsiː, -z
AM ˌɛmˌɛsˈsi, -z

MS-DOS®
BR ˌɛmɛsˈdɒs
AM ˌɛmˌɛsˈdɔs,
ˌɛmˌɛsˈdɑs

M.Tech.
BR ˌɛmˈtɛk, -s
AM ˌɛmˈtɛk, -s

mu
BR mjuː, -z
AM mju, -z

Mubarak
BR mʉˈbarak
AM məˈbɑrək

much
BR mʌtʃ
AM mətʃ

Muchinga
BR mʉˈtʃɪŋɡə(r)
AM mʊˈtʃɪŋɡə

muchly
BR ˈmʌtʃli
AM ˈmətʃli

muchness
BR ˈmʌtʃnəs
AM ˈmətʃnəs

mucilage
BR ˈmjuːsɨlɪdʒ,
ˈmjuːslɪdʒ
AM ˈmjus(ə)lɪdʒ

mucilaginous
BR ˌmjuːsɪˈladʒɪnəs
AM ˈmjusəˈlædʒənəs

mucin
BR ˈmjuːsɪn, -z
AM ˈmjusən, -z

muck
BR mʌk, -s, -ɪŋ, -t
AM mək, -s, -ɪŋ, -t

mucker
BR ˈmʌkə(r), -z
AM ˈməkər, -z

muckerish
BR ˈmʌk(ə)rɪʃ
AM ˈmək(ə)rɪʃ

muckheap
BR ˈmʌkhiːp, -s
AM ˈməkˌ(h)ip, -s

muckily
BR ˈmʌkɨli
AM ˈməkəli

muckiness
BR ˈmʌkɪnɨs
AM ˈməkinɨs

muckle
BR ˈmʌkl, -z
AM ˈməkəl, -z

muckrake
BR ˈmʌkreɪk, -s, -ɪŋ, -t

AM ˈmək,reɪk, -s, -ɪŋ, -t
muckraker
BR ˈmʌk,reɪkə(r), -z
AM ˈmək,reɪkər, -z
muckworm
BR ˈmʌkwəːm, -z
AM ˈmək,wərm, -z
mucky
BR ˈmʌk|i, -ɪə(r), -ɪɪst
AM ˈməki, -ər, -ɪst
mucopoly-saccharide
BR ˌmjuːkəʊ,pɒlɪˈsakərʌɪd, -z
AM ˌmjukoʊ,pɑliˈsækə,raɪd, -z
mucosa
BR mjuːˈkəʊzə(r)
AM mjuˈkoʊzə
mucosity
BR mjuːˈkɒsɪti
AM ˌmjuˈkɑsədi
mucous
BR ˈmjuːkəs
AM ˈmjukəs
mucro
BR ˈmjuːkrəʊ, -z
AM ˈmjukroʊ, -z
mucronate
BR ˈmjuːkrəneɪt, ˈmjuːkrənət
AM ˈmjukrənət, ˈmjukrə,neɪt
mucus
BR ˈmjuːkəs
AM ˈmjukəs
mud
BR mʌd
AM məd
mudbank
BR ˈmʌdbaŋk, -s
AM ˈməd,bæŋk, -s
mudbath
BR ˈmʌd|bɑːθ, ˈmʌd|baθ, -bɑːðz\-bɑːθs\-baθs
AM ˈməd,bæ|θ, -θs\-ðz
mudbrick
BR ˈmʌdbrɪk, -s
AM ˈməd,brɪk, -s
muddily
BR ˈmʌdɪli
AM ˈmədəli
muddiness
BR ˈmʌdɪnɪs
AM ˈmədinɪs
muddle
BR ˈmʌd|l, -lz, -l̩ɪŋ\-lɪŋ, -ld
AM ˈməd|əl, -əlz, -(ə)lɪŋ, -əld
muddler
BR ˈmʌdl̩ə(r), ˈmʌdlə(r), -z
AM ˈməd(ə)lər, -z
muddlingly
BR ˈmʌdl̩ɪŋli, ˈmʌdlɪŋli
AM ˈmədl̩ɪŋli
muddy
BR ˈmʌd|i, -ɪz, -ɪɪŋ, -ɪd, -ɪə(r), -ɪɪst
AM ˈmədi, -z, -ɪŋ, -d, -ər, -ɪst
Mudeford
BR ˈmʌdɪfəd
AM ˈmədəfərd
Mudéjar
BR ˌmuːˈdeɪhɑː(r)
AM muˈdɛ,hɑr
Mudéjares
BR ˌmuːˈdeɪhɑːrɛs
AM muˈdɛhɑr,ɛs
mudfish
BR ˈmʌdfɪʃ, -ɪz
AM ˈməd,fɪʃ, -ɪz
mudflap
BR ˈmʌdflap, -s
AM ˈməd,flæp, -s
mudflat
BR ˈmʌdflat, -s
AM ˈməd,flæt, -s
mudflow
BR ˈmʌdfləʊ, -z
AM ˈməd,floʊ, -z
Mudge
BR mʌdʒ
AM mədʒ
mudguard
BR ˈmʌdgɑːd, -z
AM ˈməd,gɑrd, -z
Mudie
BR ˈmjuːdi
AM ˈm(j)udi
mudlark
BR ˈmʌdlɑːk, -s
AM ˈməd,lɑrk, -s
mudpack
BR ˈmʌdpak, -s
AM ˈməd,pæk, -s
mudroom
BR ˈmʌdruːm, ˈmʌdrʊm, -z
AM ˈməd,rum, ˈməd,rʊm, -z
mudskipper
BR ˈmʌd,skɪpə(r), -z
AM ˈməd,skɪpər, -z
mudslinger
BR ˈmʌd,slɪŋə(r), -z
AM ˈməd,slɪŋər, -z
mudslinging
BR ˈmʌd,slɪŋɪŋ
AM ˈməd,slɪŋɪŋ
mudstone
BR ˈmʌdstəʊn, -z
AM ˈməd,stoʊn, -z
mud volcano
BR ˌmʌd vɒlˈkeɪnəʊ
AM ˈməd vɑlˈkeɪnoʊ
Mueller
BR ˈmʊlə(r), ˈm(j)uːlə(r)
AM ˈm(j)ulər
Muenster
BR ˈmʌnstə(r)
AM ˈmənstər
muesli
BR ˈm(j)uːzli
AM ˈmjuzli
muezzin
BR mʊˈɛzɪn, -z
AM m(j)uˈɛzn, ˈmuəzən, -z
muff
BR mʌf, -s, -ɪŋ, -t
AM məf, -s, -ɪŋ, -t
muffetee
BR ˌmʌfɪˈtiː, -z
AM ˈməfiti, -z
muffin
BR ˈmʌfɪn, -z
AM ˈməfən, -z
muffineer
BR ˌmʌfɪˈnɪə(r), -z
AM ˌməfəˈnɪ(ə)r, -z
muffish
BR ˈmʌfɪʃ
AM ˈməfɪʃ
muffle
BR ˈmʌf|l, -lz, -l̩ɪŋ\-lɪŋ, -ld
AM ˈməf|əl, -əlz, -(ə)lɪŋ, -əld
muffler
BR ˈmʌflə(r), -z
AM ˈməf(ə)lər, -z
mufti
BR ˈmʌfti
AM ˈməfti
mug
BR mʌg, -z, -ɪŋ, -d
AM məg, -z, -ɪŋ, -d
Mugabe
BR mʊˈgɑːbi
AM muˈgɑbi
mugful
BR ˈmʌgfʊl, -z
AM ˈməg,fʊl, -z
mugger
BR ˈmʌgə(r), -z
AM ˈməgər, -z
Muggeridge
BR ˈmʌg(ə)rɪdʒ
AM ˈməgərɪdʒ
mugginess
BR ˈmʌgɪnɪs
AM ˈməginɪs
mugging
BR ˈmʌgɪŋ, -z
AM ˈməgɪŋ, -z
muggins
BR ˈmʌgɪnz, -ɪz
AM ˈməgɪnz, -ɪz
muggy
BR ˈmʌg|i, -ɪə(r), -ɪɪst
AM ˈməgi, -ər, -ɪst
Mughal
BR ˈmʊg(ə)l, ˈmuːg(ə)l, -z
AM ˈməgəl, -z
mugshot
BR ˈmʌgʃɒt, -s
AM ˈməg,ʃɑt, -s
mugwort
BR ˈmʌgwəːt, -s
AM ˈməg,wərt, ˈməg,wɔ(ə)rt, -s
mugwump
BR ˈmʌgwʌmp, -s
AM ˈməg,wəmp, -s
Muhammad
BR mʊˈhaməd
AM moʊˈhɑməd, məˈhɑməd
Muhammadanism
BR mʊˈhamədənɪz(ə)m
AM moʊˈhɑmədn̩,ɪzəm, moʊˈhɑmədə,nɪzəm, məˈhɑmədn̩,ɪzəm, məˈhɑmədə,nɪzəm
Muhammed
BR mʊˈhamɪd
AM moʊˈhɑməd, məˈhɑməd
Muhammedan
BR mʊˈhamɪd(ə)n, -z
AM moʊˈhɑmədən, məˈhɑmədən, -z
Muir
BR ˈmjʊə(r), mjɔː(r)
AM ˈmju(ə)r
Muirhead
BR ˈmjʊəhɛd, ˈmjɔːhɛd
AM ˈmjʊ(ə)r,hɛd
mujahadeen
BR ˌmʊdʒəhəˈdiːn, ˌmuːdʒəhəˈdiːn
AM ˌmʊdʒəhəˈdin, ˌmudʒəhəˈdin
mujaheddin
BR ˌmʊdʒəhɪˈdiːn, ˌmuːdʒəhɪˈdiːn
AM ˌmʊdʒəhəˈdin, ˌmudʒəhəˈdin
mujahedin
BR ˌmʊdʒəhɪˈdiːn, ˌmuːdʒəhɪˈdiːn
AM ˌmʊdʒəhəˈdin, ˌmudʒəhəˈdin
mujahidin
BR ˌmʊdʒəhəˈdiːn, ˌmuːdʒəhəˈdiːn
AM ˌmʊdʒəhɪˈdin, ˌmudʒəhɪˈdin
Mukden
BR ˈmʊkdən
AM ˈmʊkdən
mukluk
BR ˈmʌklʌk, -s
AM ˈmək,lək, -s
mulatto
BR mjuːˈlatəʊ, mjʊˈlatəʊ, -z
AM m(j)ʊˈlɑdoʊ, m(j)ʊˈlædoʊ, -z
mulberry
BR ˈmʌlb(ə)r|i, -ɪz
AM ˈməl,bɛri, -z

Mulcaghey
BR mʌl'kaxi, mʌl'kahi
AM məl'keɪhi

Mulcahy
BR mʌl'kahi
AM məl'keɪhi

mulch
BR mʌl(t)ʃ, -ɪz, -ɪŋ, -t
AM məltʃ, -əz, -ɪŋ, -t

mulct
BR mʌlkt, -s, -ɪŋ, -ɪd
AM məlk|(t), -(t)s, -tɪŋ, -təd

Muldoon
BR mʌl'du:n
AM məl'dun

mule
BR mju:l, -z
AM mjul, -z

muleteer
BR ˌmju:lɪ'tɪə(r), -z
AM ˌmjul(ə)'tɪ(ə)r, -z

mulga
BR 'mʌlgə(r), -z
AM 'məlgə, -z

Mulhearn
BR mʌl'hə:n
AM məl'hərn

Mulholland
BR mʌl'hɒlənd
AM məl'hɑlən(d)

muli
BR 'mu:l|i, -ɪz
AM 'mjuli, -z

muliebrity
BR ˌmju:lɪ'ɛbrɪti
AM ˌmjuli'ɛbrədi

mulish
BR 'mju:lɪʃ
AM 'mjulɪʃ

mulishly
BR 'mju:lɪʃli
AM 'mjulɪʃli

mulishness
BR 'mju:lɪʃnɪs
AM 'mjulɪʃnɪs

mull
BR mʌl, -z, -ɪŋ, -d
AM məl, -z, -ɪŋ, -d

mulla
BR 'mʌlə(r), 'mʊlə(r), -z
AM 'mʊlə, 'mulə, -z

mullah
BR 'mʌlə(r), 'mʊlə(r), -z
AM 'mʊlə, 'mulə, -z

Mullan
BR 'mʌlən
AM 'mələn

mullein
BR 'mʌlɪn, 'mʌleɪn, -z
AM 'mələn, -z

Mullen
BR 'mʌlən
AM 'mələn

Muller
BR 'mʌlə(r)
AM 'mələr

Müller
BR 'mʊlə(r)
AM 'm(j)ʊlər
GER 'mʏlɐ

muller
BR 'mʌlə(r), -z
AM 'mələr, -z

mullet
BR 'mʌlɪt, -s
AM 'mələt, -s

Mulley
BR 'mʌli
AM 'məli

mulligan
BR 'mʌlɪg(ə)n, -z
AM 'mələgən, -z

mulligatawny
BR ˌmʌlɪgə'tɔ:ni
AM ˌmələgə'tɔni, ˌmələgə'tɑni

mulligrubs
BR 'mʌlɪgrʌbz
AM 'məliˌgrəbz

Mullins
BR 'mʌlɪnz
AM 'mələnz

mullion
BR 'mʌlɪən, -z, -d
AM 'məljən, 'məliən, -z, -d

mullock
BR 'mʌlək
AM 'mələk

mulloway
BR 'mʌləweɪ, -z
AM 'mələˌweɪ, -z

Mulroney
BR mʌl'rəʊni
AM məl'roʊni

se**multangular**
BR mʌl'taŋgjʊlə(r)
AM ˌməl'tæŋ(g)jələr

multiaxial
BR ˌmʌltɪ'aksɪəl
AM ˌməlti'æksiəl, ˌməlˌtaɪ'æksiəl

multicellular
BR ˌmʌltɪ'sɛljʊlə(r)
AM ˌməlti'sɛljələr, ˌməltə'sɛljələr, ˌməlˌtaɪ'sɛljələr

multichannel
BR ˌmʌltɪ'tʃanl
AM ˌməltiˌtʃænəl, ˌməltəˌtʃænəl, ˌməlˌtaɪˌtʃænəl

multicolor
BR 'mʌltɪˌkʌlə(r), ˌmʌltɪ'kʌlə(r)
AM ˌməlti'kələr, ˌməltə'kələr, ˌməlˌtaɪ'kələr

multicolored
BR ˌmʌltɪ'kʌləd
AM ˌməlti'kələrd, ˌməltə'kələrd, ˌməlˌtaɪ'kələrd

multicolour
BR 'mʌltɪˌkʌlə(r), ˌmʌltɪ'kʌlə(r)
AM ˌməlti'kələr, ˌməltə'kələr, ˌməlˌtaɪ'kələr

multicoloured
BR ˌmʌltɪ'kʌləd
AM ˌməlti'kələrd, ˌməltə'kələrd, ˌməlˌtaɪ'kələrd

multicultural
BR ˌmʌltɪ'kʌltʃ(ə)rəl, ˌmʌltɪ'kʌltʃ(ə)rl̩
AM ˌməlti'kəl(t)ʃ(ə)rəl, ˌməltə'kəl(t)ʃ(ə)rəl, ˌməlˌtaɪ'kəl(t)ʃ(ə)rəl

multiculturalism
BR ˌmʌltɪ'kʌltʃ(ə)rəlɪz(ə)m, ˌmʌltɪ'kʌltʃ(ə)rl̩ɪz(ə)m
AM ˌməlti'kəl(t)ʃ(ə)rəˌlɪzəm, ˌməltə'kəl(t)ʃ(ə)rəˌlɪzəm, ˌməlˌtaɪ'kəl(t)ʃ(ə)rəˌlɪzəm

multiculturalist
BR ˌmʌltɪ'kʌltʃ(ə)rəlɪst, ˌmʌltɪ'kʌltʃ(ə)rl̩ɪst, -s
AM ˌməlti'kəl(t)ʃ(ə)rələst, ˌməltə'kəl(t)ʃ(ə)rələst, ˌməlˌtaɪ'kəl(t)ʃ(ə)rələst, -s

multiculturally
BR ˌmʌltɪ'kʌltʃ(ə)rəli, ˌmʌltɪ'kʌltʃ(ə)rl̩i
AM ˌməlti'kəl(t)ʃ(ə)rəli, ˌməltə'kəl(t)ʃ(ə)rəli, ˌməlˌtaɪ'kəl(t)ʃ(ə)rəli

multidimensional
BR ˌmʌltɪdʌɪ'mɛnʃn̩(ə)l, ˌmʌltɪdʌɪ'mɛnʃən(ə)l, ˌmʌltɪdɪ'mɛnʃn̩əl, ˌmʌltɪdɪ'mɛnʃənəl
AM ˌməltidə'mɛn(t)ʃ(ə)nəl, ˌməltədə'mɛn(t)ʃ(ə)nəl, ˌməltiˌdaɪ'mɛn(t)ʃ(ə)nəl, ˌməltəˌdaɪ'mɛn(t)ʃ(ə)nəl, ˌməlˌtaɪdə'mɛn(t)ʃ(ə)nəl

multidimensionality
BR ˌmʌltɪdʌɪˌmɛnʃə'nalɪti, ˌmʌltɪdɪˌmɛnʃə'nalɪti
AM ˌməltidəˌmɛn(t)ʃə'nælədi, ˌməltidəˌmɛn(t)ʃn̩'ælədi, ˌməltiˌdaɪˌmɛn(t)ʃə'nælədi, ˌməltiˌdaɪˌmɛn(t)ʃn̩'ælədi, ˌməltəˌdaɪˌmɛn(t)ʃə'nælədi, ˌməltəˌdaɪˌmɛn(t)ʃn̩'ælədi, ˌməltədəˌmɛn(t)ʃə'nælədi, ˌməltədəˌmɛn(t)ʃn̩'ælədi, ˌməlˌtaɪdəˌmɛn(t)ʃə'nælədi, ˌməlˌtaɪdəˌmɛn(t)ʃn̩'ælədi

multidimensionally
BR ˌmʌltɪdʌɪ'mɛnʃn̩əli, ˌmʌltɪdʌɪ'mɛnʃ(ə)nəli, ˌmʌltɪdɪ'mɛnʃn̩əli, ˌmʌltɪdɪ'mɛnʃ(ə)nəli, ˌmʌltɪdʌɪ'mɛnʃn̩li, ˌmʌltɪdʌɪ'mɛnʃənli
AM ˌməltidə'mɛn(t)ʃ(ə)nəli, ˌməltiˌdaɪ'mɛn(t)ʃ(ə)nəli, ˌməltədə'mɛn(t)ʃ(ə)nəli, ˌməltəˌdaɪ'mɛn(t)ʃ(ə)nəli, ˌməlˌtaɪdə'mɛn(t)ʃ(ə)nəli

multidirectional
BR ˌmʌltɪdɪ'rɛkʃn̩(ə)l, ˌmʌltɪdɪ'rɛkʃən(ə)l, ˌmʌltɪdʌɪ'rɛkʃn̩(ə)l, ˌmʌltɪdʌɪ'rɛkʃən(ə)l
AM ˌməltidə'rɛkʃ(ə)nəl, ˌməltiˌdaɪ'rɛkʃ(ə)nəl, ˌməltədə'rɛkʃ(ə)nəl, ˌməltəˌdaɪ'rɛkʃ(ə)nəl, ˌməlˌtaɪdə'rɛkʃ(ə)nəl

multi-ethnic
BR ˌmʌltɪ'ɛθnɪk
AM ˌməlti'ɛθnɪk, ˌməlˌtaɪ'ɛθnɪk

multifaceted
BR ˌmʌltɪ'fasɪtɪd
AM ˌməlti'fæsədəd, ˌməltə'fæsədəd, ˌməlˌtaɪ'fæsədəd

multifarious
BR ˌmʌltɪ'fɛ:rɪəs
AM ˌməlti'fɛriəs, ˌməltə'fɛriəs

multifariously
BR ˌmʌltɪ'fɛ:rɪəsli
AM ˌməlti'fɛriəsli, ˌməltə'fɛriəsli

multifariousness
BR ˌmʌltɪ'fɛ:rɪəsnəs
AM ˌməlti'fɛriəsnəs, ˌməltə'fɛriəsnəs

multifid
BR 'mʌltɪfɪd
AM 'məltiˌfɪd, 'məltəˌfɪd, 'məlˌtaɪˌfɪd

multifoil
BR 'mʌltɪfɔɪl

AM ˈməltiˌfɔɪl, ˈməltəˌfɔɪl, ˈməlˌtaɪˌfɔɪl

multiform
BR ˈmʌltɪfɔːm
AM ˈməltiˌfɔ(ə)rm, ˈməltəˌfɔ(ə)rm, ˈməlˌtaɪˌfɔ(ə)rm

multiformity
BR ˌmʌltɪˈfɔːmɪt|i, -ɪz
AM ˌməltiˈfɔrmədi, ˌməltəˈfɔrmədi, -z

multifunction
BR ˌmʌltɪˈfʌŋ(k)ʃn
AM ˌməltiˈfənkʃən, ˌməltəˈfənkʃən, ˌməlˌtaɪˈfənkʃən

multifunctional
BR ˌmʌltɪˈfʌŋ(k)ʃn̩(ə)l, ˌmʌltɪˈfʌŋ(k)ʃən(ə)l
AM ˌməltiˈfənkʃ(ə)nəl, ˌməltəˈfənkʃ(ə)nəl, ˌməlˌtaɪˈfənkʃ(ə)nəl

multigrade
BR ˈmʌltɪgreɪd, -z
AM ˈməltiˌgreɪd, ˈməltəˌgreɪd, ˈməlˌtaɪˌgreɪd, -z

multihull
BR ˈmʌltɪhʌl, -z
AM ˈməltiˌhəl, ˈməltəˌhəl, ˈməlˌtaɪˌhəl, -z

multilateral
BR ˌmʌltɪˈlat(ə)rəl, ˌmʌltɪˈlat(ə)rl̩
AM ˌməltiˈlædərəl, ˌməltiˈlætrəl, ˌməltəˈlædərəl, ˌməltəˈlætrəl, ˌməlˌtaɪˈlædərəl, ˌməlˌtaɪˈlætrəl

multilateralism
BR ˌmʌltɪˈlat(ə)rəlɪz(ə)m, ˌmʌltɪˈlat(ə)rl̩ɪz(ə)m
AM ˈməltilætərəlɪzəm, ˈməltəlætərəlɪzəm, ˈməlˌtaɪlætərəlɪzəm

multilateralist
BR ˌmʌltɪˈlat(ə)rəlɪst, ˌmʌltɪˈlatrl̩ɪst, -s
AM ˈməltilætərələst, ˈməltəlætərələst, ˈməlˌtaɪlætərələst, -s

multilaterally
BR ˌmʌltɪˈlat(ə)rəli, ˌmʌltɪˈlat(ə)rl̩i
AM ˌməltiˈlædərəli, ˌməltiˈlætrəli, ˌməltəˈlædərəli, ˌməltəˈlætrəli, ˌməlˌtaɪˈlædərəli, ˌməlˌtaɪˈlætrəli

multi-layered
BR ˌmʌltɪˈleɪəd
AM ˌməltiˈleɪərd, ˌməltəˈleɪərd, ˌməlˌtaɪˈleɪərd

multilevel
BR ˌmʌltɪˈlɛvl
AM ˌməltiˈlɛvəl, ˌməltəˈlɛvəl, ˌməlˌtaɪˈlɛvəl

multilingual
BR ˌmʌltɪˈlɪŋgw(ə)l
AM ˌməltiˈlɪŋgwəl, ˌməltəˈlɪŋgwəl, ˌməlˌtaɪˈlɪŋgwəl

multilingualism
BR ˌmʌltɪˈlɪŋgwəlɪz(ə)m, ˌmʌltɪˈlɪŋgwl̩ɪz(ə)m
AM ˌməltiˈlɪŋgwəˌlɪzəm, ˌməltəˈlɪŋgwəˌlɪzəm, ˌməlˌtaɪˈlɪŋgwəˌlɪzəm

multilingually
BR ˌmʌltɪˈlɪŋgwəli, ˌmʌltɪˈlɪŋgwl̩i
AM ˌməltiˈlɪŋgwəli, ˌməltəˈlɪŋgwəli, ˌməlˌtaɪˈlɪŋgwəli

multimedia
BR ˌmʌltɪˈmiːdɪə(r)
AM ˌməltiˈmidiə, ˌməltəˈmidiə

multimillion
BR ˌmʌltɪˈmɪljən, -z
AM ˌməltiˈmɪljən, ˌməltəˈmɪljən, -z

multimillionaire
BR ˌmʌltɪˌmɪljəˈnɛː(r), -z
AM ˌməltiˌmɪljəˈnɛ(ə)r, ˌməltəˌmɪljəˈnɛ(ə)r, ˌməlˌtaɪˌmɪljəˈnɛ(ə)r, -z

multimillionnaire
BR ˌmʌltɪˌmɪljəˈnɛː(r), -z
AM ˌməltiˌmɪljəˈnɛ(ə)r, ˌməltəˌmɪljəˈnɛ(ə)r, ˌməlˌtaɪˌmɪljəˈnɛ(ə)r, -z

multinational
BR ˌmʌltɪˈnaʃn̩(ə)l, ˌmʌltɪˈnaʃən(ə)l, -z
AM ˌməltiˈnæʃ(ə)nəl, ˌməltəˈnæʃ(ə)nəl, ˌməlˌtaɪˈnæʃ(ə)nəl, -z

multinationally
BR ˌmʌltɪˈnaʃn̩əli, ˌmʌltɪˈnaʃn̩l̩i, ˌmʌltɪˈnaʃənl̩i, ˌmʌltɪˈnaʃ(ə)nəli
AM ˌməltiˈnæʃ(ə)nəli, ˌməltəˈnæʃ(ə)nəli, ˌməlˌtaɪˈnæʃ(ə)nəli

multinomial
BR ˌmʌltɪˈnəʊmɪəl, -z
AM ˌməltiˈnoʊmiəl, ˌməltəˈnoʊmiəl, -z

multiparous
BR mʌlˈtɪp(ə)rəs
AM ˌməlˈtɪpərəs

multipartite
BR ˌmʌltɪˈpɑːtʌɪt
AM ˌməltiˈpɑrˌtaɪt, ˌməltəˈpɑrˌtaɪt, ˌməlˌtaɪˈpɑrˌtaɪt

multi-party
BR ˌmʌltɪˈpɑːti
AM ˌməltiˈpɑrdi, ˌməltəˈpɑrdi, ˌməlˌtaɪˈpɑrdi

multiphase
BR ˈmʌltɪfeɪz, -ɪz
AM ˌməltiˈfeɪz, ˌməltəˈfeɪz, ˌməlˌtaɪˈfeɪz, -ɪz

multiple
BR ˈmʌltɪpl, -z
AM ˈməltəpəl, -z

multiplex
BR ˈmʌltɪplɛks
AM ˈməltiˌplɛks, ˈməltəˌplɛks

multiplexer
BR ˈmʌltɪplɛksə(r), -z
AM ˈməltiˌplɛksər, ˈməltəˌplɛksər, -z

multiplexor
BR ˈmʌltɪplɛksə(r), -z
AM ˈməltiˌplɛksər, ˈməltəˌplɛksər, -z

multipliable
BR ˈmʌltɪplʌɪəbl
AM ˈməltəplaɪəbəl, ˈməltiplaɪəbəl

multiplicable
BR ˈmʌltɪplɪkəbl
AM ˌməltəˈplɪkəbəl, ˌməltiˈplɪkəbəl

multiplicand
BR ˌmʌltɪplɪˈkand, ˈmʌltɪplɪkand, -z
AM ˌməltəpləˈkænd, -z

multiplication
BR ˌmʌltɪplɪˈkeɪʃn
AM ˌməltəpləˈkeɪʃən

multiplicative
BR ˈmʌltɪplɪkətɪv
AM ˈməltəpləˌkeɪdɪv, ˌməltəˈplɪkədɪv

multiplicity
BR ˌmʌltɪˈplɪsɪti
AM ˌməltəˈplɪsɪdi

multiplier
BR ˈmʌltɪplʌɪə(r), -z
AM ˈməltəˌplaɪər, -z

multiply
BR ˈmʌltɪplʌɪ, -z, -ɪŋ, -d
AM ˈməltəˌplaɪ, -z, -ɪŋ, -d

multipolar
BR ˌmʌltɪˈpəʊlə(r)
AM ˌməltiˈpoʊlər, ˌməltəˈpoʊlər, ˌməlˌtaɪˈpoʊlər

multiprocessing
BR ˌmʌltɪˈprəʊsɛsɪŋ, -z
AM ˌməltiˈprɑsəsɪŋ, ˌməltəˈprɑsəsɪŋ, ˌməlˌtaɪˈprɑsəsɪŋ, ˌmɛltiˈprɑˌsɛsɪŋ, ˌməltəˈprɑˌsɛsɪŋ, ˌməltaɪˈprɑˌsɛsɪŋ-z

multiprocessor
BR ˌmʌltɪˈprəʊsɛsə(r), -z
AM ˌməltiˈprɑsəsər, ˌməltəˈprɑsəsər, ˌməltiˈprɑˌsɛsər, ˌməltəˈprɑˌsɛsər, -z

multiprogramming
BR ˌmʌltɪˈprəʊgramɪŋ, -z
AM ˌməltiˈproʊˌgræmɪŋ, ˌməltəˈproʊˌgræmɪŋ, ˌməlˌtaɪˈproʊˌgræmɪŋ, -z

multipurpose
BR ˌmʌltɪˈpəːpəs
AM ˌməltiˌpərpəs, ˌməltəˌpərpəs, ˌməlˌtaɪˌpərpəs

multiracial
BR ˌmʌltɪˈreɪʃl
AM ˌməltiˈreɪʃəl, ˌməltəˈreɪʃəl, ˌməlˌtaɪˈreɪʃəl

multiracially
BR ˌmʌltɪˈreɪʃl̩i, ˌmʌltɪˈreɪʃəli
AM ˌməltiˈreɪʃəli, ˌməltəˈreɪʃəli, ˌməlˌtaɪˈreɪʃəli

multistage
BR ˌmʌltɪˈsteɪdʒ
AM ˌməltiˈsteɪdʒ, ˌməltəˈsteɪdʒ, ˌməlˌtaɪˈsteɪdʒ

multistorey
BR ˌmʌltɪˈstɔːri
AM ˌməltiˌstɔri, ˌməltəˌstɔri, ˌməlˌtaɪˌstɔri

multitude
BR ˈmʌltɪtjuːd, ˈmʌltɪtʃuːd, -z
AM ˈməltəˌt(j)ud, -z

multitudinous
BR ˌmʌltɪˈtjuːdɪnəs, ˌmʌltɪˈtʃuːdɪnəs
AM ˌməltəˈt(j)udn̩əs

multitudinously
BR ˌmʌltɪˈtjuːdɪnəsli, ˌmʌltɪˈtʃuːdɪnəsli
AM ˌməltəˌt(j)udn̩əsli

multitudinousness
BR ˌmʌltɪˈtjuːdɪnəsnəs, ˌmʌltɪˈtʃuːdɪnəsnəs
AM ˌməltəˌt(j)udn̩əsnəs

multivalency
BR ˌmʌltɪˈveɪləns|i, ˌmʌltɪˈveɪln̩s|i, -ɪz
AM ˌməltiˈveɪlənsi, ˌməltəˈveɪlənsi, ˌməlˌtaɪˈveɪlənsi, -z

multivalent
BR ˌmʌltɪˈveɪlənt, ˌmʌltɪˈveɪln̩t

AM ˌməlti'veɪlənt, ˌməltə'veɪlənt, ˌməlˌtaɪ'veɪlənt

multivalve
BR ˌmʌltɪ'valv
AM ˌməlti'vælv, ˌməltə'vælv, ˌməlˌtaɪ'vælv

multivariate
BR ˌmʌltɪ'vɛːrɪət
AM ˌməlti'vɛriət, ˌməltə'vɛriət, ˌməlˌtaɪ'vɛriət

multiversity
BR ˌmʌltɪ'vəːsɪt|i, -ɪz
AM ˌməlti'vərsədi, ˌməltə'vərsədi, -z

multivocal
BR ˌmʌltɪ'vəʊkl
AM ˌməlti'voʊkəl, ˌməltə'voʊkəl, ˌməlˌtaɪ'voʊkəl

multum in parvo
BR ˌmʌltəm ɪn 'pɑːvəʊ
AM ˌmʊltəm ɪn 'pɑrvoʊ

multure
BR 'mʌltʃə(r), -z
AM 'məltʃər, -z

mum
BR mʌm, -z, -ɪŋ, -d
AM məm, -z, -ɪŋ, -d

mumble
BR 'mʌmb|l, -lz, -l̩ɪŋ\-lɪŋ, -ld
AM 'məmbəl, -əlz, -(ə)lɪŋ, -əld

mumbler
BR 'mʌmbl̩ə(r), 'mʌmblə(r), -z
AM 'məmb(ə)lər, -z

Mumbles
BR 'mʌmblz
AM 'məmblz

mumbling
BR 'mʌmbl̩ɪŋ, 'mʌmblɪŋ, -z
AM 'məmb(ə)lɪŋ, -z

mumblingly
BR 'mʌmbl̩ɪŋli, 'mʌmblɪŋli
AM 'məmbəlɪŋli

mumbo-jumbo
BR ˌmʌmbəʊ'dʒʌmbəʊ, -z
AM 'məmboʊ'dʒəmboʊ, -z

mumchance
BR 'mʌmtʃɑːns, 'mʌmtʃans, -ɪz
AM 'məmˌtʃæns, -əz

mu-meson
BR ˌmjuː'miːzɒn, ˌmjuː'miːsɒn, ˌmjuː'mɛzɒn, ˌmjuː'mɛsɒn, ˌmjuː'meɪzɒn, -z
AM 'mjuˌmeɪˌzɑn, 'mjuˌmeɪˌsɑn, -z

Mumford
BR 'mʌmfəd
AM 'məmfərd

mummer
BR 'mʌmə(r), -z
AM 'məmər, -z

mummery
BR 'mʌm(ə)ri
AM 'məməri

mummification
BR ˌmʌmɨfɪ'keɪʃn
AM ˌməməfə'keɪʃən

mummify
BR mʌmɨfʌɪ, -z, -ɪŋ, -d
AM 'məməˌfaɪ, -z, -ɪŋ, -d

mumming
BR 'mʌmɪŋ
AM 'məmɪŋ

mummy
BR 'mʌm|i, -ɪz
AM 'məmi, -z

mumpish
BR 'mʌmpɪʃ
AM 'məmpɪʃ

mumps
BR mʌmps
AM məmps

Munch
BR mʊŋk
AM məŋk, mʊŋk

munch
BR mʌn(t)ʃ, -ɪz, -ɪŋ, -t
AM mən(t)ʃ, -əz, -ɪŋ, -t

Munchausen
BR 'mʊntʃaʊzn
AM 'mʊnˌ(t)ʃaʊzn

München
BR 'mʊn(t)ʃ(ə)n
AM 'mʊntʃən
GER 'mʏnçn̩

munchies
BR 'mʌn(t)ʃɪz
AM 'mən(t)ʃiz

Muncie
BR 'mʌnsi
AM 'mənsi

Munda
BR 'mʊndə(*r*), -z
AM 'mʊndə, -z

mundane
BR ˌmʌn'deɪn
AM ˌmən'deɪn

mundanely
BR ˌmʌn'deɪnli
AM ˌmən'deɪnli

mundaneness
BR ˌmʌn'deɪnnɪs
AM ˌmən'deɪ(n)nɪs

mundanity
BR ˌmʌn'deɪnɪt|i, -ɪz
AM ˌmən'deɪnɪdi, -z

mung
BR mʌŋ, muːŋ
AM məŋ

mungo
BR 'mʌŋgəʊ
AM 'məŋgoʊ

Munich
BR 'mjuːnɪk, 'mjuːnɪx
AM 'mjunɪk

municipal
BR mjʊ'nɪsɪpl
AM mju'nɪsəpəl, mjə'nɪsəpəl

municipalisation
BR mjʊˌnɪsɪpəlʌɪ'zeɪʃn, mjʊˌnɪsɪpl̩ʌɪ'zeɪʃn
AM mjuˌnɪsəpələ'zeɪʃən, mjəˌnɪsəpələ'zeɪʃən, mjuˌnɪsəpəˌlaɪ'zeɪʃən, mjəˌnɪsəpəˌlaɪ'zeɪʃən

municipalise
BR mjʊ'nɪsɪpəlʌɪz, mjʊ'nɪsɪpl̩ʌɪz, -ɪz, -ɪŋ, -d
AM mju'nɪsəpəˌlaɪz, mjə'nɪsəpəˌlaɪz, -ɪz, -ɪŋ, -d

municipality
BR mjʊˌnɪsɪ'palɪt|i, ˌmjuːnɪsɪ'palɪt|i, -ɪz
AM mjuˌnɪsə'pælədi, mjəˌnɪsə'pælədi, -z

municipalization
BR mjʊˌnɪsɪpəlʌɪ'zeɪʃn, mjʊˌnɪsɪpl̩ʌɪ'zeɪʃn
AM mjuˌnɪsəpələ'zeɪʃən, mjəˌnɪsəpələ'zeɪʃən, mjuˌnɪsəpəˌlaɪ'zeɪʃən, mjəˌnɪsəpəˌlaɪ'zeɪʃən

municipalize
BR mjʊ'nɪsɪpəlʌɪz, mjʊ'nɪsɪpl̩ʌɪz, -ɪz, -ɪŋ, -d
AM mju'nɪsəpəˌlaɪz, mjə'nɪsəpəˌlaɪz, -ɪz, -ɪŋ, -d

municipally
BR mjʊ'nɪsɪpl̩i, mjʊ'nɪsɪpəli
AM mju'nɪsəpəli, mjə'nɪsəpəli

munificence
BR mjʊ'nɪfɪsns
AM mju'nɪfəsəns, mjə'nɪfəsəns

munificent
BR mjʊ'nɪfɪsnt
AM mju'nɪfəsənt, mjə'nɪfəsənt

munificently
BR mjʊ'nɪfɪsntli
AM mju'nɪfəsəntli, mjə'nɪfəsən(t)li

muniment
BR mjuːnɪm(ə)nt, -s
AM 'mjunəmənt, -s

munition
BR mjʊ'nɪʃn, -z
AM mju'nɪʃən, mjə'nɪʃən, -z

munitioner
BR mjʊ'nɪʃn̩ə(r), mjʊ'nɪʃənə(r), -z
AM mju'nɪʃənər, mjə'nɪʃənər, -z

munnion
BR 'mʌnjən, -z
AM 'mənjən, -z

Muñoz
BR 'muːnjəʊz
AM 'munjoʊz
SP mu'ɲoθ, mu'ɲos

Munro
BR mən'rəʊ, mʌn'rəʊ
AM mən'roʊ

munshi
BR 'muːnʃiː, -z
AM 'mənʃi, -z

Munster
BR 'mʌnstə(r)
AM 'mənstər

Münster
BR 'mʊnstə(r)
AM 'mʊnstər
GER 'mʏnstɐ

munt
BR mʊnt, -s
AM mʊnt, -s

muntjac
BR 'mʌntdʒak, -s
AM 'mənt,dʒæk, -s

muntjak
BR 'mʌntdʒak, -s
AM 'mənt,dʒæk, -s

Muntz metal
BR 'mʌnts ˌmɛtl
AM 'mən(t)s ˌmɛdl

muon
BR 'mjuːɒn, -z
AM 'mjuˌɑn, -z

muonic
BR mjuː'ɒnɪk
AM mju'ɑnɪk, mjə'wɑnɪk

murage
BR 'mjʊər|ɪdʒ, 'mjɔːr|ɪdʒ, -ɪdʒɪz
AM 'mjʊrɪdʒ, -ɪz

mural
BR 'mjʊərəl, 'mjʊərl̩, 'mjɔːrəl, 'mjɔːrl̩, -z
AM 'mjʊrəl, -z

muralist
BR 'mjʊərl̩ɪst, 'mjʊərəlɪst, 'mjɔːrl̩ɪst, 'mjɔːrəlɪst, -s
AM 'mjʊrələst, -s

Murchison
BR 'məːtʃɪs(ə)n
AM 'mərtʃəzən

murder
BR 'məːd|ə(r), -əz, -(ə)rɪŋ, -əd
AM 'mərdər, -z, -ɪŋ, -d

murderer
BR ˈməːd(ə)rə(r), -z
AM ˈmərdərər, -z

murderess
BR ˈməːdərɛs, ˈməːd(ə)rɪs, ˌməːdəˈrɛs, -ɪz
AM ˈmərdərəs, -əz

murderous
BR ˈməːd(ə)rəs
AM ˈmərd(ə)rəs

murderously
BR ˈməːd(ə)rəsli
AM ˈmərd(ə)rəsli

murderousness
BR ˈməːd(ə)rəsnəs
AM ˈmərd(ə)rəsnəs

Murdo
BR ˈməːdəʊ
AM ˈmərdoʊ

Murdoch
BR ˈməːdɒk, ˈməːdəx
AM ˈmərdɑk, ˈmərdək

mure
BR mjʊə(r), mjɔː(r), -z, -ɪŋ, -d
AM mjʊ(ə)r, -z, -ɪŋ, -d

murex
BR ˈmjʊərɛks, ˈmjɔːrɛks
AM ˈmjʊˌrɛks

Murgatroyd
BR ˈməːgətrɔɪd
AM ˈmərgəˌtrɔɪd

muriatic
BR ˌmjʊərɪˈatɪk, ˌmjɔːrɪˈatɪk
AM ˌmjʊriˈædɪk

Muriel
BR ˈmjʊərɪəl, ˈmjɔːrɪəl
AM ˈmjʊriəl

Murillo
BR mjʊˈrɪləʊ
AM m(j)ʊˈriljoʊ
SP muˈrijo

murine
BR ˈmjʊərʌɪn, ˈmjʊərɪn, ˈmjɔːrʌɪn, ˈmjɔːrɪn
AM ˈmjuˌraɪn, ˈmjurən, ˈmjuˌrin

murk
BR məːk
AM mərk

murkily
BR ˈməːkɪli
AM ˈmərkəli

murkiness
BR ˈməːkɪnɪs
AM ˈmərkinɪs

murky
BR ˈməːk|i, -ɪə(r), -ɪɪst
AM ˈmərki, -ər, -ɪst

Murmansk
BR məːˈmansk
AM mʊrˈmænsk, ˈmʊrˌmænsk
RUS ˈmurmənsk

murmur
BR ˈməːm|ə(r), -əz, -(ə)rɪŋ, -əd
AM ˈmərm|ər, -ərz, -(ə)rɪŋ, -ərd

murmurer
BR ˈməːm(ə)rə(r), -z
AM ˈmərmərər, -z

murmuringly
BR ˈməːm(ə)rɪŋli
AM ˈmərm(ə)rɪŋli

murmurous
BR ˈməːm(ə)rəs
AM ˈmərm(ə)rəs

murphy
BR ˈməːf|i, -ɪz
AM ˈmərfi, -z

murrain
BR ˈmʌrɪn, ˈmʌrn̩, ˈmʌreɪn, -z
AM ˈmərən, -z

Murray
BR ˈmʌri
AM ˈməri

murre
BR məː(r), -z
AM mər, -z

murrelet
BR ˈməːlɪt, -s
AM ˈmərlət, -s

murrey
BR ˈmʌr|i, -ɪz
AM ˈməri, -z

murrhine
BR ˈmʌrɪn, ˈmʌrn̩, ˈmʌrʌɪn, -z
AM ˈmərən, ˈməˌraɪn, -z

Murrow
BR ˈmʌrəʊ
AM ˈməroʊ

Murrumbidgee
BR ˌmʌrəmˈbɪdʒiː
AM ˌmərəmˈbɪdʒi

Murtagh
BR ˈməːtə(*r*)
AM ˈmərˌtɔ

murther
BR ˈməːð|ə(r), -əz, -(ə)rɪŋ, -əd
AM ˈmərð|ər, -ərz, -(ə)rɪŋ, -ərd

Mururoa
BR ˌm(j)ʊərəˈrəʊə(*r*)
AM ˌmjʊrəˈroʊə

musaceous
BR mjuːˈzeɪʃəs, mjʊˈzeɪʃəs
AM mjuˈzeɪʃəs

Musala
BR mjuːˈsɑːlə(*r*)
AM mjuˈsɑlə

muscadel
BR ˌmʌskəˈdɛl, -z
AM ˈməskəˈdɛl, -z

Muscadet
BR ˈmʌskədeɪ, ˌmʌskəˈdeɪ, -z
AM ˈməskəˌdɛt, -s

muscadine
BR ˈmʌskədʌɪn, ˈmʌskədɪn, -z
AM ˈməskəˌdaɪn, -z

muscarine
BR ˈmʌskəriːn, ˈmʌskərɪn, -z
AM ˈməskərən, ˈməskəˌrin, -z

muscat
BR ˈmʌskat, -s
AM ˈməˌskæt, -s

muscatel
BR ˌmʌskəˈtɛl, -z
AM ˈməskəˈtɛl, -z

muscle
BR ˈmʌs|l, -lz, -l̩ɪŋ\-lɪŋ, -ld
AM ˈməs|əl, -əlz, -(ə)lɪŋ, -əld

muscleless
BR ˈmʌsl̩ləs
AM ˈməs(l)ləs

muscly
BR ˈmʌsl̩i
AM ˈməsl̩i

muscologist
BR mʌˈskɒlədʒɪst, -s
AM məsˈkɑlədʒəst, -s

muscology
BR mʌˈskɒlədʒi
AM məsˈkɑlədʒi

muscovado
BR ˌmʌskəˈvɑːdəʊ, -z
AM ˌməskəˈveɪdoʊ, ˌməskəˈvɑdoʊ, -z

Muscovite
BR ˈmʌskəvʌɪt, -s
AM ˈməskəˌvaɪt, -s

Muscovy
BR ˈmʌskəvi
AM ˈməskəvi

muscular
BR ˈmʌskjʊlə(r)
AM ˈməskjələr

muscularity
BR ˌmʌskjʊˈlarɪti
AM ˌməskjəˈlɛrədi

muscularly
BR ˈmʌskjʊləli
AM ˈməskjələrli

musculature
BR ˈmʌskjʊlətʃə(r)
AM ˈməskjələtʃər

musculoskeletal
BR ˌmʌskjʊləʊˈskɛlɪtl
AM ˈməskjələˈskɛlətl

muse
BR mjuːz, -ɪz, -ɪŋ, -d
AM mjuz, -əz, -ɪŋ, -d

museology
BR ˌmjuːzɪˈɒlədʒi
AM ˌmjuziˈɑlədʒi

musette
BR mjuːˈzɛt, mjʊˈzɛt, -s
AM mjuˈzɛt, -s

museum
BR mjuːˈziːəm, mjʊˈziːəm, -z
AM mjuˈziəm, -z

Musgrave
BR ˈmʌzgreɪv
AM ˈməsgreɪv

Musgrove
BR ˈmʌzgrəʊv
AM ˈməsgroʊv

mush[1]
noun, man
BR mʊʃ, -ɪz
AM məʃ, -əz

mush[2]
verb
BR mʌʃ, -ɪz, -ɪŋ, -t
AM məʃ, -əz, -ɪŋ, -t

mushily
BR ˈmʌʃɪli
AM ˈməʃəli

mushiness
BR ˈmʌʃɪnɪs
AM ˈməʃinɪs

mushroom
BR ˈmʌʃruːm, ˈmʌʃrʊm, -z
AM ˈməʃˌrum, ˈməʃˌrʊm, -z

mushroomy
BR ˈmʌʃruːmi, ˈmʌʃrʊmi
AM ˈməʃˌrumi, ˈməʃˌrʊmi

mushy
BR ˈmʌʃ|i, -ɪə(r), -ɪɪst
AM ˈməʃi, -ər, -ɪst

music
BR ˈmjuːzɪk
AM ˈmjuzɪk

musical
BR ˈmjuːzɪkl, -z
AM ˈmjuzəkəl, -z

musicale
BR ˌmjuːzɪˈkɑːl, ˌmjuːzɪˈkal, -z
AM ˌmjuzəˈkæl, -z

musicalise
BR ˈmjuːzɪkəlʌɪz, ˈmjuːzɪkl̩ʌɪz, -ɪz, -ɪŋ, -d
AM ˈmjuzəkəˌlaɪz, -ɪz, -ɪŋ, -d

musicality
BR ˌmjuːzɪˈkalɪti
AM ˌmjuzəˈkælədi

musicalize
BR ˈmjuːzɪkəlʌɪz, ˈmjuːzɪkl̩ʌɪz, -ɪz, -ɪŋ, -d
AM ˈmjuzəkəˌlaɪz, -ɪz, -ɪŋ, -d

musically
BR ˈmjuːzɪkl̩i, ˈmjuːzɪkli
AM ˈmjuzək(ə)li

musicalness
BR ˈmjuːzɪklnəs

AM 'mjuzəkəlnəs

musician
BR mjuː'zɪʃn, mjʊ'zɪʃn, -z
AM mju'zɪʃən, -z

musicianly
BR mjuː'zɪʃnli, mjʊ'zɪʃnli
AM mju'zɪʃənli

musicianship
BR mjuː'zɪʃnʃɪp, mjʊ'zɪʃnʃɪp
AM mju'zɪʃən,ʃɪp

musicological
BR ,mjuːzɪkə'lɒdʒɪkl
AM ¦mjuzəkə'lɑdʒəkl

musicologically
BR ,mjuːzɪkə'lɒdʒɪkli
AM ¦mjuzəkə'lɑdʒ(ə)kli

musicologist
BR ,mjuːzɪ'kɒlədʒɪst, -s
AM ,mjuzə'kɑlədʒəst, -s

musicology
BR ,mjuːzɪ'kɒlədʒi
AM ,mjuzə'kɑlədʒi

musing
BR 'mjuːzɪŋ, -z
AM 'mjuzɪŋ, -z

musingly
BR 'mjuːzɪŋli
AM 'mjuzɪŋli

musique concrète
BR mjuː,ziːk kɒŋ'krɛt, mjʊ,ziːk +
AM mʊ¦zik kɑn'krɛt

musk
BR mʌsk
AM məsk

muskeg
BR 'mʌskɛg
AM 'məs,kɛg

muskellunge
BR 'mʌskəlʌn(d)ʒ, -ɪz
AM 'məskə,ləndʒ, -əz

musket
BR 'mʌskɪt, -s
AM 'məskət, -s

musketeer
BR ,mʌskɪ'tɪə(r), -z
AM ,məskə'tɪ(ə)r, -z

musketoon
BR ,mʌskɪ'tuːn, -z
AM ,məskə'tun, -z

musketry
BR 'mʌskɪtri
AM 'məskətri

muskie
BR 'mʌski
AM 'məski

muskiness
BR 'mʌskɪnɪs
AM 'məskinɪs

muskmelon
BR 'mʌsk,mɛlən, -z
AM 'məsk,mɛlən, 'məʃ,mɛlən, -z

Muskogean
BR mʌ'skəʊgiən, -z
AM mə'skoʊgiən, ,mə'skoʊgiən, -z

muskrat
BR 'mʌskrat, -s
AM 'mə,skræt, -s

muskwood
BR 'mʌskwʊd
AM 'məsk,wʊd

musky
BR 'mʌski
AM 'məski

Muslim
BR 'mʊzlɪm, 'mʌzlɪm, 'mʊslɪm, -z
AM 'məzləm, 'mʊzləm, -z

muslin
BR 'mʌzlɪn, -d
AM 'məzlən, -d

musmon
BR 'mʌsmən, 'mʌzmən, -z
AM 'məzmən, -z

muso
BR 'mjuːzəʊ, -z
AM 'mjuzoʊ, -z

musquash
BR 'mʌskwɒʃ, -ɪz
AM 'mə,skwɔʃ, 'mə,skwɑʃ, -əz

muss
BR mʌs, -ɪz, -ɪŋ, -t
AM məs, -əz, -ɪŋ, -t

mussel
BR 'mʌsl, -z
AM 'məsəl, -z

Musselburgh
BR 'mʌslb(ə)rə(r)
AM 'məsl,bərg, 'məsl,bərə

Mussolini
BR ,mʊsə'liːni, ,mʌsə'liːni
AM ,musə'lini

Mussorgsky
BR mʊ'sɔːgski, mʊ'zɔːgski
AM mə'sɔrgski
RUS 'musərkskʲij

Mussulman
BR 'mʌs(ə)lmən, -z
AM 'məsəlmən, -z

Mussulmen
BR 'mʌs(ə)lmən
AM 'məsəlmən

mussy
BR 'mʌsi
AM 'məsi

must
BR mʌst
AM məst

mustache
BR mə'stɑːʃ, -ɪz, -t
AM 'mə,stæʃ, mə'stæʃ, -əz, -t

mustachio
BR mə'stɑːʃ(ɪ)əʊ, mə'staʃ(ɪ)əʊ, -z, -d
AM mə'stæʃioʊ, -z, -d

Mustafa
BR 'mʊstəfə(r), 'mʌstəfə(r), mʊ'stɑːfə(r), mʊ'stafə(r)
AM 'mʊstəfə, mʊs'tɑfə

mustang
BR 'mʌstaŋ, -z
AM 'mə,stæŋ, -z

Mustapha
BR 'mʊstəfə(r), 'mʌstəfə(r), mʊ'stɑːfə(r), mʊ'stafə(r)
AM 'mʊstəfə, mʊs'tɑfə

mustard
BR 'mʌstəd
AM 'məstərd

muster
BR 'mʌst|ə(r), -əz, -(ə)rɪŋ, -əd
AM 'məst|ər, -ərz, -(ə)rɪŋ, -ərd

musterer
BR 'mʌst(ə)rə(r), -z
AM 'məst(ə)rər, -z

musth
BR mʌst
AM məst

mustily
BR 'mʌstɪli
AM 'məstəli

mustiness
BR 'mʌstɪnɪs
AM 'məstinɪs

Mustique
BR mʊ'stiːk
AM mə'stik

mustn't
BR 'mʌsnt
AM 'məsnt

musty
BR 'mʌst|i, -ɪə(r), -ɪɪst
AM 'məsti, -ər, -ɪst

Mut
BR mʌt
AM mət

mutability
BR ,mjuːtə'bɪlɪti
AM ,mjudə'bɪlɪdi

mutable
BR 'mjuːtəbl
AM 'mjudəbəl

mutagen
BR 'mjuːtədʒ(ə)n
AM 'mjudə,dʒɛn, 'mjudədʒən

mutagenesis
BR ,mjuːtə'dʒɛnɪsɪs
AM ,mjudə'dʒɛnəsəs

mutagenic
BR ,mjuːtə'dʒɛnɪk
AM ,mjudə'dʒɛnɪk

mutant
BR 'mjuːt(ə)nt, -s
AM 'mjutnt, -s

mutate
BR mjuː'teɪt, -s, -ɪŋ, -ɪd
AM 'mju,teɪ|t, -ts, -dɪŋ, -dɪd

mutation
BR mjuː'teɪʃn, -z
AM mju'teɪʃən, -z

mutational
BR mjuː'teɪʃn̩(ə)l, mjuː'teɪʃən(ə)l
AM ,mju'teɪʃ(ə)nəl

mutationally
BR mjuː'teɪʃn̩əli, mjuː'teɪʃn̩l̩i, mjuː'teɪʃənl̩i, mjuː'teɪʃ(ə)nəli
AM mju'teɪʃ(ə)nəli

mutatis mutandis
BR m(j)uː,tɑːtɪs m(j)uː'tandɪs
AM m(j)u,tɑdəs m(j)u'tɑndəs, + m(j)u'tændəs

mutch
BR mʌtʃ, -ɪz
AM mətʃ, -əz

mute
BR mjuːt, -s, -ɪŋ, -ɪd
AM mju|t, -ts, -dɪŋ, -dəd

mutely
BR 'mjuːtli
AM 'mjutli

muteness
BR 'mjuːtnəs
AM 'mjutnəs

mutilate
BR 'mjuːtɪleɪt, 'mjuːtl̩eɪt, -s, -ɪŋ, -ɪd
AM 'mjudl,eɪ|t, -ts, -dɪŋ, -dɪd

mutilation
BR ,mjuːtɪ'leɪʃn, ,mjuːtl̩'eɪʃn, -z
AM ,mjudl'eɪʃən, -z

mutilative
BR 'mjuːtɪlətɪv, 'mjuːtl̩ətɪv
AM 'mjudl,eɪdɪv

mutilator
BR 'mjuːtɪleɪtə(r), 'mjuːtl̩eɪtə(r), -z
AM 'mjudl,eɪdər, -z

mutineer
BR ,mjuːtɪ'nɪə(r), -z
AM ,mjutn'ɪ(ə)r, -z

mutinous
BR 'mjuːtɪnəs
AM 'mjutn̩əs

mutinously
BR 'mjuːtɪnəsli
AM 'mjutn̩əsli

mutiny
BR ˈmjuːtɪn|i, -ɪz, -ɪɪŋ, -ɪd
AM ˈmjutn̩i, -z, -ɪŋ, -d

mutism
BR ˈmjuːtɪz(ə)m
AM ˈmjuˌtɪzəm, ˈmjudɪzəm

muton
BR ˈmjuːtɒn, -z
AM ˈmjutn, -z

mutt
BR mʌt, -s
AM mət, -s

mutter
BR ˈmʌt|ə(r), -əz, -(ə)rɪŋ, -əd
AM ˈmə|dər, -dərz, -dərɪŋ\-trɪŋ, -dərd

mutterer
BR ˈmʌt(ə)rə(r), -z
AM ˈmədərər, -z

muttering
BR ˈmʌt(ə)rɪŋ, -z
AM ˈmədərɪŋ, ˈmətrɪŋ, -z

mutteringly
BR ˈmʌt(ə)rɪŋli
AM ˈmədərɪŋli, ˈmətrɪŋli

mutton
BR ˈmʌtn
AM ˈmətn

muttonchop
BR ˌmʌtnˈtʃɒp, -s
AM ˈmətnˌtʃɑp, -s

muttonhead
BR ˈmʌtnhɛd, -z
AM ˈmətnˌ(h)ɛd, -z

muttony
BR ˈmʌtn̩i
AM ˈmətn̩i

mutual
BR ˈmjuːtʃʊəl, ˈmjuːtʃ(ʉ)l, ˈmjuːtjʊəl, ˈmjuːtjʉl
AM ˈmjutʃ(əw)əl

mutualism
BR ˈmjuːtʃʊəlɪz(ə)m, ˈmjuːtʃʉlɪz(ə)m, ˈmjuːtʃl̩ɪz(ə)m, ˈmjuːtjʊəlɪz(ə)m, ˈmjuːtjʉlɪz(ə)m
AM ˈmjutʃ(u)wəˌlɪzəm

mutualist
BR ˈmjuːtʃʊəlɪst, ˈmjuːtʃʉlɪst, ˈmjuːtʃl̩ɪst, ˈmjuːtjʊəlɪst, ˈmjuːtjʉlɪst, -s
AM ˈmjutʃ(əw)ələst, -s

mutualistic
BR ˌmjuːtʃʊəˈlɪstɪk, ˌmjuːtʃʉˈlɪstɪk, ˌmjuːtʃl̩ˈɪstɪk, ˌmjuːtjʊəˈlɪstɪk, ˌmjuːtjʉˈlɪstɪk
AM ˌmjutʃ(u)wəˈlɪstɪk

mutualistically
BR ˌmjuːtʃʊəˈlɪstɪkli, ˌmjuːtʃʉˈlɪstɪkli, ˌmjuːtʃl̩ˈɪstɪkli, ˌmjuːtjʊəˈlɪstɪkli, ˌmjuːtjʉˈlɪstɪkli
AM ˌmjutʃ(u)wəˈlɪstək(ə)li

mutuality
BR ˌmjuːtʃʊˈalɪti, ˌmjuːtjʊˈalɪti
AM ˌmjutʃəˈwælədi

mutually
BR ˈmjuːtʃʊəli, ˈmjuːtʃʉli, ˈmjuːtʃl̩i, ˈmjuːtjʊəli, ˈmjuːtjʉli
AM ˈmjutʃ(əw)əli

mutuel
BR ˈmjuːtʃʊəl, ˈmjuːtjʊəl, -z
AM ˈmjutʃ(ə)wəl, -z

mutule
BR ˈmjuːtʃuːl, ˈmjuːtjuːl, -z
AM ˈmjuˌtʃul, -z

muu-muu
BR ˈmuːmuː, -z
AM ˈmuˌmu, -z

Muzak®
BR ˈmjuːzak
AM ˈmjuzæk

muzhik
BR ˈmuː(d)ʒɪk, -s
AM muˈʒɪk, -s
RUS muˈʒɪk

muzz
BR mʌz, -ɪz, -ɪŋ, -d
AM məz, -əz, -ɪŋ, -d

muzzily
BR ˈmʌzɪli
AM ˈməzəli

muzziness
BR ˈmʌzɪnɪs
AM ˈməzinɪs

muzzle
BR ˈmʌz|l, -lz, -l̩ɪŋ\-lɪŋ, -ld
AM ˈməz|əl, -əlz, -(ə)lɪŋ, -əld

muzzler
BR ˈmʌzl̩ə(r), ˈmʌzlə(r), -z
AM ˈməz(ə)lər, -z

muzzy
BR ˈmʌz|i, -ɪə(r), -ɪɪst
AM ˈməzi, -ər, -ɪst

my
BR mʌɪ
AM maɪ

myalgia
BR mʌɪˈaldʒ(ɪ)ə(r)
AM maɪˈældʒ(i)ə

myalgic
BR mʌɪˈaldʒɪk
AM maɪˈældʒɪk

myalism
BR ˈmʌɪəlɪz(ə)m
AM ˈmaɪəlɪzəm

myall
BR ˈmʌɪəl, -z
AM ˈmaɪˌɔl, ˈmaɪˌɑl, -z

myasthenia
BR ˌmʌɪəsˈθiːnɪə(r)
AM ˌmaɪəsˈθiniə

myasthenic
BR ˌmʌɪəsˈθɛnɪk
AM ˌmaɪəsˈθɛnɪk

mycelia
BR mʌɪˈsiːlɪə(r)
AM maɪˈsiljə, maɪˈsiliə

mycelial
BR mʌɪˈsiːlɪəl
AM maɪˈsiliəl

mycelium
BR mʌɪˈsiːlɪəm
AM maɪˈsiliəm

Mycenae
BR mʌɪˈsiːniː
AM maɪˈsini

Mycenaean
BR mʌɪˈsiːnɪən, -z
AM maɪˈsiniən, -z

mycological
BR ˌmʌɪkəˈlɒdʒɪkl
AM ˌmaɪkəˈlɑdʒəkəl

mycologically
BR ˌmʌɪkəˈlɒdʒɪkli
AM ˌmaɪkəˈlɑdʒək(ə)li

mycologist
BR mʌɪˈkɒlədʒɪst, -s
AM maɪˈkɑlədʒəst, -s

mycology
BR mʌɪˈkɒlədʒi
AM maɪˈkɑlədʒi

mycorrhiza
BR ˌmʌɪkə(ʊ)ˈrʌɪzə(r)
AM ˌmaɪkəˈraɪzə

mycorrhizae
BR ˌmʌɪkə(ʊ)ˈrʌɪziː
AM ˌmaɪkəˈraɪzi

mycorrhizal
BR ˌmʌɪkə(ʊ)ˈrʌɪzl
AM ˌmaɪkəˈraɪzəl

mycosis
BR mʌɪˈkəʊsɪs
AM maɪˈkoʊsəs

mycotic
BR mʌɪˈkɒtɪk
AM maɪˈkɑdɪk

mycotoxin
BR ˌmʌɪkə(ʊ)ˈtɒksɪn, -z
AM ˌmaɪkəˈtɑksən, -z

mycotrophy
BR mʌɪˈkɒtrəfi
AM maɪˈkɑtrəfi

mydriasis
BR mʌɪˈdrʌɪəsɪs, mɪˈdrʌɪəsɪs, ˌmɪdrɪˈeɪsɪs
AM maɪˈdraɪəsəs

myelin
BR ˈmʌɪɪlɪn
AM ˈmaɪələn

myelination
BR ˌmʌɪɪlɪˈneɪʃn
AM ˌmaɪələˈneɪʃən

myelitis
BR ˌmʌɪəˈlʌɪtɪs
AM ˌmaɪəˈlaɪdɪs

myeloid
BR ˈmʌɪəlɔɪd
AM ˈmaɪəˌlɔɪd

myeloma
BR ˌmʌɪəˈləʊmə(r), -z
AM ˌmaɪəˈloʊmə, -z

myelomata
BR ˌmʌɪəˈləʊmətə(r)
AM ˌmaɪəˈloʊmədə

Myers
BR ˈmʌɪəz
AM ˈmaɪərz

Myfanwy
BR mɪˈvanwi
AM məˈvɑnwi
WE mʌˈvanwi

Mykonos
BR ˈmɪkənɒs
AM ˈmɪkəˌnɔs, ˈmɪkəˌnɑs

Mylar
BR ˈmʌɪlɑː(r)
AM ˈmaɪˌlɑr

Myles
BR mʌɪlz
AM maɪlz

mylodon
BR ˈmʌɪlədɒn, ˈmʌɪləd(ə)n, -z
AM ˈmaɪləˌdɑn, -z

mylonite
BR ˈmʌɪlənʌɪt, ˈmɪlənʌɪt
AM ˈmaɪləˌnaɪt, ˈmɪləˌnaɪt

myna
BR ˈmʌɪnə(r), -z
AM ˈmaɪnə, -z

mynah
BR ˈmʌɪnə(r), -z
AM ˈmaɪnə, -z

Mynd
BR mɪnd
AM mɪnd

Mynett
BR ˈmʌɪnɪt, mʌɪˈnɛt
AM ˈmaɪnət, ˈmɪnət

Mynott
BR ˈmʌɪnət
AM ˈmaɪnət, ˈmaɪˌnɑt

Mynwy
BR ˈmʌnwi
AM ˈmɑnwi

myocardia
BR ˌmʌɪə(ʊ)ˈkɑːdɪə(r)
AM ˌmaɪəˈkɑrdiə

myocardial
BR ˌmʌɪə(ʊ)ˈkɑːdɪəl
AM ˌmaɪəˈkɑrdiəl

myocardiogram
BR ˌmʌɪə(ʊ)ˈkɑːdɪəgram, -z
AM ˌmaɪəˈkɑrdiəˌgræm, -z

myocarditis
BR ˌmʌɪə(ʊ)kɑːˈdʌɪtɨs
AM ˌmaɪəˌkɑrˈdaɪdɨs

myocardium
BR ˌmʌɪə(ʊ)ˈkɑːdɪəm
AM ˌmaɪəˈkɑrdiəm

myofibril
BR ˌmʌɪə(ʊ)ˈfʌɪbrɪl, ˌmʌɪə(ʊ)ˈfɪbrɪl, -z
AM ˌmaɪəˈfɪbrəl, -z

myogenic
BR ˌmʌɪə(ʊ)ˈdʒɛnɪk
AM ˌmaɪəˈdʒɛnɪk

myoglobin
BR ˌmʌɪə(ʊ)ˈgləʊbɪn, -z
AM ˌmaɪəˈgloʊbən, -z

myology
BR mʌɪˈɒlədʒi
AM maɪˈɑlədʒi

myope
BR ˈmʌɪəʊp, -s
AM ˈmaɪˌoʊp, -s

myopia
BR mʌɪˈəʊpɪə(r)
AM maɪˈoʊpiə

myopic
BR mʌɪˈɒpɪk
AM maɪˈɑpɪk

myopically
BR mʌɪˈɒpɨkli
AM maɪˈɑpək(ə)li

myosis
BR mʌɪˈəʊsɪs
AM maɪˈoʊsəs

myositis
BR ˌmʌɪəˈsʌɪtɨs
AM ˌmaɪəˈsaɪdɨs

myosote
BR ˈmʌɪə(ʊ)səʊt, -s
AM ˈmaɪəˌsoʊt, -s

myosotis
BR ˌmʌɪə(ʊ)ˈsəʊtɪs, -ɨz
AM ˌmaɪəˈsoʊdəs, -əz

myotonia
BR ˌmʌɪə(ʊ)ˈtəʊnɪə(r)
AM ˌmaɪəˈtoʊniə

myotonic
BR mʌɪə(ʊ)ˈtɒnɪk
AM ˌmaɪəˈtɑnɪk

Myra
BR ˈmʌɪrə(r)
AM ˈmaɪrə

Myrdal
BR ˈmɪədɑːl
AM ˈmɪrˌdɑl

myriad
BR ˈmɪrɪəd, -z
AM ˈmɪriəd, -z

myriapod
BR ˈmɪrɪəpɒd, -z
AM ˈmɪriəˌpɑd, -z

myrmecology
BR ˌməːmɪˈkɒlədʒi
AM ˌmərməˈkɑlədʒi

myrmecophile
BR ˈməːmɪkəfʌɪl, məˈmɪkəfʌɪl, -z
AM ˈmərməkəˌfaɪl, -z

Myrmidon
BR ˈməːmɨd(ə)n, -z
AM ˈmərməˌdɑn, -z

Myrna
BR ˈməːnə(r)
AM ˈmərnə

myrobalan
BR mʌɪˈrɒbələn, mʌɪˈrɒbl̩ən, -z
AM maɪˈrɑbələn, məˈrɑbələn, -z

Myron
BR ˈmʌɪrən, ˈmʌɪrn̩
AM ˈmaɪrən

myrrh
BR məː(r)
AM mər

myrrhic
BR ˈməːrɪk
AM ˈmərɪk

myrrhy
BR ˈməːri
AM ˈməri

myrtaceous
BR məːˈteɪʃəs
AM mərˈteɪʃəs

myrtle
BR ˈməːtl
AM ˈmərdəl

myself
BR mʌɪˈsɛlf, məˈsɛlf
AM maɪˈsɛlf, məˈsɛlf

Mysia
BR ˈmɪsɪə(r)
AM ˈmɪʃiə

Mysian
BR ˈmɪsɪən, -z
AM ˈmɪʃiən, -z

Mysore
BR (ˌ)mʌɪˈsɔː(r)
AM maɪˈsɔ(ə)r

mystagogic
BR ˌmɪstəˈgɒdʒɪk
AM ˌmɪstəˈgɑdʒɪk

mystagogical
BR ˌmɪstəˈgɒdʒɨkl
AM ˌmɪstəˈgɑdʒəkəl

mystagogue
BR ˈmɪstəgɒg, -z
AM ˈmɪstəˌgɑg, -z

mysterious
BR mɨˈstɪərɪəs
AM məˈstɪriəs

mysteriously
BR mɨˈstɪərɪəsli
AM məˈstɪriəsli

mysteriousness
BR mɨˈstɪərɪəsnəs
AM məˈstɪriəsnəs

mystery
BR ˈmɪst(ə)r|i, -ɪz
AM ˈmɪst(ə)ri, -z

mystic
BR ˈmɪstɪk, -s
AM ˈmɪstɪk, -s

mystical
BR ˈmɪstɨkl
AM ˈmɪstəkəl

mystically
BR ˈmɪstɨkli
AM ˈmɪstək(ə)li

mysticism
BR ˈmɪstɨsɪz(ə)m
AM ˈmɪstəˌsɪzəm

mystification
BR ˌmɪstɨfɨˈkeɪʃn
AM ˌmɪstəfəˈkeɪʃən

mystify
BR ˈmɪstɨfʌɪ, -z, -ɪŋ, -d
AM ˈmɪstəˌfaɪ, -z, -ɪŋ, -d

mystifyingly
BR ˈmɪstɨfʌɪɪŋli
AM ˈmɪstəˌfaɪɪŋli

mystique
BR mɨˈstiːk
AM mɪˈstik

myth
BR mɪθ, -s
AM mɪθ, -s

mythi
BR ˈmʌɪθʌɪ, ˈmɪθiː
AM ˈmaɪθi

mythic
BR ˈmɪθɪk
AM ˈmɪθɪk

mythical
BR ˈmɪθɨkl
AM ˈmɪθəkəl

mythically
BR ˈmɪθɨkli
AM ˈmɪθək(ə)li

mythicise
BR ˈmɪθɨsʌɪz, -ɨz, -ɪŋ, -d
AM ˈmɪθəˌsaɪz, -ɨz, -ɪŋ, -d

mythicism
BR ˈmɪθɨsɪz(ə)m
AM ˈmɪθəˌsɪzəm

mythicist
BR ˈmɪθɨsɪst, -s
AM ˈmɪθəsəst, -s

mythicize
BR ˈmɪθɨsʌɪz, -ɨz, -ɪŋ, -d
AM ˈmɪθəˌsaɪz, -ɨz, -ɪŋ, -d

mythogenesis
BR ˌmɪθə(ʊ)ˈdʒɛnɨsɪs
AM ˌmɪθəˈdʒɛnəsəs

mythographer
BR mɨˈθɒgrəfə(r), -z
AM məˈθɑgrəfər, -z

mythography
BR mɨˈθɒgrəfi
AM məˈθɑgrəfi

Mytholmroyd
BR ˈmʌɪð(ə)mrɔɪd
AM ˈmɪðəmˌrɔɪd

mythologer
BR mɨˈθɒlədʒə(r), -z
AM məˈθɑlədʒər, -z

mythologic
BR ˌmɪθəˈlɒdʒɪk
AM ˌmɪθəˈlɑdʒɪk

mythological
BR ˌmɪθəˈlɒdʒɨkl
AM ˌmɪθəˈlɑdʒəkəl

mythologically
BR ˌmɪθəˈlɒdʒɨkli
AM ˌmɪθəˈlɑdʒək(ə)li

mythologise
BR mɨˈθɒlədʒʌɪz, -ɨz, -ɪŋ, -d
AM məˈθɑləˌdʒaɪz, -ɨz, -ɪŋ, -d

mythologiser
BR mɨˈθɒlədʒʌɪzə(r), -z
AM məˈθɑləˌdʒaɪzər, -z

mythologist
BR mɨˈθɒlədʒɪst, -s
AM məˈθɑlədʒəst, -s

mythologize
BR mɨˈθɒlədʒʌɪz, -ɨz, -ɪŋ, -d
AM məˈθɑləˌdʒaɪz, -ɨz, -ɪŋ, -d

mythologizer
BR mɨˈθɒlədʒʌɪzə(r), -z
AM məˈθɑləˌdʒaɪzər, -z

mythology
BR mɨˈθɒlədʒ|i, -ɪz
AM məˈθɑlədʒi, -z

mythomania
BR ˌmɪθə(ʊ)ˈmeɪnɪə(r), -z
AM ˌmɪθəˈmeɪniə, -z

mythomaniac
BR ˌmɪθə(ʊ)ˈmeɪnɪak, -s
AM ˌmɪθəˈmeɪniˌæk, -s

mythopoeia
BR ˌmɪθə(ʊ)ˈpiːə(r), -z
AM ˌmɪθəˈpiə, -z

mythopoeic
BR ˌmɪθə(ʊ)ˈpiːɪk
AM ˌmɪθəˈpiɪk

mythus
BR ˈmʌɪθəs, ˈmɪθəs
AM ˈmaɪθəs, ˈmɪθəʃ

Mytilene
BR ˈmɪtɨliːn, ˈmɪtl̩iːn
AM ˈmɪtl̩in

myxedema
BR ˌmɪksɨˈdiːmə(r)
AM ˌmɪksəˈdimə

myxoedema
BR ˌmɪksɨˈdiːmə(r)
AM ˌmɪksəˈdimə

myxoma
BR mɪkˈsəʊmə(r), -z
AM mɪkˈsoʊmə, -z

myxomata
BR mɪk'səʊmətə(r)
AM mɪk'soʊmədə

myxomatosis
BR ˌmɪksəmə'təʊsɪs
AM mɪkˌsoʊmə'toʊsəs

myxomycete
BR ˌmɪksə(ʊ)'mʌɪsiːt, -s
AM ˈmɪksə'maɪˌsit, -s

myxovirus
BR 'mɪksəʊˌvʌɪrəs, -ɪz
AM 'mɪksoʊˌvaɪrəs, -ɪz

Nn

n
BR ɛn, -z
AM ɛn, -z
'n
and
BR (ə)n
AM (ə)n
na
BR nə(*r*)
AM nə
NAAFI
BR 'naf|i, -ɪz
AM 'næˌfi, 'nɑˌfi, -z
nab
BR nab, -z, -ɪŋ, -d
AM næb, -z, -ɪŋ, -d
Nabarro
BR nə'bɑːrəʊ
AM nə'bɑroʊ
Nabataean
BR ˌnabə'tiːən, -z
AM ˌnæbə'tiən, -z
Nabi
BR 'nɑːbiː, -z
AM 'nɑbi, -z
Nabisco®
BR nə'bɪskəʊ
AM nə'bɪskoʊ
Nablus
BR 'nabləs, 'nɑːbləs
AM 'nɑbləs, 'næbləs
nabob
BR 'neɪbɒb, -z
AM 'neɪˌbɑb, -z
Nabokov
BR 'nabəkɒv
AM 'nɑbəˌkɔv, nə'bɔˌkɔf, 'nɑbəˌkɑv, nə'bɑˌkɑf
Naboth
BR 'neɪbɒθ
AM 'neɪbɑθ
nacarat
BR 'nakərat
AM 'nækəˌræt
nacelle
BR nə'sɛl, -z
AM nə'sɛl, neɪ'sɛl, -z
nacho
BR 'nɑːtʃəʊ, 'natʃəʊ, -z
AM 'nɑtʃoʊ, -z
NACODS
BR 'neɪkɒdz
AM 'neɪˌkɑdz
nacre
BR 'neɪkə(r)
AM 'neɪkər
nacred
BR 'neɪkəd
AM 'neɪkərd
nacreous
BR 'neɪkrɪəs
AM 'neɪkriəs
NACRO
BR 'nakrəʊ
AM 'nækroʊ
nacrous
BR 'neɪkrəs
AM 'neɪkrəs
Na-Dene
BR ˌnɑːdeɪ'neɪ, ˌnɑː'deɪneɪ, ˌnɑː'deɪni, ˌnɑː'dɛni
AM ˌnɑˈdeɪˈneɪ, ˌnɑ'dɛˌni
Nader
BR 'neɪdə(r)
AM 'neɪdər
Nadia
BR 'nɑːdɪə(*r*), 'neɪdɪə(*r*)
AM 'nɑdiə
Nadine
BR neɪ'diːn, nə'diːn
AM neɪ'din, nə'din
nadir
BR 'neɪdɪə(r), -z
AM 'neɪdər, 'neɪˌdɪ(ə)r, -z
nae
BR neɪ
AM neɪ
naevae
BR 'niːvʌɪ
AM 'niˌvaɪ
naevoid
BR 'niːvɔɪd
AM 'niˌvɔɪd
naevus
BR 'niːvəs
AM 'nivəs
naff
BR naf
AM næf
Naffy
BR 'nafi
AM 'næfi
nag
BR nag, -z, -ɪŋ, -d
AM næg, -z, -ɪŋ, -d
naga
BR 'nɑːgə(*r*), -z
AM 'nɑgə, -z
Nagaland
BR 'nɑːgəland
AM 'nɑgəˌlænd
nagana
BR nə'gɑːnə(*r*)
AM nə'gɑnə
Nagasaki
BR ˌnagə'sɑːki
AM ˌnɑgə'sɑki
nagger
BR 'nagə(r), -z
AM 'nægər, -z
naggingly
BR 'nagɪŋli
AM 'nægɪŋli
Nagle
BR 'neɪgl
AM 'neɪgəl
nagor
BR 'neɪgɔː(r), -z
AM 'nægər, -z
Nagorno-Karabakh
BR nəˌgɔːnəʊˌkarə'bak
AM nəˈgɔrnoʊˌkɛrə'bɑk
Nagoya
BR nə'gɔɪə(*r*)
AM nə'gɔɪə
Nagpur
BR ˌnag'pʊə(r)
AM ˌnæg'pʊ(ə)r
Nahuatl
BR 'nɑːwɑːtl, nɑː'wɑːtl, -z
AM ˈnɑˈwɑtl, -z
Nahuatlan
BR 'nɑːwɑːtlən, nɑː'wɑːtlən
AM nɑ'wɑtlən
Nahum
BR 'neɪhəm
AM 'neɪhəm
naiad
BR 'nʌɪad, -z
AM 'neɪˌæd, 'naɪˌæd, 'neɪəd, 'naɪəd, -z
naiant
BR 'neɪənt
AM 'neɪənt
naif
BR nʌɪ'iːf, nɑː'iːf, -s
AM naɪ'if, nɑ'if, -s
nail
BR neɪl, -z, -ɪŋ, -d
AM neɪl, -z, -ɪŋ, -d
nailbrush
BR 'neɪlbrʌʃ, -ɨz
AM 'neɪlˌbrəʃ, -əz
nailer
BR 'neɪlə(r), -z
AM 'neɪlər, -z
nailery
BR 'neɪlər|i, -ɪz
AM 'neɪləri, -z
nailless
BR 'neɪlɨs
AM 'neɪlɨs
nainsook
BR 'neɪnsʊk, -s
AM 'neɪnˌsʊk, -s
Naipaul
BR nʌɪ'pɔːl, 'nʌɪpɔːl
AM 'naɪˌpɔl, 'naɪˌpɑl
naira
BR 'nʌɪrə(*r*)
AM 'naɪrə
Nairn
BR nɛːn
AM nɛrn
Nairobi
BR nʌɪ'rəʊbi
AM naɪ'roʊbi
Naismith
BR 'neɪsmɪθ
AM 'neɪˌsmɪθ
naive
BR nʌɪ'iːv, nɑː'iːv
AM nɑ'iv
naively
BR nʌɪ'iːvli, nɑː'iːvli
AM nɑ'ivli
naiveness
BR nʌɪ'iːvnɨs, nɑː'iːvnɨs
AM nɑ'ivnɨs
naiveté
BR nʌɪ'iːv(ɨ)teɪ, nɑː'iːv(ɨ)teɪ
AM ˌnɑˌiv(ə)'teɪ, nɑ'iv(ə)ˌteɪ
naivety
BR nʌɪ'iːv(ɨ)ti, nɑː'iːv(ɨ)ti
AM nɑ'ivədi, nɑ'ivti
Najaf
BR na'dʒaf
AM nə'dʒɑf
naked
BR 'neɪkɨd
AM 'neɪkɨd
nakedly
BR 'neɪkɨdli
AM 'neɪkɨdli
nakedness
BR 'neɪkɨdnɨs
AM 'neɪkɨdnɨs
naker
BR 'neɪkə(r), -z
AM 'neɪkər, -z
Nakuru
BR na'kuːruː
AM nə'kuru
NALGO
BR 'nalgəʊ
AM 'nælˌgoʊ
'Nam
BR nam, nɑːm
AM nɑm, næm
Namaqualand
BR nə'mɑːkwəland
AM nə'mɑkwəˌlænd
namby-pamby
BR ˌnambɪ'pambi
AM ˈnæmbi'pæmbi
name
BR neɪm, -z, -ɪŋ, -d
AM neɪm, -z, -ɪŋ, -d
nameable
BR 'neɪməbl
AM 'neɪməbəl
namedrop
BR 'neɪmdrɒp, -s, -ɪŋ, -t
AM 'neɪmˌdrɑp, -s, -ɪŋ, -t
name-dropper
BR 'neɪmˌdrɒpə(r), -z
AM 'neɪmˌdrɑpər, -z

nameless
BR 'neɪmlɨs
AM 'neɪmlɨs

namelessly
BR 'neɪmlɨsli
AM 'neɪmlɨsli

namelessness
BR 'neɪmlɨsnɨs
AM 'neɪmlɨnɨs

namely
BR 'neɪmli
AM 'neɪmli

nameplate
BR 'neɪmpleɪt, -s
AM 'neɪm,pleɪt, -s

namesake
BR 'neɪmseɪk, -s
AM 'neɪm,seɪk, -s

Namibia
BR nə'mɪbɪə(*r*)
AM nə'mɪbiə

Namibian
BR nə'mɪbɪən, -z
AM nə'mɪbiən, -z

namma
BR 'namə(*r*), -z
AM 'nɑmə, -z

Namur
BR nə'mjʊə(r)
AM nə'm(j)ʊ(ə)r
FR namyʀ

nan
BR nan, -z
AM næn, -z

nana[1]
foolish person
BR 'nɑːnə(*r*), -z
AM 'nɑnə, -z

nana[2]
grandmother
BR 'nanə(*r*), -z
AM 'nɑnə, 'nænə, -z

Nanaimo
BR nə'nʌɪməʊ
AM nə'naɪ,moʊ

Nanak
BR 'nɑːnak
AM 'nɑnək, 'nɑ,næk

Nancarrow
BR nan'karəʊ
AM næn'kɛroʊ

nance
BR nans, -ɨz
AM næns, -əz

Nanchang
BR nan'tʃaŋ
AM næn'tʃæŋ

Nancy
city
BR 'nansi
AM 'nansi, nɑn'si
FR nɑ̃si

nancy
BR 'nans|i, -ɪz
AM 'nænsi, -z

NAND
BR nand
AM nænd

Nandi
BR 'nandi
AM 'nɑndi

Nanette
BR na'nɛt
AM nə'nɛt

Nanga Parbat
BR ,naŋgə 'pɑːbat
AM ',nɑŋgə 'pɑrbət

Nanjing
BR nan'dʒɪŋ
AM næn'dʒɪŋ

nankeen
BR nan'kiːn, naŋ'kiːn
AM næn'kin

Nanking
BR nan'kɪŋ, naŋ'kɪŋ
AM næn'kɪŋ

nanna
BR 'nanə(*r*), -z
AM 'nænə, 'nɑnə, -z

nanny
BR 'nan|i, -ɪz, -ɪɪŋ, -ɪd
AM 'næni, -z, -ɪŋ, -d

nannygoat
BR 'nanɪgəʊt, -s
AM 'næni,goʊt, -s

nannyish
BR 'nanɪɪʃ
AM 'næniɪʃ

nanogram
BR 'nanə(ʊ)gram, -z
AM 'nænə,græm, -z

nanometer
BR 'nanə(ʊ),miːtə(r), -z
AM 'nænə,midər, -z

nanometre
BR 'nanə(ʊ),miːtə(r), -z
AM 'nænə,midər, -z

nanosecond
BR 'nanə(ʊ),sɛknd, -z
AM 'nænə,sɛkənd, -z

nanotechnology
BR ,nanə(ʊ)tɛk'nɒlədʒi
AM ',nænoʊ,tɛk'nɑlədʒi

Nansen
BR 'nansn
AM 'nænsən

Nantes
BR nɑːnt, nɒnt
AM nɑnt

Nantgaredig
BR ,nantgə'rɛdɪg
AM ,næntgə'rɛdɪg

Nantucket
BR nan'tʌkɪt
AM næn'təkət

Nantwich
BR 'nantwɪtʃ
AM 'næntwɪtʃ

Nant-y-glo
BR ,nantə'gləʊ
AM ,næn(t)ə'gloʊ
WE ,nant ʌ 'glɒ

naoi
BR 'neɪɔɪ
AM 'neɪ,ɔɪ

Naomi
BR neɪ'əʊmi
AM neɪ'oʊmi, naɪ'oʊmi

naos
BR 'neɪɒs
AM 'neɪ,ɑs

nap
BR nap, -s, -ɪŋ, -t
AM næp, -s, -ɪŋ, -t

napa
BR 'napə(*r*), -z
AM 'næpə, -z

napalm
BR 'neɪpɑːm
AM 'neɪ,pɑ(l)m

Napa Valley
BR ,napə 'vali
AM ',næpə 'væli

nape
BR neɪp, -s
AM neɪp, -s

napery
BR 'neɪp(ə)ri
AM 'neɪp(ə)ri

Naphtali
BR 'naftəlʌɪ
AM 'næftə,laɪ, 'næptə,laɪ

naphtha
BR 'nafθə(*r*), 'napθə(*r*)
AM 'næpθə, 'næfθə

naphthalene
BR 'nafθəliːn, 'napθəliːn
AM 'næpθə,lin, 'næfθə,lin

naphthalic
BR naf'θalɪk, nap'θalɪk
AM næp'θælɪk, næf'θælɪk

naphthene
BR 'nafθiːn, 'napθiːn, -z
AM 'næp,θin, 'næf,θin, -z

naphthenic
BR naf'θiːnɪk, nap'θiːnɪk, naf'θɛnɪk, nap'θɛnɪk
AM næp'θɛnɪk, næp'θinɪk, næf'θɛnɪk, næf'θinɪk

naphthol
BR 'nafθɒl, 'napθɒl
AM 'næp,θɔl, 'næp,θɑl, 'næp,θoʊl, 'næf,θɔl, 'næf,θɑl, 'næf,θoʊl

Napier
BR 'neɪpɪə(r)
AM 'neɪpi(ə)r

Napierian
BR neɪ'pɪərɪən, nə'pɪərɪən
AM neɪ'pɪrɪən

napkin
BR 'napkɪn, -z
AM 'næpkɪn, -z

Naples
BR 'neɪplz
AM 'neɪpəlz

napoleon
BR nə'pəʊlɪən, -z
AM nə'poʊliən, nə'poʊljən, -z

Napoleonic
BR nə,pəʊlɪ'ɒnɪk
AM nə'poʊli'ɑnɪk

nappa
BR 'napə(*r*), -z
AM 'næpə, -z

nappe
BR nap, -s
AM næp, -s

napper
BR 'napə(r), -z
AM 'næpər, -z

nappy
BR 'nap|i, -ɪz
AM 'næpi, -z

Nara
BR 'nɑːrə(*r*)
AM 'nɑrə

Narayan
BR nə'rʌɪən
AM nə'raɪən

Narberth
BR 'nɑːbəθ
AM 'nɑr,bərθ

Narbonne
BR nɑː'bɒn
AM nɑr'bən

narc
BR nɑːk, -s
AM nɑrk, -s

narcissi
BR nɑː'sɪsʌɪ
AM nɑr'sɪ,saɪ

narcissism
BR 'nɑːsɪsɪz(ə)m
AM 'nɑrsə,sɪzəm

narcissist
BR 'nɑːsɪsɪst, -s
AM 'nɑrsəsəst, -s

narcissistic
BR ,nɑːsɪ'sɪstɪk
AM ,nɑrsə'sɪstɪk

narcissistically
BR ,nɑːsɪ'sɪstɨkli
AM ',nɑrsə'sɪstək(ə)li

narcissus
BR nɑː'sɪsəs, -ɨz
AM nɑr'sɪsəs, -əz

narcolepsy
BR 'nɑːkə(ʊ)lɛpsi
AM 'nɑrkə,lɛpsi

narcoleptic
BR ,nɑːkə(ʊ)'lɛptɪk
AM ,nɑrkə'lɛptɪk

narcosis
BR nɑː'kəʊsɪs
AM nɑr'koʊsəs

narcoterrorism
BR ˌnɑːkəʊˈtɛrərɪz(ə)m
AM ˈnɑrkoʊˈtɛrəˌrɪzəm
narcoterrorist
BR ˌnɑːkəʊˈtɛrərɪst, -s
AM ˈnɑrkoʊˈtɛrərəst, -s
narcotic
BR nɑːˈkɒtɪk, -s
AM nɑrˈkɑdɪk, -s
narcotically
BR nɑːˈkɒtɨkli
AM nɑrˈkɑdək(ə)li
narcotisation
BR ˌnɑːkɑːtʌɪˈzeɪʃn
AM ˌnɑrkədəˈzeɪʃən, ˌnɑrkəˌtaɪˈzeɪʃən
narcotise
BR ˈnɑːkətʌɪz, -ɨz, -ɪŋ, -d
AM ˈnɑrkəˌtaɪz, -ɨz, -ɪŋ, -d
narcotism
BR ˈnɑːkətɪz(ə)m
AM ˈnɑrkəˌtɪzəm
narcotization
BR ˌnɑːkətʌɪˈzeɪʃn
AM ˌnɑrkədəˈzeɪʃən, ˌnɑrkəˌtaɪˈzeɪʃən
narcotize
BR ˈnɑːkətʌɪz, -ɨz, -ɪŋ, -d
AM ˈnɑrkəˌtaɪz, -ɨz, -ɪŋ, -d
nard
BR nɑːd
AM nɑrd
nardoo
BR ˌnɑːˈduː, ˈnɑːduː, -z
AM ˈnɑrˈdu, -z
nareal
BR ˈnɛːrɪəl
AM ˈnɛriəl
nares
BR ˈnɛːriːz
AM ˈnɛriz, nɛrz
nargile
BR ˈnɑːgɪl|eɪ, ˈnɑːgɨl|i, -eɪz\-ɪz
AM ˈnɑrgəli, -ɪz
nargileh
BR ˈnɑːgɪl|eɪ, ˈnɑːgɨl|i, -eɪz\-ɪz
AM ˈnɑrgəli, -ɪz
narial
BR ˈnɛːrɪəl
AM ˈnɛriəl
nark
BR nɑːk, -s, -ɪŋ, -t
AM nɑrk, -s, -ɪŋ, -t
narky
BR ˈnɑːk|i, -ɪə(r), -ɪɪst
AM ˈnɑrki, -ər, -ɨst
Narnia
BR ˈnɑːnɪə(r)
AM ˈnɑrniə
Narragansett
BR ˌnaraˈgansɪt
AM ˌnɛrəˈgænsət
narratable
BR nəˈreɪtəbl
AM nəˈreɪdəbəl
narrate
BR nəˈreɪt, -s, -ɪŋ, -ɨd
AM ˈnɛˌreɪ|t, -ts, -dɪŋ, -dɨd
narration
BR nəˈreɪʃn, -z
AM nɛˈreɪʃən, -z
narrational
BR nəˈreɪʃn̩(ə)l, nəˈreɪʃən(ə)l
AM nəˈreɪʃ(ə)nəl
narrative
BR ˈnarətɪv, -z
AM ˈnɛrədɪv, -z
narratively
BR ˈnarətɨvli
AM ˈnɛrədəvli
narrator
BR nəˈreɪtə(r), -z
AM ˈnɛˌreɪdər, -z
narrow
BR ˈnarəʊ, -z, -ɪŋ, -d, -ə(r), -ɨst
AM ˈnɛr|oʊ, -oʊz, -əwɪŋ, -oʊd, -əwər, -əwəst
narrowcast
BR ˈnarəʊkɑːst, ˈnarəʊkast, -s
AM ˈnɛroʊˌkæst, -s
narrowcaster
BR ˈnarəʊˌkɑːstə(r), ˈnarəʊˌkastə(r), -z
AM ˈnæroʊˌkæstər, -z
narrowcasting
BR ˈnarəʊˌkɑːstɪŋ, ˈnarəʊˌkastɪŋ
AM ˈnɛroʊˌkæstɪŋ
narrowish
BR ˈnarəʊɪʃ
AM ˈnɛrəwɪʃ
narrowly
BR ˈnarəʊli
AM ˈnɛroʊli
narrowness
BR ˈnarəʊnəs
AM ˈnɛroʊnəs
narthex
BR ˈnɑːθɛks, -ɨz
AM ˈnɑrˌθɛks, -əz
Narvik
BR ˈnɑːvɪk
AM ˈnɑrˌvɪk
narwhal
BR ˈnɑːw(ə)l, -z
AM ˈnɑrˌ(h)wɑl, ˈnɑrwəl, -z
nary
BR ˈnɛːri
AM ˈnɛri
NASA
BR ˈnasə(r)
AM ˈnæsə
nasal
BR ˈneɪzl
AM ˈneɪzəl
nasalisation
BR ˌneɪzəlʌɪˈzeɪʃn, ˌneɪzl̩ʌɪˈzeɪʃn, -z
AM ˌneɪzələˈzeɪʃən, ˌneɪzəˌlaɪˈzeɪʃən, -z
nasalise
BR ˈneɪzəlʌɪz, ˈneɪzl̩ʌɪz, -ɨz, -ɪŋ, -d
AM ˈneɪzəˌlaɪz, -ɨz, -ɪŋ, -d
nasality
BR neɪˈzalɨti
AM ˌneɪˈzælədi
nasalization
BR ˌneɪzəlʌɪˈzeɪʃn, ˌneɪzl̩ʌɪˈzeɪʃn, -z
AM ˌneɪzələˈzeɪʃən, ˌneɪzəˌlaɪˈzeɪʃən, -z
nasalize
BR ˈneɪzəlʌɪz, ˈneɪzl̩ʌɪz, -ɨz, -ɪŋ, -d
AM ˈneɪzəˌlaɪz, -ɨz, -ɪŋ, -d
nasally
BR ˈneɪzl̩i, ˈneɪzəli
AM ˈneɪzəli
NASCAR
BR ˈnaskɑː(r)
AM ˈnæsˌkɑr
nascency
BR ˈnasnsi, ˈneɪsnsi
AM ˈneɪsənsi
nascent
BR ˈnasnt, ˈneɪsnt
AM ˈneɪsənt
NASDAQ
BR ˈnazdak
AM ˈnæzˌdæk
naseberry
BR ˈneɪzb(ə)r|i, -ɪz
AM ˈneɪsˌbɛri, -z
Naseby
BR ˈneɪzbi
AM ˈneɪzbi
Nash
BR naʃ
AM næʃ
Nashe
BR naʃ
AM næʃ
Nashua
BR ˈnaʃʊə(r)
AM ˈnæʃəwə
Nashville
BR ˈnaʃvɪl
AM ˈnæʃˌvɪl, ˈnæʃvəl
nasion
BR ˈneɪzɪən, -z
AM ˈneɪˌzaɪən, -z
Nasmyth
BR ˈneɪsmɪθ
AM ˈneɪˌsmɪθ
naso-frontal
BR ˌneɪzəʊˈfrʌntl
AM ˈneɪzoʊˈfrən(t)l
Nassau[1]
Bahamas
BR ˈnasɔː(r)
AM ˈnæˌsɔ
Nassau[2]
Germany
BR ˈnasaʊ
AM ˈnɑˌsaʊ
Nasser
BR ˈnasə(r)
AM ˈnæsər
Nastase
BR nəˈstɑːzi
AM nəˈstɑzi, nəˈstɑsi
nastic
BR ˈnastɪk
AM ˈnæstɪk
nastily
BR ˈnɑːstɨli, ˈnastɨli
AM ˈnæstəli
nastiness
BR ˈnɑːstɪnɪs, ˈnastɪnɪs
AM ˈnæstinɨs
nasturtium
BR nəˈstəːʃ(ə)m, -z
AM næˈstərʃəm, nəˈstərʃəm, -z
nasty
BR ˈnɑːst|i, ˈnast|i, -ɪə(r), -ɪɪst
AM ˈnæsti, -ər, -ɨst
Nat
BR nat
AM næt
Natal
BR nəˈtal, nəˈtɑːl
AM nəˈtɑl
natal
BR ˈneɪtl
AM ˈneɪdl
Natalie
BR ˈnatəli
AM ˈnædli
natality
BR nəˈtalɨt|i, -ɪz
AM nəˈtælədi, neɪˈtælədi, -z
Natasha
BR nəˈtaʃə(r)
AM nəˈtɑʃə, nəˈtæʃə
natation
BR nəˈteɪʃn
AM nɑˈteɪʃən, neɪˈteɪʃən
natatoria
BR ˌneɪtəˈtɔːrɪʌ(r)
AM ˌneɪdəˈtɔriə, ˈnædəˈtɔriə
natatorial
BR ˌneɪtəˈtɔːrɪəl
AM ˈneɪdəˌtɔriəl, ˈnædəˈtɔriəl
natatorium
BR ˌneɪtəˈtɔːrɪʌm, -z
AM ˌneɪdəˈtɔriəm, ˌnædəˈtɔriəm, -z

natatory
BR 'neɪtətri
AM 'neɪdə,tɔri, 'nædə,tɔri

natch
BR natʃ
AM nætʃ

nates
plural noun
BR 'neɪtiːz
AM 'neɪ,tiz

Nathalie
BR 'natəli
AM 'nædl̩i

Nathan
BR 'neɪθn
AM 'neɪθən

Nathaniel
BR nə'θanɪəl
AM nə'θænjəl

nation
BR 'neɪʃn, -z
AM 'neɪʃən, -z

national
BR 'naʃn̩(ə)l, 'naʃən(ə)l
AM 'næʃ(ə)nəl

nationalisation
BR ,naʃn̩əlʌɪ'zeɪʃn, ,naʃn̩l̩ʌɪ'zeɪʃn, ,naʃənl̩ʌɪ'zeɪʃn, ,naʃ(ə)nəlʌɪ'zeɪʃn
AM ,næʃ(ə)nələ'zeɪʃən, ,næʃ(ə)nə,laɪ'zeɪʃən

nationalise
BR 'naʃn̩əlʌɪz, 'naʃn̩l̩ʌɪz, 'naʃənl̩ʌɪz, 'naʃ(ə)nəlʌɪz, -ɪz, -ɪŋ, -d
AM 'næʃ(ə)nə,laɪz, -ɪz, -ɪŋ, -d

nationaliser
BR 'naʃn̩əlʌɪzə(r), 'naʃn̩l̩ʌɪzə(r), 'naʃənl̩ʌɪzə(r), 'naʃ(ə)nəlʌɪzə(r), -z
AM 'næʃ(ə)nə,laɪzər, -z

nationalism
BR 'naʃn̩əlɪz(ə)m, 'naʃn̩l̩ɪz(ə)m, 'naʃənl̩ɪz(ə)m, 'naʃ(ə)nəlɪz(ə)m
AM 'næʃ(ə)nə,lɪzəm

nationalist
BR 'naʃn̩əlɪst, 'naʃn̩l̩ɪst, 'naʃənl̩ɪst, 'naʃ(ə)nəlɪst, -s
AM 'næʃ(ə)nələst, -s

nationalistic
BR ,naʃn̩ə'lɪstɪk, ,naʃn̩l̩'ɪstɪk, ,naʃənl̩'ɪstɪk, ,naʃ(ə)nə'lɪstɪk
AM ,næʃ(ə)nə'lɪstɪk

nationalistically
BR ,naʃn̩ə'lɪstɨkli, ,naʃn̩l̩'ɪstɨkli, ,naʃənl̩'ɪstɨkli, ,naʃ(ə)nə'lɪstɨkli, ,naʃn̩ə'lɪstɨkli, ,naʃn̩l̩'ɪstɨkli
AM ,næʃ(ə)nə'lɪstək(ə)li

nationality
BR ,naʃ(ə)'nalɪt|i, -ɪz
AM ,næʃə'nælədi, -z

nationalization
BR ,naʃn̩əlʌɪ'zeɪʃn, ,naʃn̩l̩ʌɪ'zeɪʃn, ,naʃənl̩ʌɪ'zeɪʃn, ,naʃ(ə)nəlʌɪ'zeɪʃn
AM ,næʃ(ə)nələ'zeɪʃən, ,næʃ(ə)nə,laɪ'zeɪʃən

nationalize
BR 'naʃn̩əlʌɪz, 'naʃn̩l̩ʌɪz, 'naʃənl̩ʌɪz, 'naʃ(ə)nəlʌɪz, -ɪz, -ɪŋ, -d
AM 'næʃ(ə)nə,laɪz, -ɪz, -ɪŋ, -d

nationalizer
BR 'naʃn̩əlʌɪzə(r), 'nasn̩l̩ʌɪzə(r), 'naʃənl̩ʌɪzə(r), 'naʃ(ə)nəlʌɪzə(r), -z
AM 'næʃ(ə)nə,laɪzər, -z

nationally
BR 'naʃn̩əli, 'naʃn̩li, 'naʃənl̩i, 'naʃ(ə)nəli
AM 'næʃ(ə)nəli

nationhood
BR 'neɪʃnhʊd
AM 'neɪʃən,(h)ʊd

nationwide
BR ,neɪʃn'wʌɪd
AM ',neɪʃən',waɪd

native
BR 'neɪtɪv, -z
AM 'neɪdɪv, -z

natively
BR 'neɪtɨvli
AM 'neɪdɨvli

nativeness
BR 'neɪtɨvnɨs
AM 'neɪdɪvnɨs

nativism
BR 'neɪtɨvɪz(ə)m
AM 'neɪdə,vɪzəm

nativist
BR 'neɪtɨvɪst, -s
AM 'neɪdəvəst, -s

nativity
BR nə'tɪvɪt|i, -ɪz
AM nə'tɪvɨdi, -z

NATO
BR 'neɪtəʊ
AM 'neɪ,doʊ

natriuresis
BR ,neɪtrijʊ(ə)'riːsɪs, ,natrijʊ(ə)'riːsɪs
AM ,neɪtriju'risɪs

natriuretic
BR ,neɪtrijʊ(ə)'rɛtɪk, ,natrɪjʊ(ə)'rɛtɪk
AM ,neɪtriju'rɛdɪk

natron
BR 'neɪtrɒn, 'neɪtr(ə)n
AM 'neɪ,trɑn, 'neɪtrən

NATSOPA
BR nat'səʊpə(*r*)
AM næt'soʊpə

natter
BR 'nat|ə(r), -əz, -(ə)rɪŋ, -əd
AM 'nædər, -z, -ɪŋ, -d

natterer
BR 'nat(ə)rə(r), -z
AM 'nædərər, -z

natterjack
BR 'natədʒak, -s
AM 'nædər,dʒæk, -s

nattier blue
BR ,natjeɪ 'bluː
AM ,nædiər 'blu

nattily
BR 'natɨli
AM 'nædəli

nattiness
BR 'natɪnɨs
AM 'nædinɨs

natty
BR 'nat|i, -ɪə(r), -ɪɨst
AM 'nædi, -ər, -ɨst

Natufian
BR nɑː'tuːfɪən, -z
AM nə'tufiən, -z

natural
BR 'natʃ(ə)rəl, 'natʃ(ə)rl̩, -z
AM 'nætʃ(ə)rəl, -z

naturalisation
BR ,natʃ(ə)rəlʌɪ'zeɪʃn, ,natʃ(ə)rl̩ʌɪ'zeɪʃn
AM ,nætʃ(ə)rələ'zeɪʃən, ,nætʃ(ə)rə,laɪ'zeɪʃən

naturalise
BR 'natʃ(ə)rəlʌɪz, 'natʃ(ə)rl̩ʌɪz, -ɪz, -ɪŋ, -d
AM 'nætʃ(ə)rə,laɪz, -ɪz, -ɪŋ, -d

naturalism
BR 'natʃ(ə)rəlɪz(ə)m, 'natʃ(ə)rl̩ɪz(ə)m
AM 'nætʃ(ə)rə,lɪzəm

naturalist
BR 'natʃ(ə)rəlɪst, 'natʃ(ə)rl̩ɪst, -s
AM 'nætʃ(ə)rələst, -s

naturalistic
BR ,natʃ(ə)rə'lɪstɪk, ,natʃ(ə)rl̩'ɪstɪk
AM ,nætʃ(ə)rə'lɪstɪk

naturalistically
BR ,natʃ(ə)rə'lɪstɨkli, ,natʃ(ə)rl̩'ɪstɨkli
AM ,nætʃ(ə)rə'lɪstək(ə)li

naturalization
BR ,natʃ(ə)rəlʌɪ'zeɪʃn, ,natʃ(ə)rl̩ʌɪ'zeɪʃn
AM ,nætʃ(ə)rələ'zeɪʃən, ,nætʃ(ə)rə,laɪ'zeɪʃən

naturalize
BR 'natʃ(ə)rəlʌɪz, 'natʃ(ə)rl̩ʌɪz, -ɪz, -ɪŋ, -d
AM 'nætʃ(ə)rə,laɪz, -ɪz, -ɪŋ, -d

naturally
BR 'natʃ(ə)rəli, 'natʃ(ə)rl̩i
AM 'nætʃ(ə)rəli

naturalness
BR 'natʃ(ə)rəlnəs, 'natʃ(ə)rl̩nəs
AM 'nætʃ(ə)rəlnəs

nature
BR 'neɪtʃə(r), -z
AM 'neɪtʃər, -z

natured
BR 'neɪtʃəd
AM 'neɪtʃərd

naturism
BR 'neɪtʃ(ə)rɪz(ə)m
AM 'neɪtʃə,rɪzəm

naturist
BR 'neɪtʃ(ə)rɪst, -s
AM 'neɪtʃərəst, -s

naturopath
BR 'neɪtʃ(ə)rəpaθ, 'natʃ(ə)rəpaθ, -s
AM 'neɪtʃərə,pæθ, 'nætʃərə,pæθ, -s

naturopathic
BR ,neɪtʃ(ə)rə'paθɪk, ,natʃ(ə)rə'paθɪk
AM ',neɪtʃərə'pæθɪk, ',nætʃərə'pæθɪk

naturopathically
BR ,neɪtʃ(ə)rə'paθɨkli, ,natʃ(ə)rə'paθɨkli
AM ',neɪtʃərə'pæθək(ə)li, ',nætʃərə'pæθək(ə)li

naturopathy
BR ,neɪtʃə'rɒpəθi, ,natʃə'rɒpəθi
AM ,neɪtʃə'rɑpəθi, ,nætʃə'rɑpəθi

NatWest®
BR ,nat'wɛst
AM ,næt'wɛst

naugahyde
BR 'nɔːgəhʌɪd
AM 'nɔgə,haɪd, 'nɑgə,haɪd

naught
BR nɔːt, -s
AM nɔt, nɑt, -s

Naughtie
BR 'nɒxti
AM 'nɔdi, 'nɑdi

naughtily
BR 'nɔːtɨli
AM 'nɔdəli, 'nɑdəli

naughtiness
BR 'nɔːtɪnɨs, -ɪz
AM 'nɔdinɨs, 'nɑdinɨs, -ɪz

Naughton
BR 'nɔːt(ə)n

AM 'nɔtn, 'nɑtn

naughty
BR 'nɔːt|i, -ɪə(r), -ɪɪst
AM 'nɔdi, 'nɑdi, -ər, -ɨst

nauplii
BR 'nɔːplɪʌɪ, 'nɔːpliː
AM 'nɔpli,aɪ, 'nɑpli,aɪ

nauplius
BR 'nɔːplɪəs
AM 'nɔpliəs, 'nɑpliəs

Nauru
BR nɑː'uːruː, naʊ'ruː, nɑː'ruː
AM nɑ'uru

Nauruan
BR nɑː'uːruːən, naʊ'ruːən, nɑː'ruːən, -z
AM nɑ'uruwən, -z

nausea
BR 'nɔːsɪə(r), 'nɔːzɪə(r)
AM 'nɔziə, 'nɔʒə, 'nɑziə, 'nɑʒə

nauseate
BR 'nɔːsɪeɪt, 'nɔːzɪeɪt, -s, -ɪŋ, -ɨd
AM 'nɔzi,eɪ|t, 'nɔʒi,eɪ|t, 'nɑzi,eɪ|t, 'nɑʒi,eɪ|t, -ts, -dɪŋ, -dɨd

nauseatingly
BR 'nɔːsɪeɪtɪŋli, 'nɔːzɪeɪtɪŋli
AM 'nɔzi,eɪdɪŋli, 'nɔʒi,eɪdɪŋli, 'nɑzi,eɪdɪŋli, 'nɑʒi,eɪdɪŋli

nauseous
BR 'nɔːsɪəs, 'nɔːzɪəs
AM 'nɔʃəs, 'nɔʒəs, 'nɑʃəs, 'nɑʒəs

nauseously
BR 'nɔːsɪəsli, 'nɔːzɪəsli
AM 'nɔʃəsli, 'nɔʒəsli, 'nɑʃəsli, 'nɑʒəsli

nauseousness
BR 'nɔːsɪəsnəs, 'nɔːzɪəsnəs
AM 'nɔʃəsnəs, 'nɔʒəsnəs, 'nɑʃəsnəs, 'nɑʒəsnəs

Nausicaa
BR nɔː'sɪkɪə(r), nɔː'sɪkeɪə(r)
AM nɔ'sɪkiə, nɔ'sɪkeɪə, nɑ'sɪkiə, nɑ'sɪkeɪə

nautch
BR nɔːtʃ, -ɨz
AM nɔtʃ, nɑtʃ, -əz

nautical
BR 'nɔːtɨkl
AM 'nɔdəkəl, 'nɑdəkəl

nautically
BR 'nɔːtɨkli
AM 'nɔdək(ə)li, 'nɑdək(ə)li

nautilus
BR 'nɔːtɨləs, 'nɔːtl̩əs, -ɨz
AM 'nɔdl̩əs, 'nɑdl̩əs, -əz

Navaho
BR 'navəhəʊ, -z
AM 'nɑvə,hoʊ, 'nævə,hoʊ, -z

Navajo
BR 'navəhəʊ, -z
AM 'nɑvə,hoʊ, 'nævə,hoʊ, -z

naval
BR 'neɪvl
AM 'neɪvəl

navally
BR 'neɪvl̩i, 'neɪvəli
AM 'neɪvəli

navarin
BR 'nav(ə)rɪn, 'nav(ə)rn̩
AM 'nævərən

Navarino
BR ,navə'riːnəʊ
AM ,nævə'rinoʊ

Navarone
BR ,navə'rəʊn
AM ,nævə'roʊn

Navarre
BR nə'vɑː(r)
AM nə'vɑr

nave
BR neɪv, -z
AM neɪv, -z

navel
BR 'neɪvl, -z
AM 'neɪvəl, -z

navelwort
BR 'neɪvlwəːt, -s
AM 'neɪvəl,wərt, 'neɪvəl,wɔ(ə)rt, -s

navicular
BR nə'vɪkjʉlə(r), -z
AM nə'vɪkjələr, -z

navigability
BR ,navɨgə'bɪlɨti
AM ,nævəgə'bɪlɨdi

navigable
BR 'navɨgəbl
AM 'nævəgəbəl

navigableness
BR 'navɨgəblnəs
AM 'nævəgəbəlnəs

navigate
BR 'navɨgeɪt, -s, -ɪŋ, -ɨd
AM 'nævə,geɪ|t, -ts, -dɪŋ, -dɨd

navigation
BR ,navɨ'geɪʃn, -z
AM ,nævə'geɪʃən, -z

navigational
BR ,navɨ'geɪʃn̩(ə)l, ,navɨ'geɪʃən(ə)l
AM ¦nævə'geɪʃ(ə)nəl

navigator
BR 'navɨgeɪtə(r), -z
AM 'nævə,geɪdər, -z

Navrátilová
BR ,navratɪ'ləʊvə(r)
AM ,nɑvrədə'loʊvə
CZ 'nʌvrɑːtjlɔvɑː

navvy
BR 'nav|i, -ɪz
AM 'nævi, -z

navy
BR 'neɪv|i, -ɪz
AM 'neɪvi, -z

nawab
BR nə'wɑːb, nə'wɔːb, -z
AM nə'wɔb, nə'wɑb, -z

Náxos
BR 'naksɒs
AM 'næk,sɔs, 'næk,sɑs

nay
BR neɪ, -z
AM neɪ, -z

Nayland
BR 'neɪlənd
AM 'neɪlənd

Naylor
BR 'neɪlə(r)
AM 'neɪlər

naysay
BR 'neɪseɪ, -z, -ɪŋ, -d
AM 'neɪ,seɪ, -z, -ɪŋ, -d

naysayer
BR 'neɪ,seɪə(r), -z
AM 'neɪ,seɪər, -z

Nazarene
BR ,nazə'riːn, 'nazəriːn, -z
AM 'næzə,rin, -z

Nazareth
BR 'naz(ə)rəθ
AM 'næz(ə)rəθ

Nazarite
BR 'nazərʌɪt, -s
AM 'næzə,raɪt, -s

Nazca Lines
BR 'nazkə lʌɪnz, 'naskə +
AM 'nɑskə ,laɪnz

naze
BR neɪz, -ɨz
AM neɪz, -ɨz

Nazi
BR 'nɑːts|i, 'nats|i, -ɪz
AM 'nɑtsi, 'nætsi, -z

Nazidom
BR 'nɑːtsɪdəm, 'natsɪdəm
AM 'nɑtsidəm, 'nætsidəm

Nazification
BR ,nɑːtsɨfɨ'keɪʃn, ,natsɨfɨ'keɪʃn
AM ,nɑtsəfə'keɪʃən, ,nætsəfə'keɪʃən

Nazify
BR 'nɑːtsɨfʌɪ, 'natsɨfʌɪ, -z, -ɪŋ, -d
AM 'nɑtʃə,faɪ, 'nætsə,faɪ, -z, -ɪŋ, -d

Naziism
BR 'nɑːtsɪɪz(ə)m, 'natsɪɪz(ə)m
AM 'nɑtsi,ɪzəm, 'nætsi,ɪzəm

Nazirite
BR 'nazɨrʌɪt
AM 'næzə,raɪt

Nazism
BR 'nɑːtsɪz(ə)m, 'natsɪz(ə)m
AM 'nɑt,sɪzəm, 'næt,sɪzəm

Ndebele
BR n̩dɪ'biːli, (n)dɪ'beɪli
AM (n)də'bili

N'Djamena
BR n̩dʒə'meɪnə(r)
AM (n)'dʒɑmənə

Ndola
BR n̩'dəʊlə(r)
AM '(n)doʊlə

né
BR neɪ
AM neɪ

Neagh
BR neɪ
AM neɪ

Neal
BR niːl
AM nil

Neale
BR niːl
AM nil

neanderthal
BR nɪ'andətɑːl, -z
AM ni'ændər,θɔl, ni'ændər,θɑl, -z

neap
BR niːp, -s
AM nip, -s

Neapolitan
BR nɪə'pɒlɨt(ə)n, ,niːə'pɒlɨt(ə)n, -z
AM ¦niə'pɑlətn̩, ¦niə'pɑlədən, -z

near
BR nɪə(r)
AM nɪ(ə)r

nearby
BR ,nɪə'bʌɪ
AM ¦nɪr'baɪ

Nearctic
BR ,niː'ɑːktɪk
AM ni'ɑr(k)tɪk, ni'ɑrdɪk

nearish
BR 'nɪərɪʃ
AM 'nɪrɪʃ

nearly
BR 'nɪəli
AM 'nɪrli

nearness
BR 'nɪənəs
AM 'nɪrnəs

nearside
BR 'nɪəsʌɪd
AM 'nɪr¦saɪd

Neasden
BR ˈniːzd(ə)n
AM ˈnizdən
neat
BR niːt, -ə(r), -ɪst
AM ni|t, -dər, -dɪst
neaten
BR ˈniːtn̩, -z, -ɪŋ, -d
AM ˈnitn, -z, -ɪŋ, -d
neath
BR niːθ
AM niθ
neatly
BR ˈniːtli
AM ˈnitli
neatness
BR ˈniːtnɨs
AM ˈnitnɨs
Neave
BR niːv
AM niv
nebbish
BR ˈnɛb|ɪʃ, -ɪʃɪz
AM ˈnɛbɪʃ, -ɪz
Nebraska
BR nəˈbraskə(r)
AM nəˈbræskə
Nebraskan
BR nɪˈbraskən, -z
AM nəˈbræskən, -z
Nebuchadnezzar
BR ˌnɛbjʉkədˈnɛzə(r), -z
AM ˌnɛb(j)əkə(d)ˈnɛzər, -z
nebula
BR ˈnɛbjʉlə(r), -z
AM ˈnɛbjələ, -z
nebulae
BR ˈnɛbjʉliː
AM ˈnɛbjəli, ˈnɛbjəˌlaɪ
nebular
BR ˈnɛbjʉlə(r)
AM ˈnɛbjələr
nebuliser
BR ˈnɛbjʉlʌɪzə(r), -z
AM ˈnɛbjəˌlaɪzər, -z
nebulizer
BR ˈnɛbjʉlʌɪzə(r), -z
AM ˈnɛbjəˌlaɪzər, -z
nebulosity
BR ˌnɛbjʉˈlɒsɪti
AM ˌnɛbjəˈlɑsədi
nebulous
BR ˈnɛbjʉləs
AM ˈnɛbjələs
nebulously
BR ˈnɛbjʉləsli
AM ˈnɛbjələsli
nebulousness
BR ˈnɛbjʉləsnəs
AM ˈnɛbjələsnəs
nebuly
BR ˈnɛbjʉli
AM ˈnɛbjəli
necessarian
BR ˌnɛsɪˈsɛːrɪən, -z
AM ˌnɛsəˈsɛriən, -z
necessarianism
BR ˌnɛsɪˈsɛːrɪənɪz(ə)m
AM ˌnɛsəˈsɛriəˌnɪzəm
necessarily
BR ˈnɛsɪs(ə)rɪli, ˌnɛsəˈsɛrɪli
AM ˌnɛsəˈsɛrəli
necessariness
BR ˈnɛsɪs(ə)rɪnɪs
AM ˈnɛsəˌsɛrinɪs
necessary
BR ˈnɛsɪs(ə)r|i, -ɪz
AM ˈnɛsəˌsɛri, -z
necessitarian
BR nɪˌsɛsɪˈtɛːrɪən, -z
AM nəˌsɛsəˈtɛriən, -z
necessitarianism
BR nɪˌsɛsɪˈtɛːrɪənɪz(ə)m
AM nəˌsɛsəˈtɛriəˌnɪzəm
necessitate
BR nɪˈsɛsɪteɪt, -s, -ɪŋ, -ɪd
AM nəˈsɛsəˌteɪ|t, -ts, -dɪŋ, -dɪd
necessitous
BR nɪˈsɛsɪtəs
AM nəˈsɛsədəs
necessitously
BR nɪˈsɛsɪtəsli
AM nəˈsɛsədəsli
necessitousness
BR nɪˈsɛsɪtəsnəs
AM nəˈsɛsədəsnəs
necessity
BR nɪˈsɛsɪt|i, -ɪz
AM nəˈsɛsədi, -z
neck
BR nɛk, -s, -ɪŋ, -t
AM nɛk, -s, -ɪŋ, -t
neck-and-neck
BR ˌnɛk(ə)n(d)ˈnɛk
AM ˈnɛkənˈnɛk
Neckar
BR ˈnɛkə(r), ˈnɛkɑː(r)
AM ˈnɛkər
neckband
BR ˈnɛkband, -z
AM ˈnɛkˌbænd, -z
Necker
BR ˈnɛkə(r)
AM ˈnɛkər
neckerchief
BR ˈnɛkətʃɪf, ˈnɛkətʃiːf, -s
AM ˈnɛkərˌtʃɪf, ˈnɛkərˌtʃif, -s
necklace
BR ˈnɛklɪs, -ɪz
AM ˈnɛkləs, -əz
necklet
BR ˈnɛklɪt, -s
AM ˈnɛklət, -s
neckline
BR ˈnɛklʌɪn, -z
AM ˈnɛkˌlaɪn, -z
necktie
BR ˈnɛktʌɪ, -z
AM ˈnɛkˌtaɪ, -z
neckwear
BR ˈnɛkwɛː(r)
AM ˈnɛkˌwɛ(ə)r
necrobiosis
BR ˌnɛkrə(ʊ)bʌɪˈəʊsɪs
AM ˌnɛkrəˈbaɪəsəs
necrobiotic
BR ˌnɛkrə(ʊ)bʌɪˈɒtɪk
AM ˈnɛkrəˌbaɪˈɑdɪk
necrogenic
BR ˌnɛkrə(ʊ)ˈdʒɛnɪk
AM ˌnɛkrəˈdʒɛnɪk
necrolatry
BR nɪˈkrɒlətri, nɛˈkrɒlətri
AM nəˈkrɑlətri, nɛˈkrɑlətri
necrological
BR ˌnɛkrəˈlɒdʒɪkl
AM ˌnɛkrəˈlɑdʒəkəl
necrologist
BR nɪˈkrɒlədʒɪst, nɛˈkrɒlədʒɪst, -s
AM nəˈkrɑlədʒəst, nɛˈkrɑlədʒəst, -s
necrology
BR nɪˈkrɒlədʒ|i, nɛˈkrɒlədʒ|i, -ɪz
AM nəˈkrɑlədʒi, nɛˈkrɑlədʒi, -z
necromancer
BR ˈnɛkrə(ʊ)mansə(r), -z
AM ˈnɛkrəˌmænsər, -z
necromancy
BR ˈnɛkrə(ʊ)mansi
AM ˈnɛkrəˌmænsi
necromantic
BR ˌnɛkrə(ʊ)ˈmantɪk, -s
AM ˌnɛkrəˈmæn(t)ɪk, -s
necrophagous
BR nɪˈkrɒfəgəs, nɛˈkrɒfəgəs
AM nəˈkrɑfəgəs, nɛˈkrɑfəgəs
necrophil
BR ˈnɛkrə(ʊ)fɪl, -z
AM ˈnɛkrəˌfɪl, -z
necrophile
BR ˈnɛkrə(ʊ)fʌɪl, -z
AM ˈnɛkrəˌfaɪl, -z
necrophilia
BR ˌnɛkrə(ʊ)ˈfɪlɪə(r)
AM ˌnɛkrəˈfɪljə, ˌnɛkrəˈfɪliə
necrophiliac
BR ˌnɛkrə(ʊ)ˈfɪlɪak, -s
AM ˈnɛkrəˈfɪliˌæk, -s
necrophilic
BR ˌnɛkrə(ʊ)ˈfɪlɪk
AM ˌnɛkrəˈfɪlɪk
necrophilism
BR nɪˈkrɒfɪlɪz(ə)m, nɛˈkrɒfɪlɪz(ə)m
AM nəˈkrɑfəˌlɪzəm, nɛˈkrɑfəˌlɪzəm
necrophilist
BR nɪˈkrɒfɪlɪst, nɛˈkrɒfɪlɪst, -s
AM nəˈkrɑfələst, nɛˈkrɑfələst, -s
necrophily
BR nɪˈkrɒfɪli, nɛˈkrɒfɪli
AM nəˈkrɑfəli, nɛˈkrɑfəli
necrophobia
BR ˌnɛkrə(ʊ)ˈfəʊbɪə(r)
AM ˌnɛkrəˈfoʊbiə
necropolis
BR nɪˈkrɒpəlɪs, nɪˈkrɒpl̩ɪs, nɛˈkrɒpəlɪs, nɛˈkrɒpl̩ɪs, -ɪz
AM nəˈkrɑpələs, nɛˈkrɑpələs, -əz
necropsy
BR ˈnɛkrɒpsi, nɪˈkrɒpsi, nɛˈkrɒpsi
AM nəˈkrɑpsi, ˈnɛˌkrɑpsi
necroscopic
BR ˌnɛkrə(ʊ)ˈskɒpɪk
AM ˌnɛkrəˈskɑpɪk
necroscopy
BR nɪˈkrɒskəp|i, nɛˈkrɒskəpi, -ɪz
AM nəˈkrɑskəpi, nɛˈkrɑskəpi, -z
necrose
BR ˈnɛkrəʊs, nɪˈkrəʊs, nɛˈkrəʊs
AM ˈnɛˌkroʊs, nəˈkroʊs, nɛˈkroʊs
necrosis
BR nɪˈkrəʊsɪs, nɛˈkrəʊsɪs
AM nəˈkroʊsəs, nɛˈkroʊsəs
necrotic
BR nɪˈkrɒtɪk, nɛˈkrɒtɪk
AM nəˈkrɑdɪk, nɛˈkrɑdɪk
necrotise
BR ˈnɛkrə(ʊ)tʌɪz, -ɪz, -ɪŋ, -d
AM ˈnɛkrəˌtaɪz, -ɪz, -ɪŋ, -d
necrotize
BR ˈnɛkrə(ʊ)tʌɪz, -ɪz, -ɪŋ, -d
AM ˈnɛkrəˌtaɪz, -ɪz, -ɪŋ, -d
nectar
BR ˈnɛktə(r)
AM ˈnɛktər
nectarean
BR nɛkˈtɛːrɪən

AM nɛk'tɛriən

nectared
BR 'nɛktəd
AM 'nɛktərd

nectareous
BR nɛk'tɛːrɪəs
AM nɛk'tɛriəs

nectariferous
BR ˌnɛktə'rɪf(ə)rəs
AM ˌnɛktə'rɪf(ə)rəs

nectarine
BR 'nɛktəriːn, 'nɛktərɪn, -z
AM ¦nɛktə¦rin, -z

nectarous
BR 'nɛkt(ə)rəs
AM 'nɛktərəs

nectary
BR 'nɛkt(ə)r|i, -ɪz
AM 'nɛktəri, -z

Ned
BR nɛd
AM nɛd

neddy
BR 'nɛd|i, -ɪz
AM 'nɛdi, -z

nee
BR neɪ
AM neɪ

née
BR neɪ
AM neɪ

need
BR niːd, -z, -ɪŋ, -ɨd
AM nid, -z, -ɪŋ, -ɨd

needful
BR 'niːdf(ʊ)l
AM 'nidfəl

needfully
BR 'niːdfʊli, 'niːdfḷi
AM 'nidfəli

needfulness
BR 'niːdf(ʊ)lnəs
AM 'nidfəlnəs

Needham
BR 'niːdəm
AM 'nidəm

needily
BR 'niːdɪli
AM 'nidɨli

neediness
BR 'niːdɪnɪs
AM 'nidinɪs

needle
BR 'niːd|l, -lz, -ḷɪŋ\-lɪŋ, -ld
AM 'nid|əl, -əlz, -(ə)lɪŋ, -əld

needlecord
BR 'niːdlkɔːd
AM 'nidlˌkɔrd

needlecraft
BR 'niːdlkrɑːft, 'niːdlkraft
AM 'nidlˌkræft

needleful
BR 'niːdlfʊl, -z
AM 'nidlˌfʊl, -z

needlepoint
BR 'niːdlpɔɪnt
AM 'nidlˌpɔɪnt

Needles
BR 'niːdlz
AM 'nidlz

needless
BR 'niːdlɨs
AM 'nidlɨs

needlessly
BR 'niːdlɨsli
AM 'nidlɨsli

needlessness
BR 'niːdlɨsnɨs
AM 'nidlɪnɪs

needlewoman
BR 'niːdlˌwʊmən
AM 'nidlˌwʊmən

needlewomen
BR 'niːdlˌwɪmɪn
AM 'nidlˌwɪmɪn

needlework
BR 'niːdlwəːk
AM 'nidlˌwərk

needn't
BR 'niːdnt
AM 'nidnt

needy
BR 'niːd|i, -ɪə(r), -ɪɪst
AM 'nidi, -ər, -ɪst

neep
BR niːp, -s
AM nip, -s

ne'er
BR nɛː(r)
AM nɛ(ə)r

ne'er-do-well
BR 'nɛːdʊwɛl, -z
AM 'nɛrduˌwɛl, 'nɛrdəˌwɛl, -z

nefarious
BR nɪ'fɛːrɪəs
AM nə'fɛriəs

nefariously
BR nɪ'fɛːrɪəsli
AM nə'fɛriəsli

nefariousness
BR nɪ'fɛːrɪəsnəs
AM nə'fɛriəsnəs

Nefertiti
BR ˌnɛfə'tiːti
AM ˌnɛfər'tidi

Neff®
BR nɛf
AM nɛf

Nefyn
BR 'nɛv(ɪ)n
AM 'nɛvən

neg.
negative
BR nɛg
AM nɛg

negate
BR nɪ'geɪt, -s, -ɪŋ, -ɨd
AM nə'geɪ|t, -ts, -dɪŋ, -dɨd

negation
BR nɪ'geɪʃn, -z
AM nə'geɪʃən, -z

negationist
BR nɪ'geɪʃn̩ɪst, -s
AM nə'geɪʃ(ə)nəst, -s

negative
BR 'nɛgətɪv, -z
AM 'nɛgədɪv, -z

negatively
BR 'nɛgətɨvli
AM 'nɛgədɨvli

negativeness
BR 'nɛgətɨvnɨs
AM 'nɛgədɪvnɨs

negativism
BR 'nɛgətɨvɪz(ə)m
AM 'nɛgədəvˌɪzəm

negativist
BR 'nɛgətɨvɪst, -s
AM 'nɛgədəvəst, -s

negativistic
BR ˌnɛgətɪ'vɪstɪk
AM ˌnɛgədə'vɪstɪk

negativity
BR ˌnɛgə'tɪvɨti
AM ˌnɛgə'tɪvɨdi

negator
BR nɪ'geɪtə(r), -z
AM nə'geɪdər, -z

negatory
BR 'nɛgət(ə)ri
AM 'nɛgəˌtɔri

Negev
BR 'nɛgɛv
AM 'nɛˌgɛv

neglect
BR nɪ'glɛkt, -s, -ɪŋ, -ɨd
AM nə'glɛk|(t), -(t)s, -tɪŋ, -təd

neglectful
BR nɪ'glɛk(t)f(ʊ)l
AM nə'glɛk(t)fəl

neglectfully
BR nɪ'glɛk(t)fʊli, nɪ'glɛk(t)fḷi
AM nə'glɛk(t)fəli

neglectfulness
BR nɪ'glɛk(t)f(ʊ)lnəs
AM nə'glɛk(t)fəlnəs

negligee
BR 'nɛglɪʒeɪ, -z
AM 'nɛgləˌʒeɪ, ˌnɛglə'ʒeɪ, -z

negligence
BR 'nɛglɪdʒ(ə)ns
AM 'nɛglədʒəns

negligent
BR 'nɛglɪdʒ(ə)nt
AM 'nɛglədʒənt

negligently
BR 'nɛglɪdʒ(ə)ntli
AM 'nɛglədʒən(t)li

negligibility
BR ˌnɛglɪdʒɪ'bɪlɨti
AM ˌnɛglədʒə'bɪlɨdi

negligible
BR 'nɛglɪdʒɪbl
AM 'nɛglədʒəbəl

negligibly
BR 'nɛglɪdʒɪbli
AM 'nɛglədʒəbli

Negombo
BR nɪ'gɒmbəʊ
AM nə'gɔmˌboʊ, nə'gɑmˌboʊ

negotiability
BR nɪˌgəʊʃ(ɪ)ə'bɪlɨti
AM nəˌgoʊʃ(i)ə'bɪlɨdi

negotiable
BR nɪ'gəʊʃ(ɪ)əbl
AM nə'goʊʃ(i)əbəl

negotiant
BR nɪ'gəʊʃɪənt, nɪ'gəʊʃ(ə)nt, -s
AM nə'goʊʃ(i)ənt, -s

negotiate
BR nɪ'gəʊʃɪeɪt, nɪ'gəʊsɪeɪt, -s, -ɪŋ, -ɨd
AM nə'goʊʃiˌeɪ|t, nə'goʊsiˌeɪ|t, -ts, -dɪŋ, -dɨd

negotiation
BR nɪˌgəʊʃɪ'eɪʃn, nɪˌgəʊsɪ'eɪʃn, -z
AM nəˌgoʊʃi'eɪʃən, nəˌgoʊsi'eɪʃən, -z

negotiator
BR nɪ'gəʊʃɪeɪtə(r), nɪ'gəʊsɪeɪtə(r), -z
AM nə'goʊʃiˌeɪdər, nə'goʊsiˌeɪdər, -z

Negress
BR 'niːgrɪs, 'niːgrɛs, -ɨz
AM 'nigrɪs, -əz

Negrillo
BR nɪ'grɪləʊ, -z
AM nə'grɪloʊ, -z

Negrito
BR nɪ'griːtəʊ, -z
AM nə'gridoʊ, -z

negritude
BR 'nɛgrɪtjuːd, 'nɛgrɪtʃuːd
AM 'nɛgrəˌt(j)ud

Negro
BR 'niːgrəʊ, -z
AM 'nigroʊ, -z

negroid
BR 'niːgrɔɪd
AM 'niˌgrɔɪd

Negroism
BR 'niːgrəʊɪz(ə)m
AM 'nigrəˌwɪzəm

Negrophobia
BR ˌniːgrə(ʊ)'fəʊbɪə(r)
AM ˌnigrə'foʊbiə

Negrophobic
BR ˌniːgrə(ʊ)'fəʊbɪk
AM ˌnigrə'foʊbɪk

negus
BR 'niːgəs
AM 'nigəs

Nehemiah
BR ˌniːɪˈmʌɪə(r)
AM ˌniəˈmaɪə

Nehru
BR ˈnɛːruː
AM ˈneɪru

neigh
BR neɪ, -z, -ɪŋ, -d
AM neɪ, -z, -ɪŋ, -d

neighbor
BR ˈneɪb|ə(r), -əz, -(ə)rɪŋ, -əd
AM ˈneɪbər, -z, -ɪŋ, -d

neighborhood
BR ˈneɪbəhʊd, -z
AM ˈneɪbərˌ(h)ʊd, -z

neighborliness
BR ˈneɪbəlɪnɨs
AM ˈneɪbərlinɨs

neighborly
BR ˈneɪbəli
AM ˈneɪbərli

neighbour
BR ˈneɪb|ə(r), -əz, -(ə)rɪŋ, -əd
AM ˈneɪbər, -z, -ɪŋ, -d

neighbourhood
BR ˈneɪbəhʊd, -z
AM ˈneɪbərˌ(h)ʊd, -z

neighbourliness
BR ˈneɪbəlɪnɨs
AM ˈneɪbərlinɨs

neighbourly
BR ˈneɪbəli
AM ˈneɪbərli

Neil
BR niːl
AM nil

Neill
BR niːl
AM nil

Neilson
BR ˈniːls(ə)n
AM ˈnilsən

neither
BR ˈnʌɪðə(r), ˈniːðə(r)
AM ˈniðər, ˈnaɪðər

nekton
BR ˈnɛkt(ə)n, ˈnɛktɒn
AM ˈnɛktən, ˈnɛkˌtɑn

Nell
BR nɛl
AM nɛl

Nellie
BR ˈnɛli
AM ˈnɛli

nelly
BR ˈnɛl|i, -ɪz
AM ˈnɛli, -z

Nelson
BR ˈnɛlsn
AM ˈnɛlsən

nelumbo
BR nɪˈlʌmbəʊ, -z
AM nəˈləmboʊ, -z

nematocyst
BR nɪˈmatə(ʊ)sɪst, ˈnɛmətəsɪst, -s
AM ˈnimədəˌsɪst, nəˈmædəˌsɪst, -s

nematode
BR ˈnɛmətəʊd, -z
AM ˈniməˌtoʊd, -z

Nembutal®
BR ˈnɛmbjʉtal, ˈnɛmbjʉtɒl
AM ˈnɛmbjəˌtɔl, ˈnɛmbjəˌtɑl, ˈnɛmbjəˌtæl

nem con
BR ˌnɛm ˈkɒn
AM ˌnɛm ˈkɑn

nemertean
BR nɪˈməːtɪən, ˌnɛməˈtiːən, ˈnɛmətiːn, -z
AM nəˈmərdiən, -z

nemertine
BR nɪˈməːtʌɪn, nɪˈmətiːn, ˈnɛmətʌɪn, ˈnɛmətiːn
AM ˈnɛmərˌtin

nemeses
BR ˈnɛmɪsiːz
AM ˈnɛməˌsiz

nemesia
BR nɪˈmiːʒ(ɪ)ə(r)
AM nəˈmiʒ(i)ə, nəˈmiziə

nemesis
BR ˈnɛmɪsɪs
AM ˈnɛməsəs

Nemo
BR ˈniːməʊ
AM ˈnimoʊ

Nene[1]
river at Northampton, UK
BR nɛn
AM nɛn

Nene[2]
river at Peterborough, Norfolk and Lincolnshire, UK
BR niːn
AM nin

nene
BR ˈneɪneɪ, -z
AM ˈneɪˌneɪ, -z

Nennius
BR ˈnɛnɪəs
AM ˈnɛniəs

nenuphar
BR ˈnɛnjʉfɑː(r), -z
AM ˈnɛnjəˌfɑr, -z

neo-Cambrian
BR ˌniːə(ʊ)ˈkambrɪən
AM ˌnioʊˈkæmbriən

Neocene
BR ˈnɪə(ʊ)siːn
AM ˈniəˌsin

neoclassic
BR ˌniːə(ʊ)ˈklasɪk
AM ¦nioʊˈklæsɪk

neoclassical
BR ˌniːə(ʊ)ˈklasɪkl
AM ¦nioʊˈklæsəkəl

neoclassicism
BR ˌniːə(ʊ)ˈklasɪsɪz(ə)m
AM ¦nioʊˈklæsəˌsɪzəm

neoclassicist
BR ˌniːə(ʊ)ˈklasɪsɪst, -s
AM ¦nioʊˈklæsəsəst, -s

neocolonial
BR ˌniːəʊkəˈləʊnɪəl
AM ¦nioʊkəˈloʊnjəl, ¦nioʊkəˈloʊniəl

neocolonialism
BR ˌniːəʊkəˈləʊnɪəlɪz(ə)m
AM ¦nioʊkəˈloʊnjəˌlɪzəm, ¦nioʊkəˈloʊniəˌlɪzəm

neocolonialist
BR ˌniːəʊkəˈləʊnɪəlɪst, -s
AM ¦nioʊkəˈloʊnjələst, ¦nioʊkəˈloʊniələst, -s

neodymium
BR ˌnɪə(ʊ)ˈdɪmɪəm
AM ˌnioʊˈdɪmiəm

neolithic
BR ˌniːəˈlɪθɪk
AM ¦niəˈlɪθɪk

neologian
BR ˌniːəˈləʊdʒɪən, ˌniːəˈləʊdʒ(ə)n, -z
AM ¦nioʊˈloʊdʒ(i)ən, -z

neologise
BR nɪˈɒlədʒʌɪz, -ɪz, -ɪŋ, -d
AM niˈɑləˌdʒaɪz, -ɪz, -ɪŋ, -d

neologism
BR nɪˈɒlədʒɪz(ə)m, -z
AM niˈɑləˌdʒɪzəm, -z

neologist
BR nɪˈɒlədʒɪst, -s
AM niˈɑlədʒəst, -s

neologize
BR nɪˈɒlədʒʌɪz, -ɪz, -ɪŋ, -d
AM niˈɑləˌdʒaɪz, -ɪz, -ɪŋ, -d

neology
BR nɪˈɒlədʒ|i, -ɪz
AM niˈɑlədʒi, -z

neomycin
BR ˌnɪə(ʊ)ˈmʌɪsɪn
AM ˌnioʊˈmaɪsən

neon
BR ˈniːɒn
AM ˈniˌɑn

neonatal
BR ˌnɪə(ʊ)ˈneɪtl
AM ˌnioʊˈneɪdəl

neonate
BR ˈnɪə(ʊ)neɪt, -s
AM ˈniəˌneɪt, -s

neonatology
BR ˌnɪə(ʊ)neɪˈtɒlədʒi
AM ˌnioʊˌneɪˈtɑlədʒi

neontologist
BR ˌnɪɒnˈtɒlədʒɪst, -s
AM ˌniˌɑnˈtɑlədʒəst, -s

neontology
BR ˌnɪɒnˈtɒlədʒi
AM ˌniˌɑnˈtɑlədʒi

neopentane
BR ˌniːə(ʊ)ˈpɛnteɪn
AM ¦nioʊˈpɛnˌteɪn

neophobia
BR ˌniːə(ʊ)ˈfəʊbɪə(r)
AM ¦nioʊˈfoʊbiə

neophron
BR ˈnɪə(ʊ)frɒn, -z
AM ˈniəˌfrɑn, -z

neophyte
BR ˈnɪə(ʊ)fʌɪt, -s
AM ˈniəˌfaɪt, -s

neoplasm
BR ˈnɪə(ʊ)plaz(ə)m, -z
AM ˈniəˌplæzəm, -z

neoplastic
BR ˌniːə(ʊ)ˈplastɪk
AM ¦niəˈplæstɪk

neo-plasticism
BR ˌniːə(ʊ)ˈplastɪsɪz(ə)m
AM ˌniəˈplæstəˌsɪzəm

Neoplatonic
BR ˌniːə(ʊ)pləˈtɒnɪk
AM ¦nioʊpləˈtɑnɪk

Neoplatonism
BR ˌniːə(ʊ)ˈpleɪtənɪz(ə)m, ˌniːəʊˈpleɪtn̩ɪz(ə)m
AM ˌniəˈpleɪtn̩ˌɪzəm

Neoplatonist
BR ˌniːə(ʊ)ˈpleɪtənɪst, ˌniːəʊˈpleɪtn̩ɪst, -s
AM ˌniəˈpleɪtn̩əst, -s

neoprene
BR ˈnɪə(ʊ)priːn
AM ˈniəˌprin

neostigmine
BR ˌniːə(ʊ)ˈstɪgmiːn
AM ˌnioʊˈstɪgmin

neotenic
BR ˌniːə(ʊ)ˈtɛnɪk
AM ˌnioʊˈtɛnɪk, ˌnioʊˈtinɪk

neotenous
BR nɪˈɒtɪnəs, nɪˈɒtn̩əs
AM ˌnioʊˈtinəs

neoteny
BR nɪˈɒtɪni, nɪˈɒtn̩i
AM niˈɑt(ɪ)ni

neoteric
BR ˌniːə(ʊ)ˈtɛrɪk
AM ˌniəˈtɛrɪk

neotropical
BR ˌniːə(ʊ)ˈtrɒpɪkl
AM ¦nioʊˈtrɑpəkəl

Neozoic
BR ˌniːə(ʊ)ˈzəʊɪk
AM ˌniəˈzoʊɪk

Nepal
BR nɪˈpɔːl
AM ˌneɪˈpɑl
Nepalese
BR ˌnɛpəˈliːz
AM ˌnɛpəˈliz
Nepali
BR nɪˈpɔːl|i, -ɪz
AM nəˈpɔli, nəˈpɑli, -z
nepenthe
BR nɪˈpɛnθi
AM nəˈpɛnθi
nepenthes
BR nɪˈpɛnθiːz
AM nəˈpɛnθiz
nepeta
BR nɪˈpiːtə(r), -z
AM nəˈpidə, -z
nepheline
BR ˈnɛfəliːn, ˈnɛflḭːn
AM ˈnɛfəˌlin
nephelometer
BR ˌnɛfɪˈlɒmɪtə(r), -z
AM ˌnɛfəˈlɑmədər, -z
nephelometric
BR ˌnɛfələ(ʊ)ˈmɛtrɪk, ˌnɛflə(ʊ)ˈmɛtrɪk
AM ˌnɛfəloʊˈmɛtrɪk
nephelometry
BR ˌnɛfəˈlɒmɪtri
AM ˌnɛfəˈlɑmətri
nephew
BR ˈnɛfjuː, ˈnɛvjuː, -z
AM ˈnɛfju, -z
nephology
BR nɪˈfɒlədʒi, nɛˈfɒlədʒi
AM nəˈfɑlədʒi, nɛˈfɑlədʒi
nephrectomy
BR nɪˈfrɛktəm|i, nɛˈfrɛktəmi, -ɪz
AM nəˈfrɛktəmi, -z
nephridia
BR nɪˈfrɪdɪə(r)
AM nəˈfrɪdiə
nephridiopore
BR nɪˈfrɪdɪəpɔː(r), -z
AM nəˈfrɪdiəˌpɔ(ə)r, -z
nephridium
BR nɪˈfrɪdɪəm
AM nəˈfrɪdiəm
nephrite
BR ˈnɛfrʌɪt
AM ˈnɛˌfraɪt
nephritic
BR nɪˈfrɪtɪk, nɛˈfrɪtɪk
AM nəˈfrɪdɪk
nephritis
BR nɪˈfrʌɪtɪs, nɛˈfrʌɪtɪs
AM nəˈfraɪdɪs
nephrology
BR nɪˈfrɒlədʒi, nɛˈfrɒlədʒi
AM nəˈfrɑlədʒi, nɛˈfrɑlədʒi
nephron
BR ˈnɛfrɒn, -z
AM ˈnɛˌfrɑn, -z
nephropathy
BR nɪˈfrɒpəθi, nɛˈfrɒpəθi
AM nəˈfrɑpəθi, nɛˈfrɑpəθi
nephrosis
BR nɪˈfrəʊsɪs
AM nəˈfroʊsəs
nephrotomy
BR nɪˈfrɒtəm|i, nɛˈfrɒtəmi, -ɪz
AM nəˈfrɑdəmi, nɛˈfrɑdəmi, -z
ne plus ultra
BR ˌneɪ plʌs ˈʌltrə(r), ˌniː +, + plʊs +, + ˈʊltrɑː(r)
AM ˌni ˌpləs ˈəltrə, ˌneɪ ˌplʊs ˈʊltrə
nepotism
BR ˈnɛpətɪz(ə)m
AM ˈnɛpəˌtɪzəm
nepotist
BR ˈnɛpətɪst, -s
AM ˈnɛpədəst, -s
nepotistic
BR ˌnɛpəˈtɪstɪk
AM ˌnɛpəˈtɪstɪk
Neptune
BR ˈnɛptjuːn, ˈnɛptʃuːn
AM ˈnɛpˌt(j)un
Neptunian
BR nɛpˈtjuːnɪən, nɛpˈtʃuːnɪən
AM nɛpˈt(j)uniən
Neptunist
BR ˈnɛptjuːnɪst, ˈnɛptʃuːnɪst, -s
AM nɛpˈt(j)unəst, -s
neptunium
BR nɛpˈtjuːnɪəm, nɛpˈtʃuːnɪəm
AM nɛpˈt(j)uniəm
nerd
BR nəːd, -z
AM nərd, -z
nerdy
BR ˈnəːd|i, -ɪə(r), -ɪɪst
AM ˈnərdi, -ər, -əst
nereid
BR ˈnɪərɪɪd, -z
AM ˈnɪriɨd, ˈnɛriɨd, -z
Nereus
BR ˈnɪərɪəs
AM ˈnɛriəs, ˈnɪ(ə)rjəs
nerine
BR nɪˈrʌɪn|i, nɪˈriːn|i, -ɪz
AM nəˈrini, -z
Nerissa
BR nɪˈriːsə(r)
AM nəˈrisə, nəˈrɪsə
nerka
BR ˈnəːkə(r), -z
AM ˈnərkə, -z
Nernst
BR nəːnst
AM nərnst
Nero
BR ˈnɪərəʊ
AM ˈnɪroʊ, ˈniroʊ
neroli
BR ˈnɪərəli
AM ˈnɛrəli
Neronian
BR nɪˈrəʊnɪən
AM nəˈroʊniən
Neruda
BR nəˈruːdə(r)
AM nəˈrudə
Nerva
BR ˈnəːvə(r)
AM ˈnərvə
nervate
BR ˈnəːveɪt
AM ˈnərˌveɪt
nervation
BR nə(ː)ˈveɪʃn, -z
AM ˌnərˈveɪʃən, -z
nerve
BR nəːv, -z, -ɪŋ, -d
AM nərv, -z, -ɪŋ, -d
nerveless
BR ˈnəːvləs
AM ˈnərvləs
nervelessly
BR ˈnəːvləsli
AM ˈnərvləsli
nervelessness
BR ˈnəːvləsnəs
AM ˈnərvləsnəs
nerve-racking
BR ˈnəːvˌrakɪŋ
AM ˈnərvˌrækɪng
nerve-wracking
BR ˈnəːvˌrakɪŋ
AM ˈnərvˌrækɪŋ
Nervi
BR ˈnəːvi
AM ˈnərvi
nervily
BR ˈnəːvɪli
AM ˈnərvəli
nervine
BR ˈnəːvʌɪn, ˈnəːviːn, -z
AM ˈnərˌvin, -z
nerviness
BR ˈnəːvɪnɪs
AM ˈnərvinɨs
nervous
BR ˈnəːvəs
AM ˈnərvəs
nervously
BR ˈnəːvəsli
AM ˈnərvəsli
nervousness
BR ˈnəːvəsnəs
AM ˈnərvəsnəs
nervure
BR ˈnəːvj(ʊ)ə(r), -z
AM ˈnərvjər, ˈnərˌvjʊ(ə)r, -z
nervy
BR ˈnəːv|i, -ɪə(r), -ɪɪst
AM ˈnərvi, -ər, -ɨst
Nerys
BR ˈnɛrɪs
AM ˈnɛrɨs
Nesbit
BR ˈnɛzbɪt
AM ˈnɛzbət
Nesbitt
BR ˈnɛzbɪt
AM ˈnɛzbət
Nescafé®
BR ˈnɛskəfeɪ
AM ˈnɛskəˌfeɪ
nescience
BR ˈnɛsɪəns
AM ˈnɛʃ(i)əns, ˈnɛsiəns
nescient
BR ˈnɛsɪənt
AM ˈnɛʃ(i)ənt, ˈnɛsiənt
nesh
BR nɛʃ
AM nɛʃ
ness
BR nɛs, -ɪz
AM nɛs, -ɨz
Nessa
BR ˈnɛsə(r)
AM ˈnɛsə
Nessie
BR ˈnɛsi
AM ˈnɛsi
nest
BR nɛst, -s, -ɪŋ, -ɪd
AM nɛst, -s, -ɪŋ, -əd
Nesta
BR ˈnɛstə(r)
AM ˈnɛstə
nestful
BR ˈnɛstfʊl, -z
AM ˈnɛs(t)ˌfʊl, -z
Nestlé®
BR ˈnɛsleɪ, ˈnɛsl
AM ˈnɛsli
nestle
BR ˈnɛs|l, -lz, -l̩ɪŋ\-lɪŋ, -ld
AM ˈnɛs|əl, -əlz, -(ə)lɪŋ, -əld
nestlike
BR ˈnɛs(t)lʌɪk
AM ˈnɛs(t)ˌlaɪk
nestling
BR ˈnɛs(t)lɪŋ, -z
AM ˈnɛs(t)lɪŋ, -z
Nestor
BR ˈnɛstə(r)
AM ˈnɛstər
Nestorian
BR nɛˈstɔːrɪən
AM nɛsˈtɔriən
Nestorianism
BR nɛˈstɔːrɪənɪz(ə)m

AM nɛs'tɔriə,nɪzəm

Nestorius
BR nɛ'stɔːrɪəs
AM nɛ'stɔriəs

net
BR nɛt, -s, -ɪŋ, -ɪd
AM nɛ|t, -ts, -dɪŋ, -dəd

netball
BR 'nɛtbɔːl
AM 'nɛt,bɔl, 'nɛt,bɑl

netful
BR 'nɛtfʊl, -z
AM 'nɛt,fʊl, -z

nether
BR 'nɛðə(r)
AM 'nɛðər

Netherlander
BR 'nɛðə,landə(r), -z
AM 'nɛðər,lændər, -z

Netherlandish
BR 'nɛðə,landɪʃ
AM 'nɛðər,lændɪʃ

Netherlands
BR ðə 'nɛðəːlən(d)z
AM 'nɛðərlən(d)z

nethermost
BR 'nɛðəməʊst
AM 'nɛðər,moʊst

netherworld
BR 'nɛðəwəːld
AM 'nɛðər,wərld

netsuke
BR 'nɛts(ʊ)k|i, -ɪz
AM 'nɛts(ʊ)ki, -z

nett
BR nɛt
AM nɛt

Nettie
BR 'nɛti
AM 'nɛdi

nettle
BR 'nɛt|l, -lz, -l̩ɪŋ\-lɪŋ, -ld
AM 'nɛdəl, -z, -ɪŋ, -d

Nettlefold
BR 'nɛtlfəʊld
AM 'nɛdl,foʊld

nettlesome
BR 'nɛtls(ə)m
AM 'nɛdlsəm

network
BR 'nɛtwəːk, -s, -ɪŋ, -t
AM 'nɛt,wərk, -s, -ɪŋ, -t

networker
BR 'nɛtwəːkə(r), -z
AM 'nɛt,wərkər, -z

neum
BR njuːm, -z
AM n(j)um, -z

Neumann
BR 'njuːmən
AM 'n(j)umən

neume
BR njuːm, -z
AM n(j)um, -z

neural
BR 'njʊərəl, 'njʊər l̩
AM 'n(j)ʊrəl, 'n(j)urəl

neuralgia
BR njʉ'raldʒə(r), njʊə'raldʒə(r)
AM n(j)u'rældʒə, n(j)ə'rældʒə

neuralgic
BR njʉ'raldʒɪk, njʊə'raldʒɪk
AM n(j)u'rældʒɪk, n(j)ə'rældʒɪk

neurally
BR 'njʊərl̩i, 'njʊərəli
AM 'n(j)ʊrəli, 'n(j)urəli

neurasthenia
BR ,njʊərəs'θiːnɪə(r)
AM ',n(j)ʊrəs'θiniə

neurasthenic
BR ,njʊərəs'θɛnɪk, -s
AM ',n(j)ʊrəs'θɛnɪk, -s

neuration
BR njʉ'reɪʃn, njʊə'reɪʃn, -z
AM nju'reɪʃən, njə'reɪʃən, -z

neuritic
BR njʉ'rɪtɪk, njʊə'rɪtɪk
AM n(j)u'rɪdɪk, n(j)ə'rɪdɪk

neuritis
BR njʉ'rʌɪtɪs, njʊə'rʌɪtɪs
AM n(j)u'raɪdɨs, n(j)ə'raɪdɨs

neuroanatomical
BR ,njʊərəʊ,anə'tɒmɪkl
AM ',n(j)uroʊ,ænə'tɑməkəl, ',n(j)əroʊ,ænə'tɑməkəl

neuroanatomy
BR ,njʊərəʊə'natəmi
AM ,n(j)uroʊə'nædəmi, ,n(j)əroʊə'nædəmi

neurobiological
BR ,njʊərəʊ,bʌɪə'lɒdʒɪkl
AM ',n(j)uroʊbaɪə'lɑdʒəkəl, ',n(j)ərəbaɪə'lɑdʒəkəl

neurobiology
BR ,njʊərəʊbʌɪ'ɒlədʒi
AM ,n(j)uroʊbaɪ'ɑlədʒi, ,n(j)ərəbaɪ'ɑlədʒi

neurofibroma
BR ,njʊərəʊfʌɪ'brəʊmə(r), -z
AM ,n(j)ʊroʊfaɪ'broʊmə, -z

neurofibromata
BR ,njʊərəʊfʌɪ'brəʊmətə(r)
AM ,n(j)ʊroʊ,faɪbroʊ'mɑdə

neurofibromatosis
BR ,njʊərəʊfʌɪ,brəʊmə'təʊsɪs
AM ,n(j)ʊroʊ,faɪbroʊmə'toʊsəs

neurogenesis
BR ,njʊərə(ʊ)'dʒɛnɪsɪs, -ɪz
AM ,n(j)uroʊ'dʒɛnəsəs, ,n(j)ərə'dʒɛnəsəs, -əz

neurogenic
BR ,njʊərə(ʊ)'dʒɛnɪk
AM ,n(j)uroʊ'dʒɛnɪk, ,n(j)ərə'dʒɛnɪk

neuroglia
BR njʉ'rɒglɪə(r), njʊə'rɒglɪə(r)
AM n(j)u'rɑgliə, n(j)ə'rɑgliə

neurohormone
BR ,njʊərə'hɔːməʊn, 'njʊərə(ʊ),hɔːməʊn, -z
AM ,n(j)uroʊ'hɔr,moʊn, ,n(j)ərə'hɔr,moʊn, -z

neurolinguistic
BR ,njʊərəʊlɪŋ'gwɪstɪk
AM ,n(j)uroʊ,lɪŋ'gwɪstɪk, ,n(j)ərə,lɪŋ'gwɪstɪk

neurological
BR ,njʊərə'lɒdʒɪkl
AM ,n(j)urə'lɑdʒəkəl, ,n(j)ərə'lɑdʒəkəl

neurologically
BR ,njʊərə'lɒdʒɪkli
AM ,n(j)urə'lɑdʒək(ə)li, ,n(j)ərə'lɑdʒək(ə)li

neurologist
BR njʉ'rɒlədʒɪst, njʊə'rɒlədʒɪst, -s
AM n(j)u'rɑlədʒəst, n(j)ə'rɑlədʒəst, -s

neurology
BR njʉ'rɒlədʒi, njʊə'rɒlədʒi
AM n(j)u'rɑlədʒi, n(j)ə'rɑlədʒi

neuroma
BR njʉ'rəʊmə(r), njʊə'rəʊmə(r), -z
AM n(j)u'roʊmə, -z

neuromata
BR njʉ'rəʊmətə(r), njʊə'rəʊmətə(r)
AM n(j)u'roʊmədə

neuromuscular
BR ,njʊərəʊ'mʌskjʉlə(r)
AM ,n(j)uroʊ'məskjələr, ,n(j)ərə'məskjələr

neuron
BR 'njʊərɒn, -z
AM 'n(j)u,rɑn, 'n(j)ʊ,rɑn, -z

neuronal
BR 'njʊərənl, njʉ'rəʊnl, njʊə'rəʊnl
AM 'n(j)uroʊnl, 'n(j)ʊrənl, n(j)u'roʊnəl

neurone
BR 'njʊərəʊn, -z
AM 'n(j)u,roʊn, 'n(j)ʊ,roʊn, -z

neuronic
BR njʉ'rɒnɪk, njʊə'rɒnɪk
AM n(j)u'rɑnɪk

neuropath
BR 'njʊərəpaθ, -s
AM 'n(j)uroʊ,pæθ, 'n(j)ərə,pæθ, -s

neuropathic
BR ,njʊərə(ʊ)'paθɪk
AM ,n(j)uroʊ'pæθɪk, ,n(j)ərə'pæθɪk

neuropathologist
BR ,njʊərəʊpə'θɒlədʒɪst, -s
AM ,n(j)uroʊpə'θɑlədʒəst, ,n(j)ərəpə'θɑlədʒəst, -s

neuropathology
BR ,njʊərəʊpə'θɒlədʒi
AM ,n(j)uroʊpə'θɑlədʒi, ,n(j)ərəpə'θɑlədʒi

neuropathy
BR njʉ'rɒpəθi, njʊə'rɒpəθi
AM n(j)u'rɑpəθi, n(j)ə'rɑpəθi

neurophysiological
BR ,njʊərəʊfɪzɪə'lɒdʒɪkl
AM ',n(j)uroʊ,fiziə'lɑdʒəkəl, ',n(j)ərə,fiziə'lɑdʒəkəl

neurophysiologist
BR ,njʊərəʊfɪzɪ'ɒlədʒɪst, -s
AM ',n(j)uroʊ,fizi'ɑlədʒəst, ',n(j)ərə,fizi'ɑlədʒəst, -s

neurophysiology
BR ,njʊərəʊfɪzɪ'ɒlədʒi
AM ',n(j)uroʊ,fizi'ɑlədʒi, ',n(j)ərə,fizi'ɑlədʒi

neuropsychological
BR ,njʊərəʊsʌɪkə'lɒdʒɪkl
AM ',n(j)uroʊ,saɪkə'lɑdʒəkəl, ',n(j)ərə,saɪkə'lɑdʒəkəl

neuropsychology
BR ,njʊərəʊsʌɪ'kɒlədʒi
AM ',n(j)uroʊ,saɪ'kɑlədʒi, ',n(j)ərə,saɪ'kɑlədʒi

Neuroptera
BR njʉ'rɒpt(ə)rə(r), njʊə'rɒpt(ə)rə(r)
AM n(j)u'rɑptərə, n(j)ʊ'rɑptərə

neuropteran
BR njʉ'rɒpt(ə)rən, njʊə'rɒpt(ə)rən, -z
AM n(j)u'rɑptərən, n(j)ʊ'rɑptərən, -z

neuropterous
BR njʉ'rɒpt(ə)rəs, njʊə'rɒpt(ə)rəs
AM n(j)u'rɑptərəs, n(j)ʊ'rɑptərəs

neuroscience
BR ˌnjʊərəʊˈsʌɪəns, ˈnjʊərə(ʊ)ˌsʌɪəns
AM ˈn(j)uroʊˌsaɪəns, ˈn(j)ərəˌsaɪəns

neuroscientist
BR ˌnjʊərəʊˈsʌɪəntɪst, ˈnjʊərə(ʊ)ˌsʌɪəntɪst, -s
AM ˈn(j)uroʊˌsaɪən(t)əst, ˈn(j)ərəˌsaɪən(t)əst, -s

neuroses
BR njʊˈrəʊsiːz, njʊəˈrəʊsiːz
AM n(j)uˈroʊsiz, n(j)əˈroʊsiz

neurosis
BR njʊˈrəʊsɪs, njʊəˈrəʊsɪs
AM n(j)uˈroʊsəz, n(j)əˈroʊsəz

neurosurgeon
BR ˈnjʊərə(ʊ)ˌsəːdʒ(ə)n, -z
AM ˈn(j)uroʊˌsərdʒən, ˈn(j)ərəˌsərdʒən, -z

neurosurgery
BR ˈnjʊərə(ʊ)ˌsəːdʒ(ə)ri, -ɪz
AM ˌn(j)uroʊˈsərdʒəri, ˌn(j)ərəˈsərdʒəri, -z

neurosurgical
BR ˌnjʊərə(ʊ)ˈsəːdʒɪkl
AM ˌn(j)uroʊˈsərdʒəkəl, ˌn(j)ərəˈsərdʒəkəl

neurotic
BR njʊˈrɒtɪk, njʊəˈrɒtɪk, -s
AM n(j)uˈrɑdɪk, n(j)əˈrɑdɪk, -s

neurotically
BR njʊˈrɒtɪkli, njʊəˈrɒtɪkli
AM n(j)uˈrɑdək(ə)li, n(j)əˈrɑdək(ə)li

neuroticism
BR njʊˈrɒtɪsɪz(ə)m, njʊəˈrɒtɪsɪz(ə)m
AM n(j)uˈrɑdəˌsɪzəm, n(j)əˈrɑdəˌsɪzəm

neurotomy
BR njʊˈrɒtəm|i, njʊəˈrɒtəm|i, -ɪz
AM n(j)uˈrɑdəmi, n(j)əˈrɑdəmi, -z

neurotoxin
BR ˈnjʊərəʊˌtɒksɪn, -z
AM ˌn(j)uroʊˈtɑksən, ˌn(j)ərəˈtɑksən, -z

neurotransmitter
BR ˌnjʊərəʊtranzˈmɪtə(r), -z
AM ˌn(j)uroʊˈtrænzmɪdər, ˌn(j)ərəˈtrænzmɪdər, -z

neuston
BR ˈnjuːstɒn
AM ˈn(j)ustən

neuter
BR ˈnjuːt|ə(r), -əz, -(ə)rɪŋ, -əd
AM ˈn(j)udər, -z, -ɪŋ, -d

neutral
BR ˈnjuːtr(ə)l, -z
AM ˈn(j)utrəl, -z

neutralisation
BR ˌnjuːtrəlʌɪˈzeɪʃn, ˌnjuːtrl̩ʌɪˈzeɪʃn, -z
AM ˌnjutrələˈzeɪʃən, ˌnjutrəˌlaɪˈzeɪʃən, -z

neutralise
BR ˈnjuːtrəlʌɪz, ˈnjuːtrl̩ʌɪz, -ɪz, -ɪŋ, -d
AM ˈn(j)utrəˌlaɪz, -ɪz, -ɪŋ, -d

neutraliser
BR ˈnjuːtrəlʌɪzə(r), ˈnjuːtrl̩ʌɪzə(r), -z
AM ˈn(j)utrəˌlaɪzər, -z

neutralism
BR ˈnjuːtrəlɪz(ə)m, ˈnjuːtrl̩ɪz(ə)m
AM ˈn(j)utrəˌlɪzəm

neutralist
BR ˈnjuːtrəlɪst, ˈnjuːtrl̩ɪst, -s
AM ˈn(j)utrələst, -s

neutrality
BR njuːˈtralɪti
AM n(j)uˈtrælədi

neutralization
BR ˌnjuːtrəlʌɪˈzeɪʃən, ˌnjuːtrl̩ʌɪˈzeɪʃn, -z
AM ˌn(j)utrələˈzeɪʃən, ˌn(j)utrəˌlaɪˈzeɪʃən, -z

neutralize
BR ˈnjuːtrəlʌɪz, ˈnjuːtrl̩ʌɪz, -ɪz, -ɪŋ, -d
AM ˈn(j)utrəˌlaɪz, -ɪz, -ɪŋ, -d

neutralizer
BR ˈnjuːtrəlʌɪzə(r), ˈnjuːtrl̩ʌɪzə(r), -z
AM ˈn(j)utrəˌlaɪzər, -z

neutrally
BR ˈnjuːtrəli
AM ˈn(j)utrəli

neutrino
BR njuːˈtriːnəʊ, -z
AM n(j)uˈtrinoʊ, -z

neutron
BR ˈnjuːtrɒn, -z
AM ˈn(j)uˌtrɑn, -z

neutropenia
BR ˌnjuːtrə(ʊ)ˈpiːnɪə(r)
AM ˌn(j)utrəˈpiniə

neutrophil
BR ˈnjuːtrəfɪl, -z
AM ˈn(j)utrəˌfɪl, -z

Neva
BR ˈniːvə(r), ˈneɪvə(r)
AM ˈnivə
RUS nʲiˈva

Nevada
BR nɪˈvɑːdə(r)
AM nəˈvædə

Nevadan
BR nɪˈvɑːd(ə)n, -z
AM nəˈvædən, -z

Neve
BR niːv
AM niv

névé
BR ˈnɛveɪ
AM neɪˈveɪ

never
BR ˈnɛvə(r)
AM ˈnɛvər

nevermore
BR ˌnɛvəˈmɔː(r), ˈnɛvəmɔː(r)
AM ˈnɛvərˈmɔ(ə)r

never-never
BR ˌnɛvəˈnɛvə(r)
AM ˈnɛvərˈnɛvər

nevertheless
BR ˌnɛvəðəˈlɛs
AM ˈnɛvərðəˈlɛs

nevi
BR ˈniːvʌɪ
AM ˈniˌvaɪ

Neville
BR ˈnɛvɪl
AM ˈnɛvəl

Nevin
BR ˈnɛv(ɪ)n
AM ˈnɛvən

Nevis[1]
Scotland
BR ˈnɛvɪs
AM ˈnɛvəs

Nevis[2]
West Indies
BR ˈniːvɪs
AM ˈnivəs, ˈnɛvəs

nevoid
BR ˈnɛvɔɪd
AM ˈnɛvɔɪd

Nevsky
BR ˈnɛvski
AM ˈnɛvski
RUS ˈnʲefskʲij

nevus
BR ˈniːvəs
AM ˈnivəs

new
BR njuː, -ə(r), -ɪst
AM n(j)|u, -uər\-ʊ(ə)r, -uəst

Newark[1]
New Jersey
BR ˈnjʊək
AM ˈn(j)uwərk

Newark[2]
Delaware
BR njuːˈɑːk
AM n(j)uˈɑrk

Newbiggin
BR ˈnjuːbɪg(ɪ)n
AM ˈn(j)uˌbɪgɪn

Newbold
BR ˈnjuːbəʊld
AM ˈn(j)uˌboʊld

Newbolt
BR ˈnjuːbəʊlt
AM ˈn(j)uˌboʊlt

newborn[1]
adjective
BR ˌnjuːˈbɔːn
AM ˈn(j)uˌbɔ(ə)rn

newborn[2]
noun
BR ˈnjuːbɔːn, -z
AM ˈn(j)uˌbɔ(ə)rn, -z

Newborough
BR ˈnjuːb(ə)rə(r)
AM ˈn(j)uˌbərə

Newbould
BR ˈnjuːbəʊld
AM ˈn(j)uˌboʊld

Newbridge
BR ˈnjuːbrɪdʒ
AM ˈn(j)uˌbrɪdʒ

Newburg
BR ˈnjuːbəːg
AM ˈn(j)uˌbərg

Newburgh
BR ˈnjuːb(ə)rə(r)
AM ˈn(j)uˌbərə

Newbury
BR ˈnjuːb(ə)ri
AM ˈn(j)uˌbɛri

Newby
BR ˈnjuːbi
AM ˈn(j)ubi

Newcastle
BR ˈnjuːkɑːsl, ˈnjuːkasl
AM ˈn(j)uˌkæsəl

Newcastle upon Tyne
BR ˈnjuːkasl əˌpɒn ˈtʌɪn, njʊˈkasl +, ˈnjuːkɑːsl +
AM ˈn(j)uˌkæsəl əˌpɑn ˈtaɪn

Newcomb
BR ˈnjuːkəm
AM ˈn(j)ukəm

Newcombe
BR ˈnjuːkəm
AM ˈn(j)ukəm

Newcome
BR ˈnjuːkəm
AM ˈn(j)ukəm

Newcomen
BR ˈnjuːkʌmən
AM ˈn(j)uˌkəmən

newcomer
BR ˈnjuːkʌmə(r), -z
AM ˈn(j)uˌkəmər, -z

Newdigate
BR ˈnjuːdɪgeɪt
AM ˈn(j)udəˌgeɪt

newel
BR ˈnjuːəl, -z
AM ˈn(j)uwəl, -z

Newell
BR ˈnjuːəl
AM ˈn(j)uəl
newelpost
BR ˈnjuːəlpəʊst, -s
AM ˈn(j)uwəlˌpoʊst, -s
newfangled
BR ˌnjuːˈfaŋgld
AM ˌn(j)uˈfæŋgəld
Newfoundland
BR ˈnjuːfn(d)lənd, ˌnjuːˈfaʊn(d)lənd
AM ˈn(j)ufən(d)lən(d), ˈn(j)ufən(d)ˌlænd, ˌn(j)uˈfaʊn(d)lənd, ˌn(j)ufənˈlænd
Newfoundlander
BR ˈnjuːfn(d)ləndə(r), ˌnjuːˈfaʊn(d)ləndə(r), -z
AM ˈn(j)ufən(d)ləndər, ˈn(j)ufən(d)ˌlændər, ˌn(j)uˈfaʊn(d)ləndər, ˌn(j)ufənˈlændər, -z
Newgate
BR ˈnjuːgeɪt
AM ˈn(j)uˌgeɪt
Newham
BR ˈnjuːəm
AM ˈn(j)uəm
Newhaven
BR ˈnjuːˌheɪvn
AM ˌn(j)uˈheɪvən
Ne Win
BR ˌneɪ ˈwɪn
AM ˌnɛ ˈwɪn
Newington
BR ˈnjuːɪŋt(ə)n
AM ˈn(j)uɪŋtən
newish
BR ˈnjuːɪʃ
AM ˈn(j)uɪʃ
newlaid
BR ˌnjuːˈleɪd
AM ˌn(j)uˈleɪd
Newlands
BR ˈnjuːlən(d)z
AM ˈn(j)ulən(d)z
newly
BR ˈnjuːli
AM ˈn(j)uli
Newlyn
BR ˈnjuːlɪn
AM ˈn(j)ulən
newlywed
BR ˈnjuːlɪwɛd, -z
AM ˈn(j)uliˌwɛd, -z
Newman
BR ˈnjuːmən
AM ˈn(j)umən
Newmark
BR ˈnjuːmɑːk
AM ˈn(j)uˌmɑrk
Newmarket
BR ˈnjuːˌmɑːkɪt
AM ˈn(j)uˌmɑrkət
new-mown
BR ˌnjuːˈməʊn
AM ˌn(j)uˈmoʊn
Newnes
BR njuːnz
AM ˈn(j)unəs
newness
BR ˈnjuːnəs
AM ˈn(j)unəs
Newnham
BR ˈnjuːnəm
AM ˈn(j)unəm
New Orleans
BR ˌnjuː ɔːˈliːənz
AM ˌn(j)u ˈɔrlənz, ˌn(j)u ərˈlinz
Newport
BR ˈnjuːpɔːt
AM ˈn(j)uˌpɔ(ə)rt
Newquay
BR ˈnjuːkiː
AM ˈn(j)uˌki
Newry
BR ˈnjʊəri
AM ˈn(j)uri
news
BR njuːz
AM n(j)uz
newsagent
BR ˈnjuːzˌeɪdʒ(ə)nt, -s
AM ˈn(j)uzˌeɪdʒənt, -s
newsboy
BR ˈnjuːzbɔɪ, -z
AM ˈn(j)uzˌbɔɪ, -z
newsbrief
BR ˈnjuːzbriːf, -s
AM ˈn(j)uzˌbrif, -s
newscast
BR ˈnjuːzkɑːst, ˈnjuːzkast, -s, -ɪŋ
AM ˈn(j)uzˌkæst, -s, -ɪŋ
newscaster
BR ˈnjuːzˌkɑːstə(r), ˈnjuːzˌkastə(r), -z
AM ˈn(j)uzˌkæstər, -z
newsdealer
BR ˈnjuːzˌdiːlə(r), -z
AM ˈn(j)uzˌdilər, -z
newsflash
BR ˈnjuːzflaʃ, -ɪz
AM ˈn(j)uzˌflæʃ, -əz
newsgirl
BR ˈnjuːzgəːl, -z
AM ˈn(j)uzˌgərl, -z
newshound
BR ˈnjuːzhaʊnd, -z
AM ˈn(j)uzˌ(h)aʊnd, -z
newsiness
BR ˈnjuːzɪnɪs
AM ˈn(j)uzinɪs
newsless
BR ˈnjuːzləs
AM ˈn(j)uzləs
newsletter
BR ˈnjuːzˌlɛtə(r), -z
AM ˈn(j)uzˌlɛdər, -z
newsman
BR ˈnjuːzman
AM ˈn(j)uzˌmæn
newsmen
BR ˈnjuːzmɛn
AM ˈn(j)uzˌmɛn
newsmonger
BR ˈnjuːzˌmʌŋgə(r), -z
AM ˈn(j)uzˌmɑŋgər, ˈn(j)uzˌməŋgər, -z
Newsom
BR ˈnjuːs(ə)m
AM ˈn(j)usəm
Newsome[1]
place in UK
BR ˈnjuːz(ə)m
AM ˈn(j)uzəm
Newsome[2]
surname
BR ˈnjuːs(ə)m
AM ˈn(j)usəm
New South Wales
BR ˌnjuː saʊθ ˈweɪlz
AM ˌn(j)u ˌsaʊθ ˈweɪlz
newspaper
BR njuːzˌpeɪpə(r), -z
AM ˈn(j)uzˌpeɪpər, -z
newspaperman
BR ˈnjuːzpeɪpəˌman
AM ˈn(j)uzˌpeɪpərˌmæn
newspapermen
BR ˈnjuːzpeɪpəˌmɛn
AM ˈn(j)uzˌpeɪpərˌmɛn
newspeak
BR ˈnjuːspiːk
AM ˈn(j)uˌspik
newsprint
BR ˈnjuːzprɪnt
AM ˈn(j)uzˌprɪnt
newsreader
BR ˈnjuːzˌriːdə(r), -z
AM ˈn(j)uzˌridər, -z
newsreel
BR ˈnjuːzriːl, -z
AM ˈn(j)uzˌril, -z
newsroom
BR ˈnjuːzruːm, ˈnjuːzrʊm
AM ˈn(j)uzˌrum, ˈn(j)uzˌrʊm
newssheet
BR ˈnjuːzʃiːt, -s
AM ˈn(j)uzˌʃit, -s
newsstand
BR ˈnjuːzstand, -z
AM ˈn(j)uzˌstænd, -z
Newstead
BR ˈnjuːstɪd, ˈnjuːstɛd
AM ˈn(j)uˌstɛd
newsvendor
BR ˈnjuːzˌvɛndə(r), -z
AM ˈn(j)uzˌvɛndər, -z
newsworthiness
BR ˈnjuːzˌwəːðɪnɪs
AM ˈn(j)uzˌwərðinɪs
newsworthy
BR ˈnjuːzˌwəːði
AM ˈn(j)uzˌwərði
newsy
BR ˈnjuːzi
AM ˈn(j)uzi
newt
BR njuːt, -s
AM n(j)ut, -s
newton
BR ˈnjuːtn, -z
AM ˈn(j)utn, -z
Newton Abbott
BR ˌnjuːtn ˈabət
AM ˌn(j)utn ˈæbət
Newtonian
BR njʊˈtəʊnɪən, njuːˈtəʊnɪən
AM n(j)uˈtoʊniən
Newtonmore
BR ˌnjuːtnˈmɔː(r)
AM ˌn(j)utnˈmɔ(ə)r
Newtown
BR ˈnjuːtaʊn
AM ˈn(j)uˌtaʊn
Newtownabbey
BR ˌnjuːtnˈabi
AM ˌn(j)utnˈæbi
next
BR nɛkst
AM nɛkst
nexus
BR ˈnɛksəs, -ɪz
AM ˈnɛksəs, -ɪz
Ney
BR neɪ
AM neɪ
Nez Percé
BR ˌnɛz ˈpəːs
AM ˌnɛz ˈpərs
ngaio
BR ˈnʌɪəʊ, -z
AM ˈnaɪoʊ, -z
Ngamiland
BR (ə)ŋˈgɑːmɪland
AM (ə)ŋˈgɑmiˌlænd
Ngorungoro Crater
BR (ə)ŋˌgɒrəŋgɒrə(ʊ) ˈkreɪtə(r)
AM (ə)ŋˌgɔrəŋˈgɔroʊ ˌkreɪdər
Nguni
BR (ə)ŋˈguːni
AM (ə)ŋˈguni
Nguyen
BR ˌnɔɪˈɛn
AM ˌnuˈjɛn
niacin
BR ˈnʌɪəsɪn
AM ˈnaɪəsən
Niagara
BR nʌɪˈagrə(r)
AM naɪˈæg(ə)rə
Niall
BR ˈnʌɪəl
AM ˈnaɪəl
Niamey
BR nɪˈɑːmeɪ, ˌnɪəˈmeɪ
AM niˈɑˌmeɪ
nib
BR nɪb, -z

AM nɪb, -z

nibble
BR 'nɪb|l, -lz, -l̩ɪŋ\-lɪŋ, -ld
AM 'nɪbəl, -əlz, -(ə)lɪŋ, -əld

nibbler
BR 'nɪbl̩ə(r), 'nɪblə(r), -z
AM 'nɪb(ə)lər, -z

Nibelung
BR 'ni:bəlʊŋ
AM 'nibəˌlʊŋ

Nibelungenlied
BR 'ni:bəlʊŋ(g)ənˌli:d
AM ˈnibə'lʊŋ(g)ənˌlid

niblick
BR 'nɪblɪk, -s
AM 'nɪblɪk, -s

nicad
BR 'nʌɪkad
AM 'naɪˌkæd

Nicaea
BR nʌɪ'si:ə(r)
AM naɪ'siə

Nicam
BR 'nʌɪkam
AM 'naɪˌkæm

Nicaragua
BR ˌnɪkə'ragjʊə(r)
AM ˌnɪkə'rɑgwə

Nicaraguan
BR ˌnɪkə'ragjʊən, -z
AM ˌnɪkə'rɑgwən, -z

Nice
place in France
BR ni:s
AM nis

nice
BR nʌɪs, -ə(r), -ɪst
AM naɪs, -ər, -ɪst

niceish
BR 'nʌɪsɪʃ
AM 'naɪsɪʃ

nicely
BR 'nʌɪsli
AM 'naɪsli

Nicene
BR ˌnʌɪ'si:n
AM 'naɪˌsin, ˌnaɪ'sin

niceness
BR 'nʌɪsnɨs
AM 'naɪsnɨs

nicety
BR 'nʌɪsɪt|i, -ɪz
AM 'naɪsɨdi, -z

niche
BR ni:ʃ, nɪtʃ, -ɪz
AM nɪtʃ, -ɪz

Nichol
BR 'nɪkl
AM 'nɪkəl

Nichola
BR 'nɪkələ(r), 'nɪkl̩ə(r)
AM 'nɪkələ

Nicholas
BR 'nɪk(ə)ləs, 'nɪkl̩əs
AM 'nɪk(ə)ləs

Nicholls
BR 'nɪklz
AM 'nɪkəlz

Nichols
BR 'nɪklz
AM 'nɪkəlz

Nicholson
BR 'nɪkls(ə)n
AM 'nɪkəlsən

Nichrome®
BR 'nʌɪkrəʊm
AM 'naɪˌkroʊm

nicish
BR 'nʌɪsɪʃ
AM 'naɪsɪʃ

nick
BR nɪk, -s, -ɪŋ, -t
AM nɪk, -s, -ɪŋ, -t

nickel
BR 'nɪkl, -z
AM 'nɪkəl, -z

nickelic
BR 'nɪkəlɪk
AM nɪ'kɛlɪk, 'nɪkəlɪk

nickelodeon
BR ˌnɪkə'ləʊdɪən, ˌnɪkl'əʊdɪən, -z
AM ˌnɪkə'loʊdiən, -z

nickelous
BR 'nɪkl̩əs, 'nɪkələs
AM 'nɪkələs

nicker
BR 'nɪk|ə(r), -əz, -(ə)rɪŋ, -əd
AM 'nɪkər, -z, -ɪŋ, -d

Nicki
BR 'nɪki
AM 'nɪki

Nicklaus
BR 'nɪkləs
AM 'nɪkləs

Nickleby
BR 'nɪklbi
AM 'nɪkəlbi

nicknack
BR 'nɪknak, -s
AM 'nɪkˌnæk, -s

nickname
BR 'nɪkneɪm, -z
AM 'nɪkˌneɪm, -z

Nicky
BR 'nɪki
AM 'nɪki

Nicobar Islands
BR 'nɪkə(ʊ)bɑ:r ˌʌɪlən(d)z
AM 'nɪkəbɑr ˈaɪlən(d)z

Nicodemus
BR ˌnɪkə'di:məs
AM ˌnɪkə'diməs

nicol
BR 'nɪkl, -z
AM 'nɪkəl, -z

Nicola
BR 'nɪkələ(r), 'nɪkl̩ə(r)
AM 'nɪkələ

Nicole
BR nɪ'kəʊl
AM nə'koʊl

Nicolet
BR ˌnɪkə'leɪ
AM ˌnɪkə'leɪ

Nicolette
BR ˌnɪkə'lɛt
AM ˌnɪkə'lɛt

Nicoll
BR 'nɪkl
AM 'nɪkəl

Nicolson
BR 'nɪkls(ə)n
AM 'nɪkəlsən

Nicomachean
BR nʌɪˌkɒmə'ki:ən, ˌnʌɪkəmə'ki:ən
AM ˌnɪkəmə'kiən

Nicomachus
BR nʌɪ'kɒməkəs
AM ˌnɪkə'mɑkəs

Nicosia
BR ˌnɪkə'si:ə(r)
AM ˌnɪkə'siə

nicotiana
BR nɪˌkɒtɪ'ɑ:nə(r), nɪˌkəʊʃɪ'ɑ:nə(r), ˌnɪkɒtɪ'ɑ:nə(r), ˌnɪkəʊʃɪ'ɑ:nə(r)
AM nɪˌkoʊʃi'ɑnə, nɪˌkɑdi'ɑnə

nicotinamide
BR ˌnɪkə'tɪnəmʌɪd
AM ˌnɪkə'tɪnəˌmaɪd

nicotine
BR 'nɪkəti:n
AM 'nɪkəˌtin, ˌnɪkə'tin

nicotinic
BR ˌnɪkə'tɪnɪk
AM ˌnɪkə'tinɪk

nicotinise
BR 'nɪkətɪnʌɪz, -ɪz, -ɪŋ, -d
AM 'nɪkədnˌaɪz, -ɪz, -ɪŋ, -d

nicotinism
BR 'nɪkətɪnɪz(ə)m
AM 'nɪkədnˌɪzəm

nicotinize
BR 'nɪkətɪnʌɪz, -ɪz, -ɪŋ, -d
AM 'nɪkədnˌaɪz, -ɪz, -ɪŋ, -d

nictitate
BR 'nɪktɪteɪt, -s, -ɪŋ, -ɪd
AM 'nɪktəˌteɪ|t, -ts, -dɪŋ, -dɪd

nictitation
BR ˌnɪktɪ'teɪʃn
AM ˌnɪktə'teɪʃən

nidamental
BR ˌnʌɪdə'mɛntl
AM ˌnaɪdə'mɛn(t)l

nide
BR nʌɪd, -z
AM naɪd, -z

nidi
BR 'nʌɪdʌɪ
AM 'naɪˌdaɪ

nidificate
BR 'nɪdɪfɪkeɪt, -s, -ɪŋ, -ɪd
AM 'nɪdəfəˌkeɪ|t, -ts, -dɪŋ, -dɪd

nidification
BR ˌnɪdɪfɪ'keɪʃn
AM ˌnɪdəfə'keɪʃən

nidifugous
BR nɪ'dɪfjʊgəs
AM nə'dɪfjəgəs

nidify
BR 'nɪdɪfʌɪ, -z, -ɪŋ, -d
AM 'nɪdəˌfaɪ, -z, -ɪŋ, -d

nidus
BR 'nʌɪdəs, -ɪz
AM 'naɪdəs, -əz

niece
BR ni:s, -ɪz
AM nis, -ɪz

niello
BR nɪ'ɛləʊ, -z, -ɪŋ, -d
AM ni'ɛloʊ, -z, -ɪŋ, -d

nielsbohrium
BR ˌni:lz'bɔ:rɪəm
AM ˌnilz'bɔriəm

Nielsen
BR 'ni:ls(ə)n
AM 'nilsən

Niemann
BR 'ni:mən
AM 'nimən

Niemeyer
BR 'ni:mʌɪə(r)
AM 'niˌmaɪər

Niemöller
BR 'ni:mʊlə(r)
AM 'niˌmoʊlər
GER 'ni:mœlɐ

Niersteiner
BR 'nɪəstʌɪnə(r), 'nɪəʃtʌɪnə(r)
AM 'nɪrˌstaɪnər

Nietzsche
BR 'ni:tʃə(r)
AM 'nitʃə

Nietzschean
BR 'ni:tʃɪən
AM 'nitʃiən

niff
BR nɪf, -s, -ɪŋ, -t
AM nɪf, -s, -ɪŋ, -t

niffy
BR 'nɪf|i, -ɪə(r), -ɪɪst
AM 'nɪfi, -ər, -ɪst

Niflheim
BR 'nɪflhʌɪm
AM 'nɪfəlˌ(h)aɪm

niftily
BR 'nɪftɪli
AM 'nɪftɪli

niftiness
BR ˈnɪftɪnɨs
AM ˈnɪftinɨs

nifty
BR ˈnɪft|i, -ɪə(r), -ɪɪst
AM ˈnɪfti, -ər, -ɨst

Nigel
BR ˈnʌɪdʒl
AM ˈnaɪdʒəl

Nigella
BR nʌɪˈdʒɛlə(*r*)
AM naɪˈgɛlə

Niger[1]
country
BR niːˈʒɛː(r), nɪˈʒɛː(r), ˈnʌɪdʒə(r)
AM ˈnaɪdʒər

Niger[2]
river
BR ˈnʌɪdʒə(r)
AM ˈnaɪdʒər

Niger-Congo
BR ˈnʌɪdʒəˈkɒŋgəʊ
AM ˈnaɪdʒərˈkɔŋˌgoʊ, ˈnaɪdʒərˈkɑŋˌgoʊ

Nigeria
BR nʌɪˈdʒɪərɪə(*r*)
AM naɪˈdʒɪriə

Nigerian
BR nʌɪˈdʒɪərɪən, -z
AM naɪˈdʒɪriən, -z

Nigerien
BR nʌɪˈdʒɪərɪən, -z
AM naɪˈdʒɪriən, -z

niggard
BR ˈnɪgəd, -z
AM ˈnɪgərd, -z

niggardliness
BR ˈnɪgədlɪnɨs
AM ˈnɪgərdlinɨs

niggardly
BR ˈnɪgədli
AM ˈnɪgərdli

nigger
BR ˈnɪgə(r), -z
AM ˈnɪgər, -z

niggle
BR ˈnɪg|l, -lz, -l̩ɪŋ\-lɪŋ, -ld
AM ˈnɪg|əl, -əlz, -(ə)lɪŋ, -əld

niggler
BR ˈnɪgl̩ə(r), ˈnɪglə(r), -z
AM ˈnɪg(ə)lər, -z

niggliness
BR ˈnɪglɪnɨs
AM ˈnɪglinɨs, ˈnɪgl̩inɨs

nigglingly
BR ˈnɪgl̩ɪŋli, ˈnɪglɪŋli
AM ˈnɪg(ə)lɪŋli

niggly
BR ˈnɪgli
AM ˈnɪgli, ˈnɪgl̩i

nigh
BR nʌɪ
AM naɪ

night
BR nʌɪt, -s
AM naɪt, -s

nightbird
BR ˈnʌɪtbəːd, -z
AM ˈnaɪtˌbərd, -z

nightcap
BR ˈnʌɪtkap, -s
AM ˈnaɪtˌkæp, -s

nightclothes
BR ˈnʌɪtkləʊ(ð)z
AM ˈnaɪtˌkloʊðz

nightclub
BR ˈnʌɪtklʌb, -z, -ɪŋ, -d
AM ˈnaɪtˌkləb, -z, -ɪŋ, -d

nightcrawler
BR ˈnʌɪtˌkrɔːlə(r), -z
AM ˈnaɪtˌkrɔlər, ˈnaɪtˌkrɑlər, -z

nightdress
BR ˈnʌɪtdrɛs, -ɨz
AM ˈnaɪtˌdrɛs, -əz

nightfall
BR ˈnʌɪtfɔːl
AM ˈnaɪtˌfɔl, ˈnaɪtˌfɑl

nightgown
BR ˈnʌɪtgaʊn, -z
AM ˈnaɪtˌgaʊn, -z

nighthawk
BR ˈnʌɪthɔːk, -s
AM ˈnaɪtˌ(h)ɔk, ˈnaɪtˌ(h)ɑk, -s

nightie
BR ˈnʌɪt|i, -ɪz
AM ˈnaɪdi, -z

nightingale
BR ˈnʌɪtɨŋgeɪl, -z
AM ˈnaɪtn̩ˌgeɪl, -z

nightjar
BR ˈnʌɪtdʒɑː(r), -z
AM ˈnaɪtˌdʒɑr, -z

nightlife
BR ˈnʌɪtlʌɪf
AM ˈnaɪtˌlaɪf

nightlight
BR ˈnʌɪtlʌɪt, -s
AM ˈnaɪtˌlaɪt, -s

nightline
BR ˈnʌɪtlʌɪn, -z
AM ˈnaɪtˌlaɪn, -z

nightlong
BR ˌnʌɪtˈlɒŋ
AM ˈnaɪtˌlɔŋ, ˈnaɪtˌlɑŋ

nightly
BR ˈnʌɪtli
AM ˈnaɪtli

nightman
BR ˈnʌɪtman
AM ˈnaɪtˌmæn

nightmare
BR ˈnʌɪtmɛː(r), -z
AM ˈnaɪtˌmɛ(ə)r, -z

nightmarish
BR ˈnʌɪtmɛːrɪʃ
AM ˈnaɪtˌmɛrɪʃ

nightmarishly
BR ˈnʌɪtmɛːrɨʃli
AM ˈnaɪtˌmɛrɨʃli

nightmarishness
BR ˈnʌɪtmɛːrɪʃnɨs
AM ˈnaɪtˌmɛrɪʃnɨs

nightmen
BR ˈnʌɪtmɛn
AM ˈnaɪtˌmɛn

nightrider
BR ˈnʌɪtˌrʌɪdə(r), -z
AM ˈnaɪtˌraɪdər, -z

nightshade
BR ˈnʌɪtʃeɪd
AM ˈnaɪtˌʃeɪd

nightshirt
BR ˈnʌɪtʃəːt, -s
AM ˈnaɪtˌʃərt, -s

nightspot
BR ˈnʌɪtspɒt, -s
AM ˈnaɪtˌspɑt, -s

nightstick
BR ˈnʌɪtstɪk, -s
AM ˈnaɪtˌstɪk, -s

nighttime
BR ˈnʌɪttʌɪm
AM ˈnaɪtˌtaɪm

nightwear
BR ˈnʌɪtwɛː(r)
AM ˈnaɪtˌwɛ(ə)r

nigrescence
BR nɨˈgrɛsns
AM naɪˈgrɛsəns

nigrescent
BR nɨˈgrɛsnt
AM naɪˈgrɛsənt

nigritude
BR ˈnɪgrɨtjuːd, ˈnɪgrɨtʃuːd
AM ˈnɪgrəˌt(j)ud

nihilism
BR ˈnʌɪ(h)ɨlɪz(ə)m, ˈniː(h)ɨlɪz(ə)m, ˈnɪhɨlɪz(ə)m
AM ˈnaɪəˌlɪzəm, ˈniəˌlɪzəm, ˈnɪhɨˌlɪzəm

nihilist
BR ˈnʌɪ(h)ɨlɪst, ˈniː(h)ɨlɪst, ˈnɪhɨlɪst, -s
AM ˈnaɪələst, ˈniəlɨst, ˈnɪhɨlɪst, -s

nihilistic
BR ˌnʌɪ(h)ɪˈlɪstɪk, ˌniː(h)ɪˈlɪstɪk, ˌnɪhɪˈlɪstɪk
AM ˌnaɪəˈlɪstɪk, ˌniəˈlɪstɪk, ˌnɪhɪˈlɪstɪk

nihility
BR nʌɪˈ(h)ɪlɨt|i, niːˈ(h)ɪlɨti, nɪˈhɪlɨti, -ɪz
AM naɪˈhɪlɨdi, -z

nihilo
BR ˈnʌɪ(h)ɨləʊ, ˈniː(h)ɨləʊ, ˈnɪhɨləʊ
AM ˈnaɪhəˌloʊ

nihil obstat
BR ˌnʌɪhɨl ˈɒbstat, ˌnɪhɨl +
AM ˌnaɪhɨl ˈɑbzˌtæt, + ˈɑbˌstæt

Nijinsky
BR nɪˈʒɪnski
AM nəˈʒɪnski

Nijmegen
BR ˈnʌɪmeɪg(ə)n
AM ˈnaɪˌmeɪgən
DU ˈnɛimexə(n)

Nike
BR ˈnʌɪki
AM ˈnaɪki

Nikkei index
BR ˌnɪkeɪ ˈɪndɛks
AM ˈnɪˌkeɪ ˈɪndɛks

Nikki
BR ˈnɪki
AM ˈnɪki

Nikon®
BR ˈnɪkɒn
AM ˈnaɪˌkɑn

nil
BR nɪl
AM nɪl

nil desperandum
BR ˌnɪl ˌdɛspəˈrandəm
AM ˌnɪl ˌdɛspəˈrɑndəm

Nile
BR nʌɪl
AM naɪl

nilgai
BR ˈnɪlgʌɪ, -z
AM ˈnɪlˌgaɪ, -z

Nilotic
BR nʌɪˈlɒtɪk
AM naɪˈlɑdɪk

Nilsson
BR ˈnɪls(ə)n
AM ˈnɪlsən

nim
BR nɪm
AM nɪm

nimbi
BR ˈnɪmbʌɪ
AM ˈnɪmˌbaɪ

nimble
BR ˈnɪmbl̩, -ə(r), -ɪst
AM ˈnɪmb|əl, -(ə)lər, -(ə)ləst

nimbleness
BR ˈnɪmblnəs
AM ˈnɪmbəlnəs

nimbly
BR ˈnɪmbli
AM ˈnɪmbli, ˈnɪmbl̩i

nimbostrati
BR ˌnɪmbəʊˈstrɑːtʌɪ, ˌnɪmbəʊˈstreɪtʌɪ
AM ˌnɪmboʊˈstrædˌaɪ

nimbostratus
BR ˌnɪmbəʊˈstrɑːtəs, ˌnɪmbəʊˈstreɪtəs
AM ˌnɪmboʊˈstrædəs

nimbus
BR ˈnɪmbəs, -ɪz, -t
AM ˈnɪmbəs, -əz, -t
nimby
BR ˈnɪmb|i, -ɪz
AM ˈnɪmbi, -z
Nîmes
BR niːm
AM nim
niminy-piminy
BR ˌnɪmɨnɪˈpɪmɨni
AM ˈnɪmɨniˈpɪmɨni
Nimitz
BR ˈnɪmɨts
AM ˈnɪmɨts
Nimmo
BR ˈnɪməʊ
AM ˈnɪmoʊ
Nimrod
BR ˈnɪmrɒd
AM ˈnɪmˌrɑd
Nina
BR ˈniːnə(r)
AM ˈninə
nincompoop
BR ˈnɪŋkəmpuːp, -s
AM ˈnɪnkəmˌpup, ˈnɪŋkəmˌpup, -s
nine
BR nʌɪn, -z
AM naɪn, -z
ninefold
BR ˈnʌɪnfəʊld
AM ˈnaɪnˌfoʊld
ninepin
BR ˈnʌɪnpɪn, -z
AM ˈnaɪnˌpɪn, -z
nineteen
BR ˌnʌɪnˈtiːn
AM ˈnaɪnˈtin
nineteenth
BR ˌnʌɪnˈtiːnθ, -s
AM ˈnaɪnˈtinθ, -s
ninetieth
BR ˈnʌɪntɪɨθ
AM ˈnaɪn(t)iɨθ
ninety
BR ˈnʌɪnt|i, -ɪz
AM ˈnaɪn(t)i, -z
ninetyfold
BR ˈnʌɪntɪfəʊld
AM ˈnaɪn(t)iˌfoʊld
Nineveh
BR ˈnɪnɨvə(r)
AM ˈnɪnɨvə
Ninian
BR ˈnɪnɪən
AM ˈnɪnjən, ˈnɪniən
ninja
BR ˈnɪndʒə(r), -z
AM ˈnɪndʒə, -z
ninjutsu
BR nɪnˈdʒʌtsuː
AM nɪnˈdʒətˌsu
ninny
BR ˈnɪn|i, -ɪz
AM ˈnɪni, -z
ninon
BR ˈniːnɒn
AM ˈniˌnɑn
Nintendo®
BR nɪnˈtɛndəʊ
AM nɪnˈtɛndoʊ
ninth
BR nʌɪnθ
AM naɪnθ
ninthly
BR ˈnʌɪnθli
AM ˈnaɪnθli
Niobe
BR ˈnʌɪəbi
AM naɪˈoʊbi
niobic
BR nʌɪˈəʊbɪk
AM naɪˈoʊbɪk
niobium
BR nʌɪˈəʊbɪəm
AM naɪˈoʊbiəm
niobous
BR ˈnʌɪəbəs
AM ˈnaɪəbəs
nip
BR nɪp, -s, -ɪŋ, -t
AM nɪp, -s, -ɪŋ, -t
nipa
BR ˈniːpə(r), ˈnʌɪpə(r), -z
AM ˈnipə, -z
nipper
BR ˈnɪpə(r), -z
AM ˈnɪpər, -z
nippily
BR ˈnɪpɨli
AM ˈnɪpɨli
nippiness
BR ˈnɪpɪnɨs
AM ˈnɪpinɨs
nipple
BR ˈnɪpl, -z
AM ˈnɪpl, -z
nipplewort
BR ˈnɪplwəːt, -s
AM ˈnɪplˌwərt, ˈnɪplˌwɔ(ə)rt, -s
Nippon
BR ˈnɪpɒn
AM ˈnɪˌpɑn
Nipponese
BR ˌnɪpəˈniːz
AM ˌnɪpəˈniz
nippy
BR ˈnɪp|i, -ɪə(r), -ɪɨst
AM ˈnɪpi, -ər, -ɨst
NIREX
BR ˈnʌɪrɛks
AM ˈnaɪˌrɛks
nirvana
BR nɪəˈvɑːnə(r), nə(ː)ˈvɑːnə(r)
AM nərˈvɑnə, nɪrˈvɑnə
Nisan
BR ˈniːsɑːn, ˈnɪsɑːn, ˈnʌɪsan, ˈnɪs(ə)n
AM ˈnɪsɑn, niˈsɑn
Nisbet
BR ˈnɪzbɪt
AM ˈnɪzbət
Nisbett
BR ˈnɪzbɪt
AM ˈnɪzbət
nisei
BR ˈniːseɪ, -z
AM niˈseɪ, -z
nisi
BR ˈnʌɪsʌɪ
AM ˈnaɪˌsaɪ
Nissan®
BR ˈnɪsan, -z
AM ˈnɪˌsɑn, -z
Nissen
BR ˈnɪsn
AM ˈnɪsən
nit
BR nɪt, -s
AM nɪt, -s
nite
BR nʌɪt, -s
AM naɪt, -s
niter
BR ˈnʌɪtə(r)
AM ˈnaɪdər
niterie
BR ˈnʌɪt(ə)r|i, -ɪz
AM ˈnaɪdəri, -z
nitid
BR ˈnɪtɪd
AM ˈnɪdɨd
nitinol
BR ˈnɪtɨnɒl
AM ˈnaɪdəˌnɑl, ˈnɪtn̩ˌɑl
nitpick
BR ˈnɪtpɪk, -s, -ɪŋ, -t
AM ˈnɪtˌpɪk, -s, -ɪŋ, -t
nitrate
BR ˈnʌɪtreɪt, -s
AM ˈnaɪˌtreɪt, -s
nitration
BR nʌɪˈtreɪʃn, -z
AM naɪˈtreɪʃən, -z
nitrazepam
BR nʌɪˈtreɪzɨpam, nʌɪˈtrazɨpam
AM naɪˈtræzəˌpæm
nitre
BR ˈnʌɪtə(r)
AM ˈnaɪdər
nitric
BR ˈnʌɪtrɪk
AM ˈnaɪtrɪk
nitride
BR ˈnʌɪtrʌɪd, -z
AM ˈnaɪˌtraɪd, -z
nitrifiable
BR ˈnʌɪtrɪfʌɪəbl
AM ˈnaɪtrəˌfaɪəbəl
nitrification
BR ˌnʌɪtrɪfɪˈkeɪʃn, -z
AM ˌnaɪtrəfəˈkeɪʃən, -z
nitrify
BR ˈnʌɪtrɪfʌɪ, -z, -ɪŋ, -d
AM ˈnaɪtrəˌfaɪ, -z, -ɪŋ, -d
nitrile
BR ˈnʌɪtrʌɪl, -z
AM ˈnaɪtrɨl, ˈnaɪˌtraɪl, -z
nitrite
BR ˈnʌɪtrʌɪt, -s
AM ˈnaɪˌtraɪt, -s
nitro
BR ˈnʌɪtrəʊ
AM ˈnaɪtroʊ
nitrobenzene
BR ˌnʌɪtrəʊˈbɛnziːn
AM ˈnaɪtroʊˈbɛnzin
nitrocellulose
BR ˌnʌɪtrəʊˈsɛljʉləʊs, ˌnʌɪtrəʊˈsɛljʉləʊz
AM ˈnaɪtroʊˈsɛljəˌloʊs, ˈnaɪtroʊˈsɛljəˌloʊz
nitrogen
BR ˈnʌɪtrədʒ(ə)n
AM ˈnaɪtrədʒən
nitrogenous
BR nʌɪˈtrɒdʒɪnəs
AM naɪˈtrɑdʒənəs
nitroglycerin
BR ˌnʌɪtrəʊˈglɪs(ə)riːn, ˌnʌɪtrəʊˈglɪs(ə)rɪn
AM ˈnaɪtroʊˈglɪsərən
nitroglycerine
BR ˌnʌɪtrəʊˈglɪs(ə)riːn, ˌnʌɪtrəʊˈglɪs(ə)rɪn
AM ˈnaɪtroʊˈglɪsərən
nitrosamine
BR nʌɪˈtrəʊsəmiːn
AM naɪˈtroʊsəˌmin
nitrous
BR ˈnʌɪtrəs
AM ˈnaɪtrəs
nitty-gritty
BR ˌnɪtɪˈgrɪti
AM ˈnɪdiˈgrɪdi
nitwit
BR ˈnɪtwɪt, -s
AM ˈnɪtˌwɪt, -s
nitwitted
BR ˌnɪtˈwɪtɨd
AM ˈnɪtˌwɪdɨd
nitwittedness
BR ˌnɪtˈwɪtɨdnɨs
AM ˈnɪtˈwɪdɨdnɨs
nitwittery
BR ˈnɪtˌwɪt(ə)ri
AM ˌnɪtˈwɪdəri
Niue
BR ˈnjuːeɪ
AM ˈnjuˌ(w)eɪ
Niu Gini
BR ˌnjuː ˈgɪni
AM ˌnu ˈgɪni
nival
BR ˈnʌɪvl
AM ˈnaɪvəl
nivation
BR nʌɪˈveɪʃn
AM naɪˈveɪʃən
Nivea®
BR ˈnɪviːə(r)

AM 'nɪviə

Niven
BR 'nɪvn
AM 'nɪvən

niveous
BR 'nɪvɪəs
AM 'nɪviəs

nix
BR nɪks, -ɪz, -ɪŋ, -t
AM nɪks, -ɪz, -ɪŋ, -t

Nixdorf®
BR 'nɪksdɔːf
AM 'nɪks,dɔ(ə)rf

Nixon
BR 'nɪks(ə)n
AM 'nɪksən

Nizari
BR nɪ'zaːr|i, -ɪz
AM nə'zari, -z

Nizhni Novgorod
BR ,nɪʒnɪ 'nɒvgərɒd
AM ,nɪʒni 'nɔv,gɔrəd, ,nɪʒni 'nɑv,gɔrəd

Njanja
BR nɪ'an(d)ʒə(r), 'njan(d)ʒə(r)
AM nə'jændʒə

Nkomo
BR (ə)ŋ'kəʊməʊ
AM (ə)ŋ'kɔmoʊ, (ə)ŋ'koʊmoʊ

Nkrumah
BR (ə)ŋ'kruːmə(r)
AM (ə)ŋ'krumə

no
BR nəʊ, -z
AM noʊ, -z

no-account
BR ,nəʊə'kaʊnt, -s
AM 'noʊə,kaʊnt, -s

Noah
BR 'nəʊə(r), nɔː(r)
AM 'noʊə

Noakes
BR nəʊks
AM noʊks

Noam
BR 'nəʊ(ə)m
AM 'noʊəm

nob
BR nɒb, -z
AM nɑb, -z

no-ball
BR 'nəʊbɔːl, -z, -ɪŋ, -d
AM 'noʊ,bɔl, 'noʊ,bɑl, -z, -ɪŋ, -d

nobble
BR 'nɒb|l, -lz, -l̩ɪŋ\-lɪŋ, -ld
AM 'nɑbəl, -əlz, -(ə)lɪŋ, -əld

nobbler
BR 'nɒbl̩ə(r), 'nɒblə(r), -z
AM 'nɑb(ə)lər, -z

nobbut
BR 'nɒbət
AM 'nɑbət

Nobel
BR nəʊ'bɛl
AM noʊ'bɛl

nobelium
BR nə(ʊ)'biːlɪəm, nə(ʊ)'bɛlɪəm
AM noʊ'bɛliəm

Nobel prize
BR ,nəʊbɛl 'prʌɪz, -ɪz
AM noʊ'bɛl 'praɪz, 'noʊbɛl +, -ɪz

nobiliary
BR nə(ʊ)'bɪlɪəri
AM noʊ'bɪli,ɛri, noʊ'bɪljəri

nobility
BR nə(ʊ)'bɪlɪti
AM noʊ'bɪlɪdi

noble
BR 'nəʊbl, -z, -ə(r), -ɪst
AM 'noʊb|əl, -əlz, -lər, -ləst

nobleman
BR 'nəʊblmən
AM 'noʊbəlmən

noblemen
BR 'nəʊblmən
AM 'noʊbəlmən

nobleness
BR 'nəʊblnəs
AM 'noʊbəlnəs

noblesse
BR nə(ʊ)'blɛs
AM noʊ'blɛs

noblesse oblige
BR nə(ʊ),blɛs ə(ʊ)'bliːʒ, + ɒ'bliːʒ
AM noʊ'blɛs ə'bliʒ

noblewoman
BR 'nəʊbl,wʊmən
AM 'noʊbəl,wʊmən

noblewomen
BR 'nəʊbl,wɪmɪn
AM 'noʊbəl,wɪmɪn

nobly
BR 'nəʊbli
AM 'noʊbli

nobody
BR 'nəʊbəd|i, -ɪz
AM 'noʊ,bɑdi, 'noʊbədi, -z

nociceptor
BR 'nəʊsɪsɛptə(r), -z
AM 'noʊsə,sɛptər, -z

nock
BR nɒk, -s
AM nɑk, -s

no-claim bonus
BR ,nəʊkleɪm 'bəʊnəs, -ɪz
AM ,noʊ,kleɪm 'boʊnəs, -əz

no-claims bonus
BR ,nəʊkleɪmz 'bəʊnəs, -ɪz
AM ,noʊ,kleɪmz 'boʊnəs, -əz

noctambulism
BR nɒk'tambjʊlɪz(ə)m
AM nɑk'tæmbjə,lɪzəm

noctambulist
BR nɒk'tambjʊlɪst, -s
AM nɑk'tæmbjələst, -s

noctiluca
BR ,nɒktɪ'luːkə(r)
AM ,nɑktə'lukə

noctilucae
BR ,nɒktɪ'luːkiː
AM ,nɑktə'luki

noctilucent
BR ,nɒktɪ'luːsnt
AM ,nɑktə'lusnt

noctivagant
BR nɒk'tɪvəg(ə)nt
AM nɑk'tɪvəgənt

noctivagous
BR nɒk'tɪvəgəs
AM nɑk'tɪvəgəs

noctuid
BR 'nɒktjʊɪd, 'nɒktʃʊɪd, -z
AM 'nɑk,tʃuɪd, -z

noctule
BR 'nɒktjuːl, 'nɒktʃuːl, -z
AM 'nɑk,tʃul, -z

nocturn
BR 'nɒktəːn, ,nɒk'təːn, -z
AM 'nɑktərn, -z

nocturnal
BR nɒk'təːnl
AM nɑk'tərnəl

nocturnally
BR nɒk'təːnli, nɒk'təːnəli
AM nɑk'tərnəli

nocturne
BR 'nɒktəːn, ,nɒk'təːn, -z
AM 'nɑktərn, -z

nocuous
BR 'nɒkjʊəs
AM 'nɑkjəwəs

nod
BR nɒd, -z, -ɪŋ, -ɪd
AM nɑd, -z, -ɪŋ, -əd

nodal
BR 'nəʊdl
AM 'noʊdəl

noddle
BR 'nɒdl, -z
AM 'nɑdəl, -z

noddy
BR 'nɒd|i, -ɪz
AM 'nɑdi, -z

node
BR nəʊd, -z
AM noʊd, -z

nodi
BR 'nəʊdʌɪ
AM 'noʊ,daɪ

nodical
BR 'nəʊdɪkl
AM 'nɑdəkəl, 'noʊdəkəl

nodose
BR nə(ʊ)'dəʊs
AM 'noʊ,doʊs, 'noʊ,doʊz

nodosity
BR nə(ʊ)'dɒsɪti
AM noʊ'dɑsədi

nodular
BR 'nɒdjʊlə(r), 'nɒdʒʊlə(r)
AM 'nɑdʒələr, 'nɑdjələr

nodulated
BR 'nɒdjʊleɪtɪd, 'nɒdʒʊleɪtɪd
AM 'nɑdʒə,leɪdɪd, 'nɑdjə,leɪdɪd

nodulation
BR ,nɒdjʊ'leɪʃn, ,nɒdʒʊ'leɪʃn
AM ,nɑdʒə'leɪʃən, ,nɑdjə'leɪʃən

nodule
BR 'nɒdjuːl, 'nɒdʒuːl, 'nɒdʒʊl, -z
AM 'nɑ,dʒul, 'nɑ,djul, -z

nodulose
BR 'nɒdjʊləʊs, 'nɒdʒʊləʊs
AM 'nɑdʒəloʊs, 'nɑdʒəloʊz

nodulous
BR 'nɒdjʊləs, 'nɒdʒʊləs
AM 'nɑdʒələs

nodus
BR 'nəʊdəs
AM 'noʊdəs

Noel¹
Christmas
BR nəʊ'ɛl
AM noʊ'ɛl

Noel²
forename
BR 'nəʊ(ə)l
AM 'noʊ(ə)l

Noelle
BR nəʊ'ɛl
AM noʊ'ɛl

noes
BR nəʊz
AM noʊz

noesis
BR nəʊ'iːsɪs
AM noʊ'isɪs

noetic
BR nəʊ'ɛtɪk
AM noʊ'ɛdɪk

nog
BR nɒg
AM nɑg

noggin
BR 'nɒgɪn, -z
AM 'nɑgən, -z

nogging
BR 'nɒɡɪŋ, -z
AM 'nɑɡɪŋ, -z

Noguchi
BR nɒ'ɡuːtʃi, nə'ɡuːtʃi
AM noʊ'ɡutʃi

Noh
BR nəʊ
AM noʊ

no-hoper
BR ˌnəʊ'həʊpə(r), -z
AM ˈnoʊ'hoʊpər, -z

nohow
BR 'nəʊhaʊ
AM 'noʊˌhaʊ

noil
BR nɔɪl, -z
AM nɔɪl, -z

noise
BR nɔɪz, -ɪz, -ɪŋ, -d
AM nɔɪz, -ɪz, -ɪŋ, -d

noiseless
BR 'nɔɪzlɨs
AM 'nɔɪzlɨs

noiselessly
BR 'nɔɪzlɨsli
AM 'nɔɪzlɨsli

noiselessness
BR 'nɔɪzlɨsnɨs
AM 'nɔɪzlɨsnɨs

noisemaker
BR 'nɔɪzˌmeɪkə(r), -z
AM 'nɔɪzˌmeɪkər, -z

noisette
BR nwɑː'zɛt, nwɒ'zɛt, -s
AM nwɑ'zɛt, -s

noisily
BR 'nɔɪzɨli
AM 'nɔɪzɨli

noisiness
BR 'nɔɪzɪnɨs
AM 'nɔɪzɪnɨs

noisome
BR 'nɔɪs(ə)m
AM 'nɔɪsəm

noisomely
BR 'nɔɪs(ə)mli
AM 'nɔɪsəmli

noisomeness
BR 'nɔɪs(ə)mnəs
AM 'nɔɪsəmnəs

noisy
BR 'nɔɪz|i, -ɪə(r), -ɪɪst
AM 'nɔɪzi, -ər, -ɪst

Nok
BR nɒk
AM nɑk

Nola
BR 'nəʊlə(*r*)
AM 'noʊlə

Nolan
BR 'nəʊlən
AM 'noʊl(ə)n

nolens volens
BR ˌnəʊlɛnz 'vəʊlɛnz
AM 'noʊlənz 'voʊlənz

nolle prosequi
BR ˌnɒli 'prɒsɨkwʌɪ
AM 'noʊli 'prɑsəˌkwaɪ

nomad
BR 'nəʊmad, -z
AM 'noʊˌmæd, -z

nomadic
BR nə(ʊ)'madɪk
AM noʊ'mædɪk

nomadically
BR nə(ʊ)'madɨkli
AM noʊ'mædək(ə)li

nomadise
BR 'nəʊmədʌɪz, -ɨz, -ɪŋ, -d
AM 'noʊˌmædˌaɪz, 'noʊməˌdaɪz, -ɨz, -ɪŋ, -d

nomadism
BR 'nəʊmədɪz(ə)m
AM 'noʊməˌdɪzəm

nomadize
BR 'nəʊmədʌɪz, -ɨz, -ɪŋ, -d
AM 'noʊˌmædˌaɪz, 'noʊməˌdaɪz, -ɨz, -ɪŋ, -d

no-man's-land
BR 'nəʊmanzland
AM 'noʊˌmænzˌlæn(d)

nombril
BR 'nɒmbrɨl, -z
AM 'nɑmbrəl, -z

nom de guerre
BR ˌnɒm də 'ɡɛː(r)
AM ˌnɔm də 'ɡɛ(ə)r

nom de plume
BR ˌnɒm də 'pluːm
AM ˌnɔm də 'plum

Nome
BR nəʊm
AM noʊm

nomen
BR 'nəʊmɛn, 'nəʊmən
AM 'noʊmən

nomenclative
BR 'nəʊmənˌkleɪtɪv
AM 'noʊmənˌkleɪdɪv

nomenclatural
BR ˌnəʊmən'klatʃ(ə)rəl, ˌnəʊmən'klatʃ(ə)rl̩
AM ˈnoʊmənˈkleɪtʃ(ə)rəl

nomenclature
BR nə(ʊ)'mɛŋklətʃə(r), -z
AM 'noʊmənˌkleɪtʃər, -z

nomenklatura
BR nɒˌmɛnklə'tjʊərə(*r*), nɒˌmɛŋklə'tʃʊərə(*r*)
AM ˌnoʊmənˌklə't(j)ʊrə
RUS naˌmjɛnkla'tura

nomina
BR 'nɒmɨnə(*r*)
AM 'nɑmənə

nominal
BR 'nɒmɨnl
AM 'nɑmənəl

nominalisation
BR ˌnɒmɨnl̩ʌɪ'zeɪʃn, ˌnɒmɨnəlʌɪ'zeɪʃn, -z
AM 'nɑmənlə'zeɪʃən, 'nɑmənələ'zeɪʃən, 'nɑmənlˌaɪ'zeɪʃən, 'nɑmənəˌlaɪ'zeɪʃən, -z

nominalise
BR 'nɒmɨnl̩ʌɪz, 'nɒmɨnəlʌɪz, -ɨz, -ɪŋ, -d
AM 'nɑmənlˌaɪz, 'nɑmənəˌlaɪz, -ɨz, -ɪŋ, -d

nominalism
BR 'nɒmɨnl̩ɪz(ə)m, 'nɒmɨnəlɪz(ə)m
AM 'nɑmənlˌɪzəm, 'nɑmənəˌlɪzəm

nominalist
BR 'nɒmɨnl̩ɪst, 'nɒmɨnəlɪst, -s
AM 'nɑmənləst, 'nɑmənələst, -s

nominalistic
BR ˌnɒmɨnl'ɪstɪk, ˌnɒmɨnə'lɪstɪk
AM ˌnɑmənə'lɪstɪk

nominalization
BR ˌnɒmɨnl̩ʌɪ'zeɪʃn, ˌnɒmɨnəlʌɪ'zeɪʃn, -z
AM 'nɑmənlə'zeɪʃən, 'nɑmənələ'zeɪʃən, 'nɑmənlˌaɪ'zeɪʃən, 'nɑmənəˌlaɪ'zeɪʃən, -z

nominalize
BR 'nɒmɨnl̩ʌɪz, 'nɒmɨnəlʌɪz, -ɨz, -ɪŋ, -d
AM 'nɑmənlˌaɪz, 'nɑmənəˌlaɪz, -ɨz, -ɪŋ, -d

nominally
BR 'nɒmɨnl̩i, 'nɒmɨnəli
AM 'nɑmənl̩i, 'nɑmənəli

nominate
BR 'nɒmɨneɪt, -s, -ɪŋ, -ɨd
AM 'nɑməˌneɪ|t, -ts, -dɪŋ, -dɨd

nomination
BR ˌnɒmɨ'neɪʃn, -z
AM ˌnɑmə'neɪʃən, -z

nominatival
BR ˌnɒm(ɨ)nə'tʌɪvl, ˌnɒmn̩ə'tʌɪvl
AM 'nɑm(ə)nəˌtaɪvəl

nominative
BR 'nɒm(ɨ)nətɪv, 'nɒmn̩ətɪv, -z
AM 'nɑm(ə)nədɪv, -z

nominator
BR 'nɒmɨneɪtə(r), 'nɒmn̩eɪtə(r), -z
AM 'nɑməˌneɪdər, -z

nominee
BR ˌnɒmɨ'niː, -z
AM ˌnɑmə'ni, -z

nomogram
BR 'nɒməɡram, 'nəʊməɡram, -z
AM 'nɑməˌɡræm, 'noʊməˌɡræm, -z

nomograph
BR 'nɒməɡrɑːf, 'nɒməɡraf, 'nəʊməɡrɑːf, 'nəʊməɡraf, -s
AM 'nɑməˌɡræf, 'noʊməˌɡræf, -s

nomographic
BR ˌnɒmə'ɡrafɪk, ˌnəʊmə'ɡrafɪk
AM ˌnɑmə'ɡræfɪk, ˌnoʊmə'ɡræf

nomographically
BR ˌnɒmə'ɡrafɨkli, ˌnəʊmə'ɡrafɨkli
AM ˌnɑmə'ɡræfək(ə)li, ˌnoʊmə'ɡræfək(ə)li

nomography
BR nə'mɒɡrəfi
AM nə'mɑɡrəfi

nomothetic
BR ˌnɒmə'θɛtɪk, ˌnəʊmə'θɛtɪk
AM ˌnɑmə'θɛdɪk, ˌnoʊmə'θɛdɪk

noms de guerre
BR ˌnɒm(z) də 'ɡɛː(r)
AM ˌnɔm(z) də 'ɡɛ(ə)r

noms de plume
BR ˌnɒm(z) də 'pluːm
AM ˌnɔm(z) də 'plum

non
BR nɒn
AM nɑn

nonacceptance
BR ˌnɒnək'sɛpt(ə)ns
AM ˈnɑnək'sɛptns

nonage
BR 'nəʊnɪdʒ, 'nɒnɪdʒ
AM 'nɑnɪdʒ, 'noʊnɪdʒ

nonagenarian
BR ˌnɒnədʒɨ'nɛːrɪən, ˌnəʊnədʒɨ'nɛːrɪən, -z
AM ˌnɑnədʒə'nɛriən, ˌnoʊnədʒə'nɛriən, -z

nonaggressive
BR ˌnɒnə'ɡrɛsɪv
AM ˌnɑnə'ɡrɛsɪv

nonagon
BR 'nɒnəɡɒn, 'nɒnəɡ(ə)n, -z
AM 'nɑnəˌɡɑn, 'noʊnəˌɡɑn, -z

nonagression
BR ˌnɒnə'ɡrɛʃn
AM ˈnɑnə'ɡrɛʃən

nonalcoholic
BR ˌnɒnalkə'hɒlɪk
AM ˈnɑnˌælkə'hɔlɪk, ˈnɑnˌælkə'hɑlɪk

nonaligned
BR ˌnɒnə'lʌɪnd

AM ˌnɑnəˈlaɪnd
nonalignment
BR ˌnɒnəˈlʌɪnm(ə)nt
AM ˌnɑnəˈlaɪnmənt
nonappearance
BR ˌnɒnəˈpɪərəns, ˌnɒnəˈpɪərn̩s
AM ˌnɑnəˈpɪrəns
nonary
BR ˈnəʊnəri
AM ˈnoʊnəri
nonassertive
BR ˌnɒnəˈsəːtɪv
AM ˌnɑnəˈsərdɪv
nonassertively
BR ˌnɒnəˈsəːtɪvli
AM ˌnɑnəˈsərdɪvli
nonattendance
BR ˌnɒnəˈtɛnd(ə)ns
AM ˌnɑnəˈtɛndns
nonavailability
BR ˌnɒnəveɪləˈbɪlɪti
AM ˌnɑnəveɪləˈbɪlɪdi
nonbelligerency
BR ˌnɒnbɪˈlɪdʒ(ə)rənsi, ˌnɒnbɪˈlɪdʒ(ə)rn̩si
AM ˌnɑnbəˈlɪdʒərənsi
nonbelligerent
BR ˌnɒnbɪˈlɪdʒ(ə)rənt, ˌnɒnbɪˈlɪdʒ(ə)rn̩t, -s
AM ˌnɑnbəˈlɪdʒərənt, -s
nonbiodegradable
BR ˌnɒnˌbʌɪə(ʊ)dɪˈgreɪdəbl
AM ˌnɑnˌbaɪoʊdəˈgreɪdəbəl
non-biological
BR ˌnɒnbʌɪəˈlɒdʒɪkl
AM ˌnɑnˌbaɪəˈlɑdʒəkəl
nonce
BR nɒns
AM nɑns
nonchalance
BR ˈnɒnʃəl(ə)ns, ˈnɒnʃl̩(ə)ns
AM ˌnɑnʃəˌlɑns
nonchalant
BR ˈnɒnʃəl(ə)nt, ˈnɒnʃl̩(ə)nt
AM ˌnɑnʃəˈlɑnt
nonchalantly
BR ˈnɒntʃəl(ə)ntli, ˈnɒnʃl̩(ə)ntli
AM ˌnɑn(t)ʃəˈlɑn(t)li
non-com
BR ˈnɒnˌkɒm, -z
AM ˈnɑnˌkɑm, -z
non compos mentis
BR ˌnɒn ˌkɒmpəs ˈmɛntɪs
AM ˌnɑn ˌkɑmpəs ˈmɛn(t)əs
nonconformism
BR ˌnɒnkənˈfɔːmɪz(ə)m
AM ˌnɑnkənˈfɔrˌmɪzəm
nonconformist
BR ˌnɒnkənˈfɔːmɪst, -s
AM ˌnɑnkənˈfɔrməst, -s
nonconformity
BR ˌnɒnkənˈfɔːmɪti
AM ˌnɑnkənˈfɔrmədi
nonda
BR ˈnɒndə(r), -z
AM ˈnɑndə, -z
nondescriminatory
BR ˌnɒndɪˈskrɪmɪnətri
AM ˌnɑndəˈskrɪmɪnəˌtɔri
nondescript
BR ˈnɒndɪskrɪpt
AM ˌnɑndəˈskrɪpt
nondescriptly
BR ˈnɒndɪskrɪp(t)li
AM ˌnɑndəˈskrɪp(t)li
nondescriptness
BR ˈnɒndɪskrɪp(t)nɪs
AM ˌnɑndəˈskrɪp(t)nɪs
none
BR nʌn
AM nən
nonentity
BR nɒˈnɛntɪt|i, nəˈnɛntɪti, -ɪz
AM nɑnˈɛn(t)ədi, -z
nones
BR nəʊnz
AM noʊnz
nonessential
BR ˌnɒnɪˈsɛnʃl, -z
AM ˌnɑnəˈsɛn(t)ʃəl, ˌnɑniˈsɛn(t)ʃəl, -z
nonesuch
BR ˈnʌnsʌtʃ, -ɪz
AM ˈnənˌsətʃ, -əz
nonet
BR nəʊˈnɛt, nɒˈnɛt, -s
AM noʊˈnɛt, -s
nonetheless
BR ˌnʌnðəˈlɛs
AM ˌnənðəˈlɛs
nonexistent
BR ˌnɒnɪgˈzɪst(ə)nt
AM ˌnɑnəgˈzɪstənt
nonfeasance
BR ˌnɒnˈfiːz(ə)ns
AM nɑnˈfizəns
nonfiction
BR ˌnɒnˈfɪkʃn
AM ˌnɑnˈfɪkʃən
nong
BR nɒŋ, -z
AM nɔŋ, nɑŋ, -z
noninvolvement
BR ˌnɒnɪnˈvɒlvm(ə)nt
AM ˌnɑnənˈvɔlvmənt, ˌnɑnənˈvɑlvmənt
nonjoinder
BR ˌnɒnˈdʒɔɪndə(r), -z
AM ˌnɑnˈdʒɔɪndər, -z
nonjuring
BR ˌnɒnˈdʒʊərɪŋ
AM ˌnɑnˈdʒʊrɪŋ
nonjuror
BR ˌnɒnˈdʒʊərə(r), -z
AM ˌnɑnˈdʒʊrər, ˌnɑnˈdʒʊˌrɔ(ə)r, ˌnɑnˈdʒurər, ˌnɑnˈdʒurɔ(ə)r, -z
non-jury
BR ˌnɒnˈdʒʊəri
AM ˌnɑnˈdʒʊri, ˌnɑnˈdʒuri
non-material
BR ˌnɒnməˈtɪərɪəl
AM ˌnɑnməˈtɪriəl
no-no
BR ˈnəʊnəʊ, -z
AM ˈnoʊˌnoʊ, -z
nonpareil
BR ˌnɒnpəˈreɪl, ˈnɒnp(ə)rəl, ˈnɒnp(ə)rl, ˈnɒmp(ə)rəl, ˈnɒnp(ə)rl̩
AM ˌnɑnpəˌrɛl
non placet
BR ˌnɒn ˈpleɪsɛt, + ˈplakɛt, -s
AM ˌnɑn ˈpleɪsɪt, -s
nonplus
BR ˌnɒnˈplʌs, -ɪz, -ɪŋ, -t
AM nɑnˈpləs, -əz, -ɪŋ, -t
non possumus
BR ˌnɒn ˈpɒsjʉməs
AM ˌnɑn ˈpɑs(j)əməs
nonrestrictive
BR ˌnɒnrɪˈstrɪktɪv
AM ˌnɑnrəˈstrɪktɪv, ˈˌnɑnriˈstrɪktɪv
nonreturnable
BR ˌnɒnrɪˈtəːnəbl
AM ˌnɑnrəˈtərnəbəl, ˌnɑnriˈtərnəbəl
nonsense
BR ˈnɒns(ə)ns, -ɪz
AM ˈnɑnˌsɛns, ˈnɑnsəns, -əz
nonsensical
BR nɒnˈsɛnsɪkl
AM nɑnˈsɛnsəkəl
nonsensicality
BR ˌnɒnsɛnsɪˈkalɪt|i, -ɪz
AM nənˌsɛnsəˈkælədi, -z
nonsensically
BR nɒnˈsɛnsɪkli
AM nɑnˈsɛnsək(ə)li
non sequitur
BR ˌnɒn ˈsɛkwɪtə(r), -z
AM ˌnɑn ˈsɛkwədər, -z
nonstandard
BR ˌnɒnˈstandəd
AM ˌnɑnˈstændərd
nonstick
BR ˌnɒnˈstɪk
AM ˌnɑnˈstɪk
nonstop
BR ˌnɒnˈstɒp
AM ˌnɑnˌstɑp
nonsuch
BR ˈnɒnsʌtʃ, ˈnʌnsʌtʃ, -ɪz
AM ˈnənˌsətʃ, -əz
nonsuit
BR ˌnɒnˈsuːt, ˌnɒnˈsjuːt, -s, -ɪŋ, -ɪd
AM ˌnɑnˈs(j)u|t, -ts, -dɪŋ, -dəd
nontheless
BR ˌnʌnðəˈlɛs
AM ˌnənðəˈlɛs
non-U
BR ˌnɒnˈjuː
AM ˌnɑnˈju
nonviolence
BR ˌnɒnˈvʌɪəl(ə)ns
AM nɑnˈvaɪələns
nonviolent
BR ˌnɒnˈvʌɪəl(ə)nt
AM ˌnɑnˈvaɪələnt
noodle
BR ˈnuːdl, -z
AM ˈnudəl, -z
nook
BR nʊk, -s
AM nʊk, -s
nookie
BR ˈnʊki
AM ˈnʊki
nooky
BR ˈnʊki
AM ˈnʊki
noon
BR nuːn, -z
AM nun, -z
Noonan
BR ˈnuːnən
AM ˈnunən
noonday
BR ˈnuːndeɪ
AM ˈnunˌdeɪ
no one
BR ˈnəʊ wʌn
AM ˈnoʊ ˌwən
noontide
BR ˈnuːntʌɪd
AM ˈnunˌtaɪd
noontime
BR ˈnuːntʌɪm
AM ˈnunˌtaɪm
noose
BR nuːs, -ɪz
AM nus, -əz
Nootka
BR ˈnuːtkə(r), ˈnʊtkə(r), -z
AM ˈnutkə, -z
nopal
BR ˈnəʊpl, -z
AM ˈnoʊpəl, -z
nope
BR nəʊp
AM noʊp

noplace
BR ˈnəʊpleɪs
AM ˈnoʊˌpleɪs

nor
BR nɔː(r)
AM nɔ(ə)r

Nora
BR ˈnɔːrə(r)
AM ˈnɔrə

NORAD
BR ˈnɔːrad
AM ˈnɔrˌæd

noradrenalin
BR ˌnɔːrəˈdrɛnəlɪn, ˌnɔːrəˈdrɛnl̩ɪn
AM ˌnɔrəˈdrɛnələn

noradrenaline
BR ˌnɔːrəˈdrɛnəlɪn, ˌnɔːrəˈdrɛnl̩ɪn
AM ˌnɔrəˈdrɛnələn

Norah
BR ˈnɔːrə(r)
AM ˈnɔrə

Noraid
BR ˈnɔːreɪd
AM ˈnɔˌreɪd

Norbert
BR ˈnɔːbət
AM ˈnɔrbərt

Norden
BR ˈnɔːdn
AM ˈnɔrdən

Nordic
BR ˈnɔːdɪk
AM ˈnɔrdɪk

Nordkinn
BR ˈnɔːdkɪn
AM ˈnɔrdkɪn
NO ˈnuːrçin

Nore
BR nɔː(r)
AM nɔ(ə)r

Noreen
BR ˈnɔːriːn
AM nɔˈrin

Norfolk
BR ˈnɔːfək
AM ˈnɔrfək

Noriega
BR ˌnɒrɪˈeɪɡə(r)
AM ˌnɔriˈeɪɡə

nork
BR nɔːk, -s
AM nɔ(ə)rk, -s

norland
BR ˈnɔːlənd, -z
AM ˈnɔrlən(d), -z

norm
BR nɔːm, -z
AM nɔ(ə)rm, -z

Norma
BR ˈnɔːmə(r)
AM ˈnɔrmə

normal
BR ˈnɔːml
AM ˈnɔrməl

normalcy
BR ˈnɔːmlsi
AM ˈnɔrməlsi

normalisation
BR ˌnɔːməlʌɪˈzeɪʃn, ˌnɔːml̩ʌɪˈzeɪʃn
AM ˌnɔrmələˈzeɪʃən, ˌnɔrməˌlaɪˈzeɪʃən

normalise
BR ˈnɔːməlʌɪz, ˈnɔːml̩ʌɪz, -ɨz, -ɪŋ, -d
AM ˈnɔrməˌlaɪz, -ɨz, -ɪŋ, -d

normaliser
BR ˈnɔːməlʌɪzə(r), ˈnɔːml̩ʌɪz, -z
AM ˈnɔrməˌlaɪzər, -z

normality
BR nɔːˈmalɨti
AM nɔrˈmælədi

normalization
BR ˌnɔːməlʌɪˈzeɪʃn, ˌnɔːml̩ʌɪˈzeɪʃn
AM ˌnɔrmələˈzeɪʃən, ˌnɔrməˌlaɪˈzeɪʃən

normalize
BR ˈnɔːməlʌɪz, ˈnɔːml̩ʌɪzə(r), -ɨz, -ɪŋ, -d
AM ˈnɔrməˌlaɪz, -ɨz, -ɪŋ, -d

normalizer
BR ˈnɔːməlʌɪzə(r), ˈnɔːml̩ʌɪzə(r), -z
AM ˈnɔrməˌlaɪzər, -z

normally
BR ˈnɔːməli, ˈnɔːml̩i
AM ˈnɔrməli

Norman
BR ˈnɔːmən, -z
AM ˈnɔrmən, -z

Normandy
BR ˈnɔːməndi
AM ˈnɔrməndi

Normanesque
BR ˌnɔːməˈnɛsk
AM ˌnɔrməˈnɛsk

Normanise
BR ˈnɔːmənʌɪz, -ɨz, -ɪŋ, -d
AM ˈnɔrməˌnaɪz, -ɨz, -ɪŋ, -d

Normanism
BR ˈnɔːmənɪz(ə)m, -z
AM ˈnɔrməˌnɪzəm, -z

Normanize
BR ˈnɔːmanʌɪz, -ɨz, -ɪŋ, -d
AM ˈnɔrməˌnaɪz, -ɨz, -ɪŋ, -d

Normanton
BR ˈnɔːməntən
AM ˈnɔrməntən

normative
BR ˈnɔːmətɪv
AM ˈnɔrmədɪv

normatively
BR ˈnɔːmətɨvli
AM ˈnɔrmədɨvli

normativeness
BR ˈnɔːmətɨvnɨs
AM ˈnɔrmədɨvnɨs

Norn
BR nɔːn, -z
AM nɔ(ə)rn, -z

Norris
BR ˈnɒrɪs
AM ˈnɔrəs

Norrköping
BR ˈnɔːkəːpɪŋ
AM ˈnɔrkəpɪŋ
SW nɒrˈʃəːpɪŋ

Norroy
BR ˈnɒrɔɪ
AM ˈnɔˌrɔɪ

Norse
BR nɔːs
AM nɔ(ə)rs

Norseman
BR ˈnɔːsmən
AM ˈnɔrsmən

Norsemen
BR ˈnɔːsmən, ˈnɔːsmɛn
AM ˈnɔrsmən, ˈnɔrsˌmɛn

north
BR nɔːθ
AM nɔrθ

Northallerton
BR nɔːθˈalət(ə)n
AM nɔrˈθælərtən

Northampton
BR nɔːˈθam(p)t(ə)n
AM nɔrˈθæm(p)tən

Northamptonshire
BR nɔːˈθam(p)tənʃ(ɪ)ə(r)
AM nɔrˈθæm(p)tənˌʃɪ(ə)r

Northanger
BR ˈnɔːθaŋɡə(r), nɔːˈθaŋɡə(r)
AM ˈnɔrθæŋər, nɔrˈθæŋər

Northants
BR nɔːˈθants, ˈnɔːθants
AM ˈnɔrˌθæn(t)s

northbound
BR ˈnɔːθbaʊnd
AM ˈnɔrθˌbaʊnd

Northcliffe
BR ˈnɔːθklɪf
AM ˈnɔrθˌklɪf

North Dakota
BR ˌnɔːθ dəˈkəʊtə(r)
AM ˈnɔrθ dəˈkoʊdə

northeast
BR ˌnɔːθˈiːst
AM ˌnɔrθˈist

northeaster
BR ˌnɔːθˈiːstə(r), -z
AM ˌnɔrθˈistər, -z

northeasterly
BR ˌnɔːθˈiːstəl|i, -ɪz
AM ˌnɔrθˈistərli, -z

northeastern
BR ˌnɔːθˈiːst(ə)n
AM ˌnɔrθˈistərn

northeastward
BR ˌnɔːθˈiːstwəd, -z
AM ˌnɔrθˈistwərd, -z

Northenden
BR ˈnɔːðndən
AM ˈnɔrðəndən

norther
BR ˈnɔːðə(r), -z
AM ˈnɔrðər, -z

northerly
BR ˈnɔːðəl|i, -ɪz
AM ˈnɔrðərli, -z

northern
BR ˈnɔːðn
AM ˈnɔrðərn

northerner
BR ˈnɔːðn̩ə(r), ˈnɔːðənə(r), -z
AM ˈnɔrðərnər, -z

northernmost
BR ˈnɔːðnməʊst
AM ˈnɔrðərnˌmoʊst

Northfleet
BR ˈnɔːθfliːt
AM ˈnɔrθˌflit

northing
BR ˈnɔːθɪŋ, ˈnɔːðɪŋ, -z
AM ˈnɔrθɪŋ, ˈnɔrðɪŋ, -z

Northland
BR ˈnɔːθlənd
AM ˈnɔrθlən(d), ˈnɔrθˌlænd

Northman
BR ˈnɔːθmən
AM ˈnɔrθmən

Northmen
BR ˈnɔːθmən, ˈnɔːθmɛn
AM ˈnɔrθmən

north-northeast[1]
BR ˌnɔːθnɔːθˈiːst
AM ˌnɔrθˌnɔrθˈist

north-northeast[2]
nautical use
BR ˌnɔːnɔːrˈiːst
AM ˌnɔrˌnɔrˈist

north-northwest[1]
BR ˌnɔːθnɔːθˈwɛst
AM ˌnɔrθˌnɔrθˈwɛst

north-northwest[2]
nautical use
BR ˌnɔːnɔːˈwɛst
AM ˌnɔrˌnɔrˈwɛst

Northolt
BR ˈnɔːθəʊlt
AM ˈnɔrθˌ(h)oʊlt

North Pole
BR ˌnɔːθ ˈpəʊl
AM ˌnɔrθ ˈpoʊl

North Rhine-Westphalia
BR ˌnɔːθ ˈrʌɪnwɛstˈfeɪlɪə(r)
AM ˌnɔrθ ˈraɪnˌwɛstˈfɑljə, ˌnɔrθ ˈraɪnˌwɛstˈfɑliə

Northrop
BR 'nɔːθrəp
AM 'nɔrθrəp

Northrup
BR 'nɔːθrəp
AM 'nɔrθrəp

Northumberland
BR nɔː'θʌmbələnd
AM nɔr'θəmbərlən(d)

Northumbria
BR nɔː'θʌmbrɪə(r)
AM nɔr'θəmbriə

Northumbrian
BR nɔː'θʌmbrɪən, -z
AM nɔr'θəmbriən, -z

North Utsire
BR ˌnɔːθ ʊt'sɪərə(r)
AM ˌnɔrθ ʊt'sɪ(ə)r

northward
BR 'nɔːθwəd, -z
AM 'nɔrθwərd, -z

northwest
BR ˌnɔːθ'wɛst
AM ˌnɔrθ'wɛst

northwester
BR ˌnɔːθ'wɛstə(r), -z
AM ˌnɔrθ'wɛstər, -z

northwesterly
BR ˌnɔːθ'wɛstəl|i, -ɪz
AM ˌnɔrθ'wɛstərli, -z

northwestern
BR ˌnɔːθ'wɛst(ə)n
AM ˌnɔrθ'wɛstərn

North-West Frontier
BR ˌnɔːθwɛst 'frʌntɪə(r), + frʌn'tɪə(r)
AM ˌnɔrθˌwɛst frən'tiər

northwestward
BR ˌnɔːθ'wɛstwəd, -z
AM ˌnɔrθ'wɛs(t)wərd, -z

Northwich
BR 'nɔːθwɪtʃ
AM 'nɔrθwɪtʃ

Norton
BR 'nɔːtn
AM 'nɔrtən

Norvic
BR 'nɔːvɪk
AM 'nɔrvɨk

Norway
BR 'nɔːweɪ
AM 'nɔrweɪ

Norwegian
BR nɔː'wiːdʒ(ə)n, -z
AM ˌnɔr'widʒən, -z

nor'-wester
BR ˌnɔː'wɛstə(r), -z
AM ˌnɔr'wɛstər, -z

Norwich
BR 'nɒrɪdʒ, 'nɒrɪtʃ
AM 'nɔr(w)ɪtʃ, 'nɔrɪdʒ

Norwood
BR 'nɔːwʊd
AM 'nɔrˌwʊd

nos
numbers
BR 'nʌmbəz
AM 'nəmbərz

nose
BR nəʊz, -ɪz, -ɪŋ, -d
AM noʊz, -əz, -ɪŋ, -d

nosebag
BR 'nəʊzbag, -z
AM 'noʊzˌbæg, -z

noseband
BR 'nəʊzband, -z
AM 'noʊzˌbænd, -z

nosebleed
BR 'nəʊzbliːd, -z
AM 'noʊzˌblid, -z

nosecone
BR 'nəʊzkəʊn, -z
AM 'noʊzˌkoʊn, -z

nosedive
BR 'nəʊzdʌɪv, -z, -ɪŋ, -d
AM 'noʊzˌdaɪv, -z, -ɪŋ, -d

nosegay
BR 'nəʊzgeɪ, -z
AM 'noʊzˌgeɪ, -z

noseless
BR 'nəʊzləs
AM 'noʊzləs

nosepipe
BR 'nəʊzpʌɪp, -s
AM 'noʊzˌpaɪp, -s

nosering
BR 'nəʊzrɪŋ, -z
AM 'noʊzˌrɪŋ, -z

nosey
BR 'nəʊz|i, -ɪə(r), -ɪɪst
AM 'noʊzi, -ər, -ɪst

nosey parker
BR ˌnəʊzɪ 'pɑːkə(r), -z
AM 'noʊzi 'pɑrkər, -z

Nosferatu
BR ˌnɒsfə'rɑːtuː
AM ˌnɔsfə'rɑtu, ˌnɑsfə'rɑtu

nosh
BR nɒʃ, -ɪz, -ɪŋ, -t
AM nɑʃ, -əz, -ɪŋ, -t

noshery
BR 'nɒʃ(ə)r|i, -ɪz
AM 'nɑʃəri, -z

no-show
BR ˌnəʊ'ʃəʊ, 'nəʊʃəʊ, -z
AM 'noʊˌʃoʊ, -z

nosh-up
BR 'nɒʃʌp, -s
AM 'nɑʃəp, -s

nosily
BR 'nəʊzɪli
AM 'noʊzɨli

nosiness
BR 'nəʊzɪnɪs
AM 'noʊzinɪs

nosocomial
BR ˌnɒsə(ʊ)'kəʊmɪəl
AM ˌnoʊzoʊ'koʊmiəl

nosography
BR nəʊ'sɒgrəfi
AM noʊ'sɑgrəfi

nosological
BR ˌnɒsə'lɒdʒɪkl
AM ˌnɑsə'lɑdʒəkəl

nosology
BR nɒ'sɒlədʒi
AM noʊ'sɑlədʒi

nostalgia
BR nɒ'staldʒ(ɪ)ə(r)
AM nə'stældʒə, nɔs'tældʒə, nɑs'tældʒə

nostalgic
BR nɒ'staldʒɪk
AM nə'stældʒɪk, nɔs'tældʒɪk, nɑs'tældʒɪk

nostalgically
BR nɒ'staldʒɪkli
AM nə'stældʒək(ə)li, nɔs'tældʒək(ə)li, nɑs'tældʒək(ə)li

nostoc
BR 'nɒstɒk, -s
AM 'nɑˌstɑk, -s

Nostradamus
BR ˌnɒstrə'dɑːməs
AM ˌnɔstrə'dɑməs, ˌnɑstrə'dɑməs

nostril
BR 'nɒstr(ɪ)l, -z
AM 'nɑstrəl, -z

nostrum
BR 'nɒstrəm, -z
AM 'nɑstrəm, -z

nosy
BR 'nəʊz|i, -ɪə(r), -ɪɪst
AM 'noʊzi, -ər, -ɪst

nosy parker
BR ˌnəʊzɪ 'pɑːkə(r), -z
AM 'noʊzi 'pɑrkər, -z

not
BR nɒt
AM nɑt

nota bene
BR ˌnəʊtə 'bɛneɪ, + 'bɛni
AM ˌnoʊdə 'bɛni, + 'bɛneɪ

notability
BR ˌnəʊtə'bɪlɪt|i, -ɪz
AM ˌnoʊdə'bɪlɨdi, -z

notable
BR 'nəʊtəbl
AM 'noʊdəbəl

notableness
BR 'nəʊtəblnəs
AM 'noʊdəbəlnəs

notably
BR 'nəʊtəbli
AM 'noʊdəbli

notarial
BR nəʊ'tɛːrɪəl
AM noʊ'tɛriəl

notarially
BR nəʊ'tɛːrɪəli
AM noʊ'tɛriəli

notarise
BR 'nəʊtərʌɪz, -ɪz, -ɪŋ, -d
AM 'noʊdəˌraɪz, -ɪz, -ɪŋ, -d

notarization
BR ˌnəʊtərʌɪ'zeɪʃn
AM ˌnoʊdərə'zeɪʃən, ˌnoʊdəraɪ'zeɪʃən

notarize
BR 'nəʊtərʌɪz, -ɪz, -ɪŋ, -d
AM 'noʊdəˌraɪz, -ɪz, -ɪŋ, -d

notary
BR 'nəʊt(ə)r|i, -ɪz
AM 'noʊdəri, -z

notate
BR nə(ʊ)'teɪt, -s, -ɪŋ, -ɪd
AM 'noʊˌteɪ|t, -ts, -dɪŋ, -dɨd

notation
BR nə(ʊ)'teɪʃn, -z
AM noʊ'teɪʃən, -z

notational
BR nə(ʊ)'teɪʃn̩(ə)l, nə(ʊ)'teɪʃən(ə)l
AM noʊ'teɪʃ(ə)nəl

notch
BR nɒtʃ, -ɪz, -ɪŋ, -t
AM nɑtʃ, -əz, -ɪŋ, -t

notcher
BR 'nɒtʃə(r), -z
AM 'nɑtʃər, -z

notchy
BR 'nɒtʃ|i, -ɪə(r), -ɪɪst
AM 'nɑtʃi, -ər, -əst

note
BR nəʊt, -s, -ɪŋ, -ɪd
AM noʊ|t, -ts, -dɪŋ, -dəd

notebook
BR 'nəʊtbʊk, -s
AM 'noʊtˌbʊk, -s

notecase
BR 'nəʊtkeɪs, -ɪz
AM 'noʊtˌkeɪs, -ɪz

noteless
BR 'nəʊtləs
AM 'noʊtləs

notelet
BR 'nəʊtlɪt, -s
AM 'noʊtlət, -s

notepad
BR 'nəʊtpad, -z
AM 'noʊtˌpæd, -z

notepaper
BR 'nəʊtˌpeɪpə(r)
AM 'noʊtˌpeɪpər

note-row
BR 'nəʊtrəʊ, -z
AM 'noʊtˌroʊ, -z

noteworthiness
BR 'nəʊtˌwəːðɪnɪs
AM 'noʊtˌwərðinɪs

noteworthy
BR 'nəʊtˌwəːði

AM ˈnoʊtˌwərði

nothing
BR ˈnʌθɪŋ, -z
AM ˈnəθɪŋ, -z

nothingness
BR ˈnʌθɪŋnɪs
AM ˈnəθɪŋnɪs

notice
BR ˈnəʊtɪs, -ɪz, -ɪŋ, -t
AM ˈnoʊdəs, -əz, -ɪŋ, -t

noticeable
BR ˈnəʊtɪsəbl
AM ˈnoʊdəsəbəl

noticeably
BR ˈnəʊtɪsəbli
AM ˈnoʊdəsəbli

noticeboard
BR ˈnəʊtɪsbɔːd, -z
AM ˈnoʊdəsˌbɔ(ə)rd, -z

notifiable
BR ˈnəʊtɪfʌɪəbl
AM ˌnoʊdəˈfaɪəbəl

notification
BR ˌnəʊtɪfɪˈkeɪʃn
AM ˌnoʊdəfəˈkeɪʃən

notify
BR ˈnəʊtɪfʌɪ, -z, -ɪŋ, -d
AM ˈnoʊdəˌfaɪ, -z, -ɪŋ, -d

notion
BR ˈnəʊʃn, -z
AM ˈnoʊʃən, -z

notional
BR ˈnəʊʃn(ə)l, ˈnəʊʃən(ə)l
AM ˈnoʊʃ(ə)nəl

notionalist
BR ˈnəʊʃn̩əlɪst, ˈnəʊʃn̩l̩ɪst, ˈnəʊʃənl̩ɪst, ˈnəʊʃ(ə)nəlɪst, -s
AM ˈnoʊʃənələst, ˈnoʊʃnələst, -s

notionally
BR ˈnəʊʃn̩əli, ˈnəʊʃn̩l̩i, ˈnəʊʃənl̩i, ˈnəʊʃ(ə)nəli
AM ˈnoʊʃ(ə)nəli

notochord
BR ˈnəʊtəkɔːd, -z
AM ˈnoʊdəˌkɔ(ə)rd, -z

notoriety
BR ˌnəʊtəˈrʌɪɪti
AM ˌnoʊdəˈraɪɪdi

notorious
BR nə(ʊ)ˈtɔːrɪəs
AM nəˈtɔriəs, noʊˈtɔriəs

notoriously
BR nə(ʊ)ˈtɔːrɪəsli
AM nəˈtɔriəsli, noʊˈtɔriəsli

notoriousness
BR nə(ʊ)ˈtɔːrɪəsnəs
AM nəˈtɔriəsnəs, noʊˈtɔriəsnəs

Notre-Dame[1]
church in Paris
BR ˌnɒtrə ˈdɑːm, ˌnəʊtrə +
AM ˌnoʊtrə ˈdɑm, ˈnoʊdər ˈdɑm

Notre Dame[2]
US university
BR ˌnɒtrə ˈdɑːm, ˈnəʊtrə +, + ˈdeɪm
AM ˌnoʊdər ˈdeɪm

no-trump
BR ˌnəʊˈtrʌmp
AM ˈnoʊˌtrəmp

no-trumper
BR ˌnəʊˈtrʌmpə(r), -z
AM ˈnoʊˌtrəmpər, -z

Nott
BR nɒt
AM nɑt

Nottingham
BR ˈnɒtɪŋəm
AM ˈnɑdɪŋˌhæm, ˈnɑdɪŋəm

Nottinghamshire
BR ˈnɒtɪŋəmʃ(ɪ)ə(r)
AM ˈnɑdɪŋəmˌʃɪ(ə)r, ˈnɑdɪŋˌhæmˌʃɪ(ə)r

Notting Hill
BR ˌnɒtɪŋ ˈhɪl
AM ˌnɑdɪŋ ˈhɪl

Notts.
Nottinghamshire
BR nɒts
AM nɑts

notwithstanding
BR ˌnɒtwɪðˈstandɪŋ, ˌnɒtwɪθˈstandɪŋ
AM ˌnɑtwɪ(θ)ˈstændɪŋ, ˌnɑtwɪðˈstændɪŋ

nougat
BR ˈnuːɡɑː(r), ˈnʌɡɪt
AM ˈnuɡət

nougatine
BR ˌnuːɡəˈtiːn, ˈnuːɡətiːn
AM ˈnuɡəˌtin

nought
BR nɔːt, -s
AM nɔt, nɑt, -s

Nouméa
BR nuːˈmeɪə(r)
AM nuˈmeɪə

noumena
BR ˈnuːmɪnə(r), ˈnaʊmɪnə(r)
AM ˈnumənə

noumenal
BR ˈnuːmɪnl, ˈnaʊmɪnl
AM ˈnumənəl

noumenally
BR ˈnuːmɪnl̩i, ˈnuːmɪnəli, ˈnaʊmɪnl̩i, ˈnaʊmɪnəli
AM ˈnumənəli

noumenon
BR ˈnuːmɪnɒn, ˈnaʊmɪnɒn
AM ˈnuməˌnɑn

noun
BR naʊn, -z
AM naʊn, -z

nounal
BR ˈnaʊnl
AM ˈnaʊnəl

nourish
BR ˈnʌr|ɪʃ, -ɪʃɪz, -ɪʃɪŋ, -ɪʃt
AM ˈnərɪʃ, ˈnʊrɪʃ, -ɪz, -ɪŋ, -t

nourisher
BR ˈnʌrɪʃə(r), -z
AM ˈnərɪʃər, ˈnʊrɪʃər, -z

nourishingly
BR ˈnʌrɪʃɪŋli
AM ˈnərɪʃɪŋli, ˈnʊrɪʃɪŋli

nourishment
BR ˈnʌrɪʃm(ə)nt, -s
AM ˈnərɪʃmənt, ˈnʊrɪʃmənt, -s

nous
BR naʊs
AM nus

nouveau riche
BR ˌnuːvəʊ ˈriːʃ
AM ˌnuˌvoʊ ˈriʃ

nouveau roman
BR ˌnuːvəʊ rə(ʊ)ˈmɑːn, -z
AM ˌnuˌvoʊ roʊˈmɑn, -z

nouveaux riches
BR ˌnuːvəʊ ˈriːʃ
AM ˌnuˌvoʊ ˈriʃ

nova
BR ˈnəʊvə(r), -z
AM ˈnoʊvə, -z

novae
BR ˈnəʊviː
AM ˈnoʊvi

Novak
BR ˈnəʊvak
AM ˈnoʊvæk

Nova Lisboa
BR ˌnəʊvə lɪzˈbəʊə(r)
AM ˌnoʊvə lɪzˈboʊə

Nova Scotia
BR ˌnəʊvə ˈskəʊʃə(r)
AM ˌnoʊvə ˈskoʊʃə

Nova Scotian
BR ˌnəʊvə ˈskəʊʃ(ə)n, -z
AM ˌnoʊvə ˈskoʊʃən, -z

Novaya Zemlya
BR ˌnəʊvʌɪə ˈzɛmlɪə(r)
AM ˌnoʊvəjə ˌzɛmˈl(j)ɑ
RUS ˌnovəjə zʲinʲˈlʲa

novel
BR ˈnɒvl, -z
AM ˈnɑvəl, -z

novelese
BR ˌnɒvəˈliːz, ˌnɒvlˈiːz
AM ˌnɑvəˈliz

novelesque
BR ˌnɒvəˈlɛsk, ˌnɒvlˈɛsk
AM ˌnɑvəˈlɛsk

novelette
BR ˌnɒvəˈlɛt, ˌnɒvlˈɛt, -s
AM ˌnɑvəˈlɛt, -s

novelettish
BR ˌnɒvəˈlɛtɪʃ, ˌnɒvlˈɛtɪʃ
AM ˌnɑvəˈlɛdɪʃ

novelisation
BR ˌnɒvəlʌɪˈzeɪʃn, ˌnɒvl̩ʌɪˈzeɪʃn, -z
AM ˌnɑvələˈzeɪʃən, ˌnɑvəˌlaɪˈzeɪʃən, -z

novelise
BR ˈnɒvəlʌɪz, ˈnɒvl̩ʌɪz, -ɪz, -ɪŋ, -d
AM ˈnɑvəˌlaɪz, -ɪz, -ɪŋ, -d

novelist
BR ˈnɒvəlɪst, ˈnɒvl̩ɪst, -s
AM ˈnɑvələst, -s

novelistic
BR ˌnɒvəˈlɪstɪk, ˌnɒvlˈɪstɪk
AM ˌnɑvəˈlɪstɪk

novelization
BR ˌnɒvəlʌɪˈzeɪʃn, ˌnɒvl̩ʌɪˈzeɪʃn, -z
AM ˌnɑvələˈzeɪʃən, ˌnɑvəˌlaɪˈzeɪʃən, -z

novelize
BR ˈnɒvəlʌɪz, ˈnɒvl̩ʌɪz, -ɪz, -ɪŋ, -d
AM ˈnɑvəˌlaɪz, -ɪz, -ɪŋ, -d

novella
BR nə(ʊ)ˈvɛlə(r), -z
AM noʊˈvɛlə, -z

novelle
BR nə(ʊ)ˈvɛliː
AM noʊˈvɛli

Novello
BR nəˈvɛləʊ
AM noʊˈvɛloʊ

novelty
BR ˈnɒvlt|i, -ɪz
AM ˈnɑvəlti, -z

November
BR nə(ʊ)ˈvɛmbə(r), -z
AM noʊˈvɛmbər, nəˈvɛmbər, -z

novena
BR nə(ʊ)ˈviːnə(r), -z
AM noʊˈvinə, -z

Novgorod
BR ˈnɒvɡərɒd
AM ˈnɑvɡəˌrɑd
RUS ˈnovɡərət

novice
BR ˈnɒvɪs, -ɪz
AM ˈnɑvəs, -əz

Novi Sad
BR ˌnəʊvɪ ˈsad

AM ˌnoʊvi ˈsæd

novitiate
BR nəˈvɪʃɪət, -s
AM noʊˈvɪʃət, nəˈvɪʃət, -s

Novocain
BR ˈnəʊvə(ʊ)keɪn
AM ˈnoʊvəˌkeɪn

Novocaine®
BR ˈnəʊvə(ʊ)keɪn
AM ˈnoʊvəˌkeɪn

Novokuznetsk
BR ˌnəʊvə(ʊ)kʊz-ˈn(j)ɛtsk
AM ˌnoʊvəkʊzˈn(j)ɛtsk

Novosibirsk
BR ˌnəʊvə(ʊ)sɪˈbɪəsk
AM ˌnoʊvəsɪˈbərsk
RUS nəvəsʲiˈbʲirsk

Novotel
BR ˈnəʊvə(ʊ)tɛl
AM ˈnoʊvəˌtɛl

Novotný
BR nəˈvɒtni
AM nəˈvɔtni, nəˈvɑtni
CZ ˈnɔvɔtniː

now
BR naʊ
AM naʊ

nowaday
BR ˈnaʊədeɪ
AM ˈnaʊəˌdeɪ

nowadays
BR ˈnaʊədeɪz
AM ˈnaʊəˌdeɪz

noway
BR ˌnəʊˈweɪ, -z
AM ˌnoʊˌweɪ, -z

Nowel
BR nəʊˈɛl
AM ˈnoʊəl

Nowell¹
Christmas
BR nəʊˈɛl
AM noʊˈwɛl

Nowell²
forename
BR ˈnəʊ(ə)l
AM ˈnoʊ(ə)l

nowhere
BR ˈnəʊwɛː(r)
AM ˈnoʊˌ(h)wɛ(ə)r

no-win
BR ˌnəʊˈwɪn
AM ˈnoʊˈwɪn

nowise
BR ˈnəʊwʌɪz
AM ˈnoʊˌwaɪz

nowt
BR naʊt
AM naʊt

noxious
BR ˈnɒkʃəs
AM ˈnɔkʃəs, ˈnɑkʃəs

noxiously
BR ˈnɒkʃəsli
AM ˈnɔkʃəsli, ˈnɑkʃəsli

noxiousness
BR ˈnɒkʃəsnəs
AM ˈnɔkʃəsnəs, ˈnɑkʃəsnəs

noyau
BR ˌnwɑːˈjəʊ
AM ˌnwɑˈjoʊ

noyaux
BR ˌnwɑːˈjəʊ(z)
AM ˌnwɑˈjoʊ(z)

Noyes
BR nɔɪz
AM nɔɪz

nozzle
BR ˈnɒzl, -z
AM ˈnɑzəl, -z

n't
BR n̩t
AM n̩t

nth
BR ɛnθ
AM ɛnθ

nu
BR njuː
AM n(j)u

nuance
BR ˈnjuːɑːns, -ɪz
AM ˈn(j)uˌɑns, -əz

nub
BR nʌb, -z
AM nəb, -z

Nuba
BR ˈnjuːbə(r)
AM ˈnubə

nubble
BR ˈnʌbl, -z
AM ˈnəbəl, -z

nubbly
BR ˈnʌbli
AM ˈnəbl̩i

nubby
BR ˈnʌbi
AM ˈnəbi

Nubia
BR ˈnjuːbɪə(r)
AM ˈn(j)ubiə

Nubian
BR ˈnjuːbɪən, -z
AM ˈn(j)ubiən, -z

nubile
BR ˈnjuːbʌɪl
AM ˈn(j)uˌbaɪl, ˈn(j)ubəl

nubility
BR ˌnjuːˈbɪlɨti
AM ˌn(j)uˈbɪlɨdi

nuchal
BR ˈnjuːkl
AM ˈn(j)ukəl

nuciferous
BR ˌnjuːˈsɪf(ə)rəs
AM ˌn(j)uˈsɪf(ə)rəs

nucivorous
BR ˌnjuːˈsɪv(ə)rəs
AM ˌn(j)uˈsɪv(ə)rəs

nuclear
BR ˈnjuːklɪə(r)
AM ˈn(j)ukliər, ˈn(j)ukjələr

nuclease
BR ˈnjuːklɪeɪz, -ɪz
AM ˈn(j)ukliˌeɪz, -ɪz

nucleate
BR ˈnjuːklɪeɪt, -s, -ɪŋ, -ɨd
AM ˈn(j)ukliˌeɪ|t, -ts, -dɪŋ, -dɨd

nucleation
BR ˌnjuːklɪˈeɪʃn, -z
AM ˌn(j)ukliˈeɪʃən, -z

nuclei
BR ˈnjuːklɪʌɪ
AM ˈn(j)ukliˌaɪ

nucleic
BR njuːˈkliːɪk, njuːˈkleɪɪk
AM n(j)uˈkliɨk, n(j)uˈkleɪɨk

nucleolar
BR njuːˈklɪələ(r), ˌnjuːklɪˈəʊlə(r)
AM ˌn(j)ukliˈoʊlər, ˌn(j)uˈkliələr

nucleoli
BR njuːˈklɪəlʌɪ, ˌnjuːklɪˈəʊlʌɪ
AM ˌn(j)ukliˈoʊlaɪ, ˌn(j)uˈklieˌlaɪ

nucleolus
BR njuːˈklɪələs, ˌnjuːklɪˈəʊləs
AM ˌn(j)ukliˈoʊləs, ˌn(j)uˈkliələs

nucleon
BR ˈnjuːklɪɒn, -z
AM ˈn(j)ukliəˌɑn, -z

nucleonic
BR ˌnjuːklɪˈɒnɪk, -s
AM ˌn(j)ukliˈɑnɪk, -s

nucleoprotein
BR ˌnjuːklɪəˈprəʊtiːn, -z
AM ˌn(j)ukliəʊˈproʊˌtin, -z

nucleoside
BR ˈnjuːklɪəsʌɪd, -z
AM ˈn(j)ukliəˌsaɪd, -z

nucleotide
BR ˈnjuːklɪətʌɪd, -z
AM ˈn(j)ukliəˌtaɪd, -z

nucleus
BR ˈnjuːklɪəs
AM ˈn(j)ukliəs

nuclide
BR ˈnjuːklʌɪd, -z
AM ˈn(j)uˌklaɪd, -z

nuclidic
BR njuːˈklɪdɪk
AM n(j)uˈklɪdɪk

nuddy
BR ˈnʌdi
AM ˈnədi

nude
BR njuːd, -z
AM n(j)ud, -z

nudge
BR nʌdʒ, -ɪz, -ɪŋ, -d
AM nədʒ, -əz, -ɪŋ, -d

nudger
BR ˈnʌdʒə(r), -z
AM ˈnədʒər, -z

nudism
BR ˈnjuːdɪz(ə)m
AM ˈn(j)uˌdɪzəm

nudist
BR ˈnjuːdɪst, -s
AM ˈn(j)udəst, -s

nudity
BR ˈnjuːdɨti
AM ˈn(j)udədi

nudnik
BR ˈnʊdnɪk, -s
AM ˈnʊdˌnɪk, -s

nuée ardente
BR ˌnjʊeɪ ɑːˈdɒ̃t
AM ˌnueɪ ˌɑrˈdɑnt

Nuer
BR ˈnuːə(r)
AM ˈnuər

Nuevo León
BR ˌnweɪvəʊ liːˈɒn
AM ˌnwɛvoʊ liˈoʊn
SP ˌnweβo leˈon

Nuffield
BR ˈnʌfiːld
AM ˈnəfild

nugatory
BR ˈnjuːgət(ə)ri, njuːˈgeɪt(ə)ri
AM ˈnugəˌtɔri

Nugent
BR ˈnjuːdʒ(ə)nt
AM ˈnudʒənt

nugget
BR ˈnʌgɪt, -s
AM ˈnəgət, -s

nuisance
BR ˈnjuːsns, -ɪz
AM ˈn(j)usns, -əz

Nuits-Saint-George
BR ˌnwiːsanˈʒɔːʒ
AM ˌnwisænˈ(d)ʒɔr(d)ʒ

nuke
BR njuːk, -s, -ɪŋ, -t
AM n(j)uk, -s, -ɪŋ, -t

Nuku'alofa
BR ˌnuːkuːəˈləʊfə(r)
AM ˌnukuəˈlɔfə, ˌnukuəˈloʊfə

null
BR nʌl
AM nəl

nullah
BR ˈnʌlə(r), -z
AM ˈnələ, -z

nulla-nulla
BR ˈnʌlənʌlə(r), -z
AM ˌnələˈnələ, -z

Nullarbor Plain
BR ˌnʌləbɔː ˈpleɪn
AM nəlˌɑrbər ˈpleɪn
nullification
BR ˌnʌlɨfɨˈkeɪʃn
AM ˌnələfəˈkeɪʃən
nullifidian
BR ˌnʌlɪˈfɪdɪən, -z
AM ˌnələˈfɪdiən, -z
nullifier
BR ˈnʌlɨfʌɪə(r), -z
AM ˈnələˌfaɪər, -z
nullify
BR ˈnʌlɨfʌɪ, -z, -ɪŋ, -d
AM ˈnələˌfaɪ, -z, -ɪŋ, -d
nullipara
BR nʌˈlɪp(ə)rə(*r*), -z
AM nəˈlɪpərə, -z
nulliparous
BR nʌˈlɪp(ə)rəs
AM nəˈlɪp(ə)rəs
nullipore
BR ˈnʌlɨpɔː(r), -z
AM ˈnələˌpɔ(ə)r, -z
nullity
BR ˈnʌlɨt|i, -ɪz
AM ˈnələdi, -z
numb
BR nʌm, -z, -ɪŋ, -d
AM nəm, -z, -ɪŋ, -d
numbat
BR ˈnʌmbat, -s
AM ˈnəmˌbæt, -s
number
BR ˈnʌmb|ə(r), -əz, -(ə)rɪŋ, -əd
AM ˈnəmb|ər, -ərz, -(ə)rɪŋ, -ərd
numberless
BR ˈnʌmbələs
AM ˈnəmbərləs
numberplate
BR ˈnʌmbəpleɪt, -s
AM ˈnəmbərˌpleɪt, -s
numbingly
BR ˈnʌmɪŋli
AM ˈnəmɪŋli
numbly
BR ˈnʌmli
AM ˈnəmli
numbness
BR ˈnʌmnəs
AM ˈnəmnəs
numbskull
BR ˈnʌmskʌl, -z
AM ˈnəmˌskəl, -z
numdah
BR ˈnʌmdə(*r*), -z
AM ˈnəmdə, -z
numen
BR ˈnjuːmən
AM ˈn(j)umən
numerable
BR ˈnjuːm(ə)rəbl
AM ˈn(j)um(ə)rəbəl
numerably
BR ˈnjuːm(ə)rəbli
AM ˈn(j)um(ə)rəbli
numeracy
BR ˈnjuːm(ə)rəsi
AM ˈn(j)um(ə)rəsi
numeral
BR ˈnjuːm(ə)rəl, ˈnjuːm(ə)rl̩, -z
AM ˈn(j)um(ə)rəl, -z
numerate
BR ˈnjuːm(ə)rət
AM ˈn(j)um(ə)rət
numeration
BR ˌnjuːməˈreɪʃn
AM ˌn(j)uməˈreɪʃən
numerative
BR ˈnjuːm(ə)rətɪv
AM ˈn(j)uməˌreɪdɪv
numerator
BR ˈnjuːməreɪtə(r), -z
AM ˈn(j)uməˌreɪdər, -z
numeric
BR njuːˈmɛrɪk, njʊˈmɛrɪk
AM n(j)uˈmɛrɪk
numerical
BR njuːˈmɛrɪkl, njʊˈmɛrɪkl
AM n(j)uˈmɛrɪkəl
numerically
BR njuːˈmɛrɨkli, njʊˈmɛrɨkli
AM n(j)uˈmɛrək(ə)li
numerological
BR ˌnjuːm(ə)rəˈlɒdʒɨkl
AM ˌn(j)umərəˈlɑdʒəkəl
numerologist
BR ˌnjuːməˈrɒlədʒɪst, -s
AM ˌn(j)uməˈrɑlədʒəst, -s
numerology
BR ˌnjuːməˈrɒlədʒi
AM ˌn(j)uməˈrɑlədʒi
numerous
BR ˈnjuːm(ə)rəs
AM ˈn(j)um(ə)rəs
numerously
BR ˈnjuːm(ə)rəsli
AM ˈn(j)um(ə)rəsli
numerousness
BR ˈnjuːm(ə)rəsnəs
AM ˈn(j)um(ə)rəsnəs
numerus clausus
BR ˌnjuːmərəs ˈklaʊsəs
AM ˌn(j)umərəs ˈklaʊsəs
Numidia
BR njuːˈmɪdɪə(*r*), njʊˈmɪdɪə(*r*)
AM n(j)uˈmɪdiə
Numidian
BR njuːˈmɪdɪən, njʊˈmɪdɪən, -z
AM n(j)uˈmɪdiən, -z
numina
BR ˈnjuːmɨnə(*r*)
AM ˈn(j)umənə
numinous
BR ˈnjuːmɨnəs
AM ˈn(j)umənəs
numinously
BR ˈnjuːmɨnəsli
AM ˈn(j)umənəsli
numinousness
BR ˈnjuːmɨnəsnəs
AM ˈn(j)umənəsnəs
numismatic
BR ˌnjuːmɪzˈmatɪk, -s
AM ˌ¦n(j)uməzˈmædɪk, ¦n(j)uməsˈmædɪk, -s
numismatically
BR ˌnjuːmɪzˈmatɨkli
AM ¦n(j)uməzˈmædək(ə)li, ¦n(j)uməsˈmædək(ə)li
numismatist
BR njuːˈmɪzmətɪst, njʊˈmɪzmətɪst, -s
AM n(j)uˈmɪzmədəst, n(j)uˈmɪsmədəst, -s
numismatology
BR njuːˌmɪzməˈtɒlədʒi, njʊˌmɪzməˈtɒlədʒi
AM n(j)uˌmɪzməˈtɑlədʒi, n(j)uˌmɪsməˈtɑlədʒi
nummary
BR ˈnʌm(ə)ri
AM ˈnəməri
nummular
BR ˈnʌmjʊlə(r)
AM ˈnəmjələr
nummulite
BR ˈnʌmjʊlʌɪt, -s
AM ˈnəmjəˌlaɪt, -s
numnah
BR ˈnʌmnə(*r*), -z
AM ˈnəmnə, -z
numskull
BR ˈnʌmskʌl, -z
AM ˈnəmˌskəl, -z
nun
BR nʌn, -z
AM nən, -z
nunatak
BR ˈnʌnətak, -s
AM ˈnənəˌtæk, -s
nun-buoy
BR ˈnʌnbɔɪ, -z
AM ˈnənˌbuɪ, ˈnənˌbɔɪ, -z
Nunc Dimittis
BR ˌnʌŋk dɪˈmɪtɪs, ˌnʊŋk +
AM ˌnəŋk dəˈmɪdəs
nunchaks
BR ˈnʌntʃaks
AM ˈnənˌtʃæks
nunchaku
BR nʌnˈtʃakuː, -z
AM nənˈtʃɑku, -z
nunciature
BR ˈnʌnsɪətjʊə(r), ˈnʌnsɪətʃə(r), -z
AM ˈnənsiəˌtʃʊ(ə)r, nənsiətʃər, -z
nuncio
BR ˈnʌnsɪəʊ, -z
AM ˈnənsioʊ, -z
nuncupate
BR ˈnʌŋkjʊpeɪt, -s, -ɪŋ, -ɨd
AM ˈnəŋkjəˌpeɪ|t, -ts, -dɪŋ, -dɨd
nuncupation
BR ˌnʌŋkjʊˈpeɪʃn, -z
AM ˌnəŋkjəˈpeɪʃən, -z
nuncupative
BR ˈnʌŋkjʊpətɪv
AM ˈnəŋkjəˌpeɪdɪv
Nuneaton
BR nʌnˈiːtn
AM nənˈitn
nunhood
BR ˈnʌnhʊd, -z
AM ˈnənˌ(h)ʊd, -z
nunlike
BR ˈnʌnlʌɪk
AM ˈnənˌlaɪk
Nunn
BR nʌn
AM nən
nunnery
BR ˈnʌn(ə)r|i, -ɪz
AM ˈnənəri, -z
nunnish
BR ˈnʌnɪʃ
AM ˈnənɪʃ
NUPE
BR ˈnjuːpi
AM ˈn(j)upi
Nupe
language
BR ˈnuːpeɪ
AM ˈnupeɪ
nuptial
BR ˈnʌpʃl, ˈnʌptʃ(ə)l, -z
AM ˈnəp(t)ʃəl, -z
nurd
BR nəːd, -z
AM nərd, -z
Nuremberg
BR ˈnjʊərəmbəːg
AM ˈnʊr(ə)mˌbərg
Nureyev
BR ˈnjʊəreɪɛf, ˈnjʊəreɪɛv, njʊˈreɪɛf, njʊˈreɪɛv
AM nʊˈreɪɛv, ˈnʊrəjɛv
Nuristan
BR ˌnʊərɪˈstɑːn, ˌnʊərɪˈstan
AM ˈnʊrəˌstæn
Nurofen®
BR ˈnjʊərə(ʊ)fɛn
AM ˈn(j)ʊrəˌfɛn
nurse
BR nəːs, -ɨz, -ɪŋ, -t
AM nərs, -əz, -ɪŋ, -t
nurseling
BR ˈnəːslɪŋ, -z
AM ˈnərslɪŋ, -z

nursemaid
BR 'nə:smeɪd, -z
AM 'nərs,meɪd, -z

nursery
BR 'nə:s(ə)r|i, -ɪz
AM 'nərs(ə)ri, -z

nurseryman
BR 'nə:s(ə)rɪmən
AM 'nərs(ə)rimæn, 'nərs(ə)rimən

nurserymen
BR 'nə:s(ə)rɪmən
AM 'nərs(ə)rimən

nursling
BR 'nə:slɪŋ, -z
AM 'nərslɪŋ, -z

nurture
BR 'nə:tʃ|ə(r), -əz, -(ə)rɪŋ, -əd
AM 'nərtʃər, -z, -ɪŋ, -d

nurturer
BR 'nə:tʃ(ə)rə(r), -z
AM 'nərtʃərər, -z

NUT
BR ˌɛnju:'ti:
AM ˌɛn,ju'ti

nut
BR nʌt, -s, -ɪŋ, -ɨd
AM nə|t, -ts, -dɪŋ, -dəd

nutant
BR 'nju:t(ə)nt
AM 'n(j)utnt

nutation
BR nju:'teɪʃn, njʊ'teɪʃn, -z
AM n(j)u'teɪʃən, -z

nutcase
BR 'nʌtkeɪs, -ɨz
AM 'nət,keɪs, -ɨz

nutcracker
BR 'nʌt,krakə(r), -z
AM 'nət,krækər, -z

nutgall
BR 'nʌtgɔ:l, -z
AM 'nət,gɔl, 'nət,gɑl, -z

nuthatch
BR 'nʌthatʃ, -ɨz
AM 'nət,(h)ætʃ, -əz

nuthouse
BR 'nʌthaʊ|s, -zɨz
AM 'nət,(h)aʊ|s, -zəz

nutlet
BR 'nʌtlɨt, -s
AM 'nətlət, -s

nutlike
BR 'nʌtlʌɪk
AM 'nət,laɪk

nutmeat
BR 'nʌtmi:t, -s
AM 'nət,mit, -s

nutmeg
BR 'nʌtmɛg, -z
AM 'nət,mɛg, -z

nutpick
BR 'nʌtpɪk, -s
AM 'nət,pɪk, -s

Nutrasweet®
BR 'nju:trəswi:t
AM 'n(j)utrə,swit

nutria
BR 'nju:trɪə(*r*)
AM 'n(j)utriə

nutrient
BR 'nju:trɪənt, -s
AM 'n(j)utriənt, -s

nutriment
BR 'nju:trɪm(ə)nt
AM 'n(j)utrəmənt

nutrimental
BR ˌnju:trɪ'mɛntl
AM ˌn(j)utrə'mɛn(t)l

nutrition
BR nju:'trɪʃn, njʊ'trɪʃn
AM n(j)u'trɪʃən

nutritional
BR nju:'trɪʃn̩(ə)l, njʊ'trɪʃən(ə)l
AM n(j)u'trɪʃ(ə)nəl

nutritionally
BR nju:'trɪʃn̩əli, njʊ'trɪʃn̩əli, nju:'trɪʃ(ə)nəli, njʊ'trɪʃ(ə)nəli
AM n(j)u'trɪʃ(ə)nəli

nutritionist
BR nju:'trɪʃn̩ɪst, njʊ'trɪʃn̩ɪst, nju:'trɪʃənɪst, njʊ'trɪʃənɪst, -s
AM n(j)u'trɪʃənəst, -s

nutritious
BR nju:'trɪʃəs, njʊ'trɪʃəs
AM n(j)u'trɪʃəs

nutritiously
BR nju:'trɪʃəsli, njʊ'trɪʃəsli
AM n(j)u'trɪʃəsli

nutritiousness
BR nju:'trɪʃəsnəs, njʊ'trɪʃəsnəs
AM n(j)u'trɪʃəsnəs

nutritive
BR 'nju:trətɪv
AM 'n(j)utrədɪv

nutshell
BR 'nʌtʃɛl, -z
AM 'nət,ʃɛl, -z

Nuttall
BR 'nʌtɔ:l
AM 'nədɔl, 'nədɑl

nutter
BR 'nʌtə(r), -z
AM 'nədər, -z

nuttiness
BR 'nʌtɪnɨs
AM 'nədinɨs

Nutting
BR 'nʌtɪŋ
AM 'nədɪŋ

nutty
BR 'nʌt|i, -ɪə(r), -ɪɨst
AM 'nədi, -ər, -ɨst

nux vomica
BR ˌnʌks 'vɒmɪkə(*r*), -z
AM ˌnəks 'vɑməkə, -z

nuzzle
BR 'nʌz|l, -lz, -lɪŋ\-lɪŋ, -ld
AM 'nəz|əl, -əlz, -(ə)lɪŋ, -əld

nyala
BR 'njɑ:lə(*r*), -z
AM 'njɑlə, -z

Nyasa
BR nʌɪ'asə(*r*), nɪ'asə(*r*)
AM 'njɑsə, ni'ɑsə

Nyasaland
BR nʌɪ'asəland, nɪ'asəland
AM 'njɑsələnd, ni'ɑsələnd

nyctalopia
BR ˌnɪktə'ləʊpɪə(*r*)
AM ˌnɪktə'loʊpiə

nyctitropic
BR ˌnɪktɪ'trɒpɪk, ˌnɪktɪ'trəʊpɪk
AM ˌnɪktə'trɑpɪk

Nye
BR nʌɪ
AM naɪ

Nyerere
BR njə'rɛ:ri
AM njə'rɛri

nylghau
BR 'nɪlgɔ:(*r*), -z
AM 'nɪl,gɔ, -z

nylon
BR 'nʌɪlɒn, -z
AM 'naɪ,lɑn, -z

nymph
BR nɪmf, -s
AM nɪmf, -s

nympha
BR 'nɪmfə(*r*)
AM nɪmfə

nymphae
BR 'nɪmfi:
AM 'nɪmfi, 'nɪm,faɪ

nymphal
BR 'nɪmfl
AM 'nɪmfəl

nymphean
BR 'nɪmfɪən
AM 'nɪmfiən

nymphet
BR nɪm'fɛt, -s
AM nɪm'fɛt, -s

nymphlike
BR 'nɪmflʌɪk
AM 'nɪmf,laɪk

nympho
BR 'nɪmfəʊ, -z
AM 'nɪm,foʊ, -z

nympholepsy
BR ˌnɪmfəlɛpsi
AM 'nɪmfə,lɛpsi

nympholept
BR 'nɪmfəlɛpt, -s
AM 'nɪmfə,lɛpt, -s

nympholeptic
BR ˌnɪmfə'lɛptɪk
AM ˌnɪmfə'lɛptɪk

nymphomania
BR ˌnɪmfə'meɪnɪə(*r*)
AM nɪmfə'meɪniə

nymphomaniac
BR ˌnɪmfə'meɪnɪak, -s
AM nɪmfə'meɪni,æk, -s

Nynorsk
BR 'nju:nɔ:sk, 'nʌɪnɔ:sk
AM 'n(j)u,nɔrsk
NOR 'ny:nɔrsk

Nyree
BR 'nʌɪri:
AM 'naɪri

nystagmic
BR nɪ'stagmɪk
AM nə'stægmɪk

nystagmus
BR nɪ'stagməs
AM nə'stægməs

Nyx
BR nɪks
AM nɪks

Oo

O'
BR əʊ, ə
AM ə, oʊ

o
BR əʊ, -z
AM oʊ, -z

o'
BR ə
AM ə, oʊ

Oadby
BR 'əʊdbi
AM 'oʊdbi

oaf
BR əʊf, -s
AM oʊf, -s

oafish
BR 'əʊfɪʃ
AM 'oʊfɪʃ

oafishly
BR 'əʊfɪʃli
AM 'oʊfɪʃli

oafishness
BR 'əʊfɪʃnɪs
AM 'oʊfɪʃnɪs

Oahu
BR əʊ'ɑːhuː
AM oʊ'wɑhu

oak
BR əʊk, -s
AM oʊk, -s

oaken
BR 'əʊk(ə)n
AM 'oʊkən

Oakes
BR əʊks
AM oʊks

Oakham
BR 'əʊkəm
AM 'oʊkəm

Oakland
BR 'əʊklənd
AM 'oʊklən(d)

Oakley
BR 'əʊkli
AM 'oʊkli

Oaks
BR əʊks
AM oʊks

Oaksey
BR 'əʊksi
AM 'oʊksi

oakum
BR 'əʊkəm
AM 'oʊkəm

Oakville
BR 'əʊkvɪl
AM 'oʊkˌvɪl

OAP
BR ˌəʊeɪ'piː, -z
AM ˌoʊˌeɪ'pi, -z

OAPEC
BR 'əʊpɛk
AM 'oʊˌpɛk

oar
BR ɔː(r), -z, -d
AM ɔ(ə)r, -z, -d

oarfish
BR 'ɔːfɪʃ
AM 'ɔrˌfɪʃ

oarless
BR 'ɔːləs
AM 'ɔrləs

oarlock
BR 'ɔːlɒk, -s
AM 'ɔrˌlɑk, -s

oarsman
BR 'ɔːzmən
AM 'ɔrzmən

oarsmanship
BR 'ɔːzmənʃɪp
AM 'ɔrzmənˌʃɪp

oarsmen
BR 'ɔːzmən
AM 'ɔrzmən

oarswoman
BR 'ɔːzˌwʊmən
AM 'ɔrzˌwʊmən

oarswomen
BR 'ɔːzˌwɪmɪn
AM 'ɔrzˌwɪmɨn

oarweed
BR 'ɔːwiːd
AM 'ɔrˌwid

oases
BR əʊ'eɪsiːz
AM oʊ'eɪsiz

oasis
BR əʊ'eɪsɪs
AM oʊ'eɪsɪs

oast
BR əʊst, -s
AM oʊst, -s

oasthouse
BR 'əʊsthaʊ|s, -zɪz
AM 'oʊstˌ(h)aʊ|s, -zəz

oat
BR əʊt, -s
AM oʊt, -s

oatcake
BR 'əʊtkeɪk, -s
AM 'oʊtˌkeɪk, -s

oaten
BR 'əʊtn
AM 'oʊtn

Oates
BR əʊts
AM oʊts

oath
BR əʊ|θ, -ðz\-θs
AM oʊθ, -s

oatmeal
BR 'əʊtmiːl
AM 'oʊtˌmil

oaty
BR 'əʊti
AM 'oʊdi

Oaxaca
BR wɑː'hɑːkə(r)
AM wɑ'hɑkə

Ob
BR ɒb
AM ɑb, ɔb

Obadiah
BR ˌəʊbə'dʌɪə(r)
AM ˌoʊbə'daɪə

obbligati
BR ˌɒblɪ'gɑːti(ː)
AM ˌɑblə'gɑdi

obbligato
BR ˌɒblɪ'gɑːtəʊ, -z
AM ˌɑblə'gɑdoʊ, -z

obconic
BR ɒb'kɒnɪk
AM ɑb'kɑnɪk

obconical
BR ɒb'kɒnɪkl
AM ɑb'kɑnəkəl

obcordate
BR ɒb'kɔːdeɪt
AM ɑb'kɔrˌdeɪt

obduracy
BR 'ɒbdjʊrəsi,
'ɒbdʒʊrəsi
AM 'ɑbd(j)ərəsi

obdurate
BR 'ɒbdjʊrət,
'ɒbdʒʊrət
AM 'ɑbd(j)ərət

obdurately
BR 'ɒbdjʊrətli,
'ɒbdʒʊrətli
AM 'ɑbd(j)ərətli

obdurateness
BR 'ɒbdjʊrətnəs,
'ɒbdʒʊrətnəs
AM 'ɑbd(j)ərətnəs

OBE
BR 'əʊbiː'iː, -z
AM ˌoʊˌbi'i, -z

obeah
BR 'əʊbɪə(r)
AM 'oʊbiə

obeche
BR əʊ'biːtʃ|i, -ɪz
AM oʊ'bitʃi, -z

obedience
BR ə(ʊ)'biːdɪəns
AM ə'bidiəns,
oʊ'bidiəns

obedient
BR ə(ʊ)'biːdɪənt
AM ə'bidiənt,
oʊ'bidiənt

obediently
BR ə(ʊ)'biːdɪəntli
AM ə'bidiən(t)li,
oʊ'bidiən(t)li

obeisance
BR ə(ʊ)'beɪsns,
ə(ʊ)'biːsns, -ɪz
AM oʊ'beɪsəns,
ə'beɪsns, oʊ'bisəns,
ə'bisəns, -ɨz

obeisant
BR ə(ʊ)'beɪsnt,
ə(ʊ)'biːsnt
AM oʊ'beɪsənt,
ə'beɪsənt, oʊ'bisənt,
ə'bisənt

obeisantly
BR ə(ʊ)'beɪsntli,
ə(ʊ)'biːsntli
AM oʊ'beɪsntli,
ə'beɪsn(t)li,
oʊ'bisn(t)li,
ə'bisn(t)li

obeli
BR 'ɒbɪlʌɪ, 'ɒbl̩ʌɪ
AM 'ɑbəˌlaɪ

obelise
BR 'ɒbɪlʌɪz, 'ɒbl̩ʌɪz,
-ɪz, -ɪŋ, -d
AM 'ɑbəˌlaɪz, -ɨz, -ɪŋ, -d

obelisk
BR 'ɒbɪlɪsk, 'ɒblɪsk, -s
AM 'ɑbəˌlɪsk, -s

obelize
BR 'ɒbɪlʌɪz, 'ɒbl̩ʌɪz,
-ɪz, -ɪŋ, -d
AM 'ɑbəˌlaɪz, -ɨz, -ɪŋ, -d

obelus
BR 'ɒbɪləs, 'ɒbl̩əs
AM 'ɑbələs

Oberammergau
BR ˌəʊbər'aməgaʊ
AM ˌoʊbər'ɑmərgaʊ

Oberland
BR 'əʊbəland
AM 'oʊbərˌlænd

Oberon
BR 'əʊbərɒn
AM 'oʊbəˌrɑn

Oberösterreich
BR ˌəʊbər'ɔːstərʌɪk,
ˌəʊbər'ɔːstərʌɪx
AM ˌoʊbər'ɔstəˌraɪk

obese
BR ə(ʊ)'biːs
AM oʊ'bis

obeseness
BR ə(ʊ)'biːsnɪs
AM oʊ'bisnɪs

obesity
BR ə(ʊ)'biːsɪti
AM oʊ'bisɨdi

obey
BR ə(ʊ)'beɪ, -z, -ɪŋ, -d
AM ə'beɪ, oʊ'beɪ, -z, -ɪŋ,
-d

obeyer
BR ə(ʊ)'beɪə(r), -z
AM ə'beɪər, oʊ'beɪər, -z

obfuscate
BR 'ɒbfʌskeɪt,
'ɒbfəskeɪt, -s, -ɪŋ, -ɨd
AM 'ɑbfəˌskeɪ|t, -ts,
-dɪŋ, -dɨd

obfuscation
BR ˌɒbfʌ'skeɪʃn,
ˌɒbfə'skeɪʃn, -z
AM ˌɑbfə'skeɪʃən, -z

obfuscatory
BR ɒb'fʌskət(ə)ri, əb'fʌskət(ə)ri
AM ɑb'fəskəˌtɔri

obi
BR 'əʊb|i, -ɪz
AM 'oʊbi, -z

obit
BR 'ɒbɪt, 'əʊbɪt, -s
AM 'oʊbət, oʊ'bɪt, -s

obiter
BR 'ɒbɨtə(r), 'əʊbɨtə(r)
AM 'oʊbɪdər

obiter dicta
BR ˌɒbɨtə 'dɪktə(r), ˌəʊbɪtə +
AM ˌoʊbɪdər 'dɪktə

obiter dictum
BR ˌɒbɨtə 'dɪktəm, ˌəʊbɪtə +
AM ˌoʊbɪdər 'dɪktəm

obituarial
BR əˌbɪtʃʊ'ɛːrɪəl, əˌbɪtjʊ'ɛːrɪəl
AM ə'bɪtʃəˌwɛriəl, oʊ'bɪtʃəˌwɛriəl

obituarist
BR ə'bɪtʃ(ʊ)ərɪst, ə'bɪtj(ʊ)ərɪst, -s
AM ə'bɪtʃəˌwɛrəst, oʊ'bɪtʃəˌwɛrəst, -s

obituary
BR ə'bɪtʃʊər|i, ə'bɪtʃ(ʉ)r|i, ə'bɪtjʊər|i, ə'bɪtjʉr|i, -ɪz
AM ə'bɪtʃəˌwɛri, oʊ'bɪtʃəˌwɛri, -z

object¹
noun
BR 'ɒbdʒɪkt, 'ɒbdʒɛkt, -s
AM 'ɑbdʒək(t), -s

object²
verb
BR əb'dʒɛkt, -s, -ɪŋ, -ɨd
AM əb'dʒɛk|(t), ɑb'dʒɛk|(t), -(t)s, -tɪŋ, -təd

objectification
BR əbˌdʒɛktɨfɨ'keɪʃn, -z
AM əbˌdʒɛktəfə'keɪʃən, ɑbˌdʒɛktəfə'keɪʃən, -z

objectify
BR əb'dʒɛktɨfʌɪ, -z, -ɪŋ, -d
AM əb'dʒɛktəˌfaɪ, ɑb'dʒɛktəˌfaɪ, -z, -ɪŋ, -d

objection
BR əb'dʒɛkʃn, -z
AM əb'dʒɛkʃən, ɑb'dʒɛkʃən, -z

objectionable
BR əb'dʒɛkʃn̩əbl, əb'dʒɛkʃ(ə)nəbl
AM əb'dʒɛkʃ(ə)nəbəl, ɑb'dʒɛkʃ(ə)nəbəl

objectionableness
BR əb'dʒɛkʃn̩əblnəs, əb'dʒɛkʃ(ə)nəblnəs
AM əb'dʒɛkʃ(ə)nəbəlnəs, ɑb'dʒɛkʃ(ə)nəbəlnəs

objectionably
BR əb'dʒɛkʃn̩əbli, əb'dʒɛkʃ(ə)nəbli
AM əb'dʒɛkʃ(ə)nəbli, ɑb'dʒɛkʃ(ə)nəbli

objectival
BR ˌɒbdʒɪk'tʌɪvl, ˌɒbdʒɛk'tʌɪvl
AM ˌɑbdʒək'taɪvəl

objective
BR əb'dʒɛktɪv, -z
AM əb'dʒɛktɪv, ɑb'dʒɛktɪv, -z

objectively
BR əb'dʒɛktɨvli
AM əb'dʒɛktɨvli, ɑb'dʒɛktɨvli

objectiveness
BR əb'dʒɛktɨvnɨs
AM əb'dʒɛktɪvnɨs, ɑb'dʒɛktɪvnɨs

objectivisation
BR əbˌdʒɛktɨvʌɪ'zeɪʃn
AM əbˌdʒɛktəvə'zeɪʃən, ɑbˌdʒɛktəvə'zeɪʃən, əbˌdʒɛktəˌvaɪ'zeɪʃən, ɑbˌdʒɛktəˌvaɪ'zeɪʃən

objectivise
BR əb'dʒɛktɨvʌɪz, -ɨz, -ɪŋ, -d
AM əb'dʒɛktəˌvaɪz, ɑb'dʒɛktəˌvaɪz, -ɨz, -ɪŋ, -d

objectivism
BR əb'dʒɛktɨvɪz(ə)m
AM əb'dʒɛktəˌvɪzəm, ɑb'dʒɛktəˌvɪzəm

objectivist
BR əb'dʒɛktɨvɪst, -s
AM əb'dʒɛktəvəst, ɑb'dʒɛktəvəst, -s

objectivistic
BR əbˌdʒɛktɪ'vɪstɪk
AM əbˌdʒɛktə'vɪstɪk, ɑbˌdʒɛktə'vɪstɪk

objectivity
BR ˌɒbjɛk'tɪvɨti, ˌɒbdʒɪk'tɪvɨti
AM ˌɑbjɛk'tɪvɨdi

objectivization
BR əbˌdʒɛktɨvʌɪ'zeɪʃn
AM əbˌdʒɛktəvə'zeɪʃən, ɑbˌdʒɛktəvə'zeɪʃən, əbˌdʒɛktəˌvaɪ'zeɪʃən, ɑbˌdʒɛktəˌvaɪ'zeɪʃən

objectivize
BR əb'dʒɛktɨvʌɪz, -ɨz, -ɪŋ, -d
AM əb'dʒɛktəˌvaɪz, ɑb'dʒɛktəˌvaɪz, -ɨz, -ɪŋ, -d

objectless
BR 'ɒbdʒɪk(t)lɨs, 'ɒbdʒɛk(t)ləs
AM 'ɑbdʒək(t)ləs

objector
BR əb'dʒɛktə(r), -z
AM əb'dʒɛktər, ɑb'dʒɛktər, -z

objet d'art
BR ˌɒbʒeɪ 'dɑː(r)
AM ˌɑbˌʒeɪ 'dɑr

objets d'art
BR ˌɒbʒeɪ 'dɑː(r)
AM ˌɑbˌʒeɪ 'dɑr

objurgate
BR 'ɒbdʒəgeɪt, -s, -ɪŋ, -ɨd
AM 'ɑbdʒərˌgeɪ|t, -ts, -dɪŋ, -dɨd

objurgation
BR ˌɒbdʒə'geɪʃn
AM ˌɑbdʒər'geɪʃən

objurgatory
BR əb'dʒəːgət(ə)ri
AM əb'dʒərgəˌtɔri, ɑb'dʒərgəˌtɔri

oblanceolate
BR əb'lɑːnsɪələt, əb'lansɪələt
AM əb'lænsiəˌleɪt, ɑb'lænsiəˌleɪt

oblast
BR 'ɒblast, -s
AM 'ɑblæst, 'ɑblɑst, -s

oblate¹
adjective
BR 'ɒbleɪt, ɒ'bleɪt, ə(ʊ)'bleɪt, -s
AM 'ɑbˌleɪt, ˌoʊ'bleɪt, -s

oblate²
person
BR 'ɒbleɪt, ɒ'bleɪt, ə(ʊ)'bleɪt, -s
AM 'ɑbˌleɪt, -s

oblation
BR ə(ʊ)'bleɪʃn, ɒ'bleɪʃn, -z
AM ə'bleɪʃən, oʊ'bleɪʃən, -z

oblational
BR ə(ʊ)'bleɪʃn̩(ə)l, ə(ʊ)'bleɪʃən(ə)l, ɒ'bleɪʃn̩(ə)l, ɒ'bleɪʃən(ə)l
AM ə'bleɪʃ(ə)nəl, oʊ'bleɪʃ(ə)nəl

oblatory
BR 'ɒblət(ə)ri
AM 'ɑbləˌtɔri

obligate
BR 'ɒblɨgeɪt, -s, -ɪŋ, -ɨd
AM 'ɑbləˌgeɪt, -ts, -dɪŋ, -dɨd

obligation
BR ˌɒblɪ'geɪʃn, -z
AM ˌɑblə'geɪʃən, -z

obligational
BR ˌɒblɪ'geɪʃn̩(ə)l, ˌɒblɪ'geɪʃən(ə)l
AM ˌɑblə'geɪʃ(ə)nəl

obligator
BR 'ɒblɨgeɪtə(r), -z
AM 'ɑbləˌgeɪdər, -z

obligatorily
BR ə'blɪgət(ə)rɨli
AM əˌblɪgə'tɔrəli

obligatory
BR ə'blɪgət(ə)ri
AM ə'blɪgəˌtɔri

oblige
BR ə'blʌɪdʒ, -ɨz, -ɪŋ, -d
AM ə'blaɪdʒ, -ɨz, -ɪŋ, -d

obligee
BR ˌɒblɪ'dʒiː, -z
AM ˌɑblə'dʒi, ˌɑbˌlaɪ'dʒi, -z

obliger
BR ə'blʌɪdʒə(r), -z
AM ə'blaɪdʒər, -z

obliging
BR ə'blʌɪdʒɪŋ
AM ə'blaɪdʒɪŋ

obligingly
BR ə'blʌɪdʒɪŋli
AM ə'blaɪdʒɪŋli

obligingness
BR ə'blʌɪdʒɪŋnɨs
AM ə'blaɪdʒɪŋnɨs

obligor
BR ˌɒblɪ'gɔː(r), -z
AM ˌɑblə'gɔ(ə)r, -z

oblique
BR ə(ʊ)'bliːk
AM ə'blik, oʊ'blik

obliquely
BR ə(ʊ)'bliːkli
AM ə'blikli, oʊ'blikli

obliqueness
BR ə(ʊ)'bliːknɨs
AM ə'bliknɨs, oʊ'bliknɨs

obliquity
BR ə(ʊ)'blɪkwɪt|i, -ɪz
AM ə'blɪkwɨdi, oʊ'blɪkwɨdi, -z

obliterate
BR ə'blɪtəreɪt, -s, -ɪŋ, -ɨd
AM ə'blɪdəˌreɪ|t, oʊ'blɪdəˌreɪ|t, -ts, -dɪŋ, -dɨd

obliteration
BR əˌblɪtə'reɪʃn
AM əˌblɪdə'reɪʃən, oʊˌblɪdə'reɪʃən

obliterative
BR ə'blɪt(ə)rətɪv
AM ə'blɪdəˌreɪdɪv, oʊ'blɪdəˌreɪdɪv

obliterator
BR ə'blɪtəreɪtə(r), -z
AM ə'blɪdəˌreɪdər, oʊ'blɪdəˌreɪdər, -z

oblivion
BR əˈblɪvɪən
AM əˈblɪviən, oʊˈblɪviən
oblivious
BR əˈblɪvɪəs
AM əˈblɪviəs, oʊˈblɪviəs
obliviously
BR əˈblɪvɪəsli
AM əˈblɪviəsli, oʊˈblɪviəsli
obliviousness
BR əˈblɪvɪəsnəs
AM əˈblɪviəsnəs, oʊˈblɪviəsnəs
oblong
BR ˈɒblɒŋ, -z
AM ˈɑbˌlɔŋ, ˈɑbˌlɑŋ, -z
obloquy
BR ˈɒbləkwi
AM ˈɑbləkwi
obnoxious
BR əbˈnɒkʃəs, ɒbˈnɒkʃəs
AM əbˈnɑkʃəs
obnoxiously
BR əbˈnɒkʃəsli, ɒbˈnɒkʃəsli
AM əbˈnɑkʃəsli
obnoxiousness
BR əbˈnɒkʃəsnəs, ɒbˈnɒkʃəsnəs
AM əbˈnɑkʃəsnəs
oboe
BR ˈəʊbəʊ, -z
AM ˈoʊboʊ, -z
oboe d'amore
BR ˌəʊbəʊ daˈmɔːreɪ
AM ˈoʊboʊ dɑˈmɔreɪ
oboes d'amore
BR ˌəʊbəʊz daˈmɔːreɪ
AM ˈoʊboʊz dɑˈmɔreɪ
oboist
BR ˈəʊbəʊɪst, -s
AM ˈoʊboʊwəst, ˈoʊbəwəst, -s
obol
BR ˈɒb(ɒ)l, -z
AM ˈɔˌbɔl, ˈɑˌbɑl, -z
obovate
BR ɒbˈəʊveɪt
AM ɑbˈoʊˌveɪt
O'Boyle
BR əʊˈbɔɪl
AM oʊˈbɔɪl
O'Brady
BR ə(ʊ)ˈbreɪdi, ə(ʊ)ˈbrɔːdi
AM oʊˈbreɪdi
O'Brien
BR ə(ʊ)ˈbrʌɪən
AM əˈbraɪən, oʊˈbraɪən
obscene
BR əbˈsiːn
AM əbˈsin
obscenely
BR əbˈsiːnli
AM əbˈsinli
obsceneness
BR əbˈsiːnnɨs
AM əbˈsi(n)nɨs
obscenity
BR əbˈsɛnɪt|i, -ɪz
AM əbˈsɛnədi, ɑbˈsɛnədi, -z
obscurant
BR ˈɒbskjʉrənt, -s
AM ˈɑbskjərənt, -s
obscurantism
BR ˌɒbskjʉˈrantɪz(ə)m
AM əbˈskjʊrənˌtɪzəm, ɑbˈskjʊrənˌtɪzəm, ˌɑbskjəˈrænˌtɪzəm
obscurantist
BR ˌɒbskjʉˈrantɪst, -s
AM əbˈskjʊrəntəst, ɑbˈskjʊrəntəst, ˌɑbskjəˈræntəst, -s
obscuration
BR ˌɒbskjʉˈreɪʃn, -z
AM ˌɑbskjəˈreɪʃən, -z
obscure
BR əbˈskjʊə(r), əbˈskjɔː(r), -z, -ɪŋ, -d, -ə(r), -ɨst
AM əbˈskjʊ(ə)r, ɑbˈskjʊ(ə)r, -z, -ɪŋ, -d, -ər, -əst
obscurely
BR əbˈskjʊəli, əbˈskjɔːli
AM əbˈskjʊrli, ɑbˈskjʊrli
obscurity
BR əbˈskjʊərɪt|i, əbˈskjɔːrɪti, -ɪz
AM əbˈskjʊrədi, ɑbˈskjʊrədi, -z
obsecrate
BR ˈɒbsɪkreɪt, -s, -ɪŋ, -ɨd
AM ˈɑbsəˌkreɪ|t, -ts, -dɪŋ, -dɨd
obsecration
BR ˌɒbsɪˈkreɪʃn, -z
AM ˌɑbsəˈkreɪʃən, -z
obsequial
BR əbˈsiːkwɪəl
AM əbˈsikwiəl
obsequies
BR ˈɒbsɪkwɪz
AM ˈɑbsəkwiz
obsequious
BR əbˈsiːkwɪəs
AM əbˈsikwiəs
obsequiously
BR əbˈsiːkwɪəsli
AM əbˈsikwiəsli
obsequiousness
BR əbˈsiːkwɪəsnəs
AM əbˈsikwiəsnəs
observable
BR əbˈzəːvəbl
AM əbˈzərvəbəl
observably
BR əbˈzəːvəbli
AM əbˈzərvəbli
observance
BR əbˈzəːvns, -ɪz
AM əbˈzərvəns, -əz
observant
BR əbˈzəːvnt
AM əbˈzərvənt
observantly
BR əbˈzəːvntli
AM əbˈzərvən(t)li
observation
BR ˌɒbzəˈveɪʃn, -z
AM ˌɑbzərˈveɪʃən, -z
observational
BR ˌɒbzəˈveɪʃn̩(ə)l, ˌɒbzəˈveɪʃən(ə)l
AM ˌɑbzərˈveɪʃ(ə)nəl
observationally
BR ˌɒbzəˈveɪʃn̩əli, ˌɒbzəˈveɪʃn̩li, ˌɒbzəˈveɪʃənl̩i, ˌɒbzəˈveɪʃ(ə)nəli
AM ˌɑbzərˈveɪʃ(ə)nəli
observatory
BR əbˈzəːvət(ə)r|i, -ɪz
AM əbˈzərvəˌtɔri, -z
observe
BR əbˈzəːv, -z, -ɪŋ, -d
AM əbˈzərv, -z, -ɪŋ, -d
observer
BR əbˈzəːvə(r), -z
AM əbˈzərvər, -z
obsess
BR əbˈsɛs, -ɪz, -ɪŋ, -t
AM əbˈsɛs, ɑbˈsɛs, -əz, -ɪŋ, -t
obsession
BR əbˈsɛʃn, -z
AM əbˈsɛʃən, ɑbˈsɛʃən, -z
obsessional
BR əbˈsɛʃn̩(ə)l, əbˈsɛʃən(ə)l, -z
AM əbˈsɛʃ(ə)nəl, ɑbˈsɛʃ(ə)nəl, -z
obsessionalism
BR əbˈsɛʃn̩əlɪz(ə)m, əbˈsɛʃn̩l̩ɪz(ə)m, əbˈsɛʃənl̩ɪz(ə)m, əbˈsɛʃ(ə)nəlɪz(ə)m
AM əbˈsɛʃənlˌɪzəm, əbˈsɛʃnəˌlɪzəm, ɑbˈsɛʃənlˌɪzəm, ɑbˈsɛʃnəˌlɪzəm
obsessionally
BR əbˈsɛʃn̩əli, əbˈsɛʃn̩li, əbˈsɛʃənl̩i, əbˈsɛʃ(ə)nəli
AM əbˈsɛʃ(ə)nəli, ɑbˈsɛʃ(ə)nəli
obsessive
BR əbˈsɛsɪv, -z
AM əbˈsɛsɪv, ɑbˈsɛsɪv, -z
obsessively
BR əbˈsɛsɪvli
AM əbˈsɛsɪvli, ɑbˈsɛsɪvli
obsessiveness
BR əbˈsɛsɪvnɨs
AM əbˈsɛsɪvnɨs, ɑbˈsɛsɪvnɨs
obsidian
BR əbˈsɪdɪən
AM əbˈsɪdiən, ɑbˈsɪdiən
obsolescence
BR ˌɒbsəˈlɛsns
AM ˌɑbsəˈlɛsəns
obsolescent
BR ˌɒbsəˈlɛsnt
AM ˌɑbsəˈlɛsənt
obsolete
BR ˈɒbsəliːt, ˌɒbsəˈliːt
AM ˌɑbsəˈlit
obsoletely
BR ˈɒbsəliːtli, ˌɒbsəˈliːtli
AM ˌɑbsəˈlitli
obsoleteness
BR ˈɒbsəliːtnɨs, ˌɒbsəˈliːtnɨs
AM ˌɑbsəˈlitnɨs
obsoletism
BR ˈɒbsəliːtɪz(ə)m, ˌɒbsəˈliːtɪz(ə)m
AM ˌɑbsəˈliˌtɪzəm
obstacle
BR ˈɒbstəkl, -z
AM ˈɑbztəkəl, ˈɑbstəkəl, -z
obstetric
BR əbˈstɛtrɪk, ɒbˈstɛtrɪk, -s
AM əbˈstɛtrɪk, ɑbˈstɛtrɪk, -s
obstetrical
BR əbˈstɛtrɪkl, ɒbˈstɛtrɪkl
AM əbˈstɛtrəkəl, ɑbˈstɛtrəkəl
obstetrically
BR əbˈstɛtrɪkli, ɒbˈstɛtrɪkli
AM əbˈstɛtrək(ə)li, ɑbˈstɛtrək(ə)li
obstetrician
BR ˌɒbstɪˈtrɪʃn, ˌɒbstɛˈtrɪʃn, -z
AM ˌɑbztəˈtrɪʃən, ˌɑbstəˈtrɪʃən, -z
obstinacy
BR ˈɒbstɪnəsi
AM ˈɑbztənəsi, ˈɑbstənəsi
obstinate
BR ˈɒbstɪnət
AM ˈɑbztənət, ˈɑbstənət
obstinately
BR ˈɒbstɪnətli
AM ˈɑbztənətli, ˈɑbstənətli

obstreperous
BR əb'strɛp(ə)rəs, ɒb'strɛp(ə)rəs
AM əb'strɛp(ə)rəs, ɑb'strɛp(ə)rəs

obstreperously
BR əb'strɛp(ə)rəsli, ɒb'strɛp(ə)rəsli
AM əb'strɛp(ə)rəsli, ɑb'strɛp(ə)rəsli

obstreperousness
BR əb'strɛp(ə)rəsnəs, ɒb'strɛp(ə)rəsnəs
AM əb'strɛp(ə)rəsnəs, ɑb'strɛp(ə)rəsnəs

obstruct
BR əb'strʌkt, -s, -ɪŋ, -ɨd
AM əb'strək|(t), ɑb'strək|(t), -(t)s, -tɪŋ, -təd

obstruction
BR əb'strʌkʃn, -z
AM əb'strəkʃən, əb'strəkʃən, -z

obstructionism
BR əb'strʌkʃn̩ɪz(ə)m, əb'strʌkʃənɪz(ə)m
AM əb'strəkʃəˌnɪzəm, ɑb'strəkʃəˌnɪzəm

obstructionist
BR əb'strʌkʃn̩ɪst, əb'strʌkʃənɪst, -s
AM əb'strəkʃənəst, əb'strəkʃənəst, -s

obstructive
BR əb'strʌktɪv
AM əb'strəktɪv, ɑb'strəktɪv

obstructively
BR əb'strʌktɨvli
AM əb'strəktɨvli, ɑb'strəktɨvli

obstructiveness
BR əb'strʌktɨvnɨs
AM əb'strəktɪvnɨs, ɑb'strəktɪvnɨs

obstructor
BR əb'strʌktə(r), -z
AM əb'strəktər, ɑb'strəktər, -z

obstupefaction
BR əbˌstju:pɪ'fakʃn, əbˌstʃu:pɪ'fakʃn
AM əbˌst(j)upə'fækʃən, ɑbˌst(j)upə'fækʃən

obstupefy
BR əb'stju:pɨfʌɪ, əb'stʃu:pɨfʌɪ, -z, -ɪŋ, -d
AM əb'st(j)upəˌfaɪ, ɑb'st(j)upəˌfaɪ, -z, -ɪŋ, -d

obtain
BR əb'teɪn, -z, -ɪŋ, -d
AM əb'teɪn, ɑb'teɪn, -z, -ɪŋ, -d

obtainability
BR əbˌteɪnə'bɪlɨti
AM əb'teɪnə'bɪlɨdi, ɑb'teɪnə'bɪlɨdi

obtainable
BR əb'teɪnəbl
AM əb'teɪnəbəl, ɑb'teɪnəbəl

obtainer
BR əb'teɪnə(r), -z
AM əb'teɪnər, ɑb'teɪnər, -z

obtainment
BR əb'teɪnm(ə)nt, -s
AM əb'teɪnmənt, ɑb'teɪnmənt, -s

obtention
BR əb'tɛnʃn, -z
AM əb'tɛn(t)ʃən, ɑb'tɛn(t)ʃən, -z

obtrude
BR əb'tru:d, ɒb'tru:d, -z, -ɪŋ, -ɨd
AM əb'trud, ɑb'trud, -z, -ɪŋ, -əd

obtruder
BR əb'tru:də(r), ɒb'tru:də(r), -z
AM əb'trudər, ɑb'trudər, -z

obtrusion
BR əb'tru:ʒn, ɒb'tru:ʒn, -z
AM əb'truʒən, ɑb'truʒən, -z

obtrusive
BR əb'tru:sɪv, ɒb'tru:sɪv
AM əb'trusɪv, ɑb'trusɪv

obtrusively
BR əb'tru:sɨvli, ɒb'tru:sɨvli
AM əb'trusɨvli, ɑb'trusɨvli

obtrusiveness
BR əb'tru:sɪvnɨs, ɒb'tru:sɪvnɨs
AM əb'trusɪvnɨs, ɑb'trusɪvnɨs

obtund
BR əb'tʌnd, ɒb'tʌnd, -z, -ɪŋ, -ɨd
AM əb'tənd, ɑb'tənd, -z, -ɪŋ, -əd

obturate
BR 'ɒbtjʊreɪt, 'ɒbtʃʊreɪt, -s, -ɪŋ, -ɨd
AM 'ɑbt(j)əˌreɪ|t, -ts, -dɪŋ, -dɨd

obturation
BR ˌɒbtjʊ'reɪʃn, ˌɒbtʃʊ'reɪʃn, -z
AM ˌɑbt(j)ə'reɪʃən, -z

obturator
BR 'ɒbtjʊreɪtə(r), 'ɒbtʃʊreɪtə(r), -z
AM 'ɑbt(j)əˌreɪdər, -z

obtuse
BR əb'tju:s, ɒb'tju:s, əb'tʃu:s, ɒb'tʃu:s
AM əb't(j)us, ɑb't(j)us

obtusely
BR əb'tju:sli, ɒb'tju:sli, əb'tʃu:sli, ɒb'tʃu:sli
AM əb't(j)usli, ɑb't(j)usli

obtuseness
BR əb'tju:snəs, ɒb'tju:snəs, əb'tʃu:snəs, ɒb'tʃu:snəs
AM əb't(j)usnəs, ɑb't(j)usnəs

obtusity
BR əb'tju:sɪti, ɒb'tju:sɪti, əb'tʃu:sɪti, ɒb'tʃu:sɪti
AM əb't(j)usədi, ɑb't(j)usədi

obverse[1]
adjective
BR 'ɒbvə:s
AM əb'vərs, ɑb'vərs

obverse[2]
noun
BR 'ɒbvə:s, -ɨz
AM 'ɑbˌvərs, -əz

obversely
BR 'ɒbvə:sli
AM əb'vərsli, ɑb'vərsli

obversion
BR əb'və:ʃn, ɒb'və:ʃn, -z
AM əb'vərʒən, ɑb'vərʒən, əb'vərʃən, ɑb'vərʃən, -z

obvert
BR əb'və:t, ɒb'və:t, -s, -ɪŋ, -ɨd
AM əb'vərt, ɑb'vər|t, -ts, -dɪŋ, -dəd

obviate
BR 'ɒbvɪeɪt, -s, -ɪŋ, -ɨd
AM 'ɑbviˌeɪ|t, -ts, -dɪŋ, -dɨd

obviation
BR ˌɒbvɪ'eɪʃn
AM ˌɑbvi'eɪʃən

obvious
BR 'ɒbvɪəs
AM 'ɑbviəs

obviously
BR 'ɒbvɪəsli
AM 'ɑbviəsli

obviousness
BR 'ɒbvɪəsnəs
AM 'ɑbviəsnəs

O'Byrne
BR ə(ʊ)'bə:n
AM oʊ'bərn

O'Callaghan
BR ə(ʊ)'kaləhən, ə(ʊ)'kaləhan
AM oʊ'kæləhæn

ocarina
BR ˌɒkə'ri:nə(r), -z
AM ˌɑkə'rinə, -z

O'Carroll
BR ə(ʊ)'karəl, ə(ʊ)'karl̩
AM oʊ'kɛrəl

O'Casey
BR ə(ʊ)'keɪsi
AM ə'keɪsi, oʊ'keɪsi

Occam
BR 'ɒkəm, -z
AM 'ɑkəm, -z

occasion
BR ə'keɪʒn, -z
AM ə'keɪʒən, -z

occasional
BR ə'keɪʒn̩(ə)l, ə'keɪʒən(ə)l
AM ə'keɪʒ(ə)nəl

occasionalism
BR ə'keɪʒn̩əlɪz(ə)m, ə'keɪʒn̩l̩ɪz(ə)m, ə'keɪʒənl̩ɪz(ə)m, ə'keɪʒ(ə)nəlɪz(ə)m
AM ə'keɪʒənlˌɪzəm, ə'keɪʒnəˌlɪzəm

occasionalist
BR ə'keɪʒn̩əlɪst, ə'keɪʒn̩l̩ɪst, ə'keɪʒənl̩ɪst, ə'keɪʒ(ə)nəlɪst, -s
AM ə'keɪʒənl̩əst, ə'keɪʒnələst, -s

occasionality
BR əˌkeɪʒə'nalɪti
AM əˌkeɪʒə'nælədi

occasionally
BR ə'keɪʒn̩əli, ə'keɪʒn̩l̩i, ə'keɪʒənl̩i, ə'keɪʒ(ə)nəli
AM ə'keɪʒ(ə)nəli

occident
BR 'ɒksɪd(ə)nt
AM 'ɑksədnt

occidental
BR ˌɒksɪ'dɛntl, -z
AM ¦ɑksə'dɛn(t)l, -z

occidentalise
BR ˌɒksɪ'dɛntl̩ʌɪz, -ɨz, -ɪŋ, -d
AM ¦ɑksə'dɛn(t)lˌʌɪz, -ɨz, -ɪŋ, -d

occidentalism
BR ˌɒksɪ'dɛntl̩ɪz(ə)m
AM ¦ɑksə'dɛn(t)lˌɪzəm

occidentalist
BR ˌɒksɪ'dɛntl̩ɪst, -s
AM ¦ɑksə'dɛn(t)l̩əst, -s

occidentalize
BR ˌɒksɪ'dɛntl̩ʌɪz, -ɨz, -ɪŋ, -d
AM ¦ɑksə'dɛn(t)lˌʌɪz, -ɨz, -ɪŋ, -d

occidentally
BR ˌɒksɪ'dɛntl̩i, ˌɒksɪ'dɛnt(ə)li
AM ¦ɑksə'dɛn(t)l̩i

occipital
BR ɒk'sɪpɪtl
AM ɑk'sɪpɪdl
occipitally
BR ɒk'sɪpɪtl̩i, ɒk'sɪpɪtəli
AM ɑk'sɪpɪdli
occiput
BR 'ɒksɪpʌt, 'ɒksɪpət, -s
AM 'ɑksəpət, -s
Occitan
BR 'ɒksɪtn
AM 'ɑksəˌtɑn, 'ɑksətn
Occitanian
BR ˌɒksɪ'teɪnɪən, -z
AM ˌɑksə'teɪniən, -z
occlude
BR ə'kluːd, -z, -ɪŋ, -ɪd
AM ə'klud, -z, -ɪŋ, -əd
occlusion
BR ə'kluːʒn, -z
AM ə'kluʒən, -z
occlusive
BR ə'kluːsɪv, -z
AM ə'klusɪv, -z
occult
BR 'ɒkʌlt, ə'kʌlt
AM ə'kəlt
occultation
BR ˌɒk(ʌ)l'teɪʃn, -z
AM ˌɑkəl'teɪʃən, -z
occultism
BR 'ɒk(ʌ)ltɪz(ə)m
AM ə'kəlˌtɪzəm
occultist
BR 'ɒk(ʌ)ltɪst, -s
AM ə'kəltəst, -s
occultly
BR 'ɒk(ʌ)ltli, ə'kʌltli
AM ə'kəltli
occultness
BR 'ɒk(ʌ)ltnəs, ə'kʌltnəs
AM ə'kəltnəs
occupancy
BR 'ɒkjʉp(ə)nsi
AM 'ɑkjəpənsi
occupant
BR 'ɒkjʉp(ə)nt, -s
AM 'ɑkjəpənt, -s
occupation
BR ˌɒkjʉ'peɪʃn, -z
AM ˌɑkjə'peɪʃən, -z
occupational
BR ˌɒkjʉ'peɪʃn̩(ə)l, ˌɒkjʉ'peɪʃən(ə)l
AM ˌɑkjə'peɪʃ(ə)nəl
occupationally
BR ˌɒkjʉ'peɪʃn̩əli, ˌɒkjʉ'peɪʃn̩l̩i, ˌɒkjʉ'peɪʃənl̩i, ˌɒkjʉ'peɪʃ(ə)nəli
AM ˌɑkjə'peɪʃ(ə)nəli
occupier
BR 'ɒkjʉpʌɪə(r), -z
AM 'ɑkjəˌpaɪər, -z
occupy
BR 'ɒkjʉpʌɪ, -z, -ɪŋ, -d
AM 'ɑkjəˌpaɪ, -z, -ɪŋ, -d
occur
BR ə'kəː(r), -z, -ɪŋ, -d
AM ə'kər, -z, -ɪŋ, -d
occurrence
BR ə'kʌrəns, ə'kʌrn̩s, -ɪz
AM ə'kərəns, -əz
occurrent
BR ə'kʌrənt, ə'kʌrn̩t
AM ə'kərənt
ocean
BR 'əʊʃn, -z
AM 'oʊʃən, -z
oceanaria
BR ˌəʊʃə'nɛːrɪə(r)
AM ˌoʊʃə'nɛriə
oceanarium
BR ˌəʊʃə'nɛːrɪəm, -z
AM ˌoʊʃə'nɛriəm, -z
oceanfront
BR 'əʊʃnfrʌnt
AM 'oʊʃənˌfrənt
ocean-going
BR ˌəʊʃn'gəʊɪŋ
AM 'oʊʃənˌgoʊɪŋ
Oceania
BR ˌəʊsɪ'ɑːnɪə(r), ˌəʊʃɪ'ɑːnɪə(r), ˌəʊsɪ'eɪnɪə(r), ˌəʊʃɪ'eɪnɪə(r)
AM ˌoʊʃi'æniə
Oceanian
BR ˌəʊsɪ'ɑːnɪən, ˌəʊʃɪ'ɑːnɪən, ˌəʊsɪ'eɪnɪən, ˌəʊʃɪ'eɪnɪən, -z
AM ˌoʊʃi'æniən, -z
oceanic
BR ˌəʊʃɪ'anɪk, ˌəʊsɪ'anɪk
AM ˌoʊʃi'ænɪk
Oceanid
BR əʊ'siːənɪd, 'əʊʃn̩ɪd, -z
AM oʊ'siənɪd, -z
oceanographer
BR ˌəʊʃə'nɒgrəfə(r), -z
AM ˌoʊʃə'nɑgrəfər, -z
oceanographic
BR ˌəʊʃ(ə)nə'grafɪk, ˌəʊʃn̩ə'grafɪk
AM ˌoʊʃənə'græfɪk
oceanographical
BR ˌəʊʃ(ə)nə'grafɪkl, ˌəʊʃn̩ə'grafɪkl
AM ˌoʊʃənə'græfəkəl
oceanography
BR ˌəʊʃə'nɒgrəfi
AM ˌoʊʃə'nɑgrəfi
Oceanus
BR əʊ'siːənəs, əʊ'ʃiːənəs
AM oʊ'siənəs
oceanward
BR 'əʊʃnwəd
AM 'oʊʃənwərd
ocellar
BR ə(ʊ)'sɛlə(r), ɒ'sɛlə(r)
AM oʊ'sɛlər
ocellate
BR 'ɒsɪlət
AM oʊ'sɛˌleɪt, oʊ'sɛlət, 'ɑsələt
ocellated
BR 'ɒsɪleɪtɪd
AM 'ɑsəˌleɪdəd
ocelli
BR ə(ʊ)'sɛlʌɪ, ɒ'sɛlʌɪ
AM oʊ'sɛˌlaɪ
ocellus
BR ə(ʊ)'sɛləs, ɒ'sɛləs
AM oʊ'sɛləs
ocelot
BR 'ɒsɪlɒt, 'ɒsl̩ɒt, -s
AM 'ɑsəˌlɑt, 'oʊsəˌlɑt, -s
och
BR ɒx
AM ɑx
oche
BR 'ɒk|i, -ɪz
AM 'ɑki, -z
ocher
BR 'əʊkə(r)
AM 'oʊkər
Ochil
BR 'əʊxl, 'əʊkl
AM 'oʊkəl
ochlocracy
BR ɒk'lɒkrəs|i, -ɪz
AM ɑk'lɑkrəsi, -z
ochlocrat
BR 'ɒkləkrat, -s
AM 'ɑkləˌkræt, -s
ochlocratic
BR ˌɒklə'kratɪk
AM ˌɑklə'krædɪk
ochone
BR əʊ'həʊn, ɒ'xəʊn
AM oʊ'hoʊn
ochre
BR 'əʊkə(r)
AM 'oʊkər
ochrea
BR 'ɒkrɪə(r), -z
AM 'ɑkriə, -z
ochreae
BR 'ɒkrɪiː
AM 'ɑkrii
ochreish
BR 'əʊk(ə)rɪʃ
AM 'oʊk(ə)rɪʃ
ochreous
BR 'əʊkrɪəs, 'əʊk(ə)rəs
AM 'oʊk(ə)rəs
ochrous
BR 'əʊkrəs
AM 'oʊk(ə)rəs
ochry
BR 'əʊkri
AM 'oʊk(ə)ri
ocker
BR 'ɒkə(r), -z
AM 'ɑkər, -z
o'clock
BR ə'klɒk
AM ə'klɑk
O'Connell
BR ə(ʊ)'kɒnl
AM ə'kɑnəl, oʊ'kɑnəl
O'Connor
BR ə(ʊ)'kɒnə(r)
AM ə'kɑnər, oʊ'kɑnər
Ocracoke
BR 'əʊkrəkəʊk
AM 'oʊkrəˌkoʊk
octachord
BR 'ɒktəkɔːd, -z
AM 'ɑktəˌkɔ(ə)rd, -z
octad
BR 'ɒktad, -z
AM 'ɑkˌtæd, -z
octagon
BR 'ɒktəg(ə)n, -z
AM 'ɑktəˌgɑn, 'ɑktəgən, -z
octagonal
BR ɒk'tagn̩(ə)l
AM ɑk'tægənəl
octagonally
BR ɒk'tagn̩l̩i, ɒk'tagn̩əli
AM ɑk'tægənəli
octahedra
BR ˌɒktə'hiːdrə(r)
AM ˌɑktə'hidrə
octahedral
BR ˌɒktə'hiːdr(ə)l
AM ˌɑktə'hidrəl
octahedron
BR ˌɒktə'hiːdrən, -z
AM ˌɑktə'hidrən, -z
octal
BR 'ɒktl, -z
AM 'ɑktl, -z
octamerous
BR ɒk'tam(ə)rəs
AM ɑk'tæm(ə)rəs
octameter
BR ɒk'tamɪtə(r), -z
AM ɑk'tæmədər, -z
octane
BR 'ɒkteɪn
AM 'ɑkˌteɪn
Octans
BR 'ɒktanz
AM 'ɑktənz
octant
BR 'ɒkt(ə)nt, -s
AM 'ɑktnt, -s
octarchy
BR 'ɒktɑːk|i, -ɪz
AM 'ɑkˌtɑrki, -z
octaroon
BR ˌɒktə'ruːn, -z
AM ˌɑktə'run, -z
octastyle
BR 'ɒktəstʌɪl, -z

AM 'ɑktəˌstaɪl, -z
Octateuch
BR 'ɒktətjuːk, 'ɒktətʃuːk
AM 'ɑktəˌt(j)uk
octavalent
BR ˌɒktə'veɪlənt, ˌɒktə'veɪln̩t
AM ˌɑktə'veɪlənt
octave
BR 'ɒktɪv, 'ɒkteɪv, -z
AM 'ɑktəv, 'ɑkˌteɪv, -z
Octavia
BR ɒk'teɪvɪə(r)
AM ɑk'teɪviə
Octavian
BR ɒk'teɪvɪən
AM ɑk'teɪviən
Octavius
BR ɒk'teɪvɪəs
AM ɑk'teɪviəs
8vo
octavo
BR ɒk'tɑːvəʊ
AM ɑk'tɑvoʊ
octavo
BR ɒk'tɑːvəʊ, ɒk'teɪvəʊ, -z
AM ɑk'tɑvoʊ, -z
octennial
BR ɒk'tɛnɪəl
AM ɑk'tɛniəl
octennially
BR ɒk'tɛnɪəli
AM ɑk'tɛniəli
octet
BR ɒk'tɛt, -s
AM ɑk'tɛt, -s
octette
BR ɒk'tɛt, -s
AM ɑk'tɛt, -s
October
BR ɒk'təʊbə(r), -z
AM ɑk'toʊbər, -z
Octobrist
BR ɒk'təʊbrɪst, -s
AM ɑk'toʊbrəst, -s
octocentenary
BR ˌɒktəʊsɛn'tiːn(ə)r|i, ˌɒktəʊsɛn'tɛn(ə)r|i, -ɪz
AM ˌɑktoʊˌsɛn'tɛnəri, -z
octodecimo
BR ˌɒktəʊ'dɛsɪməʊ, -z
AM ˌɑktoʊ'dɛsəˌmoʊ, -z
octogenarian
BR ˌɒktədʒɪ'nɛːrɪən, -z
AM ˌɑktədʒə'nɛriən, -z
octonarian
BR ˌɒktə(ʊ)'nɛːrɪən, -z
AM ˌɑktə'nɛriən, -z
octonarii
BR ˌɒktə(ʊ)'nɛːrɪʌɪ
AM ˌɑktə'nɛriˌaɪ
octonarius
BR ˌɒktə(ʊ)'nɛːrɪəs
AM ˌɑktə'nɛriəs
octonary
BR 'ɒktə(ʊ)n(ə)r|i, -ɪz
AM 'ɑktəˌnɛri, -z
octopod
BR 'ɒktəpɒd, -z
AM 'ɑktəˌpɑd, -z
octopus
BR 'ɒktəpəs, -ɪz
AM 'ɑktəpəs, -əz
octoroon
BR ˌɒktə'ruːn, -z
AM ˌɑktə'run, -z
octosyllabic
BR ˌɒktəʊsɪ'labɪk
AM ˌɑktəsə'læbɪk, ˌɑktoʊsə'læbɪk
octosyllable
BR 'ɒktəʊˌsɪləbl, ˌɒktəʊ'sɪləbl, -z
AM ˌɑktə'sɪləbəl, -z
octroi
BR 'ɒktrwɑː, -z
AM ɑk'trwɑ, 'ɑk'trɔɪ, -z
octuple
BR 'ɒktjʊpl, ɒk'tjuːpl, -z
AM ɑk't(j)əpəl, -z
octyl
BR 'ɒktʌɪl, 'ɒktɪl
AM 'ɑktl
ocular
BR 'ɒkjʊlə(r)
AM 'ɑkjələr
ocularist
BR 'ɒkjʊlərɪst, -s
AM 'ɑkjələrəst, -s
ocularly
BR 'ɒkjʊləli
AM 'ɑkjələrli
ocular spectra
BR ˌɒkjʊlə 'spɛktrə(r)
AM ˌɑkjələr 'spɛktrə
ocular spectrum
BR ˌɒkjʊlə 'spɛktrəm
AM ˌɑkjələr 'spɛktrəm
oculate
BR 'ɒkjʊlət
AM 'ɑkjələt, 'ɑkjəˌleɪt
oculist
BR 'ɒkjʊlɪst, -s
AM 'ɑkjələst, -s
oculistic
BR ˌɒkjʊ'lɪstɪk
AM ˌɑkjə'lɪstɪk
oculonasal
BR ˌɒkjʊləʊ'neɪzl
AM ˌɑkjələ'neɪzəl
OD
BR ˌəʊ'diː, -z, -ɪŋ, -d
AM ˌoʊ'di, -z, -ɪŋ, -d
od
God
BR ɒd
AM ɑd, ɔd
odal
BR 'əʊdl, -z
AM 'oʊdəl, -z
odalisk
BR 'əʊdəlɪsk, 'əʊdl̩ɪsk, 'ɒdəlɪsk, 'ɒdl̩ɪsk, -s
AM 'oʊdlˌɪsk, ˌoʊdl'ɪsk, -s
odalisque
BR 'əʊdəlɪsk, 'əʊdl̩ɪsk, 'ɒdəlɪsk, 'ɒdl̩ɪsk, -s
AM 'oʊdlˌɪsk, ˌoʊdl'ɪsk, -s
odd
BR ɒd, -z, -ə(r), -ɪst
AM ɑd, -z, -ər, -əst
oddball
BR 'ɒdbɔːl, -z
AM 'ɔdˌbɔl, 'ɑdˌbɑl, -z
Oddfellow
BR 'ɒdˌfɛləʊ, -z
AM 'ɑdˌfɛloʊ, -z
Oddie
BR 'ɒdi
AM 'ɑdi
oddish
BR 'ɒdɪʃ
AM 'ɑdɪʃ
oddity
BR 'ɒdɪt|i, -ɪz
AM 'ɑdədi, -z
oddly
BR 'ɒdli
AM 'ɑdli
oddment
BR 'ɒdm(ə)nt, -s
AM 'ɑdmənt, -s
oddness
BR 'ɒdnəs
AM 'ɑdnəs
odds and ends
BR ˌɒdz(ə)n(d)'ɛndz
AM ˌɑdzən'ɛn(d)z
odds-on
BR ˌɒdz'ɒn
AM ˌɑdz'ɑn
ode
BR əʊd, -z
AM oʊd, -z
O'Dea
BR ə(ʊ)'deɪ, ə(ʊ)'diː
AM oʊ'deɪ
odea
BR 'əʊdɪə(r)
AM 'oʊdiə
Odell
BR ə(ʊ)'dɛl, 'əʊdl
AM ə'dɛl, oʊ'dɛl
Odense
BR 'əʊdənsə(r)
AM 'oʊdənsə
DAN 'oːˀðənsə
Odeon
BR 'əʊdɪən, -z
AM 'oʊdiˌɑn, -z
Oder
BR 'əʊdə(r)
AM 'oʊdər
Odessa
BR ə(ʊ)'dɛsə(r)
AM oʊ'dɛsə
RUS a'dʲesə
Odets
BR 'əʊdɛts
AM oʊ'dɛts
Odette
BR ə(ʊ)'dɛt
AM ɔ'dɛt, oʊ'dɛt
odeum
BR 'əʊdɪəm
AM 'oʊdiəm
Odham
BR 'ɒdəm
AM 'ɑdəm
Odiham
BR 'əʊdɪ(h)əm
AM 'oʊdiəm
Odin
BR 'əʊdɪn
AM 'oʊdən
odious
BR 'əʊdɪəs
AM 'oʊdiəs
odiously
BR 'əʊdɪəsli
AM 'oʊdiəsli
odiousness
BR 'əʊdɪəsnəs
AM 'oʊdiəsnəs
odium
BR 'əʊdɪəm
AM 'oʊdiəm
Odo
BR 'əʊdəʊ
AM 'oʊdoʊ
O'Doherty
BR ə(ʊ)'dɒxəti, ə(ʊ)'dɒhəti, ə(ʊ)'dɒkəti
AM oʊ'dɔrdi
Odom
BR 'əʊdəm
AM 'oʊdəm
odometer
BR ə(ʊ)'dɒmɪtə(r), -z
AM oʊ'dɑmədər, -z
odometry
BR ə(ʊ)'dɒmɪtri
AM oʊ'dɑmətri
Odonata
BR ˌəʊdə'nɑːtə(r)
AM ˌoʊdn̩'ɑdə, oʊ'dɑnədə
odonate
BR 'əʊdəneɪt, -s
AM 'oʊdn̩ət, 'oʊdnˌeɪt, -s
O'Donnell
BR ə(ʊ)'dɒnl
AM ə'dɑnəl, oʊ'dɑnəl
O'Donoghue
BR ə(ʊ)'dɒnəhjuː
AM oʊ'dɑnəhju

O'Donovan
BR ə(ʊ)'dɒnəv(ə)n, ə(ʊ)'dʌnəv(ə)n
AM oʊ'dɑnəvən

odontoglossum
BR ɒ,dɒntə'glɒsəm, əʊ,dɒntə'glɒsəm, -z
AM oʊ,dɑn(t)ə'glɑsəm, -z

odontoid
BR ɒ'dɒntɔɪd, əʊ'dɒntɔɪd
AM oʊ'dɑn,tɔɪd

odontological
BR ɒ,dɒntə'lɒdʒɪkl, əʊ,dɒntə'lɒdʒɪkl
AM oʊ,dɑn(t)ə'lɑdʒəkəl

odontologist
BR ,ɒdɒn'tɒlədʒɪst, ,əʊdɒn'tɒlədʒɪst, -s
AM oʊdn'tɑlədʒəst, -s

odontology
BR ,ɒdɒn'tɒlədʒi, ,əʊdɒn'tɒlədʒi
AM ,oʊdn'tɑlədʒi

odontorhynchous
BR ɒ,dɒntə'rɪŋkəs, əʊ,dɒntə'rɪŋkəs
AM oʊ¦dɑn(t)ə¦rɪŋkəs

odor
BR 'əʊdə(r), -z
AM 'oʊdər, -z

odoriferous
BR ,əʊdə'rɪf(ə)rəs
AM ¦oʊdə'rɪf(ə)rəs

odoriferously
BR ,əʊdə'rɪf(ə)rəsli
AM ¦oʊdə'rɪf(ə)rəsli

odoriferousness
BR ,əʊdə'rɪf(ə)rəsnəs
AM ¦oʊdə'rɪf(ə)rəsnəs

odorless
BR 'əʊdələs
AM 'oʊdərləs

Odo-Ro-No
BR ,əʊdə(ʊ)'rəʊnəʊ
AM ,oʊdoʊ'roʊnoʊ

odorous
BR 'əʊd(ə)rəs
AM 'oʊdərəs

odorously
BR 'əʊd(ə)rəsli
AM 'oʊdərəsli

odorousness
BR 'əʊd(ə)rəsnəs
AM 'oʊdərəsnəs

odour
BR 'əʊdə(r), -z
AM 'oʊdər, -z

odourless
BR 'əʊdələs
AM 'oʊdərləs

O'Dowd
BR ə(ʊ)'daʊd
AM oʊ'daʊd

O'Driscoll
BR ə(ʊ)'drɪskl
AM oʊ'drɪskəl

O'Dwyer
BR ə(ʊ)'dwʌɪə(r)
AM oʊ'dwaɪər

Odyssean
BR ə(ʊ)'dɪsɪən, ɒ'dɪsɪən
AM ə'disiən

Odysseus
BR ə(ʊ)'dɪsjuːs, ɒ'dɪsjuːs, ə(ʊ)'dɪsɪəs, ɒ'dɪsɪəs
AM ə'disiəs

odyssey
BR 'ɒdɪs|i, -ɪz
AM 'ɑdəsi, -z

oecist
BR 'iːsɪst, 'iːkɪst, -s
AM 'isɪst, -s

oecumenical
BR ,iːkjʊ'mɛnɪkl, ,ɛkjʊ'mɛnɪkl
AM ¦ɛkjə'mɛnəkəl

oecumenicalism
BR ,iːkjʊ'mɛnɪkəlɪz(ə)m, ,iːkjʊ'mɛnɪkl̩ɪz(ə)m, ,ɛkjʊ'mɛnɪkəlɪz(ə)m, ,ɛkjʊ'mɛnɪkl̩ɪz(ə)m
AM ,ɛkjə'mɛnəkə,lɪzəm

oecumenically
BR ,iːkjʊ'mɛnɪkli, ,ɛkjʊ'mɛnɪkli
AM ¦ɛkjə'mɛnək(ə)li

oecumenicity
BR ɪ,kjuːmə'nɪsɪti
AM ,ɛkjəmə'nɪsɪdi

oecumenism
BR ɪ'kjuːmənɪz(ə)m
AM 'ɛkjəmə,nɪzəm, ɛ'kjʊmə,nɪzəm

oedema
BR ɪ'diːmə(r), iː'diːmə(r), -z
AM ə'dimə, i'dimə, -z

oedematose
BR ɪ'diːmətəʊs, iː'diːmətəʊs
AM ə'dimə,toʊs, ə'dimə,toʊz

oedematous
BR ɪ'diːmətəs, iː'diːmətəs
AM ə'dɛmədəs

Oedipal
BR 'iːdɪpl
AM 'ɛdəpəl, 'idəpəl

Oedipus
BR 'iːdɪpəs
AM 'ɛdəpəs, 'idəpəs

œillade
BR əː'jɑːd, -z
AM ə'jɑd, eɪ'jɑd, -z

oenological
BR ,iːnə'lɒdʒɪkl
AM ,inə'lɑdʒəkəl

oenologist
BR iː'nɒlədʒɪst
AM i'nɑlədʒəst

oenology
BR iː'nɒlədʒi
AM i'nɑlədʒi

Oenone
BR 'iːnəʊn
AM i'noʊni

oenophile
BR 'iːnəfʌɪl
AM 'inə,faɪl

oenophilist
BR iː'nɒfɪlɪst
AM i'nɑfələst

o'er
BR 'əʊə(r)
AM 'oʊ(ə)r

Oerlikon®
BR 'əːlɪkɒn, 'əːlɪk(ə)n
AM 'ərləkən, 'ərlə,kɑn

oersted
BR 'əːstɪd, 'əːstɛd, -z
AM 'ər,stɛd, -z

oesophageal
BR ɪ,sɒfə'dʒiːəl, iː,sɒfə'dʒiːəl
AM ə¦sɑfə'dʒiəl

oesophagi
BR ɪ'sɒfəgʌɪ, iː'sɒfəgʌɪ, ɪ'sɒfədʒʌɪ, iː'sɒfədʒʌɪ
AM ə'sɑfə,gaɪ, ə'sɑfə,dʒaɪ

oesophagus
BR ɪ'sɒfəgəs, iː'sɒfəgəs, -ɪz
AM ə'sɑfəgəs, -əz

oestral
BR 'iːstr(ə)l, 'ɛstr(ə)l
AM 'ɛstrəl

oestrogen
BR 'iːstrədʒ(ə)n, 'ɛstrədʒ(ə)n
AM 'ɛstrədʒən

oestrogenic
BR ,iːstrə'dʒɛnɪk, ,ɛstrə'dʒɛnɪk
AM ,ɛstrə'dʒɛnɪk

oestrogenically
BR ,iːstrə'dʒɛnɪkli, ,ɛstrə'dʒɛnɪkli
AM ,ɛstrə'dʒɛnək(ə)li

oestrous
BR 'iːstrəs, 'ɛstrəs
AM 'ɛstrəs

oestrum
BR 'iːstrəm, 'ɛstrəm
AM 'ɛstrəm

oestrus
BR 'iːstrəs, 'ɛstrəs
AM 'ɛstrəs

oeuvre
BR 'əːvrə(r)
AM 'ʊvrə

of[1]
strong form
BR ɒv
AM əv

of[2]
weak form
BR əv, ə
AM əv, ə

O'Faolain
BR ə(ʊ)'feɪlən, ə(ʊ)'falən
AM oʊ'feɪlən

ofay
BR 'əʊfeɪ, -z
AM 'oʊ,feɪ, -z

off
BR ɒf
AM ɔf, ɑf

Offa
BR 'ɒfə(r)
AM 'ɔfə, 'ɑfə

offal
BR 'ɒfl
AM 'ɔfəl, 'ɑfəl

Offaly
BR 'ɒfl̩i, 'ɒfəli
AM 'ɔfəli, 'ɑfəli

off and on
BR ,ɒf (ə)n(d) 'ɒn
AM ¦ɔf ən 'ɔn, ¦ɑf ən 'ɑn

offbeat
noun
BR 'ɒfbiːt, -s
AM 'ɔf,bit, 'ɑf,bit, -s

off-beat
adjective
BR 'ɒfbiːt
AM ¦ɔf'bit, ,ɑf'bit

off-cast
BR 'ɒfkɑːst, 'ɒfkast, -s
AM 'ɔf,kæst, 'ɑf,kæst, -s

off-chance
BR 'ɒftʃɑːns, 'ɒftʃans
AM ¦ɔf,tʃæns, ¦ɑf,tʃæns

offcut
BR 'ɒfkʌt, -s
AM 'ɔf,kət, 'ɑf,kət, -s

Offenbach
BR 'ɒfnbɑːk
AM 'ɔfən,bɑk, 'ɑfən,bɑk

offence
BR ə'fɛns, -ɪz
AM ə'fɛns, 'ɔ,fɛns, 'ɑ,fɛns, -əz

offenceless
BR ə'fɛnsləs
AM ə'fɛnsləs, 'ɔ,fɛnsləs, 'ɑ,fɛnsləs

offend
BR ə'fɛnd, -z, -ɪŋ, -ɪd
AM ə'fɛnd, -z, -ɪŋ, -əd

offendedly
BR ə'fɛndɪdli
AM ə'fɛndədli

offender
BR ə'fɛndə(r), -z
AM ə'fɛndər, -z

offense
BR ə'fɛns, -ɪz

AM ə'fɛns, 'ɔˌfɛns, 'ɑˌfɛns, -əz

offenseless
BR ə'fɛnsləs
AM ə'fɛnsləs, 'ɔˌfɛnsləs, 'ɑˌfɛnsləs

offensive
BR ə'fɛnsɪv
AM ə'fɛnsɪv, 'ɔˌfɛnsɪv, 'ɑˌfɛnsɪv

offensively
BR ə'fɛnsɨvli
AM ə'fɛnsɨvli, 'ɔˌfɛnsɨvli, 'ɑˌfɛnsɨvli

offensiveness
BR ə'fɛnsɨvnɨs
AM ə'fɛnsɪvnɨs, 'ɔˌfɛnsɪvnɨs, 'ɑˌfɛnsɪvnɨs

offer
BR 'ɒf|ə(r), -əz, -(ə)rɪŋ, -əd
AM 'ɔf|ər, 'ɑf|ər, -ərz, -(ə)rɪŋ, -ərd

offerer
BR 'ɒf(ə)rə(r), -z
AM 'ɔf(ə)rər, 'ɑf(ə)rər, -z

offering
BR 'ɒf(ə)rɪŋ, -z
AM 'ɔf(ə)rɪŋ, ɑf(ə)rɪŋ, -z

offeror
BR 'ɒf(ə)rə(r), -z
AM 'ɔf(ə)rər, 'ɑf(ə)rər, -z

offertory
BR 'ɒfət(ə)r|i, -ɪz
AM 'ɔfərˌtɔri, 'ɑfərˌtɔri, -z

offhand
BR ˌɒf'hand
AM ¦ɔf¦hænd, ¦ɑf¦hænd

offhanded
BR ˌɒf'handɨd
AM 'ɔf¦hæn(d)əd, 'ɑf¦hæn(d)əd

offhandedly
BR ˌɒf'handɨdli
AM 'ɔf¦hæn(d)ədli, 'ɑf¦hæn(d)ədli

offhandedness
BR ˌɒf'handɨdnɨs
AM 'ɔf¦hæn(d)ədnəs, 'ɑf¦hændə(d)nəs

office
BR 'ɒf|ɪs, -ɨsɨz
AM 'ɔfəs, 'ɑfəs, -əz

officeholder
BR 'ɒfɪsˌhəʊldə(r), -z
AM 'ɔfəsˌ(h)oʊldər, 'ɑfəsˌ(h)oʊldər, -z

officer
BR 'ɒfɪsə(r), -z
AM 'ɔfəsər, 'ɑfəsər, -z

official
BR ə'fɪʃl, -z
AM ə'fɪʃəl, oʊ'fɪʃəl, -z

officialdom
BR ə'fɪʃldəm
AM ə'fɪʃəldəm, oʊ'fɪʃəldəm

officialese
BR əˌfɪʃə'liːz, əˌfɪʃl'iːz
AM əˌfɪʃə¦liz, oʊˌfɪʃə¦liz

officialism
BR ə'fɪʃl̩ɪz(ə)m
AM ə'fɪʃəˌlɪzəm, oʊ'fɪʃəˌlɪzəm

officially
BR ə'fɪʃl̩i, ə'fɪʃəli
AM ə'fɪʃəli, oʊ'fɪʃəli

officiant
BR ə'fɪʃɪənt, -s
AM ə'fɪʃiənt, oʊ'fɪʃiənt, -s

officiate
BR ə'fɪʃɪeɪt, -s, -ɪŋ, -ɨd
AM ə'fɪʃiˌeɪ|t, oʊ'fɪʃiˌeɪ|t, -ts, -dɪŋ, -dɨd

officiation
BR əˌfɪʃɪ'eɪʃn
AM əˌfɪʃi'eɪʃən, oʊˌfɪʃi'eɪʃən

officiator
BR ə'fɪʃɪeɪtə(r), -z
AM ə'fɪʃiˌeɪdər, oʊ'fɪʃiˌeɪdər, -z

officinal
BR ˌɒfɪ'siːnl, ə'fɪsɪnl
AM ə'fɪsənəl

officinally
BR ˌɒfɪ'siːnl̩i, ˌɒfɪ'siːnəli, ə'fɪsɪnl̩i, ə'fɪsɪnəli
AM ə'fɪsənəli

officious
BR ə'fɪʃəs
AM ə'fɪʃəs

officiously
BR ə'fɪʃəsli
AM ə'fɪʃəsli

officiousness
BR ə'fɪʃəsnəs
AM ə'fɪʃəsnəs

offing
BR 'ɒfɪŋ
AM 'ɔfɪŋ, 'ɑfɪŋ

offish
BR 'ɒfɪʃ
AM 'ɔfɪʃ, 'ɑfɪʃ

offishly
BR 'ɒfɨʃli
AM 'ɔfɨʃli, 'ɑfɨʃli

offishness
BR 'ɒfɨʃnɨs
AM 'ɔfɨʃnɨs, 'ɑfɨʃnɨs

offload
BR ˌɒfl'əʊd, -z, -ɪŋ, -ɨd
AM ¦ɔfˌloʊd, ¦ɑfˌloʊd, -z, -ɪŋ, -əd

offprint
BR 'ɒfprɪnt, -s
AM 'ɔfˌprɪnt, 'ɑfˌprɪnt, -s

off-putting
BR 'ɒfˌpʊtɪŋ, ˌɒf'pʊtɪŋ
AM 'ɔfˌpʊdɪŋ, 'ɑfˌpʊdɪŋ

off-puttingly
BR 'ɒfˌpʊtɪŋli, ˌɒf'pʊtɪŋli
AM 'ɔfˌpʊdɪŋli, 'ɑfˌpʊdɪŋli

offset[1]
noun
BR 'ɒfsɛt, -s
AM 'ɔfˌsɛt, 'ɑfˌsɛt, -s

offset[2]
verb
BR 'ɒfsɛt, ˌɒf'sɛt, -s, -ɪŋ
AM ˌɔf'sɛ|t, ˌɑf'sɛ|t, -ts, -dɪŋ

offshoot
BR 'ɒfʃuːt, -s
AM 'ɔfˌʃut, 'ɑfˌʃut, -s

offshore
BR ˌɒf'ʃɔː(r)
AM ¦ɔf¦ʃɔ(ə)r, ¦ɑf¦ʃɔ(ə)r

offside
BR ˌɒf'sʌɪd, -z
AM ¦ɔf¦saɪd, ¦ɑf¦saɪd, -z

offsider
BR ˌɒ'fsʌɪdə(r), -z
AM ¦ɔf¦saɪdər, ¦ɑf¦saɪdər, -z

offspring
BR 'ɒfsprɪŋ, -z
AM 'ɔfˌsprɪŋ, 'ɑfˌsprɪŋ, -z

offstage
BR ˌɒf'steɪdʒ
AM ¦ɔf'steɪdʒ, ¦ɑf'steɪdʒ

off stage
adverbial
BR ˌɒf 'steɪdʒ
AM ¦ɔf 'steɪdʒ, ¦ɑf +

Ofgas
BR 'ɒfgas
AM 'ɔfˌgæs, 'ɑfˌgæs

O'Flaherty
BR ə(ʊ)'flɑː(h)əti
AM oʊ'flɛrdi

O'Flynn
BR ə(ʊ)'flɪn
AM oʊ'flɪn

oft
BR ɒft
AM ɔft, ɑft

Oftel
BR 'ɒftɛl
AM 'ɔfˌtɛl, 'ɑfˌtɛl

often
BR 'ɒf(t)n̩, 'ɒftən, -ə(r), -ɨst
AM 'ɔf(t)ən, 'ɑf(t)ən, -ər, -əst

oftentimes
BR 'ɒfntʌɪmz, 'ɒft(ə)ntʌɪmz
AM 'ɔf(t)ənˌtaɪmz, 'ɑf(t)ənˌtaɪmz

Ofwat
BR 'ɒfwɒt
AM 'ɔfˌwɑt, 'ɑfˌwɑt

Ogaden
BR ˌɒgə'dɛn
AM ˌɔgə'dɛn, ˌɑgə'dɛn

ogam
BR 'ɒgəm, -z
AM 'ɑgəm, -z

Ogden
BR 'ɒgdən
AM 'ɑgdən

ogdoad
BR 'ɒgdəʊad, -z
AM 'ɑgdəˌwɑd, -z

Ogdon
BR 'ɒgdən
AM 'ɑgdən

ogee
BR 'əʊdʒiː, -z, -d
AM 'oʊdʒi, -z, -d

ogham
BR 'ɒgəm, -z
AM 'ɑgəm, -z

Ogilvie
BR 'əʊglvi
AM 'oʊgəlvi

Ogilvy
BR 'əʊglvi
AM 'oʊgəlvi

ogival
BR 'əʊdʒʌɪvl, əʊ'dʒʌɪvl
AM oʊ'dʒaɪvəl

ogive
BR 'əʊdʒʌɪv, əʊ'dʒʌɪv, -z
AM oʊ'dʒaɪv, -z

ogle
BR 'əʊg|l, -lz, -l̩ɪŋ\-lɪŋ, -ld
AM 'oʊg|əl, 'ɑg|əl, -əlz, -(ə)lɪŋ, -əld

ogler
BR 'əʊglə(r), 'əʊgl̩ə(r), -z
AM 'oʊg(ə)lər, 'ɑg(ə)lər, -z

Oglethorpe
BR 'əʊglθɔːp
AM 'oʊgəlˌθɔ(ə)rp

Ogmore
BR 'ɒgmɔː(r)
AM 'ɑgˌmɔ(ə)r

O'Gorman
BR ə(ʊ)'gɔːmən
AM oʊ'gɔrmən

OGPU
BR ˌəʊdʒiːpiː'juː, 'ɒgpuː
AM ˌoʊˌdʒiˌpi'ju, 'ɑgˌpu

O'Grady
BR ə(ʊ)'greɪdi
AM oʊ'greɪdi

ogre
BR 'əʊgə(r), -z
AM 'oʊgər, -z

ogreish
BR 'əʊg(ə)rɪʃ

AM ˈoʊɡ(ə)rɪʃ

ogreishly
BR ˈəʊɡ(ə)rɪʃli
AM ˈoʊɡ(ə)rɪʃli

ogress
BR ˈəʊɡrɪs, ˈəʊɡrɛs, -ɪz
AM ˈoʊɡrəs, -əz

ogrish
BR ˈəʊɡ(ə)rɪʃ
AM ˈoʊɡ(ə)rɪʃ

Ogwen
BR ˈɒɡwɛn, ˈɒɡwən
AM ˈɑɡwən
WE ˈɒɡwen

Ogygian
BR əʊˈdʒɪdʒɪən
AM oʊˈdʒɪdʒiən

oh
BR əʊ
AM oʊ

O'Hagan
BR ə(ʊ)ˈheɪɡ(ə)n
AM oʊˈheɪɡən

O'Halloran
BR ə(ʊ)ˈhalərən, ə(ʊ)ˈhalərn̩
AM oʊˈhælərən

O'Hanlon
BR ə(ʊ)ˈhanlən
AM oʊˈhænlən

O'Hara
BR ə(ʊ)ˈhɑːrə(r)
AM oʊˈhɛrə

O'Hare
BR ə(ʊ)ˈhɛː(r)
AM oʊˈhɛ(ə)r

O'Higgins
BR ə(ʊ)ˈhɪɡɪnz
AM oʊˈhɪɡɪnz

Ohio
BR ə(ʊ)ˈhʌɪəʊ
AM oʊˈhaɪoʊ

Ohioan
BR ə(ʊ)ˈhʌɪəʊən, -z
AM oʊˈhaɪoʊən, -z

ohm
BR əʊm, -z
AM oʊm, -z

ohmage
BR ˈəʊmɪdʒ
AM ˈoʊmɪdʒ

ohmic
BR ˈəʊmɪk
AM ˈoʊmɪk

ohmmeter
BR ˈəʊmˌmiːtə(r), -z
AM ˈoʊ(m)ˌmidər, -z

oho
BR ə(ʊ)ˈhəʊ
AM oʊˈhoʊ

OHP
BR ˌəʊeɪtʃˈpiː, -z
AM ˌoʊˌeɪtʃˈpi, -z

oi
BR ɔɪ
AM ɔɪ

oick
BR ɔɪk, -s
AM ɔɪk, -s

oidia
BR əʊˈɪdɪə(r)
AM oʊˈɪdiə

oidium
BR əʊˈɪdɪəm
AM oʊˈɪdiəm

oik
BR ɔɪk, -s
AM ɔɪk, -s

oil
BR ɔɪl, -z, -ɪŋ, -d
AM ɔɪl, -z, -ɪŋ, -d

oilcake
BR ˈɔɪlkeɪk
AM ˈɔɪlˌkeɪk

oilcan
BR ˈɔɪlkan, -z
AM ˈɔɪlˌkæn, -z

oilcloth
BR ˈɔɪlklɒθ
AM ˈɔɪlˌklɔθ, ˈɔɪlˌklɑθ

oiler
BR ˈɔɪlə(r), -z
AM ˈɔɪlər, -z

oilfield
BR ˈɔɪlfiːld, -z
AM ˈɔɪlˌfild, -z

oilily
BR ˈɔɪlɨli
AM ˈɔɪlɨli

oiliness
BR ˈɔɪlɪnɨs
AM ˈɔɪlinɨs

oilless
BR ˈɔɪllɨs
AM ˈɔɪ(l)lɨs

oilman
BR ˈɔɪlman
AM ˈɔɪlˌmæn, ɔɪlmən

oilmen
BR ˈɔɪlmɛn
AM ˈɔɪlˌmɛn, ˈɔɪlmən

oilrig
BR ˈɔɪlrɪɡ, -z
AM ˈɔɪlˌrɪɡ, -z

oilseed
BR ˈɔɪlsiːd, -z
AM ˈɔɪlˌsid, -z

oilskin
BR ˈɔɪlskɪn, -z
AM ˈɔɪlˌskɪn, -z

oilstone
BR ˈɔɪlstəʊn, -z
AM ˈɔɪlˌstoʊn, -z

oily
BR ˈɔɪl|i, -ɪə(r), -ɪɨst
AM ˈɔɪli, -ər, -ɨst

oink
BR ɔɪŋ|k, -ks, -kɪŋ, -(k)t
AM ɔɪŋ|k, -ks, -kɪŋ, -(k)t

ointment
BR ˈɔɪntm(ə)nt, -s
AM ˈɔɪntmənt, -s

Oireachtas
BR ˈɛrəktəs, ˈɛrəxtəs
AM ˈɛrəkθəs
IR ˈorʲəxtəs

Oistrakh
BR ˈɔɪstrɑːk, ˈɔɪstrɑːx
AM ˈɔɪstrɑk

Ojibwa
BR ə(ʊ)ˈdʒɪbwə(r), -z
AM əˈdʒɪbwə, -z

Ojibway
BR ə(ʊ)ˈdʒɪbweɪ, -z
AM oʊˈdʒɪbweɪ, -z

OK
BR (ˌ)əʊˈkeɪ, -z, -ɪŋ, -d
AM ˌoʊˈkeɪ, -z, -ɪŋ, -d

okapi
BR ə(ʊ)ˈkɑːp|i, -ɪz
AM oʊˈkɑpi, -z

Okavango
BR ˌɒkəˈvaŋɡəʊ
AM ˌoʊkəˈvɑŋɡoʊ

okay
BR (ˌ)əʊˈkeɪ, -z, -ɪŋ, -d
AM ˌoʊˈkeɪ, -z, -ɪŋ, -d

O'Keefe
BR ə(ʊ)ˈkiːf
AM oʊˈkif

O'Keeffe
BR ə(ʊ)ˈkiːf
AM oʊˈkif

Okefenokee
BR ˌəʊkɪfɪˈnəʊki
AM ˌoʊkifəˈnoʊki

Okehampton
BR ˌəʊkˈham(p)t(ə)n
AM ˌoʊkˈhæm(p)tən

O'Kelly
BR ə(ʊ)ˈkɛli
AM oʊˈkɛli

okey-doke
BR ˌəʊkɪˈdəʊk
AM ˌoʊkiˈdoʊk

okey-dokey
BR ˌəʊkɪˈdəʊki
AM ˌoʊkiˈdoʊki

Okhotsk
BR əʊˈkɒtsk, ˈəʊkɒtsk
AM ˈɑˌkɑtsk

Okie
BR ˈəʊk|i, -ɪz
AM ˈoʊki, -z

Okinawa
BR ˌɒkɪˈnɑːwə(r), ˌəʊkɪˈnɑːwə(r)
AM ˌoʊkəˈnɑwə

Oklahoma
BR ˌəʊkləˈhəʊmə(r)
AM ˌoʊkləˈhoʊmə

Oklahoman
BR ˌəʊkləˈhəʊmən, -z
AM ˌoʊkləˈhoʊmən, -z

okra
BR ˈəʊkrə(r), ˈɒkrə(r)
AM ˈoʊkrə

okta
BR ˈɒktə(r), -z
AM ˈɑktə, -z

Olaf
BR ˈəʊlaf, ˈəʊləf
AM ˈoʊˌlɑf

Öland
BR ˈəːland
AM ˈəˌlɑnd
SW ˈəːlʌnd

Olav
BR ˈəʊlav, ˈəʊləv
AM ˈoʊləv

Olave
BR ˈəʊləv, ˈəʊleɪv
AM ˈoʊləv, ˈoʊleɪv

Olbers
BR ˈɒlbəz
AM ˈɔlbərz, ˈɑlbərz

old
BR əʊld, -ə(r), -ɨst
AM oʊld, -ər, -əst

Oldbury
BR ˈəʊl(d)b(ə)ri
AM ˈoʊl(d)ˌbɛri

Oldcastle
BR ˈəʊl(d)ˌkɑːsl, ˈəʊl(d)ˌkasl
AM ˈoʊl(d)ˌkæsəl

Old Dominion
BR ˌəʊl(d) dəˈmɪnjən
AM ˌoʊl(d) dəˈmɪnjən

olden
BR ˈəʊld(ə)n
AM ˈoʊldən

Oldenburg
BR ˈəʊld(ə)nbəːɡ
AM ˈoʊldənˌbərɡ

olde worlde
BR ˌəʊldɪ ˈwəːldi
AM ˈoʊl(d) ˈwərld(i)

old-fashioned
BR ˌəʊl(d)ˈfaʃnd
AM ˌoʊl(d)ˈfæʃənd

Oldfield
BR ˈəʊl(d)fiːld
AM ˈoʊl(d)ˌfild

Oldham
BR ˈəʊldəm
AM ˈoʊldˌhæm, ˈoʊldəm

oldie
BR ˈəʊld|i, -ɪz
AM ˈoʊldi, -z

oldish
BR ˈəʊldɪʃ
AM ˈoʊldɪʃ

old-maidish
BR ˌəʊl(d)ˈmeɪdɪʃ
AM ˌoʊl(d)ˈmeɪdɪʃ

oldness
BR ˈəʊldnəs
AM ˈoʊl(d)nəs

Old Sarum
BR ˌəʊl(d) ˈsɛːrəm
AM ˌoʊl(d) ˈsɛrəm

Oldsmobile
BR ˈəʊl(d)zməbiːl, -z
AM ˈoʊl(d)zməˌbil, -z

old-stager
BR ˌəʊl(d)ˈsteɪdʒə(r), -z
AM ˈoʊl(d)ˌsteɪdʒər, -z

oldster
BR ˈəʊldstə(r), -z
AM ˈoʊl(d)stər, -z

old-timer
BR ˌəʊl(d)ˈtʌɪmə(r), -z
AM ˈoʊl(d)ˌtaɪmər, -z

Olduvai Gorge
BR ˌɒldʉvʌɪ ˈɡɔːdʒ
AM ˈɔldəˌvaɪ ˌɡɔ(ə)rdʒ, ˈoʊldəˌvaɪ ˈɡɔ(ə)rdʒ

Old Vic
BR ˌəʊl(d) ˈvɪk
AM ˌoʊl(d) vɪk

olé
BR əʊˈleɪ
AM oʊˈleɪ

olea
BR ˈəʊlɪə(r)
AM ˈoʊliə

oleaceous
BR ˌəʊlɪˈeɪʃəs
AM ˌoʊliˈeɪʃəs

oleaginous
BR ˌəʊlɪˈadʒɪnəs
AM ˌoʊliˈædʒənəs

oleander
BR ˌəʊlɪˈandə(r), -z
AM ˈoʊliˌændər, -z

O'Leary
BR ə(ʊ)ˈlɪəri
AM oʊˈlɪri

oleaster
BR ˌəʊlɪˈastə(r), -z
AM ˈoʊliˌæstər, -z

oleate
BR ˈəʊlɪeɪt, -s
AM ˈoʊliˌeɪt, -s

olecranon
BR əʊˈlɛkrənɒn, ˌəʊlɪˈkreɪnɒn, -z
AM oʊˈlɛkrəˌnɑn, ˌoʊləˈkreɪˌnɑn, -z

olefin
BR ˈəʊlɪfɪn, -z
AM ˈoʊləfən, -z

olefine
BR ˈəʊlɪfiːn, ˈəʊlɪfɪn, -z
AM ˈoʊləfən, -z

Oleg
BR ˈəʊlɛɡ
AM ˈoʊlɛɡ

oleiferous
BR ˌəʊlɪˈɪf(ə)rəs
AM ˌoʊliˈɪf(ə)rəs

oleo
BR ˈəʊlɪəʊ
AM ˈoʊlioʊ

oleograph
BR ˈəʊlɪəɡrɑːf, ˈəʊlɪəɡraf, -s
AM ˈoʊlioʊˌɡræf, -s

oleomargarine
BR ˌəʊlɪəʊˌmɑːdʒəˈriːn, ˌəʊlɪəʊˌmɑːɡəˈriːn
AM ˌoʊlioʊˈmɑrdʒ(ə)rən

oleometer
BR ˌəʊlɪˈɒmɪtə(r), -z
AM ˌoʊliˈɑmədər, -z

oleo-resin
BR ˌəʊlɪəʊˈrɛzɪn, -z
AM ˈoʊlioʊˈrɛzən, -z

oleum
BR ˈəʊlɪəm
AM ˈoʊliəm

olfaction
BR ɒlˈfakʃn
AM ɑlˈfækʃən, oʊlˈfækʃən

olfactive
BR ɒlˈfaktɪv
AM ɑlˈfæktɪv, oʊlˈfæktɪv

olfactometer
BR ˌɒlfakˈtɒmɪtə(r), -z
AM ˌɑlfækˈtɑmədər, -z

olfactory
BR ɒlˈfakt(ə)ri
AM ɑlˈfækt(ə)ri, oʊlˈfækt(ə)ri

Olga
BR ˈɒlɡə(r)
AM ˈoʊlɡə

olibanum
BR ɒˈlɪbənəm
AM oʊˈlɪbənəm

Olifant
BR ˈɒlɪf(ə)nt
AM ˈɑləfənt

oligarch
BR ˈɒlɪɡɑːk, -s
AM ˈɑləˌɡɑrk, ˈoʊləˌɡɑrk, -s

oligarchic
BR ˌɒlɪˈɡɑːkɪk
AM ˈɑləˈɡɑrkɪk, ˈoʊləˈɡɑrkɪk

oligarchical
BR ˌɒlɪˈɡɑːkɪkl
AM ˈɑləˈɡɑrkəkəl, ˈoʊləˈɡɑrkəkəl

oligarchically
BR ˌɒlɪˈɡɑːkɪkli
AM ˈɑləˈɡɑrkək(ə)li, ˈoʊləˈɡɑrkək(ə)li

oligarchy
BR ˈɒlɪɡɑːk|i, -ɪz
AM ˈɑləˌɡɑrki, ˈoʊləˌɡɑrki, -z

oligocarpous
BR ˌɒlɪɡə(ʊ)ˈkɑːpəs
AM ˌɑləɡoʊˈkɑrpəs

Oligocene
BR ˈɒlɪɡə(ʊ)siːn, ɒˈlɪɡə(ʊ)siːn
AM ˈɑləɡoʊˌsin, əˈlɪɡəˌsin

oligoclase
BR ˈɒlɪɡə(ʊ)kleɪz
AM ˈɑləɡoʊˌkleɪs

oligodendrocyte
BR ˌɒlɪɡəʊˈdɛndrəsʌɪt, -s
AM ˈɑləɡoʊˈdɛndrəˌsaɪt, -s

oligodendroglia
BR ˌɒlɪɡə(ʊ)ˌdɛndrəˈɡlʌɪə(r)
AM ˌɑləɡoʊˌdɛndrəˈɡliə

oligomer
BR ˌɒlɪˈɡəʊmə(r), əˈlɪɡəmə(r), ɒˈlɪɡəmə(r), ˈɒlɪɡəmə(r), -z
AM ˈɑləɡəˌmɛ(ə)r, əˈlɪɡəˌmɛ(ə)r, -z

oligomerise
BR əˈlɪɡəmərʌɪz, -ɪz, -ɪŋ, -d
AM əˈlɪɡəməˌraɪz, -ɪz, -ɪŋ, -d

oligomerize
BR əˈlɪɡəmərʌɪz, -ɪz, -ɪŋ, -d
AM əˈlɪɡəməˌraɪz, -ɪz, -ɪŋ, -d

oligomerous
BR ˌɒlɪˈɡɒm(ə)rəs
AM ˌɑləˈɡɑm(ə)rəs

oligonucleotide
BR ˌɒlɪɡə(ʊ)ˈnjuːklɪətʌɪd
AM ˌɑləɡoʊˈn(j)ukliəˌtaɪd

oligopeptide
BR ˌɒlɪɡə(ʊ)ˈpɛptʌɪd
AM ˌɑləɡoʊˈpɛpˌtaɪd

oligopolist
BR ˌɒlɪˈɡɒpəlɪst, -s
AM ˌɑləˈɡɑpələst, -s

oligopolistic
BR ˌɒlɪˌɡɒpəˈlɪstɪk
AM ˌɑləɡəpəˈlɪstɪk

oligopoly
BR ˌɒlɪˈɡɒpəl|i, ˌɒlɪˈɡɒpl|i, -ɪz
AM ˌɑləˈɡɑpəli, -z

oligopsony
BR ˌɒlɪˈɡɒpsən|i, ˌɒlɪˈɡɒpsn̩|i, -ɪz
AM ˌɑləˈɡɑpsəni, -z

oligosaccharide
BR ˌɒlɪɡə(ʊ)ˈsakərʌɪd, -z
AM ˌɑləɡəˈsækəˌraɪd, -z

oligotrophic
BR ˌɒlɪɡəˈtrɒfɪk, ˌɒlɪɡəˈtrəʊfɪk
AM ˌɑləɡəˈtrɑfɪk

oligotrophy
BR ˌɒlɪˈɡɒtrəfi
AM ˌɑləˈɡɑtrəfi

olingo
BR ɒˈlɪŋɡəʊ, -z
AM əˈlɪŋɡoʊ, -z

olio
BR ˈəʊlɪəʊ, -z
AM ˈoʊlioʊ, -z

Oliphant
BR ˈɒlɪf(ə)nt
AM ˈɑləfənt

olivaceous
BR ˌɒlɪˈveɪʃəs
AM ˌɑləˈveɪʃəs

olivary
BR ˈɒlɪv(ə)ri
AM ˈɑləˌvɛri

olive
BR ˈɒlɪv, -z
AM ˈɑləv, -z

Oliver
BR ˈɒlɪvə(r)
AM ˈɑləvər

Olivet
BR ˈɒlɪvɛt, ˈɒlɪvɪt
AM ˌɑləˈvɛt

Olivetti®
BR ˌɒlɪˈvɛti
AM ˌɑləˈvɛdi

Olivia
BR əˈlɪvɪə(r), ɒˈlɪvɪə(r)
AM əˈlɪviə

Olivier
BR əˈlɪvɪeɪ, ɒˈlɪvɪeɪ, əˈlɪvɪə(r), ɒˈlɪvɪə(r)
AM əˈlɪvieɪ, oʊˈlɪvieɪ

olivine
BR ˈɒlɪviːn, ˌɒlɪˈviːn, -z
AM ˈɑləˌvin, -z

olla podrida
BR ˌɒlə pəˈdriːdə(r), -z
AM ˌɑlə pəˈdridə, ˌɔ(l)jə +, -z

Ollerenshaw
BR ˈɒl(ə)rənʃɔː(r), ˈɒl(ə)rn̩ʃɔː(r)
AM ˈɑlərənˌʃɔ

Ollerton
BR ˈɒlət(ə)n
AM ˈɑlərtən

Ollie
BR ˈɒli
AM ˈɑli

olm
BR ɒlm, əʊlm, -z
AM ɑlm, oʊlm, -z

Olmec
BR ˈɒlmɛk
AM ˈɑlˌmɛk

Olmsted
BR ˈɒmstɛd
AM ˈoʊmˌstɛd

ology
BR ˈɒlədʒ|i, -ɪz
AM ˈɑlədʒi, -z

oloroso
BR ˌɒləˈrəʊsəʊ, -z
AM ˌoʊləˈroʊˌsoʊ, -z

O'Loughlin
BR ə(ʊ)ˈlɒxlɪn, ə(ʊ)ˈlɒklɪn
AM oʊˈlɔflən, oʊˈlɑflən

Olsen
BR ˈɒls(ə)n

AM ˈoʊlsən

Olson
BR ˈɒls(ə)n
AM ˈoʊlsən

Olwen
BR ˈɒlwɪn
AM ˈɑlwən

Olympia
BR əˈlɪmpɪə(r)
AM əˈlɪmpiə

Olympiad
BR əˈlɪmpɪəd, əˈlɪmpɪad, -z
AM oʊˈlɪmpiˌæd, əˈlɪmpiəd, -z

Olympian
BR əˈlɪmpɪən, -z
AM əˈlɪmpiən, oʊˈlɪmpiən, -z

Olympic
BR əˈlɪmpɪk, -s
AM əˈlɪmpɪk, oʊˈlɪmpɪk, -s

Olympus
BR əˈlɪmpəs
AM əˈlɪmpəs

om
BR əʊm, ɒm
AM ɔm, oʊm, ɑm

Omagh
BR ˈəʊmə(r), əʊˈmɑː(r)
AM oʊˈmɑ

Omaha
BR ˈəʊməhɑː(r)
AM ˈoʊməˌhɑ

O'Mahoney
BR ə(ʊ)ˈmɑː(h)əni
AM ˌoʊməˈhoʊni

O'Mahony
BR ə(ʊ)ˈmɑː(h)əni
AM ˌoʊməˈhoʊni

O'Malley
BR ə(ʊ)ˈmali
AM oʊˈmæli

Oman[1]
country
BR əʊˈmɑːn
AM oʊˈmɑn

Oman[2]
surname
BR ˈəʊmən
AM ˈoʊmən

Omani
BR əʊˈmɑːn|i, -ɪz
AM oʊˈmɑni, -z

O'Mara
BR ə(ʊ)ˈmɑːrə(r)
AM oʊˈmɛrə

Omar Khayyám
BR ˌəʊmɑː kʌɪˈam, + kʌɪˈɑːm
AM ˌoʊmɑr kaɪˈɑm

omasa
BR əʊˈmeɪsə(r)
AM oʊˈmeɪsə

omasum
BR əʊˈmeɪsəm
AM oʊˈmeɪsəm

ombre
BR ˈɒmbə(r), -z
AM ˈɑmbər, -z

ombré
BR ˈɒmbreɪ, ˈɒ̃breɪ, -z
AM ˈɑmˌbreɪ, -z

ombrology
BR ɒmˈbrɒlədʒi
AM ɑmˈbrɑlədʒi

ombrometer
BR ɒmˈbrɒmɪtə(r), -z
AM ɑmˈbrɑmədər, -z

ombudsman
BR ˈɒmbʊdzmən
AM ˈɑmˌbədzmən, ˈɑmˌbʊdzmən

ombudsmen
BR ˈɒmbʊdzmən
AM ˈɑmˌbədzmən, ˈɑmˌbʊdzmən

Omdurman
BR ˈɒmdəmən, ˌɒmdəˈmɑːn, ˌɒmdəˈman
AM ˌɔmdərˈmɑn, ˌɑmdərˈmɑn, ˌɔmdərˈmɑn, ˌɑmdərˈmɑn

O'Meara
BR ə(ʊ)ˈmɑːrə(r), ə(ʊ)ˈmɛːrə(r), ə(ʊ)ˈmɪərə(r)
AM oʊˈmɪrə

omega
BR ˈəʊmɪɡə(r), -z
AM oʊˈmeɪɡə, oʊˈmɛɡə, -z

omelet
BR ˈɒmlɪt, -s
AM ˈɑmlət, -s

omelette
BR ˈɒmlɪt, -s
AM ˈɑmlət, -s

omen
BR ˈəʊmən, -z
AM ˈoʊmən, -z

omenta
BR əʊˈmɛntə(r)
AM oʊˈmɛn(t)ə

omental
BR əʊˈmɛntl
AM oʊˈmɛn(t)l

omentum
BR əʊˈmɛntəm
AM oʊˈmɛn(t)əm

omer
BR ˈəʊmə(r), -z
AM ˈoʊmər, -z

omicron
BR ə(ʊ)ˈmʌɪkrɒn, ə(ʊ)ˈmʌɪkr(ə)n, ˈɒmɪkrɒn, ˈɒmɪkr(ə)n, -z
AM ˈɑməˌkrɑn, ˈoʊməˌkrɑn, -z

ominous
BR ˈɒmɪnəs
AM ˈɑmənəs

ominously
BR ˈɒmɪnəsli
AM ˈɑmənəsli

ominousness
BR ˈɒmɪnəsnəs
AM ˈɑmənəsnəs

omissible
BR ə(ʊ)ˈmɪsɪbl
AM oʊˈmɪsəbəl

omission
BR ə(ʊ)ˈmɪʃn, -z
AM oʊˈmɪʃən, əˈmɪʃən, -z

omissive
BR ə(ʊ)ˈmɪsɪv
AM oʊˈmɪsɪv, əˈmɪsɪv

omit
BR ə(ʊ)ˈmɪt, -s, -ɪŋ, -ɪd
AM oʊˈmɪ|t, əˈmɪ|t, -ts, -dɪŋ, -dɪd

ommatidia
BR ˌɒməˈtɪdɪə(r)
AM ˌɑməˈtɪdiə

ommatidium
BR ˌɒməˈtɪdɪəm
AM ˌɑməˈtɪdiəm

omnibus
BR ˈɒmnɪbəs, ˈɒmnɪbʌs, -ɪz
AM ˈɑmnəˌbəs, -əz

omnicompetence
BR ˌɒmnɪˈkɒmpɪt(ə)ns
AM ˌɑmnəˈkɑmpətns

omnicompetent
BR ˌɒmnɪˈkɒmpɪt(ə)nt
AM ˌɑmnəˈkɑmpədnt

omnidirectional
BR ˌɒmnɪdɪˈrɛkʃn̩(ə)l, ˌɒmnɪdɪˈrɛkʃən(ə)l, ˌɒmnɪdʌɪˈrɛkʃn̩(ə)l, ˌɒmnɪdʌɪˈrɛkʃən(ə)l
AM ˌɑmnəˌdaɪˈrɛkʃ(ə)nəl, ˌɑmnədəˈrɛkʃ(ə)nəl

omnifarious
BR ˌɒmnɪˈfɛːrɪəs
AM ˌɑmnəˈfɛriəs

omnific
BR ɒmˈnɪfɪk
AM ɑmˈnɪfɪk

omnigenous
BR ɒmˈnɪdʒɪnəs
AM ɑmˈnɪdʒənəs

omnipotence
BR ɒmˈnɪpət(ə)ns
AM ɑmˈnɪpədəns, əmˈnɪpədəns, ɑmˈnɪpətns, əmˈnɪpətns

omnipotent
BR ɒmˈnɪpət(ə)nt
AM ɑmˈnɪpədnt, əmˈnɪpədnt

omnipotently
BR ɒmˈnɪpət(ə)ntli
AM ɑmˈnɪpədən(t)li, əmˈnɪpədən(t)li, ɑmˈnɪpətn(t)li, əmˈnɪpətn(t)li

omnipresence
BR ˌɒmnɪˈprɛzns
AM ˌɑmnəˈprɛzns

omnipresent
BR ˌɒmnɪˈprɛznt
AM ˌɑmnəˌprɛznt

omniscience
BR ɒmˈnɪsɪəns
AM ɑmˈnɪʃəns

omniscient
BR ɒmˈnɪsɪənt
AM ɑmˈnɪʃənt

omnisciently
BR ɒmˈnɪsɪəntli
AM ɑmˈnɪʃən(t)li

omnivore
BR ˈɒmnɪvɔː(r), -z
AM ˈɑmnəˌvɔ(ə)r, -z

omnivorous
BR ɒmˈnɪv(ə)rəs
AM ɑmˈnɪv(ə)rəs

omnivorously
BR ɒmˈnɪv(ə)rəsli
AM ɑmˈnɪv(ə)rəsli

omnivorousness
BR ɒmˈnɪv(ə)rəsnəs
AM ɑmˈnɪv(ə)rəsnəs

omphaloi
BR ˈɒmfəlɔɪ
AM ˈɑmfəˌlɔɪ

omphalos
BR ˈɒmfəlɒs
AM ˈɔmfələs, ˈɔmfələs, ˈɑmfələs, ˈɑmfələs

omphalotomy
BR ˌɒmfəˈlɒtəm|i, -ɪz
AM ˌɑmfəˈlɑdəmi, ˌɑmpəˈlɑdəmi, -z

Omsk
BR ɒmsk
AM ɑmsk

on
BR ɒn
AM ɔn, ɑn

onager
BR ˈɒnədʒə(r), ˈɒnəɡə(r), -z
AM ˈɔnədʒər, ˈɑnədʒər, -z

Onan
BR ˈəʊnən, ˈəʊnan
AM ˈoʊnən

onanism
BR ˈəʊnənɪz(ə)m
AM ˈoʊnəˌnɪzəm

onanist
BR ˈəʊnənɪst, -s
AM ˈoʊnənəst, -s

onanistic
BR ˌəʊnəˈnɪstɪk
AM ˌoʊnəˈnɪstɪk

Onassis
BR ə(ʊ)ˈnasɪs
AM əˈnæsəs, oʊˈnæsəs

ONC
BR ˌəʊɛnˈsiː, -z
AM ˌoʊɛnˈsi, -z

once
BR wʌns
AM wəns

once-over
BR ˈwʌnsˌəʊvə(r)
AM ¦wəns¦oʊvər

oncer
BR ˈwʌnsə(r), -z
AM ˈwənsər, -z

oncogene
BR ˈɒŋkə(ʊ)dʒiːn, -z
AM ˈɔnkoʊˌdʒin, ˈɔŋkoʊˌdʒin, ˈɑnkoʊˌdʒin, ˈɑŋkoʊˌdʒin, -z

oncogenic
BR ˌɒŋkə(ʊ)ˈdʒɛnɪk
AM ˌɔnkoʊˈdʒɛnɪk, ˌɔŋkoʊˈdʒɛnɪk, ˌɑnkoʊˈdʒɛnɪk, ˌɑŋkoʊˈdʒɛnɪk

oncogenous
BR ɒŋˈkɒdʒɪnəs
AM ɔnˈkɑdʒənəs, ɔŋˈkɑdʒənəs, ɑnˈkɑdʒənəs, ɑŋˈkɑdʒənəs

oncologist
BR ɒŋˈkɒlədʒɪst, -s
AM ɔnˈkɑlədʒəst, ɔŋˈkɑlədʒəst, ɑnˈkɑlədʒəst, ɑŋˈkɑlədʒəst, -s

oncology
BR ɒŋˈkɒlədʒi
AM ɔnˈkɑlədʒi, ɔŋˈkɑlədʒi, ɑnˈkɑlədʒi, ɑŋˈkɑlədʒi

oncoming
BR ˈɒnˌkʌmɪŋ
AM ˈɔnˌkəmɪŋ, ˈɑnˌkəmɪŋ

oncost
BR ˈɒnkɒst, -s
AM ɔnˈkɔst, ɑnˈkɑst, -s

OND
BR ˌəʊɛnˈdiː, -z
AM ˌoʊɛnˈdi, -z

one
BR wʌn
AM wən

O'Neal
BR ə(ʊ)ˈniːl
AM oʊˈnil

onefold
BR ˈwʌnfəʊld
AM ˈwənˌfoʊld

Oneida
BR əʊˈnʌɪdə(r)
AM oʊˈnaɪdə

O'Neil
BR ə(ʊ)ˈniːl
AM oʊˈnil

O'Neill
BR ə(ʊ)ˈniːl
AM oʊˈnil

oneiric
BR ə(ʊ)ˈnʌɪrɪk
AM oʊˈnaɪrɪk

oneirocritic
BR ə(ʊ)ˌnʌɪrəˈkrɪtɪk, -s
AM oʊˌnaɪroʊˈkrɪdɪk, -s

oneirologist
BR ə(ʊ)ˌnʌɪˈrɒlədʒɪst, -s
AM oʊˌnaɪˈrɑlədʒəst, -s

oneirology
BR ə(ʊ)ˌnʌɪˈrɒlədʒi
AM oʊˌnaɪˈrɑlədʒi

oneiromancer
BR ə(ʊ)ˈnʌɪrəmansə(r), -z
AM oʊˈnaɪrəˌmænsər, -z

oneiromancy
BR ə(ʊ)ˈnʌɪrəmansi
AM oʊˈnaɪroʊˌmænsi

oneness
BR ˈwʌnnəs
AM ˈwə(n)nəs

oner
BR ˈwʌnə(r), -z
AM ˈwənər, -z

onerous
BR ˈəʊn(ə)rəs, ˈɒn(ə)rəs
AM ˈoʊnərəs, ˈɑnərəs

onerously
BR ˈəʊn(ə)rəsli, ˈɒn(ə)rəsli
AM ˈoʊnərəsli, ˈɑnərəsli

onerousness
BR ˈəʊn(ə)rəsnəs, ˈɒn(ə)rəsnəs
AM ˈoʊnərəsnəs, ˈɑnərəsnəs

oneself
BR ˌwʌnˈsɛlf
AM ˌwənˈsɛlf

one-sided
BR ˌwʌnˈsʌɪdɪd
AM ¦wən¦saɪdɪd

one-sidedly
BR ˌwʌnˈsʌɪdɪdli
AM ¦wən¦saɪdɪdli

one-sidedness
BR ˌwʌnˈsʌɪdɪdnɪs
AM ¦wən¦saɪdɪdnɪs

Onesimus
BR əʊˈniːsɪməs, əʊˈnɛsɪməs
AM oʊˈnisɪməs, oʊˈnɛsɪməs

one-step
BR ˈwʌnstɛp, -s, -ɪŋ, -t
AM ˈwən¦stɛp, -s, -ɪŋ, -t

one-time
adjective
BR ˈwʌntʌɪm
AM ˈwən¦taɪm

one-to-one
BR ˌwʌntəˈwʌn
AM ˈwən(t)əˈwən

one-upmanship
BR (ˌ)wʌnˈʌpmənʃɪp
AM wənˈəp(s)mənˌʃɪp

onflow
BR ˈɒnfləʊ, -z
AM ˈɔnˌfloʊ, ˈɑnˌfloʊ, -z

onglaze
BR ˈɒngleɪz
AM ˈɔnˌgleɪz, ˈɑnˌgleɪz

ongoing
BR ˈɒngəʊɪŋ, ˌɒnˈgəʊɪŋ
AM ˈɔnˌgoʊɪŋ, ˈɑnˌgoʊɪŋ

ongoingness
BR ˈɒngəʊɪŋnɪs, ˌɒnˈgəʊɪŋnɪs
AM ˈɔngoʊɪŋnɪs, ˈɑngoʊɪŋnɪs

onion
BR ˈʌnjən, -z
AM ˈənjən, -z

Onions
BR ˈʌnjənz, ə(ʊ)ˈnʌɪənz
AM ˈənjənz

onionskin
BR ˈʌnjənskɪn, -z
AM ˈənjənˌskɪn, -z

oniony
BR ˈʌnjəni
AM ˈənjəni

on-line
BR ˌɒnˈlʌɪn
AM ¦ɔn¦laɪn, ¦ɑn¦laɪn

onlooker
BR ˈɒnˌlʊkə(r), -z
AM ˈɔnˌlʊkər, ˈɑnˌlʊkər, -z

onlooking
BR ˈɒnˌlʊkɪŋ
AM ˈɔnˌlʊkɪŋ, ˈɑnˌlʊkɪŋ

only
BR ˈəʊnli
AM ˈoʊnli

only-begotten
BR ˌəʊnlɪbɪˈgɒtn
AM ¦oʊnlibəˈgɑtn, ¦oʊnlibiˈgɑtn

on-off
BR ˌɒnˈɒf
AM ¦ɔnˈɔf, ¦ɑnˈɑf

onomasiology
BR ˌɒnəmeɪsɪˈɒlədʒi, ˌɒnəmeɪzɪˈɒlədʒi
AM ˌɔnəˌmeɪsiˈɑlədʒi, ˌɔnəˌmeɪziˈɑlədʒi, ˌɑnəˌmeɪsiˈɑlədʒi, ˌɑnəˌmeɪziˈɑlədʒi

onomast
BR ˈɒnəmast, -s
AM ˈɑnəˌmæst, -s

onomastic
BR ˌɒnəˈmastɪk, -s
AM ˌɔnəˈmæstɪk, ˌɑnəˈmæstɪk, -s

onomatopoeia
BR ˌɒnəmatəˈpiːə(r)
AM ˌɔnəˌmædəˈpiə, ˌɑnəˌmædəˈpiə

onomatopoeic
BR ˌɒnəmatəˈpiːɪk
AM ˌɔnəˌmædəˈpiɪk, ˌɑnəˌmædəˈpiɪk

onomatopoeically
BR ˌɒnəmatəˈpiːɪkli
AM ˌɑnəˌmædəˈpiɪk(ə)li

onomatopoetic
BR ˌɒnəmatəˌpəʊˈɛtɪk
AM ˌɔnəˌmædəpoʊˈɛdɪk, ˌɑnəˌmædəpoʊˈɛdɪk

Onondaga
BR ˌɒnənˈdɑːgə(r), -z
AM ˌɔnənˈdɑgə, ˌɑnənˈdɑgə, -z

onrush
BR ˈɒnrʌʃ, -ɪz
AM ˈɔnˌrəʃ, ˈɑnˌrəʃ, -əz

onrushing
BR ˈɒnˌrʌʃɪŋ
AM ˈɔnˌrəʃɪŋ, ˈɑnˌrəʃɪŋ

onset
noun
BR ˈɒnsɛt, -s
AM ˈɔnˌsɛt, ˈɑnˌsɛt, -s

on-set
adjective, adverb
BR ˌɒnˈsɛt
AM ¦ɔnˈsɛt, ¦ɑnˈsɛt

onshore
BR ˌɒnˈʃɔː(r)
AM ¦ɔnˈʃɔ(ə)r, ¦ɑnˈʃɔ(ə)r

onside
BR ˌɒnˈsʌɪd
AM ¦ɔnˈsaɪd, ¦ɑnˈsaɪd

onslaught
BR ˈɒnslɔːt, -s
AM ˈɔnˌslɔt, ˈɑnˌslɔt, -s

Onslow
BR ˈɒnzləʊ
AM ˈɑnzloʊ

onstream
BR ˌɒnˈstriːm
AM ¦ɔnˈstrim, ¦ɑnˈstrim

Ontario
BR ɒnˈtɛːrɪəʊ
AM ɔnˈtɛrioʊ, ɑnˈtɛrioʊ

on-the-spot
BR ˌɒnðəˈspɒt
AM ˌɔnðəˈspɑt, ˌɑnðəˈspɑt

onto
BR ˈɒntʉ
AM ˈɔnˌtʊ, ˈɑnˌtʊ

ontogenesis
BR ˌɒntə(ʊ)ˈdʒɛnɪsɪs

AM ˌɔnˌtoʊˈdʒɛnəsəs, ˌɑnˌtoʊˈdʒɛnəsəs
ontogenetic
BR ˌɒntəʊdʒɪˈnɛtɪk
AM ˌɔnˌtoʊdʒəˈnɛdɪk, ˌɑnˌtoʊdʒəˈnɛdɪk
ontogenetically
BR ˌɒntəʊdʒɪˈnɛtɨkli
AM ˌɔnˌtoʊdʒəˈnɛdək(ə)li, ˌɑnˌtoʊdʒəˈnɛdək(ə)li
ontogenic
BR ˌɒntə(ʊ)ˈdʒɛnɪk
AM ˌɔnˌtoʊˈdʒɛnɪk, ˌɑnˌtoʊˈdʒɛnɪk
ontogenically
BR ˌɒntə(ʊ)ˈdʒɛnɨkli
AM ˌɔnˌtoʊˈdʒɛnək(ə)li, ˌɑnˌtoʊˈdʒɛnək(ə)li
ontogeny
BR ɒnˈtɒdʒɪni, ɒnˈtɒdʒn̩i
AM ɔnˈtɑdʒəni, ɑnˈtɑdʒəni
ontological
BR ˌɒntəˈlɒdʒɨkl
AM ˌɔn(t)əˈlɑdʒəkəl, ˌɑn(t)əˈlɑdʒəkəl
ontologically
BR ˌɒntəˈlɒdʒɨkli
AM ˌɔn(t)əˈlɑdʒək(ə)li, ˌɑn(t)əˈlɑdʒək(ə)li
ontologist
BR ɒnˈtɒlədʒɪst, -s
AM ɔnˈtɑlədʒəst, ɑnˈtɑlədʒəst, -s
ontology
BR ɒnˈtɒlədʒi
AM ɔnˈtɑlədʒi, ɑnˈtɑlədʒi
onus
BR ˈəʊnəs
AM ˈoʊnəs
onward
BR ˈɒnwəd, -z
AM ˈɔnwərd, ˈɑnwərd, -z
onymous
BR ˈɒnɨməs
AM ˈɔnəməs, ˈɑnəməs
onyx
BR ˈɒnɪks, -ɨz
AM ˈɔnɪks, ˈɑnɪks, -ɨz
oocyte
BR ˈəʊəsʌɪt
AM ˈoʊəˌsaɪt
oodles
BR ˈuːdlz
AM ˈudlz
oof
BR uːf
AM uf
oofiness
BR ˈuːfɪnɨs
AM ˈufinɨs
oofy
BR ˈuːf|i, -ɪə(r), -ɪɨst
AM ˈufi, -ər, -əst
oogamous
BR əʊˈɒgəməs
AM oʊˈ(w)ɑgəməs
oogamy
BR əʊˈɒgəmi
AM oʊˈ(w)ɑgəmi
oogenesis
BR əʊə(ʊ)ˈdʒɛnɪsɪs
AM ˌoʊəˈdʒɛnəsəs
oogenetic
BR ˌəʊə(ʊ)dʒɪˈnɛtɪk
AM ˌoʊədʒəˈnɛdɪk
ooh
BR uː, -z, -ɪŋ, -d
AM u, -z, -ɪŋ, -d
oolite
BR ˈəʊəlʌɪt, -s
AM ˈoʊəˌlaɪt, -s
oolith
BR ˈəʊəlɪθ, -s
AM ˈoʊəˌlɪθ, -s
oolitic
BR ˌəʊəˈlɪtɪk
AM ˌoʊəˈlɪdɪk
oological
BR ˌəʊəˈlɒdʒɨkl
AM ˌoʊəˈlɑdʒəkəl
oologist
BR əʊˈɒlədʒɪst, -s
AM oʊˈ(w)ɑlədʒəst, -s
oology
BR əʊˈɒlədʒi
AM oʊˈ(w)ɑlədʒi
oolong
BR ˈuːlɒŋ
AM ˈuˌlɔŋ, ˈuˌlɑŋ
oomiak
BR ˈuːmɪak, -s
AM ˈumiək, ˈumiˌæk, -s
oompah
BR ˈʊmpɑː(r), ˈuːmpɑː(r)
AM ˈumˌpɑ, ˈʊmˌpɑ
oomph
BR ʊmf, uːmf
AM ʊmf, umf
Oona
BR ˈuːnə(r)
AM ˈunə
Oonagh
BR ˈuːnə(r)
AM ˈunə
oophorectomy
BR ˌəʊəfəˈrɛktəm|i, -ɪz
AM ˌoʊfəˈrɛktəmi, -z
oops
BR (w)ʊps
AM (w)ʊps, ups
oops-a-daisy
BR ˌ(w)ʊpsəˈdeɪzi, ˌ(w)uːpsəˈdeɪzi
AM ˈ(w)ʊpsəˌdeɪzi, ˈ(w)upsəˌdeɪzi
Oort
BR ɔːt, ʊət
AM ɔ(ə)rt
oosperm
BR ˈəʊə(ʊ)spəːm, -z
AM ˈoʊəˌspərm, -z
Oostende
BR ɒˈstɛnd
AM ˈɔˌstɛnd, ˈoʊˌstɛnd
FL oːstˈɛndə
Oosterhuis
BR ˈəʊstəhaʊs, ˈuːstəhaʊs
AM ˈustərˌ(h)aʊs
ooze
BR uːz, -ɨz, -ɪŋ, -d
AM uz, -əz, -ɪŋ, -d
oozily
BR ˈuːzɨli
AM ˈuzəli
ooziness
BR ˈuːzɪnɨs
AM ˈuzinɨs
oozy
BR ˈuːz|i, -ɪə(r), -ɪɨst
AM ˈuzi, -ər, -ɨst
op
BR ɒp, -s
AM ɑp, -s
op.
opus, operator
BR ɒp
AM ɑp
opacifier
BR əʊˈpasɪfʌɪə(r), -z
AM oʊˈpæsəˌfaɪər, -z
opacify
BR əʊˈpasɪfʌɪ, -z, -ɪŋ, -d
AM oʊˈpæsəˌfaɪ, -z, -ɪŋ, -d
opacity
BR ə(ʊ)ˈpasɨti
AM oʊˈpæsədi
opah
BR ˈəʊpə(r), -z
AM ˈoʊpə, -z
opal
BR ˈəʊpl, -z
AM ˈoʊpəl, -z
opalesce
BR ˌəʊpəˈlɛs, -ɨz, -ɪŋ, -t
AM ˌoʊpəˈlɛs, -əz, -ɪŋ, -t
opalescence
BR ˌəʊpəˈlɛsns
AM ˌoʊpəˈlɛsəns
opalescent
BR ˌəʊpəˈlɛsnt
AM ˌoʊpəˈlɛsənt
opaline
BR ˈəʊpəlʌɪn
AM ˈoʊpəˌlin, ˈoʊpəˌlaɪn
opaque
BR ə(ʊ)ˈpeɪk
AM oʊˈpeɪk
opaquely
BR ə(ʊ)ˈpeɪkli
AM oʊˈpeɪkli
opaqueness
BR ə(ʊ)ˈpeɪknɨs
AM oʊˈpeɪknɨs
op art
BR ˈɒp ɑːt
AM ˈɑp ˌɑrt
op. cit.
BR ˌɒp ˈsɪt
AM ˈɑp ˌsɪt
ope
BR əʊp, -s, -ɪŋ, -t
AM oʊp, -s, -ɪŋ, -t
OPEC
BR ˈəʊpɛk
AM ˈoʊpɛk
Op-Ed
BR ˌɒpˈɛd
AM ˌɑpˈɛd
Opel®
BR ˈəʊpl, -z
AM ˈoʊpɛl, -z
open
BR ˈəʊp|(ə)n, -(ə)nz, -(ə)nɪŋ\-n̩ɪŋ, -(ə)nd
AM ˈoʊp|ən, -ənz, -(ə)nɪŋ, -ənd\-n̩d
openable
BR ˈəʊp(ə)nəbl, ˈəʊpn̩əbl
AM ˈoʊp(ə)nəbəl
opencast
BR ˈəʊp(ə)nkɑːst, ˈəʊp(ə)nkast
AM ˈoʊpənˌkæst
opener
BR ˈəʊp(ə)nə(r), ˈəʊpn̩ə(r), -z
AM ˈoʊp(ə)nər, -z
opening
BR ˈəʊp(ə)nɪŋ, ˈəʊpn̩ɪŋ, -z
AM ˈoʊp(ə)nɪŋ, -z
openly
BR ˈəʊp(ə)nli
AM ˈoʊpənli
openness
BR ˈəʊp(ə)nnəs
AM ˈoʊpə(n)nəs
Openshaw
BR ˈəʊp(ə)nʃɔː(r)
AM ˈoʊpənˌʃɔ
openwork
BR ˈəʊp(ə)nwəːk
AM ˈoʊpənˌwərk
opera
BR ˈɒp(ə)rə(r), -z
AM ˈɑp(ə)rə, -z
operability
BR ˌɒp(ə)rəˈbɪlɨti
AM ˌɑp(ə)rəˈbɪlɨdi
operable
BR ˈɒp(ə)rəbl
AM ˈɑp(ə)rəbəl
operably
BR ˈɒp(ə)rəbli
AM ˈɑp(ə)rəbli
opera buffa
BR ˌɒp(ə)rə ˈbuːfə(r)
AM ˈoʊp(ə)rə ˈbufə

opéra comique
BR ˌɒp(ə)rə kɒˈmiːk, -s
AM ¦oʊp(ə)rə kɔˈmik, -s

operand
BR ˈɒpərand, ˈɒp(ə)rənd, ˈɒp(ə)rn̩d, -z
AM ˈɑpəˌrænd, -z

operant
BR ˈɒp(ə)rənt, ˈɒp(ə)rn̩t, -s
AM ˈɑpərənt, -s

operas buffa
BR ˌɒp(ə)rəz ˈbuːfə(r)
AM ¦oʊp(ə)rəz ˈbufə

opera seria
BR ˌɒp(ə)rə ˈsɪərɪə(r)
AM ¦oʊp(ə)rə ˈsɪriə

operas seria
BR ˌɒp(ə)rəz ˈsɪərɪə(r)
AM ¦oʊp(ə)rəz ˈsɪriə

operate
BR ˈɒpəreɪt, -s, -ɪŋ, -ɨd
AM ˈɑpəˌreɪ|t, -ts, -dɪŋ, -dɨd

operatic
BR ˌɒpəˈratɪk, -s
AM ¦ɑpəˈrædɪk, -s

operatically
BR ˌɒpəˈratɨkli
AM ¦ɑpəˈrædək(ə)li

operation
BR ˌɒpəˈreɪʃn, -z
AM ˌɑpəˈreɪʃən, -z

operational
BR ˌɒpəˈreɪʃn̩(ə)l, ˌɒpəˈreɪʃən(ə)l
AM ˌɑpəˈreɪʃ(ə)nəl

operationalise
BR ˌɒpəˈreɪʃn̩əlʌɪz, ˌɒpəˈreɪʃn̩l̩ʌɪz, ˌɒpəˈreɪʃənl̩ʌɪz, ˌɒpəˈreɪʃ(ə)nəlʌɪz, -ɨz, -ɪŋ, -d
AM ˌɑpəˈreɪʃənlˌaɪz, ˌɑpəˈreɪʃnəˌlaɪz, -ɨz, -ɪŋ, -d

operationalize
BR ˌɒpəˈreɪʃn̩əlʌɪz, ˌɒpəˈreɪʃn̩l̩ʌɪz, ˌɒpəˈreɪʃənl̩ʌɪz, ˌɒpəˈreɪʃ(ə)nəlʌɪz, -ɨz, -ɪŋ, -d
AM ˌɑpəˈreɪʃənlˌaɪz, ˌɑpəˈreɪʃnəˌlaɪz, -ɨz, -ɪŋ, -d

operationally
BR ˌɒpəˈreɪʃn̩əli, ˌɒpəˈreɪʃn̩l̩i, ˌɒpəˈreɪʃənl̩i, ˌɒpəˈreɪʃ(ə)nəli
AM ˌɑpəˈreɪʃ(ə)nəli

operative
BR ˈɒp(ə)rətɪv, -z
AM ˈɑp(ə)rədɪv, -z

operatively
BR ˈɒp(ə)rətɨvli
AM ˈɑp(ə)rədɨvli

operativeness
BR ˈɒp(ə)rətɨvnɨs
AM ˈɑp(ə)rədɪvnɨs

operator
BR ˈɒpəreɪtə(r), -z
AM ˈɑpəˌreɪdər, -z

opercula
BR ə(ʊ)ˈpəːkjʊlə(r), ɒˈpəːkjʊlə(r)
AM oʊˈpərkjələ

opercular
BR ə(ʊ)ˈpəːkjʊlə(r), ɒˈpəːkjʊlə(r)
AM oʊˈpərkjələr

operculate
BR əʊˈpəːkjʊlət, ɒˈpəːkjʊlət
AM oʊˈpərkjəˌleɪt

operculum
BR ə(ʊ)ˈpəːkjʊləm, ɒˈpəːkjʊləm
AM oʊˈpərkjələm

opere buffe
BR ˌɒp(ə)reɪ ˈbuːfeɪ
AM ¦oʊp(ə)reɪ ˈbufeɪ

opere serie
BR ˌɒp(ə)reɪ ˈsɪərɪeɪ
AM ¦oʊp(ə)rə ˈsɪrieɪ

operetta
BR ˌɒpəˈrɛtə(r), -z
AM ˌɑpəˈrɛdə, -z

operon
BR ˈɒpərɒn, -z
AM ˈɑpərɑn, -z

Ophelia
BR ə(ʊ)ˈfiːlɪə(r), ɒˈfiːlɪə(r)
AM oʊˈfiljə, əˈfiljə, oʊˈfiliə, əˈfiliə

ophicleide
BR ˈɒfɪklʌɪd, -z
AM ˈɑfəˌklaɪd, ˈoʊfəˌklaɪd, -z

ophidia
BR ɒˈfɪdɪə(r), ə(ʊ)ˈfɪdɪə(r)
AM oʊˈfɪdiə

ophidian
BR ɒˈfɪdɪən, ə(ʊ)ˈfɪdɪən, -z
AM oʊˈfɪdiən, -z

ophiolatry
BR ˌɒfɪˈɒlətri
AM ˌɑfiˈɑlətri, ˌoʊfiˈɑlətri

ophiolite
BR ˈɒfɪəlʌɪt
AM ˈɑfiəˌlaɪt

ophiologist
BR ˌɒfɪˈɒlədʒɪst, -s
AM ˌɑfiˈɑlədʒəst, ˌoʊfiˈɑlədʒəst, -s

ophiology
BR ˌɒfɪˈɒlədʒi
AM ˌɑfiˈɑlədʒi, ˌoʊfiˈɑlədʒi

Ophir
BR ˈəʊfə(r)
AM ˈoʊfər

ophite
BR ˈɒfʌɪt, ˈəʊfʌɪt, -s
AM ˈoʊˌfaɪt, -s

ophitic
BR ɒˈfɪtɪk, əʊˈfɪtɪk
AM oʊˈfɪdɪk

Ophiuchus
BR ɒˈfjuːkəs, ˌɒfɪˈuːkəs
AM ɑˈfjukəs

ophthalmia
BR ɒfˈθalmɪə(r), ɒpˈθalmɪə(r)
AM ɑpˈθælmiə, ɑfˈθælmiə

ophthalmic
BR ɒfˈθalmɪk, ɒpˈθalmɪk
AM ɑpˈθælmɪk, ɑfˈθælmɪk

ophthalmitis
BR ˌɒfθalˈmʌɪtɪs, ˌɒpθalˈmʌɪtɪs
AM ˌɑpθə(l)ˈmaɪdɪs, ˌɑfθə(l)ˈmaɪdɪs

ophthalmological
BR ˌɒfθaləˈlɒdʒɪkl, ˌɒpθaləˈlɒdʒɪkl
AM ˌɑpθə(l)məˈlɑdʒəkəl, ˌɑfθə(l)məˈlɑdʒəkəl

ophthalmologist
BR ˌɒfθalˈmɒlədʒɪst, ˌɒpθalˈmɒlədʒɪst, -s
AM ˌɑpθə(l)ˈmɑlədʒəst, ˌɑfθə(l)ˈmɑlədʒəst, ˌɑpθə(l)ˈmɑlədʒəst, -s

ophthalmology
BR ˌɒfθalˈmɒlədʒi, ˌɒpθalˈmɒlədʒi
AM ˌɑpθə(l)ˈmɑlədʒi, ˌɑfθə(l)ˈmɑlədʒi

ophthalmoscope
BR ɒfˈθalməskəʊp, ɒpˈθalməskəʊp, -s
AM ɑpˈθælməˌskoʊp, ɑfˈθælməˌskoʊp, -s

ophthalmoscopic
BR ɒfˌθalməˈskɒpɪk, ɒpˌθalməˈskɒpɪk
AM ¦ɑpθə(l)məˈskɑpɪk, ¦ɑfθə(l)məˈskɑpɪk

ophthalmoscopically
BR ɒfˌθalməˈskɒpɨkli, ɒpˌθalməˈskɒpɨkli
AM ¦ɑpθə(l)məˈskɑpək(ə)li, ¦ɑfθə(l)məˈskɑpək(ə)li

ophthalmoscopy
BR ˌɒfθalˈmɒskəpi, ˌɒpθalˈmɒskəpi
AM ˌɑpθə(l)ˈmɑskəpi, ˌɑfθə(l)ˈmɑskəpi

opiate
BR ˈəʊpɪət, -s
AM ˈoʊpiɪt, -s

Opie
BR ˈəʊpi
AM ˈoʊpi

opine
BR ə(ʊ)ˈpʌɪn, -z, -ɪŋ, -d
AM oʊˈpaɪn, -z, -ɪŋ, -d

opinion
BR əˈpɪnjən, -z
AM əˈpɪnjən, -z

opinionated
BR əˈpɪnjəneɪtɨd
AM əˈpɪnjəˌneɪdɨd

opinionatedly
BR əˈpɪnjəneɪtɨdli
AM əˈpɪnjəˌneɪdɨdli

opinionatedness
BR əˈpɪnjəneɪtɨdnɨs
AM əˈpɪnjəˌneɪdɨdnɨs

opinionative
BR əˈpɪnjənətɪv
AM əˈpɪnjəˌneɪdɪv

opioid
BR ˈəʊpɪɔɪd, -z
AM ˈoʊpiɔɪd, -z

opisometer
BR ˌɒpɪˈsɒmɨtə(r), -z
AM ˌɑpəˈsɑmədər, -z

opisthograph
BR əˈpɪsθəgrɑːf, əˈpɪsθəgraf, -s
AM əˈpɪsθəˌgræf, -s

opisthography
BR ˌɒpɪsˈθɒgrəfi
AM ˌɑpəsˈθɑgrəfi

opisthosoma
BR əˌpɪsθəˈsəʊmə(r), -z
AM əˌpɪsθəˈsoʊmə, -z

opium
BR ˈəʊpɪəm
AM ˈoʊpiəm

opiumise
BR ˈəʊpɪəmʌɪz, -ɨz, -ɪŋ, -d
AM ˈoʊpiəˌmaɪz, ˈoʊpjəˌmaɪz, -ɨz, -ɪŋ, -d

opiumize
BR ˈəʊpɪəmʌɪz, -ɨz, -ɪŋ, -d
AM ˈoʊpiəˌmaɪz, ˈoʊpjəˌmaɪz, -ɨz, -ɪŋ, -d

opodeldoc
BR ˌɒpə(ʊ)ˈdɛldɒk
AM ˌɑpəˈdɛlˌdɑk

opopanax
BR ə(ʊ)ˈpɒpənaks
AM əˈpɑpəˌnæks

Oporto
BR ə(ʊ)ˈpɔːtəʊ, ɒˈpɔːtəʊ
AM əˈpɔrdoʊ, ɔˈpɔrˌtoʊ, ɑˈpɔrˌtoʊ

opossum
BR əˈpɒsəm, -z
AM (ə)ˈpɑsəm, -z

Oppenheim
BR ˈɒp(ə)nhʌɪm
AM ˈɑpənhaɪm

Oppenheimer
BR 'ɒp(ə)nhʌɪmə(r)
AM 'ɑp(ə)nˌ(h)aɪmər
oppidan
BR 'ɒpɨd(ə)n, -z
AM 'ɑpədən, -z
oppo
BR 'ɒpəʊ, -z
AM 'ɑˌpoʊ, -z
opponency
BR ə'pəʊnənsi
AM ə'poʊnənsi
opponent
BR ə'pəʊnənt, -s
AM ə'poʊnənt, -s
opportune
BR 'ɒpətjuːn, 'ɒpətʃuːn, ˌɒpə'tjuːn, ˌɒpə'tʃuːn
AM ¦ɑpər¦t(j)un
opportunely
BR 'ɒpətjuːnli, 'ɒpətʃuːnli, ˌɒpə'tjuːnli, ˌɒpə'tʃuːnli
AM ˌɑpər't(j)unli
opportuneness
BR 'ɒpətjuːnnəs, 'ɒpətʃuːnnəs, ˌɒpə'tjuːnnəs, ˌɒpə'tʃuːnnəs
AM ˌɑpər't(j)u(n)nəs
opportunism
BR 'ɒpətjuːnɪz(ə)m, 'ɒpətʃuːnɪz(ə)m, ˌɒpə'tjuːnɪz(ə)m, ˌɒpə'tʃuːnɪz(ə)m
AM ¦ɑpər¦t(j)uˌnɪzəm
opportunist
BR 'ɒpətjuːnɪst, 'ɒpətʃuːnɪst, ˌɒpə'tjuːnɪst, ˌɒpə'tʃuːnɪst, -s
AM ˌɑpər't(j)unəst, -s
opportunistic
BR ˌɒpətjuː'nɪstɪk, ˌɒpətʃuː'nɪstɪk
AM ˌɑpərt(j)u'nɪstɪk
opportunistically
BR ˌɒpətjuː'nɪstɪkli, ˌɒpətʃuː'nɪstɪkli
AM ¦ɑpərt(j)u'nɪstək(ə)li
opportunity
BR ˌɒpə'tjuːnɪt|i, ˌɒpə'tʃuːnɪt|i, -ɪz
AM ˌɑpər't(j)unədi, -z
opposable
BR ə'pəʊzəbl
AM ə'poʊzəbəl
oppose
BR ə'pəʊz, -ɪz, -ɪŋ, -d
AM ə'poʊz, -əz, -ɪŋ, -d
opposer
BR ə'pəʊzə(r), -z
AM ə'poʊzər, -z
opposite
BR 'ɒpəzɪt, 'ɒpəsɪt, -s
AM 'ɑpəzət, -s
oppositely
BR 'ɒpəzɪtli, 'ɒpəsɪtli
AM 'ɑpɑzətli
oppositeness
BR 'ɒpəzɪtnɪs, 'ɒpəsɪtnɪs
AM 'ɑpɑzətnəs
opposition
BR ˌɒpə'zɪʃn, -z
AM ˌɑpə'zɪʃən, -z
oppositional
BR ˌɒpə'zɪʃn̩(ə)l, ˌɒpə'zɪʃən(ə)l
AM ˌɑpə'zɪʃ(ə)nəl
oppositive
BR ə'pɒzɪtɪv
AM ə'pɑzədɪv
oppress
BR ə'prɛs, -ɪz, -ɪŋ, -t
AM ə'prɛs, -əz, -ɪŋ, -t
oppression
BR ə'prɛʃn
AM ə'prɛʃən
oppressive
BR ə'prɛsɪv
AM ə'prɛsɪv
oppressively
BR ə'prɛsɪvli
AM ə'prɛsɪvli
oppressiveness
BR ə'prɛsɪvnɪs
AM ə'prɛsɪvnɪs
oppressor
BR ə'prɛsə(r), -z
AM ə'prɛsər, -z
opprobrious
BR ə'prəʊbrɪəs
AM ə'proʊbriəs
opprobriously
BR ə'prəʊbrɪəsli
AM ə'proʊbriəsli
opprobriousness
BR ə'prəʊbrɪəsnəs
AM ə'proʊbriəsnəs
opprobrium
BR ə'prəʊbrɪəm
AM ə'proʊbriəm
oppugn
BR ə'pjuːn, -z, -ɪŋ, -d
AM ə'pjun, -z, -ɪŋ, -d
oppugnance
BR ə'pʌgnəns
AM ə'pəgnəns
oppugnancy
BR ə'pʌgnənsi
AM ə'pəgnənsi
oppugnant
BR ə'pʌgnənt
AM ə'pəgnənt
oppugnation
BR ˌɒpʌg'neɪʃn
AM ˌɑpəg'neɪʃən
oppugner
BR ə'pjuːnə(r), -z
AM ə'pjunər, -z
Oprah
BR 'əʊprə(*r*)
AM 'oʊprə
Opren®
BR 'əʊpr(ə)n, 'əʊprɛn
AM 'oʊprən
opsimath
BR 'ɒpsɪmaθ, -s
AM 'ɑpsəˌmæθ, -s
opsimathy
BR ɒp'sɪməθi
AM ɑp'sɪməθi
opsonic
BR ɒp'sɒnɪk
AM ɑp'sɑnɪk
opsonin
BR 'ɒpsənɪn, -z
AM 'ɑpsənən, -z
opt
BR ɒpt, -s, -ɪŋ, -ɪd
AM ɑpt, -s, -ɪŋ, -əd
Optacon
BR 'ɒptək(ə)n
AM 'ɑptəˌkɑn
optant
BR 'ɒpt(ə)nt, -s
AM 'ɑptnt, -s
optative
BR 'ɒptətɪv, -z
AM 'ɑptədɪv, -z
optatively
BR 'ɒptətɪvli
AM 'ɑptədɪvli
optic
BR 'ɒptɪk, -s
AM 'ɑptɪk, -s
optical
BR 'ɒptɪkl
AM 'ɑptəkəl
optically
BR 'ɒptɪkli
AM 'ɑptək(ə)li
optician
BR ɒp'tɪʃn, -z
AM ɑp'tɪʃən, -z
optima
BR 'ɒptɪmə(*r*)
AM 'ɑptəmə
optimal
BR 'ɒptɪml
AM 'ɑptəməl
optimality
BR ˌɒptɪ'malɪti
AM ˌɑptə'mælədi
optimally
BR 'ɒptɪməli, 'ɒptɪml̩i
AM 'ɑptəm(ə)li
optimisation
BR ˌɒptɪmʌɪ'zeɪʃn, -z
AM ˌɑptəmə'zeɪʃən, ˌɑptəˌmaɪ'zeɪʃən, -z
optimise
BR 'ɒptɪmʌɪz, -ɪz, -ɪŋ, -d
AM 'ɑptəˌmaɪz, -ɪz, -ɪŋ, -d
optimism
BR 'ɒptɪmɪz(ə)m
AM 'ɑptəˌmɪzəm
optimist
BR 'ɒptɪmɪst, -s
AM 'ɑptəməst, -s
optimistic
BR ˌɒptɪ'mɪstɪk
AM ˌɑptə'mɪstɪk
optimistically
BR ˌɒptɪ'mɪstɪkli
AM ˌɑptə'mɪstɪk(ə)li
optimization
BR ˌɒptɪmʌɪ'zeɪʃn, -z
AM ˌɑptəmə'zeɪʃən, ˌɑptəˌmaɪ'zeɪʃən, -z
optimize
BR 'ɒptɪmʌɪz, -ɪz, -ɪŋ, -d
AM 'ɑptəˌmaɪz, -ɪz, -ɪŋ, -d
optimum
BR 'ɒptɪməm, -z
AM 'ɑptəməm, -z
option
BR 'ɒpʃn, -z
AM 'ɑpʃən, -z
optional
BR 'ɒpʃn̩(ə)l, 'ɒpʃən(ə)l
AM 'ɑpʃ(ə)nəl
optionality
BR ˌɒpʃə'nalɪti
AM ˌɑpʃə'nælədi
optionally
BR 'ɒpʃn̩əli, 'ɒpʃn̩l̩i, 'ɒpʃənl̩i, 'ɒpʃ(ə)nəli
AM 'ɑpʃ(ə)nəli
optometer
BR ɒp'tɒmɪtə(r), -z
AM ɑp'tɑmədər, -z
optometric
BR ˌɒptə'mɛtrɪk
AM ˌɑptə'mɛtrɪk
optometrist
BR ɒp'tɒmɪtrɪst, -s
AM ɑp'tɑmətrəst, -s
optometry
BR ɒp'tɒmɪtri
AM ɑp'tɑmətri
optophone
BR 'ɒptəfəʊn, -z
AM 'ɑptəˌfoʊn, -z
opt-out
BR 'ɒptaʊt, -s
AM 'ɑpˌtaʊt, -s
Optrex®
BR 'ɒptrɛks
AM 'ɑptrɛks
opulence
BR 'ɒpjʊləns, 'ɒpjʊln̩s
AM 'ɑpjələns, 'oʊpjələns
opulent
BR 'ɒpjʊlənt, 'ɒpjʊln̩t
AM 'ɑpjələnt, 'oʊpjələnt
opulently
BR 'ɒpjʊləntli, 'ɒpjʊln̩tli

AM 'ɑpjələn(t)li, 'oʊpjələn(t)li
opuntia
BR ə(ʊ)'pʌnʃ(ɪ)ə(r), ɒ'pʌnʃ(ɪ)ə(r), -z
AM oʊ'pənʃ(i)ə, -z
opus
BR 'əʊpəs, -ɪz
AM 'oʊpəs, -əz
opuscule
BR ə'pʌskju:l, -z
AM oʊ'pəskjul, -z
or¹
strong
BR ɔ:(r)
AM ɔ(ə)r
or²
weak
BR ə(r)
AM ə(r)
orach
BR 'ɒrətʃ, -ɪz
AM 'ɔrətʃ, 'ɑrətʃ, -əz
orache
BR 'ɒrətʃ, -ɪz
AM 'ɔrətʃ, 'ɑrətʃ, -əz
oracle
BR 'ɒrəkl, -z
AM 'ɔrəkəl, -z
oracular
BR ɒ'rakjʉlə(r), ə'rakjʉlə(r), ɔ:'rakjʉlə(r)
AM ɔ'rækjələr, ə'rækjələr
oracularity
BR ɒˌrakjʉ'larɪti, əˌrakjʉ'larɪti, ɔ:ˌrakjʉ'larɪti
AM ɔˌrækjə'lɛrədi, əˌrækjə'lɛrədi
oracularly
BR ə'rakjʉləli, ɒ'rakjʉləli, ɔ:'rakjʉləli
AM ɔ'rækjələrli, ə'rækjələrli
oracy
BR 'ɔ:rəsi
AM 'ɔrəsi, 'oʊrəsi
oral
BR 'ɔ:rəl, 'ɔ:rl̩, -z
AM 'ɔrəl, 'oʊrəl, -z
oralism
BR 'ɔ:rəlɪz(ə)m, 'ɔ:rl̩ɪz(ə)m
AM 'ɔrəˌlɪzəm, 'ɔrəˌlɪzəm
oralist
BR 'ɔ:rəlɪst, 'ɔ:rl̩ɪst, -s
AM 'ɔrələst, 'oʊrələst, -s
orality
BR ɔ:'ralɪti
AM ɔ'rælədi, oʊ'rælədi
orally
BR 'ɔ:rəli, 'ɔ:rl̩i
AM 'ɔrəli, 'oʊrəli
Oran
BR ə'ran, ə'rɑ:n
AM oʊ'rɑn
orange
BR 'ɒrɪn(d)ʒ, -ɪz
AM 'ɔrəndʒ, -ɪz
orangeade
BR ˌɒrɪn(d)ʒ'eɪd, -z
AM 'ɔrəndʒˌeɪd, -z
Orangeism
BR 'ɒrɪn(d)ʒɪz(ə)m
AM 'ɔrəndʒˌɪzm
Orangeman
BR 'ɒrɪn(d)ʒmən
AM 'ɔrəndʒmən
Orangemen
BR 'ɒrɪn(d)ʒmən
AM 'ɔrəndʒmən
orangery
BR 'ɒrɪn(d)ʒ(ə)r|i, -ɪz
AM 'ɔrəndʒri, -z
orang-outang
BR ə'raŋətaŋ, ɔ:'raŋətaŋ, ɒ'raŋətaŋ, ˌɔ:raŋ'u:taŋ, -z
AM ə'ræŋ(g)əˌtæŋ, oʊ'ræŋ(g)əˌtæŋ, -z
orangutan
BR ə'raŋətan, ə'raŋətaŋ, ɔ:'raŋətan, ɔ:'raŋətaŋ, ɒ'raŋətan, ɒ'raŋətaŋ, ˌɔ:raŋ'u:tan, -z
AM ə'ræŋ(g)əˌtæŋ, oʊ'ræŋ(g)əˌtæŋ, -z
orangutang
BR ə'raŋətaŋ, ɔ:'raŋətaŋ, ɒ'raŋətaŋ, ˌɔ:raŋ'u:taŋ, -z
AM ə'ræŋ(g)əˌtæŋ, oʊ'ræŋ(g)əˌtæŋ, -z
orate
BR ɔ:'reɪt, ɒ'reɪt, ə'reɪt, -s, -ɪŋ, -ɪd
AM ɔ'reɪ|t, 'ɔrˌeɪ|t, -ts, -dɪŋ, -dɪd
oration
BR ə'reɪʃn, ɒ'reɪʃn, -z
AM ɔ'reɪʃən, ə'reɪʃən, -z
orator
BR 'ɒrətə(r), -z
AM 'ɔrədər, -z
oratorial
BR ˌɒrə'tɔ:rɪəl
AM ˌɔrə'tɔriəl
oratorian
BR ˌɒrə'tɔ:rɪən, -z
AM ˌɔrə'tɔriən, -z
oratorical
BR ˌɒrə'tɒrɪkl
AM ˌɔrə'tɔrəkəl
oratorically
BR ˌɒrə'tɒrɪkli
AM ˌɔrə'tɔrək(ə)li
oratorio
BR ˌɒrə'tɔ:rɪəʊ, -z
AM ˌɔrə'tɔrioʊ, -z
oratory
BR 'ɒrət(ə)ri
AM 'ɔrəˌtɔri
orb
BR ɔ:b, -z
AM ɔ(ə)rb, -z
Orbach
BR 'ɔ:bak
AM 'ɔrˌbɑk
orbicular
BR ɔ:'bɪkjʉlə(r)
AM ɔr'bɪkjələr
orbicularity
BR ɔ:ˌbɪkjʉ'larɪti
AM ɔrˌbɪkjə'lɛrədi
orbicularly
BR ɔ:'bɪkjʉləli
AM ɔr'bɪkjələrli
orbiculate
BR ɔ:'bɪkjʉlət
AM ɔr'bɪkjələt, ɔr'bɪkjəˌleɪt
orbit
BR 'ɔ:b|ɪt, -ɪts, -ɪtɪŋ, -ɪtɪd
AM 'ɔrbə|t, -ts, -dɪŋ, -dəd
orbital
BR 'ɔ:bɪtl
AM 'ɔrbədəl
orbiter
BR 'ɔ:bɪtə(r), -z
AM 'ɔrbədər, -z
orc
BR ɔ:k, -s
AM ɔ(ə)rk, -s
orca
BR 'ɔ:kə(r), -z
AM 'ɔrkə, -z
Orcadian
BR ɔ:'keɪdɪən, -z
AM ɔr'keɪdiən, -z
orchard
BR 'ɔ:tʃəd, -z
AM 'ɔrtʃərd, -z
orcharding
BR 'ɔ:tʃədɪŋ
AM 'ɔrtʃərdɪŋ
orchardist
BR 'ɔ:tʃədɪst, -s
AM 'ɔrtʃərdəst, -s
orchardman
BR 'ɔ:tʃədmən
AM 'ɔrtʃərdˌmæn
orchardmen
BR 'ɔ:tʃədmən
AM 'ɔrtʃərdˌmɛn
orchestic
BR ɔ:'kɛstɪk
AM ɔr'kɛstɪk
orchestra
BR 'ɔ:kɪstrə(r), 'ɔ:kɛstrə(r), -z
AM 'ɔrkəstrə, 'ɔrˌkɛstrə, -z
orchestral
BR ɔ:'kɛstr(ə)l
AM ɔr'kɛstrəl
orchestrally
BR ɔ:'kɛstrl̩i, ɔ:'kɛstrəli
AM ɔr'kɛstrəli
orchestrate
BR 'ɔ:kɪstreɪt, 'ɔ:kɛstreɪt, -s, -ɪŋ, -ɪd
AM 'ɔrkəˌstreɪ|t, -ts, -dɪŋ, -dɪd
orchestration
BR ˌɔ:kɪ'streɪʃn, ˌɔ:kɛ'streɪʃn, -z
AM ˌɔrkə'streɪʃən, -z
orchestrator
BR 'ɔ:kɪstreɪtə(r), 'ɔ:kɛstreɪtə(r), -z
AM 'ɔrkəˌstreɪdər, -z
orchestrina
BR ˌɔ:kɪ'stri:nə(r), ˌɔ:kɛ'stri:nə(r), -z
AM ˌɔrkə'strinə, -z
orchid
BR 'ɔ:kɪd, -z
AM 'ɔrkəd, -z
orchidaceous
BR ˌɔ:kɪ'deɪʃəs
AM ˌɔrkə'deɪʃəs
orchidist
BR 'ɔ:kɪdɪst, -s
AM 'ɔrkədəst, -s
orchidology
BR ˌɔ:kɪ'dɒlədʒi
AM ˌɔrkə'dɑlədʒi
orchil
BR 'ɔ:kɪl, 'ɔ:tʃɪl, -z
AM 'ɔrkəl, -z
orchilla
BR ɔ:'kɪlə(r), ɔ:'tʃɪlə(r), -z
AM 'ɔrkələ, -z
orchis
BR 'ɔ:k|ɪs, -ɪsɪz
AM 'ɔrkəs, -əz
orchitis
BR ɔ:'kʌɪtɪs
AM ɔr'kaɪdəs
orcin
BR 'ɔ:sɪn
AM 'ɔrsən
orcinol
BR 'ɔ:sɪnɒl
AM 'ɔrsəˌnɑl, 'ɔrsənəl
Orcus
BR 'ɔ:kəs
AM 'ɔrkəs
Orczy
BR 'ɔ:tsi, 'ɔ:ksi
AM 'ɔrtsi
ordain
BR ɔ:'deɪn, -z, -ɪŋ, -d
AM ɔr'deɪn, -z, -ɪŋ, -d

ordainer
BR ɔːˈdeɪnə(r), -z
AM ɔrˈdeɪnər, -z

ordainment
BR ɔːˈdeɪnm(ə)nt, -s
AM ɔrˈdeɪnmənt, -s

ordeal
BR ɔːˈdiːl, -z
AM ɔrˈdil, -z

order
BR ˈɔːd|ə(r), -əz, -(ə)rɪŋ, -əd
AM ˈɔrdər, -z, -ɪŋ, -d

orderer
BR ˈɔːd(ə)rə(r), -z
AM ˈɔrdərər, -z

ordering
BR ˈɔːd(ə)rɪŋ, -z
AM ˈɔrd(ə)rɪŋ, -z

orderliness
BR ˈɔːdəlɪnɨs
AM ˈɔrdərlinɨs

orderly
BR ˈɔːdəl|i, -ɪz
AM ˈɔrdərli, -z

ordinaire
BR ˌɔːdɪˈnɛː(r)
AM ˌɔrdəˈnɛ(ə)r

ordinal
BR ˈɔːdɪnl, ˈɔːdn̩l, -z
AM ˈɔrdnl, -z

ordinance
BR ˈɔːd(ɪ)nəns, ˈɔːdn̩əns, -ɨz
AM ˈɔrdn̩əns, -əz

ordinand
BR ˈɔːdɪnand, ˈɔːdɪnənd, -z
AM ˈɔrdəˌnænd, -z

ordinarily
BR ˈɔːdɪn(ə)rəli, ˈɔːdn̩(ə)rəli
AM ˌɔrdnˈɛrəli

ordinariness
BR ˈɔːdɪn(ə)rɪnɨs, ˈɔːdn̩(ə)rɪnɨs
AM ˈɔrdnˌɛrinɨs

ordinary
BR ˈɔːdɪn(ə)ri, ˈɔːdn̩(ə)ri
AM ˈɔrdnˌɛri

ordinate
BR ˈɔːdɪnət, ˈɔːdn̩ət, -s
AM ˈɔrdn̩ət, -s

ordination
BR ˌɔːdɪˈneɪʃn, -z
AM ˌɔrdnˈeɪʃən, -z

ordnance
BR ˈɔːdnəns
AM ˈɔrdn̩əns

ordonnance
BR ˈɔːdənəns, -ɨz
AM ˈɔrdn̩əns, -əz

Ordovician
BR ˌɔːdə(ʊ)ˈvɪʃɪən, ˌɔːdə(ʊ)ˈvɪsɪən
AM ˌɔrdəˈvɪʃən

ordure
BR ˈɔːdj(ʊ)ə(r), ˈɔːdʒə(r)
AM ˈɔrdʒər

ore
BR ɔː(r), -z
AM ɔ(ə)r, -z

öre
BR ˈəːrə(r)
AM ˈərə
SW ˈøːrɛ

øre
BR ˈəːrə(r)
AM ˈərə
DAN ˈœːʌ
NO ˈœːrə

oread
BR ˈɔːrɪad, -z
AM ˈɔriˌæd, -z

orectic
BR ɒˈrɛktɪk
AM oʊˈrɛktɪk

oregano
BR ˌɒrɪˈgɑːnəʊ, əˈrɛgənəʊ
AM əˈrɛgəˌnoʊ

Oregon
BR ˈɒrɪg(ə)n
AM ˈɔrəˌgɑn, ˈɔrəgən

Oregonian
BR ˌɒrɪˈgəʊnɪən, -z
AM ˌɔrəˈgoʊniən, -z

O'Reilly
BR ə(ʊ)ˈrʌɪli
AM oʊˈraɪli

Orenburg
BR ˈɒrənbəːg
AM ˈɔrənˌbərg

Oreo®
BR ˈɔːrɪəʊ, -z
AM ˈɔrioʊ, -z

oreography
BR ˌɒrɪˈɒgrəfi
AM ˌɔriˈɑgrəfi

Oresteia
BR ˌɒrɪˈstʌɪə(r), ˌɒrɪˈstiːə(r), ˌɒrɪˈsteɪə(r), ˌɔːrɪˈstʌɪə(r), ˌɔːrɪˈstiːə(r), ˌɔːrɪˈsteɪə(r)
AM ˌɔrəsˈtaɪə

Orestes
BR ɒˈrɛstiːz
AM ɔˈrɛstiz

oreweed
BR ˈɔːwiːd
AM ˈɔrˌwid

orfe
BR ɔːf, -s
AM ɔ(ə)rf, -s

Orff
BR ɔːf
AM ɔ(ə)rf

Orford
BR ˈɔːfəd
AM ˈɔrfərd

organ
BR ˈɔːg(ə)n, -z
AM ˈɔrgən, -z

organa
BR ˈɔːgənə(r), ˈɔːgn̩ə(r)
AM ˈɔrgənə

organdie
BR ˈɔːg(ə)nd|i, -ɪz
AM ˈɔrgəndi, -z

organdy
BR ˈɔːg(ə)nd|i, -ɪz
AM ˈɔrgəndi, -z

organelle
BR ˌɔːgəˈnɛl, -z
AM ˌɔrgəˈnɛl, -z

organic
BR ɔːˈganɪk
AM ɔrˈgænɪk

organically
BR ɔːˈganɪkli
AM ɔrˈgænək(ə)li

organisable
BR ˈɔːgənʌɪzəbl, ˈɔːgn̩ʌɪzəbl
AM ˌɔrgəˌnaɪzəbəl

organisation
BR ˌɔːgənʌɪˈzeɪʃn, ˌɔːgn̩ʌɪˈzeɪʃn, -z
AM ˌɔrgənəˈzeɪʃən, ˌɔrgəˌnaɪˈzeɪʃən, -z

organisational
BR ˌɔːgənʌɪˈzeɪʃn̩(ə)l, ˌɔːgənʌɪˈzeɪʃən(ə)l, ˌɔːgn̩ʌɪˈzeɪʃn̩(ə)l, ˌɔːgn̩ʌɪˈzeɪʃən(ə)l
AM ˌɔrgənəˈzeɪʃ(ə)nəl, ˌɔrgəˌnaɪˈzeɪʃ(ə)nəl

organisationally
BR ˌɔːgənʌɪˈzeɪʃn̩əli, ˌɔːgənʌɪˈzeɪʃn̩l̩i, ˌɔːgənʌɪˈzeɪʃənl̩i, ˌɔːgənʌɪˈzeɪʃ(ə)nəli, ˌɔːgn̩ʌɪˈzeɪʃn̩əli, ˌɔːgn̩ʌɪˈzeɪʃn̩l̩i, ˌɔːgn̩ʌɪˈzeɪʃənl̩i, ˌɔːgn̩ʌɪˈzeɪʃ(ə)nəli
AM ˌɔrgənəˈzeɪʃ(ə)nəli, ˌɔrgəˌnaɪˈzeɪʃ(ə)nəli

organise
BR ˈɔːgənʌɪz, ˈɔːgn̩ʌɪz, -ɨz, -ɪŋ, -d
AM ˈɔrgəˌnaɪz, -ɨz, -ɪŋ, -d

organiser
BR ˈɔːgənʌɪzə(r), ˈɔːgn̩ʌɪzə(r), -z
AM ˈɔrgəˌnaɪzər, -z

organism
BR ˈɔːgənɪz(ə)m, ˈɔːgn̩ɪz(ə)m, -z
AM ˈɔrgəˌnɪzəm, -z

organist
BR ˈɔːgənɪst, ˈɔːgn̩ɪst, -s
AM ˈɔrgənəst, -s

organizable
BR ˈɔːgənʌɪzəbl, ˈɔːgn̩ʌɪzəbl
AM ˌɔrgəˌnaɪzəbəl

organization
BR ˌɔːgənʌɪˈzeɪʃn, ˌɔːgn̩ʌɪˈzeɪʃn, -z
AM ˌɔrgənəˈzeɪʃən, ˌɔrgəˌnaɪˈzeɪʃən, -z

organizational
BR ˌɔːgənʌɪˈzeɪʃn̩(ə)l, ˌɔːgənʌɪˈzeɪʃən(ə)l, ˌɔːgn̩ʌɪˈzeɪʃn̩(ə)l, ˌɔːgn̩ʌɪˈzeɪʃən(ə)l
AM ˌɔrgənəˈzeɪʃ(ə)nəl, ˌɔrgəˌnaɪˈzeɪʃ(ə)nəl

organizationally
BR ˌɔːgənʌɪˈzeɪʃn̩əli, ˌɔːgənʌɪˈzeɪʃn̩l̩i, ˌɔːgənʌɪˈzeɪʃənl̩i, ˌɔːgənʌɪˈzeɪʃ(ə)nəli, ˌɔːgn̩ʌɪˈzeɪʃn̩əli, ˌɔːgn̩ʌɪˈzeɪʃn̩l̩i, ˌɔːgn̩ʌɪˈzeɪʃənl̩i, ˌɔːgn̩ʌɪˈzeɪʃ(ə)nəli
AM ˌɔrgənəˈzeɪʃ(ə)nəli, ˌɔrgəˌnaɪˈzeɪʃ(ə)nəli

organize
BR ˈɔːgənʌɪz, ˈɔːgn̩ʌɪz, -ɨz, -ɪŋ, -d
AM ˈɔrgəˌnaɪz, -ɨz, -ɪŋ, -d

organizer
BR ˈɔːgənʌɪzə(r), ˈɔːgn̩ʌɪzə(r), -z
AM ˈɔrgəˌnaɪzər, -z

organochlorine
BR ɔːˌganəʊˈklɔːriːn, ˌɔːgənəʊˈklɔːriːn, ˌɔːgn̩əʊˈklɔːriːn, -z
AM ˌɔrgənoʊˈklɔrin, ɔrˌgænoʊˈklɔrin, -z

organoleptic
BR ɔːˌganə(ʊ)ˈlɛptɪk, ˌɔːgənə(ʊ)ˈlɛptɪk, ˌɔːgn̩ə(ʊ)ˈlɛptɪk
AM ˌɔrgənoʊˈlɛptɪk

organometallic
BR ɔːˌganəʊmɪˈtalɪk, ˌɔːgənəʊmɪˈtalɪk, ˌɔːgn̩əʊmɪˈtalɪk
AM ˌɔrgənoʊməˈtælɪk

organon
BR ˈɔːgənɒn, ˈɔːgn̩ɒn, -z
AM ˈɔrgəˌnɑn, -z

organophosphate
BR ɔːˌganəʊˈfɒsfeɪt, ˌɔːgənəʊˈfɒsfeɪt, ˌɔːgn̩əʊˈfɒsfeɪt, -s
AM ˌɔrgənəˈfɑsˌfeɪt, ɔrˌgænoʊˈfɑsˌfeɪt, -s

organophosphorus
BR ɔːˌganəʊˈfɒsf(ə)rəs, ˌɔːgənəʊˈfɒsf(ə)rəs, ˌɔːgn̩əʊˈfɒsf(ə)rəs
AM ˌɔrgənəˈfɑsf(ə)rəs, ɔrˌgænoʊˈfɑsf(ə)rəs

organotherapy
BR ˌɔːgənəʊˈθɛrəpi, ˌɔːgn̩əʊˈθɛrəpi
AM ˌɔrgənəˈθɛrəpi, ɔrˌgænoʊˈθɛrəpi

organum
BR ˈɔːɡənəm, ˈɔːɡn̩əm
AM ˈɔrɡənəm

organza
BR ɔːˈɡanzə(r), -z
AM ɔrˈɡænzə, -z

organzine
BR ˈɔːɡ(ə)nziːn,
ɔːˈɡanziːn, -z
AM ˈɔrɡənˌzin, -z

orgasm
BR ˈɔːɡaz(ə)m, -z
AM ˈɔrˌɡæzəm, -z

orgasmic
BR ɔːˈɡazmɪk
AM ɔrˈɡæzmɪk

orgasmically
BR ɔːˈɡazmɨkli
AM ɔrˈɡæzmək(ə)li

orgastic
BR ɔːˈɡastɪk
AM ɔrˈɡæstɪk

orgastically
BR ɔːˈɡastɨkli
AM ɔrˈɡæstək(ə)li

orgeat
BR ˈɔːdʒɪət, -s
AM ˈɔrˌʒɑt, -s

orgiastic
BR ˌɔːdʒɪˈastɪk
AM ˌɔrdʒiˈæstɪk

orgiastically
BR ˌɔːdʒɪˈastɨkli
AM ˌɔrdʒiˈæstək(ə)li

orgone
BR ˈɔːɡəʊn
AM ˈɔrˌɡoʊn

Orgreave
BR ˈɔːɡriːv
AM ˈɔrˌɡriv

orgulous
BR ˈɔːɡjʉləs
AM ˈɔrɡ(j)ələs

orgy
BR ˈɔːdʒ|i, -ɪz
AM ˈɔrdʒi, -z

Oriana
BR ˌɒrɪˈɑːnə(r),
ˌɔːrɪˈɑːnə(r)
AM ˌɔriˈɑnə

oribi
BR ˈɒrɨb|i, -ɪz
AM ˈɔrəbi, -z

oriel
BR ˈɔːrɪəl, -z
AM ˈɔriəl, -z

Orient
BR ˈɔːrɪənt, ˈɒrɪənt
AM ˈɔriənt

orient
verb
BR ˈɔːrɪɛnt, ˈɒrɪɛnt, -s,
-ɪŋ, -ɨd
AM ˈɔriˌɛn|t, -ts, -(t)ɪŋ,
-(t)əd

Oriental
BR ˌɔːrɪˈɛntl, ˌɒrɪˈɛntl,
-z
AM ˌɔriˈɛn(t)l, -z

orientalise
BR ˌɔːrɪˈɛntl̩ʌɪz,
ˌɔːrɪˈɛntəlʌɪz,
ˌɒrɪˈɛntl̩ʌɪz,
ˌɒrɪˈɛntəlʌɪz, -ɨz, -ɪŋ, -d
AM ˌɔriˈɛn(t)lˌaɪz, -ɨz,
-ɪŋ, -d

orientalism
BR ˌɔːrɪˈɛntl̩ɪz(ə)m,
ˌɔːrɪˈɛntəlɪz(ə)m,
ˌɒrɪˈɛntl̩ɪz(ə)m,
ˌɒrɪˈɛntəlɪz(ə)m
AM ˌɔriˈɛn(t)lˌɪzəm

orientalist
BR ˌɔːrɪˈɛntl̩ɪst,
ˌɔːrɪˈɛntəlɪst,
ˌɒrɪˈɛntl̩ɪst,
ˌɒrɪˈɛntəlɪst, -s
AM ˌɔriˈɛn(t)l̩əst, -s

orientalize
BR ˌɔːrɪˈɛntl̩ʌɪz,
ˌɔːrɪˈɛntəlʌɪz,
ˌɒrɪˈɛntl̩ʌɪz,
ˌɒrɪˈɛntəlʌɪz, -ɨz, -ɪŋ, -d
AM ˌɔriˈɛn(t)lˌaɪz, -ɨz,
-ɪŋ, -d

orientally
BR ˌɔːrɪˈɛntl̩i,
ˌɔːrɪˈɛntəli, ˌɒrɪˈɛntl̩i,
ˌɒrɪˈɛntəli
AM ˌɔriˈɛn(t)l̩i

orientate
BR ˈɔːrɪənteɪt,
ˈɔːrɪɛnteɪt, ˈɒrɪənteɪt,
ˈɒrɪɛnteɪt, -s
AM ˈɔriənˌteɪt, -s

orientation
BR ˌɔːrɪənˈteɪʃn,
ˌɔːrɪɛnˈteɪʃn,
ˌɒrɪənˈteɪʃn,
ˌɒrɪɛnˈteɪʃn, -z
AM ˌɔriənˈteɪʃən, -z

orientational
BR ˌɔːrɪənˈteɪʃn̩(ə)l,
ˌɔːrɪənˈteɪʃən(ə)l,
ˌɔːrɪɛnˈteɪʃn̩(ə)l,
ˌɔːrɪɛnˈteɪʃən(ə)l,
ˌɒrɪənˈteɪʃn̩(ə)l,
ˌɒrɪənˈteɪʃən(ə)l,
ˌɒrɪɛnˈteɪʃn̩(ə)l,
ˌɒrɪɛnˈteɪʃən(ə)l
AM ˌɔriənˈteɪʃ(ə)nəl

orienteer
BR ˌɔːrɪənˈtɪə(r),
ˌɔːrɪɛnˈtɪə(r),
ˌɒrɪənˈtɪə(r),
ˌɒrɪɛnˈtɪə(r), -z
AM ˌɔriənˈtɪ(ə)r, -z

orienteering
BR ˌɔːrɪənˈtɪərɪŋ,
ˌɔːrɪɛnˈtɪərɪŋ,
ˌɒrɪənˈtɪərɪŋ,
ˌɒrɪɛnˈtɪərɪŋ
AM ˌɔriənˈtɪrɪŋ

orifice
BR ˈɒrɨf|ɪs, -ɨsɪz
AM ˈɔrəfəs, -əz

oriflamme
BR ˈɒrɨflam, -z
AM ˈɔrəˌflæm, -z

origami
BR ˌɒrɨˈɡɑːmi
AM ˌɔrəˈɡɑmi

origan
BR ˈɒrɨɡ(ə)n, -z
AM ˈɔrəɡən, -z

origanum
BR əˈrɪɡənəm,
əˈrɪɡn̩əm, ɒˈrɪɡənəm,
ɒˈrɪɡn̩əm, -z
AM əˈrɪɡənəm, -z

Origen
BR ˈɒrɪdʒɛn
AM ˈɔriˌdʒɛn

origin
BR ˈɒrɨdʒ(ɨ)n, -z
AM ˈɔrədʒən, -z

original
BR əˈrɪdʒn̩l, əˈrɪdʒɨnl,
-z
AM əˈrɪdʒ(ə)nəl, -z

originality
BR əˌrɪdʒɨˈnalɨti
AM əˌrɪdʒəˈnælədi

originally
BR əˈrɪdʒn̩l̩i,
əˈrɪdʒn̩əli, əˈrɪdʒɨnl̩i,
əˈrɪdʒɨnəli
AM əˈrɪdʒ(ə)nəli

originate
BR əˈrɪdʒɨneɪt, -s, -ɪŋ,
-ɪd
AM əˈrɪdʒəˌneɪ|t, -ts,
-dɪŋ, -dɨd

origination
BR əˌrɪdʒɨˈneɪʃn, -z
AM əˌrɪdʒəˈneɪʃən, -z

originative
BR əˈrɪdʒɨnətɪv
AM əˈrɪdʒəˌneɪdɪv

originator
BR əˈrɪdʒɨneɪtə(r), -z
AM əˈrɪdʒəˌneɪdər, -z

orinasal
BR ˌɔːrɪˈneɪzl
AM ˌɔrəˈneɪzəl

O-ring
BR ˈəʊrɪŋ, -z
AM ˈoʊˌrɪŋ, -z

Orinoco
BR ˌɒrɨˈnəʊkəʊ
AM ˌɔrəˈnoʊkoʊ

Orinthia
BR əˈrɪnθɪə(r),
ɒˈrɪnθɪə(r)
AM əˈrɪnθiə

oriole
BR ˈɔːrɪəʊl, -z
AM ˈɔriˌoʊl, -z

Orion
BR əˈrʌɪən
AM əˈraɪən, oʊˈraɪən

O'Riordan
BR ə(ʊ)ˈrɪədn
AM oʊˈrɪrdən

orison
BR ˈɒrɨzn, -z
AM ˈɔrəsən, ˈɔrəzn, -z

Orissa
BR ɒˈrɪsə(r)
AM ɔˈrɪsə

Oriya
BR ɒˈriːə(r), -z
AM ɔˈriə, -z

ork
BR ɔːk, -s
AM ɔ(ə)rk, -s

Orkney
BR ˈɔːkn|i, -ɪz
AM ˈɔrkni, -z

Orlando
BR ɔːˈlandəʊ
AM ɔrˈlændoʊ

orle
BR ɔːl, -z
AM ˈɔr(ə)l, -z

Orleanist
BR ɔːˈlɪənɪst, -s
AM ɔrˈliənəst, -s

Orléans
BR ɔːˈliːənz, ˈɔːlɪənz
AM ˈɔrliən(z),
ɔrˈliən(z)
FR ɔʀleɑ̃

Orlon®
BR ˈɔːlɒn
AM ˈɔrˌlɑn

orlop
BR ˈɔːlɒp, -s
AM ˈɔrˌlɑp, -s

Orm
BR ɔːm
AM ɔ(ə)rm
DAN ˈoːˀʌm

Orme
BR ɔːm
AM ɔ(ə)rm

ormer
BR ˈɔːmə(r), -z
AM ˈɔrmər, -z

Ormerod
BR ˈɔːm(ə)rɒd
AM ˈɔrmˌrɑd

Ormesby
BR ˈɔːmzbi
AM ˈɔrmzbi

ormolu
BR ˈɔːməluː
AM ˈɔrməˌlu

Ormond
BR ˈɔːm(ə)nd
AM ˈɔrmənd

Ormonde
BR ˈɔːm(ə)nd
AM ˈɔrmənd

Ormrod
BR ˈɔːmrɒd
AM ˈɔrmˌrɑd

Ormsby
BR 'ɔːmzbi
AM 'ɔrmzbi
Ormskirk
BR 'ɔːmzkəːk
AM 'ɔrmzˌkərk
Ormuz
BR 'ɔːmʌz
AM 'ɔrməz
ornament[1]
noun
BR 'ɔːnəm(ə)nt
AM 'ɔrnəmənt
ornament[2]
verb
BR 'ɔːnəmɛnt, -s, -ɪŋ, -ɨd
AM 'ɔrnəˌmɛn|t, -ts, -(t)ɪŋ, -(t)əd
ornamental
BR ˌɔːnə'mɛntl
AM ˌɔrnə'mɛn(t)l
ornamentalism
BR ˌɔːnə'mɛntl̩ɪz(ə)m, ˌɔːnə'mɛntəlɪz(ə)m
AM ˌɔrnə'mɛn(t)lˌɪzəm
ornamentalist
BR ˌɔːnə'mɛntl̩ɪst, ˌɔːnə'mɛntəlɪst, -s
AM ˌɔrnə'mɛn(t)l̩əst, -s
ornamentally
BR ˌɔːnə'mɛntl̩i, ˌɔːnə'mɛntəli
AM ˌɔrnə'mɛn(t)l̩i
ornamentation
BR ˌɔːnəmɛn'teɪʃn, ˌɔːnəm(ə)n'teɪʃn
AM ˌɔrnəˌmɛn'teɪʃən
ornate
BR ɔː'neɪt
AM ɔr'neɪt
ornately
BR ɔː'neɪtli
AM ɔr'neɪtli
ornateness
BR ɔː'neɪtnɨs
AM ɔr'neɪtnɨs
orneriness
BR 'ɔːn(ə)rɪnɨs
AM 'ɔrn(ə)rinɨs
ornery
BR 'ɔːn(ə)ri
AM 'ɔrn(ə)ri
ornithic
BR ɔː'nɪθɪk
AM ɔr'nɪθɪk
ornithischian
BR ˌɔːnɪ'θɪʃɪən, ˌɔːnɪ'θɪskɪən, -z
AM ˌɔrnə'θɪskiən, ˌɔrnə'θɪʃ(i)ən, -z
ornithological
BR ˌɔːnɪθə'lɒdʒɪkl
AM ɔrˌnɪθə'lɑdʒəkəl
ornithologically
BR ˌɔːnɪθə'lɒdʒɪkli
AM ɔrˌnɪθə'lɑdʒək(ə)li
ornithologist
BR ˌɔːnɪ'θɒlədʒɪst, -s
AM ˌɔrnə'θɑlədʒəst, -s
ornithology
BR ˌɔːnɪ'θɒlədʒi
AM ˌɔrnə'θɑlədʒi
ornithorhynchus
BR ˌɔːnɪθə(ʊ)'rɪŋkəs, -ɪz
AM ɔrˌnɪθə'rɪŋkəs, ˌɔrnəθə'rɪŋkəs, -əz
ornithoscopy
BR ˌɔːnɪ'θɒskəpi
AM ˌɔrnə'θɑskəpi
orogenesis
BR ˌɒrə(ʊ)'dʒɛnɨsɪs, ˌɔːrə(ʊ)'dʒɛnɨsɪs
AM ˌɔroʊ'dʒɛnəsəs
orogenetic
BR ˌɒrəʊdʒɪ'nɛtɪk, ˌɔːrəʊdʒɪ'nɛtɪk
AM ˌɔroʊdʒə'nɛdɪk
orogenic
BR ˌɒrə(ʊ)'dʒɛnɪk, ˌɔːrə(ʊ)'dʒɛnɪk
AM ˌɔroʊ'dʒɛnɪk
orogeny
BR ɒ'rɒdʒɨni, ə'rɒdʒɨni, ɔː'rɒdʒɨni
AM ɔ'rɑdʒ(ə)ni
orographic
BR ˌɒrə'grafɪk, ˌɔːrə'grafɪk
AM ˌɔrə'græfɪk
orographical
BR ˌɒrə'grafɪkl, ˌɔːrə'grafɪkl
AM ˌɔrə'græfəkəl
orography
BR ɒ'rɒgrəfi, ə'rɒgrəfi, ɔː'rɒgrəfi
AM ɔ'rɑgrəfi
oroide
BR 'ɒrəʊʌɪd, -z
AM 'ɔrəˌwaɪd, -z
orological
BR ˌɒrə'lɒdʒɪkl
AM ˌɔrə'lɑdʒəkəl
orologist
BR ɒ'rɒlədʒɪst, ə'rɒlədʒɪst, ɔː'rɒlədɪst, -s
AM ɔ'rɑlədʒəst, -s
orology
BR ɒ'rɒlədʒi, ə'rɒlədʒi, ɔː'rɒlədʒi
AM ɔ'rɑlədʒi
Oronsay
BR 'ɒrənseɪ, 'ɒrn̩seɪ, 'ɒrənzeɪ, 'ɒrn̩zeɪ
AM 'ɔrənˌseɪ
Orontes
BR ə'rɒntiːz, ɒ'rɒntiːz
AM ɔ'rɔn(t)iz, ɔ'rɑn(t)iz
oropendola
BR ˌɒrə'pɛndələ(*r*), ˌɒrə'pɛndl̩ə(*r*), -z
AM ˌɔrə'pɛndələ, -z
oropharynges
BR ˌɔːrəʊfə'rɪn(d)ʒiːz
AM ˌɔroʊfə'rɪndʒiz
oropharynx
BR ˌɔːrəʊ'farɪŋks, -ɨz
AM ˌɔroʊ'fɛrɪŋks, -ɨz
orotund
BR 'ɒrətʌnd
AM 'ɔrəˌtənd
O'Rourke
BR ə(ʊ)'rɔːk
AM oʊ'rɔ(ə)rk
orphan
BR 'ɔːf|n, -nz, -n̩ɪŋ, -nd
AM 'ɔrf|ən, -ənz, -(ə)nɪŋ, -ənd
orphanage
BR 'ɔːfn̩|ɪdʒ, 'ɔːfən|ɪdʒ, -ɨdʒɨz
AM 'ɔrf(ə)nɪdʒ, -ɨz
orphanhood
BR 'ɔːfnhʊd
AM 'ɔrfənˌ(h)ʊd
orphanise
BR 'ɔːfn̩ʌɪz, 'ɔːfənʌɪz, -ɨz, -ɪŋ, -d
AM 'ɔrfəˌnaɪz, -ɨz, -ɪŋ, -d
orphanize
BR 'ɔːfn̩ʌɪz, 'ɔːfənʌɪz, -ɨz, -ɪŋ, -d
AM 'ɔrfəˌnaɪz, -ɨz, -ɪŋ, -d
Orphean
BR ɔː'fiːən, 'ɔːfɪən
AM 'ɔrfiən
Orpheus
BR 'ɔːfɪəs
AM 'ɔrfiəs
Orphic
BR 'ɔːfɪk
AM 'ɔrfɪk
Orphism
BR 'ɔːfɪz(ə)m
AM 'ɔrˌfɪzəm
orphrey
BR 'ɔːfr|i, -ɪz
AM 'ɔrfri, -z
orpiment
BR 'ɔːpɪm(ə)nt, -s
AM 'ɔrpəmənt, -s
orpin
BR 'ɔːpɪn, -z
AM 'ɔrpən, -z
orpine
BR 'ɔːpʌɪn, 'ɔːpɪn, -z
AM 'ɔrpən, -z
Orpington
BR 'ɔːpɪŋt(ə)n
AM 'ɔrpɪŋtən
Orr
BR ɔː(r)
AM ɔ(ə)r
orra
BR 'ɒrə(*r*)
AM 'ɔrə
Orrell
BR 'ɒrəl, 'ɒrl̩
AM 'ɔrəl
orrery
BR 'ɒrər|i, -ɪz
AM 'ɔrəri, -z
orris
BR 'ɒr|ɪs, -ɨsɪz
AM 'ɔrəs, -əz
Orsino
BR ɔː'siːnəʊ
AM ɔr'sinoʊ
Orson
BR 'ɔːsn
AM 'ɔrsən
ortanique
BR ˌɔːtə'niːk, -s
AM ˌɔrtə'nik, -s
Ortega
BR ɔː'teɪgə(*r*), ɔː'tiːgə(*r*)
AM ɔr'teɪgə
orthocephalic
BR ˌɔːθəʊsɪ'falɪk, ˌɔːθəʊkɛ'falɪk
AM ˌɔrθoʊsə'fælɪk
orthochromatic
BR ˌɔːθəʊkrə'matɪk
AM ˌɔrθoʊkrə'mædɪk
orthoclase
BR 'ɔːθə(ʊ)kleɪz, 'ɔːθə(ʊ)kleɪs, -ɨz
AM 'ɔrθəˌkleɪs, 'ɔrθəˌkleɪz, -ɨz
orthodontia
BR ˌɔːθə'dɒntɪə(*r*)
AM ˌɔrθə'dɑn(t)ʃ(i)ə
orthodontic
BR ˌɔːθə'dɒntɪk, -s
AM ˌɔrθə'dɑn(t)ɪk, -s
orthodontist
BR ˌɔːθə'dɒntɪst, -s
AM ˌɔrθəˌdɑn(t)əst, -s
orthodox
BR 'ɔːθədɒks
AM 'ɔrθəˌdɑks
orthodoxly
BR 'ɔːθədɒksli
AM 'ɔrθəˌdɑksli
orthodoxy
BR 'ɔːθədɒks|i, -ɪz
AM 'ɔrθəˌdɑksi, -z
orthoepic
BR ˌɔːθəʊ'ɛpɪk
AM ˌɔrθoʊ'ɛpɪk
orthoepist
BR 'ɔːθəʊˌɛpɪst, ˌɔːθəʊ'ɛpɪst, 'ɔːθəʊˌiːpɪst, ˌɔːθəʊ'iːpɪst, ɔː'θəʊɪpɪst, -s
AM ɔr'θoʊəpəst, -s
orthoepy
BR 'ɔːθəʊˌiːpi, 'ɔːθəʊˌɛpi, 'ɔːθəʊɪpi, ɔː'θəʊɪpi
AM ɔr'θoʊəpi
orthogenesis
BR ˌɔːθə(ʊ)'dʒɛnɨsɪs
AM ˌɔrθoʊ'dʒɛnəsəs

orthogenetic
BR ˌɔːθəʊdʒɪˈnɛtɪk
AM ˌ͵ɔrθoʊdʒəˈnɛdɪk
orthogenetically
BR ˌɔːθəʊdʒɪˈnɛtɪkli
AM ˌ͵ɔrθoʊdʒəˈnɛdək(ə)li
orthognathous
BR ɔːˈθɒgnəθəs
AM ɔrˈθɑgnəθəs
orthogonal
BR ɔːˈθɒgənl, ɔˈθɒgn̩l
AM ɔrˈθɑgənəl
orthogonally
BR ɔːˈθɒg(ə)nl̩i, ɔːθɒgn̩l̩i, ɔːˈθɒg(ə)nəli, ɔːθɒgn̩əli
AM ɔrˈθɑg(ə)nəli
orthographer
BR ɔːˈθɒgrəfə(r), -z
AM ɔrˈθɑgrəfər, -z
orthographic
BR ˌɔːθəˈgrafɪk
AM ˌ͵ɔrθəˈgræfɪk
orthographical
BR ˌɔːθəˈgrafɪkl
AM ˌ͵ɔrθəˈgræfəkəl
orthographically
BR ˌɔːθəˈgrafɪkli
AM ˌ͵ɔrθəˈgræfək(ə)li
orthography
BR ɔːˈθɒgrəfi
AM ɔrˈθɑgrəfi
ortho-hydrogen
BR ˌɔːθəʊˈhʌɪdrədʒ(ə)n
AM ˈɔrθoʊˈhaɪdrədʒən
orthopaedic
BR ˌɔːθəˈpiːdɪk, -s
AM ˌ͵ɔrθəˈpidɪk, -s
orthopaedist
BR ˌɔːθəˈpiːdɪst, -s
AM ˌ͵ɔrθəˈpidɪst, -s
orthopedic
BR ˌɔːθəˈpiːdɪk, -s
AM ˌ͵ɔrθəˈpidɪk, -s
orthopedist
BR ˌɔːθəˈpiːdɪst, -s
AM ˌ͵ɔrθəˈpidɪst, -s
Orthoptera
BR ɔːˈθɒpt(ə)rə(*r*)
AM ɔrˈθɑptərə
orthopteran
BR ɔːˈθɒpt(ə)rən, ɔːˈθɒpt(ə)rn̩
AM ɔrˈθɑptərən
orthopterous
BR ɔːˈθɒpt(ə)rəs
AM ɔrˈθɑptərəs
orthoptic
BR ɔːˈθɒptɪk, -s
AM ɔrˈθɑptɪk, -s
orthoptist
BR ˈɔːθɒptɪst, -s
AM ɔrˈθɑptəst, -s
orthorhombic
BR ˌɔːθəˈrɒmbɪk
AM ˌɔrθəˈrɑmbɪk
orthostatic
BR ˌɔːθəˈstatɪk
AM ˌɔrθəˈstædɪk
orthotone
BR ˈɔːθətəʊn, -z
AM ˈɔrθəˌtoʊn, -z
Ortiz
BR ɔːˈtiːz
AM ɔrˈtiz
SP orˈtiθ, orˈtis
ortolan
BR ˈɔːtələn, ˈɔːtl̩ən, -z
AM ˈɔrdl̩ən, -z
Orton
BR ˈɔːtn
AM ˈɔrtən
orts
BR ɔːts
AM ɔ(ə)rts
Oruro
BR ɔːˈrʊərəʊ
AM ɔˈruroʊ
Orvieto
BR ɔːˈvjɛtəʊ
AM ɔrˈvjɛdoʊ
Orville
BR ˈɔːv(ɪ)l
AM ˈɔrvəl
Orwell
BR ˈɔːw(ɛ)l
AM ˈɔrˌwɛl
Orwellian
BR ɔːˈwɛlɪən
AM ɔrˈwɛljən, ɔrˈwɛliən
oryx
BR ˈɒr|ɪks, -ɪksɪz
AM ˈɔrɪks, -ɪz
Osage
BR əʊˈseɪdʒ, ˈəʊseɪdʒ
AM ˈoʊˌseɪdʒ
Osaka
BR əʊˈsɑːkə(*r*)
AM oʊˈsɑkə
Osbert
BR ˈɒzbət, ˈɒzbəːt
AM ˈɑzbərt
Osborn
BR ˈɒzbɔːn
AM ˈɑzˌbɔ(ə)rn, ˈɑzbərn
Osborne
BR ˈɒzbɔːn
AM ˈɑzˌbɔ(ə)rn, ˈɑzbərn
Oscar
BR ˈɒskə(r), -z
AM ˈɑskər, -z
oscillate
BR ˈɒsɪleɪt, -s, -ɪŋ, -ɪd
AM ˈɑsəˌleɪ|t, -ts, -dɪŋ, -dɪd
oscillation
BR ˌɒsɪˈleɪʃn, -z
AM ˌɑsəˈleɪʃən, -z
oscillator
BR ˈɒsɪleɪtə(r), -z
AM ˈɑsəˌleɪdər, -z
oscillatory
BR əˈsɪlət(ə)ri, ɒˈsɪlət(ə)ri
AM əˈsɪləˌtɔri
oscillogram
BR əˈsɪləgram, ɒˈsɪləgram, -z
AM əˈsɪləˌgræm, -z
oscillograph
BR əˈsɪləgrɑːf, ɒˈsɪləgrɑːf, əˈsɪləgraf, ɒˈsɪləgraf, -s
AM əˈsɪləˌgræf, -s
oscillographic
BR əˌsɪləˈgrafɪk, ɒˌsɪləˈgrafɪk
AM əˌsɪləˈgræfɪk
oscillography
BR ˌɒsɪˈlɒgrəfi
AM ˌɑsəˈlɑgrəfi
oscilloscope
BR əˈsɪləskəʊp, ɒˈsɪləskəʊp, -s
AM əˈsɪləˌskoʊp, -s
oscilloscopic
BR əˌsɪləˈskɒpɪk, ɒˌsɪləˈskɒpɪk
AM əˌsɪləˈskɑpɪk
oscine
BR ˈɒsʌɪn, ˈɒsɪn
AM ˈɑsn, ˈɑˌsaɪn
oscinine
BR ˈɒsɪnʌɪn, ˈɒsɪniːn
AM ˈɑsəˌnaɪn, ˈɑsənən
oscitation
BR ˌɒsɪˈteɪʃn, -z
AM ˌɑsəˈteɪʃən, -z
oscula
BR ˈɒskjʉlə(*r*)
AM ˈɑskjələ
osculant
BR ˈɒskjʉlənt, ˈɒskjʉln̩t
AM ˈɑskjələnt
oscular
BR ˈɒskjʉlə(r)
AM ˈɑskjələr
osculate
BR ˈɒskjʉleɪt, -s, -ɪŋ, -ɪd
AM ˈɑskjəˌleɪ|t, -ts, -dɪŋ, -dɪd
osculation
BR ˌɒskjʉˈleɪʃn, -z
AM ˌɑskjəˈleɪʃən, -z
osculatory
BR ˈɒskjʉlət(ə)ri
AM ˈɑskjələˌtɔri
osculum
BR ˈɒskjʉləm
AM ˈɑskjələm
Osgood
BR ˈɒzgʊd
AM ˈɑzˌgʊd
OSHA
BR ˈəʊʃə(*r*)
AM ˈoʊʃə
O'Shaughnessy
BR ə(ʊ)ˈʃɔːnɪsi
AM oʊˈʃɔnəsi, oʊˈʃɑnəsi
O'Shea
BR ə(ʊ)ˈʃeɪ, ə(ʊ)ˈʃiː
AM oʊˈʃeɪ
osier
BR ˈəʊzɪə(r), ˈəʊʒ(ɪ)ə(r), -z
AM ˈoʊʒər, -z
Osiris
BR ə(ʊ)ˈsʌɪrɪs
AM oʊˈsaɪrɪs
Osler
BR ˈɒslə(r)
AM ˈɑslər
Oslo
BR ˈɒzləʊ
AM ˈɑzˌloʊ
NO ˈuslu
Osman
BR ˈɒzmən, ˈɒsmən
AM ˈɑzmən, ˈɑzˌmɑn
Osmanli
BR ɒzˈmanl|i, ɒsˈmanl|i, ɒzˈmɑːnl|i, ɒsˈmɑːnl|i, -ɪz
AM ˈɑzmənli, ˈɑzˌmɑnli, -z
osmic
BR ˈɒzmɪk
AM ˈɑzmɪk
osmically
BR ˈɒzmɪkli
AM ˈɑzmək(ə)li
Osmiroid
BR ˈɒzmɪrɔɪd
AM ˈɑzməˌrɔɪd
osmium
BR ˈɒzmɪəm
AM ˈɑzmiəm
osmolality
BR ˌɒzməˈlalɪti
AM ˌɑzməˈlælədi
osmolarity
BR ˌɒzməˈlarɪti
AM ˌɑzməˈlɛrədi
Osmond
BR ˈɒzmənd
AM ˈɑzmən(d)
osmosis
BR ɒzˈməʊsɪs
AM ɑzˈmoʊsəs, ɑˈsmoʊsəs
Osmotherley
BR ɒzˈmʌðəli
AM ɑzˈməðərli
Osmotherly
BR ɒzˈmʌðəli
AM ɑzˈməðərli
osmotic
BR ɒzˈmɒtɪk
AM ɑzˈmɑdɪk, ɑˈsmɑdɪk
osmotically
BR ɒzˈmɒtɪkli

AM ɑz'madək(ə)li, ɑ'smadək(ə)li

osmund
BR 'ɒzmənd, -z
AM 'ɑzmən(d), -z

osmunda
BR ɒz'mʌndə(r), -z
AM ɑz'məndə, -z

Osnabrück
BR 'ɒznəbrʊk
AM 'ɑsnə,brʊk
GER ɔsnə'brʏk

osnaburg
BR 'ɒznəbəːg
AM 'ɑznə,bərg

osprey
BR 'ɒspreɪ, -z
AM 'ɑspri, -z

Ossa
BR 'ɒsə(r)
AM 'ɑsə

ossein
BR 'ɒsɪɪn
AM 'ɑsiɪn

osseous
BR 'ɒsɪəs
AM 'ɑsiəs

Ossetia
BR ɒ'sɛtɪə(r), ɒ'siːʃə(r)
AM ɔ'siʃə, ɔ'sɛdiə, ɑ'siʃə, ɑ'sɛdiə

Ossetic
BR ɒ'sɛtɪk
AM ɔ'sɛdɪk, ɑ'sɛdɪk

Ossett
BR 'ɒsɪt
AM 'ɑsət

ossia
BR ɒ'siːə(r), 'ɒsjə(r)
AM oʊ'siə

Ossian
BR 'ɒsɪən
AM 'ɑsiən

Ossianic
BR ,ɒsɪ'anɪk
AM ,ɑsi'ænɪk, ,ɑʃi'ænɪk

ossicle
BR 'ɒsɪkl, -z
AM 'ɑsəkəl, -z

Ossie
BR 'ɒs|i, -ɪz
AM 'ɑsi, -z

ossific
BR ɒ'sɪfɪk
AM ɑ'sɪfɪk

ossification
BR ,ɒsɪfɪ'keɪʃn
AM ,ɑsəfə'keɪʃən

ossifrage
BR 'ɒsɪfr|ɪdʒ, -ɪdʒɪz
AM 'ɑsə,frɪdʒ, -ɪz

ossify
BR 'ɒsɪfʌɪ, -z, -ɪŋ, -d
AM 'ɑsə,faɪ, -z, -ɪŋ, -d

osso buco
BR ,ɒsəʊ 'bʊkəʊ, + 'buːkəʊ
AM ˌɑsoʊ 'bʊko

ossuary
BR 'ɒsjʊər|i, -ɪz
AM 'ɑʃə,wɛri, 'ɑs(j)ə,wɛri, -z

Ostade
BR 'ɒstɑːd
AM 'ɑs,tɑd

osteitis
BR ,ɒstɪ'ʌɪtɪs
AM ,ɑsti'aɪdəs

Ostend
BR ɒ'stɛnd
AM ɔ'stɛnd, ɑ'stɛnd

ostensible
BR ɒ'stɛnsɪbl
AM ə'stɛnsəbəl

ostensibly
BR ɒ'stɛnsɪbli
AM ə'stɛnsɪbli

ostensive
BR ɒ'stɛnsɪv
AM ə'stɛnsɪv

ostensively
BR ɒ'stɛnsɪvli
AM ə'stɛnsɪvli

ostensiveness
BR ɒ'stɛnsɪvnɪs
AM ə'stɛnsɪvnɪs

ostensory
BR ɒ'stɛns(ə)r|i, -ɪz
AM ə'stɛnsəri, -z

ostentation
BR ,ɒstɛn'teɪʃn, ,ɒst(ə)n'teɪʃn
AM ,ɑstən'teɪʃən

ostentatious
BR ,ɒstɛn'teɪʃəs, ,ɒst(ə)n'teɪʃəs
AM ,ɑstən'teɪʃəs

ostentatiously
BR ,ɒstɛn'teɪʃəsli, ,ɒst(ə)n'teɪʃəsli
AM ,ɑstən'teɪʃəsli

osteoarthritic
BR ,ɒstɪəʊɑː'θrɪtɪk
AM ˌɑstioʊ,ɑr'θrɪdɪk

osteoarthritis
BR ,ɒstɪəʊɑː'θrʌɪtɪs
AM ˌɑstioʊ,ɑr'θraɪdɪs

osteogenesis
BR ,ɒstɪəʊ'dʒɛnɪsɪs
AM ˌɑstioʊ'dʒɛnəsəs

osteogenetic
BR ,ɒstɪəʊdʒɪ'nɛtɪk
AM ˌɑstioʊdʒə'nɛdɪk

osteogeny
BR ,ɒstɪ'ɒdʒɪni
AM ,ɑsti'ɑdʒɛni

osteography
BR ,ɒstɪ'ɒgrəfi
AM ,ɑsti'ɑgrəfi

osteological
BR ,ɒstɪə'lɒdʒɪkl
AM ˌɑstiə'lɑdʒəkəl

osteologically
BR ,ɒstɪə'lɒdʒɪkli
AM ˌɑstiə'lɑdʒək(ə)li

osteologist
BR ,ɒstɪ'ɒlədʒɪst, -s
AM ,ɑsti'ɑlədʒəst, -s

osteology
BR ,ɒstɪ'ɒlədʒi
AM ,ɑsti'ɑlədʒi

osteomalacia
BR ,ɒstɪəʊmə'leɪʃ(ɪ)ə(r)
AM ,ɑstioʊmə'leɪʃ(i)ə

osteomalacic
BR ,ɒstɪəʊmə'lasɪk
AM ,ɑstioʊmə'læsɪk

osteomyelitis
BR ,ɒstɪəʊ,mʌɪə'lʌɪtɪs
AM ˌɑstioʊ,maɪ(ə)'laɪdɪs

osteopath
BR 'ɒstɪəpaθ, -s
AM 'ɑstiə,pæθ, -s

osteopathic
BR ,ɒstɪə'paθɪk
AM ˌɑstiə'pæθɪk

osteopathically
BR ,ɒstɪə'paθɪkli
AM ˌɑstiə'pæθək(ə)li

osteopathy
BR ,ɒstɪ'ɒpəθi
AM ,ɑsti'ɑpəθi

osteophyte
BR ,ɒstɪəfʌɪt, -s
AM 'ɑstiə,faɪt, -s

osteoporosis
BR ,ɒstɪəʊpə'rəʊsɪs
AM ,ɑstioʊpə'roʊsəs

Ostermilk
BR 'ɒstəmɪlk
AM 'ɑstər,mɪlk, 'oʊstər,mɪlk

Österreich
BR 'əːstərʌɪk, 'əːstərʌɪx
AM 'əstə,raɪk

Ostia
BR 'ɒstɪə(r)
AM 'ɑstiə

ostinato
BR ,ɒstɪ'nɑːtəʊ, -z
AM ,ɑstə'nɑdoʊ, ,ɑsti'nɑdoʊ, -z

ostler
BR 'ɒslə(r), -z
AM 'ɑslər, -z

Ostmark
BR 'ɒstmɑːk
AM 'ɑs(t),mɑrk

ostomy
BR 'ɒstəmi
AM 'ɑstəmi

Ostpolitik
BR 'ɒstpɒlɪ,tiːk
AM ˌɑs(t),pɑlə'tik

ostraca
BR 'ɒstrəkə(r)
AM 'ɑstrəkə

ostracise
BR 'ɒstrəsʌɪz, -ɪz, -ɪŋ, -d
AM 'ɑstrə,saɪz, -ɪz, -ɪŋ, -d

ostracism
BR 'ɒstrəsɪz(ə)m
AM 'ɑstrə,sɪzəm

ostracize
BR 'ɒstrəsʌɪz, -ɪz, -ɪŋ, -d
AM 'ɑstrə,saɪz, -ɪz, -ɪŋ, -d

ostracoderm
BR ɒ'strakədəːm, -z
AM ə'strækə,dərm, -z

ostracon
BR 'ɒstrəkɒn
AM 'ɑstrə,kɑn

Ostrava
BR 'ɒstrəvə(r)
AM 'ɔstrəvə, 'ɑstrəvə

ostrich
BR 'ɒstrɪtʃ, 'ɒstrɪdʒ, -ɪz
AM 'ɑstrɪtʃ, -ɪz

Ostrogoth
BR 'ɒstrəgɒθ, -s
AM 'ɑstrə,gɑθ, -s

Ostrogothic
BR ,ɒstrə'gɒθɪk
AM ,ɑstrə'gɑθɪk

Ostwald
BR 'ɒs(t)w(ə)ld
AM 'ɑs(t),wɑld
GER 'ɔstvalt

O'Sullivan
BR ə(ʊ)'sʌlɪv(ə)n
AM oʊ'sələvən

Oswald
BR 'ɒzw(ə)ld
AM 'ɑz,wɑld

Oswaldtwistle
BR 'ɒzw(ə)l(d),twɪsl
AM 'ɑzwəl(d),twɪsəl

Oswego
BR ɒs'wiːgəʊ
AM ɑs'wigoʊ

Oswestry
BR 'ɒzwɪstri
AM 'ɑzwəstri

Osyth
BR 'əʊzɪθ, 'əʊsɪθ
AM 'oʊzɪθ, 'oʊsɪθ

Otago
BR ə(ʊ)'tɑːgəʊ, ɒ'tɑːgəʊ
AM oʊ'teɪgoʊ

otary
BR 'əʊt(ə)r|i, -ɪz
AM 'oʊdəri, -z

Otello
BR ə(ʊ)'tɛləʊ
AM oʊ'tɛloʊ, ə'tɛloʊ

Othello
BR ə'θɛləʊ
AM oʊ'θɛloʊ, ə'θɛloʊ

other
BR 'ʌðə(r), -z
AM 'əðər, -z

otherness
BR 'ʌðənəs
AM 'əðərnəs
otherwhere
BR 'ʌðəwɛː(r)
AM 'əðər,(h)wɛ(ə)r
otherwise
BR 'ʌðəwʌɪz
AM 'əðər,waɪz
Othman
BR 'ɒθmən, ɒθ'mɑːn
AM 'ɑθmən, ɑθ'mɑn
Otho
BR 'əʊθəʊ
AM 'oʊθoʊ
otic
BR 'əʊtɪk, 'ɒtɪk
AM 'oʊdɪk, 'ɑdɪk
otiose
BR 'əʊtɪəʊs, 'əʊʃɪəʊs, 'əʊtɪəʊz, 'əʊʃɪəʊz
AM 'oʊdi,oʊz, 'oʊʃi,oʊz, 'oʊdi,oʊs, 'oʊʃi,oʊs
otiosely
BR 'əʊtɪəʊsli, 'əʊʃɪəʊsli, 'əʊtɪəʊzli, 'əʊʃɪəʊzli
AM 'oʊdi,oʊzli, 'oʊʃi,oʊzli, 'oʊdi,oʊsli, 'oʊʃi,oʊsli
otioseness
BR 'əʊtɪəʊsnəs, 'əʊʃɪəʊsnəs. 'əʊtɪəʊznəs, 'əʊʃɪəʊznəs
AM 'oʊdi,oʊznəs, 'oʊʃi,oʊznəs, 'oʊdi,oʊsnəs, 'oʊʃi,oʊsnəs
Otis
BR 'əʊtɪs
AM 'oʊdəs
otitis
BR əʊ'tʌɪtɪs
AM oʊ'taɪdɪs
Otley
BR 'ɒtli
AM 'ɑtli
otolaryngological
BR ,əʊtəʊ,larɪŋgə'lɒdʒɪkl
AM ˌoʊdoʊ,lɛrəngə'lɑdʒəkəl
otolaryngologist
BR ,əʊtəʊ,larɪŋ'gɒlədʒɪst, -s
AM 'oʊdoʊ,lɛrən'gɑlədʒəst, -s
otolaryngology
BR ,əʊtəʊ,larɪŋ'gɒlədʒi
AM 'oʊdoʊ,lɛrən'gɑlədʒi
otolith
BR 'əʊtəlɪθ, -s
AM 'oʊdl,ɪθ, -s
otolithic
BR ,əʊtə'lɪθɪk
AM ,oʊdl'ɪθɪk
otological
BR ,əʊtə'lɒdʒɪkl
AM ,oʊdə'lɑdʒəkəl
otologist
BR əʊ'tɒlədʒɪst, -s
AM oʊ'tɑlədʒəst, -s
otology
BR əʊ'tɒlədʒi
AM oʊ'tɑlədʒi
Otomi
BR ,əʊtə'miː
AM ,oʊdə'mi
O'Toole
BR ə(ʊ)'tuːl
AM oʊ'tul
otoplasty
BR 'əʊtə(ʊ)plast|i, -ɪz
AM 'oʊdoʊ,plæsti, -z
otorhinolaryngologist
BR ,əʊtəʊ,rʌɪnəʊ,larɪŋ'gɒlədʒɪst, -s
AM 'oʊdoʊ,raɪnoʊ,lɛrən'gɑlədʒəst, -s
otorhinolaryngology
BR ,əʊtəʊ,rʌɪnəʊ,larɪŋ'gɒlədʒi
AM 'oʊdoʊ,raɪnoʊ,lɛrən'gɑlədʒi
otoscope
BR 'əʊtəskəʊp, -s
AM 'oʊdə,skoʊp, -s
otoscopic
BR ,əʊtə'skɒpɪk
AM ,oʊdə'skɑpɪk
Otranto
BR ə'trantəʊ
AM ,oʊ'træn(t)oʊ
Ott
BR ɒt
AM ɑt
ottar
BR 'ɒtə(r)
AM 'ɑdər
ottava rima
BR ə(ʊ),tɑːvə 'riːmə(*r*)
AM ə'tɑvə 'rimə, oʊ'tɑvə +
Ottawa
BR 'ɒtəwə(*r*)
AM 'ɑdə,wɑ
otter
BR 'ɒtə(r), -z
AM 'ɑdər, -z
Otterburn
BR 'ɒtəbəːn
AM 'ɑdər,bərn
Ottery
BR 'ɒt(ə)ri
AM 'ɑdəri
Otto
BR 'ɒtəʊ, -z
AM 'ɑdoʊ, -z
Ottoline
BR 'ɒtəlɪn, 'ɒtl̩ɪn
AM 'ɑdə,laɪn
ottoman
BR 'ɒtəmən, -z
AM 'ɑdəmən, -z
Otway
BR 'ɒtweɪ
AM 'ɑtweɪ
Ouagadougou
BR ,wɑːgə'duːguː, ,wagə'duːguː
AM ˌwɑgə'dugu
ouananiche
BR ,wanə'niːʃ
AM ,wɑnə'niʃ
oubliette
BR ,uːblɪ'ɛt, -s
AM ,ubli'ɛt, -s
ouch
BR aʊtʃ
AM aʊtʃ
oud
BR uːd, -z
AM ud, -z
Oudenarde
BR 'uːdənɑːd, 'ʊdn̩ɑːd
AM ,udə'nɑrd
Oudh
BR uːd
AM ud
ought
BR ɔːt
AM ɔt, ɑt
oughtn't
BR 'ɔːtnt
AM 'ɔtnt, 'ɑtnt
ougiya
BR uː'giːjə(*r*), -z
AM u'dʒiə, -z
ouguiya
BR uː'giːjə(*r*), -z
AM u'giə, -z
Ouida
BR 'wiːdə(*r*)
AM 'widə
ouija board
BR 'wiːdʒə ,bɔːd, 'wiːdʒɪ +, -z
AM 'widʒə ,bɔ(ə)rd, 'widʒi +, -z
Ould
BR əʊld, uːld
AM oʊld
Oulton
BR 'əʊlt(ə)n
AM 'oʊlt(ə)n
Oulu
BR 'əʊluː
AM 'oʊ,lu
ounce
BR aʊns, -ɪz
AM aʊns, -əz
Oundle
BR 'aʊndl
AM 'aʊndəl
our[1]
strong form
BR 'aʊə(r)
AM 'aʊ(ə)r
our[2]
weak form
BR ɑː(r)
AM ɑr
ours[1]
strong form
BR 'aʊəz
AM 'aʊ(ə)rz
ours[2]
weak form
BR ɑːz
AM ɑrz
ourself[1]
strong form
BR aʊə'sɛlf
AM aʊr'sɛlf
ourself[2]
weak form
BR ɑː'sɛlf
AM ɑr'sɛlf
ourselves[1]
strong form
BR aʊə'sɛlvz
AM aʊr'sɛlvz
ourselves[2]
weak form
BR ɑː'sɛlvz
AM ɑr'sɛlvz
Ouse
BR uːz
AM uz
ousel
BR 'uːzl, -z
AM 'uzəl, -z
oust
BR aʊst, -s, -ɪŋ, -ɪd
AM aʊst, -s, -ɪŋ, -əd
ouster
BR 'aʊstə(r), -z
AM 'aʊstər, -z
out
BR aʊt
AM aʊt
outact
BR ,aʊt'akt, -s, -ɪŋ, -ɪd
AM ,aʊt'æk|(t), -(t)s, -tɪŋ, -təd
outage
BR 'aʊt|ɪdʒ, -ɪdʒɪz
AM 'aʊdɪdʒ, -ɪz
out-and-out
BR ,aʊt(ə)n(d)'aʊt
AM 'aʊdən'aʊt, 'aʊtn'aʊt
out-and-outer
BR ,aʊt(ə)n(d)'aʊtə(r), -z
AM 'aʊdən'aʊdər, 'aʊtn'aʊdər-z
outback[1]
BR 'aʊtbak
AM ˌaʊt'bæk
outback[2]
Australia
AM 'aʊtbak
BR 'aʊt,bæk

outbacker
BR 'aʊt,bakə(r), -z
AM ¦aʊt¦bækər, -z
outbalance
BR ,aʊt'baləns, ,aʊt'balṇs, -ɪz, -ɪŋ, -t
AM ,aʊt'bæləns, -əz, -ɪŋ, -t
outbid
BR ,aʊt'bɪd, -z, -ɪŋ
AM ,aʊt'bɪd, -z, -ɪŋ
outbidder
BR ,aʊt'bɪdə(r), -z
AM ,aʊt'bɪdər, -z
outblaze
BR ,aʊt'bleɪz, -ɨz, -ɪŋ, -d
AM ,aʊt'bleɪz, -ɨz, -ɪŋ, -d
outboard
BR 'aʊtbɔːd, -z
AM 'aʊt,bɔ(ə)rd, -z
outbound
BR 'aʊtbaʊnd
AM 'aʊt,baʊnd
outbrave
BR ,aʊt'breɪv, -z, -ɪŋ, -d
AM ,aʊt'breɪv, -z, -ɪŋ, -d
outbreak
BR 'aʊtbreɪk, -s
AM 'aʊt,breɪk, -s
outbred
BR ,aʊt'brɛd, -z, -ɪŋ
AM ,aʊt'brɛd, -z, -ɪŋ
outbreed
BR ,aʊt'briːd, -z, -ɪŋ
AM ,aʊt'brid, -z, -ɪŋ
outbuilding
BR 'aʊt,bɪldɪŋ, -z
AM 'aʊt,bɪldɪŋ, -z
outburst
BR 'aʊtbəːst, -s
AM 'aʊt,bərst, -s
outcast
BR 'aʊtkɑːst, 'aʊtkast, -s
AM 'aʊt,kæst, -s
outcaste
BR 'aʊtkɑːst, 'aʊtkast, -s
AM 'aʊt,kæst, -s
outclass
BR ,aʊt'klɑːs, ,aʊt'klas, -ɨz, -ɪŋ, -t
AM ,aʊt'klæs, -əz, -ɪŋ, -t
outcome
BR 'aʊtkʌm, -z
AM 'aʊt,kəm, -z
outcompete
BR ,aʊtkəm'piːt, -s, -ɪŋ, -ɪd
AM ,aʊtkəm'pi|t, -ts, -dɪŋ, -dɨd
outcrop
BR 'aʊtkrɒp, -s, -ɪŋ
AM 'aʊt,krɑp, -s, -ɪŋ
outcry
BR 'aʊtkrʌɪ, -z
AM 'aʊt,kraɪ, -z
outdance
BR ,aʊt'dɑːns, ,aʊt'dans, -ɨz, -ɪŋ, -t
AM ,aʊt'dæns, -əz, -ɪŋ, -t
outdare
BR ,aʊt'dɛː(r), -z, -ɪŋ, -d
AM ,aʊt'dɛ(ə)r, -z, -ɪŋ, -d
outdated
BR ,aʊt'deɪtɨd
AM ¦aʊt¦deɪdɨd
outdatedness
BR ,aʊt'deɪtɨdnɨs
AM ¦aʊt¦deɪdɨdnɨs
outdid
BR ,aʊt'dɪd
AM ,aʊt'dɪd
outdistance
BR ,aʊt'dɪst(ə)ns, -ɨz, -ɪŋ, -t
AM ,aʊt'dɪstəns, -əz, -ɪŋ, -t
outdo
BR ,aʊt'duː, -ɪŋ
AM ,aʊt'du, -ɪŋ
outdoes
BR ,aʊt'dʌz
AM ,aʊt'dəz
outdone
BR ,aʊt'dʌn
AM ,aʊt'dən
outdoor
BR ,aʊt'dɔː(r), -z
AM ¦aʊt¦dɔ(ə)r, -z
outdoorsman
BR aʊt'dɔːzmən
AM aʊt'dɔrzmən
outdoorsmen
BR aʊt'dɔːzmən
AM aʊt'dɔrzmən
outer
BR 'aʊtə(r)
AM 'aʊdər
outermost
BR 'aʊtəməʊst
AM 'aʊdər,moʊst
outerwear
BR 'aʊtəwɛː(r)
AM 'aʊdər,wɛ(ə)r
outface
BR ,aʊt'feɪs, -ɨz, -ɪŋ, -t
AM ,aʊt'feɪs, -ɨz, -ɪŋ, -t
outfall
BR 'aʊtfɔːl, -z
AM 'aʊt,fɔl, 'aʊt,fɑl, -z
outfield
BR 'aʊtfiːld, -z
AM 'aʊt,fild, -z
outfielder
BR 'aʊtfiːldə(r), -z
AM 'aʊt,fildər, -z
outfight
BR ,aʊt'fʌɪt, -s, -ɪŋ
AM ,aʊt'faɪ|t, -ts, -dɪŋ
outfit
BR 'aʊtfɪt, -s, -ɪŋ, -ɨd
AM 'aʊt,fɪ|t, -ts, -dɪŋ, -dɨd
outfitter
BR 'aʊtfɪtə(r), -z
AM 'aʊt,fɪdər, -z
outflank
BR ,aʊt'flaŋ|k, -ks, -kɪŋ, -(k)t
AM ,aʊt'flæŋ|k, -ks, -kɪŋ, -(k)t
outflew
BR ,aʊt'fluː
AM ,aʊt'flu
outflow
BR 'aʊtfləʊ, -z
AM 'aʊt,floʊ, -z
outflown
BR ,aʊt'fləʊn
AM ,aʊt'floʊn
outflung
BR ,aʊt'flʌŋ
AM ,aʊt'fləŋ
outfly
BR ,aʊt'flʌɪ, -z, -ɪŋ
AM ,aʊt'flaɪ, -z, -ɪŋ
outfought
BR ,aʊt'fɔːt
AM ,aʊt'fɔt, ,aʊt'fɑt
outfox
BR ,aʊt'fɒks, -ɨz, -ɪŋ, -t
AM ,aʊt'fɑks, -əz, -ɪŋ, -t
outgas
BR ,aʊt'gas, -ɨz, -ɪŋ, -t
AM ,aʊt'gæs, -əz, -ɪŋ, -t
outgeneral
BR ,aʊt'dʒɛn(ə)rəl, ,aʊt'dʒɛn(ə)rḷ, -z, -ɪŋ, -d
AM ,aʊt'dʒɛn(ə)rəl, -z, -ɪŋ, -d
outgo
BR ,aʊt'gəʊ, -z, -ɪŋ
AM ,aʊt'goʊ, -z, -ɪŋ
outgoing[1]
adjective
BR ,aʊt'gəʊɪŋ
AM ¦aʊt¦goʊɪŋ
outgoing[2]
noun
BR 'aʊt,gəʊɪŋ, -z
AM 'aʊt,goʊɪŋ, -z
outgone
BR ,aʊt'gɒn
AM ,aʊt'gɔn, ,aʊt'gɑn
outgrew
BR ,aʊt'gruː
AM ,aʊt'gru
outgrow
BR ,aʊt'grəʊ, -z, -ɪŋ
AM ,aʊt'groʊ, -z, -ɪŋ
outgrown
BR ,aʊt'grəʊn
AM ,aʊt'groʊn
outgrowth
BR 'aʊtgrəʊθ, -s
AM 'aʊt,groʊθ, -s
outguess
BR ,aʊt'gɛs, -ɨz, -ɪŋ, -t
AM ,aʊt'gɛs, -əz, -ɪŋ, -t
outgun
BR ,aʊt'gʌn, -z, -ɪŋ, -d
AM ,aʊt'gən, -z, -ɪŋ, -d
outhouse
BR 'aʊthaʊ|s, -zɨz
AM 'aʊt,(h)aʊ|s, -zəz
outie
BR 'aʊt|i, -ɪz
AM 'aʊdi, -z
outing
BR 'aʊtɪŋ, -z
AM 'aʊdɪŋ, -z
outjockey
BR ,aʊt'dʒɒk|i, -ɪz, -ɪɪŋ, -ɪd
AM ,aʊt'dʒɑki, -z, -ɪŋ, -d
outjump
BR ,aʊt'dʒʌmp, -s, -ɪŋ, -t
AM ,aʊt'dʒəmp, -s, -ɪŋ, -t
outlander
BR 'aʊt,landə(r), -z
AM 'aʊt,lændər, -z
outlandish
BR (,)aʊt'landɪʃ
AM aʊt'lændɪʃ
outlandishly
BR (,)aʊt'landɨʃli
AM aʊt'lændɨʃli
outlandishness
BR (,)aʊt'landɨʃnɨs
AM aʊt'lændɪʃnɪs
outlast
BR ,aʊt'lɑːst, ,aʊt'last, -s, -ɪŋ, -ɨd
AM ,aʊt'læst, -s, -ɪŋ, -əd
outlaw
BR 'aʊtlɔː(*r*), -z, -ɪŋ, -d
AM 'aʊt,lɔ, 'aʊt,lɑ, -z, -ɪŋ, -d
outlawry
BR 'aʊtlɔːri
AM 'aʊt,lɔri
outlay[1]
noun
BR 'aʊtleɪ, -z
AM 'aʊt,leɪ, -z
outlay[2]
verb
BR ,aʊt'leɪ, -z, -ɪŋ, -d
AM ¦aʊt¦leɪ, -z, -ɪŋ, -d
outlet
BR 'aʊtlɛt, -s
AM 'aʊt,lɛt, 'aʊtlət, -s
outlier
BR 'aʊt,lʌɪə(r), -z
AM 'aʊt,laɪ(ə)r, -z
outline
BR 'aʊtlʌɪn, -z, -ɪŋ, -d
AM 'aʊt,laɪn, -z, -ɪŋ, -d
outlive
BR ,aʊt'lɪv, -z, -ɪŋ, -d
AM ,aʊt'lɪv, -z, -ɪŋ, -d
outlook
BR 'aʊtlʊk, -s
AM 'aʊt,lʊk, -s
outlying
BR 'aʊt,lʌɪɪŋ

AM ˈaʊtˌlaɪŋ

outmaneuver
BR ˌaʊtməˈnuːv|ə(r), -əz, -(ə)rɪŋ, -əd
AM ¦aʊtməˌn(j)uv|ər, -ərz, -(ə)rɪŋ, -ərd

outmanoeuvre
BR ˌaʊtməˈnuːv|ə(r), -əz, -(ə)rɪŋ, -əd
AM ¦aʊtməˌn(j)uv|ər, -ərz, -(ə)rɪŋ, -ərd

outmatch
BR ˌaʊtˈmatʃ, -ɪz, -ɪŋ, -t
AM ˌaʊtˈmætʃ, -əz, -ɪŋ, -t

outmeasure
BR ˌaʊtˈmɛʒ|ə(r), -əz, -(ə)rɪŋ, -əd
AM ˌaʊtˈmɛʒ|ər, -ərz, -(ə)rɪŋ, -ərd

outmoded
BR ˌaʊtˈməʊdɪd
AM ˌaʊtˈmoʊdəd

outmodedly
BR ˌaʊtˈməʊdɪdli
AM ˌaʊtˈmoʊdədli

outmodedness
BR ˌaʊtˈməʊdɪdnɨs
AM ˌaʊtˈmoʊdədnəs

outmost
BR ˈaʊtməʊst
AM ˈaʊtˌmoʊst

outnumber
BR ˌaʊtˈnʌmb|ə(r), -əz, -(ə)rɪŋ, -əd
AM ˌaʊtˈnəmbər, -ərz, -(ə)rɪŋ, -ərd

outpace
BR ˌaʊtˈpeɪs, -ɪz, -ɪŋ, -t
AM ˌaʊtˈpeɪs, -ɪz, -ɪŋ, -t

outpatient
BR ˈaʊtˌpeɪʃnt, -s
AM ˈaʊtˌpeɪʃənt, -s

outperform
BR ˌaʊtpəˈfɔːm, -z, -ɪŋ, -d
AM ˌaʊtpərˈfɔ(ə)rm, -z, -ɪŋ, -d

outperformance
BR ˌaʊtpəˈfɔːməns, -ɪz
AM ˌaʊtpərˈfɔrməns, -əz

outplacement
BR ˈaʊtˌpleɪsm(ə)nt, -s
AM ˈaʊtˌpleɪsmənt, -s

outplay
BR ˌaʊtˈpleɪ, -z, -ɪŋ, -d
AM ˌaʊtˈpleɪ, -z, -ɪŋ, -d

outpoint
BR ˌaʊtˈpɔɪnt, -s, -ɪŋ, -ɪd
AM ˌaʊtˈpɔɪn|t, -ts, -(t)ɪŋ, -(t)ɨd

outport
BR ˈaʊtpɔːt, -s
AM ˈaʊtˌpɔ(ə)rt, -s

outpost
BR ˈaʊtpəʊst, -s
AM ˈaʊtˌpoʊst, -s

outpouring
BR ˈaʊtˌpɔːrɪŋ, -z
AM ˈaʊtˌpɔrɪŋ, -z

output
BR ˈaʊtpʊt, -s
AM ˈaʊtˌpʊt, -s

outrage
BR ˈaʊtreɪdʒ, -ɪz, -ɪŋ, -d
AM ˈaʊtˌreɪdʒ, -ɪz, -ɪŋ, -d

outrageous
BR (ˌ)aʊtˈreɪdʒəs
AM aʊtˈreɪdʒəs

outrageously
BR (ˌ)aʊtˈreɪdʒəsli
AM aʊtˈreɪdʒəsli

outrageousness
BR (ˌ)aʊtˈreɪdʒəsnəs
AM aʊtˈreɪdʒəsnəs

Outram
BR ˈuːtr(ə)m, ˈaʊtr(ə)m
AM ˈutrəm, ˈaʊtrəm

outran
BR ˌaʊtˈran
AM ˌaʊtˈræn

outrange
BR ˌaʊtˈreɪn(d)ʒ, -ɪz, -ɪŋ, -d
AM ˌaʊtˈreɪndʒ, -ɪz, -ɪŋ, -d

outrank
BR ˌaʊtˈraŋ|k, -ks, -kɪŋ, -(k)t
AM ˌaʊtˈræŋ|k, -ks, -kɪŋ, -(k)t

outré
BR ˈuːtreɪ
AM uˈtreɪ

outreach¹
noun
BR ˈaʊtriːtʃ
AM ˈaʊtˌritʃ

outreach²
verb
BR ˌaʊtˈriːtʃ, -ɪz, -ɪŋ, -t
AM ˌaʊtˈritʃ, -ɪz, -ɪŋ, -t

outridden
BR ˌaʊtˈrɪdn
AM ˌaʊtˈrɪdən

outride
BR ˌaʊtˈrʌɪd, -z, -ɪŋ
AM ˌaʊtˈraɪd, -z, -ɪŋ

outrider
BR ˈaʊtˌrʌɪdə(r), -z
AM ˈaʊtˌraɪdər, -z

outrigged
BR ˈaʊtrɪgd
AM ˈaʊtˌrɪgd

outrigger
BR ˈaʊtˌrɪgə(r), -z
AM ˈaʊtˌrɪgər, -z

outright
BR (ˌ)aʊtˈrʌɪt, ˈaʊtrʌɪt
AM ¦aʊtˌraɪt

outrightness
BR ˈaʊtrʌɪtnɨs
AM ¦aʊtˌraɪtnəs

outrival
BR ˌaʊtˈrʌɪv|l, -lz, -l̩ɪŋ\-əlɪŋ, -ld
AM ˌaʊtˈraɪv|əl, -əlz, -(ə)lɪŋ, -əld

outrode
BR ˌaʊtˈrəʊd
AM ˌaʊtˈroʊd

outrun¹
noun
BR ˈaʊtrʌn, -z
AM ˈaʊtˌrən, -z

outrun²
verb
BR ˌaʊtˈrʌn, -z, -ɪŋ
AM ˌaʊtˈrən, -z, -ɪŋ

outrush
BR ˈaʊtrʌʃ, -ɪz
AM ˌaʊtˈrəʃ, -əz

outsail
BR ˌaʊtˈseɪl, -z, -ɪŋ, -d
AM ˌaʊtˈseɪl, -z, -ɪŋ, -d

outsat
BR ˌaʊtˈsat
AM ˌaʊtˈsæt

outsell
BR ˌaʊtˈsɛl, -z, -ɪŋ
AM ˌaʊtˈsɛl, -z, -ɪŋ

outset
BR ˈaʊtsɛt
AM ˈaʊtˌsɛt

outshine
BR ˌaʊtˈʃʌɪn
AM ˌaʊtˈʃaɪn

outshone
BR ˌaʊtˈʃɒn
AM ˌaʊtˈʃoʊn

outshoot
BR ˌaʊtˈʃuːt, -s, -ɪŋ
AM ˌaʊtˈʃu|t, -ts, -dɪŋ

outshot
BR ˌaʊtˈʃɒt
AM ˌaʊtˈʃɑt

outside
BR ˌaʊtˈsʌɪd
AM ¦aʊtˌsaɪd

outsider
BR ˌaʊtˈsʌɪdə(r), -z
AM ¦aʊtˌsaɪdər, -z

outsit
BR ˌaʊtˈsɪt, -s, -ɪŋ
AM ˌaʊtˈsɪ|t, -ts, -dɪŋ

outsize
BR ˌaʊtˈsʌɪz, -ɪz, -ɪŋ, -d
AM ˌaʊtˈsaɪz, -ɪz, -ɪŋ, -d

outsizeness
BR ˈaʊtsʌɪznɨs
AM ˈaʊtˌsaɪznɨs

outskirts
BR ˈaʊtskəːts
AM ˈaʊtˌskərts

outsmart
BR ˌaʊtˈsmɑːt, -s, -ɪŋ, -ɨd
AM ˌaʊtˈsmɑr|t, -ts, -dɪŋ, -dəd

outsold
BR ˌaʊtˈsəʊld
AM ˌaʊtˈsoʊld

outsource
BR ˈaʊtsɔːs, -ɪz, -ɪŋ, -t
AM ˈaʊtˌsɔ(ə)rs, -əz, -ɪŋ, -t

outspan¹
noun
BR ˈaʊtspan, -z
AM ˈaʊtˌspæn, -z

outspan²
verb
BR ˌaʊtˈspan, -z, -ɪŋ, -d
AM ˌaʊtˈspæn, -z, -ɪŋ, -d

outspend
BR ˌaʊtˈspɛnd, -z, -ɪŋ
AM ˌaʊtˈspɛnd, -z, -ɪŋ

outspent
BR ˌaʊtˈspɛnt
AM ˌaʊtˈspɛnt

outspoken
BR ˌaʊtˈspəʊk(ə)n
AM ˌaʊtˈspoʊkən

outspokenly
BR ˌaʊtˈspəʊk(ə)nli
AM ˌaʊtˈspoʊkənli

outspokenness
BR ˌaʊtˈspəʊk(ə)nnəs
AM ˌaʊtˈspoʊkə(n)nəs

outspread
BR ˌaʊtˈsprɛd
AM ˌaʊtˈsprɛd

outstanding¹
exceptional
BR (ˌ)aʊtˈstandɪŋ
AM ˌaʊtˈstændɪŋ

outstanding²
sticking out
BR (ˌ)aʊtˈstandɪŋ
AM ˈaʊtˌstændɪŋ

outstandingly
BR ˌaʊtˈstandɪŋli
AM ˌaʊtˈstændɪŋli

outstare
BR ˌaʊtˈstɛː(r), -z, -ɪŋ, -d
AM ˌaʊtˈstɛ(ə)r, -z, -ɪŋ, -d

outstation
BR ˈaʊtˌsteɪʃn, -z
AM ˈaʊtˌsteɪʃən, -z

outstay
BR ˌaʊtˈsteɪ, -z, -ɪŋ, -d
AM ˌaʊtˈsteɪ, -z, -ɪŋ, -d

outstep
BR ˌaʊtˈstɛp, -s, -ɪŋ, -t
AM ˌaʊtˈstɛp, -s, -ɪŋ, -t

outstretch
BR ˌaʊtˈstrɛtʃ, -ɪz, -ɪŋ
AM ˌaʊtˈstrɛtʃ, -ɪz, -ɪŋ

outstretched
BR ˌaʊtˈstrɛtʃt
AM ¦aʊtˌstrɛtʃt

outstrip
BR ˌaʊtˈstrɪp, -s, -ɪŋ, -t
AM ˌaʊtˈstrɪp, -s, -ɪŋ, -t

outswing
BR 'aʊtswɪŋ, -z
AM 'aʊtˌswɪŋ, -z

out-swinger
BR 'aʊtˌswɪŋə(r), -z
AM 'aʊtˌswɪŋər, -z

out-take
BR 'aʊtteɪk, -s
AM 'aʊtˌteɪk, -s

outtalk
BR ˌaʊt'tɔːk, -s, -ɪŋ, -t
AM ˌaʊt'tɔk, ˌaʊt'tɑk, -s, -ɪŋ, -t

outvalue
BR ˌaʊt'valjuː, -z, -ɪŋ, -d
AM ˌaʊt'væl|ju, -juz, -jəwɪŋ, -jud

outvote
BR ˌaʊt'vəʊt, -s, -ɪŋ, -ɪd
AM ˌaʊt'voʊ|t, -ts, -dɪŋ, -dəd

outwalk
BR ˌaʊt'wɔːk, -s, -ɪŋ, -t
AM ˌaʊt'wɔk, ˌaʊt'wɑk, -s, -ɪŋ, -t

outward
BR 'aʊtwəd, -z
AM 'aʊtwərd, -z

outwardly
BR 'aʊtwədli
AM 'aʊtwərdli

outwardness
BR 'aʊtwədnəs
AM 'aʊtwərdnəs

outwash
BR 'aʊtwɒʃ, -ɪz
AM ¦aʊt¦wɔʃ, ¦aʊt¦wɑʃ, -əz

outwatch
BR ˌaʊt'wɒtʃ, -ɪz, -ɪŋ, -t
AM ˌaʊt'wɑtʃ, ˌaʊt'wɔtʃ, -əz, -ɪŋ, -t

outwear
BR ˌaʊt'wɛː(r), -z, -ɪŋ
AM ˌaʊt'wɛ(ə)r, -z, -ɪŋ

outweigh
BR ˌaʊt'weɪ, -z, -ɪŋ, -d
AM ˌaʊt'weɪ, -z, -ɪŋ, -d

outwent
BR ˌaʊt'wɛnt
AM ˌaʊt'wɛnt

outwit
BR ˌaʊt'wɪt, -s, -ɪŋ, -ɪd
AM ˌaʊt'wɪ|t, -ts, -dɪŋ, -dɪd

outwith
BR ˌaʊt'wɪθ, ˌaʊt'wɪð
AM ˌaʊt'wɪθ

outwore
BR ˌaʊt'wɔː(r)
AM ˌaʊt'wɔ(ə)r

outwork[1]
noun
BR 'aʊtwəːk, -s
AM 'aʊtˌwərk, -s

outwork[2]
verb
BR ˌaʊt'wəːk, -s, -ɪŋ, -t
AM ˌaʊt'wərk, -s, -ɪŋ, -t

outworker
BR 'aʊtˌwəːkə(r), -z
AM 'aʊtˌwərkər, -z

outworking
noun
BR 'aʊtˌwəːkɪŋ
AM ˌaʊt'wərkɪŋ

outworn
BR ˌaʊt'wɔːn
AM ˌaʊt'wɔ(ə)rn

ouzel
BR 'uːzl, -z
AM 'uzəl, -z

ouzo
BR 'uːzəʊ
AM 'uzoʊ

ova
BR 'əʊvə(*r*)
AM 'oʊvə

oval
BR 'əʊvl, -z
AM 'oʊvəl, -z

ovality
BR əʊ'valɪti
AM oʊ'vælədi

ovally
BR 'əʊvḷi
AM 'oʊvəli

ovalness
BR 'əʊvlnəs
AM 'oʊvəlnəs

Ovaltine®
BR 'əʊvltiːn
AM 'oʊvəlˌtin

Ovambo
BR ə(ʊ)'vambəʊ, -z
AM oʊ'væmboʊ, -z

Ovamboland
BR ə(ʊ)'vambəʊland
AM oʊ'væmboʊˌlænd

ovarian
BR ə(ʊ)'vɛːrɪən
AM oʊ'vɛriən

ovariectomy
BR ə(ʊ)ˌvɛːrɪ'ɛktəm|i, -ɪz
AM oʊˌvɛri'ɛktəmi, -z

ovariotomy
BR ə(ʊ)ˌvɛːrɪ'ɒtəm|i, -ɪz
AM oʊˌvɛri'ɑdəmi, -z

ovaritis
BR ˌəʊvə'rʌɪtɪs
AM ˌoʊvə'raɪdɪs

ovary
BR 'əʊv(ə)r|i, -ɪz
AM 'oʊv(ə)ri, -z

ovate
BR 'əʊveɪt
AM 'oʊˌveɪt

ovation
BR ə(ʊ)'veɪʃn, -z
AM oʊ'veɪʃən, -z

ovational
BR ə(ʊ)'veɪʃṇ(ə)l, ə(ʊ)'veɪʃən(ə)l
AM oʊ'veɪʃ(ə)nəl

oven
BR 'ʌvn, -z
AM 'əvən, -z

ovenbird
BR 'ʌvnbəːd, -z
AM 'əvənˌbərd, -z

Ovenden
BR 'ɒvndən, 'əʊvndən
AM 'əvəndən

ovenproof
BR 'ʌvnpruːf
AM 'əvənˌpruf

oven-ready
BR ˌʌvn'rɛdi
AM ¦əvən¦rɛdi

Ovens
BR 'ʌvnz
AM 'əvənz

ovenware
BR 'ʌvnwɛː(r)
AM 'əvənˌwɛ(ə)r

over
BR 'əʊvə(r), -z
AM 'oʊvər, -z

overabundance
BR ˌəʊv(ə)rə'bʌnd(ə)ns, -ɪz
AM ¦oʊvərə¦bəndns, -əz

overabundant
BR ˌəʊv(ə)rə'bʌnd(ə)nt
AM ¦oʊvərə¦bəndnt

overabundantly
BR ˌəʊv(ə)rə'bʌnd(ə)nt-li
AM ¦oʊvərə¦bəndən(t)li

overachieve
BR ˌəʊv(ə)rə'tʃiːv, -z, -ɪŋ, -d
AM ˌoʊvərə'tʃiv, -z, -ɪŋ, -d

overachievement
BR ˌəʊv(ə)rə'tʃiːv-m(ə)nt, -s
AM ˌoʊvərə'tʃivmənt, -s

overachiever
BR ˌəʊv(ə)rə'tʃiːvə(r), -z
AM ˌoʊvərə'tʃivər, -z

overact
BR ˌəʊvər'akt, -s, -ɪŋ, -ɪd
AM ˌoʊvər'æk|(t), -(t)s, -tɪŋ, -təd

overactive
BR ˌəʊvər'aktɪv
AM ¦oʊvər'æktɪv

overactivity
BR ˌəʊv(ə)rak'tɪvɪti
AM ¦oʊvərˌæk'tɪvɪdi

overage[1]
adjective
BR ˌəʊvər'eɪdʒ
AM ¦oʊvər¦eɪdʒ

overage[2]
noun
BR 'əʊv(ə)r|ɪdʒ, -ɪdʒɪz
AM 'oʊv(ə)rɪdʒ, -ɪz

overall[1]
adjective, adverb
BR ˌəʊvər'ɔːl
AM ¦oʊvə¦rɔl, ¦oʊvə¦rɑl

overall[2]
noun
BR 'əʊvərɔːl, -z, -d
AM 'oʊvəˌrɔl, 'oʊvəˌrɑl, -z, -d

overambition
BR ˌəʊv(ə)ram'bɪʃn
AM ˌoʊvərəm'bɪʃən, ˌoʊvərˌæm'bɪʃən

overambitious
BR ˌəʊv(ə)ram'bɪʃəs
AM 'oʊvərəm'bɪʃəs, 'oʊvərˌæm'bɪʃəs

overambitiously
BR ˌəʊv(ə)ram'bɪʃəsli
AM 'oʊvərəm'bɪʃəsli, 'oʊvərˌæm'bɪʃəsli

over-and-over
BR ˌəʊv(ə)rən(d)'əʊvə(r), ˌəʊv(ə)rṇ(d)'əʊvə(r)
AM 'oʊv(ə)rən'oʊvər

overanxiety
BR ˌəʊv(ə)raŋ'zʌɪɪti
AM ¦oʊvəræŋ'zaɪɪdi

overanxious
BR ˌəʊvər'aŋ(k)ʃəs
AM ¦oʊvər'æŋ(k)ʃəs

overanxiously
BR ˌəʊvər'aŋ(k)ʃəsli
AM ¦oʊvər'æŋ(k)ʃəsli

overarch
BR ˌəʊvər'ɑːtʃ, -ɪz, -ɪŋ, -t
AM ˌoʊvər'ɑrtʃ, -əz, -ɪŋ, -t

overarm
BR 'əʊvərɑːm
AM 'oʊvərˌɑrm

overate
from verb 'overeat'
BR ˌəʊvər'ɛt, ˌəʊvər'eɪt
AM ˌoʊvər'eɪt

overattentive
BR ˌəʊv(ə)rə'tɛntɪv
AM ¦oʊvərə'tɛn(t)ɪv

overawe
BR ˌəʊvər'ɔː(*r*), -z, -ɪŋ, -d
AM ¦oʊvər'ɔ, ¦oʊvər'ɑ, -z, -ɪŋ, -d

overbalance
BR ˌəʊvə'baləns, ˌəʊvə'balṇs, -ɪz, -ɪŋ, -t
AM ˌoʊvər'bæləns, -ɪz, -ɪŋ, -t

overbear
BR ˌəʊvə'bɛː(r), -z, -ɪŋ
AM ˌoʊvər'bɛ(ə)r, -z, -ɪŋ

overbearing
BR ˌəʊvəˈbɛːrɪŋ
AM ˌoʊvərˈbɛrɪŋ

overbearingly
BR ˌəʊvəˈbɛːrɪŋli
AM ˌoʊvərˈbɛrɪŋli

overbearingness
BR ˌəʊvəˈbɛːrɪŋnɨs
AM ˌoʊvərˈbɛrɪŋnɨs

overbid
BR ˌəʊvəˈbɪd, -z, -ɪŋ
AM ˌoʊvərˌbɪd, -z, -ɪŋ

overbidder
BR ˌəʊvəˈbɪdə(r), -z
AM ˌoʊvərˌbɪdər, -z

overblew
BR ˌəʊvəˈbluː
AM ˌoʊvərˈblu

overblouse
BR ˈəʊvəblaʊz, -ɨz
AM ˈoʊvərˌblaʊs, ˈoʊvərˌblaʊz, -əz

overblow
BR ˌəʊvəˈbləʊ, -z, -ɪŋ
AM ˌoʊvərˈbloʊ, -z, -ɪŋ

overblown
BR ˌəʊvəˈbləʊn
AM ˌoʊvərˈbloʊn

overboard
BR ˈəʊvəbɔːd
AM ˈoʊvərˌbɔ(ə)rd

overbold
BR ˌəʊvəˈbəʊld
AM ˌoʊvərˈboʊld

overboldly
BR ˌəʊvəˈbəʊldli
AM ˌoʊvərˈboʊldli

overbook
BR ˌəʊvəˈbʊk, -s, -ɪŋ, -t
AM ˌoʊvərˈbʊk, -s, -ɪŋ, -t

overboot
BR ˈəʊvəbuːt, -s
AM ˈoʊvərˌbut, -s

overborne
BR ˌəʊvəˈbɔːn
AM ˌoʊvərˌbɔ(ə)rn

overbought
BR ˌəʊvəˈbɔːt
AM ˌoʊvərˈbɔt, ˌoʊvərˈbɑt

overbred
BR ˌəʊvəˈbrɛd
AM ˌoʊvərˈbrɛd

overbreed
BR ˌəʊvəˈbriːd, -z, -ɪŋ
AM ˌoʊvərˈbrid, -z, -ɪŋ

overbrim
BR ˌəʊvəˈbrɪm, -z, -ɪŋ, -d
AM ˌoʊvərˈbrɪm, -z, -ɪŋ, -d

overbuild
BR ˌəʊvəˈbɪld, -z, -ɪŋ
AM ˌoʊvərˈbɪld, -z, -ɪŋ

overbuilt
BR ˌəʊvəˈbɪlt
AM ˌoʊvərˈbɪlt

overburden
BR ˌəʊvəˈbəːd|n, -nz, -n̩ɪŋ\-nɪŋ, -nd
AM ˌoʊvərˌbərdən, -z, -ɪŋ, -d

overburdensome
BR ˌəʊvəˈbəːdns(ə)m
AM ˌoʊvərˌbərdnsəm

Overbury
BR ˈəʊvəb(ə)ri
AM ˈoʊvərˌbɛri

overbusy
BR ˌəʊvəˈbɪzi
AM ˌoʊvərˈbɪzi

overbuy
BR ˌəʊvəˈbʌɪ, -z, -ɪŋ
AM ˌoʊvərˈbaɪ, -z, -ɪŋ

overcall[1]
noun
BR ˈəʊvəkɔːl, -z
AM ˈoʊvərˌkɔl, ˈoʊvərˌkɑl, -z

overcall[2]
verb
BR ˌəʊvəˈkɔːl, -z, -ɪŋ, -d
AM ˌoʊvərˈkɔl, ˌoʊvərˈkɑl, -z, -ɪŋ, -d

overcame
BR ˌəʊvəˈkeɪm
AM ˌoʊvərˈkeɪm

overcapacity
BR ˌəʊvəkəˈpasɪti
AM ˌoʊvərkəˈpæsədi

overcapitalize
BR ˌəʊvəˈkapɪtl̩ʌɪz, ˌəʊvəˈkapɪtəlʌɪz, -ɨz, -ɪŋ, -d
AM ˌoʊvərˈkæpədlˌaɪz, -ɨz, -ɪŋ, -d

overcareful
BR ˌəʊvəˈkɛːf(ʊ)l
AM ˌoʊvərˈkɛrfəl

overcarefully
BR ˌəʊvəˈkɛːfʊli, ˌəʊvəˈkɛːfl̩i
AM ˌoʊvərˈkɛrfəli

overcast
BR ˌəʊvəˈkɑːst, ˌəʊvəˈkast, ˈəʊvəkɑːst, ˈəʊvəkast
AM ˈoʊvərˌkæst

overcaution
BR ˌəʊvəˈkɔːʃn
AM ˌoʊvərˈkɔʃən, ˌoʊvərˈkɑʃən

overcautious
BR ˌəʊvəˈkɔːʃəs
AM ˌoʊvərˈkɔʃəs, ˌoʊvərˈkɑʃəs

overcautiously
BR ˌəʊvəˈkɔːʃəsli
AM ˌoʊvərˈkɔʃəsli, ˌoʊvərˈkɑʃəsli

overcautiousness
BR ˌəʊvəˈkɔːʃəsnəs
AM ˌoʊvərˈkɔʃəsnəs, ˌoʊvərˈkɑʃəsnəs

overcharge[1]
noun
BR ˈəʊvətʃɑːdʒ
AM ˌoʊvərˌtʃɑrdʒ

overcharge[2]
verb
BR ˌəʊvəˈtʃɑːdʒ, -ɨz, -ɪŋ, -d
AM ˌoʊvərˌtʃɑrdʒ, -əz, -ɪŋ, -d

overcheck
BR ˈəʊvətʃɛk, -s
AM ˈoʊvərˌtʃɛk, -s

overcloud
BR ˌəʊvəˈklaʊd, -z, -ɪŋ, -ɨd
AM ˌoʊvərˈklaʊd, -z, -ɪŋ, -ɨd

overcoat
BR ˈəʊvəkəʊt, -s
AM ˈoʊvərˌkoʊt, -s

overcome
BR ˌəʊvəˈkʌm, -z, -ɪŋ
AM ˌoʊvərˈkəm, -z, -ɪŋ

overcommit
BR ˌəʊvəkəˈmɪt, -s, -ɪŋ, -ɨd
AM ˌoʊvərkəˈmɪ|t, -ts, -dɪŋ, -dɨd

overcompensate
BR ˌəʊvəˈkɒmp(ə)nseɪt, ˌəʊvəˈkɒmpɛnseɪt, -s, -ɪŋ, -ɨd
AM ˌoʊvərˈkɑmpənˌseɪ|t, -ts, -dɪŋ, -dɨd

overcompensation
BR ˌəʊvəˌkɒmp(ə)nˈseɪʃn, ˌəʊvəˌkɒmpɛnˈseɪʃn
AM ˌoʊvərˌkɑmpənˈseɪʃən

overcompensatory
BR ˌəʊvəˌkɒmp(ə)nˈseɪt(ə)ri, ˌəʊvəˌkɒmpɛnˈseɪt(ə)ri
AM ˌoʊvərkəmˈpɛnsəˌtɔri

overconfidence
BR ˌəʊvəˈkɒnfɪd(ə)ns
AM ˌoʊvərˈkɑnfədəns

overconfident
BR ˌəʊvəˈkɒnfɪd(ə)nt
AM ˌoʊvərˈkɑnfədnt

overconfidently
BR ˌəʊvəˈkɒnfɪd(ə)ntli
AM ˌoʊvərˈkɑnfədən(t)li

overcook
BR ˌəʊvəˈkʊk, -s, -ɪŋ, -t
AM ˌoʊvərˈkʊk, -s, -ɪŋ, -t

overcritical
BR ˌəʊvəˈkrɪtɪkl
AM ˌoʊvərˈkrɪdəkəl

overcrop
BR ˌəʊvəˈkrɒp, -s, -ɪŋ, -t
AM ˌoʊvərˈkrɑp, -s, -ɪŋ, -t

overcrowd
BR ˌəʊvəˈkraʊd, -z, -ɪŋ, -ɨd
AM ˌoʊvərˈkraʊd, -z, -ɪŋ, -əd

overdetermination
BR ˌəʊvədɪˌtəːmɪˈneɪʃn
AM ˌoʊvərdəˌtərməˈneɪʃən

overdetermine
BR ˌəʊvədɪˈtəːmɪn, -z, -ɪŋ, -d
AM ˌoʊvərdəˈtərmən, -z, -ɪŋ, -d

overdevelop
BR ˌəʊvədɪˈvɛləp, -s, -ɪŋ, -t
AM ˌoʊvərdəˌvɛləp, -s, -ɪŋ, -t

overdid
BR ˌəʊvəˈdɪd
AM ˌoʊvərˈdɪd

overdo
BR ˌəʊvəˈduː, -ɪŋ
AM ˌoʊvərˈdu, -ɪŋ

overdoes
BR ˌəʊvəˈdʌz
AM ˌoʊvərˈdəz

overdone
BR ˌəʊvəˈdʌn
AM ˌoʊvərˌdən

overdosage
BR ˌəʊvəˈdəʊs|ɪdʒ, -ɪdʒɪz
AM ˈoʊvərˌdoʊsɪdʒ, -ɨz

overdose[1]
noun, verb, drug abuse
BR ˈəʊvədəʊs, -ɨz, -ɪŋ, -t
AM ˈoʊvərˌdoʊs, -ɨz, -ɪŋ, -t

overdose[2]
verb, by mistake
BR ˌəʊvəˈdəʊs, -ɨz, -ɪŋ, -t
AM ˌoʊvərˌdoʊs, -ɨz, -ɪŋ, -t

overdraft
BR ˈəʊvədrɑːft, ˈəʊvədraft, -s
AM ˈoʊvərˌdræft, -s

overdramatise
BR ˌəʊvəˈdramətʌɪz, -ɨz, -ɪŋ, -d
AM ˌoʊvərˈdræməˌtaɪz, ˌoʊvərˈdrɑməˌtaɪz, -ɨz, -ɪŋ, -d

overdramatize
BR ˌəʊvəˈdramətʌɪz, -ɨz, -ɪŋ, -d
AM ˌoʊvərˈdræməˌtaɪz, ˌoʊvərˈdrɑməˌtaɪz, -ɨz, -ɪŋ, -d

overdrank
BR ˌəʊvəˈdraŋk
AM ˌoʊvərˈdræŋk

overdraw
BR ˌəʊvəˈdrɔː(r), -z, -ɪŋ

AM ˌoʊvərˈdrɔ, ˌoʊvərˈdrɑ, -z, -ɪŋ

overdrawer
BR ˌəʊvəˈdrɔː(r)ə(r), -z
AM ¦oʊvərˈdrɔ(ə)r, -z

overdrawn
BR ˌəʊvəˈdrɔːn
AM ˌoʊvərˈdrɔn, ˌoʊvərˈdrɑn

overdress
BR ˌəʊvəˈdrɛs, -ɪz, -ɪŋ, -t
AM ˌoʊvərˈdrɛs, -əz, -ɪŋ, -t

overdrew
BR ˌəʊvəˈdruː
AM ˌoʊvərˈdru

overdrink
BR ˌəʊvəˈdrɪŋk, -s, -ɪŋ
AM ˌoʊvərˈdrɪŋk, -s, -ɪŋ

overdrive
BR ˈəʊvədrʌɪv, -z
AM ˈoʊvərˌdraɪv, -z

overdrunk
BR ˌəʊvəˈdrʌŋk
AM ˌoʊvərˈdrəŋk

overdub
BR ˌəʊvəˈdʌb, -z, -ɪŋ, -d
AM ˌoʊvərˈdəb, -z, -ɪŋ, -d

overdue
BR ˌəʊvəˈdjuː, ˌəʊvəˈdʒuː
AM ˌoʊvərˈd(j)u

overeager
BR ˌəʊvərˈiːɡə(r)
AM ¦oʊvərˈiɡər

overeagerly
BR ˌəʊvərˈiːɡəli
AM ¦oʊvərˈiɡərli

overeagerness
BR ˌəʊvərˈiːɡənəs
AM ¦oʊvərˈiɡərnəs

overeat
BR ˌəʊvərˈiːt, -s, -ɪŋ
AM ˌoʊvərˈi|t, -ts, -dɪŋ

overeaten
BR ˌəʊvərˈiːtn
AM ˌoʊvərˈitn

overemphases
BR ˌəʊvərˈɛmfəsiːz
AM ˌoʊvərˈɛmfəsiz

overemphasis
BR ˌəʊvərˈɛmfəsɪs
AM ˌoʊvərˈɛmfəsəs

overemphasise
BR ˌəʊvərˈɛmfəsʌɪz, -ɪz, -ɪŋ, -d
AM ˌoʊvərˈɛmfəˌsaɪz, -ɪz, -ɪŋ, -d

overemphasize
BR ˌəʊvərˈɛmfəsʌɪz, -ɪz, -ɪŋ, -d
AM ˌoʊvərˈɛmfəˌsaɪz, -ɪz, -ɪŋ, -d

overenthusiasm
BR ˌəʊv(ə)rɪnˈθjuːzɪaz(ə)m, ˌəʊv(ə)rɛnˈθjuːzɪaz(ə)m
AM ¦oʊvərənˈθ(j)uziˌæzəm

overenthusiastic
BR ˌəʊv(ə)rɪnˌθjuːzɪˈastɪk, ˌəʊv(ə)rɛnˌθjuːzɪˈastɪk
AM ¦oʊvərənˌθjuziˈæstɪk

overenthusiastically
BR ˌəʊv(ə)rɪnˌθjuːzɪˈastɪkli, ˌəʊv(ə)rɛnˌθjuːzɪˈastɪkli
AM ¦oʊvərən¦θjuziˈæstək(ə)li

overestimate¹
noun
BR ˌəʊvərˈɛstɪmət, -s
AM ˌoʊvərˈɛstəmət, -s

overestimate²
verb
BR ˌəʊvərˈɛstɪmeɪt, -s, -ɪŋ, -ɪd
AM ¦oʊvər¦ɛstəˌmeɪ|t, -ts, -dɪŋ, -dɪd

overestimation
BR ˌəʊvərˌɛstɪˈmeɪʃn
AM ¦oʊvərˌɛstəˈmeɪʃən

overexcite
BR ˌəʊv(ə)rɪkˈsʌɪt, ˌəʊv(ə)rɛkˈsʌɪt, -s, -ɪŋ, -ɪd
AM ¦oʊvərɪk¦saɪ|t, ¦oʊvərɛk¦saɪ|t, -ts, -dɪŋ, -dɪd

overexcitement
BR ˌəʊv(ə)rɪkˈsʌɪtm(ə)nt, ˌəʊv(ə)rɛkˈsʌɪtm(ə)nt
AM ¦oʊvərɪkˈsaɪtmənt, ¦oʊvərɛkˈsaɪtmənt

overexert
BR ˌəʊv(ə)rɪɡˈzəːt, ˌəʊv(ə)rɛɡˈzəːt, -s, -ɪŋ, -ɪd
AM ¦oʊvərɪɡˈzər|t, ¦oʊvərɛɡˈzərt, -ts, -dɪŋ, -dəd

overexertion
BR ˌəʊv(ə)rɪɡˈzəːʃn, ˌəʊv(ə)rɛɡˈzəːʃn
AM ¦oʊvərɪɡˈzərʃən, ¦oʊvərɛɡˈzərʃən

overexpose
BR ˌəʊv(ə)rɪkˈspəʊz, ˌəʊv(ə)rɛkˈspəʊz, -ɪz, -ɪŋ, -d
AM ¦oʊvərɪkˈspoʊz, ¦oʊvərɛkˈspoʊz, -ɪz, -ɪŋ, -d

overexposure
BR ˌəʊv(ə)rɪkˈspəʊʒə(r), ˌəʊv(ə)rɛkˈspəʊʒə(r)
AM ¦oʊvərɪkˈspoʊʒər, ¦oʊvərɛkˈspoʊʒər

overextend
BR ˌəʊvərɪkˈstɛnd, ˌəʊvərɛkˈstɛnd, -z, -ɪŋ, -ɪd
AM ¦oʊvərɪkˈstɛnd, ¦oʊvərɛkˈstɛnd, -z, -ɪŋ, -əd

overfall
BR ˈəʊvəfɔːl, -z
AM ˈoʊvərˌfɔl, ˈoʊvərˌfɑl, -z

overfamiliar
BR ˌəʊvəfəˈmɪlɪə(r)
AM ¦oʊvərfəˌmɪljər, ¦oʊvərfəˈmɪliər

overfamiliarity
BR ˌəʊvəfəˌmɪlɪˈarɪti
AM ¦oʊvərfəˌmɪliˈɛrədi

overfatigue
BR ˌəʊvəfəˈtiːɡ, -z, -ɪŋ, -d
AM ¦oʊvərfəˈtiɡ, -z, -ɪŋ, -d

overfed
BR ˌəʊvəˈfɛd
AM ¦oʊvərˈfɛd

overfeed
BR ˌəʊvəˈfiːd, -z, -ɪŋ
AM ˌoʊvərˈfid, -z, -ɪŋ

overfill
BR ˌəʊvəˈfɪl, -z, -ɪŋ, -d
AM ˌoʊvərˈfɪl, -z, -ɪŋ, -d

overfine
BR ˌəʊvəˈfʌɪn
AM ˌoʊvərˈfaɪn

overfish
BR ˌəʊvəˈfɪʃ, -ɪz, -ɪŋ, -t
AM ˌoʊvərˈfɪʃ, -ɪz, -ɪŋ, -t

overflew
BR ˌəʊvəˈfluː
AM ˌoʊvərˈflu

overflight
BR ˈəʊvəflʌɪt, -s
AM ˈoʊvərˌflaɪt, -s

overflow¹
noun
BR ˈəʊvəfləʊ, -z
AM ˈoʊvərˌfloʊ, -z

overflow²
verb
BR ˌəʊvəˈfləʊ, -z, -ɪŋ, -d
AM ˌoʊvərˈfloʊ, -z, -ɪŋ, -d

overflown
BR ˌəʊvəˈfləʊn
AM ˌoʊvərˈfloʊn

overfly
BR ˌəʊvəˈflʌɪ, -z, -ɪŋ
AM ˌoʊvərˈflaɪ, -z, -ɪŋ

overfold
BR ˈəʊvəfəʊld, -z
AM ˈoʊvərˌfoʊld, -z

overfond
BR ˌəʊvəˈfɒnd
AM ¦oʊvərˈfɑnd

overfondly
BR ˌəʊvəˈfɒndli
AM ¦oʊvərˈfɑn(d)li

overfondness
BR ˌəʊvəˈfɒn(d)nəs
AM ¦oʊvərˈfɑn(d)nəs

overfulfil
BR ˌəʊvəfʊlˈfɪl, -z, -ɪŋ, -d
AM ¦oʊvərˌfʊ(l)ˈfɪl, -z, -ɪŋ, -d

overfulfill
BR ˌəʊvəfʊlˈfɪl, -z, -ɪŋ, -d
AM ¦oʊvərˌfʊ(l)ˈfɪl, -z, -ɪŋ, -d

overfulfillment
BR ˌəʊvəfʊlˈfɪlm(ə)nt
AM ¦oʊvərˌfʊ(l)ˈfɪlmənt

overfulfilment
BR ˌəʊvəfʊlˈfɪlm(ə)nt
AM ¦oʊvərˌfʊ(l)ˈfɪlmənt

overfull
BR ˌəʊvəˈfʊl
AM ¦oʊvərˈfʊl

overgarment
BR ˈəʊvəˌɡɑːm(ə)nt, -s
AM ˈoʊvərˌɡɑrmənt, -s

overgeneralisation
BR ˌəʊvəˌdʒɛn(ə)rəlʌɪˈzeɪʃn, ˌəʊvəˌdʒɛn(ə)rl̩ʌɪˈzeɪʃn, -z
AM ¦oʊvərˌdʒɛn(ə)rələˈzeɪʃən, ¦oʊvərˌdʒɛn(ə)rəˌlaɪˈzeɪʃən, -z

overgeneralise
BR ˌəʊvəˈdʒɛn(ə)rəlʌɪz, ˌəʊvəˈdʒɛn(ə)rl̩ʌɪz, -ɪz, -ɪŋ, -d
AM ¦oʊvərˈdʒɛn(ə)rəˌlaɪz, -ɪz, -ɪŋ, -d

overgeneralization
BR ˌəʊvəˌdʒɛn(ə)rəlʌɪˈzeɪʃn, ˌəʊvəˌdʒɛn(ə)rl̩ʌɪˈzeɪʃn, -z
AM ¦oʊvərˌdʒɛn(ə)rələˈzeɪʃən, ¦oʊvərˌdʒɛn(ə)rəˌlaɪˈzeɪʃən, -z

overgeneralize
BR ˌəʊvəˈdʒɛn(ə)rəlʌɪz, ˌəʊvəˈdʒɛn(ə)rl̩ʌɪz, -ɪz, -ɪŋ, -d
AM ¦oʊvərˈdʒɛn(ə)rəˌlaɪz, -ɪz, -ɪŋ, -d

overgenerous
BR ˌəʊvəˈdʒɛn(ə)rəs
AM ˌoʊvərˈdʒɛn(ə)rəs

overgenerously
BR ˌəʊvəˈdʒɛn(ə)rəsli
AM ˌoʊvərˈdʒɛn(ə)rəsli

overglaze
BR ˌəʊvəˈɡleɪz, -ɪz, -ɪŋ, -d
AM ˌoʊvərˈɡleɪz, -ɪz, -ɪŋ, -d

overgraze
BR ˌəʊvəˈɡreɪz, -ɪz, -ɪŋ, -d
AM ˌoʊvərˈɡreɪz, -ɪz, -ɪŋ, -d

overgrew
BR ˌəʊvəˈgruː
AM ˌoʊvərˈgru

overground
BR ˈəʊvəgraʊnd
AM ˈoʊvərˌgraʊnd

overgrow
BR ˌəʊvəˈgrəʊ, -z, -ɪŋ
AM ˌoʊvərˈgroʊ, -z, -ɪŋ

overgrown
BR ˌəʊvəˈgrəʊn
AM ˈoʊvərˌgroʊn

overgrowth
BR ˈəʊvəgrəʊθ
AM ˈoʊvərˌgroʊθ

overhand
BR ˈəʊvəhand
AM ˈoʊvərˌ(h)ænd

overhang[1]
noun
BR ˈəʊvəhaŋ, -z
AM ˈoʊvərˌ(h)æŋ, -z

overhang[2]
verb
BR ˌəʊvəˈhaŋ, -z, -ɪŋ
AM ˈoʊvərˈhæŋ, -z, -ɪŋ

overhanging
BR ˌəʊvəˈhaŋɪŋ
AM ˈoʊvərˈhæŋɪŋ

overhaste
BR ˌəʊvəˈheɪst
AM ˈoʊvərˈheɪst

overhastily
BR ˌəʊvəˈheɪstɨli
AM ˈoʊvərˈheɪstɨli

overhasty
BR ˌəʊvəˈheɪsti
AM ˈoʊvərˈheɪsti

overhaul[1]
noun
BR ˈəʊvəhɔːl, -z
AM ˈoʊvərˌ(h)ɔl,
ˈoʊvərˌ(h)ɑl, -z

overhaul[2]
verb
BR ˈəʊvəhɔːl,
ˌəʊvəˈhɔːl, -z, -ɪŋ, -d
AM ˈoʊvərˈhɔl,
ˈoʊvərˈhɑl, -z, -ɪŋ, -d

overhead[1]
adjective
BR ˌəʊvəˈhɛd
AM ˌoʊvərˈhɛd

overhead[2]
adverb
BR ˈəʊvəːhɛd
AM ˌoʊvərˈhɛd

overhead[3]
noun
BR ˈəʊvəhɛd, -z
AM ˈoʊvərˌ(h)ɛd, -z

overhear
BR ˌəʊvəˈhɪə(r), -z, -ɪŋ
AM ˌoʊvərˈhɪ(ə)r, -z, -ɪŋ

overheard
BR ˌəʊvəˈhəːd
AM ˌoʊvərˈhərd

overheat
BR ˌəʊvəˈhiːt, -s, -ɪŋ, -ɨd
AM ˌoʊvərˈhi|t, -ts, -dɪŋ,
-dɨd

overhung
BR ˌəʊvəˈhʌŋ
AM ˈoʊvərˈhəŋ

overindulge
BR ˌəʊv(ə)rɪnˈdʌldʒ,
-ɪz, -ɪŋ, -d
AM ˈoʊvərənˈdəldʒ, -əz,
-ɪŋ, -d

overindulgence
BR ˌəʊv(ə)rɪnˈdʌldʒ(ə)ns
AM ˈoʊvərənˈdəldʒəns

overindulgent
BR ˌəʊv(ə)rɪnˈdʌldʒ(ə)nt
AM ˈoʊvərənˈdəldʒənt

overindulgently
BR ˌəʊv(ə)rɪnˈdʌldʒ-
(ə)ntli
AM ˈoʊvərənˈdəldʒ-
ən(t)li

over-inflated
BR ˌəʊv(ə)rɪnˈfleɪtɪd
AM ˈoʊvərənˈfleɪdɨd

overinsurance
BR ˌəʊv(ə)rɪnˈʃʊərəns,
ˌəʊvərɪnˈʃʊərn̩s,
ˌəʊv(ə)rɪnˈʃɔːrəns,
ˌəʊvərɪnˈʃɔːrn̩s
AM ˈoʊvərənˈʃʊrəns

overinsure
BR ˌəʊv(ə)rɪnˈʃʊə(r),
ˌəʊv(ə)rɪnˈʃɔː(r), -z,
-ɪŋ, -d
AM ˈoʊvərənˈʃʊ(ə)r, -z,
-ɪŋ, -d

overissue
BR ˌəʊvərˈɪʃ(j)uː,
ˌəʊvərˈɪsjuː, -z, -ɪŋ, -d
AM ˌoʊvərˈɪʃu, -z, -ɪŋ, -d

overjoyed
BR ˌəʊvəˈdʒɔɪd
AM ˈoʊvərˈjɔɪd

overkill
BR ˈəʊvəkɪl
AM ˈoʊvərˌkɪl

overladen
BR ˌəʊvəˈleɪdn
AM ˌoʊvərˈleɪdən

overlaid
BR ˌəʊvəˈleɪd
AM ˌoʊvərˈleɪd

overlain
BR ˌəʊvəˈleɪn
AM ˌoʊvərˈleɪn

overland
BR ˈəʊvəland,
ˌəʊvəˈland
AM ˈoʊvərˌlænd

overlander
BR ˈəʊvəˌlandə(r), -z
AM ˈoʊvərˌlændər, -z

overlap[1]
noun
BR ˈəʊvəlap, -s
AM ˈoʊvərˌlæp, -s

overlap[2]
verb
BR ˌəʊvəˈlap, -s, -ɪŋ, -t
AM ˌoʊvərˈlæp, -s, -ɪŋ, -t

overlarge
BR ˌəʊvəˈlɑːdʒ
AM ˈoʊvərˈlɑrdʒ

overlay[1]
noun
BR ˈəʊvəleɪ, -z
AM ˈoʊvərˌleɪ, -z

overlay[2]
verb
BR ˌəʊvəˈleɪ, -z, -ɪŋ, -d
AM ˌoʊvərˈleɪ, -z, -ɪŋ, -d

overleaf
BR ˌəʊvəˈliːf
AM ˈoʊvərˈlif

overleap
BR ˌəʊvərˈliːp, -s, -ɪŋ
AM ˌoʊvərˈlip, -s, -ɪŋ

overleaped
BR ˌəʊvəˈlɛpt
AM ˌoʊvərˈlipt

overlept
BR ˌəʊvərˈlɛpt
AM ˌoʊvərˈlɛpt

overlie
BR ˌəʊvəˈlʌɪ, -z
AM ˌoʊvərˈlaɪ, -z

overload[1]
noun
BR ˈəʊvələʊd, -z
AM ˈoʊvərˌloʊd, -z

overload[2]
verb
BR ˌəʊvəˈləʊd, -z, -ɪŋ,
-ɨd
AM ˈoʊvərˈloʊd, -z, -ɪŋ,
-əd

overlong
BR ˌəʊvəˈlɒŋ
AM ˈoʊvərˈlɔŋ,
ˈoʊvərˈlɑŋ

overlook
BR ˌəʊvəˈlʊk, -s, -ɪŋ, -t
AM ˈoʊvərˈlʊk, -s, -ɪŋ, -t

overlooker
BR ˈəʊvəˌlʊkə(r), -z
AM ˌoʊvərˈlʊkər, -z

overlord
BR ˈəʊvəlɔːd, -z
AM ˈoʊvərˌlɔ(ə)rd, -z

overlordship
BR ˈəʊvəˌlɔːdʃɪp, -s
AM ˈoʊvərˌlɔrdˌʃɪp, -s

overly
BR ˈəʊvəli
AM ˈoʊvərli

overlying
BR ˌəʊvəˈlʌɪɪŋ
AM ˈoʊvərˈlaɪ(ɪ)ŋ

overman[1]
noun
BR ˈəʊvəmən,
ˈəʊvəman
AM ˈoʊvərˌmæn

overman[2]
verb
BR ˌəʊvəˈman, -z, -ɪŋ, -d
AM ˌoʊvərˈmæn, -z, -ɪŋ,
-d

overmantel
BR ˈəʊvəˌmantl, -z
AM ˈoʊvərˌmæn(t)l, -z

over-many
BR ˌəʊvəˈmɛni
AM ˈoʊvərˈmɛni

overmaster
BR ˌəʊvəˈmɑːst|ə(r),
ˌəʊvəˈmast|ə(r), -əz,
-(ə)rɪŋ, -əd
AM ˌoʊvərˈmæst|ər,
-ərz, -(ə)rɪŋ, -ərd

overmastery
BR ˌəʊvəˈmɑːst(ə)ri,
ˌəʊvəˈmast(ə)ri
AM ˌoʊvərˈmæstəri

overmatch
BR ˌəʊvəˈmatʃ, -ɪz, -ɪŋ,
-t
AM ˌoʊvərˈmætʃ, -əz,
-ɪŋ, -t

overmeasure
BR ˌəʊvəˈmɛʒ|ə(r), -əz,
-(ə)rɪŋ, -əd
AM ˌoʊvərˈmɛʒər, -z,
-ɪŋ, -d

overmen
BR ˈəʊvəmən,
ˈəʊvəmɛn
AM ˈoʊvərˌmɛn

over-mighty
BR ˌəʊvəˈmʌɪti
AM ˈoʊvərˈmaɪdi

overmuch
BR ˌəʊvəˈmʌtʃ
AM ˈoʊvərˈmətʃ

overnight
BR ˌəʊvəˈnʌɪt
AM ˈoʊvərˈnaɪt

overnighter
BR ˌəʊvəˈnʌɪtə(r), -z
AM ˌoʊvərˈnaɪdər, -z

overpaid
BR ˌəʊvəˈpeɪd
AM ˈoʊvərˈpeɪd

overpaint
BR ˌəʊvəˈpeɪnt, -s, -ɪŋ,
-ɨd
AM ˌoʊvərˈpeɪn|t, -ts,
-dɪŋ, -dɨd

overparted
BR ˌəʊvəˈpɑːtɨd
AM ˈoʊvərˈpɑrdəd

overpass[1]
noun
BR ˈəʊvəpɑːs,
ˈəʊvəpas, -ɪz
AM ˈoʊvərˌpæs, -əz

overpass[2]
verb
BR ˌəʊvəˈpɑːs,
ˌəʊvəˈpas, -ɪz, -ɪŋ, -t

AM ˌoʊvər'pæs, -əz, -ɪŋ, -t

overpay
BR ˌəʊvə'peɪ, -z, -ɪŋ, -d
AM ˌoʊvər'peɪ, -z, -ɪŋ, -d

overpayed
adjective
BR ˌəʊvə'peɪd
AM ¦oʊvər'peɪd

overpayment
BR 'əʊvəˌpeɪm(ə)nt, ˌəʊvə'peɪm(ə)nt, -s
AM ¦oʊvərˌpeɪmənt, -s

overpersuade
BR ˌəʊvəpə'sweɪd, -z, -ɪŋ, -ɨd
AM ¦oʊvərpər'sweɪd, -z, -ɪŋ, -ɨd

overpitch
BR ˌəʊvə'pɪtʃ, -ɨz, -ɪŋ, -t
AM ˌoʊvər'pɪtʃ, -ɨz, -ɪŋ, -t

overplay
BR ˌəʊvə'pleɪ, -z, -ɪŋ, -d
AM ¦oʊvər'pleɪ, -z, -ɪŋ, -d

overplus
BR 'əʊvəplʌs, -ɨz
AM ¦oʊvər¦pləs, -əz

overpopulate
BR ˌəʊvə'pɒpjʉleɪt, -s, -ɪŋ, -ɨd
AM ¦oʊvər¦pɑpjəˌleɪ|t, -ts, -dɪŋ, -dɨd

overpopulation
BR ˌəʊvəˌpɒpjʉ'leɪʃn
AM ¦oʊvərˌpɑpjə'leɪʃən

overpower
BR ˌəʊvə'paʊə(r), -z, -ɪŋ, -d
AM ˌoʊvər'paʊ(ə)r, -z, -ɪŋ, -d

overpoweringly
BR ˌəʊvə'paʊərɪŋli
AM ˌoʊvər'paʊrɪŋli

overpraise
BR ˌəʊvə'preɪz, -ɨz, -ɪŋ, -d
AM ¦oʊvər'preɪz, -ɨz, -ɪŋ, -d

overprice
BR ˌəʊvə'prʌɪs, -ɨz, -ɪŋ, -t
AM ¦oʊvər'praɪs, -ɨz, -ɪŋ, -t

overprint[1]
noun
BR 'əʊvəprɪnt, -s
AM 'oʊvərˌprɪnt, -s

overprint[2]
verb
BR ˌəʊvə'prɪnt, -s, -ɪŋ, -ɨd
AM ¦oʊvər¦prɪn|t, -ts, -(t)ɪŋ, -(t)əd

overproduce
BR ˌəʊvəprə'djuːs, ˌəʊvəprə'dʒuːs, -ɨz, -ɪŋ, -t
AM ¦oʊvərprə'd(j)us, -ɨz, -ɪŋ, -t

overproduction
BR ˌəʊvəprə'dʌkʃn
AM ¦oʊvərprə'dəkʃən

overproof
BR ˌəʊvə'pruːf
AM ¦oʊvər'pruf

overprotective
BR ˌəʊvəprə'tɛktɪv
AM ¦oʊvərprə'tɛktɪv

overqualified
BR ˌəʊvə'kwɒlɨfʌɪd
AM ¦oʊvər'kwɔləˌfaɪd, ¦oʊvər'kwɑləˌfaɪd

overran
BR ˌəʊvə'ran
AM ¦oʊvə(r)'ræn

overrate
BR ˌəʊvə'reɪt, -s, -ɪŋ, -ɨd
AM ¦oʊvə(r)¦reɪ|t, -ts, -dɪŋ, -dɨd

overreach
BR ˌəʊvə'riːtʃ, -ɨz, -ɪŋ, -d
AM ¦oʊvə(r)'ritʃ, -ɨz, -ɪŋ, -d

overreact
BR ˌəʊvərɪ'akt, -s, -ɪŋ, -d
AM ¦oʊvə(r)ri'æk|(t), -(t)s, -tɪŋ, -təd

overreaction
BR ˌəʊvərɪ'akʃn, -z
AM ¦oʊvə(r)ri'ækʃən, -z

overridden
BR ˌəʊvə'rɪdn
AM ¦oʊvə(r)'rɪdən

override
BR ˌəʊvə'rʌɪd, -z, -ɪŋ
AM ¦oʊvə(r)¦raɪd, -z, -ɪŋ

overrider
BR 'əʊvəˌrʌɪdə(r), -z
AM ¦oʊvə(r)¦raɪdər, -z

overripe
BR ˌəʊvə'rʌɪp
AM ¦oʊvə(r)¦raɪp

overripen
BR ˌəʊvə'rʌɪp|n, -nz, -n̩ɪŋ\-nɪŋ, -nd
AM ¦oʊvə(r)¦raɪp|ən, -ənz, -(ə)nɪŋ, -ənd

overripeness
BR ˌəʊvə'rʌɪpnɨs
AM ¦oʊvə(r)¦raɪpnɨs

overrode
BR ˌəʊvə'rəʊd
AM ¦oʊvə(r)¦roʊd

overruff[1]
noun
BR 'əʊvərʌf, -s
AM 'oʊvə(r)ˌrəf, -s

overruff[2]
verb
BR ˌəʊvə'rʌf, -s, -ɪŋ, -d
AM ¦oʊvə(r)¦rəf, -s, -ɪŋ, -d

overrule
BR ˌəʊvə'ruːl, -z, -ɪŋ, -d
AM ¦oʊvə(r)'rul, -z, -ɪŋ, -d

overrun
BR ˌəʊvə'rʌn, -z, -ɪŋ
AM ¦oʊvə(r)¦rən, -z, -ɪŋ

oversailing
BR ˌəʊvə'seɪlɪŋ
AM ¦oʊvər'seɪlɪŋ

oversaw
BR ˌəʊvə'sɔː(r)
AM ˌoʊvər'sɔ

overscrupulous
BR ˌəʊvə'skruːpjʉləs
AM ¦oʊvər'skrupjələs

oversea
BR ˌəʊvə'siː, -z
AM ¦oʊvər'si, -z

oversee
BR ˌəʊvə'siː, -z, -ɪŋ
AM ¦oʊvər'si, -z, -ɪŋ

overseen
BR ˌəʊvə'siːn
AM ¦oʊvər'sin

overseer
BR 'əʊvəsɪə(r), -z
AM ¦oʊvər¦sɪ(ə)r, -z

oversell
BR ˌəʊvə'sɛl, -z, -ɪŋ
AM ¦oʊvər'sɛl, -z, -ɪŋ

overset
BR ˌəʊvə'sɛt, -s, -ɪŋ
AM ˌoʊvər'sɛ|t, -ts, -dɪŋ

oversew
BR ˌəʊvə'səʊ, -z, -ɪŋ, -d
AM ¦oʊvər'soʊ, -z, -ɪŋ, -d

oversexed
BR ˌəʊvə'sɛkst
AM ¦oʊvər'sɛkst

overshadow
BR ˌəʊvə'ʃadəʊ, -z, -ɪŋ, -d
AM ¦oʊvər¦ʃæd|oʊ, -oʊz, -əwɪŋ, -oʊd

overshoe
BR 'əʊvəʃuː, -z
AM 'oʊvərˌʃu, -z

overshoot
BR ˌəʊvə'ʃuːt, -s, -ɪŋ
AM ˌoʊvər'ʃu|t, -ts, -dɪŋ

overshot
BR ˌəʊvə'ʃɒt
AM ¦oʊvər'ʃɑt

overside
BR 'əʊvəsʌɪd
AM 'oʊvərˌsaɪd

oversight
BR 'əʊvəsʌɪt, -s
AM 'oʊvərˌsaɪt, -s

oversimplification
BR ˌəʊvəˌsɪmplɨfɪ'keɪʃn, -z
AM ¦oʊvərˌsɪmpləfə'keɪʃən, -z

oversimplify
BR ˌəʊvə'sɪmplɨfʌɪ, -z, -ɪŋ, -d
AM ¦oʊvər'sɪmpləˌfaɪ, -z, -ɪŋ, -d

oversize
BR ˌəʊvə'sʌɪz, -d
AM ¦oʊvər¦saɪz, -d

overskirt
BR 'əʊvəskəːt, -s
AM 'oʊvərˌskərt, -s

overslaugh
BR ˌəʊvə'slɔː(r), -z, -ɪŋ, -d
AM ˌoʊvər'slɔ, ˌoʊvər'slɑ, -z, -ɪŋ, -d

oversleep
BR ˌəʊvə'sliːp, -s, -ɪŋ
AM ˌoʊvər'slip, -s, -ɪŋ

oversleeve
BR 'əʊvəsliːv, -z
AM 'oʊvərˌsliv, -z

overslept
BR ˌəʊvə'slɛpt
AM ˌoʊvər'slɛpt

oversold
BR ˌəʊvə'səʊld
AM ¦oʊvər'soʊld

oversolicitous
BR ˌəʊvəsə'lɪsɪtəs
AM ¦oʊvərsə'lɪsədəs

oversolicitude
BR ˌəʊvəsə'lɪsɪtjuːd, ˌəʊvəsə'lɪsɪtʃuːd
AM ¦oʊvərsə'lɪsəˌt(j)ud

oversoul
BR 'əʊvəsəʊl
AM 'oʊvərˌsoʊl

overspecialisation
BR ˌəʊvəˌspɛʃəlʌɪ'zeɪʃn, ˌəʊvəˌspɛʃl̩ʌɪ'zeɪʃn
AM ¦oʊvərˌspɛʃ(ə)lə'zeɪʃən, ¦oʊvərˌspɛʃ(ə)ˌlaɪ'zeɪʃən

overspecialise
BR ˌəʊvə'spɛʃəlʌɪz, ˌəʊvə'spɛʃl̩ʌɪz, -ɨz, -ɪŋ, -d
AM ˌoʊvər'spɛʃ(ə)ˌlaɪz, -ɨz, -ɪŋ, -d

overspecialization
BR ˌəʊvəˌspɛʃəlʌɪ'zeɪʃn, ˌəʊvəˌspɛʃl̩ʌɪ'zeɪʃn
AM ¦oʊvərˌspɛʃ(ə)lə'zeɪʃən, ¦oʊvərˌspɛʃ(ə)ˌlaɪ'zeɪʃən

overspecialize
BR ˌəʊvə'spɛʃəlʌɪz, ˌəʊvə'spɛʃl̩ʌɪz, -ɨz, -ɪŋ, -d
AM ˌoʊvər'spɛʃ(ə)ˌlaɪz, -ɨz, -ɪŋ, -d

overspend[1]
noun
BR 'əʊvəspɛnd, -z

AM ˈoʊvərˌspɛnd, -z

overspend²
verb
BR ˌəʊvəˈspɛnd, -z, -ɪŋ
AM ˌoʊvərˈspɛnd, -z, -ɪŋ

overspent
BR ˌəʊvəˈspɛnt
AM ˌoʊvərˈspɛnt

overspill
BR ˈəʊvəspɪl
AM ˈoʊvərˈspɪl

overspread
BR ˌəʊvəˈsprɛd, -z, -ɪŋ
AM ˌoʊvərˈsprɛd, -z, -ɪŋ

overstaff
BR ˌəʊvəˈstɑːf, ˌəʊvəˈstaf, -s, -ɪŋ, -t
AM ˈoʊvərˈstæf, -s, -ɪŋ, -t

overstate
BR ˌəʊvəˈsteɪt, -s, -ɪŋ, -ɪd
AM ˈoʊvərˈsteɪ|t, -ts, -dɪŋ, -dɪd

overstatement
BR ˌəʊvəˈsteɪtm(ə)nt, ˈəʊvəˌsteɪtm(ə)nt, -s
AM ˈoʊvərˈsteɪtmənt, -s

overstay
BR ˌəʊvəˈsteɪ, -z, -ɪŋ, -d
AM ˌoʊvərˈsteɪ, -z, -ɪŋ, -d

oversteer¹
noun
BR ˈəʊvəstɪə(r)
AM ˈoʊvərˌstɪ(ə)r

oversteer²
verb
BR ˌəʊvəˈstɪə(r), -z, -ɪŋ, -d
AM ˈoʊvərˈstɪ(ə)r, -z, -ɪŋ, -d

overstep
BR ˌəʊvəˈstɛp, -s, -ɪŋ, -t
AM ˈoʊvərˈstɛp, -s, -ɪŋ, -t

overstock
BR ˌəʊvəˈstɒk, -s, -ɪŋ, -t
AM ˈoʊvərˈstɑk, -s, -ɪŋ, -t

overstrain
verb
BR ˌəʊvəˈstreɪn, -z, -ɪŋ, -d
AM ˈoʊvərˈstreɪn, -z, -ɪŋ, -d

overstress
BR ˌəʊvəˈstrɛs, -ɪz, -ɪŋ, -t
AM ˈoʊvərˈstrɛs, -əz, -ɪŋ, -t

overstretch
BR ˌəʊvəˈstrɛtʃ, -ɪz, -ɪŋ, -t
AM ˈoʊvərˈstrɛtʃ, -əz, -ɪŋ, -t

overstrong
BR ˌəʊvəˈstrɒŋ
AM ˈoʊvərˈstrɔŋ, ˈoʊvərˈstrɑŋ

overstrung
BR ˌəʊvəˈstrʌŋ
AM ˈoʊvərˈstrəŋ

overstudy
BR ˌəʊvəˈstʌd|i, -ɪz, -ɪɪŋ, -ɪd
AM ˌoʊvərˈstədi, -z, -ɪŋ, -d

overstuff
BR ˌəʊvəˈstʌf, -s, -ɪŋ, -d
AM ˌoʊvərˈstəf, -s, -ɪŋ, -d

oversubscribe
BR ˌəʊvəsəbˈskrʌɪb, -z, -ɪŋ, -d
AM ˈoʊvərsəbˈskraɪb, -z, -ɪŋ, -d

oversubtle
BR ˌəʊvəˈsʌtl
AM ˈoʊvərˈsədəl

oversupply
BR ˌəʊvəsəˈplʌɪ, -z, -ɪŋ, -d
AM ˈoʊvərsəˈplaɪ, -z, -ɪŋ, -d

oversusceptible
BR ˌəʊvəsəˈsɛptɪbl
AM ˈoʊvərsəˈsɛptəbəl

overt
BR ə(ʊ)ˈvəːt, ˈəʊvəːt
AM oʊˈvərt, ˈoʊvərt

overtake
BR ˌəʊvəˈteɪk, -s, -ɪŋ
AM ˈoʊvərˈteɪk, -s, -ɪŋ

overtaken
BR ˌəʊvəˈteɪk(ə)n
AM ˈoʊvərˈteɪkən

overtask
BR ˌəʊvəˈtɑːsk, ˌəʊvəˈtask, -s, -ɪŋ, -t
AM ˈoʊvərˈtæsk, -s, -ɪŋ, -t

overtax
BR ˌəʊvəˈtaks
AM ˈoʊvərˈtæks

over-the-counter
BR ˌəʊvəðəˈkaʊntə(r)
AM ˈoʊvərðəˈkaʊn(t)ər

over-the-top
BR ˌəʊvəðəˈtɒp
AM ˈoʊvərðəˈtɑp

overthrew
BR ˌəʊvəˈθruː
AM ˈoʊvərˈθru

overthrow¹
noun
BR ˈəʊvəθrəʊ, -z
AM ˈoʊvərˌθroʊ, -z

overthrow²
verb
BR ˌəʊvəˈθrəʊ, -z, -ɪŋ
AM ˈoʊvərˈθroʊ, -z, -ɪŋ

overthrown
BR ˌəʊvəˈθrəʊn
AM ˈoʊvərˈθroʊn

overthrust
BR ˈəʊvəθrʌst, -s
AM ˈoʊvərˌθrəst, -s

overtime
BR ˈəʊvətʌɪm
AM ˈoʊvərˌtaɪm

overtire
BR ˌəʊvəˈtʌɪə(r), -z, -ɪŋ, -d
AM ˌoʊvərˈtaɪ(ə)r, -z, -ɪŋ, -d

overtly
BR ə(ʊ)ˈvəːtli, ˈəʊvəːtli
AM oʊˈvərtli, ˈoʊvərtli

overtness
BR ə(ʊ)ˈvəːtnəs, ˈəʊvəːtnəs
AM oʊˈvərtnəs, ˈoʊvərtnəs

Overton
BR ˈəʊvət(ə)n
AM ˈoʊvərt(ə)n

overtone
BR ˈəʊvətəʊn, -z
AM ˈoʊvərˌtoʊn, -z

overtook
BR ˌəʊvəˈtʊk
AM ˈoʊvərˈtʊk

overtop
BR ˌəʊvəˈtɒp, -s, -ɪŋ, -t
AM ˈoʊvərˈtɑp, -s, -ɪŋ, -t

overtrain
BR ˌəʊvəˈtreɪn, -z, -ɪŋ, -d
AM ˌoʊvərˈtreɪn, -z, -ɪŋ, -d

overtrick
BR ˈəʊvətrɪk, -s
AM ˈoʊvərˌtrɪk, -s

overtrump
BR ˌəʊvəˈtrʌmp, -s, -ɪŋ, -t
AM ˈoʊvərˈtrəmp, -s, -ɪŋ, -t

overture
BR ˈəʊvətjʊə(r), ˈəʊvətʃ(ʊ)ə(r), -z
AM ˈoʊvərˌtʃʊ(ə)r, ˈoʊvərˌtʃər, -z

overturn
BR ˌəʊvəˈtəːn, -z, -ɪŋ, -d
AM ˌoʊvərˈtərn, -z, -ɪŋ, -d

overuse¹
noun
BR ˌəʊvəˈjuːs
AM ˈoʊvərˈjus

overuse²
verb
BR ˌəʊvəˈjuːz, -ɪz, -ɪŋ, -d
AM ˈoʊvərˈjuz, -əz, -ɪŋ, -d

overvaluation
BR ˌəʊvəˌvaljuˈeɪʃn, -z
AM ˈoʊvərəˌvæljəˈweɪʃən, -z

overvalue
BR ˌəʊvəˈvaljuː, -z, -ɪŋ, -d
AM ˈoʊvərˈvælju, -z, -ɪŋ, -d

overview
BR ˈəʊvəvjuː, -z
AM ˈoʊvərˌvju, -z

overwater
BR ˌəʊvəˈwɔːt|ə(r), -əz, -(ə)rɪŋ, -əd
AM ˈoʊvərˈwɔdər, ˈoʊvərˈwɑdər, -z, -ɪŋ, -d

overweening
BR ˌəʊvəˈwiːnɪŋ
AM ˈoʊvərˈwinɪŋ

overweeningly
BR ˌəʊvəˈwiːnɪŋli
AM ˈoʊvərˈwinɪŋli

overweeningness
BR ˌəʊvəˈwiːnɪŋnɪs
AM ˈoʊvərˈwinɪŋnɪs

overweight
BR ˌəʊvəˈweɪt
AM ˈoʊvərˈweɪt

overwhelm
BR ˌəʊvəˈwɛlm, -z, -ɪŋ, -d
AM ˈoʊvərˈ(h)wɛlm, -z, -ɪŋ, -d

overwhelmingly
BR ˌəʊvəˈwɛlmɪŋli
AM ˈoʊvərˈ(h)wɛlmɪŋli

overwhelmingness
BR ˌəʊvəˈwɛlmɪŋnɪs
AM ˈoʊvərˈ(h)wɛlmɪŋnɪs

overwind
BR ˌəʊvəˈwʌɪnd, -z, -ɪŋ
AM ˈoʊvərˈwaɪnd, -z, -ɪŋ

overwinter
BR ˌəʊvəˈwɪnt|ə(r), -əz, -(ə)rɪŋ, -əd
AM ˈoʊvərˈwɪn(t)ər, -z, -ɪŋ, -d

overwork
BR ˌəʊvəˈwəːk, -s, -ɪŋ, -t
AM ˈoʊvərˈwərk, -s, -ɪŋ, -t

overwound
BR ˌəʊvəˈwaʊnd
AM ˈoʊvərˈwaʊnd

overwrite
BR ˌəʊvəˈrʌɪt, -s, -ɪŋ
AM ˈoʊvəˈraɪ|t, -ts, -dɪŋ

overwritten
BR ˌəʊvəˈrɪtn
AM ˈoʊvəˈrɪtn

overwrote
BR ˌəʊvəˈrəʊt
AM ˈoʊvəˈroʊt

overwrought
BR ˌəʊvəˈrɔːt
AM ˈoʊvəˈrɔt, ˈoʊvəˈrɑt

overzeal
BR ˌəʊvəˈziːl
AM ˈoʊvərˌzil

overzealous
BR ˌəʊvəˈzɛləs
AM ˈoʊvərˈzɛləs

Ovett
BR ˈəʊvɪt, ˈəʊvɛt, əʊˈvɛt
AM oʊˈvɛt, ˈoʊvət

ovibovine
BR ˌəʊvɪˈbəʊvʌɪn, -z
AM ˈoʊviˈboʊvaɪn, -z

ovicide
BR ˈəʊvɨsʌɪd, ˈɒvɨsʌɪd
AM ˈoʊvəˌsaɪd, ˈɑvəˌsaɪd

Ovid
BR ˈɒvɪd
AM ˈɑvɪd

oviducal
BR ˌəʊvɪˈdjuːkl, ˌəʊvɪˈdʒuːkl
AM ˌoʊvəˈdukəl

oviduct
BR ˈəʊvɪdʌkt, -s
AM ˈoʊvəˌdək(t), -(t)s

oviductal
BR ˌəʊvɪˈdʌktl
AM ˌoʊvəˈdəktəl

Oviedo
BR ˌɒvɪˈeɪdəʊ
AM ɔˈvjɛdoʊ, ɑˈvjɛdoʊ
SP oˈβjeðo

oviform
BR ˈəʊvɪfɔːm
AM ˈoʊvəˌfɔ(ə)rm

ovine
BR ˈəʊvʌɪn
AM ˈoʊˌvaɪn

oviparity
BR ˌəʊvɪˈparɨti
AM ˌoʊvəˈpɛrədi

oviparous
BR əʊˈvɪp(ə)rəs
AM oʊˈvɪpərəs

oviparously
BR əʊˈvɪp(ə)rəsli
AM oʊˈvɪpərəsli

oviposit
BR ˌəʊvɪˈpɒz|ɪt, -ɪts, -ɨtɪŋ, -ɨtɨd
AM ˈoʊvəˌpɑzə|t, -ts, -dɪŋ, -dəd

oviposition
BR ˌəʊvɪpəˈzɪʃn
AM ˌoʊvəpəˈzɪʃən

ovipositor
BR ˌəʊvɪˈpɒzɨtə(r), -z
AM ˈoʊvəˌpɑzədər, -z

ovoid
BR ˈəʊvɔɪd
AM ˈoʊˌvɔɪd

ovoli
BR ˈəʊvəliː
AM ˈoʊvəlaɪ, ˈɔvəˌlaɪ

ovolo
BR ˈəʊvələʊ
AM ˈoʊvəloʊ, ˈɔvəˌloʊ

ovotestes
BR ˌəʊvəʊˈtɛstiːz
AM ˌoʊvoʊˈtɛstiz

ovotestis
BR ˌəʊvəʊˈtɛstɪs
AM ˌoʊvoʊˈtɛstəs

ovoviviparity
BR ˌəʊvəʊˌvɪvɨˈparɨti
AM oʊˌvoʊˌvɪvɨˈpɛrədi

ovoviviparous
BR ˌəʊvəʊvɪˈvɪp(ə)rəs, ˌəʊvəʊvʌɪˈvɪp(ə)rəs
AM oʊˌvoʊvəˈvɪp(ə)rəs

ovular
BR ˈɒvjʉlə(r)
AM ˈoʊvjələr, ˈɑvjələr

ovulate
BR ˈɒvjʉleɪt, -s, -ɪŋ, -ɨd
AM ˈoʊvjəˌleɪ|t, ˈɑvjəˌleɪ|t, -ts, -dɪŋ, -dɨd

ovulation
BR ˌɒvjʉˈleɪʃn, -z
AM ˌoʊvjəˈleɪʃən, ˌɑvjəˈleɪʃən, -z

ovulatory
BR ˈɒvjʉlət(ə)ri
AM ˈoʊvjələˌtɔri, ˈɑvjələˌtɔri

ovule
BR ˈɒvjuːl, -z
AM ˈoʊvjul, ˈɑvjul, -z

ovum
BR ˈəʊvəm
AM ˈoʊvəm

ow!
BR aʊ
AM aʊ

Owain
BR ˈəʊʌɪn
AM ˈoʊweɪn

owe
BR əʊ, -z, -ɪŋ, -d
AM oʊ, -z, -(w)ɪŋ, -d

Owen
BR ˈəʊɪn
AM ˈoʊ(w)ən

Owens
BR ˈəʊɪnz
AM ˈoʊ(w)ənz

owl
BR aʊl, -z
AM aʊl, -z

owlery
BR ˈaʊlər|i, -ɪz
AM ˈaʊləri, -z

owlet
BR ˈaʊlɪt, -s
AM ˈaʊlət, -s

owlish
BR ˈaʊlɪʃ
AM ˈaʊlɪʃ

owlishly
BR ˈaʊlɪʃli
AM ˈaʊlɪʃli

owlishness
BR ˈaʊlɪʃnɪs
AM ˈaʊlɪʃnɪs

own
BR əʊn, -z, -ɪŋ, -d
AM oʊn, -z, -ɪŋ, -d

own brand
BR ˌəʊn ˈbrand, ˈəʊn brand, -z
AM ˈoʊn ˌbrænd, -z

owner
BR ˈəʊnə(r), -z
AM ˈoʊnər, -z

ownerless
BR ˈəʊnələs
AM ˈoʊnərləs

ownership
BR ˈəʊnəʃɪp
AM ˈoʊnərˌʃɪp

owt
BR aʊt
AM aʊt

ox
BR ɒks
AM ɑks

oxalate
BR ˈɒksəleɪt, -s
AM ˈɑksəˌleɪt, -s

oxalic
BR ɒkˈsalɪk
AM ɑkˈsælɪk

oxalis
BR ˈɒksəlɪs, ɒkˈsalɪs, ɒkˈsɑːlɪs
AM ˈɑksələs, ɑkˈsæləs

oxbow
BR ˈɒksbəʊ, -z
AM ˈɑksˌboʊ, -z

Oxbridge
BR ˈɒksbrɪdʒ
AM ˈɑksˌbrɪdʒ

oxcart
BR ˈɒkskɑːt, -s
AM ˈɑksˌkɑrt, -s

oxen
BR ˈɒksn
AM ˈɑksən

Oxenden
BR ˈɒksndən
AM ˈɑksəndən

Oxenford
BR ˈɒksnfɔːd
AM ˈɑksənfərd

Oxenholme
BR ˈɒksnhəʊm
AM ˈɑksənˌ(h)oʊm

oxer
BR ˈɒksə(r), -z
AM ˈɑksər, -z

Oxfam
BR ˈɒksfam
AM ˈɑksfæm

Oxford
BR ˈɒksfəd
AM ˈɑksfərd

Oxfordshire
BR ˈɒksfədʃ(ɪ)ə(r)
AM ˈɑksfərdˌʃɪ(ə)r

oxheart
BR ˈɒkshɑːt, -s
AM ˈɑksˌ(h)ɑrt, -s

oxherd
BR ˈɒkshəːd, -z
AM ˈɑksˌ(h)ərd, -z

Oxhey
BR ˈɒksi, ˈɒksheɪ
AM ˈɑksi

oxhide
BR ˈɒkshʌɪd
AM ˈɑksˌ(h)aɪd

oxidant
BR ˈɒksɪd(ə)nt, -s
AM ˈɑksədnt, -s

oxidate
BR ˈɒksɨdeɪt, -s, -ɪŋ, -ɨd
AM ˈɑksəˌdeɪ|t, -ts, -dɪŋ, -dɨd

oxidation
BR ˌɒksɨˈdeɪʃn
AM ˌɑksəˈdeɪʃən

oxidational
BR ˌɒksɨˈdeɪʃn̩(ə)l, ˌɒksɨˈdeɪʃən(ə)l
AM ˌɑksəˈdeɪʃ(ə)nəl

oxidative
BR ˈɒksɨdeɪtɪv
AM ˈɑksəˌdeɪdɪv

oxide
BR ˈɒksʌɪd, -z
AM ˈɑkˌsaɪd, -z

oxidisable
BR ˈɒksɨdʌɪzəbl
AM ˈɑksəˌdaɪzəbəl

oxidisation
BR ˌɒksɨdʌɪˈzeɪʃn
AM ˌɑksəˌdaɪˈzeɪʃən, ˌɑksədəˈzeɪʃən

oxidise
BR ˈɒksɨdʌɪz, -ɨz, -ɪŋ, -d
AM ˈɑksəˌdaɪz, -ɨz, -ɪŋ, -d

oxidiser
BR ˈɒksɨdʌɪzə(r), -z
AM ˈɑksəˌdaɪzər, -z

oxidizable
BR ˈɒksɨdʌɪzəbl
AM ˈɑksəˌdaɪzəbəl

oxidization
BR ˌɒksɨdʌɪˈzeɪʃn
AM ˌɑksəˌdaɪˈzeɪʃən, ˌɑksədəˈzeɪʃən

oxidize
BR ˈɒksɨdʌɪz, -ɨz, -ɪŋ, -d
AM ˈɑksəˌdaɪz, -ɨz, -ɪŋ, -d

oxidizer
BR ˈɒksɨdʌɪzə(r), -z
AM ˈɑksəˌdaɪzər, -z

Oxley
BR ˈɒksli
AM ˈɑksli

oxlip
BR ˈɒkslɪp, -s
AM ˈɑksˌlɪp, -s

Oxnard
BR 'ɒksnɑːd, 'ɒksnəd
AM 'ɑksˌnɑrd

oxo
BR 'ɒksəʊ
AM 'ɑksoʊ

Oxon
BR 'ɒks(ɒ)n
AM 'ɑksˌɑn

Oxonian
BR ɒk'səʊnɪən, -z
AM ɑk'soʊniən, ɑk'soʊnjən, -z

oxonium
BR ɒk'səʊnɪəm
AM ɑk'soʊniəm

Oxshott
BR 'ɒk(s)ʃɒt
AM 'ɑkˌʃɑt

oxslip
BR 'ɒkslɪp, -s
AM 'ɑksˌlɪp, -s

oxtail
BR 'ɒksteɪl, -z
AM 'ɑksˌteɪl, -z

oxter
BR 'ɒkstə(r), -z
AM 'ɑkstər, -z

Oxton
BR 'ɒkst(ə)n
AM 'ɑkstən

oxtongue
BR 'ɒkstʌŋ, -z
AM 'ɑksˌtəŋ, -z

Oxus
BR 'ɒksəs
AM 'ɑksəs

oxyacetylene
BR ˌɒksɪə'sɛtɨliːn, ˌɒksɪə'sɛtl̩iːn, ˌɒksɪə'sɛtɨlɪn, ˌɒksɪə'sɛtl̩ɪn
AM ˌɑksiə'sɛdl̩ən, ˌɑksiə'sɛdlˌin

oxyacid
BR ˌɒksɪ'asɪd, -z
AM ˌɑksi'æsəd, -z

oxycarpous
BR ˌɒksɪ'kɑːpəs
AM ˌɑksi'kɑrpəs

Oxydol
BR 'ɒksɪdɒl
AM 'ɑksɨˌdɔl, 'ɑksɨˌdɑl

oxygen
BR 'ɒksɪdʒ(ə)n
AM 'ɑksədʒən

oxygenate
BR 'ɒksɪdʒɪneɪt, ɒk'sɪdʒəneɪt, -s, -ɪŋ, -ɪd
AM 'ɑksədʒəˌneɪ|t, -ts, -dɪŋ, -dɨd

oxygenation
BR ˌɒksɪdʒɪ'neɪʃn
AM ˌɑksədʒə'neɪʃən

oxygenator
BR 'ɒksɪdʒɪneɪtə(r), ɒk'sɪdʒəneɪtə(r), -z
AM 'ɑksədʒəˌneɪdər, -z

oxygenise
BR 'ɒksɪdʒɪnʌɪz, -ɪz, -ɪŋ, -d
AM 'ɑksədʒəˌnaɪz, -ɨz, -ɪŋ, -d

oxygenize
BR 'ɒksɪdʒɪnʌɪz, -ɪz, -ɪŋ, -d
AM 'ɑksədʒəˌnaɪz, -ɨz, -ɪŋ, -d

oxygenous
BR ɒk'sɪdʒɪnəs
AM ɑk'sɪdʒənəs

oxyhaemoglobin
BR ˌɒksɪˌhiːmə'gləʊbɪn
AM ˌɑksiˈhiməˌgloʊbən

oxyhemoglobin
BR ˌɒksɪˌhiːmə'gləʊbɪn
AM ˌɑksiˈhiməˌgloʊbən

oxy-hydrogen
BR ˌɒksɪ'hʌɪdrədʒ(ə)n
AM ˌɑksi'haɪdrədʒən

oxymoron
BR ˌɒksɪ'mɔːrɒn, -z
AM ˌɑksə'mɔrˌɑn, -z

oxyopia
BR ˌɒksɪ'əʊpɪə(*r*)
AM ˌɑksi'oʊpiə

Oxyrhynchus
BR ˌɒksɪ'rɪŋkəs
AM ˌɑksə'rɪŋkəs

oxysalt
BR ˌɒksɪ'sɔːlt, ˌɒksɪ'sɒlt, 'ɒksɪsɔːlt, 'ɒksɪsɒlt, -s
AM 'ɑksiˌsɔlt, 'ɑksiˌsɑlt, -s

oxytocin
BR ˌɒksɪ'təʊsɪn, -z
AM ˌɑksə'toʊsn, -z

oxytone
BR 'ɒksɪtəʊn, -z
AM 'ɑksəˌtoʊn, -z

oyes
BR əʊ'jeɪ, əʊ'jɛz, əʊ'jɛs
AM oʊ'jeɪ, oʊ'jɛz

oyez
BR əʊ'jeɪ, əʊ'jɛz, əʊ'jɛs
AM oʊ'jeɪ, oʊ'jɛz

oyster
BR 'ɔɪstə(r), -z
AM 'ɔɪstər, -z

oystercatcher
BR 'ɔɪstəˌkatʃə(r), -z
AM 'ɔɪstərˌkætʃər, -z

Oystermouth
BR 'ɔɪstəmaʊθ
AM 'ɔɪstərməθ

oystershell
BR 'ɔɪstəʃɛl
AM 'ɔɪstərˌʃɛl

Oz
BR ɒz
AM ɑz

oz.
BR aʊns, -ɪz
AM aʊns, -ɪz

Ozalid®
BR 'ɒzəlɪd, 'ɒzl̩ɪd, 'əʊzəlɪd, 'əʊzl̩ɪd
AM 'oʊzəˌlɪd, 'ɑzəˌlɪd

Ozark
BR 'əʊzɑːk, -s
AM 'oʊˌzɑrk, -s

Ozawa
BR ɒ'zɑːwə(*r*)
AM oʊ'zɑwə

ozocerite
BR əʊ'zɒsərʌɪt, əʊ'zəʊsərʌɪt, ˌəʊzə(ʊ)'sɪərʌɪt
AM oʊ'zoʊkəˌraɪt

ozokerite
BR əʊ'zɒkərʌɪt, əʊ'zəʊkərʌɪt, ˌəʊzə(ʊ)'kɪərʌɪt
AM oʊ'zoʊkəˌraɪt

ozone
BR 'əʊzəʊn
AM 'oʊˌzoʊn

ozonic
BR əʊ'zɒnɪk
AM oʊ'zɑnɪk

ozonisation
BR ˌəʊzə(ʊ)nʌɪ'zeɪʃn
AM ˌoʊzənə'zeɪʃən, ˌoʊzəˌnaɪ'zeɪʃən

ozonise
BR 'əʊzə(ʊ)nʌɪz, -ɪz, -ɪŋ, -d
AM 'oʊzəˌnaɪz, -ɨz, -ɪŋ, -d

ozonization
BR ˌəʊzə(ʊ)nʌɪ'zeɪʃn
AM ˌoʊzənə'zeɪʃən, ˌoʊzəˌnaɪ'zeɪʃən

ozonize
BR 'əʊzə(ʊ)nʌɪz, -ɪz, -ɪŋ, -d
AM 'oʊzəˌnaɪz, -ɨz, -ɪŋ, -d

Ozymandias
BR ˌɒzɪ'mandɪəs, ˌɒzɪ'mandɪas
AM ˌoʊzə'mændiəs

Ozzie
BR 'ɒzi
AM 'ɑzi

Pp

p
BR piː, -z
AM pi, -z
PA
BR ˌpiːˈeɪ, -z
AM ˌpiˈeɪ, -z
pa
BR pɑː(*r*), -z
AM pɑ, -z
Paarl
BR pɑːl
AM pɑrl
Pablo
BR ˈpabləʊ
AM ˈpɑbloʊ
Pablum®
BR ˈpabləm
AM ˈpæbləm
pabulum
BR ˈpabjʊləm
AM ˈpæb(jə)ləm
paca
BR ˈpakə(*r*), ˈpɑːkə(*r*), -z
AM ˈpɑkə, ˈpækə, -z
pacarana
BR ˌpakəˈrɑːnə(*r*), -z
AM ˌpɑkəˈrɑnə, -z
pace¹
noun, verb
BR peɪs, -ɪz, -ɪŋ, -t
AM peɪs, -ɪz, -ɪŋ, -t
pace²
preposition, with respect to
BR ˈpeɪsi, ˈpɑːtʃeɪ, ˈpɑːkeɪ
AM ˈpeɪˌsi, ˈpɑˌtʃeɪ
pacemaker
BR ˈpeɪsˌmeɪkə(r), -z
AM ˈpeɪsˌmeɪkər, -z
pacemaking
BR ˈpeɪsˌmeɪkɪŋ
AM ˈpeɪsˌmeɪkɪŋ
paceman
BR ˈpeɪsmən, ˈpeɪsman
AM ˈpeɪsˌmæn, ˈpeɪsmən
pacemen
BR ˈpeɪsmən, ˈpeɪsmɛn
AM ˈpeɪsmən, ˈpeɪsˌmɛn
pacer
BR ˈpeɪsə(r), -z
AM ˈpeɪsər, -z
pacesetter
BR ˈpeɪsˌsɛtə(r), -z
AM ˈpeɪ(s)ˌsɛdər, -z
pace-setting
BR ˈpeɪsˌsɛtɪŋ
AM ˈpeɪ(s)ˌsɛdɪŋ
pacey
BR ˈpeɪsi
AM ˈpeɪsi
pacha
BR ˈpɑːʃə(*r*), ˈpaʃə(*r*), -z
AM ˈpɑʃə, -z
Pachelbel
BR ˈpaklbɛl, paxlbɛl
AM ˈpɑkəlˌbɛl
pachinko
BR pəˈtʃɪŋkəʊ
AM pəˈtʃɪŋkoʊ
pachisi
BR pəˈtʃiːzi
AM pəˈtʃizi
pachuco
BR pəˈtʃuːkəʊ, -z
AM pəˈtʃʊkoʊ, -z
pachyderm
BR ˈpakɪdəːm, -z
AM ˈpækəˌdərm, -z
pachydermal
BR ˌpakɪˈdəːml
AM ˌpækəˈdərməl
pachydermatous
BR ˌpakɪˈdəːmətəs
AM ˌpækəˈdərmədəs
pachysandra
BR ˌpakɪˈsandrə(*r*)
AM ˌpækəˈsændrə
pachytene
BR ˈpakɪtiːn
AM ˈpækəˌtin
pacific
BR pəˈsɪfɪk
AM pəˈsɪfɪk
pacifically
BR pəˈsɪfɪkli
AM pəˈsɪfək(ə)li
pacification
BR ˌpasɪfɪˈkeɪʃn, -z
AM ˌpæsəfəˈkeɪʃən, -z
pacificatory
BR pəˈsɪfɪkət(ə)ri, ˌpasɪfɪˈkeɪt(ə)ri
AM pəˈsɪfɪkəˌtɔri
Pacific Ocean
BR pəˌsɪfɪk ˈəʊʃn
AM pəˌsɪfɪk ˈoʊʃən
pacifier
BR ˈpasɪfʌɪə(r), -z
AM ˈpæsəˌfaɪ(ə)r, -z
pacifism
BR ˈpasɪfɪz(ə)m
AM ˈpæsəˌfɪzəm
pacifist
BR ˈpasɪfɪst, -s
AM ˈpæsəfəst, -s
pacify
BR ˈpasɪfʌɪ, -z, -ɪŋ, -d
AM ˈpæsəˌfaɪ, -z, -ɪŋ, -d
Pacino
BR pəˈtʃiːnəʊ
AM pəˈtʃinoʊ
pack
BR pak, -s, -ɪŋ, -t
AM pæk, -s, -ɪŋ, -t
packable
BR ˈpakəbl
AM ˈpækəbəl
package
BR ˈpak|ɪdʒ, -ɪdʒɪz, -ɪdʒɪŋ, -ɪdʒd
AM ˈpækɪdʒ, -ɪz, -ɪŋ, -d
packager
BR ˈpakɪdʒə(r), -z
AM ˈpækɪdʒər, -z
Packard
BR ˈpakɑːd
AM ˈpækərd
packer
BR ˈpakə(r), -z
AM ˈpækər, -z
packet
BR ˈpak|ɪt, -ɪts, -ɪtɪŋ, -ɪtɪd
AM ˈpækə|t, -ts, -dɪŋ, -dəd
packhorse
BR ˈpakhɔːs, -ɪz
AM ˈpækˌ(h)ɔ(ə)rs, -əz
packice
BR ˈpakʌɪs
AM ˈpækˌaɪs
packing
BR ˈpakɪŋ, -z
AM ˈpækɪŋ, -z
packingcase
BR ˈpakɪŋkeɪs, -ɪz
AM ˈpækɪŋˌkeɪs, -ɪz
packman
BR ˈpakman, ˈpakmən
AM ˈpækˌmæn, ˈpækmən
packmen
BR ˈpakmɛn, ˈpakmən
AM ˈpækˌmɛn, ˈpækmən
packsaddle
BR ˈpakˌsadl, -z
AM ˈpækˌsædəl, -z
packthread
BR ˈpakθrɛd
AM ˈpækˌθrɛd
Pac-man®
BR ˈpakman
AM ˈpækˌmæn
pact
BR pakt, -s
AM pæk(t), -(t)s
pacy
BR ˈpeɪs|i, -ɪə(r), -ɪɪst
AM ˈpeɪsi, -ər, -əst
pad
BR pad, -z, -ɪŋ, -ɪd
AM pæd, -z, -ɪŋ, -əd
Padbury
BR ˈpadb(ə)ri
AM ˈpædˌbɛri
Paddington
BR ˈpadɪŋt(ə)n
AM ˈpædɪŋtən
paddle
BR ˈpad|l, -lz, -lɪŋ\-əlɪŋ, -ld
AM ˈpæd|əl, -əlz, -(ə)lɪŋ, -əld
paddleball
BR ˈpadlbɔːl
AM ˈpædlˌbɔl, ˈpædlˌbɑl
paddler
BR ˈpadlə(r), -z
AM ˈpæd(ə)lər, -z
paddock
BR ˈpadək, -s
AM ˈpædək, -s
paddy
BR ˈpad|i, -ɪz
AM ˈpædi, -z
paddywack
BR ˈpadɪwak, -s
AM ˈpædiˌ(h)wæk, -s
paddywhack
BR ˈpadɪwak, -s
AM ˈpædiˌ(h)wæk, -s
pademelon
BR ˈpadɪˌmɛlən, -z
AM ˈpædiˌmɛlən, -z
Paderewski
BR ˌpadəˈrɛfski, ˌpadəˈrɛvski
AM ˌpædəˈrɛfski
Padfield
BR ˈpadfiːld
AM ˈpædˌfild
Padiham
BR ˈpadɪəm
AM ˈpædiəm
Padilla
BR pəˈdɪlə(*r*)
AM pəˈdɪlə
padlock
BR ˈpadlɒk, -s, -ɪŋ, -t
AM ˈpædˌlɑk, -s, -ɪŋ, -t
padloper
BR ˈpatˌləʊpə(r), -z
AM ˈpædˌloʊpər, -z
Padma
BR ˈpadmə(*r*)
AM ˈpædmə
Padmore
BR ˈpadmɔː(r)
AM ˈpædˌmɔ(ə)r
padouk
BR pəˈdaʊk, -s
AM pəˈdaʊk, -s
padre
BR ˈpɑːdreɪ, -z
AM ˈpɑˌdreɪ, -z
padrone
BR pəˈdrəʊn|i, -ɪz
AM pəˈdroʊn(eɪ), -z
padsaw
BR ˈpadsɔː(*r*), -z
AM ˈpædˌsɔ, ˈpædˌsɑ, -z

Padstow
BR ˈpadstəʊ
AM ˈpædˌstoʊ
Padua
BR ˈpadjʊə(r), ˈpadʒʊə(r)
AM ˈpædʒʊə
Paduan
BR ˈpadjʊən, ˈpadʒʊən, -z
AM ˈpædʒʊən, -z
Paducah
BR pəˈd(j)uːkə(r)
AM pəˈd(j)ukə
paean
BR ˈpiːən, -z
AM ˈpiən, -z
paederast
BR ˈpɛdərast, -s
AM ˈpɛdəˌræst, -s
paederastic
BR ˌpɛdəˈrastɪk
AM ˌpɛdəˈræstɪk
paederasty
BR ˈpɛdərasti
AM ˈpɛdəˌræsti
paediatric
BR ˌpiːdɪˈatrɪk, -s
AM ˌpidiˈætrɪk, -s
paediatrician
BR ˌpiːdɪəˈtrɪʃn, -z
AM ˌpidiəˈtrɪʃən, -z
paediatrist
BR ˌpiːˈdʌɪətrɪst, ˌpiːdɪˈatrɪst, -s
AM ˌpidiˈætrəst, -s
paedophile
BR ˈpiːdəfʌɪl
AM ˈpɛdəˌfaɪl
paedophilia
BR ˌpiːdəˈfɪlɪə(r)
AM ˌpɛdəˈfɪljə, ˌpidəˈfɪljə, ˌpɛdəˈfɪliə, ˌpidəˈfɪliə
paedophiliac
BR ˌpiːdəˈfɪlɪak
AM ˌpidəˈfɪliˌæk, -s
paella
BR pʌɪˈɛlə(r)
AM pəˈɛlə, paɪˈɛlə
paeon
BR ˈpiːən, -z
AM ˈpiən, -z
paeonic
BR ˌpiːˈɒnɪk
AM piˈɑnɪk
paeony
BR ˈpiːən|i, -ɪz
AM ˈpiəni, -z
Pagalu
BR ˈpagəluː
AM ˈpægəlu
pagan
BR ˈpeɪg(ə)n, -z
AM ˈpeɪgən, -z
Paganini
BR ˌpagəˈniːni
AM ˌpægəˈnini
paganise
BR ˈpeɪgənʌɪz, ˈpeɪgn̩ʌɪz, -ɪz, -ɪŋ, -d
AM ˈpeɪgəˌnaɪz, -ɪz, -ɪŋ, -d
paganish
BR ˈpeɪgənɪʃ, ˈpeɪgn̩ɪʃ
AM ˈpeɪgənɪʃ
paganism
BR ˈpeɪgənɪz(ə)m, ˈpeɪgn̩ɪz(ə)m
AM ˈpeɪgəˌnɪzəm
paganize
BR ˈpeɪgənʌɪz, ˈpeɪgn̩ʌɪz, -ɪz, -ɪŋ, -d
AM ˈpeɪgəˌnaɪz, -ɪz, -ɪŋ, -d
page
BR peɪdʒ, -ɪz, -ɪŋ, -d
AM peɪdʒ, -ɪz, -ɪŋ, -d
pageant
BR ˈpadʒ(ə)nt, -s
AM ˈpædʒənt, -s
pageantry
BR ˈpadʒ(ə)ntri
AM ˈpædʒəntri
pageboy
BR ˈpeɪdʒbɔɪ, -z
AM ˈpeɪdʒˌbɔɪ, -z
pager
BR ˈpeɪdʒə(r), -z
AM ˈpeɪdʒər, -z
Paget
BR ˈpadʒɪt
AM ˈpædʒət
paginal
BR ˈpadʒɪnl
AM ˈpædʒənəl
paginary
BR ˈpadʒɪn(ə)ri
AM ˈpædʒəˌnɛri
paginate
BR ˈpadʒɪneɪt, -s, -ɪŋ, -ɪd
AM ˈpædʒəˌneɪ|t, -ts, -dɪŋ, -dɪd
pagination
BR ˌpadʒɪˈneɪʃn
AM ˌpædʒəˈneɪʃən
Pagliacci
BR ˌpalɪˈɑːtʃi
AM ˌpæ(g)liˈɑtʃi
IT paʎˈʎattʃi
Pagnell
BR ˈpagnl
AM ˈpægnəl
pagoda
BR pəˈgəʊdə(r), -z
AM pəˈgoʊdə, -z
pah
BR pɑː(r)
AM pɑ
Pahang
BR pəˈhaŋ, pəˈhʌŋ
AM pəˈhæŋ
Pahlavi
BR ˈpɑːləvi
AM ˈpɑləvi
pahoehoe
BR pəˈhəʊɪˌhəʊi
AM pəˈhoʊˌiˈhoʊˌi
paid
BR peɪd
AM peɪd
Paige
BR peɪdʒ
AM peɪdʒ
Paignton
BR ˈpeɪntən
AM ˈpeɪn(t)ən
pail
BR peɪl, -z
AM peɪl, -z
pailful
BR ˈpeɪlfʊl, -z
AM ˈpeɪlˌfʊl, -z
paillasse
BR ˈpalɪas, ˌpalɪˈas, -ɪz
AM paɪˈ(j)ɑs, ˌpæliˌæs, pælˈjæs, -ɪəz
paillette
BR palˈjɛt, ˌpalɪˈɛt, -s
AM paɪˈ(j)ɛt, pɑˈ(j)ɛt, pəˈlɛt, -s
pain
BR peɪn, -z, -ɪŋ, -d
AM peɪn, -z, -ɪŋ, -d
Paine
BR peɪn
AM peɪn
painful
BR ˈpeɪnf(ʊ)l
AM ˈpeɪnfəl
painfully
BR ˈpeɪnfʊli, ˈpeɪnfl̩i
AM ˈpeɪnfəli
painfulness
BR ˈpeɪnf(ʊ)lnəs
AM ˈpeɪnfəlnəs
painkiller
BR ˈpeɪnˌkɪlə(r), -z
AM ˈpeɪnˌkɪlər, -z
painkilling
BR ˈpeɪnˌkɪlɪŋ
AM ˈpeɪnˌkɪlɪŋ
painless
BR ˈpeɪnlɪs
AM ˈpeɪnlɪs
painlessly
BR ˈpeɪnlɪsli
AM ˈpeɪnlɪsli
painlessness
BR ˈpeɪnlɪsnɪs
AM ˈpeɪnlɪnɪs
painstaking
BR ˈpeɪnzˌteɪkɪŋ
AM ˈpeɪnˌsteɪkɪŋ
painstakingly
BR ˈpeɪnzˌteɪkɪŋli
AM ˈpeɪnˌsteɪkɪŋli
painstakingness
BR ˈpeɪnzˌteɪkɪŋnɪs
AM ˈpeɪnˌstækɪŋnɪs
paint
BR peɪnt, -s, -ɪŋ, -ɪd
AM peɪn|t, -ts, -(t)ɪŋ, -(t)əd
paintable
BR ˈpeɪntəbl
AM ˈpeɪn(t)əbəl
paintball
BR ˈpeɪntbɔːl
AM ˈpeɪntˌbɔl, ˈpeɪntˌbɑl
paintbox
BR ˈpeɪntbɒks, -ɪz
AM ˈpeɪntˌbɑks, -əz
paintbrush
BR ˈpeɪntbrʌʃ, -ɪz
AM ˈpeɪntˌbrəʃ, -əz
painter
BR ˈpeɪntə(r), -z
AM ˈpeɪn(t)ər, -z
painterliness
BR ˈpeɪntəlɪnɪs
AM ˈpeɪn(t)ərlinɪs
painterly
BR ˈpeɪntəli
AM ˈpeɪn(t)ərli
painting
BR ˈpeɪntɪŋ, -z
AM ˈpeɪn(t)ɪŋ, -z
paintstick
BR ˈpeɪntstɪk, -s
AM ˈpeɪntˌstɪk, -s
paintwork
BR ˈpeɪntwəːk
AM ˈpeɪntˌwərk
painty
BR ˈpeɪnti
AM ˈpeɪn(t)i
pair
BR pɛː(r), -z, -ɪŋ, -d
AM pɛ(ə)r, -z, -ɪŋ, -d
pairing
BR ˈpɛːrɪŋ, -z
AM ˈpɛrɪŋ, -z
pairwork
BR ˈpɛːwəːk
AM ˈpɛrˌwərk
paisa
BR ˈpʌɪsɑː(r), ˈpʌɪsə(r)
AM ˈpaɪsə
paise
BR ˈpʌɪsə(r)
AM ˈpaɪsə
Paish
BR peɪʃ
AM peɪʃ
paisley
BR ˈpeɪzli
AM ˈpeɪzli
Paisleyite
BR ˈpeɪzlɪʌɪt, -s
AM ˈpeɪzliˌaɪt, -s
Paiute
BR ˈpʌɪuːt, ˌpʌɪˈ(j)uːt, -s

AM 'paɪˌ(j)ut, ˌpaɪ'(j)ut, -s

pajama
BR pə'dʒɑːmə(*r*), -z
AM pə'dʒɑmə, pə'dʒæmə, -z

pakapoo
BR ˌpakə'puː, 'pakəpuː
AM ˌpækəˌpu

pakapu
BR ˌpakə'puː, 'pakəpuː
AM ˌpækəˌpu

pakeha
BR 'pɑːkɪhɑː(*r*), -z
AM 'pɑkəˌhɑ, 'pɑkiˌɑ, -z

Pakenham[1]
surname
BR 'pak(ə)nəm, 'paknṃ
AM 'pæknṃ

Pakenham[2]
UK placename
BR 'peɪkənəm, 'peɪknṃ
AM 'peɪknṃ

Paki
BR 'pak|i, -ɪz
AM 'pæki, -z

Pakistan
BR ˌpɑːkɪ'stɑːn, ˌpakɪ'stan
AM 'pækəˌstæn

Pakistani
BR ˌpɑːkɪ'stɑːn|i, ˌpakɪ'stan|i, -ɪz
AM ˌpækə'stɑni, -z

pakora
BR pə'kɔːrə(*r*)
AM pə'kɔrə

pal
BR pal, -z, -ɪŋ, -d
AM pæl, -z, -ɪŋ, -d

palace
BR 'palɪs, -ɪz
AM 'pæləs, -əz

paladin
BR 'palədɪn, -z
AM 'pælədn, 'pælədən, -z

Palaearctic
BR ˌpalɪ'ɑːktɪk, ˌpeɪlɪ'ɑːktɪk
AM ˌpeɪli'ɑr(k)tɪk, ˌpæli'ɑr(k)tɪk

palaeoanthropological
BR ˌpalɪəʊˌanθrəpə'lɒdʒɪkl, ˌpeɪlɪəʊˌanθrəpə'lɒdʒɪkl
AM ˌpeɪlioʊˌænθrəpə'lɑdʒəkəl

palaeoanthropologist
BR ˌpalɪəʊˌanθrə'pɒlədʒɪst, ˌpeɪlɪəʊˌanθrə'pɒlədʒɪst, -s
AM ˌpeɪlioʊˌænθrə'pɑlədʒəst, -s

palaeoanthropology
BR ˌpalɪəʊˌanθrə'pɒlədʒi, ˌpeɪlɪəʊˌanθrə'pɒlədʒi
AM ˌpeɪlioʊˌænθrə'pɑlədʒi

palaeobotany
BR ˌpalɪəʊ'bɒtəni, ˌpalɪəʊ'bɒtṇi, ˌpeɪlɪəʊ'bɒtəni, ˌpeɪlɪəʊ'bɒtṇi
AM ˌpeɪlioʊ'bɑtṇi

Palaeocene
BR 'palɪə(ʊ)siːn, 'peɪlɪə(ʊ)siːn
AM 'peɪliəˌsin

palaeoclimatology
BR ˌpalɪəʊˌklʌɪmə'tɒlədʒi, ˌpeɪlɪəʊˌklʌɪmə'tɒlədʒi
AM ˌpeɪlioʊˌklaɪmə'tɑlədʒi

palaeoecological
BR ˌpalɪəʊˌiːkə'lɒdʒɪkl, ˌpalɪəʊˌɛkə'lɒdʒɪkl, ˌpeɪlɪəʊˌiːkə'lɒdʒɪkl, ˌpeɪlɪəʊˌɛkə'lɒdʒɪkl
AM ˌpeɪlioʊˌɛkə'lɑdʒəkəl, ˌpeɪlioʊˌikə'lɑdʒəkəl

palaeoecologist
BR ˌpalɪəʊɪ'kɒlədʒɪst, ˌpeɪlɪəʊɪ'kɒlədʒɪst, -s
AM ˌpeɪlioʊˌɛ'kɑlədʒəst, ˌpeɪlioʊˌi'kɑlədʒəst, -s

palaeoecology
BR ˌpalɪəʊɪ'kɒlədʒi, ˌpalɪəʊɛ'kɒlədʒi, ˌpeɪlɪəʊɪ'kɒlədʒi, ˌpeɪlɪəʊɛ'kɒlədʒi
AM ˌpeɪlioʊˌɛ'kɑlədʒi, ˌpeɪlioʊˌi'kɑlədʒi

palaeogeography
BR ˌpalɪəʊdʒɪ'ɒgrəfi, ˌpalɪəʊ'dʒɒgrəfi, ˌpeɪlɪəʊdʒɪ'ɒgrəfi, ˌpeɪlɪəʊ'dʒɒgrəfi
AM ˌpeɪlioʊdʒi'ɑgrəfi

palaeographer
BR ˌpalɪ'ɒgrəfə(r), ˌpeɪlɪ'ɒgrəfə(r), -z
AM ˌpeɪli'ɑgrəfər, -z

palaeographic
BR ˌpalɪə'grafɪk, ˌpeɪlɪə'grafɪk
AM ˌpeɪliə'græfɪk

palaeographical
BR ˌpalɪə'grafɪkl, ˌpeɪlɪə'grafɪkl
AM ˌpeɪliə'græfəkəl

palaeographically
BR ˌpalɪə'grafɪkli, ˌpeɪlɪə'grafɪkli
AM ˌpeɪliə'græfək(ə)li

palaeography
BR ˌpalɪ'ɒgrəfi, ˌpeɪlɪ'ɒgrəfi
AM ˌpeɪli'ɑgrəfi

Palaeolithic
BR ˌpalɪə'lɪθɪk, ˌpeɪlɪə'lɪθɪk
AM ˌpeɪliə'lɪθɪk

palaeomagnetism
BR ˌpalɪəʊ'magnɪtɪz(ə)m, ˌpeɪlɪəʊ'magnɪtɪz(ə)m
AM ˌpeɪlioʊ'mægnəˌtɪzəm

palaeontological
BR ˌpalɪˌɒntə'lɒdʒɪkl, ˌpeɪlɪˌɒntə'lɒdʒɪkl
AM ˌpeɪliˌɑntə'lɑdʒəkəl

palaeontologist
BR ˌpalɪən'tɒlədʒɪst, ˌpeɪlɪən'tɒlədʒɪst, -s
AM ˌpeɪliˌən'tɑlədʒəst, -s

palaeontology
BR ˌpalɪən'tɒlədʒi, ˌpeɪlɪən'tɒlədʒi
AM ˌpeɪliˌən'tɑlədʒi

Palaeozoic
BR ˌpalɪə'zəʊɪk, ˌpeɪlɪə'zəʊɪk
AM ˌpeɪliə'zoʊɪk

palaestra
BR pə'liːstrə(*r*), pə'lʌɪstrə(*r*), -z
AM pə'lɛstrə, -z

palais
BR 'pal|eɪ, 'pal|i, -eɪz\-ɪz
AM pæ'leɪ, -z

palankeen
BR ˌpalən'kiːn, -z
AM ˌpælən'k(w)in, ˌpæ'læŋk(w)ən, -z

palanquin
BR ˌpalən'kiːn, 'palənkwɪn, -z
AM ˌpælən'k(w)in, ˌpæ'læŋk(w)ən, -z

palapa
BR pə'lapə(*r*), -z
AM pə'lɑpə, -z

palatability
BR ˌpalɪtə'bɪlɪti
AM ˌpælədə'bɪlɪdi

palatable
BR 'palɪtəbl
AM 'pælədəbəl

palatableness
BR 'palɪtəblnəs
AM 'pælədəbəlnəs

palatably
BR 'palɪtəbli
AM 'pælədəbli

palatal
BR 'palətl, pə'leɪtl, -z
AM 'pælədl, -z

palatalisation
BR ˌpalətəlʌɪ'zeɪʃn, ˌpalətḷʌɪ'zeɪʃn
AM ˌpælədḷə'zeɪʃən, ˌpælədlˌaɪ'zeɪʃən

palatalise
BR 'palətəlʌɪz, 'palətḷʌɪz, -ɪz, -ɪŋ, -d
AM 'pælədlˌaɪz, -ɪz, -ɪŋ, -d

palatalization
BR ˌpalətəlʌɪ'zeɪʃn, ˌpalətḷʌɪ'zeɪʃn
AM ˌpælədḷə'zeɪʃən, ˌpælədlˌaɪ'zeɪʃən

palatalize
BR 'palətəlʌɪz, 'palətḷʌɪz, -ɪz, -ɪŋ, -d
AM 'pælədlˌaɪz, -ɪz, -ɪŋ, -d

palatally
BR 'palətḷi, 'palətəli, pə'leɪtḷi, pə'leɪtəli
AM 'pælədḷi

palate
BR 'palət, -s
AM 'pælət, -s

palatial
BR pə'leɪʃl
AM pə'leɪʃəl

palatially
BR pə'leɪʃḷi, pə'leɪʃəli
AM pə'leɪʃəli

Palatinate
BR pə'latɪnət, pə'latṇət, -s
AM pə'lætṇət, pə'lætnˌeɪt, -s

Palatine
BR 'palətʌɪn
AM 'pæləˌtaɪn

Palau
BR pə'laʊ, pa'laʊ
AM pə'laʊ, pæ'laʊ

palaver
BR pə'lɑːv|ə(r), -əz, -(ə)rɪŋ, -əd
AM pə'lævər, pə'lɑvər, -z, -ɪŋ, -d

Palawan
BR pa'laʊən, -z
AM pə'laʊən, pɑ'laʊən, -z

pale
BR peɪl, -z, -ɪŋ, -d
AM peɪl, -z, -ɪŋ, -d

palea
BR 'peɪlɪə(*r*), -z
AM 'peɪliə, -z

paleae
BR 'peɪlɪiː
AM 'peɪliˌi, 'peɪliˌaɪ

Palearctic
BR ˌpalɪ'ɑːktɪk, ˌpeɪlɪ'ɑːktɪk
AM ˌpeɪli'ɑr(k)tɪk, ˌpæli'ɑr(k)tɪk

paleface
BR ˈpeɪlfeɪs, -ɪz
AM ˈpeɪlˌfeɪs, -ɪz

pale-faced
BR ˌpeɪlˈfeɪst
AM ˈpeɪlˌfeɪst

Palekh
BR ˈpɑːlɛk
AM ˈpɑlɛk

palely
BR ˈpeɪ(l)li
AM ˈpeɪ(l)li

Palembang
BR pɑːˈlɛmbaŋ, paˈlɛmbaŋ
AM pɑˈlɛmˌbæŋ

paleness
BR ˈpeɪlnɨs
AM ˈpeɪlnɨs

Palenque
BR pəˈlɛŋki
AM pəˈlɛŋki, pæˈlɛŋki

paleoanthropological
BR ˌpalɪəʊˌanθrəpəˈlɒdʒɪkl, ˌpeɪlɪəʊˌanθrəpəˈlɒdʒɪkl
AM ˈpeɪlioʊˌænθrəpəˈlɑdʒəkəl

paleoanthropologist
BR ˌpalɪəʊˌanθrəˈpɒlədʒɪst, ˌpeɪlɪəʊˌanθrəˈpɒlədʒɪst, -s
AM ˌpeɪlioʊˌænθrəˈpɑlədʒəst, -s

paleoanthropology
BR ˌpalɪəʊˌanθrəˈpɒlədʒi, ˌpeɪlɪəʊˌanθrəˈpɒlədʒi
AM ˌpeɪlioʊˌænθrəˈpɑlədʒi

paleobotany
BR ˌpalɪəʊˈbɒtəni, ˌpalɪəʊˈbɒtn̩i, ˌpeɪlɪəʊˈbɒtəni, ˌpeɪlɪəʊˈbɒtn̩i
AM ˌpeɪlioʊˈbɑtni

Paleocene
BR ˈpalɪə(ʊ)siːn, ˈpeɪlɪə(ʊ)siːn
AM ˈpeɪliəˌsin

paleoclimatology
BR ˌpalɪəʊˌklʌɪməˈtɒlədʒi, ˌpeɪlɪəʊˌklʌɪməˈtɒlədʒi
AM ˌpeɪlioʊˌklaɪməˈtɑlədʒi

paleoecological
BR ˌpalɪəʊˌiːkəˈlɒdʒɪkl, ˌpalɪəʊˌɛkəˈlɒdʒɪkl, ˌpeɪlɪəʊˌiːkəˈlɒdʒɪkl, ˌpeɪlɪəʊˌɛkəˈlɒdʒɪkl
AM ˈpeɪlioʊˌɛkəˈlɑdʒəkəl, ˈpeɪlioʊˌikəˈlɑdʒəkəl

paleoecologist
BR ˌpalɪəʊɪˈkɒlədʒɪst, ˌpalɪəʊɛˈkɒlədʒɪst, ˌpeɪlɪəʊɪˈkɒlədʒɪst, ˌpeɪlɪəʊɛˈkɒlədʒɪst, -s
AM ˌpeɪlioʊˌɛˈkɑlədʒəst, ˌpeɪlioʊˌiˈkɑlədʒəst, -s

paleoecology
BR ˌpalɪəʊɪˈkɒlədʒi, ˌpalɪəʊɛˈkɒlədʒi, ˌpeɪlɪəʊɪˈkɒlədʒi, ˌpeɪlɪəʊɛˈkɒlədʒi
AM ˌpeɪlioʊˌɛˈkɑlədʒi, ˌpeɪlioʊˌiˈkɑlədʒi

paleogeography
BR ˌpalɪəʊdʒɪˈɒɡrəfi, ˌpalɪəʊˈdʒɒɡrəfi, ˌpeɪlɪəʊdʒɪˈɒɡrəfi, ˌpeɪlɪəʊˈdʒɒɡrəfi
AM ˌpeɪlioʊdʒiˈɑɡrəfi

paleographer
BR ˌpalɪˈɒɡrəfə(r), ˌpeɪlɪˈɒɡrəfə(r), -z
AM ˌpeɪliˈɑɡrəfər, -z

paleographic
BR ˌpalɪəˈɡrafɪk, ˌpeɪlɪəˈɡrafɪk
AM ˈpeɪliəˈɡræfɪk

paleographical
BR ˌpalɪəˈɡrafɪkl, ˌpeɪlɪəˈɡrafɪkl
AM ˈpeɪliəˈɡræfəkəl

paleographically
BR ˌpalɪəˈɡrafɪkli, ˌpeɪlɪəˈɡrafɪkli
AM ˈpeɪliəˈɡræfək(ə)li

paleography
BR ˌpalɪˈɒɡrəfi, ˌpeɪlɪˈɒɡrəfi
AM ˌpeɪliˈɑɡrəfi

Paleolithic
BR ˌpalɪəˈlɪθɪk, ˌpeɪlɪəˈlɪθɪk
AM ˈpeɪliəˈlɪθɪk

paleomagnetism
BR ˌpalɪəʊˈmaɡnɪtɪz(ə)m, ˌpeɪlɪəʊˈmaɡnɪtɪz(ə)m
AM ˌpeɪlioʊˈmæɡnəˌtɪzəm

paleontological
BR ˌpalɪˌɒntəˈlɒdʒɪkl, ˌpeɪlɪˌɒntəˈlɒdʒɪkl
AM ˈpeɪliˌɑntəˈlɑdʒəkəl

paleontologist
BR ˌpalɪənˈtɒlədʒɪst, ˌpeɪlɪənˈtɒlədʒɪst, -s
AM ˌpeɪliˌənˈtɑlədʒəst, -s

paleontology
BR ˌpalɪənˈtɒlədʒi, ˌpeɪlɪənˈtɒlədʒi
AM ˌpeɪliˌənˈtɑlədʒi

Paleozoic
BR ˌpalɪəˈzəʊɪk, ˌpeɪlɪəˈzəʊɪk
AM ˌpeɪliəˈzoʊɪk

Palermo
BR pəˈlɛːməʊ, pəˈləːməʊ
AM pəˈlərˌmoʊ, pəˈlɛrˌmoʊ

Palestine
BR ˈpalɨstʌɪn
AM ˈpæləˌstaɪn

Palestinian
BR ˌpalɨˈstɪnɪən, -z
AM ˌpæləˈstɪniən, -z

palestra
BR pəˈlɛstrə(r), -z
AM pəˈlɛstrə, -z

Palestrina
BR ˌpalɨˈstriːnə(r)
AM ˌpæləˈstrinə

Palethorp
BR ˈpeɪlθɔːp
AM ˈpeɪlˌθɔ(ə)rp

Palethorpe
BR ˈpeɪlθɔːp
AM ˈpeɪlˌθɔ(ə)rp

paletot
BR ˈpalɨtəʊ, -z
AM ˈpæl(ə)ˌtoʊ, -z

palette
BR ˈpalɨt, -s
AM ˈpælət, -s

palfrey
BR ˈpɔːlfr|i, ˈpɒlfr|i, -ɪz
AM ˈpɔlfri, ˈpɑlfri, -z

Palfreyman
BR ˈpɔːlfrɪmən, ˈpɒlfrɪmən
AM ˈpɔlfrimən, ˈpɑlfrimən

Palgrave
BR ˈpɔːlɡreɪv, ˈpalɡreɪv
AM ˈpɔlˌɡreɪv, ˈpɑlˌɡreɪv

Pali
BR ˈpɑːli
AM ˈpɑˌli

palilalia
BR ˌpalɨˈleɪlɪə(r)
AM ˌpɑləˈleɪliə

palimony
BR ˈpalɨmən|i
AM ˈpæləˌmoʊni

palimpsest
BR ˈpalɪm(p)sɛst, -s
AM ˈpæləm(p)ˌsɛst, -s

Palin
BR ˈpeɪlɪn
AM ˈpeɪlən

palindrome
BR ˈpalɪndrəʊm, -z
AM ˈpælənˌdroʊm, -z

palindromic
BR ˌpalɪnˈdrɒmɪk
AM ˈpælənˈdrɑmɪk

palindromist
BR pəˈlɪndrəmɪst, -s
AM pəˈlɪndrəməst, -s

paling
BR ˈpeɪlɪŋ, -z
AM ˈpeɪlɪŋ, -z

palingenesis
BR ˌpalɪnˈdʒɛnɨsɪs
AM ˌpælənˈdʒɛnəsəs

palingenetic
BR ˌpalɪndʒɪˈnɛtɪk
AM ˈpæləndʒəˈnɛdɪk

palinode
BR ˈpalɪnəʊd, -z
AM ˈpæləˌnoʊd, -z

palisade
BR ˌpalɨˈseɪd, -z, -ɪŋ, -ɨd
AM ˌpæləˈseɪd, -z, -ɪŋ, -əd

Palisades
BR ˈpalɨseɪdz
AM ˌpæləˈseɪdz

palish
BR ˈpeɪlɪʃ
AM ˈpeɪlɪʃ

Palissy
BR ˈpalɨsi
AM ˈpæləsi

pall
BR pɔːl, -z
AM pɔl, pɑl, -z

Palladian
BR pəˈleɪdɪən
AM pəˈleɪdiən

Palladianism
BR pəˈleɪdɪənɪz(ə)m
AM pəˈleɪdiəˌnɪzəm

Palladio
BR pəˈladɪəʊ, pəˈlɑːdɪəʊ
AM pəˈlɑdioʊ

palladium
BR pəˈleɪdɪəm, -z
AM pəˈleɪdiəm, -z

Pallas
BR ˈpaləs, ˈpalas
AM ˈpæləs

pallbearer
BR ˈpɔːlˌbɛːrə(r), -z
AM ˈpɔlˌbɛrər, ˈpɑlˌbɛrər, -z

pallet
BR ˈpalɨt, -s
AM ˈpælət, -s

palletisation
BR ˌpalɨtʌɪˈzeɪʃn
AM ˌpælədəˈzeɪʃən, ˌpæləˌtaɪˈzeɪʃən

palletise
BR ˈpalɨtʌɪz, -ɪz, -ɪŋ, -d
AM ˈpæləˌtaɪz, -ɪz, -ɪŋ, -d

palletization
BR ˌpalɨtʌɪˈzeɪʃn
AM ˌpælədəˈzeɪʃən, ˌpæləˌtaɪˈzeɪʃən

palletize
BR ˈpalɨtʌɪz, -ɪz, -ɪŋ, -d
AM ˈpæləˌtaɪz, -ɪz, -ɪŋ, -d

pallia
BR 'palɪə(r)
AM 'pæljə, 'pæliə

pallial
BR 'palɪəl
AM 'pæljəl, 'pæliəl

palliasse
BR 'palɪas, -ɪz
AM ˌpæliˈæs, pælˈjæs, -əz

palliate
BR 'palɪeɪt, -s, -ɪŋ, -ɨd
AM 'pæli,eɪ|t, -ts, -dɪŋ, -dɨd

palliation
BR ˌpalɪˈeɪʃn
AM ˌpæliˈeɪʃən

palliative
BR 'palɪətɪv, -z
AM 'pæli,eɪdɪv, 'pæljədɪv, -z

palliatively
BR 'palɪətɨvli
AM 'pæljədɨvli, 'pæli,eɪdɨvli

palliator
BR 'palɪeɪtə(r), -z
AM 'pæli,eɪdər, -z

pallid
BR 'palɪd
AM 'pæləd

pallidity
BR pəˈlɪdɪti
AM pəˈlɪdɨdi, pæˈlɪdɨdi

pallidly
BR 'palɨdli
AM 'pælədli

pallidness
BR 'palɨdnɨs
AM 'pælədnəs

pallium
BR 'palɪəm, -z
AM 'pæliəm, -z

Pall Mall
BR ˌpal ˈmal
AM ˌpɑl ˈmɑl

pall-mall
BR ˌpalˈmal
AM 'pɛlˈmɛl, 'pɔlˈmɔl, 'pɑlˈmɑl

pallor
BR 'palə(r)
AM 'pælər

pally
BR 'pal|i, -ɪə(r), -ɪɨst
AM 'pæli, -ər, -əst

palm
BR pɑːm, -z, -ɪŋ, -d
AM pɑ(l)m, -z, -ɪŋ, -d

Palma
BR 'palmə(r), 'pɑːmə(r)
AM 'pɑlmə

palmaceous
BR palˈmeɪʃəs, pɑːˈmeɪʃəs
AM pælˈmeɪʃəs, pɑˈmeɪʃəs

palmar
BR 'palmə(r), 'palmɑː(r), -z
AM 'pælmər, 'pɑ(l)mər, -z

palmate
BR 'palmeɪt, 'pɑːmeɪt
AM 'pæl,meɪt, 'pɑ(l),meɪt

palmer
BR 'pɑːmə(r), -z
AM 'pɑ(l)mər, -z

Palmerston
BR 'pɑːməst(ə)n
AM 'pɑ(l)mərstən

Palmerston North
BR ˌpɑːməst(ə)n ˈnɔːθ
AM ˌpɑ(l)mərstən ˈnɔ(ə)rθ

palmette
BR palˈmɛt, pɑːˈmɛt, -s
AM ˌpælˈmɛt, ˌpɑ(l)ˈmɛt, -s

palmetto
BR palˈmɛtəʊ, pɑːˈmɛtəʊ, -z
AM ˌpɑ(l)ˈmɛdoʊ, -z

palmful
BR 'pɑːmfʊl, -z
AM 'pɑ(l)m,fʊl, -z

palmiped
BR 'palmɪpɛd, -z
AM 'pælmə,pɛd, 'pɔlmə,pɛd, 'pɑlmə,pɛd, -z

palmipede
BR 'palmɪpiːd, -z
AM 'pælmə,pid, 'pɔlmə,pid, 'pɑlmə,pid, -z

palmist
BR 'pɑːmɪst, -s
AM 'pɑ(l)məst, -s

palmistry
BR 'pɑːmɪstri
AM 'pɑ(l)məstri

palmitate
BR 'palmɪteɪt, 'pɑːmɪteɪt, -s, -ɪŋ, -ɨd
AM 'pɑ(l)mə,teɪ|t, -ts, -dɪŋ, -dɨd

palmitic
BR palˈmɪtɪk, pɑːˈmɪtɪk
AM pɑ(l)ˈmɪdɪk

palm-oil
BR 'pɑːmɔɪl
AM 'pɑ(l)m,ɔɪl

Palmolive®
BR ˌpɑːmˈɒlɪv
AM pɔ(l)ˈmɑlɪv, pɑ(l)ˈmɑlɪv

Palm Springs
BR ˌpɑːm ˈsprɪŋz
AM ˌpɑ(l)m ˈsprɪŋz

palmtop
BR 'pɑːmtɒp, -s
AM 'pɑ(l)m,tɑp, -s

palmy
BR 'pɑːm|i, -ɪə(r), -ɪɨst
AM 'pɑ(l)mi, -ər, -əst

palmyra
BR palˈmʌɪrə(r), -z
AM pælˈmaɪrə, -z

Palo Alto
BR ˌpaləʊ ˈaltəʊ
AM 'pæ,loʊ ˈæl,toʊ

palolo
BR pəˈləʊləʊ, -z
AM pəˈloʊ,loʊ, -z

Palomar
BR 'paləmɑː(r)
AM 'pælə,mɑr

palomino
BR ˌpaləˈmiːnəʊ, -z
AM ˌpæləˈminoʊ, -z

palooka
BR pəˈluːkə(r), -z
AM pəˈlukə, -z

Palouse
BR pəˈluːs
AM pəˈlus

paloverde
BR ˌpalə(ʊ)ˈvəːd|i, -ɪz
AM ˌpæloʊˈvərdi, -z

palp
BR palp, -s
AM pælp, -s

palpability
BR ˌpalpəˈbɪlɨti
AM ˌpælpəˈbɪlɨdi

palpable
BR 'palpəbl
AM 'pælpəbəl

palpably
BR 'palpəbli
AM 'pælpəbli

palpal
BR 'palpl
AM 'pælpəl

palpate
BR 'palpeɪt, palˈpeɪt, -s, -ɪŋ, -ɨd
AM 'pæl,peɪ|t, -ts, -dɪŋ, -dɨd

palpation
BR palˈpeɪʃn
AM pælˈpeɪʃən

palpebral
BR 'palpəbr(ə)l
AM 'pælpəbrəl, pælˈpibrəl

palpitant
BR 'palpɪt(ə)nt
AM 'pælpədənt, 'pælpətnt

palpitate
BR 'palpɪteɪt, -s, -ɪŋ, -ɨd
AM 'pælpə,teɪ|t, -ts, -dɪŋ, -dɨd

palpitation
BR ˌpalpɪˈteɪʃn
AM ˌpælpəˈteɪʃən

palpus
BR 'palpəs
AM 'pælpəs

palsgrave
BR 'pɔːlzgreɪv, 'pɒlzgreɪv, -z
AM 'pɔlz,greɪv, 'pɑlz,greɪv, -z

palsied
BR 'pɔːlzɪd, 'pɒlzɪd
AM 'pɔlzid, 'pɑlzid

palstave
BR 'pɔːlsteɪv, 'pɒlsteɪv, -z
AM 'pɔl,steɪv, 'pɑl,steɪv, -z

palsy
BR 'pɔːlz|i, 'pɒlz|i, -ɪz
AM 'pɔlzi, 'pɑlzi, -z

palsy-walsy
BR ˌpalzɪˈwalzi
AM ˌpælziˈwælzi

palter
BR 'pɔːlt|ə(r), 'pɒlt|ə(r), -əz, -(ə)rɪŋ, -əd
AM 'pɔltər, 'pɑltər, -z, -ɪŋ, -d

palterer
BR 'pɔːlt(ə)rə(r), 'pɒlt(ə)rə(r), -z
AM 'pɔltərər, 'pɑltərər, -z

paltrily
BR 'pɔːltrɨli, 'pɒltrɨli
AM 'pɔltrəli, 'pɑltrəli

paltriness
BR 'pɔːltrɪnɨs, 'pɒltrɪnɨs
AM 'pɔltrinɨs, 'pɑltrinɨs

paltry
BR 'pɔːltr|i, 'pɒltr|i, -ɪə(r), -ɪɨst
AM 'pɔltri, 'pɑltri, -ər, -ɨst

paludism
BR 'paljʉdɪz(ə)m
AM 'pæljə,dɪzəm

Paludrine®
BR 'paljʉdrɪn
AM 'pæljədrən

paly
BR 'peɪli
AM 'peɪli

palynological
BR ˌpalɪnəˈlɒdʒɪkl
AM ˌpælənəˈlɑdʒəkəl

palynologist
BR ˌpalɪˈnɒlədʒɪst, -s
AM ˌpæləˈnɑlədʒəst, -s

palynology
BR ˌpalɪˈnɒlədʒi
AM ˌpæləˈnɑlədʒi

Pam
BR pam
AM pæm

Pamela
BR 'pam(ɪ)lə(r), 'pamḷə(r)
AM 'pæmələ

Pamirs
BR pə'mɪəz
AM pə'mɪərz

pampas
BR 'pampəs
AM 'pæmpəz, 'pɑmpəz

pamper
BR 'pamp|ə(r), -əz, -(ə)rɪŋ, -əd
AM 'pæmp|ər, -ərz, -(ə)rɪŋ, -ərd

pamperer
BR 'pamp(ə)rə(r), -z
AM 'pæmpərər, -z

pampero
BR pam'pɛːrəʊ, -z
AM pæm'pɛroʊ, -z

Pampers®
BR 'pampəz
AM 'pæmpərz

pamphlet
BR 'pamflɪt, -s
AM 'pæmflət, -s

pamphleteer
BR ˌpamflɪ'tɪə(r), -z, -ɪŋ, -d
AM ˌpæmflə'tɪ(ə)r, -z, -ɪŋ, -d

Pamphylia
BR pam'fɪlɪə(r)
AM pæm'fɪljə, pæm'fɪliə

Pamphylian
BR pam'fɪlɪən, -z
AM pæm'fɪliən, -z

Pamplona
BR pam'pləʊnə(r)
AM pæm'ploʊnə

Pan
BR pan
AM pæn

pan¹
betel leaf
BR pɑːn
AM pɑn

pan²
noun, verb
BR pan, -z, -ɪŋ, -d
AM pæn, -z, -ɪŋ, -d

panacea
BR ˌpanə'sɪə(r), ˌpanə'siːə(r), -z
AM ˌpænə'siə, -z

panacean
BR ˌpanə'sɪən, ˌpanə'siːən
AM ˌpænə'siən

panache
BR pə'naʃ
AM pə'næʃ, pə'nɑʃ

panada
BR pə'nɑːdə(r)
AM pə'nɑdə, pə'neɪdə

Panadol®
BR 'panədɒl
AM 'pænəˌdɔl, 'pænəˌdɑl

Pan-African
BR ˌpan'afrɪk(ə)n
AM ˌpæn'æfrəkən

Panaji
BR pə'nɑːdʒi
AM pɑ'nɑdʒi

Pan-Am
BR ˌpan'am
AM ˌpæn'æm

Panama
BR ˌpanə'mɑː(r), 'panəmɑː(r)
AM 'pænəˌmɑ

Panamanian
BR ˌpanə'meɪnɪən, -z
AM ˌpænə'meɪniən, -z

Pan-American
BR ˌpanə'mɛrɪk(ə)n
AM ˌpænə'mɛrəkən

Pan-Anglican
BR ˌpan'aŋglɪk(ə)n
AM ˌpæn'æŋgləkən

Panasonic
BR ˌpanə'sɒnɪk
AM ˌpænə'sɑnɪk

panatela
BR ˌpanə'tɛlə(r), -z
AM ˌpænə'tɛlə, -z

panatella
BR ˌpanə'tɛlə(r), -z
AM ˌpænə'tɛlə, -z

pancake
BR 'pankeɪk, 'paŋkeɪk, -s, -ɪŋ, -t
AM 'pænˌkeɪk, -s, -ɪŋ, -t

panchayat
BR pʌn'tʃʌɪjət, -s
AM pæn'tʃaɪət, -s

Panchen lama
BR ˌpantʃən 'lɑːmə(r), -z
AM 'pæn(t)ʃən ˌlɑmə, -z

panchromatic
BR ˌpankrə'matɪk
AM ˌpænkroʊ'mædɪk, ˌpænkrə'mædɪk

pancosmism
BR ˌpan'kɒzmɪz(ə)m
AM ˌpæn'kɑzˌmɪzəm

Pancras
BR 'paŋkrəs
AM 'pæŋkrəs, 'pænkrəs

pancreas
BR 'paŋkrɪəs, -ɪz
AM 'pæŋkriəs, 'pænkriəs, -əz

pancreatic
BR ˌpaŋkrɪ'atɪk
AM ˌpæŋkri'ædɪk, ˌpænkri'ædɪk

pancreatin
BR 'paŋkrɪətɪn
AM 'pæŋkriətn, 'pænkriətn

pancreatitis
BR ˌpaŋkrɪə'tʌɪtɪs
AM ˌpæŋkriə'taɪdɪs, ˌpænkriə'taɪdɪs

panda
BR 'pandə(r), -z
AM 'pændə, -z

pandanus
BR pan'danəs, -ɪz
AM pæn'deɪnəs, pæn'dænəs, -əz

Pandarus
BR 'pand(ə)rəs
AM 'pændərəs

pandean
BR 'pandɪən, -z
AM 'pændiən, -z

pandect
BR 'pandɛkt, -s
AM 'pænˌdɛk|(t), -(t)s

pandemic
BR (ˌ)pan'dɛmɪk, -s
AM pæn'dɛmɪk, -s

pandemonium
BR ˌpandɪ'məʊnɪəm, -z
AM ˌpændə'moʊniəm, -z

pander
BR 'pand|ə(r), -əz, -(ə)rɪŋ, -əd
AM 'pænd|ər, -ərz, -(ə)rɪŋ, -ərd

pandit
BR 'pandɪt, 'pʌndɪt, -s
AM 'pændət, 'pəndət, -s

Pandora
BR pan'dɔːrə(r)
AM pæn'dɔrə

pandowdy
BR pan'daʊd|i, -ɪz
AM pæn'daʊdi, -z

pane
BR peɪn, -z, -d
AM peɪn, -z, -d

paneer
BR pa'nɪə(r)
AM pə'nɪ(ə)r

panegyric
BR ˌpanɪ'dʒɪrɪk, -s
AM ˌpænə'dʒɪrɪk, -s

panegyrical
BR ˌpanɪ'dʒɪrɪkl
AM ˌpænə'dʒɪrəkəl

panegyrise
BR 'panɪdʒɪrʌɪz, -ɪz, -ɪŋ, -d
AM 'pænədʒəˌraɪz, -ɪz, -ɪŋ, -d

panegyrist
BR ˌpanɪ'dʒɪrɪst, -s
AM ˌpænə'dʒɪrɪst, ˌpænə'dʒaɪrɪst, -s

panegyrize
BR 'panɪdʒɪrʌɪz, -ɪz, -ɪŋ, -d
AM 'pænədʒəˌraɪz, -ɪz, -ɪŋ, -d

panel
BR 'pan|l, -lz, -ḷɪŋ\-əlɪŋ, -ld
AM 'pænəl, -z, -ɪŋ, -d

panelist
BR 'panḷɪst, -s
AM 'pænḷəst, -s

panellist
BR 'panḷɪst, -s
AM 'pænḷəst, -s

panettone
BR ˌpanɪ'təʊn|eɪ, ˌpanɪ'təʊn|i, -ɪz
AM ˌpænə'toʊni, -z

panettoni
BR ˌpanɪ'təʊniː
AM ˌpænə'toʊni

pan-European
BR ˌpanˌjʊərə'piːən, ˌpanˌjɔːrə'piːən
AM ˌpænˌjʊrə'piən, ˌpænˌjurə'piən

panfish
BR 'panfɪʃ
AM 'pænˌfɪʃ

panforte
BR ˌpan'fɔːteɪ, ˌpan'fɔːti
AM ˌpæn'fɔrˌteɪ

pan-fried
BR ˌpan'frʌɪd
AM 'pænˌfraɪd

panfry
BR 'panfrʌɪ, -z, -ɪŋ, -d
AM 'pænˌfraɪ, -z, -ɪŋ, -d

panful
BR 'panfʊl, -z
AM 'pænˌfʊl, -z

pang
BR paŋ, -z
AM pæŋ, -z

panga
BR 'paŋgə(r), -z
AM 'pæŋgə, -z

Pangaea
BR pan'dʒiːə(r)
AM pæn'dʒiə

Pangbourne
BR 'paŋbɔːn
AM 'pæŋˌbɔ(ə)rn

pangolin
BR paŋ'gəʊlɪn, 'paŋgəlɪn, -z
AM 'pæŋgələn, pæŋ'goʊlən, -z

panhandle
BR 'panˌhand|l, -lz, -ḷɪŋ\-əlɪŋ, -ld
AM 'pænˌ(h)æn(d)əl, -z, -ɪŋ, -d

panhandler
BR 'panˌhandḷə(r), -z
AM 'pænˌ(h)æn(d)ələr, -z

pan-Hellenic
BR ˌpanhɛˈlɛnɪk, ˌpanhɪˈlɛnɪk
AM ¦ˌpænˌ(h)ɛˈlɛnɪk

pan-Hellenism
BR ˌpanˈhɛlɪnɪz(ə)m
AM ˈpænˈhɛləˌnɪzəm

panic
BR ˈpan|ɪk, -ɪks, -ɨkɪŋ, -ɪkt
AM ˈpænɪk, -ɪks, -ɨkɪŋ, -ɪkt

panicky
BR ˈpanɨki
AM ˈpænəki

panicle
BR ˈpanɨkl, -z, -d
AM ˈpænəkəl, -z, -d

Panini[1]
Italian name
BR pəˈniːni
AM pəˈnini

Panini[2]
Sanskrit name
BR ˈpanɪniː
AM ˈpænɪni

Panjabi
BR pʌnˈdʒɑːb|i, pənˈdʒɑːb|i, -ɪz
AM pənˈdʒɑbi, -z

panjandrum
BR panˈdʒandrəm, -z
AM pænˈdʒændrəm, -z

Pankhurst
BR ˈpaŋkhəːst
AM ˈpæŋkˌ(h)ərst

panlike
BR ˈpanlʌɪk
AM ˈpænˌlaɪk

Panmunjom
BR ˌpanmʊnˈdʒɒm
AM ¦ˌpæn¦mʊnˈdʒɔm, ¦ˌpæn¦mʊnˈdʒɑm

pannage
BR ˈpanɪdʒ
AM ˈpænɪdʒ

Pannal
BR ˈpanl
AM ˈpænəl

panne
BR pan
AM pæn

Pannell
BR ˈpanl
AM ˈpænəl, pəˈnɛl

panner
BR ˈpanə(r), -z
AM ˈpænər, -z

pannier
BR ˈpanɪə(r), -z
AM ˈpænjər, ˈpæniər, -z

pannikin
BR ˈpanɨkɪn, -z
AM ˈpænəkən, -z

pannus
BR ˈpanəs
AM ˈpɑnəs

panoplied
BR ˈpanəplɪd
AM ˈpænəplid

panoply
BR ˈpanəpl|i, -ɪz
AM ˈpænəpli, -z

panoptic
BR pəˈnɒptɪk, (ˌ)panˈɒptɪk
AM pæˈnɑptɪk, pəˈnɑptɪk

panorama
BR ˌpanəˈrɑːmə(*r*), -z
AM ˌpænəˈræmə, ˌpænəˈrɑmə, -z

panoramic
BR ˌpanəˈramɪk
AM ¦ˌpænəˈræmɪk

panoramically
BR ˌpanəˈramɨkli
AM ¦ˌpænəˈræmək(ə)li

panpipe
BR ˈpanpʌɪp, -s
AM ˈpænˌpaɪp, -s

panpsychism
BR panˈsʌɪkɪz(ə)m
AM pænˈsaɪkɪzəm

panslavism
BR panˈslɑːvɪz(ə)m
AM pænˈslɑvɪzəm

panspermia
BR panˈspəːmɪə(*r*)
AM pænˈspərmiə

panstick
BR ˈpanstɪk
AM ˈpænˌstɪk

pansy
BR ˈpanz|i, -ɪz
AM ˈpænzi, -z

pant
BR pant, -s, -ɪŋ, -ɨd
AM pæn|t, -(t)s, -(t)ɪŋ, -(t)əd

pantagraph
BR ˈpantəgrɑːf, ˈpantəgraf, -s
AM ˈpæn(t)əˌgræf, -s

Pantagruel
BR ˌpantəgrʊˈɛl, ˈpantəgrʊəl
AM ˌpæn(t)əgrʊˈɛl, ˈpæn(t)əˌgruəl

pantalets
BR ˌpantəˈlɛts, ˌpantlˈɛts
AM ˌpæn(t)lˈɛts

pantalettes
BR ˌpantəˈlɛts, ˌpantlˈɛts
AM ˌpæn(t)lˈɛts

pantaloon
BR ˌpantəˈluːn, -z
AM ˌpæn(t)lˈun, ˌpæn(t)əˈlun, -z

pantechnicon
BR panˈtɛknɨk(ə)n, -z
AM pænˈtɛknəkən, pænˈtɛknəˌkɑn, -z

Pantelleria
BR ˌpantələˈriːə(*r*)
AM ¦ˌpæn(t)ələˈriə

Panthalassa
BR ˌpanθəˈlasə(*r*)
AM ˌpænθəˈlæsə

pantheism
BR ˈpanθɪɪz(ə)m
AM ˈpænθiˌɪzəm

pantheist
BR ˈpanθɪɪst, -s
AM ˈpænθiɨst, -s

pantheistic
BR ˌpanθɪˈɪstɪk
AM ˌpænθiˈɪstɪk

pantheistical
BR ˌpanθɪˈɪstɨkl
AM ˌpænθiˈɪstɨkəl

pantheistically
BR ˌpanθɪˈɪstɨkli
AM ˌpænθiˈɪstɨk(ə)li

pantheon
BR ˈpanθɪən, -z
AM ˈpænθiˌɑn, ˈpænθiən, -z

panther
BR ˈpanθə(r), -z
AM ˈpænθər, -z

pantie-girdle
BR ˈpantɪˌgəːdl, -z
AM ˈpæn(t)iˌgərdəl, -z

panties
BR ˈpantɪz
AM ˈpæn(t)iz

pantihose
BR ˈpantɪhəʊz
AM ˈpæn(t)iˌhoʊz

pantile
BR ˈpantʌɪl, -z, -d
AM ˈpænˌtaɪl, -z, -d

pantingly
BR ˈpantɪŋli
AM ˈpæn(t)ɪŋli

panto
BR ˈpantəʊ, -z
AM ˈpænˌtoʊ, -z

pantograph
BR ˈpantəgrɑːf, ˈpantəgraf, -s
AM ˈpæn(t)əˌgræf, -s

pantographic
BR ˌpantəˈgrafɪk
AM ¦ˌpæn(t)əˈgræfɪk

pantologic
BR ˌpantəˈlɒdʒɪk
AM ¦ˌpæn(t)əˈlɑdʒɪk

pantology
BR panˈtɒlədʒi
AM pænˈtɑlədʒi

pantomime
BR ˈpantəmʌɪm, -z
AM ˈpæn(t)əˌmaɪm, -z

pantomimic
BR ˌpantəˈmɪmɪk
AM ¦ˌpæn(t)əˈmɪmɪk

pantomimist
BR ˈpantəmʌɪmɪst, -s
AM ˈpæn(t)əˌmaɪmɨst, -s

pantomorphic
BR ˌpantə(ʊ)ˈmɔːfɪk
AM ˌpæn(t)əˈmɔrfɪk

pantoscopic
BR ˌpantəˈskɒpɪk
AM ˌpæn(t)əˈskɑpɪk

pantothenic
BR ˌpantəˈθɛnɪk
AM ¦ˌpæn(t)əˈθɛnɪk

pantry
BR ˈpantr|i, -ɪz
AM ˈpæntri, -z

pantryman
BR ˈpantrɪmən
AM ˈpæntrimən

pantrymen
BR ˈpantrɪmən
AM ˈpæntrimən

pants
BR pants
AM pæn(t)s

pantsuit
BR ˈpantsuːt, -s
AM ˈpæntˌsut, -s

pantyhose
BR ˈpantɪhəʊz
AM ˈpæn(t)iˌhoʊz

pantywaist
BR ˈpantɪweɪst, -s
AM ˈpæn(t)iˌweɪst, -s

Panzer
BR ˈpanzə(r), -z
AM ˈpænzər, ˈpɑn(t)sər, -z

pap
BR pap, -s
AM pæp, -s

papa
BR pəˈpɑː(*r*), -z
AM ˈpɑpə, -z

papabile
BR pəˈpɑːbɪleɪ
AM pəˈpɑbəˌleɪ

papacy
BR ˈpeɪpəs|i, -ɪz
AM ˈpeɪpəsi, -z

papain
BR pəˈpeɪɪn, pəˈpʌɪɪn
AM ˈpæˌpeɪn, pəˈpeɪn

papal
BR ˈpeɪpl
AM ˈpeɪpəl

papalism
BR ˈpeɪpl̩ɪz(ə)m, ˈpeɪpəlɪz(ə)m
AM ˈpeɪpəˌlɪzəm

papalist
BR ˈpeɪpl̩ɪst, ˈpeɪpəlɪst, -s
AM ˈpeɪpələst, -s

papally
BR ˈpeɪpl̩i, ˈpeɪpəli
AM ˈpeɪpəli

paparazzi
BR ˌpapəˈratsiː

AM ˌpɑpəˈrɑtˌsi
paparazzo
BR ˌpapəˈratsəʊ
AM ˌpɑpəˈrɑtˌsoʊ
papaveraceous
BR pəˌpeɪvəˈreɪʃəs
AM pəˌpævəˈreɪʃəs
papaverine
BR pəˈpeɪvəriːn, pəˈpavəriːn, pəˈpeɪvərɪn, pəˈpavərɪn
AM pəˈpævəˌrin, pəˈpævərən
papaw
BR ˈpɔːpɔː(r), pəˈpɔː(r), -z
AM pəˈpɔ, pəˈpɑ, -z
papaya
BR pəˈpʌɪə(r), -z
AM pəˈpaɪə, -z
Papeete
BR ˌpɑːpɪˈiːti, ˌpɑːpɪˈeɪti, ˌpapɪˈiːti, ˌpapɪˈeɪti, pəˈpiːti
AM ˌpɑpiˈiti, pəˈpidi
paper
BR ˈpeɪp|ə(r), -əz, -(ə)rɪŋ, -əd
AM ˈpeɪp|ər, -ərz, -(ə)rɪŋ, -ərd
paperback
BR ˈpeɪpəbak, -s
AM ˈpeɪpərˌbæk, -s
paperboy
BR ˈpeɪpəbɔɪ, -z
AM ˈpeɪpərˌbɔɪ, -z
paperchase
BR ˈpeɪpətʃeɪs, -ɪz
AM ˈpeɪpərˌtʃeɪs, -ɪz
paperclip
BR ˈpeɪpəklɪp, -s
AM ˈpeɪpərˌklɪp, -s
paperer
BR ˈpeɪp(ə)rə(r), -z
AM ˈpeɪpərər, -z
paperhanger
BR ˈpeɪpəˌhaŋə(r), -z
AM ˈpeɪpərˌ(h)æŋər, -z
paperknife
BR ˈpeɪpənʌɪf
AM ˈpeɪpərˌnaɪf
paperknives
BR ˈpeɪpənʌɪvz
AM ˈpeɪpərˌnaɪvz
paperless
BR ˈpeɪpələs
AM ˈpæpərləs
papermaker
BR ˈpeɪpəˌmeɪkə(r), -z
AM ˈpeɪpərˌmeɪkər, -z
papermaking
BR ˈpeɪpəˌmeɪkɪŋ
AM ˈpeɪpərˌmeɪkɪŋ
paperweight
BR ˈpeɪpəweɪt, -s
AM ˈpeɪpərˌweɪt, -s
paperwork
BR ˈpeɪpəwəːk
AM ˈpeɪpərˌwərk
papery
BR ˈpeɪp(ə)ri
AM ˈpeɪpəri
Paphlagonia
BR ˌpafləˈgəʊnɪə(r)
AM ˌpæfləˈgoʊniə
Paphlagonian
BR ˌpafləˈgəʊnɪən, -z
AM ˌpæfləˈgoʊniən, -z
papier-mâché
BR ˌpapjeɪˈmaʃeɪ
AM ˌpeɪpərməˈʃeɪ
papilionaceous
BR pəˌpɪlɪəˈneɪʃəs
AM pəˌpɪliəˈneɪʃəs
papilla
BR pəˈpɪlə(r)
AM pəˈpɪlə
papillae
BR pəˈpɪliː
AM pəˈpɪlˌi, pəˈpɪlˌaɪ
papillary
BR pəˈpɪl(ə)ri, ˈpapɪləri
AM ˈpæpəˌlɛri
papillate
BR ˈpapɪleɪt, pəˈpɪlət
AM ˈpæpəˌleɪt, pəˈpɪlɪt
papilloma
BR ˌpapɪˈləʊmə(r), -z
AM ˌpæpəˈloʊmə, -z
papillomata
BR ˌpapɪˈləʊmətə(r)
AM ˌpæpəˈloʊmədə
papillon
BR ˈpapɪlɒn, ˈpapɪjɒ̃, -z
AM ˌpɑpiˈjɔn, -z
papillose
BR ˈpapɪləʊs, ˈpapɪləʊz
AM ˈpɑpəˈloʊs, ˈpɑpəˌloʊz
papism
BR ˈpeɪpɪz(ə)m
AM ˈpeɪˌpɪzəm
papist
BR ˈpeɪpɪst, -s
AM ˈpeɪpɪst, -s
papistic
BR pəˈpɪstɪk
AM pəˈpɪstɪk
papistical
BR pəˈpɪstɪkl
AM pəˈpɪstəkəl
papistry
BR ˈpeɪpɪstri
AM ˈpeɪpɪstri
papoose
BR pəˈpuːs, -ɪz
AM pæˈpus, pəˈpus, -əz
Papp
BR pap, -s
AM pæp, -s
pappardelle
BR ˌpapɑːˈdɛleɪ
AM ˌpɑpəˈdɛli
pappi
BR ˈpapʌɪ
AM ˈpæˌpaɪ
pappose
BR paˈpəʊs
AM ˈpæˌpoʊs, ˈpæˌpoʊz
pappus
BR ˈpapəs
AM ˈpæpəs
pappy
BR ˈpap|i, -ɪə(r), -ɪɪst
AM ˈpæpi, -ər, -əst
paprika
BR ˈpaprɪkə(r), pəˈpriːkə(r)
AM pəˈprikə, pæˈprikə
Papua
BR ˈpap(j)ʊə(r), ˈpɑːpʊə(r)
AM ˈpɑpʊə, ˈpæpjʊə
Papuan
BR ˈpap(j)ʊən, ˈpɑːp(j)ʊən, -z
AM ˈpɑpʊən, ˈpæpjʊən, -z
Papua New Guinea
BR ˌpap(j)ʊə njuː ˈgɪni, ˌpɑːp(j)ʊə +
AM ˌpɑpʊə ˌn(j)u ˈgɪni, ˌpæpjʊə +
Papua New Guinean
BR ˌpap(j)ʊə njuː ˈgɪnɪən, ˌpɑːp(j)ʊə +, -z
AM ˌpɑpʊə ˌn(j)u ˈgɪniən, ˌpæpjʊə +, -z
papula
BR ˈpapjʉlə(r)
AM ˈpæpjələ
papulae
BR ˈpapjʉliː
AM ˈpæpjəˌli, ˈpæpjəˌlaɪ
papular
BR ˈpapjʉlə(r)
AM ˈpæpjələr
papule
BR ˈpapjuːl, -z
AM ˈpæpˌjul, -z
papulose
BR ˈpapjʉləʊs, ˈpapjʉləʊz
AM ˈpæpjəloʊs, ˈpæpjəloʊz
papulous
BR ˈpapjʉləs
AM ˈpæpjələs
Papworth
BR ˈpapwəθ
AM ˈpæpˌwərθ
papyraceous
BR ˌpapɪˈreɪʃəs
AM ˌpæpəˈreɪʃəs
papyri
BR pəˈpʌɪrʌɪ
AM pəˈpaɪri, pəˈpaɪˌraɪ
papyrological
BR pəˌpʌɪrəˈlɒdʒɪkl, pəˌpɪərəˈlɒdʒɪkl
AM pəˌpaɪrəˈlɑdʒəkəl, pəˌpaɪərəˈlɑdʒəkəl
papyrologist
BR ˌpapɪˈrɒlədʒɪst, -s
AM ˌpæpəˈrɑlədʒəst, -s
papyrology
BR ˌpapɪˈrɒlədʒi
AM ˌpæpəˈrɑlədʒi
papyrus
BR pəˈpʌɪrəs, -ɪz
AM pəˈpaɪrəs, -əz
par
BR pɑː(r)
AM pɑr
Pará
BR paˈrɑː(r)
AM pɑˈrɑ
para
paratrooper, paragraph
BR ˈparə(r), -z
AM ˈpɛrə, -z
parabases
BR ˌparaˈbeɪsiːz
AM ˌpɛrəˈbeɪˌsiz
parabasis
BR ˌparaˈbeɪsɪs
AM ˌpɛrəˈbeɪsɪs
parabioses
BR ˌparəbʌɪˈəʊsiːz
AM ˌpɛrəˈbaɪəˌsiz
parabiosis
BR ˌparəbʌɪˈəʊsɪs
AM ˌpɛrəˈbaɪəsəs
parabiotic
BR ˌparəbʌɪˈɒtɪk
AM ˌpɛrəbaɪˈɑdɪk
parable
BR ˈparəbl, -z
AM ˈpɛrəbəl, -z
parabola
BR pəˈrabələ(r), pəˈrablə(r), -z
AM pəˈræbələ, -z
parabolic
BR ˌparəˈbɒlɪk
AM ˌpɛrəˈbɑlɪk
parabolical
BR ˌparəˈbɒlɪkl
AM ˌpɛrəˈbɑləkəl
parabolically
BR ˌparəˈbɒlɪkli
AM ˌpɛrəˈbɑlək(ə)li
paraboloid
BR pəˈrabəlɔɪd, pəˈrablɔɪd, -z
AM pəˈræbəˌlɔɪd, -z
paraboloidal
BR pəˌrabəˈlɔɪdl
AM pəˌræbəˈlɔɪdəl
Paracelsus
BR ˌparəˈsɛlsəs
AM ˌpɛrəˈsɛlsəs

paracetamol
BR ˌparəˈsiːtəmɒl, ˌparəˈsɛtəmɒl, -z
AM ˌpɛrəˈsidəˌmɑl, ˌpɛrəˈsɛdəˌmɑl, -z
parachronism
BR pəˈrakrənɪz(ə)m, -z
AM ˌpɛrəˈkrɑˌnɪzəm, -z
parachute
BR ˈparəʃuːt, -s, -ɪŋ, -ɨd
AM ˈpɛrəˌʃu|t, -ts, -dɪŋ, -dəd
parachutist
BR ˈparəʃuːtɪst, -s
AM ˈpɛrəˌʃudəst, -s
paraclete
BR ˈparəkliːt, -s
AM ˈpɛrəˌklit, -s
parade
BR pəˈreɪd, -z, -ɪŋ, -ɨd
AM pəˈreɪd, -z, -ɪŋ, -ɨd
parader
BR pəˈreɪdə(r), -z
AM pəˈreɪdər, -z
paradichlorobenzene
BR ˌparədʌɪˌklɔːrəʊˈbɛnziːn
AM ˌ¦pɛrəˌdaɪˌklɔrəˈbɛnzin
paradiddle
BR ˈparədɪdl, ˌparəˈdɪdl, -z
AM ˈpɛrəˌdɪdəl, -z
paradigm
BR ˈparədʌɪm, -z
AM ˈpɛrəˌdaɪm, -z
paradigmatic
BR ˌparədɪɡˈmatɪk
AM ¦pɛrəˌdɪɡˈmædɪk
paradigmatical
BR ˌparədɪɡˈmatɪkl
AM ¦pɛrəˌdɪɡˈmædəkəl
paradigmatically
BR ˌparədɪɡˈmatɪkli
AM ¦pɛrəˌdɪɡˈmædək(ə)li
paradisaical
BR ˌparədɪˈsʌɪɪkl, ˌparədɪˈzʌɪɪkl
AM ¦pɛrədəˈsaɪəkəl, ¦pɛrədəˈzaɪəkəl
paradisal
BR ˌparəˈdʌɪsl, ˌparəˈdʌɪzl
AM ¦pɛrəˈdaɪzəl
paradise
BR ˈparədʌɪs, -ɨz
AM ˈpɛrəˌdaɪs, ˈpɛrəˌdaɪz, -ɨz
paradisiacal
BR ˌparədɪˈsʌɪəkl, ˌparədɪˈzʌɪəkl
AM ¦pɛrədəˈsaɪəkəl, ¦pɛrədəˈzaɪəkəl
paradisical
BR ˌparəˈdɪsɪkl, ˌparəˈdɪzɪkl
AM ¦parəˈdɪsəkəl, ¦parəˈdɪzəkəl
parador
BR ˈparədɔː(r), -z
AM ˈpɛ(ə)rəˌdɔ(ə)r, -z
parados
BR ˈparədɒs, -ɨz
AM ˈpɛrəˌdɑs, -əz
paradox
BR ˈparədɒks, -ɨz
AM ˈpɛrəˌdɑks, -əz
paradoxical
BR ˌparəˈdɒksɨkl
AM ¦pɛrəˈdɑksəkəl
paradoxically
BR ˌparəˈdɒksɨkli
AM ¦pɛrəˈdɑksək(ə)li
paradoxure
BR ˌparəˈdɒksjʊə(r), -z
AM ¦pɛrə¦dɑkʃər, -z
paradrop
BR ˈparədrɒp, -s
AM ˈpɛrəˌdrɑp, -s
paraffin
BR ˈparəfɪn
AM ˈpɛrəfən
paraglide
BR ˈparəɡlʌɪd
AM ˈpɛrəˌɡlaɪd
paraglider
BR ˈparəˌɡlʌɪdə(r), -z
AM ˈpɛrəˌɡlaɪdər, -z
paragliding
BR ˈparəˌɡlʌɪdɪŋ
AM ˈpɛrəˌɡlaɪdɪŋ
paragoge
BR ˌparəˈɡəʊdʒi
AM ˈpɛrəˌɡoʊdʒi
paragogic
BR ˌparəˈɡɒdʒɪk
AM ˌpɛrəˈɡɑdʒɪk
paragon
BR ˈparəɡ(ə)n, -z
AM ˈpɛrəˌɡɑn, ˈpɛrəɡən, -z
paragraph
BR ˈparəɡrɑːf, ˈparəɡraf, -s, -ɪŋ, -t
AM ˈpɛrəˌɡræf, -s, -ɪŋ, -t
paragraphic
BR ˌparəˈɡrafɪk
AM ¦pɛrəˈɡræfɪk
paragraphist
BR ˈparəˌɡrafɪst, -s
AM ˈpɛrəˌɡræfəst, -s
Paraguay
BR ˈparəɡwʌɪ, ˌparəˈɡwʌɪ
AM ˈpɛrəˌɡwaɪ
SP paraˈɣwaj
Paraguayan
BR ˌparəˈɡwʌɪən, -z
AM ¦pɛrəˈɡwaɪən, -z
parahydrogen
BR ˌparəˈhʌɪdrədʒ(ə)n
AM ¦pɛrəˈhaɪdrədʒən
parakeet
BR ˈparəkiːt, ˌparəˈkiːt, -s
AM ˈpɛrəˌkit, -s
paralanguage
BR ˈparəˌlaŋɡwɪdʒ
AM ˈpɛrəˌlæŋɡwɪdʒ
paraldehyde
BR pəˈraldɨhʌɪd
AM ¦pɛrˈældəˌhaɪd
paralegal
BR ˌparəˈliːɡl
AM ¦pɛrəˈliɡəl
paraleipomena
BR ˌparəlʌɪˈpɒmɨnə(r), ˌparəlɪˈpɒmɨnə(r)
AM ¦pɛrəˌlaɪˈpɑmənə, ¦pɛrələˈpɑmənə
paraleipses
BR ˌparəˈlʌɪpsiːz
AM ¦pɛrəˈlaɪpsiz
paraleipsis
BR ˌparəˈlʌɪpsɪs
AM ¦pɛrəˈlaɪpsɨs
paralinguistic
BR ˌparəlɪŋˈɡwɪstɪk
AM ˌpɛrəˌlɪŋˈɡwɪstɪk
paralipomena
BR ˌparəlʌɪˈpɒmɨnə(r), ˌparəlɪˈpɒmɨnə(r)
AM ¦pɛrəˌlaɪˈpɑmənə, ¦pɛrələˈpɑmənə
paralipses
BR ˌparəˈlɪpsiːz
AM ¦pɛrəˈlɪpˌsiz
paralipsis
BR ˌparəˈlɪpsɪs
AM ¦pɛrəˈlɪpsɨs
parallactic
BR ˌparəˈlaktɪk
AM ¦pɛrəˈlæktɪk
parallax
BR ˈparəlaks, -ɨz
AM ˈpɛrəˌlæks, -əz
parallel
BR ˈparəlɛl, -z, -ɪŋ, -d
AM ˈpɛrəˌlɛl, -z, -ɪŋ, -d
parallelepiped
BR ˌparəlɛləˈpʌɪpɛd, -z
AM ¦pɛrəˌlɛləˈpaɪpɨd, -z
parallelism
BR ˈparəlɛlɪz(ə)m
AM ˈpɛrəˌlɛlˌɪzəm
parallelogram
BR ˌparəˈlɛləɡram, -z
AM ¦pɛrəˈlɛləˌɡræm, -z
paralogise
BR pəˈralədʒʌɪz, -ɨz, -ɪŋ, -d
AM pəˈræləˌdʒaɪz, -ɨz, -ɪŋ, -d
paralogism
BR pəˈralədʒɪz(ə)m, -z
AM pəˈræləˌdʒɪzəm, -z
paralogist
BR pəˈralədʒɪst, -s
AM pəˈrælədʒəst, -s
paralogize
BR pəˈralədʒʌɪz, -ɨz, -ɪŋ, -d
AM pəˈræləˌdʒaɪz, -ɨz, -ɪŋ, -d
Paralympics
BR ˌparəˈlɪmpɪks
AM ˌpɛrəˈlɪmpɪks
paralysation
BR ˌparəlʌɪˈzeɪʃn
AM ˌpɛrələˈzeɪʃən, ˌpɛrəˌlaɪˈzeɪʃən
paralyse
BR ˈparəlʌɪz, -ɨz, -ɪŋ, -d
AM ˈpɛrəˌlaɪz, -ɨz, -ɪŋ, -d
paralyses
noun plural
BR pəˈralɨsiːz
AM pəˈræləˌsiz
paralysingly
BR ˈparəlʌɪzɪŋli
AM ˈpɛrəˌlaɪzɪŋli
paralysis
BR pəˈralɨsɪs
AM pəˈræləsəs
paralytic
BR ˌparəˈlɪtɪk
AM ¦pɛrəˈlɪdɪk
paralytically
BR ˌparəˈlɪtɨkli
AM ¦pɛrəˈlɪdək(ə)li
paralyzation
BR ˌparəlʌɪˈzeɪʃn
AM ˌpɛrələˈzeɪʃən, ˌpɛrəˌlaɪˈzeɪʃən
paralyze
BR ˈparəlʌɪz, -ɨz, -ɪŋ, -d
AM ˈpɛrəˌlaɪz, -ɨz, -ɪŋ, -d
paralyzingly
BR ˈparəlʌɪzɪŋli
AM ˈpɛrəˌlaɪzɪŋli
paramagnetic
BR ˌparəmaɡˈnɛtɪk
AM ¦pɛrəmæɡˈnɛdɪk
paramagnetism
BR ˌparəˈmaɡnɨtɪz(ə)m
AM ¦pɛrəˈmæɡnəˌtɪzəm
paramatta
BR ˌparəˈmatə(r)
AM ˌpɛrəˈmædə
paramecia
BR ˌparəˈmiːsɪə(r)
AM ˌpɛrəˈmisiə
paramecium
BR ˌparəˈmiːsɪəm
AM ˌpɛrəˈmisiəm
paramedic
BR ˌparəˈmɛdɪk, -s
AM ¦pɛrəˈmɛdɪk, -s
paramedical
BR ˌparəˈmɛdɪkl
AM ¦pɛrəˈmɛdəkəl
parameter
BR pəˈramɨtə(r), -z
AM pəˈræmədər, -z
parametric
BR ˌparəˈmɛtrɪk

AM ˌpɛrəˈmɛtrɪk

parametrise
BR pəˈramɪtrʌɪz, -ɪz, -ɪŋ, -d
AM pəˈræməˌtraɪz, -ɪz, -ɪŋ, -d

parametrize
BR pəˈramɪtrʌɪz, -ɪz, -ɪŋ, -d
AM pəˈræməˌtraɪz, -ɪz, -ɪŋ, -d

paramilitary
BR ˌparəˈmɪlɪt(ə)ri
AM ˌpɛrəˈmɪləˌtɛri

paramnesia
BR ˌparəmˈniːzɪə(r), ˌparəmˈniːʒə(r)
AM ˌpɛˌræmˈniʒ(i)ə, ˌpɛrəmˈniʒ(i)ə, ˌpɛˌræmˈniziə, ˌpɛrəmˈniziə

paramo
BR ˈparəməʊ, -z
AM ˈpɛrəˌmoʊ, -z

paramoecia
BR ˌparəˈmiːʃ(ɪ)ə(r), -z
AM ˌpɛrəˈmiʃ(i)ə, -z

paramoecium
BR ˌparəˈmiːʃ(ɪ)əm, -z
AM ˌpɛrəˈmiʃ(i)əm, -z

paramount
BR ˈparəmaʊnt
AM ˈpɛrəˌmaʊnt

paramountcy
BR ˈparəmaʊn(t)si
AM ˈpɛrəˌmaʊn(t)si

paramountly
BR ˈparəmaʊntli
AM ˈpɛrəˌmaʊn(t)li

paramour
BR ˈparəmʊə(r), ˈparəmɔː(r), -z
AM ˈpɛrəˌmʊ(ə)r, ˈpɛrəˌmɔ(ə)r, -z

Paraná
BR ˌparəˈnɑː(r)
AM ˌpɑrəˈnɑ

parang
BR pəˈraŋ, -z
AM pəˈrɑŋ, -z

paranoia
BR ˌparəˈnɔɪə(r)
AM ˌpɛrəˈnɔɪə

paranoiac
BR ˌparəˈnɔɪak, -s
AM ˌpɛrəˈnɔɪɪk, -s

paranoiacally
BR ˌparəˈnɔɪəkli
AM ˌpɛrəˈnɔɪɪk(ə)li

paranoic
BR ˌparəˈnɔɪɪk
AM ˌpɛrəˈnɔɪɪk

paranoically
BR ˌparəˈnɔɪɪkli
AM ˌpɛrəˈnɔɪɪk(ə)li

paranoid
BR ˈparənɔɪd
AM ˈpɛrəˌnɔɪd

paranormal
BR ˌparəˈnɔːml
AM ¦pɛrəˈnɔrməl

paranormally
BR ˌparəˈnɔːmḷi, ˌparəˈnɔːməli
AM ¦pɛrəˈnɔrməli

Paranthropus
BR pəˈranθrəpəs, ˌparənˈθrəʊpəs
AM pəˈrænθrəpəs

parapet
BR ˈparəpɪt, -s, -ɪd
AM ˈpɛrəpə|t, -ts, -dɪd

paraph
BR ˈparaf, ˈparəf, -s
AM ˈpɛrəf, pəˈræf, -s

paraphernalia
BR ˌparəfəˈneɪlɪə(r)
AM ˌpɛrəfə(r)ˈneɪljə, ˌpɛrəfə(r)ˈneɪliə

paraphrase
BR ˈparəfreɪz, -ɪz, -ɪŋ, -d
AM ˈpɛrəˌfreɪz, -ɪz, -ɪŋ, -d

paraphrastic
BR ˌparəˈfrastɪk
AM ¦pɛrəˈfræstɪk

paraphrastically
BR ˌparəˈfrastɪkli
AM ¦pɛrəˈfræstək(ə)li

paraplegia
BR ˌparəˈpliːdʒə(r)
AM ˌpɛrəˈplidʒ(i)ə

paraplegic
BR ˌparəˈpliːdʒɪk, -s
AM ¦pɛrəˈplidʒɪk, -s

paraprofessional
BR ˌparəprəˈfɛʃn̩(ə)l, ˌparəprəˈfɛʃən(ə)l
AM ˌpɛrəprəˈfɛʃ(ə)nəl

parapsychological
BR ˌparəˌsʌɪkəˈlɒdʒɪkl
AM ¦pɛrəˌsaɪkəˈlɑdʒəkəl

parapsychologically
BR ˌparəˌsʌɪkəˈlɒdʒɪkli
AM ¦pɛrəˌsaɪkəˈlɑdʒək(ə)li

parapsychologist
BR ˌparəsʌɪˈkɒlədʒɪst, -s
AM ¦pɛrəsaɪˈkɑlədʒəst, -s

parapsychology
BR ˌparəsʌɪˈkɒlədʒi
AM ¦pɛrəsaɪˈkɑlədʒi

paraquat
BR ˈparəkwɒt, ˈparəkwat
AM ˈpɛrəˌkwɑt

pararhyme
BR ˈparərʌɪm
AM ˈpɛrəˌraɪm

parasailer
BR ˈparəˌseɪlə(r), -z
AM ˈpɛrəˌseɪlər, -z

parasailing
BR ˈparəˌseɪlɪŋ
AM ˈpɛrəˌseɪlɪŋ

parasailor
BR ˈparəˌseɪlə(r), -z
AM ˈpɛrəˌseɪlər, -z

parasang
BR ˈparəsaŋ, -z
AM ˈpɛrəˌsæŋ, -z

parascend
BR ˈparəsɛnd, -z, -ɪŋ, -ɪd
AM ˈpɛrəˌsɛnd, -z, -ɪŋ, -əd

parascender
BR ˈparəˌsɛndə(r), -z
AM ˈpɛrəˌsɛndər, -z

paraselenae
BR ˌparəsɪˈliːniː
AM ˌpɛrəsəˈlini, ˌpɛrəsəˈlinaɪ

paraselene
BR ˌparəsɪˈliːni
AM ˌpɛrəsəˈlini

parasitaemia
BR ˌparəsɪˈtiːmɪə(r)
AM ˌpɛrəsəˈtimiə

parasite
BR ˈparəsʌɪt, -s
AM ˈpɛrəˌsaɪt, -s

parasitemia
BR ˌparəsɪˈtiːmɪə(r)
AM ˌpɛrəsəˈtimiə

parasitic
BR ˌparəˈsɪtɪk
AM ˌpɛrəˈsɪdɪk

parasitical
BR ˌparəˈsɪtɪkl
AM ˌpɛrəˈsɪdɪkəl

parasitically
BR ˌparəˈsɪtɪkli
AM ˌpɛrəˈsɪdɪk(ə)li

parasiticide
BR ˌparəˈsɪtɪsʌɪd
AM ˌpɛrəˈsɪdɪˌsaɪd

parasitisation
BR ˌparəsɪtʌɪˈzeɪʃn
AM ˌpɛrəsədəˈzeɪʃən, ˌpɛrəsəˌtaɪˈzeɪʃən

parasitise
BR ˈparəsɪtʌɪz, -ɪz, -ɪŋ, -d
AM ˈpɛrəsəˌtaɪz, ˈpɛrəsaɪˌtaɪz, -ɪz, -ɪŋ, -d

parasitism
BR ˈparəsɪtɪz(ə)m
AM ˈpɛrəsəˌtɪzəm, ˈpɛrəˌsaɪˌtɪzəm

parasitization
BR ˌparəsɪtʌɪˈzeɪʃn
AM ˌpɛrəsədəˈzeɪʃən, ˌpɛrəsəˌtaɪˈzeɪʃən

parasitize
BR ˈparəsɪtʌɪz, -ɪz, -ɪŋ, -d
AM ˈpɛrəsəˌtaɪz, ˈpɛrəsaɪˌtaɪz, -ɪz, -ɪŋ, -d

parasitoid
BR ˈparəsɪtɔɪd, -z
AM ˈpɛrəsəˌtɔɪd, ˈpɛrəˌsaɪˌtɔɪd, -z

parasitologist
BR ˌparəsɪˈtɒlədʒɪst, ˌparəsʌɪˈtɒlədʒɪst, -s
AM ˌpɛrəsəˈtɑlədʒəst, ˌpɛrəsaɪˈtɑlədʒəst, -s

parasitology
BR ˌparəsɪˈtɒlədʒi, ˌparəsʌɪˈtɒlədʒi
AM ˌpɛrəsəˈtɑlədʒi, ˌpɛrəsaɪˈtɑlədʒi

parasol
BR ˈparəsɒl, -z
AM ˈpɛrəˌsɔl, ˈpɛrəˌsɑl, -z

parasuicide
BR ˌparəˈs(j)uːɪsʌɪd, -z
AM ˌpɛrəˈsʊ(w)əˌsaɪd, -z

parasympathetic
BR ˌparəˌsɪmpəˈθɛtɪk
AM ˌpɛrəˌsɪmpəˈθɛdɪk

parasyntheses
BR ˌparəˈsɪnθɪsiːz
AM ˌpɛrəˈsɪnθəsiz

parasynthesis
BR ˌparəˈsɪnθɪsɪs
AM ˌpɛrəˈsɪnθəsəs

parasynthetic
BR ˌparəsɪnˈθɛtɪk
AM ¦pɛrəˌsɪnˈθɛdɪk

paratactic
BR ˌparəˈtaktɪk
AM ˌpɛrəˈtæktɪk

paratactically
BR ˌparəˈtaktɪkli
AM ˌpɛrəˈtæktək(ə)li

parataxis
BR ˌparəˈtaksɪs
AM ˌpɛrəˈtæksəs

parathion
BR ˌparəˈθʌɪɒn
AM ˌpɛrəˈθaɪˌɑn

parathyroid
BR ˌparəˈθʌɪrɔɪd
AM ˌpɛrəˈθaɪˌrɔɪd

paratroop
BR ˈparətruːp, -s
AM ˈpɛrəˌtrup, -s

paratrooper
BR ˈparətruːpə(r), -z
AM ˈpɛrəˌtrupər, -z

paratroops
BR ˈparətruːps
AM ˈpɛrəˌtrups

paratyphoid
BR ˌparəˈtʌɪfɔɪd
AM ˌpɛrəˈtaɪˌfɔɪd

paravane
BR ˈparəveɪn, -z
AM ˈpɛrəˌveɪn, -z

par avion
BR ˌpɑːr ˈavjɔ̃
AM ˌpɑr ɑˈvjɔn

parboil
BR ˈpɑːbɔɪl, -z, -ɪŋ, -d
AM ˈpɑrˌbɔɪl, -z, -ɪŋ, -d

parbuckle
BR ˈpɑːˌbʌk|l, -lz, -l̩ɪŋ\-lɪŋ, -ld
AM ˈpɑrˌbək|əl, -əlz, -(ə)lɪŋ, -əld

Parcae
BR ˈpɑːsi
AM ˈpɑrsi, ˈpɑrˌkaɪ

parcel
BR ˈpɑːs|l, -lz, -l̩ɪŋ\-əlɪŋ, -ld
AM ˈpɑrs|əl, -əlz, -(ə)lɪŋ, -əld

parch
BR pɑːtʃ, -ɪz, -ɪŋ, -t
AM pɑrtʃ, -əz, -ɪŋ, -t

Parcheesi®
BR pɑːˈtʃiːzi
AM pɑrˈtʃizi

parchment
BR ˈpɑːtʃm(ə)nt, -s
AM ˈpɑrtʃmənt, -s

parclose
BR ˈpɑːkləʊz, -ɪz
AM ˈpɑrˌkloʊz, -əz

pard
BR pɑːd, -z
AM pɑrd, -z

pardalote
BR ˈpɑːdələʊt, ˈpɑːdl̩əʊt, -s
AM ˈpɑrdlˌoʊt, -s

pardner
BR ˈpɑːdnə(r), -z
AM ˈpɑrdnər, -z

Pardoe
BR ˈpɑːdəʊ
AM ˈpɑrdoʊ

pardon
BR ˈpɑːd|n, -nz, -n̩ɪŋ\-nɪŋ, -nd
AM ˈpɑrdən, -z, -ɪŋ, -d

pardonable
BR ˈpɑːdn̩əbl, ˈpɑːdnəbl
AM ˈpɑrdn̩əbəl

pardonably
BR ˈpɑːdn̩əbli, ˈpɑːdnəbli
AM ˈpɑrdn̩əbli

pardoner
BR ˈpɑːdn̩ə(r), ˈpɑːdnə(r), -z
AM ˈpɑrdn̩ər, -z

pare
BR pɛː(r), -z, -ɪŋ, -d
AM pɛ(ə)r, -z, -ɪŋ, -d

paregoric
BR ˌparəˈɡɒrɪk
AM ˌpɛrəˈɡɔrɪk

pareira
BR pəˈrɛːrə(r)
AM pəˈrɛrə, pəˈreɪrə

paren
BR pəˈrɛn, -z
AM ˈpɛrɛn, ˈpɛrən, -z

parenchyma
BR pəˈrɛŋkɪmə(r)
AM pəˈrɛŋkəmə

parenchymal
BR pəˈrɛŋkɪml
AM pəˈrɛŋkəməl

parenchymatous
BR ˌparənˈkɪmətəs, ˌparn̩ˈkɪmətəs
AM ˌpɛrənˌkɪmədəs

parent
BR ˈpɛːrənt, ˈpɛːrn̩t, -s, -ɪŋ, -ɪd
AM ˈpɛrənt, -s, -ɪŋ, -ɪd

parentage
BR ˈpɛːrəntɪdʒ, ˈpɛːrn̩tɪdʒ
AM ˈpɛrən(t)ədʒ

parental
BR pəˈrɛntl
AM pəˈrɛn(t)l

parentally
BR pəˈrɛntl̩i, pəˈrɛntəli
AM pəˈrɛn(t)li

parenteral
BR pəˈrɛnt(ə)rəl, pəˈrɛnt(ə)rl̩
AM pəˈrɛn(t)ərəl

parenterally
BR pəˈrɛnt(ə)rəli, pəˈrɛnt(ə)rl̩i
AM pəˈrɛn(t)ərəli

parentheses
BR pəˈrɛnθɪsiːz
AM pəˈrɛnθəsiz

parenthesis
BR pəˈrɛnθɪsɪs
AM pəˈrɛnθəsəs

parenthesise
BR pəˈrɛnθɪsʌɪz, -ɪz, -ɪŋ, -d
AM pəˈrɛnθəˌsaɪz, -ɪz, -ɪŋ, -d

parenthesize
BR pəˈrɛnθɪsʌɪz, -ɪz, -ɪŋ, -d
AM pəˈrɛnθəˌsaɪz, -ɪz, -ɪŋ, -d

parenthetic
BR ˌparənˈθɛtɪk, ˌparn̩ˈθɛtɪk
AM ˌpɛrənˈθɛdɪk

parenthetical
BR ˌparənˈθɛtɪkl, ˌparn̩ˈθɛtɪkl
AM ˌpɛrənˈθɛdəkəl

parenthetically
BR ˌparənˈθɛtɪkli, ˌparn̩ˈθɛtɪkli
AM ˌpɛrənˈθɛdək(ə)li

parenthood
BR ˈpɛːrənthʊd, ˈpɛːrn̩thʊd
AM ˈpɛrən(t)ˌ(h)ʊd

parentless
BR ˈpɛːrəntləs, ˈpɛːrn̩tləs
AM ˈpɛrən(t)ləs

parer
BR ˈpɛːrə(r), -z
AM ˈpɛrər, -z

parerga
BR pəˈrəːɡə(r)
AM pəˈrərɡə

parergon
BR pəˈrəːɡɒn
AM pəˈrərˌɡɑn

paresis
BR pəˈriːsɪs
AM pəˈrisɪs

paresthesia
BR ˌparəsˈθiːzɪə(r), ˌparəsˈθiːʒə(r)
AM ˌpɛrəsˈθiʒ(i)ə, ˌpɛrəsˈθiziə

paresthetic
BR ˌparəsˈθɛtɪk
AM ˌpɛrəsˈθɛdɪk

paretic
BR pəˈrɛtɪk
AM pəˈrɛdɪk

par excellence
BR ˌpɑːr ˌɛksəˈlɑːns, + ˈɛksəlɑːns, ˌɛksəˈlɒ̃s, ˈɛksəlɒ̃s
AM ˌpɑr ˌɛksəˈlɑns

parfait
BR ˈpɑːfeɪ, -z
AM pɑrˈfeɪ, -z

Parfitt
BR ˈpɑːfɪt
AM ˈpɑrfɪt

parfleche
BR ˈpɑːflɛʃ
AM ˈpɑrˌflɛʃ

parfumerie
BR pɑːˈfjuːmər|i, -ɪz
AM pɑrˌfjuməˈri, -z

parget
BR ˈpɑːdʒ|ɪt, -ɪts, -ɪtɪŋ, -ɪtɪd
AM ˈpɑrdʒət, -s, -ɪŋ, -əd

Pargiter
BR ˈpɑːdʒɪtə(r)
AM ˈpɑrdʒɪdər

parhelia
BR pɑːˈhiːlɪə(r)
AM pɑrˈhiljə, pɑrˈhiliə

parheliacal
BR ˌpɑːhɪˈlʌɪəkl, ˌpɑːhɛˈlʌɪəkl
AM ˌpɑrhəˈlaɪəkəl, ˌpɑrhiˈlaɪəkəl

parhelic
BR ˌpɑːˈhiːlɪk
AM ˌpɑrˈhɛlɪk, ˌpɑrˈhilɪk

parhelical
BR ˌpɑːˈhiːlɪkl
AM ˌpɑrˈhɛləkəl, ˌpɑrˈhilɪkəl

parhelion
BR pɑːˈhiːlɪən
AM pɑrˈhiliən, pɑrˈhiliˌɑn

pariah
BR pəˈrʌɪə(r), -z
AM pəˈraɪə, -z

Parian
BR ˈpɛːrɪən, -z
AM ˈpɛriən, -z

parietal
BR pəˈrʌɪɪtl
AM pəˈraɪədəl

pari-mutuel
BR ˌparɪˈmjuːtʃʊəl, ˌparɪˈmjuːtʃ(ʉ)l, ˌparɪˈmjuːtjʊəl, ˌparɪˈmjuːtjʉl
AM ˌpɛrəˈmjutʃə(wə)l

paring
BR ˈpɛːrɪŋ, -z
AM ˈpɛrɪŋ, -z

pari passu
BR ˌparɪ ˈpɑːsuː, ˌpɑːrɪ +
AM ˌpari ˈpɑˌsu, ˌpɑrə +

Paris
BR ˈparɪs
AM ˈpɛrəs

parish
BR ˈpar|ɪʃ, -ɪʃɪz
AM ˈpɛrɪʃ, -ɪz

parishioner
BR pəˈrɪʃ(ə)nə(r), pəˈrɪʃn̩ə(r), -z
AM pəˈrɪʃ(ə)nər, -z

Parisian
BR pəˈrɪzɪən, -z
AM pəˈriʒən, -z

parison
BR ˈparɪsn, -z
AM ˈpɛrəsən, -z

parisyllabic
BR ˌparɪsɪˈlabɪk
AM ˌpɛrəsəˈlæbɪk

parity
BR ˈparɪti
AM ˈpɛrədi

park
BR pɑːk, -s, -ɪŋ, -t
AM pɑrk, -s, -ɪŋ, -t

parka
BR ˈpɑːkə(r), -z
AM ˈpɑrkə, -z

park and ride
BR ˌpɑːk (ə)n(d) ˈrʌɪd, -z
AM ˈpɑrk ən ˌraɪd, -z

Parke
BR pɑːk
AM pɑrk

parker
BR ˈpɑːkə(r), -z
AM ˈpɑrkər, -z

Parkes
BR pɑːks
AM pɑrks

Parkeston
BR 'pɑːkst(ə)n
AM 'pɑrkstən
Parkhouse
BR 'pɑːkhaʊs
AM 'pɑrk,(h)aʊs
parkin
BR 'pɑːkɪn
AM 'pɑrkɪn
Parkinson
BR 'pɑːkɪns(ə)n
AM 'pɑrkənsən
Parkinsonism
BR 'pɑːkɪnsənɪz(ə)m, 'pɑːkɪnsn̩ɪz(ə)m
AM 'pɑrkənsə,nɪzəm
parkland
BR 'pɑːklənd, 'pɑːkland, -z
AM 'pɑrk,lænd, -z
Parks
BR pɑːks
AM pɑrks
Parkstone
BR 'pɑːkst(ə)n
AM 'pɑrk,stoʊn
parkway
BR 'pɑːkweɪ, -z
AM 'pɑrk,weɪ, -z
parky
BR 'pɑːk|i, -ɪə(r), -ɪɪst
AM 'pɑrki, -ər, -ɪst
parlance
BR 'pɑːləns, 'pɑːln̩s
AM 'pɑrləns
parlay
BR 'pɑːleɪ, -z, -ɪŋ, -d
AM 'pɑr,leɪ, -z, -ɪŋ, -d
parley
BR 'pɑːl|i, -ɪz, -ɪɪŋ, -ɪd
AM 'pɑrli, -z, -ɪŋ, -d
parliament
BR 'pɑːlɪm(ə)nt, -s
AM 'pɑrləmənt, -s
parliamentarian
BR ,pɑːləmɛn'tɛːrɪən, ,pɑːləm(ə)n'tɛːrɪən, -z
AM ,pɑrlə,mɛn'tɛriən, ,pɑrləmən'tɛriən, -z
parliamentary
BR ,pɑːlə'mɛnt(ə)ri
AM ,pɑrlə'mɛnt(ə)ri, ,pɑrlə'mɛnəri
Parlophone
BR 'pɑːləfəʊn
AM 'pɑrlə,fon
parlor
BR 'pɑːlə(r), -z
AM 'pɑrlər, -z
parlormaid
BR 'pɑːləmeɪd, -z
AM 'pɑrlər,meɪd, -z
parlour
BR 'pɑːlə(r), -z
AM 'pɑrlər, -z
parlourmaid
BR 'pɑːləmeɪd, -z
AM 'pɑrlər,meɪd, -z
parlous
BR 'pɑːləs
AM 'pɑrləs
parlously
BR 'pɑːləsli
AM 'pɑrləsli
parlousness
BR 'pɑːləsnəs
AM 'pɑrləsnəs
Parma
BR 'pɑːmə(*r*)
AM 'pɑrmə
Parmenides
BR pɑː'mɛnɪdiːz
AM pɑr'mɛnə,diz
Parmenter
BR 'pɑːmɪntə(r)
AM 'pɑrmən(t)ər
Parmentier
BR pɑː'mɛntɪə(r), pɑː'mɒntɪeɪ
AM 'pɑrmən(t)ər, ,pɑrmən(t)i'eɪ
parmesan
BR ,pɑːmɪ'zan
AM 'pɑrmə,zɑn
Parmigianino
BR ,pɑːmɪdʒə'niːnəʊ
AM ,pɑrmədʒə'ni,noʊ
Parmigiano
BR ,pɑːmɪ'dʒɑːnəʊ
AM ,pɑrmə'dʒɑnoʊ, ,pɑrmi'dʒɑ,noʊ
Parmiter
BR 'pɑːmɪtə(r)
AM 'pɑrmədər
Parnassian
BR pɑː'nasɪən, -z
AM pɑr'næsiən, pɑr'næsjən, -z
Parnassus
BR pɑː'nasəs
AM pɑr'næsəs
Parnell
BR pɑː'nɛl
AM pɑr'nɛl
Parnes
BR pɑːnz
AM pɑrnz
parochial
BR pə'rəʊkɪəl
AM pə'roʊkiəl, pə'roʊkjəl
parochialism
BR pə'rəʊkɪəlɪz(ə)m
AM pə'roʊkiə,lɪzəm, pə'roʊkjə,lɪzəm
parochiality
BR pə,rəʊkɪ'alɪti
AM pə,roʊki'ælədi
parochially
BR pə'rəʊkɪəli
AM pə'roʊkiəli, pə'roʊkjəli
parodic
BR pə'rɒdɪk
AM pə'rɑdɪk
parodist
BR 'parədɪst, -s
AM 'pɛrədəst, -s
parody
BR 'parəd|i, -ɪz
AM 'pɛrədi, -z
paroecious
BR pə'riːʃəs
AM pə'riʃəs
parol
BR pə'rəʊl, 'parəl, 'parl̩, -z
AM pə'roʊl, 'pɛrəl, -z
parole
BR pə'rəʊl, -z, -ɪŋ, -d
AM pə'roʊl, -z, -ɪŋ, -d
parolee
BR pə,rəʊ'liː, -z
AM pə,roʊ'li, -z
paronomasia
BR ,parənə(ʊ)'meɪzɪə(*r*), ,parn̩ə(ʊ)'meɪzɪə(*r*)
AM ,pɛrənoʊ'meɪʒ(i)ə, ,pɛrənoʊ'meɪziə
paronym
BR 'parənɪm, -z
AM 'pɛrə,nɪm, -z
paronymous
BR pə'rɒnɪməs
AM pə'rɑnəməs
parotid
BR pə'rɒtɪd, -z
AM pə'rɑdəd, -z
parotitis
BR ,parə'tʌɪtɪs
AM ,pɛrə'taɪdəs
paroxysm
BR 'parəksɪz(ə)m, -z
AM 'pɛrək,sɪzəm, pə'rɑk,sɪzəm, -z
paroxysmal
BR ,parək'sɪzm(ə)l
AM ,pɛrək'sɪzməl, pə'rɑk,sɪzməl
paroxytone
BR pə'rɒksɪtəʊn, pa'rɒksɪtəʊn, -z
AM pɛr'ɑksə,toʊn, -z
parozone
BR 'parəzəʊn
AM 'pɛrə,zoʊn
parpen
BR 'pɑːp(ə)n, -z
AM 'pɑrpən, -z
parquet
BR 'pɑːkeɪ, -z
AM pɑr'keɪ, -z
parquetry
BR 'pɑːkɪtri
AM 'pɑrkətri
parr
BR pɑː(r)
AM pɑr
Parramatta
BR ,parə'matə(*r*)
AM ,pɛrə'mædə
parricidal
BR ,parɪ'sʌɪdl
AM ,pɛrə'saɪdəl
parricide
BR 'parɪsʌɪd, -z
AM 'pɛrə,saɪd, -z
Parrish
BR 'parɪʃ
AM 'pɛrɪʃ
parrot
BR 'parət, -s
AM 'pɛrət, -s
parrotfish
BR 'parətfɪʃ, -ɪz
AM 'pɛrət,fɪʃ, -ɪz
Parrott
BR 'parət
AM 'pɛrət
parry
BR 'par|i, -ɪz, -ɪɪŋ, -ɪd
AM 'pɛri, -z, -ɪŋ, -d
parse
BR pɑːz, -ɪz, -ɪŋ, -d
AM pɑrs, -əz, -ɪŋ, -d
parsec
BR 'pɑːsɛk, -s
AM 'pɑr,sɛk, -s
Parsee
BR ,pɑː'siː, 'pɑːsiː, -z
AM ,pɑr'si, 'pɑrsi, -z
Parseeism
BR ,pɑː'siːɪz(ə)m, 'pɑːsiːɪz(ə)m
AM ,pɑr'si,ɪzəm, 'pɑrsi,ɪzəm
parser
BR 'pɑːzə(r), -z
AM 'pɑrsər, -z
Parsifal
BR 'pɑːsɪf(a)l
AM 'pɑrsəfəl, 'pɑr(t)sə,fɑl
parsimonious
BR ,pɑːsɪ'məʊnɪəs
AM ¦pɑrsə'moʊniəs, ¦pɑrsə'moʊnjəs
parsimoniously
BR ,pɑːsɪ'məʊnɪəsli
AM ¦pɑrsə'moʊniəsli, ¦pɑrsə'moʊnjəsli
parsimoniousness
BR ,pɑːsɪ'məʊnɪəsnəs
AM ¦pɑrsə'moʊniəsnəs, ¦pɑrsə'moʊnjəsnəs
parsimony
BR 'pɑːsɪməni
AM 'pɑrsə,moʊni
Parsley
surname
BR 'pɑːzli
AM 'pɑrzli
parsley
BR 'pɑːsli
AM 'pɑrsli
parsley-piert
BR ,pɑːslɪ'pɪət, -s
AM 'pɑrsli,pɪ(ə)rt, -s

parsnip
BR 'pɑːsnɪp, -s
AM 'pɑrsnəp, -s

parson
BR 'pɑːsn, -z
AM 'pɑrsən, -z

parsonage
BR 'pɑːsn̩|ɪdʒ, -ɪdʒɪz
AM 'pɑrsn̩ɪdʒ, -ɪz

parsonical
BR pɑː'sɒnɪkl
AM pɑr'sɑnəkəl

Parsons
BR 'pɑːsnz
AM 'pɑrsənz

part
BR pɑːt, -s, -ɪŋ, -ɪd
AM pɑr|t, -ts, -dɪŋ, -dəd

partakable
BR pɑː'teɪkəbl
AM pɑr'teɪkəbəl

partake
BR pɑː'teɪk, -s, -ɪŋ
AM pɑr'teɪk, -s, -ɪŋ

partaken
BR pɑː'teɪk(ə)n
AM pɑr'teɪkən

partaker
BR pɑː'teɪkə(r), -z
AM pɑr'teɪkər, -z

partan
BR 'pɑːt(ə)n, -z
AM 'pɑrdn, -z

parterre
BR pɑː'tɛː(r), -z
AM pɑr'tɛ(ə)r, -z

part-exchange
BR ˌpɑːtɪks'tʃeɪn(d)ʒ, ˌpɑːtɛks'tʃeɪn(d)ʒ, -ɪz, -ɪŋ, -d
AM ˌpɑrdɪks'tʃeɪndʒ, ˌpɑrdɛks'tʃeɪndʒ, -ɪz, -ɪŋ, -d

parthenogenesis
BR ˌpɑːθɪnə(ʊ)'dʒɛnɪsɪs
AM ˌpɑrθənoʊ'dʒɛnəsəs

parthenogenetic
BR ˌpɑːθɪnə(ʊ)dʒɪ'nɛtɪk, ˌpɑːθn̩ə(ʊ)dʒɪ'nɛtɪk
AM ˌpɑrθənoʊdʒə'nɛdɪk

parthenogenetically
BR ˌpɑːθɪnə(ʊ)dʒɪ'nɛtɪkli
AM ˌpɑrθənoʊdʒə'nɛdək(ə)li

Parthenon
BR 'pɑːθɪnən, 'pɑːθn̩ən, 'pɑːθɪnɒn, 'pɑːθn̩ɒn
AM 'pɑrθəˌnɑn

Parthia
BR 'pɑːθɪə(r)
AM 'pɑrθiə

Parthian
BR 'pɑːθɪən, -z
AM 'pɑrθiən, -z

parti
BR 'pɑːt|i, -ɪz
AM 'pɑrdi, -z

partial
BR 'pɑːʃl
AM 'pɑrʃəl

partiality
BR ˌpɑːʃɪ'alɪti
AM ˌpɑrʃi'ælədi

partially
BR 'pɑːʃl̩i, 'pɑːʃəli
AM 'pɑrʃəli

partialness
BR 'pɑːʃlnəs
AM 'pɑrʃəlnəs

partible
BR 'pɑːtɪbl
AM 'pɑrdəbəl

participant
BR pɑː'tɪsɪp(ə)nt, -s
AM pɑr'tɪsɪpənt, -s

participate
BR pɑː'tɪsɪpeɪt, -s, -ɪŋ, -ɪd
AM pɑr'tɪsɪˌpeɪ|t, -ts, -dɪŋ, -dɪd

participation
BR pɑːˌtɪsɪ'peɪʃn, ˌpɑːtɪsɪ'peɪʃn
AM pɑrˌtɪsɪ'peɪʃən

participative
BR pɑː'tɪsɪpətɪv
AM pɑr'tɪsɪˌpeɪdɪv, pɑr'tɪsɪpədɪv

participator
BR pɑː'tɪsɪpeɪtə(r), -z
AM pɑr'tɪsɪˌpeɪdər, -z

participatory
BR pɑːˌtɪsɪ'peɪt(ə)ri, ˌpɑːtɪsɪ'peɪt(ə)ri, pɑː'tɪsɪpət(ə)ri
AM pɑr'tɪsəpəˌtɔri

participial
BR ˌpɑːtɪ'sɪpɪəl
AM ˌpɑrdə'sɪpiəl

participially
BR ˌpɑːtɪ'sɪpɪəli
AM ˌpɑrdə'sɪpiəli

participle
BR 'pɑːtɪsɪpl, pɑː'tɪsɪpl, pə'tɪsɪpl, -z
AM 'pɑrdəˌsɪpəl, -z

Partick
BR 'pɑːtɪk
AM 'pɑrdək

particle
BR 'pɑːtɪkl, -z
AM 'pɑrdəkəl, -z

particolored
BR ˌpɑːtɪ'kʌləd
AM 'pɑrdiˌkələrd

particoloured
BR ˌpɑːtɪ'kʌləd
AM 'pɑrdiˌkələrd

particular
BR pə'tɪkjʉlə(r), -z
AM pə(r)'tɪkjələr, pɑr'tɪkjələr, -z

particularisation
BR pəˌtɪkjʉlərʌɪ'zeɪʃn
AM pə(r)ˌtɪkjələrə'zeɪʃən, pə(r)ˌtɪkjələˌraɪ'zeɪʃən

particularise
BR pə'tɪkjʉlərʌɪz, -ɪz, -ɪŋ, -d
AM pə(r)'tɪkjələˌraɪz, pɑr'tɪkjələˌraɪz, -ɪz, -ɪŋ, -d

particularism
BR pə'tɪkjʉlərɪz(ə)m
AM pə(r)'tɪkjələˌrɪzəm

particularist
BR pə'tɪkjʉlərɪst, -s
AM pə(r)'tɪkjələrəst, -s

particularity
BR pəˌtɪkjʉ'larɪti
AM pə(r)ˌtɪkjə'lɛrədi, pɑrˌtɪkjə'lɛrədi

particularization
BR pəˌtɪkjʉlərʌɪ'zeɪʃn
AM pə(r)ˌtɪkjələrə'zeɪʃən, pə(r)ˌtɪkjələˌraɪ'zeɪʃən

particularize
BR pə'tɪkjʉlərʌɪz, -ɪz, -ɪŋ, -d
AM pə(r)'tɪkjələˌraɪz, pɑr'tɪkjələˌraɪz, -ɪz, -ɪŋ, -d

particularly
BR pə'tɪkjʉləli
AM pə(r)'tɪkjələrli, pɑr'tɪkjələrli

particulate
BR pɑː'tɪkjʉleɪt, pɑː'tɪkjʉlət, pə'tɪkjʉleɪt, pə'tɪkjʉlət, -s
AM pə(r)'tɪkjələt, pə(r)'tɪkjəˌleɪt, pɑr'tɪkjələt, pɑr'tɪkjəˌleɪt, -s

parting
BR 'pɑːtɪŋ, -z
AM 'pɑrdɪŋ, -z

Partington
BR 'pɑːtɪŋt(ə)n
AM 'pɑrdɪŋtən

parti pris
BR ˌpɑːtɪ 'priː, -z
AM ˌpɑrdi 'pri, -z

partisan
BR ˌpɑːtɪ'zan, 'pɑːtɪz(ə)n, -z
AM 'pɑrdəzn, 'pɑrdəˌzæn, -z

partisanship
BR ˌpɑːtɪ'zanʃɪp, 'pɑːtɪz(ə)nʃɪp
AM 'pɑrdəzənˌʃɪp

partita
BR pɑː'tiːtə(r)
AM pɑr'tidə

partite
BR 'pɑːtʌɪt
AM 'pɑrˌtaɪt

partition
BR pɑː'tɪʃn, pə'tɪʃn, -z
AM pɑr'tɪʃən, -z

partitioner
BR pɑː'tɪʃn̩ə(r), pə'tɪʃn̩ə(r), -z
AM pɑr'tɪʃənər, -z

partitionist
BR pɑː'tɪʃn̩ɪst, pə'tɪʃn̩ɪst, -s
AM pɑr'tɪʃənəst, -s

partitive
BR 'pɑːtɪtɪv
AM 'pɑrdədɪv

partitively
BR 'pɑːtɪtɪvli
AM 'pɑrdədɪvli

partizan
BR ˌpɑːtɪ'zan, 'pɑːtɪz(ə)n, -z
AM 'pɑrdəzən, 'pɑrdəˌzæn, -z

partly
BR 'pɑːtli
AM 'pɑrtli

partner
BR 'pɑːtnə(r), -z
AM 'pɑrtnər, -z

partnerless
BR 'pɑːtnələs
AM 'pɑrtnərləs

partnership
BR 'pɑːtnəʃɪp, -s
AM 'pɑrtnərˌʃɪp, -s

Parton
BR 'pɑːtn
AM 'pɑrtn

partook
BR pɑː'tʊk
AM pɑr'tʊk

partridge
BR 'pɑːtr|ɪdʒ, -ɪdʒɪz
AM 'pɑrtrɪdʒ, -ɪz

part-singing
BR 'pɑːtˌsɪŋɪŋ
AM 'pɑrtˌsɪŋɪŋ

part-song
BR 'pɑːtsɒŋ, -z
AM 'pɑrtˌsɔŋ, 'pɑrtˌsɑŋ, -z

part-time
BR ˌpɑːt'tʌɪm
AM ˌpɑr(t)ˌtaɪm

part-timer
BR ˌpɑːt'tʌɪmə(r), -z
AM ˌpɑr(t)ˌtaɪmər, -z

parturient
BR pɑː'tjʊərɪənt
AM pɑr't(j)ʊriənt

parturition
BR ˌpɑːtjʉ'rɪʃn, ˌpɑːtʃʉ'rɪʃn
AM ˌpɑrdə'rɪʃən, ˌpɑrˌtʊ'rɪʃən, ˌpɑrtʃə'rɪʃən, ˌpɑrtjə'rɪʃən

part-way
BR ˌpɑːtˈweɪ
AM ˈpɑrtˌweɪ

part-work
BR ˈpɑːtwəːk
AM ˈpɑrtˌwərk

party
BR ˈpɑːt|i, -ɪz
AM ˈpɑrdi, -z

party line¹
in politics
BR ˌpɑːtɪ ˈlʌɪn, -z
AM ˈpɑrdi ˈlaɪn, -z

party line²
telephone
BR ˈpɑːtɪ lʌɪn, -z
AM ˈpɑrdi ˌlaɪn, -z

party-pooper
BR ˈpɑːtɪˌpuːpə(r), -z
AM ˈpɑrdiˌpupər, -z

parvenu
BR ˈpɑːvən(j)uː, -z
AM ˈpɑrvəˌn(j)u, -z

parvenue
BR ˈpɑːvən(j)uː, -z
AM ˈpɑrvəˌn(j)u, -z

parvis
BR ˈpɑːvɪs, -ɪz
AM ˈpɑrvəs, -əz

parvise
BR ˈpɑːvɪs, -ɪz
AM ˈpɑrvəs, -əz

parvovirus
BR ˈpɑːvəʊˌvʌɪrəs, -ɪz
AM ˈpɑrvəˌvaɪrəs, -əz

pas
BR pɑː(r)
AM pɑ

Pasadena
BR ˌpasəˈdiːnə(r)
AM ˌpæsəˈdinə

Pascal
BR paˈskɑːl, ˈpaskɑːl, paˈskal, ˈpaskal
AM pəˈskæl, pæsˈkæl

pascal
BR paˈskɑːl, ˈpaskɑːl, paˈskal, ˈpaskal, -z
AM pəˈskæl, pæsˈkæl, -z

Pascale
BR paˈskɑːl
AM pæˈskæl

paschal
BR ˈpask(ə)l
AM ˈpæskəl, ˈpæʃəl

Pasco
BR ˈpaskəʊ
AM ˈpæskoʊ

Pascoe
BR ˈpaskəʊ
AM ˈpæskoʊ

pas de chat
BR ˌpɑː də ˈʃɑː(r)
AM ˌpɑ də ˈʃɑ

pas de deux
BR ˌpɑː də ˈdəː(r), -z
AM ˌpɑdəˈdə, -z

paseo
BR pəˈseɪəʊ, -z
AM pəˈseɪoʊ, -z

pas glissé
BR ˌpɑː glɪˈseɪ
AM ˌpɑ gliˈseɪ

pash
BR paʃ, -ɪz
AM pæʃ, -əz

pasha
BR ˈpaʃə(r), -z
AM ˈpɑʃə, ˈpæʃə, -z

pashalic
BR ˈpɑːʃəlɪk, pəˈʃɑːlɪk, -s
AM pəˈʃælɪk, -s

pashm
BR ˈpaʃ(ə)m
AM ˈpæʃəm

Pashto
BR ˈpʌʃtəʊ, ˈpaʃtəʊ
AM ˈpæʃˌtoʊ

Pasiphaë
BR pəˈsɪfɪiː, pəˈsɪfeɪiː
AM pəˈsɪfəˌi

Pasmore
BR ˈpɑːsmɔː(r), ˈpasmɔː(r)
AM ˈpæsˌmɔ(ə)r

paso doble
BR ˌpasə ˈdəʊbleɪ, -z
AM ˌpæsoʊ ˈdoʊbleɪ, -z

paspalum
BR ˈpaspələm
AM ˈpæspələm

pasque flower
BR ˈpask ˌflaʊə(r), -z
AM ˈpæsk ˌflaʊər, -z

pasquinade
BR ˌpaskwɪˈneɪd, -z
AM ˌpæskwəˈneɪd, -z

pass
BR pɑːs, pas, -ɪz, -ɪŋ, -t
AM pæs, -əz, -ɪŋ, -t

passable
BR ˈpɑːsəbl, ˈpasəbl
AM ˈpæsəbəl

passableness
BR ˈpɑːsəblnəs, ˈpasəblnəs
AM ˈpæsəbəlnəs

passably
BR ˈpɑːsəbli, ˈpasəbli
AM ˈpæsəbli

passacaglia
BR ˌpasəˈkɑːlɪə(r), -z
AM ˌpɑsəˈkɑljə, ˌpɑsəˈkɑliə, -z

passade
BR pəˈseɪd, paˈseɪd
AM pəˈseɪd

passage
BR ˈpas|ɪdʒ, -ɪdʒɪz
AM ˈpæsɪdʒ, -ɪz

passageway
BR ˈpasɪdʒweɪ, -z
AM ˈpæsədʒˌweɪ, -z

Passamaquoddy
BR ˌpasəməˈkwɒdi
AM ˌpæsəməˈkwɑdi

passant¹
chess
BR ˈpasɒ̃t
AM pəˈsɑnt

passant²
heraldry
BR ˈpas(ə)nt
AM ˈpæsnt

Passat®
BR paˈsat
AM pəˈsɑt

passata
BR pəˈsɑːtə(r)
AM pəˈsɑdə

passband
BR ˈpɑːsband, ˈpasband, -z
AM ˈpæsˌbænd, -z

passbook
BR ˈpɑːsbʊk, ˈpasbʊk, -s
AM ˈpæsˌbʊk, -s

Passchendaele
BR ˈpaʃndeɪl
AM ˈpæʃənˌdeɪl
FL ˈpɑsxəndɑːlə

passé
BR ˈpɑːseɪ, ˈpaseɪ, paˈseɪ
AM pæˈseɪ

passée
BR ˈpɑːseɪ, ˈpaseɪ, paˈseɪ
AM pæˈseɪ

passel
BR ˈpasl, -z
AM ˈpæsəl, -z

passementerie
BR ˈpasm(ə)ntri
AM ˌpɑsəˌmənˈtri

passenger
BR ˈpas(ɪ)n(d)ʒə(r), -z
AM ˈpæsndʒər, -z

passe-partout
BR ˈpas pɑːtuː, ˈpas pətuː, ˌpas pɑːˈtuː, ˌpas pəˈtuː, -z
AM ˌpæs pərˈtu, ˌpɑs pɑrˈtu, -z

passer
BR ˈpɑːsə(r), ˈpasə(r), -z
AM ˈpæsər, -z

passer-by
BR ˌpɑːsəˈbʌɪ, ˌpasəˈbʌɪ
AM ˈpæsərˈbaɪ

passerine
BR ˈpasərʌɪn
AM ˈpæsərən, ˈpæsəˌraɪn, ˈpæsəˌrin

passers-by
BR ˌpɑːsəzˈbʌɪ, ˌpasəzˈbʌɪ
AM ˈpæsərzˈbaɪ

pas seul
BR ˌpɑː ˈsəːl, -z
AM ˌpɑ ˈsəl, -z

passibility
BR ˌpasɪˈbɪlɪti
AM ˌpæsəˈbɪlɪdi

passible
BR ˈpasɪbl
AM ˈpæsəbəl

passim
BR ˈpasɪm
AM ˈpæsəm, ˈpæsˌɪm

passing
BR ˈpɑːsɪŋ, ˈpasɪŋ, -z
AM ˈpæsɪŋ, -z

passingly
BR ˈpɑːsɪŋli, ˈpasɪŋli
AM ˈpæsɪŋli

passing-out
BR ˌpɑːsɪŋˈaʊt, ˌpasɪŋˈaʊt
AM ˈpæsɪŋˈaʊt

passion
BR ˈpaʃn, -z
AM ˈpæʃən, -z

passional
BR ˈpaʃn̩(ə)l, ˈpaʃən(ə)l, -z
AM ˈpæʃ(ə)nəl, -z

passionate
BR ˈpaʃn̩ət, ˈpaʃənət
AM ˈpæʃ(ə)nət

passionately
BR ˈpaʃn̩ətli, ˈpaʃənətli
AM ˈpæʃ(ə)nətli

passionateness
BR ˈpaʃn̩ətnəs, ˈpaʃənətnəs
AM ˈpæʃ(ə)nətnəs

passionflower
BR ˈpaʃnˌflaʊə(r), -z
AM ˈpæʃənˌflaʊ(ə)r, -z

passionfruit
BR ˈpaʃnfruːt, -s
AM ˈpæʃənˌfrut, -s

Passionist
BR ˈpaʃn̩ɪst, ˈpaʃənɪst, -s
AM ˈpæʃənəst, -s

passionless
BR ˈpaʃnləs
AM ˈpæʃənləs

Passiontide
BR ˈpaʃntʌɪd
AM ˈpæʃənˌtaɪd

passivate
BR ˈpasɪveɪt, -s, -ɪŋ, -ɪd
AM ˈpæsəˌveɪ|t, -ts, -dɪŋ, -dɪd

passivation
BR ˌpasɪˈveɪʃn
AM ˌpæsəˈveɪʃən

passive
BR ˈpasɪv
AM ˈpæsɪv

passively
BR ˈpasɨvli
AM ˈpæsɨvli

passiveness
BR ˈpasɨvnɨs
AM ˈpæsɪvnɨs

passivity
BR pəˈsɪvɨti
AM pæˈsɪvɨdi,
pəˈsɪvɨdi

passkey
BR ˈpɑːskiː, ˈpaskiː, -z
AM ˈpæsˌki, -z

Passover
BR ˈpɑːsˌəʊvə(r),
ˈpasˌəʊvə(r)
AM ˈpæsˌoʊvər

passport
BR ˈpɑːspɔːt, ˈpaspɔːt,
-s
AM ˈpæsˌpɔ(ə)rt, -s

password
BR ˈpɑːswəːd,
ˈpaswəːd, -z
AM ˈpæsˌwərd, -z

past
BR pɑːst, past
AM pæst

pasta
BR ˈpastə(*r*)
AM ˈpɑstə

paste
BR peɪst, -s, -ɪŋ, -ɨd
AM peɪst, -s, -ɪŋ, -ɨd

pasteboard
BR ˈpeɪs(t)bɔːd
AM ˈpeɪs(t)ˌbɔ(ə)rd

pastedown
BR ˈpeɪs(t)daʊn
AM ˈpeɪs(t)ˌdaʊn

pastel
BR ˈpastl
AM pæˈstɛl

pastelist
BR ˈpastəlɪst, ˈpastl̩ɪst,
-s
AM pæˈstɛləst, -s

pastellist
BR ˈpastəlɪst, ˈpastl̩ɪst,
-s
AM pæˈstɛləst, -s

pastern
BR ˈpastn, ˈpastəːn, -z
AM ˈpæstərn, -z

Pasternak
BR ˈpastənak
AM ˈpæstərˌnæk

Pasteur
BR paˈstəː(r)
AM pæsˈtər

pasteurisation
BR ˌpɑːst(ʃ)ərʌɪˈzeɪʃn,
ˌpast(ʃ)ərʌɪˈzeɪʃn,
ˌpɑːstjərʌɪˈzeɪʃn,
ˌpastjərʌɪˈzeɪʃn
AM ˌpæstʃərəˈzeɪʃən,
ˌpæstərəˈzeɪʃən,
ˌpæstʃəˌraɪˈzeɪʃən,
ˌpæstəˌraɪˈzeɪʃən

pasteurise
BR ˈpɑːst(ʃ)ərʌɪz,
ˈpast(ʃ)ərʌɪz,
ˈpɑːstjərʌɪz,
ˈpastjərʌɪz, -ɨz, -ɪŋ, -d
AM ˈpæstʃəˌraɪz,
ˈpæʃtʃəˌraɪz,
ˈpæstəˌraɪz, -ɨz, -ɪŋ, -d

pasteuriser
BR ˈpɑːst(ʃ)ərʌɪzə(r),
ˈpast(ʃ)ərʌɪzə(r),
ˈpɑːstjərʌɪzə(r),
ˈpastjərʌɪzə(r), -z
AM ˈpæstʃəˌraɪzər,
ˈpæʃtʃəˌraɪzər,
ˈpæstəˌraɪzər, -z

pasteurization
BR ˌpɑːst(ʃ)ərʌɪˈzeɪʃn,
ˌpast(ʃ)ərʌɪˈzeɪʃn,
ˌpɑːstjərʌɪˈzeɪʃn,
ˌpastjərʌɪˈzeɪʃn
AM ˌpæstʃərəˈzeɪʃən,
ˌpæstərəˈzeɪʃən,
ˌpæstʃəˌraɪˈzeɪʃən,
ˌpæstəˌraɪˈzeɪʃən

pasteurize
BR ˈpɑːst(ʃ)ərʌɪz,
ˈpast(ʃ)ərʌɪz,
ˈpɑːstjərʌɪz,
ˈpastjərʌɪz, -ɨz, -ɪŋ, -d
AM ˈpæstʃəˌraɪz,
ˈpæʃtʃəˌraɪz,
ˈpæstəˌraɪz, -ɨz, -ɪŋ, -d

pasteurizer
BR ˈpɑːst(ʃ)ərʌɪzə(r),
ˈpast(ʃ)ərʌɪzə(r),
ˈpɑːstjərʌɪzə(r),
ˈpastjərʌɪzə(r), -z
AM ˈpæstʃəˌraɪzər,
ˈpæʃtʃəˌraɪzər,
ˈpæstəˌraɪzər, -z

pasticcio
BR paˈstiːtʃəʊ, -z
AM pɑˈsti(t)ʃ(i)oʊ, -z

pastiche
BR paˈstiːʃ, -ɨz
AM pæˈstiʃ, pɑˈstiʃ, -ɨz

pastie
BR ˈpeɪsti, -ɪz
AM ˈpeɪsti, -ɪz

pastil
BR ˈpast(ɪ)l, -z
AM ˈpæstəl, -z

pastile
BR ˈpast(ɪ)l, -z
AM ˈpæstəl, -z

pastille
BR ˈpast(ɪ)l, -z
AM pæˈstil, -z

pastily
BR ˈpeɪstɨli
AM ˈpeɪstɨli

pastime
BR ˈpɑːstʌɪm,
ˈpastʌɪm, -z
AM ˈpæsˌtaɪm, -z

pastiness
BR ˈpeɪstɪnɨs
AM ˈpeɪstinɨs

pasting
BR ˈpeɪstɪŋ, -z
AM ˈpeɪstɪŋ, -z

pastis
BR ˈpastɪs, paˈstiːs
AM pɑˈstis

pastmaster
BR ˈpɑːs(t)ˌmɑːstə(r),
ˈpas(t)ˌmastə(r), -z
AM ˌpæstˌmæstər, -z

Paston[1]
BR ˈpast(ə)n
AM ˈpæstən

Paston[2]
BR ˈpast(ə)n
AM ˈpæstən

pastor
BR ˈpɑːstə(r),
ˈpastə(r), -z
AM ˈpæstər, -z

pastoral
BR ˈpɑːst(ə)rəl,
ˈpɑːst(ə)rl,
ˈpast(ə)rəl, ˈpast(ə)rl̩,
-z
AM ˈpæstərəl,
pæsˈtɔrəl, -z

pastorale
BR ˌpastəˈrɑːl,
ˌpastəˈrɑːli, -lz\-lɪz
AM ˌpæstəˈrɑl,
ˌpæstəˈræl, -z

pastoralism
BR ˈpɑːst(ə)rəlɪz(ə)m,
ˈpast(ə)rəlɪz(ə)m
AM ˈpæst(ə)rəˌlɪzəm

pastoralist
BR ˈpɑːst(ə)rəlɪst,
ˈpast(ə)rəlɪst, -s
AM ˈpæst(ə)rələst, -s

pastorality
BR ˌpastəˈralɨti
AM ˌpæstəˈrælədi

pastorally
BR ˈpɑːst(ə)rəli,
ˈpɑːst(ə)rl̩i,
ˈpast(ə)rəli,
ˈpast(ə)rl̩i
AM ˈpæstərəli,
pæsˈtɔrəli

pastorate
BR ˈpɑːst(ə)rət,
ˈpast(ə)rət, -s
AM ˈpæst(ə)rət, -s

pastorship
BR ˈpɑːstəʃɪp,
ˈpastəʃɪp, -s
AM ˈpæstərˌʃɪp, -s

pastrami
BR pəˈstrɑːmi
AM pəˈstrɑmi

pastry
BR ˈpeɪstr|i, -ɪz
AM ˈpeɪstri, -z

pastrycook
BR ˈpeɪstrɪkʊk, -s
AM ˈpeɪstriˌkʊk, -s

pasturage
BR ˈpɑːstʃ(ə)rɪdʒ,
ˈpastʃ(ə)rɪdʒ,
ˈpɑːstjʊrɪdʒ,
ˈpastjʊrɪdʒ
AM ˈpæstʃərədʒ,
ˈpæʃtʃərədʒ

pasture
BR ˈpɑːstʃə(r),
ˈpastʃə(r), -z, -ɪŋ, -d
AM ˈpæstʃər, ˈpæʃtʃər,
-z, -ɪŋ, -d

pastureland
BR ˈpɑːstʃəland,
ˈpastʃəland, -z
AM ˈpæstʃərˌlænd,
ˈpæʃtʃərˌlænd, -z

pasty[1]
adjective
BR ˈpeɪst|i, -ɪə(r), -ɪɪst
AM ˈpeɪsti, -ər, -ɨst

pasty[2]
noun
BR ˈpast|i, -ɪz
AM ˈpæsti, -z

pat
BR pat, -s, -ɪŋ, -ɨd
AM pæ|t, -ts, -dɪŋ, -dəd

pat-a-cake
BR ˈpatəkeɪk
AM ˈpædəˌkeɪk

patagia
BR ˌpatəˈdʒʌɪə(*r*)
AM pəˈteɪdʒiə

patagium
BR ˌpatəˈdʒʌɪəm
AM pəˈteɪdʒiəm

Patagonia
BR ˌpatəˈgəʊnɪə(*r*)
AM ˌpædəˈgoʊniə

Patagonian
BR ˌpatəˈgəʊnɪən, -z
AM ˌpædəˈgoʊniən, -z

Patavinity
BR ˌpatəˈvɪnɨti
AM ˌpædəˈvɪnɨdi

patball
BR ˈpatbɔːl
AM ˈpætˌbɔl, ˈpætˌbɑl

patch
BR patʃ, -ɨz, -ɪŋ, -t
AM pætʃ, -əz, -ɪŋ, -t

patchboard
BR ˈpatʃbɔːd, -z
AM ˈpætʃˌbɔ(ə)rd, -z

patcher
BR ˈpatʃə(r), -z
AM ˈpætʃər, -z

patchily
BR ˈpatʃɨli
AM ˈpætʃɨli

patchiness
BR ˈpatʃɪnɨs
AM ˈpætʃinɨs

patchouli
BR 'patʃʊli, pə'tʃuːli
AM pə'tʃuli

patchwork
BR 'patʃwəːk, -s
AM 'pætʃˌwərk, -s

patchy
BR 'patʃ|i, -ɪə(r), -ɪɪst
AM 'pætʃi, -ər, -ɪst

Pate
BR peɪt
AM peɪt

pate
top of head
BR peɪt, -s
AM peɪt, -s

paté
of a cross
BR 'pateɪ, 'pati
AM pə'teɪ

pâte
BR pɑːt, -s
AM pɑt, -s

pâté
meat spread
BR 'pateɪ, -z
AM pɑ'teɪ, pæ'teɪ, -z

pâté de foie gras
BR ˌpateɪ də ˌfwɑː 'grɑː(r)
AM ˈpɑteɪ də ˌfwɑ 'grɑ

patée
of a cross
BR 'pateɪ, 'pati
AM pə'teɪ

Patel
BR pə'tɛl
AM pə'tɛl

Pateley
BR 'peɪtli
AM 'peɪtli

patella
BR pə'tɛlə(r), -z
AM pə'tɛlə, -z

patellae
BR pə'tɛliː
AM pə'tɛˌli, pə'tɛˌlaɪ

patellar
BR pə'tɛlə(r)
AM pə'tɛlər

patellate
BR pə'tɛlət
AM pə'tɛlət, pə'tɛˌleɪt

paten
BR 'patn, -z
AM 'pætn, -z

patency
BR 'peɪtnsi
AM 'pætnsi, 'peɪtnsi

patent[1]
adjective, open
BR 'peɪtnt
AM 'peɪtnt

patent[2]
inventions, legal etc
BR 'patnt, 'peɪtnt, -s, -ɪŋ, -ɪd
AM 'pætnt, -s, -ɪŋ, -əd

patent[3]
leather
BR 'peɪtnt
AM 'pætnt

patentable
BR 'patntəbl, 'peɪtntəbl
AM 'pætntəbəl, 'pætn̩əbəl

patentee
BR ˌpatn'tiː, ˌpeɪtn'tiː, -z
AM ˌpætn'ti, -z

patently
BR 'peɪtntli
AM 'pætn(t)li, 'peɪtn(t)li

patentor
BR 'patntə(r), 'peɪtntə(r), -z
AM 'pætntər, 'pætn̩ər, -z

Pater
BR 'peɪtə(r)
AM 'peɪdər

pater
BR 'peɪtə(r), -z
AM 'peɪdər, 'pɑdər, -z

paterfamilias
BR ˌpeɪtəfə'mɪlɪas, ˌpatəfə'mɪlɪas, -ɪz
AM ˌpædərfə'mɪliəs, ˌpɑdərfə'mɪliəs, -əz

paternal
BR pə'təːnl
AM pə'tərnəl

paternalism
BR pə'təːnəlɪz(ə)m, pə'təːnl̩ɪz(ə)m
AM pə'tərnlˌɪzəm

paternalist
BR pə'təːnəlɪst, pə'təːnl̩ɪst, -s
AM pə'tərnl̩əst, -s

paternalistic
BR pəˌtəːnə'lɪstɪk, pəˌtəːnl'ɪstɪk
AM pəˌtərnl'ɪstɪk

paternalistically
BR pəˌtəːnə'lɪstɪkli, pəˌtəːnl'ɪstɪkli
AM pəˌtərnl'ɪstək(ə)li

paternally
BR pə'təːnəli, pə'təːnl̩i
AM pə'tərnəli

paternity
BR pə'təːnɪti
AM pə'tərnədi

paternoster
BR ˌpatə'nɒstə(r), -z
AM 'pædərˌnɑstər, 'pɑdərˌnɑstər, -z

Paterson
BR 'patəs(ə)n
AM 'pædərsən

path
BR pɑːθ, paθ, pɑːðz\paðz\paθs
AM pæ|θ, -ðz\-θs

Pathan
BR pə'tɑːn, -z
AM pə'tɑn, -z

Pathé
BR 'paθeɪ
AM pɑ'teɪ

pathetic
BR pə'θɛtɪk
AM pə'θɛdɪk

pathetically
BR pə'θɛtɪkli
AM pə'θɛdək(ə)li

pathfinder
BR 'pɑːθˌfʌɪndə(r), 'paθˌfʌɪndə(r), -z
AM 'pæθˌfaɪndər, -z

pathic
BR 'paθɪk, -s
AM 'pæθɪk, -s

pathless
BR 'pɑːθləs, 'paθləs
AM 'pæθləs

pathogen
BR 'paθədʒɛn, 'paθədʒ(ə)n
AM 'pæθəˌdʒɛn, 'pæθədʒən

pathogenesis
BR ˌpaθə'dʒɛnɪsɪs
AM ˌpæθə'dʒɛnəsəs

pathogenetic
BR ˌpaθədʒɪ'nɛtɪk
AM ˈpæθədʒə'nɛdɪk

pathogenic
BR ˌpaθə'dʒɛnɪk
AM ˈpæθə'dʒɛnɪk

pathogenous
BR pə'θɒdʒɪnəs
AM pə'θɑdʒɛnəs

pathogeny
BR pə'θɒdʒɪni
AM 'pə'θɑdʒəni

pathognomonic
BR ˌpaθəgnə'mɒnɪk, -s
AM pəˌθɑgnə'mɑnɪk, ˌpæθəgnə'mɑnɪk, -s

pathognomy
BR pə'θɒgnəmi
AM pə'θɑgnəmi

pathologic
BR ˌpaθə'lɒdʒɪk
AM ˈpæθə'lɑdʒɪk

pathological
BR ˌpaθə'lɒdʒɪkl
AM ˈpæθə'lɑdʒəkəl

pathologically
BR ˌpaθə'lɒdʒɪkli
AM ˈpæθə'lɑdʒək(ə)li

pathologist
BR pə'θɒlədʒɪst, -s
AM pə'θɑlədʒəst, -s

pathology
BR pə'θɒlədʒi
AM pə'θɑlədʒi

pathos
BR 'peɪθɒs
AM 'peɪˌθɔs, 'peɪˌθɑs, 'pæˌθɑs, 'pæˌθɔs

pathway
BR 'pɑːθweɪ, 'paθweɪ, -z
AM 'pæθˌweɪ, -z

patience
BR 'peɪʃns
AM 'peɪʃəns

patient
BR 'peɪʃnt
AM 'peɪʃənt

patiently
BR 'peɪʃntli
AM 'peɪʃən(t)li

patina
BR 'patɪnə(r), pə'tiːnə(r), -z
AM pə'tinə, -z

patinaed
BR 'patɪnəd, pə'tiːnəd
AM pə'tinəd

patinated
BR 'patɪneɪtɪd
AM 'pædəˌneɪdɪd, 'pætnˌeɪdɪd

patination
BR ˌpatɪ'neɪʃn
AM ˌpædə'neɪʃən, ˌpætn'eɪʃən

patinous
BR 'patɪnəs
AM 'pædənəs, 'pætn̩əs

patio
BR 'patɪəʊ, -z
AM 'pædioʊ, -z

pâtisserie
BR pə'tɪs(ə)r|i, -ɪz
AM pə'tɪsəri, -z

patly
BR 'patli
AM 'pætli

Patmore
BR 'patmɔː(r)
AM 'pætˌmɔ(ə)r

Pátmos
BR 'patmɒs
AM 'pætˌmɔs, 'pætˌmɑs

Patna
BR 'patnə(r)
AM 'pætnə

patness
BR 'patnəs
AM 'pætnəs

patois[1]
singular
BR 'patwɑː(r)
AM 'pæˌtwɑ, 'pɑˌtwɑ

patois[2]
plural
BR 'patwɑːz
AM 'pæˌtwɑz, 'pɑˌtwɑz

Paton
BR 'peɪtn
AM 'peɪtn

patrial
BR 'peɪtrɪəl, 'patrɪəl, -z
AM 'peɪtriəl, -z

patriality
BR ˌpeɪtrɪ'alɪti, ˌpatrɪ'alɪti
AM ˌpeɪtri'ælədi

patriarch
BR 'peɪtrɪɑːk, 'patrɪɑːk, -s
AM 'peɪtriˌɑrk, -s

patriarchal
BR ˌpeɪtrɪ'ɑːkl, ˌpatrɪ'ɑːkl
AM ˌpeɪtri'ɑrkəl

patriarchally
BR ˌpeɪtrɪ'ɑːkl̩i, ˌpeɪtrɪ'ɑːkəli, ˌpatrɪ'ɑːkl̩i, ˌpatrɪ'ɑːkəli
AM ˌpeɪtri'ɑrkəli

patriarchate
BR 'peɪtrɪɑːkət, 'patrɪɑːkət, -s
AM ˌpeɪtri'ɑrkət, ˌpeɪtri'ɑrˌkeɪt, -s

patriarchism
BR 'peɪtrɪɑːkɪz(ə)m, 'patrɪɑːkɪz(ə)m
AM 'peɪtriˌɑrˌkɪzəm

patriarchy
BR 'peɪtrɪɑːk|i, 'patrɪɑːk|i, -ɪz
AM 'peɪtriˌɑrki, -z

Patrice
BR pa'triːs, pə'triːs
AM pə'tris

Patricia
BR pə'trɪʃə(r)
AM pə'trɪʃə

patrician
BR pə'trɪʃn, -z
AM pə'trɪʃən, -z

patriciate
BR pə'trɪʃɪət, -s
AM pə'trɪʃ(i)ɪt, pə'trɪʃiˌeɪt, -s

patricidal
BR ˌpatrɪ'sʌɪdl
AM ˌpætrə'saɪdəl

patricide
BR 'patrɪsʌɪd, -z
AM 'pætrəˌsaɪd, -z

Patrick
BR 'patrɪk
AM 'pætrɪk

patrilineal
BR ˌpatrɪ'lɪnɪəl
AM ˌpætrə'lɪniəl, ˌpætrə'lɪnjəl

patrimonial
BR ˌpatrɪ'məʊnɪəl
AM ˌpætrə'moʊniəl, ˌpætrə'moʊnjəl

patrimonially
BR ˌpatrɪ'məʊnɪəli
AM ˌpætrə'moʊniəli, ˌpætrə'moʊnjəli

patrimony
BR 'patrɪmən|i, -ɪz
AM 'pætrəˌmoʊni, -z

patriot
BR 'patrɪət, 'peɪtrɪət, -s
AM 'peɪtriət, -s

patriotic
BR ˌpatrɪ'ɒtɪk, ˌpeɪtrɪ'ɒtɪk
AM ˌpeɪtri'ɑdɪk

patriotically
BR ˌpatrɪ'ɒtɪkli, ˌpeɪtrɪ'ɒtɪkli
AM ˌpeɪtri'ɑdək(ə)li

patriotism
BR 'patrɪətɪz(ə)m, 'peɪtrɪətɪz(ə)m
AM 'peɪtriəˌtɪzəm

patristic
BR pə'trɪstɪk, -s
AM pə'trɪstɪk, -s

Patroclus
BR pə'trɒkləs
AM pə'trɑkləs

patrol
BR pə'trəʊl, -z, -ɪŋ, -d
AM pə'troʊl, -z, -ɪŋ, -d

patroller
BR pə'trəʊlə(r), -z
AM pə'troʊlər, -z

patrolman
BR pə'trəʊlman, pə'trəʊlmən
AM pə'troʊlmən

patrolmen
BR pə'trəʊlmɛn, pə'trəʊlmən
AM pə'troʊlmən

patrological
BR ˌpatrə'lɒdʒɪkl
AM ˌpætrə'lɑdʒəkəl

patrologist
BR pə'trɒlədʒɪst, -s
AM pə'trɑlədʒəst, -s

patrology
BR pə'trɒlədʒi
AM pə'trɑlədʒi

patron
BR 'peɪtr(ə)n, -z
AM 'peɪtrən, -z

patronage
BR 'patrənɪdʒ, 'patrn̩ɪdʒ
AM 'pætrənədʒ, 'peɪtrənədʒ

patronal
BR pə'trəʊnl
AM 'peɪtrənəl

patroness
BR 'peɪtrənɪs, 'peɪtrn̩ɪs, ˌpeɪtrə'nɛs, -ɪz
AM 'peɪtrənəs, -əz

patronisation
BR ˌpatrənʌɪ'zeɪʃn
AM ˌpeɪtrənə'zeɪʃən, ˌpeɪtrəˌnaɪ'zeɪʃən, ˌpætrənə'zeɪʃən, ˌpætrəˌnaɪ'zeɪʃən

patronise
BR 'patrənʌɪz, -ɪz, -ɪŋ, -d
AM 'peɪtrəˌnaɪz, 'pætrəˌnaɪz, -ɪz, -ɪŋ, -d

patroniser
BR 'patrənʌɪzə(r), -z
AM 'peɪtrəˌnaɪzər, 'pætrəˌnaɪzər, -z

patronisingly
BR 'patrənʌɪzɪŋli
AM 'peɪtrəˌnaɪzɪŋli, 'pætrəˌnaɪzɪŋli

patronization
BR ˌpatrənʌɪ'zeɪʃn
AM ˌpeɪtrənə'zeɪʃən, ˌpeɪtrəˌnaɪ'zeɪʃən, ˌpætrənə'zeɪʃən, ˌpætrəˌnaɪ'zeɪʃən

patronize
BR 'patrənʌɪz, -ɪz, -ɪŋ, -d
AM 'peɪtrəˌnaɪz, 'pætrəˌnaɪz, -ɪz, -ɪŋ, -d

patronizer
BR 'patrənʌɪzə(r), -z
AM 'peɪtrəˌnaɪzər, 'pætrəˌnaɪzər, -z

patronizingly
BR 'patrənʌɪzɪŋli
AM 'peɪtrəˌnaɪzɪŋli, 'pætrəˌnaɪzɪŋli

patronymic
BR ˌpatrə'nɪmɪk, -s
AM ˌpætrə'nɪmɪk, -s

patronymically
BR ˌpatrə'nɪmɪkli
AM ˌpætrə'nɪmək(ə)li

patroon
BR pə'truːn, -z
AM pə'trun, -z

patsy
BR 'pats|i, -ɪz
AM 'pætsi, -z

pattée
of a cross
BR 'pateɪ, 'pati
AM pə'teɪ

patten
BR 'patn, -z
AM 'pætn, -z

patter
BR 'pat|ə(r), -əz, -(ə)rɪŋ, -əd
AM 'pædər, -z, -ɪŋ, -d

Patterdale
BR 'patədeɪl
AM 'pædərˌdeɪl

pattern
BR 'patn, -nz, -n̩ɪŋ\-ənɪŋ, -nd
AM 'pædərn, -z, -ɪŋ, -d

Patterson
BR 'patəs(ə)n
AM 'pædərsən

Patti
BR 'pati
AM 'pædi

Pattie
BR 'pati
AM 'pædi

Pattison
BR 'patɪs(ə)n
AM 'pædəsən

Patton
BR 'patn
AM 'pætn

patty
BR 'pat|i, -ɪz
AM 'pædi, -z

pattypan
BR 'patɪpan, -z
AM 'pædiˌpæn, -z

patulous
BR 'patjʊləs
AM 'pætʃələs

patulously
BR 'patjʊləsli
AM 'pætʃələsli

patulousness
BR 'patjʊləsnəs, 'patʃʊləsnəs
AM 'pætʃələsnəs

Patuxent
BR pə'tʌksnt
AM pə'təksənt

paua
BR 'paʊə(r), -z
AM 'paʊə, -z

paucity
BR 'pɔːsɪti
AM 'pɔsədi, 'pɑsədi

Paul
BR pɔːl
AM pɔl, pɑl

Paula
BR 'pɔːlə(r)
AM 'pɔlə, 'pɑlə

Paulette
BR pɔː'lɛt
AM pɔ'lɛt, pɑ'lɛt

Pauli
BR 'paʊli
AM 'paʊli

Pauline[1]
of St Paul
BR 'pɔːlʌɪn
AM 'pɔˌlaɪn, 'pɔˌlin, 'pɑˌlaɪn, 'pɑˌlin

Pauline[2]
forename
BR 'pɔːliːn
AM pɔ'lin, pɑ'lin

Pauling
BR 'pɔːlɪŋ
AM 'pɔlɪŋ, 'pɑlɪŋ

paulownia
BR pɔː'ləʊnɪə(r), -z
AM pɔ'loʊniə, pɑ'loʊniə, -z

paunch
BR pɔːn(t)ʃ, -ɪz, -ɪŋ, -t

AM pɔn(t)ʃ, pɑn(t)ʃ, -əz, -ɪŋ, -t
paunchiness
BR 'pɔːn(t)ʃɪnɨs
AM 'pɔntʃinɨs, 'pɑntʃinɨs
paunchy
BR 'pɔːn(t)ʃ|i, -ɪə(r), -ɪɪst
AM 'pɔntʃi, 'pɑntʃi, -ər, -əst
pauper
BR 'pɔːpə(r), -z
AM 'pɔpər, 'pɑpər, -z
pauperdom
BR 'pɔːpədəm
AM 'pɔpərdəm, 'pɑpərdəm
pauperisation
BR ˌpɔːp(ə)rʌɪ'zeɪʃn
AM ˌpɔpərə'zeɪʃən, ˌpɔpəˌraɪ'zeɪʃən, ˌpɑpərə'zeɪʃən, ˌpɑpəˌraɪ'zeɪʃən
pauperise
BR 'pɔːp(ə)rʌɪz, -ɨz, -ɪŋ, -d
AM 'pɔpəˌraɪz, 'pɑpəˌraɪz, -ɨz, -ɪŋ, -d
pauperism
BR 'pɔːp(ə)rɪz(ə)m
AM 'pɔpəˌrɪzəm, 'pɑpəˌrɪzəm
pauperization
BR ˌpɔːp(ə)rʌɪ'zeɪʃn
AM ˌpɔpərə'zeɪʃən, ˌpɔpəˌraɪ'zeɪʃən, ˌpɑpərə'zeɪʃən, ˌpɑpəˌraɪ'zeɪʃən
pauperize
BR 'pɔːp(ə)rʌɪz, -ɨz, -ɪŋ, -d
AM 'pɔpəˌraɪz, 'pɑpəˌraɪz, -ɨz, -ɪŋ, -d
paupiette
BR pɔː'pjɛt, -s
AM poʊ'piɛt, -z
Pausanias
BR pɔː'seɪnɪəs
AM pɔ'seɪniəs, pɑ'seɪniəs
pause
BR pɔːz, -ɨz, -ɪŋ, -d
AM pɔz, pɑz, -ɨz, -ɪŋ, -d
pavage
BR 'peɪvɪdʒ
AM 'peɪvɪdʒ
pavan
BR pə'van, pə'vɑːn, 'pavn, -z
AM pə'vɑn, -z
pavane
BR pə'van, pə'vɑːn, 'pavn, -z
AM pə'vɑn, -z
Pavarotti
BR ˌpavə'rɒti
AM ˌpɑvə'rɑdi, ˌpævə'rɑdi
pave
BR peɪv, -z, -ɪŋ, -d
AM peɪv, -z, -ɪŋ, -d
pavé
noun
BR 'paveɪ, -z
AM pə'veɪ, pæ'veɪ, -z
pavement
BR 'peɪvm(ə)nt, -s
AM 'peɪvmənt, -s
paver
BR 'peɪvə(r), -z
AM 'peɪvər, -z
Pavey
BR 'peɪvi
AM 'peɪvi
pavilion
BR pə'vɪlɪən, -z
AM pə'vɪljən, -z
paving
BR 'peɪvɪŋ, -z
AM 'peɪvɪŋ, -z
pavior
BR 'peɪvɪə(r), -z
AM 'peɪviər, -z
paviour
BR 'peɪvɪə(r), -z
AM 'peɪviər, -z
Pavlov
BR 'pavlɒv
AM 'pɑvˌlɔv, 'pɑvˌlɑv
Pavlova
BR pav'ləʊvə(*r*), 'pavləvə(*r*)
AM pɑv'loʊvə
Pavlovian
BR pav'ləʊvɪən
AM pɑv'loʊviən, pɑv'lɔviən, pɑv'lɑviən
pavonine
BR 'pavənʌɪn
AM 'pævəˌnaɪn
paw
BR pɔː(*r*), -z, -ɪŋ, -d
AM pɔ, pɑ, -z, -ɪŋ, -d
pawkily
BR 'pɔːkɨli
AM 'pɔkəli, 'pɑkəli
pawkiness
BR 'pɔːkɪnɨs
AM 'pɔkinɨs, 'pɑkinɨs
pawky
BR 'pɔːk|i, -ɪə(r), -ɪɪst
AM 'pɔki, 'pɑki, -ər, -ɨst
pawl
BR pɔːl, -z, -ɪŋ, -d
AM pɔl, pɑl, -z, -ɪŋ, -d
pawn
BR pɔːn, -z, -ɪŋ, -d
AM pɔn, pɑn, -z, -ɪŋ, -d
pawnbroker
BR 'pɔːnˌbrəʊkə(r), -z
AM 'pɔnˌbroʊkər, 'pɑnˌbroʊkər, -z
pawnbroking
BR 'pɔːnˌbrəʊkɪŋ
AM 'pɔnˌbroʊkɪŋ, 'pɑnˌbroʊkɪŋ
Pawnee
BR pɔː'niː, -z
AM pɔ'ni, pɑ'ni, -z
pawnshop
BR 'pɔːnʃɒp, -s
AM 'pɔnˌʃɑp, 'pɑnˌʃɑp, -s
pawpaw
BR 'pɔːpɔː(*r*), -z
AM 'pɔpɔ, 'pɑpɑ, -z
pax
BR paks
AM pæks, pɑks
Paxo®
BR 'paksəʊ
AM 'pæksoʊ
Paxton
BR 'pakstən
AM 'pækstən
pay
BR peɪ, -z, -ɪŋ, -d
AM peɪ, -z, -ɪŋ, -d
payable
BR 'peɪəbl
AM 'peɪəbəl
pay-as-you-earn
BR ˌpeɪəzjuː'əːn
AM ˌpeɪəzˌju'ərn
payback
BR 'peɪbak, -s
AM 'peɪˌbæk, -s
paycheck
BR 'peɪtʃɛk, -s
AM 'peɪˌtʃɛk, -s
paycheque
BR 'peɪtʃɛk, -s
AM 'peɪˌtʃɛk, -s
payday
BR 'peɪdeɪ, -z
AM 'peɪˌdeɪ, -z
paydirt
BR 'peɪdəːt
AM 'peɪˌdərt
PAYE
BR ˌpiːeɪwʌɪ'iː
AM 'piˌeɪˌwaɪ'i
payee
BR ˌpeɪ'iː, -z
AM peɪ'i, -z
payer
BR 'peɪə(r), -z
AM 'peɪər, -z
payload
BR 'peɪləʊd, -z
AM 'peɪˌloʊd, -z
paymaster
BR 'peɪˌmɑːstə(r), 'peɪˌmastə(r), -z
AM 'peɪˌmæstər, -z
payment
BR 'peɪm(ə)nt, -s
AM 'peɪmənt, -s
Payn
BR peɪn
AM peɪn
Payne
BR peɪn
AM peɪn
paynim
BR 'peɪnɪm
AM 'peɪnɨm
payoff
BR 'peɪɒf, -s
AM 'peɪˌɔf, 'peɪˌɑf, -s
payola
BR peɪ'əʊlə(*r*), -z
AM peɪ'oʊlə, -z
payout
BR 'peɪaʊt, -s
AM 'peɪˌaʊt, -s
paypacket
BR 'peɪˌpakɪt, -s
AM 'peɪˌpækət, -s
payphone
BR 'peɪfəʊn, -z
AM 'peɪˌfoʊn, -z
payroll
BR 'peɪrəʊl, -z
AM 'peɪˌroʊl, -z
paysage
BR ˌpeɪ'zɑːʒ, 'peɪzɑː(d)ʒ, -ɨz
AM ˌpeɪ(i)'z|ɑʒ, -əz
payslip
BR 'peɪslɪp, -s
AM 'peɪˌslɪp, -s
Payton
BR 'peɪtn
AM 'peɪtn
Paz
BR pɑːz
AM pɑz
pea
BR piː, -z
AM pi, -z
Peabody
BR 'piːˌbɒdi, 'piːbədi
AM 'piˌbɑdi
peace
BR piːs
AM pis
peaceable
BR 'piːsəbl
AM 'pisəbəl
peaceableness
BR 'piːsəblnəs
AM 'pisəblnɨs
peaceably
BR 'piːsəbli
AM 'pisəbli
peaceful
BR 'piːsf(ʊ)l
AM 'pisfəl
peacefully
BR 'piːsfʊli, 'piːsfl̩i
AM 'pisfəli
peacefulness
BR 'piːsf(ʊ)lnəs
AM 'pisfəlnəs

peacekeeper
BR ˈpiːsˌkiːpə(r), -z
AM ˈpisˌkipər, -z

peacekeeping
BR ˈpiːsˌkiːpɪŋ
AM ˈpisˌkipɪŋ

peacemaker
BR ˈpiːsˌmeɪkə(r), -z
AM ˈpisˌmeɪkər, -z

peacemaking
BR ˈpiːsˌmeɪkɪŋ
AM ˈpisˌmeɪkɪŋ

peacenik
BR ˈpiːsnɪk, -s
AM ˈpisˌnɪk, -s

peacetime
BR ˈpiːstʌɪm
AM ˈpisˌtaɪm

peach
BR piːtʃ, -ɪz, -ɪŋ, -t
AM pitʃ, -ɪz, -ɪŋ, -t

Peachey
BR ˈpiːtʃi
AM ˈpitʃi

peachick
BR ˈpiːtʃɪk, -s
AM ˈpiˌtʃɪk, -s

peachiness
BR ˈpiːtʃɪnɪs
AM ˈpitʃinɪs

peachy
BR ˈpiːtʃ|i, -ɪə(r), -ɪɪst
AM ˈpitʃi, -ər, -əst

peacock
BR ˈpiːkɒk, -s
AM ˈpiˌkɑk, -s

peacockery
BR ˈpiːkɒk(ə)ri
AM ˌpiˈkɑk(ə)ri

peafowl
BR ˈpiːfaʊl, -z
AM ˈpiˌfaʊl, -z

peahen
BR ˈpiːhɛn, -z
AM ˈpiˌhɛn, -z

peak
BR piːk, -s, -ɪŋ, -t
AM pik, -s, -ɪŋ, -t

Peak District
BR ˈpiːk ˌdɪstrɪkt
AM ˈpik ˌdɪstrɪk(t)

Peake
BR piːk
AM pik

peakiness
BR ˈpiːkɪnɪs
AM ˈpikinɪs

peakish
BR ˈpiːkɪʃ
AM ˈpikɪʃ

peakload
BR ˈpiːkləʊd, -z
AM ˌpikˈloʊd, -z

peaky
BR ˈpiːki
AM ˈpiki

peal
BR piːl, -z, -ɪŋ, -d
AM pil, -z, -ɪŋ, -d

pean
BR ˈpiːən
AM ˈpiən

peanut
BR ˈpiːnʌt, -s
AM ˈpinət, -s

pear
BR pɛː(r), -z
AM pɛ(ə)r, -z

Pearce
BR pɪəs
AM pɪ(ə)rs

pearl
BR pəːl, -z, -ɪŋ, -d
AM pərl, -z, -ɪŋ, -d

pearler
BR ˈpəːlə(r), -z
AM ˈpərlər, -z

pearlescent
BR pəːˈlɛsnt
AM pərˈlɛsənt

Pearl Harbor
BR ˌpəːl ˈhɑːbə(r)
AM ˌpərl ˈhɑrbər

pearliness
BR ˈpəːlɪnɪs
AM ˈpərlinɪs

pearlised
BR ˈpəːlʌɪzd
AM ˈpərˌlaɪzd

pearlite
BR ˈpəːlʌɪt
AM ˈpərˌlaɪt

pearlized
BR ˈpəːlʌɪzd
AM ˈpərˌlaɪzd

pearlware
BR ˈpəːlwɛː(r)
AM ˈpərlˌwɛ(ə)r

pearlwort
BR ˈpəːlwəːt
AM ˈpərlˌwərt, ˈpərlˌwɔ(ə)rt

pearly
BR ˈpəːl|i, -ɪz, -ɪə(r), -ɪɪst
AM ˈpərli, -z, -ər, -ɪst

pearmain
BR ˈpəːmeɪn, ˈpɛːmeɪn, pəˈmeɪn
AM ˈpɛrˌmeɪn, pərˈmeɪn

Pears[1]®
soap brand
BR pɛːz
AM pɛrz

Pears[2]
surname
BR pɪəz, pɛːz
AM pɛrz

Pearsall
BR ˈpɪəsl
AM ˈpɪrˌsɔl, ˈpɪrˌsɑl

pearshaped
BR ˈpɛːʃeɪpt
AM ˈpɛrˌʃeɪpt

Pearson
BR ˈpɪəsn
AM ˈpɪrsən

peart
BR ˈpɪət
AM ˈpɪ(ə)rt

Peary
BR ˈpɪəri
AM ˈpɪri

peasant
BR ˈpɛznt, -s
AM ˈpɛznt, -s

peasantry
BR ˈpɛzntri
AM ˈpɛzntri

peasanty
BR ˈpɛznti
AM ˈpɛzn(t)i

peascod
BR ˈpiːzkɒd, -z
AM ˈpizˌkɑd, -z

pease
BR piːz
AM piz

peasecod
BR ˈpiːzkɒd, -z
AM ˈpizˌkɑd, -z

peasepudding
BR ˌpiːzˈpʊdɪŋ
AM ˌpizˈpʊdɪŋ

peashooter
BR ˈpiːˌʃuːtə(r), -z
AM ˈpiˌʃudər, -z

pea-soup
BR ˌpiːˈsuːp
AM ˌpiˈsup

pea-souper
BR ˌpiːˈsuːpə(r), -z
AM ˌpiˈsupər, -z

pea stick
BR ˈpiː stɪk, -s
AM ˈpi ˌstɪk, -s

peat
BR piːt
AM pit

peatbog
BR ˈpiːtbɒg, -z
AM ˈpitˌbɔg, ˈpitˌbɑg, -z

peatiness
BR ˈpiːtɪnɪs
AM ˈpidinɪs

peatland
BR ˈpiːtland, -z
AM ˈpitˌlænd, -z

peatmoss
BR ˈpiːtmɒs, -ɪz
AM ˈpitˌmɔs, ˈpitˌmɑs, -əz

peaty
BR ˈpiːt|i, -ɪə(r), -ɪɪst
AM ˈpidi, -ər, -ɪst

peau-de-soie
BR ˌpəʊdəˈswɑː(*r*)
AM ˌpoʊdəˈswɑ

Peaudouce®
BR pəʊˈd(j)uːs
AM poʊˈd(j)us

peavey
BR ˈpiːv|i, -ɪz
AM ˈpivi, -z

peavy
BR ˈpiːv|i, -ɪz
AM ˈpivi, -z

pebble
BR ˈpɛbl, -z, -d
AM ˈpɛbəl, -z, -d

pebbledash
BR ˈpɛbldaʃ, -t
AM ˈpɛbəlˌdæʃ, -t

pebbly
BR ˈpɛbl̩i, ˈpɛbli
AM ˈpɛb(ə)li

pec
BR pɛk, -s
AM pɛk, -s

pecan
BR pɪˈkan, ˈpiːk(ə)n, -z
AM pəˈkɑn, pəˈkæn, ˈpiˌkɑn, ˈpiˌkæn, -z

peccability
BR ˌpɛkəˈbɪlɪti
AM ˌpɛkəˈbɪlɪdi

peccable
BR ˈpɛkəbl
AM ˈpɛkəbəl

peccadillo
BR ˌpɛkəˈdɪləʊ, -z
AM ˌpɛkəˈdɪloʊ, -z

peccancy
BR ˈpɛk(ə)nsi
AM ˈpɛkənsi

peccant
BR ˈpɛk(ə)nt
AM ˈpɛkənt

peccary
BR ˈpɛk(ə)r|i, -ɪz
AM ˈpɛkəri, -z

peccavi
BR pɛˈkɑːviː, pəˈkɑːvi
AM pəˈkɑvi

pêche Melba
BR ˌpɛʃ ˈmɛlbə(*r*), -z
AM ˌpɛʃ ˈmɛlbə, -z

peck
BR pɛk, -s, -ɪŋ, -t
AM pɛk, -s, -ɪŋ, -t

pecker
BR ˈpɛkə(r), -z
AM ˈpɛkər, -z

Peckham
BR ˈpɛkəm
AM ˈpɛkəm

peckish
BR ˈpɛkɪʃ
AM ˈpɛkɪʃ

peckishly
BR ˈpɛkɪʃli
AM ˈpɛkɪʃli

peckishness
BR ˈpɛkɪʃnɪs
AM ˈpɛkɪʃnɪs

Pecksniff
BR 'pɛksnɪf
AM 'pɛkˌsnɪf

pecorino
BR ˌpɛkə'riːnəʊ
AM ˌpɛkə'riˌnoʊ

Pecos
BR 'peɪkəs, 'peɪkɒs
AM 'peɪˌkoʊs, 'peɪkəs

pecten
BR 'pɛktɪn, 'pɛktɛn, -z
AM 'pɛktən, -z

pectic
BR 'pɛktɪk
AM 'pɛktɪk

pectin
BR 'pɛktɪn
AM 'pɛktən

pectinate
BR 'pɛktɪnət
AM 'pɛktənət, 'pɛktəˌneɪt

pectinated
BR 'pɛktɪneɪtɪd
AM 'pɛktəˌneɪdɪd

pectination
BR ˌpɛktɪ'neɪʃn
AM ˌpɛktə'neɪʃən

pectines
BR 'pɛktɪniːz
AM 'pɛktəˌniz

pectoral
BR 'pɛkt(ə)rəl, 'pɛkt(ə)rl̩
AM 'pɛkt(ə)rəl

pectose
BR 'pɛktəʊs, 'pɛktəʊz
AM 'pɛktoʊs, 'pɛktoʊz

peculate
BR 'pɛkjʉleɪt, -s, -ɪŋ, -ɪd
AM 'pɛkjəˌleɪ|t, -ts, -dɪŋ, -dɪd

peculation
BR ˌpɛkjʉ'leɪʃn, -z
AM ˌpɛkjə'leɪʃən, -z

peculator
BR 'pɛkjʉleɪtə(r), -z
AM 'pɛkjəˌleɪdər, -z

peculiar
BR pɪ'kjuːlɪə(r)
AM pə'kjuljər

peculiarity
BR pɪˌkjuːlɪ'arɪt|i, -ɪz
AM pəˌkjul'jɛrədi, pəˌkjuli'ɛrədi, -z

peculiarly
BR pɪ'kjuːlɪəli
AM pə'kjuljərli

pecuniarily
BR pɪ'kjuːn(jə)rɪli
AM pəˌkjuni'ɛrəli

pecuniary
BR pɪ'kjuːn(jə)ri
AM pə'kjuniˌɛri

pedagogic
BR ˌpɛdə'gɒdʒɪk, ˌpɛdə'gɒgɪk, -s
AM ˌpɛdə'gɑdʒɪk, -s

pedagogical
BR ˌpɛdə'gɒdʒɪkl, ˌpɛdə'gɒgɪkl
AM ˌpɛdə'gɑdʒəkəl

pedagogically
BR ˌpɛdə'gɒdʒɪkli, ˌpɛdə'gɒgɪkli
AM ˌpɛdə'gɑdʒək(ə)li

pedagogism
BR 'pɛdəgɒgɪz(ə)m, 'pɛdəgɒdʒɪz(ə)m
AM 'pɛdəˌgɑˌgɪzəm, 'pɛdəˌgɑˌdʒɪzəm

pedagogue
BR 'pɛdəgɒg, -z
AM 'pɛdəˌgɑg, -z

pedagoguism
BR 'pɛdəgɒgɪz(ə)m, 'pɛdəgɒdʒɪz(ə)m
AM 'pɛdəˌgɑˌgɪzəm

pedagogy
BR 'pɛdəgɒdʒi, 'pɛdəgɒgi
AM 'pɛdəˌgɑdʒi

pedal[1]
adjective, of the foot
BR 'pɛdl, 'piːdl
AM 'pidəl, 'pɛdəl

pedal[2]
noun, verb
BR 'pɛd|l, -lz, -l̩ɪŋ\-lɪŋ, -ld
AM 'pɛdəl, -z, -ɪŋ, -d

pedalo
BR 'pɛdələʊ, 'pɛdl̩əʊ, -z
AM 'pɛdlˌoʊ, -z

pedant
BR 'pɛdnt, -s
AM 'pɛdnt, -s

pedantic
BR pɪ'dantɪk
AM pə'dæn(t)ɪk

pedantically
BR pɪ'dantɪkli
AM pə'dæn(t)ək(ə)li

pedantry
BR 'pɛdntri
AM 'pɛdntri

pedate
BR 'pɛdət, 'pɛdeɪt
AM 'pɛˌdeɪt, 'pɛdət

peddle
BR 'pɛd|l, -lz, -l̩ɪŋ\-lɪŋ, -ld
AM 'pɛd|əl, -əlz, -(ə)lɪŋ, -əld

peddler
BR 'pɛdlə(r), -z
AM 'pɛd(ə)lər, -z

pederast
BR 'pɛdərast, -s
AM 'pɛdəˌræst, -s

pederastic
BR ˌpɛdə'rastɪk
AM ˌpɛdə'ræstɪk

pederasty
BR 'pɛdərasti
AM 'pɛdəˌræsti

pedestal
BR 'pɛdɪstl, -z
AM 'pɛdəstl, -z

pedestrian
BR pɪ'dɛstrɪən, -z
AM pə'dɛstriən, -z

pedestrianisation
BR pɪˌdɛstrɪənʌɪ'zeɪʃn
AM pəˌdɛstriənə'zeɪʃən, pəˌdɛstriəˌnaɪ'zeɪʃən

pedestrianise
BR pɪ'dɛstrɪənʌɪz, -ɪz, -ɪŋ, -d
AM pə'dɛstriəˌnaɪz, -ɪz, -ɪŋ, -d

pedestrianism
BR pɪ'dɛstrɪənɪz(ə)m
AM pə'dɛstriəˌnɪzəm

pedestrianization
BR pɪˌdɛstrɪənʌɪ'zeɪʃn
AM pəˌdɛstriənə'zeɪʃən, pəˌdɛstriəˌnaɪ'zeɪʃən

pedestrianize
BR pɪ'dɛstrɪənʌɪz, -ɪz, -ɪŋ, -d
AM pə'dɛstriəˌnaɪz, -ɪz, -ɪŋ, -d

pediatric
BR ˌpiːdɪ'atrɪk, -s
AM ˌpidi'ætrɪk, -s

pediatrician
BR ˌpiːdɪə'trɪʃn, -z
AM ˌpidiə'trɪʃən, -z

pediatrist
BR ˌpiː'dʌɪətrɪst, ˌpiːdɪ'atrɪst
AM ˌpidi'ætrəst

pedicab
BR 'pɛdɪkab, -z
AM 'pɛdɪkæb, -z

pedicel
BR 'pɛdɪs(ɛ)l, -z
AM 'pɛdəˌsɛl, -z

pedicellate
BR 'pɛdɪsɪleɪt, 'pɛdɪsl̩eɪt
AM ˌpɛdi'sɛlət, ˌpɛdi'sɛˌleɪt

pedicle
BR 'pɛdɪkl, -z
AM 'pɛdəkəl, -z

pedicular
BR pɪ'dɪkjʉlə(r), pɛ'dɪkjʉlə(r)
AM pə'dɪkjələr

pediculate
BR pɪ'dɪkjʉlət, pɛ'dɪkjʉlət
AM pə'dɪkjələt, pə'dɪkjəˌleɪt

pediculosis
BR pɪˌdɪkjʉ'ləʊsɪs, pɛˌdɪkjʉ'ləʊsɪs
AM pəˌdɪkjə'loʊsəs

pediculous
BR pɪ'dɪkjʉləs, pɛ'dɪkjʉləs
AM pə'dɪkjələs

pedicure
BR 'pɛdɪkjʊə(r), 'pɛdɪkjɔː(r), -z
AM 'pɛdəˌkjʊ(ə)r, -z

pedicurist
BR 'pɛdɪkjʊərɪst, 'pɛdɪkjɔːrɪst, -s
AM 'pɛdəˌkjʊrəst, -s

pediform
BR 'pɛdɪfɔːm
AM 'pɛdəˌfɔ(ə)rm

pedigree
BR 'pɛdɪgriː, -z, -d
AM 'pɛdəˌgri, -z, -d

pediment
BR 'pɛdɪm(ə)nt, -s, -ɪd
AM 'pɛdəmən|t, -ts, -ɪd

pedimental
BR ˌpɛdɪ'mɛntl
AM ˌpɛdə'mɛn(t)l

pedlar
BR 'pɛdlə(r), -z
AM 'pɛdlər, -z

pedlary
BR 'pɛdləri
AM 'pɛdləri

pedological[1]
child study
BR ˌpiːdə'lɒdʒɪkl
AM ˌpɛdə'lɑdʒəkəl, ˌpidə'lɑdʒəkəl

pedological[2]
soil science
BR ˌpɛdə'lɒdʒɪkl
AM ˌpɛdə'lɑdʒəkəl

pedologist
BR pɪ'dɒlədʒɪst, pɛ'dɒlədʒɪst, -s
AM pə'dɑlədʒəst, -s

pedology
BR pɪ'dɒlədʒi, pɛ'dɒlədʒi
AM pə'dɑlədʒi

pedometer
BR pɪ'dɒmɪtə(r), pɛ'dɒmɪtə(r), -z
AM pə'dɑmədər, -z

pedophile
BR 'piːdəfʌɪl, -z
AM 'pɛdəˌfaɪl, 'pidəˌfaɪl, -z

pedophilia
BR ˌpiːdə'fɪlɪə(r)
AM ˌpɛdə'fɪljə, ˌpidə'fɪljə, ˌpɛdə'fɪliə, ˌpidə'fɪliə

pedophiliac
BR ˌpiːdə'fɪlɪak, -s
AM ˌpɛdə'fɪliˌæk, ˌpidə'fɪliˌæk, -s

pedophiliad
BR ˌpiːdə'fɪlɪad
AM ˌpɛdə'fɪliˌæd, ˌpidə'fɪliˌæd

Pedro
BR 'pɛdrəʊ
AM 'peɪdroʊ

peduncle
BR pɪˈdʌŋkl, -z
AM ˈpiˌdəŋkəl, piˈdəŋkəl, -z

peduncular
BR pɪˈdʌŋkjʊlə(r)
AM pəˈdəŋkjələr

pedunculate
BR pɪˈdʌŋkjʊleɪt, pɪˈdʌŋkjʊlət
AM pəˈdəŋkjəˌleɪt, pəˈdəŋkjələt

pee
BR piː, -z, -ɪŋ, -d
AM pi, -z, -ɪŋ, -d

Peebles
BR ˈpiːblz
AM ˈpibəlz

peek
BR piːk, -s, -ɪŋ, -t
AM pik, -s, -ɪŋ, -t

peekaboo
BR ˌpiːkəˈbuː
AM ˈpikəˌbu

peekily
BR ˈpiːkɨli
AM ˈpikɨli

peekiness
BR ˈpiːkɪnɨs
AM ˈpikinɨs

peeky
BR ˈpiːk|i, -ɪə(r), -ɪɪst
AM ˈpiki, -ər, -ɨst

peel
BR piːl, -z, -ɪŋ, -d
AM pil, -z, -ɪŋ, -d

peeler
BR ˈpiːlə(r), -z
AM ˈpilər, -z

peeling
BR ˈpiːlɪŋ, -z
AM ˈpilɪŋ, -z

Peelite
BR ˈpiːlʌɪt, -s
AM ˈpiˌlaɪt, -s

peen
BR piːn, -z
AM pin, -z

Peenemunde
BR ˈpiːnəˌmʊndə(*r*)
AM ˌpinəˈmʊndə
GER ˈpeːnəmʏndə

peep
BR piːp, -s, -ɪŋ, -t
AM pip, -s, -ɪŋ, -t

peep-bo
BR ˈpiːp(b)əʊ
AM ˈpipˌboʊ

peeper
BR ˈpiːpə(r), -z
AM ˈpipər, -z

peephole
BR ˈpiːphəʊl, -z
AM ˈpipˌ(h)oʊl, -z

peepshow
BR ˈpiːpʃəʊ, -z
AM ˈpipˌʃoʊ, -z

peepul
BR ˈpiːpl, -z
AM ˈpipəl, -z

peer
BR pɪə(r), -z
AM pɪ(ə)r, -z

peerage
BR ˈpɪər|ɪdʒ, -ɨdʒɨz
AM ˈpɪrɪdʒ, -ɨz

peeress
BR ˈpɪərɪs, ˌpɪəˈrɛs, -ɨz
AM ˈpɪrɨs, -ɨz

peer-group
BR ˈpɪəgruːp
AM ˈpɪrˌgrup

peerless
BR ˈpɪələs
AM ˈpɪrlɨs

peerlessly
BR ˈpɪələsli
AM ˈpɪrlɨsli

peerlessness
BR ˈpɪələsnəs
AM ˈpɪrlɨsnɨs

peeve
BR piːv, -z, -ɪŋ, -d
AM piv, -z, -ɪŋ, -d

peevish
BR ˈpiːvɪʃ
AM ˈpivɪʃ

peevishly
BR ˈpiːvɨʃli
AM ˈpivɨʃli

peevishness
BR ˈpiːvɨʃnɨs
AM ˈpivɪʃnɨs

peewee
BR ˈpiːwiː, -z
AM ˈpiˌwi, -z

peewit
BR ˈpiːwɪt, -s
AM ˈpiwɨt, ˈpiˌwɪt, -s

peg
BR pɛg, -z, -ɪŋ, -d
AM pɛg, -z, -ɪŋ, -d

Pegasean
BR ˌpɛgəˈsiːən
AM ˌpɛgəˌsiən

Pegasus
BR ˈpɛgəsəs
AM ˈpɛgəsəs

pegboard
BR ˈpɛgbɔːd, -z
AM ˈpɛgˌbɔ(ə)rd, -z

Pegg
BR pɛg
AM pɛg

Peggie
BR ˈpɛgi
AM ˈpɛgi

Peggotty
BR ˈpɛgəti
AM ˈpɛgədi

Peggy
BR ˈpɛgi
AM ˈpɛgi

peg-leg
BR ˈpɛglɛg, -z
AM ˈpɛgˌlɛg, -z

pegmatite
BR ˈpɛgmətʌɪt
AM ˈpɛgməˌtaɪt

pegtop
BR ˈpɛgtɒp, -s
AM ˈpɛgˌtɑp, -s

Pegu
BR ˈpɛgjuː, -z
AM pɛˈgu, -z

Pei
BR peɪ
AM peɪ

peignoir
BR ˈpeɪnwɑː(r), -z
AM ˌpeɪnˈwɑr, -z

Peirce
BR pɪəs
AM pɪ(ə)rs

pejoration
BR ˌpɛdʒəˈreɪʃn
AM ˌpɛdʒəˈreɪʃən, ˌpeɪəˈreɪʃən

pejorative
BR pɪˈdʒɒrətɪv, -z
AM pəˈdʒɔrədɪv, ˈpɛdʒəˌreɪdɪv, -z

pejoratively
BR pɪˈdʒɒrətɨvli
AM pəˈdʒɔrədɨvli, ˈpɛdʒəˌreɪdɨvli

pekan
BR ˈpɛk(ə)n
AM pəˈkɑn, pəˈkæn, ˈpiˌkɑn, ˈpiˌkæn

peke
BR piːk, -s
AM pik, -s

Pekin
BR ˌpiːˈkɪn
AM ˈpikɪn

Pekinese
BR ˌpiːkɪˈniːz
AM ˈpikɪnˌiz

Peking
BR ˌpiːˈkɪŋ
AM ˌpiˈkɪŋ, ˌpeɪˈkɪŋ

pekingese
BR ˌpiːkɪˈniːz, -ɨz
AM ˈpikɪnˌiz, -ɨz

pekoe
BR ˈpiːkəʊ
AM ˈpiˌkoʊ

pelage
BR ˈpɛl|ɪdʒ, -ɨdʒɨz
AM ˈpɛlɪdʒ, -ɨz

Pelagian
BR pɪˈleɪdʒɪən, pɪˈleɪdʒ(ə)n, -z
AM pəˈleɪdʒiən, -z

Pelagianism
BR pɪˈleɪdʒ(ɪ)ənɪz(ə)m, pɪˈleɪdʒn̩ɪz(ə)m
AM pəˈleɪdʒ(i)əˌnɪzəm

pelagic
BR pɪˈladʒɪk
AM pəˈlædʒɪk

Pelagius
BR pɪˈleɪdʒɪəs
AM pəˈleɪdʒ(i)əs

pelargonium
BR ˌpɛləˈgəʊnɪəm, -z
AM ˌpɛˌlɑrˈgoʊniəm, ˌpɛlərˈgoʊniəm, -z

Pelasgian
BR pɪˈlazdʒɪən, pɛˈlazdʒɪən, pɪˈlazgɪən, pɛˈlazgɪən, -z
AM pəˈlæzdʒiən, pəˈlæzgiən, -z

Pelasgic
BR pɪˈlazdʒɪk, pɛˈlazdʒɪk, pɪˈlazgɪk, pɛˈlazgɪk
AM pəˈlæzdʒɪk, pəˈlæzgɪk

Pelé
BR ˈpɛleɪ
AM ˈpɛˌleɪ

pele
BR piːl, -z
AM pil, -z

pelerine
BR ˈpɛlərɪn, ˈpɛləriːn, -z
AM ˌpɛləˈrin, -z

Peleus
BR ˈpɛljəs, ˈpiːljəs, ˈpɛlɪəs, ˈpiːlɪəs
AM ˈpɛliəs, ˈpiliəs, ˈpɛljəs, ˈpiljəs

pelf
BR pɛlf
AM pɛlf

pelham
BR ˈpɛləm, -z
AM ˈpɛləm, -z

Pelias
BR ˈpiːlɪas, ˈpɛlɪas
AM ˈpɛliəs

pelican
BR ˈpɛlɪk(ə)n, -z
AM ˈpɛləkən, -z

Pelion
BR ˈpiːlɪən, ˈpiːlɪɒn
AM ˈpiliən, ˈpiljən

pelisse
BR pɪˈliːs, -ɨz
AM pəˈlis, -ɨz

pelite
BR ˈpiːlʌɪt
AM ˈpiˌlaɪt

pellagra
BR pɪˈlagrə(*r*), pɛˈlagrə(*r*), pɪˈleɪgrə(*r*), pɛˈleɪgrə(*r*)
AM pəˈleɪgrə, pəˈlægrə

pellagrous
BR pɪˈlagrəs, pɪˈleɪgrəs

AM pəˈleɪɡrəs, pəˈlæɡrəs

pellet
BR ˈpɛlɪt, -s
AM ˈpɛlət, -s

pelletise
BR ˈpɛlɨtʌɪz, -ɨz, -ɪŋ, -d
AM ˈpɛləˌtaɪz, -ɨz, -ɪŋ, -d

pelletize
BR ˈpɛlɨtʌɪz, -ɨz, -ɪŋ, -d
AM ˈpɛləˌtaɪz, -ɨz, -ɪŋ, -d

pellicle
BR ˈpɛlɨkl, -z
AM ˈpɛləkəl, -z

pellicular
BR pɨˈlɪkjʉlə(r)
AM pəˈlɪkjələr

pellitory
BR ˈpɛlɨt(ə)r|i, -ɪz
AM ˈpɛləˌtɔri, -z

pell-mell
BR ˌpɛlˈmɛl
AM ˌpɛlˈmɛl

pellucid
BR pɨˈl(j)uːsɪd, pɛˈl(j)uːsɪd
AM pəˈlusəd, pəlˈjusəd

pellucidity
BR ˌpɛljʉˈsɪdɨti
AM ˌpɛljəˈsɪdɨdi

pellucidly
BR pɨˈl(j)uːsɪdli, pɛˈl(j)uːsɪdli
AM pəˈlusədli, pəlˈjusədli

pellucidness
BR pɨˈl(j)uːsɪdnɨs, pɛˈl(j)uːsɪdnɨs
AM pəˈlusədnəs, pəlˈjusədnəs

Pelmanise
BR ˈpɛlmənʌɪz, -ɨz, -ɪŋ, -d
AM ˈpɛlməˌnaɪz, -ɨz, -ɪŋ, -d

Pelmanism
BR ˈpɛlmənɪz(ə)m
AM ˈpɛlməˌnɪzəm

Pelmanize
BR ˈpɛlmənʌɪz, -ɨz, -ɪŋ, -d
AM ˈpɛlməˌnaɪz, -ɨz, -ɪŋ, -d

pelmet
BR ˈpɛlmɪt, -s
AM ˈpɛlmət, -s

Peloponnese
BR ˌpɛləpəˈniːz
AM ˌpɛləpəˈniz

Peloponnesian
BR ˌpɛləpəˈniːzj(ə)n, ˌpɛləpəˈniːʒn, -z
AM ˌpɛləpəˈniʒən, ˌpɛləpəˈniʃən, -z

Pelops
BR ˈpiːlɒps, ˈpɛlɒps
AM ˈpɛˌlɑps

pelorus
BR pɨˈlɔːrəs, -ɨz
AM pəˈlɔrəs, -əz

pelota
BR pɨˈlɒtə(r), pɛˈlɒtə(r), pɨˈləʊtə(r), pɛˈləʊtə(r)
AM pəˈloʊdə

pelt
BR pɛlt, -s, -ɪŋ, -ɨd
AM pɛlt, -s, -ɪŋ, -əd

pelta
BR ˈpɛltə(r)
AM ˈpɛltə

peltae
BR ˈpɛltiː
AM ˈpɛlti, ˈpɛlˌtaɪ

peltate
BR ˈpɛlteɪt
AM ˈpɛlˌteɪt

peltry
BR ˈpɛltri
AM ˈpɛltri

pelvic
BR ˈpɛlvɪk
AM ˈpɛlvɪk

pelvis
BR ˈpɛlvɪs, -ɨz
AM ˈpɛlvəs, -əz

Pemba
BR ˈpɛmbə(r)
AM ˈpɛmbə

Pemberton
BR ˈpɛmbət(ə)n
AM ˈpɛmbərtən

Pembroke
BR ˈpɛmbrʊk, ˈpɛmbrəʊk
AM ˈpɛmˌbroʊk, ˈpɛmˌbrʊk

pemican
BR ˈpɛmɨk(ə)n
AM ˈpɛməkən

pemmican
BR ˈpɛmɨk(ə)n
AM ˈpɛməkən

pemphigoid
BR ˈpɛmfɨɡɔɪd
AM ˈpɛm(p)fəˌɡɔɪd

pemphigous
BR ˈpɛmfɨɡəs
AM ˈpɛm(p)fəɡəs, pɛmˈfaɪɡəs

pemphigus
BR ˈpɛmfɨɡəs
AM ˈpɛm(p)fəɡəs, pɛmˈfaɪɡəs

pen
BR pɛn, -z, -ɪŋ, -d
AM pɛn, -z, -ɪŋ, -d

Peña
BR ˈpeɪnjə(r)
AM ˈpeɪnjə

penal
BR ˈpiːnl
AM ˈpinəl

penalisation
BR ˌpiːnəlʌɪˈzeɪʃn, ˌpiːnl̩ʌɪˈzeɪʃn
AM ˌpɛnləˈzeɪʃən, ˌpinləˈzeɪʃən, ˌpɛnlˌaɪˈzeɪʃən, ˌpinlˌaɪˈzeɪʃən

penalise
BR ˈpiːnəlʌɪz, ˈpiːnl̩ʌɪz, -ɨz, -ɪŋ, -d
AM ˈpɛnlˌaɪz, ˈpinlˌaɪz, -ɨz, -ɪŋ, -d

penalization
BR ˌpiːnəlʌɪˈzeɪʃn, ˌpiːnl̩ʌɪˈzeɪʃn
AM ˌpɛnləˈzeɪʃən, ˌpinləˈzeɪʃən, ˌpɛnlˌaɪˈzeɪʃən, ˌpinlˌaɪˈzeɪʃən

penalize
BR ˈpiːnəlʌɪz, ˈpiːnl̩ʌɪz, -ɨz, -ɪŋ, -d
AM ˈpɛnlˌaɪz, ˈpinlˌaɪz, -ɨz, -ɪŋ, -d

penally
BR ˈpiːnl̩i, ˈpiːnəli
AM ˈpinəli

penalty
BR ˈpɛnlt|i, -ɪz
AM ˈpɛnlti, -z

penance
BR ˈpɛnəns, -ɨz
AM ˈpɛnəns, -əz

pen-and-ink
BR ˌpɛnən(d)ˈɪŋk
AM ˌpɛnənˈɪŋk

Penang
BR pɨˈnaŋ, pɛˈnaŋ
AM pəˈnæŋ

penannular
BR pɛnˈanjʉlə(r)
AM pɛnˈænjələr

Penarth
BR pɛˈnɑːθ
AM pəˈnɑrθ

penates
BR pɨˈnɑːtiːz, pɨˈnɑːteɪz, pɨˈneɪtiːz, pɛˈnɑːtiːz, pɛˈnɑːteɪz, pɛˈneɪtiːz
AM pəˈneɪdiz, pəˈnɑdiz

pence
BR pɛns
AM pɛns

penchant
BR ˈpɒ̃ʃɒ̃, -z
AM ˈpɛn(t)ʃənt, -s

pencil
BR ˈpɛns|l, -lz, -l̩ɪŋ\-əlɪŋ, -ld
AM ˈpɛns|əl, -əlz, -(ə)lɪŋ, -əld

penciller
BR ˈpɛnsl̩ə(r), ˈpɛnsələ(r), -z
AM ˈpɛnsələr, -z

pend
BR pɛnd, -z, -ɪŋ, -ɨd
AM pɛnd, -z, -ɪŋ, -əd

pendant
BR ˈpɛnd(ə)nt, -s
AM ˈpɛndnt, -s

pendency
BR ˈpɛnd(ə)nsi
AM ˈpɛndnsi

Pendennis
BR pɛnˈdɛnɪs
AM pɛnˈdɛnəs

pendent
BR ˈpɛnd(ə)nt, -s
AM ˈpɛndnt, -s

pendentive
BR pɛnˈdɛntɪv, -z
AM pɛnˈdɛn(t)ɪv, -z

Penderecki
BR ˌpɛndəˈrɛtski
AM ˌpɛndəˈrɛtski

Pendine
BR pɛnˈdʌɪn
AM pɛnˈdaɪn

Pendle
BR ˈpɛndl
AM ˈpɛndəl

Pendlebury
BR ˈpɛndlb(ə)ri
AM ˈpɛndəlˌbɛri

Pendleton
BR ˈpɛndlt(ə)n
AM ˈpɛn(d)əltən

pendragon
BR pɛnˈdraɡ(ə)n, -z
AM ˌpɛnˈdræɡən, -z

pendulate
BR ˈpɛndjʉleɪt, ˈpɛndʒʉleɪt, -s, -ɪŋ, -ɨd
AM ˈpɛndʒəˌleɪ|t, ˈpɛnd(j)əˌleɪ|t, -ts, -dɪŋ, -dɨd

penduline
BR ˈpɛndjʉlʌɪn, ˈpɛndʒʉlʌɪn
AM ˈpɛndʒələn, ˈpɛndʒəˌlaɪn

pendulous
BR ˈpɛndjʉləs, ˈpɛndʒʉləs
AM ˈpɛndʒələs, ˈpɛndjələs

pendulously
BR ˈpɛndjʉləsli, ˈpɛndʒʉləsli
AM ˈpɛndʒələsli, ˈpɛndjələsli

pendulum
BR ˈpɛndjʉləm, ˈpɛndʒʉləm, -z
AM ˈpɛndʒələm, ˈpɛndjələm, -z

Penelope
BR pɨˈnɛləpi
AM pəˈnɛləpi

peneplain
BR ˈpiːnɨpleɪn, ˈpɛnɨpleɪn, ˌpiːnɨˈpleɪn, ˌpɛnɨˈpleɪn, -z

AM 'pinə,pleɪn, -z
penetrability
BR ,pɛnɨtrə'bɪlɨti
AM ,pɛnətrə'bɪlɨdi
penetrable
BR 'pɛnɨtrəbl
AM 'pɛnətrəbəl
penetralia
BR ,pɛnɨ'treɪlɪə(r)
AM ,pɛnə'treɪljə, ,pɛnə'treɪliə
penetrance
BR 'pɛnɨtr(ə)ns
AM 'pɛnətrəns
penetrant
BR 'pɛnɨtr(ə)nt, -s
AM 'pɛnətrənt, -s
penetrate
BR 'pɛnɨtreɪt, -s, -ɪŋ, -ɨd
AM 'pɛnə,treɪ|t, -ts, -dɪŋ, -dɨd
penetratingly
BR 'pɛnɨ,treɪtɪŋli
AM 'pɛnə,treɪdɪŋli
penetration
BR ,pɛnɨ'treɪʃn, -z
AM ,pɛnə'treɪʃən, -z
penetrative
BR 'pɛnɨtrətɪv
AM 'pɛnə,treɪdɪv, 'pɛnətrədɪv
penetratively
BR 'pɛnɨtrətɪvli
AM ',pɛnə',treɪdɪvli, 'pɛnətrədɪvli
penetrator
BR 'pɛnɨtreɪtə(r), -z
AM 'pɛnə,treɪdər, -z
pen-feather
BR 'pɛn,fɛðə(r), -z
AM 'pɛn,fɛðər, -z
Penfold
BR 'pɛnfəʊld
AM 'pɛn,foʊld
penfriend
BR 'pɛnfrɛnd, -z
AM 'pɛn,frɛnd, -z
Pengam
BR 'pɛŋgəm
AM 'pɛŋəm
Penge
BR pɛn(d)ʒ
AM pɛn(d)ʒ
Pengelly
BR pɛn'gɛli
AM pɛn'gɛli
penguin
BR 'pɛŋgwɪn, -z
AM 'pɛŋgwən, -z
Penhaligon
BR pɛn'halɨg(ə)n
AM pɛn'hæləgən
penicillate
BR 'pɛnɨ,sɪlət, ,pɛnɪ'sɪlət
AM ,pɛnə'sɪlɪt, ,pɛnə'sɪleɪt
penicillia
BR ,pɛnɪ'sɪlɪə(r)
AM ,pɛnə'sɪljə, ,pɛnə'sɪliə
penicillin
BR ,pɛnɪ'sɪlɪn
AM ,pɛnə'sɪlɨn
penicillium
BR ,pɛnɪ'sɪlɪəm
AM ,pɛnə'sɪliəm
penile
BR 'piːnʌɪl
AM 'pinaɪl, 'pinl
penillion
BR pɛ'nɪɬɪən, pɛ'nɪθlɪən
AM pə'nɪljən
peninsula
BR pɪ'nɪnsjʉlə(r), -z
AM pə'nɪns(ə)lə, -z
peninsular
BR pɪ'nɪnsjʉlə(r)
AM pə'nɪns(ə)lər
penis
BR 'piːn|ɪs, -ɨsɨz
AM 'pinɨs, -ɨz
Penistone
BR 'pɛnɪst(ə)n
AM 'pɛnəstən
penitence
BR 'pɛnɨt(ə)ns
AM 'pɛnədəns, 'pɛnətns
penitent
BR 'pɛnɨt(ə)nt, -s
AM 'pɛnədnt, -s
penitential
BR ,pɛnɪ'tɛnʃl
AM ,pɛnə'tɛn(t)ʃəl
penitentially
BR ,pɛnɪ'tɛnʃli, ,pɛnɪ'tɛnʃəli
AM ,pɛnə'tɛn(t)ʃəli
penitentiary
BR ,pɛnɪ'tɛnʃ(ə)r|i, -ɪz
AM ,pɛnə'tɛn(t)ʃ(ə)ri, -z
penitently
BR 'pɛnɨt(ə)ntli
AM 'pɛnədən(t)li, 'pɛnətn̩(t)li
penknife
BR 'pɛnnʌɪf
AM 'pɛn,naɪf
penknives
BR 'pɛnnʌɪvz
AM 'pɛn,naɪvz
penlight
BR 'pɛnlʌɪt, -s
AM 'pɛn,laɪt, -s
Penmaenmawr
BR ,pɛnmʌɪn'maʊə(r), ,pɛnmə(n)'maʊə(r)
AM ,pɛnmaɪn'maʊ(ə)r
WE ,penmaɪn'maʊr
penman
BR 'pɛnmən
AM 'pɛn,mæn
penmanship
BR 'pɛnmənʃɪp
AM 'pɛnmən,ʃɪp
penmen
BR 'pɛnmən
AM 'pɛn,mɛn
Penn
BR pɛn
AM pɛn
pennant
BR 'pɛnənt, -s
AM 'pɛnənt, -s
penne
BR 'pɛni
AM 'pɛneɪ, 'pɛnə
penni
BR 'pɛni
AM 'pɛni
penniä
BR 'pɛnɪɑː(r)
AM 'pɛniə
pennies
BR 'pɛnɪz
AM 'pɛniz
penniless
BR 'pɛnɨlɨs, 'pɛnl̩əs
AM 'pɛnl̩əs, 'pɛnilɨs
pennilessly
BR 'pɛnɨlɨsli, 'pɛnl̩əsli
AM 'pɛnl̩əsli, 'pɛnilɨsli
pennilessness
BR 'pɛnɨlɨsnɨs, 'pɛnl̩əsnəs
AM 'pɛnl̩əsnəs, 'pɛnilɨsnɨs
pennill
BR 'pɛnɪɬ
AM 'pɛ,nɪl
Pennine
BR 'pɛnʌɪn, -z
AM 'pɛ,naɪn, -z
Pennington
BR 'pɛnɪŋt(ə)n
AM 'pɛnɪŋtən
pennon
BR 'pɛnən, -z, -d
AM 'pɛnən, -z, -d
penn'orth
BR 'pɛnəθ
AM 'pɛnərθ
Pennsylvania
BR ,pɛns(ɪ)l'veɪnɪə(r)
AM ',pɛnsəl'veɪnjə
Pennsylvanian
BR ,pɛns(ɪ)l'veɪnɪən, -z
AM ',pɛnsəl'veɪnjən, -z
penny
BR 'pɛn|i, -ɪz
AM 'pɛni, -z
penny-ante
BR ,pɛnɪ'anti
AM ',pɛni'æn(t)i
Pennycuick
BR 'pɛnɪkʊk, 'pɛnɪkjuːk, 'pɛnɪkwɪk
AM 'pɛni,kʊk, 'pɛni,kwɪk
pennyfarthing
BR ,pɛnɪ'fɑːθɪŋ, -z
AM ',pɛni'fɑrðɪŋ, -z
Pennyfeather
BR 'pɛnɪ,fɛðə(r)
AM 'pɛni,fɛðər
pennyroyal
BR ,pɛnɪ'rɔɪəl
AM ',pɛni',rɔɪ(ə)l
pennyweight
BR 'pɛnɪweɪt, -s
AM 'pɛni,weɪt, -s
pennywort
BR 'pɛnɪwəːt, -s
AM 'pɛniwərt, 'pɛniwɔ(ə)rt, -s
pennyworth
BR 'pɛnəθ, 'pɛnɪwəθ, 'pɛnɪwəːθ
AM 'pɛni,wərth
penological
BR ,piːnə'lɒdʒɪkl
AM ',pinl'ɑdʒəkəl
penologist
BR piː'nɒlədʒɪst, pɪ'nɒlədʒɪst, -s
AM pi'nɑlədʒəst, pə'nɑlədʒəst, -s
penology
BR piː'nɒlədʒi, pɪ'nɒlədʒi
AM pi'nɑlədʒi, pə'nɑlədʒi
penpusher
BR 'pɛn,pʊʃə(r), -z
AM 'pɛn,pʊʃər, -z
Penrhos
BR (,)pɛn'rəʊs, 'pɛnrəʊs
AM pɛn'roʊs, 'pɛn,roʊs
WE 'penrɔs
Penrhyn
BR (,)pɛn'rɪn, 'pɛnrɪn
AM pɛn'rɪn, 'pɛnrən
Pensacola
BR ,pɛnsə'kəʊlə(r)
AM ,pɛnsə'koʊlə
pensée
BR 'pɒ̃seɪ, pɒ̃'seɪ, -z
AM ,pɑn'seɪ, -z
Penshurst
BR 'pɛnzhəːst
AM 'pɛnz,(h)ərst
pensile
BR 'pɛnsʌɪl
AM 'pɛnsəl
pension¹
hotel
BR 'pɒ̃sjɒ̃, -z
AM ,pɑnsi'ɔn, ,pɑnsi'ɑn, -z
pension²
money
BR 'pɛnʃ|n, -nz, -n̩ɪŋ\-ənɪŋ, -ənd

AM ˈpɛnʃ|ən, -ənz, -(ə)nɪŋ, -ənd
pensionability
BR ˌpɛnʃn̩əˈbɪlɨti, ˌpɛnʃənəˈbɪlɨti
AM ˌpɛnʃ(ə)nəˈbɪlɨdi
pensionable
BR ˈpɛnʃn̩əbl, ˈpɛnʃənəbl
AM ˈpɛnʃ(ə)nəbəl
pensionary
BR ˈpɛnʃn̩(ə)r|i, ˈpɛnʃən(ə)ri, -ɪz
AM ˈpɛnʃəˌnɛri, -z
pensioner
BR ˈpɛnʃn̩ə(r), ˈpɛnʃənə(r), -z
AM ˈpɛnʃ(ə)nər, -z
pensionless
BR ˈpɛnʃnləs
AM ˈpɛnʃənləs
pensive
BR ˈpɛnsɪv
AM ˈpɛnsɪv
pensively
BR ˈpɛnsɨvli
AM ˈpɛnsɨvli
pensiveness
BR ˈpɛnsɪvnɨs
AM ˈpɛnsɪvnɨs
penstemon
BR pɛnˈstiːmən, ˈpɛn(t)stɪmən, -z
AM pɛnˈstimən, ˈpɛnstəmən, -z
penstock
BR ˈpɛnstɒk, -s
AM ˈpɛnˌstɑk, -s
pent
BR pɛnt
AM pɛnt
pentachord
BR ˈpɛntəkɔːd, -z
AM ˈpɛn(t)əˌkɔ(ə)rd, -z
pentacle
BR ˈpɛntəkl, -z
AM ˈpɛn(t)əkəl, -z
pentad
BR ˈpɛntad, -z
AM ˈpɛnˌtæd, -z
pentadactyl
BR ˌpɛntəˈdakt(ɪ)l, -z
AM ˌpɛn(t)əˈdæktl, -z
pentagon
BR ˈpɛntəg(ə)n, -z
AM ˈpɛn(t)əˌgɑn, -z
pentagonal
BR pɛnˈtagənl, pɛnˈtagn̩l
AM pɛnˈtægənəl
pentagonally
BR pɛnˈtagənl̩i, pɛnˈtagənəli, pɛnˈtagn̩l̩i, pɛnˈtagn̩əli
AM pɛnˈtæg(ə)nəli
pentagram
BR ˈpɛntəgram, -z
AM ˈpɛn(t)əˌgræm, -z
pentagynous
BR pɛnˈtadʒɪnəs
AM pɛnˈtædʒənəs
pentahedra
BR ˌpɛntəˈhiːdrə(r)
AM ˌpɛn(t)əˈhidrə
pentahedral
BR ˌpɛntəˈhiːdr(ə)l
AM ˌpɛn(t)əˈhidrəl
pentahedron
BR ˌpɛntəˈhiːdrən
AM ˌpɛn(t)əˈhidrən
pentamerous
BR pɛnˈtam(ə)rəs
AM pɛnˈtæmərəs
pentameter
BR pɛnˈtamɪtə(r), -z
AM pɛnˈtæmədər, -z
pentamidine
BR pɛnˈtamɨdiːn
AM pɛnˈtæməˌdin
pentandrous
BR pɛnˈtandrəs
AM pɛnˈtændrəs
pentane
BR ˈpɛnteɪn
AM ˈpɛnˌteɪn
pentangle
BR ˈpɛntaŋgl, -z
AM ˈpɛnˌtæŋgəl, -z
pentanoic acid
BR ˌpɛntənəʊɪk ˈasɪd
AM ˌpɛn(t)əˈnoʊɪk ˈæsəd
pentaprism
BR ˈpɛntəˌprɪz(ə)m, -z
AM ˈpɛn(t)əˌprɪzəm, -z
Pentateuch
BR ˈpɛntətjuːk, ˈpɛntətʃuːk
AM ˈpɛn(t)əˌt(j)uk
pentateuchal
BR ˌpɛntəˈtjuːkl, ˌpɛntəˈtʃuːkl
AM ˌpɛn(t)əˌt(j)ukəl
pentathlete
BR pɛnˈtaθliːt, -s
AM pɛnˈtæθˌlit, -s
pentathlon
BR pɛnˈtaθlən, pɛnˈtaθlɒn, -z
AM pɛnˈtæθ(ə)lən, pɛnˈtæθ(ə)ˌlɑn, -z
pentatonic
BR ˌpɛntəˈtɒnɪk
AM ˌpɛn(t)əˈtɑnɪk
pentavalent
BR ˌpɛntəˈveɪlənt, ˌpɛntəˈveɪln̩t
AM ˌpɛn(t)əˈveɪlənt
Pentax®
BR ˈpɛntaks
AM ˈpɛntæks
Pentecost
BR ˈpɛntɨkɒst
AM ˈpɛn(t)əˌkɔst, ˈpɛn(t)əˌkɑst
Pentecostal
BR ˌpɛntɪˈkɒstl, -z
AM ˌpɛn(t)əˈkɔstl, ˌpɛn(t)əˈkɑstl, -z
Pentecostalism
BR ˌpɛntɪˈkɒstl̩ɪz(ə)m
AM ˌpɛn(t)əˈkɔstlˌɪzəm, ˌpɛn(t)əˈkɑstlˌɪzəm
Pentecostalist
BR ˌpɛntɪˈkɒstl̩ɪst, -s
AM ˌpɛn(t)əˈkɔstl̩əst, ˌpɛn(t)əˈkɑstl̩əst, -s
Pentel®
BR ˈpɛntɛl
AM ˈpɛnˌtɛl
Penthesilea
BR ˌpɛnθɛsɪˈleɪə(r), ˌpɛnθɪsɪˈleɪə(r)
AM ˌpɛnθəˈsɪliə
penthouse
BR ˈpɛnthaʊ|s, -zɪz
AM ˈpɛn(t)ˌ(h)aʊ|s, -zəz
pentimenti
BR ˌpɛntɪˈmɛnti
AM ˌpɛn(t)əˈmɛnˌti
pentimento
BR ˌpɛntɪˈmɛntəʊ
AM ˌpɛn(t)əˈmɛnˌtoʊ
Pentire
BR pɛnˈtʌɪə(r)
AM pɛnˈtaɪ(ə)r
Pentland
BR ˈpɛntlənd
AM ˈpɛn(t)lənd
pentobarbital
BR ˌpɛntə(ʊ)ˈbɑːbɪtl
AM ˌpɛn(t)əˈbɑrbədl, ˌpɛn(t)əˈbɑrbəˌtɔl, ˌpɛn(t)əˈbɑrbəˌtɑl
pentobarbitol
BR ˌpɛntə(ʊ)ˈbɑːbɪtɒl
AM ˌpɛn(t)əˈbɑrbədl, ˌpɛn(t)əˈbɑrbəˌtɔl, ˌpɛn(t)əˈbɑrbəˌtɑl
pentobarbitone
BR ˌpɛntə(ʊ)ˈbɑːbɪtəʊn
AM ˌpɛn(t)əˈbɑrbəˌtoʊn
pentode
BR ˈpɛntəʊd, -z
AM ˈpɛnˌtoʊd, -z
Pentonville
BR ˈpɛntənvɪl
AM ˈpɛntnˌvɪl
pentose
BR ˈpɛntəʊz, ˈpɛntəʊs, -ɪz
AM ˈpɛnˌtoʊs, ˈpɛnˌtoʊz, -əz
Pentothal®
BR ˈpɛntəθal
AM ˈpɛn(t)əˌθɔl, ˈpɛn(θ)əˌθɑl
pent-roof
BR ˈpɛntruːf, ˈpɛntrʊf, -s
AM ˈpɛn(t)ˌruf, -s
pentstemon
BR pɛn(t)ˈstiːmən, ˈpɛn(t)stɪmən, -z
AM pɛn(t)ˈstimən, ˈpɛn(t)stəmən, -z
pentyl
BR ˈpɛntʌɪl
AM ˈpɛn(t)əl
penuche
BR pɪˈnuːtʃi
AM pəˈnutʃi
penult
BR pɪˈnʌlt, ˈpɛnʌlt, -s
AM ˈpiˌnəlt, pəˈnəlt, -s
penultimate
BR pɪˈnʌltɪmət, pɛˈnʌltɪmət, -s
AM pəˈnəltəmət, -s
penultimately
BR pɪˈnʌltɪmətli, pɛˈnʌltɪmətli
AM pəˈnəltəmətli
penumbra
BR pɪˈnʌmbrə(r), pɛˈnʌmbrə(r), -z
AM pəˈnəmbrə, -z
penumbrae
BR pɪˈnʌmbriː, pɛˈnʌmbriː
AM pəˈnəmˌbri, pəˈnəmˌbraɪ
penumbral
BR pɪˈnʌmbr(ə)l, pɛˈnʌmbr(ə)l
AM pəˈnəmbrəl
penurious
BR pɪˈnjʊərɪəs, pɛˈnjʊərɪəs, pɪˈnjɔːrɪəs, pɛˈnjɔːrɪəs
AM pəˈn(j)ʊriəs
penuriously
BR pɪˈnjʊərɪəsli, pɛˈnjʊərɪəsli, pɪˈnjɔːrɪəs, pɛˈnjɔːrɪəs
AM pəˈn(j)ʊriəsli
penuriousness
BR pɪˈnjʊərɪəsnəs, pɛˈnjʊərɪəsnəs, pɪˈnjɔːrɪəsnəs, pɛˈnjɔːrɪəsnəs
AM pəˈn(j)ʊriəsnəs
penury
BR ˈpɛnjʊri
AM ˈpɛnjəri
Penybont
BR ˌpɛnɪˈbɒnt
AM ˌpɛniˈbɔnt, ˌpɛniˈbɑnt
WE ˌpɛnʌˈbɒnt
Penyghent
BR ˌpɛnɪˈgɛnt
AM ˌpɛniˈgɛnt
Penza
BR ˈp(j)ɛnzə(r)
AM ˈpɛnzə

Penzance
BR pɛn'zans
AM pɛn'zæns

peon
BR 'piːən, 'piːɒn, -z
AM 'piˌɑn, 'piən, -z

peonage
BR 'piːənɪdʒ
AM 'piənɪdʒ

peony
BR 'piːən|i, -ɪz
AM 'piəni, -z

people
BR 'piːp|l, -lz, -l̩ɪŋ\-lɪŋ, -ld
AM 'pip|əl, -əlz, -(ə)lɪŋ, -əld

pep
BR pɛp, -s, -ɪŋ, -t
AM pɛp, -s, -ɪŋ, -t

Pepe
BR 'pɛpeɪ
AM 'pɛpeɪ

peperino
BR ˌpɛpə'riːnəʊ
AM ˌpɛpə'riˌnoʊ

peperoni
BR ˌpɛpə'rəʊn|i, -ɪz
AM ˌpɛpə'roʊni, -z

Pepin
BR 'pɛpɪn
AM 'pɛpən

pepla
BR 'pɛplə(r)
AM 'pɛplə

peplum
BR 'pɛpləm, -z
AM 'pɛpləm, -z

pepo
BR 'pɛpəʊ, -z
AM 'pɛˌpoʊ, -z

Peppard
BR 'pɛpɑːd
AM pə'pɑrd, 'pɛpərd

pepper
BR 'pɛp|ə(r), -əz, -(ə)rɪŋ, -əd
AM 'pɛpər, -z, -ɪŋ, -d

pepperbox
BR 'pɛpəbɒks, -ɨz
AM 'pɛpərˌbɑks, -əz

peppercorn
BR 'pɛpəkɔːn, -z
AM 'pɛpərˌkɔ(ə)rn, -z

pepperiness
BR 'pɛp(ə)rɪnɨs
AM 'pɛp(ə)rinɨs

peppermint
BR 'pɛpəmɪnt, -s
AM 'pɛpərˌmɪnt, -s

pepperminty
BR 'pɛpəmɪnti
AM 'pɛpərˌmɪn(t)i

pepperoni
BR ˌpɛpə'rəʊni
AM ˌpɛpə'roʊni

pepperpot
BR 'pɛpəpɒt, -s
AM 'pɛpərˌpɑt, -s

pepperwort
BR 'pɛpəwəːt, -s
AM 'pɛpərwərt, 'pɛpərwɔ(ə)rt, -s

peppery
BR 'pɛp(ə)ri
AM 'pɛp(ə)ri

peppily
BR 'pɛpɨli
AM 'pɛpəli

peppiness
BR 'pɛpɪnɨs
AM 'pɛpinɨs

peppy
BR 'pɛp|i, -ɪə(r), -ɪɪst
AM 'pɛpi, -ər, -ɨst

Pepsi®
BR 'pɛpsi
AM 'pɛpsi

Pepsi-Cola®
BR ˌpɛpsɪ'kəʊlə(r)
AM ˌpɛpsə'koʊlə

pepsin
BR 'pɛpsɪn, -z
AM 'pɛpsən, -z

Pepsodent®
BR 'pɛpsədɛnt, 'pɛpsəd(ə)nt
AM 'pɛpsədnt

peptalk
BR 'pɛptɔːk, -s
AM 'pɛpˌtɔk, 'pɛpˌtɑk, -s

peptic
BR 'pɛptɪk
AM 'pɛptɪk

peptide
BR 'pɛptʌɪd
AM 'pɛpˌtaɪd

peptone
BR 'pɛptəʊn, -z
AM 'pɛpˌtoʊn, -z

peptonise
BR 'pɛptənʌɪz, -ɨz, -ɪŋ, -d
AM 'pɛptəˌnaɪz, -ɨz, -ɪŋ, -d

peptonize
BR 'pɛptənʌɪz, -ɨz, -ɪŋ, -d
AM 'pɛptəˌnaɪz, -ɨz, -ɪŋ, -d

Pepys
BR piːps, 'pɛp(ɪ)s
AM pips

per[1]
strong form
BR pəː(r)
AM pər

per[2]
weak form
BR pə(r)
AM pər

peradventure
BR ˌpəːrəd'vɛntʃə(r), p(ə)rəd'vɛntʃə(r)
AM ˌpərəd'vɛn(t)ʃər, ˌpɛrəd'vɛn(t)ʃər

Perak
BR 'pɛːrə(r), 'pɪərə(r), pɛ'rak
AM 'pɛræk, pə'ræk

perambulate
BR pə'rambjʉleɪt, -s, -ɪŋ, -ɨd
AM pə'ræmbjəˌleɪ|t, -ts, -dɪŋ, -dɨd

perambulation
BR pəˌrambjʊ'leɪʃn, -z
AM pəˌræmbjə'leɪʃən, -z

perambulator
BR pə'rambjʉleɪtə(r), -z
AM pə'ræmbjəˌleɪdər, -z

perambulatory
BR pə'rambjʉlət(ə)ri
AM pə'ræmbjələˌtɔri

per annum
BR pər 'anəm, pəːr +
AM pə 'rænəm

percale
BR pə'keɪl, pə'kɑːl
AM pər'keɪ(ə)l

per capita
BR pə 'kapɨtə(r), pəː +
AM pər 'kæpədə

per caput
BR pə 'kapʊt, pəː +
AM pər 'kæpət

perceivable
BR pə'siːvəbl
AM pər'sivəbəl

perceivably
BR pə'siːvəbli
AM pər'sivəbli

perceive
BR pə'siːv, -z, -ɪŋ, -d
AM pər'siv, -z, -ɪŋ, -d

perceiver
BR pə'siːvə(r), -z
AM pər'sivər, -z

percent
BR pə'sɛnt
AM pər'sɛnt

percentage
BR pə'sɛnt|ɪdʒ, -ɨdʒɨz
AM pər'sɛn(t)ɪdʒ, -ɨz

percentile
BR pə'sɛntʌɪl
AM pər'sɛnˌtaɪl

percept
BR 'pəːsɛpt, -s
AM 'pərˌsɛpt, -s

perceptibility
BR pəˌsɛptɪ'bɪlɨti
AM pərˌsɛptə'bɪlɨdi

perceptible
BR pə'sɛptɨbl
AM pər'sɛptəbəl

perceptibly
BR pə'sɛptɨbli
AM pər'sɛptəbli

perception
BR pə'sɛpʃn, -z
AM pər'sɛpʃən, -z

perceptional
BR pə'sɛpʃn̩(ə)l, pə'sɛpʃən(ə)l
AM pər'sɛpʃ(ə)nəl

perceptive
BR pə'sɛptɪv
AM pər'sɛptɪv

perceptively
BR pə'sɛptɨvli
AM pər'sɛptɨvli

perceptiveness
BR pə'sɛptɨvnɨs
AM pər'sɛptɪvnɨs

perceptivity
BR ˌpəːsɛp'tɪvɨti
AM ˌpərsɛp'tɪvɨdi

perceptual
BR pə'sɛptʃʊəl, pə'sɛptʃ(ʉ)l, pə'sɛptjʊəl, pə'sɛptjʉl
AM pər'sɛp(t)ʃ(əw)əl

perceptually
BR pə'sɛptʃʊəli, pə'sɛptʃʉli, pə'sɛptʃli, pə'sɛptjʊəli, pə'sɛptjʉli
AM pər'sɛp(t)ʃ(əw)əli

Perceval
BR 'pəːsɪvl
AM 'pərsəvəl

perch
BR pəːtʃ, -ɨz, -ɪŋ, -t
AM pərtʃ, -əz, -ɪŋ, -t

perchance
BR pə'tʃɑːns, pə'tʃans
AM pər'tʃæns

percher
BR 'pəːtʃə(r), -z
AM 'pərtʃər, -z

Percheron
BR 'pəːʃ(ə)rɒn, -z
AM 'pɛr(t)ʃəˌrɑn, -z

perchlorate
BR pə'klɔːreɪt, -s
AM pər'klɔˌreɪt, -s

perchloric acid
BR pəˌklɔːrɪk 'asɪd, pəˌklɒrɪk +
AM pərˌklɔrɪk 'æsəd

perchloroethylene
BR pəˌklɔːrəʊ'ɛθɨliːn
AM pərˌklɔroʊ'ɛθəˌlin

percipience
BR pə'sɪpɪəns
AM pər'sɪpiəns

percipient
BR pə'sɪpɪənt
AM pər'sɪpiənt

percipiently
BR pə'sɪpɪəntli

AM pər'sɪpiən(t)li

Percival
BR 'pəːsɪvl
AM 'pərsəvəl

percoid
BR 'pəːkɔɪd, -z
AM 'pərkɔɪd, -z

percolate
BR 'pəːkəleɪt, -s, -ɪŋ, -ɪd
AM 'pərkəˌleɪ|t, -ts, -dɪŋ, -dɪd

percolation
BR ˌpəːkə'leɪʃn
AM ˌpərkə'leɪʃən

percolator
BR 'pəːkəleɪtə(r), -z
AM 'pərkəˌleɪdər, -z

per contra
BR pəː 'kɒntrə(r)
AM pər 'kɔntrə, pər 'kɑntrə

percuss
BR pə'kʌs, -ɪz, -ɪŋ, -t
AM pər'kəs, -əz, -ɪŋ, -t

percussion
BR pə'kʌʃn
AM pər'kəʃən

percussionist
BR pə'kʌʃn̩ɪst, -s
AM pər'kəʃənəst, -s

percussive
BR pə'kʌsɪv
AM pər'kəsɪv

percussively
BR pə'kʌsɪvli
AM pər'kəsɪvli

percussiveness
BR pə'kʌsɪvnɪs
AM pər'kəsɪvnɪs

percutaneous
BR ˌpəːkjʊ'teɪnɪəs
AM ˌpərkjə'teɪniəs

percutaneously
BR ˌpəːkjʊ'teɪnɪəsli
AM ˌpərkjə'teɪniəsli

Percy
BR 'pəːsi
AM 'pərsi

per diem
BR pəː 'diːɛm, -z
AM pər 'diəm, -z

Perdita
BR 'pəːdɪtə(r)
AM pər'didə

perdition
BR pə'dɪʃn
AM pər'dɪʃən

perdurability
BR pəˌdjʊərə'bɪlɪti, pəˌdjɔːrə'bɪlɪti, pəˌdʒʊərə'bɪlɪti, pəˌdʒɔːrə'bɪlɪti
AM pərˌd(j)ʊrə'bɪlɪdi

perdurable
BR pə'djʊərəbl, pə'djɔːrəbl, pə'dʒʊərəbl, pə'dʒɔːrəbl
AM pər'd(j)ʊrəbəl

perdurably
BR pə'djʊərəbli, pə'djɔːrəbli, pə'dʒʊərəbli, pə'dʒɔːrəbli
AM pər'd(j)ʊrəbli

père
BR pɛː(r)
AM pɛ(ə)r

peregrinate
BR 'pɛrɪɡrɪneɪt, -s, -ɪŋ, -ɪd
AM 'pɛrəɡrəˌneɪ|t, -ts, -dɪŋ, -dɪd

peregrination
BR ˌpɛrɪɡrɪ'neɪʃn, -z
AM ˌpɛrəɡrə'neɪʃən, -z

peregrinator
BR 'pɛrɪɡrɪneɪtə(r), -z
AM 'pɛrəɡrəˌneɪdər, -z

peregrine
BR 'pɛrɪɡrɪn, -z
AM 'pɛrəɡrən, -z

pereira
BR pə'rɛːrə(r), pə'rɪərə(r)
AM pə'rɛrə

Perelman
BR 'pəːlmən
AM 'pər(ə)lmən

peremptorily
BR pə'rɛm(p)t(ə)rɪli
AM pə'rɛm(p)t(ə)rəli

peremptoriness
BR pə'rɛm(p)t(ə)rɪnɪs
AM pə'rɛm(p)t(ə)rinɪs

peremptory
BR pə'rɛm(p)t(ə)ri
AM pə'rɛm(p)t(ə)ri

perennial
BR pə'rɛnɪəl, -z
AM pə'rɛnjəl, pə'rɛniəl, -z

perenniality
BR pəˌrɛnɪ'alɪti
AM pəˌrɛni'ælədi

perennially
BR pə'rɛnɪəli
AM pə'rɛnjəli, pə'rɛniəli

Peres
BR 'pɛrɛz
AM 'pɛrəs, 'pɛˌrɛz

perestroika
BR ˌpɛrɪ'strɔɪ(ɪ)kə(r)
AM ˌpɛrə'strɔɪkə

Pérez
BR 'pɛrɛz
AM pə'rɛz, 'pɛrəz
SP 'pereθ, 'peres

perfect¹
adjective
BR 'pəːfɪkt
AM 'pərfək(t)

perfect²
verb
BR pə'fɛkt, -s, -ɪŋ, -ɪd
AM pər'fɛk|(t), -(t)s, -tɪŋ, -təd

perfecta
BR pə'fɛktə(r)
AM pər'fɛktə

perfecter
BR pə'fɛktə(r), -z
AM pər'fɛktər, -z

perfectibility
BR pəˌfɛktɪ'bɪlɪti
AM pərˌfɛktə'bɪlɪdi

perfectible
BR pə'fɛktɪbl
AM pər'fɛktəbəl

perfection
BR pə'fɛkʃn
AM pər'fɛkʃən

perfectionism
BR pə'fɛkʃn̩ɪz(ə)m, pə'fɛkʃənɪz(ə)m
AM pər'fɛkʃəˌnɪzəm

perfectionist
BR pə'fɛkʃn̩ɪst, pə'fɛkʃənɪst, -s
AM pər'fɛkʃ(ə)nəst, -s

perfective
BR pə'fɛktɪv
AM pər'fɛktɪv

perfectly
BR 'pəːfɪk(t)li
AM 'pərfək(t)li

perfectness
BR 'pəːfɪk(t)nɪs
AM 'pərfək(t)nəs

perfecto
BR pə'fɛktəʊ
AM pər'fɛkˌtoʊ

perfervid
BR pəː'fəːvɪd, pə'fəːvɪd
AM ˌpər'fərvɪd

perfervidly
BR pəː'fəːvɪdli, pə'fəːvɪdli
AM ˌpər'fərvɪdli

perfervidness
BR pəː'fəːvɪdnɪs, pə'fəːvɪdnɪs
AM ˌpər'fərvɪdnɪs

perfidious
BR pə'fɪdɪəs
AM pər'fɪdiəs

perfidiously
BR pə'fɪdɪəsli
AM pər'fɪdiəsli

perfidiousness
BR pə'fɪdɪəsnəs
AM pər'fɪdiəsnəs

perfidy
BR 'pəːfɪd|i, -ɪz
AM 'pərfədi, -z

perfin
BR 'pəːfɪn, -z
AM 'pərfɪn, -z

perfoliate
BR pə'fəʊlɪət
AM pər'foʊliˌeɪt, pər'foʊliət

perforate¹
adjective
BR 'pəːf(ə)rət
AM 'pərf(ə)rət, 'pərfəˌreɪt

perforate²
verb
BR 'pəːfəreɪt, -s, -ɪŋ, -ɪd
AM 'pərfəˌreɪ|t, -ts, -dɪŋ, -dɪd

perforation
BR ˌpəːfə'reɪʃn, -z
AM ˌpərfə'reɪʃən, -z

perforative
BR 'pəːf(ə)rətɪv
AM 'pərfəˌreɪdɪv, 'pərfərədɪv

perforator
BR 'pəːfəreɪtə(r), -z
AM 'pərfəˌreɪdər, -z

perforce
BR pə'fɔːs
AM pər'fɔ(ə)rs

perforin
BR 'pəːf(ə)rɪn
AM 'pərfərɪn

perform
BR pə'fɔːm, -z, -ɪŋ, -d
AM pər'fɔ(ə)rm, -z, -ɪŋ, -d

performability
BR pəˌfɔːmə'bɪlɪti
AM pərˌfɔrmə'bɪlɪdi

performable
BR pə'fɔːməbl
AM pər'fɔrməbəl

performance
BR pə'fɔːməns, -ɪz
AM pər'fɔrməns, -ɪz

performative
BR pə'fɔːmətɪv, -z
AM pər'fɔrmədɪv, -z

performatory
BR pə'fɔːmət(ə)r|i, -ɪz
AM pər'fɔrməˌtɔri, -z

performer
BR pə'fɔːmə(r), -z
AM pər'fɔrmər, -z

perfume¹
noun
BR 'pəːfjuːm, -z
AM 'pərˌfjum, ˌpər'fjum, -z

perfume²
verb
BR pə'fjuːm, 'pəːfjuːm, -z, -ɪŋ, -d
AM ˌpər'fjum, 'pərˌfjum, -z, -ɪŋ, -d

perfumer
BR pə'fjuːmə(r), -z
AM pər'fjumər, -z

perfumery
BR pə'fjuːm(ə)r|i, -ɪz

AM pər'fjum(ə)ri, -z
perfumier
BR pə'fju:mɪə(r), -z
AM pər'fjumɪ(ə)r, -z
perfumy
BR 'pə:fju:mi
AM 'pər,fjumi, ,pər'fjumi
perfunctorily
BR pə'fʌŋ(k)t(ə)rɨli
AM pər'fəŋ(k)t(ə)rəli
perfunctoriness
BR pə'fʌŋ(k)t(ə)rɪnɨs
AM pər'fəŋ(k)t(ə)rinɨs
perfunctory
BR pə'fʌŋ(k)t(ə)ri
AM pər'fəŋ(k)t(ə)ri
perfuse
BR pə'fju:z, -ɨz, -ɪŋ, -d
AM pər'fjuz, -əz, -ɪŋ, -d
perfusion
BR pə'fju:ʒn, -z
AM pər'fjuʒən, -z
perfusive
BR pə'fju:zɪv
AM pər'fjuzɪv
Pergamene
BR 'pə:gəmi:n, ,pə:gə'mi:n, -z
AM 'pərgə,min, -z
Pergamon
BR 'pə:gəmən
AM 'pərgəmən
Pergamum
BR 'pə:gəməm
AM 'pərgəməm
pergola
BR 'pə:gələ(*r*), 'pə:gl̩ə(*r*), -z
AM 'pərgələ, -z
perhaps
BR pə'haps, praps
AM pər'(h)æps
peri
BR 'pɪər|i, -ɪz
AM 'pɪəri, -z
perianth
BR 'pɛrɪanθ, -s
AM 'pɛri,ænθ, -s
periapses
BR ,pɛrɪ'apsi:z
AM ,pɛri'æpsiz
periapsis
BR ,pɛrɪ'apsɪs
AM ,pɛri'æpsɪs
periapt
BR 'pɛrɪapt, -s
AM 'pɛri,æpt, -s
pericardia
BR ,pɛrɪ'kɑ:dɪə(*r*)
AM ,pɛrə'kɑrdiə
pericardiac
BR ,pɛrɪ'kɑ:dɪak
AM ,pɛrə'kɑrdi,æk
pericardial
BR ,pɛrɪ'kɑ:dɪəl
AM ,pɛrə'kɑrdiəl
pericarditis
BR ,pɛrɪkɑ:'dʌɪtɪs
AM ,pɛrə,kɑr'daɪdɪs
pericardium
BR ,pɛrɪ'kɑ:dɪəm, -z
AM ,pɛrə'kɑrdiəm, -z
pericarp
BR 'pɛrɪkɑ:p, -s
AM 'pɛrə,kɑrp, -s
perichondria
BR ,pɛrɪ'kɒndrɪə(*r*)
AM ,pɛrə'kɑndriə
perichondrium
BR ,pɛrɪ'kɒndrɪəm
AM ,pɛrə'kɑndriəm
periclase
BR 'pɛrɨkleɪz, 'pɛrɨkleɪs
AM 'pɛrə,kleɪs, 'pɛrə,kleɪz
Periclean
BR ,pɛrɨ'kli:ən
AM ,pɛrə'kliən
Pericles
BR 'pɛrɨkli:z
AM 'pɛrə,kliz
periclinal
BR ,pɛrɪ'klʌɪnl
AM ¦pɛrə¦klaɪnəl
pericope
BR pɨ'rɪkəpi
AM pə'rɪkəpi
pericrania
BR ,pɛrɪ'kreɪnɪə(*r*)
AM ,pɛrə'kreɪniə
pericranium
BR ,pɛrɪ'kreɪnɪəm, -z
AM ,pɛrə'kreɪniəm, -z
peridia
BR pɨ'rɪdɪə(*r*)
AM pə'rɪdiə
peridium
BR pɨ'rɪdɪəm
AM pə'rɪdiəm
peridot
BR 'pɛrɪdɒt
AM 'pɛri,dɑt
peridotite
BR 'pɛrɨdətʌɪt
AM pə'rɪdə,taɪt
perigean
BR ,pɛrɨ'dʒi:ən
AM ,pɛrə'dʒiən
perigee
BR 'pɛrɨdʒi:, -z
AM 'pɛrədʒi, -z
periglacial
BR ,pɛrɪ'gleɪʃl, ,pɛrɪ'gleɪsɪəl
AM ,pɛrə'gleɪʃəl
perigynous
BR pɨ'rɪdʒɨnəs
AM pə'rɪdʒənəs
perihelion
BR ,pɛrɪ'hi:lɪən
AM ,pɛrə'hiljən, ,pɛrə'hiliən
peril
BR 'pɛrɪl, pɛrl̩, -z
AM 'pɛrəl, -z
perilous
BR 'pɛrɨləs, 'pɛrl̩əs
AM 'pɛrələs
perilously
BR 'pɛrɨləsli, 'pɛrl̩əsli
AM 'pɛrələsli
perilousness
BR 'pɛrɨləsnəs, 'pɛrl̩əsnəs
AM 'pɛrələsnəs
perilune
BR 'pɛrɪl(j)u:n
AM 'pɛrə,lun
perilymph
BR 'pɛrɪlɪmf
AM 'pɛrə,lɪmf
perimeter
BR pɨ'rɪmɨtə(r), -z
AM pə'rɪmɨdər, -z
perimetric
BR ,pɛrɨ'mɛtrɪk
AM ,pɛrə'mɛtrɪk
perimysium
BR ,pɛrɨ'mɪsɪəm
AM ,pɛrə'mɪʒ(i)əm
perinatal
BR ,pɛrɪ'neɪtl
AM ¦pɛrə'neɪdl
perinea
BR ,pɛrɨ'ni:ə(*r*)
AM ,pɛrə'niə
perineal
BR ,pɛrɨ'ni:əl
AM ,pɛrə'niəl
perineum
BR ,pɛrɨ'ni:əm, -z
AM ,pɛrə'niəm, -z
period
BR 'pɪərɪəd, -z
AM 'pɪriəd, -z
periodate
BR pə'rʌɪədeɪt, -s
AM pər'aɪə,deɪt, -s
periodic
BR ,pɪərɪ'ɒdɪk
AM ¦pɪri'ɑdɪk
periodical
BR ,pɪərɪ'ɒdɨkl, -z
AM ¦pɪri'ɑdəkəl, -z
periodically
BR ,pɪərɪ'ɒdɨkli
AM ¦pɪri'ɑdək(ə)li
periodicity
BR ,pɪərɪə'dɪsɨti
AM ,pɪriə'dɪsɨdi
periodisation
BR ,pɪərɪədʌɪ'zeɪʃn
AM ,pɛriədə'zeɪʃən, ,pɛriə,daɪ'zeɪʃən
periodise
BR 'pɪərɪədʌɪz, -ɨz, -ɪŋ, -d
AM 'piriɑdaɪz, -ɨz, -ɪŋ, -d
periodization
BR ,pɪərɪədʌɪ'zeɪʃn
AM ,pɛriədə'zeɪʃən, ,pɛriə,daɪ'zeɪʃən
periodize
BR 'pɪərɪədʌɪz, -ɨz, -ɪŋ, -d
AM 'piriɑdaɪz, -ɨz, -ɪŋ, -d
periodontal
BR ,pɛrɪə'dɒntl
AM ,pɛrioʊ'dɑn(t)l
periodontics
BR ,pɛrɪə'dɒntɪks
AM ,pɛrioʊ'dɑn(t)ɪks
periodontist
BR ,pɛrɪə'dɒntɪst, -s
AM ,pɛrioʊ'dɑn(t)əst, -s
periodontology
BR ,pɛrɪədɒn'tɒlədʒi
AM ,pɛrioʊ,dɑn'tɑlədʒi
periostea
BR ,pɛrɪ'ɒstɪə(*r*)
AM ,pɛri'ɑstiə
periosteal
BR ,pɛrɪ'ɒstɪəl
AM ,pɛri'ɑstiəl
periosteum
BR ,pɛrɪ'ɒstɪəm
AM ,pɛri'ɑstiəm
periostitis
BR ,pɛrɪə'stʌɪtɪs
AM ,pɛri,ɑs'taɪdɪs, ,pɛriə'staɪdɪs
peripatetic
BR ,pɛrɨpə'tɛtɪk
AM ,pɛrəpə'tɛdɪk
peripatetically
BR ,pɛrɨpə'tɛtɨkli
AM ,pɛrəpə'tɛdək(ə)li
peripateticism
BR ,pɛrɨpə'tɛtɪsɪz(ə)m
AM ,pɛrəpə'tɛdə,sɪzəm
peripeteia
BR ,pɛrɨpɨ'tʌɪə(*r*), ,pɛrɨpɨ'tɪə(*r*)
AM ,pɛrəpə'ti(j)ə, ,pɛrəpə'taɪə
peripheral
BR pɨ'rɪf(ə)rəl, pɨ'rɪf(ə)rl̩
AM pə'rɪf(ə)rəl
peripherality
BR pɨ,rɪfə'ralɨti
AM pə,rɪfə'rælədi
peripherally
BR pɨ'rɪf(ə)rəli, pɨ'rɪf(ə)rl̩i
AM pə'rɪf(ə)rəli
periphery
BR pɨ'rɪf(ə)r|i, -ɪz
AM pə'rɪf(ə)ri, -z
periphrases
BR pɨ'rɪfrəsi:z
AM pə'rɪfrə,siz
periphrasis
BR pɨ'rɪfrəsɪs

AM pəˈrɪfrəsəz
periphrastic
BR ˌpɛrɪˈfrastɪk
AM ˌpɛrəˈfræstɪk
periphrastically
BR ˌpɛrɪˈfrastɪkli
AM ˌpɛrəˈfræstək(ə)li
peripteral
BR pɪˈrɪpt(ə)rəl, pɪˈrɪpt(ə)rl̩
AM pəˈrɪpt(ə)rəl
perique
BR pəˈriːk
AM pəˈrik
periscope
BR ˈpɛrɪskəʊp, -s
AM ˈpɛrəˌskoʊp, -s
periscopic
BR ˌpɛrɪˈskɒpɪk
AM ˌpɛrəˈskɑpɪk
periscopically
BR ˌpɛrɪˈskɒpɪkli
AM ˌpɛrəˈskɑpək(ə)li
perish
BR ˈpɛr|ɪʃ, -ɪʃɪz, -ɪʃɪŋ, -ɪʃt
AM ˈpɛrɪʃ, -ɪz, -ɪŋ, -t
perishability
BR ˌpɛrɪʃəˈbɪlɪti
AM ˌpɛrəʃəˈbɪlɪdi
perishable
BR ˈpɛrɪʃəbl, -z
AM ˈpɛrəʃəbəl, -z
perishableness
BR ˈpɛrɪʃəblnəs
AM ˈpɛrəʃəbəlnəs
perishably
BR ˈpɛrɪʃəbli
AM ˈpɛrəʃəbli
perisher
BR ˈpɛrɪʃə(r), -z
AM ˈpɛrɪʃər, -z
perishingly
BR ˈpɛrɪʃɪŋli
AM ˈpɛrɪʃɪŋli
perishless
BR ˈpɛrɪʃlɪs
AM ˈpɛrɪʃləs
perisperm
BR ˈpɛrɪspəːm, -z
AM ˈpɛrəˌspərm, -z
perissodactyl
BR pɪˌrɪsə(ʊ)ˈdakt(ɪ)l, -z
AM pəˌrɪsəˈdæktl, -z
Perissodactyla
BR ˌpɛrɪsəˈdaktɪlə(r)
AM pəˌrɪsəˈdæktələ
peristalith
BR pɪˈrɪstəlɪθ, -s
AM pəˈrɪstəˌlɪθ, -s
peristalsis
BR ˌpɛrɪˈstalsɪs
AM ˌpɛrəˈstɔlsəs, ˌpɛrəˈstɑlsəs
peristaltic
BR ˌpɛrɪˈstaltɪk
AM ˌpɛrəˈstɔltɪk, ˌpɛrəˈstɑltɪk
peristaltically
BR ˌpɛrɪˈstaltɪkli
AM ˌpɛrəˈstɔltək(ə)li, ˌpɛrəˈstɑltək(ə)li
peristome
BR ˈpɛrɪstəʊm, -z
AM ˈpɛrəˌstoʊm, -z
peristyle
BR ˈpɛrɪstʌɪl, -z
AM ˈpɛrəˌstaɪl, -z
peritonea
BR ˌpɛrɪtəˈniːə(r)
AM ˌpɛrətnˈiə
peritoneal
BR ˌpɛrɪtəˈniːəl
AM ˌpɛrətnˈiəl
peritoneum
BR ˌpɛrɪtəˈniːəm, -z
AM ˌpɛrətnˈiəm, -z
peritonitis
BR ˌpɛrɪtəˈnʌɪtɪs
AM ˌpɛrətnˈaɪdɪs
Perivale
BR ˈpɛrɪveɪl
AM ˈpɛrəˌveɪl
periwig
BR ˈpɛrɪwɪɡ, -z, -d
AM ˈpɛrəˌwɪɡ, ˈpɛriˌwɪɡ, -z, -d
periwinkle
BR ˈpɛrɪˌwɪŋkl, -z
AM ˈpɛrəˌwɪŋkəl, ˈpɛriˌwɪŋkəl, -z
perjure
BR ˈpəːdʒ|ə(r), -əz, -(ə)rɪŋ, -əd
AM ˈpərdʒ|ər, -ərz, -(ə)rɪŋ, -ərd
perjurer
BR ˈpəːdʒ(ə)rə(r), -z
AM ˈpərdʒərər, -z
perjurious
BR pəːˈdʒʊərɪəs
AM pərˈdʒʊriəs
perjury
BR ˈpəːdʒ(ə)r|i, -ɪz
AM ˈpərdʒ(ə)ri, -z
perk
BR pəːk, -s, -ɪŋ, -t
AM pərk, -s, -ɪŋ, -t
perkily
BR ˈpəːkɪli
AM ˈpərkəli
Perkin
BR ˈpəːkɪn
AM ˈpərkən
perkiness
BR ˈpəːkɪnɪs
AM ˈpərkinɪs
Perkins
BR ˈpəːkɪnz
AM ˈpərkənz
Perks
BR pəːks
AM pərks
perky
BR ˈpəːk|i, -ɪə(r), -ɪɪst
AM ˈpərki, -ər, -ɪst
Perlis
BR ˈpəːlɪs
AM ˈpərləs
perlite
BR ˈpəːlʌɪt, -s
AM ˈpərˌlaɪt, -s
perlocution
BR ˌpəːləˈkjuːʃn
AM ˌpərləˈkjuʃən
perm
BR pəːm, -z, -ɪŋ, -d
AM pərm, -z, -ɪŋ, -d
permafrost
BR ˈpəːməfrɒst
AM ˈpərməˌfrɔst, ˈpərməˌfrɑst
Permalloy
BR ˈpəːməlɔɪ
AM ˈpərməˌlɔɪ
permanence
BR ˈpəːmənəns, ˈpəːmn̩əns
AM ˈpərm(ə)nəns
permanency
BR ˈpəːmənəns|i, ˈpəːmn̩əns|i, -ɪz
AM ˈpərm(ə)nənsi, -z
permanent
BR ˈpəːmənənt, ˈpəːmn̩ənt
AM ˈpərm(ə)nənt
permanentise
BR ˈpəːmənəntʌɪz, ˈpəːmn̩əntʌɪz, -ɪz, -ɪŋ, -d
AM ˈpərm(ə)nənˌtaɪz, -ɪz, -ɪŋ, -d
permanentize
BR ˈpəːmənəntʌɪz, ˈpəːmn̩əntʌɪz, -ɪz, -ɪŋ, -d
AM ˈpərm(ə)nənˌtaɪz, -ɪz, -ɪŋ, -d
permanently
BR ˈpəːmənəntli, ˈpəːmn̩əntli
AM ˈpərm(ə)nən(t)li
permanganate
BR pəˈmaŋɡəneɪt, pəˈmaŋɡənət
AM ˌpərˈmæŋɡəˌneɪt, ˌpərˈmæŋɡənət
permanganic acid
BR ˌpəːmaŋɡanɪk ˈasɪd
AM pərˌmænˌɡænɪk ˈæsəd
permeability
BR ˌpəːmɪəˈbɪlɪti
AM ˌpərmiəˈbɪlɪdi
permeable
BR ˈpəːmɪəbl
AM ˈpərmiəbəl
permeance
BR ˈpəːmɪəns
AM ˈpərmiəns
permeant
BR ˈpəːmɪənt
AM ˈpərmiənt
permeate
BR ˈpəːmɪeɪt, -s, -ɪŋ, -ɪd
AM ˈpərmiˌeɪ|t, -ts, -dɪŋ, -dɪd
permeation
BR ˌpəːmɪˈeɪʃn
AM ˌpərmiˈeɪʃən
permeator
BR ˈpəːmɪeɪtə(r), -z
AM ˈpərmiˌeɪdər, -z
Permian
BR ˈpəːmɪən
AM ˈpərmiən
per mil
BR pəː ˈmɪl
AM pər ˈmɪl
per mille
BR pəː ˈmɪl
AM pər ˈmɪl
permissibility
BR pəˌmɪsɪˈbɪlɪti
AM pərˌmɪsəˈbɪlɪdi
permissible
BR pəˈmɪsɪbl
AM pərˈmɪsəbəl
permissibleness
BR pəˈmɪsɪblnəs
AM pərˈmɪsəbəlnəs
permissibly
BR pəˈmɪsɪbli
AM pərˈmɪsəbli
permission
BR pəˈmɪʃn
AM pərˈmɪʃən
permissive
BR pəˈmɪsɪv
AM pərˈmɪsɪv
permissively
BR pəˈmɪsɪvli
AM pərˈmɪsɪvli
permissiveness
BR pəˈmɪsɪvnɪs
AM pərˈmɪsɪvnɪs
permit[1]
noun
BR ˈpəːmɪt, -s
AM ˈpərmɪt, -s
permit[2]
verb
BR pəˈmɪt, -s, -ɪŋ, -ɪd
AM pərˈmɪ|t, -ts, -dɪŋ, -dɪd
permittee
BR ˌpəːmɪˈtiː, -z
AM ˌpərməˈti, -z
permitter
BR pəˈmɪtə(r), -z
AM pərˈmɪdər, -z
permittivity
BR ˌpəːmɪˈtɪvɪti
AM ˌpərməˈtɪvɪdi

permutable
BR pə'mjuːtəbl
AM pər'mjudəbəl

permutate
BR 'pəːmjʊteɪt, -s, -ɪŋ, -ɪd
AM 'pərmjəˌteɪ|t, -ts, -dɪŋ, -dɪd

permutation
BR ˌpəːmjʊ'teɪʃn, -z
AM ˌpərmjə'teɪʃən, ˌpərmju'teɪʃən, -z

permutational
BR ˌpəːmjʊ'teɪʃn̩(ə)l, ˌpəːmjʊ'teɪʃən(ə)l
AM ˌpərmjə'teɪʃ(ə)nəl

permute
BR pə'mjuːt, -s, -ɪŋ, -ɪd
AM pər'mju|t, -ts, -dɪŋ, -dəd

Pernambuco
BR ˌpəːnəm'b(j)uːkəʊ, ˌpəːnam'b(j)uːkəʊ
AM ˌpərnəm'bjuˌkoʊ

pernicious
BR pə'nɪʃəs
AM pər'nɪʃəs

perniciously
BR pə'nɪʃəsli
AM pər'nɪʃəsli

perniciousness
BR pə'nɪʃəsnəs
AM pər'nɪʃəsnəs

pernicketiness
BR pə'nɪkɪtɪnɪs
AM pər'nɪkɨdinɪs

pernickety
BR pə'nɪkɪti
AM pər'nɪkɨdi

pernoctate
BR 'pəːnɒkteɪt, -s, -ɪŋ, -d
AM pər'nɑkˌteɪ|t, -ts, -dɪŋ, -dɪd

pernoctation
BR ˌpəːnɒk'teɪʃn
AM pərˌnɑk'teɪʃən

Pernod®
BR 'pɛːnəʊ, 'pəːnəʊ
AM pɛr'noʊ

Perón
BR pɛ'rɒn
AM pɛ'roʊn

peroneal
BR ˌpɛrə(ʊ)'niːəl
AM ˌpɛrə'niəl

Peronism
BR 'pɛrənɪz(ə)m
AM pə'roʊnɪzəm

Peronist
BR 'pɛrənɪst, -s
AM pə'roʊnəst, -s

perorate
BR 'pɛrəreɪt, -s, -ɪŋ, -ɪd
AM 'pɛrəˌreɪ|t, -ts, -dɪŋ, -dɪd

peroration
BR ˌpɛrə'reɪʃn, -z
AM ˌpɛrə'reɪʃən, pərˌɔr'eɪʃən, -z

Perot
BR pə'rəʊ
AM pə'roʊ

peroxidase
BR pə'rɒksɪdeɪz, -ɪz
AM pə'rɑksəˌdeɪz, -ɪz

peroxide
BR pə'rɒksʌɪd, -z
AM pə'rɑkˌsaɪd, -z

perpend
BR pə'pɛnd, -z, -ɪŋ, -ɪd
AM pər'pɛnd, -z, -ɪŋ, -əd

perpendicular
BR ˌpəːp(ə)n'dɪkjʊlə(r), -z
AM ˌpərpən'dɪkjələr, -z

perpendicularity
BR ˌpəːp(ə)nˌdɪkjʊ'larɪti
AM ˌpərpənˌdɪkjə'lɛrədi

perpendicularly
BR ˌpəːp(ə)n'dɪkjʊləli
AM ˌpərpən'dɪkjələrli

perpetrable
BR 'pəːpətrəbl
AM 'pərpətrəbəl

perpetrate
BR 'pəːpɪtreɪt, -s, -ɪŋ, -ɪd
AM 'pərpəˌtreɪ|t, -ts, -dɪŋ, -dɪd

perpetration
BR ˌpəːpɪ'treɪʃn
AM ˌpərpə'treɪʃən

perpetrator
BR 'pəːpɪtreɪtə(r), -z
AM 'pərpəˌtreɪdər, -z

perpetual
BR pə'pɛtʃʊəl, pə'pɛtʃ(ʊ)l, pə'pɛtjʊəl, pə'pɛtjʊl
AM pər'pɛtʃ(əw)əl

perpetualism
BR pə'pɛtʃʊəlɪz(ə)m, pə'pɛtʃʊlɪz(ə)m, pə'pɛtʃl̩ɪz(ə)m, pə'pɛtjʊəlɪz(ə)m, pə'pɛtjʊlɪz(ə)m
AM pər'pɛtʃ(əw)əˌlɪzəm

perpetually
BR pə'pɛtʃʊəli, pə'pɛtʃʊli, pə'pɛtʃl̩i, pə'pɛtjʊəli, pə'pɛtjʊli
AM pər'pɛtʃ(əw)əli

perpetuance
BR pə'pɛtʃʊəns, pə'pɛtjʊəns
AM pər'pɛtʃəwəns

perpetuate
BR pə'pɛtʃʊeɪt, pə'pɛtjʊeɪt, -s, -ɪŋ, -ɪd
AM pər'pɛtʃəˌweɪ|t, -ts, -dɪŋ, -dɪd

perpetuation
BR pəˌpɛtʃʊ'eɪʃn, pəˌpɛtjʊ'eɪʃn
AM pərˌpɛtʃə'weɪʃən

perpetuator
BR pə'pɛtʃʊeɪtə(r), pə'pɛtjʊeɪtə(r), -z
AM pər'pɛtʃəˌweɪdər, -z

perpetuity
BR ˌpəːpɪ'tjuːɪti, ˌpəːpɪ'tʃuːɪti
AM ˌpərpə't(j)uədi

perpetuum mobile
BR pəˌpɛtjʊəm 'məʊbɪli, pəˌpɛtʃʊəm +
AM pər'pɛtʃəwəm 'moʊbəli, + 'moʊbəˌleɪ

perplex
BR pə'plɛks, -ɪz, -ɪŋ, -t
AM pər'plɛks, -əz, -ɪŋ, -t

perplexedly
BR pə'plɛksɪdli
AM pər'plɛksədli

perplexingly
BR pə'plɛksɪŋli
AM pər'plɛksɪŋli

perplexity
BR pə'plɛksɪt|i, -ɪz
AM pər'plɛksədi, -z

per pro.
BR pəː 'prəʊ
AM pər 'proʊ

perquisite
BR 'pəːkwɪzɪt, -s
AM 'pərkwəzət, -s

Perranporth
BR ˌpɛrən'pɔːθ, ˌpɛrn̩'pɔːθ, 'pɛrənpɔːθ, 'pɛrn̩pɔːθ
AM ˌpɛrən'pɔ(ə)rθ

Perrault
BR pɛ'rəʊ, 'pɛrəʊ
AM pə'roʊ

Perrier®
BR 'pɛrɪeɪ
AM ˌpɛri'jeɪ, 'pɛriˌjeɪ

Perrin¹
BR 'pɛrɪn
AM 'pɛrən

Perrin²
French
BR 'pɛrã
AM 'pɛrən

perron
BR 'pɛrən, 'pɛrɒ̃, -z
AM 'pɛrən, pə'rɔn, pə'rɑn, -z

perruquier
BR pə'ruːkɪeɪ, pɛ'ruːkɪeɪ, -z
AM pəˌruki'eɪ, -z

perry
BR 'pɛr|i, -ɪz
AM 'pɛri, -z

perse
BR pəːs
AM pərs

per se
BR pəː 'seɪ
AM pər 'seɪ

persecute
BR 'pəːsɪkjuːt, -s, -ɪŋ, -ɪd
AM 'pərsəˌkju|t, -ts, -dɪŋ, -dəd

persecution
BR ˌpəːsɪ'kjuːʃn, -z
AM ˌpərsə'kjuʃən, -z

persecutor
BR 'pəːsɪkjuːtə(r), -z
AM 'pərsəˌkjudər, -z

persecutory
BR 'pəːsɪkjuːt(ə)ri
AM 'pərsəkjəˌtɔri, pər'sɛkjəˌtɔri

Perseids
BR 'pəːsɪɪdz
AM 'pərsiɨdz

Persephone
BR pə'sɛfəni, pə'sɛfn̩i
AM pər'sɛfəni

Persepolis
BR pə'sɛpəlɪs, pə'sɛpl̩ɪs
AM pər'sɛpələs

Perseus
BR 'pəːsɪəs
AM 'pərsiəs

perseverance
BR ˌpəːsɪ'vɪərəns, ˌpəːsɪ'vɪərn̩s
AM ˌpərsə'vɪrəns

perseverate
BR pə'sɛvəreɪt, -s, -ɪŋ, -ɪd
AM pər'sɛvəˌreɪ|t, -ts, -dɪŋ, -dɪd

perseveration
BR pəˌsɛvə'reɪʃn
AM pərˌsɛvə'reɪʃən

persevere
BR ˌpəːsɪ'vɪə(r), -z, -ɪŋ, -d
AM ˌpərsə'vɪ(ə)r, -z, -ɪŋ, -d

Pershing
BR 'pəːʃɪŋ
AM 'pərʃɪŋ, 'pərʒɪŋ

Persia
BR 'pəːʃə(r), 'pəːʒə(*r*)
AM 'pərʒə

Persian
BR 'pəːʃn, 'pəːʒn, -z
AM 'pərʒən, -z

persiennes
BR ˌpəːsɪ'ɛn(z)
AM ˌpərzi'ɛn(z)

persiflage
BR 'pəːsɪflɑːʒ, ˌpəːsɪ'flɑːʒ
AM 'pərsəˌflɑʒ

Persil®
BR 'pəːs(ɪ)l
AM 'pərsəl

persimmon
BR pə:ˈsɪmən, -z
AM pərˈsɪmən, -z

persist
BR pəˈsɪst, -s, -ɪŋ, -ɨd
AM pərˈsɪst, -s, -ɪŋ, -ɨd

persistence
BR pəˈsɪst(ə)ns
AM pərˈsɪstəns

persistency
BR pəˈsɪst(ə)nsi
AM pərˈsɪstnsi

persistent
BR pəˈsɪst(ə)nt
AM pərˈsɪstənt

persistently
BR pəˈsɪst(ə)ntli
AM pərˈsɪst(ə)n(t)li

person
BR ˈpə:sn, -z
AM ˈpərsən, -z

persona
BR pəˈsəʊnə(r), -z
AM ˌpərˈsoʊnə, -z

personable
BR ˈpə:sn̩əbl, ˈpə:s(ə)nəbl
AM ˈpərs(ə)nəbəl

personableness
BR ˈpə:sn̩əblnəs, ˈpə:s(ə)nəblnəs
AM ˈpərs(ə)nəbəlnəs

personably
BR ˈpə:sn̩əbli, ˈpə:s(ə)nəbli
AM ˈpərs(ə)nəbli

personae
BR pəˈsəʊnʌɪ, pəˈsəʊni:
AM ˌpərˈsoʊni, ˌpərˈsoʊˌnaɪ

personage
BR ˈpə:sn̩|ɪdʒ, ˈpə:sən|ɪdʒ, -ɨdʒɨz
AM ˈpərsənɪdʒ, -ɨz

persona grata
BR pəˌsəʊnə ˈgrɑ:tə(r)
AM ˌpərˈsoʊnə ˈgrɑdə

personal
BR ˈpə:sn̩(ə)l, ˈpə:sən(ə)l
AM ˈpərs(ə)nəl

personalisation
BR ˌpə:sn̩əlʌɪˈzeɪʃn, ˌpə:sn̩l̩ʌɪˈzeɪʃn, ˌpə:sənl̩ʌɪˈzeɪʃn, ˌpə:s(ə)nəlʌɪˈzeɪʃn
AM ˌpərsn(ə)ləˈzeɪʃən, ˌpərs(ə)nəˌlaɪˈzeɪʃən

personalise
BR ˈpə:sn̩əlʌɪz, ˈpə:sn̩l̩ʌɪz, ˈpə:sənl̩ʌɪz, ˈpə:s(ə)nəlʌɪz, -ɨz, -ɪŋ, -d
AM ˈpərs(ə)nəˌlaɪz, -ɨz, -ɪŋ, -d

personality
BR ˌpə:səˈnalɪt|i, -ɪz
AM ˌpərsnˈælədi, -z

personalization
BR ˌpə:sn̩əlʌɪˈzeɪʃn, ˌpə:sn̩l̩ʌɪˈzeɪʃn, ˌpə:sənl̩ʌɪˈzeɪʃn, ˌpə:s(ə)nəlʌɪˈzeɪʃn
AM ˌpərsn(ə)ləˈzeɪʃən, ˌpərs(ə)nəˌlaɪˈzeɪʃən

personalize
BR ˈpə:sn̩əlʌɪz, ˈpə:sn̩l̩ʌɪz, ˈpə:sənl̩ʌɪz, ˈpə:s(ə)nəlʌɪz, -ɨz, -ɪŋ, -d
AM ˈpərs(ə)nəˌlaɪz, -ɨz, -ɪŋ, -d

personally
BR ˈpə:sn̩əli, ˈpə:sn̩l̩i, ˈpə:sənl̩i, ˈpə:s(ə)nəli
AM ˈpərs(ə)nəli

personalty
BR ˈpə:sn̩lt|i, ˈpə:s(ə)nl̩t|i, -ɪz
AM ˈpərs(ə)nəlti, -z

persona non grata
BR pəˌsəʊnə nɒn ˈgrɑ:tə(r)
AM ˌpərˌsoʊnə ˌnɑn ˈgrɑdə, + ˌnoʊn ˈgrɑdə

personate
BR ˈpə:sn̩eɪt, ˈpə:səneɪt, -s, -ɪŋ, -ɨd
AM ˈpərsnˌeɪ|t, -ts, -dɪŋ, -dɨd

personation
BR ˌpə:səˈneɪʃn, ˌpə:snˈeɪʃn, -z
AM ˌpərsnˈeɪʃən, -z

personator
BR ˈpə:səneɪtə(r), ˈpə:sn̩eɪtə(r)
AM ˈpərsnˌeɪdər

personhood
BR ˈpə:snhʊd
AM ˈpərsənˌ(h)ʊd

personification
BR pəˌsɒnɨfɨˈkeɪʃn, -z
AM pərˌsɑnəfəˈkeɪʃən, -z

personifier
BR pəˈsɒnɨfʌɪə(r), -z
AM pərˈsɑnəˌfaɪ(ə)r, -z

personify
BR pəˈsɒnɨfʌɪ, -z, -ɪŋ, -d
AM pərˈsɑnəˌfaɪ, -z, -ɪŋ, -d

personnel
BR ˌpə:səˈnɛl, ˌpə:snˈɛl
AM ˌpərsnˈɛl

person-to-person
BR ˌpə:sntəˈpə:sn
AM ˈˌpərsn(t)əˈpərsən

perspectival
BR pəˈspɛktɨvl
AM pərˈspɛktɨvəl

perspective
BR pəˈspɛktɪv, -z
AM pərˈspɛktɪv, -z

perspectively
BR pəˈspɛktɨvli
AM pərˈspɛktɨvli

perspex
BR ˈpə:spɛks
AM ˈpərˌspɛks

perspicacious
BR ˌpə:spɪˈkeɪʃəs
AM ˈˌpərspəˈkeɪʃəs

perspicaciously
BR ˌpə:spɪˈkeɪʃəsli
AM ˈˌpərspəˈkeɪʃəsli

perspicaciousness
BR ˌpə:spɪˈkeɪʃəsnəs
AM ˈˌpərspəˈkeɪʃəsnəs

perspicacity
BR ˌpə:spɪˈkasɪti
AM ˌpərspəˈkæsədi

perspicuity
BR ˌpə:spɪˈkju:ɪti
AM ˌpərspəˈkjuədi

perspicuous
BR pəˈspɪkjʊəs
AM pərˈspɪkjəwəs

perspicuously
BR pəˈspɪkjʊəsli
AM pərˈspɪkjəwəsli

perspicuousness
BR pəˈspɪkjʊəsnəs
AM pərˈspɪkjəwəsnəs

perspiration
BR ˌpə:spəˈreɪʃn
AM ˌpərspəˈreɪʃən

perspiratory
BR pəˈspʌɪrət(ə)ri
AM pərˈspaɪrəˌtɔri

perspire
BR pəˈspʌɪə(r), -z, -ɪŋ, -d
AM pərˈspaɪ(ə)r, -z, -ɪŋ, -d

persuadability
BR pəˌsweɪdəˈbɪlɪti
AM pərˌsweɪdəˈbɪlɨdi

persuadable
BR pəˈsweɪdəbl
AM pərˈsweɪdəbəl

persuade
BR pəˈsweɪd, -z, -ɪŋ, -ɨd
AM pərˈsweɪd, -z, -ɪŋ, -ɨd

persuader
BR pəˈsweɪdə(r), -z
AM pərˈsweɪdər, -z

persuasible
BR pəˈsweɪzɨbl
AM pərˈsweɪzəbəl

persuasion
BR pəˈsweɪʒn, -z
AM pərˈsweɪʒən, -z

persuasive
BR pəˈsweɪsɪv, pəˈsweɪzɪv
AM pərˈsweɪsɪv, pərˈsweɪzɪv

persuasively
BR pəˈsweɪsɨvli, pəˈsweɪzɨvli
AM pərˈsweɪsɨvli, pərˈsweɪzɨvli

persuasiveness
BR pəˈsweɪsɨvnɨs, pəˈsweɪzɨvnɨs
AM pərˈsweɪsɪvnɨs, pərˈsweɪzɪvnɨs

pert
BR pə:t
AM pərt

pertain
BR pəˈteɪn, -z, -ɪŋ, -d
AM pərˈteɪn, -z, -ɪŋ, -d

Perth
BR pə:θ
AM pərθ

pertinacious
BR ˌpə:tɪˈneɪʃəs
AM ˈˌpərtnˈeɪʃəs

pertinaciously
BR ˌpə:tɪˈneɪʃəsli
AM ˈˌpərtnˈeɪʃəsli

pertinaciousness
BR ˌpə:tɪˈneɪʃəsnəs
AM ˈˌpərtnˈeɪʃəsnəs

pertinacity
BR ˌpə:tɪˈnasɪti
AM ˌpərtnˈæsədi

pertinence
BR ˈpə:tɪnəns
AM ˈpərtn̩əns

pertinency
BR ˈpə:tɪnənsi
AM ˈpərtn̩ənsi

pertinent
BR ˈpə:tɪnənt
AM ˈpərtn̩ənt

pertinently
BR ˈpə:tɪnəntli
AM ˈpərtn̩ən(t)li

pertly
BR ˈpə:tli
AM ˈpərtli

pertness
BR ˈpə:tnəs
AM ˈpərtnəs

perturb
BR pəˈtə:b, -z, -ɪŋ, -d
AM pərˈtərb, -z, -ɪŋ, -d

perturbable
BR pəˈtə:bəbl
AM pərˈtərbəbəl

perturbation
BR ˌpə:təˈbeɪʃn, -z
AM ˌpərdərˈbeɪʃən, -z

perturbative
BR pəˈtə:bətɪv
AM pərˈtərbədɪv, ˈpərdərˌbeɪdɪv

perturbingly
BR pəˈtə:bɪŋli
AM pərˈtərbɪŋli

pertussis
BR pə'tʌsɪs
AM pər'təsəs

Pertwee
BR 'pə:twi:
AM 'pərt,wi

Peru
BR pə'ru:
AM pə'ru

Perugia
BR pə'ru:dʒ(ɪ)ə(r)
AM pə'rudʒə

peruke
BR pə'ru:k, -s
AM pə'ruk, -s

perusal
BR pə'ru:zl, -z
AM pə'ruzəl, -z

peruse
BR pə'ru:z, -ɨz, -ɪŋ, -d
AM pə'ruz, -əz, -ɪŋ, -d

peruser
BR pə'ru:zə(r), -z
AM pə'ruzər, -z

Perutz
BR pə'rʊts
AM pə'rʊtz

Peruvian
BR pə'ru:vɪən, -z
AM pə'ruviən, -z

perv
BR pə:v, -z, -ɪŋ, -d
AM pərv, -z, -ɪŋ, -d

pervade
BR pə'veɪd, -z, -ɪŋ, -ɨd
AM pər'veɪd, -z, -ɪŋ, -ɨd

pervasion
BR pə'veɪʒn
AM pər'veɪʒən

pervasive
BR pə'veɪsɪv, pə'veɪzɪv
AM pər'veɪsɪv

pervasively
BR pə'veɪsɨvli, pə'veɪzɨvli
AM pər'veɪsɨvli

pervasiveness
BR pə'veɪsɨvnɨs, pə'veɪzɨvnɨs
AM pər'veɪsɪvnɨs

perve
BR pə:v, -z, -ɪŋ, -d
AM pərv, -z, -ɪŋ, -d

perverse
BR pə'və:s
AM pər'vərs

perversely
BR pə'və:sli
AM pər'vərsli

perverseness
BR pə'və:snəs
AM pər'vərsnəs

perversion
BR pə'və:ʃn, pə'və:ʒn, -z
AM pər'vərʒən, -z

perversity
BR pə'və:sɨti
AM pər'vərsədi

perversive
BR pə'və:sɪv
AM pər'vərsɪv

pervert[1]
noun
BR 'pə:və:t, -s
AM 'pər,vərt, -s

pervert[2]
verb
BR pə'və:t, -s, -ɪŋ, -ɨd
AM pər'vər|t, -ts, -dɪŋ, -dəd

pervertedly
BR pə'və:tɨdli
AM pər'vərdədli

perverter
BR pə'və:tə(r), -z
AM pər'vərdər, -z

pervious
BR 'pə:vɪəs
AM 'pərviəs

perviously
BR 'pə:vɪəsli
AM 'pərviəsli

perviousness
BR 'pə:vɪəsnəs
AM 'pərviəsnəs

Pery
BR 'pɪəri, 'pɛ:ri, 'pɛri
AM 'pɛri

Pesach
BR 'peɪsɑ:k, 'peɪsɑ:x
AM 'peɪ,sɑk

peseta
BR pə'seɪtə(r), -z
AM pə'seɪdə, -z

Peshitta
BR pə'ʃi:tə(r)
AM pə'ʃidə

peskily
BR 'pɛskɨli
AM 'pɛskəli

peskiness
BR 'pɛskɪnɨs
AM 'pɛskinɨs

pesky
BR 'pɛsk|i, -ɪə(r), -ɪɨst
AM 'pɛski, -ər, -ɨst

peso
BR 'peɪsəʊ, -z
AM 'peɪsoʊ, -z

pessary
BR 'pɛs(ə)r|i, -ɪz
AM 'pɛsəri, -z

pessimism
BR 'pɛsɨmɪz(ə)m
AM 'pɛsə,mɪzəm

pessimist
BR 'pɛsɨmɪst, -s
AM 'pɛsəməst, -s

pessimistic
BR ,pɛsɨ'mɪstɪk
AM ,pɛsə'mɪstɪk

pessimistically
BR ,pɛsɨ'mɪstɨkli
AM ,pɛsə'mɪstɪk(ə)li

pest
BR pɛst, -s
AM pɛst, -s

Pestalozzi
BR ,pɛstə'lɒtsi
AM ,pɛstə'lɑtsi

pester
BR 'pɛst|ə(r), -əz, -(ə)rɪŋ, -əd
AM 'pɛstər, -z, -ɪŋ, -d

pesterer
BR 'pɛst(ə)rə(r), -z
AM 'pɛstərər, -z

pesthole
BR 'pɛsthəʊl, -z
AM 'pɛst,(h)oʊl, -z

pesticidal
BR ,pɛstɨ'sʌɪdl
AM ,pɛstə'saɪdəl

pesticide
BR 'pɛstɨsʌɪd, -z
AM 'pɛstə,saɪd, -z

pestiferous
BR pɛ'stɪf(ə)rəs
AM pɛ'stɪf(ə)rəs

pestiferously
BR pɛ'stɪf(ə)rəsli
AM pɛ'stɪf(ə)rəsli

pestilence
BR 'pɛstɨləns, 'pɛstɨlns, -ɪz
AM 'pɛstələns, -ɪz

pestilent
BR 'pɛstɨlənt, 'pɛstɨlnt
AM 'pɛstələnt

pestilential
BR ,pɛstɨ'lɛnʃl
AM ,pɛstə'lɛn(t)ʃəl

pestilentially
BR ,pɛstɨ'lɛnʃli, ,pɛstɨ'lɛnʃəli
AM ,pɛstə'lɛn(t)ʃəli

pestilently
BR 'pɛstɨləntli, 'pɛstɨlntli
AM 'pɛstələn(t)li

pestle
BR 'pɛs(t)l, -z
AM 'pɛstəl, 'pɛsəl, -z

pesto
BR 'pɛstəʊ
AM 'pɛstoʊ

pestological
BR ,pɛstə'lɒdʒɨkl
AM ,pɛstə'lɑdʒəkəl

pestologist
BR pɛ'stɒlədʒɪst, -s
AM pɛs'tɑlədʒəst, -s

pestology
BR pɛ'stɒlədʒi
AM pɛs'tɑlədʒi

PET
positron emission tomography, polyethylene terephthalate
BR ,pi:i:'ti:, pɛt
AM ,pii'ti, pɛt

pet
BR pɛt, -s, -ɪŋ, -ɨd
AM pɛ|t, -ts, -dɪŋ, -dəd

Peta
BR 'pi:tə(r)
AM 'peɪdə, 'pidə

Pétain
BR pɛ'tã
AM pɛ'tɛn

petal
BR 'pɛtl, -z, -d
AM 'pɛdl, -z, -d

petaline
BR 'pɛtəlʌɪn, 'pɛtlʌɪn
AM 'pɛdl,aɪn, 'pɛdlən

petal-like
BR 'pɛtllʌɪk
AM 'pɛdl,laɪk

petaloid
BR 'pɛtlɔɪd
AM 'pɛdl,ɔɪd

petalon
BR 'pɛtəlɒn, 'pɛtələn
AM 'pɛdl,ɑn

pétanque
BR ,peɪ'tɒŋk
AM ,peɪ'tɑŋk

petard
BR pɨ'tɑ:d, -z
AM pə'tɑrd, -z

petasus
BR 'pɛtəsəs, -ɪz
AM 'pɛdəsəs, -əz

petaurist
BR pɨ'tɔ:rɪst, -s
AM pə'tɔrəst, -s

petcock
BR 'pɛtkɒk, -s
AM 'pɛt,kɑk, -s

Pete
BR pi:t
AM pit

petechia
BR pɨ'ti:kɪə(r)
AM pə'tikiə

petechiae
BR pə'ti:kɪi:
AM pə'tiki,aɪ, pə'tiki,i

petechial
BR pɨ'ti:kɪəl
AM pə'tikiəl

peter
BR 'pi:t|ə(r), -əz, -(ə)rɪŋ, -əd
AM 'pidər, -z, -ɪŋ, -d

Peterborough
BR 'pi:təb(ə)rə(r)
AM 'pidər,bərə

Peterhead
BR ,pi:tə'hɛd
AM ,pidər'hɛd

Peterkin
BR 'pi:təkɪn

AM ˈpidərkən

Peterlee
BR ˌpiːtəˈliː
AM ˌpidərˈli

Peterloo
BR ˌpiːtəˈluː
AM ˌpidərˈlu

peterman
BR ˈpiːtəmən
AM ˈpidərmən

petermen
BR ˈpiːtəmən
AM ˈpidərmən

Peter Pan
BR ˌpiːtə ˈpan
AM ˌpidər ˈpæn

Peters
BR ˈpiːtəz
AM ˈpidərz

Petersburg
BR ˈpiːtəzbəːg
AM ˈpidərzˌbərg

Petersen
BR ˈpiːtəs(ə)n
AM ˈpidərsən
DAN ˈpeːˀdʌsən

Petersfield
BR ˈpiːtəzfiːld
AM ˈpidərzˌfild

petersham
BR ˈpiːtəʃ(ə)m, -z
AM ˈpidəˌrʃæm, -z

Peterson
BR ˈpiːtəs(ə)n
AM ˈpidərsən

Petherick
BR ˈpɛθ(ə)rɪk
AM ˈpɛθ(ə)rək

pethidine
BR ˈpɛθɪdiːn
AM ˈpɛθəˌdin

petiolar
BR ˈpɛtɪəʊlə(r)
AM ˌpidiˈoʊlər

petiolate
BR ˈpɛtɪələt
AM ˌpidiˈoʊlət, ˈpidiəˌleɪt

petiole
BR ˈpɛtɪəʊl, -z
AM ˈpidiˌoʊl, -z

petit
BR ˈpɛti, pəˈtiː
AM ˈpɛdi, pəˈti(t)

petit bourgeois
BR ˌpɛtɪ ˈbʊəʒwɑː(*r*), pəˌtiː +, + ˈbɔːʒwɑː(*r*), -z
AM ˌpɛdi bʊrˈʒwɑ, pəˌti(t) +, -z

petite
BR pəˈtiːt
AM pəˈtit

petite bourgeoisie
BR pəˌtiːt ˌbʊəʒwɑːˈziː, + ˌbɔːʒwɑːˈziː
AM ˌpɛdi ˌbʊrˌʒwɑˈzi, pəˌti(t) +

petit four
BR ˌpɛtɪ ˈfɔː(r), -z
AM ˈpɛdi ˌfɔ(ə)r, -z

petition
BR pɪˈtɪʃ|n, -nz, -n̩ɪŋ\-ənɪŋ, -nd
AM pəˈtɪʃ|ən, -ənz, -(ə)nɪŋ, -ənd

petitionable
BR pɪˈtɪʃn̩əbl, pɪˈtɪʃənəbl
AM pəˈtɪʃ(ə)nəbəl

petitionary
BR pɪˈtɪʃ(ə)nər|i, -ɪz
AM pəˈtɪʃəˌnɛri, -z

petitioner
BR pəˈtɪʃn̩ə(r), pəˈtɪʃənə(r), -z
AM pəˈtɪʃənər, -z

petitio principii
BR pɪˈtɪʃɪəʊ prɪnˈsɪpɪʌɪ, + prɪŋˈkɪpɪʌɪ
AM pəˌtɪʃioʊ prɪnˈsɪpiˌi

petit jury
BR ˌpɛtɪ ˈdʒʊər|i, -ɪz
AM ˈpɛdi ˌdʒʊri, -z

petit-maître
BR ˌpɛtɪˈmeɪtrə(*r*), -z
AM ˌpɛdiˈmeɪtrə, -z

petit mal
BR ˌpɛtɪ ˈmal
AM ˈpɛdi ˌmɑl

petit point
BR ˌpɛt ˈpɔɪnt
AM ˈpɛdi ˌpɔɪnt

petits pois
plural noun
BR ˌpɛtɪ ˈpwɑː(*r*)
AM ˌpɛdi ˈpwɑ

petnapper
BR ˈpɛtˌnapə(r), -z
AM ˈpɛtˌnæpər, -z

petnapping
BR ˈpɛtˌnapɪŋ
AM ˈpɛtˌnæpɪŋ

Peto
BR ˈpiːtəʊ
AM ˈpidoʊ

Petra
BR ˈpɛtrə(*r*)
AM ˈpɛtrə

Petrarch
BR ˈpɛtrɑːk
AM ˈpɛˌtrɑrk

Petrarchan
BR pɪˈtrɑːk(ə)n
AM pəˈtrɑrkən

petrel
BR ˈpɛtr(ə)l, -z
AM ˈpɛtrəl, -z

Petri dish
BR ˈpɛtrɪ ˌdɪʃ, ˈpiːtrɪ +, -ɪz
AM ˈpitri ˌdɪʃ, -ɪz

Petrie
BR ˈpiːtri
AM ˈpɛtri, ˈpitri

petrifaction
BR ˌpɛtrɪˈfakʃn
AM ˌpɛtrəˈfækʃən

petrification
BR ˌpɛtrɪfɪˈkeɪʃn
AM ˌpɛtrəfəˈkeɪʃən

petrify
BR ˈpɛtrɪfʌɪ, -z, -ɪŋ, -d
AM ˈpɛtrəˌfaɪ, -z, -ɪŋ, -d

petrochemical
BR ˌpɛtrəʊˈkɛmɪkl
AM ˌpɛtroʊˈkɛməkəl

petrochemistry
BR ˌpɛtrəʊˈkɛmɪstri
AM ˌpɛtroʊˈkɛməstri

petrodollar
BR ˈpɛtrə(ʊ)ˌdɒlə(r), -z
AM ˈpɛtroʊˌdɑlər, -z

Petrofina
BR ˌpɛtrə(ʊ)ˈfiːnə(*r*)
AM ˌpɛtrəˈfinə

petrogenesis
BR ˌpɛtrə(ʊ)ˈdʒɛnɪsɪs
AM ˌpɛtroʊˈdʒɛnəsəs

petroglyph
BR ˈpɛtrə(ʊ)glɪf, -s
AM ˈpɛtrəˌglɪf, -s

Petrograd
BR ˈpɛtrəgrad
AM ˈpɛtrəˌgræd
RUS pʲitraˈgrat

petrographer
BR pɪˈtrɒgrəfə(r), -z
AM pəˈtrɑgrəfər, -z

petrographic
BR ˌpɛtrəˈgrafɪk
AM ˌpɛtrəˈgræfɪk

petrographical
BR ˌpɛtrəˈgrafɪkl
AM ˌpɛtrəˈgræfəkəl

petrography
BR pɪˈtrɒgrəfi
AM pəˈtrɑgrəfi

petrol
BR ˈpɛtr(ə)l
AM ˈpɛtrəl

petrolatum
BR ˌpɛtrəˈleɪtəm
AM ˌpɛtroʊˈleɪdəm

petroleum
BR pɪˈtrəʊlɪəm
AM pəˈtroʊliəm

petrolic
BR pɪˈtrɒlɪk
AM pəˈtrɑlɪk

petrologic
BR ˌpɛtrəˈlɒdʒɪk
AM ˌpɛtrəˈlɑdʒɪk

petrological
BR ˌpɛtrəˈlɒdʒɪkl
AM ˌpɛtrəˈlɑdʒəkəl

petrologist
BR pɪˈtrɒlədʒɪst, -s
AM pəˈtrɑlədʒəst, -s

petrology
BR pɪˈtrɒlədʒi
AM pəˈtrɑlədʒi

petronel
BR ˈpɛtrənl, -z
AM ˈpɛtrənəl, -z

Petronella
BR ˌpɛtrəˈnɛlə(*r*)
AM ˌpɛtrəˈnɛlə

Petronius
BR pɪˈtrəʊnɪəs
AM pəˈtroʊniəs

petrous
BR ˈpɛtrəs
AM ˈpɛtrəs, ˈpitrəs

petter
BR ˈpɛtə(r), -z
AM ˈpɛdər, -z

petticoat
BR ˈpɛtɪkəʊt, -s
AM ˈpɛdiˌkoʊ|t, ˈpɛdəˌkoʊ|t, -ts

Pettifer
BR ˈpɛtɪfə(r)
AM ˈpɛdəfər

pettifog
BR ˈpɛtɪfɒg, -z, -ɪŋ, -d
AM ˈpɛdiˌfɔg, ˈpɛdiˌfɑg, -z, -ɪŋ, -d

pettifogger
BR ˈpɛtɪˌfɒgə(r), -z
AM ˈpɛdiˌfɔgər, ˈpɛdiˌfɑgər, -z

pettifoggery
BR ˈpɛtɪˌfɒg(ə)ri
AM ˌpɛdiˈfɔgəri, ˌpɛdiˈfɑgəri

Pettigrew
BR ˈpɛtɪgruː
AM ˈpɛdəˌgru

pettily
BR ˈpɛtɪli
AM ˈpɛdəli

pettiness
BR ˈpɛtɪnɪs
AM ˈpɛdinɪs

pettish
BR ˈpɛtɪʃ
AM ˈpɛdɪʃ

pettishly
BR ˈpɛtɪʃli
AM ˈpɛdɪʃli

pettishness
BR ˈpɛtɪʃnɪs
AM ˈpɛdɪʃnɪs

Pettit
BR ˈpɛtɪt
AM ˈpɛdɪt

pettitoe
BR ˈpɛtɪtəʊ, -z
AM ˈpɛdiˌtoʊ, -z

Pettitt
BR ˈpɛtɪt
AM ˈpɛdɪt

petty
BR ˈpɛt|i, -ɪə(r), -ɪɪst
AM ˈpɛdi, -ər, -ɪst

petty bourgeois
BR ˌpɛtɪ ˈbʊəʒwɑː(r), + ˈbɔːʒwɑː(r), -z
AM ˈpɛdi bʊrˈʒwɑ, -z

petty bourgeoisie
BR ˌpɛtɪ ˌbʊəʒwɑːˈziː, + ˌbɔːʒwɑːˈziː
AM ˈpɛdi ˌbʊrˌʒwɑˈzi

Petula
BR pɪˈtjuːlə(r), pɪˈtʃuːlə(r)
AM pəˈt(j)ulə, pəˈtʃulə

petulance
BR ˈpɛtjʊləns, ˈpɛtjʊlṇs, ˈpɛtʃʊləns, ˈpɛtʃʊlṇs
AM ˈpɛtʃələns

petulant
BR ˈpɛtjʊlənt, ˈpɛtjʊlṇt, ˈpɛtʃʊlənt, ˈpɛtʃʊlṇt
AM ˈpɛtʃələnt

petulantly
BR ˈpɛtjʊləntli, ˈpɛtjʊlṇtli, ˈpɛtʃʊləntli, ˈpɛtʃʊlṇtli
AM ˈpɛtʃələn(t)li

Petulengro
BR ˌpɛtjʊˈlɛŋgrəʊ, ˌpɛtʃəˈlɛŋgrəʊ
AM ˌpɛt(j)əˈlɛŋgroʊ, ˌpɛtʃəˈlɛŋgroʊ

petunia
BR pɪˈtjuːnɪə(r), pɪˈtʃuːnɪə(r), -z
AM pəˈt(j)uniə, pəˈt(j)unjə, -z

petuntse
BR peɪˈtʊntsə(r), pɪˈtʌntsə(r)
AM pəˈtʊn(t)sə

Petworth
BR ˈpɛtwəːθ, ˈpɛtwəθ
AM ˈpɛtˌwərθ

Peugeot®
BR ˈpəːʒəʊ, ˈpjuːʒəʊ, -z
AM p(j)əˈʒoʊ, ˈpjʊˌʒoʊ, -z

Pevensey
BR ˈpɛvnzi
AM ˈpɛvənsi

Peveril
BR ˈpɛv(ə)rɪl, ˈpɛv(ə)rḷ
AM ˈpɛv(ə)rəl

Pevsner
BR ˈpɛvznə(r)
AM ˈpɛvznər

pew
BR pjuː, -z
AM pju, -z

pewage
BR ˈpjuːɪdʒ
AM ˈpjuɪdʒ

pewee
BR ˈpiːwiː, -z
AM ˈpiˌwi, -z

pewit
BR ˈpiːwɪt, -s
AM ˈpiwɨt, ˈpjuət, -s

pewless
BR ˈpjuːləs
AM ˈpjuləs

Pewsey
BR ˈpjuːzi
AM ˈpjuzi

pewter
BR ˈpjuːtə(r)
AM ˈpjudər

pewterer
BR ˈpjuːt(ə)rə(r), -z
AM ˈpjudərər, -z

peyote
BR peɪˈəʊti, pɪˈəʊti
AM peɪˈoʊdi

peyotism
BR peɪˈəʊtɪz(ə)m, pɪˈəʊtɪz(ə)m
AM peɪˈoʊˌtɪzəm

Peyton
BR ˈpeɪtn
AM ˈpeɪtn

Pfennig
BR ˈ(p)fɛnɪg, -z
AM ˈ(p)fɛnɪg, -z

pH
BR ˌpiːˈeɪtʃ
AM ˌpiˈeɪtʃ

Phaedo
BR ˈfiːdəʊ
AM ˈfeɪdoʊ

Phaedra
BR ˈfeɪdrə(r)
AM ˈfeɪdrə

Phaedrus
BR ˈfiːdrəs
AM ˈfeɪdrəs

Phaethon
BR ˈfeɪɪθ(ə)n
AM ˈfeɪ(ə)tn

phaeton
BR ˈfeɪtn, -z
AM ˈfeɪ(ə)tn, -z

phage
BR feɪdʒ, -ɪz
AM feɪdʒ, -ɨz

phagedaena
BR ˌfadʒɪˈdiːnə(r)
AM ˌfædʒəˈdinə

phagedaenic
BR ˌfadʒɪˈdiːnɪk
AM ˌfædʒəˈdinɪk

phagedena
BR ˌfadʒɪˈdiːnə(r)
AM ˌfædʒəˈdinə

phagedenic
BR ˌfadʒɪˈdiːnɪk
AM ˌfædʒəˈdinɪk

phagocyte
BR ˈfagəsʌɪt, -s
AM ˈfægəˌsaɪt, -s

phagocytic
BR ˌfagəˈsɪtɪk
AM ˌfægəˈsɪdɪk

phagocytise
BR ˈfagəsʌɪtʌɪz, -ɪz, -ɪŋ, -d
AM ˈfægəsəˌtaɪz, -ɨz, -ɪŋ, -d

phagocytize
BR ˈfagəsʌɪtʌɪz, -ɪz, -ɪŋ, -d
AM ˈfægəsəˌtaɪz, -ɨz, -ɪŋ, -d

phagocytose
BR ˈfagəsʌɪtəʊz, -ɪz, -ɪŋ, -d
AM ˈfægəˌsaɪˌtoʊs, ˈfægəˌsaɪˌtoʊz, -əz, -ɪŋ, -d

phagocytosis
BR ˌfagəsʌɪˈtəʊsɪs
AM ˌfægəˌsaɪˈtoʊsəs

Phaidon
BR ˈfʌɪdn
AM ˈfaɪdən

Phalange
BR fəˈlan(d)ʒ
AM fəˈlændʒ

phalangeal
BR fəˈlan(d)ʒɪəl
AM ˈfeɪˌlændʒ(i)əl, fəˈlændʒ(i)əl

phalanger
BR fəˈlan(d)ʒə(r), -z
AM ˈfeɪˌlændʒər, fəˈlændʒər, -z

phalanges
bones, plural of phalanx
BR fəˈlan(d)ʒiːz
AM fəˈlændʒiz, feɪˈlændʒiz

phalangist
BR fəˈlan(d)ʒɪst, -s
AM fəˈlændʒəst, feɪˈlændʒəst, -s

phalansterian
BR ˌfalənˈstɪərɪən, ˌfalṇˈstɪərɪən
AM ˌfælənˈstɪriən

phalanstery
BR ˈfalənst(ə)r|i, ˈfalṇst(ə)r|i, -ɪz
AM ˈfælənˌstɛri, -z

phalanx
BR ˈfalaŋks, -ɪz
AM ˈfeɪˌlæŋks, -əz

phalarope
BR ˈfalərəʊp, -s
AM ˈfæləˌroʊp, -s

phalli
BR ˈfalʌɪ, ˈfaliː
AM ˈfæˌlaɪ

phallic
BR ˈfalɪk
AM ˈfælɪk

phallically
BR ˈfalɨkli
AM ˈfælək(ə)li

phallicism
BR ˈfalɪsɪz(ə)m
AM ˈfæləˌsɪzəm

phallism
BR ˈfalɪz(ə)m
AM ˈfæˌlɪzəm

phallocentric
BR ˌfalə(ʊ)ˈsɛntrɪk
AM ˈfæloʊˈsɛntrɪk

phallocentricity
BR ˌfalə(ʊ)sɛnˈtrɪsɪti
AM ˈfæloʊˌsɛnˈtrɪsədi

phallocentrism
BR ˌfalə(ʊ)ˈsɛntrɪz(ə)m
AM ˈfæloʊˈsɛnˌtrɪzəm

phallus
BR ˈfaləs, -ɪz
AM ˈfæləs, -əz

phanariot
BR fəˈnarɪət, -s
AM fəˈnɛriət, fəˈnɛriˌɑt, -s

phanerogam
BR ˈfan(ə)rə(ʊ)gam, -z
AM ˈfænərəˌgæm, -z

phanerogamic
BR ˌfan(ə)rəˈgamɪk
AM ˈfænərəˈgæmɪk

phanerogamous
BR ˌfanəˈrɒgəməs
AM ˌfænəˈrɑgəməs

Phanerozoic
BR ˌfan(ə)rəˈzəʊɪk
AM ˌfæn(ə)rəˈzoʊɪk

phantasise
BR ˈfantəsʌɪz, -ɪz, -ɪŋ, -d
AM ˈfæn(t)əˌsaɪz, -ɨz, -ɪŋ, -d

phantasize
BR ˈfantəsʌɪz, -ɪz, -ɪŋ, -d
AM ˈfæn(t)əˌsaɪz, -ɨz, -ɪŋ, -d

phantasm
BR ˈfantaz(ə)m, -z
AM ˈfænˌtæzəm, -z

phantasmagoria
BR ˌfantazməˈgɔːrɪə(r), fanˌtazməˈgɔːrɪə(r)
AM ˌfænˌtæzməˈgɔriə

phantasmagoric
BR ˌfantazməˈgɒrɪk, fanˌtazməˈgɒrɪk
AM fænˌtæzməˈgɔrɪk

phantasmagorical
BR ˌfantazməˈgɒrɪkl, fanˌtazməˈgɒrɪkl
AM fænˌtæzməˈgɔrəkəl

phantasmal
BR fanˈtazml
AM fænˈtæzməl

phantasmally
BR fanˈtazmḷi, fanˈtazməli
AM fænˈtæzməli

phantasmic
BR fanˈtazmɪk
AM fænˈtæzmɪk

phantast
BR 'fantast, -s
AM 'fæn,tæst, -s
phantasy
BR 'fantəs|i, -ɪz
AM 'fæn(t)əsi, -z
phantom
BR 'fantəm, -z
AM 'fæn(t)əm, -z
pharanges
BR fə'ran(d)ʒiːz
AM fə'randʒiz
Pharaoh
BR 'fɛːrəʊ, -z
AM 'fɛroʊ, -z
Pharaonic
BR ˌfɛːreɪ'ɒnɪk
AM ˌfɛreɪ'ɑnɪk
Pharisaic
BR ˌfarɪ'seɪɪk
AM ¦fɛrə'seɪɪk
Pharisaical
BR ˌfarɪ'seɪɪkl
AM ¦fɛrə'seɪɪkəl
Pharisaically
BR ˌfarɪ'seɪɪkli
AM ¦fɛrə'seɪɪk(ə)li
Pharisaicalness
BR ˌfarɪ'seɪɪklnɨs
AM ¦fɛrə'seɪɪkəlnəs
Pharisaism
BR 'farɪseɪɪz(ə)m
AM 'fɛrəˌseɪˌɪzəm
Pharisee
BR 'farɪsiː, -z
AM 'fɛrəˌsi, -z
pharmaceutic
BR ˌfɑːmə's(j)uːtɪk, -s
AM ˌfɑrmə'sudɪk, -s
pharmaceutical
BR ˌfɑːmə's(j)uːtɪkl, -z
AM ˌfɑrmə'sudəkəl, -z
pharmaceutically
BR ˌfɑːmə's(j)uːtɪkli
AM ˌfɑrmə'sudək(ə)li
pharmacist
BR 'fɑːməsɪst, -s
AM 'fɑrməsəst, -s
pharmacognosy
BR ˌfɑːmə'kɒgnəsi
AM ˌfɑrmə'kɑgnəsi
pharmacological
BR ˌfɑːməkə'lɒdʒɪkl
AM ¦fɑrməkə'lɑdʒəkəl
pharmacologically
BR ˌfɑːməkə'lɒdʒɪkli
AM ¦fɑrməkə'lɑdʒək(ə)li
pharmacologist
BR ˌfɑːmə'kɒlədʒɪst, -s
AM ˌfɑrmə'kɑlədʒəst, -s
pharmacology
BR ˌfɑːmə'kɒlədʒi
AM ˌfɑrmə'kɑlədʒi
pharmacopeia
BR ˌfɑːməkə'piːə(*r*), -z
AM ˌfɑrməkə'pi(j)ə, ˌfɑrmə'koʊpi(j)ə, -z
pharmacopeial
BR ˌfɑːməkə'piːəl, -z
AM ˌfɑrməkə'pi(j)əl, ˌfɑrmə'koʊpi(j)əl, -z
pharmacopoeia
BR ˌfɑːməkə'piːə(*r*), -z
AM ˌfɑrməkə'pi(j)ə, ˌfɑrmə'koʊpi(j)ə, -z
pharmacopoeial
BR ˌfɑːməkə'piːəl, -z
AM ˌfɑrmə'koʊpi(j)əl, -z
pharmacy
BR 'fɑːməs|i, -ɪz
AM 'fɑrməsi, -z
Pharoah
BR 'fɛːrəʊ, -z
AM 'fɛroʊ, -z
pharos
BR 'fɛːrɒs, -ɨz
AM 'fɛˌrɔs, 'fɛrɑs, -əz
Pharsala
BR fɑː'sɑːlə(*r*), fɑː'seɪlə(*r*)
AM fɑr'sɑlə
pharyngal
BR fə'rɪŋgl, -z
AM fə'rɪŋgəl, -z
pharyngeal
BR fə'rɪn(d)ʒɪəl, ˌfarɪn'dʒiːəl, ˌfarn̩'dʒiːəl
AM fə'rɪndʒ(i)əl, ˌfɛrən'dʒiəl
pharyngitis
BR ˌfarɪn'dʒʌɪtɪs, ˌfarn̩'dʒʌɪtɪs
AM ˌfɛrən'dʒaɪdɨs
pharyngoscope
BR fə'rɪŋgəskəʊp, -s
AM fə'rɪŋgəˌskoʊp, -s
pharyngotomy
BR ˌfarɪŋ'gɒtəm|i, -ɪz
AM ˌfɛrɪŋ'gɑdəmi, -z
pharynx
BR 'farɪŋks, -ɨz
AM 'fɛrɪŋ(k)s, -ɨz
phase
BR feɪz, -ɨz, -ɪŋ, -d
AM feɪz, -ɨz, -ɪŋ, -d
phasedown
BR 'feɪzdaʊn, -z
AM 'feɪzˌdaʊn, -z
phaseout
BR 'feɪzaʊt, -s
AM 'feɪzˌaʊt, -s
phasic
BR 'feɪzɪk
AM 'feɪzɪk
phasmid
BR 'fazmɪd, -z
AM 'fæzməd, -z
Phasmida
BR 'fazmɪdə(*r*)
AM 'fæzmədə
phatic
BR 'fatɪk
AM 'fædɪk
Ph.D.
BR ˌpiːeɪtʃ'diː, -z
AM ˌpieɪtʃ'di, -z
pheasant
BR 'fɛznt, -s
AM 'fɛznt, -s
pheasantry
BR 'fɛzntr|i, -ɪz
AM 'fɛzntri, -z
Pheidippides
BR fʌɪ'dɪpɪdiːz
AM faɪ'dɪpəˌdiz
Phelan
BR 'fiːlən
AM 'feɪlən
Phelps
BR fɛlps
AM fɛlps
phenacetin
BR fɪ'nasɪtɪn
AM fi'næsədən, fɛ'næsədən
phenobarbital
BR ˌfiːnə(ʊ)'bɑːbɪtl
AM ¦finoʊ'bɑrbəˌtɔl, ¦finoʊ'bɑrbəˌtɑl
phenobarbitone
BR ˌfiːnə(ʊ)'bɑːbɪtəʊn
AM ¦finoʊ'bɑrbəˌtoʊn
phenocryst
BR 'fiːnə(ʊ)krɪst, 'fɛnə(ʊ)krɪst, -s
AM 'finəˌkrɪst, 'fɛnəˌkrɪst, -s
phenol
BR 'fiːnɒl
AM 'fiˌnɔl, 'fiˌnɑl
phenolic
BR fɪ'nɒlɪk
AM fə'nɑlɪk, fi'nɑlɪk
phenological
BR ˌfiːnə'lɒdʒɪkl
AM ˌfinə'lɑdʒəkəl
phenologist
BR fɪ'nɒlədʒɪst, -s
AM fə'nɑlədʒəst, -s
phenology
BR fɪ'nɒlədʒi
AM fə'nɑlədʒi
phenolphthalein
BR ˌfiːnɒl'(f)θeɪlɪɪn, ˌfiːnɒl'(f)θalɪɪn, ˌfiːnɒl'(f)θeɪliːn, ˌfiːnɒl'(f)θaliːn
AM ¦finəl'θeɪˌli(ə)n
phenomena
BR fɪ'nɒmɪnə(*r*)
AM fə'nɑmənə
phenomenal
BR fɪ'nɒmɪnl
AM fə'nɑmənəl
phenomenalise
BR fɪ'nɒmɪnl̩ʌɪz, fɪ'nɒmɪnəlʌɪz, -ɨz, -ɪŋ, -d
AM fə'nɑmənəˌlaɪz, -ɨz, -ɪŋ, -d
phenomenalism
BR fɪ'nɒmɪnl̩ɪz(ə)m, fɪ'nɒmɪnəlɪz(ə)m
AM fə'nɑmənəˌlɪzəm
phenomenalist
BR fɪ'nɒmɪnl̩ɪst, fɪ'nɒmɪnəlɪst, -s
AM fə'nɑmənələst, -s
phenomenalistic
BR fɪˌnɒmɪnə'lɪstɪk, fɪˌnɒmɪnl'ɪstɪk
AM fɪˌnɑmənə'lɪstɪk
phenomenalize
BR fɪ'nɒmɪnl̩ʌɪz, fɪ'nɒmɪnəlʌɪz, -ɨz, -ɪŋ, -d
AM fə'nɑmənəˌlaɪz, -ɨz, -ɪŋ, -d
phenomenally
BR fɪ'nɒmɪnl̩i, fɪ'nɒmɪnəli
AM fə'nɑm(ə)n(ə)li
phenomenological
BR fɪˌnɒmɪnə'lɒdʒɪkl
AM fəˌnɑmənə'lɑdʒəkəl
phenomenologically
BR fɪˌnɒmɪnə'lɒdʒɪkli
AM fə¦nɑmənə'lɑdʒək(ə)li
phenomenologist
BR fɪˌnɒmɪ'nɒlədʒɪst, -s
AM fəˌnɑmə'nɑlədʒəst, -s
phenomenology
BR fɪˌnɒmɪ'nɒlədʒi
AM fəˌnɑmə'nɑlədʒi
phenomenon
BR fɪ'nɒmɪnən
AM fə'nɑməˌnɑn, fə'nɑmənən
phenotype
BR 'fiːnə(ʊ)tʌɪp, -s
AM 'finəˌtaɪp, -s
phenotypic
BR ˌfiːnə(ʊ)'tɪpɪk
AM ˌfinə'tɪpɪk
phenotypical
BR ˌfiːnə(ʊ)'tɪpɪkl
AM ˌfinə'tɪpɪkəl
phenotypically
BR ˌfiːnə(ʊ)'tɪpɪkli
AM ˌfinə'tɪpɪk(ə)li
Phensic
BR 'fɛnzɪk, 'fɛnsɪk
AM 'fɛnzɪk, 'fɛnsɪk
phenyl
BR 'fiːnʌɪl, 'fɛnʌɪl, 'fiːn(ɪ)l, 'fɛn(ɪ)l, -z
AM 'fɛnəl, 'finəl, -z
phenylalanine
BR ˌfiːnʌɪl'aləniːn, ˌfiːn(ɪ)l'aləniːn, ˌfiːnʌɪl'alənʌɪn, ˌfiːn(ɪ)l'alənʌɪn

AM ˈfɛnəlˈæləˌnin, ˈfinəlˈæləˌnin

phenylketonuria
BR ˌfiːnʌɪlˌkiːtəˈnjʊərɪə(r), ˌfiːn(ɪ)lˌkiːtəˈnjʊərɪə(r)
AM ˈfɛnəlˌkitəˈn(j)uriə, ˈfinəlˌkitəˈn(j)uriə

pheromonal
BR ˌfɛrəˈməʊnl, ˈfɛrəməʊnl
AM ˈfɛrəmoʊnəl

pheromone
BR ˈfɛrəməʊn, -z
AM ˈfɛrəˌmoʊn, -z

phew
BR ɸː, fjuː
AM fju

phi
BR fʌɪ, -z
AM faɪ, -z

phial
BR ˈfʌɪəl, -z
AM ˈfaɪ(ə)l, -z

Phi Beta Kappa
BR ˌfʌɪ ˌbeɪtə ˈkapə(r), + ˌbiːtə +, -z
AM ˈfaɪ ˈbeɪdə ˈkæpə, -z

Phidias
BR ˈfɪdɪas
AM ˈfɪdiəs

Phil
BR fɪl
AM fɪl

philabeg
BR ˈfɪləbɛg, -z
AM ˈfɪləˌbɛg, -z

Philadelphia
BR ˌfɪləˈdɛlfɪə(r)
AM ˌfɪləˈdɛlfiə

Philadelphian
BR ˌfɪləˈdɛlfɪən, -z
AM ˌfɪləˈdɛlfiən, -z

philadelphus
BR ˌfɪləˈdɛlfəs
AM ˌfɪləˈdɛlfəs

philander
BR fɪˈland|ə(r), -əz, -(ə)rɪŋ, -əd
AM fəˈlænd|ər, -ərz, -(ə)rɪŋ, -ərd

philanderer
BR fɪˈland(ə)rə(r), -z
AM fəˈlændərər, -z

philanthrope
BR ˈfɪlənθrəʊp, -s
AM ˈfilənˌθroʊp, -s

philanthropic
BR ˌfɪlənˈθrɒpɪk
AM ˈfɪlənˈθrɑpɪk

philanthropically
BR ˌfɪlənˈθrɒpɪkli
AM ˈfɪlənˈθrɑpək(ə)li

philanthropise
BR fɪˈlanθrəpʌɪz, -ɪz, -ɪŋ, -d
AM fəˈlænθrəˌpaɪz, -ɪz, -ɪŋ, -d

philanthropism
BR fɪˈlanθrəpɪz(ə)m
AM fəˈlænθrəˌpɪzəm

philanthropist
BR fɪˈlanθrəpɪst, -s
AM fəˈlænθrəpəst, -s

philanthropize
BR fɪˈlanθrəpʌɪz, -ɪz, -ɪŋ, -d
AM fəˈlænθrəˌpaɪz, -ɪz, -ɪŋ, -d

philanthropy
BR fɪˈlanθrəpi
AM fəˈlænθrəpi

philatelic
BR ˌfɪləˈtɛlɪk
AM ˈfɪləˈtɛlɪk

philatelically
BR ˌfɪləˈtɛlɪkli
AM ˈfɪləˈtɛlək(ə)li

philatelist
BR fɪˈlatəlɪst, fɪˈlatl̩ɪst, -s
AM fəˈlædl̩əst, -s

philately
BR fɪˈlatəli, fɪˈlatl̩i
AM fəˈlædli

Philbin
BR ˈfɪlbɪn
AM ˈfɪlbɪn

Philby
BR ˈfɪlbi
AM ˈfɪlbi

Philemon
BR fʌɪˈliːmən
AM fəˈlimən, faɪˈlimən

philharmonia
BR ˌfɪl(h)ɑːˈməʊnɪə(r), ˌfɪləˈməʊnɪə(r)
AM ˌfɪl(h)ɑrˈmoʊniə

philharmonic
BR ˌfɪl(h)ɑːˈmɒnɪk, ˌfɪləˈmɒnɪk, -s
AM ˈfɪlərˈmɑnɪk, ˈfɪlˌ(h)ɑrˈmɑnɪk, -s

philhellene
BR fɪlˈhɛliːn, -z
AM fɪlˈhɛlin, -z

philhellenic
BR ˌfɪlhɛˈliːnɪk, ˌfɪlhəˈliːnɪk, ˌfɪlhɛˈlɛnɪk, ˌfɪlhəˈlɛnɪk
AM ˌfɪlˌ(h)ɛˈlɛnɪk

philhellenism
BR fɪlˈhɛlɪnɪz(ə)m
AM fɪlˈhɛləˌnɪzəm

philhellenist
BR fɪlˈhɛlɪnɪst, -s
AM fɪlˈhɛlɛnəst, -s

Philip
BR ˈfɪlɪp
AM ˈfɪlɪp

Philippa
BR ˈfɪlɪpə(r)
AM fəˈlɪpə

Philippi
BR ˈfɪlɪpʌɪ
AM fəˈlɪpi

Philippian
BR fɪˈlɪpɪən, -z
AM fəˈlɪpiən, -z

philippic
BR fɪˈlɪpɪk, -s
AM fəˈlɪpɪk, -s

philippina
BR ˌfɪlɪˈpiːnə(r), -z
AM ˈfɪləˌpinə, -z

Philippine
BR ˈfɪlɪpiːn, -z
AM ˈfɪləˌpin, -z

Philippino
BR ˌfɪlɪˈpiːnəʊ, -z
AM ˌfɪləˈpinoʊ, -z

Philips
BR ˈfɪlɪps
AM ˈfɪlɪps

Philistine
BR ˈfɪlɪstʌɪn, -z
AM ˈfɪləˌstin, ˈfɪləˌstaɪn, -z

Philistinism
BR ˈfɪlɪstɪnɪz(ə)m
AM ˈfɪləˌstiˌnɪzəm, ˈfɪləˌstaɪˌnɪzəm

Phillida
BR ˈfɪlɪdə(r)
AM ˈfɪlədə

Phillip
BR ˈfɪlɪp
AM ˈfɪlɪp

Phillipines
BR ˈfɪlɪpiːnz
AM ˈfɪləˌpinz

Phillips
BR ˈfɪlɪps
AM ˈfɪlɪps

Phillpot
BR ˈfɪlpɒt
AM ˈfɪlˌpɑt

Phillpott
BR ˈfɪlpɒt
AM ˈfɪlˌpɑt

phillumenist
BR fɪˈl(j)uːmɪnɪst, -s
AM fəˈl(j)umənəst, -s

phillumeny
BR fɪˈl(j)uːmɪni
AM fəˈl(j)uməni

Philly
BR ˈfɪli
AM ˈfɪli

Philoctetes
BR ˌfɪləkˈtiːtiːz
AM ˌfɪləkˈtidiz

philodendron
BR ˌfɪləˈdɛndr(ə)n, -z
AM ˌfɪləˈdɛndrən, -z

philogynist
BR fɪˈlɒdʒɪnɪst, -s
AM fəˈlɑdʒənəst, -s

philologer
BR fɪˈlɒlədʒə(r), -z
AM fəˈlɑlədʒər, -z

philologian
BR ˌfɪləˈləʊdʒɪən, -z
AM ˌfɪləˈloʊdʒiən, -z

philologic
BR ˌfɪləˈlɒdʒɪk
AM ˈfɪləˈlɑdʒɪk

philological
BR ˌfɪləˈlɒdʒɪkl
AM ˈfɪləˈlɑdʒəkəl

philologically
BR ˌfɪləˈlɒdʒɪkli
AM ˈfɪləˈlɑdʒək(ə)li

philologise
BR fɪˈlɒlədʒʌɪz, -ɪz, -ɪŋ, -d
AM fəˈlɑləˌdʒaɪz, -ɪz, -ɪŋ, -d

philologist
BR fɪˈlɒlədʒɪst, -s
AM fəˈlɑlədʒəst, -s

philologize
BR fɪˈlɒlədʒʌɪz, -ɪz, -ɪŋ, -d
AM fəˈlɑləˌdʒaɪz, -ɪz, -ɪŋ, -d

philology
BR fɪˈlɒlədʒi
AM fəˈlɑlədʒi

philomel
BR ˈfɪləmɛl, -z
AM ˈfɪləˌmɛl, -z

Philomela
BR ˌfɪləˈmiːlə(r)
AM ˌfɪləˈmilə

Philomena
BR ˌfɪləˈmiːnə(r)
AM ˌfɪləˈminə

philoprogenitive
BR ˌfɪlə(ʊ)prə(ʊ)ˈdʒɛnɪtɪv
AM ˈfɪləproʊˈdʒɛnədɪv

philosophaster
BR fɪˈlɒsəfastə(r), fɪˌlɒsəˈfastə(r), -z
AM fəˌlɑsəˈfæstər, -z

philosopher
BR fɪˈlɒsəfə(r), -z
AM fəˈlɑs(ə)fər, -z

philosophic
BR ˌfɪləˈsɒfɪk
AM ˈfɪləˈsɑfɪk

philosophical
BR ˌfɪləˈsɒfɪkl
AM ˈfɪləˈsɑfəkəl

philosophically
BR ˌfɪləˈsɒfɪkli
AM ˈfɪləˈsɑfək(ə)li

philosophise
BR fɪˈlɒsəfʌɪz, -ɪz, -ɪŋ, -d
AM fəˈlɑsəˌfaɪz, -ɪz, -ɪŋ, -d

philosophiser
BR fɪˈlɒsəfʌɪzə(r), -z
AM fəˈlɑsəˌfaɪzər, -z

philosophize
BR fɪˈlɒsəfʌɪz, -ɪz, -ɪŋ, -d

AM fə'lɑsə,faɪz, -ɨz, -ɪŋ, -d

philosophizer
BR fɪ'lɒsəfʌɪzə(r), -z
AM fə'lɑsə,faɪzər, -z

philosophy
BR fɪ'lɒsəf|i, -ɪz
AM fə'lɑsəfi, -z

Philostratus
BR fɪ'lɒstrətəs
AM fɪ'lɑstrədəs, ,fɪlə'strɑdəs

Philpot
BR 'fɪlpɒt
AM 'fɪl,pɑt

philter
BR 'fɪltə(r), -z
AM 'fɪltər, -z

philtre
BR 'fɪltə(r), -z
AM 'fɪltər, -z

phimosis
BR fʌɪ'məʊsɪs
AM faɪ'moʊsəs

phimotic
BR fʌɪ'mɒtɪk
AM faɪ'mɑdɪk

Phineas
BR 'fɪnɪəs
AM 'fɪniəs

Phipps
BR fɪps
AM fɪps

phiz
BR fɪz, -ɨz
AM fɪz, -ɨz

phizog
BR 'fɪzɒg, -z
AM 'fɪz,ɑg, -z

phlebitic
BR flɪ'bɪtɪk
AM flə'bɪdɪk

phlebitis
BR flɪ'bʌɪtɪs
AM flə'baɪdɪs

phlebotomise
BR flɪ'bɒtəmʌɪz, -ɨz, -ɪŋ, -d
AM flə'bɑdə,maɪz, -ɨz, -ɪŋ, -d

phlebotomist
BR flɪ'bɒtəmɪst, -s
AM flə'bɑdəməst, -s

phlebotomize
BR flɪ'bɒtəmʌɪz, -ɨz, -ɪŋ, -d
AM flə'bɑdə,maɪz, -ɨz, -ɪŋ, -d

phlebotomy
BR flɪ'bɒtəm|i, -ɪz
AM flə'bɑdəmi, -z

phlegm
BR flɛm
AM flɛm

phlegmatic
BR flɛg'matɪk
AM flɛg'mædɪk

phlegmatically
BR flɛg'matɪkli
AM flɛg'mædək(ə)li

phlegmy
BR 'flɛmi
AM 'flɛmi

phloem
BR 'fləʊɛm
AM 'floʊ,ɛm, 'floʊəm

phlogistic
BR flə'dʒɪstɪk
AM flə'dʒɪstɪk

phlogiston
BR flə'dʒɪstɒn, flə'dʒɪst(ə)n
AM floʊ'dʒɪstən

phlox
BR flɒks, -ɨz
AM flɑks, -əz

Phnom Penh
BR ,(p)nɒm 'pɛn
AM ,(p)nɑm 'pɛn

phobia
BR 'fəʊbɪə(r), -z
AM 'foʊbiə, -z

phobic
BR 'fəʊbɪk
AM 'foʊbɪk

Phobos
BR 'fəʊbɒs
AM 'foʊ,bɔs, 'foʊ,bɑs

Phocaea
BR fə(ʊ)'siːə(r)
AM foʊ'siə

Phocian
BR 'fəʊʃɪən, 'fəʊsɪən
AM 'foʊsiən

Phocis
BR 'fəʊsɪs
AM 'foʊsəs

phoebe
BR 'fiːb|i, -ɪz
AM 'fi,bi, -z

Phoebus
BR 'fiːbəs
AM 'fibəs

Phoenicia
BR fɪ'nɪʃə(r), fɪ'niːʃə(r)
AM fə'nɪʃə, fə'niʃə

Phoenician
BR fɪ'nɪʃn, fɪ'niːʃn, -z
AM fə'nɪʃən, fə'niʃən, -z

phoenix
BR 'fiːnɪks, -ɨz
AM 'finɪks, -ɨz

pholas
BR 'fəʊləs
AM 'foʊləs

phon
BR fɒn, -z
AM fɑn, -z

phonaesthesia
BR ,fɒnəs'θiːzɪə(r), ,fɒnəs'θiːʒə(r)
AM ,foʊnəs'θiz(i)ə

phonate
BR fə'neɪt, -s, -ɪŋ, -ɨd
AM 'foʊ,neɪ|t, -ts, -dɪŋ, -dɨd

phonation
BR fə'neɪʃn
AM foʊ'neɪʃən

phonatory
BR 'fəʊnət(ə)ri
AM 'foʊnə,tɔri

phonautograph
BR fə(ʊ)'nɔːtəgrɑːf, fə(ʊ)'nɔːtəgraf, -s
AM foʊ'nɔdə,græf, foʊ'nɑdə,græf, -s

phone
BR fəʊn, -z, -ɪŋ, -d
AM foʊn, -z, -ɪŋ, -d

phonecard
BR 'fəʊnkɑːd, -z
AM 'foʊn,kɑrd, -z

phone-in
BR 'fəʊnɪn, -z
AM 'foʊn,ɪn, -z

phoneme
BR 'fəʊniːm, -z
AM 'foʊ,nim, -z

phonemic
BR fə'niːmɪk, -s
AM foʊ'nimɪk, fə'nimɪk, -s

phonemicisation
BR fə,niːmɪsʌɪ'zeɪʃn
AM foʊ,nimәsә'zeɪʃən, fə,nimәsә'zeɪʃən, foʊ,nimə,saɪ'zeɪʃən, fə,nimə,saɪ'zeɪʃən

phonemicise
BR fə'niːmɪsʌɪz, -ɨz, -ɪŋ, -d
AM foʊ'nimə,saɪz, fə'nimə,saɪz, -ɨz, -ɪŋ, -d

phonemicist
BR fə'niːmɪsɪst, -s
AM foʊ'nimɪsəst, -s

phonemicization
BR fə,niːmɪsʌɪ'zeɪʃn
AM foʊ,nimәsә'zeɪʃən, fə,nimәsә'zeɪʃən, foʊ,nimə,saɪ'zeɪʃən, fə,nimə,saɪ'zeɪʃən

phonemicize
BR fə'niːmɪsʌɪz, -ɨz, -ɪŋ, -d
AM foʊ'nimə,saɪz, fə'nimə,saɪz, -ɨz, -ɪŋ, -d

phonendoscope
BR ,fəʊn'ɛndəskəʊp, -s
AM ,foʊn'ɛndə,skoʊp, -s

phonesthesia
BR ,fɒnəs'θiːzɪə(r), ,fɒnəs'θiːʒə(r)
AM ,foʊnəs'θiz(i)ə

phonetapping
BR 'fəʊn,tapɪŋ, -z
AM 'foʊn,tæpɪŋ, -z

phonetic
BR fə'nɛtɪk, -s
AM foʊ'nɛdɪk, fə'nɛdɪk, -s

phonetically
BR fə'nɛtɪkli
AM foʊ'nɛdək(ə)li, fə'nɛdək(ə)li

phonetician
BR ,fɒnə'tɪʃn, ,fəʊnə'tɪʃn, -z
AM ,foʊnə'tɪʃən, -z

phoneticise
BR fə'nɛtɪsʌɪz, -ɨz, -ɪŋ, -d
AM foʊ'nɛdə,saɪz, fə'nɛdə,saɪz, -ɨz, -ɪŋ, -d

phoneticism
BR fə'nɛtɪsɪz(ə)m
AM foʊ'nɛdə,sɪzəm, fə'nɛdə,sɪzəm

phoneticist
BR fə'nɛtɪsɪst, -s
AM foʊ'nɛdəsəst, fə'nɛdəsəst, -s

phoneticization
BR fə,nɛtɪsʌɪ'zeɪʃn
AM foʊ,nɛtəsə'zeɪʃən, fə,nɛtəsə'zeɪʃən, foʊ,nɛtə,saɪ'zeɪʃən, fə,nɛtə,saɪ'zeɪʃən

phoneticize
BR fə'nɛtɪsʌɪz, -ɨz, -ɪŋ, -d
AM foʊ'nɛdə,saɪz, fə'nɛdə,saɪz, -ɨz, -ɪŋ, -d

phonetist
BR fə'nɛtɪst, -s
AM foʊ'nɛdəst, fə'nɛdəst, -s

phoney
BR 'fəʊn|i, -ɪz
AM 'foʊni, -z

phonic
BR 'fɒnɪk, 'fəʊnɪk, -s
AM 'fɑnɪk, -s

phonically
BR 'fɒnɪkli, 'fəʊnɪkli
AM 'fɑnək(ə)li

phonily
BR 'fəʊnɪli
AM 'foʊnəli

phoniness
BR 'fəʊnɪnɪs
AM 'foʊninɪs

phono
BR 'fəʊnə(ʊ), 'fɒnə(ʊ)
AM 'foʊnoʊ

phonogram
BR 'fəʊnəgram, -z
AM 'foʊnə,græm, -z

phonograph
BR 'fəʊnəgrɑːf, 'fəʊnəgraf, -s
AM 'foʊnə,græf, -s

phonographer
BR fə'nɒgrəfə(r), -z

AM fə'nagrəfər, foʊ'nagrəfər, -z

phonographic
BR ˌfəʊnə'grafɪk
AM ˌfoʊnə'græfɪk

phonographical
BR ˌfəʊnə'grafɪkl
AM ˌfoʊnə'græfəkəl

phonographically
BR ˌfəʊnə'grafɪkli
AM ˌfoʊnə'græfək(ə)li

phonography
BR fə'nɒgrəfi
AM fə'nagrəfi

phonolite
BR 'fəʊnəlʌɪt, -s
AM 'foʊnəˌlaɪt, -s

phonological
BR ˌfɒnə'lɒdʒɪkl, ˌfəʊnə'lɒdɪkl
AM ˌfanl'adʒəkəl, ˌfoʊnl'adʒəkəl

phonologically
BR ˌfɒnə'lɒdʒɪkli, ˌfəʊnə'lɒdʒɪkli
AM ˌfanl'adʒək(ə)li, ˌfoʊnl'adʒək(ə)li

phonologist
BR fə'nɒlədʒɪst, -s
AM fə'nalədʒəst, foʊ'nalədʒəst, -s

phonology
BR fə'nɒlədʒi
AM fə'nalədʒi, foʊ'nalədʒi

phonometer
BR fə(ʊ)'nɒmɪtə(r), -z
AM foʊ'namədər, -z

phonon
BR 'fəʊnɒn, -z
AM 'foʊˌnan, -z

phonoscope
BR 'fəʊnəskəʊp, -s
AM 'foʊnəˌskoʊp, -s

phonotype
BR 'fəʊnətʌɪp, -s
AM 'foʊnəˌtaɪp, -s

phony
BR 'fəʊn|i, -ɪz
AM 'foʊni, -z

phooey
BR 'fuːi
AM 'fui

phoresy
BR 'fɔːrəsi
AM 'fɔrəsi

phoretic
BR fə'rɛtɪk
AM fə'rɛdɪk

phormium
BR 'fɔːmɪəm
AM 'fɔrmiəm

phosgene
BR 'fɒzdʒiːn
AM 'fazˌdʒin

phosphatase
BR 'fɒsfəteɪz, 'fɒsfəteɪs
AM 'fasfəˌteɪs, 'fasfəˌteɪz

phosphate
BR 'fɒsfeɪt, -s
AM 'fasˌfeɪt, -s

phosphatic
BR fɒs'fatɪk
AM fas'fædɪk

phosphene
BR 'fɒsfiːn
AM 'fasˌfin

phosphide
BR 'fɒsfʌɪd, -z
AM 'fasˌfaɪd, -z

phosphine
BR 'fɒsfiːn
AM 'fasˌfin

phosphinic
BR fɒs'fɪnɪk
AM fas'fɪnɪk

phosphite
BR 'fɒsfʌɪt, -s
AM 'fasˌfaɪt, -s

phospholipid
BR ˌfɒsfə(ʊ)'lɪpɪd, -z
AM ˌfasfoʊ'lɪpɪd, -z

phosphor
BR 'fɒsfə(r)
AM 'fasfər

phosphorate
BR 'fɒsfəreɪt, -s, -ɪŋ, -ɪd
AM 'fasfəˌreɪ|t, -ts, -dɪŋ, -dɪd

phosphoresce
BR ˌfɒsfə'rɛs, -ɪz, -ɪŋ, -t
AM ˌfasfə'rɛs, -əz, -ɪŋ, -t

phosphorescence
BR ˌfɒsfə'rɛsns
AM ˌfasfə'rɛsəns

phosphorescent
BR ˌfɒsfə'rɛsnt
AM ˌfasfə'rɛsənt

phosphoric
BR fɒs'fɒrɪk
AM fas'fɔrɪk

phosphorite
BR 'fɒsfərʌɪt
AM 'fasfəˌraɪt

phosphorous
BR 'fɒsf(ə)rəs
AM 'fasf(ə)rəs

phosphorus
BR 'fɒsf(ə)rəs
AM 'fasf(ə)rəs

phosphorylate
BR fɒs'fɒrɪleɪt, -s, -ɪŋ, -ɪd
AM fas'fɔrəˌleɪ|t, -ts, -dɪŋ, -dɪd

phosphorylation
BR ˌfɒsfɒrɪ'leɪʃn
AM fasˌfɔrə'leɪʃən

phossy
BR 'fɒsi
AM 'fɔsi, 'fasi

phot
BR fəʊt, -s
AM foʊt, fat, -s

photic
BR 'fəʊtɪk
AM 'foʊdɪk

photism
BR 'fəʊtɪz(ə)m, -z
AM 'foʊˌtɪzəm, -z

Photius
BR 'fəʊtɪəs
AM 'foʊdiəs

photo
BR 'fəʊtəʊ, -z
AM 'foʊdoʊ, -z

photobiology
BR ˌfəʊtəʊbʌɪ'ɒlədʒi
AM ˌfoʊdoʊˌbaɪ'alədʒi

photocall
BR 'fəʊtə(ʊ)kɔːl
AM 'foʊdoʊˌkɔl, 'foʊdoʊˌkal

photocell
BR 'fəʊtə(ʊ)sɛl, -z
AM 'foʊdəˌsɛl, -z

photochemical
BR ˌfəʊtə(ʊ)'kɛmɪkl
AM ˌfoʊdə'kɛməkəl

photochemistry
BR ˌfəʊtə(ʊ)'kɛmɪstri
AM ˌfoʊdə'kɛməstri

photochromic
BR ˌfəʊtə(ʊ)'krəʊmɪk
AM ˌfoʊdə'kroʊmɪk

photocomposition
BR ˌfəʊtəʊˌkɒmpə'zɪʃn
AM ˌfoʊdəˌkampə'zɪʃən

photoconductive
BR ˌfəʊtəʊkən'dʌktɪv
AM ˌfoʊdəkən'dəktɪv

photoconductivity
BR ˌfəʊtəʊˌkɒndʌk'tɪvɪti
AM ˌfoʊdoʊˌkandək'tɪvɪdi

photoconductor
BR 'fəʊtə(ʊ)kənˌdʌktə(r), -z
AM ˌfoʊdəkən'dəktər, -z

photocopiable
BR 'fəʊtə(ʊ)ˌkɒpɪəbl
AM 'foʊdəˌkapiəbəl

photocopier
BR 'fəʊtə(ʊ)ˌkɒpɪə(r), -z
AM 'foʊdəˌkoʊpiər, -z

photocopy
BR 'fəʊtə(ʊ)ˌkɒp|i, -ɪz, -ɪɪŋ, -ɪd
AM 'foʊdəˌkapi, -z, -ɪŋ, -d

photodegradable
BR ˌfəʊtəʊdɪ'greɪdəbl
AM ˌfoʊdoʊdə'greɪdəbəl, ˌfoʊdoʊdi'greɪdəbəl

photodiode
BR 'fəʊtəʊˌdʌɪəʊd, -z
AM 'foʊdoʊˌdaɪoʊd, -z

photoduplicate
BR ˌfəʊtə(ʊ)'djuːplɪkeɪt, ˌfəʊtə(ʊ)'dʒuːplɪkeɪt, -s, -ɪŋ, -ɪd
AM ˌfoʊdə'd(j)upləˌkeɪ|t, -ts, -dɪŋ, -dɪd

photoduplication
BR ˌfəʊtə(ʊ)ˌdjuːplɪ'keɪʃn, ˌfəʊtə(ʊ)ˌdʒuːplɪ'keɪʃn
AM ˌfoʊdəˌd(j)uplə'keɪʃən

photodynamic
BR ˌfəʊtə(ʊ)dʌɪ'namɪk
AM ˌfoʊdəˌdaɪ'næmɪk

photoelectric
BR ˌfəʊtəʊɪ'lɛktrɪk
AM ˌfoʊdoʊi'lɛktrɪk, ˌfoʊdoʊə'lɛktrɪk

photoelectricity
BR ˌfəʊtəʊɪˌlɛk'trɪsɪti, ˌfəʊtəʊˌɛlɛk'trɪsɪti, ˌfəʊtəʊˌɛlɪk'trɪsɪti, ˌfəʊtəʊˌɪlɛk'trɪsɪti, ˌfəʊtəʊˌiːlɛk'trɪsɪti
AM ˌfoʊdoʊəˌlɛk'trɪsədi, ˌfoʊdoʊiˌlɛk'trɪsədi

photoelectron
BR ˌfəʊtəʊɪ'lɛktrɒn, -z
AM ˌfoʊdoʊə'lɛkˌtran, ˌfoʊdoʊi'lɛkˌtran, -z

photoemission
BR ˌfəʊtəʊɪ'mɪʃn, -z
AM ˌfoʊdoʊə'mɪʃən, ˌfoʊdoʊi'mɪʃən, -z

photoemitter
BR ˌfəʊtəʊɪ'mɪtə(r), -z
AM ˌfoʊdoʊə'mɪdər, ˌfoʊdoʊi'mɪdər, -z

photoengraving
BR ˌfəʊtəʊɪn'greɪvɪŋ, ˌfəʊtəʊɛn'greɪvɪŋ
AM ˌfoʊdoʊɪn'greɪvɪŋ, ˌfoʊdoʊɛn'greɪvɪŋ

photo finish
BR ˌfəʊtəʊ 'fɪnɪʃ
AM ˌfoʊdoʊ 'fɪnɪʃ

photofit
BR 'fəʊtə(ʊ)fɪt, -s
AM 'foʊdəˌfɪt, -s

photogenic
BR ˌfəʊtə'dʒɛnɪk, ˌfəʊtə'dʒiːnɪk
AM ˌfoʊdə'dʒɛnɪk

photogenically
BR ˌfəʊtə'dʒɛnɪkli, ˌfəʊtə'dʒiːnɪkli
AM ˌfoʊdə'dʒɛnək(ə)li

photogram
BR 'fəʊtəgram, -z
AM 'foʊdəˌgræm, -z

photogrammetrist
BR ˌfəʊtə(ʊ)'gramɪtrɪst, -s
AM ˌfoʊdə'græmətrəst, -s

photogrammetry
BR ˌfəʊtə(ʊ)'gramɪtri
AM ˌfoʊdə'græmətri

photograph
BR 'fəʊtəgrɑːf, 'fəʊtəgraf, -s, -ɪŋ, -t
AM 'foʊdəˌgræf, -s, -ɪŋ, -t

photographable
BR 'fəʊtəgrɑːfəbl, 'fəʊtəgrafəbl
AM 'foʊdəˌgræfəbəl

photographer
BR fə'tɒgrəfə(r), -z
AM fə'tɑgrəfər, -z

photographic
BR ˌfəʊtə'grafɪk
AM ˌfoʊdə'græfɪk

photographical
BR ˌfəʊtə'grafɪkl
AM ˌfoʊdə'græfəkəl

photographically
BR ˌfəʊtə'grafɪkli
AM ˌfoʊdə'græfək(ə)li

photography
BR fə'tɒgrəfi
AM fə'tɑgrəfi

photogravure
BR ˌfəʊtə(ʊ)grə'vjʊə(r), -z
AM ˌfoʊdəgrəˌvju(ə)r, -z

photojournalism
BR ˌfəʊtəʊ'dʒəːnəlɪz(ə)m, ˌfəʊtəʊ'dʒəːnl̩ɪz(ə)m
AM ˌfoʊdə'dʒərnəˌlɪzəm

photojournalist
BR ˌfəʊtəʊ'jəːnəlɪst, ˌfəʊtəʊ'jəːnl̩ɪst, -s
AM ˌfoʊdə'dʒərnələst, -s

photokinetic
BR ˌfəʊtə(ʊ)kɪ'nɛtɪk
AM ˌfoʊdəkə'nɛdɪk

photolithographer
BR ˌfəʊtəʊlɪ'θɒgrəfə(r), -z
AM ˌfoʊdoʊˌlɪ'θɑgrəfər, -z

photolithographic
BR ˌfəʊtəʊˌlɪθə'grafɪk
AM ˌfoʊdəˌlɪθə'græfɪk

photolithographically
BR ˌfəʊtəʊˌlɪθə'grafɪkli
AM ˌfoʊdəˌlɪθə'græfək(ə)li

photolithography
BR ˌfəʊtə(ʊ)lɪ'θɒgrəfi
AM ˌfoʊdəˌlɪ'θɑgrəfi

photolyse
BR 'fəʊtəlʌɪz, 'fəʊtl̩ʌɪz, -ɨz, -ɪŋ, -d
AM 'foʊdl̩aɪz, -ɨz, -ɪŋ, -d

photolysis
BR fə(ʊ)'tɒlɪsɪs
AM foʊ'tɑləsəs

photolytic
BR ˌfəʊtə'lɪtɪk
AM ˌfoʊdə'lɪdɪk

photolyze
BR 'fəʊtəlʌɪz, 'fəʊtl̩ʌɪz, -ɨz, -ɪŋ, -d
AM 'foʊdl̩aɪz, -ɨz, -ɪŋ, -d

photomechanical
BR ˌfəʊtəʊmɪ'kanɪkl
AM ˌfoʊdəmə'kænəkəl

photomechanically
BR ˌfəʊtəʊmɪ'kanɪkli
AM ˌfoʊdoʊmə'kænək(ə)li

photometer
BR fə(ʊ)'tɒmɪtə(r), -z
AM fə'tɑmədər, -z

photometric
BR ˌfəʊtə'mɛtrɪk
AM ˌfoʊdə'mɛtrɪk

photometry
BR fə(ʊ)'tɒmɪtri
AM fə'tɑmətri

photomicrograph
BR ˌfəʊtəʊ'mʌɪkrəgrɑːf, ˌfəʊtəʊ'mʌɪkrəgraf, -s
AM ˌfoʊdə'maɪkroʊˌgræf, -s

photomicrography
BR ˌfəʊtə(ʊ)mʌɪ'krɒgrəfi
AM ˌfoʊdəˌmaɪ'krɑgrəfi

photomontage
BR ˌfəʊtəʊ'mɒntɑːʒ, ˌfəʊtə(ʊ)mɒn'tɑːʒ
AM ˌfoʊdoʊˌmɑn'tɑʒ

photon
BR 'fəʊtɒn, -z
AM 'foʊˌtɑn, -z

photonics
BR fəʊ'tɒnɪks
AM foʊ'tɑnɪks

photonovel
BR 'fəʊtəʊˌnɒvl, -z
AM 'foʊdoʊˌnɑvəl, -z

photo-offset
BR ˌfəʊtəʊ'ɒfsɛt
AM ˌfoʊdoʊ'ɔfˌsɛt, ˌfoʊdoʊ'ɑfˌsɛt

photoperiod
BR 'fəʊtəʊˌpɪərɪəd, -z
AM 'foʊdoʊˌpɪriəd, -z

photoperiodic
BR ˌfəʊtəʊˌpɪərɪ'ɒdɪk
AM ˌfoʊdoʊˌpɪri'ɑdɪk

photoperiodism
BR ˌfəʊtə(ʊ)'pɪərɪədɪz(ə)m
AM ˌfoʊdoʊ'pɪriəˌdɪzəm

photophobia
BR ˌfəʊtə(ʊ)'fəʊbɪə(r)
AM ˌfoʊdə'foʊbiə

photophobic
BR ˌfəʊtə(ʊ)'fəʊbɪk
AM ˌfoʊdə'foʊbɪk

photopic
BR fəʊ'tɒpɪk, fəʊ'təʊpɪk
AM fə'tɑpɪk, ˌfoʊ'tɑpɪk

photorealism
BR ˌfəʊtəʊ'rɪəlɪz(ə)m
AM 'foʊdoʊ'ri(ə)lɪzəm

photoreception
BR ˌfəʊtə(ʊ)rɪ'sɛpʃn
AM ˌfoʊdərə'sɛpʃən

photoreceptor
BR ˌfəʊtə(ʊ)rɪ'sɛptə(r), -z
AM ˌfoʊdərə'sɛptər, -z

photosensitive
BR ˌfəʊtəʊ'sɛnsɪtɪv
AM ˌfoʊdə'sɛnsədɪv

photosensitivity
BR ˌfəʊtəʊˌsɛnsɪ'tɪvɪti
AM ˌfoʊdəˌsɛnsə'tɪvɨdi

photosensitize
BR ˌfəʊtəʊ'sɛnsɪtʌɪz, -ɨz, -ɪŋ, -d
AM ˌfoʊdə'sɛnsəˌtaɪz, -ɨz, -ɪŋ, -d

photoset
BR 'fəʊtə(ʊ)sɛt, -s, -ɪŋ
AM 'foʊdəˌsɛ|t, -ts, -dɪŋ

photosetter
BR 'fəʊtəʊˌsɛtə(r), -z
AM 'foʊdəˌsɛdər, -z

photosetting
BR 'fəʊtəʊˌsɛtɪŋ
AM 'foʊdəˌsɛdɪŋ

photosphere
BR 'fəʊtəsfɪə(r), -z
AM 'foʊdəˌsfɪ(ə)r, -z

photospheric
BR ˌfəʊtə'sfɛrɪk
AM ˌfoʊdə'sfɛrɪk

photostat®
BR 'fəʊtəstat, -s, -ɪŋ, -ɨd
AM 'foʊdəˌstæ|t, -ts, -dɪŋ, -dəd

photostatic
BR ˌfəʊtə'statɪk
AM ˌfoʊdə'stædɪk

photosynthesis
BR ˌfəʊtə(ʊ)'sɪnθɨsɪs
AM ˌfoʊdə'sɪnθəsəs

photosynthesise
BR ˌfəʊtə(ʊ)'sɪnθɨsʌɪz, -ɨz, -ɪŋ, -d
AM ˌfoʊdə'sɪnθəˌsaɪz, -ɨz, -ɪŋ, -d

photosynthesize
BR ˌfəʊtə(ʊ)'sɪnθɨsʌɪz, -ɨz, -ɪŋ, -d
AM ˌfoʊdə'sɪnθəˌsaɪz, -ɨz, -ɪŋ, -d

photosynthetic
BR ˌfəʊtə(ʊ)sɪn'θɛtɪk
AM ˌfoʊdəˌsɪn'θɛdɪk

photosynthetically
BR ˌfəʊtə(ʊ)sɪn'θɛtɪkli
AM ˌfoʊdəˌsɪn'θɛdək(ə)li

phototransistor
BR ˌfəʊtə(ʊ)tran'zɪstə(r), ˌfəʊtə(ʊ)trɑːn'zɪstə(r), ˌfəʊtə(ʊ)tran'sɪstə(r), ˌfəʊtə(ʊ)trɑːn'sɪstə(r), -z
AM ˌfoʊdoʊˌtræn'zɪstər, -z

phototropic
BR ˌfəʊtə(ʊ)'trɒpɪk, ˌfəʊtə(ʊ)'trəʊpɪk
AM ˌfoʊdə'trɑpɪk

phototropism
BR ˌfəʊtə(ʊ)'trəʊpɪz(ə)m
AM ˌfoʊdə'troʊˌpɪzəm

phototypesetter
BR ˌfəʊtə(ʊ)'tʌɪpsɛtə(r), -z
AM ˌfoʊdoʊ'taɪpˌsɛdər, -z

phototypesetting
BR ˌfəʊtə(ʊ)'tʌɪpsɛtɪŋ
AM ˌfoʊdoʊ'taɪpˌsɛdɪŋ

photovoltaic
BR ˌfəʊtə(ʊ)vɒl'teɪɪk
AM ˌfoʊdoʊˌvoʊl'teɪɪk

phrasal
BR 'freɪzl
AM 'freɪzəl

phrase
BR freɪz, -ɨz, -ɪŋ, -d
AM freɪz, -ɨz, -ɪŋ, -d

phrasebook
BR 'freɪzbʊk, -s
AM 'freɪzˌbʊk, -s

phraseogram
BR 'freɪzɪəgram, -z
AM 'freɪziəˌgræm, -z

phraseological
BR ˌfreɪzɪə'lɒdʒɪkl
AM ˌfreɪziə'lɑdʒəkəl

phraseology
BR ˌfreɪzɪ'ɒlədʒ|i, -ɪz
AM ˌfreɪzi'ɑlədʒi, -z

phrasing
BR 'freɪzɪŋ, -z
AM 'freɪzɪŋ, -z

phratry
BR 'freɪtr|i, -ɪz
AM 'freɪtri, -z

phreatic
BR frɪ'atɪk
AM fri'ædɪk

phrenetic
BR frɪ'nɛtɪk
AM frə'nɛdɪk

phrenetically
BR frɪ'nɛtɪkli
AM frə'nɛdək(ə)li

phrenic
BR 'frɛnɪk
AM 'frɛnɪk

phrenological
BR ˌfrɛnə'lɒdʒɪkl
AM ˌfrɛnə'lɑdʒəkəl

phrenologically
BR ˌfrɛnə'lɒdʒɪkli
AM ˌfrɛnə'lɑdʒək(ə)li

phrenologist
BR frɪ'nɒlədʒɪst, -s
AM frə'nɑlədʒəst, -s

phrenology
BR frɪ'nɒlədʒi

AM frəˈnɑlədʒi

Phrygia
BR ˈfrɪdʒɪə(r)
AM ˈfrɪdʒiə

Phrygian
BR ˈfrɪdʒɪən, -z
AM ˈfrɪdʒiən, -z

phthalate
BR ˈ(f)θaleɪt, -s
AM ˈθæˌleɪt, -s

phthalic acid
BR ˌ(f)θalɪk ˈasɪd
AM ˌθælɪk ˈæsəd

phthisic
BR ˈ(f)θʌɪsɪk, ˈtʌɪsɪk
AM ˈtɪzɪk, ˈθaɪsɪk, ˈtaɪsɪk

phthisical
BR ˈ(f)θʌɪsɨkl, ˈtʌɪsɨkl
AM ˈtɪzɨkəl, ˈθaɪsɨkəl, ˈtaɪsɨkəl

phthisis
BR ˈ(f)θʌɪsɪs, ˈtʌɪsɪs
AM ˈθaɪsəs, ˈtaɪsəs

Phuket
BR ˌpuːˈkɛt
AM ˌpuˈkɛt

phut
BR fʌt
AM fət

phut-phut
BR ˈfʌtfʌt
AM ˈfətˌfət

phutt
BR fʌt
AM fət

phycological
BR ˌfʌɪkəˈlɒdʒɨkl
AM ˌfaɪkəˈlɑdʒəkəl

phycologist
BR fʌɪˈkɒlədʒɪst, -s
AM faɪˈkɑlədʒəst, -s

phycology
BR fʌɪˈkɒlədʒi
AM faɪˈkɑlədʒi

phycomycete
BR ˌfʌɪkə(ʊ)ˈmʌɪsiːt, -s
AM ˈfaɪkəˈmaɪˌsit, -s

phyla
BR ˈfʌɪlə(r)
AM ˈfaɪlə

phylactery
BR fɨˈlakt(ə)r|i, -ɪz
AM fəˈlækt(ə)ri, -z

phyletic
BR fʌɪˈlɛtɪk
AM faɪˈlɛdɪk

phyletically
BR fʌɪˈlɛtɨkli
AM faɪˈlɛdək(ə)li

Phyllida
BR ˈfɪlɨdə(r)
AM ˈfɪlədə

Phyllis
BR ˈfɪlɪs
AM ˈfɪlɪs

phyllite
BR ˈfɪlʌɪt
AM ˈfɪlaɪt

phyllode
BR ˈfɪləʊd, -z
AM ˈfɪˌloʊd, -z

phyllophagous
BR fɨˈlɒfəgəs
AM fəˈlɑfəgəs

phyllopod
BR ˈfɪləpɒd, -z
AM ˈfɪləˌpɑd, -z

phylloquinone
BR ˌfʌɪləʊˈkwɪnəʊn
AM ˌfɪloʊˈkwaɪˌnoʊn

Phyllosan
BR ˈfɪlə(ʊ)san
AM ˈfɪləsən

phyllostome
BR ˈfɪləstəʊm, -z
AM ˈfɪləˌstoʊm, -z

phyllotactic
BR ˌfɪlə(ʊ)ˈtaktɪk
AM ˌfɪləˈtæktɪk

phyllotaxis
BR ˌfɪlə(ʊ)ˈtaksɪs, ˈfɪlə(ʊ)ˌtaksɪs
AM ˈfɪləˈtæksəs

phyllotaxy
BR ˈfɪlə(ʊ)ˌtaksi
AM ˈfɪləˌtæksi

phylloxera
BR fɨˈlɒks(ə)rə(r), ˌfɪlɒkˈsɪərə(r)
AM fəˈlɑksərə, ˌfɪləkˈsirə

phylogenesis
BR ˌfʌɪlə(ʊ)ˈdʒɛnɪsɪs
AM ˌfaɪloʊˈdʒɛnəsəs

phylogenetic
BR ˌfʌɪlə(ʊ)dʒɨˈnɛtɪk
AM ˌfaɪloʊdʒəˈnɛdɪk

phylogenetically
BR ˌfʌɪlə(ʊ)dʒɨˈnɛtɨkli
AM ˌfaɪloʊdʒəˈnɛdək(ə)li

phylogenic
BR ˌfʌɪlə(ʊ)ˈdʒɛnɪk
AM ˌfaɪloʊˈdʒɛnɪk

phylogeny
BR fʌɪˈlɒdʒɨni, fʌɪˈlɒdʒni
AM ˌfaɪˈlɑdʒəni

phyloxera
BR fɨˈlɒks(ə)rə(r), ˌfɪlɒkˈsɪərə(r)
AM fəˈlɑksərə, ˌfɪləkˈsirə

phylum
BR ˈfʌɪləm
AM ˈfaɪləm

physalis
BR ˈfʌɪsəlɪs, ˈfɪsəlɪs, fʌɪˈseɪlɪs
AM ˈfaɪsələs, ˈfɪsələs, faɪˈsæləs

physic
BR ˈfɪzɪk, -s, -ɪŋ, -t
AM ˈfɪzɪk, -s, -ɪŋ, -t

physical
BR ˈfɪzɨkl
AM ˈfɪzəkəl

physicalism
BR ˈfɪzɨkl̩ɪz(ə)m, ˈfɪzɨkəlɪz(ə)m
AM ˈfɪzəkəˌlɪzəm

physicalist
BR ˈfɪzɨkl̩ɪst, ˈfɪzɨkəlɪst, -s
AM ˈfɪzəkələst, -s

physicalistic
BR ˌfɪzɨkəˈlɪstɪk, ˌfɪzɨklˈɪstɪk
AM ˌfɪzəkəˈlɪstɪk

physicality
BR ˌfɪzɪˈkalɨti
AM ˌfɪzəˈkælədi

physically
BR ˈfɪzɨkli
AM ˈfɪzək(ə)li

physicalness
BR ˈfɪzɨklnəs
AM ˈfɪzəkəlnəs

physician
BR fɨˈzɪʃn, -z
AM fəˈzɪʃən, -z

physicist
BR ˈfɪzɪsɪst, -s
AM ˈfɪzəsəst, -s

physicky
BR ˈfɪzɨki
AM ˈfɪzɨki

physico-chemical
BR ˌfɪzɨkəʊˈkɛmɨkl
AM ˈfɪzəkoʊˈkɛməkəl

physio
BR ˈfɪzɪəʊ, -z
AM ˈfɪzioʊ, -z

physiocracy
BR ˌfɪzɪˈɒkrəs|i, -ɪz
AM ˌfɪziˈɑkrəsi, -z

physiocrat
BR ˈfɪzɪəkrat, -s
AM ˈfɪziəˌkræt, -s

physiocratic
BR ˌfɪzɪəˈkratɪk
AM ˌfɪzɪəˈkrædɪk

physiognomic
BR ˌfɪzɪəˈnɒmɪk
AM ˈfɪziəˈnɑmɪk

physiognomical
BR ˌfɪzɪəˈnɒmɨkl
AM ˈfɪziəˈnɑməkəl

physiognomically
BR ˌfɪzɪəˈnɒmɨkli
AM ˈfɪziəˈnɑmək(ə)li

physiognomist
BR ˌfɪzɪˈɒnəmɪst, -s
AM ˌfɪziˈɑ(g)nəməst, -s

physiognomy
BR ˌfɪzɪˈɒnəm|i, -ɪz
AM ˌfɪziˈɑ(g)nəmi, -z

physiographer
BR ˌfɪzɪˈɒgrəfə(r), -z
AM ˌfɪziˈɑgrəfər, -z

physiographic
BR ˌfɪzɪəˈgrafɪk
AM ˈfɪziəˈgræfɪk

physiographical
BR ˌfɪzɪəˈgrafɨkl
AM ˈfɪziəˈgræfəkəl

physiographically
BR ˌfɪzɪəˈgrafɨkli
AM ˈfɪziəˈgræfək(ə)li

physiography
BR ˌfɪzɪˈɒgrəfi
AM ˌfɪziˈɑgrəfi

physiological
BR ˌfɪzɪəˈlɒdʒɨkl
AM ˈfɪziəˈlɑdʒəkəl

physiologically
BR ˌfɪzɪəˈlɒdʒɨkli
AM ˈfɪziəˈlɑdʒək(ə)li

physiologist
BR ˌfɪzɪˈɒlədʒɪst, -s
AM ˌfɪziˈɑlədʒəst, -s

physiology
BR ˌfɪzɪˈɒlədʒi
AM ˌfɪziˈɑlədʒi

physiotherapist
BR ˌfɪzɪə(ʊ)ˈθɛrəpɪst, -s
AM ˈfɪzioʊˈθɛrəpɪst, -s

physiotherapy
BR ˌfɪzɪə(ʊ)ˈθɛrəpi
AM ˈfɪzioʊˈθɛrəpi

physique
BR fɨˈziːk
AM fəˈzik

physostigmine
BR ˌfʌɪsəʊˈstɪgmiːn
AM ˌfaɪzəˈstɪgˌmin

phytoalexin
BR ˌfʌɪtəʊəˈlɛksɪn
AM ˌfaɪdoʊəˈlɛksɪn

phytochemical
BR ˌfʌɪtəʊˈkɛmɨkl
AM ˌfaɪdəˈkɛməkəl

phytochemist
BR ˌfʌɪtəʊˈkɛmɪst
AM ˈfaɪdəˈkɛməst

phytochemistry
BR ˌfʌɪtəʊˈkɛmɪstri
AM ˈfaɪdəˈkɛməstri

phytochrome
BR ˈfʌɪtəkrəʊm
AM ˈfaɪdəˌkroʊm

phytogenesis
BR ˌfʌɪtəʊˈdʒɛnɪsɪs
AM ˌfaɪdəˈdʒɛnəsəs

phytogeny
BR fʌɪˈtɒdʒɨni
AM faɪˈtɑdʒəni

phytogeography
BR ˌfʌɪtəʊdʒɪˈɒgrəfi, ˌfʌɪtəʊˈdʒɒgrəfi
AM ˌfaɪdədʒiˈɑgrəfi

phytography
BR fʌɪˈtɒgrəfi
AM faɪˈtɑgrəfi

phytolith
BR ˈfʌɪtəlɪθ, -s
AM ˈfaɪdəˌlɪθ, -s

phytopathology
BR ˌfʌɪtəʊpəˈθɒlədʒi
AM ˌfaɪdəpəˈθɑlədʒi

phytophagous
BR fʌɪˈtɒfəgəs
AM faɪˈtɑfəgəs

phytoplankton
BR ˈfʌɪtəʊˌplaŋ(k)tən
AM ˌfaɪdəˈplæŋktən

phytotomy
BR fʌɪˈtɒtəmi
AM faɪˈtɑdəmi

phytotoxic
BR ˌfʌɪtə(ʊ)ˈtɒksɪk
AM ˌfaɪdəˈtɑksɪk

phytotoxin
BR ˈfʌɪtəˌtɒksɪn, -z
AM ˈfaɪdəˌtɑksən, -z

pi
BR pʌɪ, -z
AM paɪ, -z

piacular
BR pʌɪˈakjʉlə(r)
AM paɪˈækjələr

Piaf
BR ˈpiːaf
AM ˈpiɑf

piaffe
BR pɪˈaf, -s, -ɪŋ, -t
AM piˈæf, pjæf, -s, -ɪŋ, -t

Piaget
BR pɪˈaʒeɪ
AM ˌpiɑˈʒeɪ

pia mater
BR ˌpʌɪə ˈmeɪtə(r), ˌpiːə +
AM ˌpiə ˈmɑdər, ˌpaɪə ˈmeɪdər

pianism
BR ˈpɪənɪz(ə)m
AM ˈpiəˌnɪzəm

pianissimo
BR ˌpɪəˈnɪsɪməʊ, -z
AM ˌpiəˈnɪsəˌmoʊ, -z

pianist
BR ˈpɪənɪst, -s
AM ˈpiənəst, -s

pianistic
BR ˌpɪəˈnɪstɪk
AM ˌpiəˈnɪstɪk

pianistically
BR ˌpɪəˈnɪstɪkli
AM ˌpiəˈnɪstək(ə)li

piano¹
instrument
BR pɪˈanəʊ, -z
AM piˈænoʊ, -z

piano²
softly
BR ˈpjɑːnəʊ, pɪˈɑːnəʊ
AM piˈɑnoʊ

piano-accordion
BR pɪˌanəʊəˈkɔːdɪən, -z
AM piˌænoʊəˈkɔrdiən, -z

pianoforte
BR pɪˌanəʊˈfɔːt|i, pɪˌanəʊˈfɔːt|eɪ, -ɪz\-eɪz
AM piˈænəˌfɔrdi, -z

pianola®
BR ˌpɪəˈnəʊlə(r), -z
AM ˌpiəˈnoʊlə, -z

piano nobile
BR ˌpjɑːnəʊ ˈnəʊbɪleɪ, -z
AM ˌpjɑˌnoʊ ˈnoʊbiˌleɪ, -z

piasava
BR ˌpiːəˈsɑːvə(r), -z
AM ˌpiəˈsɑvə, -z

piassava
BR ˌpiːəˈsɑːvə(r), -z
AM ˌpiəˈsɑvə, -z

piaster
BR pɪˈastə(r), -z
AM piˈæstər, -z

piastre
BR pɪˈastə(r), -z
AM piˈæstər, -z

Piat
BR ˈpiːət, -s
AM ˈpiət, -s

piazza
BR pɪˈatsə(r), -z
AM piˈɑtsə, piˈæzə, -z

pibroch
BR ˈpiːbrɒk, ˈpiːbrɒx, -s
AM ˈpiˌbrɑx, ˈpiˌbrɑk, -s

PIBS
permanent interest-bearing share
BR pɪbz
AM pɪbz

pic
BR pɪk, -s
AM pɪk, -s

pica
BR ˈpʌɪkə(r)
AM ˈpaɪkə

picador
BR ˈpɪkədɔː(r), -z
AM ˈpɪkəˌdɔ(ə)r, -z

picadore
BR ˈpɪkədɔː(r), -z
AM ˈpɪkəˌdɔ(ə)r, -z

picaninny
BR ˈpɪkənɪn|i, ˌpɪkəˈnɪn|i, -ɪz
AM ˈpɪkəˌnɪni, -z

Picard
BR ˈpɪkɑːd, pɪˈkɑːd
AM pəˈkɑrd

Picardy
BR ˈpɪkədi
AM ˈpɪkərdi

picaresque
BR ˌpɪkəˈrɛsk
AM ˌpɪkəˈrɛsk

picaroon
BR ˌpɪkəˈruːn, -z
AM ˌpɪkəˈrun, -z

Picasso
BR pɪˈkasəʊ, pɪˈkɑːsəʊ
AM pəˈkɑsoʊ

picayune
BR ˌpɪkəˈjuːn, -z
AM ˌpɪkəˈjun, ˌpɪkiˈjun, -z

Piccadilly
BR ˌpɪkəˈdɪli
AM ˈpɪkəˌdɪli

piccalilli
BR ˌpɪkəˈlɪli
AM ˈpɪkəˌlɪli

piccaninny
BR ˈpɪkənɪn|i, ˌpɪkəˈnɪn|i, -ɪz
AM ˈpɪkəˌnɪni, -z

piccolo
BR ˈpɪkələʊ, -z
AM ˈpɪkəˌloʊ, -z

pice
BR pʌɪs
AM paɪs

pichiciago
BR ˌpɪtʃɪˈsjeɪgəʊ, -z
AM ˌpitʃisiˈeɪgoʊ, -z

pick
BR pɪk, -s, -ɪŋ, -t
AM pɪk, -s, -ɪŋ, -t

pickaback
BR ˈpɪkəbak, -s
AM ˈpɪkəˌbæk, -s

pickable
BR ˈpɪkəbl
AM ˈpɪkəbəl

pickaninny
BR ˈpɪkənɪn|i, ˌpɪkəˈnɪn|i, -ɪz
AM ˈpɪkəˌnɪni, -z

pickax
BR ˈpɪkaks, -ɪz, -ɪŋ, -t
AM ˈpɪkˌæks, -əz, -ɪŋ, -t

pickaxe
BR ˈpɪkaks, -ɪz, -ɪŋ, -t
AM ˈpɪkˌæks, -əz, -ɪŋ, -t

Pickelhaube
BR ˈpɪklˌhaʊbə(r), -z
AM ˈpɪklˌ(h)aʊbə, -z

picker
BR ˈpɪkə(r), -z
AM ˈpɪkər, -z

pickerel
BR ˈpɪk(ə)rəl, ˈpɪk(ə)rl̩, -z
AM ˈpɪk(ə)rəl, -z

Pickering
BR ˈpɪk(ə)rɪŋ
AM ˈpɪk(ə)rɪŋ

picket
BR ˈpɪk|ɪt, -ɪts, -ɪtɪŋ, -ɪtɪd
AM ˈpɪkɪ|t, -ts, -dɪŋ, -dɪd

picketer
BR ˈpɪkɪtə(r), -z
AM ˈpɪkɪdər, -z

Pickett
BR ˈpɪkɪt
AM ˈpɪkɪt

Pickford
BR ˈpɪkfəd
AM ˈpɪkfərd

pickiness
BR ˈpɪkɪnɪs
AM ˈpɪkinɪs

pickings
BR ˈpɪkɪŋz
AM ˈpɪkɪŋz

pickle
BR ˈpɪk|l, -lz, -l̩ɪŋ\-lɪŋ, -ld
AM ˈpɪk|əl, -əlz, -(ə)lɪŋ, -əld

pickler
BR ˈpɪkl̩ə(r), ˈpɪklə(r), -z
AM ˈpɪk(ə)lər, -z

Pickles
BR ˈpɪklz
AM ˈpɪkəlz

picklock
BR ˈpɪklɒk, -s
AM ˈpɪkˌlɑk, -s

pick-me-up
BR ˈpɪkmɪʌp, -s
AM ˈpɪkmiˌəp, -s

pickoff
BR ˈpɪkɒf, -s
AM ˈpɪkˌɔf, ˈpɪkˌɑf, -s

pickpocket
BR ˈpɪkˌpɒk|ɪt, -s, -ɪtɪŋ, -ɪdɪd
AM ˈpɪkˌpɑkə|t, -ts, -dɪŋ, -dəd

pickpocketing
BR ˈpɪkˌpɒkɪtɪŋ
AM ˈpɪkˌpɑkədɪŋ

Pickthorne
BR ˈpɪkθɔːn
AM ˈpɪkˌθɔ(ə)rn

pickup
BR ˈpɪkʌp, -s
AM ˈpɪkˌəp, -s

Pickwick
BR ˈpɪkwɪk
AM ˈpɪkˌwɪk

Pickwickian
BR pɪkˈwɪkɪən
AM pɪkˈwɪkiən

picky
BR ˈpɪk|i, -ɪə(r), -ɪɪst
AM ˈpɪki, -ər, -ɪst

pick-your-own
BR ˌpɪkjərˈəʊn, -z
AM ˈpɪkˌjəˈroʊn, -z

picnic
BR ˈpɪkn|ɪk, -ɪks, -ɪkɪŋ, -ɪkt
AM ˈpɪkˌnɪk, -s, -ɪŋ, -t

picnicker
BR ˈpɪknɪkə(r), -z
AM ˈpɪkˌnɪkər, -z

picnicky
BR 'pɪknɨki
AM 'pɪkˌnɪki

Pico
BR 'piːkəʊ
AM 'pikoʊ

picosecond
BR 'piːkəʊˌsɛk(ə)nd, 'pʌɪkəʊˌsɛk(ə)nd, -z
AM 'paɪkoʊˌsɛkənd, -z

picot
BR 'piːkəʊ, -z, -ɪŋ, -d
AM 'piˌkoʊ, -z, -ɪŋ, -d

picotee
BR ˌpɪkə'tiː, -z
AM ˌpɪkə'ti, -z

picquet¹
picket
BR 'pɪkɪt, -s
AM 'pɪkɨt, -s

picquet²
piquet
BR pɪ'kɛt
AM pə'keɪ

picrate
BR 'pɪkreɪt, -s
AM 'pɪˌkreɪt, -s

picric acid
BR ˌpɪkrɪk 'asɪd
AM 'pɪˌkrɪk 'æsəd

Pict
BR pɪkt, -s
AM pɪk|(t), -(t)s

Pictish
BR 'pɪktɪʃ
AM 'pɪktɪʃ

pictogram
BR 'pɪktəgram, -z
AM 'pɪktəˌgræm, -z

pictograph
BR 'pɪktəgrɑːf, 'pɪktəgraf, -s
AM 'pɪktəˌgræf, -s

pictographic
BR ˌpɪktə'grafɪk
AM ˌpɪktə'græfɪk

pictography
BR pɪk'tɒgrəfi
AM pɪk'tɑgrəfi

pictorial
BR pɪk'tɔːrɪəl
AM pɪk'tɔriəl

pictorially
BR pɪk'tɔːrɪəli
AM pɪk'tɔriəli

picture
BR 'pɪktʃ|ə(r), -əz, -(ə)rɪŋ, -əd
AM 'pɪk(t)ʃər, -z, -ɪŋ, -d

picturebook
BR 'pɪktʃəbʊk, -s
AM 'pɪk(t)ʃərˌbʊk, -s

picturegoer
BR 'pɪktʃəˌgəʊə(r), -z
AM 'pɪk(t)ʃərˌgoʊər, -z

picturesque
BR ˌpɪktʃə'rɛsk
AM ¦pɪk(t)ʃə'rɛsk

picturesquely
BR ˌpɪktʃə'rɛskli
AM ¦pɪk(t)ʃə'rɛskli

picturesqueness
BR ˌpɪktʃə'rɛsknəs
AM ¦pɪk(t)ʃə'rɛsknəs

piddle
BR 'pɪd|l, -lz, -ļɪŋ\-lɪŋ, -ld
AM 'pɪd|əl, -əlz, -(ə)lɪŋ, -əld

piddler
BR 'pɪdļə(r), 'pɪdlə(r), -z
AM 'pɪd(ə)lər, -z

piddock
BR 'pɪdək, -s
AM 'pɪdək, -s

pidgin
BR 'pɪdʒ(ɨ)n, -z
AM 'pɪdʒɨn, -z

pidginisation
BR ˌpɪdʒɨnʌɪ'zeɪʃn, ˌpɪdʒņʌɪ'zeɪʃn
AM ˌpɪdʒɨnə'zeɪʃən, ˌpɪdʒɨˌnaɪ'zeɪʃən

pidginise
BR 'pɪdʒɨnʌɪz, 'pɪdʒņʌɪz, -ɨz, -ɪŋ, -d
AM 'pɪdʒɨnˌaɪz, -ɨz, -ɪŋ, -d

pidginization
BR ˌpɪdʒɨnʌɪ'zeɪʃn, ˌpɪdʒņʌɪ'zeɪʃn
AM ˌpɪdʒɨnə'zeɪʃən, ˌpɪdʒɨˌnaɪ'zeɪʃən

pidginize
BR 'pɪdʒɨnʌɪz, 'pɪdʒņʌɪz, -ɨz, -ɪŋ, -d
AM 'pɪdʒɨnˌaɪz, -ɨz, -ɪŋ, -d

pi-dog
BR 'pʌɪdɒg, -z
AM 'paiˌdɔg, 'paiˌdɑg, -z

pie
BR pʌɪ, -z
AM paɪ, -z

piebald
BR 'pʌɪbɔːld, -z
AM 'paɪˌbɔld, 'paɪˌbɑld, -z

piece
BR piːs, -ɨz, -ɪŋ, -t
AM pis, -ɨz, -ɪŋ, -t

pièce de résistance
BR piːˌɛs də rɪ'zɪstɒ̃s, + rɛ'zɪstɒ̃s, + ˌrɛzɪ'stɒ̃s
AM piˌɛs də rəˌzi'stɑns, + reɪˌzi'stɑns

piece-goods
BR 'piːsgʊdz
AM 'pisˌgʊdz

piecemeal
BR 'piːsmiːl
AM 'pisˌmil

piecer
BR 'piːsə(r), -z
AM 'pisər, -z

piece-rate
BR 'piːsreɪt, -s
AM 'pisˌreɪt, -s

pièces de résistance
BR piːˌɛs də rɪ'zɪstɒ̃s, + rɛ'zɪstɒ̃s, + ˌrɛzɪ'stɒ̃s
AM piˌɛs də rəˌzi'stɑns, + reɪˌzi'stɑns

piecework
BR 'piːswəːk
AM 'pisˌwərk

piecrust
BR 'pʌɪkrʌst, -s
AM 'paɪˌkrəst, -s

pied
BR pʌɪd
AM paɪd

pied-à-terre
BR ˌpjɛdə'tɛː(r), ˌpjeɪdə'tɛː(r), -z
AM piˌeɪdə'tɛ(ə)r, -z

piedmont
BR 'piːdmɒnt, -s
AM 'pidˌmɑnt, -s

Piedmontese
BR ˌpiːdmɒn'tiːz, ˌpiːdmən'tiːz
AM ˌpidmɑn'tiz

pie-dog
BR 'pʌɪdɒg, -z
AM 'paɪˌdɔg, 'paɪˌdɑg, -z

Pied Piper
BR ˌpʌɪd 'pʌɪpə(r)
AM ¦paɪd 'paɪpər

pie-eater
BR 'pʌɪˌiːtə(r), -z
AM 'paɪˌidər, -z

pie-eyed
BR ˌpʌɪ'ʌɪd
AM 'paɪˌaɪd

pie in the sky
BR ˌpʌɪ ɪn ðə 'skʌɪ
AM ¦paɪ ɪn ðə 'skaɪ

pieman
BR 'pʌɪmən
AM 'paɪmən, 'paɪˌmæn

piemen
BR 'pʌɪmən
AM 'paɪmən, 'paɪˌmɛn

pier
BR pɪə(r), -z
AM pɪ(ə)r, -z

pierce
BR pɪəs, -ɨz, -ɪŋ, -t
AM pɪ(ə)rs, -ɨz, -ɪŋ, -t

piercer
BR 'pɪəsə(r), -z
AM 'pɪrsər, -z

piercingly
BR 'pɪəsɪŋli
AM 'pɪrsɪŋli

Piercy
BR 'pɪəsi
AM 'pɪrsi

Pierian
BR pʌɪ'ɪərɪən, pʌɪ'ɛːrɪən
AM paɪ'ɪriən

pierogi
BR pɪə'rəʊg|i, pə'rəʊg|i, -ɪz
AM pə'roʊgi, pɪr'oʊgi, -z

Pierre¹
city in S. Dakota
BR 'pɪə(r)
AM 'pɪ(ə)r

Pierre²
French forename
BR pɪ'ɛː(r), pjɛː(r)
AM pi'ɛ(ə)r, 'pjɛ(ə)r

Pierrot
BR 'pɪərəʊ, -z
AM 'piəˌroʊ, 'pɪˌroʊ, -z

Piers
BR pɪəz
AM pɪ(ə)rz

Pierson
BR 'pɪəsn
AM 'pɪrsən

pieta
BR ˌpiːɛ'tɑː(*r*), ˌpiːeɪ'tɑː(*r*), -z
AM ¦pieɪ'tɑ, -z

pietà
BR ˌpiːɛ'tɑː(*r*), ˌpiːeɪ'tɑː(*r*), -z
AM ¦pieɪ'tɑ, -z

Pietermaritzburg
BR ˌpiːtə'marɪtsbəːg
AM ˌpidər'mɛrətsˌbərg
AFK ˌpiːtərma'rətsbərx

Pietism
BR 'pʌɪɨtɪz(ə)m
AM 'paɪəˌtɪzəm

pietist
BR 'pʌɪɨtɪst, -s
AM 'paɪədəst, -s

pietistic
BR ˌpʌɪɨ'tɪstɪk
AM ˌpaɪə'tɪstɪk

pietistical
BR ˌpʌɪɨ'tɪstɨkl
AM ˌpaɪə'tɪstəkəl

pietra dura
BR ˌpjɛtrə 'duːrə(*r*)
AM ˌpieɪtrə 'd(j)ʊrə

piety
BR 'pʌɪɨti
AM 'paɪədi

piezoelectric
BR ˌpiːzəʊɪ'lɛktrɪk, ˌpiːtsəʊɪ'lɛktrɪk, pɪˌɛtsəʊɪ'lɛktrɪk, pʌɪˌiːzəʊɪ'lɛktrɪk, pʌɪˌiːtsəʊɪ'lɛktrɪk, ˌpʌɪɨzəʊɪ'lɛktrɪk
AM piˌeɪzoʊə'lɛktrɪk, piˌeɪtsoʊə'lɛktrɪk

piezoelectrically
BR ˌpiːzəʊɪˈlɛktrɪkli, ˌpiːtsəʊɪˈlɛktrɪkli, pɪˌɛtsəʊɪˈlɛktrɪkli, pʌɪˌiːzəʊɪˈlɛktrɪkli, pʌɪˌiːtsəʊɪˈlɛktrɪkli, ˌpʌɪɪzəʊɪˈlɛktrɪkli
AM piˌeɪzoʊəˈlɛktrək(ə)li, piˌeɪtsoʊəˈlɛktrək(ə)li

piezoelectricity
BR ˌpiːzəʊɪlɛkˈtrɪsɪti, ˌpiːtsəʊɪlɛkˈtrɪsɪti, pɪˌɛtsəʊɪlɛkˈtrɪsɪti, pʌɪˌiːzəʊɪlɛkˈtrɪsɪti, pʌɪˌiːtsəʊɪlɛkˈtrɪsɪti, ˌpʌɪɪzəʊɪlɛkˈtrɪsɪti
AM piˌeɪzoʊˌɛlɛkˈtrɪsɪdi, piˌeɪtsoʊˌɛlɛkˈtrɪsɪdi

piezometer
BR ˌpiːɪˈzɒmɪtə(r), ˌpʌɪɪˈzɒmɪtə(r), -z
AM piəˈzɑmədər, -z

piffle
BR ˈpɪfl
AM ˈpɪfəl

piffler
BR ˈpɪfl̩ə(r), ˈpɪflə(r), -z
AM ˈpɪf(ə)lər, -z

piffling
BR ˈpɪflɪŋ
AM ˈpɪf(ə)lɪŋ

pig
BR pɪɡ, -z
AM pɪɡ, -z

pigeon
BR ˈpɪdʒ(ɪ)n, -z
AM ˈpɪdʒən, -z

pigeonhole
BR ˈpɪdʒ(ɪ)nhəʊl, -z, -ɪŋ, -d
AM ˈpɪdʒənˌ(h)oʊl, -z, -ɪŋ, -d

pigeon pair
BR ˌpɪdʒ(ɪ)n ˈpɛː(r), -z
AM ˈpɪdʒən ˌpɛ(ə)r, -z

pigeonry
BR ˈpɪdʒ(ɪ)nr|i, -ɪz
AM ˈpɪdʒənri, -z

piggery
BR ˈpɪɡ(ə)r|i, -ɪz
AM ˈpɪɡ(ə)ri, -z

piggin
BR ˈpɪɡɪn, -z
AM ˈpɪɡɪn, -z

piggish
BR ˈpɪɡɪʃ
AM ˈpɪɡɪʃ

piggishly
BR ˈpɪɡɪʃli
AM ˈpɪɡɪʃli

piggishness
BR ˈpɪɡɪʃnɪs
AM ˈpɪɡɪʃnɪs

Piggott
BR ˈpɪɡət
AM ˈpɪɡət

piggy
BR ˈpɪɡ|i, -ɪz
AM ˈpɪɡi, -z

piggyback
BR ˈpɪɡɪbak, -s
AM ˈpɪɡiˌbæk, -s

piggybank
BR ˈpɪɡɪbaŋk, -s
AM ˈpɪɡiˌbæŋk, -s

piggy in the middle
BR ˌpɪɡɪ ɪn ðə ˈmɪdl
AM ˈpɪɡi ɪn(ð)ə ˈmɪdəl

piggywig
BR ˈpɪɡɪwɪɡ, -z
AM ˈpɪɡiˌwɪɡ, -z

pigheaded
BR ˌpɪɡˈhɛdɪd
AM ˈpɪɡˌ(h)ɛdəd

pig in the middle
BR ˌpɪɡ ɪn ðə ˈmɪdl
AM ˈpɪɡ ən(ð)ə ˈmɪdəl

piglet
BR ˈpɪɡlɪt, -s
AM ˈpɪɡlɪt, -s

piglike
BR ˈpɪɡlʌɪk
AM ˈpɪɡˌlaɪk

pigling
BR ˈpɪɡlɪŋ, -z
AM ˈpɪɡ(ə)lɪŋ, -z

pigmaean
BR pɪɡˈmiːən
AM ˈpɪɡmiən, pɪɡˈmiən

pigmean
BR pɪɡˈmiːən
AM ˈpɪɡmiən, pɪɡˈmiən

pigmeat
BR ˈpɪɡmiːt
AM ˈpɪɡˌmit

pigment[1]
noun
BR ˈpɪɡm(ə)nt, -s
AM ˈpɪɡmənt, -s

pigment[2]
verb
BR pɪɡˈmɛnt, ˈpɪɡm(ə)nt, -s, -ɪŋ, -ɪd
AM pɪɡˈmɛnt, ˈpɪɡmənt, -s, -ɪŋ, -ɪd

pigmental
BR pɪɡˈmɛntl
AM pɪɡˈmɛn(t)l

pigmentary
BR ˈpɪɡmənt(ə)ri
AM ˈpɪɡmənˌtɛri

pigmentation
BR ˌpɪɡmɛnˈteɪʃn, ˌpɪɡm(ə)nˈteɪʃn
AM ˌpɪɡmənˈteɪʃən, ˌpɪɡˌmɛnˈteɪʃən

pigmentosa
BR ˌpɪɡm(ə)nˈtəʊsə(r)
AM ˌpɪɡmənˈtoʊsə, ˌpɪɡˌmɛnˈtoʊsə

pigmy
BR ˈpɪɡmi, -ɪz
AM ˈpɪɡmi, -z

pignut
BR ˈpɪɡnʌt, -s
AM ˈpɪɡˌnət, -s

pig-out
BR ˌpɪɡˈaʊt
AM ˈpɪɡˈaʊt

pigpen
BR ˈpɪɡpɛn, -z
AM ˈpɪɡˌpɛn, -z

pigskin
BR ˈpɪɡskɪn, -z
AM ˈpɪɡˌskɪn, -z

pigsticker
BR ˈpɪɡˌstɪkə(r), -z
AM ˈpɪɡˌstɪkər, -z

pigsticking
BR ˈpɪɡˌstɪkɪŋ
AM ˈpɪɡˌstɪkɪŋ

pigsty
BR ˈpɪɡstʌɪ, -z
AM ˈpɪɡˌstaɪ, -z

pigswill
BR ˈpɪɡswɪl
AM ˈpɪɡˌswɪl

pigtail
BR ˈpɪɡteɪl, -z, -d
AM ˈpɪɡˌteɪl, -z, -d

pigwash
BR ˈpɪɡwɒʃ
AM ˈpɪɡˌwɔʃ, ˈpɪɡˌwɑʃ

pigweed
BR ˈpɪɡwiːd, -z
AM ˈpɪɡˌwid, -z

pi jaw
BR ˈpʌɪ dʒɔː(*r*)
AM ˈpaɪ ˌdʒɔ, ˈpaɪˌdʒɑ

pika
BR ˈpʌɪkə(*r*), ˈpiːkə(*r*), -z
AM ˈpaɪkə, ˈpikə, -z

pike
BR pʌɪk, -s
AM paɪk, -s

pikelet
BR ˈpʌɪklɪt, -s
AM ˈpaɪklət, -s

pikeman
BR ˈpʌɪkmən
AM ˈpaɪkmən

pikemen
BR ˈpʌɪkmən
AM ˈpaɪkmən

pikeperch
BR ˈpʌɪkpəːtʃ
AM ˈpaɪkˌpərtʃ

piker
BR ˈpʌɪkə(r), -z
AM ˈpaɪkər, -z

pikestaff
BR ˈpʌɪkstɑːf, ˈpʌɪkstaf, -s
AM ˈpaɪkˌstæf, -s

pilaf
BR ˈpɪlaf, ˈpiːlaf, pɪˈlaf, -s
AM ˈpiˌlɑf, pəˈlɑf, -s

pilaff
BR ˈpɪlaf, ˈpiːlaf, pɪˈlaf, -s
AM ˈpiˌlɑf, pəˈlɑf, -s

pilaster
BR pɪˈlastə(r), -z, -d
AM pəˈlæstər, -z, -d

Pilate
BR ˈpʌɪlət
AM ˈpaɪlət

Pilatus
BR pɪˈlɑːtəs
AM pəˈlɑdəs

pilau
BR pɪˈlaʊ, ˈpiːlaʊ, -z
AM pəˈlaʊ, piˈlaʊ, -z

pilaw
BR pɪˈlaʊ, ˈpiːlaʊ, -z
AM pəˈlaʊ, piˈlaʊ, -z

pilch
BR pɪltʃ, -ɪz
AM pɪltʃ, -ɪz

pilchard
BR ˈpɪltʃəd, -z
AM ˈpɪltʃərd, -z

pile
BR pʌɪl, -z, -ɪŋ, -d
AM paɪl, -z, -ɪŋ, -d

pileate
BR ˈpɪlɪət, ˈpʌɪlɪət
AM ˈpaɪliət, ˈpɪliət

pileated
BR ˈpɪlɪeɪtɪd, ˈpʌɪlɪeɪtɪd
AM ˈpaɪliˌeɪdɪd, ˈpɪliˌeɪdɪd

piledriver
BR ˈpʌɪlˌdrʌɪvə(r), -z
AM ˈpaɪlˌdraɪvər, -z

piledriving
BR ˈpʌɪlˌdrʌɪvɪŋ
AM ˈpaɪlˌdrɪvɪŋ

pilei
BR ˈpʌɪlɪʌɪ
AM ˈpaɪliˌaɪ

pileup
BR ˈpʌɪlʌp, -s
AM ˈpaɪlˌəp, -s

pileus
BR ˈpʌɪlɪəs
AM ˈpaɪliəs

pilewort
BR ˈpʌɪlwəːt
AM ˈpaɪlwərt, ˈpaɪlwɔ(ə)rt

pilfer
BR ˈpɪlf|ə(r), -əz, -(ə)rɪŋ, -əd
AM ˈpɪlfər, -z, -ɪŋ, -d

pilferage
BR ˈpɪlf(ə)rɪdʒ
AM ˈpɪlf(ə)rɪdʒ

pilferer
BR ˈpɪlf(ə)rə(r), -z
AM ˈpɪlf(ə)rər, -z

pilgrim
BR ˈpɪlɡrɪm, -z

AM ˈpɪlgrɪm, -z
pilgrimage
BR ˈpɪlgrɪm|ɪdʒ, -ɨdʒɪz
AM ˈpɪlgrəmɪdʒ, -ɪz
pilgrimise
BR ˈpɪlgrɪmʌɪz, -ɪz, -ɪŋ, -d
AM ˈpɪlgrəˌmaɪz, -ɪz, -ɪŋ, -d
pilgrimize
BR ˈpɪlgrɪmʌɪz, -ɪz, -ɪŋ, -d
AM ˈpɪlgrəˌmaɪz, -ɪz, -ɪŋ, -d
piliferous
BR pʌɪˈlɪf(ə)rəs
AM paɪˈlɪf(ə)rəs
piliform
BR ˈpʌɪlɨfɔːm
AM ˈpaɪləˌfɔ(ə)rm
piling
BR ˈpʌɪlɪŋ, -z
AM ˈpaɪlɪŋ, -z
Pilipino
BR ˌpɪlɪˈpiːnəʊ
AM ˌpɪləˈpiˌnoʊ
Pilkington
BR ˈpɪlkɪŋt(ə)n
AM ˈpɪlkɪŋtən
pill
BR pɪl, -z, -ɪŋ, -d
AM pɪl, -z, -ɪŋ, -d
pillage
BR ˈpɪl|ɪdʒ, -ɨdʒɪz, -ɨdʒɪŋ, -ɪdʒd
AM ˈpɪlɪdʒ, -ɪz, -ɪŋ, -d
pillager
BR ˈpɪlɪdʒə(r), -z
AM ˈpɪlədʒər, -z
pillar
BR ˈpɪlə(r), -z, -d
AM ˈpɪlər, -z, -d
pillarbox
BR ˈpɪləbɒks, -ɪz
AM ˈpɪlərˌbɑks, -əz
pillaret
BR ˌpɪləˈrɛt, -s
AM ˌpɪləˈrɛt, -s
pillbox
BR ˈpɪlbɒks, -ɪz
AM ˈpɪlˌbɑks, -əz
Pilling
BR ˈpɪlɪŋ
AM ˈpɪlɪŋ
pillion
BR ˈpɪljən, ˈpɪlɪən, -z, -ɪŋ, -d
AM ˈpɪljən, -z, -ɪŋ, -d
pilliwinks
BR ˈpɪlɪwɪŋks
AM ˈpɪliˌwɪŋks
pillock
BR ˈpɪlək, -s
AM ˈpɪlək, -s
pillory
BR ˈpɪl(ə)r|i, -ɪz, -ɪɪŋ, -ɪd
AM ˈpɪləri, -z, -ɪŋ, -d
pillow
BR ˈpɪləʊ, -z, -ɪŋ, -d
AM ˈpɪloʊ, -z, -ɪŋ, -d
pillowcase
BR ˈpɪlə(ʊ)keɪs, -ɪz
AM ˈpɪloʊˌkeɪs, -ɪz
pillowslip
BR ˈpɪlə(ʊ)slɪp, -s
AM ˈpɪloʊˌslɪp, -s
pillowy
BR ˈpɪləʊi
AM ˈpɪloʊi
pillular
BR ˈpɪljʉlə(r)
AM ˈpɪljələr
pillule
BR ˈpɪljuːl, -z
AM ˈpɪlˌjul, -z
pillwort
BR ˈpɪlwəːt, -s
AM ˈpɪlwərt, ˈpɪlwɔ(ə)rt, -s
pilose
BR ˈpʌɪləʊz, ˈpʌɪləʊs
AM ˈpaɪˌloʊs, ˈpaɪˌloʊz
pilosity
BR pʌɪˈlɒsɪti
AM paɪˈlɑsədi
pilot
BR ˈpʌɪlət, -s, -ɪŋ, -ɪd
AM ˈpaɪlə|t, -ts, -dɪŋ, -dəd
pilotage
BR ˈpʌɪlətɪdʒ
AM ˈpaɪlədɪdʒ
pilothouse
BR ˈpʌɪləthaʊ|s, -zɪz
AM ˈpaɪlətˌ(h)aʊ|s, -zəz
pilot-jacket
BR ˈpʌɪlətˌdʒakɪt, -s
AM ˈpaɪlətˌdʒækət, -s
pilotless
BR ˈpʌɪlətləs
AM ˈpaɪlətləs
pilous
BR ˈpʌɪləs
AM ˈpaɪləs
Pilsen
BR ˈpɪlzn, ˈpɪlsn
AM ˈpɪlzən, ˈpɪlsən
pilsener
BR ˈpɪlznə(r), ˈpɪlsnə(r)
AM ˈpɪlz(ə)nər, ˈpɪlsnər
pilsner
BR ˈpɪlznə(r), ˈpɪlsnə(r)
AM ˈpɪlz(ə)nər, ˈpɪlsnər
Piltdown
BR ˈpɪltdaʊn
AM ˈpɪltˌdaʊn
Pilton
BR ˈpɪlt(ə)n
AM ˈpɪltən
pilular
BR ˈpɪljʉlə(r)
AM ˈpɪljələr
pilule
BR ˈpɪljuːl, -z
AM ˈpɪlˌjul, -z
pilulous
BR ˈpɪljʉləs
AM ˈpɪljələs
Pima
BR ˈpiːmə(r), -z
AM ˈpimə, -z
Piman
BR ˈpiːmən
AM ˈpimən
pimento
BR pɪˈmɛntəʊ, -z
AM pəˈmɛn(t)oʊ, -z
pi-meson
BR ˌpʌɪˈmiːzɒn, ˌpʌɪˈmiːsɒn, ˌpʌɪˈmɛzɒn, ˌpʌɪˈmɛsɒn, ˌpʌɪˈmeɪzɒn
AM ˈpaɪˌmeɪˌsɑn, ˈpaɪˌmeɪˌzɑn
pimiento
BR ˌpɪmɪˈɛntəʊ, pɪmˈjɛntəʊ, -z
AM pəˈm(j)ɛn(t)oʊ, -z
Pimlico
BR ˈpɪmlɪkəʊ
AM ˈpɪmlɪˌkoʊ
Pimm
BR pɪm, -z
AM pɪm, -z
pimp
BR pɪm|p, -(p)s, -pɪŋ, -(p)t
AM pɪmp, -s, -ɪŋ, -t
pimpernel
BR ˈpɪmpənɛl, -z
AM ˈpɪmpərˌnɛl, ˈpɪmpərnəl, -z
pimple
BR ˈpɪmpl, -z, -d
AM ˈpɪmpəl, -z, -d
pimpliness
BR ˈpɪmplɪnɪs
AM ˈpɪmp(ə)linɪs
pimply
BR ˈpɪmpli
AM ˈpɪmp(ə)li
PIN
BR pɪn
AM pɪn
pin
BR pɪn, -z, -ɪŋ, -d
AM pɪn, -z, -ɪŋ, -d
piña colada
BR ˌpɪnjə kəˈlɑːdə(r), ˌpiːnə +
AM ˈpinjə kəˈlɑdə
pinafore
BR ˈpɪnəfɔː(r), -z
AM ˈpɪnəˌfɔ(ə)r, -z
Pinang
BR pɪˈnaŋ
AM pəˈnæŋ
pinaster
BR pʌɪˈnastə(r), pɪˈnastə(r), -z
AM paɪˈnæstər, -z
piñata
BR pɪˈn(j)ɑːtə(r), -z
AM pɪnˈjɑdə, -z
pinball
BR ˈpɪnbɔːl
AM ˈpinˌbɔl, ˈpinˌbɑl
PINC
BR pɪŋk
AM pɪŋk
pince-nez[1]
singular
BR ˌpansˈneɪ, ˌpãsˈneɪ
AM ˌpɪn(t)ˈsneɪ
pince-nez[2]
plural
BR ˌpansˈneɪz, ˌpãsˈneɪz
AM ˌpɪn(t)ˈsneɪz
pincer
BR ˈpɪnsə(r), -z
AM ˈpɪntʃər, ˈpɪn(t)sər, -z
pincette
BR pɪnˈsɛt, pãˈsɛt, -s
AM pɪnˈsɛt, -s
pinch
BR pɪn(t)ʃ, -ɪz, -ɪŋ, -t
AM pɪn(t)ʃ, -ɪz, -ɪŋ, -t
pinchbeck
BR ˈpɪn(t)ʃbɛk, -s
AM ˈpɪn(t)ʃˌbɛk, -s
Pincher
BR ˈpɪn(t)ʃə(r)
AM ˈpɪn(t)ʃər
pinch-hit
BR ˌpɪn(t)ʃˈhɪt, -s, -ɪŋ
AM ˈ¦pɪn(t)ʃˈhɪ|t, -ts, -dɪŋ
pinch-hitter
BR ˌpɪn(t)ʃˈhɪtə(r), -z
AM ¦pɪn(t)ʃˈhɪdər, -z
pinchpenny
BR ˈpɪn(t)ʃˌpɛn|i, -ɪz
AM ˈpɪn(t)ʃˌpɛni, -z
pinch-run
BR ˌpɪn(t)ʃˈrʌn, -z, -ɪŋ
AM ¦pɪn(t)ʃˈrən, -z, -ɪŋ
pinch-runner
BR ˌpɪn(t)ʃˈrʌnə(r), -z
AM ¦pɪn(t)ʃˈrənər, -z
Pincus
BR ˈpɪŋkəs
AM ˈpɪŋkəs
pincushion
BR ˈpɪnˌkʊʃn
AM ˈpɪnˌkʊʃən
Pindar
BR ˈpɪndɑː(r)
AM ˈpɪnˌdɑr
Pindaric
BR (ˌ)pɪnˈdarɪk
AM pɪnˈdɛrɪk

pin-down
noun
BR 'pɪndaʊn
AM 'pɪn,daʊn
Pindus
BR 'pɪndəs
AM 'pɪndəs
pine
BR pʌɪn, -z, -ɪŋ, -d
AM paɪn, -z, -ɪŋ, -d
pineal
BR 'pɪnɪəl, pʌɪ'ni:əl
AM 'paɪniəl, paɪ'niəl
pineapple
BR 'pʌɪn,apl, -z
AM 'paɪ,næpəl, -z
pinecone
BR 'pʌɪnkəʊn, -z
AM 'paɪn,koʊn, -z
pine marten
BR 'pʌɪn ,mɑ:t(ɪ)n, -z
AM 'paɪn ,mɑrtən, -z
Pinero
BR pɪ'nɪərəʊ, pɪ'nɛ:rəʊ
AM pə'nɪroʊ, pə'nɛroʊ
pinery
BR 'pʌɪn(ə)r|i, -ɪz
AM 'paɪnəri, -z
pineta
BR pʌɪ'ni:tə(r)
AM paɪ'nidə
pinetree
BR 'pʌɪntri:, -z
AM 'paɪn,tri, -z
pinetum
BR pʌɪ'ni:təm
AM paɪ'nidəm
pinewood
BR 'pʌɪnwʊd, -z
AM 'paɪn,wʊd, -z
pinfeather
BR 'pɪn,fɛðə(r), -z
AM 'pɪn,fɛðər, -z
pinfold
BR 'pɪnfəʊld, -z, -ɪŋ, -ɪd
AM 'pɪn,foʊld, -z, -ɪŋ, -əd
ping
BR pɪŋ, -z, -ɪŋ, -d
AM pɪŋ, -z, -ɪŋ, -d
pinger
BR 'pɪŋə(r), -z
AM 'pɪŋ(g)ər, -z
pingo
BR 'pɪŋgəʊ, -z
AM 'pɪŋ(g)oʊ, -z
pingpong
BR 'pɪŋpɒŋ
AM 'pɪŋ,pɔŋ, 'pɪŋ,pɑŋ
pinguid
BR 'pɪŋgwɪd
AM 'pɪŋgwɪd
pinguin
BR 'pɪŋgwɪn, -z
AM 'pɪŋgwɪn, -z
pinhead
BR 'pɪnhɛd, -z
AM 'pɪn,(h)ɛd, -z
pinheaded
BR ,pɪn'hɛdɪd
AM 'pɪn¦hɛdəd
pinheadedness
BR ,pɪn'hɛdɪdnɪs
AM 'pɪn¦hɛdədnəs
pinhole
BR 'pɪnhəʊl, -z
AM 'pɪn,(h)oʊl, -z
pinion
BR 'pɪnjən, -z, -ɪŋ, -d
AM 'pɪnjən, -z, -ɪŋ, -d
pink
BR pɪŋ|k, -ks, -kɪŋ, -(k)t
AM pɪŋ|k, -ks, -kɪŋ, -(k)t
Pinkerton
BR 'pɪŋkət(ə)n
AM 'pɪŋkərtən
pinkeye
BR 'pɪŋkʌɪ
AM 'pɪŋk,aɪ
Pink Floyd
BR ,pɪŋk 'flɔɪd
AM ,pɪŋk 'flɔɪd
pinkie
BR 'pɪŋk|i, -ɪz
AM 'pɪŋki, -z
pinkish
BR 'pɪŋkɪʃ
AM 'pɪŋkɪʃ
pinkly
BR 'pɪŋkli
AM 'pɪŋkli
pinkness
BR 'pɪŋknɪs
AM 'pɪŋknɪs
pinko
BR 'pɪŋkəʊ, -z
AM 'pɪŋkoʊ, -z
Pinkster
BR 'pɪŋkstə(r)
AM 'pɪŋkstər
pinky
BR 'pɪŋk|i, -ɪz
AM 'pɪŋki, -z
pinna
BR 'pɪnə(r), -z
AM 'pɪnə, -z
pinnace
BR 'pɪnɪs, -ɪz
AM 'pɪnɪs, -ɪz
pinnacle
BR 'pɪnɪkl, -z
AM 'pɪnɪkəl, -z
pinnae
BR 'pɪni:
AM 'pɪni, 'pɪ,naɪ
pinnate
BR 'pɪneɪt, 'pɪnət
AM 'pɪ,neɪt, 'pɪnɪt
pinnated
BR 'pɪneɪtɪd, 'pɪnətɪd
AM 'pɪ,neɪdɪd, 'pɪnɪdɪd
pinnately
BR 'pɪneɪtli, 'pɪnətli
AM 'pɪ,neɪtli, 'pɪnɪtli
pinnation
BR pɪ'neɪʃn
AM pə'neɪʃən
Pinner
BR 'pɪnə(r)
AM 'pɪnər
Pinney
BR 'pɪni
AM 'pɪni
pinnigrade
BR 'pɪnɪgreɪd
AM 'pɪnə,greɪd
pinniped
BR 'pɪnɪpɛd, -z
AM 'pɪni,pɛd, -z
pinnular
BR 'pɪnjʉlə(r)
AM 'pɪnjələr
pinnule
BR 'pɪnju:l, -z
AM 'pɪn,jul, -z
pinny
BR 'pɪn|i, -ɪz
AM 'pɪni, -z
Pinocchio
BR pɪ'nəʊkɪəʊ, pɪ'nɒkɪəʊ
AM pə'noʊkioʊ
Pinochet
BR 'pɪnəʃeɪ
AM ,pinə'ʃeɪ
pinochle
BR 'pi:,nʌkl, 'pi:,nɒkl
AM 'pi,nəkəl, 'pi,nɑkl
pinocle
BR 'pi:,nʌkl, 'pi:,nɒkl
AM 'pi,nəkəl, 'pi,nɑkl
pinol
BR 'pʌɪnɒl, 'pʌɪnəʊl
AM 'paɪ,nɔl, 'paɪ,nɑl
pinole[1]
kind of flour
BR pɪ'nəʊli, pɪ'nəʊleɪ
AM pə'noʊli
pinole[2]
liquid ether
BR 'pʌɪnəʊl
AM 'paɪ,noʊl
piñon
BR pi:'njɒn, 'pɪnjən, -z
AM pin'jɑn, 'pɪnjən, -z
Pinot Blanc
BR ,pi:nəʊ 'blɒ̃, -z
AM ,pinoʊ 'blaŋk, -s
Pinot Noir
BR ,pi:nəʊ 'nwɑ:(r), -z
AM ,pinoʊ 'nwɑr, -z
pinpoint
BR 'pɪnpɔɪnt, -s, -ɪŋ, -ɪd
AM 'pɪn,pɔɪn|t, -ts, -(t)ɪŋ, -(t)ɪd
pinprick
BR 'pɪnprɪk, -s
AM 'pɪn,prɪk, -s
pinsetter
BR 'pɪn,sɛtə(r), -z
AM 'pɪn,sɛdər, -z
pinspotter
BR 'pɪn,spɒtə(r), -z
AM 'pɪn,spɑdər, -z
pinstripe
BR 'pɪnstrʌɪp, -s, -t
AM 'pɪn,straɪp, -s, -t
pint
BR pʌɪnt, -s
AM paɪnt, -s
Pinta
Columbus ship
BR 'pɪntə(r)
AM 'pɪn(t)ə
pinta[1]
disease
BR 'pɪntə(r)
AM 'pɪn(t)ə
pinta[2]
pint of
BR 'pʌɪntə(r), -z
AM 'paɪn(t)ə, -z
pintable
BR 'pɪn,teɪbl, -z
AM 'pɪn,teɪbəl, -z
pintado
BR pɪn'tɑ:dəʊ, -z
AM pɪn'tɑ,doʊ, -z
pintail
BR 'pɪnteɪl, -z
AM 'pɪn,teɪl, -z
Pinter
BR 'pɪntə(r)
AM 'pɪn(t)ər
pintle
BR 'pɪntl, -z
AM 'pɪn(t)əl, -z
pinto
BR 'pɪntəʊ, -z
AM 'pɪn(t)oʊ, -z
pinup
BR 'pɪnʌp, -s
AM 'pɪn,əp, -s
pinwheel
BR 'pɪnwi:l, -z
AM 'pɪn,(h)wil, -z
pinworm
BR 'pɪnwə:m, -z
AM 'pɪn,wərm, -z
piny
BR 'pʌɪni
AM 'paɪni
Pinyin
BR ,pɪn'jɪn
AM 'pɪn'jɪn
piolet
BR 'pi:əleɪ, -z
AM ,piə'leɪ, -z
pion
BR 'pʌɪɒn, -z
AM 'paɪ,ɑn, -z
pioneer
BR ,pʌɪə'nɪə(r), -z, -ɪŋ, -d
AM ,paɪə'nɪ(ə)r, -z, -ɪŋ, -d

pionic
BR pʌɪˈɒnɪk
AM paɪˈɑnɪk
pious
BR ˈpʌɪəs
AM ˈpaɪəs
piously
BR ˈpʌɪəsli
AM ˈpaɪəsli
piousness
BR ˈpʌɪəsnəs
AM ˈpaɪəsnəs
pip
BR pɪp, -s, -ɪŋ, -t
AM pɪp, -s, -ɪŋ, -t
pipa
BR pɪˈpɑː(r), ˈpʌɪpə(r), -z
AM ˈpipə, -z
pipal
BR ˈpiːpl, -z
AM ˈpipəl, -z
pipe
BR pʌɪp, -s, -ɪŋ, -t
AM paɪp, -s, -ɪŋ, -t
pipeclay
BR ˈpʌɪpkleɪ
AM ˈpaɪpˌkleɪ
pipecleaner
BR ˈpʌɪpˌkliːnə(r), -z
AM ˈpaɪpˌklinər, -z
pipefish
BR ˈpʌɪpfɪʃ, -ɨz
AM ˈpaɪpˌfɪʃ, -ɨz
pipefitting
BR ˈpʌɪpˌfɪtɪŋ
AM ˈpaɪpˌfɪdɪŋ
pipeful
BR ˈpʌɪpfʊl, -z
AM ˈpaɪpˌfʊl, -z
pipeless
BR ˈpʌɪplɨs
AM ˈpaɪplɨs
pipeline
BR ˈpʌɪplʌɪn, -z
AM ˈpaɪpˌlaɪn, -z
pip emma
BR ˌpɪp ˈɛmə(r)
AM ˈpɪp ˈɛmə
piper
BR ˈpʌɪpə(r), -z
AM ˈpaɪpər, -z
piperade
BR ˌpɪpəˈrɑːd, ˌpiːpəˈrɑːd, -z
AM ˌpɪpəˈrɑd, -z
piperidine
BR pɪˈpɛrɨdiːn, pɪˈpɛrɨdɪn, pʌɪˈpɛrɨdiːn, pʌɪˈpɛrɨdɪn
AM pəˈpɛrəˌdin, paɪˈpɛrəˌdin, paɪˈpɛrədn, pəˈpɛrədn
pipette
BR pɪˈpɛt, -s
AM paɪˈpɛt, -s
pipework
BR ˈpʌɪpwəːk
AM ˈpaɪpˌwərk
pipistrelle
BR ˈpɪpɨstrɛl, -z
AM ˈpɪpəˌstrɛl, -z
pipit
BR ˈpɪpɪt, -s
pipkin
BR ˈpɪpkɪn, -z
AM ˈpɪpkɨn, -z
pipless
BR ˈpɪplɨs
AM ˈpɪplɨs
Pippa
BR ˈpɪpə(r)
AM ˈpɪpə
pippin
BR ˈpɪpɪn, -z
AM ˈpɪpɨn, -z
pipsqueak
BR ˈpɪpskwiːk, -s
AM ˈpɪpˌskwik, -s
pipy
BR ˈpʌɪpi
AM ˈpaɪpi
piquancy
BR ˈpiːk(ə)nsi
AM ˈpik(w)ənsi
piquant
BR ˈpiːk(ə)nt
AM ˈpik(w)ənt
piquantly
BR ˈpiːk(ə)ntli
AM ˈpik(w)ən(t)li
pique
BR piːk
AM pik
piqué
BR ˈpiːkeɪ, -z
AM piˈkeɪ, -z
piquet[1]
card game
BR pɪˈkɛt, pɪˈkeɪ
AM piˈkeɪ, pəˈkeɪ
piquet[2]
group of people
BR ˈpɪkɪt, -s
AM ˈpɪkɨt, -s
piracy
BR ˈpʌɪrəsi
AM ˈpaɪrəsi
Piraeus
BR pʌɪˈriːəs, pɪˈreɪəs
AM pəˈreɪəs, paɪˈriəs
piragua
BR pɪˈragwə(r), -z
AM pəˈrɑgwə, -z
piraña
BR pɪˈrɑːnə(r), -z
AM pəˈrɑn(j)ə, -z
Pirandello
BR ˌpɪrənˈdɛləʊ, ˌpɪrn̩ˈdɛləʊ
AM ˌpɪrənˈdɛloʊ
Piranesi
BR ˌpɪrəˈneɪzi
AM ˌpɪrəˈnɛzɪ
piranha
BR pɪˈrɑːnə(r), -z
AM pəˈrɑn(j)ə, -z
pirate
BR ˈpʌɪrət, -s, -ɪŋ, -ɨd
AM ˈpaɪrə|t, -ts, -dɪŋ, -dəd
piratic
BR pʌɪˈratɪk, pɪˈratɪk
AM paɪˈrædɪk, pəˈrædɪk
piratical
BR pʌɪˈratɨkl, pɪˈratɨkl
AM paɪˈrædəkəl, pəˈrædəkəl
piratically
BR pʌɪˈratɨkli, pɪˈratɨkli
AM paɪˈrædək(ə)li, pəˈrædək(ə)li
Pirie
BR ˈpɪri
AM ˈpɪri
piripiri
BR ˈpɪrɪˌpɪri
AM ˈpɪriˈpɪri
pirog
BR pɪˈrəʊg, -z
AM piˈroʊg, pɪˈroʊg, -z
pirogue
BR pɪˈrəʊg, -z
AM piˈroʊg, pɪˈroʊg, -z
pirouette
BR ˌpɪrʊˈɛt, -s, -ɪŋ, -ɨd
AM ˌpɪrəˈwɛ|t, -ts, -dɪŋ, -dəd
Pisa
BR ˈpiːzə(r)
AM ˈpizə
pis aller
BR ˌpiːz ˈaleɪ, -z
AM ˌpiz əˈleɪ, + æˈleɪ, -z
Pisan
BR ˈpiːzn, -z
AM ˈpizn, -z
Pisano
BR pɪˈzɑːnəʊ
AM pəˈzɑnoʊ
piscary
BR ˈpɪsk(ə)r|i, -ɪz
AM ˈpɪskəri, -z
piscatorial
BR ˌpɪskəˈtɔːrɪəl
AM ˈpɪskəˈtɔriəl
piscatorially
BR ˌpɪskəˈtɔːrɪəli
AM ˈpɪskəˈtɔriəli
piscatory
BR ˈpɪskət(ə)ri
AM ˈpɪskəˌtɔri
Piscean
astrology
BR ˈpʌɪsɪən
AM ˈpaɪsiən
piscean
biology
BR pɪˈsiːən, ˈpɪs(k)ɪən
AM ˈpɪs(k)iən, pəˈsiən
Pisces
BR ˈpʌɪsiːz
AM ˈpaɪsiz
piscicultural
BR ˌpɪsɪˈkʌltʃ(ə)rəl, ˌpɪsɪˈkʌltʃ(ə)rl̩
AM ˈpɪsəˈkəltʃ(ə)rəl
pisciculture
BR ˈpɪsɨˌkʌltʃə(r)
AM ˈpɪsəˈkəltʃər
pisciculturist
BR ˌpɪsɪˈkʌltʃ(ə)rɪst, -s
AM ˌpɪsəˈkəltʃ(ə)rəst, -s
piscina
BR pɪˈsiːnə(r), -z
AM pəˈsnə, pəˈsaɪnə, -z
piscine[1]
adjective
BR ˈpɪs(k)ʌɪn, ˈpɪs(k)iːn
AM ˈpɪsin, ˈpɪsaɪn
piscine[2]
noun
BR ˈpɪsiːn, pɪˈsiːn, -z
AM pəˈsin, ˈpɪsin, -z
piscivorous
BR pɪˈsɪv(ə)rəs
AM pəˈsɪv(ə)rəs
pisco
BR ˈpɪskəʊ
AM ˈpɪskoʊ
Pisgah
BR ˈpɪzgə(r)
AM ˈpɪzgə
pish
BR pɪʃ
AM pɪʃ
Pisidia
BR pʌɪˈsɪdɪə(r)
AM pəˈsɪdiə, paɪˈsɪdiə
Pisidian
BR pʌɪˈsɪdɪən, -z
AM pəˈsɪdiən, paɪˈsɪdiən, -z
pisiform
BR ˈpɪsɪfɔːm
AM ˈpaɪsəˌfɔ(ə)rm, ˈpaɪzəˌfɔ(ə)rm
pismire
BR ˈpɪsˌmʌɪə(r), -z
AM ˈpɪsˌmaɪ(ə)r, ˈpɪzˌmaɪ(ə)r, -z
piss
BR pɪs, -ɪz, -ɪŋ, -t
AM pɪs, -ɪz, -ɪŋ, -t
Pissarro
BR pɪˈsɑːrəʊ
AM pɪˈsɑˌroʊ
pissoir
BR ˈpɪswɑː(r), -z
AM pɪˈswɑr, -z
pisspot
BR ˈpɪspɒt, -s

AM 'pɪsˌpɑt, -s

piss-taker
BR 'pɪsˌteɪkə(r), -z
AM 'pɪsˌteɪkər, -z

piss-taking
BR 'pɪsˌteɪkɪŋ
AM 'pɪsˌteɪkɪŋ

piss-up
BR 'pɪsʌp, -s
AM 'pɪsəp, -s

pistachio
BR pɪ'stɑː(t)ʃɪəʊ, pɪ'sta(t)ʃɪəʊ, -z
AM pə'stæʃioʊ, pə'stɑʃioʊ, -z

piste
BR piːst, -s
AM pist, -s

pisteur
BR piː'stəː(r), -z
AM pi'stər, -z

pistil
BR 'pɪst(ɪ)l, -z
AM 'pɪstl, -z

pistillary
BR 'pɪstɪl(ə)ri, 'pɪstl̩(ə)ri
AM 'pɪstəˌlɛri

pistillate
BR 'pɪstɪlət, 'pɪstl̩ət, 'pɪstɪleɪt, 'pɪstl̩eɪt
AM 'pɪstəˌleɪt, 'pɪstələt

pistilliferous
BR ˌpɪstɪ'lɪf(ə)rəs
AM ˌpɪstə'lɪf(ə)rəs

pistilline
BR 'pɪstɪlɪn, 'pɪstl̩ɪn, 'pɪstɪliːn, 'pɪstl̩iːn
AM 'pɪstələn, 'pɪstəˌlaɪn

pistol
BR 'pɪstl, -z
AM 'pɪstl, -z

pistole
BR 'pɪstəʊl, pɪ'stəʊl, -z
AM pə'stoʊl, -z

pistoleer
BR ˌpɪstə'lɪə(r), -z
AM ˌpɪstə'lɪ(ə)r, -z

piston
BR 'pɪst(ə)n, -z
AM 'pɪstən, -z

pistou
BR 'piːstuː
AM pi'stu

pit
BR pɪt, -s, -ɪŋ, -ɪd
AM pɪ|t, -ts, -dɪŋ, -dɪd

pita
BR 'pɪtə(r), 'piːtə(r)
AM 'pidə

pit-a-pat
BR ˌpɪtə'pat, 'pɪtəpat
AM 'pɪdəˌpæt

Pitcairn
BR 'pɪtkɛːn
AM 'pɪtˌkɛrn

pitch
BR pɪtʃ, -ɪz, -ɪŋ, -t
AM pɪtʃ, -ɪz, -ɪŋ, -t

pitchblack
BR ˌpɪtʃ'blak
AM 'pɪtʃ'blæk

pitchblende
BR 'pɪtʃblɛnd
AM 'pɪtʃˌblɛnd

pitcher
BR 'pɪtʃə(r), -z
AM 'pɪtʃər, -z

pitcherful
BR 'pɪtʃəfʊl, -z
AM 'pɪtʃərˌfʊl, -z

pitchfork
BR 'pɪtʃfɔːk, -s, -ɪŋ, -t
AM 'pɪtʃˌfɔ(ə)rk, -s, -ɪŋ, -t

pitchman
BR 'pɪtʃmən
AM 'pɪtʃmən

pitchmen
BR 'pɪtʃmən
AM 'pɪtʃmən

pitchout
BR 'pɪtʃaʊt, -s
AM 'pɪtʃˌaʊt, -s

pitchpine
BR 'pɪtʃpʌɪn
AM 'pɪtʃˌpaɪn

pitchpipe
BR 'pɪtʃpʌɪp, -s
AM 'pɪtʃˌpaɪp, -s

pitchstone
BR 'pɪtʃstəʊn
AM 'pɪtʃˌstoʊn

pitchy
BR 'pɪtʃi
AM 'pɪtʃi

piteous
BR 'pɪtɪəs
AM 'pɪdiəs

piteously
BR 'pɪtɪəsli
AM 'pɪdiəsli

piteousness
BR 'pɪtɪəsnəs
AM 'pɪdiəsnəs

pitfall
BR 'pɪtfɔːl, -z
AM 'pɪtˌfɔl, 'pɪtˌfɑl, -z

pith
BR pɪθ
AM pɪθ

pithead
BR 'pɪthɛd, -z
AM 'pɪtˌ(h)ɛd, -z

Pithecanthropus
BR ˌpɪθɪ'kanθrəpəs
AM ˌpɪθə'kænθrəpəs, ˌpɪθəˌkæn'θroʊpəs

pithecoid
BR 'pɪθɪkɔɪd, -z
AM 'pɪθəˌkɔɪd, -z

pithily
BR 'pɪθɪli
AM 'pɪθɪli

pithiness
BR 'pɪθɪnɪs
AM 'pɪθinɪs

pithless
BR 'pɪθləs
AM 'pɪθləs

pithoi
BR 'pɪθɔɪ, 'pʌɪθɔɪ
AM 'pɪˌθɔɪ, 'paɪˌθɔɪ

pithos
BR 'pɪθɒs, 'pʌɪθɒs
AM 'pɪˌθɔs, 'paɪˌθɔs, 'pɪˌθɑs, 'paɪˌθɑs

pithy
BR 'pɪθi
AM 'pɪθi

pitiable
BR 'pɪtɪəbl
AM 'pɪdiəbəl

pitiableness
BR 'pɪtɪəblnəs
AM 'pɪdiəbəlnəs

pitiably
BR 'pɪtɪəbli
AM 'pɪdiəbli

pitiful
BR 'pɪtɪf(ʊ)l
AM 'pɪdifəl

pitifully
BR 'pɪtɪfʊli, 'pɪtɪfl̩i
AM 'pɪdifəli

pitifulness
BR 'pɪtɪf(ʊ)lnəs
AM 'pɪdifəlnəs

pitiless
BR 'pɪtɪlɪs
AM 'pɪdilɪs

pitilessly
BR 'pɪtɪlɪsli
AM 'pɪdilɪsli

pitilessness
BR 'pɪtɪlɪsnɪs
AM 'pɪdilɪsnɪs

Pitlochry
BR pɪt'lɒxri, pɪt'lɒkri
AM pɪt'lɑkri

pitman
BR 'pɪtmən
AM 'pɪtmən

pitmen
BR 'pɪtmən
AM 'pɪtmən

Pitney
BR 'pɪtni
AM 'pɪtni

piton
BR 'piːtɒn, 'piːtõ, -z
AM 'piˌtɑn, -z

Pitot tube
BR 'piːtəʊ tjuːb, + tʃuːb, -z
AM pi'toʊ ˌt(j)ub, 'pidoʊ +, -z

pitpan
BR 'pɪtpan, -z
AM 'pɪtˌpæn, -z

Pitsea
BR 'pɪtsiː
AM 'pɪtsi

Pitt
BR pɪt
AM pɪt

pitta
BR 'pɪtə(*r*)
AM 'pɪdə

pittance
BR 'pɪt(ə)ns, -ɪz
AM 'pɪtn̩s, -ɪz

Pittenweem
BR ˌpɪtn'wiːm
AM ˌpɪtn'wim

pitter-patter
BR 'pɪtəˌpatə(r), ˌpɪtə'patə(r)
AM 'pɪdər'pædər

Pitti
BR 'pɪti
AM 'pɪdi

Pittman
BR 'pɪtmən
AM 'pɪtmən

pittosporum
BR pɪ'tɒsp(ə)rəm, -z
AM pə'tɑspərəm, ˌpɪdə'spɔrəm, -z

Pitt-Rivers
BR ˌpɪt'rɪvəz
AM 'pɪt'rɪvərz

Pitts
BR pɪts
AM pɪts

Pittsburgh
BR 'pɪtsbəːg
AM 'pɪtsˌbərg

pituitary
BR pɪ'tjuːɪt(ə)ri, pɪ'tʃuːɪt(ə)ri
AM pə't(j)uəˌtɛri

pituri
BR 'pɪtjʊəri, 'pɪtjʊri, 'pɪtʃ(ə)ri
AM 'pɪtʃəri

pity
BR 'pɪt|i, -ɪz, -ɪɪŋ, -ɪd
AM 'pɪdi, -z, -ɪŋ, -d

pityingly
BR 'pɪtɪɪŋli
AM 'pɪdiɪŋli

pityriasis
BR ˌpɪtɪ'rʌɪəsɪs
AM ˌpɪdə'raɪəsəs

più
BR pjuː
AM pju, pi'u

Pius
BR 'pʌɪəs
AM 'paɪəs

pivot
BR 'pɪvət, -s, -ɪŋ, -ɪd
AM 'pɪvə|t, -ts, -dɪŋ, -dəd

pivotability
BR ˌpɪvətə'bɪlɪti

AM ˌpɪvədəˈbɪlɨdi

pivotable
BR ˈpɪvətəbl
AM ˈpɪvədəbəl

pivotal
BR ˈpɪvətl
AM ˈpɪvədl

pix
BR pɪks
AM pɪks

pixel
BR ˈpɪksl, -z
AM ˈpɪksəl, -z

pixie
BR ˈpɪks|i, -ɪz
AM ˈpɪksi, -z

pixilated
BR ˈpɪksɨleɪtɨd
AM ˈpɪksəˌleɪdɨd

pixy
BR ˈpɪks|i, -ɪz
AM ˈpɪksi, -z

Pizarro
BR pɪˈzɑːrəʊ
AM pəˈzɑroʊ

pizazz
BR pɪˈzaz
AM pəˈzæz

pizza
BR ˈpiːtsə(r), -z
AM ˈpitsə, -z

pizzazz
BR pɪˈzaz
AM pəˈzæz

pizzeria
BR ˌpiːtsəˈriːə(r), ˌpɪtsəˈriːə(r), -z
AM ˌpitsəˈriə, -z

Pizzey
BR ˈpɪtsi, ˈpɪzi
AM ˈpɪtsi, ˈpɪzi

pizzicato
BR ˌpɪtsɪˈkɑːtəʊ, -z
AM ˌpɪtsəˈkɑdoʊ, -z

pizzle
BR ˈpɪzl, -z
AM ˈpɪzl, -z

PJ's
BR ˌpiːˈdʒeɪz
AM ˈpiˌdʒeɪz

placability
BR ˌplakəˈbɪlɨti
AM ˌplækəˈbɪlɨdi

placable
BR ˈplakəbl
AM ˈplækəbəl

placableness
BR ˈplakəblnəs
AM ˈplækəbəlnəs

placably
BR ˈplakəbli
AM ˈplækəbli

placard
BR ˈplakɑːd, -z
AM ˈplækərd, ˈplæˌkɑrd, -z

placate
BR pləˈkeɪt, -s, -ɪŋ, -ɨd
AM ˈpleɪˌkeɪ|t, -ts, -dɪŋ, -dɨd

placatingly
BR pləˈkeɪtɪŋli
AM pləˈkeɪdɪŋli

placation
BR pləˈkeɪʃn
AM pləˈkeɪʃən

placatory
BR pləˈkeɪt(ə)ri, ˈplakət(ə)ri
AM ˈpleɪkəˌtɔri, ˈplækəˌtɔri

place
BR pleɪs, -ɨz, -ɪŋ, -t
AM pleɪs, -ɨz, -ɪŋ, -t

placebo
BR pləˈsiːbəʊ, -z
AM pləˈsiboʊ, -z

placeholder
BR ˈpleɪsˌhəʊldə(r), -z
AM ˈpleɪsˌ(h)oʊldər, -z

placeless
BR ˈpleɪslɨs
AM ˈpleɪslɨs

placement
BR ˈpleɪsm(ə)nt, -s
AM ˈpleɪsmənt, -s

placenta
BR pləˈsɛntə(r), -z
AM pləˈsɛn(t)ə, -z

placental
BR pləˈsɛntl, -z
AM pləˈsɛn(t)l, -z

placer
BR ˈpleɪsə(r), -z
AM ˈpleɪsər, -z

placet
BR ˈpleɪsɛt, ˈpleɪsɪt, -s
AM ˈpleɪsɨt, -s

placid
BR ˈplasɪd
AM ˈplæsəd

placidity
BR pləˈsɪdɨti
AM plæˈsɪdɨdi, pləˈsɪdɨdi

placidly
BR ˈplasɨdli
AM ˈplæsədli

placidness
BR ˈplasɪdnɨs
AM ˈplæsədnəs

placing
BR ˈpleɪsɪŋ, -z
AM ˈpleɪsɪŋ, -z

placket
BR ˈplakɪt, -s
AM ˈplækət, -s

placoid
BR ˈplakɔɪd, -z
AM ˈplæˌkɔɪd, -z

plafond
BR plaˈfɔ̃, plaˈfɒnd, -z
AM pləˈfɑnd, -z

plagal
BR ˈpleɪgl
AM ˈpleɪgəl

plage
BR plɑːʒ, -ɨz
AM plɑʒ, -əz

plagiarise
BR ˈpleɪdʒ(ɪ)ərʌɪz, -ɨz, -ɪŋ, -d
AM ˈpleɪdʒəˌraɪz, -ɨz, -ɪŋ, -d

plagiariser
BR ˈpleɪdʒ(ɪ)ərʌɪzə(r), -z
AM ˈpleɪdʒəˌraɪzər, -z

plagiarism
BR ˈpleɪdʒ(ɪ)ərɪz(ə)m
AM ˈpleɪdʒəˌrɪzəm

plagiarist
BR ˈpleɪdʒ(ɪ)ərɪst, -s
AM ˈpleɪdʒərəst, -s

plagiaristic
BR ˌpleɪdʒ(ɪ)əˈrɪstɪk
AM ˌpleɪdʒəˈrɪstɪk

plagiarize
BR ˈpleɪdʒ(ɪ)ərʌɪz, -ɨz, -ɪŋ, -d
AM ˈpleɪdʒəˌraɪz, -ɨz, -ɪŋ, -d

plagiarizer
BR ˈpleɪdʒ(ɪ)ərʌɪzə(r), -z
AM ˈpleɪdʒəˌraɪzər, -z

plagiocephalic
BR ˌpleɪdʒɪəʊsɪˈfalɪk, ˌpleɪdʒɪəʊkɛˈfalɪk
AM ˌpleɪdʒiəsəˈfælɪk

plagioclase
BR ˈpleɪdʒɪəkleɪz, pleɪdʒɪəkleɪs, -ɨz
AM ˈpleɪdʒiəˌkleɪs, ˈpleɪdʒiəˌkleɪz, -ɨz

plagioclastic
BR ˌpleɪdʒɪəˈklastɪk
AM ˌpleɪdʒiəˈklæstɪk

plagiostome
BR ˈpleɪdʒɪəstəʊm, -z
AM ˈpleɪdʒiəˌstoʊm, -z

plague
BR pleɪg, -z, -ɪŋ, -d
AM pleɪg, -z, -ɪŋ, -d

plagueily
BR ˈpleɪgɨli
AM ˈpleɪgɨli

plagueiness
BR ˈpleɪgɪnɨs
AM ˈpleɪginɨs

plaguesome
BR ˈpleɪgs(ə)m
AM ˈpleɪgsəm

plaguey
BR ˈpleɪgi
AM ˈpleɪgi

plaguily
BR ˈpleɪgɨli
AM ˈpleɪgɨli

plaguiness
BR ˈpleɪgɪnɨs
AM ˈpleɪginɨs

plaguy
BR ˈpleɪgi
AM ˈpleɪgi

plaice
BR pleɪs
AM pleɪs

plaid
BR plad, -z
AM plæd, -z

Plaid Cymru
BR ˌplʌɪd ˈkʌmri, + ˈkʌmri
AM ˈplaɪd ˈkʊmri

plaided
BR ˈpladɨd
AM ˈplædəd

plain
BR pleɪn, -z, -ə(r), -ɨst
AM pleɪn, -z, -ər, -ɨst

plainchant
BR ˈpleɪntʃɑːnt, ˈpleɪntʃant, -s
AM ˈpleɪnˌtʃænt, -s

plainclothes
BR ˌpleɪnˈkləʊ(ð)z
AM ˈpleɪnˈkloʊ(ð)z

plainly
BR ˈpleɪnli
AM ˈpleɪnli

plainness
BR ˈpleɪnnɨs
AM ˈpleɪ(n)nɨs

plainsman
BR ˈpleɪnzmən
AM ˈpleɪnzmən

plainsmen
BR ˈpleɪnzmən
AM ˈpleɪnzmən

plainsong
BR ˈpleɪnsɒŋ
AM ˈpleɪnˌsɔŋ, ˈpleɪnˌsɑŋ

plainspoken
BR ˌpleɪnˈspəʊk(ə)n
AM ˈpleɪnˈspoʊkən

plainswoman
BR ˈpleɪnzˌwʊmən
AM ˈpleɪnzˌwʊmən

plainswomen
BR ˈpleɪnzˌwɪmɪn
AM ˈpleɪnzˌwɪmɨn

plaint
BR pleɪnt, -s
AM pleɪnt, -s

plaintiff
BR ˈpleɪntɪf, -s
AM ˈpleɪn(t)ɨf, -s

plaintive
BR ˈpleɪntɪv
AM ˈpleɪn(t)ɪv

plaintively
BR ˈpleɪntɨvli
AM ˈpleɪn(t)ɨvli

plaintiveness
BR ˈpleɪntɨvnɨs
AM ˈpleɪn(t)ɨvnɨs

Plaistow[1]
place in U.K.
BR 'plɑːstəʊ, 'plastəʊ
AM 'plæstoʊ

Plaistow[2]
surname
BR 'plɑːstəʊ, 'plastəʊ, 'pleɪstəʊ
AM 'plæstoʊ, 'pleɪstoʊ

plait
BR plat, -s, -ɪŋ, -ɨd
AM pleɪ|t, plæ|t, -ts, -dɪŋ, -dɨd\-dəd

plan
BR plan, -z, -ɪŋ, -d
AM plæn, -z, -ɪŋ, -d

planar
BR 'pleɪnə(r)
AM 'pleɪnər

planarian
BR plə'nɛːrɪən, -z
AM plə'nɛriən, -z

planchet
BR 'plan(t)ʃɪt, -s
AM 'plæn(t)ʃət, -s

planchette
BR plɑːn'ʃɛt, plan'ʃɛt, plɒ̃'ʃɛt, -s
AM plæn'ʃɛt, -s

Planck
BR plaŋk
AM plæŋk

plane
BR pleɪn, -z, -ɪŋ, -d
AM pleɪn, -z, -ɪŋ, -d

planeload
BR 'pleɪnləʊd, -z
AM 'pleɪn,loʊd, -z

planemaker
BR 'pleɪn,meɪkə(r), -z
AM 'pleɪn,meɪkər, -z

planemaking
BR 'pleɪn,meɪkɪŋ
AM 'pleɪn,meɪkɪŋ

planer
BR 'pleɪnə(r), -z
AM 'pleɪnər, -z

planet
BR 'planɪt, -s
AM 'plænət, -s

planetaria
BR ,planɪ'tɛːrɪə(r)
AM ,plænə'tɛriə

planetarium
BR ,planɪ'tɛːrɪəm, -z
AM ,plænə'tɛriəm, -z

planetary
BR 'planɪt(ə)ri
AM 'plænə,tɛri

planetesimal
BR ,planɪ'tɛsɪml
AM ,plænə'tɛsəməl

planetoid
BR 'planɪtɔɪd, -z
AM 'plænə,tɔɪd, -z

planetologist
BR ,planɪ'tɒlədʒɪst, -s
AM ,plænə'tɑlədʒəst, -s

planetology
BR ,planɪ'tɒlədʒi
AM ,plænə'tɑlədʒi

plangency
BR 'plan(d)ʒ(ə)nsi
AM 'plændʒənsi

plangent
BR 'plan(d)ʒ(ə)nt
AM 'plændʒənt

plangently
BR 'plan(d)ʒ(ə)ntli
AM 'plændʒəntli

planimeter
BR pla'nɪmɪtə(r), plə'nɪmɪtə(r), -z
AM plə'nɪmədər, -z

planimetric
BR ,pleɪnɪ'mɛtrɪk
AM ,pleɪnə'mɛtrɪk

planimetrical
BR ,pleɪnɪ'mɛtrɪkl
AM ,pleɪnə'mɛtrəkəl

planimetry
BR pla'nɪmɪtri, plə'nɪmɪtri
AM plə'nɪmətri

planish
BR 'plan|ɪʃ, -ɪʃɪz, -ɪʃɪŋ, -ɪʃt
AM 'plænɪʃ, -ɪz, -ɪŋ, -t

planisher
BR 'planɪʃə(r), -z
AM 'plænɪʃər, -z

planisphere
BR 'planɪsfɪə(r), -z
AM 'plænə,sfɪ(ə)r, -z

planispheric
BR ,planɪ'sfɛrɪk
AM ,plænə'sfɛrɪk

plank
BR plaŋ|k, -ks, -kɪŋ, -(k)t
AM plæŋ|k, -ks, -kɪŋ, -(k)t

plankton
BR 'plaŋ(k)tən
AM 'plæŋktən

planktonic
BR plaŋ(k)'tɒnɪk
AM plæŋk'tɑnɪk

planner
BR 'planə(r), -z
AM 'plænər, -z

planoconcave
BR ,pleɪnəʊ'kɒnkeɪv, ,pleɪnəʊ'kɒŋkeɪv
AM ,pleɪnoʊ'kɑn,keɪv

planoconvex
BR 'pleɪnəʊ'kɒnvɛks
AM ,pleɪnoʊ,kɑn'vɛks

planographic
BR ,planə'grafɪk
AM ,plænə'græfɪk

planography
BR pla'nɒgrəfi, plə'nɒgrəfi
AM plə'nɑgrəfi

planometer
BR pla'nɒmɪtə(r), plə'nɒmɪtə(r), -z
AM plə'nɑmədər, -z

plant
BR plɑːnt, plant, -s, -ɪŋ, -ɨd
AM plæn|t, -ts, -(t)ɪŋ, -(t)əd

plantable
BR 'plɑːntəbl, 'plantəbl
AM 'plæn(t)əbəl

Plantagenet
BR plan'tadʒɪnɪt, plan'tadʒṇɪt, -s
AM plæn'tædʒənət, -s

plantain
BR 'plantɪn, 'planteɪn, -z
AM 'plænt(ə)n, -z

plantar
BR 'plantə(r), 'plantɑː(r)
AM 'plæn(t)ər

plantation
BR plɑːn'teɪʃn, plan'teɪʃn, -z
AM plæn'teɪʃən, -z

planter
BR 'plɑːntə(r), 'plantə(r), -z
AM 'plæn(t)ər, -z

plantigrade
BR 'plantɪgreɪd, -z
AM 'plæn(t)ə,greɪd, -z

Plantin
BR 'plantɪn
AM 'plæntn

planting
BR 'plɑːntɪŋ, 'plantɪŋ, -z
AM 'plæn(t)ɪŋ, -z

plantlet
BR 'plɑːntlɨt, 'plantlɨt, -s
AM 'plæn(t)lət, -s

plantlike
BR 'plɑːntlʌɪk, 'plantlʌɪk
AM 'plænt,laɪk

plaque
BR plak, plɑːk
AM plæk

plaquette
BR pla'kɛt, -s
AM plæ'kɛt, -s

plash
BR plaʃ, -ɪz, -ɪŋ, -t
AM plæʃ, -əz, -ɪŋ, -t

plashy
BR 'plaʃi
AM 'plæʃi

plasm
BR 'plaz(ə)m
AM 'plæzəm

plasma
BR 'plazmə(r)
AM 'plæzmə

plasmacyte
BR 'plazməsʌɪt, -s
AM 'plæzmə,saɪt, -s

plasmagel
BR 'plazmədʒɛl
AM 'plæzmə,dʒɛl

plasmagene
BR 'plazmədʒiːn, -z
AM 'plæzmə,dʒin, -z

plasmapheresis
BR ,plazmə'fɛrɪsɪs, ,plazməfə'riːsɪs
AM ,plæzməfə'risɪs, ,plæzmə'fɛrəsɪs

plasmasol
BR 'plazməsɒl
AM 'plæzmə,sɔl, 'plæzmə,sɑl

plasmatic
BR plaz'matɪk
AM plæz'mædɪk

plasmic
BR 'plazmɪk
AM 'plæzmɪk

plasmid
BR 'plazmɪd, -z
AM 'plæzmɪd, -z

plasmodesma
BR ,plazmə'dɛzmə(r)
AM ,plæzmə'dɛzmə

plasmodesmata
BR ,plazmə'dɛzmətə(r)
AM ,plæzmə'dɛzmədə

plasmodia
BR plaz'məʊdɪə(r)
AM plæz'moʊdiə

plasmodial
BR plaz'məʊdɪəl
AM plæz'moʊdiəl

plasmodium
BR plaz'məʊdɪəm
AM plæz'moʊdiəm

plasmolyse
BR 'plazməlʌɪz, -ɪz, -ɪŋ, -t
AM 'plæzmə,laɪz, -ɪz, -ɪŋ, -t

plasmolysis
BR plaz'mɒlɪsɪs
AM plæz'mɑləsəs

plasmolyze
BR 'plazməlʌɪz, -ɪz, -ɪŋ, -d
AM 'plæzmə,laɪz, -ɪz, -ɪŋ, -d

Plassey
BR 'plasi
AM 'plæsi

plaster
BR 'plɑːst|ə(r), 'plast|ə(r), -əz, -(ə)rɪŋ, -əd

AM ˈplæst|ər, -ərz, -(ə)rɪŋ, -ərd

plasterboard
BR ˈplɑːstəbɔːd, ˈplastəbɔːd
AM ˈplæstərˌbɔ(ə)rd

plasterer
BR ˈplɑːst(ə)rə(r), ˈplast(ə)rə(r), -z
AM ˈplæstərər, -z

plasterwork
BR ˈplɑːstəwəːk, ˈplastəwəːk
AM ˈplæstərˌwərk

plastery
BR ˈplɑːst(ə)ri, ˈplast(ə)ri
AM ˈplæst(ə)ri

plastic
BR ˈplastɪk, -s
AM ˈplæstɪk, -s

plastically
BR ˈplastɪkli
AM ˈplæstək(ə)li

Plasticine®
BR ˈplastəsiːn, ˈplɑːstəsiːn
AM ˈplæstəˌsin

plasticisation
BR ˌplastɪsʌɪˈzeɪʃn
AM ˌplæstəsəˈzeɪʃən, ˌplæstəˌsaɪˈzeɪʃən

plasticise
BR ˈplastɪsʌɪz, -ɪz, -ɪŋ, -d
AM ˈplæstəˌsaɪz, -ɪz, -ɪŋ, -d

plasticiser
BR ˈplastɪsʌɪzə(r)
AM ˈplæstəˌsaɪzər

plasticity
BR plaˈstɪsɨti
AM plæˈstɪsɨdi

plasticization
BR ˌplastɪsʌɪˈzeɪʃn
AM ˌplæstəsəˈzeɪʃən, ˌplæstəˌsaɪˈzeɪʃən

plasticize
BR ˈplastɪsʌɪz, -ɪz, -ɪŋ, -d
AM ˈplæstəˌsaɪz, -ɪz, -ɪŋ, -d

plasticizer
BR ˈplastɪsʌɪzə(r), -z
AM ˈplæstəˌsaɪzər, -z

plasticky
BR ˈplastɪki
AM ˈplæstɪki

plastid
BR ˈplastɪd, -z
AM ˈplæstəd, -z

plastral
BR ˈplastr(ə)l
AM ˈplæstrəl

plastron
BR ˈplastr(ə)n, -z
AM ˈplæstrən, -z

plat
BR plat, -s
AM plæt, -s

Plataea
BR pləˈtiːə(r)
AM pləˈtiə

platan
BR ˈplat(ə)n, -z
AM ˈplætn, -z

plat du jour
BR ˌplɑː də ˈʒʊə(r), + duː +
AM ˌplɑ də ˈʒʊ(ə)r

plate
BR pleɪt, -s, -ɪŋ, -ɨd
AM pleɪ|t, -ts, -dɪŋ, -dɨd

plateau
BR ˈplatəʊ, plaˈtəʊ, pləˈtəʊ, -z
AM plæˈtoʊ, -z

plateaux
BR ˈplatəʊz, plaˈtəʊz, pləˈtəʊz
AM plæˈtoʊ

plateful
BR ˈpleɪtfʊl, -z
AM ˈpleɪtˌfʊl, -z

platelayer
BR ˈpleɪtˌleɪə(r), -z
AM ˈpleɪtˌleɪər, -z

plateless
BR ˈpleɪtlɨs
AM ˈpleɪtlɨs

platelet
BR ˈpleɪtlɨt, -s
AM ˈpleɪtlɨt, -s

platen
BR ˈplatn, -z
AM ˈplætn, -z

plater
BR ˈpleɪtə(r), -z
AM ˈpleɪdər, -z

plateresque
BR ˌplatərˈɛsk
AM ˌplædəˈrɛsk

platform
BR ˈplatfɔːm, -z
AM ˈplætˌfɔ(ə)rm, -z

Plath
BR plaθ
AM plæθ

plating
BR ˈpleɪtɪŋ, -z
AM ˈpleɪdɪŋ, -z

platinic
BR pləˈtɪnɪk
AM pləˈtɪnɪk

platinisation
BR ˌplatɪnʌɪˈzeɪʃn, ˌplatn̩ʌɪˈzeɪʃn
AM ˌplætn̩əˈzeɪʃən, ˌplætn̩ˌaɪˈzeɪʃən

platinise
BR ˈplatɪnʌɪz, ˈplatn̩ʌɪz, -ɪz, -ɪŋ, -d
AM ˈplætn̩ˌaɪz, -ɪz, -ɪŋ, -d

platinization
BR ˌplatɪnʌɪˈzeɪʃn, ˌplatn̩ʌɪˈzeɪʃn
AM ˌplætn̩əˈzeɪʃən, ˌplætn̩ˌaɪˈzeɪʃən

platinize
BR ˈplatɪnʌɪz, ˈplatn̩ʌɪz, -ɪz, -ɪŋ, -d
AM ˈplætn̩ˌaɪz, -ɪz, -ɪŋ, -d

platinoid
BR ˈplatɪnɔɪd, ˈplatn̩ɔɪd, -z
AM ˈplætn̩ˌɔɪd, -z

platinotype
BR ˈplatɪnəʊtʌɪp, ˈplatn̩əʊtʌɪp, -s
AM ˈplætn̩oʊˌtaɪp, -s

platinum
BR ˈplatɪnəm, ˈplatn̩əm
AM ˈplædənəm, ˈplætn̩əm, ˈplætnəm

platitude
BR ˈplatɪtjuːd, ˈplatɪtʃuːd, -z
AM ˈplædəˌt(j)ud, -z

platitudinarian
BR ˌplatɪˌtjuːdɪˈnɛːrɪən, ˌplatɪˌtʃuːdɪˈnɛːrɪən, -z
AM ¦plædəˌt(j)udn¦ɛriən, -z

platitudinise
BR ˌplatɪˈtjuːdɪnʌɪz, ˌplatɪˈtʃuːdɪnʌɪz, -ɪz, -ɪŋ, -d
AM ˌplædəˈt(j)udnˌaɪz, -ɪz, -ɪŋ, -d

platitudinize
BR ˌplatɪˈtjuːdɪnʌɪz, ˌplatɪˈtʃuːdɪnʌɪz, -ɪz, -ɪŋ, -d
AM ˌplædəˈt(j)udn̩ˌaɪz, -ɪz, -ɪŋ, -d

platitudinous
BR ˌplatɪˈtjuːdɪnəs, ˌplatɪˈtʃuːdɪnəs
AM ˌplædəˈt(j)udn̩əs

Plato
BR ˈpleɪtəʊ
AM ˈpleɪdoʊ

Platonic
BR pləˈtɒnɪk
AM pləˈtɑnɪk

platonical
BR pləˈtɒnɪkl
AM pləˈtɑnəkəl

Platonically
BR pləˈtɒnɪkli
AM pləˈtɑnək(ə)li

Platonism
BR ˈpleɪtənɪz(ə)m, ˈpleɪtn̩ɪz(ə)m
AM ˈpleɪtnˌɪzəm

Platonist
BR ˈpleɪtənɪst, ˈpleɪtn̩ɪst, -s
AM ˈpleɪtn̩əst, -s

platoon
BR pləˈtuːn, -z
AM pləˈtun, -z

plats du jour
BR ˌplɑː də ˈʒʊə(r), + duː +
AM ˌplɑ də ˈʒʊ(ə)r

Platt
BR plat
AM plæt

Plattdeutsch
BR ˈplatdɔɪtʃ
AM ˈplætˌdɔɪtʃ

platteland
BR ˈplatəland
AM ˈplædəˌlænd

plattelander
BR ˈplatˌlandə(r), -z
AM ˈplætˌlændər, -z

platter
BR ˈplatə(r), -z
AM ˈplædər, -z

platy
BR ˈpleɪti
AM ˈpleɪdi

platyhelminth
BR ˌplatɪˈhɛlmɪnθ, -s
AM ˌplædiˈhɛlmənθ, -s

platypus
BR ˈplatɪpəs, ˈplatɪpʊs, -ɪz
AM ˈplædəpəs, ˈplædəˌpʊs, -əz

platyrrhine
BR ˈplatɪrʌɪn, -z
AM ˈplædəˌraɪn, ˈplædərən, -z

plaudit
BR ˈplɔːdɪt, -s
AM ˈplɔdət, ˈplɑdət, -s

plausibility
BR ˌplɔːzɪˈbɪlɨti
AM ˌplɔzəˈbɪlɨdi, ˌplɑzəˈbɪlɨdi

plausible
BR ˈplɔːzɪbl
AM ˈplɔzəbəl, ˈplɑzəbəl

plausibly
BR ˈplɔːzɪbli
AM ˈplɔzəbli, ˈplɑzəbli

Plautus
BR ˈplɔːtəs
AM ˈplɔdəs, ˈplɑdəs

play
BR pleɪ, -z, -ɪŋ, -d
AM pleɪ, -z, -ɪŋ, -d

playa
BR ˈplʌɪə(r), -z
AM ˈplaɪə, -z

playability
BR ˌpleɪəˈbɪlɨti
AM ˌpleɪəˈbɪlɨdi

playable
BR ˈpleɪəbl
AM ˈpleɪəbəl

play-act
BR ˈpleɪakt, -s, -ɪŋ, -ɨd

AM ˈpleɪˌæk|(t), -(t)s, -tɪŋ, -təd

play-actor
BR ˈpleɪˌaktə(r), -z
AM ˈpleɪˌæktər, -z

playback
BR ˈpleɪbak, -s
AM ˈpleɪˌbæk, -s

playbill
BR ˈpleɪbɪl, -z
AM ˈpleɪˌbɪl, -z

playbook
BR ˈpleɪbʊk, -s
AM ˈpleɪˌbʊk, -s

playboy
BR ˈpleɪbɔɪ, -z
AM ˈpleɪˌbɔɪ, -z

player
BR ˈpleɪə(r), -z
AM ˈpleɪər, -z

player-piano
BR ˌpleɪəpɪˈanəʊ, -z
AM ˈpleɪərpiˌænoʊ, -z

Playfair
BR ˈpleɪfɛː(r)
AM ˈpleɪˌfɛ(ə)r

playfellow
BR ˈpleɪˌfɛləʊ, -z
AM ˈpleɪˌfɛloʊ, -z

playful
BR ˈpleɪf(ʊ)l
AM ˈpleɪfəl

playfully
BR ˈpleɪfʊli, ˈpleɪfl̩i
AM ˈpleɪfəli

playfulness
BR ˈpleɪf(ʊ)lnəs
AM ˈpleɪfəlnəs

playgirl
BR ˈpleɪgəːl, -z
AM ˈpleɪˌgərl, -z

playgoer
BR ˈpleɪˌgəʊə(r), -z
AM ˈpleɪˌgoʊər, -z

playground
BR ˈpleɪgraʊnd, -z
AM ˈpleɪˌgraʊnd, -z

playgroup
BR ˈpleɪgruːp, -s
AM ˈpleɪˌgrup, -s

playhouse
BR ˈpleɪhaʊ|s, -zɪz
AM ˈpleɪˌhaʊ|s, -zəz

playlet
BR ˈpleɪlɪt, -s
AM ˈpleɪlət, -s

playlist
BR ˈpleɪlɪst, -s
AM ˈpleɪˌlɪst, -s

playmaker
BR ˈpleɪˌmeɪkə(r), -z
AM ˈpleɪˌmeɪkər, -z

playmate
BR ˈpleɪmeɪt, -s
AM ˈpleɪˌmeɪt, -s

playoff
BR ˈpleɪɒf
AM ˈpleɪˌɔf, ˈpleɪˌɑf

playpen
BR ˈpleɪpɛn, -z
AM ˈpleɪˌpɛn, -z

playroom
BR ˈpleɪruːm, ˈpleɪrʊm, -z
AM ˈpleɪˌrum, ˈpleɪˌrʊm, -z

playschool
BR ˈpleɪskuːl, -z
AM ˈpleɪˌskul, -z

playsuit
BR ˈpleɪs(j)uːt, -s
AM ˈpleɪˌsut, -s

Playtex®
BR ˈpleɪtɛks
AM ˈpleɪˌtɛks

plaything
BR ˈpleɪθɪŋ, -z
AM ˈpleɪˌθɪŋ, -z

playtime
BR ˈpleɪtʌɪm
AM ˈpleɪˌtaɪm

playwear
BR ˈpleɪwɛː(r)
AM ˈpleɪˌwɛ(ə)r

playwright
BR ˈpleɪrʌɪt, -s
AM ˈpleɪˌraɪt, -s

playwriting
BR ˈpleɪˌrʌɪtɪŋ
AM ˈpleɪˌraɪdɪŋ

plaza
BR ˈplɑːzə(r), -z
AM ˈplɑzə, ˈplæzə, -z

plc
BR ˌpiːɛlˈsiː, -z
AM ˌpiˌɛlˈsi, -z

plea
BR pliː, -z
AM pli, -z

pleach
BR pliːtʃ, -ɪz, -ɪŋ, -t
AM plitʃ, -ɪz, -ɪŋ, -t

plead
BR pliːd, -z, -ɪŋ, -ɪd
AM plid, -z, -ɪŋ, -ɪd

pleadable
BR ˈpliːdəbl
AM ˈplidəbəl

pleader
BR ˈpliːdə(r), -z
AM ˈplidər, -z

pleading
BR ˈpliːdɪŋ, -z
AM ˈplidɪŋ, -z

pleadingly
BR ˈpliːdɪŋli
AM ˈplidɪŋli

pleasance
BR ˈplɛzns, -ɪz
AM ˈplɛzns, -əz

pleasant
BR ˈplɛznt
AM ˈplɛznt

pleasantly
BR ˈplɛzntli
AM ˈplɛzn(t)li

pleasantness
BR ˈplɛzntnəs
AM ˈplɛzn(t)nəs

pleasantry
BR ˈplɛzntr|i, -ɪz
AM ˈplɛzntri, -z

pleasaunce
BR ˈplɛzns
AM ˈplɛzns

please
BR pliːz, -ɪz, -ɪŋ, -d
AM pliz, -ɪz, -ɪŋ, -d

pleasingly
BR ˈpliːzɪŋli
AM ˈplizɪŋli

pleasurable
BR ˈplɛʒ(ə)rəbl
AM ˈplɛʒ(ə)r(ə)bəl

pleasurableness
BR ˈplɛʒ(ə)rəblnəs
AM ˈplɛʒ(ə)rəbəlnəs, ˈplɛʒərbəlnəs

pleasurably
BR ˈplɛʒ(ə)rəbli
AM ˈplɛʒ(ə)rəbli, ˈplɛʒərbli

pleasure
BR ˈplɛʒə(r), -z
AM ˈplɛʒər, -z

pleat
BR pliːt, -s, -ɪŋ, -ɪd
AM pli|t, -ts, -dɪŋ, -dɪd

pleb
BR plɛb, -z
AM plɛb, -z

plebby
BR ˈplɛbi
AM ˈplɛbi

plebe
BR pliːb, -z
AM plib, -z

plebeian
BR plɪˈbiːən, -z
AM pləˈbiən, -z

plebeianism
BR plɪˈbiːənɪz(ə)m
AM pləˈbiəˌnɪzəm

plebiscitary
BR plɪˈbɪsɪt(ə)ri
AM pləˈbɪsəˌtɛri

plebiscite
BR ˈplɛbɪsɪt, ˈplɛbɪsʌɪt, -s
AM ˈplɛbəˌsaɪt, -s

plectra
BR ˈplɛktrə(r)
AM ˈplɛktrə

plectron
BR ˈplɛktr(ə)n
AM ˈplɛktr(ə)n

plectrum
BR ˈplɛktrəm, -z
AM ˈplɛktrəm, -z

pled
BR plɛd
AM plɛd

pledge
BR plɛdʒ, -ɪz, -ɪŋ, -d
AM plɛdʒ, -əz, -ɪŋ, -d

pledgeable
BR ˈplɛdʒəbl
AM ˈplɛdʒəbəl

pledgee
BR plɛˈdʒiː, -z
AM plɛˈdʒi, -z

pledger
BR ˈplɛdʒə(r), -z
AM ˈplɛdʒər, -z

pledget
BR ˈplɛdʒɪt, -s
AM ˈplɛdʒət, -s

pledgor
BR ˈplɛdʒə(r), -z
AM ˈplɛdʒər, -z

pleiad
BR ˈplʌɪəd, -z
AM ˈpliəd, -z

Pleiades
BR ˈplʌɪədiːz
AM ˈpliədiz

plein-air
BR ˌpleɪnˈɛː(r)
AM ˌpleɪnˈɛ(ə)r

plein-airist
BR ˌpleɪnˈɛːrɪst, -s
AM ˌpleɪnˈɛrəst, -s

pleiotropic
BR ˌplʌɪəˈtrəʊpɪk, ˌplʌɪəˈtrɒpɪk
AM ˌplaɪəˈtroʊpɪk, ˌplaɪəˈtrɑpɪk

pleiotropism
BR ˌplʌɪəˈtrəʊpɪz(ə)m
AM ˌplaɪəˈtroʊpɪzm

pleiotropy
BR plʌɪˈɒtrəpi
AM ˌplaɪˈɑtrəpi

Pleistocene
BR ˈplʌɪstəsiːn
AM ˈplaɪstəˌsin

plena
BR ˈpliːnə(r)
AM ˈplɛnə, ˈplinə

plenarily
BR ˈpliːn(ə)rɪli
AM ˈplɛnər(ə)li, pləˈnɛrəli

plenary
BR ˈpliːn(ə)r|i, -ɪz
AM ˈplɛnəri, -z

plenipotentiary
BR ˌplɛnɪpəˈtɛnʃ(ə)r|i, -ɪz
AM ˌplɛnəpəˈtɛn(t)ʃəri, -z

plenitude
BR ˈplɛnɪtjuːd, ˈplɛnɪtʃuːd
AM ˈplɛnəˌt(j)ud

plenteous
BR 'plɛntɪəs
AM 'plɛn(t)iəs
plenteously
BR 'plɛntɪəsli
AM 'plɛn(t)iəsli
plenteousness
BR 'plɛntɪəsnəs
AM 'plɛn(t)iəsnəs
plentiful
BR 'plɛntɪf(ʊ)l
AM 'plɛn(t)əfəl
plentifully
BR 'plɛntɪfʊli, 'plɛntɪfl̩i
AM 'plɛn(t)əfəli
plentifulness
BR 'plɛntɪf(ʊ)lnəs
AM 'plɛn(t)əfəlnəs
plenty
BR 'plɛnti
AM 'plɛn(t)i
plenum
BR 'pliːnəm, -z
AM 'plɛnəm, 'plinəm, -z
pleochroic
BR ˌplɪə'krəʊɪk
AM ˌpliə'kroʊɪk
pleochroism
BR ˌplɪə'krəʊɪz(ə)m
AM ˌpliə'kroʊˌɪzəm
pleomorphic
BR ˌplɪə'mɔːfɪk
AM ˌpliə'mɔrfɪk
pleomorphism
BR ˌplɪə'mɔːfɪz(ə)m
AM ˌpliə'mɔrˌfɪzəm
pleonasm
BR 'pliːənaz(ə)m, -z
AM 'pliəˌnæzəm, -z
pleonastic
BR ˌplɪə'nastɪk
AM ˌpliə'næstɪk
pleonastically
BR ˌplɪə'nastɪkli
AM ˌpliə'næstək(ə)li
plesiosaur
BR 'pliːzɪəsɔː(r), -z
AM 'plisiəˌsɔ(ə)r, -z
plesiosauri
BR ˌpliːzɪə'sɔːrʌɪ
AM ˌplisiə'sɔˌraɪ
plesiosaurus
BR ˌpliːzɪə'sɔːrəs, -ɪz
AM ˌplisiə'sɔrəs, -əz
plessor
BR 'plɛsə(r), -z
AM 'plɛsər, -z
plethora
BR 'plɛθ(ə)rə(*r*)
AM 'plɛθərə
plethoric
BR 'plɛθ(ə)rɪk, plɛ'θɒrɪk, plɪ'θɒrɪk
AM 'plɛθərɪk, plə'θɔrɪk
plethorically
BR plɛ'θɒrɪkli, plɪ'θɒrɪkli
AM plə'θɔrək(ə)li
pleura
BR 'plʊərə(*r*), 'plɔːrə(*r*)
AM 'plʊrə
pleural
BR 'plʊərəl, 'plʊərl 'plɔːrəl, 'plɔːrl̩
AM 'plʊrəl
pleurisy
BR 'plʊərəsi, 'plɔːrəsi
AM 'plurəsi, 'plʊrəsi
pleuritic
BR plʊə'rɪtɪk, plʊ'rɪtɪk
AM plu'rɪdɪk, plʊ'rɪdɪk, plə'rɪdɪk
pleurodynia
BR ˌplʊərə'dɪnɪə(*r*), ˌplɔːrə'dɪnɪə(*r*)
AM ˌplʊrə'dɪniə
pleuron
BR 'plʊərɒn, 'plɔːrɒn
AM 'plʊˌrɑn
pleuropneumonia
BR ˌplʊərəʊnjuː'məʊnɪə(*r*), ˌplɔːrəʊnjuː'məʊnɪə(*r*)
AM ˌplurəˌn(j)u'moʊniə
Pleven
BR 'plɛvn
AM 'plɛvən
plew
BR pluː, -z
AM plu, -z
plexiform
BR 'plɛksɪfɔːm
AM 'plɛksəˌfɔ(ə)rm
Plexiglass®
BR 'plɛksɪglɑːs, 'plɛksɪglas
AM 'plɛksəˌglæs
plexor
BR 'plɛksə(r), -z
AM 'plɛksər, -z
plexus
BR 'plɛksəs, -ɪz
AM 'plɛksəs, -ɪz
pliability
BR ˌplʌɪə'bɪlɪti
AM ˌplaɪə'bɪlɪdi
pliable
BR 'plʌɪəbl
AM 'plaɪəbəl
pliableness
BR 'plʌɪəblnəs
AM 'plaɪəbəlnəs
pliably
BR 'plʌɪəbli
AM 'plaɪəbli
pliancy
BR 'plʌɪənsi
AM 'plaɪənsi
pliant
BR 'plʌɪənt
AM 'plaɪənt
pliantly
BR 'plʌɪəntli
AM 'plaɪən(t)li
pliantness
BR 'plʌɪəntnəs
AM 'plaɪən(t)nəs
plicate
BR 'plʌɪkət, 'plʌɪkeɪt
AM 'plaɪˌkeɪt, 'plaɪkɪt
plicated
BR plɪ'keɪtɪd, plʌɪ'keɪtɪd
AM 'plaɪˌkeɪdɪd, 'plaɪkɪdɪd
plication
BR plɪ'keɪʃn, plʌɪ'keɪʃn, -z
AM plaɪ'keɪʃən, -z
plié
BR 'pliːeɪ, -z
AM pli'eɪ, -z
pliers
BR 'plʌɪəz
AM 'plaɪərz
plight
BR plʌɪt, -s, -ɪŋ, -ɪd
AM plaɪ|t, -ts, -dɪŋ, -dɪd
plimsole
BR 'plɪmsl, 'plɪmsəʊl, -z
AM 'plɪmsəl, 'plɪmˌsɔl, 'plɪmˌsɑl, -z
plimsoll
BR 'plɪmsl, -z
AM 'plɪmsəl, 'plɪmˌsɔl, 'plɪmˌsɑl, -z
pling
BR plɪŋ, -z
AM plɪŋ, -z
plink
BR plɪŋk, -s
AM plɪŋk, -s
Plinlimmon
BR plɪn'lɪmən
AM plɪn'lɪmən
plinth
BR plɪnθ, -s
AM plɪnθ, -s
Pliny
BR 'plɪni
AM 'plɪni, 'plaɪni
Pliocene
BR 'plʌɪə(ʊ)siːn
AM 'plaɪəˌsin
plissé
BR 'pliːseɪ
AM pli'seɪ, plə'seɪ
plod
BR plɒd, -z, -ɪŋ, -ɪd
AM plɑd, -z, -ɪŋ, -əd
plodder
BR 'plɒdə(r), -z
AM 'plɑdər, -z
ploddingly
BR 'plɒdɪŋli
AM 'plɑdɪŋli
ploidy
BR 'plɔɪd|i, -ɪz
AM 'plɔɪdi, -z
Plomer
BR 'pluːmə(r), 'pləʊmə(r)
AM 'ploʊmər
Plomley
BR 'plʌmli
AM 'pləmli
plonk
BR plɒŋ|k, -ks, -kɪŋ, -(k)t
AM plɑŋ|k, -ks, -kɪŋ, -(k)t
plonker
BR 'plɒŋkə(r), -z
AM 'plɑŋkər, -z
plonko
BR 'plɒŋkəʊ, -z
AM 'plɑŋˌkoʊ, -z
plop
BR plɒp, -s, -ɪŋ, -t
AM plɑp, -s, -ɪŋ, -t
plosion
BR 'pləʊʒn, -z
AM 'ploʊʒən, -z
plosive
BR 'pləʊsɪv, -z
AM 'ploʊzɪv, 'ploʊsɪv, -z
plot
BR plɒt, -s, -ɪŋ, -ɪd
AM plɑ|t, -ts, -dɪŋ, -dəd
Plotinus
BR plɒ'tʌɪnəs, plə'tʌɪnəs
AM plə'taɪnəs, plɔ'taɪnəs, plɑ'taɪnəs
plotless
BR 'plɒtləs
AM 'plɑtləs
plotlessness
BR 'plɒtləsnəs
AM 'plɑtləsnəs
plotter
BR 'plɒtə(r), -z
AM 'plɑdər, -z
plough
BR plaʊ, -z, -ɪŋ, -d
AM plaʊ, -z, -ɪŋ, -d
ploughable
BR 'plaʊəbl
AM 'plaʊəbəl
ploughboy
BR 'plaʊbɔɪ, -z
AM 'plaʊˌbɔɪ, -z
plougher
BR 'plaʊə(r), -z
AM 'plaʊər, -z
ploughland
BR 'plaʊland
AM 'plaʊˌlænd
ploughman
BR 'plaʊmən
AM 'plaʊmən

ploughmen
BR 'plaʊmən
AM 'plaʊmən

ploughshare
BR 'plaʊʃɛː(r), -z
AM 'plaʊˌʃɛ(ə)r, -z

Plouviez
BR 'pluːvɪeɪ
AM 'pluvieɪ, ˌpluvi'eɪ

plover
BR 'plʌvə(r), -z
AM 'pləvər, 'ploʊvər, -z

plow
BR plaʊ, -z, -ɪŋ, -d
AM plaʊ, -z, -ɪŋ, -d

plowable
BR 'plaʊəbl
AM 'plaʊəbəl

plowboy
BR 'plaʊbɔɪ, -z
AM 'plaʊˌbɔɪ, -z

Plowden
BR 'plaʊdn
AM 'plaʊdən

plower
BR 'plaʊə(r)
AM 'plaʊər

plowland
BR 'plaʊland
AM 'plaʊˌlænd

plowman
BR 'plaʊmən
AM 'plaʊmən

plowmen
BR 'plaʊmən
AM 'plaʊmən

Plowright
BR 'plaʊrʌɪt
AM 'plaʊˌraɪt

plowshare
BR 'plaʊʃɛː(r), -z
AM 'plaʊˌʃɛ(ə)r, -z

ploy
BR plɔɪ, -z
AM plɔɪ, -z

pluck
BR plʌk, -s, -ɪŋ, -t
AM plək, -s, -ɪŋ, -t

plucker
BR 'plʌkə(r), -z
AM 'plәkər, -z

pluckily
BR 'plʌkɨli
AM 'pləkəli

pluckiness
BR 'plʌkɪnɨs
AM 'pləkinɨs

pluckless
BR 'plʌkləs
AM 'pləkləs

plucky
BR 'plʌk|i, -ɪə(r), -ɪɪst
AM 'pləki, -ər, -ɨst

plug
BR plʌg, -z, -ɪŋ, -d
AM pləg, -z, -ɪŋ, -d

plugger
BR 'plʌgə(r), -z
AM 'pləgər, -z

plughole
BR 'plʌghəʊl, -z
AM 'pləgˌ(h)oʊl, -z

plugola
BR plʌ'gəʊlə(r)
AM plə'goʊlə

plug-ugly
BR ˌplʌg'ʌgli
AM 'pləg'əgli

plum
BR plʌm, -z
AM pləm, -z

plumage
BR 'pluːm|ɪdʒ, -ɨdʒɪz, -ɪdʒd
AM 'plumɪdʒ, -ɨz, -d

plumassier
BR ˌpluːmə'sɪə(r), -z
AM ˌplumə'sɪ(ə)r, -z

plumb
BR plʌm, -z, -ɪŋ, -d
AM pləm, -z, -ɪŋ, -d

plumbaginous
BR plʌm'badʒɪnəs
AM ˌpləm'bædʒənəs

plumbago
BR plʌm'beɪgəʊ
AM ˌpləm'beɪgoʊ

plumbate
BR 'plʌmbeɪt, -s
AM 'pləmˌbeɪt, -s

plumbeous
BR 'plʌmbɪəs
AM 'pləmbiəs

plumber
BR 'plʌmə(r), -z
AM 'pləmər, -z

plumbic
BR 'plʌmbɪk
AM 'pləmbɪk

plumbiferous
BR plʌm'bɪf(ə)rəs
AM ˌpləm'bɪfərəs

plumbism
BR 'plʌmbɪz(ə)m
AM 'pləmˌbɪzəm

plumbless
BR 'plʌmləs
AM 'pləmləs

plumbline
BR 'plʌmlʌɪn, -z
AM 'pləmˌlaɪn, -z

plumbous
BR 'plʌmbəs
AM 'pləmbəs

plumbum
BR 'plʌmbəm
AM 'pləmbəm

plume
BR pluːm, -z
AM plum, -z

plumeless
BR 'pluːmləs
AM 'plumləs

plumelike
BR 'pluːmlʌɪk
AM 'plumˌlaɪk

plumery
BR 'pluːm(ə)ri
AM 'pluməri

Plummer
BR 'plʌmə(r)
AM 'pləmər

plummet
BR 'plʌm|ɪt, -ɪts, -ɨtɪŋ, -ɨtɨd
AM 'pləmə|t, -ts, -dɪŋ, -dəd

plummily
BR 'plʌmɨli
AM 'pləməli

plumminess
BR 'plʌmɪnɨs
AM 'pləminɨs

plummy
BR 'plʌm|i, -ɪə(r), -ɪɪst
AM 'pləmi, -ər, -ɨst

plumose
BR 'pluːməʊs, pluː'məʊs
AM 'pluˌmoʊs, 'pluˌmoʊz

plump
BR plʌm|p, -(p)s, -pɪŋ, -(p)t, -pə(r), -pɨst
AM pləmp, -s, -ɪŋ, -t, -ər, -əst

plumpish
BR 'plʌmpɪʃ
AM 'pləmpɪʃ

plumply
BR 'plʌmpli
AM 'pləmpli

plumpness
BR 'plʌmpnəs
AM 'pləmpnəs

Plumpton
BR 'plʌm(p)tən
AM 'pləm(p)tən

Plumptre
BR 'plʌm(p)triː
AM 'pləm(p)tri

plumpy
BR 'plʌmpi
AM 'pləmpi

Plumstead
BR 'plʌmstɨd, 'plʌmstɛd
AM 'pləmˌstɛd

Plumtre
BR 'plʌmtriː
AM 'pləmˌtri

plumulaceous
BR ˌpluːmjʊ'leɪʃəs
AM ˌplumjə'leɪʃəs

plumular
BR 'pluːmjʊlə(r)
AM 'plumjələr

plumule
BR 'pluːmjuːl, -z
AM 'plumˌjul, -z

plumy
BR 'pluːm|i, -ɪə(r), -ɪɪst
AM 'plumi, -ər, -ɨst

plunder
BR 'plʌnd|ə(r), -əz, -(ə)rɪŋ, -əd
AM 'plənd|ər, -ərz, -(ə)rɪŋ, -ərd

plunderer
BR 'plʌnd(ə)rə(r), -z
AM 'plənd(ə)rər, -z

plundering
BR 'plʌnd(ə)rɪŋ, -z
AM 'plənd(ə)rɪŋ, -z

plunderous
BR 'plʌnd(ə)rəs
AM 'plənd(ə)rəs

plunge
BR plʌn(d)ʒ, -ɨz, -ɪŋ, -d
AM pləndʒ, -əz, -ɪŋ, -d

plunger
BR 'plʌn(d)ʒə(r), -z
AM 'pləndʒər, -z

plunk
BR plʌŋk, -s
AM pləŋk, -s

Plunket
BR 'plʌŋkɪt
AM 'pləŋkət

Plunkett
BR 'plʌŋkɪt
AM 'pləŋkət

pluperfect
BR ˌpluː'pəːfɪkt, -s
AM ˌplu'pərfək(t), -(t)s

plural
BR 'plʊərəl, 'plʊərl̩, 'plɔːrəl, 'plɔːrl̩, -z
AM 'plʊrəl, -z

pluralisation
BR ˌplʊərəlʌɪ'zeɪʃn, ˌplʊərl̩ʌɪ'zeɪʃn, ˌplɔːrəlʌɪ'zeɪʃn, ˌplɔːrl̩ʌɪ'zeɪʃn
AM ˌplʊrələ'zeɪʃən, ˌplʊrəˌlaɪ'zeɪʃən

pluralise
BR 'plʊərəlʌɪz, 'plʊərl̩ʌɪz, 'plɔːrəlʌɪz, 'plɔːrl̩ʌɪz, -ɨz, -ɪŋ, -d
AM 'plʊrəˌlaɪz, -ɨz, -ɪŋ, -d

pluralism
BR 'plʊərəlɪz(ə)m, 'plʊərl̩ɪz(ə)m, 'plɔːrəlɪz(ə)m, 'plɔːrl̩ɪz(ə)m
AM 'plʊrəˌlɪzəm

pluralist
BR 'plʊərəlɪst, 'plʊərl̩ɪst, 'plɔːrəlɪst, 'plɔːrl̩ɪst, -s
AM 'plʊrələst, -s

pluralistic
BR ˌplʊərə'lɪstɪk, ˌplʊərl̩'ɪstɪk,

ˌplɔːrəˈlɪstɪk,
ˌplɔːrl̩ˈɪstɪk
AM ˌplʊrəˈlɪstɪk

pluralistically
BR ˌplʊərəˈlɪstɨkli,
ˌplʊərl̩ˈɪstɨkli,
ˌplɔːrəˈlɪstɨkli,
ˌplɔːrl̩ˈɪstɨkli
AM ˌplʊrəˈlɪstək(ə)li

plurality
BR plʊəˈralɨti,
plɔːˈralɨti, plʉˈralɨti
AM plʊˈrælədi,
pləˈrælədi

pluralization
BR ˌplʊərəlʌɪˈzeɪʃn,
ˌplʊərl̩ʌɪˈzeɪʃn,
ˌplɔːrəlʌɪˈzeɪʃn,
ˌplɔːrl̩ʌɪˈzeɪʃn
AM ˌplʊrələˈzeɪʃən,
ˌplʊrəˌlaɪˈzeɪʃən

pluralize
BR ˈplʊərəlʌɪz,
ˈplʊərl̩ʌɪz,
ˈplɔːrəlʌɪz, ˈplɔːrl̩ʌɪz,
-ɨz, -ɪŋ, -d
AM ˈplʊrəˌlaɪz, -ɨz, -ɪŋ,
-d

plurally
BR ˈplʊərəli, ˈplʊərl̩i,
ˈplɔːrəli, ˈplɔːrl̩i
AM ˈplʊrəli

pluripotential
BR ˌplʊərɪpəˈtɛnʃl,
ˌplɔːrɪpəˈtɛnʃl
AM ˌplʊrəpəˈtɛn(t)ʃəl

pluripresence
BR ˌplʊərɪˈprɛzns,
ˌplɔːrɪˈprɛzns
AM ˌplʊrəˈprɛzns

plurry
BR ˈplʌri
AM ˈpləri

plus
BR plʌs, -ɨz
AM pləs, -əz

plus ça change
BR ˌpluː sa ˈʃɒ̃ʒ
AM ˌplu sɑ ˈʃɒnʒ, ˌplu
sɑ ˈʃɑnʒ

plus-fours
BR ˌplʌsˈfɔːz
AM ˌpləsˈfɔ(ə)rz

plush
BR plʌʃ, -ə(r), -ɪst
AM pləʃ, -ər, -əst

plushily
BR ˈplʌʃɨli
AM ˈpləʃəli

plushiness
BR ˈplʌʃɪnɨs
AM ˈpləʃinɨs

plushly
BR ˈplʌʃli
AM ˈpləʃli

plushness
BR ˈplʌʃnəs
AM ˈpləʃnəs

plushy
BR ˈplʌʃ|i, -ɪə(r), -ɪɨst
AM ˈpləʃi, -ər, -ɨst

Plutarch
BR ˈpluːtɑːk
AM ˈpluˌtɑrk

plutarchy
BR ˈpluːtɑːk|i, -ɪz
AM ˈpluˌtɑrki, -z

Pluto
BR ˈpluːtəʊ
AM ˈpludoʊ

plutocracy
BR pluːˈtɒkrəs|i, -ɪz
AM pluˈtɑkrəsi, -z

plutocrat
BR ˈpluːtəkrat, -s
AM ˈpludəˌkræt, -s

plutocratic
BR ˌpluːtəˈkratɪk
AM ˌpludəˈkrædɪk

plutocratically
BR ˌpluːtəˈkratɨkli
AM ˌpludəˈkrædək(ə)li

plutolatry
BR pluːˈtɒlətri
AM pluˈtɑlətri

pluton
BR ˈpluːtɒn, -z
AM ˈpluˌtɑn, -z

Plutonian
BR pluːˈtəʊnɪən
AM pluˈtoʊniən

Plutonic
BR pluːˈtɒnɪk
AM pluˈtɑnɪk

Plutonism
BR ˈpluːtənɪz(ə)m,
ˈpluːtn̩ɪz(ə)m
AM ˈplutnˌɪzəm

plutonium
BR pluːˈtəʊnɪəm
AM pluˈtoʊniəm

pluvial
BR ˈpluːvɪəl
AM ˈpluviəl

pluviometer
BR ˌpluːvɪˈɒmɨtə(r), -z
AM ˌpluviˈɑmədər, -z

pluviometric
BR ˌpluːvɪə(ʊ)ˈmɛtrɪk
AM ˌpluvioʊˈmɛtrɪk

pluviometrical
BR ˌpluːvɪə(ʊ)ˈmɛtrɪkl
AM ˌpluvioʊˈmɛtrəkəl

pluviometrically
BR ˌpluːvɪə(ʊ)ˈmɛtrɪkli
AM ˌpluvioʊˈmɛtrək(ə)li

pluvious
BR ˈpluːvɪəs
AM ˈpluviəs

ply
BR plʌɪ, -z, -ɪŋ, -d
AM plaɪ, -z, -ɪŋ, -d

Plymouth
BR ˈplɪməθ
AM ˈplɪməθ

Plynlimon
BR plɪnˈlɪmən
AM plɪnˈlɪmən

plywood
BR ˈplʌɪwʊd
AM ˈplaɪˌwʊd

pneumatic
BR njuːˈmatɪk,
njʉˈmatɪk, -s
AM n(j)uˈmædɪk, -s

pneumatically
BR njuːˈmatɨkli,
njʉˈmatɨkli
AM n(j)uˈmædək(ə)li

pneumaticity
BR ˌnjuːməˈtɪsɨti
AM ˌn(j)uməˈtɪsɨdi

pneumatocyst
BR ˈnjuːmətəsɪst,
njuːˈmatəsɪst,
njʉˈmatəsɪst, -s
AM ˌn(j)uˈmædəˌsɪst,
-s

pneumatological
BR ˌnjuːmətəˈlɒdʒɪkl
AM ˌn(j)umədəˈlɑdʒəkəl

pneumatology
BR ˌnjuːməˈtɒlədʒi
AM ˌn(j)uməˈtɑlədʒi

pneumatophore
BR ˈnjuːmətəfɔː(r),
njuːˈmatəfɔː(r),
njʉˈmatəfɔː(r), -z
AM ˌn(j)uˈmædəˌfɔ(ə)r,
-z

pneumococcus
BR ˌnjuːmə(ʊ)ˈkɒkəs
AM ˌn(j)umoʊˈkɑkəs

pneumoconiosis
BR ˌnjuːmə(ʊ)ˌkəʊnɪ-
ˈəʊsɪs
AM ˌn(j)umoʊˌkoʊni-
ˈoʊsəs

pneumocystis
BR ˌnjuːmə(ʊ)ˈsɪstɪs
AM ˈn(j)umoʊˌsɪstɪs

pneumogastric
BR ˌnjuːmə(ʊ)ˈgastrɪk
AM ˌn(j)umoʊˈgæstrɪk

pneumonectomy
BR ˌnjuːmə(ʊ)ˈnɛktəm|i,
-ɪz
AM ˌn(j)umoʊˈnɛktəmi,
-z

pneumonia
BR njuːˈməʊnɪə(*r*),
njʉˈməʊnɪə(*r*)
AM nəˈmoʊnjə,
n(j)uˈmoʊnjə

pneumonic
BR njuːˈmɒnɪk,
njʉˈmɒnɪk
AM n(j)uˈmɑnɪk

pneumonitis
BR ˌnjuːməˈnʌɪtɨs
AM ˌn(j)uməˈnaɪdɨs

pneumothorax
BR ˌnjuːməʊˈθɔːraks
AM ˌn(j)umoʊˈθɔræks

Pnyx
BR (p)nɪks
AM (p)niks

PO
BR ˌpiːˈəʊ, -z
AM ˌpiˈoʊ, -z

po
BR pəʊ
AM poʊ

poach
BR pəʊtʃ, -ɨz, -ɪŋ, -t
AM poʊtʃ, -ɨz, -ɪŋ, -t

poacher
BR ˈpəʊtʃə(r), -z
AM ˈpoʊtʃər, -z

poblano
BR pɒˈblɑːnəʊ, -z
AM pəˈblanoʊ, -z

Pocahontas
BR ˌpɒkəˈhɒntəs
AM ˌpoʊkəˈhɑn(t)əs

pochard
BR ˈpɒtʃəd, ˈpəʊtʃəd, -z
AM ˈpoʊtʃərd, -z

pochette
BR pɒˈʃɛt, -s
AM poʊˈʃɛt, -s

pock
BR pɒk, -s, -ɪŋ, -t
AM pɑk, -s, -ɪŋ, -t

pocket
BR ˈpɒk|ɪt, -ɪts, -ɨtɪŋ,
-ɨtɨd
AM ˈpɑkə|t, -ts, -dɪŋ,
-dəd

pocketable
BR ˈpɒkɪtəbl
AM ˈpɑkətəbəl

pocketbook
BR ˈpɒkɪtbʊk, -s
AM ˈpɑkə(t)ˌbʊk, -s

pocketful
BR ˈpɒkɪtfʊl, -z
AM ˈpɑkətˌfʊl, -z

pocketless
BR ˈpɒkɪtlɨs
AM ˈpɑkətləs

pockety
BR ˈpɒkɨti
AM ˈpɑkədi

Pocklington
BR ˈpɒklɪŋt(ə)n
AM ˈpɑklɪŋtən

pockmark
BR ˈpɒkmɑːk, -s, -ɪŋ, -t
AM ˈpɑkˌmɑrk, -s, -ɪŋ, -t

pocky
BR ˈpɒki
AM ˈpɑki

poco
BR ˈpəʊkəʊ
AM ˈpoʊkoʊ

Pocock
BR ˈpəʊkɒk
AM ˈpoʊˌkɑk

pococurante
BR ˌpəʊkəʊkjʊˈrant|i, -ɪz
AM ˌpoʊkoʊkjəˈræn(t)i, -z

pococuranteism
BR ˌpəʊkəʊkjʊˈrantɪ-ɪz(ə)m
AM ˌpoʊkoʊkjəˈræn(t)i-ˌɪzəm

pococurantism
BR ˌpəʊkəʊkjʊˈrant-ɪz(ə)m
AM ˌpoʊkoʊkjə-ˈrænˌtɪzəm

Pocono
BR ˈpəʊkənəʊ, -z
AM ˈpoʊkəˌnoʊ, -z

pod
BR pɒd, -z
AM pɑd, -z

podagra
BR pɒˈdagrə(r), pəˈdagrə(r)
AM pəˈdægrə, ˈpɑdəgrə

podagral
BR pɒˈdagr(ə)l, pəˈdagr(ə)l
AM pəˈdægrə, ˈpɑdəgrəl

podagric
BR pɒˈdagrɪk, pəˈdagrɪk
AM pəˈdægrɪk, ˈpɑdəgrɪk

podagrous
BR pɒˈdagrəs, pəˈdagrəs
AM pəˈdægrəs, ˈpɑdəgrəs

poddy
BR ˈpɒd|i, -ɪz
AM ˈpɑdi, -z

podestà
BR ˌpəʊdəˈstɑː(r)
AM ˌpoʊdəˈstɑ

podgily
BR ˈpɒdʒɨli
AM ˈpɑdʒəli

podginess
BR ˈpɒdʒɪnɨs
AM ˈpɑdʒinɨs

podgy
BR ˈpɒdʒ|i, -ɪə(r), -ɪɪst
AM ˈpɑdʒi, -ər, -ɨst

podia
BR ˈpəʊdɪə(r)
AM ˈpoʊdiə

podiatrist
BR pə(ʊ)ˈdʌɪətrɪst, -s
AM pəˈdaɪətrəst, -s

podiatry
BR pə(ʊ)ˈdʌɪətri
AM pəˈdaɪətri

podium
BR ˈpəʊdɪəm, -z
AM ˈpoʊdiəm, -z

podophyllin
BR ˌpɒdəˈfɪlɪn
AM ˌpɑdəˈfɪlɨn

podsol
BR ˈpɒdsɒl, -z
AM ˈpɑdˌsɔl, ˈpɑdˌsɑl, -z

podunk
BR ˈpəʊdʌŋk, -s
AM ˈpoʊˌdəŋk, -s

podzol
BR ˈpɒdzɒl, -z
AM ˈpɑdˌsɔl, ˈpɑdˌsɑl, -z

podzolisation
BR ˌpɒdzəlʌɪˈzeɪʃn, ˌpɒdzl̩ʌɪˈzeɪʃn
AM ˌpɑdzələˈzeɪʃən, ˌpɑdzəˌlaɪˈzeɪʃən

podzolise
BR ˈpɒdzəlʌɪz, ˈpɒdzl̩ʌɪz, -ɪz, -ɪŋ, -d
AM ˈpɑdzəˌlaɪz, -ɪz, -ɪŋ, -d

podzolization
BR ˌpɒdzəlʌɪˈzeɪʃn, ˌpɒdzl̩ʌɪˈzeɪʃn
AM ˌpɑdzələˈzeɪʃən, ˌpɑdzəˌlaɪˈzeɪʃən

podzolize
BR ˈpɒdzəlʌɪz, ˈpɒdzl̩ʌɪz, -ɪz, -ɪŋ, -d
AM ˈpɑdzəˌlaɪz, -ɪz, -ɪŋ, -d

Poe
BR pəʊ
AM poʊ

poem
BR ˈpəʊɪm, -z
AM ˈpoʊ(ə)m, -z

poesy
BR ˈpəʊɪzi
AM ˈpoʊəzi, ˈpoʊəsi

poet
BR ˈpəʊɪt, -s
AM ˈpoʊət, -s

poetaster
BR ˌpəʊɪˈtastə(r), ˈpəʊɪtastə(r), ˌpəʊɪˈteɪstə(r), ˈpəʊɪteɪstə(r), -z
AM ˈpoʊəˌtæstər, -z

poetess
BR ˈpəʊɪtɪs, ˌpəʊɪˈtɛs, -ɪz
AM ˈpoʊədəs, -əz

poetic
BR pəʊˈɛtɪk, -s
AM poʊˈɛdɪk, -s

poetical
BR pəʊˈɛtɪkl
AM poʊˈɛdəkəl

poetically
BR pəʊˈɛtɪkli
AM poʊˈɛdək(ə)li

poeticise
BR pəʊˈɛtɪsʌɪz, -ɪz, -ɪŋ, -d
AM poʊˈɛdəˌsaɪz, -ɪz, -ɪŋ, -d

poeticize
BR pəʊˈɛtɪsʌɪz, -ɪz, -ɪŋ, -d
AM poʊˈɛdəˌsaɪz, -ɪz, -ɪŋ, -d

poetise
BR ˈpəʊɪtʌɪz, -ɪz, -ɪŋ, -d
AM ˈpoʊəˌtaɪz, -ɪz, -ɪŋ, -d

poetize
BR ˈpəʊɪtʌɪz, -ɪz, -ɪŋ, -d
AM ˈpoʊəˌtaɪz, -ɪz, -ɪŋ, -d

Poet Laureate
BR ˌpəʊɪt ˈlɔːrɪət, + ˈlɒrɪət, -s
AM ˌpoʊət ˈlɔriɨt, -s

poetry
BR ˈpəʊɪtri
AM ˈpoʊətri

po-faced
BR ˌpəʊˈfeɪst
AM ˈpoʊˌfeɪst

pogey
BR ˈpəʊgi
AM ˈpoʊgi

pogo
BR ˈpəʊgəʊ, -z, -ɪŋ, -d
AM ˈpoʊgoʊ, -z, -ɪŋ, -d

pogrom
BR ˈpɒgrəm, ˈpɒgrɒm, -z
AM poʊˈgrəm, -z

Pogue
BR pəʊg, -z
AM poʊg, -z

poi
BR pɔɪ
AM pɔɪ

poignance
BR ˈpɔɪnjəns
AM ˈpɔɪn(j)əns

poignancy
BR ˈpɔɪnjənsi
AM ˈpɔɪn(j)ənsi

poignant
BR ˈpɔɪnjənt
AM ˈpɔɪn(j)ənt

poignantly
BR ˈpɔɪnjəntli
AM ˈpɔɪn(j)ən(t)li

poikilotherm
BR ˈpɔɪkɪləˌθəːm, -z
AM pɔɪˈkɪləˌθərm, ˈpɔɪkəloʊˌθərm, -z

poikilothermal
BR ˌpɔɪkɪləˈθəːml
AM pɔɪˌkɪləˈθərml, ˌpɔɪkəloʊˈθərml

poikilothermia
BR ˌpɔɪkɪləˈθəːmɪə(r)
AM pɔɪˌkɪləˈθərmiə, ˌpɔɪkəloʊˈθərmiə

poikilothermic
BR ˌpɔɪkɪləˈθəːmɪk
AM pɔɪˌkɪləˈθərmɪk, ˌpɔɪkəloʊˈθərmɪk

poikilothermy
BR ˈpɔɪkɪləˌθəːmi
AM pɔɪˈkɪləˌθərmi, ˈpɔɪkəloʊˌθərmi

poilu
BR ˈpwɑːluː, ˌpwɑːˈluː, -z
AM pwɑˈlu, -z

poinciana
BR ˌpɔɪnsɪˈɑːnə(r), -z
AM ˌpɔɪnsiˈɑnə, -z

poind
BR pɔɪnd, pɪnd, -z, -ɪŋ, -ɨd
AM pɪnd, -z, -ɪŋ, -ɨd

Poindexter
BR ˈpɔɪnˌdɛkstə(r)
AM ˈpɔɪnˌdɛkstər

poinsettia
BR pɔɪnˈsɛtɪə(r)
AM pɔɪnˈsɛd(i)ə

point
BR pɔɪnt, -s, -ɪŋ, -ɨd
AM pɔɪn|t, -ts, -(t)ɪŋ, -(t)ɨd

point-blank
BR ˌpɔɪntˈblaŋk
AM ˌpɔɪn(t)ˈblæŋk

point duty
BR ˈpɔɪnt ˌdjuːti, + ˌdʒuːti
AM ˈpɔɪnt ˌd(j)udi

pointe
BR pwãt
AM pwɑnt

pointedly
BR ˈpɔɪntɨdli
AM ˈpɔɪn(t)ɨdli

pointedness
BR ˈpɔɪntɨdnɨs
AM ˈpɔɪn(t)ɨdnɨs

pointer
BR ˈpɔɪntə(r), -z
AM ˈpɔɪn(t)ər, -z

pointes
BR pwãt
AM pwɑnt(s)

pointillism
BR ˈpwãtɪjɪz(ə)m, ˈpɔɪntɪlɪz(ə)m
AM ˈpwɑn(t)l̩ˌɪzəm

pointillist
BR ˈpwãtɪjɪst, ˈpɔɪntɪlɪst
AM ˈpwɑn(t)l̩əst

pointillistic
BR ˌpwãtɪˈjɪstɪk, ˌpɔɪntɪˈlɪstɪk
AM ˌpwɑn(t)lˈɪstɪk

pointless
BR ˈpɔɪntlɨs
AM ˈpɔɪn(t)lɨs

pointlessly
BR ˈpɔɪntlɨsli
AM ˈpɔɪn(t)lɨsli

pointlessness
BR ˈpɔɪntlɨsnɨs
AM ˈpɔɪn(t)lɨsnɨs

Pointon
BR ˈpɔɪntən
AM ˈpɔɪn(t)ən

pointsman
BR ˈpɔɪntsmən
AM ˈpɔɪn(t)smən

pointsmen
BR ˈpɔɪntsmən
AM ˈpɔɪn(t)smən

point-to-point
BR ˌpɔɪnt(t)əˈpɔɪnt, -s
AM ˌpɔɪn(t)təˈpɔɪnt, -s

pointy
BR ˈpɔɪnt|i, -ɪə(r), -ɪɪst
AM ˈpɔɪn(t)i, -ər, -ɪst

Poirot
BR ˈpwɑːrəʊ
AM pwɑˈroʊ

poise
BR pɔɪz, -ɪz, -ɪŋ, -d
AM pɔɪz, -ɪz, -ɪŋ, -d

poison
BR ˈpɔɪz|n, -nz, -n̩ɪŋ\-nɪŋ, -nd
AM ˈpɔɪzn̩, -z, -ɪŋ, -d

poisoner
BR ˈpɔɪzn̩ə(r), ˈpɔɪznə(r), -z
AM ˈpɔɪzn̩ər, -z

poisoning
BR ˈpɔɪzn̩ɪŋ, ˈpɔɪznɪŋ, -z
AM ˈpɔɪzn̩ɪŋ, -z

poisonous
BR ˈpɔɪzn̩əs, ˈpɔɪznəs
AM ˈpɔɪzn̩əs, ˈpɔɪznəs

poisonously
BR ˈpɔɪzn̩əsli, ˈpɔɪznəsli
AM ˈpɔɪzn̩əsli, ˈpɔɪznəsli

poisonousness
BR ˈpɔɪzn̩əsnəs, ˈpɔɪznəsnəs
AM ˈpɔɪzn̩əsnəs, ˈpɔɪznəsnəs

Poisson distribution
BR ˌpwɑːsɒn ˌdɪstrɪˈbjuːʃn, ˌpwasɒn +, ˌpwɑːsɒ̃ +, ˌpwasɒ̃ +, -z
AM ˌpwɑˈsɑn ˌdɪstrəˌbjuʃən, -z

Poitier
BR ˈpwɒtɪeɪ, ˈpwɑːtɪeɪ
AM ˌpwɑdiˈeɪ

Poitiers
BR ˈpwɒtɪeɪ
AM ˌpwɑdiˈeɪ

Poitou
BR ˌpwɒˈtuː
AM ˌpwɑˈtu

poke
BR pəʊk, -s, -ɪŋ, -t
AM poʊk, -s, -ɪŋ, -t

poker
BR ˈpəʊkə(r), -z
AM ˈpoʊkər, -z

pokerwork
BR ˈpəʊkəwəːk
AM ˈpoʊkərˌwərk

pokeweed
BR ˈpəʊkwiːd, -z
AM ˈpoʊkˌwid, -z

pokey
BR ˈpəʊk|i, -ɪə(r), -ɪɪst
AM ˈpoʊki, -ər, -ɪst

pokily
BR ˈpəʊkɪli
AM ˈpoʊkəli

pokiness
BR ˈpəʊkɪnɪs
AM ˈpoʊkinɪs

poky
BR ˈpəʊk|i, -ɪə(r), -ɪɪst
AM ˈpoʊki, -ər, -ɪst

pol
BR pɒl, -z
AM pɑl, -z

polacca
BR pə(ʊ)ˈlakə(r), -z
AM poʊˈlɑkə, -z

Polack
BR ˈpəʊlak, -s
AM ˈpoʊˌlɑk, -s

polacre
BR pə(ʊ)ˈlɑːkə(r), -z
AM poʊˈlækər, -z

Polak
BR ˈpəʊlak, -s
AM ˈpoʊˌlɑk, -s

Poland
BR ˈpəʊlənd
AM ˈpoʊlənd

Polanski
BR pəˈlanski
AM pəˈlænski

polar
BR ˈpəʊlə(r)
AM ˈpoʊlər

polarimeter
BR ˌpəʊləˈrɪmɪtə(r), -z
AM ˌpoʊləˈrɪmədər, -z

polarimetric
BR ˌpəʊlərɪˈmɛtrɪk
AM ˌpoʊlərəˈmɛtrɪk

polarimetry
BR ˌpəʊləˈrɪmɪtri
AM ˌpoʊləˈrɪmətri

Polaris
BR pəˈlɑːrɪs
AM pəˈlɛrəs

polarisable
BR ˈpəʊlərʌɪzəbl
AM ˈpoʊləˌraɪzəbəl

polarisation
BR ˌpəʊlərʌɪˈzeɪʃn
AM ˌpoʊlərəˈzeɪʃən, ˌpoʊləˌraɪˈzeɪʃən

polariscope
BR pəˈlarɪskəʊp, -s
AM pəˈlɛrəˌskoʊp, poʊˈlɛrəˌskoʊp, -s

polariscopic
BR pəˌlarɪˈskɒpɪk
AM poʊˌlɛrəˈskɑpɪk

polarise
BR ˈpəʊlərʌɪz, -ɪz, -ɪŋ, -d
AM ˈpoʊləˌraɪz, -ɪz, -ɪŋ, -d

polariser
BR ˈpəʊlərʌɪzə(r), -z
AM ˈpoʊləˌraɪzər, -z

polarity
BR pə(ʊ)ˈlarɪti
AM pəˈlɛrədi, poʊˈlɛrədi

polarizable
BR ˈpəʊlərʌɪzəbl
AM ˈpoʊləˌraɪzəbəl

polarization
BR ˌpəʊlərʌɪˈzeɪʃn
AM ˌpoʊlərəˈzeɪʃən, ˌpoʊləˌraɪˈzeɪʃən

polarize
BR ˈpəʊlərʌɪz, -ɪz, -ɪŋ, -d
AM ˈpoʊləˌraɪz, -ɪz, -ɪŋ, -d

polarizer
BR ˈpəʊlərʌɪzə(r), -z
AM ˈpoʊləˌraɪzər, -z

polarly
BR ˈpəʊləli
AM ˈpoʊlərli

polarographic
BR ˌpəʊlərəˈgrafɪk
AM ˌpoʊlərəˈgræfɪk, poʊˌlɛrəˈgræfɪk

polarography
BR ˌpəʊləˈrɒgrəfi
AM ˌpoʊləˈrɑgrəfi

Polaroid®
BR ˈpəʊlərɔɪd, -z
AM ˈpoʊləˌrɔɪd, -z

polder
BR ˈpəʊldə(r), ˈpɒldə(r), -z
AM ˈpoʊldər, -z

pole
BR pəʊl, -z, -ɪŋ, -d
AM poʊl, -z, -ɪŋ, -d

poleax
BR ˈpəʊlaks, -ɪz, -ɪŋ, -t
AM ˈpoʊˌlæks, -ɪz, -ɪŋ, -t

pole-axe
BR ˈpəʊlaks, -ɪz, -ɪŋ, -t
AM ˈpoʊˌlæks, -ɪz, -ɪŋ, -t

polecat
BR ˈpəʊlkat, -s
AM ˈpoʊlˌkæt, -s

Polegate
BR ˈpəʊlgeɪt
AM ˈpoʊlˌgeɪt

polemic
BR pəˈlɛmɪk, -s
AM pəˈlɛmɪk, -s

polemical
BR pəˈlɛmɪkl
AM pəˈlɛməkəl

polemically
BR pəˈlɛmɪkli
AM pəˈlɛmək(ə)li

polemicise
BR pəˈlɛmɪsʌɪz, -ɪz, -ɪŋ, -d
AM pəˈlɛməˌsaɪz, -ɪz, -ɪŋ, -d

polemicist
BR pəˈlɛmɪsɪst, -s
AM pəˈlɛməsəst, -s

polemicize
BR pəˈlɛmɪsʌɪz, -ɪz, -ɪŋ, -d
AM pəˈlɛməˌsaɪz, -ɪz, -ɪŋ, -d

polenta
BR pəˈlɛntə(*r*)
AM poʊˈlɛn(t)ə

polestar
BR ˈpəʊlstɑː(r)
AM ˈpoʊlˌstɑr

polevault
BR ˈpəʊlvɔːlt, ˈpəʊlvɒlt, -s, -ɪŋ, -ɪd
AM ˈpoʊlˌvɔlt, ˈpoʊlˌvɑlt, -s, -ɪŋ, -əd

pole-vaulter
BR ˈpəʊlˌvɔːltə(r), ˈpəʊlˌvɒltə(r), -z
AM ˈpoʊlˌvɔltər, ˈpoʊlˌvɑltər, -z

poleward
BR ˈpəʊlwəd, -z
AM ˈpoʊlwərd, -z

police
BR pəˈliːs, pliːs, -ɪz, -ɪŋ, -t
AM pəˈlis, -ɪz, -ɪŋ, -t

policeman
BR pəˈliːsmən, ˈpliːsmən
AM pəˈlismən

policemen
BR pəˈliːsmən, ˈpliːsmən
AM pəˈlismən

policewoman
BR pəˈliːsˌwʊmən, ˈpliːsˌwʊmən
AM pəˈlisˌwʊmən

policewomen
BR pəˈliːsˌwɪmɪn, ˈpliːsˌwɪmɪn
AM pəˈlisˌwɪmɪn

policlinic
BR ˌpɒlɪˈklɪnɪk, -s
AM ˌpɑləˈklɪnɪk, -s

policy
BR ˈpɒlɪs|i, -ɪz
AM ˈpɑləsi, -z

policyholder
BR ˈpɒlɪsɪˌhəʊldə(r), -z
AM ˈpɑləsiˌhoʊldər, -z

polimorphism
BR ˌpɒlɪˈmɔːfɪz(ə)m
AM ˌpɑliˈmɔrˌfɪzəm

polio
BR ˈpəʊlɪəʊ
AM ˈpoʊlioʊ

poliomyelitis
BR ˌpəʊlɪəʊˌmʌɪəˈlʌɪtɪs
AM ˌpoʊlioʊˌmaɪəˈlaɪdɪs

polis
police
BR ˈpɒlɪs
AM ˈpoʊləs, ˈpoʊlis

Polisario
BR ˌpɒlɪˈsɑːrɪəʊ
AM ˌpɔləˈsɑrioʊ, ˌpɑləˈsɑrioʊ

Polish
adjective 'of Poland'
BR ˈpəʊlɪʃ
AM ˈpoʊlɪʃ

polish
noun, verb
BR ˈpɒl|ɪʃ, -ɪʃɪz, -ɪʃɪŋ, -ɪʃt
AM ˈpɑlɪʃ, -ɪz, -ɪŋ, -t

polishable
BR ˈpɒlɪʃəbl
AM ˈpɑləʃəbəl

polisher
BR ˈpɒlɪʃə(r), -z
AM ˈpɑlɪʃər, -z

Politburo
BR ˈpɒlɪtˌbjʊərəʊ, ˈpɒlɪtˌbjɔːrəʊ
AM ˈpɑlətˌbjʊroʊ, ˈpoʊlətˌbjʊroʊ
RUS pəlʲitbʲuˈro

polite
BR pəˈlʌɪt
AM pəˈlaɪt

politely
BR pəˈlʌɪtli
AM pəˈlaɪtli

politeness
BR pəˈlʌɪtnɪs, -ɪz
AM pəˈlaɪtnɪs, -ɪz

politesse
BR ˌpɒlɪˈtɛs
AM ˌpɑləˈtɛs

politic
BR ˈpɒlɪtɪk, -s, -ɪŋ, -t
AM ˈpɑlətɪk, -s, -ɪŋ, -t

political
BR pəˈlɪtɪkl
AM pəˈlɪdɪkəl

politically
BR pəˈlɪtɪkli
AM pəˈlɪdɪk(ə)li

politician
BR ˌpɒlɪˈtɪʃn, -z
AM ˌpɑləˈtɪʃən, -z

politicisation
BR pəˌlɪtɪsʌɪˈzeɪʃn
AM pəˌlɪdɪsɪˈzeɪʃən, pəˌlɪdɪˌsaɪˈzeɪʃən

politicise
BR pəˈlɪtɪsʌɪz, -ɪz, -ɪŋ, -d
AM pəˈlɪdɪˌsaɪz, -ɪz, -ɪŋ, -d

politicization
BR pəˌlɪtɪsʌɪˈzeɪʃn
AM pəˌlɪdɪsɪˈzeɪʃən, pəˌlɪdɪˌsaɪˈzeɪʃən

politicize
BR pəˈlɪtɪsʌɪz, -ɪz, -ɪŋ, -d
AM pəˈlɪdɪˌsaɪz, -ɪz, -ɪŋ, -d

politicking
BR ˈpɒlɪtɪkɪŋ
AM ˈpɑlətɪkɪŋ

politicly
BR ˈpɒlɪtɪkli
AM ˈpɑləˌtɪkli

politico
BR pəˈlɪtɪkəʊ, -z
AM pəˈlɪdɪkoʊ, -z

polity
BR ˈpɒlɪt|i, -ɪz
AM ˈpɑlədi, -z

polje
BR ˈpɒljə(r), -z
AM ˈpɑljə, -z

Polk
BR pəʊk
AM poʊk

polka
BR ˈpɒlkə(r), -z
AM ˈpoʊ(l)kə, -z

polkadot
BR ˈpɒlkədɒt, -s
AM ˈpoʊkəˌdɑt, -s

poll[1]
vote
BR pəʊl, -z, -ɪŋ, -d
AM poʊl, -z, -ɪŋ, -d

poll[2]
parrot
BR pɒl
AM pɑl

pollack
BR ˈpɒlək, -s
AM ˈpɑlək, -s

pollan
BR ˈpɒlən, -z
AM ˈpɑlən, -z

pollard
BR ˈpɒləd, ˈpɒlɑːd, -z, -ɪŋ, -ɪd
AM ˈpɑlərd, -z, -ɪŋ, -ɪd

pollee
BR pəʊlˈiː, -z
AM poʊˈli, -z

pollen
BR ˈpɒlən, -z
AM ˈpɑlən, -z

pollenless
BR ˈpɒlənləs
AM ˈpɑlənləs

pollex
BR ˈpɒlɛks, -ɪz
AM ˈpɑˌlɛks, -əz

pollicitation
BR ˌpɒlɪsɪˈteɪʃn
AM pəˌlɪsəˈteɪʃən

pollie
BR ˈpɒl|i, -ɪz
AM ˈpɑli, -z

pollinate
BR ˈpɒlɪneɪt, -s, -ɪŋ, -ɪd
AM ˈpɑləˌneɪ|t, -ts, -dɪŋ, -dɪd

pollination
BR ˌpɒlɪˈneɪʃn
AM ˌpɑləˈneɪʃən

pollinator
BR ˈpɒlɪneɪtə(r), -z
AM ˈpɑləˌneɪdər, -z

pollinia
BR pəˈlɪnɪə(r)
AM pəˈlɪniə

pollinic
BR pəˈlɪnɪk
AM pəˈlɪnɪk

polliniferous
BR ˌpɒlɪˈnɪf(ə)rəs
AM ˌpɑləˈnɪf(ə)rəs

pollinium
BR pəˈlɪnɪəm
AM pəˈlɪniəm

Pollitt
BR ˈpɒlɪt
AM ˈpɑlət

polliwog
BR ˈpɒlɪwɒg, -z
AM ˈpɑliˌwɔg, ˈpɑliˌwɑg, -z

pollock
BR ˈpɒlək, -s
AM ˈpɑlək, -s

pollster
BR ˈpəʊlstə(r), -z
AM ˈpoʊlztər, ˈpoʊlstər, -z

pollutant
BR pəˈl(j)uːtnt, -s
AM pəˈlutnt, -s

pollute
BR pəˈl(j)uːt, -s, -ɪŋ, -ɪd
AM pəˈlu|t, -ts, -dɪŋ, -dəd

polluter
BR pəˈl(j)uːtə(r), -z
AM pəˈludər, -z

pollution
BR pəˈl(j)uːʃn
AM pəˈluʃən

Pollux
BR ˈpɒləks
AM ˈpɑləks

polly
BR ˈpɒl|i, -ɪz
AM ˈpɑli, -z

Pollyanna
BR ˌpɒlɪˈanə(r), -z
AM ˌpɑliˈænə, -z

Pollyannaish
BR ˌpɒlɪˈanə(r)ɪʃ
AM ˌpɑliˈænɪʃ

Pollyannaism
BR ˌpɒlɪˈanə(r)ɪz(ə)m
AM ˌpɑliˈænəˌɪzəm

pollywog
BR ˈpɒlɪwɒg, -z
AM ˈpɑliˌwɔg, ˈpɑliˌwɑg, -z

polo
BR ˈpəʊləʊ
AM ˈpoʊloʊ

polocrosse
BR ˈpəʊləʊkrɒs
AM ˈpoʊloʊˌkrɔs, ˈpoʊloʊˌkrɑs

polonaise
BR ˌpɒləˈneɪz, -ɪz
AM ˌpɑləˈneɪz, ˌpoʊləˈneɪz, -ɪz

polonium
BR pəˈləʊnɪəm
AM pəˈloʊniəm

Polonius
BR pəˈləʊnɪəs
AM pəˈloʊniəs

polony
BR pəˈləʊn|i, -ɪz
AM pəˈloʊni, -z

Polperro
BR pɒlˈpɛrəʊ
AM ˌpɔlˈpɛroʊ, ˌpɑlˈpɛroʊ

poltergeist
BR ˈpɒltəgʌɪst, -s
AM ˈpoʊltərˌgaɪst, -s

poltroon
BR pɒlˈtruːn, -z
AM pɑlˈtrun, poʊlˈtrun, -z

poltroonery
BR pɒlˈtruːn(ə)ri
AM pɑlˈtrunəri, poʊlˈtrunəri

poly
BR ˈpɒl|i, -ɪz
AM ˈpɑli, -z

polyadelphous
BR ˌpɒlɪəˈdɛlfəs
AM ˌpɑliəˈdɛlfəs

polyamide
BR ˌpɒlɪˈamʌɪd, -z
AM ˌpɑliˈæmaɪd, -z

polyandrous
BR ˌpɒlɪˈandrəs
AM ˌpɑliˈændrəs

polyandry
BR ˈpɒlɪandri, ˌpɒlɪˈandri
AM ˈpɑliˌændri

polyantha
BR ˌpɒlɪˈanθə(r), -z
AM ˌpɑliˈænθə, -z

polyanthus
BR ˌpɒlɪˈanθəs, -ɪz
AM ˌpɑliˈænθəs, -əz

polyatomic
BR ˌpɒlɪəˈtɒmɪk
AM ˌpɑliəˈtɑmɪk

polybag
BR ˈpɒlɪbag, -z
AM ˈpɑliˌbæg, -z

polybasic
BR ˌpɒlɪˈbeɪsɪk
AM ˌpɑliˈbeɪsɪk

Polybius
BR pəˈlɪbɪəs, pɒˈlɪbɪəs
AM pəˈlɪbiəs

polycarbonate
BR ˌpɒlɪˈkɑːbəneɪt, ˌpɒlɪˈkɑːbənət, -s
AM ˌpɑliˈkɑrbənət, -s

Polycarp
BR ˈpɒlɪkɑːp
AM ˈpɑliˌkɑrp

Polycell®
BR ˈpɒlɪsɛl
AM ˈpɑliˌsɛl

polychaetan
BR ˌpɒlɪˈkiːtn
AM ˌpɑliˈkitn

polychaete
BR ˈpɒlɪkiːt, -s
AM ˈpɑliˌkit, -s

polychaetous
BR ˌpɒlɪˈkiːtəs
AM ˌpɑliˈkidəs

polychlorinated
BR ˌpɒlɪˈklɔːrɨneɪtɨd, ˌpɒlɪˈklɒrɨneɪtɨd
AM ¦pɑliˈklɔrəˌneɪdɨd

polychromatic
BR ˌpɒlɨkrəˈmatɪk
AM ¦pɑlikrəˈmædɪk, ¦pɑlikroʊˈmædɪk

polychromatism
BR ˌpɒlɪˈkrəʊmətɪz(ə)m
AM ¦pɑliˈkroʊməˌtɪzəm

polychrome
BR ˈpɒlɪkrəʊm
AM ˈpɑliˌkroʊm

polychromic
BR ˌpɒlɪˈkrəʊmɪk
AM ˌpɑliˈkroʊmɪk

polychromous
BR ˌpɒlɪˈkrəʊməs
AM ˌpɑliˈkroʊməs

polychromy
BR ˈpɒlɪˌkrəʊmi
AM ˈpɑliˌkroʊmi

polyclinic
BR ˌpɒlɪˈklɪnɪk, -s
AM ˌpɑliˈklɪnɪk, -s

Polyclitus
BR ˌpɒlɪˈklʌɪtəs
AM ˌpɑliˈklaɪdɪs

polycotton
BR ˌpɒlɪˈkɒtn
AM ¦pɑliˈkɑtn

Polycrates
BR pəˈlɪkrətiːz, pɒˈlɪkrətiːz
AM pəˈlɪkrətiz

polycrystal
BR ˈpɒlɪˌkrɪstl, -z
AM ˈpɑliˌkrɪstəl, -z

polycrystalline
BR ˌpɒlɪˈkrɪstəlʌɪn, ˌpɒlɪˈkrɪstl̩ʌɪn
AM ¦pɑliˈkrɪstələn, ¦pɑliˈkrɪstəˌlaɪn

polycyclic
BR ˌpɒlɪˈsʌɪklɪk, -s
AM ˌpɑliˈsɪklɪk, ˌpɑliˈsaɪklɪk, -s

polycythaemia
BR ˌpɒlɪsʌɪˈθiːmɪə(r)
AM ˌpɑliˌsaɪˈθimiə

polycythemia
BR ˌpɒlɪsʌɪˈθiːmɪə(r)
AM ˌpɑliˌsaɪˈθimiə

polydactyl
BR ˌpɒlɪˈdakt(ɪ)l, -z
AM ¦pɑli¦dæktl, -z

polydaemonism
BR ˌpɒlɪˈdiːmənɪz(ə)m
AM ˌpɑliˈdiməˌnɪzəm

polydipsia
BR ˌpɒlɪˈdɪpsɪə(r)
AM ˌpɑliˈdɪpsiə

polyester
BR ˌpɒlɪˈɛstə(r)
AM ¦pɑli¦ɛstər

polyethene
BR ˈpɒlɪˌɛθiːn
AM ˈpɑliəˌθin

polyethylene
BR ˌpɒlɪˈɛθɨliːn, ˌpɒlɪˈɛθl̩iːn
AM ˌpɑliˈɛθəlin

Polyfilla®
BR ˈpɒlɪˌfɪlə(r)
AM ˈpɑliˌfɪlə

polygamic
BR ˌpɒlɪˈgamɪk
AM ˌpɑliˈgæmɪk

polygamist
BR pəˈlɪgəmɪst, pɒˈlɪgəmɪst, -s
AM pəˈlɪgəməst, -s

polygamous
BR pəˈlɪgəməs, pɒˈlɪgəməs
AM pəˈlɪgəməs

polygamously
BR pəˈlɪgəməsli, pɒˈlɪgəməsli
AM pəˈlɪgəməsli

polygamy
BR pəˈlɪgəmi, pɒˈlɪgəmi
AM pəˈlɪgəmi

polygene
BR ˈpɒlɪdʒiːn, -z
AM ˈpɑliˌdʒin, -z

polygenesis
BR ˌpɒlɪˈdʒɛnɨsɪs
AM ˌpɑliˈdʒɛnəsəs

polygenetic
BR ˌpɒlɪdʒɪˈnɛtɪk
AM ¦pɑlidʒəˈnɛdɪk

polygenic
BR ˌpɒlɪˈdʒɛnɪk
AM ˌpɑliˈdʒɛnɪk

polygenism
BR pəˈlɪdʒɨnɪz(ə)m, pəˈlɪdʒn̩ɪz(ə)m, pɒˈlɪdʒɨnɪz(ə)m, pɒˈlɪdʒn̩ɪz(ə)m
AM pəˈlɪdʒəˌnɪzəm

polygenist
BR pəˈlɪdʒɨnɪst, pəˈlɪdʒn̩ɪst, pɒˈlɪdʒɨnɪst, pɒˈlɪdʒn̩ɪst, -s
AM ˌpəˈlɪdʒənəst, -s

polygeny
BR pəˈlɪdʒɨni, pəˈlɪdʒn̩i, pɒˈlɪdʒɨni, pɒˈlɪdʒn̩i
AM pəˈlɪdʒəni

polyglot
BR ˈpɒlɪglɒt, -s
AM ˈpɑliˌglɑt, -s

polyglottal
BR ˌpɒlɪˈglɒtl
AM ¦pɑli¦glɑdl

polyglottic
BR ˌpɒlɪˈglɒtɪk
AM ˌpɑliˈglɑdɪk

polyglottism
BR ˈpɒlɪglɒtɪz(ə)m
AM ˌpɑliˈglɑˌtɪzəm

polygon
BR ˈpɒlɨg(ə)n, ˈpɒlɨgɒn, -z
AM ˈpɑliˌgɑn, -z

polygonal
BR pəˈlɪgənl, pəˈlɪgn̩l, pɒˈlɪgənl, pɒˈlɪgn̩l
AM pəˈlɪgənəl

polygonum
BR pəˈlɪgənəm, pəˈlɪgn̩əm, pɒˈlɪgənəm, pɒˈlɪgn̩əm
AM pəˈlɪgənəm

polygraph
BR ˈpɒlɪgrɑːf, ˈpɒlɪgraf, -s
AM ˈpɑliˌgræf, -s

polygynous
BR pəˈlɪdʒɨnəs, pɒˈlɪdʒɨnəs
AM pəˈlɪdʒɨnəs

polygyny
BR pəˈlɪdʒɨni, pɒˈlɪdʒɨni
AM pəˈlɪdʒɨni

polyhedra
BR ˌpɒlɪˈhiːdrə(r)
AM ˌpɑliˈhidrə

polyhedral
BR ˌpɒlɪˈhiːdr(ə)l
AM ˌpɑliˈhidrəl

polyhedric
BR ˌpɒlɪˈhiːdrɪk
AM ˌpɑliˈhidrɪk

polyhedron
BR ˌpɒlɪˈhiːdr(ə)n, -z
AM ˌpɑliˈhidrən, -z

polyhistor
BR ˌpɒlɪˈhɪstə(r), -z
AM ¦pɑli¦hɪstər, -z

Polyhymnia
BR ˌpɒlɪˈhɪmnɪə(r)
AM ˌpɑliˈhɪmniə

polymath
BR ˈpɒlɪmaθ, -s
AM ˈpɑliˌmæθ, -s

polymathic
BR ˌpɒlɪˈmaθɪk
AM ˌpɑliˈmæθɪk

polymathy
BR pəˈlɪməθi, pɒˈlɪməθi
AM pəˈlɪməθi

polymer
BR ˈpɒlɨmə(r), -z
AM ˈpɑləmər, -z

polymerase
BR ˈpɒlɨməreɪz, pəˈlɪməreɪz, pɒˈlɪməreɪz, -ɨz
AM pəˈlɪməˌreɪz, -ɨz

polymeric
BR ˌpɒlɪˈmɛrɪk
AM ˌpɑliˈmɛrɪk

polymerisation
BR ˌpɒlɨmərʌɪˈzeɪʃn
AM pəˌlɪmərəˈzeɪʃən, ˌpɑləmərəˈzeɪʃən, ˌpɑləməˌraɪˈzeɪʃən

polymerise
BR ˈpɒlɨmərʌɪz, -ɨz, -ɪŋ, -d
AM pəˈlɪməˌraɪz, ˈpɑləməˌraɪz, -ɨz, -ɪŋ, -d

polymerism
BR ˈpɒlɨmərɪz(ə)m
AM ˈpɑləməˌrɪzəm, pəˈlɪməˌrɪzəm

polymerization
BR ˌpɒlɨmərʌɪˈzeɪʃn
AM pəˌlɪmərəˈzeɪʃən, ˌpɑləmərəˈzeɪʃən, ˌpɑləməˌraɪˈzeɪʃən

polymerize
BR ˈpɒlɨmərʌɪz, -ɨz, -ɪŋ, -d
AM pəˈlɪməˌraɪz, ˈpɑləməˌraɪz, -ɨz, -ɪŋ, -d

polymerous
BR pəˈlɪm(ə)rəs, pɒˈlɪm(ə)rəs
AM pəˈlɪmərəs

polymorph
BR ˈpɒlɪmɔːf, -s
AM ˈpɑliˌmɔ(ə)rf, -s

polymorphic
BR ˌpɒlɪˈmɔːfɪk
AM ˌpɑliˈmɔrfɪk

polymorphism
BR ˌpɒlɪˈmɔːfɪz(ə)m
AM ˌpɑliˈmɔrˌfɪzəm

polymorphous
BR ˌpɒlɪˈmɔːfəs

AM ˌpɑliˈmɔrfəs
Polynesia
BR ˌpɒlɪˈniːzjə(r), ˌpɒlɪˈniːʒə(r)
AM ˌpɑləˈniʒə, ˌpɑləˈniʃə
Polynesian
BR ˌpɒlɪˈniːzj(ə)n, ˌpɒlɪˈniːʒ(ə)n, -z
AM ˌpɑləˈniʒən, ˌpɑləˈniʃən, -z
polyneuritic
BR ˌpɒlɪnjʊˈrɪtɪk, ˌpɒlɪnjʊəˈrɪtɪk
AM ˌpɑlən(j)uˈrɪdɪk, ˌpɑlən(j)əˈrɪdɪk
polyneuritis
BR ˌpɒlɪnjʊˈrʌɪtɪs, ˌpɒlɪnjʊəˈrʌɪtɪs
AM ˌpɑlən(j)uˈraɪdɪs, ˌpɑlən(j)əˈraɪdɪs
Polynices
BR ˌpɒlɪˈnʌɪsiːz
AM ˌpɑliˈnaɪsiz
polynomial
BR ˌpɒlɪˈnəʊmɪəl, -z
AM ˌpɑliˈnoʊmiəl, ˌpɑləˈnoʊmiəl, -z
polynya
BR pə(ʊ)ˈlɪnjə(r)
AM ˌpɑlənˈjɑ
polyopia
BR ˌpɒlɪˈəʊpɪə(r)
AM ˌpɑliˈoʊpiə
polyp
BR ˈpɒlɪp, -s
AM ˈpɑləp, -s
polypary
BR ˈpɒlɪp(ə)r|i, -ɪz
AM ˈpɑləˌpɛri, -z
polypeptide
BR ˌpɒlɪˈpɛptʌɪd
AM ˌpɑliˈpɛpˌtaɪd
polyphagous
BR pəˈlɪfəgəs
AM pəˈlɪfəgəs
polyphase
BR ˈpɒlɪfeɪz, -ɪz
AM ˈpɑliˌfeɪz, -ɪz
polyphasic
BR ˌpɒlɪˈfeɪzɪk
AM ˌpɑliˈfeɪzɪk
Polyphemus
BR ˌpɒlɪˈfiːməs
AM ˌpɑliˈfiməs
polyphone
BR ˈpɒlɪfəʊn, -z
AM ˈpɑliˌfoʊn, -z
polyphonic
BR ˌpɒlɪˈfɒnɪk
AM ˌpɑliˈfɑnɪk, ˌpɑləˈfɑnɪk
polyphonically
BR ˌpɒlɪˈfɒnɪkli
AM ˌpɑliˈfɑnək(ə)li, ˌpɑləˈfɑnək(ə)li
polyphonous
BR pəˈlɪfənəs, pəˈlɪfn̩əs, pɒˈlɪfənəs, pɒˈlɪfn̩əs
AM pəˈlɪfənəs
polyphony
BR pəˈlɪfəni, pəˈlɪfn̩i, pɒˈlɪfəni, pɒˈlɪfn̩i
AM pəˈlɪfəni
polyphosphate
BR ˌpɒlɪˈfɒsfeɪt, -s
AM ˌpɑliˈfɑsfeɪt, -s
polyphyletic
BR ˌpɒlɪfʌɪˈlɛtɪk
AM ˌpɑlifaɪˈlɛdɪk
polypi
BR ˈpɒlɪpʌɪ
AM ˈpɑləˌpaɪ
polyploid
BR ˈpɒlɪplɔɪd, -z
AM ˈpɑləˌplɔɪd, -z
polyploidy
BR ˈpɒlɪplɔɪdi
AM ˈpɑləplɔɪdi
polypod
BR ˈpɒlɪpɒd
AM ˈpɑləˌpɑd
polypody
BR ˈpɒlɪpəʊd|i, -ɪz
AM ˈpɑliˌpoʊdi, -z
polypoid
BR ˈpɒlɪpɔɪd
AM ˈpɑləˌpɔɪd
polyposis
BR ˌpɒlɪˈpəʊsɪs
AM ˌpɑləˈpoʊsɪs
polypous
BR ˈpɒlɪpəs
AM ˈpɑləpəs
polypropene
BR ˌpɒlɪˈprəʊpiːn, -z
AM ˌpɑliˈproʊˌpin, -z
polypropylene
BR ˌpɒlɪˈprəʊpɪliːn
AM ˌpɑləˈproʊpəˌlin
polyptych
BR ˈpɒlɪptɪk, -s
AM ˈpɑlɪpˌtɪk, pəˈlɪptɪk, -s
polypus
BR ˈpɒlɪpəs
AM ˈpɑləpəs
polyrhythm
BR ˈpɒlɪˌrɪð(ə)m, -z
AM ˈpɑliˌrɪðəm, -z
polysaccharide
BR ˌpɒlɪˈsakərʌɪd, -z
AM ˌpɑliˈsækəˌraɪd, -z
polysemic
BR ˌpɒlɪˈsiːmɪk
AM ˌpɑliˈsimɪk
polysemous
BR ˌpɒlɪˈsiːməs
AM ˌpɑliˌsiməs, ˌpɑləˌsiməs
polysemy
BR pəˈlɪsɪmi, ˈpɒlɪˌsiːmi
AM pəˈlɪsɪmi
polystyrene
BR ˌpɒlɪˈstʌɪriːn
AM ˌpɑliˈstaɪˌrin, ˌpɑləˈstaɪˌrin
polysyllabic
BR ˌpɒlɪsɪˈlabɪk
AM ˌpɑlisəˈlæbɪk, ˌpɑləsəˈlæbɪk
polysyllabically
BR ˌpɒlɪsɪˈlabɪkli
AM ˌpɑlisəˈlæbək(ə)li, ˌpɑləsəˈlæbək(ə)li
polysyllable
BR ˈpɒlɪˌsɪləbl, -z
AM ˌpɑliˈsɪləbəl, ˌpɑləˈsɪləbəl, -z
polysynthetic
BR ˌpɒlɪsɪnˈθɛtɪk
AM ˌpɑləsɪnˈθɛdɪk, ˌpɑliˌsɪnˈθɛdɪk
polytechnic
BR ˌpɒlɪˈtɛknɪk, -s
AM ˌpɑləˈtɛknɪk, -s
polytetrafluoroethylene
BR ˌpɒlɪtɛtrəˌflʊərəʊˈɛθɪliːn, ˌpɒlɪtɛtrəˌflɔːrəʊˈɛθɪliːn
AM ˌpɑliˌtɛtrəˌflʊroʊˈɛθəˌlin
polytheism
BR ˈpɒlɪθiːɪz(ə)m, ˈpɒlɪˌθiːɪz(ə)m
AM ˈpɑliθiˌɪzəm, ˈpɑləθiˌɪzəm, ˌpɑliˈθiɪzəm
polytheist
BR ˈpɒlɪθiːɪst, ˈpɒlɪˌθiːɪst, -s
AM ˌpɑliˈθiɪst, -s
polytheistic
BR ˌpɒlɪθɪˈɪstɪk
AM ˌpɑliˌθiˈɪstɪk, ˌpɑləθiˈɪstɪk
polythene
BR ˈpɒlɪθiːn
AM ˈpɑləθin
polytonal
BR ˌpɒlɪˈtəʊnl
AM ˌpɑliˈtoʊnəl
polytonality
BR ˌpɒlɪtə(ʊ)ˈnalɪti
AM ˌpɑliˌtoʊˈnælədi
polyunsaturate
BR ˌpɒlɪʌnˈsatʃʊreɪt, ˌpɒlɪʌnˈsatjʊreɪt, -ɪd
AM ˌpɑliənˈsætʃəˌreɪ|t, -dɨd
polyunsaturates
BR ˌpɒlɪʌnˈsatʃʊrəts, ˌpɒlɪʌnˈsatjʊrəts
AM ˌpɑliənˈsætʃ(ə)rəts
polyurethane
BR ˌpɒlɪˈjʊərɪθeɪn, ˌpɒlɪˈjɔːrɪθeɪn
AM ˌpɑliˈjʊrəˌθeɪn, ˌpɑləˈjʊrəˌθeɪn
polyvalence
BR ˌpɒlɪˈveɪləns, ˌpɒlɪˈveɪln̩s
AM ˌpɑliˈveɪləns, ˌpɑləˈveɪləns
polyvalent
BR ˌpɒlɪˈveɪlənt, ˌpɒlɪˈveɪln̩t
AM ˌpɑliˈveɪlənt, ˌpɑləˈveɪlənt
polyvinyl
BR ˌpɒlɪˈvʌɪn(ɪ)l
AM ˌpɑliˈvaɪnl, ˌpɑləˈvaɪnl
polyzoan
BR ˌpɒlɪˈzəʊən, -z
AM ˌpɑliˈzoʊən, -z
Polzeath
BR pɒlˈzɛθ, pɒlˈziːθ
AM ˈpɔlziθ, ˈpɑlziθ
pom
BR pɒm, -z
AM pɑm, -z
pomace
BR ˈpʌmɪs, ˈpɒmɪs, -ɪz
AM ˈpəməs, -ɪz
pomade
BR pəˈmɑːd, -z
AM pəˈmeɪd, poʊˈmeɪd, -z
Pomagne®
BR pə(ʊ)ˈmeɪn
AM poʊˈmeɪn
pomander
BR ˈpɒmandə(r), ˈpəʊmandə(r), pəˈmandə(r), -z
AM poʊˈmændər, -z
pomatum
BR pə(ʊ)ˈmeɪtəm, -z, -ɪŋ, -d
AM pəˈmɑdəm, pəˈmeɪdəm, pəˈmɑdəm, -z, -ɪŋ, -d
pombe
BR ˈpɒmbeɪ
AM ˈpɑmˌbeɪ
pome
BR pəʊm, -z
AM poʊm, -z
pomegranate
BR ˈpɒmɪgranɪt, -s
AM ˈpɑməˌgrænət, -s
pomelo
BR ˈpɒmɪləʊ, ˈpʌmɪləʊ, pəˈmɛləʊ, -z
AM ˈpɑməloʊ, -z
Pomerania
BR ˌpɒməˈreɪnɪə(r)
AM ˌpɑməˈreɪniə
Pomeranian
BR ˌpɒməˈreɪnɪən, -z
AM ˌpɑməˈreɪniən, -z

Pomeroy
BR 'pɒmərɔɪ, 'pəʊmərɔɪ
AM 'pɑmə,rɔɪ

pomfret
BR 'pɒmfrɪt
AM 'pɑmfrət

pomiculture
BR 'pɒmɪ,kʌltʃə(r)
AM 'pɑmə,kəltʃər

pomiferous
BR pə'mɪf(ə)rəs
AM pə'mɪf(ə)rəs

pommel[1]
noun, part of saddle
BR 'pʌml, 'pɒml, -z
AM 'pɑməl, -z

pommel[2]
verb
BR 'pʌm|l, -lz, -l̩ɪŋ\-əlɪŋ, -ld
AM 'pəm|əl, -əlz, -(ə)lɪŋ, -əld

pommie
BR 'pɒm|i, -ɪz
AM 'pɑmi, -z

pommy
BR 'pɒm|i, -ɪz
AM 'pɑmi, -z

pomological
BR ,pɒmə'lɒdʒɨkl
AM ,pɑmə'lɑdʒəkəl

pomologist
BR pə(ʊ)'mɒlədʒɪst, pɒ'mɒlədʒɪst, -s
AM pə'mɑlədʒəst, -s

pomology
BR pə(ʊ)'mɒlədʒi, pɒ'mɒlədʒi
AM pə'mɑlədʒi

Pomona
BR pə'məʊnə(*r*)
AM pə'moʊnə

pomp
BR pɒmp
AM pɑmp

Pompadour
BR ,pɒmpə'dʊə(r), 'pɒmpədɔː(r)
AM ,pɑmpə'dɔ(ə)r, ,pɑmpə'dʊ(ə)r

pompano
BR 'pɒmpənəʊ, -z
AM 'pɑmpə,noʊ, -z

Pompeii
BR pɒm'peɪ(i)
AM pɑm'peɪ(i)

Pompey
BR 'pɒmpi
AM 'pɑmpi

Pompidou
BR 'pɒmpɪduː
AM 'pɑmpə,du, 'pɑmpi,du

pompom
BR 'pɒmpɒm, -z
AM 'pɑm,pɑm, -z

pompon
BR 'pɒmpɒn, -z
AM 'pɑm,pɑn, -z

pomposity
BR pɒm'pɒsɪti
AM pɑm'pɑsədi

pompous
BR 'pɒmpəs
AM 'pɑmpəs

pompously
BR 'pɒmpəsli
AM 'pɑmpəsli

pompousness
BR 'pɒmpəsnəs
AM 'pɑmpəsnəs

'pon
upon
BR pɒn, pən
AM pɑn, pən

ponce
BR pɒns, -ɪz, -ɪŋ, -t
AM pɑns, -əz, -ɪŋ, -t

ponceau
BR 'pɒnsəʊ, -z
AM pɑn'soʊ, -z

ponceaux
BR 'pɒnsəʊz
AM pɑn'soʊ

poncey
BR 'pɒns|i, -ɪə(r), -ɪɪst
AM 'pɑnsi, -ər, -ɨst

poncho
BR 'pɒn(t)ʃəʊ, -z
AM 'pɑn(t)ʃoʊ, -z

poncy
BR 'pɒns|i, -ɪə(r), -ɪɪst
AM 'pɑnsi, -ər, -ɨst

pond
BR pɒnd, -z
AM pɑnd, -z

pondage
BR 'pɒndɪdʒ
AM 'pɑndɪdʒ

ponder
BR 'pɒnd|ə(r), -əz, -(ə)rɪŋ, -əd
AM 'pɑnd|ər, -ərz, -(ə)rɪŋ, -ərd

ponderability
BR ,pɒnd(ə)rə'bɪlɪti
AM ,pɑnd(ə)rə'bɪlɨdi

ponderable
BR 'pɒnd(ə)rəbl
AM 'pɑnd(ə)rəbəl

ponderation
BR ,pɒndə'reɪʃn
AM ,pɑndə'reɪʃən

pondering
BR 'pɒnd(ə)rɪŋ, -z
AM 'pənd(ə)rɪŋ, -z

ponderosa
BR ,pɒndə'rəʊzə(*r*), ,pɒndə'rəʊsə(*r*), -z
AM ,pɑndə'roʊsə, -z

ponderosity
BR ,pɒndə'rɒsɪti
AM ,pəndə'rɑsədi

ponderous
BR 'pɒnd(ə)rəs
AM 'pɑnd(ə)rəs

ponderously
BR 'pɒnd(ə)rəsli
AM 'pɑnd(ə)rəsli

ponderousness
BR 'pɒnd(ə)rəsnəs
AM 'pɑnd(ə)rəsnəs

Pondicherry
BR ,pɒndɪ'tʃɛri
AM ,pɑndə'tʃɛri

pondweed
BR 'pɒndwiːd
AM 'pɑn(d),wid

pone
BR pəʊn
AM poʊn

pong
BR pɒŋ, -z, -ɪŋ, -d
AM pɔŋ, pɑŋ, -z, -ɪŋ, -d

ponga
BR 'pʌŋə(*r*), -z
AM 'pɑŋə, -z

pongal
BR 'pɒŋgl
AM 'pɔŋ(g)əl, 'pɑŋ(g)əl

pongee
BR pɒn'dʒiː, 'pɒndʒiː, -z
AM 'pɑndʒi, pɑn'dʒi, -z

pongid
BR 'pɒn(d)ʒɪd, -z
AM 'pɑndʒəd, -z

pongo
BR 'pɒŋgəʊ, -z
AM 'pɔŋgoʊ, 'pɑŋgoʊ, -z

pongy
BR 'pɒŋ|i, -ɪə(r), -ɪɪst
AM 'pɑŋi, -ər, -ɨst

poniard
BR 'pɒnjəd, 'pɒnjɑːd, -z
AM 'pɑnjərd, -z

pons
BR pɒnz, -ɪz
AM pɑnz, -əz

pons asinorum
BR ,pɒnz ,asɪ'nɔːrəm
AM 'pɑnz ,æsn'ɔrəm

Ponsonby
BR 'pɒns(ə)nbi
AM 'pɑnsənbi

pons Varolii
BR ,pɒnz və'rəʊlɪʌɪ
AM 'pɑnz və'roʊli,aɪ

pont
BR pɒnt, -s
AM pɑnt, -s

Pontardawe
BR ,pɒntə'daʊi
AM ,pɑn(t)ər'daʊi
WE ,pɒntar'dawe

Pontardulais
BR ,pɒntə'dɪləs
AM ,pɑn(t)ər'dɪləs
WE ,pɒntar'dɪlaɪs

Pontefract
BR 'pɒntɪfrakt
AM 'pɑn(t)ə,fræk(t)

Ponteland
BR pɒn'tiːlənd
AM pɑn'tɪlənd

pontes
BR 'pɒntiːz
AM 'pɑn,tiz

pontes asinorum
BR ,pɒntiːz ,asɪ'nɔːrəm
AM 'pɑn,tiz ,æsn'ɔrəm

pontes Varolii
BR ,pɒntiːz və'rəʊlɪʌɪ
AM 'pɑn,tiz və'roʊli,aɪ

Pontiac
BR 'pɒntɪak, -s
AM 'pɑn(t)i,æk, -s

Pontianak
BR ,pɒntɪ'ɑːnak, ,pɒntɪ'anak
AM ,pɑn(t)i'ɑnək

pontifex
BR 'pɒntɪfɛks
AM 'pɑn(t)ə,fɛks

pontiff
BR 'pɒntɪf, -s
AM 'pɑn(t)əf, -s

pontific
BR pɒn'tɪfɪk
AM pɑn'tɪfɪk

pontifical
BR pɒn'tɪfɪkl, -z
AM pɑn'tɪfɨkəl, -z

pontificalia
BR ,pɒntɪfɪ'keɪlɪə(*r*)
AM pɑn,tɪfə'keɪljə, ,pɑn(t)əfə'keɪljə, pɑn,tɪfə'keɪliə, ,pɑn(t)əfə'keɪliə

pontifically
BR pɒn'tɪfɪkli
AM pɑn'tɪfɪk(ə)li

pontificate[1]
noun
BR pɒn'tɪfɪkət, -s
AM pɑn'tɪfɨkət, -s

pontificate[2]
verb
BR pɒn'tɪfɪkeɪt, -s, -ɪŋ, -ɪd
AM pɑn'tɪfɪ,keɪ|t, -ts, -dɪŋ, -dɨd

pontification
BR pɒn,tɪfɪ'keɪʃn, ,pɒntɪfɪ'keɪʃn
AM ,pɑn,tɪfə'keɪʃən, ,pɑn(t)əfə'keɪʃən

pontifices
BR pɒn'tɪfɪsiːz
AM pɑn'tɪfə,siz

Pontin
BR 'pɒntɪn
AM 'pɑntn

Pontine Marshes
BR ,pɒntʌɪn 'mɑːʃɪz

AM 'pɑn,tin mɑr∫əz, 'pɑn,taɪn +

Ponting
BR 'pɒntɪŋ
AM 'pɑn(t)ɪŋ

Pontius
BR 'pɒntɪəs, 'pɒn(t)∫əs
AM 'pɑn(t)∫əs

pontoon
BR pɒn'tuːn, -z
AM ˌpɑn'tun, -z

Pontormo
BR pɒn'tɔːməʊ
AM pɔn'tɔrˌmoʊ, pɑn'tɔrˌmoʊ

Pontus
BR 'pɒntəs
AM 'pɑn(t)əs

Pontypool
BR ˌpɒntɪ'puːl
AM ˌpɑn(t)i'pul

Pontypridd
BR ˌpɒntɪ'priːð
AM ˌpɑn(t)i'prɪð
WE ˌpɒntʌ'prið

pony
BR 'pəʊn|i, -ɪz
AM 'poʊni, -z

ponytail
BR 'pəʊnɪteɪl, -z
AM 'poʊniˌteɪl, -z

Ponzi scheme
BR 'pɒnzɪ skiːm, -z
AM 'pɑnzi ˌskim, -z

poo
BR puː, -z, -ɪŋ, -d
AM pu, -z, -ɪŋ, -d

pooch
BR puːt∫, -ɪz
AM put∫, -əz

poodle
BR 'puːdl, -z
AM 'pudəl, -z

poof
BR pʊf, puːf, -s
AM puf, -s

poofter
BR 'pʊftə(r), 'puːftə(r), -z
AM 'puftər, -z

poofy
BR 'puːf|i, -ɪə(r), -ɪɪst
AM 'pufi, -ər, -ɪst

pooh
BR p(h)uː, -z, -ɪŋ, -d
AM pu, -z, -ɪŋ, -d

pooh-bah
BR ˌpuː'bɑː(r), -z
AM 'puˌbɑ, -z

pooh-pooh
BR ˌpuː'puː, -z, -ɪŋ, -d
AM ˌpu'pu, -z, -ɪŋ, -d

pooja
BR 'puːdʒə(r), -z
AM 'pudʒə, -z

poojah
BR 'puːdʒə(r), -z
AM 'pudʒə, -z

Pook
BR puːk
AM puk

pooka
BR 'puːkə(r), -z
AM 'pukə, -z

pool
BR puːl, -z, -ɪŋ, -d
AM pul, -z, -ɪŋ, -d

Poole
BR puːl
AM pul

Pooley
BR 'puːli
AM 'puli

poolroom
BR 'puːlruːm, 'puːlrʊm, -z
AM 'pulˌrum, 'pulˌrʊm, -z

poolside
BR 'puːlsʌɪd
AM 'pulˌsaɪd

poon
BR puːn, -z
AM pun, -z

Poona
BR 'puːnə(r)
AM 'punə

poop
BR puːp, -s, -t
AM pup, -s, -t

pooper-scooper
BR 'puːpəˌskuːpə(r), -z
AM 'pupərˌskupər, -z

poo-poo
BR 'puːpuː, -z
AM ˌpu'pu, -z

poor
BR pɔː(r), pʊə(r), -ə(r), -ɪst
AM pʊ(ə)r, pɔ(ə)r, -ər, -əst

poorboy
BR 'pɔːbɔɪ, -z
AM 'pʊrˌbɔɪ, 'pɔrˌbɔɪ, -z

poorhouse
BR 'pɔːhaʊ|s, 'pʊəhaʊ|s, -zɪz
AM 'pʊrˌ(h)aʊ|s, ˌpɔrˌ(h)aʊ|s, -zəz

poorly
BR 'pɔːli, 'pʊəli
AM 'pʊrli, 'pɔrli

poorness
BR 'pɔːnəs, 'pʊənəs
AM 'pʊrnəs, 'pɔrnəs

Pooter
BR 'puːtə(r)
AM 'pudər

Pooterish
BR 'puːt(ə)rɪ∫
AM 'pudərɪ∫

pootle
BR 'puːt|l, -lz, -l̩ɪŋ\-lɪŋ, -ld
AM 'pudəl, -z, -ɪŋ, -d

poove
BR puːv, -z
AM puv, -z

pop
BR pɒp, -s, -ɪŋ, -t
AM pɑp, -s, -ɪŋ, -t

popadom
BR 'pɒpədəm, -z
AM 'pɑpədəm, -z

popadum
BR 'pɒpədəm, -z
AM 'pɑpədəm, -z

popcorn
BR 'pɒpkɔːn
AM 'pɑpˌkɔ(ə)rn

pope
BR pəʊp, -s
AM poʊp, -s

popedom
BR 'pəʊpdəm
AM 'poʊpdəm

popeless
BR 'pəʊpləs
AM 'poʊpləs

Popemobile
BR 'pəʊpmə(ʊ)biːl, -z
AM 'poʊpməˌbil, -z

popery
BR 'pəʊp(ə)ri
AM 'poʊp(ə)ri

Popeye
BR 'pɒpʌɪ
AM 'pɑpaɪ

popeyed
BR ˌpɒp'ʌɪd
AM 'pɑpaɪd

popgun
BR 'pɒpgʌn, -z
AM 'pɑpˌgən, -z

Popham
BR 'pɒpəm
AM 'pɑpəm

popinjay
BR 'pɒpɪndʒeɪ, -z
AM 'pɑpənˌdʒeɪ, -z

popish
BR 'pəʊpɪ∫
AM 'poʊpɪ∫

popishly
BR 'pəʊpɪ∫li
AM 'poʊpɪ∫li

popishness
BR 'pəʊpɪ∫nɪs
AM 'poʊpɪ∫nɪs

poplar
BR 'pɒplə(r), -z
AM 'pɑplər, -z

poplin
BR 'pɒplɪn
AM 'pɑplən

popliteal
BR ˌpɒplɪ'tiːəl
AM ˌpɑplə'tiəl

Popocatépetl
BR ˌpɒpəˌkatə'pɛtl
AM ˌpoʊpəˌkædə'pɛdl

popover
BR 'pɒpˌəʊvə(r), -z
AM 'pɑpˌoʊvər, -z

poppa
BR 'pɒpə(r), -z
AM 'pɑpə, -z

poppadom
BR 'pɒpədəm, -z
AM 'pɑpədəm, -z

poppadum
BR 'pɒpədəm, -z
AM 'pɑpədəm, -z

popper
BR 'pɒpə(r), -z
AM 'pɑpər, -z

poppet
BR 'pɒpɪt, -s
AM 'pɑpət, -s

poppied
BR 'pɒpɪd
AM 'pɑpid

popple
BR 'pɒp|l, -lz, -l̩ɪŋ\-lɪŋ, -ld
AM 'pɑpəl, -z, -ɪŋ, -d

Poppleton
BR 'pɒplt(ə)n
AM 'pɑpəltən

Popplewell
BR 'pɒplwɛl
AM 'pɑplˌwɛl

popply
BR 'pɒpl̩i, 'pɒpli
AM 'pɑpl̩i, 'pɑpli

poppy
BR 'pɒp|i, -ɪz
AM 'pɑpi, -z

poppycock
BR 'pɒpɪkɒk
AM 'pɑpiˌkɑk

Popsicle®
BR 'pɒpsɪkl, -z
AM 'pɑpsəkəl, 'pɑpˌsɪkəl, -z

popsie
BR 'pɒps|i, -ɪz
AM 'pɑpsi, -z

popsy
BR 'pɒps|i, -ɪz
AM 'pɑpsi, -z

populace
BR 'pɒpjʊləs
AM 'pɑpjələs

popular
BR 'pɒpjʊlə(r)
AM 'pɑpjələr

popularisation
BR ˌpɒpjʊlərʌɪ'zeɪ∫n, -z
AM ˌpɑpjələrə'zeɪ∫ən, ˌpɑpjələˌraɪ'zeɪ∫ən, -z

popularise
BR 'pɒpjʊlərʌɪz, -ɪz, -ɪŋ, -d
AM 'pɑpjələˌraɪz, -ɪz, -ɪŋ, -d

populariser
BR ˈpɒpjʊlərʌɪzə(r), -z
AM ˈpɑpjələˌraɪzər, -z

popularism
BR ˈpɒpjʊlərɪz(ə)m
AM ˈpɑpjələˌrɪzəm

popularity
BR ˌpɒpjʊˈlarɪti
AM ˌpɑpjəˈlɛrədi

popularization
BR ˌpɒpjʊlərʌɪˈzeɪʃn, -z
AM ˌpɑpjələrəˈzeɪʃən, ˌpɑpjələˌraɪˈzeɪʃən, -z

popularize
BR ˈpɒpjʊlərʌɪz, -ɪz, -ɪŋ, -d
AM ˈpɑpjələˌraɪz, -ɪz, -ɪŋ, -d

popularizer
BR ˈpɒpjʊlərʌɪzə(r), -z
AM ˈpɑpjələˌraɪzər, -z

popularly
BR ˈpɒpjʊləli
AM ˈpɑpjələrli

populate
BR ˈpɒpjʊleɪt, -s, -ɪŋ, -ɪd
AM ˈpɑpjəˌleɪ|t, -ts, -dɪŋ, -dɪd

population
BR ˌpɒpjʊˈleɪʃn, -z
AM ˌpɑpjəˈleɪʃən, -z

populism
BR ˈpɒpjʊlɪz(ə)m
AM ˈpɑpjəˌlɪzəm

populist
BR ˈpɒpjʊlɪst, -s
AM ˈpɑpjələst, -s

populistic
BR ˌpɒpjʊˈlɪstɪk
AM ˌpɑpjəˈlɪstɪk

populous
BR ˈpɒpjʊləs
AM ˈpɑpjələs

populously
BR ˈpɒpjʊləsli
AM ˈpɑpjələsli

populousness
BR ˈpɒpjʊləsnəs
AM ˈpɑpjələsnəs

porbeagle
BR ˈpɔːˌbiːgl, -z
AM ˈpɔrˌbigəl, -z

porcelain
BR ˈpɔːsl̩ɪn, ˈpɔːs(ə)lɪn, ˈpɔːsl̩eɪn, ˈpɔːs(ə)leɪn
AM ˈpɔrs(ə)lən

porcellaneous
BR ˌpɔːsɪˈleɪnɪəs
AM ˌpɔrsəˈleɪniəs

porcellanous
BR pɔːˈsɛlənəs
AM ˈpɔrs(ə)lənəs

porch
BR pɔːtʃ, -ɪz, -t
AM pɔrtʃ, -əz, -t

Porchester
BR ˈpɔːtʃɪstə(r)
AM ˈpɔrtʃəstər

porchless
BR ˈpɔːtʃləs
AM ˈpɔrtʃləs

porcine
BR ˈpɔːsʌɪn
AM ˈpɔrˌsaɪn, ˈpɔrˌsin, ˈpɔrsn̩

porcini
BR pɔːˈtʃiːniː
AM ˌpɔrˈtʃini

porcupine
BR ˈpɔːkjʊpʌɪn, -z
AM ˈpɔrkjəˌpaɪn, ˈpɔrkiˌpaɪn, -z

porcupinish
BR ˈpɔːkjʊpʌɪnɪʃ
AM ˈpɔrkjəˌpaɪnɪʃ, ˈpɔrkiˌpaɪnɪʃ

porcupiny
BR ˈpɔːkjʊpʌɪni
AM ˈpɔrkjəˌpaɪni, ˈpɔrkiˌpaɪni

pore
BR pɔː(r), -z, -ɪŋ, -d
AM pɔ(ə)r, -z, -ɪŋ, -d

porgy
BR ˈpɔːg|i, -ɪz
AM ˈpɔrgi, -z

Pori
BR ˈpɔːri
AM ˈpɔri

porifer
BR ˈpɔːrɪfə(r), -z
AM ˈpɔrəfər, -z

poriferan
BR pəˈrɪf(ə)rən, pəˈrɪf(ə)rn̩, -z
AM pəˈrɪf(ə)rən, -z

porism
BR ˈpɔːrɪz(ə)m, ˈpɒrɪz(ə)m, -z
AM ˈpɔˌrɪzəm, -z

porismatic
BR ˌpɔːrɪzˈmatɪk, ˌpɒrɪzˈmatɪk
AM ˌpɔrəzˈmædɪk

pork
BR pɔːk
AM pɔ(ə)rk

porker
BR ˈpɔːkə(r), -z
AM ˈpɔrkər, -z

porkling
BR ˈpɔːklɪŋ, -z
AM ˈpɔrklɪŋ, -z

porky
BR ˈpɔːk|i, -ɪə(r), -ɪɪst
AM ˈpɔrki, -ər, -ɪst

Porlock
BR ˈpɔːlɒk
AM ˈpɔrˌlɑk

porn
BR pɔːn
AM pɔ(ə)rn

porno
BR ˈpɔːnəʊ
AM ˈpɔrnoʊ

pornographer
BR pɔːˈnɒgrəfə(r), -z
AM pɔrˈnɑgrəfər, -z

pornographic
BR ˌpɔːnəˈgrafɪk
AM ˌpɔrnəˈgræfɪk

pornographically
BR ˌpɔːnəˈgrafɪkli
AM ˌpɔrnəˈgræfək(ə)li

pornography
BR pɔːˈnɒgrəfi
AM pɔrˈnɑgrəfi

poroplastic
BR ˌpɒrəˈplastɪk
AM ˌpɔrəˈplæstɪk

porosity
BR pɔːˈrɒsɪti
AM pəˈrɑsədi, poʊˈrɑsədi

porous
BR ˈpɔːrəs
AM ˈpɔrəs

porously
BR ˈpɔːrəsli
AM ˈpɔrəsli

porousness
BR ˈpɔːrəsnəs
AM ˈpɔrəsnəs

porphyria
BR pɔːˈfɪrɪə(*r*)
AM pɔrˈfɪriə

porphyrin
BR ˈpɔːf(ɪ)rɪn, -z
AM ˈpɔrfərɪn, -z

porphyritic
BR ˌpɔːfɪˈrɪtɪk
AM ˌpɔrfəˈrɪdɪk

porphyrogenite
BR ˌpɔːfɪˈrɒdʒɪnʌɪt, -s
AM ˌpɔrfəˈrɑdʒəˌnaɪt, ˌpɔrfərəˈdʒɛˌnaɪt, -s

porphyry
BR ˈpɔːf(ɪ)ri
AM ˈpɔrfəri

porpoise
BR ˈpɔːpəs, -ɪz
AM ˈpɔrpəs, -əz

porrect
BR pəˈrɛkt, -s, -ɪŋ, -ɪd
AM pəˈrɛk|(t), pɔˈrɛk|(t), -(t)s, -tɪŋ, -tɪd

porridge
BR ˈpɒrɪdʒ
AM ˈpɔrɪdʒ

porridgy
BR ˈpɒrɪdʒi
AM ˈpɔrɪdʒi

porringer
BR ˈpɒrɪn(d)ʒə(r), -z
AM ˈpɔrəndʒər, -z

Porsche®
BR pɔːʃ, ˈpɔːʃ|ə(*r*), -ɪz
AM ˈpɔrʃ|(ə), -əz

Porsena
BR ˈpɔːsɪnə(*r*), ˈpɔːsn̩ə(*r*)
AM ˈpɔrsənə

Porson
BR ˈpɔːsn
AM ˈpɔrsən

port
BR pɔːt, -s, -ɪŋ, -ɪd
AM pɔ(ə)rt, -ts, ˈpɔrdɪŋ, ˈpɔrdəd

portability
BR ˌpɔːtəˈbɪlɪti
AM ˌpɔrdəˈbɪlɪdi

portable
BR ˈpɔːtəbl
AM ˈpɔrdəbəl

portableness
BR ˈpɔːtəblnəs
AM ˈpɔrdəbəlnəs

portably
BR ˈpɔːtəbli
AM ˈpɔrdəbli

portage
BR ˈpɔːt|ɪdʒ, -ɪdʒɪz, -ɪdʒɪŋ, -ɪdʒd
AM ˈpɔrdɪdʒ, -ɪz, -ɪŋ, -d

Portakabin®
BR ˈpɔːtəˌkabɪn, -z
AM ˈpɔrdəˌkæbən, -z

portal
BR ˈpɔːtl, -z
AM ˈpɔrdl, -z

portamenti
BR ˌpɔːtəˈmɛntiː
AM ˌpɔrdəˈmɛn(t)i

portamento
BR ˌpɔːtəˈmɛntəʊ, -z
AM ˌpɔrdəˈmɛn(t)oʊ, -z

portative
BR ˈpɔːtətɪv
AM ˈpɔrdədɪv

Port-au-Prince
BR ˌpɔːtəʊˈprɪns
AM ˌpɔrdəˈprɪns

portcullis
BR pɔːtˈkʌlɪs, -ɪz, -t
AM pɔrtˈkələs, -ɪz, -t

Porte
BR pɔːt
AM pɔ(ə)rt

porte-cochère
BR ˌpɔːtkɒˈʃɛː(r), -z
AM ˌpɔrtkoʊˈʃɛ(ə)r, -z

portend
BR pɔːˈtɛnd, -z, -ɪŋ, -ɪd
AM pɔrˈtɛnd, -z, -ɪŋ, -əd

portent
BR ˈpɔːtɛnt, ˈpɔːt(ə)nt, -s
AM ˈpɔrˌtɛnt, -s

portentous
BR pɔːˈtɛntəs
AM pɔrˈtɛn(t)əs

portentously
BR pɔːˈtɛntəsli
AM pɔrˈtɛn(t)əsli

portentousness
BR pɔːˈtɛntəsnəs
AM pɔrˈtɛn(t)əsnəs

Porteous
BR ˈpɔːtɪəs
AM ˈpɔrdiəs

porter
BR ˈpɔːtə(r), -z
AM ˈpɔrdər, -z

porterage
BR ˈpɔːt(ə)rɪdʒ
AM ˈpɔrdərədʒ

porterhouse
BR ˈpɔːtəhaʊ|s, -zɪz
AM ˈpɔrdər,(h)aʊ|s, -zəz

Porteus
BR ˈpɔːtɪəs
AM ˈpɔrdiəs

portfire
BR ˈpɔːt,fʌɪə(r), -z
AM ˈpɔrt,faɪ(ə)r, -z

portfolio
BR pɔːtˈfəʊlɪəʊ, -z
AM pɔrtˈfoʊlioʊ, -z

Porth
BR pɔːθ
AM pɔ(ə)rθ

Port Harcourt
BR ,pɔːt ˈhɑːkɔːt
AM ˌpɔrt ˈhɑr,kɔ(ə)rt

Porthcawl
BR ,pɔːθˈkɔːl
AM ,pɔrθˈkɔl, ,pɔrθˈkɑl

Port Hedland
BR ,pɔːt ˈhɛdlənd
AM ˌpɔ(ə)rt ˈhɛdlənd

Porthmadog
BR ,pɔːθˈmadəg, ,pɔːθˈmadɒg
AM ,pɔrθˈmɑdəg

porthole
BR ˈpɔːthəʊl, -z
AM ˈpɔrt,(h)oʊl, -z

Portia
BR ˈpɔːʃə(r)
AM ˈpɔrʃə

portico
BR ˈpɔːtɪkəʊ, -z, -d
AM ˈpɔrdə,koʊ, -z, -d

portière
BR ,pɔːtɪˈɛː(r), -z
AM ,pɔrdiˈɛ(ə)r, -z

portion
BR ˈpɔːʃ|n, -nz, -n̩ɪŋ\-ənɪŋ, -nd
AM ˈpɔrʃ|ən, -ənz, -(ə)nɪŋ, -ənd

portionless
BR ˈpɔːʃnləs, ˈpɔːʃənləs
AM ˈpɔrʃənləs

Portishead
BR ˈpɔːtɪshɛd
AM ˈpɔrdəs,(h)ɛd

Portland
BR ˈpɔːtlənd
AM ˈpɔrtlən(d)

portliness
BR ˈpɔːtlɪnɪs
AM ˈpɔrtlinɪs

portly
BR ˈpɔːtl|i, -ɪə(r), -ɪɪst
AM ˈpɔrtli, -ər, -ɪst

Portmadoc
BR ,pɔːtˈmadək
AM ,pɔrtˈmædək

portmanteau
BR pɔːtˈmantəʊ, -z
AM ,pɔrtmænˈtoʊ, pɔrtˈmæntoʊ, -z

portmanteaux
BR pɔːtˈmantəʊz
AM ,pɔrtmænˈtoʊ, pɔrtˈmæntoʊ

Portmeirion
BR ,pɔːtˈmɛrɪən
AM ,pɔrtˈmɛriən
WE pɒrtˈmeɪrjɒn

Port Moresby
BR ,pɔːt ˈmɔːzbi
AM ˌpɔrt ˈmɔrzbi

Portnoy
BR ˈpɔːtnɔɪ
AM ˈpɔrt,nɔɪ

Porto
BR ˈpɔːtəʊ
AM ˈpɔr,toʊ, ˈpɔrdoʊ

Porto Alegre
BR ,pɔːtəʊ əˈlɛgrə(r)
AM ˌpɔrdoʊ əˈlɛgrə

Portobello
BR ,pɔːtəˈbɛləʊ
AM ,pɔrdəˈbɛloʊ

Port-of-Spain
BR ,pɔːtəvˈspeɪn
AM ˌpɔrdə(v)ˈspeɪn

portolan
BR ˈpɔːtələn, ˈpɔːtl̩ən, -z
AM ˈpɔrdl̩ən, -z

portolano
BR ,pɔːtəˈlɑːnəʊ, ,pɔːtl̩ˈɑːnəʊ, -z
AM ,pɔrdlˈɑnoʊ, -z

Porton
BR ˈpɔːtn
AM ˈpɔrtən

Porto Novo
BR ,pɔːtəʊ ˈnəʊvəʊ
AM ˈpɔrdoʊ ˈnoʊ,voʊ

Porto Rican
BR ,pɔːtə ˈriːkən, -z
AM ,pɔrdə ˈrikən, -z

Porto Rico
BR ,pɔːtə ˈriːkəʊ
AM ,pɔrdə ˈrikoʊ

portrait
BR ˈpɔːtreɪt, ˈpɔːtrɪt, -s
AM ˈpɔrtrət, -s

portraitist
BR ˈpɔːtrɪtɪst, ˈpɔːtreɪtɪst, -s
AM ˈpɔrtrədəst, -s

portraiture
BR ˈpɔːtrɪtʃə(r)
AM ˈpɔrtrətʃər, ˈpɔrtrə,tʃʊ(ə)r, ˈpɔrtrə,t(j)ʊ(ə)r

portray
BR pɔːˈtreɪ, -z, -ɪŋ, -d
AM pɔrˈtreɪ, -z, -ɪŋ, -d

portrayable
BR pɔːˈtreɪəbl
AM pɔrˈtreɪəbəl

portrayal
BR pɔːˈtreɪəl, -z
AM pɔrˈtreɪ(ə)l, -z

portrayer
BR pɔːˈtreɪə(r), -z
AM pɔrˈtreɪər, -z

Portreath
BR pɔːˈtriːθ
AM pɔrˈtriθ

Portree
BR pɔːˈtriː
AM pɔrˈtri

portreeve
BR ˈpɔːtriːv, -z
AM ˈpɔrt,riv, -z

Port Said
BR ,pɔːt ˈsʌɪd
AM ˌpɔrt saɪˈid

Portsmouth
BR ˈpɔːtsməθ
AM ˈpɔrtsməθ

Port Stanley
BR ,pɔːt ˈstanli
AM ,pɔrt ˈstænli

Port Sudan
BR ,pɔːt sʊˈdɑːn, + sʊˈdan
AM ˌpɔrt suˈdæn

Port Talbot
BR ,pɔː(t) ˈtɔːlbət, + ˈtalbət, + ˈtɒlbət
AM ,pɔrt ˈtælbət

Portugal
BR ˈpɔːtʃʊgl, ˈpɔːtjʊgl
AM ˈpɔrtʃəgəl

Portuguese
BR ,pɔːtʃʊˈgiːz, ,pɔːtjʊˈgiːz
AM ˈpɔrtʃə,giz

pose
BR pəʊz, -ɪz, -ɪŋ, -d
AM poʊz, -əz, -ɪŋ, -d

Poseidon
BR pəˈsʌɪdn, pɒˈsʌɪdn
AM pəˈsaɪdn, poʊˈsaɪdn

poser
BR ˈpəʊzə(r), -z
AM ˈpoʊzər, -z

poseur
BR pəʊˈzəː(r), -z
AM poʊˈzər, -z

poseuse
BR pəʊˈzəːz
AM poʊˈzəz

poseuses
BR pəʊˈzəːz
AM poʊˈzʊz

posey
BR ˈpəʊzi
AM ˈpoʊzi

posh
BR pɒʃ, -ə(r), -ɪst
AM pɑʃ, -ər, -əst

poshly
BR ˈpɒʃli
AM ˈpɑʃli

poshness
BR ˈpɒʃnəs
AM ˈpɑʃnəs

posit
BR ˈpɒz|ɪt, -ɪts, -ɪtɪŋ, -ɪtɪd
AM ˈpɑzə|t, -ts, -dɪŋ, -dəd

position
BR pəˈzɪʃ|n, -nz, -n̩ɪŋ\-ənɪŋ, -nd
AM pəˈzɪʃ|ən, -ənz, -(ə)nɪŋ, -ənd

positional
BR pəˈzɪʃn̩(ə)l, pəˈzɪʃən(ə)l
AM pəˈzɪʃ(ə)nəl

positionally
BR pəˈzɪʃn̩əli, pəˈzɪʃn̩l̩i, pəˈzɪʃənl̩i, pəˈzɪʃ(ə)nəli
AM pəˈzɪʃ(ə)nəli

positioner
BR pəˈzɪʃn̩ə(r), pəˈzɪʃ(ə)nə(r), -z
AM pəˈzɪʃ(ə)nər, -z

positive
BR ˈpɒzɪtɪv, -z
AM ˈpɑzədɪv, ˈpɑztɪv, -z

positively
BR ˈpɒzɪtɪvli
AM ˈpɑzədɪvli, ˈpɑztɪvli

positiveness
BR ˈpɒzɪtɪvnɪs
AM ˈpɑzədɪvnɪs, ˈpɑztɪvnɪs

positivism
BR ˈpɒzɪtɪvɪz(ə)m
AM ˈpɑzədɪ,vɪzəm

positivist
BR ˈpɒsɪtɪvɪst, -s
AM ˈpɑzədɪ,vɪst, -s

positivistic
BR ,pɒzɪtɪˈvɪstɪk
AM ,pɑzədəˈvɪstɪk

positivistically
BR ,pɒzɪtɪˈvɪstɪkli
AM ,pɑzədəˈvɪstɪk(ə)li

positivity
BR ,pɒzɪˈtɪvɪti
AM ,pɑzəˈtɪvɪdi

positron
BR ˈpɒzɪtrɒn, -z
AM ˈpɑzə,trɑn, -z

positronic
BR ˌpɒzɪˈtrɒnɪk
AM ˌpɑzəˈtrɑnɪk

positronium
BR ˌpɒzɪˈtrəʊnɪəm, -z
AM ˌpɑzəˈtroʊniəm, -z

posological
BR ˌpɒsəˈlɒdʒɪkl
AM ˌpɑzəˈlɑdʒəkəl

posology
BR pə(ʊ)ˈsɒlədʒi
AM pəˈzɑlədʒi

poss.
BR pɒs
AM pɑs

posse
BR ˈpɒs|i, -ɪz
AM ˈpɑsi, -z

posse comitatus
BR ˌpɒsɪ ˌkɒmɪˈtɑːtəs, -ɪz
AM ˌpɑsi ˌkɑməˈtɑdəs, -əz

possess
BR pəˈzɛs, -ɪz, -ɪŋ, -t
AM pəˈzɛs, -əz, -ɪŋ, -t

possession
BR pəˈzɛʃn, -z
AM pəˈzɛʃən, -z

possessionless
BR pəˈzɛʃnləs
AM pəˈzɛʃənləs

possessive
BR pəˈzɛsɪv
AM pəˈzɛsɪv

possessively
BR pəˈzɛsɪvli
AM pəˈzɛsɪvli

possessiveness
BR pəˈzɛsɪvnɪs
AM pəˈzɛsɪvnɪs

possessor
BR pəˈzɛsə(r), -z
AM pəˈzɛsər, -z

possessory
BR pəˈzɛs(ə)ri
AM pəˈzɛsəri

posset
BR ˈpɒs|ɪt, -ɪts, -ɪtɪŋ, -ɪtɪd
AM ˈpɑsə|t, -ts, -dɪŋ, -dəd

possibility
BR ˌpɒsɪˈbɪlɪt|i, -ɪz
AM ˌpɑsəˈbɪlɪdi, -z

possible
BR ˈpɒsɪbl
AM ˈpɑsəbəl

possibly
BR ˈpɒsɪbli
AM ˈpɑsəbli

possum
BR ˈpɒsəm, -z
AM ˈpɑsəm, -z

post
BR pəʊst, -s, -ɪŋ, -ɪd
AM poʊst, -s, -ɪŋ, -əd

postage
BR ˈpəʊstɪdʒ
AM ˈpoʊstɪdʒ

postal
BR ˈpəʊstl
AM ˈpoʊstəl

postally
BR ˈpəʊstl̩i, ˈpəʊstəli
AM ˈpoʊstəli

postbag
BR ˈpəʊs(t)bag, -z
AM ˈpoʊs(t)ˌbæg, -z

postbox
BR ˈpəʊs(t)bɒks, -ɪz
AM ˈpoʊs(t)ˌbɑks, -əz

postbus
BR ˈpəʊs(t)bʌs, -ɪz
AM ˈpoʊs(t)ˌbəs, -əz

postcard
BR ˈpəʊs(t)kɑːd, -z
AM ˈpoʊs(t)ˌkɑrd, -z

post-chaise
BR ˈpəʊs(t)ʃeɪz, -ɪz
AM ˈpoʊs(t)ˌʃeɪz, -ɪz

postcode
BR ˈpəʊs(t)kəʊd, -z
AM ˈpoʊs(t)ˌkoʊd, -z

postdate
BR ˌpəʊs(t)ˈdeɪt, -s, -ɪŋ, -ɪd
AM ˌpoʊs(t)ˈdeɪ|t, -ts, -dɪŋ, -dɪd

postdoc
BR ˈpəʊs(t)dɒk, -s
AM ˈpoʊs(t)ˌdɑk, -s

postdoctoral
BR ˌpəʊs(t)ˈdɒkt(ə)rəl, ˌpəʊs(t)ˈdɒkt(ə)rl̩
AM ˌpoʊs(t)ˈdɑkt(ə)rəl

poster
BR ˈpəʊstə(r), -z
AM ˈpoʊstər, -z

poste restante
BR ˌpəʊst ˈrɛstɒnt
AM ˌpoʊs(t)ˌrɛˈstɑnt

posterior
BR pɒˈstɪərɪə(r), -z
AM pɑˈstɪriər, poʊˈstɪriər, -z

posteriority
BR pɒˌstɪərɪˈɒrɪti
AM pɑˌstɪriˈɔrədi

posteriorly
BR pɒˈstɪərɪəli
AM pɑˈstɪriərli, poʊˈstɪriərli

posterity
BR pɒˈstɛrɪti
AM pɑˈstɛrədi

postern
BR ˈpɒst(ə)n, ˈpəʊst(ə)n, -z
AM ˈpoʊstərn, ˈpɑstərn, -z

postface
BR ˈpəʊs(t)feɪs, -ɪz
AM ˈpoʊs(t)ˌfeɪs, -ɪz

postfix
BR ˌpəʊs(t)ˈfɪks, -ɪz, -ɪŋ, -t
AM ˌpoʊs(t)ˈfɪks, -ɪz, -ɪŋ, -t

Postgate
BR ˈpəʊs(t)geɪt
AM ˈpoʊs(t)ˌgeɪt

postglacial
BR ˌpəʊs(t)ˈgleɪʃl, ˌpəʊs(t)ˈgleɪsɪəl
AM ˌpoʊs(t)ˈgleɪʃəl

postgrad
BR ˌpəʊs(t)ˈgrad, -z
AM ˌpoʊs(t)ˈgræd, -z

postgraduate
BR ˌpəʊs(t)ˈgradʒʊət, ˌpəʊs(t)ˈgradjʊət, -s
AM ˌpoʊs(t)ˈgrædʒəwət, -s

posthaste
BR ˌpəʊstˈheɪst
AM ˌpoʊs(t)ˈheɪst

post hoc
BR ˌpəʊst ˈhɒk
AM ˌpoʊs(t) ˈhɑk

posthole
BR ˈpəʊsthəʊl, -z
AM ˈpoʊs(t)ˌ(h)oʊl, -z

posthorn
BR ˈpəʊsthɔːn, -z
AM ˈpoʊs(t)ˌ(h)ɔ(ə)rn, -z

posthumous
BR ˈpɒstʃʉməs, ˈpɒstjʉməs
AM ˈpɑstʃəməs, pɑˈst(j)uməs

posthumously
BR ˈpɒstʃʉməsli, ˈpɒstjʉməsli
AM ˈpɑstʃəməsli, pɑˈst(j)uməsli

postiche
BR pɒˈstiːʃ, -ɪz
AM pɑˈstiʃ, ˈpɑˌstiʃ, -ɪz

postie
BR ˈpəʊst|i, -ɪz
AM ˈpoʊsti, -z

postil
BR ˈpɒstɪl, -z
AM ˈpɑstl, -z

postilion
BR pɒˈstɪlɪən, pəˈstɪlɪən, -z
AM pəˈstɪljən, poʊˈstɪljən, -z

postillion
BR pɒˈstɪlɪən, pəˈstɪlɪən, -z
AM pəˈstɪljən, poʊˈstɪljən, -z

posting
BR ˈpəʊstɪŋ, -z
AM ˈpoʊstɪŋ, -z

Postlethwaite
BR ˈpɒslθweɪt
AM ˈpɑsəlˌweɪt

postliminy
BR ˌpəʊs(t)ˈlɪmɪn|i, -ɪz
AM ˌpoʊs(t)ˈlɪməni, -z

postlude
BR ˈpəʊs(t)luːd, -z
AM ˈpoʊs(t)ˌlud, -z

postman
BR ˈpəʊs(t)mən
AM ˈpoʊs(t)mən

postman's knock
BR ˌpəʊs(t)mənz ˈnɒk
AM ˌpoʊs(t)mənz ˈnɑk

postmark
BR ˈpəʊs(t)mɑːk, -s, -ɪŋ, -t
AM ˈpoʊs(t)ˌmɑrk, -s, -ɪŋ, -t

postmaster
BR ˈpəʊs(t)ˌmɑːstə(r), ˈpəʊs(t)ˌmastə(r), -z
AM ˈpoʊs(t)ˌmæstər, -z

postmen
BR ˈpəʊs(t)mən
AM ˈpoʊs(t)mən

post meridian
BR ˌpəʊs(t) mɪˈrɪdɪən
AM ˌpoʊs(t) məˈrɪdiən

post meridiem
BR pəʊs(t) mɪˈrɪdɪəm
AM ˌpoʊs(t) məˈrɪdiəm

postmistress
BR ˈpəʊs(t)ˌmɪstrɪs, -ɪz
AM ˈpoʊs(t)ˌmɪstrɪs, -ɪz

postmodern
BR ˌpəʊs(t)ˈmɒd(ə)n
AM ˌpoʊs(t)ˈmɑdərn

postmodernism
BR ˌpəʊs(t)ˈmɒdn̩ɪz(ə)m, ˌpəʊs(t)ˈmɒdənɪz(ə)m
AM ˌpoʊs(t)ˈmɑdərnˌɪzəm

postmodernist
BR ˌpəʊs(t)ˈmɒdn̩ɪst, ˌpəʊs(t)ˈmɒdənɪst, -s
AM ˌpoʊs(t)ˈmɑdərnəst, -s

postmodernity
BR ˌpəʊs(t)məˈdəːnɪti, ˌpəʊs(t)mɒˈdəːnɪti
AM ˌpoʊs(t)məˈdərnədi, ˌpoʊs(t)moʊˈdərnədi, ˌpoʊs(t)mɑˈdɛrnədi, ˌpoʊs(t)məˈdɛrnədi

postmortem
BR ˌpəʊs(t)ˈmɔːtəm, -z
AM ˌpous(t)ˈmɔrtəm, -z

postop
BR ˌpəʊstˈɒp
AM ˈpoʊsˌtɑp

postoperative
BR ˌpəʊstˈɒp(ə)rətɪv
AM ˌpoʊsˈtɑpərədɪv

postpaid
BR ˌpəʊs(t)ˈpeɪd
AM ˌpoʊs(t)ˈpeɪd

post-partum
BR ˌpəʊs(t)ˈpɑːtəm
AM ˌpoʊs(t)ˈpɑrdəm

postponable
BR pə'spəʊnəbl, ˌpəʊs(t)'pəʊnəbl
AM ˌpoʊs(t)'poʊnəbəl, pə'spoʊnəbəl

postpone
BR pə'spəʊn, ˌpəʊs(t)'pəʊn, -z, -ɪŋ, -d
AM ˌpoʊs(t)'poʊn, pə'spoʊn, -z, -ɪŋ, -d

postponement
BR pə'spəʊnm(ə)nt, ˌpəʊs(t)'pəʊnm(ə)nt, -s
AM ˌpoʊs(t)'poʊnmənt, pə'spoʊnmənt, -s

postponer
BR pə'spəʊnə(r), ˌpəʊs(t)'pəʊnə(r), -z
AM ˌpoʊs(t)'poʊnər, pə'spoʊnər, -z

postposition
BR ˌpəʊs(t)pə'zɪʃn, -z
AM ˌpoʊs(t)pə'zɪʃən, -z

postpositional
BR ˌpəʊs(t)pə'zɪʃn̩(ə)l, ˌpəʊs(t)pə'zɪʃən(ə)l
AM ˌpoʊs(t)pə'zɪʃ(ə)nəl

postpositive
BR ˌpəʊs(t)'pɒzɨtɪv
AM ˌpoʊs(t)'pɑzədɪv

postpositively
BR ˌpəʊs(t)'pɒzɨtɨvli
AM ˌpoʊs(t)'pɑzədɨvli

postprandial
BR ˌpəʊs(t)'prandɪəl
AM ˌpoʊs(t)'prændiəl

post room
BR 'pəʊst ruːm, + rʊm, -z
AM 'poʊs(t) ˌrum, + ˌrʊm, -z

postscript
BR 'pəʊs(t)skrɪpt, -s
AM 'poʊs(t)ˌskrɪpt, -s

postulant
BR 'pɒstjʉlənt, 'pɒstjʉln̩t, 'pɒstʃʉlənt, 'pɒstʃʉln̩t, -s
AM 'pɑstʃələnt, -s

postulate[1]
noun
BR 'pɒstjʉlət, 'pɒstʃʉlət, -s
AM 'pɑstʃələt, -s

postulate[2]
verb
BR 'pɒstjʉleɪt, 'pɒstʃʉleɪt, -s, -ɪŋ, -ɪd
AM 'pɑstʃəˌleɪ|t, -ts, -dɪŋ, -dɪd

postulation
BR ˌpɒstjʉ'leɪʃn, ˌpɒstʃʉ'leɪʃn, -z
AM ˌpɑstʃə'leɪʃən, -z

postulator
BR 'pɒstjʉleɪtə(r), 'pɒstʃʉleɪtə(r), -z
AM 'pɑstʃəˌleɪdər, -z

postural
BR 'pɒstʃʉrəl, 'pɒstʃʉrl̩
AM 'pɑstʃərəl

posture
BR 'pɒstʃ|ə(r), -əz, -(ə)rɪŋ, -əd
AM 'pɑstʃər, -z, -ɪŋ, -d

posturer
BR 'pɒstʃ(ə)rə(r), -z
AM 'pɑstʃərər, -z

posturing
BR 'pɒstʃ(ə)rɪŋ, -z
AM 'pɑstʃərɪŋ, -z

postvocalic
BR ˌpəʊs(t)və'kalɪk
AM ˌpoʊs(t)voʊ'kælɪk

postwar
BR ˌpəʊs(t)'wɔː(r)
AM ˈpoʊs(t)'wɔ(ə)r

postwoman
BR 'pəʊs(t)ˌwʊmən
AM 'poʊs(t)ˌwʊmən

postwomen
BR 'pəʊs(t)ˌwɪmɪn
AM 'poʊs(t)ˌwɪmɨn

posy
BR 'pəʊz|i, -ɪz
AM 'poʊzi, -z

pot
BR pɒt, -s, -ɪŋ, -ɨd
AM pɑ|t, -ts, -dɪŋ, -dəd

potability
BR ˌpəʊtə'bɪlɨti
AM ˌpoʊdə'bɪlɨdi

potable
BR 'pəʊtəbl
AM 'poʊdəbəl

potableness
BR 'pəʊtəblnəs
AM 'poʊdəbəlnəs

potage
BR pɒ'tɑːʒ, 'pɒtɑːʒ, -ɪz
AM poʊ'tɑʒ, -əz

potager
BR 'pɒtədʒə(r), -z
AM poʊ'tɑʒər, -z

potamic
BR pə'tamɪk, pɒ'tamɪk
AM pə'tæmɪk

potamology
BR ˌpɒtə'mɒlədʒi
AM ˌpɑdə'mɑlədʒi

potash
BR 'pɒtaʃ
AM 'pɑdˌæʃ

potassic
BR pə'tasɪk
AM pə'tæsɪk

potassium
BR pə'tasɪəm
AM pə'tæsiəm, poʊ'tæsiəm

potation
BR pə(ʊ)'teɪʃn, -z
AM poʊ'teɪʃən, -z

potato
BR pə'teɪtəʊ, -z
AM pə'teɪdoʊ, -z

potatory
BR 'pəʊtət(ə)ri
AM 'poʊdəˌtɔri

pot-au-feu
BR ˌpɒtɔː'fəː(r), -z
AM ˈpɔdˌoʊ'fə, -z

potbelly
BR 'pɒtˌbɛl|i, ˌpɒt'bɛl|i, -ɪz
AM 'pɑtˌbɛli, -z

potboiler
BR 'pɒtˌbɔɪlə(r), -z
AM 'pɑtˌbɔɪlər, -z

potbound
BR 'pɒtbaʊnd
AM 'pɑtˌbaʊnd

potch
BR pɒtʃ, -ɪz
AM pɑtʃ, -əz

poteen
BR pɒ't(ʃ)iːn, pə't(ʃ)iːn
AM pɑ'tin, poʊ'tin

Potemkin
BR pə'tɛmkɪn
AM pə'tɛm(p)kən

potence
BR 'pəʊtns
AM 'poʊtns

potency
BR 'pəʊtnsi
AM 'poʊtnsi

potent
BR 'pəʊtnt
AM 'poʊtnt

potentate
BR 'pəʊtnteɪt, -s
AM 'poʊtnˌteɪt, -s

potential
BR pə'tɛnʃl, -z
AM pə'tɛn(t)ʃəl, -z

potentiality
BR pəˌtɛnʃɪ'alɨt|i, -ɪz
AM pəˌtɛn(t)ʃi'ælədi, -z

potentially
BR pə'tɛnʃl̩i, pə'tɛnʃəli
AM pə'tɛn(t)ʃəli

potentiate
BR pə'tɛnʃɪeɪt, -s, -ɪŋ, -ɨd
AM pə'tɛn(t)ʃieɪ|t, -ts, -dɪŋ, -dɨd

potentilla
BR ˌpəʊt(ə)n'tɪlə(r), -z
AM ˌpoʊtn'tɪlə, -z

potentiometer
BR pəˌtɛnʃɪ'ɒmɨtə(r), -z
AM pəˌtɛn(t)ʃi'ɑmədər, -z

potentiometric
BR pəˌtɛnʃɪə'mɛtrɪk
AM pəˌtɛn(t)ʃiə'mɛtrɪk

potentiometry
BR pəˌtɛnʃɪ'ɒmɨtri
AM pəˌtɛn(t)ʃi'ɑmətri

potentisation
BR ˌpəʊtntʌɪ'zeɪʃn
AM ˌpoʊtn(t)ə'zeɪʃən, ˌpoʊtnˌ(t)aɪ'zeɪʃən

potentise
BR 'pəʊtntʌɪz, -ɨz, -ɪŋ, -d
AM 'poʊtnˌtaɪz, -ɨz, -ɪŋ, -d

potentization
BR ˌpəʊtntʌɪ'zeɪʃn
AM ˌpoʊtn(t)ə'zeɪʃən, ˌpoʊtnˌ(t)aɪ'zeɪʃən

potentize
BR 'pəʊtntʌɪz, -ɨz, -ɪŋ, -d
AM 'poʊtnˌtaɪz, -ɨz, -ɪŋ, -d

potently
BR 'pəʊtntli
AM 'poʊtn(t)li

potful
BR 'pɒtfʊl, -z
AM 'pɑtˌfʊl, -z

pothead
BR 'pɒthɛd, -z
AM 'pɑtˌ(h)ɛd, -z

potheen
BR pɒ't(ʃ)iːn, pə't(ʃ)iːn
AM pɑ'tin, poʊ'tin

pother
BR 'pɒð|ə(r), -əz, -(ə)rɪŋ, -əd
AM 'pɑðər, -z, -ɪŋ, -d

potherb
BR 'pɒthəːb, -z
AM 'pɑtˌ(h)ərb, -z

pothole
BR 'pɒthəʊl, -z, -ɪŋ, -d
AM 'pɑtˌ(h)oʊl, -z, -ɪŋ, -d

potholer
BR 'pɒthəʊlə(r), -z
AM 'pɑtˌ(h)oʊlər, -z

pothook
BR 'pɒthʊk, -s
AM 'pɑtˌ(h)ʊk, -s

pothouse
BR 'pɒthaʊ|s, -zɨz
AM 'pɑtˌ(h)aʊ|s, -zəz

potiche
BR pɒ'tiːʃ, pə'tiːʃ, -ɨz
AM poʊ'tiʃ, -ɨz

potion
BR 'pəʊʃn, -z
AM 'poʊʃən, -z

Potiphar
BR 'pɒtɪfə(r), 'pɒtɪfɑː(r)
AM 'pɑdəfər

potlatch
BR ˈpɒtlatʃ, -ɪz
AM ˈpɑtˌlætʃ, -əz

potlatching
BR ˈpɒtˌlatʃɪŋ
AM ˈpɑtˌlætʃɪŋ

Potomac
BR pəˈtəʊmak
AM pəˈtoʊmək

potoroo
BR ˌpəʊtəˈruː, ˌpɒtəˈruː, -z
AM ˌpoʊdəˈru, -z

potpie
BR ˈpɒtpʌɪ
AM ˈpɑtˈpaɪ

potpourri
BR ˌpəʊˈpʊriː, ˌpəʊpʊˈriː, -z
AM ˌpoʊpəˈri, -z

potrero
BR pəˈtrɛːrəʊ, -z
AM pəˈtrɛˌroʊ, -z

Potsdam
BR ˈpɒtsdam
AM ˈpɑtsˌdæm

potsherd
BR ˈpɒt-ʃəːd, -z
AM ˈpɑtˌʃərd, -z

potshot
BR ˈpɒt-ʃɒt, -s
AM ˈpɑtˌʃɑt, -s

potstone
BR ˈpɒtstəʊn
AM ˈpɑtˌstoʊn

pottage
BR ˈpɒtɪdʒ
AM ˈpɑdɪdʒ

potter
BR ˈpɒt|ə(r), -əz, -(ə)rɪŋ, -əd
AM ˈpɑdər, -z, -ɪŋ, -d

potterer
BR ˈpɒt(ə)rə(r), -z
AM ˈpɑdərər, -z

Potteries
BR ˈpɒt(ə)rɪz
AM ˈpɑdəriz

pottery
BR ˈpɒt(ə)r|i, -ɪz
AM ˈpɑdəri, -z

pottiness
BR ˈpɒtɪnɨs
AM ˈpɑdinɨs

pottle
BR ˈpɒtl, -z
AM ˈpɑdəl, -z

potto
BR ˈpɒtəʊ, -z
AM ˈpɑˌdoʊ, -z

Potts
BR pɒts
AM pɑts

potty
BR ˈpɒt|i, -ɪz, -ɪə(r), -ɪɪst
AM ˈpɑdi, -z, -ər, -ɨst

pouch
BR paʊtʃ, -ɪz, -ɪŋ, -t
AM paʊtʃ, -əz, -ɪŋ, -t

pouchy
BR ˈpaʊtʃ|i, -ɪə(r), -ɪɪst
AM ˈpaʊtʃi, -ər, -ɨst

pouf¹
homosexual
BR pʊf, puːf, -s
AM puf, -s

pouf²
seat, hair
BR puːf, -s
AM puf, -s

pouffe¹
homosexual
BR pʊf, puːf, -s
AM puf, -s

pouffe²
seat, hair
BR puːf, -s
AM puf, -s

Poughkeepsie
BR pəˈkɪpsi
AM pəˈkɪpsi

poulard
BR puːˈlɑːd, -z
AM puˈlɑrd, -z

Poulenc
BR ˈpuːlaŋk
AM puˈlɛŋk

Poulson
BR ˈpəʊls(ə)n
AM ˈpɔlsən, ˈpoʊlsən

poult¹
chicken
BR pəʊlt, -s
AM poʊlt, -s

poult²
fabric
BR puːlt, pʊlt
AM pu(lt)

poult-de-soie
BR ˌpuːdəˈswɑː(*r*)
AM ˌpudəˈswɑ

Poulteney
BR ˈpəʊltni
AM ˈpoʊltni

Poulter
BR ˈpəʊltə(r)
AM ˈpoʊltər

poulterer
BR ˈpəʊlt(ə)rə(r), -z
AM ˈpoʊltərər, -z

poultice
BR ˈpəʊltɪs, -ɪz
AM ˈpoʊltəs, -ɪz

Poultney
BR ˈpəʊltni
AM ˈpoʊltni

Poulton
BR ˈpəʊlt(ə)n
AM ˈpoʊltən

poultry
BR ˈpəʊltri
AM ˈpoʊltri

poultryman
BR ˈpəʊltrɪmən
AM ˈpoʊltrimən

poultrymen
BR ˈpəʊltrɪmən
AM ˈpoʊltrimən

pounce
BR paʊns, -ɪz, -ɪŋ, -t
AM paʊns, -əz, -ɪŋ, -t

pouncer
BR ˈpaʊnsə(r), -z
AM ˈpaʊnsər, -z

pouncet-box
BR ˈpaʊnsɪtbɒks, -ɪz
AM ˈpaʊnsətˌbɑks, -əz

pound
BR paʊnd, -z, -ɪŋ, -ɨd
AM paʊnd, -z, -ɪŋ, -əd

poundage
BR ˈpaʊnd|ɪdʒ, -ɨdʒɪz
AM ˈpaʊndɪdʒ, -ɪz

poundal
BR ˈpaʊndl, -z
AM ˈpaʊndəl, -z

pounder
BR ˈpaʊndə(r), -z
AM ˈpaʊndər, -z

Pountney
BR ˈpaʊntni
AM ˈpoʊn(t)ni

pour
BR pɔː(r), -z, -ɪŋ, -d
AM pɔ(ə)r, -z, -ɪŋ, -d

pourable
BR ˈpɔːrəbl
AM ˈpɔrəbəl

pourboire
BR ˈpʊəbwɑː(r), ˈpɔːbwɑː(r), -z
AM pʊrˈbwɑr, -z

pourer
BR ˈpɔːrə(r), -z
AM ˈpɔrər, -z

pourparler
BR ˌpʊəˈpɑːleɪ, ˌpɔːˈpɑːleɪ, -z
AM ˈpʊrˌpɑrˈleɪ, -z

pousada
BR pə(ʊ)ˈsɑːdə(*r*), -z
AM poʊˈsadə, -z

poussette
BR puːˈsɛt, -s, -ɪŋ, -ɨd
AM puˈsɛ|t, -ts, -dɪŋ, -dɨd

Poussin
BR ˈpuːsan, ˈpuːsã
AM pʊˈsɛn

pout
BR paʊt, -s, -ɪŋ, -ɨd
AM paʊ|t, -ts, -dɪŋ, -dəd

pouter
BR ˈpaʊtə(r), -z
AM ˈpaʊdər, -z

poutingly
BR ˈpaʊtɪŋli
AM ˈpaʊdɪŋli

pouty
BR ˈpaʊt|i, -ɪə(r), -ɪɪst
AM ˈpaʊdi, -ər, -ɨst

poverty
BR ˈpɒvəti
AM ˈpɑvərdi

Povey
BR ˈpəʊvi
AM ˈpoʊvi

pow!
BR paʊ
AM paʊ

powan
BR ˈpəʊən, -z
AM ˈpoʊən, -z

powder
BR ˈpaʊd|ə(r), -əz, -(ə)rɪŋ, -əd
AM ˈpaʊdər, -z, -ɪŋ, -d

powderiness
BR ˈpaʊd(ə)rɪnɪs
AM ˈpaʊdərinɨs

powderpuff
BR ˈpaʊdəpʌf, -s
AM ˈpaʊdərˌpəf, -s

powdery
BR ˈpaʊd(ə)ri
AM ˈpaʊdəri

Powell
BR ˈpaʊ(ə)l, ˈpəʊ(ə)l
AM ˈpaʊəl

power
BR ˈpaʊə(r), -z, -ɪŋ, -d
AM ˈpaʊ(ə)r, -z, -ɪŋ, -d

powerboat
BR ˈpaʊəbəʊt, -s
AM ˈpaʊ(ə)rˌboʊt, -s

powerful
BR ˈpaʊəf(ʊ)l
AM ˈpaʊ(ə)rfəl

powerfully
BR ˈpaʊəfʊli, ˈpaʊəfl̩i
AM ˈpaʊ(ə)rfəli

powerfulness
BR ˈpaʊəf(ʊ)lnəs
AM ˈpaʊ(ə)rfəlnəs

powerhouse
BR ˈpaʊəhaʊ|s, -zɪz
AM ˈpaʊ(ə)rˌ(h)aʊ|s, -zəz

powerless
BR ˈpaʊələs
AM ˈpaʊ(ə)rləs

powerlessly
BR ˈpaʊələsli
AM ˈpaʊ(ə)rləsli

powerlessness
BR ˈpaʊələsnəs
AM ˈpaʊ(ə)rləsnəs

powerpack
BR ˈpaʊəpak, -s
AM ˈpaʊ(ə)rˌpæk, -s

powerpoint
BR ˈpaʊəpɔɪnt, -s
AM ˈpaʊ(ə)rˌpɔɪnt, -s

Powers
BR ˈpaʊəz

AM 'paʊərz

Powhatan
BR paʊ'hatn, 'paʊəˌtan
AM paʊ'hætn

Powis
BR 'pəʊɪs, 'paʊɪs
AM 'paʊɪs, 'poʊəs

powwow
BR 'paʊwaʊ, -z
AM 'paʊˌwaʊ, -z

Powys[1]
surname
BR 'pəʊɪs, 'paʊɪs
AM 'poʊəs
WE 'poʊɪs

Powys[2]
Welsh county
BR 'paʊɪs
AM 'paʊɪs
WE 'poʊɪs

pox
BR pɒks
AM pɑks

poxy
BR 'pɒks|i, -ɪə(r), -ɪɪst
AM 'pɑksi, -ər, -ɪst

Poznań
BR 'pɒznan
AM 'pɑznæn, 'poʊznæn
POL 'pɒznanʲ

pozzolana
BR ˌpɒtsə'lɑːnə(r)
AM ˌpɑtʃə'lɑnə

praam
BR pram, prɑːm, -z
AM præm, -z

practicability
BR ˌpraktɪkə'bɪlɪti
AM ˌpræktəkə'bɪlɨdi

practicable
BR 'praktɪkəbl
AM 'præktəkəbəl

practicableness
BR 'praktɪkəblnəs
AM 'præktəkəbəlnəs

practicably
BR 'praktɪkəbli
AM 'præktəkəbli

practical
BR 'praktɪkl
AM 'præktəkəl

practicality
BR ˌpraktɪ'kalɪt|i, -ɪz
AM ˌpræktə'kælədi, -z

practically[1]
almost
BR 'praktɪkli
AM 'præktək(ə)li

practically[2]
in a practical way
BR 'praktɪk(ə)li, 'praktɪkḷi
AM 'præktək(ə)li

practicalness
BR 'praktɪklnəs
AM 'præktəkəlnəs

practice
BR 'prakt|ɪs, -ɪsɪz
AM 'præktəs, -əz

practicer
BR 'praktɪsə(r), -z
AM 'præktəsər, -z

practicum
BR 'praktɪkəm, -z
AM 'præktəkəm, -z

practise
BR 'prakt|ɪs, -ɪsɪz, -ɪsɪŋ, -ɪst
AM 'præktəs, -əz, -ɪŋ, -t

practiser
BR 'praktɪsə(r), -z
AM 'præktəsər, -z

practitioner
BR prak'tɪʃn̩ə(r), prak'tɪʃ(ə)nə(r), -z
AM præk'tɪʃ(ə)nər, -z

prad
BR prad, -z
AM præd, -z

Prado
BR 'prɑːdəʊ
AM 'prɑˌdoʊ

praecipe
BR 'priːsɪp|i, -ɪz
AM 'prisəpi, -z

praecocial
BR prɪ'kəʊʃl
AM pri'koʊʃəl

praecox
BR 'priːkɒks
AM 'priˌkɑks

praedial
BR 'priːdɪəl
AM 'pridiəl

praemunire
BR ˌpriːmjuː'nɪəri, ˌpriːmjʊ'nɪəri
AM ˌprimjə'naɪri

praenomen
BR ˌpriː'nəʊmɛn, ˌpriː'nəʊmən, -z
AM pri'noʊmən, -z

praepostor
BR ˌpriː'pɒstə(r), -z
AM pri'pɑstər, -z

praesidia
BR prɪ'sɪdɪə(r), prɪ'zɪdɪə(r), prʌɪ'sɪdɪə(r), prʌɪ'zɪdɪə(r)
AM prə'sɪdiə, prə'zɪdiə

Praesidium
BR prɪ'sɪdɪəm, prɪ'zɪdɪəm, prʌɪ'sɪdɪəm, prʌɪ'zɪdɪəm, -z
AM prə'sɪdiəm, prə'zɪdiəm, -z

praetor
BR 'priːtə(r), 'priːtɔː(r), -z
AM 'pridər, -z

praetoria
BR prɪ'tɔːrɪə(r), priː'tɔːrɪə(r), prʌɪ'tɔːrɪə(r)
AM prə'tɔriə

praetorian
BR prɪ'tɔːrɪən, priː'tɔːrɪən, prʌɪ'tɔːrɪən
AM prə'tɔriən

praetorium
BR prɪ'tɔːrɪəm, priː'tɔːrɪəm, prʌɪ'tɔːrɪəm, -z
AM prə'tɔriəm, -z

praetorship
BR 'priːtəʃɪp, 'priːtɔːʃɪp, -s
AM 'pridərˌʃɪp, -s

pragmatic
BR prag'matɪk, -s
AM præg'mædɪk, -s

pragmatical
BR prag'matɪkl
AM præg'mædəkəl

pragmaticality
BR pragˌmatɪ'kalɪti
AM prægˌmædə'kælədi

pragmatically
BR prag'matɪkli
AM præg'mædək(ə)li

pragmatise
BR 'pragmətʌɪz, -ɪz, -ɪŋ, -d
AM 'prægməˌtaɪz, -ɪz, -ɪŋ, -d

pragmatism
BR 'pragmətɪz(ə)m
AM 'prægməˌtɪzəm

pragmatist
BR 'pragmətɪst, -s
AM 'prægmədəst, -s

pragmatistic
BR ˌpragmə'tɪstɪk
AM ˌprægmə'tɪstɪk

pragmatize
BR 'pragmətʌɪz, -ɪz, -ɪŋ, -d
AM 'prægməˌtaɪz, -ɪz, -ɪŋ, -d

Prague
BR prɑːg
AM prɑg

Praha
BR 'prɑːhɑː(r)
AM 'prɑˌhɑ
CZ 'prʌhʌ

prahu
BR 'prɑːhuː, -z
AM 'prɑˌhu, -z

Praia
BR 'prʌɪə(r)
AM 'praɪə

prairie
BR 'prɛːr|i, -ɪz
AM 'prɛri, -z

praise
BR preɪz, -ɪz, -ɪŋ, -d
AM preɪz, -ɪz, -ɪŋ, -d

praiseful
BR 'preɪzf(ʊ)l
AM 'preɪzfəl

praiser
BR 'preɪzə(r), -z
AM 'preɪzər, -z

praiseworthily
BR 'preɪzˌwəːðɪli
AM 'preɪzˌwərðəli

praiseworthiness
BR 'preɪzˌwəːðɪnɪs
AM 'preɪzˌwərðinɨs

praiseworthy
BR 'preɪzˌwəːði
AM 'preɪzˌwərði

Prakrit
BR 'prɑːkrɪt, -s
AM 'prɑˌkrɪt, -s

praline
BR 'prɑːliːn, 'preɪliːn, -z
AM 'preɪˌlin, -z

pralltriller
BR 'prɑːlˌtrɪlə(r), -z
AM 'prɑlˌtrɪlər, -z

pram
BR pram, -z
AM præm, -z

prana
BR 'prɑːnə(r)
AM 'prɑnə

pranayama
BR ˌprɑːnʌ'jɑːmə(r), ˌprɑːnə'jɑːmə(r)
AM ˌprɑnə'jɑmə

prance
BR prɑːns, prans, -ɪz, -ɪŋ, -t
AM præns, -əz, -ɪŋ, -t

prancer
BR 'prɑːnsə(r), 'pransə(r), -z
AM 'prænsər, -z

prandial
BR 'prandɪəl
AM 'prændiəl

Prandtl
BR 'prantl
AM 'prændl

prang
BR praŋ, -z, -ɪŋ, -d
AM præŋ, -z, -ɪŋ, -d

prank
BR praŋk, -s
AM præŋk, -s

prankful
BR 'praŋkf(ʊ)l
AM 'præŋkfəl

prankish
BR 'praŋkɪʃ
AM 'præŋkɪʃ

pranksome
BR 'praŋks(ə)m
AM 'præŋksəm

prankster
BR 'praŋkstə(r), -z

AM ˈpræŋkstər, -z

prase
BR preɪz
AM preɪz

praseodymium
BR ˌpreɪzɪə(ʊ)ˈdɪmɪəm
AM ˌpreɪzioʊˈdɪmiəm

prat
BR prat, -s
AM præt, -s

prate
BR preɪt, -s, -ɪŋ, -ɪd
AM preɪ|t, -ts, -dɪŋ, -dɪd

prater
BR ˈpreɪtə(r), -z
AM ˈpreɪdər, -z

pratfall
BR ˈpratfɔːl, -z
AM ˈprætˌfɔl, ˈprætˌfɑl, -z

pratie
BR ˈpreɪt|i, -ɪz
AM ˈpreɪdi, -z

pratincole
BR ˈpratɪŋkəʊl, -z
AM ˈprætnˌkoʊl, ˈprædɪŋˌkoʊl, -z

pratique
BR praˈtiːk, -s
AM præˈtik, prəˈtik, -s

Pratt
BR prat
AM præt

prattle
BR ˈprat|l, -lz, -l̩ɪŋ\-lɪŋ, -ld
AM ˈprædəl, -z, -ɪŋ, -d

prattler
BR ˈpratl̩ə(r), ˈpratlə(r), -z
AM ˈprædlər, -z

prau
BR prɑːuː, -z
AM praʊ, -z

Pravda
BR ˈprɑːvdə(r)
AM ˈprɑvdə

prawn
BR prɔːn, -z
AM prɔn, prɑn, -z

praxes
BR ˈpraksiːz
AM ˈprækˌsiz

praxis
BR ˈpraksɪs
AM ˈpræksəs

Praxiteles
BR prakˈsɪtɪliːz, prakˈsɪtl̩iːz
AM ˌprækˈsɪdəˌliz

pray
BR preɪ, -z, -ɪŋ, -d
AM preɪ, -z, -ɪŋ, -d

prayer[1]
person praying
BR ˈpreɪə(r), -z
AM ˈpreɪər, -z

prayer[2]
what is said to God
BR prɛː(r), -z
AM prɛ(ə)r, -z

prayerbook
BR ˈprɛːbʊk, -s
AM ˈprɛrˌbʊk, -s

prayerful
BR ˈprɛːf(ʉ)l
AM ˈprɛrfəl

prayerfully
BR ˈprɛːfʉli, ˈprɛːfl̩i
AM ˈprɛrfəli

prayerfulness
BR ˈprɛːf(ʉ)lnəs
AM ˈprɛrfəlnəs

prayerless
BR ˈprɛːləs
AM ˈprɛrləs

preach
BR priːtʃ, -ɪz, -ɪŋ, -t
AM pritʃ, -ɪz, -ɪŋ, -t

preachable
BR ˈpriːtʃəbl
AM ˈpritʃəbəl

preacher
BR ˈpriːtʃə(r), -z
AM ˈpritʃər, -z

preachify
BR ˈpriːtʃɪfʌɪ, -z, -ɪŋ, -d
AM ˈpritʃəˌfaɪ, -z, -ɪŋ, -d

preachiness
BR ˈpriːtʃɪnɪs
AM ˈpritʃinɪs

preaching
BR ˈpriːtʃɪŋ, -z
AM ˈpritʃɪŋ, -z

preachment
BR ˈpriːtʃm(ə)nt, -s
AM ˈpritʃmənt, -s

preachy
BR ˈpriːtʃi
AM ˈpritʃi

pre-adamite
BR ˌpriːˈadəmʌɪt
AM ˌpriˈædəˌmaɪt

pre-adolescence
BR ˌpriːadəˈlɛsns
AM ˌpriˌædəˈlɛsəns

pre-adolescent
BR ˌpriːadəˈlɛsnt, -s
AM ˌpriˌædəˈlɛsənt, -s

preamble
BR ˈpriːambl, prɪˈambl, -z
AM ˈpriˌæmbəl, -z

preambular
BR (ˌ)priːˈambjʉlə(r)
AM ˌpriˈæmbjələr

preamp
BR ˈpriːamp, -s
AM ˈpriˌæmp, -s

preamplified
BR (ˌ)priːˈamplɪfʌɪd
AM ˌpriˈæmpləˌfaɪd

preamplifier
BR (ˌ)priːˈamplɪfʌɪə(r), -z
AM ˌpriˈæmpləˌfaɪər, -z

preamplify
BR (ˌ)priːˈamplɪfʌɪ, -z, -ɪŋ, -d
AM ˌpriˈæmpləˌfaɪ, -z, -ɪŋ, -d

prearrange
BR ˌpriːəˈreɪn(d)ʒ, -ɪz, -ɪŋ, -d
AM ˌpriəˈreɪndʒ, -ɪz, -ɪŋ, -d

prearrangement
BR ˌpriːəˈreɪn(d)ʒm(ə)nt
AM ˌpriəˈreɪndʒmənt

preatomic
BR ˌpriːəˈtɒmɪk
AM ˌpriəˈtɑmɪk

prebend
BR ˈprɛb(ə)nd, -z
AM ˈprɛbənd, -z

prebendal
BR ˈprɛb(ə)ndl
AM ˈprɛbəndəl

prebendary
BR ˈprɛb(ə)nd(ə)r|i, -ɪz
AM ˈprɛbənˌdɛri, -z

prebendaryship
BR ˈprɛb(ə)nd(ə)rɪʃɪp, -s
AM ˈprɛbənˌdɛriˌʃɪp, -s

pre-book
BR ˌpriːˈbʊk, -s, -ɪŋ, -t
AM ˌpriˈbʊk, -s, -ɪŋ, -t

pre-bookable
BR ˌpriːˈbʊkəbl
AM ˌpriˈbʊkəbəl

Precambrian
BR (ˌ)priːˈkambrɪən
AM ˌpriˈkæmbriən

precancerous
BR ˌpriːˈkans(ə)rəs
AM ˌpriˈkæns(ə)rəs

precancerously
BR ˌpriːˈkans(ə)rəsli
AM ˌpriˈkæns(ə)rəsli

precarious
BR prɪˈkɛːrɪəs
AM prəˈkɛriəs

precariously
BR prɪˈkɛːrɪəsli
AM prəˈkɛriəsli

precariousness
BR prɪˈkɛːrɪəsnəs
AM prəˈkɛriəsnəs

precast
BR ˌpriːˈkɑːst, ˌpriːˈkast
AM ˈpriˌkæst

precative
BR ˈprɛkətɪv, -z
AM ˈprɛkədɪv, -z

precatory
BR ˈprɛkət(ə)ri
AM ˈprɛkəˌtɔri

precaution
BR prɪˈkɔːʃn, -z
AM priˈkɔʃən, prəˈkɔʃən, priˈkɑʃən, prəˈkɑʃən, -z

precautionary
BR prɪˈkɔːʃn̩(ə)ri
AM priˈkɔʃəˌnɛri, prəˈkɔʃəˌnɛri, priˈkɑʃəˌnɛri, prəˈkɑʃəˌnɛri

precede
BR ˌpriːˈsiːd, prɪˈsiːd
AM priˈsid, prəˈsid

precedence
BR ˈprɛsɪd(ə)ns
AM ˈprɛsədəns

precedency
BR ˈprɛsɪd(ə)ns|i, -ɪz
AM ˈprɛsədnsi, -z

precedent[1]
adjective
BR prɪˈsiːd(ə)nt
AM priˈsidnt, ˈprɛsədənt

precedent[2]
noun
BR ˈprɛsɪd(ə)nt, -s
AM ˈprɛsədnt, -s

precedented
BR ˈprɛsɪdɛntɪd
AM ˈprɛsəˌdɛn(t)əd

precedently
BR ˈprɛsɪd(ə)ntli
AM ˈprɛsəd(ə)n(t)li

precent
BR prɪˈsɛnt, ˌpriːˈsɛnt, -s, -ɪŋ, -ɪd
AM priˈsɛn|t, -ts, -(t)ɪŋ, -(t)əd

precentor
BR prɪˈsɛntə(r), ˌpriːˈsɛntə(r), -z
AM prəˈsɛn(t)ər, -z

precentorship
BR prɪˈsɛntəʃɪp, ˌpriːˈsɛntəʃɪp, -s
AM prəˈsɛn(t)ərˌʃɪp, -s

precentrices
BR prɪˈsɛntrɪsiːz, priːˈsɛntrɪsiːz
AM prəˈsɛntrəˌsiz

precentrix
BR prɪˈsɛntrɪks, ˌpriːˈsɛntrɪks, -ɪz
AM prəˈsɛntrɪks, -ɪz

precept
BR ˈpriːsɛpt, -s
AM ˈpriˌsɛpt, -s

preceptive
BR prɪˈsɛptɪv
AM prəˈsɛptɪv

preceptor
BR prɪˈsɛptə(r), -z
AM ˈpriˌsɛptər, -z

preceptorial
BR ˌpriːsɛpˈtɔːrɪəl, prɪˌsɛpˈtɔːrɪəl

AM priˌsɛp'tɔriəl
preceptorship
BR prɪ'sɛptəʃɪp, -s
AM 'priˌsɛptərˌʃɪp, -s
preceptress
BR prɪ'sɛptrɪs, -ɪz
AM pri'sɛptrəs, -əz
precession
BR prɪ'sɛʃn, -z
AM prə'sɛʃən, -z
processional
BR prɪ'sɛʃn̩(ə)l, prɪ'sɛʃən(ə)l
AM prə'sɛʃ(ə)nəl
precinct
BR 'priːsɪŋ(k)t, -s
AM 'priˌsɪŋ(k)t, 'priˌsɪŋk(t), -(t)s
preciosity
BR ˌprɛʃɪ'ɒsɪti, ˌprɛsɪ'ɒsɪti
AM ˌprɛʃi'ɑsədi
precious
BR 'prɛʃəs
AM 'prɛʃəs
preciously
BR 'prɛʃəsli
AM 'prɛʃəsli
preciousness
BR 'prɛʃəsnəs
AM 'prɛʃəsnəs
precipice
BR 'prɛsɪpɪs, -ɪz
AM 'prɛsəpəs, -əz
precipitability
BR prɪˌsɪpɪtə'bɪlɪti
AM ˌprɛsəˌpɪdə'bɪlɪdi
precipitable
BR prɪ'sɪpɪtəbl
AM prə'sɪpədəbəl
precipitance
BR prɪ'sɪpɪt(ə)ns
AM pri'sɪpədəns, prə'sɪpədns
precipitancy
BR prɪ'sɪpɪt(ə)nsi
AM pri'sɪpədənsi, prə'sɪpədnsi
precipitant
BR prɪ'sɪpɪt(ə)nt
AM pri'sɪpədənt, prə'sɪpədnt
precipitantly
BR prɪ'sɪpɪt(ə)ntli
AM pri'sɪpədən(t)li, prə'sɪpədən(t)li
precipitate[1]
adjective
BR prɪ'sɪpɪtət
AM pri'sɪpədət, prə'sɪpədət
precipitate[2]
verb
BR prɪ'sɪpɪteɪt, -s, -ɪŋ, -ɪd
AM pri'sɪpəˌteɪ|t, prə'sɪpəˌteɪ|t, -ts, -dɪŋ, -dɪd
precipitately
BR prɪ'sɪpɪtətli
AM pri'sɪpədətli, prə'sɪpədətli
precipitateness
BR prɪ'sɪpɪtətnəs
AM pri'sɪpədətnəs, prə'sɪpədətnəs
precipitation
BR prɪˌsɪpɪ'teɪʃn
AM priˌsɪpə'teɪʃən, prəˌsɪpə'teɪʃən
precipitator
BR prɪ'sɪpɪteɪtə(r), -z
AM pri'sɪpəˌteɪdər, prə'sɪpəˌteɪdər, -z
precipitin
BR prɪ'sɪpɪtɪn
AM prə'sɪpɪdɪn
precipitous
BR prɪ'sɪpɪtəs
AM pri'sɪpədəs, prə'sɪpədəs
precipitously
BR prɪ'sɪpɪtəsli
AM pri'sɪpədəsli, prə'sɪpədəsli
precipitousness
BR prɪ'sɪpɪtəsnəs
AM pri'sɪpədəsnəs, prə'sɪpədəsnəs
precis
singular noun, verb
BR 'preɪsiː, -z, -ɪŋ, -d
AM 'preɪsi, -z, -ɪŋ, -d
precise
BR prɪ'sʌɪs
AM pri'saɪs, prə'saɪs
precisely
BR prɪ'sʌɪsli
AM pri'saɪsli, prə'saɪsli
preciseness
BR prɪ'sʌɪsnɪs
AM pri'saɪsnɪs, prə'saɪsnɪs
precisian
BR prɪ'sɪʒn, -z
AM pri'sɪʒən, prə'sɪʒən, -z
precisianism
BR prɪ'sɪʒn̩ɪz(ə)m, prɪ'sɪʒənɪz(ə)m
AM pri'sɪʒəˌnɪzəm, prə'sɪʒəˌnɪzəm
precision
BR prɪ'sɪʒn
AM pri'sɪʒən, prə'sɪʒən
precisionism
BR prɪ'sɪʒn̩ɪz(ə)m, prɪ'sɪʒənɪz(ə)m
AM pri'sɪʒəˌnɪzəm, prə'sɪʒəˌnɪzəm
precisionist
BR prɪ'sɪʒn̩ɪst, prɪ'sɪʒənɪst, -s
AM pri'sɪʒənəst, prə'sɪʒənəst, -s
preclassical
BR ˌpriː'klasɪkl
AM prə'klæsəkəl
preclinical
BR ˌpriː'klɪnɪkl
AM prə'klɪnɪkəl
preclude
BR prɪ'kluːd, -z, -ɪŋ, -ɪd
AM pri'klud, prə'klud, -z, -ɪŋ, -əd
preclusion
BR prɪ'kluːʒn
AM pri'kluʒən, prə'kluʒən
preclusive
BR prɪ'kluːsɪv
AM pri'klusɪv, prə'klusɪv
precocial
BR prɪ'kəʊʃl, -z
AM prə'koʊʃəl, -z
precocious
BR prɪ'kəʊʃəs
AM prə'koʊʃəs
precociously
BR prɪ'kəʊʃəsli
AM prə'koʊʃəsli
precociousness
BR prɪ'kəʊʃəsnəs
AM prə'koʊʃəsnəs
precocity
BR prɪ'kɒsɪti
AM prə'kɑsədi
precognition
BR ˌpriːkɒg'nɪʃn, ˌpriːkəg'nɪʃn
AM ˌpriˌkɑg'nɪʃən
precognitive
BR ˌpriː'kɒgnɪtɪv
AM ˌpri'kɑgnədɪv
pre-coital
BR ˌpriː'kəʊɪtl, ˌpriː'kɔɪ(ɪ)tl
AM ˌpri'koʊədl
pre-coitally
BR ˌpriː'kəʊɪtl̩i, ˌpriː'kəʊɪtəli, ˌpriː'kɔɪ(ɪ)tl̩i, ˌpriː'kɔɪ(ɪ)təli
AM ˌpri'koʊədl̩i
pre-Columbian
BR ˌpriːkə'lʌmbɪən
AM ˌprikə'ləmbiən
precompensation
BR ˌpriːkɒmp(ə)n'seɪʃn, ˌpriːkɒmpɛn'seɪʃn
AM ˌpriˌkɑmpən'seɪʃən
preconceive
BR ˌpriːkən'siːv, -z, -ɪŋ, -d
AM ˌprikən'siv, -z, -ɪŋ, -d
preconception
BR ˌpriːkən'sɛpʃn, -z
AM ˌprikən'sɛpʃən, -z
preconcert
BR ˌpriːkən'səːt, -s, -ɪŋ, -ɪd
AM ˌpri'kɑnsər|t, -ts, -dɪŋ, -dəd
precondition
BR ˌpriːkən'dɪʃ|n, -nz, -n̩ɪŋ\-(ə)nɪŋ, -nd
AM ˌprikən'dɪʃən, -z, -ɪŋ, -d
preconisation
BR ˌpriːkənʌɪ'zeɪʃn
AM ˌprɛkənə'zeɪʃən, ˌprɛkəˌnaɪ'zeɪʃən
preconise
BR 'priːkənʌɪz, -ɪz, -ɪŋ, -d
AM 'prɛkəˌnaɪz, -ɪz, -ɪŋ, -d
preconization
BR ˌpriːkənʌɪ'zeɪʃn
AM ˌprɛkənə'zeɪʃən, ˌprɛkəˌnaɪ'zeɪʃən
preconize
BR 'priːkənʌɪz, -ɪz, -ɪŋ, -d
AM 'prɛkəˌnaɪz, -ɪz, -ɪŋ, -d
preconscious
BR ˌpriː'kɒnʃəs
AM pri'kɑnʃəs
preconsciousness
BR ˌpriː'kɒnʃəsnəs
AM pri'kɑnʃəsnəs
precook
BR ˌpriː'kʊk, -s, -ɪŋ, -t
AM ˌpri'kʊk, -s, -ɪŋ, -t
pre-cool
BR ˌpriː'kuːl, -z, -ɪŋ, -d
AM ˌpri'kul, -z, -ɪŋ, -d
precordial
BR ˌpriː'kɔːdɪəl
AM pri'kɔrdiəl
precostal
BR ˌpriː'kɒstl
AM pri'koʊstəl
precursive
BR prɪ'kəːsɪv, ˌpriː'kəːsɪv
AM pri'kərsɪv, prə'kərsɪv
precursor
BR prɪ'kəːsə(r), ˌpriː'kəːsə(r), -z
AM 'priˌkərsər, -z
precursory
BR prɪ'kəːs(ə)ri, ˌpriː'kəːs(ə)ri
AM pri'kərsəri, prə'kərsəri
pre-cut[1]
adjective
BR ˌpriː'kʌt
AM ˌpri'kət
pre-cut[2]
verb
BR ˌpriː'kʌt, -s, -ɪŋ
AM ˌpri'kə|t, -ts, -dɪŋ

predacious
BR prɪˈdeɪʃəs
AM prəˈdeɪʃəs
predaciousness
BR prɪˈdeɪʃəsnəs
AM prəˈdeɪʃəsnəs
predacity
BR prɪˈdasɨti
AM prəˈdæsədi
predate
prey upon
BR prɪˈdeɪt, -s, -ɪŋ, -ɨd
AM ˈprɛˌdeɪ|t, -ts, -dɪŋ, -dɨd
pre-date
give an earlier date
BR (ˌ)priːˈdeɪt, -s, -ɪŋ, -ɨd
AM ˈpriˌdeɪ|t, -ts, -dɪŋ, -dɨd
predation
BR prɪˈdeɪʃn
AM prəˈdeɪʃən
predator
BR ˈprɛdətə(r), -z
AM ˈprɛdədər, -z
predatorily
BR ˈprɛdət(ə)rɪli
AM ˈprɛdəˌtɔrəli
predatoriness
BR ˈprɛdət(ə)rɪnɪs
AM ˈprɛdəˌtɔrinɨs
predatory
BR ˈprɛdət(ə)ri
AM ˈprɛdəˌtɔri
predecease
BR ˌpriːdɪˈsiːs, -ɨz, -ɪŋ, -t
AM ˌpridəˈsis, -ɨz, -ɪŋ, -t
predecessor
BR ˈpriːdɪsɛsə(r), -z
AM ˈprɛdəˌsɛsər, ˈpridəˌsɛsər, -z
predella
BR prɪˈdɛlə(*r*), -z
AM prəˈdɛlə, -z
predestinarian
BR ˌpriːdɛstɪˈnɛːrɪən, -z
AM ˌpriˌdɛstəˈnɛriən, -z
predestinate
BR ˌpriːˈdɛstɨneɪt, prɪˈdɛstɨneɪt, -s, -ɪŋ, -ɨd
AM priˈdɛstəˌneɪ|t, -ts, -dɪŋ, -dɨd
predestination
BR priːˌdɛstɪˈneɪʃn, prɪˌdɛstɪˈneɪʃn, ˌpriːdɛstɪˈneɪʃn
AM priˌdɛstəˈneɪʃən
predestine
BR ˌpriːˈdɛst|(ɪ)n, prɪˈdɛst|(ɪ)n, -(ɪ)nz, -n̩ɪŋ\-ɨnɪŋ, -(ɪ)nd
AM priˈdɛstən, -z, -ɪŋ, -d
predeterminable
BR ˌpriːdɪˈtəːmɨnəbl
AM ˌpridəˈtərmənəbəl
predeterminate
BR ˌpriːdɪˈtəːmɨnət
AM ˌpridəˈtərmənət
predetermination
BR ˌpriːdɪˌtəːmɪˈneɪʃn
AM ˌpridəˌtɛrməˈneɪʃən
predetermine
BR ˌpriːdɪˈtəːmɪn, -z, -ɪŋ, -d
AM ˌpridəˈtɛrmən, -z, -ɪŋ, -d
predial
BR ˌpriːˈdʌɪəl, -z
AM priˈdaɪəl, -z
predicability
BR ˌprɛdɪkəˈbɪlɨti
AM ˌprɛdɪkəˈbɪlɨdi
predicable
BR ˈprɛdɪkəbl
AM ˈprɛdəkəbəl
predicament
BR prɪˈdɪkəm(ə)nt, -s
AM priˈdɪkəmənt, prəˈdɪkəmənt, -s
predicant
BR ˈprɛdɪk(ə)nt, -s
AM ˈprɛdəkənt, -s
predicate¹
noun
BR ˈprɛdɪkət, -s
AM ˈprɛdəkət, -s
predicate²
verb
BR ˈprɛdɪkeɪt, -s, -ɪŋ, -ɨd
AM ˈprɛdəˌkeɪ|t, -ts, -dɪŋ, -dɨd
predication
BR ˌprɛdɪˈkeɪʃn, -z
AM ˌprɛdəˈkeɪʃən, -z
predicative
BR prɪˈdɪkətɪv, -z
AM ˈprɛdəˌkeɪdɪv, ˈprɛdəkədɪv, -z
predicatively
BR prɪˈdɪkətɪvli
AM ˈprɛdəˌkeɪdɨvli, ˈprɛdəkədɨvli
predicator
BR ˈprɛdɪkeɪtə(r), -z
AM ˈprɛdəˌkeɪdər, -z
predicatory
BR ˈprɛdɪkət(ə)ri
AM ˈprɛdəkəˌtɔri
predict
BR prɪˈdɪkt, -s, -ɪŋ, -ɨd
AM priˈdɪk|(t), prəˈdɪk|(t), -(t)s, -tɪŋ, -tɨd
predictability
BR prɪˌdɪktəˈbɪlɨti
AM priˌdɪktəˈbɪlɨdi, prəˌdɪktəˈbɪlɨdi
predictable
BR prɪˈdɪktəbl
AM priˈdɪktəbəl, prəˈdɪktəbəl
predictably
BR prɪˈdɪktəbli
AM priˈdɪktəbli, prəˈdɪktəbli
prediction
BR prɪˈdɪkʃn, -z
AM priˈdɪkʃən, prəˈdɪkʃən, -z
predictive
BR prɪˈdɪktɪv
AM priˈdɪktɪv, prəˈdɪktɪv
predictively
BR prɪˈdɪktɨvli
AM priˈdɪktɨvli, prəˈdɪktɨvli
predictor
BR prɪˈdɪktə(r), -z
AM priˈdɪktər, prəˈdɪktər, -z
predigest
BR ˌpriːdʌɪˈdʒɛst, -s, -ɪŋ
AM ˌpridaɪˈdʒɛst, ˌpridəˈdʒɛst, -s, -ɪŋ
predigested
BR ˌpriːdʌɪˈdʒɛstɨd
AM ˌpridaɪˈdʒɛstəd, ˌpridəˈdʒɛst
predigestion
BR ˌpriːdʌɪˈdʒɛstʃn
AM ˌpridaɪˈdʒɛstʃən, ˌpridaɪˈdʒɛʃtʃən, ˌpridəˈdʒɛʃtʃən, ˌpridəˈdʒɛstʃən
predikant
BR ˌprɛdɪˈkant, -s
AM ˈprɛdəkənt, -s
predilection
BR ˌpriːdɪˈlɛkʃn
AM ˌprɛdlˈɛkʃən, ˌprɛdəˈlɛkʃən, ˌpridlˈɛkʃən, ˌpridəˈlɛkʃən
predispose
BR ˌpriːdɪˈspəʊz, -ɨz, -ɪŋ, -d
AM ˌpridəˈspoʊz, -əz, -ɪŋ, -d
predisposition
BR ˌpriːdɪspəˈzɪʃn, -z
AM ˌpridɪspəˈzɪʃən, -z
prednisone
BR ˈprɛdnɪzəʊn
AM ˈprɛdnəˌzoʊn, ˈprɛdnəˌsoʊn
predominance
BR prɪˈdɒmɨnəns
AM priˈdɑmənəns, prəˈdɑmənəns
predominant
BR prɪˈdɒmɨnənt
AM priˈdɑmənənt, prəˈdɑmənənt
predominantly
BR prɪˈdɒmɨnəntli
AM priˈdɑmənən(t)li, prəˈdɑmənən(t)li
predominate
BR prɪˈdɒmɨneɪt, -s, -ɪŋ, -ɨd
AM priˈdɑməˌneɪ|t, prəˈdɑməˌneɪ|t, -ts, -dɪŋ, -dɨd
predominately
BR prɪˈdɒmɨnətli
AM priˈdɑmənətli, prəˈdɑmənətli
predomination
BR prɪˌdɒmɪˈneɪʃn
AM prəˌdɑməˈneɪʃən, priˌdɑməˈneɪʃən
predoom
BR ˌpriːˈduːm, -z, -ɪŋ, -d
AM priˈdum, -z, -ɪŋ, -d
predorsal
BR ˌpriːˈdɔːsl
AM priˈdɔrsəl
predynastic
BR ˌpriːdɪˈnastɪk
AM ˌpriˌdaɪˈnæstɪk, ˌpridəˈnæstɪk
Preece
BR priːs
AM pris
pre-echo
BR ˌpriːˈɛkəʊ, -z, -ɪŋ, -d
AM priˈɛkoʊ, -z, -ɪŋ, -d
pre-eclampsia
BR ˌpriːɪˈklam(p)sɪə(*r*)
AM ˌpriˌɪˈklæm(p)siə
pre-eclamptic
BR ˌpriːɪˈklam(p)tɪk
AM ˌpriˌɪˈklæm(p)tɪk
Preedy
BR ˈpriːdi
AM ˈpridi
pre-elect
BR ˌpriːɪˈlɛkt, -s, -ɪŋ, -d
AM ˌpriəˈlɛk|(t), ˌpriˌiˈlɛk|(t), -(t)s, -tɪŋ, -əd
pre-election
BR ˌpriːɪˈlɛkʃn, -z
AM ˌpriəˈlɛkʃən, ˌpriˌiˈlɛkʃən, -z
pre-embryonic
BR ˌpriːɛmbrɪˈɒnɪk
AM ˌpriˌɛmbriˈɑnɪk
preemie
BR ˈpriːm|i, -ɪz
AM ˈprimi, -z
preeminence
BR ˌpriːˈɛmɨnəns, prɪˈɛmɨnəns
AM priˈɛmənəns
preeminent
BR ˌpriːˈɛmɨnənt, prɪˈɛmɨnənt
AM priˈɛmənənt
preeminently
BR ˌpriːˈɛmɨnəntli, prɪˈɛmɨnəntli
AM priˈɛmənən(t)li

preempt
BR ˌpriːˈɛm(p)t, prɪˈɛm(p)t, -s, -ɪŋ, -ɪd
AM priˈɛm(p)t, -s, -ɪŋ, -əd

preemption
BR ˌpriːˈɛm(p)ʃn, prɪˈɛm(p)ʃn
AM priˈɛm(p)ʃən

preemptive
BR ˌpriːˈɛm(p)tɪv, prɪˈɛm(p)tɪv
AM priˈɛm(p)tɪv

preemptively
BR ˌpriːˈɛm(p)tɨvli, prɪˈɛm(p)tɨvli
AM priˈɛm(p)tɨvli

preemptor
BR ˌpriːˈɛm(p)tə(r), prɪˈɛm(p)tə(r), -z
AM priˈɛm(p)tər, -z

preemptory
BR ˌpriːˈɛm(p)t(ə)r|i, prɪˈɛm(p)t(ə)r|i, -ɪz
AM priˈɛm(p)təri, -z

preen
BR priːn, -z, -ɪŋ, -d
AM prin, -z, -ɪŋ, -d

preener
BR ˈpriːnə(r), -z
AM ˈprinər, -z

pre-engage
BR ˌpriːɪnˈgeɪdʒ, ˌpriːɛnˈgeɪdʒ, ˌpriːɪŋˈgeɪdʒ, ˌpriːɛŋˈgeɪdʒ, -ɪz, -ɪŋ, -d
AM ˈˌpriɪnˈgeɪdʒ, -ɪz, -ɪŋ, -d

preengagement
BR ˌpriːɪnˈgeɪdʒm(ə)nt, ˌpriːɛnˈgeɪdʒm(ə)nt, ˌpriːɪŋˈgeɪdʒm(ə)nt, ˌpriːɛŋˈgeɪdʒm(ə)nt, -s
AM ˈˌpriɪnˈgeɪdʒmənt, -s

pre-establish
BR ˌpriːɪˈstablˌɪʃ, -ɪʃɪz, -ɪʃɪŋ, -ɪʃt
AM ˈˌpriɪˈstæblɪʃ, -ɪz, -ɪŋ, -t

preexist
BR ˌpriːɪgˈzɪst, ˌpriːɛgˈzɪst, -s, -ɪŋ, -ɪd
AM ˈˌpriɪgˈzɪst, -s, -ɪŋ, -ɪd

preexistence
BR ˌpriːɪgˈzɪst(ə)ns, ˌpriːɛgˈzɪst(ə)ns
AM ˈˌpriɪgˈzɪstəns

preexistent
BR ˌpriːɪgˈzɪst(ə)nt, ˌpriːɛgˈzɪst(ə)nt
AM ˈˌpriɪgˈzɪstənt

prefab
BR ˈpriːfab, -z
AM priˈfæb, ˈpriˌfæb, -z

prefabricate
BR ˌpriːˈfabrɪkeɪt, -s, -ɪŋ, -ɪd
AM priˈfæbrəˌkeɪ|t, -ts, -dɪŋ, -dɪd

prefabrication
BR ˌpriːfabrɪˈkeɪʃn, prɪˌfabrɪˈkeɪʃn
AM ˈˌpriˌfæbrəˈkeɪʃən

preface
BR ˈprɛfɪs, -ɪz, -ɪŋ, -t
AM ˈprɛfəs, -əz, -ɪŋ, -t

prefatorial
BR ˌprɛfəˈtɔːrɪəl
AM ˌprɛfəˈtɔriəl

prefatory
BR ˈprɛfət(ə)ri
AM ˈprɛfəˌtɔri

prefect
BR ˈpriːfɛkt, -s
AM ˈpriˌfɛk(t), -(t)s

prefectoral
BR prɪˈfɛkt(ə)rəl, prɪˈfɛkt(ə)rl̩
AM priˈfɛkt(ə)rəl

prefectorial
BR ˌpriːfɛkˈtɔːrɪəl
AM ˈˌpriˌfɛkˈtɔriəl

prefectural
BR prɪˈfɛktʃ(ə)rəl, prɪˈfɛktʃ(ə)rl̩
AM priˈfɛk(t)ʃ(ə)rəl

prefecture
BR ˈpriːfɛktʃ(ʊ)ə(r), -z
AM ˈpriˌfɛktʃər, -z

prefer
BR prɪˈfəː(r), -z, -ɪŋ, -d
AM priˈfər, prəˈfər, -z, -ɪŋ, -d

preferability
BR ˌprɛf(ə)rəˈbɪlɨti
AM ˌprɛf(ə)rəˈbɪlɨdi

preferable
BR ˈprɛf(ə)rəbl
AM ˈprɛf(ə)rəbəl

preferably
BR ˈprɛf(ə)rəbli
AM ˈprɛf(ə)rəbli, ˈprɛfərbli

preference
BR ˈprɛf(ə)rəns, ˈprɛf(ə)rn̩s, -ɪz
AM ˈprɛf(ə)rəns, -əz

preferential
BR ˌprɛfəˈrɛnʃl
AM ˌprɛfəˈrɛn(t)ʃəl

preferentially
BR ˌprɛfəˈrɛnʃl̩i, ˌprɛfəˈrɛnʃəli
AM ˌprɛfəˈrɛn(t)ʃəli

preferment
BR prɪˈfəːm(ə)nt, -s
AM priˈfərmənt, prəˈfərmənt, -s

prefiguration
BR ˌpriːfɪgəˈreɪʃn, ˌpriːfɪgjʊˈreɪʃn, priːˌfɪgəˈreɪʃn, priːˌfɪgjʊˈreɪʃn
AM priˌfɪgjəˈreɪʃən

prefigurative
BR (ˌ)priːˈfɪg(ə)rətɪv, (ˌ)priːˈfɪgjʊrətɪv
AM priˈfɪgjərədɪv, priˈfɪgjəˌreɪdɪv

prefigure
BR (ˌ)priːˈfɪg|ə(r), -əz, -(ə)rɪŋ, -əd
AM priˈfɪgjər, -z, -ɪŋ, -d

prefigurement
BR (ˌ)priːˈfɪgəm(ə)nt
AM priˈfɪgjərmənt

prefix
BR ˈpriːfɪks, -ɪz, -ɪŋ, -t
AM ˈpriˌfɪks, -ɪz, -ɪŋ, -t

prefixation
BR ˌpriːfɪkˈseɪʃn
AM ˌprifɪkˈseɪʃən

prefixion
BR (ˌ)priːˈfɪkʃn
AM priˈfɪkʃən

prefixture
BR (ˌ)priːˈfɪkstʃə(r)
AM priˈfɪk(st)ʃər

preflight
BR ˌpriːˈflʌɪt, -s, -ɪŋ, -ɪd
AM ˈpriˈflaɪ|t, -ts, -dɪŋ, -dɪd

preform
BR ˌpriːˈfɔːm, -z, -ɪŋ, -d
AM priˈfɔ(ə)rm, -z, -ɪŋ, -d

preformation
BR ˌpriːfɔːˈmeɪʃn
AM ˈˌpriˌfɔrˈmeɪʃən

preformationist
BR ˌpriːfɔːˈmeɪʃn̩ɪst, ˌpriːfɔːˈmeɪʃənɪst, -s
AM ˈˌpriˌfɔrˈmeɪʃənəst, -s

preformative
BR ˌpriːˈfɔːmətɪv, -z
AM priˈfɔrmədɪv, -z

prefrontal
BR ˌpriːˈfrʌntl
AM priˈfrən(t)l

preglacial
BR ˌpriːˈgleɪʃl, ˌpriːˈgleɪsɪəl
AM priˈgleɪʃəl

pregnable
BR ˈprɛgnəbl
AM ˈprɛgnəbəl

pregnancy
BR ˈprɛgnəns|i, -ɪz
AM ˈprɛgnənsi, -z

pregnant
BR ˈprɛgnənt
AM ˈprɛgnənt

pregnantly
BR ˈprɛgnəntli
AM ˈprɛgnən(t)li

preheat
BR ˌpriːˈhiːt, -s, -ɪŋ, -ɪd
AM priˈhi|t, -ts, -dɪŋ, -dɪd

prehensile
BR ˌpriːˈhɛnsʌɪl, prɪˈhɛnsʌɪl
AM priˈhɛnsəl, prəˈhɛnsəl

prehensility
BR ˌpriːhɛnˈsɪlɨti
AM ˈˌpriˌhɛnˈsɪlɨdi

prehension
BR prɪˈhɛnʃn
AM priˈhɛn(t)ʃən

prehistorian
BR ˌpriːhɪˈstɔːrɪən, -z
AM ˈˌprihɪˈstɔriən, -z

prehistoric
BR ˌpriːhɪˈstɒrɪk
AM ˈˌprihɪˈstɔrɪk

prehistorically
BR ˌpriːhɪˈstɒrɪkli
AM ˈˌpri(h)ɪˈstɔrək(ə)li

prehistory
BR ˌpriːˈhɪst(ə)ri
AM priˈhɪstəri

prejudge
BR ˌpriːˈdʒʌdʒ, -ɪz, -ɪŋ, -d
AM priˈdʒədʒ, -əz, -ɪŋ, -d

prejudgement
BR ˌpriːˈdʒʌdʒm(ə)nt, -s
AM priˈdʒədʒmənt, -s

prejudgment
BR ˌpriːˈdʒʌdʒm(ə)nt, -s
AM priˈdʒədʒmənt, -s

prejudice
BR ˈprɛdʒʊd|ɪs, -ɪsɪz, -ɪsɪŋ, -ɪst
AM ˈprɛdʒədəs, -əz, -ɪŋ, -t

prejudicial
BR ˌprɛdʒʊˈdɪʃl
AM ˌprɛdʒəˈdɪʃəl

prejudicially
BR ˌprɛdʒʊˈdɪʃl̩i, ˌprɛdʒʊˈdɪʃəli
AM ˌprɛdʒəˈdɪʃəli

prelacy
BR ˈprɛləs|i, -ɪz
AM ˈprɛləsi, -z

prelapsarian
BR ˌpriːlapˈsɛːrɪən
AM ˌpriˌlæpˈsɛriən

prelate
BR ˈprɛlət, -s
AM ˈprɛlət, -s

prelatic
BR prɪˈlatɪk
AM prəˈlædɪk

prelatical
BR prɪˈlatɪkl
AM prəˈlædəkəl

prelature
BR ˈprɛlətʃə(r), -z

AM 'prɛlətʃər, 'prɛlətʃʊ(ə)r, -z

prelect
BR prɪ'lɛkt, -s, -ɪŋ, -d
AM pri'lɛk|(t), -(t)s, -tɪŋ, -əd

prelection
BR prɪ'lɛkʃn, -z
AM pri'lɛkʃən, -z

prelector
BR prɪ'lɛktə(r), -z
AM pri'lɛktər, -z

prelibation
BR ˌpriːlʌɪ'beɪʃn, -z
AM ˌpriˌlaɪ'beɪʃən, -z

prelim
BR 'priːlɪm, prɪ'lɪm, -z
AM 'priˌlɪm, -z

preliminarily
BR prɪ'lɪmɪn(ə)rɪli
AM prəˌlɪmə'nɛrəli

preliminary
BR prɪ'lɪmɪn(ə)r|i, -ɪz
AM prə'lɪməˌnɛri, pri'lɪməˌnɛri, -z

preliterate
BR ˌpriː'lɪt(ə)rət
AM pri'lɪdərət

prelude
BR 'prɛljuːd, -z
AM 'prɛlˌjud, 'preɪˌlud, -z

preludial
BR prɪ'l(j)uːdɪəl
AM prə'l(j)udiəl

premarital
BR ˌpriː'marɪtl
AM pri'mɛrədl

premaritally
BR ˌpriː'marɪtl̩i, ˌpriː'marɪtəli
AM pri'mɛrədl̩i

premature
BR 'prɛmətʃə(r), 'prɛmətʃʊə(r), 'prɛmətjʊə(r), 'prɛmətʃɔː(r), 'prɛmətjɔː(r), ˌprɛmə'tʃɔː(r), ˌprɛmə'tjɔː(r)
AM ˌprimə'tʃər, ˌprimə'tʃʊ(ə)r

prematurely
BR 'prɛmətʃəli, 'prɛmətʃʊəli, 'prɛmətjʊəli, 'prɛmətʃɔːli, 'prɛmətjɔːli, ˌprɛmə'tʃɔːli, ˌprɛmə'tjɔːli
AM ˌprimə'tʃərli, ˌprimə'tʃʊrli

prematureness
BR 'prɛmətʃənəs, 'prɛmətʃʊənəs, 'prɛmətjʊənəs, 'prɛmətʃɔːnəs, 'prɛmətjɔːnəs, ˌprɛmə'tʃɔːnəs, ˌprɛmə'tjɔːnəs
AM ˌprimə'tʃərnəs, ˌprimə'tʃʊrnəs

prematurity
BR ˌprɛmə'tʃʊərɪti, ˌprɛmə'tjʊərɪti, ˌprɛmə'tʃɔːrɪti, ˌprɛmə'tjɔːrɪti
AM ˌprimə'tʃərədi, ˌprɛmə'tʃʊrədi

premaxillary
BR ˌpriːmak'sɪl(ə)ri
AM pri'mæksəˌlɛri

premed
BR ˌpriː'mɛd, -z
AM ˌpri'mɛd, -z

premedical
BR ˌpriː'mɛdɪkl
AM pri'mɛdəkəl

premedication
BR ˌpriːmɛdɪ'keɪʃn, prɪˌmɛdɪ'keɪʃn
AM ˌpriˌmɛdə'keɪʃən

premeditate
BR ˌpriː'mɛdɪteɪt, prɪ'mɛdɪteɪt, -s, -ɪŋ, -ɪd
AM pri'mɛdəˌteɪ|t, -ts, -dɪŋ, -dɪd

premeditatedly
BR ˌpriː'mɛdɪteɪtɪdli, prɪ'mɛdɪteɪtɪdli
AM pri'mɛdəˌteɪdɪdli

premeditation
BR ˌpriːmɛdɪ'teɪʃn, prɪˌmɛdɪ'teɪʃn
AM priˌmɛdə'teɪʃən

premenstrual
BR ˌpriː'mɛnstrʊəl, ˌpriː'mɛntrʊl
AM pri'mɛnztr(əw)əl, pri'mɛnstr(əw)əl

premenstrually
BR ˌpriː'mɛnstrʊəli, ˌpriː'mɛntrʊli
AM pri'mɛnztr(əw)əli, pri'mɛnstr(əw)əli

premia
BR 'priːmɪə(r)
AM 'primiə

premie
BR 'priːm|i, -ɪz
AM 'primi, -z

premier
BR 'prɛmɪə(r), -z
AM pri'mɪ(ə)r, prə'mɪ(ə)r, -z

première
BR 'prɛmɪɛː(r), -z, -ɪŋ, -d
AM pri'mɪ(ə)r, prə'mɪ(ə)r, -z, -ɪŋ, -d

premiership
BR 'prɛmɪəʃɪp, -s
AM pri'mɪrˌʃɪp, prə'mɪrˌʃɪp, -s

premillennial
BR ˌpriːmɪ'lɛnɪəl
AM ˌprimə'lɛniəl

premillennialism
BR ˌpriːmɪ'lɛnɪəlɪz(ə)m
AM ˌprimə'lɛniəˌlɪzəm

premillennialist
BR ˌpriːmɪ'lɛnɪəlɪst, -s
AM ˌprimə'lɛniələst, -s

premise[1]
noun
BR 'prɛm|ɪs, -ɪsɪz
AM 'prɛməs, -əz

premise[2]
verb
BR 'prɛm|ɪs, prɪ'mʌɪz, 'prɛmɪsɪz\prɪ'mʌɪzɪz, 'prɛmɪsɪŋ\prɪ'mʌɪzɪŋ, 'prɛmɪst\prɪ'mʌɪzd
AM 'prɛməs, -əz, -ɪŋ, -t

premises
plural noun
BR 'prɛmɪsɪz
AM 'prɛməsəz

premiss
BR 'prɛm|ɪs, -ɪsɪz
AM 'prɛməs, -əz

premium
BR 'priːmɪəm, -z
AM 'primiəm, -z

premolar
BR ˌpriː'məʊlə(r), -z
AM pri'moʊlər, -z

premonition
BR ˌprɛmə'nɪʃn, ˌpriːmə'nɪʃn, -z
AM ˌprimə'nɪʃən, ˌprɛmə'nɪʃən, -z

premonitor
BR prɪ'mɒnɪtə(r), -z
AM pri'mɑnədər, -z

premonitorily
BR prɪ'mɒnɪt(ə)rɪli
AM pri'mɑnəˌtɔrəli

premonitory
BR prɪ'mɒnɪt(ə)ri
AM pri'mɑnəˌtɔri

Premonstratensian
BR ˌpriːmɒnstrə'tɛnsɪən, -z
AM ˌprimɔnstrə'tɛnsiən, ˌprimɑnstrə'tɛnsiən, -z

premorse
BR ˌpriː'mɔːs
AM pri'mɔ(ə)rs

premotion
BR ˌpriː'məʊʃn
AM pri'moʊʃən

prenatal
BR ˌpriː'neɪtl
AM pri'neɪdl

prenatally
BR ˌpriː'neɪtl̩i
AM pri'neɪdl̩i

Prendergast
BR 'prɛndəgɑːst, 'prɛndəgast
AM 'prɛndərˌgæst

prentice
BR 'prɛnt|ɪs, -ɪsɪz
AM 'prɛn(t)əs, -əz

prenticeship
BR 'prɛntɪsʃɪp, -s
AM 'prɛn(t)əsˌʃɪp, -s

Prentiss
BR 'prɛntɪs
AM 'prɛn(t)əs

prenuptial
BR ˌpriː'nʌpʃl
AM pri'nəpʃəl

preoccupation
BR prɪˌɒkjʊ'peɪʃn, ˌpriːɒkjʊ'peɪʃn, -z
AM ˌpriˌɑkjə'peɪʃən, -z

preoccupy
BR prɪ'ɒkjʊpʌɪ, ˌpriː'ɒkjʊpʌɪ, -z, -ɪŋ, -d
AM pri'ɑkjəˌpaɪ, -z, -ɪŋ, -d

preocular
BR prɪ'ɒkjʊlə(r), ˌpriː'ɒkjʊlə(r)
AM pri'ɑkjələr

preop
BR ˌpriː'ɒp, -s
AM 'priˌɑp, -s

preoperative
BR ˌpriː'ɒp(ə)rətɪv
AM pri'ɑp(ə)rədɪv

preordain
BR ˌpriːɔː'deɪn, -z, -ɪŋ, -d
AM ˌpriɔr'deɪn, -z, -ɪŋ, -d

pre-owned
BR ˌpriː'əʊnd
AM ˌpri'oʊnd

prep
BR prɛp
AM prɛp

prepack
BR ˌpriː'pak, -s, -ɪŋ, -t
AM pri'pæk, -s, -ɪŋ, -t

prepackage
BR ˌpriː'pak|ɪdʒ, -ɪdʒɪz, -ɪdʒɪŋ, -ɪdʒd
AM pri'pækɪdʒ, -ɪz, -ɪŋ, -d

preparation
BR ˌprɛpə'reɪʃn, -z
AM ˌprɛpə'reɪʃən, -z

preparative
BR prɪ'parətɪv
AM pri'pɛrədɪv, 'prɛp(ə)rədɪv

preparatively
BR prɪ'parətɪvli
AM pri'pɛrədɪvli, 'prɛp(ə)rədɪvli

preparatorily
BR prɪ'parət(ə)rɪli
AM priˌpɛrə'tɔrəli, prəˌpɛrə'tɔrəli

preparatory
BR prɪ'parət(ə)ri

AM pri'pɛrəˌtɔri, prə'pɛrəˌtɔri

prepare
BR prɪ'pɛː(r), -z, -ɪŋ, -d
AM pri'pɛ(ə)r, prə'pɛ(ə)r, -z, -ɪŋ, -d

preparedness
BR prɪ'pɛːrɪdnɪs
AM prə'pɛr(ə)dnəs

preparer
BR prɪ'pɛːrə(r)
AM pri'pɛrər, prə'pɛrər

prepay
BR ˌpriː'peɪ, -z, -ɪŋ, -d
AM ˌpri'peɪ, -z, -ɪŋ, -d

pre-payable
BR ˌpriː'peɪəbl
AM ˌpri'peɪəbəl

prepayment
BR ˌpriː'peɪm(ə)nt, -s
AM pri'peɪmənt, -s

prepense
BR prɪ'pɛns
AM pri'pɛns

prepensely
BR prɪ'pɛnsli
AM pri'pɛnsli

pre-plan
BR ˌpriː'plan, -z, -ɪŋ, -d
AM pri'plæn, -z, -ɪŋ, -d

preponderance
BR prɪ'pɒnd(ə)rəns, prɪ'pɒnd(ə)rn̩s
AM prə'pɑnd(ə)rəns

preponderant
BR prɪ'pɒnd(ə)rənt, prɪ'pɒnd(ə)rn̩t
AM prə'pɑnd(ə)rənt

preponderantly
BR prɪ'pɒnd(ə)rəntli, prɪ'pɒnd(ə)rn̩tli
AM prə'pɑnd(ə)rən(t)li

preponderate
BR prɪ'pɒndəreɪt, -s, -ɪŋ, -ɪd
AM prə'pɑnd(ə)ˌreɪ|t, -ts, -dɪŋ, -dɪd

prepose
BR ˌpriː'pəʊz, -ɪz, -ɪŋ, -d
AM ˌpri'poʊz, -əz, -ɪŋ, -d

preposition
BR ˌprɛpə'zɪʃn, -z
AM ˌprɛpə'zɪʃən, -z

pre-position
BR ˌpriːpə'zɪʃ|n, -nz, -n̩ɪŋ\-nɪŋ, -nd
AM ˌpripə'zɪʃən, -z, -ɪŋ, -d

prepositional
BR ˌprɛpə'zɪʃn̩(ə)l, ˌprɛpə'zɪʃən(ə)l
AM ˌprɛpə'zɪʃ(ə)nəl

prepositionally
BR ˌprɛpə'zɪʃn̩əli, ˌprɛpə'zɪʃn̩l̩i, ˌprɛpə'zɪʃənl̩i, ˌprɛpə'zɪʃ(ə)nəli
AM ˌprɛpə'zɪʃ(ə)nəli

prepositive
BR (ˌ)priː'pɒzɪtɪv
AM pri'pɑzədɪv

prepossess
BR ˌpriːpə'zɛs, -ɪz, -ɪŋ, -t
AM ˌpripə'zɛs, -əz, -ɪŋ, -t

prepossession
BR ˌpriːpə'zɛʃn, -z
AM ˌpripə'zɛʃən, -z

preposterous
BR prɪ'pɒst(ə)rəs
AM prə'pɑst(ə)rəs

preposterously
BR prɪ'pɒst(ə)rəsli
AM prə'pɑst(ə)rəsli

preposterousness
BR prɪ'pɒst(ə)rəsnəs
AM prə'pɑst(ə)rəsnəs

prepostor
BR prɪ'pɒstə(r), -z
AM prə'pɑstər, -z

prepotence
BR ˌpriː'pəʊtns
AM pri'poʊtns

prepotency
BR ˌpriː'pəʊtnsi
AM pri'poʊtnsi

prepotent
BR ˌpriː'pəʊtnt
AM ˌpriː'poʊtnt

preppie
BR 'prɛp|i, -ɪz
AM 'prɛpi, -z

preppy
BR 'prɛp|i, -ɪz, -ɪə(r), -ɪɪst
AM 'prɛpi, -z, -ər, -ɪst

preprandial
BR ˌpriː'prandɪəl
AM pri'prændiəl

pre-preference
BR ˌpriː'prɛf(ə)rəns, ˌpriː'prɛf(ə)rn̩s
AM pri'prɛf(ə)rəns

preprint[1]
noun
BR 'priːprɪnt, -s
AM 'priˌprɪnt, -s

preprint[2]
verb
BR ˌpriː'prɪnt, -s, -ɪŋ, -ɪd
AM pri'prin|t, -ts, -(t)ɪŋ, -(t)ɪd

preprocess
BR ˌpriː'prəʊsɛs, -ɪz, -ɪŋ, -t
AM pri'prɑsəs, -əz, -ɪŋ, -t

pre-processor
BR ˌpriː'prəʊsɛsə(r), -z
AM pri'prɑsəsər, -z

pre-production
BR ˌpriːprə'dʌkʃn
AM ˌpriprə'dəkʃən

preprofessional
BR ˌpriːprə'fɛʃn̩(ə)l, ˌpriːprə'fɛʃən(ə)l
AM ˌpriprə'fɛʃ(ə)nəl

pre-programme
BR ˌpriː'prəʊgrəm, -z, -ɪŋ, -d
AM pri'proʊgrəm, -z, -ɪŋ, -d

pre-pubertal
BR ˌpriː'pjuːbətl
AM pri'pjubərdl

pre-puberty
BR ˌpriː'pjuːbəti
AM pri'pjubərdi

prepubescence
BR ˌpriːpjuː'bɛsns, ˌpriːpjʉ'bɛsns
AM ˌpripju'bɛsəns

prepubescent
BR ˌpriːpjuː'bɛsnt, ˌpriːpjʉ'bɛsnt, -s
AM ˌpripju'bɛsənt, -s

pre-publication
BR ˌpriːpʌblɪ'keɪʃn
AM priˌpəblə'keɪʃən

prepuce
BR 'priːpjuːs, -ɪz
AM 'priˌpjus, -əz

preputial
BR ˌpriː'pjuːʃl
AM pri'pjuʃəl

prequel
BR 'priːkw(ə)l, -z
AM 'prikwəl, -z

Pre-Raphaelism
BR (ˌ)priː'raf(ɪ)əlɪz(ə)m
AM pri'rɑfiəˌlɪzəm, pri'ræfiəˌlɪzəm

Pre-Raphaelite
BR (ˌ)priː'raf(ɪ)əlʌɪt, -s
AM pri'rɑfiəˌlaɪt, pri'ræfiəˌlaɪt, -s

Pre-Raphaelitism
BR (ˌ)priː'raf(ɪ)əlʌɪtɪz(ə)m
AM pri'rɑfiəˌlaɪˌtɪzəm, pri'rɑfiəˌlaɪdɪzəm, pri'ræfiəˌlaɪˌtɪzəm, pri'ræfiəˌlaɪdɪzəm

prerecord
BR ˌpriːrɪ'kɔːd, -z, -ɪŋ, -ɪd
AM ˌprirə'kɔ(ə)rd, -z, -ɪŋ, -əd

preregister
BR ˌpriː'rɛdʒɪst|ə(r), -əz, -(ə)rɪŋ, -əd
AM ˌpri'rɛdʒəst|ər, -ərz, -(ə)rɪŋ, -ərd

preregistration
BR ˌpriːrɛdʒɪ'streɪʃn
AM ˌpriˌrɛdʒəs'treɪʃən

prerequisite
BR (ˌ)priː'rɛkwɪzɪt, -s
AM pri'rɛkwəzət, prə'rɛkwəzət, -s

pre-revolutionary
BR ˌpriːrɛvə'l(j)uːʃn̩(ə)ri
AM priˌrɛvə'luʃəˌnɛri

prerogative
BR prɪ'rɒgətɪv, -z
AM pə'rɑgədɪv, prə'rɑgədɪv, -z

presage
BR 'prɛs|ɪdʒ, -ɪdʒɪz, -ɪdʒɪŋ, -ɪdʒd
AM pri'seɪdʒ, 'prɛsɪdʒ, -ɪz, -ɪŋ, -d

presager
BR 'prɛsɪdʒə(r), -z
AM pri'seɪdʒər, 'prɛsɪdʒər, -z

presbyopia
BR ˌprɛzbɪ'əʊpɪə(*r*), ˌprɛsbɪ'əʊpɪə(*r*)
AM ˌprɛzbi'oʊpiə, ˌprɛsbi'oʊpiə

presbyopic
BR ˌprɛzbɪ'ɒpɪk, ˌprɛsbɪ'ɒpɪk
AM ˌprɛzbi'ɑpɪk, ˌprɛsbi'ɑpɪk

presbyter
BR 'prɛzbɪtə(r), 'prɛsbɪtə(r), -z
AM 'prɛzbədər, 'prɛsbədər, -z

presbyteral
BR prɛz'bɪt(ə)rəl, prɛz'bɪt(ə)rl̩, prɛs'bɪt(ə)rəl, prɛs'bɪt(ə)rl̩
AM prɛs'bɪtrəl, prɛz'bɪtrəl, prɛs'bɪdərəl, prɛz'bɪdərəl

presbyterate
BR prɛz'bɪt(ə)rət, prɛs'bɪt(ə)rət, -s
AM prɛs'bɪtrət, prɛz'bɪtrət, prɛs'bɪdərət, prɛz'bɪdərət, prɛs'bɪdəˌreɪt, prɛz'bɪdəˌreɪt, -s

presbyterial
BR ˌprɛzbɪ'tɪərɪəl, ˌprɛsbɪ'tɪərɪəl
AM ˌprɛzbə'tɪriəl, ˌprɛsbə'tɪriəl

Presbyterian
BR ˌprɛzbɪ'tɪərɪən, ˌprɛsbɪ'tɪərɪən, -z
AM ˌprɛzbə'tɪriən, ˌprɛsbə'tɪriən, -z

Presbyterianism
BR ˌprɛzbɪ'tɪərɪənɪz(ə)m, ˌprɛsbɪ'tɪərɪənɪz(ə)m
AM ˌprɛzbə'tɪriəˌnɪzəm, ˌprɛsbə'tɪriəˌnɪzəm

presbytership
BR 'prɛzbɪtəʃɪp, 'prɛsbɪtəʃɪp, -s
AM 'prɛzbədər,ʃɪp, 'prɛsbədər,ʃɪp, -s

presbytery
BR 'prɛzbɪt(ə)r|i, 'prɛsbɪt(ə)r|i, -ɪz
AM 'prɛzbə,tɛri, 'prɛsbə,tɛri, -z

Prescely
BR prɪ'sɛli
AM prə'sɛli

preschool¹
adjective
BR ,pri:'sku:l
AM 'pri,skul

preschool²
noun
BR 'pri:sku:l, -z
AM 'pri,skul, -z

pre-schooler
BR 'pri:,sku:lə(r), -z
AM 'pri,skulər, -z

prescience
BR 'prɛsɪəns
AM 'prɛʃ(i)əns

prescient
BR 'prɛsɪənt
AM 'prɛʃ(i)ənt

presciently
BR 'prɛsɪəntli
AM 'prɛʃ(i)ən(t)li

prescind
BR prɪ'sɪnd, ,pri:'sɪnd, -z, -ɪŋ, -ɪd
AM pri'sɪnd, -z, -ɪŋ, -ɪd

Prescot
BR 'prɛskət, 'prɛskɒt
AM 'prɛs,kɑt, 'prɛskət

Prescott
BR 'prɛskət, 'prɛskɒt
AM 'prɛs,kɑt, 'prɛskət

prescribe
BR prɪ'skrʌɪb, -z, -ɪŋ, -d
AM pri'skraɪb, prə'skraɪb, -z, -ɪŋ, -d

prescriber
BR prɪ'skrʌɪbə(r), -z
AM pri'skraɪbər, prə'skraɪbər, -z

prescript
BR 'pri:skrɪpt, -s
AM 'pri,skrɪpt, pri'skrɪpt, -s

prescription
BR prɪ'skrɪpʃn, -z
AM pri'skrɪpʃən, prə'skrɪpʃən, pər'skrɪpʃən, -z

prescriptive
BR prɪ'skrɪptɪv
AM pri'skrɪptɪv, prə'skrɪptɪv

prescriptively
BR prɪ'skrɪptɪvli
AM pri'skrɪptɪvli, prə'skrɪptɪvli

prescriptiveness
BR prɪ'skrɪptɪvnɪs
AM pri'skrɪptɪvnɪs, prə'skrɪptɪvnɪs

prescriptivism
BR prɪ'skrɪptɪvɪz(ə)m
AM pri'skrɪptə,vɪzəm, prə'skrɪptə,vɪzəm

prescriptivist
BR prɪ'skrɪptɪvɪst, -s
AM pri'skrɪptəvəst, prə'skrɪptəvəst, -s

pre-season
BR ,pri:'si:zn
AM pri'sizn

Preseli
BR prɪ'sɛli
AM prə'sɛli
WE pre'seli

presence
BR 'prɛzns, -ɪz
AM 'prɛzns, -əz

present¹
military noun, verb
BR prɪ'zɛnt, -s, -ɪŋ, -ɪd
AM pri'zɛn|t, prə'zɛn|t, -ts, -(t)ɪŋ, -(t)əd

present²
non-military noun, adjective
BR 'prɛznt
AM 'prɛznt

presentability
BR prɪ,zɛntə'bɪlɪti
AM prə,zɛn(t)ə'bɪlɪdi, pri,zɛn(t)ə'bɪlɪdi

presentable
BR prɪ'zɛntəbl
AM prə'zɛn(t)əbəl, pri'zɛn(t)əbəl

presentableness
BR prɪ'zɛntəblnəs
AM prə'zɛn(t)əbəlnəs, pri'zɛn(t)əbəlnəs

presentably
BR prɪ'zɛntəbli
AM prə'zɛn(t)əbli, pri'zɛn(t)əbli

presentation
BR ,prɛzn'teɪʃn, -z
AM ,prɛzn'teɪʃən, ,pri,zɛn'teɪʃən, ,prizn'teɪʃən, -z

presentational
BR ,prɛzn'teɪʃn̩(ə)l, ,prɛzn'teɪʃən(ə)l
AM ,prɛzn'teɪʃ(ə)nəl, ,pri,zɛn'teɪʃ(ə)nəl, ,prizn'teɪʃ(ə)nəl

presentationally
BR ,prɛzn'teɪʃn̩əli, ,prɛzn'teɪʃn̩l̩i, ,prɛzn'teɪʃənl̩i, ,prɛzn'teɪʃ(ə)nəli
AM ,prɛzn'teɪʃ(ə)nəli, ,pri,zɛn'teɪʃ(ə)nəli, ,prizn'teɪʃ(ə)nəli

presentationism
BR ,prɛzn'teɪʃn̩ɪz(ə)m, ,prɛzn'teɪʃənɪz(ə)m
AM ,prɛzn'teɪʃə,nɪzəm, ,pri,zɛn'teɪʃə,nɪzəm, ,prizn'teɪʃə,nɪzəm

presentationist
BR ,prɛzn'teɪʃn̩ɪst, ,prɛzn'teɪʃənɪst, -s
AM ,prɛzn'teɪʃənəst, ,pri,zɛn'teɪʃənəst, ,prizn'teɪʃənəst, -s

presentative
BR prɪ'zɛntətɪv
AM prə'zɛn(t)ədɪv, pri'zɛn(t)ədɪv

present-day
BR ,prɛznt'deɪ
AM 'prɛzn(t)'deɪ

presentee
BR ,prɛzn'ti:, -z
AM ,prɛzn'ti, -z

presenter
BR prɪ'zɛntə(r), -z
AM prə'zɛn(t)ər, pri'zɛn(t)ər, -z

presentient
BR prɪ'sɛnʃnt, prɪ'sɛnʃɪənt, prɪ'sɛntɪənt
AM pri'sɛn(t)ʃənt

presentiment
BR prɪ'zɛntɪm(ə)nt, -s
AM pri'zɛn(t)əmənt, prə'zɛn(t)əmənt, -s

presently
BR 'prɛzntli
AM 'prɛzn(t)li

presentment
BR prɪ'zɛntm(ə)nt, -s
AM pri'zɛntmənt, prə'zɛntmənt, -s

presentness
BR 'prɛzntnəs
AM 'prɛzn(t)nəs

preservable
BR prɪ'zə:vəbl
AM pri'zərvəbəl, prə'zərvəbəl

preservation
BR ,prɛzə'veɪʃn
AM ,prɛzər'veɪʃən

preservationist
BR ,prɛzə'veɪʃənɪst, ,prɛzə'veɪʃn̩ɪst, -s
AM ,prɛzər'veɪʃənəst, -s

preservative
BR prɪ'zə:vətɪv, -z
AM prə'zərvədɪv, pri'zərvədɪv, -z

preserve
BR prɪ'zə:v, -z, -ɪŋ, -d
AM prə'zərv, pri'zərv, -z, -ɪŋ, -d

preserver
BR prɪ'zə:və(r), -z
AM prə'zərvər, pri'zərvər, -z

preset¹
noun
BR 'pri:sɛt, -s
AM 'pri,sɛt, -s

preset²
verb
BR ,pri:'sɛt, -s, -ɪŋ
AM pri'sɛ|t, -ts, -dɪŋ

preshrunk
BR ,pri:'ʃrʌŋk
AM pri'ʃrəŋk

preside
BR prɪ'zʌɪd, -z, -ɪŋ, -ɪd
AM prə'zaɪd, pri'zaɪd, -z, -ɪŋ, -ɪd

presidency
BR 'prɛzɪd(ə)ns|i, -ɪz
AM 'prɛz(ə)dənsi, 'prɛzədnsi, 'prɛzə,dɛnsi, -z

president
BR 'prɛzɪd(ə)nt, -s
AM 'prɛz(ə)dnt, 'prɛzə,dɛnt, -s

president-elect
BR ,prɛzɪd(ə)ntɪ'lɛkt
AM ¦prɛz(ə)dən(t)ə'lɛk(t), ¦prɛzədn(t)ə'lɛk(t), ¦prɛzə,dɛn(t)ə'lɛk(t)

presidential
BR ,prɛzɪ'dɛnʃl
AM ¦prɛzə'dɛn(t)ʃəl

presidentially
BR ,prɛzɪ'dɛnʃl̩i, ,prɛzɪ'dɛnʃəli
AM ¦prɛzə'dɛn(t)ʃəli

presidents-elect
BR ,prɛzɪd(ə)ntsɪ'lɛkt
AM ¦prɛz(ə)dən(t)sə'lɛk(t), ¦prɛzədn(t)sə'lɛk(t), ¦prɛzə,dɛn(t)sə'lɛk(t)

presidentship
BR 'prɛzɪd(ə)ntʃɪp, -s
AM 'prɛz(ə)dənt,ʃɪp, 'prɛzədnt,ʃɪp, 'prɛzə,dɛnt,ʃɪp, -s

presidiary
BR prɪ'sɪdɪəri, prɪ'zɪdɪəri
AM prə'sɪdi,ɛri

presidio
BR prɪ'sɪdɪəʊ, prɪ'zɪdɪəʊ
AM prə'sɪdioʊ

Presidium
BR prɪ'sɪdɪəm, prɪ'zɪdɪəm, -z
AM prə'sɪdiəm, -z

Presley
BR 'prɛzli
AM 'prɛzli, 'prɛsli

presoak¹
noun
BR 'pri:səʊk, -s

AM ˈpriˌsoʊk, -s
presoak²
verb
BR ˌpriːˈsəʊk, -s, -ɪŋ, -t
AM priˈsoʊk, -s, -ɪŋ, -t
pre-Socratic
BR ˌpriːsəˈkratɪk
AM ¦prisəˈkrædək
press
BR prɛs, -ɪz, -ɪŋ, -t
AM prɛs, -əz, -ɪŋ, -t
pressboard
BR ˈprɛsbɔːd
AM ˈprɛsˌbɔ(ə)rd
Pressburg
BR ˈprɛsbəːg
AM ˈprɛsˌbərg
pressgang
BR ˈprɛsgaŋ, -z, -ɪŋ, -d
AM ˈprɛsˌgæŋ, -z, -ɪŋ, -d
pressie
BR ˈprɛz|i, -ɪz
AM ˈprɛsi, ˈprɛzi, -z
pressing
BR ˈprɛsɪŋ, -z
AM ˈprɛsɪŋ, -z
pressingly
BR ˈprɛsɪŋli
AM ˈprɛsɪŋli
pressman
BR ˈprɛsmən, ˈprɛsman
AM ˈprɛsˌmæn
pressmark
BR ˈprɛsmɑːk, -s
AM ˈprɛsˌmɑrk, -s
pressmen
BR ˈprɛsmən, ˈprɛsmɛn
AM ˈprɛsmən
pressroom
BR ˈprɛsruːm, ˈprɛsrʊm, -z
AM ˈprɛsˌrum, ˈprɛsˌrʊm, -z
pressrun
BR ˈprɛsrʌn, -z
AM ˈprɛsˌrən, -z
press-up
BR ˈprɛsʌp, -s
AM ˈprɛsəp, -s
pressure
BR ˈprɛʃ|ə(r), -əz, -(ə)rɪŋ, -əd
AM ˈprɛʃər, -z, -ɪŋ, -d
pressurisation
BR ˌprɛʃ(ə)rʌɪˈzeɪʃn
AM ˌprɛʃərəˈzeɪʃən, ˌprɛʃəˌraɪˈzeɪʃən
pressurise
BR ˈprɛʃərʌɪz, -ɪz, -ɪŋ, -d
AM ˈprɛʃəˌraɪz, -ɪz, -ɪŋ, -d
pressurization
BR ˌprɛʃ(ə)rʌɪˈzeɪʃn
AM ˌprɛʃərəˈzeɪʃən, ˌprɛʃəˌraɪˈzeɪʃən
pressurize
BR ˈprɛʃərʌɪz, -ɪz, -ɪŋ, -d
AM ˈprɛʃəˌraɪz, -ɪz, -ɪŋ, -d
Prestatyn
BR prɛˈstatɪn
AM prɛˈstædən
Prestcold
BR ˈprɛs(t)kəʊld
AM ˈprɛs(t)ˌkoʊld
Presteigne
BR prɛˈstiːn
AM prɛˈstin
Prestel®
BR ˈprɛstɛl
AM ˈprɛsˌtɛl
Prester
BR ˈprɛstə(r)
AM ˈprɛstər
prestidigitation
BR ˌprɛstɪˌdɪdʒɪˈteɪʃn
AM ˌprɛstəˌdɪdʒəˈteɪʃən
prestidigitator
BR ˌprɛstɪˈdɪdʒɪteɪtə(r), -z
AM ˌprɛstəˈdɪdʒəˌteɪdər, -z
prestige
BR prɛˈstiː(d)ʒ
AM prɛˈsti(d)ʒ
prestigeful
BR prɛˈstiː(d)ʒf(ʊ)l
AM prɛˈsti(d)ʒˌfʊl
prestigious
BR prɛˈstɪdʒəs, prɪˈstɪdʒəs
AM prɛˈstɪdʒ(i)əs
prestigiously
BR prɛˈstɪdʒəsli, prɪˈstɪdʒəsli
AM prɛˈstɪdʒ(i)əsli
prestigiousness
BR prɛˈstɪdʒəsnəs, prɪˈstɪdʒəsnəs
AM prɛˈstɪdʒ(i)əsnəs
prestissimo
BR prɛˈstɪsɪməʊ
AM prɛˈstɪsəˌmoʊ
presto
BR ˈprɛstəʊ, -z
AM ˈprɛstoʊ, -z
Preston
BR ˈprɛst(ə)n
AM ˈprɛstən
Prestonpans
BR ˌprɛst(ə)nˈpanz
AM ˌprɛstnˈpænz
prestressed
BR ˌpriːˈstrɛst
AM priˈstrɛs(t)
Prestwich
BR ˈprɛstwɪtʃ
AM ˈprɛs(t)ˌwɪtʃ
Prestwick
BR ˈprɛstwɪk
AM ˈprɛs(t)ˌwɪk
presumable
BR prɪˈzjuːməbl
AM priˈz(j)uməbəl, prəˈz(j)uməbəl
presumably
BR prɪˈzjuːməbli
AM priˈz(j)uməbli, prəˈz(j)uməbli
presume
BR prɪˈzjuːm, -z, -ɪŋ, -d
AM priˈz(j)um, prəˈz(j)um, -z, -ɪŋ, -d
presumedly
BR prɪˈzjuːmɪdli
AM priˈz(j)um(ə)dli, prəˈz(j)um(ə)dli
presumingly
BR prɪˈzjuːmɪŋli
AM priˈz(j)umɪŋli, prəˈz(j)umɪŋli
presumingness
BR prɪˈzjuːmɪŋnɪs
AM priˈz(j)umɪŋnɪs, prəˈz(j)umɪŋnɪs
presumption
BR prɪˈzʌm(p)ʃn, -z
AM priˈzəm(p)ʃən, prəˈzəm(p)ʃən, -z
presumptive
BR prɪˈzʌm(p)tɪv
AM priˈzəm(p)tɪv, prəˈzəm(p)tɪv
presumptively
BR prɪˈzʌm(p)tɪvli
AM priˈzəm(p)tɪvli, prəˈzəm(p)tɪvli
presumptuous
BR prɪˈzʌm(p)tʃʊəs, prɪˈzʌm(p)tjʊəs
AM priˈzəm(p)(t)ʃ(əw)əs, prəˈzəm(p)(t)ʃ(əw)əs
presumptuously
BR prɪˈzʌm(p)tʃʊəsli, prɪˈzʌm(p)tjʊəsli
AM priˈzəm(p)(t)ʃ(əw)əsli, prəˈzəm(p)(t)ʃ(əw)əsli
presumptuousness
BR prɪˈzʌm(p)tʃʊəsnəs, prɪˈzʌm(p)tjʊəsnəs
AM priˈzəm(p)(t)ʃ(əw)əsnəs, prəˈzəm(p)(t)ʃ(əw)əsnəs
presuppose
BR ˌpriːsəˈpəʊz, -ɪz, -ɪŋ, -d
AM ˌprisəˈpoʊz, -əz, -ɪŋ, -d
presupposition
BR ˌpriːsʌpəˈzɪʃn, -z
AM ˌpriˌsəpəˈzɪʃən, -z
prêt-à-porter
BR ˌprɛtəˈpɔːteɪ
AM ˌprɛdəˈpɔrteɪ
pretax
BR ˌpriːˈtaks, -ɪz, -ɪŋ, -t
AM ¦priˈtæks, -əz, -ɪŋ, -t
preteen
BR ˌpriːˈtiːn, -z
AM ¦priˈtin, -z
pretence
BR prɪˈtɛns, -ɪz
AM priˈtɛns, prəˈtɛns, ˈpriˌtɛns, -əz
pretend
BR prɪˈtɛnd, -z, -ɪŋ, -ɪd
AM priˈtɛnd, prəˈtɛnd, -z, -ɪŋ, -əd
pretender
BR prɪˈtɛndə(r), -z
AM prəˈtɛndər, priˈtɛndər, -z
pretense
BR prɪˈtɛns, -ɪz
AM priˈtɛns, prəˈtɛns, ˈpriˌtɛns, -əz
pretension
BR prɪˈtɛnʃn, -z
AM priˈtɛn(t)ʃən, prəˈtɛn(t)ʃən, -z
pretentious
BR prɪˈtɛnʃəs
AM priˈtɛn(t)ʃəs, prəˈtɛn(t)ʃəs
pretentiously
BR prɪˈtɛnʃəsli
AM priˈtɛn(t)ʃəsli, prəˈtɛn(t)ʃəsli
pretentiousness
BR prɪˈtɛnʃəsnəs
AM priˈtɛn(t)ʃəsnəs, prəˈtɛn(t)ʃəsnəs
preterhuman
BR ˌpriːtəˈhjuːmən
AM ¦prɛdərˈ(h)jumən, ¦pridərˈ(h)jumən
preterit
BR ˈprɛt(ə)rɪt, -s
AM ˈprɛdərət, -s
preterite
BR ˈprɛt(ə)rɪt, -s
AM ˈprɛdərət, -s
preterition
BR ˌpriːtəˈrɪʃn, -z
AM ˌprɛdəˈrɪʃən, -z
pre-term
BR ˌpriːˈtəːm
AM priˈtərm
pretermission
BR ˌpriːtəˈmɪʃn
AM ˌpridərˈmɪʃən
pretermit
BR ˌpriːtəˈmɪt, -s, -ɪŋ, -ɪd
AM priˈtərmə|t, -ts, -dɪŋ, -dəd
preternatural
BR ˌpriːtəˈnatʃ(ə)rəl, ˌpriːtəˈnatʃ(ə)rl̩
AM ¦prɛdərˈnætʃ(ə)rəl, ¦pridərˈnætʃ(ə)rəl

preternaturalism
BR ˌpriːtəˈnatʃ(ə)rəlɪz(ə)m, ˌpriːtəˈnatʃ(ə)rl̩ɪz(ə)m, -z
AM ˌprɛdərˈnætʃ(ə)rəˌlɪzəm, ˌpridərˈnætʃ(ə)rəˌlɪzəm, -z

preternaturally
BR ˌpriːtəˈnatʃ(ə)rəli, ˌpriːtəˈnatʃ(ə)rl̩i
AM ˌprɛdərˈnætʃ(ə)rəli, ˌpridərˈnætʃ(ə)rəli

preternaturalness
BR ˌpriːtəˈnatʃ(ə)rəlnəs, ˌpriːtəˈnatʃ(ə)rl̩nəs
AM ˌprɛdərˈnætʃ(ə)rəlnəs, ˌpridərˈnætʃ(ə)rəlnəs

pretest
BR ˌpriːˈtɛst, -s, -ɪŋ, -ɪd
AM ˌpriˌtɛs|t, -s, -ɪŋ, -əd

pretext
BR ˈpriːtɛkst, -s
AM ˈpriˌtɛkst, -s

pretone
BR ˌpriːˈtəʊn, -z
AM priˈtoʊn, -z

pretonic
BR ˌpriːˈtɒnɪk, -s
AM priˈtɑnɪk, -s

pretor
BR ˈpriːtə(r), ˈpriːtɔː(r), -z
AM ˈpridər, -z

Pretoria
BR prɪˈtɔːrɪə(r)
AM prəˈtɔriə

pretorian
BR prɪˈtɔːrɪən, -z
AM prəˈtɔriən, -z

pretorship
BR ˈpriːtəʃɪp, ˈpriːtɔːʃɪp
AM ˈpridərˌʃɪp

pretreat
BR ˌpriːˈtriːt, -s, -ɪŋ, -ɪd
AM priˈtri|t, -ts, -dɪŋ, -dɪd

pretreatment
BR ˌpriːˈtriːtm(ə)nt, -s
AM priˈtritmənt, -s

pretrial[1]
adjective
BR ˌpriːˈtrʌɪəl
AM ˌpriˌtraɪəl

pretrial[2]
noun
BR ˈpriːtrʌɪəl, -z
AM ˌpriˌtraɪəl, -z

prettification
BR ˌprɪtɪfɪˈkeɪʃn
AM ˌprɪdəfəˈkeɪʃən

prettifier
BR ˈprɪtɪfʌɪə(r), -z
AM ˈprɪdəˌfaɪər, -z

prettify
BR ˈprɪtɪfʌɪ, -z, -ɪŋ, -d
AM ˈprɪdəˌfaɪ, -z, -ɪŋ, -d

prettily
BR ˈprɪtɪli
AM ˈprɪdɪli

prettiness
BR ˈprɪtɪnɪs
AM ˈprɪdinɪs

pretty
BR ˈprɪt|i, -ɪə(r), -ɪɪst
AM ˈprɪdi, -ər, -ɪst

prettyish
BR ˈprɪtɪɪʃ
AM ˈprɪdiɪʃ

prettyism
BR ˈprɪtɪɪz(ə)m
AM ˈprɪdiˌɪzəm

pretty-pretty
BR ˌprɪtɪˈprɪti
AM ˌprɪdiˌprɪdi

pretzel
BR ˈprɛtsl, -z
AM ˈprɛtsəl, -z

prevail
BR prɪˈveɪl, -z, -ɪŋ, -d
AM priˈveɪl, prəˈveɪl, -z, -ɪŋ, -d

prevailingly
BR prɪˈveɪlɪŋli
AM priˈveɪlɪŋli, prəˈveɪlɪŋli

prevalence
BR ˈprɛvələns, ˈprɛvəl̩ns, ˈprɛvl̩(ə)ns
AM ˈprɛv(ə)ləns

prevalent
BR ˈprɛvələnt, ˈprɛvəl̩nt, ˈprɛvl̩(ə)nt
AM ˈprɛv(ə)lənt

prevalently
BR ˈprɛvələntli, ˈprɛvəl̩ntli, ˈprɛvl̩(ə)ntli
AM ˈprɛv(ə)lən(t)li

prevaricate
BR prɪˈvarɪkeɪt, -s, -ɪŋ, -ɪd
AM priˈvɛrəˌkeɪ|t, prəˈvɛrəˌkeɪ|t, -ts, -dɪŋ, -dɪd

prevarication
BR prɪˌvarɪˈkeɪʃn, -z
AM priˌvɛrəˈkeɪʃən, prəˌvɛrəˈkeɪʃən, -z

prevaricator
BR prɪˈvarɪkeɪtə(r), -z
AM priˈvɛrəˌkeɪdər, prəˈvɛrəˌkeɪdər, -z

prevenient
BR prɪˈviːnɪənt, (ˌ)priːˈviːnɪənt
AM priˈviniənt, prəˈviniənt

preveniently
BR prɪˈviːnɪəntli, (ˌ)priːˈviːnɪəntli
AM priˈviniən(t)li, prəˈviniən(t)li

prevent
BR prɪˈvɛnt, -s, -ɪŋ, -ɪd
AM priˈvɛn|t, prəˈvɛn|t, -ts, -(t)ɪŋ, -(t)əd

preventability
BR prɪˌvɛntəˈbɪlɪti
AM priˌvɛn(t)əˈbɪlɪdi, prəˌvɛn(t)əˈbɪlɪdi

preventable
BR prɪˈvɛntəbl
AM priˈvɛn(t)əbəl, prəˈvɛn(t)əbəl

preventative
BR prɪˈvɛntətɪv, -z
AM priˈvɛn(t)ədɪv, prəˈvɛn(t)ədɪv, -z

preventatively
BR prɪˈvɛntətɪvli
AM priˈvɛn(t)ədɪvli, prəˈvɛn(t)ədɪvli

preventer
BR prɪˈvɛntə(r), -z
AM priˈvɛn(t)ər, prəˈvɛn(t)ər, -z

prevention
BR prɪˈvɛnʃn
AM priˈvɛn(t)ʃən, prəˈvɛn(t)ʃən

preventive
BR prɪˈvɛntɪv
AM priˈvɛn(t)ɪv, prəˈvɛn(t)ɪv

preventively
BR prɪˈvɛntɪvli
AM priˈvɛn(t)ɪvli, prəˈvɛn(t)ɪvli

preverbal
BR ˌpriːˈvəːbl
AM ˌpriˈvərbəl

preverbally
BR ˌpriːˈvəːbl̩i, ˌpriːˈvəːbəli
AM ˌpriˈvərbəli

preview
BR ˈpriːvjuː, -z, -ɪŋ, -d
AM ˈpriˌvju, -z, -ɪŋ, -d

Previn
BR ˈprɛvɪn
AM ˈprɛvən

previous
BR ˈpriːvɪəs
AM ˈpriviəs

previously
BR ˈpriːvɪəsli
AM ˈpriviəsli

previousness
BR ˈpriːvɪəsnəs
AM ˈpriviəsnəs

previse
BR prɪˈvʌɪz, -ɪz, -ɪŋ, -d
AM priˈvaɪz, prəˈvaɪz, -ɪz, -ɪŋ, -d

prevision
BR prɪˈvɪʒn
AM priˈvɪʒən, prəˈvɪʒən

previsional
BR prɪˈvɪʒn̩(ə)l, prɪˈvɪʒən(ə)l
AM priˈvɪʒ(ə)nəl, prəˈvɪʒ(ə)nəl

prevocalic
BR ˌpriːvə(ʊ)ˈkalɪk
AM ˌprivoʊˈkælɪk

pre-vocational
BR ˌpriːvə(ʊ)ˈkeɪʃn̩(ə)l, ˌpriːvə(ʊ)ˈkeɪʃən(ə)l
AM priˌvoʊˈkeɪʃ(ə)nəl

prevue
BR ˈpriːvjuː, -z
AM ˈpriˌvju, -z

prewar
BR ˌpriːˈwɔː(r)
AM priˈwɔ(ə)r

pre-wash
BR ˌpriːˈwɒʃ, -ɪz, -ɪŋ, -t
AM priˈwɔʃ, priˈwɑʃ, -əz, -ɪŋ, -t

prex
BR prɛks, -ɪz
AM prɛks, -əz

prexy
BR ˈprɛks|i, -ɪz
AM ˈprɛksi, -z

prey
BR preɪ, -z, -ɪŋ, -d
AM preɪ, -z, -ɪŋ, -d

preyer
BR ˈpreɪə(r), -z
AM ˈpreɪər, -z

prezzie
BR ˈprɛz|i, -ɪz
AM ˈprɛzi, -z

Priam
BR ˈprʌɪam, ˈprʌɪəm
AM ˈpraɪəm

priapic
BR prʌɪˈapɪk
AM praɪˈæpɪk

priapism
BR ˈprʌɪəpɪz(ə)m
AM ˈpraɪəˌpɪzəm

Priapus
BR prʌɪˈeɪpəs
AM praɪˈeɪpəs

price
BR prʌɪs, -ɪz, -ɪŋ, -t
AM praɪs, -ɪz, -ɪŋ, -t

priceless
BR ˈprʌɪslɪs
AM ˈpraɪslɪs

pricelessly
BR ˈprʌɪslɪsli
AM ˈpraɪslɪsli

pricelessness
BR ˈprʌɪslɪsnɪs
AM ˈpraɪslɪsnɪs

pricer
BR ˈprʌɪsə(r), -z
AM ˈpraɪsər, -z

pricey
BR ˈprʌɪs|i, -ɪə(r), -ɪɪst
AM ˈpraɪsi, -ər, -ɪst

priciness
BR ˈprɪsɪnɨs
AM ˈprɪsinɨs

prick
BR prɪk, -s, -ɪŋ, -t
AM prɪk, -s, -ɪŋ, -t

pricker
BR ˈprɪkə(r), -z
AM ˈprɪkər, -z

pricket
BR ˈprɪkɪt, -s
AM ˈprɪkɪt, -s

prickle
BR ˈprɪk|l, -lz, -l̩ɪŋ\-lɪŋ, -ld
AM ˈprɪk|əl, -əlz, -(ə)lɪŋ, -əld

prickliness
BR ˈprɪklɪnɨs
AM ˈprɪk(ə)linɨs

prickly
BR ˈprɪkl|i, -ɪə(r), -ɪɪst
AM ˈprɪk(ə)li, -ər, -ɪst

pricy
BR ˈprʌɪs|i, -ɪə(r), -ɪɪst
AM ˈpraɪsi, -ər, -ɪst

pride
BR prʌɪd, -z
AM praɪd, -z

prideful
BR ˈprʌɪdf(ʊ)l
AM ˈpraɪdfəl

pridefully
BR ˈprʌɪdfʊli, ˈprʌɪdfl̩i
AM ˈpraɪdfəli

prideless
BR ˈprʌɪdlɨs
AM ˈpraɪdlɨs

prie-dieu
BR ˌpriːˈdjəː(r), -z
AM priˈdjə, -z

prie-dieux
BR ˌpriːˈdjəː(r), ˌpriːˈdjəːz
AM priˈdjə

priest
BR priːst
AM prist

priestcraft
BR ˈpriːs(t)krɑːft, ˈpriːs(t)kraft
AM ˈpris(t)ˌkræft

priestess
BR ˌpriːˈstɛs, ˈpriːstɛs, ˈpriːstɨs, -ɪz
AM ˈpristɨs, -əz

priesthole
BR ˈpriːsthəʊl, -z
AM ˈpristˌ(h)oʊl, -z

priesthood
BR ˈpriːsthʊd
AM ˈpristˌ(h)ʊd

Priestland
BR ˈpriːs(t)lənd
AM ˈpris(t)ˌlænd

priestless
BR ˈpriːs(t)lɨs
AM ˈpris(t)lɨs

Priestley
BR ˈpriːs(t)li
AM ˈpris(t)li

priestlike
BR ˈpriːs(t)lʌɪk
AM ˈpris(t)ˌlaɪk

priestliness
BR ˈpriːs(t)lɪnɨs
AM ˈpris(t)linɨs

priestling
BR ˈpriːs(t)lɪŋ, -z
AM ˈpris(t)lɪŋ, -z

priestly
BR ˈpriːs(t)li
AM ˈpris(t)li

priests-in-charge
BR ˈpriːstsɪnˈtʃɑːdʒ
AM ˈpris(ts)ənˈtʃardʒ

prig
BR prɪɡ, -z
AM prɪɡ, -z

priggery
BR ˈprɪɡ(ə)ri
AM ˈprɪɡəri

priggish
BR ˈprɪɡɪʃ
AM ˈprɪɡɪʃ

priggishly
BR ˈprɪɡɨʃli
AM ˈprɪɡɨʃli

priggishness
BR ˈprɪɡɨʃnɨs
AM ˈprɪɡɪʃnɨs

priggism
BR ˈprɪɡɪz(ə)m
AM ˈprɪˌɡɪzəm

prim
BR prɪm
AM prɪm

prima ballerina
BR ˌpriːmə ˌbaləˈriːnə(r), -z
AM ˈpriməˌbæləˈrinə, -z

primacy
BR ˈprʌɪməsi
AM ˈpraɪməsi

prima donna
BR ˌpriːmə ˈdɒnə(r), -z
AM ˌprɪmə ˈdɑnə, ˌprimə +, -z

prima donna-ish
BR ˌpriːmə ˈdɒnə(r)ɪʃ
AM ˌprɪmə ˈdɑnəɪʃ, ˌprimə +

primaeval
BR prʌɪˈmiːvl
AM praɪˈmivəl

prima facie
BR ˌprʌɪmə ˈfeɪʃ(ɪ)iː
AM ˌprimə ˌfeɪʃi(ˌi), + ˌfeɪʃə

prima inter pares
BR ˌpriːmə(r) ˌɪntə ˈpɑːriːz, ˌprʌɪmə(r) +
AM ˌprimə ˌɪntər ˈpeɪˌriz

primal
BR ˈprʌɪml
AM ˈpraɪməl

primally
BR ˈprʌɪml̩i, ˈprʌɪməli
AM ˈpraɪməli

primarily
BR ˈprʌɪm(ə)rɨli, ˈprʌɪm(ə)rl̩i, prʌɪˈmɛrɨli
AM praɪˈmɛrəli, prəˈmɛrəli

primary
BR ˈprʌɪm(ə)r|i, -ɪz
AM ˈpraɪˌmɛri, ˈpraɪm(ə)ri, -z

primate[1]
archbishop
BR ˈprʌɪmət, ˈprʌɪmeɪt, -s
AM ˈpraɪmɪt, ˈpraɪˌmeɪt, -s

primate[2]
higher mammal
BR ˈprʌɪmeɪt, -s
AM ˈpraɪˌmeɪt, ˈpraɪmɪt, -s

primateship
BR ˈprʌɪmət-ʃɪp, ˈprʌɪmeɪt-ʃɪp, -s
AM ˈpraɪmɪtˌʃɪp, ˈpraɪˌmeɪtˌʃɪp, -s

primatial
BR prʌɪˈmeɪʃl
AM praɪˈmeɪʃəl

primatologist
BR ˌprʌɪməˈtɒlədʒɪst, -s
AM ˌpraɪməˈtɑlədʒəst, -s

primatology
BR ˌprʌɪməˈtɒlədʒi
AM ˌpraɪməˈtɑlədʒi

primavera
BR ˌpriːməˈvɛːrə(r), -z
AM ˌpriməˈvɛrə, -z

prime
BR prʌɪm, -z, -ɪŋ, -d
AM praɪm, -z, -ɪŋ, -d

primeness
BR ˈprʌɪmnɨs
AM ˈpraɪmnɨs

primer
BR ˈprʌɪmə(r), -z
AM ˈpraɪmər, -z

primeval
BR prʌɪˈmiːvl
AM praɪˈmivəl

primevally
BR prʌɪˈmiːvl̩i, prʌɪˈmiːvəli
AM praɪˈmivəli

primigravida
BR ˌprʌɪmɪˈɡravɪdə(r), ˌpriːmɪˈɡravɪdə(r), -z
AM ˌpraɪməˈɡrævədə, -z

primigravidae
BR ˌprʌɪmɪˈɡravɪdiː, ˌpriːmɪˈɡravɪdiː
AM ˌpraɪməˈɡrævədi, ˌpraɪməˈɡrævəˌdaɪ

primipara
BR prʌɪˈmɪp(ə)rə(r)
AM praɪˈmɪpərə

primiparae
BR prʌɪˈmɪp(ə)riː
AM praɪˈmɪpəri

primiparous
BR prʌɪˈmɪp(ə)rəs
AM praɪˈmɪpərəs

primitive
BR ˈprɪmɪtɪv, -z
AM ˈprɪmədɪv, -z

primitively
BR ˈprɪmɪtɪvli
AM ˈprɪmədɪvli

primitiveness
BR ˈprɪmɪtɪvnɨs
AM ˈprɪmədɪvnɨs

primitivism
BR ˈprɪmɪtɪvɪz(ə)m
AM ˈprɪmədəˌvɪzəm

primitivist
BR ˈprɪmɪtɪvɪst, -s
AM ˈprɪmədəvəst, -s

primly
BR ˈprɪmli
AM ˈprɪmli

primness
BR ˈprɪmnɨs
AM ˈprɪmnɨs

primo
BR ˈpriːməʊ, -z
AM ˈprimoʊ, -z

primogenital
BR ˌprʌɪmə(ʊ)ˈdʒɛnɪtl
AM ˌprʌɪmoʊˈdʒɛnədl

primogenitary
BR ˌprʌɪmə(ʊ)ˈdʒɛnɪt(ə)ri
AM ˌpraɪmoʊˈdʒɛnəˌtɛri

primogenitor
BR ˌprʌɪmə(ʊ)ˈdʒɛnɪtə(r), -z
AM ˌprʌɪmoʊˈdʒɛnədər, -z

primogeniture
BR ˌprʌɪmə(ʊ)ˈdʒɛnɪtʃə(r)
AM ˌpraɪmoʊˌdʒɛnəˌtʃʊ(ə)r

primordia
BR prʌɪˈmɔːdɪə(r)
AM praɪˈmɔrdiə

primordial
BR prʌɪˈmɔːdɪəl, -z
AM praɪˈmɔrdiəl, -z

primordiality
BR prʌɪˌmɔːdɪˈalɪti, ˌprʌɪmɔːdɪˈalɪti
AM ˌpraɪˌmɔrdiˈælədi

primordially
BR prʌɪˈmɔːdɪəli
AM praɪˈmɔrdiəli

primordium
BR prʌɪˈmɔːdɪəm
AM praɪˈmɔrdiəm

primp
BR prɪm|p, -ps, -pɪŋ, -(p)t
AM prɪmp, -s, -ɪŋ, -t

primrose
BR ˈprɪmrəʊz, -ɪz
AM ˈprɪmˌroʊz, -əz

primula
BR ˈprɪmjʊlə(r), -z
AM ˈprɪmjələ, -z

primum mobile
BR ˌprʌɪməm ˈməʊbɪl|i, ˌpriːməm +, + ˈməʊbl̩|i, -ɪz
AM ˌpraɪməm ˈmoʊbəˌli, -z

primus
BR ˈprʌɪməs, -ɪz
AM ˈpraɪməs, -əz

primus inter pares
BR ˌpriːməs ˌɪntə ˈpɑːriːz, ˌprʌɪməs +
AM ˌpraɪməs ˌɪntər ˈpeɪˌriz

prince
BR prɪns, -ɪz
AM prɪns, -ɪz

princedom
BR ˈprɪnsdəm, -z
AM ˈprɪnsdəm, -z

princelike
BR ˈprɪnslʌɪk
AM ˈprɪnsəˌlaɪk

princeliness
BR ˈprɪnslɪnɪs
AM ˈprɪnslinɪs

princeling
BR ˈprɪnslɪŋ, -z
AM ˈprɪnslɪŋ, -z

princely
BR ˈprɪnsl|i, -ɪə(r), -ɪɪst
AM ˈprɪnsli, -ər, -ɪst

princeship
BR ˈprɪnsʃɪp, -s
AM ˈprɪnsˌʃɪp, -s

princess
BR ˌprɪnˈsɛs, ˈprɪnsɪs, ˈprɪnsɛs, -ɪz
AM ˈprɪnsɪs, ˈprɪnˌsɛs, prɪnˈsɛs, -əz

Princeton
BR ˈprɪnstən
AM ˈprɪnstən

Princetown
BR ˈprɪnstaʊn
AM ˈprɪnsˌtoʊn

principal
BR ˈprɪnsɪpl, -z
AM ˈprɪnsəpəl, -z

principality
BR ˌprɪnsɪˈpalɪt|i, -ɪz
AM ˌprɪnsəˈpælədi, -z

principally
BR ˈprɪnsɪpl̩i, ˈprɪnsɪp(ə)li
AM ˈprɪnsəp(ə)li

principalship
BR ˈprɪnsɪplʃɪp, -s
AM ˈprɪnsəpəlˌʃɪp, -s

principate
BR ˈprɪnsɪpət, -s
AM ˈprɪnsəˌpeɪt, ˈprɪnsəpət, -s

Príncipe
BR ˈprɪnsɪpeɪ, ˈprɪnsɪpi
AM ˈprɪn(t)səpi

Principia
BR prɪnˈsɪpɪə(r)
AM ˌprɪnˈsɪpiə

principle
BR ˈprɪnsɪpl, -z, -d
AM ˈprɪnsəpəl, -z, -d

Pringle
BR ˈprɪŋgl
AM ˈprɪŋgəl

prink
BR prɪŋ|k, -ks, -kɪŋ, -(k)t
AM prɪŋ|k, -ks, -kɪŋ, -(k)t

Prinknash
BR ˈprɪnɪdʒ
AM ˈprɪnədʒ

print
BR prɪnt, -s, -ɪŋ, -ɪd
AM prɪn|t, -ts, -(t)ɪŋ, -(t)ɪd

printability
BR ˌprɪntəˈbɪlɪti
AM ˌprɪn(t)əˈbɪlɪdi

printable
BR ˈprɪntəbl
AM ˈprɪn(t)əbəl

printer
BR ˈprɪntə(r), -z
AM ˈprɪn(t)ər, -z

printery
BR ˈprɪnt(ə)r|i, -ɪz
AM ˈprɪn(t)əri, -z

printhead
BR ˈprɪnthɛd, -z
AM ˈprɪntˌ(h)ɛd, -z

printing
BR ˈprɪntɪŋ, -z
AM ˈprɪn(t)ɪŋ, -z

printless
BR ˈprɪntlɪs
AM ˈprɪn(t)lɪs

printmaker
BR ˈprɪntˌmeɪkə(r), -z
AM ˈprɪntˌmeɪkər, -z

printmaking
BR ˈprɪntˌmeɪkɪŋ
AM ˈprɪntˌmeɪkɪŋ

printout
BR ˈprɪntaʊt, -s
AM ˈprɪnˌtaʊt, ˈprɪn(t)ˌaʊt, -s

printwheel
BR ˈprɪntwiːl, -z
AM ˈprɪntˌ(h)wil, -z

printworks
BR ˈprɪntwəːks
AM ˈprɪntˌwərks

prion[1]
bird
BR ˈprʌɪən, -z
AM ˈpraɪˌɑn, -z

prion[2]
infectious particle
BR ˈpriːɒn, -z
AM ˈpriˌɑn, -z

prior
BR ˈprʌɪə(r), -z
AM ˈpraɪ(ə)r, -z

priorate
BR ˈprʌɪərət, -s
AM ˈpraɪərət, -s

prioress
BR ˈprʌɪərɪs, ˌprʌɪəˈrɛs, -ɪz
AM ˈpraɪ(ə)rəs, -əz

prioritisation
BR prʌɪˌɒrɪtʌɪˈzeɪʃn, ˌprʌɪərɪtʌɪˈzeɪʃn
AM ˌpraɪˌɔrədəˈzeɪʃən, ˌpraɪˌɔrəˌtaɪˈzeɪʃən

prioritise
BR prʌɪˈɒrɪtʌɪz, ˈprʌɪərɪtʌɪz, -ɪz, -ɪŋ, -d
AM praɪˈɔrəˌtaɪz, ˈpraɪərəˌtaɪz, -ɪz, -ɪŋ, -d

prioritization
BR prʌɪˌɒrɪtʌɪˈzeɪʃn, ˌprʌɪərɪtʌɪˈzeɪʃn
AM ˌpraɪˌɔrədəˈzeɪʃən, ˌpraɪˌɔrəˌtaɪˈzeɪʃən

prioritize
BR prʌɪˈɒrɪtʌɪz, ˈprʌɪərɪtʌɪz, -ɪz, -ɪŋ, -d
AM praɪˈɔrəˌtaɪz, ˈpraɪərəˌtaɪz, -ɪz, -ɪŋ, -d

priority
BR prʌɪˈɒrɪt|i, -ɪz
AM praɪˈɔrədi, -z

priorship
BR ˈprʌɪəʃɪp, -s
AM ˈpraɪərˌʃɪp, -s

priory
BR ˈprʌɪər|i, -ɪz
AM ˈpraɪ(ə)ri, -z

Priscian
BR ˈprɪʃɪən, ˈprɪʃn
AM ˈprɪʃən

Priscilla
BR prɪˈsɪlə(r)
AM prəˈsɪlə

prise
BR prʌɪz, -ɪz, -ɪŋ, -d
AM praɪz, -ɪz, -ɪŋ, -d

prism
BR ˈprɪz(ə)m, -z
AM ˈprɪzəm, -z

prismal
BR ˈprɪzml
AM ˈprɪzməl

prismatic
BR prɪzˈmatɪk
AM prɪzˈmædɪk

prismatically
BR prɪzˈmatɪkli
AM prɪzˈmædək(ə)li

prismoid
BR ˈprɪzmɔɪd, -z
AM ˈprɪzˌmɔɪd, -z

prismoidal
BR prɪzˈmɔɪdl
AM prɪzˈmɔɪdəl

prison
BR ˈprɪzn, -z
AM ˈprɪzn, -z

prisoner
BR ˈprɪznə(r), ˈprɪzn̩ə(r), -z
AM ˈprɪznər, ˈprɪzn̩ər, -z

prissily
BR ˈprɪsɪli
AM ˈprɪsɪli

prissiness
BR ˈprɪsɪnɪs
AM ˈprɪsinɪs

prissy
BR ˈprɪs|i, -ɪə(r), -ɪɪst
AM ˈprɪsi, -ər, -ɪst

Priština
BR ˈprɪʃtɪnə(r)
AM ˈprɪʃtɪnə

pristine
BR ˈprɪstiːn
AM ˈprɪˌstin, prɪˈstin

Pritchard
BR ˈprɪtʃəd, ˈprɪtʃɑːd
AM ˈprɪtʃərd

Pritchett
BR ˈprɪtʃɪt
AM ˈprɪtʃɪt

prithee
BR ˈprɪðiː
AM ˈprɪði

Pritt
BR prɪt
AM prɪt

privacy
BR ˈprɪvəsi, ˈprʌɪvəsi
AM ˈpraɪvəsi

private
BR ˈprʌɪvɪt, -s
AM ˈpraɪvɪt, -s

privateer
BR ˌprʌɪvɪˈtɪə(r), -z, -ɪŋ
AM ˌpraɪvəˈtɪ(ə)r, -z, -ɪŋ

privateering
BR ˌprʌɪvɪˈtɪərɪŋ
AM ˌpraɪvəˈtɪrɪŋ
privateersman
BR ˌprʌɪvɪˈtɪəzmən
AM ˌpraɪvəˈtɪrzmən
privateersmen
BR ˌprʌɪvɪˈtɪəzmən
AM ˌpraɪvəˈtɪrzmən
privately
BR ˈprʌɪvɪtli
AM ˈpraɪvɪtli
privation
BR prʌɪˈveɪʃn, -z
AM praɪˈveɪʃən, -z
privatisation
BR ˌprʌɪvɪtʌɪˈzeɪʃn, -z
AM ˌpraɪvədəˈzeɪʃən, ˌpraɪvəˌtaɪˈzeɪʃən, -z
privatise
BR ˈprʌɪvɪtʌɪz, -ɪz, -ɪŋ, -d
AM ˈpraɪvəˌtaɪz, -ɪz, -ɪŋ, -d
privatiser
BR ˈprʌɪvɪtʌɪzə(r), -z
AM ˈpraɪvəˌtaɪzər, -z
privative
BR ˈprʌɪvɪtɪv
AM ˈpraɪvədɪv
privatively
BR ˈprʌɪvɪtɪvli
AM ˈpraɪvədɪvli
privatization
BR ˌprʌɪvɪtʌɪˈzeɪʃn, -z
AM ˌpraɪvədəˈzeɪʃən, ˌpraɪvəˌtaɪˈzeɪʃən, -z
privatize
BR ˈprʌɪvɪtʌɪz, -ɪz, -ɪŋ, -d
AM ˈpraɪvəˌtaɪz, -ɪz, -ɪŋ, -d
privatizer
BR ˈprʌɪvɪtʌɪzə(r), -z
AM ˈpraɪvəˌtaɪzər, -z
privet
BR ˈprɪvɪt, -s
AM ˈprɪvɪt, -s
privilege
BR ˈprɪv(ɪ)l|ɪdʒ, ˈprɪvl̩|ɪdʒ, -ɪdʒɪz
AM ˈprɪv(ə)lɪdʒ, -ɪz
privileged
BR ˈprɪv(ɪ)lɪdʒd, ˈprɪvl̩ɪdʒd
AM ˈprɪv(ə)lɪdʒd
privily
BR ˈprɪvɪli
AM ˈprɪvɪli
privity
BR ˈprɪvɪt|i, -ɪz
AM ˈprɪvɪdi, -z
privy
BR ˈprɪv|i, -ɪz
AM ˈprɪvi, -z
prix[1]
singular
BR priː
AM pri
prix[2]
plural
BR priː, priːz
AM pri, priz
prix fixe
BR ˌpriː ˈfɪks, + ˈfiːks
AM ˈpri ˈfiks
Prix Goncourt
BR ˌpriː ɡɒ̃ˈkʊə(r), + ɡɒ̃ˈkɔː(r)
AM ˈpri ˌɡɔnˈkʊ(ə)r, ˈpri ˌɡɑnˈkʊ(ə)r
prize
BR prʌɪz, -ɪz, -ɪŋ, -d
AM praɪz, -ɪz, -ɪŋ, -d
prizefight
BR ˈprʌɪzfʌɪt, -s
AM ˈpraɪzˌfaɪt, -s
prizefighter
BR ˈprʌɪzˌfʌɪtə(r), -z
AM ˈpraɪzˌfaɪdər, -z
prizefighting
BR ˈprʌɪzˌfʌɪtɪŋ
AM ˈpraɪzˌfaɪdɪŋ
prizeman
BR ˈprʌɪzmən
AM ˈpraɪzmən
prizemen
BR ˈprʌɪzmən
AM ˈpraɪzmən
prizewinner
BR ˈprʌɪzˌwɪnə(r), -z
AM ˈpraɪzˌwɪnər, -z
prizewinning
BR ˈprʌɪzˌwɪnɪŋ
AM ˈpraɪzˌwɪnɪŋ
PRO
BR ˌpiːɑːrˈəʊ, -z
AM ˌpiˌɑrˈoʊ, -z
pro
BR prəʊ, -z
AM proʊ, -z
proa
BR ˈprəʊə(r), -z
AM ˈproʊə, -z
proaction
BR (ˌ)prəʊˈakʃn
AM proʊˈækʃən
proactive
BR (ˌ)prəʊˈaktɪv
AM proʊˈæktɪv
proactively
BR (ˌ)prəʊˈaktɪvli
AM proʊˈæktɪvli
proactivity
BR ˌprəʊakˈtɪvɪti
AM ˌproʊˌækˈtɪvɪdi
pro-am
BR ˌprəʊˈam, -z
AM ˌproʊˈæm, -z
probabilism
BR ˈprɒbəbɪlɪz(ə)m, ˈprɒbəbl̩ɪz(ə)m
AM ˈprɑbəbəˌlɪzəm
probabilist
BR ˈprɒbəbɪlɪst, ˈprɒbəbl̩ɪst, -s
AM ˈprɑbəbələst, -s
probabilistic
BR ˌprɒbəbɪˈlɪstɪk, ˌprɒbəblˈɪstɪk
AM ˌprɑbəbəˈlɪstɪk
probability
BR ˌprɒbəˈbɪlɪt|i, -ɪz
AM ˌprɑbəˈbɪlɪdi, -z
probable
BR ˈprɒbəbl
AM ˈprɑbəbəl
probably
BR ˈprɒbəbli
AM ˈprɑbəbli
proband
BR ˈprəʊband, ˈprəʊbənd, -z
AM ˈproʊˌbænd, -z
probang
BR ˈprəʊbaŋ, -z
AM ˈproʊˌbæŋ, -z
probate
BR ˈprəʊbeɪt, -s
AM ˈproʊˌbeɪt, -s
probation
BR prəˈbeɪʃn
AM proʊˈbeɪʃən
probational
BR prəˈbeɪʃn̩(ə)l, prəˈbeɪʃən(ə)l
AM proʊˈbeɪʃ(ə)nəl
probationary
BR prəˈbeɪʃn̩(ə)ri
AM proʊˈbeɪʃəˌnɛri
probationer
BR prəˈbeɪʃn̩ə(r), prəˈbeɪʃ(ə)nə(r), -z
AM proʊˈbeɪʃ(ə)nər, -z
probationership
BR prəˈbeɪʃn̩əʃɪp, prəˈbeɪʃ(ə)nəʃɪp, -s
AM proʊˈbeɪʃ(ə)nərˌʃɪp, -s
probative
BR ˈprəʊbətɪv
AM ˈproʊbədɪv
probe
BR prəʊb, -z, -ɪŋ, -d
AM proʊb, -z, -ɪŋ, -d
probeable
BR ˈprəʊbəbl
AM ˈproʊbəbəl
prober
BR ˈprəʊbə(r), -z
AM ˈproʊbər, -z
probing
BR ˈprəʊbɪŋ, -z
AM ˈproʊbɪŋ, -z
probingly
BR ˈprəʊbɪŋli
AM ˈproʊbɪŋli
probit
BR ˈprɒbɪt, -s
AM ˈprɑbət, -s
probity
BR ˈprəʊbɪti
AM ˈproʊbədi
problem
BR ˈprɒbləm, -z
AM ˈprɑbləm, -z
problematic
BR ˌprɒbləˈmatɪk
AM ˈprɑbləˈmædɪk
problematical
BR ˌprɒbləˈmatɪkl
AM ˌprɑbləˈmædəkəl
problematically
BR ˌprɒbləˈmatɪkli
AM ˌprɑbləˈmædək(ə)li
problematisation
BR ˌprɒbləmətʌɪˈzeɪʃn
AM ˌprɑbləmədəˈzeɪʃən, ˌprɑbləməˌtaɪˈzeɪʃən
problematise
BR ˈprɒbləmətʌɪz, -ɪz, -ɪŋ, -d
AM ˈprɑbləməˌtaɪz, -ɪz, -ɪŋ, -d
problematization
BR ˌprɒbləmətʌɪˈzeɪʃn
AM ˌprɑbləmədəˈzeɪʃən, ˌprɑbləməˌtaɪˈzeɪʃən
problematize
BR ˈprɒbləmətʌɪz, -ɪz, -ɪŋ, -d
AM ˈprɑbləməˌtaɪz, -ɪz, -ɪŋ, -d
probosces
BR prəˈbɒsiːz
AM proʊˈbɑsiz
proboscidean
BR ˌprɒbəˈsɪdɪən, -z
AM ˌproʊbəˈsɪdiən, proʊˌbɑsəˈdiən, -z
proboscidian
BR ˌprɒbəˈsɪdɪən, -z
AM ˌproʊbəˈsɪdiən, proʊˌbɑsəˈdiən, -z
proboscidiferous
BR prəˌbɒsɪˈdɪf(ə)rəs
AM proʊˌbɑsəˈdɪf(ə)rəs
proboscidiform
BR ˌprɒbəˈsɪdɪfɔːm
AM ˌproʊbəˈsɪdəˌfɔ(ə)rm
proboscis
BR prəˈbɒs|ɪs, -ɪsɪz
AM proʊˈbɑs|əz, proʊˈbɑs|kəs, -ɪsiz\-ɪsiz
Probyn
BR ˈprəʊbɪn
AM ˈproʊbən
procain
BR ˈprəʊkeɪn
AM ˈproʊˌkeɪn
procaine
BR ˈprəʊkeɪn
AM ˈproʊˌkeɪn
procaryote
BR prəʊˈkarɪəʊt, prəʊˈkarɪɒt, -s
AM proʊˈkɛrioʊt, -s

procaryotic
BR prəʊˌkarɪˈɒtɪk, ˌprəʊkarɪˈɒtɪk
AM proʊˌkɛriˈɑdɪk

Procea
BR ˈprəʊsɪə(r)
AM ˈproʊsie

procedural
BR prəˈsiːdʒ(ə)rəl, prəˈsiːdʒ(ə)rl̩
AM prəˈsidʒərəl, proʊˈsidʒərəl

procedurally
BR prəˈsiːdʒ(ə)rəli, prəˈsiːdʒ(ə)rl̩i
AM prəˈsidʒərəli, proʊˈsidʒərəli

procedure
BR prəˈsiːdʒə(r), -z
AM prəˈsidʒər, proʊˈsidʒər, -z

proceed
verb
BR prəˈsiːd, -z, -ɪŋ, -ɨd
AM prəˈsid, proʊˈsid, -z, -ɪŋ, -ɨd

proceedings
BR prəˈsiːdɪŋz
AM prəˈsidɪŋz, proʊˈsidɪŋz

proceeds
noun
BR ˈprəʊsiːdz
AM ˈproʊˌsidz

process¹
noun, verb, treat in a process
BR ˈprəʊsɛs, -ɪz, -ɪŋ, -t
AM ˈprɑˌsɛs, -əz, -ɪŋ, -t

process²
verb, walk in procession
BR prəˈsɛs, -ɪz, -ɪŋ, -t
AM prəˈsɛs, -əz, -ɪŋ, -t

processable
BR ˈprəʊsɛsəbl, ˈprəʊsɛsəbl
AM ˈprɑsɛsəbəl

procession
BR prəˈsɛʃn, -z
AM prəˈsɛʃən, -z

processional
BR prəˈsɛʃn̩(ə)l, prəˈsɛʃən(ə)l, -z
AM prəˈsɛʃ(ə)nəl, -z

processionary
BR prəˈsɛʃn̩(ə)ri
AM prəˈsɛʃənri, prəˈsɛʃnɛri

processionist
BR prəˈsɛʃn̩ɪst, prəˈsɛʃənɪst, -s
AM prəˈsɛʃ(ə)nəst, -s

processor
BR ˈprəʊsɛsə(r), -z
AM ˈprɑˌsɛsər, -z

procès-verbal
BR ˌprɒseɪvəːˈbɑːl, -z
AM ˌproʊˌseɪˌvərˈbɑl, -z

procès-verbaux
BR ˌprɒseɪvəːˈbəʊ
AM ˌproʊˌseɪˌvərˈboʊ

pro-choice
BR ˌprəʊˈtʃɔɪs
AM ˌproʊˈtʃɔɪs

prochronism
BR ˈprəʊkrənɪz(ə)m, -z
AM ˈproʊkrəˌnɪzəm, ˈprɑkrəˌnɪzəm, -z

proclaim
BR prəˈkleɪm, -z, -ɪŋ, -d
AM prəˈkleɪm, proʊˈkleɪm, -z, -ɪŋ, -d

proclaimer
BR prəˈkleɪmə(r), -z
AM prəˈkleɪmər, -z

proclamation
BR ˌprɒkləˈmeɪʃn, -z
AM ˌprɑkləˈmeɪʃən, -z

proclamatory
BR prə(ʊ)ˈklamət(ə)ri
AM prəˈklæməˌtɔri

proclitic
BR prə(ʊ)ˈklɪtɪk, -s
AM proʊˈklɪdɪk, -s

proclitically
BR prəˈklɪtɨkli
AM proʊˈklɪdɨk(ə)li

proclivity
BR prəˈklɪvɪt|i, -ɪz
AM prəˈklɪvɨdi, proʊˈklɪvɨdi, -z

Procne
BR ˈprɒkni
AM ˈprɑkni

proconsul
BR ˌprəʊˈkɒnsl
AM proʊˈkɑnsəl

proconsular
BR ˌprəʊˈkɒnsjʉlə(r)
AM proʊˈkɑns(j)(ə)lər

proconsulate
BR ˌprəʊˈkɒnsjʉlət, -s
AM proʊˈkɑns(j)(ə)lət, -s

proconsulship
BR ˌprəʊˈkɒnslʃɪp, -s
AM proʊˈkɑnsəlˌʃɪp, -s

Procopius
BR prəʊˈkəʊpɪəs
AM proʊˈkoʊpiəs

procrastinate
BR prə(ʊ)ˈkrastɨneɪt, -s, -ɪŋ, -ɨd
AM prəˈkræstəˌneɪ|t, proʊˈkræstəˌneɪ|t, -ts, -dɪŋ, -dɨd

procrastination
BR prə(ʊ)ˌkrastɪˈneɪʃn
AM prəˌkræstəˈneɪʃən, proʊˌkræstəˈneɪʃən

procrastinative
BR prə(ʊ)ˈkrastɨnətɪv
AM prəˈkræstəˌneɪdɪv, proʊˈkræstəˌneɪdɪv

procrastinator
BR prə(ʊ)ˈkrastɨneɪtə(r), -z
AM prəˈkræstəˌneɪdər, proʊˈkræstəˌneɪdər, -z

procrastinatory
BR prə(ʊ)ˈkrastɨnət(ə)ri
AM prəˈkræstənəˌtɔri, proʊˈkræstənəˌtɔri

procreant
BR ˈprəʊkrɪənt
AM ˈproʊkriənt

procreate
BR ˈprəʊkrɪeɪt, -s, -ɪŋ, -ɨd
AM ˈproʊkriˌeɪ|t, -ts, -dɪŋ, -dɨd

procreation
BR ˌprəʊkrɪˈeɪʃn
AM ˌproʊkriˈeɪʃən

procreative
BR ˈprəʊkrɪeɪtɪv, ˈprəʊkrɪətɪv
AM ˈproʊkriˌeɪdɪv

procreator
BR ˈprəʊkrɪeɪtə(r), -z
AM ˈproʊkriˌeɪdər, -z

Procrustean
BR prə(ʊ)ˈkrʌstɪən
AM proʊˈkrəstiən

Procrustes
BR prə(ʊ)ˈkrʌstiːz
AM proʊˈkrəstiz

Procter
BR ˈprɒktə(r)
AM ˈprɑktər

proctological
BR ˌprɒktəˈlɒdʒɪkl
AM ˌprɑktəˈlɑdʒəkəl

proctologist
BR prɒkˈtɒlədʒɪst, -s
AM prɑkˈtɑlədʒəst, -s

proctology
BR prɒkˈtɒlədʒi
AM prɑkˈtɑlədʒi

proctor
BR ˈprɒktə(r), -z
AM ˈprɑktər, -z

proctorial
BR prɒkˈtɔːrɪəl
AM prɑkˈtɔriəl

proctorship
BR ˈprɒktəʃɪp, -s
AM ˈprɑktərˌʃɪp, -s

proctoscope
BR ˈprɒktəskəʊp, -s
AM ˈprɑktəˌskoʊp, -s

procumbent
BR prə(ʊ)ˈkʌmb(ə)nt
AM proʊˈkəmbənt

procurable
BR prəˈkjʊərəbl, prəˈkjɔːrəbl
AM prəˈkjʊrəbəl

procural
BR prəˈkjʊərəl, prəˈkjʊərl̩, prəˈkjɔːrəl, prəˈkjɔːrl̩
AM prəˈkjərəl

procurance
BR prəˈkjʊərəns, prəˈkjʊərn̩s, prəˈkjɔːrəns, prəˈkjɔːrn̩s
AM prəˈkjʊrəns

procuration
BR ˌprɒkjʉˈreɪʃn, -z
AM ˌprɑkjəˈreɪʃən, -z

procurator
BR ˈprɒkjʉreɪtə(r), -z
AM ˈprɑkjəˌreɪdər, -z

procurator fiscal
BR ˌprɒkjʉreɪtə ˈfɪskl
AM ˌprɑkjəˌreɪdər ˈfɪskəl

procuratorial
BR ˌprɒkjʉrəˈtɔːrɪəl
AM ˌprɑkjərəˈtɔriəl

procurators fiscal
BR ˌprɒkjʉreɪtəz ˈfɪskl
AM ˌprɑkjəˌreɪdərz ˈfɪskəl

procuratorship
BR ˈprɒkjʉreɪtəʃɪp, -s
AM ˈprɑkjəreɪdərˌʃɪp, -s

procuratory
BR ˈprɒkjʉrət(ə)ri
AM ˈprɑkjərəˌtɔri

procure
BR prəˈkjʊə(r), prəˈkjɔː(r), -z, -ɪŋ, -d
AM prəˈkju(ə)r, proʊˈkjʊ(ə)r, -z, -ɪŋ, -d

procurement
BR prəˈkjʊəm(ə)nt, prəˈkjɔːm(ə)nt, -s
AM prəˈkjʊrmənt, proʊˈkjʊrmənt, -s

procurer
BR prəˈkjʊərə(r), prəˈkjɔːrə(r), -z
AM prəˈkjurər, proʊˈkjʊrər, -z

procuress
BR prəˈkjʊərɛs, prəˈkjʊərɪs, prəˈkjɔːrɛs, prəˈkjɔːrɪs, -ɪz
AM prəˈkjurəs, proʊˈkjʊrəs, -əz

Procyon
BR ˈprəʊsɪən
AM ˈproʊsiən

prod
BR prɒd, -z, -ɪŋ, -ɨd
AM prɑd, -z, -ɪŋ, -əd

prodder
BR ˈprɒdə(r), -z
AM ˈprɑdər, -z

prodigal
BR 'prɒdɪgl, -z
AM 'prɑdəgəl, -z
prodigalise
BR 'prɒdɪgl̩ʌɪz, 'prɒdɪgəlʌɪz, -ɪz, -ɪŋ, -d
AM 'prɑdɪgəˌlaɪz, -ɪz, -ɪŋ, -d
prodigality
BR ˌprɒdɪ'galɪti
AM ˌprɑdə'gælədi
prodigalize
BR 'prɒdɪgl̩ʌɪz, 'prɒdɪgəlʌɪz, -ɪz, -ɪŋ, -d
AM 'prɑdəgəˌlaɪz, -ɪz, -ɪŋ, -d
prodigally
BR 'prɒdɪgl̩i, 'prɒdɪgəli
AM 'prɑdəgəli
prodigalness
BR 'prɒdɪglnəs
AM 'prɑdəgəlnəs
prodigious
BR prə'dɪdʒəs
AM prə'dɪdʒəs, proʊ'dɪdʒəs
prodigiously
BR prə'dɪdʒəsli
AM prə'dɪdʒəsli, proʊ'dɪdʒəsli
prodigiousness
BR prə'dɪdʒəsnəs
AM prə'dɪdʒəsnəs, proʊ'dɪdʒəsnəs
prodigy
BR 'prɒdɪdʒ|i, -ɪz
AM 'prɑdədʒi, -z
prodromal
BR 'prɒdrəʊml, prə(ʊ)'drəʊml
AM proʊ'droʊməl
prodrome
BR 'prəʊdrəʊm, -z
AM 'proʊˌdroʊm, -z
prodromic
BR prə(ʊ)'drɒmɪk
AM proʊ'drɑmɪk
produce[1]
noun
BR 'prɒdjuːs, 'prɒdʒuːs
AM 'prɑˌdus, 'proʊˌdus
produce[2]
verb
BR prə'djuːs, prə'dʒuːs, -ɪz, -ɪŋ, -t
AM prə'd(j)us, proʊ'd(j)us, -əz, -ɪŋ, -t
producer
BR prə'djuːsə(r), prə'dʒuːsə(r), -z
AM prə'd(j)usər, proʊ'd(j)usər, -z
producibility
BR prəˌdjuːsɪ'bɪlɪti, prəˌdʒuːsɪ'bɪlɪti
AM prəˌd(j)usə'bɪlɨdi, proʊˌd(j)usə'bɪlɨdi
producible
BR prə'djuːsɪbl, prə'dʒuːsɪbl
AM prə'd(j)usəbəl, proʊ'd(j)usəbəl
product
BR 'prɒdʌkt, -s
AM 'prɑdək(t), -(t)s
production
BR prə'dʌkʃn, -z
AM prə'dəkʃən, proʊ'dəkʃən, -z
productional
BR prə'dʌkʃn̩(ə)l, prə'dʌkʃən(ə)l
AM prə'dəkʃ(ə)nəl, proʊ'dəkʃ(ə)nəl
productive
BR prə'dʌktɪv
AM prə'dəktɪv, proʊ'dəktɪv
productively
BR prə'dʌktɪvli
AM prə'dəktɪvli, proʊ'dəktɪvli
productiveness
BR prə'dʌktɪvnɪs
AM prə'dəktɪvnɪs, proʊ'dəktɪvnɪs
productivity
BR ˌprɒdʌk'tɪvɪti
AM prɑˌdək'tɪvɨdi, ˌproʊˌdək'tɪvɨdi
proem
BR 'prəʊɛm, -z
AM 'proʊˌɛm, -z
proemial
BR prəʊ'ɛmɪəl
AM proʊ'ɛmiəl
Prof.
BR prɒf, -s
AM prɔf, prɑf, -s
profanation
BR ˌprɒfə'neɪʃn, -z
AM ˌprɑfə'neɪʃən, -z
profane
BR prə'feɪn, -ə(r), -ɪst
AM prə'feɪn, proʊ'feɪn, -ər, -ɪst
profanely
BR prə'feɪnli
AM prə'feɪnli, proʊ'feɪnli
profaneness
BR prə'feɪnnɪs
AM prə'feɪ(n)nɪs, proʊ'feɪ(n)nɪs
profaner
BR prə'feɪnə(r), -z
AM prə'feɪnər, proʊ'feɪnər, -z
profanity
BR prə'fanɪt|i, -ɪz
AM prə'fænədi, proʊ'fænədi, -z
profess
BR prə'fɛs, -ɪz, -ɪŋ, -t
AM prə'fɛs, proʊ'fɛs, -əz, -ɪŋ, -t
professedly
BR prə'fɛsɪdli
AM prə'fɛsədli, proʊ'fɛsədli
profession
BR prə'fɛʃn, -z
AM prə'fɛʃən, proʊ'fɛʃən, -z
professional
BR prə'fɛʃn̩(ə)l, prə'fɛʃ(ə)n(ə)l, -z
AM prə'fɛʃ(ə)nəl, proʊ'fɛʃ(ə)nəl, -z
professionalisation
BR prəˌfɛʃn̩əlʌɪ'zeɪʃn, prəˌfɛʃn̩l̩ʌɪ'zeɪʃn, prəˌfɛʃənl̩ʌɪ'zeɪʃn, prəˌfɛʃ(ə)nəlʌɪ'zeɪʃn
AM prəˌfɛʃənl̩ə'zeɪʃən, proʊˌfɛʃənl̩ə'zeɪʃən, prəˌfɛʃnələ'zeɪʃən, proʊˌfɛʃnələ'zeɪʃən, prəˌfɛʃənlˌaɪ'zeɪʃən, proʊˌfɛʃənlˌaɪ'zeɪʃən, prəˌfɛʃnəˌlaɪ'zeɪʃən, proʊˌfɛʃnəˌlaɪ'zeɪʃən
professionalise
BR prə'fɛʃn̩əlʌɪz, prə'fɛʃn̩l̩ʌɪz, prə'fɛʃənl̩ʌɪz, prə'fɛʃ(ə)nəlʌɪz, -ɪz, -ɪŋ, -d
AM prə'fɛʃənlˌaɪz, proʊ'fɛʃənlˌaɪz, prə'fɛʃnəˌlaɪz, proʊ'fɛʃnəˌlaɪz, -ɪz, -ɪŋ, -d
professionalism
BR prə'fɛʃn̩əlɪz(ə)m, prə'fɛʃn̩l̩ɪz(ə)m, prə'fɛʃənl̩ɪz(ə)m, prə'fɛʃ(ə)nəlɪz(ə)m
AM prə'fɛʃənlˌɪzəm, proʊ'fɛʃənlˌɪzəm, prə'fɛʃnəˌlɪzəm, proʊ'fɛʃnəˌlɪzəm
professionalization
BR prəˌfɛʃn̩əlʌɪ'zeɪʃn, prəˌfɛʃn̩l̩ʌɪ'zeɪʃn, prəˌfɛʃənl̩ʌɪ'zeɪʃn, prəˌfɛʃ(ə)nəlʌɪ'zeɪʃn
AM prəˌfɛʃənl̩ə'zeɪʃən, proʊˌfɛʃənl̩ə'zeɪʃən, prəˌfɛʃnələ'zeɪʃən, proʊˌfɛʃnələ'zeɪʃən, prəˌfɛʃənlˌaɪ'zeɪʃən, proʊˌfɛʃənlˌaɪ'zeɪʃən, prəˌfɛʃnəˌlaɪ'zeɪʃən, proʊˌfɛʃnəˌlaɪ'zeɪʃən
professionalize
BR prə'fɛʃn̩əlʌɪz, prə'fɛʃn̩l̩ʌɪz, prə'fɛʃənl̩ʌɪz, prə'fɛʃ(ə)nəlʌɪz, -ɪz, -ɪŋ, -d
AM prə'fɛʃənlˌaɪz, proʊ'fɛʃənlˌaɪz, prə'fɛʃnəˌlaɪz, proʊ'fɛʃnəˌlaɪz, -ɪz, -ɪŋ, -d
professionally
BR prə'fɛʃn̩əli, prə'fɛʃn̩l̩i, prə'fɛʃənl̩i, prə'fɛʃ(ə)nəli
AM prə'fɛʃ(ə)nəli, proʊ'fɛʃ(ə)nəli
professionless
BR prə'fɛʃnləs
AM prə'fɛʃənləs, proʊ'fɛʃənləs
professor
BR prə'fɛsə(r), -z
AM prə'fɛsər, proʊ'fɛsər, -z
professorate
BR prə'fɛs(ə)rət, -s
AM prə'fɛsərət, proʊ'fɛsərət, -s
professorial
BR ˌprɒfɪ'sɔːrɪəl
AM ¦prɑfə¦sɔriəl, ¦proʊfə¦sɔriəl
professorially
BR ˌprɒfɪ'sɔːrɪəli
AM ¦prɑfə¦sɔriəli, ¦proʊfə¦sɔriəli
professoriate
BR ˌprɒfɪ'sɔːrɪət
AM ˌprɑfə'sɔriət, ˌproʊfə'sɔriət
professorship
BR prə'fɛsəʃɪp, -s
AM prə'fɛsərˌʃɪp, proʊ'fɛsərˌʃɪp, -s
proffer
BR 'prɒf|ə(r), -əz, -(ə)rɪŋ, -əd
AM 'prɑf|ər, -ərz, -(ə)rɪŋ, -ərd
proficiency
BR prə'fɪʃnsi
AM prə'fɪʃənsi, proʊ'fɪʃənsi
proficient
BR prə'fɪʃnt
AM prə'fɪʃənt, proʊ'fɪʃənt
proficiently
BR prə'fɪʃntli
AM prə'fɪʃən(t)li, proʊ'fɪʃən(t)li
profile
BR 'prəʊfʌɪl, -z, -ɪŋ, -d
AM 'proʊˌfaɪl, -z, -ɪŋ, -d
profiler
BR 'prəʊfʌɪlə(r), -z
AM 'proʊˌfaɪlər, -z
profilist
BR 'prəʊfʌɪlɪst, -s
AM 'proʊˌfaɪlɪst, -s

profit
BR ˈprɒf|ɪt, -ɪts, -ɨtɪŋ, -ɨtɨd
AM ˈprɑfə|t, -ts, -dɪŋ, -dəd

profitability
BR ˌprɒfɨtəˈbɪlɨt|i, -ɪz
AM ˌprɑfədəˈbɪlɨdi, -z

profitable
BR ˈprɒfɨtəbl
AM ˈprɑfədəbəl, ˈprɑftəbəl

profitableness
BR ˈprɒfɨtəblnəs
AM ˈprɑfədəbəlnəs, ˈprɑftəbəlnəs

profitably
BR ˈprɒfɨtəbli
AM ˈprɑfədəbli, ˈprɑftəbli

profiteer
BR ˌprɒfɨˈtɪə(r), -z, -ɪŋ, -d
AM ˌprɑfəˌtɪ(ə)r, -z, -ɪŋ, -d

profiterole
BR prəˈfɪtərəʊl, -z
AM prəˈfɪdəˌroʊl, -z

profitless
BR ˈprɒfɨtlɨs
AM ˈprɑfətləs

profligacy
BR ˈprɒflɨgəsi
AM ˈprɑfləgəsi

profligate
BR ˈprɒflɨgət, -s
AM ˈprɑfləgət, ˈprɑfləˌgeɪt, -s

profligately
BR ˈprɒflɨgətli
AM ˈprɑfləgətli

profligateness
BR ˈprɒflɨgətnəs
AM ˈprɑfləgətnəs

pro-forma
BR (ˌ)prəʊˈfɔːmə(*r*)
AM proʊˈfɔrmə

profound
BR prəˈfaʊnd, -ə(r), -ɨst
AM prəˈfaʊnd, proʊˈfaʊnd, -ər, -əst

profoundly
BR prəˈfaʊndli
AM prəˈfaʊn(d)li, proʊˈfaʊn(d)li

profoundness
BR prəˈfaʊn(d)nəs
AM prəˈfaʊn(d)nəs, proʊˈfaʊn(d)nəs

Profumo
BR prəˈfjuːməʊ
AM prəˈf(j)umoʊ

profundity
BR prəˈfʌndɪt|i, -ɪz
AM prəˈfəndədi, proʊˈfəndədi, -z

profuse
BR prəˈfjuːs, -ɨst
AM prəˈfjus, proʊˈfjus, -əst

profusely
BR prəˈfjuːsli
AM prəˈfjusli, proʊˈfjusli

profuseness
BR prəˈfjuːsnəs
AM prəˈfjusnəs, proʊˈfjusnəs

profusion
BR prəˈfjuːʒn, -z
AM prəˈfjuʒən, proʊˈfjuʒən, -z

prog
BR prɒg, -z
AM prɑg, -z

progenitive
BR prə(ʊ)ˈdʒɛnɨtɪv
AM prəˈdʒɛnədɪv, proʊˈdʒɛnədɪv

progenitor
BR prə(ʊ)ˈdʒɛnɨtə(r), -z
AM prəˈdʒɛnədər, proʊˈdʒɛnədər, -z

progenitorial
BR ˌprəʊdʒɛnɨˈtɔːrɪəl, prə(ʊ)ˌdʒɛnɨˈtɔːrɪəl
AM prəˌdʒɛnəˈtɔriəl, proʊˌdʒɛnəˈtɔriəl

progenitorship
BR prə(ʊ)ˈdʒɛnɨtəʃɪp, -s
AM prəˈdʒɛnədərˌʃɪp, proʊˈdʒɛnədərˌʃɪp, -s

progenitress
BR prə(ʊ)ˈdʒɛnɨtrɛs, prə(ʊ)ˈdʒɛnɨtrɪs, -ɪz
AM prəˈdʒɛnətrəs, proʊˈdʒɛnətrəs, -əz

progenitrices
BR prə(ʊ)ˈdʒɛnɨtrɪsiːz
AM proʊˈdʒɛnɨtrɪsiz

progenitrix
BR prə(ʊ)ˈdʒɛnɨtrɪks, -ɪz
AM prəˈdʒɛnətrɪks, proʊˈdʒɛnətrɪks, -ɪz

progeniture
BR prə(ʊ)ˈdʒɛnɨtʃə(r)
AM prəˈdʒɛnətʃər, proʊˈdʒɛnətʃər, proʊˈdʒɛnətʃʊ(ə)r

progeny
BR ˈprɒdʒɪn|i, -ɪz
AM ˈprɑdʒəni, -z

progesterone
BR prəˈdʒɛstərəʊn
AM proʊˈdʒɛstəˌroʊn

progestogen
BR prəˈdʒɛstədʒ(ə)n, -z
AM proʊˈdʒɛstədʒən, -z

proglottid
BR prə(ʊ)ˈglɒtɪd, -z
AM ˌproʊˈglɑdɪd, -z

proglottis
BR prəʊˈglɒtɪs, -ɪz
AM proʊˈglɑdəs, -əz

prognathic
BR prɒgˈnaθɪk
AM prɑgˈnæθɪk

prognathism
BR ˈprɒgnəθɪz(ə)m
AM ˈprɑgnəˌθɪzəm

prognathous
BR prɒgˈneɪθəs, ˈprɒgnəθəs
AM ˈprɑgnəθəs

prognoses
BR prɒgˈnəʊsiːz
AM prɑgˈnoʊˌsiz

prognosis
BR prɒgˈnəʊsɪs
AM prɑgˈnoʊsəs

prognostic
BR prɒgˈnɒstɪk
AM prɑgˈnɑstɪk

prognosticable
BR prɒgˈnɒstɪkəbl
AM prɑgˈnɑstəkəbəl

prognostically
BR prɒgˈnɒstɪkli
AM prɑgˈnɑstək(ə)li

prognosticate
BR prɒgˈnɒstɪkeɪt, -s, -ɪŋ, -ɨd
AM prɑgˈnɑstəˌkeɪ|t, -ts, -dɪŋ, -dɨd

prognostication
BR prɒgˌnɒstɪˈkeɪʃn, -z
AM prɑgˌnɑstəˈkeɪʃən, -z

prognosticative
BR prɒgˈnɒstɪkətɪv
AM prɑgˈnɑstəˌkeɪdɪv, prɑgˈnɑstəkədɪv

prognosticator
BR prɒgˈnɒstɪkeɪtə(r), -z
AM prɑgˈnɑstəˌkeɪdər, -z

prognosticatory
BR prɒgˈnɒstɪkət(ə)ri
AM prɑgˈnɑstəkəˌtɔri

program
BR ˈprəʊgram, -z, -ɪŋ, -d
AM ˈproʊˌgræm, -z, -ɪŋ, -d

programable
BR ˈprəʊgraməbl, prə(ʊ)ˈgraməbl
AM proʊˈgræməbəl

programmability
BR ˌprəʊgraməˈbɪlɪti, prə(ʊ)ˌgraməˈbɪlɪti
AM proʊˌgræməˈbɪlɨdi

programmable
BR ˈprəʊgraməbl, prə(ʊ)ˈgraməbl
AM proʊˈgræməbəl

programmatic
BR ˌprəʊgrəˈmatɪk
AM ˌproʊgrəˈmædɪk

programmatically
BR ˌprəʊgrəˈmatɪkli
AM ˌproʊgrəˈmædək(ə)li

programme
BR ˈprəʊgram, -z, -ɪŋ, -d
AM ˈproʊˌgræm, -z, -ɪŋ, -d

programmer
BR ˈprəʊgramə(r), -z
AM ˈproʊˌgræmər, -z

progress[1]
noun
BR ˈprəʊgrɛs, -ɪz
AM ˈprɑgrəs, -əz

progress[2]
verb
BR prə(ʊ)ˈgrɛs, ˈprəʊgrɛs, -ɪz, -ɪŋ, -d
AM prəˈgrɛs, proʊˈgrɛs, -əz, -ɪŋ, -d

progression
BR prəˈgrɛʃn, -z
AM prəˈgrɛʃən, proʊˈgrɛʃən, -z

progressional
BR prəˈgrɛʃn̩(ə)l, prəˈgrɛʃən(ə)l
AM prəˈgrɛʃ(ə)nəl, proʊˈgrɛʃ(ə)nəl

progressionist
BR prəˈgrɛʃn̩ɪst, prəˈgrɛʃənɪst, -s
AM prəˈgrɛʃənəst, -s

progressive
BR prəˈgrɛsɪv, -z
AM prəˈgrɛsɪv, prouˈgrɛsɪv, -z

progressively
BR prəˈgrɛsɪvli
AM prəˈgrɛsɪvli, prouˈgrɛsɪvli

progressiveness
BR prəˈgrɛsɪvnɪs
AM prəˈgrɛsɪvnɪs, prouˈgrɛsɪvɪs

progressivism
BR prəˈgrɛsɪvɪz(ə)m
AM prəˈgrɛsəˌvɪzəm, prouˈgrɛsəˌvɪzəm

progressivist
BR prəˈgrɛsɪvɪst, -s
AM prəˈgrɛsəvəst, prouˈgrɛsəvəst, -s

pro hac vice
BR ˌprəʊ hɑːk ˈvʌɪsi, + hak +, + ˈviːkeɪ
AM ˌproʊ ˌhæk ˈvaɪsi

prohibit
BR prə(ʊ)ˈhɪb|ɪt, -ɪts, -ɨtɪŋ, -ɨtɨd
AM prəˈhɪbɨ|t, proʊˈhɪbɨ|t, -ts, -dɪŋ, -dɨd

prohibiter
BR prə(ʊ)'hɪbɪtə(r), -z
AM prə'hɪbɪdər, proʊ'hibɪdər, -z

prohibition
BR ˌprəʊ(h)ɪ'bɪʃn, -z
AM ˌproʊ(h)ə'bɪʃən, -z

prohibitionary
BR ˌprəʊ(h)ɪ'bɪʃn̩(ə)ri
AM ˌproʊ(h)ə'bɪʃəˌnɛri

prohibitionism
BR ˌprəʊ(h)ɪ'bɪʃn̩ɪz(ə)m, ˌprəʊ(h)ɪ'bɪʃənɪz(ə)m
AM ˌproʊ(h)ə'bɪʃəˌnɪz-əm

prohibitionist
BR ˌprəʊ(h)ɪ'bɪʃn̩ɪst, ˌprəʊ(h)ɪ'bɪʃənɪst, -s
AM ˌproʊ(h)ə'bɪʃ(ə)nəst, -s

prohibitive
BR prə(ʊ)'hɪbɪtɪv
AM prə'hɪbədɪv, proʊ'hɪbədɪv

prohibitively
BR prə(ʊ)'hɪbɪtɪvli
AM prə'hɪbədɪvli, proʊ'hɪbədɪvli

prohibitiveness
BR prə(ʊ)'hɪbɪtɪvnɪs
AM prə'hɪbədɪvnɪs, proʊ'hɪbədɪvnɪs

prohibitor
BR prə(ʊ)'hɪbɪtə(r), -z
AM prə'hɪbɪdər, proʊ'hibɪdər, -z

prohibitory
BR prə(ʊ)'hɪbɪt(ə)ri
AM prə'hɪbɪˌtɔri, proʊ'hibɪˌtɔri

project[1]
noun
BR 'prɒdʒɛkt, -s
AM 'prɑˌdʒɛk(t), -s

project[2]
verb
BR prə'dʒɛkt, -s, -ɪŋ, -ɪd
AM prə'dʒɛk|(t), proʊ'dʒɛk|(t), -(t)s, -tɪŋ, -təd

projectile
BR prə'dʒɛktʌɪl, -z
AM prə'dʒɛktl, prə'dʒɛkˌtaɪl, proʊ'dʒɛktl, proʊ'dʒɛkˌtaɪl, -z

projection
BR prə'dʒɛkʃn, -z
AM prə'dʒɛkʃən, proʊ'dʒɛkʃən, -z

projectionist
BR prə'dʒɛkʃn̩ɪst, prə'dʒɛkʃənɪst, -s
AM prə'dʒɛkʃənəst, proʊ'dʒɛkʃənəst, -s

projective
BR prə'dʒɛktɪv
AM prə'dʒɛktɪv, proʊ'dʒɛktɪv

projectively
BR prə'dʒɛktɪvli
AM prə'dʒɛktɪvli, proʊ'dʒɛktɪvli

projector
BR prə'dʒɛktə(r), -z
AM prə'dʒɛktər, proʊ'dʒɛktər, -z

prokaryote
BR prəʊ'karɪəʊt, prəʊ'karɪɒt, -s
AM proʊ'kɛrioʊt, -s

prokaryotic
BR prəʊˌkarɪ'ɒtɪk, ˌprəʊkarɪ'ɒtɪk
AM proʊˌkɛri'ɑdɪk

Prokofiev
BR prə'kɒfɪɛf
AM proʊ'kɔfiˌɛf, proʊ'kɑfiˌɛf

prolactin
BR prəʊ'laktɪn
AM proʊ'lækt(ə)n

prolapse
BR 'prəʊlaps, -ɪz, -ɪŋ, -t
AM proʊ'læps, 'proʊˌlæps, -əz, -ɪŋ, -t

prolapsus
BR prəʊ'lapsəs
AM proʊ'læpsəs, 'proʊˌlæpsəs

prolate
BR 'prəʊleɪt, prəʊ'leɪt
AM proʊ'leɪt, 'proʊˌleɪt

prolately
BR 'prəʊleɪtli, prə(ʊ)'leɪtli
AM proʊ'leɪtli, 'proʊˌleɪtli

prolative
BR 'prəʊlətɪv, prə(ʊ)'leɪtɪv
AM 'proʊlədɪv, proʊ'leɪdɪv, 'proʊˌleɪdɪv

prole
BR prəʊl, -z
AM proʊl, -z

proleg
BR 'prəʊlɛg, -z
AM 'proʊˌlɛg, -z

prolegomena
BR ˌprəʊlɛ'gɒmɪnə(*r*), ˌprəʊlɪ'gɒmɪnə(*r*)
AM ˌproʊlə'gɑmənə

prolegomenary
BR ˌprəʊlɛ'gɒmɪn(ə)ri, ˌprəʊlɪ'gɒmɪn(ə)ri
AM ˌproʊlə'gɑməˌnɛri

prolegomenon
BR ˌprəʊlɛ'gɒmɪnən, ˌprəʊlɪ'gɒmɪnən
AM ˌproʊlə'gɑməˌnɑn, ˌproʊlə'gɑmənən

prolegomenous
BR ˌprəʊlɛ'gɒmɪnəs, ˌprəʊlɪ'gɒmɪnəs
AM ˌproʊlə'gɑmənəs

prolepses
BR prə(ʊ)'lɛpsiːz
AM proʊ'lɛpˌsiz

prolepsis
BR prə(ʊ)'lɛpsɪs
AM proʊ'lɛpsəs

proleptic
BR prə(ʊ)'lɛptɪk
AM proʊ'lɛptɪk

proletarian
BR ˌprəʊlɪ'tɛːrɪən, -z
AM ˌproʊlə'tɛriən, -z

proletarianisation
BR ˌprəʊlɪˌtɛːrɪənʌɪ'zeɪʃn
AM ˌproʊləˌtɛriənə'zeɪʃən, ˌproʊləˌtɛriəˌnaɪ'zeɪʃən

proletarianise
BR ˌprəʊlɪ'tɛːrɪənʌɪz, -ɪz, -ɪŋ, -d
AM ˌproʊlə'tɛriəˌnaɪz, -ɪz, -ɪŋ, -d

proletarianism
BR ˌprəʊlɪ'tɛːrɪənɪz(ə)m
AM ˌproʊlə'tɛriəˌnɪzəm

proletarianization
BR ˌprəʊlɪˌtɛːrɪənʌɪ'zeɪʃn
AM ˌproʊləˌtɛriənə'zeɪʃən, ˌproʊləˌtɛriəˌnaɪ'zeɪʃən

proletarianize
BR ˌprəʊlɪ'tɛːrɪənʌɪz, -ɪz, -ɪŋ, -d
AM ˌproʊlə'tɛriəˌnaɪz, -ɪz, -ɪŋ, -d

proletariat
BR ˌprəʊlɪ'tɛːrɪət
AM ˌproʊlə'tɛriət

pro-life
BR ˌprəʊ'lʌɪf
AM ˌproʊ'laɪf

proliferate
BR prə'lɪfəreɪt, -s, -ɪŋ, -ɪd
AM prə'lɪfəˌreɪ|t, proʊ'lɪfəˌreɪ|t, -ts, -dɪŋ, -dɪd

proliferation
BR prəˌlɪfə'reɪʃn
AM prəˌlɪfə'reɪʃən, proʊˌlɪfə'reɪʃən

proliferative
BR prə'lɪf(ə)rətɪv
AM prə'lɪfərədɪv, proʊ'lɪfərədɪv, prə'lɪfəˌreɪdɪv, proʊ'lɪfəˌreɪdɪv

proliferator
BR prə'lɪfəreɪtə(r), -z
AM prə'lɪfəˌreɪdər, proʊ'lɪfəˌreɪdər, -z

proliferous
BR prə'lɪf(ə)rəs
AM prə'lɪf(ə)rəs, proʊ'lɪf(ə)rəs

prolific
BR prə'lɪfɪk
AM prə'lɪfɪk, proʊ'lɪfɪk

prolificacy
BR prə'lɪfɪkəsi
AM prə'lɪfɪkəsi, proʊ'lɪfɪkəsi

prolifically
BR prə'lɪfɪkli
AM prə'lɪfɪk(ə)li, proʊ'lɪfɪk(ə)li

prolificity
BR ˌprəʊlɪ'fɪsɪti
AM ˌproʊlə'fɪsɪdi

prolificness
BR prə'lɪfɪknɪs
AM prə'lɪfɪknɪs, proʊ'lɪfɪknɪs

proline
BR 'prəʊliːn, -z
AM 'proʊˌlin, 'proʊlən, -z

prolix
BR 'prəʊlɪks
AM proʊ'lɪks, 'proʊˌlɪks

prolixity
BR prə'lɪksɪti
AM proʊ'lɪksɪdi

prolixly
BR 'prəʊlɪksli
AM proʊ'lɪksli, 'proʊˌlɪksli

prolocutor
BR prəʊ'lɒkjʊtə(r), -z
AM proʊ'lɑkjədər, -z

prolocutorship
BR prəʊ'lɒkjʊtəʃɪp, -s
AM proʊ'lɑkjədərˌʃɪp, -s

PROLOG
BR 'prəʊlɒg
AM 'proʊˌlɔg, 'proʊˌlɑg

prolog
BR 'prəʊlɒg, -z
AM 'proʊˌlɔg, 'proʊˌlɑg, -z

prologise
BR 'prəʊləgʌɪz, -ɪz, -ɪŋ, -d
AM 'proʊləˌgaɪz, -ɪz, -ɪŋ, -d

prologize
BR 'prəʊləgʌɪz, -ɪz, -ɪŋ, -d
AM 'proʊləˌgaɪz, -ɪz, -ɪŋ, -d

prologue
BR 'prəʊlɒg, -z
AM 'proʊˌlɔg, 'proʊˌlɑg, -z

prolong
BR prə'lɒŋ, -z, -ɪŋ, -d

AM prə'lɔŋ, proʊ'lɔŋ, prə'lɑŋ, proʊ'lɑŋ, -z, -ɪŋ, -d
prolongation
BR ˌprəʊlɒŋ'geɪʃn, ˌprɒlɒŋ'geɪʃn
AM proʊˌlɔŋ'(g)eɪʃən, prəˌlɔŋ'(g)eɪʃən, proʊˌlɑŋ'(g)eɪʃən, prəˌlɑŋ'(g)eɪʃən
prolonger
BR prə'lɒŋə(r), -z
AM prə'lɔŋər, proʊ'lɔŋər, prə'lɑŋər, proʊ'lɑŋər, -z
prolusion
BR prə'l(j)u:ʒn
AM proʊ'l(j)uʒən
prolusory
BR prə'l(j)u:z(ə)ri
AM proʊ'l(j)uzəri
prom
BR prɒm, -z
AM prɑm, -z
promenade
BR ˌprɒmə'nɑ:d, 'prɒmənɑ:d, -z, -ɪŋ, -ɨd
AM ¦prɑmə¦neɪd, ¦prɑmə¦nɑd, -z, -ɪŋ, -əd
promenader
BR ˌprɒmə'nɑ:də(r), 'prɒmənɑ:də(r), -z
AM ¦prɑmə¦neɪdər, ¦prɑmə¦nɑdər, -z
promethazine
BR prə(ʊ)'mɛθəzi:n
AM proʊ'mɛθəˌzin, proʊ'mɛθəzən
Promethean
BR prə'mi:θɪən
AM prə'miθiən, proʊ'miθiən
Prometheus
BR prə'mi:θɪəs
AM prə'miθiəs, proʊ'miθiəs
promethium
BR prə'mi:θɪəm
AM proʊ'miθiəm
prominence
BR 'prɒmɨnəns, -ɨz
AM 'prɑmənəns, -əz
prominency
BR 'prɒmɨnənsi
AM 'prɑmənənsi
prominent
BR 'prɒmɨnənt
AM 'prɑmənənt
prominenti
BR ˌprɒmɨ'nɛnti(:)
AM ˌprɑmə'nɛn(t)i
prominently
BR 'prɒmɨnəntli
AM 'prɑmənən(t)li
promiscuity
BR ˌprɒmɨ'skju:ɪti
AM ˌprɑmə'skjuədi, ˌproʊˌmɪ'skjuədi
promiscuous
BR prə'mɪskjʊəs
AM prə'mɪskjəwəs
promiscuously
BR prə'mɪskjʊəsli
AM prə'mɪskjəwəsli
promiscuousness
BR prə'mɪskjʊəsnəs
AM prə'mɪskjəwəsnəs
promise
BR 'prɒm|ɪs, -ɨsɨz, -ɨsɪŋ, -ɪst
AM 'prɑməs, -əz, -ɪŋ, -t
promisee
BR ˌprɒmɨ'si:, -z
AM ˌprɑmə'si, -z
promiser
BR 'prɒmɨsə(r), -z
AM 'prɑməsər, -z
promisingly
BR 'prɒmɨsɪŋli
AM 'prɑməsɪŋli
promisor
BR 'prɒmɨsə(r), -z
AM 'prɑməsər, -z
promissory
BR 'prɒmɪs(ə)ri
AM 'prɑməˌsɔri
prommer
BR 'prɒmə(r), -z
AM 'prɑmər, -z
promo
BR 'prəʊməʊ, -z
AM 'proʊˌmoʊ, -z
promontory
BR 'prɒm(ə)nt(ə)r|i, -ɪz
AM 'prɑmənˌtɔri, -z
promotability
BR prəˌməʊtə'bɪlɪti
AM prəˌmoʊdə'bɪlɨdi
promotable
BR prə'məʊtəbl
AM prə'moʊdəbəl
promote
BR prə'məʊt, -s, -ɪŋ, -ɨd
AM prə'moʊ|t, -ts, -dɪŋ, -dəd
promoter
BR prə'məʊtə(r), -z
AM prə'moʊdər, -z
promotion
BR prə'məʊʃn, -z
AM prə'moʊʃən, -z
promotional
BR prə'məʊʃn̩(ə)l, prə'məʊʃən(ə)l
AM prə'moʊʃ(ə)nəl
promotive
BR prə'məʊtɪv
AM prə'moʊdɪv
prompt
BR prɒm(p)t, -s, -ɪŋ, -ɨd, -ə(r), -ɨst
AM prɑm(p)t, -s, -ɪŋ, -əd, -ər, -əst
prompter
BR 'prɒm(p)tə(r), -z
AM 'prɑm(p)tər, -z
prompting
BR 'prɒm(p)tɪŋ, -z
AM 'prɑm(p)tɪŋ, -z
promptitude
BR 'prɒm(p)tɪtju:d, 'prɒm(p)tɪtʃu:d
AM 'prɑm(p)təˌtud
promptly
BR 'prɒm(p)tli
AM 'prɑm(p)tli, 'prɑmp(t)li
promptness
BR 'prɒmp(t)nəs
AM 'prɑmp(t)nəs
promulgate
BR 'prɒmlgeɪt, -s, -ɪŋ, -ɨd
AM 'prɑməlˌgeɪ|t, -ts, -dɪŋ, -dɨd
promulgation
BR ˌprɒml'geɪʃn, -z
AM ˌprɑməl'geɪʃən, ˌproʊməl'geɪʃən, -z
promulgator
BR 'prɒmlgeɪtə(r), -z
AM 'prɑməlˌgeɪdər, -z
promulge
BR prə'mʌldʒ, -ɨz, -ɪŋ, -d
AM proʊ'məldʒ, -əz, -ɪŋ, -d
pronaoi
BR prəʊ'neɪɔɪ
AM proʊ'neɪˌɔɪ
pronaos
BR prəʊ'neɪɒs
AM proʊ'neɪəs
pronate
BR 'prəʊneɪt, -s, -ɪŋ, -ɨd
AM 'proʊˌneɪ|t, -ts, -dɪŋ, -dɨd
pronation
BR prəʊ'neɪʃn
AM proʊ'neɪʃən
pronator
BR prəʊ'neɪtə(r), -z
AM 'proʊˌneɪdər, -z
prone
BR prəʊn, -ə(r), -ɨst
AM proʊn, -ər, -əst
pronely
BR 'prəʊnli
AM 'proʊnli
proneness
BR 'prəʊnnəs
AM 'proʊ(n)nəs
proneur
BR prəʊ'nə:(r), -z
AM proʊ'nər, -z
prong
BR prɒŋ, -z, -d
AM prɔŋ, prɑŋ, -z, -d
pronghorn
BR 'prɒŋhɔ:n, -z
AM 'prɔŋˌ(h)ɔ(ə)rn, 'prɑŋˌ(h)ɔ(ə)rn, -z
pronominal
BR prə(ʊ)'nɒmɨnl
AM prə'nɑmənəl, proʊ'nɑmənəl
pronominalise
BR prə(ʊ)'nɒmɨnl̩ʌɪz, prə(ʊ)'nɒmɨnəlʌɪz, -ɨz, -ɪŋ, -d
AM prə'nɑmənəˌlaɪz, proʊ'nɑmənəˌlaɪz, -ɨz, -ɪŋ, -d
pronominalize
BR prə(ʊ)'nɒmɨnl̩ʌɪz, prə(ʊ)'nɒmɨnəlʌɪz, -ɨz, -ɪŋ, -d
AM prə'nɑmənəˌlaɪz, proʊ'nɑmənəˌlaɪz, -ɨz, -ɪŋ, -d
pronominally
BR prə(ʊ)'nɒmɨnl̩i, prə(ʊ)'nɒmɨnəli
AM prə'nɑmənəli, proʊ'nɑmənəli
pronoun
BR 'prəʊnaʊn, -z
AM 'proʊˌnaʊn, -z
pronounce
BR prə'naʊns, -ɨz, -ɪŋ, -t
AM prə'naʊns, -əz, -ɪŋ, -t
pronounceable
BR prə'naʊnsəbl
AM prə'naʊnsəbəl
pronouncedly
BR prə'naʊnsɨdli
AM prə'naʊnsədli
pronouncement
BR prə'naʊnsm(ə)nt, -s
AM prə'naʊnsmənt, -s
pronouncer
BR prə'naʊnsə(r), -z
AM prə'naʊnsər, -z
pronto
BR 'prɒntəʊ
AM 'prɑn(t)oʊ
pronunciamento
BR prəˌnʌnsɪə'mɛntəʊ, prəˌnʌnʃ(ɪ)ə'mɛntəʊ, -z
AM proʊˌnən(t)ʃ(i)ə-'mɛn(t)oʊ, -z
pronunciation
BR prəˌnʌnsɪ'eɪʃn, -z
AM prəˌnənsi'eɪʃən, -z
proof
BR pru:f, -s, -ɪŋ, -t
AM pruf, -s, -ɪŋ, -t
proofless
BR 'pru:fləs
AM 'prufləs
proofmark
BR 'pru:fmɑ:k, -s
AM 'prufˌmɑrk, -s
proof-plane
BR 'pru:fpleɪn, -z

AM ˈpruf,pleɪn, -z
proofread¹
present tense
BR ˈpruːfriːd, -z, -ɪŋ
AM ˈpruf,rid, -z, -ɪŋ
proofread²
past tense
BR ˈpruːfrɛd
AM ˈpruf,rɛd
proofreader
BR ˈpruːf,riːdə(r), -z
AM ˈpruf,ridər, -z
prop
BR prɒp, -s, -ɪŋ, -t
AM prɑp, -s, -ɪŋ, -t
propaedeutic
BR ˌprəʊpiːˈdjuːtɪk, ˌprəʊpiːˈdʒuːtɪk, -s
AM ˌproʊpiˈd(j)udɪk, -s
propaedeutical
BR ˌprəʊpiːˈdjuːtɪkl, ˌprəʊpiːˈdʒuːtɪkl
AM ˌproʊpiˈd(j)udəkəl
propaganda
BR ˌprɒpəˈgandə(r)
AM ˌprɑpəˈgændə
propagandise
BR ˌprɒpəˈgandʌɪz, -ɪz, -ɪŋ, -d
AM ˌprɑpəˈgæn,daɪz, -ɪz, -ɪŋ, -d
propagandism
BR ˌprɒpəˈgandɪz(ə)m
AM ˌprɑpəˈgæn,dɪzəm
propagandist
BR ˌprɒpəˈgandɪst, -s
AM ˌprɑpəˈgændəst, -s
propagandistic
BR ˌprɒpəganˈdɪstɪk
AM ˌprɑpə,gænˈdɪstɪk
propagandistically
BR ˌprɒpəganˈdɪstɪkli
AM ˌprɑpə,gænˈdɪstək(ə)li
propagandize
BR ˌprɒpəˈgandʌɪz, -ɪz, -ɪŋ, -d
AM ˌprɑpəˈgæn,daɪz, -ɪz, -ɪŋ, -d
propagate
BR ˈprɒpəgeɪt, -s, -ɪŋ, -ɪd
AM ˈprɑpə,geɪ|t, -ts, -dɪŋ, -dɪd
propagation
BR ˌprɒpəˈgeɪʃn
AM ˌprɑpəˈgeɪʃən
propagative
BR ˈprɒpəgeɪtɪv
AM ˈprɑpə,geɪdɪv
propagatively
BR ˈprɒpəgeɪtɪvli
AM ˈprɑpə,geɪdɪvli
propagator
BR ˈprɒpəgeɪtə(r), -z
AM ˈprɑpə,geɪdər, -z
propane
BR ˈprəʊpeɪn
AM ˈproʊ,peɪn
propanoic acid
BR ˌprəʊpənəʊɪk ˈasɪd
AM ˌproʊpəˈnoʊɪk ˈæsəd
propanone
BR ˈprəʊpənəʊn
AM ˈproʊpə,noʊn
proparoxytone
BR ˌprəʊpəˈrɒksɪtəʊn, -z
AM ˌproʊpəˈrɑksə,toʊn, -z
propel
BR prəˈpɛl, -z, -ɪŋ, -d
AM prəˈpɛl, proʊˈpɛl, -z, -ɪŋ, -d
propellant
BR prəˈpɛlənt, prəˈpɛlnt, -s
AM prəˈpɛlənt, proʊˈpɛlənt, -s
propellent
BR prəˈpɛlənt, prəˈpɛlnt
AM prəˈpɛlənt, proʊˈpɛlənt
propeller
BR prəˈpɛlə(r), -z
AM prəˈpɛlər, proʊˈpɛlər, -z
propene
BR ˈprəʊpiːn
AM ˈproʊ,pin
propensity
BR prəˈpɛnsɪt|i, -ɪz
AM prəˈpɛnsədi, proʊˈpɛnsədi, -z
proper
BR ˈprɒpə(r)
AM ˈprɑpər
properispomena
BR prə(ʊ),pɛrɪˈspɒmɪnə(r)
AM proʊ,pɛriˈspoʊmənə, proʊ,pɛriˈspɑmənə
properispomenon
BR prə(ʊ),pɛrɪˈspɒmɪnɒn
AM proʊ,pɛriˈspoʊmə,nɑn, proʊ,pɛriˈspɑmə,nɑn, proʊ,pɛriˈspoʊmənən, proʊ,pɛriˈspɑmənən
properly
BR ˈprɒp(ə)li
AM ˈprɑpərli
properness
BR ˈprɒpənəs
AM ˈprɑpərnəs
propertied
BR ˈprɒpətɪd
AM ˈprɑpərdid
Propertius
BR prə(ʊ)ˈpəːʃ(ɪ)əs
AM proʊˈpərʃ(i)əs
property
BR ˈprɒpət|i, -ɪz
AM ˈprɑpərdi, -z
prophase
BR ˈprəʊfeɪz, -ɪz
AM ˈproʊ,feɪz, -ɪz
prophecy
BR ˈprɒfɪs|i, -ɪz
AM ˈprɑfəsi, -z
prophesier
BR ˈprɒfɪsʌɪə(r), -z
AM ˈprɑfə,saɪ(ə)r, -z
prophesy
BR ˈprɒfɪsʌɪ, -z, -ɪŋ, -d
AM ˈprɑfə,saɪ, -z, -ɪŋ, -d
prophet
BR ˈprɒfɪt, -s
AM ˈprɑfət, -s
prophetess
BR ˌprɒfɪˈtɛs, ˈprɒfɪtɪs, -ɪz
AM ˈprɑfədəs, -əz
prophethood
BR ˈprɒfɪthʊd
AM ˈprɑfət,(h)ʊd
prophetic
BR prəˈfɛtɪk
AM prəˈfɛdɪk, proʊˈfɛdɪk
prophetical
BR prəˈfɛtɪkl
AM prəˈfɛdəkəl, proʊˈfɛdəkəl
prophetically
BR prəˈfɛtɪkli
AM prəˈfɛdək(ə)li, proʊˈfɛdək(ə)li
propheticism
BR prəˈfɛtɪsɪz(ə)m, -z
AM prəˈfɛdə,sɪzəm, proʊˈfɛdə,sɪzəm, -z
prophetism
BR ˈprɒfɪtɪz(ə)m
AM ˈprɑfə,tɪzəm
prophetship
BR ˈprɒfɪtʃɪp
AM ˈprɑfət,ʃɪp
prophylactic
BR ˌprɒfɪˈlaktɪk, -s
AM ˌproʊfəˈlæktɪk, -s
prophylaxis
BR ˌprɒfɪˈlaksɪs
AM ˌproʊfəˈlæksəs
propinquity
BR prəˈpɪŋkwɪti
AM prəˈpɪŋkwɪdi, proʊˈpɪŋkwɪdi
propionate
BR ˈprəʊpɪəneɪt, -s
AM ˈproʊpiə,neɪt, -s
propionic acid
BR ˌprəʊpɪanɪk ˈasɪd
AM ˌproʊpiˈænɪk ˌæsəd
propitiate
BR prəˈpɪʃɪeɪt, -s, -ɪŋ, -ɪd
AM prəˈpɪʃi,eɪ|t, proʊˈpɪʃi,eɪ|t, -ts, -dɪŋ, -dɪd
propitiation
BR prə,pɪʃɪˈeɪʃn, -z
AM prə,pɪʃiˈeɪʃən, proʊ,pɪʃiˈeɪʃən, -z
propitiator
BR prəˈpɪʃɪeɪtə(r), -z
AM prəˈpɪʃi,eɪdər, proʊˈpɪʃi,eɪdər, -z
propitiatorily
BR prə,pɪʃɪəˈtɔːrɪli
AM prə,pɪʃiəˈtɔrəli, proʊ,pɪʃiəˈtɔrəli
propitiatory
BR prəˈpɪʃɪət(ə)ri
AM prəˈpɪʃiə,tɔri, proʊˈpɪʃiə,tɔri
propitious
BR prəˈpɪʃəs
AM prəˈpɪʃəs, proʊˈpɪʃəs
propitiously
BR prəˈpɪʃəsli
AM prəˈpɪʃəsli, proʊˈpɪʃəsli
propitiousness
BR prəˈpɪʃəsnəs
AM prəˈpɪʃəsnəs, proʊˈpɪʃəsnəs
propjet
BR ˈprɒpdʒɛt, -s
AM ˈprɑp,dʒɛt, -s
propolis
BR ˈprɒpəlɪs
AM ˈprɑpələs
proponent
BR prəˈpəʊnənt, -s
AM prəˈpoʊnənt, proʊˈpoʊnənt, -s
Propontis
BR prə(ʊ)ˈpɒntɪs
AM prəˈpɑn(t)əs
proportion
BR prəˈpɔːʃ|n, -nz, -n̩ɪŋ \ -(ə)nɪŋ, -nd
AM prəˈpɔrʃ|ən, pərˈpɔrʃ|ən, -ənz, -(ə)nɪŋ, -ənd
proportionable
BR prəˈpɔːʃn̩əbl, prəˈpɔːʃ(ə)nəbl
AM prəˈpɔrʃənəbəl, pərˈpɔrʃənəbəl
proportionably
BR prəˈpɔːʃn̩əbli, prəˈpɔːʃ(ə)nəbli
AM prəˈpɔrʃənəbli, pərˈpɔrʃənəbli
proportional
BR prəˈpɔːʃn̩(ə)l, prəˈpɔːʃən(ə)l
AM prəˈpɔrʃ(ə)nəl, pərˈpɔrʃ(ə)nəl
proportionalist
BR prəˈpɔːʃn̩əlɪst, prəˈpɔːʃn̩lɪst,

prə'pɔːʃənḷɪst, prə'pɔːʃ(ə)nəlɪst, -s
AM prə'pɔrʃənləst, pər'pɔrʃənləst, prə'pɔrʃnələst, pər'pɔrʃnələst, -s

proportionality
BR prəˌpɔːʃə'nalɪti
AM prəˌpɔrʃə'nælədi, pərˌpɔrʃə'nælədi

proportionally
BR prə'pɔːʃṇəli, prə'pɔːʃṇḷi, prə'pɔːʃənḷi, prə'pɔːʃ(ə)nəli
AM prə'pɔrʃ(ə)nəli, pər'pɔrʃ(ə)nəli

proportionate
BR prə'pɔːʃənət, prə'pɔːʃṇət
AM prə'pɔrʃ(ə)nət, pər'pɔrʃ(ə)nət

proportionately
BR prə'pɔːʃənətli, prə'pɔːʃṇətli
AM prə'pɔrʃ(ə)nətli, pər'pɔrʃ(ə)nətli

proportionless
BR prə'pɔːʃnləs
AM prə'pɔrʃənləs, pər'pɔrʃənləs

proportionment
BR prə'pɔːʃnm(ə)nt
AM prə'pɔrʃənmənt, pər'pɔrʃənmənt

proposal
BR prə'pəʊzl, -z
AM prə'poʊzəl, -z

propose
BR prə'pəʊz, -ɪz, -ɪŋ, -d
AM prə'poʊz, -əz, -ɪŋ, -d

proposer
BR prə'pəʊzə(r), -z
AM prə'poʊzər, -z

proposition
BR ˌprɒpə'zɪʃ|n, -nz, -ṇɪŋ\-nɪŋ, -nd
AM ˌprɑpə'zɪʃən, -z, -ɪŋ, -d

propositional
BR ˌprɒpə'zɪʃṇ(ə)l, ˌprɒpə'zɪʃən(ə)l
AM ˌprɑpə'zɪʃ(ə)nəl

propositionally
BR ˌprɒpə'zɪʃṇəli, ˌprɒpə'zɪʃṇḷi, ˌprɒpə'zɪʃənḷi, ˌprɒpə'zɪʃ(ə)nəli
AM ˌprɑpə'zɪʃ(ə)nəli

propound
BR prə'paʊnd, -z, -ɪŋ, -ɪd
AM prə'paʊnd, -z, -ɪŋ, -əd

propounder
BR prə'paʊndə(r), -z
AM prə'paʊndər, -z

propraetor
BR prəʊ'priːtə(r), -z
AM proʊ'pridər, -z

proprietary
BR prə'prʌɪət(ə)ri
AM p(r)ə'praɪəˌtɛri

proprietor
BR prə'prʌɪətə(r), -z
AM p(r)ə'praɪədər, -z

proprietorial
BR prəˌprʌɪə'tɔːrɪəl
AM p(r)əˌpraɪə'tɔriəl

proprietorially
BR prəˌprʌɪə'tɔːrɪəli
AM p(r)əˌpraɪə'tɔriəli

proprietorship
BR prə'prʌɪətəʃɪp, -s
AM p(r)ə'praɪədərˌʃɪp, -s

proprietress
BR prə'prʌɪətrɪs, -ɪz
AM p(r)ə'praɪətrəs, -əz

propriety
BR prə'prʌɪəti
AM p(r)ə'praɪədi

proprioception
BR ˌprə(ʊ)prɪə'sɛpʃn
AM ˌproʊpriə'sɛpʃən

proprioceptive
BR ˌprə(ʊ)prɪə'sɛptɪv
AM ˌproʊpriə'sɛptɪv

pro-proctor
BR prəʊ'prɒktə(r), -z
AM proʊ'prɑktər, -z

proptoses
BR prɒp'təʊsiːz
AM ˌprɑp'toʊˌsiz

proptosis
BR prɒp'təʊsɪs
AM ˌprɑp'toʊsəs

propulsion
BR prə'pʌlʃn
AM prə'pəlʃən

propulsive
BR prə'pʌlsɪv
AM prə'pəlsɪv

propulsor
BR prə'pʌlsə(r), -z
AM prə'pəlsər, -z

propyl
BR 'prəʊp(ɪ)l
AM 'proʊpəl

propyla
BR 'prɒpɪlə(*r*), 'prəʊpɪlə(*r*), -z
AM 'prɑpələ, -z

propylaea
BR ˌprɒpɪ'liːə(*r*), ˌprəʊpɪ'liːə(*r*)
AM ˌprɑpə'liə

propylaeum
BR ˌprɒpɪ'liːəm, ˌprəʊpɪ'liːəm
AM ˌprɑpə'liəm

propylene
BR 'prəʊpɪliːn, 'prɒpɪliːn
AM 'proʊpəˌlin

propylon
BR 'prɒpɪlɒn, 'prəʊpɪlɒn, -z
AM 'prɑpəˌlɑn, -z

pro rata
BR (ˌ)prəʊ 'rɑːtə(*r*)
AM proʊ 'reɪdə, proʊ 'rɑdə, proʊ 'rædə

prorate
BR ˌprəʊ'reɪt, -s, -ɪŋ, -ɪd
AM ˈproʊˈreɪ|t, -ts, -dɪŋ, -dɪd

proration
BR prə(ʊ)'reɪʃn
AM proʊ'reɪʃən

prorogation
BR ˌprəʊrə(ʊ)'geɪʃn, -z
AM ˌproʊrə'geɪʃən, -z

prorogue
BR prə(ʊ)'rəʊg, -z, -ɪŋ, -d
AM proʊ'roʊg, prə'roʊg, -z, -ɪŋ, -d

pros
plural of pro
BR prəʊz
AM proʊz

prosaic
BR prə(ʊ)'zeɪɪk
AM prə'zeɪɪk, proʊ'zeɪɪk

prosaically
BR prə(ʊ)'zeɪɪkli
AM prə'zeɪɪk(ə)li, proʊ'zeɪɪk(ə)li

prosaicness
BR prə(ʊ)'zeɪɪknɪs
AM prə'zeɪɪknɪs, proʊ'zeɪɪknɪs

prosaism
BR 'prəʊzeɪɪz(ə)m, -z
AM 'proʊzeɪˌɪzəm, -z

prosaist
BR 'prəʊzeɪɪst, -s
AM 'proʊzeɪɪst, -s

proscenia
BR prə'siːnɪə(*r*)
AM prə'siniə, proʊ'siniə

proscenium
BR prə'siːnɪəm, -z
AM prə'siniəm, proʊ'siniəm, -z

prosciutto
BR prə'ʃuːtəʊ
AM prə'ʃudoʊ, proʊ'ʃudoʊ

proscribe
BR prə(ʊ)'skrʌɪb, -z, -ɪŋ, -d
AM proʊ'skraɪb, -z, -ɪŋ, -d

proscription
BR prə(ʊ)ˌskrɪpʃn, -z
AM proʊ'skrɪpʃən, -z

proscriptive
BR prə(ʊ)'skrɪptɪv
AM proʊ'skrɪptɪv

prose
BR prəʊz
AM proʊz

prosector
BR prə(ʊ)'sɛktə(r), -z
AM proʊ'sɛktər, -z

prosecutable
BR 'prɒsɪkjuːtəbl
AM 'prɑsəˌkjudəbəl

prosecute
BR 'prɒsɪkjuːt, -s, -ɪŋ, -ɪd
AM 'prɑsəˌkju|t, -ts, -dɪŋ, -dəd

prosecution
BR ˌprɒsɪ'kjuːʃn, -z
AM ˌprɑsə'kjuʃən, -z

prosecutor
BR 'prɒsɪkjuːtə(r), -z
AM 'prɑsəˌkjudər, -z

prosecutorial
BR ˌprɒsɪkjʊ'tɔːrɪəl
AM ˈprɑsəkjə'tɔriəl

prosecutrices
BR ˌprɒsɪ'kjuːtrɪsiːz
AM ˌprɑsə'kjutrɪsiz

prosecutrix
BR 'prɒsɪkjuːtrɪks, ˌprɒsɪ'kjuːtrɪks, -ɪz
AM 'prɑsəkjutrɪks, -ɪz

proselyte
BR 'prɒsɪlʌɪt, -s
AM 'prɑsəˌlaɪt, -s

proselytise
BR 'prɒsɪlɪtʌɪz, 'prɒsḷɪtʌɪz, -ɪz, -ɪŋ, -d
AM 'prɑs(ə)ləˌtaɪz, -ɪz, -ɪŋ, -d

proselytiser
BR 'prɒsɪlɪtʌɪzə(r), 'prɒsḷɪtʌɪzə(r), -z
AM 'prɑs(ə)ləˌtaɪzər, -z

proselytism
BR 'prɒsɪlɪtɪz(ə)m, 'prɒsḷɪtɪz(ə)m
AM 'prɑs(ə)ləˌtɪzəm

proselytize
BR 'prɒsɪlɪtʌɪz, 'prɒsḷɪtʌɪz, -ɪz, -ɪŋ, -d
AM 'prɑs(ə)ləˌtaɪz, -ɪz, -ɪŋ, -d

proselytizer
BR 'prɒsɪlɪtʌɪzə(r), 'prɒsḷɪtʌɪzə(r), -z
AM 'prɑs(ə)ləˌtaɪzər, -z

proseminar
BR ˌprəʊ'sɛmɪnɑː(r), -z
AM ˌproʊ'sɛməˌnɑr, -z

prosencephalon
BR ˌprɒsɛn'sɛfəlɒn, ˌprɒsɛn'sɛfḷɒn, ˌprɒsɛn'kɛfəlɒn, ˌprɒsɛn'kɛfḷɒn
AM ˌprɑsn'sɛfəˌlɑn

prosenchyma
BR prɒ'sɛŋkɪmə(*r*)
AM prɑ'sɛŋkəmə

prosenchymal
BR prɒˈsɛŋkɪml
AM prɑˈsɛŋkəməl
prosenchymata
BR ˌprɒsɛnˈkɪmətə(r)
AM ˌprɑsnˈkɪmədə
prosenchymatous
BR ˌprɒsɛnˈkɪmətəs
AM ˌprɑsnˈkɪmədəs
proser
BR ˈprəʊzə(r), -z
AM ˈproʊzər, -z
Proserpina
BR prə(ʊ)ˈsəːpɪnə(r)
AM proʊˈsərpənə
Proserpine
BR ˈprɒsəpʌɪn
AM proʊˈsərpəni, ˈprɑsərˌpaɪn
prosify
BR ˈprəʊzɪfʌɪ, -z, -ɪŋ, -d
AM ˈproʊzəˌfaɪ, -z, -ɪŋ, -d
prosily
BR ˈprəʊzɪli
AM ˈproʊzəli
prosimian
BR prəʊˈsɪmɪən, -z
AM proʊˈsɪmiən, -z
prosiness
BR ˈprəʊzɪnɪs
AM ˈproʊzinɪs
prosodic
BR prə(ʊ)ˈsɒdɪk, prə(ʊ)ˈzɒdɪk
AM prəˈsɑdɪk, proʊˈzɑdɪk
prosodically
BR prə(ʊ)ˈsɒdɪkli, prə(ʊ)ˈzɒdɪkli
AM prəˈsɑdək(ə)li, proʊˈzɑdək(ə)li
prosodist
BR ˈprɒsədɪst, ˈprɒzədɪst, ˈprəʊzədɪst, -s
AM ˈprɑsədəst, -s
prosody
BR ˈprɒsədi, ˈprɒzədi, ˈprəʊzədi
AM ˈprɑsədi
prosopographer
BR ˌprɒsə(ʊ)ˈpɒgrəfə(r), -z
AM ˌprɑsəˈpɑgrəfər, -z
prosopographic
BR ˌprɒsə(ʊ)pəˈgrafɪk
AM ˌprɑsəpəˈgræfɪk
prosopographical
BR ˌprɒsə(ʊ)pəˈgrafɪkl
AM ˌprɑsəpəˈgræfəkəl
prosopography
BR ˌprɒsə(ʊ)ˈpɒgrəfi
AM ˌprɑsəˈpɑgrəfi
prosopopoeia
BR ˌprɒsə(ʊ)pəˈpiːə(r)
AM prəˌsoʊpəˈpiə, ˌprɑsəpəˈpiə
prospect[1]
noun
BR ˈprɒspɛkt, -s
AM ˈprɑˌspɛk(t), -s
prospect[2]
verb
BR prəˈspɛkt, prɒˈspɛkt, ˈprɒspɛkt, -s, -ɪŋ, -ɪd
AM ˈprɑˌspɛk|(t), -(t)s, -tɪŋ, -təd
prospective
BR prəˈspɛktɪv
AM prəˈspɛktɪv, prɑˈspɛktɪv
prospectively
BR prəˈspɛktɪvli
AM prəˈspɛktɪvli, prɑˈspɛktɪvli
prospectiveness
BR prəˈspɛktɪvnɪs
AM prəˈspɛktɪvnɪs, prɑˈspɛktɪvnɪs
prospectless
BR ˈprɒspɛk(t)ləs
AM ˈprɑˌspɛk(t)ləs
prospector
BR prəˈspɛktə(r), prɒˈspɛktə(r), ˈprɒspɛktə(r), -z
AM ˈprɑˌspɛktə(r), -z
prospectus
BR prəˈspɛktəs, -ɪz
AM prəˈspɛktəs, -əz
prosper
BR ˈprɒsp|ə(r), -əz, -(ə)rɪŋ, -əd
AM ˈprɑsp|ər, -ərz, -(ə)rɪŋ, -ərd
prosperity
BR prɒˈspɛrɪti, prəˈspɛrɪti
AM prɑˈspɛrədi
Prospero
BR ˈprɒsp(ə)rəʊ
AM ˈprɑspəroʊ
prosperous
BR ˈprɒsp(ə)rəs
AM ˈprɑsp(ə)rəs
prosperously
BR ˈprɒsp(ə)rəsli
AM ˈprɑsp(ə)rəsli
prosperousness
BR ˈprɒsp(ə)rəsnəs
AM ˈprɑsp(ə)rəsnəs
Prosser
BR ˈprɒsə(r)
AM ˈprɔsər, ˈprɑsər
Prost
BR prɒst
AM prɔst, prɑst
prostaglandin
BR ˌprɒstəˈglandɪn, -z
AM ˌprɑstəˈglændən, -z
prostate
BR ˈprɒsteɪt, -s
AM ˈprɑsˌteɪt, -s
prostatectomy
BR ˌprɒstəˈtɛktəm|i, -ɪz
AM ˌprɑstəˈtɛktəmi, -z
prostatic
BR prɒˈstatɪk
AM prɑˈstædɪk
prosthesis
BR (ˌ)prɒsˈθiːsɪs, prəsˈθiːsɪs
AM prɑsˈθisɪs
prosthetic
BR (ˌ)prɒsˈθɛtɪk, prəsˈθɛtɪk, -s
AM prɑsˈθɛdɪk, -s
prosthetically
BR (ˌ)prɒsˈθɛtɪkli, prəsˈθɛtɪkli
AM prɑsˈθɛdək(ə)li
prostitute
BR ˈprɒstɪtjuːt, ˈprɒstɪtʃuːt, -s
AM ˈprɑstəˌt(j)ut, -s
prostitution
BR ˌprɒstɪˈtjuːʃn, ˌprɒstɪˈtʃuːʃn
AM ˌprɑstəˈt(j)uʃən
prostitutional
BR ˌprɒstɪˈtjuːʃn̩(ə)l, ˌprɒstɪˈtjuːʃən(ə)l, ˌprɒstɪˈtʃuːʃn̩(ə)l, ˌprɒstɪˈtʃuːʃən(ə)l
AM ˌprɑstəˈt(j)uʃ(ə)nəl
prostitutor
BR ˈprɒstɪtjuːtə(r), ˈprɒstɪtʃuːtə(r), -z
AM ˈprɑstəˌt(j)udər, -z
prostrate[1]
adjective
BR ˈprɒstreɪt
AM ˈprɑˌstreɪt
prostrate[2]
verb
BR prɒˈstreɪt, prəˈstreɪt, -s, -ɪŋ, -ɪd
AM ˈprɑˌstreɪ|t, -ts, -dɪŋ, -dɪd
prostration
BR prɒˈstreɪʃn, prəˈstreɪʃn
AM prɑˈstreɪʃən
prostyle
BR ˈprəʊstʌɪl, -z
AM ˈproʊˌstaɪl, -z
prosy
BR ˈprəʊz|i, -ɪə(r), -ɪɪst
AM ˈproʊzi, -ər, -ɪst
protactinium
BR ˌprəʊtakˈtɪnɪəm
AM ˌproʊˌtækˈtɪniəm
protagonist
BR prə(ʊ)ˈtagənɪst, prə(ʊ)ˈtagn̩ɪst, -s
AM prəˈtægənəst, proʊˈtægənəst, -s
Protagoras
BR prə(ʊ)ˈtagəras, prə(ʊ)ˈtag(ə)rəs
AM prəˈtægərəs, proʊˈtægərəs
protamine
BR ˈprəʊtəmiːn, -z
AM ˈproʊdəˌmin, ˈproʊdəmən, -z
protandrous
BR prə(ʊ)ˈtandrəs
AM ˌproʊˈtændrəs
protanope
BR ˈprəʊtənəʊp, -s
AM ˈproʊdəˌnoʊp, -s
protanopia
BR ˌprəʊtəˈnəʊpɪə(r)
AM ˌproʊdəˈnoʊpiə
protases
BR ˈprɒtəsiːz
AM ˈprɑdəˌsiz
protasis
BR ˈprɒtəsɪs
AM ˈprɑdəsəs
protatic
BR prə(ʊ)ˈtatɪk
AM proʊˈtædɪk
protea
BR ˈprəʊtɪə(r), -z
AM ˈproʊdiə, -z
protean
BR ˈprəʊtɪən, prəʊˈtiːən
AM ˈproʊdiən, proʊˈtiən
protease
BR ˈprəʊtɪeɪz, ˈprəʊtɪeɪs, -ɪz
AM ˈproʊdiˌeɪz, ˈproʊdiˌeɪs, -ɪz
protect
BR prəˈtɛkt, -s, -ɪŋ, -ɪd
AM prəˈtɛk|(t), -(t)s, -tɪŋ, -təd
protectant
BR prəˈtɛkt(ə)nt, -s
AM prəˈtɛktnt, -s
protection
BR prəˈtɛkʃn
AM prəˈtɛkʃən
protectionism
BR prəˈtɛkʃn̩ɪz(ə)m, prəˈtɛkʃənɪz(ə)m
AM prəˈtɛkʃəˌnɪzəm
protectionist
BR prəˈtɛkʃn̩ɪst, prəˈtɛkʃənɪst, -s
AM prəˈtɛkʃ(ə)nəst, -s
protective
BR prəˈtɛktɪv
AM prəˈtɛktɪv
protectively
BR prəˈtɛktɪvli
AM prəˈtɛktɪvli
protectiveness
BR prəˈtɛktɪvnɪs
AM prəˈtɛktɪvnɪs
protector
BR prəˈtɛktə(r), -z
AM prəˈtɛktər, -z

protectoral
BR prəˈtɛkt(ə)rəl, prəˈtɛkt(ə)rl
AM prəˈtɛkt(ə)rəl

protectorate
BR prəˈtɛkt(ə)rət, -s
AM prəˈtɛkt(ə)rət, -s

protectorship
BR prəˈtɛktəʃɪp
AM prəˈtɛktərˌʃɪp

protectress
BR prə(ʊ)ˈtɛktrɛs, prə(ʊ)ˈtɛktrɪs, -ɪz
AM ˈproʊtɛktrɛs, -əz

protégé
masculine
BR ˈprɒtɪʒeɪ, -z
AM ˈproʊdəˌʒeɪ, -z

protégée
feminine
BR ˈprɒtɪʒeɪ, -z
AM ˈproʊdəˌʒeɪ, -z

proteiform
BR ˈprəʊtɪɪfɔːm
AM ˈproʊdiəˌfɔ(ə)rm

protein
BR ˈprəʊtiːn, -z
AM ˈproʊˌtin, -z

proteinaceous
BR ˌprəʊtɪˈneɪʃəs
AM ˌproʊˌtiˈneɪʃəs, ˌproʊdəˈneɪʃəs

proteinic
BR prəʊˈtiːnɪk
AM proʊˈtinɪk

proteinous
BR prəʊˈtiː(ɪ)nəs
AM proʊˈti(ə)nəs

pro tem
BR (ˌ)prəʊ ˈtɛm
AM ˌproʊ ˈtɛm

pro tempore
BR (ˌ)prəʊ ˈtɛmp(ə)reɪ, + ˈtɛmp(ə)ri
AM ˌproʊ ˈtɛmpəˌreɪ

proteolyses
BR ˌprəʊtɪˈɒlɪsiːz
AM ˌproʊdiˈɑləˌsiz

proteolysis
BR ˌprəʊtɪˈɒlɪsɪs
AM ˌproʊdiˈɑləsəs

proteolytic
BR ˌprəʊtiəˈlɪtɪk
AM ˌproʊdiəˈlɪdɪk

Proterozoic
BR ˌprəʊt(ə)rəˈzəʊɪk
AM ˌproʊtərəˈzoʊɪk

protest¹
noun
BR ˈprəʊtɛst, -s
AM ˈproʊˌtɛst, -s

protest²
verb
BR prəˈtɛst, -s, -ɪŋ, -ɪd
AM prəˈtɛst, proʊˈtɛst, -s, -ɪŋ, -əd

Protestant
BR ˈprɒtɪst(ə)nt, -s
AM ˈprɑdəstənt, -s

Protestantise
BR ˈprɒtɪst(ə)ntʌɪz, -ɪz, -ɪŋ, -d
AM ˈprɑdəstənˌtaɪz, -ɪz, -ɪŋ, -d

Protestantism
BR ˈprɒtɪst(ə)ntɪz(ə)m
AM ˈprɑdəstənˌtɪzəm

Protestantize
BR ˈprɒtɪst(ə)ntʌɪz, -ɪz, -ɪŋ, -d
AM ˈprɑdəstənˌtaɪz, -ɪz, -ɪŋ, -d

protestation
BR ˌprɒtɪˈsteɪʃn, -z
AM ˌprɑdəˈsteɪʃən, -z

protester
BR prəˈtɛstə(r), -z
AM ˈproʊˌtɛstər, -z

protestingly
BR prəˈtɛstɪŋli
AM prəˈtɛstɪŋli, proʊˈtɛstɪŋli

protestor
BR prəˈtɛstə(r), -z
AM ˈproʊˌtɛstər, -z

Proteus
BR ˈprəʊtiəs
AM ˈproʊdiəs

prothalamia
BR ˌprəʊθəˈleɪmɪə(r)
AM ˌproʊθəˈleɪmiə

prothalamion
BR ˌprəʊθəˈleɪmɪən
AM ˌproʊθəˈleɪmiən

prothalamium
BR ˌprəʊθəˈleɪmɪəm
AM ˌproʊθəˈleɪmiəm

prothalli
BR prəʊˈθalʌɪ, prəʊˈθaliː
AM proʊˈθæˌlaɪ

prothallia
BR prəʊˈθalɪə(r)
AM proʊˈθæljə, proʊˈθæliə

prothallium
BR prəʊˈθalɪəm
AM proʊˈθæliəm

prothallus
BR prəʊˈθaləs
AM proʊˈθæləs

Prothero
BR ˈprɒðərəʊ
AM ˈproʊˌθ(ə)roʊ

Protheroe
BR ˈprɒðərəʊ
AM ˈproʊˌθ(ə)roʊ

protheses
BR ˈprɒθɪsiːz
AM ˈprɑθəˌsiz

prothesis
BR ˈprɒθɪsɪs
AM ˈprɑθəsəs

prothetic
BR prə(ʊ)ˈθɛtɪk
AM prəˈθɛdɪk

prothetically
BR prə(ʊ)ˈθɛtɪkli
AM prəˈθɛdək(ə)li

prothonotary
BR ˌprəʊθəˈnəʊt(ə)r|i, prə(ʊ)ˈθɒnət(ə)r|i, -ɪz
AM prəˈθɑnəˌtɛri, ˌproʊθəˈnɑdəri, -z

protist
BR ˈprəʊtɪst, -s
AM ˈproʊdəst, -s

protistology
BR ˌprəʊtɪsˈtɒlədʒi
AM ˌproʊdəˈstɑlədʒi

protium
BR ˈprəʊtɪəm
AM ˈproʊdiəm, ˈproʊʃəm

protocol
BR ˈprəʊtəkɒl, -z
AM ˈproʊdəˌkɔl, ˈproʊdəˌkɑl, -z

protogynous
BR prə(ʊ)ˈtɒdʒɪnəs
AM proʊˈtɑdʒənəs

protomartyr
BR ˌprəʊtəʊˈmɑːtə(r), -z
AM ˌproʊdoʊˈmɑrdər, -z

proton
BR ˈprəʊtɒn, -z
AM ˈproʊˌtɑn, -z

protonate
BR ˈprəʊtəneɪt, -s, -ɪŋ, -ɪd
AM ˈproʊdəˌneɪt, -s, -ɪŋ, -ɪd

protonic
BR prəʊˈtɒnɪk
AM proʊˈtɑnɪk

protonotary
BR ˌprəʊtəˈnəʊt(ə)r|i, prə(ʊ)ˈtɒnət(ə)r|i, -ɪz
AM ˌproʊdəˈnoʊdəri, -z

protopectin
BR ˌprəʊtə(ʊ)ˈpɛktɪn, -z
AM ˌproʊdəˈpɛktən, -z

protophyte
BR ˈprəʊtəfʌɪt, -s
AM ˈproʊdəˌfaɪt, -s

protoplasm
BR ˈprəʊtə(ʊ)plaz(ə)m
AM ˈproʊdəˌplæzəm

protoplasmal
BR ˌprəʊtə(ʊ)ˈplazml
AM ˈproʊdəˌplæzməl

protoplasmatic
BR ˌprəʊtə(ʊ)plazˈmatɪk
AM ˌproʊdəˌplæzˈmædɪk

protoplasmic
BR ˌprəʊtə(ʊ)ˈplazmɪk
AM ˌproʊdəˈplæzmɪk

protoplast
BR ˈprəʊtə(ʊ)plast, -s
AM ˈproʊdəˌplæst, -s

protoplastic
BR ˌprəʊtə(ʊ)ˈplastɪk
AM ˌproʊdəˈplæstɪk

prototheria
BR ˌprəʊtə(ʊ)ˈθɪərɪə(r)
AM ˌproʊdəˈθɪriə

prototherian
BR ˌprəʊtə(ʊ)ˈθɪərɪən, -z
AM ˌproʊdəˈθɪriən, -z

prototypal
BR ˈprəʊtətʌɪpl, ˌprəʊtə(ʊ)ˈtʌɪpl
AM ˌproʊdəˌtaɪpəl

prototype
BR ˈprəʊtətʌɪp, -s, -ɪŋ, -t
AM ˈproʊdəˌtaɪp, -s, -ɪŋ, -t

prototypic
BR ˌprəʊtə(ʊ)ˈtɪpɪk
AM ˌproʊdəˈtɪpɪk

prototypical
BR ˌprəʊtə(ʊ)ˈtɪpɪkl
AM ˌproʊdəˈtɪpəkəl

prototypically
BR ˌprəʊtə(ʊ)ˈtɪpɪkli
AM ˌproʊdəˈtɪpɪk(ə)li

protozoa
BR ˌprəʊtə(ʊ)ˈzəʊə(r)
AM ˌproʊdəˈzoʊə

protozoal
BR ˌprəʊtə(ʊ)ˈzəʊəl
AM ˌproʊdəˈzoʊəl

protozoan
BR ˌprəʊtə(ʊ)ˈzəʊən
AM ˌproʊdəˈzoʊən

protozoic
BR ˌprəʊtə(ʊ)ˈzəʊɪk
AM ˌproʊdəˈzoʊɪk

protozoology
BR ˌprəʊtə(ʊ)zuːˈɒlədʒi, ˌprəʊtə(ʊ)zəʊˈɒlədʒi
AM ˌproʊdoʊˌzoʊˈwɑlədʒi, ˌproʊdoʊzəˈwɑlədʒi

protozoon
BR ˌprəʊtə(ʊ)ˈzəʊən, ˌprəʊtə(ʊ)ˈzəʊɒn
AM ˌproʊdəˈzoʊən

protract
BR prəˈtrakt, -s, -ɪŋ, -ɪd
AM prəˈtræk|(t), proʊˈtræk|(t), -(t)s, -tɪŋ, -təd

protracted
BR prəˈtraktɪd
AM prəˈtræktəd, proʊˈtræktəd

protractedly
BR prəˈtraktɪdli
AM prəˈtræktədli, proʊˈtræktədli

protractedness
BR prəˈtraktɪdnɪs
AM prəˈtræktədnəs, proʊˈtræktədnəs

protractile
BR prəˈtraktʌɪl
AM prəˈtræktəl, proʊˈtræktəl, proʊˈtræk,taɪl, prəˈtræk,taɪl

protraction
BR prəˈtrakʃn, -z
AM prəˈtrækʃən, proʊˈtrækʃən, -z

protractor
BR prəˈtraktə(r), -z
AM ˈproʊ,træktər, -z

protrude
BR prəˈtruːd, -z, -ɪŋ, -ɨd
AM prəˈtrud, proʊˈtrud, -z, -ɪŋ, -əd

protrudent
BR prəˈtruːdnt
AM prəˈtrudnt, proʊˈtrudnt

protrusible
BR prəˈtruːsɨbl
AM prəˈtrusəbəl, proʊˈtrusəbəl

protrusile
BR prəˈtruːsʌɪl
AM prəˈtrusəl, proʊˈtrusəl, proʊˈtru,saɪl

protrusion
BR prəˈtruːʒn, -z
AM prəˈtruʒən, proʊˈtruʒən, -z

protrusive
BR prəˈtruːsɪv
AM prəˈtrusɪv, proʊˈtrusɪv

protrusively
BR prəˈtruːsɪvli
AM prəˈtrusɪvli, proʊˈtrusɪvli

protrusiveness
BR prəˈtruːsɪvnɨs
AM prəˈtrusɪvnɨs, proʊˈtrusɪvnɨs

protuberance
BR prəˈtjuːb(ə)rəns, prəˈtjuːb(ə)rn̩s, prəˈtʃuːb(ə)rəns, prəˈtʃuːb(ə)rn̩s, -ɨz
AM prəˈt(j)ub(ə)rəns, proʊˈt(j)ub(ə)rəns, -əz

protuberant
BR prəˈtjuːb(ə)rənt, prəˈtjuːb(ə)rn̩t, prəˈtʃuːb(ə)rənt, prəˈtʃuːb(ə)rn̩t
AM prəˈt(j)ub(ə)rənt, proʊˈt(j)ub(ə)rənt

protuberantly
BR prəˈtjuːb(ə)rəntli, prəˈtjuːb(ə)rn̩tli, prəˈtʃuːb(ə)rəntli, prəˈtʃuːb(ə)rn̩tli
AM prəˈt(j)ub(ə)rən(t)li, proʊˈt(j)ub(ə)rən(t)li

proud
BR praʊd, -ə(r), -ɨst
AM praʊd, -ər, -əst

Proudhon
BR ˈpruːdɒn
AM prʊˈdɔn
FR pʀudɔ̃

proudly
BR ˈpraʊdli
AM ˈpraʊdli

proudness
BR ˈpraʊdnəs
AM ˈpraʊdnəs

Proust
BR pruːst
AM prust

Prout
BR praʊt
AM praʊt

provability
BR ˌpruːvəˈbɪlɨti
AM ˌpruvəˈbɪlɨdi

provable
BR ˈpruːvəbl
AM ˈpruvəbəl

provableness
BR ˈpruːvəblnəs
AM ˈpruvəbəlnəs

provably
BR ˈpruːvəbli
AM ˈpruvəbli

prove
BR pruːv, -z, -ɪŋ, -d
AM pruv, -z, -ɪŋ, -d

proven
BR ˈpruːvn, ˈprəʊvn
AM ˈpruvən

provenance
BR ˈprɒvɨnəns, ˈprɒvn̩əns, -t
AM ˈprɑvənəns, -t

Provençal
BR ˌprɒvnˈsɑːl
AM ˌproʊvənˈsɑl, ˌprɑvənˈsɑl

Provence
BR prɒˈvɑːns, prɒˈvɒ̃s
AM proʊˈvɑns

provender
BR ˈprɒv(ɨ)ndə(r)
AM ˈprɑvəndər

provenience
BR prəˈviːnɪəns
AM prəˈvɪnjəns

proverb
BR ˈprɒvəːb, -z
AM ˈprɑ,vərb, -z

pro-verb
BR ˈprəʊvəːb, -z
AM ˈproʊ,vərb, -z

proverbial
BR prəˈvəːbɪəl
AM prəˈvərbiəl

proverbiality
BR prə,vəːbɪˈalɨti
AM prə,vərbiˈælədi

proverbially
BR prəˈvəːbɪəli
AM prəˈvərbiəli

Proverbs
BR ˈprɒvəːbz
AM ˈprɑ,vərbz

provide
BR prəˈvʌɪd, -z, -ɪŋ, -ɨd
AM prəˈvaɪd, proʊˈvaɪd, -z, -ɪŋ, -ɨd

providence
BR ˈprɒvɨd(ə)ns
AM ˈprɑvə,dɛns, ˈprɑvədns

provident
BR ˈprɒvɨd(ə)nt
AM ˈprɑvədnt, ˈprɑvə,dɛnt

providential
BR ˌprɒvɪˈdɛnʃl
AM ˌprɑvəˈdɛn(t)ʃəl

providentially
BR ˌprɒvɪˈdɛnʃl̩i, ˌprɒvɪˈdɛnʃəli
AM ˌprɑvəˈdɛn(t)ʃəli

providently
BR ˈprɒvɨd(ə)ntli
AM ˈprɑvə,dɛn(t)li, ˈprɑvədn(t)li

provider
BR prəˈvʌɪdə(r), -z
AM prəˈvaɪdər, proʊˈvaɪdər, -z

province
BR ˈprɒv|ɪns, -ɨnsɨz
AM ˈprɑvəns, -əz

provincial
BR prəˈvɪnʃl, -z
AM prəˈvɪn(t)ʃəl, proʊˈvɪn(t)ʃəl, -z

provincialise
BR prəˈvɪnʃl̩ʌɪz, prəˈvɪnʃəlʌɪz, -ɨz, -ɪŋ, -d
AM prəˈvɪn(t)ʃə,laɪz, proʊˈvɪn(t)ʃə,laɪz, -ɨz, -ɪŋ, -d

provincialism
BR prəˈvɪnʃl̩ɪz(ə)m, prəˈvɪnʃəlɪz(ə)m, -z
AM prəˈvɪn(t)ʃə,lɪzəm, proʊˈvɪn(t)ʃə,lɪzəm, -z

provincialist
BR prəˈvɪnʃl̩ɪst, prəˈvɪnʃəlɪst, -s
AM prəˈvɪn(t)ʃələst, proʊˈvɪn(t)ʃələst, -s

provinciality
BR prə,vɪnʃɪˈalɨti
AM prə,vɪn(t)ʃiˈælədi, proʊ,vɪn(t)ʃiˈælədi

provincialize
BR prəˈvɪnʃl̩ʌɪz, prəˈvɪnʃəlʌɪz, -ɨz, -ɪŋ, -d
AM prəˈvɪn(t)ʃə,laɪz, proʊˈvɪn(t)ʃə,laɪz, -ɨz, -ɪŋ, -d

provincially
BR prəˈvɪnʃl̩i, prəˈvɪnʃəli
AM prəˈvɪn(t)ʃəli, proʊˈvɪn(t)ʃəli

provision
BR prəˈvɪʒ|n, -nz, -n̩ɪŋ\-ənɪŋ, -nd
AM prəˈvɪʒən, proʊˈvɪʒən, -z, -ɪŋ, -d

provisional
BR prəˈvɪʒn̩(ə)l, prəˈvɪʒən(ə)l, -z
AM prəˈvɪʒ(ə)nəl, proʊˈvɪʒ(ə)nəl, -z

provisionality
BR prə,vɪʒəˈnalɨti
AM prə,vɪʒəˈnælədi, proʊ,vɪʒəˈnælədi

provisionally
BR prəˈvɪʒn̩əli, prəˈvɪʒn̩l̩i, prəˈvɪʒənl̩i, prəˈvɪʒ(ə)nəli
AM prəˈvɪʒ(ə)nəli, proʊˈvɪʒ(ə)nəli

provisionalness
BR prəˈvɪʒn̩(ə)lnəs, prəˈvɪʒən(ə)lnəs
AM prəˈvɪʒənlnəs, proʊˈvɪʒənlnəs, prəˈvɪʒnəlnəs, proʊˈvɪʒnəlnəs

provisioner
BR prəˈvɪʒn̩ə(r), prəˈvɪʒənə(r), -z
AM prəˈvɪʒənər, proʊˈvɪʒənər, -z

provisionless
BR prəˈvɪʒnləs
AM prəˈvɪʒənləs, proʊˈvɪʒənləs

provisionment
BR prəˈvɪʒnm(ə)nt
AM prəˈvɪʒənmənt, proʊˈvɪʒənmənt

proviso
BR prəˈvʌɪzəʊ, -z
AM prəˈvaɪzoʊ, proʊˈvaɪzoʊ, -z

provisor
BR prəˈvʌɪzə(r), -z
AM prəˈvaɪzər, proʊˈvaɪzər, -z

provisorily
BR prəˈvʌɪz(ə)rɨli
AM prəˈvaɪzərəli, proʊˈvaɪzərəli

provisory
BR prəˈvʌɪz(ə)ri
AM prəˈvaɪzəri, proʊˈvaɪzəri

Provo
BR ˈprəʊvəʊ, -z
AM ˈproʊvoʊ, -z

provocateur
BR prəˌvɒkəˈtəː(r)
AM prəˌvɑkəˈtər

provocation
BR ˌprɒvəˈkeɪʃn, -z
AM ˌprɑvəˈkeɪʃən, -z

provocative
BR prəˈvɒkətɪv
AM prəˈvɑkədɪv, proʊˈvɑkədɪv

provocatively
BR prəˈvɒkətɪvli
AM prəˈvɑkədɪvli, proʊˈvɑkədɪvli

provocativeness
BR prəˈvɒkətɪvnɪs
AM prəˈvɑkədɪvnɪs, proʊˈvɑkədɪvnɪs

provokable
BR prəˈvəʊkəbl
AM prəˈvoʊkəbəl, proʊˈvoʊkəbəl

provoke
BR prəˈvəʊk, -s, -ɪŋ, -t
AM prəˈvoʊk, proʊˈvoʊk, -s, -ɪŋ, -t

provoker
BR prəˈvəʊkə(r), -z
AM prəˈvoʊkər, proʊˈvoʊkər, -z

provokingly
BR prəˈvəʊkɪŋli
AM prəˈvoʊkɪŋli, proʊˈvoʊkɪŋli

provost
BR ˈprɒvəst, ˈprɒvɒst, -s
AM ˈproʊˌvoʊst, ˈproʊvəst, -s

provost-marshall
BR prəˌvəʊˈmɑːʃl, -z
AM ˈproʊvoʊˈmɑrʃəl, -z

provostship
BR ˈprɒvəstʃɪp, ˈprɒvɒstʃɪp
AM ˈproʊˌvoʊstˌʃɪp, ˈproʊvəstˌʃɪp

prow
BR praʊ, -z
AM praʊ, -z

prowess
BR ˈpraʊɪs, ˈpraʊɛs, praʊˈɛs
AM ˈpraʊ(w)əs

prowl
BR praʊl, -z, -ɪŋ, -d
AM ˈpraʊ(wə)l, -z, -ɪŋ, -d

prowler
BR ˈpraʊlə(r), -z
AM ˈpraʊ(wə)lər, -z

Prowse
BR praʊz, praʊs
AM praʊz

prox.
BR prɒks
AM prɑks

proxemic
BR prɒkˈsiːmɪk, -s
AM prɑkˈsimɪk, -s

Proxima Centauri
BR ˌprɒksɪmə sɛnˈtɔːrʌɪ, + sɛnˈtɔːriː
AM ˈprɑksəmə ˌsɛnˈtɔˌraɪ

proximal
BR ˈprɒksɪml
AM ˈprɑksəməl

proximally
BR ˈprɒksɪml̩i, ˈprɒksɪməli
AM ˈprɑksəməli

proximate
BR ˈprɒksɪmət
AM ˈprɑksəmət

proximately
BR ˈprɒksɪmətli
AM ˈprɑksəmətli

proxime accessit
BR ˌprɒksɪmɪ akˈsɛsɪt, ˌprɒksɪmeɪ +
AM ˈprɑksəmə ækˈsɛsət

proximity
BR prɒkˈsɪmɪti
AM prɑkˈsɪmɪdi

proximo
BR ˈprɒksɪməʊ
AM ˈprɑksəˌmoʊ

proxy
BR ˈprɒks|i, -ɪz
AM ˈprɑksi, -z

Prozac®
BR ˈprəʊzak
AM ˈproʊzæk

Pru
BR pruː
AM pru

prude
BR pruːd, -z
AM prud, -z

prudence
BR ˈpruːdns
AM ˈprudns

prudent
BR ˈpruːdnt
AM ˈprudnt

prudential
BR prʊˈdɛnʃl
AM pruˈdɛn(t)ʃəl

prudentialism
BR prʊˈdɛnʃl̩ɪz(ə)m, prʊˈdɛnʃəlɪz(ə)m
AM pruˈdɛn(t)ʃəˌlɪzəm

prudentialist
BR prʊˈdɛnʃl̩ɪst, prʊˈdɛnʃəlɪst, -s
AM pruˈdɛn(t)ʃələst, -s

prudentially
BR prʊˈdɛnʃl̩i, prʊˈdɛnʃəli
AM pruˈdɛn(t)ʃəli

prudently
BR ˈpruːdntli
AM ˈprudn(t)li

prudery
BR ˈpruːd(ə)ri
AM ˈprudəri

Prudhoe
place in UK
BR ˈprʌdəʊ
AM ˈprədoʊ

Prudhoe Bay
BR ˌpruːdəʊ ˈbeɪ
AM ˈprud(h)oʊ ˈbeɪ

prudish
BR ˈpruːdɪʃ
AM ˈprudɪʃ

prudishly
BR ˈpruːdɪʃli
AM ˈprudɪʃli

prudishness
BR ˈpruːdɪʃnɪs
AM ˈprudɪʃnɪs

Prue
BR pruː
AM pru

Prufrock
BR ˈpruːfrɒk
AM ˈprufˌrɑk

pruinose
BR ˈpruːɪnəʊs
AM ˈpruəˌnoʊs, ˈpruəˌnoʊz

Pruitt
BR ˈpruːɪt
AM ˈpruɪt

prune
BR pruːn, -z, -ɪŋ, -d
AM prun, -z, -ɪŋ, -d

prunella
BR prʊˈnɛlə(r), -z
AM pruˈnɛlə, -z

pruner
BR ˈpruːnə(r), -z
AM ˈprunər, -z

prurience
BR ˈprʊərɪəns
AM ˈprʊriəns, ˈpruriəns

pruriency
BR ˈprʊərɪənsi
AM ˈprʊriənsi, ˈpruriənsi

prurient
BR ˈprʊərɪənt
AM ˈprʊriənt, ˈpruriənt

pruriently
BR ˈprʊərɪəntli
AM ˈprʊriən(t)li, ˈpruriən(t)li

pruriginous
BR prʊəˈrɪdʒɪnəs
AM prʊˈrɪdʒənəs

prurigo
BR prʊəˈrʌɪɡəʊ
AM prʊˈraɪˌɡoʊ

pruritic
BR prʊəˈrɪtɪk
AM prʊˈrɪdɪk

pruritis
BR prʊəˈrʌɪtɪs
AM prʊˈraɪdɪs

prusik
BR ˈprʌs|ɪk, -ɪks, -ɪkɪŋ, -ɪkt
AM ˈprəsɪk, -s, -ɪŋ, -t

Prussia
BR ˈprʌʃə(r)
AM ˈprəʃə

Prussian
BR ˈprʌʃn, -z
AM ˈprəʃən, -z

prussic
BR ˈprʌsɪk
AM ˈprəsɪk

pry
BR prʌɪ, -z, -ɪŋ, -d
AM praɪ, -z, -ɪŋ, -d

Pryce
BR prʌɪs
AM praɪs

Pryde
BR prʌɪd
AM praɪd

pryingly
BR ˈprʌɪɪŋli
AM ˈpraɪɪŋli

Prynne
BR prɪn
AM prɪn

prytany
BR ˈprɪtən|i, -ɪz
AM ˈprɪdəni, -z

Przewalski
BR ˌprəʒɪˈvalski, ˌprəʒɪˈwɒlski
AM ˌprəʒəˈwɔlski, ˌprəʒəˈwɑlski
RUS prʒɪˈvalʲskʲij

psalm
BR sɑːm, -z
AM sɑ(l)m, -z

psalmbook
BR ˈsɑːmbʊk, -s
AM ˈsɑ(l)mˌbʊk, -s

psalmic
BR ˈsɑːmɪk
AM ˈsɑ(l)mɪk

psalmist
BR ˈsɑːmɪst, -s
AM ˈsɑ(l)məst, -s

psalmodic
BR salˈmɒdɪk
AM sɑ(l)ˈmɑdɪk

psalmodise
BR ˈsalmədʌɪz, ˈsɑːmədʌɪz, -ɪz, -ɪŋ, -d
AM ˈsɑ(l)məˌdaɪz, -ɪz, -ɪŋ, -d

psalmodist
BR ˈsɑːmədɪst, ˈsalmədɪst, -s
AM ˈsɑ(l)mədəst, -s

psalmodize
BR ˈsalmədʌɪz, ˈsɑːmədʌɪz, -ɪz, -ɪŋ, -d
AM ˈsɑ(l)məˌdaɪz, -ɪz, -ɪŋ, -d

psalmody
BR ˈsɑːmədi, ˈsalmədi
AM ˈsɑ(l)mədi

psalter
BR ˈsɔːltə(r), ˈsɒltə(r), -z
AM ˈsɔltər, ˈsɑltər, -z

psalteria
BR sɔːlˈtɪərɪə(r), sɒlˈtɪərɪə(r)
AM ˌsɔlˈtɪriə

psalterium
BR sɔːlˈtɪərɪəm, sɒlˈtɪərɪəm, -z
AM ˌsɔlˈtɪriəm, ˌsɑlˈtɪriəm, -z

psaltery
BR ˈsɔːlt(ə)r|i, ˈsɒlt(ə)r|i, -ɪz
AM ˈsɔltəri, ˈsɑltəri, -z

psephological
BR ˌsiːfəˈlɒdʒɨkl, ˌsɛfəˈlɒdʒɨkl
AM ˌsifəˈlɑdʒəkəl

psephologically
BR ˌsiːfəˈlɒdʒɨkli, ˌsɛfəˈlɒdʒɨkli
AM ˌsifəˈlɑdʒək(ə)li

psephologist
BR sɪˈfɒlədʒɪst, siːˈfɒlədʒɪst, sɛˈfɒlədʒɪst, -s
AM siˈfɑlədʒəst, -s

psephology
BR sɪˈfɒlədʒi, siːˈfɒlədʒi, sɛˈfɒlədʒi
AM siˈfɑlədʒi

pseud
BR s(j)uːd, -z
AM sud, -z

pseudepigrapha
BR ˌs(j)uːdɪˈpɪɡrəfə(r)
AM ˌsudəˈpɪɡrəfə

pseudepigraphal
BR ˌs(j)uːdɪˈpɪɡrəfl
AM ˌsudəˈpɪɡrəfəl

pseudepigraphic
BR ˌs(j)uːdɪpɪˈɡrafɪk
AM ˈsudˌɛpəˈɡræfɪk

pseudepigraphical
BR ˌs(j)uːdɪpɪˈɡrafɪkl
AM ˈsudˌɛpəˈɡræfəkəl

pseudo
BR ˈs(j)uːdəʊ, -z
AM ˈsudoʊ, -z

pseudocarp
BR ˈs(j)uːdə(ʊ)kɑːp, -s
AM ˈsudoʊˌkɑrp, -s

pseudograph
BR ˈs(j)uːdə(ʊ)ɡrɑːf, ˈs(j)uːdə(ʊ)ɡraf, -s
AM ˈsudoʊˌɡræf, -s

pseudomorph
BR ˈs(j)uːdə(ʊ)mɔːf, -s
AM ˈsudoʊˌmɔ(ə)rf, -s

pseudomorphic
BR ˌs(j)uːdə(ʊ)ˈmɔːfɪk
AM ˌsudoʊˈmɔrfɪk

pseudomorphism
BR ˌs(j)uːdə(ʊ)ˈmɔːfɪz(ə)m
AM ˌsudoʊˈmɔrˌfɪzəm

pseudomorphous
BR ˌs(j)uːdə(ʊ)ˈmɔːfəs
AM ˌsudoʊˈmɔrfəs

pseudonym
BR ˈs(j)uːdənɪm, -z
AM ˈsudn̩ɪm, -z

pseudonymity
BR ˌs(j)uːdəˈnɪmɨti
AM ˌsudəˈnɪmɨdi

pseudonymous
BR ˈs(j)uːˈdɒnɨməs
AM suˈdɑnəməs

pseudonymously
BR ˈs(j)uːˈdɒnɨməsli
AM suˈdɑnəməsli

pseudopod
BR ˈs(j)uːdə(ʊ)pɒd, -z
AM ˈsudəˌpɑd, -z

pseudopodia
BR ˌs(j)uːdə(ʊ)ˈpəʊdɪə(r)
AM ˌsudəˈpoʊdiə

pseudopodium
BR ˌs(j)uːdə(ʊ)ˈpəʊdɪəm
AM ˌsudəˈpoʊdiəm

pseudo-science
BR ˈs(j)uːdəʊˌsʌɪəns, ˌs(j)uːdəʊˈsʌɪəns, -ɪz
AM ˈsudoʊˌsaɪəns, -əz

pseudo-scientific
BR ˌs(j)uːdəʊˌsʌɪənˈtɪfɪk
AM ˈsudoʊˌsaɪənˈtɪfɪk

pshaw
BR pɸ, (p)ʃɔː(r)
AM (p)ʃɔ

psi
BR (p)sʌɪ
AM (p)saɪ

p.s.i.
pounds per square inch
BR ˌpiːɛsˈʌɪ
AM ˌpiˌɛsˈaɪ

psilanthropic
BR ˌsʌɪlanˈθrɒpɪk, ˌsʌɪlənˈθrɒpɪk
AM ˌsaɪlənˈθrɑpɪk, ˌsaɪˌlænˈθrɑpɪk

psilanthropism
BR sʌɪˈlanθrəpɪz(ə)m
AM saɪˈlænθrəˌpɪzəm

psilanthropist
BR sʌɪˈlanθrəpɪst, -s
AM saɪˈlænθrəpəst, -s

psilocybin
BR ˌsʌɪlə(ʊ)ˈsʌɪbɪn, -z
AM ˌsɪloʊˈsaɪbɪn, ˌsaɪloʊˈsaɪbɪn, -z

psilosis
BR sʌɪˈləʊsɪs
AM saɪˈloʊsəs

Psion®
BR ˈsʌɪɒn
AM ˈsaɪˌɑn

psionic
BR sʌɪˈɒnɪk
AM saɪˈɑnɪk

psionically
BR sʌɪˈɒnɨkli
AM saɪˈɑnəkli

psittacine
BR ˈsɪtəsʌɪn
AM ˈsɪdəˌsaɪn

psittacosis
BR ˌsɪtəˈkəʊsɪs
AM ˌsɪdəˈkoʊsəs

psoae
BR ˈsəʊʌɪ
AM ˈsoʊˌaɪ

psoai
BR ˈsəʊiː
AM ˈsoʊˌi

psoas
BR ˈsəʊas, ˈsəʊəs, -ɪz
AM ˈsoʊəs, -əz

psoriasis
BR səˈrʌɪəsɪs
AM səˈraɪəsəs, sɔrˈaɪəsəs

psoriatic
BR ˌsɒrɪˈatɪk
AM ˌsɔriˈædɪk

psst
BR pst
AM pst

psych
BR sʌɪk, -s, -ɪŋ, -t
AM saɪk, -s, -ɪŋ, -t

psyche[1]
noun
BR ˈsʌɪk|i, -ɪz
AM ˈsaɪki, -z

psyche[2]
verb
BR sʌɪk, -s, -ɪŋ, -t
AM saɪk, -s, -ɪŋ, -t

psychedelia
BR ˌsʌɪkɪˈdiːlɪə(r)
AM ˌsaɪkəˈdiljə, ˌsaɪkəˈdiliə

psychedelic
BR ˌsʌɪkɪˈdɛlɪk
AM ˌsaɪkəˈdɛlɪk

psychedelically
BR ˌsʌɪkɪˈdɛlɨkli
AM ˌsaɪkəˈdɛlək(ə)li

psychiatric
BR ˌsʌɪkɪˈatrɪk
AM ˈsaɪkiˈætrɪk

psychiatrical
BR ˌsʌɪkɪˈatrɪkl
AM ˈsaɪkiˈætrəkəl

psychiatrically
BR ˌsʌɪkɪˈatrɨkli
AM ˈsaɪkiˈætrək(ə)li

psychiatrist
BR sʌɪˈkʌɪətrɪst, səˈkʌɪətrɪst, -s
AM səˈkaɪətrəst, saɪˈkaɪətrəst, -s

psychiatry
BR sʌɪˈkʌɪətri, səˈkʌɪətri
AM səˈkaɪətri, saɪˈkaɪətri

psychic
BR ˈsʌɪkɪk, -s
AM ˈsaɪkɪk, -s

psychical
BR ˈsʌɪkɨkl
AM ˈsaɪkɨkəl

psychically
BR ˈsʌɪkɨkli
AM ˈsaɪkɨk(ə)li

psychicism
BR ˈsʌɪkɨsɪz(ə)m
AM ˈsaɪkəˌsɪzəm

psychicist
BR ˈsʌɪkɨsɪst, -s
AM ˈsaɪkəsəst, -s

psycho
BR ˈsʌɪkəʊ, -z
AM ˈsaɪkoʊ, -z

psychoactive
BR ˌsʌɪkəʊˈaktɪv
AM ˌsaɪkoʊˈæktɪv

psychoanalyse
BR ˌsʌɪkəʊˈanəlʌɪz, ˌsʌɪkəʊˈanl̩ʌɪz, -ɪz, -ɪŋ, -d
AM ˌsaɪkoʊˈænəˌlaɪz, -ɪz, -ɪŋ, -d

psychoanalysis
BR ˌsʌɪkəʊəˈnalɨsɪs
AM ˈsaɪkoʊəˈnæləsəs

psychoanalyst
BR ˌsʌɪkəʊˈanəlɪst, ˌsʌɪkəʊˈanl̩ɪst, -s
AM ˈsaɪkoʊˈænələst, -s

psychoanalytic
BR ˌsʌɪkəʊˌanəˈlɪtɪk
AM ˈsaɪkoʊˌænəˈlɪdɪk

psychoanalytical
BR ˌsʌɪkəʊˌanəˈlɪtɨkl
AM ˈsaɪkoʊˌænəˈlɪdɨkəl

psychoanalytically
BR ˌsʌɪkəʊˌanəˈlɪtɨkli
AM ˈsaɪkoʊˌænəˈlɪdɨk(ə)li

psychoanalyze
BR ˌsʌɪkəʊˈanəlʌɪz, ˌsʌɪkəʊˈanl̩ʌɪz, -ɪz, -ɪŋ, -d
AM ˌsaɪkoʊˈænəˌlaɪz, -ɪz, -ɪŋ, -d

psychobabble
BR ˈsʌɪkəʊˌbabl
AM ˈsaɪkoʊˌbæbəl

psychobiological
BR ˌsʌɪkəʊˌbʌɪəˈlɒdʒɨkl
AM ˈsaɪkoʊˌbaɪəˈlɑdʒəkəl

psychobiologist
BR ˌsʌɪkəʊbʌɪˈɒlədʒɪst, -s
AM ˌsaɪkoʊˌbaɪˈɑlədʒəst, -s

psychobiology
BR ˌsʌɪkəʊbʌɪˈɒlədʒi
AM ˌsaɪkoʊˌbaɪˈɑlədʒi

psychodrama
BR ˈsʌɪkə(ʊ)ˌdrɑːmə(r), -z
AM ˈsaɪkoʊˌdrɑmə, -z

psychodynamic
BR ˌsʌɪkə(ʊ)dʌɪˈnamɪk, -s
AM ¦saɪkoʊdaɪˈnæmɪk, -s

psychodynamically
BR ˌsʌɪkə(ʊ)dʌɪˈnamɨkli
AM ¦saɪkoʊˌdaɪˈnæmək(ə)li

psychogenesis
BR ˌsʌɪkəʊˈdʒɛnɨsɪs
AM ˌsaɪkoʊˈdʒɛnəsəs

psychogenic
BR ˌsʌɪkə(ʊ)ˈdʒɛnɪk
AM ˌsaɪkoʊˈdʒɛnɪk

psychograph
BR ˈsʌɪkə(ʊ)ɡrɑːf, ˈsʌɪkə(ʊ)ɡraf, -s
AM ˈsaɪkəˌɡræf, -s

psychokinesis
BR ˌsʌɪkəʊkɪˈniːsɪs, ˌsʌɪkəʊkʌɪˈniːsɪs
AM ¦saɪkoʊkəˈnisɨs, ¦saɪkoʊˌkaɪˈnisɨs

psychokinetic
BR ˌsʌɪkəʊkɪˈnɛtɪk, ˌsʌɪkəʊkʌɪˈnɛtɪk
AM ¦saɪkoʊkəˈnɛdɪk

psycholinguist
BR ˌsʌɪkəʊˈlɪŋɡwɪst, -s
AM ˌsaɪkoʊˈlɪŋɡwɨst, -s

psycholinguistic
BR ˌsʌɪkəʊlɪŋˈɡwɪstɪk, -s
AM ˌsaɪkoʊˌlɪŋˈɡwɪstɪk, -s

psychological
BR ˌsʌɪkəˈlɒdʒɨkl
AM ˌsaɪkəˈlɑdʒəkəl

psychologically
BR ˌsʌɪkəˈlɒdʒɨkli
AM ˌsaɪkəˈlɑdʒək(ə)li

psychologise
BR sʌɪˈkɒlədʒʌɪz, -ɨz, -ɪŋ, -d
AM saɪˈkɑləˌdʒaɪz, -ɨz, -ɪŋ, -d

psychologist
BR sʌɪˈkɒlədʒɪst, -s
AM saɪˈkɑlədʒəst, -s

psychologize
BR sʌɪˈkɒlədʒʌɪz, -ɨz, -ɪŋ, -d
AM saɪˈkɑləˌdʒaɪz, -ɨz, -ɪŋ, -d

psychology
BR sʌɪˈkɒlədʒi
AM saɪˈkɑlədʒi

psychometric
BR ˌsʌɪkəˈmɛtrɪk, -s
AM ˌsaɪkəˈmɛtrɪk, -s

psychometrically
BR ˌsʌɪkəˈmɛtrɨkli
AM ˌsaɪkəˈmɛtrək(ə)li

psychometrist
BR sʌɪˈkɒmɨtrɪst, -s
AM saɪˈkɑmətrəst, -s

psychometry
BR sʌɪˈkɒmɨtri
AM saɪˈkɑmətri

psychomotor
BR ˌsʌɪkəʊˈməʊtə(r)
AM ˌsaɪkoʊˈmoʊdər

psychoneuroses
BR ˌsʌɪkəʊnjʉˈrəʊsiːz, ˌsʌɪkəʊnjʊəˈrəʊsiːz
AM ¦saɪkoʊˌn(j)uˈroʊˌsiz, ¦saɪkoʊˌn(j)əˈroʊsiz

psychoneurosis
BR ˌsʌɪkəʊnjʉˈrəʊsɪs, ˌsʌɪkəʊnjʊəˈrəʊsɪs
AM ¦saɪkoʊˌn(j)uˈroʊsəs, ¦saɪkoʊˌn(j)əˈroʊsəs

psychoneurotic
BR ˌsʌɪkəʊnjʉˈrɒtɪk, ˌsʌɪkəʊnjʊəˈrɒtɪk
AM ¦saɪkoʊˌn(j)uˈrɑdɪk, ¦saɪkoʊˌn(j)əˈrɑdɪk

psychopath
BR ˈsʌɪkəpaθ, -s
AM ˈsaɪkəˌpæθ, -s

psychopathic
BR ˌsʌɪkəˈpaθɪk
AM ˌsaɪkəˈpæθɪk

psychopathically
BR ˌsʌɪkəˈpaθɨkli
AM ˌsaɪkəˈpæθək(ə)li

psychopathological
BR ˌsʌɪkə(ʊ)ˌpaθəˈlɒdʒɨkl
AM ¦saɪkəpæθəˈlɑdʒəkəl

psychopathology
BR ˌsʌɪkəʊpəˈθɒlədʒi
AM ˌsaɪkoʊpəˈθɑlədʒi

psychopathy
BR sʌɪˈkɒpəθi
AM saɪˈkɑpəθi

psychopharmacology
BR ˌsʌɪkəʊˌfɑːməˈkɒlədʒi
AM ˌsaɪkoʊˌfɑrməˈkɑlədʒi

psychophysical
BR ˌsʌɪkəʊˈfɪzɨkl
AM ˌsaɪkəˈfɪzɨkəl

psychophysics
BR ˌsʌɪkəʊˈfɪzɪks
AM ˌsaɪkəˈfɪzɪks

psychophysiological
BR ˌsʌɪkəʊˌfɪzɪəˈlɒdʒɨkl
AM ¦saɪkəˌfɪziəˈlɑdʒəkəl

psychophysiology
BR ˌsʌɪkəʊˌfɪzɪˈɒlədʒi
AM ˌsaɪkoʊˌfɪziˈɑlədʒi

psychoses
BR sʌɪˈkəʊsiːz
AM saɪˈkoʊˌsiz

psychosexual
BR ˌsʌɪkəʊˈsɛkʃʊəl, ˌsʌɪkəʊˈsɛkʃ(ʉ)l, ˌsʌɪkəʊˈsɛksjʊ(ə)l
AM ˌsaɪkoʊˈsɛkʃ(əw)əl

psychosexually
BR ˌsʌɪkəʊˈsɛkʃʊəli, ˌsʌɪkəʊˈsɛkʃʉli, ˌsʌɪkəʊˈsɛkʃl̩i, ˌsʌɪkəʊˈsɛksjʊ(ə)li
AM ˌsaɪkoʊˈsɛkʃ(əw)əli

psychosis
BR sʌɪˈkəʊsɪs
AM saɪˈkoʊsəs

psychosocial
BR ˌsʌɪkəʊˈsəʊʃl
AM ˌsaɪkoʊˈsoʊʃəl

psychosocially
BR ˌsʌɪkəʊˈsəʊʃl̩i, ˌsʌɪkəʊˈsəʊʃəli
AM ˌsaɪkəˈsoʊʃəli

psychosomatic
BR ˌsʌɪkə(ʊ)səˈmatɪk
AM ¦saɪkoʊsəˈmædɪk

psychosomatically
BR ˌsʌɪkə(ʊ)səˈmatɨkli
AM ¦saɪkoʊsəˈmædək(ə)li

psychosurgery
BR ˌsʌɪkəʊˈsəːdʒ(ə)ri
AM ˌsaɪkoʊˈsərdʒəri

psychosurgical
BR ˌsʌɪkəʊˈsəːdʒɨkl
AM ¦saɪkəˈsərdʒəkəl

psychotherapeutic
BR ˌsʌɪkəʊˌθɛrəˈpjuːtɪk
AM ¦saɪkəˌθɛrəˈpjudɪk

psychotherapist
BR ˌsʌɪkə(ʊ)ˈθɛrəpɪst, -s
AM ¦saɪkoʊˈθɛrəpəst, -s

psychotherapy
BR ˌsʌɪkə(ʊ)ˈθɛrəpi
AM ¦saɪkoʊˈθɛrəpi

psychotic
BR sʌɪˈkɒtɪk, -s
AM saɪˈkɑdɪk, -s

psychotically
BR sʌɪˈkɒtɨkli
AM saɪˈkɑdək(ə)li

psychotropic
BR ˌsʌɪkə(ʊ)ˈtrɒpɪk, ˌsʌɪkə(ʊ)ˈtrəʊpɪk
AM ˌsaɪkəˈtrɑpɪk

psychrometer
BR sʌɪˈkrɒmɨtə(r), -z
AM saɪˈkrɑmədər, -z

psylla
BR ˈsɪlə(r)
AM ˈsɪlə

psyllid
BR ˈsɪlɪd
AM ˈsɪlɨd

psyllium
BR ˈsɪlɪəm
AM ˈsɪliəm

ptarmigan
BR ˈtɑːmɨɡ(ə)n, -z
AM ˈtɑrməɡən, -z

pteranodon
BR təˈranədɒn, təˈranədən, -z
AM təˈrænəˌdɑn, -z

pteridological
BR ˌtɛrɨdəˈlɒdʒɨkl
AM ¦tɛrədəˈlɑdʒəkəl

pteridologist
BR ˌtɛrɨˈdɒlədʒɪst, -s
AM ˌtɛrəˈdɑlədʒəst, -s

pteridology
BR ˌtɛrɨˈdɒlədʒi
AM ˌtɛrəˈdɑlədʒi

pteridophyte
BR tɪˈrɪdəfʌɪt, -s
AM təˈrɪdəˌfaɪt, ˈtɛrədəˌfaɪt, -s

pterodactyl
BR ˌtɛrəˈdakt(ɨ)l, -z
AM ¦tɛrəˈdæktəl, -z

pteropod
BR ˈtɛrəpɒd, -z
AM ˈtɛrəˌpɑd, -z

pterosaur
BR ˈtɛrəsɔː(r), -z
AM ˈtɛrəˌsɔ(ə)r, -z

pteroylglutamic acid
BR ˌtɛrəʊɪlɡluːˌtamɪk ˈasɪd
AM ¦tɛrəwəlˌɡluˈtæmɪk ˈæsəd

pterygoid process
BR ˈtɛrɨɡɔɪd ˌprəʊsɛs, -ɨz
AM ˈtɛrəˌɡɔɪd ˌprɑˌsɛs, + ˌproʊˌsɛs, -əz

ptisan
BR tɪˈzan, -z
AM təˈzæn, ˈtɪzn, -z

Ptolemaic
BR ˌtɒləˈmeɪɪk
AM ¦tɑləˈmeɪɪk

Ptolemy
BR ˈtɒləmi
AM ˈtɑləmi

ptomain
BR ˈtəʊmeɪn, tə(ʊ)ˈmeɪn
AM ¦toʊ¦meɪn

ptomaine
BR 'təʊmeɪn, tə(ʊ)'meɪn
AM ˌtoʊˌmeɪn
ptosed
BR təʊzd
AM toʊzd
ptosis
BR 'təʊsɪs
AM 'toʊsəs
ptotic
BR 'təʊtɪk
AM 'toʊdɪk
ptyalin
BR 'tʌɪəlɪn
AM 'taɪələn
pub
BR pʌb, -z
AM pəb, -z
pubcrawl
BR 'pʌbkrɔːl, -z, -ɪŋ, -d
AM 'pəbˌkrɔl, 'pəbˌkrɑl, -z, -ɪŋ, -d
pubertal
BR 'pjuːbətl
AM 'pjubərdəl
puberty
BR 'pjuːbəti
AM 'pjubərdi
pubes
BR 'pjuːbiːz
AM 'pjubiz
pubescence
BR pjʊ'bɛsns
AM pju'bɛsəns
pubescent
BR pjʊ'bɛsnt
AM pju'bɛsənt
pubic
BR 'pjuːbɪk
AM 'pjubɪk
pubis
BR 'pjuːbɪs
AM 'pjubəs
public
BR 'pʌblɪk
AM 'pəblɪk
publically
BR 'pʌblɨkli
AM 'pəblək(ə)li
publican
BR 'pʌblɪk(ə)n, -z
AM 'pəbləkən, -z
publication
BR ˌpʌblɪ'keɪʃn, -z
AM ˌpəblə'keɪʃən, -z
publicise
BR 'pʌblɪsʌɪz, -ɪz, -ɪŋ, -d
AM 'pəbləˌsaɪz, -ɪz, -ɪŋ, -d
publicism
BR 'pʌblɪsɪz(ə)m
AM 'pəbləˌsɪzəm
publicist
BR 'pʌblɪsɪst, -s
AM 'pəbləsəst, -s
publicistic
BR ˌpʌblɪ'sɪstɪk
AM ˌpəblə'sɪstɪk
publicity
BR pʌb'lɪsɪti
AM pə'blɪsɨdi
publicize
BR 'pʌblɪsʌɪz, -ɪz, -ɪŋ, -d
AM 'pəbləˌsaɪz, -ɪz, -ɪŋ, -d
publicly
BR 'pʌblɨkli
AM 'pəblɨk(ə)li
publish
BR 'pʌbl|ɪʃ, -ɨʃɨz, -ɨʃɪŋ, -ɪʃt
AM 'pəblɪʃ, -ɪz, -ɪŋ, -t
publishable
BR 'pʌblɨʃəbl
AM 'pəblɨʃəbəl
publisher
BR 'pʌblɨʃə(r), -z
AM 'pəblɨʃər, -z
Publius
BR 'pʌbliəs
AM 'pəbliəs, 'pʊbliəs
Puccini
BR pʊ'tʃiːni
AM pʊ'tʃini
puccoon
BR pə'kuːn, pʌ'kuːn, -z
AM pə'kun, -z
puce
BR pjuːs
AM pjus
puck
BR pʌk, -s
AM pək, -s
pucka
BR 'pʌkə(*r*)
AM 'pəkə
pucker
BR 'pʌk|ə(r), -əz, -(ə)rɪŋ, -əd
AM 'pəkər, -z, -ɪŋ, -d
puckery
BR 'pʌk(ə)ri
AM 'pəkəri
Puckett
BR 'pʌkɪt
AM 'pəkət
puckish
BR 'pʌkɪʃ
AM 'pəkɪʃ
puckishly
BR 'pʌkɨʃli
AM 'pəkɨʃli
puckishness
BR 'pʌkɨʃnɨs
AM 'pəkɪʃnɨs
pucklike
BR 'pʌklʌɪk
AM 'pəkˌlaɪk
pud
BR pʊd, -z
AM pəd, pʊd, -z
pudding
BR 'pʊdɪŋ, -z
AM 'pʊdɪŋ, -z
puddingy
BR 'pʊdɪŋi
AM 'pʊdɪŋ(g)i
puddle
BR 'pʌd|l, -lz, -l̩ɪŋ\-lɪŋ, -ld
AM 'pəd|əl, -əlz, -(ə)lɪŋ, -əld
puddler
BR 'pʌdl̩ə(r), 'pʌdlə(r), -z
AM 'pəd(ə)lər, -z
puddly
BR 'pʌdl̩i, 'pʌdli
AM 'pədli
puddock
BR 'pʌdək, -s
AM 'pədək, -s
pudency
BR 'pjuːdnsi
AM 'pjudnsi
pudenda
BR pjʊ'dɛndə(*r*)
AM pju'dɛndə
pudendal
BR pjʊ'dɛndl
AM pju'dɛndəl
pudendum
BR pjʊ'dɛndəm
AM pju'dɛndəm
pudeur
BR pjuː'dəː(r)
AM pju'dər
pudge
BR pʌdʒ, -ɪz
AM pədʒ, -əz
pudgily
BR 'pʌdʒɨli
AM 'pədʒəli
pudginess
BR 'pʌdʒɪnɪs
AM 'pədʒinɨs
pudgy
BR 'pʌdʒ|i, -ɪə(r), -ɪɪst
AM 'pədʒi, -ər, -ɨst
pudic
BR 'pjuːdɪk
AM 'pjudɪk
Pudsey
BR 'pʌdzi, 'pʌdsi
AM 'pədzi, 'pədsi
pudu
BR 'puːduː, -z
AM 'pudu, -z
Puebla
BR 'pwɛblə(*r*), 'pweɪblə(*r*)
AM 'pwɛblə
pueblo
BR 'pwɛbləʊ, 'pweɪbləʊ, -z
AM 'pwɛbloʊ, -z
puerile
BR 'pjʊərʌɪl, 'pjɔːrʌɪl
AM 'pjurəl, 'pjuˌraɪl
puerilely
BR 'pjʊərʌɪl(l)i, 'pjɔːrʌɪl(l)i
AM 'pjurəli, 'pjuˌraɪli
puerility
BR pjʊə'rɪlɪt|i, pjɔː'rɪlɪti, -ɪz
AM ˌpju'rɪlɨdi, -z
puerperal
BR pjuː'əːp(ə)rəl, pjuː'əːp(ə)rl̩
AM pju'ərp(ə)rəl
Puerto Rican
BR ˌpwəːtə(ʊ) 'riːk(ə)n, ˌpwɛːtə(ʊ) +, ˌpɔːtə(ʊ) +, -z
AM ˌpɔrdə 'rɪkən, ˌpwɛrdə +, -z
Puerto Rico
BR ˌpwɛːtə(ʊ) 'riːkəʊ, ˌpwɛːtə(ʊ) +, ˌpɔːtə(ʊ) +
AM ˌpɔrdə 'rɪkoʊ, ˌpwɛrdə +
puff
BR pʌf, -s, -ɪŋ, -t
AM pəf, -s, -ɪŋ, -t
puffball
BR 'pʌfbɔːl, -z
AM 'pəfˌbɔl, 'pəfˌbɑl, -z
puffer
BR 'pʌfə(r), -z
AM 'pəfər, -z
puffery
BR 'pʌf(ə)ri
AM 'pəfəri
puffily
BR 'pʌfɨli
AM 'pəfəli
puffin
BR 'pʌfɪn, -z
AM 'pəfən, -z
puffiness
BR 'pʌfɪnɪs
AM 'pəfinɨs
puff-puff
BR 'pʌfpʌf, -s
AM 'pəfˌpəf, -s
puffy
BR 'pʌf|i, -ɪə(r), -ɪɪst
AM 'pəfi, -ər, -ɨst
pug
BR pʌg, -z
AM pəg, -z
pugaree
BR 'pʌg(ə)r|i, -ɪz
AM 'pəg(ə)ri, -z
Puget Sound
BR ˌpjuːdʒɪt 'saʊnd
AM ˌpjudʒət 'saʊnd
puggaree
BR 'pʌg(ə)r|i, -ɪz
AM 'pəg(ə)ri, -z
puggish
BR 'pʌgɪʃ
AM 'pəgɪʃ

puggy
BR ˈpʌgi
AM ˈpəgi
Pugh
BR pjuː
AM pju
Pughe
BR pjuː
AM pju
pugilism
BR ˈpjuːdʒᵻlɪz(ə)m
AM ˈpjudʒəˌlɪzəm
pugilist
BR ˈpjuːdʒᵻlɪst, -s
AM ˈpjudʒələst, -s
pugilistic
BR ˌpjuːdʒᵻˈlɪstɪk
AM ˌpjudʒəˈlɪstɪk
Pugin
BR ˈpjuːdʒɪn
AM ˈpjudʒən
pugnacious
BR pʌgˈneɪʃəs
AM pəgˈneɪʃəs
pugnaciously
BR pʌgˈneɪʃəsli
AM pəgˈneɪʃəsli
pugnaciousness
BR pʌgˈneɪʃəsnəs
AM pəgˈneɪʃəsnəs
pugnacity
BR pʌgˈnasᵻti
AM ˌpəgˈnæsədi
Pugwash
BR ˈpʌgwɒʃ
AM ˈpəgˌwɔʃ, ˈpəgˌwɑʃ
puisne
BR ˈpjuːni
AM ˈpjuni
puissance[1]
general use
BR ˈpjuːɪsns, ˈpwɪsns
AM ˈpwɪsəns, ˈpjuəsəns, pjuˈɪsəns
puissance[2]
show-jumping
BR ˈpwiːsns, ˈpwiːsɒ̃s
AM ˈpwɪsəns, ˌpwiˈsɑns
puissant
BR ˈpjuːɪsnt, ˈpwɪsnt
AM ˈpwɪsnt, ˈpjuəsnt, pjuˈɪsnt
puissantly
BR ˈpjuːɪsntli, ˈpwɪsntli
AM ˈpwɪsn(t)li, ˈpjuəsn(t)li, pjuˈɪsn(t)li
puja
BR ˈpuːdʒə(r), -z
AM ˈpudʒə, -z
puke
BR pjuːk, -s, -ɪŋ, -t
AM pjuk, -s, -ɪŋ, -t
pukeko
BR ˈpuːkɛkəʊ, -z
AM puˈkeɪˌkoʊ, -z
pukey
BR ˈpjuːki
AM ˈpjuki
pukka
BR ˈpʌkə(r)
AM ˈpəkə
pukkah
BR ˈpʌkə(r)
AM ˈpəkə
puku
BR ˈpuːkuː, -z
AM ˈpuˌku, -z
pul
BR puːl, -z
AM pul, -z
pula
BR ˈpʊlə(r), -z
AM ˈpʊlə, -z
pulao
BR pəˈlaʊ, -z
AM pəˈlaʊ, -z
Pulaski
BR pəˈlaski
AM pəˈlæski
Pulborough
BR ˈpʊlb(ə)rə(r)
AM ˈpʊlbərə
pulchritude
BR ˈpʌlkrᵻtjuːd, ˈpʌlkrᵻtʃuːd
AM ˈpəlkrəˌt(j)ud
pulchritudinous
BR ˌpʌlkrᵻˈtjuːdᵻnəs, ˌpʌlkrᵻˈtʃuːdᵻnəs
AM ˌpəlkrəˈt(j)udn̩əs
pule
BR pjuːl, -z, -ɪŋ, -d
AM pjul, -z, -ɪŋ, -d
puli
BR ˈpuːli
AM ˈpuli
Pulitzer
BR ˈpʊlᵻtsə(r), ˈpjuːlɪtsə(r)
AM ˈpʊlətsər, ˈpjulətsər
pull
BR pʊl, -z, -ɪŋ, -d
AM pʊl, -z, -ɪŋ, -d
pullback
BR ˈpʊlbak, -s
AM ˈpʊlˌbæk, -s
pulldown
BR ˈpʊldaʊn
AM ˈpʊlˌdaʊn
Pullen
BR ˈpʊlɪn
AM ˈpʊlən
puller
BR ˈpʊlə(r), -z
AM ˈpʊlər, -z
pullet
BR ˈpʊlɪt, -s
AM ˈpʊlət, -s
pulley
BR ˈpʊl|i, -ɪz
AM ˈpʊli, -z
Pullman
BR ˈpʊlmən, -z
AM ˈpʊlmən, -z
pullout
BR ˈpʊlaʊt, -s
AM ˈpʊlˌaʊt, -s
pullover
BR ˈpʊlˌəʊvə(r), -z
AM ˈpʊlˌoʊvər, -z
pullthrough
BR ˈpʊlθruː, -z
AM ˈpʊlˌθru, -z
pullulant
BR ˈpʌljʉlənt, ˈpʌljʉln̩t
AM ˈpəljələnt
pullulate
BR ˈpʌljʉleɪt, -s, -ɪŋ, -ᵻd
AM ˈpəljəˌleɪ|t, -ts, -dɪŋ, -dᵻd
pullulation
BR ˌpʌljʉˈleɪʃn, -z
AM ˌpəljəˈleɪʃən, -z
pull-up
BR ˈpʊlʌp, -s
AM ˈpʊləp, -s
Pulman
BR ˈpʊlmən
AM ˈpʊlmən
pulmonaria
BR ˌpʌlməˈnɛːrɪə(r)
AM ˌpəlməˈnɛriə
pulmonary
BR ˈpʌlmən(ə)ri, ˈpʊlmən(ə)ri
AM ˈpəlməˌnɛri
pulmonate
BR ˈpʌlmənət, ˈpʊlmənət
AM ˈpəlməˌneɪt, ˈpəlmənət
pulmonic
BR pʌlˈmɒnɪk, pʊlˈmɒnɪk
AM pəlˈmɑnɪk
pulmonically
BR pʌlˈmɒnᵻkli, pʊlˈmɒnᵻkli
AM pəlˈmɑnək(ə)li
pulp
BR pʌlp, -s, -ɪŋ, -t
AM pəlp, -s, -ɪŋ, -t
pulper
BR ˈpʌlpə(r), -z
AM ˈpəlpər, -z
pulpiness
BR ˈpʌlpɪnᵻs
AM ˈpəlpinᵻs
pulpit
BR ˈpʊlpɪt, -s
AM ˈpəlpət, ˈpʊlpət, -s
pulpiteer
BR ˌpʊlpᵻˈtɪə(r), -z, -ɪŋ, -d
AM ˌpʊlpəˈtɪ(ə)r, ˌpəlpəˈtɪ(ə)r, -z, -ɪŋ, -d
pulpless
BR ˈpʌlpləs
AM ˈpəlpləs
pulpous
BR ˈpʌlpəs
AM ˈpəlpəs
pulpwood
BR ˈpʌlpwʊd
AM ˈpəlpˌwʊd
pulpy
BR ˈpʌlp|i, -ɪə(r), -ɪɪst
AM ˈpəlpi, -ər, -ɪst
pulque
BR ˈpʊlki, ˈpʊlkeɪ
AM ˈpʊlkeɪ, ˈpʊlki
pulsar
BR ˈpʌlsɑː(r), -z
AM ˈpəlˌsɑr, -z
pulsate
BR pʌlˈseɪt, -s, -ɪŋ, -ᵻd
AM ˈpəlˌseɪ|t, -ts, -dɪŋ, -dᵻd
pulsatile
BR ˈpʌlsətʌɪl
AM ˈpəlsədl, ˈpəlsəˌtaɪl
pulsatilla
BR ˌpʌlsəˈtɪlə(r), -z
AM ˌpəlsəˈtɪlə, -z
pulsation
BR pʌlˈseɪʃn, -z
AM ˌpəlˈseɪʃən, -z
pulsative
BR ˈpʌlsətɪv
AM ˈpəlsədɪv
pulsator
BR pʌlˈseɪtə(r), -z
AM ˈpəlˌseɪdər, -z
pulsatory
BR pʌlˈseɪt(ə)ri
AM ˈpəlsəˌtɔri
pulse
BR pʌls, -ɪz
AM pəls, -əz
pulseless
BR ˈpʌlsləs
AM ˈpəlsləs
pulsimeter
BR pʌlˈsɪmᵻtə(r), -z
AM ˌpəlˈsɪmədər, -z
Pulsometer
BR pʌlˈsɒmᵻtə(r), -z
AM ˌpəlˈsɑmədər, -z
pultrude
BR pʊlˈtruːd, pʌlˈtruːd, -z, -ɪŋ, -ᵻd
AM pəlˈtrud, -z, -ɪŋ, -ᵻd
pulverisable
BR ˈpʌlvərʌɪzəbl
AM ˈpəlvəˌraɪzəbəl
pulverisation
BR ˌpʌlv(ə)rʌɪˈzeɪʃn
AM ˌpəlvərəˈzeɪʃən, ˌpəlvəˌraɪˈzeɪʃən
pulverisator
BR ˈpʌlv(ə)rʌɪzeɪtə(r), -z
AM ˈpəlvərəˌzeɪdər, ˈpəlvəˌraɪˌzeɪdər, -z

pulverise
BR ˈpʌlvərʌɪz, -ɨz, -ɪŋ, -d
AM ˈpəlvəˌraɪz, -ɨz, -ɪŋ, -d

pulveriser
BR ˈpʌlvərʌɪzə(r), -z
AM ˈpəlvəˌraɪzər, -z

pulverizable
BR ˈpʌlvərʌɪzəbl
AM ˈpəlvəˌraɪzəbəl

pulverization
BR ˌpʌlv(ə)rʌɪˈzeɪʃn
AM ˌpəlvərəˈzeɪʃən, ˌpəlvəˌraɪˈzeɪʃən

pulverizator
BR ˈpʌlv(ə)rʌɪzeɪtə(r), -z
AM ˈpəlvərəˌzeɪdər, ˈpəlvəˌraɪˌzeɪdər, -z

pulverize
BR ˈpʌlvərʌɪz, -ɨz, -ɪŋ, -d
AM ˈpəlvəˌraɪz, -ɨz, -ɪŋ, -d

pulverizer
BR ˈpʌlvərʌɪzə(r), -z
AM ˈpəlvəˌraɪzər, -z

pulverulent
BR pʌlˈvɛr(j)ʉlənt, pʌlˈvɛr(j)ʉln̩t
AM pəlˈvɛrjələnt

pulvinate
BR ˈpʌlvɨneɪt, -s, -ɪŋ, -ɨd
AM ˈpəlvəˌneɪ|t, -ts, -dɪŋ, -dɨd

puma
BR ˈpjuːmə(*r*), -z
AM ˈpjumə, -z

pumice
BR ˈpʌmɪs
AM ˈpəməs

pumiceous
BR pjuːˈmɪʃəs
AM pjuˈmɪʃəs

pummel
BR ˈpʌm|l, -lz, -l̩ɪŋ\-əlɪŋ, -ld
AM ˈpəm|əl, -əlz, -(ə)lɪŋ, -əld

pump
BR pʌm|p, -ps, -pɪŋ, -(p)t
AM pəmp, -s, -ɪŋ, -t

pumpernickel
BR ˈpʌmpəˌnɪkl, ˈpʊmpəˌnɪkl
AM ˈpəmpərˌnɪkəl

Pumphrey
BR ˈpʌmfri
AM ˈpəmfri

pumpkin
BR ˈpʌm(p)kɪn, -z
AM ˈpəm(p)kən, -z

pumpkinseed
BR ˈpʌm(p)kɪnsiːd, -z
AM ˈpəm(p)kənˌsid, -z

pun
BR pʌn, -z, -ɪŋ, -d
AM pən, -z, -ɪŋ, -d

puna
BR ˈpuːnə(*r*), -z
AM ˈpunə, -z

punch
BR pʌn(t)ʃ, -ɨz, -ɪŋ, -t
AM pən(t)ʃ, -əz, -ɪŋ, -t

Punch and Judy
BR ˌpʌn(t)ʃ (ə)n(d) ˈdʒuːdi
AM ˈpən(t)ʃ ən ˈdʒudi

punchbag
BR ˈpʌn(t)ʃbag, -z
AM ˈpən(t)ʃˌbæg, -z

punchball
BR ˈpʌn(t)ʃbɔːl, -z
AM ˈpəntʃˌbɔl, ˈpəntʃˌbɑl, -z

punchbowl
BR ˈpʌn(t)ʃbəʊl, -z
AM ˈpən(t)ʃˌboʊl, -z

punchcard
BR ˈpʌn(t)ʃkɑːd, -z
AM ˈpən(t)ʃˌkɑrd, -z

punchdrunk
BR ˈpʌn(t)ʃdrʌŋk, ˌpʌn(t)ʃˈdrʌŋk
AM ˈpən(t)ʃˌdrəŋk

puncheon
BR ˈpʌn(t)ʃ(ə)n, -z
AM pən(t)ʃən, -z

puncher
BR ˈpʌn(t)ʃə(r), -z
AM ˈpən(t)ʃər, -z

punchily
BR ˈpʌn(t)ʃɨli
AM ˈpən(t)ʃəli

Punchinello
BR ˌpʌn(t)ʃɪˈnɛləʊ, -z
AM ˌpən(t)ʃəˈnɛloʊ, -z

punchiness
BR ˈpʌn(t)ʃɪnɪs
AM ˈpən(t)ʃinɪs

punchline
BR ˈpʌn(t)ʃlʌɪn, -z
AM ˈpən(t)ʃˌlaɪn, -z

punchup
BR ˈpʌn(t)ʃʌp, -s
AM ˈpən(t)ʃˌəp, -s

punchy
BR ˈpʌn(t)ʃ|i, -ɪə(r), -ɪɪst
AM ˈpən(t)ʃi, -ər, -ɨst

puncta
BR ˈpʌŋ(k)tə(*r*)
AM ˈpəŋ(k)tə

punctate
BR ˈpʌŋ(k)teɪt
AM ˈpəŋ(k)ˌteɪt

punctation
BR ˌpʌŋ(k)ˈteɪʃn
AM ˌpəŋ(k)ˈteɪʃən

punctilio
BR ˌpʌŋ(k)ˈtɪlɪəʊ
AM ˌpəŋ(k)ˈtɪlioʊ

punctilious
BR ˌpʌŋ(k)ˈtɪlɪəs
AM ˌpəŋ(k)ˈtɪliəs

punctiliously
BR ˌpʌŋ(k)ˈtɪlɪəsli
AM ˌpəŋ(k)ˈtɪliəsli

punctiliousness
BR ˌpʌŋ(k)ˈtɪlɪəsnəs
AM ˌpəŋ(k)ˈtɪliəsnəs

punctual
BR ˈpʌŋ(k)tʃʊəl, ˈpʌŋ(k)tʃ(ʉ)l, ˈpʌŋ(k)tjʊəl, ˈpʌŋ(k)tjʉl
AM ˈpəŋ(k)(t)ʃ(əw)əl

punctuality
BR ˌpʌŋ(k)tʃʊˈalɨti, ˌpʌŋ(k)tjʊˈalɨti
AM ˌpəŋ(k)(t)ʃəˈwælədi

punctually
BR ˈpʌŋ(k)tʃʊəli, ˈpʌŋ(k)tʃʉli, ˈpʌŋ(k)tʃl̩i, ˈpʌŋ(k)tjʊəli, ˈpʌŋ(k)tjʉli
AM ˈpəŋ(k)(t)ʃ(əw)əli

punctuate
BR ˈpʌŋ(k)tʃʊeɪt, ˈpʌŋ(k)tjʊeɪt, -s, -ɪŋ, -ɨd
AM ˈpəŋ(k)(t)ʃəˌweɪ|t, -ts, -dɪŋ, -dɨd

punctuation
BR ˌpʌŋ(k)tʃʊˈeɪʃn, ˌpʌŋ(k)tjʊˈeɪʃn
AM ˌpəŋ(k)(t)ʃəˈweɪʃən

punctum
BR ˈpʌŋ(k)təm
AM ˈpəŋ(k)təm

puncture
BR ˈpʌŋ(k)tʃ|ə(r), -əz, -(ə)rɪŋ, -əd
AM ˈpəŋ(k)(t)ʃər, -z, -ɪŋ, -d

pundit
BR ˈpʌndɪt, -s
AM ˈpəndət, -s

punditry
BR ˈpʌndɨtri
AM ˈpəndətri

pungency
BR ˈpʌn(d)ʒ(ə)nsi
AM ˈpəndʒənsi

pungent
BR ˈpʌn(d)ʒ(ə)nt
AM ˈpəndʒənt

pungently
BR ˈpʌn(d)ʒ(ə)ntli
AM ˈpəndʒən(t)li

Punic
BR ˈpjuːnɪk
AM ˈpjunɪk

punily
BR ˈpjuːnɨli
AM ˈpjunəli

puniness
BR ˈpjuːnɪnɪs
AM ˈpjuninɪs

punish
BR ˈpʌn|ɪʃ, -ɨʃɪz, -ɨʃɪŋ, -ɪʃt
AM ˈpənɪʃ, -ɨz, -ɪŋ, -t

punishable
BR ˈpʌnɨʃəbl
AM ˈpənɪʃəbəl

punisher
BR ˈpʌnɨʃə(r), -z
AM ˈpənɪʃər, -z

punishingly
BR ˈpʌnɨʃɪŋli
AM ˈpənɪʃɪŋli

punishment
BR ˈpʌnɨʃm(ə)nt, -s
AM ˈpənɪʃmənt, -s

punitive
BR ˈpjuːnɨtɪv
AM ˈpjunədɪv

punitively
BR ˈpjuːnɨtɨvli
AM ˈpjunədɨvli

punitiveness
BR ˈpjuːnɨtɨvnɨs
AM ˈpjunədɨvnɨs

punitory
BR ˈpjuːnɨt(ə)ri
AM ˈpjunəˌtɔri

Punjab
BR pʌnˈdʒɑːb, ˈpʌndʒɑːb, pʊnˈdʒɑːb, ˈpʊndʒɑːb
AM ˈpənˌdʒɑb

Punjabi
BR pʌnˈdʒɑːbi, pʊnˈdʒɑːbi
AM pənˈdʒɑbi

punk
BR pʌŋk, -s
AM pəŋk, -s

punka
BR ˈpʌŋkə(*r*), -z
AM ˈpəŋkə, -z

punkah
BR ˈpʌŋkə(*r*), -z
AM ˈpəŋkə, -z

punkah-wallah
BR ˈpʌŋkəˌwɒlə(*r*), -z
AM ˈpəŋkəˈwɔlə, ˈpəŋkəˈwɑlə, -z

punkish
BR ˈpʌŋkɪʃ
AM ˈpəŋkɪʃ

punky
BR ˈpʌŋk|i, -ɪə(r), -ɪɪst
AM ˈpəŋki, -ər, -ɨst

punner
BR ˈpʌnə(r), -z
AM ˈpənər, -z

punnet
BR ˈpʌnɪt, -s
AM ˈpənət, -s

punningly
BR ˈpʌnɪŋli
AM ˈpənɪŋli

punster
BR ˈpʌnstə(r), -z

AM 'pənstər, -z

punt¹
gambling, kicking, boating
BR pʌnt, -s, -ɪŋ, -ɨd
AM pən|t, -ts, -(t)ɪŋ, -(t)əd

punt²
Irish pound
BR pʊnt, -s
AM pʊnt, -s

Punta Arenas
BR ˌpʊntə(r) ə'reɪnəs
AM ˌpʊn(tə) ə'reɪnəs

punter
BR 'pʌntə(r), -z
AM 'pən(t)ər, -z

puny
BR 'pju:n|i, -ɪə(r), -ɪɪst
AM 'pjuni, -ər, -ɨst

pup
BR pʌp, -s
AM pəp, -s

pupa
BR 'pju:pə(r), -z
AM 'pjupə, -z

pupae
BR 'pju:pi:
AM 'pjupi, 'pjuˌpaɪ, 'pjupeɪ

pupal
BR 'pju:pl
AM 'pjupəl

pupate
BR pju:'peɪt, -s, -ɪŋ, -ɨd
AM 'pjuˌpeɪ|t, -ts, -dɪŋ, -dɨd

pupation
BR pju:'peɪʃn
AM ˌpju'peɪʃən

pupil
BR 'pju:pl, -z
AM 'pjupəl, -z

pupilage
BR 'pju:pɨl|ɪdʒ, 'pju:pḷ|ɪdʒ, -ɨdʒɨz
AM 'pjupəlɪdʒ, -ɨz

pupilar
BR 'pju:pɨlə(r), 'pju:pḷə(r)
AM 'pjupələr

pupilarity
BR ˌpju:pɨ'larɨti
AM ˌpjupə'lɛrədi

pupilary
BR 'pju:pɨl(ə)ri, 'pju:pḷ(ə)ri
AM 'pjupəˌlɛri

pupillage
BR 'pju:pɨlɪdʒ, 'pju:pḷɪdʒ
AM 'pjupəlɪdʒ

pupillar
BR 'pju:pɨlə(r), 'pju:pḷə(r)
AM 'pjupələr

pupillarity
BR ˌpju:pɨ'larɨti
AM ˌpjupə'lɛrədi

pupillary
BR 'pju:pɨl(ə)ri, 'pju:pḷ(ə)ri
AM 'pjupəˌlɛri

pupiparous
BR pju:'pɪp(ə)rəs
AM pju'pɪpərəs

puppet
BR 'pʌpɪt, -s
AM 'pəpət, -s

puppeteer
BR ˌpʌpɨ'tɪə(r), -z
AM ˌpəpə'tɪ(ə)r, -z

puppeteering
BR 'pʌpɨtɪərɪŋ
AM 'pəpəˌtɪrɪŋ

puppetry
BR 'pʌpɨtri
AM 'pəpətri

puppy
BR 'pʌp|i, -ɪz
AM 'pəpi, -z

puppyhood
BR 'pʌpɪhʊd
AM 'pəpiˌhʊd

puppyish
BR 'pʌpi:ɪʃ
AM 'pəpiɪʃ

Purana
BR pʊ'rɑ:nə(r), -z
AM pʊ'rɑnə, -z

Puranic
BR pʊ'ranɪk
AM pʊ'rɑnɪk

Purbeck
BR 'pə:bɛk
AM 'pərˌbɛk

purblind
BR 'pə:blʌɪnd
AM 'pərˌblaɪnd

purblindness
BR 'pə:blʌɪn(d)nɨs
AM 'pərˌblaɪn(d)nɨs

Purcell
BR 'pə:sl, pə:'sɛl
AM pər'sɛl

purchasable
BR 'pə:tʃɨsəbl
AM 'pərtʃəsəbəl

purchase
BR 'pə:tʃɪs, -ɨz, -ɪŋ, -t
AM 'pərtʃəs, -əz, -ɪŋ, -t

purchaseable
BR 'pə:tʃɪsəbl
AM 'pərtʃəsəbəl

purchaser
BR 'pə:tʃɪsə(r), -z
AM 'pərtʃəsər, -z

purda
BR 'pə:dɑ:(r), 'pə:də(r)
AM 'pərdə

purdah
BR 'pə:dɑ:(r), 'pə:də(r)
AM 'pərdə

Purdie
BR 'pə:di
AM 'pərdi

Purdon
BR 'pə:dn
AM 'pərdən

Purdue
BR 'pə:dju:
AM pər'd(j)u

Purdy
BR 'pə:di
AM 'pərdi

pure
BR pjʊə(r), pjɔ:(r), -ə(r), -ɨst
AM pjʊ(ə)r, -ər, -əst

pureblood
BR 'pjʊəblʌd, 'pjɔ:blʌd
AM 'pjʊrˌbləd

pureblooded
BR ˌpjʊə'blʌdɨd, ˌpjɔ:'blʌdɨd
AM ˌpjʊrˌblədəd

purebred¹
adjective
BR ˌpjʊə'brɛd, ˌpjɔ:'brɛd
AM ˌpjʊrˌbrɛd

purebred²
noun
BR 'pjʊəbrɛd, 'pjɔ:brɛd, -z
AM 'pjʊrˌbrɛd, -z

purée
BR 'pjʊəreɪ, 'pjɔ:reɪ, -z
AM pjʊ'reɪ, pjə'reɪ, -z

purely
BR 'pjʊəli, 'pjɔ:li
AM 'pjʊrli

pureness
BR 'pjʊənəs, 'pjɔ:nəs
AM 'pjʊrnəs

purfle
BR 'pə:fl, -lz, -ḷɪŋ\-lɪŋ, -ld
AM 'pərfəl, -z, -ɪŋ, -d

Purfleet
BR 'pə:fli:t
AM 'pərˌflit

purgation
BR pə:'geɪʃn
AM ˌpər'geɪʃən

purgative
BR 'pə:gətɪv, -z
AM 'pərgədɪv, -z

purgatorial
BR ˌpə:gə'tɔ:rɪəl
AM ˌpərgə'tɔriəl

purgatory
BR 'pə:gət(ə)ri
AM 'pərgəˌtɔri

purge
BR pə:dʒ, -ɨz, -ɪŋ, -d
AM pərdʒ, -əz, -ɪŋ, -d

purger
BR 'pə:dʒə(r), -z
AM 'pərdʒər, -z

purification
BR ˌpjʊərɪfɪ'keɪʃn, ˌpjɔ:rɪfɪ'keɪʃn
AM ˌpjurəfə'keɪʃən

purificator
BR 'pjʊərɪfɪkeɪtə(r), 'pjɔ:rɪfɪkeɪtə(r), -z
AM 'pjurəfəˌkeɪdər, -z

purificatory
BR ˌpjʊərɪfɪ'keɪt(ə)ri, ˌpjɔ:rɪfɪ'keɪt(ə)ri
AM pju'rɪfəkəˌtɔri

purifier
BR 'pjʊərɪfʌɪə(r), 'pjɔ:rɪfʌɪə(r), -z
AM 'pjurəˌfaɪər, -z

purify
BR 'pjʊərɪfʌɪ, 'pjɔ:rɪfʌɪ, -z, -ɪŋ, -d
AM 'pjurəˌfaɪ, -z, -ɪŋ, -d

Purim
BR 'p(j)ʊərɪm, pʊ'ri:m
AM 'pʊrəm, 'purəm, pu'rɪm

purine
BR 'p(j)ʊəri:n, 'pjɔ:ri:n, -z
AM 'pjʊˌrin, 'pjurən, -z

purism
BR 'pjʊərɪz(ə)m, 'pjɔ:rɪz(ə)m
AM 'pjʊˌrɪzəm

purist
BR 'pjʊərɪst, 'pjɔ:rɪst, -s
AM 'pjʊrəst, -s

puristic
BR pjʊə'rɪstɪk, pjɔ:'rɪstɪk
AM pjʊ'rɪstɪk, pjə'rɪstɪk

puritan
BR 'pjʊərɪt(ə)n, 'pjɔ:rɪt(ə)n, -z
AM 'pjʊrətn̩, 'pjʊrədən, -z

puritanic
BR ˌpjʊərɪ'tanɪk, ˌpjɔ:rɪ'tanɪk
AM ˌpjʊrə'tænɪk

puritanical
BR ˌpjʊərɪ'tanɪkl, ˌpjɔ:rɪ'tanɪkl
AM ˌpjʊrə'tænəkəl

puritanically
BR ˌpjʊərɪ'tanɪkli, ˌpjɔ:rɪ'tanɪkli
AM ˌpjʊrəˌtænək(ə)li

puritanism
BR 'pjʊərɪtənɪz(ə)m, 'pjʊərɪtn̩ɪz(ə)m, 'pjɔ:rɪtənɪz(ə)m, 'pjɔ:rɪtn̩ɪz(ə)m
AM 'pjʊrətnˌɪzəm, 'pjʊrətdəˌnɪzəm

purity
BR 'pjʊərɪti, 'pjɔ:rɪti
AM 'pjʊrədi

purl
BR pəːl, -z, -ɪŋ, -d
AM pərl, -z, -ɪŋ, -d

purler
BR 'pəːlə(r), -z
AM 'pərlər, -z

Purley
BR 'pəːli
AM 'pərli

purlieu
BR 'pəːljuː, -z
AM 'pərl(j)u, -z

purlieux
BR 'pəːljuːz
AM 'pərl(j)u

purlin
BR 'pəːlɪn, -z
AM 'pərlən, -z

purline
BR 'pəːlɪn, -z
AM 'pərlən, -z

purloin
BR pəː'lɔɪn, -z, -ɪŋ, -d
AM pər'lɔɪn, -z, -ɪŋ, -d

purloiner
BR pəː'lɔɪnə(r), -z
AM pər'lɔɪnər, -z

Purnell
BR pəː'nɛl
AM pər'nɛl

purple
BR 'pəːpl
AM 'pərpəl

purpleness
BR 'pəːplnəs
AM 'pərpəlnəs

purplish
BR 'pəːplɪʃ, 'pəːplɪʃ
AM 'pərp(ə)lɪʃ

purply
BR 'pəːpli, 'pəːpli
AM 'pərp(ə)li

purport[1]
noun
BR 'pəːpɔːt, 'pəːpət
AM 'pər,pɔ(ə)rt

purport[2]
verb
BR pəː'pɔːt, -s, -ɪŋ, -ɪd
AM pər'pɔ(ə)rt, -ts, -'pɔrdɪŋ, -'pɔrdəd

purportedly
BR pəː'pɔːtɪdli
AM pər'pɔrdədli

purpose
BR 'pəːpəs, -ɪz, -ɪŋ, -t
AM 'pərpəs, -əz, -ɪŋ, -t

purposeful
BR 'pəːpəsf(ʊ)l
AM 'pərpəsfəl

purposefully
BR 'pəːpəsfʊli, 'pəːpəsfli
AM 'pərpəsfəli

purposefulness
BR 'pəːpəsf(ʊ)lnəs
AM 'pərpəsfəlnəs

purposeless
BR 'pəːpəsləs
AM 'pərpəsləs

purposelessly
BR 'pəːpəsləsli
AM 'pərpəsləsli

purposelessness
BR 'pəːpəsləsnəs
AM 'pərpəsləsnəs

purposely
BR 'pəːpəsli
AM 'pərpəsli

purposive
BR 'pəːpəsɪv
AM 'pərpəsɪv

purposively
BR 'pəːpəsɪvli
AM 'pərpəsɪvli

purposiveness
BR 'pəːpəsɪvnɪs
AM 'pərpəsɪvnɪs

purpura
BR 'pəːpjʊrə(r)
AM 'pərp(j)ərə

purpure
BR 'pəːpjʊə(r)
AM 'pərp(j)ər

purpuric
BR pəː'pjʊərɪk, pəː'pjɔːrɪk
AM pər'p(j)ʊrɪk

purpurin
BR 'pəːpjʊrɪn
AM 'pərp(j)ərən

purr
BR pəː(r), -z, -ɪŋ, -d
AM pər, -z, -ɪŋ, -d

purse
BR pəːs, -ɪz, -ɪŋ, -t
AM pərs, -əz, -ɪŋ, -t

purseful
BR 'pəːsfʊl, -z
AM 'pərsfəl, -z

purser
BR 'pəːsə(r), -z
AM 'pərsər, -z

pursership
BR 'pəːsəʃɪp
AM 'pərsər,ʃɪp

purse-seine
BR 'pəːssеɪn, -z
AM 'pər(s),seɪn, -z

purse-seiner
BR 'pəːs,seɪnə(r), -z
AM 'pər(s),seɪnər, -z

purse-strings
BR 'pəːsstrɪŋz
AM 'pər(s),strɪŋz

pursiness
BR 'pəːsɪnɪs
AM 'pərsinɪs

purslane
BR 'pəːslɪn, 'pəːsleɪn
AM 'pərslən, 'pər,sleɪn

pursuable
BR pə'sjuːəbl
AM pər's(j)uəbəl

pursuance
BR pə'sjuːəns
AM pər's(j)uəns

pursuant
BR pə'sjuːənt
AM pər's(j)uənt

pursuantly
BR pə'sjuːəntli
AM pər's(j)uən(t)li

pursue
BR pə'sjuː, -z, -ɪŋ, -d
AM pər's(j)u, -z, -ɪŋ, -d

pursuer
BR pə'sjuːə(r), -z
AM pər's(j)uər, -z

pursuit
BR pə'sjuːt, -s
AM pər's(j)ut, -s

pursuivant
BR 'pəːs(w)ɪv(ə)nt, -s
AM 'pərs(w)əvənt, 'pərs(w)ivənt, -s

pursy
BR 'pəːsi
AM 'pərsi

purulence
BR 'pjʊər(j)ʊləns, 'pjʊər(j)ʊlns
AM 'pjʊr(j)ələns

purulency
BR 'pjʊər(j)ʊlənsi, 'pjʊər(j)ʊlnsi
AM 'pjʊr(j)ələnsi

purulent
BR 'pjʊər(j)ʊlənt, 'pjʊər(j)ʊlnt
AM 'pjʊr(j)ələnt

purulently
BR 'pjʊər(j)ʊləntli, 'pjʊər(j)ʊlntli
AM 'pjʊr(j)ələntli

Purves
BR 'pəːvɪs
AM 'pərvəs

purvey
BR pəː'veɪ, -z, -ɪŋ, -d
AM pər'veɪ, -z, -ɪŋ, -d

purveyance
BR pəː'veɪəns
AM pər'veɪəns

purveyor
BR pəː'veɪə(r), -z
AM pər'veɪər, -z

purview
BR 'pəːvjuː, -z
AM 'pər,vju, -z

Purvis
BR 'pəːvɪs
AM 'pərvəs

pus
BR pʌs
AM pəs

Pusan
BR ,puː'san
AM ,pu'sæn

Pusey
BR 'pjuːzi
AM 'pjuzi

push
BR pʊʃ, -ɪz, -ɪŋ, -t
AM pʊʃ, -əz, -ɪŋ, -t

pushbike
BR 'pʊʃbʌɪk, -s
AM 'pʊʃ,baɪk, -s

pushbroom
BR 'pʊʃbruːm, 'pʊʃbrʊm, -z
AM 'pʊʃ,brʊm, 'pʊʃ,brum, -z

pushbutton
BR 'pʊʃ,bʌtn, -z
AM 'pʊʃ,bətn, -z

pushcart
BR 'pʊʃkɑːt, -s
AM 'pʊʃ,kɑrt, -s

push-chain
BR 'pʊʃtʃeɪn, -z
AM 'pʊʃ,tʃeɪn, -z

pushchair
BR 'pʊʃtʃɛː(r), -z
AM 'pʊʃ,tʃɛ(ə)r, -z

pushdown
BR 'pʊʃdaʊn, -z
AM 'pʊʃ,daʊn, -z

pusher
BR 'pʊʃə(r), -z
AM 'pʊʃər, -z

pushful
BR 'pʊʃf(ʊ)l
AM 'pʊʃfəl

pushfully
BR 'pʊʃfʊli, 'pʊʃfli
AM 'pʊʃfəli

pushfulnes
BR 'pʊʃf(ʊ)lnəs
AM 'pʊʃfəlnəs

pushily
BR 'pʊʃɪli
AM 'pʊʃəli

pushiness
BR 'pʊʃɪnɪs
AM 'pʊʃinɪs

pushingly
BR 'pʊʃɪŋli
AM 'pʊʃɪŋli

Pushkin
BR 'pʊʃkɪn
AM 'pʊʃkɪn
RUS 'puʃkʲin

pushover
BR 'pʊʃ,əʊvə(r), -z
AM 'pʊʃ,oʊvər, -z

pushpin
BR 'pʊʃpɪn, -z
AM 'pʊʃ,pɪn, -z

push-pull
BR ,pʊʃ'pʊl
AM ,pʊʃ'pʊl

pushrod
BR 'pʊʃrɒd, -z
AM 'pʊʃ,rɑd, -z

pushstart
BR 'pʊʃstɑːt, -s, -ɪŋ, -ɪd

AM 'pʊʃˌstɑr|t, -ts, -dɪŋ, -dəd

Pushto
BR 'pʌʃtəʊ
AM 'pəʃtoʊ

Pushtu
BR 'pʌʃtuː
AM 'pəʃtu

pushy
BR 'pʊʃ|i, -ɪə(r), -ɪɪst
AM 'pʊʃi, -ər, -ɪst

pusillanimity
BR ˌpjuːsɪlə'nɪmɪti, ˌpjuːsḷə'nɪmɪti, ˌpjuːzɪlə'nɪmɪti, ˌpjuːzlə'nɪmɪti
AM ˌpjusələ'nɪmɪdi

pusillanimous
BR ˌpjuːsɪ'lanɪməs, ˌpjuːzɪ'lanɪməs
AM ¦pjusə'lænəməs

pusillanimously
BR ˌpjuːsɪ'lanɪməsli, ˌpjuːzɪ'lanɪməsli
AM ¦pjusə'lænəməsli

pusillanimousness
BR ˌpjuːsɪ'lanɪməsnəs, ˌpjuːzɪ'lanɪməsnəs
AM ¦pjusə'lænəməsnəs

puss
BR pʊs, -ɪz
AM pʊs, -əz

pussy
BR 'pʊs|i, -ɪz
AM 'pʊsi, -z

pussycat
BR 'pʊsɪkat, -s
AM 'pʊsiˌkæt, -s

pussyfoot
BR 'pʊsɪfʊt, -s, -ɪŋ, -ɪd
AM 'pʊsiˌfʊ|t, -ts, -dɪŋ, -dəd

pussyfooter
BR 'pʊsɪˌfʊtə(r), -z
AM 'pʊsiˌfʊdər, -z

pustulant
BR 'pʌstjʉlənt, 'pʌstjʉlṇt, 'pʌstʃʉlənt, 'pʌstʃʉlṇt
AM 'pəstʃələnt, 'pəstjələnt

pustular
BR 'pʌstjʉlə(r), 'pʌstʃʉlə(r)
AM 'pəstʃələr, pə'stjələr

pustulate
BR 'pʌstjʉleɪt, 'pʌstʃʉleɪt, -s, -ɪŋ, -d
AM 'pəstʃəˌleɪ|t, 'pəstjəˌleɪ|t, -ts, -dɪŋ, -dɪd

pustulation
BR ˌpʌsjʉ'leɪʃn, 'pʌstʃʉ'leɪʃn
AM ˌpəstʃə'leɪʃən, ˌpəstjə'leɪʃən

pustule
BR 'pʌstjuːl, 'pʌstʃuːl, -z
AM 'pəstʃəl, pə'stjul, -z

pustulous
BR 'pʌstjʉləs, 'pʌstʃʉləs
AM 'pəstʃələs, pə'stjələs

put
BR pʊt, -s, -ɪŋ
AM pʊ|t, -ts, -dɪŋ

putative
BR 'pjuːtətɪv
AM 'pjudədɪv

putatively
BR 'pjuːtətɪvli
AM 'pjudədɪvli

putdown
BR 'pʊtdaʊn, -z
AM 'pʊtˌdaʊn, -z

putlock
BR 'pʊtlɒk, -s
AM 'pʊtˌlɑk, -s

putlog
BR 'pʊtlɒg, -z
AM 'pʊtˌlɑg, -z

Putnam
BR 'pʌtnəm
AM 'pətnəm

Putney
BR 'pʌtni
AM 'pətni

put-put
BR ˌpʌt'pʌt, -s, -ɪŋ, -ɪd
AM 'pət'pə|t, -ts, -dɪŋ, -dəd

putrefacient
BR ˌpjuːtrɪ'feɪʃnt
AM ˌpjutrə'feɪʃənt

putrefaction
BR ˌpjuːtrɪ'fakʃn
AM ˌpjutrə'fækʃən

putrefactive
BR ˌpjuːtrɪ'faktɪv
AM ˌpjutrə'fæktɪv

putrefy
BR 'pjuːtrɪfʌɪ, -z, -ɪŋ, -d
AM 'pjutrəˌfaɪ, -z, -ɪŋ, -d

putrescence
BR pjuː'trɛsns
AM pju'trɛsəns

putrescent
BR pjuː'trɛsnt
AM pju'trɛsənt

putrescible
BR pjuː'trɛsɪbl
AM pju'trɛsəbəl

putrid
BR 'pjuːtrɪd
AM 'pjutrɪd

putridity
BR pjuː'trɪdɪti
AM pju'trɪdɪdi

putridly
BR 'pjuːtrɪdli
AM 'pjutrɪdli

putridness
BR 'pjuːtrɪdnɪs
AM 'pjutrɪdnɪs

putsch
BR pʊtʃ, -ɪz
AM pʊtʃ, -əz

putt
BR pʌt, -s, -ɪŋ, -ɪd
AM pə|t, -ts, -dɪŋ, -dəd

puttee
BR 'pʌtiː, pʌ'tiː, -z
AM ˌpə'ti, -z

Puttenham
BR 'pʌtṇəm
AM 'pətṇəm

putter[1]
noun, someone who puts
BR 'pʊtə(r), -z
AM 'pʊdər, -z

putter[2]
noun, someone who putts
BR 'pʌtə(r), -z
AM 'pədər, -z

putter[3]
verb
BR 'pʌt|ə(r), -əz, -(ə)rɪŋ, -əd
AM 'pədər, -z, -ɪŋ, -d

putti
BR 'pʊtiː
AM 'pudi

putting-green
BR 'pʌtɪŋɡriːn, -z
AM 'pədɪŋˌɡrin, -z

Puttnam
BR 'pʌtnəm
AM 'pətnəm

putto
BR 'pʊtəʊ
AM 'pudoʊ

putt-putt
BR ˌpʌt'pʌt, -s, -ɪŋ, -ɪd
AM 'pət'pə|t, -ts, -dɪŋ, -dəd

putty
BR 'pʌt|i, -ɪz, -ɪɪŋ, -ɪd
AM 'pədi, -z, -ɪŋ, -d

putz
BR pʊts, pʌts, -ɪz
AM pəts, -əz

puy
BR pwiː, -z
AM pwi, -z

puzzle
BR 'pʌz|l, -lz, -ḷɪŋ\-lɪŋ, -ld
AM 'pəz|əl, -əlz, -(ə)lɪŋ, -əld

puzzlement
BR 'pʌzlm(ə)nt, -s
AM 'pəzlmənt, -s

puzzler
BR 'pʌzlə(r), 'pʌzḷə(r), -z
AM 'pəz(ə)lər, -z

puzzling
BR 'pʌzlɪŋ, 'pʌzḷɪŋ
AM 'pəz(ə)lɪŋ

puzzlingly
BR 'pʌzlɪŋli, 'pʌzḷɪŋli
AM 'pəz(ə)lɪŋli

puzzolana
BR ˌpʊtsə'lɑːnə(r)
AM ˌpʊtsə'lɑnə

Pwllheli
BR pʉ'ɬɛli, pʉ'θɛli
AM pʊ'θɛli
WE pʊ'ɬeli

pya
BR pjɑː(*r*), -z
AM pi'ɑ, pjɑ, -z

pyaemia
BR pʌɪ'iːmɪə(*r*)
AM paɪ'imiə

pyaemic
BR pʌɪ'iːmɪk
AM paɪ'imɪk

pycnic
BR 'pɪknɪk, -s
AM 'pɪkˌnɪk, -s

Pye
BR pʌɪ
AM paɪ

pye-dog
BR 'pʌɪdɒg, -z
AM 'paɪˌdɔg, 'paɪˌdɑg, -z

pyelitis
BR ˌpʌɪə'lʌɪtɪs
AM ˌpaɪə'laɪdɪs

pyelogram
BR 'pʌɪələ(ʊ)gram, -z
AM 'paɪəloʊˌgræm, paɪ'ɛləˌgræm, -z

pyelonephritis
BR ˌpʌɪələʊnɪ'frʌɪtɪs
AM ˌpaɪloʊnə'fraɪdəs

pyemia
BR pʌɪ'iːmɪə(*r*)
AM paɪ'imiə

pyemic
BR pʌɪ'iːmɪk
AM paɪ'imɪk

pygmaean
BR pɪg'miːən
AM 'pɪgmiən, pɪg'miən

Pygmalion
BR pɪg'meɪlɪən
AM pɪg'meɪliən

pygmean
BR pɪg'miːən
AM 'pɪgmiən, pɪg'miən

pygmy
BR 'pɪgm|i, -ɪz
AM 'pɪgmi, -z

pyjama
BR pə'dʒɑːmə(*r*), -z
AM pə'dʒɑmə, -z

pyknic
BR 'pɪknɪk, -s
AM 'pɪkˌnɪk, -s

Pyle
BR pʌɪl

AM paɪl

pylon
BR 'pʌɪlən, 'pʌɪlɒn, -z
AM 'paɪˌlɑn, -z

pylori
BR pʌɪ'lɔːrʌɪ
AM paɪ'lɔˌraɪ

pyloric
BR pʌɪ'lɒrɪk
AM paɪ'lɔrɪk

pylorus
BR pʌɪ'lɔːrəs
AM paɪ'lɔrəs

Pylos
BR 'pʌɪlɒs
AM 'paɪlɔs, 'paɪlɑs

Pym
BR pɪm
AM pɪm

Pymm
BR pɪm
AM pɪm

pyoid
BR 'pʌɪɔɪd
AM 'paɪˌɔɪd

Pyongyang
BR ˌpjɒŋ'jaŋ
AM 'pjɔŋ'jæŋ, 'pjɑŋ'jæŋ

pyorrhea
BR ˌpʌɪə'riːə(r)
AM ˌpaɪə'riə

pyorrhoea
BR ˌpʌɪə'riːə(r)
AM ˌpaɪə'riə

pyosis
BR pʌɪ'əʊsɪs
AM paɪ'oʊsəs

pyracantha
BR ˌpʌɪrə'kanθə(r), -z
AM ˌpaɪrə'kænθə, -z

Pyrah
BR 'pʌɪrə(r)
AM 'paɪrə

pyralid
BR pʌɪ'ralɪd, pʌɪ'reɪlɪd, -z
AM 'pɪrəˌlɪd, -z

pyramid
BR 'pɪrəmɪd, -z
AM 'pɪrəˌmɪd, -z

pyramidal
BR pɨ'ramɨdl
AM pə'ræmədəl, ˌpɪrə'mɪdəl

pyramidally
BR pɨ'ramɨdḷi, pɨ'ramɨdəli
AM ˌpɪrə'mɪdḷi, pə'ræmədli

pyramidic
BR ˌpɪrə'mɪdɪk
AM ˌpɪrə'mɪdɪk

pyramidically
BR ˌpɪrə'mɪdɪkli
AM ˌpɪrə'mɪdɪk(ə)li

Pyramus
BR 'pɪrəməs
AM 'pɪrəməs

pyre
BR 'pʌɪə(r), -z
AM 'paɪ(ə)r, -z

Pyrenean
BR ˌpɪrə'niːən, -z
AM ˌpɪrə'niən, -z

Pyrenees
BR ˌpɪrə'niːz
AM 'pɪrəˌniz

pyrethrin
BR pʌɪ'riːθrɪn
AM paɪ'riθrən, paɪ'rɛθrən

pyrethroid
BR pʌɪ'riːθrɔɪd, -z
AM paɪ'riˌθrɔɪd, -z

pyrethrum
BR pʌɪ'riːθrəm
AM paɪ'riθrəm, paɪ'rɛθrəm

pyretic
BR pʌɪ'rɛtɪk, pɨ'rɛtɪk
AM paɪ'rɛdɪk

Pyrex®
BR 'pʌɪrɛks
AM 'paɪˌrɛks

pyrexia
BR pʌɪ'rɛksɪə(r)
AM paɪ'rɛksiə

pyrexial
BR pʌɪ'rɛksɪəl
AM paɪ'rɛksiəl

pyrexic
BR pʌɪ'rɛksɪk
AM paɪ'rɛksɪk

pyrexical
BR pʌɪ'rɛksɨkl
AM paɪ'rɛksəkəl

pyrheliometer
BR pəːˌhiːlɪ'ɒmɨtə(r), -z
AM ˌpaɪ(ə)rˌ(h)ili'ɑmədər, -z

pyridine
BR 'pɪrɨdiːn
AM 'pɪrəˌdin, 'pɪrədn

pyridoxal
BR ˌpɪrɨ'dɒksl
AM ˌpɪrɨ'dɑksəl

pyridoxine
BR ˌpɪrɨ'dɒksiːn, ˌpɪrɨ'dɒksɪn
AM ˌpɪrə'dɑksin, ˌpɪrə'dɑksən

pyrimidine
BR pʌɪ'rɪmɨdiːn, pɨ'rɪmɨdiːn, -z
AM pə'rɪməˌdin, paɪ'rɪməˌdin, paɪ'rɪmədn, -z

pyrite
BR 'pʌɪrʌɪt
AM 'paɪˌraɪt

pyrites
BR pʌɪ'rʌɪtiːz, pɨ'rʌɪtiːz
AM pə'raɪdiz, paɪ'raɪdiz

pyritic
BR pʌɪ'rɪtɪk
AM paɪ'rɪdɪk, pə'rɪdɪk

pyritiferous
BR ˌpʌɪrʌɪ'tɪf(ə)rəs, ˌpʌɪrɨ'tɪf(ə)rəs
AM ˌpaɪˌraɪd'ɪf(ə)rəs

pyritise
BR 'pʌɪrʌɪtʌɪz, 'pʌɪrɨtʌɪz, -ɨz, -ɪŋ, -d
AM 'paɪˌraɪdˌaɪz, -ɨz, -ɪŋ, -d

pyritize
BR 'pʌɪrʌɪtʌɪz, 'pʌɪrɨtʌɪz, -ɨz, -ɪŋ, -d
AM 'paɪˌraɪdˌaɪz, -ɨz, -ɪŋ, -d

pyritous
BR 'pʌɪrɨtəs, pʌɪ'rʌɪtəs
AM pə'raɪdəs, paɪ'raɪdəs

pyro
BR 'pʌɪrəʊ
AM 'paɪˌroʊ

pyroclast
BR 'pʌɪrə(ʊ)klɑːst, 'pʌɪrə(ʊ)klast, -s
AM 'paɪroʊˌklæst, -s

pyroclastic
BR ˌpʌɪrə(ʊ)'klastɪk, -s
AM ˌpaɪroʊ'klæstɪk, -s

pyroelectric
BR ˌpʌɪrəʊɨ'lɛktrɪk
AM ˌpaɪroʊə'lɛktrɪk, ˌpaɪroʊi'lɛktrɪk

pyroelectricity
BR ˌpʌɪrəʊɨˌlɛk'trɪsɪti, ˌpʌɪrəʊˌɛlɛk'trɪsɪti, ˌpʌɪrəʊˌɛlɪk'trɪsɪti, ˌpʌɪrəʊˌɪlɛk'trɪsɪti, ˌpʌɪrəʊˌiːlɛk'trɪsɪti
AM ˌpaɪroʊəˌlɛk'trɪsɨdi, ˌpaɪroʊiˌlɛk'trɪsɨdi

pyrogallic acid
BR ˌpʌɪrə(ʊ)galɪk 'asɪd
AM ˌpaɪroʊ'gælɪk 'æsəd

pyrogallol
BR ˌpʌɪrə(ʊ)'galɒl
AM ˌpaɪroʊ'gæˌlɔl, ˌpaɪroʊ'gæˌlɑl

pyrogenic
BR ˌpʌɪrə(ʊ)'dʒɛnɪk
AM ˌpaɪroʊ'dʒɛnɪk

pyrogenous
BR pʌɪ'rɒdʒɪnəs
AM paɪ'rɑdʒənəs

pyrography
BR pʌɪ'rɒgrəfi
AM paɪ'rɑgrəfi

pyrolatry
BR pʌɪ'rɒlətri
AM paɪ'rɑlətri

pyroligneous
BR ˌpʌɪrə'lɪgnɪəs
AM ˌpaɪrə'lɪgniəs

pyrolyse
BR 'pʌɪrəlʌɪz, -ɨz, -ɪŋ, -t
AM 'paɪrəˌlaɪz, -ɨz, -ɪŋ, -t

pyrolysis
BR pʌɪ'rɒlɨsɪs
AM paɪ'rɑləsəs

pyrolytic
BR ˌpʌɪrə'lɪtɪk
AM ˌpaɪrə'lɪdɪk

pyrolyze
BR 'pʌɪrəlʌɪz, -ɨz, -ɪŋ, -d
AM 'paɪrəˌlaɪz, -ɨz, -ɪŋ, -d

pyromancy
BR 'pʌɪrə(ʊ)ˌmansi
AM 'paɪroʊˌmænsi

pyromania
BR ˌpʌɪrə(ʊ)'meɪnɪə(r)
AM ˌpaɪroʊ'meɪniə

pyromaniac
BR ˌpʌɪrə(ʊ)'meɪnɪak, -s
AM ˌpaɪroʊ'meɪniˌæk, -s

pyrometer
BR pʌɪ'rɒmɨtə(r), -z
AM paɪ'rɑmədər, -z

pyrometric
BR ˌpʌɪrə(ʊ)'mɛtrɪk
AM ˌpaɪroʊ'mɛtrɪk

pyrometrically
BR ˌpʌɪrə(ʊ)'mɛtrɨkli
AM ˌpaɪroʊ'mɛtrək(ə)li

pyrometry
BR pʌɪ'rɒmɪtri
AM paɪ'rɑmətri

pyrope
BR 'pʌɪrəʊp, -s
AM 'paɪˌroʊp, -s

pyrophoric
BR ˌpʌɪrə(ʊ)'fɒrɪk
AM ˌpaɪroʊ'fɔrɪk

pyrosis
BR pʌɪ'rəʊsɪs
AM paɪ'roʊsəs

pyrotechnic
BR ˌpʌɪrə(ʊ)'tɛknɪk, -s
AM ˌpaɪroʊ'tɛknɪk, -s

pyrotechnical
BR ˌpʌɪrə(ʊ)'tɛknɨkl
AM ˌpaɪroʊ'tɛknəkəl

pyrotechnically
BR ˌpʌɪrə(ʊ)'tɛknɨkli
AM ˌpaɪroʊ'tɛknək(ə)li

pyrotechnist
BR ˌpʌɪrə(ʊ)'tɛknɪst, -s
AM ˌpaɪroʊ'tɛknəst, -s

pyrotechny
BR 'pʌɪrə(ʊ)ˌtɛkni
AM 'paɪroʊˌtɛkni

pyroxene
BR pʌɪ'rɒksiːn, -z
AM paɪ'rɑkˌsin, pə'rɑkˌsin, -z

pyroxylin
BR pʌɪ'rɒksɪlɪn, pʌɪ'rɒksl̩ɪn
AM paɪ'rɑksələn, pə'rɑksələn

Pyrrha
BR 'pɪrə(r)
AM 'pɪrə

Pyrrhic
BR 'pɪrɪk, -s
AM 'pɪrɪk, -s

Pyrrho
BR 'pɪrəʊ
AM 'pɪroʊ

Pyrrhonian
BR pɪ'rəʊnɪən
AM pə'roʊniən

Pyrrhonic
BR pɪ'rɒnɪk
AM pə'rɑnɪk

Pyrrhonism
BR 'pɪrənɪz(ə)m
AM 'pɪrənɪzəm

Pyrrhonist
BR 'pɪrənɪst, -s
AM 'pɪrənəst, -s

Pyrrhus
BR 'pɪrəs
AM 'pɪrəs

pyruvate
BR pʌɪ'ruːveɪt
AM paɪ'ruˌveɪt, pə'ruˌveɪt

pyruvic acid
BR pʌɪˌruːvɪk 'asɪd
AM paɪ'ruvɪk 'æsəd, pə'ruvɪk +

Pythagoras
BR pʌɪ'θag(ə)rəs
AM paɪ'θægərəs, pə'θægərəs

Pythagorean
BR ˌpʌɪθagə'riːən, pʌɪˌθagə'riːən
AM pəˌθægə'riən, paɪˌθægə'riən

Pythia
BR 'pɪθɪə(r)
AM 'pɪθiə

Pythian
BR 'pɪθɪən
AM 'pɪθiən

Pythias
BR 'pɪθɪəs
AM 'pɪθiəs

python
BR 'pʌɪθn, -z
AM 'paɪˌθɑn, 'paɪθən, -z

Pythonesque
BR ˌpʌɪθə'nɛsk
AM ˌpaɪθə'nɛsk

pythonic
BR pʌɪ'θɒnɪk
AM paɪ'θɑnɪk

pyuria
BR pʌɪ'jʊərɪə(r)
AM paɪ'jʊriə

pyx
BR pɪks, -ɪz
AM pɪks, -ɪz

pyxides
BR 'pɪksɪdiːz
AM 'pɪksɪˌdiz

pyxidia
BR pɪk'sɪdɪə(r)
AM pɪk'sɪdiə

pyxidium
BR pɪk'sɪdɪəm
AM pɪk'sɪdiəm

pyxie
BR 'pɪks|i, -ɪz
AM 'pɪksi, -z

pyxis
BR 'pɪksɪs
AM 'pɪksɪs

pzazz
BR pə'zaz
AM pə'zæz

Qq

q
BR kjuː, -z
AM kju, -z

Qantas®
BR 'kwɒntəs
AM 'kwɑn(t)əs

Qatar
BR 'katɑː(r), 'gatɑː(r), 'kʌtɑː(r), 'gʌtɑː(r), kə'tɑː(r)
AM 'kɑˌtɑr, kə'tɑr

Qatari
BR ka'tɑːr|i, ga'tɑːr|i, kʌ'tɑːr|i, gʌ'tɑːr|i, kə'tɑːr|i, -ɪz
AM kɑ'tɑri, kə'tɑri, -z

Qattara
BR ka'tɑːrə(r), kʌ'tɑːrə(r), kə'tɑːrə(r)
AM kɑ'tɑrə, kə'tɑrə

Q-boat
BR 'kjuːbəʊt, -s
AM 'kjuˌboʊt, -s

Q.C.
BR ˌkjuː'siː, -z
AM ˌkju'si, -z

QED
BR ˌkjuːiː'diː
AM ˌkjuˌi'di

Q fever
BR 'kjuː ˌfiːvə(r)
AM 'kju ˌfivər

qibla
BR 'kɪblə(r)
AM 'kɪblə

Qinghai
BR ˌtʃɪŋ'hʌɪ
AM 'tʃɪŋ'haɪ

Q-ship
BR 'kjuːʃɪp, -s
AM 'kjuˌʃɪp, -s

q.t.
BR ˌkjuː'tiː
AM ˌkju'ti

qua
BR kweɪ, kwɑː(r)
AM kwɑ, kweɪ

Quaalude®
BR 'kweɪluːd, -z
AM 'kweɪˌlud, -z

quack
BR kwak, -s, -ɪŋ, -t
AM kwæk, -s, -ɪŋ, -t

quackery
BR 'kwak(ə)ri
AM 'kwækəri

quackish
BR 'kwakɪʃ
AM 'kwækɪʃ

quad
BR kwɒd, -z
AM kwɑd, -z

quadragenarian
BR ˌkwɒdrədʒɪ'nɛːrɪən, -z
AM ˌkwɑdrədʒə'nɛriən, -z

Quadragesima
BR ˌkwɒdrə'dʒɛsɪmə(r)
AM ˌkwɑdrə'dʒɛsəmə

quadragesimal
BR ˌkwɒdrə'dʒɛsɪml
AM ˌkwɑdrə'dʒɛsəməl

quadrangle
BR 'kwɒdraŋgl, -z
AM 'kwɑˌdræŋgəl, -z

quadrangular
BR kwɒ'draŋgjʊlə(r), kwə'draŋgjʊlə(r)
AM kwɑ'dræŋgjələr

quadrant
BR 'kwɒdr(ə)nt, -s
AM 'kwɑdrənt, -s

quadrantal
BR kwɒ'drantl
AM kwɑ'dræn(t)l

quadraphonic
BR ˌkwɒdrə'fɒnɪk, -s
AM ˌkwɑdrə'fɑnɪk, -s

quadraphonically
BR ˌkwɒdrə'fɒnɪkli
AM ˌkwɑdrə'fɑnək(ə)li

quadraphony
BR kwɒ'drɒfəni, kwɒ'drɒfn̩i, 'kwɒdrəˌfɒni
AM kwɑ'drɑfəni

quadrat
BR 'kwɒdrət, 'kwɒdrat, -s
AM 'kwɑdræt, 'kwɑdrət, -s

quadrate¹
noun, adjective
BR 'kwɒdreɪt, 'kwɒdrət, -s
AM 'kwɑdˌreɪt, 'kwɑdrət, -s

quadrate²
verb
BR kwɒ'dreɪt, kwə'dreɪt, -s, -ɪŋ, -ɨd
AM 'kwɑdˌreɪ|t, -ts, -dɪŋ, -dɨd

quadratic
BR kwɒ'dratɪk, kwə'dratɪk, -s
AM kwɑ'drædɪk, -s

quadrature
BR 'kwɒdrətʃə(r)
AM 'kwɑdrətʃər, 'kwɑdrətʃʊ(ə)r

quadrennia
BR kwɒ'drɛnɪə(r), kwə'drɛnɪə(r)
AM kwɑ'drɛniə

quadrennial
BR kwɒ'drɛnɪəl, kwə'drɛnɪəl
AM kwɑ'drɛniəl

quadrennially
BR kwɒ'drɛnɪəli, kwə'drɛnɪəli
AM kwɑ'drɛniəli

quadrennium
BR kwɒ'drɛnɪəm, kwə'drɛnɪəm
AM kwɑ'drɛniəm

quadric
BR 'kwɒdrɪk
AM 'kwɑdrɪk

quadriceps
BR 'kwɒdrɪsɛps
AM 'kwɑdrəˌsɛps

quadrifid
BR 'kwɒdrɪfɪd
AM 'kwɑdrəˌfɪd

quadriga
BR kwɒ'driːgə(r), kwə'driːgə(r), kwɒ'drʌɪgə(r), kwə'drʌɪgə(r), -z
AM kwɑ'draɪgə, -z

quadrilateral
BR ˌkwɒdrɪ'lat(ə)rəl, ˌkwɒdrɪ'lat(ə)rl̩, -z
AM ˌkwɑdrə'lædərəl, ˌkwɑdrə'lætrəl, -z

quadrilingual
BR ˌkwɒdrɪ'lɪŋgw(ə)l
AM ˌkwɑdrə'lɪŋgwəl

quadrille
BR kwɒ'drɪl, kwə'drɪl, -z
AM kwɑ'drɪl, k(w)ə'drɪl, -z

quadrillion
BR kwɒ'drɪljən, kwə'drɪljən, -z
AM kwɑ'drɪljən, -z

quadrinomial
BR ˌkwɒdrɪ'nəʊmɪəl, -z
AM ˌkwɑdrə'noʊmiəl, -z

quadripartite
BR ˌkwɒdrɪ'pɑːtʌɪt
AM ˌkwɑdrə'pɑrtaɪt

quadriplegia
BR ˌkwɒdrɪ'pliːdʒ(ɪ)ə(r)
AM ˌkwɑdrə'pli(d)ʒə

quadriplegic
BR ˌkwɒdrɪ'pliːdʒɪk, -s
AM ˌkwɑdrə'plidʒɪk, -s

quadrireme
BR 'kwɒdrɪriːm, -z
AM 'kwɑdrəˌrim, -z

quadrisyllabic
BR ˌkwɒdrɪsɪ'labɪk
AM ˌkwɑdrəsə'læbɪk

quadrisyllable
BR 'kwɒdrɪˌsɪləbl, -z
AM ˌkwɑdrə'sɪləbəl, -z

quadrivalent
BR ˌkwɒdrɪ'veɪlənt, ˌkwɒdrɪ'veɪln̩t
AM ˌkwɑdrə'veɪlənt

quadrivia
BR kwɒ'drɪvɪə(r), kwə'drɪvɪə(r)
AM kwɑ'drɪviə

quadrivium
BR kwɒ'drɪvɪəm, kwə'drɪvɪəm
AM kwɑ'drɪviəm

quadroon
BR kwɒ'druːn, kwə'druːn, -z
AM kwɑ'drun, -z

quadrophonic
BR ˌkwɒdrə'fɒnɪk, -s
AM ˌkwɑdrə'fɑnɪk, -s

quadrophonically
BR ˌkwɒdrə'fɒnɪkli
AM ˌkwɑdrə'fɑnək(ə)li

quadrophony
BR kwɒ'drɒfəni, kwɒ'drɒfn̩i, kwə'drɒfəni, kwə'drɒfn̩i
AM kwɑ'drɑfəni

quadrumanous
BR kwɒ'druːmənəs, kwə'druːmənəs
AM kwɑ'drumənəs

quadruped
BR 'kwɒdrʊpɛd, -z
AM 'kwɑdrəˌpɛd, -z

quadrupedal
BR kwɒ'druːpɪdl, kwə'druːpɪdl, ˌkwɒdrʊ'piːdl, ˌkwɒdrʊ'pɛdl
AM ˌkwɑdrə'pɛdəl, kwɑ'drupədəl

quadruple
BR 'kwɒdrʊp|l, kwɒ'druːp|l, kwə'druːp|l, -lz, -l̩ɪŋ\-lɪŋ, -ld
AM kwɑ'drup|əl, kwə'drup|əl, kwɑ'drəp|əl, kwə'drəp|əl, -əlz, -(ə)lɪŋ, -əld

quadruplet
BR 'kwɒdrʊplɪt, kwɒ'druːplɪt, kwə'druːplɪt, -s
AM kwɑ'drəplət, kwə'drəplət, kwɑ'druplət, kwə'druplət, -s

quadruplicate¹
noun, adjective
BR kwɒ'druːplɪkət, kwə'druːplɪkət, -s
AM kwɑ'drupləkət, kwə'drupləkət, -s

quadruplicate²
verb
BR kwɒˈdruːplɨkeɪt, kwəˈdruːplɨkeɪt, -s, -ɪŋ, -ɨd
AM kwɑˈdrupləˌkeɪ|t, kwəˈdrupləˌkeɪ|t, -ts, -dɪŋ, -dɨd

quadruplication
BR kwɒˌdruːplɨˈkeɪʃn, kwəˌdruːplɨˈkeɪʃn, -z
AM kwɑˌdrupləˈkeɪʃən, kwəˌdrupləˈkeɪʃən, -z

quadruplicity
BR ˌkwɒdrʊˈplɪsɨti
AM ˌkwɑdrəˈplɪsɨdi

quadruply
BR ˈkwɒdrʊpli, kwɒˈdruːpli, kwəˈdruːpli
AM kwɑˈdrup(ə)li, kwəˈdrup(ə)li, kwɑˈdrəp(ə)li

quadrupole
BR ˈkwɒdrʊpəʊl, -z
AM ˈkwɑdrəˌpoʊl, -z

quaere
BR ˈkwɪər|i, -ɪz, -ɪɪŋ, -ɪd
AM ˈkwɪri, -z, -ɪŋ, -d

quaestor
BR ˈkwiːstə(r), ˈkwiːstɔː(r), ˈkwʌɪstə(r), ˈkwʌɪstɔː(r), -z
AM ˈkwɛstər, -z

quaestorial
BR kwiːˈstɔːrɪəl, kwʌɪˈstɔːrɪəl
AM kwɛˈstɔriəl

quaestorship
BR ˈkwiːstəʃɪp, ˈkwʌɪstəʃɪp, -s
AM ˈkwɛstərʃɪp, -s

quaff
BR kwɒf, -s, -ɪŋ, -t
AM kwɑf, -s, -ɪŋ, -t

quaffable
BR ˈkwɒfəbl
AM ˈkwɑfəbəl

quaffer
BR ˈkwɒfə(r), -z
AM ˈkwɑfər, -z

quag
BR kwag, kwɒg, -z
AM kwæg, kwɑg, -z

quagga
BR ˈkwagə(*r*), -z
AM ˈkwægə, -z

quaggy
BR ˈkwag|i, ˈkwɒg|i, -ɪə(r), -ɪɪst
AM ˈkwægi, -ər, -ɨst

Quaglino's®
BR kwagˈliːnəʊz
AM kwɑgˈlinoʊz

quagmare
BR ˈkwagmʌɪə(r), ˈkwɒgmʌɪə(r), -z
AM ˈkwægˌmaɪ(ə)r, -z

quahaug
BR ˈkwɔːhɒg, ˈkwɑːhɒg, k(w)əˈhɔːg, -z
AM ˈkwɔˌhɔg, ˈkwɑˌhɑg, -z

quahog
BR ˈkwɔːhɒg, ˈkwɑːhɒg, k(w)əˈhɔːg, -z
AM ˈkwɔˌhɔg, ˈkwɑˌhɑg, -z

quaich
BR kweɪx, kweɪk, -ɨz
AM kweɪk, -ɨz

Quaid
BR kweɪd
AM kweɪd

Quai d'Orsay
BR ˌkeɪ dɔːˈseɪ
AM ˌki dɔrˈseɪ

quail
BR kweɪl, -z, -ɪŋ, -d
AM kweɪl, -z, -ɪŋ, -d

quailery
BR ˈkweɪl(ə)r|i, -ɪz
AM ˈkweɪləri, -z

quaint
BR kweɪnt, -ə(r), -ɨst
AM kweɪn|t, -(t)ər, -(t)ɨst

quaintly
BR ˈkweɪntli
AM ˈkweɪn(t)li

quaintness
BR ˈkweɪntnɨs
AM ˈkweɪn(t)nɨs

quake
BR kweɪk, -s, -ɪŋ, -t
AM kweɪk, -s, -ɪŋ, -t

Quaker
BR ˈkweɪkə(r), -z
AM ˈkweɪkər, -z

Quakerish
BR ˈkweɪk(ə)rɪʃ
AM ˈkweɪkərɪʃ

Quakerism
BR ˈkweɪk(ə)rɪz(ə)m, -z
AM ˈkweɪkəˌrɪzəm, -z

Quakerly
BR ˈkweɪkəli
AM ˈkweɪkərli

quakily
BR ˈkweɪkɨli
AM ˈkweɪkɨli

quakiness
BR ˈkweɪkɪnɪs
AM ˈkweɪkinɨs

quaky
BR ˈkweɪk|i, -ɪə(r), -ɪɪst
AM ˈkweɪki, -ər, -ɨst

Qualcast®
BR ˈkwɒlkɑːst, ˈkwɒlkast
AM ˈkwɑlˌkæst, ˈkwɔlˌkæst

qualifiable
BR ˈkwɒlɨfʌɪəbl
AM ˌkwɑləˈfaɪəbəl, ˌkwɔləˈfaɪəbəl

qualification
BR ˌkwɒlɨfɨˈkeɪʃn, -z
AM ˌkwɑləfəˈkeɪʃən, ˌkwɔləfəˈkeɪʃən, -z

qualificatory
BR ˈkwɒlɨfɨkət(ə)ri, ˌkwɒlɨfɨˈkeɪt(ə)ri
AM ˈkwɑləfəkəˌtɔri, ˈkwɔləfəkəˌtɔri

qualifier
BR ˈkwɒlɨfaɪə(r), -z
AM ˈkwɑləˌfaɪər, -z, ˈkwɔləˌfaɪər

qualify
BR ˈkwɒlɨfʌɪ, -z, -ɪŋ, -d
AM ˈkwɑləˌfaɪ, ˈkwɔləˌfaɪ, -z, -ɪŋ, -d

qualitative
BR ˈkwɒlɨtətɪv, ˈkwɒlɨteɪtɪv
AM ˈkwɑləˌteɪdɪv, ˈkwɔləˌteɪdɪv

qualitatively
BR ˈkwɒlɨtətɨvli, ˈkwɒlɨteɪtɨvli
AM ˈkwɑləˌteɪdɨvli, ˈkwɔləˌteɪdɨvli

quality
BR ˈkwɒlɨt|i, -ɪz
AM ˈkwɔlədi, ˈkwɑlədi, -z

qualm
BR kwɑːm, -z
AM kwɑ(l)m, -z, kwɔ(l)m

qualmish
BR ˈkwɑːmɪʃ
AM ˈkwɑ(l)mɪʃ, ˈkwɔ(l)mɪʃ

quamash
BR kwəˈmaʃ, ˈkwɒməʃ, -ɨz
AM kwəˈmæʃ, ˈkwɔˌmæʃ, ˈkwɑˌmæʃ

quandary
BR ˈkwɒnd(ə)r|i, -ɪz
AM ˈkwɑnd(ə)ri, -z

quango
BR ˈkwaŋgəʊ, -z
AM ˈkwæŋgoʊ, -z

quant
BR kwɒnt, -s, -ɪŋ, -ɨd
AM kwɑn|t, -ts, -(d)ɪŋ, -(d)əd

quanta
BR ˈkwɒntə(*r*)
AM ˈkwɑn(t)ə

quantal
BR ˈkwɒntl
AM ˈkwɑn(t)əl

quantally
BR ˈkwɒntl̩i, ˈkwɒntəli
AM ˈkwɑn(t)l̩i

Quantel
BR ˌkwɒnˈtɛl, ˈkwɒntɛl
AM ˌkwɑnˈtɛl, ˈkwɑnˌtɛl

quantic
BR ˈkwɒntɪk
AM ˈkwɑn(t)ɪk

quantifiability
BR ˌkwɒntɨˌfʌɪəˈbɪlɨti
AM ˌkwɑn(t)əˌfaɪəˈbɪlɨdi

quantifiable
BR ˈkwɒntɨfʌɪəbl
AM ˈkwɑn(t)əˌfaɪəbəl

quantification
BR ˌkwɒntɨfɨˈkeɪʃn
AM ˌkwɑn(t)əfəˈkeɪʃən

quantifier
BR ˈkwɒntɨfʌɪə(r), -z
AM ˈkwɑn(t)əˌfaɪər, -z

quantify
BR ˈkwɒntɨfʌɪ, -z, -ɪŋ, -d
AM ˈkwɑn(t)əˌfaɪ, -z, -ɪŋ, -d

quantisation
BR ˌkwɒntʌɪˈzeɪʃn, -z
AM ˌkwɑn(t)əˈzeɪʃən, ˌkwɑnˌtaɪˈzeɪʃən, -z

quantise
BR ˈkwɒntʌɪz, -ɨz, -ɪŋ, -d
AM ˈkwɑnˌtaɪz, -ɨz, -ɪŋ, -d

quantitative
BR ˈkwɒntɨtətɪv, ˈkwɒntɨteɪtɪv
AM ˈkwɑn(t)əˌteɪdɪv

quantitatively
BR ˈkwɒntɨtətɨvli, ˈkwɒntɨteɪtɨvli
AM ˈkwɑn(t)əˌteɪdɨvli

quantitive
BR ˈkwɒntɨtɪv
AM ˈkwɑn(t)ədɪv

quantitively
BR ˈkwɒntɨtɨvli
AM ˈkwɑn(t)ədɨvli

quantity
BR ˈkwɒntɨt|i, -ɪz
AM ˈkwɑn(t)ədi, -z

quantization
BR ˌkwɒntʌɪˈzeɪʃn, -z
AM ˌkwɑn(t)əˈzeɪʃən, ˌkwɑnˌtaɪˈzeɪʃən, -z

quantize
BR ˈkwɒntʌɪz, -ɨz, -ɪŋ, -d
AM ˈkwɑnˌtaɪz, -ɨz, -ɪŋ, -d

Quantock
BR ˈkwɒntək, ˈkwɒntɒk, -s
AM ˈkwɑn(t)ək, -s

quantum
BR ˈkwɒntəm
AM ˈkwɑn(t)əm

quaquaversal
BR ˌkweɪkwəˈvəːsl
AM ˌkweɪkwəˈvərsəl

quarantine
BR 'kwɒrəntiːn, 'kwɒrn̩tiːn, -z, -ɪŋ, -d
AM 'kwɔrən,tin, -z, -ɪŋ, -d

quark¹
subatomic particle
BR kwɑːk, -s
AM kwɑrk, -s

quark²
soft cheese
BR kwɑːk
AM kwɑrk

Quarndon
BR 'k(w)ɔːndən
AM 'kwɔrndən

quarrel
BR 'kwɒrəl, 'kwɒrl̩, -z, -ɪŋ, -d
AM 'kwɔrəl, -z, -ɪŋ, -d

quarreler
BR 'kwɒrələ(r), 'kwɒrl̩ə(r), -z
AM 'kwɔr(ə)lər, -z

quarreller
BR 'kwɒrələ(r), 'kwɒrl̩ə(r), -z
AM 'kwɔr(ə)lər, -z

quarrelsome
BR 'kwɒrəls(ə)m, 'kwɒrl̩s(ə)m
AM 'kwɔr(ə)lsəm

quarrelsomely
BR 'kwɒrəls(ə)mli, 'kwɒrl̩s(ə)mli
AM 'kwɔr(ə)lsəmli

quarrelsomeness
BR 'kwɒrəls(ə)mnəs, 'kwɒrl̩s(ə)mnəs
AM 'kwɔr(ə)lsəmnəs

quarrian
BR 'kwɒrɪən, -z
AM 'kwɔriən, -z

quarry
BR 'kwɒr|i, -ɪz, -ɪɪŋ, -ɪd
AM 'kwɔri, -z, -ɪn, -d

quarryman
BR 'kwɒrɪmən
AM 'kwɔrimən

quarrymen
BR 'kwɒrɪmən
AM 'kwɔrimən

quart
BR kwɔːt, -s
AM kwɔ(ə)rt, -s

quartan
BR 'kwɔːtn
AM 'kwɔrtn

quartation
BR kwɔː'teɪʃn, -z
AM kwɔr'teɪʃən, -z

quarte
BR kɑːt
AM kɑrt

quarter
BR 'kwɔːt|ə(r), -əz, -(ə)rɪŋ, -əd
AM 'kwɔrdər, -z, -ɪŋ, -d

quarterage
BR 'kwɔːt(ə)r|ɪdʒ, -ɨdʒɨz
AM 'kwɔrdərɪdʒ, -ɨz

quarterback
BR 'kwɔːtəbak, -s
AM 'kwɔrdər,bæk, -s

quarterdeck
BR 'kwɔːtədɛk, -s
AM 'kwɔrdər,dɛk, -s

quarterfinal
BR 'kwɔːtə,fʌɪnl, ,kwɔːtə'fʌɪnl, -z
AM ¦kwɔrdər¦faɪnəl, -z

quarter-hour
BR ,kwɔːtər'aʊə(r), -z
AM ,kwɔrdər'aʊər, -z

quartering
BR 'kwɔːt(ə)rɪŋ, -z
AM 'kwɔrdərɪŋ, -z

quarterlight
BR 'kwɔːtəlʌɪt, -s
AM 'kwɔrdər,laɪt, -s

quarter-line
BR 'kwɔːtəlʌɪn, -z
AM 'kwɔrdər,laɪn, -z

quarterly
BR 'kwɔːtəli
AM 'kwɔrdərli

Quartermaine
BR 'kwɔːtəmeɪn
AM 'kwɔrdər,meɪn

Quarterman
BR 'kwɔːtəmən
AM 'kwɔrdərmən

quartermaster
BR 'kwɔːtə,mɑːstə(r), 'kwɔːtə,mastə(r), -z
AM 'kwɔrdər,mæstər, -z

Quartermaster General
BR ,kwɔːtəmɑːstə 'dʒɛn(ə)rəl, ,kwɔːtəmastə +, + 'dʒɛn(ə)rl̩, -z
AM ¦kwɔrdər,mæstər 'dʒɛn(ə)rəl, -z

quartern
BR 'kwɔːt(ə)n, -z
AM 'kwɔrdərn, -z

quarterstaff
BR 'kwɔːtəstɑːf, 'kwɔːtəstaf, -s
AM 'kwɔrdər,stæf, -s

quartet
BR kwɔː'tɛt, -s
AM kwɔr'tɛt, -s

quartette
BR kwɔː'tɛt, -s
AM kwɔr'tɛt, -s

quartic
BR 'kwɔːtɪk, -s
AM 'kwɔrdɪk, -s

quartile
BR 'kwɔːtʌɪl, -z
AM 'kwɔr,taɪl, 'kwɔrdl, -z

4to
quarto
BR 'kwɔːtəʊ
AM 'kwɔrdoʊ

quarto
BR 'kwɔːtəʊ, -z
AM 'kwɔrdoʊ, -z

quartz
BR kwɔːts
AM kwɔrts

quartzite
BR 'kwɔːtsʌɪt
AM 'kwɔrt,saɪt

quasar
BR 'kweɪzɑː(r), -z
AM 'kweɪ,zɑr, -z

quash
BR kwɒʃ, -ɨz, -ɪŋ, -t
AM kwɔʃ, kwɑʃ, -əz, -ɪŋ, -t

quasi
BR 'kweɪzʌɪ, 'kwɑːzi
AM 'kwɑzi, 'kweɪ,zaɪ

Quasimodo
BR ,kwɒzɪ'məʊdəʊ, ,kwɑːzɪ'məʊdəʊ, ,kwazɪ'məʊdəʊ
AM ,kwɑzi'moʊ,doʊ

quassia
BR 'kwɒʃ(ɪ)ə(*r*), 'kwaʃ(ɪ)ə(*r*), 'kwasɪə(*r*), -z
AM 'kwɑʃ(i)ə, 'kwɑsiə, -z

quatercentenary
BR ,kwatəsɛn'tiːn(ə)r|i, ,kwatəsɛn'tɛn(ə)r|i, ,kwɒtəsɛn'tiːn(ə)r|i, ,kwɒtəsɛn'tɛn(ə)r|i, ,kwatə'sɛntɪnər|i, ,kwɒtə'sɛntɪnər|i, -ɪz
AM ¦kwɑdərsɛn'tɛnəri, ¦kwɑdər'sɛntn,ɛri, -z

Quatermass
BR 'kweɪtəmas
AM 'kweɪtər,mæs

quaternary
BR kwə'təːn(ə)r|i, -ɪz
AM 'kwɑdər,nɛri, -z

quaternion
BR kwə'təːnɪən, -z
AM kwə'tərniən, kwɑ'tɛrniən, -z

quaternity
BR kwə'təːnɪt|i, -ɪz
AM kwɑ'tərnədi, -z

quatorzain
BR 'katəzeɪn, -z
AM kə'tɔr,zeɪn, 'kædər,zeɪn, kə'tɔrzən, -z

quatorze
BR kə'tɔːz, -ɨz
AM kə'tɔ(ə)rz, -əz

quatrain
BR 'kwɒtreɪn, -z
AM 'kwɑ,treɪn, -z

quatrefoil
BR 'katrəfɔɪl, -z
AM 'kædər,fɔɪl, 'kætrə,fɔɪl, -z

quatrillion
BR kwɒ'trɪljən, kwə'trɪljən, -z
AM kwɑ'trɪljən, -z

Quattro
BR 'kwɒtrəʊ, 'kwatrəʊ, -z
AM 'kwɑtroʊ, -z

quattrocentist
BR ,kwatrə(ʊ)'tʃɛntɪst, ,kwɒtrə(ʊ)'tʃɛntɪst, -s
AM ,kwɑ,troʊ'(t)ʃɛn(t)əst, -s

quattrocento
BR ,kwatrə(ʊ)'tʃɛntəʊ, ,kwɒtrə(ʊ)'tʃɛntəʊ
AM ,kwɑ,troʊ'(t)ʃɛntoʊ

quaver
BR 'kweɪv|ə(r), -əz, -(ə)rɪŋ, -əd
AM 'kweɪv|ər, -ərz, -(ə)rɪŋ, -ərd

quaveriness
BR 'kweɪv(ə)rɪnɪs
AM 'kweɪv(ə)rinɨs

quaveringly
BR 'kweɪv(ə)rɪŋli
AM 'kweɪv(ə)rɪŋli

quavery
BR 'kweɪv(ə)ri
AM 'kweɪv(ə)ri

quay
BR kiː, -z
AM ki, -z

quayage
BR 'kiː|ɪdʒ, -ɨdʒɨz
AM 'kiɪdʒ, -ɨz

Quayle
BR kweɪl
AM kweɪl

quayside
BR 'kiːsʌɪd
AM 'ki,saɪd

quean
BR kwiːn, -z
AM kwin, -z

queasily
BR 'kwiːzɪli
AM 'kwizɨli

queasiness
BR 'kwiːzɪnɪs
AM 'kwizinɨs

queasy
BR 'kwiːzi
AM 'kwizi

Québec
BR kwɪ'bɛk
AM k(w)ə'bɛk, keɪ'bɛk
FR kebɛk

Quebecer
BR kwɪ'bɛkə(r), -z
AM k(w)ə'bɛkər, keɪ'bɛkər, -z

Quebecker
BR kwɪ'bɛkə(r), -z
AM k(w)ə'bɛkər, keɪ'bɛkər, -z

Québecois
BR ˌkeɪbɛ'kwɑː(r)
AM ˌkeɪbɛ'kwɑ
FR kebekwa

quebracho
BR keɪ'brɑːtʃəʊ, kɪ'brɑːtʃəʊ, -z
AM keɪ'brɑtʃoʊ, kə'brɑtʃoʊ, -z

Quechua
BR 'kɛtʃwə(r)
AM 'kɛtʃwə

Quechuan
BR 'kɛtʃwən, -z
AM 'kɛtʃwən, -z

queen
BR kwiːn, -z, -ɪŋ, -d
AM kwin, -z, -ɪŋ, -d

Queenborough
BR 'kwiːnb(ə)rə(r)
AM 'kwinˌbərə

queendom
BR 'kwiːndəm, -z
AM 'kwindəm, -z

queenhood
BR 'kwiːnhʊd, -z
AM 'kwinˌ(h)ʊd, -z

queenie
BR 'kwiːn|i, -ɪz
AM 'kwini, -z

queenless
BR 'kwiːnlɨs
AM 'kwinləs

queenlike
BR 'kwiːnlʌɪk
AM 'kwinˌlaɪk

queenliness
BR 'kwiːnlɪnɨs
AM 'kwinlinɨs

queenly
BR 'kwiːnl|i, -ɪə(r), -ɪɪst
AM 'kwinli, -ər, -ɨst

Queens
BR kwiːnz
AM kwinz

Queensberry
BR 'kwiːnsb(ə)ri
AM 'kwinsbəri

Queensferry
BR 'kwiːnzˌfɛri
AM 'kwinzˌfɛri

queenship
BR 'kwiːnʃɪp
AM 'kwinˌʃɪp

queen-size
BR 'kwiːnsʌɪz
AM 'kwinˌsaɪz

Queensland
BR 'kwiːnzlənd, 'kwiːnzland
AM 'kwinzlənd, 'kwinzˌlænd

Queenslander
BR 'kwiːnzləndə(r), 'kwiːnslandə(r), -z
AM 'kwinzləndər, 'kwinzˌlændər, -z

Queenstown
BR 'kwiːnztaʊn
AM 'kwinzˌtaʊn

Queensway
BR 'kwiːnzweɪ
AM 'kwinzˌweɪ

queer
BR kwɪə(r), -z, -ɪŋ, -d, -ə(r), -ɨst
AM kwɪ(ə)r, -z, -ɪŋ, -d, -ər, -ɨst

queerish
BR 'kwɪərɪʃ
AM 'kwirɪʃ

queerly
BR 'kwɪəli
AM 'kwirli

queerness
BR 'kwɪənəs
AM 'kwirnəs

quelia
BR 'kwiːlɪə(r), -z
AM 'kwiliə, -z

quell
BR kwɛl, -z, -ɪŋ, -d
AM kwɛl, -z, -ɪŋ, -d

queller
BR 'kwɛlə(r), -z
AM 'kwɛlər, -z

Quemoy
BR kɪ'mɔɪ
AM ki'mɔɪ

quench
BR kwɛn(t)ʃ, -ɨz, -ɪŋ, -t
AM kwɛn(t)ʃ, -ɨz, -ɪŋ, -t

quenchable
BR 'kwɛn(t)ʃəbl
AM 'kwɛn(t)ʃəbəl

quencher
BR 'kwɛn(t)ʃə(r), -z
AM 'kwɛn(t)ʃər, -z

quenchless
BR 'kwɛn(t)ʃləs
AM 'kwɛn(t)ʃləs

quenelle
BR kə'nɛl, -z
AM kə'nɛl, -z

Quentin
BR 'kwɛntɪn
AM 'kwɛntn

Quercia
BR 'kwəːʃə(r)
AM 'kwərʃə

querist
BR 'kwɪərɪst, -s
AM 'kwɪrəst, 'kwɛrəst, -s

quern
BR kwəːn, -z
AM kwərn, -z

querulous
BR 'kwɛr(j)ʊləs
AM 'kwɛr(j)ələs

querulously
BR 'kwɛr(j)ʊləsli
AM 'kwɛrələsli

querulousness
BR 'kwɛr(j)ʊləsnəs
AM 'kwɛrələsnəs

query
BR 'kwɪər|i, -ɪz, -ɪɪŋ, -ɪd
AM 'kwɪri, 'kwɛri, -z, -ɪŋ, -d

quest
BR kwɛst, -s, -ɪŋ, -ɨd
AM kwɛst, -s, -ɪŋ, -ɨd

Quested
BR 'kwɛstɨd
AM 'kwɛstəd

quester
BR 'kwɛstə(r), -z
AM 'kwɛstər, -z

questingly
BR 'kwɛstɪŋli
AM 'kwɛstɪŋli

question
BR 'kwɛstʃ|(ə)n, -(ə)nz, -ənɪŋ\-n̩ɪŋ, -(ə)nd
AM 'kwɛstʃ|ən, 'kwɛʃtʃ|ən, -ənz, -(ə)nɪŋ, -ənd

questionability
BR ˌkwɛstʃənə'bɪlɨti, ˌkwɛstʃn̩ə'bɪlɨti
AM ˌkwɛstʃənə'bɪlɨdi, ˌkwɛʃtʃənə'bɪlɨdi

questionable
BR 'kwɛstʃənəbl, 'kwɛstʃn̩əbl
AM 'kwɛstʃənəbəl, 'kwɛʃtʃənəbəl

questionableness
BR 'kwɛstʃənəblnəs, 'kwɛstʃn̩əblnəs
AM 'kwɛstʃənəbəlnəs

questionably
BR 'kwɛstʃənəbli, 'kwɛstʃn̩əbli
AM 'kwɛstʃənəbli

questionary
BR 'kwɛstʃən(ə)r|i, 'kwɛstʃn̩(ə)r|i, -ɪz
AM 'kwɛstʃənɛri, -z

questioner
BR 'kwɛstʃənə(r), 'kwɛstʃn̩ə(r), -z
AM 'kwɛstʃənər, -z

questioningly
BR 'kwɛstʃənɪŋli, 'kwɛstʃn̩ɪŋ
AM 'kwɛstʃənɪŋli

questionless
BR 'kwɛstʃ(ə)nləs
AM 'kwɛstʃənl, 'kwɛstʃənləs

questionnaire
BR ˌk(w)ɛstʃə'nɛː(r), -z
AM ˌkwɛstʃə'nɛ(ə)r, ˌkwɛʃtʃə'nɛ(ə)r, -z

questor
BR 'kwɛstə(r), 'kwɛstɔː(r), 'kwiːstə(r), -z
AM 'kwɛstər, -z

Quetta
BR 'kwɛtə(r)
AM 'kwɛdə

quetzal
BR 'k(w)ɛtsl, kɛt'sal, -z
AM kɛt'sɑl, -z

Quetzalcóatl
BR 'kɛtslkəʊ'atl
AM ˌkɛtzəlkoʊ'ɑtl

queue
BR kjuː, -z, -ɪŋ, -d
AM kju, -z, -ɪŋ, -d

Quezon
BR 'keɪzɒn, 'keɪsɒn
AM 'keɪzɑn

quibble
BR 'kwɪb|l, -lz, -l̩ɪŋ\-lɪŋ, -ld
AM 'kwɪbəl, -əlz, -(ə)lɪŋ, -əld

quibbler
BR 'kwɪbl̩ə(r), 'kwɪblə(r), -z
AM 'kwɪb(ə)lər, -z

quibblingly
BR 'kwɪbl̩ɪŋli, 'kwɪblɪŋli
AM 'kwɪb(ə)lɪŋli

quiche
BR kiːʃ, -ɨz
AM kiʃ, -ɨz

Quichua
BR 'kɪtʃwə(r)
AM 'kɪtʃwə

quick
BR kwɪk, -ə(r), -ɨst
AM kwɪk, -ər, -ɨst

quicken
BR 'kwɪk|(ə)n, -(ə)nz, -n̩ɪŋ\-(ə)nɪŋ, -(ə)nd
AM 'kwɪk|ən, -ənz, -(ə)nɪŋ, -ənd

quickie
BR 'kwɪk|i, -ɪz
AM 'kwɪki, -z

quicklime
BR 'kwɪklʌɪm
AM 'kwɪkˌlaɪm

quickly
BR 'kwɪkli
AM 'kwɪkli

quickness
BR 'kwɪknɨs
AM 'kwɪknəs

quicksand
BR 'kwɪksand, -z
AM 'kwɪkˌsænd, -z

quickset
BR ˌkwɪk'sɛt
AM 'kwɪkˌsɛt

quicksilver
BR 'kwɪkˌsɪlvə(r)
AM 'kwɪkˌsɪlvər

quickstep
BR ˈkwɪkstɛp, -s
AM ˈkwɪkˌstɛp, -s
quickthorn
BR ˈkwɪkθɔːn, -z
AM ˈkwɪkˌθɔ(ə)rn, -z
quick-witted
BR ˌkwɪkˈwɪtɨd
AM ¦kwɪk¦wɪdɨd
quick-wittedness
BR ˌkwɪkˈwɪtɨdnɨs
AM ¦kwɪk¦wɪdɨdnɨs
quid
BR kwɪd, -z
AM kwɪd, -z
quiddity
BR ˈkwɪdɪt|i, -ɪz
AM ˈkwɪdɨdi, -z
quidnunc
BR ˈkwɪdnʌŋk, -s
AM ˈkwɪdˌnəŋk, -s
quid pro quo
BR ˌkwɪd prəʊ ˈkwəʊ, -z
AM ¦kwɪd ˌproʊ ¦kwoʊ, -z
quiescence
BR kwɪˈɛsns, kwʌɪˈɛsns
AM kwaɪˈɛsəns, kwiˈɛsəns
quiescency
BR kwɪˈɛsnsi, kwʌɪˈɛsnsi
AM ˌkwaɪˈɛsənsi, kwiˈɛsənsi
quiescent
BR kwɪˈɛsnt, kwʌɪˈɛsnt
AM kwaɪˈɛsənt, kwiˈɛsənt
quiescently
BR kwɪˈɛsntli, kwʌɪˈɛsntli
AM ˌkwaɪˈɛsn(t)li, kwiˈɛsn(t)li
quiet
BR ˈkwʌɪət, -s, -ɪŋ, -ɨd, -ə(r), -ɨst
AM ˈkwaɪə|t, -ts, -dɪŋ, -dəd, -dər, -dəst
quieten
BR ˈkwʌɪət|n, -nz, -n̩ɪŋ\-nɪŋ, -nd
AM ˈkwaɪətn, -z, -ɪŋ, -d
quietism
BR ˈkwʌɪɨtɪz(ə)m
AM ˈkwaɪəˌtɪzəm
quietist
BR ˈkwʌɪɨtɪst, -s
AM ˈkwaɪədəst, -s
quietistic
BR ˌkwʌɪɨˈtɪstɪk
AM ˌkwaɪəˈtɪstɪk
quietly
BR ˈkwʌɪətli
AM ˈkwaɪətli
quietness
BR ˈkwʌɪətnəs
AM ˈkwaɪətnəs
quietude
BR ˈkwʌɪɨtjuːd, ˈkwʌɪɨtʃuːd
AM ˈkwaɪəˌt(j)ud
quietus
BR kwʌɪˈiːtəs, kwʌɪˈeɪtəs, kwɪˈeɪtəs
AM ˈkwaɪədəs
quiff
BR kwɪf, -s
AM kwɪf, -s
Quigley
BR ˈkwɪgli
AM ˈkwɪgli
quill
BR kwɪl, -z
AM kwɪl, -z
quill-coverts
BR ˈkwɪlˌkʌvəts
AM ˈkwɪlˌkəvərts
Quiller-Couch
BR ˌkwɪləːˈkuːtʃ
AM ˌkwɪlərˈkaʊtʃ
quilling
BR ˈkwɪlɪŋ
AM ˈkwɪlɪŋ
Quilp
BR kwɪlp
AM kwɪlp
quilt
BR kwɪlt, -s, -ɪŋ, -ɨd
AM kwɪlt, -s, -ɪŋ, -ɨd
quilter
BR ˈkwɪltə(r), -z
AM ˈkwɪltər, -z
quim
BR kwɪm, -z
AM kwɪm, -z
quin
BR kwɪn, -z
AM kwɪn, -z
quinacrine
BR ˈkwɪnəkriːn, ˈkwɪnəkrɪn
AM ˈkwɪnəˌkrɪn
quinary
BR ˈkwʌɪn(ə)ri
AM ˈkwaɪˌnɛri
quinate
BR ˈkwʌɪneɪt
AM ˈkwaɪˌneɪt
quince
BR kwɪns, -ɨz
AM kwɪns, -ɨz
quincentenary
BR ˌkwɪnsɛnˈtiːn(ə)r|i, ˌkwɪnsɛnˈtɛn(ə)r|i, -ɪz
AM ˌkwɪnˌsɛnˈtɛnəri, -z
quincentennial
BR ˌkwɪnsɛnˈtɛnɪəl
AM ˌkwɪnˌsɛnˈtɛniəl
Quincey
BR ˈkwɪnsi
AM ˈkwɪnsi
quincuncial
BR kwɪnˈkʌnʃl, kwɪŋˈkʌnʃl
AM ˌkwɪnˈkənʃl
quincuncially
BR kwɪnˈkʌnʃl̩i, kwɪnˈkʌnʃəli, kwɪŋˈkʌnʃl̩i, kwɪŋˈkʌnʃəli
AM ˌkwɪnˈkənʃəli
quincunx
BR ˈkwɪnkʌŋks, ˈkwɪŋkʌŋks, -ɨz
AM ˈkwɪnˌkəŋ(k)s, -ɨz
quinella
BR kwɪˈnɛlə(r), -z
AM kwɪˈnɛlə, -z
quingentenary
BR ˌkwɪn(d)ʒ(ə)nˈtiːn(ə)r|i, ˌkwɪn(d)ʒ(ə)nˈtɛn(ə)r|i, -ɪz
AM ˌkwɪnˌgɛnˈtɛnəri, -z
quinine
BR ˈkwɪniːn, kwɪˈniːn
AM ˈkwaɪˌnaɪn
Quink®
BR kwɪŋk
AM kwɪŋk
Quinlan
BR ˈkwɪnlən
AM ˈkwɪnlən
Quinn
BR kwɪn
AM kwɪn
quinol
BR ˈkwɪnɒl
AM ˈkwɪnɔl, ˈkwɪnɑl
quinoline
BR ˈkwɪnəliːn, ˈkwɪnl̩iːn, ˈkwɪnəlɪn, ˈkwɪnl̩ɪn, -z
AM ˈkwɪnəlɪn, -z
quinone
BR ˈkwɪnəʊn, -z
AM ˈkwɪnoʊn, -z
quinquagenarian
BR ˌkwɪŋkwədʒɪˈnɛːrɪən, -z
AM ˌkwɪŋkwəˌdʒəˈnɛriən, -z
quinquagenary
BR kwɪŋˈkwadʒɪn(ə)r|i, kwɪnˈkwadʒɪn(ə)r|i, -ɪz
AM ˌkwɪŋˈkwædʒənɛri, -z
Quinquagesima
BR ˌkwɪŋkwəˈdʒɛsɪmə(r)
AM ˌkwɪŋkwəˈdʒɛsəmə
quinquelateral
BR ˌkwɪŋkwɪˈlat(ə)rəl, ˌkwɪŋkwɪˈlat(ə)rl̩
AM ˌkwɪŋkwəˈlædərəl
quinquennia
BR kwɪŋˈkwɛnɪə(r), kwɪnˈkwɛnɪə(r)
AM kwɪŋˈkwɛniə
quinquennial
BR kwɪŋˈkwɛnɪəl, kwɪnˈkwɛnɪəl
AM kwɪŋˈkwɛniəl
quinquennially
BR kwɪŋˈkwɛnɪəli, kwɪnˈkwɛnɪəli
AM ˈkwɪŋkwɛniəli
quinquennium
BR kwɪŋˈkwɛnɪəm, kwɪnˈkwɛnɪəm, -z
AM kwɪŋˈkwɛniəm, -z
quinquereme
BR ˈkwɪŋkwɪriːm, -z
AM ˈkwɪŋkwəˌrim, -z
quinquevalent
BR ˌkwɪŋkwɪˈveɪlənt, ˌkwɪŋkwɪˈveɪln̩t
AM ˌkwɪŋkwəˈveɪlənt
quinsied
BR ˈkwɪnzɪd
AM ˈkwɪnzid
quinsy
BR ˈkwɪnzi
AM ˈkwɪnzi
quint
BR k(w)ɪnt, -s
AM kwɪnt, -s
quinta
BR ˈk(w)ɪntə(r), -z
AM ˈkwɪn(t)ə, -z
quintain
BR ˈkwɪntɪn, -z
AM ˈkwɪntn, -z
quintal
BR ˈkwɪntl, -z
AM ˈkwɪn(t)l, -z
quintan
BR ˈkwɪntən, -z
AM ˈkwɪntn, -z
quinte
BR kãt
AM kwɪnt
quintessence
BR kwɪnˈtɛsns
AM kwɪnˈtɛsəns
quintessential
BR ˌkwɪntɪˈsɛnʃl
AM ¦kwɪn(t)əˈsɛn(t)ʃəl
quintessentially
BR ˌkwɪntɪˈsɛnʃl̩i, ˌkwɪntɪˈsɛnʃəli
AM kwɪn(t)əˈsɛn(t)ʃəli
quintet
BR kwɪnˈtɛt, -s
AM kwɪnˈtɛt, -s
quintile
BR ˈkwɪnt(ɪ)l, ˈkwɪntʌɪl, -z
AM ːkwɪnˌtaɪl, ˈkwɪntl, -z
Quintilian
BR kwɪnˈtɪlɪən

AM kwɪn'tɪljən, kwɪn'tɪliən
quintillion
BR kwɪn'tɪljən
AM kwɪn'tɪljən
quintillionth
BR kwɪn'tɪljənθ
AM kwɪn'tɪljənθ
Quintin
BR 'kwɪntɪn
AM 'kwɪntn
Quinton
BR 'kwɪntən
AM 'kwɪn(t)ən
quintuple
BR 'kwɪntjʊp|l, 'kwɪntʃʊp|l, kwɪn'tjuːp|l, kwɪn'tʃuːp|l, -lz, -l̩ɪŋ\-əlɪŋ, -ld
AM kwɪn't(j)up|əl, kwɪn'təp|əl, -əlz, -(ə)lɪŋ, -əld
quintuplet
BR 'kwɪntjʊplɪt, 'kwɪntʃʊplɪt, kwɪn'tjuːplɪt, kwɪn'tʃuːplɪt, -s
AM kwɪn'təplət, kwɪn't(j)uplət, -s
quintuplicate
BR kwɪn'tjuːplɪkeɪt, kwɪn'tʃuːplɪkeɪt, -s, -ɪŋ, -ɪd
AM kwɪn'təplə,keɪ|t, kwɪn't(j)uplə,keɪ|t, -ts, -dɪŋ, -dɪd
quintuplication
BR kwɪn,tjuːplɪ'keɪʃn, kwɪn,tʃuːplɪ'keɪʃn, -z
AM kwɪn,təplə'keɪʃən, kwɪn,t(j)uplə'keɪʃən, -z
quintuply
BR 'kwɪntjʊpli, 'kwɪntʃʊpli
AM kwɪn't(j)up(ə)li
Quintus
BR 'kwɪntəs
AM 'kwɪn(t)əs
quip
BR kwɪp, -s, -ɪŋ, -t
AM kwɪp, -s, -ɪŋ, -t
quipster
BR 'kwɪpstə(r), -z
AM 'kwɪpstər, -z
quipu
BR 'kiːpuː, 'kwɪpuː, -z
AM 'kipu, 'kwɪpu, -z
quire
BR 'kwʌɪə(r), -z
AM 'kwaɪ(ə)r, -z
Quirinus
BR kwɪ'rʌɪnəs
AM kwə'raɪnəs
quirk
BR kwəːk, -s
AM kwərk, -s
Quirke
BR kwəːk
AM kwərk
quirkily
BR 'kwəːkɪli
AM 'kwərkəli
quirkiness
BR 'kwəːkɪnɪs
AM 'kwərkinɪs
quirkish
BR 'kwəːkɪʃ
AM 'kwərkɪʃ
quirky
BR 'kwəːk|i, -ɪə(r), -ɪɪst
AM 'kwərki, -ər, -ɪst
quirt
BR kwəːt, -s
AM kwərt, -s
quisling
BR 'kwɪzlɪŋ, -z
AM 'kwɪzlɪŋ, -z
quislingite
BR 'kwɪzlɪŋʌɪt, -s
AM 'kwɪzlɪŋ,aɪt, -s
quit
BR kwɪt, -s, -ɪŋ, -ɪd
AM kwɪ|t, -ts, -dɪŋ, -dɪd
quitch
BR kwɪtʃ
AM kwɪtʃ
quitclaim
BR 'kwɪtkleɪm, -z, -ɪŋ, -d
AM 'kwɪt,kleɪm, -z, -ɪŋ, -d
quite
BR kwʌɪt
AM kwaɪt
Quito
BR 'kiːtəʊ
AM 'kidoʊ
quitrent
BR 'kwɪtrɛnt, -s
AM 'kwɪt,rɛnt, -s
quittance
BR 'kwɪt(ə)ns, -ɪz
AM 'kwɪtns, -ɪz
quitter
BR 'kwɪtə(r), -z
AM 'kwɪdər, -z
quiver
BR 'kwɪv|ə(r), -əz, -(ə)rɪŋ, -əd
AM 'kwɪv|ər, -ərz, -(ə)rɪŋ, -ərd
quiverful
BR 'kwɪvəfʊl, -z
AM 'kwɪvər,fʊl, -z
quivering
BR 'kwɪv(ə)rɪŋ, -z
AM 'kwɪvərɪŋ, -z
quiveringly
BR 'kwɪv(ə)rɪŋli
AM 'kwɪvərɪŋli
quivery
BR 'kwɪv(ə)ri
AM 'kwɪv(ə)ri
qui vive
BR ,kiː 'viːv
AM ,ki 'viv
Quixote
BR 'kwɪksət, 'kwɪksəʊt, kɪ'həʊti
AM ki'(h)oʊdi, ki'hoʊ,teɪ
quixotic
BR kwɪk'sɒtɪk
AM kwɪk'sɑdɪk
quixotically
BR kwɪk'sɒtɪkli
AM kwɪk'sɑdək(ə)li
quixotise
BR 'kwɪksətʌɪz, -ɪz, -ɪŋ, -d
AM 'kwɪksə,taɪz, -ɪz, -ɪŋ, -d
quixotism
BR 'kwɪksətɪz(ə)m
AM 'kwɪksə,tɪzəm
quixotize
BR 'kwɪksətʌɪz, -ɪz, -ɪŋ, -d
AM 'kwɪksə,taɪz, -ɪz, -ɪŋ, -d
quixotry
BR 'kwɪksɒtri
AM 'kwɪksətri
quiz
BR kwɪz, -ɪz, -ɪŋ, -d
AM kwɪz, -ɪz, -ɪŋ, -d
quizmaster
BR 'kwɪz,mɑːstə(r), 'kwɪz,mastə(r), -z
AM 'kwɪz,mæstər, -z
quizshow
BR 'kwɪzʃəʊ, -z
AM 'kwɪz,ʃoʊ, -z
quizzer
BR 'kwɪzə(r), -z
AM 'kwɪzər, -z
quizzical
BR 'kwɪzɪkl
AM 'kwɪzəkəl
quizzicality
BR ,kwɪzɪ'kalɪti
AM ,kwɪzɪ'kælədi
quizzically
BR 'kwɪzɪkli
AM 'kwɪzək(ə)li
quizzicalness
BR 'kwɪzɪklnəs
AM 'kwɪzɪkəlnəs
Qum
BR kʊm
AM kʊm
Qumran
BR kʊm'rɑːn
AM kʊm'ræn
quod
BR kwɒd, -z, -ɪŋ, -ɪd
AM kwɑd, -z, -ɪŋ, -ɪd
quodlibet
BR 'kwɒdlɪbɛt, -s
AM 'kwɑdlə,bɛt, -s
quodlibetarian
BR ,kwɒdlɪbɪ'tɛːrɪən, -z
AM ,kwɑdləbə'tɛriən, -z
quodlibetical
BR ,kwɒdlɪ'bɛtɪkl
AM ,kwɑdlə'bɛdəkəl
quodlibetically
BR ,kwɒdlɪ'bɛtɪkli
AM ,kwɑdlə'bɛdək(ə)li
quoin
BR k(w)ɔɪn, -z, -ɪŋ, -d
AM k(w)ɔɪn, -z, -ɪŋ, -d
quoit
BR k(w)ɔɪt, -s
AM k(w)ɔɪt, kweɪt, -s
quokka
BR 'kwɒkə(r), -z
AM 'kwɑkə, -z
quondam
BR 'kwɒndam, 'kwɒndəm
AM 'kwɑndəm, 'kwɑn,dæm, 'kwɑn,dɑm
Quonset®
BR 'kwɒnsɪt, -s
AM 'kwɔnsət, 'kwɑnsət, -s
quorate
BR 'kwɔːreɪt
AM 'kwɔ,reɪt, 'kwɑ,reɪt
Quorn®
BR kwɔːn
AM kwɔ(ə)rn
quorum
BR 'kwɔːrəm, -z
AM 'kwɔrəm, -z
Quosh
BR kwɒʃ
AM kwɔʃ, kwɑʃ
quota
BR 'kwəʊtə(r), -z
AM 'kwoʊdə, -z
quotability
BR ,kwəʊtə'bɪlɪti
AM ,kwoʊdə'bɪlɪdi
quotable
BR 'kwəʊtəbl
AM 'kwoʊdəbəl
quotation
BR kwə(ʊ)'teɪʃn, -z
AM ,kwoʊ'teɪʃən, -z
quotative
BR 'kwəʊtətɪv
AM 'kwoʊdədɪv
quote
BR kwəʊt, -s, -ɪŋ, -ɪd
AM kwoʊ|t, -ts, -dɪŋ, -dəd
quoth
BR kwəʊθ
AM kwoʊθ

quotha
BR 'kwəʊθə(*r*)
AM 'kwoʊθə

quotidian
BR kwə'tɪdɪən, kwɒ'tɪdɪən
AM kwoʊ'tɪdiən

quotient
BR 'kwəʊʃnt, -s
AM 'kwoʊʃənt, -s

Quran
BR kɔː'rɑːn, kə'rɑːn
AM kɔ'ræn, kə'ræn

Quranic
BR kɔː'ranɪk, kə'ranɪk
AM kɔ'rænɪk, kə'rænɪk

q.v.
BR ˌkjuː'viː
AM ˌkju'vi

Qwaqwa
BR 'kwɑːkwə(*r*)
AM 'kwɑkwə

QWERTY
BR 'kwəːti
AM 'kwərdi

Rr

r
BR ɑː(r), -z
AM ɑr, -z

Raasey
BR 'rɑːseɪ
AM 'rɑseɪ

Rabat
BR rə'bat, rə'bɑːt
AM rə'bɑt

Rabaul
BR rə'baʊl
AM rɑ'baʊl

rabbet
BR 'rab|ɪt, -ɪts, -ɪtɪŋ, -ɪtɪd
AM 'ræbə|t, -ts, -dɪŋ, -dəd

rabbi
BR 'rabʌɪ, -z
AM 'ræˌbaɪ, -z

Rabbie
BR 'rabi
AM 'rɑbi

rabbin
BR 'rabɪn, -z
AM 'ræbən, -z

rabbinate
BR 'rabɪnət, 'rabɪneɪt, -s
AM 'ræbəˌneɪt, 'ræbənət, -s

rabbinic
BR rə'bɪnɪk
AM rə'bɪnɪk

rabbinical
BR rə'bɪnɪkl
AM rə'bɪnəkəl

rabbinically
BR rə'bɪnɪkli
AM rə'bɪnək(ə)li

rabbinism
BR 'rabɪnɪz(ə)m
AM 'ræbəˌnɪzəm

rabbinist
BR 'rabɪnɪst, -s
AM 'ræbənəst, -s

rabbit
BR 'rab|ɪt, -ɪts, -ɪtɪŋ, -ɪtɪd
AM 'ræbə|t, -ts, -dɪŋ, -dəd

rabbity
BR 'rabɪti
AM 'ræbədi

rabble
BR 'rabl, -z
AM 'ræbəl, -z

rabble-rouser
BR 'rablˌraʊzə(r), -z
AM 'ræbəlˌraʊzər, -z

Rabelais
BR 'rabəleɪ
AM 'ræbəˌleɪ, ˌræbə'leɪ

Rabelaisian
BR ˌrabə'leɪzɪən, ˌrabə'leɪʒn
AM ˌræbə'leɪziən, ˌræbə'leɪʒən

rabi
BR 'rabiː, 'rʌbiː
AM 'rɑbi

rabid
BR 'rabɪd, 'reɪbɪd
AM 'ræbəd

rabidity
BR rə'bɪdɪti
AM rə'bɪdɪdi

rabidly
BR 'rabɪdli, 'reɪbɪdli
AM 'ræbədli

rabidness
BR 'rabɪdnɪs, 'reɪbɪdnɪs
AM 'ræbədnəs

rabies
BR 'reɪbiːz, 'reɪbɪz
AM 'reɪbiz

Rabin
BR ra'biːn
AM rɑ'bin

Rabindranath
BR rə'bɪndrənɑːθ
AM rə'bɪndrənəθ

Rabinowitz
BR rə'bɪnəwɪts, rə'bɪnəvɪts
AM rə'bɪnəˌwɪts

raccoon
BR rə'kuːn, ra'kuːn, -z
AM ræ'kun, rə'kun, -z

race
BR reɪs, -ɪz, -ɪŋ, -t
AM reɪs, -ɪz, -ɪŋ, -t

racecard
BR 'reɪskɑːd, -z
AM 'reɪsˌkɑrd, -z

racecourse
BR 'reɪskɔːs, -ɪz
AM 'reɪsˌkɔ(ə)rs, -əz

racegoer
BR 'reɪsˌgəʊə(r), -z
AM 'reɪsˌgoʊər, -z

racegoing
BR 'reɪsˌgəʊɪŋ
AM 'reɪsˌgoʊɪŋ

racehorse
BR 'reɪshɔːs, -ɪz
AM 'reɪsˌ(h)ɔ(ə)rs, -əz

racemate
BR 'reɪsmeɪt, -s
AM 'reɪsˌmeɪt, -s

raceme
BR 'rasiːm, rə'siːm, ra'siːm, -z
AM reɪ'sim, rə'sim, -z

racemic
BR rə'siːmɪk, ra'siːmɪk
AM reɪ'simɪk, rə'simɪk

racemise
BR 'rasɪmʌɪz, -ɪz, -ɪŋ, -d
AM 'ræsəˌmaɪz, reɪ'siˌmaɪz, rə'siˌmaɪz, -ɪz, -ɪŋ, -d

racemize
BR 'rasɪmʌɪz, -ɪz, -ɪŋ, -d
AM 'ræsəˌmaɪz, reɪ'siˌmaɪz, rə'siˌmaɪz, -ɪz, -ɪŋ, -d

racemose
BR 'rasɪməʊs
AM 'ræsəˌmoʊs, 'ræsəˌmoʊz

racer
BR 'reɪsə(r), -z
AM 'reɪsər, -z

racetrack
BR 'reɪstrak, -s
AM 'reɪsˌtræk, -s

raceway
BR 'reɪsweɪ, -z
AM 'reɪsˌweɪ, -z

Rachael
BR 'reɪtʃl
AM 'reɪtʃəl

Rachel
BR 'reɪtʃl
AM 'reɪtʃəl

rachel
BR rə'ʃɛl
AM rə'ʃɛl

rachidial
BR rə'kɪdɪəl
AM rə'kɪdiəl

rachis
BR 'reɪkɪs
AM 'reɪkɪs

rachitic
BR rə'kɪtɪk, ra'kɪtɪk
AM rə'kɪdɪk

rachitis
BR rə'kʌɪtɪs, ra'kʌɪtɪs
AM rə'kaɪdɪs

Rachmaninov
BR rak'manɪnɒf
AM rɑk'mɑnənɔf, rɑk'mɑnənɑf

Rachmanism
BR 'rakmənɪz(ə)m
AM 'rɑkməˌnɪzəm

racial
BR 'reɪʃl
AM 'reɪʃəl

racialism
BR 'reɪʃəlɪz(ə)m, 'reɪʃl̩ɪz(ə)m
AM 'reɪʃəˌlɪzəm

racialist
BR 'reɪʃəlɪst, 'reɪʃl̩ɪst, -s
AM 'reɪʃələst, -s

racially
BR 'reɪʃl̩i, 'reɪʃəli
AM 'reɪʃəli

racily
BR 'reɪsɪli
AM 'reɪsɪli

Racine
BR ra'siːn
AM rə'sin

raciness
BR 'reɪsɪnɪs
AM 'reɪsinɪs

racism
BR 'reɪsɪz(ə)m
AM 'reɪˌsɪzəm

racist
BR 'reɪsɪst, -s
AM 'reɪsɪst, -s

rack
BR rak, -s, -ɪŋ, -t
AM ræk, -s, -ɪŋ, -t

rack-and-pinion
BR ˌrak(ə)n(d)'pɪnjən
AM ˌrækən'pɪniən

racket
BR 'rak|ɪt, -ɪts, -ɪtɪŋ, -ɪtɪd
AM 'rækə|t, -ts, -dɪŋ, -dəd

racketball
BR 'rakɪtbɔːl
AM 'rækətˌbɔl, 'rækətˌbɑl

racketeer
BR ˌrakɪ'tɪə(r), -z, -ɪŋ
AM ˌrækə'tɪ(ə)r, -z, -ɪŋ

rackety
BR 'rakɪti
AM 'rækədi

Rackham
BR 'rakəm
AM 'rækəm

raclette
BR ra'klɛt, -s
AM rə'klɛt, -s

racon
BR 'reɪkɒn, -z
AM 'reɪˌkɑn, 'reɪkən, -z

raconteur
BR ˌrakɒn'təː(r), -z
AM ˌrɑˌkɑn'tər, -z

raconteuse
BR ˌrakɒn'təːz
AM ˌrɑˌkɑn'təz

racoon
BR rə'kuːn, -z
AM ræ'kun, rə'kun, -z

racquet
BR 'rakɪt, -s
AM 'rækət, -s

racquetball
BR 'rakɪtbɔːl
AM 'rækətˌbɔl, 'rækətˌbɑl

racy
BR 'reɪs|i, -ɪə(r), -ɪɪst
AM 'reɪsi, -ər, -ɪst

rad
BR rad, -z

AM ræd, -z
RADA
BR 'rɑːdə(r)
AM 'rɑdə
radar
BR 'reɪdɑː(r)
AM 'reɪˌdɑr
Radcliff
BR 'radklɪf
AM 'rædˌklɪf
Radcliffe
BR 'radklɪf
AM 'rædˌklɪf
Radclyffe
BR 'radklɪf
AM 'rædˌklɪf
raddle
BR 'rad|l, -lz, -l̩ɪŋ\-lɪŋ, -ld
AM 'ræd|əl, -əlz, -(ə)lɪŋ, -əld
Radetsky
BR rə'dɛtski
AM rə'dɛtski
Radford
BR 'radfəd
AM 'rædfərd
radial
BR 'reɪdɪəl
AM 'reɪdiəl
radially
BR 'reɪdɪəli
AM 'reɪdiəli
radian
BR 'reɪdɪən, -z
AM 'reɪdiən, -z
radiance
BR 'reɪdɪəns
AM 'reɪdiəns
radiancy
BR 'reɪdɪəns|i, -ɪz
AM 'reɪdiənsi, -z
radiant
BR 'reɪdɪənt
AM 'reɪdiənt
radiantly
BR 'reɪdɪəntli
AM 'reɪdiən(t)li
radiate
BR 'reɪdɪeɪt, -s, -ɪŋ, -ɪd
AM 'reɪdiˌeɪ|t, -ts, -dɪŋ, -dɪd
radiately
BR 'reɪdɪeɪ(t)li
AM 'reɪdiɪ(t)li
radiation
BR ˌreɪdɪ'eɪʃn, -z
AM ˌreɪdi'eɪʃən, -z
radiational
BR ˌreɪdɪ'eɪʃn̩(ə)l, ˌreɪdɪ'eɪʃən(ə)l
AM ˌreɪdi'eɪʃ(ə)nəl
radiationally
BR ˌreɪdɪ'eɪʃn̩əli, ˌreɪdɪ'eɪʃn̩li, ˌreɪdɪ'eɪʃənli, ˌreɪdɪ'eɪʃ(ə)nəli
AM ˌreɪdi'eɪʃ(ə)nəli
radiative
BR 'reɪdɪətɪv
AM 'reɪdiədɪv, 'reɪdiˌeɪdɪv
radiator
BR 'reɪdɪeɪtə(r), -z
AM 'reɪdiˌeɪdər, -z
radical
BR 'radɪkl, -z
AM 'rædəkəl, -z
radicalisation
BR ˌradɪkəlʌɪ'zeɪʃn, ˌradɪkl̩ʌɪ'zeɪʃn
AM ˌrædəkələ'zeɪʃən, ˌrædəkəˌlaɪ'zeɪʃən
radicalise
BR 'radɪkəlʌɪz, 'radɪkl̩ʌɪz, -ɪz, -ɪŋ, -d
AM 'rædəkəˌlaɪz, 'rædəklˌaɪz, -ɪz, -ɪŋ, -d
radicalism
BR 'radɪkəlɪz(ə)m, 'radɪkl̩ɪz(ə)m
AM 'rædəkəˌlɪzəm
radicalization
BR ˌradɪkəlʌɪ'zeɪʃn, ˌradɪkl̩ʌɪ'zeɪʃn
AM ˌrædəkələ'zeɪʃən, ˌrædəkəˌlaɪ'zeɪʃən
radicalize
BR 'radɪkəlʌɪz, 'radɪkl̩ʌɪz, -ɪz, -ɪŋ, -d
AM 'rædəkəˌlaɪz, 'rædəklˌaɪz, -ɪz, -ɪŋ, -d
radically
BR 'radɪkli
AM 'rædək(ə)li
radicalness
BR 'radɪklnəs
AM 'rædəkəlnəs
radicchio
BR ra'diːkɪəʊ
AM ræ'dɪkioʊ, rə'dɪkioʊ
Radice
BR rə'diːtʃi
AM rə'dɪtʃi
radices
BR 'radɪsiːz, 'reɪdɪsiːz
AM 'rædəˌsiz, 'reɪdəˌsiz
radicle
BR 'radɪkl, -z
AM 'rædəkəl, -z
radicular
BR ra'dɪkjʊlə(r), rə'dɪkjʊlə(r)
AM rə'dɪkjələr
radii
BR 'reɪdɪʌɪ
AM 'reɪdiˌaɪ
radio
BR 'reɪdɪəʊ, -z, -ɪŋ, -d
AM 'reɪdioʊ, -z, -ɪŋ, -d
radioactive
BR ˌreɪdɪəʊ'aktɪv
AM ¦reɪdioʊ'æktɪv
radioactively
BR ˌreɪdɪəʊ'aktɪvli
AM ¦reɪdioʊ'æktɪvli
radioactivity
BR ˌreɪdɪəʊak'tɪvɪti
AM ˌreɪdioʊæk'tɪvɪdi
radio-assay
BR ˌreɪdɪəʊə'seɪ, ˌreɪdɪəʊ'aseɪ, -z, -ɪŋ, -d
AM ¦reɪdioʊ'æˌseɪ, -z, -ɪŋ, -d
radiobiological
BR ˌreɪdɪəʊˌbʌɪə'lɒdʒɪkl
AM ¦reɪdioʊˌbaɪə'lɑdʒəkəl
radiobiologically
BR ˌreɪdɪəʊˌbʌɪə'lɒdʒɪkli
AM ¦reɪdioʊˌbaɪə'lɑdʒək(ə)li
radiobiologist
BR ˌreɪdɪəʊbʌɪ'ɒlədʒɪst, -s
AM ¦reɪdioʊˌbaɪ'ɑlədʒəst, -s
radiobiology
BR ˌreɪdɪəʊbʌɪ'ɒlədʒi
AM ¦reɪdioʊˌbaɪ'ɑlədʒi
radiocarbon
BR ˌreɪdɪəʊ'kɑːb(ə)n
AM ¦reɪdioʊ'kɑrbən
radiochemical
BR ˌreɪdɪəʊ'kɛmɪkl
AM ¦reɪdioʊ'kɛməkəl
radiochemist
BR ˌreɪdɪəʊ'kɛmɪst, -s
AM ¦reɪdioʊ'kɛməst, -s
radiochemistry
BR ˌreɪdɪəʊ'kɛmɪstri
AM ¦reɪdioʊ'kɛmɪstri
radiogenic
BR ˌreɪdɪəʊ'dʒɛnɪk
AM ¦reɪdioʊ'dʒɛnɪk
radiogenically
BR ˌreɪdɪəʊ'dʒɛnɪkli
AM ¦reɪdioʊ'dʒɛnək(ə)li
radio-goniometer
BR ˌreɪdɪəʊˌgəʊnɪ'ɒmɪtə(r), -z
AM ¦reɪdioʊˌgoʊni'ɑmədər, -z
radiogram
BR 'reɪdɪə(ʊ)gram, -z
AM 'reɪdiəˌgræm, 'reɪdioʊˌgræm, -z
radiograph
BR 'reɪdɪə(ʊ)grɑːf, 'reɪdɪə(ʊ)graf, -s
AM 'reɪdiəˌgræf, 'reɪdioʊˌgræf, -s
radiographer
BR ˌreɪdɪ'ɒgrəfə(r), -z
AM ˌreɪdi'ɑgrəfər, -z
radiographic
BR ˌreɪdɪə'grafɪk
AM ¦reɪdiə'græfɪk, ¦reɪdioʊ'græfɪk
radiographically
BR ˌreɪdɪə'grafɪkli
AM ¦reɪdiə'græfək(ə)li, ¦reɪdioʊ'græfək(ə)li
radiography
BR ˌreɪdɪ'ɒgrəfi
AM ˌreɪdi'ɑgrəfi
radioimmunology
BR ˌreɪdɪəʊˌɪmjʊ'nɒlədʒi
AM ¦reɪdioʊˌɪmjə'nɑlədʒi
radioisotope
BR ˌreɪdɪəʊ'ʌɪsətəʊp, -s
AM ¦reɪdioʊ'aɪsəˌtoʊp, -s
radioisotopic
BR ˌreɪdɪəʊˌʌɪsə'tɒpɪk
AM ¦reɪdioʊˌaɪsə'tɑpɪk
radioisotopically
BR ˌreɪdɪəʊˌʌɪsə'tɒpɪkli
AM ¦reɪdioʊˌaɪsə'tɑpək(ə)li
radiolaria
BR ˌreɪdɪə(ʊ)'lɛːrɪə(r)
AM ˌreɪdiə'lɛriə
radiolarian
BR ˌreɪdɪə(ʊ)'lɛːrɪən, -z
AM ¦reɪdiə'lɛriən, ¦reɪdioʊ'lɛriən, -z
radiolocation
BR ˌreɪdɪəʊlə(ʊ)'keɪʃn
AM ¦reɪdioʊˌloʊ'keɪʃən
radiologic
BR ˌreɪdɪə'lɒdʒɪk
AM ¦reɪdiə'lɑdʒɪk
radiological
BR ˌreɪdɪə'lɒdʒɪkl
AM ¦reɪdiə'lɑdʒəkəl
radiologist
BR ˌreɪdɪ'ɒlədʒɪst, -s
AM ˌreɪdi'ɑlədʒəst, -s
radiology
BR ˌreɪdɪ'ɒlədʒi
AM ˌreɪdi'ɑlədʒi
radiometer
BR ˌreɪdɪ'ɒmɪtə(r), -z
AM ˌreɪdi'ɑmədər, -z
radiometric
BR ˌreɪdɪə'mɛtrɪk
AM ¦reɪdiə'mɛtrɪk
radiometry
BR ˌreɪdɪ'ɒmɪtri
AM ˌreɪdi'ɑmətri
radionics
BR ˌreɪdɪ'ɒnɪks
AM ˌreɪdi'ɑnɪks
radionuclide
BR ˌreɪdɪəʊ'njuːklʌɪd, -z
AM ¦reɪdioʊ'n(j)uˌklaɪd, -z
radio-opaque
BR ˌreɪdɪəʊə(ʊ)'peɪk
AM ¦reɪdioʊˌoʊ'peɪk
radiopacity
BR ˌreɪdɪəʊə(ʊ)'pasɪti
AM ¦reɪdioʊˌoʊ'pæsədi

radiopaging
BR ˈreɪdɪəʊˌpeɪdʒɪŋ
AM ˌreɪdioʊˈpeɪdʒɪŋ

radiopaque
BR ˌreɪdɪə(ʊ)ˈpeɪk
AM ˌreɪdioʊˈpeɪk

radiophonic
BR ˌreɪdɪə(ʊ)ˈfɒnɪk
AM ˌreɪdiəˈfɑnɪk

radioscopic
BR ˌreɪdɪə(ʊ)ˈskɒpɪk
AM ˌreɪdiəˈskɑpɪk

radioscopy
BR ˌreɪdɪˈɒskəpi
AM ˌreɪdiˈɑskəpi

radiosonde
BR ˈreɪdɪə(ʊ)sɒnd, -z
AM ˈreɪdioʊˌsɑnd, -z

radiotelegraphy
BR ˌreɪdɪəʊtɪˈlɛɡrəfi
AM ˌreɪdioʊtəˈlɛɡrəfi

radiotelephone
BR ˌreɪdɪəʊˈtɛlɪfəʊn, -z
AM ˌreɪdioʊˈtɛləˌfoʊn, -z

radio-telephonic
BR ˌreɪdɪəʊˌtɛlɪˈfɒnɪk
AM ˌreɪdioʊˌtɛləˈfɑnɪk

radio-telephony
BR ˌreɪdɪəʊtɪˈlɛfəni, ˌreɪdɪəʊtɪˈlɛfn̩i
AM ˌreɪdioʊtəˈlɛfəni

radiotelex
BR ˌreɪdɪəʊˈtɛlɛks, -ɪz
AM ˌreɪdioʊˈtɛˌlɛks, -əz

radiotherapeutic
BR ˌreɪdɪəʊˌθɛrəˈpjuːtɪk
AM ˌreɪdioʊˌθɛrəˈpjudɪk

radiotherapist
BR ˌreɪdɪəʊˈθɛrəpɪst, -s
AM ˌreɪdioʊˈθɛrəpəst, -s

radiotherapy
BR ˌreɪdɪəʊˈθɛrəpi
AM ˌreɪdioʊˈθɛrəpi

radish
BR ˈrad|ɪʃ, -ɪʃɪz
AM ˈrædɪʃ, -ɪz

radium
BR ˈreɪdɪəm
AM ˈreɪdiəm

radius
BR ˈreɪdɪəs, -t
AM ˈreɪdiəs, -t

radix
BR ˈrad|ɪks, ˈreɪd|ɪks, -ɪksɪz
AM ˈrædɪks, ˈreɪdɪks, -ɪz

Radlett
BR ˈradlɪt
AM ˈrædlət

Radley
BR ˈradli
AM ˈrædli

Radner
BR ˈradnə(r)
AM ˈrædnər

Radnor
BR ˈradnə(r)
AM ˈrædnər

Radnorshire
BR ˈradnəʃ(ɪ)ə(r)
AM ˈrædnərʃɪ(ə)r

radome
BR ˈreɪdəʊm, -z
AM ˈreɪˌdoʊm, -z

radon
BR ˈreɪdɒn
AM ˈreɪˌdɑn

Radox®
BR ˈreɪdɒks
AM ˈreɪˌdɑks

radula
BR ˈradjʉlə(*r*), ˈradʒʉlə(*r*)
AM ˈrædʒələ

radulae
BR ˈradjʉliː, ˈradʒʉliː
AM ˈrædʒəli, ˈrædʒəˌlaɪ

radular
BR ˈradjʉlə(r), ˈradʒʉlə(r)
AM ˈrædʒələr

Rae
BR reɪ
AM reɪ

Raeburn
BR ˈreɪbəːn
AM ˈreɪˌbərn

Rael-Brook
BR ˈreɪlbrʊk, ˌreɪlˈbrʊk
AM ˈreɪlˌbrʊk

Raelene
BR ˈreɪliːn
AM ˈreɪlin, reɪˈlin

RAF
BR ˌɑːreɪˈɛf, raf
AM ˌɑˌreɪˈɛf

Rafe
BR reɪf
AM reɪf

Rafferty
BR ˈrafəti
AM ˈræfərdi

Raffi
BR ˈrafi
AM ˈræfi

raffia
BR ˈrafɪə(*r*)
AM ˈræfiə

raffinate
BR ˈrafɪneɪt, -s
AM ˈræfəˌneɪt, -s

raffinose
BR ˈrafɪnəʊz, ˈrafɪnəʊs
AM ˈræfəˌnoʊs, ˈræfəˌnoʊz

raffish
BR ˈrafɪʃ
AM ˈræfɪʃ

raffishly
BR ˈrafɪʃli
AM ˈræfɪʃli

raffishness
BR ˈrafɪʃnɪs
AM ˈræfɪʃnɪs

raffle
BR ˈraf|l, -lz, -lɪŋ\-lɪŋ, -ld
AM ˈræf|əl, -əlz, -(ə)lɪŋ, -əld

Raffles
BR ˈraflz
AM ˈræfəlz

rafflesia
BR rəˈfliːʒɪə(*r*), rəˈfliːzɪə(*r*)
AM rəˈfliʒ(i)ə, rəˈfliziə

Rafsanjani
BR ˌrafsanˈdʒɑːni
AM ˌrɑfsɑnˈdʒɑni

raft
BR rɑːft, raft, -s, -ɪŋ, -ɪd
AM ræft, -s, -ɪŋ, -əd

rafter
BR ˈrɑːftə(r), ˈraftə(r), -z, -d
AM ˈræftər, -z, -d

raftsman
BR ˈrɑːf(t)smən, ˈraf(t)smən
AM ˈræf(t)smən

raftsmen
BR ˈrɑːf(t)smən, ˈraf(t)smən
AM ˈræf(t)smən

rag
BR raɡ, -z, -ɪŋ, -d
AM ræɡ, -z, -ɪŋ, -d

raga
BR ˈrɑːɡə(*r*), -z
AM ˈrɑɡə, -z

ragamuffin
BR ˈraɡəˌmʌfɪn, -z
AM ˈræɡəˌməfən, -z

rag-and-bone
BR ˌraɡ(ə)n(d)ˈbəʊn
AM ˌræɡənˈboʊn

ragbag
BR ˈraɡbaɡ, -z
AM ˈræɡˌbæɡ, -z

Ragdoll
BR ˈraɡdɒl, -z
AM ˈræɡˌdɑl, -z

rag doll
BR ˌraɡ ˈdɒl, -z
AM ˈræɡ ˌdɑl, -z

rage
BR reɪdʒ, -ɪz, -ɪŋ, -d
AM reɪdʒ, -ɪz, -ɪŋ, -d

ragee
BR ˈrɑːɡiː
AM ˈræɡi

ragged
BR ˈraɡɪd, -ɪst
AM ˈræɡəd, -əst

raggedly
BR ˈraɡɪdli
AM ˈræɡədli

raggedness
BR ˈraɡɪdnɪs
AM ˈræɡədnəs

raggedy
BR ˈraɡɪdi
AM ˈræɡədi

raggee
BR ˈrɑːɡiː
AM ˈræɡi

raggle
BR ˈraɡl, -z
AM ˈræɡəl, -z

raggle-taggle
BR ˌraɡlˈtaɡl, ˈraɡlˌtaɡl
AM ˌræɡəlˌtæɡəl

raglan
BR ˈraɡlən
AM ˈræɡlən

ragman
BR ˈraɡman, ˈraɡmən
AM ˈræɡˌmæn, ˈræɡmən

ragmen
BR ˈraɡmɛn, ˈraɡmən
AM ˈræɡˌmɛn, ˈræɡmən

Ragnarök
BR ˈraɡnərɒk, ˈraɡnərəːk
AM ˈrɑɡnəˌrɔk, ˈrɑɡnəˌrɑk

ragout
BR ˈraɡuː, raˈɡuː, -z
AM ræˈɡu, -z

ragstone
BR ˈraɡstəʊn
AM ˈræɡˌstoʊn

rags-to-riches
BR ˌraɡztəˈrɪtʃɪz
AM ˌræɡztəˈrɪtʃɪz

ragtag
BR ˈraɡtaɡ
AM ˈræɡˌtæɡ

ragtime
BR ˈraɡtʌɪm
AM ˈræɡˌtaɪm

ragtop
BR ˈraɡtɒp, -s
AM ˈræɡˌtɑp, -s

raguly
BR ˈraɡjʉli
AM ˈræɡjəli

ragweed
BR ˈraɡwiːd, -z
AM ˈræɡˌwid, -z

ragworm
BR ˈraɡwəːm, -z
AM ˈræɡˌwərm, -z

ragwort
BR ˈraɡwəːt, -s
AM ˈræɡˌwərt, ˈræɡˌwɔ(ə)rt, -s

rah
BR rɑː(*r*), -z

AM rɑ, -z

Rahman
BR ˈrɑːmən
AM ˈrɑmən

rah-rah
BR ˈrɑːrɑː(r), -z
AM ˌrɑˈrɑ, -z

rai
BR rʌɪ
AM raɪ

raid
BR reɪd, -z, -ɪŋ, -ɨd
AM reɪd, -z, -ɪŋ, -ɨd

raider
BR ˈreɪdə(r), -z
AM ˈreɪdər, -z

Raikes
BR reɪks
AM reɪks

rail
BR reɪl, -z, -ɪŋ, -d
AM reɪl, -z, -ɪŋ, -d

railage
BR ˈreɪlɪdʒ
AM ˈreɪlɪdʒ

railcar
BR ˈreɪlkɑː(r), -z
AM ˈreɪlˌkɑr, -z

railcard
BR ˈreɪlkɑːd, -z
AM ˈreɪlˌkɑrd, -z

railer
BR ˈreɪlə(r), -z
AM ˈreɪlər, -z

rail fence
BR ˈreɪl fɛns, ˌreɪl ˈfɛns, -ɨz
AM ˈreɪl ˌfɛns, -əz

railhead
BR ˈreɪlhɛd, -z
AM ˈreɪlˌ(h)ɛd, -z

railing
BR ˈreɪlɪŋ, -z
AM ˈreɪlɪŋ, -z

raillery
BR ˈreɪlər|i, -ɪz
AM ˈreɪləri, -z

railless
BR ˈreɪ(l)lɨs
AM ˈreɪ(l)lɨs

railman
BR ˈreɪlmən
AM ˈreɪlmən

railmen
BR ˈreɪlmən
AM ˈreɪlmən

railroad
BR ˈreɪlrəʊd, -z, -ɪŋ, -ɨd
AM ˈreɪlˌroʊd, -z, -ɪŋ, -əd

railway
BR ˈreɪlweɪ, -z
AM ˈreɪlˌweɪ, -z

railwayman
BR ˈreɪlweɪmən, ˈreɪlwəmən
AM ˈreɪlˌweɪmən

railwaymen
BR ˈreɪlweɪmən, ˈreɪlwəmən
AM ˈreɪlˌweɪmən

raiment
BR ˈreɪm(ə)nt
AM ˈreɪmənt

rain
BR reɪn, -z, -ɪŋ, -d
AM reɪn, -z, -ɪŋ, -d

Raina
BR rʌɪˈiːnə(r), ˈreɪnə(r)
AM ˈreɪnə

rainbird
BR ˈreɪnbəːd, -z
AM ˈreɪnˌbərd, -z

rainbow
BR ˈreɪnbəʊ, -z
AM ˈreɪnˌboʊ, -z

raincoat
BR ˈreɪnkəʊt, -s
AM ˈreɪnˌkoʊt, -s

raindrop
BR ˈreɪndrɒp, -s
AM ˈreɪnˌdrɑp, -s

Raine
BR reɪn
AM reɪn

rainfall
BR ˈreɪnfɔːl
AM ˈreɪnˌfɔl, ˈreɪnˌfɑl

Rainford
BR ˈreɪnfəd
AM ˈreɪnfərd

rainforest
BR ˈreɪnˌfɒrɪst, -s
AM ˈreɪnˌfɔrəst, -s

raingauge
BR ˈreɪngeɪdʒ, -ɨz
AM ˈreɪnˌgeɪdʒ, -ɨz

Rainhill
BR ˌreɪnˈhɪl
AM ˌreɪnˈhɪl

Rainier[1]
mountain
BR ˈreɪnɪə(r), rəˈnɪə(r)
AM ˈreɪniər, rəˈnɪ(ə)r

Rainier[2]
prince of Monaco
BR ˈreɪnɪeɪ
AM ˈreɪniər

rainily
BR ˈreɪnɨli
AM ˈreɪnɨli

raininess
BR ˈreɪnɪnɨs
AM ˈreɪninɨs

rainless
BR ˈreɪnlɨs
AM ˈreɪnlɨs

rainmaker
BR ˈreɪnˌmeɪkə(r), -z
AM ˈreɪnˌmeɪkər, -z

rainmaking
BR ˈreɪnˌmeɪkɪŋ
AM ˈreɪnˌmeɪkɪŋ

rainproof
BR ˈreɪnpruːf, -s, -ɪŋ, -t
AM ˈreɪnˌpruf, -s, -ɪŋ, -t

rainstorm
BR ˈreɪnstɔːm, -z
AM ˈreɪnˌstɔ(ə)rm, -z

rainswept
BR ˈreɪnswɛpt
AM ˈreɪnˌswɛpt

rainwater
BR ˈreɪnˌwɔːtə(r)
AM ˈreɪnˌwɔdər, ˈreɪnˌwɑdər

rainwear
BR ˈreɪnwɛː(r)
AM ˈreɪnˌwɛ(ə)r

rainy
BR ˈreɪn|i, -ɪə(r), -ɪɨst
AM ˈreɪni, -ər, -ɨst

Raisa
BR rʌɪˈiːsə(r), rɑːˈiːsə(r)
AM rɑˈisə

raisable
BR ˈreɪzəbl
AM ˈreɪzəbəl

raise
BR reɪz, -ɨz, -ɪŋ, -d
AM reɪz, -ɨz, -ɪŋ, -d

raisin
BR ˈreɪzn, -z
AM ˈreɪzn, -z

raisiny
BR ˈreɪzn̩i, ˈreɪzɨni
AM ˈreɪzn̩i

Raison
BR ˈreɪzn
AM ˈreɪzn

raison d'être
BR ˌreɪzɒ̃ ˈdɛtr(ər), ˌreɪz(ɒ)n +
AM ˈreɪˌzɔn ˈdɛtrə

raisons d'être
BR ˌreɪzɒ̃ ˈdɛtr(ər), ˌreɪz(ɒ)n
AM ˈreɪˌzɔn(z) ˈdɛtrə

Raistrick
BR ˈreɪstrɪk
AM ˈreɪstrɪk

raj
BR rɑː(d)ʒ
AM rɑdʒ

raja
BR ˈrɑːdʒə(r), -z
AM ˈrɑ(d)ʒə, -z

rajah
BR ˈrɑːdʒə(r), -z
AM ˈrɑ(d)ʒə, -z

rajaship
BR ˈrɑːdʒəʃɪp, -s
AM ˈrɑ(d)ʒəˌʃɪp, -s

Rajasthan
BR ˌrɑːdʒəˈstɑːn
AM ˌrɑdʒəˈstɑn

Rajasthani
BR ˌrɑːdʒəˈstɑːn|i, -ɪz
AM ˈrɑdʒəˈstɑni, -z

Rajneesh
BR ˌrɑːdʒˈniːʃ
AM ˌrɑdʒˈniʃ

Rajpoot
BR ˈrɑːdʒpʊt
AM ˈrɑdʒˌpʊt

Rajput
BR ˈrɑːdʒpʊt
AM ˈrɑdʒˌpʊt

Rajputana
BR ˌrɑːdʒpʊˈtɑːnə(r)
AM ˌrɑdʒpəˈtɑnə

Rajshahi
BR ˌrɑːdʒˈʃɑːhi
AM ˌrɑdʒˈʃɑˌ(h)i

rake
BR reɪk, -s, -ɪŋ, -t
AM reɪk, -s, -ɪŋ, -t

raker
BR ˈreɪkə(r), -z
AM ˈreɪkər, -z

raki
BR ˈrɑːki, ˈraki, rəˈkiː
AM ˈreɪki, ˈrɑki

rakish
BR ˈreɪkɪʃ
AM ˈreɪkɪʃ

rakishly
BR ˈreɪkɨʃli
AM ˈreɪkɨʃli

rakishness
BR ˈreɪkɨʃnɨs
AM ˈreɪkɪʃnɨs

raku
BR ˈrɑːkuː
AM ˈrɑˌku

rale
BR rɑːl, ral, -z
AM rɑl, ræl, -z

Ralegh
BR ˈrali, ˈrɑːli, ˈrɔːli
AM ˈrɑli

Raleigh
BR ˈrali, ˈrɑːli, ˈrɔːli
AM ˈrɑli

Ralf
BR ralf, reɪf
AM rælf

rallentando
BR ˌralənˈtandəʊ, ˌraln̩ˈtandəʊ, -z
AM ˌrɑlənˈtɑndoʊ, ˌrælənˈtændoʊ, -z

rallier
BR ˈralɪə(r), -z
AM ˈræliər, -z

ralline
BR ˈralʌɪn
AM ˈræˌlaɪn

rally
BR ˈral|i, -ɪz, -ɪɪŋ, -ɪd
AM ˈræli, -z, -ɪŋ, -d

rallycross
BR ˈralɪkrɒs
AM ˈræliˌkrɔs, ˈræliˌkrɑs

Ralph
BR ralf, reɪf
AM rælf

ram
BR ram, -z, -ɪŋ, -d
AM ræm, -z, -ɪŋ, -d

Rama
BR 'rɑːmə(r)
AM 'rɑmə

Ramadan
BR 'ramədan, ˌramə'dan, ˌramə'dɑːn
AM ˌrɑmə'dɑn

Ramadhan
BR 'ramədan, ˌramə'dan, ˌramə'dɑːn
AM ˌrɑmə'dɑn

Ramakrishna
BR ˌrɑːmə'krɪʃnə(r)
AM ˌrɑmə'krɪʃnə

ramal
BR 'reɪml
AM 'reɪməl

Raman effect
BR 'rɑːmən ɪˌfɛkt
AM 'rɑmən əˌfɛk(t), + iˌfɛk(t)

Ramayana
BR rə'mɑːjənə(r)
AM ˌrɑmə'jɑnə

Rambert
BR 'rɒmbɛː(r), 'rɒ̃bɛː(r)
AM 'rɑmˌbɛ(ə)r

ramble
BR 'ramb|l, -lz, -l̩ɪŋ\-lɪŋ, -ld
AM 'ræmbəl, -əlz, -(ə)lɪŋ, -əld

rambler
BR 'ramblə(r), 'rambl̩ə(r), -z
AM 'ræmb(ə)lər, -z

rambling
BR 'ramblɪŋ, 'rambl̩ɪŋ, -z
AM 'ræmb(ə)lɪŋ, -z

ramblingly
BR 'ramblɪŋli, 'rambl̩ɪŋli
AM 'ræmb(ə)lɪŋli

Rambo
BR 'rambəʊ
AM 'ræmboʊ

rambunctious
BR ram'bʌŋ(k)ʃəs
AM ræm'bəŋ(k)ʃəs

rambunctiously
BR ram'bʌŋ(k)ʃəsli
AM ræm'bəŋ(k)ʃəsli

rambunctiousness
BR ram'bʌŋ(k)ʃəsnəs
AM ræm'bəŋ(k)ʃəsnəs

rambutan
BR ram'buːtn, -z
AM ræm'butn, -z

Rameau
BR 'rɑːməʊ, 'raməʊ
AM rɑ'moʊ

ramee
BR 'ram|i, -ɪz
AM 'ræmi, 'reɪmi, -z

ramekin
BR 'ram(ɪ)kɪn, -z
AM 'ræməkən, -z

ramen
BR 'rɑːmɛn
AM 'rɑˌmɛn

Rameses
BR 'ram(ɪ)siːz
AM 'ræm(ə)ˌsiz

rami
BR 'reɪmʌɪ, 'reɪmiː
AM 'reɪˌmaɪ

ramie
BR 'ram|i, -ɪz
AM 'rami, 'reɪmi, -z

ramification
BR ˌramɪfɪ'keɪʃn, -z
AM ˌræməfə'keɪʃən, -z

ramify
BR 'ramɪfʌɪ, -z, -ɪŋ, -d
AM 'ræməˌfaɪ, -z, -ɪŋ, -d

Ramillies
BR 'ramɪliːz, 'raml̩iːz
AM 'ræməˌliz

ramin
BR ra'miːn, -z
AM ræ'min, -z

Ramírez
BR rə'mɪərɛz, ra'mɪərɛz
AM rə'mɪ(ə)rɛz

ramjet
BR 'ramdʒɛt, -s
AM 'ræmˌdʒɛt, -s

rammer
BR 'ramə(r), -z
AM 'ræmər, -z

rammy
BR 'ram|i, -ɪz
AM 'ræmi, -z

Ramón
BR rə'mɒn, ra'mɒn
AM rə'moʊn

Ramona
BR rə'məʊnə(r)
AM rə'moʊnə

Ramos
BR 'ramɒs
AM 'rɑmoʊs

ramose
BR 'raməʊs, 'reɪməʊs
AM 'ræˌmoʊs, 'ræˌmoʊz

ramp
BR ram|p, -ps, -pɪŋ, -(p)t
AM ræmp, -s, -ɪŋ, -t

rampage¹
noun
BR 'rampeɪdʒ, -ɪz
AM 'ræmˌpeɪdʒ, -ɪz

rampage²
verb
BR ram'peɪdʒ, 'rampeɪdʒ, -ɪz, -ɪŋ, -d
AM ˌræmˌpeɪdʒ, -ɪz, -ɪŋ, -d

rampageous
BR ram'peɪdʒəs
AM ˌræm'peɪdʒəs

rampageously
BR ram'peɪdʒəsli
AM ˌræm'peɪdʒəsli

rampageousness
BR ram'peɪdʒəsnəs
AM ˌræm'peɪdʒəsnəs

rampager
BR ram'peɪdʒə(r), 'ramˌpeɪdʒə(r), -z
AM ˌræm'peɪdʒər, -z

rampancy
BR 'ramp(ə)nsi
AM 'ræmpənsi

rampant
BR 'ramp(ə)nt
AM 'ræmpənt

rampantly
BR 'ramp(ə)ntli
AM 'ræmpən(t)li

rampart
BR 'rampɑːt, -s
AM 'ræmˌpɑrt, -s

rampion
BR 'rampɪən, -z
AM 'ræmpiən, -z

Rampton
BR 'ram(p)tən
AM 'ræm(p)tən

Rampur
BR 'rampʊə(r)
AM 'ræmˌpʊ(ə)r

ram-raid
BR 'ramreɪd, -z, -ɪŋ, -ɪd
AM 'ræmˌreɪd, -z, -ɪŋ, -ɪd

ramrod
BR 'ramrɒd, -z
AM 'ræmˌrɑd, -z

Ramsaran
BR 'rɑːms(ə)rən, 'rɑːms(ə)rn̩
AM 'ræmsərən

Ramsay
BR 'ramzi
AM 'ræmzi

Ramsbotham
BR 'ramzˌbɒtəm, 'ramzˌbɒθəm
AM 'ræmzˌbɑdəm

Ramsbottom
BR 'ramzˌbɒtəm
AM 'ræmzˌbɑdəm

Ramsden
BR 'ramzdən
AM 'ræmzdən

Ramsey
BR 'ramzi
AM 'ræmzi

Ramsgate
BR 'ramzgeɪt
AM 'ræmzˌgeɪt

ramshackle
BR 'ramˌʃakl
AM 'ræmˌʃækəl

ramson
BR 'ramz(ə)n, 'rams(ə)n, -z
AM 'ræmzn, 'ræm(p)sən, -z

ramus
BR 'reɪməs
AM 'reɪməs

ran
BR ran
AM ræn

rance
BR rans
AM ræns

ranch
BR rɑːn(t)ʃ, ran(t)ʃ, -ɪz, -ɪŋ, -t
AM ræn(t)ʃ, -əz, -ɪŋ, -t

rancher
BR 'rɑːn(t)ʃə(r), 'ran(t)ʃə(r), -z
AM 'ræn(t)ʃər, -z

ranchero
BR rɑːn'tʃɛːrəʊ, ran'tʃɛːrəʊ, -z
AM ræn'tʃɛroʊ, -z

Ranchi
BR 'rɑːn(t)ʃi, 'ran(t)ʃi
AM 'ræn(t)ʃi

rancho
BR 'rɑːn(t)ʃəʊ, 'ran(t)ʃəʊ, -z
AM 'ræn(t)ʃoʊ, -z

rancid
BR 'ransɪd
AM 'rænsəd

rancidity
BR ran'sɪdɪti
AM ræn'sɪdɪdi

rancidness
BR 'ransɪdnɪs
AM 'rænsədnəs

rancor
BR 'raŋkə(r)
AM 'ræŋkər

rancorous
BR 'raŋk(ə)rəs
AM 'ræŋk(ə)rəs

rancorously
BR 'raŋk(ə)rəsli
AM 'ræŋk(ə)rəsli

rancour
BR 'raŋkə(r)
AM 'ræŋkər

rand
BR ran|d, rɑːn|t, ran|t, rɒn|t, -dz\-ts
AM rænd, -s

Randal
BR 'randl
AM 'rændəl

Randall
BR 'randl
AM 'rændl
randan
BR ˌran'dan, -z
AM 'ræn,dæn, ræn'dæn, -z
R and B
BR ˌɑːr ən(d) 'biː, + n̩(d) +
AM ˌɑr ən 'bi
R and D
BR ˌɑːr ən(d) 'diː, + n̩(d) +
AM ˌɑr ən 'di
Randers
BR 'randəz
AM 'rændərz
randily
BR 'randɨli
AM 'rændɨli
randiness
BR 'randɪnɨs
AM 'rændinɨs
Randolf
BR 'randɒlf
AM 'ræn,dɔlf, 'ræn,dɑlf
Randolph
BR 'randɒlf
AM 'ræn,dɔlf, 'ræn,dɑlf
random
BR 'randəm
AM 'rændəm
randomisation
BR ˌrandəmʌɪ'zeɪʃn
AM ˌrændəmə'zeɪʃən, ˌrændə,maɪ'zeɪʃən
randomise
BR 'randəmʌɪz, -ɨz, -ɪŋ, -d
AM 'rændə,maɪz, -ɪz, -ɪŋ, -d
randomization
BR ˌrandəmʌɪ'zeɪʃn
AM ˌrændəmə'zeɪʃən, ˌrændə,maɪ'zeɪʃən
randomize
BR 'randəmʌɪz, -ɨz, -ɪŋ, -d
AM 'rændə,maɪz, -ɨz, -ɪŋ, -d
randomly
BR 'randəmli
AM 'rændəmli
randomness
BR 'randəmnəs
AM 'rændəmnəs
Randstad
BR 'randstat
AM 'ræn(d),stæt
randy
BR 'rand|i, -ɪə(r), -ɪɨst
AM 'rændi, -ər, -ɨst
ranee
BR 'rɑːniː, ˌrɑː'niː, -z
AM 'rɑni, rɑ'ni, -z
Ranelagh
BR 'ranɨlə(*r*), 'ranl̩ə(*r*)
AM 'rænələ
rang
BR raŋ
AM ræŋ
rangatira
BR ˌraŋgə'tɪərə(*r*), -z
AM ˌræŋgə'tɪ(ə)rə, -z
range
BR reɪn(d)ʒ, -ɨz, -ɪŋ, -d
AM reɪndʒ, -ɨz, -ɪŋ, -d
rangé
BR rɒ̃'ʒeɪ
AM rɑn'ʒeɪ
rangefinder
BR 'reɪn(d)ʒ,fʌɪndə(r), -z
AM 'reɪndʒ,faɪndər, -z
rangeland
BR 'reɪn(d)ʒland, -z
AM 'reɪndʒ,lænd, -z
ranger
BR 'reɪn(d)ʒə(r), -z
AM 'reɪndʒər, -z
rangership
BR 'reɪn(d)ʒəʃɪp, -s
AM 'reɪndʒər,ʃɪp, -s
ranginess
BR 'reɪn(d)ʒɪnɨs
AM 'reɪndʒinɨs
Rangoon
BR raŋ'guːn
AM ræŋ'gun
rangy
BR 'reɪn(d)ʒ|i, -ɪə(r), -ɪɨst
AM 'reɪndʒi, -ər, -ɨst
rani
BR 'rɑːniː, ˌrɑː'niː, -z
AM 'rɑni, rɑ'ni, -z
Ranjit Singh
BR ˌran(d)ʒɪt 'sɪŋ
AM ˌrændʒət 'sɪŋ
Ranjitsinhji
BR ˌran(d)ʒɪt'sɪn(d)ʒi
AM ˌrændʒət,sɪndʒi
rank
BR raŋ|k, -ks, -kɪŋ, -(k)t, -kə(r), -kɨst
AM ræŋ|k, -ks, -kɪŋ, -(k)t, -kər, -kəst
rank-and-file
BR ˌraŋk(ə)n(d)'fʌɪl
AM ˌræŋkən'faɪl
ranker
BR 'raŋkə(r), -z
AM 'ræŋkər, -z
Rankin
BR 'raŋkɪn
AM 'ræŋkən
ranking
BR 'raŋkɪŋ, -z
AM 'ræŋkɪŋ, -z
rankle
BR 'raŋk|l, -lz, -l̩ɪŋ\-lɪŋ, -ld
AM 'ræŋk|əl, -əlz, -(ə)lɪŋ, -əld
rankly
BR 'raŋkli
AM 'ræŋkli
rankness
BR 'raŋknəs
AM 'ræŋknəs
Rannoch
BR 'ranəx, 'ranək
AM 'rænək
ransack
BR 'ransak, -s, -ɪŋ, -t
AM 'ræn,sæk, -s, -ɪŋ, -t
ransacker
BR 'ransakə(r), -z
AM 'ræn,sækər, -z
ransom
BR 'rans|(ə)m, -(ə)mz, -əmɪŋ\-m̩ɪŋ, -(ə)md
AM 'rænsəm, -z, -ɪŋ, -d
Ransome
BR 'rans(ə)m
AM 'rænsəm
ransomer
BR 'ransəmə(r), 'ransm̩ə(r), -z
AM 'rænsəmər, -z
rant
BR rant, -s, -ɪŋ, -ɨd
AM ræn|t, -ts, -(t)ɪŋ, -(t)əd
ranter
BR 'rantə(r), -z
AM 'ræn(t)ər, -z
ranting
BR 'rantɪŋ, -z
AM 'ræn(t)ɪŋ, -z
rantingly
BR 'rantɪŋli
AM 'ræn(t)ɪŋli
rantipole
BR 'rantɪpəʊl, -z, -ɪŋ, -d
AM 'ræn(t)i,poʊl, -z, -ɪŋ, -d
Ranulf
BR 'ranəlf, 'ranʌlf
AM 'rænəlf
Ranulph
BR 'ranəlf, 'ranʌlf
AM 'rænəlf
ranunculaceous
BR rəˌnʌŋkjʊ'leɪʃəs
AM rəˌnənkjə'leɪʃəs
ranunculi
BR rə'nʌŋkjʊlʌɪ, rə'nʌŋkjʊliː
AM rə'nəŋkjə,laɪ
ranunculus
BR rə'nʌŋkjʊləs, -ɨz
AM rə'nəŋkjələs, -əz
Raoul
BR raʊ'uːl, rɑː'uːl
AM rɑ'ul
rap
BR rap, -s, -ɪŋ, -t
AM ræp, -s, -ɪŋ, -t
rapacious
BR rə'peɪʃəs
AM rə'peɪʃəs
rapaciously
BR rə'peɪʃəsli
AM rə'peɪʃəsli
rapaciousness
BR rə'peɪʃəsnəs
AM rə'peɪʃəsnəs
rapacity
BR rə'pasɨti
AM rə'pæsədi
rape
BR reɪp, -s, -ɪŋ, -t
AM reɪp, -s, -ɪŋ, -t
raper
BR 'reɪpə(r), -z
AM 'reɪpər, -z
rapeseed
BR 'reɪpsiːd
AM 'reɪp,sid
Raphael[1]
Italian artist
BR 'rafeɪ(ə)l, 'rafʌɪɛl
AM ˌrɑfaɪ'ɛl
Raphael[2]
BR 'rafeɪ(ə)l
AM 'ræfiəl, 'reɪfiəl, ˌræfi'ɛl, ˌræfaɪ'ɛl
raphia
BR 'rafɪə(*r*), -z
AM 'reɪfiə, 'ræfiə, -z
raphide
BR 'reɪfʌɪd, -z
AM 'reɪfɨd, 'reɪ,fɨd, -z
rapid
BR 'rap|ɪd, -ɪdz, -ɨdɪst
AM 'ræpəd, -z, -ɨst
rapid-fire
BR ˌrapɪd'fʌɪə(r)
AM 'ræpəd'faɪ(ə)r
rapidity
BR rə'pɪdɨti
AM rə'pɪdɨdi, ræ'pɪdɨdi
rapidly
BR 'rapɪdli
AM 'ræpədli
rapidness
BR 'rapɪdnɨs
AM 'ræpədnəs
rapier
BR 'reɪpɪə(r), -z
AM 'reɪpiər, -z
rapine
BR 'rapʌɪn, 'rapɪn
AM 'ræpən, 'ræ,paɪn, 'reɪ,paɪn
rapist
BR 'reɪpɪst, -s
AM 'reɪpɨst, -s
Rappahannock
BR ˌrapə'hanək
AM ˌræpə'hænək

rapparee
BR ˌrapəˈriː, -z
AM ˌræpəˈri, -z
rappee
BR raˈpiː
AM ræˈpi
rappel
BR raˈpɛl, rəˈpɛl, -z, -ɪŋ, -d
AM rəˈpɛl, -z, -ɪŋ, -d
rapper
BR ˈrapə(r), -z
AM ˈræpər, -z
rapport
BR raˈpɔː(r), rəˈpɔː(r)
AM ræˈpɔ(ə)r, rəˈpɔ(ə)r
rapporteur
BR ˌrapɔːˈtəː(r), -z
AM ˌræˌpɔrˈtər, -z
rapprochement
BR rəˈprɒʃmɒ̃, raˈprɒʃmɒ̃, -z
AM ˈræˌprɔʃˈmɑnt, ˈrɑˌprɔʃˈmɑnt, -z
rapscallion
BR rapˈskalɪən, -z
AM ræpˈskæljən, ræpˈskæliən, -z
rapt
BR rapt
AM ræp(t)
raptly
BR ˈraptli
AM ˈræp(t)li
raptness
BR ˈrap(t)nəs
AM ˈræp(t)nəs
raptor
BR ˈraptə(r), -z
AM ˈræptər, -z
raptorial
BR rapˈtɔːrɪəl
AM ræpˈtɔriəl
rapture
BR ˈraptʃə(r), -z, -d
AM ˈræp(t)ʃər, -z, -d
rapturous
BR ˈraptʃ(ə)rəs
AM ˈræp(t)ʃərəs
rapturously
BR ˈraptʃ(ə)rəsli
AM ˈræp(t)ʃərəsli
rapturousness
BR ˈraptʃ(ə)rəsnəs
AM ˈræp(t)ʃərəsnəs
Rapunzel
BR rəˈpʌnzl
AM rəˈpənzəl
Raquel
BR raˈkɛl, rəˈkɛl
AM rəˈkɛl, ˌræˈkɛl
rara avis
BR ˌrɑːrə ˈeɪvɪs, ˌrɛːrə +, + ˈɑːvɪs, + ˈavɪs
AM ˈrɑrə ˈeɪvɪs
rare
BR rɛː(r), -ə(r), -ɨst
AM rɛ(ə)r, -ər, -əst
rarebit
BR ˈrɛːbɪt, ˈrabɪt, -s
AM ˈrɛrbət, -s
raree-show
BR ˈrɛːrɪʃəʊ, -z
AM ˈrɛriˌʃoʊ, -z
rarefaction
BR ˌrɛːrɪˈfakʃn
AM ˌrɛrəˈfækʃən
rarefactive
BR ˌrɛːrɪˈfaktɪv
AM ˌrɛrəˈfæktɪv
rarefication
BR ˌrɛːrɪfɪˈkeɪʃn
AM ˌrɛrəfəˈkeɪʃən
rarefy
BR ˈrɛːrɪfʌɪ, -z, -ɪŋ, -d
AM ˈrɛrəˌfaɪ, -z, -ɪŋ, -d
rarely
BR ˈrɛːli
AM ˈrɛrli
rareness
BR ˈrɛːnəs
AM ˈrɛrnəs
rarify
BR ˈrɛːrɪfʌɪ, -z, -ɪŋ, -d
AM ˈrɛrəˌfaɪ, -z, -ɪŋ, -d
raring
BR ˈrɛːrɪŋ
AM ˈrɛrɪŋ
rarity
BR ˈrɛːrɪt|i, -ɪz
AM ˈrɛrədi, -z
Rarotonga
BR ˌrɛːrəˈtɒŋgə(*r*), ˌrarəˈtɒŋgə(*r*)
AM ˌrɛrəˈtɔŋgə, ˌrɛrəˈtɑŋgə
Rarotongan
BR ˌrɛːrəˈtɒŋg(ə)n, ˌrarəˈtɒŋg(ə)n, -z
AM ˌrɛrəˈtɔŋgən, ˌrɛrəˈtɑŋgən, -z
rascal
BR ˈrɑːskl, ˈraskl, -z
AM ˈræskəl, -z
rascaldom
BR ˈrɑːskldəm, ˈraskldəm
AM ˈræskəldəm
rascalism
BR ˈrɑːskl̩ɪz(ə)m, ˈrɑːskəlɪz(ə)m, ˈraskl̩ɪz(ə)m, ˈraskəlɪz(ə)m
AM ˈræskəˌlɪzəm
rascality
BR rasˈkalɪt|i, -ɪz
AM ræsˈkælədi, -z
rascally
BR ˈrɑːskl̩i, ˈrɑːskəli, ˈraskl̩i, ˈraskəli
AM ˈræsk(ə)li
raschel
BR ˈraʃl, -z
AM rɑˈʃɛl, -z
rase
BR reɪz, -ɪz, -ɪŋ, -d
AM reɪz, -ɪz, -ɪŋ, -d
rash
BR raʃ, -ə(r), -ɨst
AM ræʃ, -ə(r), -ɪst
rasher
BR ˈraʃə(r), -z
AM ˈræʃər, -z
Rashid
BR raˈʃiːd
AM rəˈʃid
rashly
BR ˈraʃli
AM ˈræʃli
rashness
BR ˈraʃnəs
AM ˈræʃnəs
Rasmussen
BR ˈrazmʉsn, ˈrasmʉsn
AM ˈræsˌmʊsən, ˈræsməsən
rasp
BR rɑːsp, rasp, -s, -ɪŋ, -t
AM ræsp, -s, -ɪŋ, -t
raspatory
BR ˈrɑːspət(ə)ri, ˈraspət(ə)r|i, -ɪz
AM ˈræspəˌtɔri, -z
raspberry
BR ˈrɑːzb(ə)r|i, ˈrazb(ə)r|i, -ɪz
AM ˈræzˌbɛri, -z
rasper
BR ˈrɑːspə(r), ˈraspə(r), -z
AM ˈræspər, -z
raspingly
BR ˈrɑːspɪŋli, ˈraspɪŋli
AM ˈræspɪŋli
Rasputin
BR raˈspjuːtɪn
AM ræˈspjutn
raspy
BR ˈrɑːspi, ˈraspi
AM ˈræspi
Rasta
BR ˈrastə(*r*), -z
AM ˈræstə, -z
Rastafari
BR ˌrastəˈfɑːr|i, -ɪz
AM ˌræstəˈfɛri, -z
Rastafarian
BR ˌrastəˈfɛːrɪən, ˌrastəˈfɑːrɪən, -z
AM ˌræstəˈfɛriən, -z
Rastafarianism
BR ˌrastəˈfɛːrɪənɪz(ə)m, ˌrastəˈfɑːrɪənɪz(ə)m
AM ˌræstəˈfɛriəˌnɪzəm
raster
BR ˈrastə(r), -z
AM ˈræstər, -z
rasterisation
BR ˌrast(ə)rʌɪˈzeɪʃn
AM ˌræstərəˈzeɪʃən, ˌræstəˌraɪˈzeɪʃən
rasterise
BR ˈrast(ə)rʌɪz, -ɪz, -ɪŋ, -d
AM ˈræstəˌraɪz, -ɪz, -ɪŋ, -d
rasteriser
BR ˈrast(ə)rʌɪzə(r), -z
AM ˈræstəˌraɪzər, -z
rasterization
BR ˌrast(ə)rʌɪˈzeɪʃn
AM ˌræstərəˈzeɪʃən, ˌræstəˌraɪˈzeɪʃən
rasterize
BR ˈrast(ə)rʌɪz, -ɪz, -ɪŋ, -d
AM ˈræstəˌraɪz, -ɪz, -ɪŋ, -d
rasterizer
BR ˈrast(ə)rʌɪzə(r), -z
AM ˈræstəˌraɪzər, -z
Rastrick
BR ˈrastrɪk
AM ˈræstrɪk
Rastus
BR ˈrastəs
AM ˈræstəs
rat
BR rat, -s, -ɪŋ, -ɨd
AM ræ|t, -ts, -dɪŋ, -dəd
rata[1]
in pro rata
BR ˈrɑːtə(*r*)
AM ˈrædə, ˈrɑdə
rata[2]
tree
BR ˈrɑːtə(*r*), -z
AM ˈrɑdə, -z
ratability
BR ˌreɪtəˈbɪlɨti
AM ˌreɪdəˈbɪlɨdi
ratable
BR ˈreɪtəbl
AM ˈreɪdəbəl
ratably
BR ˈreɪtəbli
AM ˈreɪdəbli
ratafia
BR ˌratəˈfɪə(*r*), ˌratəˈfiːə(*r*), -z
AM ˌrædəˈfiə, -z
ratan
BR rəˈtan, raˈtan, -z
AM ræˈtæn, rəˈtæn, -z
rataplan
BR ˌratəˈplan, -z, -ɪŋ, -d
AM ˈrɑdəˌplæn, -z, -ɪŋ, -d
rat-arsed
BR ˌratˈɑːst, ˈratɑːst
AM ˈrædˌɑrst
rat-a-tat
BR ˌratəˈtat, -s
AM ˈrædəˈtæt, -s
rat-a-tat-tat
BR ˌratətatˈtat
AM ˈrædəˌtæ(t)ˈtæt

ratatouille
BR ˌratəˈtwiː, -z
AM ˌrædəˈtui, -z

ratbag
BR ˈratbag, -z
AM ˈrætˌbæg, -z

ratcatcher
BR ˈratˌkatʃə(r), -z
AM ˈrætˌkɛtʃər, -z

ratch
BR ratʃ, -ɨz
AM rætʃ, -əz

ratchet
BR ˈratʃɪt, -s
AM ˈrætʃət, -s

Ratcliff
BR ˈratklɪf
AM ˈrætˌklɪf

Ratcliffe
BR ˈratklɪf
AM ˈrætˌklɪf

rate
BR reɪt, -s, -ɪŋ, -ɨd
AM reɪ|t, -ts, -dɪŋ, -dɨd

rateability
BR ˌreɪtəˈbɪlɪti
AM ˌreɪdəˈbɪlɨdi

rateable
BR ˈreɪtəbl
AM ˈreɪdəbəl

rateably
BR ˈreɪtəbli
AM ˈreɪdɨbli

ratecap
BR ˈreɪtkap, -s, -ɪŋ, -t
AM ˈreɪtˌkæp, -s, -ɪŋ, -t

ratel
BR ˈreɪtl, ˈrɑːtl, -z
AM ˈreɪdl, ˈrɑdl, -z

ratepayer
BR ˈreɪtˌpeɪə(r), -z
AM ˈreɪtˌpeɪər, -z

ratfink
BR ˈratfɪŋk, -s
AM ˈrætˌfɪŋk, -s

Rathbone
BR ˈraθbəʊn
AM ˈræθˌboʊn

rathe
BR reɪð
AM reɪð, ræθ

rather
BR ˈrɑːðə(r)
AM ˈræðər

rathe-ripe
BR ˈreɪðrʌɪp, -s
AM ˈreɪðˌraɪp, -s

Rathlin
BR ˈraθlɪn
AM ˈræθlən

rathole
BR ˈrathəʊl, -z
AM ˈrætˌ(h)oʊl, -z

rathskeller
BR ˈrɑːtˌskɛlə(r), -z
AM ˈrɑtˌskɛlər, ˈrætˌskɛlər, -z

ratifiable
BR ˈratɪfʌɪəbl
AM ˈrædəˌfaɪəbəl

ratification
BR ˌratɪfɪˈkeɪʃn, -z
AM ˌrædəfəˈkeɪʃən, -z

ratifier
BR ˈratɪfʌɪə(r), -z
AM ˈrædəˌfaɪər, -z

ratify
BR ˈratɪfʌɪ, -z, -ɪŋ, -d
AM ˈrædəˌfaɪ, -z, -ɪŋ, -d

rating
BR ˈreɪtɪŋ, -z
AM ˈreɪdɪŋ, -z

ratio
BR ˈreɪʃɪəʊ, -z
AM ˈreɪʃ(i)oʊ, -z

ratiocinate
BR ˌratɪˈɒsɨneɪt, ˌraʃɪˈɒsɨneɪt, -s, -ɪŋ, -ɨd
AM ˌreɪdiˈoʊsnˌeɪ|t, ˌræʃiˈoʊsnˌeɪ|t, -ts, -dɪŋ, -dɨd

ratiocination
BR ˌratɪˌɒsɨˈneɪʃn, ˌraʃɪˌɒsɨˈneɪʃn, -z
AM ˌræʃiˌoʊsnˈeɪʃən, -z

ratiocinative
BR ˌratɪˈɒsɨnətɪv, ˌraʃɪˈɒsɨnətɪv
AM ˌræʃiˈoʊsəˌneɪdɪv

ratiocinator
BR ˌratɪˈɒsɨneɪtə(r), ˌraʃɪˈɒsɨneɪtə(r), -z
AM ˌræʃiˈoʊsəˌneɪdər, -z

ration
BR ˈraʃ|n, -nz, -n̩ɪŋ\-(ə)nɪŋ, -nd
AM ˈræʃ|ən, ˈreɪʃ|ən, -ənz, -(ə)nɪŋ, -ənd

rational
BR ˈraʃn̩(ə)l, ˈraʃən(ə)l
AM ˈræʃ(ə)nəl

rationale
BR ˌraʃəˈnɑːl, ˌraʃəˈnal, -z
AM ˌræʃəˈnæl, -z

rationalisation
BR ˌraʃn̩əlʌɪˈzeɪʃn, ˌraʃn̩l̩ʌɪˈzeɪʃn, ˌraʃənl̩ʌɪˈzeɪʃn, ˌraʃ(ə)nəlʌɪˈzeɪʃn
AM ˌræʃənləˈzeɪʃən, ˌræʃnələˈzeɪʃən, ˌræʃənlˌaɪˈzeɪʃən, ˌræʃnəˌlaɪˈzeɪʃən

rationalise
BR ˈraʃn̩əlʌɪz, ˈraʃn̩l̩ʌɪz, ˈraʃənl̩ʌɪz, ˈraʃ(ə)nəlʌɪz, -ɨz, -ɪŋ, -d
AM ˈræʃənlˌaɪz, ˈræʃnəˌlaɪz, -ɨz, -ɪŋ, -d

rationaliser
BR ˈraʃn̩əlʌɪzə(r), ˈraʃn̩l̩ʌɪzə(r), ˈraʃənl̩ʌɪzə(r), ˈraʃ(ə)nəlʌɪzə(r), -z
AM ˈræʃənlˌaɪzər, ˈræʃnəˌlaɪzər, -z

rationalism
BR ˈraʃn̩əlɪz(ə)m, ˈraʃn̩l̩ɪz(ə)m, ˈraʃənl̩ɪz(ə)m, ˈraʃ(ə)nəlɪz(ə)m
AM ˈræʃənlˌɪzəm, ˈræʃnəˌlɪzəm

rationalist
BR ˈraʃn̩əlɪst, ˈraʃn̩l̩ɪst, ˈraʃənl̩ɪst, ˈraʃ(ə)nəlɪst, -s
AM ˈræʃənləst, ˈræʃnələst, -s

rationalistic
BR ˌraʃn̩əˈlɪstɪk, ˌraʃn̩lˈɪstɪk, ˌraʃənlˈɪstɪk, ˌraʃ(ə)nəˈlɪstɪk
AM ˌræʃənlˈɪstɪk, ˌræʃnəˈlɪstɪk

rationalistically
BR ˌraʃn̩əˈlɪstɪkli, ˌraʃn̩lˈɪstɪkli, ˌraʃənlˈɪstɪkli, ˌraʃ(ə)nəˈlɪstɪkli
AM ˌræʃənlˈɪstək(ə)li, ˌræʃnəˈlɪstək(ə)li

rationality
BR ˌraʃəˈnalɨti
AM ˌræʃəˈnælədi

rationalization
BR ˌraʃn̩əlʌɪˈzeɪʃn, ˌraʃn̩l̩ʌɪˈzeɪʃn, ˌraʃənl̩ʌɪˈzeɪʃn, ˌraʃ(ə)nəlʌɪˈzeɪʃn
AM ˌræʃənləˈzeɪʃən, ˌræʃnələˈzeɪʃən, ˌræʃənlˌaɪˈzeɪʃən, ˌræʃnəˌlaɪˈzeɪʃən

rationalize
BR ˈraʃn̩əlʌɪz, ˈraʃn̩l̩ʌɪz, ˈraʃənl̩ʌɪz, ˈraʃ(ə)nəlʌɪz, -ɨz, -ɪŋ, -d
AM ˈræʃənlˌaɪz, ˈræʃnəˌlaɪz, -ɨz, -ɪŋ, -d

rationalizer
BR ˈraʃn̩əlʌɪzə(r), ˈraʃn̩l̩ʌɪzə(r), ˈraʃənl̩ʌɪzə(r), ˈraʃ(ə)nəlʌɪzə(r), -z
AM ˈræʃənlˌaɪzər, ˈræʃnəˌlaɪzər, -z

rationally
BR ˈraʃn̩əli, ˈraʃn̩l̩i, ˈraʃənl̩i, ˈraʃ(ə)nəli
AM ˈræʃ(ə)nəli

ratite
BR ˈratʌɪt, -s
AM ˈræˌtaɪt, -s

ratlin
BR ˈratlɪn, -z
AM ˈrætlən, -z

ratline
BR ˈratlɪn, -z
AM ˈrætlən, -z

Ratner
BR ˈratnə(r)
AM ˈrætnər

ratoon
BR rəˈtuːn, raˈtuːn, -z, -ɪŋ, -d
AM rəˈtun, -z, -ɪŋ, -d

ratrace
BR ˈratreɪs
AM ˈrætˌreɪs

ratsbane
BR ˈratsbeɪn, -z
AM ˈrætsˌbeɪn, -z

Ratskeller
BR ˈratˌskɛlə(r), -z
AM ˈrɑtˌskɛlər, ˈrætˌskɛlər, -z

rat's-tail
BR ˈratsteɪl
AM ˈrætsˌteɪl

rattan
BR rəˈtan, raˈtan, -z
AM ræˈtæn, rəˈtæn, -z

rat-tat
BR ˌratˈtat
AM ˌrætˈtæt

Rattenbury
BR ˈratnb(ə)ri
AM ˈrætnˌbɛri

ratter
BR ˈratə(r), -z
AM ˈrædər, -z

Rattigan
BR ˈratɪg(ə)n
AM ˈrædəgən

rattily
BR ˈratɨli
AM ˈrædəli

rattiness
BR ˈratɪnɨs
AM ˈrædinɨs

rattle
BR ˈrat|l, -lz, -l̩ɪŋ\-lɪŋ, -ld
AM ˈrædəl, -z, -ɪŋ, -d

rattlebox
BR ˈratlbɒks, -ɨz
AM ˈrædlˌbɑks, -əz

rattler
BR ˈratl̩ə(r), ˈratlə(r), -z
AM ˈrædlər, ˈrætlər, -z

rattlesnake
BR ˈratlsneɪk, -s
AM ˈrædlˌsneɪk, -s

rattletrap
BR ˈratltrap, -s
AM ˈrædlˌtræp, -s

rattling
BR ˈratl̩ɪŋ, ˈratlɪŋ, -z
AM ˈrædlɪŋ, -z

rattly
BR ˈratl̩i, ˈratli

AM 'rædli
Rattray
BR 'ratri, 'ratreɪ
AM 'rætreɪ
ratty
BR 'rat|i, -ɪə(r), -ɪɪst
AM 'rædi, -ər, -ɪst
raucous
BR 'rɔːkəs
AM 'rɔkəs, 'rɑkəs
raucously
BR 'rɔːkəsli
AM 'rɔkəsli, 'rɑkəsli
raucousness
BR 'rɔːkəsnəs
AM 'rɔkəsnəs, 'rɑkəsnəs
raunch
BR rɔːn(t)ʃ
AM rɔn(t)ʃ, rɑn(t)ʃ
raunchily
BR 'rɔːn(t)ʃɪli
AM 'rɔn(t)ʃəli, 'rɑn(t)ʃəli
raunchiness
BR 'rɔːn(t)ʃɪnɪs
AM 'rɔn(t)ʃinɪs, 'rɑn(t)ʃinɪs
raunchy
BR 'rɔːn(t)ʃ|i, -ɪə(r), -ɪɪst
AM 'rɔn(t)ʃi, 'rɑn(t)ʃi, -ər, -ɪst
ravage
BR 'rav|ɪdʒ, -ɪdʒɪz, -ɪdʒɪŋ, -ɪdʒd
AM 'rævɪdʒ, -ɪz, -ɪŋ, -d
ravager
BR 'ravɪdʒə(r), -z
AM 'rævɪdʒər, -z
rave
BR reɪv, -z, -ɪŋ, -d
AM reɪv, -z, -ɪŋ, -d
Ravel
BR rə'vɛl
AM rə'vɛl
ravel
BR 'rav|l, -lz, -l̩ɪŋ\-(ə)lɪŋ, -ld
AM 'ræv|əl, -əlz, -(ə)lɪŋ, -əld
ravelin
BR 'ravl̩ɪn, 'rav(ə)lɪn, -z
AM 'rævlən, -z
raven[1]
noun, adjective
BR 'reɪvn, -z
AM 'reɪvən, -z
raven[2]
verb
BR 'rav|n, -nz, -n̩ɪŋ\-(ə)nɪŋ, -nd
AM 'ræv|ən, -ənz, -(ə)nɪŋ, -ənd
Ravenglass
BR 'reɪvnglɑːs, 'reɪvŋglɑːs, 'reɪvnglas, 'reɪvŋglas
AM 'reɪvən,glæs
Ravenna
BR rə'vɛnə(*r*)
AM rə'vɛnə
ravenous
BR 'ravn̩əs, 'ravənəs
AM 'ræv(ə)nəs
ravenously
BR 'ravn̩əsli, 'ravənəsli
AM 'ræv(ə)nəsli
ravenousness
BR 'ravn̩əsnəs, 'ravənəsnəs
AM 'ræv(ə)nəsnəs
raver
BR 'reɪvə(r), -z
AM 'reɪvər, -z
rave-up
BR 'reɪvʌp, -s
AM 'reɪv,əp, -s
ravin
BR 'ravɪn, -z
AM 'rævən, -z
ravine[1]
plunder
BR 'ravɪn, -z
AM 'rævən, -z
ravine[2]
valley
BR rə'viːn, -z, -d
AM rə'vin, -z, -d
raving
BR 'reɪvɪŋ, -z
AM 'reɪvɪŋ, -z
ravingly
BR 'reɪvɪŋli
AM 'reɪvɪŋli
ravioli
BR ,ravɪ'əʊli
AM ,rævi'oʊli
ravish
BR 'rav|ɪʃ, -ɪʃɪz, -ɪʃɪŋ, -ɪʃt
AM 'rævɪʃ, -ɪz, -ɪŋ, -t
ravisher
BR 'ravɪʃə(r), -z
AM 'rævɪʃər, -z
ravishing
BR 'ravɪʃɪŋ
AM 'rævɪʃɪŋ
ravishingly
BR 'ravɪʃɪŋli
AM 'rævɪʃɪŋli
ravishment
BR 'ravɪʃm(ə)nt
AM 'rævɪʃmənt
raw
BR rɔː(*r*), -ə(r), -ɪst
AM rɔ, rɑ, -ər, -əst
Rawalpindi
BR ,rɔːl'pɪndi, ,rɔːw(ə)l'pɪndi, ,rɑːw(ə)l'pɪndi
AM ,rɑw(ə)l'pɪndi
Rawdon
BR 'rɔːdn
AM 'rɔdən, 'rɑdən
rawhide
BR 'rɔːhʌɪd, -z
AM 'rɔ,(h)aɪd, 'rɑ,(h)aɪd, -z
Rawle
BR rɔːl
AM rɔl, rɑl
Rawlings
BR 'rɔːlɪŋz
AM 'rɔlɪŋz, 'rɑlɪŋz
Rawlins
BR 'rɔːlɪnz
AM 'rɔlɪnz, 'rɑlɪnz
Rawlinson
BR 'rɔːlɪns(ə)n
AM 'rɔlɪnsən, 'rɑlɪnsən
Rawlplug®
BR 'rɔːlplʌg, -z
AM 'rɔl,pləg, 'rɑl,pləg, -z
Rawls
BR rɔːlz
AM rɔlz, rɑlz
rawly
BR 'rɔːli
AM 'rɔli, 'rɑli
rawness
BR 'rɔːnəs
AM 'rɔnəs, 'rɑnəs
Rawson
BR 'rɔːsn
AM 'rɔsən, 'rɑsən
Rawtenstall
BR 'rɒtnstɔːl, 'rɔːtnstɔːl
AM 'rɔtn,stɔl, 'rɑtn,stɑl
ray
BR reɪ, -z
AM reɪ, -z
rayah
BR 'rʌɪə(*r*), -z
AM 'raɪə, -z
Rayburn
BR 'reɪbəːn
AM 'reɪ,bərn
Rayleen
BR 'reɪliːn
AM 'reɪlin
Rayleigh
BR 'reɪli
AM 'reɪli
rayless
BR 'reɪlɪs
AM 'reɪləs
raylet
BR 'reɪlɪt, -s
AM 'reɪlət, -s
Raymond
BR 'reɪmənd
AM 'reɪmən(d)
Rayner
BR 'reɪnə(r)
AM 'reɪnər
Raynes
BR reɪnz
AM reɪnz
rayon
BR 'reɪɒn, 'reɪən
AM 'reɪ,ɑn
raze
BR reɪz, -ɪz, -ɪŋ, -d
AM reɪz, -ɪz, -ɪŋ, -d
razoo
BR rɑː'zʊ, rə'zuː, 'rɑːzʊ, -z
AM rə'zu, -z
razor
BR 'reɪz|ə(r), -əz, -(ə)rɪŋ, -əd
AM 'reɪzər, -z, -ɪŋ, -d
razorback
BR 'reɪzəbak, -s
AM 'reɪzər,bæk, -s
razorbill
BR 'reɪzəbɪl, -z
AM 'reɪzər,bɪl, -z
razorblade
BR 'reɪzəbleɪd, -z
AM 'reɪzər,bleɪd, -z
razorshell
BR 'reɪzəʃɛl, -z
AM 'reɪzər,ʃɛl, -z
razz
BR raz, -ɪz, -ɪŋ, -d
AM ræz, -ɪz, -ɪŋ, -d
razzamatazz
BR 'raz(ə)mətaz, ,raz(ə)mə'taz
AM 'ræz(ə)mə,tæz
razzamattazz
BR 'raz(ə)mətaz, ,raz(ə)mə'taz
AM 'ræz(ə)mə,tæz
razzia
BR 'razɪə(*r*), -z
AM 'ræziə, -z
razzle
BR 'razl
AM 'ræzəl
razzle-dazzle
BR 'razl,dazl, ,razl'dazl
AM ',ræzəl'dæzəl
razzmatazz
BR 'razmətaz, ,razmə'taz
AM 'ræz(ə)mə,tæz
razzmattazz
BR 'razmətaz, ,razmə'taz
AM 'ræzmə,tæz
re[1]
preposition
BR reɪ, riː
AM reɪ, ri
re[2]
Tonic Sol-fa
BR reɪ

AM reɪ

Rea
BR reɪ, riː, ˈriːə(r)
AM ˈri(ə)

reabsorb
BR ˌriːəbˈzɔːb, ˌriːəbˈsɔːb, -z, -ɪŋ, -d
AM ˌriəbˈsɔ(ə)rb, ˌriəbˈzɔ(ə)rb, -z, -ɪŋ, -d

reabsorption
BR ˌriːəbˈsɔːpʃn, ˌriːəbˈzɔːpʃn, -z
AM ˌriəbˈsɔrpʃən, ˌriəbˈzɔrpʃən, -z

reaccept
BR ˌriːəkˈsɛpt, -s, -ɪŋ, -d
AM ˌriəkˈsɛpt, -s, -ɪŋ, -d

reacceptance
BR ˌriːəkˈsɛpt(ə)ns, -ɪz
AM ˌriəkˈsɛptns, -əz

reaccustom
BR ˌriːəˈkʌstəm, -z, -ɪŋ, -d
AM ˌriəˈkəstəm, -z, -ɪŋ, -d

reach
BR riːtʃ, -ɪz, -ɪŋ, -t
AM ritʃ, -ɪz, -ɪŋ, -t

reachable
BR ˈriːtʃəbl
AM ˈritʃəbəl

reacher
BR ˈriːtʃə(r), -z
AM ˈritʃər, -z

reacquaint
BR ˌriːəˈkweɪnt, -s, -ɪŋ, -ɨd
AM ˌriəˈkweɪn|t, -ts, -(t)ɪŋ, -(t)ɨd

reacquaintance
BR ˌriːəˈkweɪnt(ə)ns, -ɪz
AM ˌriəˈkweɪn(t)ns, -əz

reacquire
BR ˌriːəˈkwʌɪə(r), -z, -ɪŋ, -d
AM ˌriəˈkwaɪ(ə)r, -z, -ɪŋ, -d

reacquisition
BR ˌriːakwɪˈzɪʃn, -z
AM riˌækwəˈzɪʃən, -z

react
BR rɪˈakt, -s, -ɪŋ, -ɨd
AM riˈæk|(t), -(t)s, -tɪŋ, -təd

reactance
BR rɪˈakt(ə)ns, -ɪz
AM riˈæktns, -əz

reactant
BR rɪˈakt(ə)nt, -s
AM riˈæktnt, -s

reaction
BR rɪˈakʃn, -z
AM riˈækʃən, -z

reactionary
BR rɪˈakʃn̩(ə)r|i, -ɪz
AM riˈækʃəˌnɛri, -z

reactionist
BR rɪˈakʃnɪst, rɪˈakʃənɪst, -s
AM riˈækʃənəst, -s

reactivate
BR rɪˈaktɪveɪt, -s, -ɪŋ, -ɨd
AM riˈæktəˌveɪ|t, -ts, -dɪŋ, -dɨd

reactivation
BR rɪˌaktɪˈveɪʃn
AM riˌæktəˈveɪʃən

reactive
BR rɪˈaktɪv
AM riˈæktɪv

reactively
BR rɪˈaktɪvli
AM riˈæktɪvli

reactivity
BR ˌriːakˈtɪvɪt|i, -ɪz
AM ˌriˌækˈtɪvɨdi, -z

reactor
BR rɪˈaktə(r), -z
AM riˈæktər, -z

Read
BR riːd
AM rid

read[1]
present tense
BR riːd, -z, -ɪŋ
AM rid, -z, -ɪŋ

read[2]
past tense
BR rɛd
AM rɛd

readability
BR ˌriːdəˈbɪlɪti
AM ˌridəˈbɪlɨdi

readable
BR ˈriːdəbl
AM ˈridəbəl

readableness
BR ˈriːdəblnəs
AM ˈridəbəlnəs

readably
BR ˈriːdəbli
AM ˈridəbli

readapt
BR ˌriːəˈdapt, -s, -ɪŋ, -d
AM ˌriəˈdæpt, -s, -ɪŋ, -d

readaptation
BR ˌriːadəpˈteɪʃn, ˌriːadapˈteɪʃn, -z
AM riˌædəpˈteɪʃən, -z

readdress
BR ˌriːəˈdrɛs, -ɪz, -ɪŋ, -t
AM ˌriəˈdrɛs, -ɪz, -ɪŋ, -t

Reade
BR riːd
AM rid

reader
BR ˈriːdə(r), -z
AM ˈridər, -z

readership
BR ˈriːdəʃɪp, -s
AM ˈridərˌʃɪp, -s

readily
BR ˈrɛdɪli
AM ˈrɛdəli

read-in
BR ˈriːdɪn, -z
AM ˈridˌɪn, -z

readiness
BR ˈrɛdɪnɨs
AM ˈrɛdinɨs

Reading
UK town
BR ˈrɛdɪŋ
AM ˈrɛdɪŋ

reading
BR ˈriːdɪŋ, -z
AM ˈridɪŋ, -z

readjust
BR ˌriːəˈdʒʌst, -s, -ɪŋ, -ɨd
AM ˌriəˈdʒəst, -s, -ɪŋ, -ɨd

readjustment
BR ˌriːəˈdʒʌs(t)m(ə)nt, -s
AM ˌriəˈdʒəs(t)mənt, -s

Readman
BR ˈrɛdmən
AM ˈrɛdmən

readmission
BR ˌriːədˈmɪʃn, -z
AM ˌriədˈmɪʃən, -z

readmit
BR ˌriːədˈmɪt, -s, -ɪŋ, -ɨd
AM ˌriədˈmɪ|t, -ts, -dɪŋ, -dɨd

readmittance
BR ˌriːədˈmɪtns
AM ˌriədˈmɪtns

read-only memory
BR ˌriːdəʊnli ˈmɛm(ə)r|i, -ɪz
AM ˈridˌoʊnli ˈmɛm(ə)ri, -z

readopt
BR ˌriːəˈdɒpt, -s, -ɪŋ, -d
AM ˌriəˈdɑpt, -s, -ɪŋ, -d

readoption
BR ˌriːəˈdɒpʃn, -z
AM ˌriəˈdɑpʃən, -z

readout
BR ˈriːdaʊt, -s
AM ˈriˌdaʊt, -s

readthrough
BR ˈriːdθruː, -z
AM ˈridˌθru, -z

re-advertise
BR rɪˈadvətʌɪz, -ɪz, -ɪŋ, -d
AM riˈædvərˌtaɪz, -ɪz, -ɪŋ, -d

re-advertisement
BR ˌriːədˈvəːtɪsm(ə)nt, ˌriːədˈvəːtɪzm(ə)nt, -s
AM riˈædvərˌtaɪzmənt, -s

read-write
BR ˌriːdˈrʌɪt
AM ˈridˈraɪt

ready
BR ˈrɛd|i, -ɪə(r), -ɪɪst
AM ˈrɛdi, -ər, -ɨst

ready-to-serve
BR ˌrɛdɪtəˈsəːv
AM ˌrɛdidəˈsərv

ready-to-wear
BR ˌrɛdɪtəˈwɛː(r)
AM ˌrɛdidəˈwɛ(ə)r

reaffirm
BR ˌriːəˈfəːm, -z, -ɪŋ, -d
AM ˌriəˈfərm, -z, -ɪŋ, -d

reaffirmation
BR ˌriːafəˈmeɪʃn, rɪˌafəˈmeɪʃn, -z
AM ˌriˌæfərˈmeɪʃən, -z

reafforest
BR ˌriːəˈfɒrɪst, -s, -ɪŋ, -ɨd
AM ˌriəˈfɔrəst, -s, -ɪŋ, -əd

reafforestation
BR ˌriːəˌfɒrɪˈsteɪʃn
AM ˌriəˌfɔrəsˈteɪʃən

Reagan
BR ˈreɪg(ə)n
AM ˈreɪgən

reagency
BR rɪˈeɪdʒ(ə)ns|i, -ɪz
AM riˈeɪdʒənsi, -z

reagent
BR rɪˈeɪdʒ(ə)nt, -s
AM riˈeɪdʒənt, -s

real[1]
adjective
BR rɪəl
AM ri(ə)l

real[2]
money
BR reɪˈɑːl, -z
AM reɪˈɑl, riˈɑl, -z

realgar
BR rɪˈalgə(r), rɪˈalgɑː(r), -z
AM riˈælgər, riˈælˌgɑr, -z

realign
BR ˌriːəˈlʌɪn, -z, -ɪŋ, -d
AM ˌriəˈlaɪn, -z, -ɪŋ, -d

realignment
BR ˌriːəˈlʌɪnm(ə)nt, -s
AM ˌriəˈlaɪnmənt, -s

realisability
BR ˌriːəlʌɪzəˈbɪlɪt|i, -ɪz
AM ˌriəlaɪzəˈbɪlɨdi, -z

realisable
BR ˈrɪəlʌɪzəbl
AM ˌriəˈlaɪzəbəl

realisation
BR ˌrɪəlʌɪˈzeɪʃn, ˌrɪəlɪˈzeɪʃn, -z
AM ˌri(ə)ləˈzeɪʃən, -z

realise
BR ˈrɪəlʌɪz, -ɪz, -ɪŋ, -d
AM ˈri(ə)ˌlaɪz, -ɪz, -ɪŋ, -d

realiser
BR 'rɪəlʌɪzə(r), -z
AM 'ri(ə)ˌlaɪzər, -z

realism
BR 'rɪəlɪz(ə)m
AM 'riəˌlɪzəm

realist
BR 'rɪəlɪst, -s
AM 'riələst, -s

realistic
BR ˌrɪə'lɪstɪk
AM ˌriə'lɪstɪk

realistically
BR ˌrɪə'lɪstɨkli
AM ˌriə'lɪstɨk(ə)li

reality
BR rɪ'alɨt|i, -ɪz
AM ri'ælədi, -z

realizability
BR ˌrɪəlʌɪzə'bɪlɨt|i, -ɪz
AM ˌriəlaɪzə'bɪlɨdi, -z

realizable
BR 'rɪəlʌɪzəbl
AM ˌriə'laɪzəbəl

realization
BR ˌrɪəlʌɪ'zeɪʃn, ˌrɪəlɪ'zeɪʃn, -z
AM ˌri(ə)lə'zeɪʃən, -z

realize
BR 'rɪəlʌɪz, -ɨz, -ɪŋ, -d
AM 'ri(ə)ˌlaɪz, -ɨz, -ɪŋ, -d

realizer
BR 'rɪəlʌɪzə(r), -z
AM 'ri(ə)ˌlaɪzər, -z

reallocate
BR ˌriː'aləkeɪt, -s, -ɪŋ, -ɨd
AM ri'æləˌkeɪ|t, -ts, -dɪŋ, -dəd

reallocation
BR ˌriːalə'keɪʃn, rɪˌalə'keɪʃn
AM ˌriˌælə'keɪʃən

reallot
BR ˌriːə'lɒt, -s, -ɪŋ, -ɨd
AM ˌriə'lɑ|t, -ts, -dɪŋ, -dəd

reallotment
BR ˌriːə'lɒtm(ə)nt, -s
AM ˌriə'lɑtmənt, -s

really
BR 'rɪəli, 'riːli
AM 'ri(ə)li

realm
BR rɛlm, -z
AM rɛlm, -z

realness
BR 'rɪəlnəs
AM 'ri(ə)lnəs

Realpolitik
BR reɪ'ɑːlpɒlɨˌtiːk
AM reɪ'ɑlˌpɔlɨˌtik, reɪ'ɑlˌpɑlɨˌtik

realtor
BR 'rɪəltə(r), 'rɪəltɔː(r), -z
AM 'ri(ə)ltər, 'ri(ə)lˌtɔ(ə)r, -z

realty
BR 'rɪəlti
AM 'ri(ə)lti

ream
BR riːm, -z
AM rim, -z

reamer
BR 'riːmə(r), -z
AM 'rimər, -z

reanalyse
BR (ˌ)riː'anl̩ʌɪz, (ˌ)riː'anəlʌɪz, -ɨz, -ɪŋ, -d
AM ri'ænlˌaɪz, ri'ænəˌlaɪz, -ɨz, -ɪŋ, -d

reanalyses
BR ˌriːə'nalɨsiːz
AM ˌriə'næləsiz

reanalysis
BR ˌriːə'nalɨsɪs
AM ˌriə'næləsɪs

reanalyze
BR (ˌ)riː'anl̩ʌɪz, (ˌ)riː'anəlʌɪz, -ɨz, -ɪŋ, -d
AM ri'ænlˌaɪz, ri'ænəˌlaɪz, -ɨz, -ɪŋ, -d

reanimate
BR (ˌ)riː'anɪmeɪt, -s, -ɪŋ, -ɨd
AM ri'ænəˌmeɪ|t, -ts, -dɪŋ, -dɨd

reanimation
BR ˌriːanɪ'meɪʃn, riːˌanɪ'meɪʃn
AM ˌriˌænə'meɪʃən

reap
BR riːp, -s, -ɪŋ, -t
AM rip, -s, -ɪŋ, -t

reaper
BR 'riːpə(r), -z
AM 'ripər, -z

reappear
BR ˌriːə'pɪə(r), -z, -ɪŋ, -d
AM ˌriə'pɪ(ə)r, -z, -ɪŋ, -d

reappearance
BR ˌriːə'pɪərəns, ˌriːə'pɪərn̩s, -ɨz
AM ˌriə'pɪrəns, -əz

reapplication
BR ˌriːaplɪ'keɪʃn, -z
AM ˌriˌæplə'keɪʃən, -z

reapply
BR ˌriːə'plʌɪ, -z, -ɪŋ, -d
AM ˌriə'plaɪ, -z, -ɪŋ, -d

reappoint
BR ˌriːə'pɔɪnt, -s, -ɪŋ, -ɨd
AM ˌriə'pɔɪn|t, -ts, -(t)ɪŋ, -(t)ɨd

reappointment
BR ˌriːə'pɔɪntm(ə)nt, -s
AM ˌriə'pɔɪntmənt, -s

reapportion
BR ˌriːə'pɔːʃn, -z, -ɪŋ, -d
AM ˌriə'pɔrʃən, -z, -ɪŋ, -d

reapportionment
BR ˌriːə'pɔːʃnm(ə)nt, -s
AM ˌriə'pɔrʃənmənt, -s

reappraisal
BR ˌriːə'preɪzl, -z
AM ˌriə'preɪzəl, -z

reappraise
BR ˌriːə'preɪz, -ɨz, -ɪŋ, -d
AM ˌriə'preɪz, -ɨz, -ɪŋ, -d

rear
BR rɪə(r), -z, -ɪŋ, -d
AM rɪ(ə)r, -z, -ɪŋ, -d

Reardon
BR 'rɪəd(ə)n
AM 'rɪrdən

rearer
BR 'rɪərə(r), -z
AM 'rɪrər, -z

rearm
BR ˌriː'ɑːm, rɪ'ɑːm, -z, -ɪŋ, -d
AM ri'ɑrm, -z, -ɪŋ, -d

rearmament
BR ˌriː'ɑːməm(ə)nt, rɪ'ɑːməm(ə)nt
AM ri'ɑrməmənt

rearmost
BR 'rɪəməʊst
AM 'rɪrˌmoʊst

rearrange
BR ˌriːə'reɪn(d)ʒ, -ɨz, -ɪŋ, -d
AM ˌriə'reɪndʒ, -ɨz, -ɪŋ, -d

rearrangement
BR ˌriːə'reɪn(d)ʒm(ə)nt, -s
AM ˌriə'reɪndʒmənt, -s

rearrest
BR ˌriːə'rɛst, -s, -ɪŋ, -ɨd
AM ˌriə'rɛst, -s, -ɪŋ, -əd

rearview
BR ˌrɪə'vjuː
AM 'rɪrˌvju

rearward
BR 'rɪəwəd
AM 'rɪrwərd

rear-wheel drive
BR ˌrɪəwiːl 'drʌɪv
AM 'rɪrˌ(h)wil ˌdraɪv

reascend
BR ˌriːə'sɛnd, -z, -ɪŋ, -ɨd
AM ˌriə'sɛnd, -z, -ɪŋ, -əd

reascension
BR ˌriːə'sɛnʃn, -z
AM ˌriə'sɛn(t)ʃən, -z

reason
BR 'riːz|n, -nz, -n̩ɪŋ\-(ə)nɪŋ, -nd
AM 'rizn̩, -z, -ɪŋ, -d

reasonable
BR 'riːzn̩əbl, 'riːz(ə)nəbl
AM 'rizn̩əbəl, 'riznəbəl

reasonableness
BR 'riːzn̩əblnəs, 'riːz(ə)nəblnəs
AM 'rizn̩əbəlnəs, 'riznəbəlnəs

reasonably
BR 'riːzn̩əbli, 'riːz(ə)nəbli
AM 'rizn̩əbli, 'riznəbli

reasoner
BR 'riːzn̩ə(r), 'riːz(ə)nə(r), -z
AM 'rizn̩ər, 'riznər, -z

reasoning
BR 'riːzn̩ɪŋ, 'riːz(ə)nɪŋ, -z
AM 'rizn̩ɪŋ, 'riznɪŋ, -z

reasonless
BR 'riːznləs
AM 'riznləs

reassemble
BR ˌriːə'sɛmb|l, -lz, -l̩ɪŋ\-lɪŋ, -ld
AM ˌriə'sɛmbəl, -z, -ɪŋ, -d

reassembly
BR ˌriːə'sɛmbl|i, -ɪz
AM ˌriə'sɛmbli, -z

reassert
BR ˌriːə'səːt, -s, -ɪŋ, -ɨd
AM ˌriə'sər|t, -ts, -dɪŋ, -dəd

reassertion
BR ˌriːə'səːʃn
AM ˌriə'sərʃən

reassess
BR ˌriːə'sɛs, -ɨz, -ɪŋ, -t
AM ˌriə'sɛs, -əz, -ɪŋ, -t

reassessment
BR ˌriːə'sɛsm(ə)nt, -s
AM ˌriə'sɛsmənt, -s

reassign
BR ˌriːə'sʌɪn, -z, -ɪŋ, -d
AM ˌriə'saɪn, -z, -ɪŋ, -d

reassignment
BR ˌriːə'sʌɪnm(ə)nt, -s
AM ˌriə'saɪnmənt, -s

reassume
BR ˌriːə'sjuːm, -z, -ɪŋ, -d
AM ˌriə's(j)um, -z, -ɪŋ, -d

reassumption
BR ˌriːə'sʌm(p)ʃn, -z
AM ˌriə'səm(p)ʃən, -z

reassurance
BR ˌriːə'ʃʊərəns, ˌriːə'ʃʊərn̩s, ˌriːə'ʃɔːrəns, ˌriːə'ʃɔːrn̩s
AM ˌriə'ʃʊrəns

reassure
BR ˌriːə'ʃʊə(r), ˌriːə'ʃɔː(r), -z, -ɪŋ, -d
AM ˌriə'ʃʊ(ə)r, -z, -ɪŋ, -d

reassurer
BR ˌriːə'ʃʊərə(r), ˌriːə'ʃɔːrə(r), -z
AM ˌriə'ʃʊrər, -z

reassuring
BR ˌriːə'ʃʊərɪŋ, ˌriːə'ʃɔːrɪŋ
AM ˌriə'ʃʊrɪŋ

reassuringly
BR ˌriːəˈʃʊərɪŋli, ˌriːəˈʃɔːrɪŋli
AM ˈriəˈʃʊrɪŋli

reattach
BR ˌriːəˈtatʃ, -ɨz, -ɪŋ, -t
AM ˈriəˈtætʃ, -əz, -ɪŋ, -t

reattachment
BR ˌriːəˈtatʃm(ə)nt, -s
AM ˈriəˈtætʃmənt, -s

reattain
BR ˌriːəˈteɪn, -z, -ɪŋ, -d
AM ˈriəˈteɪn, -z, -ɪŋ, -d

reattainment
BR ˌriːəˈteɪnm(ə)nt, -s
AM ˈriəˈteɪnmənt, -s

reattempt
BR ˌriːəˈtɛm(p)t, -s, -ɪŋ, -ɨd
AM ˈriəˈtɛm(p)t, -s, -ɪŋ, -əd

reave
BR riːv, -z, -ɪŋ, -d
AM riv, -z, -ɪŋ, -d

reawaken
BR ˌriːəˈweɪk|(ə)n, -(ə)nz, -(ə)nɪŋ\-n̩ɪŋ, -(ə)nd
AM ˈriəˈweɪk|ən, -ənz, -(ə)nɪŋ, -ənd

Reay
BR reɪ
AM reɪ

reb
BR rɛb, -z
AM rɛb, -z

rebadge
BR ˌriːˈbadʒ, -ɨz, -ɪŋ, -d
AM ˌriˈbædʒ, -ɨz, -ɪŋ, -d

rebalance
BR ˌriːˈbaləns, ˌriːˈbaln̩s, -ɨz, -ɪŋ, -t
AM rəˈbæləns, riˈbæləns, -əz, -ɪŋ, -t

rebaptise
BR ˌriːbapˈtʌɪz, -ɨz, -ɪŋ, -d
AM rəˈbæpˌtaɪz, ˌriˈbæpˌtaɪz, -ɨz, -ɪŋ, -d

rebaptize
BR ˌriːbapˈtʌɪz, -ɨz, -ɪŋ, -d
AM rəˈbæpˌtaɪz, ˌriˈbæpˌtaɪz, -ɨz, -ɪŋ, -d

rebar
noun
BR ˈriːbɑː(r)
AM ˈribar

rebarbative
BR rɪˈbɑːbətɪv
AM rəˈbɑrbədɪv

rebase
BR ˌriːˈbeɪs, -ɨz, -ɪŋ, -t
AM rəˈbeɪs, riˈbeɪs, -ɨz, -ɪŋ, -t

rebatable
BR ˈriːbeɪtəbl
AM ˈriˌbeɪdəbəl

rebate[1]
finance
BR ˈriːbeɪt, -s
AM ˈriˌbeɪt, -s

rebate[2]
joint
BR ˈriːbeɪt, ˈrabɪt, -s, -ɪŋ, -ɨd
AM ˈræbɪt, ˈriˌbeɪ|t, -ts, -dɪŋ, -dɨd

rebater
BR ˈriːbeɪtə(r), -z
AM ˈriˌbeɪdər, -z

rebbe
BR ˈrɛbə(*r*), -z
AM ˈrɛbə, -z

rebbetzin
BR ˈrɛbɨtsɪn, -z
AM ˈrɛbətsɪn, -z

rebec
BR ˈriːbɛk, -s
AM ˈrɛbək, ˈriˌbɛk, -s

Rebecca
BR rɪˈbɛkə(*r*)
AM rəˈbɛkə

rebeck
BR ˈriːbɛk, -s
AM ˈrɛbək, ˈriˌbɛk, -s

rebel[1]
noun
BR ˈrɛbl, -z
AM ˈrɛbəl, -z

rebel[2]
verb
BR rɪˈbɛl, -z, -ɪŋ, -d
AM rəˈbɛl, -z, -ɪŋ, -d

rebellion
BR rɪˈbɛljən, -z
AM rəˈbɛljən, riˈbɛljən, -z

rebellious
BR rɪˈbɛljəs
AM rəˈbɛljəs, riˈbɛljəs

rebelliously
BR rɪˈbɛljəsli
AM rəˈbɛljəsli, riˈbɛljəsli

rebelliousness
BR rɪˈbɛljəsnəs
AM rəˈbɛljəsnəs, riˈbɛljəsnəs

rebid[1]
noun
BR ˈriːbɪd, -z
AM ˈriˌbɪd, -z

rebid[2]
verb
BR ˌriːˈbɪd, -z, -ɪŋ
AM ˌriˈbɪd, -z, -ɪŋ

rebind
BR ˌriːˈbʌɪnd, -z, -ɪŋ
AM ˌriˈbaɪnd, -z, -ɪŋ

rebirth
BR ˌriːˈbəːθ, ˈriːbəːθ, -s
AM riˈbərθ, -s

rebirther
BR ˌriːˈbəːθə(r), ˈriːbəːθə(r), -z
AM riˈbərθər, -z

rebirthing
BR ˌriːˈbəːθɪŋ, ˈriːbəːθɪŋ, -z
AM riˈbərθɪŋ, -z

reboot
BR ˌriːˈbuːt, -s, -ɪŋ, -ɨd
AM ˌriˈbu|t, -ts, -dɪŋ, -dəd

rebore
BR ˌriːˈbɔː(r), -z, -ɪŋ, -d
AM ˌriˈbɔ(ə)r, -z, -ɪŋ, -d

reborn
BR ˌriːˈbɔːn
AM riˈbɔ(ə)rn

rebound[1]
adjective
BR ˌriːˈbaʊnd
AM ˈriˌbaʊnd

rebound[2]
noun
BR ˈriːbaʊnd
AM ˈriˌbaʊnd

rebound[3]
past tense of rebind
BR ˌriːˈbaʊnd
AM ˌriˈbaʊnd

rebound[4]
verb, of basketball
BR rɪˈbaʊnd, -z, -ɪŋ, -ɨd
AM ˈriˌbaʊnd, -z, -ɪŋ, -əd

rebounder
BR rɪˈbaʊndə(r), -z
AM ˈriˌbaʊndər, -z

rebozo
BR rɪˈbəʊzəʊ, -z
AM rəˈboʊzoʊ, -z

rebroadcast
BR ˌriːˈbrɔːdkɑːst, ˌriːˈbrɔːdkast, -s, -ɪŋ
AM ˈriˈbrɔdˌkæst, ˈriˈbrɑdˌkæst, -s, -ɪŋ

rebuff
BR rɪˈbʌf, -s, -ɪŋ, -t
AM rəˈbəf, riˈbəf, -s, -ɪŋ, -t

rebuild[1]
noun
BR ˈriːbɪld, -z
AM ˈriˌbɪld, -z

rebuild[2]
verb
BR (ˌ)riːˈbɪld, -z, -ɪŋ
AM riˈbɪld, -z, -ɪŋ

rebuilder
BR (ˌ)riːˈbɪldə(r), -z
AM riˈbɪldər, -z

rebuilding
BR (ˌ)riːˈbɪldɪŋ, -z
AM riˈbɪldɪŋ, -z

rebuilt
BR (ˌ)riːˈbɪlt
AM riˈbɪlt, ˈriˈbɪlt

rebuke
BR rɪˈbjuːk, -s, -ɪŋ, -t
AM rəˈbjuk, riˈbjuk, -s, -ɪŋ, -t

rebuker
BR rɪˈbjuːkə(r), -z
AM rəˈbjukər, riˈbjukər, -z

rebukingly
BR rɪˈbjuːkɪŋli
AM rəˈbjukɪŋli, riˈbjukɪŋli

reburial
BR ˌriːˈbɛrɪəl, -z
AM riˈbɛriəl, -z

rebury
BR ˌriːˈbɛr|i, -ɪz, -ɪɪŋ, -ɪd
AM ˌriˈbɛri, -z, -ɪŋ, -d

rebus
BR ˈriːbəs, -ɨz
AM ˈribəs, -əz

rebut
BR rɪˈbʌt, -s, -ɪŋ, -ɨd
AM rəˈbə|t, riˈbə|t, -ts, -dɪŋ, -dəd

rebutment
BR rɪˈbʌtm(ə)nt, -s
AM rəˈbətmənt, riˈbətmənt, -s

rebuttable
BR rɪˈbʌtəbl
AM rəˈbədəbəl, riˈbədəbəl

rebuttal
BR rɪˈbʌtl, -z
AM rəˈbədl, riˈbədl, -z

rebutter
BR rɪˈbʌtə(r), -z
AM rəˈbədər, riˈbədər, -z

rec
BR rɛk
AM rɛk

recalcitrance
BR rɪˈkalsɪtr(ə)ns
AM rəˈkælsətrəns, riˈkælsətrəns

recalcitrant
BR rɪˈkalsɪtr(ə)nt, -s
AM rəˈkælsətrənt, riˈkælsətrənt, -s

recalcitrantly
BR rɪˈkalsɪtr(ə)ntli
AM rəˈkælsətrən(t)li, riˈkælsətrən(t)li

recalculate
BR ˌriːˈkalkjʊleɪt, -s, -ɪŋ, -ɨd
AM rəˈkælkjəˌleɪ|t, riˈkælkjəˌleɪ|t, -ts, -dɪŋ, -dɨd

recalculation
BR ˌriːkalkjʊˈleɪʃn, -z
AM rəˌkælkjəˈleɪʃən, riˌkælkjəˈleɪʃən, -z

recalesce
BR ˌriːkəˈlɛs, -ɨz, -ɪŋ, -t
AM ˌrikəˈlɛs, -əz, -ɪŋ, -t

recalescence
BR ˌriːkəˈlɛsns
AM ˌrikəˈlɛsns

recall[1]
noun, something called back for correction
BR 'ri:kɔ:l, -z
AM 'riˌkɔl, 'riˌkɑl, -z

recall[2]
noun, something remembered
BR rɪ'kɔ:l, 'ri:kɔ:l
AM 'riˌkɔl, rə'kɔl, ri'kɔl, 'riˌkɑl, rə'kɑl, ri'kɑl

recall[3]
verb
BR rɪ'kɔ:l, -z, -ɪŋ, -d
AM rə'kɔl, ri'kɔl, rə'kɑl, ri'kɑl, -z, -ɪŋ, -d

recallable
BR rɪ'kɔ:ləbl
AM rə'kɔləbəl, ri'kɔləbəl, rə'kɑləbəl, ri'kɑləbəl

recant
BR rɪ'kant, -s, -ɪŋ, -ɪd
AM rə'kæn|t, ri'kæn|t, -ts, -(t)ɪŋ, -(t)əd

recantation
BR ˌri:kan'teɪʃn, -z
AM ˌriˌkæn'teɪʃən, -z

recanter
BR rɪ'kantə(r), -z
AM rə'kæn(t)ər, ri'kæn(t)ər, -z

recap[1]
noun
BR 'ri:kap, -s
AM 'riˌkæp, -s

recap[2]
verb
BR ˌri:'kap, 'ri:kap, -s, -ɪŋ, -t
AM ri'kæp, -s, -ɪŋ, -t

recapitalisation
BR (ˌ)ri:ˌkapɪtl̩ʌɪ'zeɪʃn
AM rəˌkæpədlə'zeɪʃən, riˌkæpədlə'zeɪʃən, rəˌkæpədlˌaɪ'zeɪʃən, riˌkæpədlˌaɪ'zeɪʃən, rəˌkæpədələ'zeɪʃən, riˌkæpədələ'zeɪʃən, rəˌkæpədəˌlaɪ'zeɪʃən, riˌkæpədəˌlaɪ'zeɪʃən

recapitalise
BR (ˌ)ri:'kapɪtl̩ʌɪz, -ɪz, -ɪŋ, -d
AM rə'kæpədlˌaɪz, ri'kæpədlˌaɪz, rə'kæpədəˌlaɪz, ri'kæpədəˌlaɪz, -ɪz, -ɪŋ, -d

recapitalization
BR (ˌ)ri:ˌkapɪtl̩ʌɪ'zeɪʃn
AM rəˌkæpədlə'zeɪʃən, riˌkæpədlə'zeɪʃən, rəˌkæpədlˌaɪ'zeɪʃən, riˌkæpədlˌaɪ'zeɪʃən, rəˌkæpədələ'zeɪʃən, riˌkæpədələ'zeɪʃən, rəˌkæpədəˌlaɪ'zeɪʃən, riˌkæpədəˌlaɪ'zeɪʃən

recapitalize
BR (ˌ)ri:'kapɪtl̩ʌɪz, -ɪz, -ɪŋ, -d
AM rə'kæpədlˌaɪz, ri'kæpədlˌaɪz, rə'kæpədəˌlaɪz, ri'kæpədəˌlaɪz, -ɪz, -ɪŋ, -d

recapitulate
BR ˌri:kə'pɪtʃʊleɪt, ˌri:kə'pɪtjʊleɪt, -s, -ɪŋ, -ɪd
AM ˌrikə'pɪtʃəˌleɪ|t, -ts, -dɪŋ, -dɪd

recapitulation
BR ˌri:kəˌpɪtʃʊ'leɪʃn, ˌri:kəˌpɪtjʊ'leɪʃn, -z
AM ˌrikəˌpɪtʃə'leɪʃən, -z

recapitulative
BR ˌri:kə'pɪtʃʊlətɪv, ˌri:kə'pɪtjʊlətɪv
AM ˌrikə'pɪtʃələdɪv, ˌrikə'pɪtʃəˌleɪdɪv

recapitulatory
BR ˌri:kə'pɪtʃʊlət(ə)ri, ˌri:kə'pɪtjʊlət(ə)ri
AM ˌrikə'pɪtʃələˌtɔri

recapture
BR (ˌ)ri:'kaptʃ|ə(r), -əz, -(ə)rɪŋ, -əd
AM ri'kæptʃ|ər, -ərz, -(ə)rɪŋ, -ərd

recast
BR ˌri:'kɑ:st, ˌri:'kast, -s, -ɪŋ
AM ri'kæst, -s, -ɪŋ

recce
BR 'rɛk|i, -ɪz, -ɪɪŋ, -ɪd
AM 'rɛki, -z, -ɪŋ, -d

recede
BR rɪ'si:d, -z, -ɪŋ, -ɪd
AM rə'sid, ri'sid, -z, -ɪŋ, -ɪd

re-cede
BR ˌri:'si:d, -z, -ɪŋ, -ɪd
AM ˌri'sid, -z, -ɪŋ, -ɪd

receipt
BR rɪ'si:t, -s, -ɪŋ, -ɪd
AM rə'si|t, ri'si|t, -ts, -dɪŋ, -dɪd

receivable
BR rɪ'si:vəbl
AM rə'sivəbəl, ri'sivəbəl

receive
BR rɪ'si:v, -z, -ɪŋ, -d
AM rə'siv, ri'siv, -z, -ɪŋ, -d

receiver
BR rɪ'si:və(r), -z
AM rə'sivər, ri'sivər, -z

receivership
BR rɪ'si:vəʃɪp, -s
AM rə'sivərˌʃɪp, ri'sivərˌʃɪp, -s

recency
BR 'ri:snsi
AM 'risənsi

recension
BR rɪ'sɛnʃn, -z
AM rə'sɛnʃən, ri'sɛnʃən, -z

recent
BR 'ri:snt
AM 'risənt

recently
BR 'ri:sntli
AM 'risn(t)li

recentness
BR 'ri:sntnəs
AM 'risn(t)nɪs

recep
BR rɪ'sɛp, -s
AM 'riˌsɛp, -s

receptacle
BR rɪ'sɛptəkl, -z
AM rə'sɛptəkəl, ri'sɛptəkəl, -z

reception
BR rɪ'sɛpʃn, -z
AM rə'sɛpʃən, ri'sɛpʃən, -z

receptionist
BR rɪ'sɛpʃn̩ɪst, rɪ'sɛpʃənɪst, -s
AM rə'sɛpʃənəst, ri'sɛpʃənəst, -s

receptive
BR rɪ'sɛptɪv
AM rə'sɛptɪv, ri'sɛptɪv

receptively
BR rɪ'sɛptɪvli
AM rə'sɛptɪvli, ri'sɛptɪvli

receptiveness
BR rɪ'sɛptɪvnɪs
AM rə'sɛptɪvnɪs, ri'sɛptɪvnɪs

receptivity
BR ˌri:sɛp'tɪvɪti
AM ˌriˌsɛp'tɪvɪdi

receptor
BR rɪ'sɛptə(r), -z
AM ri'sɛptər, -z

recess[1]
noun
BR rɪ'sɛs, 'ri:sɛs, -ɪz
AM 'riˌsɛs, rə'sɛs, ri'sɛs, -əz

recess[2]
verb
BR rɪ'sɛs, -ɪz, -ɪŋ, -t
AM 'riˌsɛs, rə'sɛs, ri'sɛs, -əz, -ɪŋ, -t

recession
BR rɪ'sɛʃn, -z
AM rə'sɛʃən, ri'sɛʃən, -z

recessional
BR rɪ'sɛʃn̩(ə)l, rɪ'sɛʃən(ə)l, -z
AM rə'sɛʃ(ə)nəl, ri'sɛʃ(ə)nəl, -z

recessionary
BR rɪ'sɛʃn̩(ə)ri
AM rə'sɛʃəˌnɛri, ri'sɛʃəˌnɛri

recessive
BR rɪ'sɛsɪv
AM rə'sɛsɪv, ri'sɛsɪv

recessively
BR rɪ'sɛsɪvli
AM rə'sɛsɪvli, ri'sɛsɪvli

recessiveness
BR rɪ'sɛsɪvnɪs
AM rə'sɛsɪvnɪs, ri'sɛsɪvnɪs

Rechabite
BR 'rɛkəbʌɪt, -s
AM 'rɛkəˌbaɪt, -s

recharge
BR ˌri:'tʃɑ:dʒ, -ɪz, -ɪŋ, -d
AM ri'tʃɑrdʒ, -əz, -ɪŋ, -d

rechargeable
BR ˌri:'tʃɑ:dʒəbl
AM ri'tʃɑrdʒəbəl

recharger
BR ˌri:'tʃɑ:dʒə(r), -z
AM ri'tʃɑrdʒər, -z

réchauffé
BR reɪ'ʃəʊfeɪ, -z
AM ˌreɪˌʃoʊ'feɪ, -z

recheck
BR ˌri:'tʃɛk, -s, -ɪŋ, -t
AM ri'tʃɛk, -s, -ɪŋ, -t

recherché
BR rə'ʃɛ:ʃeɪ
AM rəˌʃɛr'ʃeɪ

rechristen
BR ˌri:'krɪs|n, -nz, -n̩ɪŋ\-(ə)nɪŋ, -nd
AM ri'krɪsn, -z, -ɪŋ, -d

recidivism
BR rɪ'sɪdɪvɪz(ə)m
AM rə'sɪdəˌvɪzəm, ri'sɪdəˌvɪzəm

recidivist
BR rɪ'sɪdɪvɪst, -s
AM rə'sɪdəvəst, ri'sɪdəvəst, -s

recidivistic
BR rɪˌsɪdɪ'vɪstɪk
AM rəˌsɪdə'vɪstɪk, riˌsɪdə'vɪstɪk

Recife
BR rɛ'si:feɪ
AM rɛ'sifeɪ
B PORT xe'sifi
L PORT ʀə'sifə

recipe
BR 'rɛsɪp|i, -ɪz
AM 'rɛsəˌpi, -z

recipiency
BR rɪ'sɪpɪənsi
AM rə'sɪpiənsi, ri'sɪpiənsi

recipient
BR rɪ'sɪpɪənt, -s

AM rə'sɪpiənt, ri'sɪpiənt, -s

reciprocal
BR rɪ'sɪprəkl, -z
AM rə'sɪprəkəl, ri'sɪprəkəl, -z

reciprocality
BR rɪˌsɪprə'kalɪt|i, -ɪz
AM rəˌsɪprə'kælədi, riˌsɪprə'kælədi, -z

reciprocally
BR rɪ'sɪprəkl̩i, rɪ'sɪprəkəli
AM rə'sɪprək(ə)li, ri'sɪprək(ə)li

reciprocalness
BR rɪ'sɪprəklnəs
AM rə'sɪprəkəlnəs, ri'sɪprəkəlnəs

reciprocate
BR rɪ'sɪprəkeɪt, -s, -ɪŋ, -ɪd
AM rə'sɪprəˌkeɪ|t, ri'sɪprəˌkeɪ|t, -ts, -dɪŋ, -dɪd

reciprocation
BR rɪˌsɪprə'keɪʃn
AM rəˌsɪprə'keɪʃən, riˌsɪprə'keɪʃən

reciprocator
BR rɪ'sɪprəkeɪtə(r), -z
AM rə'sɪprəˌkeɪdər, ri'sɪprəˌkeɪdər, -z

reciprocity
BR ˌrɛsɪ'prɒsɪti
AM ˌrɛsə'prɑsədi

recirculate
BR ˌriː'səːkjʊleɪt, -s, -ɪŋ, -ɪd
AM rə'sərkjəˌleɪ|t, ri'sərkjəˌleɪ|t, -ts, -dɪŋ, -dɪd

recirculation
BR riːˌsəːkjʊ'leɪʃn, -z
AM rəˌsərkjə'leɪʃən, riˌsərkjə'leɪʃən, -z

recision
BR rɪ'sɪʒn, -z
AM ri'sɪʒən, rə'sɪʒən, -z

recital
BR rɪ'sʌɪtl, -z
AM rə'saɪdl, ri'saɪdl, -z

recitalist
BR rɪ'sʌɪtl̩ɪst, -s
AM rə'saɪdl̩əst, ri'saɪdl̩əst, -s

recitation
BR ˌrɛsɪ'teɪʃn, -z
AM ˌrɛsə'teɪʃən, -z

recitative
BR ˌrɛsɪtə'tiːv, -z
AM ˌrɛsədə'tiv, -z

recite
BR rɪ'sʌɪt, -s, -ɪŋ, -ɪd
AM rə'saɪ|t, ri'saɪ|t, -ts, -dɪŋ, -dɪd

reciter
BR rɪ'sʌɪtə(r), -z
AM rə'saɪdər, ri'saɪdər, -z

reck
BR rɛk, -s, -ɪŋ, -t
AM rɛk, -s, -ɪŋ, -t

reckless
BR 'rɛkləs
AM 'rɛkləs

recklessly
BR 'rɛkləsli
AM 'rɛkləsli

recklessness
BR 'rɛkləsnəs
AM 'rɛkləsnəs

reckon
BR 'rɛk|(ə)n, -(ə)nz, -(ə)nɪŋ\-n̩ɪŋ, -(ə)nd
AM 'rɛk|ən, -ənz, -(ə)nɪŋ, -ənd

reckoner
BR 'rɛk(ə)nə(r), 'rɛkn̩ə(r), -z
AM 'rɛk(ə)nər, -z

reckoning
BR 'rɛk(ə)nɪŋ, 'rɛkn̩ɪŋ, -z
AM 'rɛk(ə)nɪŋ, -z

reclaim
BR rɪ'kleɪm, ˌriː'kleɪm, -z, -ɪŋ, -d
AM rə'kleɪm, ri'kleɪm, -z, -ɪŋ, -d

reclaimable
BR rɪ'kleɪməbl, ˌriː'kleɪməbl
AM rə'kleɪməbəl, ri'kleɪməbəl

reclaimer
BR rɪ'kleɪmə(r), ˌriː'kleɪmə(r), -z
AM rə'kleɪmər, ri'kleɪmər, -z

reclamation
BR ˌrɛklə'meɪʃn
AM ˌrɛklə'meɪʃən

reclassification
BR riːˌklasɪfɪ'keɪʃn, -z
AM rəˌklæsəfə'keɪʃən, riˌklæsəfə'keɪʃən, -z

reclassify
BR ˌriː'klasɪfʌɪ, -z, -ɪŋ, -d
AM rə'klæsəˌfaɪ, ri'klæsəˌfaɪ, -z, -ɪŋ, -d

reclinable
BR rɪ'klʌɪnəbl
AM rə'klaɪnəbəl, ri'klaɪnəbəl

reclinate
BR 'rɛklɪneɪt
AM 'rɛkləˌneɪt, 'rɛklənət

recline
BR rɪ'klʌɪn, -z, -ɪŋ, -d
AM rə'klaɪn, ri'klaɪn, -z, -ɪŋ, -d

recliner
BR rɪ'klʌɪnə(r), -z
AM rə'klaɪnər, ri'klaɪnər, -z

reclosable
BR ˌriː'kləʊzəbl
AM ri'kloʊzəbəl

reclothe
BR ˌriː'kləʊð, -z, -ɪŋ, -d
AM ˌri'kloʊ|ð, -(ð)z, -ðɪŋ, -ðd

recluse
BR rɪ'kluːs, -ɪz
AM 'rɛˌklus, rə'klus, ri'klus, 'rɛˌkluz, rə'kluz, ri'kluz, -əz

reclusion
BR rɪ'kluːʒn
AM rə'kluʒən, ri'kluʒən

reclusive
BR rɪ'kluːsɪv
AM rə'klusɪv, rə'kluzɪv

reclusiveness
BR rɪ'kluːsɪvnɪs
AM rə'klusɪvnɪs, rə'kluzɪvnɪs

recode
BR ˌriː'kəʊd, -z, -ɪŋ, -ɪd
AM ˌri'koʊd, -z, -ɪŋ, -əd

recognisability
BR ˌrɛkəgˌnʌɪzə'bɪlɪti
AM ˌrɛkə(g)ˌnaɪzə'bɪlɪdi

recognisable
BR 'rɛkəgnʌɪzəbl, ˌrɛkəg'nʌɪzəbl
AM ˌrɛkə(g)'naɪzəbəl

recognisably
BR 'rɛkəgnʌɪzəbli, ˌrɛkəg'nʌɪzəbli
AM ˌrɛkə(g)'naɪzəbli

recognisance
BR rɪ'kɒgnɪz(ə)ns, -ɪz
AM rə'kɑgnəzəns, ri'kɑgnəzəns, -əz

recognisant
BR rɪ'kɒgnɪz(ə)nt
AM rə'kɑgnəznt, ri'kɑgnəznt

recognise
BR 'rɛkəgnʌɪz, -ɪz, -ɪŋ, -d
AM 'rɛkə(g)ˌnaɪz, -ɪz, -ɪŋ, -d

recogniser
BR 'rɛkəgnʌɪzə(r), -z
AM 'rɛkə(g)ˌnaɪzər, -z

recognition
BR ˌrɛkəg'nɪʃn
AM ˌrɛkəg'nɪʃən

recognitory
BR rɪ'kɒgnɪt(ə)ri
AM rə'kɑgnəˌtɔri, ri'kɑgnəˌtɔri

recognizability
BR ˌrɛkəgˌnʌɪzə'bɪlɪti
AM ˌrɛkə(g)ˌnaɪzə'bɪlɪdi

recognizable
BR 'rɛkəgnʌɪzəbl, ˌrɛkəg'nʌɪzəbl
AM ˌrɛkə(g)'naɪzəbəl

recognizably
BR 'rɛkəgnʌɪzəbli, ˌrɛkəg'nʌɪzəbli
AM ˌrɛkə(g)'naɪzəbli

recognizance
BR rɪ'kɒgnɪz(ə)ns, -ɪz
AM rə'kɑgnəzəns, ri'kɑgnəzns, -əz

recognizant
BR rɪ'kɒgnɪz(ə)nt
AM rə'kɑgnəznt, ri'kɑgnəznt

recognize
BR 'rɛkəgnʌɪz, -ɪz, -ɪŋ, -d
AM 'rɛkə(g)ˌnaɪz, -ɪz, -ɪŋ, -d

recognizer
BR 'rɛkəgnʌɪzə(r), -z
AM 'rɛkə(g)ˌnaɪzər, -z

recoil[1]
noun
BR 'riːkɔɪl, -z
AM 'riˌkɔɪl, -z

recoil[2]
verb
BR rɪ'kɔɪl, -z, -ɪŋ, -d
AM rə'kɔɪl, ri'kɔɪl, -z, -ɪŋ, -d

recoilless
BR rɪ'kɔɪlɪs, 'riːkɔɪlɪs
AM rə'kɔɪlɪs, ri'kɔɪlɪs

recoin
BR ˌriː'kɔɪn, -z, -ɪŋ, -d
AM ˌri'kɔɪn, -z, -ɪŋ, -d

recollect[1]
collect again
BR ˌriːkə'lɛkt, -s, -ɪŋ, -ɪd
AM ˌrikə'lɛk|(t), -(t)s, -tɪŋ, -təd

recollect[2]
remember
BR ˌrɛkə'lɛkt, -s, -ɪŋ, -ɪd
AM ˌrɛkə'lɛk|(t), -(t)s, -tɪŋ, -təd

recollection
BR ˌrɛkə'lɛkʃn, -z
AM ˌrɛkə'lɛkʃən, -z

recollective
BR ˌrɛkə'lɛktɪv
AM ˌrɛkə'lɛktɪv

recolonisation
BR (ˌ)riːˌkɒlənʌɪ'zeɪʃn, -z
AM riˌkɑlənə'zeɪʃən, riˌkɑləˌnaɪ'zeɪʃən, -z

recolonise
BR (ˌ)riː'kɒlənʌɪz, -ɪz, -ɪŋ, -d
AM ˌri'kɑləˌnaɪz, -ɪz, -ɪŋ, -d

recolonization
BR (ˌ)riːˌkɒlənʌɪ'zeɪʃn, -z

AM riˌkɑlənəˈzeɪʃən, riˌkɑləˌnaɪˈzeɪʃən, -z

recolonize
BR (ˌ)riːˈkɒlənʌɪz, -ɨz, -ɪŋ, -d
AM ˈriˈkɑləˌnaɪz, -ɨz, -ɪŋ, -d

recolor
BR ˌriːˈkʌlə(r), -z, -ɪŋ, -d
AM ˈriˈkələr, -z, -ɪŋ, -d

recolour
BR ˌriːˈkʌlə(r), -z, -ɪŋ, -d
AM ˈriˈkələr, -z, -ɪŋ, -d

recombinant
BR (ˌ)riːˈkɒmbɪnənt, rɪˈkɒmbɪnənt, -s
AM riˈkɑmbənənt, -s

recombination
BR ˌriːkɒmbɪˈneɪʃn, -z
AM ˈriˌkɑmbəˈneɪʃən, -z

recombine
BR ˌriːkəmˈbʌɪn, -z, -ɪŋ, -d
AM ˌrikəmˈbaɪn, -z, -ɪŋ, -d

recommence
BR ˌriːkəˈmɛns, ˌrɛkəˈmɛns, -ɨz, -ɪŋ, -t
AM ˈrikəˈmɛns, -əz, -ɪŋ, -t

recommencement
BR ˌriːkəˈmɛnsm(ə)nt, ˌrɛkəˈmɛnsm(ə)nt, -s
AM ˈrikəˈmɛnsmənt, -s

recommend
BR ˌrɛkəˈmɛnd, -z, -ɪŋ, -ɨd
AM ˌrɛkəˈmɛnd, -z, -ɪŋ, -əd

recommendable
BR ˌrɛkəˈmɛndəbl
AM ˌrɛkəˈmɛndəbəl

recommendation
BR ˌrɛkəmɛnˈdeɪʃn, ˌrɛkəm(ə)nˈdeɪʃn, -z
AM ˌrɛkəmənˈdeɪʃən, ˌrɛkəˌmɛnˈdeɪʃən, -z

recommendatory
BR ˌrɛkəˈmɛndət(ə)ri
AM ˌrɛkəˈmɛndəˌtɔri

recommender
BR ˌrɛkəˈmɛndə(r), -z
AM ˌrɛkəˈmɛndər, -z

recommission
BR ˌriːkəˈmɪʃ|n, -nz, -n̩ɪŋ\-nɪŋ, -nd
AM ˈrikəˈmɪʃən, -z, -ɪŋ, -d

recommit
BR ˌriːkəˈmɪt, -s, -ɪŋ, -ɨd
AM ˈrikəˈmɪ|t, -ts, -dɪŋ, -dɨd

recommitment
BR ˌriːkəˈmɪtm(ə)nt, -s
AM ˈrikəˈmɪtmənt, -s

recommittal
BR ˌriːkəˈmɪtl, -z
AM ˈrikəˈmɪdl, -z

recompense
BR ˈrɛkəmpɛns, -ɨz, -ɪŋ, -t
AM ˈrɛkəmˌpɛns, -əz, -ɪŋ, -t

recompose
BR ˌriːkəmˈpəʊz, -ɨz, -ɪŋ, -d
AM ˈrikəmˈpoʊz, -əz, -ɪŋ, -d

reconcilability
BR ˌrɛk(ə)nˌsʌɪləˈbɪlɨti
AM ˈrɛkənˌsaɪləˈbɪlɨdi

reconcilable
BR ˈrɛk(ə)nsʌɪləbl, ˌrɛk(ə)nˈsʌɪləbl
AM ˌrɛkənˈsaɪləbəl

reconcilably
BR ˈrɛk(ə)nsʌɪləbli, ˌrɛk(ə)nˈsʌɪləbli
AM ˌrɛkənˈsaɪləbli

reconcile
BR ˈrɛk(ə)nsʌɪl, -z, -ɪŋ, -d
AM ˈrɛkənˌsaɪl, -z, -ɪŋ, -d

reconcilement
BR ˈrɛk(ə)nsʌɪlm(ə)nt, -s
AM ˈrɛkənˌsaɪlmənt, -s

reconciler
BR ˈrɛk(ə)nsʌɪlə(r), -z
AM ˈrɛkənˌsaɪlər, -z

reconciliation
BR ˌrɛk(ə)nsɪlɪˈeɪʃn, -z
AM ˌrɛkənˌsɪliˈeɪʃən, -z

reconciliatory
BR ˌrɛk(ə)nˈsɪlɪət(ə)ri
AM ˌrɛkənˈsɪliəˌtɔri

recondite
BR ˈrɛk(ə)ndʌɪt, rɪˈkɒndʌɪt
AM ˈrɛkənˌdaɪt, rəˈkɑnˌdaɪt, riˈkɑnˌdaɪt

reconditely
BR ˈrɛk(ə)ndʌɪtli, rɪˈkɒndʌɪtli
AM ˈrɛkənˌdaɪtli, rəˈkɑnˌdaɪtli, riˈkɑnˌdaɪtli

reconditeness
BR ˈrɛk(ə)ndʌɪtnɨs, rɪˈkɒndʌɪtnɨs
AM ˈrɛkənˌdaɪtnɨs, rəˈkɑnˌdaɪtnɨs, riˈkɑnˌdaɪtnɨs

recondition
BR ˌriːkənˈdɪʃ|n, -nz, -n̩ɪŋ\-nɪŋ, -nd
AM ˈrikənˈdɪʃ|ən, -ənz, -(ə)nɪŋ, -ənd

reconditioner
BR ˌriːkənˈdɪʃn̩ə(r), ˌriːkənˈdɪʃ(ə)nə(r), -z
AM ˈrikənˈdɪʃ(ə)nər, -z

reconduct
BR ˌriːkənˈdʌkt, -s, -ɪŋ, -ɨd
AM ˈrikənˈdək|(t), -(t)s, -tɪŋ, -təd

reconfiguration
BR ˌriːkənˌfɪɡəˈreɪʃn, ˌriːkənˌfɪɡjʊˈreɪʃn, -z
AM ˈrikənˌfɪɡ(j)əˈreɪʃən, -z

reconfigure
BR ˌriːkənˈfɪɡə(r), -z, -ɪŋ, -d
AM ˌrikənˈfɪɡjər, -z, -ɪŋ, -d

reconfirm
BR ˌriːkənˈfəːm, -z, -ɪŋ, -d
AM ˌrikənˈfərm, -z, -ɪŋ, -d

reconfirmation
BR ˌriːkɒnfəˈmeɪʃn, -z
AM ˌriˌkɑnfərˈmeɪʃən, -z

reconnaissance
BR rɪˈkɒnɪs(ə)ns, -ɨz
AM riˈkɑnəsəns, rəˈkɑnəsəns, -ɨz

reconnect
BR ˌriːkəˈnɛkt, -s, -ɪŋ, -ɨd
AM ˌrikəˈnɛk|(t), -(t)s, -tɪŋ, -təd

reconnection
BR ˌriːkəˈnɛkʃn, -z
AM ˌrikəˈnɛkʃən, -z

reconnoiter
BR ˌrɛkəˈnɔɪt|ə(r), -əz, -(ə)rɪŋ, -əd
AM ˌrɛkəˈnɔɪ|dər, ˌrikəˈnɔɪ|dər, -dərz, -dərɪŋ\-trɪŋ, -dərd

reconnoitre
BR ˌrɛkəˈnɔɪt|ə(r), -əz, -(ə)rɪŋ, -əd
AM ˌrɛkəˈnɔɪ|dər, ˌrikəˈnɔɪ|dər, -dərz, -dərɪŋ\-trɪŋ, -dərd

reconquer
BR ˌriːˈkɒŋk|ə(r), -əz, -(ə)rɪŋ, -əd
AM riˈkɑŋk|ər, -ərz, -(ə)rɪŋ, -ərd

reconquest
BR ˌriːˈkɒŋkwɛst, -s
AM riˈkɑŋkwəst, -s

reconsecrate
BR ˌriːˈkɒnsɪkreɪt, -s, -ɪŋ, -ɨd
AM ˌriˈkɑnsɛˌkreɪ|t, -ts, -dɪŋ, -dɨd

reconsecration
BR ˌriːkɒnsɪˈkreɪʃn
AM ˈriˌkɑnsəˈkreɪʃən

reconsider
BR ˌriːkənˈsɪd|ə(r), -əz, -(ə)rɪŋ, -əd
AM ˈrikənˈsɪdər, -z, -ɪŋ, -d

reconsideration
BR ˌriːkənˌsɪdəˈreɪʃn
AM ˈrikənˌsɪdəˈreɪʃən

reconsign
BR ˌriːkənˈsʌɪn, -z, -ɪŋ, -d
AM ˈrikənˈsaɪn, -z, -ɪŋ, -d

reconsignment
BR ˌriːkənˈsʌɪnm(ə)nt, -s
AM ˌrikənˈsaɪnmənt, -s

reconsolidate
BR ˌriːkənˈsɒlɨdeɪt, -s, -ɪŋ, -ɨd
AM ˈrikənˈsɑləˌdeɪ|t, -ts, -dɪŋ, -dɨd

reconsolidation
BR ˌriːkənˌsɒlɪˈdeɪʃn, -z
AM ˈrikənˌsɑləˈdeɪʃən, -z

reconstitute
BR ˌriːˈkɒnstɪtjuːt, ˌriːˈkɒnstɪtʃuːt, -s, -ɪŋ, -ɨd
AM riˈkɑnstəˌt(j)u|t, -ts, -dɪŋ, -dəd

reconstitution
BR ˌriːkɒnstɪˈtjuːʃn, ˌriːkɒnstɪˈtʃuːʃn
AM ˈriˌkɑnstəˈt(j)uʃən

reconstruct
BR ˌriːkənˈstrʌkt, -s, -ɪŋ, -ɨd
AM ˈrikənˈstrək|(t), -(t)s, -tɪŋ, -təd

reconstructable
BR ˌriːkənˈstrʌktəbl
AM ˈrikənˈstrəktəbəl

reconstruction
BR ˌriːkənˈstrʌkʃn, -z
AM ˈrikənˈstrəkʃən, -z

reconstructive
BR ˌriːkənˈstrʌktɪv
AM ˈrikənˈstrəktɪv

reconstructor
BR ˌriːkənˈstrʌktə(r), -z
AM ˈrikənˈstrəktər, -z

reconvene
BR ˌriːkənˈviːn, -z, -ɪŋ, -d
AM ˈrikənˈvin, -z, -ɪŋ, -d

reconversion
BR ˌriːkənˈvəːʃn, -z
AM ˈrikənˈvərʒən, -z

reconvert
BR ˌriːkənˈvəːt, -s, -ɪŋ, -ɨd
AM ˈrikənˈvər|t, -ts, -dɪŋ, -dəd

record[1]
noun
BR ˈrɛkɔːd, -z
AM ˈrɛkərd, -z

record²
verb
BR rɪ'kɔːd, -z, -ɪŋ, -ɪd
AM rə'kɔ(ə)rd, ri'kɔ(ə)rd, -z, -ɪŋ, -əd

recordable
BR rɪ'kɔːdəbl
AM rə'kɔrdəbəl, ri'kɔrdəbəl

recorder
BR rɪ'kɔːdə(r), -z
AM rə'kɔrdər, ri'kɔrdər, -z

recordership
BR rɪ'kɔːdəʃɪp, -s
AM rə'kɔrdər,ʃɪp, ri'kɔrdər,ʃɪp, -s

recording
BR rɪ'kɔːdɪŋ, -z
AM rə'kɔrdɪŋ, ri'kɔrdɪŋ, -z

recordist
BR rɪ'kɔːdɪst, -s
AM rə'kɔrdəst, ri'kɔrdəst, -s

record-player
BR 'rɛkɔːd,pleɪə(r), -z
AM 'rɛkərd,pleɪər, -z

recount¹
noun
BR 'riːkaʊnt, -s
AM 'ri,kaʊnt, -s

recount²
verb, count again
BR ,riː'kaʊnt, -s, -ɪŋ, -ɪd
AM ,ri'kaʊn|t, rə'kaʊn|t, -ts, -(t)ɪŋ, -(t)əd

recount³
verb, tell
BR rɪ'kaʊnt, -s, -ɪŋ, -ɪd
AM ri'kaʊn|t, rə'kaʊn|t, -ts, -(t)ɪŋ, -(t)əd

recoup
BR rɪ'kuːp, -s, -ɪŋ, -t
AM ri'kup, rə'kup, -s, -ɪŋ, -t

recoupable
BR rɪ'kuːpəbl
AM ri'kupəbəl, rə'kupəbəl

recoupment
BR rɪ'kuːpm(ə)nt, -s
AM ri'kupmənt, rə'kupmənt, -s

recourse
BR rɪ'kɔːs
AM 'ri,kɔ(ə)rs, ri'kɔ(ə)rs

recover¹
cover again
BR ,riː'kʌv|ə(r), -əz, -(ə)rɪŋ, -əd
AM ri'kəv|ər, -ərz, -(ə)rɪŋ, -ərd

recover²
regain
BR rɪ'kʌv|ə(r), -əz, -(ə)rɪŋ, -əd
AM rə'kəv|ər, ri'kəv|ər, -ərz, -(ə)rɪŋ, -ərd

recoverability
BR rɪ,kʌv(ə)rə'bɪlɪt|i, -ɪz
AM ˌri,kəv(ə)rə'bɪlɪdi, -z

recoverable
BR rɪ'kʌv(ə)rəbl
AM rə'kəv(ə)rəbəl, ri'kəv(ə)rəbəl

recoverer
BR rɪ'kʌv(ə)rə(r), -z
AM rə'kəv(ə)rər, ri'kəv(ə)rər, -z

recovery
BR rɪ'kʌv(ə)r|i, -ɪz
AM rə'kəv(ə)ri, ri'kəv(ə)ri, -z

recreancy
BR 'rɛkrɪənsi
AM 'rɛkriənsi

recreant
BR 'rɛkrɪənt, -s
AM 'rɛkriənt, -s

recreantly
BR 'rɛkrɪəntli
AM 'rɛkriən(t)li

recreate¹
create again
BR ,riːkrɪ'eɪt, -s, -ɪŋ, -ɪd
AM ˌrikri'eɪ|t, -ts, -dɪŋ, -dɪd

recreate²
refresh, enliven
BR 'rɛkrɪeɪt, -s, -ɪŋ, -ɪd
AM 'rɛkri,eɪ|t, -ts, -dɪŋ, -dɪd

recreation¹
creating again
BR ,riːkrɪ'eɪʃn, -z
AM ˌrikri'eɪʃən, -z

recreation²
exercise, refreshment
BR ,rɛkrɪ'eɪʃn, -z
AM ,rɛkri'eɪʃən, -z

recreational
BR ,rɛkrɪ'eɪʃn̩(ə)l, ,rɛkrɪ'eɪʃən(ə)l
AM ˌrɛkri'eɪʃ(ə)nəl

recreationally
BR ,rɛkrɪ'eɪʃn̩əli, ,rɛkrɪ'eɪʃn̩li, ,rɛkrɪ'eɪʃənl̩i, ,rɛkrɪ'eɪʃ(ə)nəli
AM ˌrɛkri'eɪʃ(ə)nəli

recreative
BR 'rɛkrɪeɪtɪv, 'rɛkrɪətɪv
AM ˌrɛkri'eɪdɪv

recriminate
BR rɪ'krɪmɪneɪt, -s, -ɪŋ, -ɪd
AM rə'krɪmə,neɪ|t, ri'krɪmə,neɪ|t, -ts, -dɪŋ, -dɪd

recrimination
BR rɪ,krɪmɪ'neɪʃn, -z
AM rə,krɪmə'neɪʃən, ri,krɪmə'neɪʃən, -z

recriminative
BR rɪ'krɪmɪnətɪv
AM rə'krɪmənədɪv, ri'krɪmənədɪv, rə'krɪmə,neɪdɪv, ri'krɪmə,neɪdɪv

recriminatory
BR rɪ'krɪmɪnət(ə)ri
AM rə'krɪmənə,tɔri, ri'krɪmənə,tɔri

recross
BR ,riː'krɒs, -ɪz, -ɪŋ, -t
AM ,ri'krɔs, ,ri'krɑs, -əz, -ɪŋ, -t

recrudesce
BR ,riːkruː'dɛs, ,rɛkruː'dɛs, -ɪz, -ɪŋ, -t
AM ,rikru'dɛs, -ɪz, -ɪŋ, -t

recrudescence
BR ,riːkruː'dɛsns, ,rɛkruː'dɛsns
AM ,rikru'dɛsəns

recrudescent
BR ,riːkruː'dɛsnt, ,rɛkruː'dɛsnt
AM ,rikru'dɛsənt

recruit
BR rɪ'kruːt, -s, -ɪŋ, -ɪd
AM rə'kru|t, ri'kru|t, -ts, -dɪŋ, -dəd

recruitable
BR rɪ'kruːtəbl
AM rə'krudəbəl, ri'krudəbəl

recruital
BR rɪ'kruːtl, -z
AM rə'krudl, ri'krudl, -z

recruiter
BR rɪ'kruːtə(r), -z
AM rə'krudər, ri'krudər, -z

recruitment
BR rɪ'kruːtm(ə)nt
AM rə'krutmənt, ri'krutmənt

recrystallisation
BR ,riː,krɪstl̩ʌɪ'zeɪʃn, ,riː,krɪstəlʌɪ'zeɪʃn
AM ˌri,krɪstələ'zeɪʃən, ˌri,krɪstə,laɪ'zeɪʃən

recrystallise
BR ,riː'krɪstl̩ʌɪz, ,riː'krɪstəlʌɪz, -ɪz, -ɪŋ, -d
AM ˌri'krɪstə,laɪz, -ɪz, -ɪŋ, -d

recrystallization
BR ,riː,krɪstl̩ʌɪ'zeɪʃn, ,riː,krɪstəlʌɪ'zeɪʃn, -z
AM ˌri,krɪstələ'zeɪʃən, ˌri,krɪstə,laɪ'zeɪʃən, -z

recrystallize
BR ,riː'krɪstl̩ʌɪz, ,riː'krɪstəlʌɪz, -ɪz, -ɪŋ, -d
AM ˌri'krɪstə,laɪz, -ɪz, -ɪŋ, -d

recta
BR 'rɛktə(*r*)
AM 'rɛktə

rectal
BR 'rɛktl
AM 'rɛkt(ə)l

rectally
BR 'rɛktl̩i, 'rɛktəli
AM 'rɛkt(ə)li

rectangle
BR 'rɛktaŋgl
AM 'rɛk,tæŋgəl

rectangular
BR rɛk'taŋgjʉlə(r)
AM rɛk'tæŋgjələr

rectangularity
BR rɛk,taŋgjʉ'larɪti
AM rɛk,tæŋgjə'lɛrədi

rectangularly
BR rɛk'taŋgjʉləli
AM 'rɛktæŋgjələrli

recti
BR 'rɛktʌɪ
AM 'rɛk,taɪ

rectifiable
BR 'rɛktɪfʌɪəbl
AM 'rɛktə,faɪəbəl

rectification
BR ,rɛktɪfɪ'keɪʃn, -z
AM ,rɛktəfə'keɪʃən, -z

rectifier
BR 'rɛktɪfʌɪə(r), -z
AM 'rɛktə,faɪər, -z

rectify
BR 'rɛktɪfʌɪ, -z, -ɪŋ, -d
AM 'rɛktə,faɪ, -z, -ɪŋ, -d

rectilineal
BR ,rɛktɪ'lɪnɪəl
AM ˌrɛktə'lɪniəl

rectilinear
BR ,rɛktɪ'lɪnɪə(r)
AM ˌrɛktə'lɪniər

rectilinearity
BR ,rɛktɪ,lɪnɪ'arɪti
AM ˌrɛktə,lɪni'ɛrədi

rectilinearly
BR ,rɛktɪ'lɪnɪəli
AM ˌrɛktə'lɪniərli

rectitude
BR 'rɛktɪtjuːd, 'rɛktɪtʃuːd
AM 'rɛktə,t(j)ud

recto
BR 'rɛktəʊ
AM 'rɛktoʊ

rector
BR 'rɛktə(r), -z
AM 'rɛktər, -z

rectoral
BR 'rɛkt(ə)rəl, 'rɛkt(ə)rl̩
AM 'rɛkt(ə)rəl

rectorate
BR 'rɛkt(ə)rət, -s
AM 'rɛkt(ə)rət, -s

rectorial
BR rɛk'tɔːrɪəl
AM rɛk'tɔriəl

rectorship
BR 'rɛktəʃɪp, -s
AM 'rɛktərˌʃɪp, -s

rectory
BR 'rɛkt(ə)r|i, -ɪz
AM 'rɛkt(ə)ri, -z

rectrices
BR 'rɛktrɪsiːz
AM 'rɛktrəˌsiz

rectrix
BR 'rɛktrɪks, -ɪz
AM 'rɛkˌtrɪks, -ɪz

rectum
BR 'rɛktəm, -z
AM 'rɛktəm, -z

rectus
BR 'rɛktəs
AM 'rɛktəs

recumbence
BR rɪ'kʌmb(ə)ns
AM rə'kəmbəns, ri'kəmbəns

recumbency
BR rɪ'kʌmb(ə)nsi
AM rə'kəmbənsi, ri'kəmbənsi

recumbent
BR rɪ'kʌmb(ə)nt
AM rə'kəmbənt, ri'kəmbənt

recumbently
BR rɪ'kʌmb(ə)ntli
AM rə'kəmbən(t)li, ri'kəmbən(t)li

recuperable
BR rɪ'k(j)uːp(ə)rəbl
AM rə'kupərəbəl, ri'kupərəbəl

recuperate
BR rɪ'k(j)uːpəreɪt, -s, -ɪŋ, -ɪd
AM rə'kupəˌreɪ|t, ri'kupəˌreɪ|t, -ts, -dɪŋ, -dɪd

recuperation
BR rɪˌk(j)uːpə'reɪʃn
AM rəˌkupə'reɪʃən, riˌkupə'reɪʃən

recuperative
BR rɪ'k(j)uːp(ə)rətɪv
AM rə'kupəˌreɪdɪv, ri'kupəˌreɪdɪv, rə'kup(ə)rədɪv, ri'kup(ə)rədɪv

recuperator
BR rɪ'k(j)uːpəreɪtə(r), -z
AM rə'kupəˌreɪdər, ri'kupəˌreɪdər, -z

recur
BR rɪ'kəː(r), -z, -ɪŋ, -d
AM rə'kər, ri'kər, -z, -ɪŋ, -d

recurrence
BR rɪ'kʌrəns, rɪ'kʌrn̩s, -ɪz
AM rə'kərəns, ri'kərəns, -əz

recurrent
BR rɪ'kʌrənt, rɪ'kʌrn̩t
AM rə'kərənt, ri'kərənt

recurrently
BR rɪ'kʌrəntli, rɪ'kʌrn̩tli
AM rə'kərən(t)li, ri'kərən(t)li

recursion
BR rɪ'kəːʃn, rɪ'kəːʒn, -z
AM rə'kərʒən, -z

recursive
BR rɪ'kəːsɪv, -z
AM rə'kərsɪv, ri'kərsɪv, -z

recursively
BR rɪ'kəːsɪvli
AM rə'kərsɪvli, ri'kərsɪvli

recurvate
BR rɪ'kəːveɪt
AM rə'kərˌveɪt, ri'kərˌveɪt, rə'kərvət, ri'kərvət

recurvature
BR rɪ'kəːvətʃə(r), -z
AM ri'kərvətʃər, ri'kərvətʃʊ(ə)r, -z

recurve
BR ˌriː'kəːv, -z, -ɪŋ, -d
AM rə'kərv, ri'kərv, -z, -ɪŋ, -d

recusance
BR 'rɛkjʊz(ə)ns
AM rə'kjuzns

recusancy
BR 'rɛkjʊz(ə)nsi
AM rə'kjuznsi

recusant
BR 'rɛkjʊz(ə)nt, -s
AM rə'kjuznt, -s

recyclable
BR ˌriː'sʌɪkləbl
AM ri'saɪkləbəl

recycle
BR ˌriː'sʌɪk|l, -lz, -lɪŋ, -ld
AM ri'saɪk|əl, -əlz, -(ə)lɪŋ, -əld

recycler
BR ˌriː'sʌɪklə(r), -z
AM ri'saɪklər, -z

red
BR rɛd, -z, -ə(r), -ɪst
AM rɛd, -z, -ər, -əst

redact
BR rɪ'dakt, -s, -ɪŋ, -ɪd
AM rə'dæk|(t), ri'dæk|(t), -(t)s, -tɪŋ, -təd

redaction
BR rɪ'dakʃn, -z
AM rə'dækʃən, ri'dækʃən, -z

redactional
BR rɪ'dakʃn̩(ə)l, rɪ'dakʃən(ə)l
AM rə'dækʃ(ə)nəl, ri'dækʃ(ə)nəl

redactor
BR rɪ'daktə(r), -z
AM rə'dæktər, ri'dæktər, -z

redan
BR rɪ'dan, -z
AM rə'dæn, -z

redback
BR 'rɛdbak, -s
AM 'rɛdˌbæk, -s

red bark
BR ˌrɛd 'bɑːk
AM ˈrɛd 'bɑrk

red-blooded
BR ˌrɛd'blʌdɪd
AM 'rɛd'blədəd

red-bloodedness
BR ˌrɛd'blʌdɪdnɪs
AM 'rɛd'blədədnəs

redbreast
BR 'rɛdbrɛst, -s
AM 'rɛdˌbrɛst, -s

redbrick
adjective
BR 'rɛdbrɪk, ˌrɛd'brɪk
AM 'rɛdˈbrɪk

Redbridge
BR 'rɛdbrɪdʒ
AM 'rɛdˌbrɪdʒ

redbud
BR 'rɛdbʌd, -z
AM 'rɛdˌbəd, -z

redcap
BR 'rɛdkap, -s
AM 'rɛdˌkæp, -s

Redcar
BR 'rɛdkə(r), 'rɛdkɑː(r)
AM 'rɛdkər, 'rɛdˌkɑr

redcoat
BR 'rɛdkəʊt, -s
AM 'rɛdˌkoʊt, -s

redcurrant
BR ˌrɛd'kʌrənt, ˌrɛd'kʌrn̩t, -s
AM ˈrɛd'kərənt, -s

redd
BR rɛd, -z, -ɪŋ, -ɪd
AM rɛd, -z, -ɪŋ, -əd

Reddaway
BR 'rɛdəweɪ
AM 'rɛdəˌweɪ

redden
BR 'rɛd|n, -nz, -n̩ɪŋ\-nɪŋ, -nd
AM rɛdən, -z, -ɪŋ, -d

reddish
BR 'rɛdɪʃ
AM 'rɛdɪʃ

reddishness
BR 'rɛdɪʃnɪs
AM 'rɛdɪʃnɪs

Redditch
BR 'rɛdɪtʃ
AM 'rɛdɪtʃ

reddle
BR 'rɛdl
AM 'rɛdəl

red-dog
BR 'rɛddɒg
AM 'rɛdˌdɔg, 'rɛdˌdɑg

reddy
BR 'rɛdi
AM 'rɛdi

rede
BR riːd, -z, -ɪŋ, -ɪd
AM rid, -z, -ɪŋ, -ɪd

redecorate
BR (ˌ)riː'dɛkəreɪt, -s, -ɪŋ, -ɪd
AM ri'dɛkəˌreɪ|t, -ts, -dɪŋ, -dɪd

redecoration
BR ˌriːdɛkə'reɪʃn, riːˌdɛkə'reɪʃn
AM ˈriˌdɛkə'reɪʃən

rededicate
BR (ˌ)riː'dɛdɪkeɪt, -s, -ɪŋ, -ɪd
AM ˈri'dɛdəˌkeɪ|t, -ts, -dɪŋ, -dɪd

rededication
BR ˌriːdɛdɪ'keɪʃn, riːˌdɛdɪ'keɪʃn
AM ˈriˌdɛdə'keɪʃən

redeem
BR rɪ'diːm, -z, -ɪŋ, -d
AM rə'dim, ri'dim, -z, -ɪŋ, -d

redeemable
BR rɪ'diːməbl
AM rə'diməbəl, ri'diməbəl

redeemer
BR rɪ'diːmə(r), -z
AM rə'dimər, ri'dimər, -z

redefine
BR ˌriːdɪ'fʌɪn, -z, -ɪŋ, -d
AM ˌridə'faɪn, -z, -ɪŋ, -d

redefinition
BR ˌriːdɛfɪ'nɪʃn, -z
AM ˈriˌdɛfə'nɪʃən, -z

redemption
BR rɪ'dɛm(p)ʃn, -z
AM rə'dɛm(p)ʃən, ri'dɛm(p)ʃən, -z

redemptive
BR rɪ'dɛm(p)tɪv

AM rə'dɛm(p)tɪv, ri'dɛm(p)tɪv

Redemptorist
BR rɪ'dɛm(p)t(ə)rɪst, -s
AM rə'dɛm(p)tərəst, ri'dɛm(p)tərəst, -s

redeploy
BR ˌri:dɪ'plɔɪ, -z, -ɪŋ, -d
AM ˈridə'plɔɪ, -z, -ɪŋ, -d

redeployment
BR ˌri:dɪ'plɔɪm(ə)nt, -s
AM ˌridə'plɔɪmənt, -s

redescend
BR ˌri:dɪ'sɛnd, -z, -ɪŋ, -ɪd
AM ˌridə'sɛnd, -z, -ɪŋ, -əd

Redesdale
BR 'ri:dzdeɪl
AM 'ridzˌdeɪl

redesign
BR ˌri:dɪ'zʌɪn, -z, -ɪŋ, -d
AM ˌridə'zaɪn, -z, -ɪŋ, -d

redesignate
BR ˌri:'dɛzɪgneɪt, -s, -ɪŋ, -ɪd
AM ˌri'dɛzəgˌneɪ|t, -ts, -dɪŋ, -dɪd

redesignation
BR ˌri:dɛzɪg'neɪʃn
AM ˈriˌdɛzəg'neɪʃən

redetermination
BR ˌri:dɪˌtə:mɪ'neɪʃn, -z
AM ˈridəˌtərmə'neɪʃən, -z

redetermine
BR ˌri:dɪ'tə:mɪn, -z, -ɪŋ, -d
AM ˈridə'tərmən, -z, -ɪŋ, -d

redevelop
BR ˌri:dɪ'vɛləp, -s, -ɪŋ, -t
AM ˌridə'vɛləp, -s, -ɪŋ, -t

redeveloper
BR ˌri:dɪ'vɛləpə(r), -z
AM ˌridə'vɛləpər, -z

redevelopment
BR ˌri:dɪ'vɛləpm(ə)nt, -s
AM ˌridə'vɛləpmənt, -s

red-eye
BR 'rɛdʌɪ
AM 'rɛdˌaɪ

red-faced
BR ˌrɛd'feɪst
AM ˈrɛd'feɪst

Redfearn
BR 'rɛdfə:n
AM 'rɛdˌfərn

Redfern
BR 'rɛdfə:n
AM 'rɛdˌfərn

redfish
BR 'rɛdfɪʃ, -ɪz
AM 'rɛdˌfɪʃ, -ɪz

Redford
BR 'rɛdfəd
AM 'rɛdfərd

Redgrave
BR 'rɛdgreɪv
AM 'rɛdˌgreɪv

redhanded
BR ˌrɛd'handɪd
AM ˈrɛd'hændəd

redhead
BR 'rɛdhɛd, -z
AM 'rɛdˌ(h)ɛd, -z

Redhill
BR ˌrɛd'hɪl
AM 'rɛdˌ(h)ɪl

redial
BR ˌri:'dʌɪ(ə)l, -z, -ɪŋ, -d
AM ri'daɪəl, -z, -ɪŋ, -d

redid
BR ˌri:'dɪd
AM ri'dɪd

rediffuse
BR ˌri:dɪ'fju:z, -ɪz, -ɪŋ, -d
AM ˌridə'fjuz, -əz, -ɪŋ, -d

rediffusion
BR ˌri:dɪ'fju:ʒn
AM ˈridə'fjuʒən

redingote
BR 'rɛdɪŋgəʊt, -s
AM 'rɛdɪŋˌgoʊt, -s

redintegrate
BR rɪ'dɪntɪgreɪt, -s, -ɪŋ, -ɪd
AM rə'dɪn(t)əˌgreɪ|t, ri'dɪn(t)əˌgreɪ|t, -ts, -dɪŋ, -dɪd

redintegration
BR rɪˌdɪntɪ'greɪʃn, -z
AM rəˌdɪn(t)ə'greɪʃən, riˌdɪn(t)ə'greɪʃən, -z

redintegrative
BR rɪ'dɪntɪˌgreɪtɪv
AM rə'dɪn(t)əˌgreɪdɪv, ri'dɪn(t)əˌgreɪdɪv

redirect
BR ˌri:dɪ'rɛkt, ˌri:dʌɪ'rɛkt, -s, -ɪŋ, -ɪd
AM ˈridə'rɛk|(t), ˈriˌdaɪ'rɛk|(t), -(t)s, -tɪŋ, -təd

redirection
BR ˌri:dɪ'rɛkʃn, ˌri:dʌɪ'rɛkʃn
AM ˈridə'rɛkʃən, ˈriˌdaɪ'rɛkʃən

rediscover
BR ˌri:dɪ'skʌv|ə(r), -əz, -(ə)rɪŋ, -əd
AM ˈridə'skəv|ər, -ərz, -(ə)rɪŋ, -ərd

rediscoverer
BR ˌri:dɪ'skʌv(ə)rə(r), -z
AM ˈridə'skəv(ə)rər, -z

rediscovery
BR ˌri:dɪ'skʌv(ə)ri
AM ˈridə'skəv(ə)ri

redissolution
BR ˌri:dɪsə'l(j)u:ʃn, -z
AM ˈriˌdɪsə'luʃən, -z

redissolve
BR ˌri:dɪ'zɒlv, -z, -ɪŋ, -d
AM ˌridə'zɔlv, ˌridə'zɑlv, -z, -ɪŋ, -d

redistribute
BR ˌri:dɪ'strɪbju:t, ri:'dɪstrɪbju:t, -s, -ɪŋ, -ɪd
AM ˈridə'strɪˌbju|t, -ts, -dɪŋ, -dəd

redistribution
BR ˌri:dɪstrɪ'bju:ʃn
AM ˈridəstrə'bjuʃən

redistributive
BR ˌri:dɪ'strɪbju:tɪv, ri:'dɪstrɪbju:tɪv
AM ˈridə'strɪˌbjudɪv

redivide
BR ˌri:dɪ'vʌɪd, -z, -ɪŋ, -ɪd
AM ˌridə'vaɪd, -z, -ɪŋ, -ɪd

redivision
BR ˌri:dɪ'vɪʒn, -z
AM ˌridə'vɪʒən, -z

redivivus
BR ˌrɛdɪ'vʌɪvəs, ˌrɛdɪ'vi:vəs
AM ˌrɛdə'vaɪvəs, ˌrɛdə'vɪvəs

redleg
BR 'rɛdlɛg, -z
AM 'rɛdˌlɛg, -z

redline
BR 'rɛdlʌɪn, -z
AM 'rɛdˌlaɪn, -z

redly
BR 'rɛdli
AM 'rɛdli

Redmond
BR 'rɛdmənd
AM 'rɛdmən(d)

redneck
BR 'rɛdnɛk, -s
AM 'rɛdˌnɛk, -s

redness
BR 'rɛdnəs
AM 'rɛdnəs

redo
BR ˌri:'du:, -ɪŋ
AM ri'du, -ɪŋ

redoes
BR ˌri:'dʌz
AM ri'dəz

redolence
BR 'rɛdələns, 'rɛdəl̩ns, 'rɛdl̩(ə)ns
AM 'rɛdl̩əns

redolent
BR 'rɛdələnt, 'rɛdəl̩nt, 'rɛdl̩(ə)nt
AM 'rɛdl̩ənt

redolently
BR 'rɛdələntli, 'rɛdəl̩ntli, 'rɛdl̩(ə)ntli
AM 'rɛdlən(t)li

redone
BR ˌri:'dʌn
AM ri'dən

redouble
BR ˌri:'dʌb|l, rɪ'dʌb|l, -lz, -l̩ɪŋ\-lɪŋ, -ld
AM ri'dəbəl, -əlz, -(ə)lɪŋ, -əld

redoubt
BR rɪ'daʊt, -s
AM rə'daʊt, ri'daʊt, -s

redoubtable
BR rɪ'daʊtəbl
AM rə'daʊdəbəl, ri'daʊdəbəl

redoubtably
BR rɪ'daʊtəbli
AM rə'daʊdəbli, ri'daʊdəbli

redound
BR rɪ'daʊnd, -z, -ɪŋ, -ɪd
AM rə'daʊnd, ri'daʊnd, -z, -ɪŋ, -ɪd

redox
BR 'ri:dɒks
AM 'riˌdɑks

redpoll
BR 'rɛdpəʊl, 'rɛdpɒl, -z
AM 'rɛdˌpoʊl, -z

redraft
BR ˌri:'drɑ:ft, ˌri:'draft, -s, -ɪŋ, -ɪd
AM ri'dræft, -s, -ɪŋ, -ɪd

redraw
BR ˌri:'drɔ:(r), -z, -ɪŋ
AM ri'drɔ, rə'drɑ, -z, -ɪŋ

redrawn
BR ˌri:'drɔ:n
AM ri'drɔn, ri'drɑn

redress[1]
correct, amend
BR rɪ'drɛs, -ɪz, -ɪŋ, -t
AM rə'drɛs, ri'drɛs, -əz, -ɪŋ, -t

redress[2]
dress again
BR ˌri:'drɛs, -ɪz, -ɪŋ, -t
AM ri'drɛs, -əz, -ɪŋ, -t

redressable
BR rɪ'drɛsəbl
AM rə'drɛsəbəl, ri'drɛsəbəl

redressal
BR rɪ'drɛsl, -z
AM rə'drɛsəl, ri'drɛsəl, -z

redresser
BR rɪ'drɛsə(r), -z
AM rə'drɛsər, ri'drɛsər, -z

redressment
BR rɪ'drɛsm(ə)nt, -s
AM rə'drɛsmənt, ri'drɛsmənt, -s

redrew
BR ˌri:'dru:
AM rə'dru, ri'dru

Redruth
BR ˌrɛdˈruːθ, ˈrɛdruːθ
AM ˌrɛdˈruθ
redshank
BR ˈrɛdʃaŋk, -s
AM ˈrɛdˌʃæŋk, -s
redshirt
BR ˈrɛdʃəːt, -s
AM ˈrɛdˌʃərt, -s
redskin
BR ˈrɛdskɪn, -z
AM ˈrɛdˌskɪn, -z
redstart
BR ˈrɛdstɑːt, -s
AM ˈrɛdˌstɑrt, -s
reduce
BR rɪˈdjuːs, rɪˈdʒuːs, -ɪz, -ɪŋ, -t
AM rəˈd(j)us, riˈd(j)us, -əz, -ɪŋ, -t
reducer
BR rɪˈdjuːsə(r), rɪˈdʒuːsə(r), -z
AM rəˈd(j)usər, riˈd(j)usər, -z
reducibility
BR rɪˌdjuːsɪˈbɪlɪti, rɪˌdʒuːsɪˈbɪlɪti
AM rəˌd(j)usəˈbɪlɪdi, riˌd(j)usəˈbɪlɪdi
reducible
BR rɪˈdjuːsɪbl, rɪˈdʒuːsɪbl
AM rəˈd(j)usəbəl, riˈd(j)usəbəl
reductio ad absurdum
BR rɪˌdʌktɪəʊ ad əbˈsəːdəm, + abˈsəːdəm
AM rəˌdəkʃioʊ æd əbˈsərdəm, riˌdəkʃioʊ +, rəˈdəktioʊ +, riˈdəktioʊ +
reduction
BR rɪˈdʌkʃn, -z
AM rəˈdəkʃən, riˈdəkʃən, -z
reductionism
BR rɪˈdʌkʃn̩ɪz(ə)m, rɪˈdʌkʃənɪz(ə)m
AM rəˈdəkʃəˌnɪzəm, riˈdəkʃəˌnɪzəm
reductionist
BR rɪˈdʌkʃn̩ɪst, rɪˈdʌkʃənɪst, -s
AM rəˈdəkʃənəst, riˈdəkʃənəst, -s
reductionistic
BR rɪˌdʌkʃəˈnɪstɪk
AM rəˌdəkʃəˈnɪstɪk, riˌdəkʃəˈnɪstɪk
reductive
BR rɪˈdʌktɪv
AM rəˈdəktɪv, riˈdəktɪv
redundance
BR rɪˈdʌnd(ə)ns
AM rəˈdənd(ə)ns, riˈdənd(ə)ns
redundancy
BR rɪˈdʌnd(ə)ns|i, -ɪz
AM rəˈdənd(ə)nsi, riˈdənd(ə)nsi, -z
redundant
BR rɪˈdʌnd(ə)nt
AM rəˈdənd(ə)nt, riˈdənd(ə)nt
redundantly
BR rɪˈdʌnd(ə)ntli
AM rəˈdənd(ə)n(t)li, riˈdənd(ə)n(t)li
reduplicate
BR rɪˈdjuːplɪkeɪt, ˌriːˈdjuːplɪkeɪt, rɪˈdʒuːplɪkeɪt, ˌriːˈdʒuːplɪkeɪt, -s, -ɪŋ, -ɪd
AM riˈd(j)upləˌkeɪ|t, rəˈd(j)upləˌkeɪ|t, -ts, -dɪŋ, -dɪd
reduplication
BR rɪˌdjuːplɪˈkeɪʃn, rɪˌdʒuːplɪˈkeɪʃn
AM ˈriˌd(j)upləˈkeɪʃən, rəˌd(j)upləˈkeɪʃən
reduplicative
BR rɪˈdjuːplɪkətɪv, rɪˈdʒuːplɪkətɪv
AM riˈd(j)upləˌkeɪdɪv, rəˈd(j)upləˌkeɪdɪv
redux
BR ˈriːdʌks
AM ˈriˈdəks
Redvers
BR ˈrɛdvəz
AM ˈrɛdvərz
redwing
BR ˈrɛdwɪŋ, -z
AM ˈrɛdˌwɪŋ, -z
redwood
BR ˈrɛdwʊd, -z
AM ˈrɛdˌwʊd, -z
redye
BR ˌriːˈdʌɪ, -z, -ɪŋ, -d
AM riˈdaɪ, -z, -ɪŋ, -d
reebok
BR ˈriːbɒk, -s
AM ˈriˌbɑk, -s
Reece
BR riːs
AM ris
re-echo
BR ˌriːˈɛkəʊ, rɪˈɛkəʊ, -z, -ɪŋ, -d
AM riˈɛkoʊ, -z, -ɪŋ, -d
reed
BR riːd, -z
AM rid, -z
reed-bed
BR ˈriːdbɛd, -z
AM ˈridˌbɛd, -z
reedbuck
BR ˈriːdbʌk, -s
AM ˈridˌbək, -s
reeded
BR ˈriːdɪd
AM ˈridɪd
reedification
BR rɪˌɛdɪfɪˈkeɪʃn
AM riˌɛdəfəˈkeɪʃən
reedify
BR ˌriːˈɛdɪfʌɪ, -z, -ɪŋ, -d
AM riˈɛdəˌfaɪ, -z, -ɪŋ, -d
reedily
BR ˈriːdɪli
AM ˈridɪli
reediness
BR ˈriːdɪnɪs
AM ˈridinɪs
reeding
BR ˈriːdɪŋ, -z
AM ˈridɪŋ, -z
re-edit
BR ˌriːˈɛd|ɪt, rɪˈɛd|ɪt, -ɪts, -ɪtɪŋ, -ɪtɪd
AM riˈɛdə|t, -ts, -dɪŋ, -dəd
re-edition
BR ˌriːɪˈdɪʃn, -z
AM ˈriˌɛˈdɪʃən, -z
reedling
BR ˈriːdlɪŋ, -z
AM ˈridlɪŋ, -z
re-educate
BR ˌriːˈɛdjʊkeɪt, rɪˈɛdjʊkeɪt, ˌriːˈɛdʒʊkeɪt, rɪˈɛdʒʊkeɪt, -s, -ɪŋ, -ɪd
AM riˈɛdʒəˌkeɪ|t, -ts, -dɪŋ, -dɪd
re-education
BR ˌriːɛdjʊˈkeɪʃn, rɪˌɛdjʊˈkeɪʃn, ˌriːɛdʒʊˈkeɪʃn, rɪˌɛdʒʊˈkeɪʃn
AM riˌɛdʒəˈkeɪʃən
reed-warbler
BR ˈriːdˌwɔːblə(r), -z
AM ˈridˌwɔrblər, -z
reedy
BR ˈriːd|i, -ɪə(r), -ɪɪst
AM ˈridi, -ər, -ɪst
reef
BR riːf, -s, -ɪŋ, -t
AM rif, -s, -ɪŋ, -t
reefer
BR ˈriːfə(r), -z
AM ˈrifər, -z
reefpoint
BR ˈriːfpɔɪnt, -s
AM ˈrifˌpɔɪnt, -s
reek
BR riːk, -s, -ɪŋ, -t
AM rik, -s, -ɪŋ, -t
reeky
BR ˈriːk|i, -ɪə(r), -ɪɪst
AM ˈriki, -ər, -ɪst
reel
BR riːl, -z, -ɪŋ, -d
AM ril, -z, -ɪŋ, -d
re-elect
BR ˌriːɪˈlɛkt, -s, -ɪŋ, -ɪd
AM ˈriəˈlɛk|(t), -(t)s, -tɪŋ, -təd
re-election
BR ˌriːɪˈlɛkʃn, -z
AM ˈriəˈlɛkʃən, -z
reeler
BR ˈriːlə(r), -z
AM ˈrilər, -z
re-eligible
BR ˌriːˈɛlɪdʒɪbl
AM riˈɛlədʒəbəl
re-embark
BR ˌriːɪmˈbɑːk, -s, -ɪŋ, -t
AM ˈriəmˈbɑrk, ˈriˌɛmˈbɑrk, -s, -ɪŋ, -t
re-embarkation
BR ˌriːɛmbɑːˈkeɪʃn, -z
AM ˈriˌɛmbɑrˈkeɪʃən, -z
re-emerge
BR ˌriːɪˈməːdʒ, -ɪz, -ɪŋ, -d
AM ˈriəˈmərdʒ, ˈriˌiˈmərdʒ, -əz, -ɪŋ, -d
re-emergence
BR ˌriːɪˈməːdʒ(ə)ns, -ɪz
AM ˈriəˈmərdʒəns, ˈriˌiˈmərdʒəns, -əz
re-emergent
BR ˌriːɪˈməːdʒ(ə)nt
AM ˈriəˈmərdʒənt, ˈriˌiˈmərdʒənt
re-emphases
BR (ˌ)riːˈɛmfəsiːz
AM riˈɛmfəsiz
re-emphasis
BR (ˌ)riːˈɛmfəsɪs
AM riˈɛmfəsəs
re-emphasise
BR (ˌ)riːˈɛmfəsʌɪz, -ɪz, -ɪŋ, -d
AM riˈɛmfəˌsaɪz, -ɪz, -ɪŋ, -d
re-emphasize
BR (ˌ)riːˈɛmfəsʌɪz, -ɪz, -ɪŋ, -d
AM riˈɛmfəˌsaɪz, -ɪz, -ɪŋ, -d
re-employ
BR ˌriːɪmˈplɔɪ, ˌriːɛmˈplɔɪ, -z, -ɪŋ, -d
AM ˈriəmˈplɔɪ, ˈriˌɛmˈplɔɪ, -z, -ɪŋ, -d
re-employment
BR ˌriːɪmˈplɔɪm(ə)nt, ˌriːɛmˈplɔɪm(ə)nt, -s
AM ˈriəmˈplɔɪmənt, ˈriˌɛmˈplɔɪmənt, -s
re-enact
BR ˌriːɪˈnakt, -s, -ɪŋ, -ɪd
AM ˈriəˈnæk|(t), -(t)s, -tɪŋ, -təd
re-enactment
BR ˌriːɪˈnak(t)m(ə)nt, -s
AM ˈriəˈnæk(t)mənt, -s
re-enforce
BR ˌriːɪnˈfɔːs, -ɪz, -ɪŋ, -t

AM ˌriənˈfɔ(ə)rs, -əz, -ɪŋ, -t

re-enforcement
BR ˌriːɪnˈfɔːsm(ə)nt
AM ˌriənˈfɔrsmənt

re-engage
BR ˌriːɪnˈgeɪdʒ, ˌriːɛnˈgeɪdʒ, ˌriːɪŋˈgeɪdʒ, ˌriːɛŋˈgeɪdʒ, -ɪz, -ɪŋ, -d
AM ˌriənˈgeɪdʒ, -ɪz, -ɪŋ, -d

re-engagement
BR ˌriːɪnˈgeɪdʒm(ə)nt, ˌriːɛnˈgeɪdʒm(ə)nt, ˌriːɪŋˈgeɪdʒm(ə)nt, ˌriːɛŋˈgeɪdʒm(ə)nt, -s
AM ˌriənˈgeɪdʒmənt, -s

re-engineer
BR ˌriːɛn(d)ʒɪˈnɪə(r), -z, -ɪŋ, -d
AM riˌɛndʒəˈnɪ(ə)r, -z, -ɪŋ, -d

re-enlist
BR ˌriːɪnˈlɪst, -s, -ɪŋ, -ɪd
AM ˌriənˈlɪst, -s, -ɪŋ, -ɪd

re-enlister
BR ˌriːɪnˈlɪstə(r), -z
AM ˌriənˈlɪstər, -z

re-enlistment
BR ˌriːɪnˈlɪs(t)m(ə)nt, -s
AM ˌriənˈlɪs(t)mənt, -s

re-enter
BR ˌriːˈɛnt|ə(r), rɪˈɛnt|ə(r), -əz, -(ə)rɪŋ, -əd
AM riˈɛn(t)|ər, -ərz, -(ə)rɪŋ, -ərd

re-entrance
BR ˌriːˈɛntr(ə)ns, rɪˈɛntr(ə)ns, -ɪz
AM riˈɛntrəns, -əz

re-entrant
BR ˌriːˈɛntr(ə)nt, rɪˈɛntr(ə)nt, -s
AM riˈɛntrənt, -s

re-entry
BR ˌriːˈɛntr|i, rɪˈɛntr|i, -ɪz
AM riˈɛntri, -z

re-equip
BR ˌriːɪˈkwɪp, -s, -ɪŋ, -t
AM ˌriəˈkwɪp, -s, -ɪŋ, -t

re-erect
BR ˌriːɪˈrɛkt, -s, -ɪŋ, -d
AM ˌriəˈrɛk|(t), -(t)s, -tɪŋ, -təd

re-erection
BR ˌriːɪˈrɛkʃn
AM ˌriəˈrɛkʃən

Rees
BR riːs
AM ris

Reese
BR riːs
AM ris

re-establish
BR ˌriːɪˈstabl|ɪʃ, -ɪʃɪz, -ɪʃɪŋ, -ɪʃt
AM ˌriəsˈtæblɪʃ, ˌriɛsˈtæblɪʃ, -ɪz, -ɪŋ, -t

re-establishment
BR ˌriːɪˈstablɪʃm(ə)nt, -s
AM ˌriəsˈtæblɪʃmənt, ˌriɛsˈtæblɪʃmənt, -s

re-evaluate
BR ˌriːɪˈvaljʊeɪt, -s, -ɪŋ, -ɪd
AM ˌriəˈvæljəˌweɪ|t, -ts, -dɪŋ, -dɪd

re-evaluation
BR ˌriːɪˌvaljʊˈeɪʃn, -z
AM ˌriəˌvæljəˈweɪʃən, -z

reeve
BR riːv, -z
AM riv, -z

Reeves
BR riːvz
AM rivz

re-examination
BR ˌriːɪgˌzamɪˈneɪʃn, -z
AM ˌriɪgˌzæməˈneɪʃən, ˌriɛgˌzæməˈneɪʃən, -z

re-examine
BR ˌriːɪgˈzam|ɪn, -ɪnz, -ɪnɪŋ, -ɪnd
AM ˌriɪgˈzæmən, ˌriɛgˈzæmən, -z, -ɪŋ, -d

re-export
BR ˌriːˈɛkspɔːt, rɪˈɛkspɔːt, -s, -ɪŋ, -ɪd
AM ˌriˈɛkspɔ(ə)rt, -ts, -pɔrdɪŋ, -pɔrdəd

re-exportation
BR ˌriːɛkspɔːˈteɪʃn, -z
AM ˌriˌɛkspɔrˈteɪʃən, -z

re-exporter
BR ˌriːˈɛkspɔːtə(r), rɪˈɛkspɔːtə(r), -z
AM ˌriˈɛkspɔrdər, -z

ref
BR rɛf, -s
AM rɛf, -s

reface
BR (ˌ)riːˈfeɪs, -ɪz, -ɪŋ, -t
AM riˈfeɪs, -ɪz, -ɪŋ, -t

refashion
BR (ˌ)riːˈfaʃ|n, -nz, -ənɪŋ\-n̩ɪŋ, -nd
AM riˈfæʃ|ən, -ənz, -(ə)nɪŋ, -ənd

refection
BR rɪˈfɛkʃn
AM rəˈfɛkʃən, riˈfɛkʃən

refectory
BR rɪˈfɛkt(ə)r|i, -ɪz
AM rəˈfɛkt(ə)ri, riˈfɛkt(ə)ri, -z

refer
BR rɪˈfəː(r), -z, -ɪŋ, -d
AM rəˈfər, riˈfər, -z, -ɪŋ, -d

referable
BR rɪˈfəːrəbl, ˈrɛf(ə)rəbl
AM rəˈfərəbəl, riˈfərəbəl, ˈrɛf(ə)rəbəl

referee
BR ˌrɛfəˈriː, -z
AM ˌrɛfəˈri, -z

reference
BR ˈrɛf(ə)rəns, ˈrɛr(ə)rn̩s, -ɪz
AM ˈrɛf(ə)rəns, -əz

referenda
BR ˌrɛfəˈrɛndə(r)
AM ˌrɛfəˈrɛndə

referendum
BR ˌrɛfəˈrɛndəm, -z
AM ˌrɛfəˈrɛndəm, -z

referent
BR ˈrɛf(ə)rənt, ˈrɛf(ə)rn̩t, -s
AM ˈrɛf(ə)rənt, -s

referential
BR ˌrɛfəˈrɛnʃl
AM ˌrɛfəˈrɛn(t)ʃəl

referentiality
BR ˌrɛfəˌrɛnʃɪˈalɪti
AM ˌrɛfəˌrɛn(t)ʃiˈælədi

referentially
BR ˌrɛfəˈrɛnʃl̩i, ˌrɛfəˈrɛnʃəli
AM ˌrɛfəˈrɛn(t)ʃəli

referral
BR rɪˈfəːrəl, rɪˈfəːrl̩, -z
AM rəˈfərəl, riˈfərəl, -z

referrer
BR rɪˈfəːrə(r), -z
AM rəˈfərər, riˈfərər, -z

refill[1]
noun
BR ˈriːfɪl, -z
AM ˈriˌfɪl, -z

refill[2]
verb
BR ˌriːˈfɪl, -z, -ɪŋ, -d
AM riˈfɪl, -z, -ɪŋ, -d

refillable
BR ˌriːˈfɪləbl
AM riˈfɪləbəl

refinable
BR rɪˈfʌɪnəbl
AM rəˈfaɪnəbəl, riˈfaɪnəbəl

refinance
BR ˌriːfʌɪˈnans, ˌriːfɪˈnans, ˌriːˈfʌɪnans, -ɪz, -ɪŋ, -d
AM ˌrifəˈnæns, riˈfaɪˌnæns, -əz, -ɪŋ, -d

refine
BR rɪˈfʌɪn, -z, -ɪŋ, -d
AM rəˈfaɪn, riˈfaɪn, -z, -ɪŋ, -d

refinement
BR rɪˈfʌɪnm(ə)nt, -s
AM rəˈfaɪnmənt, riˈfaɪnmənt, -s

refiner
BR rɪˈfʌɪnə(r), -z
AM rəˈfaɪnər, riˈfaɪnər, -z

refinery
BR rɪˈfʌɪn(ə)r|i, -ɪz
AM rəˈfaɪn(ə)ri, riˈfaɪn(ə)ri, -z

refinish
BR ˌriːˈfɪn|ɪʃ, -ɪʃɪz, -ɪʃɪŋ, -ɪʃt
AM rəˈfɪnɪʃ, riˈfɪnɪʃ, -ɪz, -ɪŋ, -t

refit[1]
noun
BR ˈriːfɪt, -s
AM ˈriˌfɪt, -s

refit[2]
verb
BR ˌriːˈfɪt, -s, -ɪŋ, -ɪd
AM riˈfɪ|t, -ts, -dɪŋ, -dɪd

refitment
BR ˌriːˈfɪtm(ə)nt, -s
AM riˈfɪtmənt, -s

reflag
BR ˌriːˈflag, -z, -ɪŋ, -d
AM riˈflæg, -z, -ɪŋ, -d

reflate
BR ˌriːˈfleɪt, rɪˈfleɪt, -s, -ɪŋ, -ɪd
AM rəˈfleɪ|t, riˈfleɪ|t, -ts, -dɪŋ, -dɪd

reflation
BR ˌriːˈfleɪʃn, rɪˈfleɪʃn
AM rəˈfleɪʃən, riˈfleɪʃən

reflationary
BR ˌriːˈfleɪʃn̩(ə)ri, rɪˈfleɪʃn̩(ə)ri
AM rəˈfleɪʃəˌnɛri, riˈfleɪʃəˌnɛri

reflect
BR rɪˈflɛkt, -s, -ɪŋ, -ɪd
AM rəˈflɛk|(t), riˈflɛk|(t), -(t)s, -tɪŋ, -təd

reflectance
BR rɪˈflɛkt(ə)ns, -ɪz
AM rəˈflɛkt(ə)ns, riˈflɛkt(ə)ns, -əz

reflection
BR rɪˈflɛkʃn, -z
AM rəˈflɛkʃən, riˈflɛkʃən, -z

reflectional
BR rɪˈflɛkʃn̩(ə)l, rɪˈflɛkʃən(ə)l
AM rəˈflɛkʃ(ə)nəl, riˈflɛkʃ(ə)nəl

reflective
BR rɪˈflɛktɪv
AM rəˈflɛktɪv, riˈflɛktɪv

reflectively
BR rɪˈflɛktɪvli

AM rəˈflɛktɨvli, riˈflɛktɨvli

reflectiveness
BR rɪˈflɛktɨvnɨs
AM rəˈflɛktɪvnɨs, riˈflɛktɪvnɨs

reflectivity
BR ˌriːflɛkˈtɪvɨti, rɪˌflɛkˈtɪvɨt|i, -ɪz
AM rəˌflɛkˈtɪvɨdi, riˌflɛkˈtɪvɨdi, -z

reflector
BR rɪˈflɛktə(r), -z
AM rəˈflɛktər, riˈflɛktər, -z

reflet
BR rɪˈfleɪ
AM rəˈfleɪ, riˈfleɪ-z

reflex
BR ˈriːflɛks, -ɨz, -t
AM ˈriˌflɛks, -əz, -t

reflexibility
BR ˌriːflɛksɪˈbɪlɨti, rɪˌflɛksɪˈbɪlɨti
AM ˌriflɛksəˈbɪlɨdi

reflexible
BR rɪˈflɛksɨbl
AM rəˈflɛksəbəl, riˈflɛksəbəl

reflexion
BR rɪˈflɛkʃn, -z
AM rəˈflɛkʃən, riˈflɛkʃən, -z

reflexive
BR rɪˈflɛksɪv, -z
AM rəˈflɛksɪv, riˈflɛksɪv, -z

reflexively
BR rɪˈflɛksɨvli
AM rəˈflɛksɨvli, riˈflɛksɨvli

reflexiveness
BR rɪˈflɛksɪvnɨs
AM rəˈflɛksɪvnɨs, riˈflɛksɪvnɨs

reflexivity
BR ˌriːflɛkˈsɪvɨti
AM ˌriflɛkˈsɪvɨdi

reflexologist
BR ˌriːflɛkˈsɒlədʒɪst, -s
AM ˌriflɛkˈsɑlədʒəst, -s

reflexology
BR ˌriːflɛkˈsɒlədʒi
AM ˌriflɛkˈsɑlədʒi

refloat
BR ˌriːˈfləʊt, -s, -ɪŋ, -ɨd
AM riˈfloʊ|t, -ts, -dɪŋ, -dəd

refluence
BR ˈrɛflʊəns, -ɨz
AM ˈrɛˌfluəns, -əz

refluent
BR ˈrɛflʊənt
AM ˈrɛˌfluənt

reflux
BR ˈriːflʌks, -ɨz
AM ˈriˌfləks, -əz

refocus
BR ˌriːˈfəʊkəs, -ɨz, -ɪŋ, -t
AM riˈfoʊkəs, -əz, -ɪŋ, -t

refold
BR ˌriːˈfəʊld, -z, -ɪŋ, -ɨd
AM riˈfoʊld, -z, -ɪŋ, -əd

reforest
BR (ˌ)riːˈfɒrɪst, -s, -ɪŋ, -ɨd
AM riˈfɔrəst, -s, -ɪŋ, -ɨd

reforestation
BR ˌriːfɒrɪˈsteɪʃn, riːˌfɒrɪˈsteɪʃn
AM riˌfɔrəˈsteɪʃən

reforge
BR ˌriːˈfɔːdʒ, -ɨz, -ɪŋ, -d
AM riˈfɔrdʒ, -əz, -ɪŋ, -d

reform[1]
correct, make better
BR rɪˈfɔːm, -z, -ɪŋ, -d
AM rəˈfɔ(ə)rm, riˈfɔ(ə)rm, -z, -ɪŋ, -d

reform[2]
form again
BR ˌriːˈfɔːm, -z, -ɪŋ, -d
AM riˈfɔ(ə)rm, -z, -ɪŋ, -d

reformable
BR rɪˈfɔːməbl
AM rəˈfɔrməbəl, riˈfɔrməbəl

reformat
BR ˌriːˈfɔːmat, -s, -ɪŋ, -ɨd
AM riˈfɔrˌmæ|t, -ts, -dɪŋ, -dəd

reformation
BR ˌrɛfəˈmeɪʃn, -z
AM ˌrɛfərˈmeɪʃən, -z

re-formation
BR ˌriːfɔːˈmeɪʃn, -z
AM ˈriˌfɔrˈmeɪʃən, -z

reformational
BR ˌrɛfəˈmeɪʃn̩(ə)l, ˌrɛfəˈmeɪʃən(ə)l
AM ˌrɛfərˈmeɪʃ(ə)nəl

reformative
BR rɪˈfɔːmətɪv
AM rəˈfɔrmədɪv, riˈfɔrmədɪv

reformatory
BR rɪˈfɔːmət(ə)r|i, -ɪz
AM rəˈfɔrməˌtɔri, riˈfɔrməˌtɔri, -z

reformer
BR rɪˈfɔːmə(r), -z
AM rəˈfɔrmər, riˈfɔrmər, -z

reformism
BR rɪˈfɔːmɪz(ə)m
AM rəˈfɔrˌmɪzəm, riˈfɔrˌmɪzəm

reformist
BR rɪˈfɔːmɪst
AM rəˈfɔrməst, riˈfɔrməst

reformulate
BR ˌriːˈfɔːmjʊleɪt, -s, -ɪŋ, -ɨd
AM rəˈfɔrmjəˌleɪ|t, riˈfɔrmjəˌleɪ|t, -ts, -dɪŋ, -dɨd

reformulation
BR ˌriːfɔːmjʊˈleɪʃn, -z
AM rəˌfɔrmjəˈleɪʃən, riˌfɔrmjəˈleɪʃən, -z

refract
BR rɪˈfrakt, -s, -ɪŋ, -ɨd
AM rəˈfræk|(t), riˈfræk|(t), -(t)s, -tɪŋ, -təd

refraction
BR rɪˈfrakʃn
AM rəˈfrækʃən, riˈfrækʃən

refractive
BR rɪˈfraktɪv
AM rəˈfræktɪv, riˈfræktɪv

refractometer
BR ˌriːfrakˈtɒmɨtə(r), rɪˌfrakˈtɒmɨtə(r), -z
AM rəˌfrækˈtɑmədər, riˌfrækˈtɑmədər, -z

refractometric
BR rɪˌfraktəˈmɛtrɪk
AM rəˌfræktəˈmɛtrɪk, riˌfræktəˈmɛtrɪk

refractometry
BR ˌriːfrakˈtɒmɨtri, rɪˌfrakˈtɒmɨtri
AM rəˌfrækˈtɑmətri, riˌfrækˈtɑmətri

refractor
BR rɪˈfraktə(r), -z
AM rəˈfræktər, riˈfræktər, -z

refractorily
BR rɪˈfrakt(ə)rɨli
AM rəˈfrækˌtɔrəli, riˈfrækˌtɔrəli

refractoriness
BR rɪˈfrakt(ə)rɪnɨs
AM rəˈfrækˌtɔrinɨs, riˈfrækˌtɔrinəs

refractory
BR rɪˈfrakt(ə)ri
AM rəˈfrækˌtɔri, riˈfrækˌtɔri

refrain
BR rɪˈfreɪn, -z, -ɪŋ, -d
AM rəˈfreɪn, riˈfreɪn, -z, -ɪŋ, -d

refrainment
BR rɪˈfreɪnm(ə)nt, -s
AM rəˈfreɪnmənt, riˈfreɪnmənt, -s

refrangibility
BR rɪˌfran(d)ʒɪˈbɪlɨti
AM rəˌfrændʒəˈbɪlɨdi, riˌfrændʒəˈbɪlɨdi

refrangible
BR rɪˈfran(d)ʒɨbl
AM rəˈfrandʒəbəl, riˈfrandʒəbəl

refreeze
BR ˌriːˈfriːz, -ɨz, -ɪŋ
AM rəˈfriz, riˈfriz, -ɨz, -ɪŋ

refresh
BR rɪˈfrɛʃ, -ɨz, -ɪŋ, -d
AM rəˈfrɛʃ, riˈfrɛʃ, -əz, -ɪŋ, -t

refresher
BR rɪˈfrɛʃə(r), -z
AM rəˈfrɛʃər, riˈfrɛʃər, -z

refreshingly
BR rɪˈfrɛʃɪŋli
AM rəˈfrɛʃɪŋli, riˈfrɛʃɪŋli

refreshment
BR rɪˈfrɛʃm(ə)nt, -s
AM rəˈfrɛʃmənt, riˈfrɛʃmənt, -s

refried
BR ˌriːˈfrʌɪd
AM ˈriˌfraɪd

refrigerant
BR rɪˈfrɪdʒ(ə)rənt, rɪˈfrɪdʒ(ə)rn̩t, -s
AM rəˈfrɪdʒ(ə)rənt, riˈfrɪdʒ(ə)rənt, -s

refrigerate
BR rɪˈfrɪdʒəreɪt, -s, -ɪŋ, -ɨd
AM rəˈfrɪdʒəˌreɪ|t, riˈfrɪdʒəˌreɪ|t, -ts, -dɪŋ, -dɨd

refrigeration
BR rɪˌfrɪdʒəˈreɪʃn
AM rəˌfrɪdʒəˈreɪʃən, riˌfrɪdʒəˈreɪʃən

refrigerative
BR rɪˈfrɪdʒ(ə)rətɪv
AM rəˈfrɪdʒərədɪv, riˈfrɪdʒərədɪv

refrigerator
BR rɪˈfrɪdʒəreɪtə(r), -z
AM rəˈfrɪdʒəˌreɪdər, riˈfrɪdʒəˌreɪdər, -z

refrigeratory
BR rɪˈfrɪdʒ(ə)rət(ə)ri
AM rəˈfrɪdʒ(ə)rəˌtɔri, riˈfrɪdʒ(ə)rəˌtɔri

refringent
BR rɪˈfrɪn(d)ʒ(ə)nt
AM rəˈfrɪndʒənt, riˈfrɪndʒənt

refroze
BR ˌriːˈfrəʊz
AM rəˈfroʊz, riˈfroʊz

refrozen
BR ˌriːˈfrəʊzn
AM rəˈfroʊzən, ˌriˈfroʊzən

reft
BR rɛft
AM rɛft

refuel
BR ˌriːˈfjuːəl, -z, -ɪŋ, -d
AM riˈfju(ə)l, -z, -ɪŋ, -d

refuge
BR ˈrɛfjuːdʒ, -ɨz
AM ˈrɛfjudʒ, -ɨz

refugee
BR ˌrɛfjʊˈdʒiː, ˌrɛfjuːˈdʒiː, -z
AM ˈˌrɛfjəˈˌdʒi, -z

refulgence
BR rɪˈfʌldʒ(ə)ns
AM rəˈfəldʒəns, riˈfəldʒəns

refulgent
BR rɪˈfʌldʒ(ə)nt
AM rəˈfəldʒənt, riˈfəldʒənt

refulgently
BR rɪˈfʌldʒ(ə)ntli
AM rəˈfəldʒən(t)li, riˈfəldʒən(t)li

refund[1]
noun
BR ˈriːfʌnd, -z
AM ˈriˌfənd, -z

refund[2]
verb
BR (ˌ)riːˈfʌnd, rɪˈfʌnd, ˈriːfʌnd, -z, -ɪŋ, -ɪd
AM rəˈfənd, riˈfənd, -z, -ɪŋ, -əd

re-fund
BR ˌriːˈfʌnd, ˈriːfʌnd, -z, -ɪŋ, -ɪd
AM riˈfənd, -z, -ɪŋ, -əd

refundable
BR (ˌ)riːˈfʌndəbl, rɪˈfʌndəbl, ˈriːfʌndəbl
AM rəˈfəndəbəl, riˈfəndəbəl

refunder
BR (ˌ)riːˈfʌndə(r), rɪˈfʌndə(r), ˈriːfʌndə(r), -z
AM ˈriˌfəndər

refundment
BR (ˌ)riːˈfʌndm(ə)nt, rɪˈfʌndm(ə)nt, ˈriːfʌndm(ə)nt, -s
AM rəˈfən(d)mənt, riˈfən(d)mənt, -s

refurbish
BR (ˌ)riːˈfəːb|ɪʃ, -ɪʃɪz, -ɪʃɪŋ, -ɪʃt
AM riˈfərbɪʃ, -ɪz, -ɪŋ, -t

refurbishment
BR (ˌ)riːˈfəːbɪʃm(ə)nt, -s
AM riˈfərbɪʃmənt, -s

refurnish
BR (ˌ)riːˈfəːn|ɪʃ, -ɪʃɪz, -ɪʃɪŋ, -ɪʃt
AM riˈfərnɪʃ, -ɪz, -ɪŋ, -t

refusable
BR rɪˈfjuːzəbl
AM rəˈfjuzəbəl, riˈfjuzəbəl

refusal
BR rɪˈfjuːzl, -z
AM rəˈfjuzəl, riˈfjuzəl, -z

refuse[1]
noun
BR ˈrɛfjuːs
AM ˈrɛˌfjuz

refuse[2]
verb
BR rɪˈfjuːz, -ɪz, -ɪŋ, -d
AM rəˈfjuz, riˈfjuz, -əz, -ɪŋ, -d

refusenik
BR rɪˈfjuːznɪk, -s
AM rəˈfjuznɪk, riˈfjuznɪk, -s

refuser
BR rɪˈfjuːzə(r), -z
AM rəˈfjuzər, riˈfjuzər, -z

refutability
BR rɪˌfjuːtəˈbɪlɪti, ˌrɛfjʊtəˈbɪlɪti
AM rəˌfjudəˈbɪlɪdi, riˌfjudəˈbɪlɪdi, ˌrɛfjədəˈbɪlɪdi

refutable
BR rɪˈfjuːtəbl, ˈrɛfjʊtəbl
AM rəˈfjudəbəl, riˈfjudəbəl, ˈrɛfjədəbəl

refutal
BR rɪˈfjuːtl, -z
AM rəˈfjudl, riˈfjudl, -z

refutation
BR ˌrɛfjʊˈteɪʃn, -z
AM ˌrɛfjəˈteɪʃən, -z

refute
BR rɪˈfjuːt, -s, -ɪŋ, -ɪd
AM rəˈfju|t, riˈfju|t, -ts, -dɪŋ, -dəd

refuter
BR rɪˈfjuːtə(r), -z
AM rəˈfjudər, riˈfjudər, -z

reg
BR rɛdʒ
AM rɛdʒ

regain
BR rɪˈgeɪn, ˌriːˈgeɪn, -z, -ɪŋ, -d
AM riˈgeɪn, rəˈgeɪn, -z, -ɪŋ, -d

regal
BR ˈriːgl
AM ˈrigəl

regale
BR rɪˈgeɪl, -z, -ɪŋ, -d
AM rəˈgeɪl, riˈgeɪl, -z, -ɪŋ, -d

regalement
BR rɪˈgeɪlm(ə)nt, -s
AM rəˈgeɪlmənt, riˈgeɪlmənt, -s

regalia
BR rɪˈgeɪlɪə(*r*)
AM rəˈgeɪljə, rəˈgeɪliə

regalism
BR ˈriːgḷɪz(ə)m, ˈriːgəlɪz(ə)m
AM ˈrigəˌlɪzəm

regality
BR riːˈgalɪt|i, -ɪz
AM riˈgælədi, -z

regally
BR ˈriːgḷi, ˈriːgəli
AM ˈrigəli

Regan
BR ˈriːg(ə)n
AM ˈrigən, ˈreɪgən

regard
BR rɪˈgɑːd, -z, -ɪŋ, -ɪd
AM rəˈgɑrd, riˈgɑrd, -z, -ɪŋ, -əd

regardant
BR rɪˈgɑːdnt
AM rəˈgɑrdnt, riˈgɑrdnt

regardful
BR rɪˈgɑːdf(ʊ)l
AM rəˈgɑrdfəl, riˈgɑrdfəl

regardfully
BR rɪˈgɑːdfʊli, rɪˈgɑːdfḷi
AM rəˈgɑrdfəli, riˈgɑrdfəli

regardfulness
BR rɪˈgɑːdf(ʊ)lnəs
AM rəˈgɑrdfəlnəs, riˈgɑrdfəlnəs

regardless
BR rɪˈgɑːdləs
AM rəˈgɑrdləs, riˈgɑrdləs

regardlessly
BR rɪˈgɑːdləsli
AM rəˈgɑrdləsli, riˈgɑrdləsli

regardlessness
BR rɪˈgɑːdləsnəs
AM rəˈgɑrdləsnəs, riˈgɑrdləsnəs

regather
BR ˌriːˈgað|ə(r), -əz, -(ə)rɪŋ, -əd
AM riˈgæð|ər, -ərz, -(ə)rɪŋ, -ərd

regatta
BR rɪˈgatə(*r*), -z
AM rəˈgædə, rəˈgɑdə, -z

regelate
BR ˌriːdʒɪˈleɪt, -s, -ɪŋ, -ɪd
AM ˌriˈdʒəˌleɪ|t, -ts, -dɪŋ, -dɪd

regelation
BR ˌriːdʒɪˈleɪʃn, -z
AM ˌridʒəˈleɪʃən, -z

regency
BR ˈriːdʒ(ə)ns|i, -ɪz
AM ˈridʒənsi, -z

regenerate[1]
adjective
BR rɪˈdʒɛn(ə)rət
AM riˈdʒɛn(ə)rət, rəˈdʒɛn(ə)rət

regenerate[2]
verb
BR rɪˈdʒɛnəreɪt, ˌriːˈdʒɛnəreɪt, -s, -ɪŋ, -ɪd
AM riˈdʒɛnəˌreɪ|t, rəˈdʒɛnəˌreɪ|t, -ts, -dɪŋ, -dɪd

regeneration
BR rɪˌdʒɛnəˈreɪʃn, ˌriːdʒɛnəˈreɪʃn
AM riˌdʒɛnəˈreɪʃən, rəˌdʒɛnəˈreɪʃən

regenerative
BR rɪˈdʒɛn(ə)rətɪv
AM riˈdʒɛnərədɪv, rəˈdʒɛnərədɪv

regeneratively
BR rɪˈdʒɛn(ə)rətɪvli
AM riˈdʒɛnərədɪvli, rəˈdʒɛnərədɪvli

regenerator
BR rɪˈdʒɛnəreɪtə(r), ˌriːˈdʒɛnəreɪtə(r), -z
AM riˈdʒɛnəˌreɪdər, rəˈdʒɛnəˌreɪdər, -z

regeneses
BR ˌriːˈdʒɛnɪsiːz
AM riˈdʒɛnəˌsiz

regenesis
BR ˌriːˈdʒɛnɪsɪs
AM riˈdʒɛnəsəs

regent
BR ˈriːdʒ(ə)nt, -s
AM ˈridʒənt, -s

regentship
BR ˈriːdʒ(ə)ntʃɪp, -s
AM ˈridʒəntˌʃɪp, -s

regerminate
BR ˌriːˈdʒəːmɪneɪt, -s, -ɪŋ, -ɪd
AM riˈdʒərməˌneɪ|t, -ts, -dɪŋ, -dɪd

regermination
BR ˌriːdʒəːmɪˈneɪʃn, -z
AM ˈriˌdʒərməˈneɪʃən, -z

reggae
BR ˈrɛgeɪ
AM ˈrɛgeɪ

regicidal
BR ˌrɛdʒɪˈsʌɪdl
AM ˈˌrɛdʒəˈsaɪdəl

regicide
BR ˈrɛdʒɪsʌɪd, -z
AM ˈrɛdʒəˌsaɪd, -z

regild
BR ˌriːˈgɪld, -z, -ɪŋ, -ɪd
AM riˈgɪld, -z, -ɪŋ, -ɪd

regilt
BR ˌriːˈgɪlt
AM riˈgɪlt

régime
BR reɪˈʒiːm, rɛˈʒiːm, rəˈʒiːm, -z
AM reɪˈʒim, rəˈʒim, -z

regimen
BR 'rɛdʒɪmən, 'rɛʒɪmɛn, -z
AM 'rɛdʒəmən, 'rɛdʒə,mɛn, -z

regiment[1]
noun
BR 'rɛdʒɪm(ə)nt, -s
AM 'rɛdʒəmənt, -s

regiment[2]
verb
BR 'rɛdʒɪmɛnt, -s, -ɪŋ, -ɨd
AM 'rɛdʒə,mɛn|t, -ts, -(t)ɪŋ, -(t)əd

regimental
BR ,rɛdʒɪ'mɛntl, -z
AM ¦rɛdʒə¦mɛn(t)l, -z

regimentally
BR ,rɛdʒɪ'mɛntḷi
AM 'ridʒɪmən(t)ḷi

regimentation
BR ,rɛdʒɪmɛn'teɪʃn, ,rɛdʒɪm(ə)n'teɪʃn
AM ,rɛdʒəmən'teɪʃən, ,rɛdʒə,mɛn'teɪʃən

Regina
BR rɪ'dʒʌɪnə(r)
AM rə'dʒinə

Reginald
BR 'rɛdʒɪnld
AM 'rɛdʒənld

region
BR 'ri:dʒ(ə)n, -z
AM 'ridʒən, -z

regional
BR 'ri:dʒṇ(ə)l, 'ri:dʒən(ə)l
AM 'ridʒ(ə)nəl

regionalisation
BR ,ri:dʒṇəlʌɪ'zeɪʃn, ,ri:dʒṇḷʌɪ'zeɪʃn, ,ri:dʒənḷʌɪ'zeɪʃn, ,ri:dʒ(ə)nəlʌɪ'zeɪʃn
AM ,ridʒənḷə'zeɪʃən, ,ridʒnələ'zeɪʃən, ,ridʒənl,aɪ'zeɪʃən, ,ridʒnə,laɪ'zeɪʃən

regionalise
BR 'ri:dʒṇəlʌɪz, 'ri:dʒṇḷʌɪz, 'ri:dʒənḷʌɪz, 'ri:dʒ(ə)nəlʌɪz, -ɨz, -ɪŋ, -d
AM 'ridʒənl,aɪz, 'ridʒnə,laɪz, -ɨz, -ɪŋ, -d

regionalism
BR 'ri:dʒṇəlɪz(ə)m, 'ri:dʒṇḷɪz(ə)m, 'ri:dʒənḷɪz(ə)m, 'ri:dʒ(ə)nəlɪz(ə)m
AM 'ridʒənl,ɪsəm, 'ridʒnə,lɪsəm

regionalist
BR 'ri:dʒṇəlɪst, 'ri:dʒṇḷɪst, 'ri:dʒənḷɪst, 'ri:dʒ(ə)nəlɪst, -s
AM 'ridʒənləst, 'ridʒnələst, -s

regionalization
BR ,ri:dʒṇəlʌɪ'zeɪʃn, ,ri:dʒṇḷʌɪ'zeɪʃn, ,ri:dʒənḷʌɪ'zeɪʃn, ,ri:dʒ(ə)nəlʌɪ'zeɪʃn
AM ,ridʒənḷə'zeɪʃən, ,ridʒnələ'zeɪʃən, ,ridʒənl,aɪ'zeɪʃən, ,ridʒnə,laɪ'zeɪʃən

regionalize
BR 'ri:dʒṇəlʌɪz, 'ri:dʒṇḷʌɪz, 'ri:dʒənḷʌɪz, 'ri:dʒ(ə)nəlʌɪz, -ɨz, -ɪŋ, -d
AM 'ridʒənl,aɪz, 'ridʒnə,laɪz, -ɨz, -ɪŋ, -d

regionally
BR 'ri:dʒṇəli, 'ri:dʒṇḷi, 'ri:dʒənḷi, 'ri:dʒ(ə)nəli
AM 'ridʒ(ə)nəli

Regis
BR 'ri:dʒɪs
AM 'ridʒɪs

régisseur
BR ,reɪʒɪ'sə:(r), -z
AM ,reɪdʒɪ'sər, -z

register
BR 'rɛdʒɪst|ə(r), -əz, -(ə)rɪŋ, -əd
AM 'rɛdʒəst|ər, -ərz, -(ə)rɪŋ, -ərd

registrable
BR 'rɛdʒɪstrəbl
AM 'rɛdʒəstrəbəl

registrant
BR 'rɛdʒɪstr(ə)nt, -s
AM 'rɛdʒəstrənt, -s

registrar
BR ,rɛdʒɪ'strɑ:(r), 'rɛdʒɪstrɑ:(r), -z
AM 'rɛdʒə,strɑr, -z

Registrar General
BR ,rɛdʒɪstrɑ: 'dʒɛn(ə)rəl, + 'dʒɛn(ə)rḷ, -z
AM 'rɛdʒə,strɑr 'dʒɛn(ə)rəl, -z

registrarship
BR ,rɛdʒɪ'strɑ:ʃɪp, 'rɛdʒɪstrɑ:ʃɪp, -s
AM 'rɛdʒə,strɑr,ʃɪp, -s

registrary
BR 'rɛdʒɪstrər|i, -ɪz
AM 'rɛdʒə,strɛri, -z

registration
BR ,rɛdʒɪ'streɪʃn, -z
AM ,rɛdʒə'streɪʃən, -z

registry
BR 'rɛdʒɪstr|i, -ɪz
AM 'rɛdʒəstri, -z

Regius
BR 'ri:dʒ(ɪ)əs
AM 'ridʒ(i)əs

reglaze
BR ,ri:'gleɪz, -ɨz, -ɪŋ, -d
AM ri'gleɪz, -ɨz, -ɪŋ, -d

reglet
BR 'rɛglɪt, -s
AM 'rɛglət, -s

regnal
BR 'rɛgnl
AM 'rɛgnəl

regnant
BR 'rɛgnənt
AM 'rɛgnənt

regolith
BR 'rɛgəlɪθ, -s
AM 'rɛgə,lɪθ, -s

regorge
BR ,ri:'gɔ:dʒ, -ɨz, -ɪŋ, -d
AM ri'gɔrdʒ, -əz, -ɪŋ, -d

regrade
BR ,ri:'greɪd, -z, -ɪŋ, -ɨd
AM ri'greɪd, -z, -ɪŋ, -ɨd

regrate
BR ,ri:'greɪt, -s, -ɪŋ, -ɨd
AM ri'greɪ|t, -ts, -dɪŋ, -dɨd

regreen
BR ,ri:'gri:n, -z, -ɪŋ, -d
AM ri'grin, -z, -ɪŋ, -d

regress[1]
noun
BR 'ri:grɛs
AM 'ri,grɛs

regress[2]
verb
BR rɪ'grɛs, ,ri:'grɛs, -ɨz, -ɪŋ, -t
AM rə'grɛs, ri'grɛs, -əz, -ɪŋ, -t

regression
BR rɪ'grɛʃn, ,ri:'grɛʃn, -z
AM rə'grɛʃən, ri'grɛʃən, -z

regressive
BR rɪ'grɛsɪv, ,ri:'grɛsɪv
AM rə'grɛsɪv, ri'grɛsɪv

regressively
BR rɪ'grɛsɪvli, ,ri:'grɛsɪvli
AM rə'grɛsɪvli, ri'grɛsɪvli

regressiveness
BR rɪ'grɛsɪvnɨs, ,ri:'grɛsɪvnɨs
AM rə'grɛsɪvnɨs, ri'grɛsɪvnɨs

regret
BR rɪ'grɛt, -s, -ɪŋ, -ɨd
AM rə'grɛ|t, ri'grɛ|t, -ts, -dɪŋ, -dəd

regretful
BR rɪ'grɛtf(ʉ)l
AM rə'grɛtfəl, ri'grɛtfəl

regretfully
BR rɪ'grɛtfʉli, rɪ'grɛtfḷi
AM rə'grɛtfəli, ri'grɛtfəli

regretfulness
BR rɪ'grɛtf(ʉ)lnəs
AM rə'grɛtfəlnəs, ri'grɛtfəlnəs

regrettable
BR rɪ'grɛtəbl
AM rə'grɛdəbəl, ri'grɛdəbəl

regrettably
BR rɪ'grɛtəbli
AM rə'grɛdəbli, ri'grɛdəbli

regrew
BR ,ri:'gru:
AM ri'gru

regroup
BR ,ri:'gru:p, -s, -ɪŋ, -t
AM ri'grup, -s, -ɪŋ, -t

regroupment
BR ,ri:'gru:pm(ə)nt, -s
AM ri'grupmənt, -s

regrow
BR ,ri:'grəʊ, -z, -ɪŋ
AM ri'groʊ, -z, -ɪŋ

regrown
BR ,ri:'grəʊn
AM ri'groʊn

regrowth
BR ,ri:'grəʊθ, -s
AM ri'groʊθ, -s

regulable
BR 'rɛgjʉləbl
AM 'rɛgjələbəl

regular
BR 'rɛgjʉlə(r), -z
AM 'rɛg(jə)lər, -z

regularisation
BR ,rɛgjʉlərʌɪ'zeɪʃn
AM ,rɛgjələrə'zeɪʃən, ,rɛgjələ,raɪ'zeɪʃən

regularise
BR 'rɛgjʉlərʌɪz, -ɨz, -ɪŋ, -d
AM 'rɛgjələ,raɪz, -ɨz, -ɪŋ, -d

regularity
BR ,rɛgjʉ'larɪti
AM ,rɛgjə'lɛrədi

regularization
BR ,rɛgjʉlərʌɪ'zeɪʃn
AM ,rɛgjələrə'zeɪʃən, ,rɛgjələ,raɪ'zeɪʃən

regularize
BR 'rɛgjʉlərʌɪz, -ɨz, -ɪŋ, -d
AM 'rɛgjələ,raɪz, -ɨz, -ɪŋ, -d

regularly
BR 'rɛgjʉləli
AM 'rɛg(jə)lərli

regulate
BR 'rɛgjʉleɪt, -s, -ɪŋ, -ɨd
AM 'rɛgjə,leɪ|t, -ts, -dɪŋ, -dɨd

regulation
BR ,rɛgjʉ'leɪʃn, -z

AM ˌrɛg(j)əˈleɪʃən, -z

regulative
BR ˈrɛgjʉlətɪv
AM ˈrɛgjələdɪv, ˈrɛgjəˌleɪdɪv

regulator
BR ˈrɛgjʉleɪtə(r), -z
AM ˈrɛgjəˌleɪdər, -z

regulatory
BR ˈrɛgjʉlət(ə)ri, ˌrɛgjʉˈleɪt(ə)ri
AM ˈrɛgjələˌtɔri

reguli
BR ˈrɛgjʉlʌɪ, ˈrɛgjʉliː
AM ˈrɛgjəˌlaɪ

reguline
BR ˈrɛgjʉlʌɪn
AM ˈrɛgjələn, ˈrɛgjəˌlaɪn

regulo
BR ˈrɛgjʉləʊ, -z
AM ˈrɛgjəloʊ, -z

regulus
BR ˈrɛgjʉləs, -ɪz
AM ˈrɛgjələs, -əz

regurgitate
BR rɪˈgəːdʒɪteɪt, ˌriːˈgəːdʒɪteɪt, -s, -ɪŋ, -ɪd
AM rəˈgərdʒəˌteɪ|t, riˈgərdʒəˌteɪ|t, -ts, -dɪŋ, -dɪd

regurgitation
BR rɪˌgəːdʒɪˈteɪʃn, ˌriːgəːdʒɪˈteɪʃn
AM rəˌgərdʒəˈteɪʃən, riˌgərdʒəˈteɪʃən

rehab
BR ˈriːhab
AM ˈriˌhæb

rehabilitate
BR ˌriː(h)əˈbɪlɪteɪt, -s, -ɪŋ, -ɪd
AM ˌri(h)əˈbɪləˌteɪ|t, -ts, -dɪŋ, -dɪd

rehabilitation
BR ˌriː(h)əˌbɪlɪˈteɪʃn
AM ˌri(h)əˌbɪliˈteɪʃən

rehabilitative
BR ˌriː(h)əˈbɪlɪtətɪv
AM ˌri(h)əˈbɪləˌteɪdɪv

rehandle
BR ˌriːˈhand|l, -lz, -ḷɪŋ\-lɪŋ, -ld
AM riˈhæn(d)əl, -z, -ɪŋ, -d

rehang
BR (ˌ)riːˈhaŋ, -z, -ɪŋ
AM riˈhæŋ, -z, -ɪŋ

rehash¹
noun
BR ˈriːhaʃ, -ɪz
AM ˈriˌhæʃ, -ɪz

rehash²
verb
BR (ˌ)riːˈhaʃ, -ɪz, -ɪŋ, -t
AM riˈhæʃ, -ɪz, -ɪŋ, -t

rehear
BR ˌriːˈhɪə(r), -z, -ɪŋ
AM riˈhɪ(ə)r, -z, -ɪŋ

reheard
BR ˌriːˈhəːd
AM riˈhərd

rehearsal
BR rɪˈhəːsl, -z
AM rəˈhərsəl, riˈhərsəl, -z

rehearse
BR rɪˈhəːs, -ɪz, -ɪŋ, -t
AM rəˈhərs, riˈhərs, -əz, -ɪŋ, -t

rehearser
BR rɪˈhəːsə(r), -z
AM rəˈhərsər, ˈrihərsər, -z

reheat
BR ˌriːˈhiːt, -s, -ɪŋ, -ɪd
AM riˈhi|t, -ts, -dɪŋ, -dɪd

reheater
BR ˌriːˈhiːtə(r), -z
AM riˈhidər, -z

reheel
BR ˌriːˈhiːl, -z, -ɪŋ, -d
AM riˈhil, -z, -ɪŋ, -d

Rehnquist
BR ˈrɛnkwɪst
AM ˈrɛnˌkwist
SW reːnˈkvɪst

Rehoboam
BR ˌriː(h)əˈbəʊəm, -z
AM ˌri(h)əˈboʊəm, -z

rehome
BR ˌriːˈhəʊm, -z, -ɪŋ, -d
AM riˈhoʊm, -z, -ɪŋ, -d

rehouse
BR ˌriːˈhaʊz, -ɪz, -ɪŋ, -d
AM riˈhaʊz, -əz, -ɪŋ, -d

rehung
BR (ˌ)riːˈhʌŋ
AM riˈhəŋ

rehydratable
BR ˌriːhʌɪˈdreɪtəbl
AM riˈhaɪˌdreɪdəbəl

rehydrate
BR ˌriːhʌɪˈdreɪt, -s, -ɪŋ, -ɪd
AM riˈhaɪˌdreɪ|t, -ts, -dɪŋ, -dɪd

rehydration
BR ˌriːhʌɪˈdreɪʃn
AM ˈriˌhaɪˈdreɪʃən

Reich
BR rʌɪx, rʌɪk
AM raɪk

Reichstag
BR ˈrʌɪxstɑːg, ˈrʌɪʃstɑːg, ˈrʌɪkstɑːg
AM ˈraɪkˌstæg

Reid
BR riːd
AM rid

reification
BR ˌreɪɪfɪˈkeɪʃn, ˌriːɪfɪˈkeɪʃn
AM ˌriəfəˈkeɪʃən, ˌreɪəfəˈkeɪʃən

reificatory
BR ˌreɪɪfɪˈkeɪt(ə)ri, ˌriːɪfɪˈkeɪt(ə)ri
AM reɪˈɪfəkəˌtɔri, riˈɪfəkəˌtɔri

reify
BR ˈreɪɪfʌɪ, ˈriːɪfʌɪ, -z, -ɪŋ, -d
AM ˈriəˌfaɪ, -z, -ɪŋ, -d

Reigate
BR ˈrʌɪgeɪt, ˈrʌɪgət
AM ˈraɪˌgeɪt

reign
BR reɪn, -z, -ɪŋ, -d
AM reɪn, -z, -ɪŋ, -d

reignite
BR ˌriːɪgˈnʌɪt, -s, -ɪŋ, -ɪd
AM ˌriɪgˈnaɪ|t, -ts, -dɪŋ, -dɪd

Reilly
BR ˈrʌɪli
AM ˈraɪli

reimbursable
BR ˌriːɪmˈbəːsəbl
AM ˈriɪmˈbərsəbəl

reimburse
BR ˌriːɪmˈbəːs, -ɪz, -ɪŋ, -t
AM ˈriɪmˈbərs, -əz, -ɪŋ, -t

reimbursement
BR ˌriːɪmˈbəːsm(ə)nt, -s
AM ˈriɪmˈbərsmənt, -s

reimburser
BR ˌriːɪmˈbəːsə(r), -z
AM ˈriɪmˈbərsər, -z

reimport
BR ˌriːɪmˈpɔːt, -s, -ɪŋ, -ɪd
AM riˈɪmˌpɔ(ə)rt, riɪmˈpɔ(ə)rt, -ts, -pɔrdɪŋ, -pɔrdəd

reimportation
BR ˌriːɪmpɔːˈteɪʃn
AM ˈriˌɪmpɔrˈteɪʃən

reimpose
BR ˌriːɪmˈpəʊz, -ɪz, -ɪŋ, -d
AM ˈriɪmˈpoʊz, -əz, -ɪŋ, -d

reimposition
BR ˌriːɪmpəˈzɪʃn
AM ˈriˌɪmpəˈzɪʃən

Reims
BR riːmz
AM rimz
FR rɛ̃s

rein
BR reɪn, -z, -ɪŋ, -d
AM reɪn, -z, -ɪŋ, -d

reincarnate¹
adjective
BR ˌriːɪnˈkɑːnət, ˌriːɪŋˈkɑːnət
AM ˈriɪnˈkɑrnət, ˈriɪŋˈkɑrˌnət

reincarnate²
verb
BR ˌriːɪnˈkɑːneɪt, ˌriːɪŋˈkɑːneɪt, -s, -ɪŋ, -ɪd
AM ˈriɪnˈkɑrˌneɪ|t, ˈriɪŋˈkɑrˌneɪ|t, -ts, -dɪŋ, -dɪd

reincarnation
BR ˌriːɪnkɑːˈneɪʃn, ˌriːɪŋkɑːˈneɪʃn, -z
AM ˈriɪnˌkɑrˈneɪʃən, ˈriɪŋˌkɑrˈneɪʃən, -z

reincorporate
BR ˌriːɪnˈkɔːpəreɪt, ˌriːɪŋˈkɔːpəreɪt, -s, -ɪŋ, -ɪd
AM ˈriɪnˈkɔrpəˌreɪ|t, ˈriɪŋˈkɔrpəreɪ|t, -ts, -dɪŋ, -dɪd

reincorporation
BR ˌriːɪnˌkɔːpəˈreɪʃn, ˌriːɪŋˌkɔːpəˈreɪʃn
AM ˈriɪnˌkɔrpəˈreɪʃən, ˈriɪŋˌkɔrpəˈreɪʃən

reindeer
BR ˈreɪndɪə(r), -z
AM ˈreɪnˌdɪ(ə)r, -z

reinfect
BR ˌriːɪnˈfɛkt, -s, -ɪŋ, -ɪd
AM ˈriɪnˈfɛk|(t), -(t)s, -tɪŋ, -təd

reinfection
BR ˌriːɪnˈfɛkʃn, -z
AM ˈriɪnˈfɛkʃən, -z

reinforce
BR ˌriːɪnˈfɔːs, -ɪz, -ɪŋ, -t
AM ˈriɪnˈfɔ(ə)rs, -əz, -ɪŋ, -t

reinforcement
BR ˌriːɪnˈfɔːsm(ə)nt, -s
AM ˈriɪnˈfɔrsmənt, -s

reinforcer
BR ˌriːɪnˈfɔːsə(r), -z
AM ˈriɪnˈfɔrsər, -z

Reinhardt
BR ˈrʌɪnhɑːt
AM ˈraɪnˌ(h)ɑrt

reinject
BR ˌriːɪnˈdʒɛkt, -s, -ɪŋ, -ɪd
AM ˈriɪnˈdʒɛk|(t), -(t)s, -tɪŋ, -təd

reinless
BR ˈreɪnlɪs
AM ˈreɪnlɪs

reinsert
BR ˌriːɪnˈsəːt, -s, -ɪŋ, -ɪd
AM ˈriɪnˈsər|t, -ts, -dɪŋ, -dəd

reinsertion
BR ˌriːɪnˈsəːʃn, -z
AM ˈriɪnˈsərʃən, -z

reinspect
BR ˌriːɪnˈspɛkt, -s, -ɪŋ, -ɪd

AM ˌriɨnzˈpɛk|(t), ˌriːɪnˈspɛk|(t), -(t)s, -tɪŋ, -təd

reinstal
BR ˌriːɪnˈstɔːl, -z, -ɪŋ, -d
AM ˌriɨnzˈtɔl, ˌriɨnˈstɔl, ˌriɨnzˈtɑl, ˌriɨnˈstɑl, -z, -ɪŋ, -d

reinstall
BR ˌriːɪnˈstɔːl, -z, -ɪŋ, -d
AM ˌriɨnzˈtɔl, ˌriɨnˈstɔl, ˌriɨnzˈtɑl, ˌriɨnˈstɑl, -z, -ɪŋ, -d

reinstate
BR ˌriːɪnˈsteɪt, -s, -ɪŋ, -ɨd
AM ˌriɨnˈsteɪ|t, -ts, -dɪŋ, -dɨd

reinstatement
BR ˌriːɪnˈsteɪtm(ə)nt, -s
AM ˌriɨnˈsteɪtmənt, -s

reinstitute
BR ˌriːˈɪnstɨtjuːt, ˌriːˈɪnstɨtʃuːt, -s, -ɪŋ, -d
AM ˌriˈɪnstəˌt(j)u|t, -ts, -dɪŋ, -dɨd

reinstitution
BR ˌriːɪnstɨˈtjuːʃn, ˌriːɪnstɨˈtʃuːʃn
AM ˌriˌɪnstəˈt(j)uʃən

reinsurance
BR ˌriːɪnˈʃʊərəns, ˌriːɪnˈʃʊərn̩s, ˌriːɪnˈʃɔːrəns, ˌriːɪnˈʃɔːrn̩s
AM ˌriɨnʃʊrəns

reinsure
BR ˌriːɪnˈʃʊə(r), ˌriːɪnˈʃɔː(r), -z, -ɪŋ, -d
AM ˌriɨnˈʃʊ(ə)r, -z, -ɪŋ, -d

reinsurer
BR ˌriːɪnˈʃʊərə(r), ˌriːɪnˈʃɔːrə(r), -z
AM ˌriɨnˈʃʊrər, -z

reintegrate
BR ˌriːˈɪntɨɡreɪt, -s, -ɪŋ, -ɨd
AM ˌriˈɪn(t)əˌɡreɪ|t, -ts, -dɪŋ, -dɨd

reintegration
BR ˌriːɪntɨˈɡreɪʃn
AM ˌriˌɪn(t)əˈɡreɪʃən

reinter
BR ˌriːɪnˈtəː(r), -z, -ɪŋ, -d
AM ˌriɨnˈtər, -z, -ɪŋ, -d

reinterment
BR ˌriːɪnˈtəːm(ə)nt, -s
AM ˌriɨnˈtərmənt, -s

reinterpret
BR ˌriːɪnˈtəːprɪt, -s, -ɪŋ, -ɨd
AM ˌriɨnˈtərprə|t, -ts, -dɪŋ, -dəd

reinterpretation
BR ˌriːɪnˌtəːprɨˈteɪʃn, -z
AM ˌriɨnˌtərprəˈteɪʃən, -z

reintroduce
BR ˌriːɪntrəˈdjuːs, ˌriːɪntrəˈdʒuːs, -ɨz, -ɪŋ, -t
AM ˌriɨntrəˈd(j)us, -ɨz, -ɪŋ, -t

reintroduction
BR ˌriːɪntrəˈdʌkʃn
AM ˌriɨntrəˈdəkʃən

reinvent
BR ˌriːɪnˈvɛnt, -s, -ɪŋ, -ɨd
AM ˌriɨnˈvɛn|t, -ts, -(t)ɪŋ, -(t)əd

reinvention
BR ˌriːɪnˈvɛnʃn
AM ˌriɨnˈvɛnʃən

reinvest
BR ˌriːɪnˈvɛst, -s, -ɪŋ, -ɨd
AM ˌriɨnˈvɛst, -s, -ɪŋ, -ɨd

reinvestigate
BR ˌriːɪnˈvɛstɨɡeɪt, -s, -ɪŋ, -d
AM ˌriɨnˈvɛstəˌɡeɪ|t, -ts, -dɪŋ, -dɨd

reinvestigation
BR ˌriːɪnˌvɛstɨˈɡeɪʃn, -z
AM ˌriɨnˌvɛstəˈɡeɪʃən, -z

reinvestment
BR ˌriːɪnˈvɛs(t)m(ə)nt, -s
AM ˌriɨnˈvɛstmənt, -s

reinvigorate
BR ˌriːɪnˈvɪɡəreɪt, -s, -ɪŋ, -ɨd
AM ˌriɨnˈvɪɡəˌreɪ|t, -ts, -dɪŋ, -dɨd

reinvigoration
BR ˌriːɪnˌvɪɡəˈreɪʃn
AM ˌriɨnˌvɪɡəˈreɪʃən

reissue
BR ˌriːˈɪʃ(j)uː, ˌriːˈɪsjuː, -z, -ɪŋ, -d
AM riˈɪʃu, -z, -ɪŋ, -d

reiterate
BR rɪˈɪtəreɪt, ˌriːˈɪtəreɪt, -s, -ɪŋ, -ɨd
AM riˈɪdəˌreɪ|t, -ts, -dɪŋ, -dɨd

reiteration
BR rɪˌɪtəˈreɪʃn, ˌriːˌɪtəˈreɪʃn
AM riˌɪdəˈreɪʃən

reiterative
BR rɪˈɪt(ə)rətɪv, ˌriːˈɪt(ə)rətɪv
AM riˈɪdəˌreɪdɪv, riˈɪdərədɪv

Reith
BR riːθ
AM riθ

reive
BR riːv, -z, -ɪŋ, -d
AM riv, -z, -ɪŋ, -d

reiver
BR ˈriːvə(r), -z
AM ˈrivər, -z

reject[1]
noun
BR ˈriːdʒɛkt, -s
AM ˈriˌdʒɛk(t), -s

reject[2]
verb
BR rɨˈdʒɛkt, -s, -ɪŋ, -ɨd
AM rəˈdʒɛk|(t), riˈdʒɛk|(t), -(t)s, -tɪŋ, -təd

rejectable
BR rɨˈdʒɛktəbl
AM rəˈdʒɛktəbəl, riˈdʒɛktəbəl

rejectamenta
BR rɨˌdʒɛktəˈmɛntə(r)
AM rəˌdʒɛktəˈmɛn(t)ə, riˌdʒɛktəˈmɛn(t)ə

rejecter
BR rɨˈdʒɛktə(r), -z
AM rəˈdʒɛktər, riˈdʒɛktər, -z

rejection
BR rɨˈdʒɛkʃn, -z
AM rəˈdʒɛkʃən, riˈdʒɛkʃən, -z

rejectionist
BR rɨˈdʒɛkʃn̩ɪst, rɨˈdʒɛkʃənɪst, -s
AM rəˈdʒɛkʃənəst, rəˈdʒɛkʃn̩əst, riˈdʒɛkʃənəst, riˈdʒɛkʃn̩əst, -s

rejective
BR rɨˈdʒɛktɪv
AM rəˈdʒɛktɪv, riˈdʒɛktɪv

rejector
BR rɨˈdʒɛktə(r), -z
AM rəˈdʒɛktər, riˈdʒɛktər, -z

rejig
BR ˌriːˈdʒɪɡ, -z, -ɪŋ, -d
AM riˈdʒɪɡ, -z, -ɪŋ, -d

rejoice
BR rɨˈdʒɔɪs, -ɨz, -ɪŋ, -t
AM rəˈdʒɔɪs, riˈdʒɔɪs, -ɨz, -ɪŋ, -t

rejoicer
BR rɨˈdʒɔɪsə(r), -z
AM rəˈdʒɔɪsər, riˈdʒɔɪsər, -z

rejoicing
BR rɨˈdʒɔɪsɪŋ, -z
AM rəˈdʒɔɪsɪŋ, riˈdʒɔɪsɪŋ, -z

rejoicingly
BR rɨˈdʒɔɪsɪŋli
AM rəˈdʒɔɪsɪŋli, riˈdʒɔɪsɪŋli

rejoin[1]
answer
BR rɨˈdʒɔɪn, -z, -ɪŋ, -d
AM rəˈdʒɔɪn, riˈdʒɔɪn, -z, -ɪŋ, -d

rejoin[2]
join again
BR ˌriːˈdʒɔɪn, -z, -ɪŋ, -d
AM riˈdʒɔɪn, -z, -ɪŋ, -d

rejoinder
BR rɨˈdʒɔɪndə(r), -z
AM rəˈdʒɔɪndər, riˈdʒɔɪndər, -z

rejuvenate
BR rɨˈdʒuːvɨneɪt, -s, -ɪŋ, -ɨd
AM rəˈdʒuvəˌneɪ|t, riˈdʒuvəˌneɪ|t, -ts, -dɪŋ, -dɨd

rejuvenation
BR rɨˌdʒuːvɨˈneɪʃn
AM rəˌdʒuvəˈneɪʃən, riˌdʒuvəˈneɪʃən

rejuvenator
BR rɨˈdʒuːvɨneɪtə(r), -z
AM rəˈdʒuvəˌneɪdər, riˈdʒuvəˌneɪdər, -z

rejuvenesce
BR ˌriːdʒuːvɨˈnɛs, rɨˌdʒuːvɨˈnɛs, -ɨz, -ɪŋ, -t
AM rəˌdʒuvəˈnɛs, riˌdʒuvəˈnɛs, -əz, -ɪŋ, -t

rejuvenescence
BR ˌriːdʒuːvɨˈnɛsns, rɨˌdʒuːvɨˈnɛsns
AM rəˌdʒuvəˈnɛsəns, riˌdʒuvəˈnɛsəns

rejuvenescent
BR ˌriːdʒuːvɨˈnɛsnt, rɨˌdʒuːvɨˈnɛsnt
AM rəˌdʒuvəˈnɛsənt, riˌdʒuvəˈnɛsənt

rekindle
BR (ˌ)riːˈkɪnd|l, -lz, -l̩ɪŋ\-lɪŋ, -ld
AM riˈkɪn|dəl, -dəlz, -(d)(ə)lɪŋ, -dəld

relabel
BR (ˌ)riːˈleɪb|l, -lz, -l̩ɪŋ\-lɪŋ, -ld
AM riˈleɪbəl, -z, -ɪŋ, -d

relapse[1]
noun
BR rɨˈlaps, ˈriːlaps, -ɨz
AM ˈriˌlæps, -əz

relapse[2]
verb
BR rɨˈlaps, -ɨz, -ɪŋ, -t
AM rəˈlæps, riˈlæps, ˈriˌlæps, -əz, -ɪŋ, -t

relapser
BR rɨˈlapsə(r), -z
AM rəˈlæpsər, riˈlæpsər, ˈriˌlæpsər, -z

relatable
BR rɨˈleɪtəbl

AM rə'leɪdəbəl, ri'leɪdəbəl
relate
BR rɪ'leɪt, -s, -ɪŋ, -ɪd
AM rə'leɪ|t, ri'leɪ|t, -ts, -dɪŋ, -dɪd
relatedness
BR rɪ'leɪtɪdnɪs
AM rə'leɪdɪdnɪs, ri'leɪdɪdnɪs
relater
BR rɪ'leɪtə(r), -z
AM rə'leɪdər, ri'leɪdər, -z
relation
BR rɪ'leɪʃn, -z
AM rə'leɪʃən, ri'leɪʃən, -z
relational
BR rɪ'leɪʃn̩(ə)l, rɪ'leɪʃən(ə)l
AM rə'leɪʃ(ə)nəl, ri'leɪʃ(ə)nəl
relationally
BR rɪ'leɪʃn̩əli, rɪ'leɪʃn̩l̩i, rɪ'leɪʃənl̩i, rɪ'leɪʃ(ə)nəli
AM rə'leɪʃ(ə)nəli, ri'leɪʃ(ə)nəli
relationism
BR rɪ'leɪʃn̩ɪz(ə)m, rɪ'leɪʃənɪz(ə)m
AM rə'leɪʃəˌnɪzəm, ri'leɪʃəˌnɪzəm
relationist
BR rɪ'leɪʃn̩ɪst, rɪ'leɪʃənɪst, -s
AM rə'leɪʃənəst, ri'leɪʃənəst, -s
relationship
BR rɪ'leɪʃn̩ʃɪp, -s
AM rə'leɪʃənˌʃɪp, ri'leɪʃənˌʃɪp, -s
relatival
BR ˌrɛlə'tʌɪvl
AM ˌrɛlə'taɪvəl
relative
BR 'rɛlətɪv, -z
AM 'rɛlədɪv, -z
relatively
BR 'rɛlətɪvli
AM 'rɛlədɪvli
relativeness
BR 'rɛlətɪvnɪs
AM 'rɛlədɪvnɪs
relativisation
BR ˌrɛlətɪvʌɪ'zeɪʃn
AM ˌrɛlədəvə'zeɪʃən, ˌrɛlədəˌvaɪ'zeɪʃən
relativise
BR 'rɛlətɪvʌɪz, -ɪz, -ɪŋ, -d
AM 'rɛlədəˌvaɪz, -ɪz, -ɪŋ, -d
relativism
BR 'rɛlətɪvɪz(ə)m
AM 'rɛlədəˌvɪzəm
relativist
BR 'rɛlətɪvɪst, -s
AM 'rɛlədəvəst, -s
relativistic
BR ˌrɛlətɪ'vɪstɪk
AM ˌrɛlədə'vɪstɪk
relativistically
BR ˌrɛlətɪ'vɪstɪkli
AM ˌrɛlədə'vɪstək(ə)li
relativity
BR ˌrɛlə'tɪvɪti
AM ˌrɛlə'tɪvɪdi
relativization
BR ˌrɛlətɪvʌɪ'zeɪʃn
AM ˌrɛlədəvə'zeɪʃən, ˌrɛlədəˌvaɪ'zeɪʃən
relativize
BR 'rɛlətɪvʌɪz, -ɪz, -ɪŋ, -d
AM 'rɛlədəˌvaɪz, -ɪz, -ɪŋ, -d
relator
BR rɪ'leɪtə(r), -z
AM rə'leɪdər, ri'leɪdər, -z
relaunch[1]
noun
BR 'riːlɔːn(t)ʃ, -ɪz
AM ri'lɔn(t)ʃ, ri'lɑn(t)ʃ, -əz
relaunch[2]
verb
BR ˌriː'lɔːn(t)ʃ, -ɪz, -ɪŋ, -t
AM ri'lɔn(t)ʃ, ri'lɑn(t)ʃ, -əz, -ɪŋ, -t
relax
BR rɪ'laks, -ɪz, -ɪŋ, -t
AM rə'læks, ri'læks, -əz, -ɪŋ, -t
relaxant
BR rɪ'laksnt, -s
AM rə'læksənt, -s
relaxation
BR ˌriːlak'seɪʃn, -z
AM rəˌlæk'seɪʃən, riˌlæk'seɪʃən, -z
relaxedly
BR rɪ'laksɪdli
AM rə'læksədli, ri'læksədli
relaxedness
BR rɪ'laksɪdnɪs
AM rə'læksədnəs, ri'læksədnəs
relaxer
BR rɪ'laksə(r), -z
AM rə'læksər, ri'læksər, -z
relay[1]
noun
BR 'riːleɪ, -z
AM 'riˌleɪ, -z
relay[2]
verb, broadcast
BR 'riːleɪ, -z, -ɪŋ, -d
AM ri'leɪ, rə'leɪ, 'riˌleɪ, -z, -ɪŋ, -d
relay[3]
verb, lay again
BR ˌriː'leɪ, -z, -ɪŋ, -d
AM ri'leɪ, -z, -ɪŋ, -d
relearn
BR ˌriː'ləːn, -z, -ɪŋ, -d
AM ri'lərn, -z, -ɪŋ, -d
releasable
BR rɪ'liːsəbl
AM rə'lisəbəl, ri'lisəbəl
release[1]
noun new lease
BR ˌriː'liːs, -ɪz
AM ri'lis, -z
release[2]
noun, verb, freedom/free
BR rɪ'liːs, -ɪz, -ɪŋ, -t
AM rə'lis, ri'lis, -ɪz, -ɪŋ, -t
releasee
BR rɪˌliː'siː, -z
AM rəˌli'si, riˌli'si, -z
releaser
BR rɪ'liːsə(r), -z
AM rə'lisər, ri'lisər, -z
releasor
BR rɪ'liːsə(r), -z
AM rə'lisər, ri'lisər, -z
relegable
BR 'rɛlɪgəbl
AM 'rɛləgəbəl
relegate
BR 'rɛlɪgeɪt, -s, -ɪŋ, -ɪd
AM 'rɛləˌgeɪ|t, -ts, -dɪŋ, -dɪd
relegation
BR ˌrɛlɪ'geɪʃn
AM ˌrɛlə'geɪʃən
relent
BR rɪ'lɛnt, -s, -ɪŋ, -ɪd
AM rə'lɛn|t, ri'lɛn|t, -ts, -(t)ɪŋ, -(t)əd
relentless
BR rɪ'lɛntləs
AM rə'lɛn(t)ləs, ri'lɛn(t)ləs
relentlessly
BR rɪ'lɛntləsli
AM rə'lɛn(t)ləsli, ri'lɛn(t)ləsli
relentlessness
BR rɪ'lɛntləsnəs
AM rə'lɛn(t)ləsnəs, ri'lɛn(t)ləsnəs
relet
BR ˌriː'lɛt, -s, -ɪŋ
AM ri'lɛ|t, -ts, -dɪŋ
relevance
BR 'rɛlɪv(ə)ns
AM 'rɛləvəns
relevancy
BR 'rɛlɪv(ə)nsi
AM 'rɛləvənsi
relevant
BR 'rɛlɪv(ə)nt
AM 'rɛləvənt
relevantly
BR 'rɛlɛv(ə)ntli
AM 'rɛləvən(t)li
relevé
BR ˌrələ'veɪ, -z
AM ˌrələ'veɪ, -z
reliability
BR rɪˌlʌɪə'bɪlɪti
AM rəˌlaɪə'bɪlɪdi, riˌlaɪə'bɪlɪdi
reliable
BR rɪ'lʌɪəbl
AM rə'laɪəbəl, ri'laɪəbəl
reliableness
BR rɪ'lʌɪəblnəs
AM rə'laɪəbəlnəs, ri'laɪəbəlnəs
reliably
BR rɪ'lʌɪəbli
AM rə'laɪəbli, ri'laɪəbli
reliance
BR rɪ'lʌɪəns
AM rə'laɪəns, ri'laɪəns
reliant
BR rɪ'lʌɪənt
AM rə'laɪənt, ri'laɪənt
relic
BR 'rɛlɪk, -s
AM 'rɛlɪk, -s
relict
BR 'rɛlɪkt, -s
AM 'rɛlɪk|(t), -(t)s
relief
BR rɪ'liːf, -s
AM rə'lif, ri'lif, -s
relievable
BR rɪ'liːvəbl
AM rə'livəbəl, ri'livəbəl
relieve
BR rɪ'liːv, -z, -ɪŋ, -d
AM rə'liv, ri'liv, -z, -ɪŋ, -d
reliever
BR rɪ'liːvə(r), -z
AM rə'livər, ri'livər, -z
relievo
BR rɪ'liːvəʊ, ˌrɛlɪ'eɪvəʊ, -z
AM ri'livoʊ, -z
relight
BR ˌriː'lʌɪt, -s, -ɪŋ, -ɪd
AM ri'laɪ|t, -ts, -dɪŋ, -dɪd
religion
BR rɪ'lɪdʒ(ə)n, -z
AM rə'lɪdʒən, ri'lɪdʒən, -z
religioner
BR rɪ'lɪdʒ(ə)nə(r), rɪ'lɪdʒn̩ə(r), -z
AM rə'lɪdʒənər, ri'lɪdʒənər, -z
religionism
BR rɪ'lɪdʒn̩ɪz(ə)m, rɪ'lɪdʒənɪz(ə)m

AM rəˈlɪdʒəˌnɪzəm, riˈlɪdʒəˌnɪzəm
religionist
BR rɪˈlɪdʒənɪst, rɪˈlɪdʒn̩ɪst, -s
AM rəˈlɪdʒənəst, riˈlɪdʒənəst, -s
religionless
BR rɪˈlɪdʒənləs, rɪˈlɪdʒn̩ləs
AM rəˈlɪdʒənləs, riˈlɪdʒənləs
religiose
BR rɪˈlɪdʒɪəʊs
AM rəˌlɪdʒiˈoʊs
religiosity
BR rɪˌlɪdʒɪˈɒsɪti
AM rəˌlɪdʒiˈɑsədi
religious
BR rɪˈlɪdʒəs
AM rəˈlɪdʒəs, riˈlɪdʒəs
religiously
BR rɪˈlɪdʒəsli
AM rəˈlɪdʒəsli, riˈlɪdʒəsli
religiousness
BR rɪˈlɪdʒəsnəs
AM rəˈlɪdʒəsnəs, riˈlɪdʒəsnəs
reline
BR ˌriːˈlʌɪn, -z, -ɪŋ, -d
AM riˈlaɪn, -z, -ɪŋ, -d
relinquish
BR rɪˈlɪŋkw|ɪʃ, -ɪʃɪz, -ɪʃɪŋ, -ɪʃt
AM rəˈlɪŋkwɪʃ, riˈlɪŋkwɪʃ, -ɪz, -ɪŋ, -t
relinquishment
BR rɪˈlɪŋkwɪʃm(ə)nt, -s
AM rəˈlɪŋkwɪʃmənt, riˈlɪŋkwɪʃmənt, -s
reliquary
BR ˈrɛlɪkwər|i, -ɪz
AM ˈrɛləˌkwɛri, -z
reliquiae
BR rɪˈlɪkwɪiː
AM rəˈlɪkwiˌi, rəˈlɪkwiˌaɪ
relish
BR ˈrɛl|ɪʃ, -ɪʃɪz, -ɪʃɪŋ, -ɪʃt
AM ˈrɛlɪʃ, -ɪz, -ɪŋ, -t
relishable
BR ˈrɛlɪʃəbl
AM ˈrɛləʃəbəl
relit
BR ˌriːˈlɪt
AM riˈlɪt
relive
BR ˌriːˈlɪv, -z, -ɪŋ, -d
AM riˈlɪv, -z, -ɪŋ, -d
reload
BR ˌriːˈləʊd, -z, -ɪŋ, -ɪd
AM riˈloʊd, -z, -ɪŋ, -əd
relocate
BR ˌriːlə(ʊ)ˈkeɪt, -s, -ɪŋ, -ɪd
AM riˈloʊˌkeɪ|t, ˌriloʊˈkeɪ|t, -ts, -dɪŋ, -dɪd
relocation
BR ˌriːlə(ʊ)ˈkeɪʃn
AM ˌriloʊˈkeɪʃən
relucent
BR ˌriːˈluːs(ə)nt
AM riˈlusənt
reluctance
BR rɪˈlʌkt(ə)ns
AM rəˈləkt(ə)ns, riˈləkt(ə)ns
reluctant
BR rɪˈlʌkt(ə)nt
AM rəˈləktnt, riˈləktnt
reluctantly
BR rɪˈlʌkt(ə)ntli
AM rəˈləktən(t)li, riˈləktən(t)li
rely
BR rɪˈlʌɪ, -z, -ɪŋ, -d
AM rəˈlaɪ, riˈlaɪ, -z, -ɪŋ, -d
REM
BR ˌɑːriːˈɛm
AM ˌɑrˌiˈɛm
rem
BR rɛm, -z
AM rɛm, -z
remade
BR ˌriːˈmeɪd
AM riˈmeɪd
remain
BR rɪˈmeɪn, -z, -ɪŋ, -d
AM rəˈmeɪn, riˈmeɪn, -z, -ɪŋ, -d
remainder
BR rɪˈmeɪnd|ə(r), -əz, -(ə)rɪŋ, -əd
AM rəˈmeɪnd|ər, riˈmeɪnd|ər, -ərz, -(ə)rɪŋ, -ərd
remake[1]
noun
BR ˈriːmeɪk, -s
AM ˈriˌmeɪk, -s
remake[2]
verb
BR ˌriːˈmeɪk, -s, -ɪŋ
AM riˈmeɪk, -s, -ɪŋ
reman
BR ˌriːˈman, -z, -ɪŋ, -d
AM riˈmæn, -z, -ɪŋ, -d
remand
BR rɪˈmɑːnd, rɪˈmand, -z, -ɪŋ, -ɪd
AM rəˈmænd, riˈmænd, -z, -ɪŋ, -əd
remanence
BR ˈrɛmənəns, -ɪz
AM ˈrɛmənəns, -əz
remanent
BR ˈrɛmənənt
AM ˈrɛmənənt
remark[1]
comment, notice
BR rɪˈmɑːk, -s, -ɪŋ, -t
AM rəˈmɑrk, riˈmɑrk, -s, -ɪŋ, -t
remark[2]
mark again
BR ˌriːˈmɑːk, -s, -ɪŋ, -t
AM riˈmɑrk, -s, -ɪŋ, -t
remarkable
BR rɪˈmɑːkəbl
AM rəˈmɑrkəbəl, riˈmɑrkəbəl
remarkableness
BR rɪˈmɑːkəblnəs
AM rəˈmɑrkəbəlnəs, riˈmɑrkəbəlnəs
remarkably
BR rɪˈmɑːkəbli
AM rəˈmɑrkəbli, riˈmɑrkəbli
remarriage
BR ˌriːˈmar|ɪdʒ, -ɪdʒɪz
AM riˈmɛrɪdʒ, -ɪz
remarry
BR ˌriːˈmar|i, -ɪz, -ɪɪŋ, -ɪd
AM riˈmɛri, -z, -ɪŋ, -d
remaster
BR ˌriːˈmɑːst|ə(r), ˌriːˈmast|ə(r), -əz, -(ə)rɪŋ, -əd
AM riˈmæstər, -z, -ɪŋ, -d
rematch[1]
noun
BR ˈriːmatʃ, -ɪz
AM ˈriˌmætʃ, -əz
rematch[2]
verb
BR ˌriːˈmatʃ, -ɪz, -ɪŋ, -t
AM riˈmætʃ, -əz, -ɪŋ, -t
Rembrandt
BR ˈrɛmbrant, -s
AM ˈrɛmˌbrænt, -s
REME
BR ˈriːmi
AM ˈrimi
remeasure
BR ˌriːˈmɛʒ|ə(r), -əz, -(ə)rɪŋ, -əd
AM riˈmɛʒər, -z, -ɪŋ, -d
remeasurement
BR ˌriːˈmɛʒəm(ə)nt, -s
AM riˈmɛʒərmənt, -s
remediable
BR rɪˈmiːdɪəbl
AM rəˈmidiəbəl, riˈmidiəbəl
remedial
BR rɪˈmiːdɪəl
AM rəˈmidiəl, riˈmidiəl
remedially
BR rɪˈmiːdɪəli
AM rəˈmidiəli, riˈmidiəli
remediless
BR ˈrɛmɪdɪlɪs
AM ˈrɛmədilɪs
remedy
BR ˈrɛmɪd|i, -ɪz, -ɪɪŋ, -ɪd
AM ˈrɛmədi, -z, -ɪŋ, -d
remember
BR rɪˈmɛmb|ə(r), -əz, -(ə)rɪŋ, -əd
AM rəˈmɛmb|ər, riˈmɛmb|ər, -ərz, -(ə)rɪŋ, -ərd
rememberable
BR rɪˈmɛmb(ə)rəbl
AM rəˈmɛmb(ə)rəbəl, riˈmɛmb(ə)rəbəl
rememberer
BR rɪˈmɛmb(ə)rə(r), -z
AM rəˈmɛmb(ə)rər, riˈmɛmb(ə)rər, -z
remembrance
BR rɪˈmɛmbr(ə)ns, -ɪz
AM rəˈmɛmbrəns, riˈmɛmbrəns, -əz
remembrancer
BR rɪˈmɛmbr(ə)nsə(r), -z
AM rəˈmɛmbrənsər, riˈmɛmbrənsər, -z
remex
BR ˈriːmɛks, -ɪz
AM ˈriˌmɛks, -əz
remind
BR rɪˈmʌɪnd, -z, -ɪŋ, -ɪd
AM rəˈmaɪnd, riˈmaɪnd, -z, -ɪŋ, -ɪd
reminder
BR rɪˈmʌɪndə(r), -z
AM rəˈmaɪndər, riˈmaɪndər, -z
remindful
BR rɪˈmʌɪn(d)f(ʊ)l
AM rəˈmaɪn(d)fəl, riˈmaɪn(d)fəl
Remington®
BR ˈrɛmɪŋt(ə)n
AM ˈrɛmɪŋtən
reminisce
BR ˌrɛmɪˈnɪs, -ɪz, -ɪŋ, -t
AM ˌrɛməˈnɪs, -ɪz, -ɪŋ, -t
reminiscence
BR ˌrɛmɪˈnɪsns, -ɪz
AM ˌrɛməˈnɪsəns, -ɪz
reminiscent
BR ˌrɛmɪˈnɪsnt
AM ˌrɛməˈnɪsənt
reminiscential
BR ˌrɛmɪnɪˈsɛnʃl
AM ˌrɛmənəˈsɛn(t)ʃəl
reminiscently
BR ˌrɛmɪˈnɪsntli
AM ˌrɛməˈnɪsn(t)li
reminiscer
BR ˌrɛmɪˈnɪsə(r), -z
AM ˌrɛməˈnɪsər, -z
remint
BR ˌriːˈmɪnt, -s, -ɪŋ, -ɪd
AM riˈmɪn|t, -ts, -(t)ɪŋ, -(t)ɪd
remise
BR rɪˈmʌɪz, -ɪz, -ɪŋ, -d
AM rəˈmaɪz, riˈmaɪz, -ɪz, -ɪŋ, -d

remiss
BR rɪ'mɪs
AM rə'mɪs, ri'mɪs

remissible
BR rɪ'mɪsɪbl
AM rə'mɪsɪbəl, ri'mɪsɪbəl

remission
BR rɪ'mɪʃn, -z
AM rə'mɪʃən, ri'mɪʃən, -z

remissive
BR rɪ'mɪsɪv
AM rə'mɪsɪv, ri'mɪsɪv

remissly
BR rɪ'mɪsli
AM rə'mɪsli, ri'mɪsli

remissness
BR rɪ'mɪsnɪs
AM rə'mɪsnɪs, ri'mɪsnɪs

remit¹
noun
BR 'ri:mɪt, -s
AM rə'mɪt, ri'mɪt, 'ri,mɪt, -s

remit²
verb
BR rɪ'mɪt, -s, -ɪŋ, -ɪd
AM rə'mɪ|t, ri'mɪ|t, -ts, -dɪŋ, -dɪd

remittable
BR rɪ'mɪtəbl
AM rə'mɪdəbəl, ri'mɪdəbəl

remittal
BR rɪ'mɪtl, -z
AM rə'mɪdl, ri'mɪdl, -z

remittance
BR rɪ'mɪt(ə)ns, -ɪz
AM rə'mɪtns, ri'mɪtns, -ɪz

remittee
BR rɪ,mɪ'ti:, -z
AM rə,mɪ'ti, ri,mɪ'ti, -z

remittent
BR rɪ'mɪt(ə)nt
AM rə'mɪtnt, ri'mɪtnt

remitter
BR rɪ'mɪtə(r), -z
AM rə'mɪdər, ri'mɪdər, -z

remix
BR ,ri:'mɪks, -ɪz, -ɪŋ, -t
AM ri'mɪks, -əz, -ɪŋ, -t

remixer
BR ,ri:'mɪksə(r), -z
AM ri'mɪksər, -z

remnant
BR 'rɛmnənt, -s
AM 'rɛmnənt, -s

remodel
BR (,)ri:'mɒd|l, -lz, -lɪŋ\-lɪŋ, -ld
AM ri'mɑdəl, -əlz, -(ə)lɪŋ, -əld

remodification
BR ,ri:mɒdɪfɪ'keɪʃn, -z
AM ,ri,mɑdəfə'keɪʃən, -z

remodify
BR ,ri:'mɒdɪfʌɪ, -z, -ɪŋ, -d
AM ri'mɑdə,faɪ, -z, -ɪŋ, -d

remold¹
noun
BR 'ri:məʊld, -z
AM 'ri,moʊld, -z

remold²
verb
BR ,ri:'məʊld, -z, -ɪŋ, -ɪd
AM ri'moʊld, -z, -ɪŋ, -əd

remonetisation
BR ,ri:mʌnɪtʌɪ'zeɪʃn
AM ri,mɑnədə'zeɪʃən, ri,mɑnə,taɪ'zeɪʃən

remonetise
BR ,ri:'mʌnɪtʌɪz, -ɪz, -ɪŋ, -d
AM ri'mɑnə,taɪz, -ɪz, -ɪŋ, -d

remonetization
BR ,ri:mʌnɪtʌɪ'zeɪʃn
AM ri,mɑnədə'zeɪʃən, ri,mɑnə,taɪ'zeɪʃən

remonetize
BR ,ri:'mʌnɪtʌɪz, -ɪz, -ɪŋ, -d
AM ri'mɑnə,taɪz, -ɪz, -ɪŋ, -d

remonstrance
BR rɪ'mɒnstr(ə)ns, -ɪz
AM rə'mɑnstrəns, ri'mɑnstrəns, -əz

remonstrant
BR rɪ'mɒnstr(ə)nt
AM rə'mɑnstrənt, ri'mɑnstrənt

remonstrantly
BR rɪ'mɒnstr(ə)ntli
AM rə'mɑnstrən(t)li, ri'mɑnstrən(t)li

remonstrate
BR 'rɛmənstreɪt, -s, -ɪŋ, -ɪd
AM rə'mɑn,streɪ|t, ri'mɑn,streɪ|t, 'rɛmən,streɪ|t, -ts, -dɪŋ, -dɪd

remonstration
BR ,rɛmən'streɪʃn, -z
AM rə,mɑn'streɪʃən, ri,mɑn'streɪʃən, ,rɛmən'streɪʃən, -z

remonstrative
BR rɪ'mɒnstrətɪv
AM rə'mɑnstrədɪv, ri'mɑnstrədɪv, 'rɛmən,streɪdɪv

remonstrator
BR 'rɛmənstreɪtə(r), -z
AM rə'mɑn,streɪdər, ri'mɑn,streɪdər, 'rɛmən,streɪdər, -z

remontant
BR rɪ'mɒnt(ə)nt, -s
AM rə'mɑntnt, ri'mɑntnt, -s

remora
BR 'rɛm(ə)rə(r), rɪ'mɔ:rə(r), -z
AM 'rɛmərə, -z

remorse
BR rɪ'mɔ:s
AM rə'mɔ(ə)rs, ri'mɔ(ə)rs

remorseful
BR rɪ'mɔ:sf(ʊ)l
AM rə'mɔrsfəl, ri'mɔrsfəl

remorsefully
BR rɪ'mɔ:sfʊli, rɪ'mɔ:sfḷi
AM rə'mɔrsfəli, ri'mɔrsfəli

remorsefulness
BR rɪ'mɔ:sf(ʊ)lnəs
AM rə'mɔrsfəlnəs, ri'mɔrsfəlnəs

remorseless
BR rɪ'mɔ:sləs
AM rə'mɔrsləs, ri'mɔrsləs

remorselessly
BR rɪ'mɔ:sləsli
AM rə'mɔrsləsli, ri'mɔrsləsli

remorselessness
BR rɪ'mɔ:sləsnəs
AM rə'mɔrsləsnəs, ri'mɔrsləsnəs

remortgage
BR ,ri:'mɔ:g|ɪdʒ, -ɪdʒɪz, -ɪdʒɪŋ, -ɪdʒd
AM ri'mɔrgɪdʒ, -ɪz, -ɪŋ, -d

remote
BR rɪ'məʊt, -ə(r), -ɪst
AM rə'moʊ|t, ri'moʊ|t, -dər, -dəst

remotely
BR rɪ'məʊtli
AM rə'moʊtli, ri'moʊtli

remoteness
BR rɪ'məʊtnəs
AM rə'moʊtnəs, ri'moʊtnəs

remould¹
noun
BR 'ri:məʊld, -z
AM 'ri,moʊld, -z

remould²
verb
BR ,ri:'məʊld, -z, -ɪŋ, -ɪd
AM rə'moʊld, ri'moʊld, -z, -ɪŋ, -əd

remount¹
noun
BR 'ri:maʊnt, -s
AM 'ri,maʊnt, -s

remount²
verb
BR ,ri:'maʊnt, -s, -ɪŋ, -ɪd
AM rə'maʊn|t, ri'maʊn|t, -ts, -(t)ɪŋ, -(t)əd

removability
BR rɪ,mu:və'bɪlɪti
AM rə,muvə'bɪlɪdi, ri,muvə'bɪlɪdi

removable
BR rɪ'mu:vəbl
AM rə'muvəbəl, ri'muvəbəl

removal
BR rɪ'mu:vl, -z
AM rə'muvəl, ri'muvəl, -z

remove
BR rɪ'mu:v, -z, -ɪŋ, -d
AM rə'muv, ri'muv, -z, -ɪŋ, -d

removeable
BR rɪ'mu:vəbl
AM rə'muvəbəl, ri'muvəbəl

remover
BR rɪ'mu:və(r), -z
AM rə'muvər, ri'muvər, -z

Remploy®
BR 'rɛmplɔɪ
AM 'rɛmplɔɪ

remunerate
BR rɪ'mju:nəreɪt, -s, -ɪŋ, -ɪd
AM rə'mjunə,reɪ|t, ri'mjunə,reɪ|t, -ts, -dɪŋ, -dɪd

remuneration
BR rɪ,mju:nə'reɪʃn
AM rə,mjunə'reɪʃən, ri,mjunə'reɪʃən

remunerative
BR rɪ'mju:n(ə)rətɪv
AM rə'mjun(ə)rədɪv, ri'mjun(ə)rədɪv, rə'mjunə,reɪdɪv, ri'mjunə,reɪdɪv

remuneratory
BR rɪ'mju:n(ə)rət(ə)ri
AM rə'mjun(ə)rə,tɔri, ri'mjun(ə)rə,tɔri

Remus
BR 'ri:məs
AM 'riməs

Renaissance
BR rɪ'neɪs(ə)ns, rɪ'neɪsɑ:ns, -ɪz
AM ',rɛnə',sɑns, -əz

renal
BR 'ri:nl
AM 'rinəl

rename
BR (,)ri:'neɪm, -z, -ɪŋ, -d
AM ri'neɪm, -z, -ɪŋ, -d

renascence
BR rɪ'nasns, rɪ'neɪsns, -ɪz
AM rə'neɪsəns, ri'neɪsəns, ˌrə'næsəns, ri'næsns, -əz

renascent
BR rɪ'nasnt, rɪ'neɪsnt
AM rə'neɪsənt, ri'neɪsənt, rə'næsənt, ri'næsənt

Renata
BR rɪ'nɑːtə(r)
AM rə'nɑdə

renationalisation
BR ˌriːnaʃn̩əlʌɪ'zeɪʃn, ˌriːnaʃn̩lʌɪ'zeɪʃn, ˌriːnaʃənl̩ʌɪ'zeɪʃn, ˌriːnaʃ(ə)nəlʌɪ'zeɪʃn
AM ˌriˌnæʃənl̩ə'zeɪʃən, ˌriˌnæʃnələ'zeɪʃən, ˌriˌnæʃənlˌaɪ'zeɪʃən, ˌriˌnæʃnəˌlaɪ'zeɪʃən

renationalise
BR ˌriː'naʃn̩əlʌɪz, ˌriː'naʃn̩lʌɪz, ˌriː'naʃənl̩ʌɪz, ˌriː'naʃ(ə)nəlʌɪz, -ɪz, -ɪŋ, -d
AM ˌri'næʃənlˌaɪz, ˌri'næʃnəˌlaɪz, -ɪz, -ɪŋ, -d

renationalization
BR ˌriːnaʃn̩əlʌɪ'zeɪʃn, ˌriːnaʃn̩lʌɪ'zeɪʃn, ˌriːnaʃənl̩ʌɪ'zeɪʃn, ˌriːnaʃ(ə)nəlʌɪ'zeɪʃn
AM ˌriˌnæʃənl̩ə'zeɪʃən, ˌriˌnæʃnələ'zeɪʃən, ˌriˌnæʃənlˌaɪ'zeɪʃən, ˌriˌnæʃnəˌlaɪ'zeɪʃən

renationalize
BR ˌriː'naʃn̩əlʌɪz, ˌriː'naʃn̩lʌɪz, ˌriː'naʃənl̩ʌɪz, ˌriː'naʃ(ə)nəlʌɪz, -ɪz, -ɪŋ, -d
AM ˌri'næʃənlˌaɪz, ˌri'næʃnəˌlaɪz, -ɪz, -ɪŋ, -d

Renault®
BR 'rɛnəʊ, -z
AM rə'noʊ, rə'nɔl|t, rə'nɑlt, -z\-ts

rencontre
BR rɛn'kɒntə(r), -z
AM rɛn'kɑn(t)ər, -z

rencounter
BR rɛn'kaʊnt|ə(r), -əz, -(ə)rɪŋ, -əd
AM rɛn'kaʊn(t)ər, -z, -ɪŋ, -d

rend
BR rɛnd, -z, -ɪŋ
AM rɛnd, -z, -ɪŋ

Rendall
BR 'rɛndl
AM 'rɛndəl

Rendell
BR 'rɛndl
AM 'rɛndəl

render
BR 'rɛnd|ə(r), -əz, -(ə)rɪŋ, -əd
AM 'rɛnd|ər, -ərz, -(ə)rɪŋ, -ərd

renderer
BR 'rɛnd(ə)rə(r), -z
AM 'rɛndərər, -z

rendering
BR 'rɛnd(ə)rɪŋ, -z
AM 'rɛnd(ə)rɪŋ, -z

render-set
BR 'rɛndəsɛt, -s, -ɪŋ
AM 'rɛndərˌsɛ|t, -ts, -dɪŋ

rendezvous
BR 'rɒndɪvuː, 'rɒndeɪvuː, -z, -ɪŋ, -d
AM 'rɑndəˌvu, 'rɑndeɪˌvu, -z, -ɪŋ, -d

rendition
BR rɛn'dɪʃn, -z
AM rɛn'dɪʃən, -z

rendzina
BR rɛn(d)'ziːnə(r)
AM rɛn(d)'zinə

René
BR 'rɛneɪ, 'rəneɪ, rə'neɪ
AM rə'neɪ

Renée
BR 'rɛneɪ, 'rəneɪ, rə'neɪ, 'riːni
AM rə'neɪ

renegade
BR 'rɛnɪgeɪd, -z
AM 'rɛnəˌgeɪd, -z

renegado
BR ˌrɛnɪ'gɑːdəʊ, -z
AM ˌrɛnə'gɑˌdoʊ, -z

renege
BR rɪ'niːg, rɪ'neɪg, -z, -ɪŋ, -d
AM rə'nɛg, ri'nɛg, -z, -ɪŋ, -d

reneger
BR rɪ'niːgə(r), rɪ'neɪgə(r), -z
AM rə'nɛgər, ri'nɛgər, -z

renegotiable
BR ˌriːnɪ'gəʊʃ(ɪ)əbl
AM ˌrinə'goʊʃ(i)əbəl

renegotiate
BR ˌriːnɪ'gəʊʃɪeɪt, ˌriːnɪ'gəʊsɪeɪt, -s, -ɪŋ, -ɪd
AM ˌrinə'goʊʃiˌeɪ|t, -ts, -dɪŋ, -dɪd

renegotiation
BR ˌriːnɪˌgəʊʃɪ'eɪʃn, ˌriːnɪˌgəʊsɪ'eɪʃn, -z
AM ˌrinəˌgoʊʃi'eɪʃən, ˌrinəˌgoʊsi'eɪʃən, -z

renegue
BR rɪ'niːg, rɪ'neɪg, -z, -ɪŋ, -d
AM rə'nɛg, ri'nɛg, -z, -ɪŋ, -d

reneguer
BR rɪ'niːgə(r), rɪ'neɪgə(r), -z
AM rə'nɛgər, ri'nɛgər, -z

renew
BR rɪ'njuː, -z, -ɪŋ, -d
AM rə'n(j)u, ri'n(j)u, -z, -ɪŋ, -d

renewability
BR rɪˌnjuːə'bɪlɪti
AM rəˌn(j)uə'bɪlɪdi, riˌn(j)uə'bɪlɪdi

renewable
BR rɪ'njuːəbl
AM rə'n(j)uəbəl, ri'n(j)uəbəl

renewal
BR rɪ'njuːəl, -z
AM rə'n(j)uəl, ri'n(j)uəl, -z

renewer
BR rɪ'njuːə(r), -z
AM rə'n(j)uər, ri'n(j)uər, -z

Renfrew
BR 'rɛnfruː
AM 'rɛnfru

reniform
BR 'rɛnɪfɔːm
AM 'rɛnəˌfɔ(ə)rm, 'reɪnəˌfɔ(ə)rm

renitence
BR 'rɛnɪtns
AM 'rɛnətns

renitency
BR 'rɛnɪtnsi
AM 'rɛnətnsi

renitent
BR 'rɛnɪtnt
AM 'rɛnətnt

renminbi
BR 'rɛnmɪnbi
AM 'rɛnmɪnbi

Rennes
BR rɛn
AM rɛn(s)

rennet
BR 'rɛnɪt
AM 'rɛnət

Rennie
BR 'rɛni
AM 'rɛni

rennin
BR 'rɛnɪn
AM 'rɛnən

Reno
BR 'riːnəʊ
AM 'rinoʊ

Renoir
BR 'rɛnwɑː(r), rə'nwɑː(r), -z
AM 'rɛnˌwɑr, rə'nwɑr, -z

renominate
BR ˌriː'nɒmɪneɪt, -s, -ɪŋ, -ɪd
AM ri'nɑməˌneɪ|t, -ts, -dɪŋ, -dɪd

renomination
BR ˌriːnɒmɪ'neɪʃn, -z
AM ˌriˌnɑmə'neɪʃən, -z

renounce
BR rɪ'naʊns, -ɪz, -ɪŋ, -t
AM rə'naʊns, ri'naʊns, -əz, -ɪŋ, -t

renounceable
BR rɪ'naʊnsəbl
AM rə'naʊnsəbəl, ri'naʊnsəbəl

renouncement
BR rɪ'naʊnsm(ə)nt, -s
AM rə'naʊnsmənt, ri'naʊnsmənt, -s

renouncer
BR rɪ'naʊnsə(r), -z
AM rə'naʊnsər, ri'naʊnsər, -z

renovate
BR 'rɛnəveɪt, -s, -ɪŋ, -ɪd
AM 'rɛnəˌveɪ|t, -ts, -dɪŋ, -dɪd

renovation
BR ˌrɛnə'veɪʃn, -z
AM ˌrɛnə'veɪʃən, -z

renovative
BR 'rɛnəveɪtɪv
AM 'rɛnəˌveɪdɪv

renovator
BR 'rɛnəveɪtə(r), -z
AM 'rɛnəˌveɪdər, -z

renown
BR rɪ'naʊn, -d
AM rə'naʊn, ri'naʊn, -d

Renshaw
BR 'rɛnʃɔː(r)
AM 'rɛnˌʃɔ

rent
BR rɛnt, -s, -ɪŋ, -ɪd
AM rɛn|t, -ts, -(t)ɪŋ, -(t)əd

rentability
BR ˌrɛntə'bɪlɪti
AM ˌrɛn(t)ə'bɪlɪdi

rentable
BR 'rɛntəbl
AM 'rɛn(t)əbəl

rent-a-car
BR 'rɛntəkɑː(r)
AM 'rɛn(t)əˌkɑr

rental
BR 'rɛntl, -z
AM 'rɛn(t)l, -z

rentboy
BR 'rɛntbɔɪ, -z
AM 'rɛntˌbɔɪ, -z

renter
BR 'rɛntə(r), -z
AM 'rɛn(t)ər, -z

rentier
BR ˈrɒntɪeɪ, -z
AM ˌrɑnˈtjeɪ, -z

Rentokil®
BR ˈrɛntə(ʊ)kɪl
AM ˈrɛn(t)əˌkɪl

Renton
BR ˈrɛntən
AM ˈrɛn(t)ən

renumber
BR ˌriːˈnʌmb|ə(r), -əz, -(ə)rɪŋ, -əd
AM riˈnəmbər, -z, -ɪŋ, -d

renunciant
BR rɪˈnʌnsɪənt, -s
AM rəˈnənsiənt, riˈnənsiənt, -s

renunciation
BR rɪˌnʌnsɪˈeɪʃn, -z
AM rəˌnənsiˈeɪʃən, riˌnənsiˈeɪʃən, -z

renunciative
BR rɪˈnʌnsɪətɪv
AM rəˈnənsiədɪv, riˈnənsiədɪv, rəˈnənsiˌeɪdɪv, riˈnənsiˌeɪdɪv

renunciatory
BR rɪˈnʌnsɪət(ə)ri
AM rəˈnənsiəˌtɔri, riˈnənsiəˌtɔri

renvoi
BR ˈrɒnvwɑː(r), -z
AM rɛnˈvɔɪ, -z

Renwick
BR ˈrɛn(w)ɪk
AM ˈrɛnwɪk

reoccupation
BR ˌriːɒkjʊˈpeɪʃn, rɪˌɒkjʊˈpeɪʃn, -z
AM ˌriˌɑkjəˈpeɪʃən, -z

reoccupy
BR ˌriːˈɒkjʊpʌɪ, rɪˈɒkjʊpʌɪ, -z, -ɪŋ, -d
AM riˈɑkjəˌpaɪ, -z, -ɪŋ, -d

reoccur
BR ˌriːəˈkəː(r), -z, -ɪŋ, -d
AM ˌriəˈkər, -z, -ɪŋ, -d

reoccurrence
BR ˌriːəˈkʌrəns, ˌriːəˈkʌrn̩s, -ɪz
AM ˌriəˈkərəns, -əz

reoffend
BR ˌriːəˈfɛnd, -z, -ɪŋ, -ɪd
AM ˌriəˈfɛnd, -z, -ɪŋ, -əd

reopen
BR ˌriːˈəʊp|(ə)n, rɪˈəʊp|(ə)n, -(ə)nz, -(ə)nɪŋ\-n̩ɪŋ, -nd
AM riˈoʊp|ən, -ənz, -(ə)nɪŋ, -(ə)nd

reopening
BR ˌriːˈəʊp(ə)nɪŋ, rɪˈəʊp(ə)nɪŋ, ˌriːˈəʊpn̩ɪŋ, rɪˈəʊpn̩ɪŋ, -z
AM riˈoʊp(ə)nɪŋ, -z

reorder
BR ˌriːˈɔːd|ə(r), rɪˈɔːdə(r), -əz, -(ə)rɪŋ, -əd
AM riˈɔrdər, -z, -ɪŋ, -d

reorganisation
BR rɪˌɔːɡənʌɪˈzeɪʃn, rɪˌɔːɡn̩ʌɪˈzeɪʃn, ˌriːɔːɡənʌɪˈzeɪʃn, ˌriːɔːɡn̩ʌɪˈzeɪʃn
AM ˈriˌɔrɡənəˈzeɪʃən, ˈriˌɔrɡəˌnaɪˈzeɪʃən

reorganise
BR rɪˈɔːɡənʌɪz, rɪˈɔːɡn̩ʌɪz, ˌriːˈɔːɡənʌɪz, ˌriːˈɔːɡn̩ʌɪz, -ɪz, -ɪŋ, -d
AM riˈɔrɡəˌnaɪz, -ɪz, -ɪŋ, -d

reorganiser
BR rɪˈɔːɡənʌɪzə(r), rɪˈɔːɡn̩ʌɪzə(r), ˌriːˈɔːɡənʌɪzə(r), ˌriːˈɔːɡn̩ʌɪzə(r), -z
AM riˈɔrɡəˌnaɪzər, -z

reorganization
BR rɪˌɔːɡənʌɪˈzeɪʃn, rɪˌɔːɡn̩ʌɪˈzeɪʃn, ˌriːɔːɡənʌɪˈzeɪʃn, ˌriːɔːɡn̩ʌɪˈzeɪʃn
AM ˈriˌɔrɡənəˈzeɪʃən, ˈriˌɔrɡəˌnaɪˈzeɪʃən

reorganize
BR rɪˈɔːɡənʌɪz, rɪˈɔːɡn̩ʌɪz, ˌriːˈɔːɡənʌɪz, ˌriːˈɔːɡn̩ʌɪz, -ɪz, -ɪŋ, -d
AM riˈɔrɡəˌnaɪz, -ɪz, -ɪŋ, -d

reorganizer
BR rɪˈɔːɡənʌɪzə(r), rɪˈɔːɡn̩ʌɪzə(r), ˌriːˈɔːɡənʌɪzə(r), ˌriːˈɔːɡn̩ʌɪzə(r), -z
AM riˈɔrɡəˌnaɪzər, -z

reorient
BR rɪˈɔːrɪɛnt, rɪˈɒrɪɛnt, ˌriːˈɔːrɪɛnt, ˌriːˈɒrɪɛnt, -s, -ɪŋ, -ɪd
AM riˈɔriən|t, -ts, -(t)ɪŋ, -(t)əd

reorientate
BR rɪˈɔːrɪənteɪt, ˌriːˈɔːrɪənteɪt, rɪˈɒrɪənteɪt, ˌriːˈɒrɪənteɪt, -s, -ɪŋ, -ɪd
AM riˈɔriənˌteɪ|t, -ts, -dɪŋ, -dɪd

reorientation
BR rɪˌɔːrɪənˈteɪʃn, ˌriːɔːrɪənˈteɪʃn, rɪˌɒrɪənˈteɪʃn, ˌriːɒrɪənˈteɪʃn
AM ˈriˌɔriənˈteɪʃən

rep
BR rɛp, -s
AM rɛp, -s

repack
BR ˌriːˈpak, -s, -ɪŋ, -t
AM riˈpæk, -s, -ɪŋ, -t

repackage
BR ˌriːˈpak|ɪdʒ, -ɪdʒɪz, -ɪdʒɪŋ, -ɪdʒd
AM riˈpækɪdʒ, -ɪz, -ɪŋ, -d

repaginate
BR ˌriːˈpadʒɪneɪt, -s, -ɪŋ, -ɪd
AM riˈpædʒəˌneɪ|t, -ts, -dɪŋ, -dɪd

repagination
BR ˌriːpadʒɪˈneɪʃn, riːˌpadʒɪˈneɪʃn, -z
AM riˌpædʒəˈneɪʃən, -z

repaid¹
paid again
BR ˌriːˈpeɪd
AM riˈpeɪd

repaid²
paid back
BR rɪˈpeɪd, (ˌ)riːˈpeɪd
AM rəˈpeɪd, riˈpeɪd

repaint
BR ˌriːˈpeɪnt, -s, -ɪŋ, -ɪd
AM riˈpeɪn|t, -ts, -(t)ɪŋ, -(t)ɪd

repair
BR rɪˈpɛː(r), -z, -ɪŋ, -d
AM rəˈpɛ(ə)r, riˈpɛ(ə)r, -z, -ɪŋ, -d

repairable
BR rɪˈpɛːrəbl
AM rəˈpɛrəbəl, riˈpɛrəbəl

repairer
BR rɪˈpɛːrə(r), -z
AM rəˈpɛrər, riˈpɛrər, -z

repairman
BR rɪˈpɛːman
AM rəˈpɛrˌmæn, riˈpɛrˌmæn

repairmen
BR rɪˈpɛːmɛn
AM rəˈpɛrˌmɛn, riˈpɛrˌmɛn

repand
BR rɪˈpand
AM rəˈpænd, riˈpænd

repaper
BR ˌriːˈpeɪp|ə(r), -əz, -(ə)rɪŋ, -əd
AM riˈpeɪpər, -z, -ɪŋ, -d

reparability
BR ˌrɛp(ə)rəˈbɪlɪti
AM ˌrɛp(ə)rəˈbɪlɪdi

reparable
BR ˈrɛp(ə)rəbl
AM ˈrɛp(ə)rəbəl

reparably
BR ˈrɛp(ə)rəbli
AM ˈrɛp(ə)rəbli

reparation
BR ˌrɛpəˈreɪʃn, -z
AM ˌrɛpəˈreɪʃən, -z

reparative
BR rɪˈparətɪv, ˈrɛp(ə)rətɪv
AM rəˈpɛrədɪv, riˈpɛrədɪv

repartee
BR ˌrɛpɑːˈtiː
AM ˈrɛˌpɑrˈti, ˈrɛpərˈti

repartition
BR ˌriːpɑːˈtɪʃ|n, -nz, -n̩ɪŋ\-ənɪŋ, -nd
AM ˈriˌpɑrˈtɪʃən, -z, -ɪŋ, -d

repass
BR ˌriːˈpɑːs, ˌriːˈpas, -ɪz, -ɪŋ, -t
AM riˈpæs, -əz, -ɪŋ, -t

repast
BR rɪˈpɑːst, rɪˈpast, -s
AM rəˈpæst, riˈpæst, -s

repat
noun, repatriate
BR ˈriːpat, -s
AM ˈriˌpæt, -s

repatriate
BR ˌriːˈpatrɪeɪt, rɪˈpatrɪeɪt, -s, -ɪŋ, -ɪd
AM riˈpeɪtriˌeɪ|t, riˈpætriˌeɪ|t, -ts, -dɪŋ, -dɪd

repatriation
BR ˌriːpatrɪˈeɪʃn, rɪˌpatrɪˈeɪʃn, -z
AM riˌpeɪtriˈeɪʃən, riˌpætriˈeɪʃən, -z

repay¹
pay again
BR ˌriːˈpeɪ, -z, -ɪŋ, -d
AM riˈpeɪ, -z, -ɪŋ, -d

repay²
pay back
BR rɪˈpeɪ, (ˌ)riːˈpeɪ, -z, -ɪŋ, -d
AM riˈpeɪ, rəˈpeɪ, -z, -ɪŋ, -d

repayable
BR rɪˈpeɪəbl, (ˌ)riːˈpeɪəbl
AM riˈpeɪəbəl, rəˈpeɪəbəl

repayment
BR rɪˈpeɪm(ə)nt, (ˌ)riːˈpeɪm(ə)nt, -s
AM riˈpeɪmənt, rəˈpeɪmənt, -s

repeal
BR rɪˈpiːl, -z, -ɪŋ, -d
AM rəˈpil, riˈpil, -z, -ɪŋ, -d

repealable
BR rɪˈpiːləbl
AM rəˈpiləbəl, riˈpiləbəl

repeat
BR rɪˈpiːt, -s, -ɪŋ, -ɪd
AM rəˈpi|t, riˈpi|t, -ts, -dɪŋ, -dɪd

repeatability
BR rɪˌpiːtəˈbɪlɪti
AM rəˌpidəˈbɪlɨdi, riˌpidəˈbɪlɨdi
repeatable
BR rɪˈpiːtəbl
AM rəˈpidəbəl, riˈpidəbəl
repeatedly
BR rɪˈpiːtɨdli
AM rəˈpidɨdli, riˈpidɨdli
repeater
BR rɪˈpiːtə(r), -z
AM rəˈpidər, riˈpidər, -z
repêchage
BR ˈrɛpɪʃɑːʒ, ˌrɛpɪˈʃɑːʒ, -ɪz
AM ˌrɛpəˈʃɑʒ, -əz
repel
BR rɪˈpɛl, -z, -ɪŋ, -d
AM rəˈpɛl, riˈpɛl, -z, -ɪŋ, -d
repellence
BR rɪˈpɛləns, rɪˈpɛlns
AM rəˈpɛləns, riˈpɛləns
repellency
BR rɪˈpɛlənsi, rɪˈpɛlnsi
AM rəˈpɛlənsi, riˈpɛlənsi
repellent
BR rɪˈpɛlənt, rɪˈpɛlnt
AM rəˈpɛlənt, riˈpɛlənt
repellently
BR rɪˈpɛləntli, rɪˈpɛlntli
AM rəˈpɛlən(t)li, riˈpɛlən(t)li
repeller
BR rɪˈpɛlə(r), -z
AM rəˈpɛlər, riˈpɛlər, -z
repent
BR rɪˈpɛnt, -s, -ɪŋ, -ɨd
AM rəˈpɛn|t, riˈpɛn|t, -ts, -(t)ɪŋ, -(t)əd
repentance
BR rɪˈpɛnt(ə)ns, -ɨz
AM rəˈpɛntns, riˈpɛntns, -əz
repentant
BR rɪˈpɛnt(ə)nt
AM rəˈpɛn(t)nt, riˈpɛn(t)nt
repentantly
BR rɪˈpɛnt(ə)ntli
AM rəˈpɛntn(t)li, riˈpɛntn(t)li
repenter
BR rɪˈpɛntə(r), -z
AM rəˈpɛn(t)ər, riˈpɛn(t)ər, -z
repeople
BR ˌriːˈpiːp|l, -lz, -lɪŋ\-lɪŋ, -ld
AM riˈpip|əl, -əlz, -(ə)lɪŋ, -əld
repercussion
BR ˌriːpəˈkʌʃn, -z
AM ˌripərˈkəʃən, ˌrɛpərˈkəʃən, -z
repercussive
BR ˌriːpəˈkʌsɪv
AM ˌripərˈkəsɪv, ˌrɛpərˈkəsɪv
repertoire
BR ˈrɛpətwɑː(r), -z
AM ˈrɛpə(r)ˌtwɑr, -z
repertory
BR ˈrɛpət(ə)r|i, -ɪz
AM ˈrɛpə(r)ˌtɔri, -z
repetend
BR ˈrɛpɪtɛnd, ˌrɛpɪˈtɛnd, -z
AM ˈrɛpəˌtɛnd, -z
répétiteur
BR rɪˌpɛtɪˈtəː(r), -z
AM rəˌpɛdiˈtər, -z
repetition
BR ˌrɛpɪˈtɪʃn, -z
AM ˌrɛpəˈtɪʃən, -z
repetitional
BR ˌrɛpɪˈtɪʃn(ə)l, ˌrɛpɪˈtɪʃən(ə)l
AM ˌrɛpəˈtɪʃ(ə)nəl
repetitionary
BR ˌrɛpəˈtɪʃn(ə)ri
AM ˌrɛpəˈtɪʃəˌnɛri
repetitious
BR ˌrɛpɪˈtɪʃəs
AM ˌrɛpəˈtɪʃəs
repetitiously
BR ˌrɛpɪˈtɪʃəsli
AM ˌrɛpəˈtɪʃəsli
repetitiousness
BR ˌrɛpɪˈtɪʃəsnəs
AM ˌrɛpəˈtɪʃəsnəs
repetitive
BR rɪˈpɛtɪtɪv
AM rəˈpɛdədɪv, riˈpɛdədɪv
repetitively
BR rɪˈpɛtɪtɪvli
AM rəˈpɛdədɨvli, riˈpɛdədɨvli
repetitiveness
BR rɪˈpɛtɪtɪvnɪs
AM rəˈpɛdədɪvnɪs, riˈpɛdədɪvnɪs
rephrase
BR ˌriːˈfreɪz, -ɨz, -ɪŋ, -d
AM riˈfreɪz, -ɨz, -ɪŋ, -d
repine
BR rɪˈpʌɪn, -z, -ɪŋ, -d
AM rəˈpaɪn, riˈpaɪn, -z, -ɪŋ, -d
repique
BR rɪˈpiːk, -s, -ɪŋ, -t
AM riˈpik, rəˈpik, -s, -ɪŋ, -t
replace
BR rɪˈpleɪs, (ˌ)riːˈpleɪs, -ɨz, -ɪŋ, -t
AM rəˈpleɪs, riˈpleɪs, -ɨz, -ɪŋ, -t
replaceable
BR rɪˈpleɪsəbl, (ˌ)riːˈpleɪsəbl
AM rəˈpleɪsəbəl, riˈpleɪsəbəl
replacement
BR rɪˈpleɪsm(ə)nt, (ˌ)riːˈpleɪsm(ə)nt, -s
AM rəˈpleɪsmənt, riˈpleɪsmənt, -s
replacer
BR rɪˈpleɪsə(r), (ˌ)riːˈpleɪsə(r), -z
AM rəˈpleɪsər, riˈpleɪsər, -z
replan
BR ˌriːˈplan, -z, -ɪŋ, -d
AM riˈplæn, -z, -ɪŋ, -d
replant
BR ˌriːˈplɑːnt, ˌriːˈplant, -s, -ɪŋ, -ɨd
AM riˈplæn|t, -ts, -(t)ɪŋ, -(t)əd
replay[1]
noun
BR ˈriːpleɪ, -z
AM ˈriˌpleɪ, -z
replay[2]
verb
BR ˌriːˈpleɪ, -z, -ɪŋ, -d
AM riˈpleɪ, -z, -ɪŋ, -d
replenish
BR rɪˈplɛn|ɪʃ, -ɨʃɨz, -ɨʃɪŋ, -ɪʃt
AM rəˈplɛnɪʃ, riˈplɛnɪʃ, -ɨz, -ɪŋ, -t
replenisher
BR rɪˈplɛnɨʃə(r), -z
AM rəˈplɛnɪʃər, riˈplɛnɪʃər, -z
replenishment
BR rɪˈplɛnɨʃm(ə)nt, -s
AM rəˈplɛnɪʃmənt, riˈplɛnɪʃmənt, -s
replete
BR rɪˈpliːt
AM rəˈplit, riˈplit
repleteness
BR rɪˈpliːtnɪs
AM rəˈplitnɪs, riˈplitnɪs
repletion
BR rɪˈpliːʃn
AM rəˈpliʃən, riˈpliʃən
replevin
BR rɪˈplɛvɪn
AM rəˈplɛvən, riˈplɛvən
replevy
BR rɪˈplɛv|i, -ɪz, -ɪɪŋ, -ɪd
AM rəˈplɛvi, riˈplɛvi, -z, -ɪŋ, -d
replica
BR ˈrɛplɪkə(*r*), -z
AM ˈrɛpləkə, -z
replicability
BR ˌrɛplɪkəˈbɪlɪti
AM ˌrɛpləkəˈbɪlɨdi
replicable
BR ˈrɛplɪkəbl
AM ˈrɛpləkəbəl
replicate
BR ˈrɛplɪkeɪt, -s, -ɪŋ, -ɨd
AM ˈrɛpləˌkeɪ|t, -ts, -dɪŋ, -dɨd
replication
BR ˌrɛplɪˈkeɪʃn
AM ˌrɛpləˈkeɪʃən
replicative
BR ˈrɛplɪkətɪv
AM ˈrɛpləˌkeɪdɪv, ˈrɛpləkədɪv
replicator
BR ˈrɛplɪkeɪtə(r), -z
AM ˈrɛpləˌkeɪdər, -z
replier
BR rɪˈplʌɪə(r), -z
AM rəˈplaɪər, riˈplaɪər, -z
reply
BR rɪˈplʌɪ, -z, -ɪŋ, -d
AM rəˈplaɪ, riˈplaɪ, -z, -ɪŋ, -d
reply-paid
BR rɪˌplʌɪˈpeɪd
AM rəˌplaɪˈpeɪd, riˌplaɪˈpeɪd
repo
BR ˈriːpəʊ, -z
AM ˈriˌpoʊ, -z
repoint
BR ˌriːˈpɔɪnt, -s, -ɪŋ, -ɨd
AM riˈpɔɪn|t, -ts, -(t)ɪŋ, -(t)ɨd
repolish
BR ˌriːˈpɒl|ɪʃ, -ɨʃɨz, -ɨʃɪŋ, -ɪʃt
AM riˈpɑlɪʃ, -ɨz, -ɪŋ, -t
repopulate
BR ˌriːˈpɒpjʊleɪt, -s, -ɪŋ, -ɨd
AM riˈpɑpjəˌleɪ|t, -ts, -dɪŋ, -dɨd
repopulation
BR ˌriːpɒpjʊˈleɪʃn, riːˌpɒpjʊˈleɪʃn
AM ˌriˌpɑpjəˈleɪʃən
report
BR rɪˈpɔːt, -s, -ɪŋ, -ɨd
AM rəˈpɔ(ə)rt, riˈpɔ(ə)rt, -ts, -ˈpɔrdɪŋ, -ˈpɔrdəd
reportable
BR rɪˈpɔːtəbl
AM rəˈpɔrdəbəl, riˈpɔrdəbəl
reportage
BR ˌrɛpɔːˈtɑː(d)ʒ, rɪˈpɔːtɪdʒ
AM rəˈpɔrdɪdʒ, riˈpɔrdɪdʒ
reportedly
BR rɪˈpɔːtɨdli

AM rə'pɔrdədli, ri'pɔrdədli
reporter
BR rɪ'pɔːtə(r), -z
AM rə'pɔrdər, ri'pɔrdər, -z
reportorial
BR ˌrɛpɔː'tɔːrɪəl, ˌriːpɔː'tɔːrɪəl
AM ˌrɛpər'tɔriəl
reportorially
BR ˌrɛpɔː'tɔːrɪəli, ˌriːpɔː'tɔːrɪəli
AM ˌrɛpər'tɔriəli
reposal
BR rɪ'pəʊzl, -z
AM rə'poʊzəl, ri'poʊzəl, -z
repose
BR rɪ'pəʊz, -ɪz, -ɪŋ, -d
AM rə'poʊz, ri'poʊz, -əz, -ɪŋ, -d
reposeful
BR rɪ'pəʊzf(ʊ)l
AM rə'poʊzfəl, ri'poʊzfəl
reposefully
BR rɪ'pəʊzfʊli, rɪ'pəʊzfl̩i
AM rə'poʊzfəli, ri'poʊzfəli
reposefulness
BR rɪ'pəʊzf(ʊ)lnəs
AM rə'poʊzfəlnəs, ri'poʊzfəlnəs
reposition
BR ˌriːpə'zɪʃ|n, -nz, -n̩ɪŋ\-nɪŋ, -nd
AM ˌripə'zɪʃ|ən, -ənz, -(ə)nɪŋ, -ənd
repository
BR rɪ'pɒzɪt(ə)r|i, -ɪz
AM rə'pɑzəˌtɔri, ri'pɑzəˌtɔri, -z
repossess
BR ˌriːpə'zɛs, -ɪz, -ɪŋ, -t
AM ˌripə'zɛs, -ɪz, -ɪŋ, -t
repossession
BR ˌriːpə'zɛʃn, -z
AM ˌripə'zɛʃən, -z
repossessor
BR ˌriːpə'zɛsə(r), -z
AM ˌripə'zɛsər, -z
repot
BR ˌriː'pɒt, -s, -ɪŋ, -ɪd
AM ri'pɑ|t, -ts, -dɪŋ, -dəd
repoussé
BR rɪ'puːseɪ
AM rəˌpu'seɪ
repp
BR rɛp, -s, -t
AM rɛp, -s, -t
reprehend
BR ˌrɛprɪ'hɛnd, -z, -ɪŋ, -ɪd
AM ˌrɛprə'hɛnd, -z, -ɪŋ, -ed
reprehensibility
BR ˌrɛprɪˌhɛnsɪ'bɪlɪti
AM ˌrɛprəˌhɛnsə'bɪlɪdi
reprehensible
BR ˌrɛprɪ'hɛnsɪbl
AM ˌrɛprə'hɛnsəbəl
reprehensibly
BR ˌrɛprɪ'hɛnsɪbli
AM ˌrɛprə'hɛnsəbli
reprehension
BR ˌrɛprɪ'hɛnʃn
AM ˌrɛprə'hɛnʃən
represent
BR ˌrɛprɪ'zɛnt, -s, -ɪŋ, -ɪd
AM ˌrɛprə'zɛn|t, -ts, -(t)ɪŋ, -(t)əd
re-present
BR ˌriːprɪ'zɛnt, -s, -ɪŋ, -ɪd
AM ˌriprə'zɛn|t, -ts, -(t)ɪŋ, -(t)ɪd
representability
BR ˌrɛprɪˌzɛntə'bɪlɪti
AM ˌrɛprəˌzɛn(t)ə'bɪɪədi
representable
BR ˌrɛprɪ'zɛntəbl
AM ˌrɛprə'zɛn(t)əbəl
representation
BR ˌrɛprɪz(ɛ)n'teɪʃn, -z
AM ˌrɛprəˌzɛn'teɪʃən, ˌrɛprəzən'teɪʃən, -z
re-presentation
BR ˌriːˌprɛz(ɛ)n'teɪʃn
AM ˌriˌprɛzn'teɪʃən, ˌriˌpriˌzɛn'teɪʃən
representational
BR ˌrɛprɪz(ɛ)n'teɪʃn̩(ə)l, ˌrɛprɪz(ɛ)n'teɪʃən(ə)l
AM ˌrɛprəˌzɛn'teɪʃ(ə)nəl, ˌrɛprəzən'teɪʃ(ə)nəl
representationalism
BR ˌrɛprɪz(ɛ)n'teɪʃn̩əlɪz(ə)m, ˌrɛprɪz(ɛ)n'teɪʃn̩l̩ɪz(ə)m, ˌrɛprɪz(ɛ)n'teɪʃənl̩ɪz(ə)m, ˌrɛprɪz(ɛ)n'teɪʃ(ə)nəlɪz(ə)m
AM ˌrɛprəˌzɛn'teɪʃənl̩ˌɪzəm, ˌrɛprəzən'teɪʃənl̩ˌɪzəm, ˌrɛprəˌzɛn'teɪʃnəˌlɪzəm, ˌrɛprəzən'teɪʃnəˌlɪzəm
representationalist
BR ˌrɛprɪz(ɛ)n'teɪʃn̩əlɪst, ˌrɛprɪz(ɛ)n'teɪʃn̩l̩ɪst, ˌrɛprɪz(ɛ)n'teɪʃənl̩ɪst, ˌrɛprɪz(ɛ)n'teɪʃ(ə)nəlɪst, -s
AM ˌrɛprəˌzɛn'teɪʃənl̩əst, ˌrɛprəzən'teɪʃənl̩əst, ˌrɛprəˌzɛn'teɪʃnələst, ˌrɛprəzən'teɪʃnələst, -s
representationism
BR ˌrɛprɪz(ɛ)n'teɪʃn̩ɪz(ə)m, ˌrɛprɪz(ɛ)n'teɪʃənɪz(ə)m
AM ˌrɛprəˌzɛn'teɪʃəˌnɪzəm, ˌrɛprəzən'teɪʃəˌnɪzəm
representationist
BR ˌrɛprɪz(ɛ)n'teɪʃn̩ɪst, ˌrɛprɪz(ɛ)n'teɪʃənɪst, -s
AM ˌrɛprəˌzɛn'teɪʃənəst, ˌrɛprəzən'teɪʃənəst, -s
representative
BR ˌrɛprɪ'zɛntətɪv, -z
AM ˌrɛprə'zɛn(t)ədɪv, -z
representatively
BR ˌrɛprɪ'zɛntətɪvli
AM ˌrɛprə'zɛn(t)ədɪvli
representativeness
BR ˌrɛprɪ'zɛntətɪvnɪs
AM ˌrɛprə'zɛn(t)ədɪvnɪs
repress
BR rɪ'prɛs, -ɪz, -ɪŋ, -t
AM rə'prɛs, ri'prɛs, -əz, -ɪŋ, -t
represser
BR rɪ'prɛsə(r), -z
AM rə'prɛsər, ri'prɛsər, -z
repressible
BR rɪ'prɛsɪbl
AM rə'prɛsəbəl, ri'prɛsəbəl
repression
BR rɪ'prɛʃn, -z
AM rə'prɛʃən, ri'prɛʃən, -z
repressive
BR rɪ'prɛsɪv
AM rə'prɛsɪv, ri'prɛsɪv
repressively
BR rɪ'prɛsɪvli
AM rə'prɛsɪvli, ri'prɛsɪvli
repressiveness
BR rɪ'prɛsɪvnɪs
AM rə'prɛsɪvnɪs, ri'prɛsɪvnɪs
repressor
BR rɪ'prɛsə(r), -z
AM rə'prɛsər, ri'prɛsər, -z
repressurisation
BR ˌriːprɛʃ(ə)rʌɪ'zeɪʃn
AM ˌriˌprɛʃərə'zeɪʃən, ˌriˌprɛʃəˌraɪ'zeɪʃən
repressurise
BR ˌriː'prɛʃərʌɪz, -ɪz, -ɪŋ, -d
AM ri'prɛʃəˌraɪz, -ɪz, -ɪŋ, -d
repressurization
BR ˌriːprɛʃ(ə)rʌɪ'zeɪʃn
AM ˌriˌprɛʃərə'zeɪʃən, ˌriˌprɛʃəˌraɪ'zeɪʃən
repressurize
BR ˌriː'prɛʃərʌɪz, -ɪz, -ɪŋ, -d
AM ri'prɛʃəˌraɪz, -ɪz, -ɪŋ, -d
reprice
BR ˌriː'prʌɪs, -ɪz, -ɪŋ, -t
AM ri'praɪs, -ɪz, -ɪŋ, -t
reprieve
BR rɪ'priːv, -z, -ɪŋ, -d
AM rə'priv, ri'priv, -z, -ɪŋ, -d
reprimand
BR 'rɛprɪmɑːnd, 'rɛprɪmand, -z, -ɪŋ, -ɪd
AM 'rɛprəˌmænd, -z, -ɪŋ, -əd
reprint[1]
noun
BR 'riːprɪnt, -s
AM 'riˌprɪnt, -s
reprint[2]
verb
BR ˌriː'prɪnt, -s, -ɪŋ, -ɪd
AM ri'prɪn|t, -ts, -(t)ɪŋ, -(t)ɪd
reprinter
BR ˌriː'prɪntə(r), -z
AM ri'prɪn(t)ər, -z
reprinting
BR ˌriː'prɪntɪŋ, -z
AM ri'prɪn(t)ɪŋ, -z
reprisal
BR rɪ'prʌɪzl, -z
AM rə'praɪzəl, ri'praɪzəl, -z
reprise
BR rɪ'priːz, -ɪz
AM rə'praɪz, ri'praɪz, -ɪz
repro
BR 'riːprəʊ, -z
AM 'riˌproʊ, -z
reproach
BR rɪ'prəʊtʃ, -ɪz, -ɪŋ, -t
AM rə'proʊtʃ, ri'proʊtʃ, -əz, -ɪŋ, -t
reproachable
BR rɪ'prəʊtʃəbl
AM rə'proʊtʃəbəl, ri'proʊtʃəbəl
reproacher
BR rɪ'prəʊtʃə(r), -z
AM rə'proʊtʃər, ri'proʊtʃər, -z
reproachful
BR rɪ'prəʊtʃf(ʊ)l
AM rə'proʊtʃfəl, ri'proʊtʃfəl
reproachfully
BR rɪ'prəʊtʃfʊli, rɪ'pəʊtʃfl̩i

AM rə'proʊtʃfəli, ri'proʊtʃfəli

reproachfulness
BR rɪ'prəʊtʃf(ʊ)lnəs
AM rə'proʊtʃfəlnəs, ri'proʊtʃfəlnəs

reproachingly
BR rɪ'prəʊtʃɪŋli
AM rə'proʊtʃɪŋli, ri'proʊtʃɪŋli

reprobate
BR 'rɛprəbeɪt, -s, -ɪŋ, -ɨd
AM 'rɛprə,beɪ|t, -ts, -dɪŋ, -dɨd

reprobation
BR ,rɛprə'beɪʃn
AM ,rɛprə'beɪʃən

reprocess
BR ,riː'prəʊsɛs, -ɨz, -ɪŋ, -t
AM ri'prɑ,sɛs, -əz, -ɪŋ, -t

reproduce
BR ,riːprə'djuːs, ,riːprə'dʒuːs, -ɨz, -ɪŋ, -t
AM ¦riprə'd(j)us, ¦riprə'dʒus, -əz, -ɪŋ, -t

reproducer
BR ,riːprə'djuːsə(r), ,riːprə'dʒuːsə(r), -z
AM ¦riprə'd(j)usər, ¦riprə'dʒusər, -z

reproducibility
BR ,riːprə,djuːsɪ'bɪlɨti, ,riːprə,dʒuːsɪ'bɪlɨti
AM ¦riprə,d(j)usə'bɪlɨdi, ¦riprə,dʒusə'bɪlɨdi

reproducible
BR ,riːprə'djuːsɨbl, ,riːprə'dʒuːsɨbl
AM ¦riprə'd(j)usəbəl, ¦riprə'dʒusəbəl

reproducibly
BR ,riːprə'djuːsɨbli, ,riːprə'dʒuːsɨbli
AM ¦riprə'd(j)usəbli, ¦riprə'dʒusəbli

reproduction
BR ,riːprə'dʌkʃn, -z
AM ¦riprə'dəkʃən, -z

reproductive
BR ,riːprə'dʌktɪv
AM ¦riprə'dəktɪv

reproductively
BR ,riːprə'dʌktɨvli
AM ¦riprə'dəktɨvli

reproductiveness
BR ,riːprə'dʌktɨvnɨs
AM ¦riprə'dəktɪvnɨs

reprogram
BR ,riː'prəʊgram, -z, -ɪŋ, -d
AM ri'proʊ,græm, -z, -ɪŋ, -d

reprogrammable
BR ,riː'prəʊgraməbl
AM ri,proʊ'græməbəl, ri'proʊgrəməbəl

reprographer
BR rɪ'prɒgrəfə(r), -z
AM rə'prɑgrəfər, ri'prɑgrəfər, -z

reprographic
BR ,riːprə'grafɪk, ,rɛprə'grafɪk, -s
AM ¦rɛprə'græfɪk, ¦riprə'græfɪk, -s

reprographically
BR ,riːprə'grafɨkli, ,rɛprə'grafɨkli
AM ¦rɛprə'græfək(ə)li, ¦riprə'græfək(ə)li

reprography
BR rɪ'prɒgrəfi
AM rə'prɑgrəfi, ri'prɑgrəfi

reproof[1]
noun
BR rɪ'pruːf, -s
AM rə'pruf, ri'pruf, -s

reproof[2]
verb
BR ,riː'pruːf, -s, -ɪŋ, -t
AM ri'pruf, -s, -ɪŋ, -t

reprovable
BR rɪ'pruːvəbl
AM rə'pruvəbəl, ri'pruvəbəl

reproval
BR rɪ'pruːvl, -z
AM rə'pruvəl, ri'pruvəl, -z

reprove
BR rɪ'pruːv, -z, -ɪŋ, -d
AM rə'pruv, ri'pruv, -z, -ɪŋ, -d

reprover
BR rɪ'pruːvə(r), -z
AM rə'pruvər, ri'pruvər, -z

reproving
BR rɪ'pruːvɪŋ
AM rə'pruvɪŋ, ri'pruvɪŋ

reprovingly
BR rɪ'pruːvɪŋli
AM rə'pruvɪŋli, ri'pruvɪŋli

reptant
BR 'rɛptənt
AM 'rɛptnt

reptile
BR 'rɛptʌɪl, -z
AM 'rɛptl, 'rɛp,taɪl, -z

reptilian
BR rɛp'tɪlɪən, -z
AM rɛp'tɪljən, rɛp'tɪliən, -z

Repton
BR 'rɛpt(ə)n
AM 'rɛptən

republic
BR rɪ'pʌblɪk, -s
AM rə'pəblɪk, ri'pəblɪk, -s

republican
BR rɪ'pʌblɪk(ə)n, -z
AM rə'pəbləkən, ri'pəbləkən, -z

republicanism
BR rɪ'pʌblɪkənɪz(ə)m, rɪ'pʌblɪknɪz(ə)m
AM rə'pəbləkə,nɪzəm, ri'pəbləkə,nɪzəm

republication
BR ,riːpʌblɪ'keɪʃn, -z
AM ri,pəblə'keɪʃən, rə,pəblə'keɪʃən, -z

republish
BR ,riː'pʌbl|ɪʃ, -ɪʃɨz, -ɪʃɪŋ, -ɪʃt
AM ri'pəblɪʃ, rə'pəblɪʃ, -ɨz, -ɪŋ, -t

repudiable
BR rɪ'pjuːdɪəbl
AM rə'pjudiəbəl, ri'pjudiəbəl

repudiate
BR rɪ'pjuːdɪeɪt, -s, -ɪŋ, -ɨd
AM rə'pjudi,eɪ|t, ri'pjudi,eɪ|t, -ts, -dɪŋ, -dɨd

repudiation
BR rɪ,pjuːdɪ'eɪʃn
AM rə,pjudi'eɪʃən, ri,pjudi'eɪʃən

repudiator
BR rɪ'pjuːdɪeɪtə(r), -z
AM rə'pjudi,eɪdər, ri'pjudi,eɪdər, -z

repugnance
BR rɪ'pʌgnəns
AM rə'pəgnəns, ri'pəgnəns

repugnant
BR rɪ'pʌgnənt
AM rə'pəgnənt, ri'pəgnənt

repugnantly
BR rɪ'pʌgnəntli
AM rə'pəgnən(t)li, ri'pəgnən(t)li

repulse
BR rɪ'pʌls, -ɨz, -ɪŋ, -t
AM rə'pəls, ri'pəls, -əz, -ɪŋ, -t

repulsion
BR rɪ'pʌlʃn
AM rə'pəlʃən, ri'pəlʃən

repulsive
BR rɪ'pʌlsɪv
AM rə'pəlsɪv, ri'pəlsɪv

repulsively
BR rɪ'pʌlsɨvli
AM rə'pəlsɨvli, ri'pəlsɨvli

repulsiveness
BR rɪ'pʌlsɪvnɨs
AM rə'pəlsɪvnɨs, ri'pəlsɪvnɨs

repurchase
BR ,riː'pəːtʃɪs, -ɨz, -ɪŋ, -t
AM ri'pərtʃəs, -əz, -ɪŋ, -t

repurification
BR ,riːpjʊərɪfɪ'keɪʃn, ,riːpjɔːrɪfɪ'keɪʃn, -z
AM rə,pjʊrəfə'keɪʃən, ri,pjʊrəfə'keɪʃən, -z

repurify
BR ,riː'pjʊərɪfʌɪ, ,riː'pjɔːrɪfʌɪ, -z, -ɪŋ, -d
AM ri'pjʊrə,faɪ, -z, -ɪŋ, -d

reputability
BR ,rɛpjʊtə'bɪlɨti
AM ,rɛpjədə'bɪlɨdi

reputable
BR 'rɛpjʊtəbl
AM 'rɛpjədəbəl

reputably
BR 'rɛpjʊtəbli
AM 'rɛpjədəbli

reputation
BR ,rɛpjʊ'teɪʃn, -z
AM ,rɛpjə'teɪʃən, -z

repute
BR rɪ'pjuːt
AM rə'pjut, ri'pjut

reputed
BR rɪ'pjuːtɪd
AM rə'pjudəd, ri'pjudəd

reputedly
BR rɪ'pjuːtɨdli
AM rə'pjudədli, ri'pjudədli

request
BR rɪ'kwɛst, -s, -ɪŋ, -ɨd
AM rə'kwɛst, ri'kwɛst, -s, -ɪŋ, -əd

requester
BR rɪ'kwɛstə(r), -z
AM rə'kwɛstər, ri'kwɛstər, -z

requicken
BR ,riː'kwɪk|(ə)n, -(ə)nz, -ŋɪŋ\-(ə)nɪŋ, -(ə)nd
AM ri'kwɪk|ən, -ənz, -(ə)nɪŋ, -ənd

requiem
BR 'rɛkwɪəm, 'rɛkwɪɛm, -z
AM 'rɛkwiəm, 'reɪkwiəm, -z

requiescat
BR ,rɛkwɪ'ɛskat, -s
AM ,rɛkwi'ɛs,kɑt, -s

require
BR rɪ'kwʌɪə(r), -z, -ɪŋ, -d
AM rə'kwaɪ(ə)r, ri'kwaɪ(ə)r, -z, -ɪŋ, -d

requirement
BR rɪ'kwʌɪəm(ə)nt, -s
AM rə'kwaɪ(ə)rmənt, ri'kwaɪ(ə)rmənt, -s

requirer
BR rɪˈkwʌɪərə(r), -z
AM rəˈkwaɪ(ə)rər, riˈkwaɪ(ə)rər, -z

requisite
BR ˈrɛkwɪzɪt, -s
AM ˈrɛkwəzət, -s

requisitely
BR ˈrɛkwɪzɪtli
AM ˈrɛkwəzətli

requisiteness
BR ˈrɛkwɪzɪtnɪs
AM ˈrɛkwəzətnəs

requisition
BR ˌrɛkwɪˈzɪʃ|n, -nz, -n̩ɪŋ, -nd
AM ˌrɛkwəˈzɪʃ|ən, -ənz, -(ə)nɪŋ, -ənd

requisitioner
BR ˌrɛkwɪˈzɪʃn̩ə(r), -z
AM ˌrɛkwəˈzɪʃ(ə)nər, -z

requisitionist
BR ˌrɛkwɪˈzɪʃn̩ɪst, -s
AM ˌrɛkwəˈzɪʃ(ə)nəst, -s

requital
BR rɪˈkwʌɪtl
AM rəˈkwaɪdl, riˈkwaɪdl

requite
BR rɪˈkwʌɪt, -s, -ɪŋ, -ɪd
AM rəˈkwaɪ|t, riˈkwaɪ|t, -ts, -dɪŋ, -dɪd

reran
BR (ˌ)riːˈran
AM riˈræn

rerate
BR ˌriːˈreɪt, -s, -ɪŋ, -ɪd
AM riˈreɪ|t, -ts, -dɪŋ, -dɪd

re-read¹
present tense
BR (ˌ)riːˈriːd, -z, -ɪŋ
AM riˈrid, -z, -ɪŋ

re-read²
past tense
BR (ˌ)riːˈrɛd
AM riˈrɛd

re-readable
BR (ˌ)riːˈriːdəbl
AM riˈridəbəl

re-record
BR ˌriːrɪˈkɔːd, -z, -ɪŋ, -ɪd
AM ˈrirəˈkɔ(ə)rd, -z, -ɪŋ, -əd

reredos
BR ˈrɪədɒs, -ɪz
AM ˈrɛrəˌdɑs, ˈrɪrəˌdɑs, -əz

re-release
BR ˌriːrɪˈliːs, -ɪz, -ɪŋ, -t
AM ˈrirəˈlis, -ɪz, -ɪŋ, -t

re-roof
BR ˌriːˈruːf, ˌriːˈrʊf, -s, -ɪŋ, -t
AM riˈruf, riˈrʊf, -s, -ɪŋ, -t

re-route
BR ˌriːˈruːt, -s, -ɪŋ, -ɪd
AM riˈraʊ|t, riˈru|t, -ts, -dɪŋ, -dəd

rerun
noun
BR ˈriːrʌn, -z
AM ˈriˌrən, -z

re-run
verb
BR (ˌ)riːˈrʌn, -z, -ɪŋ
AM riˈrən, -z, -ɪŋ

res
BR reɪz, riːz
AM reɪs

resalable
BR ˌriːˈseɪləbl
AM riˈseɪləbəl

resale
BR ˈriːseɪl, -z
AM ˈriˌseɪl, -z

resaleable
BR ˌriːˈseɪləbl
AM riˈseɪləbəl

resat
BR ˌriːˈsat
AM riˈsæt

reschedule
BR ˌriːˈʃɛdjʉl, ˌriːˈʃɛdjuːl, ˌriːˈʃɛdʒʉl, ˌriːˈskɛdjʉl, ˌriːˈskɛdjuːl, -z, -ɪŋ, -d
AM riˈskɛdʒəl, -z, -ɪŋ, -d

rescind
BR rɪˈsɪnd, -z, -ɪŋ, -ɪd
AM rəˈsɪnd, riˈsɪnd, -z, -ɪŋ, -ɪd

rescindable
BR rɪˈsɪndəbl
AM rəˈsɪndəbəl, riˈsɪndəbəl

rescindment
BR rɪˈsɪn(d)m(ə)nt, -s
AM rəˈsɪn(d)mənt, riˈsɪn(d)mənt, -s

rescission
BR rɪˈsɪʒn
AM rəˈsɪʒən, riˈsɪʒən

rescript
BR ˈriːskrɪpt, -s
AM ˈriˌskrɪpt, -s

rescuable
BR ˈrɛskjʊəbl
AM ˈrɛskjuəbəl, ˈrɛskjəwəbəl

rescue
BR ˈrɛskjuː, -z, -ɪŋ, -d
AM ˈrɛskj|u, -uz, -uɪŋ\-əwɪŋ, -ud

rescuer
BR ˈrɛskjuːə(r), -z
AM ˈrɛskjuər, ˈrɛskjəwər, -z

reseal
BR ˌriːˈsiːl, -z, -ɪŋ, -d
AM riˈsil, -z, -ɪŋ, -d

resealable
BR ˌriːˈsiːləbl
AM riˈsiləbəl

research¹
noun
BR rɪˈsəːtʃ, ˈriːsəːtʃ, -ɪz
AM ˈriˌsərtʃ, rəˈsərtʃ, riˈsərtʃ, -əz

research²
verb
BR rɪˈsəːtʃ, -ɪz, -ɪŋ, -t
AM rəˈsərtʃ, riˈsərtʃ, ˈriˌsərtʃ, -əz, -ɪŋ, -t

researchable
BR rɪˈsəːtʃəbl
AM rəˈsərtʃəbəl, riˈsərtʃəbəl, ˈriˌsərtʃəbəl

researcher
BR rɪˈsəːtʃə(r), ˈriːsəːtʃə(r), -z
AM rəˈsərtʃər, riˈsərtʃər, ˈriˌsərtʃər, -z

reseat
BR ˌriːˈsiːt, -s, -ɪŋ, -ɪd
AM rəˈsi|t, riˈsi|t, -ts, -dɪŋ, -dɪd

resect
BR rɪˈsɛkt, -s, -ɪŋ, -ɪd
AM rəˈsɛk|(t), riˈsɛk|(t), -(t)s, -tɪŋ, -təd

resection
BR rɪˈsɛkʃn, -z
AM rəˈsɛkʃən, riˈsɛkʃən, -z

resectional
BR rɪˈsɛkʃn̩(ə)l, rɪˈsɛkʃən(ə)l
AM rəˈsɛkʃ(ə)nəl, riˈsɛkʃ(ə)nəl

resectionist
BR rɪˈsɛkʃn̩ɪst, rɪˈsɛkʃənɪst, -s
AM rəˈsɛkʃənəst, riˈsɛkʃənəst, -s

reseda
BR ˈrɛsɪdə(r), rɪˈsiːdə(r), -z
AM rəˈsidə, -z

reseed
BR ˌriːˈsiːd, -z, -ɪŋ, -ɪd
AM riˈsid, -z, -ɪŋ, -ɪd

reselect
BR ˌriːsɪˈlɛkt, -s, -ɪŋ, -ɪd
AM ˈrisəˈlɛk|(t), -(t)s, -tɪŋ, -təd

reselection
BR ˌriːsɪˈlɛkʃn, -z
AM ˈrisəˈlɛkʃən, -z

resell
BR ˌriːˈsɛl, -z, -ɪŋ
AM riˈsɛl, -z, -ɪŋ

reseller
BR ˌriːˈsɛlə(r), -z
AM riˈsɛlər, -z

resemblance
BR rɪˈzɛmbl(ə)ns, -ɪz
AM rəˈzɛmbləns, riˈzɛmbləns, -əz

resemblant
BR rɪˈzɛmbl(ə)nt
AM rəˈzɛmblənt, riˈzɛmblənt

resemble
BR rɪˈzɛmb|l, -lz, -l̩ɪŋ\-lɪŋ, -ld
AM rəˈzɛmbəl, riˈzɛmbəl, -əlz, -(ə)lɪŋ, -əld

resembler
BR rɪˈzɛmblə(r), -z
AM rəˈzɛmblər, riˈzɛmblər, -z

resent
BR rɪˈzɛnt, -s, -ɪŋ, -ɪd
AM rəˈzɛn|t, riˈzɛn|t, -ts, -(t)ɪŋ, -(t)əd

resentful
BR rɪˈzɛntf(ʊ)l
AM rəˈzɛntfəl, riˈzɛntfəl

resentfully
BR rɪˈzɛntfʊli, rɪˈzɛntfl̩i
AM rəˈzɛntfəli, riˈzɛntfəli

resentfulness
BR rɪˈzɛntf(ʊ)lnəs
AM rəˈzɛntfəlnəs, riˈzɛntfəlnəs

resentment
BR rɪˈzɛntm(ə)nt, -s
AM rəˈzɛntmənt, riˈzɛntmənt, -s

reserpine
BR ˈrɛsəpiːn, ˈrɛsəpɪn, rɪˈsəːpiːn
AM rəˈsərpən, riˈsərpən, rəˈsərˌpin, riˈsərˌpin, ˈrɛsərˌpin, ˈrɛsərpən

reservable
BR rɪˈzəːvəbl
AM rəˈzərvəbəl, riˈzərvəbəl

reservation
BR ˌrɛzəˈveɪʃn, -z
AM ˌrɛzərˈveɪʃən, -z

reserve
BR rɪˈzəːv, -z, -ɪŋ, -d
AM rəˈzərv, riˈzərv, -z, -ɪŋ, -d

re-serve
BR ˌriːˈsəːv, -z, -ɪŋ, -d
AM riˈsərv, -z, -ɪŋ, -d

reservedly
BR rɪˈzəːvɪdli
AM rəˈzərvədli, riˈzərvədli

reservedness
BR rɪˈzəːvɪdnɪs
AM rəˈzərvədnəs, riˈzərvədnəs

reserver
BR rɪ'zəːvə(r), -z
AM rə'zərvər, ri'zərvər, -z

reservist
BR rɪ'zəːvɪst, -s
AM rə'zərvəst, ri'zərvəst, -s

reservoir
BR 'rɛzəvwɑː(r), -z
AM 'rɛzə(r),vwɑr, -z

reset
BR ˌriː'sɛt, -s, -ɪŋ
AM ri'sɛ|t, -ts, -dɪŋ

resettability
BR ˌriːsɛtə'bɪlɨti, rɪˌsɛtə'bɪlɨti
AM ˌriˌsɛdə'bɪlɨdi

resettable
BR ˌriː'sɛtəbl
AM ri'sɛdəbəl

resettle
BR (ˌ)riː'sɛt|l, -lz, -l̩ɪŋ\-lɪŋ, -ld
AM ri'sɛdəl, -z, -ɪŋ, -d

resettlement
BR (ˌ)riː'sɛtlm(ə)nt
AM ri'sɛdlmənt

reshape
BR ˌriː'ʃeɪp, -s, -ɪŋ, -t
AM ri'ʃeɪp, -s, -ɪŋ, -t

reship
BR ˌriː'ʃɪp, -s, -ɪŋ, -t
AM ri'ʃɪp, -s, -ɪŋ, -t

reshuffle[1]
noun
BR 'riːʃʌfl, -z
AM ri'ʃəfəl, -z

reshuffle[2]
verb
BR ˌriː'ʃʌf|l, -lz, -l̩ɪŋ\-lɪŋ, -ld
AM ri'ʃəf|əl, -əlz, -(ə)lɪŋ, -əld

reside
BR rɪ'zʌɪd, -z, -ɪŋ, -ɨd
AM rə'zaɪd, ri'zaɪd, -z, -ɪŋ, -ɨd

residence
BR 'rɛzɨd(ə)ns, -ɨz
AM 'rɛz(ə)d(ə)ns, -əz

residency
BR 'rɛzɨd(ə)ns|i, -ɪz
AM 'rɛz(ə)d(ə)nsi, -z

resident
BR 'rɛzɨd(ə)nt, -s
AM 'rɛz(ə)d(ə)nt, -s

residential
BR ˌrɛzɪ'dɛnʃl
AM ˌrɛzə'dɛn(t)ʃəl

residentially
BR ˌrɛzɪ'dɛnʃl̩i, ˌrɛzɪ'dɛnʃəli
AM ˌrɛzə'dɛn(t)ʃəli

residentiary
BR ˌrɛzɪ'dɛnʃ(ə)r|i, -ɪz
AM ˌrɛzɪ'dɛn(t)ʃiˌɛri, ˌrɛzɪ'dɛn(t)ʃiˌɛri, ˌrɛzɪ'dɛn(t)ʃəri, -z

residentship
BR 'rɛzɨd(ə)ntʃɪp, -s
AM 'rɛz(ə)dəntˌʃɪp, 'rɛzədntˌʃɪp, -s

residua
BR rɪ'zɪdjʊə(*r*), rɪ'zɪdʒʊə(*r*)
AM rə'sɪdʒ(ə)wə, ri'sɪdʒ(ə)wə

residual
BR rɪ'zɪdjʉl, rɪ'zɪdjʊəl, rɪ'zɪdʒ(ʉ)l, rɪ'zɪdʒʊəl, -z
AM rə'sɪdʒ(ə)wəl, ri'sɪdʒ(ə)wəl, rə'sɪdʒəl, ri'sɪdʒəl, -z

residually
BR rɪ'zɪdjʉli, rɪ'zɪdjʊəli, rɪ'zɪdʒʉli, rɪ'zɪdʒl̩i, rɪ'zɪdʒʊəli
AM rə'sɪdʒ(ə)wəli, ri'sɪdʒ(ə)wəli, rə'sɪdʒəli, ri'sɪdʒəli

residuary
BR rɪ'zɪdjʉri, rɪ'zɪdjʊəri, rɪ'zɪdʒ(ʉ)ri, rɪ'zɪdʒʊəri
AM rə'sɪdʒəˌwɛri, ri'sɪdʒəˌwɛri

residue
BR 'rɛzɨdjuː, 'rɛzɨdʒuː, -z
AM 'rɛzəˌd(j)u, -z

residuum
BR rɪ'zɪdjʊəm, rɪ'zɪdʒʊəm
AM rə'sɪdʒ(ə)wəm, ri'sɪdʒ(ə)wəm

resign[1]
give up
BR rɪ'zʌɪn, -z, -ɪŋ, -d
AM rə'zaɪn, ri'zaɪn, -z, -ɪŋ, -d

resign[2]
sign again
BR ˌriː'sʌɪn, -z, -ɪŋ, -d
AM ri'saɪn, -z, -ɪŋ, -d

resignal
BR ˌriː'sɪgnl, -z, -ɪŋ, -d
AM ri'sɪgnəl, -z, -ɪŋ, -d

resignation
BR ˌrɛzɪg'neɪʃn, -z
AM ˌrɛzəg'neɪʃən, -z

resigned
BR rɪ'zʌɪnd
AM rə'zaɪnd, ri'zaɪnd

resignedly
BR rɪ'zʌɪnɨdli
AM rə'zaɪnədli, ri'zaɪnədli

resignedness
BR rɪ'zʌɪnɨdnɨs
AM rə'zaɪnədnəs, ri'zaɪnədnəs

resigner
BR rɪ'zʌɪnə(r), -z
AM rə'zaɪnər, ri'zaɪnər, -z

resile
BR rɪ'zʌɪl, -z, -ɪŋ, -d
AM rə'zaɪl, ri'zaɪl, -z, -ɪŋ, -d

resilience
BR rɪ'zɪlɪəns
AM rə'zɪliəns, rə'zɪljəns

resiliency
BR rɪ'zɪlɪənsi
AM rə'zɪliənsi, rə'zɪljənsi

resilient
BR rɪ'zɪlɪənt
AM rə'zɪliənt, rə'zɪljənt

resiliently
BR rɪ'zɪlɪəntli
AM rə'zɪliən(t)li, rə'zɪljən(t)li

re-silver
BR ˌriː'sɪlv|ə(r), -əz, -(ə)rɪŋ, -əd
AM ri'sɪlvər, -z, -ɪŋ, -d

resin
BR 'rɛzɪn, -z
AM 'rɛzən, -z

resinate
BR 'rɛzɨneɪt, 'rɛzn̩eɪt, -s, -ɪŋ, -ɨd
AM 'rɛzəˌneɪ|t, -ts, -dɪŋ, -dɨd

resiniferous
BR ˌrɛzɪ'nɪf(ə)rəs, ˌrɛzn'ɪf(ə)rəs
AM ˌrɛzə'nɪf(ə)rəs

resinification
BR ˌrɛzɪnɪfɪ'keɪʃn, ˌrɛzn̩ɪfɪ'keɪʃn
AM ˌrɛzənəfə'keɪʃən

resiniform
BR 'rɛzɨnɪfɔːm, 'rɛzn̩ɪfɔːm
AM 'rɛzənəˌfɔ(ə)rm

resinify
BR 'rɛzɨnɪfʌɪ, 'rɛzn̩ɪfʌɪ, -z, -ɪŋ, -d
AM 'rɛzənəˌfaɪ, -z, -ɪŋ, -d

resinoid
BR 'rɛzɪnɔɪd, 'rɛzn̩ɔɪd, -z
AM 'rɛzəˌnɔɪd, -z

resinous
BR 'rɛzɪnəs, 'rɛzn̩əs
AM 'rɛzənəs

resist
BR rɪ'zɪst, -s, -ɪŋ, -ɨd
AM rə'zɪst, ri'zɪst, -s, -ɪŋ, -ɨd

resistance
BR rɪ'zɪst(ə)ns, -ɨz
AM rə'zɪstəns, ri'zɪstəns, -əz

resistant
BR rɪ'zɪst(ə)nt
AM rə'zɪstənt, ri'zɪstənt

resister
BR rɪ'zɪstə(r), -z
AM rə'zɪstər, ri'zɪstər, -z

resistibility
BR rɪˌzɪstɪ'bɪlɨti
AM rəˌzɪstə'bɪlɨdi, riˌzɪstə'bɪlɨdi

resistible
BR rɪ'zɪstɨbl
AM rə'zɪstəbəl, ri'zɪstəbəl

resistibly
BR rɪ'zɪstɨbli
AM rə'zɪstəbli, ri'zɪstəbli

resistive
BR rɪ'zɪstɪv
AM rə'zɪstɪv, ri'zɪstɪv

resistivity
BR ˌriːzɪ'stɪvɨti, ˌrɛzɪ'stɪvɨti, rɪˌzɪs'tɪvɨti
AM rəˌzɪs'tɪvɨdi, riˌzɪs'tɪvɨdi

resistless
BR rɪ'zɪs(t)lɨs
AM rə'zɪs(t)lɨs, ri'zɪs(t)lɨs

resistlessly
BR rɪ'zɪs(t)lɨsli
AM rə'zɪs(t)lɨsli, ri'zɪs(t)lɨsli

resistor
BR rɪ'zɪstə(r), -z
AM rə'zɪstər, ri'zɪstər, -z

resit[1]
noun
BR 'riːsɪt, -s
AM 'riˌsɪt, -s

resit[2]
verb
BR ˌriː'sɪt, -s, -ɪŋ
AM ri'sɪ|t, -ts, -dɪŋ

resite
BR ˌriː'sʌɪt, -s, -ɪŋ, -ɨd
AM ri'saɪ|t, -ts, -dɪŋ, -dɨd

resize
BR ˌriː'sʌɪz, -ɨz, -ɪŋ, -d
AM ri'saɪz, -ɨz, -ɪŋ, -d

resold
BR ˌriː'səʊld
AM ri'soʊld

resole
BR ˌriː'səʊl, -z, -ɪŋ, -d
AM ri'soʊl, -z, -ɪŋ, -d

resoluble
BR ˌriː'sɒljʉbl
AM rə'zɑljəbəl, ri'zɑljəbəl

resolute
BR 'rɛzəl(j)uːt

AM 'rɛzə,l(j)ut

resolutely
BR 'rɛzəl(j)u:tli
AM 'rɛzə,l(j)utli

resoluteness
BR 'rɛzəl(j)u:tnəs
AM 'rɛzə,l(j)utnəs

resolution
BR ,rɛzə'l(j)u:ʃn, -z
AM ,rɛzə'luʃən, -z

resolutive
BR 'rɛzəl(j)u:tɪv
AM rə'zɑljədɪv, 'rɛzə,ludɪv

resolvability
BR rɪ,zɒlvə'bɪlɪti
AM rə,zɔlvə'bɪlɨdi, ri,zɔlvə'bɪlɨdi, rə,zɑlvə'bɪlɨdi, ri,zɑlvə'bɪlɨdi

resolvable
BR rɪ'zɒlvəbl
AM rə'zɔlvəbəl, ri'zɔlvəbəl, rə'zɑlvəbəl, ri'zɑlvəbəl

resolve
BR rɪ'zɒlv, -z, -ɪŋ, -d
AM rə'zɔlv, ri'zɔlv, rə'zɑlv, ri'zɑlv, -z, -ɪŋ, -d

resolvedly
BR rɪ'zɒlvɪdli
AM rə'zɔlvədli, ri'zɔlvədli, rə'zɑlvədli, ri'zɑlvədli

resolvedness
BR rɪ'zɒlvɪdnɪs
AM rə'zɔlvədnəs, ri'zɔlvədnəs, rə'zɑlvədnəs, ri'zɑlvədnəs

Resolven
BR rɪ'zɒlv(ə)n
AM rə'zɔlvən, rə'zɑlvən

resolvent
BR rɪ'zɒlv(ə)nt, -s
AM rə'zɔlvənt, ri'zɔlvənt, rə'zɑlvənt, ri'zɑlvənt, -s

resolver
BR rɪ'zɒlvə(r), -z
AM rə'zɔlvər, ri'zɔlvər, rə'zɑlvər, ri'zɑlvər, -z

resonance
BR 'rɛzənəns, 'rɛzn̩əns, -ɪz
AM 'rɛzənəns, 'rɛzn̩əns, -əz

resonant
BR 'rɛzənənt, 'rɛzn̩ənt
AM 'rɛzənənt, 'rɛzn̩ənt

resonantly
BR 'rɛzənəntli, 'rɛzn̩əntli
AM 'rɛzənən(t)li, 'rɛzn̩ən(t)li

resonate
BR 'rɛzəneɪt, 'rɛzn̩eɪt, -s, -ɪŋ, -ɨd
AM 'rɛzn,eɪ|t, -ts, -dɪŋ, -dɨd

resonator
BR 'rɛzəneɪtə(r), 'rɛzn̩eɪtə(r), -z
AM 'rɛzn,eɪdər, -z

resorb
BR rɪ'sɔ:b, rɪ'zɔ:b, -z, -ɪŋ, -d
AM rə'sɔ(ə)rb, ri'sɔ(ə)rb, rə'zɔ(ə)rb, ri'zɔ(ə)rb, -z, -ɪŋ, -d

resorbence
BR rɪ'sɔ:b(ə)ns, rɪ'zɔ:b(ə)ns
AM rə'sɔrbəns, ri'sɔrbəns, rə'zɔrbəns, ri'zɔrbəns

resorbent
BR rɪ'sɔ:b(ə)nt, rɪ'zɔ:b(ə)nt
AM rə'sɔrbənt, ri'sɔrbənt, rə'zɔrbənt, ri'zɔrbənt

resorcin
BR rɪ'zɔ:sɪn
AM rə'zɔrsən, ri'zɔrsən

resorcinol
BR rɪ'zɔ:sɪnɒl
AM rə'zɔrsə,nɑl, ri'zɔrsə,nɑl

resorption
BR rɪ'sɔ:pʃn, rɪ'zɔ:pʃn
AM rə'sɔrpʃən, rə'zɔrpʃən, ri'sɔrpʃən, ri'zɔrpʃən

resorptive
BR rɪ'sɔ:ptɪv, rɪ'zɔ:ptɪv
AM rə'sɔrptɪv, rə'zɔrptɪv, ri'sɔrptɪv, ri'zɔrptɪv

resort[1]
noun, verb, make use of, visit
BR rɪ'zɔ:t, -s, -ɪŋ, -ɨd
AM rə'zɔ(ə)rt, ri'zɔ(ə)rt, -ts, -'zɔrdɪŋ, -'zɔrdəd

resort[2]
verb, sort again
BR ,ri:'sɔ:t, -s, -ɪŋ, -ɨd
AM ri'sɔ(ə)rt, -ts, -'sɔrdɪŋ, -'sɔrdəd

resorter
BR rɪ'zɔ:tə(r), -z
AM rə'zɔrdər, ri'zɔrdər, -z

resound
BR rɪ'zaʊnd, -z, -ɪŋ, -ɨd
AM rə'zaʊnd, ri'zaʊnd, -z, -ɪŋ, -əd

resoundingly
BR rɪ'zaʊndɪŋli
AM rə'zaʊndɪŋli, ri'zaʊndɪŋli

resource
BR rɪ'zɔ:s, rɪ'sɔ:s, -ɪz
AM 'ri,sɔ(ə)rs, rə'sɔ(ə)rs, ri'sɔ(ə)rs, -əz

resourceful
BR rɪ'zɔ:sf(ʊ)l, rɪ'sɔ:sf(ʊ)l
AM rə'sɔrsfəl, ri'sɔrsfəl

resourcefully
BR rɪ'zɔ:sfʊli, rɪ'zɔ:sfl̩i, rɪ'sɔ:sfʊli, rɪ'sɔ:sfl̩i
AM rə'sɔrsfəli, ri'sɔrsfəli

resourcefulness
BR rɪ'zɔ:sf(ʊ)lnəs, rɪ'sɔ:sf(ʊ)lnəs
AM rə'sɔrsfəlnəs, ri'sɔrsfəlsnəs

resourceless
BR rɪ'zɔ:sləs, rɪ'sɔ:sləs
AM 'ri,sɔrsləs, rə'sɔrsləs, ri'sɔrsləs

resourcelessness
BR rɪ'zɔ:sləsnəs, rɪ'sɔ:sləsnəs
AM 'ri,sɔrsləsnəs, rə'sɔrsləsnəs, ri'sɔrsləsnəs

respect
BR rɪ'spɛkt, -s, -ɪŋ, -ɨd
AM rə'spɛk|(t), ri'spɛk|(t), -(t)s, -tɪŋ, -təd

respectability
BR rɪ,spɛktə'bɪlɪti
AM rə,spɛktə'bɪlɨdi, ri,spɛktə'bɪlɨdi

respectable
BR rɪ'spɛktəbl
AM rə'spɛktəbəl, ri'spɛktəbəl

respectableness
BR rɪ'spɛktəblnəs
AM rə'spɛktəbəlnəs, ri'spɛktəbəlnəs

respectably
BR rɪ'spɛktəbli
AM rə'spɛktəbli, ri'spɛktəbli

respecter
BR rɪ'spɛktə(r), -z
AM rə'spɛktər, ri'spɛktər, -z

respectful
BR rɪ'spɛk(t)f(ʊ)l
AM rə'spɛk(t)fəl, ri'spɛk(t)fəl

respectfully
BR rɪ'spɛk(t)fʊli, rɪ'spɛk(t)fl̩i
AM rə'spɛk(t)fəli, ri'spɛk(t)fəli

respectfulness
BR rɪ'spɛk(t)f(ʊ)lnəs
AM rə'spɛk(t)fəlnəs, ri'spɛk(t)fəlnəs

respective
BR rɪ'spɛktɪv
AM rə'spɛktɪv, ri'spɛktɪv

respectively
BR rɪ'spɛktɨvli
AM rə'spɛktɨvli, ri'spɛktɨvli

respell
BR ,ri:'spɛl, -z, -ɪŋ, -d
AM ri'spɛl, -z, -ɪŋ, -d

Respighi
BR rɪ'spi:gi, rɛ'spi:gi
AM rə'spɪgi

respirable
BR 'rɛsp(ɪ)rəbl
AM 'rɛspərəbəl

respirate
BR 'rɛspɪreɪt, -s, -ɪŋ, -ɨd
AM 'rɛspə,reɪ|t, -ts, -dɪŋ, -dɨd

respiration
BR ,rɛspɪ'reɪʃn
AM ,rɛspə'reɪʃən

respirator
BR 'rɛspɪreɪtə(r), -z
AM ,rɛspə'reɪdər, -z

respiratory
BR 'rɛspɪrət(ə)ri, rɪ'spɪrət(ə)ri, rɪ'spʌɪ(ə)rət(ə)ri
AM 'rɛsp(ə)rə,tɔri, rə'spaɪrə,tɔri

respire
BR rɪ'spʌɪə(r), -z, -ɪŋ, -d
AM rə'spaɪ(ə)r, ri'spaɪ(ə)r, -z, -ɪŋ, -d

respite
BR 'rɛspʌɪt, 'rɛspɪt, -s, -ɪŋ, -ɨd
AM 'rɛspə|t, -ts, -dɪŋ, -dəd

resplendence
BR rɪ'splɛnd(ə)ns
AM rə'splɛnd(ə)ns, ri'splɛnd(ə)ns

resplendency
BR rɪ'splɛnd(ə)nsi
AM rə'splɛnd(ə)nsi, ri'splɛnd(ə)nsi

resplendent
BR rɪ'splɛnd(ə)nt
AM rə'splɛndənt, ri'splɛndənt

resplendently
BR rɪ'splɛnd(ə)ntli
AM rə'splɛndən(t)li, ri'splɛndən(t)li

respond
BR rɪ'spɒnd, -z, -ɪŋ, -ɨd
AM rə'spɑnd, ri'spɑnd, -z, -ɪŋ, -əd

respondence
BR rɪ'spɒnd(ə)ns, -ɪz
AM rə'spand(ə)ns, ri'spand(ə)ns, -əz
respondency
BR rɪ'spɒnd(ə)nsi
AM rə'spand(ə)nsi, ri'spand(ə)nsi
respondent
BR rɪ'spɒnd(ə)nt, -s
AM rə'spandənt, ri'spandənt, -s
responder
BR rɪ'spɒndə(r), -z
AM rə'spandər, ri'spandər, -z
response
BR rɪ'spɒns, -ɪz
AM rə'spans, ri'spans, -əz
responsibility
BR rɪ,spɒnsɪ'bɪlɪt|i, -ɪz
AM rə,spansə'bɪlɪdi, ri,spansə'bɪlɪdi, -z
responsible
BR rɪ'spɒnsɪbl
AM rə'spansəbəl, ri'spansəbəl
responsibleness
BR rɪ'spɒnsɪblnəs
AM rə'spansəbəlnəs, ri'spansəbəlnəs
responsibly
BR rɪ'spɒnsɪbli
AM rə'spansəbli, ri'spansəbli
responsive
BR rɪ'spɒnsɪv
AM rə'spansɪv, ri'spansɪv
responsively
BR rɪ'spɒnsɪvli
AM rə'spansɪvli, ri'spansɪvli
responsiveness
BR rɪ'spɒnsɪvnɪs
AM rə'spansɪvnɪs, ri'spansɪvnɪs
responsory
BR rɪ'spɒns(ə)r|i, -ɪz
AM rə'spansəri, ri'spansəri, -z
respray[1]
noun
BR 'riːspreɪ, -z
AM 'ri,spreɪ, -z
respray[2]
verb
BR ,riː'spreɪ, -z, -ɪŋ, -d
AM ri'spreɪ, -z, -ɪŋ, -d
res publica
BR (,)reɪz 'pʊblɪkə(*r*), + 'pʌblɪkə(*r*)
AM ,reɪs 'pʊbləkə
rest
BR rɛst, -s, -ɪŋ, -ɪd
AM rɛst, -s, -ɪŋ, -əd
restage
BR ,riː'steɪdʒ, -ɪz, -ɪŋ, -d
AM ri'steɪdʒ, -ɪz, -ɪŋ, -d
restart[1]
noun
BR 'riːstɑːt, -s
AM 'ri,stɑrt, -s
restart[2]
verb
BR ,riː'stɑːt, -s, -ɪŋ, -ɪd
AM ri'stɑr|t, -ts, -dɪŋ, -dəd
restate
BR ,riː'steɪt, -s, -ɪŋ, -ɪd
AM ri'steɪ|t, -ts, -dɪŋ, -dɪd
restatement
BR ,riː'steɪtm(ə)nt, -s
AM ri'steɪtmənt, -s
restaurant
BR 'rɛst(ʃ)(ə)rɑːnt, 'rɛst(ʃ)(ə)rɒnt, 'rɛst(ʃ)(ə)rənt, 'rɛst(ʃ)(ə)rn̩t, 'rɛst(ʃ)(ə)rɒ̃, -s
AM 'rɛst(ə)rənt, 'rɛstə,rɑnt, 'rɛ,strɑnt, -s
restauranteur
BR ,rɛstərɑːn'təː(r), ,rɛst(ʃ)ərɒn'təː(r), ,rɛst(ʃ)(ə)rən'təː(r), ,rɛst(ʃ)(ə)rn̩'təː(r), ,rɛst(ʃ)ərɒ̃'təː(r), -z
AM ¦rɛstərən'tər, ¦rɛstə,rɑn'tər, -z
restaurateur
BR ,rɛst(ə)rə'təː(r), -z
AM ¦rɛstərə'tər, ¦rɛstə,rɑ'tər, -z
restful
BR 'rɛs(t)f(ʊ)l
AM 'rɛs(t)fəl
restfully
BR 'rɛs(t)fʊli, 'rɛs(t)fl̩i
AM 'rɛs(t)fəli
restfulness
BR 'rɛs(t)f(ʊ)lnəs
AM 'rɛs(t)fəlnəs
resthouse
BR 'rɛsthaʊ|s, -zɪz
AM 'rɛst,(h)aʊ|s, -zəz
resting-place
BR 'rɛstɪŋpleɪs, -ɪz
AM 'rɛstɪŋ,pleɪs, -ɪz
restitution
BR ,rɛstɪ'tjuːʃn, ,rɛstɪ'tʃuːʃn
AM ,rɛstə't(j)uʃən
restitutive
BR 'rɛstɪtjuːtɪv, 'rɛstɪtʃuːtɪv
AM 'rɛstə,t(j)utɪv
restive
BR 'rɛstɪv
AM 'rɛstɪv
restively
BR 'rɛstɪvli
AM 'rɛstɪvli
restiveness
BR 'rɛstɪvnɪs
AM 'rɛstɪvnɪs
restless
BR 'rɛs(t)ləs
AM 'rɛs(t)ləs
restlessly
BR 'rɛs(t)ləsli
AM 'rɛs(t)ləsli
restlessness
BR 'rɛs(t)ləsnəs
AM 'rɛs(t)ləsnəs
restock
BR ,riː'stɒk, -s, -ɪŋ, -t
AM ri'stɑk, -s, -ɪŋ, -t
restorable
BR rɪ'stɔːrəbl
AM rə'stɔrəbəl, ri'stɔrəbəl
restoration
BR ,rɛstə'reɪʃn, -z
AM ,rɛstə'reɪʃən, -z
restorationism
BR ,rɛstə'reɪʃn̩ɪz(ə)m, ,rɛstə'reɪʃənɪz(ə)m
AM ,rɛstə'reɪʃə,nɪzəm
restorationist
BR ,rɛstə'reɪʃn̩ɪst, ,rɛstə'reɪʃənɪst, -s
AM ,rɛstə'reɪʃənəst, -s
restorative
BR rɪ'stɒrətɪv, rɪ'stɔːrətɪv, -z
AM rə'stɔrədɪv, -z
restoratively
BR rɪ'stɒrətɪvli, rɪ'stɔːrətɪvli
AM rə'stɔrədɪvli
restore
BR rɪ'stɔː(r), -z, -ɪŋ, -d
AM rə'stɔ(ə)r, ri'stɔ(ə)r, -z, -ɪŋ, -d
restorer
BR rɪ'stɔːrə(r), -z
AM rə'stɔrər, ri'stɔrər, -z
restrain[1]
hold back
BR rɪ'streɪn, -z, -ɪŋ, -d
AM rə'streɪn, ri'streɪn, -z, -ɪŋ, -d
restrain[2]
strain again
BR ,riː'streɪn, -z, -ɪŋ, -d
AM ri'streɪn, -z, -ɪŋ, -d
restrainable
BR rɪ'streɪnəbl
AM rə'streɪnəbəl, ri'streɪnəbəl
restrainedly
BR rɪ'streɪnɪdli
AM rə'streɪnɪdli, ri'streɪnɪdli
restrainer
BR rɪ'streɪnə(r), -z
AM rə'streɪnər, ri'streɪnər, -z
restraint
BR rɪ'streɪnt, -s
AM rə'streɪnt, ri'streɪnt, -s
restrict
BR rɪ'strɪkt, -s, -ɪŋ, -ɪd
AM rə'strɪk|(t), ri'strɪk|(t), -(t)s, -tɪŋ, -tɪd
restrictedly
BR rɪ'strɪktɪdli
AM rə'strɪktɪdli, ri'strɪktɪdli
restrictedness
BR rɪ'strɪktɪdnɪs
AM rə'strɪktɪdnɪs, ri'strɪktɪdnɪs
restriction
BR rɪ'strɪkʃn, -z
AM rə'strɪkʃən, ri'strɪkʃən, -z
restrictionist
BR rɪ'strɪkʃn̩ɪst, rɪ'strɪkʃənɪst, -s
AM rə'strɪkʃənəst, ri'strɪkʃənəst, -s
restrictive
BR rɪ'strɪktɪv
AM rə'strɪktɪv, ri'strɪktɪv
restrictively
BR rɪ'strɪktɪvli
AM rə'strɪktɪvli, ri'strɪktɪvli
restrictiveness
BR rɪ'strɪktɪvnɪs
AM rə'strɪktɪvnɪs, ri'strɪktɪvnɪs
restring
BR ,riː'strɪŋ, -z, -ɪŋ
AM ri'strɪŋ, -z, -ɪŋ
restroom
BR 'rɛstruːm, 'rɛstrʊm, -z
AM 'rɛs(t),rum, 'rɛs(t),rʊm, -z
restructure
BR ,riː'strʌktʃ|ə(r), -əz, -(ə)rɪŋ, -əd
AM ri'strək(t)ʃər, -z, -ɪŋ, -d
restructuring
BR ,riː'strʌktʃ(ə)rɪŋ, -z
AM ri'strək(t)ʃərɪŋ, -z
restrung
BR ,riː'strʌŋ
AM ri'strəŋ
restudy
BR ,riː'stʌd|i, -ɪz, -ɪɪŋ, -ɪd
AM ri'stədi, -z, -ɪŋ, -d
restyle
BR ,riː'stʌɪl, -z, -ɪŋ, -d
AM ri'staɪl, -z, -ɪŋ, -d

resubmit
BR ˌriːsəbˈmɪt, -s, -ɪŋ, -ɨd
AM ˈrisəbˈmɪ|t, -ts, -dɪŋ, -dɨd

result
BR rɪˈzʌlt, -s, -ɪŋ, -ɨd
AM rəˈzəlt, riˈzəlt, -s, -ɪŋ, -əd

resultant
BR rɪˈzʌlt(ə)nt
AM rəˈzəltnt, riˈzəltnt

resultful
BR rɪˈzʌltf(ʊ)l
AM rəˈzəltfəl, riˈzəltfəl

resultless
BR rɪˈzʌltləs
AM rəˈzəltləs, riˈzəltləs

resumable
BR rɪˈzjuːməbl
AM rəˈz(j)uməbəl, riˈz(j)uməbəl

resume[1]
noun
BR ˈrɛzjʊmeɪ, ˈreɪzjʊmeɪ, rɪˈzjuːmeɪ, -z
AM ˈrɛzəˌmeɪ, -z

resume[2]
verb
BR rɪˈzjuːm, -z, -ɪŋ, -d
AM rəˈz(j)um, riˈz(j)um, -z, -ɪŋ, -d

résumé
BR ˈrɛzjʊmeɪ, ˈreɪzjʊmeɪ, rɪˈzjuːmeɪ, -z
AM ˈrɛzəˌmeɪ, -z

resumption
BR rɪˈzʌm(p)ʃn, -z
AM rəˈzəm(p)ʃən, riˈzəm(p)ʃən, -z

resumptive
BR rɪˈzʌm(p)tɪv
AM rəˈzəm(p)tɪv, riˈzəm(p)tɪv

resupinate
BR ˌriːˈsjuːpɨnət
AM riˈs(j)upəˌneɪt, riˈs(j)upənət

resupply
BR ˌriːsəˈplʌɪ, -z, -ɪŋ, -d
AM ˌrisəˈplaɪ, -z, -ɪŋ, -d

resurface
BR ˌriːˈsəːfɪs, -ɨz, -ɪŋ, -t
AM riˈsərfəs, -əz, -ɪŋ, -t

resurgence
BR rɪˈsəːdʒ(ə)ns
AM rəˈsərdʒəns, riˈsərdʒəns

resurgent
BR rɪˈsəːdʒ(ə)nt
AM rəˈsərdʒənt, riˈsərdʒənt

resurrect
BR ˌrɛzəˈrɛkt, -s, -ɪŋ, -ɨd
AM ˈrɛzəˈrɛk|(t), ˈrɛʒəˈrɛk|(t), -(t)s, -tɪŋ, -təd

resurrection
BR ˌrɛzəˈrɛkʃn, -z
AM ˌrɛzəˈrɛkʃən, ˌrɛʒəˈrɛkʃən, -z

resurrectional
BR ˌrɛzəˈrɛkʃn̩(ə)l, ˌrɛzəˈrɛkʃən(ə)l
AM ˌrɛzəˈrɛkʃ(ə)nəl

resurvey
BR ˌriːsəˈveɪ, ˌriːˈsəːveɪ, -z, -ɪŋ, -d
AM riˈsərˌveɪ, riˌsərˈveɪ, -z, -ɪŋ, -d

resuscitate
BR rɪˈsʌsɪteɪt, -s, -ɪŋ, -ɨd
AM rəˈsəsəˌteɪ|t, riˈsəsəˌteɪ|t, -ts, -dɪŋ, -dɨd

resuscitation
BR rɪˌsʌsɪˈteɪʃn
AM rəˌsəsəˈteɪʃən, riˌsəsəˈteɪʃən

resuscitative
BR rɪˈsʌsɪtətɪv
AM rəˈsəsəˌteɪdɪv, riˈsəsəˌteɪdɪv

resuscitator
BR rɪˈsʌsɪteɪtə(r), -z
AM rəˈsəsəˌteɪdər, riˈsəsəˌteɪdər, -z

ret
BR rɛt, -s, -ɪŋ, -ɨd
AM rɛ|t, -ts, -dɪŋ, -dəd

retable
BR rɪˈteɪbl, -z
AM rəˈteɪbəl, riˈteɪbəl, -z

retail[1]
selling
BR ˈriːteɪl, -z, -ɪŋ, -d
AM ˈriˌteɪl, -z, -ɪŋ, -d

retail[2]
tell
BR rɪˈteɪl, -z, -ɪŋ, -d
AM rəˈteɪl, riˈteɪl, -z, -ɪŋ, -d

retailer[1]
seller
BR ˈriːteɪlə(r), -z
AM ˈriˌteɪlər, -z

retailer[2]
teller
BR rɪˈteɪlə(r), -z
AM rəˈteɪlər, riˈteɪlər, -z

retain
BR rɪˈteɪn, -z, -ɪŋ, -d
AM rəˈteɪn, riˈteɪn, -z, -ɪŋ, -d

retainability
BR rɪˌteɪnəˈbɪlɨti
AM rəˌteɪnəˈbɪlɨdi, riˌteɪnəˈbɪlɨdi

retainable
BR rɪˈteɪnəbl
AM rəˈteɪnəbəl, riˈteɪnəbəl

retainer
BR rɪˈteɪnə(r), -z
AM rəˈteɪnər, riˈteɪnər, -z

retainment
BR rɪˈteɪnm(ə)nt, -s
AM rəˈteɪnmənt, riˈteɪnmənt, -s

retake[1]
noun
BR ˈriːteɪk, -s
AM ˈriˌteɪk, -s

retake[2]
verb
BR (ˌ)riːˈteɪk, -s, -ɪŋ
AM rəˈteɪk, riˈteɪk, -s, -ɪŋ

retaken
BR (ˌ)riːˈteɪk(ə)n
AM rəˈteɪkən, riˈteɪkən

retaliate
BR rɪˈtalɪeɪt, -s, -ɪŋ, -ɨd
AM rəˈtæliˌeɪ|t, riˈtæliˌeɪ|t, -ts, -dɪŋ, -dɨd

retaliation
BR rɪˌtalɪˈeɪʃn
AM rəˌtæliˈeɪʃən, riˌtæliˈeɪʃən

retaliative
BR rɪˈtalɪətɪv
AM rəˈtæliədɪv, riˈtæliədɪv

retaliator
BR rɪˈtalɪeɪtə(r), -z
AM rəˈtæliˌeɪdər, riˈtæliˌeɪdər, -z

retaliatory
BR rɪˈtalɪət(ə)ri
AM rəˈtæliəˌtɔri, riˈtæliəˌtɔri, rəˈtæljəˌtɔri, riˈtæljəˌtɔri

retard[1]
noun, retarded person
BR ˈriːtɑːd, -z
AM ˈritɑrd, -z

retard[2]
verb, noun, slowdown
BR rɪˈtɑːd, -z, -ɪŋ, -ɨd
AM rəˈtɑrd, riˈtɑrd, -z, -ɪŋ, -əd

retardant
BR rɪˈtɑːd(ə)nt, -s
AM rəˈtɑrdənt, riˈtɑrdənt, -s

retardate
BR rɪˈtɑːdeɪt, -s
AM rəˈtɑrˌdeɪt, riˈtɑrˌdeɪt, -s

retardation
BR ˌriːtɑːˈdeɪʃn
AM ˌriˌtɑrˈdeɪʃən

retardative
BR rɪˈtɑːdətɪv
AM rəˈtɑrdədɪv, riˈtɑrdədɪv

retardatory
BR rɪˈtɑːdət(ə)ri
AM rəˈtɑrdəˌtɔri, riˈtɑrdəˌtɔri

retarded
BR rɪˈtɑːdɨd
AM rəˈtɑrdəd, riˈtɑrdəd

retarder
BR rɪˈtɑːdə(r), -z
AM rəˈtɑrdər, riˈtɑrdər, -z

retardment
BR rɪˈtɑːdm(ə)nt, -s
AM rəˈtɑrdmənt, riˈtɑrdmənt, -s

retaught
BR ˌriːˈtɔːt
AM riˈtɔt, riˈtɑt

retch
BR rɛtʃ, -ɨz, -ɪŋ, -t
AM rɛtʃ, -əz, -ɪŋ, -t

rete
BR ˈriːti
AM ˈridi

reteach
BR ˌriːˈtiːtʃ, -ɨz, -ɪŋ
AM riˈtitʃ, -ɨz, -ɪŋ

retell
BR ˌriːˈtɛl, -z, -ɪŋ
AM riˈtɛl, -z, -ɪŋ

retention
BR rɪˈtɛnʃn
AM rəˈtɛnʃən, riˈtɛnʃən

retentive
BR rɪˈtɛntɪv
AM rəˈtɛn(t)ɪv, riˈtɛn(t)ɪv

retentively
BR rɪˈtɛntɨvli
AM rəˈtɛn(t)ɨvli, riˈtɛn(t)ɨvli

retentiveness
BR rɪˈtɛntɪvnɨs
AM rəˈtɛn(t)ɪvnɨs, riˈtɛn(t)ɪvnɨs

retest[1]
noun
BR ˈriːtɛst, -s
AM ˈriˌtɛst, -s

retest[2]
verb
BR ˌriːˈtɛst, -s, -ɪŋ, -ɨd
AM riˈtɛst, -s, -ɪŋ, -əd

retexture
BR ˌriːˈtɛkstʃ|ə(r), -əz, -(ə)rɪŋ, -əd
AM riˈtɛk(st)ʃər, -z, -ɪŋ, -d

Retford
BR ˈrɛtfəd
AM ˈrɛtfərd

rethink¹
noun
BR 'riːθɪŋk, -s
AM 'riˌθɪŋk, -s

rethink²
verb
BR ˌriː'θɪŋk, -s, -ɪŋ
AM ri'θɪŋk, -s, -ɪŋ

rethought
BR ˌriː'θɔːt
AM ri'θɔt, ri'θɑt

retia
BR 'riːʃ(ɪ)ə(r), 'riːtɪə(r)
AM 'riʃ(i)ə, 'ridiə

retiarii
BR ˌrɛtɪ'ɑːrɪiː, ˌrɛtɪ'ɑːrɪʌɪ, ˌrɛtɪ'ɛːrɪiː, ˌrɛtɪ'ɛːrɪʌɪ
AM ˌriʃi'ɛriaɪ

retiarius
BR ˌrɛtɪ'ɑːrɪəs, ˌrɛtɪ'ɛːrɪəs
AM ˌriʃi'ɛriəs

retiary
BR 'riːʃɪər|i, -ɪz
AM 'riʃiˌɛri, -z

reticence
BR 'rɛtɪs(ə)ns
AM 'rɛdəsəns

reticent
BR 'rɛtɪs(ə)nt
AM 'rɛdəsənt

reticently
BR 'rɛtɪs(ə)ntli
AM 'rɛdəsən(t)li

reticle
BR 'rɛtɪkl, -z
AM 'rɛdəkəl, -z

reticula
BR rɪ'tɪkjʉlə(r)
AM rə'tɪkjələ

reticular
BR rɪ'tɪkjʉlə(r)
AM rə'tɪkjələr

reticulate¹
adjective
BR rɪ'tɪkjʉlət
AM rə'tɪkjələt, ri'tɪkjələt, rə'tɪkjəˌleɪt, ri'tɪkjəˌleɪt

reticulate²
verb
BR rɪ'tɪkjʉleɪt, -s, -ɪŋ, -ɪd
AM rə'tɪkjəˌleɪ|t, ri'tɪkjə'leɪ|t, -ts, -dɪŋ, -dɪd

reticulately
BR rɪ'tɪkjʉlətli
AM rə'tɪkjələtli, ri'tɪkjələtli, rə'tɪkjəˌleɪtli, ri'tɪkjəˌleɪtli

reticulation
BR rɪˌtɪkjʉ'leɪʃn
AM rəˌtɪkjə'leɪʃən, riˌtɪkjə'leɪʃən

reticule
BR 'rɛtɪkjuːl, -z
AM 'rɛdəˌkjul, -z

reticulocyte
BR rɪ'tɪkjʉləsʌɪt, -s
AM rə'tɪkjələˌsaɪt, -s

reticulose
BR rɪ'tɪkjʉləʊs
AM rə'tɪkjəˌloʊs, rə'tɪkjəˌloʊz

reticulum
BR rɪ'tɪkjʉləm
AM rə'tɪkjələm

retie
BR ˌriː'tʌɪ, -z, -ɪŋ, -d
AM ri'taɪ, -z, -ɪŋ, -d

retiform
BR 'rɛtɪfɔːm
AM 'rɛdəˌfɔ(ə)rm

retina
BR 'rɛtɪnə(r), -z
AM 'rɛtn̩ə, -z

retinae
BR 'rɛtɪniː
AM 'rɛtnˌi, 'rɛtn̩ˌaɪ

retinal
BR 'rɛtɪnl
AM 'rɛtn̩l

retinitis
BR ˌrɛtɪ'nʌɪtɪs
AM ˌrɛtn'aɪdɪs

retinitis pigmentosa
BR ˌrɛtɪˌnʌɪtɪs ˌpɪgmɛn'təʊzə(r)
AM ˌrɛtn'aɪdɪs ˌpɪgmən'toʊzə

retinoid
BR 'rɛtɪnɔɪd, -z
AM 'rɛtnˌɔɪd, -z

retinol
BR 'rɛtɪnɒl
AM 'rɛtn̩ɑl

retinopathy
BR ˌrɛtɪ'nɒpəθi
AM ˌrɛtn'ɑpəθi

retinue
BR 'rɛtɪnjuː, -z
AM 'rɛtnˌ(j)u, -z

retiracy
BR rɪ'tʌɪərəsi
AM rə'taɪ(ə)rəsi

retiral
BR rɪ'tʌɪərəl, rɪ'tʌɪərl̩, -z
AM rə'taɪrəl, -z

retire
BR rɪ'tʌɪə(r), -z, -ɪŋ, -d
AM rə'taɪ(ə)r, ri'taɪ(ə)r, -z, -ɪŋ, -d

retiredness
BR rɪ'tʌɪədnəs
AM rə'taɪrdnəs, ri'taɪrdnəs

retiree
BR ˌriːtʌɪə'riː, -z
AM riˌtaɪ'ri, rə'taɪˌri, -z

retirement
BR rɪ'tʌɪəm(ə)nt, -s
AM rə'taɪrmənt, ri'taɪrmənt, -s

retirer
BR rɪ'tʌɪərə(r), -z
AM rə'taɪrər, ri'taɪrər, -z

retiring
BR rɪ'tʌɪərɪŋ
AM rə'taɪrɪŋ, ri'taɪrɪŋ

retiringly
BR rɪ'tʌɪərɪŋli
AM rə'taɪrɪŋli, ri'taɪrɪŋli

retitle
BR ˌriː'tʌɪt|l, -lz, -l̩ɪŋ\-lɪŋ, -ld
AM ri'taɪdəl, -z, -ɪŋ, -d

retold
BR ˌriː'təʊld
AM ri'toʊld

retook
BR (ˌ)riː'tʊk
AM ri'tʊk

retool
BR ˌriː'tuːl, -z, -ɪŋ, -d
AM ri'tul, -z, -ɪŋ, -d

retort
BR rɪ'tɔːt, -s, -ɪŋ, -ɪd
AM rə'tɔ(ə)rt, ri'tɔ(ə)rt, -ts, -'tɔrdɪŋ, -'tɔrdəd

retortion
BR rɪ'tɔːʃn, -z
AM rə'tɔrʃən, ri'tɔrʃən, -z

retouch
BR ˌriː'tʌtʃ, -ɪz, -ɪŋ, -t
AM ri'tətʃ, -əz, -ɪŋ, -t

retoucher
BR ˌriː'tʌtʃə(r), -z
AM ri'tətʃər, -z

retrace
BR ˌriː'treɪs, rɪ'treɪs, -ɪz, -ɪŋ, -t
AM ri'treɪs, -ɪz, -ɪŋ, -t

retract
BR rɪ'trakt, -s, -ɪŋ, -ɪd
AM rə'træk|(t), ri'træk|(t), -(t)s, -tɪŋ, -təd

retractable
BR rɪ'traktəbl
AM rə'træktəbəl, ri'træktəbəl

retractation
BR ˌriːtrak'teɪʃn
AM ˌriˌtræk'teɪʃən

retractible
BR rɪ'traktəbl
AM rə'træktəbəl, ri'træktəbəl

retractile
BR rɪ'traktʌɪl
AM rə'træktl

retractility
BR rɪˌtrak'tɪlɪti
AM rəˌtræk'tɪlɪdi, riˌtræk'tɪlɪdi

retraction
BR rɪ'trakʃn, -z
AM rə'trækʃən, ri'trækʃən, -z

retractive
BR rɪ'traktɪv
AM rə'træktɪv, ri'træktɪv

retractor
BR rɪ'traktə(r), -z
AM rə'træktər, ri'træktər, -z

retrain
BR ˌriː'treɪn, -z, -ɪŋ, -d
AM ri'treɪn, -z, -ɪŋ, -d

retral
BR 'riːtr(ə)l
AM 'ritrəl

retranslate
BR ˌriːtrans'leɪt, ˌriːtrɑːns'leɪt, ˌriːtranz'leɪt, ˌriːtrɑːnz'leɪt, -s, -ɪŋ, -ɪd
AM ˌri'trænz'leɪ|t, ˌriˌtrænz'leɪ|t, -ts, -dɪŋ, -dɪd

retranslation
BR ˌriːtrans'leɪʃn, ˌriːtrɑːns'leɪʃn, ˌriːtranz'leɪʃn, ˌriːtrɑːnz'leɪʃn, -z
AM ˌriˌtrænz'leɪʃən, -z

retransmission
BR ˌriːtranz'mɪʃn, ˌriːtrɑːnz'mɪʃn, ˌriːtrans'mɪʃn, ˌriːtrɑːns'mɪʃn, -z
AM ¦riˌtræn'smɪʃən, -z

retransmit
BR ˌriːtranz'mɪt, ˌriːtrɑːnz'mɪt, ˌriːtrans'mɪt, ˌriːtrɑːns'mɪt, -s, -ɪŋ, -ɪd
AM ¦riːˌtræn'smɪ|t, -ts, -dɪŋ, -dɪd

retread¹
noun
BR 'riːtrɛd, -z
AM 'riˌtrɛd, -z

retread²
verb
BR ˌriː'trɛd, -z, -ɪŋ
AM ri'trɛd, -z, -ɪŋ

retreat
BR rɪ'triːt, -s, -ɪŋ, -ɪd
AM rə'tri|t, ri'tri|t, -ts, -dɪŋ, -dɪd

retrench
BR rɪ'trɛn(t)ʃ, -ɪz, -ɪŋ, -t
AM rə'trɛn(t)ʃ, ri'trɛn(t)ʃ, -əz, -ɪŋ, -t

retrenchment
BR rɪ'trɛn(t)ʃm(ə)nt, -s
AM rə'trɛn(t)ʃmənt, ri'trɛn(t)ʃmənt, -z

retrial
BR ˌriː'trʌɪəl, 'riːtrʌɪəl, -z
AM ˈriˌtraɪəl, -z

retribution
BR ˌrɛtrɪ'bjuːʃn
AM ˌrɛtrə'bjuʃən

retributive
BR rɪ'trɪbjʉtɪv
AM rə'trɪbjədɪv, ri'trɪbjədɪv

retributively
BR rɪ'trɪbjʉtɪvli
AM rə'trɪbjədɪvli, ri'trɪbjədɪvli

retributory
BR rɪ'trɪbjʉt(ə)ri
AM rə'trɪbjəˌtɔri, ri'trɪbjəˌtɔri

retrievable
BR rɪ'triːvəbl
AM rə'trivəbəl, ri'trivəbəl

retrievableness
BR rɪ'triːvəblnəs
AM rə'trivəbəlnəs, ri'trivəbəlnəs

retrievably
BR rɪ'triːvəbli
AM rə'trivəbli, ri'trivəbli

retrieval
BR rɪ'triːvl
AM rə'trivəl, ri'trivəl

retrieve
BR rɪ'triːv, -z, -ɪŋ, -d
AM rə'triv, ri'triv, -z, -ɪŋ, -d

retriever
BR rɪ'triːvə(r), -z
AM rə'trivər, ri'trivər, -z

retrim
BR ˌriː'trɪm, -z, -ɪŋ, -d
AM ri'trɪm, -z, -ɪŋ, -d

retro
BR 'rɛtrəʊ, -z
AM 'rɛtroʊ, -z

retroact
BR ˌrɛtrəʊ'akt, -s, -ɪŋ, -ɨd
AM ˈrɛtroʊ'æk|(t), -(t)s, -tɪŋ, -təd

retroaction
BR ˌrɛtrəʊ'akʃn, -z
AM ˈrɛtroʊ'ækʃən, -z

retroactive
BR ˌrɛtrəʊ'aktɪv
AM ˈrɛtroʊ'æktɪv

retroactively
BR ˌrɛtrəʊ'aktɪvli
AM ˈrɛtroʊ'æktɪvli

retroactivity
BR ˌrɛtrəʊak'tɪvɪti
AM ˈrɛtroʊˌæk'tɪvɨdi

retrocede
BR ˌrɛtrə(ʊ)'siːd, -z, -ɪŋ, -ɨd
AM ˌrɛtrə'sid, -z, -ɪŋ, -ɨd

retrocedence
BR ˌrɛtrə(ʊ)'siːdns
AM ˌrɛtroʊ'sidns

retrocedent
BR ˌrɛtrə(ʊ)'siːdnt
AM ˌrɛtroʊ'sidnt

retrocession
BR ˌrɛtrə(ʊ)'sɛʃn, -z
AM ˌrɛtrə'sɛʃən, -z

retrocessive
BR ˌrɛtrə(ʊ)'sɛsɪv
AM ˌrɛtroʊ'sɛsɪv

retrochoir
BR 'rɛtrəʊˌkwʌɪə(r), -z
AM 'rɛtroʊˌkwaɪ(ə)r, -z

retrod
BR ˌriː'trɒd
AM ri'trɑd

retrodden
BR ˌriː'trɒdn
AM ri'trɑdən

retrofit
BR ˌrɛtrəʊ'fɪt, -s, -ɪŋ, -ɨd
AM ˌrɛtroʊ'fɪ|t, -ts, -dɪŋ, -dɨd

retroflection
BR ˌrɛtrə(ʊ)'flɛkʃn
AM ˌrɛtrə'flɛkʃən

retroflex
BR 'rɛtrə(ʊ)flɛks, -t
AM 'rɛtrəˌflɛks, -t

retroflexion
BR ˌrɛtrə(ʊ)'flɛkʃn
AM ˌrɛtrə'flɛkʃən

retrogradation
BR ˌrɛtrəʊgrə'deɪʃn, -z
AM ˈrɛtroʊgreɪ'deɪʃən, -z

retrograde
BR 'rɛtrə(ʊ)greɪd
AM 'rɛtrəˌgreɪd

retrogradely
BR 'rɛtrə(ʊ)greɪdli
AM 'rɛtrəˌgreɪdli

retrogress
BR ˌrɛtrə(ʊ)'grɛs, -ɪz, -ɪŋ, -t
AM ˌrɛtrə'grɛs, -əz, -ɪŋ, -t

retrogression
BR ˌrɛtrə(ʊ)'grɛʃn
AM ˌrɛtrə'grɛʃən

retrogressive
BR ˌrɛtrə(ʊ)'grɛsɪv
AM ˌrɛtrə'grɛsɪv

retrogressively
BR ˌrɛtrə(ʊ)'grɛsɪvli
AM ˌrɛtrə'grɛsɪvli

retroject
BR 'rɛtrə(ʊ)dʒɛkt, -s, -ɪŋ, -ɨd
AM 'rɛtrəˌdʒɛk|(t), -(t)s, -tɪŋ, -təd

retro-rocket
BR 'rɛtrəʊˌrɒkɪt, -s
AM 'rɛtroʊˌrɑkət, -s

retrorse
BR rɪ'trɔːs
AM rə'trɔ(ə)rs

retrorsely
BR rɪ'trɔːsli
AM rə'trɔrsli

retrospect
BR 'rɛtrəspɛkt, -s
AM 'rɛtrəˌspɛk(t), -s

retrospection
BR ˌrɛtrə(ʊ)'spɛkʃn
AM ˌrɛtrə'spɛkʃən

retrospective
BR ˌrɛtrə(ʊ)'spɛktɪv
AM ˌrɛtrə'spɛktɪv

retrospectively
BR ˌrɛtrə(ʊ)'spɛktɪvli
AM ˌrɛtrə'spɛktɪvli

retrosternal
BR ˌrɛtrəʊ'stəːnl
AM ˈrɛtroʊ'stərnəl

retroussé
BR rɪ'truːseɪ
AM ˌrɛtrʊ'seɪ

retroversion
BR ˌrɛtrə(ʊ)'vəːʃn
AM ˌrɛtrə'vərʒən

retrovert[1]
noun
BR 'rɛtrəvəːt, -s
AM 'rɛtrəˌvərt, -s

retrovert[2]
verb
BR ˌrɛtrə(ʊ)'vəːt, -s, -ɪŋ, -ɨd
AM ˌrɛtrə'vər|t, -ts, -dɪŋ, -dəd

Retrovir
BR 'rɛtrə(ʊ)vɪə(r)
AM 'rɛtroʊˌvɪ(ə)r

retrovirus
BR 'rɛtrəʊˌvʌɪrəs, -ɪz
AM ˈrɛtroʊ'vaɪrəs, -ɪz

retry
BR ˌriː'trʌɪ, -z, -ɪŋ, -d
AM ri'traɪ, -z, -ɪŋ, -d

retsina
BR rɛt'siːnə(*r*), 'rɛtsɪnə(*r*)
AM 'rɛtsənə

Rett
BR rɛt
AM rɛt

rettery
BR 'rɛt(ə)r|i, -ɪz
AM 'rɛdəri, -z

retune
BR ˌriː'tjuːn, ˌriː'tʃuːn, -z, -ɪŋ, -d
AM ri't(j)un, -z, -ɪŋ, -d

returf
BR ˌriː'təːf, -s, -ɪŋ, -t
AM ri'tərf, -s, -ɪŋ, -t

return
BR rɪ'təːn, -z, -ɪŋ, -d
AM rə'tərn, ri'tərn, -z, -ɪŋ, -d

returnable
BR rɪ'təːnəbl
AM rə'tərnəbəl, ri'tərnəbəl

returnee
BR rɪˌtəː'niː, ˌriːtəː'niː, -z
AM rəˌtər'ni, riˌtər'ni, -z

returner
BR rɪ'təːnə(r), -z
AM rə'tərnər, ri'tərnər, -z

returning officer
BR rɪ'təːnɪŋ ˌɒfɪsə(r), -z
AM rəˌtərnɪŋ ˈɔfəsər, + ˈɑfəsər, -z

returnless
BR rɪ'təːnləs
AM rə'tərnləs, ri'tərnləs

retuse
BR rɪ'tjuːs, rɪ'tʃuːs
AM 'rə't(j)uz

retying
BR ˌriː'tʌɪɪŋ
AM ri'taɪɪŋ

retype
BR ˌriː'tʌɪp, -s, -ɪŋ, -t
AM ri'taɪp, -s, -ɪŋ, -t

Reuben
BR 'ruːb(ɪ)n
AM 'rubən

reunification
BR ˌriːjuːnɪfɪ'keɪʃn, rɪˌjuːnɪfɪ'keɪʃn
AM ˈriˌjunəfə'keɪʃən

reunify
BR (ˌ)riː'juːnɪfʌɪ, -z, -ɪŋ, -d
AM ri'junəˌfaɪ, -z, -ɪŋ, -d

Réunion
BR riː'juːnɪən
AM ri'junjən
FR ʀeynjɔ̃

reunion
BR (ˌ)riː'juːnɪən, -z
AM ri'junjən, -z

reunite
BR ˌriːjʊ'nʌɪt, ˌriːjuː'nʌɪt, -s, -ɪŋ, -ɨd
AM ˈriju'naɪ|t, -ts, -dɪŋ, -dɨd

reupholster
BR ˌriːʌp'həʊlst|ə(r), -əz, -(ə)rɪŋ, -əd
AM ˈriˌəp'(h)oʊlstər, -z, -ɪŋ, -d

reupholstery
BR ˌriːʌp'həʊlst(ə)ri

AM ˌriˌəpˈ(h)oʊlstəri

reurge
BR ˌriːˈəːdʒ, -ɨz, -ɪŋ, -d
AM riˈərdʒ, -əz, -ɪŋ, -d

reusable
BR ˌriːˈjuːzəbl
AM riˈjuzəbəl

re-use[1]
noun
BR ˌriːˈjuːs
AM riˈjus

re-use[2]
verb
BR ˌriːˈjuːz, -ɨz, -ɪŋ, -d
AM riˈjuz, -əz, -ɪŋ, -d

reuseable
BR ˌriːˈjuːzəbl
AM riˈjuzəbəl

Reuter
BR ˈrɔɪtə(r), -z
AM ˈrɔɪdər, -z

reutilisation
BR ˌriːjuːtɨlʌɪˈzeɪʃn, ˌriːjuːtl̩ʌɪˈzeɪʃn, rɪˌjuːtɨlʌɪˈzeɪʃn, rɪˌjuːtl̩ʌɪˈzeɪʃn
AM ˈriˌjudləˈzeɪʃən, ˈriˌjudlaɪˈzeɪʃən

reutilise
BR ˌriːˈjuːtɨlʌɪz, ˌriːˈjuːtl̩ʌɪz, rɪˈjuːtɨlʌɪz, rɪˈjuːtl̩ʌɪz, -ɨz, -ɪŋ, -d
AM riˈjudlˌaɪz, -ɨz, -ɪŋ, -d

reutilization
BR ˌriːjuːtɨlʌɪˈzeɪʃn, ˌriːjuːtl̩ʌɪˈzeɪʃn, rɪˌjuːtɨlʌɪˈzeɪʃn, rɪˌjuːtl̩ʌɪˈzeɪʃn
AM ˈriˌjudləˈzeɪʃən, ˈriˌjudlaɪˈzeɪʃən

reutilize
BR ˌriːˈjuːtɨlʌɪz, rɪˈjuːtɨlʌɪz, rɪˈjuːtɨlʌɪz, rɪˈjuːtl̩ʌɪz, -ɨz, -ɪŋ, -d
AM riˈjudlˌaɪz, -ɨz, -ɪŋ, -d

Rev.
BR rɛv, ˈrɛv(ə)rənd, ˈrɛv(ə)rn̩d
AM ˈrɛvərnd, ˈrɛv(ə)rənd

rev
BR rɛv, -z, -ɪŋ, -d
AM rɛv, -z, -ɪŋ, -d

revaccinate
BR ˌriːˈvaksɨneɪt, -s, -ɪŋ, -ɨd
AM riˈvæksəˌneɪ|t, -ts, -dɪŋ, -dɨd

revaccination
BR ˌriːvaksɨˈneɪʃn, -z
AM ˈriˌvæksəˈneɪʃən, -z

revalorisation
BR ˌriːvalərʌɪˈzeɪʃn, -z
AM ˈriˌvælərəˈzeɪʃən, ˈriˌvæləˌraɪˈzeɪʃən, -z

revalorise
BR ˌriːˈvalərʌɪz, -ɨz, -ɪŋ, -d
AM riˈvæləˌraɪz, -ɨz, -ɪŋ, -d

revalorization
BR ˌriːvalərʌɪˈzeɪʃn, -z
AM ˈriˌvælərəˈzeɪʃən, ˈriˌvæləˌraɪˈzeɪʃən, -z

revalorize
BR ˌriːˈvalərʌɪz, -ɨz, -ɪŋ, -d
AM riˈvæləˌraɪz, -ɨz, -ɪŋ, -d

revaluation
BR ˌriːvaljʊˈeɪʃn, -z
AM ˌriˌvæljəˈweɪʃən, -z

revalue
BR ˌriːˈvalj|uː, -uːz, -ʊɪŋ, -uːd
AM riˈvælj|u, -uz, -əwɪŋ, -ud

revamp
BR (ˌ)riːˈvam|p, -ps, -pɪŋ, -(p)t
AM riˈvæmp, -s, -ɪŋ, -t

revanchism
BR rɪˈvan(t)ʃɪz(ə)m
AM rəˈvɑn(t)ʃˌɪzəm

revanchist
BR rɪˈvan(t)ʃɪst, -s
AM rəˈvɑn(t)ʃəst, -s

revarnish
BR ˌriːˈvɑːn|ɪʃ, -ɨʃɨz, -ɨʃɪŋ, -ɪʃt
AM riˈvɑrnɪʃ, -ɨz, -ɪŋ, -t

revcounter
BR ˈrɛvˌkaʊntə(r), -z
AM ˈrɛvˌkaʊn(t)ər, -z

reveal
BR rɪˈviːl, -z, -ɪŋ, -d
AM rəˈvil, riˈvil, -z, -ɪŋ, -d

revealable
BR rɪˈviːləbl
AM rəˈviləbəl, riˈviləbəl

revealer
BR rɪˈviːlə(r), -z
AM rəˈvilər, riˈvilər, -z

revealing
BR rɪˈviːlɪŋ
AM rəˈvilɪŋ, riˈvilɪŋ

revealingly
BR rɪˈviːlɪŋli
AM rəˈvilɪŋli, riˈvilɪŋli

reveille
BR rɪˈval|i, -ɪz
AM ˈrɛvəli, -z

revel
BR ˈrɛv|l, -lz, -l̩ɪŋ \-lɪŋ, -ld
AM ˈrɛv|əl, -əlz, -(ə)lɪŋ, -əld

revelation
BR ˌrɛvəˈleɪʃn, -z
AM ˌrɛvəˈleɪʃən, -z

revelational
BR ˌrɛvəˈleɪʃn̩(ə)l, ˌrɛvəˈleɪʃən(ə)l
AM ˌrɛvəˈleɪʃ(ə)nəl

revelationist
BR ˌrɛvəˈleɪʃn̩ɪst, ˌrɛvəˈleɪʃənɪst, -s
AM ˌrɛvəˈleɪʃənəst, -z

revelatory
BR ˌrɛvəˈleɪt(ə)ri, ˈrɛvələt(ə)ri, ˈrɛvl̩ət(ə)ri
AM rəˈvɛləˌtɔri

reveler
BR ˈrɛvl̩ə(r), ˈrɛvlə(r), -z
AM ˈrɛv(ə)lər, -z

reveller
BR ˈrɛvl̩ə(r), ˈrɛvlə(r), -z
AM ˈrɛv(ə)lər, -z

revelry
BR ˈrɛvlr|i, -ɪz
AM ˈrɛvəlri, -z

revenant
BR ˈrɛvɨnənt, -s
AM ˈrɛvənənt, ˈrɛvəˌnɑnt, -z

revendication
BR rɪˌvɛndɪˈkeɪʃn, -z
AM rəˌvɛndəˈkeɪʃən, -z

revenge
BR rɪˈvɛn(d)ʒ, -ɨz, -ɪŋ, -d
AM rəˈvɛndʒ, riˈvɛndʒ, -əz, -ɪŋ, -d

revengeful
BR rɪˈvɛn(d)ʒf(ʊ)l
AM rəˈvɛndʒfəl, riˈvɛndʒfəl

revengefully
BR rɪˈvɛn(d)ʒfʊli, rɪˈvɛn(d)ʒfl̩i
AM rəˈvɛndʒfəli, riˈvɛndʒfəli

revengefulness
BR rɪˈvɛn(d)ʒf(ʊ)lnəs
AM rəˈvɛndʒfəlnəs, riˈvɛndʒfəlnəs

revenger
BR rɪˈvɛn(d)ʒə(r), -z
AM rəˈvɛndʒər, riˈvɛndʒər, -z

revenue
BR ˈrɛvɨnjuː, -z
AM ˈrɛvəˌn(j)u, -z

reverb
reverberation
BR rɪˈvəːb, -z
AM rəˈvərb, -z

reverberant
BR rɪˈvəːb(ə)rənt, rɪˈvəːb(ə)rn̩t
AM rəˈvərb(ə)rənt, riˈvərb(ə)rənt

reverberantly
BR rɪˈvəːb(ə)rəntli, rɪˈvəːb(ə)rn̩tli
AM rəˈvərb(ə)rən(t)li, riˈvərb(ə)rən(t)li

reverberate
BR rɪˈvəːbəreɪt, -s, -ɪŋ, -ɨd
AM rəˈvərbəˌreɪ|t, riˈvərbəˌreɪ|t, -ts, -dɪŋ, -dɨd

reverberation
BR rɪˌvəːbəˈreɪʃn, -z
AM rəˌvərbəˈreɪʃən, riˌvərbəˈreɪʃən, -z

reverberative
BR rɪˈvəːb(ə)rətɪv
AM rəˈvərbərədɪv, riˈvərbərədɪv, rəˈvərbəˌreɪdɪv, riˈvərbəˌreɪdɪv

reverberator
BR rɪˈvəːbəreɪtə(r), -z
AM rəˈvərbəˌreɪdər, riˈvərbəˌreɪdər, -z

reverberatory
BR rɪˈvəːb(ə)rət(ə)ri, rɪˈvəːbəreɪt(ə)ri
AM rəˈvərb(ə)rəˌtɔri, riˈvərb(ə)rəˌtɔri

revere
BR rɪˈvɪə(r), -z, -ɪŋ, -d
AM rəˈvɪ(ə)r, riˈvɪ(ə)r, -z, -ɪŋ, -d

reverence
BR ˈrɛv(ə)rəns, ˈrɛv(ə)rn̩s, -ɨz, -ɪŋ, -t
AM ˈrɛvərn̩s, ˈrɛv(ə)rəns, -əz, -ɪŋ, -t

reverend
BR ˈrɛv(ə)rənd, ˈrɛv(ə)rn̩d, -z
AM ˈrɛvərn̩d, ˈrɛv(ə)rənd, -z

reverent
BR ˈrɛv(ə)rənt, ˈrɛv(ə)rn̩t
AM ˈrɛv(ə)rənt

reverential
BR ˌrɛvəˈrɛnʃl
AM ˈrɛvəˈrɛn(t)ʃəl

reverentially
BR ˌrɛvəˈrɛnʃl̩i, ˌrɛvəˈrɛnʃəli
AM ˈrɛvəˈrɛn(t)ʃəli

reverently
BR ˈrɛv(ə)rəntli, ˈrɛvərn̩tli
AM ˈrɛvərn̩(t)li, ˈrɛv(ə)rən(t)li

reverie
BR ˈrɛv(ə)r|i, -ɪz
AM ˈrɛv(ə)ri, -z

revers[1]
singular
BR rɪˈvɪə(r)
AM rəˈvɪ(ə)r, riˈvɪ(ə)r, rəˈvɛ(ə)r, riˈvɛ(ə)r

revers²
plural
BR rɪ'vɪəz
AM rə'vɪ(ə)rz, ri'vɪ(ə)rz, rə'vɛ(ə)rz, ri'vɛ(ə)rz
reversal
BR rɪ'vəːsl, -z
AM rə'vərsəl, ri'vərsəl, -z
reverse¹
noun
BR rɪ'vəːs
AM rə'vərs, 'rivərs
reverse²
noun, contrasted with obverse
BR 'riːvəːs
AM rə'vərs, ri'vərs
reverse³
verb, adjective
BR rɪ'vəːs, -ɪz, -ɪŋ, -t
AM rə'vərs, ri'vərs, -əz, -ɪŋ, -t
reversely
BR rɪ'vəːsli
AM rə'vərsli, ri'vərsli
reverser
BR rɪ'vəːsə(r), -z
AM rə'vərsər, ri'vərsər, -z
reversibility
BR rɪˌvəːsə'bɪlɪti
AM rəˌvərsə'bɪlɨdi, riˌvərsə'bɪlɨdi
reversible
BR rɪ'vəːsɪbl
AM rə'vərsəbəl, ri'vərsəbəl
reversibleness
BR rɪ'vəːsɪblnəs
AM rə'vərsəbəlnəs, ri'vərsəbəlnəs
reversibly
BR rɪ'vəːsɪbli
AM rə'vərsəbli, ri'vərsəbli
reversion
BR rɪ'vəːʃn, -z
AM rə'vərʒən, ri'vərʒən, rə'vərʃən, ri'vərʃən, -z
reversional
BR rɪ'vəːʃn̩(ə)l, rɪ'vəːʃən(ə)l
AM rə'vərʒ(ə)nəl, ri'vərʒ(ə)nəl, rə'vərʃ(ə)nəl, ri'vərʃ(ə)nəl
reversionary
BR rɪ'vəːʃn̩(ə)ri
AM rə'vərʒəˌnɛri, ri'vərʒəˌnɛri, rə'vərʃəˌnɛri, ri'vərʃəˌnɛri
reversioner
BR rɪ'vəːʃn̩ə(r), -z
AM rə'vərʒənər, ri'vərʒənər, rə'vərʃənər, ri'vərʃənər, -z
revert
BR rɪ'vəːt, -s, -ɪŋ, -ɪd
AM rə'vər|t, ri'vər|t, -ts, -dɪŋ, -dəd
reverter
BR rɪ'vəːtə(r), -z
AM rə'vərdər, ri'vərdər, -z
revertible
BR rɪ'vəːtɪbl
AM rə'vərdəbəl, ri'vərdəbəl
revet
BR rɪ'vɛt, -s, -ɪŋ, -ɪd
AM rə'vɛ|t, ri'vɛ|t, -ts, -dɪŋ, -dəd
revetment
BR rɪ'vɛtm(ə)nt, -s
AM rə'vɛtmənt, ri'vɛtmənt, -s
revictual
BR ˌriː'vɪt|l, -lz, -l̩ɪŋ\-lɪŋ, -ld
AM ri'vɪdl, -z, -ɪŋ, -d
Revie
BR 'riːvi
AM 'rivi
review
BR rɪ'vjuː, -z, -ɪŋ, -d
AM rə'vju, ri'vju, -z, -ɪŋ, -d
reviewable
BR rɪ'vjuːəbl
AM rə'vjuəbəl, ri'vjuəbəl
reviewal
BR rɪ'vjuːəl, -z
AM rə'vjuəl, ri'vjuəl, -z
reviewer
BR rɪ'vjuːə(r), -z
AM rə'vjuər, ri'vjuər, -z
revile
BR rɪ'vʌɪl, -z, -ɪŋ, -d
AM rə'vaɪl, ri'vaɪl, -z, -ɪŋ, -d
revilement
BR rɪ'vʌɪlm(ə)nt, -s
AM rə'vaɪlmənt, ri'vaɪlmənt, -z
reviler
BR rɪ'vʌɪlə(r), -z
AM rə'vaɪlər, ri'vaɪlər, -z
reviling
BR rɪ'vʌɪlɪŋ, -z
AM rə'vaɪlɪŋ, ri'vaɪlɪŋ, -z
revisable
BR rɪ'vʌɪzəbl
AM rə'vaɪzəbəl, ri'vaɪzəbəl
revisal
BR rɪ'vʌɪzl, -z
AM rə'vaɪzəl, ri'vaɪzəl, -z
revise
BR rɪ'vʌɪz, -ɪz, -ɪŋ, -d
AM rə'vaɪz, ri'vaɪz, -ɪz, -ɪŋ, -d
Revised Standard Version
BR rɪˌvʌɪzd 'standəd ˌvəːʃn, + ˌvəːʒn
AM rəˌvaɪzd 'stændərd ˌvərʒən, riˌvaɪzd +
reviser
BR rɪ'vʌɪzə(r), -z
AM rə'vaɪzər, ri'vaɪzər, -z
revision
BR rɪ'vɪʒn, -z
AM rə'vɪʒən, ri'vɪʒən, -z
revisionary
BR rɪ'vɪʒn̩(ə)ri
AM rə'vɪʒəˌnɛri, ri'vɪʒəˌnɛri
revisionism
BR rɪ'vɪʒn̩ɪz(ə)m
AM rə'vɪʒəˌnɪzəm, ri'vɪʒəˌnɪzəm
revisionist
BR rɪ'vɪʒn̩ɪst, -s
AM rə'vɪʒ(ə)nəst, ri'vɪʒ(ə)nəst, -s
revisit
BR ˌriː'vɪz|ɪt, -ɪts, -ɪtɪŋ, -ɪtɪd
AM ri'vɪzɨ|t, -s, -ɪŋ, -ɨd
revisory
BR rɪ'vʌɪz(ə)ri
AM rə'vaɪzəri, ri'vaɪzəri
revitalisation
BR ˌriːvʌɪtl̩ʌɪ'zeɪʃn, ˌriːvʌɪtəlʌɪ'zeɪʃn, riːˌvʌɪtl̩ʌɪ'zeɪʃn, riːˌvʌɪtəlʌɪ'zeɪʃn
AM riˌvaɪdl̩ə'zeɪʃən, riˌvaɪdlˌaɪ'zeɪʃən
revitalise
BR (ˌ)riː'vʌɪtl̩ʌɪz, (ˌ)riː'vʌɪtəlʌɪz, -ɪz, -ɪŋ, -d
AM ri'vaɪdəˌlaɪz, -ɪz, -ɪŋ, -d
revitalization
BR ˌriːvʌɪtl̩ʌɪ'zeɪʃn, ˌriːvʌɪtəlʌɪ'zeɪʃn, riːˌvʌɪtl̩ʌɪ'zeɪʃn, riːˌvʌɪtəlʌɪ'zeɪʃn
AM riˌvaɪdl̩ə'zeɪʃən, riˌvaɪdlˌaɪ'zeɪʃən
revitalize
BR (ˌ)riː'vʌɪtl̩ʌɪz, (ˌ)riː'vʌɪtəlʌɪz, -ɪz, -ɪŋ, -d
AM ri'vaɪdəˌlaɪz, -ɪz, -ɪŋ, -d
revivable
BR rɪ'vʌɪvəbl
AM rə'vaɪvəbəl, ri'vaɪvəbəl
revival
BR rɪ'vʌɪvl, -z
AM rə'vaɪvəl, ri'vaɪvəl, -z
revivalism
BR rɪ'vʌɪvl̩ɪz(ə)m, rɪ'vʌɪvəlɪz(ə)m
AM rə'vaɪvəˌlɪzəm, ri'vaɪvəˌlɪzəm
revivalist
BR rɪ'vʌɪvl̩ɪst, rɪ'vʌɪvəlɪst, -s
AM rə'vaɪv(ə)ləst, ri'vaɪv(ə)ləst, -s
revivalistic
BR rɪˌvʌɪvl̩'ɪstɪk, rɪˌvʌɪvə'lɪstɪk
AM ˌrəˌvaɪvə'lɪstɪk, ˌriˌvaɪvə'lɪstɪk
revive
BR rɪ'vʌɪv, -z, -ɪŋ, -d
AM rə'vaɪv, ri'vaɪv, -z, -ɪŋ, -d
reviver
BR rɪ'vʌɪvə(r), -z
AM rə'vaɪvər, ri'vaɪvər, -z
revivification
BR ˌriːvɪvɪfɪ'keɪʃn, riːˌvɪvɪfɪ'keɪʃn
AM ˌriˌvɪvəfə'keɪʃən
revivify
BR (ˌ)riː'vɪvɪfʌɪ, -z, -ɪŋ, -d
AM ri'vɪvəˌfaɪ, -z, -ɪŋ, -d
reviviscence
BR ˌrɛvɪ'vɪsns
AM ˌrɛvə'vɪsəns
reviviscent
BR ˌrɛvɪ'vɪsnt
AM ˌrɛvə'vɪsənt
Revlon®
BR 'rɛvlɒn
AM 'rɛvˌlɑn
revocability
BR ˌrɛvəkə'bɪlɪti
AM ˌrɛvəkə'bɪlɨdi, rəˌvoʊkə'bɪlɨdi, riˌvoʊkə'bɪlɨdi
revocable
BR 'rɛvəkəbl
AM 'rɛvəkəbəl, rə'voʊkəbəl, ri'voʊkəbəl
revocation
BR ˌrɛvə'keɪʃn, -z
AM ˌrɛvə'keɪʃən, riˌvoʊ'keɪʃən, -z
revocatory
BR 'rɛvəkət(ə)ri
AM 'rɛvəkəˌtɔri, rə'voʊkəˌtɔri, ri'voʊkəˌtɔri

revoke
BR rɪ'vəʊk, -s, -ɪŋ, -t
AM rə'voʊk, ri'voʊk, -s, -ɪŋ, -t

revoker
BR rɪ'vəʊkə(r), -z
AM rə'voʊkər, ri'voʊkər, -z

revolt
BR rɪ'vəʊlt, -s, -ɪŋ, -ɪd
AM rə'voʊlt, ri'voʊlt, -s, -ɪŋ, -əd

revolting
BR rɪ'vəʊltɪŋ
AM rə'voʊltɪŋ, ri'voʊltɪŋ

revoltingly
BR rɪ'vəʊltɪŋli
AM rə'voʊltɪŋli, ri'voʊltɪŋli

revolute
adjective
BR 'rɛvəl(j)uːt
AM 'rɛvəˌl(j)ut

revolution
BR ˌrɛvə'l(j)uːʃn, -z
AM ˌrɛvə'luʃən, -z

revolutionary
BR ˌrɛvə'l(j)uːʃn̩(ə)r|i, -ɪz
AM ˌrɛvəˈluʃəˌnɛri, -z

revolutionise
BR ˌrɛvə'l(j)uːʃn̩ʌɪz, ˌrɛvə'l(j)uːʃənʌɪz, -ɪz, -ɪŋ, -d
AM ˌrɛvə'luʃəˌnaɪz, -ɪz, -ɪŋ, -d

revolutionism
BR ˌrɛvə'l(j)uːʃn̩ɪz(ə)m, ˌrɛvə'l(j)uːʃənɪz(ə)m
AM ˌrɛvə'luʃəˌnɪzəm

revolutionist
BR ˌrɛvə'l(j)uːʃn̩ɪst, ˌrɛvə'l(j)uːʃənɪst, -s
AM ˌrɛvə'luʃənəst, -s

revolutionize
BR ˌrɛvə'l(j)uːʃn̩ʌɪz, ˌrɛvə'l(j)uːʃənʌɪz, -ɪz, -ɪŋ, -d
AM ˌrɛvə'luʃəˌnaɪz, -ɪz, -ɪŋ, -d

revolvable
BR rɪ'vɒlvəbl
AM rə'vɔlvəbəl, ri'vɔlvəbəl, rə'vɑlvəbəl, ri'vɑlvəbəl

revolve
BR rɪ'vɒlv, -z, -ɪŋ, -d
AM rə'vɔlv, ri'vɔlv, rə'vɑlv, ri'vɑlv, -z, -ɪŋ, -d

revolver
BR rɪ'vɒlvə(r), -z
AM rə'vɔlvər, ri'vɔlvər, rə'vɑlvər, ri'vɑlvər, -z

revue
BR rɪ'vjuː, -z
AM rə'vju, ri'vju, -z

revulsion
BR rɪ'vʌlʃn
AM rə'vəlʃən, ri'vəlʃən

revulsive
BR rɪ'vʌlsɪv
AM rə'vəlsɪv, ri'vəlsɪv

reward
BR rɪ'wɔːd, -z, -ɪŋ, -ɪd
AM rə'wɔ(ə)rd, ri'wɔ(ə)rd, -z, -ɪŋ, -əd

rewardingly
BR rɪ'wɔːdɪŋli
AM rə'wɔrdɪŋli, ri'wɔrdɪŋli

rewardless
BR rɪ'wɔːdləs
AM rə'wɔrdləs, ri'wɔrdləs

rewarewa
BR ˌreɪwə'reɪwə(*r*), -z
AM 'reɪwə'reɪwə, -z

rewash
BR ˌriː'wɒʃ, -ɪz, -ɪŋ, -t
AM ri'wɔʃ, ri'wɑʃ, -əz, -ɪŋ, -t

reweigh
BR ˌriː'weɪ, -z, -ɪŋ, -d
AM ri'weɪ, -z, -ɪŋ, -d

rewind[1]
noun
BR 'riːwʌɪnd, -z
AM 'riˌwaɪnd, -z

rewind[2]
verb
BR (ˌ)riː'wʌɪnd, -z, -ɪŋ
AM ri'waɪnd, -z, -ɪŋ

rewinder
BR (ˌ)riː'wʌɪndə(r), -z
AM ri'waɪndər, -z

rewirable
BR ˌriː'wʌɪərəbl
AM ri'waɪrəbəl

rewire
BR ˌriː'wʌɪə(r), -z, -ɪŋ, -d
AM ri'waɪ(ə)r, -z, -ɪŋ, -d

reword
BR ˌriː'wəːd, -z, -ɪŋ, -ɪd
AM ri'wɔ(ə)rd, -z, -ɪŋ, -əd

rework
BR ˌriː'wəːk, -s, -ɪŋ, -t
AM ri'wərk, -s, -ɪŋ, -t

reworking
BR ˌriː'wəːkɪŋ, -z
AM ri'wərkɪŋ, -z

rewound
BR (ˌ)riː'waʊnd
AM ri'waʊnd

rewrap
BR ˌriː'rap, -s, -ɪŋ, -t
AM ri'ræp, -s, -ɪŋ, -t

rewrite
BR ˌriː'rʌɪt, -s, -ɪŋ
AM ri'raɪ|t, -ts, -dɪŋ

rewritten
BR ˌriː'rɪtn
AM ri'rɪtn

rewrote
BR ˌriː'rəʊt
AM ri'roʊt

Rex
BR rɛks
AM rɛks

Rexine®
BR 'rɛksiːn
AM 'rɛkˌsin, 'rɛksən

Rey
BR reɪ
AM reɪ

Reyes
BR rʌɪz, reɪz
AM 'reɪəs

Reykjavik
BR 'rɛkjəvɪk, 'reɪkjəvɪk
AM 'reɪkjəˌvɪk

reynard
BR 'reɪnɑːd, 'rɛnəd, -z
AM reɪ'nɑrd, 'rɛˌnɑrd, 'reɪnərd, 'rɛnərd, -z

Reynolds
BR 'rɛnldz
AM 'rɛnəl(d)z

Rh
BR ˌɑːr'eɪtʃ
AM ˌɑr'eɪtʃ

rhabdomancy
BR 'rabdəˌmansi
AM 'ræbdəˌmænsi

Rhadamanthine
BR ˌradə'manθʌɪn
AM ˌrædə'mænˌθin, ˌrædə'mænˌθaɪn

Rhadamanthus
BR ˌradə'manθəs
AM ˌrædə'mænθəs

Rhaetian
BR 'riːʃn, 'riːʃɪən, -z
AM 'reɪʃ(i)ən, -z

Rhaetic
BR 'riːtɪk, -s
AM 'reɪdɪk, -z

Rhaeto-Romance
BR ˌriːtəʊrə(ʊ)'mans, -ɪz
AM ˌridoʊˌroʊ'mæns, -əz

Rhaeto-Romanic
BR ˌriːtəʊrə(ʊ)'manɪk, -s
AM ˌridoʊˌroʊ'mænɪk, -z

rhapsode
BR 'rapsəʊd, -z
AM 'ræpˌsoʊd, -z

rhapsodic
BR rap'sɒdɪk
AM (h)ræp'sɑdɪk

rhapsodical
BR rap'sɒdɪkl
AM (h)ræp'sɑdəkəl

rhapsodically
BR rap'sɒdɪkli
AM (h)ræp'sɑdək(ə)li

rhapsodise
BR 'rapsədʌɪz, -ɪz, -ɪŋ, -d
AM '(h)ræpsəˌdaɪz, -ɪz, -ɪŋ, -d

rhapsodist
BR 'rapsədɪst, -s
AM '(h)ræpsədəst, -z

rhapsodize
BR 'rapsədʌɪz, -ɪz, -ɪŋ, -d
AM '(h)ræpsəˌdaɪz, -ɪz, -ɪŋ, -d

rhapsody
BR 'rapsəd|i, -ɪz
AM '(h)ræpsədi, -z

rhatany
BR 'ratəni, 'ratn̩i, -ɪz
AM 'rætni

Rhayader
BR 'rʌɪədə(r)
AM 'raɪədər

rhea
BR rɪə(*r*), 'riːə(*r*), -z
AM 'riə, -z

rhebok
BR 'riːbɒk, -s
AM 'riˌbɑk, -s

Rheims
BR riːmz
AM rimz
FR Rɛ̃s

Rhein
BR rʌɪn
AM raɪn

rheme
BR riːm, -z
AM rim, -z

Rhemish
BR 'riːmɪʃ
AM 'rimɪʃ

Rhenish
BR 'rɛnɪʃ
AM 'rɛnɪʃ

rhenium
BR 'riːnɪəm
AM 'riniəm

rheological
BR ˌrɪə'lɒdʒɪkl
AM ˌriə'lɑdʒəkəl

rheologist
BR ˌriː'ɒlədʒɪst, -s
AM ri'ɑlədʒəst, -z

rheology
BR riː'ɒlədʒi
AM ri'ɑlədʒi

rheostat
BR 'riːəstat, -s
AM 'riəˌstæt, -s

rheostatic
BR ˌriːə(ʊ)'statɪk
AM ˌriə'stædɪk

rheotropic
BR ˌriːə(ʊ)ˈtrɒpɪk, ˌriːə(ʊ)ˈtrəʊpɪk
AM ˌriəˈtrɑpɪk

rheotropism
BR ˌriːə(ʊ)ˈtrəʊpɪz(ə)m
AM ˌriəˈtrɑˌpɪzəm

rhesus
BR ˈriːsəs, -ɪz
AM ˈrisəs, -əz

rhesus-negative
BR ˌriːsəsˈnɛɡətɪv
AM ¦risəsˈnɛɡədɪv

rhesus-positive
BR ˌriːsəsˈpɒzɪtɪv
AM ¦risəsˈpɑzədɪv

rhetor
BR ˈriːtə(r)
AM ˈrɛdər

rhetoric
BR ˈrɛtərɪk
AM ˈrɛdərɪk

rhetorical
BR rɪˈtɒrɪkl
AM rəˈtɔrəkəl

rhetorically
BR rɪˈtɒrɪkli
AM rəˈtɔrək(ə)li

rhetorician
BR ˌrɛtəˈrɪʃn, -z
AM ˌrɛdəˈrɪʃən, -z

Rhett
BR rɛt
AM rɛt

rheum
BR ruːm
AM (h)rum

rheumatic
BR ruːˈmatɪk, -s
AM ruˈmædɪk, -s

rheumatically
BR ruːˈmatɪkli
AM ruˈmædək(ə)li

rheumatic fever
BR ruːˌmatɪk ˈfiːvə(r)
AM ru¦mædɪk ˈfivər

rheumaticky
BR ruːˈmatɪki
AM ruˈmædəki, rəˈmædəki

rheumatism
BR ˈruːmətɪz(ə)m
AM ˈruməˌtɪzəm

rheumatoid
BR ˈruːmətɔɪd
AM ˈruməˌtɔɪd

rheumatological
BR ˌruːmətəˈlɒdʒɪkl
AM ¦rumədəˈlɑdʒəkəl

rheumatologist
BR ˌruːməˈtɒlədʒɪst, -s
AM ˌruməˈtɑlədʒəst, -s

rheumatology
BR ˌruːməˈtɒlədʒi
AM ˌruməˈtɑlədʒi

rheumy
BR ˈruːmi
AM ˈrumi

Rhiannon
BR rɪˈanən, rɪˈanɒn
AM riˈænən

rhinal
BR ˈrʌɪnl
AM ˈraɪnəl

Rhine
BR rʌɪn
AM raɪn

Rhineland
BR ˈrʌɪnland
AM ˈraɪnˌlænd

Rhineland-Palatinate
BR ˌrʌɪnlandpəˈlatɪnət
AM ˈraɪnˌlændpəˈlætn̩ət, ˈraɪnˌlændpəˈlætn̩eɪt

rhinestone
BR ˈrʌɪnstəʊn, -z
AM ˈraɪnˌstoʊn, -z

rhinitis
BR rʌɪˈnʌɪtɪs
AM raɪˈnaɪdɪs

rhino
BR ˈrʌɪnəʊ, -z
AM ˈraɪnoʊ, -z

rhinoceros
BR rʌɪˈnɒs(ə)rəs, -ɪz
AM raɪˈnɑs(ə)rəs, -ɪz

rhinocerotic
BR rʌɪˌnɒsəˈrɒtɪk
AM raɪˌnɑsəˈrɑdɪk, ˌraɪnəsəˈrɑdɪk

rhinopharyngeal
BR ˌrʌɪnəʊfəˈrɪn(d)ʒ(ɪ)əl, ˌrʌɪnəʊfəˈrɪn(d)ʒl
AM ˌraɪnoʊfəˈrɪn(d)ʒ(i)əl

rhinoplastic
BR ˌrʌɪnə(ʊ)ˈplastɪk
AM ˌraɪnoʊˈplæstɪk

rhinoplasty
BR ˈrʌɪnə(ʊ)ˌplasti
AM ˈraɪnoʊˌplæsti

rhinoscope
BR ˈrʌɪnəskəʊp, -s
AM ˈraɪnəˌskoʊp, -z

rhizocarp
BR ˈrʌɪzəʊkɑːp, -s
AM ˈraɪzoʊˌkɑrp, -z

rhizoid
BR ˈrʌɪzɔɪd
AM ˈraɪˌzɔɪd

rhizome
BR ˈrʌɪzəʊm, -z
AM ˈraɪˌzoʊm, -z

rhizopod
BR ˈrʌɪzə(ʊ)pɒd, -z
AM ˈraɪzəˌpɑd, -z

rho
BR rəʊ
AM roʊ

Rhoda
BR ˈrəʊdə(r)
AM ˈroʊdə

rhodamine
BR ˈrəʊdəmiːn, -z
AM ˈroʊdəˌmin, ˈroʊdəmən, -z

Rhode Island
BR ˌrəʊd ˈʌɪlənd
AM roʊˈdaɪlənd

Rhodes
BR rəʊdz
AM roʊdz

Rhodesia
BR rə(ʊ)ˈdiːʃə(r), rə(ʊ)ˈdiːʒə(r)
AM roʊˈdiʒə

Rhodesian
BR rə(ʊ)ˈdiːʃn, rə(ʊ)ˈdiːʒn, -z
AM roʊˈdiʒən, -z

Rhodian
BR ˈrəʊdiən, -z
AM ˈroʊdiən, -z

rhodium
BR ˈrəʊdiəm
AM ˈroʊdiəm

rhodochrosite
BR ˌrəʊdəˈkrəʊsʌɪt
AM ˌroʊdəˈkroʊˌsaɪt, roʊˈdɑkrəˌsaɪt

rhododendron
BR ˌrəʊdəˈdɛndr(ə)n, -z
AM ˌroʊdəˈdɛndrən, -z

Rhodope
BR ˈrɒdəpi, rɒˈdəʊpi
AM ˈrɑdəpi

Rhodophyta
BR ˌrəʊdə(ʊ)ˈfʌɪtə(r)
AM ˌroʊdoʊˈfaɪdə

rhodopsin
BR rə(ʊ)ˈdɒpsɪn
AM roʊˈdɑpsən

rhodora
BR rə(ʊ)ˈdɔːrə(r), -z
AM rəˈdɔrə, -z

Rhodri
BR ˈrɒdri
AM ˈrɑdri

rhomb
BR rɒm(b), -z
AM rɑm(b), -z

rhombi
BR ˈrɒmbʌɪ
AM ˈrɑmˌbaɪ

rhombic
BR ˈrɒmbɪk
AM ˈrɑmbɪk

rhombohedra
BR ˌrɒmbəˈhiːdrə(r)
AM ˌrɑmboʊˈhidrə

rhombohedral
BR ˌrɒmbəˈhiːdr(ə)l
AM ˌrɑmboʊˈhidrəl

rhombohedron
BR ˌrɒmbəˈhiːdrən, -z
AM ˌrɑmboʊˈhidrən, ˌrɑmboʊˈhiˌdrɑn, -z

rhomboid
BR ˈrɒmbɔɪd, -z
AM ˈrɑmˌbɔɪd, -z

rhomboidal
BR rɒmˈbɔɪdl
AM rɑmˈbɔɪdəl

rhomboidally
BR rɒmˈbɔɪdl̩i
AM rɑmˈbɔɪd(ə)li

rhomboidei
BR rɒmˈbɔɪdɪʌɪ
AM rɑmˈbɔɪdiˌi

rhomboideus
BR rɒmˈbɔɪdɪəs
AM rɑmˈbɔɪdiəs

rhombus
BR ˈrɒmbəs, -ɪz
AM ˈrɑmbəs, -əz

rhona
BR ˈrəʊnə(r)
AM ˈroʊnə

Rhondda
BR ˈrɒnðə(r), ˈrɒndə(r)
AM ˈrɑndə
WE ˈrɒnða

Rhône
BR rəʊn
AM roʊn

Rhoose
BR ruːs
AM rus

Rhos
BR rəʊs
AM roʊs
WE ros

Rhossili
BR rɒˈsɪli
AM rəˈsɪli

rhotic
BR ˈrəʊtɪk, -s
AM ˈroʊdɪk, -s

rhoticity
BR rə(ʊ)ˈtɪsɪti
AM roʊˈtɪsɪdi

rhubarb
BR ˈruːbɑːb
AM ˈruˌbɑrb

Rhuddlan
BR ˈrɪðlən, ˈrʌðlən
AM ˈrɪðlən
WE ˈrɪðlan

Rhum
BR rʌm
AM rʊm

rhumb
BR rʌm, -z
AM rəm, -z

rhumba
BR ˈrʌmbə(r), -z, -ɪŋ, -d
AM ˈrəmbə, -z, -ɪŋ, -d

rhumb-line
BR ˈrʌmlʌɪn, -z
AM ˈrəmˌlaɪn, -z

Rhydderch
BR ˈrʌðəx, ˈrʌðək
AM ˈrəðək

WE 'rʌðerx
Rhydding
BR 'rɪdɪŋ
AM 'rɪdɪŋ
Rhyl
BR rɪl
AM rɪl
rhyme
BR rʌɪm, -z, -ɪŋ, -d
AM raɪm, -z, -ɪŋ, -d
rhymeless
BR 'rʌɪmlɨs
AM 'raɪmlɨs
rhymer
BR 'rʌɪmə(r), -z
AM 'raɪmər, -z
rhymester
BR 'rʌɪmstə(r), -z
AM 'raɪmstər, -z
rhymist
BR 'rʌɪmɪst, -s
AM 'raɪmɪst, -z
Rhymney
BR 'rʌmni
AM 'rʊmni
rhyolite
BR 'rʌɪəlʌɪt, -s
AM 'raɪə,laɪt, -s
Rhys
BR riːs
AM rɪs
rhythm
BR 'rɪð(ə)m, -z
AM 'rɪðəm, -z
rhythm-and-blues
BR ,rɪðm̩(ə)n(d)'bluːz, ,rɪðəm(ə)n(d)'bluːz
AM 'rɪðəmən,bluz
rhythmic
BR 'rɪðmɪk
AM 'rɪðmɪk
rhythmical
BR 'rɪðmɨkl
AM 'rɪðmɨkəl
rhythmically
BR 'rɪðmɨkli
AM 'rɪðmɨk(ə)li
rhythmicity
BR ,rɪð'mɪsɨti
AM ,rɪð'mɪsɨdi
rhythmist
BR 'rɪðmɪst, -s
AM 'rɪðmɪst, -z
rhythmless
BR 'rɪð(ə)mləs
AM 'rɪðəmləs
ria
BR 'riːə(r), -z
AM 'riə, -z
rial
BR rɪ'ɑːl, 'riːɑːl, -z
AM ri'(j)ɑl, -z
rialto
BR rɪ'altəʊ, -z
AM ri'æl,toʊ, -z
rib
BR rɪb, -z, -ɪŋ, -d
AM rɪb, -z, -ɪŋ, -d
ribald
BR 'rɪbld, 'rɪbɔːld
AM 'rɪbəld, 'rɪ,bɔld, 'raɪ,bɔld, 'rɪ,bɑld, 'raɪ,bɑld
ribaldry
BR 'rɪbldri
AM 'rɪbəldri, 'rɪ,bɔldri, 'raɪ,bɔldri, 'rɪ,bɑldri, 'raɪ,bɑldri
riband
BR 'rɪb(ə)nd, -z
AM 'rɪbən(d), -z
Ribbentrop
BR 'rɪbntrɒp
AM 'rɪb(ə)n,trɑp
ribber
BR 'rɪbə(r), -z
AM 'rɪbər, -z
ribbing
BR 'rɪbɪŋ, -z
AM 'rɪbɪŋ, -z
Ribble
BR 'rɪbl
AM 'rɪbəl
ribbon
BR 'rɪb(ə)n, -z, -d
AM 'rɪbən, -z, -d
ribbonfish
BR 'rɪb(ə)nfɪʃ
AM 'rɪbən,fɪʃ
ribcage
BR 'rɪbkeɪdʒ, -ɨz
AM 'rɪb,keɪdʒ, -ɨz
Ribena®
BR rʌɪ'biːnə(r)
AM raɪ'binə
ribless
BR 'rɪblɨs
AM 'rɪblɨs
riboflavin
BR ,rʌɪbə(ʊ)'fleɪvɪn
AM ,raɪbə'fleɪvɨn
riboflavine
BR ,rʌɪbə(ʊ)'fleɪviːn
AM ,raɪbə'fleɪvin
ribonucleic
BR ,rʌɪbə(ʊ)njuː'kleɪɪk
AM ,raɪboʊn(j)u'kliɪk
ribose
BR 'rʌɪbəʊz, 'rʌɪbəʊs, -ɨz
AM 'raɪ,boʊz, 'raɪ,boʊs, -əz
ribosomal
BR ,rʌɪbə(ʊ)'səʊml
AM raɪ'bɑsəməl
ribosome
BR 'rʌɪbəsəʊm, -z
AM 'raɪbə,soʊm, -z
ribwort
BR 'rɪbwəːt, -s
AM 'rɪbwərt, 'rɪb,wɔ(ə)rt, -z
Ricardo
BR rɪ'kɑːdəʊ
AM rə'kardoʊ
rice
BR rʌɪs
AM raɪs
ricer
BR 'rʌɪsə(r), -z
AM 'raɪsər, -z
ricercar
BR ,riːtʃə'kɑː(r), 'riːtʃəkɑː(r), -z
AM ,ritʃər'kar, -z
ricercare
BR ,riːtʃə'kɑːreɪ, ,riːtʃə'kɑːr|i, 'riːtʃəkɑːreɪ, 'riːtʃəkɑːr|i, -ɪz
AM ,ritʃər'ka,reɪ, -z
rich
BR rɪtʃ, -ɨz, -ə(r), -ɨst
AM rɪtʃ, -ɨz, -ə(r), -ɨst
Richard
BR 'rɪtʃəd
AM 'rɪtʃərd
Richards
BR 'rɪtʃədz
AM 'rɪtʃərdz
Richardson
BR 'rɪtʃəds(ə)n
AM 'rɪtʃərdsən
Richelieu
BR 'riːʃ(ə)ljəː(r), 'rɪʃ(ə)ljəː(r)
AM 'rɪʃəl(j)u, rɪʃəl'ju
richen
BR 'rɪtʃ|n, -nz, -n̩ɪŋ\-(ə)nɪŋ, -d
AM 'rɪtʃən, -z, -ɪŋ, -d
Richie
BR 'rɪtʃi
AM 'rɪtʃi
richly
BR 'rɪtʃli
AM 'rɪtʃli
Richmal
BR 'rɪtʃml
AM 'rɪtʃməl
Richmond
BR 'rɪtʃm(ə)nd
AM 'rɪtʃmən(d)
richness
BR 'rɪtʃnɨs
AM 'rɪtʃnɨs
Richter
BR 'rɪktə(r)
AM 'rɪktər
ricin
BR 'rʌɪsɪn, 'rɪsɪn
AM 'raɪsən, 'rɪsən
rick
BR rɪk, -s
AM rɪk, -s
Rickard
BR 'rɪkɑːd
AM 'rɪkərd
Rickards
BR 'rɪkɑːdz
AM 'rɪkərdz
Rickenbacker
BR 'rɪk(ə)nbakə(r)
AM 'rɪkən,bækər
ricketily
BR 'rɪkɪtɨli
AM 'rɪkɨdɨli
ricketiness
BR 'rɪkɪtɪnɨs
AM 'rɪkɨdinɨs
rickets
BR 'rɪkɪts
AM 'rɪkɨts
Rickett
BR 'rɪkɪt
AM 'rɪkɨt
Ricketts
BR 'rɪkɪts
AM 'rɪkɨts
rickettsia
BR rɪ'kɛtsɪə(r), -z
AM rə'kɛtsiə, -z
rickettsiae
BR rɪ'kɛtsɪiː
AM rə'kɛtsi,i, rə'kɛtsi,aɪ
rickettsial
BR rɪ'kɛtsɪəl
AM rə'kɛtsiəl
rickety
BR 'rɪkɪt|i, -ɪə(r), -ɪɨst
AM 'rɪkɨdi, -ər, -ɨst
rickey
BR 'rɪk|i, -ɪz
AM 'rɪki, -z
Rickmansworth
BR 'rɪkmənzwəːθ
AM 'rɪkmənz,wərθ
Rickover
BR 'rɪkəʊvə(r)
AM 'rɪk,oʊvər
rickrack
BR 'rɪkrak
AM 'rɪk,ræk
Ricks
BR rɪks
AM rɪks
ricksha
BR 'rɪkʃɔː(r), -z
AM 'rɪk,ʃɔ, 'rɪk,ʃɑ, -z
rickshaw
BR 'rɪkʃɔː(r), -z
AM 'rɪk,ʃɔ, 'rɪk,ʃɑ, -z
Ricky
BR 'rɪki
AM 'rɪki
ricochet
BR 'rɪkəʃ|eɪ, 'rɪkəʃ|ɛt, -eɪz\-ɛts, -eɪɪŋ\-ɛtɪŋ, -eɪd\-ɛtɨd
AM 'rɪkə,ʃeɪ, -z, -ɪŋ, -d
Ricoh
BR 'riːkəʊ
AM 'rikoʊ

ricotta
BR rɪˈkɒtə(r)
AM rəˈkɑdə

ricrac
BR ˈrɪkrak, -s
AM ˈrɪkˌræk, -z

rictal
BR ˈrɪktl
AM ˈrɪktl

rictus
BR ˈrɪktəs
AM ˈrɪktəs

rid
BR rɪd, -z, -ɪŋ
AM rɪd, -z, -ɪŋ

ridable
BR ˈrʌɪdəbl
AM ˈraɪdəbəl

riddance
BR ˈrɪd(ə)ns
AM ˈrɪdns

Riddell
BR rɪˈdɛl, ˈrɪdl
AM ˈrɪdəl, rəˈdɛl

ridden
BR ˈrɪdn
AM ˈrɪdən

Ridding
BR ˈrɪdɪŋ
AM ˈrɪdɪŋ

riddle
BR ˈrɪd|l, -lz, -l̩ɪŋ\-lɪŋ, -ld
AM ˈrɪd|əl, -əlz, -(ə)lɪŋ, -əld

riddler
BR ˈrɪdl̩ə(r), ˈrɪdlə(r), -z
AM ˈrɪd(ə)lər, -z

riddlingly
BR ˈrɪdl̩ɪŋli, ˈrɪdlɪŋli
AM ˈrɪd(ə)lɪŋli

ride
BR rʌɪd, -z, -ɪŋ
AM raɪd, -z, -ɪŋ

rideable
BR ˈrʌɪdəbl
AM ˈraɪdəbəl

Rideout
BR ˈrʌɪdaʊt
AM ˈraɪˌdaʊt

rider
BR ˈrʌɪdə(r), -z
AM ˈraɪdər, -z

riderless
BR ˈrʌɪdələs
AM ˈraɪdərləs

ridge
BR rɪdʒ, -ɨz, -ɪŋ, -d
AM rɪdʒ, -ɨz, -ɪŋ, -d

ridgel
BR ˈrɪdʒl, -z
AM ˈrɪdʒəl, -z

ridgepole
BR ˈrɪdʒpəʊl, -z
AM ˈrɪdʒˌpoʊl, -z

ridgeway
BR ˈrɪdʒweɪ, -z
AM ˈrɪdʒˌweɪ, -z

Ridgway
BR ˈrɪdʒweɪ
AM ˈrɪdʒˌweɪ

ridgy
BR ˈrɪdʒ|i, -ɪə(r), -ɪɪst
AM ˈrɪdʒi, -ər, -ɨst

ridicule
BR ˈrɪdɨkjuːl, -z, -ɪŋ, -d
AM ˈrɪdɨˌkjul, -z, -ɪŋ, -d

ridiculous
BR rɪˈdɪkjʉləs
AM rəˈdɪkjələs

ridiculously
BR rɪˈdɪkjʉləsli
AM rəˈdɪkjələsli

ridiculousness
BR rɪˈdɪkjʉləsnəs
AM rəˈdɪkjələsnəs

riding
BR ˈrʌɪdɪŋ, -z
AM ˈraɪdɪŋ, -z

Ridley
BR ˈrɪdli
AM ˈrɪdli

Riemann
BR ˈriːmən
AM ˈrimən

Riesling
BR ˈriːzlɪŋ, ˈriːslɪŋ
AM ˈrizlɪŋ, ˈrisˌlɪŋ

Rievaulx
BR ˈriːvəʊ, ˈrɪvəz
AM riˈvoʊ, ˈrivoʊ

Rif
BR rɪf
AM rɪf

rifampicin
BR rɪˈfampɪsɪn
AM rəˈfæmpəsɪn

rifampin
BR rɪˈfampɪn
AM rəˈfæmpɪn

rife
BR rʌɪf
AM raɪf

rifeness
BR ˈrʌɪfnɨs
AM ˈraɪfnɨs

riff
BR rɪf, -s
AM rɪf, -s

riffle
BR ˈrɪf|l, -lz, -l̩ɪŋ\-lɪŋ, -ld
AM ˈrɪf|əl, -əlz, -(ə)lɪŋ, -əld

riffraff
BR ˈrɪfraf
AM ˈrɪˌfræf

Rifkind
BR ˈrɪfkɪnd
AM ˈrɪfkɪnd

rifle
BR ˈrʌɪf|l, -lz, -l̩ɪŋ\-lɪŋ, -ld
AM ˈraɪf|əl, -əlz, -(ə)lɪŋ, -əld

rifleman
BR ˈrʌɪflmən
AM ˈraɪfəlmən

riflemen
BR ˈrʌɪflmən
AM ˈraɪfəlmən

riflescope
BR ˈrʌɪflskəʊp, -s
AM ˈraɪflˌskoʊp, -z

rifling
BR ˈrʌɪfl̩ɪŋ, ˈrʌɪflɪŋ, -z
AM ˈraɪf(ə)lɪŋ, -z

rift
BR rɪft, -s
AM rɪft, -s

riftless
BR ˈrɪftlɨs
AM ˈrɪf(t)lɨs

rifty
BR ˈrɪft|i, -ɪə(r), -ɪɪst
AM ˈrɪfti, -ər, -ɨst

rig
BR rɪg, -z, -ɪŋ, -d
AM rɪg, -z, -ɪŋ, -d

Riga
BR ˈriːgə(r)
AM ˈrigə

rigadoon
BR ˌrɪgəˈduːn, -z
AM ˌrɪgəˈdun, -z

rigamarole
BR ˈrɪg(ə)mərəʊl, -z
AM ˈrɪg(ə)məˌroʊl, -z

rigatoni
BR ˌrɪgəˈtəʊni
AM ˌrɪgəˈtoʊni

Rigby
BR ˈrɪgbi
AM ˈrɪgbi

Rigel
BR ˈrʌɪgl, ˈrʌɪdʒl
AM ˈraɪdʒəl

Rigg
BR rɪg
AM rɪg

rigger
BR ˈrɪgə(r), -z
AM ˈrɪgər, -z

rigging
BR ˈrɪgɪŋ, -z
AM ˈrɪgɪŋ, -z

Riggs
BR rɪgz
AM rɪgz

right
BR rʌɪt, -s, -ɪŋ, -ɨd
AM raɪ|t, -ts, -dɪŋ, -dɨd

rightable
BR ˈrʌɪtəbl
AM ˈraɪdəbəl

rightabout
BR ˌrʌɪtəˈbaʊt
AM ˈraɪdəˌbaʊt

rightangle
BR ˈrʌɪtˌaŋgl, -z, -d
AM ˌraɪtˈæŋgəl, -z, -d

right-back
BR ˈrʌɪtbak, ˌrʌɪtˈbak, -s
AM ˈraɪtˌbæk, -z

righten
BR ˈrʌɪt|n, -nz, -n̩ɪŋ\-nɪŋ, -nd
AM ˈraɪtn, -z, -ɪŋ, -d

righteous
BR ˈrʌɪtʃəs
AM ˈraɪtʃəs

righteously
BR ˈrʌɪtʃəsli
AM ˈraɪtʃəsli

righteousness
BR ˈrʌɪtʃəsnəs
AM ˈraɪtʃəsnəs

righter
BR ˈrʌɪtə(r), -z
AM ˈraɪdər, -z

rightful
BR ˈrʌɪtf(ʊ)l
AM ˈraɪtfəl

rightfully
BR ˈrʌɪtfʊli, ˈrʌɪtfl̩i
AM ˈraɪtfəli

rightfulness
BR ˈrʌɪtf(ʊ)lnəs
AM ˈraɪtfəlnəs

righthand
BR ˌrʌɪtˈhand
AM ˌraɪtˈhænd, ˈraɪdænd

right-handed
BR ˌrʌɪtˈhandɪd
AM ˌraɪtˈhæn(d)əd, ˈraɪdæn(d)əd

right-handedly
BR ˌrʌɪtˈhandɪdli
AM ˌraɪtˈhæn(d)ədli, ˈraɪdæn(d)ədli

right-handedness
BR ˌrʌɪtˈhandɪdnɨs
AM ˌraɪtˈhæn(d)ədnəs, ˈraɪdæn(d)ədnəs

right-hander
BR ˌrʌɪtˈhandə(r)
AM ˌraɪtˈhændər, ˈraɪdændər

rightho
BR ˌrʌɪtˈ(h)əʊ
AM ˌraɪtˈ(h)oʊ

rightish
BR ˈrʌɪtɪʃ
AM ˈraɪdɪʃ

rightism
BR ˈrʌɪtɪz(ə)m
AM ˈraɪˌtɪzəm

rightist
BR ˈrʌɪtɪst, -s
AM ˈraɪdɪst, -s

rightless
BR 'rʌɪtlɨs
AM 'raɪtlɨs
rightlessness
BR 'rʌɪtlɨsnɨs
AM 'raɪtlɨsnɨs
rightly
BR 'rʌɪtli
AM 'raɪtli
rightmost
BR 'rʌɪtməʊst
AM 'raɪt,moʊst
rightness
BR 'rʌɪtnɨs
AM 'raɪtnəs
righto
BR ,rʌɪt'əʊ
AM ,raɪ'doʊ
rightward
BR 'rʌɪtwəd, -z
AM 'raɪtwərd, -z
rigid
BR 'rɪdʒɪd
AM 'rɪdʒɨd
rigidify
BR rɪ'dʒɪdɪfʌɪ, -z, -ɪŋ, -d
AM rə'dʒɪdə,faɪ, -z, -ɪŋ, -d
rigidity
BR rɪ'dʒɪdɪti
AM rə'dʒɪdɨdi
rigidly
BR 'rɪdʒɨdli
AM 'rɪdʒɨdli
rigidness
BR 'rɪdʒɨdnɨs
AM 'rɪdʒɨdnɨs
rigmarole
BR 'rɪgmərəʊl, -z
AM 'rɪg(ə)mə,roʊl, -z
rigor[1]
shivering
BR 'rʌɪgɔː(r), 'rɪgə(r)
AM 'rɪgər
rigor[2]
BR 'rɪgə(r), -z
AM 'rɪgər, -z
rigorism
BR 'rɪg(ə)rɪz(ə)m
AM 'rɪgə,rɪzəm
rigor mortis
BR ,rɪgə 'mɔːtɪs
AM ,rɪgər 'mɔrdəs
rigorous
BR 'rɪg(ə)rəs
AM 'rɪg(ə)rəs
rigorously
BR 'rɪg(ə)rəsli
AM 'rɪg(ə)rəsli
rigorousness
BR 'rɪg(ə)rəsnəs
AM 'rɪg(ə)rəsnəs
rigour
BR 'rɪgə(r), -z
AM 'rɪgər, -z
Rigsby
BR 'rɪgzbi
AM 'rɪgzbi
Rigveda
BR ,rɪg'veɪdə(r)
AM ,rɪg'veɪdə
Rijeka
BR rɪ'jɛkə(r)
AM rɪ'jɛkə
Rijksmuseum
BR 'rʌɪksmjuː,ziːəm
AM 'raɪks,muziəm
DU 'rɛiksmyzeəm
Rikki
BR 'rɪki
AM 'rɪki
Rikki-Tiki-Tavi
BR ,rɪkɪ,tɪkɪ'tɑːvi, ,rɪkɪ,tɪkɪ'teɪvi
AM ,rɪki,tɪki'tævi
rile
BR rʌɪl, -z, -ɪŋ, -d
AM raɪl, -z, -ɪŋ, -d
Riley
BR 'rʌɪli
AM 'raɪli
rilievo
BR rɪ'ljeɪvəʊ, -z
AM ri'li(eɪ)voʊ, -z
Rilke
BR 'rɪlkə(r)
AM 'rɪlkə
rill
BR rɪl, -z
AM rɪl, -z
rille
BR rɪl, -z
AM 'rɪlə, -z
rillettes
BR 'riːjɛt
AM ri'jɛt(s)
rim
BR rɪm, -z, -d
AM rɪm, -z, -d
Rimbaud
BR 'rambəʊ
AM ræm'boʊ
rime
BR rʌɪm
AM raɪm
rimester
BR 'rʌɪmstə(r), -z
AM 'raɪmstər, -z
rimfire
BR 'rɪmfʌɪə(r)
AM 'rɪm,faɪ(ə)r
Rimini
BR 'rɪmɨni
AM 'rɪmɨni
rimless
BR 'rɪmlɨs
AM 'rɪmlɨs
Rimmer
BR 'rɪmə(r)
AM 'rɪmər
Rimmon
BR 'rɪmən
AM 'rɪmən
rimose
BR rʌɪ'məʊs
AM raɪ'moʊs, raɪ'moʊz
rimous
BR 'rʌɪməs
AM 'raɪməs
rimrock
BR 'rɪmrɒk, -s
AM 'rɪm,rɑk, -s
Rimsky-Korsakov
BR ,rɪmskɪ'kɔːsəkɒf
AM 'rɪmski'kɔrsə,kɔf, 'rɪmski'kɔrsə,kɑf
rimu
BR 'riːmuː, -z
AM 'rɪmu, -z
rimy
BR 'rʌɪm|i, -ɪə(r), -ɪɨst
AM 'raɪmi, -ər, -ɨst
rind
BR rʌɪnd, -z
AM raɪnd, -z
rinderpest
BR 'rɪndəpɛst
AM 'rɪndər,pɛst
rindless
BR 'rʌɪndlɨs
AM 'raɪn(d)lɨs
ring
BR rɪŋ, -z, -ɪŋ, -d
AM rɪŋ, -z, -ɪŋ, -d
ringbark
BR 'rɪŋbɑːk, -s, -ɪŋ, -t
AM 'rɪŋ,bɑrk, -s, -ɪŋ, -t
ringbinder
BR ,rɪŋ'bʌɪndə(r), 'rɪŋ,bʌɪndə(r), -z
AM 'rɪŋ,baɪndər, -z
ringbolt
BR 'rɪŋbəʊlt, -s
AM 'rɪŋ,boʊlt, -z
ring-dove
BR 'rɪŋdʌv, -z
AM 'rɪŋ,dəv, -z
ringent
BR 'rɪn(d)ʒ(ə)nt
AM 'rɪndʒənt
ringer
BR 'rɪŋə(r), -z
AM 'rɪŋər, -z
ring-fence
BR 'rɪŋfɛns, ,rɪŋ'fɛns, -ɪz, -ɪŋ, -t
AM 'rɪŋ,fɛns, -əz, -ɪŋ, -t
ringhals
BR 'rɪŋhals, -ɪz
AM 'rɪŋ,(h)ælz, -əz
ringingly
BR 'rɪŋɪŋli
AM 'rɪŋɪŋli
ringleader
BR 'rɪŋ,liːdə(r), -z
AM 'rɪŋ,lidər, -z
ringless
BR 'rɪŋlɨs
AM 'rɪŋlɨs
ringlet
BR 'rɪŋlɨt, -s
AM 'rɪŋlɨt, -s
ringleted
BR 'rɪŋlɨtɨd
AM 'rɪŋlɨdɨd
ringletted
BR 'rɪŋlɨtɨd
AM 'rɪŋlɨdɨd
ringlety
BR 'rɪŋlɨti
AM 'rɪŋlɨdi
ringmaster
BR 'rɪŋ,mɑːstə(r), 'rɪŋ,mastə(r), -z
AM 'rɪŋ,mæstər, -z
ringpull
BR 'rɪŋpʊl, -z
AM 'rɪŋ,pʊl, -z
ringside
BR 'rɪŋsʌɪd
AM 'rɪŋ,saɪd
ringsider
BR 'rɪŋsʌɪdə(r), -z
AM 'rɪŋ,saɪdər, -z
ringster
BR 'rɪŋstə(r), -z
AM 'rɪŋstər, -z
ringtail
BR 'rɪŋteɪl, -z
AM 'rɪŋ,teɪl, -z
Ringwood
BR 'rɪŋwʊd
AM 'rɪŋ,wʊd
ringworm
BR 'rɪŋwəːm
AM 'rɪŋ,wərm
rink
BR rɪŋk, -s
AM rɪŋk, -s
rinkhals
BR 'rɪŋ(k)hals, -ɪz
AM 'rɪŋ(k),(h)ælz, -əz
rinky-dink
BR 'rɪŋkɪdɪŋk
AM ¦rɪŋki¦dɪŋk
rinse
BR rɪns, -ɪz, -ɪŋ, -t
AM rɪns, -əz, -ɪŋ, -t
rinser
BR 'rɪnsə(r), -z
AM 'rɪnsər, -z
Rintoul
BR rɪn'tuːl, 'rɪntuːl
AM rɪn'tul, 'rɪn,tul
Rio
BR 'riːəʊ
AM 'rioʊ
Rio de Janeiro
BR ,riːəʊ də (d)ʒə'nɪərəʊ
AM 'rioʊ ,deɪ (d)ʒə'nɛroʊ, 'rioʊ ,di (d)ʒə'nɛroʊ
B PORT ,xiu de ʒɑ'nejru
L PORT ,Riu də ʒɑ'nɑjru

Río de la Plata
BR ˌriːəʊ də lə ˈplɑːtə(r), + ˈplatə(r)
AM ˈrioʊ ˌdeɪ lə ˈplɑdə

Río de Oro
BR ˌriːəʊ dɪ ˈɔːrəʊ
AM ˈrioʊ di ˈɔˌroʊ

Río Grande
BR ˌriːəʊ ˈgrand(i)
AM ¦rioʊ ˈgrænd

Rioja
BR rɪˈəʊkə(r), rɪˈɒkə(r), rɪˈəʊxə(r), rɪˈɒxə(r)
AM riˈoʊhɑ

Río Muni
BR ˌriːəʊ ˈm(j)uːni
AM ¦rioʊ ˈm(j)uni

Riordan
BR ˈrɪəd(ə)n
AM ˈrɪ(ə)rdən

Ríos
BR ˈriːəʊs
AM ˈrioʊs

riot
BR ˈrʌɪət, -s, -ɪŋ, -ɨd
AM ˈraɪə|t, -ts, -dɪŋ, -dəd

rioter
BR ˈrʌɪətə(r), -z
AM ˈraɪədər, -z

riotless
BR ˈrɪətləs
AM ˈraɪətləs

riotous
BR ˈrʌɪətəs
AM ˈraɪədəs

riotously
BR ˈrʌɪətəsli
AM ˈraɪədəsli

riotousness
BR ˈrʌɪətəsnəs
AM ˈraɪədəsnəs

RIP
BR ˌɑːrʌɪˈpiː
AM ˌɑrˌaɪˈpi

rip
BR rɪp, -s, -ɪŋ, -t
AM rɪp, -s, -ɪŋ, -t

riparian
BR rʌɪˈpɛːrɪən, rɪˈpɛːrɪən
AM rəˈpɛriən, raɪˈpɛriən

ripcord
BR ˈrɪpkɔːd, -z
AM ˈrɪpˌkɔ(ə)rd, -z

ripe
BR rʌɪp, -ə(r), -ɨst
AM raɪp, -ər, -ɪst

ripely
BR ˈrʌɪpli
AM ˈraɪpli

ripen
BR ˈrʌɪp|(ə)n, -(ə)nz, -(ə)nɪŋ\-n̩ɪŋ, -nd
AM ˈraɪp|ən, -ənz, -(ə)nɪŋ, -ənd

ripeness
BR ˈrʌɪpnɨs
AM ˈraɪpnɨs

ripieno
BR ˌrɪpɪˈeɪnəʊ, -z
AM rəpˈjeɪnoʊ, -z

Ripley
BR ˈrɪpli
AM ˈrɪpli

rip-off
BR ˈrɪpɒf, -s
AM ˈrɪpˌɔf, ˈrɪpˌɑf, -s

Ripon
BR ˈrɪp(ə)n
AM ˈrɪpən

ripost
BR rɪˈpɒst, -s, -ɪŋ, -ɨd
AM rəˈpoʊst, riˈpoʊst, -s, -ɪŋ, -əd

riposte
BR rɪˈpɒst, -s, -ɪŋ, -ɨd
AM rəˈpoʊst, riˈpoʊst, -s, -ɪŋ, -əd

ripper
BR ˈrɪpə(r), -z
AM ˈrɪpər, -z

ripple
BR ˈrɪp|l, -lz, -lɪŋ\-lɪŋ, -ld
AM ˈrɪp|əl, -əlz, -(ə)lɪŋ, -əld

ripplet
BR ˈrɪplɨt, -s
AM ˈrɪplɨt, -z

ripply
BR ˈrɪpl̩i, ˈrɪpli
AM ˈrɪp(ə)li

Rippon
BR ˈrɪp(ə)n
AM ˈrɪpən

riprap
BR ˈrɪprap, -s, -ɪŋ, -t
AM ˈrɪpˌræp, -s, -ɪŋ, -t

riproaring
BR ˌrɪpˈrɔːrɪŋ
AM ¦rɪpˈrɔrɪŋ

riproaringly
BR ˌrɪpˈrɔːrɪŋli
AM ¦rɪpˈrɔrɪŋli

ripsaw
BR ˈrɪpsɔː(r), -z
AM ˈrɪpˌsɔ, ˈrɪpˌsɑ, -z

ripsnorter
BR ˈrɪpˌsnɔːtə(r), -z
AM ¦rɪpˈsnɔrdər, -z

ripsnorting
BR ˈrɪpˌsnɔːtɪŋ
AM ¦rɪpˈsnɔrdɪŋ

ripsnortingly
BR ˈrɪpˌsnɔːtɪŋli
AM ¦rɪpˈsnɔrdɪŋli

ripstop
BR ˈrɪpstɒp, -s
AM ˈrɪpˌstɑp, -s

riptide
BR ˈrɪptʌɪd, -z
AM ˈrɪpˌtaɪd, -z

Ripuarian
BR ˌrɪpjʊˈɛːrɪən, -z
AM ¦rɪp(j)əˈwɛriən, -z

Rip van Winkle
BR ˌrɪp van ˈwɪŋkl
AM ˌrɪp ˌvæn ˈwɪŋkəl

Risborough
BR ˈrɪzb(ə)rə(r)
AM ˈrɪzˌbərə

RISC
BR rɪsk
AM rɪsk

Risca
BR ˈrɪskə(r)
AM ˈrɪskə

rise
BR rʌɪz, -ɨz, -ɪŋ
AM raɪz, -ɨz, -ɪŋ

risen
BR ˈrɪzn
AM ˈrɪzn

riser
BR ˈrʌɪzə(r), -z
AM ˈraɪzər, -z

rishi
BR ˈrɪʃ|i, -ɪz
AM ˈrɪʃi, -z

risibility
BR ˌrɪzɨˈbɪlɨti, ˌrʌɪzɨˈbɪlɨti
AM ˌrɪzəˈbɪlɨdi

risible
BR ˈrɪzɨbl, ˈrʌɪzɨbl
AM ˈrɪzəbəl

risibly
BR ˈrɪzɨbli, ˈrʌɪzɨbli
AM ˈrɪzəbli

rising
BR ˈrʌɪzɪŋ, -z
AM ˈraɪzɪŋ, -z

risk
BR rɪsk, -s, -ɪŋ, -t
AM rɪsk, -s, -ɪŋ, -t

riskily
BR ˈrɪskɨli
AM ˈrɪskɨli

riskiness
BR ˈrɪskɪnɨs
AM ˈrɪskinɨs

risky
BR ˈrɪsk|i, -ɪə(r), -ɪɨst
AM ˈrɪski, -ər, -ɨst

Risorgimento
BR rɪˌsɔːdʒɪˈmɛntəʊ
AM riˌsɔrdʒəˈmɛnˌ(t)oʊ

risotto
BR rɪˈzɒtəʊ, -z
AM rəˈzɔdoʊ, rəˈsɔdoʊ, rəˈzɑdoʊ, rəˈsɑdoʊ, -z

risqué
BR ˈrɪskeɪ, rɪˈskeɪ
AM rəˈskeɪ, rɪˈskeɪ

rissole
BR ˈrɪsəʊl, -z
AM rəˈsoʊl, ˈrɪˌsoʊl, -z

rit.
BR rɪt
AM rɪt

Rita
BR ˈriːtə(r)
AM ˈridə

Ritalin®
BR ˈrɪtəlɪn
AM ˈrɪdəlɪn

ritardando
BR ˌrɪtɑːˈdandəʊ, -z
AM ˌriˌtɑrˈdɑnˌdoʊ, -z

Ritchie
BR ˈrɪtʃi
AM ˈrɪtʃi

rite
BR rʌɪt, -s
AM raɪt, -s

riteless
BR ˈrʌɪtlɨs
AM ˈraɪtlɨs

ritenuti
BR ˌrɪtəˈn(j)uːtiː
AM ˌridəˈnudi

ritenuto
BR ˌrɪtəˈn(j)uːtəʊ, -z
AM ˌridəˈnudoʊ, -z

ritornelli
BR ˌrɪtəˈnɛliː, ˌrɪtɔːˈnɛliː
AM ˌridərˈnɛli

ritornello
BR ˌrɪtəˈnɛləʊ, ˌrɪtɔːˈnɛləʊ, -z
AM ˌridərˈnɛloʊ, -z

Ritson
BR ˈrɪts(ə)n
AM ˈrɪtsən

Ritter
BR ˈrɪtə(r)
AM ˈrɪdər

ritual
BR ˈrɪtʃʊəl, ˈrɪtʃ(ʉ)l, ˈrɪtjʊəl, ˈrɪtjʉl, -z
AM ˈrɪtʃ(əw)əl, -z

ritualisation
BR ˌrɪtʃʊəlʌɪˈzeɪʃn, ˌrɪtʃʉlʌɪˈzeɪʃn, ˌrɪtʃl̩ʌɪˈzeɪʃn, ˌrɪtjʊəlʌɪˈzeɪʃn, ˌrɪtjʉlʌɪˈzeɪʃn
AM ˌrɪtʃ(əw)ələˈzeɪʃən, ˌrɪtʃ(əw)əˌlaɪˈzeɪʃən

ritualise
BR ˈrɪtʃʊəlʌɪz, ˈrɪtʃʉlʌɪz, ˈrɪtʃl̩ʌɪz, ˈrɪtjʊəlʌɪz, ˈrɪtjʉlʌɪz, -ɨz, -ɪŋ, -d
AM ˈrɪtʃ(əw)əˌlaɪz, -ɨz, -ɪŋ, -d

ritualism
BR ˈrɪtʃʊəlɪz(ə)m, ˈrɪtʃʉlɪz(ə)m, ˈrɪtʃl̩ɪz(ə)m, ˈrɪtjʊəlɪz(ə)m, ˈrɪtjʉlɪz(ə)m
AM ˈrɪtʃ(əw)əˌlɪzəm

ritualistic
BR ˌrɪtʃʊəˈlɪstɪk, ˌrɪtʃʉˈlɪstɪk,

ˌrɪtʃl'ɪstɪk, ˌrɪtjʊə'lɪstɪk, ˌrɪtjʉ'lɪstɪk
AM ˌrɪtʃ(əw)ə'lɪstɪk

ritualistically
BR rɪtʃʊə'lɪstɨkli, ˌrɪtʃʉ'lɪstɨkli, ˌrɪtʃl'ɪstɨkli, ˌrɪtjʊə'lɪstɪk, ˌrɪtjʉ'lɪstɪkli
AM ˌrɪtʃ(əw)ə'lɪstək(ə)li

ritualization
BR ˌrɪtʃʊəlʌɪ'zeɪʃn, ˌrɪtʃʉlʌɪ'zeɪʃn, ˌrɪtʃl̩ʌɪ'zeɪʃn, ˌrɪtjʊəlʌɪ'zeɪʃn, ˌrɪtjʉlʌɪ'zeɪʃn
AM ˌrɪtʃ(əw)ələ'zeɪʃən, ˌrɪtʃ(əw)əˌlaɪ'zeɪʃən

ritualize
BR 'rɪtʃʊəlʌɪz, 'rɪtʃʉlʌɪz, 'rɪtʃl̩ʌɪz, 'rɪtjʊəlʌɪz, 'rɪtjʉlʌɪz, -ɨz, -ɪŋ, -d
AM 'rɪtʃ(əw)əˌlaɪz, -ɨz, -ɪŋ, -d

ritually
BR 'rɪtʃʊəli, 'rɪtʃʉli, 'rɪtʃl̩i, 'rɪtjʊəli, 'rɪtjʉli
AM 'rɪtʃ(əw)əli

Ritz
BR rɪts
AM rɪts

ritzily
BR 'rɪtsɨli
AM 'rɪtsɨli

ritziness
BR 'rɪtsɪnɨs
AM 'rɪtsinɨs

ritzy
BR 'rɪts|i, -ɪə(r), -ɪɨst
AM 'rɪtsi, -ər, -ɨst

rival
BR 'rʌɪv|l, -lz, -l̩ɪŋ\-əlɪŋ, -ld
AM 'raɪv|əl, -əlz, -(ə)lɪŋ, -əld

rivalry
BR 'rʌɪvlr|i, -ɪz
AM 'raɪvəlri, -z

rive
BR rʌɪv, -z, -ɪŋ, -d
AM raɪv, -z, -ɪŋ, -d

Rivelin
BR 'rɪvl̩ɪn, 'rɪvlɪn
AM 'rɪvələn

riven
BR 'rɪvn
AM 'rɪvən

river[1]
one who rives
BR 'rʌɪvə(r), -z
AM 'raɪvər, -z

river[2]
water
BR 'rɪvə(r), -z, -d
AM 'rɪvər, -z, -d

Rivera
BR rɪ'vɛːrə(r)
AM rə'vɛrə

riverain
BR 'rɪvəreɪn, -z
AM 'rɪvəˌreɪn, -z

riverbank
BR 'rɪvəbaŋk, -s
AM 'rɪvərˌbæŋk, -s

riverbed
BR 'rɪvəbɛd, -z
AM 'rɪvərˌbɛd, -z

riverboat
BR 'rɪvəbəʊt, -s
AM 'rɪvərˌboʊt, -s

riverfront
BR 'rɪvəfrʌnt, -s
AM 'rɪvərˌfrənt, -s

Riverina
BR ˌrɪvə'riːnə(r)
AM ˌrɪvə'rinə

riverine
BR 'rɪvərʌɪn
AM 'rɪvəˌraɪn, 'rɪvərən

riverless
BR 'rɪvələs
AM 'rɪvərləs

Rivers
BR 'rɪvəz
AM 'rɪvərz

riverside
BR 'rɪvəsʌɪd
AM 'rɪvərˌsaɪd

rivet
BR 'rɪv|ɪt, -ɪts, -ɨtɪŋ, -ɨtɨd
AM 'rɪvɨ|t, -ts, -dɪŋ, -dɨd

riveter
BR 'rɪvɨtə(r), -z
AM 'rɪvɨdər, -z

Riviera
BR ˌrɪvɪ'ɛːrə(r)
AM ˌrɪvi'ɛrə, rɪ'vjɛrə

rivière
BR ˌrɪvɪ'ɛː(r), -ɪz
AM ˌrɪvi'ɛ(ə)r, rɪ'vjɛr, -z

rivulet
BR 'rɪvjʉlɨt, 'rɪvjʉlɛt, -s
AM 'rɪv(j)ələt, -s

Rix
BR rɪks
AM rɪks

Riyadh
BR rɪ'jad, 'riːad, rɪ'jɑːd
AM ri'jɑd

riyal
BR rɪ'ɑːl, rɪ'al, 'riːɑːl, 'riːal, -z
AM ri'(j)ɔl, ri'(j)ɑl, -z

Rizla®
BR 'rɪzlə(r)
AM 'rɪzlər

roach
BR rəʊtʃ, -ɨz
AM roʊtʃ, -əz

road
BR rəʊd, -z
AM roʊd, -z

roadability
BR ˌrəʊdə'bɪlɨti
AM ˌroʊdə'bɪlɨdi

roadbed
BR 'rəʊdbɛd, -z
AM 'roʊdˌbɛd, -z

roadblock
BR 'rəʊdblɒk, -s
AM 'roʊdˌblɑk, -s

roadhog
BR 'rəʊdhɒg, -z
AM 'roʊdˌ(h)ɔg, 'roʊdˌ(h)ɑg, -z

roadholding
BR 'rəʊdˌhəʊldɪŋ
AM 'roʊdˌ(h)oʊldɪŋ

roadhouse
BR 'rəʊdhaʊ|s, -zɨz
AM 'roʊdˌ(h)aʊ|s, -zəz

roadie
BR 'rəʊd|i, -ɪz
AM 'roʊdi, -z

roadless
BR 'rəʊdləs
AM 'roʊdləs

roadliner
BR 'rəʊdˌlʌɪnə(r), -z
AM 'roʊdˌlaɪnər, -z

roadman
BR 'rəʊdman, 'rəʊdmən
AM 'roʊdˌmæn, 'roʊdmən

roadmen
BR 'rəʊdmɛn, 'rəʊdmən
AM 'roʊdˌmɛn, 'roʊdmən

roadroller
BR 'rəʊdˌrəʊlə(r), -z
AM 'roʊdˌroʊlər, -z

roadrunner
BR 'rəʊdˌrʌnə(r), -z
AM 'roʊdˌrənər, -z

roadshow
BR 'rəʊdʃəʊ, -z
AM 'roʊdˌʃoʊ, -z

roadside
BR 'rəʊdsʌɪd
AM 'roʊdˌsaɪd

roadstead
BR 'rəʊdstɛd, -z
AM 'roʊdˌstɛd, -z

roadster
BR 'rəʊdstə(r), -z
AM 'roʊdstər, -z

roadtest
BR 'rəʊdtɛst, -s, -ɪŋ, -ɨd
AM 'roʊdˌtɛst, -s, -ɪŋ, -əd

roadway
BR 'rəʊdweɪ, -z
AM 'roʊdˌweɪ, -z

roadwork
BR 'rəʊdwəːk, -s
AM 'roʊdˌwərk, -s

roadworthiness
BR 'rəʊdˌwəːðɪnɨs
AM 'roʊdˌwərðinɨs

roadworthy
BR 'rəʊdˌwəːði
AM 'roʊdˌwərði

Roald
BR 'rəʊəld
AM 'roʊəld
NO 'ruːal

roam
BR rəʊm, -z, -ɪŋ, -d
AM roʊm, -z, -ɪŋ, -d

roamer
BR 'rəʊmə(r), -z
AM 'roʊmər, -z

roan
BR rəʊn, -z
AM roʊn, -z

Roanoke
BR 'rəʊənəʊk
AM 'roʊəˌnoʊk

roar
BR rɔː(r), -z, -ɪŋ, -d
AM rɔ(ə)r, -z, -ɪŋ, -d

roarer
BR 'rɔːrə(r), -z
AM 'rɔrər, -z

roaring
BR 'rɔːrɪŋ, -z
AM 'rɔrɪŋ, -z

roaringly
BR 'rɔːrɪŋli
AM 'rɔrɪŋli

roast
BR rəʊst, -s, -ɪŋ, -ɨd
AM roʊst, -s, -ɪŋ, -əd

roaster
BR 'rəʊstə(r), -z
AM 'roʊstər, -z

roasting
BR 'rəʊstɪŋ, -z
AM 'roʊstɪŋ, -z

Roath
BR rəʊθ
AM roʊθ

rob
BR rɒb, -z, -ɪŋ, -d
AM rɑb, -z, -ɪŋ, -d

Robb
BR rɒb
AM rɑb

Robben Island
BR ˌrɒb(ɨ)n 'ʌɪlənd
AM ˌrɑbən 'aɪlənd

robber
BR 'rɒbə(r), -z
AM 'rɑbər, -z

robbery
BR 'rɒb(ə)r|i, -ɪz
AM 'rɑb(ə)ri, -z

Robbia
della Robbia
BR 'rɒbɪə(r)

AM ˈroʊbiə
Robbie
BR ˈrɒbi
AM ˈrɑbi
Robbins
BR ˈrɒbɪnz
AM ˈrɑbənz
robe
BR rəʊb, -z, -ɪŋ, -d
AM roʊb, -z, -ɪŋ, -d
Robens
BR ˈrəʊb(ɪ)nz
AM ˈroʊbənz
Roberson
BR ˈrəʊbəs(ə)n
AM ˈroʊbərsən
Robert
BR ˈrɒbət
AM ˈrɑbərt
Roberta
BR rə(ʊ)ˈbəːtə(*r*), rɒˈbəːtə(*r*)
AM rəˈbərdə
Roberts
BR ˈrɒbəts
AM ˈrɑbərts
Robertson
BR ˈrɒbəts(ə)n
AM ˈrɑbərtsən
Robeson
BR ˈrəʊbs(ə)n
AM ˈroʊb(ə)sən
Robespierre
BR ˈrəʊbzpɪɛː(r), ˈrəʊbzpɪə(r)
AM ˌroʊbzˈspjeɪ
Robey
BR ˈrəʊbi
AM ˈroʊbi
robin
BR ˈrɒbɪn, -z
AM ˈrɑbən, -z
Robina
BR rə(ʊ)ˈbiːnə(*r*), rɒˈbiːnə(*r*)
AM rɑˈbinə
Robin Goodfellow
BR ˌrɒbɪn ˈgʊdˌfɛləʊ
AM ˌrɑbən ˈgʊdˌfɛloʊ
Robin Hood
BR ˌrɒbɪn ˈhʊd
AM ˈrɑbən ˌ(h)ʊd
robinia
BR rə(ʊ)ˈbɪnɪə(*r*), rɒˈbɪnɪə(*r*), -z
AM roʊˈbɪniə, -z
Robins
BR ˈrɒbɪnz, ˈrəʊbɪnz
AM ˈrɑbənz
Robinson
BR ˈrɒbɪns(ə)n
AM ˈrɑbənsən
Robinson Crusoe
BR ˌrɒbɪns(ə)n ˈkruːsəʊ
AM ˌrɑbənsən ˈkruˌsoʊ
roborant
BR ˈrəʊb(ə)rənt, ˈrəʊb(ə)rn̩t, ˈrɒb(ə)rənt, ˈrɒb(ə)rn̩t, -s
AM ˈrɑbərənt, ˈroʊbərənt, -z
robot
BR ˈrəʊbɒt, -s
AM ˈroʊˌbɑt, ˈroʊbət, -s
robotic
BR rə(ʊ)ˈbɒtɪk, -s
AM roʊˈbɑdɪk, -s
robotically
BR rə(ʊ)ˈbɒtɨkli
AM roʊˈbɑdək(ə)li
robotisation
BR ˌrəʊbətʌɪˈzeɪʃn
AM ˌroʊbədəˈzeɪʃən, ˌroʊbəˌtaɪˈzeɪʃən
robotise
BR ˈrəʊbətʌɪz, -ɪz, -ɪŋ, -d
AM ˈroʊbəˌtaɪz, -ɪz, -ɪŋ, -d
robotization
BR ˌrəʊbətʌɪˈzeɪʃn
AM ˌroʊbədəˈzeɪʃən, ˌroʊbəˌtaɪˈzeɪʃən
robotize
BR ˈrəʊbətʌɪz, -ɪz, -ɪŋ, -d
AM ˈroʊbəˌtaɪz, -ɪz, -ɪŋ, -d
Rob Roy
BR ˌrɒb ˈrɔɪ
AM ˌrɑb ˈrɔɪ
Robsart
BR ˈrɒbsɑːt
AM ˈrɑbˌsɑrt
Robson
BR ˈrɒbs(ə)n
AM ˈrɑbsən
robust
BR rə(ʊ)ˈbʌst, ˈrəʊbʌst
AM roʊˈbəst, ˈroʊˌbəst
robustious
BR rə(ʊ)ˈbʌstɪəs, rə(ʊ)ˈbʌstʃəs
AM roʊˈbəstʃəs, rəˈbəstʃəs
robustly
BR rə(ʊ)ˈbʌstli, ˈrəʊbʌstli
AM roʊˈbəs(t)li, ˈroʊˌbəs(t)li
robustness
BR rə(ʊ)ˈbʌs(t)nəs, ˈrəʊbʌs(t)nəs
AM roʊˈbəs(t)nəs, ˈroʊˌbəs(t)nəs
Roby
BR ˈrəʊbi
AM ˈroʊbi
roc
BR rɒk, -s
AM rɑk, -s
rocaille
BR rə(ʊ)ˈkʌɪ
AM roʊˈkaɪ
rocambole
BR ˈrɒk(ə)mbəʊl, -z
AM ˈrɑkəmˌboʊl, -z
Rocco
BR ˈrɒkəʊ
AM ˈrɑkoʊ
Rochdale
BR ˈrɒtʃdeɪl
AM ˈrɑtʃˌdeɪl
Roche
BR rəʊ(t)ʃ, rɒʃ
AM roʊʃ
Rochelle
BR rɒˈʃɛl, rəˈʃɛl
AM rəˈʃɛl
roche moutonnée
BR ˌrɒʃ muːˈtɒneɪ, -z
AM ˈrɔʃ ˌmutnˈeɪ, -z
Rochester
BR ˈrɒtʃɪstə(r)
AM ˈrɑtˌʃəstər
rochet
BR ˈrɒtʃɪt, -s
AM ˈrɑtʃət, -s
Rochford
BR ˈrɒtʃfəd
AM ˈrɑtʃfə(r)d
rock
BR rɒk, -s, -ɪŋ, -t
AM rɑk, -s, -ɪŋ, -t
rockabilly
BR ˈrɒkəˌbɪli
AM ˈrɑkəˌbɪli
Rockall
BR ˈrɒkɔːl
AM ˈrɑkˌɔl, ˈrɑkˌɑl
rock and roll
BR ˌrɒk (ə)n(d) ˈrəʊl
AM ˈrɑk ən ˈroʊl
rock and roller
BR ˌrɒk (ə)n(d) ˈrəʊlə(r), -z
AM ˈrɑk ən ˈroʊlər, -z
rock-bed
BR ˈrɒkbɛd, -z
AM ˈrɑkˌbɛd, -z
rock-bottom
BR ˌrɒkˈbɒtəm
AM ˈrɑkˈbadəm
rockbound
BR ˈrɒkbaʊnd
AM ˈrɑkˌbaʊnd
rockburst
BR ˈrɒkbəːst, -s
AM ˈrɑkˌbərst, -z
rock-cake
BR ˈrɒkkeɪk, -s
AM ˈrɑ(k)ˌkeɪk, -z
rock-candy
BR ˌrɒkˈkandi
AM ˌrɑ(k)ˈkændi
Rockefeller
BR ˈrɒkəˌfɛlə(r)
AM ˈrɑkəˌfɛlər
rocker
BR ˈrɒkə(r), -z
AM ˈrɑkər, -z
rockery
BR ˈrɒk(ə)r|i, -ɪz
AM ˈrɑkəri, -z
rocket
BR ˈrɒk|ɪt, -ɪts, -ɪtɪŋ, -ɪtɪd
AM ˈrɑkə|t, -ts, -dɪŋ, -dəd
rocketeer
BR ˌrɒkɪˈtɪə(r), -z
AM ˌrɑkəˈtɪ(ə)r, -z
rocketry
BR ˈrɒkɪtri
AM ˈrɑkətri
rocketship
BR ˈrɒkɪtʃɪp, -s
AM ˈrɑkətˌʃɪp, -s
rockfall
BR ˈrɒkfɔːl, -z
AM ˈrɑkˌfɔl, ˈrɑkˌfɑl, -z
rockfish
BR ˈrɒkfɪʃ
AM ˈrɑkˌfɪʃ
Rockhampton
BR rɒkˈham(p)tən
AM rɑkˈhæm(p)tən
rockhopper
BR ˈrɒkˌhɒpə(r), -z
AM ˈrɑkˌ(h)ɑpər, -z
Rockies
BR ˈrɒkɪz
AM ˈrɑkiz
rockily
BR ˈrɒkɪli
AM ˈrɑkəli
rockiness
BR ˈrɒkɪnɪs
AM ˈrɑkinɪs
rockless
BR ˈrɒkləs
AM ˈrɑkləs
rocklet
BR ˈrɒklɪt, -s
AM ˈrɑklət, -z
rocklike
BR ˈrɒklʌɪk
AM ˈrɑkˌlaɪk
rockling
BR ˈrɒklɪŋ, -z
AM ˈrɑklɪŋ, -z
Rockne
BR ˈrɒkni
AM ˈrɑkni
rock 'n roll
BR ˌrɒk (ə)n ˈrəʊl
AM ˈrɑk ən ˈroʊl
rock 'n roller
BR ˌrɒk (ə)n ˈrəʊlə(r)
AM ˈrɑk ən ˈroʊlər
Rockwell
BR ˈrɒkw(ɛ)l
AM ˈrɑkˌwɛl

rock-wool
BR 'rɒkwʊl
AM 'rɑk,wʊl
rocky
BR 'rɒk|i, -ɪə(r), -ɪɪst
AM 'rɑki, -ər, -ɨst
Rocky Mountains
BR ,rɒkɪ 'maʊntɪnz
AM ,rɑki 'maʊn(tə)nz
rococo
BR rə'kəʊkəʊ
AM rə'koʊkoʊ, roʊ'koʊkoʊ, 'roʊkə,koʊ
rod
BR rɒd, -z
AM rɑd, -z
Roddenberry
BR 'rɒdnb(ə)ri
AM 'rɑdn,bɛri
Roddick
BR 'rɒdɪk
AM 'rɑdək
Roddy
BR 'rɒdi
AM 'rɑdi
rode
BR rəʊd
AM roʊd
rodent
BR 'rəʊdnt, -s
AM 'roʊdnt, -s
rodential
BR rə(ʊ)'dɛnʃl
AM roʊ'dɛn(t)ʃəl
rodenticide
BR rə(ʊ)'dɛntɪsʌɪd, -z
AM roʊ'dɛn(t)ə,saɪd, -z
rodeo
BR 'rəʊdɪəʊ, rə(ʊ)'deɪəʊ, -z
AM 'roʊdi,oʊ, roʊ'deɪoʊ, -z
Roderick
BR 'rɒd(ə)rɪk
AM 'rɑd(ə)rɪk
Rodger
BR 'rɒdʒə(r)
AM 'rɑdʒər
Rodgers
BR 'rɒdʒəz
AM 'rɑdʒərz
rodham
BR 'rɒdəm, -z
AM 'rɑdəm, -z
Rodin
BR 'rəʊdan, 'rəʊdã
AM roʊ'dæn
rodless
BR 'rɒdləs
AM 'rɑdləs
rodlet
BR 'rɒdlɪt, -s
AM 'rɑdlət, -z
rodlike
BR 'rɒdlʌɪk
AM 'rɑd,laɪk
Rodney
BR 'rɒdni
AM 'rɑdni
rodomontade
BR ,rɒdəmɒn'tɑːd, ,rɒdəmɒn'teɪd, -z
AM ,rɑdəmən'teɪd, ,rɑdə,mɑn'teɪd, ,rɑdəmən'tɑd, ,rɑdə,mɑn'tɑd, -z
Rodrigues
BR rɒ'driːgɛz
AM ,rɑd'rigəs, ,rɑd'ri,gɛz
Rodriguez
BR rɒ'driːgɛz
AM ,rɑd'rigəs, ,rɑd'ri,gɛz
Rodriquez
BR rɒ'driːkɛz
AM ,rɑd'rik(w)əs, ,rɑd'ri,k(w)ɛz
roe
BR rəʊ, -z, -d
AM roʊ, -z, -d
roebuck
BR 'rəʊbʌk, -s
AM 'roʊ,bək, -s
Roedean
BR 'rəʊdiːn
AM 'roʊ,din
roe-deer
BR 'rəʊdɪə(r)
AM 'roʊ,dɪ(ə)r
Roehampton
BR rəʊ'ham(p)tən, 'rəʊham(p)tən
AM ,roʊ'hæm(p)tən, 'roʊ,(h)æm(p)tən
roentgen
BR 'rʌntjən, 'rəːntjən, 'rɒntjən, 'rʌntgən, 'rəːntgən, 'rɒntgən
AM 'rɛntgən, 'rɛntdʒən
roentgenography
BR ,rʌntjə'nɒgrəfi, ,rəːntjə'nɒgrəfi, ,rɒntjə'nɒgrəfi, ,rʌntgə'nɒgrəfi, ,rəːntgə'nɒgrəfi, ,rɒntgə'nɒgrəfi
AM ,rɛntgə'nɑgrəfi, ,rɛntdʒə'nɑgrəfi
roentgenology
BR ,rʌntjə'nɒlədʒi, ,rəːntjə'nɒlədʒi, ,rɒntjə'nɒlədʒi, ,rʌntgə'nɒlədʒi, ,rəːntgə'nɒlədʒi, ,rɒntgə'nɒlədʒi
AM ,rɛntgə'nɑlədʒi, ,rɛntdʒə'nɑlədʒi
Roffey
BR 'rɒfi
AM 'rɔfi, 'rɑfi
rogation
BR rə(ʊ)'geɪʃn, -z
AM roʊ'geɪʃən, -z
rogational
BR rə(ʊ)'geɪʃn̩(ə)l, rə(ʊ)'geɪʃən(ə)l
AM roʊ'geɪʃ(ə)nəl
Rogationtide
BR rə(ʊ)'geɪʃntʌɪd
AM roʊ'geɪʃən,taɪd
roger
BR 'rɒdʒ|ə(r), -əz, -(ə)rɪŋ, -əd
AM 'rɑdʒər, -z, -ɪŋ, -d
Rogers
BR 'rɒdʒəz
AM 'rɑdʒərz
Roget
BR 'rɒʒeɪ
AM ,roʊ'ʒeɪ
rogue
BR rəʊg, -z
AM roʊg, -z
roguery
BR 'rəʊg(ə)r|i, -ɪz
AM 'roʊgəri, -z
roguish
BR 'rəʊgɪʃ
AM 'roʊgɪʃ
roguishly
BR 'rəʊgɪʃli
AM 'roʊgɪʃli
roguishness
BR 'rəʊgɪʃnɪs
AM 'roʊgɪʃnɪs
Rohan
BR 'rəʊən
AM 'roʊ,hæn, 'roʊən
roil
BR rɔɪl, -z, -ɪŋ, -d
AM rɔɪl, -z, -ɪŋ, -d
roister
BR 'rɔɪst|ə(r), -əz, -(ə)rɪŋ, -əd
AM 'rɔɪst|ər, -ərz, -(ə)rɪŋ, -ərd
roisterer
BR 'rɔɪst(ə)rə(r), -z
AM 'rɔɪst(ə)rər, -z
roistering
BR 'rɔɪst(ə)rɪŋ, -z
AM 'rɔɪst(ə)rɪŋ, -z
roisterous
BR 'rɔɪst(ə)rəs
AM 'rɔɪst(ə)rəs
Rojas
BR 'rəʊhas
AM 'roʊ,hɑs
Rokeby
BR 'rəʊkbi
AM 'roʊkbi
Roker
BR 'rəʊkə(r)
AM 'roʊkər
Roland
BR 'rəʊlənd
AM 'roʊlən(d)
rôle
BR rəʊl, -z
AM roʊl, -z
role-play
BR 'rəʊlpleɪ, -z
AM 'roʊl,pleɪ, -z
Rolex®
BR 'rəʊlɛks
AM 'roʊ,lɛks
Rolf
BR rɒlf
AM rɔlf, rɑlf
Rolfe
BR rɒlf
AM rɔlf, rɑlf
roll
BR rəʊl, -z, -ɪŋ, -d
AM roʊl, -z, -ɪŋ, -d
rollable
BR 'rəʊləbl
AM 'roʊləbəl
rollaway
BR 'rəʊləweɪ, -z
AM 'roʊlə,weɪ, -z
rollback
BR 'rəʊlbak, -s
AM 'roʊl,bæk, -s
rollbar
BR 'rəʊlbɑː(r), -z
AM 'roʊl,bɑr, -z
rollcall
BR 'rəʊlkɔːl, -z
AM 'roʊl,kɔl, 'roʊl,kɑl, -z
Rollei
BR 'rəʊlʌɪ
AM 'roʊlaɪ
roller
BR 'rəʊlə(r), -z
AM 'roʊlər, -z
rollerball
BR 'rəʊləbɔːl, -z
AM 'roʊlər,bɔl, 'roʊlər,bɑl, -z
rollerblade
BR 'rəʊləbleɪd, -z, -ɪŋ, -ɨd
AM 'roʊlər,bleɪd, -z, -ɪŋ, -ɨd
rollerblader
BR 'rəʊlə,bleɪdə(r), -z
AM 'roʊlər,bleɪdər, -z
rollick
BR 'rɒl|ɪk, -ɪks, -ɨkɪŋ, -ɪkt
AM 'rɑlɪk, -s, -ɪŋ, -t
rollickingly
BR 'rɒlɨkɪŋli
AM 'rɑlɪkɪŋli
Rollins
BR 'rɒlɪnz
AM 'rɑlənz
rollmop
BR 'rəʊlmɒp, -s
AM 'roʊl,mɑp, -s
Rollo
BR 'rɒləʊ
AM 'rɑloʊ

roll-on
BR 'rəʊlɒn, -z
AM 'roʊlˌɑn, -z

roll-on roll-off
BR ˌrəʊlɒnˌrəʊl'ɒf
AM ˌroʊlˌɑn'roʊl'ɑf

Rolls
BR rəʊlz
AM roʊlz

Rolls-Royce®
BR ˌrəʊlz'rɔɪs, -ɪz
AM ˌroʊlz'rɔɪs, -ɪz

rolltop
BR ˌrəʊl'tɒp
AM 'roʊlˌtɑp, -s

Rolo®
BR 'rəʊləʊ, -z
AM 'roʊloʊ, -z

roly-poly
BR ˌrəʊlɪ'pəʊl|i, -ɪz
AM 'roʊli'poʊli, -z

ROM
BR rɒm
AM rɑm

Rom
BR rɒm, rəʊm, -z
AM roʊm, -z

Roma
BR 'rəʊmə(*r*)
AM 'roʊmə

Romaic
BR rə(ʊ)'meɪɪk
AM roʊ'meɪɪk

romaine
BR rə(ʊ)'meɪn
AM roʊ'meɪn

romaji
BR 'rəʊmədʒi
AM 'roʊmədʒi

Roman
BR 'rəʊmən, -z
AM 'roʊmən, -z

roman-à-clef
BR ˌrəʊmɑːnɑː'kleɪ, rə(ʊ)ˌmɑːnɑː'kleɪ, -z
AM ˌroʊˌmɑnə'kleɪ, -z

Roman Catholic
BR ˌrəʊmən 'kaθ(ə)lɪk, ˌrəʊmən 'kaθlɪk, -s
AM ˌroʊmən 'kæθ(ə)lɪk, -s

Roman Catholicism
BR ˌrəʊmən kə'θɒlɪsɪz(ə)m
AM ˌroʊmən kə'θɑləˌsɪzəm

Romance
noun, language
BR rə(ʊ)'mans
AM roʊ'mæns, 'roʊˌmæns

romance¹
noun, love, fantasy
BR rə(ʊ)'mans, 'rəʊmans, -ɪz
AM roʊ'mæns, 'roʊˌmæns, -əz

romance²
verb
BR rə(ʊ)'mans, 'rəʊmans, -ɪz, -ɪŋ, -t
AM roʊ'mæns, 'roʊˌmæns, -əz, -ɪŋ, -t

romancer
BR rə(ʊ)'mansə(r), 'rəʊmansə(r), -z
AM roʊ'mænsər, 'roʊˌmænsər, -z

Romanesque
BR ˌrəʊmə'nɛsk
AM ˌroʊmə'nɛsk

roman-fleuve
BR ˌrəʊmɑːn'fləːv, rə(ʊ)ˌmɑːn'fləːv, -z
AM ˌroʊˌmɑn'fləv, -z

Romania
BR ruː'meɪnɪə(*r*), rʊ'meɪnɪə(*r*), rə(ʊ)'meɪnɪə(*r*)
AM roʊ'meɪniə, ru'meɪniə

Romanian
BR ruː'meɪnɪən, rʊ'meɪnɪən, rə(ʊ)'meɪnɪən, -z
AM roʊ'meɪniən, ru'meɪniən, -z

Romanic
BR rə(ʊ)'manɪk
AM roʊ'mænɪk

romanisation
BR ˌrəʊmənʌɪ'zeɪʃn
AM ˌroʊmənə'zeɪʃən, ˌroʊməˌnaɪ'zeɪʃən

romanise
BR 'rəʊmənʌɪz, -ɪz, -ɪŋ, -d
AM 'roʊməˌnaɪz, -ɪz, -ɪŋ, -d

Romanish
BR 'rəʊmənɪʃ
AM 'roʊmənɪʃ

Romanism
BR 'rəʊmənɪz(ə)m
AM 'roʊməˌnɪzəm

Romanist
BR 'rəʊmənɪst, -s
AM 'roʊmənəst, -s

romanization
BR ˌrəʊmənʌɪ'zeɪʃn
AM ˌroʊmənə'zeɪʃən, ˌroʊməˌnaɪ'zeɪʃən

romanize
BR 'rəʊmənʌɪz, -ɪz, -ɪŋ, -d
AM 'roʊməˌnaɪz, -ɪz, -ɪŋ, -d

Romano
BR rə(ʊ)'mɑːnəʊ, 'rəʊmənəʊ, -z
AM roʊ'mɑnoʊ, -z

Romano-
BR rə(ʊ)'mɑːnəʊ, 'rəʊmənəʊ
AM roʊ'mɑnoʊ

Romano-British
BR rə(ʊ)ˌmɑːnəʊ'brɪtɪʃ, ˌrəʊmənəʊ'brɪtɪʃ
AM roʊˌmɑnoʊ'brɪdɪʃ

Romanov
BR 'rəʊmənɒf, 'rəʊmənɒv
AM 'roʊməˌnɔv, 'roʊməˌnɔf, 'roʊməˌnɑv, 'roʊməˌnɑf
RUS ra'manəf

romans-à-clef
BR ˌrəʊmɑːnɑː'kleɪ, rə(ʊ)ˌmɑːnɑː'kleɪ
AM ˌroʊˌmɑnə'kleɪ

Romansh
BR rə(ʊ)'manʃ
AM roʊ'mɑn(t)ʃ, roʊ'mæn(t)ʃ

romantic
BR rə(ʊ)'mantɪk, -s
AM roʊ'mæn(t)ɪk, -s

romantical
BR rə(ʊ)'mantɪkl
AM roʊ'mæn(t)əkəl

romantically
BR rə(ʊ)'mantɪkli
AM roʊ'mæn(t)ək(ə)li

romanticisation
BR rə(ʊ)ˌmantɪsʌɪ'zeɪʃn
AM roʊˌmæn(t)əsə'zeɪʃən, roʊˌmæn(t)əˌsaɪ'zeɪʃən

romanticise
BR rə(ʊ)'mantɪsʌɪz, -ɪz, -ɪŋ, -d
AM roʊ'mæn(t)əˌsaɪz, -ɪz, -ɪŋ, -d

romanticism
BR 'rə(ʊ)'mantɪsɪz(ə)m
AM roʊ'mæn(t)əˌsɪzəm

romanticist
BR rə(ʊ)'mantɪsɪst, -s
AM roʊ'mæn(t)əsəst, -s

romanticization
BR rə(ʊ)ˌmantɪsʌɪ'zeɪʃn
AM roʊˌmæn(t)əsə'zeɪʃən, roʊˌmæn(t)əˌsaɪ'zeɪʃən

romanticize
BR rə(ʊ)'mantɪsʌɪz, -ɪz, -ɪŋ, -d
AM roʊ'mæn(t)əˌsaɪz, -ɪz, -ɪŋ, -d

Romany
BR 'rəʊmən|i, -ɪz
AM 'roʊməni, 'rɑməni, -z

Romberg
BR 'rɒmbəːg
AM 'rɑmˌbərg

Rome
BR rəʊm
AM roʊm

Romeo
BR 'rəʊmɪəʊ, -z
AM 'roʊmioʊ, -z

romer
BR 'rəʊmə(r), -z
AM 'roʊmər, -z

Romero
BR rɒ'mɛːrəʊ, rə'mɛːrəʊ
AM rə'mɛroʊ, roʊ'mɛroʊ

Romish
BR 'rəʊmɪʃ
AM 'roʊmɪʃ

Rommel
BR 'rɒml
AM 'rɑməl

Romney
BR 'rɒmni
AM 'rɑmni

romneya
BR 'rɒmnɪə(*r*), -z
AM 'rɑmniə, -z

romp
BR rɒm|p, -ps, -pɪŋ, -(p)t
AM rɑmp, -s, -ɪŋ, -t

romper
BR 'rɒmpə(r), -z
AM 'rɑmpər, -z

rompingly
BR 'rɒmpɪŋli
AM 'rɑmpɪŋli

rompy
BR 'rɒmp|i, -ɪə(r), -ɪɪst
AM 'rɑmpi, -ər, -ɪst

Romsey
BR 'rɒmzi
AM 'rɑmzi

Romulus
BR 'rɒmjʉləs
AM 'rɑmjələs

Ron
BR rɒn
AM rɑn

rona
BR 'rəʊnə(*r*)
AM 'roʊnə

Ronald
BR 'rɒnld
AM 'rɑnəl(d)

Ronaldsay
BR 'rɒnl(d)seɪ
AM 'rɑnəl(d)ˌseɪ

Ronaldsway
BR 'rɒnl(d)zweɪ
AM 'rɑnəl(d)ˌzweɪ

Ronan
BR 'rəʊnən
AM 'roʊnən

Roncesvalles
BR 'rɒ̃səvɑːl, 'rɒ̃səval
AM ˌrɔnsə'vɑl(z), ˌrɑnsə'vɑl(z)

rondavel
BR rɒn'dɑːvl, -z
AM 'rɑndəˌvɛl, -z

ronde
BR rɒnd, -z

AM rɑnd, -z
rondeau
BR 'rɒndəʊ, -z
AM ˌrɑnˌdoʊ, -z
rondeaux
BR 'rɒndəʊ(z)
AM ˌrɑnˌdoʊ
rondel
BR 'rɒndl, -z
AM 'rɑndəl, ˌrɑn'dɛl, -z
rondo
BR 'rɒndəʊ, -z
AM 'rɑnˌdoʊ, -z
Rondônia
BR rɒn'dəʊnɪə(r)
AM rɔn'doʊniə, rɑn'doʊniə
rone
BR rəʊn, -z
AM roʊn, -z
roneo
BR 'rəʊnɪəʊ, -z, -ɪŋ, -d
AM 'roʊnioʊ, -z, -ɪŋ, -d
ronggeng
BR 'rɒŋgɛŋ, -z
AM 'rɔŋgɛŋ, 'rɑŋgɛŋ, -z
ronin
BR 'rəʊnɪn, -z
AM 'roʊnən, -z
Ronnie
BR 'rɒni
AM 'rɑni
Ronsard
BR rɒn'sɑː(r)
AM rɔn'sɑr, rɑn'sɑr
Ronson®
BR 'rɒns(ə)n
AM 'rɑnsən
röntgen
BR 'rʌntjən, 'rəːntjən, 'rɒntjən, 'rʌntgən, 'rəːntgən, 'rɒntgən
AM 'rɛntgən, 'rɛntdʒən
röntgenography
BR ˌrʌntjə'nɒgrəfi, ˌrəːntjə'nɒgrəfi, ˌrɒntjə'nɒgrəfi, ˌrʌntgə'nɒgrəfi, ˌrəːntgə'nɒgrəfi, ˌrɒntgə'nɒgrəfi
AM ˌrɛntgə'nɑgrəfi, ˌrɛntdʒə'nɑgrəfi
röntgenology
BR ˌrʌntjə'nɒlədʒi, ˌrəːntjə'nɒlədʒi, ˌrɒntjə'nɒlədʒi, ˌrʌntgə'nɒlədʒi, ˌrəːntgə'nɒlədʒi, ˌrɒntgə'nɒlədʒi
AM ˌrɛntgə'nɑlədʒi, ˌrɛntdʒə'nɑlədʒi
roo
BR ruː, -z
AM ru, -z
rood
BR ruːd, -z
AM rud, -z
roodscreen
BR 'ruːdskriːn, -z
AM 'rudˌskrin, -z
roof
BR ruːf, rʊf, ruːfs\ruːvz\rʊfs, 'ruːfɪŋ\'ruːvɪŋ\'rʊfɪŋ, ruːft\ruːvd\rʊft
AM ruf, rʊf, -s, -ɪŋ, -t
roofage
BR 'ruːf|ɪdʒ, -ɨdʒɪz
AM 'rufɪdʒ, 'rʊfɪdʒ, -ɪz
roofer
BR 'ruːfə(r), 'rʊfə(r), -z
AM 'rufər, 'rʊfər, -z
roofing
BR 'ruːfɪŋ, 'ruːvɪŋ, 'rʊfɪŋ
AM 'rufɪŋ, 'rʊfɪŋ
roofless
BR 'ruːfləs, 'rʊfləs
AM 'rufləs, 'rʊfləs
roofline
BR 'ruːflʌɪn, 'rʊflʌɪn, -z
AM 'rufˌlaɪn, 'rʊfˌlaɪn, -z
roofscape
BR 'ruːfskeɪp, 'rʊfskeɪp, -s
AM 'rufˌskeɪp, 'rʊfˌskeɪp, -z
rooftop
BR 'ruːftɒp, 'rʊftɒp, -s
AM 'rufˌtɑp, 'rʊfˌtɑp, -s
rooftree
BR 'ruːftriː, 'rʊftriː, -z
AM 'rufˌtri, 'rʊfˌtri, -z
rooibos
BR 'rɔɪbɒs, -ɨz
AM 'rɔɪbɑs, -əz
rooinek
BR 'rɔɪnɛk, -s
AM 'rɔɪnɛk, -s
rook
BR rʊk, -s, -ɪŋ, -t
AM rʊk, -s, -ɪŋ, -t
Rooke
BR rʊk
AM rʊk
rookery
BR 'rʊk(ə)r|i, -ɪz
AM 'rʊkəri, -z
rookie
BR 'rʊk|i, -ɪz
AM 'rʊki, -z
rooklet
BR 'rʊklɨt, -s
AM 'rʊklət, -s
rookling
BR 'rʊklɪŋ, -z
AM 'rʊklɪŋ, -z
rooky
BR 'rʊk|i, -ɪz
AM 'rʊki, -z
room
BR ruːm, rʊm, -z
AM rum, rʊm, -z
Roome
BR ruːm
AM rum, rʊm
roomer
BR 'ruːmə(r), 'rʊmə(r), -z
AM 'rumər, 'rʊmər, -z
roomette
BR ruː'mɛt, rʊ'mɛt, -s
AM ru'mɛt, rʊ'mɛt, -s
roomful
BR 'ruːmfʊl, 'rʊmfʊl, -z
AM 'rumˌfʊl, 'rʊmˌfʊl, -z
roomie
BR 'ruːm|i, 'rʊm|i, -ɪz
AM 'rumi, 'rʊmi, -z
roomily
BR 'ruːmɨli, 'rʊmɨli
AM 'ruməli, 'rʊməli
roominess
BR 'ruːmɪnɨs, 'rʊmɪnɨs
AM 'ruminɨs, 'rʊminɨs
roommate
BR 'ruːmmeɪt, 'rʊmmeɪt, -s
AM 'ru(m)ˌmeɪt, 'rʊ(m)ˌmeɪt, -s
roomy
BR 'ruːm|i, 'rʊm|i, -ɪə(r), -ɪɨst
AM 'rumi, 'rʊmi, -ər, -ɨst
Rooney
BR 'ruːni
AM 'runi
Roosevelt
BR 'rəʊzəvɛlt, 'ruːzəvɛlt
AM 'roʊzəˌvɛlt
roost
BR ruːst, -s, -ɪŋ, -ɨd
AM rust, -s, -ɪŋ, -əd
rooster
BR 'ruːstə(r), -z
AM 'rustər, -z
root
BR ruːt, -s, -ɪŋ, -ɨd
AM ru|t, rʊ|t, -ts, -dɪŋ, -dəd
rootage
BR 'ruːt|ɪdʒ, -ɨdʒɪz
AM 'rudɪdʒ, 'rʊdɪdʒ, -ɪz
rootbeer
BR 'ruːtbɪə(r)
AM 'rutˌbɪ(ə)r, 'rʊtˌbɪ(ə)r
rootedness
BR 'ruːtɨdnɨs
AM 'rudədnəs, 'rʊdədnəs
rooter
BR 'ruːtə(r), -z
AM 'rudər, 'rʊdər, -z
Rootes
BR ruːts
AM ruts, rʊts
rootle
BR 'ruːt|l, -lz, -l̩ɪŋ\-lɪŋ, -ld
AM 'rudəl, 'rʊdəl, -z, -ɪŋ, -d
rootless
BR 'ruːtləs
AM 'rutləs, 'rʊtləs
rootlessness
BR 'ruːtləsnəs
AM 'rutləsnəs, 'rʊtləsnəs
rootlet
BR 'ruːtlɨt, -s
AM 'rutlət, 'rʊtlət, -z
rootlike
BR 'ruːtlʌɪk
AM 'rutˌlaɪk, 'rʊtˌlaɪk
root-mean-square
BR ˌruːtˌmiːn'skwɛː(r), -z
AM ˌrutˌmin'skwɛ(ə)r, ˌrʊtˌmin'skwɛ(ə)r, -z
rootstock
BR 'ruːtstɒk, -s
AM 'rutˌstɑk, 'rʊtˌstɑk, -s
rootsy
BR 'ruːts|i, -ɪə(r), -ɪɨst
AM 'rutsi, 'rʊtsi, -ər, -ɨst
rooty
BR 'ruːt|i, -ɪə(r), -ɪɨst
AM 'rudi, 'rʊdi, -ər, -ɨst
rooves
BR ruːvz
AM ruvz
rope
BR rəʊp, -s, -ɪŋ, -t
AM roʊp, -s, -ɪŋ, -t
ropeable
BR 'rəʊpəbl
AM 'roʊpəbəl
ropedancer
BR 'rəʊpˌdɑːnsə(r), 'rəʊpˌdansə(r), -z
AM 'roʊpˌdænsər, -z
ropemanship
BR 'rəʊpmənʃɪp
AM 'roʊpmənˌʃɪp
Roper
BR 'rəʊpə(r)
AM 'roʊpər
ropewalk
BR 'rəʊpwɔːk, -s
AM 'roʊpˌwɔk, 'roʊpˌwɑk, -s
ropeway
BR 'rəʊpweɪ, -z
AM 'roʊpˌweɪ, -z
ropey
BR 'rəʊp|i, -ɪə(r), -ɪɨst
AM 'roʊpi, -ər, -ɨst
ropily
BR 'rəʊpɨli
AM 'roʊpəli

ropiness
BR ˈrəʊpɪnɪs
AM ˈroʊpinɨs

roping
BR ˈrəʊpɪŋ, -z
AM ˈroʊpɪŋ, -z

ropy
BR ˈrəʊp|i, -ɪə(r), -ɪɪst
AM ˈroʊpi, -ər, -ɨst

roque
BR rəʊk
AM roʊk

Roquefort®
BR ˈrɒkfɔː(r), -z
AM ˈroʊkfərt, -s

roquelaure
BR ˈrɒk(ə)lɔː(r), -z
AM ˈrɔkəˌlɔ(ə)r,
ˈroʊkəˌlɔ(ə)r, -z

roquet
BR ˈrəʊk|i, ˈrəʊk|eɪ,
-ɪz\-eɪz, -ɪɪŋ\-eɪɪŋ,
-ɪd\-eɪd
AM roʊˈkeɪ, -z, -ɪŋ, -d

Roraima
BR rɒˈrʌɪmə(r)
AM rɔˈraɪmə

Rorke
BR rɔːk
AM rɔ(ə)rk

ro-ro
BR ˈrəʊrəʊ, -z
AM ˈroʊˌroʊ, -z

rorqual
BR ˈrɔːkw(ə)l, -z
AM ˈrɔrkwəl, -z

Rorschach test
BR ˈrɔːʃɑːk tɛst,
ˈrɔːʃak +, -s
AM ˈrɔrˌʃɑk ˌtɛst,
ˈrɔrˌʒɑk +, -s

rort
BR rɔːt, -s
AM rɔ(ə)rt, -s

rorty
BR ˈrɔːt|i, -ɪə(r), -ɪɪst
AM ˈrɔrdi, -ər, -ɨst

Rory
BR ˈrɔːri
AM ˈrɔri

Ros
BR rɒz
AM rɑz

Rosa
BR ˈrəʊzə(r)
AM ˈroʊzə

rosace
BR ˈrəʊzeɪs, -ɪz
AM ˈroʊzeɪs, ˈroʊzɑs,
-əs

rosaceous
BR rə(ʊ)ˈzeɪʃəs
AM roʊˈzeɪʃəs

Rosaleen
BR ˈrɒzəliːn, ˈrəʊzəliːn
AM ˈroʊzəˌlin

Rosalie
BR ˈrəʊzəli
AM ˈroʊzəli

Rosalind
BR ˈrɒzəlɪnd
AM ˈroʊz(ə)lən(d),
ˈrɑz(ə)lən(d)

rosaline
BR ˈrəʊzəliːn, -z
AM ˈroʊzəˌlin,
ˈroʊz(ə)lən, -z

Rosalyn
BR ˈrɒzəlɪn
AM ˈroʊz(ə)lən,
ˈrɑz(ə)lən

Rosamond
BR ˈrɒzəmʌnd
AM ˈroʊzəmən(d)

Rosamund
BR ˈrɒzəmʌnd
AM ˈroʊzəmən(d)

rosaniline
BR rə(ʊ)ˈzanɨliːn,
rə(ʊ)ˈzanl̩iːn,
rə(ʊ)ˈzanɨlʌɪn,
rə(ʊ)ˈzanl̩ʌɪn,
rə(ʊ)ˈzanɨlɪn,
rə(ʊ)ˈzanl̩ɪn
AM roʊˈzænəˌlaɪn,
roʊˈzænələn

Rosanna
BR rə(ʊ)ˈzanə(r)
AM roʊˈzænə

Rosanne
BR rə(ʊ)ˈzan
AM roʊˈzæn

rosaria
BR rə(ʊ)ˈzɛːrɪə(r)
AM roʊˈzɛriə

rosarian
BR rə(ʊ)ˈzɛːrɪən, -z
AM roʊˈzɛriən, -z

Rosario
BR rə(ʊ)ˈzɑːrɪəʊ
AM roʊˈsɑrioʊ

rosarium
BR rə(ʊ)ˈzɛːrɪəm
AM roʊˈzɛriəm

rosary
BR ˈrəʊz(ə)r|i, -ɪz
AM ˈroʊz(ə)ri, -z

Roscian
BR ˈrɒsɪən, ˈrɒʃɪən,
ˈrɒʃ(ə)n
AM ˈrɑʃ(i)ən

Roscius
BR ˈrɒsɪəs, ˈrɒʃɪəs
AM ˈrɑsiəs, ˈrɑʃiəs

roscoe
BR ˈrɒskəʊ, -z
AM ˈrɑskoʊ, -z

Roscommon
BR rɒsˈkɒmən
AM rɑsˈkɑmən

rose
BR rəʊz, -ɪz
AM roʊz, -əz

rosé
BR ˈrəʊzeɪ
AM roʊˈzeɪ

Roseanne
BR rə(ʊ)ˈzan
AM roʊˈzæn

roseate
BR ˈrəʊzɪət, ˈrəʊzɪeɪt
AM ˈroʊziɨt, ˈroʊziˌeɪt

rosebay
BR ˈrəʊzbeɪ
AM ˈroʊzˌbeɪ

Rosebery
BR ˈrəʊzb(ə)ri
AM ˈroʊzˌbɛri

rosebowl
BR ˈrəʊzbəʊl, -z
AM ˈroʊzˌboʊl, -z

rosebud
BR ˈrəʊzbʌd, -z
AM ˈroʊzˌbəd, -z

rosebush
BR ˈrəʊzbʊʃ, -ɪz
AM ˈroʊzˌbʊʃ, -əz

rose-chafer
BR ˈrəʊzˌtʃeɪfə(r), -z
AM ˈroʊzˌtʃeɪfər, -z

rosehip
BR ˈrəʊzhɪp, -s
AM ˈroʊzˌ(h)ɪp, -s

roseless
BR ˈrəʊzləs
AM ˈroʊzləs

roselike
BR ˈrəʊzlʌɪk
AM ˈroʊzˌlaɪk

rosella
BR rə(ʊ)ˈzɛlə(r)
AM roʊˈzɛlə

rosemaling
BR ˈrəʊzəˌmɑːlɪŋ,
ˈrəʊzəˌmɔːlɪŋ,
ˈrəʊsəˌmɑːlɪŋ,
ˈrəʊsəˌmɔːlɪŋ
AM ˈroʊzəˌmɑlɪŋ

rosemary
BR ˈrəʊzm(ə)r|i, -ɪz
AM ˈroʊzˌmɛri, -z

Rosen
BR ˈrəʊzn
AM ˈroʊzn

Rosenberg
BR ˈrəʊznbəːg
AM ˈroʊzənˌbərg

Rosencrantz
BR ˈrəʊznkran(t)s
AM ˈroʊzənˌkræn(t)s

Rosenthal
BR ˈrəʊzntɑːl,
ˈrəʊznθɔːl
AM ˈroʊzənˌθɔl,
ˈroʊzənˌθɑl

Rosenwald
BR ˈrəʊznwɔːld
AM ˈroʊzənˌwɑld

roseola
BR rə(ʊ)ˈziːələ(r),
ˌrəʊzɪˈəʊlə(r), -z
AM ˌroʊziˈoʊlə,
roʊˈziələ, -z

roseolar
BR rə(ʊ)ˈziːələ(r),
ˌrəʊzɪˈəʊlə(r)
AM ˌroʊziˈoʊlər,
roʊˈziələr

roseolous
BR rə(ʊ)ˈziːələs,
ˌrəʊzɪˈəʊləs
AM ˌroʊziˈoʊləs,
roʊˈziələs

rosery
BR ˈrəʊz(ə)r|i, -ɪz
AM ˈroʊzəri, -z

Rosetta Stone
BR rə(ʊ)ˈzɛtə stəʊn
AM roʊˈzɛdə ˌstoʊn

rosette
BR rə(ʊ)ˈzɛt, -s
AM roʊˈzɛt, -s

rosetted
BR rə(ʊ)ˈzɛtɨd
AM roʊˈzɛdəd

Rosewall
BR ˈrəʊzwɔːl
AM ˈroʊzˌwɔl,
ˈroʊzˌwɑl

rosewater
BR ˈrəʊzˌwɔːtə(r)
AM ˈroʊzˌwɔdər,
ˈroʊzˌwɑdər

rosewood
BR ˈrəʊzwʊd
AM ˈroʊzˌwʊd

Rosh Hashana
BR ˌrɒʃ həˈʃɑːnə(r)
AM ˌrɔʃ(hə)ˈʃɑnə,
ˌrɑʃ(hə)ˈʃɑnə

Rosh Hashanah
BR ˌrɒʃ həˈʃɑːnə(r)
AM ˌrɔʃ(hə)ˈʃɑnə,
ˌrɑʃ(hə)ˈʃɑnə

Rosicrucian
BR ˌrəʊzɨˈkruːʃn, -z
AM ˌroʊzəˈkruʃən,
ˌrɑzəˈkruʃən, -z

Rosicrucianism
BR ˌrəʊzɨˈkruːʃn̩ɪz(ə)m,
ˌrəʊzɨˈkruːʃənɪz(ə)m
AM ˌroʊzəˈkruʃəˌnɪzəm,
ˌrɑzəˈkruʃəˌnɪzəm

Rosie
BR ˈrəʊzi
AM ˈroʊzi

rosily
BR ˈrəʊzɨli
AM ˈroʊzəli

rosin
BR ˈrɒzɪn
AM ˈrɑzn

rosiness
BR ˈrəʊzɪnɪs
AM ˈroʊzinɨs

rosiny
BR 'rɒzɪni, 'rɒzn̩i
AM 'rɑzn̩i

Roskilde
BR 'rɒskɪld
AM 'rɑs,kɪld(ə)
DAN 'ʀʌs,kilə

Roslea
BR (,)rɒs'leɪ
AM rɔs'leɪ, rɑs'leɪ

rosoglio
BR rə(ʊ)'zəʊlɪəʊ, rɒ'zəʊlɪəʊ, -z
AM roʊ'zoʊlioʊ, rɔ'zoʊlioʊ, -z

rosolio
BR rə(ʊ)'zəʊlɪəʊ, rɒ'zəʊlɪəʊ, -z
AM roʊ'zoʊlioʊ, rɔ'zoʊlioʊ, -z

ROSPA, RoSPA
BR 'rɒspə(r)
AM 'rɑspə

Ross
BR rɒs
AM rɔs, rɑs

Rossellini
BR ,rɒsə'li:ni
AM ,rɔsə'lini, ,rɑsə'lini

Rossendale
BR 'rɒsndeɪl
AM 'rɔsən,deɪl, 'rɑsən,deɪl

Rosser
BR 'rɒsə(r)
AM 'rɔsər, 'rɑsər

Rossetti
BR rə'zɛti, rɒ'zɛti
AM rə'zɛdi, ,roʊ'zɛdi

Rossi
BR 'rɒsi
AM 'rɔsi, 'rɑsi

Rossini
BR rɒ'si:ni, rə'si:ni
AM rə'sini

Rossiter
BR 'rɒsɪtə(r)
AM 'rɔsədər, 'rɑsədər

Rosslare
BR ,rɒs'lɛ:(r)
AM ,rɑs'lɛ(ə)r

Rosslyn
BR 'rɒslɪn
AM 'rɔslən, 'rɑslən

Ross-on-Wye
BR ,rɒsɒn'wʌɪ
AM ,rɔs,ɑn'waɪ, ,rɑs,ɑn'waɪ

roster
BR 'rɒst|ə(r), -əz, -(ə)rɪŋ, -əd
AM 'rɔst|ər, 'rɑst|ər, -ərz, -(ə)rɪŋ, -ərd

Rostock
BR 'rɒstɒk
AM 'rɑstɑk

rostra
BR 'rɒstrə(r)
AM 'rɔstrə, 'rɑstrə

rostral
BR 'rɒstr(ə)l
AM 'rɔstrəl, 'rɑstrəl

rostrally
BR 'rɒstrəli, 'rɒstrl̩i
AM 'rɔstrəli, 'rɑstrəli

rostrate
BR 'rɒstrət, 'rɒstreɪt
AM 'rɔs,treɪt, 'rɑs,treɪt

rostrated
BR rɒ'streɪtɨd
AM 'rɔs,treɪdɨd, 'rɑs,treɪdɨd

Rostrevor
BR (,)rɒs'trɛvə(r)
AM rɔs'trɛvər, rɑs'trɛvər

rostriferous
BR rɒ'strɪf(ə)rəs
AM rɔs'trɪf(ə)rəs, rɑs'trɪf(ə)rəs

rostriform
BR 'rɒstrɪfɔ:m
AM 'rɑstrə,fɔ(ə)rm, 'rɔstrə,fɔ(ə)rm

Rostropovich
BR ,rɒstrə'pəʊvɪtʃ
AM ,rɔstrə'poʊvɪtʃ, ,rɑstrə'poʊvɪtʃ

rostrum
BR 'rɒstrəm, -z
AM 'rɔstrəm, 'rɑstrəm, -z

Roswell
BR 'rɒzwɛl
AM 'rɑz,wɛl

rosy
BR 'rəʊz|i, -ɪə(r), -ɪɪst
AM 'roʊzi, -ər, -ɪst

Rosyth
BR rɒ'sʌɪθ, rə'sʌɪθ
AM rə'saɪθ

rot
BR rɒt, -s, -ɪŋ, -ɨd
AM rɑ|t, -ts, -dɪŋ, -dəd

rota
BR 'rəʊtə(r), -z, -d
AM 'roʊdə, -z, -d

Rotarian
BR rə(ʊ)'tɛ:rɪən, -z
AM roʊ'tɛriən, -z

rotary
BR 'rəʊt(ə)r|i, -ɪz
AM 'roʊdəri, -z

rotatable
BR rə(ʊ)'teɪtəbl
AM 'roʊ,teɪdəbəl, roʊ'teɪdəbəl

rotate
BR rə(ʊ)'teɪt, -s, -ɪŋ, -ɨd
AM 'roʊ,teɪ|t, -ts, -dɪŋ, -dɨd

rotation
BR rə(ʊ)'teɪʃn, -z
AM roʊ'teɪʃən, -z

rotational
BR rə(ʊ)'teɪʃn̩(ə)l, rə(ʊ)'teɪʃən(ə)l
AM roʊ'teɪʃ(ə)nəl

rotationally
BR rə(ʊ)'teɪʃn̩əli, rə(ʊ)'teɪʃn̩li, rə(ʊ)'teɪʃənl̩i, rə(ʊ)'teɪʃ(ə)nəli
AM roʊ'teɪʃ(ə)nəli

rotative
BR rə(ʊ)'teɪtɪv, 'rəʊtətɪv
AM 'roʊdədɪv, roʊ'teɪdɪv

rotatively
BR rə(ʊ)'teɪtɨvli, 'rəʊtətɨvli
AM 'roʊdədɨvli, roʊ'teɪdɨvli

rotator
BR rə(ʊ)'teɪtə(r), -z
AM 'roʊ,teɪdər, -z

rotatory
BR rə(ʊ)'teɪt(ə)ri, 'rəʊtət(ə)ri
AM 'roʊdə,tɔri

rotavate
BR 'rəʊtəveɪt, -s, -ɪŋ, -ɨd
AM 'roʊdə,veɪ|t, -ts, -dɪŋ, -dɨd

Rotavator®
BR 'rəʊtəveɪtə(r), -z
AM 'roʊdə,veɪdər, -z

rotavirus
BR 'rəʊtə,vʌɪrəs, -ɪz
AM 'roʊdə,vaɪrəs, -əz

rote
BR rəʊt
AM roʊt

rotenone
BR 'rəʊtɪnəʊn
AM 'roʊtn,oʊn

rotgut
BR 'rɒtgʌt
AM 'rɑt,gət

Roth
BR rɒθ, rəʊθ
AM rɔθ, rɑθ

Rothamsted
BR 'rɒθ(ə)mstɛd
AM 'rɑθəm,stɛd

Rother
BR 'rɒðə(r)
AM 'rɑðər

Rotherham
BR 'rɒð(ə)rəm
AM 'rɑðərəm

Rotherhithe
BR 'rɒðəhʌɪð
AM 'rɑðər,(h)aɪð

Rothermere
BR 'rɒðəmɪə(r)
AM 'rɑðər,mɪ(ə)r

Rothesay
BR 'rɒθsi, 'rɒθseɪ
AM 'rɑθsi

Rothko
BR 'rɒθkəʊ
AM 'rɔθkoʊ, 'rɑθkoʊ

Rothman
BR 'rɒθmən
AM 'rɑθmən

Rothschild
BR 'rɒθ(s)tʃʌɪld
AM 'rɔθ,tʃaɪld, 'rɑθ,tʃaɪld

Rothwell
BR 'rɒθw(ɛ)l
AM 'rɑθ,wɛl

roti
BR 'rəʊt|i, -ɪz
AM 'roʊdi, -z

rotifer
BR 'rəʊtɪfə(r), -z
AM 'roʊdəfər, -z

Rotifera
BR rəʊ'tɪf(ə)rə(r)
AM roʊ'tɪfərə

rotisserie
BR rə(ʊ)'tɪs(ə)r|i, -ɪz
AM roʊ'tɪsəri, -z

rotogravure
BR ,rəʊtə(ʊ)grə'vjʊə(r)
AM ¦roʊdəgrə'vjʊ(ə)r

rotor
BR 'rəʊtə(r), -z
AM 'roʊdər, -z

rotorscope
BR 'rəʊtəskəʊp, -s, -ɪŋ, -t
AM 'roʊdər,skoʊp, -s, -ɪŋ, -t

Rotorua
BR ,rəʊtə'ru:ə(r)
AM ,roʊdə'ruə

rotovate
BR 'rəʊtəveɪt, -s, -ɪŋ, -ɨd
AM 'roʊdə,veɪ|t, -ts, -dɪŋ, -dəd

Rotovator
BR 'rəʊtəveɪtə(r), -z
AM 'roʊdə,veɪdər, -z

rot-proof
BR 'rɒtpru:f
AM 'rɑt'pruf

rotten
BR 'rɒtn̩, -ɪst
AM 'rɑtn̩, -ɪst

rottenly
BR 'rɒtnli
AM 'rɑtnli

rottenness
BR 'rɒtnnəs
AM 'rɑt(n)nəs

rotter
BR 'rɒtə(r), -z
AM 'rɑdər, -z

Rotterdam
BR 'rɒtədam
AM 'rɑdər,dæm

Rottingdean
BR 'rɒtɪŋdi:n, ,rɒtɪŋ'di:n

AM 'rɑdɪŋ,din
Rottweiler
BR 'rɒt,wʌɪlə(r), -z
AM 'rɑt,waɪlər, -z
rotund
BR rə(ʊ)'tʌnd
AM roʊ'tənd
rotunda
BR rə(ʊ)'tʌndə(r), -z
AM roʊ'təndə, -z
rotundity
BR rə(ʊ)'tʌndɨti
AM roʊ'təndədi
rotundly
BR rə(ʊ)'tʌndli
AM roʊ'tən(d)li
rotundness
BR rə(ʊ)'tʌn(d)nəs
AM roʊ'tən(d)nəs
Rouault
BR ,ru:'əʊ
AM ru'oʊ
rouble
BR 'ru:bl, -z
AM 'rubəl, -z
roucou
BR ,ru:'ku:, -z
AM 'ru,ku, -z
roué
BR 'ru:eɪ, -z
AM ru'eɪ, -z
Rouen
BR 'ru:ɒ̃
AM 'rwɑn
rouge
BR ru:ʒ, -ɪz, -ɪŋ, -d
AM ruʒ, -əz, -ɪŋ, -d
rouge-et-noir
BR ,ru:ʒeɪ'nwɑ:(r)
AM ,ruʒeɪ'nwɑr
rough
BR rʌf, -s, -ɪŋ, -t, -ə(r), -ɨst
AM rəf, -s, -ɪŋ, -t, -ər, -əst
roughage
BR 'rʌfɪdʒ
AM 'rəfɪdʒ
rough-and-ready
BR ,rʌf(ə)n(d)'rɛdi
AM ,rəfən'rɛdi
rough-and-tumble
BR ,rʌf(ə)n(d)'tʌmbl
AM ,rəfən'təmbəl
roughcast
BR 'rʌfkɑ:st, 'rʌfkast
AM 'rəf,kæst
roughen
BR 'rʌf|n, -nz, -n̩ɪŋ\-nɪŋ, -nd
AM 'rəfən, -z, -ɪŋ, -d
roughhouse
BR 'rʌfhaʊ|s, -zɪz, -sɪŋ\-zɪŋ, -st\-zd
AM 'rəf,(h)aʊ|s, -zəz, -zɪŋ, -zd
roughie
BR 'rʌf|i, -ɪz
AM 'rəfi, -z
roughish
BR 'rʌfɪʃ
AM 'rəfɪʃ
roughly
BR 'rʌfli
AM 'rəfli
roughneck
BR 'rʌknɛk, -s
AM 'rəf,nɛk, -s
roughness
BR 'rʌfnəs
AM 'rəfnəs
roughrider
BR 'rʌf,rʌɪdə(r), -z
AM 'rəf,raɪdər, -z
roughshod
BR 'rʌfʃɒd
AM 'rəf,ʃɑd
Rough Tor
BR ,raʊ 'tɔ:(r)
AM ,raʊ 'tɔ(ə)r
roughy
BR 'rʌf|i, -ɪz
AM 'rəfi, -z
rouille
BR 'ru:i
AM 'rui
roulade
BR rʊ'lɑ:d, -z
AM ,ru'lɑd, -z
rouleau
BR 'ru:ləʊ, rʊ'ləʊ, -z
AM ru'loʊ, -z
rouleaux
BR 'ru:ləʊz, rʊ'ləʊz
AM ru'loʊ
roulement
BR 'ru:lmɒ̃
AM 'rulmən(t)
roulette
BR ru:'lɛt, rʊ'lɛt
AM ru'lɛt
Roumania
BR ru:'meɪnɪə(r), rʉ'meɪnɪə(r)
AM roʊ'meɪniə, ru'meɪniə
Roumanian
BR ru:'meɪnɪən, rʉ'meɪnɪən, -z
AM roʊ'meɪniən, ru'meɪniən, -z
Roumelia
BR ru:'mi:lɪə(r), rʉ'mi:lɪə(r)
AM ru'miljə, ru'miliə
round
BR raʊnd, -z, -ɪŋ, -ɨd, -ə(r), -ɨst
AM raʊnd, -z, -ɪŋ, -əd, -ər, -əst
roundabout
BR 'raʊndəbaʊt, -s
AM 'raʊndə,baʊt, -s
round-arm
BR 'raʊndɑ:m
AM 'raʊn,dɑrm
roundel
BR 'raʊndl, -z
AM 'raʊndəl, roʊn'dɛl, -z
roundelay
BR 'raʊndɨleɪ, -z
AM 'raʊndə,leɪ, 'rɑndə,leɪ, -z
rounder
BR 'raʊndə(r), -z
AM 'raʊndər, -z
Roundhay
BR 'raʊnd(h)eɪ
AM 'raʊnd(h)eɪ
Roundhead
BR 'raʊndhɛd, -z
AM 'raʊnd,(h)ɛd, -z
roundhouse
BR 'raʊndhaʊ|s, -zɪz
AM 'raʊnd,(h)aʊ|s, -zəz
roundish
BR 'raʊndɪʃ
AM 'raʊndɪʃ
roundly
BR 'raʊndli
AM 'raʊn(d)li
roundness
BR 'raʊn(d)nəs
AM 'raʊn(d)nəs
round robin
BR ,raʊnd 'rɒbɪn, -z
AM ',raʊn(d) ',rɑbən, -z
round-shouldered
BR ,raʊn(d)'ʃəʊldəd
AM 'raʊn(d),ʃoʊldərd
roundsman
BR 'raʊn(d)zmən
AM 'raʊn(d)zmən
roundsmen
BR 'raʊn(d)zmən
AM 'raʊn(d)zmən
roundup
BR 'raʊndʌp, -s
AM 'raʊnd,əp, -s
roundworm
BR 'raʊn(d)wə:m, -z
AM 'raʊn(d),wərm, -z
Rountree
BR 'raʊntri:
AM 'raʊn,tri
roup
BR ru:p
AM rup
roupy
BR 'ru:pi
AM 'rupi
Rourke
BR rɔ:k
AM rɔ(ə)rk
Rous
BR raʊs
AM raʊs, raʊz
rousable
BR 'raʊzəbl
AM 'raʊzəbəl
Rouse
BR raʊs
AM raʊs, raʊz
rouse
BR raʊz, -ɪz, -ɪŋ, -d
AM raʊz, -əz, -ɪŋ, -d
rouseabout
BR 'raʊzəbaʊt, -s
AM 'raʊzə,baʊt, -z
rouser
BR 'raʊzə(r), -z
AM 'raʊzər, -z
rousingly
BR 'raʊzɪŋli
AM 'raʊzɪŋli
Rousse
BR ru:s
AM rus
Rousseau
BR 'ru:səʊ
AM ru'soʊ
Roussillon
BR 'ru:sɪjɒ̃
AM ,rusi'jɔn
roust
BR raʊst, -s
AM raʊst, -s
roustabout
BR 'raʊstəbaʊt, -s
AM 'raʊstə,baʊt, -s
rout
BR raʊt, -s, -ɪŋ, -ɨd
AM raʊ|t, -ts, -dɪŋ, -dəd
route
BR ru:t, -s, -ɪŋ, -ɨd
AM ru|t, raʊ|t, -ts, -dɪŋ, -dəd
router
BR 'ru:tə(r), -z
AM 'raʊdər, -z
Routh
BR raʊθ
AM raʊθ
routine
BR ru:'ti:n, rʊ'ti:n, -z
AM ru'tin, -z
routinely
BR ru:'ti:nli, rʊ'ti:nli
AM ru'tinli
routinisation
BR ru:,ti:nʌɪ'zeɪʃn, rʊ,ti:nʌɪ'zeɪʃn
AM ,rutn̩ə'zeɪʃən, ,rutn,aɪ'zeɪʃən
routinise
BR ru:'ti:nʌɪz, rʊ'ti:nʌɪz, -ɪz, -ɪŋ, -d
AM 'rutn,aɪz, -ɪz, -ɪŋ, -d
routinism
BR ru:'ti:nɪz(ə)m, rʊ'ti:nɪz(ə)m
AM 'rutn,ɪzəm

routinist
BR ruːˈtiːnɪst,
rʊˈtiːnɪst, -s
AM ˈrutn̩əst, -s
routinization
BR ruːˌtiːnʌɪˈzeɪʃn,
rʊˌtiːnʌɪˈzeɪʃn
AM ˌrutn̩əˈzeɪʃən,
ˌrutnˌaɪˈzeɪʃən
routinize
BR ruːˈtiːnʌɪz,
rʊˈtiːnʌɪz, -ɨz, -ɪŋ, -d
AM ˈrutnˌaɪz, -ɨz, -ɪŋ, -d
Routledge
BR ˈraʊtlɪdʒ, ˈrʌtlɪdʒ
AM ˈraʊtlɨdʒ
roux[1]
singular
BR ruː
AM ru
roux[2]
plural
BR ruːz
AM ru(z)
rove
BR rəʊv, -z, -ɪŋ, -d
AM roʊv, -z, -ɪŋ, -d
rover
BR ˈrəʊvə(r), -z
AM ˈroʊvər, -z
row[1]
noise, argument
BR raʊ, -z, -ɪŋ, -d
AM raʊ, -z, -ɪŋ, -d
row[2]
noun, things in a line; verb propel a boat with oars
BR rəʊ, -z, -ɪŋ, -d
AM roʊ, -z, -ɪŋ, -d
Rowallan
BR rəʊˈalən
AM roʊˈælən
rowan
BR ˈrəʊən, ˈraʊən, -z
AM ˈraʊən, ˈroʊən, -z
rowboat
BR ˈrəʊbəʊt, -s
AM ˈroʊˌboʊt, -s
Rowbotham
BR ˈrəʊˌbɒtəm
AM ˈroʊˌbɑdəm
Rowbottom
BR ˈrəʊˌbɒtəm
AM ˈroʊˌbɑdəm
rowdily
BR ˈraʊdɪli
AM ˈraʊdəli
rowdiness
BR ˈraʊdɪnɪs
AM ˈraʊdinɨs
rowdy
BR ˈraʊd|i, -ɪə(r), -ɪɪst
AM ˈraʊdi, -ər, -ɨst
rowdyism
BR ˈraʊdɪɪz(ə)m
AM ˈraʊdiˌɪzəm
Rowe
BR rəʊ
AM roʊ
rowel
BR ˈraʊ(ə)l, -z
AM ˈraʊ(ə)l, -z
rowen
BR ˈraʊən
AM ˈraʊən, ˈroʊən
Rowena
BR rəʊˈiːnə(r)
AM roʊˈinə
Rowenta®
BR rəʊˈɛntə(r)
AM roʊˈɛn(t)ə
rower
BR ˈrəʊə(r), -z
AM ˈroʊər, -z
rowhouse
BR ˈrəʊhaʊ|s, -zɪz
AM ˈroʊˌhaʊ|s, -zəz
Rowland
BR ˈrəʊlənd
AM ˈroʊlən(d)
Rowlands
BR ˈrəʊlən(d)z
AM ˈroʊlən(d)s
Rowlandson
BR ˈrəʊlən(d)s(ə)n
AM ˈroʊlən(d)sən
Rowley
BR ˈrəʊli
AM ˈroʊli
rowlock
BR ˈrɒlək, ˈrəʊlɒk, -s
AM ˈroʊˌlɑk, -s
Rowntree
BR ˈraʊntriː
AM ˈraʊnˌtri
Rowse
BR raʊs
AM raʊz
Rowton
BR ˈraʊtn
AM ˈraʊtn
Roxana
BR rɒkˈsɑːnə(r)
AM rɑkˈsænə
Roxanna
BR rɒkˈsanə(r)
AM rɑkˈsænə
Roxanne
BR rɒkˈsan
AM rɑkˈsæn
Roxburgh
BR ˈrɒksb(ə)rə(r)
AM ˈrɑkˌbərə
Roxy
BR ˈrɒksi
AM ˈrɑksi
Roy
BR rɔɪ
AM rɔɪ
royal
BR ˈrɔɪəl, -z
AM ˈrɔɪ(ə)l, -z
royalism
BR ˈrɔɪəlɪz(ə)m
AM ˈrɔɪəlɪzəm
royalist
BR ˈrɔɪəlɪst, -s
AM ˈrɔɪələst, -s
royalistic
BR ˌrɔɪəˈlɪstɪk
AM ˌrɔɪəˈlɪstɪk
royally
BR ˈrɔɪəli
AM ˈrɔɪəli
royalty
BR ˈrɔɪəlt|i, -ɪz
AM ˈrɔɪ(ə)lti, -z
Royce
BR rɔɪs
AM rɔɪs
Royle
BR rɔɪl
AM rɔɪl
Royston
BR ˈrɔɪst(ə)n
AM ˈrɔɪstən
Roz
BR rɒz
AM rɑz
rozzer
BR ˈrɒzə(r), -z
AM ˈrɑzər, -z
Ruabon
BR rʊˈab(ə)n
AM ruˈɑbəb
WE rʊˈabɒn
Ruanda
BR rʊˈandə(r)
AM ruˈɑndə
Ruandan
BR rʊˈandən, -z
AM ruˈɑndən, -z
Ruaridh
BR ˈrʊəri, ˈrɔːri
AM ˈrʊəri
IR ˈruəriː
rub
BR rʌb, -z, -ɪŋ, -d
AM rəb, -z, -ɪŋ, -d
rub-a-dub
BR ˈrʌbəˌdʌb,
ˌrʌbəˈdʌb, -z, -ɪŋ, -d
AM ˈrəbəˈdəb, -z, -ɪŋ, -d
rub-a-dub-dub
BR ˌrʌbədʌbˈdʌb
AM ˈrəbəˌdəbˈdəb
Rubáiyát
BR ˈruːbʌɪ(j)at,
ruːˈbʌɪ(j)at
AM ˈrubiˌ(j)ɑt,
ˈruˌbaɪˌ(j)ɑt
rubato
BR rʊˈbɑːtəʊ, -z
AM ruˈbɑdoʊ, -z
rubber
BR ˈrʌbə(r), -z
AM ˈrəbər, -z
rubberiness
BR ˈrʌb(ə)rɪnɪs
AM ˈrəbərinɨs
rubberise
BR ˈrʌbərʌɪz, -ɨz, -ɪŋ, -d
AM ˈrəbəˌraɪz, -ɨz, -ɪŋ, -d
rubberize
BR ˈrʌbərʌɪz, -ɨz, -ɪŋ, -d
AM ˈrəbəˌraɪz, -ɨz, -ɪŋ, -d
rubberneck
BR ˈrʌbənɛk, -s, -ɪŋ, -t
AM ˈrəbərˌnɛk, -s, -ɪŋ, -t
rubbery
BR ˈrʌb(ə)ri
AM ˈrəbəri
rubbing
BR ˈrʌbɪŋ, -z
AM ˈrəbɪŋ, -z
rubbish
BR ˈrʌb|ɪʃ, -ɨʃɪz, -ɨʃɪŋ,
-ɪʃt
AM ˈrəbɪʃ, -ɨʃɪz, -ɨʃɪŋ,
-ɪʃt
rubbishy
BR ˈrʌbɨʃi
AM ˈrəbəʃi
rubbity
BR ˌrʌbɨt|i, -ɪz
AM ˌrəbədi, -z
rubble
BR ˈrʌbl
AM ˈrəbəl
rubblework
BR ˈrʌblwəːk
AM ˈrəbəlˌwərk
rubbly
BR ˈrʌbl̩i
AM ˈrəb(ə)li
Rubbra
BR ˈrʌbrə(r)
AM ˈrəbrə
rubdown
BR ˈrʌbdaʊn, -z
AM ˈrəbˌdaʊn, -z
rube
BR ruːb, -z
AM rub, -z
rubefacient
BR ˌruːbɪˈfeɪʃnt, -s
AM ˌrubəˈfeɪʃənt, -s
rubefaction
BR ˌruːbɪˈfakʃn
AM ˌrubəˈfækʃən
rubefy
BR ˈruːbɨfʌɪ, -z, -ɪŋ, -d
AM ˈrubəˌfaɪ, -z, -ɪŋ, -d
rubella
BR ruːˈbɛlə(r),
rʊˈbɛlə(r)
AM ruˈbɛlə
rubellite
BR ˈruːbɨlʌɪt, -s
AM ˈrubəˌlaɪt, -s
Ruben
BR ˈruːb(ɪ)n
AM ˈrubən
rubenesque
BR ˌruːbɪˈnɛsk
AM ˌrubəˈnɛsk

Rubens
BR 'ru:b(ɪ)nz
AM 'rubɛnz

rubeola
BR rʊ'bi:ələ(r), ˌru:bɪ'əʊlə(r)
AM ˌrubi'oʊlə

Rubery
BR 'ru:b(ə)ri
AM 'rubəri

Rubicon
BR 'ru:bɪk(ə)n, 'ru:bɪkɒn
AM 'rubəˌkɑn

rubicund
BR 'ru:bɪk(ə)nd, 'ru:bɪkʌnd
AM 'rubəkənd

rubicundity
BR ˌru:bɪ'kʌndɪti
AM ˌrubə'kəndədi

rubidium
BR ru:'bɪdɪəm, rʊ'bɪdɪəm
AM ru'bɪdiəm

rubify
BR 'ru:bɪfʌɪ, -z, -ɪŋ, -d
AM 'rubəˌfaɪ, -z, -ɪŋ, -d

rubiginous
BR ru:'bɪdʒɪnəs, rʊ'bɪdʒɪnəs
AM ˌru'bɪdʒɪnɪs

Rubik
BR 'ru:bɪk
AM 'rubɪk

Rubin
BR 'ru:bɪn
AM 'rubən

Rubinstein
BR 'ru:b(ɪ)nstʌɪn
AM 'rubənˌstin, 'rubənˌstaɪn

ruble
BR 'ru:bl, -z
AM 'rubəl, -z

rubric
BR 'ru:brɪk, -s
AM 'ruˌbrɪk, -s

rubrical
BR 'ru:brɪkl
AM 'rubrəkəl

rubricate
BR 'ru:brɪkeɪt, -s, -ɪŋ, -ɪd
AM 'rubrəˌkeɪ|t, -ts, -dɪŋ, -dɪd

rubrication
BR ˌru:brɪ'keɪʃn
AM ˌrubrə'keɪʃən

rubricator
BR 'rʌbrɪkeɪtə(r), -z
AM 'rubrəˌkeɪdər, -z

rubrician
BR ru:'brɪʃn, -z
AM ru'brɪʃən, -z

rubricism
BR 'ru:brɪsɪz(ə)m
AM 'rubrəˌsɪzəm

rubricist
BR 'ru:brɪsɪst, -s
AM 'rubrəsəst, -s

ruby
BR 'ru:b|i, -ɪz
AM 'rubi, -z

ruche
BR ru:ʃ, -ɪz, -ɪŋ, -t
AM ruʃ, -ɪz, -ɪŋ, -t

ruck
BR rʌk, -s, -ɪŋ, -t
AM rək, -s, -ɪŋ, -t

ruckle
BR 'rʌkl, -z, -ɪŋ, -d
AM 'rəkəl, -z, -ɪŋ, -d

rucksack
BR 'rʌksak, -s
AM 'rəkˌsæk, 'rʊkˌsæk, -s

ruckus
BR 'rʌkəs, -ɪz
AM 'rəkəs, -ɪz

rucola
BR 'ru:kələ(r)
AM 'rukələ

ruction
BR 'rʌkʃn, -z
AM 'rəkʃən, -z

rudaceous
BR rʊ'deɪʃəs
AM ru'deɪʃəs

rudbeckia
BR rʌd'bɛkɪə(r), ˌru:d'bɛkɪə(r), -z
AM ˌrud'bɛkiə, -z

rudd
BR rʌd, -z
AM rəd, -z

rudder
BR 'rʌdə(r), -z
AM 'rədər, -z

rudderless
BR 'rʌdələs
AM 'rədərləs

Ruddigore
BR 'rʌdɪgɔ:(r)
AM 'rʊdəˌgɔ(ə)r

ruddily
BR 'rʌdɪli
AM 'rədəli

ruddiness
BR 'rʌdɪnɪs
AM 'rədinɪs

ruddle
BR 'rʌd|l, -lz, -lɪŋ\-lɪŋ, -ld
AM 'rəd|əl, -əlz, -(ə)lɪŋ, -əld

ruddock
BR 'rʌdək, -s
AM 'rədək, -s

ruddy
BR 'rʌd|i, -ɪə(r), -ɪɪst
AM 'rədi, -ər, -ɪst

rude
BR ru:d, -ə(r), -ɪst
AM rud, -ər, -əst

rudely
BR 'ru:dli
AM 'rudli

rudeness
BR 'ru:dnəs
AM 'rudnəs

ruderal
BR 'ru:d(ə)rəl, 'ru:d(ə)rl, -z
AM 'rudərəl, -z

rudery
BR 'ru:dər|i, -ɪz
AM 'rudəri, -z

Rudge
BR rʌdʒ
AM rədʒ

Rudi
BR 'ru:di
AM 'rudi

rudiment
BR 'ru:dɪm(ə)nt, -s
AM 'rudəmənt, -s

rudimental
BR ˌru:dɪ'mɛntl
AM ˌrudə'mɛn(t)l

rudimentarily
BR ˌru:dɪ'mɛnt(ə)rɪli
AM ˌrudəmən'tɛrəli

rudimentariness
BR ˌru:dɪ'mɛnt(ə)rɪnɪs
AM ˌrudə'mɛn(t)ərinɪs

rudimentary
BR ˌru:dɪ'mɛnt(ə)ri
AM ˌrudə'mɛn(t)əri

rudish
BR 'ru:dɪʃ
AM 'rudɪʃ

Rudolf
BR 'ru:dɒlf
AM 'rudɔlf, 'rudɑlf

Rudolph
BR 'ru:dɒlf
AM 'rudɔlf, 'rudɑlf

Rudy
BR 'ru:di
AM 'rudi

Rudyard
BR 'rʌdjəd, 'rʌdʒəd, 'rʌdjɑ:d
AM 'rədjərd

rue
BR ru:, -z, -ɪŋ, -d
AM ru, -z, -ɪŋ, -d

rueful
BR 'ru:f(ʊ)l
AM 'rufəl

ruefully
BR 'ru:fʊli, 'ru:fli
AM 'rufəli

ruefulness
BR 'ru:f(ʊ)lnəs
AM 'rufəlnəs

rufescence
BR ru:'fɛsns
AM ru'fɛsəns

rufescent
BR ru:'fɛsnt
AM ru'fɛsənt

ruff
BR rʌf, -s, -ɪŋ, -t
AM rəf, -s, -ɪŋ, -t

ruffian
BR 'rʌfɪən, -z
AM 'rəfiən, -z

ruffianism
BR 'rʌfɪənɪz(ə)m
AM 'rəfiənɪzəm

ruffianly
BR 'rʌfɪənli
AM 'rəfiənli

ruffle
BR 'rʌf|l, -lz, -lɪŋ\-lɪŋ, -ld
AM 'rəf|əl, -əlz, -(ə)lɪŋ, -əld

rufflike
BR 'rʌflʌɪk
AM 'rəfˌlaɪk

Rufford
BR 'rʌfəd
AM 'rəfərd

rufous
BR 'ru:fəs
AM 'rufəs

Rufus
BR 'ru:fəs
AM 'rufəs

rug
BR rʌg, -z
AM rəg, -z

Rugbeian
BR rʌg'bi:ən, -z
AM 'rəgbiən, -z

rugby
BR 'rʌgbi
AM 'rəgbi

Rugeley
BR 'ru:dʒli
AM 'rudʒli

Rügen
BR 'ru:dʒ(ə)n
AM 'rudʒɛn
GER 'ʀʏgn

rugged
BR 'rʌgɪd
AM 'rəgəd

ruggedly
BR 'rʌgɪdli
AM 'rəgədli

ruggedness
BR 'rʌgɪdnɪs
AM 'rəgədnəs

rugger
BR 'rʌgə(r)
AM 'rəgər

rugola
BR 'ru:gələ(r)
AM 'rugələ

rugosa
BR ru:'gəʊzə(r), -z
AM ru'goʊzə, -z

rugose
BR 'ru:gəʊs, 'ru:gəʊz, rʊ'gəʊs

AM 'rugoʊz, 'rugoʊs

rugosely
BR 'ruːgəʊsli, 'ruːgəʊzli, rʊ'gəʊsli
AM ru'goʊzli, ru'goʊsli

rugosity
BR ruː'gɒsɨti, rʊ'gɒsɨti
AM ru'gɑsədi

Ruhr
BR 'rʊə(r)
AM 'rʊ(ə)r

ruin
BR 'ruː|ɪn, -ɪnz, -ɨnɪŋ, -ɪnd
AM 'ruən, 'ruˌɪn, -z, -ɪŋ, -d

ruination
BR ˌruːɪ'neɪʃn
AM ˌruə'neɪʃən

ruinous
BR 'ruːɨnəs
AM 'ruənəs

ruinously
BR 'ruːɨnəsli
AM 'ruənəsli

ruinousness
BR 'ruːɨnəsnəs
AM 'ruənəsnəs

Ruislip
BR 'rʌɪslɪp
AM 'raɪsləp

Ruiz
BR 'ruːɪz
AM ru'iz
SP 'rrwiθ, 'rrwis

rule
BR ruːl, -z, -ɪŋ, -d
AM rul, -z, -ɪŋ, -d

rulebook
BR 'ruːlbʊk, -s
AM 'rulˌbʊk, -s

ruleless
BR 'ruːl(l)əs
AM 'ru(l)ləs

ruler
BR 'ruːlə(r), -z
AM 'rulər, -z

rulership
BR 'ruːləʃɪp, -s
AM 'rulərˌʃɪp, -s

ruling
BR 'ruːlɪŋ, -z
AM 'rulɪŋ, -z

rum
BR rʌm, -ə(r), -ɨst
AM rəm, -ər, -əst

Rumania
BR ruː'meɪnɪə(*r*), rʊ'meɪnɪə(*r*)
AM roʊ'meɪniə, ru'meɪniə

Rumanian
BR ruː'meɪnɪən, rʊ'meɪnɪən
AM roʊ'meɪniən, ru'meɪniən

Rumansh
BR rʊ'manʃ, rʊ'mɑːnʃ
AM ro'mɑnʃ, ru'mɑnʃ

rumba
BR 'rʌmbə(*r*), -z
AM 'rəmbə, -z

rum baba
BR ˌrʌm 'bɑːbə(*r*), -z
AM ˌrəm 'bɑbə, -z

Rumbelow
BR 'rʌmbɨləʊ
AM 'rəmbəˌloʊ

rumble
BR 'rʌmb|l, -lz, -l̩ɪŋ\-lɪŋ, -ld
AM 'rəmbəl, -əlz, -(ə)lɪŋ, -əld

rumbler
BR 'rʌmbl̩ə(r), 'rʌmblə(r), -z
AM 'rəmb(ə)lər, -z

rumbling
BR 'rʌmbl̩ɪŋ, 'rʌmblɪŋ, -z
AM 'rəmb(ə)lɪŋ, -z

Rumbold
BR 'rʌmbəʊld
AM 'rəmˌboʊld

rumbustious
BR rʌm'bʌstʃəs, rʌm'bʌstɪəs
AM ˌrəm'bəstʃəs

rumbustiously
BR rʌm'bʌsʃəsli, rʌm'bʌstɪəsli
AM rəm'bəstʃəsli, rəm'bəsdiəsli

rumbustiousness
BR rʌm'bʌstʃəsnəs, rʌm'bʌstɪəsnəs
AM rəm'bəstʃəsnəs, rəm'bəsdiəsnəs

Rumelia
BR rʊ'miːlɪə(*r*)
AM ru'miljə, ru'miliə

rumen
BR 'ruːmɛn, 'ruːmɨn, -z
AM 'rumən, -z

Rumi
BR 'ruːmi
AM 'rumi

rumina
BR 'ruːmɨnə(*r*)
AM 'rumənə

ruminant
BR 'ruːmɨnənt, -s
AM 'rumənənt, -s

ruminate
BR 'ruːmɨneɪt, -s, -ɪŋ, -ɨd
AM 'ruməˌneɪ|t, -ts, -dɪŋ, -dəd

rumination
BR ˌruːmɪ'neɪʃn, -z
AM ˌrumə'neɪʃən, -z

ruminative
BR 'ruːmɨnətɪv
AM 'ruməˌneɪdɪv, 'rumənədɪv

ruminatively
BR 'ruːmɨnətɨvli
AM 'ruməˌneɪdɨvli, 'rumənəˌdɨvli

ruminator
BR 'ruːmɪneɪtə(r), -z
AM 'ruməˌneɪdər, -z

rumly
BR 'rʌmli
AM 'rəmli

rummage
BR 'rʌm|ɪdʒ, -ɨdʒɪz, -ɨdʒɪŋ, -ɪdʒd
AM 'rəmədʒ, -əz, -ɪŋ, -d

rummager
BR 'rʌmɨdʒə(r), -z
AM 'rəmədʒər, -z

rummer
BR 'rʌmə(r), -z
AM 'rəmər, -z

rummily
BR 'rʌmɨli
AM 'rəməli

rumminess
BR 'rʌmɪnɪs
AM 'rəminɪs

rummy
BR 'rʌm|i, -ɪə(r), -ɪɪst
AM 'rəmi, -ər, -ɨst

rumness
BR 'rʌmnəs
AM 'rəmnəs

rumor
BR 'ruːmə(r), -z, -d
AM 'rumər, -z, -d

rumour
BR 'ruːmə(r), -z, -d
AM 'rumər, -z, -d

rump
BR rʌmp, -s
AM rəmp, -s

Rumpelstiltskin
BR ˌrʌmpl'stɪltskɪn
AM ˌrəmpl'stɪl(t)skɨn

rumple
BR 'rʌmp|l, -lz, -l̩ɪŋ\-lɪŋ, -ld
AM 'rəmp|əl, -əlz, -(ə)lɪŋ, -əld

rumpless
BR 'rʌmpləs
AM 'rəmpləs

rumply
BR 'rʌmpl̩i
AM 'rəmp(ə)li

Rumpole
BR 'rʌmpəʊl
AM 'rəmˌpoʊl

rumpus
BR 'rʌmpəs, -ɨz
AM 'rəmpəs, -ɨz

rumpy
BR 'rʌmp|i, -ɪz
AM 'rəmpi, -z

rumpy-pumpy
BR ˌrʌmpɪ'pʌmpi
AM ¦rəmpi¦pəmpi

rumrunner
BR 'rʌmˌrʌnə(r), -z
AM 'rəmˌrənər, -z

run
BR rʌn, -z, -ɪŋ
AM rən, -z, -ɪŋ

runabout
BR 'rʌnəbaʊt, -s
AM 'rənəˌbaʊt, -s

runagate
BR 'rʌnəgeɪt, -s
AM 'rənəˌgeɪt, -s

runaround
BR 'rʌnəraʊnd
AM 'rənəˌraʊnd

runaway
BR 'rʌnəweɪ, -z
AM 'rənəˌweɪ, -z

runback
BR 'rʌnbak, -s
AM 'rənˌbæk, -s

runcible
BR 'rʌnsɨbl
AM 'rənsəbəl

Runcie
BR 'rʌnsi
AM 'rənsi

Runciman
BR 'rʌnsɪmən
AM 'rənsəmən

runcinate
BR 'rʌnsɨnət
AM 'rənsəˌneɪt

Runcorn
BR 'rʌnkɔːn, 'rʌŋkɔːn
AM 'rənˌkɔ(ə)rn

rundale
BR 'rʌndeɪl, -z
AM 'rənˌdeɪl, -z

Rundle
BR 'rʌndl
AM 'rənd(ə)l

rundown
noun
BR 'rʌndaʊn, -z
AM 'rənˌdaʊn, -z

run-down
adjective
BR ˌrʌn'daʊn
AM ¦rən'daʊn

rune
BR ruːn, -z
AM run, -z

rung
BR rʌŋ, -z, -d
AM rəŋ, -z, -d

rungless
BR 'rʌŋləs
AM 'rəŋləs

runic
BR 'ruːnɪk
AM 'runɪk

run-in
BR 'rʌnɪn, -z

AM 'rən,ɪn, -z
runlet
BR 'rʌnlɨt, -s
AM 'rənlət, -s
runnable
BR 'rʌnəbl
AM 'rənəbəl
runnel
BR 'rʌnl, -z
AM 'rənəl, -z
runner
BR 'rʌnə(r), -z
AM 'rənər, -z
runniness
BR 'rʌnɪnɨs
AM 'rəninɨs
runningboard
BR 'rʌnɪŋbɔːd, -z
AM 'rənɪŋ,bɔ(ə)rd, -z
runny
BR 'rʌn|i, -ɪə(r), -ɪɨst
AM 'rəni, -ər, -ɨst
Runnymede
BR 'rʌnɪmiːd
AM 'rəni,mid
runt
BR rʌnt, -s
AM rənt, -s
runthrough
BR 'rʌnθruː, -z
AM 'rən,θru, -z
runty
BR 'rʌnti
AM 'rən(t)i
runup
BR 'rʌnʌp, -s
AM 'rən,əp, -s
runway
BR 'rʌnweɪ, -z
AM 'rən,weɪ, -z
Runyon
BR 'rʌnjən
AM 'rənjən
rupee
BR ,ruː'piː, rʊ'piː, -z
AM ru'pi, 'rupi, -z
Rupert
BR 'ruːpət
AM 'rupərt
rupiah
BR rʊ'piːə(r), -z
AM ru'piə, -z
rupturable
BR 'rʌptʃ(ə)rəbl
AM 'rəp(t)ʃərəbəl
rupture
BR 'rʌptʃ|ə(r), -əz, -(ə)rɪŋ, -əd
AM 'rəp(t)ʃ|ər, -ərz, -(ə)rɪŋ, -ərd
rural
BR 'rʊərəl, 'rʊərl̩
AM 'rʊrəl
ruralisation
BR ,rʊərəlʌɪ'zeɪʃn, ,rʊərl̩ʌɪ'zeɪʃn
AM ,rʊrələ'zeɪʃən, ,rʊrə,laɪ'zeɪʃən
ruralise
BR 'rʊərəlʌɪz, 'rʊərl̩ʌɪz, -ɨz, -ɪŋ, -d
AM 'rʊrə,laɪz, -ɨz, -ɪŋ, -d
ruralism
BR 'rʊərəlɪz(ə)m, 'rʊərl̩ɪz(ə)m
AM 'rʊrə,lɪzəm
ruralist
BR 'rʊərəlɪst, 'rʊərl̩ɪst, -s
AM 'rʊrələst, -s
rurality
BR rʊ'ralɨt|i, -ɪz
AM ,rʊ'rælədi, -z
ruralization
BR ,rʊərəlʌɪ'zeɪʃn, ,rʊərl̩ʌɪ'zeɪʃn
AM ,rʊrələ'zeɪʃən, ,rʊrə,laɪ'zeɪʃən
ruralize
BR 'rʊərəlʌɪz, 'rʊərl̩ʌɪz, -ɨz, -ɪŋ, -d
AM 'rʊrə,laɪz, -ɨz, -ɪŋ, -d
rurally
BR 'rʊərəli, 'rʊərl̩i
AM 'rʊrəli
ruridecanal
BR ,rʊərɪdɪ'keɪnl, ,rʊərɪ'dɛkənl, ,rʊərɪ'dɛkn̩l
AM ,rʊrə'dɛkənəl
Rurik
BR 'rʊərɪk
AM 'rʊrɪk
RUS 'rʲurʲik
Ruritania
BR ,rʊərɪ'teɪnɪə(r)
AM ,rʊrə'teɪniə
Ruritanian
BR ,rʊərɪ'teɪnɪən, -z
AM ,rʊrə'teɪniən, -z
rusa
BR 'ruːsə(r), -z
AM 'rusə, -z
ruse
BR ruːz, -ɨz
AM ruz, rus, -ɨz
rush
BR rʌʃ, -ɨz, -ɪŋ, -t
AM rəʃ, -ɨz, -ɪŋ, -t
Rushdie
BR 'rʊʃdi, 'rʌʃdi
AM 'rəʃdi
rushee
BR rʌ'ʃiː, -z
AM rə'ʃi, -z
rusher
BR 'rʌʃə(r), -z
AM 'rəʃər, -z
rush-hour
BR 'rʌʃaʊə(r), -z
AM 'rəʃ,aʊ(ə)r, -z
rushingly
BR 'rʌʃɪŋli
AM 'rəʃɪŋli
rushlight
BR 'rʌʃlʌɪt, -s
AM 'rəʃ,laɪt, -s
rushlike
BR 'rʌʃlʌɪk
AM 'rəʃ,laɪk
Rushmore
BR 'rʌʃmɔː(r)
AM 'rəʃmɔ(ə)r
Rusholme
BR 'rʌʃhəʊm
AM 'rəʃ,(h)oʊm
Rushton
BR 'rʌʃt(ə)n
AM 'rəʃtən
Rushworth
BR 'rʌʃwəːθ, 'rʌʃwəθ
AM 'rəʃ,wərθ
rushy
BR 'rʌʃ|i, -ɪə(r), -ɪɨst
AM 'rəʃi, -ər, -ɨst
rusk
BR rʌsk, -s
AM rəsk, -s
Ruski
BR 'rʌsk|i, -ɪz
AM 'rəski, 'rʊski, -z
Ruskin
BR 'rʌskɪn
AM 'rəskən
Rusky
BR 'rʌsk|i, -ɪz
AM 'rəski, 'rʊski, -z
Russ
BR rʌs
AM rəs
russe
BR ruːs
AM rus
Russell
BR 'rʌsl
AM 'rəsɛl
russet
BR 'rʌsɪt, -s
AM 'rəsət, -s
russety
BR 'rʌsɨti
AM 'rəsədi
Russia
BR 'rʌʃə(r)
AM 'rəʃə
Russian
BR 'rʌʃn, -z
AM 'rəʃən, -z
Russianisation
BR ,rʌʃn̩ʌɪ'zeɪʃn, ,rʌʃənʌɪ'zeɪʃn
AM ,rəʃənə'zeɪʃən, ,rəʃə,naɪ'zeɪʃən
Russianise
BR 'rʌʃn̩ʌɪz, 'rʌʃənʌɪz, -ɨz, -ɪŋ, -d
AM 'rəʃə,naɪz, -ɨz, -ɪŋ, -d
Russianization
BR ,rʌʃn̩ʌɪ'zeɪʃn, ,rʌʃənʌɪ'zeɪʃn
AM ,rəʃənə'zeɪʃən, ,rəʃə,naɪ'zeɪʃən
Russianize
BR 'rʌʃn̩ʌɪz, 'rʌʃənʌɪz, -ɨz, -ɪŋ, -d
AM 'rəʃə,naɪz, -ɨz, -ɪŋ, -d
Russianness
BR 'rʌʃ(ə)nnəs
AM 'rəʃə(n)nəs
Russification
BR ,rʌsɨfɪ'keɪʃn
AM ,rəsəfə'keɪʃən
Russify
BR 'rʌsɨfʌɪ, -z, -ɪŋ, -d
AM 'rəsə,faɪ, -z, -ɪŋ, -d
Russki
BR 'rʌsk|i, -ɪz
AM 'rəski, 'rʊski, -z
Russky
BR 'rʌsk|i, -ɪz
AM 'rəski, 'rʊski, -z
Russo
BR 'rʌsəʊ
AM 'rəsoʊ, 'rʊsoʊ
Russo-
BR 'rʌsəʊ
AM 'rəsoʊ
Russophile
BR 'rʌsə(ʊ)fʌɪl, -z
AM 'rəsə,faɪl, -z
Russophobe
BR 'rʌsə(ʊ)fəʊb, -z
AM 'rəsə,foʊb, -z
Russophobia
BR ,rʌsəʊ'fəʊbɪə(r)
AM ,rəsə'foʊbiə
rust
BR rʌst, -s, -ɪŋ, -ɨd
AM rəst, -s, -ɪŋ, -ɨd
rust-belt
BR 'rʌs(t)bɛlt
AM 'rəs(t),bɛlt
rustbucket
BR 'rʌs(t),bʌkɪt, -s
AM 'rəs(t),bəkət, -s
rustic
BR 'rʌstɪk, -s
AM 'rəstɪk, -s
rustically
BR 'rʌstɪkli
AM 'rəstək(ə)li
rusticate
BR 'rʌstɪkeɪt, -s, -ɪŋ, -ɨd
AM 'rəstə,keɪ|t, -ts, -dɪŋ, -dɨd
rustication
BR ,rʌstɪ'keɪʃn
AM ,rəstə'keɪʃən
rusticity
BR rʌ'stɪsɨti
AM rə'stɪsɨdi
rustily
BR 'rʌstɨli
AM 'rəstəli
rustiness
BR 'rʌstɪnɨs

AM 'rəstinɪs

rustle
BR 'rʌs|l, -lz, -ḷɪŋ\-lɪŋ, -ld
AM 'rəs|əl, -əlz, -(ə)lɪŋ, -əld

rustler
BR 'rʌslə(r), -z
AM 'rəslər, -z

rustless
BR 'rʌstləs
AM 'rəs(t)ləs

rustling
BR 'rʌsḷɪŋ, 'rʌslɪŋ, -z
AM 'rəs(t)lɪŋ, -z

rustproof
BR 'rʌs(t)pruːf, -s, -ɪŋ, -t
AM 'rəs(t),pruf, -s, -ɪŋ, -t

rustre
BR 'rʌstə(r), -z
AM 'rəstər, -z

rusty
BR 'rʌst|i, -ɪə(r), -ɪɪst
AM 'rəsti, -ər, -ɨst

rut
BR rʌt, -s, -ɪŋ, -ɨd
AM rə|t, -ts, -dɪŋ, -dəd

rutabaga
BR ˌruːtə'beɪgə(r), 'ruːtəˌbeɪgə(r), -z
AM 'rudəˌbeɪgə, -z

Rutgers
BR 'rʌtgəz
AM 'rətgərz

ruth
BR ruːθ
AM rʊθ

Ruthenia
BR rʊ'θiːnɪə(r)
AM ru'θiniə

ruthenium
BR rʊ'θiːnɪəm
AM ru'θiniəm

Rutherford
BR 'rʌðəfəd
AM 'rəðərfərd

rutherfordium
BR ˌrʌðə'fɔːdɪəm
AM ˌrəðər'fɔrdiəm

ruthful
BR 'ruːθf(ʊ)l
AM 'ruθfəl

ruthfully
BR 'ruːθfʊli, 'ruːθfḷi
AM 'ruθfəli

ruthfulness
BR 'ruːθf(ʊ)lnəs
AM 'ruθfəlnəs

ruthless
BR 'ruːθləs
AM 'ruθləs

ruthlessly
BR 'ruːθləsli
AM 'ruθləsli

ruthlessness
BR 'ruːθləsnəs
AM 'ruθləsnəs

Ruthven
BR 'rɪvn, 'rʌθv(ə)n, 'ruːθv(ə)n
AM 'ruθvən

rutile
BR 'ruːtʌɪl, -z
AM 'ruˌtil, 'ruˌtaɪl, -z

rutin
BR 'ruːtɪn
AM 'rudɪn

Rutland
BR 'rʌtlənd
AM 'rətlənd

Rutledge
BR 'rʌtlɪdʒ
AM 'rətlədʒ

ruttish
BR 'rʌtɪʃ
AM 'rədɪʃ

rutty
BR 'rʌti
AM 'rədi

Ruwenzori
BR ˌruːən'zɔːri
AM ˌruwən'zɔri

R-value
BR 'ɑːˌvaljuː
AM 'ɑrˌvælju

Rwanda
BR rʊ'andə(r)
AM rʊ'ɑndə, rə'wɑndə

Rwandan
BR rʊ'andən, -z
AM ru'ɑndən, rə'wɑndən, -z

Rwandese
BR rʊˌan'diːz
AM ruˌɑn'diz, rəˌwɑn'diz

Rx
BR ˌɑːr'ɛks
AM ˌɑr'ɛks

Ryan
BR 'rʌɪən
AM 'raɪən

Rycroft
BR 'rʌɪkrɒft
AM 'raɪˌkrɔft, 'raɪˌkrɑft

Rydal
BR 'rʌɪdl
AM 'raɪd(ə)l

Ryde
BR rʌɪd
AM raɪd

Ryder
BR 'rʌɪdə(r)
AM 'raɪdər

rye
BR rʌɪ
AM raɪ

ryegrass
BR 'rʌɪgrɑːs, 'rʌɪgras
AM 'raɪˌgræs

Ryland
BR 'rʌɪlənd
AM 'raɪlən(d)

Rylands
BR 'rʌɪlən(d)z
AM 'raɪlən(d)z

Ryle
BR rʌɪl
AM raɪl

Ryles
BR rʌɪlz
AM raɪlz

Ryman
BR 'rʌɪmən
AM 'raɪmən

ryokan
BR rɪ'əʊkən, rɪ'əʊkan, -z
AM ri'oʊkən, -z

ryot
BR 'rʌɪət, -s
AM 'raɪət, -s

Ryton
BR 'rʌɪtn
AM 'raɪtn

ryu
BR rɪ'uː, -z
AM ri'u, -z

Ryvita®
BR (ˌ)rʌɪ'viːtə(r)
AM raɪ'vidə

Ss

s
BR ɛs, -ɪz
AM ɛs, -əz

Saab®
BR sɑːb, -z
AM sɑb, -z

Saadi
BR 'sɑːdi
AM 'sɑdi

Saar
BR sɑː(r)
AM sɑr

Saarbrücken
BR 'sɑːˌbrʊk(ə)n
AM 'sɑrˌbrʊkən
GER ˌzaːɐ'brykn

Saarinen
BR 'sɑːrɪnən
AM 'sɑrənən

Saarland
BR 'sɑːland
AM 'sɑrˌlænd

Saba
BR 'sɑːbə(r)
AM 'sɑbə

sabadilla
BR ˌsabə'dɪlə(r)
AM ˌsæbə'dɪlə

Sabaean
BR sə'biːən, -z
AM sə'biən, 'sɑbiən, -z

Sabah
BR 'sɑːbə(r)
AM 'sɑbɑ

Sabaism
BR 'sɑːbə(r)ɪz(ə)m
AM 'sɑbəˌɪzəm

Sabaoth
BR 'sabeɪɒθ, sə'beɪɒθ
AM 'sæbeɪˌɑθ

Sabatier
BR sə'batɪeɪ
AM səˌbɑdi'eɪ

sabayon
BR 'sabʌɪjɒ̃
AM sɑbaɪ'ɔn

sabbatarian
BR ˌsabə'tɛːrɪən, -z
AM ˌsæbə'tɛriən, -z

sabbatarianism
BR ˌsabə'tɛːrɪənɪz(ə)m
AM ˌsæbə'tɛriəˌnɪzəm

sabbath
BR 'sabəθ, -s
AM 'sæbəθ, -s

sabbatic
BR sə'batɪk, -s
AM sə'bædɪk, -s

sabbatical
BR sə'batɪkl, -z
AM sə'bædəkəl, -z

sabbatically
BR sə'batɪkli
AM sə'bædək(ə)li

sabbatisation
BR ˌsabətʌɪ'zeɪʃn
AM ˌsæbədə'zeɪʃən, ˌsæbəˌtaɪ'zeɪʃən

sabbatise
BR 'sabətʌɪz, -ɪz, -ɪŋ, -d
AM 'sæbəˌtaɪz, -ɪz, -ɪŋ, -d

sabbatization
BR ˌsabətʌɪ'zeɪʃn
AM ˌsæbədə'zeɪʃən, ˌsæbəˌtaɪ'zeɪʃən

sabbatize
BR 'sabətʌɪz, -ɪz, -ɪŋ, -d
AM 'sæbəˌtaɪz, -ɪz, -ɪŋ, -d

Sabellian
BR sə'bɛlɪən, -z
AM sə'bɛljən, sə'bɛliən, -z

saber
BR 'seɪb|ə(r), -əz, -(ə)rɪŋ, -əd
AM 'seɪb|ər, -ərz, -(ə)rɪŋ, -ərd

sabertooth
BR 'seɪbətuːθ
AM 'seɪbərˌtuθ

Sabian
BR 'seɪbɪən, -z
AM 'seɪbiən, -z

sabicu
BR ˌsabɪ'kuː, -z
AM 'sæbəˌku, -z

Sabin
BR 'seɪbɪn, 'sabɪn
AM 'seɪbən

Sabina
BR sə'biːnə(r)
AM sə'biːnə

Sabine[1]
people
BR 'sabʌɪn, -z
AM 'seɪˌbaɪn, 'seɪˌbin, -z

Sabine[2]
surname
BR 'sabʌɪn, 'seɪbʌɪn, 'seɪbɪn
AM 'seɪbən, 'seɪˌbin

Sabine[3]
U.S. river and lake
BR sə'biːn
AM sə'bin

sabir
BR sə'bɪə(r)
AM sə'bɪ(ə)r

sable
BR 'seɪbl, -z, -d
AM 'seɪbəl, -z, -d

sably
BR 'seɪbli
AM 'seɪb(ə)li

sabot
BR 'sabəʊ, -z, -d
AM ˌsæ'boʊ, -z, -d

sabotage
BR 'sabətɑː(d)ʒ, -ɪz, -ɪŋ, -d
AM 'sæbəˌtɑʒ, -əz, -ɪŋ, -d

saboteur
BR ˌsabə'təː(r), -z
AM ˌsæbə'tər, -z

sabra
BR 'sɑːbrə(r), 'sabrə(r), -z
AM 'sɑbrə, -z

sabre
BR 'seɪb|ə(r), -əz, -(ə)rɪŋ, -əd
AM 'seɪb|ər, -ərz, -(ə)rɪŋ, -ərd

sabretache
BR 'seɪbətaʃ, -ɪz
AM 'seɪbərˌtæʃ, -əz

sabretooth
BR 'seɪbətuːθ
AM 'seɪbərˌtuθ

sabreur
BR sə'brəː(r), -z
AM sə'brər, sɑ'brər, -z

Sabrina
BR sə'briːnə(r)
AM sə'brinə

sac
BR sak, -s
AM sæk, -s

saccade
BR sə'kɑːd, sa'kɑːd, -z
AM sə'kɑd, sæ'kɑd, -z

saccadic
BR sə'kadɪk
AM sə'kædɪk, sæ'kædɪk

saccate
BR 'sakeɪt
AM 'sæˌkeɪt

saccharide
BR 'sakərʌɪd, -z
AM 'sækəˌraɪd, -z

saccharimeter
BR ˌsakə'rɪmɪtə(r), -z
AM ˌsækə'rɪmədər, -z

saccharimetry
BR ˌsakə'rɪmɪtri
AM ˌsækə'rɪmətri

saccharin
BR 'sak(ə)rɪn, 'sakəriːn, -z
AM 'sæk(ə)rən, -z

saccharine
BR 'sak(ə)rɪn, 'sakəriːn, -z
AM 'sæk(ə)rən, -z

saccharogenic
BR ˌsak(ə)rə(ʊ)'dʒɛnɪk
AM ˌsækəroʊ'dʒɛnɪk

saccharometer
BR ˌsakə'rɒmɪtə(r), -z
AM ˌsækə'rɑmədər, -z

saccharometry
BR ˌsakə'rɒmɪtri
AM ˌsækə'rɑmətri

saccharose
BR 'sakərəʊz, 'sakərəʊs
AM 'sækəˌroʊs, 'sækəˌroʊz

sacciform
BR 'saksɪfɔːm
AM 'sæk(s)əˌfɔ(ə)rm

saccular
BR 'sakjʊlə(r)
AM 'sækjələr

sacculate
BR 'sakjʊleɪt, -ɪd
AM 'sækjəˌleɪ|t, -dɪd

sacculation
BR ˌsakjʊ'leɪʃn, -z
AM ˌsækjə'leɪʃən, -z

saccule
BR 'sakjuːl, -z
AM 'sæˌkjul, -z

sacerdotage
BR ˌsakə'dəʊtɪdʒ
AM ˌsæsər'doʊdɪdʒ, ˌsækər'doʊdɪdʒ

sacerdotal
BR ˌsakə'dəʊtl
AM ˌsæsər'doʊdl, ˌsækər'doʊdl

sacerdotalism
BR ˌsakə'dəʊtl̩ɪz(ə)m
AM ˌsæsər'doʊdlˌɪzəm, ˌsækər'doʊdlˌɪzəm

sacerdotalist
BR ˌsakə'dəʊtl̩ɪst, -s
AM ˌsæsər'doʊdləst, ˌsækər'doʊdləst, -s

sacerdotally
BR ˌsakə'dəʊtl̩i, ˌsakə'dəʊtəli
AM ˌsæsər'doʊdl̩i, ˌsækər'doʊdli

Sacha
BR 'saʃə(r)
AM 'sɑʃə, 'sætʃə

sachem
BR 'seɪtʃəm, -z
AM 'seɪtʃəm, -z

Sachertorte
BR 'zakəˌtɔːtə(r)
AM 'sɑkərˌtɔ(ə)rt, 'sækərˌtɔ(ə)rt

Sachertorten
BR 'zakəˌtɔːt(ə)n
AM 'sɑkərˌtɔ(ə)rtn, 'sækərˌtɔ(ə)rtn

sachet
BR 'saʃeɪ, -z
AM sæ'ʃeɪ, -z

Sacheverell
BR sə'ʃɛvr(ə)l
AM səˌʃɛvə'rɛl

Sachs
BR saks
AM sæks

Sachsen
BR 'saks(ə)n
AM 'sæksən
sack
BR sak, -s, -ɪŋ, -t
AM sæk, -s, -ɪŋ, -t
sackable
BR 'sakəbl
AM 'sækəbəl
sackbut
BR 'sakbʌt, -s
AM 'sæk,bət, -s
sackcloth
BR 'sakklɒθ
AM 'sæk,clɔθ, 'sæk,clɑθ
sacker
BR 'sakə(r), -z
AM 'sækər, -z
sackful
BR 'sakfʊl, -z
AM 'sæk,fʊl, -z
sacking
BR 'sakɪŋ, -z
AM 'sækɪŋ, -z
sackless
BR 'sakləs
AM 'sækləs
sacklike
BR 'saklʌɪk
AM 'sæk,laɪk
Sackville
BR 'sakvɪl
AM 'sæk,vɪl
sacra
BR 'seɪkrə(*r*), 'sakrə(*r*)
AM 'sækrə, 'seɪkrə
sacral
BR 'seɪkr(ə)l, 'sakr(ə)l
AM 'sækrəl, 'seɪkrəl
sacrament
BR 'sakrəm(ə)nt, -s
AM 'sækrəmənt, -s
sacramental
BR ˌsakrə'mɛntl
AM ˌsækrə'mɛn(t)l
sacramentalism
BR ˌsakrə'mɛntḷɪz(ə)m
AM ˌsækrə'mɛn(t)l,ɪzəm
sacramentalist
BR ˌsakrə'mɛntḷɪst, -s
AM ˌsækrə'mɛn(t)ḷəst, -s
sacramentality
BR ˌsakrəmən'talɪti, ˌsakrəmɛn'talɪti
AM ˌsækrəmən'tælədi, ˌsækrə,mɛn'tælədi
sacramentally
BR ˌsakrə'mɛntḷi, ˌsakrə'mɛntəli
AM ˌsækrə'mɛn(t)ḷi
sacramentarian
BR ˌsakrəmən'tɛːrɪən, ˌsakrəmɛn'tɛːrɪən, -z
AM ˌsækrəmən'tɛriən, ˌsækrə,mɛn'tɛriən, -z
Sacramento
BR ˌsakrə'mɛntəʊ
AM ˌsækrə'mɛn(t)oʊ
sacraria
BR sə'krɛːrɪə(*r*)
AM sə'krɛriə
sacrarium
BR sə'krɛːrɪəm
AM sə'krɛriəm
sacred
BR 'seɪkrɪd
AM 'seɪkrɪd
sacredly
BR 'seɪkrɪdli
AM 'seɪkrɪdli
sacredness
BR 'seɪkrɪdnɪs
AM 'seɪkrɪdnɪs
sacrementality
BR ˌsakrəm(ə)n'talɪti, ˌsakrəmɛn'talɪti
AM ˌsækrəmən'tælədi, ˌsækrə,mɛn'tælədi
sacrifice
BR 'sakrɪfʌɪs, -ɪz, -ɪŋ, -t
AM 'sækrə,faɪs, -ɪz, -ɪŋ, -t
sacrificial
BR ˌsakrɪ'fɪʃl
AM ˌsækrə'fɪʃəl
sacrificially
BR ˌsakrɪ'fɪʃḷi, ˌsakrɪ'fɪʃəli
AM ˌsækrə'fɪʃəli
sacrilege
BR 'sakrɪlɪdʒ
AM 'sækrəlɪdʒ
sacrilegious
BR ˌsakrɪ'lɪdʒəs
AM ˌsækrə'lɪdʒəs
sacrilegiously
BR ˌsakrɪ'lɪdʒəsli
AM ˌsækrə'lɪdʒəsli
sacriligious
BR ˌsakrɪ'lɪdʒəs
AM ˌsækrə'lɪdʒəs
sacriligiously
BR ˌsakrɪ'lɪdʒəsli
AM ˌsækrə'lɪdʒəsli
sacring
BR 'seɪkrɪŋ
AM 'seɪkrɪŋ
sacrist
BR 'seɪkrɪst, 'sakrɪst, -s
AM 'seɪkrəst, 'sækrəst, -s
sacristan
BR 'sakrɪst(ə)n, -z
AM 'sækrəstən, -z
sacristy
BR 'sakrɪst|i, -ɪz
AM 'sækrəsti, -z
sacroiliac
BR ˌsakrəʊ'ɪlɪak, ˌseɪkrəʊ'ɪlɪak
AM ˌsækroʊ'ɪli,æk
sacrosanct
BR 'sakrə(ʊ)saŋ(k)t
AM 'sækroʊ,sæŋ(k)t, 'sækrə,sæŋ(k)t, 'sækroʊ,sæŋk(t), 'sækrə,sæŋk(t)
sacrosanctity
BR ˌsakrə'saŋ(k)tɪti
AM ˌsækroʊ'sæŋ(k)tədi
sacrum
BR 'seɪkrəm, 'sakrəm, -z
AM 'sækrəm, 'seɪkrəm, -z
sad
BR sad, -ə(r), -ɪst
AM sæd, -ər, -əst
Sadat
BR sə'dat
AM sə'dɑt
sadden
BR 'sadn, -z, -ɪŋ, -d
AM 'sædən, -z, -ɪŋ, -d
saddish
BR 'sadɪʃ
AM 'sædɪʃ
saddle
BR 'sad|l, -lz, -ḷɪŋ\-lɪŋ, -ld
AM 'sæd|əl, -əlz, -(ə)lɪŋ, -əld
saddleback
BR 'sadlbak, -s, -t
AM 'sædl,bæk, -s, -t
saddlebag
BR 'sadlbag, -z
AM 'sædl,bæg, -z
saddle bow
BR 'sadəl bəʊ, -z
AM 'sædəl ,boʊ, -z
saddlecloth
BR 'sadlklɒ|θ, -θs\-ðz
AM 'sædl,klɔ|θ, 'sædl,klɑ|θ, -θs\-ðz
saddleless
BR 'sadlləs
AM 'sædlləs
saddler
BR 'sadlə(r), -z
AM 'sæd(ə)lər, -z
saddlery
BR 'sadləri
AM 'sædəlri, 'sædləri
Sadducean
BR ˌsadjʉ'siːən, ˌsadʒʉ'siːən
AM ˌsædʒə'siən, ˌsædjə'siən
Sadducee
BR 'sadjʉsiː, 'sadʒʉsiː, -z
AM 'sædʒə,si, 'sædjə,si, -z
Sadduceeism
BR 'sadjʉsiːɪz(ə)m, 'sadʒʉsiːɪz(ə)m
AM 'sædʒə,si,ɪzəm, 'sædjə,si,ɪzəm
Sade
writer
BR sɑːd
AM sɑd
sadhu
BR 'sɑːduː, -z
AM 'sɑ,du, -z
Sadie
BR 'seɪdi
AM 'seɪdi
sad-iron
BR 'sad,ʌɪən, -z
AM 'sæd,aɪ(ə)rn, -z
sadism
BR 'seɪdɪz(ə)m
AM 'seɪ,dɪzəm
sadist
BR 'seɪdɪst, -s
AM 'seɪdɪst, -s
sadistic
BR sə'dɪstɪk
AM sə'dɪstɪk
sadistically
BR sə'dɪstɪkli
AM sə'dɪstək(ə)li
Sadler
BR 'sadlə(r)
AM 'sæd(ə)lər
sadly
BR 'sadli
AM 'sædli
sadness
BR 'sadnəs, -ɪz
AM 'sædnəs, -əz
sadomasochism
BR ˌseɪdəʊ'masəkɪz(ə)m
AM ˌsædoʊ'mæsə,kɪzəm, ˌseɪdoʊ'mæsə,kɪzəm
sadomasochist
BR ˌseɪdəʊ'masəkɪst, -s
AM ˌsædoʊ'mæsəkəst, ˌseɪdoʊ'mæsəkəst, -s
sadomasochistic
BR ˌseɪdəʊ,masə'kɪstɪk
AM ˌsædoʊ,mæsə'kɪstɪk, ˌseɪdoʊ,mæsə'kɪstɪk
s.a.e.
BR ˌɛseɪ'iː, -z
AM ˌɛs,eɪ'i, -z
saeter
BR 'seɪtə(r), 'sɛtə(r), -z
AM 'sɛdər, 'seɪdər, -z
safari
BR sə'fɑːr|i, -ɪz
AM sə'fɑri, -z
safe
BR seɪf, -ə(r), -ɪst
AM seɪf, -ər, -ɪst
safebreaker
BR 'seɪf,breɪkə(r), -z
AM 'seɪf,breɪkər, -z
safe-conduct
BR ˌseɪf'kɒndʌkt, -s
AM ˌseɪf'kɑndək|(t), -(t)s

safecracker
BR ˈseɪfˌkrakə(r), -z
AM ˈseɪfˌkrækər, -z

safeguard
BR ˈseɪfɡɑːd, -z, -ɪŋ, -ɨd
AM ˈseɪfˌɡɑrd, -z, -ɪŋ, -əd

safekeeping
BR ˌseɪfˈkiːpɪŋ
AM ˈseɪfˈkipɪŋ

safely
BR ˈseɪfli
AM ˈseɪfli

safeness
BR ˈseɪfnɪs
AM ˈseɪfnɪs

safety
BR ˈseɪfti
AM ˈseɪfti

safety-first
BR ˌseɪftɪˈfəːst
AM ˈseɪftiˈfərst

safetyman
BR ˈseɪftɪman
AM ˈseɪftiˌmæn

safetymen
BR ˈseɪftɪmɛn
AM ˈseɪftiˌmɛn

Safeway
BR ˈseɪfweɪ
AM ˈseɪfˌweɪ

safflower
BR ˈsaflaʊə(r), -z
AM ˈsæfˌlaʊər, -z

saffron
BR ˈsafrən
AM ˈsæfrən

saffrony
BR ˈsafrəni
AM ˈsæfrəni

safranin
BR ˈsafrənɪn, ˈsafrəniːn, -z
AM ˈsæfrəˌnin, ˈsæfrənən, -z

safranine
BR ˈsafrəniːn, -z
AM ˈsæfrəˌnin, ˈsæfrənən, -z

sag
BR saɡ, -z, -ɪŋ, -d
AM sæɡ, -z, -ɪŋ, -d

saga
BR ˈsɑːɡə(r), -z
AM ˈsɑɡə, -z

sagacious
BR səˈɡeɪʃəs
AM səˈɡeɪʃəs

sagaciously
BR səˈɡeɪʃəsli
AM səˈɡeɪʃəsli

sagaciousness
BR səˈɡeɪʃəsnəs
AM səˈɡeɪʃəsnəs

sagacity
BR səˈɡasɪti
AM səˈɡæsədi

sagamore
BR ˈsaɡəmɔː(r), -z
AM ˈsæɡəˌmɔ(ə)r, -z

Sagan
BR saˈɡan
AM ˈseɪɡən

Sagar
BR ˈseɪɡə(r)
AM ˈseɪɡər

sage
BR seɪdʒ, -ɪz
AM seɪdʒ, -ɪz

sagebrush
BR ˈseɪdʒbrʌʃ
AM ˈseɪdʒˌbrəʃ

sagely
BR ˈseɪdʒli
AM ˈseɪdʒli

sageness
BR ˈseɪdʒnɪs
AM ˈseɪdʒnɪs

Sager
BR ˈseɪɡə(r)
AM ˈseɪɡər

sageship
BR ˈseɪdʒʃɪp, -s
AM ˈseɪdʒˌʃɪp, -s

saggar
BR ˈsaɡə(r), -z
AM ˈsæɡər, -z

saggy
BR ˈsaɡ|i, -ɪə(r), -ɪɪst
AM ˈsæɡi, -ər, -ɪst

Saginaw
BR ˈsaɡɪnɔː(r)
AM ˈsæɡəˌnɔ, ˈsæɡəˌnɑ

sagitta
BR səˈdʒɪtə(r), səˈɡɪtə(r), ˈsadʒɪtə(r), -z
AM səˈdʒɪdə, ˈsædʒədə, -z

sagittal
BR ˈsadʒɪtl
AM ˈsædʒədl

Sagittarian
BR ˌsadʒɪˈtɛːrɪən, -z
AM ˌsædʒəˈtɛriən, -z

Sagittarius
BR ˌsadʒɪˈtɛːrɪəs
AM ˌsædʒəˈtɛriəs

sagittate
BR ˈsadʒɪteɪt
AM ˈsædʒəˌteɪt

sago
BR ˈseɪɡəʊ
AM ˈseɪɡoʊ

saguaro
BR səˈɡwɑːrəʊ, -z
AM səˈ(ɡ)wɑroʊ, -z

sagy
BR ˈseɪdʒi
AM ˈseɪdʒi

Sahara
BR səˈhɑːrə(r)
AM səˈhɛrə, səˈhɑrə

Saharan
BR səˈhɑːrən, -z
AM səˈhɛrən, səˈhɑrən, -z

Sahel
BR səˈhɛl, sɑːˈhɛl
AM səˈhɛl

Sahelian
BR səˈhiːlɪən, sɑːˈhiːlɪən
AM səˈhiliən

sahib
BR sɑːb, ˈsɑː(h)ɪb, -z
AM ˈsɑˈ(h)ɪb, -z

sahuaro
BR səˈwɑːrəʊ, -z
AM səˈ(h)wɑroʊ, -z

Said
BR sʌɪd
AM saɪid

said
BR sɛd
AM sɛd

Saida
BR ˈsʌɪdə(r)
AM ˈsaɪdə

saiga
BR ˈsʌɪɡə(r), ˈseɪɡə(r), -z
AM ˈsaɪɡə, -z

Saigon
BR sʌɪˈɡɒn
AM saɪˈɡɑn

sail
BR seɪl, -z, -ɪŋ, -d
AM seɪl, -z, -ɪŋ, -d

sailable
BR ˈseɪləbl
AM ˈseɪləbəl

sailbag
BR ˈseɪlbaɡ, -z
AM ˈseɪlˌbæɡ, -z

sailboard
BR ˈseɪlbɔːd, -z
AM ˈseɪlˌbɔ(ə)rd, -z

sailboarder
BR ˈseɪlbɔːdə(r), -z
AM ˈseɪlˌbɔrdər, -z

sailboarding
BR ˈseɪlbɔːdɪŋ
AM ˈseɪlˌbɔrdɪŋ

sailboat
BR ˈseɪlbəʊt, -s
AM ˈseɪlˌboʊt, -s

sailcloth
BR ˈseɪlklɒθ
AM ˈseɪlˌklɔθ, ˈseɪlˌklɑθ

sailer
BR ˈseɪlə(r), -z
AM ˈseɪlər, -z

sailfish
BR ˈseɪlfɪʃ
AM ˈseɪlˌfɪʃ

sail-fluke
BR ˈseɪlfluːk, -s
AM ˈseɪlˌfluk, -s

sailing
BR ˈseɪlɪŋ, -z
AM ˈseɪlɪŋ, -z

sailless
BR ˈseɪllɪs
AM ˈseɪ(l)lɪs

sailmaker
BR ˈseɪlˌmeɪkə(r), -z
AM ˈseɪlˌmeɪkər, -z

sailor
BR ˈseɪlə(r), -z
AM ˈseɪlər, -z

sailoring
BR ˈseɪlərɪŋ
AM ˈseɪlərɪŋ

sailorless
BR ˈseɪlələs
AM ˈseɪlərləs

sailorly
BR ˈseɪləli
AM ˈseɪlərli

sailplane
BR ˈseɪlpleɪn, -z
AM ˈseɪlˌpleɪn, -z

sainfoin
BR ˈsanfɔɪn, ˈseɪnfɔɪn
AM ˈseɪnˌfɔɪn

Sainsbury
BR ˈseɪnzb(ə)ri
AM ˈseɪnzˌbɛri

saint
BR seɪnt, -s
AM seɪnt, -s

saintdom
BR ˈseɪntdəm, -z
AM ˈseɪntdəm, -z

sainted
BR ˈseɪntɪd
AM ˈseɪn(t)ɪd

Saint Elmo's fire
BR snt ˌɛlməʊz ˈfʌɪə(r)
AM ˈseɪn(t) ˈɛlmoʊz ˈfaɪ(ə)r

Saint-Étienne
BR ˌsãtɛˈtjɛn
AM sɛn(t)ˌeɪˈtjɛn

sainthood
BR ˈseɪnthʊd
AM ˈseɪn(t)ˌ(h)ʊd

saintlike
BR ˈseɪntlʌɪk
AM ˈseɪntˌlaɪk

saintliness
BR ˈseɪntlɪnɪs
AM ˈseɪntlinɪs

saintling
BR ˈseɪntlɪŋ, -z
AM ˈseɪntlɪŋ, -z

saintly
BR ˈseɪntl|i, -ɪə(r), -ɪɪst
AM ˈseɪn(t)li, -ər, -ɪst

Saint-Malo
BR s(ə)nt ˈmɑːləʊ
AM ˌsɑn məˈloʊ

Saint-Moritz
BR ˌsan məˈrɪts, s(ə)nt ˈmɒrɪts

AM seɪn(t) mə'rɪts

saintpaulia
BR ˌseɪnt'pɔːlɪə(r), -z
AM ˌseɪnt'pɔljə, ˌseɪnt'pɑljə, ˌseɪnt'pɔliə, ˌseɪnt'pɑliə, -z

Saint-Saëns
BR ˌsã'sɔ̃(s), ˌsã'sɔ̃z
AM ˌsæn'sɑnz

saintship
BR 'seɪntʃɪp, -s
AM 'seɪntˌʃɪp, -s

Saint-Tropez
BR ˌsã trɒ'peɪ
AM ˌsɑn trə'peɪ

Saipan
BR ˌsʌɪ'pan
AM ˈsaɪˈpæn

Saisho
BR 'seɪʃəʊ
AM 'seɪˌʃoʊ

saith
BR sɛθ
AM sɛθ, 'seɪɨθ

saithe
BR seɪθ, seɪð
AM seɪð

Sajama
BR sə'hɑːmə(r)
AM sə'hɑmə

Sakai
BR 'sɑːkʌɪ
AM 'sɑkˌaɪ

sake
BR seɪk, -s
AM seɪk, -s

saké
BR 'sɑːki, 'sakeɪ
AM 'sɑki

saker
BR 'seɪkə(r), -z
AM 'seɪkər, -z

sakeret
BR 'seɪkərɪt, -s
AM 'seɪkərət, -s

Sakhalin
BR 'sakəliːn, 'sakəlɪn, ˌsakə'liːn, ˌsakə'lɪn
AM 'sækəˌlin

Sakharov
BR 'sakərɒf, 'sakərɒv
AM 'sækəˌrɔv, 'sækəˌrɑf, 'sækəˌrɑv

saki
BR 'sɑːk|i, -ɪz
AM 'sɑki, -z

Sakta
BR 'ʃɑːktə(r), -z
AM 'ʃɑktə, -z

Sakti
BR 'ʃakti
AM 'ʃɑkti

Saktism
BR 'ʃɑːktɪz(ə)m
AM 'ʃɑkˌtɪzəm

sal
BR sal
AM sæl

salaam
BR sə'lɑːm, -z, -ɪŋ, -d
AM sə'lɑm, -z, -ɪŋ, -d

salability
BR ˌseɪlə'bɪlɨti
AM ˌseɪlə'bɪlɨdi

salable
BR 'seɪləbl
AM 'seɪləbəl

salacious
BR sə'leɪʃəs
AM sə'leɪʃəs

salaciously
BR sə'leɪʃəsli
AM sə'leɪʃəsli

salaciousness
BR sə'leɪʃəsnəs
AM sə'leɪʃəsnəs

salacity
BR sə'lasɪti
AM sə'læsədi

salad
BR 'saləd, -z
AM 'sæləd, -z

salade
BR sə'lɑːd, -z
AM sə'lɑd, -z

Saladin
BR 'salədɪn
AM 'sælədn

Salamanca
BR ˌsalə'maŋkə(r)
AM ˌsælə'mæŋkə

salamander
BR 'saləmandə(r), -z
AM 'sæləˌmændər, -z

salamandrian
BR ˌsalə'mandrɪən
AM ˌsælə'mændriən

salamandrine
BR ˌsalə'mandrʌɪn, ˌsalə'mandrɪn
AM ˌsælə'mændrən

salamandroid
BR ˌsalə'mandrɔɪd, -z
AM ˌsælə'mænˌdrɔɪd, -z

salami
BR sə'lɑːmi
AM sə'lɑmi

Salamis
BR 'saləmɪs
AM 'sɑləməs

sal ammoniac
BR ˌsal ə'məʊnɪak
AM ˈsæl ə'moʊniˌæk

Salang
BR sa'laŋ
AM sɑ'lɑŋ

salangane
BR 'saləŋgeɪn, -z
AM 'sælənˌgæn, 'sælənˌgeɪn, -z

salariat
BR sə'lɛːrɪət
AM sə'lɛriət, sə'lɛriˌæt

salary
BR 'sal(ə)r|i, -ɪz, -ɪd
AM 'sæl(ə)ri, -z, -d

salaryman
BR 'sal(ə)rɪmən
AM 'sæl(ə)rimən

salarymen
BR 'sal(ə)rɪmən
AM 'sæl(ə)rimən

salat
BR sa'lɑːt
AM sɑ'lɑt

Salazar
BR ˌsalə'zɑː(r)
AM 'sæləˌzɑr

salbutamol
BR sal'bjuːtəmɒl
AM sæl'bjutəmɔl, sæl'bjutəmɑl

salchow
BR 'salkəʊ, -z
AM 'sɑlkoʊ, -z

Salcombe
BR 'sɔːlkəm, 'sɒlkəm
AM 'sɔlkəm, 'sɑlkəm

sale
BR seɪl, -z
AM seɪl, -z

saleability
BR ˌseɪlə'bɪlɨti
AM ˌseɪlə'bɪlɨdi

saleable
BR 'seɪləbl
AM 'seɪləbəl

Salem
BR 'seɪləm
AM 'seɪləm

salep
BR 'salɛp, 'saləp
AM 'sæləp, sə'lɛp

saleratus
BR ˌsalə'reɪtəs
AM ˌsælə'reɪdəs

Salerno
BR sə'ləːnəʊ
AM sə'lərnoʊ, sə'lɛrnoʊ

saleroom
BR 'seɪlruːm, 'seɪlrʊm, -z
AM 'seɪlˌrum, 'seɪlˌrʊm, -z

salesclerk
BR 'seɪlzklɑːk, -s
AM 'seɪlzˌklərk, -s

salesgirl
BR 'seɪlzgəːl, -z
AM 'seɪlzˌgərl, -z

Salesian
BR sə'liːzɪən, sə'liːʒn, -z
AM sə'liʒən, -z

saleslady
BR 'seɪlzˌleɪd|i, -ɪz
AM 'seɪlzˌleɪdi, -z

salesman
BR 'seɪlzmən
AM 'seɪlzmən

salesmanship
BR 'seɪlzmənʃɪp
AM 'seɪlzmənˌʃɪp

salesmen
BR 'seɪlzmən
AM 'seɪlzmən

salesperson
BR 'seɪlzˌpəːsn
AM 'seɪlzˌpərsən

salesroom
BR 'seɪlzruːm, 'seɪlzrʊm, -z
AM 'seɪlzˌrum, 'seɪlzˌrʊm, -z

saleswoman
BR 'seɪlzˌwʊmən
AM 'seɪlzˌwʊmən

saleswomen
BR 'seɪlzˌwɪmɪn
AM 'seɪlzˌwɪmɨn

Salford
BR 'sɔːlfəd, 'sɒlfəd
AM 'sɔlfərd, 'sælfərd, 'sɑlfərd

Salian
BR 'seɪlɪən, -z
AM 'seɪljən, 'seɪliən, -z

Salic
BR 'salɪk, 'seɪlɪk
AM 'seɪlɪk, 'sælɪk

salicet
BR 'salɪsɛt, -s
AM 'sæləˌsɛt, -s

salicin
BR 'salɪsɪn
AM 'sæləsən

salicine
BR 'salɪsiːn, 'salɪsɪn
AM 'sæləˌsin, 'sæləsən

salicional
BR sə'lɪʃn̩(ə)l, sə'lɪʃən(ə)l, -z
AM sə'lɪʃ(ə)nəl, -z

salicylate
BR sə'lɪsɪleɪt, -s
AM sə'lɪsəˌleɪt, sə'lɪsələt, -s

salicylic
BR ˌsalɪ'sɪlɪk
AM ˌsælə'sɪlɪk

salicylic acid
BR ˌsaləsɪlɪk 'asɪd
AM ˈsælə'sɪlɪk 'æsəd

salience
BR 'seɪlɪəns
AM 'seɪljəns, 'seɪliəns

saliency
BR 'seɪlɪənsi
AM 'seɪljənsi, 'seɪliənsi

salient
BR 'seɪlɪənt, -s

AM ˈseɪljənt, ˈseɪliənt, -s
salientian
BR ˌseɪlɪˈɛnʃn, -z
AM ˌseɪliˈɛn(t)ʃən, -z
saliently
BR ˈseɪlɪəntli
AM ˈseɪljən(t)li, ˈseɪliən(t)li
Salieri
BR ˌsalɪˈɛːri
AM ˌsɑliˈɛri
saliferous
BR səˈlɪf(ə)rəs
AM səˈlɪf(ə)rəs
salify
BR ˈsalɪfʌɪ, -z, -ɪŋ, -d
AM ˈsæləˌfaɪ, -z, -ɪŋ, -d
Salina
BR səˈlʌɪnə(r)
AM səˈlinə
salina
BR səˈlʌɪnə(r), -z
AM səˈlinə, səˈlaɪnə, -z
Salinas
BR səˈliːnəs
AM səˈlinəs
saline
BR ˈseɪlʌɪn
AM ˈseɪˌlin
Salinger
BR ˈsalɪn(d)ʒə(r)
AM ˈsæləndʒər
salinisation
BR ˌsalɪnʌɪˈzeɪʃn
AM ˌsælənəˈzeɪʃən, ˌsæləˌnaɪˈzeɪʃən
salinity
BR səˈlɪnɪti
AM seɪˈlɪnɪdi, səˈlɪnɪdi
salinization
BR ˌsalɪnʌɪˈzeɪʃn
AM ˌsælənəˈzeɪʃən, ˌsæləˌnaɪˈzeɪʃən
salinometer
BR ˌsalɪˈnɒmɪtə(r), -z
AM ˌsæləˈnɑmədər, -z
Salisbury
BR ˈsɔːlzb(ə)ri, ˈsɒlzb(ə)ri
AM ˈsɔlzˌbɛri, ˈsɔlzb(ə)ri, ˈsɑlzˌbɛri, ˈsɑlzb(ə)ri
Salish
BR ˈseɪlɪʃ
AM ˈseɪlɪʃ
saliva
BR səˈlʌɪvə(r)
AM səˈlaɪvə
salivary
BR səˈlʌɪv(ə)ri
AM ˈsæləˌvɛri
salivate
BR ˈsalɪveɪt, -s, -ɪŋ, -ɪd
AM ˈsæləˌveɪ|t, -ts, -dɪŋ, -dɨd
salivation
BR ˌsalɪˈveɪʃn
AM ˌsæləˈveɪʃən
Salkeld
BR ˈsɔːlkɛld, ˈsɒlkɛld
AM ˈsɔlˌkɛld, ˈsɑlˌkɛld
Salk vaccine
BR ˈsɔːlk ˌvaksiːn
AM ˈsɔk vækˈsin, ˈsɑk vækˈsin
sallee
BR ˈsal|i, -ɪz
AM ˈsæli, -z
sallenders
BR ˈsalɪndəz
AM ˈsæləndərz
sallet
BR ˈsalɪt, -s
AM ˈsælət, -s
Sallis
BR ˈsalɪs
AM ˈsæləs
sallow
BR ˈsaləʊ, -z, -d
AM ˈsæloʊ, -z, -d
sallowish
BR ˈsaləʊɪʃ
AM ˈsæləwɪʃ
sallowness
BR ˈsaləʊnəs
AM ˈsæloʊnəs
sallowy
BR ˈsaləʊi
AM ˈsæləwi
Sallust
BR ˈsaləst
AM ˈsæləst
sally
BR ˈsal|i, -ɪz, -ɪɪŋ, -ɪd
AM ˈsæli, -z, -ɪŋ, -d
Sally Lunn
BR ˌsalɪ ˈlʌn, -z
AM ˌsæli ˈlən, -z
sallyport
BR ˈsalɪpɔːt, -s
AM ˈsæliˌpɔ(ə)rt, -s
salmagundi
BR ˌsalməˈɡʌnd|i, -ɪz
AM ˌsælməˈɡəndi, -z
salmanazar
BR ˌsalməˈneɪzə(r), -z
AM ˌsælməˈnæzər, ˌsælməˈnɑzər, -z
salmis
BR ˈsalm|i, -ɪz
AM ˈsælmi, -z
salmon
BR ˈsamən
AM ˈsæ(l)mən
salmonella
BR ˌsalməˈnɛlə(r)
AM ˌsælməˈnɛlə
salmonellosis
BR ˌsalmənɛˈləʊsɪs
AM ˌsælməˌnɛˈloʊsəs
salmonid
BR ˈsamənɪd, -z
AM ˈsæ(l)mənəd, ˈsæ(l)məˌnɪd, -z
salmonoid
BR ˈsamənɔɪd, -z
AM ˈsæ(l)məˌnɔɪd, -z
salmony
BR ˈsaməni
AM ˈsæ(l)məni
Salome
BR səˈləʊmi
AM ˌsɑləˈmeɪ, səˈloʊmi
salon
BR ˈsalɒ̃, ˈsalɒn, -z
AM səˈlɑn, -z
Salonica
BR səˈlɒnɪkə(r)
AM səˈlɔnəkə, səˈlɑnəkə
saloon
BR səˈluːn, -z
AM səˈlun, -z
Salop
BR ˈsaləp
AM ˈsæləp
salopette
BR ˌsaləˈpɛt, ˈsaləpɛt, -s
AM ˌsæləˈpɛt, -s
Salopian
BR səˈləʊpɪən, -z
AM səˈloʊpiən, -z
salpiglossis
BR ˌsalpɪˈɡlɒsɪs
AM ˌsælpəˈɡlɑsəs, ˌsælpəˈɡlɔsəs
salpingectomy
BR ˌsalpɪnˈdʒɛktəm|i, -ɪz
AM ˌsælpənˈdʒɛktəmi, -z
salpingitis
BR ˌsalpɪnˈdʒʌɪtɪs
AM ˌsælpənˈdʒaɪdɪs
salsa
BR ˈsalsə(r)
AM ˈsɑlsə
salsify
BR ˈsalsɪfi
AM ˈsælsəfi, ˈsælsəˌfaɪ
salt
BR sɔːlt, sɒlt, -s, -ɪŋ, -ɪd
AM sɔlt, sɑlt, -s, -ɪŋ, -əd
Saltaire
BR sɔːlˈtɛː(r), sɒlˈtɛː(r)
AM sɔlˈtɛ(ə)r, sɑlˈtɛ(ə)r
salt-and-pepper
BR ˌsɔːlt(ə)n(d)ˈpɛpə(r)
AM ˈsɔltnˈpɛpər, ˈsɑltnˈpɛpər
saltarelli
BR ˌsaltəˈrɛliː, ˌsɔːltəˈrɛliː, ˌsɒltəˈrɛliː
AM ˌsɔltəˈrɛli, ˌsɑltəˈrɛli, ˌsæltəˈrɛli
saltarello
BR ˌsaltəˈrɛləʊ, ˌsɔːltəˈrɛləʊ, ˌsɒltəˈrɛləʊ, -z
AM ˌsɔltəˈrɛˌloʊ, ˌsɑltəˈrɛˌloʊ, ˌsæltəˈrɛˌloʊ, -z
Saltash
BR ˈsɔːltaʃ, ˈsɒltaʃ
AM ˈsɔlˌtæʃ, ˈsɑlˌtæʃ
saltation
BR salˈteɪʃn, sɔːlˈteɪʃn, sɒlˈteɪʃn, -z
AM ˌsɔlˈteɪʃən, ˌsɑlˈteɪʃən, -z
saltatorial
BR ˌsaltəˈtɔːrɪəl, ˌsɔːltəˈtɔːrɪəl, ˌsɒltəˈtɔːrɪəl
AM ˌsɔltəˈtɔriəl, ˌsɑltəˈtɔriəl, ˌsæltəˈtɔriəl
saltatory
BR ˈsaltət(ə)ri, ˈsɔːltət(ə)ri, ˈsɒltət(ə)ri
AM ˈsɔltəˌtɔri, ˈsɑltəˌtɔri, ˈsæltəˌtɔri
saltbox
BR ˈsɔːltbɒks, ˈsɒltbɒks, -ɪz
AM ˈsɔltˌbɑks, ˈsɑltˌbɑks, -əz
Saltburn
BR ˈsɔːltbəːn, ˈsɒltbəːn
AM ˈsɔltˌbərn, ˈsɑltˌbərn
saltbush
BR ˈsɔːltbʊʃ, ˈsɒltbʊʃ, -ɪz
AM ˈsɔltˌbʊʃ, ˈsɑltˌbʊʃ, -əz
saltcellar
BR ˈsɔːltˌsɛlə(r), ˈsɒltˌsɛlə(r), -z
AM ˈsɔltˌsɛlər, ˈsɑltˌsɛlər, -z
salter
BR ˈsɔːltə(r), ˈsɒltə(r), -z
AM ˈsɔltər, ˈsɑltər, -z
saltern
BR ˈsɔːltən, ˈsɒltən, -z
AM ˈsɔltərn, ˈsɑltərn, -z
Salterton
BR ˈsɔːltət(ə)n, ˈsɒltət(ə)n
AM ˈsɔltərtən, ˈsɑltərtən
Salthouse
BR ˈsɔːlthaʊs, ˈsɒlthaʊs
AM ˈsɔltˌ(h)aʊs, ˈsɑltˌ(h)aʊs
saltigrade
BR ˈsaltɪɡreɪd, ˈsɔːltɪɡreɪd, ˈsɒltɪɡreɪd, -z

AM 'sɔltəˌgreɪd, 'sɑltəˌgreɪd, -z

saltimbocca
BR ˌsaltɪm'bɒkə(r)
AM ˌsɑltəm'boʊkə, ˌsɔltəm'boʊkə

saltine
BR sɔːl'tiːn, sɒl'tiːn, -z
AM sɔl'tin, sɑl'tin, -z

saltiness
BR 'sɔːltɪnɨs, 'sɒltɪnɨs
AM 'sɔltinɨs, 'sɑltinɨs

salting
BR 'sɔːltɪŋ, 'sɒltɪŋ, -z
AM 'sɔltɪŋ, 'sɑltɪŋ, -z

saltire
BR 'sɔːltʌɪə(r), 'sɒltʌɪə(r), -z
AM 'sɔlˌtaɪ(ə)r 'sɑlˌtaɪ(ə)r, 'sælˌtaɪ(ə)r, -z

saltirewise
BR 'sɔːltʌɪəwʌɪz, 'sɒltʌɪəwʌɪz
AM 'sɔlˌtaɪ(ə)rˌwaɪz, 'sɑlˌtaɪ(ə)rˌwaɪz, 'sælˌtaɪ(ə)rˌwaɪz

saltish
BR 'sɔːltɪʃ, 'sɒltɪʃ
AM 'sɔltɪʃ, 'sɑltɪʃ

Salt Lake City
BR ˌsɔːlt leɪk 'sɪti, ˌsɒlt +
AM ˌsɔl(t) ˌleɪk 'sɪdi, ˌsɑl(t) ˌleɪk 'sɪdi

saltless
BR 'sɔːltləs, 'sɒltləs
AM 'sɔltləs, 'sɑltləs

Saltley
BR 'sɔːltli, 'sɒltli
AM 'sɔltli, 'sɑltli

saltlick
BR 'sɔːltlɪk, 'sɒltlɪk, -s
AM 'sɔltˌlɪk, 'sɑltˌlɪk, -s

saltly
BR 'sɔːltli, 'sɒltli
AM 'sɔltli, 'sɑltli

Saltmarsh
BR 'sɔːltmɑːʃ, 'sɒltmɑːʃ
AM 'sɔltˌmɑrʃ, 'sɑltˌmɑrʃ

saltness
BR 'sɔːltnəs, 'sɒltnəs
AM 'sɔltnəs, 'sɑltnəs

saltpan
BR 'sɔːltpan, 'sɒltpan, -z
AM 'sɔltˌpæn, 'sɑltˌpæn, -z

saltpeter
BR ˌsɔːlt'piːtə(r), ˌsɒlt'piːtə(r)
AM ˌsɔlt'pidər, ˌsɑlt'pidər

saltpetre
BR ˌsɔːlt'piːtə(r), ˌsɒlt'piːtə(r)
AM ˌsɔlt'pidər, ˌsɑlt'pidər

saltshaker
BR 'sɔːltˌʃeɪkə(r), 'sɒltˌʃeɪkə(r), -z
AM 'sɔltˌʃeɪkər, 'sɑltˌʃeɪkər, -z

saltus
BR 'saltəs, -ɪz
AM 'sæltəs, 'sɔltəs, 'sɑltəs, -əz

saltwater
BR 'sɔːltˌwɔːtə(r), 'sɒltˌwɔːtə(r)
AM 'sɔltˌwɔdər, 'sɑltˌwɑdər

saltwort
BR 'sɔːltwəːt, 'sɒltwəːt, -s
AM 'sɔltwərt, 'sɔltwɔ(ə)rt, 'sɑltwərt, 'sɑltwɔ(ə)rt, -s

salty
BR 'sɔːlt|i, 'sɒlt|i, -ɪə(r), -ɪɨst
AM 'sɔlti, 'sɑlti, -ər, -ɨst

salubrious
BR sə'l(j)uːbrɪəs
AM sə'lubriəs

salubriously
BR sə'l(j)uːbrɪəsli
AM sə'lubriəsli

salubriousness
BR sə'l(j)uːbrɪəsnəs
AM sə'lubriəsnəs

salubrity
BR sə'l(j)uːbrɪti
AM sə'lubrədi

saluki
BR sə'luːk|i, -ɪz
AM sə'luki, -z

salutarily
BR 'saljʊtrɪli
AM ˌsæljəˌtɛrəli

salutary
BR 'saljʊt(ə)ri
AM 'sæljəˌtɛri

salutation
BR ˌsaljʊ'teɪʃn, -z
AM ˌsæljə'teɪʃən, -z

salutational
BR ˌsaljʊ'teɪʃn̩(ə)l, ˌsaljʊ'teɪʃən(ə)l
AM ˌsæljə'teɪʃ(ə)nəl

salutatorian
BR səˌl(j)uːtə'tɔːrɪən, -z
AM səˌludə'tɔriən, ˌsælədə'tɔriən, -z

salutatory
BR sə'l(j)uːtət(ə)ri
AM sə'ludəˌtɔri

salute
BR sə'l(j)uːt, -s, -ɪŋ, -ɨd
AM sə'lu|t, -ts, -dɪŋ, -dəd

saluter
BR sə'l(j)uːtə(r), -z
AM sə'ludər, -z

salvable
BR 'salvəbl
AM 'sælvəbəl

Salvador
BR 'salvədɔː(r), ˌsalvə'dɔː(r)
AM 'sælvəˌdɔ(ə)r

Salvadoran
BR ˌsalvə'dɔːrən, -z
AM ˌsælvə'dɔrən, -z

Salvadorean
BR ˌsalvə'dɔːrɪən, -z
AM ˌsælvə'dɔriən, -z

Salvadorian
BR ˌsalvə'dɔːrɪən, -z
AM ˌsælvə'dɔriən, -z

salvage
BR 'salv|ɪdʒ, -ɨdʒɪz, -ɨdʒɪŋ, -ɪdʒd
AM 'sælvɪdʒ, -ɪz, -ɪŋ, -d

salvageable
BR 'salvɨdʒəbl
AM 'sælvədʒəbəl

salvager
BR 'salvɨdʒə(r), -z
AM 'sælvədʒər, -z

Salvarsan
BR 'salvəsan
AM 'sælvərˌsæn

salvation
BR sal'veɪʃn, -z
AM sæl'veɪʃən, -z

Salvation Army
BR salˌveɪʃn 'ɑːmi
AM salˌveɪʃən 'ɑrmi

salvationism
BR sal'veɪʃn̩ɪz(ə)m, sal'veɪʃənɪz(ə)m
AM sæl'veɪʃ(ə)ˌnɪzəm

salvationist
BR sal'veɪʃn̩ɪst, sal'veɪʃənɪst, -s
AM sæl'veɪʃ(ə)nəst, -s

salve
BR salv, -z, -ɪŋ, -d
AM sæ(l)v, -z, -ɪŋ, -d

salver
BR 'salvə(r), -z
AM 'sælvər, -z

Salvesen
BR 'salvɨs(ə)n
AM 'sælvəsən

Salveson
BR 'salvɨs(ə)n
AM 'sælvəsən

salvia
BR 'salvɪə(r), -z
AM 'sælviə, -z

salvo
BR 'salvəʊ, -z
AM 'sælˌvoʊ, -z

sal volatile
BR ˌsal və'latəli, + və'latl̩i
AM ˌsæl və'lɑdl̩i

salvor
BR 'salvə(r), -z
AM 'sælvər, -z

Salyut
BR sal'juːt, -s
AM 'sælˌjut, -s

Salzburg
BR 'saltsbəːg, 'sɔːltsbəːg, 'sɒltsbəːg
AM 'sɔlzˌbərg, 'sɑlzˌbərg, 'sɔltsˌbərg, 'sɑltsˌbərg

Sam
BR sam
AM sæm

samadhi
BR sə'mɑːdi
AM sə'mɑdi

Samantha
BR sə'manθə(r)
AM sə'mænθə

Samar
BR 'sɑːmə(r)
AM sə'mɑr, 'sɑˌmɑr

Samara
BR sə'mɑːrə(r)
AM sə'mɑrə

samara
BR sə'mɑːrə(r), -z
AM 'sæmərə, sə'mɛrə, -z

Samaria
BR sə'mɛːrɪə(r)
AM sə'mɛriə

Samaritan
BR sə'marɪt(ə)n, -z
AM sə'mɛrətn, sə'mɛrədən, -z

Samaritanism
BR sə'marɪtənɪz(ə)m, sə'marɪtn̩ɪz(ə)m
AM sə'mɛrətnˌɪzəm, sə'mɛrədəˌnɪzəm

samarium
BR sə'mɛːrɪəm, -z
AM sə'mɛriəm, -z

Samarkand
BR ˌsamɑː'kand, 'saməkand
AM 'sæmərˌkænd, ˌsæmɑr'kænd

Samarra
BR sə'mɑːrə(r)
AM sə'mɑrə

Sama-Veda
BR ˌsɑːmə'veɪdə(r)
AM 'sɑmə'veɪdə

samba
BR 'sambə(r), -z
AM 'sɑmbə, -z

sambar
BR 'sɑːmbə(r), 'sambə(r), -z
AM 'sɑmbər, 'sæmbər, -z

sambhar
BR 'sɑːmbə(r), 'sambə(r), -z
AM 'sɑmbər, 'sæmbər, -z

sambo
BR 'sambəʊ, -z
AM 'sæmboʊ, -z

sambur
BR 'sɑːmbə(r), 'sambə(r), -z
AM 'sɑmbər, 'sæmbər, -z

same
BR seɪm
AM seɪm

same-day
BR ˌseɪm'deɪ
AM ¦seɪm¦deɪ

samel
BR 'sam(ə)l
AM 'sæməl

sameness
BR 'seɪmnɨs
AM 'seɪmnɨs

same-sex
BR ˌseɪm'sɛks
AM ¦seɪm¦sɛks

samey
BR 'seɪmi
AM 'seɪmi

sameyness
BR 'seɪmɪnɨs
AM 'seɪminɨs

samfu
BR 'samfuː, -z
AM 'sæmˌfu, -z

Samhain
BR 'saʊɪn, 'sawɪn, -z
AM 'saʊən, -z
IR 'səunʲ

Samian
BR 'seɪmɪən, -z
AM 'seɪmiən, -z

samisen
BR 'samɪsɛn, -z
AM 'sæməˌsɛn, -z

samite
BR 'samʌɪt, 'seɪmʌɪt, -s
AM 'sæˌmaɪt, 'seɪˌmaɪt, -s

samizdat
BR 'samɪzdat, ˌsamɪz'dat
AM 'sɑmiz¦dæt

Samlesbury
BR 'samzb(ə)ri, 'sɑːmzb(ə)ri
AM 'sæmzˌbɛri

samlet
BR 'samlɨt, -s
AM 'sæmlət, -s

Sammy
BR 'sami
AM 'sæmi

Samnite
BR 'samnʌɪt, -s
AM 'sæmˌnaɪt, -s

Samoa
BR sə'məʊə(r)
AM sə'moʊə

Samoan
BR sə'məʊən, -z
AM sə'moʊən, -z

Sámos
BR 'seɪmɒs, 'samɒs
AM 'seɪˌmɔs, 'seɪˌmɑs

samosa
BR sə'məʊsə(r), sə'muːsə(r), -z
AM sə'moʊsə, -z

Samothrace
BR 'samə(ʊ)θreɪs
AM 'sæməˌθreɪs

samovar
BR 'saməvɑː(r), ˌsamə'vɑː(r), -z
AM 'sæməˌvɑr, -z

samoyed
BR ˌsamɔɪ'ɛd, sə'mɔɪɛd, -z
AM 'sæməˌjɛd, 'sæmɔɪˌjɛd, -z

Samoyedic
BR ˌsamɔɪ'ɛdɪk, ˌsamə'jɛdɪk
AM ˌsæmə'jɛdɪk

samp
BR samp
AM sæmp

sampan
BR 'sampan, -z
AM 'sæmˌpæn, -z

samphire
BR 'samfʌɪə(r)
AM 'sæmˌfaɪ(ə)r

sample
BR 'sɑːmp|l, 'samp|l, -lz, -l̩ɪŋ\-lɪŋ, -ld
AM 'sæmp|əl, -əlz, -(ə)lɪŋ, -əld

sampler
BR 'sɑːmplə(r), 'samplə(r), -z
AM 'sæmp(ə)lər, -z

sampling
BR 'sɑːmplɪŋ, 'sɑːmpl̩ɪŋ, 'samplɪŋ, 'sampl̩ɪŋ, -z
AM 'sæmp(ə)lɪŋ, -z

Sampson
BR 'sam(p)s(ə)n
AM 'sæm(p)sən

samsara
BR səm'sɑːrə(r)
AM səm'sɑrə

samsaric
BR sam'sarɪk
AM sæm'sɛrɪk

samskara
BR səm'skɑːrə(r), -z
AM sæm'skɑrə, -z

Samson
BR 'sams(ə)n
AM 'sæmsən

Samsung
BR 'samsʌŋ, 'samsʊŋ
AM 'sæmˌsəŋ

Samuel
BR 'samjʊəl, 'samjʉl
AM 'sæmjə(wə)l

Samuels
BR 'samjʊəlz, 'samjʉlz
AM 'sæmj(u)əlz

samurai
BR 'sam(j)ʉrʌɪ, -z
AM 'sæməˌraɪ, -z

san
sanatorium
BR san, -z
AM sæn, -z

Sana'a
BR sɑː'nɑː(r)
AM sɑ'nɑ

San Andreas
BR ˌsan anˌdreɪəs
AM ˌsæn ˌæn'dreɪəz

San Antonio
BR ˌsan an'təʊnɪəʊ
AM ˌsæn ˌən'toʊnioʊ, ˌsæn ˌæn'toʊnioʊ

sanataria
BR ˌsanə'tɛːrɪə(r)
AM ˌsænə'tɛriə

sanatarium
BR ˌsanə'tɛːrɪəm, -z
AM ˌsænə'tɛriəm, -z

sanative
BR 'sanətɪv
AM 'sænədɪv

Sanatogen®
BR sə'natədʒ(ə)n, sə'natədʒɛn
AM sə'nædədʒən

sanatoria
BR ˌsanə'tɔːrɪə(r)
AM ˌsænə'tɔriə

sanatorium
BR ˌsanə'tɔːrɪəm, -z
AM ˌsænə'tɔriəm, -z

sanatory
BR 'sanət(ə)ri
AM 'sænəˌtɔri

sanbenito
BR ˌsanbə'niːtəʊ, -z
AM ˌsænbə'nidoʊ, -z

San Bernardino
BR ˌsan ˌbəːnə'diːnəʊ
AM ˌsæn bərnə'dinoʊ

Sánchez
BR 'santʃɛz
AM 'sæn(t)ʃɛz

Sancho
BR 'san(t)ʃəʊ
AM 'sɑn(t)ʃoʊ

San Clemente
BR ˌsan klɪ'mɛnti
AM ˌsæn klə'mɛn(t)i

sancta
BR 'saŋ(k)tə(r)
AM 'sæŋ(k)tə

sancta sanctorum
BR ˌsaŋ(k)tə saŋ(k)'tɔːrəm
AM ¦sæŋ(k)tə ˌsæŋ(k)'tɔrəm

sanctification
BR ˌsaŋ(k)tɪfɪ'keɪʃn
AM ˌsæŋ(k)təfə'keɪʃən

sanctifier
BR 'saŋ(k)tɪfʌɪə(r), -z
AM 'sæŋ(k)təˌfaɪər, -z

sanctify
BR 'saŋ(k)tɪfʌɪ, -z, -ɪŋ, -d
AM 'sæŋ(k)təˌfaɪ, -z, -ɪŋ, -d

sanctimonious
BR ˌsaŋ(k)tɪ'məʊnɪəs
AM ˌsæŋ(k)tə'moʊniəs

sanctimoniously
BR ˌsaŋ(k)tɪ'məʊnɪəsli
AM ˌsæŋ(k)tə'moʊniəsli

sanctimoniousness
BR ˌsaŋ(k)tɪ'məʊnɪəsnəs
AM ˌsæŋ(k)tə'moʊniəsnəs

sanctimony
BR 'saŋ(k)tɪməni, 'saŋ(k)tɪməʊni
AM 'sæŋ(k)təˌmoʊni

sanction
BR 'saŋ(k)ʃ|n, -nz, -n̩ɪŋ\-ənɪŋ, -nd
AM 'sæŋ(k)ʃ|ən, -ənz, -(ə)nɪŋ, -ənd

sanctionable
BR 'saŋ(k)ʃn̩əbl, 'saŋ(k)ʃənəbl
AM 'sæŋ(k)ʃənəbəl

sanctitude
BR 'saŋ(k)tɪtjuːd, 'saŋ(k)tɪtʃuːd
AM 'sæŋ(k)təˌt(j)ud

sanctity
BR 'saŋ(k)tɪt|i, -ɪz
AM 'sæŋ(k)tədi, -z

sanctuary
BR 'saŋ(k)tʃʊər|i, 'saŋ(k)tʃʉr|i, 'saŋ(k)tjʊər|i, 'saŋ(k)tjʉr|i, -ɪz
AM 'sæŋk(t)ʃəˌwɛri, -ɪz

sanctum
BR 'saŋ(k)təm, -z
AM 'sæŋ(k)təm, -z

sanctum sanctorum
BR ˌsaŋ(k)təm saŋ(k)'tɔːrəm, -z
AM ¦sæŋ(k)təm ˌsæŋ(k)'tɔrəm, -z

Sanctus
BR 'saŋ(k)təs, -ɪz
AM 'sæŋ(k)təs, -əz

Sand
George, French writer
BR sɔ̃
AM sɑn

sand
BR sand, -z, -ɪŋ, -ɪd
AM sænd, -z, -ɪŋ, -əd

sandal
BR 'sandl, -z
AM 'sændəl, -z

sandalwood
BR 'sandlwʊd
AM 'sændl,wʊd

sandarac
BR 'sandərak, -s
AM 'sændə,ræk, -s

sandarach
BR 'sandərak, -s
AM 'sændə,ræk, -s

Sandbach
BR 'san(d)batʃ
AM 'sæn(d),bɑk

sandbag
BR 'san(d)bag, -z, -ɪŋ, -d
AM 'sæn(d),bæg, -z, -ɪŋ, -d

sandbagger
BR 'san(d)bagə(r), -z
AM 'sæn(d)bægər, -z

sandbank
BR 'san(d)baŋk, -s
AM 'sæn(d),bæŋk, -s

sandbar
BR 'san(d)bɑː(r), -z
AM 'sæn(d),bɑr, -z

sand-bath
BR 'san(d)|bɑːθ, 'san(d)|baθ, -bɑːðz\-bɑːθs\-baθs
AM 'sæn(d),bæθ, -s, -ðz

sandblast
BR 'san(d)blɑːst, 'san(d)blast, -s, -ɪŋ, -ɪd
AM 'sæn(d),blæst, -s, -ɪŋ, -əd

sandblaster
BR 'san(d),blɑːstə(r), 'san(d),blastə(r), -z
AM 'sæn(d),blæstər, -z

sandbox
BR 'san(d)bɒks, -ɪz
AM 'sæn(d),bɑks, -əz

sandboy
BR 'san(d)bɔɪ, -z
AM 'sæn(d),bɔɪ, -z

Sandburg
BR 'san(d)bəːg
AM 'sæn(d),bərg

sandcastle
BR 'san(d),kɑːsl, 'san(d),kasl, -z
AM 'sæn(d),kæsəl, -z

sander
BR 'sandə(r), -z
AM 'sændər, -z

sanderling
BR 'sandəlɪŋ, -z
AM 'sændərlɪŋ, -z

sanders
BR 'sandəz, -ɪz
AM 'sændərz, -əz

Sanderson
BR 'sɑːndəs(ə)n, 'sandəs(ə)n
AM 'sændərsən

Sanderstead
BR 'sɑːndəstɛd, 'sɑːndəstɪd, 'sɑːndəstɛd, 'sandəstɛd
AM 'sændər,stɛd

Sandes
BR 'sandz
AM 'sæn(d)z

sandfly
BR 'san(d)flʌɪ, -z
AM 'sæn(d),flaɪ, -z

Sandford
BR 'san(d)fəd
AM 'sæn(d)fərd

Sandgate
BR 'san(d)geɪt
AM 'sæn(d),geɪt

sandglass
BR 'san(d)glɑːs, 'san(d)glas, -ɪz
AM 'sæn(d),glæs, -əz

sandgrouse
BR 'san(d)graʊs
AM 'sæn(d),graʊs

sandhi
BR 'sandi, 'sandhiː
AM 'sændi, 'sɑndi

sandhog
BR 'sandhɒg, -z
AM 'sæn(d),(h)ɔg, 'sæn(d),(h)ɑg, -z

Sandhurst
BR 'sandhəːst
AM 'sæn(d),(h)ərst

San Diego
BR ,san dɪ'eɪgəʊ
AM ,sæn di'eɪgoʊ

sandiness
BR 'sandɪnɪs
AM 'sændinɪs

Sandinista
BR ,sandɪ'nɪstə(*r*), -z
AM ,sændə'nistə, -z

sandiver
BR 'sandɪvə(r)
AM 'sændəvər

sandlike
BR 'sandlʌɪk
AM 'sæn(d),laɪk

sandlot
BR 'sandlɒt, -s
AM 'sæn(d),lɑt, -s

sandman
BR 'san(d)man
AM 'sæn(d),mæn

Sandoval
BR 'sandəval
AM 'sændə,vɑl

Sandown
BR 'sandaʊn
AM 'sæn,daʊn

Sandoz
BR 'sandɒz
AM 'sændoʊz

sandpaper
BR 'san(d),peɪp|ə(r), -əz, -(ə)rɪŋ, -əd
AM 'sæn(d),peɪp|ər, -ərz, -(ə)rɪŋ, -ərd

sandpiper
BR 'san(d),pʌɪpə(r), -z
AM 'sæn(d),paɪpər, -z

sandpit
BR 'san(d)pɪt, -s
AM 'sæn(d),pɪt, -s

Sandra
BR 'sandrə(*r*), 'sɑːndrə(*r*)
AM 'sændrə

Sandringham
BR 'sandrɪŋəm
AM 'sændrɪŋəm

Sands
BR sandz
AM sæn(d)z

sandshoe
BR 'san(d)ʃuː, -z
AM 'sæn(d),ʃu, -z

sandsoap
BR 'san(d)səʊp, -s
AM 'sæn(d),soʊp, -s

sandstock
BR 'san(d)stɒk, -s
AM 'sæn(d),stɑk, -s

sandstone
BR 'san(d)stəʊn
AM 'sæn(d),stoʊn

sandstorm
BR 'san(d)stɔːm, -z
AM 'sæn(d),stɔ(ə)rm, -z

Sandwich
town
BR 'san(d)wɪtʃ, 'san(d)wɪdʒ
AM 'sæn,(d)wɪtʃ

sandwich
BR 'sanwɪdʒ, 'samwɪdʒ, 'sanwɪtʃ, 'samwɪtʃ, -ɪz, -ɪŋ, -t
AM 'sæn,(d)wɪ|tʃ, -tʃɪz\-dʒɪz, -tʃɪŋ\-dʒɪŋ, -tʃt

sandwich-board
BR 'sanwɪdʒ bɔːd, 'samwɪdʒ bɔːd, 'sanwɪtʃ bɔːd, 'samwɪtʃ bɔːd, -z
AM 'sæn,(d)wɪtʃ, bɔ(ə)rd, -z

sandwich-man
BR 'sanwɪdʒman, 'samwɪdʒman, 'sanwɪtʃman, 'samwɪtʃman
AM 'sæn,(d)wɪdʒ,mæn

sandwich-men
BR 'sanwɪdʒmɛn, 'samwɪdʒmɛn, 'sanwɪtʃmɛn, 'samwɪtʃmɛn
AM 'sæn,(d)wɪdʒ,mɛn

sandwort
BR 'san(d)wəːt, -s
AM 'sæn(d)wərt, 'sæn(d),wɔ(ə)rt, -s

sandy
BR 'sand|i, -ɪə(r), -ɪɪst
AM 'sændi, -ər, -ɪst

sandyish
BR 'sandɪɪʃ
AM 'sændiɪʃ

Sandys
BR sandz
AM sæn(d)z

sane
BR seɪn, -ə(r), -ɪst
AM seɪn, -ər, -ɪst

sanely
BR 'seɪnli
AM 'seɪnli

saneness
BR 'seɪnnɪs
AM 'seɪ(n)nɪs

San Fernando
BR ,san fə'nandəʊ
AM ,sæn fər'nændoʊ

Sanford
BR 'sanfəd
AM 'sænfərd

sanforise
BR 'sanfərʌɪz, -ɪz, -ɪŋ, -d
AM 'sænfə,raɪz, -ɪz, -ɪŋ, -d

sanforize
BR 'sanfərʌɪz, -ɪz, -ɪŋ, -d
AM 'sænfə,raɪz, -ɪz, -ɪŋ, -d

San Francisco
BR ,san fr(ə)n'sɪskəʊ
AM ,sæn frən'sɪskoʊ, ,sæn ,fræn'sɪskoʊ

sang
BR saŋ
AM sæŋ

sanga
BR 'saŋgə(*r*), -z
AM 'sæŋgə, -z

sangar
BR 'saŋgə(r), -z
AM 'sæŋgər, -z

sangaree
BR ,saŋgə'riː
AM ,sæŋgə'ri

sang-de-bœuf
BR ,saŋdə'bəːf
AM ,sæŋdə'bəf

Sanger
BR 'saŋə(r)

AM 'sæŋ(g)ər

sang-froid
BR ˌsɒŋ'frwɑː(r), ˌsɑːŋ'frwɑː(r), ˌsaŋ'frwɑː(r)
AM sæŋ'f(r)wɑ, sɑŋ'f(r)wɑ

sangha
BR 'sʌŋgə(r), 'saŋgə(r), -z
AM 'sɑŋ(g)ə, -z

Sango
BR 'saŋgəʊ, 'sɑːŋgəʊ
AM 'sɑŋˌgoʊ

sangrail
BR saŋ'greɪl
AM sæŋ'greɪl

sangría
BR san'griːə(r), 'saŋgrɪə(r)
AM sæŋ'griə

Sangster
BR 'saŋstə(r)
AM 'sæŋstər

sanguification
BR ˌsaŋgwɪfɪ'keɪʃn
AM ˌsæŋgwəfə'keɪʃən

sanguinarily
BR 'saŋgwɪn(ə)rɨli
AM 'sæŋgwəˌnɛrəli

sanguinariness
BR 'saŋgwɪn(ə)rɪnɨs
AM 'sæŋgwəˌnɛrinɨs

sanguinary
BR 'saŋgwɪn(ə)ri
AM 'sæŋgwəˌnɛri

sanguine
BR 'saŋgwɪn
AM 'sæŋgwən

sanguinely
BR 'saŋgwɪnli
AM 'sæŋgwənli

sanguineness
BR 'saŋgwɪnnɨs
AM 'sæŋgwə(n)nɨs

sanguineous
BR saŋ'gwɪnɪəs
AM sæŋ'gwɪniəs

sanguinity
BR saŋ'gwɪnɪti
AM sæŋ'gwɪnɨdi

Sanhedrim
BR san'hɛdrɪm, san'hiːdrɪm, 'sanɨdrɪm
AM sæn'hidrɪm, sɑn'hidrɪm, sæn'hɛdrəm, sɑn'hɛdrəm

Sanhedrin
BR san'hɛdrɪn, san'hiːdrɪn, 'sanɨdrɪn
AM sæn'hidrɪn, sɑn'hidrɪn, sæn'hɛdrən, sɑn'hɛdrən

sanicle
BR 'sanɨkl, -z
AM 'sænəkl, -z

sanidine
BR 'sanɨdiːn
AM 'sænəˌdin

sanies
BR 'seɪnɪiːz
AM 'seɪniˌiz

sanify
BR 'sanɨfʌɪ, -z, -ɪŋ, -d
AM 'sænəˌfaɪ, -z, -ɪŋ, -d

sanious
BR 'seɪnɪəs
AM 'seɪniəs

sanitaria
BR ˌsanɪ'tɛːrɪə(r)
AM ˌsænə'tɛriə

sanitarian
BR ˌsanɪ'tɛːrɪən, -z
AM ˌsænə'tɛriən, -z

sanitarily
BR 'sanɪtrɨli
AM 'sænəˌtɛrəli

sanitariness
BR 'sanɪtrɪnɨs
AM 'sænəˌtɛrinɨs

sanitarium
BR ˌsanɪ'tɛːrɪəm, -z
AM ˌsænə'tɛriəm, -z

sanitary
BR 'sanɪt(ə)ri
AM 'sænəˌtɛri

sanitate
BR 'sanɪteɪt, -s, -ɪŋ, -ɨd
AM 'sænəˌteɪ|t, -ts, -dɪŋ, -dɨd

sanitation
BR ˌsanɪ'teɪʃn
AM ˌsænə'teɪʃən

sanitationist
BR ˌsanɪ'teɪʃṇɪst, ˌsanɪ'teɪʃənɪst, -s
AM ˌsænə'teɪʃənəst, -s

sanitisation
BR ˌsanɪtʌɪ'zeɪʃn
AM ˌsænədə'zeɪʃən, ˌsænəˌtaɪ'zeɪʃən

sanitise
BR 'sanɪtʌɪz, -ɨz, -ɪŋ, -d
AM 'sænəˌtaɪz, -ɨz, -ɪŋ, -d

sanitiser
BR 'sanɪtʌɪzə(r), -z
AM 'sænəˌtaɪzər, -z

sanitization
BR ˌsanɪtʌɪ'zeɪʃn
AM ˌsænədə'zeɪʃən, ˌsænəˌtaɪ'zeɪʃən

sanitize
BR 'sanɪtʌɪz, -ɨz, -ɪŋ, -d
AM 'sænəˌtaɪz, -ɨz, -ɪŋ, -d

sanitizer
BR 'sanɪtʌɪzə(r), -z
AM 'sænəˌtaɪzər, -z

sanitoria
BR ˌsanɪ'tɔːrɪə(r)
AM ˌsænə'tɔriə

sanitorium
BR ˌsanɪ'tɔːrɪəm, -z
AM ˌsænə'tɔriəm, -z

sanity
BR 'sanɪti
AM 'sænədi

San Jacinto
BR ˌsan dʒə'sɪntəʊ
AM ˌsæn dʒə'sɪn(t)oʊ

San José
BR ˌsan hə(ʊ)'zeɪ
AM ˌsæn (h)oʊ'zeɪ

San Juan
BR san '(h)wɑːn
AM ˌsæn '(h)wɑn

sank
BR saŋk
AM sæŋk

Sankey
BR 'saŋki
AM 'sæŋki

San Marino
BR ˌsan mə'riːnəʊ
AM ˌsæn mə'rinoʊ

sannyasi
BR sən'jɑːsi
AM sən'jɑsi

sanpro
sanitary protection
BR 'sanprəʊ
AM 'sænˌproʊ

San Quentin
BR san 'kwɛntɪn
AM ˌsæn 'kwɛntn

sans
BR sanz
AM sænz

San Salvador
BR san 'salvədɔː(r)
AM ˌsæn 'sælvəˌdɔ(ə)r
SP san salβa'ðor

sans-culotte
BR ˌsan(z)kjʊ'lɒt, -s
AM ˌsæn(z)kjə'lɑt, -s

sans-culottism
BR ˌsan(z)kjʊ'lɒtɪz(ə)m
AM ˌsæn(z)kjə'lɑˌtɪzəm

sanserif
BR ˌsan(z)'sɛrɪf
AM ˌsæn'sɛrəf

Sanskrit
BR 'sanskrɪt
AM 'sænˌskrɪt

Sanskritic
BR san'skrɪtɪk
AM sæn'skrɪdɪk

Sanskritist
BR 'sanskrɪtɪst, -s
AM 'sænskrətəst, -s

Sansom
BR 'sans(ə)m
AM 'sænsəm

Sanson
BR 'sansn
AM 'sænsən

Sansovino
BR ˌsansə'viːnəʊ
AM ˌsænsə'vinoʊ

sans serif
BR ˌsan(z) 'sɛrɪf
AM ˌsæn(z) 'sɛrəf

Santa
BR 'santə(r), -z
AM 'sæn(t)ə, -z

Santa Ana
BR ˌsantə(r) 'anə(r)
AM ˌsæn(t)ə 'ænə

Santa Catarina
BR ˌsantə ˌkatə'riːnə(r)
AM ˌsæn(t)ə ˌkædə'rinə

Santa Claus
BR ˌsantə 'klɔːz, 'santə klɔːz, -ɨz
AM 'sæn(t)ə ˌklɔz, 'sæn(t)ə ˌklɑz, -əz

Santa Cruz
BR ˌsantə 'kruːz
AM ˌsæn(t)ə 'kruz

Santa Fé
BR ˌsantə 'feɪ
AM ˌsæn(t)ə 'feɪ

Santander
BR ˌsantan'dɛː(r), ˌsantən'dɛː(r), san'tandə(r)
AM ˌsɑnˌtɑn'dɛ(ə)r

Santayana
BR ˌsantə'jɑːnə(r)
AM ˌsɑntə'jɑnɑ

Santiago
BR ˌsantɪ'ɑːgəʊ
AM ˌsæn(t)i'ɑgoʊ

Santiago de Compostela
BR ˌsantɪ'ɑːgəʊ də ˌkɒmpə'stɛlə(r)
AM ˌsæn(t)i'ɑgoʊ də ˌkɑmpə'stɛlə

Santo Domingo
BR ˌsantəʊ də'mɪŋgəʊ
AM ˌsæn(t)oʊ də'mɪŋgoʊ

santolina
BR ˌsantə'liːnə(r), -z
AM ˌsæn(t)ə'linə, -z

santonica
BR san'tɒnɪkə(r), -z
AM sæn'tɑnəkə, -z

santonin
BR 'santənɪn
AM 'sæntn̩ən

Santorini
BR ˌsantə'riːni
AM ˌsæn(t)ə'rini

Santos
BR 'santɒs
AM 'sæntoʊs

sanyasi
BR sən'jɑːsi
AM sən'jɑːsi

Sanyo®
BR 'sanjəʊ
AM 'sænjoʊ
São Paulo
BR saʊ(m) 'paʊləʊ
AM ˌsaʊ(m) 'paʊloʊ
São Tomé
BR ˌsaʊ(n) təʊ'meɪ
AM ˌsaʊ toʊ'meɪ
sap
BR sap, -s, -ɪŋ, -t
AM sæp, -s, -ɪŋ, -t
sapajou
BR 'sapədʒuː, -z
AM 'sæpəˌ(d)ʒu, ˌsæpə'(d)ʒu, -z
sapan
BR 'sapan
AM sə'pæn, 'sæˌpæn
sapanwood
BR 'sapanwʊd
AM sə'pænˌwʊd, 'sæˌpænˌwʊd
sapele
BR sə'piːli
AM sə'pili
sapful
BR 'sapf(ʊ)l
AM 'sæpfəl
saphenous
BR sə'fiːnəs
AM sə'finəs
sapid
BR 'sapɪd
AM 'sæpəd
sapidity
BR sə'pɪdɪti
AM sə'pɪdɪdi
sapience
BR 'seɪpɪəns
AM 'seɪpiəns, 'sæpiəns
sapiens
BR 'sapɪɛnz
AM 'seɪpiəns, 'sæpiəns
sapient
BR 'seɪpɪənt
AM 'seɪpiənt, 'sæpiəntli
sapiential
BR ˌseɪpɪ'ɛnʃl
AM ˌseɪpiˌɛn(t)ʃəl, ˌsæpiˌɛn(t)ʃəl
sapiently
BR 'seɪpɪəntli
AM 'seɪpiən(t)li, 'sæpiən(t)li
Sapir
BR sə'pɪə(r), 'seɪpɪə(r)
AM sə'pɪ(ə)r
sapless
BR 'sapləs
AM 'sæpləs
sapling
BR 'saplɪŋ, -z
AM 'sæplɪŋ, -z
sapodilla
BR ˌsapə'dɪlə(r), -z
AM ˌsæpə'dɪlə, -z
saponaceous
BR ˌsapə'neɪʃəs
AM ˌsæpə'neɪʃəs
saponifiable
BR sə'pɒnɪfʌɪəbl
AM sə'pɑnəˌfaɪəbəl
saponification
BR səˌpɒnɪfɪ'keɪʃn
AM səˌpɑnəfə'keɪʃən
saponify
BR sə'pɒnɪfʌɪ, -z, -ɪŋ, -d
AM sə'pɑnəˌfaɪ, -z, -ɪŋ, -d
saponin
BR 'sapənɪn, -z
AM 'sæpənən, -z
sapor
BR 'seɪpɔː(r), 'seɪpə(r), -z
AM 'seɪpər, -z
sappanwood
BR 'sapənwʊd
AM sə'pænˌwʊd, 'sæˌpænˌwʊd
sapper
BR 'sapə(r), -z
AM 'sæpər, -z
Sapphic
BR 'safɪk, -s
AM 'sæfɪk, -s
sapphire
BR 'safʌɪə(r), -z
AM 'sæˌfaɪ(ə)r, -z
sapphirine
BR 'safɪrʌɪn, 'safɪrɪn, -z
AM 'sæfərən, 'sæfəˌrin, 'sæfəˌraɪn, -z
Sapphism
BR 'safɪz(ə)m
AM 'sæˌfɪzəm
Sappho
BR 'safəʊ
AM 'sæfoʊ
sappily
BR 'sapɪli
AM 'sæpɪli
sappiness
BR 'sapɪnɪs
AM 'sæpinɪs
Sapporo
BR sə'pɔːrəʊ
AM sə'pɔroʊ
sappy
BR 'sapi
AM 'sæpi
saprogenic
BR ˌsaprə(ʊ)'dʒɛnɪk
AM ˌsæproʊ'dʒɛnɪk
saprophagous
BR sə'prɒfəgəs
AM sə'prɑfəgəs
saprophile
BR 'saprə(ʊ)fʌɪl, -z
AM 'sæprəˌfaɪl, -z
saprophilous
BR sə'prɒfɪləs
AM sə'prɑfələs
saprophyte
BR 'saprə(ʊ)fʌɪt, -s
AM 'sæprəˌfaɪt, -s
saprophytic
BR ˌsaprə'fɪtɪk
AM ˌsæprə'fɪdɪk
sapsucker
BR 'sapˌsʌkə(r), -z
AM 'sæpˌsəkər, -z
sapwood
BR 'sapwʊd
AM 'sæpˌwʊd
Sara
BR 'sɛːrə(*r*), 'sɑːrə(*r*)
AM 'sɛrə
saraband
BR 'sarəband, -z
AM 'sɛrəˌbænd, -z
sarabande
BR 'sarəband, -z
AM 'sɛrəˌbænd, -z
Saracen
BR 'sarəsn, -z
AM 'sɛrəsən, -z
Saracenic
BR ˌsarə'sɛnɪk
AM ˌsɛrə'sɛnɪk
Saragossa
BR ˌsarə'gɒsə(*r*)
AM ˌsɛrə'gɔsə, ˌsɛrə'gɑsə
Sarah
BR 'sɛːrə(*r*)
AM 'sɛrə
Sarajevo
BR ˌsarə'jeɪvəʊ
AM ˌsɑrə'jeɪvoʊ
saran
BR sə'ran
AM sə'ræn
sarangi
BR sɑː'rʌŋg|i, sə'raŋg|i, -ɪz
AM sə'rɑŋgi, sə'ræŋgi, -z
Saransk
BR sə'ransk
AM sə'rɑnsk
Saranwrap
BR sə'ranrap
AM sə'rænˌræp
sarape
BR sɛ'rɑːp|eɪ, sə'rɑːp|i, -eɪz\-ɪz
AM sə'rɑpi, sə'rɑpeɪ, -z
Saratoga
BR ˌsarə'təʊgə(*r*)
AM ˌsɛrə'toʊgə
Sarawak
BR sə'rɑːwak
AM sə'rɑwæk
sarcasm
BR sɑːkaz(ə)m
AM 'sɑrˌkæzəm
sarcastic
BR sɑː'kastɪk
AM sɑr'kæstɪk
sarcastically
BR sɑː'kastɪkli
AM sɑr'kæstək(ə)li
sarcelle
BR sɑː'sɛl, -z
AM sɑr'sɛl, -z
sarcenet
BR 'sɑːsnɪt
AM 'sɑrsnət
sarcoma
BR sɑː'kəʊmə(*r*), -z
AM sɑr'koʊmə, -z
sarcomata
BR sɑː'kəʊmətə(*r*)
AM sɑr'koʊmədə
sarcomatosis
BR sɑːˌkəʊmə'təʊsɪs
AM sɑrˌkoʊmə'toʊsəs
sarcomatous
BR sɑː'kəʊmətəs
AM sɑr'koʊmədəs
sarcophagi
BR sɑː'kɒfəgʌɪ, sɑː'kɒfədʒʌɪ
AM sɑr'kɑfəˌgaɪ, sɑr'kɑfəˌdʒaɪ
sarcophagus
BR sɑː'kɒfəgəs, -ɪz
AM sɑr'kɑfəgəs, -əz
sarcoplasm
BR 'sɑːkəplaz(ə)m
AM 'sɑrkəˌplæzəm
sarcoptic
BR sɑː'kɒptɪk
AM sɑr'kɑptɪk
sarcous
BR 'sɑːkəs
AM 'sɑrkəs
sard
BR sɑːd, -z
AM sɑrd, -z
Sardanapalian
BR ˌsɑːdənə'peɪlɪən, ˌsɑːdn̩ə'peɪlɪən
AM ˌsɑrdn̩əˌpeɪliən, ˌsɑrdn̩əˌpeɪljən, ˌsɑrdn̩əˌpɑliən, ˌsɑrdn̩əˌpɑljən
Sardanapalus
BR ˌsɑːdə'napələs, ˌsɑːdn̩'apələs, ˌsɑːdə'napl̩əs
AM ˌsɑrdn̩'æpələs
Sardegna
BR sɑː'dɛnjə(*r*)
AM sɑr'dɛnjə
sardelle
BR sɑː'dɛl, -z
AM sɑr'dɛl(ə), -z
sardine[1]
fish
BR sɑː'diːn, -z
AM sɑr'din, -z

sardine²
stone
BR 'sɑːdʌɪn
AM 'sɑrˌdaɪn, 'sɑrdn
Sardinia
BR sɑː'dɪnɪə(r)
AM sɑr'dɪniə
Sardinian
BR sɑː'dɪnɪən, -z
AM sɑr'dɪniən, -z
Sardis
BR 'sɑːdɪs
AM 'sɑrdəs
sardius
BR 'sɑːdɪəs, -ɪz
AM 'sɑrdiəs, -əz
sardonic
BR sɑː'dɒnɪk
AM sɑr'dɑnɪk
sardonically
BR sɑː'dɒnɪkli
AM sɑr'dɑnək(ə)li
sardonicism
BR sɑː'dɒnɪsɪz(ə)m, -z
AM sɑr'dɑnəˌsɪzəm, -z
sardonyx
BR 'sɑːdənɪks, sɑː'dɒnɪks, -ɪz
AM sɑr'dɑnɪks, -ɪz
saree
BR 'sɑːr|i, -ɪz
AM 'sɑri, -z
Sargant
BR 'sɑːdʒ(ə)nt
AM 'sɑrdʒənt
Sargasso
BR sɑː'gasəʊ
AM sɑr'gæsoʊ
sarge
BR sɑːdʒ
AM sɑrdʒ
Sargent
BR 'sɑːdʒnt
AM 'sɑrdʒənt
Sargodha
BR sɑː'gəʊdə(r)
AM sɑr'goʊdə
Sargon
BR 'sɑːgɒn
AM 'sɑrˌgɔn, 'sɑrˌgɑn
sari
BR 'sɑːr|i, -ɪz
AM 'sɑri, -z
sarin
BR sɑː'riːn, 'sarɪn
AM sɑ'rin
sark
BR sɑːk, -s
AM sɑrk, -s
sarkily
BR 'sɑːkɨli
AM 'sɑrkəli
sarkiness
BR 'sɑːkɪnɨs
AM 'sɑrkinɨs
sarking
BR 'sɑːkɪŋ
AM 'sɑrkɪŋ
sarky
BR 'sɑːk|i, -ɪə(r), -ɪɨst
AM 'sɑrki, -ər, -ɨst
Sarmatia
BR sɑː'meɪʃ(ɪ)ə(r)
AM sɑr'meɪʃ(i)ə
Sarmatian
BR sɑː'meɪʃn, -z
AM sɑr'meɪʃən, -z
sarmentose
BR 'sɑːm(ə)ntəʊs, ˌsɑːm(ə)n'təʊs, 'sɑːm(ə)ntəʊz, ˌsɑːm(ə)n'təʊz
AM sɑr'mɛnˌtoʊz, 'sɑrmənˌtoʊz, sɑr'mɛnˌtoʊs, 'sɑrmənˌtoʊs
sarmentous
BR sɑː'mɛntəs
AM sɑr'mɛn(t)əs
sarnie
sandwich
BR 'sɑːn|i, -ɪz
AM 'sɑrni, -z
sarod
BR sə'rəʊd, -z
AM sə'roʊd, -z
sarong
BR sə'rɒŋ, -z
AM sə'rɔŋ, sə'rɑŋ, -z
Saronic
BR sə'rɒnɪk
AM sə'rɑnɪk
Saros
BR 'sɛːrɒs
AM 'sɛrɔs, 'sɛrɑs
Saroyan
BR sə'rɔɪən
AM sə'rɔɪən
sarracenia
BR ˌsarə'siːnɪə(r)
AM ˌsɛrə'siniə
Sarre
BR sɑː(r)
AM sɑr
sarrusophone
BR sə'ruːzəfəʊn, -z
AM sə'ruzəˌfoʊn, sə'rəsəˌfoʊn, -z
sarsaparilla
BR ˌsɑːs(ə)pə'rɪlə(r), ˌsas(ə)pə'rɪlə(r), -z
AM ˌsɑrs(ə)pə'rɪlə, ˌsæspə'rɪlə, -z
sarsen
BR 'sɑːsn, -z
AM 'sɑrsən, -z
sarsenet
BR 'sɑːs(ə)nɪt, 'sɑːsn̩ɪt
AM 'sɑrsn̩ət
Sarson
BR 'sɑːsn
AM 'sɑrsən
Sarto
BR 'sɑːtəʊ
AM 'sɑrˌtoʊ
sartorial
BR sɑː'tɔːrɪəl
AM sɑr'tɔriəl
sartorially
BR sɑː'tɔːrɪəli
AM sɑr'tɔriəli
sartorii
BR sɑː'tɔːrɪʌɪ
AM sɑr'tɔriˌaɪ
sartorius
BR sɑː'tɔːrɪəs
AM sɑr'tɔriəs
Sartre
BR 'sɑːtrə(r)
AM 'sɑrtr(ə)
Sartrean
BR 'sɑːtrɪən, -z
AM 'sɑrtriən, -z
Sarum
BR 'sɛːrəm
AM 'sɛrəm
SAS¹
computer program
BR sas
AM sæs
SAS²
military unit, airline
BR ˌɛseɪ'ɛs
AM ˌɛsˌeɪ'ɛs
sash
BR saʃ, -ɪz, -t
AM sæʃ, -əz, -t
Sasha
BR 'saʃə(r)
AM 'sɑʃə
sashay
BR 'saʃeɪ, -z, -ɪŋ, -d
AM sæ'ʃeɪ, -z, -ɪŋ, -d
sashimi
BR 'saʃɪmi
AM sɑ'ʃimi
sasin
BR 'sasɪn, -z
AM 'seɪsn, 'sæsn, -z
sasine
BR 'seɪsɪn, -z
AM 'seɪsn, -z
Saskatchewan
BR sə'skatʃʊən
AM sə'skætʃəwən, sæ'skætʃəwən
Saskatoon
BR ˌsaskə'tuːn
AM ˌsæskə'tun
Saskia
BR 'saskɪə(r)
AM 'sæskiə
sasquatch
BR 'saskwatʃ, 'saskwɒtʃ
AM 'sæsˌkwætʃ, 'sæsˌkwɑtʃ
sass
BR sas, -ɪz, -ɪŋ, -t
AM sæs, -əz, -ɪŋ, -t
sassaby
BR 'sasəb|i, -ɪz
AM 'sæsəbi, -z
sassafras
BR 'sasəfras, -ɪz
AM 'sæs(ə)ˌfræs, -əz
Sassanian
BR sa'seɪnɪən, -z
AM sə'sæniən, sə'seɪniən, -z
Sassanid
BR 'sasənɪd, -z
AM 'sæsənəd, sə'sænəd, -z
Sassenach
BR 'sasənax, 'sasənak, -s
AM 'sæsəˌnæk, -s
sassily
BR 'sasɨli
AM 'sæsəli
sassiness
BR 'sasɪnɨs
AM 'sæsinɨs
Sassoon
BR sə'suːn
AM sə'sun, ˌsæ'sun
sassy
BR 'sas|i, -ɪə(r), -ɪɨst
AM 'sæsi, -ər, -ɨst
sastrugi
BR sə'struːgi, sa'struːgi
AM sə'strugi, sæ'strugi, 'zæstrəgi, 'sæstrəgi
SAT®
BR ˌɛseɪ'tiː
AM ˌɛsˌeɪ'ti
sat
BR sat
AM sæt
Satan
BR 'seɪtn
AM 'seɪtn
satang
BR sa'taŋ, -z
AM sə'tɑŋ, -z
satanic
BR sə'tanɪk
AM sə'tænɪk, seɪ'tænɪk
satanically
BR sə'tanɪkli
AM sə'tænək(ə)li, seɪ'tænək(ə)li
satanise
BR 'seɪtn̩ʌɪz, -ɪz, -ɪŋ, -d
AM 'seɪtnˌaɪz, -ɪz, -ɪŋ, -d
satanism
BR 'seɪtn̩ɪz(ə)m
AM 'seɪtnˌɪzəm
satanist
BR 'seɪtn̩ɪst, -s
AM 'seɪtn̩əst, -s
satanize
BR 'seɪtn̩ʌɪz, -ɪz, -ɪŋ, -d
AM 'seɪtnˌaɪz, -ɪz, -ɪŋ, -d

satanology
BR ˌseɪtn̩ˈɒlədʒi
AM ˌseɪtnˈɑlədʒi

satay
BR ˈsateɪ, -z
AM ˈsæˌteɪ, -z

satchel
BR ˈsatʃl, -z
AM ˈsætʃəl, -z

satcom
BR ˈsatkɒm
AM ˈsætkɑm

sate
BR seɪt, -s, -ɪŋ, -ɨd
AM seɪ|t, -ts, -dɪŋ, -dɨd

saté
BR ˈsateɪ, -z
AM ˈsæˌteɪ, -z

sateen
BR saˈtiːn, səˈtiːn, -z
AM sæˈtin, səˈtin, -z

sateless
BR ˈseɪtlɨs
AM ˈseɪtlɨs

satellite
BR ˈsatəlʌɪt, ˈsatl̩ʌɪt, -s
AM ˈsædlˌaɪt, -s

satellitic
BR ˌsatəˈlɪtɪk, ˌsatlˈɪtɪk
AM ˌsædlˈɪdɪk

satellitism
BR ˈsatəlʌɪtɪz(ə)m, ˈsatl̩ʌɪtɪz(ə)m
AM ˈsædlˌaɪˌtɪzəm

satem
BR ˈsɑːtəm, ˈsatəm, ˈseɪtəm
AM ˈsɑdəm

sati
BR sʌˈtiː, ˈsʌtiː, -z
AM ˌsəˈti, ˈsəˌti, -z

satiable
BR ˈseɪʃəbl
AM ˈseɪʃəbəl

satiate[1]
adjective
BR ˈseɪʃɪət
AM ˈseɪʃiət

satiate[2]
verb
BR ˈseɪʃɪeɪt, -s, -ɪŋ, -ɨd
AM ˈseɪʃiˌeɪ|t, -ts, -dɪŋ, -dɨd

satiation
BR ˌseɪʃɪˈeɪʃn
AM ˌseɪʃiˈeɪʃən

Satie
BR ˈsati
AM sɑˈti

satiety
BR səˈtʌɪɨti
AM səˈtaɪədi

satin
BR ˈsatɪn, -z
AM ˈsætn, -z

satinet
BR ˌsatɪˈnɛt, -s
AM ˌsætnˈɛt, -s

satinette
BR ˌsatɪˈnɛt
AM ˌsætnˈɛt

satinflower
BR ˈsatɪnˌflaʊə(r)
AM ˈsætnˌflaʊ(ə)r

satinised
BR ˈsatɨnʌɪzd
AM ˈsætnˌaɪzd

satinized
BR ˈsatɨnʌɪzd
AM ˈsætnˌaɪzd

satinwood
BR ˈsatɪnwʊd
AM ˈsætnˌwʊd

satiny
BR ˈsatɨni
AM ˈsætn̩i

satire
BR ˈsatʌɪə(r), -z
AM ˈsæˌtaɪ(ə)r, -z

satiric
BR səˈtɪrɪk
AM səˈtɪrɪk

satirical
BR səˈtɪrɨkl
AM səˈtɪrəkəl

satirically
BR səˈtɪrɨkli
AM səˈtɪrək(ə)li

satirisation
BR ˌsatɪrʌɪˈzeɪʃn
AM ˌsædərəˈzeɪʃən, ˌsædəˌraɪˈzeɪʃən

satirise
BR ˈsatɪrʌɪz, -ɨz, -ɪŋ, -d
AM ˈsædəˌraɪz, -ɨz, -ɪŋ, -d

satirist
BR ˈsatɪrɪst, -s
AM ˈsædərəst, -s

satirization
BR ˌsatɪrʌɪˈzeɪʃn
AM ˌsædərəˈzeɪʃən, ˌsædəˌraɪˈzeɪʃən

satirize
BR ˈsatɪrʌɪz, -ɨz, -ɪŋ, -d
AM ˈsædəˌraɪz, -ɨz, -ɪŋ, -d

satisfaction
BR ˌsatɪsˈfakʃn
AM ˌsædəˈsfækʃən

satisfactorily
BR ˌsatɪsˈfakt(ə)rɨli
AM ˌsædəˈsfæktərəli

satisfactoriness
BR ˌsatɪsˈfakt(ə)rɪnɨs
AM ˌsædəˈsfæktərinɨs

satisfactory
BR ˌsatɪsˈfakt(ə)ri
AM ˌsædəˈsfæktəri

satisfiability
BR ˌsatɪsfʌɪəˈbɪlɨti
AM ˌsædəˌsfaɪəˈbɪlɨdi

satisfiable
BR ˈsatɪsfʌɪəbl
AM ˈsædəˌsfaɪəbəl

satisfiedly
BR ˈsatɪsfʌɪdli
AM ˈsædəˌsfaɪ(ə)dli

satisfy
BR ˈsatɪsfʌɪ, -z, -ɪŋ, -d
AM ˈsædəˌsfaɪ, -z, -ɪŋ, -d

satisfyingly
BR ˈsatɪsfʌɪɪŋli
AM ˈsædəˌsfaɪɪŋli

satnav
satellite navigation
BR ˈsatnav
AM ˈsætˌnæv

satori
BR səˈtɔːri
AM səˈtɔri

satranji
BR ʃəˈtran(d)ʒ|i, -ɪz
AM səˈtrɑndʒi, -z

satrap
BR ˈsatrəp, ˈsatrap, -s
AM ˈseɪˌtræp, ˈsæˌtræp, -s

satrapy
BR ˈsatrəp|i, -ɪz
AM ˈseɪtrəpi, ˈsætrəpi, -z

satsuma
BR satˈsuːmə(r), -z
AM sætˈsumə, ˈsætsəmə, -z

Satterfield
BR ˈsatəfiːld
AM ˈsædərˌfild

Satterthwaite
BR ˈsatəθweɪt
AM ˈsædərˌθweɪt

saturable
BR ˈsatʃ(ə)rəbl, ˈsatjʊrəbl
AM ˈsætʃər(ə)bəl

saturant
BR ˈsatʃ(ə)rənt, ˈsatʃ(ə)rn̩t, ˈsatjʊrənt, ˈsatjʊrn̩t, -s
AM ˈsætʃərənt, -s

saturate
BR ˈsatʃəreɪt, ˈsatjʊreɪt, -s, -ɪŋ, -ɨd
AM ˈsætʃəˌreɪ|t, -ts, -dɪŋ, -dɨd

saturation
BR ˌsatʃəˈreɪʃn, ˌsatjʊˈreɪʃn
AM ˌsætʃəˈreɪʃən

Saturday
BR ˈsatəd|eɪ, ˈsatəd|i, -eɪz\-ɪz
AM ˈsædərˌdeɪ, ˈsædərdi, -z

Saturn
BR ˈsat(ə)n
AM ˈsædərn

saturnalia
BR ˌsatəˈneɪlɪə(r)
AM ˌsædərˈneɪljə, ˌsædərˈneɪliə

saturnalian
BR ˌsatəˈneɪlɪən
AM ˌsædərˈneɪljən, ˌsædərˈneɪliən

Saturnian
BR səˈtəːnɪən
AM səˈtərniən

saturnic
BR səˈtəːnɪk
AM səˈtərnɪk

saturniid
BR səˈtəːnɪɪd, -z
AM səˈtərniɨd, -z

saturnine
BR ˈsatənʌɪn
AM ˈsædərˌnaɪn, ˈsædərˌnin

saturnism
BR ˈsatənɪz(ə)m
AM ˈsædərˌnɪzəm

satyagraha
BR sʌˈtjɑːɡrəhɑː(r)
AM səˈtjɑɡrəhə, ˈsətjəˌɡrɑ(h)ə

satyr
BR ˈsatə(r), -z
AM ˈsædər, ˈseɪdər, -z

satyriasis
BR ˌsatɪˈrʌɪəsɪs
AM ˌsædəˈraɪəsəs, ˌseɪdəˈraɪəsəs

satyric
BR səˈtɪrɪk
AM səˈtɪrɪk, seɪˈtɪrɪk

satyrid
BR ˈsatɪrɪd, -z
AM ˈsædərəd, ˈseɪdərəd, -z

sauce
BR sɔːs, -ɨz
AM sɔs, sɑs, -əz

sauceboat
BR ˈsɔːsbəʊt, -s
AM ˈsɔsˌboʊt, ˈsɑsˌboʊt, -s

saucebox
BR ˈsɔːsbɒks, -ɨz
AM ˈsɔsˌbɑks, ˈsɑsˌbɑks, -əz

sauceless
BR ˈsɔːsləs
AM ˈsɔsləs, ˈsɑsləs

saucepan
BR ˈsɔːspən, -z
AM ˈsɔsˌpæn, ˈsɑsˌpæn, -z

saucepanful
BR ˈsɔːspənfʊl, -z
AM ˈsɔsˌpænˌfʊl, ˈsɑsˌpænˌfʊl, -z

saucepot
BR ˈsɔːspɒt, -s
AM ˈsɔsˌpɑt, ˈsɑsˌpɑt, -s

saucer
BR ˈsɔːsə(r), -z
AM ˈsɔsər, ˈsɑsər, -z

saucerful
BR 'sɔːsəfʊl, -z
AM 'sɔsər,fʊl, 'sɑsər,fʊl, -z

saucerless
BR 'sɔːsələs
AM 'sɔsərləs, 'sɑsərləs

Sauchiehall
BR ˌsɒkɪ'hɔːl, ˌsɒxɪ'hɔːl
AM ˌsɔki'hɔl, ˌsɑki'hɑl

saucily
BR 'sɔːsɨli
AM 'sɔsəli, 'sɑsəli

sauciness
BR 'sɔːsɪnɨs
AM 'sɔsinɨs, 'sɑsinɨs

saucy
BR 'sɔːs|i, -ɪə(r), -ɪɨst
AM 'sɔsi, 'sɑsi, -ər, -ɨst

Saud
BR saʊd
AM saʊd

Saudi
BR 'saʊd|i, -ɪz
AM 'saʊdi, 'sɔdi, 'sɑdi, -z

Saudi Arabia
BR ˌsaʊdɪ ə'reɪbɪə(r)
AM 'saʊdi ə'reɪbiə, 'sɔdi +, 'sɑdi +

Saudi Arabian
BR ˌsaʊdɪ ə'reɪbɪən, -z
AM 'saʊdi ə'reɪbiən, 'sɔdi +, 'sɑdi +, -z

sauerbraten
BR 'saʊə,brɑːtn
AM 'saʊ(ə)r,brɑtn

sauerkraut
BR 'saʊəkraʊt
AM 'saʊ(ə)r,kraʊt

sauger
BR 'sɔːgə(r), -z
AM 'sɔgər, 'sɑgər, -z

Saul
BR sɔːl
AM sɔl, sɑl

sault¹
a leap
BR səʊ
AM soʊ

sault²
fast water, waterfall
BR səʊ, suː, -z
AM su, -z

Saumur
BR 'səʊmjʊə(r), -z
AM 'sɔmər, 'sɑmər, -z

sauna
BR 'sɔːnə(r), 'saʊnə(r), -z
AM 'sɔnə, 'sɑnə, 'saʊnə, -z

Saunders
BR 'sɔːndəz
AM 'sɔndərz

Saundersfoot
BR 'sɔːndəzfʊt
AM 'sɔndərz,fʊt, 'sɑndərz,fʊt

saunter
BR 'sɔːnt|ə(r), -əz, -(ə)rɪŋ, -əd
AM 'sɔn|(t)ər, 'sɑn|(t)ər, -(t)ərz, -(t)ərɪŋ\-trɪŋ, -(t)ərd

saunterer
BR 'sɔːnt(ə)rə(r), -z
AM 'sɔn(t)ərər, 'sɔntrər, 'sɑn(t)ərər, 'sɑntrər, -z

saurian
BR 'sɔːrɪən, -z
AM 'sɔriən, -z

saurischian
BR sɔː'rɪskɪən, -z
AM sɔ'rɪskiən, -z

sauropod
BR 'sɔːrəpɒd, -z
AM 'sɔrə,pɑd, -z

saury
BR 'sɔːr|i, -ɪz
AM 'sɔri, -z

sausage
BR 'sɒs|ɪdʒ, -ɨdʒɪz
AM 'sɔsɪdʒ, 'sɑsɪdʒ, -ɨz

Saussure
BR sə(ʊ)'s(j)ʊə(r)
AM soʊ'sʊ(ə)r, soʊ'ʃʊ(ə)r

sauté
BR 'səʊteɪ, -z, -ɪŋ, -d
AM sɔ'teɪ, soʊ'teɪ, -z, -ɪŋ, -d

Sauterne
BR səʊ'təːn, -z
AM soʊ'tərn, sɔ'tərn, -z

Sauternes
BR səʊ'təːn, -z
AM soʊ'tərn, sɔ'tərn, -z

sauve qui peut
BR ˌsəʊv kɪ 'pəː(r)
AM ˌsoʊv ˌki ˌpə

Sauveterrian
BR ˌsəʊvə'tɛːrɪən, -z
AM ˌsoʊvə'tɛriən, -z

Sauvignon
BR 'səʊviːnjɒn, 'səʊvɪnjɒn, 'səʊviːnjɔ̃, 'səʊvɪnjɔ̃, -z
AM ˌsoʊvə'njɔn, ˌsoʊvə'njɑn, -z

savable
BR 'seɪvəbl
AM 'seɪvəbəl

savage
BR 'sav|ɪdʒ, -ɨdʒɪz, -ɨdʒɪŋ, -ɪdʒd
AM 'sævɪdʒ, -ɨz, -ɪŋ, -d

savagedom
BR 'savɨdʒdəm
AM 'sævɪdʒdəm

savagely
BR 'savɨdʒli
AM 'sævɨdʒli

savageness
BR 'savɨdʒnɨs
AM 'sævɪdʒnɨs

savagery
BR 'savɨdʒ(ə)ri
AM 'sævədʒ(ə)ri

savanna
BR sə'vanə(r), -z
AM sə'vænə, -z

savannah
BR sə'vanə(r), -z
AM sə'vænə, -z

savant
BR 'savnt, -s
AM sæ'vɑn(t), sɑ'vɑnt, sə'vɑnt, -s

savante
BR 'savnt, -s
AM sæ'vɑn(t), sɑ'vɑnt, sə'vɑnt, -s

savarin
BR 'savərɪn, -z
AM 'sævərən, -z

savate
BR sə'vɑːt
AM sə'væt

save
BR seɪv, -z, -ɪŋ, -d
AM seɪv, -z, -ɪŋ, -d

saveloy
BR 'savəlɔɪ, -z
AM 'sævə,lɔɪ, -z

saver
BR 'seɪvə(r), -z
AM 'seɪvər, -z

Savernake
BR 'savənak
AM 'sævər,næk

Savery
BR 'seɪv(ə)ri
AM 'seɪv(ə)ri

Savile
BR 'sav(ɪ)l
AM sə'vɪl, 'sævəl

savin
BR 'savɪn, -z
AM 'sævɪn, -z

savine
BR 'savɪn, -z
AM 'sævɪn, -z

saving
BR 'seɪvɪŋ, -z
AM 'seɪvɪŋ, -z

savior
BR 'seɪvjə(r), -z
AM 'seɪvjər, -z

saviour
BR 'seɪvjə(r), -z
AM 'seɪvjər, -z

Savlon®
BR 'savlɒn
AM 'sæv(ə)lɑn

savoir faire
BR ˌsavwɑː 'fɛː(r)
AM ˌsæv,wɑr 'fɛ(ə)r

savoir vivre
BR ˌsavwɑː 'viːvrə(r)
AM ˌsæv,wɑr 'vivrə

Savonarola
BR ˌsavənə'rəʊlə(r), ˌsavn̩ə'rəʊlə(r)
AM ˌsævənə'rɔlə, ˌsævənə'roʊlə

Savonlinna
BR ˌsav(ə)n'lɪnə(r)
AM ˌsævən'lɪnə

Savonnerie
BR 'savɒnri, -ɪz
AM 'sævənri, -z

savor
BR 'seɪv|ə(r), -əz, -(ə)rɪŋ, -əd
AM 'seɪv|ər, -ərz, -(ə)rɪŋ, -ərd

savorily
BR 'seɪv(ə)rɨli
AM 'seɪv(ə)rəli

savoriness
BR 'seɪv(ə)rɪnɨs
AM 'seɪv(ə)rinɨs

savorless
BR 'seɪvələs
AM 'seɪvərləs

savory
BR 'seɪv(ə)r|i, -ɪz
AM 'seɪv(ə)ri, -z

savour
BR 'seɪv|ə(r), -əz, -(ə)rɪŋ, -əd
AM 'seɪv|ər, -ərz, -(ə)rɪŋ, -ərd

savourily
BR 'seɪv(ə)rɨli
AM 'seɪv(ə)rəli

savouriness
BR 'seɪv(ə)rɪnɨs
AM 'seɪv(ə)rinɨs

savourless
BR 'seɪvələs
AM 'seɪvərləs

savoury
BR 'seɪv(ə)r|i, -ɪz
AM 'seɪv(ə)ri, -z

savoy
BR sə'vɔɪ
AM 'sæ,vɔɪ, sə'vɔɪ

Savoyard
BR sə'vɔɪɑːd, ˌsavɔɪ'ɑːd, -z
AM sə'vɔɪərd, ˌsæ,vɔɪ'(j)ɑrd, -z

savvy
BR 'savi
AM 'sævi

saw
BR sɔː(r), -z, -ɪŋ, -d
AM sɔ, sɑ, -z, -ɪŋ, -d

sawbench
BR 'sɔːbɛn(t)ʃ, -ɪz
AM 'sɔ,bɛntʃ, 'sɑ,bɛntʃ, -əz

sawbill
BR 'sɔːbɪl, -z
AM 'sɔ,bɪl, 'sɑ,bɪl, -z

sawbones
BR ˈsɔːbəʊnz
AM ˈsɔˌboʊnz, ˈsɑˌboʊnz
Sawbridgeworth
BR ˈsɔːbrɪdʒwəːθ, ˈsɔːbrɪdʒwəθ
AM ˈsɔbrɪdʒˌwərθ, ˈsɑbrɪdʒˌwərθ
sawbuck
BR ˈsɔːbʌk, -s
AM ˈsɔˌbək, ˈsɑˌbək, -s
sawcut
BR ˈsɔːkʌt, -s
AM ˈsɔˌkət, ˈsɑˌkət, -s
sawdust
BR ˈsɔːdʌst
AM ˈsɔˌdəst, ˈsɑˌdəst
sawfish
BR ˈsɔːfɪʃ
AM ˈsɔˌfɪʃ, ˈsɑˌfɪʃ
sawfly
BR ˈsɔːflʌɪ, -z
AM ˈsɔˌflaɪ, ˈsɑˌflaɪ, -z
sawgrass
BR ˈsɔːɡrɑːs, ˈsɔːɡras, -ɪz
AM ˈsɔˌɡræs, ˈsɑˌɡræs, -əz
sawhorse
BR ˈsɔːhɔːs, -ɪz
AM ˈsɔˌhɔ(ə)rs, ˈsɑˌhɔ(ə)rs, -əz
sawlike
BR ˈsɔːlʌɪk
AM ˈsɔˌlaɪk, ˈsɑˌlaɪk
sawmill
BR ˈsɔːmɪl, -z
AM ˈsɔˌmɪl, ˈsɑˌmɪl, -z
sawn
BR sɔːn
AM sɔn, sɑn
sawpit
BR ˈsɔːpɪt, -s
AM ˈsɔˌpɪt, ˈsɑˌpɪt, -s
sawtooth
BR ˈsɔːtuːθ, ˈsɔːtʊθ
AM ˈsɔˌtuθ, ˈsɑˌtuθ
sawtoothed
BR ˌsɔːˈtuːθt, ˌsɔːˈtʊθt
AM ˈsɔˌtuθt, ˈsɑˌtuθt
sawyer
BR ˈsɔːjə(r), ˈsɔɪə(r), -z
AM ˈsɔjər, ˈsɔɪər, -z
sax
BR saks, -ɪz
AM sæks, -əz
Saxa
BR ˈsaksə(r)
AM ˈsæksə
saxatile
BR ˈsaksətʌɪl, ˈsaksətɪl
AM ˈsæksəˌtaɪl, ˈsæksədl
saxboard
BR ˈsaksbɔːd, -z
AM ˈsæksˌbɔ(ə)rd, -z
Saxby
BR ˈsaksbi
AM ˈsæksbi
saxe
BR saks, -ɪz
AM sæks, -əz
Saxe-Coburg-Gotha
BR saksˌkəʊbəːɡˈɡəʊtə(r)
AM ˌsæksˈkoʊbərɡˈɡoʊθə
saxhorn
BR ˈsakshɔːn, -z
AM ˈsæksˌ(h)ɔ(ə)rn, -z
saxicoline
BR sakˈsɪkəlʌɪn, sakˈsɪkl̩ʌɪn
AM sækˈsɪkəˌlaɪn, sækˈsɪkələn
saxicolous
BR sakˈsɪkələs, sakˈsɪkl̩əs
AM sækˈsɪkələs
saxifrage
BR ˈsaksɪfreɪ(d)ʒ, -ɪz
AM ˈsæksəˌfreɪ(d)ʒ, -ɪz
saxist
BR ˈsaksɪst, -s
AM ˈsæksəst, -s
Saxmundham
BR saksˈmʌndəm
AM sæksˈməndəm
Saxo
BR ˈsaksəʊ
AM ˈsæksoʊ
Saxon
BR ˈsaksn, -z
AM ˈsæksən, -z
Saxondom
BR ˈsaksndəm
AM ˈsæksəndəm
Saxone
BR ˌsakˈsəʊn, ˈsaksəʊn
AM ˌsækˈsoʊn, ˈsækˌsoʊn
Saxonise
BR ˈsaksn̩ʌɪz, -ɪz, -ɪŋ, -d
AM ˈsæksəˌnaɪz, -ɪz, -ɪŋ, -d
Saxonism
BR ˈsaksn̩ɪz(ə)m
AM ˈsæksəˌnɪzəm
Saxonist
BR ˈsaksn̩ɪst, -s
AM ˈsæksənəst, -s
Saxonize
BR ˈsaksn̩ʌɪz, -ɪz, -ɪŋ, -d
AM ˈsæksəˌnaɪz, -ɪz, -ɪŋ, -d
saxony
BR ˈsaksən|i, ˈsaksn̩|i, -ɪz
AM ˈsæksəni, -z
saxophone
BR ˈsaksəfəʊn, -z
AM ˈsæksəˌfoʊn, -z
saxophonic
BR ˌsaksəˈfɒnɪk
AM ˌsæksəˈfɑnɪk
saxophonist
BR sakˈsɒfənɪst, sakˈsɒfn̩ɪst, -s
AM ˈsæksəˌfoʊnəst, -s
Saxton
BR ˈsakst(ə)n
AM ˈsækstən
say
BR seɪ, -ɪŋ
AM seɪ, -ɪŋ
sayable
BR ˈseɪəbl
AM ˈseɪəbəl
Sayce
BR seɪs
AM seɪs
sayer
BR ˈseɪə(r), -z
AM ˈseɪər, -z
Sayers
BR ˈseɪəz
AM ˈseɪərz
saying
BR ˈseɪɪŋ, -z
AM ˈseɪɪŋ, -z
says
BR sɛz
AM sɛz
say-so
BR ˈseɪsəʊ
AM ˈseɪˌsoʊ
S-bend
BR ˈɛsbɛnd, -z
AM ˈɛsˌbɛnd, -z
scab
BR skab, -z, -ɪŋ, -d
AM skæb, -z, -ɪŋ, -d
scabbard
BR ˈskabəd, -z
AM ˈskæbərd, -z
scabbard-fish
BR ˈskabədfɪʃ, -ɪz
AM ˈskæbərdˌfɪʃ, -ɪz
scabbiness
BR ˈskabɪnɪs
AM ˈskæbinɪs
scabby
BR ˈskabi
AM ˈskæbi
scabies
BR ˈskeɪbɪz, ˈskeɪbiːz
AM ˈskeɪbiz
scabious
BR ˈskeɪbɪəs, -ɪz
AM ˈskeɪbiəs, -əz
scablike
BR ˈskablʌɪk
AM ˈskæbˌlaɪk
scabrous
BR ˈskeɪbrəs, ˈskabrəs
AM ˈskæbrəs
scabrously
BR ˈskeɪbrəsli, ˈskabrəsli
AM ˈskæbrəsli
scabrousness
BR ˈskeɪbrəsnəs, ˈskabrəsnəs
AM ˈskæbrəsnəs
scad
BR skad, -z
AM skæd, -z
Scafell
BR skɔːˈfɛl
AM ˈskæfəl, skɔˈfɛl, skɑˈfɛl
scaffold
BR ˈskafəʊld, ˈskafld, -z
AM ˈskæfəld, ˈskæˌfoʊld, -z
scaffolder
BR ˈskafldə(r), -z
AM ˈskæfəldər, ˈskæˌfoʊldər, -z
scaffolding
BR ˈskafldɪŋ, -z
AM ˈskæfəldɪŋ, ˈskæˌfoʊldɪŋ, -z
scagliola
BR skalˈjəʊlə(r)
AM skælˈjoʊlə
scalability
BR ˌskeɪləˈbɪlɪti
AM ˌskeɪləˈbɪlɪdi
scalable
BR ˈskeɪləbl
AM ˈskeɪləbəl
scalar
BR ˈskeɪlə(r), -z
AM ˈskeɪlər, -z
scalariform
BR skəˈlarɪfɔːm
AM skəˈlɛrəˌfɔ(ə)rm
scalawag
BR ˈskalɪwaɡ, -z
AM ˈskæləˌwæɡ, ˈskæliˌwæɡ, -z
scald
BR skɔːld, -z, -ɪŋ, -ɪd
AM skɔld, skɑld, -z, -ɪŋ, -əd
scalder
BR ˈskɔːldə(r), -z
AM ˈskɔldər, ˈskɑldər, -z
scale
BR skeɪl, -z, -ɪŋ, -d
AM skeɪl, -z, -ɪŋ, -d
scaleless
BR ˈskeɪllɪs
AM ˈskeɪ(l)lɪs
scalelike
BR ˈskeɪllʌɪk
AM ˈskeɪlˌlaɪk
scale-moss
BR ˈskeɪlmɒs, -ɪz
AM ˈskeɪlˌmɔs, ˈskeɪlˌmɑs, -əz
scalene
BR ˈskeɪliːn
AM ˈskeɪˌlin

scaleni
BR skeɪˈliːnʌɪ
AM skeɪˈliˌnaɪ
scalenus
BR skeɪˈliːnəs
AM skeɪˈlinəs
scaler
BR ˈskeɪlə(r), -z
AM ˈskeɪlər, -z
Scalextric
BR skəˈlɛkstrɪk
AM skəˈlɛkstrɪk
Scaliger
BR ˈskalɨdʒə(r)
AM ˈskælədʒər
scaliness
BR ˈskeɪlɪnɨs
AM ˈskeɪlinɨs
scallawag
BR ˈskalɪwag, -z
AM ˈskæləˌwæg, ˈskæliˌwæg, -z
scallion
BR ˈskalɪən, -z
AM ˈskæljən, ˈskæliən, -z
scallop
BR ˈskɒləp, ˈskaləp, -s, -ɪŋ, -t
AM ˈskɑləp, ˈskæləp, -s, -ɪŋ, -t
scalloper
BR ˈskɒləpə(r), ˈskaləpə(r), -z
AM ˈskɑləpər, ˈskæləpər, -z
scallywag
BR ˈskalɪwag, -z
AM ˈskæləˌwæg, ˈskæliˌwæg, -z
scaloppine
BR ˌskalə(ʊ)ˈpiːn|i, -ɪz
AM ˌskæləˈpini, -z
scalp
BR skalp, -s, -ɪŋ, -t
AM skælp, -s, -ɪŋ, -t
scalpel
BR ˈskalpl, -z
AM ˈskælpəl, -z
scalper
BR ˈskalpə(r), -z
AM ˈskælpər, -z
scalpless
BR ˈskalpləs
AM ˈskælpləs
scalpriform
BR ˈskalprɪfɔːm
AM ˈskælprəˌfɔ(ə)rm
scaly
BR ˈskeɪl|i, -ɪə(r), -ɪɨst
AM ˈskeɪli, -ər, -ɨst
scam
BR skam, -z, -ɪŋ, -d
AM skæm, -z, -ɪŋ, -d
Scammell
BR ˈskaml
AM ˈskæməl
scammony
BR ˈskamən|i, -ɪz
AM ˈskæməni, -z
scamp
BR skamp, -s
AM skæmp, -s
scamper
BR ˈskamp|ə(r), -əz, -(ə)rɪŋ, -əd
AM ˈskæmp|ər, -ərz, -(ə)rɪŋ, -ərd
scampi
BR ˈskampi
AM ˈskæmpi
scampish
BR ˈskampɪʃ
AM ˈskæmpɪʃ
scan
BR skan, -z, -ɪŋ, -d
AM skæn, -z, -ɪŋ, -d
scandal
BR ˈskandl, -z
AM ˈskændəl, -z
scandalise
BR ˈskandəlʌɪz, ˈskandl̩ʌɪz, -ɨz, -ɪŋ, -d
AM ˈskændlˌaɪz, -ɨz, -ɪŋ, -d
scandalize
BR ˈskandəlʌɪz, ˈskandl̩ʌɪz, -ɨz, -ɪŋ, -d
AM ˈskændlˌaɪz, -ɨz, -ɪŋ, -d
scandalmonger
BR ˈskandlˌmʌŋgə(r), -z
AM ˈskændlˌmɑŋgər, ˈskændlˌməŋgər, -z
scandalous
BR ˈskandələs, ˈskandl̩əs
AM ˈskændl̩əs
scandalously
BR ˈskandələsli, ˈskandl̩əsli
AM ˈskændl̩əsli
scandalousness
BR ˈskandələsnəs, ˈskandl̩əsnəs
AM ˈskændl̩əsnəs
scandent
BR ˈskandənt
AM ˈskændnt
Scanderbeg
BR ˈskandəbɛg
AM ˈskændəˌbɛrg
Scandia
BR ˈskandɪə(*r*)
AM ˈskændiə
Scandinavia
BR ˌskandɪˈneɪvɪə(*r*)
AM ˌskændəˈneɪviə
Scandinavian
BR ˌskandɪˈneɪvɪən, -z
AM ˌskændəˈneɪviən, -z
scandium
BR ˈskandɪəm
AM ˈskændiəm
Scanlon
BR ˈskanlən
AM ˈskænlən
scannable
BR ˈskanəbl
AM ˈskænəbəl
scanner
BR ˈskanə(r), -z
AM ˈskænər, -z
scansion
BR ˈskanʃn
AM ˈskænʃən
scansorial
BR skanˈsɔːrɪəl
AM skænˈsɔriəl
scant
BR skant
AM skænt
scanties
BR ˈskantɪz
AM ˈskæn(t)iz
scantily
BR ˈskantɨli
AM ˈskæn(t)əli
scantiness
BR ˈskantɪnɨs
AM ˈskæn(t)inɨs
scantling
BR ˈskantlɪŋ, -z
AM ˈskæn(t)lɪŋ, -z
scantly
BR ˈskantli
AM ˈskæn(t)li
scantness
BR ˈskantnəs
AM ˈskæn(t)nəs
scanty
BR ˈskant|i, -ɪz, -ɪə(r), -ɪɨst
AM ˈskæn(t)i, -z, -ər, -ɨst
Scapa Flow
BR ˌskɑːpə ˈfləʊ, ˌskapə +
AM ˌskæpə ˈfloʊ
scape
BR skeɪp, -s
AM skeɪp, -s
scapegoat
BR ˈskeɪpgəʊt, -s
AM ˈskeɪpˌgoʊt, -s
scapegoater
BR ˈskeɪpgəʊtə(r), -z
AM ˈskeɪpˌgoʊdər, -z
scapegrace
BR ˈskeɪpgreɪs, -ɨz
AM ˈskeɪpˌgreɪs, -ɨz
scaphoid
BR ˈskafɔɪd, -z
AM ˈskæˌfɔɪd, -z
scapula
BR ˈskapjʉlə(*r*), -z
AM ˈskæpjələ, -z
scapulae
BR ˈskapjʉliː
AM ˈskæpjəˌli, ˈskæpjəˌlaɪ
scapular
BR ˈskapjʉlə(r)
AM ˈskæpjələr
scapulary
BR ˈskapjʉlər|i, -ɪz
AM ˈskæpjəˌlɛri, -z
scar
BR skɑː(r), -z, -ɪŋ, -d
AM skɑr, -z, -ɪŋ, -d
scarab
BR ˈskarəb, -z
AM ˈskɛrəb, -z
scarabaei
BR ˌskarəˈbiːʌɪ
AM ˌskɛrəˈbiˌaɪ
scarabaeid
BR ˌskarəˈbiːɪd, -z
AM ˌskɛrəˈbiɨd, -z
scarabaeus
BR ˌskarəˈbiːəs
AM ˌskɛrəˈbiəs
scaramouch
BR ˈskarəmuːʃ, -ɨz
AM ˈskɛrəˌmu(t)ʃ, -əz
scaramouche
BR ˈskarəmuːʃ, -ɨz
AM ˈskɛrəˌmu(t)ʃ, -əz
Scarborough
BR ˈskɑːb(ə)rə(*r*)
AM ˈskɑrb(ə)rə
scarce
BR skɛːs, -ə(r), -ɨst
AM skɛ(ə)rs, -ər, -əst
scarcely
BR ˈskɛːsli
AM ˈskɛrsli
scarceness
BR ˈskɛːsnəs
AM ˈskɛrsnəs
scarcity
BR ˈskɛːsɪt|i, -ɪz
AM ˈskɛrsədi, -z
scare
BR skɛː(r), -z, -ɪŋ, -d
AM skɛ(ə)r, -z, -ɪŋ, -d
scarecrow
BR ˈskɛːkrəʊ, -z
AM ˈskɛrˌkroʊ, -z
scaredy-cat
BR ˈskɛːdɪkat, -s
AM ˈskɛrdiˌkæt, -s
scaremonger
BR ˈskɛːˌmʌŋgə(r), -z
AM ˈskɛrˌmɑŋgər, ˈskɛrˌməŋgər, -z
scaremongering
BR ˈskɛːˌmʌŋg(ə)rɪŋ, -z
AM ˈskɛrˌmɑŋg(ə)rɪŋ, ˈskɛrˌməŋg(ə)rɪŋ, -z
scarer
BR ˈskɛːrə(r), -z
AM ˈskɛrər, -z
scarf
BR skɑːf, -t

AM skɑrf, -t

Scarfe
BR skɑːf
AM skɑrf

Scargill
BR ˈskɑːɡɪl
AM ˈskɑrˌɡɪl

scarification
BR ˌskarɪfɪˈkeɪʃn, ˌskɛːrɪfɪˈkeɪʃn
AM ˌskɛrəfəˈkeɪʃən

scarificator
BR ˈskarɪfɪkeɪtə(r), ˈskɛːrɪfɪkeɪtə(r), -z
AM ˈskɛrəfəˌkeɪdər, -z

scarifier
BR ˈskarɪfʌɪə(r), ˈskɛːrɪfʌɪə(r), -z
AM ˈskɛrəˌfaɪər, -z

scarify[1]
cut
BR ˈskarɪfʌɪ, ˈskɛːrɪfʌɪ, -z, -ɪŋ, -d
AM ˈskɛrəˌfaɪ, -z, -ɪŋ, -d

scarify[2]
frighten
BR ˈskɛːrɪfʌɪ, -z, -ɪŋ, -d
AM ˈskɛrəfaɪ, -z, -ɪŋ, -d

scarily
BR ˈskɛːrɪli
AM ˈskɛrəli

scariness
BR ˈskɛːrɪnɪs
AM ˈskɛrinɪs

scarious
BR ˈskɛːrɪəs
AM ˈskɛriəs

Scarisbrick
BR ˈskɛːzbrɪk
AM ˈskɛrzˌbrɪk

scarlatina
BR ˌskɑːləˈtiːnə(r)
AM ˌskɑrləˈtinə

Scarlatti
BR skɑːˈlati
AM skɑrˈlɑdi

scarless
BR ˈskɑːləs
AM ˈskɑrləs

scarlet
BR ˈskɑːlɪt
AM ˈskɑrlət

Scarlett
BR ˈskɑːlɪt
AM ˈskɑrlət

Scarman
BR ˈskɑːmən
AM ˈskɑrmən

scaroid
BR ˈskarɔɪd, ˈskɛːrɔɪd, -z
AM ˈskɛˌrɔɪd, -z

scarp
BR skɑːp, -s
AM skɑrp, -s

scarper
BR ˈskɑːp|ə(r), -əz, -(ə)rɪŋ, -əd
AM ˈskɑrpər, -z, -ɪŋ, -d

Scart
BR skɑːt
AM skɑrt

scarus
BR ˈskɛːrəs, -ɪz
AM ˈskɛrəs, -əz

scarves
BR skɑːvz
AM skɑrvz

scary
BR ˈskɛːr|i, -ɪə(r), -ɪɪst
AM ˈskɛri, -ər, -ɪst

Scase
BR skeɪs
AM skeɪs

scat
BR skat, -s, -ɪŋ, -ɪd
AM skæ|t, -ts, -dɪŋ, -dəd

scathe
BR skeɪð, -z, -ɪŋ, -d
AM skeɪð, -z, -ɪŋ, -d

scatheless
BR ˈskeɪðlɪs
AM ˈskeɪðlɪs

scathing
BR ˈskeɪðɪŋ
AM ˈskeɪðɪŋ

scathingly
BR ˈskeɪðɪŋli
AM ˈskeɪðɪŋli

scatological
BR ˌskatəˈlɒdʒɪkl
AM ˌskædlˈɑdʒəkəl

scatologist
BR skaˈtɒlədʒɪst, skəˈtɒlədʒɪst, -s
AM skəˈtɑlədʒəst, skæˈtɑlədʒəst, -s

scatology
BR skaˈtɒlədʒi, skəˈtɒlədʒi
AM skəˈtɑlədʒi, skæˈtɑlədʒi

scatophagous
BR skaˈtɒfəɡəs, skəˈtɒfəɡəs
AM skəˈtɑfəɡəs, skæˈtɑfəɡəs

scatter
BR ˈskat|ə(r), -əz, -(ə)rɪŋ, -əd
AM ˈskæd|ər, -ərz, -(ə)rɪŋ, -ərd

scatterbrain
BR ˈskatəbreɪn, -z, -d
AM ˈskædərˌbreɪn, -z, -d

scatterer
BR ˈskat(ə)rə(r), -z
AM ˈskædərər, -z

scattergram
BR ˈskatəɡram, -z
AM ˈskædərˌɡræm, -z

scattergun
BR ˈskatəɡʌn, -z
AM ˈskædərˌɡən, -z

scatterplot
BR ˈskatəplɒt, -s
AM ˈskædərˌplɑt, -s

scattershot
BR ˈskatəʃɒt, -s
AM ˈskædərˌʃɑt, -s

scattily
BR ˈskatɪli
AM ˈskædəli

scattiness
BR ˈskatɪnɪs
AM ˈskædinɪs

scatty
BR ˈskat|i, -ɪə(r), -ɪɪst
AM ˈskædi, -ər, -ɪst

scaup
BR skɔːp, -s
AM skɔp, skɑp, -s

scauper
BR ˈskɔːpə(r), -z
AM ˈskɔpər, ˈskɑpər, -z

scaur
BR skɔː(r)
AM skɑr

scavenge
BR ˈskav(ɪ)n(d)ʒ, -ɪz, -ɪŋ, -d
AM ˈskævəndʒ, -əz, -ɪŋ, -d

scavenger
BR ˈskav(ɪ)n(d)ʒə(r), -z
AM ˈskævəndʒər, -z

scavengery
BR ˈskav(ɪ)n(d)ʒ(ə)ri
AM ˈskævəndʒ(ə)ri

scazon
BR ˈskeɪzn, ˈskazn, -z
AM ˈskeɪzən, -z

scean dhu
BR ˌskiːən ˈduː, -z
AM ˌskiən ˈdu, -z

scena
BR ˈʃeɪnə(r), -z
AM ˈʃeɪnə, -z

scenario
BR sɪˈnɑːrɪəʊ, sɪˈnɛːrɪəʊ, -z
AM səˈnɛrioʊ, -z

scenarist
BR sɪˈnɑːrɪst, ˈsiːn(ə)rɪst, -s
AM səˈnɛrəst, -s

scend
BR sɛnd, -z, -ɪŋ, -ɪd
AM sɛnd, -z, -ɪŋ, -əd

scene
BR siːn, -z
AM sin, -z

scenery
BR ˈsiːn(ə)ri
AM ˈsin(ə)ri

sceneshifter
BR ˈsiːnˌʃɪftə(r), -z
AM ˈsinˌʃɪftər, -z

scenester
BR ˈsiːnstə(r), -z
AM ˈsinstər, -z

scenic
BR ˈsiːnɪk
AM ˈsinɪk

scenically
BR ˈsiːnɪkli
AM ˈsinɪk(ə)li

scent
BR sɛnt, -s, -ɪŋ, -ɪd
AM sɛn|t, -ts, -(t)ɪŋ, -(t)əd

scentless
BR ˈsɛntləs
AM ˈsɛn(t)ləs

scepsis
BR ˈskɛpsɪs
AM ˈskɛpsəs

scepter
BR ˈsɛptə(r), -z, -d
AM ˈsɛptər, -z, -d

sceptic
BR ˈskɛptɪk, -s
AM ˈskɛptɪk, -s

sceptical
BR ˈskɛptɪkl
AM ˈskɛptəkəl

sceptically
BR ˈskɛptɪkli
AM ˈskɛptək(ə)li

scepticism
BR ˈskɛptɪsɪz(ə)m
AM ˈskɛptəˌsɪzəm

sceptre
BR ˈsɛptə(r), -z, -d
AM ˈsɛptər, -z, -d

Schadenfreude
BR ˈʃɑːdnˌfrɔɪdə(r)
AM ˈʃɑdənˌfrɔɪdə

Schaefer
BR ˈʃeɪfə(r)
AM ˈʃeɪfər

Schaeffer
BR ˈʃeɪfə(r)
AM ˈʃeɪfər

Schafer
BR ˈʃeɪfə(r)
AM ˈʃeɪfər

Schapiro
BR ʃəˈpɪərəʊ
AM ʃəˈpɪroʊ

schappe
BR ʃap, ˈʃapə(r), -s
AM ˈʃɑpə, -s

schedule
BR ˈʃɛdjʊl, ˈʃɛdjuːl, ˈʃɛdʒʊl, ˈskɛdjʊl, ˈskɛdjuːl, ˈskɛdʒʊl, -z, -ɪŋ, -d
AM ˈskɛdʒəl, -z, -ɪŋ, -d

scheduler
BR ˈʃɛdjʊlə(r), ˈʃɛdjuːlə(r),

ˈʃɛdʒʉlə(r), ˈskɛdjʉlə(r), ˈskɛdjuːlə(r), ˈskɛdʒʉlə(r), -z
AM ˈskɛdʒələr, -z

Scheele
BR ˈʃeɪlə(r)
AM ˈʃeɪlə

scheelite
BR ˈʃiːlʌɪt, -s
AM ˈʃeɪˌlaɪt, -s

Scheherazade
BR ʃəˌhɛrəˈzɑːdə(r)
AM ʃəˌhɛrəˈzɑd

Schelde
BR ˈʃɛldə, skɛld
AM ˈʃɛldə, skɛld

Scheldt
BR ʃɛlt, skɛlt
AM ʃɛlt, skɛlt

Schelling
BR ˈʃɛlɪŋ
AM ˈʃɛlɪŋ

schema
BR ˈskiːmə(r), -z
AM ˈskimə, -z

schemata
BR ˈskiːmətə(r)
AM ˈskimədə

schematic
BR skiːˈmatɪk, skɪˈmatɪk
AM skəˈmædɪk, skiˈmædɪk

schematically
BR skiːˈmatɪkli, skɪˈmatɪkli
AM skəˈmædək(ə)li, skiˈmædək(ə)li

schematisation
BR ˌskiːmətʌɪˈzeɪʃn, -z
AM ˌskimədəˈzeɪʃən, ˌskiməˌtaɪˈzeɪʃən, -z

schematise
BR ˈskiːmətʌɪz, -ɪz, -ɪŋ, -d
AM ˈskiməˌtaɪz, -ɪz, -ɪŋ, -d

schematism
BR ˈskiːmətɪz(ə)m, -z
AM ˈskiməˌtɪzəm, -z

schematization
BR ˌskiːmətʌɪˈzeɪʃn, -z
AM ˌskimədəˈzeɪʃən, ˌskiməˌtaɪˈzeɪʃən, -z

schematize
BR ˈskiːmətʌɪz, -ɪz, -ɪŋ, -d
AM ˈskiməˌtaɪz, -ɪz, -ɪŋ, -d

scheme
BR skiːm, -z, -ɪŋ, -d
AM skim, -z, -ɪŋ, -d

schemer
BR ˈskiːmə(r), -z
AM ˈskimər, -z

scheming
BR ˈskiːmɪŋ, -z
AM ˈskimɪŋ, -z

schemingly
BR ˈskiːmɪŋli
AM ˈskimɪŋli

schemozzle
BR ʃɪˈmɒzl, -z
AM ʃəˈmɑzl, -z

Schenectady
BR skɪˈnɛktədi
AM skəˈnɛktədi

scherzando
BR skɛːtˈsandəʊ, skəːtˈsandəʊ, -z
AM skərtˈsɑndoʊ, -z

scherzo
BR ˈskɛːtsəʊ, ˈskəːtsəʊ, -z
AM ˈskɛrtsoʊ, -z

Schiaparelli
BR ˌʃapəˈrɛli
AM ˌʃɑpəˈrɛli
IT skjapaˈrɛlli

Schick
BR ʃɪk
AM ʃɪk

Schiedam
BR skɪˈdam
AM skiˈdæm
DU ˈsxiːdɑm

Schiele
BR ˈʃiːlə(r)
AM ˈʃilə

Schiller
BR ˈʃɪlə(r)
AM ˈʃɪlər

Schilling
BR ˈʃɪlɪŋ, -z
AM ˈʃɪlɪŋ, -z

schipperke
BR ˈskɪpək|i, ˈʃɪpək|i, -ɪz
AM ˈskɪpərki, -z

schism
BR ˈs(k)ɪz(ə)m, -z
AM ˈs(k)ɪzəm, ˈʃɪzəm, -z

schismatic
BR s(k)ɪzˈmatɪk, -s
AM s(k)ɪzˈmædɪk, -s

schismatical
BR s(k)ɪzˈmatɪkl
AM s(k)ɪzˈmædəkəl

schismatically
BR s(k)ɪzˈmatɪkli
AM s(k)ɪzˈmædək(ə)li

schismatise
BR ˈs(k)ɪzmətʌɪz, -ɪz, -ɪŋ, -d
AM ˈs(k)ɪzməˌtaɪz, -ɪz, -ɪŋ, -d

schismatize
BR ˈs(k)ɪzmətʌɪz, -ɪz, -ɪŋ, -d
AM ˈs(k)ɪzməˌtaɪz, -ɪz, -ɪŋ, -d

schist
BR ʃɪst, -s
AM ʃɪst, -s

schistose
BR ˈʃɪstəʊs
AM ˈʃɪstoʊs, ˈʃɪstoʊz

schistosome
BR ˈʃɪstəsəʊm, -z
AM ˈʃɪstəˌsoʊm, -z

schistosomiases
BR ˌʃɪstə(ʊ)səˈmʌɪəsiːz
AM ˌʃɪstoʊsəˈmaɪəˌsiz

schistosomiasis
BR ˌʃɪstə(ʊ)səˈmʌɪəsɪs
AM ˌʃɪstoʊsəˈmaɪəsəs

schizanthus
BR skɪˈzanθəs, -ɪz
AM skəˈzænθəs, -əz

schizo
BR ˈskɪtsəʊ, -z
AM ˈskɪtsoʊ, -z

schizocarp
BR ˈskɪtsə(ʊ)kɑːp, ˈskʌɪzə(ʊ)kɑːp, -s
AM ˈskɪtsoʊˌkɑrp, -s

schizocarpic
BR ˌskɪtsə(ʊ)ˈkɑːpɪk, ˌskʌɪzə(ʊ)ˈkɑːpɪk
AM ˌskɪtsəˈkɑrpɪk

schizocarpous
BR ˌskɪtsə(ʊ)ˈkɑːpəs, ˌskʌɪzə(ʊ)ˈkɑːpəs
AM ˌskɪtsəˈkɑrpəs

schizogenous
BR skɪtˈsɒdʒɪnəs, ʃʌɪˈzɒdʒɪnəs
AM skɪtˈsɑdʒənəs

schizogeny
BR skɪtˈsɒdʒəni, ʃʌɪˈzɒdʒəni
AM skɪtˈsɑdʒəni

schizoid
BR ˈskɪtsɔɪd
AM ˈskɪtˌsɔɪd

schizomycete
BR ˌskɪtsə(ʊ)ˈmʌɪsiːt, ˌskɪtsə(ʊ)ˈmʌɪsiːt, -s
AM ˌskɪtsoʊˈmaɪˌsit, -s

schizont
BR ˈskɪzɒnt, ˈʃʌɪzɒnt, -s
AM ˈskɪzɑnt, -s

schizophrenia
BR ˌskɪtsəˈfriːnɪə(r)
AM ˌskɪtsəˈfrɛniə, ˌskɪtsəˈfriniə

schizophrenic
BR ˌskɪtsəˈfrɛnɪk, -s
AM ˌskɪtsəˈfrɛnɪk, ˌskɪtsəˈfrinɪk, -s

schizostylis
BR ˌskɪtsə(ʊ)ˈstʌɪlɪs, ˌʃʌɪzə(ʊ)ˈstʌɪlɪs
AM ˌskɪtsoʊˈstaɪlɪs

schizothymia
BR ˌskɪtsə(ʊ)ˈθʌɪmɪə(r)
AM ˌskɪtsoʊˈθaɪmiə

schizothymic
BR ˌskɪtsə(ʊ)ˈθʌɪmɪk
AM ˌskɪtsoʊˈθaɪmɪk

schizotype
BR ˈskɪtsə(ʊ)tʌɪp, -s
AM ˈskɪtsəˌtaɪp, -s

Schlegel
BR ˈʃleɪgl
AM ˈʃleɪgəl

Schleicher
BR ˈʃlʌɪkə(r), ˈʃlʌɪxə(r)
AM ˈʃlaɪkər

schlemiel
BR ʃləˈmiːl, -z
AM ʃləˈmi(ə)l, -z

schlepp
BR ʃlɛp, -s, -ɪŋ, -t
AM ʃlɛp, -s, -ɪŋ, -t

Schlesinger
BR ˈʃlɛsɪn(d)ʒə(r)
AM ˈʃlɛsɪndʒər, ˈʃlɛsɪŋər

Schleswig
BR ˈʃlɛzvɪg, ˈʃlɛsvɪg, ˈʃlɛzwɪg
AM ˈʃlɛzwɪg

Schliemann
BR ˈʃliːmən
AM ˈʃlimɑn

schlieren
BR ˈʃlɪərən, ˈʃlɪərn̩, -z
AM ˈʃlɪrən, -z

schlock
BR ʃlɒk, -s
AM ʃlɑk, -s

schlocky
BR ˈʃlɒki
AM ˈʃlɑki

schmaltz
BR ʃmɔːlts
AM ʃmɔlts, ʃmɑlts

schmaltzy
BR ˈʃmɔːltsi, -ɪə(r), -ɪɪst
AM ˈʃmɔltsi, ˈʃmɑltsi, -ər, -ɪst

schmalz
BR ʃmɔːlts
AM ʃmɔlts, ʃmɑlts

schmalzy
BR ˈʃmɔːltsi, -ɪə(r), -ɪɪst
AM ˈʃmɔltsi, ˈʃmɑltsi, -ər, -ɪst

Schmidt
BR ʃmɪt
AM ʃmɪt

Schmitt
BR ʃmɪt
AM ʃmɪt

schmo
BR ʃməʊ, -z
AM ʃmoʊ, -z

schmoe
BR ʃməʊ, -z
AM ʃmoʊ, -z

schmooze
BR ʃmuːz, -ɪz, -ɪŋ, -d
AM ʃmuz, -əz, -ɪŋ, -d

schmuck
BR ʃmʌk, -s
AM ʃmək, -s
schnapps
BR ʃnaps
AM ʃnɑps
schnauzer
BR ˈʃnaʊtsə(r), ˈʃnaʊzə(r), -z
AM ˈʃnaʊzər, -z
Schneider
BR ˈʃnʌɪdə(r)
AM ˈsnaɪdər, ˈʃnaɪdər
schnitzel
BR ˈʃnɪtsl, -z
AM ˈʃnɪtsəl, -z
schnook
BR ʃnʊk, -s
AM ʃnʊk, -s
schnorkel
BR ˈʃnɔːk|l, ˈsnɔːk|l, -lz, -l̩ɪŋ\-lɪŋ, -ld
AM ˈʃnɔrk|əl, ˈsnɔrk|əl, -əlz, -(ə)lɪŋ, -əld
schnorrer
BR ˈʃnɒrə(r), ˈʃnɔːrə(r), -z
AM ˈʃnɔrər, -z
schnozz
BR ʃnɒz, -ɪz
AM ʃnɑz, -əz
schnozzle
BR ˈʃnɒzl, -z
AM ˈʃnɑzəl, -z
Schoenberg
BR ˈʃəːnbəːg
AM ˈʃənbərg, ˈʃoʊnbərg
Schofield
BR ˈskəʊfiːld
AM ˈskoʊˌfild
scholar
BR ˈskɒlə(r), -z
AM ˈskɑlər, -z
scholarliness
BR ˈskɒləlɪnɪs
AM ˈskɑlərlinɪs
scholarly
BR ˈskɒləli
AM ˈskɑlərli
scholarship
BR ˈskɒləʃɪp, -s
AM ˈskɑlərˌʃɪp, -s
scholastic
BR skəˈlastɪk
AM skəˈlæstɪk
scholastically
BR skəˈlastɪkli
AM skəˈlæstək(ə)li
scholasticism
BR skəˈlastɪsɪz(ə)m
AM skəˈlæstəˌsɪzəm
Scholefield
BR ˈskəʊlfiːld
AM ˈskoʊ(l)ˌfild
Scholes
BR skəʊlz
AM skoʊlz
Scholfield
BR ˈskəʊ(l)fiːld
AM ˈskoʊ(l)ˌfild
scholia
BR ˈskəʊlɪə(r)
AM ˈskoʊljə, ˈskoʊliə
scholiast
BR ˈskəʊlɪast, -s
AM ˈskoʊliˌæst, -s
scholiastic
BR ˌskəʊlɪˈastɪk
AM ˌskoʊliˈæstɪk
scholium
BR ˈskəʊlɪəm, -z
AM ˈskoʊliəm, -z
Scholl
BR ʃɒl, ʃəʊl
AM ʃoʊl, ʃɔl, ʃɑl
Schönberg
BR ˈʃəːnbəːg
AM ˈʃənbərg, ˈʃoʊnbərg
Schonfield
BR ˈskɒnfiːld
AM ˈskɑnˌfild
school
BR skuːl, -z, -ɪŋ, -d
AM skul, -z, -ɪŋ, -d
schoolable
BR ˈskuːləbl
AM ˈskuləbəl
school-age
BR ˈskuːleɪdʒ, ˌskuːlˈeɪdʒ
AM ˈskulˌeɪdʒ
schoolbook
BR ˈskuːlbʊk, -s
AM ˈskulˌbʊk, -s
schoolboy
BR ˈskuːlbɔɪ, -z
AM ˈskulˌbɔɪ, -z
schoolbus
BR ˌskuːlˈbʌs, ˈskuːlbʌs, -ɪz
AM ˈskulˌbəs, -əz
schoolchild
BR ˈskuːltʃʌɪld
AM ˈskulˌtʃaɪld
schoolchildren
BR ˈskuːlˌtʃɪldr(ə)n
AM ˈskulˌtʃɪldrən
schooldays
BR ˈskuːldeɪz
AM ˈskulˌdeɪz
schoolfellow
BR ˈskuːlˌfɛləʊ, -z
AM ˈskulˌfɛloʊ, -z
schoolgirl
BR ˈskuːlgəːl, -z
AM ˈskulˌgərl, -z
schoolhouse
BR ˈskuːlhaʊ|s, -zɪz
AM ˈskulˌ(h)aʊ|s, -zəz
schoolie
BR ˈskuːl|i, -ɪz
AM ˈskuli, -z
schooling
BR ˈskuːlɪŋ
AM ˈskulɪŋ
schoolkid
BR ˈskuːlkɪd, -z
AM ˈskulˌkɪd, -z
schoolman
BR ˈskuːlman, ˈskuːlmən
AM ˈskulmən, ˈskulˌmæn
schoolmarm
BR ˈskuːlmɑːm, -z
AM ˈskulˌmɑ(r)m, -z
schoolmarmish
BR ˈskuːlmɑːmɪʃ
AM ˈskulˌmɑ(r)mɪʃ
schoolmaster
BR ˈskuːlˌmɑːstə(r), ˈskuːlˌmastə(r), -z
AM ˈskulˌmæstər, -z
schoolmastering
BR ˈskuːlˌmɑːst(ə)rɪŋ, ˈskuːlˌmast(ə)rɪŋ
AM ˈskulˌmæst(ə)rɪŋ
schoolmasterly
BR ˈskuːlˌmɑːstəli, ˈskuːlˌmastəli
AM ˈskulˌmæstərli
schoolmate
BR ˈskuːlmeɪt, -s
AM ˈskulˌmeɪt, -s
schoolmen
BR ˈskuːlmɛn, ˈskuːlmən
AM ˈskulmən, ˈskulˌmɛn
schoolmistress
BR ˈskuːlˌmɪstrɪs, -ɪz
AM ˈskulˌmɪstrɪs, -ɪz
schoolmistressy
BR ˈskuːlˌmɪstrɪsi
AM ˈskulˌmɪstrɪsi
schoolroom
BR ˈskuːlruːm, ˈskuːlrʊm, -z
AM ˈskulˌrum, ˈskulˌrʊm, -z
schoolteacher
BR ˈskuːlˌtiːtʃə(r), -z
AM ˈskulˌtitʃər, -z
schoolteaching
BR ˈskuːlˌtiːtʃɪŋ
AM ˈskulˌtitʃɪŋ
schooltime
BR ˈskuːltʌɪm
AM ˈskulˌtaɪm
schoolwork
BR ˈskuːlwəːk
AM ˈskulˌwərk
schoolyard
BR ˈskuːljɑːd, -z
AM ˈskulˌjɑrd, -z
schooner
BR ˈskuːnə(r), -z
AM ˈskunər, -z
Schopenhauer
BR ˈʃəʊp(ə)nhaʊə(r), ˈʃɒp(ə)nhaʊə(r)
AM ˈʃoʊpənˌ(h)aʊər
schorl
BR ʃɔːl
AM ʃɔrl
schottische
BR ʃɒˈtiːʃ, ʃəˈtiːʃ, -ɪz
AM ˈʃɑdɪʃ, -ɪʃɪz
Schreiber
BR ˈʃrʌɪbə(r)
AM ˈʃraɪbər
Schroder
BR ˈʃrəʊdə(r)
AM ˈʃroʊdər
Schrödinger
BR ˈʃrəːdɪŋə(r), ˈʃrəʊdɪŋə(r)
AM ˈʃreɪdɪŋ(g)ər, ˈʃroʊdɪŋ(g)ər
Schroeder
BR ˈʃrəʊdə(r), ˈʃrəːdə(r)
AM ˈʃroʊdər, ˈʃreɪdər
schtick
BR ʃtɪk
AM ʃtɪk
schtuck
BR ʃtʊk
AM ʃtʊk
Schubert
BR ˈʃuːbət
AM ˈʃubərt
Schubertian
BR ʃuːˈbəːtɪən, -z
AM ʃuˈbərdiən, -z
Schultz
BR ʃʊlts
AM ʃʊlts
Schulz
BR ʃʊlts
AM ʃʊlts
Schumacher
BR ˈʃuːmakə(r)
AM ˈʃuˌmɑkər
Schumann
BR ˈʃuːmən
AM ˈʃumən, ˈʃuˌmɑn
schuss
BR ʃʊs, ʃuːs, -ɪz, -ɪŋ, -t
AM ʃus, ʃʊs, -əz, -ɪŋ, -t
Schütz
BR ʃuːts
AM ʃʊts
Schuyler
BR ˈskʌɪlə(r)
AM ˈskaɪlər
schwa
BR ʃwɑː(*r*), ʃvɑː(*r*), -z
AM ʃwɑ, -z
Schwann
BR ʃwɒn, ʃvan
AM ʃwɑn
Schwartz
BR ʃwɔːts
AM ʃwɔ(ə)rts

Schwarz
BR ʃwɔːts
AM ʃwɔ(ə)rts
Schwarzkopf
BR ˈʃvɑːtskɒ(p)f, ˈʃwɑːtskɒ(p)f, ˈʃwɔːtskɒ(p)f
AM ˈʃwɔ(ə)rtsˌkɔ(p)f
Schwarzwald
BR ˈʃvɑːtsvald
AM ˈʃwɔ(ə)rtsˌwɑld
Schweitzer
BR ˈʃwʌɪtsə(r), ˈʃvʌɪtsə(r)
AM ˈʃwaɪtsər
Schweppes®
BR ʃwɛps
AM ʃwɛps
Schyler
BR ˈskʌɪlə(r)
AM ˈskaɪlər
sciagram
BR ˈsʌɪəgram, -z
AM ˈsaɪəˌgræm, -z
sciagraph
BR ˈsʌɪəgrɑːf, ˈsʌɪəgraf, -s, -ɪŋ, -t
AM ˈsaɪəˌgræf, -s, -ɪŋ, -t
sciagraphic
BR ˌsʌɪəˈgrafɪk
AM ˌsaɪəˈgræfɪk
sciagraphy
BR sʌɪˈagrəfi
AM saɪˈægrəfi
sciamachy
BR sʌɪˈaməki
AM saɪˈæməki
sciatic
BR sʌɪˈatɪk
AM saɪˈædɪk
sciatica
BR sʌɪˈatɪkə(r)
AM saɪˈædəkə
sciatically
BR sʌɪˈatɪkli
AM saɪˈædək(ə)li
science
BR ˈsʌɪəns, -ɪz
AM ˈsaɪəns, -əz
scienter
adverb
BR sʌɪˈɛntə(r)
AM saɪˈɛn(t)ər
sciential
BR sʌɪˈɛnʃl, -z
AM saɪˈɛn(t)ʃəl, -z
scientific
BR ˌsʌɪənˈtɪfɪk
AM ˌsaɪənˈtɪfɪk
scientifically
BR ˌsʌɪənˈtɪfɪkli
AM ˌsaɪənˈtɪfɪk(ə)li
scientism
BR ˈsʌɪəntɪz(ə)m
AM ˈsaɪənˌtɪzəm
scientist
BR ˈsʌɪəntɪst, -s
AM ˈsaɪən(t)əst, -s
scientistic
BR ˌsʌɪənˈtɪstɪk
AM ˌsaɪənˈtɪstɪk
Scientologist
BR ˌsʌɪənˈtɒlədʒɪst, -s
AM ˌsaɪənˈtɑlədʒəst, -s
Scientology®
BR ˌsʌɪənˈtɒlədʒi
AM ˌsaɪənˈtɑlədʒi
sci-fi
BR ˈsʌɪfʌɪ
AM ˈsaɪˈfaɪ
scilicet
BR ˈsɪlɪsɛt, ˈsʌɪlɪsɛt, ˈskiːlɪkɛt
AM ˈsɪləˌsɛt, ˈskiləˌkɛt
scilla
BR ˈsɪlə(r), -z
AM ˈsɪlə, -z
Scillies
BR ˈsɪlɪz
AM ˈsɪliz
Scillonian
BR sɪˈləʊnɪən, -z
AM səˈloʊniən, -z
Scilly
BR ˈsɪli
AM ˈsɪli
scimitar
BR ˈsɪmɪtə(r), -z
AM ˈsɪmədər, ˈsɪməˌtɑr, -z
scintigram
BR ˈsɪntɪgram, -z
AM ˈsɪn(t)əˌgræm, -z
scintigraphy
BR sɪnˈtɪgrəfi
AM sɪnˈtɪgrəfi
scintilla
BR s(ɪ)nˈtɪlə(r), -z
AM sɪnˈtɪlə, -z
scintillant
adjective
BR ˈsɪntɪlənt, ˈsɪntɪln̩t
AM ˈsɪn(t)lənt
scintillate
BR ˈsɪntɪleɪt, -s, -ɪŋ, -ɪd
AM ˈsɪn(t)lˌeɪ|t, -ts, -dɪŋ, -dɪd
scintillatingly
BR ˈsɪntɪleɪtɪŋli
AM ˈsɪn(t)lˌeɪdɪŋli
scintillation
BR ˌsɪntɪˈleɪʃn
AM ˌsɪn(t)lˈeɪʃən
scintiscan
BR ˈsɪntɪskan, -z
AM ˈsɪn(t)əˌskæn, -z
sciolism
BR ˈsʌɪəlɪz(ə)m
AM ˈsaɪəˌlɪzəm
sciolist
BR ˈsʌɪəlɪst, -s
AM ˈsaɪələst, -s
sciolistic
BR ˌsʌɪəˈlɪstɪk
AM ˌsaɪəˈlɪstɪk
scion
BR ˈsʌɪən, -z
AM ˈsaɪən, -z
Scipio
BR ˈskɪpɪəʊ, ˈsɪpɪəʊ
AM ˈs(k)ɪpioʊ
scire facias
BR ˌsʌɪri ˈfeɪʃɪas, + ˈfeɪʃɪəs
AM ˌsaɪri ˈfeɪʃ(i)əs
scirocco
BR sɪˈrɒkəʊ, -z
AM səˈrɑkoʊ, ʃəˈrɑkoʊ, -z
scirrhi
BR ˈsɪrʌɪ
AM ˈs(k)ɪˌraɪ, ˈskɪˌri
scirrhoid
BR ˈsɪrɔɪd
AM ˈs(k)ɪˌrɔɪd
scirrhosity
BR sɪˈrɒsɪti
AM s(k)ɪˈrɑsədi
scirrhous
BR ˈsɪrəs
AM ˈs(k)ɪrəs
scirrhus
BR ˈsɪrəs
AM ˈs(k)ɪrəs
scissel
BR ˈskɪsl
AM ˈsɪsəl, ˈsɪzəl
scissile
BR ˈsɪsʌɪl, ˈsɪs(ɪ)l
AM ˈsɪsəl, ˈsɪˌsaɪl
scission
BR ˈsɪʒn, ˈsɪʃn, -z
AM ˈsɪʒən, ˈsɪʃən, -z
scissor
BR ˈsɪz|ə(r), -əz, -(ə)rɪŋ, -əd
AM ˈsɪz|ər, -ərz, -(ə)rɪŋ, -ərd
scissorwise
BR ˈsɪzəwʌɪz
AM ˈsɪzərˌwaɪz
sciurine
BR ˈsʌɪjʊrʌɪn, ˈsaɪjʊrɪn
AM ˈsaɪ(j)əˌrin, ˈsaɪ(j)ərən
sciuroid
BR ˈsʌɪjʊrɔɪd
AM ˈsaɪ(j)əˌrɔɪd
sclera
BR ˈsklɪərə(r)
AM ˈsklɛrə
scleral
BR ˈsklɪərəl, ˈsklɪərl̩
AM ˈsklɛrəl
sclerenchyma
BR sklɪəˈrɛŋkɪmə(r), sklɪˈrɛŋkɪmə(r), -z
AM skləˈrɛŋkəmə, -z
sclerenchymata
BR sklɪəˈrɛŋkɪmətə(r), sklɪˈrɛŋkɪmətə(r)
AM skləˌrɛŋkəˈmɑdə
sclerite
BR ˈsklɪərʌɪt, ˈsklɛrʌɪt
AM ˈskliˌraɪt, ˈsklɛˌraɪt
scleritis
BR sklɪəˈrʌɪtɪs, sklɪˈrʌɪtɪs
AM skləˈraɪdɪs
scleroderma
BR ˌsklɪərə(ʊ)ˈdəːmə(r), ˌsklɛrəˈdəːmə(r)
AM ˌsklɛrəˈdərmə
scleroid
BR ˈsklɪərɔɪd, ˈsklɛrɔɪd
AM ˈsklɛˌrɔɪd
scleroma
BR sklɪˈrəʊmə(r)
AM skləˈroʊmə
scleromata
BR sklɪˈrəʊmətə(r)
AM skləˈroʊmədə
sclerometer
BR sklɪˈrɒmɪtə(r), -z
AM skləˈrɑmədər, -z
sclerophyll
BR ˈsklɪərə(ʊ)fɪl, ˈsklɛrə(ʊ)fɪl, -z
AM ˈsklɛrəˌfɪl, -z
sclerophyllous
BR sklɪˈrɒfɪləs
AM skləˈrɑfələs
scleroprotein
BR ˌsklɪərə(ʊ)ˈprəʊtiːn, ˌsklɛrə(ʊ)ˈprəʊtiːn, -z
AM ˌsklɛroʊˈproʊˌtin, -z
sclerosed
BR ˈsklɪərəʊzd, ˈsklɛrəʊzd
AM ˈsklɛˌroʊzd
scleroses
BR sklɪˈrəʊsiːz
AM skləˈroʊˌsiz
sclerosis
BR sklɪˈrəʊsɪs
AM skləˈroʊsəz
sclerotherapy
BR ˌsklɪərəʊˈθɛrəpi, ˌsklɛrəʊˈθɛrəpi
AM ˌsklɛrəˈθɛrəpi
sclerotic
BR sklɪˈrɒtɪk
AM skləˈrɑdɪk
sclerotin
BR ˈsklɪərətɪn, ˈsklɛrətɪn
AM ˈsklɛrətɪn
sclerotised
BR ˈsklɪərətʌɪzd, ˈsklɛrətʌɪzd
AM ˈsklɛrəˌtaɪzd
sclerotitis
BR ˌsklɪərə(ʊ)ˈtʌɪtɪs, ˌsklɛrə(ʊ)ˈtʌɪtɪs

AM ˌsklɛrəˈtaɪdɪs

sclerotium
BR sklɪˈrəʊtɪəm
AM skləˈroʊtiəm

sclerotized
BR ˈsklɪərətʌɪzd, ˈsklɛrətʌɪzd
AM ˈsklɛrəˌtaɪzd

sclerotomy
BR sklɪˈrɒtəm|i, -ɪz
AM skləˈrɑdəmi, -z

sclerous
BR ˈsklɪərəs, ˈsklɛrəs
AM ˈsklɛrəs

Scobie
BR ˈskəʊbi
AM ˈskoʊbi

Scoby
BR ˈskəʊbi
AM ˈskoʊbi

scoff
BR skɒf, -s, -ɪŋ, -t
AM skɔf, skɑf, -s, -ɪŋ, -t

scoffer
BR ˈskɒfə(r), -z
AM ˈskɔfər, ˈskɑfər, -z

scoffingly
BR ˈskɒfɪŋli
AM ˈskɔfɪŋli, ˈskɑfɪŋli

Scofield
BR ˈskəʊfiːld
AM ˈskoʊˌfild

scold
BR skəʊld, -z, -ɪŋ, -ɪd
AM skoʊld, -z, -ɪŋ, -əd

scolder
BR ˈskəʊldə(r), -z
AM ˈskoʊldər, -z

scolding
BR ˈskəʊldɪŋ, -z
AM ˈskoʊldɪŋ, -z

scolex
BR ˈskəʊlɛks, -ɪz
AM ˈskoʊˌlɛks, -əz

scolices
BR ˈskəʊlɪsiːz
AM ˈskoʊləsiz

scoliosis
BR ˌskɒlɪˈəʊsɪs
AM ˌskoʊliˈoʊsəs

scoliotic
BR ˌskɒlɪˈɒtɪk
AM ˌskoʊliˈɑdɪk

scollop
BR ˈskɒləp, -s, -ɪŋ, -t
AM ˈskɑləp, ˈskæləp, -s, -ɪŋ, -t

scolopendria
BR ˌskɒləˈpɛndrɪə(r)
AM ˌskɑləˈpɛndriə

scolopendrium
BR ˌskɒləˈpɛndrɪəm
AM ˌskɑləˈpɛndriəm

scomber
BR ˈskɒmbə(r), -z
AM ˈskɑmbər, -z

scombrid
BR ˈskɒmbrɪd, -z
AM ˈskɑmbrəd, -z

scombroid
BR ˈskɒmbrɔɪd, -z
AM ˈskɑmˌbrɔɪd, -z

sconce
BR skɒns, -ɪz
AM skɑns, -əz

Scone
place in Scotland
BR skuːn
AM skun, skoʊn

scone
BR skɒn, skəʊn, -z
AM skoʊn, -z

scoop
BR skuːp, -s, -ɪŋ, -t
AM skup, -s, -ɪŋ, -t

scooper
BR ˈskuːpə(r), -z
AM ˈskupər, -z

scoopful
BR ˈskuːpfʊl, -z
AM ˈskupˌfʊl, -z

scoot
BR skuːt, -s, -ɪŋ, -ɪd
AM sku|t, -ts, -dɪŋ, -dəd

scooter
BR ˈskuːt|ə(r), -əz, -(ə)rɪŋ, -əd
AM ˈskudər, -z, -ɪŋ, -d

scooterist
BR ˈskuːt(ə)rɪst, -s
AM ˈskudərəst, -s

scopa
BR ˈskəʊpə(r)
AM ˈskoʊpə

scopae
BR ˈskəʊpiː
AM ˈskoʊpi

scope
BR skəʊp, -s
AM skoʊp, -s

scopolamine
BR skəˈpɒləmiːn, skəˈpɒləmɪn
AM skəˈpɑləˌmin

scopula
BR ˈskɒpjʉlə(r)
AM ˈskɑpjələ

scopulae
BR ˈskɒpjʉliː
AM ˈskɑpjəli, ˈskɑpjəˌlaɪ

Scopus
BR ˈskəʊpəs
AM ˈskoʊpəs

scorbutic
BR skɔːˈbjuːtɪk
AM skɔrˈbjudɪk

scorbutically
BR skɔːˈbjuːtɪkli
AM skɔrˈbjudək(ə)li

scorch
BR skɔːtʃ, -ɪz, -ɪŋ, -t
AM skɔrtʃ, -əz, -ɪŋ, -t

scorcher
BR ˈskɔːtʃə(r), -z
AM ˈskɔrtʃər, -z

scorchingly
BR ˈskɔːtʃɪŋli
AM ˈskɔrtʃɪŋli

scordatura
BR ˌskɔːdəˈtjʊərə(r), ˌskɔːdəˈtʃʊərə(r)
AM ˌskɔrdəˈt(j)ʊrə

score
BR skɔː(r), -z, -ɪŋ, -d
AM skɔ(ə)r, -z, -ɪŋ, -d

scoreboard
BR ˈskɔːbɔːd, -z
AM ˈskɔrˌbɔ(ə)rd, -z

scorebook
BR ˈskɔːbʊk, -s
AM ˈskɔrˌbʊk, -s

scorecard
BR ˈskɔːkɑːd, -z
AM ˈskɔrˌkɑrd, -z

scoreine
BR ˈskɔːriːn, -z
AM ˈskɔrin, -z

scorekeeper
BR ˈskɔːˌkiːpə(r), -z
AM ˈskɔrˌkipər, -z

scoreless
BR ˈskɔːləs
AM ˈskɔrləs

scorer
BR ˈskɔːrə(r), -z
AM ˈskɔrər, -z

score sheet
BR ˈskɔː ʃiːt, -s
AM ˈskɔr ˌʃit, -s

scoria
BR ˈskɔːrɪə(r)
AM ˈskɔriə

scoriaceous
BR ˌskɔːrɪˈeɪʃəs
AM ˌskɔriˈeɪʃəs

scoriae
BR ˈskɔːriː
AM ˈskɔriaɪ, ˈskɔrii

scorification
BR ˌskɔːrɪfɪˈkeɪʃn
AM ˌskɔrəfəˈkeɪʃən

scorifier
BR ˈskɔːrɪfʌɪə(r)
AM ˈskɔrəˌfaɪər

scorify
BR ˈskɔːrɪfʌɪ, -z, -ɪŋ, -d
AM ˈskɔrəˌfaɪ, -z, -ɪŋ, -d

scoring
BR ˈskɔːrɪŋ
AM ˈskɔrɪŋ

scorn
BR skɔːn, -z, -ɪŋ, -d
AM skɔ(ə)rn, -z, -ɪŋ, -d

scorner
BR ˈskɔːnə(r), -z
AM ˈskɔrnər, -z

scornful
BR ˈskɔːnf(ʉ)l
AM ˈskɔrnfəl

scornfully
BR ˈskɔːnfʉli, ˈskɔːnfl̩i
AM ˈskɔrnfəli

scornfulness
BR ˈskɔːnf(ʉ)lnəs
AM ˈskɔrnfəlnəs

scorp
BR skɔːp, -s
AM skɔ(ə)rp, -s

scorper
BR ˈskɔːpə(r), -z
AM ˈskɔrpər, -z

Scorpian
BR ˈskɔːpɪən, -z
AM ˈskɔrpiən, -z

Scorpio
BR ˈskɔːpɪəʊ, -z
AM ˈskɔrpioʊ, -z

scorpioid
BR ˈskɔːpɪɔɪd, -z
AM ˈskɔrpiˌɔɪd, -z

scorpion
BR ˈskɔːpɪən, -z
AM ˈskɔrpiən, -z

Scorpius
BR ˈskɔːpɪəs
AM ˈskɔrpiəs

scorzonera
BR ˌskɔːtsəˈnɪərə(r)
AM ˌskɔrzəˈnɪrə

Scot
BR skɒt, -s
AM skɑt, -s

scotch
BR skɒtʃ, -ɪz, -ɪŋ, -t
AM skɑtʃ, -əz, -ɪŋ, -t

Scotchman
BR ˈskɒtʃmən
AM ˈskɑtʃmən

Scotchmen
BR ˈskɒtʃmən
AM ˈskɑtʃmən

Scotchwoman
BR ˈskɒtʃˌwʊmən
AM ˈskɑtʃˌwʊmən

Scotchwomen
BR ˈskɒtʃˌwɪmɪn
AM ˈskɑtʃˌwɪmɪn

scoter
BR ˈskəʊtə(r), -z
AM ˈskoʊdər, -z

scot-free
BR ˌskɒtˈfriː
AM ˈskɑtˈfri

Scotia
BR ˈskəʊʃə(r)
AM ˈskoʊʃə

Scoticise
BR ˈskɒtɪsʌɪz, -ɪz, -ɪŋ, -d
AM ˈskɑdəˌsaɪz, -ɪz, -ɪŋ, -d

Scoticism
BR ˈskɒtɪsɪz(ə)m, -z
AM ˈskɑdəˌsɪzəm, -z

Scoticize
BR ˈskɒtɪsʌɪz, -ɪz, -ɪŋ, -d

AM 'skadə,saɪz, -ɨz, -ɪŋ, -d
Scotism
BR 'skɒtɪz(ə)m, -z
AM 'ska,tɪzəm, -z
Scotist
BR 'skɒtɪst, -s
AM 'skadəst, -s
Scotland
BR 'skɒtlənd
AM 'skatlən(d)
scotoma
BR skə'təʊmə(r), -z
AM skə'toʊmə, -z
scotomata
BR skə'təʊmətə(r)
AM skə'toʊmədə
Scots
BR skɒts
AM skats
Scotsman
BR 'skɒtsmən
AM 'skatsmən
Scotsmen
BR 'skɒtsmən
AM 'skatsmən
Scotswoman
BR 'skɒts,wʊmən
AM 'skats,wʊmən
Scotswomen
BR 'skɒts,wɪmɪn
AM 'skats,wɪmɪn
Scott
BR skɒt
AM skat
Scotticise
BR 'skɒtɪsʌɪz, -ɨz, -ɪŋ, -d
AM 'skadə,saɪz, -ɨz, -ɪŋ, -d
Scotticism
BR 'skɒtɪsɪz(ə)m, -z
AM 'skadə,sɪzəm, -z
Scotticize
BR 'skɒtɪsʌɪz, -ɨz, -ɪŋ, -d
AM 'skadə,saɪz, -ɨz, -ɪŋ, -d
Scottie
BR 'skɒt|i, -ɪz
AM 'skadi, -z
Scottish
BR 'skɒtɪʃ
AM 'skadɪʃ
Scottishness
BR 'skɒtɪʃnɨs
AM 'skadɪʃnɨs
Scotty
BR 'skɒt|i, -ɪz
AM 'skadi, -z
scoundrel
BR 'skaʊndr(ə)l, -z
AM 'skaʊndrəl, -z
scoundreldom
BR 'skaʊndr(ə)ld(ə)m
AM 'skaʊndreldəm
scoundrelism
BR 'skaʊndrəlɪz(ə)m, 'skaʊndr̩lɪz(ə)m
AM 'skaʊndrə,lɪzəm
scoundrelly
BR 'skaʊndrəli, 'skaʊndr̩li
AM 'skaʊndrəli
scour
BR 'skaʊə(r), -z, -ɪŋ, -d
AM 'skaʊ(ə)r, -z, -ɪŋ, -d
scourer
BR 'skaʊərə(r), -z
AM 'skaʊ(ə)rər, -z
Scourfield
BR 'skaʊəfiːld
AM 'skaʊ(ə)r,fild
scourge
BR skəːdʒ, -ɨz, -ɪŋ, -d
AM skərdʒ, -əz, -ɪŋ, -d
scourger
BR 'skəːdʒə(r), -z
AM 'skərdʒər, -z
scourings
BR 'skaʊərɪŋz
AM 'skaʊ(ə)rɪŋz
Scouser
BR 'skaʊsə(r), -z
AM 'skaʊsər, -z
Scout
BR skaʊt, -s
AM skaʊt, -s
scout
BR skaʊt, -s, -ɪŋ, -ɨd
AM skaʊ|t, -ts, -dɪŋ, -dəd
scouter
BR 'skaʊtə(r), -z
AM 'skaʊdər, -z
Scoutmaster
BR 'skaʊt,mɑːstə(r), 'skaʊt,mastə(r), -z
AM 'skaʊt,mæstər, -z
scow
BR skaʊ, -z
AM skaʊ, -z
scowl
BR skaʊl, -z, -ɪŋ, -d
AM skaʊl, -z, -ɪŋ, -d
scowler
BR 'skaʊlə(r), -z
AM 'skaʊlər, -z
scrabble
BR 'skrab|l, -lz, -l̩ɪŋ\-lɪŋ, -ld
AM 'skræbəl, -əlz, -(ə)lɪŋ, -əld
scrag
BR skrag, -z, -ɪŋ, -d
AM skræg, -z, -ɪŋ, -d
scrag-end
BR ,skrag'ɛnd, -z
AM 'skræg'ɛnd, -z
scraggily
BR 'skragɨli
AM 'skrægəli
scragginess
BR 'skragɪnɨs
AM 'skræginɨs
scraggly
BR 'skragli, 'skragl̩i
AM 'skræg(ə)li
scraggy
BR 'skrag|i, -ɪə(r), -ɪɨst
AM 'skrægi, -ər, -ɨst
scram
BR skram, -z, -ɪŋ, -d
AM skræm, -z, -ɪŋ, -d
scramble
BR 'skramb|l, -lz, -l̩ɪŋ\-lɪŋ, -ld
AM 'skræmbəl, -əlz, -(ə)lɪŋ, -əld
scrambler
BR 'skramblə(r), -z
AM 'skræmb(ə)lər, -z
scramjet
BR 'skramdʒɛt, -s
AM 'skræmdʒɛt, -s
scran
BR skran
AM skræn
Scranton
BR 'skrantən
AM 'skræn(t)ən
scrap
BR skrap, -s, -ɪŋ, -t
AM skræp, -s, -ɪŋ, -t
scrapbook
BR 'skrapbʊk, -s
AM 'skræp,bʊk, -s
scrape
BR skreɪp, -s, -ɪŋ, -t
AM skreɪp, -s, -ɪŋ, -t
scraper
BR 'skreɪpə(r), -z
AM 'skreɪpər, -z
scraperboard
BR 'skreɪpəbɔːd, -z
AM 'screɪpər,bɔ(ə)rd, -z
scrapheap
BR 'skraphiːp, -s
AM 'skræp,(h)ip, -s
scrapie
BR 'skreɪpi
AM 'skreɪpi
scraping
BR 'skreɪpɪŋ, -z
AM 'skreɪpɪŋ, -z
scrapper
BR 'skrapə(r), -z
AM 'skræpər, -z
scrappily
BR 'skrapɨli
AM 'skræpəli
scrappiness
BR 'skrapɪnɨs
AM 'skræpinɨs
scrapple
BR 'skrapl
AM 'skræpəl
scrappy
BR 'skrap|i, -ɪə(r), -ɪɨst
AM 'skræpi, -ər, -ɨst
scrapyard
BR 'skrapjɑːd, -z
AM 'skræp,jɑrd, -z
scratch
BR skratʃ, -ɨz, -ɪŋ, -t
AM skrætʃ, -əz, -ɪŋ, -t
scratchboard
BR 'skratʃbɔːd, -z
AM 'skrætʃ,bɔ(ə)rd, -z
scratcher
BR 'skratʃə(r), -z
AM 'skrætʃər, -z
scratchily
BR 'skratʃɨli
AM 'skrætʃəli
scratchiness
BR 'skratʃɪnɨs
AM 'skrætʃinɨs
scratchings
BR 'skratʃɪŋz
AM 'skrætʃɪŋz
scratchpad
BR 'skratʃpad, -z
AM 'skrætʃ,pæd, -z
Scratchwood
BR 'skratʃwʊd
AM 'skrætʃ,wʊd
scratchy
BR 'skratʃ|i, -ɪə(r), -ɪɨst
AM 'skrætʃi, -ər, -ɨst
scrawl
BR skrɔːl, -z, -ɪŋ, -d
AM skrɔl, skrɑl, -z, -ɪŋ, -d
scrawly
BR 'skrɔːli
AM 'skrɔli, 'skrɑli
scrawniness
BR 'skrɔːnɪnɨs
AM 'skrɔninɨs, 'skrɑninɨs
scrawny
BR 'skrɔːn|i, -ɪə(r), -ɪɨst
AM 'skrɔni, 'skrɑni, -ər, -ɨst
scream
BR skriːm, -z, -ɪŋ, -d
AM skrim, -z, -ɪŋ, -d
screamer
BR 'skriːmə(r), -z
AM 'skrimər, -z
screamingly
BR 'skriːmɪŋli
AM 'skrimɪŋli
scree
BR skriː, -z
AM skri, -z
screech
BR skriːtʃ, -ɨz, -ɪŋ, -t
AM skritʃ, -ɨz, -ɪŋ, -t
screecher
BR 'skriːtʃə(r), -z
AM 'skritʃər, -z
screechy
BR 'skriːtʃ|i, -ɪə(r), -ɪɨst
AM 'skritʃi, -ər, -ɨst

screed
BR skriːd, -z
AM skrid, -z
screen
BR skriːn, -z, -ɪŋ, -d
AM skrin, -z, -ɪŋ, -d
screenable
BR 'skriːnəbl
AM 'skrinəbəl
screener
BR 'skriːnə(r), -z
AM 'skrinər, -z
screening
BR 'skriːnɪŋ, -z
AM 'skrinɪŋ, -z
screenplay
BR 'skriːnpleɪ, -z
AM 'skrin,pleɪ, -z
screen-print
BR 'skriːnprɪnt, -s, -ɪŋ, -ɪd
AM 'skrin,prɪn|t, -ts, -(t)ɪŋ, -(t)ɪd
screenwriter
BR 'skriːn,rʌɪtə(r), -z
AM 'skrin,raɪdər, -z
screenwriting
BR 'skriːn,rʌɪtɪŋ
AM 'skrin,raɪdɪŋ
screw
BR skruː, -z, -ɪŋ, -d
AM skru, -z, -ɪŋ, -d
screwable
BR 'skruːəbl
AM 'skruəbəl
screwball
BR 'skruːbɔːl, -z
AM 'skru,bɔl, 'skru,bɑl, -z
screwdriver
BR 'skruː,drʌɪvə(r), -z
AM 'skru,draɪvər, -z
screwer
BR 'skruːə(r), -z
AM 'skru(ə)r, -z
screwiness
BR 'skruːɪnɪs
AM 'skruinɪs
screwtop
noun
BR 'skruːtɒp, ,skruː'tɒp, -s
AM 'skru,tɑp, -s
screw-top
adjective
BR ,skruː'tɒp
AM 'skru,tɑp
screwup
BR 'skruːʌp, -s
AM 'skru,əp, -s
screwworm
BR 'skruːwəːm, -z
AM 'skru,wərm, -z
screwy
BR 'skruː|i, -ɪə(r), -ɪɪst
AM 'skrui, -ər, -ɪst
Scriabin
BR skrɪ'abɪn, skrɪ'ɑːbɪn
AM skri'ɑbən
RUS 'skrʲabʲin
scribal
BR 'skrʌɪbl
AM 'skraɪbəl
scribble
BR 'skrɪb|l, -lz, -l̩ɪŋ\-lɪŋ, -ld
AM 'skrɪbəl, -əlz, -(ə)lɪŋ, -əld
scribbler
BR 'skrɪbl̩ə(r), 'skrɪblə(r), -z
AM 'skrɪb(ə)lər, -z
scribbling
BR 'skrɪbl̩ɪŋ, 'skrɪblɪŋ, -z
AM 'skrɪb(ə)lɪŋ, -z
scribbling-pad
BR 'skrɪbl̩ɪŋpad, 'skrɪblɪŋpad, -z
AM 'skrɪblɪŋ,pæd, -z
scribbly
BR 'skrɪbl̩i, 'skrɪbli
AM 'skrɪbli
scribe
BR skrʌɪb, -z, -ɪŋ, -d
AM skraɪb, -z, -ɪŋ, -d
scriber
BR 'skrʌɪbə(r), -z
AM 'skraɪbər, -z
scrim
BR skrɪm, -z
AM skrɪm, -z
Scrimgeour
BR 'skrɪmdʒə(r)
AM 'skrɪndʒər
Scrimger
BR 'skrɪmdʒə(r)
AM 'skrɪndʒər
scrimmage
BR 'skrɪm|ɪdʒ, -ɪdʒɪz
AM 'skrɪmɪdʒ, -ɪz
scrimmager
BR 'skrɪmɪdʒə(r), -z
AM 'skrɪmədʒər, -z
scrimp
BR skrɪm|p, -ps, -pɪŋ, -(p)t
AM skrɪm|p, -ps, -pɪŋ, -(p)t
scrimpy
BR 'skrɪmp|i, -ɪə(r), -ɪɪst
AM 'skrɪmpi, -ər, -ɪst
scrimshank
BR 'skrɪmʃaŋ|k, -ks, -kɪŋ, -(k)t
AM 'skrɪm,ʃæŋ|k, -ks, -kɪŋ, -(k)t
scrimshanker
BR 'skrɪmʃaŋkə(r), -z
AM 'skrɪm,ʃæŋkər, -z
scrimshaw
BR 'skrɪmʃɔː(*r*), -z, -ɪŋ, -d
AM 'skrɪm,ʃɔ, 'skrɪm,ʃɑ, -z, -ɪŋ, -d
scrip
BR skrɪp, -s
AM skrɪp, -s
scripsit
BR 'skrɪpsɪt
AM 'skrɪpsɪt
script
BR skrɪp|t, -(t)s, -tɪŋ, -tɪd
AM skrɪp|(t), -(t)s, -tɪŋ, -tɪd
scriptoria
BR skrɪp'tɔːrɪə(*r*)
AM ,skrɪp'tɔriə
scriptorial
BR skrɪp'tɔːrɪəl
AM ,skrɪp'tɔriəl
scriptorium
BR skrɪp'tɔːrɪəm, -z
AM ,skrɪp'tɔriəm, -z
scriptory
BR 'skrɪpt(ə)r|i, -ɪz
AM 'skrɪptəri, -z
scriptural
BR 'skrɪptʃ(ə)rəl, 'skrɪptʃ(ə)rl̩
AM 'skrɪp(t)ʃ(ə)rəl
scripturalism
BR 'skrɪptʃ(ə)rəlɪz(ə)m, 'skrɪptʃ(ə)rl̩ɪz(ə)m
AM 'skrɪp(t)ʃ(ə)rə,lɪz-əm
scripturalist
BR 'skrɪptʃ(ə)rəlɪst, 'skrɪptʃ(ə)rl̩ɪst, -s
AM 'skrɪp(t)ʃ(ə)rələst, -s
scripturally
BR 'skrɪptʃ(ə)rəli, 'skrɪptʃ(ə)rl̩i
AM 'skrɪp(t)ʃ(ə)rəli
scripture
BR 'skrɪptʃə(r), -z
AM 'skrɪp(t)ʃər, -z
Scriptures
BR 'skrɪptʃəz
AM 'skrɪp(t)ʃərz
scriptwriter
BR 'skrɪp(t),rʌɪtə(r), -z
AM 'skrɪp(t),raɪdər, -z
scriptwriting
BR 'skrɪp(t),rʌɪtɪŋ
AM 'skrɪp(t),raɪdɪŋ
scrivener
BR 'skrɪv(ə)nə(r), 'skrɪvn̩ə(r), -z
AM 'skrɪv(ə)nər, -z
scrobiculate
BR skrə(ʊ)'bɪkjʊlət, skrə(ʊ)'bɪkjʊleɪt
AM skroʊ'bɪkjə,leɪt, skroʊ'bɪkjələt
scrod
BR skrɒd, -z
AM skrɑd, -z
scrofula
BR 'skrɒfjʊlə(*r*)
AM 'skrɔfjələ, 'skrɑfjələ
scrofulous
BR 'skrɒfjʊləs
AM 'skrɔfjələs, 'skrɑfjələs
scrofulously
BR 'skrɒfjʊləsli
AM 'skrɔfjələsli, 'skrɑfjələsli
scrofulousness
BR 'skrɒfjʊləsnəs
AM 'skrɔfjələsnəs, 'skrɑfjələsnəs
scroll
BR skrəʊl, -z, -ɪŋ, -d
AM skroʊl, -z, -ɪŋ, -d
scroller
BR 'skrəʊlə(r), -z
AM 'skroʊlər, -z
scrollwork
BR 'skrəʊlwəːk
AM 'skroʊl,wərk
scrooge
BR skruːdʒ, -ɪz
AM skrudʒ, -əz
scrota
BR 'skrəʊtə(*r*)
AM 'skroʊdə
scrotal
BR 'skrəʊtl
AM 'skroʊdl
scrotitis
BR skrəʊ'tʌɪtɪs
AM 'skroʊ,taɪdɪs
scrotocele
BR 'skrəʊtəsiːl, -z
AM 'skroʊdə,sil, -z
scrotum
BR 'skrəʊtəm, -z
AM 'skroʊdəm, -z
scrounge
BR skraʊn(d)ʒ, -ɪz, -ɪŋ, -d
AM skraʊndʒ, -əz, -ɪŋ, -d
scrounger
BR 'skraʊn(d)ʒə(r), -z
AM 'skraʊndʒər, -z
scrub
BR skrʌb, -z, -ɪŋ, -d
AM skrəb, -z, -ɪŋ, -d
scrubber
BR 'skrʌbə(r), -z
AM 'skrəbər, -z
scrubbily
BR 'skrʌbɪli
AM 'skrəbəli
scrubby
BR 'skrʌb|i, -ɪə(r), -ɪɪst
AM 'skrəbi, -ər, -ɪst

scrubland
BR ˈskrʌbland, -z
AM ˈskrəbˌlænd, -z

scrubwoman
BR ˈskrʌbˌwʊmən
AM ˈskrəbˌwʊmən

scrubwomen
BR ˈskrʌbˌwɪmɪn
AM ˈskrəbˌwɪmɨn

scruff
BR skrʌf, -s
AM skrəf, -s

scruffily
BR ˈskrʌfɨli
AM ˈskrəfəli

scruffiness
BR ˈskrʌfɪnɨs
AM ˈskrəfinɨs

scruffy
BR ˈskrʌf|i, -ɪə(r), -ɪɪst
AM ˈskrəfi, -ər, -ɨst

scrum
BR skrʌm, -z, -ɪŋ, -d
AM skrəm, -z, -ɪŋ, -d

scrum-half
BR ˌskrʌmˈhɑːf, -s
AM ˈskrəmˌ(h)æf, -s

scrummage
BR ˈskrʌm|ɪdʒ, -ɨdʒɨz, -ɨdʒɪŋ, -ɪdʒd
AM ˈskrəmɪdʒ, -ɨz, -ɪŋ, -d

scrummager
BR ˈskrʌmɨdʒə(r), -z
AM ˈskrəmədʒər, -z

scrummy
BR ˈskrʌm|i, -ɪə(r), -ɪɪst
AM ˈskrəmi, -ər, -ɨst

scrump
BR skrʌm|p, -ps, -pɪŋ, -(p)t
AM skrəm|p, -(p)s, -pɪŋ, -(p)t

scrumple
BR ˈskrʌmp|l, -lz, -l̩ɪŋ\-lɪŋ, -ld
AM ˈskrəmpəl, -z, -ɪŋ, -d

scrumptious
BR ˈskrʌm(p)ʃəs
AM ˈskrəm(p)ʃəs

scrumptiously
BR ˈskrʌm(p)ʃəsli
AM ˈskrəm(p)ʃəsli

scrumptiousness
BR ˈskrʌm(p)ʃəsnəs
AM ˈskrəm(p)ʃəsnəs

scrumpy
BR skrʌmpi
AM ˈskrəmpi

scrunch
BR skrʌn(t)ʃ, -ɨz, -ɪŋ, -t
AM skrən(t)ʃ, -əz, -ɪŋ, -t

scruple
BR ˈskruːp|l, -lz, -l̩ɪŋ\-lɪŋ, -ld
AM ˈskrup|əl, -əlz, -(ə)lɪŋ, -əld

scrupulosity
BR ˌskruːpjʊˈlɒsɪti
AM ˌskrupjəˈlɑsədi

scrupulous
BR ˈskruːpjʊləs
AM ˈskrupjələs

scrupulously
BR ˈskruːpjʊləsli
AM ˈskrupjələsli

scrupulousness
BR ˈskruːpjʊləsnəs
AM ˈskrupjələsnəs

scrutable
BR ˈskruːtəbl
AM ˈskrudəbəl

scrutator
BR skruːˈteɪtə(r), -z
AM ˈskruˌteɪdər, -z

scrutineer
BR ˌskruːtɪˈnɪə(r), ˌskruːtn̩ˈɪə(r), -z
AM ˌskrutnˈɪ(ə)r, -z

scrutinisation
BR ˌskruːtɪnʌɪˈzeɪʃn, ˌskruːtn̩ʌɪˈzeɪʃən
AM ˌskrutn̩əˈzeɪʃən, ˌskrutnˌaɪˈzeɪʃən

scrutinise
BR ˈskruːtɪnʌɪz, ˈskruːtn̩ʌɪz, -ɨz, -ɪŋ, -d
AM ˈskrutnˌaɪz, -ɨz, -ɪŋ, -d

scrutiniser
BR ˈskruːtɪnʌɪzə(r), ˈskruːtn̩ʌɪzə(r), -z
AM ˈskrutnˌaɪzər, -z

scrutinization
BR ˌskruːtɪnʌɪˈzeɪʃn, ˌskruːtn̩ʌɪˈzeɪʃn
AM ˌskrutn̩əˈzeɪʃən, ˌskrutnˌaɪˈzeɪʃən

scrutinize
BR ˈskruːtɪnʌɪz, ˈskruːtn̩ʌɪz, -ɨz, -ɪŋ, -d
AM ˈskrutnˌaɪz, -ɨz, -ɪŋ, -d

scrutinizer
BR ˈskruːtɪnʌɪzə(r), ˈskruːtn̩ʌɪzə(r), -z
AM ˈskrutnˌaɪzər, -z

scrutiny
BR ˈskruːtɪn|i, ˈskruːtn̩|i, -ɪz
AM ˈskrutn̩i, -z

Scruton
BR ˈskruːtn
AM ˈskrutn

scry
BR skrʌɪ, -z, -ɪŋ, -d
AM skraɪ, -z, -ɪŋ, -d

scryer
BR ˈskrʌɪə(r), -z
AM ˈskraɪər, -z

SCSI
BR ˈskʌzi
AM ˈskəzi

scuba
BR ˈsk(j)uːbə(r), -z
AM ˈskubə, -z

scuba-dive
BR ˈsk(j)uːbədʌɪv, -z, -ɪŋ, -d
AM ˈskubəˌdaɪv, -z, -ɪŋ, -d

scud
BR skʌd, -z, -ɪŋ, -ɪd
AM skəd, -z, -ɪŋ, -əd

Scudamore
BR ˈsk(j)uːdəmɔː(r)
AM ˈsk(j)udəˌmɔ(ə)r

scuff
BR skʌf, -s, -ɪŋ, -t
AM skəf, -s, -ɪŋ, -t

scuffle
BR ˈskʌf|l, -lz, -l̩ɪŋ\-lɪŋ, -ld
AM ˈskəf|əl, -əlz, -(ə)lɪŋ, -əld

scuffmark
BR ˈskʌfmɑːk, -s
AM ˈskəfˌmɑrk, -s

sculduggery
BR skʌlˈdʌg(ə)ri
AM skəlˈdəgəri

scull
BR skʌl, -z, -ɪŋ, -d
AM skəl, -z, -ɪŋ, -d

sculler
BR ˈskʌlə(r), -z
AM ˈskələr, -z

scullery
BR ˈskʌl(ə)r|i, -ɪz
AM ˈskəl(ə)ri, -z

scullerymaid
BR ˈskʌl(ə)rɪmeɪd, -z
AM ˈskəl(ə)riˌmeɪd, -z

Sculley
BR ˈskʌli
AM ˈskəli

scullion
BR ˈskʌlɪən, -z
AM ˈskəljən, ˈskəliən, -z

Scully
BR ˈskʌli
AM ˈskəli

sculp
BR skʌlp, -s, -ɪŋ, -t
AM skəlp, -s, -ɪŋ, -t

sculpin
BR ˈskʌlpɪn, -z
AM ˈskəlpən, -z

sculpt
BR skʌlpt, -s, -ɪŋ, -ɨd
AM skəlpt, -s, -ɪŋ, -əd

sculptor
BR ˈskʌlptə(r), -z
AM ˈskəlptər, -z

sculptress
BR ˈskʌlptrɪs, -ɨz
AM ˈskəlptrəs, -əz

sculptural
BR ˈskʌltptʃ(ə)rəl, ˈskʌlptʃ(ə)rl̩
AM ˈskəlp(t)ʃ(ə)rəl

sculpturally
BR ˈskʌltptʃ(ə)rəli, ˈskʌlptʃ(ə)rl̩i
AM ˈskəlp(t)ʃ(ə)rəli

sculpture
BR ˈskʌlptʃə(r), -z, -ɪŋ, -d
AM ˈskəlp(t)ʃər, -z, -ɪŋ, -d

sculpturesque
BR ˌskʌlptʃəˈrɛsk
AM ˌskəlp(t)ʃəˈrɛsk

scum
BR skʌm, -z, -ɪŋ, -d
AM skəm, -z, -ɪŋ, -d

scumbag
BR ˈskʌmbag, -z
AM ˈskəmˌbæg, -z

scumble
BR ˈskʌmbl̩, -z, -ɪŋ, -d
AM ˈskəmbəl, -z, -ɪŋ, -d

scummy
BR ˈskʌmi
AM ˈskəmi

scuncheon
BR ˈskʌn(t)ʃ(ə)n, -z
AM ˈskən(t)ʃən, -z

scunge
BR skʌn(d)ʒ, -ɨz
AM skəndʒ, -əz

scungy
BR ˈskʌn(d)ʒ|i, -ɪə(r), -ɪɪst
AM ˈskəndʒi, -ər, -ɨst

scunner
BR ˈskʌn|ə(r), -əz, -(ə)rɪŋ, -əd
AM ˈskənər, -z, -ɪŋ, -d

Scunthorpe
BR ˈskʌnθɔːp
AM ˈskənˌθɔ(ə)rp

scup
BR skʌp
AM skəp

scupper
BR ˈskʌp|ə(r), -əz, -(ə)rɪŋ, -əd
AM ˈskəpər, -z, -ɪŋ, -d

scurf
BR skəːf
AM skərf

scurfiness
BR ˈskəːfɪnɨs
AM ˈskərfinɨs

scurfy
BR ˈskəːfi
AM ˈskərfi

scurrility
BR skəˈrɪlɨti, skʌˈrɪlɨti
AM skəˈrɪlɨdi

scurrilous
BR ˈskʌrɨləs
AM ˈskərələs

scurrilously
BR ˈskʌrɨləsli
AM ˈskərələsli

scurrilousness
BR ˈskʌrɨləsnəs
AM ˈskərələsnəs

scurry
BR ˈskʌr|i, -ɪz, -ɪɪŋ, -ɪd
AM ˈskəri, -z, -ɪŋ, -d

scurvied
BR ˈskəːvɪd
AM ˈskərvid

scurvily
BR ˈskəːvɨli
AM ˈskərvəli

scurviness
BR ˈskəːvɪnɪs
AM ˈskərvinɨs

scurvy
BR ˈskəːv|i, -ɪə(r), -ɪɪst
AM ˈskərvi, -ər, -ɨst

'scuse
BR skjuːz
AM skjuz

scut
BR skʌt, -s
AM skət, -s

scuta
BR ˈskjuːtə(r)
AM ˈsk(j)udə

scutage
BR ˈskjuːt|ɪdʒ, -ɨdʒɨz
AM ˈsk(j)udɪdʒ, -ɨz

scutal
BR ˈskjuːtl
AM ˈsk(j)udl

Scutari
BR skʊˈtɑːri, ˈskuːt(ə)ri
AM skuˈtɑri

scutate
BR ˈskjuːteɪt
AM ˈsk(j)uˌteɪt

scutch
BR skʌtʃ, -ɨz, -ɪŋ, -t
AM skətʃ, -əz, -ɪŋ, -t

scutcheon
BR ˈskʌtʃ(ə)n, -z
AM ˈskətʃən, -z

scutcher
BR ˈskʌtʃə(r), -z
AM ˈskətʃər, -z

scute
BR skjuːt, -s
AM sk(j)ut, -s

scutella
BR skjuːˈtɛlə(r)
AM sk(j)uˈtɛlə

scutellate
BR ˈskjuːtɨleɪt, ˈskuːtɨlət
AM sk(j)uˈtɛlət, ˈsk(j)udlˌeɪt

scutellation
BR ˌskjuːtɨˈleɪʃn, -z
AM ˌsk(j)udlˈeɪʃən, -z

scutellum
BR skjuːˈtɛləm
AM sk(j)uˈtɛləm

scutiform
BR ˈskjuːtɨfɔːm
AM ˈsk(j)udəˌfɔ(ə)rm

scutter
BR ˈskʌt|ə(r), -əz, -(ə)rɪŋ, -əd
AM ˈskədər, -z, -ɪŋ, -d

scuttle
BR ˈskʌt|l, -lz, -l̩ɪŋ\-lɪŋ, -ld
AM ˈskədəl, -z, -ɪŋ, -d

scuttlebutt
BR ˈskʌtlbʌt, -s
AM ˈskədlˌbət, -s

scutum
BR ˈskjuːtəm, -z
AM ˈsk(j)udəm, -z

scuzzy
BR ˈskʌz|i, -ɪə(r), -ɪɪst
AM ˈskəzi, -ər, -ɨst

Scylla and Charybdis
BR ˌsɪlə(r) ən(d) kəˈrɪbdɪs, + n̩(d) +
AM ˈsɪl(ə) ən kəˈrɪbdɪs, + tʃəˈrɪbdɪs

scyphi
BR ˈsʌɪfʌɪ
AM ˈsaɪˌfaɪ

scyphiform
BR ˈsʌɪfɨfɔːm
AM ˈsaɪfəˌfɔ(ə)rm

scyphose
BR ˈsʌɪfəʊs
AM ˈsaɪˌfoʊs, ˈsaɪˌfoʊz

scyphozoan
BR ˌsʌɪfəˈzəʊən, -z
AM ˌsaɪfəˈzoʊən, -z

scyphus
BR ˈsʌɪfəs
AM ˈsaɪfəs

scythe
BR sʌɪð, -z, -ɪŋ, -d
AM saɪð, -z, -ɪŋ, -d

Scythia
BR ˈsɪðɪə(r)
AM ˈsɪθiə

Scythian
BR ˈsɪðɪən
AM ˈsɪθiən

'sdeath
BR zdɛθ
AM zdɛθ

sea
BR siː, -z
AM si, -z

seabag
BR ˈsiːbag, -z
AM ˈsiˌbæg, -z

seabed
BR ˈsiːbɛd
AM ˈsiˌbɛd

seabird
BR ˈsiːbəːd, -z
AM ˈsiˌbərd, -z

seaboard
BR ˈsiːbɔːd
AM ˈsiˌbɔ(ə)rd

sea-boat
BR ˈsiːbəʊt, -s
AM ˈsiˌboʊt, -s

seaboot
BR ˈsiːbuːt, -s
AM ˈsiˌbut, -s

seaborne
BR ˈsiːbɔːn
AM ˈsiˌbɔ(ə)rn

seacoast
BR ˈsiːkəʊst, -s
AM ˈsiˌkoʊst, -s

seacock
BR ˈsiːkɒk, -s
AM ˈsiˌkɑk, -s

seadog
BR ˈsiːdɒg, -z
AM ˈsiˌdɔg, ˈsiˌdɑg, -z

Sea Dyak
BR ˈsiː ˌdʌɪak
AM ˈsi ˌdaɪˌæk

seafarer
BR ˈsiːˌfɛːrə(r), -z
AM ˈsiˌfɛrər, -z

seafaring
BR ˈsiːˌfɛːrɪŋ
AM ˈsiˌfɛrɪŋ

sea floor
BR ˈsiː flɔː(r), ˌsiː ˈflɔː(r), -z
AM ˈsi ˈflɔ(ə)r, -z

seafood
BR ˈsiːfuːd
AM ˈsiˌfud

Seaford
BR ˈsiːfəd
AM ˈsifərd

Seaforth
BR ˈsiːfɔːθ
AM ˈsiˌfɔ(ə)rθ

seafront
BR ˈsiːfrʌnt, -s
AM ˈsiˌfrənt, -s

Seaga
BR sɪˈɑːgə(r)
AM siˈɑgə

seagoing
BR ˈsiːˌgəʊɪŋ
AM ˈsiˌgoʊɪŋ

seagull
BR ˈsiːgʌl, -z
AM ˈsiˌgəl, -z

seahorse
BR ˈsiːhɔːs, -ɨz
AM ˈsiˌhɔ(ə)rs, -əz

seakale
BR ˈsiːkeɪl
AM ˈsiˌkeɪl

seal
BR siːl, -z, -ɪŋ, -d
AM si(ə)l, -z, -ɪŋ, -d

sealable
BR ˈsiːləbl
AM ˈsiləbəl

sealant
BR ˈsiːlənt, ˈsiːln̩t, -s
AM ˈsilənt, -s

Seale
BR siːl
AM si(ə)l

sealed-beam
BR ˌsiːldˈbiːm
AM ˈsil(d)ˌbim

sealer
BR ˈsiːlə(r), -z
AM ˈsilər, -z

sealery
BR ˈsiːl(ə)r|i, -ɪz
AM ˈsiləri, -z

Sealey
BR ˈsiːli
AM ˈsili

Sealink
BR ˈsiːlɪŋk
AM ˈsiˌlɪŋk

sealpoint
BR ˈsiːlpɔɪnt, -s
AM ˈsi(ə)lˌpɔɪnt, -s

sealskin
BR ˈsiːlskɪn, -z
AM ˈsi(ə)lˌskɪn, -z

sealstone
BR ˈsiːlstəʊn, -z
AM ˈsi(ə)lˌstoʊn, -z

Sealyham
BR ˈsiːlɪəm, -z
AM ˈsiliəm, -z

seam
BR siːm, -z, -ɪŋ, -d
AM sim, -z, -ɪŋ, -d

seaman
BR ˈsiːmən
AM ˈsimən

seamanlike
BR ˈsiːmənlʌɪk
AM ˈsimənˌlaɪk

seamanly
BR ˈsiːmənli
AM ˈsimənli

seamanship
BR ˈsiːmənʃɪp
AM ˈsimənˌʃɪp

seamark
BR ˈsiːmɑːk, -s
AM ˈsiˌmɑrk, -s

Seamas
BR ˈʃeɪməs
AM ˈʃeɪməs

seamen
BR ˈsiːmən
AM ˈsimən

seamer
BR ˈsiːmə(r), -z
AM ˈsimər, -z

seamew
BR ˈsiːmjuː, -z
AM ˈsiˌmju, -z

seaminess
BR ˈsiːmɪnɪs
AM ˈsiminɨs

seamless
BR ˈsiːmlɨs
AM ˈsimlɨs

seamlessly
BR 'siːmlɨsli
AM 'simlɨsli
seamlessness
BR 'siːmlɨsnɨs
AM 'simlɨsnɨs
seamstress
BR 'siːmstrɪs, -ɨz
AM 'simstrɪs, -əz
Seamus
BR 'ʃeɪməs
AM 'ʃeɪməs
seamy
BR 'siːm|i, -ɪə(r), -ɪɨst
AM 'simi, -ər, -ɨst
Sean
BR ʃɔːn
AM ʃɔn, ʃɑn
Seanad
BR 'ʃanəd
AM 'ʃænəd
séance
BR 'seɪɒ̃s, 'seɪɑːns, -ɨz
AM 'seɪˌɑns, -əz
seaplane
BR 'siːpleɪn, -z
AM 'siˌpleɪn, -z
seaport
BR 'siːpɔːt, -s
AM 'siˌpɔ(ə)rt, -s
seaquake
BR 'siːkweɪk, -s
AM 'siˌkweɪk, -s
sear
BR sɪə(r), -z, -ɪŋ, -d
AM sɪ(ə)r, -z, -ɪŋ, -d
search
BR səːtʃ, -ɨz, -ɪŋ, -t
AM sərtʃ, -əz, -ɪŋ, -t
searchable
BR 'səːtʃəbl
AM 'sərtʃəbəl
searcher
BR 'səːtʃə(r), -z
AM 'sərtʃər, -z
searchingly
BR 'səːtʃɪŋli
AM 'sərtʃɪŋli
searchless
BR 'səːtʃləs
AM 'sərtʃləs
searchlight
BR 'səːtʃlʌɪt, -s
AM 'sərtʃˌlaɪt, -s
searingly
BR 'sɪərɪŋli
AM 'sɪrɪŋli
Searle
BR səːl
AM sərl
Sears
BR sɪəz
AM sɪ(ə)rz
Seascale
BR 'siːskeɪl
AM 'siˌskeɪl
seascape
BR 'siːskeɪp, -s
AM 'siˌskeɪp, -s
seashell
BR 'siːʃɛl, -z
AM 'siˌʃɛl, -z
seashore
BR 'siːʃɔː(r)
AM 'siˌʃɔ(ə)r
seasick
BR 'siːsɪk
AM 'siˌsɪk
seasickness
BR 'siːsɪknɨs
AM 'siˌsɪknɨs
seaside
BR 'siːsʌɪd
AM 'siˌsaɪd
season
BR 'siːz|n, -nz, -n̩ɪŋ\-(ə)nɪŋ, -nd
AM 'sizn̩, -z, -ɪŋ, -d
seasonable
BR 'siːzn̩əbl, 'siːz(ə)nəbl
AM 'sizn̩əbəl, 'siznəbəl
seasonableness
BR 'siːzn̩əblnəs, 'siːz(ə)nəblnəs
AM 'sizn̩əbəlnəs, 'siznəbəlnəs
seasonably
BR 'siːzn̩əbli, 'siːz(ə)nəbli
AM 'sizn̩əbli, 'siznəbli
seasonal
BR 'siːzn̩(ə)l, 'siːz(ə)n(ə)l
AM 'siz(ə)nəl
seasonality
BR ˌsiːzə'nalɪti
AM ˌsizə'nælədi
seasonally
BR 'siːzn̩l̩i, 'siːzn̩əli, 'siːz(ə)nəli
AM 'siz(ə)nəli
seasoner
BR 'siːzn̩ə(r), 'siːz(ə)nə(r), -z
AM 'sizn̩ər, -z
seasoning
BR 'siːzn̩ɪŋ, 'siːz(ə)nɪŋ, -z
AM 'sizn̩ɪŋ, 'siznɪŋ, -z
seasonless
BR 'siːznləs
AM 'siznlɨs
seat
BR siːt, -s, -ɪŋ, -ɨd
AM si|t, -ts, -dɪŋ, -dɨd
seatbelt
BR 'siːtbɛlt, -s
AM 'sitˌbɛlt, -s
seatless
BR 'siːtlɨs
AM 'sitlɨs
seatmate
BR 'siːtmeɪt, -s
AM 'sitˌmeɪt, -s
SEATO
BR 'siːtəʊ
AM 'sidoʊ
Seaton
BR 'siːtn
AM 'sitn
seatrein
BR 'siːtreɪn, -z
AM 'siˌtreɪn, -z
Seattle
BR sɪ'atl
AM si'ædəl
seawall
BR ˌsiː'wɔːl, 'siːwɔːl, -z
AM 'siˌwɔl, 'siˌwɑl, -z
seaward
BR 'siːwəd, -z
AM 'siwərd, -z
seawater
BR 'siːˌwɔːtə(r)
AM 'siˌwɔdər, 'siˌwɑdər
seaway
BR 'siːweɪ, -z
AM 'siˌweɪ, -z
seaweed
BR 'siːwiːd
AM 'siˌwid
seaworthiness
BR 'siːˌwəːðɪnɨs
AM 'siˌwərðinɨs
seaworthy
BR 'siːˌwəːði
AM 'siˌwərði
Seb
BR sɛb
AM sɛb
sebaceous
BR sɪ'beɪʃəs
AM sə'beɪʃəs
Sebastian
BR sɪ'bastɪən
AM sə'bæstʃən
Sebastopol
BR sɪ'bastəp(ɒ)l
AM sə'bæstəˌpoʊl
Sebat
BR sɪ'bat, 'siːbat
AM sə'bæt
sebesten
BR sɪ'bɛstn, -z
AM sə'bɛstən, -z
seborrhea
BR ˌsɛbə'riːə(r)
AM ˌsɛbə'riə
seborrheic
BR ˌsɛbə'riːɪk
AM ˌsɛbə'riɪk
seborrhoea
BR ˌsɛbə'riːə(r)
AM ˌsɛbə'riə
seborrhoeic
BR ˌsɛbə'riːɪk
AM ˌsɛbə'riɪk
Sebring
BR 'siːbrɪŋ
AM 'sibrɪŋ
sebum
BR 'siːbəm
AM 'sibəm
sec
BR sɛk, -s
AM sɛk, -s
secant
BR 'siːk(ə)nt, -s
AM 'siˌkænt, 'sikənt, -s
secateurs
BR ˌsɛkə'təːz, 'sɛkətəːz
AM 'sɛkəˌtərz
secco
BR 'sɛkəʊ
AM 'sɛkoʊ
secede
BR sɪ'siːd, -z, -ɪŋ, -ɨd
AM sə'sid, si'sid, -z, -ɪŋ, -ɨd
seceder
BR sɪ'siːdə(r), -z
AM sə'sidər, si'sidər, -z
secession
BR sɪ'sɛʃn, -z
AM sə'sɛʃən, -z
secessional
BR sɪ'sɛʃn̩(ə)l, sɪ'sɛʃən(ə)l
AM sə'sɛʃ(ə)nəl
secessionism
BR sɪ'sɛʃn̩ɪz(ə)m, sɪ'sɛʃənɪz(ə)m
AM sə'sɛʃəˌnɪzəm
secessionist
BR sɪ'sɛʃn̩ɪst, sɪ'sɛʃənɪst, -s
AM sə'sɛʃənəst, -s
Secker
BR 'sɛkə(r)
AM 'sɛkər
seclude
BR sɪ'kluːd, -z, -ɪŋ, -ɨd
AM sə'klud, -z, -ɪŋ, -əd
seclusion
BR sɪ'kluːʒn
AM sə'kluʒən
seclusionist
BR sɪ'kluːʒn̩ɪst, -s
AM sə'kluʒənəst, -s
seclusive
BR sɪ'kluːsɪv
AM sə'klusɪv
Secombe
BR 'siːkəm
AM 'sikəm
second[1]
number, time, support
BR 'sɛk(ə)nd, -z, -ɪŋ, -ɨd
AM 'sɛkənd, -z, -ɪŋ, -əd
second[2]
verb, move to special duties
BR sɪ'kɒnd, -z, -ɪŋ, -ɨd
AM sə'kɑnd, 'sɛkənd, -z, -ɪŋ, -əd

secondarily
BR ˈsɛk(ə)nd(ə)rɨli
AM ˌsɛkənˈdɛrəli

secondariness
BR ˈsɛk(ə)nd(ə)rɪnɨs
AM ˈsɛkənˌdɛrinɨs

secondary
BR ˈsɛk(ə)nd(ə)r|i, -ɪz
AM ˈsɛkənˌdɛri, -z

seconde
BR səˈkɔ̃d, -z
AM səˈkɑnd, -z

secondee
BR ˌsɛk(ə)nˈdiː, -z
AM ˌsɛkənˈdi, -z

seconder
BR ˈsɛk(ə)ndə(r), -z
AM ˈsɛkəndər, -z

second hand[1]
clock dial
BR ˈsɛk(ə)nd hand
AM ˈsɛkən(d) ˌ(h)ænd

second hand[2]
used
BR ˌsɛk(ə)nd ˈhand
AM ˌsɛkən(d) ˈhænd

secondi
BR sɪˈkɒndiː, sɛˈkɒndiː
AM səˈkɑndi

secondly
BR ˈsɛk(ə)ndli
AM ˈsɛkən(d)li

secondment
BR sɪˈkɒn(d)m(ə)nt, -s
AM səˈkɑn(d)mənt, ˈsɛkən(d)mənt, -s

secondo
BR sɪˈkɒndəʊ, sɛˈkɒndəʊ
AM səˈkɑndoʊ, səˈkɔndoʊ

secrecy
BR ˈsiːkrɨsi
AM ˈsikrəsi

secret
BR ˈsiːkrɨt, -s
AM ˈsikrɨt, -s

secretaire
BR ˌsɛkrɪˈtɛː(r), -z
AM ˌsɛkrəˈtɛ(ə)r, -z

secretarial
BR ˌsɛkrɪˈtɛːrɪəl
AM ˌsɛkrəˈtɛriəl

secretariat
BR ˌsɛkrɪˈtɛːrɪət, ˌsɛkrɪˈtɛːrɪat, -s
AM ˌsɛkrəˈtɛriət, -s

secretary
BR ˈsɛkrɨt(ə)r|i, ˈsɛkrɪtɛr|i, -ɪz
AM ˈsɛkrəˌtɛri, -z

secretary-general
BR ˌsɛkrɨt(ə)rɪˈdʒɛn(ə)rəl, ˌsɛkrɨt(ə)rɪˈdʒɛn(ə)rl̩, ˌsɛkrɪtɛrɪˈdʒɛn(ə)rəl, ˌsɛkrɪtɛrɪˈdʒɛn(ə)rl̩, -z
AM ˈsɛkrəˌtɛriˈdʒɛn(ə)rəl, -z

secretaryship
BR ˈsɛkrɨt(ə)rɪʃɪp, -s
AM ˈsɛkrəˌtɛriˌʃɪp, -s

secrete
BR sɪˈkriːt, -s, -ɪŋ, -ɨd
AM səˈkri|t, siˈkri|t, -ts, -dɪŋ, -dɨd

secretion
BR sɪˈkriːʃn, -z
AM səˈkrɪʃən, siˈkrɪʃən, -z

secretive
BR ˈsiːkrɨtɪv
AM ˈsikrɨdɪv

secretively
BR ˈsiːkrɨtɨvli
AM ˈsikrɨdɨvli

secretiveness
BR ˈsiːkrɨtɨvnɨs
AM ˈsikrɨdɨvnɨs

secretly
BR ˈsiːkrɨtli
AM ˈsikrɨtli

secretor
BR sɪˈkriːtə(r), -z
AM səˈkridər, siˈkridər, -z

secretory
BR sɪˈkriːt(ə)ri
AM səˈkridəri, ˈsikrəˌtɔri

sect
BR sɛkt, -s
AM sɛk(t), -(t)s

sectarian
BR sɛkˈtɛːrɪən, -z
AM sɛkˈtɛriən, -z

sectarianise
BR sɛkˈtɛːrɪənʌɪz, -ɨz, -ɪŋ, -d
AM sɛkˈtɛriəˌnaɪz, -ɨz, -ɪŋ, -d

sectarianism
BR sɛkˈtɛːrɪənɪz(ə)m
AM sɛkˈtɛriəˌnɪzəm

sectarianize
BR sɛkˈtɛːrɪənʌɪz, -ɨz, -ɪŋ, -d
AM sɛkˈtɛriəˌnaɪz, -ɨz, -ɪŋ, -d

sectary
BR ˈsɛkt(ə)r|i, -ɪz
AM ˈsɛktəri, -z

section
BR ˈsɛkʃn, -z
AM ˈsɛkʃən, -z

sectional
BR ˈsɛkʃn̩(ə)l, ˈsɛkʃən(ə)l
AM ˈsɛkʃ(ə)nəl

sectionalise
BR ˈsɛkʃn̩əlʌɪz, ˈsɛkʃn̩l̩ʌɪz, ˈsɛkʃənl̩ʌɪz, ˈsɛkʃ(ə)nəlʌɪz, -ɨz, -ɪŋ, -d
AM ˈsɛkʃənlˌaɪz, ˈsɛkʃnəˌlaɪz, -ɨz, -ɪŋ, -d

sectionalism
BR ˈsɛkʃn̩əlɪz(ə)m, ˈsɛkʃn̩l̩ɪz(ə)m, ˈsɛkʃənl̩ɪz(ə)m, ˈsɛkʃ(ə)nəlɪz(ə)m
AM ˈsɛkʃənlˌɪzəm, ˈsɛkʃnəˌlɪzəm

sectionalist
BR ˈsɛkʃn̩əlɪst, ˈsɛkʃn̩l̩ɪst, ˈsɛkʃənl̩ɪst, ˈsɛkʃ(ə)nəlɪst, -s
AM ˈsɛkʃənləst, ˈsɛkʃnələst, -s

sectionalize
BR ˈsɛkʃn̩əlʌɪz, ˈsɛkʃn̩l̩ʌɪz, ˈsɛkʃənl̩ʌɪz, ˈsɛkʃ(ə)nəlʌɪz, -ɨz, -ɪŋ, -d
AM ˈsɛkʃənlˌaɪz, ˈsɛkʃnəˌlaɪz, -ɨz, -ɪŋ, -d

sectionally
BR ˈsɛkʃn̩əli, ˈsɛkʃn̩l̩i, ˈsɛkʃənl̩i, ˈsɛkʃ(ə)nəli
AM ˈsɛkʃ(ə)nəli

sector
BR ˈsɛktə(r), -z
AM ˈsɛktər, -z

sectoral
BR ˈsɛkt(ə)rəl, ˈsɛkt(ə)rl̩
AM ˈsɛktərəl

sectorial
BR sɛkˈtɔːrɪəl
AM sɛkˈtɔriəl

secular
BR ˈsɛkjʉlə(r)
AM ˈsɛkjələr

secularisation
BR ˌsɛkjʉlərʌɪˈzeɪʃn
AM ˌsɛkjələrəˈzeɪʃən, ˌsɛkjələˌraɪˈzeɪʃən

secularise
BR ˈsɛkjʉlərʌɪz, -ɨz, -ɪŋ, -d
AM ˈsɛkjələˌraɪz, -ɨz, -ɪŋ, -d

secularism
BR ˈsɛkjʉlərɪz(ə)m
AM ˈsɛkjələˌrɪzəm

secularist
BR ˈsɛkjʉlərɪst, -s
AM ˈsɛkjələrəst, -s

secularity
BR ˌsɛkjʉˈlarɪti
AM ˌsɛkjəˈlɛrədi

secularization
BR ˌsɛkjʉlərʌɪˈzeɪʃn
AM ˌsɛkjələrəˈzeɪʃən, ˌsɛkjələˌraɪˈzeɪʃən

secularize
BR ˈsɛkjʉlərʌɪz, -ɨz, -ɪŋ, -d
AM ˈsɛkjələˌraɪz, -ɨz, -ɪŋ, -d

secularly
BR ˈsɛkjʉləli
AM ˈsɛkjələrli

secund
BR sɪˈkʌnd
AM ˈsiˌkənd, səˈkənd

Secunderabad
BR sɪˈkʌnd(ə)rəbad, sɪˈkʌnd(ə)rəbɑːd
AM səˈkənd(ə)rəˌbɑd, səˈkənd(ə)rəˌbæd

secundly
BR sɪˈkʌn(d)li
AM ˈsiˌkən(d)li, səˈkən(d)li

securable
BR sɪˈkjʊərəbl, sɪˈkjɔːrəbl
AM səˈkjʊrəbəl

secure
BR sɪˈkjʊə(r), sɪˈkjɔː(r), -z, -ɪŋ, -d, -ə(r), -ɨst
AM səˈkjʊ(ə)r, -z, -ɪŋ, -d, -ər, -əst

securely
BR sɪˈkjʊəli, sɪˈkjɔːli
AM səˈkjʊrli

securement
BR sɪˈkjʊəm(ə)nt, sɪˈkjɔːm(ə)nt, -s
AM səˈkjʊrmənt, -s

Securicor®
BR sɪˈkjʊərɪkɔː(r), sɪˈkjɔːrɪkɔː(r)
AM səˈk(j)ʊrəˌkɔ(ə)r

securitisation
BR sɪˌkjʊərɪtʌɪˈzeɪʃn, sɪˌkjɔːrɪtʌɪˈzeɪʃn
AM səˌkjʊrədəˈzeɪʃən, səˌkjʊrəˌtaɪˈzeɪʃən

securitise
BR sɪˈkjʊərɪtʌɪz, sɪˈkjɔːrɪtʌɪz, -ɨz, -ɪŋ, -d
AM səˈkjʊrəˌtaɪz, -ɨz, -ɪŋ, -d

securitization
BR sɪˌkjʊərɪtʌɪˈzeɪʃn, sɪˌkjɔːrɪtʌɪˈzeɪʃn
AM səˌkjʊrədəˈzeɪʃən, səˌkjʊrəˌtaɪˈzeɪʃən

securitize
BR sɪˈkjʊərɪtʌɪz, sɪˈkjɔːrɪtʌɪz, -ɨz, -ɪŋ, -d
AM səˈkjʊrəˌtaɪz, -ɨz, -ɪŋ, -d

security
BR sɪˈkjʊərɪti, sɪˈkjɔːrɪt|i, -ɪz
AM səˈkjʊrədi, -z

sedan
BR sɪˈdan, -z
AM səˈdæn, -z

sedate
BR sɪ'deɪt, -s, -ɪŋ, -ɪd
AM sə'deɪ|t, -ts, -dɪŋ, -dɪd

sedately
BR sɪ'deɪtli
AM sə'deɪtli

sedateness
BR sɪ'deɪtnɪs
AM sə'deɪtnɪs

sedation
BR sɪ'deɪʃn
AM sə'deɪʃən

sedative
BR 'sɛdətɪv, -z
AM 'sɛdədɪv, -z

Sedburgh
BR 'sɛdb(ə)rə(*r*), 'sɛdbə(*r*), 'sɛdbəːg
AM 'sɛd,bərə, 'sɛd,bərg

Seddon
BR 'sɛdn
AM 'sɛdən

sedentarily
BR 'sɛd(ə)nt(ə)rɪli
AM 'sɛdn,tɛrəli

sedentariness
BR 'sɛd(ə)ntrɪnɪs
AM 'sɛdn,tɛrinɪs

sedentary
BR 'sɛd(ə)nt(ə)ri
AM 'sɛdn,tɛri

Seder
BR 'seɪdə(r)
AM 'seɪdər

sederunt
BR sɪ'dɪərənt, sɪ'dɛːrənt, -s
AM sə'dɪrənt, -s

sedge
BR sɛdʒ, -ɪz
AM sɛdʒ, -əz

Sedgefield
BR 'sɛdʒfiːld
AM 'sɛdʒ,fild

Sedgemoor
BR 'sɛdʒmɔː(r)
AM 'sɛdʒ,mɔ(ə)r

Sedgewick
BR 'sɛdʒwɪk
AM 'sɛdʒ,wɪk

Sedgwick
BR 'sɛdʒwɪk
AM 'sɛdʒ,wɪk

sedgy
BR 'sɛdʒi
AM 'sɛdʒi

sedile
BR sɪ'dʌɪli
AM sə'daɪli

sedilia
BR sɪ'dɪlɪə(*r*), sɪ'diːlɪə(*r*), sɪ'dʌɪlɪə(*r*)
AM sə'dɪljə, sə'dɪliə

sediment
BR 'sɛdɪm(ə)nt, -s
AM 'sɛdəmənt, -s

sedimentary
BR ,sɛdɪ'mɛnt(ə)ri
AM ,sɛdə'mɛn(t)əri

sedimentation
BR ,sɛdɪm(ə)n'teɪʃn, -z
AM ,sɛdəmən'teɪʃən, -z

sedition
BR sɪ'dɪʃn
AM sə'dɪʃən

seditionary
BR sɪ'dɪʃn̩(ə)r|i, -ɪz
AM sə'dɪʃə,nɛri, -z

seditionist
BR sɪ'dɪʃn̩ɪst, sɪ'dɪʃənɪst, -s
AM sə'dɪʃənəst, -s

seditious
BR sɪ'dɪʃəs
AM sə'dɪʃəs

seditiously
BR sɪ'dɪʃəsli
AM sə'dɪʃəsli

seditiousness
BR sɪ'dɪʃəsnəs
AM sə'dɪʃəsnəs

seduce
BR sɪ'djuːs, sɪ'dʒuːs, -ɪz, -ɪŋ, -t
AM sə'd(j)us, -z, -ɪŋ, -t

seducer
BR sɪ'djuːsə(r), sɪ'dʒuːsə(r), -z
AM sə'd(j)usər, -z

seducible
BR sɪ'djuːsɪbl, sɪ'dʒuːsɪbl
AM sə'd(j)usəbəl

seduction
BR sɪ'dʌkʃn, -z
AM sə'dəkʃən, -z

seductive
BR sɪ'dʌktɪv
AM sə'dəktɪv

seductively
BR sɪ'dʌktɪvli
AM sə'dəktɪvli

seductiveness
BR sɪ'dʌktɪvnɪs
AM sə'dəktɪvnɪs

seductress
BR sɪ'dʌktrɪs, -ɪz
AM sə'dəktrəs, -əz

sedulity
BR sɪ'djuːlɪti, sɪ'dʒuːlɪti
AM sə'dʒulədi

sedulous
BR 'sɛdjʊləs, 'sɛdʒʊləs
AM 'sɛdʒələs

sedulously
BR 'sɛdjʊləsli, 'sɛdʒʊləsli
AM 'sɛdʒələsli

sedulousness
BR 'sɛdjʊləsnəs, 'sɛdʒʊləsnəs
AM 'sɛdʒələsnəs

sedum
BR 'siːdəm, -z
AM 'sidəm, -z

see
BR siː, -z, -ɪŋ
AM si, -z, -ɪŋ

seeable
BR 'siːəbl
AM 'siəbəl

seed
BR siːd, -z, -ɪŋ, -ɪd
AM sid, -z, -ɪŋ, -ɪd

seedbed
BR 'siːdbɛd, -z
AM 'sid,bɛd, -z

seedcake
BR 'siːdkeɪk, -s
AM 'sid,keɪk, -s

seedcorn
BR 'siːdkɔːn
AM 'sid,kɔ(ə)rn

seeder
BR 'siːdə(r), -z
AM 'sidər, -z

seedily
BR 'siːdɪli
AM 'sidɪli

seediness
BR 'siːdɪnɪs
AM 'sidinɪs

seedless
BR 'siːdlɪs
AM 'sidlɪs

seedling
BR 'siːdlɪŋ, -z
AM 'sidlɪŋ, -z

seedsman
BR 'siːdzmən
AM 'sidzmən

seedsmen
BR 'siːdzmən
AM 'sidzmən

seedy
BR 'siːd|i, -ɪə(r), -ɪɪst
AM 'sidi, -ər, -ɪst

Seeger
BR 'siːgə(r)
AM 'sigər

seeing-eye dog
BR ,siːɪŋ'ʌɪ dɒg, -z
AM ,siɪŋ'aɪ ,dɔg, ,siɪŋ'aɪ ,dɑg, -z

seek
BR siːk, -s, -ɪŋ
AM sik, -s, -ɪŋ

seeker
BR 'siːkə(r), -z
AM 'sikər, -z

seel
BR siːl, -z, -ɪŋ, -d
AM si(ə)l, -z, -ɪŋ, -d

Seeley
BR 'siːli
AM 'sili

Seely
BR 'siːli
AM 'sili

seem
BR siːm, -z, -ɪŋ, -d
AM sim, -z, -ɪŋ, -d

seemingly
BR siːmɪŋli
AM 'simɪŋli

seemliness
BR 'siːmlɪnɪs
AM 'simlinɪs

seemly
BR 'siːml|i, -ɪə(r), -ɪɪst
AM 'simli, -ər, -ɪst

seen
BR siːn
AM sin

seep
BR siːp, -s, -ɪŋ, -t
AM sip, -s, -ɪŋ, -t

seepage
BR 'siːp|ɪdʒ, -ɪdʒɪz
AM 'sipɪdʒ, -ɪz

seer[1]
prophet
BR sɪə(r), 'siːə(r), -z
AM sɪ(ə)r, -z

seer[2]
someone who sees
BR 'siːə(r), sɪə(r), -z
AM 'siər, sɪ(ə)r, -z

seersucker
BR 'sɪə,sʌkə(r)
AM 'sɪr,səkər

seesaw
BR 'siːsɔː(*r*), -z, -ɪŋ, -d
AM 'si,sɔ, 'si,sɑ, -z, -ɪŋ, -d

seethe
BR siːð, -z, -ɪŋ, -d
AM sið, -z, -ɪŋ, -d

seethingly
BR 'siːðɪŋli
AM 'siðɪŋli

see-through
BR 'siːθruː
AM 'si,θru

Seféris
BR 'sɛf(ə)rɪs
AM 'sɛf(ə)rəs
GR se'feriːs

Segal
BR 'siːgl
AM 'sigəl

segment[1]
noun
BR 'sɛgm(ə)nt, -s
AM 'sɛgmənt, -s

segment[2]
verb
BR sɛg'mɛnt, -s, -ɪŋ, -ɪd
AM 'sɛg,mɛn|t, ,sɛg'mɛn|t, -ts, -(t)ɪŋ, -(t)əd

segmental
BR sɛg'mɛntl
AM sɛg'mɛn(t)l

segmentalisation
BR sɛɡ,mɛntl̩ʌɪ'zeɪʃn
AM sɛɡ,mɛn(t)l̩ə'zeɪʃən, sɛɡ,mɛn(t)l,aɪ'zeɪʃən

segmentalise
BR sɛɡ'mɛntl̩ʌɪz, -ɨz, -ɪŋ, -d
AM sɛɡ'mɛn(t)l,aɪz, -ɨz, -ɪŋ, -d

segmentalization
BR sɛɡ,mɛntl̩ʌɪ'zeɪʃn
AM sɛɡ,mɛn(t)l̩ə'zeɪʃən, sɛɡ,mɛn(t)l,aɪ'zeɪʃən

segmentalize
BR sɛɡ'mɛntl̩ʌɪz, -ɨz, -ɪŋ, -d
AM sɛɡ'mɛn(t)l,aɪz, -ɨz, -ɪŋ, -d

segmentally
BR sɛɡ'mɛntl̩i, sɛɡ'mɛntəli
AM sɛɡ'mɛn(t)l̩i

segmentary
BR 'sɛɡmənt(ə)ri
AM 'sɛɡmən,tɛri

segmentation
BR ,sɛɡmən'teɪʃn, ,sɛɡmɛn'teɪʃn
AM ,sɛɡmən'teɪʃən, ,sɛɡ,mɛn'teɪʃən

sego
BR 'siːɡəʊ, -z
AM 'sigoʊ, -z

Segovia
BR sɨ'ɡəʊvɪə(*r*)
AM sə'ɡoʊviə
SP se'ɣoβia

Segrave
BR 'siːɡreɪv
AM 'si,ɡreɪv

segregable
BR 'sɛɡrɪɡəbl
AM 'sɛɡrəɡəbəl

segregate
BR 'sɛɡrɪɡeɪt, -s, -ɪŋ, -ɨd
AM 'sɛɡrə,ɡeɪ|t, -ts, -dɪŋ, -dɨd

segregation
BR ,sɛɡrɪ'ɡeɪʃn
AM ,sɛɡrə'ɡeɪʃən

segregational
BR ,sɛɡrɪ'ɡeɪʃn̩(ə)l, ,sɛɡrɪ'ɡeɪʃən(ə)l
AM ,sɛɡrə'ɡeɪʃ(ə)nəl

segregationist
BR ,sɛɡrɪ'ɡeɪʃn̩ɪst, ,sɛɡrɪ'ɡeɪʃənɪst, -s
AM ,sɛɡrə'ɡeɪʃənəst, -s

segregative
BR 'sɛɡrɪɡeɪtɪv
AM 'sɛɡrə,ɡeɪdɪv

segue
BR 'sɛɡw|eɪ, 'seɪɡw|eɪ, 'sɛɡw|i, 'seɪɡw|i, -eɪz\-ɪz, -eɪɪŋ\-ɪɪŋ, -eɪd\-ɪd
AM 'sɛ,ɡweɪ, 'seɪ,ɡweɪ, -z, -ɪŋ, -d

seguidilla
BR ,sɛɡɨ'diː(l)jə(*r*), -z
AM ,sɛɡi'di(j)ə, -z

Sehnsucht
BR 'zeɪnzʊkt, 'zeɪnzʊxt
AM 'seɪn,zʊkt

sei
BR seɪ
AM seɪ

seicentist
BR seɪ'tʃɛntɪst, -s
AM seɪ'(t)ʃɛn(t)əst, -s

seicento
BR seɪ'tʃɛntəʊ
AM seɪ'(t)ʃɛn,(t)oʊ

seicentoist
BR seɪ'tʃɛntəʊɪst, -s
AM seɪ'(t)ʃɛn(t)əwəst, -s

seiche
BR seɪʃ, -ɨz
AM seɪ(t)ʃ, -ɨz

seif
BR siːf, seɪf, -s
AM seɪf, sif, -s

Seifert
BR 'siːfət
AM 'sifərt, 'saɪfərt
GER 'zaɪfɐt

Seigel
BR 'siːɡl
AM 'siɡəl

seigneur
BR sɛ'njəː(r), seɪ'njəː(r), 'seɪnjə(r), -z
AM seɪn'jər, sɛn'jər, -z

seigneurial
BR sɛ'njʊərɪəl, seɪ'njʊərɪəl, sɛ'njəːrɪəl, seɪ'njəːrɪəl
AM seɪn'jʊriəl, seɪn'jəriəl, sɛn'jəriəl, sɛn'jəriəl

seigneury
BR 'seɪnjʊr|i, -ɪz
AM 'seɪnjəri, -z

seignior
BR 'seɪnjə(r), -z
AM seɪn'jər, -z

seigniorage
BR 'seɪnjər|ɪdʒ, -ɨdʒɨz
AM 'seɪnjərɪdʒ, -ɨz

seigniorial
BR sɛ'njɔːrɪəl, seɪ'njɔːrɪəl
AM seɪn'jʊriəl, seɪn'jəriəl

seigniory
BR 'seɪnjər|i, -ɪz
AM 'seɪnjəri, -z

seignorage
BR 'seɪnjər|ɪdʒ, -ɨdʒɨz
AM seɪn'jərɪdʒ, -ɨz

Seine
BR seɪn
AM sɛn, seɪn

seine
BR seɪn, -z
AM seɪn, -z

seiner
BR 'seɪnə(r), -z
AM 'seɪnər, -z

seise
BR siːz, -d
AM siz, -d

seisin
BR 'siːzɪn, -z
AM 'sizn, -z

seismal
BR 'sʌɪzml
AM 'saɪzməl

seismic
BR 'sʌɪzmɪk
AM 'saɪzmɪk

seismical
BR 'sʌɪzmɨkl
AM 'saɪzməkəl

seismically
BR 'sʌɪzmɨkli
AM 'saɪzmək(ə)li

seismicity
BR sʌɪz'mɪsɨti
AM saɪz'mɪsɨdi

seismogram
BR 'sʌɪzməɡram, -z
AM 'saɪzmə,ɡræm, -z

seismograph
BR 'sʌɪzməɡrɑːf, 'sʌɪzməɡraf, -s
AM 'saɪzmə,ɡræf, -s

seismographer
BR sʌɪz'mɒɡrəfə(r), -z
AM saɪz'mɑɡrəfər, -z

seismographic
BR ,sʌɪzmə'ɡrafɪk
AM ¦saɪzmə'ɡræfɪk

seismographical
BR ,sʌɪzmə'ɡrafɨkl
AM ¦saɪzmə'ɡræfəkəl

seismographically
BR ,sʌɪzmə'ɡrafɨkli
AM ¦saɪzmə'ɡræfək(ə)li

seismography
BR sʌɪz'mɒɡrəfi
AM saɪz'mɑɡrəfi

seismological
BR ,sʌɪzmə'lɒdʒɨkl
AM ¦saɪzmə'lɑdʒəkəl

seismologically
BR ,sʌɪzm'lɒdʒɨkli
AM ¦saɪzmə'lɑdʒək(ə)li

seismologist
BR sʌɪz'mɒlədʒɪst, -s
AM saɪz'mɑlədʒəst, -s

seismology
BR sʌɪz'mɒlədʒi
AM saɪz'mɑlədʒi

seismometer
BR sʌɪz'mɒmɨtə(r), -z
AM saɪz'mɑmədər, -z

seismometric
BR ,sʌɪzmə'mɛtrɪk
AM ¦saɪzmə'mɛtrɪk

seismometrical
BR ,sʌɪzmə'mɛtrɨkl
AM ¦saɪzmə'mɛtrəkəl

seismometry
BR sʌɪz'mɒmɨtri
AM saɪz'mɑmətri

seismoscope
BR 'sʌɪzməskəʊp, -s
AM 'saɪzmə,skoʊp, -s

seismoscopic
BR ,sʌɪzmə'skɒpɪk
AM ¦saɪzmə'skɑpɪk

seizable
BR 'siːzəbl
AM 'sizəbəl

seize
BR siːz, -ɨz, -ɪŋ, -d
AM siz, -ɨz, -ɪŋ, -d

seizer
BR 'siːzə(r), -z
AM 'sizər, -z

seizin
BR 'siːzɪn, -z
AM 'sizn, -z

seizure
BR 'siːʒə(r), -z
AM 'siʒər, -z

sejant
BR 'siːdʒ(ə)nt
AM 'sidʒənt

Sejanus
BR sɨ'dʒeɪnəs
AM sə'dʒeɪnəs

selachian
BR sɨ'leɪkɪən, -z
AM sə'leɪkiən, -z

seladang
BR sɨ'lɑːdaŋ, -z
AM sə'lɑ,dɑŋ, -z

Selborne
BR 'sɛlbɔːn
AM 'sɛl,bɔ(ə)rn

Selbourne
BR 'sɛlbɔːn
AM 'sɛl,bɔ(ə)rn

Selby
BR 'sɛlbi
AM 'sɛlbi

seldom
BR 'sɛldəm
AM 'sɛldəm

select
BR sɨ'lɛkt, -s, -ɪŋ, -ɨd
AM sə'lɛk|(t), -(t)s, -tɪŋ, -təd

selectable
BR sɨ'lɛktəbl
AM sə'lɛktəbəl

selectee
BR sə,lɛk'tiː, -z
AM sə,lɛk'ti, -z

selection
BR sɨ'lɛkʃn, -z
AM sə'lɛkʃən, -z

selectional
BR sɪˈlɛkʃn̩(ə)l, sɪˈlɛkʃən(ə)l
AM səˈlɛkʃ(ə)nəl

selectionally
BR sɪˈlɛkʃn̩əli, sɪˈlɛkʃn̩li, sɪˈlɛkʃənl̩i, sɪˈlɛkʃ(ə)nəli
AM səˈlɛkʃ(ə)nəli

selective
BR sɪˈlɛktɪv
AM səˈlɛktɪv

selectively
BR sɪˈlɛktɨvli
AM səˈlɛktɨvli

selectiveness
BR sɪˈlɛktɨvnɨs
AM səˈlɛktɪvnɨs

selectivity
BR sɪˌlɛkˈtɪvɨti, ˌsɪlɛkˈtɪvɨti, ˌsiːlɛkˈtɪvɨti, ˌsɛlɛkˈtɪvɨti
AM səˌlɛkˈtɪvɨdi

selectman
BR sɪˈlɛk(t)mən, sɪˈlɛk(t)man
AM səˈlɛk(t)mən

selectmen
BR sɪˈlɛk(t)mən, sɪˈlɛk(t)mɛn
AM səˈlɛk(t)mən

selectness
BR sɪˈlɛk(t)nəs
AM səˈlɛk(t)nəs

selector
BR sɪˈlɛktə(r), -z
AM səˈlɛktər, -z

Selena
BR sɪˈliːnə(r)
AM səˈlinə

selenate
BR ˈsɛlɨneɪt, -s
AM ˈsɛləˌneɪt, -s

Selene
BR sɪˈliːni
AM səˈlini

selenic
BR sɪˈliːnɪk, sɪˈlɛnɪk
AM səˈlɛnɪk, səˈlinɪk

selenide
BR ˈsɛlɨnʌɪd, -z
AM ˈsɛləˌnaɪd, ˈsɛlənəd, -z

selenious
BR sɪˈliːnɪəs
AM səˈliniəs

selenite
BR ˈsɛlɨnʌɪt
AM ˈsɛləˌnaɪt

selenitic
BR ˌsɛlɨˈnɪtɪk
AM ˌsɛləˈnɪdɪk

selenium
BR sɪˈliːnɪəm
AM səˈliniəm

selenocentric
BR sɪˌliːnə(ʊ)ˈsɛntrɪk
AM səˌlinoʊˈsɛntrɪk

selenodont
BR sɪˈliːnə(ʊ)dɒnt, -s
AM səˈlinəˌdɑnt, səˈlinədənt, -s

selenographer
BR ˌsɛlɨˈnɒɡrəfə(r), -z
AM ˌsɛləˈnɑɡrəfər, -z

selenographic
BR ˌsɛlɨnəˈɡrafɪk
AM ˌsɛlənəˈɡræfɪk

selenography
BR ˌsɛlɨˈnɒɡrəfi
AM ˌsɛləˈnɑɡrəfi

selenologist
BR ˌsɛlɨˈnɒlədʒɪst, -s
AM ˌsɛləˈnɑlədʒəst, -s

selenology
BR ˌsɛlɨˈnɒlədʒi
AM ˌsɛləˈnɑlədʒi

Seleucid
BR sɪˈl(j)uːsɪd, -z
AM səˈl(j)usəd, -z

self
BR sɛlf
AM sɛlf

self-abandon
BR ˌsɛlfəˈband(ə)n, -d
AM ˈsɛlfəˈbændən, -d

self-abandonment
BR ˌsɛlfəˈband(ə)nm(ə)nt
AM ˈsɛlfəˈbændənmənt

self-abasement
BR ˌsɛlfəˈbeɪsm(ə)nt
AM ˈsɛlfəˈbeɪsmənt

self-abhorrence
BR ˌsɛlfəbˈhɒrəns, ˌsɛlfəbˈhɒrn̩s
AM ˈsɛlfəbˈhɔrəns

self-abnegation
BR ˌsɛlfabnɨˈɡeɪʃn
AM ˈsɛlfˌæbnəˈɡeɪʃən

self-absorbed
BR ˌsɛlfəbˈzɔːbd
AM ˈsɛlfəbˈzɔ(ə)rbd

self-absorption
BR ˌsɛlfəbˈzɔːpʃn
AM ˈsɛlfəbˈzɔrpʃən

self-abuse
BR ˌsɛlfəˈbjuːs
AM ˈsɛlfəˈbjus

self-accusation
BR ˌsɛlfakjʉˈzeɪʃn
AM ˈsɛlfˌækjəˈzeɪʃən

self-accusatory
BR ˌsɛlfəˈkjuːzət(ə)ri
AM ˈsɛlfəˈkjuzəˌtɔri

self-acting
BR ˌsɛlfˈaktɪŋ
AM ˈsɛlfˈæktɪŋ

self-action
BR ˌsɛlfˈakʃn
AM ˈsɛlfˈækʃən

self-activity
BR ˌsɛlfakˈtɪvɨti, ˌsɛlfəkˈtɪvɨti
AM ˈsɛlfækˈtɪvɨdi

self-addressed
BR ˌsɛlfəˈdrɛst
AM ˈsɛlfəˈdrɛst

self-adhesive
BR ˌsɛlfədˈhiːsɪv, ˌsɛlfədˈhiːzɪv
AM ˈsɛlfədˈhizɪv, ˈsɛlfədˈhisɪv

self-adjusting
BR ˌsɛlfəˈdʒʌstɪŋ
AM ˈsɛlfəˈdʒəstɪŋ

self-adjustment
BR ˌsɛlfəˈdʒʌs(t)m(ə)nt
AM ˈsɛlfəˈdʒəs(t)mənt

self-admiration
BR ˌsɛlfadmɨˈreɪʃn
AM ˈsɛlfˌædməˈreɪʃən

self-advancement
BR ˌsɛlfədˈvɑːnsm(ə)nt, ˌsɛlfədˈvansm(ə)nt
AM ˈsɛlfədˈvænsmənt

self-advertisement
BR ˌsɛlfədˈvəːtɪsm(ə)nt, ˌsɛlfədˈvəːtɪzm(ə)nt
AM ˈsɛlfˈædvərˌtaɪzmənt

self-advertiser
BR ˌsɛlfˈadvətʌɪzə(r), -z
AM ˈsɛlfˈædvərˌtaɪzər, -z

self-affirmation
BR ˌsɛlfafəˈmeɪʃn
AM ˈsɛlfˌæfərˈmeɪʃən

self-aggrandisement
BR ˌsɛlfəˈɡrandɪzm(ə)nt
AM ˈsɛlfəˈɡrænˌdaɪzmənt

self-aggrandising
BR ˌsɛlfəˈɡrandʌɪzɪŋ
AM ˈsɛlfəˈɡrænˌdaɪzɪŋ

self-aggrandizement
BR ˌsɛlfəˈɡrandɪzm(ə)nt
AM ˈsɛlfəˈɡrænˌdaɪzmənt

self-aggrandizing
BR ˌsɛlfəˈɡrandʌɪzɪŋ
AM ˈsɛlfəˈɡrænˌdaɪzɪŋ

self-analysing
BR ˌsɛlfˈanəlʌɪzɪŋ, ˌsɛlfˈanl̩ʌɪzɪŋ
AM ˈsɛlfˈænəˌlaɪzɪŋ

self-analysis
BR ˌsɛlfəˈnalɪsɪs
AM ˈsɛlfəˈnæləsəs

self-appointed
BR ˌsɛlfəˈpɔɪntɨd
AM ˈsɛlfəˈpɔɪn(t)ɨd

self-appreciation
BR ˌsɛlfəˌpriːʃɪˈeɪʃn, ˌsɛlfəˌpriːsɪˈeɪʃn
AM ˈsɛlfəˌpriʃiˈeɪʃən, ˈsɛlfəˌprisiˈeɪʃən

self-approbation
BR ˌsɛlfaprəˈbeɪʃn
AM ˈsɛlfˌæprəˈbeɪʃən

self-approval
BR ˌsɛlfəˈpruːvl
AM ˈsɛlfəˈpruvəl

self-assembly
BR ˌsɛlfəˈsɛmbli
AM ˈsɛlfəˈsɛmbli

self-asserting
BR ˌsɛlfəˈsəːtɪŋ
AM ˈsɛlfəˈsərdɪŋ

self-assertion
BR ˌsɛlfəˈsəːʃn
AM ˈsɛlfəˈsərʃən

self-assertive
BR ˌsɛlfəˈsəːtɪv
AM ˈsɛlfəˈsərdɪv

self-assertiveness
BR ˌsɛlfəˈsəːtɨvnɨs
AM ˈsɛlfəˈsərdɪvnɨs

self-assurance
BR ˌsɛlfəˈʃʊərəns, ˌsɛlfəˈʃʊərn̩s, ˌsɛlfəˈʃɔːrəns, ˌsɛlfəˈʃɔːrn̩s
AM ˈsɛlfəˈʃʊrəns

self-assured
BR ˌsɛlfəˈʃʊəd, ˌsɛlfəˈʃɔːd
AM ˈsɛlfəˈʃʊ(ə)rd

self-assuredly
BR ˌsɛlfəˈʃʊədli, ˌsɛlfəˈʃɔːdli
AM ˈsɛlfəˈʃʊr(ə)dli

self-aware
BR ˌsɛlfəˈwɛː(r)
AM ˈsɛlfəˈwɛ(ə)r

self-awareness
BR ˌsɛlfəˈwɛːnəs
AM ˈsɛlfəˈwɛrnəs

self-begotten
BR ˌsɛlfbɪˈɡɒtn
AM ˈsɛlfbəˈɡɑtn

self-betrayal
BR ˌsɛlfbɪˈtreɪəl
AM ˈsɛlfbəˈtreɪəl

self-binder
BR ˌsɛlfˈbʌɪndə(r), -z
AM ˈsɛlfˈbaɪndər, -z

self-born
BR ˌsɛlfˈbɔːn
AM ˈsɛlfˈbɔ(ə)rn

self-catering
BR ˌsɛlfˈkeɪt(ə)rɪŋ
AM ˈsɛlfˈkeɪdərɪŋ, ˈsɛlfˈkeɪtrɪŋ

self-censorship
BR ˌsɛlfˈsɛnsəʃɪp
AM ˈsɛlfˈsɛnsərˌʃɪp

self-centered
BR ˌsɛlfˈsɛntəd

AM ˈsɛlfˈsɛn(t)ərd

self-centeredly
BR ˌsɛlfˈsɛntədli
AM ˈsɛlfˈsɛn(t)ərdli

self-centeredness
BR ˌsɛlfˈsɛntədnəs
AM ˈsɛlfˈsɛn(t)ərdnəs

self-centred
BR ˌsɛlfˈsɛntəd
AM ˈsɛlfˈsɛn(t)ərd

self-centredly
BR ˌsɛlfˈsɛntədli
AM ˈsɛlfˈsɛn(t)ərdli

self-centredness
BR ˌsɛlfˈsɛntədnəs
AM ˈsɛlfˈsɛn(t)ərdnəs

self-certification
BR ˌsɛlfˌsəːtɪfɪˈkeɪʃn
AM ˈsɛlfˌsərdəfəˈkeɪʃən

self-certify
BR ˌsɛlfˈsəːtɪfʌɪ, -z, -ɪŋ, -d
AM ˈsɛlfˈsərdəˌfaɪ, -z, -ɪŋ, -d

self-cleaning
BR ˌsɛlfˈkliːnɪŋ
AM ˈsɛlfˈklinɪŋ

self-closing
BR ˌsɛlfˈkləʊzɪŋ
AM ˈsɛlfˈkloʊzɪŋ

self-cocking
BR ˌsɛlfˈkɒkɪŋ
AM ˈsɛlfˈkɑkɪŋ

self-collected
BR ˌsɛlfkəˈlɛktɪd
AM ˈsɛlfkəˈlɛktəd

self-colored
BR ˌsɛlfˈkʌləd
AM ˈsɛlfˈkələrd

self-coloured
BR ˌsɛlfˈkʌləd
AM ˈsɛlfˈkələrd

self-command
BR ˌsɛlfkəˈmɑːnd
AM ˈsɛlfkəˈmænd

self-communion
BR ˌsɛlfkəˈmjuːnɪən
AM ˈsɛlfkəˈmjuniən

self-conceit
BR ˌsɛlfkənˈsiːt, -ɪd
AM ˈsɛlfkənˈsit, -ɪd

self-condemnation
BR ˌsɛlfˌkɒndɛmˈneɪʃn
AM ˈsɛlfˌkɑnˌdɛmˈneɪʃən

self-condemned
BR ˌsɛlfkənˈdɛmd
AM ˈsɛlfkənˈdɛmd

self-confessed
BR ˌsɛlfkənˈfɛst
AM ˈsɛlfkənˈfɛst

self-confidence
BR ˌsɛlfˈkɒnfɪd(ə)ns
AM ˈsɛlfˈkɑnfədns

self-confident
BR ˌsɛlfˈkɒnfɪd(ə)nt
AM ˈsɛlfˈkɑnfədnt

self-confidently
BR ˌsɛlfˈkɒnfɪd(ə)ntli
AM ˈsɛlfˈkɑnfəd(ə)n(t)li

self-congratulation
BR ˌsɛlfkənˌgratʃʊˈleɪʃn, ˌsɛlfkəŋˌgratʃʊˈleɪʃn, ˌsɛlfkənˌgratjʊˈleɪʃn, ˌsɛlfkəŋˌgratjʊˈleɪʃn
AM ˈsɛlfkəŋˌgrætʃəˈleɪʃən

self-congratulatory
BR ˌsɛlfkənˌgratʃʊˈleɪt(ə)ri, ˌsɛlfkəŋˌgratʃʊˈleɪt(ə)ri, ˌsɛlfkənˌgratjʊˈleɪt(ə)ri, ˌsɛlfkəŋˌgratjʊˈleɪt(ə)ri, ˌsɛlfkənˈgratʃʊlət(ə)ri, ˌsɛlfkəŋˈgratʃʊlət(ə)ri, ˌsɛlfkənˈgratjʊlət(ə)ri, ˌsɛlfkəŋˈgratjʊlət(ə)ri
AM ˈsɛlfkəŋˈgrætʃ(ə)ləˌtɔri

self-conquest
BR ˌsɛlfˈkɒŋkwɛst
AM ˈsɛlfˈkɑnkwəst

self-conscious
BR ˌsɛlfˈkɒnʃəs
AM ˈsɛlfˈkɑnʃəs

self-consciously
BR ˌsɛlfˈkɒnʃəsli
AM ˈsɛlfˈkɑnʃəsli

self-consciousness
BR ˌsɛlfˈkɒnʃəsnəs
AM ˈsɛlfˈkɑnʃəsnəs

self-consistency
BR ˌsɛlfkənˈsɪst(ə)nsi
AM ˈsɛlfkənˈsɪstənsi

self-consistent
BR ˌsɛlfkənˈsɪst(ə)nt
AM ˈsɛlfkənˈsɪstənt

self-constituted
BR ˌsɛlfˈkɒnstɪtjuːtɪd, ˌsɛlfˈkɒnstɪtʃuːtɪd
AM ˈsɛlfˈkɑnstəˌt(j)udəd

self-contained
BR ˌsɛlfkənˈteɪnd
AM ˈsɛlfkənˈteɪnd

self-containment
BR ˌsɛlfkənˈteɪnm(ə)nt
AM ˈsɛlfkənˈteɪnmənt

self-contempt
BR ˌsɛlfkənˈtɛm(p)t
AM ˈsɛlfkənˈtɛm(p)t

self-contemptuous
BR ˌsɛlfkənˈtɛm(p)tjʊəs, ˌsɛlfkənˈtɛm(p)tʃʊəs
AM ˈsɛlfkənˈtɛm(pt)ʃ(əw)əs

self-content
BR ˌsɛlfkənˈtɛnt
AM ˈsɛlfkənˈtɛnt

self-contented
BR ˌsɛlfkənˈtɛntɪd
AM ˈsɛlfkənˈtɛn(t)əd

self-contradiction
BR ˌsɛlfkɒntrəˈdɪkʃn, -z
AM ˈsɛlfˌkɑntrəˈdɪkʃən, -z

self-contradictory
BR ˌsɛlfkɒntrəˈdɪkt(ə)ri
AM ˈsɛlfˌkɑntrəˈdɪkt(ə)ri

self-control
BR ˌsɛlfkənˈtrəʊl
AM ˈsɛlfkənˈtroʊl

self-controlled
BR ˌsɛlfkənˈtrəʊld
AM ˈsɛlfkənˈtroʊld

self-convicted
BR ˌsɛlfkənˈvɪktɪd
AM ˈsɛlfkənˈvɪktɪd

self-correcting
BR ˌsɛlfkəˈrɛktɪŋ
AM ˈsɛlfkəˈrɛktɪŋ

self-created
BR ˌsɛlfkrɪˈeɪtɪd
AM ˈsɛlfkriˈeɪdɪd

self-creation
BR ˌsɛlfkrɪˈeɪʃn
AM ˈsɛlfkriˈeɪʃən

self-critical
BR ˌsɛlfˈkrɪtɪkl
AM ˈsɛlfˈkrɪdəkəl

self-criticism
BR ˌsɛlfˈkrɪtɪsɪz(ə)m
AM ˈsɛlfˈkrɪdəˌsɪzəm

self-deceit
BR ˌsɛlfdɪˈsiːt
AM ˈsɛlfdəˈsit

self-deceiver
BR ˌsɛlfdɪˈsiːvə(r), -z
AM ˈsɛlfdəˈsivər, -z

self-deceiving
BR ˌsɛlfdɪˈsiːvɪŋ
AM ˈsɛlfdəˈsivɪŋ

self-deception
BR ˌsɛlfdɪˈsɛpʃn
AM ˈsɛlfdəˈsɛpʃən

self-deceptive
BR ˌsɛlfdɪˈsɛptɪv
AM ˈsɛlfdəˈsɛptɪv

self-defeating
BR ˌsɛlfdɪˈfiːtɪŋ
AM ˈsɛlfdəˈfidɪŋ

self-defence
BR ˌsɛlfdɪˈfɛns
AM ˈsɛlfdəˈfɛns, ˈsɛlfdiˈfɛns

self-defense
BR ˌsɛlfdɪˈfɛns
AM ˈsɛlfdəˈfɛns, ˈsɛlfdiˈfɛns

self-defensive
BR ˌsɛlfdɪˈfɛnsɪv
AM ˈsɛlfdəˈfɛnsɪv, ˈsɛlfdiˈfɛnsɪv

self-delight
BR ˌsɛlfdɪˈlʌɪt
AM ˈsɛlfdəˈlaɪt, ˈsɛlfdiˈlaɪt

self-delusion
BR ˌsɛlfdɪˈl(j)uːʒn, -z
AM ˈsɛlfdəˈluʒən, -z

self-denial
BR ˌsɛlfdɪˈnʌɪəl
AM ˈsɛlfdəˈnaɪəl, ˈsɛlfdiˈnaɪəl

self-denying
BR ˌsɛlfdɪˈnʌɪɪŋ
AM ˈsɛlfdəˈnaɪɪŋ, ˈsɛlfdiˈnaɪɪŋ

self-dependence
BR ˌsɛlfdɪˈpɛnd(ə)ns
AM ˈsɛlfdəˈpɛndns, ˈsɛlfdiˈpɛndns

self-dependent
BR ˌsɛlfdɪˈpɛnd(ə)nt
AM ˈsɛlfdəˈpɛndnt, ˈsɛlfdiˈpɛndnt

self-deprecating
BR ˌsɛlfˈdɛprɪkeɪtɪŋ
AM ˈsɛlfˈdɛprəˌkeɪdɪŋ

self-deprecatingly
BR ˌsɛlfˈdɛprɪkeɪtɪŋli
AM ˈsɛlfˈdɛprəˌkeɪdɪŋli

self-deprecation
BR ˌsɛlfdɛprɪˈkeɪʃn
AM ˈsɛlfˌdɛprəˈkeɪʃən

self-despair
BR ˌsɛlfdɪˈspɛː(r)
AM ˈsɛlfdəˈspɛ(ə)r, ˈsɛlfdiˈspɛ(ə)r

self-destroying
BR ˌsɛlfdɪˈstrɔɪɪŋ
AM ˈsɛlfdəˈstrɔɪɪŋ, ˈsɛlfdiˈstrɔɪɪŋ

self-destruct
BR ˌsɛlfdɪˈstrʌkt, -s, -ɪŋ, -ɪd
AM ˈsɛlfdəˈstrək|(t), ˈsɛlfdiˈstrək|(t), -(t)s, -tɪŋ, -təd

self-destruction
BR ˌsɛlfdɪˈstrʌkʃn
AM ˈsɛlfdəˈstrəkʃən, ˈsɛlfdiˈstrəkʃən

self-destructive
BR ˌsɛlfdɪˈstrʌktɪv
AM ˈsɛlfdəˈstrəktɪv, ˈsɛlfdiˈstrəktɪv

self-destructively
BR ˌsɛlfdɪˈstrʌktɪvli
AM ˈsɛlfdəˈstrəktɪvli, ˈsɛlfdiˈstrəktɪvli

self-determination
BR ˌsɛlfdɪˌtəːmɪˈneɪʃn

AM ˈsɛlfdəˌtərməˈneɪʃən, ˈsɛlfdiˌtərməˈneɪʃən

self-determined
BR ˌsɛlfdɪˈtəːmɪnd
AM ˈsɛlfdəˈtərmənd, ˈsɛlfdiˈtərmənd

self-determining
BR ˌsɛlfdɪˈtəːmɪnɪŋ
AM ˈsɛlfdəˈtərmənɪŋ, ˈsɛlfdiˈtərmənɪŋ

self-development
BR ˌsɛlfdɪˈvɛləpm(ə)nt
AM ˈsɛlfdəˈvɛləpmənt, ˈsɛlfdiˈvɛləpmənt

self-devotion
BR ˌsɛlfdɪˈvəʊʃn
AM ˈsɛlfdəˈvoʊʃən, ˈsɛlfdiˈvoʊʃən

self-discipline
BR ˌsɛlfˈdɪsɪplɪn, -d
AM ˈsɛlfˈdɪsəplən, -d

self-discovery
BR ˌsɛlfdɪˈskʌv(ə)ri
AM ˈsɛlfdəˈskəv(ə)ri

self-disgust
BR ˌsɛlfdɪsˈɡʌst, ˌsɛlfdɪzˈɡʌst
AM ˈsɛlfdɪsˈɡəst, ˈsɛlfdəˈzɡəst

self-doubt
BR ˌsɛlfˈdaʊt
AM ˈsɛlfˈdaʊt

self-drive
BR ˌsɛlfˈdrʌɪv
AM ˈsɛlfˌdraɪv

self-educated
BR ˌsɛlfˈɛdjʊkeɪtɪd, ˌsɛlfˈɛdʒʊkeɪtɪd
AM ˈsɛlfˈɛdʒəˌkeɪdɪd

self-education
BR ˌsɛlfɛdjʊˈkeɪʃn, ˌsɛlfɛdʒʊˈkeɪʃn
AM ˈsɛlfˌɛdʒəˈkeɪʃən

self-effacement
BR ˌsɛlfɪˈfeɪsm(ə)nt
AM ˈsɛlfəˈfeɪsmənt

self-effacing
BR ˌsɛlfɪˈfeɪsɪŋ
AM ˈsɛlfəˈfeɪsɪŋ

self-effacingly
BR ˌsɛlfɪˈfeɪsɪŋli
AM ˈsɛlfəˈfeɪsɪŋli

self-elective
BR ˌsɛlfɪˈlɛktɪv
AM ˈsɛlfəˈlɛktɪv

self-employed
BR ˌsɛlfɪmˈplɔɪd, ˌsɛlfɛmˈplɔɪd
AM ˈsɛlfəmˈplɔɪd

self-employment
BR ˌsɛlfɪmˈplɔɪm(ə)nt, ˌsɛlfɛmˈplɔɪm(ə)nt
AM ˈsɛlfəmˈplɔɪmənt

self-esteem
BR ˌsɛlfɪˈstiːm
AM ˈsɛlfəˈstim

self-evidence
BR ˌsɛlfˈɛvɪd(ə)ns
AM ˈsɛlfˈɛvədns

self-evident
BR ˌsɛlfˈɛvɪd(ə)nt
AM ˈsɛlfˈɛvədnt

self-evidently
BR ˌsɛlfˈɛvɪd(ə)ntli
AM ˈsɛlfˈɛvədən(t)li

self-examination
BR ˌsɛlfɪɡˌzamɪˈneɪʃn, ˌsɛlfɛɡˌzamɪˈneɪʃn
AM ˈsɛlfɪɡˌzæməˈneɪʃən, ˈsɛlfɛɡˌzæməˈneɪʃən

self-executing
BR ˌsɛlfˈɛksɪkjuːtɪŋ
AM ˈsɛlfˈɛksəˌkjudɪŋ

self-existent
BR ˌsɛlfɪɡˈzɪst(ə)nt, ˌsɛlfɛɡˈzɪst(ə)nt
AM ˈsɛlfɪɡˈzɪstənt, ˈsɛlfɛɡˈzɪstənt

self-explanatory
BR ˌsɛlfɪkˈsplanət(ə)ri, ˌsɛlfɛkˈsplanət(ə)ri
AM ˈsɛlfɛkˈsplænəˌtɔri, ˈsɛlfəkˈsplænəˌtɔri

self-expression
BR ˌsɛlfɪkˈsprɛʃn, ˌsɛlfɛkˈsprɛʃn
AM ˈsɛlfɛkˈsprɛʃən, ˈsɛlfəkˈsprɛʃən

self-expressive
BR ˌsɛlfɪkˈsprɛsɪv, ˌsɛlfɛkˈsprɛsɪv
AM ˈsɛlfɛkˈsprɛsɪv, ˈsɛlfəkˈsprɛsɪv

self-faced
BR ˌsɛlfˈfeɪst
AM ˈsɛlfˈfeɪst

self-feeder
BR ˌsɛlfˈfiːdə(r), -z
AM ˈsɛlfˈfidər, -z

self-feeding
BR ˌsɛlfˈfiːdɪŋ
AM ˈsɛlfˈfidɪŋ

self-fertile
BR ˌsɛlfˈfəːtʌɪl
AM ˈsɛlfˈfərdl

self-fertilisation
BR ˌsɛl(f)fəːtɪlʌɪˈzeɪʃn, ˌsɛl(f)fəːtl̩ʌɪˈzeɪʃn
AM ˈsɛl(f)ˌfərdl̩əˈzeɪʃən, ˈsɛl(f)ˌfərdlˌaɪˈzeɪʃən

self-fertilised
BR ˌsɛlfˈfəːtɪlʌɪzd, ˌsɛlfˈfəːtl̩ʌɪzd
AM ˈsɛl(f)ˈfərdlˌaɪzd

self-fertilising
BR ˌsɛlfˈfəːtɪlʌɪzɪŋ, ˌsɛlfˈfəːtl̩ʌɪzɪŋ
AM ˈsɛl(f)ˈfərdlˌaɪzɪŋ

self-fertility
BR ˌsɛl(f)fəːˈtɪlɪti, ˌsɛl(f)fəˈtɪlɪti
AM ˌsɛl(f)fərˈtɪlɪdi

self-fertilization
BR ˌsɛl(f)fəːtɪlʌɪˈzeɪʃn, ˌsɛl(f)fəːtl̩ʌɪˈzeɪʃn
AM ˈsɛl(f)ˌfərdl̩əˈzeɪʃən, ˈsɛl(f)ˌfərdlˌaɪˈzeɪʃən

self-fertilized
BR ˌsɛlfˈfəːtɪlʌɪzd, ˌsɛlfˈfəːtl̩ʌɪzd
AM ˈsɛl(f)ˈfərdlˌaɪzd

self-fertilizing
BR ˌsɛlfˈfəːtɪlʌɪzɪŋ, ˌsɛlfˈfəːtl̩ʌɪzɪŋ
AM ˈsɛl(f)ˈfərdlˌaɪzɪŋ

self-finance
BR ˌsɛlfˈfʌɪnans, ˌsɛl(f)fʌɪˈnans, ˌsɛl(f)fɪˈnans, -ɪz, -ɪŋ, -t
AM ˈsɛl(f)ˈfaɪˌnæns, ˈsɛl(f)fɪˈnæns, -əz, -ɪŋ, -t

self-flattering
BR ˌsɛlfˈflat(ə)rɪŋ
AM ˈsɛl(f)ˈflædərɪŋ

self-flattery
BR ˌsɛlfˈflat(ə)ri
AM ˈsɛl(f)ˈflædəri

self-forgetful
BR ˌsɛl(f)fəˈɡɛtf(ʊ)l
AM ˈsɛl(f)fərˈɡɛtfəl

self-forgetfulness
BR ˌsɛl(f)fəˈɡɛtf(ʊ)lnəs
AM ˈsɛl(f)fərˈɡɛtfəlnəs

self-fulfilling
BR ˌsɛl(f)fʊlˈfɪlɪŋ
AM ˈsɛlf(f)ə(l)ˈfɪlɪŋ

self-fulfillment
BR ˌsɛl(f)fʊlˈfɪlm(ə)nt
AM ˈsɛlf(f)ə(l)ˈfɪlmənt

self-fulfilment
BR ˌsɛl(f)fʊlˈfɪlm(ə)nt
AM ˈsɛlf(f)ə(l)ˈfɪlmənt

self-generating
BR ˌsɛlfˈdʒɛnəreɪtɪŋ
AM ˈsɛlfˈdʒɛnəˌreɪdɪŋ

self-glorification
BR ˌsɛlfˌɡlɔːrɪfɪˈkeɪʃn
AM ˈsɛlfˌɡlɔrəfəˈkeɪʃən

self-governed
BR ˌsɛlfˈɡʌvənd
AM ˈsɛlfˈɡəvərnd

self-governing
BR ˌsɛlfˈɡʌvənɪŋ, ˌsɛlfˈɡʌvn̩ɪŋ
AM ˌsɛlfˈɡəvərnɪŋ

self-government
BR ˌsɛlfˈɡʌvnm(ə)nt, ˌsɛlfˈɡʌvəm(ə)nt
AM sɛlfˈɡəvər(n)mənt, + ˈɡəvə(r)mənt

self-gratification
BR ˌsɛlfˌɡratɪfɪˈkeɪʃn
AM ˈsɛlfˌɡrædəfəˈkeɪʃən

self-gratifying
BR ˌsɛlfˈɡratɪfʌɪɪŋ
AM ˈsɛlfˈɡrædəˌfaɪɪŋ

self-hate
BR ˌsɛlfˈheɪt
AM ˈsɛlfˈheɪt

self-hatred
BR ˌsɛlfˈheɪtrɪd
AM ˈsɛlfˈheɪtrəd

self-heal
BR ˌsɛlfˈhiːl, -z
AM ˈsɛlfˈhil, -z

self-help
BR ˌsɛlfˈhɛlp
AM ˈsɛlfˌhɛlp

selfhood
BR ˈsɛlfhʊd
AM ˈsɛlfˌ(h)ʊd

self-image
BR ˌsɛlfˈɪm|ɪdʒ, -ɪdʒɪz
AM ˈsɛlfˈɪmɪdʒ, -ɪz

self-immolating
BR ˌsɛlfˈɪməleɪtɪŋ
AM ˈsɛlfˈɪməˌleɪdɪŋ

self-immolation
BR ˌsɛlfɪməˈleɪʃn
AM ˈsɛlfˌɪməˈleɪʃən

self-importance
BR ˌsɛlfɪmˈpɔːt(ə)ns
AM ˈsɛlfəmˈpɔrtns

self-important
BR ˌsɛlfɪmˈpɔːt(ə)nt
AM ˈsɛlfəmˈpɔrtnt

self-importantly
BR ˌsɛlfɪmˈpɔːt(ə)ntli
AM ˈsɛlfəmˈpɔrtn(t)li

self-imposed
BR ˌsɛlfɪmˈpəʊzd
AM ˈsɛlfəmˈpoʊzd

self-improvement
BR ˌsɛlfɪmˈpruːvm(ə)nt
AM ˈsɛlfəmˈpruvmənt

self-induced
BR ˌsɛlfɪnˈdjuːst, ˌsɛlfɪnˈdʒuːst
AM ˈsɛlfənˈd(j)ust

self-inductance
BR ˌsɛlfɪnˈdʌkt(ə)ns
AM ˈsɛlfənˈdəktns

self-induction
BR ˌsɛlfɪnˈdʌkʃn
AM ˈsɛlfənˈdəkʃən

self-inductive
BR ˌsɛlfɪnˈdʌktɪv
AM ˈsɛlfənˈdəktɪv

self-indulgence
BR ˌsɛlfɪnˈdʌldʒ(ə)ns
AM ˈsɛlfənˈdəldʒəns

self-indulgent
BR ˌsɛlfɪnˈdʌldʒ(ə)nt
AM ˈsɛlfənˈdəldʒənt

self-indulgently
BR ˌsɛlfɪnˈdʌldʒ(ə)ntli
AM ˈsɛlfənˈdəldʒən(t)li

self-inflicted
BR ˌsɛlfɪnˈflɪktɪd
AM ˈsɛlfənˈflɪktɪd

self-insurance
BR ˌsɛlfɪnˈʃʊərəns, ˌsɛlfɪnˈʃʊərn̩s, ˌsɛlfɪnˈʃɔːrəns, ˌsɛlfɪnˈʃɔːrn̩s

AM ˌsɛlfən'ʃʊrəns

self-insured
BR ˌsɛlfɪn'ʃʊəd, ˌsɛlfɪn'ʃɔːd
AM ˌsɛlfən'ʃʊ(ə)rd

self-interest
BR ˌsɛlf'ɪntrɪst, ˌsɛlf'ɪnt(ə)rɛst
AM sɛlf'ɪn(t)ərəst, sɛlf'ɪntrəst

self-interested
BR ˌsɛlf'ɪntrɪstɪd, ˌsɛlf'ɪnt(ə)rɛstɪd
AM sɛlf'ɪn(t)ərəstəd, sɛlf'ɪntrəstəd

self-involvement
BR ˌsɛlfɪn'vɒlvm(ə)nt
AM ¦sɛlfən'vɔlvmənt, ¦sɛlfən'vɑlvmənt

selfish
BR 'sɛlfɪʃ
AM 'sɛlfɪʃ

selfishly
BR 'sɛlfɪʃli
AM 'sɛlfɪʃli

selfishness
BR 'sɛlfɪʃnɪs
AM 'sɛlfɪʃnɪs

self-justification
BR ˌsɛlfˌdʒʌstɪfɪ'keɪʃn
AM ¦sɛlfˌdʒəstəfə'keɪʃən

self-justifying
BR ˌsɛlf'dʒʌstɪfʌɪɪŋ
AM ¦sɛlf'dʒəstəˌfaɪɪŋ

self-knowledge
BR ˌsɛlf'nɒlɪdʒ
AM ¦sɛlf'nɑlɪdʒ

selfless
BR 'sɛlfləs
AM 'sɛlfləs

selflessly
BR 'sɛlfləsli
AM 'sɛlfləsli

selflessness
BR 'sɛlfləsnəs
AM 'sɛlfləsnəs

self-loader
BR ˌsɛlf'ləʊdə(r), -z
AM ¦sɛlf'loʊdər, -z

self-loading
BR ˌsɛlf'ləʊdɪŋ
AM ¦sɛlf'loʊdɪŋ

self-locking
BR ˌsɛlf'lɒkɪŋ
AM ¦sɛlf'lɑkɪŋ

self-love
BR ˌsɛlf'lʌv
AM ¦sɛlf'ləv

self-made
BR ˌsɛlf'meɪd
AM ¦sɛlf'meɪd

self-mastery
BR ˌsɛlf'mɑːst(ə)ri, ˌsɛlf'mast(ə)ri
AM ¦sɛlf'mæst(ə)ri

selfmate
BR ˌsɛlf'meɪt, -s
AM ¦sɛlf'meɪt, -s

self-mocking
BR ˌsɛlf'mɒkɪŋ
AM ¦sɛlf'mɑkɪŋ

self-motion
BR ˌsɛlf'məʊʃn
AM ¦sɛlf'moʊʃən

self-motivated
BR ˌsɛlf'məʊtɪveɪtɪd
AM ¦sɛlf'moʊdəˌveɪdɪd

self-motivation
BR ˌsɛlfməʊtɪ'veɪʃn
AM ¦sɛlfˌmoʊdə'veɪʃən

self-moving
BR ˌsɛlf'muːvɪŋ
AM ¦sɛlf'muvɪŋ

self-murder
BR ˌsɛlf'məːdə(r)
AM ¦sɛlf'mərdər

self-murderer
BR ˌsɛlf'məːd(ə)rə(r), -z
AM ¦sɛlf'mərd(ə)rər, -z

self-mutilation
BR ˌsɛlfmjuːtɪ'leɪʃn, -z
AM ¦sɛlfˌmjudə'leɪʃən, -z

self-neglect
BR ˌsɛlfnɪ'glɛkt
AM ¦sɛlfnə'glɛk(t)

selfness
BR 'sɛlfnəs
AM 'sɛlfnəs

self-obsessed
BR ˌsɛlfəb'sɛst
AM 'sɛlfəb'sɛst

self-opinion
BR ˌsɛlfə'pɪnjən
AM ¦sɛlfə'pɪnjən

self-opinionated
BR ˌsɛlfə'pɪnjəneɪtɪd
AM ¦sɛlfə'pɪnjəˌneɪdɪd

self-parody
BR ˌsɛlf'parədi
AM ¦sɛlf'pɛrədi

self-perpetuating
BR ˌsɛlfpə'pɛtʃʊeɪtɪŋ, ˌsɛlfpə'pɛtjʊeɪtɪŋ
AM ¦sɛlfpər'pɛtʃəˌweɪdɪŋ

self-perpetuation
BR ˌsɛlfpəˌpɛtʃʊ'eɪʃn, ˌsɛlfpəˌpɛtjʊ'eɪʃn
AM ¦sɛlfpərˌpɛtʃə'weɪʃən

self-pity
BR ˌsɛlf'pɪti
AM ¦sɛlf'pɪdi

self-pitying
BR ˌsɛlf'pɪtɪɪŋ
AM ¦sɛlf'pɪdiɪŋ

self-pityingly
BR ˌsɛlf'pɪtɪɪŋli
AM ¦sɛlf'pɪdiɪŋli

self-pollinated
BR ˌsɛlf'pɒlɪneɪtɪd
AM ¦sɛlf'pɑləˌneɪdɪd

self-pollinating
BR ˌsɛlf'pɒlɪneɪtɪŋ
AM ¦sɛlf'pɑləˌneɪdɪŋ

self-pollination
BR ˌsɛlfpɒlɪ'neɪʃn
AM ¦sɛlfˌpɑlə'neɪʃən

self-pollinator
BR ˌsɛlf'pɒlɪneɪtə(r), -z
AM ¦sɛlf'pɑləˌneɪdər, -z

self-portrait
BR ˌsɛlf'pɔːtreɪt, ˌsɛlf'pɔːtrɪt, -s
AM ¦sɛlf'pɔrtrət, -s

self-possessed
BR ˌsɛlfpə'zɛst
AM ¦sɛlfpə'zɛst

self-possession
BR ˌsɛlfpə'zɛʃn
AM ¦sɛlfpə'zɛʃən

self-praise
BR ˌsɛlf'preɪz
AM ¦sɛlf'preɪz

self-preservation
BR ˌsɛlfprɛzə'veɪʃn
AM ¦sɛlfˌprɛzər'veɪʃən

self-proclaimed
BR ˌsɛlfprə'kleɪmd
AM ¦sɛlfprə'kleɪmd

self-propagating
BR ˌsɛlf'prɒpəgeɪtɪŋ
AM ¦sɛlf'prɑpəˌgeɪdɪŋ

self-propelled
BR ˌsɛlfprə'pɛld
AM ¦sɛlfprə'pɛld

self-propelling
BR ˌsɛlfprə'pɛlɪŋ
AM ¦sɛlfprə'pɛlɪŋ

self-protection
BR ˌsɛlfprə'tɛkʃn
AM ¦sɛlfprə'tɛkʃən

self-protective
BR ˌsɛlfprə'tɛktɪv
AM ¦sɛlfprə'tɛktɪv

self-raising
BR ˌsɛlf'reɪzɪŋ
AM ¦sɛlf'reɪzɪŋ

self-realisation
BR ˌsɛlfˌrɪəlʌɪ'zeɪʃn
AM ¦sɛlfˌri(ə)lə'zeɪʃən, ¦sɛlfˌriəˌlaɪ'zeɪʃən

self-realization
BR ˌsɛlfˌrɪəlʌɪ'zeɪʃn
AM ¦sɛlfˌri(ə)lə'zeɪʃən, ¦sɛlfˌriəˌlaɪ'zeɪʃən

self-recording
BR ˌsɛlfrɪ'kɔːdɪŋ
AM ¦sɛlfrə'kɔrdɪŋ

self-regard
BR ˌsɛlfrɪ'gɑːd
AM ¦sɛlfrə'gɑrd

self-regarding
BR ˌsɛlfrɪ'gɑːdɪŋ
AM ¦sɛlfrə'gɑrdɪŋ

self-registering
BR ˌsɛlf'rɛdʒɪst(ə)rɪŋ
AM ¦sɛlf'rɛdʒəst(ə)rɪŋ

self-regulating
BR ˌsɛlf'rɛgjʉleɪtɪŋ
AM ¦sɛlf'rɛgjəˌleɪdɪŋ

self-regulation
BR ˌsɛlfrɛgjʉ'leɪʃn
AM ¦sɛlfˌrɛgjə'leɪʃən

self-regulatory
BR ˌsɛlf'rɛgjʉlət(ə)ri
AM ¦sɛlf'rɛgjələˌtɔri

self-reliance
BR ˌsɛlfrɪ'lʌɪəns
AM ¦sɛlfrə'laɪəns, ¦sɛlfri'laɪəns

self-reliant
BR ˌsɛlfrɪ'lʌɪənt
AM ¦sɛlfrə'laɪənt, ¦sɛlfri'laɪənt

self-reliantly
BR ˌsɛlfrɪ'lʌɪəntli
AM ¦sɛlfrə'laɪən(t)li, ¦sɛlfri'laɪən(t)li

self-renewal
BR ˌsɛlfrɪ'njʊəl
AM ¦sɛlfrə'njʊəl, ¦sɛlfri'njʊəl

self-renunciation
BR ˌsɛlfrɪˌnʌnsɪ'eɪʃn
AM ¦sɛlfrəˌnənsi'eɪʃən, ¦sɛlfriˌnənsi'eɪʃən

self-reproach
BR ˌsɛlfrɪ'prəʊtʃ
AM ¦sɛlfrə'proʊtʃ, ¦sɛlfri'proʊtʃ

self-reproachful
BR ˌsɛlfrɪ'prəʊtʃf(ʉ)l
AM ¦sɛlfrə'proʊtʃfəl, ¦sɛlfri'proʊtʃfəl

self-respect
BR ˌsɛlfrɪ'spɛkt
AM ¦sɛlfrə'spɛk(t), ¦sɛlfri'spɛk(t)

self-respecting
BR ˌsɛlfrɪ'spɛktɪŋ
AM ¦sɛlfrə'spɛktɪŋ, ¦sɛlfri'spɛktɪŋ

self-restrained
BR ˌsɛlfrɪ'streɪnd
AM ¦sɛlfrə'streɪnd, ¦sɛlfri'streɪnd

self-restraint
BR ˌsɛlfrɪ'streɪnt
AM ¦sɛlfrə'streɪnt, ¦sɛlfri'streɪnt

self-revealing
BR ˌsɛlfrɪ'viːlɪŋ
AM ¦sɛlfrə'vilɪŋ

self-revelation
BR ˌsɛlfrɛvə'leɪʃn
AM ¦sɛlfˌrɛvə'leɪʃən

Selfridge
BR 'sɛlfrɪdʒ
AM 'sɛlfrɪdʒ

self-righteous
BR ˌsɛlf'rʌɪtʃəs
AM ¦sɛlf'raɪtʃəs

self-righteously
BR ˌsɛlf'rʌɪtʃəsli
AM ¦sɛlf'raɪtʃəsli

self-righteousness
BR ˌsɛlfˈrʌɪtʃəsnəs
AM ˌsɛlfˈraɪtʃəsnəs
self-righting
BR ˌsɛlfˈrʌɪtɪŋ
AM ˈsɛlfˌraɪdɪŋ
self-rising
BR ˌsɛlfˈrʌɪzɪŋ
AM ˈsɛlfˈraɪzɪŋ
self-rule
BR ˌsɛlfˈruːl
AM ˈsɛlfˈrul
self-sacrifice
BR ˌsɛlfˈsakrɪfʌɪs
AM sɛlfˈsækrəˌfaɪs
self-sacrificing
BR ˌsɛlfˈsakrɪfʌɪsɪŋ
AM ˈsɛlfˈsækrəˌfaɪsɪŋ
selfsame
BR ˈsɛlfseɪm, ˌsɛlfˈseɪm
AM ˈsɛlfˌseɪm
self-satisfaction
BR ˌsɛlfsatɪsˈfakʃn
AM ˈsɛlfˌsædəsˈfækʃən
self-satisfied
BR ˌsɛlfˈsatɪsfʌɪd
AM sɛlfˈsædəˌsfaɪd
self-satisfiedly
BR ˌsɛlfˈsatɪsfʌɪdli
AM ˈsɛlfˈsædəˌsfaɪ(ə)dli
self-sealing
BR ˌsɛlfˈsiːlɪŋ
AM ˈsɛlfˈsilɪŋ
self-seed
BR ˌsɛlfˈsiːd, -z, -ɪŋ, -ɪd
AM ˈsɛlfˈsid, -z, -ɪŋ, -ɪd
self-seeker
BR ˌsɛlfˈsiːkə(r), -z
AM ˈsɛlfˌsikər, -z
self-seeking
BR ˌsɛlfˈsiːkɪŋ
AM ˈsɛlfˌsikɪŋ
self-selecting
BR ˌsɛlfsɪˈlɛktɪŋ
AM ˈsɛlfsəˈlɛktɪŋ
self-selection
BR ˌsɛlfsɪˈlɛkʃn
AM ˈsɛlfsəˈlɛkʃən
self-service
BR ˌsɛlfˈsəːvɪs
AM ˈsɛlfˈsərvəs
self-serving
BR ˌsɛlfˈsəːvɪŋ
AM ˈsɛlfˈsərvɪŋ
self-slaughter
BR ˌsɛlfˈslɔːtə(r)
AM ˈsɛlfˈslɔdər, ˈsɛlfˈslɑdər
self-sown
BR ˌsɛlfˈsəʊn
AM ˈsɛlfˈsoʊn
self-starter
BR ˌsɛlfˈstɑːtə(r), -z
AM ˈsɛlfˈstɑrdər, -z
self-sterile
BR ˌsɛlfˈstɛrʌɪl
AM ˈsɛlfˈstɛrəl
self-sterility
BR ˌsɛlfstəˈrɪlɪti
AM ˌsɛlfstəˈrɪlɪdi
self-styled
BR ˌsɛlfˈstʌɪld
AM ˈsɛlfˈstaɪld
self-sufficiency
BR ˌsɛlfsəˈfɪʃnsi
AM ˈsɛlfsəˈfɪʃənsi
self-sufficient
BR ˌsɛlfsəˈfɪʃnt
AM ˈsɛlfsəˈfɪʃənt
self-sufficiently
BR ˌsɛlfsəˈfɪʃntli
AM ˈsɛlfsəˈfɪʃən(t)li
self-sufficing
BR ˌsɛlfsəˈfʌɪsɪŋ
AM ˈsɛlfsəˈfaɪsɪŋ
self-suggestion
BR ˌsɛlfsəˈdʒɛstʃn
AM ˈsɛlfsəˈdʒɛʃtʃən, ˈsɛlfsəˈdʒɛstʃən
self-support
BR ˌsɛlfsəˈpɔːt
AM ˈsɛlfsəˈpɔ(ə)rt
self-supporting
BR ˌsɛlfsəˈpɔːtɪŋ
AM ˈsɛlfsəˈpɔrdɪŋ
self-surrender
BR ˌsɛlfsəˈrɛndə(r)
AM ˈsɛlfˌsərɛndər
self-sustained
BR ˌsɛlfsəˈsteɪnd
AM ˈsɛlfsəsˈteɪnd
self-sustaining
BR ˌsɛlfsəˈsteɪnɪŋ
AM ˈsɛlfsəsˈteɪnɪŋ
self-tapping
BR ˌsɛlfˈtapɪŋ
AM ˈsɛlfˈtæpɪŋ
self-taught
BR ˌsɛlfˈtɔːt
AM ˈsɛlfˈtɔt, ˈsɛlfˈtɑt
self-torture
BR ˌsɛlfˈtɔːtʃə(r)
AM ˈsɛlfˈtɔrtʃər
self-understanding
BR ˌsɛlfʌndəˈstandɪŋ
AM ˈsɛlfˌəndərˈstændɪŋ
self-will
BR ˌsɛlfˈwɪl
AM ˈsɛlfˈwɪl
self-willed
BR ˌsɛlfˈwɪld
AM ˈsɛlfˈwɪld
self-winding
BR ˌsɛlfˈwʌɪndɪŋ
AM ˈsɛlfˈwaɪndɪŋ
self-worth
BR ˌsɛlfˈwəːθ
AM ˈsɛlfˈwərθ
Seligman
BR ˈsɛlɪgmən
AM ˈsɛlɪgmən, ˈsilɪgmən
Seligmann
BR ˈsɛlɪgmən
AM ˈsɛlɪgmən, ˈsilɪgmən
GER ˈzeːlɪçman
Selima
BR sɪˈliːmə(r)
AM səˈlimə
Selina
BR sɪˈliːnə(r)
AM səˈlinə
Seljuk
BR sɛlˈdʒuːk, ˈsɛldʒuːk, -s
AM sɛlˈdʒuk, ˈsɛlˌdʒuk, -s
Seljukian
BR sɛlˈdʒuːkɪən, -z
AM sɛlˈdʒukiən, -z
Selkirk
BR ˈsɛlkəːk
AM ˈsɛlˌkərk
sell
BR sɛl, -z, -ɪŋ
AM sɛl, -z, -ɪŋ
sellable
BR ˈsɛləbl
AM ˈsɛləbəl
Sellafield
BR ˈsɛləfiːld
AM ˈsɛləˌfild
Sellar
BR ˈsɛlə(r)
AM ˈsɛlər
Sellars
BR ˈsɛləz
AM ˈsɛlərz
sell-by date
BR ˈsɛlbʌɪ deɪt, -s
AM ˈsɛlˌbaɪ ˌdeɪt, -s
seller
BR ˈsɛlə(r), -z
AM ˈsɛlər, -z
Sellers
BR ˈsɛləz
AM ˈsɛlərz
Sellick
BR ˈsɛlɪk
AM ˈsɛlək
sellotape®
BR ˈsɛlə(ʊ)teɪp, -s, -ɪŋ, -t
AM ˈsɛləˌteɪp, -s, -ɪŋ, -t
sellout
BR ˈsɛlaʊt, -s
AM ˈsɛlˌaʊt, -s
Selma
BR ˈsɛlmə(r)
AM ˈsɛlmə
Selous
BR səˈluː
AM səˈlu
Selsey
BR ˈsɛlsi
AM ˈsɛlsi
seltzer
BR ˈsɛltsə(r)
AM ˈsɛltsər
selvage
BR ˈsɛlv|ɪdʒ, -ɪdʒɪz
AM ˈsɛlvɪdʒ, -ɪz
Selvas
BR ˈsɛlvəs
AM ˈsɛlvəs
selvedge
BR ˈsɛlv|ɪdʒ, -ɪdʒɪz
AM ˈsɛlvɪdʒ, -ɪz
selves
BR sɛlvz
AM sɛlvz
Selwyn
BR ˈsɛlwɪn
AM ˈsɛlwən
Selznick
BR ˈsɛlznɪk
AM ˈsɛlznɪk
SEM
BR sɛm
AM sɛm
semanteme
BR sɪˈmantiːm, -z
AM səˈmænˌtim, -z
semantic
BR sɪˈmantɪk, -s
AM səˈmæn(t)ɪk, -s
semantically
BR sɪˈmantɪkli
AM səˈmæn(t)ək(ə)li
semantician
BR sɪˌmanˈtɪʃn, -z
AM səˌmænˈtɪʃn, -z
semanticise
BR sɪˈmantɪsʌɪz, -ɪz, -ɪŋ, -d
AM səˈmæn(t)əˌsaɪz, -ɪz, -ɪŋ, -d
semanticism
BR sɪˈmantɪsɪz(ə)m
AM səˈmæn(t)əˌsɪzəm
semanticist
BR sɪˈmantɪsɪst, -s
AM səˈmæn(t)əsəst, -s
semanticize
BR sɪˈmantɪsʌɪz, -ɪz, -ɪŋ, -d
AM səˈmæn(t)əˌsaɪz, -ɪz, -ɪŋ, -d
semaphore
BR ˈsɛməfɔː(r), -z, -ɪŋ, -d
AM ˈsɛməˌfɔ(ə)r, -z, -ɪŋ, -d
semaphoric
BR ˌsɛməˈfɒrɪk
AM ˌsɛməˈfɔrɪk
semaphorically
BR ˌsɛməˈfɒrɪkli
AM ˌsɛməˈfɔrək(ə)li
Semarang
BR sɪˈmɑːraŋ
AM səˈmɑˌraŋ

semasiological
BR sɪˌmeɪzɪəˈlɒdʒɪkl, sɪˌmeɪsɪəˈlɒdʒɪkl
AM səˌmeɪsiəˈlɑdʒəkəl, səˌmeɪziəˈlɑdʒəkəl

semasiology
BR sɪˌmeɪzɪˈɒlədʒi, sɪˌmeɪsɪˈɒlədʒi
AM səˌmeɪsiˈɑlədʒi, səˌmeɪziˈɑlədʒi

sematic
BR sɪˈmatɪk
AM səˈmædɪk

semblable
BR ˈsɛmbləbl, -z
AM ˈsɛmbləbəl, -z

semblance
BR ˈsɛmbl(ə)ns, -ɪz
AM ˈsɛmbləns, -əz

semé
masculine
BR ˈsɛmi, ˈsɛmeɪ
AM səˈmeɪ, ˈsɛˌmeɪ

semée
feminine
BR ˈsɛmi, ˈsɛmeɪ
AM səˈmeɪ, ˈsɛˌmeɪ

semeiology
BR ˌsɛmɪˈɒlədʒi, ˌsiːmɪˈɒlədʒi
AM ˌsiˌmiˈɑlədʒi, ˌsɛˌmiˈɑlədʒi

semeiotics
BR ˈsɛmɪˈɒtɪks, ˈsiːmɪˈɒtɪks
AM ˌsɛˌmiˈɑdɪks, ˌsiˌmiˈɑdɪks

Semele
BR ˈsɛmɨli, ˈsɛmḷi
AM ˈsɛməli

sememe
BR ˈsiːmiːm, -z
AM ˈsɛˌmim, -z

semen
BR ˈsiːmən
AM ˈsimən

Semer Water
BR ˈsɛmə ˌwɔːtə(r)
AM ˈsɛmər ˌwɔdər, + ˌwɑdər

semester
BR sɪˈmɛstə(r), -z
AM səˈmɛstər, -z

semi
BR ˈsɛm|i, -ɪz
AM ˈsɛˌmaɪ, ˈsɛmi, -z

semiaquatic
BR ˌsɛmɪəˈkwatɪk
AM ˌsɛˌmaɪəˈkwɑdɪk, ˌsɛmiəˈkwɑdɪk

semiautomatic
BR ˌsɛmɪˌɔːtəˈmatɪk, -s
AM ˌsɛˌmaɪˌɔdəˈmædɪk, ˌsɛmiˌɔdəˈmædɪk, ˌsɛˌmaɪˌɑdəˈmædɪk, ˌsɛmiˌɑdəˈmædɪk, -s

semibreve
BR ˈsɛmɪbriːv, -z
AM ˈsɛmiˌbriv, ˈsɛˌmaɪˌbriv, -z

semicircle
BR ˈsɛmɪˌsəːkl, -z
AM ˈsɛˌmaɪˌsərkəl, ˈsɛmiˌsərkəl, -z

semicircular
BR ˌsɛmɪˈsəːkjʉlə(r)
AM ˌsɛmiˈsərkjələr, ˌsɛˌmaɪˈsərkjələr

semicolon
BR ˌsɛmɪˈkəʊlən, ˌsɛmɪˈkəʊlɒn, ˈsɛmɪˌkəʊlən, ˈsɛmɪˌkəʊlɒn, -z
AM ˈsɛmiˌkoʊlən, ˈsɛmaɪˌkoʊlən, -z

semiconducting
BR ˌsɛmɪkənˈdʌktɪŋ
AM ˈsɛmikənˌdəktɪŋ, ˈsɛˌmaɪkənˌdəktɪŋ

semiconductor
BR ˈsɛmɪkənˌdʌktə(r), -z
AM ˈsɛmikənˌdəktər, ˈsɛˌmaɪkənˌdəktər, -z

semi-conscious
BR ˌsɛmɪˈkɒnʃəs
AM ˌsɛˌmaɪˈkɑnʃəs, ˌsɛmiˈkɑnʃəs

semicylinder
BR ˈsɛmɪˌsɪlɪndə(r), -z
AM ˈsɛmiˌsɪləndər, ˈsɛˌmaɪˌsɪləndər, -z

semicylindrical
BR ˌsɛmɪsɪˈlɪndrɪkl
AM ˌsɛmisəˈlɪndrɪkəl, ˌsɛˌmaɪsəˈlɪndrɪkəl

semidemisemiquaver
BR ˌsɛmɪˌdɛmɪˈsɛmɪˌkweɪvə(r), -z
AM ˌsɛmaɪˌdɛmiˈsɛmaɪˌkweɪvər, ˌsɛmiˌdɛmiˈsɛmiˌkweɪvər, -z

semidetached
BR ˌsɛmɪdɪˈtatʃt
AM ˌsɛmidəˈtætʃt, ˌsɛmidiˈtætʃt, ˌsɛˌmaɪdəˈtætʃt, ˌsɛˌmaɪdiˈtætʃt

semidiameter
BR ˌsɛmɪdʌɪˈamɪtə(r), -z
AM ˌsɛmiˌdaɪˈæmədər, ˌsɛmaɪˌdaɪˈæmədər, -z

semifinal
BR ˌsɛmɪˈfʌɪnl, ˈsɛmɪfʌɪnl, -z
AM ˌsɛˌmaɪˈfaɪnəl, ˌsɛmiˈfaɪnəl, -z

semifinalist
BR ˌsɛmɪˈfʌɪnḷɪst, ˌsɛmɪˈfʌɪnəlɪst, -s
AM ˌsɛˌmaɪˈfaɪnləst, ˌsɛmiˈfaɪnləst, -s

semigloss
BR ˈsɛmɪglɒs, -ɪz
AM ˈsɛmiˌglɔs, ˈsɛˌmaɪˌglɔs, ˈsɛmiˌglɑs, ˈsɛˌmaɪˌglɑs, -əz

Semillon
BR ˈsɛmɪjɒ̃, ˈsɛmɪlɒn, -z
AM ˈsɛmilˌjɑn, -z

seminal
BR ˈsɛmɪnl
AM ˈsɛmənəl

seminally
BR ˈsɛmɪnḷi, ˈsɛmɪnəli
AM ˈsɛm(ə)nəli

seminar
BR ˈsɛmɪnɑː(r), -z
AM ˈsɛməˌnɑr, -z

seminarian
BR ˌsɛmɪˈnɛːrɪən, -z
AM ˌsɛməˈnɛriən, -z

seminarist
BR ˈsɛmɪn(ə)rɪst, -s
AM ˈsɛməˌnɛrəst, ˈsɛmənərəst, -s

seminary
BR ˈsɛmɪn(ə)r|i, -ɪz
AM ˈsɛməˌnɛri, -z

seminiferous
BR ˌsɛmɪˈnɪf(ə)rəs
AM ˌsɛməˈnɪf(ə)rəs

Seminole
BR ˈsɛmɪnəʊl, -z
AM ˈsɛməˌnoʊl, -z

semiological
BR ˌsɛmɪəˈlɒdʒɪkl, ˌsiːmɪəˈlɒdʒɪkl
AM ˌsiˌmiəˈlɑdʒəkəl, ˌsɛˌmiəˈlɑdʒəkəl

semiologist
BR ˌsɛmɪˈɒlədʒɪst, ˌsiːmɪˈɒlədʒɪst, -s
AM ˌsiˌmiˈɑlədʒəst, ˌsɛˌmiˈɑlədʒəst, -s

semiology
BR ˌsɛmɪˈɒlədʒi, ˌsiːmɪˈɒlədʒ
AM ˌsiˌmiˈɑlədʒi, ˌsɛmiˈɑlədʒi

semiotic
BR ˌsɛmɪˈɒtɪk, ˌsiːmɪˈɒtɪk, -s
AM ˌsɛmiˈɑdɪk, ˌsimiˈɑdɪk, -s

semiotical
BR ˌsɛmɪˈɒtɪkl, ˌsiːmɪˈɒtɪkl
AM ˌsɛmiˈɑdəkəl, ˌsimiˈɑdəkəl

semiotically
BR ˌsɛmɪˈɒtɪkli, ˌsiːmɪˈɒtɪkli
AM ˌsɛmiˈɑdək(ə)li, ˌsimiˈɑdəkəli

semiotician
BR ˌsɛmɪəˈtɪʃn, ˌsiːmɪəˈtɪʃn, -z
AM ˌsɛmiəˈtɪʃən, ˌsimiəˈtɪʃən, -z

semipalmated
BR ˌsɛmɪˈpalmeɪtɪd
AM ˌsɛˌmaɪˈpælˌmeɪdɪd, ˌsɛˌmaɪˈpɑ(l)ˌmeɪdɪd, ˌsɛmiˈpælˌmeɪdɪd, ˌsɛmiˈpɑ(l)ˌmeɪdɪd

semipermeable
BR ˌsɛmɪˈpəːmɪəbl
AM ˌsɛmiˈpərmiəbəl, ˌsɛˌmaɪˈpərmiəbəl

semiprecious
BR ˌsɛmɪˈprɛʃəs
AM ˌsɛˌmaɪˈprɛʃəs, ˌsɛmiˈprɛʃəs

semiprivate
BR ˌsɛmɪˈprʌɪvɨt
AM ˌsɛmiˈpraɪvət, ˌsɛˌmaɪˈpraɪvət

semi-professional
BR ˌsɛmɪprəˈfɛʃn̩(ə)l, ˌsɛmɪprəˈfɛʃən(ə)l, -z
AM ˌsɛˌmaɪprəˈfɛʃ(ə)nəl, ˌsɛmiprəˈfɛʃ(ə)nəl, -z

semiquaver
BR ˈsɛmɪˌkweɪvə(r), -z
AM ˌsɛˌmaɪˈkweɪvər, ˌsɛmiˈkweɪvər, -z

Semiramis
BR sɛˈmɪrəmɪs, sɪˈmɪrəmɪs
AM sɛˈmɪrəməs, səˈmɪrəməs

semiretired
BR ˌsɛmɪrɪˈtʌɪəd
AM ˌsɛmirəˈtaɪ(ə)rd, ˌsɛˌmaɪrəˈtaɪ(ə)rd

semisoft
BR ˌsɛmɪˈsɒft
AM ˌsɛmiˈsɔft, ˌsɛˌmaɪˈsɔft, ˌsɛmiˈsɑft, ˌsɛˌmaɪˈsɑft

semisweet
BR ˌsɛmɪˈswiːt
AM ˌsɛmiˈswit, ˌsɛˌmaɪˈswit

Semite
BR ˈsiːmʌɪt, ˈsɛmʌɪt, -s
AM ˈsɛˌmaɪt, -s

Semitic
BR sɪˈmɪtɪk
AM səˈmɪdɪk

Semitisation
BR ˌsɛmɪtʌɪˈzeɪʃn
AM ˌsɛmədəˈzeɪʃən, ˌsɛməˌtaɪˈzeɪʃən

Semitise
BR ˈsɛmɪtʌɪz, -ɪz, -ɪŋ, -d
AM ˈsɛməˌtaɪz, -ɪz, -ɪŋ, -d

Semitism
BR ˈsɛmɪtɪz(ə)m
AM ˈsɛməˌtɪzəm

Semitist
BR ˈsɛmɪtɪst, -s

AM 'sɛmədəst, -s
Semitization
BR ˌsɛmɪtʌɪ'zeɪʃn
AM ˌsɛmədə'zeɪʃən, ˌsɛməˌtaɪ'zeɪʃən
Semitize
BR 'sɛmɪtʌɪz, -ɪz, -ɪŋ, -d
AM 'sɛməˌtaɪz, -ɪz, -ɪŋ, -d
semitone
BR 'sɛmɪtəʊn, -z
AM 'sɛmiˌtoʊn, 'sɛˌmaɪˌtoʊn, -z
semitrailer
BR 'sɛmɪˌtreɪlə(r), -z
AM ¦sɛˌmaɪ'treɪlər, ¦sɛmi'treɪlər, -z
semitropical
BR ˌsɛmɪ'trɒpɪkl
AM ¦sɛmi'trɑpəkəl, ¦sɛˌmaɪ'trɑpəkəl
semi-tropics
BR ˌsɛmɪ'trɒpɪks
AM ¦sɛmi'trɑpɪks, ¦sɛˌmaɪ'trɑpɪks
semivowel
BR 'sɛmɪˌvaʊəl, 'sɛmɪvaʊl, -z
AM ¦sɛmi'vaʊ(ə)l, ¦sɛˌmaɪ'vaʊ(ə)l, -z
semmit
BR 'sɛmɪt, -s
AM 'sɛmət, -s
semolina
BR ˌsɛmə'liːnə(r)
AM ˌsɛmə'linə
Semper
BR 'sɛmpə(r)
AM 'sɛmpər
sempervivum
BR ˌsɛmpə'vʌɪvəm
AM ˌsɛmpər'vaɪvəm
sempiternal
BR ˌsɛmpɪ'təːnl
AM ¦sɛmpə¦tərnəl
sempiternally
BR ˌsɛmpɪ'təːnəli, ˌsɛmpɪ'təːnli
AM ¦sɛmpə'tərnəli
sempiternity
BR ˌsɛmpɪ'təːnɪti
AM ˌsɛmpə'tərnədi
Semple
BR 'sɛmpl
AM 'sɛmpəl
semplice
BR 'sɛmplɪtʃi, 'sɛmplɪtʃeɪ
AM 'sɛmpləˌtʃeɪ
sempre
BR 'sɛmpreɪ
AM 'sɛmˌpreɪ
sempstress
BR 'sɛm(p)strɪs, -ɪz
AM 'sɛm(p)strəs, -əz
Semtex®
BR 'sɛmtɛks
AM 'sɛmˌtɛks
senarii
BR sɪ'nɛːrɪʌɪ
AM sə'nɛriˌaɪ, si'nɛriˌaɪ
senarius
BR sɪ'nɛːrɪəs
AM sə'nɛriəs, si'nɛriəs
senary
BR 'siːn(ə)ri, 'sɛn(ə)ri
AM 'sinəri, 'sɛnəri
senate
BR 'sɛnɪt, -s
AM 'sɛnət, -s
senator
BR 'sɛnɪtə(r), -z
AM 'sɛnədər, -z
senatorial
BR ˌsɛnɪ'tɔːrɪəl
AM ¦sɛnə'tɔriəl
senatorially
BR ˌsɛnɪ'tɔːrɪəli
AM ¦sɛnə'tɔriəli
senatorship
BR 'sɛnɪtəʃɪp, -s
AM 'sɛnədərˌʃɪp, -s
send
BR sɛnd, -z, -ɪŋ
AM sɛnd, -z, -ɪŋ
sendable
BR 'sɛndəbl
AM 'sɛndəbəl
Sendai
BR 'sɛndʌɪ
AM 'sɛnˌdaɪ
sendal
BR 'sɛndl, -z
AM 'sɛndəl, -z
sender
BR 'sɛndə(r), -z
AM 'sɛndər, -z
sending-off
BR ˌsɛndɪŋ'ɒf, -s
AM ˌsɛndɪŋ'ɔf, ˌsɛndɪŋ'ɑf, -s
Seneca
BR 'sɛnɪkə(r)
AM 'sɛnəkə
senecio
BR sɪ'niːsɪəʊ, sɪ'niːʃɪəʊ, -z
AM si'nisioʊ, si'niʃioʊ, -z
Senegal
BR ˌsɛnɪ'gɔːl
AM ¦sɛnə¦gɔl, ¦sɛnə¦gɑl
Senegalese
BR ˌsɛnɪgə'liːz
AM ¦sɛnəgə'liz
senesce
BR sɪ'nɛs, -ɪz, -ɪŋ, -t
AM sə'nɛs, -əz, -ɪŋ, -t
senescence
BR sɪ'nɛsns
AM sə'nɛsəns
senescent
BR sɪ'nɛsnt
AM sə'nɛsənt
seneschal
BR 'sɛnɪʃl, -z
AM 'sɛnəʃəl, 'sɛnəˌʃɑl, -z
Senghenydd
BR sɛŋ'hɛnɪð
AM sɛŋ'hɛnɪð
Senhor
BR sɛ'njɔː(r), sə'njɔː(r), -z
AM seɪn'jɔ(ə)r, sin'jɔ(ə)r, -z
Senhora
BR sɛ'njɔːrə(r), sə'njɔːrə(r), -z
AM seɪn'jɔrə, sin'jɔrə, -z
Senhores
BR sɛ'njɔːreɪz, sə'njɔːreɪz
AM seɪn'jɔreɪs, sin'jɔreɪs
Senhorita
BR ˌsɛnjə'riːtə(r), ˌsɛnjɔː'riːtə(r), -z
AM ¦seɪnjə'ridə, ¦sɛnjə'ridə, -z
senile
BR 'siːnʌɪl
AM 'siˌnaɪl
senility
BR sɪ'nɪlɪti
AM sə'nɪlɪdi, sɛ'nɪlɪdi
senior
BR 'siːnɪə(r), -z
AM 'sinjər, 'siniər, -z
seniority
BR ˌsiːnɪ'ɒrɪti
AM sin'jɔrədi
seniti
BR 'sɛnɪti
AM sə'nɪdi
Senlac
BR 'sɛnlak
AM 'sɛnlæk
senna
BR 'sɛnə(r)
AM 'sɛnə
Sennacherib
BR sɪ'nakərɪb, sɛ'nakərɪb
AM sə'nækəˌrɪb
sennet
BR 'sɛnɪt
AM 'sɛnət
Sennett
BR 'sɛnɪt
AM 'sɛnət
sennight
BR 'sɛnʌɪt, -s
AM 'sɛnaɪt, -s
sennit
BR 'sɛnɪt
AM 'sɛnət
señor
BR sɛ'njɔː(r), sə'njɔː(r), -z
AM seɪn'jɔ(ə)r, sin'jɔ(ə)r, -z
señora
BR sɛ'njɔːrə(r), sə'njɔːrə(r), -z
AM seɪn'jɔrə, sin'jɔrə, -z
señores
BR sɛ'njɔːreɪz, sə'njɔːreɪz
AM seɪn'jɔreɪs, sin'jɔreɪs
señorita
BR ˌsɛnjə'riːtə(r), ˌsɛnjɔː'riːtə(r), -z
AM ¦seɪnjə'ridə, ¦sɛnjə'ridə, -z
sensa
BR 'sɛnsə(r)
AM 'sɛnsə
sensate
BR 'sɛnseɪt
AM 'sɛnˌseɪt
sensation
BR s(ɛ)n'seɪʃn, -z
AM sɛn'seɪʃən, sən'seɪʃən, -z
sensational
BR s(ɛ)n'seɪʃn̩(ə)l, s(ɛ)n'seɪʃən(ə)l
AM sɛn'seɪʃ(ə)nəl, sən'seɪʃ(ə)nəl
sensationalise
BR s(ɛ)n'seɪʃn̩əlʌɪz, s(ɛ)n'seɪʃn̩l̩ʌɪz, s(ɛ)n'seɪʃənl̩ʌɪz, s(ɛ)n'seɪʃ(ə)nəlʌɪz, -ɪz, -ɪŋ, -d
AM sɛn'seɪʃənlˌaɪz, sən'seɪʃənlˌaɪz, sɛn'seɪʃnəˌlaɪz, sən'seɪʃnəˌlaɪz, -ɪz, -ɪŋ, -d
sensationalism
BR s(ɛ)n'seɪʃn̩əlɪz(ə)m, s(ɛ)n'seɪʃn̩l̩ɪz(ə)m, s(ɛ)n'seɪʃənl̩ɪz(ə)m, s(ɛ)n'seɪʃ(ə)nəlɪz(ə)m
AM sɛn'seɪʃənlˌɪzəm, sən'seɪʃənlˌɪzəm, sɛn'seɪʃnəˌlɪzəm, sən'seɪʃnəˌlɪzəm
sensationalist
BR s(ɛ)n'seɪʃn̩əlɪst, s(ɛ)n'seɪʃn̩l̩ɪst, s(ɛ)n'seɪʃənl̩ɪst, s(ɛ)n'seɪʃ(ə)nəlɪst, -s
AM sɛn'seɪʃənləst, sən'seɪʃənləst, sɛn'seɪʃnələst, sən'seɪʃnələst, -s
sensationalistic
BR s(ɛ)nˌseɪʃn̩ə'lɪstɪk, s(ɛ)nˌseɪʃn̩l̩'ɪstɪk, s(ɛ)nˌseɪʃənl̩'ɪstɪk, s(ɛ)nˌseɪʃ(ə)nə'lɪstɪk
AM sɛnˌseɪʃənl'ɪstɪk, sənˌseɪʃənl'ɪstɪk,

sɛnˌseɪʃnəˈlɪstɪk,
sənˌseɪʃnəˈlɪstɪk

sensationalize
BR s(ɛ)nˈseɪʃn̩əlʌɪz,
s(ɛ)nˈseɪʃn̩l̩ʌɪz,
s(ɛ)nˈseɪʃənl̩ʌɪz,
s(ɛ)nˈseɪʃ(ə)nəlʌɪz,
-ɪz, -ɪŋ, -d
AM sɛnˈseɪʃənlˌaɪz,
sənˈseɪʃənlˌaɪz,
sɛnˈseɪʃnəˌlaɪz,
sənˈseɪʃnəˌlaɪz, -ɪz,
-ɪŋ, -d

sensationally
BR s(ɛ)nˈseɪʃn̩əli,
s(ɛ)nˈseɪʃn̩l̩i,
s(ɛ)nˈseɪʃənl̩i,
s(ɛ)nˈseɪʃ(ə)nəli
AM sɛnˈseɪʃ(ə)nəli,
sənˈseɪʃ(ə)nəli

sense
BR sɛns, -ɪz, -ɪŋ, -t
AM sɛns, -əz, -ɪŋ, -t

senseless
BR ˈsɛnsləs
AM ˈsɛnsləs

senselessly
BR ˈsɛnsləsli
AM ˈsɛnsləsli

senselessness
BR ˈsɛnsləsnəs
AM ˈsɛnsləsnəs

sense-organ
BR ˈsɛnsˌɔːg(ə)n, -z
AM ˈsɛnsˌɔrgən, -z

sensibility
BR ˌsɛnsɪˈbɪlɪt|i, -ɪz
AM ˌsɛnsəˈbɪlɨdi, -z

sensible
BR ˈsɛnsɪbl
AM ˈsɛnsəbəl

sensibleness
BR ˈsɛnsɪblnəs
AM ˈsɛnsəbəlnəs

sensibly
BR ˈsɛnsɪbli
AM ˈsɛnsəbli

sensitisation
BR ˌsɛnsɪtʌɪˈzeɪʃn
AM ˌsɛnsədəˈzeɪʃən,
ˌsɛnsəˌtaɪˈzeɪʃən

sensitise
BR ˈsɛnsɪtʌɪz, -ɪz, -ɪŋ, -d
AM ˈsɛnsəˌtaɪz, -ɪz, -ɪŋ,
-d

sensitiser
BR ˈsɛnsɪtʌɪzə(r), -z
AM ˈsɛnsəˌtaɪzər, -z

sensitive
BR ˈsɛnsɪtɪv
AM ˈsɛnsədɪv

sensitively
BR ˈsɛnsɪtɪvli
AM ˈsɛnsədɪvli

sensitiveness
BR ˈsɛnsɪtɪvnɪs
AM ˈsɛnsədɪvnɪs

sensitivity
BR ˌsɛnsɪˈtɪvɪti
AM ˌsɛnsəˈtɪvɪdi

sensitization
BR ˌsɛnsɪtʌɪˈzeɪʃn
AM ˌsɛnsədəˈzeɪʃən,
ˌsɛnsəˌtaɪˈzeɪʃən

sensitize
BR ˈsɛnsɪtʌɪz, -ɪz, -ɪŋ, -d
AM ˈsɛnsəˌtaɪz, -ɪz, -ɪŋ,
-d

sensitizer
BR ˈsɛnsɪtʌɪzə(r), -z
AM ˈsɛnsəˌtaɪzər, -z

sensitometer
BR ˌsɛnsɪˈtɒmɪtə(r), -z
AM ˌsɛnsəˈtɑmədər, -z

Sensodyne®
BR ˈsɛnsə(ʊ)dʌɪn
AM ˈsɛnsəˌdaɪn

sensor
BR ˈsɛnsə(r), -z
AM ˈsɛnsər, -z

sensoria
BR sɛnˈsɔːrɪə(*r*)
AM sɛnˈsɔriə

sensorial
BR sɛnˈsɔːrɪəl
AM sɛnˈsɔriəl

sensorially
BR sɛnˈsɔːrɪəli
AM sɛnˈsɔriəli

sensorily
BR ˈsɛns(ə)rɪli
AM ˈsɛnsərəli,
sɛnˈsɔrəli

sensorium
BR sɛnˈsɔːrɪəm, -z
AM sɛnˈsɔriəm, -z

sensory
BR ˈsɛns(ə)ri
AM ˈsɛnsəri

sensual
BR ˈsɛnsjʊəl, ˈsɛnsjᵿl,
ˈsɛnʃʊəl, ˈsɛnʃ(ᵿ)l
AM ˈsɛn(t)ʃ(əw)əl

sensualise
BR ˈsɛnsjʊəlʌɪz,
ˈsɛnsjᵿlʌɪz,
ˈsɛnʃʊəlʌɪz,
ˈsɛnʃᵿlʌɪz, ˈsɛnʃl̩ʌɪz,
-ɪz, -ɪŋ, -d
AM ˈsɛn(t)ʃ(əw)əˌlaɪz,
-ɪz, -ɪŋ, -d

sensualism
BR ˈsɛnsjʊəlɪz(ə)m,
ˈsɛnsjᵿlɪz(ə)m,
ˈsɛnʃʊəlɪz(ə)m,
ˈsɛnʃᵿlɪz(ə)m,
ˈsɛnʃl̩ɪz(ə)m
AM ˈsɛn(t)ʃ(əw)əˌlɪzəm

sensualist
BR ˈsɛnsjʊəlɪst,
ˈsɛnsjᵿlɪst,
ˈsɛnʃʊəlɪst,
ˈsɛnʃᵿlɪst, ˈsɛnʃl̩ɪst,
-s
AM ˈsɛn(t)ʃ(əw)ələst,
-s

sensuality
BR ˌsɛnsjʊˈalɪti,
ˌsɛnʃʊˈalɪti
AM ˌsɛn(t)ʃəˈwælədi

sensualize
BR ˈsɛnsjʊəlʌɪz,
ˈsɛnsjᵿlʌɪz,
ˈsɛnʃʊəlʌɪz,
ˈsɛnʃᵿlʌɪz, ˈsɛnʃl̩ʌɪz,
-ɪz, -ɪŋ, -d
AM ˈsɛn(t)ʃ(əw)əˌlaɪz,
-ɪz, -ɪŋ, -d

sensually
BR ˈsɛnsjʊəli,
ˈsɛnsjᵿli, ˈsɛnʃʊəli,
ˈsɛnʃᵿli, ˈsɛnʃl̩i
AM ˈsɛn(t)ʃ(əw)əli

sensualness
BR ˈsɛnsjʊəlnəs,
ˈsɛnsjᵿlnəs,
ˈsɛnʃʊəlnəs,
ˈsɛnʃ(ᵿ)lnəs
AM ˈsɛn(t)ʃ(əw)əlnəs

sensum
BR ˈsɛnsəm
AM ˈsɛnsəm

sensuous
BR ˈsɛnsjʊəs, ˈsɛnʃʊəs
AM ˈsɛn(t)ʃəwəs

sensuously
BR ˈsɛnsjʊəs,
ˈsɛnʃʊəsli
AM ˈsɛn(t)ʃəwəsli

sensuousness
BR ˈsɛnsjʊəsnəs,
ˈsɛnʃʊəsnəs
AM ˈsɛn(t)ʃəwəsnəs

sensu stricto
BR ˌsɛnsuː ˈstrɪktəʊ
AM ˌsɛnsu ˈstrɪktoʊ

sent
BR sɛnt
AM sɛnt

sente
BR ˈsɛnt|i, -ɪz
AM ˈsɛnˌti, -z

sentence
BR ˈsɛnt(ə)ns, -ɪz, -ɪŋ, -t
AM ˈsɛntns, ˈsɛn(t)əns,
-əz, -ɪŋ, -t

sentential
BR sɛnˈtɛnʃl
AM sɛnˈtɛn(t)ʃəl

sententious
BR sɛnˈtɛnʃəs
AM sɛnˈtɛn(t)ʃəs

sententiously
BR sɛnˈtɛnʃəsli
AM sɛnˈtɛn(t)ʃəsli

sententiousness
BR sɛnˈtɛnʃəsnəs
AM sɛnˈtɛn(t)ʃəsnəs

sentience
BR ˈsɛnʃns, ˈsɛnʃɪəns,
ˈsɛntɪəns
AM ˈsɛn(t)ʃ(i)əns

sentiency
BR ˈsɛnʃnsi,
ˈsɛnʃɪənsi, ˈsɛntɪənsi
AM ˈsɛn(t)ʃ(i)ənsi

sentient
BR ˈsɛnʃnt, ˈsɛnʃɪənt,
ˈsɛntɪənt
AM ˈsɛn(t)ʃ(i)ənt

sentiently
BR ˈsɛnʃntli,
ˈsɛnʃɪəntli,
ˈsɛntɪəntli
AM ˈsɛn(t)ʃ(i)ən(t)li

sentiment
BR ˈsɛntɪm(ə)nt, -s
AM ˈsɛn(t)əmənt, -s

sentimental
BR ˌsɛntɪˈmɛntl
AM ˌsɛn(t)əˈmɛn(t)l

sentimentalisation
BR ˌsɛntɪmɛntl̩ʌɪˈzeɪʃn,
ˌsɛntɪmɛntəlʌɪˈzeɪʃn,
sɛntɪˌmɛntl̩ʌɪˈzeɪʃn,
sɛntɪˌmɛntəlʌɪˈzeɪʃn
AM ˌsɛn(t)əˌmɛn(t)l̩əˈzeɪʃən
ˌsɛn(t)əˌmɛn(t)lˌaɪˈzeɪʃən

sentimentalise
BR ˌsɛntɪˈmɛntl̩ʌɪz,
ˌsɛntɪˈmɛntəlʌɪz, -ɪz,
-ɪŋ, -d
AM ˌsɛn(t)əˈmɛn(t)lˌaɪz,
-ɪz, -ɪŋ, -d

sentimentalism
BR ˌsɛntɪˈmɛntl̩ɪz(ə)m,
ˌsɛntɪˈmɛntəlɪz(ə)m
AM ˌsɛn(t)əˈmɛn(t)l-
ˌɪzəm

sentimentalist
BR ˌsɛntɪˈmɛntl̩ɪst,
ˌsɛntɪˈmɛntəlɪst, -s
AM ˌsɛn(t)əˈmɛn(t)ləst,
-s

sentimentality
BR ˌsɛntɪmɛnˈtalɪti,
ˌsɛntɪm(ə)nˈtalɪti
AM ˌsɛn(t)əˌmɛnˈtælədi,
ˌsɛn(t)əmənˈtælədi

sentimentalization
BR ˌsɛntɪmɛntl̩ʌɪˈzeɪʃn,
ˌsɛntɪmɛntəlʌɪˈzeɪʃn,
sɛntɪˌmɛntl̩ʌɪˈzeɪʃn,
sɛntɪˌmɛntəlʌɪˈzeɪʃn
AM ˌsɛn(t)əˌmɛn(t)l̩ə-
ˈzeɪʃən,
ˌsɛn(t)əˌmɛn(t)lˌaɪˈzeɪ-
ʃən

sentimentalize
BR ˌsɛntɪˈmɛntl̩ʌɪz,
ˌsɛntɪˈmɛntəlʌɪz, -ɪz,
-ɪŋ, -d
AM ˌsɛn(t)əˈmɛn(t)lˌaɪz,
-ɪz, -ɪŋ, -d

sentimentally
BR ˌsɛntɪˈmɛntl̩i,
ˌsɛntɪˈmɛntəli
AM ˌsɛn(t)əˈmɛn(t)l̩i

sentinel
BR ˈsɛntɪnl, -z

AM ˈsɛntn̩əl, ˈsɛntnəl, -z
sentry
BR ˈsɛntr|i, -ɪz
AM ˈsɛntri, -z
Senussi
BR sɛˈnuːsi, sɪˈnuːsi
AM səˈnusi
Seonaid
BR ʃəˈneɪd
AM ʃəˈneɪd
Seoul
BR səʊl
AM soʊl
sepal
BR ˈsɛp(ə)l, ˈsiːp(ə)l, -z
AM ˈsipəl, ˈsɛpəl, -z
separability
BR ˌsɛp(ə)rəˈbɪlɪti
AM ˌsɛp(ə)rəˈbɪlɪdi
separable
BR ˈsɛp(ə)rəbl
AM ˈsɛp(ə)rəbəl
separableness
BR ˈsɛp(ə)rəblnəs
AM ˈsɛp(ə)rəbəlnəs
separably
BR ˈsɛp(ə)rəbli
AM ˈsɛp(ə)rəbli
separate¹
adjective
BR ˈsɛp(ə)rət
AM ˈsɛp(ə)rət
separate²
verb
BR ˈsɛpəreɪt, -s, -ɪŋ, -ɪd
AM ˈsɛpəˌreɪ|t, -ts, -dɪŋ, -dɪd
separately
BR ˈsɛp(ə)rətli
AM ˈsɛp(ə)rətli
separateness
BR ˈsɛp(ə)rətnəs
AM ˈsɛp(ə)rətnəs
separation
BR ˌsɛpəˈreɪʃn, -z
AM ˌsɛpəˈreɪʃən, -z
separatism
BR ˈsɛp(ə)rətɪz(ə)m
AM ˈsɛp(ə)rəˌtɪzəm
separatist
BR ˈsɛp(ə)rətɪst, -s
AM ˈsɛp(ə)rədəst, -s
separative
BR ˈsɛp(ə)rətɪv
AM ˈsɛp(ə)rədɪv
separator
BR ˈsɛpəreɪtə(r), -z
AM ˈsɛpəˌreɪdər, -z
separatory
BR ˈsɛp(ə)rət(ə)ri
AM ˈsɛp(ə)rəˌtɔri
Sephardi
BR sɪˈfɑːdi, sɛˈfɑːdi
AM səˈfɑrdi
Sephardic
BR sɪˈfɑːdɪk, sɛˈfɑːdɪk
AM səˈfɑrdɪk
Sephardim
BR səˈfɑːdɪm, sɛˈfɑːdɪm
AM səˈfɑrdəm, səˌfɑrˈdim
sepia
BR ˈsiːpɪə(*r*)
AM ˈsipiə
sepoy
BR ˈsiːpɔɪ, -z
AM ˈsiˌpɔɪ, -z
seppuku
BR sɛˈpuːkuː
AM ˈsɛpuˌku, səˈpuˌku
sepses
BR ˈsɛpsiːz
AM ˈsɛpˌsiz
sepsis
BR ˈsɛpsɪs
AM ˈsɛpsəs
sept
BR sɛpt, -s
AM sɛpt, -s
septa
BR ˈsɛptə(*r*)
AM ˈsɛptə
septal
BR ˈsɛptl
AM ˈsɛptl
septate
BR ˈsɛpteɪt
AM ˈsɛpˌteɪt
septation
BR sɛpˈteɪʃn
AM sɛpˈteɪʃən
septcentenary
BR ˌsɛp(t)sɛnˈtiːn(ə)r|i, ˌsɛp(t)sɛnˈtɛn(ə)r|i, sɛptˈsɛntɪn(ə)r|i, -ɪz
AM ˈsɛp(t)ˌsɛnˈtɛnəri, ˈsɛp(t)ˈsɛntnˌɛri, -z
September
BR sɛpˈtɛmbə(r), səpˈtɛmbə(r), -z
AM sɛpˈtɛmbər, səpˈtɛmbər, -z
septenarii
BR ˌsɛptɪˈnɛːrɪʌɪ
AM ˌsɛptəˈnɛriˌaɪ
septenarius
BR ˌsɛptɪˈnɛːrɪəs
AM ˌsɛptəˈnɛriəs
septenary
BR sɛpˈtiːn(ə)r|i, sɛpˈtɛn(ə)r|i, ˈsɛptɪn(ə)r|i, -ɪz
AM sɛpˈtɛn(ə)ri, ˈsɛptəˌnɛri, -z
septenate
BR sɛpˈtɛneɪt, sɛpˈtiːneɪt
AM sɛpˈtɛˌneɪt, ˈsɛptəˌneɪt
septennia
BR sɛpˈtɛnɪə(*r*)
AM sɛpˈtɛniə, sɛpˈtɛnjə
septennial
BR sɛpˈtɛnɪəl
AM sɛpˈtɛnjəl, sɛpˈtɛniəl
septennium
BR sɛpˈtɛnɪəm
AM sɛpˈtɛniəm, sɛpˈtɛnjəm
septet
BR sɛpˈtɛt, -s
AM sɛpˈtɛt, -s
septfoil
BR ˈsɛp(t)fɔɪl, -z
AM ˈsɛp(t)ˌfɔɪl, -z
septic
BR ˈsɛptɪk
AM ˈsɛptɪk
septicaemia
BR ˌsɛptɪˈsiːmɪə(*r*)
AM ˌsɛptəˈsimiə
septicaemic
BR ˌsɛptɪˈsiːmɪk
AM ˌsɛptəˈsimɪk
septically
BR ˈsɛptɪkli
AM ˈsɛptək(ə)li
septicemia
BR ˌsɛptɪˈsiːmɪə(*r*)
AM ˌsɛptəˈsimiə
septicemic
BR ˌsɛptɪˈsiːmɪk
AM ˌsɛptəˈsimɪk
septicity
BR sɛpˈtɪsɪti
AM sɛpˈtɪsɪdi
septilateral
BR ˌsɛptɪˈlat(ə)rəl, ˌsɛptɪˈlat(ə)rl̩
AM ˈsɛptəˈlædərəl, ˈsɛptəˈlætrəl
septillion
BR sɛpˈtɪljən
AM sɛpˈtɪljən
septimal
BR ˈsɛptɪml
AM ˈsɛptəməl
septime
BR ˈsɛptiːm, -z
AM ˈsɛptəm, ˈsɛpˌtim, -z
Septimus
BR ˌsɛptɪməs
AM ˈsɛptəməs
septivalent
BR ˌsɛptɪˈveɪlənt, ˌsɛptɪˈveɪln̩t
AM ˈsɛptəˈveɪlənt
septuagenarian
BR ˌsɛptjʊədʒɪˈnɛːrɪən, ˌsɛptʃ(ʊ)ədʒɪˈnɛːrɪən, -z
AM ˈsɛptʃə(wə)dʒəˈnɛr-iən, ˈsɛptʃəˌwædʒəˈnɛriən, -z
septuagenary
BR ˌsɛptjʊəˈdʒiːn(ə)ri, ˌsɛptjʊəˈdʒɛn(ə)ri, ˌsɛptʃʊəˈdʒiːn(ə)ri, ˌsɛptʃʊəˈdʒɛn(ə)r|i, -ɪz
AM ˈsɛptʃə(wə)ˈdʒɛnəri, ˈsɛptʃə(wə)dʒəˌnɛri, -z
Septuagesima
BR ˌsɛptjʊəˈdʒɛsɪmə(*r*), ˌsɛptʃʊəˈdʒɛsɪmə(*r*)
AM ˌsɛp(t)ʃəwəˈdʒɛsəmə
Septuagint
BR ˈsɛptjʊədʒɪnt, ˈsɛptʃʊədʒɪnt
AM ˈsɛp(t)ʃəwəˌdʒɪnt
septum
BR ˈsɛptəm, -z
AM ˈsɛptəm, -z
septuple
BR ˈsɛptjʉpl, ˈsɛptʃʉpl, sɛpˈtjuːpl, sɛpˈtʃuːpl
AM ˈsɛptəpəl, sɛpˈt(j)upəl
septuplet
BR ˈsɛptjʉplɪt, ˈsɛptʃʉplɪt, sɛpˈtjuːplɪt, sɛpˈtʃuːplɪt, -s
AM sɛpˈtəplət, sɛpˈt(j)uplət, -s
sepulcher
BR ˈsɛplkə(r), -z
AM ˈsɛpəlkər, -z
sepulchral
BR sɪˈpʌlkr(ə)l
AM səˈpəlkrəl, sɛˈpəlkrəl
sepulchrally
BR sɪˈpʌlkrəli
AM səˈpəlkrəli, sɛˈpəlkrəli
sepulchre
BR ˈsɛplkə(r), -z
AM ˈsɛpəlkər, -z
sepulture
BR ˈsɛpltʃə(r), ˈsɛpltjʊə(r), -z
AM ˈsɛpəltʃər, ˈsɛpəltʃʊ(ə)r, -z
Sepulveda
BR sɪˈpʌlvɪdə(*r*), sɪˈpʊlvɪdə(*r*)
AM səˈpəlvədə
sequacious
BR sɪˈkweɪʃəs
AM səˈkweɪʃəs, siˈkweɪʃəs
sequaciously
BR sɪˈkweɪʃəsli
AM səˈkweɪʃəsli, siˈkweɪʃəsli
sequacity
BR sɪˈkwasɪti
AM səˈkwæsədi, siˈkwæsədi
sequel
BR ˈsiːkw(ə)l, -z
AM ˈsikwəl, -z

sequela
BR sɪˈkwiːlə(*r*), sɪˈkwɛlə(*r*)
AM siˈkwɛlə
sequelae
BR sɪˈkwiːliː, sɪˈkwɛliː
AM siˈkwɛli, siˈkwɛˌlaɪ
sequence
BR ˈsiːkw(ə)ns, -ɪz
AM ˈsikwəns, ˈsiˌkwɛns, -əz
sequencer
BR ˈsiːkw(ə)nsə(r), -z
AM ˈsikwənsər, ˈsiˌkwɛnsər, -z
sequent
BR ˈsiːkw(ə)nt
AM ˈsikwənt, ˈsiˌkwɛnt
sequential
BR sɪˈkwɛnʃl
AM səˈkwɛn(t)ʃəl, siˈkwɛn(t)ʃəl
sequentiality
BR sɪˌkwɛnʃɪˈalɪti
AM səˌkwɛn(t)ʃiˈælədi, siˌkwɛn(t)ʃiˈælədi
sequentially
BR sɪˈkwɛnʃl̩i, sɪˈkwɛnʃəli
AM səˈkwɛn(t)ʃəli, siˈkwɛn(t)ʃəli
sequently
BR ˈsiːkw(ə)ntli
AM ˈsikwən(t)li, ˈsiˌkwɛn(t)li
sequester
BR sɪˈkwɛst|ə(r), -əz, -(ə)rɪŋ, -əd
AM səˈkwɛstər, siˈkwɛstər, -z, -ɪŋ, -d
sequestra
BR sɪˈkwɛstrə(*r*)
AM səˈkwɛstrə, siˈkwɛstrə
sequestrable
BR sɪˈkwɛstrəbl
AM səˈkwɛstrəbəl, siˈkwɛstrəbəl
sequestral
BR sɪˈkwɛstr(ə)l
AM səˈkwɛstrəl, siˈkwɛstrəl
sequestrate
BR ˈsiːkwəstreɪt, ˈsiːkwɛstreɪt, -s, -ɪŋ, -ɪd
AM ˈsikwəˌstreɪ|t, ˈsɛkwəˌstreɪ|t, səˈkwɛsˌtreɪ|t, -ts, -dɪŋ, -dɪd
sequestration
BR ˌsiːkwəˈstreɪʃn, ˌsiːkwɛˈstreɪʃn, -z
AM ˌsikwəˈstreɪʃən, ˌsɛkwəˈstreɪʃən, -z
sequestrator
BR ˈsiːkwəstreɪtə(r), ˈsiːkwɛstreɪtə(r), -z
AM ˈsikwəˌstreɪdər, ˈsɛkwəˌstreɪdər, səˈkwɛsˌtreɪdər, -z
sequestrotomy
BR ˌsiːkwəˈstrɒtəm|i, ˌsiːkwɛˈstrɒtəm|i, -ɪz
AM ˌsikwəˈstrɑdəmi, ˌsɛkwəˈstrɑdəmi, -z
sequestrum
BR sɪˈkwɛstrəm
AM səˈkwɛstrəm, siˈkwɛstrəm
sequin
BR ˈsiːkwɪn, -z, -d
AM ˈsikwɪn, -z, -d
sequitur
BR ˈsɛkwɪtə(r)
AM ˈsɛkwədər
sequoia
BR sɪˈkwɔɪə(*r*), -z
AM səˈkɔɪə, -z
sera
BR ˈsɪərə(*r*)
AM ˈsirə
serac
BR ˈsɛrak, -s
AM səˈræk, -s
seraglio
BR sɪˈrɑːlɪəʊ, -z
AM səˈrɑljoʊ, -z
serai
BR sɪˈrʌɪ, -z
AM səˈraɪ, -z
serang
BR səˈraŋ, -z
AM səˈræŋ, -z
serape
BR sɪˈrɑːp|i, -ɪz
AM səˈrɑpi, -z
seraph
BR ˈsɛrəf, -s
AM ˈsɛrəf, -s
seraphic
BR sɪˈrafɪk
AM səˈræfɪk
seraphical
BR sɪˈrafɪkl
AM səˈræfəkəl
seraphically
BR sɪˈrafɪkli
AM səˈræfək(ə)li
seraphim
BR ˈsɛrəfɪm
AM ˈsɛrəˌfɪm
Seraphina
BR ˌsɛrəˈfiːnə(*r*)
AM ˌsɛrəˈfinə
Serapis
BR ˈsɛrəpɪs, sɪˈreɪpɪs
AM səˈreɪpɪs
Serb
BR səːb, -z
AM sərb, -z
Serbia
BR ˈsəːbɪə(*r*)
AM ˈsərbiə
Serbian
BR ˈsəːbɪən, -z
AM ˈsərbiən, -z
Serbo-Croat
BR ˌsəːbəʊˈkrəʊat, -s
AM ˌsərboʊˈkroʊat, -s
Serbo-Croatian
BR ˌsəːbəʊkrəʊˈeɪʃn
AM ˌsərboʊˌkroʊˈeɪʃən
Serbonian
BR səːˈbəʊnɪən
AM sərˈboʊniən
SERC
Science and Engineering Research Council
BR ˌɛsiːɑːˈsiː
AM ˌɛsˌiˌɑrˈsi
sere
BR sɪə(r)
AM sɪ(ə)r
serein
BR səˈran, səˈrã
AM səˈrɛn
Seremban
BR ˈsɛrəmban
AM ˈsɛrəmˌbæn
Serena
BR sɪˈriːnə(*r*)
AM səˈrinə
serenade
BR ˌsɛrəˈneɪd, -z, -ɪŋ, -ɪd
AM ˌsɛrəˈneɪd, -z, -ɪŋ, -ɪd
serenader
BR ˌsɛrəˈneɪdə(r), -z
AM ˌsɛrəˈneɪdər, -z
serenata
BR ˌsɛrəˈnɑːtə(*r*), -z
AM ˌsɛrəˈnɑdə, -z
serendipitous
BR ˌsɛrənˈdɪpɪtəs, ˌsɛrn̩ˈdɪpɪtəs
AM ˌsɛrənˈdɪpədəs
serendipitously
BR ˌsɛrənˈdɪpɪtəsli, ˌsɛrn̩ˈdɪpɪtəsli
AM ˌsɛrənˈdɪpədəsli
serendipity
BR ˌsɛrənˈdɪpɪti, ˌsɛrn̩ˈdɪpɪti
AM ˌsɛrənˈdɪpɪdi
serene
BR sɪˈriːn
AM səˈrin
serenely
BR sɪˈriːnli
AM səˈrinli
sereneness
BR sɪˈriːnnɪs
AM səˈri(n)nɪs
Serengeti
BR ˌsɛrənˈɡɛti, ˌsɛrn̩ˈɡɛti
AM ˌsɛrənˈɡɛdi
serenity
BR sɪˈrɛnɪti
AM səˈrɛnədi
serf
BR səːf, -s
AM sərf, -s
serfage
BR ˈsəːfɪdʒ
AM ˈsərfɪdʒ
serfdom
BR ˈsəːfdəm
AM ˈsərfdəm
serfhood
BR ˈsəːfhʊd
AM ˈsərfˌ(h)ʊd
serge
BR səːdʒ, -ɪz
AM sərdʒ, -əz
sergeancy
BR ˈsɑːdʒ(ə)ns|i, -ɪz
AM ˈsɑrdʒənsi, -z
sergeant
BR ˈsɑːdʒ(ə)nt, -s
AM ˈsɑrdʒənt, -s
sergeant-major
BR ˌsɑːdʒ(ə)ntˈmeɪdʒə(r), -z
AM ˌsɑrdʒəntˈmeɪdʒər, -z
sergeantship
BR ˈsɑːdʒ(ə)ntʃɪp, -s
AM ˈsɑrdʒəntˌʃɪp, -s
Sergei
BR ˈsɛːɡeɪ, sɛːˈɡeɪ
AM ˈsɛrˌɡeɪ, sɛrˈɡeɪ
Sergio
BR ˈsəːdʒɪəʊ
AM ˈsərdʒioʊ
Sergius
BR ˈsəːdʒɪəs
AM ˈsərdʒiəs
serial
BR ˈsɪərɪəl, -z
AM ˈsɪriəl, -z
serialisation
BR ˌsɪərɪəlʌɪˈzeɪʃn, -z
AM ˌsɪriələˈzeɪʃən, ˌsɪriəˌlaɪˈzeɪʃən, -z
serialise
BR ˈsɪərɪəlʌɪz, -ɪz, -ɪŋ, -d
AM ˈsɪriəˌlaɪz, -ɪz, -ɪŋ, -d
serialism
BR ˈsɪərɪəlɪz(ə)m
AM ˈsɪriəˌlɪzəm
serialist
BR ˈsɪərɪəlɪst, -s
AM ˈsɪriələst, -s
seriality
BR ˌsɪərɪˈalɪti
AM ˌsɪriˈælədi
serialization
BR ˌsɪərɪəlʌɪˈzeɪʃn, -z
AM ˌsɪriələˈzeɪʃən, ˌsɪriəˌlaɪˈzeɪʃən, -z
serialize
BR ˈsɪərɪəlʌɪz, -ɪz, -ɪŋ, -d
AM ˈsɪriəˌlaɪz, -ɪz, -ɪŋ, -d

serially
BR 'sɪərɪəli
AM 'sɪriəli

seriate¹
adjective
BR 'sɪərɪət
AM 'sɪriət

seriate²
verb
BR 'sɪərɪeɪt, -s, -ɪŋ, -ɨd
AM 'sɪri,eɪ|t, -ts, -dɪŋ, -dɨd

seriatim
BR ˌsɪərɪ'eɪtɪm, ˌsɛrɪ'eɪtɪm, ˌsɪərɪ'ɑːtɪm, ˌsɛrɪ'ɑːtɪm
AM ˌsɪri'eɪdɪm, ˌsɪri'ædəm

seriation
BR ˌsɪərɪ'eɪʃn, -z
AM ˌsɪri'eɪʃən, -z

Seric
BR 'sɛrɪk
AM 'sɪrɪk, 'sɛrɪk

sericeous
BR sɪ'rɪʃəs
AM sə'rɪʃəs

sericultural
BR ˌsɪərɪ'kʌltʃ(ə)rəl, ˌsɪərɪ'kʌltʃ(ə)rl̩, ˌsɛrɪ'kʌltʃ(ə)rəl, ˌsɛrɪ'kʌltʃ(ə)rl̩
AM ˌsɛrə'kəltʃ(ə)rəl

sericulture
BR 'sɪərɪˌkʌltʃə(r), 'sɛrɪˌkʌltʃə(r)
AM 'sɛrəˌkəltʃər

sericulturist
BR ˌsɪərɪ'kʌltʃ(ə)rɪst, ˌsɛrɪ'kʌltʃ(ə)rɪst, -s
AM ˌsɛrə'kəltʃ(ə)rəst, -s

seriema
BR ˌsɛrɪ'iːmə(r), -z
AM ˌsɛri'ɛmə, ˌsɛri'eɪmə, -z

series
BR 'sɪərɪz
AM 'sɪriz

serif
BR 'sɛrɪf, -s, -t
AM 'sɛrəf, -s, -t

serigraph
BR 'sɛrɪgrɑːf, 'sɛrɪgraf, -s
AM 'sɛrəˌgræf, -s

serigrapher
BR sɪ'rɪgrəfə(r), -z
AM sə'rɪgrəfər, -z

serigraphy
BR sɪ'rɪgrəfi
AM sə'rɪgrəfi

serin
BR 'sɛrɪn, -z
AM 'sɛrən, -z

serine
BR 'sɪəriːn, 'sɪərɪn, 'sɛriːn, 'sɛrɪn
AM 'sɛˌrin, 'sɛrən

serinette
BR ˌsɛrɪ'nɛt, -s
AM ˌsɛrə'nɛt, -s

seringa
BR sɪ'rɪŋgə(r), -z
AM sə'rɪŋgə, -z

Seringapatam
BR sɪˌrɪŋgəpə'tɑːm, sɪˌrɪŋgəpə'tam
AM səˌrɪŋgəpə'tɑm

serio-comic
BR ˌsɪərɪəʊ'kɒmɪk
AM ¦sɪrioʊ'kɑmɪk

serio-comically
BR ˌsɪərɪəʊ'kɒmɪkli
AM ¦sɪrioʊ'kɑmək(ə)li

serious
BR 'sɪərɪəs
AM 'sɪriəs

seriously
BR 'sɪərɪəsli
AM 'sɪriəsli

seriousness
BR 'sɪərɪəsnəs
AM 'sɪriəsnəs

serjeant
BR 'sɑːdʒ(ə)nt, -s
AM 'sɑrdʒənt, -s

serjeantship
BR 'sɑːdʒ(ə)ntʃɪp, -s
AM 'sɑrdʒəntˌʃɪp, -s

Serkin
BR 'səːkɪn
AM 'sərkən

Serle
BR səːl
AM sərl

sermon
BR 'səːmən, -z
AM 'sərmən, -z

sermonette
BR ˌsəːmə'nɛt, -s
AM ˌsərmə'nɛt, -s

sermonise
BR 'səːmənʌɪz, -ɨz, -ɪŋ, -d
AM 'sərməˌnaɪz, -ɨz, -ɪŋ, -d

sermoniser
BR 'səːmənʌɪzə(r), -z
AM 'sərməˌnaɪzər, -z

sermonize
BR 'səːmənʌɪz, -ɨz, -ɪŋ, -d
AM 'sərməˌnaɪz, -ɨz, -ɪŋ, -d

sermonizer
BR 'səːmənʌɪzə(r), -z
AM 'sərməˌnaɪzər, -z

seroconvert
BR ˌsɪərəʊkən'vəːt, -s, -ɪŋ, -ɨd
AM ˌsɪrəkən'vər|t, -ts, -dɪŋ, -dəd

serological
BR ˌsɪərə'lɒdʒɪkl
AM ¦sɪrə'lɑdʒəkəl, ¦sɛrə'lɑdʒəkəl

serologist
BR sɪə'rɒlədʒɪst, sɪ'rɒlədʒɪst, -s
AM sɪ'rɑlədʒəst, -s

serology
BR sɪə'rɒlədʒi, sɪ'rɒlədʒi
AM sɪ'rɑlədʒi

seronegative
BR ˌsɪərəʊ'nɛgətɪv
AM ¦sɪroʊ'nɛgədɪv, ¦sɛroʊ'nɛgədɪv

seropositive
BR ˌsɪərəʊ'pɒzɪtɪv
AM ¦sɪroʊ'pɑzədɪv, ¦sɛroʊ'pɑzədɪv

serosa
BR sɪ'rəʊsə(r)
AM sə'roʊsə, sə'roʊzə

serosity
BR sɪə'rɒsɪti
AM sə'rɑsədi

Serota
BR sɪ'rəʊtə(r)
AM sə'roʊdə

serotine
BR 'sɛrə(ʊ)tʌɪn, -z
AM 'sɛrətn, 'sɛrəˌtaɪn, 'sɛrəˌtin, -z

serotonin
BR ˌsɛrə(ʊ)'təʊnɪn, -z
AM ˌsɛrə'toʊnən, ˌsɪrə'toʊnən, -z

serotype
BR 'sɪərə(ʊ)tʌɪp, 'sɛrə(ʊ)tʌɪp, -s
AM 'sɪrəˌtaɪp, 'sɛrəˌtaɪp, -s

serous
BR 'sɪərəs
AM 'sɪrəs

serow
BR 'sɛrəʊ, -z
AM sə'roʊ, -z

Serpell
BR 'səːpl
AM 'sərpəl

Serpens
BR 'səːpɛnz, 'səːp(ə)nz
AM 'sərpəns

serpent
BR 'səːp(ə)nt, -s
AM 'sərpənt, -s

serpentiform
BR səː'pɛntɪfɔːm
AM sər'pɛn(t)əˌfɔ(ə)rm

serpentine
BR 'səːp(ə)ntʌɪn
AM 'sərpənˌtin, 'sərpənˌtaɪn

serpiginous
BR səː'pɪdʒɪnəs
AM sər'pɪdʒənəs

SERPS
BR səːps
AM sərps

serpula
BR 'səːpjʉlə(r)
AM 'sərpjələ

serpulae
BR 'səːpjʉliː
AM 'sərpjəli, 'sərpjəˌlaɪ

serra
BR 'sɛrə(r)
AM 'sɛrə

serradella
BR ˌsɛrə'dɛlə(r), -z
AM ˌsərə'dɛlə, -z

serradilla
BR ˌsɛrə'dɪlə(r), -z
AM ˌsərə'dɪlə, -z

serrae
BR 'sɛriː
AM 'sɛri, 'sɛˌraɪ

serran
BR 'sɛrən, -z
AM 'sɛrən, -z

serranid
BR 'sɛrənɪd, -z
AM 'sɛrənəd, -z

serrate¹
adjective
BR 'sɛreɪt
AM 'sɛˌreɪt, 'sɛrət

serrate²
verb
BR sɪ'reɪt, -s, -ɪŋ, -ɨd
AM 'sɛˌreɪ|t, sə'reɪ|t, -ts, -dɪŋ, -dɨd

serration
BR sɪ'reɪʃn, -z
AM sɛ'reɪʃən, -z

serried
BR 'sɛrɪd
AM 'sɛrid

serrulate
BR 'sɛrjʉleɪt, 'sɛrjʉlət
AM 'sɛr(j)ələt, 'sɛr(j)əleɪt

serrulation
BR ˌsɛrjʉ'leɪʃn, -z
AM ˌsɛr(j)ə'leɪʃən, -z

serum
BR 'sɪərəm, -z
AM 'sɪrəm, -z

serval
BR 'səːvl, -z
AM 'sərvəl, sər'væl, -z

servant
BR 'səːv(ə)nt, -s
AM 'sərvənt, -s

serve
BR səːv, -z, -ɪŋ, -d
AM sərv, -z, -ɪŋ, -d

server
BR 'səːvə(r), -z
AM 'sərvər, -z

servery
BR 'səːv(ə)r|i, -ɪz

AM ˈsərvəri, -z

Servian
BR ˈsəːvɪən
AM ˈsərviən

service
BR ˈsəːv|ɪs, -ɪsɪz, -ɪsɪŋ, -ɪst
AM ˈsərvəs, -əz, -ɪŋ, -t

serviceability
BR ˌsəːvɪsəˈbɪlɪti
AM ˌsərvəsəˈbɪlɨdi

serviceable
BR ˈsəːvɪsəbl
AM ˈsərvəsəbəl

serviceableness
BR ˈsəːvɪsəblnəs
AM ˈsərvəsəbəlnəs

serviceably
BR ˈsəːvɪsəbli
AM ˈsərvəsəbli

serviceberry
BR ˈsəːvɪsˌbɛr|i, -ɪz
AM ˈsərvəsˌbɛri, -z

serviceman
BR ˈsəːvɪsmən
AM ˈsərvəsˌmæn, ˈsərvəsmən

servicemen
BR ˈsəːvɪsmən
AM ˈsərvəsˌmɛn, ˈsərvəsmən

servicewoman
BR ˈsəːvɪsˌwʊmən
AM ˈsərvəsˌwʊmən

servicewomen
BR ˈsəːvɪsˌwɪmɪn
AM ˈsərvəsˌwɪmɨn

serviette
BR ˌsəːvɪˈɛt, -s
AM ˌsərviˈɛt, -s

servile
BR ˈsəːvʌɪl
AM ˈsərvəl, ˈsərˌvaɪl

servilely
BR ˈsəːvʌɪlli
AM ˈsərvəli, ˈsərˌvaɪli

servility
BR səːˈvɪlɪti
AM sərˈvɪlɨdi

serving
BR ˈsəːvɪŋ, -z
AM ˈsərvɪŋ, -z

Servis
BR ˈsəːvɪs
AM ˈsərvəs

Servite
BR ˈsəːvʌɪt, -s
AM ˈsərˌvaɪt, -s

servitor
BR ˈsəːvɪtə(r), -z
AM ˈsərvədər, ˈsərvəˌtɔ(ə)r, -z

servitorship
BR ˈsəːvɪtəʃɪp, -s
AM ˈsərvədərˌʃɪp, ˈsərvəˌtɔrˌʃɪp, -s

servitude
BR ˈsəːvɪtjuːd, ˈsəːvɪtʃuːd
AM ˈsərvəˌt(j)ud

servo
BR ˈsəːvəʊ, -z
AM ˈsərvoʊ, -z

sesame
BR ˈsɛsəmi
AM ˈsɛsəmi

sesamoid
BR ˈsɛsəmɔɪd
AM ˈsɛsəˌmɔɪd

sesamum
BR ˈsɛsəməm
AM ˈsɛsəməm

Sesotho
BR sɪˈsəʊtəʊ, sɛˈsəʊtəʊ
AM səˈsɔdoʊ, səˈsɑdoʊ

sesquicentenary
BR ˌsɛskwɪsɛnˈtiːn(ə)r|i, ˌsɛskwɪsɛnˈtɛn(ə)r|i, -ɪz
AM ˌsɛskwəsɛnˈtɛnəri, -z

sesquicentennial
BR ˌsɛskwɪsɛnˈtɛnɪəl
AM ˌsɛskwəsɛnˈtɛniəl, ˌsɛskwəsənˈtɛniəl

sesquipedalian
BR ˌsɛskwɪpɪˈdeɪlɪən
AM ˌsɛskwəpəˈdeɪljən, ˌsɛskwəpəˈdeɪliən

sesquiplicate
BR ˈsɛskwɪplɪkeɪt, ˈsɛskwɪplɪkət
AM ˈsɛskwəˌplɪkeɪt, ˈsɛskwəˌplɪkɪt

sess
BR sɛs
AM sɛs

sessile
BR ˈsɛsʌɪl
AM ˈsɛsəl, ˈsɛˌsaɪl

session
BR ˈsɛʃn, -z
AM ˈsɛʃən, -z

sessional
BR ˈsɛʃn̩(ə)l, ˈsɛʃən(ə)l, -z
AM ˈsɛʃ(ə)nəl, -z

sesterce
BR ˈsɛst|əːs, -əːsɪz\-əsɪz\-əsiːz
AM ˈsɛstərs, -əz

sestertia
BR sɛˈstəːtɪə(r), sɛˈstəːʃ(ɪ)ə(r)
AM sɛˈstərʃ(i)ə, səˈstərʃ(i)ə

sestertii
BR sɛˈstəːtɪʌɪ, sɛˈstəːʃɪʌɪ
AM sɛˈstərʃiˌaɪ, səˈstərʃiˌaɪ

sestertium
BR sɛˈstəːtɪəm, sɛˈstəːʃ(ɪ)əm
AM sɛˈstərʃ(i)əm, səˈstərʃ(i)əm

sestertius
BR sɛˈstəːtɪəs, sɛˈstəːʃ(ɪ)əs
AM sɛˈstərʃ(i)əs, səˈstərʃ(i)əs

sestet
BR sɛsˈtɛt, -s
AM sɛsˈtɛt, -s

sestina
BR sɛˈstiːnə(r), -z
AM sɛˈstinə, ˈsɛstənə, -z

set
BR sɛt, -s, -ɪŋ
AM sɛ|t, -ts, -dɪŋ

seta
BR ˈsiːtə(r)
AM ˈsidə

setaceous
BR sɪˈteɪʃəs
AM səˈteɪʃəs

setae
BR ˈsiːtiː
AM ˈsidi, ˈsiˌtaɪ

setaside
BR ˈsɛtəsʌɪd, -z
AM ˈsɛdəˌsaɪd, -z

setback
BR ˈsɛtbak, -s
AM ˈsɛtˌbæk, -s

Seth
BR sɛθ
AM sɛθ

SETI
BR ˈsɛti
AM ˈsɛdi

setiferous
BR sɪˈtɪf(ə)rəs
AM səˈtɪf(ə)rəs

setigerous
BR sɪˈtɪdʒ(ə)rəs
AM səˈtɪdʒ(ə)rəs

seton
BR ˈsiːtn, -z
AM ˈsitn, -z

setose
BR ˈsiːtəʊs, ˈsiːtəʊz
AM ˈsiˌtoʊs, ˈsiˌtoʊz

set-piece
BR ˌsɛtˈpiːs
AM ˈsɛtˌpis

setscrew
BR ˈsɛtskruː, -z
AM ˈsɛtˌskru, -z

setsquare
BR ˈsɛtskwɛː(r), -z
AM ˈsɛtˌskwɛ(ə)r, -z

Setswana
BR sɛtˈswɑːnə(r)
AM sɛtˈswɑnə

sett
BR sɛt, -s
AM sɛt, -s

settee
BR sɛˈtiː, -z
AM sɛˈti, -z

setter
BR ˈsɛtə(r), -z
AM ˈsɛdər, -z

setterwort
BR ˈsɛtəwəːt
AM ˈsɛdərwərt, ˈsɛdərˌwɔ(ə)rt

setting
BR ˈsɛtɪŋ, -z
AM ˈsɛdɪŋ, -z

settle
BR ˈsɛt|l, -lz, -l̩ɪŋ\-lɪŋ, -ld
AM ˈsɛ|dəl, -dlz, -dlɪŋ\-tlɪŋ, -dld

settleable
BR ˈsɛtl̩əbl, ˈsɛtləbl
AM ˈsɛdl̩əbəl, ˈsɛtləbəl

settlement
BR ˈsɛtlm(ə)nt, -s
AM ˈsɛdlmənt, -s

settler
BR ˈsɛtl̩ə(r), ˈsɛtlə(r), -z
AM ˈsɛdl̩ər, ˈsɛtlər, -z

settlor
BR ˈsɛtl̩ə(r), ˈsɛtlə(r), -z
AM ˈsɛdl̩ər, ˈsɛtlər, -z

set-to
BR ˌsɛtˈtuː, ˈsɛttuː, -z
AM ˈsɛtˌtu, -z

setup
BR ˈsɛtʌp, -s
AM ˈsɛdˌəp, -s

setwall
BR ˈsɛtw(ə)l, -z
AM ˈsɛtˌwɔl, ˈsɛtˌwɑl, -z

Seurat
BR ˈsəːrɑː(r)
AM səˈrɑ

Sevastopol
BR sɛˈvastəpɒl, səˈvastəpɒl
AM sɛˈvɑstəˌpɔl, səˈvɑstəˌpɔl, sɛˈvɑstəˌpoʊl, səˈvɑstəˌpoʊl
RUS sʲivaˈstopəlʲ

seven
BR ˈsɛvn, -z
AM ˈsɛvən, -z

sevenfold
BR ˈsɛvnfəʊld
AM ˈsɛvənˌfoʊld

Sevenoaks
BR ˈsɛvn̩əʊks
AM ˈsɛvənˌoʊks

seventeen
BR ˌsɛvnˈtiːn
AM ˌsɛvənˈtin

seventeenth
BR ˌsɛvnˈtiːnθ
AM ˌsɛvənˈtinθ

seventh
BR ˈsɛvnθ, -s
AM ˈsɛvənθ, -s

seventhly
BR ˈsɛvnθli
AM ˈsɛvənθli

seventieth
BR ˈsɛvntɪɪθ, -s
AM ˈsɛvən(t)iəθ, -s

seventy
BR ˈsɛvnt|i, -ɪz
AM ˈsɛvən(t)i, -z

seventyfold
BR ˈsɛvntɪfəʊld
AM ˈsɛvən(t)iˌfoʊld

Seven Up®
BR ˌsɛvn ˈʌp, -s
AM ˌsɛvən ˈəp, -s

sever
BR ˈsɛv|ə(r), -əz, -(ə)rɪŋ, -əd
AM ˈsɛv|ər, -ərz, -(ə)rɪŋ, -ərd

severable
BR ˈsɛv(ə)rəbl
AM ˈsɛv(ə)rəbəl

several
BR ˈsɛv(ə)rəl, ˈsɛv(ə)rl̩
AM ˈsɛv(ə)rəl

severally
BR ˈsɛv(ə)rəli, ˈsɛv(ə)rl̩i
AM ˈsɛv(ə)rəli

severalty
BR ˈsɛv(ə)rəlti, ˈsɛv(ə)rl̩ti, -ɪz
AM ˈsɛv(ə)rəlti, -z

severance
BR ˈsɛv(ə)rəns, ˈsɛv(ə)rn̩s
AM ˈsɛv(ə)rəns, ˈsɛvərəns

severe
BR sɪˈvɪə(r), -ə(r), -ɪst
AM səˈvɪ(ə)r, -ər, -est

severely
BR sɪˈvɪəli
AM səˈvɪrli

severity
BR sɪˈvɛrɪt|i, -ɪz
AM səˈvɛrədi, -z

Severn
BR ˈsɛvn
AM ˈsɛvərn

Severus
BR sɪˈvɪərəs
AM səˈvɪrəs

severy
BR ˈsɛv(ə)r|i, -ɪz
AM ˈsɛv(ə)ri, -z

seviche
BR sɛˈviːtʃeɪ
AM səˈvitʃeɪ

Seville
BR sɪˈvɪl, ˈsɛv(ɪ)l
AM səˈvɪl

Sèvres
BR ˈsɛvr(ər), ˈseɪvr(ər)
AM ˈsɛvrə

sew
BR səʊ, -z, -ɪŋ, -d
AM soʊ, -z, -ɪŋ, -d

sewage
BR ˈs(j)uːɪdʒ
AM ˈsuɪdʒ

Sewall
BR ˈs(j)uːəl
AM ˈsuəl

Seward
BR ˈsiːwəd, ˈsjuːəd
AM ˈsuərd

Sewell
BR ˈs(j)uːəl
AM ˈsuəl

sewellel
BR sɪˈwɛləl, -z
AM səˈwɛləl, -z

sewen
BR ˈsjuːɪn, -z
AM ˈsuən, -z

sewer[1]
person who sews
BR ˈsəʊə(r), -z
AM ˈsoʊər, -z

sewer[2]
pipe for sewage, servant
BR ˈs(j)uːə(r), -z
AM ˈsuər, ˈsʊ(ə)r, -z

sewerage
BR ˈs(j)uːərɪdʒ
AM ˈsuərɪdʒ

sewin
BR ˈsjuːɪn, -z
AM ˈsuən, -z

sewn
BR səʊn
AM soʊn

sex
BR sɛks, -ɪz, -ɪŋ, -t
AM sɛks, -əz, -ɪŋ, -t

sexagenarian
BR ˌsɛksədʒɪˈnɛːrɪən, -z
AM ˌsɛksədʒəˈnɛriən, -z

sexagenary
BR sɛkˈsadʒɪn(ə)r|i, sɛkˈsadʒn̩(ə)r|i, -ɪz
AM sɛkˈsædʒəˌnɛri, -z

Sexagesima
BR ˌsɛksəˈdʒɛsɪmə(r)
AM ˌsɛksəˈdʒɛsəmə

sexagesimal
BR ˌsɛksəˈdʒɛsɪml, -z
AM ˌsɛksəˈdʒɛsəməl, -z

sexagesimally
BR ˌsɛksəˈdʒɛsɪml̩i, ˌsɛksəˈdʒɛsɪməli
AM ˌsɛksəˈdʒɛsəməli

sexangular
BR sɛkˈsaŋgjʊlə(r)
AM sɛkˈsæŋgjələr

sexcentenary
BR ˌsɛksɛnˈtiːn(ə)r|i, ˌsɛksɛnˈtɛn(ə)r|i, -ɪz
AM ˌsɛksɛnˈtɛnəri, ˌsɛk(s)ˈsɛntnˌɛri, -z

sexennial
BR sɛkˈsɛnɪəl
AM sɛˈksɛniəl

sexer
BR ˈsɛksə(r), -z
AM ˈsɛksər, -z

sexfoil
BR ˈsɛksfɔɪl, -z
AM ˈsɛksˌfɔɪl, -z

sexily
BR ˈsɛksɪli
AM ˈsɛksəli

sexiness
BR ˈsɛksɪnɪs
AM ˈsɛksinɪs

sexism
BR ˈsɛksɪz(ə)m
AM ˈsɛkˌsɪzəm

sexist
BR ˈsɛksɪst, -s
AM ˈsɛksəst, -s

sexisyllabic
BR ˌsɛksɪsɪˈlabɪk
AM ˌsɛksəsəˈlæbɪk

sexisyllable
BR ˈsɛksɪˌsɪləbl, ˌsɛksɪˈsɪləbl, -z
AM ˌsɛksəˈsɪləbəl, -z

sexivalent
BR ˌsɛksɪˈveɪlənt, ˌsɛksɪˈveɪln̩t
AM ˈsɛksəˌveɪlənt

sexless
BR ˈsɛksləs
AM ˈsɛksləs

sexlessly
BR ˈsɛksləsli
AM ˈsɛksləsli

sexlessness
BR ˈsɛksləsnəs
AM ˈsɛksləsnəs

sexological
BR ˌsɛksəˈlɒdʒɪkl
AM ˌsɛksəˈlɑdʒəkəl

sexologist
BR sɛkˈsɒlədʒɪst, -s
AM sɛkˈsɑlədʒəst, -s

sexology
BR sɛkˈsɒlədʒi
AM sɛkˈsɑlədʒi

sexpartite
BR sɛksˈpɑːtʌɪt
AM sɛksˈpɑrˌtaɪt

sexploitation
BR ˌsɛksplɔɪˈteɪʃn
AM ˌsɛksplɔɪˈteɪʃən

sexpot
BR ˈsɛkspɒt, -s
AM ˈsɛksˌpɑt, -s

sexstarved
BR ˈsɛk(s)stɑːvd
AM ˈsɛk(s)ˌstɑrvd

sext
BR sɛkst
AM sɛkst

sextain
BR ˈsɛksteɪn, -z
AM ˈsɛkˌsteɪn, -z

Sextans
BR ˈsɛkst(ə)nz
AM ˈsɛkstənz

sextant
BR ˈsɛkst(ə)nt, -s
AM ˈsɛkstənt, -s

sextet
BR (ˌ)sɛkˈstɛt, (ˌ)sɛksˈtɛt, -s
AM sɛkˈstɛt, -s

sextile
BR ˈsɛkstʌɪl
AM ˈsɛkˌstaɪl

sextillion
BR sɛkˈstɪljən, -z
AM sɛkˈstɪljən, -z

sextillionth
BR sɛkˈstɪljənθ, -s
AM sɛkˈstɪljənθ, -s

sexto
BR ˈsɛkstəʊ, -z
AM ˈsɛkˌstoʊ, -z

sextodecimo
BR ˌsɛkstəʊˈdɛsɪməʊ, -z
AM ˌsɛkstəˈdɛsəˌmoʊ, -z

sexton
BR ˈsɛkst(ə)n, -z
AM ˈsɛkstən, -z

sextuple
BR ˈsɛkstjʊpl, ˈsɛkstʃʊpl
AM sɛkˈst(j)upəl, ˌsɛksˈtəpəl

sextuplet
BR sɛksˈtjuːplɪt, sɛksˈtʃuːplɪt, ˈsɛkstjʊplɪt, ˈsɛkstʃʊplɪt, -s
AM sɛkˈstəplət, -s

sextuply
BR ˈsɛkstjʊpli, ˈsɛkstʃʊpli
AM sɛkˈst(j)upli, ˌsɛksˈtəpli

sexual
BR ˈsɛkʃʊəl, ˈsɛkʃ(ʊ)l, ˈsɛksjʊ(ə)l
AM ˈsɛkʃ(əw)əl

sexualise
BR ˈsɛkʃʊəlʌɪz, ˈsɛkʃʊlʌɪz, ˈsɛkʃl̩ʌɪz, ˈsɛksjʊ(ə)lʌɪz, -ɪz, -ɪŋ, -d
AM ˈsɛkʃ(əw)əˌlaɪz, -ɪz, -ɪŋ, -d

sexualist
BR ˈsɛkʃʊəlɪst, ˈsɛkʃʊlɪst, ˈsɛkʃl̩ɪst, ˈsɛksjʊ(ə)lɪst, -s
AM ˈsɛkʃ(əw)ələst, -s

sexuality
BR ˌsɛkʃʊˈalɪti, ˌsɛksjʊˈalɪti

AM ˌsɛkʃə'wælədi
sexualize
BR 'sɛkʃʊəlʌɪz, 'sɛkʃʉlʌɪz, 'sɛkʃl̩ʌɪz, 'sɛksjʊ(ə)lʌɪz, -ɪz, -ɪŋ, -d
AM 'sɛkʃ(əw)əˌlaɪz, -ɪz, -ɪŋ, -d
sexually
BR 'sɛkʃʊəli, 'sɛkʃʉli, 'sɛkʃl̩i, 'sɛksjʊ(ə)li
AM 'sɛkʃ(əw)əli
sexvalent
BR (ˌ)sɛks'veɪlənt, (ˌ)sɛks'veɪln̩t
AM ˌsɛks'veɪlənt
sexy
BR 'sɛks|i, -ɪə(r), -ɪɪst
AM 'sɛksi, -ər, -ɨst
Seychelles
BR seɪ'ʃɛlz
AM seɪ'ʃɛlz
Seychellois
BR ˌseɪʃɛl'wɑː(r)
AM ˌseɪʃɛl'wɑ
Seychelloise
BR ˌseɪʃɛl'wɑːz
AM ˌseɪʃɛl'wɑ(z)
Seyfert
BR 'siːfət, 'sʌɪfət
AM 'sifərt, 'saɪfərt
Seymour
BR 'siːmɔː(r)
AM 'siˌmɔ(ə)r
sez
BR sɛz
AM sɛz
Sfax
BR sfaks
AM sfæks
sforzandi
BR sfɔːt'sandiː
AM sfɔrt'sɑndi
sforzando
BR sfɔːt'sandəʊ, -z
AM sfɔrt'sɑndoʊ, -z
sforzato
BR sfɔːt'satəʊ
AM sfɔrt'sɑdoʊ, sfɔrt'sɑdoʊ
sfumati
BR sfuː'mɑːtiː
AM sfu'mɑdi
sfumato
BR sfuː'mɑːtəʊ
AM sfu'mɑdoʊ
sgraffiti
BR zgra'fiːtiː, skra'fiːtiː
AM zgrɑ'fidi, skrɑ'fidi
sgraffito
BR zgra'fiːtəʊ, sgra'fiːtəʊ
AM zgrɑ'fidoʊ, skrɑ'fidoʊ
Sgurr
BR 'skʊə(r)
AM 'sgʊ(ə)r
sh!
BR ʃ
AM ʃ
Shaba
BR 'ʃɑːbə(r)
AM 'ʃɑbə
shabbat
BR ʃa'bat, -s
AM ʃə'bɑt, -s
shabbily
BR 'ʃabɨli
AM 'ʃæbəli
shabbiness
BR 'ʃabɪnɪs
AM 'ʃæbinɨs
shabbos
BR 'ʃabəs, -ɪz
AM 'ʃɑbəs, -əz
shabby
BR 'ʃab|i, -ɪə(r), -ɪɪst
AM 'ʃæbi, -ər, -ɨst
shabbyish
BR 'ʃabɪɪʃ
AM 'ʃæbiɪʃ
shabrack
BR 'ʃabrak, -s
AM 'ʃæˌbræk, -s
shack
BR ʃak, -s, -ɪŋ, -t
AM ʃæk, -s, -ɪŋ, -t
shackle
BR 'ʃak|l, -lz, -l̩ɪŋ\-lɪŋ, -ld
AM 'ʃæk|əl, -əlz, -(ə)lɪŋ, -əld
Shackleton
BR 'ʃaklt(ə)n
AM 'ʃækəltən
shad
BR ʃad
AM ʃæd
Shadbolt
BR 'ʃadbəʊlt
AM 'ʃædˌboʊlt
shadbush
BR 'ʃadbʊʃ, -ɪz
AM 'ʃædˌbʊʃ, -əz
shaddock
BR 'ʃadək, -s
AM 'ʃædək, -s
shade
BR ʃeɪd, -z, -ɪŋ, -ɨd
AM ʃeɪd, -z, -ɪŋ, -ɨd
shadeless
BR 'ʃeɪdlɨs
AM 'ʃeɪdlɨs
shadily
BR 'ʃeɪdɨli
AM 'ʃeɪdɨli
shadiness
BR 'ʃeɪdɪnɪs
AM 'ʃeɪdinɨs
shading
BR 'ʃeɪdɪŋ, -z
AM 'ʃeɪdɪŋ, -z
shadoof
BR ʃə'duːf, ʃa'duːf, -s
AM ʃə'duf, ʃɑ'duf, ʃæ'duf, -s
shadow
BR 'ʃadəʊ, -z, -ɪŋ, -d
AM 'ʃæd|oʊ, -oʊz, -əwɪŋ, -oʊd
shadowbox
BR 'ʃadə(ʊ)bɒks, -ɪz, -ɪŋ, -t
AM 'ʃædəˌbɑks, 'ʃædoʊˌbɑks, -əz, -ɪŋ, -t
shadower
BR 'ʃadəʊə(r), -z
AM 'ʃædəwər, -z
shadowgraph
BR 'ʃadəʊgrɑːf, 'ʃadəʊgraf, -s
AM 'ʃædoʊˌgræf, -s
shadowiness
BR 'ʃadəʊɪnɪs
AM 'ʃædəwinɨs
shadowless
BR 'ʃadəʊləs
AM 'ʃædoʊləs
shadowy
BR 'ʃadəʊi
AM 'ʃædəwi
Shadrach
BR 'ʃadrak, 'ʃeɪdrak
AM 'ʃædˌræk
Shadwell
BR 'ʃadw(ɛ)l
AM 'ʃædˌwɛl
shady
BR 'ʃeɪd|i, -ɪə(r), -ɪɪst
AM 'ʃeɪdi, -ər, -ɨst
SHAEF
BR ʃeɪf
AM ʃeɪf
Shaeffer
BR 'ʃeɪfə(r)
AM 'ʃeɪfər
Shafer
BR 'ʃeɪfə(r)
AM 'ʃeɪfər
Shaffer
BR 'ʃafə(r)
AM 'ʃæfər
shaft
BR ʃɑːft, ʃaft, -s, -ɪŋ, -ɨd
AM ʃæft, -s, -ɪŋ, -əd
Shaftesbury
BR 'ʃɑːf(t)sb(ə)ri, 'ʃaf(t)sb(ə)ri
AM 'ʃæf(t)sˌbɛri, 'ʃæf(t)sb(ə)ri
Shafto
BR 'ʃɑːftəʊ, 'ʃaftəʊ
AM 'ʃæfˌtoʊ
Shaftoe
BR 'ʃɑːftəʊ, 'ʃaftəʊ
AM 'ʃæfˌtoʊ
shag
BR ʃag, -z, -ɪŋ, -d
AM ʃæg, -z, -ɪŋ, -d
shagbark
BR 'ʃagbɑːk, -s
AM 'ʃægˌbɑrk, -s
shagger
BR 'ʃagə(r), -z
AM 'ʃægər, -z
shaggily
BR 'ʃagɨli
AM 'ʃægəli
shagginess
BR 'ʃagɪnɪs
AM 'ʃæginɨs
shaggy
BR 'ʃag|i, -ɪə(r), -ɪɪst
AM 'ʃægi, -ər, -ɨst
shaggy-dog
BR ˌʃagɪ'dɒg
AM ˌʃægi'dɑg
shagreen
BR ʃə'griːn, ʃa'griːn
AM ʃæ'grin, ʃə'grin
shah
BR ʃɑː(r), -z
AM ʃɑ, -z
shahdom
BR 'ʃɑːdəm, -z
AM 'ʃɑdəm, -z
shaikh
BR ʃeɪk, ʃiːk, -s
AM ʃik, ʃeɪk, -s
Shaka
BR 'ʃɑːkə(r)
AM 'ʃɑkə, 'ʃækə
shake
BR ʃeɪk, -s, -ɪŋ
AM ʃeɪk, -s, -ɪŋ
shakeable
BR 'ʃeɪkəbl
AM 'ʃeɪkəbəl
shakedown
BR 'ʃeɪkdaʊn, -z
AM 'ʃeɪkˌdaʊn, -z
shaken
BR 'ʃeɪk(ə)n
AM 'ʃeɪkən
shaker
BR 'ʃeɪkə(r), -z
AM 'ʃeɪkər, -z
Shakeress
BR 'ʃeɪkərɛs, 'ʃeɪk(ə)rɪs, ˌʃeɪkər'ɛs, -ɪz
AM 'ʃeɪk(ə)rəs, -əz
Shakerism
BR 'ʃeɪk(ə)rɪz(ə)m
AM 'ʃeɪk(ə)ˌrɪzəm
Shakeshaft
BR 'ʃeɪkʃɑːft, 'ʃeɪkʃaft
AM 'ʃeɪkˌʃæft
Shakespeare
BR 'ʃeɪkspɪə(r)
AM 'ʃeɪkˌspɪ(ə)r
Shakespearean
BR ʃeɪk'spɪərɪən, -z
AM ʃeɪk'spɪriən, -z

Shakespeareana
BR ʃeɪkˌspɪərɪ'ɑːnə(r), ˌʃeɪkspɪərɪ'ɑːnə(r)
AM ʃeɪkˌspɪri'ɑnə

Shakespearian
BR ʃeɪk'spɪərɪən, -z
AM ʃeɪk'spɪriən, -z

Shakespeariana
BR ʃeɪkˌspɪərɪ'ɑːnə(r), ˌʃeɪkspɪərɪ'ɑːnə(r)
AM ʃeɪkˌspɪri'ɑnə

shakeup
BR 'ʃeɪkʌp, -s
AM 'ʃeɪkˌəp, -s

shakily
BR 'ʃeɪkɪli
AM 'ʃeɪkɨli

shakiness
BR 'ʃeɪkɪnɪs
AM 'ʃeɪkinɨs

shako
BR 'ʃeɪkəʊ, 'ʃakəʊ, -z
AM 'ʃækoʊ, 'ʃeɪkoʊ, -z

shakuhachi
BR ˌʃakuː'hɑːtʃ|i, ˌʃakʊ'hatʃ|i, -ɪz
AM 'ʃɑku'hɑtʃi, -z

shaky
BR 'ʃeɪk|i, -ɪə(r), -ɪɪst
AM 'ʃeɪki, -ər, -ɨst

Shaldon
BR 'ʃɔːld(ə)n, 'ʃɒld(ə)n, 'ʃald(ə)n
AM 'ʃɔldən, 'ʃældən, 'ʃɑldən

shale
BR ʃeɪl
AM ʃeɪl

shaley
BR 'ʃeɪli
AM 'ʃeɪli

shaliness
BR 'ʃeɪlɪnɪs
AM 'ʃeɪlinɨs

shall¹
strong form
BR ʃal
AM ʃæl

shall²
weak form
BR ʃ(ə)l
AM ʃəl

shalloon
BR ʃə'luːn, -z
AM ʃə'lun, -z

shallop
BR 'ʃaləp, -s
AM 'ʃæləp, -s

shallot
BR ʃə'lɒt, -s
AM ʃə'lɑt, 'ʃælət, -s

shallow
BR 'ʃaləʊ, -z, -ə(r), -ɪst
AM 'ʃæl|oʊ, -oʊz, -əwər, -əwəst

shallowly
BR 'ʃaləʊli
AM 'ʃæloʊli

shallowness
BR 'ʃaləʊnəs
AM 'ʃæloʊnəs

Shalmaneser
BR ˌʃalmə'niːzə(r)
AM ˌʃælmə'nizər

shalom
BR ʃə'lɒm, ʃa'lɒm, ʃə'ləʊm, ʃa'ləʊm
AM ʃə'loʊm, ʃɑ'loʊm

shalt¹
strong form
BR ʃalt
AM ʃælt

shalt²
weak form
BR ʃ(ə)lt
AM ʃəlt

shalwar
BR 'ʃʌlvɑː(r), -z
AM 'ʃɑlˌwɑr, -z

shaly
BR 'ʃeɪl|i, -ɪə(r), -ɪɪst
AM 'ʃeɪli, -ər, -ɨst

sham
BR ʃam, -z, -ɪŋ, -d
AM ʃæm, -z, -ɪŋ, -d

shaman
BR 'ʃɑːmən, 'ʃamən, 'ʃeɪmən, -z
AM 'ʃɑmən, 'ʃeɪmən, -z

shamanic
BR ʃə'manɪk, ʃeɪ'manɪk
AM ʃə'mænɪk, ʃeɪ'mænɪk

shamanism
BR 'ʃɑːmənɪz(ə)m, 'ʃamənɪz(ə)m, 'ʃeɪmənɪz(ə)m
AM 'ʃɑməˌnɪzəm, 'ʃeɪməˌnɪzəm

shamanist
BR 'ʃɑːmənɪst, 'ʃamənɪst, 'ʃeɪmənɪst, -s
AM 'ʃɑmənəst, 'ʃeɪmənəst, -s

shamanistic
BR ˌʃɑːmə'nɪstɪk, ˌʃamə'nɪstɪk, ˌʃeɪmə'nɪstɪk
AM ˌʃɑmə'nɪstɪk, ˌʃeɪmə'nɪstɪk

shamateur
BR 'ʃamət(ʃ)ə(r), ˌʃamə'təː(r), -z
AM 'ʃæmədər, 'ʃæməˌtər, ˌʃæmə'tər, ˌʃæmə't(j)ʊ(ə)r, -z

shamateurish
BR 'ʃamət(ə)rɪʃ, 'ʃamətʃ(ə)rɪʃ, ˌʃamə'təːrɪʃ
AM ¦ʃæmə'tərɪʃ, ¦ʃæmə't(j)ʊrɪʃ, ¦ʃæmə'tʃʊrɪʃ

shamateurishly
BR 'ʃamət(ə)rɪʃli, 'ʃamətʃ(ə)rɪʃli, ˌʃamə'təːrɪʃli
AM ¦ʃæmə'tərɪʃli, ¦ʃæmə't(j)ʊrɪʃli, ¦ʃæmə'tʃʊrɪʃli

shamateurishness
BR 'ʃamət(ə)rɪʃnɪs, 'ʃamətʃ(ə)rɪʃnɪs, ˌʃamə'təːrɪʃnɪs
AM ¦ʃæmə'tərɪʃnɪs, ¦ʃæmə't(j)ʊrɪʃnɪs, ¦ʃæmə'tʃʊrɪʃnɪs

shamateurism
BR 'ʃamət(ə)rɪz(ə)m, 'ʃamətʃ(ə)rɪz(ə)m, ˌʃamə'təːrɪz(ə)m
AM 'ʃæmədəˌrɪzəm, 'ʃæməˌt(j)ʊˌrɪzəm, 'ʃæməˌtʃʊˌrɪzəm

shamble
BR 'ʃamb|l, -lz, -lɪŋ\-lɪŋ, -ld
AM 'ʃæmbəl, -əlz, -(ə)lɪŋ, -əld

shambolic
BR ʃam'bɒlɪk
AM ˌʃæm'bɑlɪk

shambolically
BR ʃam'bɒlɪkli
AM ˌʃæm'bɑlək(ə)li

shame
BR ʃeɪm, -z, -ɪŋ, -d
AM ʃeɪm, -z, -ɪŋ, -d

shamefaced
BR ˌʃeɪm'feɪst
AM 'ʃeɪmˌfeɪst

shamefacedly
BR ˌʃeɪm'feɪstli, ˌʃeɪm'feɪsɪdli
AM ¦ʃeɪm¦feɪsɨdli, ¦ʃeɪm¦feɪstli

shamefacedness
BR ˌʃeɪm'feɪstnɪs, ˌʃeɪm'feɪsɪdnɪs
AM 'ʃeɪm¦feɪsɨdnɨs, 'ʃeɪm¦feɪstnɨs

shameful
BR 'ʃeɪmf(ʊ)l
AM 'ʃeɪmfəl

shamefully
BR 'ʃeɪmfʊli, 'ʃeɪmfḷi
AM 'ʃeɪmfəli

shamefulness
BR 'ʃeɪmf(ʊ)lnəs
AM 'ʃeɪmfəlnəs

shameless
BR 'ʃeɪmlɪs
AM 'ʃeɪmlɨs

shamelessly
BR 'ʃeɪmlɪsli
AM 'ʃeɪmlɨsli

shamelessness
BR 'ʃeɪmlɪsnɪs
AM 'ʃeɪmlɨsnɨs

shamingly
BR 'ʃeɪmɪŋli
AM 'ʃeɪmɪŋli

Shamir
BR ʃə'mɪə(r)
AM ʃə'mɪ(ə)r

shammer
BR 'ʃamə(r), -z
AM 'ʃæmər, -z

shammy
BR 'ʃam|i, -ɪz
AM 'ʃæmi, -z

shampoo
BR ʃam'puː, -z, -ɪŋ, -d
AM ʃæm'pu, -z, -ɪŋ, -d

shamrock
BR 'ʃamrɒk, -s
AM 'ʃæmˌrɑk, -s

Shamu
BR ʃa'muː
AM ʃæ'mu, ʃɑ'mu

shamus
BR 'ʃeɪməs, -ɪz
AM 'ʃeɪməs, -əz

Shan¹
forename
BR ʃɑːn
AM ʃæn

Shan²
people, language
BR ʃɑːn, ʃan
AM ʃæn

Shandean
BR 'ʃandɪən, -z
AM 'ʃændiən, -z

shandrydan
BR 'ʃandrɪdan, -z
AM 'ʃændriˌdæn, -z

shandy
BR 'ʃand|i, -ɪz
AM 'ʃændi, -z

shandygaff
BR 'ʃandɪgaf, -s
AM 'ʃændiˌgæf, -s

Shane
BR ʃeɪn
AM ʃeɪn

Shang
BR ʃaŋ
AM ʃæŋ

shanghai
BR ˌʃaŋ'hʌɪ, -z, -ɪŋ, -d
AM ¦ʃæŋ¦haɪ, -z, -ɪŋ, -d

Shangri-La
BR ˌʃaŋgrɪ'lɑː(r), -z
AM ¦ʃæŋgri'lɑ, -z

shank
BR ʃaŋ|k, -ks, -(k)t
AM ʃæŋ|k, -ks, -kɪŋ, -(k)t

Shankar
BR 'ʃaŋkɑː(r)
AM 'ʃæŋˌkɑr

Shankill
BR 'ʃaŋkɪl
AM 'ʃæŋkəl

Shanklin
BR 'ʃaŋklɪn
AM 'ʃæŋklən

Shankly
BR ˈʃaŋkli
AM ˈʃæŋkli
Shanks
BR ʃaŋks
AM ʃæŋks
Shannon
BR ˈʃanən
AM ˈʃænən
shanny
BR ˈʃan|i, -ɪz
AM ˈʃæni, -z
Shansi
BR ʃanˈsiː
AM ʃænˈʃi
shan't
BR ʃɑːnt
AM ʃænt
shantung
BR ˌʃanˈtʌŋ
AM ʃænˈtəŋ
shanty
BR ˈʃant|i, -ɪz
AM ˈʃæn(t)i, -z
shantyman
BR ˈʃantɪman
AM ˈʃæn(t)iˌmæn
shantymen
BR ˈʃantɪmɛn
AM ˈʃæn(t)iˌmɛn
shantytown
BR ˈʃantɪtaʊn, -z
AM ˈʃæn(t)iˌtaʊn, -z
Shanxi
BR ʃanˈsiː
AM ʃænˈʃi
shap
BR ʃap
AM ʃæp
shapable
BR ˈʃeɪpəbl
AM ˈʃeɪpəbəl
SHAPE
BR ʃeɪp
AM ʃeɪp
shape
BR ʃeɪp, -s, -ɪŋ, -t
AM ʃeɪp, -s, -ɪŋ, -t
shapeable
BR ˈʃeɪpəbl
AM ˈʃeɪpəbəl
shapechanger
BR ˈʃeɪpˌtʃeɪn(d)ʒə(r), -z
AM ˈʃeɪpˌtʃeɪndʒər, -z
shapechanging
BR ˈʃeɪpˌtʃeɪn(d)ʒɪŋ
AM ˈʃeɪpˌtʃeɪndʒɪŋ
shapeless
BR ˈʃeɪplɨs
AM ˈʃeɪplɨs
shapelessly
BR ˈʃeɪplɨsli
AM ˈʃeɪplɨsli
shapelessness
BR ˈʃeɪplɨsnɨs
AM ˈʃeɪplɨsnɨs
shapeliness
BR ˈʃeɪplɪnɪs
AM ˈʃeɪplinɪs
shapely
BR ˈʃeɪpl|i, -ɪə(r), -ɪɪst
AM ˈʃeɪpli, -ər, -ɪst
shaper
BR ˈʃeɪpə(r), -z
AM ˈʃeɪpər, -z
shaping
BR ˈʃeɪpɪŋ, -z
AM ˈʃeɪpɪŋ, -z
Shapiro
BR ʃəˈpɪərəʊ
AM ʃəˈpɪroʊ
shard
BR ʃɑːd, -z
AM ʃɑrd, -z
share
BR ʃɛː(r), -z, -ɪŋ, -d
AM ʃɛ(ə)r, -z, -ɪŋ, -d
shareable
BR ˈʃɛːrəbl
AM ˈʃɛrəbəl
sharecrop
BR ˈʃɛːkrɒp, -s, -ɪŋ, -t
AM ˈʃɛrˌkrɑp, -s, -ɪŋ, -t
sharecropper
BR ˈʃɛːˌkrɒpə(r), -z
AM ˈʃɛrˌkrɑpər, -z
share-farmer
BR ˈʃɛːˌfɑːmə(r), -z
AM ˈʃɛrˌfɑrmər, -z
shareholder
BR ˈʃɛːˌhəʊldə(r), -z
AM ˈʃɛrˌ(h)oʊldər, -z
shareholding
BR ˈʃɛːˌhəʊldɪŋ, -z
AM ˈʃɛrˌ(h)oʊldɪŋ, -z
share-out
BR ˈʃɛːraʊt, -s
AM ˈʃɛrˌaʊt, -s
sharer
BR ˈʃɛːrə(r), -z
AM ˈʃɛrər, -z
shareware
BR ˈʃɛːwɛː(r)
AM ˈʃɛrˌwɛ(ə)r
sharia
BR ʃəˈriːə(*r*), ʃɑːˈriːə(*r*)
AM ʃəˈriə
shariah
BR ʃəˈriːə(*r*), ʃɑːˈriːə(*r*)
AM ʃəˈriə
Sharif
BR ʃəˈriːf, ʃaˈriːf
AM ʃəˈrif
Sharjah
BR ˈʃɑː(d)ʒɑː(*r*), ˈʃɑː(d)ʒə(*r*)
AM ˈʃɑr(d)ʒə
shark
BR ʃɑːk, -s
AM ʃɑrk, -s
sharkskin
BR ˈʃɑːkskɪn
AM ˈʃɑrkˌskɪn
Sharman
BR ˈʃɑːmən
AM ˈʃɑrmən
Sharon[1]
personal name
BR ˈʃarən, ˈʃarn̩
AM ˈʃɛrən
Sharon[2]
placename
BR ˈʃɛːrən, ˈʃɛːrn̩, ˈʃɑːrən, ˈʃɑːrn̩, ˈʃarən, ˈʃarn̩
AM ˈʃɛrən
sharon fruit
BR ˈʃɛːrən fruːt, ˈʃɛːrn̩ +, ˈʃɑːrən +, ˈʃɑːrn̩ +, ˈʃarən +, ˈʃarn̩ +, -s
AM ˈʃɛrən ˌfrut, -s
sharp
BR ʃɑːp, -s, -ə(r), -ɪst
AM ʃɑrp, -s, -ər, -əst
Sharpe
BR ʃɑːp
AM ʃɑrp
shar-pei
BR ˌʃɑːˈpeɪ, -z
AM ˌʃɑrˈpeɪ, -z
sharpen
BR ˈʃɑːp|(ə)n, -(ə)nz, -(ə)nɪŋ\-n̩ɪŋ, -(ə)nd
AM ˈʃɑrp|ən, -ənz, -(ə)nɪŋ, -ənd
sharpener
BR ˈʃɑːp(ə)nə(r), ˈʃɑːpn̩ə(r), -z
AM ˈʃɑrp(ə)nər, -z
sharpening
BR ˈʃɑːp(ə)nɪŋ, ˈʃɑːpn̩ɪŋ, -z
AM ˈʃɑrp(ə)nɪŋ, -z
sharper
BR ˈʃɑːpə(r), -z
AM ˈʃɑrpər, -z
Sharpeville
BR ˈʃɑːpvɪl
AM ˈʃɑrpvəl, ˈʃɑrpˌvɪl
sharpie
BR ˈʃɑːp|i, -ɪz
AM ˈʃɑrpi, -z
sharpish
BR ˈʃɑːpɪʃ
AM ˈʃɑrpɪʃ
Sharples
BR ˈʃɑːplz
AM ˈʃɑrpəlz
sharply
BR ˈʃɑːpli
AM ˈʃɑrpli
sharpness
BR ˈʃɑːpnəs
AM ˈʃɑrpnəs
sharpshooter
BR ˈʃɑːpˌʃuːtə(r), -z
AM ˈʃɑrpˌʃudər, -z
sharpshooting
BR ˈʃɑːpˌʃuːtɪŋ
AM ˈʃɑrpˌʃudɪŋ
sharpy
BR ˈʃɑːp|i, -ɪz
AM ˈʃɑrpi, -z
Sharron
BR ˈʃarən, ˈʃarn̩
AM ˈʃɛrən
Sharwood
BR ˈʃɑːwʊd
AM ˈʃɑrˌwʊd
shashlik
BR ˈʃaʃlɪk, ˈʃɑːʃlɪk, -s
AM ˈʃɑʃˌlɪk, ʃɑʃˈlɪk, -s
Shasta
BR ˈʃastə(*r*), -z
AM ˈʃæstə, -z
Shastra
BR ˈʃɑːstrə(*r*), ˈʃastrə(*r*)
AM ˈʃɑstrə
shat
BR ʃat
AM ʃæt
Shatner
BR ˈʃatnə(r)
AM ˈʃætnər
Shatt al-Arab
BR ˌʃat alˈarəb
AM ˈʃæd ˌælˈɛrəb, ˈʃɑd ˌɑlˈɛrəb
shatter
BR ˈʃat|ə(r), -əz, -(ə)rɪŋ, -əd
AM ˈʃædər, -z, -ɪŋ, -d
shatterer
BR ˈʃat(ə)rə(r), -z
AM ˈʃædərər, -z
shatteringly
BR ˈʃat(ə)rɪŋli
AM ˈʃædərɪŋli
shatterproof
BR ˈʃatəpruːf
AM ˈʃædərˌpruf
Shaughnessy
BR ˈʃɔːnəsi
AM ˈʃɔnəsi, ˈʃɑnəsi
Shaun
BR ʃɔːn
AM ʃɔn, ʃɑn
shave
BR ʃeɪv, -z, -ɪŋ, -d
AM ʃeɪv, -z, -ɪŋ, -d
shaveling
BR ˈʃeɪvlɪŋ, -z
AM ˈʃeɪvlɪŋ, -z
shaven
BR ˈʃeɪvn
AM ˈʃeɪvən
shaver
BR ˈʃeɪvə(r), -z
AM ˈʃeɪvər, -z
shavetail
BR ˈʃeɪvteɪl, -z
AM ˈʃeɪvˌteɪl, -z

Shavian
BR ˈʃeɪvɪən
AM ˈʃeɪviən, ˈʃeɪvjən
shaving
BR ˈʃeɪvɪŋ, -z
AM ˈʃeɪvɪŋ, -z
Shavuot
BR ʃəˈvuːəs, ˌʃɑːvʊˈɒt
AM ʃəˈvuˌoʊt,
ʃəˈvuˌoʊθ
Shavuoth
BR ʃəˈvuːəs, ˌʃɑːvʊˈɒt
AM ʃəˈvuˌoʊt,
ʃəˈvuˌoʊθ
shaw
BR ʃɔː(r), -z
AM ʃɔ, ʃɑ, -z
Shawcross
BR ˈʃɔːkrɒs
AM ˈʃɔˌkrɔs, ˈʃɑˌkrɑs
shawl
BR ʃɔːl, -z, -d
AM ʃɔl, ʃɑl, -z, -d
shawm
BR ʃɔːm, -z
AM ʃɔm, ʃɑm, -z
Shawnee
BR ʃɔːˈniː, -z
AM ʃɔˈni, ʃɑˈni, -z
shay
BR ʃeɪ, -z
AM ʃeɪ, -z
shchi
BR ˈʃtʃiː
AM ˈʃtʃi
she[1]
strong form
BR ʃiː
AM ʃi
she[2]
weak form
BR ʃɪ
AM ʃɪ
shea
BR ʃiː, -z
AM ʃi, ʃeɪ, -z
sheading
BR ˈʃiːdɪŋ, -z
AM ˈʃidɪŋ, -z
sheaf
BR ʃiːf
AM ʃif
shealing
BR ˈʃiːlɪŋ, -z
AM ˈʃilɪŋ, -z
shear
BR ʃɪə(r), -z, -ɪŋ, -d
AM ʃɪ(ə)r, -z, -ɪŋ, -d
shearbill
BR ˈʃɪəbɪl, -z
AM ˈʃɪrˌbɪl, -z
Sheard
BR ʃɪəd, ʃəːd, ʃɛːd
AM ʃɪ(ə)rd
shearer
BR ˈʃɪərə(r), -z
AM ˈʃɪrər, -z
shearing
BR ˈʃɪərɪŋ, -z
AM ˈʃɪrɪŋ, -z
shearling
BR ˈʃɪəlɪŋ, -z
AM ˈʃɪrlɪŋ, -z
Shearman
BR ˈʃɪəmən
AM ˈʃɪrmən
shearpin
BR ˈʃɪəpɪn, -z
AM ˈʃɪrˌpɪn, -z
sheartail
BR ˈʃɪəteɪl, -z
AM ˈʃɪrˌteɪl, -z
shearwater
BR ˈʃɪəˌwɔːtə(r), -z
AM ˈʃɪrˌwɔdər,
ˈʃɪrˌwɑdər, -z
sheatfish
BR ˈʃiːtfɪʃ, -ɪz
AM ˈʃitˌfɪʃ, -ɪz
sheath
BR ʃiː|θ, -ðz\-θs
AM ʃi|θ, -ðz\-θs
sheathe
BR ʃiːð, -z, -ɪŋ, -d
AM ʃið, -z, -ɪŋ, -d
sheathing
BR ˈʃiːðɪŋ, -z
AM ˈʃiðɪŋ, -z
sheathless
BR ˈʃiːθlɪs
AM ˈʃiθlɪs
sheave
BR ʃiːv, -z, -ɪŋ, -d
AM ʃiv, -z, -ɪŋ, -d
Sheba
BR ˈʃiːbə(r)
AM ˈʃibə
shebang
BR ʃɪˈbaŋ
AM ʃəˈbæŋ
Shebat
BR ˈʃiːbat
AM ʃəˈbɑt
shebeen
BR ʃɪˈbiːn, -z
AM ʃəˈbin, -z
she-cat
BR ˈʃiːkat, -s
AM ˈʃiˌkæt, -s
Shechinah
BR ʃɛˈkʌɪnə(r),
ʃɪˈkʌɪnə(r)
AM ʃɛˈkaɪnə, ʃəˈkaɪnə
shed
BR ʃɛd, -z, -ɪŋ
AM ʃɛd, -z, -ɪŋ
she'd
BR ʃiːd, ʃɪd
AM ʃid, ʃɪd
shedder
BR ˈʃɛdə(r), -z
AM ˈʃɛdər, -z
she-devil
BR ˈʃiːˌdɛvl, -z
AM ˈʃiˌdɛvəl, -z
shedhand
BR ˈʃɛdhand, -z
AM ˈʃɛdˌ(h)ænd, -z
Sheehan
BR ˈʃiːhən
AM ˈʃiən
Sheehy
BR ˈʃiː(h)i
AM ˈʃi(h)i
Sheelagh
BR ˈʃiːlə(r)
AM ˈʃilə
sheela-na-gig
BR ˈʃiːlənəˌɡɪɡ, -z
AM ˈʃilənəˌɡɪɡ, -z
sheen
BR ʃiːn
AM ʃin
Sheena
BR ˈʃiːnə(r)
AM ˈʃinə
Sheene
BR ʃiːn
AM ʃin
sheeny
BR ˈʃiːn|i, -ɪə(r), -ɪɪst
AM ˈʃini, -ər, -ɪst
sheep
BR ʃiːp
AM ʃip
sheepdip
BR ˈʃiːpdɪp
AM ˈʃipˌdɪp
sheepdog
BR ˈʃiːpdɒɡ, -z
AM ˈʃipˌdɔɡ, ˈʃipˌdɑɡ, -z
sheepfold
BR ˈʃiːpfəʊld, -z
AM ˈʃipˌfoʊld, -z
sheepish
BR ˈʃiːpɪʃ
AM ˈʃipɪʃ
sheepishly
BR ˈʃiːpɨʃli
AM ˈʃipɨʃli
sheepishness
BR ˈʃiːpɨʃnɨs
AM ˈʃipɨʃnɨs
sheeplike
BR ˈʃiːplʌɪk
AM ˈʃipˌlaɪk
sheepmeat
BR ˈʃiːpmiːt
AM ˈʃipˌmit
sheeprun
BR ˈʃiːprʌn, -z
AM ˈʃipˌrən, -z
sheep's-bit
BR ˈʃiːpsbɪt, -s
AM ˈʃipsˌbɪt, -s
sheepshank
BR ˈʃiːpʃaŋk, -s
AM ˈʃipˌʃæŋk, -s
sheepskin
BR ˈʃiːpskɪn, -z
AM ˈʃipˌskɪn, -z
sheepwalk
BR ˈʃiːpwɔːk, -s
AM ˈʃipˌwɔk, ˈʃipˌwɑk,
-s
sheer
BR ʃɪə(r), -z, -ɪŋ, -d
AM ʃɪ(ə)r, -z, -ɪŋ, -d
sheerlegs
BR ˈʃɪəlɛɡz
AM ˈʃɪrˌlɛɡz
sheerly
BR ˈʃɪəli
AM ˈʃɪrli
sheerness
BR ˈʃɪənəs
AM ˈʃɪrnəs
sheet
BR ʃiːt, -s, -ɪŋ, -ɪd
AM ʃi|t, -ts, -dɪŋ, -dɨd
sheetfed
BR ˌʃiːtˈfɛd
AM ˈʃitˌfɛd
sheetfeeder
BR ˈʃiːtˌfiːdə(r), -z
AM ˈʃitˌfidər, -z
Sheetrock®
BR ˈʃiːtˌrɒk
AM ˈʃitˌrɑk
Sheffield
BR ˈʃɛfiːld
AM ˈʃɛfild
sheik
BR ʃeɪk, ʃiːk, -s
AM ʃik, ʃeɪk, -s
sheikdom
BR ˈʃeɪkdəm, ˈʃiːkdəm,
-z
AM ˈʃikdəm, ˈʃeɪkdəm,
-z
sheikh
BR ʃeɪk, ʃiːk, -s
AM ʃik, ʃeɪk, -s
sheikhdom
BR ˈʃeɪkdəm, ˈʃiːkdəm,
-z
AM ˈʃikdəm, ˈʃeɪkdəm,
-z
sheila
BR ˈʃiːlə(r), -z
AM ˈʃilə, -z
shekel
BR ˈʃɛkl, -z
AM ˈʃɛkəl, -z
Shekinah
BR ʃɛˈkʌɪnə(r),
ʃɪˈkʌɪnə(r)
AM ʃɛˈkaɪnə, ʃəˈkaɪnə
Shelagh
BR ˈʃiːlə(r)
AM ˈʃilə
Shelburne
BR ˈʃɛlbəːn, ˈʃɛlb(ə)n
AM ˈʃɛlbərn
Sheldon
BR ˈʃɛld(ə)n
AM ˈʃɛldən

Sheldonian
BR ʃɛl'dəʊnɪən
AM ʃɛl'doʊniən
sheldrake
BR 'ʃɛldreɪk, -s
AM 'ʃɛlˌdreɪk, -s
shelduck
BR 'ʃɛldʌk, -s
AM 'ʃɛlˌdək, -s
shelf
BR ʃɛlf
AM ʃɛlf
shelfful
BR 'ʃɛlffʊl, -z
AM 'ʃɛl(f)ˌfʊl, -z
shelf-life
BR 'ʃɛlflʌɪf
AM 'ʃɛlfˌlaɪf
shell
BR ʃɛl, -z, -ɪŋ, -d
AM ʃɛl, -z, -ɪŋ, -d
she'll[1]
strong form
BR ʃiːl
AM ʃil
she'll[2]
weak form
BR ʃɪl
AM ʃɪl
shellac
BR ʃə'lak, 'ʃɛlak, -s, -ɪŋ, -t
AM ʃə'læk, -s, -ɪŋ, -t
shellback
BR 'ʃɛlbak, -s
AM 'ʃɛlˌbæk, -s
shell-bit
BR 'ʃɛlbɪt, -s
AM 'ʃɛlˌbɪt, -s
Shelley
BR 'ʃɛli
AM 'ʃɛli
shellfire
BR 'ʃɛlˌfʌɪə(r)
AM 'ʃɛlˌfaɪ(ə)r
shellfish
BR 'ʃɛlfɪʃ
AM 'ʃɛlˌfɪʃ
shell-less
BR 'ʃɛlləs
AM 'ʃɛ(l)ləs
Shell-Mex
BR ˌʃɛl'mɛks
AM ˌʃɛl'mɛks
shellproof
BR 'ʃɛlpruːf
AM 'ʃɛlˌpruf
shellshock
BR 'ʃɛlʃɒk
AM 'ʃɛlˌʃɑk
shelly
BR 'ʃɛli
AM 'ʃɛli
Shelta
BR 'ʃɛltə(*r*)
AM 'ʃɛltə
shelter
BR 'ʃɛlt|ə(r), -əz, -(ə)rɪŋ, -əd
AM 'ʃɛlt|ər, -ərz, -(ə)rɪŋ, -ərd
shelterer
BR 'ʃɛlt(ə)rə(r), -z
AM 'ʃɛltərər, -z
shelterless
BR 'ʃɛltələs
AM 'ʃɛltərləs
sheltie
BR 'ʃɛlt|i, -ɪz
AM 'ʃɛlti, -z
Shelton
BR 'ʃɛlt(ə)n
AM 'ʃɛltən
shelty
BR 'ʃɛlt|i, -ɪz
AM 'ʃɛlti, -z
shelve
BR ʃɛlv, -z, -ɪŋ, -d
AM ʃɛlv, -z, -ɪŋ, -d
shelver
BR 'ʃɛlvə(r), -z
AM 'ʃɛlvər, -z
shelves
BR ʃɛlvz
AM ʃɛlvz
Shem
BR ʃɛm
AM ʃɛm
Shema
BR 'ʃeɪmə(*r*), ʃɛ'mɑː(*r*), -z
AM ʃə'mɑ, -z
shemozzle
BR ʃɪ'mɒzl, -z
AM ʃə'mɑzəl, -z
Shena
BR 'ʃiːnə(*r*)
AM 'ʃinə, 'ʃeɪnə
Shenandoah
BR ˌʃɛnən'dəʊə(*r*)
AM ˌʃɛnən'doʊə
shenanigan
BR ʃɪ'nanɪɡ(ə)n, -z
AM ʃə'nænəɡən, -z
Shenfield
BR 'ʃɛnfiːld
AM ˌʃɛnˌfild
Shensi
BR 'ʃɛn'siː
AM 'ʃɛn'ʃi
Shenyang
BR 'ʃɛn'jaŋ
AM 'ʃɛn'jæŋ
Shenzhen
BR 'ʃɛn'ʒɛn
AM 'ʃɛn'ʒɛn
Sheol
BR 'ʃiːəʊl, 'ʃiːɒl
AM 'ʃiˌɔl, 'ʃiˌoʊl, 'ʃiˌɑl
Shepard
BR 'ʃɛpəd
AM 'ʃɛpərd
shepherd
BR 'ʃɛpəd, -z, -ɪŋ, -ɪd
AM 'ʃɛpərd, -z, -ɪŋ, -əd
shepherdess
BR 'ʃɛpədɛs, 'ʃɛpədɪs, ˌʃɛpə'dɛs, -ɪz
AM 'ʃɛpərdəs, -əz
Sheppard
BR 'ʃɛpəd
AM 'ʃɛpərd
Sheppey
BR 'ʃɛpi
AM 'ʃɛpi
Shepshed
BR 'ʃɛpʃɛd
AM 'ʃɛpstən
Shepton
BR 'ʃɛpt(ə)n
AM 'ʃɛptn
Shepton Mallet
BR ˌʃɛpt(ə)n 'malɪt
AM ˌʃɛptn 'mælət
Sher
BR ʃəː(r), ʃɛː(r)
AM ʃər
sherardise
BR 'ʃɛrədʌɪz, -ɪz, -ɪŋ, -d
AM ʃə'rɑrˌdaɪz, 'ʃɛrərˌdaɪz, -ɪz, -ɪŋ, -d
sherardize
BR 'ʃɛrədʌɪz, -ɪz, -ɪŋ, -d
AM ʃə'rɑrˌdaɪz, 'ʃɛrərˌdaɪz, -ɪz, -ɪŋ, -d
Sheraton
BR 'ʃɛrət(ə)n
AM 'ʃɛrətn
sherbet
BR 'ʃəːbət
AM 'ʃərbə(r)t
Sherborne
BR 'ʃəːb(ə)n, 'ʃəːbɔːn
AM 'ʃərˌbɔ(ə)rn
Sherbourne
BR 'ʃəːb(ə)n, 'ʃəːbɔːn
AM 'ʃərˌbɔ(ə)rn
Sherbrooke
BR 'ʃəːbrʊk
AM 'ʃərˌbrʊk
sherd
BR ʃəːd, -z
AM ʃərd, -z
Shere
BR ʃɪə(r)
AM ʃɪ(ə)r
shereef
BR ʃə'riːf, -s
AM ʃə'rif, -s
sheria
BR ʃə'riːə(*r*)
AM ʃə'riə
Sheridan
BR 'ʃɛrɪdn
AM 'ʃɛrədən
sherif
BR ʃə'riːf, -s
AM ʃə'rif, -s
sheriff
BR 'ʃɛrɪf, -s
AM 'ʃɛrəf, -s
sheriffalty
BR 'ʃɛrɪflt|i, -ɪz
AM 'ʃɛrəfəlti, -z
sheriffdom
BR 'ʃɛrɪfdəm, -z
AM 'ʃɛrəfdəm, -z
sheriffhood
BR 'ʃɛrɪfhʊd, -z
AM 'ʃɛrəfˌ(h)ʊd, -z
sheriffship
BR 'ʃɛrɪfʃɪp, -s
AM 'ʃɛrəfˌʃɪp, -s
Sheringham
BR 'ʃɛrɪŋəm
AM 'ʃɛrɪŋəm
sherlock
BR 'ʃəːlɒk, -s
AM 'ʃərˌlɑk, -s
Sherman
BR 'ʃəːmən
AM 'ʃərmən
sherpa
BR 'ʃəːpə(*r*), -z
AM 'ʃərpə, -z
Sherrin
BR 'ʃɛrɪn
AM 'ʃɛrən
Sherrington
BR 'ʃɛrɪŋt(ə)n
AM 'ʃɛrɪŋtən
sherry
BR 'ʃɛr|i, -ɪz
AM 'ʃɛri, -z
Sherwood
BR 'ʃəːwʊd
AM 'ʃərˌwʊd
Sheryl
BR 'ʃɛrɪl, 'ʃɛrl̩
AM 'ʃɛrəl
she's[1]
strong form
BR ʃiːz
AM ʃiz
she's[2]
weak form
BR ʃɪz
AM ʃɪz
Shetland
BR 'ʃɛtlənd, -z
AM 'ʃɛtlənd, -z
Shetlander
BR 'ʃɛtləndə(r), -z
AM 'ʃɛtləndər, -z
sheva
BR ʃə'vɑː(*r*), -z
AM ʃə'vɑ, -z
Shevardnadze
BR ˌʃɛvəd'nɑːdzə(*r*)
AM ˌʃɛvərd'nɑdzə
RUS ʃɪvard'nadzʲi
Shevat
BR 'ʃiːvat
AM ʃə'vɑt

shew
BR ʃəʊ, -z, -ɪŋ, -d
AM ʃoʊ, -z, -ɪŋ, -d
shewbread
BR ˈʃəʊbrɛd
AM ˈʃoʊˌbrɛd
shewn
BR ʃəʊn
AM ʃoʊn
she-wolf
BR ˈʃiːwʊlf
AM ˈʃiˌwʊlf
she-wolves
BR ˈʃiːwʊlvz
AM ˈʃiˌwʊlvz
Shia
BR ˈʃiːə(r), -z
AM ˈʃiɑ, -z
Shi'a
BR ˈʃiːə(r), -z
AM ˈʃiɑ, -z
Shiah
BR ˈʃiːə(r), -z
AM ˈʃiɑ, -z
shiatsu
BR ʃɪˈɑːtsuː, ʃɪˈatsuː
AM ʃiˈɑtˌsu
shibboleth
BR ˈʃɪbəlɛθ, ˈʃɪbələθ, -s
AM ˈʃɪbələθ, -s
shicer
BR ˈʃʌɪsə(r), -z
AM ˈʃaɪsər, -z
shicker
BR ˈʃɪk|ə(r), -əz, -(ə)rɪŋ, -əd
AM ˈʃɪkər, -z, -ɪŋ, -d
shicksa
BR ˈʃɪksə(r), -z
AM ˈʃɪksə, -z
shied
BR ʃʌɪd
AM ʃaɪd
shield
BR ʃiːld, -z, -ɪŋ, -ɨd
AM ʃild, -z, -ɪŋ, -ɨd
shieldbug
BR ˈʃiːldbʌg
AM ˈʃil(d)ˌbəg
shieldless
BR ˈʃiːldlɨs
AM ˈʃi(ld)lɨs
Shields
BR ʃiːldz
AM ʃi(ə)l(d)z
shieling
BR ˈʃiːlɪŋ, -z
AM ˈʃilɪŋ, -z
shift
BR ʃɪft, -s, -ɪŋ, -ɨd
AM ʃɪft, -s, -ɪŋ, -ɨd
shiftable
BR ˈʃɪftəbl
AM ˈʃɪftəbəl
shifter
BR ˈʃɪftə(r), -z
AM ˈʃɪftər, -z
shiftily
BR ˈʃɪftɨli
AM ˈʃɪftɨli
shiftiness
BR ˈʃɪftɪnɨs
AM ˈʃɪftinɨs
shiftless
BR ˈʃɪftlɨs
AM ˈʃɪf(t)lɨs
shiftlessly
BR ˈʃɪftlɨsli
AM ˈʃɪf(t)lɨsli
shiftlessness
BR ˈʃɪftlɨsnɨs
AM ˈʃɪf(t)lɨsnɨs
shifty
BR ˈʃɪft|i, -ɪə(r), -ɪɨst
AM ˈʃɪfti, -ər, -ɨst
shigella
BR ʃɨˈgɛlə(r), -z
AM ʃəˈgɛlə, -z
shiglet
BR ˈʃɪglɨt
AM ˈʃɪglɨt
shih-tzu
BR ˌʃiːˈtsuː, -z
AM ˈʃiˌtsu, -z
Shiism
BR ˈʃiːɪz(ə)m
AM ˈʃiɪzəm
Shi'ism
BR ˈʃiːɪz(ə)m
AM ˈʃiɪzəm
Shiite
BR ˈʃiːʌɪt, -s
AM ˈʃiˌaɪt, -s
Shi'ite
BR ˈʃiːʌɪt, -s
AM ˈʃiˌaɪt, -s
shikar
BR ʃɨˈkɑː(r), -z, -ɪŋ, -d
AM ʃəˈkɑr, -z, -ɪŋ, -d
shikara
BR sɨˈkɑːrə(r), -z
AM ʃəˈkɑrə, -z
shikari
BR ʃɨˈkɑːr|i, -ɪz
AM ʃəˈkɑri, -z
Shikoku
BR ˈʃiːkəʊkuː
AM ʃəˈkoʊˌku, ʃəˈkɑˌku
shiksa
BR ˈʃɪksə(r), -z
AM ˈʃɪksə, -z
shill
BR ʃɪl, -z
AM ʃɪl, -z
shillelagh
BR ʃɨˈleɪl|ə(r), ʃɨˈleɪl|i, -ɪz
AM ʃəˈleɪli, -z
shilling
BR ˈʃɪlɪŋ, -z
AM ˈʃɪlɪŋ, -z
shillingsworth
BR ˈʃɪlɪŋzwəːθ, -s
AM ˈʃɪlɪŋzˌwərθ, -s
Shillong
BR ʃɪˈlɒŋ
AM ʃəˈlɔŋ, ʃəˈlɑŋ
Shilluk
BR ʃɪˈlʊk
AM ʃəˈlʊk
shilly-shallier
BR ˈʃɪlɪˌʃalɪə(r), -z
AM ˈʃɪliˌʃæliər, -z
shilly-shally
BR ˈʃɪlɪˌʃal|i, -ɪz, -ɪɪŋ, -ɪd
AM ˈʃɪliˌʃæli, -z, -ɪŋ, -d
shilly-shallyer
BR ˈʃɪlɪˌʃalɪə(r), -z
AM ˈʃɪliˌʃæliər, -z
Shiloh
BR ˈʃʌɪləʊ
AM ˈʃaɪloʊ
Shilton
BR ˈʃɪlt(ə)n
AM ˈʃɪltən
shim
BR ʃɪm, -z
AM ʃɪm, -z
shimmer
BR ˈʃɪm|ə(r), -əz, -(ə)rɪŋ, -əd
AM ˈʃɪm|ər, -ərz, -(ə)rɪŋ, -ərd
shimmeringly
BR ˈʃɪm(ə)rɪŋli
AM ˈʃɪm(ə)rɪŋli
shimmery
BR ˈʃɪm(ə)ri
AM ˈʃɪm(ə)ri
shimmy
BR ˈʃɪm|i, -ɪz, -ɪɪŋ, -ɪd
AM ˈʃɪmi, -z, -ɪŋ, -d
shin
BR ʃɪn, -z, -ɪŋ, -d
AM ʃɪn, -z, -ɪŋ, -d
shinbone
BR ˈʃɪmbəʊn, -z
AM ˈʃɪnˌboʊn, -z
shindig
BR ˈʃɪndɪg, -z
AM ˈʃɪnˌdɪg, -z
shindy
BR ˈʃɪnd|i, -ɪz
AM ˈʃɪndi, -z
shine
BR ʃʌɪn, -z, -ɪŋ, -d
AM ʃaɪn, -z, -ɪŋ, -d
shiner
BR ˈʃʌɪnə(r), -z
AM ˈʃaɪnər, -z
shingle
BR ˈʃɪŋgl, -z
AM ˈʃɪŋgəl, -z
shingly
BR ˈʃɪŋgli
AM ˈʃɪŋg(ə)li
shinily
BR ˈʃʌɪnɨli
AM ˈʃaɪnɨli
shininess
BR ˈʃʌɪnɪnɨs
AM ˈʃaɪninɨs
shiningly
BR ˈʃʌɪnɪŋli
AM ˈʃaɪnɪŋli
shinny
BR ˈʃɪn|i, -ɪz, -ɪɪŋ, -ɪd
AM ˈʃɪni, -z, -ɪŋ, -d
shinsplints
BR ˈʃɪnsplɪnts
AM ˈʃɪnˌsplɪnts
Shinto
BR ˈʃɪntəʊ
AM ˈʃɪn(t)oʊ
Shintoism
BR ˈʃɪntəʊɪz(ə)m
AM ˈʃɪn(t)oʊˌ(w)ɪzəm
Shintoist
BR ˈʃɪntəʊɪst, -s
AM ˈʃɪn(t)oʊ(w)əst, -s
shinty
BR ˈʃɪnti
AM ˈʃɪn(t)i
Shinwell
BR ˈʃɪnw(ɛ)l
AM ˈʃɪnˌwɛl
shiny
BR ˈʃʌɪn|i, -ɪə(r), -ɪɨst
AM ˈʃaɪni, -ər, -ɨst
ship
BR ʃɪp, -s, -ɪŋ, -t
AM ʃɪp, -s, -ɪŋ, -t
shipboard
BR ˈʃɪpbɔːd
AM ˈʃɪpˌbɔ(ə)rd
shipbroker
BR ˈʃɪpˌbrəʊkə(r), -z
AM ˈʃɪpˌbroʊkər, -z
shipbuilder
BR ˈʃɪpˌbɪldə(r), -z
AM ˈʃɪpˌbɪldər, -z
shipbuilding
BR ˈʃɪpˌbɪldɪŋ
AM ˈʃɪpˌbɪldɪŋ
shiplap
BR ˈʃɪplap, -s, -ɪŋ, -t
AM ˈʃɪpˌlæp, -s, -ɪŋ, -t
shipless
BR ˈʃɪplɨs
AM ˈʃɪplɨs
Shipley
BR ˈʃɪpli
AM ˈʃɪpli
shipload
BR ˈʃɪpləʊd, -z
AM ˈʃɪpˌloʊd, -z
Shipman
BR ˈʃɪpmən
AM ˈʃɪpmən
shipmaster
BR ˈʃɪpˌmɑːstə(r), ˈʃɪpˌmastə(r), -z
AM ˈʃɪpˌmæstər, -z
shipmate
BR ˈʃɪpmeɪt, -s
AM ˈʃɪpˌmeɪt, -s

shipment
BR ˈʃɪpm(ə)nt, -s
AM ˈʃɪpmənt, -s
shipowner
BR ˈʃɪpˌəʊnə(r), -z
AM ˈʃɪpˌoʊnər, -z
shippable
BR ˈʃɪpəbl
AM ˈʃɪpəbəl
Shippam
BR ˈʃɪpəm
AM ˈʃɪpəm
shipper
BR ˈʃɪpə(r), -z
AM ˈʃɪpər, -z
ship-rigged
BR ˌʃɪpˈrɪgd
AM ˈʃɪpˌrɪgd
shipshape
BR ˈʃɪpʃeɪp, ˌʃɪpˈʃeɪp
AM ˈʃɪpˌʃeɪp
Shipston
BR ˈʃɪpst(ə)n
AM ˈʃɪpstən
Shipton
BR ˈʃɪpt(ə)n
AM ˈʃɪptən
ship-to-shore
BR ˌʃɪptəˈʃɔː(r)
AM ˈʃɪptəˈʃɔ(ə)r
shipway
BR ˈʃɪpweɪ, -z
AM ˈʃɪpˌweɪ, -z
shipworm
BR ˈʃɪpwəːm, -z
AM ˈʃɪpˌwərm, -z
shipwreck
BR ˈʃɪprɛk, -s, -ɪŋ, -t
AM ˈʃɪpˌrɛk, -s, -ɪŋ, -t
shipwright
BR ˈʃɪprʌɪt, -s
AM ˈʃɪpˌraɪt, -s
shipyard
BR ˈʃɪpjɑːd, -z
AM ˈʃɪpˌjɑrd, -z
shiralee
BR ˈʃɪrəliː, -z
AM ˈʃɪrəli, -z
Shiraz
BR ˈʃɪəraz, ʃɪˈraz, -ɪz
AM ʃ(ɪ)əˈrɑz, -əz
shire
BR ˈʃʌɪə(r), -z
AM ˈʃaɪ(ə)r, -z
-shire
county suffix
BR ʃ(ɪ)ə(r)
AM ʃɪ(ə)r, ʃər, ˌʃaɪ(ə)r
shire-horse
BR ˈʃʌɪəhɔːs, -ɪz
AM ˈʃaɪ(ə)rˌ(h)ɔ(ə)rs, -əz
shirk
BR ʃəːk, -s, -ɪŋ, -t
AM ʃərk, -s, -ɪŋ, -t
shirker
BR ˈʃəːkə(r), -z
AM ˈʃərkər, -z
Shirley
BR ˈʃəːli
AM ˈʃərli
shirr
BR ʃəː(r), -z, -ɪŋ, -d
AM ʃər, -z, -ɪŋ, -d
shirt
BR ʃəːt, -s, -ɨd
AM ʃər|t, -ts, -dəd
shirtdress
BR ˈʃəːtdrɛs, -ɨz
AM ˈʃərtˌdrɛs, -əz
shirtfront
BR ˈʃəːtfrʌnt, -s
AM ˈʃərtˌfrənt, -s
shirtily
BR ˈʃəːtɨli
AM ˈʃərdəli
shirtiness
BR ˈʃəːtɪnɨs
AM ˈʃərdinɨs
shirting
BR ˈʃəːtɪŋ, -z
AM ˈʃərdɪŋ, -z
shirtless
BR ˈʃəːtləs
AM ˈʃərtləs
shirtsleeve
BR ˈʃəːtsliːv, -z, -d
AM ˈʃərtˌsliv, -z, -d
shirttail
BR ˈʃəːtteɪl, -z
AM ˈʃər(t)ˌteɪl, -z
shirtwaist
BR ˈʃəːtweɪst, -s
AM ˈʃərtˌweɪst, -s
shirtwaister
BR ˈʃəːtˌweɪstə(r), ˌʃəːtˈweɪstə(r), -z
AM ˈʃərtˌweɪstər, -z
shirty
BR ˈʃəːt|i, -ɪə(r), -ɪɨst
AM ˈʃərdi, -ər, -ɨst
shish kebab
BR ˈʃɪʃ kɨˌbab, ˌʃɪʃ kɨˈbab, -z
AM ˈʃɪʃ kəˌbɑb, -z
shit
BR ʃɪt, -s, -ɪŋ, -ɨd
AM ʃɪ|t, -ts, -dɪŋ, -dəd
shitbag
BR ˈʃɪtbag, -z
AM ˈʃɪtˌbæg, -z
shit creek
BR ˌʃɪt ˈkriːk
AM ˈʃɪt ˈkrik
shite
BR ʃʌɪt
AM ʃaɪt
shithouse
BR ˈʃɪthaʊ|s, -zɨz
AM ˈʃɪtˌ(h)aʊ|s, -zəz
shitless
BR ˈʃɪtlɨs
AM ˈʃɪtlɨs
shit-scared
BR ˌʃɪtˈskɛːd
AM ˈʃɪtˌskɛ(ə)rd
shittim
BR ˈʃɪtɪm
AM ˈʃɪdəm
shitty
BR ˈʃɪt|i, -ɪə(r), -ɪɨst
AM ˈʃɪdi, -ər, -ɨst
shiv
BR ʃɪv, -z
AM ʃɪv, -z
Shiva
BR ˈʃiːvə(*r*)
AM ˈʃivə
shivaree
BR ˌʃɪvəˈriː, -z
AM ˌʃɪvəˈri, -z
shiver
BR ˈʃɪv|ə(r), -əz, -(ə)rɪŋ, -əd
AM ˈʃɪv|ər, -ərz, -(ə)rɪŋ, -ərd
shiverer
BR ˈʃɪv(ə)rə(r), -z
AM ˈʃɪv(ə)rər, -z
shiveringly
BR ˈʃɪv(ə)rɪŋli
AM ˈʃɪv(ə)rɪŋli
shivery
BR ˈʃɪv(ə)ri
AM ˈʃɪv(ə)ri
shivoo
BR ʃɨˈvuː, -z
AM ʃəˈvu, -z
shlemiel
BR ʃlɨˈmiəl, -z
AM ʃləˈmi(ə)l, -z
shlep
BR ʃlɛp
AM ʃlɛp
Shloer®
BR ʃləː(r)
AM ʃlər, ʃlɔ(ə)r
shmear
BR ʃmɪə(r)
AM ʃmɪ(ə)r
shmuck
BR ʃmək
AM ʃmək
shoal
BR ʃəʊl, -z, -ɪŋ, -d
AM ʃoʊl, -z, -ɪŋ, -d
shoaly
BR ˈʃəʊli
AM ˈʃoʊli
shoat
BR ʃəʊt, -s
AM ʃoʊt, -s
shochet
BR ˈʃɒkɛt, ˈʃɒxɛt, -s
AM ˈʃɑkət, -s
shock
BR ʃɒk, -s, -ɪŋ, -t
AM ʃɑk, -s, -ɪŋ, -t
shockability
BR ˌʃɒkəˈbɪlɨti
AM ˌʃɑkəˈbɪlɨdi
shockable
BR ˈʃɒkəbl
AM ˈʃɑkəbəl
shocker
BR ˈʃɒkə(r), -z
AM ˈʃɑkər, -z
shocking
BR ˈʃɒkɪŋ
AM ˈʃɑkɪŋ
shockingly
BR ˈʃɒkɪŋli
AM ˈʃɑkɪŋli
shockingness
BR ˈʃɒkɪŋnɪs
AM ˈʃɑkɪŋnɪs
shockproof
BR ˈʃɒkpruːf
AM ˈʃɑkˌpruf
shod
BR ʃɒd
AM ʃɑd
shoddily
BR ˈʃɒdɨli
AM ˈʃɑdəli
shoddiness
BR ˈʃɒdɪnɪs
AM ˈʃɑdinɪs
shoddy
BR ˈʃɒd|i, -ɪə(r), -ɪɨst
AM ˈʃɑdi, -ər, -ɨst
shoe
BR ʃuː, -z, -ɪŋ, -d
AM ʃu, -z, -ɪŋ, -d
shoebill
BR ˈʃuːbɪl, -z
AM ˈʃuˌbɪl, -z
shoeblack
BR ˈʃuːblak, -s
AM ˈʃuˌblæk, -s
shoebox
BR ˈʃuːbɒks, -ɨz
AM ˈʃuˌbɑks, -əz
Shoeburyness
BR ˌʃuːb(ə)rɪˈnɛs
AM ˌʃubəriˈnɛs
shoehorn
BR ˈʃuːhɔːn, -z, -ɪŋ, -d
AM ˈʃuˌhɔ(ə)rn, -z, -ɪŋ, -d
shoelace
BR ˈʃuːleɪs, -ɨz
AM ˈʃuˌleɪs, -ɨz
shoeleather
BR ˈʃuːˌlɛðə(r)
AM ˈʃuˌlɛðər
shoeless
BR ˈʃuːləs
AM ˈʃuləs
shoemaker
BR ˈʃuːˌmeɪkə(r), -z
AM ˈʃuˌmeɪkər, -z
shoemaking
BR ˈʃuːˌmeɪkɪŋ
AM ˈʃuˌmeɪkɪŋ
shoepolish
BR ˈʃuːˌpɒlɪʃ

AM ˈʃuˌpɑlɪʃ

shoeshine
BR ˈʃuːʃʌɪn
AM ˈʃuˌʃaɪn

shoestring
BR ˈʃuːstrɪŋ
AM ˈʃuˌstrɪŋ

shoetree
BR ˈʃuːtriː, -z
AM ˈʃuˌtri, -z

shofar
BR ˈʃəʊfə(r)
AM ˈʃoʊfɑr

shofroth
BR ˈʃəʊfrəʊt
AM ʃoʊˈfrɔθ, ʃoʊˈfrɑθ

shogun
BR ˈʃəʊgʌn, ˈʃəʊg(ə)n, -z
AM ˈʃoʊgən, -z

shogunate
BR ˈʃəʊgəneɪt, ˈʃəʊgn̩eɪt, ˈʃəʊgənət, ˈʃəʊgn̩ət, -s
AM ˈʃoʊgənət, ˈʃoʊgəˌneɪt, -s

Sholokhov
BR ˈʃɒləkɒf
AM ˈʃɔləˌkɔv, ˈʃɔləˌkɔf, ˈʃɑləˌkɑv, ˈʃɑləˌkɑf

Sholto
BR ˈʃɒltəʊ
AM ˈʃɔltoʊ, ˈʃɑltoʊ

Shona[1]
African people and language
BR ˈʃɒnə(r), ˈʃəʊnə(r)
AM ˈʃoʊnə

Shona[2]
forename
BR ˈʃəʊnə(r)
AM ˈʃoʊnə, ˈʃɔnə, ˈʃɑnə

shone
BR ʃɒn
AM ʃoʊn

shonky
BR ˈʃɒŋk|i, -ɪə(r), -ɪɨst
AM ˈʃɔŋki, ˈʃɑŋki, -ər, -ɨst

shoo
BR ʃuː, -z, -ɪŋ, -d
AM ʃu, -z, -ɪŋ, -d

shoofly
BR ˈʃuːflʌɪ, -z
AM ˈʃuˌflaɪ, -z

shoo-in
BR ˈʃuːɪn, -z
AM ˈʃuˌɪn, -z

shook
BR ʃʊk
AM ʃʊk

shoot
BR ʃuːt, -s, -ɪŋ
AM ʃu|t, -ts, -dɪŋ

shootable
BR ˈʃuːtəbl
AM ˈʃudəbəl

shoot'em up
BR ˈʃuːtəm ʌp, -s
AM ˈʃudəˌm əp, -s

shooter
BR ˈʃuːtə(r), -z
AM ˈʃudər, -z

shooting
BR ˈʃuːtɪŋ, -z
AM ˈʃudɪŋ, -z

shoot-out
BR ˈʃuːtaʊt, -s
AM ˈʃuˌdaʊt, -s

shoot-up
BR ˈʃuːtʌp, -s
AM ˈʃudəp, -s

shop
BR ʃɒp, -s, -ɪŋ, -t
AM ʃɑp, -s, -ɪŋ, -t

shopaholic
BR ˌʃɒpəˈhɒlɪk, -s
AM ˌʃɑpəˈhɑlɪk, -s

shop-bought
BR ˌʃɒpˈbɔːt
AM ˈʃɑpˌbɔt, ˈʃɑpˌbɑt

shopfitter
BR ˈʃɒpˌfɪtə(r), -z
AM ˈʃɑpˌfɪdər, -z

shopfitting
BR ˈʃɒpˌfɪtɪŋ
AM ˈʃɑpˌfɪdɪŋ

shop-floor
BR ˌʃɒpˈflɔː(r), ˈʃɒpflɔː(r), -z
AM ˈʃɑpˌflɔ(ə)r, -z

shopfront
BR ˈʃɒpfrʌnt, -s
AM ˈʃɑpˌfrənt, -s

shopgirl
BR ˈʃɒpgəːl, -z
AM ˈʃɑpˌgərl, -z

shopkeeper
BR ˈʃɒpˌkiːpə(r), -z
AM ˈʃɑpˌkipər, -z

shopkeeping
BR ˈʃɒpˌkiːpɪŋ
AM ˈʃɑpˌkipɪŋ

shopless
BR ˈʃɒpləs
AM ˈʃɑpləs

shoplift
BR ˈʃɒplɪft, -s, -ɪŋ, -ɨd
AM ˈʃɑpˌlɪft, -s, -ɪŋ, -ɨd

shoplifter
BR ˈʃɒpˌlɪftə(r), -z
AM ˈʃɑpˌlɪftər, -z

shopman
BR ˈʃɒpmən
AM ˈʃɑpmən

shopmen
BR ˈʃɒpmən
AM ˈʃɑpmən

shopper
BR ˈʃɒpə(r), -z
AM ˈʃɑpər, -z

shoppy
BR ˈʃɒpi
AM ˈʃɑpi

shopsoiled
BR ˈʃɒpsɔɪld, ˌʃɒpˈsɔɪld
AM ˈʃɑpˌsɔɪld

shoptalk
BR ˈʃɒptɔːk, -s
AM ˈʃɑpˌtɔk, ˈʃɑpˌtɑk, -s

shopwalker
BR ˈʃɒpˌwɔːkə(r), -z
AM ˈʃɑpˌwɔkər, ˈʃɑpˌwɑkər, -z

shopworker
BR ˈʃɒpˌwəːkə(r), -z
AM ˈʃɑpˌwərkər, -z

shopworn
BR ˈʃɒpwɔːn
AM ˈʃɑpˌwɔ(ə)rn

shoran
BR ˈʃɔːran, ˈʃɒran
AM ˈʃɔˌræn

shore
BR ʃɔː(r), -z, -ɪŋ, -d
AM ʃɔ(ə)r, -z, -ɪŋ, -d

shore-based
BR ˌʃɔːˈbeɪst, ˈʃɔːbeɪst
AM ˈʃɔrˌbeɪst

shorebird
BR ˈʃɔːbəːd, -z
AM ˈʃɔrˌbərd, -z

Shoreditch
BR ˈʃɔːdɪtʃ
AM ˈʃɔrˌdɪtʃ

shorefront
BR ˈʃɔːfrʌnt, -s
AM ˈʃɔrˌfrənt, -s

Shoreham
BR ˈʃɔːrəm
AM ˈʃɔrəm

shoreless
BR ˈʃɔːləs
AM ˈʃɔrləs

shoreline
BR ˈʃɔːlʌɪn, -z
AM ˈʃɔrˌlaɪn, -z

shoreward
BR ˈʃɔːwəd, -z
AM ˈʃɔrwərd, -z

shoreweed
BR ˈʃɔːwiːd, -z
AM ˈʃɔrˌwid, -z

shoring
BR ˈʃɔːrɪŋ
AM ˈʃɔrɪŋ

shorn
BR ʃɔːn
AM ʃɔ(ə)rn

short
BR ʃɔːt, -s, -ɪŋ, -ɨd, -ə(r), -ɨst
AM ʃɔ(ə)rt, -ts, ˈʃɔrdɪŋ, ˈʃɔrdəd, ˈʃɔrdər, ˈʃɔrdəst

shortage
BR ˈʃɔːt|ɪdʒ, -ɨdʒɨz
AM ˈʃɔrdɪdʒ, -ɨz

short-arm
BR ˈʃɔːtɑːm, ʃɔːtˈɑːm
AM ˈʃɔrdˌɑrm

shortbread
BR ˈʃɔːtbrɛd
AM ˈʃɔrtˌbrɛd

shortcake
BR ˈʃɔːtkeɪk
AM ˈʃɔrtˌkeɪk

short-change
BR ˌʃɔːtˈtʃeɪn(d)ʒ, -ɨz, -ɪŋ, -d
AM ˈʃɔrtˈtʃeɪndʒ, -ɨz, -ɪŋ, -d

short-circuit
BR ˌʃɔːtˈsəːk|ɪt, -ɪts, -ɨtɪŋ, -ɨtɨd
AM ˈʃɔrtˈsərkə|t, -ts, -dɪŋ, -dəd

shortcoming
BR ˈʃɔːtˌkʌmɪŋ, ˌʃɔːtˈkʌmɪŋ, -z
AM ˈʃɔrtˌkəmɪŋ, -z

shortcrust
BR ˈʃɔːtkrʌst
AM ˈʃɔrtˌkrəst

shortcut
BR ˌʃɔːtˈkʌt, ˈʃɔːtkʌt, -s
AM ˈʃɔrtˌkət, -s

short-dated
BR ˌʃɔːtˈdeɪtɨd
AM ˈʃɔrtˈdeɪdɨd

short-eared owl
BR ˌʃɔːtɪəd ˈaʊl, -z
AM ˈʃɔrˌdɪ(ə)rd ˈaʊl, -z

shorten
BR ˈʃɔːt|n, -nz, -nɪŋ\-n̩ɪŋ, -nd
AM ˈʃɔrtən, -z, -ɪŋ, -d

Shorter
BR ˈʃɔːtə(r)
AM ˈʃɔrdər

shortfall
BR ˈʃɔːtfɔːl, -z
AM ˈʃɔrtˌfɔl, ˈʃɔrtˌfɑl, -z

shorthair
BR ˈʃɔːthɛː(r), -z
AM ˈʃɔrtˌ(h)ɛ(ə)r, -z

short-haired
BR ˌʃɔːtˈhɛːd
AM ˈʃɔrtˌhɛ(ə)rd

shorthand
BR ˈʃɔːthand
AM ˈʃɔrtˌ(h)ænd

shorthanded
BR ˌʃɔːtˈhandɨd
AM ˌʃɔrtˈhændəd

shorthaul
BR ˈʃɔːthɔːl, ˌʃɔːtˈhɔːl
AM ˈʃɔrtˌ(h)ɔl, ˈʃɔrtˌ(h)ɑl

short-head
BR ˌʃɔːtˈhɛd, -z, -ɪŋ, -ɨd
AM ˈʃɔrtˌ(h)ɛd, -z, -ɪŋ, -əd

shorthold
BR ˈʃɔːthəʊld
AM ˈʃɔrtˌ(h)oʊld

shorthorn
BR 'ʃɔːthɔːn, -z
AM 'ʃɔrt,(h)ɔ(ə)rn, -z
shortie
BR 'ʃɔːt|i, -ɪz
AM 'ʃɔrdi, -z
shortish
BR 'ʃɔːtɪʃ
AM 'ʃɔrdɪʃ
shortlist
BR 'ʃɔːtlɪst, -s, -ɪŋ, -ɨd
AM 'ʃɔrt,lɪst, -s, -ɪŋ, -ɨd
shortly
BR 'ʃɔːtli
AM 'ʃɔrtli
shortness
BR 'ʃɔːtnəs
AM 'ʃɔrtnəs
short-order
BR ˌʃɔːt'ɔːdə(r)
AM ˌʃɔr'dɔrdər
shortsighted
BR ˌʃɔːt'sʌɪtɨd
AM ˌʃɔrt'saɪdɨd
shortsightedly
BR ˌʃɔːt'sʌɪtɨdli
AM ˌʃɔrt'saɪdɨdli
shortsightedness
BR ˌʃɔːt'sʌɪtɨdnɨs
AM ˌʃɔrt'saɪdɨdnɨs
shortstay
BR ˌʃɔːt'steɪ
AM ˌʃɔrt'steɪ
shortstop
BR 'ʃɔːtstɒp, -s
AM 'ʃɔrt,stɑp, -s
shortwave
BR ˌʃɔːt'weɪv, 'ʃɔːtweɪv
AM ˌʃɔrt'weɪv
shortweight
BR ˌʃɔːt'weɪt
AM 'ʃɔrt,weɪt
shorty
BR 'ʃɔːt|i, -ɪz
AM 'ʃɔrdi, -z
Shoshone
BR ʃə(ʊ)'ʃəʊn|i, -ɪz
AM ʃoʊ'ʃoʊni, ʃə'ʃoʊni, -z
Shoshonean
BR ʃə(ʊ)'ʃəʊnɪən
AM ʃoʊ'ʃoʊniən, ʃə'ʃoʊniən
Shostakovich
BR ˌʃɒstə'kəʊvɪtʃ
AM ˌʃɔstə'koʊvɪtʃ, ˌʃɑstə'koʊvɪtʃ
shot
BR ʃɒt, -s
AM ʃɑt, -s
shotgun
BR 'ʃɒtgʌn, -z
AM 'ʃɑt,gən, -z
shotproof
BR 'ʃɒtpruːf
AM 'ʃɑt,pruf
shotten
BR 'ʃɒtn
AM 'ʃɑtn
should¹
strong form
BR ʃʊd
AM ʃʊd
should²
weak form
BR ʃəd
AM ʃəd
shoulder
BR 'ʃəʊld|ə(r), -əz, -(ə)rɪŋ, -əd
AM 'ʃoʊldər, -z, -ɪŋ, -d
shouldn't
BR 'ʃʊdnt
AM 'ʃʊdnt
shout
BR ʃaʊt, -s, -ɪŋ, -ɨd
AM ʃaʊ|t, -ts, -dɪŋ, -dəd
shouter
BR 'ʃaʊtə(r), -z
AM 'ʃaʊdər, -z
shove
BR ʃʌv, -z, -ɪŋ, -d
AM ʃəv, -z, -ɪŋ, -d
shove-halfpenny
BR ˌʃʌv'heɪpni
AM 'ʃəv'heɪp(ə)ni
shove-ha'penny
BR ˌʃʌv'heɪpni
AM 'ʃəv'heɪp(ə)ni
shovel
BR 'ʃʌv|l, -lz, -l̩ɪŋ\-lɪŋ, -ld
AM 'ʃəv|əl, -əlz, -(ə)lɪŋ, -əldz
shovelboard
BR 'ʃʌvlbɔːd
AM 'ʃəvəl,bɔ(ə)rd
shoveler
BR 'ʃʌvl̩ə(r), 'ʃʌvlə(r), -z
AM 'ʃəv(ə)lər, -z
shovelful
BR 'ʃʌvlfʊl, -z
AM 'ʃəvəl,fʊl, -z
shovelhead
BR 'ʃʌvlhɛd, -z
AM 'ʃəvɛl,(h)ɛd, -z
shoveller
BR 'ʃʌvl̩ə(r), 'ʃʌvlə(r), -z
AM 'ʃəv(ə)lər, -z
show
BR ʃəʊ, -z, -ɪŋ, -d
AM ʃoʊ, -z, -ɪŋ, -d
show-and-tell
BR ˌʃəʊ ən(d) 'tɛl, + n̩(d) +
AM ˌʃoʊ ən 'tɛl
showband
BR 'ʃəʊband, -z
AM 'ʃoʊ,bænd, -z
showbiz
BR 'ʃəʊbɪz
AM 'ʃoʊ,bɪz
showboat
BR 'ʃəʊbəʊt, -s
AM 'ʃoʊ,boʊt, -s
showcard
BR 'ʃəʊkɑːd, -z
AM 'ʃoʊ,kɑrd, -z
showcase
BR 'ʃəʊkeɪs, -ɪz
AM 'ʃoʊ,keɪs, -ɪz
showdown
BR 'ʃəʊdaʊn, -z
AM 'ʃoʊ,daʊn, -z
shower¹
person who shows
BR 'ʃəʊə(r), -z
AM 'ʃoʊ(ə)r, -z
shower²
rain
BR 'ʃaʊə(r), -z, -ɪŋ, -d
AM 'ʃaʊ(ə)r, -z, -ɪŋ, -d
showerproof
BR 'ʃaʊəpruːf, -t
AM 'ʃaʊ(ə)r,pruf, -t
showery
BR 'ʃaʊ(ə)ri
AM 'ʃaʊ(ə)ri
showgirl
BR 'ʃəʊgəːl, -z
AM 'ʃoʊ,gərl, -z
showground
BR 'ʃəʊgraʊnd, -z
AM 'ʃoʊ,graʊnd, -z
showily
BR 'ʃəʊɨli
AM 'ʃoʊəli
showiness
BR 'ʃəʊɪnɪs
AM 'ʃoʊinɪs
showing
BR 'ʃəʊɪŋ, -z
AM 'ʃoʊɪŋ, -z
showjump
BR 'ʃəʊdʒʌm|p, -ps, -pɪŋ, -(p)t
AM 'ʃoʊ,dʒəmp, -s, -ɪŋ, -t
showjumper
BR 'ʃəʊˌdʒʌmpə(r), -z
AM 'ʃoʊ,dʒəmpər, -z
showjumping
BR 'ʃəʊˌdʒʌmpɪŋ
AM 'ʃoʊ,dʒəmpɪŋ
showman
BR 'ʃəʊmən
AM 'ʃoʊmən
showmanship
BR 'ʃəʊmənʃɪp
AM 'ʃoʊmən,ʃɪp
showmen
BR 'ʃəʊmən
AM 'ʃoʊmən
shown
BR ʃəʊn
AM ʃoʊn
show-off
BR 'ʃəʊɒf, -s
AM 'ʃoʊ,ɔf, 'ʃoʊ,ɑf, -s
showpiece
BR 'ʃəʊpiːs, -ɪz
AM 'ʃoʊ,pis, -ɪz
showplace
BR 'ʃəʊpleɪs, -ɪz
AM 'ʃoʊ,pleɪs, -ɪz
showroom
BR 'ʃəʊruːm, 'ʃəʊrʊm, -z
AM 'ʃoʊ,rum, 'ʃoʊ,rʊm, -z
showstopper
BR 'ʃəʊˌstɒpə(r), -z
AM 'ʃoʊ,stɑpər, -z
showstopping
BR 'ʃəʊˌstɒpɪŋ
AM 'ʃoʊ,stɑpɪŋ
showtime
BR 'ʃəʊtʌɪm
AM 'ʃoʊ,taɪm
showy
BR 'ʃəʊ|i, -ɪə(r), -ɪɪst
AM 'ʃoʊi, -ər, -ɪst
shoyu
BR 'ʃəʊjuː
AM 'ʃoʊju
shrank
BR ʃraŋk
AM ʃræŋk
shrapnel
BR 'ʃrapnl
AM 'ʃræpnəl
shred
BR ʃrɛd, -z, -ɪŋ, -ɨd
AM ʃrɛd, -z, -ɪŋ, -əd
shredder
BR 'ʃrɛdə(r), -z
AM 'ʃrɛdər, -z
Shreveport
BR 'ʃriːvpɔːt
AM 'ʃriv,pɔ(ə)rt
shrew
BR ʃruː, -z
AM ʃru, -z
shrewd
BR ʃruːd, -ə(r), -ɨst
AM ʃrud, -ər, -əst
shrewdly
BR 'ʃruːdli
AM 'ʃrudli
shrewdness
BR 'ʃruːdnəs
AM 'ʃrudnəs
shrewish
BR 'ʃruːɪʃ
AM 'ʃruɪʃ
shrewishly
BR 'ʃruːɨʃli
AM 'ʃruɨʃli
shrewishness
BR 'ʃruːɨʃnɪs
AM 'ʃruɪʃnɪs
Shrewsbury
BR 'ʃrəʊzb(ə)ri, 'ʃruːzb(ə)ri
AM 'ʃruz,bɛri, 'ʃruzb(ə)ri

shriek
BR ʃriːk, -s, -ɪŋ, -t
AM ʃrik, -s, -ɪŋ, -t
shrieker
BR ˈʃriːkə(r), -z
AM ˈʃrikər, -z
shrieval
BR ˈʃriːvl
AM ˈʃrivəl
shrievalty
BR ˈʃriːvlt|i, -ɪz
AM ˈʃrivəlti, -z
shrift
BR ʃrɪft
AM ʃrɪft
shrike
BR ʃrʌɪk, -s
AM ʃraɪk, -s
shrill
BR ʃrɪl, -z, -ɪŋ, -d, -ə(r), -ɨst
AM ʃrɪl, -z, -ɪŋ, -d, -ər, -ɨst
shrillness
BR ˈʃrɪlnɨs
AM ˈʃrɪlnɨs
shrilly
BR ˈʃrɪ(l)li
AM ˈʃrɪ(l)li
shrimp
BR ʃrɪmp, -s, -ɪŋ
AM ʃrɪmp, -s, -ɪŋ
shrimper
BR ˈʃrɪmpə(r), -z
AM ˈʃrɪmpər, -z
Shrimpton
BR ˈʃrɪm(p)t(ə)n
AM ˈʃrɪm(p)tən
shrine
BR ʃrʌɪn, -z
AM ʃraɪn, -z
Shriner
BR ˈʃrʌɪnə(r)
AM ˈʃraɪnər
shrink
BR ʃrɪŋk, -s, -ɪŋ
AM ʃrɪŋk, -s, -ɪŋ
shrinkable
BR ˈʃrɪŋkəbl
AM ˈʃrɪŋkəbəl
shrinkage
BR ˈʃrɪŋkɪdʒ
AM ˈʃrɪŋkɪdʒ
shrinker
BR ˈʃrɪŋkə(r), -z
AM ˈʃrɪŋkər, -z
shrinking
BR ˈʃrɪŋkɪŋ
AM ˈʃrɪŋkɪŋ
shrinkingly
BR ˈʃrɪŋkɪŋli
AM ˈʃrɪŋkɪŋli
shrinkpack
BR ˈʃrɪŋkpak
AM ˈʃrɪŋˌpæk
shrinkproof
BR ˈʃrɪŋkpruːf
AM ˈʃrɪŋkˌpruf
shrive
BR ʃrʌɪv, -z, -ɪŋ
AM ʃraɪv, -z, -ɪŋ
shrivel
BR ˈʃrɪv|l, -lz, -l̩ɪŋ\-lɪŋ, -ld
AM ˈʃrɪv|əl, -əlz, -(ə)lɪŋ, -əld
shriven
BR ˈʃrɪvn
AM ˈʃrɪvən
Shrivenham
BR ˈʃrɪvn̩əm
AM ˈʃrɪvənəm
Shropshire
BR ˈʃrɒpʃ(ɪ)ə(r)
AM ˈʃrɑpˌʃɪ(ə)r
shroud
BR ʃraʊd, -z, -ɪŋ, -ɨd
AM ʃraʊd, -z, -ɪŋ, -əd
shroudless
BR ˈʃraʊdləs
AM ˈʃrədləs
shrove
BR ʃrəʊv
AM ʃroʊv
Shrovetide
BR ˈʃrəʊvtʌɪd
AM ˈʃroʊvˌtaɪd
shrub
BR ʃrʌb, -z
AM ʃrəb, -z
shrubbery
BR ˈʃrʌb(ə)r|i, -ɪz
AM ˈʃrəb(ə)ri, -z
shrubbiness
BR ˈʃrʌbɪnɪs
AM ˈʃrəbinɪs
shrubby
BR ˈʃrʌb|i, -ɪə(r), -ɪɨst
AM ˈʃrəbi, -ər, -ɨst
shrug
BR ʃrʌg, -z, -ɪŋ, -d
AM ʃrəg, -z, -ɪŋ, -d
shrunk
BR ʃrʌŋk
AM ʃrəŋk
shrunken
BR ˈʃrʌŋk(ə)n
AM ˈʃrəŋkən
shtick
BR ʃtɪk, -s
AM ʃtɪk, -s
shtuck
BR ʃtʊk
AM ʃtʊk
shuck
BR ʃʌk, -s, -ɪŋ, -t
AM ʃək, -s, -ɪŋ, -t
Shuckburgh
BR ˈʃʌkb(ə)rə(*r*)
AM ˈʃəkˌbərə
shucker
BR ˈʃʌkə(r), -z
AM ˈʃəkər, -z
shudder
BR ˈʃʌd|ə(r), -əz, -(ə)rɪŋ, -əd
AM ˈʃədər, -z, -ɪŋ, -d
shudderingly
BR ˈʃʌd(ə)rɪŋli
AM ˈʃəd(ə)rɪŋli
shuddery
BR ˈʃʌd(ə)ri
AM ˈʃəd(ə)ri
shuffle
BR ˈʃʌf|l, -lz, -l̩ɪŋ\-lɪŋ, -ld
AM ˈʃəf|əl, -əlz, -(ə)lɪŋ, -əld
shuffleboard
BR ˈʃʌflbɔːd, -z
AM ˈʃəfəlˌbɔ(ə)rd, -z
Shufflebottom
BR ˈʃʌflˌbɒtəm
AM ˈʃəfəlˌbɑdəm
shuffler
BR ˈʃʌfl̩ə(r), ˈʃʌflə(r), -z
AM ˈʃəf(ə)lər, -z
Shufflewick
BR ˈʃʌflwɪk
AM ˈʃəfəlˌwɪk
shuffling
BR ˈʃʌfl̩ɪŋ, ˈʃʌflɪŋ, -z
AM ˈʃəf(ə)lɪŋ, -z
shufti
BR ˈʃʊft|i, -ɪz
AM ˈʃʊfti, -z
shufty
BR ˈʃʊft|i, -ɪz
AM ˈʃʊfti, -z
shul
BR ʃuːl, ʃʊl, -z
AM ʃul, ʃʊl, -z
Shula
BR ˈʃuːlə(*r*)
AM ˈʃulə
shuln
BR ʃuːln, ʃʊln
AM ʃuln, ʃʊln
Shumen
BR ˈʃuːmɛn
AM ˈʃuˌmɛn
shun
BR ʃʌn, -z, -ɪŋ, -d
AM ʃən, -z, -ɪŋ, -d
shunt
BR ʃʌnt, -s, -ɪŋ, -ɨd
AM ʃən|t, -ts, -(t)ɪŋ, -(t)əd
shunter
BR ˈʃʌntə(r), -z
AM ˈʃən(t)ər, -z
shush
BR ʃʌʃ, ʃʊʃ
AM ʃʊʃ, ʃəʃ
Shuster
BR ˈʃʊstə(r), ˈʃuːstə(r)
AM ˈʃustər
shut
BR ʃʌt, -s, -ɪŋ
AM ʃə|t, -ts, -dɪŋ
shutdown
BR ˈʃʌtdaʊn, -z
AM ˈʃətˌdaʊn, -z
Shute
BR ʃuːt
AM ʃut
Shuter
BR ˈʃuːtə(r)
AM ˈʃudər
shut-eye
BR ˈʃʌtʌɪ
AM ˈʃədˌaɪ
shut-in
BR ˈʃʌtɪn, -z
AM ˈʃədˌɪn, -z
shut-off
BR ˈʃʌtɒf, -s
AM ˈʃədˌɔf, ˈʃədˌɑf, -s
shut-out
BR ˈʃʌtaʊt, -s
AM ˈʃədˌaʊt, -s
shutter
BR ˈʃʌt|ə(r), -əz, -(ə)rɪŋ, -əd
AM ˈʃə|dər, -dərz, -dərɪŋ\-trɪŋ, -dərd
shutterbug
BR ˈʃʌtəbʌg, -z
AM ˈʃədərˌbəg, -z
shutterless
BR ˈʃʌtələs
AM ˈʃədərləs
shuttle
BR ˈʃʌtl̩, -z, -ɪŋ, -d
AM ˈʃədəl, -z, -ɪŋ, -d
shuttlecock
BR ˈʃʌtlkɒk, -s
AM ˈʃədlˌkɑk, -s
Shuttleworth
BR ˈʃʌtlwəːθ, ˈʃʌtlwəθ
AM ˈʃədəlˌwərθ
Shuy
BR ʃʌɪ
AM ʃaɪ
shwa
BR ʃwɑː(*r*), ʃvɑː(*r*), -z
AM ʃwɑ, ʃvɑ, -z
shy
BR ʃʌɪ, -z, -ɪŋ, -d, -ə(r), -ɨst
AM ʃaɪ, -z, -ɪŋ, -d, -ər, -ɨst
shyer
BR ˈʃʌɪə(r), -z
AM ˈʃaɪər, -z
Shylock
BR ˈʃʌɪlɒk
AM ˈʃaɪˌlɑk
shyly
BR ˈʃʌɪli
AM ˈʃaɪli
shyness
BR ˈʃʌɪnɨs
AM ˈʃaɪnɨs
shyster
BR ˈʃʌɪstə(r), -z
AM ˈʃaɪstər, -z

si
BR siː
AM si
sial
BR ˈsʌɪəl
AM ˈsaɪəl
sialagogue
BR sʌɪˈaləɡɒɡ, -z
AM saɪˈæləˌɡɑɡ, -z
sialogogue
BR sʌɪˈaləɡɒɡ, -z
AM saɪˈæləˌɡɑɡ, -z
Siam
BR sʌɪˈam
AM saɪˈæm
siamang
BR ˈsiːəmaŋ, ˈsʌɪəmaŋ, -z
AM ˈsiəˌmɑŋ, -z
Siamese
BR ˌsʌɪəˈmiːz
AM ˌsaɪəˈmiz
Siân
BR ʃɑːn
AM ʃɑn
sib
BR sɪb, -z
AM sɪb, -z
Sibelius
BR sɪˈbeɪlɪəs
AM səˈbeɪliəs
Siberia
BR sʌɪˈbɪərɪə(r)
AM saɪˈbɪriə
Siberian
BR sʌɪˈbɪərɪən, -z
AM saɪˈbɪriən, -z
sibilance
BR ˈsɪbɪləns, ˈsɪbɪlns, ˈsɪbl(ə)ns
AM ˈsɪbələns
sibilancy
BR ˈsɪbɪlənsi, ˈsɪbɪlnsi, ˈsɪbl(ə)nsi
AM ˈsɪbələnsi
sibilant
BR ˈsɪbɪlənt, ˈsɪbɪlnt, ˈsɪbl(ə)nt, -s
AM ˈsɪbələnt, -s
sibilate
BR ˈsɪbɪleɪt, -s, -ɪŋ, -ɪd
AM ˈsɪbəˌleɪ|t, -ts, -dɪŋ, -dɪd
sibilation
BR ˌsɪbɪˈleɪʃn, -z
AM ˌsɪbəˈleɪʃən, -z
Sibley
BR ˈsɪbli
AM ˈsɪbli
sibling
BR ˈsɪblɪŋ, -z
AM ˈsɪblɪŋ, -z
sibship
BR ˈsɪbʃɪp, -s
AM ˈsɪbˌʃɪp, -s
sibyl
BR ˈsɪb(ɪ)l, -z
AM ˈsɪbɪl, -z
sibylline
BR ˈsɪbɪlʌɪn
AM ˈsɪbəˌlaɪn, ˈsɪbəˌlin
sic
BR sɪk
AM sɪk
siccative
BR ˈsɪkətɪv, -z
AM ˈsɪkədɪv, -z
sice
BR sʌɪs, -ɪz
AM saɪs, saɪz, -ɪz
Sichuan
BR ˌsɪtʃˈwɑːn
AM ˈsɪˈtʃwɑn
Sicilia
BR sɪˈsɪlɪə(r)
AM səˈsɪljə, səˈsɪliə
Sicilian
BR sɪˈsɪlɪən, -z
AM səˈsɪljən, səˈsɪliən, -z
siciliana
BR sɪˌsɪlɪˈɑːnə(r), -z
AM səˌsɪliˈɑnə, -z
siciliano
BR sɪˌsɪlɪˈɑːnəʊ, -z
AM səˌsɪliˈɑˌnoʊ, -z
Sicily
BR ˈsɪsɪli, ˈsɪsl̩i
AM ˈsɪsɪli
sick
BR sɪk, -ə(r), -ɪst
AM sɪk, -ər, -ɪst
sickbay
BR ˈsɪkbeɪ, -z
AM ˈsɪkˌbeɪ, -z
sickbed
BR ˈsɪkbɛd, -z
AM ˈsɪkˌbɛd, -z
sicken
BR ˈsɪk|(ə)n, -nz, -n̩ɪŋ\-(ə)nɪŋ, -nd
AM ˈsɪk|ən, -ənz, -(ə)nɪŋ, -ənd
sickener
BR ˈsɪkn̩ə(r), ˈsɪk(ə)nə(r), -z
AM ˈsɪk(ə)nər, -z
sickeningly
BR ˈsɪkn̩ɪŋli, ˈsɪk(ə)nɪŋli
AM ˈsɪk(ə)nɪŋli
Sickert
BR ˈsɪkət
AM ˈsɪkərt
sickie
BR ˈsɪk|i, -ɪz
AM ˈsɪki, -z
sickish
BR ˈsɪkɪʃ
AM ˈsɪkɪʃ
sickle
BR ˈsɪkl, -z
AM ˈsɪkəl, -z
sickliness
BR ˈsɪklɪnɪs
AM ˈsɪklinɪs
sicklist
BR ˈsɪklɪst, -s
AM ˈsɪkˌlɪst, -s
sickly
BR ˈsɪkl|i, -ɪə(r), -ɪɪst
AM ˈsɪkli, -ər, -ɪst
sickness
BR ˈsɪknɪs
AM ˈsɪknɪs
sicko
BR ˈsɪkəʊ, -z
AM ˈsɪkoʊ, -z
sickroom
BR ˈsɪkruːm, ˈsɪkrʊm, -z
AM ˈsɪkˌrum, ˈsɪkˌrʊm, -z
Sid
BR sɪd
AM sɪd
sidalcea
BR sɪˈdalsɪə(r), -z
AM saɪˈdælʃiə, səˈdælʃiə, -z
Sidcup
BR ˈsɪdkʌp, ˈsɪdkəp
AM ˈsɪdˌkəp
Siddall
BR ˈsɪdɔːl
AM ˈsɪdɔl, ˈsɪdɑl
Siddeley
BR ˈsɪdl̩i
AM ˈsɪd(ə)li
Siddons
BR ˈsɪdnz
AM ˈsɪdnz
side
BR sʌɪd, -z, -ɪŋ, -ɪd
AM saɪd, -z, -ɪŋ, -ɪd
sidearm
BR ˈsʌɪdɑːm, -z
AM ˈsaɪdˌɑrm, -z
sideband
BR ˈsʌɪdband, -z
AM ˈsaɪdˌbænd, -z
sidebar
BR ˈsʌɪdbɑː(r), -z
AM ˈsaɪdˌbɑr, -z
sideboard
BR ˈsʌɪdbɔːd, -z
AM ˈsaɪdˌbɔ(ə)rd, -z
Sidebotham
BR ˈsʌɪdˌbɒtəm, ˈsʌɪdˌbəʊθ(ə)m, ˌsɪdɪbəˈtɑːm
AM ˈsaɪdˌbɑdəm
Sidebottom
BR ˈsʌɪdˌbɒtəm, ˌsɪdɪbəˈtɑːm
AM ˈsaɪdˌbɑdəm
sideburn
BR ˈsʌɪdbəːn, -z
AM ˈsaɪdˌbərn, -z
sidecar
BR ˈsʌɪdkɑː(r), -z
AM ˈsaɪdˌkɑr, -z
sidedish
BR ˈsʌɪddɪʃ, -ɪz
AM ˈsaɪ(d)ˌdɪʃ, -ɪz
sidedness
BR ˈsʌɪdɪdnɪs
AM ˈsaɪdɪdnɪs
sidehill
BR ˈsʌɪdhɪl, -z
AM ˈsaɪdˌ(h)ɪl, -z
sidekick
BR ˈsʌɪdkɪk, -s
AM ˈsaɪdˌkɪk, -s
sidelamp
BR ˈsʌɪdlamp, -s
AM ˈsaɪdˌlæmp, -s
sideless
BR ˈsʌɪdlɪs
AM ˈsaɪdlɪs
sidelight
BR ˈsʌɪdlʌɪt, -s
AM ˈsaɪdˌlaɪt, -s
sideline
BR ˈsʌɪdlʌɪn, -z
AM ˈsaɪdˌlaɪn, -z
sidelong
BR ˈsʌɪdlɒŋ
AM ˈsaɪdˌlɔŋ, ˈsaɪdˌlɑŋ
sideman
BR ˈsʌɪdman
AM ˈsaɪdˌmæn
sidemen
BR ˈsʌɪdmɛn
AM ˈsaɪdˌmɛn
side-on
BR ˌsʌɪdˈɒn
AM ˌsaɪdˈɑn
sidepiece
BR ˈsʌɪdpiːs, -ɪz
AM ˈsaɪdˌpis, -ɪz
sidereal
BR sʌɪˈdɪərɪəl
AM saɪˈdɪriəl
siderite
BR ˈsʌɪdərʌɪt
AM ˈsɪdəˌraɪt
siderostat
BR ˈsɪd(ə)rə(ʊ)stat, -s
AM ˈsɪdərəˌstæt, -s
sidesaddle
BR ˈsʌɪdˌsadl, -z
AM ˈsaɪdˌsædəl, -z
sideshow
BR ˈsʌɪdʃəʊ, -z
AM ˈsaɪdˌʃoʊ, -z
sideslip
BR ˈsʌɪdslɪp, -s, -ɪŋ, -t
AM ˈsaɪdˌslɪp, -s, -ɪŋ, -t
sidesman
BR ˈsʌɪdzmən
AM ˈsaɪdzmən
sidesmen
BR ˈsʌɪdzmən
AM ˈsaɪdzmən

sidesplitting
BR ˈsʌɪdˌsplɪtɪŋ
AM ˈsaɪdˌsplɪdɪŋ
sidestep
BR ˈsʌɪdstɛp, -s, -ɪŋ, -t
AM ˈsaɪdˌstɛp, -s, -ɪŋ, -t
sidestepper
BR ˈsʌɪdˌstɛpə(r), -z
AM ˈsaɪdˌstɛpər, -z
sidestroke
BR ˈsʌɪdstrəʊk
AM ˈsaɪdˌstroʊk
sideswipe
BR ˈsʌɪdswʌɪp, -s, -ɪŋ, -t
AM ˈsaɪdˌswaɪp, -s, -ɪŋ, -t
sidetrack
BR ˈsʌɪdtrak, -s, -ɪŋ, -t
AM ˈsaɪ(d)ˌtræk, -s, -ɪŋ, -t
sidewalk
BR ˈsʌɪdwɔːk, -s
AM ˈsaɪdˌwɔk, ˈsaɪdˌwɑk, -s
sideward
BR ˈsʌɪdwəd, -z
AM saɪdwərd, -z
sideways
BR ˈsʌɪdweɪz
AM ˈsaɪdˌweɪz
sidewinder
BR ˈsʌɪdˌwʌɪndə(r), -z
AM ˈsaɪdˌwaɪndər, -z
sidewise
BR ˈsʌɪdwʌɪz
AM ˈsaɪdˌwaɪz
Sidgewick
BR ˈsɪdʒwɪk
AM ˈsɪdʒˌwɪk
siding
BR ˈsʌɪdɪŋ, -z
AM ˈsaɪdɪŋ, -z
sidle
BR ˈsʌɪd|l, -lz, -l̩ɪŋ\-lɪŋ, -ld
AM ˈsaɪd|əl, -əlz, -(ə)lɪŋ, -əld
Sidmouth
BR ˈsɪdməθ
AM ˈsɪdməθ
Sidney
BR ˈsɪdni
AM ˈsɪdni
Sidon
BR ˈsʌɪdn
AM ˈsaɪdn
Sidra
BR ˈsɪdrə(r)
AM ˈsɪdrə
SIDS
BR sɪdz
AM sɪdz
siege
BR siː(d)ʒ, -ɨz
AM si(d)ʒ, -ɨz
Siegel
BR ˈsiːgl
AM ˈsigəl
Siegfried
BR ˈsiːgfriːd
AM ˈsigˌfrid
Sieg Heil
BR ˌsiːg ˈhʌɪl, ˌziːg +
AM ˌsig ˈhaɪl, ˌzig +
Siemens
BR ˈsiːmənz
AM ˈsimənz
Siena
BR sɪˈɛnə(r)
AM siˈɛnə
Sienese
BR ˌsiːəˈniːz
AM ˌsiəˈniz
sienna
BR sɪˈɛnə(r), -z
AM siˈɛnə, -z
sierra
BR sɪˈɛrə(r), -z
AM siˈɛrə, -z
Sierra Leone
BR sɪˌɛrə lɪˈəʊn(i)
AM siˌɛrəliˈoʊn
Sierra Leonian
BR sɪˌɛrə lɪˈəʊnɪən, -z
AM siˌɛrə liˈoʊniən, -z
Sierra Madre
BR sɪˌɛrə ˈmadreɪ
AM siˌɛrə ˈmɑˌdreɪ
Sierra Nevada
BR sɪˌɛrə nɪˈvɑːdə(r)
AM siˌɛrə nəˈvɑdə, + nəˈvædə
siesta
BR sɪˈɛstə(r), -z
AM siˈɛstə, -z
sieve
BR sɪv, -z, -ɪŋ, -d
AM sɪv, siv, -z, -ɪŋ, -d
sievelike
BR ˈsɪvlʌɪk
AM ˈsɪvˌlaɪk, ˈsivˌlaɪk
sievert
BR ˈsiːvət, -s
AM ˈsɪvərt, ˈsivərt, -s
sifaka
BR sɪˈfakə(r), -z
AM səˈfækə, -z
siffleur
BR siːˈfləː(r), -z
AM siˈflər, -z
siffleuse
BR siːˈfləːz, -ɨz
AM siˈfləz, -əz
sift
BR sɪft, -s, -ɪŋ, -ɨd
AM sɪft, -s, -ɪŋ, -ɨd
Sifta
BR ˈsɪftə(r)
AM ˈsɪftə
sifter
BR ˈsɪftə(r), -z
AM ˈsɪftər, -z
Sigal
BR ˈsiːgl
AM ˈsigəl
sigh
BR sʌɪ, -z, -ɪŋ, -d
AM saɪ, -z, -ɪŋ, -d
sight
BR sʌɪt, -s, -ɪŋ, -ɨd
AM saɪ|t, -ts, -dɪŋ, -dɨd
sighter
BR ˈsʌɪtə(r), -z
AM ˈsaɪdər, -z
sighting
BR ˈsʌɪtɪŋ, -z
AM ˈsaɪdɪŋ, -z
sightless
BR ˈsʌɪtlɨs
AM ˈsaɪtlɨs
sightlessly
BR ˈsʌɪtlɨsli
AM ˈsaɪtlɨsli
sightlessness
BR ˈsʌɪtlɨsnɨs
AM ˈsaɪtlɨsnɨs
sightline
BR ˈsʌɪtlʌɪn, -z
AM ˈsaɪtˌlaɪn, -z
sightliness
BR ˈsʌɪtlɪnɨs
AM ˈsaɪtlinɨs
sightly
BR ˈsʌɪtli
AM ˈsaɪtli
sight-read[1]
present tense
BR ˈsʌɪtriːd, -z, -ɪŋ
AM ˈsaɪtˌrid, -z, -ɪŋ
sight-read[2]
past tense
BR ˈsʌɪtrɛd
AM ˈsaɪtˌrɛd
sight-reader
BR ˈsʌɪtˌriːdə(r), -z
AM ˈsaɪtˌridər, -z
sight-sang
BR ˈsʌɪtsaŋ
AM ˈsaɪtˌsæŋ
sightsaw
BR ˈsʌɪtsɔː(r)
AM ˈsaɪtˌsɔ
sightscreen
BR ˈsʌɪtskriːn, -z
AM ˈsaɪtˌskrin, -z
sightsee
BR ˈsʌɪtsiː, -z, -ɪŋ
AM ˈsaɪtˌsi, -z, -ɪŋ
sightseeing
BR ˈsʌɪtˌsiːɪŋ
AM ˈsaɪtˌsiɪŋ
sightseer
BR ˈsʌɪtˌsiːə(r), -z
AM ˈsaɪtˌsɪ(ə)r, -z
sight-sing
BR ˈsʌɪtsɪŋ, -z
AM ˈsaɪtˌsɪŋ, -z
sight-singing
BR ˈsʌɪtˌsɪŋɪŋ
AM ˈsaɪtˌsɪŋɪŋ
sightworthy
BR ˈsʌɪtˌwəːði
AM ˈsaɪtˌwərði
sigil
BR ˈsɪdʒ(ɨ)l, -z
AM ˈsɪdʒɨl, -z
sigillate
BR ˈsɪdʒɨleɪt
AM ˈsɪdʒəˌleɪt
Sigismond
BR ˈsɪgɪzmənd, ˈsɪgɪsmənd
AM ˈsɪgɨsmənd
Sigismund
BR ˈsɪgɪzmənd, ˈsɪgɪsmənd
AM ˈsɪgɨsmənd
sigla
BR ˈsɪglə(r)
AM ˈsɪglə
siglum
BR ˈsɪgləm
AM ˈsɪgləm
sigma
BR ˈsɪgmə(r), -z
AM ˈsɪgmə, -z
sigmate
BR ˈsɪgmeɪt
AM ˈsɪgˌmeɪt
sigmatic
BR sɪgˈmatɪk
AM sɪgˈmædɪk
sigmoid
BR ˈsɪgmɔɪd
AM ˈsɪgˌmɔɪd
sigmoidoscope
BR sɪgˈmɔɪdəskəʊp
AM sɪgˈmɔɪdəˌskoʊp
sigmoidoscopic
BR sɪgˌmɔɪdəˈskɒpɪk
AM sɪgˌmɔɪdəˈskɑpɪk
sigmoidoscopy
BR ˌsɪgmɔɪˈdɒskəpi
AM ˌsɪgmɔɪˈdɑskəpi
Sigmund
BR ˈsɪgmənd
AM ˈsɪgmənd
sign
BR sʌɪn, -z, -ɪŋ, -d
AM saɪn, -z, -ɪŋ, -d
signable
BR ˈsʌɪnəbl
AM ˈsaɪnəbəl
signal
BR ˈsɪgn|l, -lz, -l̩ɪŋ\-əlɪŋ, -ld
AM ˈsɪgnəl, -z, -ɪŋ, -d
signalise
BR ˈsɪgnəlʌɪz, ˈsɪgnl̩ʌɪz, -ɨz, -ɪŋ, -d
AM ˈsɪgnəˌlaɪz, -ɨz, -ɪŋ, -d
signalize
BR ˈsɪgnəlʌɪz, ˈsɪgnl̩ʌɪz, -ɨz, -ɪŋ, -d
AM ˈsɪgnəˌlaɪz, -ɨz, -ɪŋ, -d

signaller
BR ˈsɪgnələ(r), ˈsɪgnl̩ə(r), -z
AM ˈsɪgnələr, -z

signally
BR ˈsɪgnəli, ˈsɪgnl̩i
AM ˈsɪgnəli

signalman
BR ˈsɪgnlmən
AM ˈsɪgnəlmən

signalmen
BR ˈsɪgnlmən
AM ˈsɪgnəlmən

signary
BR ˈsɪgnər|i, -ɪz
AM ˈsɪgnəri, -z

signatory
BR ˈsɪgnət(ə)r|i, -ɪz
AM ˈsɪgnəˌtɔri, -z

signature
BR ˈsɪgnətʃə(r), -z
AM ˈsɪgnətʃər, ˈsɪgnətʃʊ(ə)r|| -z

signboard
BR ˈsʌɪnbɔːd, -z
AM ˈsaɪnˌbɔ(ə)rd, -z

signer
BR ˈsʌɪnə(r), -z
AM ˈsaɪnər, -z

signet
BR ˈsɪgnɪt, -s
AM ˈsɪgnɪt, -s

significance
BR sɪgˈnɪfɪk(ə)ns
AM sɪgˈnɪfɪkəns

significancy
BR sɪgˈnɪfɪk(ə)ns|i, -ɪz
AM sɪgˈnɪfɪkənsi, -z

significant
BR sɪgˈnɪfɪk(ə)nt
AM sɪgˈnɪfɪkənt

significantly
BR sɪgˈnɪfɪk(ə)ntli
AM sɪgˈnɪfɪkən(t)li

signification
BR ˌsɪgnɪfɪˈkeɪʃn
AM ˌsɪgnəfəˈkeɪʃən

significative
BR sɪgˈnɪfɪkətɪv
AM sɪgˈnɪfɪkədɪv

signified
BR ˈsɪgnɪfʌɪd, -z
AM ˈsɪgnəˌfaɪd, -z

signifier
BR ˈsɪgnɪfʌɪə(r), -z
AM ˈsɪgnəˌfaɪ(ə)r, -z

signify
BR ˈsɪgnɪfʌɪ, -z, -ɪŋ, -d
AM ˈsɪgnəˌfaɪ, -z, -ɪŋ, -d

signing
BR ˈsʌɪnɪŋ, -z
AM ˈsaɪnɪŋ, -z

signor
BR siːnˈjɔː(r), ˈsiːnjɔː(r), -z
AM sinˈjɔ(ə)r, -z

signora
BR siːnˈjɔːrə(*r*), -z
AM sinˈjɔrə, -z

signorina
BR ˌsiːnjɔːˈriːnə(*r*), ˌsiːnjəˈriːnə(*r*), -z
AM ˌsinjəˈrinə, -z

signory
BR ˈsiːnjəri
AM ˈsinjeri

signpost
BR ˈsʌɪnpəʊst, -s, -ɪd
AM ˈsaɪnˌpoʊst, -s, -əd

signwriter
BR ˈsʌɪnˌrʌɪtə(r), -z
AM ˈsaɪnˌraɪdər, -z

signwriting
BR ˈsʌɪnˌrʌɪtɪŋ
AM ˈsaɪnˌraɪdɪŋ

Sigurd
BR ˈsɪgəːd
AM ˈsɪgərd

Sihanouk
BR ˈsɪənʊk
AM ˈsiənʊk

Sihanoukville
BR ˈsɪənʊkvɪl
AM ˈsiənʊkˌvɪl

sika
BR ˈsiːkə(*r*), -z
AM ˈsikə, -z

Sikh
BR siːk, -s
AM sik, -s

Sikhism
BR ˈsiːkɪz(ə)m
AM ˈsiˌkɪzəm

Sikkim
BR ˈsɪkɪm
AM ˈsɪkɪm

Sikkimese
BR ˌsɪkɪˈmiːz
AM ˌsɪkɪˈmiz

Sikorsky
BR sɪˈkɔːski
AM səˈkɔrski

silage
BR ˈsʌɪlɪdʒ
AM ˈsaɪlɪdʒ

silane
BR ˈsʌɪleɪn
AM ˈsaɪleɪn

Silas
BR ˈsʌɪləs
AM ˈsaɪləs

Silchester
BR ˈsɪltʃɪstə(r), ˈsɪltʃɛstə(r)
AM ˈsɪlˌtʃɛstər

Silcox
BR ˈsɪlkɒks
AM ˈsɪlˌkɑks

sild
BR sɪld, -z
AM sɪld, -z

silence
BR ˈsʌɪləns, ˈsʌɪln̩s, -ɪz, -ɪŋ, -t
AM ˈsaɪləns, -əz, -ɪŋ, -t

silencer
BR ˈsʌɪlənsə(r), ˈsʌɪln̩sə(r), -z
AM ˈsaɪlənsər, -z

sileni
BR sʌɪˈliːnʌɪ
AM saɪˈliˌnaɪ

silent
BR ˈsʌɪlənt, ˈsʌɪln̩t
AM ˈsaɪlənt

silently
BR ˈsʌɪləntli, ˈsʌɪln̩tli
AM ˈsaɪlən(t)li

silenus
BR sʌɪˈliːnəs
AM saɪˈlinəs

Silesia
BR sʌɪˈliːzɪə(*r*), sʌɪˈliːʒə(*r*), sʌɪˈliːʃə(*r*)
AM saɪˈliʒə, saɪˈliʃə, səˈliʒə, səˈliʃə

Silesian
BR sʌɪˈliːzɪən, sʌɪˈliːʒn, sʌɪˈliːʃn, -z
AM saɪˈliʒən, saɪˈliʃən, səˈliʒən, səˈliʃən, -z

silex
BR ˈsʌɪlɛks
AM ˈsaɪˌlɛks

silhouette
BR ˌsɪlʊˈɛt, -s, -ɪŋ, -ɪd
AM ˌsɪləˈwɛ|t, -ts, -dɪŋ, -dəd

silica
BR ˈsɪlɪkə(*r*)
AM ˈsɪlɪkə

silicate
BR ˈsɪlɪkət, ˈsɪlɪkeɪt, -s
AM ˈsɪləˌkeɪt, ˈsɪlɪkɪt, -s

siliceous
BR sɪˈlɪʃəs
AM səˈlɪʃəs

silicic
BR sɪˈlɪsɪk
AM səˈlɪsɪk

silicide
BR ˈsɪlɪsʌɪd
AM ˈsɪlɪsaɪd

siliciferous
BR ˌsɪlɪˈsɪf(ə)rəs
AM ˌsɪləˈsɪf(ə)rəs

silicification
BR sɪˌlɪsɪfɪˈkeɪʃn
AM ˌsɪləsəfəˈkeɪʃən

silicify
BR sɪˈlɪsɪfʌɪ, -z, -ɪŋ, -d
AM səˈlɪsəˌfaɪ, -z, -ɪŋ, -d

silicon
BR ˈsɪlɪk(ə)n
AM ˈsɪləˌkɑn, ˈsɪlɪkən

silicone
BR ˈsɪlɪkəʊn
AM ˈsɪləˌkoʊn

Silicon Valley
BR ˌsɪlɪk(ə)n ˈvali
AM ˈsɪləˌkɑn ˈvæli, ˌsɪlɪkən +

silicosis
BR ˌsɪlɪˈkəʊsɪs
AM ˌsɪləˈkoʊsəs

silicotic
BR ˌsɪlɪˈkɒtɪk
AM ˌsɪləˈkɑdɪk

siliqua
BR ˈsɪlɪkwə(*r*)
AM ˈsɪləkwə

siliquae
BR ˈsɪlɪkwiː, ˈsɪlɪkwʌɪ
AM ˈsɪləkwi, ˈsɪləˌkwaɪ

silique
BR sɪˈliːk, -s
AM səˈlik, ˈsɪlɪk, -s

siliquose
BR ˈsɪlɪkwəʊs
AM ˈsɪləˌkwoʊs, ˈsɪləˌkwoʊz

siliquous
BR ˈsɪlɪkwəs
AM ˈsɪləkwəs

silk
BR sɪlk, -s
AM sɪlk, -s

silken
BR ˈsɪlk(ə)n
AM ˈsɪlkən

silkily
BR ˈsɪlkɪli
AM ˈsɪlkɪli

Silkin
BR ˈsɪlkɪn
AM ˈsɪlkən

silkiness
BR ˈsɪlkɪnɪs
AM ˈsɪlkinɪs

silklike
BR ˈsɪlklʌɪk
AM ˈsɪlkˌlaɪk

silkscreen
BR ˈsɪlkskriːn, -z, -ɪŋ, -d
AM ˈsɪlkˌskrin, -z, -ɪŋ, -d

silkworm
BR ˈsɪlkwəːm, -z
AM ˈsɪlkˌwərm, -z

silky
BR ˈsɪlk|i, -ɪə(r), -ɪɪst
AM ˈsɪlki, -ər, -ɪst

sill
BR sɪl, -z
AM sɪl, -z

sillabub
BR ˈsɪləbʌb, -z
AM ˈsɪləˌbəb, -z

Sillars
BR ˈsɪləz
AM ˈsɪlərz

siller
BR ˈsɪlə(r)
AM ˈsɪlər

sillily
BR ˈsɪlɨli
AM ˈsɪlɨli
sillimanite
BR ˈsɪlɨmənʌɪt, -s
AM ˈsɪləməˌnaɪt, -s
silliness
BR ˈsɪlɪnɨs
AM ˈsɪlinɨs
Sillitoe
BR ˈsɪlɪtəʊ
AM ˈsɪlɪˌtoʊ
Silloth
BR ˈsɪləθ
AM ˈsɪləθ
Sills
BR sɪlz
AM sɪlz
silly
BR ˈsɪl|i, -ɪə(r), -ɪɪst
AM ˈsɪli, -ər, -ɨst
silo
BR ˈsʌɪləʊ, -z
AM ˈsaɪloʊ, -z
Siloam
BR sʌɪˈləʊəm, sɪˈləʊəm
AM ˌsaɪˈloʊəm, ˈsaɪləm
Silsoe
BR ˈsɪlsəʊ
AM ˈsɪlˌsoʊ
silt
BR sɪlt, -s, -ɪŋ, -ɨd
AM sɪlt, -s, -ɪŋ, -ɨd
siltation
BR sɪlˈteɪʃn
AM sɪlˈteɪʃən
siltstone
BR ˈsɪltstəʊn, -z
AM ˈsɪltˌstoʊn, -z
silty
BR ˈsɪlti
AM ˈsɪlti
Silures
BR sʌɪˈl(j)ʊəriːz, sʌɪˈljɔːriːz
AM saɪˈlʊriz
Silurian
BR sʌɪˈl(j)ʊərɪən, sʌɪˈljɔːrɪən
AM səˈlʊriən, saɪˈlʊriən
Silva
BR ˈsɪlvə(r), -z
AM ˈsɪlvə, -z
silvan
BR ˈsɪlv(ə)n
AM ˈsɪlvən
Silvanus
BR sɪlˈveɪnəs
AM sɪlˈveɪnəs
silver
BR ˈsɪlv|ə(r), -əz, -(ə)rɪŋ, -əd
AM ˈsɪlv|ər, -ərz, -(ə)rɪŋ, -ərd
silver birch
BR ˌsɪlvə ˈbəːtʃ, -ɨz
AM ˈsɪlvər ˈbərtʃ, -əz
silverfish
BR ˈsɪlvəfɪʃ, -ɨz
AM ˈsɪlvərˌfɪʃ, -ɨz
silveriness
BR ˈsɪlv(ə)rɪnɨs
AM ˈsɪlv(ə)rinɨs
Silverman
BR ˈsɪlvəmən
AM ˈsɪlvərmən
silvern
BR ˈsɪlv(ə)n
AM ˈsɪlvərn
silver-plate
BR ˌsɪlvəˈpleɪt, -s, -ɪŋ, -ɨd
AM ˈsɪlvərˈpleɪ|t, -ts, -dɪŋ, -dɨd
silverside
BR ˈsɪlvəsʌɪd, -z
AM ˈsɪlvərˌsaɪd, -z
silversmith
BR ˈsɪlvəsmɪθ, -s
AM ˈsɪlvərˌsmɪθ, -s
silversmithing
BR ˈsɪlvəˌsmɪθɪŋ
AM ˈsɪlvərˌsmɪðɪŋ
Silverstone
BR ˈsɪlvəstəʊn, ˈsɪlvəstən
AM ˈsɪlvərˌstoʊn
silverware
BR ˈsɪlvəwɛː(r)
AM ˈsɪlvərˌwɛ(ə)r
silverweed
BR ˈsɪlvəwiːd, -z
AM ˈsɪlvərˌwid, -z
silvery
BR ˈsɪlv(ə)ri
AM ˈsɪlv(ə)ri
Silvester
BR ˈsɪlvɛstə(r), ˈsɪlvɪstə(r), s(ɪ)lˈvɛstə(r)
AM sɪlˈvɛstər
silvicultural
BR ˌsɪlvɪˈkʌltʃ(ə)rəl, ˌsɪlvɪˈkʌltʃ(ə)rl̩
AM ˈsɪlvəˈkəltʃ(ə)rəl
silviculture
BR ˈsɪlvɪˌkʌltʃə(r)
AM ˈsɪlvəˌkəltʃər
silviculturist
BR ˌsɪlvɪˈkʌltʃ(ə)rɪst, -s
AM ˈsɪlvəˈkəltʃ(ə)rəst, -s
Silvie
BR ˈsɪlvi
AM ˈsɪlvi
Silvikrin®
BR ˈsɪlvɪkrɪn
AM ˈsɪlvɪˌkrɪn
Sim
BR sɪm
AM sɪm
sima
BR ˈsʌɪmə(r)
AM ˈsaɪmə
simazine
BR ˈsʌɪməziːn
AM ˈsaɪməˌzin
Simca®
BR ˈsɪmkə(r), -z
AM ˈsɪmkə, -z
simcha
BR ˈsɪmtʃə(r), ˈsɪmxə(r), -z
AM ˈsɪmkə, -z
Simcox
BR ˈsɪmkɒks
AM ˈsɪmˌkɑks
Simenon
BR ˈsiːmənɒ̃, ˈsiːmənɒn
AM ˌsiməˈnɔn, ˌsiməˈnɑn
Simeon
BR ˈsɪmɪən
AM ˈsɪmiən
Simes
BR sʌɪmz
AM saɪmz
simian
BR ˈsɪmɪən, -z
AM ˈsɪmiən, -z
similar
BR ˈsɪm(ɨ)lə(r)
AM ˈsɪm(ə)lər
similarity
BR ˌsɪmɪˈlarɪt|i, -ɪz
AM ˌsɪməˈlɛrədi, -z
similarly
BR ˈsɪm(ɨ)ləli
AM ˈsɪm(ə)lərli
simile
BR ˈsɪmɨl|i, -ɪz
AM ˈsɪmɨli, -z
similitude
BR sɪˈmɪlɪtjuːd, sɪˈmɪlɪtʃuːd, -z
AM sɪˈmɪləˌt(j)ud, -z
Simla
BR ˈsɪmlə(r)
AM ˈsɪmlə
Simm
BR sɪm
AM sɪm
simmer
BR ˈsɪm|ə(r), -əz, -(ə)rɪŋ, -əd
AM ˈsɪm|ər, -ərz, -(ə)rɪŋ, -ərd
Simmonds
BR ˈsɪmən(d)z
AM ˈsɪmənz
Simmons
BR ˈsɪmənz
AM ˈsɪmənz
Simms
BR sɪmz
AM sɪmz
simnel
BR ˈsɪmnl
AM ˈsɪmnəl
simoleon
BR sɪˈməʊlɪən
AM səˈmoʊliən
Simon
BR ˈsʌɪmən
AM ˈsaɪmən
Simonds
BR ˈsɪmən(d)z, ˌsʌɪmən(d)z
AM ˈsɪmənz, ˈsaɪmənz
Simone
BR sɪˈməʊn
AM səˈmoʊn, siˈmoʊn
simoniac
BR sɪˈməʊnɪak, -s
AM səˈmoʊniˌæk, -s
simoniacal
BR ˌsɪməˈnʌɪəkl
AM ˌsaɪməˈnaɪəkəl
simoniacally
BR ˌsɪməˈnʌɪəkli
AM ˌsaɪməˈnaɪək(ə)li
Simonides
BR sʌɪˈmɒnɨdiːz
AM saɪˈmɑnəˌdiz
simonize
BR ˈsʌɪmənʌɪz, -ɪz, -ɪŋ, -d
AM ˈsaɪməˌnaɪz, -ɪz, -ɪŋ, -d
simon-pure
BR ˌsʌɪmənˈpjʊə(r), ˌsʌɪmənˈpjɔː(r)
AM ˈsaɪmənˌpjʊ(ə)r
Simons
BR ˈsʌɪmənz
AM ˈsaɪmənz
simony
BR ˈsʌɪməni, ˈsɪməni
AM ˈsaɪməni, ˈsɪməni
simoom
BR sɪˈmuːm, -z
AM səˈmum, -z
simoon
BR sɪˈmuːn, -z
AM səˈmun, -z
simp
BR sɪmp, -s
AM sɪmp, -s
simpatico
BR sɪmˈpatɪkəʊ, -z
AM sɪmˈpædəˌkoʊ, -z
simper
BR ˈsɪmp|ə(r), -əz, -(ə)rɪŋ, -əd
AM ˈsɪmp|ər, -ərz, -(ə)rɪŋ, -ərd
simperingly
BR ˈsɪmp(ə)rɪŋli
AM ˈsɪmp(ə)rɪŋli
Simpkin
BR ˈsɪm(p)kɪn
AM ˈsɪmkɨn

Simpkins
BR 'sɪm(p)kɪnz
AM 'sɪmkɪnz
Simpkinson
BR 'sɪm(p)kɪns(ə)n
AM 'sɪmkɪnsən
simple
BR 'sɪmpl, -z, -ə(r), -ɪst
AM 'sɪmp|əl, -əlz, -(ə)lər, -(ə)ləst
simple-hearted
BR ˌsɪmpl'hɑːtɪd
AM ˈsɪmpəlˈhɑrdəd
simple-minded
BR ˌsɪmpl'mʌɪndɪd
AM ˈsɪmpəlˈmaɪndɪd
simple-mindedly
BR ˌsɪmpl'mʌɪndɪdli
AM ˈsɪmpəlˈmaɪndɪdli
simple-mindedness
BR ˌsɪmpl'mʌɪndɪdnɪs
AM ˈsɪmpəlˈmaɪndɪdnɪs
simpleness
BR 'sɪmplnəs
AM 'sɪmpəlnəs
simpleton
BR 'sɪmplt(ə)n, -z
AM 'sɪmpəltən, -z
simplex
BR 'sɪmplɛks
AM 'sɪmˌplɛks
simplicity
BR sɪm'plɪsɪti
AM sɪm'plɪsɪdi
simplification
BR ˌsɪmplɪfɪ'keɪʃn, -z
AM ˌsɪmpləfə'keɪʃən, -z
simplify
BR 'sɪmplɪfʌɪ, -z, -ɪŋ, -d
AM 'sɪmpləˌfaɪ, -z, -ɪŋ, -d
simplism
BR 'sɪmplɪz(ə)m
AM 'sɪmˌplɪzəm
simplistic
BR sɪm'plɪstɪk
AM sɪm'plɪstɪk
simplistically
BR sɪm'plɪstɪkli
AM sɪm'plɪstək(ə)li
Simplon
BR 'sɪmplɒn
AM 'sɪmˌplɔn, 'sɪmˌplɑn
Simplot
BR 'sɪmplɒt
AM 'sɪmˌplɑt
simply
BR 'sɪmpli
AM 'sɪmpli
Simpson
BR 'sɪm(p)sn
AM 'sɪm(p)sən
Sims
BR sɪmz
AM sɪmz
Simson
BR 'sɪmsn
AM 'sɪmsən
simulacra
BR ˌsɪmjʊ'leɪkrə(*r*)
AM ˌsɪmjə'leɪkrə, ˌsɪmjə'lækrə
simulacrum
BR ˌsɪmjʊ'leɪkrəm
AM ˌsɪmjə'leɪkrəm, ˌsɪmjə'lækrəm
simulate
BR 'sɪmjʊleɪt, -s, -ɪŋ, -ɪd
AM 'sɪmjəˌleɪ|t, -ts, -dɪŋ, -dɪd
simulation
BR ˌsɪmjʊ'leɪʃn, -z
AM ˌsɪmjə'leɪʃən, -z
simulative
BR 'sɪmjʊlətɪv
AM 'sɪmjələdɪv, 'sɪmjəˌleɪdɪv
simulator
BR 'sɪmjʊleɪtə(r), -z
AM 'sɪmjəˌleɪdər, -z
simulcast
BR 'sɪmlkɑːst, 'sɪmlkast, -s
AM 'saɪməlˌkæst, -s
simultaneity
BR ˌsɪmltə'neɪɪti, ˌsɪmltə'niːɪti
AM ˌsaɪməltə'niɪdi
simultaneous
BR ˌsɪml'teɪnɪəs
AM ˈsaɪməl'teɪniəs
simultaneously
BR ˌsɪml'teɪnɪəsli
AM ˈsaɪməl'teɪniəsli
simultaneousness
BR ˌsɪml'teɪnɪəsnəs
AM ˈsaɪməl'teɪniəsnəs
simurg
BR sɪ'məːg, -z
AM si'mərg, -z
sin
BR sɪn, -z, -ɪŋ, -d
AM sɪn, -z, -ɪŋ, -d
Sinai
BR 'sʌɪn(ɪ)ʌɪ
AM 'saɪˌnaɪ
Sinaitic
BR ˌsʌɪneɪ'ɪtɪk, ˌsʌɪnɪ'ɪtɪk
AM ˌsɪnə'ɪdɪk
Sinanthropus
BR sɪ'nanθrəpəs
AM sɪn'ænθrəpəs, sə'nænθrəpəs
sinapism
BR 'sɪnəpɪz(ə)m, -z
AM 'sɪnəˌpɪzəm, -z
Sinatra
BR sɪ'nɑːtrə(*r*)
AM sə'nɑtrə
Sinbad
BR 'sɪnbad
AM 'sɪnˌbæd
sin-bin
BR 'sɪnbɪn, -z
AM 'sɪnˌbɪn, -z
since
BR sɪns
AM sɪns
sincere
BR s(ɪ)n'sɪə(r), -ə(r), -ɪst
AM sɪn'sɪ(ə)r, -ər, -ɪst
sincerely
BR s(ɪ)n'sɪəli
AM sɪn'sɪrli
sincereness
BR s(ɪ)n'sɪənəs
AM sɪn'sɪrnəs
sincerity
BR s(ɪ)n'sɛrɪti
AM sɪn'sɛrədi
sincipital
BR s(ɪ)n'sɪpɪtl
AM sɪn'sɪpɪdl
sinciput
BR 'sɪnsɪpʌt, -s
AM 'sɪnsəpət, -s
Sinclair
BR 'sɪŋklɛː(r), 'sɪnklɛː(r), sɪŋ'klɛː(r), sɪn'klɛː(r)
AM sɪn'klɛ(ə)r, sɪŋ'klɛ(ə)r
Sind
BR sɪnd
AM sɪnd
Sindebele
BR ˌsɪndə'biːli, ˌsɪndə'beɪli
AM ˌsɪndə'bili
Sindh
BR sɪnd
AM sɪnd
Sindhi
BR 'sɪnd|i, -ɪz
AM 'sɪndi, -z
Sindi
BR 'sɪnd|i, -ɪz
AM 'sɪndi, -z
sindonology
BR ˌsɪndə'nɒlədʒi
AM ˌsɪndə'nɑlədʒi
Sindy
BR 'sɪndi
AM 'sɪndi
sine
trigonometry
BR sʌɪn, -z
AM saɪn, -z
Sinéad
BR ʃɪ'neɪd
AM ʃə'neɪd
sinecure
BR 'sɪnɪkjʊə(r), 'sʌɪnɪkjʊə(r), 'sɪnɪkjɔː(r), 'sʌɪnɪkjɔː(r), -z
AM 'sɪnəˌkjʊ(ə)r, -z
sinecurism
BR 'sɪnɪkjʊərɪz(ə)m, 'sʌɪnɪkjʊərɪz(ə)m, 'sɪnɪkjɔːrɪz(ə)m, 'sʌɪnɪkjɔːrɪz(ə)m
AM 'sɪnəˌkjʊˌrɪzəm
sinecurist
BR 'sɪnɪkjʊərɪst, 'sʌɪnɪkjʊərɪst, 'sɪnɪkjɔːrɪst, 'sʌɪnɪkjɔːrɪst, -s
AM 'sɪnəˌkjʊrəst, -s
sine die
BR ˌsʌɪnɪ 'dʌɪiː, ˌsɪnɪ +, + diːeɪ
AM ˌsɪnə 'diə
sine qua non
BR ˌsɪnɪ kwɑː 'nɒn, ˌsʌɪnɪ +, + kweɪ +, + 'nəʊn
AM ˌsɪnə ˌkwɑ 'noʊn, + 'nɑn
sinew
BR 'sɪnjuː, -z
AM 'sɪnju, -z
sinewless
BR 'sɪnjuːləs
AM 'sɪnjuləs
sinewy
BR 'sɪnjuːi
AM 'sɪn(j)əwi
sinfonia
BR sɪn'fəʊnɪə(*r*), ˌsɪnfə'niːə(*r*), -z
AM ˌsɪnfə'niə, ˌsɪn'foʊniə, -z
sinfonietta
BR ˌsɪnfəʊnɪ'ɛtə(*r*), ˌsɪnfɒnɪ'ɛtə(*r*), -z
AM ˌsɪnfən'jɛdə, ˌsɪnfoʊn'jɛdə, -z
sinful
BR 'sɪnf(ʊ)l
AM 'sɪnfəl
sinfully
BR 'sɪnfʊli, 'sɪnfḷi
AM 'sɪnfəli
sinfulness
BR 'sɪnf(ʊ)lnəs
AM 'sɪnfəlnəs
sing
BR sɪŋ, -z, -ɪŋ
AM sɪŋ, -z, -ɪŋ
singable
BR 'sɪŋəbl
AM 'sɪŋəbəl
singalong
BR 'sɪŋəlɒŋ
AM 'sɪŋəˌlɔŋ, 'sɪŋəˌlɑŋ
Singapore
BR ˌsɪŋ(g)ə'pɔː(r)
AM 'sɪŋəˌpɔ(ə)r
Singaporean
BR ˌsɪŋ(g)ə'pɔːrɪən, -z
AM ˌsɪŋə'pɔriən, -z
singe
BR sɪn(d)ʒ, -ɪz, -ɪŋ, -d

AM sɪndʒ, -ɨz, -ɪŋ, -d

singer
BR 'sɪŋə(r), -z
AM 'sɪŋər, -z

singer-songwriter
BR ˌsɪŋə'sɒŋrʌɪtə(r), -z
AM ¦sɪŋər'sɔŋˌraɪdər, ¦sɪŋər'sɑŋˌraɪdər, -z

Singh
BR sɪŋ
AM sɪŋ

Singhalese
BR ˌsɪŋgə'liːz, ˌsɪŋ(h)ə'liːz
AM ¦sɪŋgə'liz, ¦sɪŋ(h)ə'liz

singingly
BR 'sɪŋɪŋli
AM 'sɪŋɪŋli

single
BR 'sɪŋg|l, -lz, -l̩ɪŋ\-lɪŋ, -ld
AM 'sɪŋg|əl, -əlz, -(ə)lɪŋ, -əld

single-lens reflex
BR ˌsɪŋgllɛnz 'riːflɛks, -ɨz
AM ¦sɪŋgə(l)ˌlɛnz 'riˌflɛks, -əz

single-minded
BR ˌsɪŋgl'mʌɪndɪd
AM ¦sɪŋgəl¦maɪndɨd

single-mindedly
BR ˌsɪŋgl'mʌɪndɪdli
AM ¦sɪŋgəl¦maɪndɨdli

single-mindedness
BR ˌsɪŋgl'mʌɪndɪdnɨs
AM ¦sɪŋgəl¦maɪndɨdnɨs

singleness
BR 'sɪŋglnəs
AM 'sɪŋgəlnəs

singlestick
BR 'sɪŋglstɪk, -s
AM 'sɪŋgəlˌstɪk, -s

singlet
BR 'sɪŋglɪt, -s
AM 'sɪŋglɨt, -s

singleton[1]
BR 'sɪŋglt(ə)n, -z
AM 'sɪŋgəlt(ə)n, -z

singleton[2]
BR 'sɪŋglt(ə)n, -z
AM 'sɪŋgəltən, -z

singletree
BR 'sɪŋgltriː, -z
AM 'sɪŋgəlˌtri, -z

singly
BR 'sɪŋgli
AM 'sɪŋgli

singsong
BR 'sɪŋsɒŋ, -z
AM 'sɪŋˌsɔŋ, 'sɪŋˌsɑŋ, -z

singular
BR 'sɪŋgjʉlə(r), -z
AM 'sɪŋgjələr, -z

singularisation
BR ˌsɪŋgjʉlərʌɪ'zeɪʃn
AM ˌsɪŋgjələrə'zeɪʃən, ˌsɪŋgjələˌraɪ'zeɪʃən, ˌsɪŋgjəˌlɛrə'zeɪʃən

singularise
BR 'sɪŋgjʉlərʌɪz, -ɨz, -ɪŋ, -d
AM 'sɪŋgjələˌraɪz, -ɨz, -ɪŋ, -d

singularity
BR ˌsɪŋgjʉ'larɪt|i, -ɪz
AM ˌsɪŋgjə'lɛrədi, -z

singularization
BR ˌsɪŋgjʉlərʌɪ'zeɪʃn
AM ˌsɪŋgjələrə'zeɪʃən, ˌsɪŋgjələˌraɪ'zeɪʃən, ˌsɪŋgjəˌlɛrə'zeɪʃən

singularize
BR 'sɪŋgjʉlərʌɪz, -ɨz, -ɪŋ, -d
AM 'sɪŋgjələˌraɪz, -ɨz, -ɪŋ, -d

singularly
BR 'sɪŋgjʉləli
AM 'sɪŋgjələrli

sinh
hyperbolic sine
BR ʃʌɪn, sɪn(t)ʃ, ˌsʌɪn'eɪtʃ
AM 'saɪn, ˌsaɪn'eɪtʃ

Sinhala
BR sɪn'hɑːlə(r)
AM sɪn'hɑlə

Sinhalese
BR ˌsɪn(h)ə'liːz, ˌsɪŋgə'liːz, ˌsɪŋ(h)ə'liːz
AM ¦sɪŋgə'liz, ¦sɪŋ(h)ə'liz

sinister
BR 'sɪnɪstə(r)
AM 'sɪnɪstər

sinisterly
BR 'sɪnɪstəli
AM 'sɪnɪstərli

sinisterness
BR 'sɪnɪstənəs
AM 'sɪnɪstərnəs

sinistral
BR 'sɪnɪstr(ə)l
AM 'sɪnɪstrəl, sə'nɪstrəl

sinistrality
BR ˌsɪnɪ'stralɪti
AM ˌsɪnə'strælədi

sinistrally
BR 'sɪnɪstrəli, 'sɪnɪstrl̩i
AM 'sɪnɪstrəli, sə'nɪstrəli

sinistrorse
BR 'sɪnɪstrɔːs
AM 'sɪnəˌstrɔ(ə)rs

sinistrorsely
BR 'sɪnɪstrɔːsli
AM 'sɪnəˌstrɔrsli

Sinitic
BR sʌɪ'nɪtɪk, sɪ'nɪtɪk
AM sə'nɪdɪk

sink
BR sɪŋk, -s, -ɪŋ
AM sɪŋk, -s, -ɪŋ

sinkable
BR 'sɪŋkəbl
AM 'sɪŋkəbəl

sinkage
BR 'sɪŋk|ɪdʒ, -ɪdʒɪz
AM 'sɪŋkɪdʒ, -ɨz

sinker
BR 'sɪŋkə(r), -z
AM 'sɪŋkər, -z

sinkhole
BR 'sɪŋkhəʊl, -z
AM 'sɪŋkˌ(h)oʊl, -z

Sinkiang
BR 'sɪŋ'kjaŋ
AM 'sɪŋ'kjæŋ

sinking
BR 'sɪŋkɪŋ, -z
AM 'sɪŋkɪŋ, -z

sinless
BR 'sɪnlɨs
AM 'sɪnlɨs

sinlessly
BR 'sɪnlɨsli
AM 'sɪnlɨsli

sinlessness
BR 'sɪnlɨsnɨs
AM 'sɪnlɨsnɨs

sinner
BR 'sɪnə(r), -z
AM 'sɪnər, -z

sinnet
BR 'sɪnɪt, -s
AM 'sɪnɪt, -s

Sinn Fein
BR ˌʃɪn 'feɪn
AM ˌʃɪn 'feɪn
IR ˌsʲinʲ 'fʲeːnʲ

Sinn Feiner
BR ˌʃɪn 'feɪnə(r), -z
AM ˌʃɪn 'feɪnər, -z

Sinnott
BR 'sɪnət
AM 'sɪnət

Sino-
BR 'sʌɪnəʊ
AM 'saɪnoʊ

Sino-British
BR ˌsʌɪnəʊ'brɪtɪʃ
AM ¦saɪnoʊ'brɪdɪʃ

Sino-Japanese
BR ˌsʌɪnəʊˌdʒapə'niːz
AM ¦saɪnoʊˌdʒæpə'niz

sinological
BR ˌsʌɪnə'lɒdʒɪkl, ˌsɪnə'lɒdʒɪkl
AM ¦saɪnə'lɑdʒəkəl, ¦sɪnə'lɑdʒəkəl

Sinologist
BR sʌɪ'nɒlədʒɪst, sɪ'nɒlədʒɪst, -s
AM saɪ'nɑlədʒəst, -s

Sinologue
BR 'sʌɪnəlɒg, 'sɪnəlɒg, -z
AM ˌsaɪnə'lɔg, ˌsaɪnə'lɑg, -z

Sinology
BR sʌɪ'nɒlədʒi, sɪ'nɒlədʒi
AM saɪ'nɑlədʒi

Sinomania
BR ˌsʌɪnə(ʊ)'meɪnɪə(r)
AM ˌsaɪnə'meɪniə

Sinophile
BR 'sʌɪnəfʌɪl, -z
AM 'saɪnəˌfaɪl, -z

Sinophobe
BR 'sʌɪnəfəʊb, -z
AM 'saɪnəˌfoʊb, -z

Sinophobia
BR ˌsʌɪnə(ʊ)'fəʊbɪə(r)
AM ˌsaɪnə'foʊbiə

sinopia
BR sɪ'nəʊpɪə(r)
AM sə'noʊpiə

Sino-Soviet
BR ˌsʌɪnəʊ'səʊvɪət
AM ¦saɪnoʊ'soʊviət

Sino-Tibetan
BR ˌsʌɪnəʊtɪ'bɛtn, -z
AM ¦saɪnoʊˌtə'bɛtn, -z

sinter
BR 'sɪntə(r), -z
AM 'sɪn(t)ər, -z

Sintra
BR 'sɪntrə(r)
AM 'sɪntrə

sinuate
BR 'sɪnjʊeɪt
AM 'sɪnjəweɪt

sinuosity
BR ˌsɪnjʊ'ɒsɪt|i, -ɪz
AM ˌsɪnjə'wɑsədi, -z

sinuous
BR 'sɪnjʊəs
AM 'sɪnjəwəs

sinuously
BR 'sɪnjʊəsli
AM 'sɪnjəwəsli

sinuousness
BR 'sɪnjʊəsnəs
AM 'sɪnjəwəsnəs

sinus
BR 'sʌɪnəs, -ɨz
AM 'saɪnəs, -əz

sinusitis
BR ˌsʌɪnə'sʌɪtɨs
AM ˌsaɪnə'saɪdɨs

sinusoid
BR 'sʌɪnəsɔɪd, -z
AM 'saɪnəˌsɔɪd, -z

sinusoidal
BR ˌsʌɪnə'sɔɪdl
AM ˌsaɪnə'sɔɪdəl

sinusoidally
BR ˌsʌɪnə'sɔɪdl̩i
AM ˌsaɪnə'sɔɪd(ə)li

Siobhan
BR ʃɪ'vɔːn
AM ʃə'vɑn

Sion
BR 'sʌɪən
AM 'saɪən

Sioned
BR 'ʃɒnɨd
AM 'ʃɑnəd

Siouan
BR 'suːən
AM 'suən

Sioux
BR suː
AM su

sip
BR sɪp, -s, -ɪŋ, -t
AM sɪp, -s, -ɪŋ, -t

sipe
BR sʌɪp, -s, -ɪŋ, -t
AM saɪp, -s, -ɪŋ, -t

siphon
BR 'sʌɪf|n, -nz, -n̩ɪŋ\-ənɪŋ, -nd
AM 'saɪf|ən, -ənz, -(ə)nɪŋ, -ənd

siphonage
BR 'sʌɪfənɪdʒ, 'sʌɪfn̩ɪdʒ
AM 'saɪfənɪdʒ

siphonal
BR 'sʌɪfənl, 'sʌɪfn̩l
AM 'saɪfənəl

siphonic
BR sʌɪ'fɒnɪk
AM saɪ'fɑnɪk

siphonophore
BR sʌɪ'fɒnə(ʊ)fɔː(r), -z
AM saɪ'fɑnəˌfɔ(ə)r, -z

siphuncle
BR 'sʌɪˌfʌŋkl, -z
AM 'saɪˌfəŋkəl, -z

sipper
BR 'sɪpə(r), -z
AM 'sɪpər, -z

sippet
BR 'sɪpɨt, -s
AM 'sɪpɨt, -s

sir¹
strong form
BR səː(r), -z
AM sər, -z

sir²
weak form
BR sə(r)
AM sər

sircar
BR 'səːkɑː(r), -z
AM 'sərˌkɑr, -z

sirdar
BR 'səːdɑː(r), -z
AM 'sərˌdɑr, -z

sire
BR 'sʌɪə(r), -z, -ɪŋ, -d
AM 'saɪ(ə)r, -z, -ɪŋ, -d

siren
BR 'sʌɪrən, 'sʌɪrn̩, -z
AM 'saɪrən, -z

sirenian
BR sʌɪ'riːnɪən, -z
AM saɪ'riniən, -z

sirgang
BR 'səːgaŋ, -z
AM 'sərˌgæŋ, -z

Sirhowy
BR səː'haʊi
AM sər'haʊi

Sirius
BR 'sɪrɪəs
AM 'sɪriəs

sirloin
BR 'səːlɔɪn, -z
AM 'sərˌlɔɪn, -z

sirocco
BR sɪ'rɒkəʊ, -z
AM sə'rɑkoʊ, -z

sirrah
BR 'sɪrə(r)
AM 'sɪrə

sirree
BR sə'riː
AM sə'ri

Sirte
BR 'səːti
AM 'sərdi

sirup
BR 'sɪrəp
AM 'sɪrəp, 'sərəp

sis
BR sɪs
AM sɪs

sisal
BR 'sʌɪsl, 'sʌɪzl
AM 'saɪsəl, 'saɪzəl

siskin
BR 'sɪskɪn, -z
AM 'sɪskɨn, -z

Sisley
BR 'sɪzli
AM 'sɪsli

Sissie
BR 'sɪsi
AM 'sɪsi

sissified
BR 'sɪsɨfʌɪd
AM 'sɪsəˌfaɪd

sissiness
BR 'sɪsɪnɨs
AM 'sɪsinɨs

Sissons
BR 'sɪsnz
AM 'sɪsənz

sissoo
BR 'sɪsuː, -z
AM 'sɪˌsu, -z

sissy
BR 'sɪs|i, -ɪz
AM 'sɪsi, -z

sissyish
BR 'sɪsɪɪʃ
AM 'sɪsiɪʃ

sister
BR 'sɪstə(r), -z
AM 'sɪstər, -z

sisterhood
BR 'sɪstəhʊd, -z
AM 'sɪstər,(h)ʊd, -z

sister-in-law
BR 'sɪst(ə)rɪnˌlɔː(r), -z
AM 'sɪstərənˌlɔ, 'sɪstərənˌlɑ, -z

sisterless
BR 'sɪstələs
AM 'sɪstərləs

sisterliness
BR 'sɪstəlɪnɨs
AM 'sɪstərlinɨs

sisterly
BR 'sɪstəli
AM 'sɪstərli

sisters-in-law
BR 'sɪstəzɪnˌlɔː(r)
AM 'sɪstərzənˌlɔ, 'sɪstərzənˌlɑ

Sistine
BR 'sɪstiːn
AM 'sɪˌstin

sistra
BR 'sɪstrə(r)
AM 'sɪstrə

sistroid
BR 'sɪstrɔɪd
AM 'sɪstrɔɪd

sistrum
BR 'sɪstrəm, -z
AM 'sɪstrəm, -z

Sisyphean
BR ˌsɪsɪ'fiːən
AM ˌsɪsə'fiən

Sisyphian
BR ˌsɪsɪ'fiːən
AM ˌsɪsə'fiən

Sisyphus
BR 'sɪsɨfəs
AM 'sɪsɨfəs

sit
BR sɪt, -s, -ɪŋ
AM sɪ|t, -ts, -dɪŋ

Sita
BR 'siːtə(r)
AM 'sidə

sitar
BR 'sɪtɑː(r), sɪ'tɑː(r), -z
AM sə'tɑr, 'sɪˌtɑr, -z

sitarist
BR 'sɪtɑːrɪst, sɪ'tɑːrɪst, -s
AM 'sɪˌtɑrəst, sə'tɑrəst, -s

sitatunga
BR ˌsɪtə'tʊŋgə(r)
AM ˌsɪdə'tʊŋgə

sitcom
BR 'sɪtkɒm, -z
AM 'sɪtˌkɑm, -z

sitdown
BR 'sɪtdaʊn, ˌsɪt'daʊn, -z
AM 'sɪtˌdaʊn, -z

site
BR sʌɪt, -s, -ɪŋ, -ɨd
AM saɪ|t, -ts, -dɪŋ, -dɨd

sit-fast
BR 'sɪtfɑːst, 'sɪtfast, -s
AM 'sɪtˌfæst, -s

sit-in
BR 'sɪtɪn, -z
AM 'sɪdˌɪn, -z

Sitka
BR 'sɪtkə(r), -z
AM 'sɪtkə, -z

sitophobia
BR ˌsʌɪtə'fəʊbɪə(r)
AM ˌsaɪdə'foʊbiə, ˌsaɪˌtoʊ'foʊbiə

sitrep
BR 'sɪtrɛp, -s
AM 'sɪtˌrɛp, -s

sitringee
BR sɪ'trɪn(d)ʒiː, -z
AM sə'trɪŋgi, -z

sits vac
BR ˌsɪts 'vak
AM ˌsɪts 'væk

Sittang
BR 'sɪtaŋ
AM 'sɪˌtæŋ

sitter
BR 'sɪtə(r), -z
AM 'sɪdər, -z

sitter-in
BR ˌsɪtər'ɪn
AM ˌsɪdər'ɪn

sitters-in
BR ˌsɪtəz'ɪn
AM ˌsɪdərz'ɪn

sitting
BR 'sɪtɪŋ, -z
AM 'sɪdɪŋ, -z

Sittingbourne
BR 'sɪtɪŋbɔːn
AM 'sɪdɪŋˌbɔ(ə)rn

Sitting Bull
BR ˌsɪtɪŋ 'bʊl
AM 'sɪdɪŋ 'bʊl

situ
BR 'sɪtjuː, 'sɪtʃuː
AM 'sɪˌt(j)u

situate¹
adjective
BR 'sɪtjʊət, 'sɪtjʊeɪt, 'sɪtʃʊət, 'sɪtʃʊeɪt
AM 'sɪtʃəˌweɪt, 'sɪtʃəwət

situate²
verb
BR 'sɪtjʊeɪt, 'sɪtʃʊeɪt, -s, -ɪŋ, -ɨd
AM 'sɪtʃəˌweɪ|t, -ts, -dɪŋ, -dɨd

situation
BR ˌsɪtjʊ'eɪʃn, ˌsɪtʃʊ'eɪʃn, -z
AM ˌsɪtʃə'weɪʃən, -z

situational
BR ˌsɪtjʊ'eɪʃn̩(ə)l, ˌsɪtjʊ'eɪʃən(ə)l, ˌsɪtʃʊ'eɪʃn̩(ə)l, ˌsɪtʃʊ'eɪʃən(ə)l

AM ˌsɪtʃə'weɪʃ(ə)nəl

situationally
BR ˌsɪtjʊ'eɪʃn̩əli, ˌsɪtjʊ'eɪʃ(ə)nəli, ˌsɪtʃʊ'eɪʃn̩əli, ˌsɪtʃʊ'eɪʃ(ə)nəli
AM ˌsɪtʃə'weɪʃ(ə)nəli

situationism
BR ˌsɪtjʊ'eɪʃn̩ɪz(ə)m, ˌsɪtjʊ'eɪʃənɪz(ə)m, ˌsɪtʃʊ'eɪʃn̩ɪz(ə)m, ˌsɪtʃʊ'eɪʃənɪz(ə)m
AM ˌsɪtʃə'weɪʃəˌnɪzəm

situationist
BR ˌsɪtjʊ'eɪʃn̩ɪst, ˌsɪtjʊ'eɪʃənɪst, ˌsɪtʃʊ'eɪʃn̩ɪst, ˌsɪtʃʊ'eɪʃənɪst, -s
AM ˌsɪtʃə'weɪʃənəst, -s

sit-up
BR 'sɪtʌp, -s
AM 'sɪdəp, -s

sit-upon
BR 'sɪtəpɒn, -z
AM 'sɪdəpɑn, -z

Sitwell
BR 'sɪtw(ɛ)l
AM 'sɪtˌwɛl

sitz
BR sɪts
AM sɪts

sitz-bath
BR 'sɪts|bɑːθ, 'sɪts|baθ, -bɑːðz\-bɑːθs\-baðs
AM 'sɪtsˌbæθ, -s, -ðz

Sitzkrieg
BR 'sɪtskriːg, -z
AM 'sɪtsˌkrig, -z

sitzmark
BR 'sɪtsmɑːk, -s
AM 'sɪtsˌmɑrk, -s

Siva
BR 'ʃiːvə(r), 'siːvə(r)
AM 'sivə, 'ʃivə

Sivaism
BR 'ʃiːvə(r)ɪz(ə)m, 'siːvə(r)ɪz(ə)m
AM 'sivəˌɪzəm, 'ʃivəˌɪzəm

Sivaite
BR 'ʃiːvə(r)ʌɪt, 'siːvə(r)ʌɪt, -s
AM 'sivəˌaɪt, 'ʃivəˌaɪt, -s

Sivan
BR 'ʃiːvn, 'siːvn
AM 'sivən, 'ʃivən

Siwash
BR 'sʌɪwɒʃ
AM 'saɪˌwɔʃ, 'saɪˌwɑʃ

six
BR sɪks, -ɪz
AM sɪks, -ɪz

sixain
BR 'sɪkseɪn, -z
AM 'sɪkˌseɪn, -z

sixer
BR 'sɪksə(r), -z
AM 'sɪksər, -z

sixfold
BR 'sɪksfəʊld
AM 'sɪks¦foʊld

six-footer
BR ˌsɪks'fʊtə(r), -z
AM ¦sɪks¦fʊdər, -z

sixgun
BR 'sɪksgʌn, -z
AM 'sɪksˌgən, -z

sixpence
BR 'sɪkspəns
AM 'sɪksˌpɛns, 'sɪkspəns

sixpenny
BR 'sɪkspəni
AM 'sɪksˌpɛni, 'sɪkspəni

six-shooter
BR 'sɪkˌʃuːtə(r), -z
AM 'sɪk(s)ˌʃudər, -z

sixte
BR sɪkst, -s
AM sɪkst, -s

sixteen
BR ˌsɪks'tiːn
AM ˌsɪk¦stin

sixteenmo
BR ˌsɪks'tiːnməʊ
AM ˌsɪks'tinˌmoʊ

sixteenth
BR ˌsɪks'tiːnθ, -s
AM ¦sɪk¦stinθ, -s

sixth
BR sɪksθ, -s
AM sɪksθ, -s

sixth-former
BR 'sɪksθˌfɔːmə(r), -z
AM 'sɪksθ¦fɔrmər, -z

sixthly
BR 'sɪksθli
AM 'sɪksθli

sixtieth
BR 'sɪkstɪɪθ, -s
AM 'sɪkstiɪθ, -s

Sixtine
BR 'sɪkstiːn, 'sɪkstʌɪn
AM 'sɪksˌtin

Sixtus
BR 'sɪkstəs
AM 'sɪkstəs

sixty
BR 'sɪkst|i, -ɪz
AM 'sɪksti, -z

sixtyfold
BR 'sɪkstɪfəʊld
AM ¦sɪksti¦foʊld

sixty-fourmo
BR ˌsɪkstɪ'fɔːməʊ, -z
AM ¦sɪksti'fɔrˌmoʊ, -z

sizable
BR 'sʌɪzəbl
AM 'saɪzəbəl

sizar
BR 'sʌɪzə(r), -z
AM 'saɪzər, -z

sizarship
BR 'sʌɪzəʃɪp, -s
AM 'saɪzərˌʃɪp, -s

size
BR sʌɪz, -ɪz, -ɪŋ, -d
AM saɪz, -ɪz, -ɪŋ, -d

sizeable
BR 'sʌɪzəbl
AM 'saɪzəbəl

sizeably
BR 'sʌɪzəbli
AM 'sɪzəbli

sizer
BR 'sʌɪzə(r), -z
AM 'saɪzər, -z

Sizewell
BR 'sʌɪzw(ɛ)l
AM 'saɪzˌwɛl

sizy
BR 'sʌɪzi
AM 'saɪzi

sizzle
BR 'sɪz|l, -lz, -l̩ɪŋ\-lɪŋ, -ld
AM 'sɪz|əl, -əlz, -(ə)lɪŋ, -əld

sizzler
BR 'sɪzl̩ə(r), 'sɪzlə(r), -z
AM 'sɪz(ə)lər, -z

sjambok
BR 'ʃambɒk, -s, -ɪŋ, -t
AM ʃæm'bɑk, 'ʃæmˌbɑk, 'ʃæmbək, -s, -ɪŋ, -t

ska
BR skɑː(r)
AM skɑ

Skagerrak
BR 'skagərak
AM 'skægəˌræk

Skagway
BR 'skagweɪ
AM 'skægˌweɪ

skald
BR skɔːld, skald, -z
AM skɔld, skɑld, -z

skaldic
BR 'skɔːldɪk, 'skaldɪk
AM 'skɔldɪk, 'skɑldɪk

Skanda
BR 'skandə(r)
AM 'skændə

Skara Brae
BR ˌskarə 'breɪ
AM ˌskɛrə 'breɪ

skarn
BR skɑːn
AM skɑrn

skat
BR skat
AM skæt

skate
BR skeɪt, -s, -ɪŋ, -ɪd
AM skeɪ|t, -ts, -dɪŋ, -dɪd

skateboard
BR 'skeɪtbɔːd, -z, -ɪŋ
AM 'skeɪtˌbɔ(ə)rd, -z, -ɪŋ

skateboarder
BR 'skeɪtˌbɔːdə(r), -z
AM 'skeɪtˌbɔrdər, -z

skatepark
BR 'skeɪtpɑːk, -s
AM 'skeɪtˌpɑrk, -s

skater
BR 'skeɪtə(r), -z
AM 'skeɪdər, -z

skating-rink
BR 'skeɪtɪŋrɪŋk, -s
AM 'skeɪdɪŋˌrɪŋk, -s

skean
BR 'skiːən, skiːn, -z
AM 'ski(ə)n, -z

skean dhu
BR ˌskiː(ə)n 'duː, -z
AM ˌski(ə)n 'ðu, -z

Skeat
BR skiːt
AM skit

sked
BR skɛd, -z, -ɪŋ, -ɪd
AM skɛd, -z, -ɪŋ, -əd

skedaddle
BR skɪ'dad|l, -lz, -l̩ɪŋ\-lɪŋ, -ld
AM skə'dæd|əl, -əlz, -(ə)lɪŋ, -əld

skeet
BR skiːt
AM skit

skeeter
BR 'skiːtə(r), -z, -ɪŋ, -d
AM 'skidər, -z, -ɪŋ, -d

Skeffington
BR 'skɛfɪŋt(ə)n
AM 'skɛfɪŋtən

skeg
BR skɛg, -z
AM skɛg, -z

Skegness
BR ˌskɛg'nɛs
AM ˌskɛg'nɛs

skein
BR skeɪn, -z
AM skeɪn, -z

skeletal
BR 'skɛlɪtl, skɪ'liːtl
AM 'skɛlədl

skeletally
BR 'skɛlɪtl̩i, 'skɛlɪtəli, skɪ'liːtl̩i, skɪ'liːtəli
AM 'skɛlədl̩i

skeleton
BR 'skɛlɪtn, -z
AM 'skɛlətn, -z

skeletonise
BR 'skɛlɪtn̩ʌɪz, 'skɛlɪtənʌɪz, -ɪz, -ɪŋ, -d
AM 'skɛlətnˌaɪz, -ɪz, -ɪŋ, -d

skeletonize
BR 'skɛlɪtn̩ʌɪz, 'skɛlɪtənʌɪz, -ɪz, -ɪŋ, -d

AM 'skɛlətn,aɪz, -ɨz, -ɪŋ, -d

Skelmersdale
BR 'skɛlməzdeɪl
AM 'skɛlmərz,deɪl

Skelton
BR 'skɛlt(ə)n
AM 'skɛlt(ə)n

skep
BR skɛp, -s
AM skɛp, -s

skepsis
BR 'skɛpsɪs
AM 'skɛpsəs

skeptic
BR 'skɛptɪk
AM 'skɛptɪk

skeptical
BR 'skɛptɪkl
AM 'skɛptəkəl

skeptically
BR 'skɛptɪkli
AM 'skɛptək(ə)li

skepticism
BR 'skɛptɨsɪz(ə)m
AM 'skɛptə,sɪzəm

skerrick
BR 'skɛrɪk, -s
AM 'skɛrɪk, -s

skerry
BR 'skɛr|i, -ɪz
AM 'skɛri, -z

sketch
BR skɛtʃ, -ɨz, -ɪŋ, -t
AM skɛtʃ, -əz, -ɪŋ, -t

sketchbook
BR 'skɛtʃbʊk, -s
AM 'skɛtʃ,bʊk, -s

sketcher
BR 'skɛtʃə(r), -z
AM 'skɛtʃər, -z

sketchily
BR 'skɛtʃɨli
AM 'skɛtʃəli

sketchiness
BR 'skɛtʃɪnɨs
AM 'skɛtʃinɨs

Sketchley
BR 'skɛtʃli
AM 'skɛtʃli

sketchpad
BR 'skɛtʃpad, -z
AM 'skɛtʃ,pæd, -z

sketchy
BR 'skɛtʃ|i, -ɪə(r), -ɪɪst
AM 'skɛtʃi, -ər, -ɨst

skeuomorph
BR 'skju:ə(ʊ)mɔ:f, -s
AM 'skjuə,mɔ(ə)rf, -s

skeuomorphic
BR ,skju:ə'mɔ:fɪk
AM ,skjuə'mɔrfɪk

skew
BR skju:, -z, -ɪŋ, -d
AM skju, -z, -ɪŋ, -d

skewback
BR 'skju:bak, -s
AM 'skju,bæk, -s

skewbald
BR 'skju:bɔ:ld, -z
AM 'sju,bɔld, 'sju,bɑld, -z

Skewen
BR 'skju:ɪn
AM 'skjuən

skewer
BR 'skju:ə(r), -z, -ɪŋ, -d
AM 'skju(w)ər, 'skjʊ(ə)r, -z, -ɪŋ, -d

skewness
BR 'skju:nəs
AM 'skjunəs

skew-whiff
BR ,skju:'wɪf
AM 'skju,wɪf

ski
BR ski:, -z, -ɪŋ, -d
AM ski, -z, -ɪŋ, -d

skiable
BR 'ski:əbl
AM 'skiəbəl

skiagram
BR 'skʌɪəgram, -z
AM 'skaɪə,græm, -z

skiagraph
BR 'skʌɪəgrɑ:f, 'skʌɪəgraf, -s
AM 'skaɪə,græf, -s

skiagraphy
BR skʌɪ'agrəfi
AM skaɪ'ɑgrəfi

skiamachy
BR skʌɪ'aməki
AM skaɪ'æməki

skibob
BR 'ski:bɒb, -z
AM 'ski,bɑb, -z

ski-bobber
BR 'ski:,bɒbə(r), -z
AM 'ski,bɑbər, -z

skiboot
BR 'ski:bu:t, -s
AM 'ski,but, -s

skid
BR skɪd, -z, -ɪŋ, -ɨd
AM skɪd, -z, -ɪŋ, -ɨd

Skiddaw
BR 'skɪdɔ:(*r*)
AM 'skɪdɔ, skə'dɔ, 'skɪdɑ, skə'dɑ

skiddoo
BR skɪ'du:, -z
AM skə'du, -z

skidlid
BR 'skɪdlɪd, -z
AM 'skɪd,lɪd, -z

skidmark
BR 'skɪdmɑ:k, -s
AM 'skɪd,mark, -s

skidoo
BR skɪ'du:, -z
AM skə'du, -z

skidpan
BR 'skɪdpan, -z
AM 'skɪd,pæn, -z

skidproof
BR 'skɪdpru:f
AM 'skɪd,pruf

skid row
BR ,skɪd 'rəʊ
AM 'skɪd ,roʊ

skier
BR 'ski:ə(r), -z
AM 'skiər, -z

skiff
BR skɪf, -s
AM skɪf, -s

skiffle
BR 'skɪfl
AM 'skɪfəl

ski-jorer
BR 'ski:dʒɔ:rə(r), ,ski:'dʒɔ:rə(r), -z
AM 'ski,dʒɔrər, ,ski'dʒɔrər, -z

ski-joring
BR 'ski:dʒɔ:rɪŋ, ,ski:'dʒɔ:rɪŋ
AM 'ski,dʒɔrɪŋ, ,ski'dʒɔrɪŋ

ski-jump
BR 'ski:dʒʌmp, -s
AM 'ski,dʒəmp, -s

skilful
BR 'skɪlf(ʊ)l
AM 'skɪlfəl

skilfully
BR 'skɪlfʊli, 'skɪlfḷi
AM 'skɪlf(ə)li

skilfulness
BR 'skɪlf(ʊ)lnəs
AM 'skɪlfəlnəs

skilift
BR 'ski:lɪft, -s
AM 'ski,lɪft, -s

skill
BR skɪl, -z, -d
AM skɪl, -z, -d

skillet
BR 'skɪlɨt, -s
AM 'skɪlɨt, -s

skillful
BR 'skɪlf(ʊ)l
AM 'skɪlfəl

skillfully
BR 'skɪlfʊli, 'skɪlfḷi
AM 'skɪlfəli

skillfulness
BR 'skɪlf(ʊ)lnəs
AM 'skɪlfəlnəs

skill-less
BR 'skɪllɨs
AM 'skɪ(l)ləs

skilly
BR 'skɪl|i, -ɪz
AM 'skɪli, -z

skim
BR skɪm, -z, -ɪŋ, -d
AM skɪm, -z, -ɪŋ, -d

skimmer
BR 'skɪmə(r), -z
AM 'skɪmər, -z

skimmia
BR 'skɪmɪə(*r*), -z
AM 'skɪmiə, -z

skimp
BR skɪm|p, -ps, -pɪŋ, -(p)t
AM skɪmp, -s, -ɪŋ, -t

skimpily
BR 'skɪmpɨli
AM 'skɪmpɨli

skimpiness
BR 'skɪmpɪnɨs
AM 'skɪmpinɨs

skimpy
BR 'skɪmp|i, -ɪə(r), -ɪɪst
AM 'skɪmpi, -ər, -ɨst

skin
BR skɪn, -z, -ɪŋ, -d
AM skɪn, -z, -ɪŋ, -d

skincare
BR 'skɪnkɛ:(r)
AM 'skɪn,kɛ(ə)r

skin-deep
BR ,skɪn'di:p
AM ,skɪn'dip

skin-dive
BR 'skɪndʌɪv, -z, -ɪŋ
AM 'skɪn,daɪv, -z, -ɪŋ

skinflick
BR 'skɪnflɪk, -s
AM 'skɪn,flɪk, -s

skinflint
BR 'skɪnflɪnt, -s
AM 'skɪn,flɪnt, -s

skinful
BR 'skɪnfʊl, -z
AM 'skɪn,fʊl, -z

skinhead
BR 'skɪnhɛd, -z
AM 'skɪn,(h)ɛd, -z

skink
BR skɪŋk, -s
AM skɪŋk, -s

skinless
BR 'skɪnlɨs
AM 'skɪnlɨs

skinlike
BR 'skɪnlʌɪk
AM 'skɪn,laɪk

skinner
BR 'skɪnə(r), -z
AM 'skɪnər, -z

Skinnerian
BR skɪ'nɪərɪən
AM skɪ'nɛriən

Skinnerism
BR 'skɪnərɪz(ə)m
AM 'skɪnə,rɪzəm

skinniness
BR 'skɪnɪnɨs
AM 'skɪninɨs

skinny
BR 'skɪn|i, -ɪə(r), -ɪɪst
AM 'skɪni, -ər, -ɨst

skinny-dip
BR 'skɪnɪdɪp, -s, -ɪŋ, -t

AM ˈskɪni,dɪp, -s, -ɪŋ, -t

skint
BR skɪnt
AM skɪnt

skintight
BR ˌskɪnˈtʌɪt
AM ˈskɪnˈtaɪt

skip
BR skɪp, -s, -ɪŋ, -t
AM skɪp, -s, -ɪŋ, -t

skipjack
BR ˈskɪpdʒak, -s
AM ˈskɪp,dʒæk, -s

ski-plane
BR ˈskiːpleɪn, -z
AM ˈski,pleɪn, -z

skipper
BR ˈskɪp|ə(r), -əz, -(ə)rɪŋ, -əd
AM ˈskɪpər, -z, -ɪŋ, -d

skippet
BR ˈskɪpɪt, -s
AM ˈskɪpɪt, -s

skipping-rope
BR ˈskɪpɪŋrəʊp, -s
AM ˈskɪpɪŋ,roʊp, -s

Skipton
BR ˈskɪpt(ə)n
AM ˈskɪptən

skirl
BR skəːl, -z, -ɪŋ, -d
AM skərl, -z, -ɪŋ, -d

skirmish
BR ˈskəːm|ɪʃ, -ɪʃɪz, -ɪʃɪŋ, -ɪʃt
AM ˈskərmɪʃ, -ɪz, -ɪŋ, -t

skirmisher
BR ˈskəːmɪʃə(r), -z
AM ˈskərmɪʃər, -z

skirr
BR skəː(r), -z, -ɪŋ, -d
AM skər, -z, -ɪŋ, -d

skirret
BR ˈskɪrɪt, -s
AM ˈskərət, -s

skirt
BR skəːt, -s, -ɪŋ, -ɪd
AM skər|t, -ts, -dɪŋ, -dəd

skirting
BR ˈskəːtɪŋ, -z
AM ˈskərdɪŋ, -z

skirtless
BR ˈskəːtləs
AM ˈskərtləs

skit
BR skɪt, -s
AM skɪt, -s

skite
BR skʌɪt, -s, -ɪŋ, -ɪd
AM skaɪ|t, -ts, -dɪŋ, -dɪd

skitter
BR ˈskɪt|ə(r), -əz, -(ə)rɪŋ, -əd
AM ˈskɪdər, -z, -ɪŋ, -d

skittery
BR ˈskɪt(ə)ri
AM ˈskɪdəri

skittish
BR ˈskɪtɪʃ
AM ˈskɪdɪʃ

skittishly
BR ˈskɪtɪʃli
AM ˈskɪdɪʃli

skittishness
BR ˈskɪtɪʃnɪs
AM ˈskɪdɪʃnɪs

skittle
BR ˈskɪt|l, -lz, -l̩ɪŋ\-lɪŋ, -ld
AM ˈskɪdəl, -z, -ɪŋ, -d

skive
BR skʌɪv, -z, -ɪŋ, -d
AM skaɪv, -z, -ɪŋ, -d

skiver
BR ˈskʌɪvə(r), -z
AM ˈskaɪvər, -z

Skivvies
BR ˈskɪvɪz
AM ˈskɪviz

skivvy
BR ˈskɪv|i, -ɪz, -ɪɪŋ, -ɪd
AM ˈskɪvi, -z, -ɪŋ, -d

skiwear
BR ˈskiːwɛː(r)
AM ˈski,wɛ(ə)r

skoal
BR skəʊl
AM skoʊ(ə)l

Skoda®
BR ˈskəʊdə(r), -z
AM ˈskoʊdə, -z

Skokholm
BR ˈskɒkhəʊm, ˈskəʊkəm
AM ˈskɑk,(h)oʊm, ˈskoʊkəm

skol
BR skɒl, skəʊl
AM skoʊl

skookum
BR ˈskuːkəm
AM ˈskukəm

Skryabin
BR skrɪˈabɪn, skrɪˈɑːbɪn
AM skriˈɑbən
RUS ˈskrʲabʲin

skua
BR ˈskjuːə(r), -z
AM ˈskjuə, -z

Skues
BR skjuːz
AM skjuz

skulduggery
BR skʌlˈdʌɡ(ə)ri
AM ˌskəlˈdəɡ(ə)ri

skulk
BR skʌlk, -s, -ɪŋ, -t
AM skəlk, -s, -ɪŋ, -t

skulker
BR ˈskʌlkə(r), -z
AM ˈskəlkər, -z

skull
BR skʌl, -z
AM skəl, -z

skullcap
BR ˈskʌlkap, -s
AM ˈskəl,kæp, -s

skullduggery
BR skʌlˈdʌɡ(ə)ri
AM ˌskəlˈdəɡ(ə)ri

skunk
BR skʌŋk, -s
AM skəŋk, -s

sky
BR skʌɪ, -z, -ɪŋ, -d
AM skaɪ, -z, -ɪŋ, -d

skycap
BR ˈskʌɪkap, -s
AM ˈskaɪ,kæp, -s

skydive
BR ˈskʌɪdʌɪv
AM ˈskaɪ,daɪv

skydiver
BR ˈskʌɪ,dʌɪvə(r), -z
AM ˈskaɪ,daɪvər, -z

skydiving
BR ˈskʌɪ,dʌɪvɪŋ
AM ˈskaɪ,daɪvɪŋ

Skye
BR skʌɪ
AM skaɪ

skyer
BR ˈskʌɪə(r), -z
AM ˈskaɪər, -z

skyey
BR ˈskʌɪi
AM ˈskaɪi

sky-high
BR ˌskʌɪˈhʌɪ
AM ˈskaɪˈhaɪ

skyhook
BR ˈskʌɪhʊk, -s
AM ˈskaɪ,hʊk, -s

skyjack
BR ˈskʌɪdʒak, -s, -ɪŋ, -t
AM ˈskaɪ,dʒæk, -s, -ɪŋ, -t

skyjacker
BR ˈskʌɪdʒakə(r), -z
AM ˈskaɪ,dʒækər, -z

Skylab
BR ˈskʌɪlab
AM ˈskaɪ,læb

skylark
BR ˈskʌɪlɑːk, -s, -ɪŋ, -t
AM ˈskaɪ,lɑrk, -s, -ɪŋ, -t

skyless
BR ˈskʌɪlɪs
AM ˈskaɪləs

skylight
BR ˈskʌɪlʌɪt, -s
AM ˈskaɪ,laɪt, -s

skyline
BR ˈskʌɪlʌɪn, -z
AM ˈskaɪ,laɪn, -z

skyrocket
BR ˈskʌɪ,rɒk|ɪt, -ɪts, -ɪtɪŋ, -ɪtɪd
AM ˈskaɪ,rɑkɛ|t, -ts, -dɪŋ, -dɪd

skysail
BR ˈskʌɪseɪl, -z
AM ˈskaɪ,seɪl, -z

skyscape
BR ˈskʌɪskeɪp, -s
AM ˈskaɪ,skeɪp, -s

skyscraper
BR ˈskʌɪ,skreɪpə(r), -z
AM ˈskaɪ,skreɪpər, -z

skywalk
BR ˈskʌɪwɔːk, -s, -ɪŋ, -t
AM ˈskaɪ,wɔk, ˈskaɪ,wɑk, -s, -ɪŋ, -t

skyward
BR ˈskʌɪwəd, -z
AM ˈskaɪwərd, -z

skywatch
BR ˈskʌɪwɒtʃ, -ɪz
AM ˈskaɪ,wɑtʃ, -əz

skyway
BR ˈskʌɪweɪ, -z
AM ˈskaɪ,weɪ, -z

skywriting
BR ˈskʌɪ,rʌɪtɪŋ
AM ˈskaɪ,raɪdɪŋ

slab
BR slab, -z
AM slæb, -z

slab-sided
BR ˌslabˈsʌɪdɪd
AM ˈslæbˌsaɪdɪd

slack
BR slak, -s, -ɪŋ, -t, -ɪst
AM slæk, -s, -ɪŋ, -t

slacken
BR ˈslak|(ə)n, -(ə)nz, -n̩ɪŋ\-(ə)nɪŋ, -(ə)nd
AM ˈslæk|ən, -ənz, -(ə)nɪŋ, -ənd

slacker
BR ˈslakə(r), -z
AM ˈslækər, -z

slackly
BR ˈslakli
AM ˈslækli

slackness
BR ˈslaknəs
AM ˈslæknəs

Slade
BR sleɪd
AM sleɪd

slag
BR slag, -z
AM slæɡ, -z

slaggy
BR ˈslag|i, -ɪə(r), -ɪɪst
AM ˈslæɡi, -ər, -ɪst

slagheap
BR ˈslaghiːp, -s
AM ˈslæɡ,(h)ip, -s

slain
BR sleɪn
AM sleɪn

slàinte
BR ˈslɑːn(d)ʒə(r), ˈslɑːntʃə(r)
AM ˈslɑn(d)ʒə

IR ˈslɑːnʲtʲə
Slaithwaite
BR ˈslaθweɪt, ˈslaʊɪt
AM ˈslæθˌweɪt
slake
BR sleɪk, -s, -ɪŋ, -t
AM sleɪk, -s, -ɪŋ, -t
slalom
BR ˈslɑːləm, -z
AM ˈslɑləm, -z
slam
BR slam, -z, -ɪŋ, -d
AM slæm, -z, -ɪŋ, -d
slambang
BR ˌslamˈbaŋ
AM ˈslæmˈbæŋg
slammer
BR ˈslamə(r), -z
AM ˈslæmər, -z
slander
BR ˈslɑːnd|ə(r), ˈsland|ə(r), -əz, -(ə)rɪŋ, -əd
AM ˈslænd|ər, -ərz, -(ə)rɪŋ, -ərd
slanderer
BR ˈslɑːnd(ə)rə(r), ˈsland(ə)rə(r), -z
AM ˈslænd(ə)rər, -z
slanderous
BR ˈslɑːnd(ə)rəs, ˈsland(ə)rəs
AM ˈslænd(ə)rəs
slanderously
BR ˈslɑːnd(ə)rəsli, ˈsland(ə)rəsli
AM ˈslænd(ə)rəsli
slanderousness
BR ˈslɑːnd(ə)rəsnəs, ˈsland(ə)rəsnəs
AM ˈslænd(ə)rəsnəs
slang
BR slaŋ, -z, -ɪŋ, -d
AM slæŋ, -z, -ɪŋ, -d
slangily
BR ˈslaŋɨli
AM ˈslæŋgəli
slanginess
BR ˈslaŋɪnɨs
AM ˈslæŋginɨs
slangy
BR ˈslaŋ|i, -ɪə(r), -ɪɪst
AM ˈslæŋgi, -ər, -ɨst
slant
BR slɑːnt, slant, -s, -ɪŋ, -ɨd
AM slæn|t, -ts, -(t)ɪŋ, -(t)əd
slantways
BR ˈslɑːntweɪz, ˈslantweɪz
AM ˈslæntˌweɪz
slantwise
BR ˈslɑːntwʌɪz, ˈslantwʌɪz
AM ˈslæntˌwaɪz
slap
BR slap, -s, -ɪŋ, -t
AM slæp, -s, -ɪŋ, -t
slap-bang
BR ˌslapˈbaŋ, ˈslapbaŋ
AM ˈslæpˈbæŋ
slapdash
BR ˈslapdaʃ
AM ˈslæpˌdæʃ
slaphappy
BR ˌslapˈhapi
AM ˈslæpˌ(h)æpi
slapjack
BR ˈslapdʒak, -s
AM ˈslæpˌdʒæk, -s
slapshot
BR ˈslapʃɒt, -s
AM ˈslæpˌʃɑt, -s
slapstick
BR ˈslapstɪk
AM ˈslæpˌstɪk
slap-up
BR ˈslapʌp, ˌslapˈʌp
AM ˈslæpəp
slash
BR slaʃ, -ɪz, -ɪŋ, -t
AM slæʃ, -əz, -ɪŋ, -t
slash-and-burn
BR ˌslaʃ(ə)n(d)ˈbəːn
AM ˈslæʃˌənˈbərn
slasher
BR ˈslaʃə(r), -z
AM ˈslæʃər, -z
slat
BR slat, -s
AM slæt, -s
slate
BR sleɪt, -s, -ɪŋ, -ɨd
AM sleɪ|t, -ts, -dɪŋ, -dɨd
slater
BR ˈsleɪtə(r), -z
AM ˈsleɪdər, -z
slather
BR ˈslað|ə(r), -əz, -(ə)rɪŋ, -əd
AM ˈslæð|ər, -ərz, -(ə)rɪŋ, -ərd
slating
BR ˈsleɪtɪŋ, -z
AM ˈsleɪdɪŋ, -z
slattern
BR ˈslatn, ˈslatəːn, -z
AM ˈslædərn, -z
slatternliness
BR ˈslatnlɪnɨs
AM ˈslædərnlinɨs
slatternly
BR ˈslatnli
AM ˈslædərnli
Slattery
BR ˈslat(ə)ri
AM ˈslædəri
slaty
BR ˈsleɪti
AM ˈsleɪdi
slaughter
BR ˈslɔːt|ə(r), -əz, -(ə)rɪŋ, -əd
AM ˈslɔ|dər, ˈslɑ|dər, -dərz, -ərɪŋ\-trɪŋ, -dərd
slaughterer
BR ˈslɔːt(ə)rə(r), -z
AM ˈslɔdərər, ˈslɑdərər, -z
slaughterhouse
BR ˈslɔːtəhaʊ|s, -zɪz
AM ˈslɔdərˌ(h)aʊ|s, ˈslɑdərˌ(h)aʊ|s, -zəz
slaughterous
BR ˈslɔːt(ə)rəs
AM ˈslɔtərəs, ˈslɑtərəs
Slav
BR slɑːv, -z
AM slɑv, -z
slave
BR sleɪv, -z, -ɪŋ, -d
AM sleɪv, -z, -ɪŋ, -d
slave-driver
BR ˈsleɪvˌdrʌɪvə(r), -z
AM ˈsleɪvˌdraɪvər, -z
slaveholder
BR ˈsleɪvˌhəʊldə(r), -z
AM ˈsleɪvˌ(h)oʊldər, -z
slaver[1]
noun, slave-trader
BR ˈsleɪvə(r), -z
AM ˈsleɪvər, -z
slaver[2]
verb, drool
BR ˈslav|ə(r), ˈsleɪv|ə(r), -əz, -(ə)rɪŋ, -əd
AM ˈslæv|ər, ˈsleɪvər, -ərz, -(ə)rɪŋ, -ərd
slavery
BR ˈsleɪv(ə)ri
AM ˈsleɪv(ə)ri
slavey
BR ˈsleɪvi
AM ˈsleɪvi
Slavic
BR ˈslɑːvɪk
AM ˈslɑvɪk
slavish
BR ˈsleɪvɪʃ
AM ˈsleɪvɪʃ
slavishly
BR ˈsleɪvɨʃli
AM ˈsleɪvɪʃli
slavishness
BR ˈsleɪvɨʃnɨs
AM ˈsleɪvɪʃnɨs
Slavism
BR ˈslɑːvɪz(ə)m
AM ˈslɑvɪzəm
Slavonia
BR sləˈvəʊnɪə(*r*)
AM slɑˈvoʊniə
Slavonian
BR sləˈvəʊnɪən, -z
AM sləˈvoʊniən, -z
Slavonic
BR sləˈvɒnɪk
AM sləˈvɑnɪk
Slavophile
BR ˈslɑːvəʊfʌɪl, -z
AM ˈslɑvəˌfaɪl, -z
Slavophobe
BR ˈslɑːvəʊfəʊb, -z
AM ˈslɑvəˌfoʊb, -z
slaw
BR slɔː(*r*)
AM slɔ
slay
BR sleɪ, -z, -ɪŋ, -d
AM sleɪ, -z, -ɪŋ, -d
slayer
BR ˈsleɪə(r), -z
AM ˈsleɪər, -z
slaying
BR ˈsleɪɪŋ, -z
AM ˈsleɪɪŋ, -z
Slazenger
BR ˈslaz(ɪ)n(d)ʒə(r)
AM ˈsleɪzɪndʒer, ˈsleɪzɪŋər
Sleaford
BR ˈsliːfəd
AM ˈslifərd
sleaze
BR sliːz
AM sliz
sleazily
BR ˈsliːzɨli
AM ˈslizɨli
sleaziness
BR ˈsliːzɪnɨs
AM ˈslizinɨs
sleazoid
BR ˈsliːzɔɪd, -z
AM ˈslizɔɪd, -z
sleazy
BR ˈsliːz|i, -ɪə(r), -ɪɪst
AM ˈslizi, -ər, -ɨst
sled
BR slɛd, -z, -ɪŋ, -ɨd
AM slɛd, -z, -ɪŋ, -ɨd
sledge
BR slɛdʒ, -ɪz, -ɪŋ, -d
AM slɛdʒ, -ɪz, -ɪŋ, -d
sledgehammer
BR ˈslɛdʒˌhamə(r), -z
AM ˈslɛdʒˌ(h)æmər, -z
sleek
BR sliːk, -ə(r), -ɨst
AM slik, -ər, -ɨst
sleekly
BR ˈsliːkli
AM ˈslikli
sleekness
BR ˈsliːknɨs
AM ˈsliknəs
sleeky
BR ˈsliːki
AM ˈsliki
sleep
BR sliːp, -s, -ɪŋ
AM slip, -s, -ɪŋ
Sleepeezee
BR ˌsliːpˈiːzi, ˈsliːpˌiːzi
AM ˈslipˌizi

sleeper
BR ˈsliːpə(r), -z
AM ˈslipər, -z
sleepily
BR ˈsliːpɨli
AM ˈslipɨli
sleepiness
BR ˈsliːpɪnɨs
AM ˈslipinɨs
sleepless
BR ˈsliːplɨs
AM ˈsliplɨs
sleeplessly
BR ˈsliːplɨsli
AM ˈsliplɨsli
sleeplessness
BR ˈsliːplɨsnɨs
AM ˈsliplɨsnɨs
sleepwalk
BR ˈsliːpwɔːk, -s, -ɪŋ, -t
AM ˈslipˌwɔk, ˈslipˌwɑk, -s, -ɪŋ, -t
sleepwalker
BR ˈsliːpˌwɔːkə(r), -z
AM ˈslipˌwɔkər, ˈslipˌwɑkər, -z
sleepwalking
BR ˈsliːpˌwɔːkɪŋ
AM ˈslipˌwɔkɪŋ, ˈslipˌwɑkɪŋ
sleepwear
BR ˈsliːpwɛː(r)
AM ˈslipˌwɛ(ə)r
sleepy
BR ˈsliːp|i, -ɪə(r), -ɪɨst
AM ˈslipi, -ər, -ɨst
sleepyhead
BR ˈsliːpɪhɛd, -z
AM ˈslipiˌhɛd, -z
sleet
BR sliːt, -s, -ɪŋ, -ɨd
AM sli|t, -ts, -dɪŋ, -dɨd
sleetiness
BR ˈsliːtɪnɨs
AM ˈslidinɨs
sleety
BR ˈsliːti
AM ˈslidi
sleeve
BR sliːv, -z, -d
AM sliv, -z, -d
sleeveless
BR ˈsliːvlɨs
AM ˈslivlɨs
sleeving
BR ˈsliːvɪŋ, -z
AM ˈslivɪŋ, -z
sleigh
BR sleɪ, -z, -ɪŋ, -d
AM sleɪ, -z, -ɪŋ, -d
sleight
BR slʌɪt
AM slaɪt
slender
BR ˈslɛnd|ə(r), -(ə)rə(r), -(ə)rɪst
AM ˈslɛndər, -ər, -əst
slenderise
BR ˈslɛndərʌɪz, -ɨz, -ɪŋ, -d
AM ˈslɛndəˌraɪz, -ɨz, -ɪŋ, -d
slenderize
BR ˈslɛndərʌɪz, -ɨz, -ɪŋ, -d
AM ˈslɛndəˌraɪz, -ɨz, -ɪŋ, -d
slenderly
BR ˈslɛndəli
AM ˈslɛndərli
slenderness
BR ˈslɛndənəs
AM ˈslɛndərnəs
slept
BR slɛpt
AM slɛpt
Slessor
BR ˈslɛsə(r)
AM ˈslɛsər
sleuth
BR sl(j)uːθ, -s, -ɪŋ, -t
AM sluθ, -s, -ɪŋ, -t
sleuthhound
BR ˈsl(j)uːθhaʊnd, -z
AM ˈsluθˌ(h)aʊnd, -z
slew
BR sluː, -z, -ɪŋ, -d
AM slu, -z, -ɪŋ, -d
sley
BR sleɪ, -z
AM sleɪ, -z
slice
BR slʌɪs, -ɨz, -ɪŋ, -t
AM slaɪs, -ɨz, -ɪŋ, -t
sliceable
BR ˈslʌɪsəbl
AM ˈslaɪsəbəl
slicer
BR ˈslʌɪsə(r), -z
AM ˈslaɪsər, -z
slick
BR slɪk, -s, -ɪŋ, -t, -ə(r), -ɨst
AM slɪk, -s, -ɪŋ, -t, -ər, -ɨst
slicker
BR ˈslɪkə(r), -z
AM ˈslɪkər, -z
slickly
BR ˈslɪkli
AM ˈslɪkli
slickness
BR ˈslɪknɨs
AM ˈslɪknəs
slid
BR slɪd
AM slɪd
slidable
BR ˈslʌɪdəbl
AM ˈslɪdəbəl
slidably
BR ˈslʌɪdəbli
AM ˈslɪdəbli
slide
BR slʌɪd, -z, -ɪŋ
AM slaɪd, -z, -ɪŋ
slider
BR ˈslʌɪdə(r), -z
AM ˈslaɪdər, -z
slideway
BR ˈslʌɪdweɪ, -z
AM ˈslaɪdˌweɪ, -z
slight
BR slʌɪt, -s, -ɪŋ, -ɨd, -ə(r), -ɨst
AM slaɪ|t, -ts, -dɪŋ, -dɨd, -dər, -dɨst, -tli, -tnɨs
slightingly
BR ˈslʌɪtɪŋli
AM ˈslaɪdɪŋli
slightish
BR ˈslʌɪtɪʃ
AM ˈslaɪdɪʃ
slightly
BR ˈslʌɪtli
AM ˈslaɪtli
slightness
BR ˈslʌɪtnɨs
AM ˈslaɪtnəs
Sligo
BR ˈslʌɪgəʊ
AM ˈslaɪgoʊ
slily
BR ˈslʌɪli
AM ˈslaɪli
slim
BR slɪm, -z, -ɪŋ, -d
AM slɪm, -z, -ɪŋ, -d
slime
BR slʌɪm
AM slaɪm
slimily
BR ˈslʌɪmɨli
AM ˈslaɪmɨli
sliminess
BR ˈslʌɪmɪnɨs
AM ˈslaɪminɨs
slim-jim
BR ˌslɪmˈdʒɪm, -z
AM ˈslɪmˌdʒɪm, -z
slimline
BR ˈslɪmlʌɪn
AM ˈslɪmˌlaɪn
slimly
BR ˈslɪmli
AM ˈslɪmli
slimmer
BR ˈslɪmə(r), -z
AM ˈslɪmər, -z
slimmish
BR ˈslɪmɪʃ
AM ˈslɪmɪʃ
slimness
BR ˈslɪmnɨs
AM ˈslɪmnəs
slimy
BR ˈslʌɪm|i, -ɪə(r), -ɪɨst
AM ˈslaɪmi, -ər, -ɨst
sling
BR slɪŋ, -z, -ɪŋ
AM slɪŋ, -z, -ɪŋ
slingback
BR ˈslɪŋbak, -s
AM ˈslɪŋˌbæk, -s
slinger
BR ˈslɪŋə(r), -z
AM ˈslɪŋər, -z
slingshot
BR ˈslɪŋʃɒt, -s
AM ˈslɪŋˌʃɑt, -s
slink
BR slɪŋk, -s, -ɪŋ
AM slɪŋk, -s, -ɪŋ
slinkily
BR ˈslɪŋkɨli
AM ˈslɪŋkɨli
slinkiness
BR ˈslɪŋkɪnɨs
AM ˈslɪŋkinɨs
slinkweed
BR ˈslɪŋkwiːd
AM ˈslɪŋkˌwid
slinky
BR ˈslɪŋk|i, -ɪə(r), -ɪɨst
AM ˈslɪŋki, -ər, -ɨst
slip
BR slɪp, -s, -ɪŋ, -t
AM slɪp, -s, -ɪŋ, -t
slipcase
BR ˈslɪpkeɪs, -ɨz
AM ˈslɪpˌkeɪs, -ɨz
slipcover
BR ˈslɪpˌkʌvə(r), -z
AM ˈslɪpˌkəvər, -z
slipknot
BR ˈslɪpnɒt, -s
AM ˈslɪpˌnɑt, -s
slipover
BR ˈslɪpˌəʊvə(r), -z
AM ˈslɪpˌoʊvər, -z
slippage
BR ˈslɪp|ɪdʒ, -ɨdʒɨz
AM ˈslɪpɪdʒ, -ɨz
slipper
BR ˈslɪpə(r), -z
AM ˈslɪpər, -z
slipperily
BR ˈslɪp(ə)rɨli
AM ˈslɪp(ə)rəli
slipperiness
BR ˈslɪp(ə)rɪnɨs
AM ˈslɪp(ə)rinɨs
slipperwort
BR ˈslɪpəwəːt, -s
AM ˈslɪpərwərt, ˈslɪpərwɔ(ə)rt, -s
slippery
BR ˈslɪp(ə)r|i, -ɪə(r), -ɪɨst
AM ˈslɪp(ə)ri, -ər, -ɨst
slippiness
BR ˈslɪpɪnɨs
AM ˈslɪpinɨs
slippy
BR ˈslɪp|i, -ɪə(r), -ɪɨst
AM ˈslɪpi, -ər, -ɨst

slipshod
BR ˈslɪpʃɒd
AM ˈslɪpˌʃɑd
slipstitch
BR ˈslɪpstɪtʃ, -ɪz, -ɪŋ, -t
AM ˈslɪpˌstɪtʃ, -ɪz, -ɪŋ, -t
slipstream
BR ˈslɪpstriːm, -z, -ɪŋ, -d
AM ˈslɪpˌstrim, -z, -ɪŋ, -d
slip-ware
BR ˈslɪpwɛː(r), -z
AM ˈslɪpˌwɛ(ə)r, -z
slipway
BR ˈslɪpweɪ, -z
AM ˈslɪpˌweɪ, -z
slit
BR slɪt, -s, -ɪŋ, -ɪd
AM slɪ|t, -ts, -dɪŋ, -t
slither
BR ˈslɪð|ə(r), -əz, -(ə)rɪŋ, -əd
AM ˈslɪð|ər, -ərz, -(ə)rɪŋ, -ərd
slithery
BR ˈslɪð(ə)ri
AM ˈslɪð(ə)ri
slitter
BR ˈslɪtə(r), -z
AM ˈslɪdər, -z
slitty
BR ˈslɪt|i, -ɪə(r), -ɪɪst
AM ˈslɪdi, -ər, -ɪst
sliver
BR ˈslɪv|ə(r), ˈslʌɪv|ə(r), -əz, -(ə)rɪŋ, -əd
AM ˈslɪvər, ˈslaɪvər, -z, -ɪŋ, -d
slivovitz
BR ˈslɪvəvɪts
AM ˈslɪvəˌvɪts
Sloan
BR sləʊn
AM sloʊn
Sloane
BR sləʊn, -z
AM sloʊn, -z
Sloaney
BR ˈsləʊni
AM ˈsloʊni
slob
BR slɒb, -z
AM slɑb, -z
slobber
BR ˈslɒb|ə(r), -əz, -(ə)rɪŋ, -əd
AM ˈslɑb|ər, -ərz, -(ə)rɪŋ, -ərd
slobberiness
BR ˈslɒb(ə)rɪnɪs
AM ˈslɑb(ə)rinɪs
slobbery
BR ˈslɒb(ə)ri
AM ˈslɑb(ə)ri
slobbish
BR ˈslɒbɪʃ
AM ˈslɑbɪʃ

Slocombe
BR ˈsləʊkəm
AM ˈsloʊkəm
Slocum
BR ˈsləʊkəm
AM ˈsloʊkəm
sloe
BR sləʊ, -z
AM sloʊ, -z
sloe-eyed
BR ˌsləʊˈʌɪd
AM ˈsloʊˌaɪd
slog
BR slɒg, -z, -ɪŋ, -d
AM slɑg, -z, -ɪŋ, -d
slogan
BR ˈsləʊg(ə)n, -z
AM ˈsloʊgən, -z
slogger
BR ˈslɒgə(r), -z
AM ˈslɑgər, -z
sloid
BR slɔɪd, -z
AM slɔɪd, -z
Sloman
BR ˈsləʊmən
AM ˈsloʊmən
slo-mo
BR ˈsləʊməʊ
AM ˈsloʊˈmoʊ
sloop
BR sluːp, -s
AM slup, -s
sloosh
BR sluːʃ, -ɪz, -ɪŋ, -t
AM sluʃ, -əz, -ɪŋ, -t
sloot
BR sluːt, -s
AM slut, -s
slop
BR slɒp, -s, -ɪŋ, -t
AM slɑp, -s, -ɪŋ, -t
slope
BR sləʊp, -s, -ɪŋ, -t
AM sloʊp, -s, -ɪŋ, -t
slopewise
BR ˈsləʊpwʌɪz
AM ˈsloʊpˌwaɪz
sloppily
BR ˈslɒpɪli
AM ˈslɑpəli
sloppiness
BR ˈslɒpɪnɪs
AM ˈslɑpinɪs
sloppy
BR ˈslɒp|i, -ɪə(r), -ɪɪst
AM ˈslɑpi, -ər, -ɪst
slosh
BR slɒʃ, -ɪz, -ɪŋ, -t
AM slɑʃ, -ɪz, -ɪŋ, -t
sloshy
BR ˈslɒʃ|i, -ɪə(r), -ɪɪst
AM ˈslɑʃi, -ər, -ɪst
slot
BR slɒt, -s, -ɪŋ, -ɪd
AM slɑ|t, -ts, -dɪŋ, -dəd

slotback
BR ˈslɒtbak, -s
AM ˈslɑtˌbæk, -s
slot car
BR ˈslɒt kɑː(r), -z
AM ˈslɑt ˌkɑr, -z
sloth
BR sləʊθ, -s
AM slɔθ, sloʊθ, slɑθ, -s
slothful
BR ˈsləʊθf(ʊ)l
AM ˈslɔθfəl, ˈsloʊθfəl, ˈslɑθfəl
slothfully
BR ˈsləʊθfʊli, ˈsləʊθfl̩i
AM ˈslɔθfəli, ˈslɑθfəl, ˈsloʊθfəl
slothfulness
BR ˈslɒθf(ʊ)lnəs
AM ˈslɔθfəlnəs, ˈslɑθfəlnəs, ˈsloʊθfəlnəs
slouch
BR slaʊtʃ, -ɪz, -ɪŋ, -t
AM slaʊtʃ, -ɪz, -ɪŋ, -t
slouchy
BR ˈslaʊtʃ|i, -ɪə(r), -ɪɪst
AM ˈslaʊtʃi, -ər, -ɪst
Slough
BR slaʊ
AM slaʊ
slough[1]
noun, wet place
BR slaʊ, -z
AM slu, slaʊ, -z
slough[2]
verb, shed skin of snake etc
BR slʌf, -s, -ɪŋ, -t
AM sləf, -s, -ɪŋ, -t
sloughy
BR ˈslʌf|i, -ɪə(r), -ɪɪst
AM ˈsləfi, -ər, -ɪst
Slovak
BR ˈsləʊvak, -s
AM ˈsloʊˌvɑk, ˈsloʊˌvæk, -s
Slovakia
BR slə(ʊ)ˈvakɪə(r), slə(ʊ)ˈvɑːkɪə(r)
AM sloʊˈvɑkiə
sloven
BR ˈslʌvn, -z
AM ˈsləvən, -z
Slovene
BR ˈsləʊviːn, -z
AM ˈsloʊˌvin, -z
Slovenia
BR slə(ʊ)ˈviːnɪə(r)
AM sloʊˈviniə
Slovenian
BR slə(ʊ)ˈviːnɪən, -z
AM sloʊˈviniən, -z
slovenliness
BR ˈslʌvnlɪnɪs
AM ˈsləvənlinɪs, ˈslɑvənlinɪs

slovenly
BR ˈslʌvnli
AM ˈsləvənli, ˈslɑvənli
slovenry
BR ˈslʌvnri
AM ˈsləvənri, ˈslɑvənri
slow
BR sləʊ, -z, -ɪŋ, -d, -ə(r), -ɪst
AM sloʊ, -z, -ɪŋ, -d, -ər, -əst
slowcoach
BR ˈsləʊkəʊtʃ, -ɪz
AM ˈsloʊˌkoʊtʃ, -ɪz
slowdown
BR ˈsləʊdaʊn, -z
AM ˈsloʊˌdaʊn, -z
slowish
BR ˈsləʊɪʃ
AM ˈsloʊɪʃ
slowly
BR ˈsləʊli
AM ˈsloʊli
slowness
BR ˈsləʊnəs
AM ˈsloʊnəs
slowpoke
BR ˈsləʊpəʊk, -s
AM ˈsloʊˌpoʊk, -s
slowworm
BR ˈsləʊwəːm, -z
AM ˈsloʊˌwərm, -z
slub
BR slʌb, -z, -ɪŋ, -d
AM sləb, -z, -ɪŋ, -d
sludge
BR slʌdʒ
AM slədʒ
sludgy
BR ˈslʌdʒi
AM ˈslədʒi
slue
BR sluː, -z, -ɪŋ, -d
AM slu, -z, -ɪŋ, -d
sluff
BR slʌf, -s, -ɪŋ, -t
AM sləf, -s, -ɪŋ, -t
slug
BR slʌg, -z, -ɪŋ, -d
AM sləg, -z, -ɪŋ, -d
slugabed
BR ˈslʌgəbɛd, -z
AM ˈsləgəˌbɛd, -z
slugfest
BR ˈslʌgfɛst, -s
AM ˈsləgˌfɛst, -s
sluggard
BR ˈslʌgəd, -z
AM ˈsləgərd, -z
sluggardliness
BR ˈslʌgədlɪnɪs
AM ˈsləgərdlinɪs
sluggardly
BR ˈslʌgədli
AM ˈsləgərdli

slugger
BR ˈslʌɡə(r), -z
AM ˈsləɡər, -z

sluggish
BR ˈslʌɡɪʃ
AM ˈsləɡɪʃ

sluggishly
BR ˈslʌɡᵻʃli
AM ˈsləɡᵻʃli

sluggishness
BR ˈslʌɡᵻʃnᵻs
AM ˈsləɡᵻʃnᵻs

sluice
BR sluːs, -ᵻz, -ɪŋ, -t
AM slus, -ᵻz, -ɪŋ, -t

sluicegate
BR ˈsluːsɡeɪt, -s
AM ˈslusˌɡeɪt, -s

sluiceway
BR ˈsluːsweɪ, -z
AM ˈslusˌweɪ, -z

sluit
BR ˈsluːɪt, -s
AM ˈsluɪt, -s

slum
BR slʌm, -z, -ɪŋ, -d
AM sləm, -z, -ɪŋ, -d

slumber
BR ˈslʌmb|ə(r), -əz, -(ə)rɪŋ, -əd
AM ˈsləmb|ər, -ərz, -(ə)rɪŋ, -ərd

slumberer
BR ˈslʌmb(ə)rə(r), -z
AM ˈsləmbərər, -z

slumberous
BR ˈslʌmb(ə)rəs
AM ˈsləmbərəs

slumbrous
BR ˈslʌmbrəs
AM ˈsləmbrəs

slumgullion
BR slʌmˈɡʌljən
AM ˌsləmˈɡəliən, ˌsləmˈɡəljən

slumlord
BR ˈslʌmlɔːd, -z
AM ˈsləmˌlɔ(ə)rd, -z

slumminess
BR ˈslʌmɪnɪs
AM ˈsləminɪs

slummock
BR ˈslʌmək, -s
AM ˈsləmək, -s

slummy
BR ˈslʌm|i, -ɪə(r), -ɪɪst
AM ˈsləmi, -ər, -ɪst

slump
BR slʌm|p, -ps, -pɪŋ, -(p)t
AM sləmp, -s, -ɪŋ, -t

slung
BR slʌŋ
AM sləŋ

slunk
BR slʌŋk
AM sləŋk

slur
BR sləː(r), -z, -ɪŋ, -d
AM slər, -z, -ɪŋ, -d

slurp
BR sləːp, -s, -ɪŋ, -t
AM slərp, -s, -ɪŋ, -t

slurry
BR ˈslʌri
AM ˈsləri

slush
BR slʌʃ
AM sləʃ

slushiness
BR ˈslʌʃɪnɪs
AM ˈsləʃinɪs

slushy
BR ˈslʌʃ|i, -ɪə(r), -ɪɪst
AM ˈsləʃi, -ər, -ɪst

slut
BR slʌt, -s
AM slət, -s

sluttish
BR ˈslʌtɪʃ
AM ˈslədɪʃ

sluttishly
BR ˈslʌtᵻʃli
AM ˈslədᵻʃli

sluttishness
BR ˈslʌtᵻʃnᵻs
AM ˈslədᵻʃnᵻs

sly
BR slʌɪ, -ə(r), -ɪst
AM slaɪ, -ər, -ɪst

slyboots
BR ˈslʌɪbuːts
AM ˈslaɪˌbuts

slyly
BR ˈslʌɪli
AM ˈslaɪli

slyness
BR ˈslʌɪnɪs
AM ˈslaɪnɪs

slype
BR slʌɪp, -s
AM slaɪp, -s

smack
BR smak, -s, -ɪŋ, -t
AM smæk, -s, -ɪŋ, -t

smacker
BR ˈsmakə(r), -z
AM ˈsmækər, -z

smackeroo
BR ˌsmakəˈruː, -z
AM ˌsmækəˈru, -z

Smail
BR smeɪl
AM smeɪl

Smails
BR smeɪlz
AM smeɪlz

Smale
BR smeɪl
AM smeɪl

Smales
BR smeɪlz
AM smeɪlz

small[1]
BR smɔːl, -z, -ə(r), -ɪst
AM smɔl, smɑl, -z, -ər, -əst

small[2]
BR smɔːl, -z, -ə(r), -ɪst
AM smɔl, -z, -ər, -əst

smallage
BR ˈsmɔːlɪdʒ
AM ˈsmɔlɪdʒ, ˈsmɑlɪdʒ

Smalley
BR ˈsmɔːli
AM ˈsmɔli, ˈsmɑli

smallgoods
BR ˈsmɔːlɡʊdz
AM ˈsmɔlˌɡʊdz, ˈsmɑlˌɡʊdz

smallholder
BR ˈsmɔːlˌhəʊldə(r), -z
AM ˈsmɔlˌ(h)oʊldər, ˈsmɑlˌ(h)oʊldər, -z

smallholding
BR ˈsmɔːlˌhəʊldɪŋ, -z
AM ˈsmɔlˌ(h)oʊldɪŋ, ˈsmɑlˌ(h)oʊldɪŋ, -z

smallish
BR ˈsmɔːlɪʃ
AM ˈsmɔlɪʃ, ˈsmɑlɪʃ

small-minded
BR ˌsmɔːlˈmʌɪndɪd
AM ˈsmɔlˈmaɪn(d)ɪd, ˈsmɑlˈmaɪn(d)ɪd

small-mindedly
BR ˌsmɔːlˈmʌɪndɪdli
AM ˈsmɔlˈmaɪn(d)ᵻdli, ˈsmɑlˈmaɪn(d)ᵻdli

small-mindedness
BR ˌsmɔːl ˈmʌɪndɪdnɪs
AM ˈsmɔl ˈmaɪn(d)ᵻdnɪs, ˈsmɑl +

smallness
BR ˈsmɔːlnəs
AM ˈsmɔlnəs, ˈsmɑlnəs

Smallpiece
BR ˈsmɔːlpiːs
AM ˈsmɔlˌpis, ˈsmɑlˌpis

smallpox
BR ˈsmɔːlpɒks
AM ˈsmɔlˌpɑks, ˈsmɑlˌpɑks

smalltalk
BR ˈsmɔːltɔːk
AM ˈsmɔlˌtɔk, ˈsmɑlˌtɑk

smallwares
BR ˈsmɔːlwɛːz
AM ˈsmɔlˌwɛ(ə)rz, ˈsmɑlˌwɛ(ə)rz

Smallwood
BR ˈsmɔːlwʊd
AM ˈsmɔlˌwʊd, ˈsmɑlˌwʊd

smalt
BR smɔːlt, smɒlt
AM smɔlt, smɑlt

smarm
BR smɑːm, -z, -ɪŋ, -d
AM smɑrm, -z, -ɪŋ, -d

smarmily
BR ˈsmɑːmᵻli
AM ˈsmɑrməli

smarminess
BR ˈsmɑːmɪnɪs
AM ˈsmɑrminɪs

smarmy
BR ˈsmɑːm|i, -ɪə(r), -ɪɪst
AM ˈsmɑrmi, -ər, -ɪst

smart
BR smɑːt, -s, -ɪŋ, -ɪd, -ə(r), -ɪst
AM smɑr|t, -ts, -dɪŋ, -dəd, -dər, -dəst, -tli, -tnəs

smart alec
BR ˈsmɑːt ˌalɪk, -s
AM ˈsmɑrd ˌælək, -s

smart aleck
BR ˈsmɑːt ˌalɪk, -s
AM ˈsmɑrd ˌælək, -s

smart-alecky
BR ˈsmɑːtˌalɪki
AM ˈsmɑrdˌæləki

smart alick
BR ˈsmɑːt ˌalɪk, -s
AM ˈsmɑrd ˌælək, -s

smart-arse
BR ˈsmɑːtɑːs, -ɪz
AM ˈsmɑrdˌæs, ˈsmɑrdˌɑrs, -ɪz

smart-ass
BR ˈsmɑːtɑːs, -ɪz
AM ˈsmɑrdˌæs, -ɪz

smarten
BR ˈsmɑːt|n, -nz, -n̩ɪŋ\-nɪŋ, -nd
AM ˈsmɑrtən, -z, -ɪŋ, -d

Smartie
BR ˈsmɑːt|i, -ɪz
AM ˈsmɑrdi, -z

smartingly
BR ˈsmɑːtɪŋli
AM ˈsmɑrdɪŋli

smartish
BR ˈsmɑːtɪʃ
AM ˈsmɑrdɪʃ

smartly
BR ˈsmɑːtli
AM ˈsmɑrtli

smartness
BR ˈsmɑːtnəs
AM ˈsmɑrtnəs

smartweed
BR ˈsmɑːtwiːd
AM ˈsmɑrtˌwid

smarty
BR ˈsmɑːt|i, -ɪz
AM ˈsmɑrdi, -z

smarty-boots
BR ˈsmɑːtɪbuːts
AM ˈsmɑrdiˌbuts

smarty-pants
BR 'smɑːtɪpants
AM 'smɑrdi,pæn(t)s
smash
BR smaʃ, -ɪz, -ɪŋ, -t
AM smæʃ, -əz, -ɪŋ, -t
smash-and-grab
BR ,smaʃ(ə)n(d)'grab
AM ,smæʃən'græb
smasher
BR 'smaʃə(r), -z
AM 'smæʃər, -z
smashingly
BR 'smaʃɪŋli
AM 'smæʃɪŋli
smatter
BR 'smatə(r), -z
AM 'smædər, -z
smatterer
BR 'smat(ə)rə(r), -z
AM 'smædərər, -z
smattering
BR 'smat(ə)rɪŋ, -z
AM 'smædərɪŋ, -z
smear
BR smɪə(r), -z, -ɪŋ, -d
AM smɪ(ə)r, -z, -ɪŋ, -d
smearer
BR 'smɪərə(r), -z
AM 'smɪrər, -z
smeariness
BR 'smɪərɪnɨs
AM 'smɪrinɨs
smeary
BR 'smɪəri
AM 'smɪri
smectic
BR 'smɛktɪk, -s
AM 'smɛktɪk, -s
Smedley
BR 'smɛdli
AM 'smɛdli
smegma
BR 'smɛgmə(r)
AM 'smɛgmə
smegmatic
BR smɛg'matɪk
AM ,smɛg'mædɪk
smell
BR smɛl, -z, -ɪŋ
AM smɛl, -z, -ɪŋ
smellable
BR 'smɛləbl
AM 'smɛləbəl
smeller
BR 'smɛlə(r), -z
AM 'smɛlər, -z
smelliness
BR 'smɛlɪnɨs
AM 'smɛlinɨs
smell-less
BR 'smɛlləs
AM 'smɛ(l)ləs
smelly
BR 'smɛl|i, -ɪə(r), -ɪɪst
AM 'smɛli, -ər, -ɨst
smelt
BR smɛlt, -s, -ɪŋ, -ɨd
AM smɛlt, -s, -ɪŋ, -əd
smelter
BR 'smɛltə(r), -z
AM 'smɛltər, -z
smeltery
BR 'smɛlt(ə)r|i, -ɪz
AM 'smɛlt(ə)ri, -z
Smersh
BR sməːʃ
AM smərʃ
Smetana
BR 'smɛtənə(r),
'smɛtn̩ə(r)
AM 'smɛtn̩ə
Smethurst
BR 'smɛθ(h)əːst
AM 'smɛθ,(h)ərst
Smethwick
BR 'smɛðɪk
AM 'smɛðɪk
smew
BR smjuː, -z
AM smju, -z
smidgen
BR 'smɪdʒ(ɪ)n, -z
AM 'smɪdʒɪn, -z
smidgeon
BR 'smɪdʒ(ɪ)n, -z
AM 'smɪdʒɪn, -z
smidgin
BR 'smɪdʒ(ɪ)n, -z
AM 'smɪdʒɪn, -z
Smike
BR smʌɪk
AM smaɪk
smilax
BR 'smʌɪlaks
AM 'smaɪ,læks
smile
BR smʌɪl, -z, -ɪŋ, -d
AM smaɪl, -z, -ɪŋ, -d
smileless
BR 'smʌɪllɨs
AM 'smaɪ(l)ləs
smiler
BR 'smʌɪlə(r), -z
AM 'smaɪlər, -z
Smiles
BR smʌɪlz
AM smaɪlz
smiley
BR 'smʌɪli
AM 'smaɪli
smilingly
BR 'smʌɪlɪŋli
AM 'smaɪlɪŋli
Smily
BR 'smʌɪli
AM 'smaɪli
smirch
BR sməːtʃ, -ɪz, -ɪŋ, -t
AM smərtʃ, -ɪz, -ɪŋ, -t
smirk
BR sməːk, -s, -ɪŋ, -t
AM smərk, -s, -ɪŋ, -t
smirker
BR 'sməːkə(r), -z
AM 'smərkər, -z
smirkily
BR 'sməːkɪli
AM 'smərkəli
smirkingly
BR 'sməːkɪŋli
AM 'smərkɪŋli
smirky
BR 'sməːki
AM 'smərki
smit
BR smɪt
AM smɪt
smite
BR smʌɪt, -s, -ɪŋ
AM smaɪ|t, -ts, -dɪŋ
smiter
BR 'smʌɪtə(r), -z
AM 'smaɪdər, -z
smith
BR smɪθ, -s
AM smɪθ, -s
smithereens
BR ,smɪðə'riːnz
AM ,smɪðə'rinz
Smithers
BR 'smɪðəz
AM 'smɪðərz
smithery
BR 'smɪθ(ə)r|i, -ɪz
AM 'smɪð(ə)ri, -z
Smithfield
BR 'smɪθfiːld
AM 'smɪθ,fild
Smithson
BR 'smɪθs(ə)n
AM 'smɪθsən
Smithsonian
BR smɪθ'səʊnɪən
AM ,smɪθ'soʊniən,
,smɪð'soʊniən
smithy
BR 'smɪð|i, 'smɪθ|i, -ɪz
AM 'smɪθi, -z
smitten
BR 'smɪtn
AM 'smɪtn
smock
BR smɒk, -s, -ɪŋ, -t
AM smɑk, -s, -ɪŋ, -t
smog
BR smɒg
AM smɔg, smɑg
smoggy
BR 'smɒg|i, -ɪə(r), -ɪɪst
AM 'smɔgi, 'smɑgi, -ər,
-ɨst
smokable
BR 'sməʊkəbl
AM 'smoʊkəbəl
smoke
BR sməʊk, -s, -ɪŋ, -t
AM smoʊk, -s, -ɪŋ, -t
smoke-free
BR ,sməʊk'friː
AM ,smoʊk'fri
smoke-ho
BR 'sməʊkhəʊ, -z
AM 'smoʊk,(h)oʊ, -z
smokehouse
BR 'sməʊkhaʊ|s, -zɪz
AM 'smoʊk,(h)aʊ|s,
-zəz
smokeless
BR 'sməʊkləs
AM 'smoʊkləs
smoker
BR 'sməʊkə(r), -z
AM 'smoʊkər, -z
smokescreen
BR 'sməʊkskriːn, -z
AM 'smoʊk,skrin, -z
smokestack
BR 'sməʊkstak, -s
AM 'smoʊk,stæk, -s
smokily
BR 'sməʊkɪli
AM 'smoʊkəli
smokiness
BR 'sməʊkɪnɨs
AM 'smoʊkinɨs
smoko
BR 'sməʊkəʊ, -z
AM 'smoʊkoʊ, -z
smoky
BR 'sməʊk|i, -ɪə(r),
-ɪɪst
AM 'smoʊki, -ər, -ɨst
smolder
BR 'sməʊld|ə(r), -əz,
-(ə)rɪŋ, -əd
AM 'smoʊldər, -z, -ɪŋ, -d
smolderingly
BR 'sməʊld(ə)rɪŋli
AM 'smoʊld(ə)rɪŋli
smoleable
BR 'sməʊləbl
AM 'smoʊləbəl
Smolensk
BR smə(ʊ)'lɛnsk
AM smoʊ'lɛnsk
Smollett
BR 'smɒlɪt
AM 'smɑlət
smolt
BR sməʊlt, -s
AM smoʊlt, -s
smooch
BR smuːtʃ, -ɪz, -ɪŋ, -t
AM smutʃ, -ɪz, -ɪŋ, -t
smoocher
BR 'smuːtʃə(r), -z
AM 'smutʃər, -z
smoochy
BR 'smuːtʃi
AM 'smutʃi
smoodge
BR 'smuːdʒ, -ɪz, -ɪŋ, -d
AM 'smʊdʒ, -əz, -ɪŋ, -d
smooth
BR smuːð, -z, -ɪŋ, -d,
-ə(r), -ɪst

AM smuð, -z, -ɪŋ, -d, -ər, -əst
smoothable
BR 'smuːðəbl
AM 'smuðəbəl
smooth-bore
BR ˌsmuːð'bɔː(r), -z
AM 'smuðˌbɔ(ə)r, -z
smoothe
BR smuːð, -z, -ɪŋ, -d
AM smuð, -z, -ɪŋ, -d
smoother
BR 'smuːðə(r), -z
AM 'smuðər, -z
smooth-faced
BR ˌsmuːð'feɪst
AM 'smuðˌfeɪst
smoothie
BR 'smuːð|i, -ɪz
AM 'smuði, -z
smoothish
BR 'smuːðɪʃ
AM 'smuðɪʃ
smoothly
BR 'smuːðli
AM 'smuðli
smoothness
BR 'smuːðnəs
AM 'smuðnəs
smooth-talk
BR 'smuːðtɔːk, -s, -ɪŋ, -t
AM 'smuðˌtɔk, 'smuðˌtɑk, -s, -ɪŋ, -t
smooth-tongued
BR ˌsmuːð'tʌŋd
AM 'smuðˌtəŋd
smoothy
BR 'smuːð|i, -ɪz
AM 'smuði, -z
smorgasbord
BR 'smɔːgəsbɔːd, 'smɔːgəzbɔːd, -z
AM 'smɔrgəsˌbɔ(ə)rd, -z
smorzando
BR smɔː'tsandəʊ, -z
AM smɔr'tsɑndoʊ, -z
smote
BR sməʊt
AM smoʊt
smother
BR 'smʌð|ə(r), -əz, -(ə)rɪŋ, -əd
AM 'sməð|ər, -ərz, -(ə)rɪŋ, -ərd
smothery
BR 'smʌð(ə)ri
AM 'sməðəri
smoulder
BR 'sməʊld|ə(r), -əz, -(ə)rɪŋ, -əd
AM 'smoʊldər, -z, -ɪŋ, -d
smoulderingly
BR 'sməʊld(ə)rɪŋli
AM 'smoʊld(ə)rɪŋli
smriti
BR 'smrɪti
AM 'smrɪdi
smudge
BR smʌdʒ, -ɪz, -ɪŋ, -d
AM smədʒ, -ɪz, -ɪŋ, -d
smudgeless
BR 'smʌdʒləs
AM 'smədʒləs
smudgepot
BR 'smʌdʒpɒt, -s
AM 'smədʒˌpɑt, -s
smudgily
BR 'smʌdʒɨli
AM 'smədʒəli
smudginess
BR 'smʌdʒɪnɨs
AM 'smədʒinɨs
smudgy
BR 'smʌdʒ|i, -ɪə(r), -ɪɪst
AM 'smədʒi, -ər, -ɨst
smug
BR smʌg
AM sməg
smuggle
BR 'smʌg|l, -lz, -l̩ɪŋ\-lɪŋ, -ld
AM 'sməg|əl, -əlz, -(ə)lɪŋ, -əld
smuggler
BR 'smʌgl̩ə(r), 'smʌglə(r), -z
AM 'sməg(ə)lər, -z
smugly
BR smʌgli
AM sməgli
smugness
BR 'smʌgnəs
AM 'sməgnəs
smurf
BR sməːf, -s
AM smərf, -s
smut
BR smʌt, -s
AM smət, -s
Smuts
BR smʌts
AM sməts
smuttily
BR 'smʌtɨli
AM 'smədəli
smuttiness
BR 'smʌtɪnɨs
AM 'smədinɨs
smutty
BR 'smʌt|i, -ɪə(r), -ɪɪst
AM 'smədi, -ər, -ɨst
Smyrna
BR 'sməːnə(*r*)
AM 'smɪrnə
Smyth
BR smɪθ, smʌɪθ, smʌɪð
AM smɪθ
Smythe
BR smʌɪð, smʌɪθ
AM smaɪθ, smaɪð
snack
BR snak, -s, -ɪŋ, -t
AM snæk, -s, -ɪŋ, -t
Snaefell
BR ˌsneɪ'fɛl
AM 'sneɪˌfɛl
snaffle
BR 'snaf|l, -lz, -l̩ɪŋ\-lɪŋ, -ld
AM 'snæf|əl, -əlz, -(ə)lɪŋ, -əld
snafu
BR sna'fuː, -z, -ɪŋ, -d
AM snæ'fu, -z, -ɪŋ, -d
snag
BR snag, -z, -ɪŋ, -d
AM snæg, -z, -ɪŋ, -d
Snagge
BR snag
AM snæg
snaggletooth
BR 'snagltuːθ
AM 'snægəlˌtuθ
snaggle-toothed
BR ˌsnagl'tuːθt
AM 'snægəlˌtuθt
snaggy
BR 'snagi
AM 'snægi
snail
BR sneɪl, -z
AM sneɪl, -z
Snaith
BR sneɪθ
AM sneɪθ
snake
BR sneɪk, -s, -ɪŋ, -t
AM sneɪk, -s, -ɪŋ, -t
snakebite
BR 'sneɪkbʌɪt, -s
AM 'sneɪkˌbaɪt, -s
snake-charmer
BR 'sneɪkˌtʃɑːmə(r), -z
AM 'sneɪkˌtʃɑrmər, -z
snakelike
BR 'sneɪklʌɪk
AM 'sneɪkˌlaɪk
snakeroot
BR 'sneɪkruːt, -s
AM 'snækˌrut, -s
snakeskin
BR 'sneɪkskɪn
AM 'sneɪkˌskɪn
snakily
BR 'sneɪkɨli
AM 'sneɪkɨli
snakiness
BR 'sneɪkɪnɨs
AM 'sneɪkinɨs
snaky
BR 'sneɪki
AM 'sneɪki
snap
BR snap, -s, -ɪŋ, -t
AM snæp, -s, -ɪŋ, -t
snapdragon
BR 'snapˌdrag(ə)n, -z
AM 'snæpˌdrægən, -z
Snape
BR sneɪp
AM sneɪp
snappable
BR 'snapəbl
AM 'snæpəbəl
snapper
BR 'snapə(r), -z
AM 'snæpər, -z
snappily
BR 'snapɨli
AM 'snæpəli
snappiness
BR 'snapɪnɪs
AM 'snæpinɨs
snappingly
BR 'snapɪŋli
AM 'snæpɪŋli
snappish
BR 'snapɪʃ
AM 'snæpɪʃ
snappishly
BR 'snapɨʃli
AM 'snæpɨʃli
snappishness
BR 'snapɨʃnɨs
AM 'snæpɪʃnɨs
snappy
BR 'snap|i, -ɪə(r), -ɪɪst
AM 'snæpi, -ər, -ɨst
snapshot
BR 'snapʃɒt, -s
AM 'snæpˌʃɑt, -s
snare
BR snɛː(r), -z, -ɪŋ, -d
AM snɛ(ə)r, -z, -ɪŋ, -d
snarer
BR 'snɛːrə(r), -z
AM 'snɛrər, -z
snark
BR snɑːk, -s
AM snɑrk, -s
snarl
BR snɑːl, -z, -ɪŋ, -d
AM snɑrl, -z, -ɪŋ, -d
snarler
BR 'snɑːlə(r), -z
AM 'snɑrlər, -z
snarlingly
BR 'snɑːlɪŋli
AM 'snɑrlɪŋli
snarl-up
BR 'snɑːlʌp, -s
AM 'snɑrlˌəp, -s
snarly
BR 'snɑːl|i, -ɪə(r), -ɪɪst
AM 'snɑrli, -ər, -ɨst
snatch
BR snatʃ, -ɪz, -ɪŋ, -t
AM snætʃ, -əz, -ɪŋ, -t
snatcher
BR 'snatʃə(r), -z
AM 'snætʃər, -z
snatchily
BR 'snatʃɨli
AM 'snætʃəli

snatchy
BR 'snatʃ|i, -ɪə(r), -ɪɪst
AM 'snætʃi, -ər, -ɨst

snavel
BR 'snav|l, -lz, -l̩ɪŋ\-lɪŋ, -ld
AM 'snævəl, -z, -ɪŋ, -d

snazzily
BR 'snazɨli
AM 'snæzəli

snazziness
BR 'snazɪnɨs
AM 'snæzinɨs

snazzy
BR 'snaz|i, -ɪə(r), -ɪɪst
AM 'snæzi, -ər, -ɨst

sneak
BR sni:k, -s, -ɪŋ, -t
AM snik, -s, -ɪŋ, -t

sneaker
BR 'sni:kə(r), -z
AM 'snikər, -z

sneakily
BR 'sni:kɨli
AM 'snikəli

sneakiness
BR 'sni:kɪnɨs
AM 'snikinɨs

sneakingly
BR 'sni:kɪŋli
AM 'snikɪŋli

sneak-thief
BR 'sni:kθi:f
AM 'snik,θif

sneak-thieves
BR 'sni:kθi:vz
AM 'snik,θivz

sneaky
BR 'sni:k|i, -ɪə(r), -ɪɪst
AM 'sniki, -ər, -ɨst

sneck
BR snɛk, -s, -ɪŋ, -t
AM snɛk, -s, -ɪŋ, -t

Sneddon
BR 'snɛdn
AM 'snɛdn

Sneek
BR sni:k
AM snik

sneer
BR snɪə(r), -z, -ɪŋ, -d
AM snɪ(ə)r, -z, -ɪŋ, -d

sneerer
BR 'snɪərə(r), -z
AM 'snirər, -z

sneeringly
BR 'snɪərɪŋli
AM 'snɪrɪŋli

sneeze
BR sni:z, -ɨz, -ɪŋ, -d
AM sniz, -ɨz, -ɪŋ, -d

sneezer
BR 'sni:zə(r), -z
AM 'snizər, -z

sneezeweed
BR 'sni:zwi:d, -z
AM 'sniz,wid, -z

sneezewort
BR 'sni:zwə:t
AM 'snizwərt, 'snizwɔ(ə)rt

sneezy
BR 'sni:zi
AM 'snizi

Snelgrove
BR 'snɛlgrəʊv
AM 'snɛl,groʊv

Snell
BR snɛl
AM snɛl

Snellgrove
BR 'snɛlgrəʊv
AM 'snɛl,groʊv

snib
BR snɪb, -z, -ɪŋ, -d
AM snɪb, -z, -ɪŋ, -d

snick
BR snɪk, -s, -ɪŋ, -t
AM snɪk, -s, -ɪŋ, -t

snicker
BR 'snɪk|ə(r), -əz, -(ə)rɪŋ, -əd
AM 'snɪk|ər, -ərz, -(ə)rɪŋ, -ərd

snickeringly
BR 'snɪk(ə)rɪŋli
AM 'snɪk(ə)rɪŋli

Snickers®
BR 'snɪkəz
AM 'snɪkərz

snicket
BR 'snɪkɪt, -s
AM 'snɪkɨt, -s

snide
BR snʌɪd
AM snaɪd

snidely
BR snʌɪdli
AM snaɪdli

snideness
BR snʌɪdnɨs
AM snaɪdnɨs

Snider
BR 'snʌɪdə(r)
AM 'snaɪdər

sniff
BR snɪf, -s, -ɪŋ, -t
AM snɪf, -s, -ɪŋ, -t

sniffable
BR 'snɪfəbl
AM 'snɪfəbəl

sniffer
BR 'snɪfə(r), -z
AM 'snɪfər, -z

sniffily
BR 'snɪfɨli
AM 'snɪfəli

sniffiness
BR 'snɪfɪnɨs
AM 'snɪfinɨs

sniffingly
BR 'snɪfɪŋli
AM 'snɪfɪŋli

sniffle
BR 'snɪf|l, -lz, -l̩ɪŋ\-lɪŋ, -ld
AM 'snɪf|əl, -əlz, -(ə)lɪŋ, -əld

sniffler
BR 'snɪflə(r), 'snɪfl̩ə(r), -z
AM 'snɪf(ə)lər, -z

sniffly
BR 'snɪfli, 'snɪfl̩i
AM 'snɪf(ə)li

sniffy
BR 'snɪf|i, -ɪə(r), -ɪɪst
AM 'snɪfi, -ər, -ɨst

snifter
BR 'snɪftə(r), -z
AM 'snɪftər, -z

snig
BR snɪg, -z, -ɪŋ, -d
AM snɪg, -z, -ɪŋ, -d

snigger
BR 'snɪg|ə(r), -əz, -(ə)rɪŋ, -əd
AM 'snɪg|ər, -ərz, -(ə)rɪŋ, -ərd

sniggerer
BR 'snɪg(ə)rə(r), -z
AM 'snɪg(ə)rər, -z

sniggeringly
BR 'snɪg(ə)rɪŋli
AM 'snɪg(ə)rɪŋli

sniggle
BR 'snɪg|l, -lz, -l̩ɪŋ\-lɪŋ, -ld
AM 'snɪg|əl, -əlz, -(ə)lɪŋ, -əld

snip
BR snɪp, -s, -ɪŋ, -t
AM snɪp, -s, -ɪŋ, -t

snipe
BR snʌɪp, -s, -ɪŋ, -t
AM snaɪp, -s, -ɪŋ, -t

sniper
BR 'snʌɪpə(r), -z
AM 'snaɪpər, -z

snipper
BR 'snɪpə(r), -z
AM 'snɪpər, -z

snippet
BR 'snɪpɪt, -s
AM 'snɪpɨt, -s

snippety
BR 'snɪpɨti
AM 'snɪpɨdi

snippily
BR 'snɪpɨli
AM 'snɪpɨli

snippiness
BR 'snɪpɪnɨs
AM 'snɪpinɨs

snipping
BR 'snɪpɪŋ, -z
AM 'snɪpɪŋ, -z

snippy
BR 'snɪp|i, -ɪə(r), -ɪɪst
AM 'snɪpi, -ər, -ɨst

snit
BR snɪt, -s
AM snɪt, -s

snitch
BR snɪtʃ, -ɨz, -ɪŋ, -t
AM snɪtʃ, -ɨz, -ɪŋ, -t

snitcher
BR 'snɪtʃə(r), -z
AM 'snɪtʃər, -z

snivel
BR 'snɪv|l, -lz, -l̩ɪŋ\-(ə)lɪŋ, -ld
AM 'snɪv|əl, -əlz, -(ə)lɪŋ, -əld

sniveller
BR 'snɪvl̩ə(r), 'snɪv(ə)lə(r), -z
AM 'snɪv(ə)lər, -z

snivellingly
BR 'snɪvl̩ɪŋli, 'snɪv(ə)lɪŋli
AM 'snɪv(ə)lɪŋli

snob
BR snɒb, -z
AM snɑb, -z

snobbery
BR 'snɒb(ə)ri
AM 'snɑb(ə)ri

snobbish
BR 'snɒbɪʃ
AM 'snɑbɪʃ

snobbishly
BR 'snɒbɨʃli
AM 'snɑbɨʃli

snobbishness
BR 'snɒbɨʃnɨs
AM 'snɑbɨʃnɨs

snobby
BR 'snɒb|i, -ɪə(r), -ɪɪst
AM 'snɑbi, -ər, -ɨst

SNOBOL
BR 'snəʊbɒl
AM 'snoʊ,bɔl, 'snoʊ,bɑl

Sno-Cat®
BR 'snəʊkat, -s
AM 'snoʊ,kæt, -s

Snodgrass
BR 'snɒdgrɑ:s, 'snɒdgras
AM 'snɑd,græs

snoek
BR snu:k
AM snuk

snog
BR snɒg, -z, -ɪŋ, -d
AM snɑg, -z, -ɪŋ, -d

snood
BR snu:d, -z
AM snud, -z

snook
BR snu:k, -s
AM snuk, snʊk, -s

snooker
BR 'snu:k|ə(r), -əz, -(ə)rɪŋ, -əd
AM 'snʊkər, -z, -ɪŋ, -d

snoop
BR snuːp, -s, -ɪŋ, -t
AM snup, -s, -ɪŋ, -t
snooper
BR 'snuːpə(r), -z
AM 'snupər, -z
snooperscope
BR 'snuːpəskəʊp, -s
AM 'snupərˌskoʊp, -s
snoopy
BR 'snuːpi
AM 'snupi
snoot
BR snuːt, -s
AM snut, -s
snootily
BR 'snuːtɨli
AM 'snudəli
snootiness
BR 'snuːtɪnɪs
AM 'snudinɪs
snooty
BR 'snuːt|i, -ɪə(r), -ɪɨst
AM 'snudi, -ər, -ɨst
snooze
BR snuːz, -ɨz, -ɪŋ, -d
AM snuz, -ɨz, -ɪŋ, -d
snoozer
BR 'snuːzə(r), -z
AM 'snuzər, -z
snoozy
BR 'snuːz|i, -ɪə(r), -ɪɨst
AM 'snuzi, -ər, -ɨst
snore
BR snɔː(r), -z, -ɪŋ, -d
AM snɔ(ə)r, -z, -ɪŋ, -d
snorer
BR 'snɔːrə(r), -z
AM 'snɔrər, -z
snoringly
BR 'snɔːrɪŋli
AM 'snɔrɪŋli
snorkel
BR 'snɔːk|l, -lz, -lɪŋ\-lɪŋ, -ld
AM 'snɔrk|əl, -əlz, -(ə)lɪŋ, -əld
snorkeler
BR 'snɔːkḷə(r), 'snɔːklə(r), -z
AM 'snɔrk(ə)lər, -z
snorkeller
BR 'snɔːkḷə(r), 'snɔːklə(r), -z
AM 'snɔrk(ə)lər, -z
Snorri
BR 'snɒri
AM 'snɔri
snort
BR snɔːt, -s, -ɪŋ, -ɨd
AM snɔ(ə)rt, -ts, 'snɔrdɪŋ, 'snɔrdəd
snorter
BR 'snɔːtə(r), -z
AM 'snɔrdər, -z
snot
BR snɒt
AM snɑt
snottily
BR 'snɒtɨli
AM 'snɑdəli
snottiness
BR 'snɒtɪnɪs
AM 'snɑdinɪs
snotty
BR 'snɒt|i, -ɪə(r), -ɪɨst
AM 'snɑdi, -ər, -ɨst
snotty-nosed
BR ˌsnɒtɪ'nəʊzd
AM 'snɑdiˌnoʊzd
snout
BR snaʊt, -s, -ɨd
AM snaʊ|t, -ts, -dəd
snoutlike
BR 'snaʊtlʌɪk
AM 'snaʊtˌlaɪk
snouty
BR 'snaʊti
AM 'snaʊdi
snow
BR snəʊ, -z, -ɪŋ, -d
AM snoʊ, -z, -ɪŋ, -d
snowball
BR 'snəʊbɔːl, -z, -ɪŋ, -d
AM 'snoʊˌbɔl, 'snoʊˌbɑl, -z, -ɪŋ, -d
snowbank
BR 'snəʊbaŋk, -s
AM 'snoʊˌbæŋk, -s
snowbelt
BR 'snəʊbɛlt
AM 'snoʊˌbɛlt
snowberry
BR 'snəʊb(ə)r|i, 'snəʊˌbɛr|i, -ɪz
AM 'snoʊˌbɛri, -z
snowbird
BR 'snəʊbəːd, -z
AM 'snoʊˌbərd, -z
snowblind
BR 'snəʊblʌɪnd
AM 'snoʊˌblaɪnd
snow-blindness
BR 'snəʊˌblʌɪn(d)nɪs
AM 'snoʊˌblaɪn(d)nɪs
snowblower
BR 'snəʊˌbləʊə(r), -z
AM 'snoʊˌbloʊər, -z
snowboard
BR 'snəʊbɔːd, -z
AM 'snoʊˌbɔ(ə)rd, -z
snowboarder
BR 'snəʊbɔːdə(r), -z
AM 'snoʊˌbɔrdər, -z
snowboarding
BR 'snəʊbɔːdɪŋ
AM 'snoʊˌbɔrdɪŋ
snowboot
BR 'snəʊbuːt, -s
AM 'snoʊˌbut, -s
snowbound
BR 'snəʊbaʊnd
AM 'snoʊˌbaʊnd
snow-broth
BR 'snəʊbrɒθ
AM 'snoʊˌbrɔθ, 'snoʊˌbrɑθ
snowcap
BR 'snəʊkap, -s
AM 'snoʊˌkæp, -s
snow-capped
BR 'snəʊkapt
AM 'snoʊˌkæpt
Snowcem®
BR 'snəʊsɛm
AM 'snoʊsəm
snowclad
BR 'snəʊklad
AM 'snoʊˌklæd
snowcone
BR 'snəʊkəʊn, -z
AM 'snoʊˌkoʊn, -z
Snowden
BR 'snəʊdn
AM 'snoʊdn
Snowdon
BR 'snəʊdn
AM 'snoʊdn
Snowdonia
BR snə(ʊ)'dəʊnɪə(r)
AM snoʊ'doʊniə, snoʊ'doʊnjə
snowdrift
BR 'snəʊdrɪft, -s
AM 'snoʊˌdrɪft, -s
snowdrop
BR 'snəʊdrɒp, -s
AM 'snoʊˌdrɑp, -s
snowfall
BR 'snəʊfɔːl, -z
AM 'snoʊˌfɔl, 'snoʊˌfɑl, -z
snowfield
BR 'snəʊfiːld, -z
AM 'snoʊˌfild, -z
snowflake
BR 'snəʊfleɪk, -s
AM 'snoʊˌfleɪk, -s
snowily
BR 'snəʊɨli
AM 'snoʊəli
snowiness
BR 'snəʊɪnɪs
AM 'snoʊinɪs
snowless
BR 'snəʊləs
AM 'snoʊləs
snowlike
BR 'snəʊlʌɪk
AM 'snoʊˌlaɪk
snowline
BR 'snəʊlʌɪn, -z
AM 'snoʊˌlaɪn, -z
snowmaking
BR 'snəʊˌmeɪkɪŋ
AM 'snoʊˌmeɪkɪŋ
snowman
BR 'snəʊman
AM 'snoʊˌmæn
snowmen
BR 'snəʊmɛn
AM 'snoʊˌmɛn
snowmobile
BR 'snəʊmə(ʊ)biːl, -z
AM 'snoʊməˌbil, 'snoʊmoʊˌbil, -z
snowplough
BR 'snəʊplaʊ, -z
AM 'snoʊˌplaʊ, -z
snowplow
BR 'snəʊplaʊ, -z
AM 'snoʊˌplaʊ, -z
snowscape
BR 'snəʊskeɪp, -s
AM 'snoʊˌskeɪp, -s
snowshoe
BR 'snəʊʃuː, -z
AM 'snoʊˌʃu, -z
snowshoer
BR 'snəʊˌʃuːə(r), -z
AM 'snoʊˌʃuər, -z
snowstorm
BR 'snəʊstɔːm, -z
AM 'snoʊˌstɔ(ə)rm, -z
snowsuit
BR 'snəʊs(j)uːt, -s
AM 'snoʊˌs(j)ut, -s
Snow-white
BR ˌsnəʊ'wʌɪt
AM ˌsnoʊ'(h)waɪt
snowy
BR 'snəʊi
AM 'snoʊi
snub
BR snʌb, -z, -ɪŋ, -d
AM snəb, -z, -ɪŋ, -d
snubber
BR 'snʌbə(r), -z
AM 'snəbər, -z
snubbingly
BR 'snʌbɪŋli
AM 'snəbɪŋli
snub-nosed
BR ˌsnʌb'nəʊzd
AM 'snəbˌnoʊzd
snuck
BR snʌk
AM snək
snuff
BR snʌf, -s, -ɪŋ, -t
AM snəf, -s, -ɪŋ, -t
snuffbox
BR 'snʌfbɒks, -ɪz
AM 'snəfˌbɑks, -əz
snuffer
BR 'snʌfə(r), -z
AM 'snəfər, -z
snuffle
BR 'snʌf|l, -lz, -ḷɪŋ\-lɪŋ, -ld
AM 'snəf|əl, -əlz, -(ə)lɪŋ, -əld
snuffler
BR 'snʌfḷə(r), 'snʌflə(r), -z
AM 'snəf(ə)lər, -z

snuffly
BR ˈsnʌfl̩i, ˈsnʌfli
AM ˈsnəf(ə)li

snuffy
BR ˈsnʌfi
AM ˈsnəfi

snug
BR snʌɡ, -z, -ə(r), -ɨst
AM snəɡ, -z, -ər, -əst

snuggery
BR ˈsnʌɡ(ə)r|i, -ɪz
AM ˈsnəɡ(ə)ri, -z

snuggle
BR ˈsnʌɡ|l, -lz, -l̩ɪŋ\-lɪŋ, -ld
AM ˈsnəɡ|əl, -əlz, -(ə)lɪŋ, -əld

snuggly
BR ˈsnʌɡli, ˈsnʌɡl̩i
AM ˈsnəɡli

snugly
BR ˈsnʌɡli
AM ˈsnəɡli

snugness
BR ˈsnʌɡnəs
AM ˈsnəɡnəs

Snyder
BR ˈsnʌɪdə(r)
AM ˈsnaɪdər

so
BR səʊ
AM soʊ

soak
BR səʊk, -s, -ɪŋ, -t
AM soʊk, -s, -ɪŋ, -t

soakage
BR ˈsəʊkɪdʒ
AM ˈsoʊkɪdʒ

soakaway
BR ˈsəʊkəweɪ, -z
AM ˈsoʊkəˌweɪ, -z

soaker
BR ˈsəʊkə(r), -z
AM ˈsoʊkər, -z

soaking
BR ˈsəʊkɪŋ, -z
AM ˈsoʊkɪŋ, -z

Soames
BR səʊmz
AM soʊmz

so-and-so
BR ˈsəʊənsəʊ, -z
AM ˈsoʊənˌsoʊ, -z

Soane
BR səʊn
AM soʊn

soap
BR səʊp, -s, -ɪŋ, -t
AM soʊp, -s, -ɪŋ, -t

soapbark
BR ˈsəʊpbɑːk, -s
AM ˈsoʊpˌbɑrk, -s

soapberry
BR ˈsəʊpˌbɛr|i, -ɪz
AM ˈsoʊpˌbɛri, -z

soapbox
BR ˈsəʊpbɒks, -ɪz
AM ˈsoʊpˌbɑks, -əz

soapily
BR ˈsəʊpɪli
AM ˈsoʊpəli

soapiness
BR ˈsəʊpɪnɪs
AM ˈsoʊpinɪs

soapless
BR ˈsəʊpləs
AM ˈsoʊpləs

soaplike
BR ˈsəʊplʌɪk
AM ˈsoʊpˌlaɪk

soapstone
BR ˈsəʊpstəʊn, -z
AM ˈsoʊpˌstoʊn, -z

soapsuds
BR ˈsəʊpsʌdz
AM ˈsoʊpˌsədz

soapwort
BR ˈsəʊpwəːt, -s
AM ˈsoʊpwərt, ˈsoʊpˌwɔ(ə)rt, -s

soapy
BR ˈsəʊp|i, -ɪə(r), -ɪɪst
AM ˈsoʊpi, -ər, -ɨst

soar
BR sɔː(r), -z, -ɪŋ, -d
AM sɔ(ə)r, -z, -ɪŋ, -d

soarer
BR ˈsɔːrə(r), -z
AM ˈsɔrər, -z

soaringly
BR ˈsɔːrɪŋli
AM ˈsɔrɪŋli

SOAS
BR ˈsəʊas, ˈsəʊaz
AM ˈsoʊæs

Soay
BR ˈsəʊeɪ
AM ˈsoʊeɪ

SOB
BR ˌɛsəʊˈbiː, -z
AM ˌɛˌsoʊˈbi, -z

sob
BR sɒb, -z, -ɪŋ, -d
AM sɑb, -z, -ɪŋ, -d

sobber
BR ˈsɒbə(r), -z
AM ˈsɑbər, -z

sobbingly
BR ˈsɒbɪŋli
AM ˈsɑbɪŋli

Sobell
BR ˈsəʊbɛl
AM ˈsoʊbəl

sober
BR ˈsəʊb|ə(r), -əz, -(ə)rɪŋ, -əd, -(ə)rə(r), -(ə)rɪst
AM ˈsoʊb|ər, -ərz, -(ə)rɪŋ, -ərd, -ərər, -ərəst

soberingly
BR ˈsəʊb(ə)rɪŋli
AM ˈsoʊb(ə)rɪŋli

soberly
BR ˈsəʊbəli
AM ˈsoʊbərli

Sobers
BR ˈsəʊbəz
AM ˈsoʊbərz

Sobranie®
BR sə(ʊ)ˈbrɑːni
AM soʊˈbrɑni

sobriety
BR sə(ʊ)ˈbrʌɪɪti
AM səˈbraɪədi, soʊˈbraɪədi

sobriquet
BR ˈsəʊbrɪkeɪ, -z
AM ˈsoʊbrəˌkeɪ, ˈsoʊbrəˌkɛt, -ˌkeɪz\-ˌkɛts

soca
BR ˈsəʊkə(*r*)
AM ˈsoʊkə

socage
BR ˈsɒkɪdʒ
AM ˈsɑkɪdʒ

so-called
BR ˌsəʊˈkɔːld
AM ˈsoʊˌkɔld, ˈsoʊˌkɑld

soccage
BR ˈsɒkɪdʒ
AM ˈsɑkɪdʒ

soccer
BR ˈsɒkə(r)
AM ˈsɑkər

sociability
BR ˌsəʊʃəˈbɪlɪti
AM ˌsoʊʃəˈbɪlɨdi

sociable
BR ˈsəʊʃəbl
AM ˈsoʊʃəbəl

sociableness
BR ˈsəʊʃəblnəs
AM ˈsoʊʃəbəlnəs

sociably
BR ˈsəʊʃəbli
AM ˈsoʊʃəbli

social
BR ˈsəʊʃl
AM ˈsoʊʃəl

socialisation
BR ˌsəʊʃəlʌɪˈzeɪʃn, ˌsəʊʃl̩ʌɪˈzeɪʃn
AM ˌsoʊʃələˈzeɪʃən, ˌsoʊʃəˌlaɪˈzeɪʃən

socialise
BR ˈsəʊʃəlʌɪz, ˈsəʊʃl̩ʌɪz, -ɨz, -ɪŋ, -d
AM ˈsoʊʃəˌlaɪz, -ɨz, -ɪŋ, -d

socialism
BR ˈsəʊʃəlɪz(ə)m, ˈsəʊʃl̩ɪz(ə)m
AM ˈsoʊʃəˌlɪzəm

socialist
BR ˈsəʊʃəlɪst, ˈsəʊʃl̩ɪst, -s
AM ˈsoʊʃələst, -s

socialistic
BR ˌsəʊʃəˈlɪstɪk, ˌsəʊʃlˈɪstɪk
AM ˌsoʊʃəˈlɪstɪk

socialistically
BR ˌsəʊʃəˈlɪstɪkli, ˌsəʊʃlˈɪstɪkli
AM ˌsoʊʃəˈlɪstək(ə)li

socialite
BR ˈsəʊʃəlʌɪt, ˈsəʊʃl̩ʌɪt, -s
AM ˈsoʊʃəˌlaɪt, -s

sociality
BR ˌsəʊʃɪˈalɪti
AM ˌsoʊʃiˈælədi

socialization
BR ˌsəʊʃəlʌɪˈzeɪʃn, ˌsəʊʃl̩ʌɪˈzeɪʃn
AM ˌsoʊʃələˈzeɪʃən, ˌsoʊʃəˌlaɪˈzeɪʃən

socialize
BR ˈsəʊʃəlʌɪz, ˈsəʊʃl̩ʌɪz, -ɨz, -ɪŋ, -d
AM ˈsoʊʃəˌlaɪz, -ɨz, -ɪŋ, -d

socially
BR ˈsəʊʃl̩i, ˈsəʊʃəli
AM ˈsoʊʃəli

social science
BR ˌsəʊʃl ˈsʌɪəns, -ɨz
AM ˌsoʊʃəl ˌsaɪəns, -ɨz

social security
BR ˌsəʊʃl sɪˈkjʊərɪti, + sɪˈkjɔːrɪti
AM ˌsoʊʃəl səˈkjurədi

social service
BR ˌsəʊʃl ˈsəːv|ɪs, -ɨsɨz
AM ˌsoʊʃəl ˈsərvəs, -ɨz

social studies
BR ˌsəʊʃl ˈstʌdɪz
AM ˈsoʊʃəl ˌstədiz

social work
BR ˈsəʊʃl wəːk
AM ˈsoʊʃəl ˌwərk

societal
BR səˈsʌɪətl
AM səˈsaɪədl

societally
BR səˈsʌɪətl̩i, səˈsʌɪətəli
AM səˈsaɪədl̩i

society
BR səˈsʌɪət|i, -ɪz
AM səˈsaɪədi, -z

Socinian
BR sə(ʊ)ˈsɪnɪən, -z
AM soʊˈsiniən, -z

Socinus
BR sə(ʊ)ˈsʌɪnəs
AM soʊˈsaɪnəs

sociobiological
BR ˌsəʊʃ(ɪ)əʊˌbʌɪəˈlɒdʒɪkl, ˌsəʊsɪəʊˌbʌɪəˈlɒdʒɪkl
AM ˌsoʊsioʊˌbaɪəˈlɑdʒəkəl, ˌsoʊʃ(i)oʊˌbaɪəˈlɑdʒəkəl

sociobiologically
BR ˌsəʊʃ(ɪ)əʊˌbʌɪəˈlɒdʒɨkli, ˌsəʊsɪəʊˌbʌɪəˈlɒdʒɨkli
AM ¦soʊsioʊˌbaɪəˈlɑdʒək(ə)li, ¦soʊʃ(i)oʊˌbaɪəˈlɑdʒək(ə)li

sociobiologist
BR ˌsəʊʃ(ɪ)əʊbʌɪˈɒlədʒɪst, ˌsəʊsɪəʊbʌɪˈɒlədʒɪst, -s
AM ¦soʊsioʊˌbaɪˈɑlədʒəst, ¦soʊʃ(i)oʊˌbaɪˈɑlədʒəst, -s

sociobiology
BR ˌsəʊʃ(ɪ)əʊbʌɪˈɒlədʒi, ˌsəʊsɪəʊbʌɪˈɒlədʒi
AM ¦soʊsioʊˌbaɪˈɑlədʒi, ¦soʊʃ(i)oʊˌbaɪˈɑlədʒi

socio-cultural
BR ˌsəʊʃ(ɪ)əʊˈkʌltʃ(ə)rəl, ˌsəʊʃ(ɪ)əʊˈkʌltʃ(ə)rl̩, ˌsəʊsɪəʊˈkʌltʃ(ə)rəl, ˌsəʊsɪəʊˈkʌltʃ(ə)rl̩
AM ¦soʊsioʊˈkəltʃ(ə)rəl, ¦soʊʃ(i)oʊˈkəltʃ(ə)rəl

socioculturally
BR ˌsəʊʃ(ɪ)əʊˈkʌltʃ(ə)rəli, ˌsəʊʃ(ɪ)əʊˈkʌltʃ(ə)rl̩i, ˌsəʊsɪəʊˈkʌltʃ(ə)rəli, ˌsəʊsɪəʊˈkʌltʃ(ə)rl̩i
AM ¦soʊsioʊˈkəltʃ(ə)rəli, ¦soʊʃ(i)oʊˈkəltʃ(ə)rəli

socio-economic
BR ˌsəʊʃ(ɪ)əʊˌiːkəˈnɒmɪk, ˌsəʊsɪəʊˌiːkəˈnɒmɪk, ˌsəʊʃ(ɪ)əʊˌɛkəˈnɒmɪk, ˌsəʊsɪəʊˌɛkəˈnɒmɪk, -s
AM ¦soʊsioʊˌikəˈnɑmɪk, ¦soʊʃ(i)oʊˌikəˈnɑmɪk, ¦soʊsioʊˌɛkəˈnɑmɪk, ¦soʊʃ(i)oʊˌɛkəˈnɑmɪk, -s

socio-economically
BR ˌsəʊʃ(ɪ)əʊˌiːkəˈnɒmɨkli, ˌsəʊsɪəʊˌiːkəˈnɒmɨkli, ˌsəʊʃ(ɪ)əʊˌɛkəˈnɒmɨkli, ˌsəʊsɪəʊˌɛkəˈnɒmɨkli
AM ¦soʊsioʊˌikəˈnɑmək(ə)li, ¦soʊʃ(i)oʊˌikəˈnɑmək(ə)li, ¦soʊsioʊˌɛkəˈnɑmək(ə)li, ¦soʊʃ(i)oʊˌɛkəˈnɑmək(ə)li

sociolinguist
BR ˌsəʊʃ(ɪ)əʊˈlɪŋgwɪst, ˌsəʊsɪəʊˈlɪŋgwɪst, -s
AM ¦soʊsioʊˈlɪŋgwɪst, ¦soʊʃ(i)oʊˈlɪŋgwɪst, -s

sociolinguistic
BR ˌsəʊʃ(ɪ)əʊlɪŋˈgwɪstɪk, ˌsəʊsɪəʊlɪŋˈgwɪstɪk, -s
AM ¦soʊsioʊˌlɪŋˈgwɪstɪk, ¦soʊʃ(i)oʊˌlɪŋˈgwɪstɪk, -s

sociolinguistically
BR ˌsəʊʃ(ɪ)əʊlɪŋˈgwɪstɨkli, ˌsəʊsɪəʊlɪŋˈgwɪstɨkli
AM ¦soʊsioʊlɪŋˈgwɪstək(ə)li, ¦soʊʃ(i)oʊlɪŋˈgwɪstək(ə)li

sociological
BR ˌsəʊʃ(ɪ)əˈlɒdʒɨkl, səʊsɪəˈlɒdʒɨkl
AM ¦soʊsiəˈlɑdʒəkəl, ¦soʊʃ(i)əˈlɑdʒəkəl

sociologically
BR ˌsəʊʃ(ɪ)əˈlɒdʒɨkli, səʊsɪəˈlɒdʒɨkli
AM ¦soʊsiəˈlɑdʒəkəli, ¦soʊʃ(i)əˈlɑdʒəkəli

sociologist
BR ˌsəʊʃɪˈɒlədʒɪst, ˌsəʊsɪˈɒlədʒɪst, -s
AM ˌsoʊsiˈɑlədʒəst, ˌsoʊʃ(i)ˈɑlədʒəst, -s

sociology
BR ˌsəʊʃɪˈɒlədʒi, ˌsəʊsɪˈɒlədʒi
AM ˌsoʊsiˈɑlədʒi, ˌsoʊʃ(i)ˈɑlədʒi

sociometric
BR ˌsəʊʃ(ɪ)ə(ʊ)ˈmɛtrɪk, ˌsəʊsɪə(ʊ)ˈmɛtrɪk
AM ¦soʊsioʊˈmɛtrɪk, ¦soʊʃ(i)oʊˈmɛtrɪk

sociometrically
BR ˌsəʊʃ(ɪ)ə(ʊ)ˈmɛtrɨkli, ˌsəʊsɪə(ʊ)ˈmɛtrɨkli
AM ¦soʊsioʊˈmɛtrək(ə)li, ¦soʊʃ(i)oʊˈmɛtrək(ə)li

sociometrist
BR ˌsəʊʃɪˈɒmɨtrɪst, ˌsəʊsɪˈɒmɨtrɪst, -s
AM ¦soʊsɪˈɑmətrəst, ¦soʊʃɪˈɑmətrəst, -s

sociometry
BR ˌsəʊʃɪˈɒmɨtri, ˌsəʊsɪˈɒmɨtri
AM ¦soʊsɪˈɑmətri, ¦soʊʃɪˈɑmətri

sociopath
BR ˈsəʊʃ(ɪ)ə(ʊ)paθ, ˈsəʊsɪə(ʊ)paθ, -s
AM ˈsoʊsiəˌpæθ, ˈsoʊʃ(i)əˌpæθ, -s

sociopathic
BR ˌsəʊʃ(ɪ)ə(ʊ)ˈpaθɪk, ˌsəʊsɪə(ʊ)ˈpaθɪk
AM ˌsoʊsiəˈpæθɪk, ˌsoʊʃ(i)əˈpæθɪk

sociopathology
BR ˌsəʊʃ(ɪ)əʊpəˈθɒlədʒi, ˌsəʊsɪəʊpəˈθɒlədʒi
AM ¦soʊsioʊpəˈθɑlədʒi, ¦soʊʃ(i)oʊpəθɑlədʒi

socio-political
BR ˌsəʊʃ(ɪ)əʊpəˈlɪtɪkl, ˌsəʊsɪəʊpəˈlɪtɪkl
AM ¦soʊsioʊpəˈlɪdəkəl, ¦soʊʃ(i)oʊpəˈlɪdəkəl

sock
BR sɒk, -s, -ɪŋ, -t
AM sɑk, -s, -ɪŋ, -t

socket
BR ˈsɒkɪt, -s
AM ˈsɑkət, -s

sockeye
BR ˈsɒkʌɪ, -z
AM ˈsɑkˌaɪ, -z

sockless
BR ˈsɒkləs
AM ˈsɑkləs

socko
BR ˈsɒkəʊ, -z
AM ˈsɑkoʊ, -z

socle
BR ˈsəʊkl, ˌsɒkl, -z
AM ˈsɑkəl, -z

Socotra
BR səˈkəʊtrə(r)
AM səˈkoʊtrə

Socrates
BR ˈsɒkrətiːz
AM ˈsɑkrəˌtiz

Socratic
BR səˈkratɪk
AM səˈkrædɪk

Socratically
BR səˈkratɨkli
AM səˈkrædək(ə)li

sod
BR sɒd, -z, -ɪŋ
AM sɑd, -z, -ɪŋ

soda
BR ˈsəʊdə(r), -z
AM ˈsoʊdə, -z

sodalite
BR ˈsəʊdəlʌɪt
AM ˈsoʊdəlaɪt

sodality
BR sə(ʊ)ˈdalɪt|i, -ɪz
AM soʊˈdælədi, -z

sodbuster
BR ˈsɒdˌbʌstə(r), -z
AM ˈsɑdˌbəstər, -z

sodden
BR ˈsɒdn
AM ˈsɑdən

soddenly
BR ˈsɒdnli
AM ˈsɑdnli

soddenness
BR ˈsɒdnnəs
AM ˈsɑd(n)nəs

Soddy
BR ˈsɒdi
AM ˈsɑdi

sodic
BR ˈsəʊdɪk
AM ˈsɑdɪk

sodium
BR ˈsəʊdɪəm
AM ˈsoʊdiəm

sodium bicarb
BR ˌsəʊdɪəm ˈbaɪkɑːb
AM ¦soʊdiəm ˈbaɪˌkɑrb

sodium bicarbonate
BR ˌsəʊdɪəm ˌbaɪˈkɑːbənət, +ˌbaɪˈkɑːbn̩ət
AM ¦soʊdiəm ˌbaɪˈkɑrbəˌneɪt, + ˌbaɪˈkɑrbənət

sodium carbonate
BR ˌsəʊdɪəm ˈkɑːbənət, + ˈkɑːbənət
AM ¦soʊdiəm ˈkɑrbəˌneɪt

sodium chloride
BR ˌsəʊdɪəm ˈklɔːrʌɪd
AM ¦soʊdiəm ˈklɔˌraɪd

sodium hydroxide
BR ˌsəʊdɪəm hʌɪˈdrɒksʌɪd
AM ¦soʊdiəm haɪˈdrɑkˌsaɪd

sodium nitrate
BR ˌsəʊdɪəm ˈnʌɪtreɪt
AM ¦soʊdiəm ˈnaɪˌtreɪt

Sodom
BR ˈsɒdəm
AM ˈsɑdəm

sodomise
BR ˈsɒdəmʌɪz, -ɨz, -ɪŋ, -d
AM ˈsɑdəˌmaɪz, -ɨz, -ɪŋ, -d

sodomite
BR ˈsɒdəmʌɪt, -s
AM ˈsɑdəˌmaɪt, -s

sodomize
BR ˈsɒdəmʌɪz, -ɨz, -ɪŋ, -d
AM ˈsɑdəˌmaɪz, -ɨz, -ɪŋ, -d

sodomy
BR ˈsɒdəmi
AM ˈsɑdəmi

Sodor
BR ˈsəʊdɔː(r)
AM ˈsoʊˌdɔ(ə)r

soever
BR səʊˈɛvə(r)
AM səˈwɛvər, soʊˈɛvər

sofa
BR ˈsəʊfə(r), -z
AM ˈsoʊfə, -z

sofabed
BR ˈsəʊfəbɛd, -z

AM ˈsoʊfəˌbɛd, -z

Sofar
BR ˈsəʊfɑː(r)
AM ˈsoʊˌfɑr

soffit
BR ˈsɒfɪt, -s
AM ˈsɑfət, -s

Sofia
BR ˈsəʊfɪə(r), sə(ʊ)ˈfiːə(r)
AM soʊˈfiə, ˈsoʊfiə

soft
BR sɒft, -ə(r), -ɨst
AM sɔft, sɑft, -ər, -əst

softa
BR ˈsɒftə(r), -z
AM ˈsɔftə, ˈsɑftə, -z

softback
BR ˈsɒf(t)bak, -s
AM ˈsɔf(t)ˌbæk, ˈsɑf(t)ˌbæk, -s

softball
BR ˈsɒf(t)bɔːl
AM ˈsɔf(t)ˌbɔl, ˈsɑf(t)ˌbɑl

softbound
BR ˌsɒf(t)ˈbaʊnd
AM ˈsɔf(t)ˌbaʊnd, ˈsɑf(t)ˌbaʊnd

softcore
BR ˌsɒf(t)ˈkɔː(r)
AM ˈsɔf(t)ˈkɔ(ə)r, ˈsɑf(t)ˈkɔ(ə)r

softcover
BR ˌsɒf(t)ˈkʌvə(r)
AM ˈsɔf(t)ˌkəvər, ˈsɑf(t)ˌkəvər

soft-drink
BR ˌsɒf(t)ˈdrɪŋk, -s
AM ˈsɔf(t)ˌdrɪŋk, ˈsɑf(t)ˌdrɪŋk, -s

soften
BR ˈsɒf|n, -nz, -nɪŋ\-n̩ɪŋ, -nd
AM ˈsɔf|ən, ˈsɑf|ən, -ənz, -(ə)nɪŋ, -ənd

softener
BR ˈsɔːfnə(r), ˈsɔːfn̩ə(r), -z
AM ˈsɔf(ə)nər, ˈsɑf(ə)nər, -z

softie
BR ˈsɒft|i, -ɪz
AM ˈsɔfti, ˈsɑfti, -z

softish
BR ˈsɒftɪʃ
AM ˈsɔftɪʃ, ˈsɑftɪʃ

softly
BR ˈsɒftli
AM ˈsɔf(t)li, ˈsɑf(t)li

softly-softly
adjective
BR ˈsɒftlɪˈsɒftli
AM ˈsɔf(t)liˈsɔf(t)li, ˈsɑf(t)liˈsɑf(t)li

softness
BR ˈsɒf(t)nəs
AM ˈsɔf(t)nəs, ˈsɑf(t)nəs

software
BR ˈsɒf(t)wɛː(r)
AM ˈsɔf(t)ˌwɛ(ə)r, ˈsɑf(t)ˌwɛ(ə)r

softwood
BR ˈsɒf(t)wʊd
AM ˈsɔf(t)ˌwʊd, ˈsɑf(t)ˌwʊd

softy
BR ˈsɒft|i, -ɪz
AM ˈsɔfti, ˈsɑfti, -z

SOGAT
BR ˈsəʊgat
AM ˈsoʊˌgæt

soggily
BR ˈsɒgɨli
AM ˈsɑgəli

sogginess
BR ˈsɒgɪnɪs
AM ˈsɑginɪs

soggy
BR ˈsɒg|i, -ɪə(r), -ɪɪst
AM ˈsɑgi, -ər, -ɨst

soh
BR səʊ, -z
AM soʊ, -z

Soho
BR ˈsəʊhəʊ, ˌsəʊˈhəʊ
AM ˈsoʊˌhoʊ

soi-disant
BR ˌswɑːˈdiːzɒ̃, ˌswɑːdiːˈzɒ̃
AM ˈswɑdiˈzɑn(t)

soigné
BR ˈswɑːnjeɪ
AM swɑnˈjeɪ

soignée
BR ˈswɑːnjeɪ
AM swɑnˈjeɪ

soil
BR sɔɪl, -z, -ɪŋ, -d
AM sɔɪl, -z, -ɪŋ, -d

soil-less
BR ˈsɔɪllɨs
AM ˈsɔɪ(l)lɨs

soilpipe
BR ˈsɔɪlpʌɪp, -s
AM ˈsɔɪlˌpaɪp, -s

soily
BR ˈsɔɪli
AM ˈsɔɪli

soirée
BR ˈswɑːreɪ, -z
AM swɑˈreɪ, -z

soixante-neuf
BR ˌswasɒ̃ˈnəːf
AM ˈswɑˌsɑnˈnəf

sojourn
BR ˈsɒdʒ|(ə)n, ˈsʌdʒ|(ə)n, ˈsɒdʒ|əːn, ˈsʌdʒ|əːn, -(ə)nz, -n̩ɪŋ\-ənɪŋ, -(ə)nd
AM ˈsoʊˌdʒərn, -z, -ɪŋ, -d

sojourner
BR ˈsɒdʒn̩ə(r), ˈsɒdʒənə(r), ˈsʌdʒn̩ə(r), ˈsʌdʒənə(r), -z
AM ˈsoʊˌdʒərnər, -z

soke
BR səʊk, -s
AM soʊk, -s

sol
BR sɒl, -z
AM sɔl, sɑl, -z

sola
BR ˈsəʊlə(r)
AM ˈsoʊlə

solace
BR ˈsɒlɪs, -ɪz, -ɪŋ, -t
AM ˈsɑləs, -əz, -ɪŋ, -t

solan
BR ˈsəʊlən, -z
AM ˈsoʊlən, -z

solanaceous
BR ˌsɒləˈneɪʃəs
AM ˌsɑləˈneɪʃəs

solander
BR səˈlandə(r), -z
AM səˈlændər, -z

solar
BR ˈsəʊlə(r)
AM ˈsoʊlər

solaria
BR səˈlɛːrɪə(r)
AM səˈlɛriə, soʊˈlɛriə

solarisation
BR ˌsəʊlərʌɪˈzeɪʃn
AM ˌsoʊlərəˈzeɪʃən, ˌsoʊləˌraɪˈzeɪʃən

solarise
BR ˈsəʊlərʌɪz, -ɪz, -ɪŋ, -d
AM ˈsoʊləˌraɪz, -ɪz, -ɪŋ, -d

solarism
BR ˈsəʊlərɪz(ə)m
AM ˈsoʊləˌrɪzəm

solarist
BR ˈsəʊlərɪst, -s
AM ˈsoʊlərəst, -s

solarium
BR səˈlɛːrɪəm, -z
AM səˈlɛriəm, soʊˈlɛriəm, -z

solarization
BR ˌsəʊlərʌɪˈzeɪʃn
AM ˌsoʊlərəˈzeɪʃən, ˌsoʊləˌraɪˈzeɪʃən

solarize
BR ˈsəʊlərʌɪz, -ɪz, -ɪŋ, -d
AM ˈsoʊləˌraɪz, -ɪz, -ɪŋ, -d

solar plexus
BR ˌsəʊlə ˈplɛksəs, -ɪz
AM ˌsoʊlər ˈplɛksəs, -əz

solar system
BR ˈsəʊlə ˌsɪstɪm, -z
AM ˈsoʊlər ˌsɪstəm, -z

SOLAS
BR ˈsəʊləs
AM ˈsoʊləs

solatia
BR sə(ʊ)ˈleɪʃ(ɪ)ə(r)
AM səˈleɪʃiə

solatium
BR sə(ʊ)ˈleɪʃ(ɪ)əm, -z
AM səˈleɪʃ(i)əm, -z

sold
BR səʊld
AM soʊld

soldanella
BR ˌsɒldəˈnɛlə(r), -z
AM ˌsɑldəˈnɛlə, ˌsoʊldəˈnɛlə, -z

solder
BR ˈsɒld|ə(r), ˈsəʊld|ə(r), -əz, -(ə)rɪŋ, -əd
AM ˈsɑdər, -z, -ɪŋ, -d

solderable
BR ˈsɒld(ə)rəbl, ˈsəʊld(ə)rəbl
AM ˈsɑdərəbəl

solderer
BR ˈsɒld(ə)rə(r), ˈsəʊld(ə)rə(r), -z
AM ˈsɑd(ə)rər, -z

soldier
BR ˈsəʊldʒ|ə(r), -əz, -(ə)rɪŋ, -əd
AM ˈsoʊldʒ|ər, -ərz, -(ə)rɪŋ, -ərd

soldierly
BR ˈsəʊldʒəli
AM ˈsoʊldʒərli

soldiership
BR ˈsəʊldʒəʃɪp
AM ˈsoʊldʒərˌʃɪp

soldiery
BR ˈsəʊldʒ(ə)ri
AM ˈsoʊldʒ(ə)ri

sole
BR səʊl, -z, -ɪŋ, -d
AM soʊl, -z, -ɪŋ, -d

solecism
BR ˈsɒlɪsɪz(ə)m
AM ˈsɑləˌsɪzəm, ˈsoʊləˌsɪzəm

solecist
BR ˈsɒlɪsɪst, -s
AM ˈsɑləsəst, ˈsoʊləsəst, -s

solecistic
BR ˌsɒlɪˈsɪstɪk
AM ˌsɑləˈsɪstɪk, ˌsoʊləˈsɪstɪk

Soledad
BR ˈsɒlɪdad
AM ˈsoʊləˌdæd
SP soleˈðað

solely
BR ˈsəʊ(l)li
AM ˈsoʊ(l)li

solemn
BR ˈsɒləm
AM ˈsɑləm

solemnisation
BR ˌsɒləmnʌɪˈzeɪʃn, -z

AM ˌsɑləmnəˈzeɪʃən, ˌsɑləmˌnaɪˈzeɪʃən, -z

solemnise
BR ˈsɒləmnʌɪz, -ɨz, -ɪŋ, -d
AM ˈsɑləmˌnaɪz, -ɨz, -ɪŋ, -d

solemnity
BR səˈlɛmnɨti
AM səˈlɛmnədi, -z

solemnization
BR ˌsɒləmnʌɪˈzeɪʃn, -z
AM ˌsɑləmnəˈzeɪʃən, ˌsɑləmˌnaɪˈzeɪʃən, -z

solemnize
BR ˈsɒləmnʌɪz, -ɨz, -ɪŋ, -d
AM ˈsɑləmˌnaɪz, -ɨz, -ɪŋ, -d

solemnly
BR ˈsɒləmli
AM ˈsɑləmli

solemnness
BR ˈsɒləmnəs
AM ˈsɑləmnəs

solen
BR ˈsəʊlən, -z
AM ˈsoʊlən, ˈsoʊˌlɛn, -z

solenodon
BR səˈlɛnədən, səˈliːnədən, -z
AM soʊˈlinəˌdɑn, soʊˈlɛnəˌdɑn, -z

solenoid
BR ˈsəʊlənɔɪd, -z
AM ˈsɑləˌnɔɪd, -z

solenoidal
BR ˌsəʊləˈnɔɪdl
AM ˌsɑləˈnɔɪdəl

Solent
BR ˈsəʊlənt, ˈsəʊlṇt
AM ˈsoʊlənt

soleplate
BR ˈsəʊlpleɪt, -s
AM ˈsoʊlˌpleɪt, -s

sol-fa
BR ˌsɒlˈfɑː(r)
AM ˌsoʊlˈfɑ

solfatara
BR ˈsɒlfəˈtɑːrə(r), -z
AM ˌsɑlfəˈtɛrə, ˌsoʊlfəˈtɛrə, -z

solfeggi
BR sɒlˈfɛdʒiː
AM sɑlˈfɛdʒi

solfeggio
BR sɒlˈfɛdʒɪəʊ, -z
AM sɑlˈfɛdʒioʊ, -z

soli
BR ˈsəʊli
AM ˈsoʊli

solicit
BR səˈlɪs|ɪt, -ɪts, -ɨtɪŋ, -ɨtɨd
AM səˈlɪsɨ|t, -ts, -dɪŋ, -dɨd

solicitation
BR səˌlɪsɪˈteɪʃn
AM səˌlɪsəˈteɪʃən

solicitor
BR səˈlɪsɪtə(r), -z
AM səˈlɪsədər, -z

Solicitor-General
BR səˌlɪsɪtəˈdʒɛn(ə)rəl, səˌlɪsɪtəˈdʒɛn(ə)rḷ
AM səˌlɪsɨdərˈdʒɛn(ə)rəl

Solicitors-General
BR səˌlɪsɪtəzˈdʒɛn(ə)rəl, səˌlɪsɪtəzˈdʒɛn(ə)rḷ
AM səˌlɪsɨdərzˈdʒɛn(ə)rəl

solicitous
BR səˈlɪsɪtəs
AM səˈlɪsədəs

solicitously
BR səˈlɪsɪtəsli
AM səˈlɪsədəsli

solicitousness
BR səˈlɪsɪtəsnəs
AM səˈlɪsədəsnəs

solicitude
BR səˈlɪsɪtjuːd, səˈlɪsɪtʃuːd
AM səˈlɪsəˌt(j)ud

solid
BR ˈsɒlɪd, -z
AM ˈsɑləd, -z

solidago
BR ˌsɒlɪˈdeɪgəʊ
AM ˌsɑləˈdeɪgoʊ

solidarity
BR ˌsɒlɪˈdarɪti
AM ˌsɑləˈdɛrədi

solidi
BR ˈsɒlɪdʌɪ, ˈsɒlɪdiː
AM ˈsɑləˌdaɪ

solidifiable
BR səˈlɪdɪfʌɪəbl
AM səˌlɪdəˈfaɪəbəl

solidification
BR səˌlɪdɪfɪˈkeɪʃn
AM səˌlɪdəfəˈkeɪʃən

solidifier
BR səˈlɪdɪfʌɪə(r), -z
AM səˈlɪdəˌfaɪər, -z

solidify
BR səˈlɪdɪfʌɪ, -z, -ɪŋ, -d
AM səˈlɪdəˌfaɪ, -z, -ɪŋ, -d

solidity
BR səˈlɪdɪti
AM səˈlɪdɨdi

solidly
BR ˈsɒlɪdli
AM ˈsɑlədli

solidness
BR ˈsɒlɪdnɪs
AM ˈsɑlədnɨs

solidungulate
BR ˌsɒlɪˈdʌŋgjʉlət, -s
AM ˌsɑləˈdəŋgjələt, ˌsɑləˈdəŋgjəˌleɪt, -s

solidus
BR ˈsɒlɪdəs
AM ˈsɑlədəs

solifidian
BR ˌsɒlɪˈfɪdɪən, -z
AM ˌsɑləˈfɪdiən, -z

solifluction
BR ˌsɒlɪˈflʌkʃn
AM ˌsɑləˈflәkʃən

Solihull
BR ˌsəʊlɪˈhʌl, ˌsɒlɪˈhʌl
AM ˌsɑləˈhəl, ˌsoʊləˈhəl

soliloquise
BR səˈlɪləkwʌɪz, -ɨz, -ɪŋ, -d
AM səˈlɪləˌkwaɪz, -ɨz, -ɪŋ, -d

soliloquist
BR səˈlɪləkwɪst, -s
AM səˈlɪləkwəst, -s

soliloquize
BR səˈlɪləkwʌɪz, -ɨz, -ɪŋ, -d
AM səˈlɪləˌkwaɪz, -ɨz, -ɪŋ, -d

soliloquy
BR səˈlɪləkw|i, -ɪz
AM səˈlɪləkwi, -z

soliped
BR ˈsɒlɪpɛd, -z
AM ˈsɑləˌpɛd, -z

solipsism
BR ˈsɒlɪpsɪz(ə)m, -z
AM ˈsoʊləpˌsɪzəm, ˈsɑləpˌsɪzəm, səˈlɪpˌsɪzəm, -z

solipsist
BR ˈsɒlɪpsɪst, -s
AM ˈsoʊləpsəst, ˈsɑləpsəst, səˈlɪpsɪst, -s

solipsistic
BR ˌsɒlɪpˈsɪstɪk
AM ˌsoʊləpˈsɪstɪk, ˌsɑləpˈsɪstɪk

solipsistically
BR ˌsɒlɪpˈsɪstɪkli
AM ˌsoʊləpˈsɪstək(ə)li, ˌsɑləpˈsɪstək(ə)li

solitaire
BR ˌsɒlɪˈtɛː(r), ˈsɒlɪtɛː(r)
AM ˈsɑləˌtɛ(ə)r

solitarily
BR ˈsɒlɪt(ə)rɪli
AM ˈsɑləˌtɛrəli

solitariness
BR ˈsɒlɪt(ə)rɪnɪs
AM ˈsɑləˌterinɨs

solitary
BR ˈsɒlɪt(ə)r|i, -ɪz
AM ˈsɑləˌteri, -z

solitude
BR ˈsɒlɪtjuːd, ˈsɒlɪtʃuːd
AM ˈsɑləˌt(j)ud

solleret
BR ˌsɒləˈrɛt, -s
AM ˌsɑləˈrɛt, -s

solmizate
BR ˈsɒlmɪzeɪt, -s, -ɪŋ, -ɨd
AM ˈsɑlməˌzeɪ|t, -ts, -dɪŋ, -dɨd

solmization
BR ˌsɒlmɪˈzeɪʃn
AM ˌsɑlməˈzeɪʃən

solo
BR ˈsəʊləʊ, -z, -ɪŋ, -d
AM ˈsoʊˌl|oʊ, -oʊz, -əwɪŋ\-oʊɪŋ, -oʊd

soloist
BR ˈsəʊləʊɪst, -s
AM ˈsoʊləwəst

Solomon
BR ˈsɒləmən
AM ˈsɑləmən

Solomonic
BR ˌsɒləˈmɒnɪk
AM ˌsɑləˈmɑnɪk

Solon
BR ˈsəʊlɒn, ˈsəʊlən
AM ˈsoʊlən

solstice
BR ˈsɒlstɪs, -ɨz
AM ˈsoʊlstəs, ˈsɑlstəs, -əz

solstitial
BR sɒlˈstɪʃl
AM sɑlˈstɪʃəl, soʊlˈstɪʃəl

Solti
BR ˈʃɒlti
AM ˈʃoʊlti

solubilisation
BR ˌsɒljʉbɪlʌɪˈzeɪʃn, ˌsɒljʉbḷʌɪˈzeɪʃn
AM ˌsɑljəbələˈzeɪʃən, ˌsɑljəbəˌlaɪˈzeɪʃən

solubilise
BR ˈsɒljʉbɪlʌɪz, ˈsɒljʉbḷʌɪz, -ɨz, -ɪŋ, -d
AM ˈsɑljəbəˌlaɪz, -ɨz, -ɪŋ, -d

solubility
BR ˌsɒljʉˈbɪlɪti
AM ˌsɑljəˈbɪlɨdi

solubilization
BR ˌsɒljʉbɪlʌɪˈzeɪʃn, ˌsɒljʉbḷʌɪˈzeɪʃn
AM ˌsɑljəbələˈzeɪʃən, ˌsɑljəbəˌlaɪˈzeɪʃən

solubilize
BR ˈsɒljʉbɪlʌɪz, ˈsɒljʉbḷʌɪz, -ɨz, -ɪŋ, -d
AM ˈsɑljəbəˌlaɪz, -ɨz, -ɪŋ, -d

soluble
BR ˈsɒljʉbl
AM ˈsɑljəbəl

solus
BR ˈsəʊləs
AM ˈsoʊləs

solute
BR ˈsɒljuːt, -s
AM ˈsɑlˌjut, -s

solution
BR sə'l(j)uːʃn, -z
AM sə'luʃən, -z
Solutrean
BR sə'l(j)uːtrɪən, -z
AM sə'lutriən, -z
solvability
BR ˌsɒlvə'bɪlɨti
AM ˌsɑlvə'bɪlɨdi
solvable
BR 'sɒlvəbl
AM 'sɑlvəbəl
solvate
BR 'sɒlveɪt, -s, -ɪŋ, -ɨd
AM 'sɑlˌveɪ|t, -ts, -dɪŋ, -dɨd
solvation
BR sɒl'veɪʃn, -z
AM sɑl'veɪʃən, -z
Solvay
BR 'sɒlveɪ
AM 'sɔlveɪ, 'sɑlveɪ
solve
BR sɒlv, -z, -ɪŋ, -d
AM sɑlv, -z, -ɪŋ, -d
solvency
BR 'sɒlv(ə)nsi
AM 'sɑlvənsi
solvent
BR 'sɒlv(ə)nt, -s
AM 'sɑlvənt, -s
solver
BR 'sɒlvə(r), -z
AM 'sɑlvər, -z
Solway Firth
BR ˌsɒlweɪ 'fəːθ
AM ˌsɔlweɪ 'fərθ, ˌsɑlweɪ 'fərθ
Solzhenitsyn
BR ˌsɒlʒɨ'nɪtsɪn
AM ˌsoʊlʒə'nɪtsən
soma
BR 'səʊmə(r)
AM 'soʊmə
Somali
BR sə'mɑːl|i, -ɪz
AM sə'mɑli, soʊ'mɑli, -z
Somalia
BR sə'mɑːlɪə(r)
AM sə'mɑljə, soʊ'mɑljə, sə'mɑliə, soʊ'mɑliə
Somalian
BR sə'mɑːlɪən, -z
AM sə'mɑljən, soʊ'mɑljən, sə'mɑliən, soʊ'mɑliən, -z
Somaliland
BR sə'mɑːlɪland
AM sə'mɑliˌlænd, soʊ'mɑliˌlænd
somatic
BR sə'matɪk
AM sə'mædɪk
somatically
BR sə'matɪkli
AM sə'mædək(ə)li
somatogenic
BR ˌsəʊmətə(ʊ)'dʒɛnɪk, səˌmatə'dʒɛnɪk
AM səˌmædə'dʒɛnɪk
somatology
BR ˌsəʊmə'tɒlədʒi
AM ˌsoʊmə'tɑlədʒi
somatotonic
BR ˌsəʊmətə(ʊ)'tɒnɪk, səˌmatə'tɒnɪk
AM səˌmædə'tɑnɪk
somatotrophin
BR ˌsəʊmətə(ʊ)'trə(ʊ)fɪn, səˌmatə'trəʊfɪn, -z
AM səˌmædə'troʊfən, -z
somatotropin
BR ˌsəʊmətə(ʊ)'trə(ʊ)pɪn, səˌmatə'trəʊpɪn, -z
AM səˌmædə'troʊpən, -z
somatotype
BR 'səʊmətə(ʊ)tʌɪp, sə'matətʌɪp, -s
AM sə'mædəˌtaɪp, -s
somber
BR 'sɒmbə(r)
AM 'sɑmbər
somberly
BR 'sɒmbəli
AM 'sɑmbərli
somberness
BR 'sɒmbənəs
AM 'sɑmbərnəs
sombre
BR 'sɒmbə(r)
AM 'sɑmbər
sombrely
BR 'sɒmbəli
AM 'sɑmbərli
sombreness
BR 'sɒmbənəs
AM 'sɑmbərnəs
sombrero
BR sɒm'brɛːrəʊ, -z
AM səm'brɛroʊ, sɑm'brɛroʊ, -z
sombrous
BR 'sɒmbrəs
AM 'sɑmbrəs
some[1]
strong form
BR sʌm
AM səm
some[2]
weak form
BR s(ə)m
AM s(ə)m
somebody
BR 'sʌmbəd|i, 'sʌmˌbɒd|i, -ɪz
AM 'səmˌbɑdi, 'səmbədi, -z
someday
BR 'sʌmdeɪ
AM 'səmˌdeɪ
somehow
BR 'sʌmhaʊ
AM 'səmˌ(h)aʊ
someone
BR 'sʌmwʌn
AM 'səmˌwən
someplace
BR 'sʌmpleɪs
AM 'səmˌpleɪs
Somerfield
BR 'sʌməfiːld
AM 'səmərˌfild
Somers
BR 'sʌməz
AM 'səmərz
somersault
BR 'sʌməsɔːlt, 'sʌməsɒlt, -s, -ɪŋ, -ɨd
AM 'səmərˌsɔlt, 'səmərˌsɑlt, -s, -ɪŋ, -ɨd
Somerset
BR 'sʌməsɛt
AM 'səmərˌsɛt
Somerville
BR 'sʌməvɪl
AM 'səmərˌvɪl
something
BR 'sʌmθɪŋ
AM 'səmˌθɪŋ
sometime
BR 'sʌmtʌɪm, -z
AM 'səmˌtaɪm, -z
someway
BR 'sʌmweɪ
AM 'səmˌweɪ
somewhat
BR 'sʌmwɒt
AM 'səmˌ(h)wɑt
somewhen
BR 'sʌmwɛn
AM 'səmˌ(h)wɛn
somewhere
BR 'sʌmwɛː(r)
AM 'səmˌ(h)wɛ(ə)r
somite
BR 'səʊmʌɪt, -s
AM 'soʊˌmaɪt, -s
somitic
BR sə(ʊ)'mɪtɪk
AM soʊ'mɪdɪk
Somme
BR sɒm
AM sɔm, sɑm
sommelier
BR sɒ'mɛlɪə(r), sɒ'mɛlɪeɪ, sʌ'mɛlɪə(r), sʌ'mɛlɪeɪ, ˌsʌml'jeɪ, -z
AM ˌsəməl'jeɪ, -z
somnambulant
BR sɒm'nambjʊlənt, sɒm'nambjʊln̩t, -s
AM sɑm'næmbjələnt, -s
somnambulantly
BR sɒm'nambjʊləntli, sɒm'nambjʊln̩tli
AM sɑm'næmbjələn(t)li
somnambulism
BR sɒm'nambjʊlɪz(ə)m
AM sɑm'næmbjəˌlɪzəm
somnambulist
BR sɒm'nambjʊlɪst, -s
AM sɑm'nambjələst, -s
somnambulistic
BR sɒmˌnambjʊ'lɪstɪk
AM sɑmˌnæmbjə'lɪstɪk
somnambulistically
BR sɒmˌnambjʊ'lɪstɪkli
AM sɑmˌnæmbjə'lɪstɪk(ə)li
somniferous
BR sɒm'nɪf(ə)rəs
AM sɑm'nɪf(ə)rəs
somnolence
BR 'sɒmnələns, 'sɒmnəl̩ns
AM 'sɑmnələns
somnolency
BR 'sɒmnələnsi, 'sɒmnəl̩nsi
AM 'sɑmnələnsi
somnolent
BR 'sɒmnələnt, 'sɒmnəl̩nt
AM 'sɑmnələnt
somnolently
BR 'sɒmnələntli, 'sɒmnəl̩ntli
AM 'sɑmnələn(t)li
Somoza
BR sə'məʊzə(r)
AM sə'moʊzə
son
BR sʌn, -z
AM sən, -z
sonagram
BR 'səʊnəgram, 'sɒnəgram, -z
AM 'soʊnəˌgræm, 'sɑnəˌgræm, -z
sonagraph
BR 'səʊnəgrɑːf, 'sɒnəgrɑːf, 'səʊnəgraf, 'sɒnəgraf, -s
AM 'soʊnəˌgræf, 'sɑnəˌgræf, -s
sonancy
BR 'səʊnənsi
AM 'soʊnənsi
sonant
BR 'səʊnənt, -s
AM 'soʊnənt, -s
sonar
BR 'səʊnɑː(r), -z
AM 'soʊˌnɑr, -z
sonata
BR sə'nɑːtə(r), sn'ɑːtə(r), -z
AM sə'nɑdə, -z
sonatina
BR ˌsɒnə'tiːnə(r), -z
AM ˌsɑnə'tinə, -z
sonde
BR sɒnd, -z
AM sɑnd, -z

Sondheim
BR 'sɒndhʌɪm
AM 'sɑnd,(h)aɪm

sone
BR səʊn, -z
AM soʊn, -z

son et lumière
BR ˌsɒn eɪ 'luːmɪɛː(r), -z
AM ˌsɔn eɪ ˌlum'jɛ(ə)r, -z

song
BR sɒŋ, -z
AM sɔŋ, sɑŋ, -z

songbird
BR 'sɒŋbəːd, -z
AM 'sɔŋ,bərd, 'sɑŋ,bərd, -z

songbook
BR 'sɒŋbʊk, -s
AM 'sɔŋ,bʊk, 'sɑŋ,bʊk, -s

songfest
BR 'sɒŋfɛst, -s
AM 'sɔŋ,fɛst, 'sɑŋ,fɛst, -s

songful
BR 'sɒŋf(ʊ)l
AM 'sɔŋfəl, 'sɑŋfəl

songfully
BR 'sɒŋfʊli, 'sɒŋfl̩i
AM 'sɔŋfəli, 'sɑŋfəli

songless
BR 'sɒŋləs
AM 'sɔŋləs, 'sɑŋləs

songsmith
BR 'sɒŋsmɪθ
AM 'sɔŋ,smɪθ, 'sɑŋ,smɪθ

songster
BR 'sɒŋstə(r), -z
AM 'sɔŋstər, 'sɑŋstər, -z

songstress
BR 'sɒŋstrɪs, -ɪz
AM 'sɔŋstrəs, 'sɑŋstrəs, -əz

songthrush
BR 'sɒŋθrʌʃ, -ɪz
AM 'sɔŋ,θrəʃ, 'sɑŋ,θrəʃ, -əz

songwriter
BR 'sɒŋ,rʌɪtə(r), -z
AM 'sɔŋ,raɪdər, 'sɑŋ,raɪdər, -z

songwriting
BR 'sɒŋ,rʌɪtɪŋ
AM 'sɔŋ,raɪdɪŋ, 'sɑŋ,raɪdɪŋ

Sonia
BR 'sɒnɪə(r), 'sɒnjə(r)
AM 'sɑnjə, 'soʊnjə

sonic
BR 'sɒnɪk
AM 'sɑnɪk

sonically
BR 'sʌnɪkli
AM 'sɑnək(ə)li

son-in-law
BR 'sʌnɪnlɔː(r), -z
AM 'sənən,lɔ, 'sənən,lɑ, -z

Sonja
BR 'sɒnɪə(r), 'sɒnjə(r)
AM 'sɑnjə, 'sɑndʒə

sonless
BR 'sʌnləs
AM 'sənləs

sonnet
BR 'sɒnɪt, -s
AM 'sɑnət, -s

sonneteer
BR ˌsɒnɪ'tɪə(r), -z
AM ˌsɑnə'tɪ(ə)r, -z

Sonning
BR 'sʌnɪŋ, 'sɒnɪŋ
AM 'sɑnɪŋ

sonny
BR 'sʌn|i, -ɪz
AM 'səni, -z

sonobuoy
BR 'səʊnəbɔɪ, 'sɒnəbɔɪ, -z
AM 'soʊnə,bui, 'soʊnə,bɔi, 'sɑnə,bui, 'sɑnə,bɔi, -z

son-of-a-bitch
BR ˌsʌnəvə'bɪtʃ
AM ˌsənəvə,bɪtʃ

son-of-a-gun
BR ˌsʌnəvə'gʌn
AM ˌsənəvə,gən

sonogram
BR 'səʊnəgram, 'sɒnəgram, -z
AM 'soʊnə,græm, 'sɑnə,græm, -z

sonograph
BR 'səʊnəgrɑːf, 'sɒnəgrɑːf, 'səʊnəgraf, 'sɒnəgraf, -s
AM 'soʊnə,græf, 'sɑnə,græf, -s

sonometer
BR sə'nɒmɪtə(r), -z
AM sə'nɑmədər, -z

Sonora
BR sə'nɔːrə(r)
AM sə'nɔrə

sonorant
BR 'sɒn(ə)rənt, 'sɒn(ə)rn̩t
AM 'sɑnərənt, sə'nɔrənt

sonority
BR sə'nɒrɪti
AM sə'nɔrədi

sonorous
BR 'sɒn(ə)rəs
AM 'sɑnərəs

sonorously
BR 'sɒn(ə)rəsli
AM 'sɑnərəsli

sonorousness
BR 'sɒn(ə)rəsnəs
AM 'sɑnərəsnəs

sonship
BR 'sʌnʃɪp
AM 'sən,ʃɪp

sonsie
BR 'sɒns|i, -ɪə(r), -ɪɪst
AM 'sənzi, -ər, -ɪst

sons-in-law
BR 'sʌnzɪnlɔː(r)
AM 'sənzən,lɔ, 'sənzən,lɑ

sons-of-bitches
BR ˌsʌnzəv'bɪtʃɪz
AM ˌsənzə(v)'bɪtʃɪz

sons-of-guns
BR ˌsʌnzəv'gʌnz
AM ˌsənzə(v)'gənz

sonsy
BR 'sɒns|i, -ɪə(r), -ɪɪst
AM 'sənzi, -ər, -ɪst

Sontag
BR 'sɒntag
AM 'sɑn,tæg

Sonya
BR 'sɒnɪə(r), 'sɒnjə(r)
AM 'sɑnjə, 'soʊnjə

sool
BR suːl, -z, -ɪŋ, -d
AM sul, -z, -ɪŋ, -d

sooler
BR 'suːlə(r), -z
AM 'sulər, -z

soon
BR suːn, -ə(r), -ɪst
AM sun, -ər, -əst

soonish
BR 'suːnɪʃ
AM 'sunɪʃ

soot
BR sʊt
AM sʊt

sooterkin
BR 'suːtəkɪn, -z
AM 'sʊdərkən, -z

sooth
BR suːθ
AM suθ

soothe
BR suːð, -z, -ɪŋ, -d
AM suð, -z, -ɪŋ, -d

soother
BR 'suːðə(r), -z
AM 'suðər, -z

soothingly
BR 'suːðɪŋli
AM 'suðɪŋli

soothsaid
BR 'suːθsɛd
AM 'suθ,sɛd

soothsay
BR 'suːθseɪ, -z, -ɪŋ
AM 'suθ,seɪ, -z, -ɪŋ

soothsayer
BR 'suːθ,seɪə(r), -z
AM 'suθ,seɪər, -z

sootily
BR 'sʊtɪli
AM 'sʊdəli

sootiness
BR 'sʊtɪnɪs
AM 'sʊdinɪs

sooty
BR 'sʊt|i, -ɪə(r), -ɪɪst
AM 'sʊdi, -ər, -ɪst

sop
BR sɒp, -s, -ɪŋ, -t
AM sɑp, -s, -ɪŋ, -t

Soper
BR 'səʊpə(r)
AM 'soʊpər

Sophia
BR sə(ʊ)'fʌɪə(r), sə(ʊ)'fiːə(r)
AM soʊ'fiə, 'soʊfiə

Sophie
BR 'səʊfi
AM 'soʊfi

sophism
BR 'sɒfɪz(ə)m
AM 'sɑ,fɪzəm, 'soʊ,fɪzəm

sophist
BR 'sɒfɪst, -s
AM 'sɑfəst, 'soʊfəst, -s

sophister
BR 'sɒfɪstə(r), -z
AM 'sɑfəstər, -z

sophistic
BR sə'fɪstɪk
AM sə'fɪstɪk

sophistical
BR sə'fɪstɪkl
AM sə'fɪstəkəl

sophistically
BR sə'fɪstɪkli
AM sə'fɪstək(ə)li

sophisticate[1]
noun
BR sə'fɪstɪkeɪt, sə'fɪstɪkət, -s
AM sə'fɪstə,keɪt, sə'fɪstəkət, -s

sophisticate[2]
verb
BR sə'fɪstɪkeɪt, -s, -ɪŋ, -ɪd
AM sə'fɪstə,keɪ|t, -ts, -dɪŋ, -dɪd

sophisticatedly
BR sə'fɪstɪkeɪtɪdli
AM sə'fɪstə,keɪdɪdli

sophistication
BR səˌfɪstɪ'keɪʃn
AM səˌfɪstə'keɪʃən

sophistry
BR 'sɒfɪstri
AM 'sɑfəstri, 'soʊfəstri

Sophoclean
BR ˌsɒfə'kliːən
AM ˌsɑfə'kliən

Sophocles
BR 'sɒfəkliːz
AM 'sɑfə,kliz

sophomore
BR 'sɒfəmɔː(r), -z
AM 'sɔf(ə)ˌmɔ(ə)r, 'sɑf(ə)ˌmɔ(ə)r, -z

sophomoric
BR ˌsɒfə'mɒrɪk
AM ˌsɔf(ə)'mɔrɪk, ˌsɑf(ə)'mɔrɪk

Sophy
BR 'səʊf|i, -ɪz
AM 'soʊfi, -z

soporiferous
BR ˌsɒpə'rɪf(ə)rəs
AM ˌsɑpə'rɪf(ə)rəs

soporific
BR ˌsɒpə'rɪfɪk
AM ˌsɑpə'rɪfɪk

soporifically
BR ˌsɒpə'rɪfɪkli
AM ˌsɑpə'rɪfək(ə)li

soppily
BR 'sɒpɪli
AM 'sɑpəli

soppiness
BR 'sɒpɪnɪs
AM 'sɑpinɪs

sopping
BR 'sɒpɪŋ
AM 'sɑpɪŋ

soppy
BR 'sɒp|i, -ɪə(r), -ɪɪst
AM 'sɑpi, -ər, -ɪst

sopranino
BR ˌsɒprə'niːnəʊ, -z
AM ˌsɑprə'niˌnoʊ, -z

sopranist
BR sə'prɑːnɪst, -s
AM sə'prænəst, sə'prɑnəst, -s

soprano
BR sə'prɑːnəʊ, -z
AM sə'prænoʊ, sə'prɑnoʊ, -z

Sopwith
BR 'sɒpwɪθ
AM 'sɑpˌwɪθ

sora
BR 'sɔːrə(*r*), 'səʊrə(*r*), -z
AM 'sɔrə, -z

Soraya
BR sə'rʌɪə(*r*)
AM sə'raɪə

sorb[1]
BR sɔːb, -z
AM sɔ(ə)rb, -z

sorb[2]
BR sɔːb, -z
AM sɔ(ə)rb, -z

sorbefacient
BR ˌsɔːbɪ'feɪʃ(ə)nt, -s
AM ˌsɔrbə'feɪʃənt, -s

sorbet
BR 'sɔːbeɪ, 'sɔːbɪt, -s
AM 'sɔrbət, -s

Sorbian
BR 'sɔːbɪən, -z
AM 'sɔrbiən, -z

sorbic
BR 'sɔːbɪk
AM 'sɔrbɪk

sorbitol
BR 'sɔːbɪtɒl
AM 'sɔrbəˌtɔl, 'sɔrbəˌtɑl

sorbo
BR 'sɔːbəʊ
AM 'sɔrˌboʊ

Sorbonne
BR sɔː'bɒn
AM sɔr'bən

sorbose
BR 'sɔːbəʊz, 'sɔːbəʊs
AM 'sɔrˌboʊs

sorcerer
BR 'sɔːs(ə)rə(r), -z
AM 'sɔrs(ə)rər, -z

sorceress
BR 'sɔːs(ə)rɪs, 'sɔːs(ə)rɛs, -ɪz
AM 'sɔrs(ə)rəs, -əz

sorcerous
BR 'sɔːs(ə)rəs
AM 'sɔrs(ə)rəs

sorcery
BR 'sɔːs(ə)ri
AM 'sɔrs(ə)ri

sordid
BR 'sɔːdɪd
AM 'sɔrdəd

sordidly
BR 'sɔːdɪdli
AM 'sɔrdədli

sordidness
BR 'sɔːdɪdnɪs
AM 'sɔrdədnɪs

sordini
BR sɔː'diːniː
AM sɔr'dini

sordino
BR sɔː'diːnəʊ
AM sɔr'dinoʊ

sordor
BR 'sɔːdə(r), -z
AM 'sɔrdər, 'sɔrˌdɔ(ə)r, -z

sore
BR sɔː(r), -z, -ə(r), -ɪst
AM sɔ(ə)r, -z, -ər, -əst

sorehead
BR 'sɔːhɛd, -z
AM 'sɔrˌ(h)ɛd, -z

sorel
BR 'sɒrəl, 'sɒrl̩, -z
AM 'sɔrəl, -z

sorely
BR 'sɔːli
AM 'sɔrli

soreness
BR 'sɔːnəs
AM 'sɔrnəs

Sørensen
BR 'sɒrəns(ə)n, 'sɒrn̩s(ə)n
AM 'sɔrənsən
DAN 'sœʌ'sən
NO 'sœːrensen

sorghum
BR 'sɔːgəm
AM 'sɔrgəm

sori
BR 'sɔːrʌɪ
AM 'sɔˌraɪ

sorites
BR sə'rʌɪtiːz
AM sə'raɪdiz

soritical
BR sə'rɪtɪkl
AM sə'rɪdɪkl

Soroptimist
BR sə'rɒptɪmɪst, -s
AM sə'rɑptəməst, -s

sororicidal
BR səˌrɒrɪ'sʌɪdl
AM səˌrɔrə'saɪdəl

sororicide
BR sə'rɒrɪsʌɪd, -z
AM sə'rɔrəˌsaɪd, -z

sorority
BR sə'rɒrɪt|i, -ɪz
AM sə'rɔrədi, -z

soroses
BR sə'rəʊsiːz
AM sə'roʊˌsiz

sorosis
BR sə'rəʊsɪs
AM sə'roʊsəs

sorption
BR 'sɔːpʃn
AM 'sɔrpʃən

sorrel
BR 'sɒrəl, 'sɒrl̩, -z
AM 'sɔrəl, -z

Sorrell
BR 'sɒrəl, 'sɒrl̩
AM 'sɔrəl

Sorrento
BR sə'rɛntəʊ
AM sə'rɛn(t)oʊ

sorrily
BR 'sɒrɪli
AM 'sɔrəli, 'sɑrəli

sorriness
BR 'sɒrɪnɪs
AM 'sɔrinɪs, 'sɑrinɪs

sorrow
BR 'sɒrəʊ, -z, -ɪŋ, -d
AM 'sɔroʊ, 'sɑroʊ, -z, -ɪŋ, -d

sorrower
BR 'sɒrəʊə(r), -z
AM 'sɔroʊər, 'sɑroʊər, -z

sorrowful
BR 'sɒrə(ʊ)f(ʊ)l
AM 'sɔrəfəl, 'sɑrəfəl

sorrowfully
BR 'sɒrə(ʊ)fʊli, 'sɒrə(ʊ)fl̩i
AM 'sɔrəf(ə)li, 'sɑrəf(ə)li

sorrowfulness
BR 'sɒrə(ʊ)f(ʊ)lnəs
AM 'sɔrəfəlnəs, 'sɑrəfəlnəs

sorry
BR 'sɒr|i, -ɪə(r), -ɪɪst
AM 'sɔri, 'sɑri, -ər, -ɪst

sort
BR sɔːt, -s, -ɪŋ, -ɪd
AM sɔ(ə)rt, -ts, 'sɔrdɪŋ, 'sɔrdəd

sorta
BR 'sɔːtə(*r*)
AM 'sɔrdə

sortable
BR 'sɔːtəbl
AM 'sɔrdəbəl

sortal
BR 'sɔːtl, -z
AM 'sɔrdl, -z

sorter
BR 'sɔːtə(r), -z
AM 'sɔrdər, -z

sortie
BR 'sɔːt|i, -ɪz
AM 'sɔrdi, ˌsɔr'ti, -z

sortilege
BR 'sɔːtɪlɪdʒ
AM 'sɔrdlɪdʒ

sortition
BR sɔː'tɪʃn, -z
AM sɔr'tɪʃən, -z

sorus
BR 'sɔːrəs
AM 'sɔrəs

SOS
BR ˌɛsəʊ'ɛs, -ɪz
AM ˌɛsˌoʊ'ɛs, -əz

so-so
BR 'səʊsəʊ, ˌsəʊ'səʊ
AM ˈsoʊˈsoʊ

sostenuto
BR ˌsɒstɪ'n(j)uːtəʊ
AM ˈsɔstə'nudoʊ, ˈsɑstə'nudoʊ

sot
BR sɒt, -s
AM sɑt, -s

soteriological
BR sə(ʊ)ˌtɪərɪə'lɒdʒɪkl
AM soʊˌtɪriə'lɑdʒəkəl

soteriology
BR sə(ʊ)ˌtɪərɪ'ɒlədʒi
AM soʊˌtɪri'ɑlədʒi

Sotheby
BR 'sʌðəb|i, -ɪz
AM 'səðəbi, -z

Sothic
BR 'səʊθɪk, 'sɒθɪk
AM 'soʊθɪk, 'sɑθɪk

Sotho
BR 'suːtuː, 'səʊtəʊ, -z
AM 'soʊdoʊ, 'soʊθoʊ, -z

Soto
BR 'səʊtəʊ
AM 'soʊdoʊ

sottish
BR 'sɒtɪʃ
AM 'sɑdɪʃ

sottishly
BR 'sɒtɪʃli
AM 'sɑdɪʃli

sottishness
BR 'sɒtɪʃnɨs
AM 'sɑdɪʃnɨs

sotto voce
BR ˌsɒtəʊ 'vəʊtʃi
AM ¦sɑdoʊ 'voʊtʃi, ¦soʊdoʊ +

sou
BR suː, -z
AM su, -z

soubrette
BR suː'brɛt, sʊ'brɛt, -s
AM su'brɛt, -s

soubriquet
BR 'suːbrɪkeɪ, -z
AM ¦soʊbrə|¦keɪ, ¦soʊbrə|¦kɛt, -¦keɪz\-¦kɛts

souchong
BR ˌsuː'(t)ʃɒŋ, -z
AM ¦su'tʃɔŋ, ¦su'tʃɑŋ, -z

souffle
sound
BR 'suːfl, -z
AM 'sufəl, -z

soufflé
food
BR 'suːfleɪ, -z
AM su'fleɪ, -z

Soufrière
BR ˌsuːfrɪ'ɛː(r)
AM ˌsufri'(j)ɛ(ə)r

sough
BR saʊ, sʌf, saʊz\sʌfs, saʊɪŋ\sʌfɪŋ, saʊd\sʌft
AM səf, saʊ, səfs\saʊz, səfɪŋ\saʊɪŋ, səft\saʊd

sought
BR sɔːt
AM sɔt, sɑt

sought-after
BR 'sɔːtˌɑːftə(r), 'sɔːtˌaftə(r)
AM 'sɔdˌæftər, 'sɑdˌæftər

souk
BR suːk, -s
AM suk, -s

soukous
BR 'suːkəs, 'suːkuːs
AM 'sukəs

soul
BR səʊl, -z
AM soʊl, -z

Soulbury
BR 'səʊlb(ə)ri
AM 'soʊlˌbɛri

soulful
BR 'səʊlf(ʊ)l
AM 'soʊlfəl

soulfully
BR 'səʊlfʊli, 'səʊlfl̩i
AM 'soʊlfəli

soulfulness
BR 'səʊlf(ʊ)lnəs
AM 'soʊlfəlnəs

soulless
BR 'səʊlləs
AM 'soʊ(l)ləs

soullessly
BR 'səʊlləsli
AM 'soʊ(l)ləsli

soullessness
BR 'səʊlləsnəs
AM 'soʊ(l)ləsnəs

soulmate
BR 'səʊlmeɪt, -s
AM 'soʊlˌmeɪt, -s

soulster
BR 'səʊlstə(r), -z
AM 'soʊlstər, -z

sound
BR saʊnd, -z, -ɪŋ, -ɨd, -ə(r), -ɨst
AM saʊnd, -z, -ɪŋ, -əd, -ər, -əst

soundalike
BR 'saʊndəlʌɪk, -s
AM 'saʊndəˌlaɪk, -s

soundbite
BR 'saʊn(d)bʌɪt, -s
AM 'saʊn(d)ˌbaɪt, -s

soundboard
BR 'saʊn(d)bɔːd, -z
AM 'saʊn(d)ˌbɔ(ə)rd, -z

soundbox
BR 'saʊn(d)bɒks, -ɨz
AM 'saʊn(d)ˌbɑks, -əz

soundcheck
BR 'saʊn(d)tʃɛk, -s
AM 'saʊn(d)ˌtʃɛk, -s

sounder
BR 'saʊndə(r), -z
AM 'saʊndər, -z

soundhole
BR 'saʊndhəʊl, -z
AM 'saʊn(d)ˌ(h)oʊl, -z

sounding
BR 'saʊndɪŋ, -z
AM 'saʊndɪŋ, -z

soundless
BR 'saʊndləs
AM 'saʊn(d)ləs

soundlessly
BR 'saʊndləsli
AM 'saʊn(d)ləsli

soundlessness
BR 'saʊndləsnəs
AM 'saʊn(d)ləsnəs

soundly
BR 'saʊndli
AM 'saʊn(d)li

soundness
BR 'saʊn(d)nəs
AM 'saʊn(d)nəs

soundproof
BR 'saʊn(d)pruːf, -s, -ɪŋ, -t
AM 'saʊn(d)ˌpruf, -s, -ɪŋ, -t

soundstage
BR 'saʊn(d)steɪdʒ, -ɨz
AM 'saʊn(d)ˌsteɪdʒ, -ɨz

soundtrack
BR 'saʊn(d)trak, -s
AM 'saʊn(d)ˌtræk, -s

Souness
BR 'suːnɨs
AM 'sunəs

soup
BR suːp, -s, -ɪŋ, -t
AM sup, -s, -ɪŋ, -t

soupcon
BR 'suːpsɒ̃, 'suːpsɒn, -z
AM sup'sɔn, sup'sɑn, -z

soupçon
BR 'suːpsɒ̃, 'suːpsɒn, -z
AM sup'sɔn, sup'sɑn, -z

souped-up
BR ˌsuːpt'ʌp
AM ˌsup'təp

soupily
BR 'suːpɨli
AM 'supəli

soupiness
BR 'suːpɪnɨs
AM 'supinɨs

soupspoon
BR 'suːpspuːn, -z
AM 'supˌspun, -z

soupy
BR 'suːp|i, -ɪə(r), -ɪɨst
AM 'supi, -ər, -ɨst

sour
BR 'saʊə(r), -z, -ɪŋ, -d, -ə(r), -ɨst
AM 'saʊər, -z, -ɪŋ, -d, -ər, -əst

source
BR sɔːs, -ɨz
AM sɔ(ə)rs, -əz

sourcebook
BR 'sɔːsbʊk, -s
AM 'sɔrsˌbʊk, -s

sourdough
BR 'saʊədəʊ
AM 'saʊərˌdoʊ

sour grapes
BR ˌsaʊə 'greɪps
AM ˌsaʊər 'greɪps

sourish
BR 'saʊərɪʃ
AM 'saʊərɪʃ

sourly
BR 'saʊəli
AM 'saʊərli

sourness
BR 'saʊənəs
AM 'saʊərnəs

sourpuss
BR 'saʊəpʊs, -ɨz
AM 'saʊərˌpʊs, -əz

soursop
BR 'saʊəsɒp, -s
AM 'saʊərˌsɑp, -s

Sousa
BR 'suːzə(*r*)
AM 'suzə

sousaphone
BR 'suːzəfəʊn, -z
AM 'suzəˌfoʊn, -z

sousaphonist
BR 'suːzəfəʊnɪst, -s
AM 'suzəˌfoʊnəst, -s

souse
BR saʊs, -ɨz, -ɪŋ, -t
AM saʊs, -əz, -ɪŋ, -t

souslik
BR 'suːslɪk, -s
AM 'suslɪk, -s

Sousse
BR suːs
AM sus

sous vide
BR suː 'viːd
AM su 'vid

soutache
BR suː'taʃ, -ɨz
AM su'tɑʃ, -əz

soutane
BR suː'tɑːn, suː'tan, -z
AM su'tɑn, -z

souteneur
BR ˌsuːtə'nəː(r), -z
AM ˌsudə'nər, ˌsutn'ər, -z

souter
BR 'suːtə(r), -z
AM 'sudər, -z

souterrain
BR 'suːtəreɪn, -z
AM ˌsutə'reɪn, -z

south
BR saʊθ
AM saʊθ

South Africa
BR ˌsaʊθ 'afrɪkə(*r*)
AM ˌsaʊθ 'æfrəkə

South African
BR ˌsaʊθ 'afrɪk(ə)n, -z
AM ˌsaʊθ 'æfrəkən, -z

Southall[1]
place in UK
BR 'saʊθɔːl
AM 'saʊθɔl, 'saʊθɑl

Southall[2]
surname
BR 'sʌðl, 'sʌðɔːl
AM 'səðəl

Southam
BR 'saʊð(ə)m
AM 'saʊθəm

South America
BR ˌsaʊθ ə'mɛrɪkə(*r*)
AM ˌsaʊθ ə'mɛrəkə

South American
BR ˌsaʊθ ə'mɛrɪk(ə)n, -z
AM ˌsaʊθ ə'mɛrəkən, -z

Southampton
BR ˌsaʊθˈham(p)tən, saʊˈθam(p)tən
AM ˌsaʊθˈ(h)æm(p)tən

southbound
BR ˈsaʊθbaʊnd
AM ˈsaʊθˌbaʊnd

South Carolina
BR ˌsaʊθ ˌkarəˈlʌɪnə(r)
AM ˌsaʊθ ˌkɛrəˈlaɪnə

South China Sea
BR ˌsaʊθ ˌtʃʌɪnə ˈsiː
AM ˌsaʊθ ˌtʃaɪnə ˈsi

South Dakota
BR ˌsaʊθ dəˈkəʊtə(r)
AM ˌsaʊθdəˈkoʊdə

Southdown
BR ˈsaʊθdaʊn, -z
AM ˈsaʊθˌdaʊn, -z

southeast
BR ˌsaʊθˈiːst
AM ˌsaʊθˈist

southeaster
BR ˌsaʊθˈiːstə(r), -z
AM ˌsaʊθˈistər, -z

southeasterly
BR ˌsaʊθˈiːstəl|i, -ɪz
AM ˌsaʊθˈistərli, -z

southeastern
BR ˌsaʊθˈiːst(ə)n
AM ˌsaʊθˈistərn

south-easterner
BR ˌsaʊθˈiːstənə(r), ˌsaʊθˈiːstn̩ə(r), -z
AM ˌsaʊθˈistərnər, -z

southeastward
BR ˌsaʊθˈiːstwəd, -z
AM ˌsaʊθˈis(t)wərd, -z

Southend
BR ˌsaʊθˈɛnd
AM ˌsaʊθˈɛnd

souther
BR ˈsaʊθə(r), -z
AM ˈsaʊðər, -z

southerliness
BR ˈsʌðəlɪnɨs
AM ˈsəðərlinɨs

southerly
BR ˈsʌðəli
AM ˈsəðərli

southern
BR ˈsʌðn
AM ˈsəðərn

Southerndown
BR ˈsʌðndaʊn
AM ˈsəðərnˌdaʊn

southerner
BR ˈsaʊðənə(r), ˈsaʊðn̩ə(r), -z
AM ˈsəðərnər, -z

southernmost
BR ˈsʌðnməʊst
AM ˈsəðərnˌmoʊst

southernwood
BR ˈsʌðnwʊd, -z
AM ˈsəðərnˌwʊd, -z

Southey
BR ˈsaʊði, ˈsʌði
AM ˈsaʊði, ˈsəði

southing
BR ˈsaʊðɪŋ, ˈsaʊθɪŋ, -z
AM ˈsaʊðɪŋ, -z

southland
BR ˈsaʊθland
AM ˈsaʊθˌlænd

southpaw
BR ˈsaʊθpɔː(r), -z
AM ˈsaʊθˌpɔ, ˈsaʊθˌpɑ, -z

south-southeast[1]
BR ˌsaʊθsaʊθˈiːst
AM ˈˌsaʊθˌsaʊθˈist

south-southeast[2]
nautical use
BR ˌsaʊsaʊˈiːst
AM ˈˌsaʊˌsaʊˈist

south-southwest[1]
BR ˌsaʊθsaʊθˈwɛst
AM ˈˌsaʊθˌsaʊθˈwɛst

south-southwest[2]
nautical use
BR ˌsaʊsaʊˈwɛst
AM ˈˌsaʊˌsaʊˈwɛst

South Utsire
BR ˌsaʊθ ʊtˈsɪərə(r)
AM ˌsaʊθ ʊtˈsɪ(ə)r

southward
BR ˈsaʊθwəd, -z
AM ˈsaʊθwərd, -z

southwardly
BR ˈsaʊθwədli
AM ˈsaʊθwərdli

Southwark
BR ˈsʌðək
AM ˈsəðərk, ˈsaʊθˌwərk

Southwell
BR ˈsʌðl, ˈsaʊθw(ɛ)l
AM ˈsaʊθˌwɛl

southwest
BR ˌsaʊθˈwɛst
AM ˌsaʊθˈwɛst

southwester[1]
BR ˌsaʊθˈwɛstə(r), -z
AM ˌsaʊθˈwɛstər, -z

southwester[2]
nautical use
BR ˌsaʊˈwɛstə(r), -z
AM ˌsaʊˈwɛstər, -z

southwesterly[1]
BR ˌsaʊθˈwɛstəl|i, -ɪz
AM ˌsaʊθˈwɛstərli, -z

southwesterly[2]
nautical use
BR ˌsaʊˈwɛstəl|i, -ɪz
AM ˌsaʊˈwɛstərli, -z

southwestern
BR ˌsaʊθˈwɛst(ə)n
AM ˌsaʊθˈwɛstərn

southwesterner
BR ˌsaʊθˈwɛstənə(r), ˌsaʊθˈwɛstn̩ə(r), -z
AM ˌsaʊθˈwɛstərnər, -z

southwestward
BR ˌsaʊθˈwɛstwəd, -z
AM ˌsaʊθˈwɛs(t)wərd, -z

Southwold
BR ˈsaʊθwəʊld
AM ˈsaʊθˌwoʊld

Souttar
BR ˈsuːtə(r)
AM ˈsudər

Soutter
BR ˈsuːtə(r)
AM ˈsudər

souvenir
BR ˌsuːvəˈnɪə(r), -z
AM ˌsuvəˈnɪ(ə)r, -z

souvlaki
BR suːˈvlɑːki
AM suˈvlɑki

souvlakia
BR suːˈvlɑːkɪə(r)
AM suˈvlɑkiə

sou'wester
BR ˌsaʊˈwɛstə(r), -z
AM ˌsaʊˈwɛstər, -z

sovereign
BR ˈsɒvr(ɪ)n, -z
AM ˈsɑv(ə)rən, ˈsɑvərn, -z

sovereignly
BR ˈsɒvr(ɪ)nli
AM ˈsɑv(ə)rənli, ˈsɑvərnli

sovereignty
BR ˈsɒvr(ɪ)nti
AM ˈsɑv(ə)rən(t)i, ˈsɑvərn(t)i

soviet
BR ˈsəʊvɪət, ˈsɒvɪət, -s
AM ˈsoʊviət, ˈsoʊviˌɛt, -s

Sovietisation
BR ˌsəʊvɪətʌɪˈzeɪʃn, ˌsɒvɪətʌɪˈzeɪʃn
AM ˌsoʊviədəˈzeɪʃən, ˌsoʊviəˌtaɪˈzeɪʃən

Sovietise
BR ˈsəʊvɪətʌɪz, ˈsɒvɪətʌɪz, -ɨz, -ɪŋ, -d
AM ˈsoʊviəˌtaɪz, -ɨz, -ɪŋ, -d

Sovietization
BR ˌsəʊvɪətʌɪˈzeɪʃn, ˌsɒvɪətʌɪˈzeɪʃn
AM ˌsoʊviədəˈzeɪʃən, ˌsoʊviəˌtaɪˈzeɪʃən

Sovietize
BR ˈsəʊvɪətʌɪz, ˈsɒvɪətʌɪz, -ɨz, -ɪŋ, -d
AM ˈsoʊviəˌtaɪz, -ɨz, -ɪŋ, -d

sovietologist
BR ˌsəʊvɪəˈtɒlədʒɪst, ˌsɒvɪəˈtɒlədʒɪst, -s
AM ˌsoʊviəˈtɑlədʒəst, -s

Soviet Union
BR ˌsəʊvɪət ˈjuːnɪən, ˌsɒvɪət +
AM ˌsoʊviət ˈjunjən, ˌsoʊviɛt ˈjunjən

sow[1]
noun
BR saʊ, -z
AM saʊ, -z

sow[2]
verb
BR səʊ, -z, -ɪŋ, -d
AM soʊ, -z, -ɪŋ, -d

sowback
BR ˈsaʊbak, -s
AM ˈsaʊˌbæk, -s

sowbelly
BR ˈsaʊˌbɛl|i, -ɪz
AM ˈsaʊˌbɛli, -z

sowbread
BR ˈsaʊbrɛd, -z
AM ˈsaʊˌbrɛd, -z

sower
BR ˈsəʊə(r), -z
AM ˈsoʊər, -z

Sowerby
BR ˈsaʊəbi
AM ˈsaʊərbi

Sowetan
BR səˈwɛtən, -z
AM səˈwɛtn, -z

Soweto
BR səˈwɛtəʊ
AM səˈwɛdoʊ

sowing
BR ˈsəʊɪŋ, -z
AM ˈsoʊɪŋ, -z

sown
BR səʊn
AM soʊn

sowthistle
BR ˈsaʊˌθɪsl, -z
AM ˈsaʊˌθɪsəl, -z

sox
BR sɒks
AM sɑks

soy
BR sɔɪ
AM sɔɪ

soya
BR ˈsɔɪə(r)
AM ˈsɔɪ(ə)

soybean
BR ˈsɔɪbiːn, -z
AM ˈsɔɪˌbin, -z

Soyinka
BR ʃɔɪˈɪŋkə(r)
AM sɔɪˈɪŋkə

Soyuz
BR ˈsɔɪjʊz
AM ˈsɑˌjuz, ˈsɔɪˌjuz
RUS saˈjus

sozzled
BR ˈsɒzld
AM ˈsɑzəld

spa
BR spɑː(r), -z

AM spɑ, -z

space
BR speɪs, -ɪz, -ɪŋ, -t
AM speɪs, -ɪz, -ɪŋ, -t

space-age
BR 'speɪseɪdʒ
AM 'speɪs,eɪdʒ

spacecraft
BR 'speɪskrɑːft, 'speɪskraft
AM 'speɪs,kræf(t)

spaced-out
BR ˌspeɪst'aʊt
AM 'speɪs'taʊt

spaceflight
BR 'speɪsflʌɪt, -s
AM 'speɪs,flaɪt, -s

spacelab
BR 'speɪslab, -z
AM 'speɪs,læb, -z

spaceman
BR 'speɪsman, 'speɪsmən
AM 'speɪs,mæn, 'speɪsmən

spacemen
BR 'speɪsmɛn, 'speɪsmən
AM 'speɪs,mɛn, 'speɪsmən

spacer
BR 'speɪsə(r), -z
AM 'speɪsər, -z

spaceship
BR 'speɪsʃɪp, -s
AM 'speɪ(s),ʃɪp, -s

spaceshot
BR 'speɪsʃɒt, -s
AM 'speɪ(s),ʃɑt, -s

spacesuit
BR 'speɪss(j)uːt, -s
AM 'speɪ(s),sut, -s

spacewalk
BR 'speɪswɔːk, -s
AM 'speɪs,wɔk, 'speɪs,wɑk, -s

spaceward
BR 'speɪswəd
AM 'speɪswərd

spacewoman
BR 'speɪs,wʊmən
AM 'speɪs,wʊmən

spacewomen
BR 'speɪs,wɪmɪn
AM 'speɪs,wɪmɪn

spacey
BR 'speɪs|i, -ɪə(r), -ɪɪst
AM 'speɪsi, -ər, -ɨst

spacial
BR 'speɪʃl
AM 'speɪʃəl

spacing
BR 'speɪsɪŋ, -z
AM 'speɪsɪŋ, -z

spacious
BR 'speɪʃəs
AM 'speɪʃəs

spaciously
BR 'speɪʃəsli
AM 'speɪʃəsli

spaciousness
BR 'speɪʃəsnəs
AM 'speɪʃəsnəs

spacy
BR 'speɪs|i, -ɪə(r), -ɪɪst
AM 'speɪsi, -ər, -ɨst

spade
BR speɪd, -z, -ɪŋ, -ɨd
AM speɪd, -z, -ɪŋ, -ɨd

spadeful
BR 'speɪdfʊl, -z
AM 'speɪd,fʊl, -z

spadework
BR 'speɪdwəːk
AM 'speɪd,wərk

spadiceous
BR speɪ'dɪʃəs, spə'deɪʃəs
AM speɪ'dɪʃəs, spə'dɪʃəs

spadicose
BR 'speɪdɨkəʊs
AM 'speɪdə,koʊs, 'speɪdə,koʊz

spadille
BR spə'dɪl, -z
AM spə'dɪl, -z

spadix
BR 'speɪdɪks, -ɨz
AM 'speɪdɪks, -ɨz

spado
BR 'spadəʊ, -z
AM 'spædoʊ, -z

spae
BR speɪ, -z, -ɪŋ, -d
AM speɪ, -z, -ɪŋ, -d

spaewife
BR 'speɪwʌɪf
AM 'speɪ,waɪf

spaewives
BR 'speɪwʌɪvz
AM 'speɪ,waɪvz

spaghetti
BR spə'gɛti
AM spə'gɛdi

spaghettini
BR ˌspagɛ'tiːni, ˌspagə'tiːni
AM ˌspægə'tini

spahi
BR 'spɑːhiː, -z
AM 'spɑ(h)i, -z

Spain
BR speɪn
AM speɪn

spake
BR speɪk
AM speɪk

Spalding
BR 'spɔːldɪŋ
AM 'spɔldɪŋ, 'spɑldɪŋ

spall
BR spɔːl, -z, -ɪŋ, -d
AM spɔl, spɑl, -z, -ɪŋ, -d

spallation
BR spɔː'leɪʃn, -z
AM spɔ'leɪʃən, spɑ'leɪʃən, -z

spalpeen
BR 'spalpiːn, -z
AM 'spɔl,pin, 'spɑl,pin, -z

Spam®
BR spam
AM spæm

span
BR span, -z, -ɪŋ, -d
AM spæn, -z, -ɪŋ, -d

spanakopita
BR ˌspanə'kɒpɪtə(r)
AM ˌspænə'kɔpədə, ˌspænə'kɑpədə

Spandau
BR 'spandaʊ, 'ʃpandaʊ
AM 'spændaʊ

spandrel
BR 'spandr(ə)l, -z
AM 'spændrəl, -z

spang
BR spaŋ
AM spæŋ

spangle
BR 'spaŋg|l, -lz, -l̩ɪŋ\-lɪŋ, -ld
AM 'spæŋg|əl, -əlz, -(ə)lɪŋ, -əld

Spanglish
BR 'spaŋglɪʃ
AM 'spæŋglɪʃ

spangly
BR 'spaŋgl̩|i, 'spaŋgl|i, -ɪə(r), -ɪɪst
AM 'spæŋ(ə)li, -ər, -ɨst

Spaniard
BR 'spanjəd, -z
AM 'spænjərd, -z

spaniel
BR 'spanjəl, -z
AM 'spænjəl, -z

Spanier
BR 'spanjə(r), 'spanjeɪ
AM 'spænjər

Spanish
BR 'spanɪʃ
AM 'spænɪʃ

Spanish-American
BR ˌspanɪʃə'mɛrɨk(ə)n
AM 'spænɪʃə'mɛrəkən

Spanishness
BR 'spanɨʃnɪs
AM 'spænɪʃnɪs

spank
BR spaŋ|k, -ks, -kɪŋ, -(k)t
AM spæŋ|k, -ks, -kɪŋ, -(k)t

spanker
BR 'spaŋkə(r), -z
AM 'spæŋkər, -z

spanking
BR 'spaŋkɪŋ, -z
AM 'spæŋkiŋ, -z

spanner
BR 'spanə(r), -z
AM 'spænər, -z

Spansule®
BR 'spansjuːl, -z
AM 'spæn,s(j)ul, -z

spar
BR spɑː(r), -z, -ɪŋ, -d
AM spɑr, -z, -ɪŋ, -d

sparable
BR 'sparəbl, -z
AM 'spɑrəbəl, -z

sparaxes
BR spə'raksiːz
AM spə'ræksiz

sparaxis
BR spə'raksɪs
AM spə'ræksəs

spare
BR spɛː(r), -z, -ɪŋ, -d, -ə(r), -ɨst
AM spɛ(ə)r, -z, -ɪŋ, -d, -ər, -əst

sparely
BR 'spɛːli
AM 'spɛrli

spareness
BR 'spɛːnəs
AM 'spɛrnəs

spare part
BR ˌspɛː 'pɑːt, -s
AM 'spɛr 'pɑrt, -s

sparer
BR 'spɛːrə(r), -z
AM 'spɛrər, -z

sparerib
BR 'spɛːrɪb, -z
AM 'spɛr,rɪb, -z

spare-time
BR ˌspɛː'tʌɪm
AM 'spɛr'taɪm

sparge
BR spɑːdʒ, -ɨz, -ɪŋ, -d
AM spɑrdʒ, -əz, -ɪŋ, -d

sparger
BR 'spɑːdʒə(r), -z
AM 'spɑrdʒər, -z

sparid
BR 'sparɪd, 'speɪrɪd, -z
AM 'spɛrəd, -z

sparing
BR 'spɛːrɪŋ
AM 'spɛrɪŋ

sparingly
BR 'spɛːrɪŋli
AM 'spɛrɪŋli

sparingness
BR 'spɛːrɪŋnɨs
AM 'spɛrɪŋnɪs

spark
BR spɑːk, -s, -ɪŋ, -t
AM spɑrk, -s, -ɪŋ, -t

Sparke
BR spɑːk
AM spɑrk

sparkish
BR 'spɑːkɪʃ
AM 'spɑrkɪʃ
sparkle
BR 'spɑːk|l, -lz, -l̩ɪŋ\-lɪŋ, -d
AM 'spɑrk|əl, -əlz, -(ə)lɪŋ, -əld
sparkler
BR 'spɑːklə(r), -z
AM 'spɑrk(ə)lər, -z
sparkless
BR 'spɑːkləs
AM 'spɑrkləs
sparklet
BR 'spɑːklɨt, -s
AM 'spɑrklət, -s
sparklingly
BR 'spɑːklɪŋli
AM 'spɑrk(ə)lɪŋli
sparkly
BR 'spɑːkli
AM 'spɑrk(ə)li
Sparks
BR spɑːks
AM spɑrks
sparky
BR 'spɑːk|i, -ɪz
AM 'spɑrki, -z
sparling
BR 'spɑːlɪŋ
AM 'spɑrlɪŋ
sparoid
BR 'sparɔɪd, -z
AM 'spɛˌrɔɪd, -z
sparrow
BR 'sparəʊ, -z
AM 'spɛroʊ, -z
sparrowhawk
BR 'sparə(ʊ)hɔːk, -s
AM 'spɛroʊˌhɔk, 'spɛroʊˌhɑk, -s
sparry
BR 'spɑːri
AM 'spɑri
sparse
BR spɑːs
AM spɑrs
sparsely
BR spɑːsli
AM spɑrsli
sparseness
BR spɑːsnəs
AM spɑrsnəs
sparsity
BR 'spɑːsɨti
AM 'spɑrsədi
Sparta
BR 'spɑːtə(r)
AM 'spɑrdə
Spartacist
BR 'spɑːtəsɪst, -s
AM 'spɑrdəsəst, -s
Spartacus
BR 'spɑːtəkəs
AM 'spɑrdəkəs
spartan
BR 'spɑːtn, -z
AM 'spɑrtn, -z
spasm
BR 'spaz(ə)m, -z
AM 'spæzəm, -z
spasmodic
BR spaz'mɒdɪk
AM spæz'mɑdɪk
spasmodically
BR spaz'mɒdɪkli
AM spæz'mɑdək(ə)li
spastic
BR 'spastɪk, -s
AM 'spæstɪk, -s
spastically
BR 'spastɨkli
AM 'spæstək(ə)li
spasticity
BR spa'stɪsɨti
AM spæ'stɪsɨdi
spat
BR spat, -s
AM spæt, -s
spatchcock
BR 'spatʃkɒk, -s, -ɪŋ, -t
AM 'spætʃˌkɑk, -s, -ɪŋ, -t
spate
BR speɪt, -s
AM speɪt, -s
spathaceous
BR spə'θeɪʃəs
AM spə'θeɪʃəs
spathe
BR speɪð, -z
AM speɪð, -z
spathic
BR 'spaθɪk
AM 'spæθɪk
spathose
BR 'spaθəʊs
AM 'speɪˌθoʊs, 'speɪˌθoʊz
spatial
BR 'speɪʃl
AM 'speɪʃəl
spatialise
BR 'speɪʃəlʌɪz, 'speɪʃl̩ʌɪz, -ɪz, -ɪŋ, -d
AM 'speɪʃəˌlaɪz, -ɪz, -ɪŋ, -d
spatiality
BR ˌspeɪʃɪ'alɨti
AM ˌspeɪʃi'ælədi
spatialize
BR 'speɪʃəlʌɪz, 'speɪʃl̩ʌɪz, -ɪz, -ɪŋ, -d
AM 'speɪʃəˌlaɪz, -ɪz, -ɪŋ, -d
spatially
BR 'speɪʃl̩i, 'speɪʃəli
AM 'speɪʃəli
spatio-temporal
BR ˌspeɪʃ(ɪ)əʊ'tɛmp(ə)rəl, ˌspeɪʃ(ɪ)əʊ'tɛmp(ə)rl̩
AM ˈspeɪʃ(i)oʊ'tɛmp(ə)rəl
spatio-temporally
BR ˌspeɪʃ(ɪ)əʊ'tɛmp(ə)rəli, ˌspeɪʃ(ɪ)əʊ'tɛmp(ə)rl̩i
AM ˈspeɪʃ(i)oʊ'tɛmp(ə)rəli
Spätlese
BR 'ʃpɛtˌleɪzə(r), -z
AM 'ʃpeɪtˌleɪzə, -z
Spätlesen
BR 'ʃpɛtˌleɪzn
AM 'ʃpeɪtˌleɪzn
spatter
BR 'spat|ə(r), -əz, -(ə)rɪŋ, -əd
AM 'spæd|ər, -ərz, -(ə)rɪŋ, -ərd
spatterdash
BR 'spatədaʃ, -ɨz
AM 'spædərˌdæʃ, -əz
spatula
BR 'spatjʉlə(r), 'spatʃʉlə(r), -z
AM 'spætʃələ, -z
spatulae
BR 'spatjʉliː, 'spatʃʉliː
AM 'spætʃəli, 'spætʃəˌlaɪ
spatulate
BR 'spatjʉlət, 'spatʃʉlət
AM 'spætʃələt
Spätzle
BR 'ʃpɛtslə(r), 'ʃpɛtsl
AM 'ʃpɛtsl
spavin
BR 'spav(ɪ)n, -d
AM 'spævən, -d
spawn
BR spɔːn, -z, -ɪŋ, -d
AM spɔn, spɑn, -z, -ɪŋ, -d
spawner
BR 'spɔːnə(r), -z
AM 'spɔnər, 'spɑnər, -z
spawning
BR 'spɔːnɪŋ, -z
AM 'spɔnɪŋ, 'spɑnɪŋ, -z
spay
BR speɪ, -z, -ɪŋ, -d
AM speɪ, -z, -ɪŋ, -d
Speaight
BR speɪt
AM speɪt
speak
BR spiːk, -s, -ɪŋ
AM spik, -s, -ɪŋ
speakable
BR 'spiːkəbl
AM 'spikəbəl
speakeasy
BR 'spiːkˌiːz|i, -ɪz
AM 'spikˌizi, -z
speaker
BR 'spiːkə(r), -z
AM 'spikər, -z
speakerphone
BR 'spiːkəfəʊn
AM 'spikərˌfoʊn
speakership
BR 'spiːkəʃɪp, -s
AM 'spikərˌʃɪp, -s
speaking clock
BR ˌspiːkɪŋ 'klɒk, -s
AM ˌspikɪŋ 'klɑk, -s
spear
BR spɪə(r), -z, -ɪŋ, -d
AM spɪ(ə)r, -z, -ɪŋ, -d
spearfish
BR 'spɪəfɪʃ, -ɨz
AM 'spɪrˌfɪʃ, -ɨz
speargun
BR 'spɪəgʌn, -z
AM 'spɪrˌgən, -z
spearhead
BR 'spɪəhɛd, -z, -ɪŋ, -ɨd
AM 'spɪrˌ(h)ɛd, -z, -ɪŋ, -əd
spearman
BR 'spɪəmən
AM 'spɪrmən
spearmen
BR 'spɪəmən
AM 'spɪrmən
spearmint
BR 'spɪəmɪnt
AM 'spɪrˌmɪnt
Spears
BR spɪəz
AM spɪ(ə)rz
spearwort
BR 'spɪəwəːt, -s
AM 'spɪrwərt, 'spɪrˌwɔ(ə)rt, -s
spec
BR spɛk, -s
AM spɛk, -s
special
BR 'spɛʃl, -z
AM 'spɛʃəl, -z
specialisation
BR ˌspɛʃəlʌɪ'zeɪʃn, ˌspɛʃl̩ʌɪ'zeɪʃn, -z
AM ˈspɛʃələ'zeɪʃən, ˈspɛʃəˌlaɪ'zeɪʃən, -z
specialise
BR 'spɛʃəlʌɪz, 'spɛʃl̩ʌɪz, -ɨz, -ɪŋ, -d
AM 'spɛʃəˌlaɪz, -ɨz, -ɪŋ, -d
specialism
BR 'spɛʃəlɪz(ə)m, 'spɛʃl̩ɪz(ə)m
AM 'spɛʃəˌlɪzəm
specialist
BR 'spɛʃəlɪst, 'spɛʃl̩ɪst, -s
AM 'spɛʃ(ə)ləst, -s
specialistic
BR ˌspɛʃə'lɪstɪk
AM ˌspɛʃə'lɪstɪk
speciality
BR ˌspɛʃɪ'alɨt|i, -ɪz
AM ˌspɛʃi'ælədi, -z

specialization
BR ˌspɛʃəlʌɪˈzeɪʃn, ˌspɛʃl̩ʌɪˈzeɪʃn, -z
AM ˌspɛʃələˈzeɪʃən, ˌspɛʃəˌlaɪˈzeɪʃən, -z

specialize
BR ˈspɛʃəlʌɪz, ˈspɛʃl̩ʌɪz, -ɪz, -ɪŋ, -d
AM ˈspɛʃəˌlaɪz, -ɪz, -ɪŋ, -d

specially
BR ˈspɛʃ(ə)li, ˈspɛʃl̩i
AM ˈspɛʃəli

specialness
BR ˈspɛʃlnəs
AM ˈspɛʃəlnəs

specialty
BR ˈspɛʃlt|i, -ɪz
AM ˈspɛʃəlti, -z

speciation
BR ˌspiːʃɪˈeɪʃn, -z
AM ˌspiʃiˈeɪʃən, ˌspisiˈeɪʃən, -z

specie
BR ˈspiːʃiː, ˈspiːʃi
AM ˈspiʃi, ˈspisi

species
BR ˈspiːʃɪz, ˈspiːʃiːz, ˈspiːsɪz, ˈspiːsiːz
AM ˈspiʃiz, ˈspisiz

speciesism
BR ˈspiːʃɪzɪz(ə)m, ˈspiːsɪzɪz(ə)m
AM ˈspiʃiˌzɪzəm, ˈspisiˌzɪzəm

speciesist
BR ˈspiːʃɪzɪst, ˈspiːsɪzɪst, -s
AM ˈspiʃizɪst, ˈspisizɪst, -s

specifiable
BR ˈspɛsɪfʌɪəbl
AM ˌspɛsəˈfaɪəbəl

specific
BR spɪˈsɪfɪk, -s
AM spəˈsɪfɪk, -s

specifically
BR spɪˈsɪfɪkli
AM spəˈsɪfək(ə)li

specification
BR ˌspɛsɪfɪˈkeɪʃn, -z
AM ˌspɛsəfəˈkeɪʃən, -z

specificity
BR ˌspɛsɪˈfɪsɪti
AM ˌspɛsəˈfɪsɨdi

specificness
BR spɪˈsɪfɪknɨs
AM spəˈsɪfɪknɨs

specifier
BR ˈspɛsɪfʌɪə(r), -z
AM ˈspɛsəˌfaɪər, -z

specify
BR ˈspɛsɪfʌɪ, -z, -ɪŋ, -d
AM ˈspɛsəˌfaɪ, -z, -ɪŋ, -d

specimen
BR ˈspɛsɪmɪn, -z
AM ˈspɛsəmən, -z

speciological
BR ˌspiːʃɪəˈlɒdʒɪkl, ˌspiːsɪəˈlɒdʒɪkl
AM ˌspiʃiəˈlɑdʒəkəl, ˌspisiəˈlɑdʒəkəl

speciology
BR ˌspiːʃɪˈɒlədʒi, ˌspiːsɪˈɒlədʒi
AM ˌspiʃiˈɑlədʒi, ˌspisiˈɑlədʒi

speciosity
BR ˌspiːʃɪˈɒsɪti, ˌspiːsɪˈɒsɪti
AM ˌspiʃiˈɑsədi, ˌspisiˈɑsədi

specious
BR ˈspiːʃəs
AM ˈspiʃəs

speciously
BR ˈspiːʃəsli
AM ˈspiʃəsli

speciousness
BR ˈspiːʃəsnəs
AM ˈspiʃəsnəs

speck
BR spɛk, -s
AM spɛk, -s

speckle
BR ˈspɛk|l, -lz, -l̩ɪŋ\-lɪŋ, -ld
AM ˈspɛkəl, -z, -ɪŋ, -d

speckless
BR ˈspɛkləs
AM ˈspɛkləs

specs
BR ˈspɛks
AM ˈspɛks

spectacle
BR ˈspɛktəkl, -z, -ld
AM ˈspɛktəkəl, -z, -ld

spectacular
BR spɛkˈtakjʉlə(r), -z
AM spɛkˈtækjələr, -z

spectacularly
BR spɛkˈtakjʉləli
AM spɛkˈtækjələrli

spectate
BR spɛkˈteɪt, -s, -ɪŋ, -ɨd
AM spɛkˈteɪ|t, -ts, -dɪŋ, -dɨd

spectator
BR spɛkˈteɪtə(r), -z
AM ˈspɛkˌteɪdər, -z

spectatorial
BR ˌspɛktəˈtɔːrɪəl
AM ˌspɛktəˈtɔriəl

specter
BR ˈspɛktə(r), -z
AM ˈspɛktər, -z

Spector
BR ˈspɛktə(r)
AM ˈspɛktər

spectra
BR ˈspɛktrə(*r*)
AM ˈspɛktrə

spectral
BR ˈspɛktr(ə)l
AM ˈspɛktrəl

spectrally
BR ˈspɛktrəli, ˈspɛktr̩li
AM ˈspɛktrəli

spectre
BR ˈspɛktə(r), -z
AM ˈspɛktər, -z

spectrochemistry
BR ˌspɛktrə(ʊ)ˈkɛmɨstri
AM ˌspɛktroʊˈkɛmestri

spectrogram
BR ˈspɛktrə(ʊ)gram, -z
AM ˈspɛktrəˌgræm, -z

spectrograph
BR ˈspɛktrə(ʊ)grɑːf, ˈspɛktrə(ʊ)graf, -s
AM ˈspɛktrəˌgræf, -s

spectrographic
BR ˌspɛktrəˈgrafɪk
AM ˌspɛktrəˈgræfɪk

spectrographically
BR ˌspɛktrəˈgrafɪkli
AM ˌspɛktrəˈgræfək(ə)li

spectrography
BR spɛkˈtrɒgrəfi
AM spɛkˈtrɑgrəfi

spectroheliograph
BR ˌspɛktrəʊˈhiːlɪəgrɑːf, ˌspɛktrəʊˈhiːlɪəgraf, -s
AM ˌspɛktroʊˈhiliəˌgræf, -s

spectrohelioscope
BR ˌspɛktrəʊˈhiːlɪəskəʊp, -s
AM ˌspɛktroʊˈhiliəˌskoʊp, -s

spectrometer
BR spɛkˈtrɒmɪtə(r), -z
AM spɛkˈtrɑmədər, -z

spectrometric
BR ˌspɛktrəˈmɛtrɪk
AM ˌspɛktrəˈmɛtrɪk

spectrometry
BR spɛkˈtrɒmɪtri
AM ˈspɛkˈtrɑmətri

spectrophotometer
BR ˌspɛktrə(ʊ)fəˈtɒmɪtə(r), -z
AM ˌspɛktroʊfəˈtɑmədər, -z

spectrophotometric
BR ˌspɛktrə(ʊ)ˌfəʊtəˈmɛtrɪk
AM ˌspɛktrəˌfoʊdəˈmɛtrɪk

spectrophotometry
BR ˌspɛktrə(ʊ)fəˈtɒmɪtri
AM ˌspɛktroʊfəˈtɑmətri

spectroscope
BR ˈspɛktrəskəʊp, -s
AM ˈspɛktrəˌskoʊp, -s

spectroscopic
BR ˌspɛktrəˈskɒpɪk
AM ˌspɛktrəˈskɑpɪk

spectroscopical
BR ˌspɛktrəˈskɒpɪkl
AM ˌspɛktrəˈskɑpəkəl

spectroscopist
BR spɛkˈtrɒskəpɪst, -s
AM spɛkˈtrɑskəpəst, -s

spectroscopy
BR spɛkˈtrɒskəpi
AM spɛkˈtrɑskəpi

spectrum
BR ˈspɛktrəm, -z
AM ˈspɛktrəm, -z

specula
BR ˈspɛkjʉlə(*r*)
AM ˈspɛkjələ

specular
BR ˈspɛkjʉlə(r)
AM ˈspɛkjələr

speculate
BR ˈspɛkjʉleɪt, -s, -ɪŋ, -ɨd
AM ˈspɛk(j)əˌleɪ|t, -ts, -dɪŋ, -dɨd

speculation
BR ˌspɛkjʉˈleɪʃn, -z
AM ˌspɛkjəˈleɪʃən, -z

speculative
BR ˈspɛkjʉlətɪv
AM ˈspɛkjələdɪv, ˈspɛkjəˌleɪdɪv

speculatively
BR ˈspɛkjʉlətɪvli
AM ˈspɛkjəˌleɪdɪvli, ˈspɛkjələdɪvli

speculativeness
BR ˈspɛkjʉlətɪvnɨs
AM ˈspɛkjəˌleɪdɪvnɨs, ˈspɛkjələdɪvnɨs

speculator
BR ˈspɛkjʉleɪtə(r), -z
AM ˈspɛkjəˌleɪdər, -z

speculum
BR ˈspɛkjʉləm
AM ˈspɛkjələm

sped
BR spɛd
AM spɛd

speech
BR spiːtʃ, -ɨz
AM spitʃ, -ɨz

speechful
BR ˈspiːtʃf(ʉ)l
AM ˈspitʃˌfʊl

speechification
BR ˌspiːtʃɪfɪˈkeɪʃn, -z
AM ˌspitʃəfəˈkeɪʃən, -z

speechifier
BR ˈspiːtʃɪfʌɪə(r), -z
AM ˈspitʃəˌfaɪər, -z

speechify
BR ˈspiːtʃɪfʌɪ, -z, -ɪŋ, -d
AM ˈspitʃəˌfaɪ, -z, -ɪŋ, -d

speechless
BR 'spiːtʃlɨs
AM 'spitʃlɨs
speechlessly
BR 'spiːtʃlɨsli
AM 'spitʃlɨsli
speechlessness
BR 'spiːtʃlɨsnɨs
AM 'spitʃlɨsnɨs
speed
BR spiːd, -z, -ɪŋ, -ɨd
AM spid, -z, -ɪŋ, -ɨd
speedball
BR 'spiːdbɔːl
AM 'spid,bɔl, 'spid,bɑl
speedboat
BR 'spiːdbəʊt, -s
AM 'spid,boʊt, -s
speeder
BR 'spiːdə(r), -z
AM 'spidər, -z
speedily
BR 'spiːdɨli
AM 'spidɨli
speediness
BR 'spiːdɪnɨs
AM 'spidinɨs
speedo
BR 'spiːdəʊ, -z
AM 'spidoʊ, -z
speedometer
BR spiː'dɒmɪtə(r),
spɨ'dɒmɪtə(r), -z
AM spə'dɑmədər, -z
speedster
BR 'spiːdstə(r), -z
AM 'spidstər, -z
speedway
BR 'spiːdweɪ, -z
AM 'spid,weɪ, -z
speedwell
BR 'spiːdwɛl
AM 'spid,wɛl
speedy
BR 'spiːd|i, -ɪə(r), -ɪɪst
AM 'spidi, -ər, -ɨst
Speight
BR speɪt
AM speɪt
Speir
BR spɪə(r)
AM spɪ(ə)r
speiss
BR spʌɪs
AM spaɪs
Speke
BR spiːk
AM spik
speleological
BR ,spiːlɪə'lɒdʒɪkl
AM ˌspiliə'lɑdʒəkəl
speleologist
BR ,spiːlɪ'ɒlədʒɪst, -s
AM ,spili'ɑlədʒəst, -s
speleology
BR ,spiːlɪ'ɒlədʒi
AM ,spili'ɑlədʒi
spell
BR spɛl, -z, -ɪŋ, -d
AM spɛl, -z, -ɪŋ, -d
spellable
BR 'spɛləbl
AM 'spɛləbəl
spellbind
BR 'spɛlbʌɪnd, -z, -ɪŋ
AM 'spɛl,baɪnd, -z, -ɪŋ
spellbinder
BR 'spɛl,bʌɪndə(r), -z
AM 'spɛl,baɪndər, -z
spellbindingly
BR 'spɛl,bʌɪndɪŋli
AM 'spɛl,baɪndɪŋli
spellbound
BR 'spɛlbaʊnd
AM 'spɛl,baʊnd
speller
BR 'spɛlə(r), -z
AM 'spɛlər, -z
spellican
BR 'spɛlɪk(ə)n, -z
AM 'spɛləkən, -z
spelling
BR 'spɛlɪŋ, -z
AM 'spɛlɪŋ, -z
Spellman
BR 'spɛlmən
AM 'spɛlmən
spelt
BR spɛlt
AM spɛlt
spelter
BR 'spɛltə(r)
AM 'spɛltər
spelunker
BR spɨ'lʌŋkə(r), -z
AM spə'ləŋkər,
spi'ləŋkər, -z
spelunking
BR spɨ'lʌŋkɪŋ
AM spə'ləŋkɪŋ,
spi'ləŋkɪŋ
Spen
BR spɛn
AM spɛn
Spenborough
BR 'spɛnb(ə)rə(*r*)
AM 'spɛn,bərə
spence
BR spɛns, -ɨz
AM spɛns, -əz
spencer
BR 'spɛnsə(r), -z
AM 'spɛnsər, -z
spend
BR spɛnd, -z, -ɪŋ
AM spɛnd, -z, -ɪŋ
spendable
BR 'spɛndəbl
AM 'spɛndəbəl
spender
BR 'spɛndə(r), -z
AM 'spɛndər, -z
spendthrift
BR 'spɛn(d)θrɪft, -s
AM 'spɛn(d),θrɪft, -s
Spens
BR spɛnz
AM spɛnz
Spenser
BR 'spɛnsə(r)
AM 'spɛnsər
Spenserian
BR spɛn'sɪərɪən
AM spɛn'sɪriən,
spɛn'sɛriən
spent
BR spɛnt
AM spɛnt
sperm
BR spəːm, -z
AM spərm, -z
spermaceti
BR ,spəːmə'sɛti,
,spəːmə'siːti
AM ,spərmə'sɛdi
spermacetic
BR ,spəːmə'sɛtɪk,
,spəːmə'siːtɪk
AM ,spərmə'sɛdɪk
spermary
BR 'spəːm(ə)r|i, -ɪz
AM 'spərməri, -z
spermatheca
BR ,spəːmə'θiːkə(*r*)
AM ,spərmə'θikə
spermathecae
BR ,spəːmə'θiːkiː
AM ,spərmə'θiki,
,spərmə'θikaɪ
spermatic
BR spəː'matɪk
AM spər'mædɪk
spermatid
BR 'spəːmətɪd, -z
AM 'spərmə,tɪd, -z
spermatidal
BR ,spəːmə'tʌɪdl
AM ,spərmə'taɪdəl
spermatoblast
BR 'spəːmətə(ʊ)blɑːst,
spəː'matə(ʊ)blɑːst,
'spəːmətə(ʊ)blast,
spəː'matə(ʊ)blast, -s
AM spər'mædə,blæst,
-s
spermatocyte
BR 'spəːmətə(ʊ)sʌɪt,
spəː'matə(ʊ)sʌɪt, -s
AM spər'mædə,saɪt, -s
spermatogenesis
BR ,spəːmətə(ʊ)'dʒɛnɨsɪs
AM ,spərmədə'dʒɛnəsəs
spermatogenetic
BR ,spəːmətəʊdʒɨ'nɛtɪk
AM ˌspərmədədʒə'nɛdɪk
spermatogonia
BR ,spəːmətə'gəʊnɪə(*r*)
AM spər,mædə'goʊniə
spermatogonium
BR ,spəːmətə'gəʊnɪəm
AM spər,mædə'goʊniəm
spermatophore
BR 'spəːmətə(ʊ)fɔː(r),
spəː'matəfɔː(r), -z
AM spər'mædə,fɔ(ə)r,
-z
spermatophoric
BR ,spəːmətə'fɒrɪk
AM ˌspərmədə'fɔrɪk
spermatophyte
BR 'spəːmətə(ʊ)fʌɪt,
spəː'matəfʌɪt, -s
AM spər'mædə,faɪt, -s
spermatozoa
BR ,spəːmətə'zəʊə(*r*)
AM ,spərmədə'zoʊə,
spər,mædə'zoʊə
spermatozoal
BR ,spəːmətə'zəʊəl
AM ,spərmədə'zoʊəl,
spər,mædə'zoʊəl
spermatozoan
BR ,spəːmətə'zəʊən
AM ,spərmədə'zoʊən,
spər,mædə'zoʊən
spermatozoic
BR ,spəːmətə'zəʊɪk
AM ,spərmədə'zoʊɪk,
spər,mædə'zoʊɪk
spermatozoid
BR ,spəːmətə'zəʊɪd, -z
AM ,spərmədə'zoʊəd,
spər,mædə'zoʊəd, -z
spermatozoon
BR ,spəːmətə'zəʊən,
,spəːmətə'zəʊɒn
AM ,spərmədə'zoʊən,
spər,mædə'zoʊən
spermicidal
BR ,spəːmɨ'sʌɪdl
AM ,spərmə'saɪdəl
spermicide
BR 'spəːmɪsʌɪd, -z
AM 'spərmə,saɪd, -z
spermidine
BR 'spəːmɪdiːn
AM 'spərmə,din
spermine
BR 'spəːmiːn
AM 'spərmin
spermoblast
BR 'spəːməblɑːst,
'spəːməblast, -s
AM 'spərmə,blæst, -s
spermocyte
BR 'spəːməsʌɪt, -s
AM 'spərmə,saɪt, -s
spermogenesis
BR ,spəːmə'dʒɛnɨsɪs
AM ,spərmə'dʒɛnəsəs
spermogonia
BR ,spəːmə'gəʊnɪə(*r*)
AM ,spərmə'goʊniə
spermogonium
BR ,spəːmə'gəʊnɪəm
AM ,spərmə'goʊniəm
spermophore
BR 'spəːməfɔː(r), -z
AM 'spərmə,fɔ(ə)r, -z

spermophyte
BR ˈspəːməfʌɪt, -s
AM ˈspərməˌfaɪt, -s

spermozoa
BR ˌspəːməˈzəʊə(r)
AM ˌspərməˈzoʊə

spermozoid
BR ˈspəːməzɔɪd, -z
AM ˈspərməˌzɔɪd, -z

spermozoon
BR ˌspəːməˈzəʊən, ˌspəːməˈzəʊɒn
AM ˌspərməˈzoʊən

sperm whale
BR ˈspəːm weɪl, -z
AM ˈspərm ˌweɪl, -z

spessartine
BR ˈspɛsətiːn
AM ˈspɛsərˌtin

spew
BR spjuː, -z, -ɪŋ, -d
AM spju, -z, -ɪŋ, -d

spewer
BR ˈspjuːə(r), -z
AM ˈspjuər, -z

Spey
BR speɪ
AM speɪ

sphagnum
BR ˈsfagnəm, ˈspagnəm
AM ˈsfægnəm

sphalerite
BR ˈsfalərʌɪt, -s
AM ˈsfæləˌraɪt, -s

sphene
BR sfiːn
AM sfin

sphenoid
BR ˈsfiːnɔɪd, -z
AM ˈsfiˌnɔɪd, -z

sphenoidal
BR sfɪˈnɔɪdl
AM sfiˈnɔɪdəl

spheral
BR ˈsfɪərl̩
AM ˈsfɪrəl

sphere
BR sfɪə(r), -z
AM sfɪ(ə)r, -z

spheric
BR ˈsfɛrɪk, ˈsfɪərɪk, -s
AM ˈsfɪrɪk, ˈsfɛrɪk, -s

spherical
BR ˈsfɛrɪkl
AM ˈsfɪrəkəl, ˈsfɛrəkəl

spherically
BR ˈsfɛrɪkli
AM ˈsfɪrək(ə)li, ˈsfɛrək(ə)li

sphericity
BR sfɪˈrɪsɨti, sfɛˈrɪsɨti
AM sfəˈrɪsɨdi

spheroid
BR ˈsfɪərɔɪd, ˈsfɛrɔɪd, -z
AM ˈsfɪˌrɔɪd, ˈsfɛˌrɔɪd, -z

spheroidal
BR sfɪˈrɔɪdl
AM sfɪˈrɔɪdəl, sfəˈrɔɪdəl

spheroidicity
BR ˌsfɪərɔɪˈdɪsɨti, ˌsfɛrɔɪˈdɪsɨti
AM ˌsfɪrɔɪˈdɪsɨdi, ˌsfɛrɔɪˈdɪsɨdi

spherometer
BR ˌsfɪəˈrɒmɨtə(r), -z
AM sfəˈrɑmədər, -z

spherular
BR ˈsfɛr(j)ʉlə(r)
AM ˈsfɪr(j)ulər, ˈsfɛr(j)ulər

spherule
BR ˈsfɛr(j)uːl, -z
AM ˈsfɪrul, ˈsfɛrul, -z

spherulite
BR ˈsfɛr(j)ʉlʌɪt, -s
AM ˈsfɪr(j)əˌlaɪt, ˈsfɛr(j)əˌlaɪt, -s

spherulitic
BR ˌsfɛr(j)ʉˈlɪtɪk
AM ˌsfɪr(j)əˈlɪdɪk, ˌsfɛr(j)əˈlɪdɪk

sphincter
BR ˈsfɪŋ(k)tə(r), -z, -d
AM ˈsfɪŋ(k)tər, -z, -d

sphincteral
BR ˈsfɪŋ(k)t(ə)rəl, ˈsfɪŋ(k)t(ə)rl̩
AM ˈsfɪŋ(k)t(ə)rəl

sphincterial
BR ˌsfɪŋ(k)ˈtɪərɪəl
AM ˌsfɪŋ(k)ˈtɪriəl

sphincteric
BR ˌsfɪŋ(k)ˈtɛrɪk
AM ˌsfɪŋ(k)ˈtɛrɪk

sphingid
BR ˈsfɪn(d)ʒɪd, ˈsfɪŋgɪd, -z
AM ˈsfɪndʒɨd, ˈsfɪŋgɨd, -z

sphingomyelin
BR ˌsfɪŋgə(ʊ)ˈmʌɪəlɪn
AM ˌsfɪŋgoʊˈmaɪəlɪn

sphingosine
BR ˈsfɪŋgə(ʊ)sʌɪn
AM ˈsfɪŋgoʊˌsin, ˈsfɪŋgoʊˌsaɪn

sphinx
BR sfɪŋks, -ɪz
AM sfɪŋks, -ɪz

sphragistics
BR sfrəˈdʒɪstɪks
AM sfrəˈdʒɪstɪks

sphygmogram
BR ˈsfɪgməgram, -z
AM ˈsfɪgməˌgræm, -z

sphygmograph
BR ˈsfɪgməgrɑːf, ˈsfɪgməgraf, -s
AM ˈsfɪgməˌgræf, -s

sphygmographic
BR ˌsfɪgməˈgrafɪk
AM ˌsfɪgməˈgræfɪk

sphygmographically
BR ˌsfɪgməˈgrafɨkli
AM ˌsfɪgməˈgræfək(ə)li

sphygmography
BR sfɪgˈmɒgrəfi
AM sfɪgˈmɑgrəfi

sphygmological
BR ˌsfɪgməˈlɒdʒɪkl
AM ˌsfɪgməˈlɑdʒəkəl

sphygmology
BR sfɪgˈmɒlədʒi
AM sfɪgˈmɑlədʒi

sphygmomanometer
BR ˌsfɪgməʊməˈnɒmɨtə(r), -z
AM ˌsfɪgmoʊməˈnɑmədər, -z

sphygmomanometric
BR ˌsfɪgməʊˌmanəˈmɛtrɪk
AM ˌsfɪgmoʊˌmænəˈmɛtrɪk

spic
BR spɪk, -s
AM spɪk, -s

spica
BR ˈspʌɪkə(r), -z
AM ˈspaɪkə, -z

spicate
BR ˈspʌɪkeɪt, ˈspʌɪkət
AM ˈspaɪˌkeɪt

spicated
BR spɪˈkeɪtɨd, spʌɪˈkeɪtɨd
AM ˈspaɪˌkeɪdɨd

spiccato
BR spɪˈkɑːtəʊ, -z
AM spəˈkɑdoʊ, -z

spice
BR spʌɪs, -ɪz, -ɪŋ, -t
AM spaɪs, -ɪz, -ɪŋ, -t

spiceberry
BR ˈspʌɪsˌbɛr|i, -ɪz
AM ˈspaɪsˌbɛri, -z

spicebush
BR ˈspʌɪsbʊʃ, -ɪz
AM ˈspaɪsˌbʊʃ, -əz

spicery
BR ˈspʌɪs(ə)r|i, -ɪz
AM ˈspaɪs(ə)ri, -z

spicey
BR ˈspʌɪsi
AM ˈspaɪsi

spicily
BR ˈspʌɪsɨli
AM ˈspaɪsɨli

spiciness
BR ˈspʌɪsɪnɪs
AM ˈspaɪsinɨs

spick
BR spɪk, -s
AM spɪk, -s

spick-and-span
BR ˌspɪk(ə)n(d)ˈspan
AM ˈspɪkənˈspæn

spicknel
BR ˈspɪknl, -z
AM ˈspɪknəl, -z

spicular
BR ˈspɪkjʉlə(r)
AM ˈspɪkjələr

spiculate
BR ˈspɪkjʉlət
AM ˈspɪkjələt, ˈspɪkjəˌleɪt

spicule
BR ˈspɪkjuːl, ˈspʌɪkjuːl, -z
AM ˈspɪˌkjul, -z

spicy
BR ˈspʌɪs|i, -ɪə(r), -ɪɪst
AM ˈspaɪsi, -ər, -ɨst

spider
BR ˈspʌɪdə(r), -z
AM ˈspaɪdər, -z

spiderish
BR ˈspʌɪd(ə)rɪʃ
AM ˈspaɪdərɪʃ

spiderman
BR ˈspʌɪdəman
AM ˈspaɪdərˌmæn

spidermen
BR ˈspʌɪdəmɛn
AM ˈspaɪdərˌmɛn

spiderwort
BR ˈspʌɪdəwəːt, -s
AM ˈspʌɪdərwərt, ˈspʌɪdərwɔ(ə)rt, -s

spidery
BR ˈspʌɪd(ə)ri
AM ˈspaɪdəri

Spiegal
BR ˈspiːgl, ˈʃpiːgl
AM ˈspigəl

spiegeleisen
BR ˈspiːglˌʌɪzn
AM ˈspigəˌlaɪsən

Spiegl
BR ˈspiːgl, ˈʃpiːgl
AM ˈspigəl

spiel
BR ʃpiːl, spiːl, -z
AM spi(ə)l, ʃpi(ə)l, -z

Spielberg
BR ˈspiːlbəːg
AM ˈspilˌbərg

spieler
BR ˈʃpiːlə(r), ˈspiːlə(r), -z
AM ˈspi(ə)lər, ˈʃpi(ə)lər, -z

spiffily
BR ˈspɪfɨli
AM ˈspɪfɨli

spiffiness
BR ˈspɪfɪnɪs
AM ˈspɪfinɨs

spiffing
BR ˈspɪfɪŋ
AM ˈspɪfɪŋ

spifflicate
BR ˈspɪflɨkeɪt, -s, -ɪŋ, -ɨd

AM ˈspɪf(ə)lə,keɪ|t, -ts, -dɪŋ, -dɨd
spifflication
BR ˌspɪflɪˈkeɪʃn
AM ˌspɪf(ə)ləˈkeɪʃən
spiffy
BR ˈspɪf|i, -ɪə(r), -ɪɨst
AM ˈspɪfi, -ər, -ɨst
spiflicate
BR ˈspɪflɪkeɪt, -s, -ɪŋ, -ɨd
AM ˈspɪf(ə)lə,keɪ|t, -ts, -dɪŋ, -dɨd
spiflication
BR ˌspɪflɪˈkeɪʃn
AM ˌspɪf(ə)ləˈkeɪʃən
spignel
BR ˈspɪgnl, -z
AM ˈspɪgnəl, -z
spigot
BR ˈspɪgət, -s
AM ˈspɪgət, -s
spik
BR spɪk, -s
AM spɪk, -s
spike
BR spʌɪk, -s, -ɪŋ, -t
AM spaɪk, -s, -ɪŋ, -t
spikelet
BR ˈspʌɪklɨt, -s
AM ˈspaɪklɨt, -s
spikenard
BR ˈspʌɪknɑːd
AM ˈspaɪk,nɑrd
spikily
BR ˈspʌɪkɨli
AM ˈspaɪkɨli
spikiness
BR ˈspʌɪkɪnɪs
AM ˈspaɪkinɨs
spiky
BR ˈspʌɪk|i, -ɪə(r), -ɪɨst
AM ˈspaɪki, -ər, -ɨst
spile
BR spʌɪl, -z, -ɪŋ, -d
AM spaɪl, -z, -ɪŋ, -d
spill
BR spɪl, -z, -ɪŋ, -d
AM spɪl, -z, -ɪŋ, -d
spillage
BR ˈspɪl|ɪdʒ, -ɨdʒɪz
AM ˈspɪlɪdʒ, -ɪz
Spillane
BR spɪˈleɪn
AM spəˈleɪn
spiller
BR ˈspɪlə(r), -z
AM ˈspɪlər, -z
spillikin
BR ˈspɪlɨkɪn, -z
AM ˈspɪləkɪn, -z
spillover
BR ˈspɪl,əʊvə(r), -z
AM ˈspɪl,oʊvər, -z
spillway
BR ˈspɪlweɪ, -z
AM ˈspɪl,weɪ, -z
Spilsbury
BR ˈspɪlzb(ə)ri
AM ˈspɪlz,bɛri
spilt
BR spɪlt
AM spɪlt
spilth
BR spɪlθ, -s
AM spɪlθ, -s
spin
BR spɪn, -z, -ɪŋ
AM spɪn, -z, -ɪŋ
spina bifida
BR ˌspʌɪnə ˈbɪfɨdə(r)
AM ˌspaɪnə ˈbɪfədə
spinaceous
BR spɨˈneɪʃəs
AM spəˈneɪʃəs, spɪˈneɪʃəs
spinach
BR ˈspɪnɪdʒ, ˈspɪnɪtʃ
AM ˈspɪnɪtʃ
spinachy
BR ˈspɪnɪdʒi, ˈspɪnɪtʃi
AM ˈspɪnɨtʃi
spinal
BR ˈspʌɪnl
AM ˈspaɪnəl
spinally
BR ˈspʌɪnl̩i
AM ˈspaɪnəli
spindle
BR ˈspɪndl, -z
AM ˈspɪndəl, -z
spindleshanks
BR ˈspɪndlʃaŋks
AM ˈspɪndl,ʃæŋks
spindly
BR ˈspɪndli
AM ˈspɪn(d)li
spin-drier
BR ˌspɪnˈdrʌɪə(r), ˈspɪn,drʌɪə(r), -z
AM ˈspɪn,draɪər, -z
spindrift
BR ˈspɪndrɪft
AM ˈspɪn,drɪft
spin-dry
BR ˌspɪnˈdrʌɪ, -z, -ɪŋ, -d
AM ˈspɪnˌdraɪ, -z, -ɪŋ, -d
spine
BR spʌɪn, -z, -d
AM spaɪn, -z, -d
spinel
BR spɪˈnɛl, -z
AM spəˈnɛl, -z
spineless
BR ˈspʌɪnlɨs
AM ˈspaɪnlɨs
spinelessly
BR ˈspʌɪnlɨsli
AM ˈspaɪnlɨsli
spinelessness
BR ˈspʌɪnlɨsnɨs
AM ˈspaɪnlɨsnɨs
spinet
BR spɪˈnɛt, ˈspɪnɪt, -s
AM ˈspɪnɨt, -s
spinifex
BR ˈspɪnɨfɛks
AM ˈspɪnə,fɛks
spininess
BR ˈspʌɪnɪnɨs
AM ˈspaɪninɨs
Spink
BR spɪŋk
AM spɪŋk
Spinks
BR spɪŋks
AM spɪŋks
spinnaker
BR ˈspɪnəkə(r), -z
AM ˈspɪnəkər, -z
spinner
BR ˈspɪnə(r), -z
AM ˈspɪnər, -z
spinneret
BR ˌspɪnəˈrɛt, -s
AM ˌspɪnəˈrɛt, -s
spinney
BR ˈspɪn|i, -ɪz
AM ˈspɪni, -z
spin-off
BR ˈspɪnɒf, -s
AM ˈspɪn,ɔf, ˈspɪn,ɑf, -s
spinose
BR ˈspʌɪnəʊs
AM ˈspaɪ,noʊs, ˈspaɪ,noʊz
spinous
BR ˈspʌɪnəs
AM ˈspaɪnəs
spin-out
BR ˈspɪnaʊt, -s
AM ˈspɪn,aʊt, -s
Spinoza
BR spɪˈnəʊzə(r)
AM spəˈnoʊzə
Spinozism
BR spɪˈnəʊzɪz(ə)m
AM spəˈnoʊ,zɪzəm
Spinozist
BR spɪˈnəʊzɪst, -s
AM spəˈnoʊzəst, -s
Spinozistic
BR ˌspɪnəˈzɪstɪk
AM ˌspɪnəˈzɪstɪk
spinster
BR ˈspɪnstə(r), -z
AM ˈspɪnstər, -z
spinsterhood
BR ˈspɪnstəhʊd
AM ˈspɪnstər,(h)ʊd
spinsterish
BR ˈspɪnst(ə)rɪʃ
AM ˈspɪnst(ə)rɪʃ
spinsterishness
BR ˈspɪnst(ə)rɪʃnɪs
AM ˈspɪnst(ə)rɪʃnɪs
spinthariscope
BR spɪnˈθarɪskəʊp, -s
AM spɪnˈθɛrə,skoʊp, -s
spinule
BR ˈspɪnjuːl, -z
AM ˈspaɪ,njul, ˈspɪn,jul, -z
spinulose
BR ˈspɪnjʉləʊs
AM ˈspaɪnjə,loʊs, ˈspɪnjə,loʊs ˈspaɪnjə,loʊz, ˈspɪnjə,loʊz
spinulous
BR ˈspʌɪnjʉləs
AM ˈspaɪnjələs, ˈspɪnjələs
spiny
BR ˈspʌɪni
AM ˈspaɪni
Spion Kop
BR ˌspʌɪən ˈkɒp
AM ˌspaɪən ˈkɑp
spiracle
BR ˈspʌɪrəkl, -z
AM ˈspaɪrəkəl, ˈspɪrəkəl, -z
spiracula
BR spʌɪˈrakjʉlə(r)
AM spəˈrækjələ, spaɪˈrækjələ
spiracular
BR spʌɪˈrakjʉlə(r)
AM spəˈrækjələr, spaɪˈrækjələr
spiraculum
BR spʌɪˈrakjʉləm
AM spəˈrækjələm, spaɪˈrækjələm
spiraea
BR spʌɪˈriːə(r), -z
AM spaɪˈriə, -z
spiral
BR ˈspʌɪrəl, ˈspʌɪrl̩, -z, -ɪŋ, -d
AM ˈspaɪrəl, -z, -ɪŋ, -d
spirality
BR spʌɪˈralɨti
AM ˌspaɪˈrælədi
spirally
BR ˈspʌɪrəli, ˈspʌɪrl̩i
AM ˈspaɪrəli
spirant
BR ˈspʌɪrənt, ˈspʌɪrn̩t, -s
AM ˈspaɪrənt, -s
spire
BR ˈspʌɪə(r), -z, -d
AM ˈspaɪ(ə)r, -z, -d
spirea
BR spʌɪˈriːə(r)
AM spaɪˈriə
spirilla
BR spʌɪˈrɪlə(r)
AM spaɪˈrɪlə
spirillum
BR spʌɪˈrɪləm
AM spaɪˈrɪləm
spirit
BR ˈspɪr|ɪt, -ɪts, -ɨtɪŋ, -ɨtɨd
AM ˈspɪrɨ|t, -ts, -dɪŋ, -dɨd

spiritedly
BR 'spɪrɪtɪdli
AM 'spɪrɪdɪdli

spiritedness
BR 'spɪrɪtɪdnɪs
AM 'spɪrɪdɪdnɪs

spiritism
BR 'spɪrɪtɪz(ə)m
AM 'spɪrə,tɪzəm

spiritist
BR 'spɪrɪtɪst, -s
AM 'spɪrədəst, -s

spiritless
BR 'spɪrɪtlɨs
AM 'spɪrɪtlɨs

spiritlessly
BR 'spɪrɪtlɨsli
AM 'spɪrɪtlɨsli

spiritlessness
BR 'spɪrɪtlɨsnɨs
AM 'spɪrɪtlɨsnɨs

spiritous
BR 'spɪrɪtəs
AM 'spɪrɪdəs

spiritual
BR 'spɪrɪtʃʊəl, 'spɪrɪtʃ(ʉ)l, 'spɪrɪtjʊəl, 'spɪrɪtjʉl
AM 'spɪrɪtʃ(əw)əl

spiritualisation
BR ˌspɪrɪtʃʉlʌɪ'zeɪʃn, ˌspɪrɪtʃl̩ʌɪ'zeɪʃn, ˌspɪrɪtjʉlʌɪ'zeɪʃn
AM ˌspɪrɪtʃ(əw)ələ'zeɪʃən, ˌspɪrɪtʃ(əw)əˌlaɪ'zeɪʃən

spiritualise
BR 'spɪrɪtʃʉlʌɪz, 'spɪrɪtʃl̩ʌɪz, 'spɪrɪtjʉlʌɪz, -ɪz, -ɪŋ, -d
AM 'spɪrɪtʃ(əw)əˌlaɪz, -ɪz, -ɪŋ, -d

spiritualism
BR 'spɪrɪtʃʉlɪz(ə)m, 'spɪrɪtʃl̩ɪz(ə)m, 'spɪrɪtjʉlɪz(ə)m
AM 'spɪrɪtʃ(əw)əˌlɪzəm

spiritualist
BR 'spɪrɪtʃʉlɪst, 'spɪrɪtʃl̩ɪst, 'spɪrɪtjʉlɪst, -s
AM 'spɪrɪtʃ(əw)ələst, -s

spiritualistic
BR ˌspɪrɪtʃʉ'lɪstɪk, ˌspɪrɪtʃl̩'ɪstɪk, ˌspɪrɪtjʉ'lɪstɪk
AM ˌspɪrɪtʃ(əw)ə'lɪstɪk

spirituality
BR ˌspɪrɪtʃʊ'alɨti, ˌspɪrɪtjʊ'alɨti
AM ˌspɪrɪtʃ(ə)'wælədi

spiritualization
BR ˌspɪrɪtʃʉlʌɪ'zeɪʃn, ˌspɪrɪtʃl̩ʌɪ'zeɪʃn, ˌspɪrɪtjʉlʌɪ'zeɪʃn
AM ˌspɪrɪtʃ(əw)ələ'zeɪʃən, ˌspɪrɪtʃ(əw)əˌlaɪ'zeɪʃən

spiritualize
BR 'spɪrɪtʃʉlʌɪz, 'spɪrɪtʃl̩ʌɪz, 'spɪrɪtjʉlʌɪz, -ɪz, -ɪŋ, -d
AM 'spɪrɪtʃ(əw)əˌlaɪz, -ɪz, -ɪŋ, -d

spiritually
BR 'spɪrɪtʃʊəli, 'spɪrɪtʃʉli, 'spɪrɪtʃl̩i, 'spɪrɪtjʊəli, 'spɪrɪtjʉli
AM 'spɪrɪtʃ(əw)əli

spiritualness
BR 'spɪrɪtʃʊəlnəs, 'spɪrɪtʃ(ʉ)lnəs, 'spɪrɪtjʊəlnəs, 'spɪrɪtjʉlnəs
AM 'spɪrɪtʃ(əw)əlnəs

spirituel
BR ˌspɪrɪtʃʊ'ɛl, ˌspɪrɪtjʊ'ɛl
AM ˌspɪrətʃə'wɛl

spirituelle
BR ˌspɪrɪtʃʊ'ɛl, ˌspɪrɪtjʊ'ɛl
AM ˌspɪrətʃə'wɛl

spirituous
BR 'spɪrɪtʃʊəs, 'spɪrɪtjʊəs
AM 'spɪrɪtʃ(əw)əs

spirituousness
BR 'spɪrɪtʃʊəsnəs, 'spɪrɪtjʊəsnəs
AM 'spɪrɪtʃ(əw)əsnəs

spirketing
BR 'spəːkɪtɪŋ
AM 'spərkədɪŋ

spirochaete
BR 'spʌɪrəkiːt, -s
AM 'spaɪrəˌkit, -s

spirochete
BR 'spʌɪrəkiːt, -s
AM 'spaɪrəˌkit, -s

spirograph
BR 'spʌɪrəgrɑːf, 'spʌɪrəgraf, -s
AM 'spaɪrəˌgræf, -s

spirographic
BR ˌspʌɪrə'grafɪk
AM ˌspaɪrə'græfɪk

spirographically
BR ˌspʌɪrə'grafɪkli
AM ˌspaɪrə'græfək(ə)li

spirogyra
BR ˌspʌɪrə'dʒʌɪrə(r)
AM ˌspaɪrə'dʒaɪrə

spirometer
BR spʌɪ'rɒmɪtə(r), -z
AM spaɪ'rɑmədər, -z

spirt
BR spəːt, -s, -ɪŋ, -ɪd
AM spər|t, -ts, -dɪŋ, -dəd

spiry
BR 'spʌɪ(ə)ri
AM 'spaɪri

spit
BR spɪt, -s, -ɪŋ, -ɪd
AM spɪ|t, -ts, -dɪŋ, -dɪd

Spitalfields
BR 'spɪtlfiːldz
AM 'spɪdəlˌfildz

spit-and-polish
BR ˌspɪt(ə)n(d)'pɒlɪʃ
AM ˌspɪdən'pɑlɪʃ

spitball
BR 'spɪtbɔːl, -z
AM 'spɪtˌbɔl, 'spɪtˌbɑl, -z

spitballer
BR 'spɪtˌbɔːlə(r), -z
AM 'spɪtˌbɔlər, 'spɪtˌbɑlər, -z

spitchcock
BR 'spɪtʃkɒk, -s, -ɪŋ, -t
AM 'spɪtʃˌkɑk, -s, -ɪŋ, -t

spite
BR spʌɪt, -s, -ɪŋ, -ɪd
AM spaɪ|t, -ts, -dɪŋ, -dɪd

spiteful
BR 'spʌɪtf(ʉ)l
AM 'spaɪtfəl

spitefully
BR 'spʌɪtfʉli, 'spʌɪtfl̩i
AM 'spaɪtf(ə)li

spitefulness
BR 'spʌɪtf(ʉ)lnəs
AM 'spaɪtfəlnəs

spitfire
BR 'spɪtˌfʌɪə(r), -z
AM 'spɪtˌfaɪ(ə)r, -z

Spithead
BR ˌspɪt'hɛd
AM ˌspɪt'hɛd

Spitsbergen
BR 'spɪtsˌbəːg(ə)n
AM 'spɪtsˌbərgən

spitter
BR 'spɪtə(r), -z
AM 'spɪdər, -z

spittle
BR 'spɪtl
AM 'spɪdəl

spittly
BR 'spɪtl̩i
AM 'spɪdl̩i

spittoon
BR spɪ'tuːn, -z
AM spɪ'tun, -z

spitty
BR 'spɪti
AM 'spɪdi

spitz
BR spɪts, -ɪz
AM spɪts, -ɪz

spiv
BR spɪv, -z
AM spɪv, -z

spivish
BR 'spɪvɪʃ
AM 'spɪvɪʃ

spivvery
BR 'spɪv(ə)ri
AM 'spɪv(ə)ri

spivvish
BR 'spɪvɪʃ
AM 'spɪvɪʃ

spivvy
BR 'spɪvi
AM 'spɪvi

splake
BR spleɪk, -s
AM spleɪk, -s

splanchnic
BR 'splaŋknɪk
AM 'splæŋknɪk

splanchnology
BR ˌsplaŋk'nɒlədʒi
AM ˌsplæŋk'nɑlədʒi

splanchnotomy
BR ˌsplaŋk'nɒtəm|i, -ɪz
AM ˌsplæŋk'nɑdəmi, -z

splash
BR splaʃ, -ɪz, -ɪŋ, -t
AM splæʃ, -əz, -ɪŋ, -t

splashback
BR 'splaʃbak, -s
AM 'splæʃˌbæk, -s

splashboard
BR 'splaʃbɔːd, -z
AM 'splæʃˌbɔ(ə)rd, -z

splashdown
BR 'splaʃdaʊn, -z
AM 'splæʃˌdaʊn, -z

splashily
BR 'splaʃɪli
AM 'splæʃəli

splashiness
BR 'splaʃɪnɪs
AM 'splæʃinɪs

splashy
BR 'splaʃi
AM 'splæʃi

splat
BR splat, -s
AM splæt, -s

splatter
BR 'splat|ə(r), -əz, -(ə)rɪŋ, -əd
AM 'splædər, -z, -ɪŋ, -d

splay
BR spleɪ, -z, -ɪŋ, -d
AM spleɪ, -z, -ɪŋ, -d

splay-feet
BR ˌspleɪ'fiːt
AM 'spleɪˌfit

splay-foot
BR ˌspleɪ'fʊt
AM 'spleɪˌfʊt

splay-footed
BR ˌspleɪ'fʊtɪd
AM 'spleɪˌfʊdəd

spleen
BR spliːn, -z
AM splin, -z

spleenful
BR 'spliːnf(ʉ)l
AM 'splinfəl

spleenwort
BR 'spliːnwəːt, -s
AM 'splinwərt, 'splinˌwɔ(ə)rt, -s

spleeny
BR ˈspliːn|i, -ɪə(r), -ɪɪst
AM ˈsplini, -ər, -ɨst

splendent
BR ˈsplɛnd(ə)nt
AM ˈsplɛndənt

splendid
BR ˈsplɛndɪd
AM ˈsplɛndəd

splendidly
BR ˈsplɛndɨdli
AM ˈsplɛndədli

splendidness
BR ˈsplɛndɨdnɨs
AM ˈsplɛndədnəs

splendiferous
BR splɛnˈdɪf(ə)rəs
AM splɛnˈdɪf(ə)rəs

splendiferously
BR splɛnˈdɪf(ə)rəsli
AM splɛnˈdɪf(ə)rəsli

splendiferousness
BR splɛnˈdɪf(ə)rəsnəs
AM splɛnˈdɪf(ə)rəsnəs

splendor
BR ˈsplɛndə(r), -z
AM ˈsplɛndər, -z

splendour
BR ˈsplɛndə(r), -z
AM ˈsplɛndər, -z

splenectomy
BR spliːˈnɛktəm|i, splɪˈnɛktəm|i, -ɪz
AM spləˈnɛktəmi, -z

splenetic
BR splɪˈnɛtɪk
AM spləˈnɛdɪk

splenetically
BR splɪˈnɛtɨkli
AM spləˈnɛdək(ə)li

splenial
BR ˈspliːnɪəl
AM ˈspliniəl

splenic
BR ˈspliːnɪk, ˈsplɛnɪk
AM ˈsplinɪk, ˈsplɛnɪk

splenii
BR ˈspliːnɪʌɪ
AM ˈsplini,aɪ

splenitis
BR spliːˈnʌɪtɨs, splɪˈnʌɪtɨs
AM spliˈnaɪdɨs

splenius
BR ˈspliːnɪəs
AM ˈspliniəs

splenoid
BR ˈspliːnɔɪd, ˈsplɛnɔɪd
AM ˈspli,nɔɪd, ˈsplɛ,nɔɪd

splenology
BR spliːˈnɒlədʒi, splɪˈnɒlədʒi
AM spliˈnɑlədʒi, spləˈnɑlədʒi

splenomegaly
BR ˌspliːnə(ʊ)ˈmɛgəl|i, ˌspliːnə(ʊ)ˈmɛgl̩|i, -ɪz
AM ˌsplinəˈmɛgəli, ˌsplɛnəˈmɛgəli, -z

splenotomy
BR spliːˈnɒtəm|i, splɪˈnɒtəm|i, -ɪz
AM spliˈnɑdəmi, spləˈnɑdəmi, -z

splice
BR splʌɪs, -ɨz, -ɪŋ, -t
AM splaɪs, -ɨz, -ɪŋ, -t

splicer
BR ˈsplʌɪsə(r), -z
AM ˈsplaɪsər, -z

splif
BR splɪf, -s
AM splɪf, -s

spliff
BR splɪf, -s
AM splɪf, -s

spline
BR splʌɪn, -z
AM splaɪn, -z

splint
BR splɪnt, -s, -ɪŋ, -ɨd
AM splɪn|t, -ts, -(t)ɪŋ, -(t)əd

splint-bone
BR ˈsplɪntbəʊn, -z
AM ˈsplɪnt,boʊn, -z

splint-coal
BR ˈsplɪntkəʊl, -z
AM ˈsplɪnt,koʊl, -z

splinter
BR ˈsplɪnt|ə(r), -əz, -(ə)rɪŋ, -əd
AM ˈsplɪn(t)ər, -z, -ɪŋ, -d

splintery
BR ˈsplɪnt(ə)ri
AM ˈsplɪn(t)əri

split
BR splɪt, -s, -ɪŋ, -ɨd
AM splɪ|t, -ts, -dɪŋ, -dɨd

split-level
BR ˌsplɪtˈlɛvl
AM ˈsplɪt,lɛvəl

split-second
BR ˌsplɪtˈsɛknd
AM ˈsplɪtˌsɛkənd

splitter
BR ˈsplɪtə(r), -z
AM ˈsplɪ(d)ər, -z

split-up
BR ˈsplɪtʌp, -s
AM ˈsplɪd,əp, -s

splodge
BR splɒdʒ, -ɨz
AM splɑdʒ, -əz

splodginess
BR ˈsplɒdʒɪnɨs
AM ˈsplɑdʒinɨs

splodgy
BR ˈsplɒdʒ|i, -ɪə(r), -ɪɪst
AM ˈsplɑdʒi, -ər, -ɨst

sploosh
BR spluːʃ, -ɨz, -ɪŋ, -t
AM spluʃ, -əz, -ɪŋ, -t

splosh
BR splɒʃ, -ɨz, -ɪŋ, -t
AM splɑʃ, -əz, -ɪŋ, -t

splotch
BR splɒtʃ, -ɨz
AM splɑtʃ, -əz

splotchiness
BR ˈsplɒtʃɪnɨs
AM ˈsplɑtʃinɨs

splotchy
BR ˈsplɒtʃ|i, -ɪə(r), -ɪɪst
AM ˈsplɑtʃi, -ər, -ɨst

Splott
BR splɒt
AM splɑt

splurge
BR spləːdʒ, -ɨz, -ɪŋ, -d
AM splərdʒ, -əz, -ɪŋ, -d

splutter
BR ˈsplʌt|ə(r), -əz, -(ə)rɪŋ, -əd
AM ˈsplədər, -z, -ɪŋ, -d

splutterer
BR ˈsplʌt(ə)rə(r), -z
AM ˈsplədərər, -z

splutteringly
BR ˈsplʌt(ə)rɪŋli
AM ˈsplədərɪŋli

spluttery
BR ˈsplʌt(ə)ri
AM ˈsplədəri

Spock
BR spɒk
AM spɑk

Spode®
BR spəʊd
AM spoʊd

spodosol
BR ˈspɒdəsɒl
AM ˈspɑdə,sɔl, ˈspɑdə,sɑl

spodumene
BR ˈspɒdjʉmiːn
AM ˈspɑdʒə,min

Spofforth
BR ˈspɒfəθ
AM ˈspɑfərθ

spoil
BR spɔɪl, -z, -ɪŋ, -d
AM spɔɪl, -z, -ɪŋ, -d

spoilage
BR ˈspɔɪlɪdʒ
AM ˈspɔɪlɪdʒ

spoiler
BR ˈspɔɪlə(r), -z
AM ˈspɔɪlər, -z

spoilsman
BR ˈspɔɪlzmən
AM ˈspɔɪlzmən

spoilsmen
BR ˈspɔɪlzmən
AM ˈspɔɪlzmən

spoilsport
BR ˈspɔɪlspɔːt, -s
AM ˈspɔɪl,spɔ(ə)rt, -s

spoilt
BR spɔɪlt
AM spɔɪlt

Spokane
BR spəʊˈkan
AM spoʊˈkæn

spoke
BR spəʊk, -s
AM spoʊk, -s

spoke-bone
BR ˈspəʊkbəʊn, -z
AM ˈspoʊk,boʊn, -z

spoken
BR ˈspəʊk(ə)n
AM ˈspoʊkən

spokeshave
BR ˈspəʊkʃeɪv, -z
AM ˈspoʊk,ʃeɪv, -z

spokesman
BR ˈspəʊksmən
AM ˈspoʊksmən

spokesmen
BR ˈspəʊksmən
AM ˈspoʊksmən

spokesperson
BR ˈspəʊks,pəːsn, -z
AM ˈspoʊks,pərsən, -z

spokeswoman
BR ˈspəʊks,wʊmən
AM ˈspoʊks,wʊmən

spokeswomen
BR ˈspəʊks,wɪmɪn
AM ˈspoʊks,wɪmɪn

spokewise
BR ˈspəʊkwʌɪz
AM ˈspoʊk,waɪz

spoliation
BR ˌspəʊlɪˈeɪʃn
AM ˌspoʊliˈeɪʃən

spoliator
BR ˈspəʊlɪeɪtə(r), -z
AM ˈspoʊli,eɪdər, -z

spoliatory
BR ˈspəʊlɪət(ə)ri
AM ˈspoʊliə,tɔri

spondaic
BR spɒnˈdeɪɪk
AM spɑnˈdeɪɪk

spondee
BR ˈspɒndiː, -z
AM ˈspɑndi, -z

Spondon
BR ˈspɒndən
AM ˈspɑndən

spondulicks
BR spɒnˈd(j)uːlɪks
AM spɑnˈd(j)ulɪks

spondylitis
BR ˌspɒndɪˈlʌɪtɨs
AM ˌspɑndəˈlaɪdɨs

Spong
BR spɒŋ
AM spɑŋ

sponge
BR spʌn(d)ʒ, -ɨz, -ɪŋ, -d
AM spəndʒ, -əz, -ɪŋ, -d

spongeable
BR ˈspʌn(d)ʒəbl
AM ˈspəndʒəbəl
spongelike
BR ˈspʌn(d)ʒlʌɪk
AM ˈspəndʒˌlaɪk
sponger
BR ˈspʌn(d)ʒə(r), -z
AM ˈspəndʒər, -z
spongiform
BR ˈspʌn(d)ʒɪfɔːm
AM ˈspəndʒəˌfɔ(ə)rm
spongily
BR ˈspʌn(d)ʒɨli
AM ˈspəndʒəli
sponginess
BR ˈspʌn(d)ʒɪnɪs
AM ˈspəndʒinɨs
spongy
BR ˈspʌn(d)ʒ|i, -ɪə(r), -ɪɪst
AM ˈspəndʒi, -ər, -ɨst
sponsion
BR ˈspɒnʃn
AM ˈspɑnʃən
sponson
BR ˈspɒnsn, -z
AM ˈspɑnsən, -z
sponsor
BR ˈspɒns|ə(r), -əz, -(ə)rɪŋ, -əd
AM ˈspɑn(t)sər, -z, -ɪŋ, -d
sponsorial
BR spɒnˈsɔːrɪəl
AM ˌspɑnˈsɔriəl
sponsorship
BR ˈspɒnsəʃɪp
AM ˈspɑn(t)sərˌʃɪp
spontaneity
BR ˌspɒntəˈneɪɪti, ˌspɒntəˈniːɪti
AM ˌspɑn(t)əˈniɨdi
spontaneous
BR spɒnˈteɪnɪəs
AM spɑnˈteɪniəs
spontaneously
BR spɒnˈteɪnɪəsli
AM spɑnˈteɪniəsli
spontaneousness
BR spɒnˈteɪnɪəsnəs
AM spɑnˈteɪniəsnəs
spontoon
BR spɒnˈtuːn, -z
AM ˌspɑnˈtun, -z
spoof
BR spuːf, -s, -ɪŋ, -t
AM spuf, -s, -ɪŋ, -t
spoofer
BR ˈspuːfə(r), -z
AM ˈspufər, -z
spoofery
BR ˈspuːf(ə)ri
AM ˈspufəri
spook
BR spuːk, -s, -ɪŋ, -t
AM spuk, -s, -ɪŋ, -t
spookily
BR ˈspuːkɪli
AM ˈspʊkəli
spookiness
BR ˈspuːkɪnɪs
AM ˈspʊkinɪs
spooky
BR ˈspuːk|i, -ɪə(r), -ɪɪst
AM ˈspuki, -ər, -ɨst
spool
BR spuːl, -z, -ɪŋ, -d
AM spul, -z, -ɪŋ, -d
spoon
BR spuːn, -z, -ɪŋ, -d
AM spun, -z, -ɪŋ, -d
spoonbeak
BR ˈspuːnbiːk, -s
AM ˈspunˌbik, -s
spoonbill
BR ˈspuːnbɪl, -z
AM ˈspunˌbɪl, -z
spoon-bread
BR ˈspuːnbrɛd, -z
AM ˈspunˌbrɛd, -z
spooner
BR ˈspuːnə(r), -z
AM ˈspunər, -z
spoonerism
BR ˈspuːnərɪz(ə)m, -z
AM ˈspunəˌrɪzəm, -z
spoonfed
BR ˈspuːnfɛd
AM ˈspunˌfɛd
spoonfeed
BR ˈspuːnfiːd, -z, -ɪŋ
AM ˈspunˌfid, -z, -ɪŋ
spoonful
BR ˈspuːnfʊl, -z
AM ˈspunˌfʊl, -z
spoonily
BR ˈspuːnɪli
AM ˈspunəli
spooniness
BR ˈspuːnɪnɪs
AM ˈspuninɪs
spoonsful
BR ˈspuːnzfʊl
AM ˈspunzˌfʊl
spoony
BR ˈspuːn|i, -ɪə(r), -ɪɪst
AM ˈspuni, -ər, -ɨst
spoor
BR spʊə(r), spɔː(r), -z
AM spʊ(ə)r, spɔ(ə)r, -z
spoorer
BR ˈspʊərə(r), ˈspɔːrə(r), -z
AM ˈspʊrər, ˈspɔrər, -z
Sporades
BR ˈspɒrədiːz, spəˈrɑːdiːz
AM ˈspɔrəˌdiz
sporadic
BR spəˈradɪk
AM spəˈrædɪk
sporadically
BR spəˈradɪkli
AM spəˈrædək(ə)li
sporangia
BR spəˈran(d)ʒɪə(r)
AM spəˈrændʒiə, spoʊˈrændʒiə
sporangial
BR spəˈran(d)ʒɪəl
AM spəˈrændʒiəl, spoʊˈrændʒiəl
sporangium
BR spəˈran(d)ʒɪəm
AM spəˈrændʒiəm, spoʊˈrændʒiəm
spore
BR spɔː(r), -z
AM spɔ(ə)r, -z
sporogenesis
BR ˌspɒrə(ʊ)ˈdʒɛnɪsɪs
AM ˌspɔroʊˈdʒɛnəsəs
sporogenous
BR spəˈrɒdʒɪnəs
AM spəˈrɑdʒənəs, spoʊˈrɑdʒənəs
sporophore
BR ˈspɒrəfɔː(r), ˈspɔːrəfɔː(r), -z
AM ˈspɔrəˌfɔ(ə)r, -z
sporophyte
BR ˈspɒrə(ʊ)fʌɪt, ˈspɔːrə(ʊ)fʌɪt, -s
AM ˈspɔrəˌfaɪt, -s
sporophytic
BR ˌspɒrə(ʊ)ˈfɪtɪk, ˌspɔːrə(ʊ)ˈfɪtɪk
AM ˌspɔrəˈfɪdɪk
sporophytically
BR ˌspɒrə(ʊ)ˈfɪtɪkli, ˌspɔːrə(ʊ)ˈfɪtɪkli
AM ˌspɔrəˈfɪdɪk(ə)li
sporozoite
BR ˌspɒrə(ʊ)ˈzəʊʌɪt, ˌspɔːrə(ʊ)ˈzəʊʌɪt, -s
AM ˌspɔrəˈzoʊˌaɪt, -s
sporran
BR ˈspɒrən, ˈspɒrn̩, -z
AM ˈspɑrən, -z
sport
BR spɔːt, -s, -ɪŋ, -ɨd
AM spɔ(ə)rt, -ts, ˈspɔrdɪŋ, ˈspɔrdəd
sporter
BR ˈspɔːtə(r), -z
AM ˈspɔrdər, -z
sportif
BR spɔːˈtiːf
AM spɔrˈtif
sportily
BR ˈspɔːtɨli
AM ˈspɔrdəli
sportiness
BR ˈspɔːtɪnɪs
AM ˈspɔrdinɪs
sportingly
BR ˈspɔːtɪŋli
AM ˈspɔrdɪŋli
sportive
BR ˈspɔːtɪv
AM ˈspɔrdɪv
sportively
BR ˈspɔːtɪvli
AM ˈspɔrdɪvli
sportiveness
BR ˈspɔːtɪvnɪs
AM ˈspɔrdɪvnɪs
sportscast
BR ˈspɔːtskɑːst, ˈspɔːtskast, -s, -ɪŋ
AM ˈspɔrtsˌkæst, -s, -ɪŋ
sportscaster
BR ˈspɔːtsˌkɑːstə(r), ˈspɔːtsˌkastə(r), -z
AM ˈspɔrtsˌkæstər, -z
sportshirt
BR ˈspɔːtʃəːt, -s
AM ˈspɔrtˌʃərt, -s
sportsman
BR ˈspɔːtsmən
AM ˈspɔrtsmən
sportsmanlike
BR ˈspɔːtsmənlʌɪk
AM ˈspɔrtsmənˌlaɪk
sportsmanly
BR ˈspɔːtsmənli
AM ˈspɔrtsmənli
sportsmanship
BR ˈspɔːtsmənʃɪp
AM ˈspɔrtsmənˌʃɪp
sportsmen
BR ˈspɔːtsmən
AM ˈspɔrtsmən
sportspeople
BR ˈspɔːtsˌpiːpl
AM ˈspɔrtsˌpipəl
sportsperson
BR ˈspɔːtsˌpəːsn, -z
AM ˈspɔrtsˌpərsən, -z
sportswear
BR ˈspɔːtswɛː(r)
AM ˈspɔrtsˌwɛ(ə)r
sportswoman
BR ˈspɔːtsˌwʊmən
AM ˈspɔrtsˌwʊmən
sportswomen
BR ˈspɔːtsˌwɪmɪn
AM ˈspɔrtsˌwɪmɨn
sportswriter
BR ˈspɔːtsˌrʌɪtə(r), -z
AM ˈspɔrtsˌraɪdər, -z
sporty
BR ˈspɔːti
AM ˈspɔrdi
sporular
BR ˈspɒrjʊlə(r)
AM ˈspɔrjələr
sporule
BR ˈspɒr(j)uːl, -z
AM ˈspɔrˌjul, -z
spot
BR spɒt, -s, -ɪŋ, -ɨd
AM spɑ|t, -ts, -dɪŋ, -dəd
spot-check
BR ˌspɒtˈtʃɛk, -s, -ɪŋ, -t
AM ˈspɑtˌtʃɛk, -s, -ɪŋ, -t
spotlamp
BR ˈspɒtlamp, -s

AM ˈspɑtˌlæmp, -s

spotless
BR ˈspɒtləs
AM ˈspɑtləs

spotlessly
BR ˈspɒtləsli
AM ˈspɑtləsli

spotlessness
BR ˈspɒtləsnəs
AM ˈspɑtləsnəs

spotlight
BR ˈspɒtlʌɪt, -s, -ɪŋ, -ɨd
AM ˈspɑtˌlaɪ|t, -ts, -dɪŋ, -dɨd

spot-on
BR ˌspɒtˈɒn
AM ˌspɑdˈɑn

spottedness
BR ˈspɒtɨdnɨs
AM ˈspɑdədnəs

spotter
BR ˈspɒtə(r), -z
AM ˈspɑdər, -z

spottily
BR ˈspɒtɨli
AM ˈspɑdəli

spottiness
BR ˈspɒtɪnɨs
AM ˈspɑdinɨs

Spottiswoode
BR ˈspɒt(ɨ)swʊd, ˈspɒtɪzwʊd
AM ˈspɑtsˌwʊd, ˈspɑdəsˌwʊd

spotty
BR ˈspɒt|i, -ɪə(r), -ɪɨst
AM ˈspɑdi, -ər, -ɨst

spotweld
BR ˈspɒtwɛld, -z, -ɪŋ, -ɨd
AM ˈspɑtˌwɛld, -z, -ɪŋ, -əd

spotwelder
BR ˈspɒtˌwɛldə(r), -z
AM ˈspɑtˌwɛldər, -z

spousal
BR ˈspaʊzl, -z
AM ˈspaʊzəl, -z

spouse
BR spaʊs, spaʊz, -ɪz
AM spaʊs, -əz

spout
BR spaʊt, -s, -ɪŋ, -ɨd
AM spaʊ|t, -ts, -dɪŋ, -dəd

spouter
BR ˈspaʊtə(r), -z
AM ˈspaʊdər, -z

spoutless
BR ˈspaʊtləs
AM ˈspaʊtləs

Sprachgefühl
BR ˈʃprɑːxgəfuːl, ˈʃpraxgɛfuːl
AM ˈʃprɑkgəˌf(j)ul

sprag
BR sprag, -z
AM spræg, -z

Spragge
BR sprag
AM spræg

Sprague
BR spreɪg
AM spreɪg

sprain
BR spreɪn, -z, -ɪŋ, -d
AM spreɪn, -z, -ɪŋ, -d

spraing
BR spreɪŋ
AM spreɪŋ

spraint
BR spreɪnt, -s
AM spreɪnt, -s

sprang
BR spraŋ
AM spræŋ

sprat
BR sprat, -s, -ɪŋ
AM spræ|t, -ts, -dɪŋ

Spratly Islands
BR ˈspratlɪ ˌʌɪlən(d)z
AM ˈsprætli ˌaɪlən(d)z

Spratt
BR sprat
AM spræt

spratter
BR ˈspratə(r), -z
AM ˈsprædər, -z

sprauncy
BR ˈsprɔːns|i, -ɪə(r), -ɪɨst
AM ˈsprɔnsi, ˈsprɑnsi, -ər, -ɨst

sprawl
BR sprɔːl, -z, -ɪŋ, -d
AM sprɔl, sprɑl, -z, -ɪŋ, -d

sprawler
BR ˈsprɔːlə(r), -z
AM ˈsprɔlər, ˈsprɑlər, -z

sprawlingly
BR ˈsprɔːlɪŋli
AM ˈsprɔlɪŋli, ˈsprɑlɪŋli

spray
BR spreɪ, -z, -ɪŋ, -d
AM spreɪ, -z, -ɪŋ, -d

sprayable
BR ˈspreɪəbl
AM ˈspreɪəbəl

spray-dry
BR ˈspreɪdrʌɪ, -z, -ɪŋ, -d
AM ˈspreɪˌdraɪ, -z, -ɪŋ, -d

sprayer
BR ˈspreɪə(r), -z
AM ˈspreɪər, -z

sprayey
BR ˈspreɪi
AM ˈspreɪi

spray-paint
BR ˈspreɪpeɪnt, -s, -ɪŋ, -ɨd
AM ˈspreɪˌpeɪn|t, -ts, -(t)ɪŋ, -(t)ɨd

spread
BR sprɛd, -z, -ɪŋ
AM sprɛd, -z, -ɪŋ

spreadable
BR ˈsprɛdəbl
AM ˈsprɛdəbəl

spread-eagle
BR ˌsprɛdˈiːg|l, ˈsprɛdiːg|l, -lz, -l̩ɪŋ\-lɪŋ, -ld
AM ˌsprɛdˈig|əl, -əlz, -(ə)lɪŋ, -əld

spreader
BR ˈsprɛdə(r), -z
AM ˈsprɛdər, -z

spreadsheet
BR ˈsprɛdʃiːt, -s
AM ˈsprɛdˌʃit, -s

spree
BR spriː, -z
AM spri, -z

sprig
BR sprɪg, -z
AM sprɪg, -z

spriggy
BR ˈsprɪg|i, -ɪə(r), -ɪɨst
AM ˈsprɪgi, -ər, -ɨst

sprightliness
BR ˈsprʌɪtlɪnɨs
AM ˈspraɪtlinɨs

sprightly
BR ˈsprʌɪtl|i, -ɪə(r), -ɪɨst
AM ˈspraɪtli, -ər, -ɨst

sprigtail
BR ˈsprɪgteɪl, -z
AM ˈsprɪgˌteɪl, -z

spring
BR sprɪŋ, -z, -ɪŋ
AM sprɪŋ, -z, -ɪŋ

spring balance
BR ˌsprɪŋ ˈbaləns, + ˈbaln̩s, -ɪz
AM ˈsprɪŋ ˌbæləns, -əz

springboard
BR ˈsprɪŋbɔːd, -z
AM ˈsprɪŋˌbɔ(ə)rd, -z

springbok
BR ˈsprɪŋbɒk, -s
AM ˈsprɪŋˌbɑk, -s

spring-clean[1]
noun
BR ˈsprɪŋkliːn, -z
AM ˈsprɪŋˌklin, -z

spring-clean[2]
verb
BR ˌsprɪŋˈkliːn, ˈsprɪŋkliːn, -z, -ɪŋ, -d
AM ˌsprɪŋˈklin, -z, -ɪŋ, -d

spring-cleaning
BR ˌsprɪŋˈkliːnɪŋ, ˈsprɪŋkliːnɪŋ
AM ˌsprɪŋˈklinɪŋ

springe
BR sprɪn(d)ʒ, -ɪz
AM sprɪndʒ, -ɪz

springer
BR ˈsprɪŋə(r), -z
AM ˈsprɪŋər, -z

Springfield
BR ˈsprɪŋfiːld
AM ˈsprɪŋˌfild

springform
BR ˈsprɪŋfɔːm, -z
AM ˈsprɪŋˌfɔ(ə)rm, -z

springhouse
BR ˈsprɪŋhaʊ|s, -zɪz
AM ˈsprɪŋˌ(h)aʊ|s, -zəz

springily
BR ˈsprɪŋɨli
AM ˈsprɪŋɨli

springiness
BR ˈsprɪŋɪnɨs
AM ˈsprɪŋinɨs

springless
BR ˈsprɪŋlɨs
AM ˈsprɪŋlɨs

springlet
BR ˈsprɪŋlɨt, -s
AM ˈsprɪŋlɨt, -s

springlike
BR ˈsprɪŋlʌɪk
AM ˈsprɪŋˌlaɪk

spring-loaded
BR ˌsprɪŋˈləʊdɨd
AM ˌsprɪŋˈloʊdəd

Springs
BR sprɪŋz
AM sprɪŋz

Springsteen
BR ˈsprɪŋstiːn
AM ˈsprɪŋˌstin

springtail
BR ˈsprɪŋteɪl, -z
AM ˈsprɪŋˌteɪl, -z

springtide
season of Spring
BR ˈsprɪŋtʌɪd, -z
AM ˈsprɪŋˌtaɪd, -z

springtime
BR ˈsprɪŋtʌɪm
AM ˈsprɪŋˌtaɪm

springwater
BR ˈsprɪŋˌwɔːtə(r)
AM ˈsprɪŋˌwɔdər, ˈsprɪŋˌwɑdər

springy
BR ˈsprɪŋ|i, -ɪə(r), -ɪɨst
AM ˈsprɪŋi, -ər, -ɨst

sprinkle
BR ˈsprɪŋk|l, -lz, -l̩ɪŋ\-lɪŋ, -ld
AM ˈsprɪŋkəl, -əlz, -(ə)lɪŋ, -əld

sprinkler
BR ˈsprɪŋklə(r), ˈsprɪŋkl̩ə(r), -z
AM ˈsprɪŋk(ə)lər, -z

sprinkling
BR ˈsprɪŋklɪŋ, ˈsprɪŋkl̩ɪŋ, -z
AM ˈsprɪŋk(ə)lɪŋ, -z

sprint
BR sprɪnt, -s, -ɪŋ, -ɨd
AM sprɪn|t, -ts, -(t)ɪŋ, -(t)ɨd
sprinter
BR 'sprɪntə(r), -z
AM 'sprɪn(t)ər, -z
sprit
BR sprɪt, -s
AM sprɪt, -s
sprite
BR sprʌɪt, -s
AM spraɪt, -s
spritely
BR 'sprʌɪtli
AM 'spraɪtli
spritsail
BR 'sprɪtsl, 'sprɪtseɪl, -z
AM 'sprɪtsəl, 'sprɪt,seɪl, -z
spritz
BR sprɪts, -ɨz, -ɪŋ, -t
AM sprɪts, -ɨz, -ɪŋ, -d
spritzer
BR 'sprɪtsə(r), -z
AM 'sprɪtsər, -z
sprocket
BR 'sprɒkɪt, -s
AM 'sprɑkət, -s
sprog
BR sprɒg, -z
AM sprɑg, -z
Sproughton
BR 'sprɔ:tn
AM 'sprɔtn, 'sprɑtn
Sproule
BR sprəʊl, spru:l
AM sprul
sprout
BR spraʊt, -s, -ɪŋ, -ɨd
AM spraʊ|t, -ts, -dɪŋ, -dəd
spruce
BR spru:s, -ɨz, -ə(r), -ɨst
AM sprus, -əz, -ər, -əst
sprucely
BR 'spru:sli
AM 'sprusli
spruceness
BR 'spru:snəs
AM 'sprusnəs
sprucer
BR 'spru:sə(r), -z
AM 'sprusər, -z
sprue
BR spru:, -z
AM spru, -z
spruik
BR spru:k, -s, -ɪŋ, -t
AM spruk, -s, -ɪŋ, -t
spruiker
BR 'spru:kə(r), -z
AM 'sprukər, -z
spruit
BR spreɪt, -s
AM sprut, spreɪt, -s
AFK sprœɪt
sprung
BR sprʌŋ
AM sprəŋ
spry
BR sprʌɪ, -ə(r), -ɨst
AM spraɪ, -ər, -ɨst
spryly
BR 'sprʌɪli
AM 'spraɪli
spryness
BR 'sprʌɪnɨs
AM 'spraɪnɨs
spud
BR spʌd, -z
AM spəd, -z
spue
BR spju:, -z, -ɪŋ, -d
AM spju, -z, -ɪŋ, -d
spumante
BR sp(j)ʊ'mant|i, -ɪz
AM sp(j)u'mɑn(t)i, sp(j)ə'mɑn(t)i, -z
spume
BR spju:m
AM spjum
spumoni
BR sp(j)ʊ'məʊni
AM spu'moʊni, spə'moʊni
spumous
BR 'spju:məs
AM 'spjuməs
spumy
BR 'spju:m|i, -ɪə(r), -ɪɨst
AM 'spjumi, -ər, -ɨst
spun
BR spʌn
AM spən
spunk
BR spʌŋk
AM spəŋk
spunkily
BR 'spʌŋkɨli
AM 'spəŋkəli
spunkiness
BR 'spʌŋkɪnɨs
AM 'spəŋkinɨs
spunky
BR 'spʌŋk|i, -ɪə(r), -ɪɨst
AM 'spəŋki, -ər, -ɨst
spur
BR spə:(r), -z, -ɪŋ, -d
AM spər, -z, -ɪŋ, -d
spurge
BR spə:dʒ, -ɨz
AM spərdʒ, -əz
Spurgeon
BR 'spə:dʒ(ə)n
AM 'spərdʒən
spurious
BR 'spjʊərɪəs, 'spjɔ:rɪəs
AM 'sp(j)ʊriəs, 'spjuriəs
spuriously
BR 'spjʊərɪəsli, 'spjɔ:rɪəsli
AM 'sp(j)ʊriəsli, 'spjuriəsli
spuriousness
BR 'spjʊərɪəsnəs, 'spjɔ:rɪəsnəs
AM 'sp(j)ʊriəsnəs, 'spjuriəsnəs
spurless
BR 'spə:ləs
AM 'spərləs
Spurling
BR 'spə:lɪŋ
AM 'spərlɪŋ
spurn
BR spə:n, -z, -ɪŋ, -d
AM spərn, -z, -ɪŋ, -d
spurner
BR 'spə:nə(r), -z
AM 'spərnər, -z
spur-of-the-moment
BR ˌspə:rə(v)ðə'məʊm(ə)nt
AM ˌspərə(v)ðə'moʊmənt
Spurrell
BR 'spʌrəl, 'spʌrl̩
AM 'spərəl
spurrey
BR 'spʌr|i, -ɪz
AM 'spəri, -z
spurrier
BR 'spʌrɪə(r), 'spə:rɪə(r), -z
AM 'spəriər, -z
spurry
BR 'spə:r|i, -ɪz
AM 'spəri, -z
spurt
BR spə:t, -s, -ɪŋ, -ɨd
AM spər|t, -ts, -dɪŋ, -dəd
spurwort
BR 'spə:wə:t, -s
AM 'spərwərt, 'spərwɔ(ə)rt, -s
sputa
BR 'spju:tə(*r*)
AM 'spjudə
sputnik
BR 'spʊtnɪk, 'spʌtnɪk, -s
AM 'spʊtnɪk, 'spətnɪk, -s
sputter
BR 'spʌt|ə(r), -əz, -(ə)rɪŋ, -əd
AM 'spə|dər, -dərz, -dərɪŋ\-trɪŋ, -dərd
sputterer
BR 'spʌt(ə)rə(r), -z
AM 'spədərər, -z
sputum
BR 'spju:təm
AM 'spjudəm
spy
BR spʌɪ, -z, -ɪŋ, -d
AM spaɪ, -z, -ɪŋ, -d
spycatcher
BR 'spʌɪˌkatʃə(r), -z
AM 'spaɪˌkɛtʃər, -z
spyglass
BR 'spʌɪglɑ:s, 'spʌɪglas, -ɨz
AM 'spaɪˌglæs, -əz
spyhole
BR 'spʌɪhəʊl, -z
AM 'spaɪˌhoʊl, -z
spymaster
BR 'spʌɪˌmɑ:stə(r), 'spʌɪˌmastə(r), -z
AM 'spaɪˌmæstər, -z
Sqezy
BR 'skwi:zi
AM 'skwizi
squab
BR skwɒb, -z
AM skwɑb, -z
squabble
BR 'skwɒb|l, -lz, -l̩ɪŋ\-lɪŋ, -ld
AM 'skwɑbəl, -əlz, -(ə)lɪŋ, -əld
squabbler
BR 'skwɒbl̩ə(r), 'skwɒblə(r), -z
AM 'skwɑb(ə)lər, -z
squabby
BR 'skwɒbi
AM 'skwɑbi
squab-chick
BR 'skwɒbtʃɪk, -s
AM 'skwɑbˌtʃɪk, -s
squacco
BR 'skwakəʊ, -z
AM 'skwɑkoʊ, -z
squad
BR skwɒd, -z
AM skwɑd, -z
squaddie
BR 'skwɒd|i, -ɪz
AM 'skwɑdi, -z
squaddy
BR 'skwɒd|i, -ɪz
AM 'skwɑdi, -z
squadron
BR 'skwɒdr(ə)n, -z
AM 'skwɑdrən, -z
squail
BR skweɪl, -z
AM skweɪl, -z
squalid
BR 'skwɒlɪd
AM 'skwɔlɨd, 'skwɑlɨd
squalidity
BR skwɒ'lɪdɨti
AM ˌskwɔ'lɪdɨdi, ˌskwɑ'lɪdɨdi
squalidly
BR 'skwɒlɨdli
AM 'skwɔlɨdli, 'skwɑlɨdli

squalidness
BR ˈskwɒlɨdnɨs
AM ˈskwɔlɨdnɨs, ˈskwɑlɨdnɨs

squall
BR skwɔːl, -z, -ɪŋ, -d
AM skwɔl, skwɑl, -z, -ɪŋ, -d

squally
BR ˈskwɔːli
AM ˈskwɔli, ˈskwɑli

squaloid
BR ˈskweɪlɔɪd, -z
AM ˈskweɪˌlɔɪd, -z

squalor
BR ˈskwɒlə(r)
AM ˈskwɔlər, ˈskwɑlər

squama
BR ˈskweɪmə(r)
AM ˈskweɪmə

squamae
BR ˈskweɪmiː
AM ˈskweɪmi, ˈskweɪˌmaɪ

squamate
BR ˈskweɪmət
AM ˈskweɪˌmeɪt

Squamish
BR ˈskwɑːm|ɪʃ, -ɨʃɪz
AM ˈskwɑmɪʃ, -əz

squamose
BR ˈskweɪməʊs
AM ˈskweɪˌmoʊs, ˈskweɪˌmoʊz

squamous
BR ˈskweɪməs
AM ˈskweɪməs

squamously
BR ˈskweɪməsli
AM ˈskweɪməsli

squamousness
BR ˈskweɪməsnəs
AM ˈskweɪməsnəs

squamule
BR ˈskwamjuːl, ˈskweɪmjuːl, -z
AM ˈskwæˌmjul, ˈskwɑˌmjul, ˈskweɪˌmjul, -z

squander
BR ˈskwɒnd|ə(r), -əz, -(ə)rɪŋ, -əd
AM ˈskwɑnd|ər, -ərz, -(ə)rɪŋ, -ərd

squanderer
BR ˈskwɒnd(ə)rə(r), -z
AM ˈskwɑnd(ə)rər, -z

square
BR skwɛː(r), -z, -ɪŋ, -d, -ə(r), -ɨst
AM skwɛ(ə)r, -z, -ɪŋ, -d, -ər, -əst

square-bashing
BR ˈskwɛːˌbaʃɪŋ
AM ˈskwɛrˌbæʃɪŋ

square-built
BR ˌskwɛːˈbɪlt
AM ˈskwɛrˈbɪlt

squaredance
BR ˈskwɛːdɑːns, ˈskwɛːdans, -ɨz, -ɪŋ
AM ˈskwɛrˌdæns, -əz, -ɪŋ

square deal
BR ˌskwɛː ˈdiːl, -z
AM ˈskwɛr ˈdil, -z

square-eyed
BR ˌskwɛːrˈʌɪd
AM ˈskwɛrˈaɪd

squarely
BR ˈskwɛːli
AM ˈskwɛrli

squareness
BR ˈskwɛːnəs
AM ˈskwɛrnəs

squarer
BR ˈskwɛːrə(r), -z
AM ˈskwɛrər, -z

square-rigged
BR ˌskwɛːˈrɪgd
AM ˈskwɛrˈrɪgd

square-rigger
BR ˌskwɛːˈrɪgə(r), -z
AM ˈskwɛrˈrɪgər, -z

square root
BR ˌskwɛː ˈruːt, -s
AM ˌskwɛr ˈrut, -s

Squarial
BR ˈskwɛːrɪəl, -z
AM ˈskwɛriəl, -z

squarish
BR ˈskwɛːrɪʃ
AM ˈskwɛrɪʃ

squarrose
BR ˈskwɒrəʊs, skwɒˈrəʊs, ˈskwarəʊs, skwaˈrəʊs
AM ˈskwɑˌroʊs, ˈskwɑˌroʊz

squash
BR skwɒʃ, -ɨz, -ɪŋ, -t
AM skwɔʃ, skwɑʃ, -əz, -ɪŋ, -t

squashily
BR ˈskwɒʃɨli
AM ˈskwɔʃəli, ˈskwɑʃəli

squashiness
BR ˈskwɒʃɪnɨs
AM ˈskwɔʃinɨs, ˈskwɑʃinɨs

squashy
BR ˈskwɒʃ|i, -ɪə(r), -ɪɨst
AM ˈskwɔʃi, ˈskwɑʃi, -ər, -ɨst

squat
BR skwɒt, -s, -ɪŋ, -ɨd
AM skwɑ|t, -ts, -dɪŋ, -dəd

squatly
BR ˈskwɒtli
AM ˈskwɑtli

squatness
BR ˈskwɒtnəs
AM ˈskwɑtnəs

squatter
BR ˈskwɒtə(r), -z
AM ˈskwɑdər, -z

squaw
BR skwɔː(r), -z
AM skwɔ, skwɑ, -z

squawk
BR skwɔːk, -s, -ɪŋ, -t
AM skwɔk, skwɑk, -s, -ɪŋ, -t

squawker
BR ˈskwɔːkə(r), -z
AM ˈskwɔkər, ˈskwɑkər, -z

squeak
BR skwiːk, -s, -ɪŋ, -t
AM skwik, -s, -ɪŋ, -t

squeaker
BR ˈskwiːkə(r), -z
AM ˈskwikər, -z

squeakily
BR ˈskwiːkɨli
AM ˈskwikɨli

squeakiness
BR ˈskwiːkɪnɨs
AM ˈskwikinɨs

squeaky
BR ˈskwiːk|i, -ɪə(r), -ɪɨst
AM ˈskwiki, -ər, -ɨst

squeal
BR skwiːl, -z, -ɪŋ, -d
AM skwil, -z, -ɪŋ, -d

squealer
BR ˈskwiːlə(r), -z
AM ˈskwilər, -z

squeamish
BR ˈskwiːmɪʃ
AM ˈskwimɪʃ

squeamishly
BR ˈskwiːmɨʃli
AM ˈskwimɨʃli

squeamishness
BR ˈskwiːmɨʃnɨs
AM ˈskwimɨʃnɨs

squeegee
BR ˈskwiːdʒiː, -z, -ɪŋ, -d
AM ˈskwiˌdʒi, -z, -ɪŋ, -d

Squeers
BR skwɪəz
AM skwɪ(ə)rz

squeezable
BR ˈskwiːzəbl
AM ˈskwizəbəl

squeeze
BR skwiːz, -ɨz, -ɪŋ, -d
AM skwiz, -ɨz, -ɪŋ, -d

squeezebox
BR ˈskwiːzbɒks, -ɨz
AM ˈskwizˌbɑks, -əz

squeezer
BR ˈskwiːzə(r), -z
AM ˈskwizər, -z

squelch
BR skwɛltʃ, -ɨz, -ɪŋ, -t
AM skwɛltʃ, -əz, -ɪŋ, -t

squelcher
BR ˈskwɛltʃə(r), -z
AM ˈskwɛltʃər, -z

squelchiness
BR ˈskwɛltʃɪnɨs
AM ˈskwɛltʃinɨs

squelchy
BR ˈskwɛltʃ|i, -ɪə(r), -ɪɨst
AM ˈskwɛltʃi, -ər, -ɨst

squib
BR skwɪb, -z
AM skwɪb, -z

squid
BR skwɪd, -z
AM skwɪd, -z

squidginess
BR ˈskwɪdʒɪnɨs
AM ˈskwɪdʒinɨs

squidgy
BR ˈskwɪdʒ|i, -ɪə(r), -ɪɨst
AM ˈskwɪdʒi, -ər, -ɨst

squiffed
BR ˈskwɪft
AM ˈskwɪft

squiffy
BR ˈskwɪf|i, -ɪə(r), -ɪɨst
AM ˈskwɪfi, -ər, -ɨst

squiggle
BR ˈskwɪg|l, -lz, -l̩ɪŋ\-lɪŋ, -ld
AM ˈskwɪg|əl, -əlz, -(ə)lɪŋ, -əld

squiggly
BR ˈskwɪgl̩i, ˈskwɪgli
AM ˈskwɪg(ə)li

squill
BR skwɪl, -z
AM skwɪl, -z

squillion
BR ˈskwɪljən, -z
AM ˈskwɪljən, ˈskwɪliən, -z

squinancywort
BR ˈskwɪnənsɪˌwəːt
AM ˈskwɪnɨnsiˌwərt, ˈskwɪnɨnsiˌw(ə)rt

squinch
BR skwɪn(t)ʃ, -ɨz
AM skwɪn(t)ʃ, -ɨz

squint
BR skwɪnt, -s, -ɪŋ, -ɨd
AM skwɪn|t, -ts, -(t)ɪŋ, -(t)ɨd

squinter
BR ˈskwɪntə(r), -z
AM ˈskwɪn(t)ər, -z

squinty
BR ˈskwɪnti
AM ˈskwɪn(t)i

squirarchy
BR ˈskwʌɪərɑːk|i, -ɪz
AM ˈskwaɪ(ə)ˌrɑrki, -z

squire
BR ˈskwʌɪə(r), -z, -ɪŋ, -d
AM ˈskwaɪ(ə)r, -z, -ɪŋ, -d

squirearch
BR 'skwʌɪərɑːk, -ɪz
AM 'skwaɪ(ə),rɑrk, -əz

squirearchical
BR ˌskwʌɪə'rɑːkɪkl
AM ˌskwaɪ(ə)'rɑrkəkəl

squirearchy
BR 'skwʌɪərɑːk|i, -ɪz
AM 'skwaɪ(ə),rɑrki, -z

squiredom
BR 'skwʌɪədəm, -z
AM 'skwaɪ(ə)dəm, -z

squireen
BR ˌskwʌɪə'riːn, -z
AM skwaɪ'rin, -z

squirehood
BR 'skwʌɪəhʊd, -z
AM 'skwaɪ(ə)r,(h)ʊd, -z

squirelet
BR 'skwʌɪəlɨt, -s
AM 'skwaɪ(ə)rlət, -s

squireling
BR 'skwʌɪəlɪŋ, -z
AM 'skwaɪ(ə)rlɪŋ, -z

squirely
BR 'skwʌɪəli
AM 'skwaɪ(ə)rli

squireship
BR 'skwʌɪəʃɪp, -s
AM 'skwaɪ(ə)r,ʃɪp, -s

squirl
BR skwəːl, -z
AM skwərl, -z

squirm
BR skwəːm, -z, -ɪŋ, -d
AM skwərm, -z, -ɪŋ, -d

squirmer
BR 'skwəːmə(r), -z
AM 'skwərmər, -z

squirmy
BR 'skwəːmi
AM 'skwərmi

squirrel
BR 'skwɪrəl, 'skwɪrl̩, -z
AM 'skwərəl, -z

squirrelly
BR 'skwɪrəli, 'skwɪrl̩i
AM 'skwər(ə)li

squirt
BR skwəːt, -s, -ɪŋ, -ɨd
AM skwər|t, -ts, -dɪŋ, -dəd

squirter
BR 'skwəːtə(r), -z
AM 'skwərdər, -z

squish
BR skwɪʃ, -ɪz, -ɪŋ, -t
AM skwɪʃ, -ɪz, -ɪŋ, -t

squishiness
BR 'skwɪʃɪnɪs
AM 'skwɪʃinɪs

squishy
BR 'skwɪʃ|i, -ɪə(r), -ɪɪst
AM 'skwɪʃi, -ər, -ɨst

squit
BR skwɪt, -s
AM skwɪt, -s

squitch
BR skwɪtʃ, -ɪz
AM skwɪtʃ, -ɪz

squitters
BR 'skwɪtəz
AM 'skwɪdərz

squiz
BR skwɪz
AM skwɪz

squoze
BR skwəʊz, -d
AM skwoʊz, -d

Sri Lanka
BR ˌsrɪ 'laŋkə(r), ˌsriː +, ˌʃrɪ +, ˌʃriː +
AM ˌsri 'læŋkə

Sri Lankan
BR ˌsrɪ 'laŋkən, ˌsriː +, ˌʃrɪ +, ˌʃriː +, -z
AM ˌsri 'læŋkən, -z

Srinagar
BR srɪ'nʌgə(r), sriː'nʌgə(r), ʃrɪ'nʌgə(r), ʃriː'nʌgə(r)
AM sri'nɑgər, sri'nəgər

srubbiness
BR 'skrʌbɪnɪs
AM 'skrəbinɪs

ssh
BR ʃ
AM ʃ

St
saint
BR s(ə)nt, seɪnt
AM seɪn(t), s(ə)n(t)

St.
street
BR striːt
AM strit

stab
BR stab, -z, -ɪŋ, -d
AM stæb, -z, -ɪŋ, -d

stabber
BR 'stabə(r), -z
AM 'stæbər, -z

stabbing
BR 'stabɪŋ, -z
AM 'stæbɪŋ, -z

stabile
BR 'steɪbʌɪl, -z
AM 'steɪ,bil, -z

stabilisation
BR ˌsteɪbɪlʌɪ'zeɪʃn, ˌsteɪbl̩ʌɪ'zeɪʃn
AM ˌsteɪbələ'zeɪʃən, ˌsteɪbə,laɪ'zeɪʃən

stabilise
BR 'steɪbɪlʌɪz, 'steɪbl̩ʌɪz, -ɪz, -ɪŋ, -d
AM 'steɪbə,laɪz, -ɪz, -ɪŋ, -d

stabiliser
BR 'steɪbɪlʌɪzə(r), 'steɪbl̩ʌɪzə(r), -z
AM 'steɪbə,laɪzər, -z

stability
BR stə'bɪlɨti
AM stə'bɪlɨdi

stabilization
BR ˌsteɪbɪlʌɪ'zeɪʃn, ˌsteɪbl̩ʌɪ'zeɪʃn
AM ˌsteɪbələ'zeɪʃən, ˌsteɪbə,laɪ'zeɪʃən

stabilize
BR 'steɪbɪlʌɪz, 'steɪbl̩ʌɪz, -ɪz, -ɪŋ, -d
AM 'steɪbə,laɪz, -ɪz, -ɪŋ, -d

stabilizer
BR 'steɪbɪlʌɪzə(r), 'steɪbl̩ʌɪzə(r), -z
AM 'steɪbə,laɪzər, -z

stable
BR steɪb|l, -lz, -l̩ɪŋ\-lɪŋ, -ld, -l̩ə(r)\-lə(r), -l̩ɪst\-lɪst
AM 'steɪbəl, -əlz, -(ə)lɪŋ, -əld, -(ə)lər, -(ə)ləst

stableful
BR 'steɪblfʊl, -z
AM 'steɪbəl,fʊl, -z

stableman
BR 'steɪblman
AM 'steɪbəl,mæn

stablemate
BR 'steɪblmeɪt, -s
AM 'steɪbəl,meɪt, -s

stablemen
BR 'steɪblmɛn
AM 'steɪbəl,mɛn

stableness
BR 'steɪblnəs
AM 'steɪbəlnəs

stablish
BR 'stabl|ɪʃ, -ɪʃɪz, -ɪʃɪŋ, -ɪʃt
AM 'stæblɪʃ, -ɪz, -ɪŋ, -t

stably
BR 'steɪbli, 'steɪbl̩i
AM 'steɪb(ə)li

staccato
BR stə'kɑːtəʊ
AM stə'kɑdoʊ

Stacey
BR 'steɪsi
AM 'steɪsi

stack
BR stak, -s, -ɪŋ, -t
AM stæk, -s, -ɪŋ, -t

stackable
BR 'stakəbl
AM 'stækəbəl

stacker
BR 'stakə(r), -z
AM 'stækər, -z

Stackhouse
BR 'stakhaʊs
AM 'stæk,(h)aʊs

stacte
BR 'staktiː, -z
AM 'stækti, -z

Stacy
BR 'steɪsi
AM 'steɪsi

staddle
BR 'stadl, -z
AM 'stædəl, -z

stadia
BR 'steɪdɪə(*r*)
AM 'steɪdiə

stadium
BR 'steɪdɪəm, -z
AM 'steɪdiəm, -z

stadtholder
BR 'stad,həʊldə(r), -z
AM 'stæd,(h)oʊldər, -z

stadtholdership
BR 'stad,həʊldəʃɪp, -s
AM 'stæd,(h)oʊldər,ʃɪp, -s

staff
BR stɑːf, staf, -s, -ɪŋ, -t
AM stæf, -s, -ɪŋ, -t

Staffa
BR 'stafə(*r*)
AM 'stæfə

staffage
BR 'stɑːfɪdʒ, 'stafɪdʒ
AM 'stæfɪdʒ

staffer
BR 'stɑːfə(r), 'stafə(r), -z
AM 'stæfər, -z

Stafford
BR 'stafəd
AM 'stæfərd

Staffordshire
BR 'stafədʃ(ɪ)ə(r)
AM 'stæfərd,ʃɪ(ə)r

staffroom
BR 'stɑːfruːm, 'stɑːfrʊm, 'stafruːm, -z
AM 'stæf,rum, 'stæf,rʊm, -z

Staffs.
Staffordshire
BR stafs
AM stæfs

stag
BR stag, -z
AM stæg, -z

stage
BR steɪdʒ, -ɪz, -ɪŋ, -d
AM steɪdʒ, -ɪz, -ɪŋ, -d

stageability
BR ˌsteɪdʒə'bɪlɨti
AM ˌsteɪdʒə'bɪlɨdi

stageable
BR 'steɪdʒəbl
AM 'steɪdʒəbəl

stagecoach
BR 'steɪdʒkəʊtʃ, -ɪz
AM 'steɪdʒ,koʊtʃ, -əz

stagecraft
BR 'steɪdʒkrɑːft, 'steɪdʒkraft
AM 'steɪdʒ,kræft

stagehand
BR ˈsteɪdʒhand, -z
AM ˈsteɪdʒˌ(h)ænd, -z
stage-manage
BR ˌsteɪdʒˈman|ɪdʒ, ˈsteɪdʒˌman|ɪdʒ, -ɪdʒɪz, -ɪdʒɪŋ, -ɪdʒd
AM ˈsteɪdʒˌmænɪdʒ, -ɪz, -ɪŋ, -d
stager
BR ˈsteɪdʒə(r), -z
AM ˈsteɪdʒər, -z
stagestruck
BR ˈsteɪdʒstrʌk
AM ˈsteɪdʒˌstrək
stage whisper
BR ˌsteɪdʒ ˈwɪspə(r), -z
AM ˈsteɪdʒ ˌ(h)wɪspər, -z
stagey
BR ˈsteɪdʒi
AM ˈsteɪdʒi
stagflation
BR ˌstagˈfleɪʃn
AM ˌstægˈfleɪʃən
Stagg
BR stag
AM stæg
stagger
BR ˈstag|ə(r), -əz, -(ə)rɪŋ, -əd
AM ˈstæg|ər, -ərz, -(ə)rɪŋ, -ərd
staggerer
BR ˈstag(ə)rə(r), -z
AM ˈstæg(ə)rər, -z
staggeringly
BR ˈstag(ə)rɪŋli
AM ˈstæg(ə)rɪŋli
staghound
BR ˈstaghaʊnd, -z
AM ˈstægˌ(h)aʊnd, -z
stagily
BR ˈsteɪdʒɨli
AM ˈsteɪdʒɨli
staginess
BR ˈsteɪdʒɪnɪs
AM ˈsteɪdʒinɪs
staging
BR ˈsteɪdʒɪŋ
AM ˈsteɪdʒɪŋ
stagnancy
BR ˈstagnənsi
AM ˈstægnənsi
stagnant
BR ˈstagnənt
AM ˈstægnənt
stagnantly
BR ˈstagnən(t)li
AM ˈstægnən(t)li
stagnate
BR stagˈneɪt, -s, -ɪŋ, -ɨd
AM ˈstægˌneɪ|t, -ts, -dɪŋ, -dɨd
stagnation
BR stagˈneɪʃn
AM stægˈneɪʃən
stagnicolous
BR stagˈnɪkələs, stagˈnɪkl̩əs
AM stægˈnɪkələs
stagy
BR ˈsteɪdʒ|i, -ɪə(r), -ɪɪst
AM ˈsteɪdʒi, -ər, -ɨst
staid
BR steɪd
AM steɪd
staidly
BR ˈsteɪdli
AM ˈsteɪdli
staidness
BR ˈsteɪdnɪs
AM ˈsteɪdnɪs
stain
BR steɪn, -z, -ɪŋ, -d
AM steɪn, -z, -ɪŋ, -d
stainable
BR ˈsteɪnəbl
AM ˈsteɪnəbəl
stained-glass
BR ˌsteɪndˈglɑːs, ˌsteɪndˈglas
AM ˈsteɪn(d)ˌglæs
stainer
BR ˈsteɪnə(r), -z
AM ˈsteɪnər, -z
Staines
BR steɪnz
AM steɪnz
Stainforth
BR ˈsteɪnfəθ, ˈsteɪnfɔːθ
AM ˈsteɪnˌfɔ(ə)rθ
stainless
BR ˈsteɪnlɪs
AM ˈsteɪnlɪs
stainlessly
BR ˈsteɪnlɪsli
AM ˈsteɪnlɪsli
stainlessness
BR ˈsteɪnlɪsnɪs
AM ˈsteɪnlɪsnɪs
Stainton
BR ˈsteɪntən
AM ˈsteɪn(tə)n
stair
BR stɛː(r), -z
AM stɛ(ə)r, -z
staircase
BR ˈstɛːkeɪs, -ɪz
AM ˈstɛrˌkeɪs, -ɪz
stairhead
BR ˈstɛːhɛd, -z
AM ˈstɛrˌ(h)ɛd, -z
stairlift
BR ˈstɛːlɪft, -s
AM ˈstɛrˌlɪft, -s
stairway
BR ˈstɛːweɪ, -z
AM ˈstɛrˌweɪ, -z
stairwell
BR ˈstɛːwɛl, -z
AM ˈstɛrˌwɛl, -z
staithe
BR steɪð, -z
AM steɪð, -z
stake
BR steɪk, -s, -ɪŋ, -t
AM steɪk, -s, -ɪŋ, -t
stakeboat
BR ˈsteɪkbəʊt, -s
AM ˈsteɪkˌboʊt, -s
stakebuilding
BR ˈsteɪkˌbɪldɪŋ
AM ˈsteɪkˌbɪldɪŋ
stakeholder
BR ˈsteɪkˌhəʊldə(r), -z
AM ˈsteɪkˌ(h)oʊldər, -z
stakeout
BR ˈsteɪkaʊt, -s
AM ˈsteɪkˌaʊt, -s
staker
BR ˈsteɪkə(r), -z
AM ˈsteɪkər, -z
Stakhanovism
BR stəˈkanəvɪz(ə)m, staˈkanəvɪz(ə)m
AM stəˈkɑnəˌvɪzəm
Stakhanovist
BR stəˈkanəvɪst, staˈkanəvɪst, -s
AM stəˈkɑnəvəst, -s
Stakhanovite
BR stəˈkanəvʌɪt, staˈkanəvʌɪt, -s
AM stəˈkɑnəˌvaɪt, -s
stalactic
BR stəˈlaktɪk
AM stəˈlæktɪk
stalactiform
BR stəˈlaktɨfɔːm
AM stəˈlæktəˌfɔ(ə)rm
stalactite
BR ˈstaləktʌɪt, -s
AM stəˈlækˌtaɪt, -s
stalactitic
BR ˌstalәkˈtɪtɪk
AM ˌstæləkˈtɪdɪk
Stalag
BR ˈstalag, -z
AM ˈstɑˌlɑg, -z
stalagmite
BR ˈstaləgmʌɪt, -s
AM stəˈlægˌmaɪt, -s
stalagmitic
BR ˌstaləgˈmɪtɪk
AM ˌstæləgˈmɪdɪk
St Albans
BR s(ə)nt ˈɔːlb(ə)nz, + ˈɒlb(ə)nz
AM seɪn(t) ˈɔlbənz, seɪn(t) ˈɑlbənz
stale
BR steɪl, -ə(r), -ɨst
AM steɪl, -ər, -ɨst
stalely
BR ˈsteɪ(l)li
AM ˈsteɪ(l)li
stalemate
BR ˈsteɪlmeɪt, -s, -ɪŋ, -ɨd
AM ˈsteɪlˌmeɪ|t, -ts, -dɪŋ, -dɨd
staleness
BR ˈsteɪlnɪs
AM ˈsteɪlnɪs
Stalin
BR ˈstɑːlɪn
AM ˈstɑlən
Stalingrad
BR ˈstɑːlɪngrad
AM ˈstɑlənˌgræd, ˈstɑlənˌgrɑd
RUS stəlʲinˈgrat
Stalinism
BR ˈstɑːlɪnɪz(ə)m
AM ˈstɑləˌnɪzəm
Stalinist
BR ˈstɑːlɪnɪst, -s
AM ˈstɑlənəst, -s
stalk
BR stɔːk, -s, -ɪŋ, -t
AM stɔk, stɑk, -s, -ɪŋ, -t
stalker
BR ˈstɔːkə(r), -z
AM ˈstɔkər, ˈstɑkər, -z
stalk-eyed
BR ˌstɔːkˈʌɪd
AM ˈstɔkˌaɪd, ˈstɑkˌaɪd
stalkless
BR ˈstɔːkləs
AM ˈstɔkləs, ˈstɑkləs
stalklet
BR ˈstɔːklɪt, -s
AM ˈstɔklət, ˈstɑklət, -s
stalklike
BR ˈstɔːklʌɪk
AM ˈstɔkˌlaɪk, ˈstɑkˌlaɪk
stalky
BR ˈstɔːki
AM ˈstɔki, ˈstɑki
stall
BR stɔːl, -z, -ɪŋ, -d
AM stɔl, stɑl, -z, -ɪŋ, -d
stallage
BR ˈstɔːl|ɪdʒ, -ɪdʒɪz
AM ˈstɔlɪdʒ, ˈstɑlɪdʒ, -ɪz
stallholder
BR ˈstɔːlˌhəʊldə(r), -z
AM ˈstɔlˌ(h)oʊldər, ˈstɑlˌ(h)oʊldər, -z
stallion
BR ˈstaljən, -z
AM ˈstæljən, -z
Stallybrass
BR ˈstalɪbrɑːs, ˈstalɪbras
AM ˈstæliˌbræs
stalwart
BR ˈstɔːlwət, ˈstɒlwət, -s
AM ˈstɔlwərt, ˈstɑlwərt, -s
stalwartly
BR ˈstɔːlwətli, ˈstɒlwətli
AM ˈstɔlwərtli, ˈstɑlwərtli

stalwartness
BR 'stɔːlwətnəs, 'stɒlwətnəs
AM 'stɔlwərtnəs, 'stɑlwərtnəs

Stalybridge
BR 'steɪlɪbrɪdʒ
AM 'steɪli,brɪdʒ

Stamboul
BR stam'buːl
AM stæm'bul

stamen
BR 'steɪmən, 'steɪmɛn, -z
AM 'steɪmɪn, -z

stamina
BR 'stamɪnə(r)
AM 'stæmənə

staminal
BR 'stamɪnl
AM 'stæmənəl

staminate
BR 'stamɪnət
AM 'stæmə,neɪt

staminiferous
BR ,stamɪ'nɪf(ə)rəs
AM ,stæmə'nɪf(ə)rəs

stammer
BR 'stam|ə(r), -əz, -(ə)rɪŋ, -əd
AM 'stæm|ər, -ərz, -(ə)rɪŋ, -ərd

stammerer
BR 'stam(ə)rə(r), -z
AM 'stæm(ə)rər, -z

stammeringly
BR 'stam(ə)rɪŋli
AM 'stæm(ə)rɪŋli

stamp
BR stam|p, -ps, -pɪŋ, -(p)t
AM stæmp, -s, -ɪŋ, -t

stampede
BR stam'piːd, -z, -ɪŋ, -ɪd
AM stæm'pid, -z, -ɪŋ, -ɪd

stampeder
BR stam'piːdə(r), -z
AM stæm'pidər, -z

stamper
BR 'stampə(r), -z
AM 'stæmpər, -z

Stanbury
BR 'stanb(ə)ri
AM 'stæn,bɛri

stance
BR stɑːns, stans, -ɪz
AM stæns, -əz

stanch
BR stɑːn(t)ʃ, stan(t)ʃ, -ɪz, -ɪŋ, -t
AM stɔn(t)ʃ, stɑn(t)ʃ, -əz, -ɪŋ, -t

stanchion
BR 'stanʃn, -z
AM 'stæn(t)ʃən, -z

stand
BR stand, -z, -ɪŋ
AM stænd, -z, -ɪŋ

stand-alone
BR 'standələʊn
AM 'stændə,loʊn

standard
BR 'standəd, -z
AM 'stændərd, -z

Standardbred
BR 'standədbrɛd, -z
AM 'stændərd,brɛd, -z

standardisable
BR 'standədʌɪzəbl
AM 'stændər,daɪzəbəl

standardisation
BR ,standədʌɪ'zeɪʃn
AM ,stændərdə'zeɪʃən, ,stændər,daɪ'zeɪʃən

standardise
BR 'standədʌɪz, -ɪz, -ɪŋ, -d
AM 'stændər,daɪz, -ɪz, -ɪŋ, -d

standardiser
BR 'standədʌɪzə(r), -z
AM 'stændər,daɪzər, -z

standardizable
BR 'standədʌɪzəbl
AM 'stændər,daɪzəbəl

standardization
BR ,standədʌɪ'zeɪʃn
AM ,stændərdə'zeɪʃən, ,stændər,daɪ'zeɪʃən

standardize
BR 'standədʌɪz, -ɪz, -ɪŋ, -d
AM 'stændər,daɪz, -ɪz, -ɪŋ, -d

standardizer
BR 'standədʌɪzə(r), -z
AM 'stændər,daɪzər, -z

standby
BR 'stan(d)bʌɪ, -z
AM 'stæn(d),baɪ, -z

standee
BR stan'diː, -z
AM stæn'di, -z

stander
BR 'standə(r), -z
AM 'stændər, -z

stand-in
BR 'standɪn, -z
AM 'stænd,ɪn, -z

standing
BR 'standɪŋ, -z
AM 'stændɪŋ, -z

Standish
BR 'standɪʃ
AM 'stændɪʃ

stand-off
BR 'standɒf, -s
AM 'stænd,ɔf, 'stænd,ɑf, -s

standoffish
BR ,stand'ɒfɪʃ
AM ¦stænd'ɔfɪʃ, ¦stænd'ɑfɪʃ

standoffishly
BR ,stand'ɒfɪʃli
AM ¦stænd'ɔfɪʃli, ¦stænd'ɑfɪʃli

standoffishness
BR ,stand'ɒfɪʃnɪs
AM ¦stænd'ɔfɪʃnɪs, ¦stænd'ɑfɪʃnɪs

standout
BR 'standaʊt, -s
AM 'stænd,aʊt, -s

standpipe
BR 'stan(d)pʌɪp, -s
AM 'stæn(d),paɪp, -s

standpoint
BR 'stan(d)pɔɪnt, -s
AM 'stæn(d),pɔɪnt, -s

St Andrews
BR s(ə)nt 'andruːz
AM seɪn(t) 'ændruz

standstill
BR 'stan(d)stɪl, -z
AM 'stæn(d),stɪl, -z

stand-to
BR 'stan(d)tuː, ,stan(d)'tuː
AM ¦stæn(d)¦tu

Stanford
BR 'stanfəd
AM 'stænfərd

Stanhope
BR 'stanəp, 'stanhəʊp
AM 'stæn,(h)oʊp, 'stænəp

Stanislas
BR 'stanɪslas, 'stanɪsləs, 'stanɪslɑːs
AM 'stænə,slɑs

Stanislaus
BR 'stanɪslaʊs, 'stanɪslɔːs
AM 'stænə,slɑs

Stanislavsky
BR ,stanɪ'slavski
AM ,stænə'slɑfski

stank
BR staŋk
AM stæŋk

Stanley
BR 'stanli
AM 'stænli

Stanleyville
BR 'stanlɪvɪl
AM 'stænli,vɪl

Stanmore
BR 'stanmɔː(r)
AM 'stæn,mɔ(ə)r

Stannard
BR 'stanəd
AM 'stænərd

stannary
BR 'stan(ə)r|i, -ɪz
AM 'stænəri, -z

stannate
BR 'staneɪt
AM 'stæ,neɪt

stannic
BR 'stanɪk
AM 'stænɪk

stannite
BR 'stanʌɪt, -s
AM 'stæ,naɪt, -s

stannous
BR 'stanəs
AM 'stænəs

Stansfield
BR 'stanzfiːld, 'stansfiːld
AM 'stænz,fild

Stansgate
BR 'stanzgeɪt
AM 'stænz,geɪt

Stansted
BR 'stanstɛd, 'stanstɪd
AM 'stænstəd, 'stæn,stɛd

Stanton
BR 'stantən
AM 'stæn(t)ən

Stanway
BR 'stanweɪ
AM 'stæn,weɪ

Stanwell
BR 'stanw(ɛ)l
AM 'stæn,wɛl

Stanwick
BR 'stan(w)ɪk
AM 'stæn,wɪk

stanza
BR 'stanzə(r), -z, -d
AM 'stænzə, -z, -d

stanzaic
BR stan'zeɪɪk
AM stæn'zeɪɪk

stapedes
BR stə'piːdiːz
AM stə'pi,diz

stapelia
BR stə'piːlɪə(r), -z
AM stə'piljə, stə'piliə, -z

stapes
BR 'steɪpiːz
AM 'steɪ,piz

staphylococcal
BR ,staf(ə)lə'kɒkl, ,staflə'kɒkl
AM ,stæf(ə)lə'kɑkəl

staphylococcus
BR ,staf(ə)lə'kɒkəs, ,staflə'kɒkəs
AM ,stæf(ə)lə'kɑkəs

staple
BR 'steɪp|l, -lz, -lɪŋ\-lɪŋ, -ld
AM 'steɪp|əl, -əlz, -(ə)lɪŋ, -əld

Stapleford[1]
place in UK
BR 'staplfəd
AM 'stæpəlfərd

Stapleford[2]
surname
BR 'steɪplfəd
AM 'steɪpəlfərd

Staplehurst
BR 'steɪplhəːst

AM 'steɪpəl,(h)ərst

stapler
BR 'steɪpl̩ə(r), 'steɪplə(r), -z
AM 'steɪp(ə)lər, -z

Stapleton
BR 'steɪplt(ə)n
AM 'steɪpəltən

star
BR stɑː(r), -z, -ɪŋ, -d
AM stɑr, -z, -ɪŋ, -d

Stara Zagora
BR ˌstɑːrə zə'gɔːrə(r)
AM ˌstɑrə zə'gɔrə

starboard
BR 'stɑːbəd, 'stɑːbɔːd
AM 'stɑrbərd, 'stɑrˌbɔ(ə)rd

starburst
BR 'stɑːbəːst, -s
AM 'stɑrˌbərst, -s

starch
BR stɑːtʃ, -ɨz, -ɪŋ, -t
AM stɑrtʃ, -əz, -ɪŋ, -t

starcher
BR 'stɑːtʃə(r), -z
AM 'stɑrtʃər, -z

starchily
BR 'stɑːtʃɨli
AM 'stɑrtʃəli

starchiness
BR 'stɑːtʃɪnɨs
AM 'stɑrtʃinɨs

starch-reduced
BR ˌstɑːtʃrɪ'djuːst, ˌstɑːtʃrɪ'dʒuːst
AM 'stɑrtʃrəˌd(j)ust, 'stɑrtʃriˌd(j)ust

starchy
BR 'stɑːtʃ|i, -ɪə(r), -ɪɪst
AM 'stɑrtʃi, -ər, -ɨst

star-crossed
BR 'stɑːkrɒst, ˌstɑː'krɒst
AM 'stɑrˌkrɔst, 'stɑrˌkrɑst

stardom
BR 'stɑːdəm
AM 'stɑrdəm

stardust
BR 'stɑːdʌst
AM 'stɑrˌdəst

stare
BR stɛː(r), -z, -ɪŋ, -d
AM stɛ(ə)r, -z, -ɪŋ, -d

starer
BR 'stɛːrə(r), -z
AM 'stɛrər, -z

starfish
BR 'stɑːfɪʃ, -ɨz
AM 'stɑrˌfɪʃ, -ɨz

stargaze
BR 'stɑːgeɪz, -ɨz, -ɪŋ, -d
AM 'stɑrˌgeɪz, -ɨz, -ɪŋ, -d

stargazer
BR 'stɑːˌgeɪzə(r), -z
AM 'stɑrˌgeɪzər, -z

stargazing
BR 'stɑːˌgeɪzɪŋ
AM 'stɑrˌgeɪzɪŋ

stark
BR stɑːk, -ə(r), -ɨst
AM stɑrk, -ər, -əst

starkers
BR 'stɑːkəz
AM 'stɑrkərz

Starkey
BR 'stɑːki
AM 'stɑrki

Starkie
BR 'stɑːki
AM 'stɑrki

starkly
BR 'stɑːkli
AM 'stɑrkli

starkness
BR 'stɑːknəs
AM 'stɑrknəs

starless
BR 'stɑːləs
AM 'stɑrləs

starlet
BR 'stɑːlɨt, -s
AM 'stɑrlət, -s

starlight
BR 'stɑːlʌɪt
AM 'stɑrˌlaɪt

starlike
BR 'stɑːlʌɪk
AM 'stɑrˌlaɪk

starling
BR 'stɑːlɪŋ, -z
AM 'stɑrlɪŋ, -z

starlit
BR 'stɑːlɪt
AM 'stɑrˌlɪt

Starr
BR stɑː(r)
AM stɑr

starrily
BR 'stɑːrɨli
AM 'stɑrəli

starriness
BR 'stɑːrɪnɨs
AM 'stɑrinɨs

starry
BR 'stɑːri
AM 'stɑri

starry-eyed
BR ˌstɑːrɪ'ʌɪd
AM 'stɑriˌaɪd

Stars and Bars
BR ˌstɑːz (ə)n(d) 'bɑːz
AM ˌstɑrz ən 'bɑrz

Stars and Stripes
BR ˌstɑːz (ə)n(d) 'strʌɪps
AM ˌstɑrz ən 'straɪps

starship
BR 'stɑːʃɪp, -s
AM 'stɑrˌʃɪp, -s

START
BR stɑːt
AM stɑrt

start
BR stɑːt, -s, -ɪŋ, -ɨd
AM stɑr|t, -ts, -dɪŋ, -dəd

starter
BR 'stɑːtə(r), -z
AM 'stɑrdər, -z

startle
BR 'stɑːt|l, -lz, -l̩ɪŋ\-lɪŋ, -ld
AM 'stɑrdəl, -z, -ɪŋ, -d

startler
BR 'stɑːtl̩ə(r), 'stɑːtlə(r), -z
AM 'stɑrdl̩ər, -z

startlingly
BR 'stɑːtl̩ɪŋli, 'stɑːtlɪŋli
AM 'stɑrdl̩ɪŋli

start-up
BR 'stɑːtʌp, -s
AM 'stɑrdəp, -s

star turn
BR ˌstɑː 'təːn, -z
AM 'stɑr ˌtərn, -z

starvation
BR stɑː'veɪʃn
AM stɑr'veɪʃən

starve
BR stɑːv, -z, -ɪŋ, -d
AM stɑrv, -z, -ɪŋ, -d

starveling
BR 'stɑːvlɪŋ, -z
AM 'stɑrvlɪŋ, -z

starwort
BR 'stɑːwəːt, -s
AM 'stɑrwərt, 'stɑrˌwɔ(ə)rt, -s

stases
BR 'steɪsiːz
AM 'steɪˌsiz

stash
BR staʃ, -ɨz, -ɪŋ, -t
AM stæʃ, -əz, -ɪŋ, -t

Stasi
BR 'stɑːzi
AM 'stɑzi

stasis
BR 'steɪsɪs
AM 'steɪsɨs

stat
BR stat, -s
AM stæt, -s

statable
BR 'steɪtəbl
AM 'steɪdəbəl

statal
BR 'steɪtl
AM 'steɪdl

state
BR steɪt, -s, -ɪŋ, -ɨd
AM steɪ|t, -ts, -dɪŋ, -dɨd

statecraft
BR 'steɪtkrɑːft, 'steɪtkraft
AM 'steɪtˌkræft

statedly
BR 'steɪtɨdli
AM 'steɪdɨdli

statehood
BR 'steɪthʊd
AM 'steɪtˌ(h)ʊd

statehouse
BR 'steɪthaʊ|s, -zɨz
AM 'steɪtˌ(h)aʊ|s, -zəz

stateless
BR 'steɪtlɨs
AM 'steɪtlɨs

statelessness
BR 'steɪtlɨsnɨs
AM 'steɪtlɨsnɨs

statelet
BR 'steɪtlɨt, -s
AM 'steɪtlɨt, -s

stateliness
BR 'steɪtlɪnɨs
AM 'steɪtlinɨs

stately
BR 'steɪtl|i, -ɪə(r), -ɪɪst
AM 'steɪtli, -ər, -ɨst

statement
BR 'steɪtm(ə)nt, -s
AM 'steɪtmənt, -s

Staten Island
BR ˌstatn 'ʌɪlənd
AM ˌstætn 'aɪlənd

state-of-the-art
BR ˌsteɪtə(v)ðɪ'ɑːt
AM ˌsteɪdə(v)ði'ɑrt, ˌsteɪdə(v)ðə'ɑrt

stater
BR 'steɪtə(r), -z
AM 'steɪdər, -z

stateroom
BR 'steɪtruːm, 'steɪtrʊm, -z
AM 'steɪtˌrum, 'steɪtˌrʊm, -z

stateside
BR 'steɪtsʌɪd
AM 'steɪtˌsaɪd

statesman
BR 'steɪtsmən
AM 'steɪtsmən

statesmanlike
BR 'steɪtsmənlʌɪk
AM 'steɪtsmənˌlaɪk

statesmanly
BR 'steɪtsmənli
AM 'steɪtsmənli

statesmanship
BR 'steɪtsmənʃɪp
AM 'steɪtsmənˌʃɪp

statesmen
BR 'steɪtsmən
AM 'steɪtsmən

statesperson
BR 'steɪtsˌpəːsn, -z
AM 'steɪtsˌpərsən, -z

stateswoman
BR 'steɪtsˌwʊmən
AM 'steɪtsˌwʊmən

stateswomen
BR 'steɪtsˌwɪmɪn
AM 'steɪtsˌwɪmɨn

statewide
BR ˌsteɪtˈwʌɪd
AM ˈsteɪtˈwaɪd

Statham
BR ˈsteɪθ(ə)m, ˈsteɪð(ə)m
AM ˈsteɪdəm, ˈstædəm

static
BR ˈstatɪk, -s
AM ˈstædɪk, -s

statical
BR ˈstatɨkl
AM ˈstædəkəl

statically
BR ˈstatɨkli
AM ˈstædək(ə)li

statice
BR ˈstatɪs|i, -ɪz
AM ˈstædəsi, -z

station
BR ˈsteɪʃ|n, -nz, -n̩ɪŋ\-(ə)nɪŋ, -nd
AM ˈsteɪʃən, -z, -ɪŋ, -d

stationariness
BR ˈsteɪʃn̩rɪnɨs, ˈsteɪʃən(ə)rɪnɨs
AM ˈsteɪʃəˌnɛrinɨs

stationary
BR ˈsteɪʃn̩(ə)ri, ˈsteɪʃən(ə)ri
AM ˈsteɪʃəˌnɛri

stationer
BR ˈsteɪʃn̩ə(r), ˈsteɪʃənə(r), -z
AM ˈsteɪʃ(ə)nər, -z

stationery
BR ˈsteɪʃn̩(ə)ri, ˈsteɪʃən(ə)ri
AM ˈsteɪʃəˌnɛri

station-keeping
BR ˈsteɪʃnˌkiːpɪŋ
AM ˈsteɪʃənˌkipɪŋ

statism
BR ˈsteɪtɪz(ə)m
AM ˈsteɪdɪzəm

statist
BR ˈsteɪtɪst, -s
AM ˈsteɪdɪst, -s

statistic
BR stəˈtɪstɪk, -s
AM stəˈtɪstɪk, -s

statistical
BR stəˈtɪstɨkl
AM stəˈtɪstəkəl

statistically
BR stəˈtɪstɨkli
AM stəˈtɪstək(ə)li

statistician
BR ˌstatɪˈstɪʃn, -z
AM ˌstædəˈstɪʃən, -z

Statius
BR ˈsteɪʃ(ɪ)əs, ˈsteɪtɪəs
AM ˈsteɪʃ(i)əs

stative
BR ˈsteɪtɪv
AM ˈsteɪdɪv

stator
BR ˈsteɪtə(r), -z
AM ˈsteɪdər, -z

statoscope
BR ˈstatəskəʊp, -s
AM ˈstædəˌskoʊp, -s

stats
BR stats
AM stæts

statuary
BR ˈstatʃʊəri, ˈstatʃəri, ˈstatjʊəri, ˈstatjəri
AM ˈstætʃəˌwɛri

statue
BR ˈstatʃuː, ˈstatjuː, -z, -d
AM ˈstætʃu, -z, -d

statuesque
BR ˌstatʃʊˈɛsk, ˌstatjʊˈɛsk
AM ˌstætʃəˈwɛsk

statuesquely
BR ˌstatʃʊˈɛskli, ˌstatjʊˈɛskli
AM ˌstætʃəˈwɛskli

statuesqueness
BR ˌstatʃʊˈɛsknəs, ˌstatjʊˈɛsknəs
AM ˌstætʃəˈwɛsknəs

statuette
BR ˌstatʃʊˈɛt, ˌstatjʊˈɛt, -s
AM ˌstætʃəˈwɛt, -s

stature
BR ˈstatʃə(r), ˈstatjə(r), -d
AM ˈstætʃər, -d

status
BR ˈsteɪtəs, -ɪz
AM ˈsteɪdəs, ˈstædəs, -əz

status quo
BR ˌsteɪtəs ˈkwəʊ
AM ˌsteɪdəs ˈkwoʊ, ˌstædəs +

statutable
BR ˈstatʃuːtəbl, ˈstatjuːtəbl
AM ˈstætʃudəbəl, ˈstætʃədəbəl

statutably
BR ˈstatʃuːtəbli, ˈstatjuːtəbli
AM ˈstætʃudəbli, ˈstætʃədəbli

statute
BR ˈstatʃuːt, ˈstatjuːt, -s
AM ˈstætʃut, -s

statute-barred
BR ˌstatʃuːtˈbɑːd, ˌstatjuːtˈbɑːd
AM ˈstætʃutˌbɑrd

statutorily
BR ˈstatʃʊtrɨli, ˈstatjʊtrɨli
AM ˈstætʃəˌtɔrəli

statutory
BR ˈstatʃʊt(ə)ri, ˈstatjʊt(ə)ri
AM ˈstætʃəˌtɔri

staunch
BR stɔːn(t)ʃ, -ɨz, -ɪŋ, -t, -ə(r), -ɨst
AM stɔn(t)ʃ, stɑn(t)ʃ, -əz, -ɪŋ, -t, -ər, -əst

staunchly
BR ˈstɔːn(t)ʃli
AM ˈstɔn(t)ʃli, ˈstɑn(t)ʃli

staunchness
BR ˈstɔːn(t)ʃnəs
AM ˈstɔn(t)ʃnəs, ˈstɑn(t)ʃnəs

Staunton[1]
place in UK
BR ˈstɔːnt(ə)n
AM ˈstɔn(t)ən, ˈstɑn(t)ən

Staunton[2]
place in USA
BR ˈstant(ə)n
AM ˈstæn(t)ən

staurolite
BR ˈstɔːrəlʌɪt
AM ˈstɔrəˌlaɪt

stauroscope
BR ˈstɔːrəskəʊp, -s
AM ˈstɔrəˌskoʊp, -s

stauroscopic
BR ˌstɔːrəˈskɒpɪk
AM ˈstɔrəˈskɑpɪk

stauroscopically
BR ˌstɔːrəˈskɒpɨkli
AM ˈstɔrəˈskɑpək(ə)li

Stavanger
BR stəˈvaŋə(r)
AM stəˈvæŋər

stave
BR steɪv, -z, -ɪŋ, -d
AM steɪv, -z, -ɪŋ, -d

stavesacre
BR ˈsteɪvzˌeɪkə(r), -z
AM ˈsteɪvzˌeɪkər, -z

stay
BR steɪ, -z, -ɪŋ, -d
AM steɪ, -z, -ɪŋ, -d

stay-at-home
BR ˈsteɪəthəʊm, -z
AM ˈsteɪətˌ(h)oʊm, -z

stayer
BR ˈsteɪə(r), -z
AM ˈsteɪər, -z

staysail
BR ˈsteɪsl, ˈsteɪseɪl, -z
AM ˈsteɪsəl, ˈsteɪˌseɪl, -z

St Bernard
BR s(ə)nt ˈbəːnəd, -z
AM seɪn(t) bərˈnɑrd, -z

stead
BR stɛd
AM stɛd

steadfast
BR ˈstɛdfɑːst, ˈstɛdfast, ˈstɛdfəst
AM ˈstɛdˌfæst

steadfastly
BR ˈstɛdfɑːstli, ˈstɛdfastli, ˈstɛdfəstli
AM ˈstɛdˌfæs(t)li

steadfastness
BR ˈstɛdfɑːs(t)nəs, ˈstɛdfas(t)nəs, ˈstɛdfəs(t)nəs
AM ˈstɛdˌfæs(t)nəs

steadier
BR ˈstɛdɪə(r), -z
AM ˈstɛdiər, -z

steadily
BR ˈstɛdɪli
AM ˈstɛdəli

steadiness
BR ˈstɛdɪnɨs
AM ˈstɛdinɨs

steading
BR ˈstɛdɪŋ, -z
AM ˈstɛdɪŋ, -z

Steadman
BR ˈstɛdmən
AM ˈstɛdmən

steady
BR ˈstɛd|i, -ɪz, -ɪɪŋ, -ɪd, -ɪə(r), -ɪɨst
AM ˈstɛdi, -z, -ɪŋ, -d, -ər, -ɨst

steak
BR steɪk, -s, -ɪŋ
AM steɪk, -s, -ɪŋ

steakhouse
BR ˈsteɪkhaʊ|s, -zɪz
AM ˈsteɪkˌ(h)aʊ|s, -zəz

steal
BR stiːl, -z, -ɪŋ
AM stil, -z, -ɪŋ

stealer
BR ˈstiːlə(r), -z
AM ˈstilər, -z

stealth
BR stɛlθ
AM stɛlθ

stealthily
BR ˈstɛlθɨli
AM ˈstɛlθəli

stealthiness
BR ˈstɛlθɪnɨs
AM ˈstɛlθinɨs

stealthy
BR ˈstɛlθ|i, -ɪə(r), -ɪɨst
AM ˈstɛlθi, -ər, -ɨst

steam
BR stiːm, -z, -ɪŋ, -d
AM stim, -z, -ɪŋ, -d

steamboat
BR ˈstiːmbəʊt, -s
AM ˈstimˌboʊt, -s

steamer
BR ˈstiːmə(r), -z
AM ˈstimər, -z

steamfitter
BR ˈstiːmˌfɪtə(r), -z
AM ˈstimˌfɪdər, -z

steamily
BR 'sti:mɨli
AM 'stimɨli
steaminess
BR 'sti:mɪnɪs
AM 'stiminɨs
steaming
BR 'sti:mɪŋ, -z
AM 'stimɪŋ, -z
steamroller
BR 'sti:m,rəʊlə(r), -z, -ɪŋ, -d
AM 'stim,roʊlər, -z, -ɪŋ, -d
steamship
BR 'sti:mʃɪp, -s
AM 'stim,ʃɪp, -s
steamshovel
BR 'sti:m,ʃʌvl
AM 'stim,ʃəvəl
steamy
BR 'sti:m|i, -ɪə(r), -ɪɪst
AM 'stimi, -ər, -ɨst
stearate
BR 'stɪəreɪt, -s
AM 'stɪ(ə),reɪt, -s
stearic
BR stɪ'arɪk
AM sti'ɛrɪk
stearin
BR 'stɪərɪn
AM 'stɪrɪn
Stearn
BR stə:n
AM stərn
Stearne
BR stə:n
AM stərn
steatite
BR 'stɪətʌɪt, -s
AM 'stiə,taɪt, -s
steatitic
BR ,stɪə'tɪtɪk
AM ,stiə'tɪdɪk
steatopygia
BR ,stɪətə(ʊ)'pɪdʒɪə(*r*), ,stɪətə(ʊ)'pʌɪdʒɪə(*r*)
AM ,stiədə'pɪdʒiə, ,stiədə'paɪdʒiə, ,stiədə'pɪgiə, ,stiədə'paɪgiə
steatopygous
BR ,stɪətə(ʊ)'pʌɪgəs, ,stɪə'tɒpɪgəs
AM ,stiədə'paɪgəs, ,stiə'tɑpəgəs
steatorrhoea
BR ,sti:ətə'ri:ə(*r*)
AM ,stiədə'riə
steatosis
BR ,stɪə'təʊsɪs
AM ,stiə'toʊsɪs
Stechford
BR 'stɛtʃfəd
AM 'stɛtʃfərd
stedfast
BR 'stɛdfɑ:st, 'stɛdfast, 'stɛdfəst
AM 'stɛd,fæst
stedfastly
BR 'stɛdfɑ:stli, 'stɛdfastli, 'stɛdfəstli
AM 'stɛd,fæs(t)li
stedfastness
BR 'stɛdfɑ:s(t)nəs, 'stɛdfas(t)nəs, 'stɛdfəs(t)nəs
AM 'stɛd,fæs(t)nəs
Stedman
BR 'stɛdmən
AM 'stɛdmən
steed
BR sti:d, -z
AM stid, -z
steel
BR sti:l, -z, -ɪŋ, -d
AM stil, -z, -ɪŋ, -d
Steele
BR sti:l
AM stil
steelhead
BR 'sti:lhɛd, -z
AM 'stil,(h)ɛd, -z
steeliness
BR 'sti:lɪnɪs
AM 'stilinɨs
steelwork
BR 'sti:lwə:k, -s
AM 'stil,wərk, -s
steelworker
BR 'sti:l,wə:kə(r), -z
AM 'stil,wərkər, -z
steelworks
BR 'sti:lwə:ks
AM 'stil,wərks
steely
BR 'sti:l|i, -ɪə(r), -ɪɪst
AM 'stili, -ər, -ɨst
steelyard
BR 'stɪljəd, 'sti:ljɑ:d, -z
AM 'stil,jɑrd, -z
Steen
BR sti:n
AM stin, steɪn
steenbok
BR 'sti:nbɒk, -s
AM 'stin,bɑk, -s
steenkirk
BR 'sti:nkə:k, -s
AM 'stin,kərk, -s
steep
BR sti:p, -s, -ɪŋ, -t, -ə(r), -ɨst
AM stip, -s, -ɪŋ, -t, -ər, -ɨst
steepen
BR 'sti:p|(ə)n, -(ə)nz, -(ə)nɪŋ\-n̩ɪŋ, -(ə)nd
AM 'stipən, -ənz, -(ə)nɪŋ, -ənd
steepish
BR 'sti:pɪʃ
AM 'stipɪʃ
steeple
BR 'sti:pl, -z, -d
AM 'stipəl, -z, -d
steeplechase
BR 'sti:pltʃeɪs, -ɪz
AM 'stipəl,tʃeɪs, -ɪz
steeplechaser
BR 'sti:pl,tʃeɪsə(r), -z
AM 'stipəl,tʃeɪsər, -z
steeplechasing
BR 'sti:pl,tʃeɪsɪŋ
AM 'stipəl,tʃeɪsɪŋ
steeplejack
BR 'sti:pldʒak, -s
AM 'stipəl,dʒæk, -s
steeply
BR 'sti:pli
AM 'stipli
steepness
BR 'sti:pnɪs
AM 'stipnɨs
steer
BR stɪə(r), -z, -ɪŋ, -d
AM stɪ(ə)r, -z, -ɪŋ, -d
steerable
BR 'stɪərəbl
AM 'stɪrəbəl
steerage
BR 'stɪərɪdʒ
AM 'stɪrɪdʒ
steerageway
BR 'stɪərɪdʒweɪ
AM 'stɪrɪdʒ,weɪ
steerer
BR 'stɪərə(r), -z
AM 'stɪrər, -z
steersman
BR 'stɪəzmən
AM 'stɪrzmən
steersmen
BR 'stɪəzmən
AM 'stɪrzmən
steeve
BR sti:v, -z, -ɪŋ, -d
AM stiv, -z, -ɪŋ, -d
Stefanie
BR 'stɛfəni, 'stɛfn̩i
AM 'stɛfəni
stegosaur
BR 'stɛgəsɔ:(r), -z
AM 'stɛgə,sɔ(ə)r, -z
stegosaurus
BR ,stɛgə'sɔ:rəs, -ɪz
AM ,stɛgə'sɔrəs, -əz
Steichen
BR 'stʌɪk(ə)n
AM 'staɪkən
GER 'ʃtaɪçn
Steiermark
BR 'ʃtʌɪəmɑ:k
AM 'ʃtaɪər,mɑrk
Steiger
BR 'stʌɪgə(r)
AM 'staɪgər
stein
BR stʌɪn, -z
AM staɪn, -z
Steinbeck
BR 'stʌɪnbɛk
AM 'staɪn,bɛk
Steinberg
BR 'stʌɪnbə:g
AM 'staɪn,bərg
steinbock
BR 'stʌɪnbɒk, -s
AM 'staɪn,bɑk, -s
steinbok
BR 'stʌɪnbɒk, -s
AM 'staɪn,bɑk, -s
Steiner
BR 'stʌɪnə(r)
AM 'staɪnər
Steinway®
BR 'stʌɪnweɪ, -z
AM 'staɪn,weɪ, -z
stela
BR 'sti:lə(*r*)
AM 'stilə
stelae
BR 'sti:li:
AM 'stili, 'sti,laɪ
stelar
BR 'sti:lə(r)
AM 'stilər
stele
BR sti:l, 'sti:li
AM stil, 'stili
Stella
BR 'stɛlə(*r*)
AM 'stɛlə
stellar
BR 'stɛlə(r)
AM 'stɛlər
stellate
BR 'stɛleɪt, 'stɛlət
AM 'stɛlət, 'stɛ,leɪt
stellated
BR 'stɛleɪtɪd, 'stɛlətɪd
AM 'stɛlədəd, 'stɛ,leɪdɪd
stelliform
BR 'stɛlɪfɔ:m
AM 'stɛlə,fɔ(ə)rm
stellini
BR stɛ'li:ni:, stɪ'li:ni:
AM stə'lini, stɛ'lini
stellular
BR 'stɛljʉlə(r)
AM 'stɛljələr
stem
BR stɛm, -z, -ɪŋ, -d
AM stɛm, -z, -ɪŋ, -d
stemless
BR 'stɛmləs
AM 'stɛmləs
stemlet
BR 'stɛmlɪt, -s
AM 'stɛmlət, -s
stemlike
BR 'stɛmlʌɪk
AM 'stɛm,laɪk
stemma
BR 'stɛmə(*r*), -z
AM 'stɛmə, -z
stemple
BR 'stɛmpl, -z

AM 'stɛmpəl, -z
stemware
BR 'stɛmwɛː(r)
AM 'stɛm,wɛ(ə)r
stench
BR stɛn(t)ʃ, -ɪz, -ɪŋ, -t
AM stɛn(t)ʃ, -əz, -ɪŋ, -t
stencil
BR 'stɛns|l, -lz, -l̩ɪŋ\-lɪŋ, -ld
AM 'stɛns|əl, -əlz, -(ə)lɪŋ, -əld
Stendhal
BR 'stɒndɑːl, stɛn'dɑːl
AM stɛn'dɑl
Sten gun
BR 'stɛn gʌn, -z
AM 'stɛn ,gən, -z
steno
stenographer
BR 'stɛnəʊ, -z
AM 'stɛnoʊ, -z
stenograph
BR 'stɛnəgrɑːf, 'stɛnəgraf, -s
AM 'stɛnə,græf, -s
stenographer
BR stɪ'nɒgrəfə(r), stɛ'nɒgrəfə(r), -z
AM stə'nɑgrəfər, -z
stenographic
BR ,stɛnə'grafɪk
AM ,stɛnə'græfɪk
stenography
BR stɪ'nɒgrəfi, stɛ'nɒgrəfi
AM stə'nɑgrəfi
stenoses
BR stɪ'nəʊsiːz, stɛ'nəʊsiːz
AM stə'noʊsiz
stenosis
BR stɪ'nəʊsɪs, stɛ'nəʊsɪs
AM stə'noʊsəs
stenotic
BR stɪ'nɒtɪk, stɛ'nɒtɪk
AM stə'nɑdɪk
stenotype
BR 'stɛnətʌɪp, -s
AM 'stɛnə,taɪp, -s
stenotypist
BR 'stɛnə,tʌɪpɪst, -s
AM 'stɛnə,taɪpɪst, -s
stent
BR stɛnt
AM stɛnt
stentor
BR 'stɛntɔː(r), 'stɛntə(r), -z
AM 'stɛn,tɔ(ə)r, 'stɛn(t)ər, -z
stentorian
BR stɛn'tɔːrɪən
AM stɛn'tɔriən
step
BR stɛp, -s, -ɪŋ, -t
AM stɛp, -s, -ɪŋ, -t
stepbrother
BR 'stɛp,brʌðə(r), -z
AM 'stɛp,brəðər, -z
step-by-step
BR ,stɛpbʌɪ'stɛp
AM ¦stɛpbaɪ'stɛp
stepchild
BR 'stɛptʃʌɪld
AM 'stɛp,tʃaɪld
stepchildren
BR 'stɛp,tʃɪldr(ə)n
AM 'stɛp,tʃɪldrən
stepdad
BR 'stɛpdad, -z
AM 'stɛp,dæd, -z
stepdaughter
BR 'stɛp,dɔːtə(r), -z
AM 'stɛp,dɔdər, 'stɛp,dɑdər, -z
step-down
BR 'stɛpdaʊn, -z
AM 'stɛp,daʊn, -z
stepfamily
BR 'stɛp,fam(ɪ)l|i, 'stɛp,faml̩|i, -ɪz
AM 'stɛp,fæm(ə)li, -z
stepfather
BR 'stɛp,fɑːðə(r), -z
AM 'stɛp,fɑðər, -z
Stephanie
BR 'stɛfəni, 'stɛfn̩i
AM 'stɛfəni
stephanotis
BR ,stɛfə'nəʊtɪs
AM ,stɛfə'noʊdəs
Stephen
BR 'stiːvn
AM 'stivən, 'stɛfən
Stephens
BR 'stiːvnz
AM 'stivənz
Stephenson
BR 'stiːvns(ə)n
AM 'stivənsən
stepladder
BR 'stɛp,ladə(r), -z
AM 'stɛp,lædər, -z
steplike
BR 'stɛplʌɪk
AM 'stɛp,laɪk
stepmother
BR 'stɛp,mʌðə(r), -z
AM 'stɛp,məðər, -z
Stepney
BR 'stɛpni
AM 'stɛpni
step-parent
BR 'stɛp,pɛːrənt, 'stɛp,pɛːrn̩t, -s
AM 'stɛp,pɛrənt, -s
steppe
BR stɛp, -s
AM stɛp, -s
stepping-stone
BR 'stɛpɪŋstəʊn, -z
AM 'stɛpɪŋ,stoʊn, -z
stepsister
BR 'stɛp,sɪstə(r), -z
AM 'stɛp,sɪstər, -z
stepson
BR 'stɛpsʌn, -z
AM 'stɛp,sən, -z
stepstool
BR 'stɛpstuːl, -z
AM 'stɛp,stul, -z
Steptoe
BR 'stɛptəʊ
AM 'stɛp,toʊ
stepwise
BR 'stɛpwʌɪz
AM 'stɛp,waɪz
Steradent
BR 'stɛrədɛnt
AM 'stɛrədnt
steradian
BR stə'reɪdɪən, -z
AM stə'reɪdiən, -z
stercoraceous
BR ,stəːkə'reɪʃəs
AM ¦stərkə'reɪʃəs
stercoral
BR stə'kɔːrəl, stə'kɔːrl̩
AM stər'kɔrəl
stere
BR stɪə(r), -z
AM stɪ(ə)r, -z
stereo
BR 'stɛrɪəʊ, -z
AM 'stɛrioʊ, -z
stereobate
BR 'stɛrɪə(ʊ)beɪt, -s
AM 'stɛriə,beɪt, -s
stereochemistry
BR ,stɛrɪəʊ'kɛmɪstri
AM ¦stɛriə'kɛməstri
stereograph
BR 'stɛrɪə(ʊ)grɑːf, 'stɛrɪə(ʊ)graf, -s
AM 'stɛrɪə,græf, -s
stereography
BR ,stɛrɪ'ɒgrəfi
AM ,stɛri'ɑgræfi
stereoisomer
BR ,stɛrɪəʊ'ʌɪsəmə(r), -z
AM ¦stɛrioʊ'aɪsəmər, -z
stereometry
BR ,stɛrɪ'ɒmɪtri
AM ,stɛri'ɑmətri
stereophonic
BR ,stɛrɪə(ʊ)'fɒnɪk
AM ¦stɛriə'fɑnɪk
stereophonically
BR ,stɛrɪə'fɒnɪkli
AM ¦stɛriə'fɑnək(ə)li
stereophony
BR ,stɛrɪ'ɒfəni, ,stɛrɪ'ɒfn̩i
AM ,stɛri'ɑfəni
stereopsis
BR ,stɛrɪ'ɒpsɪs
AM ,stɛri'ɑpsəs
stereoptic
BR ,stɛrɪ'ɒptɪk, -s
AM ,stɛri'ɑptɪk, -s
stereopticon
BR ,stɛrɪ'ɒptɪkɒn, -z
AM ,stɛri'ɑptə,kɑn, -z
stereoscope
BR 'stɛrɪəskəʊp, -s
AM 'stɛriə,skoʊp, -s
stereoscopic
BR ,stɛrɪə'skɒpɪk
AM ¦stɛriə'skɑpɪk
stereoscopically
BR ,stɛrɪə'skɒpɪkli
AM ¦stɛriə'skɑpək(ə)li
stereoscopy
BR ,stɛrɪ'ɒskəpi
AM ,stɛri'ɑskəpi
stereospecific
BR ,stɛrɪəʊspɪ'sɪfɪk
AM ¦stɛriəspə'sɪfɪk
stereospecifically
BR ,stɛrɪəʊspɪ'sɪfɪkli
AM ¦stɛriəspə'sɪfɪk(ə)li
stereospecificity
BR ,stɛrɪəʊ,spɛsɪ'fɪsɪti
AM ¦stɛriə,spɛsə'fɪsɪdi
stereotactic
BR ,stɛrɪə(ʊ)'taktɪk
AM ¦stɛriə'tæktɪk
stereotaxic
BR ,stɛrɪə(ʊ)'taksɪk
AM ¦stɛriə'tæksɪk
stereotaxis
BR ,stɛrɪə(ʊ)'taksɪs
AM ¦stɛriə'tæksəs
stereotaxy
BR 'stɛrɪə,taksi
AM ¦stɛriə'tæksi
stereotype
BR 'stɛrɪətʌɪp, -s, -ɪŋ, -t
AM 'stɛriə,taɪp, -s, -ɪŋ, -t
stereotypic
BR ,stɛrɪə(ʊ)'tɪpɪk
AM ¦stɛriə'tɪpɪk
stereotypical
BR ,stɛrɪə(ʊ)'tɪpɪkl
AM ¦stɛriə'tɪpɪkəl
stereotypically
BR ,stɛrɪə(ʊ)'tɪpɪkli
AM ¦stɛriə'tɪpɪk(ə)li
stereotypy
BR 'stɛrɪə,tʌɪpi
AM 'stɛriə,taɪpi
Stergene
BR 'stəːdʒiːn
AM 'stər,dʒin
steric
BR 'stɛrɪk, 'stɪərɪk
AM 'stɪrɪk
sterile
BR 'stɛrʌɪl
AM 'stɛrəl
sterilely
BR 'stɛrʌɪlli
AM 'stɛrə(l)li

sterilisable
BR ˈstɛrɨlʌɪzəbl
AM ˈstɛrəˌlaɪzəbəl

sterilisation
BR ˌstɛrɨlʌɪˈzeɪʃn, ˌstɛrl̩ʌɪˈzeɪʃn
AM ˌstɛrələˈzeɪʃən, ˌstɛrəˌlaɪˈzeɪʃən

sterilise
BR ˈstɛrɨlʌɪz, -ɨz, -ɪŋ, -d
AM ˈstɛrəˌlaɪz, -ɨz, -ɪŋ, -d

steriliser
BR ˈstɛrɨlʌɪzə(r), -z
AM ˈstɛrəˌlaɪzər, -z

sterility
BR stəˈrɪlɨti
AM stəˈrɪlɨdi, stɛˈrɪlɨdi

sterilizable
BR ˈstɛrɨlʌɪzəbl
AM ˈstɛrəˌlaɪzəbəl

sterilization
BR ˌstɛrɨlʌɪˈzeɪʃn, ˌstɛrl̩ʌɪˈzeɪʃn, -z
AM ˌstɛrələˈzeɪʃən, ˌstɛrəˌlaɪˈzeɪʃən, -z

sterilize
BR ˈstɛrɨlʌɪz, -ɨz, -ɪŋ, -d
AM ˈstɛrəˌlaɪz, -ɨz, -ɪŋ, -d

sterilizer
BR ˈstɛrɨlʌɪzə(r), -z
AM ˈstɛrəˌlaɪzər, -z

sterlet
BR ˈstəːlɨt, -s
AM ˈstərlət, -s

sterling
BR ˈstəːlɪŋ
AM ˈstərlɪŋ

sterlingness
BR ˈstəːlɪŋnɨs
AM ˈstərlɪŋnɨs

stern
BR stəːn, -z, -ə(r), -ɨst
AM stərn, -z, -ər, -əst

sterna
BR ˈstəːnə(*r*)
AM ˈstərnə

sternal
BR ˈstəːnl
AM ˈstərnəl

Sterne
BR stəːn
AM stərn

sternly
BR ˈstəːnli
AM ˈstərnli

sternmost
BR ˈstəːnməʊst
AM ˈstərnˌmoʊst

sternness
BR ˈstəːnnəs
AM ˈstər(n)nəs

Sterno®
BR ˈstəːnəʊ
AM ˈstərnoʊ

sternpost
BR ˈstəːnpəʊst, -s
AM ˈstərnˌpoʊst, -s

sternum
BR ˈstəːnəm, -z
AM ˈstərnəm, -z

sternutation
BR ˌstəːnjʉˈteɪʃn, -z
AM ˌstərnjəˈteɪʃən, -z

sternutator
BR ˈstəːnjʉteɪtə(r), -z
AM ˈstərnjəˌteɪdər, -z

sternutatory
BR stəːˈnjuːtət(ə)ri, ˌstəːnjʉˈteɪt(ə)ri
AM stərˈnjudəˌtɔri

sternward
BR ˈstəːnwəd, -z
AM ˈstərnwərd, -z

sternway
BR ˈstəːnweɪ
AM ˈstərnˌweɪ

stern-wheeler
BR ˌstəːnˈwiːlə(r), ˈstəːnˌwiːlə(r), -z
AM ˈstərnˌ(h)wilər, -z

steroid
BR ˈstɛrɔɪd, ˈstɪərɔɪd, -z
AM ˈstɛˌrɔɪd, ˈstɪˌrɔɪd, -z

steroidal
BR ˈstɛrɔɪdl, ˈstɪərɔɪdl
AM stɛˈrɔɪdəl, stɪˈrɔɪdəl

stertor
BR ˈstəːtə(r)
AM ˈstərdər

stertorous
BR ˈstəːt(ə)rəs
AM ˈstərdərəs

stertorously
BR ˈstəːt(ə)rəsli
AM ˈstərdərəsli

stertorousness
BR ˈstəːt(ə)rəsnəs
AM ˈstərdərəsnəs

stet
BR stɛt
AM stɛt

stethoscope
BR ˈstɛθəskəʊp, -s
AM ˈstɛθəˌskoʊp, -s

stethoscopic
BR ˌstɛθəˈskɒpɪk
AM ˌstɛθəˈskɑpɪk

stethoscopical
BR ˌstɛθəˈskɒpɪkl
AM ˌstɛθəˈskɑpəkəl

stethoscopically
BR ˌstɛθəˈskɒpɪkli
AM ˌstɛθəˈskɑpək(ə)li

stethoscopist
BR stɛˈθɒskəpɪst, -s
AM stɛˈθɑskəpəst, ˈʃtɛθəˌskoʊpəst, -s

stethoscopy
BR stɛˈθɒskəpi
AM stɛˈθɑskəpi, ˈʃtɛθəˌskoʊpi

Stetson®
BR ˈstɛtsn, -z
AM ˈstɛtsən, -z

Steuart
BR ˈstjuːət, ˈstʃuːət
AM ˈst(j)uərt

Steuben
BR ˈst(j)uːb(ə)n
AM ˈst(j)ubən

Stevas
BR ˈstiːvəs
AM ˈstivəs

Steve
BR stiːv
AM stiv

stevedore
BR ˈstiːvɨdɔː(r), -z, -ɪŋ
AM ˈstivəˌdɔ(ə)r, -z, -ɪŋ

Steven
BR ˈstiːvn
AM ˈstivən

Stevenage
BR ˈstiːv(ə)nɪdʒ, ˈstiːvn̩ɪdʒ
AM ˈstivənɪdʒ

stevengraph
BR ˈstiːvngrɑːf, ˈstiːvngraf, -s
AM ˈstivənˌgræf, -s

Stevens
BR ˈstiːvnz
AM ˈstivənz

Stevenson
BR ˈstiːvns(ə)n
AM ˈstivənsən

stew
BR stjuː, stʃuː, -z, -ɪŋ, -d
AM st(j)u, -z, -ɪŋ, -d

steward
BR ˈstjuːəd, ˈstʃuːəd, -z, -ɪŋ, -ɨd
AM ˈst(j)uərd, -z, -ɪŋ, -əd

stewardess
BR ˈstjuːədɪs, ˌstjuːəˈdɛs, ˈstʃuːədɪs, ˌstʃuːəˈdɛs, -ɨz
AM ˈst(j)uərdəs, -əz

stewardship
BR ˈstjuːədʃɪp, ˈstʃuːədʃɪp, -s
AM ˈst(j)uərdˌʃɪp, -s

Stewart
BR ˈstjuːət, ˈstʃuːət
AM ˈst(j)uərt

stewpan
BR ˈstjuːpan, ˈstʃuːpan, -z
AM ˈst(j)uˌpæn, -z

stewpot
BR ˈstjuːpɒt, ˈstʃuːpɒt, -s
AM ˈst(j)uˌpɑt, -s

Steyning
BR ˈstɛnɪŋ
AM ˈstɛnɪŋ

stg.
BR ˈstəːlɪŋ
AM ˈstərlɪŋ

St George
BR s(ə)nt ˈdʒɔːdʒ
AM seɪn(t) ˈdʒɔrdʒ

St Gotthard
BR s(ə)n(t) ˈgɒtəd, + ˈgɒtɑːd
AM seɪn(t) ˈgɔdərd, seɪn(t) ˈgɑdərd

St Helena
island
BR ˌsɛnt ɪˈliːnə(*r*), ˌs(ə)nt həˈliːnə(*r*)
AM seɪn(t) həˈlinə

St Helens
BR s(ə)nt ˈhɛlənz
AM seɪn(t) ˈhɛlənz

St Helier
BR s(ə)nt ˈhɛlɪə(r)
AM seɪn(t) ˈhɛliər

sthenia
BR ˈsθɛnɪə(*r*)
AM ˈsθɛniə

sthenic
BR ˈsθɛnɪk
AM ˈsθɛnɪk

stichomythia
BR ˌstɪkəˈmɪθɪə(*r*), -z
AM ˌstɪkəˈmɪθiə, -z

stick
BR stɪk, -s, -ɪŋ
AM stɪk, -s, -ɪŋ

stickability
BR ˌstɪkəˈbɪlɨti
AM ˌstɪkəˈbɪlɨdi

stickball
BR ˈstɪkbɔːl
AM ˈstɪkˌbɔl, ˈstɪkˌbɑl

sticker
BR ˈstɪkə(r), -z
AM ˈstɪkər, -z

stickily
BR ˈstɪkɨli
AM ˈstɪkɨli

stickiness
BR ˈstɪkɪnɨs
AM ˈstɪkinɨs

stick-in-the-mud
BR ˈstɪkɪnðəˌmʌd, -z
AM ˈstɪkɨnðəˌməd, -z

stickjaw
BR ˈstɪkdʒɔː(*r*), -z
AM ˈstɪkˌdʒɔ, ˈstɪkˌdʒɑ, -z

stickleback
BR ˈstɪklbak, -s
AM ˈstɪkəlˌbæk, -s

stickler
BR ˈstɪklə(r), -z
AM ˈstɪk(ə)lər, -z

stickless
BR ˈstɪklɪs

AM ˈstɪklɪs

sticklike
BR ˈstɪklʌɪk
AM ˈstɪkˌlaɪk

stickpin
BR ˈstɪkpɪn, -z
AM ˈstɪkˌpɪn, -z

stickshift
BR ˈstɪkʃɪft, -s
AM ˈstɪkˌʃɪft, -s

stick-to-it-ive
BR ˌstɪkˈtuːɪtɪv
AM ˌstɪkˈtuədɪv

stick-to-it-iveness
BR ˌstɪkˈtuːɪtɪvnɪs
AM ˌstɪkˈtuədɪvnɪs

stickum
BR ˈstɪkəm, -z
AM ˈstɪkəm, -z

stick-up
BR ˈstɪkʌp, -s
AM ˈstɪkəp, -s

stickweed
BR ˈstɪkwiːd, -z
AM ˈstɪkˌwid, -z

sticky
BR ˈstɪk|i, -ɪə(r), -ɪɪst
AM ˈstɪki, -ər, -ɪst

stickybeak
BR ˈstɪkɪbiːk, -s, -ɪŋ, -t
AM ˈstɪkiˌbik, -s, -ɪŋ, -t

Stieglitz
BR ˈstiːɡlɪts
AM ˈstiɡlɪts

stifado
BR stɪˈfɑːdəʊ
AM stəˈfadoʊ

stiff
BR stɪf, -s, -ə(r), -ɪst
AM stɪf, -s, -ər, -əst

stiffen
BR ˈstɪf|n, -nz, -n̩ɪŋ\-nɪŋ, -nd
AM ˈstɪf|ən, -ənz, -(ə)nɪŋ, -ənd

stiffener
BR ˈstɪfn̩ə(r), ˈstɪfnə(r), -z
AM ˈstɪf(ə)nər, -z

stiffening
BR ˈstɪfn̩ɪŋ, ˈstɪfnɪŋ, -z
AM ˈstɪf(ə)nɪŋ, -z

stiffish
BR ˈstɪfɪʃ
AM ˈstɪfɪʃ

Stiffkey
BR ˈstɪfkiː, ˈst(j)uːki
AM ˈstɪfki

stiffly
BR ˈstɪfli
AM ˈstɪfli

stiffness
BR ˈstɪfnɪs
AM ˈstɪfnɪs

stiffy
BR ˈstɪf|i, -ɪz
AM ˈstɪfi, -z

stifle
BR ˈstʌɪf|l, -lz, -l̩ɪŋ\-lɪŋ, -ld
AM ˈstaɪf|əl, -əlz, -(ə)lɪŋ, -əld

stifler
BR ˈstʌɪflə(r), ˈstʌɪfl̩ə(r), -z
AM ˈstaɪf(ə)lər, -z

stiflingly
BR ˈstʌɪflɪŋli, ˈstʌɪfl̩ɪŋli
AM ˈstaɪf(ə)lɪŋli

stigma
BR ˈstɪɡmə(r)
AM ˈstɪɡmə

stigmata
BR ˈstɪɡmətə(r), stɪɡˈmɑːtə(r)
AM stɪɡˈmɑdə, ˈstɪɡmədə

stigmatic
BR stɪɡˈmatɪk, -s
AM stɪɡˈmædɪk, -s

stigmatically
BR stɪɡˈmatɪkli
AM stɪɡˈmædək(ə)li

stigmatisation
BR ˌstɪɡmətʌɪˈzeɪʃn
AM ˌstɪɡmədəˈzeɪʃən, ˌstɪɡməˌtaɪˈzeɪʃən

stigmatise
BR ˈstɪɡmətʌɪz, -ɪz, -ɪŋ, -d
AM ˈstɪɡməˌtaɪz, -ɪz, -ɪŋ, -d

stigmatist
BR ˈstɪɡmətɪst, -s
AM ˈstɪɡmədəst, -s

stigmatization
BR ˌstɪɡmətʌɪˈzeɪʃn
AM ˌstɪɡmədəˈzeɪʃən, ˌstɪɡməˌtaɪˈzeɪʃən

stigmatize
BR ˈstɪɡmətʌɪz, -ɪz, -ɪŋ, -d
AM ˈstɪɡməˌtaɪz, -ɪz, -ɪŋ, -d

stilb
BR stɪlb, -z
AM stɪlb, -z

stilbene
BR ˈstɪlbiːn
AM ˈstɪlˌbin

stilbestrol
BR stɪlˈbiːstrɒl, stɪlˈbɛstrɒl, stɪlˈbiːstr(ə)l, stɪlˈbɛstr(ə)l
AM stɪlˈbɛsˌtrɔl, stɪlˈbɛsˌtrɑl

stilbite
BR ˈstɪlbʌɪt
AM ˈstɪlˌbaɪt

stilboestrol
BR stɪlˈbiːstrɒl, stɪlˈbɛstrɒl, stɪlˈbiːstr(ə)l, stɪlˈbɛstr(ə)l
AM stɪlˈbɛsˌtrɔl, stɪlˈbɛsˌtrɑl

stile
BR stʌɪl, -z
AM staɪl, -z

Stiles
BR stʌɪlz
AM staɪlz

stiletto
BR stɪˈlɛtəʊ, -z
AM stəˈlɛdoʊ, -z

Stilgoe
BR ˈstɪlɡəʊ
AM ˈstɪlɡoʊ

stili
BR ˈstʌɪlʌɪ
AM ˈstaɪˌlaɪ

Stilicho
BR ˈstɪlɪkəʊ
AM ˈstɪlɪkoʊ

still
BR stɪl, -z, -ɪŋ, -d, -ə(r), -ɪst
AM stɪl, -z, -ɪŋ, -d, -ər, -ɪst

stillage
BR ˈstɪl|ɪdʒ, -ɪdʒɪz
AM ˈstɪlɪdʒ, -ɪz

stillbirth
BR ˈstɪlbəːθ, ˌstɪlˈbəːθ, -s
AM ˈstɪlˌbərθ, -s

stillborn
BR ˈstɪlbɔːn, ˌstɪlˈbɔːn
AM ˈstɪlˌbɔ(ə)rn

stillicide
BR ˈstɪlɪsʌɪd, -z
AM ˈstɪlɪˌsaɪd, -z

still-life
BR ˌstɪlˈlʌɪf
AM ˈstɪlˌlaɪf

stillness
BR ˈstɪlnɪs, -ɪz
AM ˈstɪlnɪs, -ɪz

stillroom
BR ˈstɪlruːm, ˈstɪlrʊm, -z
AM ˈstɪlˌrum, ˈstɪlˌrʊm, -z

Stillson
BR ˈstɪls(ə)n, -z
AM ˈstɪlsən, -z

stilly[1]
adjective
BR ˈstɪli
AM ˈstɪli

stilly[2]
adverb
BR ˈstɪlli
AM ˈstɪlli

stilt
BR stɪlt, -s
AM stɪlt, -s

stilted
BR ˈstɪltɪd
AM ˈstɪltɪd

stiltedly
BR ˈstɪltɪdli
AM ˈstɪltɪdli

stiltedness
BR ˈstɪltɪdnɪs
AM ˈstɪltɪdnɪs

stiltless
BR ˈstɪltlɪs
AM ˈstɪltlɪs

Stilton®
BR ˈstɪlt(ə)n
AM ˈstɪlt(ə)n

stilus
BR ˈstʌɪləs, -ɪz
AM ˈstaɪləs, -əz

Stimson
BR ˈstɪms(ə)n
AM ˈstɪmsən

stimulant
BR ˈstɪmjʊlənt, ˈstɪmjʊlnt, -s
AM ˈstɪmjələnt, -s

stimulate
BR ˈstɪmjʊleɪt, -s, -ɪŋ, -ɪd
AM ˈstɪmjəˌleɪ|t, -ts, -dɪŋ, -dɪd

stimulatingly
BR ˈstɪmjʊleɪtɪŋli
AM ˈstɪmjəˌleɪdɪŋli

stimulation
BR ˌstɪmjʊˈleɪʃn, -z
AM ˌstɪmjəˈleɪʃən, -z

stimulative
BR ˈstɪmjʊlətɪv, -z
AM ˈstɪmjəˌleɪdɪv, ˈstɪmjələdɪv, -z

stimulator
BR ˈstɪmjʊleɪtə(r), -z
AM ˈstɪmjəˌleɪdər, -z

stimulatory
BR ˈstɪmjʊlət(ə)ri
AM ˈstɪmjələˌtɔri

stimuli
BR ˈstɪmjʊlʌɪ, ˈstɪmjʊliː
AM ˈstɪmjəˌlaɪ

stimulus
BR ˈstɪmjʊləs
AM ˈstɪmjələs

stimy
BR ˈstʌɪm|i, -ɪz, -ɪɪŋ, -ɪd
AM ˈstaɪmi, -z, -ɪŋ, -d

sting
BR stɪŋ, -z, -ɪŋ
AM stɪŋ, -z, -ɪŋ

stingaree
BR ˌstɪŋɡəˈriː, ˈstɪŋɡəriː, -z
AM ˈstɪŋəˈri, -z

stinger
BR ˈstɪŋə(r), -z
AM ˈstɪŋər, -z

stingily
BR ˈstɪn(d)ʒɪli
AM ˈstɪndʒɪli

stinginess
BR 'stɪn(d)ʒɪnɨs
AM 'stɪndʒinɨs

stingingly
BR 'stɪŋɪŋli
AM 'stɪŋɪŋli

stingless
BR 'stɪŋlɨs
AM 'stɪŋlɨs

stinglike
BR 'stɪŋlʌɪk
AM 'stɪŋ,laɪk

stingray
BR 'stɪŋreɪ, -z
AM 'stɪŋ,reɪ, -z

stingy[1]
miserly
BR 'stɪn(d)ʒ|i, -ɪə(r), -ɪɪst
AM 'stɪndʒi, -ər, -ɨst

stingy[2]
with a sting
BR 'stɪŋi
AM 'stɪŋi

stink
BR stɪŋk, -s, -ɪŋ
AM stɪŋk, -s, -ɪŋ

stinkard
BR 'stɪŋkəd, -z
AM 'stɪŋkərd, -z

stinkbomb
BR 'stɪŋkbɒm, -z
AM 'stɪŋk,bɑm, -z

stinker
BR 'stɪŋkə(r), -z
AM 'stɪŋkər, -z

stinkhorn
BR 'stɪŋkhɔːn, -z
AM 'stɪŋk,(h)ɔ(ə)rn, -z

stinkingly
BR 'stɪŋkɪŋli
AM 'stɪŋkɪŋli

stinko
BR 'stɪŋkəʊ
AM 'stɪŋkoʊ

stinkpot
BR 'stɪŋkpɒt, -s
AM 'stɪŋk,pɑt, -s

stinkweed
BR 'stɪŋkwiːd, -z
AM 'stɪŋk,wid, -z

stinkwood
BR 'stɪŋkwʊd, -z
AM 'stɪŋk,wʊd, -z

stinky
BR 'stɪŋk|i, -ɪə(r), -ɪɪst
AM 'stɪŋki, -ər, -ɨst

stint
BR stɪnt, -s, -ɪŋ, -ɨd
AM stɪn|t, -ts, -(t)ɪŋ, -(t)ɨd

stinter
BR 'stɪntə(r), -z
AM 'stɪn(t)ər, -z

stintless
BR 'stɪntlɨs
AM 'stɪn(t)lɨs

stipe
BR stʌɪp, -s
AM staɪp, -s

stipel
BR 'stʌɪpl, -z
AM 'staɪpəl, -z

stipellate
BR stɪ'pɛlət, -s
AM staɪ'pɛlət, stə'pɛlət, 'staɪpə,leɪt, -s

stipend
BR 'stʌɪpɛnd, -z
AM 'staɪ,pɛnd, 'staɪpənd, -z

stipendiary
BR stʌɪ'pɛndjər|i, -ɪz
AM staɪ'pɛndi,ɛri, -z

stipes
BR 'stʌɪpiːz
AM 'staɪ,piz

stipiform
BR 'stʌɪpɪfɔːm
AM 'staɪpə,fɔ(ə)rm

stipitate
BR 'stɪpɪtət
AM 'stɪpə,teɪt

stipitiform
BR 'stɪpɪtɪfɔːm
AM 'stɪpədə,fɔ(ə)rm

stipple
BR 'stɪp|l, -lz, -l̩ɪŋ\-lɪŋ, -ld
AM 'stɪp|əl, -əlz, -(ə)lɪŋ, -əld

stippler
BR 'stɪpl̩ə(r), 'stɪplə(r), -z
AM 'stɪp(ə)lər, -z

stipular
BR 'stɪpjʉlə(r)
AM 'stɪpjələr

stipulate
BR 'stɪpjʉleɪt, -s, -ɪŋ, -ɨd
AM 'stɪpjə,leɪ|t, -ts, -dɪŋ, -dɨd

stipulation
BR ,stɪpjʉ'leɪʃn, -z
AM ,stɪpjə'leɪʃən, -z

stipulator
BR 'stɪpjʉleɪtə(r), -z
AM 'stɪpjə,leɪdər, -z

stipulatory
BR 'stɪpjʉlət(ə)ri, ,stɪpjʉ'leɪt(ə)ri
AM 'stɪpjələ,tɔri

stipule
BR 'stɪpjuːl, -z
AM 'stɪpjul, -z

stir
BR stəː(r), -z, -ɪŋ, -d
AM stər, -z, -ɪŋ, -d

stir-crazy
BR 'stəː,kreɪzi, ,stəː'kreɪzi
AM 'stər,kreɪzi

stir-fry
BR 'stəːfrʌɪ, ,stəː'frʌɪ, -z, -ɪŋ, -d
AM 'stər,fraɪ, -z, -ɪŋ, -d

stirk
BR stəːk, -s
AM stərk, -s

stirless
BR 'stəːləs
AM 'stərləs

Stirling
BR 'stəːlɪŋ
AM 'stərlɪŋ

stirpes
BR 'stəːpiːz
AM 'stər,piz

stirpiculture
BR 'stəːpɪ,kʌltʃə(r)
AM 'stərpə,kəltʃər

stirps
BR stəːps
AM stərps

stirrer
BR 'stəːrə(r), -z
AM 'stərər, -z

stirring
BR 'stəːrɪŋ, -z
AM 'stərɪŋ, -z

stirringly
BR 'stəːrɪŋli
AM 'stərɪŋli

stirrup
BR 'stɪrəp, -s
AM 'stɪrəp, -s

stishovite
BR 'stɪʃəvʌɪt
AM 'stɪʃə,vaɪt

stitch
BR stɪtʃ, -ɪz, -ɪŋ, -t
AM stɪtʃ, -ɪz, -ɪŋ, -t

stitcher
BR 'stɪtʃə(r), -z
AM 'stɪtʃər, -z

stitchery
BR 'stɪtʃ(ə)ri
AM 'stɪtʃəri

stitchless
BR 'stɪtʃlɨs
AM 'stɪtʃlɨs

stitchwork
BR 'stɪtʃwəːk
AM 'stɪtʃ,wərk

stitchwort
BR 'stɪtʃwəːt, -s
AM 'stɪtʃwərt, 'stɪtʃ,wɔ(ə)rt, -s

stiver
BR 'stʌɪvə(r), -z
AM 'staɪvər, -z

Stivichall
BR 'stʌɪtʃl, 'stʌɪtʃɔːl
AM 'staɪtʃəl

St John
BR s(ə)nt 'dʒɒn
AM seɪn(t) 'dʒɑn

St John's
BR s(ə)nt 'dʒɒnz
AM seɪn(t) 'dʒɑnz

St Kilda
BR s(ə)nt 'kɪldə(r)
AM seɪn(t) 'kɪldə

St Kitts
BR s(ə)nt 'kɪts
AM seɪn(t) 'kɪts

St Kitts-Nevis
BR s(ə)nt ,kɪts'niːvɪs
AM seɪn(t) 'kɪts'nivɨs

St Lawrence
BR s(ə)nt 'lɒrəns, + 'lɒrn̩s
AM seɪn(t) 'lɔrəns

St Leger
BR s(ə)nt 'lɛdʒə(r)
AM seɪn(t) 'lɛdʒər

St Louis[1]
BR s(ə)nt 'luːi
AM seɪn(t) 'lui(s)

St Louis[2]
US city
BR s(ə)nt 'luːɪs
AM ˌseɪn(t)'luəs

St Lucia
BR s(ə)nt 'luːʃ(ɪ)ə(r), + 'luːsɪə(r)
AM ˌseɪnt'luʃə, ˌseɪnt,lu'siə, ˌsən(t)'luʃə, ˌsən(t),lu'siə

stoa
BR 'stəʊə(r)
AM 'stoʊə

stoat
BR stəʊt, -s
AM stoʊt, -s

stob
BR stɒb, -z
AM stɑb, -z

stochastic
BR stə'kastɪk, stɒ'kastɪk
AM stə'kæstɪk

stochastically
BR stə'kastɪkli, stɒ'kastɪkli
AM stə'kæstək(ə)li

stock
BR stɒk, -s, -ɪŋ, -t
AM stɑk, -s, -ɪŋ, -t

stockade
BR stɒ'keɪd, -z, -ɪŋ, -ɨd
AM stɑ'keɪd, -z, -ɪŋ, -ɨd

stockbreeder
BR 'stɒk,briːdə(r), -z
AM 'stɑk,bridər, -z

stockbreeding
BR 'stɒk,briːdɪŋ
AM 'stɑk,bridɪŋ

Stockbridge
BR 'stɒkbrɪdʒ
AM 'stɑk,brɪdʒ

stockbroker
BR 'stɒk,brəʊkə(r), -z
AM 'stɑk,broʊkər, -z

stockbrokerage
BR 'stɒk,brəʊk(ə)rɪdʒ
AM 'stɑk,broʊk(ə)rɪdʒ

stockbroking
BR 'stɒk,brəʊkɪŋ
AM 'stɑk,broʊkɪŋ

stockcar
BR 'stɒkkɑː(r), -z
AM 'stɑ(k),kɑr, -z

Stockdale
BR 'stɒkdeɪl
AM 'stɑk,deɪl

stocker
BR 'stɒkə(r), -z
AM 'stɑkər, -z

stock exchange
BR 'stɒk ɪks,tʃeɪn(d)ʒ, -ɪz
AM 'stɑk əks,tʃeɪndʒ, -ɪz

stockfish
BR 'stɒkfɪʃ
AM 'stɑk,fɪʃ

Stockhausen
BR 'stɒk,haʊzn, 'ʃtɒk,haʊzn
AM 'stɑk,(h)aʊzn

stockholder
BR 'stɒk,həʊldə(r), -z
AM 'stɑk,(h)oʊldər, -z

stockholding
BR 'stɒk,həʊldɪŋ, -z
AM 'stɑk,(h)oʊldɪŋ, -z

Stockholm
BR 'stɒkhəʊm
AM 'stɑk,(h)oʊ(l)m

stockily
BR 'stɒkɨli
AM 'stɑkəli

stockiness
BR 'stɒkɪnɨs
AM 'stɑkinɨs

stockinet
BR ,stɒkɪ'nɛt
AM ,stɑkə'nɛt

stockinette
BR ,stɒkɪ'nɛt
AM ,stɑkə'nɛt

stocking
BR 'stɒkɪŋ, -z, -d
AM 'stɑkɪŋ, -z, -d

stockingless
BR 'stɒkɪŋlɨs
AM 'stɑkɪŋlɨs

stock-in-trade
BR ,stɒkɪn'treɪd
AM ¦stɑkən'treɪd

stockist
BR 'stɒkɪst, -s
AM 'stɑkəst, -s

stockjobber
BR 'stɒk,dʒɒbə(r), -z
AM 'stɑk,dʒɑbər, -z

stockjobbing
BR 'stɒk,dʒɒbɪŋ
AM 'stɑk,dʒɑbɪŋ

stockless
BR 'stɒkləs
AM 'stɑkləs

stocklist
BR 'stɒklɪst, -s
AM 'stɑk,lɪst, -s

stockman
BR 'stɒkmən
AM 'stɑkmən, 'stɑk,mæn

stockmen
BR 'stɒkmən
AM 'stɑkmən, 'stɑk,mɛn

stockout
BR 'stɒkaʊt, -s
AM 'stɑk,aʊt, -s

stockpile
BR 'stɒkpʌɪl, -z, -ɪŋ, -d
AM 'stɑk,paɪl, -z, -ɪŋ, -d

stockpiler
BR 'stɒk,pʌɪlə(r), -z
AM 'stɑk,paɪlər, -z

Stockport
BR 'stɒkpɔːt
AM 'stɑk,pɔ(ə)rt

stockpot
BR 'stɒkpɒt, -s
AM 'stɑk,pɑt, -s

stockroom
BR 'stɒkruːm, 'stɒkrʊm, -z
AM 'stɑk,rum, 'stɑk,rʊm, -z

Stocks
BR stɒks
AM stɑks

Stocksbridge
BR 'stɒksbrɪdʒ
AM 'stɑks,brɪdʒ

stock-still
BR ,stɒk'stɪl
AM 'stɑk'stɪl

stocktake
BR 'stɒkteɪk, -s
AM 'stɑk,teɪk, -s

stocktaking
BR 'stɒk,teɪkɪŋ
AM 'stɑk,teɪkɪŋ

Stockton
BR 'stɒktən
AM 'stɑktən

Stockton-on-Tees
BR ,stɒktənɒn'tiːz
AM ¦stɑktənən'tiz

Stockwell
BR 'stɒkw(ɛ)l
AM 'stɑk,wɛl

Stockwood
BR 'stɒkwʊd
AM 'stɑk,wʊd

stocky
BR 'stɒk|i, -ɪə(r), -ɪɪst
AM 'stɑki, -ər, -ɨst

stockyard
BR 'stɒkjɑːd, -z
AM 'stɑk,jɑrd, -z

Stoddard
BR 'stɒdəd, 'stɒdɑːd
AM 'stɑdərd

Stoddart
BR 'stɒdət, 'stɒdɑːt
AM 'stɑdərt

stodge
BR stɒdʒ
AM stɑdʒ

stodgily
BR 'stɒdʒɨli
AM 'stɑdʒəli

stodginess
BR 'stɒdʒɪnɨs
AM 'stɑdʒinɨs

stodgy
BR 'stɒdʒ|i, -ɪə(r), -ɪɪst
AM 'stɑdʒi, -ər, -ɨst

stoep
BR stuːp, -s
AM stup, -s

stogey
BR 'stəʊg|i, -ɪz
AM 'stoʊgi, -z

stogie
BR 'stəʊg|i, -ɪz
AM 'stoʊgi, -z

Stogumber
BR stə(ʊ)'gʌmbə(r), 'stɒgəmbə(r)
AM stə'gəmbər

Stogursey
BR stə(ʊ)'gəːzi
AM stə'gərzi

stogy
BR 'stəʊg|i, -ɪz
AM 'stoʊgi, -z

Stoic
BR 'stəʊɪk, -s
AM 'stoʊɪk, -s

stoical
BR 'stəʊɨkl
AM 'stoʊəkəl

stoically
BR 'stəʊɨkli
AM 'stoʊək(ə)li

stoichiometric
BR ,stɔɪkɪə'mɛtrɪk
AM ¦stɔɪkioʊ'mɛtrɪk

stoichiometrical
BR ,stɔɪkɪə'mɛtrɪkl
AM ¦stɔɪkioʊ'mɛtrəkəl

stoichiometrically
BR ,stɔɪkɪə'mɛtrɪkli
AM ¦stɔɪkioʊ'mɛtrək(ə)li

stoichiometry
BR ,stɔɪkɪ'ɒmɪtri
AM ,stɔɪki'ɑmətri

Stoicism
BR 'stəʊɪsɪz(ə)m
AM 'stoʊə,sɪzəm

stoke
BR stəʊk, -s, -ɪŋ, -t
AM stoʊk, -s, -ɪŋ, -t

stokehold
BR 'stəʊkhəʊld, -z
AM 'stoʊk,(h)oʊld, -z

stokehole
BR 'stəʊkhəʊl, -z
AM 'stoʊk,(h)oʊl, -z

Stoke-on-Trent
BR ,stəʊkɒn'trɛnt
AM ¦stoʊkən'trɛnt

Stoker
BR 'stəʊkə(r)
AM 'stoʊkər

stoker
BR 'stəʊkə(r), -z
AM 'stoʊkər, -z

stokes
BR stəʊks
AM stoʊks

Stokowski
BR stə'kɒfski
AM stə'kaʊski

STOL
BR stɒl, 'ɛstɒl
AM stɔl, stɑl

stola
BR 'stəʊlə(*r*), -z
AM 'stoʊlə, -z

stolae
BR 'stəʊliː
AM 'stoʊli, 'stoʊ,laɪ

stole
BR stəʊl, -z
AM stoʊl, -z

stolen
BR 'stəʊlən
AM 'stoʊlən

stolid
BR 'stɒlɪd
AM 'stɑləd

stolidity
BR stə'lɪdɪti, stɒ'lɪdɪti
AM stə'lɪdɨdi

stolidly
BR 'stɒlɪdli
AM 'stɑlədli

stolidness
BR 'stɒlɪdnɪs
AM 'stɑlədnəs

Stollen
BR 'stɒlən, 'ʃtɒlən, -z
AM 'ʃtələn, 'stələn, -z

stolon
BR 'stəʊlɒn, 'stəʊlən, -z
AM 'stoʊlən, -z

stolonate
BR 'stəʊləneɪt
AM 'stoʊlənət, 'stoʊlə,neɪt

stoloniferous
BR ,stəʊlə'nɪf(ə)rəs
AM ,stoʊlə'nɪf(ə)rəs

stoma
BR 'stəʊmə(*r*), -z
AM 'stoʊmə, -z

stomach
BR 'stʌmək, -s, -ɪŋ, -t
AM 'stəmək, -s, -ɪŋ, -t

stomachache
BR 'stʌmək,eɪk, -s
AM 'stəmək,eɪk, -s

stomacher
BR 'stʌməkə(r), -z
AM 'stəməkər, -z

stomachful
BR 'stʌməkfʊl, -z
AM 'stəmək,fʊl, -z

stomachic
BR stə'makɪk
AM stə'mækɪk

stomachless
BR 'stʌmələs
AM 'stəmələs

stomal
BR 'stəʊml
AM 'stoʊməl

stomata
BR 'stəʊmətə(r), stə'mɑːtə(r)
AM 'stoʊmədə, ˌstoʊ'mɑdə

stomatal
BR 'stəʊmətl, 'stɒmətl
AM 'stoʊmədl, 'stɑmədl

stomatitis
BR ˌstəʊmə'tʌɪtɪs
AM ˌstoʊmə'taɪdɪs

stomatological
BR ˌstəʊmətə'lɒdʒɪkl
AM ˌstoʊmədə'lɑdʒəkəl

stomatologist
BR ˌstəʊmə'tɒlədʒɪst, -s
AM ˌstoʊmə'tɑlədʒəst, -s

stomatology
BR ˌstəʊmə'tɒlədʒi
AM ˌstoʊmə'tɑlədʒi

stomp
BR stɒm|p, -ps, -pɪŋ, -(p)t
AM stɔmp, stɑmp, -s, -ɪŋ, -t

stomper
BR 'stɒmpə(r), -z
AM 'stɔmpər, 'stɑmpər, -z

stone
BR stəʊn, -z, -ɪŋ, -d
AM stoʊn, -z, -ɪŋ, -d

Stonebridge
BR 'stəʊnbrɪdʒ
AM 'stoʊn,brɪdʒ

stonechat
BR 'stəʊntʃat, -s
AM 'stoʊn,tʃæt, -s

stonecrop
BR 'stəʊnkrɒp, -s
AM 'stoʊnə,krɑp, -s

stonecutter
BR 'stəʊn,kʌtə(r), -z
AM 'stoʊn,kədər, -z

stonefish
BR 'stəʊnfɪʃ, -ɪz
AM 'stoʊn,fɪʃ, -ɪz

stonefly
BR 'stəʊnflʌɪ, -z
AM 'stoʊn,flaɪ, -z

stoneground
BR ˌstəʊn'graʊnd
AM ˌstoʊn'graʊn(d)

stonehatch
BR 'stəʊnhatʃ, -ɪz
AM 'stoʊn,(h)ætʃ, -əz

Stonehaven
BR ˌstəʊn'heɪvn
AM 'stoʊn,(h)eɪvən

Stonehenge
BR ˌstəʊn'hɛn(d)ʒ
AM 'stoʊn,(h)ɛndʒ

Stonehouse
BR 'stəʊnhaʊs
AM 'stoʊn,(h)aʊs

Stoneleigh
BR 'stəʊnli
AM 'stoʊnli

stoneless
BR 'stəʊnləs
AM 'stoʊnləs

stonemason
BR 'stəʊn,meɪsn, -z
AM 'stoʊn,meɪsən, -z

stonemasonry
BR 'stəʊn,meɪsnri
AM 'stoʊn,meɪsnri

stone-pit
BR 'stəʊnpɪt, -s
AM 'stoʊn,pɪt, -s

stoner
BR 'stəʊnə(r), -z
AM 'stoʊnər, -z

stonewall
BR ˌstəʊn'wɔːl, 'stəʊnwɔːl, -z, -ɪŋ, -d
AM 'stoʊn,wɔl, 'stoʊn,wɑl, -z, -ɪŋ, -d

stonewaller
BR ˌstəʊn'wɔːlə(r), 'stəʊn,wɔːlə(r), -z
AM 'stoʊn,wɔlər, 'stoʊn,wɑlər, -z

stoneware
BR 'stəʊnwɛː(r)
AM 'stoʊn,wɛ(ə)r

stonewashed
BR 'stəʊnwɒʃt
AM 'stoʊn,wɔʃt, 'stoʊn,wɑʃt

stoneweed
BR 'stəʊnwiːd, -z
AM 'stoʊn,wid, -z

stonework
BR 'stəʊnwəːk
AM 'stoʊn,wərk

stoneworker
BR 'stəʊn,wəːkə(r), -z
AM 'stoʊn,wərkər, -z

stonewort
BR 'stəʊnwəːt, -s
AM 'stoʊnwərt, 'stoʊn,wɔ(ə)rt, -s

stonily
BR 'stəʊnɪli
AM 'stoʊnəli

stoniness
BR 'stəʊnɪnɪs
AM 'stoʊninɪs

stonker
BR 'stɒŋk|ə(r), -əz, -(ə)rɪŋ, -əd
AM 'stɔŋkər, 'stɑŋkər, -z, -ɪŋ, -d

stonking
BR 'stɒŋkɪŋ
AM 'stɔŋkɪŋ, 'stɑŋkɪŋ

Stonor
BR 'stəʊnə(r)
AM 'stoʊnər

stony
BR 'stəʊn|i, -ɪə(r), -ɪɪst
AM 'stoʊni, -ər, -ɪst

stony-broke
BR ˌstəʊnɪ'brəʊk
AM 'stoʊni,broʊk

stony-hearted
BR ˌstəʊnɪ'hɑːtɪd
AM 'stoʊni,hɑrdəd

stood
BR stʊd
AM stʊd

stooge
BR stuːdʒ, -ɪz, -ɪŋ, -d
AM studʒ, -əz, -ɪŋ, -d

stook
BR stuːk, stʊk, -s, -ɪŋ, -t
AM stʊk, stuk, -s, -ɪŋ, -t

stool
BR stuːl, -z
AM stul, -z

stoolball
BR 'stuːlbɔːl
AM 'stul,bɔl, 'stul,bɑl

stoolie
BR 'stuːl|i, -ɪz
AM 'stuli, -z

stoolpigeon
BR 'stuːl,pɪdʒɪn, -z
AM 'stul,pɪdʒɪn, -z

stoop
BR stuːp, -s, -ɪŋ, -t
AM stup, -s, -ɪŋ, -t

stop
BR stɒp, -s, -ɪŋ, -t
AM stɑp, -s, -ɪŋ, -t

stop-and-go
BR ˌstɒp(ə)n(d)'gəʊ
AM ˌstɑpən'goʊ

stopbank
BR 'stɒpbaŋk, -s
AM 'stɑp,bæŋk, -s

stopcock
BR 'stɒpkɒk, -s
AM 'stɑp,kɑk, -s

stope
BR stəʊp, -s
AM stoʊp, -s

Stopes
BR stəʊps
AM stoʊps

stopgap
BR 'stɒpgap, -s
AM 'stɑp,gæp, -s

stop-go
BR ˌstɒp'gəʊ
AM 'stɑp,goʊ

stopless
BR 'stɒpləs
AM 'stɑpləs

stoplight
BR 'stɒplʌɪt, -s
AM 'stɑp,laɪt, -s

stopoff
BR 'stɒpɒf, -s
AM 'stɑp,ɔf, 'stɑp,ɑf, -s

stopover
BR 'stɒp,əʊvə(r), -z
AM 'stɑp,oʊvər, -z

stoppable
BR 'stɒpəbl
AM 'stɑpəbəl

stoppage
BR 'stɒp|ɪdʒ, -ɪdʒɪz
AM 'stɑpɪdʒ, -ɪz

Stoppard
BR 'stɒpɑːd
AM 'stɑpərd, 'stɑ,pɑrd

stopper
BR 'stɒp|ə(r), -əz, -(ə)rɪŋ, -əd
AM 'stɑpər, -z, -ɪŋ, -d

stopping
BR 'stɒpɪŋ, -z
AM 'stɑpɪŋ, -z

stopple
BR 'stɒp|l, -lz, -l̩ɪŋ\-lɪŋ, -ld
AM 'stɑp|əl, -əlz, -(ə)lɪŋ, -əld

stop press
BR ˌstɒp 'prɛs
AM ˌstɑp 'prɛs

stop-start
BR ˌstɒp'stɑːt
AM ˌstɑp'stɑrt

stopwatch
BR 'stɒpwɒtʃ, -ɪz
AM 'stɑp,wɑtʃ, -əz

storable
BR 'stɔːrəbl
AM 'stɔrəbəl

storage
BR 'stɔːrɪdʒ
AM 'stɔrɪdʒ

storax
BR 'stɔːraks, -ɪz
AM 'stɔ,ræks, -əz

store
BR stɔː(r), -z, -ɪŋ, -d
AM stɔ(ə)r, -z, -ɪŋ, -d

storefront
BR 'stɔːfrʌnt, -s
AM 'stɔr,frənt, -s

storehouse
BR 'stɔːhaʊ|s, -zɪz
AM 'stɔr,(h)aʊ|s, -zəz

storekeeper
BR 'stɔː,kiːpə(r), -z
AM 'stɔr,kipər, -z

storeman
BR 'stɔːmən
AM 'stɔrmən

storemen
BR 'stɔːmən
AM 'stɔrmən

storer
BR 'stɔːrə(r), -z
AM 'stɔrər, -z

storeroom
BR 'stɔːruːm, 'stɔːrʊm, -z
AM 'stɔr,rum, 'stɔr,rʊm, -z

storey
BR 'stɔːr|i, -ɪz, -ɪd
AM 'stɔri, -z, -d

storiated
BR 'stɔːrɪeɪtɪd
AM 'stɔri,eɪdɪd

storiation
BR ,stɔːrɪ'eɪʃn, -z
AM ,stɔri'eɪʃən, -z

storied
BR 'stɔːrɪd
AM 'stɔrid

stork
BR stɔːk, -s
AM stɔ(ə)rk, -s

storksbill
BR 'stɔːksbɪl, -z
AM 'stɔrks,bɪl, -z

storm
BR stɔːm, -z, -ɪŋ, -d
AM stɔ(ə)rm, -z, -ɪŋ, -d

stormbound
BR 'stɔːmbaʊnd
AM 'stɔrm,baʊnd

stormdoor
BR 'stɔːmdɔː(r), -z
AM 'stɔrm'dɔ(ə)r, -z

stormer
BR 'stɔːmə(r), -z
AM 'stɔrmər, -z

stormily
BR 'stɔːmɪli
AM 'stɔrməli

storminess
BR 'stɔːmɪnɪs
AM 'stɔrminɪs

stormless
BR 'stɔːmləs
AM 'stɔrmləs

Stormont
BR 'stɔːmɒnt, 'stɔːm(ə)nt
AM 'stɔr,mɑnt

stormproof
BR 'stɔːmpruːf
AM 'stɔrm,pruf

storm-tossed
BR 'stɔːmtɒst
AM 'stɔrm,tɔst, 'stɔrm,tɑst

stormy
BR 'stɔːm|i, -ɪə(r), -ɪɪst
AM 'stɔrmi, -ər, -ɪst

stormy petrel
BR ,stɔːmɪ 'pɛtr(ə)l, -z
AM ',stɔrmi 'pɛtrəl, -z

Stornoway
BR 'stɔːnəweɪ
AM 'stɔrnə,weɪ

Storr
BR stɔː(r)
AM stɔ(ə)r

Storrs
BR stɔːz
AM stɔrz

Stortford
BR 'stɔː(t)fəd
AM 'stɔr(t)fərd

story
BR 'stɔːr|i, -ɪz
AM 'stɔri, -z

storyboard
BR 'stɔːrɪbɔːd, -z
AM 'stɔri,bɔ(ə)rd, -z

storybook
BR 'stɔːrɪbʊk, -s
AM 'stɔri,bʊk, -s

storyline
BR 'stɔːrɪlʌɪn, -z
AM 'stɔri,laɪn, -z

storyteller
BR 'stɔːrɪ,tɛlə(r), -z
AM 'stɔri,tɛlər, -z

storytelling
BR 'stɔːrɪ,tɛlɪŋ
AM 'stɔri,tɛlɪŋ

stot
BR stɒt, -s, -ɪŋ, -ɪd
AM stɑ|t, -ts, -dɪŋ, -dəd

stotinka
BR stɒ'tɪŋkə(*r*), stə'tɪŋkə(*r*)
AM stə'tɪŋkə, stɑ'tɪŋkə

stotinki
BR stɒ'tɪŋki, stə'tɪŋki
AM stə'tɪŋki, stɑ'tɪŋki

stotious
BR 'stəʊʃəs
AM 'stoʊʃəs

Stott
BR stɒt
AM stɑt

Stoughton
BR 'stəʊtn, 'staʊtn, 'stɔːtn
AM 'stɔtn, 'stɑtn

stoup
BR stuːp, -s
AM stup, -s

Stour[1]
East Anglia UK
BR stʊə(r)
AM stʊ(ə)r

Stour[2]
Warwickshire UK
BR 'staʊə(r)
AM 'staʊ(ə)r

Stour[3]
BR 'stəʊə(r)
AM stoʊr, 'staʊ(ə)r

Stourbridge
BR 'staʊəbrɪdʒ
AM 'staʊr,brɪdʒ

Stourport
BR 'staʊəpɔːt
AM 'staʊr,pɔ(ə)rt

Stourton
BR 'stəːtn
AM 'staʊrtən

stoush
BR staʊʃ, -ɪz, -ɪŋ, -t
AM staʊʃ, -əz, -ɪŋ, -t

stout
BR staʊt, -s, -ə(r), -ɪst
AM staʊ|t, -ts, -dər, -dəst

stoutish
BR 'staʊtɪʃ
AM 'staʊdɪʃ

stoutly
BR 'staʊtli
AM 'staʊtli

stoutness
BR 'staʊtnəs
AM 'staʊtnəs

stove
BR stəʊv, -z
AM stoʊv, -z

stovepipe
BR 'stəʊvpʌɪp, -s
AM 'stoʊv,paɪp, -s

stove-pipe hat
BR ,stəʊvpʌɪp 'hat, -s
AM ',stoʊv,paɪp 'hæt, -s

stow
BR stəʊ, -z, -ɪŋ, -d
AM stoʊ, -z, -ɪŋ, -d

stowage
BR 'stəʊɪdʒ
AM 'stoʊɪdʒ

stowaway
BR 'stəʊəweɪ, -z
AM 'stoʊə,weɪ, -z

Stowe
BR stəʊ
AM stoʊ

Stowmarket
BR 'stəʊ,mɑːkɪt
AM 'stoʊ,mɑrkət

Stow-on-the-Wold
BR ,stəʊɒnðə'wəʊld
AM ,stoʊɑnðə'woʊld

St Peter Port
BR s(ə)nt 'piːtə pɔːt
AM seɪn(t) 'pidər ,pɔ(ə)rt

St Petersburg
BR s(ə)nt 'piːtəzbəːg
AM seɪn(t) 'pidərz,bərg

Strabane
BR strə'ban
AM ,strə'bæn

strabismal
BR strə'bɪzml
AM strə'bɪzməl

strabismic
BR strə'bɪzmɪk
AM strə'bɪzmɪk

strabismus
BR strə'bɪzməs
AM strə'bɪzməs

Strabo
BR 'streɪbəʊ
AM 'streɪboʊ

Strachan[1]
traditionally
BR strɔːn
AM strɔn, strɑn

Strachan[2]
BR 'strak(ə)n, 'strax(ə)n
AM 'streɪkən, 'strækən

Strachey
BR 'streɪtʃi
AM 'streɪtʃi

Strad
BR strad, -z
AM stræd, -z

Stradbroke
BR 'stradbrʊk
AM 'stræd,brʊk

straddle
BR 'strad|l, -lz, -l̩ɪŋ\-lɪŋ, -ld
AM 'stræd|əl, -əlz, -(ə)lɪŋ, -əld

straddler
BR 'stradl̩ə(r), 'stradlə(r), -z
AM 'stræd(ə)lər, -z

Stradivari
BR ,stradɪ'vɑːri
AM ,strædə'vɑri

Stradivarius
BR ,stradɪ'vɛːrɪəs, ,stradɪ'vɑːrɪəs, -ɪz
AM ,strædə'vɛriəs, -əz

Stradling
BR 'stradlɪŋ
AM 'strædlɪŋ

strafe
BR strɑːf, streɪf, -s, -ɪŋ, -t
AM streɪf, -s, -ɪŋ, -t

Strafford
BR 'strafəd
AM 'stræfərd

strafing
BR 'strɑːfɪŋ, 'streɪfɪŋ, -z

AM 'streɪfɪŋ, -z
straggle
BR 'strag|l, -lz, -l̩ɪŋ\-lɪŋ, -ld
AM 'stræg|əl, -əlz, -(ə)lɪŋ, -əld
straggler
BR 'stragl̩ə(r), 'straglə(r), -z
AM 'stræg(ə)lər, -z
straggly
BR 'stragl̩|i, 'stragl|i, -ɪə(r), -ɪɪst
AM 'stræg(ə)li, -ər, -ɪst
straight
BR streɪt, -s, -ə(r), -ɪst
AM streɪ|t, -ts, -dər, -dəst
straightaway[1]
adverb
BR ˌstreɪtə'weɪ
AM ˌstreɪdə'weɪ
straightaway[2]
noun
BR 'streɪtəweɪ, -z
AM 'streɪdəˌweɪ, -z
straightedge
BR 'streɪtɛdʒ, -ɪz
AM 'streɪdˌɛdʒ, -ɪz
straight-eight
BR ˌstreɪt'eɪt, -s
AM ˌstreɪd'eɪt, -s
straighten
BR 'streɪt|n, -nz, -nɪŋ\-n̩ɪŋ, -nd
AM 'streɪt|n, -nz, -n̩ɪŋ, -nd
straightener
BR ˌstreɪtnə(r), ˌstreɪtn̩ə(r), -z
AM ˌstreɪtn̩ər, -z
straightforward
BR ˌstreɪt'fɔːwəd
AM ˌstreɪt'fɔrwərd
straightforwardly
BR ˌstreɪt'fɔːwədli
AM ˌstreɪt'fɔrwərdli
straightforward-ness
BR ˌstreɪt'fɔːwədnəs
AM ˌstreɪt'fɔrwərdnəs
straightish
BR 'streɪtɪʃ
AM 'streɪdɪʃ
straightjacket
BR 'streɪtˌdʒak|ɪt, -s, -ɪtɪŋ, -ɪtɪd
AM 'streɪtˌdʒækə|t, -ts, -dɪŋ, -dəd
straightlaced
BR ˌstreɪt'leɪst
AM 'streɪtˌleɪst
straightly
BR 'streɪtli
AM 'streɪtli
straightness
BR 'streɪtnɪs
AM 'streɪtnɪs
straight-out
BR ˌstreɪt'aʊt
AM ˌstreɪd'aʊt
straight-up
BR ˌstreɪt'ʌp
AM ˌstreɪd'əp
straightway
BR ˌstreɪt'weɪ
AM 'streɪtˌweɪ
strain
BR streɪn, -z, -ɪŋ, -d
AM streɪn, -z, -ɪŋ, -d
strainable
BR 'streɪnəbl
AM 'streɪnəbəl
strainer
BR 'streɪnə(r), -z
AM 'streɪnər, -z
strait
BR streɪt, -s
AM streɪt, -s
straiten
BR 'streɪt|n, -nz, -nɪŋ\-n̩ɪŋ, -nd
AM 'streɪt|n, -nz, -n̩ɪŋ, -nd
straitjacket
BR 'streɪtˌdʒak|ɪt, -ɪts, -ɪtɪŋ, -ɪtɪd
AM 'streɪtˌdʒækə|t, -ts, -dɪŋ, -dəd
straitlaced
BR ˌstreɪt'leɪst
AM 'streɪtˌleɪst
straitly
BR 'streɪtli
AM 'streɪtli
straitness
BR 'streɪtnɪs
AM 'streɪtnɪs
strake
BR streɪk, -s
AM streɪk, -s
stramonium
BR strə'məʊnɪəm
AM strə'moʊniəm
strand
BR strand, -z, -ɪŋ, -ɪd
AM strænd, -z, -ɪŋ, -əd
stranding
BR 'strandɪŋ, -z
AM 'strændɪŋ, -z
Strang
BR straŋ
AM stræŋ
strange
BR streɪn(d)ʒ, -ə(r), -ɪst
AM streɪndʒ, -ər, -ɪst
strangely
BR 'streɪn(d)ʒli
AM 'streɪndʒli
strangeness
BR 'streɪn(d)ʒnɪs
AM 'streɪndʒnɪs
stranger
BR 'streɪn(d)ʒə(r), -z
AM 'streɪndʒər, -z
Strangeways
BR 'streɪn(d)ʒweɪz
AM 'streɪndʒˌweɪz
Strangford
BR 'straŋfəd
AM 'stræŋfərd
strangle
BR 'straŋg|l, -lz, -l̩ɪŋ\-lɪŋ, -ld
AM 'stræŋg|əl, -əlz, -(ə)lɪŋ, -əld
stranglehold
BR 'straŋglhəʊld, -z
AM 'stræŋgəlˌ(h)oʊld, -z
strangler
BR 'straŋglə(r), -z
AM 'stræŋg(ə)lər, -z
strangling
BR 'straŋgl̩ɪŋ, 'straŋglɪŋ, -z
AM 'stræŋg(ə)lɪŋ, -z
strangulate
BR 'straŋgjʉleɪt, -s, -ɪŋ, -ɪd
AM 'stræŋgjəˌleɪ|t, -ts, -dɪŋ, -dɪd
strangulation
BR ˌstraŋgjʉ'leɪʃn, -z
AM ˌstræŋgjə'leɪʃən, -z
stranguríous
BR ˌstraŋ'gjʊərɪəs, ˌstraŋ'gjɔːrɪəs
AM ˌstræŋ'gjʊriəs
strangury
BR 'straŋgjʉr|i, -ɪz
AM 'stræŋgjəri, -z
Stranraer
BR stran'rɑː(r)
AM stræn'rɑr
strap
BR strap, -s, -ɪŋ, -t
AM stræp, -s, -ɪŋ, -t
strap-hang
BR 'straphaŋ, -z, -ɪŋ
AM 'stræpˌ(h)æŋ, -z, -ɪŋ
straphanger
BR 'strapˌhaŋə(r), -z
AM 'stræpˌ(h)æŋər, -z
straphanging
BR 'strapˌhaŋɪŋ
AM 'stræpˌ(h)æŋɪŋ
strap-hung
BR 'straphʌŋ
AM 'stræpˌ(h)ʌŋ
strapless
BR 'strapləs
AM 'stræpləs
strapline
BR 'straplʌɪn, -z
AM 'stræpˌlaɪn, -z
strappado
BR strə'pɑːdəʊ, strə'peɪdəʊ, -z
AM strə'peɪdoʊ, strə'pɑˌdoʊ, -z
strapper
BR 'strapə(r), -z
AM 'stræpər, -z
strappy
BR 'strapi
AM 'stræpi
Strasberg
BR 'strasbəːg
AM 'stræsˌbərg, 'strɑsˌbərg
Strasbourg
BR 'strazbəːg
AM 'strɑsˌbərg, 'strɑzˌbərg
strass
BR stras
AM stræs
strata
BR 'strɑːtə(r)
AM 'streɪdə, 'strɑdə, 'strædə
stratagem
BR 'stratədʒəm, 'stratədʒɛm, -z
AM 'strædəˌdʒəm, -z
stratal
BR 'strɑːtl, 'streɪtl
AM 'streɪdl, 'strɑdl, 'strædl
strategic
BR strə'tiːdʒɪk, -s
AM strə'tidʒɪk, -s
strategical
BR strə'tiːdʒɪkl
AM strə'tidʒɪkəl
strategically
BR strə'tiːdʒɪkli
AM strə'tidʒɪk(ə)li
strategist
BR 'stratɪdʒɪst, -s
AM 'strædədʒəst, -s
strategy
BR 'stratɪdʒ|i, -ɪz
AM 'strædədʒi, -z
Stratford-on-Avon
BR ˌstratfədɒn'eɪvn
AM ˌstrætfərdˌɑn'eɪvɑn
Stratford-upon-Avon
BR ˌstratfədəpɒn'eɪvn
AM 'strætfərdəˌpɑn-'eɪvɑn
strath
BR straθ, -s
AM stræθ, -s
Strathclyde
BR straθ'klʌɪd
AM stræθ'klaɪd
Strathleven
BR straθ'liːvn
AM stræθ'livən
Strathmore
BR straθ'mɔː(r)
AM stræθ'mɔ(ə)r
strathspey
BR straθ'speɪ, -z
AM stræθ'speɪ, -z

strati
BR ˈstreɪtʌɪ
AM ˈstreɪdˌaɪ

straticulate
BR strəˈtɪkjʉlət
AM strəˈtɪkjələt, strəˈtɪkjəˌleɪt

stratification
BR ˌstratɪfɪˈkeɪʃn, -z
AM ˌstrædəfəˈkeɪʃən, -z

stratificational
BR ˌstratɪfɪˈkeɪʃn̩(ə)l, ˌsratɪfɪˈkeɪʃən(ə)l
AM ˌstrædəfəˈkeɪʃ(ə)nəl

stratify
BR ˈstratɪfʌɪ, -z, -ɪŋ, -d
AM ˈstrædəˌfaɪ, -z, -ɪŋ, -d

stratigraphic
BR ˌstratɪˈgrafɪk
AM ˌstrædəˈgræfɪk

stratigraphical
BR ˌstratɪˈgrafɪkl
AM ˌstrædəˈgræfəkəl

stratigraphy
BR strəˈtɪgrəfi
AM strəˈtɪgrəfi

stratocirrus
BR ˌstratə(ʊ)ˈsɪrəs, ˌstreɪtə(ʊ)ˈsɪrəs, -ɪz
AM ˌstrædoʊˈsɪrəs, ˌstreɪdoʊˈsɪrəs, -əz

stratocracy
BR strəˈtɒkrəs|i, -ɪz
AM strəˈtɑkrəsi, -z

stratocumuli
BR ˌstratə(ʊ)ˈkjuːmjʉlʌɪ, ˌstreɪtə(ʊ)ˈkjuːmjʉlʌɪ
AM ˌstrædoʊˈkjumjəˌlaɪ, ˌstreɪdoʊˈkjumjəˌlaɪ

stratocumulus
BR ˌstratə(ʊ)ˈkjuːmjʉləs, ˌstreɪtə(ʊ)ˈkjuːmjʉləs
AM ˌstrædoʊˈkjumjələs, ˌstreɪdoʊˈkjumjələs

stratopause
BR ˈstratə(ʊ)pɔːz
AM ˈstrædəˌpɔz, ˈstrædəˌpɑz

stratosphere
BR ˈstratəsfɪə(r)
AM ˈstrædəˌsfɪ(ə)r

stratospheric
BR ˌstratəˈsfɛrɪk
AM ˌstrædəˈsfɪrɪk

stratum
BR ˈstrɑːtəm, ˈstreɪtəm
AM ˈstreɪdəm, ˈstrɑdəm, ˈstrædəm

stratus
BR ˈstrɑːtəs, ˈstreɪtəs
AM ˈstreɪdəs, ˈstrɑdəs, ˈstrædəs

Strauss
BR straʊs
AM straʊs

Stravinsky
BR strəˈvɪnski
AM strəˈvɪnski

straw
BR strɔː(r), -z
AM strɔ, strɑ, -z

strawberry
BR ˈstrɔːb(ə)r|i, -ɪz
AM ˈstrɔˌbɛri, ˈstrɔbəri, ˈstrɑˌbɛri, ˈstrɑbəri, -z

strawboard
BR ˈstrɔːbɔːd
AM ˈstrɔˌbɔ(ə)rd, ˈstrɑˌbɔ(ə)rd

strawboss
BR ˈstrɔːbɒs, -ɪz
AM ˈstrɔˌbɔs, ˈstrɑˌbɑs, -əz

strawman
BR ˈstrɔːman
AM ˈstrɔˈmæn, ˈstrɑˈmæn

strawmen
BR ˈstrɔːmɛn
AM ˈstrɔˈmɛn, ˈstrɑˈmɛn

strawy
BR ˈstrɔː(r)i
AM ˈstrɔi, ˈstrɑi

stray
BR streɪ, -z, -ɪŋ, -d
AM streɪ, -z, -ɪŋ, -d

strayer
BR ˈstreɪə(r), -z
AM ˈstreɪər, -z

streak
BR striːk, -s, -ɪŋ, -t
AM strik, -s, -ɪŋ, -t

streaker
BR ˈstriːkə(r), -z
AM ˈstrikər, -z

streakily
BR ˈstriːkɪli
AM ˈstrikɪli

streakiness
BR ˈstriːkɪnɪs
AM ˈstrikinɪs

streaky
BR ˈstriːk|i, -ɪə(r), -ɪɪst
AM ˈstriki, -ər, -ɪst

stream
BR striːm, -z, -ɪŋ, -d
AM strim, -z, -ɪŋ, -d

streambed
BR ˈstriːmbɛd, -z
AM ˈstrimˌbɛd, -z

streamer
BR ˈstriːmə(r), -z
AM ˈstrimər, -z

streamless
BR ˈstriːmlɪs
AM ˈstrimlɪs

streamlet
BR ˈstriːmlɪt, -s
AM ˈstrimlət, -s

streamline
BR ˈstriːmlʌɪn, -z, -ɪŋ, -d
AM ˈstrimˌlaɪn, -z, -ɪŋ, -d

Streatfield
BR ˈstrɛtfiːld
AM ˈstrɛtˌfild

Streatham
BR ˈstrɛtəm
AM ˈstrɛdəm

Streatley
BR ˈstriːtli
AM ˈstritli

Streep
BR striːp
AM strip

street
BR striːt, -s, -ɪd
AM stri|t, -ts, -dɪd

streetcar
BR ˈstriːtkɑː(r), -z
AM ˈstritˌkɑr, -z

street-cred
BR ˌstriːtˈkrɛd, ˈstriːtkrɛd
AM ˈstritˌkrɛd

Streeter
BR ˈstriːtə(r)
AM ˈstridər

streetlight
BR ˈstriːtlʌɪt, -s
AM ˈstritˌlaɪt, -s

streetwalker
BR ˈstriːtˌwɔːkə(r), -z
AM ˈstritˌwɔkər, ˈstritˌwɑkər, -z

streetwalking
BR ˈstriːtˌwɔːkɪŋ
AM ˈstritˌwɔkɪŋ, ˈstritˌwɑkɪŋ

streetward
BR ˈstriːtwəd
AM ˈstritwərd

streetwise
BR ˈstriːtwʌɪz
AM ˈstritˌwaɪz

Streisand
BR ˈstrʌɪsand, ˈstrʌɪsənd
AM ˈstraɪˌsæn(d)

strelitzia
BR strəˈlɪtsɪə(r), -z
AM strəˈlɪtsiə, -z

strength
BR strɛŋ(k)θ, -s
AM strɛŋ(k)θ, strɛnθ, -s

strengthen
BR ˈstrɛŋ(k)θ|n, -nz, -(ə)nɪŋ\-n̩ɪŋ, -nd
AM ˈstrɛŋ(k)θ|ən, -ənz, -(ə)nɪŋ, -ənd

strengthener
BR ˈstrɛŋ(k)θ(ə)nə(r), ˈstrɛŋ(k)θn̩ə(r), -z
AM ˈstrɛŋ(k)θ(ə)nər, -z

strengthless
BR ˈstrɛŋ(k)θləs
AM ˈstrɛŋ(k)θləs, ˈstrɛnθləs

strenuous
BR ˈstrɛnjʊəs
AM ˈstrɛnjəwəs

strenuously
BR ˈstrɛnjʊəsli
AM ˈstrɛnjəwəsli

strenuousness
BR ˈstrɛnjʊəsnəs
AM ˈstrɛnjəwəsnəs

strep
BR strɛp
AM strɛp

streptocarpi
BR ˌstrɛptə(ʊ)ˈkɑːpʌɪ
AM ˈstrɛptəˈkɑrˌpaɪ

streptocarpus
BR ˌstrɛptə(ʊ)ˈkɑːpəs
AM ˈstrɛptəˈkɑrpəs

streptococcal
BR ˌstrɛptəˈkɒkl
AM ˈstrɛptəˈkɑkəl

streptococci
BR ˌstrɛptəˈkɒkʌɪ
AM ˌstrɛptəˈkɑˌkaɪ

streptococcus
BR ˌstrɛptəˈkɒkəs
AM ˌstrɛptəˈkɑkəs

streptomycin
BR ˌstrɛptəˈmʌɪsɪn
AM ˌstrɛptəˈmaɪ(ə)sn̩

stress
BR strɛs, -ɪz, -ɪŋ, -t
AM strɛs, -əz, -ɪŋ, -t

stressful
BR ˈstrɛsf(ʉ)l
AM ˈstrɛsfəl

stressfully
BR ˈstrɛsfʉli, ˈstrɛsfl̩i
AM ˈstrɛsfəli

stressfulness
BR ˈstrɛsf(ʉ)lnəs
AM ˈstrɛsfəlnəs

stressless
BR ˈstrɛsləs
AM ˈstrɛsləs

stretch
BR strɛtʃ, -ɪz, -ɪŋ, -t
AM strɛtʃ, -əz, -ɪŋ, -t

stretchability
BR ˌstrɛtʃəˈbɪlɪti
AM ˌstrɛtʃəˈbɪlɪdi

stretchable
BR ˈstrɛtʃəbl
AM ˈstrɛtʃəbəl

stretcher
BR ˈstrɛtʃə(r), -z
AM ˈstrɛtʃər, -z

stretchiness
BR ˈstrɛtʃɪnɪs

AM 'strɛtʃinɪs

stretchy
BR 'strɛtʃ|i, -ɪə(r), -ɪɪst
AM 'strɛtʃi, -ər, -ɪst

Stretford
BR 'strɛtfəd
AM 'strɛtfərd

stretto
BR 'strɛtəʊ
AM 'strɛdoʊ

Stretton
BR 'strɛtn
AM 'strɛtn

streusel
BR 'strɔɪzl, 'stru:zl, -z
AM 'strusəl, 'struzəl, -z

Strevens
BR 'strɛvnz
AM 'strɛvənz

strew
BR stru:, -z, -ɪŋ, -d, -n
AM stru, -z, -ɪŋ, -d, -n

strewer
BR 'stru:ə(r), -z
AM 'struər, -z

strewth
BR stru:θ
AM struθ

stria
BR 'strʌɪə(*r*)
AM 'straɪə

striae
BR 'strʌɪi:
AM 'straɪ,i, 'straɪ,aɪ

striate
BR strʌɪeɪt, -s, -ɪŋ, -d
AM 'straɪ,eɪ|t, -ts, -dɪŋ, -dɨd

striated
adjective
BR strʌɪ'eɪtɨd
AM 'straɪ,eɪdɨd

striation
BR strʌɪ'eɪʃn, -z
AM straɪ'eɪʃən, -z

striature
BR 'strʌɪətʃə(r)
AM 'straɪətʃʊ(ə)r, 'straɪətʃər

strick
BR strɪk
AM strɪk

stricken
BR 'strɪk(ə)n
AM 'strɪkən

Strickland
BR 'strɪklənd
AM 'strɪklənd

strickle
BR 'strɪk|l, -lz, -l̩ɪŋ\-lɪŋ, -ld
AM 'strɪk|əl, -əlz, -(ə)lɪŋ, -əld

strict
BR strɪkt, -ə(r), -ɪst
AM strɪk|(t), -ər, -ɪst

strictly
BR 'strɪk(t)li
AM 'strɪk(t)li

strictness
BR 'strɪk(t)nəs
AM 'strɪk(t)nəs

stricture
BR 'strɪktʃə(r), -z
AM 'strɪk(t)ʃər, -z

strictured
BR 'strɪktʃəd
AM 'strɪk(t)ʃərd

stridden
BR 'strɪdn
AM 'strɪdən

stride
BR strʌɪd, -z, -ɪŋ
AM straɪd, -z, -ɪŋ

stridence
BR 'strʌɪdns
AM 'straɪdns

stridency
BR 'strʌɪdnsi
AM 'straɪdnsi

strident
BR 'strʌɪdnt
AM 'straɪdnt

stridently
BR 'strʌɪdntli
AM 'straɪdn(t)li

strider
BR 'strʌɪdə(r), -z
AM 'straɪdər, -z

stridor
BR 'strʌɪdə(r), -z
AM 'straɪdər, -z

stridulant
BR 'strɪdjʉlənt, 'strɪdjʉl̩nt, 'strɪdʒʉlənt, 'strɪdʒʉl̩nt
AM 'strɪdʒələnt

stridulate
BR 'strɪdjʉleɪt, 'strɪdʒʉleɪt, -s, -ɪŋ, -ɨd
AM 'strɪdʒə,leɪ|t, -ts, -dɪŋ, -dɨd

stridulation
BR ,strɪdjʉ'leɪʃn, ,strɪdʒʉ'leɪʃn, -z
AM ,strɪdʒə'leɪʃən, -z

strife
BR strʌɪf
AM straɪf

strigil
BR 'strɪdʒ(ɨ)l, -z
AM 'strɪdʒəl, -z

strigose
BR 'strʌɪgəʊs
AM 'straɪ,goʊs, 'straɪ,goʊz

strikable
BR 'strʌɪkəbl
AM 'straɪkəbəl

strike
BR strʌɪk, -s, -ɪŋ
AM straɪk, -s, -ɪŋ

strikebound
BR 'strʌɪkbaʊnd
AM 'straɪk,baʊnd

strikebreaker
BR 'strʌɪk,breɪkə(r), -z
AM 'straɪk,breɪkər, -z

strikebreaking
BR 'strʌɪk,breɪkɪŋ
AM 'straɪk,breɪkɪŋ

strikeout
BR strʌɪkaʊt, -s
AM 'straɪk,aʊt, -s

strikeover
BR 'strʌɪk,əʊvə(r), -z
AM 'straɪk,oʊvər, -z

striker
BR 'strʌɪkə(r), -z
AM 'straɪkər, -z

strike-slip fault
BR 'strʌɪkslɪp ,fɔ:lt, + ,fɒlt, -s
AM 'straɪk,slɪp ,fɔlt, 'straɪk,slɪp ,fɑlt, -s

strikingly
BR 'strʌɪkɪŋli
AM 'straɪkɪŋli

strikingness
BR 'strʌɪkɪŋnɪs
AM 'straɪkɪŋnɪs

strimmer®
BR 'strɪmə(r), -z
AM 'strɪmər, -z

Strindberg
BR 'strɪn(d)bə:g
AM 'strɪn(d),bərg
SW strɪnd'bɛrj

Strine
BR strʌɪn
AM straɪn

string
BR strɪŋ, -z, -ɪŋ
AM strɪŋ, -z, -ɪŋ

stringboard
BR 'strɪŋbɔ:d, -z
AM 'strɪŋ,bɔ(ə)rd, -z

stringency
BR 'strɪn(d)ʒ(ə)nsi
AM 'strɪndʒənsi

stringendo
BR strɪn'dʒɛndəʊ, -z
AM strɪn'dʒɛndoʊ, -z

stringent
BR 'strɪn(d)ʒ(ə)nt
AM 'strɪndʒənt

stringently
BR 'strɪn(d)ʒ(ə)ntli
AM 'strɪndʒən(t)li

stringer
BR 'strɪŋə(r), -z
AM 'strɪŋər, -z

stringhalt
BR 'strɪŋhɔ:lt, 'strɪŋhɒlt, -s
AM 'strɪŋ,(h)ɔlt, 'strɪŋ,(h)ɑlt, -s

stringily
BR 'strɪŋɨli
AM 'strɪŋɨli

stringiness
BR 'strɪŋɪnɪs
AM 'strɪŋinɪs

stringless
BR 'strɪŋlɪs
AM 'strɪŋlɪs

stringlike
BR 'strɪŋlʌɪk
AM 'strɪŋ,laɪk

stringy
BR 'strɪŋ|i, -ɪə(r), -ɪɪst
AM 'strɪŋi, -ər, -ɪst

stringy-bark
BR 'strɪŋɪbɑ:k, -s
AM 'strɪŋi,bɑrk, -s

strip
BR strɪp, -s, -ɪŋ, -t
AM strɪp, -s, -ɪŋ, -t

stripe
BR strʌɪp, -s, -ɪŋ, -t
AM straɪp, -s, -ɪŋ, -t

stripling
BR 'strɪplɪŋ, -z
AM 'strɪplɪŋ, -z

stripper
BR 'strɪpə(r), -z
AM 'strɪpər, -z

stripperama
BR ,strɪpə'rɑ:mə(*r*)
AM ,strɪpə'rɑmə

striptease
BR 'strɪpti:z, ,strɪp'ti:z
AM ¦strɪp'tiz

stripteaser
BR 'strɪp,ti:zə(r), ,strɪp'ti:zə(r), -z
AM ¦strɪp'tizər, -z

stripy
BR 'strʌɪp|i, -ɪə(r), -ɪɪst
AM 'straɪpi, -ər, -ɪst

strive
BR strʌɪv, -z, -ɪŋ, -d
AM straɪv, -z, -ɪŋ, -d

striver
BR 'strʌɪvə(r), -z
AM 'straɪvər, -z

strobe
BR strəʊb, -z
AM stroʊb, -z

strobila
BR strə'bʌɪlə(*r*)
AM strə'baɪlə

strobilae
BR strə'bʌɪlʌɪ, strə'bʌɪli:
AM strə'baɪli, strə'baɪ,laɪ

strobile
BR 'strəʊbʌɪl, -z
AM 'stroʊbəl, -z

strobili
BR 'strəʊbɨlʌɪ
AM 'stroʊbə,laɪ

strobilus
BR 'strəʊbɨləs
AM 'stroʊbələs

stroboscope
BR 'strəʊbəskəʊp, -s
AM 'stroʊbə,skoʊp, -s
stroboscopic
BR ,strəʊbə'skɒpɪk
AM ,stroʊbə'skɑpɪk
stroboscopical
BR ,strəʊbə'skɒpɨkl
AM ,stroʊbə'skɑpəkəl
stroboscopically
BR ,strəʊbə'skɒpɨkli
AM ,stroʊbə'skɑpək(ə)li
strode
BR strəʊd
AM stroʊd
Stroganoff
BR 'strɒgənɒf, -s
AM 'stroʊgə,nɔf, -s
stroke
BR strəʊk, -s, -ɪŋ, -t
AM stroʊk, -s, -ɪŋ, -t
strokeplay
BR 'strəʊkpleɪ
AM 'stroʊk,pleɪ
stroll
BR strəʊl, -z, -ɪŋ, -d
AM stroʊl, -z, -ɪŋ, -d
stroller
BR 'strəʊlə(r), -z
AM 'stroʊlər, -z
stroma
BR 'strəʊmə(*r*)
AM 'stroʊmə
stromata
BR 'strəʊmətə(*r*)
AM 'stroʊmədə
stromatic
BR strə(ʊ)'matɪk
AM stroʊ'mædɪk
stromatolite
BR strə(ʊ)'matəlʌɪt, -s
AM stroʊ'mædə,laɪt, -s
Stromboli
BR 'strɒmbəli,
'strɒmbḷi
AM 'strɑmbəli
Stromness
BR 'strɒmnɛs,
'strʌmnɛs
AM 'strɑm,nɛs
strong
BR strɒŋ, -gə(r), -gɪst
AM strɔŋ, strɑŋ, -gər,
-gəst
strongbox
BR 'strɒŋbɒks, -ɪz
AM 'strɔŋ,bɑks,
'strɑŋ,bɑks, -əz
stronghold
BR 'strɒŋhəʊld, -z
AM 'strɔŋ,(h)oʊld,
'strɑŋ,(h)oʊld, -z
strongish
BR 'strɒŋɪʃ
AM 'strɔŋɪʃ, 'strɑŋɪʃ
strongly
BR 'strɒŋli
AM 'strɔŋli, 'strɑŋli
strongman
BR 'strɒŋman
AM 'strɔŋ,mæn,
'strɑŋ,mæn
strongmen
BR 'strɒŋmɛn
AM 'strɔŋ,mɛn,
'strɑŋ,mɛn
strongpoint
BR 'strɒŋpɔɪnt, -s
AM 'strɔŋ,pɔɪnt,
'strɑŋ,pɔɪnt, -s
strongroom
BR 'strɒŋruːm,
'strɒŋrʊm, -z
AM 'strɔŋ,rum,
'strɔŋ,rʊm,
'strɑŋ,rum,
'strɑŋ,rʊm, -z
strongyle
BR 'strɒndʒ(ɪ)l, -z
AM 'strɔndʒəl, -z
strontia
BR 'strɒntɪə(*r*),
'strɒnʃ(ɪ)ə(*r*)
AM 'strɑnʃiə, 'strɑntiə
strontium
BR 'strɒntɪəm,
'strɒnʃ(ɪ)əm
AM 'strɑn(t)ʃiəm,
'strɑntiəm
Strood
BR struːd
AM strud
strop
BR strɒp, -s, -ɪŋ, -t
AM strɑp, -s, -ɪŋ, -t
strophanthin
BR strə(ʊ)'fanθɪn,
strɒ'fanθɪn
AM stroʊ'fænθən
strophe
BR 'strəʊf|i, 'strɒf|i, -ɪz
AM 'stroʊfi, -z
strophic
BR 'strɒfɪk, 'strəʊfɪk
AM 'stroʊfɪk, 'strɑfɪk
stroppily
BR 'strɒpɨli
AM 'strɑpəli
stroppiness
BR 'strɒpɪnɨs
AM 'strɑpinɨs
stroppy
BR 'strɒp|i, -ɪə(r), -ɪɪst
AM 'strɑpi, -ər, -ɨst
Stroud
BR straʊd
AM straʊd
strove
BR strəʊv
AM stroʊv
strow
BR strəʊ, -z, -ɪŋ, -d
AM stroʊ, -z, -ɪŋ, -d
strown
BR strəʊn
AM stroʊn
struck
BR strʌk
AM strək
structural
BR 'strʌktʃ(ə)rəl,
'strʌktʃ(ə)rḷ
AM 'strək(t)ʃ(ə)rəl
structuralism
BR 'strʌktʃ(ə)rəlɪz(ə)m,
'strʌktʃ(ə)rḷɪz(ə)m
AM 'strək(t)ʃ(ə)rə,lɪzəm
structuralist
BR 'strʌktʃ(ə)rəlɪst,
'strʌktʃ(ə)rḷɪst, -s
AM 'strək(t)ʃ(ə)rələst,
-s
structurally
BR 'strʌktʃ(ə)rəli,
'strʌktʃ(ə)rḷi
AM 'strək(t)ʃ(ə)rəli
structure
BR 'strʌktʃ|ə(r), -əz,
-(ə)rɪŋ, -əd
AM 'strək(t)ʃər, -z, -ɪŋ,
-d
structureless
BR 'strʌktʃələs
AM 'strək(t)ʃərləs
strudel
BR 'struːdl, -z
AM 'strudəl, -z
struggle
BR 'strʌg|l, -lz,
-ḷɪŋ\-lɪŋ, -ld
AM 'strəg|əl, -əlz,
-(ə)lɪŋ, -əld
struggler
BR 'strʌgḷə(r),
'strʌglə(r), -z
AM 'strəg(ə)lər, -z
strum
BR strʌm, -z, -ɪŋ, -d
AM strəm, -z, -ɪŋ, -d
struma
BR 'struːmə(*r*)
AM 'strumə
strumae
BR 'struːmiː
AM 'strumi, 'stru,maɪ
Strumble
BR 'strʌmbl
AM 'strəmbəl
strummer
BR 'strʌmə(r), -z
AM 'strəmər, -z
strumose
BR 'struːməs,
'struːməʊs
AM 'stru,moʊs,
'stru,moʊz
strumous
BR 'struːməs
AM 'struməs
strumpet
BR 'strʌmpɪt, -s
AM 'strəmpət, -s
strung
BR strʌŋ
AM strəŋ
strut
BR strʌt, -s, -ɪŋ, -ɨd
AM strə|t, -ts, -dɪŋ, -dəd
'struth
BR struːθ
AM struθ
struthious
BR 'struːθɪəs
AM 'struθiəs, 'struðiəs
Strutt
BR strʌt
AM strət
strutter
BR 'strʌtə(r), -z
AM 'strədər, -z
struttingly
BR 'strʌtɪŋli
AM 'strədɪŋli
Struwwelpeter
BR ,struːəl'piːtə(r),
'struːəl,piːtə(r)
AM 'struəl,pidər
strychnic
BR 'strɪknɪk
AM 'strɪknɪk
strychnine
BR 'strɪkniːn
AM 'strɪk,naɪn,
'strɪk,nin
strychninism
BR 'strɪknɨnɪz(ə)m
AM 'strɪknə,nɪzəm
strychnism
BR 'strɪknɪz(ə)m
AM 'strɪk,nɪzəm
St Thomas
BR s(ə)nt 'tɒməs
AM seɪn(t) 'tɑməs
Stuart
BR 'stjuːət, 'stʃuːət, -s
AM 'st(j)uərt, -s
stub
BR stʌb, -z, -ɪŋ, -d
AM stəb, -z, -ɪŋ, -d
stubbily
BR 'stʌbɨli
AM 'stəbəli
stubbiness
BR 'stʌbɪnɨs
AM 'stəbinɨs
stubble
BR 'stʌbl, -d
AM 'stəbəl, -d
stubbly
BR 'stʌbḷi
AM 'stəb(ə)li
stubborn
BR 'stʌbən, 'stʌbṇ,
-ə(r), -ɨst
AM 'stəbərn, -ər, -əst
stubbornly
BR 'stʌb(ə)nli
AM 'stəbərnli

stubbornness
BR 'stʌb(ə)nnəs
AM 'stəbər(n)nəs

Stubbs
BR stʌbz
AM stəbz

stubby
BR 'stʌb|i, -ɪə(r), -ɪɪst
AM 'stəbi, -ər, -ɪst

stucco
BR 'stʌkəʊ
AM 'stəkoʊ

stuccowork
BR 'stʌkəʊwəːk
AM 'stəkoʊˌwərk

stuck
BR stʌk
AM stək

stuck-up
BR ˌstʌk'ʌp
AM ˌstək'əp

stud
BR stʌd, -z, -ɪŋ, -ɪd
AM stəd, -z, -ɪŋ, -əd

studbook
BR 'stʌdbʊk, -s
AM 'stədˌbʊk, -s

studding-sail[1]
BR 'stʌdɪŋseɪl, -z
AM 'stədɪŋˌseɪl, -z

studding-sail[2]
nautical use
BR 'stʌnsl, -z
AM 'stənsəl, -z

Studebaker
BR 'st(j)uːdəˌbeɪkə(r)
AM 'studəˌbeɪkər

student
BR 'stjuːdnt, 'stʃuːdnt, -s
AM 'st(j)udnt, -s

studentship
BR 'stjuːdntʃɪp, 'stʃuːdntʃɪp, -s
AM 'st(j)udntˌʃɪp, -s

studiedly
BR 'stʌdɪdli
AM 'stədidli

studiedness
BR 'stʌdɪdnɪs
AM 'stədidnɪs

studio
BR 'stjuːdɪəʊ, 'stʃuːdɪəʊ, -z
AM 'st(j)udioʊ, -z

studious
BR 'stjuːdɪəs, 'stʃuːdɪəs
AM 'st(j)udiəs

studiously
BR 'stjuːdɪəs, 'stʃuːdɪəsli
AM 'st(j)udiəsli

studiousness
BR 'stjuːdɪəsnəs, 'stʃuːdɪəsnəs
AM 'st(j)udiəsnəs

Studland
BR 'stʌdlənd
AM 'stədlənd

Studley
BR 'stʌdli
AM 'stədli

study
BR 'stʌd|i, -ɪz, -ɪɪŋ, -ɪd
AM 'stədi, -z, -ɪŋ, -d

stuff
BR stʌf, -s, -ɪŋ, -t
AM stəf, -s, -ɪŋ, -t

stuffer
BR 'stʌfə(r), -z
AM 'stəfər, -z

stuffily
BR 'stʌfɪli
AM 'stəfəli

stuffiness
BR 'stʌfɪnɪs
AM 'stəfinɪs

stuffing
BR 'stʌfɪŋ, -z
AM 'stəfɪŋ, -z

stuffy
BR 'stʌf|i, -ɪə(r), -ɪɪst
AM 'stəfi, -ər, -ɪst

Stuka
BR 'stuːkə(*r*), 'ʃtuːkə(*r*), -z
AM 'stukə, 'ʃtukə, -z

stultification
BR ˌstʌltɪfɪ'keɪʃn
AM ˌstəltəfə'keɪʃən

stultifier
BR 'stʌltɪfʌɪə(r), -z
AM 'stəltəˌfaɪər, -z

stultify
BR 'stʌltɪfʌɪ, -z, -ɪŋ, -d
AM 'stəltəˌfaɪ, -z, -ɪŋ, -d

stum[1]
silent
BR ʃtʊm
AM ʃtʊm

stum[2]
BR stʌm, -z, -ɪŋ, -d
AM stəm, -z, -ɪŋ, -d

stumble
BR 'stʌmb|l, -lz, -l̩ɪŋ\-lɪŋ, -ld
AM 'stəmbəl, -əlz, -(ə)lɪŋ, -əld

stumblebum
BR 'stʌmblbʌm, -z
AM 'stəmbəlˌbəm, -z

stumbler
BR 'stʌmblə(r), -z
AM 'stəmb(ə)lər, -z

stumblingly
BR 'stʌmblɪŋli
AM 'stəmb(ə)lɪŋli

stumer
BR 'stjuːmə(*r*), 'stʃuːmə(r), -z
AM 'st(j)umər, -z

stumm
silent
BR ʃtʊm
AM ʃtʊm

stump
BR stʌm|p, -ps, -pɪŋ, -(p)t
AM stəm|p, -ps, -pɪŋ, -(p)t

stumper
BR 'stʌmpə(r), -z
AM 'stəmpər, -z

stumpily
BR 'stʌmpɪli
AM 'stəmpəli

stumpiness
BR 'stʌmpɪnɪs
AM 'stəmpinɪs

stumpy
BR stʌmp|i, -ɪə(r), -ɪɪst
AM 'stəmpi, -ər, -ɪst

stun
BR stʌn, -z, -ɪŋ, -d
AM stən, -z, -ɪŋ, -d

stung
BR stʌŋ
AM stəŋ

stunk
BR stʌŋk
AM stəŋk

stunner
BR 'stʌnə(r), -z
AM 'stənər, -z

stunningly
BR 'stʌnɪŋli
AM 'stənɪŋli

stunsail
BR 'stʌnsl, -z
AM 'stənsəl, -z

stunt
BR stʌnt, -s, -ɪŋ, -ɪd
AM stən|t, -ts, -(t)ɪŋ, -(t)əd

stuntedness
BR 'stʌntɪdnɪs
AM 'stən(t)ədnəs

stunter
BR 'stʌntə(r), -z
AM 'stən(t)ər, -z

stuntman
BR 'stʌntman
AM 'stəntˌmæn

stuntmen
BR 'stʌntmɛn
AM 'stəntˌmɛn

stupa
BR 'stuːpə(*r*), -z
AM 'st(j)upə, -z

stupe
BR stjuːp, -s, -ɪŋ, -t
AM st(j)up, -s, -ɪŋ, -t

stupefacient
BR ˌstjuːpɪ'feɪʃnt, ˌstʃuːpɪ'feɪʃnt, -s
AM ˌst(j)upə'feɪʃənt, -s

stupefaction
BR ˌstjuːpɪ'fakʃn, ˌstʃuːpɪ'fakʃn
AM ˌst(j)upə'fækʃən

stupefactive
BR ˌstjuːpɪ'faktɪv, ˌstʃuːpɪ'faktɪv
AM ˌst(j)upə'fæktɪv

stupefier
BR 'stjuːpɪfʌɪə(r), 'stʃuːpɪfʌɪə(r), -z
AM 'st(j)upəˌfaɪər, -z

stupefy
BR 'stjuːpɪfʌɪ, 'stʃuːpɪfʌɪ, -z, -ɪŋ, -d
AM 'st(j)upəˌfaɪ, -z, -ɪŋ, -d

stupefyingly
BR 'stjuːpɪfʌɪɪŋli, 'stʃuːpɪfʌɪɪŋli
AM 'st(j)upəˌfaɪɪŋli

stupendous
BR stjuː'pɛndəs, stʃuː'pɛndəs, stjʊ'pɛndəs, stʃʊ'pɛndəs
AM st(j)u'pɛndəs

stupendously
BR stjuː'pɛndəsli, stʃuː'pɛndəsli, stjʊ'pɛndəsli, stʃʊ'pɛndəsli
AM st(j)u'pɛndəsli

stupendousness
BR stjuː'pɛndəsnəs, stʃuː'pɛndəsnəs, stjʊ'pɛndəsnəs, stʃʊ'pɛndəsnəs
AM st(j)u'pɛndəsnəs

stupid
BR 'stjuːpɪd, 'stʃuːpɪd
AM 'st(j)upəd

stupidity
BR stjuː'pɪdɪti, stʃuː'pɪdɪti, stjʊ'pɪdɪt|i, stʃʊ'pɪdɪti, -ɪz
AM st(j)u'pɪdɪdi, -z

stupidly
BR 'stjuːpɪdli, 'stʃuːpɪdli
AM 'st(j)upədli

stupor
BR 'stjuːpə(r), 'stʃuːpə(r), -z
AM 'st(j)upər, -z

stuporous
BR 'stjuːp(ə)rəs, 'stʃuːp(ə)rəs
AM 'st(j)upərəs

sturdied
BR 'stəːdɪd
AM 'stərdid

sturdily
BR 'stəːdɪli
AM 'stərdəli

sturdiness
BR 'stəːdɪnɪs

AM 'stərdinᵻs

sturdy
BR 'stəːd|i, -ɪə(r), -ɪᵻst
AM 'stərdi, -ər, -ᵻst

sturgeon
BR 'stəːdʒ(ə)n, -z
AM 'stərdʒən, -z

Sturmabteilung
BR 'ʃtʊəmab,tʌɪlʊŋ
AM 'ʃtʊrməb,taɪlʊŋ

Sturminster
BR 'stəː,mɪnstə(r)
AM 'stər,mɪnstər

Sturm und Drang
BR ,ʃtʊəm ʊnt 'draŋ
AM 'ʃtʊrm ʊn(d) 'dræŋ

Sturt
BR stəːt
AM stərt

Sturtevant
BR 'stəːtɪv(ə)nt
AM 'stərdəvənt

Sturtivant
BR 'stəːtɪv(ə)nt
AM 'stərdəvənt

Stuttaford
BR 'stʌtəfəd
AM 'stədəfərd

stutter
BR 'stʌt|ə(r), -əz, -(ə)rɪŋ, -əd
AM 'stədər, -z, -ɪŋ, -d

stutterer
BR 'stʌt(ə)rə(r), -z
AM 'stədərər, -z

stutteringly
BR 'stʌt(ə)rɪŋli
AM 'stədərɪŋli

Stuttgart
BR 'stʊtgaːt, 'ʃtʊtgaːt
AM 'stʊt,gart, 'stət,gart, 'ʃtʊt,gart, 'ʃtət,gart

Stuyvesant
BR 'stʌɪvᵻs(ə)nt
AM 'staɪvəsənt, 'stɔɪvəsənt

St Valentine
BR s(ə)nt 'valəntʌɪn, + 'valn̩tʌɪn
AM ˌseɪn(t) 'vælən,taɪn

St Vincent
BR s(ə)nt 'vɪns(ə)nt
AM ,seɪn(t) 'vɪnsənt

St Vitus
BR s(ə)nt 'vʌɪtəs, -ᵻz
AM ˌseɪnt 'vaɪdəs, ˌsən(t) +, -əz

sty
BR stʌɪ, -z
AM staɪ, -z

stye
BR stʌɪ, -z
AM staɪ, -z

Stygian
BR 'stɪdʒɪən
AM 'stɪdʒ(i)ən

style
BR stʌɪl, -z, -ɪŋ, -d
AM staɪl, -z, -ɪŋ, -d

stylebook
BR 'stʌɪlbʊk, -s
AM 'staɪl,bʊk, -s

styleless
BR 'stʌɪllᵻs
AM 'staɪ(l)lᵻs

stylelessness
BR 'stʌɪllᵻsnᵻs
AM 'staɪ(l)lᵻsnᵻs

styler
BR 'stʌɪlə(r), -z
AM 'staɪlər, -z

Styles
BR stʌɪlz
AM staɪlz

stylet
BR 'stʌɪlᵻt, -s
AM ,staɪ'lɛt, 'staɪlət, -s

styli
BR 'stʌɪlʌɪ
AM 'staɪ,laɪ

stylisation
BR ,stʌɪlʌɪ'zeɪʃn
AM ,staɪlə'zeɪʃən, ,staɪ,laɪ'zeɪʃən

stylise
BR 'stʌɪlʌɪz, -ᵻz, -ɪŋ, -d
AM 'staɪ,laɪz, -ᵻz, -ɪŋ, -d

stylish
BR 'stʌɪlɪʃ
AM 'staɪlɪʃ

stylishly
BR 'stʌɪlɪʃli
AM 'staɪlɪʃli

stylishness
BR 'stʌɪlɪʃnᵻs
AM 'staɪlɪʃnᵻs

stylist
BR 'stʌɪlɪst, -s
AM 'staɪlɪst, -s

stylistic
BR stʌɪ'lɪstɪk, stə'lɪstɪk, -s
AM staɪ'lɪstɪk, -s

stylistically
BR stʌɪ'lɪstɪkli
AM staɪ'lɪstɪk(ə)li

stylite
BR 'stʌɪlʌɪt, -s
AM 'staɪ,laɪt, -s

Stylites
BR stʌɪ'lʌɪtiːz
AM staɪ'laɪdiz

stylization
BR ,stʌɪlʌɪ'zeɪʃn
AM ,staɪlə'zeɪʃən, ,staɪ,laɪ'zeɪʃən

stylize
BR 'stʌɪlʌɪz, -ᵻz, -ɪŋ, -d
AM 'staɪ,laɪz, -ᵻz, -ɪŋ, -d

stylo
BR 'stʌɪləʊ, -z
AM 'staɪloʊ, -z

stylobate
BR 'stʌɪləbeɪt, -s
AM 'staɪlə,beɪt, -s

stylograph
BR 'stʌɪləgraːf, 'stʌɪləgraf, -s
AM 'staɪlə,græf, -s

stylographic
BR ,stʌɪlə'grafɪk
AM ,staɪlə'græfɪk

styloid
BR 'stʌɪlɔɪd, -z
AM 'staɪ,lɔɪd, -z

stylus
BR 'stʌɪləs, -ᵻz
AM 'staɪləs, -əz

stymie
BR 'stʌɪm|i, -ɪz, -ɪɪŋ, -ɪd
AM 'staɪmi, -z, -ɪŋ, -d

stymy
BR 'stʌɪm|i, -ɪz, -ɪɪŋ, -ɪd
AM 'staɪmi, -z, -ɪŋ, -d

styptic
BR 'stɪptɪk
AM 'stɪptɪk

styrax
BR 'stʌɪraks
AM 'staɪ,ræks

styrene
BR 'stʌɪriːn
AM 'staɪ,rin

Styria
BR 'stɪrɪə(r)
AM 'stɪriə

Styrofoam®
BR 'stʌɪrə(ʊ)fəʊm
AM 'staɪrə,foʊm

Styron
BR 'stʌɪrɒn
AM 'staɪrən

Styx
BR stɪks
AM stɪks

Su
BR suː
AM su

suability
BR ,s(j)uːə'bɪlᵻti
AM ,suə'bɪlᵻdi

suable
BR 's(j)uːəbl
AM 'suəbəl

suasion
BR 'sweɪʒn
AM 'sweɪʒən

suasive
BR 'sweɪsɪv, 'sweɪzɪv
AM 'sweɪzɪv

suave
BR swaːv, -ə(r), -ᵻst
AM swav, -ər, -əst

suavely
BR 'swaːvli
AM 'suavli

suaveness
BR 'swaːvnəs
AM 'suavnəs

suavity
BR 'swaːvᵻti
AM 'swavədi

sub
BR sʌb, -z, -ɪŋ, -d
AM səb, -z, -ɪŋ, -d

subabdominal
BR ,sʌbəb'dɒmᵻnl
AM ,səbəb'damənəl

subacid
BR ,sʌb'asɪd
AM ,səb'æsəd

subacidity
BR ,sʌbə'sɪdᵻti
AM ,səbə'sɪdᵻdi

subacute
BR ,sʌbə'kjuːt
AM ,səbə'kjut

subacutely
BR ,sʌbə'kjuːtli
AM ,səbə'kjutli

subagency
BR ,sʌb'eɪdʒ(ə)ns|i, -ɪz
AM 'səb,eɪdʒənsi, -z

subagent
BR ,sʌb'eɪdʒ(ə)nt, -s
AM 'səb,eɪdʒənt, -s

subahdar
BR ,sʌbə'daː(r), ,suːbə'daː(r), -z
AM ,səbə'dar, -z

subalpine
BR ,sʌb'alpʌɪn
AM ,səb'æl,paɪn

subaltern
BR 'sʌblt(ə)n, -z
AM sə'bɔltərn, sə'baltərn, -z

subantarctic
BR ,sʌban'taːktɪk
AM ,subən'tarktɪk

subaqua
BR ,sʌb'akwə(r)
AM ,səb'akwə

subaquatic
BR ,sʌbə'kwatɪk
AM ,səbə'kwadɪk

subaqueous
BR ,sʌb'eɪkwɪəs, ,sʌb'akwɪəs
AM ,səb'eɪkwiəs, ,səb'ækwiəs

subarctic
BR ,sʌb'aːktɪk
AM ,səb'ar(k)tɪk

Subaru®
BR 'suːbəruː, sʊ'baːruː, -z
AM 'subə,ru, -z

subastral
BR ,sʌb'astr(ə)l
AM ,səb'æstrəl

subatomic
BR ,sʌbə'tɒmɪk

AM ˌsəbəˈtɑmɪk

subaudition
BR ˌsʌbɔːˈdɪʃn
AM ˌsəbɔˈdɪʃən, ˌsəbɑˈdɪʃən

subaxillary
BR ˌsʌbakˈsɪl(ə)ri
AM ˌsəbˈæksəˌlɛri

sub-basement
BR ˌsʌbˈbeɪsm(ə)nt, -s
AM ˈsəbˌbeɪsmənt, -s

sub-branch
BR ˈsʌbbrɑːn(t)ʃ, ˈsʌbbran(t)ʃ, -ɪz
AM ˈsəbˌbræn(t)ʃ, -əz, -ɪŋ, -t

sub-breed
BR ˈsʌbbriːd, -z
AM ˈsəbˌbrid, -z

Subbuteo®
BR səˈb(j)uːtɪəʊ
AM səˈb(j)udioʊ

subcategorisation
BR ˌsʌbkatɪɡərʌɪˈzeɪʃn, -z
AM ˈsəbˌkædəɡ(ə)rəˈzeɪʃən, ˈsəbˌkædəɡəˌraɪˈzeɪʃən, -z

subcategorise
BR ˌsʌbˈkatɪɡərʌɪz, -ɪz, -ɪŋ, -d
AM ˌsəbˈkædəɡəˌraɪz, ˌsəbˈkædəɡɔˌraɪz, -ɪz, -ɪŋ, -d

subcategorization
BR ˌsʌbkatɪɡərʌɪˈzeɪʃn, -z
AM ˈsəbˌkædəɡ(ə)rəˈzeɪʃən, ˈsəbˌkædəɡəˌraɪˈzeɪʃən, -z

subcategorize
BR ˌsʌbˈkatɪɡərʌɪz, -ɪz, -ɪŋ, -d
AM ˌsəbˈkædəɡəˌraɪz, ˌsəbˈkædəɡɔˌraɪz, -ɪz, -ɪŋ, -d

subcategory
BR ˈsʌbˌkatɪɡ(ə)r|i, -ɪz
AM ˈsəbˌkædəˌɡɔri, -z

subcaudal
BR ˌsʌbˈkɔːdl
AM ˌsəbˈkɔdəl, ˌsəbˈkɑdəl

subclass
BR ˈsʌbklɑːs, ˈsʌbklas, -ɪz
AM ˈsəbˌklæs, -əz

subclassification
BR ˌsʌbklasɪfɪˈkeɪʃn
AM ˈsəbˌklæsəfəˈkeɪʃən

sub-clause
BR ˈsʌbklɔːz, -ɪz
AM ˈsəbˌklɔz, ˈsəbˌklɑz, -əz

subclavian
BR ˌsʌbˈkleɪvɪən
AM ˌsəbˈkleɪviən

subclinical
BR ˌsʌbˈklɪnɪkl
AM ˈsəbˈklɪnɪkəl

subcommissioner
BR ˌsʌbkəˈmɪʃn̩ə(r), ˌsʌbkəˈmɪʃ(ə)nə(r), -z
AM ˌsəbkəˈmɪʃ(ə)nər, -z

subcommittee
BR ˈsʌbkəˌmɪt|i, -ɪz
AM ˈsəbkəˌmɪdi, -z

subcompact
BR ˌsʌbˈkɒmpakt, -s
AM ˌsəbˈkɑmˌpæk(t), -(t)s

subconical
BR ˌsʌbˈkɒnɪkl
AM ˌsəbˈkɑnəkəl

subconscious
BR ˌsʌbˈkɒnʃəs, səbˈkɒnʃəs
AM səbˈkɑnʃəs

subconsciously
BR ˌsʌbˈkɒnʃəsli, səbˈkɒnʃəsli
AM səbˈkɑnʃəsli

subconsciousness
BR ˌsʌbˈkɒnʃəsnəs, səbˈkɒnʃəsnəs
AM səbˈkɑnʃəsnəs

subcontinent
BR ˌsʌbˈkɒntɪnənt, ˈsʌbˌkɒntɪnənt, -s
AM ˌsəbˈkɑntn̩ənt, -s

subcontinental
BR ˌsʌbkɒntɪˈnɛntl
AM ˌsəbˌkɑn(t)əˈnɛn(t)l

subcontract
BR ˌsʌbkənˈtrakt, ˈsʌbkəntrakt, -s, -ɪŋ, -ɪd
AM ˈsəbˈkɑnˌtræk|(t), -(t)s, -tɪŋ, -təd

subcontractor
BR ˈsʌbkənˌtraktə(r), -z
AM ˈsəbˈkɑnˌtræktər, -z

subcontrary
BR ˌsʌbˈkɒntrər|i, -ɪz
AM ˌsəbˈkɑntrəri, -z

subcordate
BR ˌsʌbˈkɔːdeɪt
AM ˌsəbˈkɔrdeɪt

subcortical
BR ˌsʌbˈkɔːtɪkl
AM ˌsəbˈkɔrdəkəl

subcostal
BR ˌsʌbˈkɒstl
AM ˈsəbˈkɔstl, ˌsəbˈkɑstl

subcranial
BR ˌsʌbˈkreɪnɪəl
AM ˌsəbˈkreɪniəl

subcritical
BR ˌsʌbˈkrɪtɪkl
AM ˌsəbˈkrɪdɪkəl

subcultural
BR ˌsʌbˈkʌltʃ(ə)rəl, ˌsʌbˈkʌltʃ(ə)rl̩
AM ˈsəbˈkəltʃ(ə)rəl

subculture
BR ˈsʌbˌkʌltʃə(r), -z
AM ˈsəbˌkəltʃər, -z

subcutaneous
BR ˌsʌbkjʊˈteɪnɪəs
AM ˌsəbkjuˈteɪniəs

subcutaneously
BR ˌsʌbkjʊˈteɪnɪəsli
AM ˌsəbkjuˈteɪniəsli

subcuticular
BR ˌsʌbkjʊˈtɪkjʊlə(r)
AM ˌsəbkjəˈtɪkjələr

subdeacon
BR ˌsʌbˈdiːk(ə)n, ˈsʌbdiːk(ə)n, -z
AM ˈsəbˈdikən, -z

subdean
BR ˌsʌbˈdiːn, ˈsʌbdiːn, -z
AM ˈsəbˈdin, -z

subdeanery
BR ˌsʌbˈdiːn(ə)r|i, ˈsʌbˌdiːn(ə)r|i, -ɪz
AM ˌsəbˈdinəri, -z

subdecanal
BR ˌsʌbˈdɛkənl
AM ˌsəbˈdɛkənəl

subdeliria
BR ˌsʌbdɪˈlɪrɪə(r), ˌsʌbdɪˈlɪərɪə(r)
AM ˌsəbdəˈlɪriə, ˌsəbdiˈlɪriə

subdelirious
BR ˌsʌbdɪˈlɪrɪəs, ˌsʌbdɪˈlɪərɪəs
AM ˌsəbdəˈlɪriəs, ˈsəbdiˈlɪriəs

subdelirium
BR ˌsʌbdɪˈlɪrɪəm, ˌsʌbdɪˈlɪərɪəm
AM ˌsəbdəˈlɪriəm, ˌsəbdiˈlɪriəm

subdiaconate
BR ˌsʌbdʌɪˈakəneɪt, ˌsʌbdʌɪˈakənət, ˌsʌbdʌɪˈakn̩ət, -s
AM ˌsəbdaɪˈækənət, ˌsəbdiˈækənət, -s

subdivide
BR ˌsʌbdɪˈvʌɪd, ˈsʌbdɪvʌɪd, -z, -ɪŋ, -ɪd
AM ˈsəbdəˌvaɪd, -z, -ɪŋ, -ɪd

subdivision
BR ˈsʌbdɪˌvɪʒn, ˌsʌbdɪˈvɪʒn, -z
AM ˈsəbdəˌvɪʒən, -z

subdominant
BR ˌsʌbˈdɒmɪnənt, -s
AM ˌsəbˈdɑmənənt, -s

subduable
BR səbˈdjuːəbl, səbˈdʒuːəbl
AM səbˈd(j)uəbəl

subdual
BR səbˈdjuːəl, səbˈdʒuːəl, -z
AM səbˈd(j)uəl, -z

subduct
BR səbˈdʌkt, ˌsʌbˈdʌkt, -s, -ɪŋ, -d
AM səbˈdək|(t), -(t)s, -tɪŋ, -təd

subduction
BR səbˈdʌkʃn, ˌsʌbˈdʌkʃn
AM səbˈdəkʃən

subdue
BR səbˈdjuː, səbˈdʒuː, -z, -ɪŋ, -d
AM səbˈd(j)u, -z, -ɪŋ, -d

subdural
BR ˌsʌbˈdjʊərl̩, ˌsʌbˈdjɔːrl̩, ˌsʌbˈdʒʊərl̩, ˌsʌbˈdʒɔːrl̩
AM ˌsəbˈd(j)ʊrəl

subedit
BR ˌsʌbˈɛd|ɪt, ˈsʌbˌɛd|ɪt, -s, -ɪtɪŋ, -ɪtɪd
AM ˌsəbˈɛdə|t, -ts, -dɪŋ, -dəd

subeditor
BR ˌsʌbˈɛdɪtə(r), ˈsʌbˌɛdɪtə(r), -z
AM ˌsəbˈɛdədər, -z

sub-editorial
BR ˌsʌbɛdɪˈtɔːrɪəl
AM ˌsəbˌɛdəˈtɔriəl

subeditorship
BR ˌsʌbˈɛdɪtəʃɪp, -s
AM ˌsəbˈɛdədərˌʃɪp, -s

suberect
BR ˌsʌbɪˈrɛkt
AM ˌsubəˈrɛk(t)

subereous
BR s(j)uːˈbɪərɪəs
AM suˈbɪriəs

suberic
BR s(j)uːˈbɛrɪk
AM suˈbɛrɪk

suberose
BR ˈs(j)uːb(ə)rəʊs
AM ˈsubəˌroʊs, ˈsubəˌroʊz

subfamily
BR ˈsʌbˌfam(ɪ)l|i, ˈsʌbˌfaml̩|i, -ɪz
AM ˌsəbˈfæm(ə)li, -z

subfloor
BR ˈsʌbflɔː(r), -z
AM ˈsəbˌflɔ(ə)r, -z

subform
BR ˈsʌbfɔːm, -z
AM ˈsəbˌfɔ(ə)rm, -z

sub-frame
BR ˈsʌbfreɪm, -z
AM ˈsəbˌfreɪm, -z

subfusc
BR ˈsʌbfʌsk
AM ˈsəbˈfəsk

subgenera
BR 'sʌbˌdʒɛn(ə)rə(r)
AM 'səbˌdʒɛnərə

subgeneric
BR ˌsʌbdʒɪ'nɛrɪk
AM ˌsəbdʒə'nɛrɪk

subgenus
BR 'sʌbˌdʒiːnəs
AM 'səbˌdʒinəs

subglacial
BR ˌsʌb'gleɪʃl
AM ˌsəb'gleɪʃəl

subgroup
BR 'sʌbgruːp, -s
AM 'səbˌgrup, -s

subhead
BR 'sʌbhɛd, -z
AM 'səbˌ(h)ɛd, -z

subheading
BR 'sʌbˌhɛdɪŋ, -z
AM 'səbˌ(h)ɛdɪŋ, -z

subhuman
BR ˌsʌb'hjuːmən, -z
AM ˈsəb'(h)jumən, -z

subjacent
BR ˌsʌb'dʒeɪs(ə)nt, səb'dʒeɪs(ə)nt
AM ˌsəb'dʒeɪsnt

subject[1]
noun
BR 'sʌbdʒɪkt, 'sʌbdʒɛkt, -s
AM 'səbdʒək(t), -s

subject[2]
verb
BR səb'dʒɛkt, -s, -ɪŋ, -ɪd
AM səb'dʒɛk|(t), -(t)s, -tɪŋ, -təd

subjection
BR səb'dʒɛkʃn
AM səb'dʒɛkʃən

subjective
BR səb'dʒɛktɪv, ˌsʌb'dʒɛktɪv
AM səb'dʒɛktɪv

subjectively
BR səb'dʒɛktɪvli, ˌsʌb'dʒɛktɪvli
AM səb'dʒɛktɪvli

subjectiveness
BR səb'dʒɛktɪvnɪs, ˌsʌb'dʒɛktɪvnɪs
AM səb'dʒɛktɪvnɪs

subjectivism
BR səb'dʒɛktɪvɪz(ə)m, ˌsʌb'dʒɛktɪvɪz(ə)m
AM səb'dʒɛktəˌvɪzəm

subjectivist
BR səb'dʒɛktɪvɪst, ˌsʌb'dʒɛktɪvɪst, -s
AM səb'dʒɛktəvəst, -s

subjectivity
BR ˌsʌbdʒɛk'tɪvɪti, ˌsʌbdʒɪk'tɪvɪti
AM ˌsəbˌdʒɛk'tɪvɪdi

subjectless
BR 'sʌbdʒɪk(t)ləs, 'sʌbdʒɛk(t)ləs
AM 'səbdʒək(t)ləs

subjoin
BR ˌsʌb'dʒɔɪn, səb'dʒɔɪn, -z, -ɪŋ, -d
AM ˌsəb'dʒɔɪn, -z, -ɪŋ, -d

subjoint
BR 'sʌbdʒɔɪnt, -s
AM 'səbˌdʒɔɪnt, -s

sub judice
BR ˌsʌb 'dʒuːdɪsiː, səb +
AM ˌsəb 'judəˌkeɪ, + 'dʒudəˌsi

subjugable
BR 'sʌbdʒʊgəbl
AM 'səbdʒəgəbəl

subjugate
BR 'sʌbdʒʊgeɪt, -s, -ɪŋ, -ɪd
AM 'səbdʒəˌgeɪ|t, -ts, -dɪŋ, -dɪd

subjugation
BR ˌsʌbdʒʊ'geɪʃn
AM ˌsəbdʒə'geɪʃən

subjugator
BR 'sʌbdʒʊgeɪtə(r), -z
AM 'səbdʒəˌgeɪdər, -z

subjunctive
BR səb'dʒʌŋ(k)tɪv, -z
AM səb'dʒəŋ(k)tɪv, -z

subjunctively
BR səb'dʒʌŋ(k)tɪvli
AM səb'dʒəŋ(k)tɪvli

subkingdom
BR 'sʌbˌkɪŋdəm, -z
AM 'səbˌkɪŋdəm, -z

sublapsarian
BR ˌsʌblap'sɛːrɪən, -z
AM ˌsəblæp'sɛriən, -z

sublease[1]
noun
BR 'sʌbliːs, -ɪz
AM 'səbˌlis, -ɪz

sublease[2]
verb
BR ˌsʌb'liːs, -ɪz, -ɪŋ, -t
AM səb'lis, -ɪz, -ɪŋ, -t

sub-lessee
BR ˌsʌblɛ'siː, -z
AM ˈsəbˌlɛ'si, -z

sub-lessor
BR 'sʌbˌlɛsə(r), ˌsʌb'lɛsə(r), -z
AM ˈsəb'lɛsər, -z

sublet
BR ˌsʌb'lɛt, -s, -ɪŋ
AM ˈsəb'lɛ|t, -ts, -dɪŋ

sub-librarian
BR ˌsʌblʌɪ'brɛːrɪən, -z
AM ˌsəbˌlaɪ'brɛriən, -z

sub-licence
BR 'sʌbˌlʌɪsns, -ɪz
AM 'səbˌlaɪsəns, -əz

sub-license
BR ˌsʌb'lʌɪsns, -ɪz, -ɪŋ, -t
AM ˌsəb'laɪsns, -əz, -ɪŋ, -t

sub-licensee
BR ˌsʌblʌɪsn'siː, -z
AM ˌsəbˌlaɪsn'si, -z

sub-licensor
BR ˌsʌb'lʌɪsnsə(r), -z
AM ˌsəb'laɪsnsər, -z

sublieutenant
BR ˌsʌblɛf'tɛnənt, -s
AM ˌsəbˌlu'tɛnənt, -s

sublimate
BR 'sʌblɪmeɪt, -s, -ɪŋ, -ɪd
AM 'səbləˌmeɪ|t, -ts, -dɪŋ, -dɪd

sublimation
BR ˌsʌblɪ'meɪʃn
AM ˌsəblə'meɪʃən

sublime
BR sə'blʌɪm, -ə(r), -ɪst
AM sə'blaɪm, -ər, -ɪst

sublimely
BR sə'blʌɪmli
AM sə'blaɪmli

Sublime Porte
BR səˌblʌɪm 'pɔːt
AM səˈblaɪm 'pɔ(ə)rt

subliminal
BR ˌsʌb'lɪmɪnl, sə'blɪmɪnl
AM sə'blɪmənəl

subliminally
BR ˌsʌb'lɪmɪnl̩i, ˌsʌb'lɪmɪnəli, sə'blɪmɪnl̩i, sə'blɪmɪnəli
AM sə'blɪmənəli

sublimity
BR sə'blɪmɪti
AM sə'blɪmɪdi

sublingual
BR ˌsʌb'lɪŋgw(ə)l
AM ˌsəb'lɪŋgwəl

sublittoral
BR ˌsʌb'lɪt(ə)rəl, ˌsʌb'lɪt(ə)rl̩
AM ˌsəb'lɪdərəl

sublunary
BR ˌsʌb'luːn(ə)ri
AM ˌsəb'lunəri

subluxation
BR ˌsʌblʌk'seɪʃn, -z
AM ˌsəbˌlək'seɪʃən, -z

submachine gun
BR ˌsʌbmə'ʃiːn gʌn, -z
AM ˌsəbmə'ʃin ˌgən, -z

subman
BR 'sʌbman
AM 'səbˌmæn

submarginal
BR ˌsʌb'mɑːdʒɪnl
AM ˌsəb'mɑrdʒənəl

submarine
BR ˌsʌbmə'riːn, 'sʌbməriːn, -z
AM ˈsəbməˌrin, -z

submariner
BR ˌsʌb'marɪnə(r), -z
AM səb'mɛrənər, -z

submaster
BR 'sʌbˌmɑːstə(r), 'sʌbˌmastə(r), -z
AM 'səbˌmæstər, -z

submaxillary
BR ˌsʌb'maksɪl(ə)ri, ˌsʌbmak'sɪl(ə)ri
AM ˌsəb'mæksəˌlɛri

submediant
BR ˌsʌb'miːdɪənt, -s
AM ˌsəb'midiənt, -s

submen
BR 'sʌbmɛn
AM 'səbˌmɛn

submental
BR ˌsʌb'mɛntl
AM ˌsəb'mɛn(t)l

submerge
BR səb'məːdʒ, -ɪz, -ɪŋ, -d
AM səb'mərdʒ, -əz, -ɪŋ, -d

submergence
BR səb'məːdʒ(ə)ns
AM səb'mərdʒəns

submergible
BR səb'məːdʒɪbl
AM səb'mərdʒəbəl

submerse
BR səb'məːs, -ɪz, -ɪŋ, -t
AM səb'mərs, -əz, -ɪŋ, -t

submersible
BR səb'məːsɪbl, -z
AM səb'mərsəbəl, -z

submersion
BR səb'məːʃn, səb'məːʒn, -z
AM səb'mərʒən, səb'mərʃən, -z

submicroscopic
BR ˌsʌbmʌɪkrə'skɒpɪk
AM ˈsəbˌmaɪkrə'skɑpɪk

subminiature
BR ˌsʌb'mɪnɪtʃə(r)
AM ˌsəb'mɪn(i)əˌtʃʊ(ə)r, ˌsəb'mɪn(i)ətʃər

submission
BR səb'mɪʃn, -z
AM səb'mɪʃən, -z

submissive
BR səb'mɪsɪv
AM səb'mɪsɪv

submissively
BR səb'mɪsɪvli
AM səb'mɪsɪvli

submissiveness
BR səb'mɪsɪvnɪs
AM səb'mɪsɪvnɪs

submit
BR səb'mɪt, -s, -ɪŋ, -ɪd

AM səbˈmɪ|t, -ts, -dɪŋ, -dɨd

submittal
BR səbˈmɪtl, -z
AM səbˈmɪdl, -z

submitter
BR sʌbˈmɪtə(r), -z
AM səbˈmɪdər, -z

submultiple
BR ˌsʌbˈmʌltɨpl, -z
AM ˌsəbˈməltəpəl, -z

subnormal
BR ˌsʌbˈnɔːml
AM ˈsəbˈnɔrməl

subnormality
BR ˌsʌbnɔːˈmalɪti
AM ˈsəbˌnɔrˈmæləɾi

sub-nuclear
BR ˌsʌbˈnjuːklɪə(r)
AM ˌsəbˈn(j)ukliər

subocular
BR ˌsʌbˈɒkjʊlə(r)
AM ˌsəbˈɑkjələr

suborbital
BR ˌsʌbˈɔːbɨtl
AM ˈsəbˈɔrbədl

suborder
BR ˈsʌbˌɔːdə(r), -z
AM ˈsəbˌɔrdər, -z

subordinal
BR ˌsʌbˈɔːdɨnl
AM ˈsəbˈɔrdənəl

subordinary
BR ˌsʌbˈɔːdɨn(ə)r|i, ˌsʌbˈɔːdn̩(ə)r|i, -ɪz
AM ˌsəbˈɔrdnˌɛri, -z

subordinate¹
noun, adjective
BR səˈbɔːdɨnət, səˈbɔːdn̩ət, -s
AM səˈbɔrdn̩ət, -s

subordinate²
verb
BR səˈbɔːdɨneɪt, -s, -ɪŋ, -ɨd
AM səˈbɔrdnˌeɪ|t, -ts, -dɪŋ, -dɨd

subordinately
BR səˈbɔːdɨnətli, səˈbɔːdn̩ətli
AM səˈbɔrdn̩ətli

subordination
BR səˌbɔːdɪˈneɪʃn
AM səˌbɔrdnˈeɪʃən

subordinative
BR səˈbɔːdɨnətɪv, səˈbɔːdn̩ətɪv
AM səˈbɔrdn̩ədɪv

suborn
BR səˈbɔːn, -z, -ɪŋ, -d
AM səˈbɔ(ə)rn, -z, -ɪŋ, -d

subornation
BR ˌsʌbɔːˈneɪʃn
AM ˌsəbɔrˈneɪʃən

suborner
BR səˈbɔːnə(r), -z
AM səˈbɔrnər, -z

suboxide
BR ˌsʌbˈɒksʌɪd, -z
AM ˌsəbˈɑkˌsaɪd, -z

sub-paragraph
BR ˈsʌbˌparəgrɑːf, ˌsʌbˈparəgrɑːf, ˈsʌbˌparəgraf, ˌsʌbˈparəgraf, -s
AM ˈsəbˈpɛrəˌgræf, -s

subphyla
BR ˈsʌbˌfʌɪlə(r)
AM ˈsəbˌfaɪlə

subphylum
BR ˈsʌbˌfʌɪləm
AM ˈsəbˌfaɪləm

subplot
BR ˈsʌbplɒt, -s
AM ˈsəbˌplɑt, -s

subpoena
BR sə(b)ˈpiːnə(r), -z, -ɪŋ, -d
AM səˈpinə, -z, -ɪŋ, -d

subprior
BR ˈsʌbˌprʌɪə(r), -z
AM ˈsəbˌpraɪər, -z

subprocess
BR ˈsʌbˌprəʊsɛs, -ɨz
AM ˈsəbˌprɑsəs, -əz

subprogram
BR ˈsʌbˌprəʊgram, ˈsʌbˌprəʊgrəm, -z
AM ˈsəbˌproʊgrəm, -z

subregion
BR ˈsʌbˌriːdʒ(ə)n, -z
AM ˈsəbˌridʒən, -z

subregional
BR ˌsʌbˈriːdʒn̩(ə)l, ˌsʌbˈriːdʒən(ə)l
AM ˌsəbˈridʒ(ə)nəl

subreption
BR səˈbrɛpʃn, -z
AM səˈbrɛpʃən, -z

subrogate
BR ˈsʌbrəgeɪt, -s, -ɪŋ, -ɨd
AM ˈsəbrəˌgeɪ|t, -ts, -dɪŋ, -dɨd

subrogation
BR ˌsʌbrəˈgeɪʃn
AM ˌsəbrəˈgeɪʃən

sub rosa
BR ˌsʌb ˈrəʊzə(r)
AM ˌsəb ˈroʊzə

subroutine
BR ˈsʌbruːtiːn, ˈsʌbrʊtiːn, -z
AM ˈsəbruˌtin, -z

sub-Saharan
BR ˌsʌbsəˈhɑːrən, ˌsʌbsəˈhɑːrn̩
AM ˌsəbsəˈhɛrən

subscribe
BR səbˈskrʌɪb, -z, -ɪŋ, -d
AM səbˈskraɪb, -z, -ɪŋ, -d

subscriber
BR səbˈskrʌɪbə(r), -z
AM səbˈskraɪbər, -z

subscript
BR ˈsʌbskrɪpt, -s
AM ˈsəbˌskrɪpt, -s

subscription
BR səbˈskrɪpʃn, -z
AM səbˈskrɪpʃən, -z

subsection
BR ˈsʌbˌsɛkʃn, -z
AM ˈsəbˌsɛkʃən, -z

sub-sector
BR ˈsʌbˌsɛktə(r), -z
AM ˈsəbˌsɛktər, -z

subsellia
BR səbˈsɛlɪə(r)
AM ˌsəbˈsɛljə, ˌsəbˈsɛliə

subsellium
BR səbˈsɛlɪəm
AM ˌsəbˈsɛliəm

subsequence
BR ˈsʌbsɨkw(ə)ns
AM ˈsəbsəkwəns

sub-sequence
BR ˈsʌbˌsiːkw(ə)ns, -ɨz
AM ˈsəbˌsikwəns, -əz

subsequent
BR ˈsʌbsɨkw(ə)nt
AM ˈsəbsəkwənt

subsequently
BR ˈsʌbsɨkw(ə)ntli
AM ˈsəbsəkwən(t)li

subserve
BR səbˈsəːv, -z, -ɪŋ, -d
AM səbˈsərv, -z, -ɪŋ, -d

subservience
BR səbˈsəːvɪəns
AM səbˈsərviəns

subserviency
BR səbˈsəːvɪənsi
AM səbˈsərviənsi

subservient
BR səbˈsəːvɪənt
AM səbˈsərviənt

subserviently
BR səbˈsəːvɪəntli
AM səbˈsərviən(t)li

subset
BR ˈsʌbsɛt, -s
AM ˈsəbˌsɛt, -s

subshrub
BR ˈsʌbʃrʌb, -z
AM ˈsəbˌʃrəb, -z

subside
BR səbˈsʌɪd, -z, -ɪŋ, -ɨd
AM səbˈsaɪd, -z, -ɪŋ, -ɨd

subsidence
BR səbˈsʌɪdns, ˈsʌbsɨdns, -ɨz
AM səbˈsaɪdns, ˈsəbsədns, -ɨz

subsidiarily
BR səbˈsɪdɪərɨli
AM səbˌsɪdiˈɛrəli

subsidiariness
BR səbˈsɪdɪərɪnɪs
AM səbˈsɪdiˌɛrinɪs

subsidiarity
BR səbˌsɪdɪˈarɪti
AM səbˌsɪdiˈɛrədi

subsidiary
BR səbˈsɪdɪər|i, -ɪz
AM səbˈsɪdiˌɛri, -z

subsidisation
BR ˌsʌbsɨdʌɪˈzeɪʃn
AM ˌsəbsədəˈzeɪʃən, ˌsəbsəˌdaɪˈzeɪʃən

subsidise
BR ˈsʌbsɨdʌɪz, -ɨz, -ɪŋ, -d
AM ˈsəbsəˌdaɪz, -ɨz, -ɪŋ, -d

subsidiser
BR ˈsʌbsɨdʌɪzə(r)
AM ˈsəbsəˌdaɪzər

subsidization
BR ˌsʌbsɨdʌɪˈzeɪʃn
AM ˌsəbsədəˈzeɪʃən, ˌsəbsəˌdaɪˈzeɪʃən

subsidize
BR ˈsʌbsɨdʌɪz, -ɨz, -ɪŋ, -d
AM ˈsəbsəˌdaɪz, -ɨz, -ɪŋ, -d

subsidizer
BR ˈsʌbsɨdʌɪzə(r), -z
AM ˈsəbsəˌdaɪzər, -z

subsidy
BR ˈsʌbsɨd|i, -ɪz
AM ˈsəbsədi, -z

subsist
BR səbˈsɪst, -s, -ɪŋ, -ɨd
AM səbˈsɪst, -s, -ɪŋ, -ɨd

subsistence
BR səbˈsɪst(ə)ns
AM səbˈsɪstəns

subsistent
BR səbˈsɪst(ə)nt
AM səbˈsɪstənt

subsoil
BR ˈsʌbsɔɪl, -z
AM ˈsəbˌsɔɪl, -z

subsonic
BR ˌsʌbˈsɒnɪk
AM ˌsəbˈsɑnɪk

subsonically
BR ˌsʌbˈsɒnɨkli
AM ˌsəbˈsɑnək(ə)li

subspecies
BR ˈsʌbˌspiːʃɪz, ˈsʌbˌspiːʃiːz, ˈsʌbˌspiːsɪz, ˈsʌbˌspiːsiːz
AM ˈsəbˌspiʃiz, ˈsəbˌspisiz

subspecific
BR ˌsʌbspɨˈsɪfɪk
AM ˌsəbspəˈsɪfɪk

substance
BR ˈsʌbst(ə)ns, -ɨz
AM ˈsəbstəns, -əz

substandard
BR ˌsʌbˈstandəd
AM ˈsəbˈstændərd

substantial
BR səb'stanʃl,
səb'stɑːnʃl
AM ˌsəb'stæn(t)ʃəl

substantialise
BR səb'stanʃəlʌɪz,
səb'stanʃl̩ʌɪz,
səb'stɑːnʃəlʌɪz,
səb'stɑːnʃl̩ʌɪz, -ɪz, -ɪŋ,
-d
AM ˌsəb'stæn(t)ʃəˌlaɪz,
-ɪz, -ɪŋ, -d

substantialism
BR səb'stanʃəlɪz(ə)m,
səb'stanʃl̩ɪz(ə)m,
səb'stɑːnʃəlɪz(ə)m,
səb'stɑːnʃl̩ɪz(ə)m
AM ˌsəb'stæn(t)ʃəˌlɪzəm

substantialist
BR ˌsʌb'stanʃəlɪst,
ˌsʌb'stanʃl̩ɪst,
ˌsʌb'stɑːnʃəlɪst,
ˌsʌb'stɑːnʃl̩ɪst, -s
AM ˌsəb'stæn(t)ʃələst,
-s

substantiality
BR səbˌstanʃɪ'alɪti,
səbˌstɑːnʃɪ'alɪti
AM səbˌstæn(t)ʃi'ælədi

substantialize
BR səb'stanʃəlʌɪz,
səb'stanʃl̩ʌɪz,
səb'stɑːnʃəlʌɪz,
səb'stɑːnʃl̩ʌɪz, -ɪz, -ɪŋ,
-d
AM ˌsəb'stæn(t)ʃəˌlaɪz,
-ɪz, -ɪŋ, -d

substantially
BR səb'stanʃəli,
səb'stanʃl̩i,
səb'stɑːnʃəli,
səb'stɑːnʃl̩i
AM ˌsəb'stæn(t)ʃəli

substantialness
BR səb'stanʃlnəs,
səb'stɑːnʃlnəs
AM ˌsəb'stæn(t)ʃəlnəs

substantiate
BR səb'stanʃɪeɪt,
səb'stansɪeɪt,
səb'stɑːnʃɪeɪt,
səb'stɑːnsɪeɪt, -s, -ɪŋ,
-ɪd
AM səb'stæn(t)ʃiˌeɪ|t,
-ts, -dɪŋ, -dɪd

substantiation
BR səbˌstanʃɪ'eɪʃn,
səbˌstansɪ'eɪʃn,
səbˌstɑːnʃɪ'eɪʃn,
səbˌstɑːnsɪ'eɪʃn
AM səbˌstæn(t)ʃi'eɪʃən

substantival
BR ˌsʌbst(ə)n'tʌɪvl
AM ¦səbstən'taɪvəl

substantive[1]
noun
BR 'sʌbst(ə)ntɪv,
səb'stantɪv, -z
AM 'səbstən(t)ɪv, -z

substantive[2]
adjective
BR səb'stantɪv,
'sʌbst(ə)ntɪv
AM 'səbstən(t)ɪv,
səb'stæn(t)ɪv

substantively
BR səb'stantɪvli,
'sʌbst(ə)ntɪvli
AM 'səbstən(t)ɪvli,
səb'stæn(t)ɪvli

substantiveness
BR səb'stantɪvnɪs,
'sʌbst(ə)ntɪvnɪs
AM 'səbstən(t)ɪvnɪs,
səb'stæn(t)ɪvnɪs

substation
BR 'sʌbˌsteɪʃn, -z
AM 'səbˌsteɪʃən, -z

substituent
BR səb'stɪtjʊənt,
səb'stɪtʃʊənt, -s
AM ˌsəb'stɪtʃ(əw)ənt,
-s

substitutability
BR ˌsʌbstɪtjuːtə'bɪlɪti,
ˌsʌbstɪtʃuːtə'bɪlɪti
AM ˌsəbstəˌt(j)udə'bɪlɪdi

substitutable
BR 'sʌbstɪtjuːtəbl,
'sʌbstɪtʃuːtəbl
AM 'səbstəˌt(j)udəbəl

substitute
BR 'sʌbstɪtjuːt,
'sʌbstɪtʃuːt, -s, -ɪŋ, -ɪd
AM 'səbstəˌt(j)u|t, -ts,
-dɪŋ, -dəd

substitution
BR ˌsʌbstɪ'tjuːʃn,
ˌsʌbstɪ'tʃuːʃn, -z
AM ˌsəbstə't(j)uʃən, -z

substitutional
BR ˌsʌbstɪ'tjuːʃn̩(ə)l,
ˌsʌbstɪ'tjuːʃən(ə)l,
ˌsʌbstɪ'tʃuːʃn̩(ə)l,
ˌsʌbstɪ'tʃuːʃən(ə)l
AM ˌsəbstə't(j)uʃ(ə)nəl

substitutionary
BR ˌsʌbstɪ'tjuːʃn̩(ə)ri,
ˌsʌbstɪ'tʃuːʃn̩(ə)ri
AM ˌsəbstə't(j)uʃəˌnɛri

substitutive
BR 'sʌbstɪtjuːtɪv,
'sʌbstɪtʃuːtɪv
AM 'səbstəˌt(j)udɪv

substrata
BR 'sʌbˌstrɑːtə(r),
'sʌbˌstreɪtə(r),
ˌsʌb'strɑːtə(r),
ˌsʌb'streɪtə(r)
AM 'səbˌstreɪdə,
'səbˌstrɑdə,
'səbˌstrædə

substrate
BR 'sʌbstreɪt, -s
AM 'səbˌstreɪt, -s

substratum
BR 'sʌbˌstrɑːtəm,
'sʌbˌstreɪtəm,
ˌsʌb'strɑːtəm,
ˌsʌb'streɪtəm
AM 'səbˌstreɪdəm,
'səbˌstrɑdəm,
'səbˌstrædəm

substructural
BR ˌsʌb'strʌktʃ(ə)rəl,
ˌsʌb'strʌktʃ(ə)rl̩
AM ¦səb¦strək(t)ʃ(ə)rəl

substructure
BR 'sʌbˌstrʌktʃə(r), -z
AM 'səbˌstrək(t)ʃər, -z

subsumable
BR səb'sjuːməbl
AM səb's(j)uməbəl

subsume
BR səb'sjuːm, -z, -ɪŋ, -d
AM səb's(j)um, -z, -ɪŋ,
-d

subsumption
BR səb'sʌm(p)ʃn, -z
AM səb'səmpʃən, -z

subsurface
BR 'sʌbˌsəːfɪs, -ɪz
AM 'səbˌsərfəs, -əz

subsystem
BR 'sʌbˌsɪstɪm, -z
AM 'səbˌsɪstəm, -z

subtenancy
BR ˌsʌb'tɛnəns|i,
'sʌbˌtɛnəns|i, -ɪz
AM ˌsəb'tɛnənsi, -z

subtenant
BR ˌsʌb'tɛnənt,
'sʌbˌtɛnənt, -s
AM ˌsəb'tɛnənt, -s

subtend
BR səb'tɛnd, -z, -ɪŋ, -ɪd
AM səb'tɛnd, -z, -ɪŋ, -əd

subterfuge
BR 'sʌbtəfjuː(d)ʒ, -ɪz
AM 'səbtərˌfjudʒ, -əz

subterminal
BR ˌsʌb'təːmɪnl
AM ˌsəb'tərmənəl

subterranean
BR ˌsʌbtə'reɪnɪən
AM ˌsəbtə'reɪniən

subterraneously
BR ˌsʌbtə'reɪnɪəsli
AM ˌsəbtə'reɪniəsli

subtext
BR 'sʌbtɛkst, -s
AM 'səbˌtɛkst, -s

subtilisation
BR ˌsʌtl̩ʌɪ'zeɪʃn
AM ˌsədlə'zeɪʃən,
ˌsədlˌaɪ'zeɪʃən

subtilise
BR 'sʌtl̩ʌɪz, -ɪz, -ɪŋ, -d
AM 'sədlˌaɪz, -ɪz, -ɪŋ, -d

subtilization
BR ˌsʌtl̩ʌɪ'zeɪʃn
AM ˌsədlə'zeɪʃən,
ˌsədlˌaɪ'zeɪʃən

subtilize
BR 'sʌtl̩ʌɪz, -ɪz, -ɪŋ, -d
AM 'sədlˌaɪz, -ɪz, -ɪŋ, -d

subtitle
BR 'sʌbˌtʌɪtl, -z, -d
AM 'səbˌtaɪdəl, -z, -d

subtle
BR 'sʌt|l, -l̩ə(r)\-lə(r),
-l̩ɪst\-lɪst
AM 'sədəl, -ər, -əst

subtleness
BR 'sʌtlnəs
AM 'sədlnəs

subtlety
BR 'sʌtlt|i, -ɪz
AM 'sədldi, 'sədlti, -z

subtly
BR 'sʌtl̩i, 'sʌtli
AM 'sədli

subtonic
BR ˌsʌb'tɒnɪk, -s
AM ˌsəb'tɑnɪk, -s

subtopia
BR ˌsʌb'təʊpɪə(r), -z
AM ˌsəb'toʊpiə, -z

subtopian
BR ˌsʌb'təʊpɪən
AM ˌsəb'toʊpiən

subtotal
BR 'sʌbˌtəʊtl,
ˌsʌb'təʊtl, -z
AM ¦sub¦toʊdl, -z

subtract
BR səb'trakt, -s, -ɪŋ, -ɪd
AM səb'træk(t), -(t)s,
-tɪŋ, -təd

subtracter
BR səb'traktə(r), -z
AM səb'træktər, -z

subtraction
BR səb'trakʃn, -z
AM səb'trækʃən, -z

subtractive
BR səb'traktɪv
AM səb'træktɪv

subtractor
BR səb'traktə(r), -z
AM səb'træktər, -z

subtrahend
BR 'sʌbtrəhɛnd, -z
AM 'səbtrəˌhɛnd, -z

subtropical
BR ˌsʌb'trɒpɪkl
AM səb'trɑpəkəl

subtropics
BR 'sʌbˌtrɒpɪks,
ˌsʌb'trɒpɪks
AM ˌsəb'trɑpɪks

subtype
BR 'sʌbtʌɪp, -s
AM 'səbˌtaɪp, -s

subulate
BR 'sʌbjʊleɪt
AM 'səbjəˌleɪt,
'səbjələt

sub-unit
BR ˈsʌbˌjuːnɪt, -s
AM ˈsəbˌjunət, -s
suburb
BR ˈsʌbəːb, -z
AM ˈsəbərb, -z
suburban
BR səˈbəːb(ə)n
AM səˈbərbən
suburbanisation
BR səˌbəːbənʌɪˈzeɪʃn, səˌbəːbn̩ʌɪˈzeɪʃn
AM səˌbərbənəˈzeɪʃən, səˌbərbəˌnaɪˈzeɪʃən
suburbanise
BR səˈbəːbənʌɪz, səˈbəːbn̩ʌɪz, -ɨz, -ɪŋ, -d
AM səˈbərbəˌnaɪz, -ɨz, -ɪŋ, -d
suburbanite
BR səˈbəːbənʌɪt, səˈbəːbn̩ʌɪt, -s
AM səˈbərbəˌnaɪt, -s
suburbanization
BR səˌbəːbənʌɪˈzeɪʃn, səˌbəːbn̩ʌɪˈzeɪʃn
AM səˌbərbənəˈzeɪʃən, səˌbərbəˌnaɪˈzeɪʃən
suburbanize
BR səˈbəːbənʌɪz, səˈbəːbn̩ʌɪz, -ɨz, -ɪŋ, -d
AM səˈbərbəˌnaɪz, -ɨz, -ɪŋ, -d
suburbia
BR səˈbəːbɪə(*r*)
AM səˈbərbiə
subvariety
BR ˈsʌbvəˌrʌɪɨt|i, -ɪz
AM ˈsəbvəˌraɪədi, -z
subvention
BR səbˈvɛnʃn, -z
AM səbˈvɛn(t)ʃən, -z
subversion
BR səbˈvəːʃn, -z
AM səbˈvərʒən, səbˈvərʃən, -z
subversive
BR səbˈvəːsɪv, -z
AM səbˈvərsɪv, -z
subversively
BR səbˈvəːsɪvli
AM səbˈvərsɪvli
subversiveness
BR səbˈvəːsɪvnɪs
AM səbˈvərsɪvnɪs
subvert
BR səbˈvəːt, -s, -ɪŋ, -ɨd
AM səbˈvər|t, -ts, -dɪŋ, -dəd
subverter
BR səbˈvəːtə(r), -z
AM səbˈvərdər, -z
subway
BR ˈsʌbweɪ, -z
AM ˈsəbˌweɪ, -z
sub-zero
BR ˌsʌbˈzɪərəʊ
AM ˈsəbˈzɪroʊ, ˈsəbˈziroʊ
succedanea
BR ˌsʌksɪˈdeɪnɪə(*r*)
AM ˌsəksəˈdeɪniə
succedaneous
BR ˌsʌksɪˈdeɪnɪəs
AM ˌsəksəˈdeɪniəs
succedaneum
BR ˌsʌksɪˈdeɪnɪəm
AM ˌsəksəˈdeɪniəm
succeed
BR səkˈsiːd, -z, -ɪŋ, -ɨd
AM səkˈsid, -z, -ɪŋ, -ɨd
succeeder
BR səkˈsiːdə(r), -z
AM səkˈsidər, -z
succentor
BR səkˈsɛntə(r), -z
AM səkˈsɛn(t)ər, -z
succentorship
BR səkˈsɛntəʃɪp, -s
AM səkˈsɛn(t)ərˌʃɪp, -s
succès de scandale
BR səkˌseɪ də ˌskɒ̃ˈdɑːl
AM səkˌseɪ də ˌskɑnˈdɑl
success
BR səkˈsɛs, -ɨz
AM səkˈsɛs, -əz
successful
BR səkˈsɛsf(ʊ)l
AM səkˈsɛsfəl
successfully
BR səkˈsɛsfʊli, səkˈsɛsfl̩i
AM səkˈsɛsfəli
successfulness
BR səkˈsɛsf(ʊ)lnəs
AM səkˈsɛsfəlnəs
succession
BR səkˈsɛʃn, -z
AM səkˈsɛʃən, -z
successional
BR səkˈsɛʃn̩(ə)l, səkˈsɛʃən(ə)l
AM səkˈsɛʃ(ə)nəl
successive
BR səkˈsɛsɪv
AM səkˈsɛsɪv
successively
BR səkˈsɛsɪvli
AM səkˈsɛsɪvli
successiveness
BR səkˈsɛsɪvnɪs
AM səkˈsɛsɪvnɪs
successor
BR səkˈsɛsə(r), -z
AM səkˈsɛsər, -z
succinate
BR ˈsʌksɪneɪt
AM ˈsəksəˌneɪt
succinct
BR səkˈsɪŋ(k)t
AM sə(k)ˈsɪŋ(k)t, sə(k)ˈsɪŋk(t)
succinctly
BR səkˈsɪŋ(k)tli, səkˈsɪŋk(t)li
AM sə(k)ˈsɪŋ(k)tli, sə(k)ˈsɪŋk(t)li
succinctness
BR səkˈsɪŋ(k)tnɪs, səkˈsɪŋk(t)nɪs
AM sə(k)ˈsɪŋ(k)tnɪs, sə(k)ˈsɪŋk(t)nɪs
succinic
BR sʌkˈsɪnɪk, səkˈsɪnɪk
AM səkˈsɪnɪk
succor
BR ˈsʌk|ə(r), -əz, -(ə)rɪŋ, -əd
AM ˈsəkər, -z, -ɪŋ, -d
succorless
BR ˈsʌkələs
AM ˈsəkərləs
succory
BR ˈsʌk(ə)r|i, -ɪz
AM ˈsəkəri, -z
succotash
BR ˈsʌkətaʃ
AM ˈsəkəˌtæʃ
Succoth
BR sʊˈkəʊt, ˈsʌkəθ
AM ˈsuˈkoʊt
succour
BR ˈsʌk|ə(r), -əz, -(ə)rɪŋ, -əd
AM ˈsəkər, -z, -ɪŋ, -d
succourless
BR ˈsʌkələs
AM ˈsəkərləs
succuba
BR ˈsʌkjʊbə(*r*)
AM ˈsəkjəbə
succubae
BR ˈsʌkjʊbiː, ˈsʌkjʊbʌɪ
AM ˈsəkjəbi, ˈsəkjəˌbaɪ
succubi
BR ˈsʌkjʊbʌɪ
AM ˈsəkjəˌbaɪ
succubus
BR ˈsʌkjʊbəs
AM ˈsəkjəbəs
succulence
BR ˈsʌkjʊləns, ˈsʌkjʊln̩s
AM ˈsəkjələns
succulent
BR ˈsʌkjʊlənt, ˈsʌkjʊln̩t
AM ˈsəkjələnt
succulently
BR ˈsʌkjʊləntli, ˈsʌkjʊln̩tli
AM ˈsəkjələn(t)li
succumb
BR səˈkʌm, -z, -ɪŋ, -d
AM səˈkəm, -z, -ɪŋ, -d
succursal
BR səˈkəːsl
AM səˈkərsəl
succuss
BR ˈsʌkəs, -ɨz, -ɪŋ, -t
AM ˈsəkəs, -əz, -ɪŋ, -t
succussion
BR səˈkʌʃn, -z
AM səˈkəʃən, -z
such[1]
strong form
BR sʌtʃ
AM sətʃ
such[2]
weak form
BR sətʃ
AM sətʃ
such-and-such
BR ˈsʌtʃ(ə)n(d)sʌtʃ
AM ˈsətʃənˌsətʃ
Suchard
BR ˈsuːʃɑː(d)
AM suˈʃɑrd
Suchet
BR ˈsuːʃeɪ
AM suˈʃeɪ
suchlike
BR ˈsʌtʃlʌɪk
AM ˈsətʃˌlaɪk
suck
BR sʌk, -s, -ɪŋ, -t
AM sək, -s, -ɪŋ, -t
sucker
BR ˈsʌkə(r), -z, -d
AM ˈsəkər, -z, -d
suckle
BR ˈsʌk|l, -lz, -l̩ɪŋ\-lɪŋ, -ld
AM ˈsək|əl, -əlz, -(ə)lɪŋ, -əld
suckler
BR ˈsʌklə(r), -z
AM ˈsək(ə)lər, -z
Suckling
BR ˈsʌklɪŋ
AM ˈsəklɪŋ
suckling
noun
BR ˈsʌklɪŋ, -z
AM ˈsək(ə)lɪŋ, -z
sucre
BR ˈsuːkreɪ, -z
AM ˈsuˌkreɪ, -z
sucrose
BR ˈs(j)uːkrəʊz, ˈs(j)uːkrəʊs
AM ˈsuˌkroʊs, ˈsuˌkroʊz
suction
BR ˈsʌkʃn
AM ˈsəkʃən
suctorial
BR sʌkˈtɔːrɪəl, səkˈtɔːrɪəl
AM səkˈtɔriəl
suctorian
BR sʌkˈtɔːrɪən, səkˈtɔːrɪən, -z
AM səkˈtɔriən, -z
Sudan
BR sʊˈdɑːn, sʊˈdan

AM su'dæn
Sudanese
BR ˌsuːdə'niːz
AM ˌsudə'niz
sudaria
BR s(j)uː'dɛːrɪə(r)
AM su'dɛriə
sudarium
BR s(j)uː'dɛːrɪəm
AM su'dɛriəm
sudatoria
BR ˌs(j)uːdə'tɔːrɪə(r)
AM ˌsudə'tɔriə
sudatorium
BR ˌs(j)uːdə'tɔːrɪəm
AM ˌsudə'tɔriəm
sudatory
BR 's(j)uːdət(ə)r|i, -ɪz
AM 'sudəˌtɔri, -z
Sudbury
BR 'sʌdb(ə)ri
AM 'sədˌbɛri, 'sədbəri
sudd
BR sʌd, -z
AM səd, -z
Suddaby
BR 'sʌdəbi
AM 'sədəbi
sudden
BR 'sʌdn
AM 'sədən
suddenly
BR 'sʌdnli
AM 'sədnli
suddenness
BR 'sʌdnnəs
AM 'səd(n)nəs
Sudetenland
BR sʊ'deɪtnland
AM su'deɪtnˌlænd
sudoriferous
BR ˌs(j)uːdə'rɪf(ə)rəs
AM ˌsudə'rɪf(ə)rəs
sudorific
BR ˌs(j)uːdə'rɪfɪk, -s
AM ˌsudə'rɪfɪk, -s
Sudra
BR 'suːdrə(r), -z
AM 'sudrə, -z
suds
BR sʌdz
AM sədz
sudsy
BR 'sʌdzi
AM 'sədzi
sue
BR s(j)uː, -z, -ɪŋ, -d
AM su, -z, -ɪŋ, -d
suède
BR sweɪd
AM sweɪd
suer
BR 's(j)uːə(r), -z
AM 'suər, -z
suet
BR 's(j)uːɪt
AM 'suət
Suetonius
BR s(j)uː'təʊnɪəs
AM suə'toʊniəs
suety
BR s(j)uːɪti
AM 'suədi
Suez
BR 's(j)uːɪz
AM su'ɛz, 'suˌɛz
suffer
BR 'sʌf|ə(r), -əz, -(ə)rɪŋ, -əd
AM 'səf|ər, -ərz, -(ə)rɪŋ, -ərd
sufferable
BR 'sʌf(ə)rəbl
AM 'səf(ə)rəbəl
sufferance
BR 'sʌf(ə)rəns, 'sʌf(ə)rns
AM 'səf(ə)rəns
sufferer
BR 'sʌf(ə)rə(r), -z
AM 'səf(ə)rər, -z
suffering
BR 'sʌf(ə)rɪŋ, -z
AM 'səf(ə)rɪŋ, -z
suffice
BR sə'fʌɪs, -ɪz, -ɪŋ, -t
AM sə'faɪs, -ɪz, -ɪŋ, -t
sufficiency
BR sə'fɪʃnsi
AM sə'fɪʃənsi
sufficient
BR sə'fɪʃnt
AM sə'fɪʃənt
sufficiently
BR sə'fɪʃntli
AM sə'fɪʃən(t)li
suffix[1]
noun
BR 'sʌfɪks, -ɪksɪz, -ɪksɪŋ, -ɪkst
AM 'səfɪks, -ɪz, -ɪŋ, -t
suffix[2]
verb
BR 'sʌfɪks, sə'fɪks, 'sʌfɪksɪz, sə'fɪksɪz, 'sʌfɪksɪŋɪŋ, sə'fɪksɪŋ, 'sʌfɪkst, sə'fɪkst
AM 'səfɪks, sə'fɪks, -ɪz, -ɪŋ, -d
suffixation
BR ˌsʌfɪk'seɪʃn
AM ˌsəfək'seɪʃən
suffocate
BR 'sʌfəkeɪt, -s, -ɪŋ, -ɪd
AM 'səfəˌkeɪ|t, -ts, -dɪŋ, -dɪd
suffocating
BR 'sʌfəkeɪtɪŋ
AM 'səfəˌkeɪdɪŋ
suffocatingly
BR 'sʌfəkeɪtɪŋli
AM 'səfəˌkeɪdɪŋli
suffocation
BR ˌsʌfə'keɪʃn
AM ˌsəfə'keɪʃən
Suffolk
BR 'sʌfək
AM 'səfək
suffragan
BR 'sʌfrəg(ə)n, -z
AM 'səfrəgən, -z
suffraganship
BR 'sʌfrəg(ə)nʃɪp, -s
AM 'səfrəgənˌʃɪp, -s
suffrage
BR 'sʌfr|ɪdʒ, -ɪdʒɪz
AM 'səfrɪdʒ, -ɪz
suffragette
BR ˌsʌfrə'dʒɛt, -s
AM ˌsəfrə'dʒɛt, -s
suffragism
BR 'sʌfrədʒɪz(ə)m
AM 'səfrəˌdʒɪzəm
suffragist
BR 'sʌfrədʒɪst, -s
AM 'səfrədʒəst, -s
suffuse
BR sə'fjuːz, -ɪz, -ɪŋ, -d
AM sə'fjuz, -əz, -ɪŋ, -d
suffusion
BR sə'fjuːʒn, -z
AM sə'fjuʒən, -z
Sufi
BR 'suːf|i, -ɪz
AM 'sufi, -z
Sufic
BR 'suːfɪk
AM 'sufɪk
Sufism
BR 'suːfɪz(ə)m
AM 'suˌfɪzəm
sugar
BR 'ʃʊg|ə(r), -əz, -(ə)rɪŋ, -əd
AM 'ʃʊgər, -z, -ɪŋ, -d
sugarbeet
BR 'ʃʊgəbiːt
AM 'ʃʊgərˌbit
sugarbush
BR 'ʃʊgəbʊʃ, -ɪz
AM 'ʃʊgərˌbʊʃ, -əz
sugarcane
BR 'ʃʊgəkeɪn
AM 'ʃʊgərˌkeɪn
sugarcoated
BR ˌʃʊgə'kəʊtɪd
AM 'ʃʊgərˌkoʊdəd
sugarhouse
BR 'ʃʊgəhaʊs, -ɪz
AM 'ʃʊgərˌ(h)aʊs, -əz
sugariness
BR 'ʃʊg(ə)rɪnɪs
AM 'ʃʊgərinɪs
sugarless
BR 'ʃʊgələs
AM 'ʃʊgərləs
sugarloaf
BR 'ʃʊgələʊf
AM 'ʃʊgərˌloʊf
sugarloaves
BR 'ʃʊgələʊvz
AM 'ʃʊgərˌloʊvz
sugarplum
BR 'ʃʊgəplʌm, -z
AM 'ʃʊgərˌpləm, -z
sugary
BR 'ʃʊg(ə)ri
AM 'ʃʊgəri
suggest
BR sə'dʒɛst, -s, -ɪŋ, -ɪd
AM sə(g)'dʒɛst, -s, -ɪŋ, -əd
suggester
BR sə'dʒɛstə(r), -z
AM sə(g)'dʒɛstər, -z
suggestibility
BR səˌdʒɛstɪ'bɪlɪti
AM sə(g)ˌdʒɛstə'bɪlɪdi
suggestible
BR sə'dʒɛstɪbl
AM sə(g)'dʒɛstəbəl
suggestion
BR sə'dʒɛstʃ(ə)n, -z
AM sə(g)'dʒɛstʃən, sə(g)'dʒɛʃtʃən, -z
suggestive
BR sə'dʒɛstɪv
AM sə(g)'dʒɛstɪv
suggestively
BR sə'dʒɛstɪvli
AM sə(g)'dʒɛstɪvli
suggestiveness
BR sə'dʒɛstɪvnɪs
AM sə(g)'dʒɛstɪvnɪs
Sui
BR sweɪ
AM sweɪ
suicidal
BR ˌs(j)uːɪ'sʌɪdl
AM ˌsuə'saɪdəl
suicidally
BR ˌs(j)uːɪ'sʌɪdḷi
AM ˌsuə'saɪdḷi
suicide
BR s(j)uːɪsʌɪd, -z
AM 'suəˌsaɪd, -z
sui generis
BR ˌs(j)uːʌɪ 'dʒɛn(ə)rɪs, ˌs(j)uːiː +, + 'gɛn(ə)rɪs
AM ˌsui 'dʒɛnərəs, ˌsuˌaɪ +
sui juris
BR ˌs(j)uːʌɪ 'dʒʊərɪs, ˌs(j)uːiː +, + 'jʊərɪs
AM ˌsuˌaɪ 'dʒʊrəs, ˌsui 'jurəs
suint
BR swɪnt, 's(j)uːɪnt
AM 'suənt, swɪnt
suit
BR s(j)uːt, -s, -ɪŋ, -ɪd
AM su|t, -ts, -dɪŋ, -dəd
suitability
BR ˌs(j)uːtə'bɪlɪti
AM ˌsudə'bɪlɪdi
suitable
BR 's(j)uːtəbl
AM 'sudəbəl

suitableness
BR 'ˈs(j)uːtəblnəs
AM 'sudəbəlnəs

suitably
BR 's(j)uːtəbli
AM 'sudəbli

suitcase
BR 's(j)uːtkeɪs, -ɪz
AM 'sutˌkeɪs, -ɪz

suitcaseful
BR 's(j)uːtkeɪsfʊl, -z
AM 'surtˌkeɪsˌfʊl, -z

suite
BR swiːt, -s
AM swit, -s

suiting
BR 's(j)uːtɪŋ, -z
AM 'sudɪŋ, -z

suitor
BR 's(j)uːtə(r), -z
AM 'sudər, -z

suk
BR suːk, -s
AM suk, -s

Sukarno
BR suː'kɑːnəʊ
AM su'kɑrnoʊ

Sukey
BR 'suːki
AM 'suki

Sukhotai
BR ˌsʊkə'tʌɪ
AM ˌsʊkə'taɪ

Sukie
BR 'suːki
AM 'suki

sukiyaki
BR ˌsuːkɪ'jɑːki, ˌsʊkɪ'jɑːki, ˌsuːkɪ'jaki, ˌsʊkɪ'jaki
AM sʊki'jɑki

Sukkur
BR 'sʊkə(r)
AM 'sʊkər

Sulawesi
BR ˌsuːlə'weɪsi
AM ˌsulə'weɪsi

sulcate
BR 'sʌlkeɪt
AM 'səlˌkeɪt

sulci
BR 'sʌlsʌɪ, 'sʌlkʌɪ, 'sʌlsiː, 'sʌlkiː
AM 'səlˌsaɪ

sulcus
BR 'sʌlkəs
AM 'səlkəs

Suleiman
BR sʊ'leɪmən
AM sʊ'leɪmən, 'suleɪˌmɑn

sulfa
BR 'sʌlfə(*r*)
AM 'səlfə

sulfadimidine
BR ˌsʌlfə'dʌɪmɪdiːn
AM ˌsəlfə'daɪməˌdin

sulfa drug
BR 'sʌlfə drʌg, -z
AM 'səlfə ˌdrəg, -z

sulfamate
BR 'sʌlfəmeɪt
AM 'səlfəˌmeɪt

sulfanilamide
BR ˌsʌlfə'nɪləmʌɪd, -z
AM ˌsəlfə'nɪləˌmaɪd, -z

sulfate
BR 'sʌlfeɪt, -s
AM 'səlˌfeɪt, -s

sulfide
BR 'sʌlfʌɪd, -z
AM 'səlˌfaɪd, -z

sulfite
BR 'sʌlfʌɪt, -s
AM 'səlˌfaɪt, -s

sulfonamide
BR sʌl'fɒnəmʌɪd, -z
AM səl'fɑnəˌmaɪd, -z

sulfonate
BR 'sʌlfəneɪt
AM 'səlfəˌneɪt

sulfonation
BR ˌsʌlfə'neɪʃn
AM ˌsəlfə'neɪʃən

sulfone
BR 'sʌlfəʊn, -z
AM 'səlˌfoʊn, -z

sulfonic
BR sʌl'fɒnɪk
AM səl'fɑnɪk

sulfur
BR 'sʌlfə(r)
AM 'səlfər

sulfurate
BR 'sʌlfjʊreɪt
AM 'səlf(j)əˌreɪt

sulfuration
BR ˌsʌlfjʊ'reɪʃn
AM ˌsəlf(j)ə'reɪʃən

sulfurator
BR 'sʌlfjʊreɪtə(r)
AM 'səlf(j)əˌreɪdər

sulfureous
BR sʌl'fjʊərɪəs, sʌl'fjɔːrɪəs
AM səl'f(j)əriəs

sulfuretted
BR ˌsʌlfjʊ'rɛtɪd, 'sʌlfjʊrɛtɪd
AM ˌsəlf(j)ə'rɛdəd

sulfuric
BR sʌl'fjʊərɪk, sʌl'fjɔːrɪk
AM ˌsəl'fjʊrɪk

sulfurisation
BR ˌsʌlfjʊrʌɪ'zeɪʃn
AM ˌsəlf(j)ərə'zeɪʃən, ˌsəlf(j)əˌraɪ'zeɪʃən

sulfurise
BR 'sʌlfjʊrʌɪz
AM 'səlf(j)əˌraɪz

sulfurization
BR ˌsʌlfjʊrʌɪ'zeɪʃn
AM ˌsəlf(j)ərə'zeɪʃən, ˌsəlf(j)əˌraɪ'zeɪʃən

sulfurize
BR 'sʌlfjʊrʌɪz
AM 'səlf(j)əˌraɪz

sulfurous
BR 'sʌlf(ə)rəs, 'sʌlfjʊrəs
AM 'səlfərəs

sulfury
BR 'sʌlf(ə)ri, 'sʌlfjʊri
AM 'səlfəri

Sulgrave
BR 'sʌlgreɪv
AM 'səlˌgreɪv

sulk
BR sʌlk, -s, -ɪŋ, -t
AM səlk, -s, -ɪŋ, -t

sulker
BR 'sʌlkə(r), -z
AM 'səlkər, -z

sulkily
BR 'sʌlkɪli
AM 'səlkəli

sulkiness
BR 'sʌlkɪnɪs
AM 'səlkinɪs

sulky
BR 'sʌlk|i, -ɪə(r), -ɪɪst
AM 'səlki, -ər, -ɪst

Sulla
BR 'sʌlə(*r*), 'sʊlə(*r*)
AM 'sʊlə

sullage
BR 'sʌlɪdʒ
AM 'səlɪdʒ

sullen
BR 'sʌlən, -ɪst
AM 'sələn, -ɪst

sullenly
BR 'sʌlənli
AM 'sələnli

sullenness
BR 'sʌlənnəs
AM 'sələ(n)nəs

Sullivan
BR 'sʌlɪvn
AM 'sələvən

Sullom Voe
BR ˌsʌləm 'vəʊ, ˌsuːləm +
AM ˌsələm 'voʊ

sully
BR 'sʌl|i, -ɪz, -ɪɪŋ, -ɪd
AM 'səli, -z, -ɪŋ, -d

sulpha
BR 'sʌlfə(*r*)
AM 'səlfə

sulphadimidine
BR ˌsʌlfə'dʌɪmɪdiːn
AM ˌsəlfə'daɪməˌdin

sulphamate
BR 'sʌlfameɪt
AM 'səlfəˌmeɪt

sulphanilamide
BR ˌsʌlfə'nɪləmʌɪd, -z
AM ˌsəlfə'nɪləˌmaɪd, -z

sulphate
BR 'sʌlfeɪt, -s
AM 'səlˌfeɪt, -s

sulphide
BR 'sʌlfʌɪd, -z
AM 'səlˌfaɪd, -z

sulphite
BR 'sʌlfʌɪt, -s
AM 'səlˌfaɪt, -s

sulphonamide
BR sʌl'fɒnəmʌɪd, -z
AM səl'fɑnəˌmaɪd, -z

sulphonate
BR 'sʌlfəneɪt
AM 'səlfəˌneɪt

sulphonation
BR ˌsʌlfə'neɪʃn
AM ˌsəlfə'neɪʃən

sulphone
BR 'sʌlfəʊn, -z
AM 'səlˌfoʊn, -z

sulphonic
BR sʌl'fɒnɪk
AM səl'fɑnɪk

sulphur
BR 'sʌlfə(r)
AM 'səlfər

sulphurate
BR 'sʌlfjʊreɪt
AM 'səlf(j)əˌreɪt

sulphuration
BR ˌsʌlfjʊ'reɪʃn
AM ˌsəlf(j)ə'reɪʃən

sulphurator
BR 'sʌlfjʊreɪtə(r)
AM 'səlf(j)əˌreɪdər

sulphureous
BR sʌl'fjʊərɪəs, sʌl'fjɔːrɪəs
AM əl'f(j)əriəs

sulphuretted
BR ˌsʌlfjʊ'rɛtɪd, 'sʌlfjʊrɛtɪd
AM ˌsəlf(j)ə'rɛdəd

sulphuric
BR sʌl'fjʊərɪk, sʌl'fjɔːrɪk
AM ˌsəl'fjʊrɪk

sulphurisation
BR ˌsʌlfjʊrʌɪ'zeɪʃn
AM ˌsəlf(j)ərə'zeɪʃən, ˌsəlf(j)əˌraɪ'zeɪʃən

sulphurise
BR 'sʌlfjʊrʌɪz, -ɪz, -ɪŋ, -d
AM 'səlf(j)əˌraɪz, -ɪz, -ɪŋ, -d

sulphurization
BR ˌsʌlfjʊrʌɪ'zeɪʃn
AM ˌsəlf(j)ərə'zeɪʃən, ˌsəlf(j)əˌraɪ'zeɪʃən

sulphurize
BR 'sʌlfjʊrʌɪz, -ɪz, -ɪŋ, -d
AM 'səlf(j)əˌraɪz, -ɪz, -ɪŋ, -d

sulphurous
BR ˈsʌlf(ə)rəs, ˈsʌlfjʉrəs
AM ˈsəlfərəs

sulphury
BR ˈsʌlf(ə)ri, ˈsʌlfjʉri
AM ˈsəlfəri

sultan
BR ˈsʌlt(ə)n, -z
AM ˈsəltn̩, -z

sultana
BR s(ə)lˈtɑːnə(r), ˌsʌlˈtɑːnə(r), -z
AM ˌsəlˈtænə, səlˈtɑnə, -z

sultanate
BR ˈsʌltənət, ˈsʌltn̩ət, ˈsʌltəneɪt, ˈsʌltn̩eɪt, -s
AM ˈsəltn̩ət, ˈsəltnˌeɪt, -s

sultrily
BR ˈsʌltrɨli
AM ˈsəltrəli

sultriness
BR ˈsʌltrɪnɨs
AM ˈsəltrinɨs

sultry
BR ˈsʌltr|i, -ɪə(r), -ɪɪst
AM ˈsəltri, -ər, -ɨst

sulu
BR ˈsuːluː, -z
AM ˈsulu, -z

sum
BR sʌm, -z, -ɪŋ, -d
AM səm, -z, -ɪŋ, -d

sumac
BR ˈs(j)uːmak, ˈʃuːmak, -s
AM ˈsuˌmæk, ˈʃuˌmæk, -s

sumach
BR ˈs(j)uːmak, ˈʃuːmak, -s
AM ˈsuˌmæk, ˈʃuˌmæk, -s

Sumatra
BR sʉˈmɑːtrə(r)
AM səˈmɑtrə

Sumatran
BR sʉˈmɑːtr(ə)n, -z
AM səˈmɑtrən, -z

Sumburgh
BR ˈsʌmb(ə)rə(r)
AM ˈsəmˌbərə

Sumer
BR ˈsuːmə(r)
AM ˈsumər

Sumerian
BR s(j)ʉˈmɪərɪən, s(j)ʉˈmɛːrɪən, -z
AM səˈmɛriən, suˈmɛriən, -z

Sumitomo
BR ˌsuːmɪˈtəʊməʊ
AM ˌsuməˈtoʊmoʊ

summa
BR ˈsʌmə(r), ˈsʊmə(r)
AM ˈsəmə, ˈsʊmə, ˈsumə

summa cum laude
BR ˌsʌmə kʌm ˈlaʊdeɪ, ˌsʊmə kʊm +
AM ˌsʊmə ˌkʊm ˈlaʊdə, ˌsumə ˌkum +, + ˈlaʊdi

summarily
BR ˈsʌm(ə)rɨli
AM səˈmɛrəli, ˈsəmərəli

summariness
BR ˈsʌm(ə)rɪnɨs
AM səˈmɛrinɨs, ˈsəmərinɨs

summarisable
BR ˈsʌmərʌɪzəbl
AM ˈsəməˌraɪzəbəl

summarisation
BR ˌsʌmərʌɪˈzeɪʃn
AM ˌsəmərəˈzeɪʃən, ˌsəməˌraɪˈzeɪʃən

summarise
BR ˈsʌmərʌɪz, -ɪz, -ɪŋ, -d
AM ˈsəməˌraɪz, -ɨz, -ɪŋ, -d

summariser
BR ˈsʌmərʌɪzə(r), -z
AM ˈsəməˌraɪzər, -z

summarist
BR ˈsʌmərɪst, -s
AM ˈsəmərəst, -s

summarizable
BR ˈsʌmərʌɪzəbl
AM ˈsəməˌraɪzəbəl

summarization
BR ˌsʌmərʌɪˈzeɪʃn
AM ˌsəmərəˈzeɪʃən, ˌsəməˌraɪˈzeɪʃən

summarize
BR ˈsʌmərʌɪz, -ɪz, -ɪŋ, -d
AM ˈsəməˌraɪz, -ɨz, -ɪŋ, -d

summarizer
BR ˈsʌmərʌɪzə(r), -z
AM ˈsəməˌraɪzər, -z

summary
BR ˈsʌm(ə)r|i, -ɪz
AM ˈsəməri, -z

summation
BR sʌˈmeɪʃn, səˈmeɪʃn, -z
AM səˈmeɪʃən, -z

summational
BR səˈmeɪʃn̩(ə)l, səˈmeɪʃən(ə)l
AM səˈmeɪʃ(ə)nəl

summer
BR ˈsʌmə(r), -z
AM ˈsəmər, -z

Summerfield
BR ˈsʌməfiːld
AM ˈsəmərˌfild

Summerhayes
BR ˈsʌməheɪz
AM ˈsəmərˌ(h)eɪz

Summerhill
BR ˈsʌməhɪl
AM ˈsəmərˌ(h)ɪl

summerhouse
BR ˈsʌməhaʊ|s, -zɪz
AM ˈsəmərˌ(h)aʊ|s, -zəz

summerise
BR ˈsʌmərʌɪz, -ɪz, -ɪŋ, -d
AM ˈsəməˌraɪz, -ɨz, -ɪŋ, -d

summerize
BR ˈsʌmərʌɪz, -ɪz, -ɪŋ, -d
AM ˈsəməˌraɪz, -ɨz, -ɪŋ, -d

summerless
BR ˈsʌmələs
AM ˈsəmərləs

summerly
BR ˈsʌməli
AM ˈsəmərli

Summers
BR ˈsʌməz
AM ˈsəmərz

summersault
BR ˈsʌməsɔːlt, ˈsʌməsɒlt, -s, -ɪŋ, -ɨd
AM ˈsəmərˌsɔl|t, ˈsəmərˌsɑl|t, -ts, -dɪŋ, -dəd

summertime
BR ˈsʌmətʌɪm
AM ˈsəmərˌtaɪm

summer-weight
BR ˈsʌməweɪt
AM ˈsəmərˌweɪt

summery
BR ˈsʌm(ə)ri
AM ˈsəməri

summings-up
BR ˌsʌmɪŋzˈʌp
AM ˌsəmɪŋzˈəp

summing-up
BR ˌsʌmɪŋˈʌp
AM ˌsəmɪŋˈəp

summit
BR ˈsʌmɪt, -s
AM ˈsəmət, -s

summiteer
BR ˌsʌmɪˈtɪə(r), -z
AM ˈsəməˌtɪ(ə)r, -z

summitless
BR ˈsʌmɪtlɨs
AM ˈsəmətləs

summitry
BR ˈsʌmɨtri
AM ˈsəmətri

summon
BR sʌmən, -z, -ɪŋ, -d
AM ˈsəmən, -z, -ɪŋ, -d

summonable
BR ˈsʌmənəbl
AM ˈsəmənəbəl

summoner
BR ˈsʌmənə(r), -z
AM ˈsəmənər, -z

summons
BR ˈsʌmənz, -ɨz, -ɪŋ, -d
AM ˈsəmənz, -ɨz, -ɪŋ, -d

summum bonum
BR ˌsʌməm ˈbəʊnəm, ˌsʊməm +, + ˈbɒnəm
AM ˈsʊməm ˈboʊnəm, ˈsuməm +

Sumner
BR ˈsʌmnə(r)
AM ˈsəmnər

sumo
BR ˈsuːməʊ
AM ˈsumoʊ

sump
BR sʌmp, -s
AM səmp, -s

sumpter
BR ˈsʌm(p)tə(r), -z
AM ˈsəm(p)tər, -z

sumptuary
BR ˈsʌm(p)tʃʊəri, ˈsʌmtʃʉri, ˈsʌm(p)tjʊəri, ˈsʌm(p)tjʉri
AM ˈsəm(p)(t)ʃəˌwɛri

sumptuosity
BR ˌsʌm(p)tʃʊˈɒsɪti, ˌsʌm(p)tjʊˈɒsɪti
AM ˌsəm(p)(t)ʃəˈwɑsədi

sumptuous
BR ˈsʌm(p)tʃʊəs, ˈsʌm(p)tjʊəs
AM ˈsəm(p)(t)ʃ(əw)əs

sumptuously
BR ˈsʌm(p)tʃʊəsli, ˈsʌm(p)tjʊəsli
AM ˈsəm(p)(t)ʃ(əw)əsli

sumptuousness
BR ˈsʌm(p)tʃʊəsnəs, ˈsʌm(p)tjʊəsnəs
AM ˈsəm(p)(t)ʃ(əw)əsnəs

Sumter
BR ˈsʌmtə(r)
AM ˈsəmtər

sun
BR sʌn, -z, -ɪŋ, -d
AM sən, -z, -ɪŋ, -d

sun-baked
BR ˈsʌnbeɪkt
AM ˈsənˌbeɪkt

sunbathe
BR ˈsʌnbeɪð, -z, -ɪŋ, -d
AM ˈsənˌbeɪð, -z, -ɪŋ, -d

sunbather
BR ˈsʌnbeɪðə(r), -z
AM ˈsənˌbeɪðər, -z

sunbeam
BR ˈsʌnbiːm, -z
AM ˈsənˌbim, -z

sunbed
BR ˈsʌnbɛd, -z
AM ˈsənˌbɛd, -z

Sunbelt
BR ˈsʌnbɛlt

AM 'sən,bɛlt

sunbird
BR 'sʌnbəːd, -z
AM 'sən,bərd, -z

sunblind
BR 'sʌnblʌɪnd, -z
AM 'sən,blaɪnd, -z

sunblock
BR 'sʌnblɒk, -s
AM 'sən,blɑk, -s

sunbonnet
BR 'sʌn,bɒnɪt, -s
AM 'sən,bɑnət, -s

sunbow
BR 'sʌnbəʊ, -z
AM 'sən,boʊ, -z

sunburn
BR 'sʌnbəːn, -d
AM 'sən,bərn, -d

sunburnt
BR 'sʌnbəːnt
AM 'sən,bərnt

sunburst
BR 'sʌnbəːst, -s
AM 'sən,bərst, -s

Sunbury
BR 'sʌnb(ə)ri
AM 'sən,bɛri, 'sənbəri

Sun City
BR ,sʌn 'sɪti
AM ˌsən 'sɪdi

Sunda
BR 'sʌndə(*r*), 'sʊndə(*r*)
AM 'səndə

sundae
BR 'sʌnd|eɪ, 'sʌnd|i, -eɪz\-ɪz
AM 'sən,deɪ, -z

Sundanese
BR ,sʌndə'niːz
AM ,səndə'niz

Sunday
BR 'sʌnd|eɪ, 'sʌnd|i, -eɪz\-ɪz
AM 'sən,deɪ, 'səndi, -z

Sunday best
BR ,sʌndeɪ 'bɛst, ,sʌndi +
AM ˌsən,deɪ 'bɛst, 'səndi +

Sunday school
BR 'sʌndeɪ ,skuːl, 'sʌndɪ +, -z
AM 'sən,deɪ ,skul, 'səndi +, -z

sundeck
BR 'sʌndɛk, -s
AM 'sən,dɛk, -s

sunder
BR 'sʌnd|ə(r), -əz, -(ə)rɪŋ, -əd
AM 'sənd|ər, -ərz, -(ə)rɪŋ, -ərd

Sunderland
BR 'sʌndələnd
AM 'səndərlənd

sundew
BR 'sʌndjuː, -z
AM 'sən,d(j)u, -z

sundial
BR 'sʌn,dʌɪəl, -z
AM 'sən,daɪəl, -z

sundown
BR 'sʌndaʊn
AM 'sən,daʊn

sundowner
BR 'sʌn,daʊnə(r), -z
AM 'sən,daʊnər, -z

sundrenched
BR 'sʌndrɛn(t)ʃt
AM 'sən,drɛn(t)ʃt

sundress
BR 'sʌndrɛs, -ɪz
AM 'sən,drɛs, -əz

sun-dried
BR 'sʌndrʌɪd, ,sʌn'drʌɪd
AM 'sən,draɪd

sundriesman
BR 'sʌndrɪzmən
AM 'səndriz,mæn

sundriesmen
BR 'sʌndrɪzmən
AM 'səndriz,mɛn

sundry
noun, adjective 'various'
BR 'sʌndr|i, -ɪz
AM 'səndri, -z

sunfast
BR 'sʌnfɑːst, 'sʌnfast
AM 'sən,fæst

sunfish
BR 'sʌnfɪʃ, -ɪz
AM 'sən,fɪʃ, -ɪz

sunflower
BR 'sʌn,flaʊə(r), -z
AM 'sən,flaʊər, -z

sung
BR sʌŋ
AM səŋ

sunglasses
BR 'sʌn,glɑːsɪz, 'sʌn,glasɪz
AM 'sən,glæsəz

sun-god
BR 'sʌngɒd, -z
AM 'sən,gɑd, -z

sunhat
BR 'sʌnhat, -s
AM 'sən,(h)æt, -s

sunk
BR sʌŋk
AM səŋk

sunken
BR 'sʌŋk(ə)n
AM 'səŋkən

Sunkist
BR 'sʌnkɪst
AM 'sən,kɪst

sunlamp
BR 'sʌnlamp, -s
AM 'sən,læmp, -s

sunless
BR 'sʌnləs
AM 'sənləs

sunlessness
BR 'sʌnləsnəs
AM 'sənələsnəs

sunlight
BR 'sʌnlʌɪt
AM 'sən,laɪt

sunlike
BR 'sʌnlʌɪk
AM 'sən,laɪk

sunlit
BR 'sʌnlɪt
AM 'sən,lɪt

sunlounger
BR 'sʌn,laʊn(d)ʒə(r), -z
AM 'sən,laʊndʒər, -z

sun-lover
BR 'sʌn,lʌvə(r), -z
AM 'sən,ləvər, -z

sunn
BR sʌn
AM sən

Sunna
BR 'sʊnə(*r*), 'sʌnə(*r*)
AM 'sənə, 'sʊnə

Sunni
BR 'sʊn|i, 'sʌn|i, -ɪz
AM 'sʊni, -z

sunnily
BR 'sʌnɪli
AM 'sənəli

sunniness
BR 'sʌnɪnɪs
AM 'səninɪs

Sunningdale
BR 'sʌnɪŋdeɪl
AM 'sənɪŋ,deɪl

Sunnite
BR 'sʊnʌɪt, 'sʌnʌɪt, -s
AM 'sə,naɪt, -s

sunny
BR 'sʌn|i, -ɪə(r), -ɪɪst
AM 'səni, -ər, -ɪst

sunproof
BR 'sʌnpruːf
AM 'sən,pruf

sunray
BR 'sʌnreɪ, -z
AM 'sən,reɪ, -z

sunrise
BR 'sʌnrʌɪz, -ɪz
AM 'sən,raɪz, -ɪz

sunroof
BR 'sʌnruːf, 'sʌnrʊf, -s
AM 'sən,ruf, -s

sunroom
BR 'sʌnruːm, 'sʌnrʊm, -z
AM 'sən,rum, 'sən,rʊm, -z

sunscreen
BR 'sʌnskriːn
AM 'sən,skrin

sunset
BR 'sʌnsɛt, -s
AM 'sən,sɛt, -s

sunshade
BR 'sʌnʃeɪd, -z
AM 'sən,ʃeɪd, -z

sunshine
BR 'sʌnʃʌɪn
AM 'sən,ʃaɪn

sunshiny
BR 'sʌnʃʌɪni
AM 'sən,ʃaɪni

sunspot
BR 'sʌnspɒt, -s
AM 'sən,spɑt, -s

sunstar
BR 'sʌnstɑː(r), -z
AM 'sən,stɑr, -z

sunstone
BR 'sʌnstəʊn, -z
AM 'sən,stoʊn, -z

sunstroke
BR 'sʌnstrəʊk
AM 'sən,stroʊk

sunstruck
BR 'sʌnstrʌk
AM 'sən,strək

sunsuit
BR 'sʌns(j)uːt, -s
AM 'sən,sut, -s

suntan
BR 'sʌntan, -z, -d
AM 'sən,tæn, -z, -d

Suntory®
BR sʌn'tɔːri, 'sʌntɔːri
AM sən'tɔri

suntrap
BR 'sʌntrap, -s
AM 'sən,træp, -s

sunup
BR 'sʌnʌp, -s
AM 'sən,əp, -s

sunward
BR 'sʌnwəd, -z
AM 'sənwərd, -z

Sun Yat-sen
BR ,sʊn jat'sɛn
AM 'sʊn ,jæt'sɛn

sup
BR sʌp, -s, -ɪŋ, -t
AM səp, -s, -ɪŋ, -t

super
BR 's(j)uːpə(r)
AM 'supər

superable
BR 's(j)uːp(ə)rəbl
AM 'sup(ə)rəbəl

superableness
BR 's(j)uːp(ə)rəblnəs
AM 'sup(ə)rəbəlnəs

superabound
BR ,s(j)uːp(ə)rə'baʊnd, -z, -ɪŋ, -ɪd
AM ,supərə'baʊnd, -z, -ɪŋ, -əd

superabundance
BR ˌs(j)uːp(ə)rəˈbʌnd(ə)ns
AM ˈsupərəˈbəndns

superabundant
BR ˌs(j)uːp(ə)rəˈbʌnd(ə)nt
AM ˈsupərəˈbəndnt

superabundantly
BR ˌs(j)uːp(ə)rəˈbʌnd(ə)ntli
AM ˈsupərəˈbəndən(t)li

superadd
BR ˌs(j)uːpərˈad, -z, -ɪŋ, -ɨd
AM ˌsupərˈæd, -z, -ɪŋ, -əd

superaddition
BR ˌs(j)uːpərəˈdɪʃn, -z
AM ˌsupərəˈdɪʃən, -z

superaltar
BR ˈs(j)uːpərˌɔːltə(r), ˈs(j)uːpərˌɒltə(r), -z
AM ˌsupərˈɔltər, ˌsupərˈɑltər, -z

superannuable
BR ˌs(j)uːpərˈanjʊəbl
AM ˌsupərˈænjəwəbəl

superannuate
BR ˌs(j)uːpərˈanjʊeɪt, -s, -ɪŋ, -ɨd
AM ˌsupərˈænjəˌweɪ|t, -ts, -dɪŋ, -dɨd

superannuation
BR ˌs(j)uːpərˌanjʊˈeɪʃn
AM ˌsupərˌænjəˈweɪʃən

superaqueous
BR ˌs(j)uːpərˈakwɪəs, ˌs(j)uːpərˈeɪkwɪəs
AM ˌsupərˈɑkwiəs, ˌsupərˈækwiəs, ˌsupərˈeɪkwiəs

superb
BR s(j)uːˈpəːb, s(j)ʉˈpəːb
AM suˈpərb, səˈpərb

superbly
BR s(j)uːˈpəːbli, s(j)ʉˈpəːbli
AM suˈpərbli, səˈpərbli

superbness
BR s(j)uːˈpəːbnəs, s(j)ʉˈpəːbnəs
AM suˈpərbnəs, səˈpərbnəs

Super Bowl
BR ˈs(j)uːpə bəʊl, -z
AM ˈsupər ˌboʊl, -z

supercalender
BR ˌs(j)uːpəˈkalɪnd|ə(r), -əz, -(ə)rɪŋ, -əd
AM ˈsupərˌkæləndər, -z, -ɪŋ, -d

supercargo
BR ˈs(j)uːpəˌkɑːɡəʊ, -z
AM ˈsupərˌkɑrɡoʊ, -z

supercelestial
BR ˌs(j)uːpəsɪˈlɛstɪəl
AM ˌsupərsəˈlɛstʃəl, ˌsupərsəˈlɛsdiəl

supercharge
BR ˈs(j)uːpətʃɑːdʒ, -ɨz, -ɪŋ, -d
AM ˈsupərˌtʃɑrdʒ, -əz, -ɪŋ, -d

supercharger
BR ˈs(j)uːpəˌtʃɑːdʒə(r), -z
AM ˈsupərˌtʃɑrdʒər, -z

superciliary
BR ˌs(j)uːpəˈsɪlɪəri
AM ˌsupərˈsɪliəri

supercilious
BR ˌs(j)uːpəˈsɪlɪəs
AM ˌsupərˈsɪliəs

superciliously
BR ˌs(j)uːpəˈsɪlɪəsli
AM ˌsupərˈsɪliəsli

superciliousness
BR ˌs(j)uːpəˈsɪlɪəsnəs
AM ˌsupərˈsɪliəsnəs

superclass
BR ˈs(j)uːpəːklɑːs, ˈs(j)uːpəːklas, -ɨz
AM ˈsupərˌklæs, -əz

supercolumnar
BR ˌs(j)uːpəkəˈlʌmnə(r)
AM ˈsupərkəˈləmnər

supercolumniation
BR ˌs(j)uːpəkəˌlʌmnɪˈeɪʃn
AM ˈsupərkəˌləmniˈeɪʃən

supercomputer
BR ˈs(j)uːpəkəmˌpjuːtə(r), -z
AM ˈsupərkəmˌpjudər, -z

supercomputing
BR ˈs(j)uːpəkəmˌpjuːtɪŋ
AM ˈsupərkəmˌpjudɪŋ

superconducting
BR ˌs(j)uːpəkənˈdʌktɪŋ
AM ˈsupərkənˈdəktɪŋ

superconductive
BR ˌs(j)uːpəkənˈdʌktɪv
AM ˈsupərkənˈdəktɪv

superconductivity
BR ˌs(j)uːpəˌkɒndʌkˈtɪvɨti
AM ˈsupərˌkɑndəkˈtɪvɨdi

superconductor
BR ˈs(j)uːpəkənˌdʌktə(r), -z
AM ˈsupərkənˌdəktər, -z

superconscious
BR ˌs(j)uːpəˈkɒnʃəs
AM ˌsupərˈkɑnʃəs

superconsciously
BR ˌs(j)uːpəˈkɒnʃəsli
AM ˌsupərˈkɑnʃəsli

superconsciousness
BR ˌs(j)uːpəˈkɒnʃəsnəs
AM ˌsupərˈkɑnʃəsnəs

supercontinent
BR ˈs(j)uːpəˌkɒntɪnənt, -s
AM ˈsupərˌkɑntn̩ənt, -s

supercool
BR ˌs(j)uːpəˈkuːl, ˈs(j)uːpəkuːl, -z, -ɪŋ, -d
AM ˈsupərˈkul, -z, -ɪŋ, -d

supercritical
BR ˌs(j)uːpəˈkrɪtɨkl
AM ˌsupərˈkrɪdɨkəl

superduper
BR ˌs(j)uːpəˈduːpə(r)
AM ˈsupərˈdupər

superego
BR ˈs(j)uːpərˌiːɡəʊ, -z
AM ˈsupərˈiɡoʊ, -z

superelevation
BR ˌs(j)uːpərˌɛlɪˈveɪʃn, -z
AM ˌsupərˌɛləˈveɪʃən, -z

supereminence
BR ˌs(j)uːpərˈɛmɪnəns, -ɨz
AM ˌsupərˈɛmənəns, -əz

supereminent
BR ˌs(j)uːpərˈɛmɪnənt
AM ˌsupərˈɛmənənt

supereminently
BR ˌs(j)uːpərˈɛmɪnəntli
AM ˌsupərˈɛmənən(t)li

supererogation
BR ˌs(j)uːpərˌɛrəˈɡeɪʃn
AM ˌsupərˌɛrəˈɡeɪʃən

supererogatory
BR ˌs(j)uːpərɪˈrɒɡət(ə)ri
AM ˈsupərəˈrɑɡəˌtɔri

superexcellence
BR ˌs(j)uːpərˈɛksələns, ˌs(j)uːpərˈɛksl̩ns, ˌs(j)uːpərˈɛksl̩(ə)ns
AM ˌsuperˈɛksələns

superexcellent
BR ˌs(j)uːpərˈɛksələnt, ˌs(j)uːpərˈɛksl̩nt, ˌs(j)uːpərˈɛksl̩(ə)nt
AM ˌsuperˈɛks(ə)lənt

superexcellently
BR ˌs(j)uːpərˈɛksələntli, ˌs(j)uːpərˈɛksl̩ntli, ˌs(j)uːpərˈɛksl̩(ə)ntli
AM ˌsuperˈɛks(ə)lən(t)li

superfamily
BR ˈs(j)uːpəˌfam(ɪ)l|i, ˈs(j)uːpəˌfaml̩|i, -ɪz
AM ˈsupərˌfæm(ə)li, -z

superfatted
BR ˌs(j)uːpəˈfatɨd
AM ˌsupərˈfædəd

superfecta
BR ˌs(j)uːpəˈfɛktə(r)
AM ˌsupərˈfɛktə

superfecundation
BR ˌs(j)uːpəˌfɛk(ə)nˈdeɪʃn, ˌs(j)uːpəˌfɛkʌnˈdeɪʃn, ˌs(j)uːpəˌfiːk(ə)nˈdeɪʃn, ˌs(j)uːpəˌfiːkʌnˈdeɪʃn, -z
AM ˈsupərˌfɛkənˈdeɪʃən, -z

superfetation
BR ˌs(j)uːpəfiːˈteɪʃn, -z
AM ˈsupərˌfiˈteɪʃən, -z

superficial
BR ˌs(j)uːpəˈfɪʃl
AM ˌsupərˈfɪʃəl

superficiality
BR ˌs(j)uːpəˌfɪʃɪˈalɪt|i, -ɪz
AM ˌsupərˌfɪʃiˈælədi, -z

superficially
BR ˌs(j)uːpəˈfɪʃl̩i, ˌs(j)uːpəˈfɪʃəli
AM ˌsupərˈfɪʃəli

superficialness
BR ˌs(j)uːpəˈfɪʃlnəs
AM ˌsupərˈfɪʃəlnəs

superficies
BR ˌs(j)uːpəˈfɪʃ(ɪ)iːz
AM ˌsupərˈfɪʃiz

superfine
BR ˈs(j)uːpəfʌɪn, ˌs(j)uːpəˈfʌɪn
AM ˈsupərˈfaɪn

superfluid
BR ˈs(j)uːpəˌfluːɪd, -z
AM ˈsupərˌflu(w)əd, -z

superfluidity
BR ˌs(j)uːpəfluːˈɪdɪti
AM ˈsupərˌfluˈɪdɨdi

superfluity
BR ˌs(j)uːpəˈfluːɪt|i, -ɪz
AM ˌsupərˈfluədi, -z

superfluous
BR s(j)uːˈpəːflʊəs, s(j)ʉˈpəːflʊəs
AM suˈpərfləwəs

superfluously
BR s(j)uːˈpəːflʊəsli, s(j)ʉˈpəːflʊəsli
AM suˈpərfləwəsli

superfluousness
BR s(j)uːˈpəːflʊəsnəs, s(j)ʉˈpəːflʊəsnəs
AM suˈpərfləwəsnəs

supergiant
BR ˈs(j)uːpəˌdʒʌɪənt, -s
AM ˈsupərˌdʒaɪənt, -s

superglue
BR ˈs(j)uːpəɡluː, -z, -ɪŋ, -d
AM ˈsupərˌɡlu, -z, -ɪŋ, -d

supergrass
BR ˈs(j)uːpəɡrɑːs, ˈs(j)uːpəɡras, -ɨz
AM ˈsupərˌɡræs, -əz

supergun
BR ˈs(j)uːpəɡʌn, -z
AM ˈsupərˌɡən, -z

superheat
BR ˌs(j)uːpəˈhiːt, -s, -ɪŋ, -ɨd
AM ˌsupərˈhi|t, -ts, -dɪŋ, -dɨd

superheater
BR ˈs(j)uːpəˌhiːtə(r), -z
AM ˈsupərˌhidər, -z

superhero
BR ˈs(j)uːpəˌhɪərəʊ, -z
AM ˈsupərˌ(h)ɪroʊ, -z

superhet
BR ˈs(j)uːpəhɛt, -s
AM ˈsupərˌ(h)ɛt, -s

superheterodyne
BR ˌs(j)uːpəˈhɛt(ə)rədʌɪn, -z
AM ˌsupərˈhɛdərəˌdaɪn, -z

superhighway
BR ˈs(j)uːpəˌhʌɪweɪ, -z
AM ˈsupərˈhaɪˌweɪ, -z

superhuman
BR ˌs(j)uːpəˈhjuːmən
AM ˌsupərˈ(h)jumən

superhumanly
BR ˌs(j)uːpəˈhjuːmənli
AM ˌsupərˈ(h)jumənli

superhumeral
BR ˌs(j)uːpəˈhjuːm(ə)rəl, ˌs(j)uːpəˈhjuːm(ə)rl̩, -z
AM ˌsupərˈ(h)jumərəl, -z

superimpose
BR ˌs(j)uːp(ə)rɪmˈpəʊz, -ɪz, -ɪŋ, -d
AM ˌsup(ə)rəmˈpoʊz, -əz, -ɪŋ, -d

superimposition
BR ˌs(j)uːpərˌɪmpəˈzɪʃn, -z
AM ˈsup(ə)rəmpəˈzɪʃən, -z

superincumbent
BR ˌs(j)uːp(ə)rɪnˈkʌmb(ə)nt
AM ˈsup(ə)rɪnˈkəmbənt, ˈsup(ə)rɪŋˈkəmbənt

superinduce
BR ˌs(j)uːp(ə)rɪnˈdjuːs, ˌs(j)uːp(ə)rɪnˈdʒuːs, -ɪz, -ɪŋ, -t
AM ˈsup(ə)rɪnˈd(j)us, -əz, -ɪŋ, -t

superintend
BR ˌs(j)uːp(ə)rɪnˈtɛnd, -z, -ɪŋ, -ɨd
AM ˈsup(ə)r(ə)nˈtɛnd, -z, -ɪŋ, -əd

superintendence
BR ˌs(j)uːp(ə)rɪnˈtɛnd(ə)ns
AM ˈsup(ə)r(ə)nˈtɛndəns

superintendency
BR ˌs(j)uːp(ə)rɪnˈtɛnd(ə)nsi
AM ˈsup(ə)r(ə)nˈtɛndnsi

superintendent
BR ˌs(j)uːp(ə)rɪnˈtɛnd(ə)nt, -s
AM ˈsup(ə)rɪnˈtɛndənt, -s

superior
BR s(j)uːˈpɪərɪə(r), s(j)ʉˈpɪərɪə(r), -z
AM səˈpɪriər, -z

superioress
BR s(j)uːˈpɪərɪərɪs, s(j)ʉˈpɪərɪərɪs, -ɪz
AM səˈpɪriəˌrɛs, -əz

superiority
BR s(j)uːˌpɪərɪˈɒrɨti, s(j)ʉˌpɪərɪˈɒrɨti
AM səˌpɪriˈɔrədi

superiorly
BR s(j)uːˈpɪərɪəli, s(j)ʉˈpɪərɪəli
AM səˈpɪriərli

superjacent
BR ˌs(j)uːpəˈdʒeɪs(ə)nt
AM ˌsupərˈdʒeɪsənt

superlative
BR s(j)uːˈpəːlətɪv, s(j)ʉˈpəːlətɪv, -z
AM səˈpərlədɪv, -z

superlatively
BR s(j)uːˈpəːlətɪvli, s(j)ʉˈpəːlətɪvli
AM səˈpərlədɪvli

superlativeness
BR s(j)uːˈpəːlətɪvnɪs, s(j)ʉˈpəːlətɪvnɪs
AM səˈpərlədɪvnɪs

superluminal
BR ˌs(j)uːpəˈl(j)uːmɪnl
AM ˌsupərˈlumənəl

superlunary
BR ˌs(j)uːpəˈluːn(ə)ri
AM ˌsupərˈlunəri

Superman
BR ˈs(j)uːpəman
AM ˈsupərˌmæn

supermarket
BR ˈs(j)uːpəˌmɑːkɪt, -s
AM ˈsupərˌmɑrkət, -s

supermen
BR ˈs(j)uːpəmɛn
AM ˈsupərˌmɛn

supermini
BR ˈs(j)uːpəˌmɪn|i, -ɪz
AM ˈsupərˌmɪni, -z

supermodel
BR ˈs(j)uːpəˌmɒdl, -z
AM ˈsupərˌmɑdəl, -z

supermundane
BR ˌs(j)uːpəmʌnˈdeɪn
AM ˈsupərˌmənˈdeɪn

supernacular
BR ˌs(j)uːpəˈnakjʉlə(r)
AM ˌsupərˈnækjələr

supernaculum
BR ˌs(j)uːpəˈnakjʉləm
AM ˌsupərˈnækjələm

supernal
BR s(j)uːˈpəːnl, s(j)ʉˈpəːnl
AM səˈpərnəl

supernally
BR s(j)uːˈpəːnl̩i, s(j)uːˈpəːnəli, s(j)ʉˈpəːnl̩i, s(j)ʉˈpəːnəli
AM səˈpərnəli

supernatant
BR ˌs(j)uːpəˈneɪt(ə)nt, -s
AM ˌsupərˈneɪtnt, -s

supernatural
BR ˌs(j)uːpəˈnatʃ(ə)rəl, ˌs(j)uːpəˈnatʃ(ə)rl̩
AM ˌsupərˈnætʃ(ə)rəl

supernaturalise
BR ˌs(j)uːpəˈnatʃ(ə)rəlʌɪz, ˌs(j)uːpəˈnatʃ(ə)rl̩ʌɪz, -ɪz, -ɪŋ, -d
AM ˌsupərˈnætʃ(ə)rəˌlaɪz, -ɪz, -ɪŋ, -d

supernaturalism
BR ˌs(j)uːpəˈnatʃ(ə)rəlɪz(ə)m, ˌs(j)uːpəˈnatʃ(ə)rl̩ɪz(ə)m
AM ˌsupərˈnætʃ(ə)rəˌlɪzəm

supernaturalist
BR ˌs(j)uːpəˈnatʃ(ə)rəlɪst, ˌs(j)uːpəˈnatʃ(ə)rl̩ɪst, -s
AM ˌsupərˈnætʃ(ə)rələst, -s

supernaturalize
BR ˌs(j)uːpəˈnatʃ(ə)rəlʌɪz, ˌs(j)uːpəˈnatʃ(ə)rl̩ʌɪz, -ɪz, -ɪŋ, -d
AM ˌsupərˈnætʃ(ə)rəˌlaɪz, -ɪz, -ɪŋ, -d

supernaturally
BR ˌs(j)uːpəˈnatʃ(ə)rəli, ˌs(j)uːpəˈnatʃ(ə)rl̩i
AM ˌsupərˈnætʃ(ə)rəli

supernaturalness
BR ˌs(j)uːpəˈnatʃ(ə)rəlnəs, ˌs(j)uːpəˈnatʃ(ə)rl̩nəs
AM ˌsupərˈnætʃ(ə)rəlnəs

supernormal
BR ˌs(j)uːpəˈnɔːml
AM ˌsupərˈnɔrməl

supernormality
BR ˌs(j)uːpənɔːˈmalɪti
AM ˈsupərˌnɔrˈmælədi

supernova
BR ˈs(j)uːpəˌnəʊvə(r), ˌs(j)uːpəˈnəʊvə(r), -z
AM ˈsupərˈnoʊvə, -z

supernovae
BR ˈs(j)uːpəˌnəʊviː, ˌs(j)uːpəˈnəʊviː
AM ˈsupərˈnoʊˌvi

supernumerary
BR ˌs(j)uːpəˈnjuːmər(ər)|i, -ɪz
AM ˌsupərˈn(j)uməˌrɛri, -z

superorder
BR ˈs(j)uːpərˌɔːdə(r), -z
AM ˈsupərˌɔrdər, -z

superordinal
BR ˌs(j)uːpərˈɔːdɪnl, ˌs(j)uːpərˈɔːdn̩l
AM ˌsupərˈɔrdn̩l

superordinate
BR ˌs(j)uːpərˈɔːdɪnət, ˌs(j)uːpərˈɔːdn̩ət, -s
AM ˌsupərˈɔrd(ə)nət, -s

superphosphate
BR ˈs(j)uːpəˌfɒsfeɪt, -s
AM ˈsupərˌfɑsˌfeɪt, -s

superphysical
BR ˌs(j)uːpəˈfɪzɪkl
AM ˌsupərˈfɪzɪkəl

superpose
BR ˌs(j)uːpəˈpəʊz, -ɪz, -ɪŋ, -d
AM ˈsupərˈpoʊz, -əz, -ɪŋ, -d

superposition
BR ˌs(j)uːpəpəˈzɪʃn, -z
AM ˌsuərpəˈzɪʃən, -z

superpower
BR ˈs(j)uːpəˌpaʊə(r), -z
AM ˈsupərˌpaʊər, -z

supersaturate
BR ˌs(j)uːpəˈsatʃʊreɪt, ˌs(j)uːpəˈsatjʊreɪt, -s, -ɪŋ, -ɨd
AM ˌsupərˈsætʃəˌreɪ|t, -ts, -dɪŋ, -dɨd

supersaturation
BR ˌs(j)uːpəˌsatʃʊˈreɪʃn, ˌs(j)uːpəˌsatjʊˈreɪʃn
AM ˈsupərˌsætʃəˈreɪʃən

superscribe
BR ˌs(j)uːpəˈskrʌɪb, ˈs(j)uːpəskrʌɪb, -z, -ɪŋ, -d
AM ˈsupərˈskraɪb, -z, -ɪŋ, -d

superscript
BR ˈs(j)uːpəskrɪpt, -s
AM ˈsupərˌskrɪpt, -s

superscription
BR ˌs(j)uːpəˈskrɪpʃn, -z
AM ˌsupərˈskrɪpʃən, -z

supersede
BR ˌs(j)uːpəˈsiːd, -z, -ɪŋ, -ɨd
AM ˌsupərˈsid, -z, -ɪŋ, -ɨd

supersedence
BR ˌs(j)uːpəˈsiːdns

AM ˌsupər'sidns
supersedure
BR ˌs(j)u:pə'si:dʒə(r)
AM ˌsupər'sidʒər
supersession
BR ˌs(j)u:pə'sɛʃn
AM ˌsupər'sɛʃən
supersonic
BR ˌs(j)u:pə'sɒnɪk, -s
AM ˌsupər'sɑnɪk, -s
supersonically
BR ˌs(j)u:pə'sɒnɨkli
AM ˌsupər'sɑnək(ə)li
superstar
BR 's(j)u:pəstɑ:(r), -z
AM 'supərˌstɑr, -z
superstardom
BR 's(j)u:pəstɑ:dəm
AM 'supərˌstɑrdəm
superstate
BR 's(j)u:pəsteɪt, -s
AM 'supərˌsteɪt, -s
superstition
BR ˌs(j)u:pə'stɪʃn, -z
AM ˌsupər'stɪʃən, -z
superstitious
BR ˌs(j)u:pə'stɪʃəs
AM ˌsupər'stɪʃəs
superstitiously
BR ˌs(j)u:pə'stɪʃəsli
AM ˌsupər'stɪʃəsli
superstitiousness
BR ˌs(j)u:pə'stɪʃəsnəs
AM ˌsupər'stɪʃəsnəs
superstore
BR 's(j)u:pəstɔ:(r), -z
AM 'supərˌstɔ(ə)r, -z
superstrata
BR 's(j)u:pəˌstrɑ:tə(r), 's(j)u:pəˌstreɪtə(r)
AM 'supərˌstreɪdə, 'supərˌstrædə, 'supərˌstrɑdə
superstrate
BR 's(j)u:pəstreɪt, -s
AM 'supərˌstreɪt, -s
superstratum
BR 's(j)u:pəˌstrɑ:təm, 's(j)u:pəˌstreɪtəm
AM 'supərˌstreɪdəm, 'supərˌstrædəm, 'supərˌstrɑdəm
superstructural
BR ˌs(j)u:pə'strʌktʃ(ə)rəl, ˌs(j)u:pə'strʌktʃ(ə)rl̩
AM ˌsupər'strək(t)ʃ(ə)rəl
superstructure
BR 's(j)u:pəˌstrʌktʃə(r), -z
AM 'supərˌstrək(t)ʃər, -z
supersubtle
BR ˌs(j)u:pə'sʌtl
AM ˌsupər'sədəl
supersubtlety
BR ˌs(j)u:pə'sʌtlt|i, -ɪz
AM ˌsupər'sədlti, -z
supertanker
BR 's(j)u:pəˌtaŋkə(r), -z
AM 'supərˌtæŋkər, -z
supertax
BR 's(j)u:pətaks, -ɪz
AM 'supərˌtæks, -əz
supertemporal
BR ˌs(j)u:pə'tɛmp(ə)rəl, ˌs(j)u:pə'tɛmp(ə)rl̩
AM ˌsupər'tɛmp(ə)rəl
superterrene
BR ˌs(j)u:pə'tɛri:n, ˌs(j)u:pətə'ri:n
AM ˌsupərtə'rin
superterrestrial
BR ˌs(j)u:pətɨ'rɛstrɪəl
AM ˌsupərtə'rɛstriəl
supertitle
BR 's(j)u:pəˌtʌɪtl, -z
AM 'supərˌtaɪdəl, -z
supertonic
BR 's(j)u:pəˌtɒnɪk, -s
AM 'supərˌtɑnɪk, -s
supervene
BR ˌs(j)u:pə'vi:n, -z, -ɪŋ, -d
AM ˌsupər'vin, -z, -ɪŋ, -d
supervenient
BR ˌs(j)u:pə'vi:nɪənt
AM ˌsupər'viniənt, ˌsupər'vinjənt
supervention
BR ˌs(j)u:pə'vɛnʃn
AM ˌsupər'vɛn(t)ʃən
supervise
BR 's(j)u:pəvʌɪz, -ɪz, -ɪŋ, -d
AM 'supərˌvaɪz, -ɪz, -ɪŋ, -d
supervision
BR ˌs(j)u:pə'vɪʒn
AM ˌsupər'vɪʒən
supervisor
BR 'su:pəvʌɪzə(r), -z
AM 'supərˌvaɪzər, -z
supervisory
BR ˌs(j)u:pə'vʌɪz(ə)ri, 's(j)u:pəvʌɪz(ə)ri
AM ˌsupər'vaɪzəri
superwoman
BR 's(j)u:pəˌwʊmən
AM 'supərˌwʊmən
superwomen
BR 's(j)u:pəˌwɪmɪn
AM 'supərˌwɪmɨn
supinate
BR 's(j)u:pɨneɪt, -s, -ɪŋ, -ɨd
AM 'supəˌneɪ|t, -ts, -dɪŋ, -dɨd
supination
BR ˌs(j)u:pɨ'neɪʃn, -z
AM ˌsupə'neɪʃən, -z
supinator
BR 's(j)u:pɨneɪtə(r), -z
AM 'supəˌneɪdər, -z
supine
BR 's(j)u:pʌɪn
AM 'suˌpaɪn
supinely
BR 's(j)u:pʌɪnli
AM 'suˌpaɪnli
supineness
BR 's(j)u:pʌɪnnɨs
AM 'suˌpaɪ(n)nɨs
supper
BR 'sʌpə(r), -z
AM 'səpər, -z
supperless
BR 'sʌpələs
AM 'səpərləs
suppertime
BR 'sʌpətʌɪm, -z
AM 'səpərˌtaɪm, -z
supplant
BR sə'plɑ:nt, sə'plant, -s, -ɪŋ, -ɨd
AM sə'plæn|t, -ts, -(t)ɪŋ, -(t)əd
supplanter
BR sə'plɑ:ntə(r), sə'plantə(r), -z
AM sə'plæn(t)ər, -z
supple
BR 'sʌpl
AM 'səpəl
supplejack
BR 'sʌpldʒak, -s
AM 'səpəlɛdʒæk, -s
suppleley
BR 'sʌpl(l)i, 'sʌpl̩i
AM 'səp(ə)li
supplement[1]
noun
BR 'sʌplɨm(ə)nt, -s
AM 'səpləmənt, -s
supplement[2]
verb
BR 'sʌplɨmɛnt, -s, -ɪŋ, -ɨd
AM 'səpləˌmɛn|t, 'səpləmən|t, -ts, -(t)ɪŋ, -(t)əd
supplemental
BR ˌsʌplɨ'mɛntl
AM ˌsəplə'mɛn(t)l
supplementally
BR ˌsʌplɨ'mɛntl̩i, ˌsʌplɨ'mɛntəli
AM ˌsəplə'mɛn(t)l̩i
supplementarily
BR ˌsʌplɨ'mɛnt(ə)rɨli, ˌsʌplɨ'mɛnt(ə)rɨli
AM ˌsəpləˌmɛn'tɛrəli
supplementary
BR ˌsʌplɨ'mɛnt(ə)r|i, -ɪz
AM ˌsəplə'mɛn(t)əri, -z
supplementation
BR ˌsʌplɨmɛn'teɪʃn, ˌsʌplɨm(ə)n'teɪʃn
AM ˌsəpləˌmɛn'teɪʃən
suppleness
BR 'sʌplnəs
AM 'səpəlnəs
suppletion
BR sə'pli:ʃn
AM sə'pliʃən
suppletive
BR sə'pli:tɪv, 'sʌplɪtɪv, -z
AM sə'plidɪv, 'səplədɪv, -z
suppliant
BR 'sʌplɪənt, -s
AM 'səpliənt, -s
suppliantly
BR 'sʌplɪəntli
AM 'səpliən(t)li
supplicant
BR 'sʌplɨk(ə)nt, -s
AM 'səpləkənt, -s
supplicate
BR 'sʌplɨkeɪt, -s, -ɪŋ, -ɨd
AM 'səpləˌkeɪ|t, -ts, -dɪŋ, -dɨd
supplication
BR ˌsʌplɨ'keɪʃn, -z
AM ˌsəplə'keɪʃən, -z
supplicatory
BR 'sʌplɨkət(ə)ri, ˌsʌplɨ'keɪt(ə)ri
AM 'səpləkəˌtɔri
supplier
BR sə'plʌɪə(r), -z
AM sə'plaɪər, -z
supply
BR sə'plʌɪ, -z, -ɪŋ, -d
AM sə'plaɪ, -z, -ɪŋ, -d
support
BR sə'pɔ:t, -s, -ɪŋ, -ɨd
AM sə'pɔ(ə)rt, -ts, -'pɔrdɪŋ, -'pɔrdəd
supportability
BR səˌpɔ:tə'bɪlɨti
AM səˌpɔrdə'bɪlɨdi
supportable
BR sə'pɔ:təbl
AM sə'pɔrdəbəl
supportably
BR sə'pɔ:təbli
AM sə'pɔrdəbli
supporter
BR sə'pɔ:tə(r), -z
AM sə'pɔrdər, -z
supportingly
BR sə'pɔ:tɪŋli
AM sə'pɔrdɪŋli
supportive
BR sə'pɔ:tɪv
AM sə'pɔrdɪv
supportively
BR sə'pɔ:tɨvli
AM sə'pɔrdɨvli
supportiveness
BR sə'pɔ:tɨvnɨs
AM sə'pɔrdɪvnɨs
supportless
BR sə'pɔ:tləs
AM sə'pɔrtləs

supposable
BR sə'pəʊzəbl
AM sə'poʊzəbəl
suppose
BR sə'pəʊz, -ɪz, -ɪŋ, -d
AM sə'poʊz, -əz, -ɪŋ, -d
supposedly
BR sə'pəʊzɪdli
AM sə'poʊzədli
supposition
BR ˌsʌpə'zɪʃn, -z
AM ˌsəpə'zɪʃən, -z
suppositional
BR ˌsʌpə'zɪʃn̩(ə)l, ˌsʌpə'zɪʃən(ə)l
AM ˌsəpə'zɪʃ(ə)nəl
suppositionally
BR ˌsʌpə'zɪʃn̩əli, ˌsʌpə'zɪʃn̩l̩i, ˌsʌpə'zɪʃənl̩i, ˌsʌpə'zɪʃ(ə)nəli
AM ˌsəpə'zɪʃ(ə)nəli
suppositious
BR ˌsʌpə'zɪʃəs
AM ˌsəpə'zɪʃəs
suppositiously
BR ˌsʌpə'zɪʃəsli
AM ˌsəpə'zɪʃəsli
suppositiousness
BR ˌsʌpə'zɪʃəsnəs
AM 'səpə'zɪʃəsnəs
supposititious
BR səˌpɒzɪ'tɪʃəs
AM səˌpɑzə'tɪʃəs
supposititiously
BR səˌpɒzɪ'tɪʃəsli
AM səˌpɑzə'tɪʃəsli
supposititiousness
BR səˌpɒzɪ'tɪʃəsnəs
AM səˌpɑzə'tɪʃəsnəs
suppository
BR sə'pɒzɪt(ə)r|i, -ɪz
AM sə'pɑzəˌtɔri, -z
suppress
BR sə'prɛs, -ɪz, -ɪŋ, -t
AM sə'prɛs, -əz, -ɪŋ, -t
suppressant
BR sə'prɛs(ə)nt, -s
AM sə'prɛsənt, -s
suppressible
BR sə'prɛsɪbl
AM sə'prɛsəbəl
suppression
BR sə'prɛʃn
AM sə'prɛʃən
suppressive
BR sə'prɛsɪv
AM sə'prɛsɪv
suppressor
BR sə'prɛsə(r), -z
AM sə'prɛsər, -z
suppurate
BR 'sʌpjʊreɪt, -s, -ɪŋ, -ɪd
AM 'səpjəˌreɪ|t, -ts, -dɪŋ, -dɪd
suppuration
BR ˌsʌpjʊ'reɪʃn
AM ˌsəpjə'reɪʃən
suppurative
BR 'sʌpjʊrətɪv
AM 'səpjəˌreɪdɪv, 'səp(jə)rədɪv
supra
BR 's(j)uːprə(*r*)
AM 'suprə
supralapsarian
BR ˌs(j)uːprəlap'sɛːrɪən, -z
AM ˌsuprəˌlæp'sɛriən, -z
supramaxillary
BR ˌs(j)uːprəmak'sɪl(ə)ri
AM ˌsuprə'mæksəˌlɛri
supramundane
BR ˌs(j)uːprə'mʌndeɪn
AM ˌsuprəˌmən'deɪn
supranational
BR ˌs(j)uːprə'naʃn̩(ə)l, ˌs(j)uːprə'naʃən(ə)l
AM ˌsuprə'næʃ(ə)nəl
supranationalism
BR ˌs(j)uːprə'naʃn̩əlɪz(ə)m, ˌs(j)uːprə'naʃn̩l̩ɪz(ə)m, ˌs(j)uːprə'naʃənl̩ɪz(ə)m, ˌs(j)uːprə'naʃ(ə)nəlɪz(ə)m
AM ˌsuprə'næʃənlˌɪzəm, ˌsuprə'næʃnəlɪzəm
supranationality
BR ˌs(j)uːprəˌnaʃ(ə)'nalɪti
AM ˌsuprəˌnæʃə'nælədi
supraorbital
BR ˌs(j)uːprə(*r*)'ɔːbɪtl
AM ˌsuprə'ɔrbədl
suprarenal
BR ˌs(j)uːprə'riːnl
AM ˌsuprə'rinəl
suprasegmental
BR ˌs(j)uːprəsɛg'mɛntl
AM ˌsuprəˌsɛg'mɛn(t)l
supremacism
BR s(j)ʊ'prɛməsɪz(ə)m, s(j)uː'prɛməsɪz(ə)m
AM sə'prɛməˌsɪzəm, su'prɛməˌsɪzəm
supremacist
BR s(j)ʊ'prɛməsɪst, s(j)uː'prɛməsɪst, -s
AM sə'prɛməsəst, su'prɛməsəst, -s
supremacy
BR s(j)ʊ'prɛməsi, s(j)uː'prɛməsi
AM sə'prɛməsi, su'prɛməsi
suprematism
BR s(j)ʊ'prɛmətɪz(ə)m, s(j)uː'prɛmətɪz(ə)m
AM sə'prɛməˌtɪzəm, su'prɛməˌtɪzəm
supreme
BR s(j)ʊ'priːm, s(j)uː'priːm
AM sə'prim, su'prim
suprême
BR s(j)uː'prɛm, -z
AM sʊ'prɛm, -z
supremely
BR s(j)ʊ'priːmli, s(j)uː'priːmli
AM sə'primli, su'primli
supremeness
BR s(j)ʊ'priːmnɪs, s(j)uː'priːmnɪs
AM sə'primnɪs, su'primnɪs
supremo
BR s(j)ʊ'priːməʊ, s(j)uː'priːməʊ, -z
AM sə'primoʊ, su'primoʊ, -z
sura
BR 'sʊərə(*r*), -z
AM 'surə, -z
Surabaya
BR ˌsʊərə'bʌɪə(*r*)
AM ˌsʊrə'baɪə
surah
BR 'sʊərə(*r*), -z
AM 'surə, -z
surahi
BR sʊ'rɑːh|i, -ɪz
AM sə'rɑhi, -z
sural
BR 's(j)ʊərəl, 's(j)ʊərl̩
AM 'surəl
Surat
BR sʊ'rat, 's(j)ʊərat
AM 'sʊˌræt
Surbiton
BR 'səːbɪt(ə)n
AM 'sərbətn
surcease
BR səː'siːs, -ɪz, -ɪŋ, -t
AM ˌsər'siz, -ɪz, -ɪŋ, -t
surcharge
BR 'səːtʃɑːdʒ, -ɪz, -ɪŋ, -d
AM 'sərˌtʃɑrdʒ, -əz, -ɪŋ, -d
surcingle
BR 'səːˌsɪŋgl, -z
AM 'sərˌsɪŋgəl, -z
surcoat
BR 'səːkəʊt, -s
AM 'sərˌkoʊt, -s
surculose
BR 'səːkjʊləʊs
AM 'sərkjəˌloʊs, 'sərkjəˌloʊz
surd
BR səːd, -z
AM sərd, -z
surdity
BR 'səːdɪti
AM 'sərdədi
sure
BR ʃʊə(r), ʃɔː(r), -ə(r), -ɪst
AM ʃʊ(ə)r, -ər, -əst
sure-enough
BR ˌʃʊərɪ'nʌf, ˌʃɔːrɪ'nʌf
AM 'ʃʊr(ə)'nəf
surefire
BR 'ʃʊəˌfʌɪə(r), 'ʃɔːˌfʌɪə(r)
AM 'ʃʊrˌfaɪ(ə)r
surefooted
BR ˌʃʊə'fʊtɪd, ˌʃɔː'fʊtɪd
AM 'ʃʊrˌfʊdəd
surefootedly
BR ˌʃʊə'fʊtɪdli, ˌʃɔː'fʊtɪdli
AM 'ʃʊrˌfʊdədli
surefootedness
BR ˌʃɔː'fʊtɪdnɪs, ˌʃʊə'fʊtɪdnɪs
AM 'ʃʊrˌfʊdədnəs
surehanded
BR ˌʃʊə'handɪd, ˌʃɔː'handɪd
AM 'ʃʊrˌhæn(d)əd
surehandedly
BR ˌʃʊə'handɪdli, ˌʃɔː'handɪdli
AM 'ʃʊrˌhæn(d)ədli
surehandedness
BR ˌʃʊə'handɪdnɪs, ˌʃɔː'handɪdnɪs
AM 'ʃʊrˌhæn(d)ədnəs
surely
BR 'ʃʊəli, 'ʃɔːli
AM 'ʃʊrli
sureness
BR 'ʃʊənəs, 'ʃɔːnəs
AM 'ʃʊrnəs
surety
BR 'ʃʊərɪt|i, 'ʃɔːrɪti, -ɪz
AM 'ʃʊrədi, -z
suretyship
BR 'ʃʊərɪtɪʃɪp, 'ʃɔːrɪtɪʃɪp
AM 'ʃʊrədiˌʃɪp
surf
BR səːf, -s, -ɪŋ, -t
AM sərf, -s, -ɪŋ, -t
surface
BR 'səːfɪs, -ɪz, -ɪŋ, -t
AM 'sərfəs, -əz, -ɪŋ, -t
surfacer
BR 'səːfɪsə(r), -z
AM 'sərfəsər, -z
surface-to-air
BR ˌsəːfɪstʊ'ɛː(r)
AM ˌsərfəstə'ɛ(ə)r
surface-to-surface
BR ˌsəːfɪstə'səːfɪs
AM ˌsərfəstə'sərfəs
surfactant
BR səː'fakt(ə)nt
AM sər'fæktənt

surfbird
BR 'sə:fbə:d, -z
AM 'sərf,bərd, -z
surfboard
BR 'sə:fbɔ:d, -z
AM 'sərf,bɔ(ə)rd, -z
surfboat
BR 'sə:fbəʊt, -s
AM 'sərf,boʊt, -s
surfeit
BR 'sə:fɪt, -s, -ɪŋ, -ɨd
AM 'sərfə|t, -ts, -dɪŋ, -dəd
surfer
BR 'sə:fə(r), -z
AM 'sərfər, -z
surficial
BR sə:'fɪʃl
AM sər'fɪʃəl
surficially
BR sə:'fɪʃl̩i, sə:'fɪʃəli
AM sər'fɪʃəli
surfy
BR 'sə:f|i, -ɪə(r), -ɪɨst
AM 'sərfi, -ər, -ɨst
surge
BR sə:dʒ, -ɨz, -ɪŋ, -d
AM sərdʒ, -əz, -ɪŋ, -d
surgeon
BR 'sə:dʒ(ə)n, -z
AM 'sərdʒən, -z
surgery
BR 'sə:dʒ(ə)r|i, -ɪz
AM 'sərdʒ(ə)ri, -z
surgical
BR 'sə:dʒɪkl
AM 'sərdʒəkəl
surgically
BR 'sə:dʒɪkli
AM 'sərdʒək(ə)li
suricate
BR 's(j)ʊərɪkeɪt, -s
AM 'ʃʊrə,keɪt, -s
Surinam
BR 's(j)ʊərɪnam
AM 'sʊrə,næm, 'sʊrə,nɑm
Suriname
BR 's(j)ʊərɪnam
AM 'sʊrə,næm, 'sʊrə,nɑm
Surinamer
BR ,s(j)ʊərɪ'nɑ:mə(r), -z
AM 'sʊrə,næmər, 'sʊrə,nɑmər, -z
Surinamese
BR ,s(j)ʊərɪnə'mi:z
AM ,sʊrənə'miz
surlily
BR 'sə:lɪli
AM 'sərləli
surliness
BR 'sə:lɪnɨs
AM 'sərlinɨs
surly
BR 'sə:l|i, -ɪə(r), -ɪɨst
AM 'sərli, -ər, -ɨst
surmise[1]
noun
BR sə'mʌɪz, 'sə:mʌɪz, -ɨz
AM sər'maɪz, 'sər,maɪz, -ɨz
surmise[2]
verb
BR sə'mʌɪz, -ɨz, -ɪŋ, -d
AM sər'maɪz, -ɨz, -ɪŋ, -d
surmount
BR sə'maʊnt, -s, -ɪŋ, -ɨd
AM sər'maʊn|t, -ts, -(t)ɪŋ, -(t)əd
surmountable
BR sə'maʊntəbl
AM sər'maʊn(t)əbəl
surmullet
BR sə:'mʌlɪt
AM sər'mələt
surname
BR 'sə:neɪm, -z, -d
AM 'sər,neɪm, -z, -d
surpass
BR sə'pɑ:s, sə'pas, -ɨz, -ɪŋ, -t
AM sər'pæs, -əz, -ɪŋ, -t
surpassable
BR sə'pɑ:səbl, sə'pasəbl
AM sər'pæsəbəl
surpassing
BR sə'pɑ:sɪŋ, sə'pasɪŋ
AM sər'pæsɪŋ
surpassingly
BR sə'pɑ:sɪŋli, sə'pasɪŋli
AM sər'pæsɪŋli
surplice
BR 'sə:plɪs, -ɨz, -t
AM 'sərpləs, -əz, -t
surplus
BR 'sə:pləs, -ɨz
AM 'sərpləs, -əz
surplusage
BR 'sə:pləsɪdʒ
AM 'sərpləsɪdʒ
surprise
BR sə'prʌɪz, -ɨz, -ɪŋ, -d
AM sə(r)'praɪz, -ɨz, -ɪŋ, -d
surprisedly
BR sə'prʌɪz(ɨ)dli
AM sə(r)'praɪz(ɨ)dli
surprising
BR sə'prʌɪzɪŋ
AM sə(r)'praɪzɪŋ
surprisingly
BR sə'prʌɪzɪŋli
AM sə(r)'praɪzɪŋli
surprisingness
BR sə'prʌɪzɪŋnɨs
AM sə(r)'praɪzɪŋnɨs
surra
BR 'sʊərə(r), 'sʌrə(r)
AM 'sʊrə, 'sərə
surreal
BR sə'rɪəl
AM sə'riəl
surrealism
BR sə'rɪəlɪz(ə)m
AM sə'riə,lɪzəm
surrealist
BR sə'rɪəlɪst, -s
AM sə'riəlɨst, -s
surrealistic
BR sə,rɪə'lɪstɪk
AM sə,riə'lɪstɪk, ,səriə'lɪstɪk
surrealistically
BR sə,rɪə'lɪstɪkli
AM sə,riə'lɪstɪk(ə)li
surreality
BR ,sʌrɪ'alɨti
AM ,səri'ælədi
surreally
BR sə'rɪəli
AM sə'riəli
surrebuttal
BR ,sʌrɪ'bʌtl, -z
AM ,sərə'bətl, -z
surrebutter
BR ,sʌrɪ'bʌtə(r), -z
AM ,sərə'bədər, -z
surrejoinder
BR ,sʌrɪ'dʒɔɪndə(r), -z
AM ,sərə'dʒɔɪndər, -z
surrender
BR sə'rɛnd|ə(r), -əz, -(ə)rɪŋ, -əd
AM sə'rɛnd|ər, -ərz, -(ə)rɪŋ, -ərd
surreptitious
BR ,sʌrɪp'tɪʃəs
AM ,sərəp'tɪʃəs
surreptitiously
BR ,sʌrɪp'tɪʃəsli
AM ,sərəp'tɪʃəsli
surreptitiousness
BR ,sʌrɪp'tɪʃəsnəs
AM ,sərə'ptɪʃəsnəs
surrey
BR 'sʌr|i, -ɪz
AM 'səri, -z
Surridge
BR 'sʌrɪdʒ
AM 'sərɪdʒ
surrogacy
BR 'sʌrəgəs|i, -ɪz
AM 'sərəgəsi, -z
surrogate
BR 'sʌrəgət, 'sʌrəgeɪt, -s
AM 'sərəgət, 'sərə,geɪt, -s
surrogateship
BR 'sʌrəgətʃɪp, 'sʌrəgeɪtʃɪp, -s
AM 'sərəgət,ʃɪp, 'sərə,geɪt,ʃɪp, -s
surround
BR sə'raʊnd, -z, -ɪŋ, -ɨd
AM sə'raʊnd, -z, -ɪŋ, -əd
surrounding
BR sə'raʊndɪŋ, -z
AM sə'raʊndɪŋ, -z
surtax
BR 'sə:taks, -ɨz
AM 'sər,tæks, -əz
Surtees
BR 'sə:ti:z
AM 'sərtiz
surtitle
BR 'sə:,tʌɪtl, -z
AM sər'taɪdəl, -z
surtout
BR 'sə:tu:, -z
AM ,sər'tu(t), -z
Surtsey
BR 'sə:tsi
AM 'sərtsi
surveillance
BR sə'veɪləns, sə'veɪlns, sə:'veɪləns, sə:'veɪlns
AM sər'veɪləns
survey[1]
noun
BR 'sə:veɪ, -z
AM 'sər,veɪ, -z
survey[2]
verb
BR sə'veɪ, 'sə:veɪ, -z, -ɪŋ, -d
AM sər'veɪ, -z, -ɪŋ, -d
surveyor
BR sə'veɪə(r), -z
AM sər'veɪər, -z
surveyorship
BR sə'veɪəʃɪp, -s
AM sər'veɪər,ʃɪp, -s
survivability
BR sə,vʌɪvə'bɪlɨti
AM sər,vaɪvə'bɪlɨdi
survivable
BR sə'vʌɪvəbl
AM sər'vaɪvəbəl
survival
BR sə'vʌɪvl, -z
AM sər'vaɪvəl, -z
survivalism
BR sə'vʌɪvl̩ɪz(ə)m
AM sər'vaɪvə,lɪzəm
survivalist
BR sə'vʌɪvl̩ɪst, -s
AM sər'vaɪvələst, -s
survive
BR sə'vʌɪv, -z, -ɪŋ, -d
AM sər'vaɪv, -z, -ɪŋ, -d
survivor
BR sə'vʌɪvə(r), -z
AM sər'vaɪvər, -z
survivorship
BR sə'vʌɪvəʃɪp
AM sər'vaɪvər,ʃɪp
Surya
BR 'sʊərɪə(r)
AM 'sʊriə

sus
BR sʌs, -ɪz, -ɪŋ, -t
AM səs, -əz, -ɪŋ, -t

Susa
BR 'su:zə(r), 'su:sə(r)
AM 'suzə, 'susə

Susan
BR 'su:zn
AM 'suzn

Susanna
BR sʊ'zanə(r)
AM su'zænə

Susannah
BR sʊ'zanə(r)
AM su'zænə

Susanne
BR sʊ'zan
AM su'zæn

susceptibility
BR sə,sɛptɪ'bɪlɪti
AM sə,sɛptə'bɪlɨdi

susceptible
BR sə'sɛptɪbl
AM sə'sɛptəbəl

susceptibly
BR sə'sɛptɪbli
AM sə'sɛptəbli

susceptive
BR sə'sɛptɪv
AM sə'sɛptɪv

sushi
BR 'su:ʃi
AM 'suʃi

Susie
BR 'su:zi
AM 'suzi

suslik
BR 'sʊslɪk, 'sʌslɪk, -s
AM 'səs,lɪk, -s

suspect[1]
noun
BR 'sʌspɛkt, -s
AM 'səs,pɛk(t), -s

suspect[2]
verb
BR sə'spɛkt, -s, -ɪŋ, -ɪd
AM sə'spɛk(t), -(t)s, -tɪŋ, -təd

suspend
BR sə'spɛnd, -z, -ɪŋ, -ɪd
AM sə'spɛnd, -z, -ɪŋ, -əd

suspender
BR sə'spɛndə(r), -z
AM sə'spɛndər, -z

suspense
BR sə'spɛns
AM sə'spɛns

suspenseful
BR sə'spɛnsf(ʊ)l
AM sə'spɛnsfəl

suspensible
BR sə'spɛnsɪbl
AM sə'spɛnsəbəl

suspension
BR sə'spɛnʃn, -z
AM sə'spɛn(t)ʃən, -z

suspensive
BR sə'spɛnsɪv
AM sə'spɛnsɪv

suspensively
BR sə'spɛnsɪvli
AM sə'spɛnsɪvli

suspensiveness
BR sə'spɛnsɪvnɪs
AM sə'spɛnsɪvnɪs

suspensory
BR sə'spɛns(ə)ri
AM sə'spɛnsəri

suspicion
BR sə'spɪʃn, -z
AM sə'spɪʃən, -z

suspicious
BR sə'spɪʃəs
AM sə'spɪʃəs

suspiciously
BR sə'spɪʃəsli
AM sə'spɪʃəsli

suspiciousness
BR sə'spɪʃəsnəs
AM sə'spɪʃəsnəs

suspiration
BR ,sʌspɪ'reɪʃn, -z
AM ,səspə'reɪʃən, -z

suspire
BR sə'spʌɪə(r), -z, -ɪŋ, -d
AM sə'spaɪ(ə)r, -z, -ɪŋ, -d

Susquehanna
BR ,sʌskwɪ'hanə(r)
AM ,səskwə'hænə

suss
BR sʌs, -ɪz, -ɪŋ, -t
AM səs, -əz, -ɪŋ, -t

Sussex
BR 'sʌsɪks
AM 'səsəks

sustain
BR sə'steɪn, -z, -ɪŋ, -d
AM sə'steɪn, -z, -ɪŋ, -d

sustainability
BR sə,steɪnə'bɪlɪti
AM sə,steɪnə'bɪlɨdi

sustainable
BR sə'steɪnəbl
AM sə'steɪnəbəl

sustainably
BR sə'steɪnəbli
AM sə'steɪnəbli

sustainedly
BR sə'steɪnɪdli
AM sə'steɪnɪdli

sustainer
BR sə'steɪnə(r), -z
AM sə'steɪnər, -z

sustainment
BR sə'steɪnm(ə)nt
AM sə'steɪnmənt

sustenance
BR 'sʌstɪnəns
AM 'səstənəns

sustentation
BR ,sʌstɛn'teɪʃn, ,sʌst(ə)n'teɪʃn
AM ,səst(ə)n'teɪʃən

susurration
BR ,s(j)u:sʌ'reɪʃn, -z
AM ,sʊsə'reɪʃən, -z

susurrus
BR s(j)u:'sʌrəs
AM sʊ'sərəs

Sutch
BR sʌtʃ
AM sətʃ

Sutcliff
BR 'sʌtklɪf
AM 'sət,klɪf

Sutcliffe
BR 'sʌtklɪf
AM 'sət,klɪf

Sutherland
BR 'sʌðələnd
AM 'səðərlən(d)

Sutlej
BR 'sʌtlɪdʒ
AM 'sətlɪdʒ

sutler
BR 'sʌtlə(r), -z
AM 'sətlər, -z

sutra
BR 'su:trə(r), -z
AM 'sutrə, -z

Sutro
BR 'su:trəʊ
AM 'sutroʊ

suttee
BR sʌ'ti:, 'sʌti:, -z
AM sə'ti, 'su,ti, -z

Sutter
BR 'sʌtə(r)
AM 'sədər

Sutton
BR 'sʌtn
AM 'sətn

Sutton Coldfield
BR ,sʌtn 'kəʊl(d)fi:ld
AM ,sətn 'koʊl(d),fild

Sutton Hoo
BR ,sʌtn 'hu:
AM ,sətn 'hu

sutural
BR 'su:tʃ(ə)rəl, 'su:tʃ(ə)rl̩
AM 'sutʃərəl

suture
BR 'su:tʃə(r), -z
AM 'sutʃər, -z

Suva
BR 'su:və(r)
AM 'suvə

Suwannee
BR sʉ'wɒni, 'swɒni
AM 'swɑni, sə'wɑni

Suzanna
BR sʊ'zanə(r)
AM su'zænə

Suzanne
BR sʊ'zan
AM su'zæn

suzerain
BR 'su:zəreɪn, 'su:z(ə)rən, 'su:z(ə)rn̩, -z
AM 'suzərən, 'suzə,reɪn, -z

suzerainty
BR 'su:zəreɪnt|i, 'su:z(ə)rənt|i, 'su:z(ə)rn̩ti, -ɪz
AM 'suzərənti, 'suzə,reɪnti, -z

Suzette
BR sʊ'zɛt
AM su'zɛt, sə'zɛt

Suzie
BR 'su:zi
AM 'suzi

Suzuki®
BR sʉ'zu:k|i, -ɪz
AM sə'zuki, -z

Suzy
BR 'su:zi
AM 'suzi

Svalbard
BR 'svalbɑ:d
AM 'svɑl,bɑrd

svarabhakti
BR ,svarə'bakti:, ,svɑ:rə'bakti:, ,svʌrə'bʌkti:
AM ,sfɑrə'bɑkti

svelte
BR svɛlt
AM svɛlt, sfɛlt

Svengali
BR svɛn'gɑ:l|i, sfɛn'gɑ:l|i, -ɪz
AM svɛn'gɑli, sfɛn'gɑli, -z

Sverdlovsk
BR ,svɛ:d'lɒfsk, ,svɛ:d'lɒvsk
AM ,svərd'lɔfsk, ,svərd'lɑfsk

swab
BR swɒb, -z, -ɪŋ, -d
AM swɑb, -z, -ɪŋ, -d

swabbie
BR 'swɒb|i, -ɪz
AM 'swɑbi, -z

swabby
BR 'swɒb|i, -ɪz
AM 'swɑbi, -z

Swabia
BR 'sweɪbɪə(r)
AM 'sweɪbiə

Swabian
BR 'sweɪbɪən, -z
AM 'sweɪbiən, -z

swaddie
BR 'swɒd|i, -ɪz
AM 'swɑdi, -z

swaddle
BR 'swɒd|l, -lz, -l̩ɪŋ\-lɪŋ, -ld

AM 'swɑd|əl, -əlz, -(ə)lɪŋ, -əld
swaddy
BR 'swɒd|i, -ɪz
AM 'swɑdi, -z
Swadeshi
BR swə'deɪʃi
AM swə'deɪʃi
Swadlincote
BR 'swɒdlɪnkəʊt
AM 'swɑdlɪŋ,koʊt
Swaffer
BR 'swɒfə(r)
AM 'swɑfər
Swaffham
BR 'swɒf(ə)m
AM 'swɑfəm
swag
BR swag
AM swæg
swage
BR sweɪdʒ, -ɪz
AM sw|eɪdʒ, sw|ɛdʒ, -eɪdʒɪz\-ɛdʒəz
Swaggart
BR 'swagət
AM 'swægərt
swagger
BR 'swag|ə(r), -əz, -(ə)rɪŋ, -əd
AM 'swæg|ər, -ərz, -(ə)rɪŋ, -ərd
swaggerer
BR 'swag(ə)rə(r), -z
AM 'swæg(ə)rər, -z
swaggeringly
BR 'swag(ə)rɪŋli
AM 'swæg(ə)rɪŋli
swaggie
BR 'swag|i, -ɪz
AM 'swægi, -z
swagman
BR 'swagman
AM 'swæg,mæn
swagmen
BR 'swagmɛn
AM 'swæg,mɛn
Swahili
BR swɑː'hiːli, swə'hiːli
AM swɑ'hili
swain
BR sweɪn, -z
AM sweɪn, -z
Swainson
BR 'sweɪns(ə)n
AM 'sweɪnsən
swale
BR sweɪl, -z
AM sweɪl, -z
Swaledale
BR 'sweɪldeɪl
AM 'sweɪl,deɪl
Swales
BR sweɪlz
AM sweɪlz
swallow
BR 'swɒləʊ, -z, -ɪŋ, -d
AM 'swɑl|oʊ, -oʊz, -əwɪŋ\-oʊɪŋ, -oʊd
swallowable
BR 'swɒləʊəbl
AM 'swɑləwəbəl
swallow-dive
BR 'swɒlə(ʊ)dʌɪv, -z, -ɪŋ, -d
AM 'swɑloʊ,daɪv, -z, -ɪŋ, -d
swallower
BR 'swɒləʊə(r), -z
AM 'swɑləwər, -z
swallow-hole
BR 'swɒləʊhəʊl, -z
AM 'swɑloʊ,hoʊl, -z
swallowtail
BR 'swɒlə(ʊ)teɪl, -z, -d
AM 'swɑloʊ,teɪl, -z, -d
swam
BR swam
AM swæm
swami
BR 'swɑːm|i, -ɪz
AM 'swɑmi, -z
swamp
BR swɒm|p, -ps, -pɪŋ, -(p)t
AM swɑmp, -s, -ɪŋ, -t
swampiness
BR 'swɒmpɪnɪs
AM 'swɑmpinɪs
swampland
BR 'swɒmpland, -z
AM 'swɑmp,lænd, -z
swampy
BR 'swɒmp|i, -ɪə(r), -ɪɪst
AM 'swɑmpi, -ər, -ɪst
swan
BR swɒn, -z, -ɪŋ, -d
AM swɑn, -z, -ɪŋ, -d
Swanage
BR 'swɒnɪdʒ
AM 'swɑnɪdʒ
swandive
BR 'swɒndʌɪv, -z
AM 'swɑn,daɪv, -z
Swanee
BR 'swɒni
AM 'swɑni
swank
BR swaŋ|k, -ks, -kɪŋ, -(k)t
AM swæŋ|k, -ks, -kɪŋ, -(k)t
swankily
BR 'swaŋkɪli
AM 'swæŋkəli
swankiness
BR 'swaŋkɪnɪs
AM 'swæŋkinɪs
swankpot
BR 'swaŋkpɒt, -s
AM 'swæŋk,pɑt, -s
swanky
BR 'swaŋk|i, -ɪə(r), -ɪɪst
AM 'swæŋki, -ər, -ɪst
Swanley
BR 'swɒnli
AM 'swɑnli
swanlike
BR 'swɒnlʌɪk
AM 'swɑn,laɪk
Swann
BR swɒn
AM swɑn
swan-neck
BR 'swɒnnɛk, -s
AM 'swɑ(n),nɛk, -s
swannery
BR 'swɒn(ə)r|i, -ɪz
AM 'swɑnəri, -z
Swanscombe
BR 'swɒnzkəm
AM 'swɑnzkəm
swansdown
BR 'swɒnzdaʊn
AM 'swɑnz,daʊn
Swansea
BR 'swɒnzi
AM 'swɔnzi, 'swɑnzi
Swanson
BR 'swɒnsn
AM 'swɑnsən
swansong
BR 'swɒnsɒŋ, -z
AM 'swɑn,sɔŋ, 'swɑn,sɑŋ, -z
Swanton
BR 'swɒntən
AM 'swɑn(t)ən
swan-upping
BR ˌswɒn'ʌpɪŋ, 'swɒn,ʌpɪŋ
AM 'swɑn,əpɪŋ
swap
BR swɒp, -s, -ɪŋ, -t
AM swɑp, -s, -ɪŋ, -t
SWAPO
BR 'swɑːpəʊ
AM 'swɑ,poʊ
swapper
BR 'swɒpə(r), -z
AM 'swɑpər, -z
Swaraj
BR swə'rɑːdʒ
AM swə'rɑdʒ
Swarajist
BR swə'rɑːdʒɪst, -s
AM swə'rɑdʒəst, -s
Swarbrick
BR 'swɔːbrɪk
AM 'swɑr,brɪk
sward
BR swɔːd, -z, -ɪd
AM swɔ(ə)rd, -z, -əd
sware
BR swɛː(r)
AM swɛ(ə)r
swarf
BR swɔːf
AM swɔ(ə)rf
Swarfega®
BR swɔː'fiːgə(r)
AM swɑr'figə
swarm
BR swɔːm, -z, -ɪŋ, -d
AM swɔ(ə)rm, -z, -ɪŋ, -d
swart
BR swɔːt
AM swɔ(ə)rt
swarthily
BR 'swɔːðɪli
AM 'swɔrðəli
swarthiness
BR 'swɔːðɪnɪs
AM 'swɔrðinɪs
swarthy
BR 'swɔːð|i, -ɪə(r), -ɪɪst
AM 'swɔrði, -ər, -ɪst
Swartz
BR swɔːts
AM swɔ(ə)rts
swash
BR swɒʃ, -ɪz, -ɪŋ, -t
AM swɔʃ, swɑʃ, -əz, -ɪŋ, -t
swashbuckler
BR 'swɒʃ,bʌklə(r), -z
AM 'swɔʃ,bək(ə)lər, 'swɑʃ,bək(ə)lər, -z
swashbuckling
BR 'swɒʃ,bʌklɪŋ
AM 'swɔʃ,bək(ə)lɪŋ, 'swɑʃ,bək(ə)lɪŋ
swastika
BR 'swɒstɪkə(r), -z
AM 'swɑstəkə, -z
swat
BR swɒt, -s, -ɪŋ, -ɪd
AM swɑ|t, -ts, -dɪŋ, -dəd
swatch
BR swɒtʃ, -ɪz
AM swɑtʃ, -əz
swath
BR swɒθ, swɔːθ, -s
AM swɑθ, -s
swathe
BR sweɪð, -z, -ɪŋ, -d
AM sweɪð, -z, -ɪŋ, -d
SWAT team
BR 'swɒt tiːm, -z
AM 'swɑ(t) ,tim, -z
swatter
BR 'swɒtə(r), -z
AM 'swɑdər, -z
sway
BR sweɪ, -z, -ɪŋ, -d
AM sweɪ, -z, -ɪŋ, -d
Swazi
BR 'swɑːz|i, -ɪz
AM 'swɑzi, -z
Swaziland
BR 'swɑːzɪland
AM 'swɑzi,lænd

swear
BR swɛː(r), -z, -ɪŋ
AM swɛ(ə)r, -z, -ɪŋ
swearer
BR ˈswɛːrə(r), -z
AM ˈswɛrər, -z
swearword
BR ˈswɛːwəːd, -z
AM ˈswɛrˌwərd, -z
sweat
BR swɛt, -s, -ɪŋ, -ɨd
AM swɛ|t, -ts, -dɪŋ, -dəd
sweatband
BR ˈswɛtband, -z
AM ˈswɛtˌbænd, -z
sweatbox
BR ˈswɛtbɒks, -ɪz
AM ˈswɛtˌbɑks, -əz
sweater
BR ˈswɛtə(r), -z
AM ˈswɛdər, -z
sweatily
BR ˈswɛtɨli
AM ˈswɛdəli
sweatiness
BR ˈswɛtɪnɨs
AM ˈswɛdinɨs
sweatpants
BR ˈswɛtpants
AM ˈswɛtˌpæn(t)s
sweatshirt
BR ˈswɛtʃəːt, -s
AM ˈswɛtˌʃərt, -s
sweatshop
BR ˈswɛtʃɒp, -s
AM ˈswɛtˌʃɑp, -s
sweatsuit
BR ˈswɛtsuːt, -s
AM ˈswɛtˌsut, -s
sweaty
BR ˈswɛt|i, -ɪə(r), -ɪɨst
AM ˈswɛdi, -ər, -ɨst
Swede
BR swiːd, -z
AM swid, -z
Sweden
BR ˈswiːdn
AM ˈswidən
Swedenborg
BR ˈswiːdnbɔːɡ
AM ˈswidnˌbɔrɡ
SW ˈsveːdɛnbɒrj
Swedenborgian
BR ˌswiːdnˈbɔːɡɪən, ˌswiːdnˈbɔːdʒɪən
AM ˌswidənˈbɔrɡiən
Swedish
BR ˈswiːdɪʃ
AM ˈswidɪʃ
Sweeney
BR ˈswiːni
AM ˈswini
sweep
BR swiːp, -s, -ɪŋ
AM swip, -z, -ɪŋ
sweepback
BR ˈswiːpbak, -s
AM ˈswipˌbæk, -s
sweeper
BR ˈswiːpə(r), -z
AM ˈswipər, -z
sweeping
BR ˈswiːpɪŋ, -z
AM ˈswipɪŋ, -z
sweepingly
BR ˈswiːpɪŋli
AM ˈswipɪŋli
sweepingness
BR ˈswiːpɪŋnɨs
AM ˈswipɪŋnɨs
sweepstake
BR ˈswiːpsteɪk, -s
AM ˈswipˌsteɪk, -s
sweet
BR swiːt, -s, -ə(r), -ɨst
AM swi|t, -ts, -dər, -dɨst
sweet-and-sour
BR ˌswiːt(ə)n(d)ˈsaʊə(r)
AM ˌswidənˈsaʊ(ə)r
sweetbread
BR ˈswiːtbrɛd, -z
AM ˈswitˌbrɛd, -z
sweetbriar
BR ˈswiːtˌbrʌɪə(r), -z
AM ˈswitˌbraɪər, -z
sweetbrier
BR ˈswiːtˌbrʌɪə(r), -z
AM ˈswitˌbraɪər, -z
sweetcorn
BR ˈswiːtkɔːn
AM ˈswitˌkɔ(ə)rn
sweeten
BR ˈswiːt|n, -nz, -nɪŋ\-n̩ɪŋ, -nd
AM ˈswitn, -z, -ɪŋ, -d
sweetener
BR ˈswiːtnə(r), ˈswiːtn̩ə(r), -z
AM ˈswitn̩ər, ˈswitnər, -z
sweetening
BR ˈswiːtnɪŋ, ˈswiːtn̩ɪŋ, -z
AM ˈswitn̩ɪŋ, ˈswitnɪŋ, -z
Sweetex®
BR ˈswiːtɛks
AM ˈswiˌtɛks
sweetheart
BR ˈswiːthɑːt, -s
AM ˈswitˌ(h)ɑrt, -s
sweetie
BR ˈswiːt|i, -ɪz
AM ˈswidi, -z
sweetie-pie
BR ˈswiːtɪpʌɪ, -z
AM ˈswidiˌpaɪ, -z
sweeting
BR ˈswiːtɪŋ, -z
AM ˈswidɪŋ, -z
sweetish
BR ˈswiːtɪʃ
AM ˈswidɪʃ
sweetly
BR ˈswiːtli
AM ˈswitli
sweetmeal
BR ˈswiːtmiːl
AM ˈswitˌmil
sweetmeat
BR ˈswiːtmiːt, -s
AM ˈswitˌmit, -s
sweetness
BR ˈswiːtnɨs
AM ˈswitnɨs
sweetshop
BR ˈswiːtʃɒp, -s
AM ˈswitˌʃɑp, -s
sweetsop
BR ˈswiːtsɒp, -s
AM ˈswitˌsɑp, -s
sweet-talk
BR ˈswiːttɔːk, -s, -ɪŋ, -t
AM ˈswi(t)ˌtɔk, ˈswi(t)ˌtɑk, -s, -ɪŋ, -t
sweety
BR ˈswiːt|i, -ɪz
AM ˈswidi, -z
swell
BR swɛl, -z, -ɪŋ, -d
AM swɛl, -z, -ɪŋ, -d
swelling
BR ˈswɛlɪŋ, -z
AM ˈswɛlɪŋ, -z
swellish
BR ˈswɛlɪʃ
AM ˈswɛlɪʃ
swelter
BR ˈswɛlt|ə(r), -əz, -(ə)rɪŋ, -əd
AM ˈswɛlt|ər, -ərz, -(ə)rɪŋ, -ərd
swelteringly
BR ˈswɛlt(ə)rɪŋli
AM ˈswɛlt(ə)rɪŋli
Swenson
BR ˈswɛns(ə)nt
AM ˈswɛnsən
swept
BR swɛpt
AM swɛpt
swerve
BR swəːv, -z, -ɪŋ, -d
AM swərv, -z, -ɪŋ, -d
swerveless
BR ˈswəːvləs
AM ˈswərvləs
swerver
BR ˈswəːvə(r), -z
AM ˈswərvər, -z
swift
BR swɪft, -s, -ə(r), -ɨst
AM swɪft, -s, -ər, -ɨst
swiftie
BR ˈswɪft|i, -ɪz
AM ˈswɪfti, -z
swiftlet
BR ˈswɪftlɨt, -s
AM ˈswɪf(t)lət, -s
swiftly
BR ˈswɪftli
AM ˈswɪf(t)li
swiftness
BR ˈswɪf(t)nɨs
AM ˈswɪf(t)nɨs
swig
BR swɪɡ, -z, -ɪŋ, -d
AM swɪɡ, -z, -ɪŋ, -d
swigger
BR ˈswɪɡə(r), -z
AM ˈswɪɡər, -z
swill
BR swɪl, -z, -ɪŋ, -d
AM swɪl, -z, -ɪŋ, -d
swiller
BR ˈswɪlə(r), -z
AM ˈswɪlər, -z
swim
BR swɪm, -z, -ɪŋ
AM swɪm, -z, -ɪŋ
swimmable
BR ˈswɪməbl
AM ˈswɪməbəl
swimmer
BR ˈswɪmə(r), -z
AM ˈswɪmər, -z
swimmeret
BR ˌswɪməˈrɛt, -s
AM ˌswɪməˈrɛt, -s
swimmingly
BR ˈswɪmɪŋli
AM ˈswɪmɪŋɡli
swimsuit
BR ˈswɪms(j)uːt, -s, -ɨd
AM ˈswɪmˌsu|t, -ts, -dəd
swimwear
BR ˈswɪmwɛː(r)
AM ˈswɪmˌwɛ(ə)r
Swinburne
BR ˈswɪnbəːn
AM ˈswɪnˌbərn
swindle
BR ˈswɪnd|l, -lz, -l̩ɪŋ\-lɪŋ, -ld
AM ˈswɪn|dəl, -dəlz, -(d)(ə)lɪŋ, -dəld
swindler
BR ˈswɪndlə(r), -z
AM ˈswɪn(də)lər, -z
Swindon
BR ˈswɪndən
AM ˈswɪndən
swine
BR swʌɪn
AM swaɪn
swineherd
BR ˈswʌɪnhəːd, -z
AM ˈswaɪnˌ(h)ərd, -z
swinery
BR ˈswʌɪn(ə)r|i, -ɪz
AM ˈswaɪnəri, -z
swing
BR swɪŋ, -z, -ɪŋ
AM swɪŋ, -z, -ɪŋ
swingbin
BR ˈswɪŋbɪn, -z

AM 'swɪŋˌbɪn, -z
swingboat
BR 'swɪŋbəʊt, -s
AM 'swɪŋˌboʊt, -s
swinge
BR swɪn(d)ʒ, -ɪz, -ɪŋ, -d
AM swɪndʒ, -ɪz, -ɪŋ, -d
swingeingly
BR 'swɪn(d)ʒɪŋli
AM 'swɪndʒɪŋli
swinger
BR 'swɪŋə(r), -z
AM 'swɪŋər, -z
swingingly
BR 'swɪŋɪŋli
AM 'swɪŋɪŋli
swingle
BR 'swɪŋg|l, -lz, -l̩ɪŋ\-lɪŋ, -ld
AM 'swɪŋg|əl, -əlz, -(ə)lɪŋ, -əld
Swingler
BR 'swɪŋglə(r)
AM 'swɪŋ(g)lər
swingletree
BR 'swɪŋgltriː, -z
AM 'swɪŋglˌtri, -z
swingometer
BR swɪŋ'ɒmɪtə(r), -z
AM swɪŋ'(g)ɑmədər, -z
swingy
BR 'swɪŋ|i, -ɪə(r), -ɪɪst
AM 'swɪŋi, -ər, -ɪst
swinish
BR 'swʌɪnɪʃ
AM 'swaɪnɪʃ
swinishly
BR 'swʌɪnɪʃli
AM 'swaɪnɪʃli
swinishness
BR 'swʌɪnɪʃnɪs
AM 'swaɪnɪʃnɪs
Swinnerton
BR 'swɪnət(ə)n
AM 'swɪnərt(ə)n
Swinton
BR 'swɪntən
AM 'swɪn(t)ən
swipe
BR swʌɪp, -s, -ɪŋ, -t
AM swaɪp, -s, -ɪŋ, -t
swiper
BR 'swʌɪpə(r), -z
AM 'swaɪpər, -z
swipple
BR 'swɪpl, -z
AM 'swɪpəl, -z
swirl
BR swəːl, -z, -ɪŋ, -d
AM swərl, -z, -ɪŋ, -d
swirly
BR 'swəːl|i, -ɪə(r), -ɪɪst
AM 'swərli, -ər, -ɪst
swish
BR swɪʃ, -ɪz, -ɪŋ, -t, -ə(r), -ɪst
AM swɪʃ, -ɪz, -ɪŋ, -t, -ər, -ɪst
swishily
BR 'swɪʃɨli
AM 'swɪʃɨli
swishiness
BR 'swɪʃɪnɪs
AM 'swɪʃinɨs
swishy
BR 'swɪʃ|i, -ɪə(r), -ɪɪst
AM 'swɪʃi, -ər, -ɪst
Swiss
BR swɪs
AM swɪs
Swissair®
BR 'swɪsɛː(r)
AM ˌswɪs'ɛ(ə)r
switch
BR swɪtʃ, -ɪz, -ɪŋ, -t
AM swɪtʃ, -ɪz, -ɪŋ, -t
switchable
BR 'swɪtʃəbl
AM 'swɪtʃəbəl
switchback
BR 'swɪtʃbak, -s
AM 'swɪtʃˌbæk, -s
switchblade
BR 'swɪtʃbleɪd, -z
AM 'swɪtʃˌbleɪd, -z
switchboard
BR 'swɪtʃbɔːd, -z
AM 'swɪtʃˌbɔ(ə)rd, -z
switcher
BR 'swɪtʃə(r), -z
AM 'swɪtʃər, -z
switcheroo
BR ˌswɪtʃə'ruː, -z
AM ˌswɪtʃə'ru, -z
switchgear
BR 'swɪtʃgɪə(r)
AM 'swɪtʃˌgɪ(ə)r
switchman
BR 'swɪtʃmən
AM 'swɪtʃmən
switchmen
BR 'swɪtʃmən
AM 'swɪtʃmən
switch-over
BR 'swɪtʃˌəʊvə(r), -z
AM 'swɪtʃˌoʊvər, -z
switchyard
BR 'swɪtʃjɑːd, -z
AM 'swɪtʃˌjɑrd, -z
swither
BR 'swɪð|ə(r), -əz, -(ə)rɪŋ, -əd
AM 'swɪðər, -z, -ɪŋ, -d
Swithin
BR 'swɪð(ɪ)n
AM 'swɪðɨn
Swithun
BR 'swɪðn
AM 'swɪðɨn
Switzerland
BR 'swɪtsələnd, 'swɪtsl̩nd
AM 'swɪtsərlənd
swive
BR swʌɪv, -z, -ɪŋ, -d
AM swaɪv, -z, -ɪŋ, -d
swivel
BR 'swɪv|l, -lz, -l̩ɪŋ\-lɪŋ, -ld
AM 'swɪv|əl, -əlz, -(ə)lɪŋ, -əld
swiz
BR swɪz, -ɪz
AM swɪz, -ɪz
swizz
BR swɪz, -ɪz
AM swɪz, -ɪz
swizzle
BR 'swɪz|l, -lz, -l̩ɪŋ\-lɪŋ, -ld
AM 'swɪz|əl, -əlz, -(ə)lɪŋ, -əld
swob
BR swɒb, -z, -ɪŋ, -d
AM swɑb, -z, -ɪŋ, -d
swollen
BR 'swəʊlən
AM 'swoʊlən
swoon
BR swuːn, -z, -ɪŋ, -d
AM swun, -z, -ɪŋ, -d
swoop
BR swuːp, -s, -ɪŋ, -t
AM swup, -s, -ɪŋ, -t
swoosh
BR swuːʃ, swʊʃ, -ɪz, -ɪŋ, -t
AM swuʃ, -əz, -ɪŋ, -t
swop
BR swɒp, -s, -ɪŋ, -t
AM swɑp, -s, -ɪŋ, -t
sword
BR sɔːd, -z
AM sɔ(ə)rd, -z
swordbearer
BR 'sɔːdˌbɛːrə(r), -z
AM 'sɔrdˌbɛrər, -z
swordbelt
BR 'sɔːdbɛlt, -s
AM 'sɔrdˌbɛlt, -s
swordbill
BR 'sɔːdbɪl, -z
AM 'sɔrdˌbɪl, -z
swordfish
BR 'sɔːdfɪʃ, -ɪz
AM 'sɔrdˌfɪʃ, -ɪz
swordlike
BR 'sɔːdlʌɪk
AM 'sɔrdˌlaɪk
swordplay
BR 'sɔːdpleɪ
AM 'sɔrdˌpleɪ
swordsman
BR 'sɔːdzmən
AM 'sɔrdzmən
swordsmanship
BR 'sɔːdzmənʃɪp
AM 'sɔrdzmənˌʃɪp
swordsmen
BR 'sɔːdzmən
AM 'sɔrdzmən
swordstick
BR 'sɔːdstɪk, -s
AM 'sɔrdˌstɪk, -s
swordtail
BR 'sɔːdteɪl, -z
AM 'sɔrdˌteɪl, -z
swore
BR swɔː(r)
AM swɔ(ə)r
sworn
BR swɔːn
AM swɔ(ə)rn
swot
BR swɒt, -s, -ɪŋ, -ɪd
AM swɑ|t, -ts, -dɪŋ, -dəd
swotter
BR 'swɒtə(r), -z
AM 'swɑdər, -z
swum
BR swʌm
AM swəm
swung
BR swʌŋ
AM swəŋ
swy
BR swʌɪ, -z
AM swaɪ, -z
sybarite
BR 'sɪbərʌɪt, -s
AM 'sɪbəˌraɪt, -s
sybaritic
BR ˌsɪbə'rɪtɪk
AM ˌsɪbə'rɪdɪk
sybaritical
BR ˌsɪbə'rɪtɪkl
AM ˌsɪbə'rɪdəkəl
sybaritically
BR ˌsɪbə'rɪtɪkli
AM ˌsɪbə'rɪdək(ə)li
sybaritism
BR 'sɪbərʌɪtɪz(ə)m
AM 'sɪbəˌraɪˌtɪzəm
sybil
BR 'sɪb(ɪ)l, -z
AM 'sɪbɪl, -z
sycamine
BR 'sɪkəmɪn, 'sɪkəmʌɪn, -z
AM 'sɪkəmən, 'sɪkəˌmaɪn, -z
syce
BR sʌɪs, -ɪz
AM saɪs, -ɪz
sycomore
BR 'sɪkəmɔː(r), -z
AM 'sɪkəˌmɔ(ə)r, -z
syconia
BR sʌɪ'kəʊnɪə(*r*)
AM saɪ'koʊniə
syconium
BR sʌɪ'kəʊnɪəm
AM saɪ'koʊniəm
sycophancy
BR 'sɪkəf(ə)ns|i, -ɪz
AM 'sɪkəfənsi, 'sɪkəˌfænsi, -z

sycophant
BR ˈsɪkəf(ə)nt, ˈsɪkəfant, -s
AM ˈsɪkəfənt, ˈsɪkəˌfænt, -s

sycophantic
BR ˌsɪkəˈfantɪk
AM ˌsɪkəˈfæn(t)ɪk

sycophantically
BR ˌsɪkəˈfantɪkli
AM ˌsɪkəˈfæn(t)ək(ə)li

sycoses
BR sʌɪˈkəʊsiːz
AM saɪˈkoʊˌsiz

sycosis
BR sʌɪˈkəʊsɪs
AM saɪˈkoʊsəs

Sydney
BR ˈsɪdni
AM ˈsɪdni

Sydneysider
BR ˈsɪdnɪˌsʌɪdə(r), -z
AM ˈsɪdniˌsaɪdər, -z

syenite
BR ˈsʌɪənʌɪt, -s
AM ˈsaɪəˌnaɪt, -s

syenitic
BR ˌsʌɪəˈnɪtɪk
AM ˌsaɪəˈnɪdɪk

Sykes
BR sʌɪks
AM saɪks

syllabary
BR ˈsɪləb(ə)r|i, -ɪz
AM ˈsɪləˌbɛri, -z

syllabi
BR ˈsɪləbʌɪ
AM ˈsɪləˌbaɪ

syllabic
BR sɪˈlabɪk
AM səˈlæbɪk

syllabically
BR sɪˈlabɪkli
AM səˈlæbək(ə)li

syllabication
BR sɪˌlabɪˈkeɪʃn
AM səˌlæbəˈkeɪʃən

syllabicity
BR ˌsɪləˈbɪsɪti
AM ˌsɪləˈbɪsɪdi

syllabification
BR sɪˌlabɪfɪˈkeɪʃn
AM səˌlæbəfəˈkeɪʃən

syllabify
BR sɪˈlabɪfʌɪ, -z, -ɪŋ, -d
AM səˈlæbəˌfaɪ, -z, -ɪŋ, -d

syllabise
BR ˈsɪləbʌɪz, -ɪz, -ɪŋ, -d
AM ˈsɪləˌbaɪz, -ɪz, -ɪŋ, -d

syllabize
BR ˈsɪləbʌɪz, -ɪz, -ɪŋ, -d
AM ˈsɪləˌbaɪz, -ɪz, -ɪŋ, -d

syllable
BR ˈsɪləbl, -z
AM ˈsɪləbəl, -z

syllabub
BR ˈsɪləbʌb, -z
AM ˈsɪləˌbəb, -z

syllabus
BR ˈsɪləbəs, -ɪz
AM ˈsɪləbəs, -əz

syllepses
BR sɪˈlɛpsiːz
AM səˈlɛpsiz

syllepsis
BR sɪˈlɛpsɪs
AM səˈlɛpsəs

sylleptic
BR sɪˈlɛptɪk
AM səˈlɛptɪk

sylleptically
BR sɪˈlɛptɪkli
AM səˈlɛptək(ə)li

syllogise
BR ˈsɪlədʒʌɪz, -ɪz, -ɪŋ, -d
AM ˈsɪləˌdʒaɪz, -ɪz, -ɪŋ, -d

syllogism
BR ˈsɪləˌdʒɪz(ə)m, -z
AM ˈsɪləˌdʒɪzəm, -z

syllogistic
BR ˌsɪləˈdɪstɪk
AM ˌsɪləˈdʒɪstɪk

syllogistically
BR ˌsɪləˈdʒɪstɪkli
AM ˌsɪləˈdʒɪstək(ə)li

syllogize
BR ˈsɪlədʒʌɪz, -ɪz, -ɪŋ, -d
AM ˈsɪləˌdʒaɪz, -ɪz, -ɪŋ, -d

sylph
BR sɪlf, -s
AM sɪlf, -s

Sylphides
BR sɪlˈfiːd
AM sɪlˈfid

sylphlike
BR ˈsɪlflʌɪk
AM ˈsɪlfˌlaɪk

sylva
BR ˈsɪlvə(r), -z
AM ˈsɪlvə, -z

sylvae
BR ˈsɪlviː
AM ˈsɪlvi, ˈsɪlˌvaɪ

sylvan
BR ˈsɪlv(ə)n
AM ˈsɪlvən

sylvatic
BR s(ɪ)lˈvatɪk
AM sɪlˈvædɪk

Sylvester
BR ˈsɪlvɛstə(r), ˈsɪlvɪstə(r), s(ɪ)lˈvɛstə(r)
AM sɪlˈvɛstər

Sylvia
BR ˈsɪlvɪə(r)
AM ˈsɪlviə

sylviculture
BR ˈsɪlvɪˌkʌltʃə(r)
AM ˈsɪlvəˌkəltʃər

Sylvie
BR ˈsɪlvi
AM ˈsɪlvi

sylvine
BR ˈsɪlviːn
AM ˈsɪlvin

sylvite
BR ˈsɪlvʌɪt
AM ˈsɪlvaɪt

symbiont
BR ˈsɪmbʌɪɒnt, ˈsɪmbɪɒnt, -s
AM ˈsɪmbaɪˌɑnt, ˈsɪmbiˌɑnt, -s

symbioses
BR ˌsɪmbʌɪˈəʊsiːz, ˌsɪmbɪˈəʊsiːz
AM ˌsɪmbaɪˈoʊˌsis, ˌsɪmbiˈoʊˌsis

symbiosis
BR ˌsɪmbʌɪˈəʊsɪs, ˌsɪmbɪˈəʊsɪs
AM ˌsɪmbaɪˈoʊsəs, ˌsɪmbiˈoʊsəs

symbiotic
BR ˌsɪmbʌɪˈɒtɪk, ˌsɪmbɪˈɒtɪk
AM ˌsɪmbaɪˈɑdɪk, ˌsɪmbiˈɑdɪk

symbiotically
BR ˌsɪmbʌɪˈɒtɪkli, ˌsɪmbɪˈɒtɪkli
AM ˌsɪmbaɪˈɑdək(ə)li, ˌsɪmbiˈɑdək(ə)li

symbol
BR ˈsɪmbl, -z
AM ˈsɪmbəl, -z

symbolic
BR sɪmˈbɒlɪk, -s
AM sɪmˈbɑlɪk, -s

symbolical
BR sɪmˈbɒlɪkl
AM sɪmˈbɑləkəl

symbolically
BR sɪmˈbɒlɪkli
AM sɪmˈbɑlək(ə)li

symbolisation
BR ˌsɪmbəlʌɪˈzeɪʃn, ˌsɪmbl̩ʌɪˈzeɪʃn
AM ˌsɪmbələˈzeɪʃən, ˌsɪmbəˌlaɪˈzeɪʃən

symbolise
BR ˈsɪmbəlʌɪz, ˈsɪmbl̩ʌɪz, -ɪz, -ɪŋ, -d
AM ˈsɪmbəˌlaɪz, -ɪz, -ɪŋ, -d

symbolism
BR ˈsɪmbəlɪz(ə)m, ˈsɪmbl̩ɪz(ə)m
AM ˈsɪmbəˌlɪzəm

symbolist
BR ˈsɪmbəlɪst, ˈsɪmbl̩ɪst, -s
AM ˈsɪmbələst, -s

symbolistic
BR ˌsɪmbəˈlɪstɪk, ˌsɪmblˈɪstɪk
AM ˌsɪmbəˈlɪstɪk

symbolization
BR ˌsɪmbəlʌɪˈzeɪʃn, ˌsɪmbl̩ʌɪˈzeɪʃn
AM ˌsɪmbələˈzeɪʃən, ˌsɪmbəˌlaɪˈzeɪʃən

symbolize
BR ˈsɪmbəlʌɪz, ˈsɪmbl̩ʌɪz, -ɪz, -ɪŋ, -d
AM ˈsɪmbəˌlaɪz, -ɪz, -ɪŋ, -d

symbology
BR sɪmˈbɒlədʒi
AM sɪmˈbɑlədʒi

symbolology
BR ˌsɪmbəˈlɒlədʒi, ˌsɪmblˈɒlədʒi
AM ˌsɪmbəˈlɑlədʒi

Symes
BR sʌɪmz
AM saɪmz

Symington
BR ˈsɪmɪŋt(ə)n, ˈsʌɪmɪŋt(ə)n
AM ˈsaɪmɪŋtən

symmetric
BR sɪˈmɛtrɪk
AM səˈmɛtrɪk

symmetrical
BR sɪˈmɛtrɪkl
AM səˈmɛtrəkəl

symmetrically
BR sɪˈmɛtrɪkli
AM səˈmɛtrək(ə)li

symmetricalness
BR sɪˈmɛtrɪklnəs
AM səˈmɛtrəkəlnəs

symmetrise
BR ˈsɪmətrʌɪz, -ɪz, -ɪŋ, -d
AM ˈsɪməˌtraɪz, -ɪz, -ɪŋ, -d

symmetrize
BR ˈsɪmətrʌɪz, -ɪz, -ɪŋ, -d
AM ˈsɪməˌtraɪz, -ɪz, -ɪŋ, -d

symmetrophobia
BR ˌsɪmətrəˈfəʊbɪə(r)
AM ˌsɪmətrəˈfoʊbiə

symmetry
BR ˈsɪmɪtri
AM ˈsɪmətri

Symon
BR ˈsʌɪmən
AM ˈsaɪmən

Symonds
BR ˈsɪm(ə)n(d)z, ˈsʌɪmən(d)z
AM ˈsaɪmənz

Symonds Yat
BR ˌsɪm(ə)n(d)z ˈjat
AM ˌsaɪmənz ˈjæt

Symons
BR ˈsɪm(ə)nz, ˈsʌɪm(ə)nz
AM ˈsaɪmənz

sympathectomy
BR ˌsɪmpəˈθɛktəm|i, -ɪz
AM ˌsɪmpəˈθɛktəmi, -z

sympathetic
BR ˌsɪmpəˈθɛtɪk
AM ˌsɪmpəˈθɛdɪk

sympathetically
BR ˌsɪmpəˈθɛtɨkli
AM ˌsɪmpəˈθɛdək(ə)li

sympathise
BR ˈsɪmpəθʌɪz, -ɨz, -ɪŋ, -d
AM ˈsɪmpəˌθaɪz, -ɨz, -ɪŋ, -d

sympathiser
BR ˈsɪmpəθʌɪzə(r), -z
AM ˈsɪmpəˌθaɪzər, -z

sympathize
BR ˈsɪmpəθʌɪz, -ɨz, -ɪŋ, -d
AM ˈsɪmpəˌθaɪz, -ɨz, -ɪŋ, -d

sympathizer
BR ˈsɪmpəθʌɪzə(r), -z
AM ˈsɪmpəˌθaɪzər, -z

sympathy
BR ˈsɪmpəθ|i, -ɪz
AM ˈsɪmpəθi, -z

sympatric
BR sɪmˈpatrɪk
AM sɪmˈpætrɪk

sympetalous
BR sɪmˈpɛtl̩əs
AM sɪmˈpɛdl̩əs

symphonic
BR sɪmˈfɒnɪk
AM sɪmˈfɑnɪk

symphonically
BR sɪmˈfɒnɪkli
AM sɪmˈfɑnək(ə)li

symphonious
BR sɪmˈfəʊnɪəs
AM sɪmˈfoʊniəs

symphonist
BR ˈsɪmfənɪst, -s
AM ˈsɪmfənəst, -s

symphony
BR ˈsɪmfən|i, -ɪz
AM ˈsɪmfəni, -z

symphyllous
BR sɪmˈfɪləs
AM sɪm(p)ˈfɪləs

symphyseal
BR sɪmˈfɪzɪəl
AM sɪmˈfɪziəl

symphyses
BR ˈsɪmfɨsiːz
AM ˈsɪmfəˌsiz

symphysial
BR sɪmˈfɪzɪəl
AM sɪmˈfɪziəl

symphysis
BR ˈsɪmfɨsɪs
AM ˈsɪm(p)fəsəs

symplasm
BR ˈsɪmplaz(ə)m
AM ˈsɪmˌplæzm

symplast
BR ˈsɪmplast, -s
AM ˈsɪmˌplæst, -s

sympodia
BR sɪmˈpəʊdɪə(r)
AM sɪmˈpoʊdiə

sympodial
BR sɪmˈpəʊdɪəl
AM sɪmˈpoʊdiəl

sympodially
BR sɪmˈpəʊdɪəli
AM sɪmˈpoʊdiəli

sympodium
BR sɪmˈpəʊdɪəm
AM sɪmˈpoʊdiəm

symposia
BR sɪmˈpəʊzɪə(r)
AM sɪmˈpoʊziə

symposiac
BR sɪmˈpəʊzɪak, -s
AM sɪmˈpoʊziˌæk, -s

symposial
BR sɪmˈpəʊzɪəl
AM sɪmˈpoʊziəl

symposiarch
BR sɪmˈpəʊzɪɑːk, -s
AM sɪmˈpoʊziˌɑrk, -s

symposiast
BR sɪmˈpəʊzɪast, -s
AM sɪmˈpoʊziəst, -s

symposium
BR sɪmˈpəʊzɪəm, -z
AM sɪmˈpoʊziəm, -z

symptom
BR ˈsɪm(p)təm, -z
AM ˈsɪm(p)təm, -z

symptomatic
BR ˌsɪm(p)təˈmatɪk
AM ˌsɪm(p)təˈmædɪk

symptomatically
BR ˌsɪm(p)təˈmatɪkli
AM ˌsɪm(p)təˈmædək(ə)li

symptomatology
BR ˌsɪm(p)təməˈtɒlədʒi
AM ˌsɪm(p)təməˈtɑlədʒi

symptomless
BR ˈsɪm(p)təmləs
AM ˈsɪm(p)təmləs

synaereses
BR sɨˈnɪərəsiːz
AM səˈnɛrəˌsiz, sɨˈnɪrəˌsiz

synaeresis
BR sɨˈnɪərəsɪs
AM səˈnɛrəsəs, səˈnɪrəsəs

synaesthesia
BR ˌsɪnɨsˈθiːzɪə(r), ˌsɪnɨsˈθiːʒə(r)
AM ˌsɪnɨsˈθiʒ(i)ə, ˌsɪnɨsˈθiziə

synaesthetic
BR ˌsɪnɨsˈθɛtɪk
AM ˌsɪnɨsˈθɛdɪk

synagogal
BR ˌsɪnəˈgɒgl
AM ˌsɪnəˈgɑgəl

synagogical
BR ˌsɪnəˈgɒdʒɪkl, ˌsɪnəˈgɒgɪkl
AM ˌsɪnəˈgɑdʒəkəl

synagogue
BR ˈsɪnəgɒg, -z
AM ˈsɪnəˌgɑg, -z

synallagmatic
BR ˌsɪnəlagˈmatɪk
AM ˌsɪnəlægˈmædɪk

synantherous
BR sɨˈnanθ(ə)rəs
AM səˈnænθərəs

synanthous
BR sɨˈnanθəs
AM səˈnænθəs

synapse
BR ˈsʌɪnaps, ˈsɪnaps, -ɨz
AM ˈsɪnˌæps, -əz

synapses
BR sɨˈnapsiːz
AM səˈnæpˌsiz

synapsis
BR sɨˈnapsɪs
AM səˈnæpsəs

synaptic
BR sɨˈnaptɪk
AM səˈnæptɪk

synaptically
BR sɨˈnaptɨkli
AM səˈnæptək(ə)li

synarchy
BR ˈsɪnɑːki
AM ˈsɪnərki

synarthroses
BR ˌsɪnɑːˈθrəʊsiːz
AM ˌsɪˌnɑrˈθroʊˌsiz

synarthrosis
BR ˌsɪnɑːˈθrəʊsɪs
AM ˌsɪˌnɑrˈθroʊsəs

sync
BR sɪŋ|k, -ks, -kɪŋ, -(k)t
AM sɪŋk, -s, -ɪŋ, -t

syncarp
BR ˈsɪŋkɑːp, -s
AM ˈsɪnˌkɑrp, -s

syncarpous
BR sɪnˈkɑːpəs
AM sɪnˈkɑrpəs

synch
BR sɪŋ|k, -ks, -kɪŋ, -(k)t
AM sɪŋk, -s, -ɪŋ, -t

synchondroses
BR ˌsɪŋkɒnˈdrəʊsiːz
AM ˌsɪŋkənˈdroʊˌsiz

synchondrosis
BR ˌsɪŋkɒnˈdrəʊsɪs
AM ˌsɪŋkənˈdroʊsəs

synchro
BR ˈsɪŋkrəʊ
AM ˈsɪŋkroʊ, ˈsɪnkroʊ

synchrocyclotron
BR ˌsɪŋkrəʊˈsʌɪklətrɒn, -z
AM ˌsɪŋkrəˈsaɪkləˌtrɑn, ˌsɪkrəˈsaɪkləˌtrɑn, -z

synchroflash
BR ˈsɪŋkrəflaʃ, -ɨz
AM ˈsɪŋkroʊˌflæʃ, ˈsɪnkroʊˌflæʃ, -əz

synchromesh
BR ˈsɪŋkrəmɛʃ
AM ˈsɪŋkroʊˌmɛʃ, ˈsɪnkroʊˌmɛʃ

synchronic
BR sɪnˈkrɒnɪk, sɪŋˈkrɒnɪk
AM sɪŋˈkrɑnɪk, sɪnˈkrɑnɪk

synchronically
BR sɪnˈkrɒnɨkli, sɪŋˈkrɒnɨkli
AM sɪŋˈkrɑnək(ə)li, sɪnˈkrɑnək(ə)li

synchronicity
BR ˌsɪŋkrəˈnɪsɨti
AM ˌsɪŋkrəˈnɪsɨdi, ˌsɪnkrəˈnɪsɨdi

synchronisation
BR ˌsɪŋkrənʌɪˈzeɪʃn
AM ˌsɪŋkrənəˈzeɪʃən, ˌsɪŋkrəˌnaɪˈzeɪʃən, ˌsɪnkrənəˈzeɪʃən, ˌsɪnkrəˌnaɪˈzeɪʃən

synchronise
BR ˈsɪŋkrənʌɪz, -ɨz, -ɪŋ, -d
AM ˈsɪŋkrəˌnaɪz, ˈsɪnkrəˌnaɪz, -ɨz, -ɪŋ, -d

synchroniser
BR ˈsɪŋkrənʌɪzə(r)
AM ˈsɪŋkrəˌnaɪzər, ˈsɪnkrəˌnaɪzər

synchronism
BR ˈsɪŋkrənɪz(ə)m
AM ˈsɪŋkrəˌnɪzəm, ˈsɪnkrəˌnɪzəm

synchronistic
BR ˌsɪŋkrəˈnɪstɪk
AM ˌsɪŋkrəˈnɪstɪk, ˌsɪnkrəˈnɪstɪk

synchronistically
BR ˌsɪŋkrəˈnɪstɨkli
AM ˌsɪŋkrəˈnɪstɨk(ə)li, ˌsɪnkrəˈnɪstɨk(ə)li

synchronization
BR ˌsɪŋkrənʌɪˈzeɪʃn
AM ˌsɪŋkrənəˈzeɪʃən, ˌsɪŋkrəˌnaɪˈzeɪʃən, ˌsɪnkrənəˈzeɪʃən, ˌsɪnkrəˌnaɪˈzeɪʃən

synchronize
BR ˈsɪŋkrənʌɪz, -ɨz, -ɪŋ, -d
AM ˈsɪŋkrəˌnaɪz, ˈsɪnkrəˌnaɪz, -ɨz, -ɪŋ, -d

synchronizer
BR ˈsɪŋkrənʌɪzə(r), -z

AM ˈsɪŋkrəˌnaɪzər, ˈsɪnkrəˌnaɪzər, -z

synchronous
BR ˈsɪŋkrənəs
AM ˈsɪŋkrənəs, ˈsɪnkrənəs

synchronously
BR ˈsɪŋkrənəsli
AM ˈsɪŋkrənəsli, ˈsɪnkrənəsli

synchronousness
BR ˈsɪŋkrənəsnəs
AM ˈsɪŋkrənəsnəs, ˈsɪnkrənəsnəs

synchrony
BR ˈsɪŋkrəni
AM ˈsɪŋkrəni, ˈsɪnkrəni

synchrotron
BR ˈsɪŋkrətrɒn, -z
AM ˈsɪŋkrəˌtrɑn, ˈsɪnkrəˌtrɑn, -z

synclinal
BR sɪnˈklʌɪnl, sɪŋˈklʌɪnl
AM ˌsɪŋˈklaɪnəl

syncline
BR ˈsɪŋklʌɪn, -z
AM ˈsɪŋˌklaɪn, -z

syncopal
BR ˈsɪŋkəpl
AM ˈsɪŋkəpəl

syncopate
BR ˈsɪŋkəpeɪt, -s, -ɪŋ, -ɨd
AM ˈsɪŋkəˌpeɪ|t, -ts, -dɪŋ, -dɨd

syncopation
BR ˌsɪŋkəˈpeɪʃn
AM ˌsɪŋkəˈpeɪʃən

syncopator
BR ˈsɪŋkəpeɪtə(r), -z
AM ˈsɪŋkəˌpeɪdər, -z

syncope
BR ˈsɪŋkəpi
AM ˈsɪŋkəpi

syncretic
BR sɪnˈkrɛtɪk, sɪŋˈkrɛtɪk
AM sɪŋˈkrɛdɪk, sɪnˈkrɛdɪk

syncretise
BR ˈsɪŋkrɪtʌɪz, -ɨz, -ɪŋ, -d
AM ˈsɪŋkrəˌtaɪz, ˈsɪnkrəˌtaɪz, -ɨz, -ɪŋ, -d

syncretism
BR ˈsɪŋkrɪtɪz(ə)m
AM ˈsɪŋkrəˌtɪzəm, ˈsɪnkrəˌtɪzəm

syncretist
BR ˈsɪŋkrɪtɪst, -s
AM ˈsɪŋkrədəst, ˈsɪnkrədəst, -s

syncretistic
BR ˌsɪŋkrɪˈtɪstɪk
AM ˌsɪŋkrəˈtɪstɪk, ˌsɪnkrəˈtɪstɪk

syncretize
BR ˈsɪŋkrɪtʌɪz, -ɨz, -ɪŋ, -d
AM ˈsɪŋkrəˌtaɪz, ˈsɪnkrəˌtaɪz, -ɨz, -ɪŋ, -d

syncytia
BR sɪnˈsɪtɪə(r)
AM sɪnˈsɪʃə

syncytial
BR sɪnˈsɪʃl
AM sɪnˈsɪʃəl

syncytium
BR sɪnˈsɪtɪəm
AM sɪnˈsɪʃəm

syndactyl
BR sɪnˈdakt(ɪ)l
AM sɪnˈdæktl

syndactylism
BR sɪnˈdaktɪlɪz(ə)m, sɪnˈdaktl̩ɪz(ə)m
AM sɪnˈdæktlˌɪzəm

syndactylous
BR sɪnˈdaktɪləs, sɪnˈdaktl̩əs
AM sɪnˈdæktələs

syndactyly
BR sɪnˈdaktɪli, sɪnˈdaktl̩i
AM sɪnˈdæktəli

syndeses
BR ˈsɪndɪsiːz
AM ˈsɪndəˌsiz

syndesis
BR ˈsɪndɪsɪs
AM ˈsɪndəsəs

syndesmoses
BR ˌsɪndɛzˈməʊsiːz
AM ˌsɪnˌdɛzˈmoʊˌsiz

syndesmosis
BR ˌsɪndɛzˈməʊsɪs
AM ˌsɪnˌdɛzˈmoʊsəs

syndetic
BR sɪnˈdɛtɪk
AM sɪnˈdɛdɪk

syndic
BR ˈsɪndɪk, -s
AM ˈsɪndɪk, -s

syndical
BR ˈsɪndɪkl
AM ˈsɪndɪkəl

syndicalism
BR ˈsɪndɪkəlɪz(ə)m, ˈsɪndɪkl̩ɪz(ə)m
AM ˈsɪndəkəˌlɪzəm

syndicalist
BR ˈsɪndɪkəlɪst, ˈsɪndɪkl̩ɪst, -s
AM ˈsɪndəkələst, -s

syndicate¹
noun
BR ˈsɪndɪkət, -s
AM ˈsɪndɪkɪt, -s

syndicate²
verb
BR ˈsɪndɪkeɪt, -s, -ɪŋ, -ɨd
AM ˈsɪndəˌkeɪ|t, -ts, -dɪŋ, -dɨd

syndication
BR ˌsɪndɪˈkeɪʃn
AM ˌsɪndəˈkeɪʃən

syndrome
BR ˈsɪndrəʊm, -z
AM ˈsɪnˌdroʊm, -z

syndromic
BR sɪnˈdrɒmɪk
AM sɪnˈdrɑmɪk

syne
BR sʌɪn
AM saɪn

synecdoche
BR sɪˈnɛkdəki
AM səˈnɛkdəki

synecdochic
BR sɪˈnɛkdəkɪk
AM səˈnɛkdəkɪk

synecious
BR sɪˈniːʃəs
AM səˈniʃəs

synecological
BR ˌsiːniːkəˈlɒdʒɪkl, ˌsɪnɛkəˈlɒdʒɪkl
AM ¦sɪnˌɛkəˈlɑdʒəkəl, ¦sɪnˌikəˈlɑdʒəkəl

synecologist
BR ˌsɪnɪˈkɒlədʒɪst, -s
AM ¦sɪniˈkɑlədʒəst, ¦sɪnəˈkɑlədʒəst, -s

synecology
BR ˌsɪnɪˈkɒlədʒi
AM ¦sɪnˌiˈkɑlədʒi, ¦sɪnˌɛˈkɑlədʒi

syneresis
BR sɪˈnɪərəsiːz
AM səˈnɛrəˌsiz, sɪˈnɪrəˌsiz

syneresis
BR sɪˈnɪərəsɪs
AM səˈnɛrəsəs, səˈnɪrəsəs

synergetic
BR ˌsɪnəˈdʒɛtɪk
AM ˌsɪnərˈdʒɛdɪk

synergic
BR sɪˈnəːdʒɪk
AM səˈnərdʒɪk

synergism
BR ˈsɪnədʒɪz(ə)m
AM ˈsɪnərˌdʒɪzəm

synergist
BR ˈsɪnədʒɪst, -s
AM ˈsɪnərdʒəst, -s

synergistic
BR ˌsɪnəˈdʒɪstɪk
AM ˌsɪnərˈdʒɪstɪk

synergistically
BR ˌsɪnəˈdʒɪstɪkli
AM ¦sɪnərˈdʒɪstək(ə)li

synergy
BR ˈsɪnədʒi
AM ˈsɪnərdʒi

synesis
BR ˈsɪnɪsɪs
AM ˈsɪnəsəs

synesthesia
BR ˌsɪnɪsˈθiːzɪə(r), ˌsɪnɪsˈθiːʒə(r)
AM ˌsɪnɪsˈθiʒ(i)ə, ˌsɪnɪsˈθiziə

syngamous
BR ˈsɪŋgəməs
AM ˈsɪŋgəməs

syngamy
BR ˈsɪŋgəmi
AM ˈsɪŋgəmi

Synge
BR sɪŋ
AM sɪŋ

syngenesis
BR sɪnˈdʒɛnɪsɪs
AM sɪnˈdʒɛnəsəs

syngnathous
BR ˈsɪŋnəθəs
AM ˈsɪŋnəθəs

synizeses
BR ˌsɪnɪˈziːsiːz
AM ˌsɪnəˈziˌsiz

synizesis
BR ˌsɪnɪˈziːsɪs
AM ˌsɪnəˈzisɪs

synod
BR ˈsɪnəd, ˈsɪnɒd, -z
AM ˈsɪnəd, -z

synodal
BR ˈsɪnədl
AM ˈsɪnədəl

synodic
BR sɪˈnɒdɪk
AM səˈnɑdɪk

synodical
BR sɪˈnɒdɪkl
AM səˈnɑdəkəl

synodically
BR sɪˈnɒdɪkli
AM səˈnɑdək(ə)li

synoecious
BR sɪˈniːʃəs
AM səˈniʃəs

synonym
BR ˈsɪnənɪm, -z
AM ˈsɪnəˌnɪm, -z

synonymic
BR ˌsɪnəˈnɪmɪk
AM ˌsɪnəˈnɪmɪk

synonymity
BR ˌsɪnəˈnɪmɪti
AM ˌsɪnəˈnɪmɪdi

synonymous
BR sɪˈnɒnɪməs
AM səˈnɑnəməs

synonymously
BR sɪˈnɒnɪməsli
AM səˈnɑnəməsli

synonymousness
BR sɪˈnɒnɪməsnəs
AM səˈnɑnəməsnəs

synonymy
BR sɪˈnɒnɪmi
AM səˈnɑnəmi

synopses
BR sɪˈnɒpsiːz

AM sə'nɑpˌsiz
synopsis
BR sɪ'nɒpsɪs
AM sə'nɑpsəs
synopsise
BR sɪ'nɒpsʌɪz, -ɪz, -ɪŋ, -d
AM sə'nɑpˌsaɪz, -ɪz, -ɪŋ, -d
synopsize
BR sɪ'nɒpsʌɪz, -ɪz, -ɪŋ, -d
AM sə'nɑpˌsaɪz, -ɪz, -ɪŋ, -d
synoptic
BR sɪ'nɒptɪk, -s
AM sə'nɑptɪk, -s
synoptical
BR sɪ'nɒptɪkl
AM sə'nɑptəkəl
synoptically
BR sɪ'nɒptɪkli
AM sə'nɑptək(ə)li
synoptist
BR sɪ'nɒptɪst, -s
AM sə'nɑptəst, -s
synostoses
BR ˌsɪnɒ'stəʊsiːz
AM ˌsɪnə'stoʊsiz
synostosis
BR ˌsɪnɒ'stəʊsɪs
AM ˌsɪˌnɑ'stoʊsəs
synovia
BR sʌɪ'nəʊvɪə(*r*), sɪ'nəʊvɪə(*r*)
AM sə'noʊviə
synovial
BR sʌɪ'nəʊvɪəl, sɪ'nəʊvɪəl
AM sə'noʊviəl
synovitis
BR ˌsʌɪnə(ʊ)'vʌɪtɪs, ˌsɪnə'vʌɪtɪs
AM ˌsɪnə'vaɪdɪs
syntactic
BR sɪn'taktɪk
AM sɪn'tæktɪk
syntactical
BR sɪn'taktɪkl
AM sɪn'tæktəkəl
syntactically
BR sɪn'taktɪkli
AM sɪn'tæktək(ə)li
syntagm
BR 'sɪntam, -z
AM 'sɪnˌtæm, -z
syntagma
BR sɪn'tagmə(*r*)
AM sɪn'tægmə
syntagmata
BR sɪn'tagmətə(*r*)
AM sɪn'tægmədə
syntagmatic
BR ˌsɪntag'matɪk
AM ˌsɪnˌtæg'mædɪk
syntagmatically
BR ˌsɪntag'matɪkli
AM ˌsɪnˌtæg'mædək(ə)li
syntagmic
BR sɪn'tagmɪk
AM ˌsɪn'tægmɪk
syntax
BR 'sɪntaks
AM 'sɪnˌtæks
syntheses
BR 'sɪnθɪsiːz
AM 'sɪnθəˌsiz
synthesis
BR 'sɪnθɪsɪs
AM 'sɪnθəsəs
synthesise
BR 'sɪnθɪsʌɪz, -ɪz, -ɪŋ, -d
AM 'sɪnθəˌsaɪz, -ɪz, -ɪŋ, -d
synthesiser
BR 'sɪnθɪsʌɪzə(r), -z
AM 'sɪnθəˌsaɪzər, -z
synthesist
BR 'sɪnθɪsɪst, -s
AM 'sɪnθəsəst, -s
synthesize
BR 'sɪnθɪsʌɪz, -ɪz, -ɪŋ, -d
AM 'sɪnθəˌsaɪz, -ɪz, -ɪŋ, -d
synthesizer
BR 'sɪnθɪsʌɪzə(r), -z
AM 'sɪnθəˌsaɪzər, -z
synthetic
BR sɪn'θɛtɪk, -s
AM sɪn'θɛdɪk, -s
synthetical
BR sɪn'θɛtɪkl
AM sɪn'θɛdəkəl
synthetically
BR sɪn'θɛtɪkli
AM sɪn'θɛdək(ə)li
synthetise
BR 'sɪnθɪtʌɪz, -ɪz, -ɪŋ, -d
AM 'sɪnθəˌtaɪz, -ɪz, -ɪŋ, -d
synthetize
BR 'sɪnθɪtʌɪz, -ɪz, -ɪŋ, -d
AM 'sɪnθəˌtaɪz, -ɪz, -ɪŋ, -d
syntype
BR 'sɪntʌɪp, -s
AM 'sɪnˌtaɪp, -s
Syon
BR 'sʌɪən
AM 'saɪən
syphilis
BR 'sɪfɪlɪs, 'sɪfl̩ɪs
AM 'sɪf(ə)lɪs, 'sɪfələs
syphilise
BR 'sɪfɪlʌɪz, 'sɪfl̩ʌɪz, -ɪz, -ɪŋ, -d
AM 'sɪf(ə)ˌlaɪz, -ɪz, -ɪŋ, -d
syphilitic
BR ˌsɪfɪ'lɪtɪk
AM ˌsɪf(ə)'lɪdɪk
syphilize
BR 'sɪfɪlʌɪz, 'sɪfl̩ʌɪz, -ɪz, -ɪŋ, -d
AM 'sɪf(ə)ˌlaɪz, -ɪz, -ɪŋ, -d
syphiloid
BR 'sɪfɪlɔɪd, 'sɪfl̩ɔɪd
AM 'sɪf(ə)ˌlɔɪd
syphon
BR 'sʌɪfn̩, -nz, -n̩ɪŋ\-(ə)nɪŋ, -nd
AM 'saɪfl̩ən, -ənz, -(ə)nɪŋ, -ənd
Syracuse[1]
New York
BR 'sɪrəkjuːs, 'sɪrəkjuːz
AM 'sɪrəˌkjuz
Syracuse[2]
Sicily
BR 'sʌɪrəkjuːz, 'sʌɪrəkjuːs
AM 'sɪrəˌkjus, 'sɪrəˌkjuz
syren
BR 'sʌɪrən, -z
AM 'saɪrən, -z
syrette®
BR sɪ'rɛt, -s
AM sə'rɛt, -s
Syria
BR 'sɪrɪə(*r*)
AM 'sɪriə
Syriac
BR 'sɪrɪak
AM 'sɪriˌæk
Syrian
BR 'sɪrɪən, -z
AM 'sɪriən, -z
syringa
BR sɪ'rɪŋgə(*r*), -z
AM sə'rɪŋgə, -z
syringe
BR sɪ'rɪn(d)ʒ, -ɪz, -ɪŋ, -d
AM sə'rɪndʒ, 'sɪrɪndʒ, -ɪz, -ɪŋ, -d
syringeal
BR sɪ'rɪn(d)ʒɪəl
AM sə'rɪndʒiəl
syrinx
BR 'sɪrɪŋks, -ɪz
AM 'sɪrɪŋks, -ɪz
Syro-Phoenician
BR ˌsʌɪrəʊfɪ'nɪʃn, ˌsʌɪrəʊfɪ'niːʃn, -z
AM ˌsaɪroʊfə'nɪʃən, ˌsɪroʊfə'nɪʃən, -z
syrphid
BR 'səːfɪd, -z
AM 'sərfəd, -z
syrup
BR 'sɪrəp, -s
AM 'sɪrəp, -s
syrupy
BR 'sɪrəpi
AM 'sɪrəpi
syssarcoses
BR ˌsɪsɑː'kəʊsiːz
AM ˌsɪsɑr'koʊˌsiz
syssarcosis
BR ˌsɪsɑː'kəʊsɪs
AM ˌsɪsɑr'koʊsəs
systaltic
BR sɪ'staltɪk
AM sə'stɔltɪk, sə'stæltɪk, sə'stɑltɪk
system
BR 'sɪstɪm, -z
AM 'sɪstɪm, -z
systematic
BR ˌsɪstɪ'matɪk, -s
AM ˌsɪstə'mædɪk, -s
systematically
BR ˌsɪstɪ'matɪkli
AM ˌsɪstə'mædək(ə)li
systematisation
BR ˌsɪstɪmətʌɪ'zeɪʃn
AM ˌsɪstəmədə'zeɪʃən, ˌsɪstəməˌtaɪ'zeɪʃən
systematise
BR 'sɪstɪmətʌɪz, -ɪz, -ɪŋ, -d
AM 'sɪstəməˌtaɪz, -ɪz, -ɪŋ, -d
systematiser
BR 'sɪstɪmətʌɪzə(r)
AM 'sɪstəməˌtaɪzər
systematism
BR 'sɪstɪmətɪz(ə)m
AM 'sɪstəməˌtɪzəm
systematist
BR 'sɪstɪmətɪst, -s
AM 'sɪstəmədəst, -s
systematization
BR ˌsɪstɪmətʌɪ'zeɪʃn
AM ˌsɪstəmədə'zeɪʃən, ˌsɪstəməˌtaɪ'zeɪʃən
systematize
BR 'sɪstɪmətʌɪz, -ɪz, -ɪŋ, -d
AM 'sɪstəməˌtaɪz, -ɪz, -ɪŋ, -d
systematizer
BR 'sɪstɪmətʌɪzə(r), -z
AM 'sɪstəməˌtaɪzər, -z
systemic
BR sɪ'stiːmɪk, sɪ'stɛmɪk, -s
AM sə'stɛmɪk, -s
systemically
BR sɪ'stiːmɪkli, sɪ'stɛmɪkli
AM sə'stɛmək(ə)li
systemisation
BR ˌsɪstɪmʌɪ'zeɪʃn
AM ˌsɪstəmə'zeɪʃən, ˌsɪstəˌmaɪ'zeɪʃən
systemise
BR 'sɪstɪmʌɪz, -ɪz, -ɪŋ, -d
AM 'sɪstəˌmaɪz, -ɪz, -ɪŋ, -d
systemiser
BR 'sɪstɪmʌɪzə(r), -z
AM 'sɪstəˌmaɪzər, -z
systemization
BR ˌsɪstɪmʌɪ'zeɪʃn
AM ˌsɪstəmə'zeɪʃən, ˌsɪstəˌmaɪ'zeɪʃən

systemize
BR ˈsɪstɪmʌɪz, -ɪz, -ɪŋ, -d
AM ˈsɪstəˌmaɪz, -ɪz, -ɪŋ, -d

systemizer
BR ˈsɪstɪmʌɪzə(r), -z
AM ˈsɪstəˌmaɪzər, -z

systemless
BR ˈsɪstɪmlɪs
AM ˈsɪstɪmlɪs

systole
BR ˈsɪstəli
AM ˈsɪstəli

systolic
BR sɪˈstɒlɪk
AM səˈstɑlɪk

Syston
BR ˈsʌɪst(ə)n
AM ˈsaɪstən

syzygy
BR ˈsɪzɪdʒ|i, -ɪz
AM ˈsɪzɪdʒi, -z

Szechuan
BR ˌsɛ(t)ʃˈwɑːn
AM ˈsɛ(t)ʃˌwɑn

Szechwan
BR ˌsɛ(t)ʃˈwɑːn
AM ˈsɛ(t)ʃˈwɑn

Szeged
BR ˈsɛɡɛd
AM ˈsɛɡˌɛd

Tt

t
BR tiː, -z
AM ti, -z
't
it
BR t
AM t
TA
BR ˌtiːˈeɪ, -z
AM ˌtiˈeɪ, -z
ta
BR tɑː(r)
AM tɑ
Taal
BR tɑːl
AM tɑl
tab
BR tab, -z
AM tæb, -z
tabard
BR ˈtabəd, ˈtabɑːd, -z
AM ˈtæbərd, -z
tabaret
BR ˈtabərɪt, -s
AM ˈtæbərət, -s
Tabasco
BR təˈbaskəʊ
AM təˈbæskoʊ
tabby
BR ˈtab|i, -ɪz
AM ˈtæbi, -z
tabernacle
BR ˈtabənakl, -z, -d
AM ˈtæbərˌnækəl, -z, -d
tabes
BR ˈteɪbiːz
AM ˈteɪˌbiz
tabetic
BR təˈbɛtɪk
AM təˈbɛdɪk
tabinet
BR ˈtabɪnɪt, -s
AM ˈtæbəˌnɛt, -s
Tabitha
BR ˈtabɪθə(r)
AM ˈtæbəθə
tabla
BR ˈtablə(r), -z
AM ˈtæblə, -z
tablature
BR ˈtablətʃə(r), -z
AM ˈtæblətʃər, ˈtæblətʃʊ(ə)r, -z
table
BR ˈteɪb|l, -lz, -l̩ɪŋ\-lɪŋ, -ld
AM ˈteɪbəl, -əlz, -(ə)lɪŋ, -əld
tableau
BR ˈtabləʊ
AM ˌtæˈbloʊ, ˌtɑˈbloʊ
tableau vivant
BR ˌtabləʊ ˈviːvɒ̃, -z
AM ˌtɑˈbloʊ vɪˈvɑnt, -s
tableaux
BR ˈtabləʊz
AM ˌtæˈbloʊz, ˌtɑˈbloʊz
tableaux vivants
BR ˌtabləʊ ˈviːvɒ̃(z)
AM ˌtɑˈbloʊ vɪˈvɑnts
tablecloth
BR ˈteɪblklɒ|θ, -θs\-ðz
AM ˈteɪbəlˌklɔ|θ, ˈteɪbəlˌklɑ|θ, -θs\-ðz
table d'hôte
BR ˌtɑːbl ˈdəʊt
AM ˌtɑbəl ˈdoʊt
tableful
BR ˈteɪblfʊl, -z
AM ˈteɪbəlˌfʊl, -z
table lamp
BR ˈteɪbl lamp, -s
AM ˈteɪbəl ˌ(l)æmp, -s
tableland
BR ˈteɪblland
AM ˈteɪbəlˌ(l)ænd
Table Mountain
BR ˌteɪbl ˈmaʊntɪn
AM ˌteɪbəl ˈmaʊntn
tables d'hôte
BR ˌtɑːbl ˈdəʊt
AM ˌtɑbəl(z) ˈdoʊt
tablespoon
BR ˈteɪblspuːn, -z
AM ˈteɪbəlˌspun, -z
tablespoonful
BR ˈteɪblˌspuːnfʊl, -z
AM ˈteɪbəlˈspunˌfʊl, -z
tablespoonsful
BR ˈteɪblˌspuːnzfʊl
AM ˈteɪbəlˈspunzˌfʊl
tablet
BR ˈtablɪt, -s
AM ˈtæblət, -s
tabletop
BR ˈteɪbltɒp, -s
AM ˈteɪbəlˌtɑp, -s
tableware
BR ˈteɪblwɛː(r)
AM ˈteɪbəlˌwɛ(ə)r
tablier
BR ˈtablɪeɪ, -z
AM tɑbliˈeɪ, -z
tabloid
BR ˈtablɔɪd, -z
AM ˈtæbˌlɔɪd, -z
taboo
BR təˈbuː, -z, -ɪŋ, -d
AM təˈbu, -z, -ɪŋ, -d
tabor
BR ˈteɪbə(r), ˈteɪbɔː(r), -z
AM ˈteɪbər, -z
taboret
BR ˈtabərɪt, ˈtabəreɪ, -s
AM ˌtæbəˈrɛt, ˈtæbərət, -s
tabouret
BR ˈtabərɪt, ˈtabəreɪ, -s
AM ˌtæbəˈrɛt, ˈtæbərət, -s
Tabriz
BR təˈbriːz
AM təˈbriz
tabu
BR təˈbuː, -z
AM təˈbu, -z
tabula
BR ˈtabjʉlə(r)
AM ˈtæbjələ
tabulae
BR ˈtabjʉliː
AM ˈtæbjəli, ˈtæbjəˌlaɪ
tabular
BR ˈtabjʉlə(r)
AM ˈtæbjələr
tabula rasa
BR ˌtabjʉlə ˈrɑːzə(r)
AM ˌtɑb(j)ʊlə ˈrɑzə
tabularly
BR ˈtabjʉləli
AM ˈtæbjələrli
tabulate
BR ˈtabjʉleɪt, -s, -ɪŋ, -ɪd
AM ˈtæbjəˌleɪ|t, -ts, -dɪŋ, -dɨd
tabulation
BR ˌtabjʉˈleɪʃn, -z
AM ˌtæbjəˈleɪʃən, -z
tabulator
BR ˈtabjʉleɪtə(r), -z
AM ˈtæbjəˌleɪdər, -z
tabun
BR ˈtɑːbʊn
AM ˈtɑbʊn
tacamahac
BR ˈtak(ə)məhak, -s
AM ˈtæk(ə)məˌhæk, -s
tacet
BR ˈtasɪt, ˈteɪsɪt, -s
AM ˈteɪsət, ˈtɑˌkɛt, -s
tach
BR tak, -s
AM tæk, -s
tachism
BR ˈtaʃɪz(ə)m
AM ˈtæˌʃɪzəm
tachistoscope
BR taˈkɪstəskəʊp, təˈkɪstəskəʊp, -s
AM təˈkɪstəˌskoʊp, -s
tachistoscopic
BR taˌkɪstəˈskɒpɪk, təˌkɪstəˈskɒpɪk
AM təˌkɪstəˈskɑpɪk
tacho
tachometer
BR ˈtakəʊ, -z
AM ˈtækoʊ, -z
tachograph
BR ˈtakəgrɑːf, ˈtakəgraf, -s
AM ˈtækəˌgræf, -s
tachometer
BR taˈkɒmɪtə(r), təˈkɒmɪtə(r), -z
AM tæˈkɑmədər, təˈkɑmədər, -z
tachycardia
BR ˌtakɪˈkɑːdɪə(r)
AM ˌtækəˈkɑrdiə
tachygrapher
BR taˈkɪgrəfə(r), təˈkɪgrəfə(r), -z
AM tæˈkɪgrəfər, təˈkɪgrəfər, -z
tachygraphic
BR ˌtakɪˈgrafɪk
AM ˌtækəˈgræfɪk
tachygraphical
BR ˌtakɪˈgrafɪkl
AM ˌtækəˈgræfəkəl
tachygraphy
BR taˈkɪgrəfi, təˈkɪgrəfi
AM tæˈkɪgrəfi, təˈkɪgrəfi
tachymeter
BR taˈkɪmɪtə(r), təˈkɪmɪtə(r), -z
AM tæˈkɪmədər, təˈkɪmədər, -z
tachymetry
BR taˈkɪmɪtri, təˈkɪmɪtri
AM tæˈkɪmətri, təˈkɪmətri
tachyon
BR ˈtakɪɒn
AM ˈtækiˌɑn
tacit
BR ˈtasɪt
AM ˈtæsət
Tacitean
BR ˌtasɪˈtiːən, təˈsɪtɪən
AM ˌtæsəˈtiən, təˈsɪdiən
tacitly
BR ˈtasɪtli
AM ˈtæsətli
tacitness
BR ˈtasɪtnɪs
AM ˈtæsətnɪs
taciturn
BR ˈtasɪtəːn
AM ˈtæsəˌtərn
taciturnity
BR ˌtasɪˈtəːnɪti
AM ˌtæsəˈtərnədi
taciturnly
BR ˈtasɪtəːnli
AM ˈtæsəˌtərnli
Tacitus
BR ˈtasɪtəs
AM ˈtæsədəs
tack
BR tak, -s, -ɪŋ, -t
AM tæk, -s, -ɪŋ, -t
tackboard
BR ˈtakbɔːd, -z
AM ˈtækˌbɔ(ə)rd, -z

tacker
BR 'takə(r), -z
AM 'tækər, -z
tackily
BR 'takɨli
AM 'tækəli
tackiness
BR 'takɪnɨs
AM 'tækinɨs
tackle
BR 'tak|l, -lz, -l̩ɪŋ\-lɪŋ, -ld
AM 'tæk|əl, -əlz, -(ə)lɪŋ, -əld
tackler
BR 'takl̩ə(r) 'taklə(r), -z
AM 'tæk(ə)lər, -z
tacky
BR 'tak|i, -ɪə(r), -ɪɪst
AM 'tæki, -ər, -ɨst
taco
BR 'takəʊ, 'tɑːkəʊ, -z
AM 'tɑkoʊ, -z
Tacoma
BR tə'kəʊmə(r)
AM tə'koʊmə
taconite
BR 'takənʌɪt, -s
AM 'tækəˌnaɪt, -s
tact
BR takt
AM tæk(t)
tactful
BR 'taktf(ʊ)l
AM 'tæk(t)fəl
tactfully
BR 'taktfʊli, 'taktfl̩i
AM 'tæk(t)fəli
tactfulness
BR 'taktf(ʊ)lnəs
AM 'tæk(t)fəlnəs
tactic
BR 'taktɪk, -s
AM 'tæktɪk, -s
tactical
BR 'taktɨkl
AM 'tæktəkəl
tactically
BR 'taktɨkli
AM 'tæktək(ə)li
tactician
BR tak'tɪʃn, -z
AM tæk'tɪʃən, -z
tactile
BR 'taktʌɪl
AM 'tæktl, 'tækˌtaɪl
tactility
BR tak'tɪlɨti
AM tæk'tɪlɨdi
tactless
BR 'taktləs
AM 'tæk(t)ləs
tactlessly
BR 'taktləsli
AM 'tæk(t)ləsli
tactlessness
BR 'taktləsnəs
AM 'tæk(t)ləsnəs
tactual
BR 'taktʃʊəl, 'taktʃ(ʊ)l, 'taktjʊəl, 'taktjʊl
AM 'tæk(t)ʃ(əw)əl
tactually
BR 'taktʃʊəli, 'taktʃʊli, 'taktʃl̩i, 'taktjʊəli, 'taktjʊli
AM 'tæk(t)ʃ(əw)əli
tad
BR tad, -z
AM tæd, -z
Tadcaster
BR 'tadˌkastə(r), 'tadkəstə(r), 'tadˌkɑːstə(r)
AM 'tædˌkæstər
Tadema
BR 'tadɪmə(r)
AM 'tɑdəmə
Tadjik
BR 'tɑːdʒɪk, tɑː'dʒiːk, -s
AM tɑ'dʒɪk, -s
Tadjikistan
BR təˌdʒiːkɪ'stɑːn, təˌdʒiːkɪ'stan
AM tə'dʒikəˌstæn
tadpole
BR 'tadpəʊl, -z
AM 'tædˌpoʊl, -z
Tadzhik
BR 'tɑːdʒɪk, tɑː'dʒiːk, -s
AM tɑ'dʒɪk, -s
Tadzhikistan
BR təˌdʒiːkɪ'stɑːn, təˌdʒiːkɪ'stan
AM tə'dʒikəˌstæn
tae kwon do
BR ˌtʌɪ ˌkwɒn 'dəʊ
AM ˈtaɪ ˌkwɑn 'doʊ
ta'en
BR teɪn
AM teɪn
taenia
BR 'tiːnɪə(r)
AM 'tiniə
taeniae
BR 'tiːnɪiː
AM 'tiniˌi, 'tiniˌaɪ
taenioid
BR 'tiːnɪɔɪd
AM 'tiniˌɔɪd
Taff
BR taf, -s
AM tæf, -s
taffeta
BR 'tafɨtə(r)
AM 'tæfədə
taffrail
BR 'tafreɪl, 'tafr(ɨ)l, -z
AM 'tæfrəl, 'tæˌfreɪl, -z
taffy
BR 'taf|i, -ɪz
AM 'tæfi, -z
tafia
BR 'tafɪə(r), -z
AM 'tæfiə, -z
Taft
BR taft
AM tæft
tag
BR tag, -z, -ɪŋ, -d
AM tæg, -z, -ɪŋ, -d
Tagalog
BR tə'gɑːlɒg, tə'gɑːləg, tə'galɒg, tə'galəg
AM tə'gɑləg, 'tægəˌlɔg, 'tægəˌlɑg
tagalong
BR 'tagəlɒŋ, -z
AM 'tægəˌlɔŋ, 'tægəˌlɑŋ, -z
Taganrog
BR 'tagənrɒg
AM 'tægənˌrɔg, 'tægənˌrɑg
tag end
BR 'tag ɛnd, -z
AM 'tæg ˌɛnd, -z
tagetes
BR 'tadʒɪtiːz, tə'dʒiːtiːz
AM 'tædʒəˌtiz, tə'dʒɛdiz
Taggart
BR 'tagət
AM 'tægərt
tagliatelle
BR ˌtaljə'tɛli
AM ˌtæljə'tɛl
tagmeme
BR 'tagmiːm, -z
AM 'tægˌmim, -z
tagmemics
BR tag'miːmɪks
AM tæg'mimɪks
Tagore
BR tə'gɔː(r)
AM tə'gɔ(ə)r
Tagus
BR 'teɪgəs
AM 'teɪgəs
Tahiti
BR tɑː'hiːti, tə'hiːti
AM tə'hidi, tɑ'hidi
Tahitian
BR tɑː'hiːʃn, tə'hiːʃn, -z
AM tə'hiʃən, tɑ'hiʃən, -z
Tahoe
BR 'tɑːhəʊ
AM 'tɑˌhoʊ
tahr
BR tɑː(r), -z
AM tɑr, -z
tahsil
BR tɑː'siːl, -z
AM tɑ'si(ə)l, -z
tahsildar
BR ˌtɑːsiːl'dɑː(r), -z
AM ˌtɑsil'dɑr, -z
Tai
BR tʌɪ
AM taɪ
Tai'an
BR ˌtʌɪ'ɑːn
AM 'taɪ'ɑn
tai chi
BR ˌtʌɪ 'tʃiː
AM ˌtaɪ 'tʃi
t'ai chi
BR ˌtʌɪ 'tʃiː
AM ˌtaɪ 'tʃi
t'ai chi ch'uan
BR ˌtʌɪ ˌtʃiː 'tʃwɑːn
AM ˈtaɪ ˌtʃi 'tʃwɑn
Taichung
BR ˌtʌɪ'tʃʊŋ
AM 'taɪ'tʃʊŋ
taig
BR teɪg, -z
AM teɪg, -z
taiga
BR 'tʌɪgə(r), 'tʌɪgɑː(r), -z
AM 'taɪgə, taɪ'gɑ, -z
tail
BR teɪl, -z, -ɪŋ, -d
AM teɪl, -z, -ɪŋ, -d
tailback
BR 'teɪlbak, -s
AM 'taɪlˌbæk, -s
tailboard
BR 'teɪlbɔːd, -z
AM 'teɪlˌbɔ(ə)rd, -z
tailbone
BR 'teɪlbəʊn, -z
AM 'taɪlˌboʊn, -z
tailcoat
BR 'teɪlkəʊt, ˌteɪl'kəʊt, -s
AM 'teɪlˌkoʊt, -s
tail-end
BR ˌteɪl'ɛnd, -z
AM ˈteɪl'ɛnd, -z
tail-ender
BR ˌteɪl'ɛndə(r), -z
AM ˈteɪl'ɛndər, -z
tailgate
BR 'teɪlgeɪt, -s, -ɪŋ, -ɨd
AM 'teɪlˌgeɪ|t, -ts, -dɪŋ, -dɨd
tailgater
BR 'teɪlgeɪtə(r), -z
AM 'teɪlˌgeɪdər, -z
tailie
BR 'teɪl|i, -ɪz
AM 'teɪli, -z
tailing
BR 'teɪlɪŋ, -z
AM 'teɪlɪŋ, -z
tail lamp
BR 'teɪl lamp, -s
AM 'teɪl ˌ(l)æmp, -s
Tailleferre
BR ˌtʌɪ'fɛː(r), 'tʌɪfɛː(r)
AM ˌtaɪə'fɛ(ə)r

tailless
BR ˈteɪllɨs
AM ˈteɪ(l)ləs

taillight
BR ˈteɪllʌɪt, -s
AM ˈteɪl,(l)aɪt, -s

tailor
BR ˈteɪlə(r), -z
AM ˈteɪlər, -z

tailoress
BR ,teɪləˈrɛs, -ɪz
AM ˈteɪlərəs, -əz

tailor-made
BR ,teɪləˈmeɪd
AM ˌteɪlərˈmeɪd

tailpiece
BR ˈteɪlpiːs, -ɪz
AM ˈteɪl,pis, -ɪz

tailpipe
BR ˈteɪlpʌɪp, -s
AM ˈteɪl,paɪp, -s

tailplane
BR ˈteɪlpleɪn, -z
AM ˈteɪl,pleɪn, -z

tailspin
BR ˈteɪlspɪn, -z
AM ˈteɪl,spɪn, -z

tailstock
BR ˈteɪlstɒk, -s
AM ˈteɪl,stɑk, -s

tailwheel
BR ˈteɪlwiːl, -z
AM ˈteɪl,(h)wil, -z

tailwind
BR ˈteɪlwɪnd, -z
AM ˈteɪl,wɪnd, -z

Taimyr
BR ,tʌɪˈmɪə(r)
AM taɪˈmɪ(ə)r

Tainan
BR ,tʌɪˈnan
AM ˈtaɪˈnæn

taint
BR teɪnt, -s, -ɪŋ, -ɪd
AM teɪn|t, -ts, -(t)ɪŋ, -(t)ɪd

taintless
BR ˈteɪntlɨs
AM ˈteɪn(t)lɨs

taipan
BR ˈtʌɪpan, -z
AM ˈtaɪ,pæn, -z

Taipei
BR ,tʌɪˈpeɪ
AM ,taɪˈpeɪ

Taiping
BR ,tʌɪˈpɪŋ
AM ,taɪˈpɪŋ

Tait
BR teɪt
AM teɪt

Taiwan
BR ,tʌɪˈwɑːn, ,tʌɪˈwɒn
AM ,taɪˈwɑn

Taiwanese
BR ,tʌɪwəˈniːz
AM ,taɪ,wɑˈniz

taj
BR tɑː(d)ʒ, -ɪz
AM tɑ(d)ʒ, -əz

Tajik
BR ˈtɑːdʒɪk, tɑːˈdʒiːk, -s
AM tɑˈdʒɪk, -s

Tajikistan
BR tə,dʒiːkɪˈstɑːn, tə,dʒiːkɪˈstan
AM təˈdʒɪkə,stæn

Taj Mahal
BR ,tɑː(d)ʒ məˈhɑːl
AM ˌtɑ(d)ʒ məˈhɑl

Tajo
BR ˈtɑːhəʊ
AM ˈtɑhoʊ

taka
BR ˈtɑːkɑː(r)
AM ˈtɑkə

takable
BR ˈteɪkəbl
AM ˈteɪkəbəl

takahe
BR ˈtɑːkəh|i, -ɪz
AM təˈkaɪ, -z

take
BR teɪk, -s, -ɪŋ
AM teɪk, -s, -ɪŋ

takeaway
BR ˈteɪkəweɪ, -z
AM ˈteɪkə,weɪ, -z

takedown
BR ˈteɪkdaʊn, -z
AM ˈteɪk,daʊn, -z

take-home
BR ˈteɪkhəʊm, -z
AM ˈteɪk,(h)oʊm, -z

take-in
BR ˈteɪkɪn, -z
AM ˈteɪk,ɪn, -z

taken
BR ˈteɪk(ə)n
AM ˈteɪkən

takeoff
BR ˈteɪkɒf, -s
AM ˈteɪk,ɔf, ˈteɪk,ɑf, -s

takeout
BR ˈteɪkaʊt, -s
AM ˈteɪk,aʊt, -s

takeover
BR ˈteɪk,əʊvə(r), -z
AM ˈteɪk,oʊvər, -z

taker
BR ˈteɪkə(r), -z
AM ˈteɪkər, -z

takeup
BR ˈteɪkʌp, -s
AM ˈteɪk,əp, -s

taking
BR ˈteɪkɪŋ, -z
AM ˈteɪkɪŋ, -z

takingly
BR ˈteɪkɪŋli
AM ˈteɪkɪŋli

takingness
BR ˈteɪkɪŋnɨs
AM ˈteɪkɪŋnɨs

Taklimakan
BR ,taklɪməˈkɑːn
AM ,tɑkləməˈkɑn

tala
BR ˈtɑːlə(r), -z
AM ˈtɑːlə, -z

talapoin
BR ˈtaləpɔɪn, -z
AM ˈtælə,pɔɪn, ˈtælə,pwɑn, -z

talaria
BR təˈlɛːrɪə(r)
AM təˈlɛriə

talbot[1]
BR ˈtɔːlbət, ˈtɒlbət, -s
AM ˈtælbət, ˈtɔlbət, ˈtɑlbət, -s

talbot[2]
BR ˈtɔːlbət, ˈtɒlbət, -s
AM ˈtælbət, ˈtɔlbət, ˈtɑlbət, -s

talc
BR talk
AM tælk

talcose
BR ˈtalkəʊs, ˈtalkəʊz
AM ˈtæl,koʊs, ˈtæl,koʊz

talcous
BR ˈtalkəs
AM ˈtælkəs

talcum
BR ˈtalkəm
AM ˈtælkəm

talcy
BR ˈtalki
AM ˈtælki

tale
BR teɪl
AM teɪl

talebearer
BR ˈteɪl,bɛːrə(r), -z
AM ˈteɪl,berər, -z

talebearing
BR ˈteɪl,bɛːrɪŋ
AM ˈteɪl,berɪŋ

talent
BR ˈtalənt, ˈtaln̩t, -s, -ɪd
AM ˈtælənt, -s, -əd

talentless
BR ˈtaləntləs, ˈtaln̩tləs
AM ˈtælən(t)ləs

tales[1]
people chosen for a jury
BR ˈteɪliːz
AM ˈteɪ,liz

tales[2]
plural of tale
BR teɪlz
AM teɪlz

talesman
BR ˈteɪlzmən
AM ˈteɪlzmən

talesmen
BR ˈteɪlzmən
AM ˈteɪlzmən

taleteller
BR ˈteɪl,tɛlə(r), -z
AM ˈteɪl,tɛlər, -z

Talgarth
BR ˈtalgɑːθ
AM ˈtæl,gɑrθ

tali
BR ˈteɪlʌɪ
AM ˈteɪ,laɪ

talion
BR ˈtalɪən, -z
AM ˈtæliən, -z

talipes
BR ˈtalɪpiːz
AM ˈtælə,piz

talipot
BR ˈtalɪpɒt, -s
AM ˈtælə,pɑt, -s

talisman
BR ˈtalɪzmən, ˈtalɪsmən, -z
AM ˈtæləsmən, ˈtæləzmən, -z

talismanic
BR ,talɪzˈmanɪk
AM ,tæləzˈmænɪk

talk
BR tɔːk, -s, -ɪŋ, -t
AM tɔk, tɑk, -s, -ɪŋ, -t

talkathon
BR ˈtɔːkəθɒn, -z
AM ˈtɔkə,θɑn, ˈtɑkə,θɑn, -z

talkative
BR ˈtɔːkətɪv
AM ˈtɔkədɪv, ˈtɑkədɪv

talkatively
BR ˈtɔːkətɪvli
AM ˈtɔkədɪvli, ˈtɑkədɪvli

talkativeness
BR ˈtɔːkətɪvnɪs
AM ˈtɔkədɪvnɪs, ˈtɑkədɪvnɪs

talkback
BR ˈtɔːkbak, -s
AM ˈtɔk,bæk, ˈtɑk,bæk, -s

talker
BR ˈtɔːkə(r), -z
AM ˈtɔkər, ˈtɑkər, -z

talkfest
BR ˈtɔːkfɛst, -s
AM ˈtɔk,fɛst, ˈtɑk,fɛst, -s

talkie
BR ˈtɔːk|i, -ɪz
AM ˈtɔki, ˈtɑki, -z

tall
BR tɔːl, -ə(r), -ɪst
AM tɔl, tɑl, -ər, -əst

tallage
BR ˈtal|ɪdʒ, -ɪdʒɪz
AM ˈtælədʒ, -ɪz

Tallahassee
BR ,taləˈhasi
AM ,tæləˈhæsi

tallboy
BR 'tɔːlbɔɪ, -z
AM 'tɔl,bɔɪ, 'tɑl,bɔɪ, -z

Talley
BR 'tali
AM 'tæli

Talleyrand
BR 'talɪrand
AM 'tæli,rænd

Tallin
BR 'talɪn, ta'liːn
AM 'tælən

Tallinn
BR 'talɪn, ta'liːn
AM 'tælən

Tallis
BR 'talɪs
AM 'tæləs

tallish
BR 'tɔːlɪʃ
AM 'tɔlɪʃ, 'tɑlɪʃ

tallith
BR 'talɪθ, 'tɑːlɪθ, 'talɪs, 'tɑːlɪs
AM 'tɑləs, 'tɑləθ

tallness
BR 'tɔːlnəs
AM 'tɔlnəs, 'tɑlnəs

tallow
BR 'taləʊ
AM 'tæloʊ

tallowish
BR 'taləʊɪʃ
AM 'tæləwɪʃ

tallowy
BR 'taləʊi
AM 'tæləwi

Tallulah
BR tə'luːlə(r)
AM tə'lulə

tally
BR 'tal|i, -ɪz, -ɪɪŋ, -ɪd
AM 'tæli, -z, -ɪŋ, -d

tally-ho
BR ,talɪ'həʊ, -z
AM ,tæli'hoʊ, -z

tallyman
BR 'talɪmən, 'talɪman
AM 'tæli,mæn

tallymen
BR 'talɪmən, 'talɪmɛn
AM 'tæli,mɛn

Talmud
BR 'talmʊd, 'talmʌd
AM 'tɑl,mʊd, 'tælməd

Talmudic
BR tal'mʊdɪk, tal'mʌdɪk
AM tæl'm(j)udɪk, tæl'mʊdɪk, tɑl'm(j)udɪk, tɑl'mʊdɪk

Talmudical
BR tal'mʊdɪkl, tal'mʌdɪkl
AM tæl'm(j)udəkəl, tæl'mʊdəkəl, tɑl'm(j)udəkəl, tɑl'mʊdəkəl

Talmudist
BR 'talmʊdɪst, 'talmʌdɪst, -s
AM 'tɑl,mʊdəst, 'tælmədəst, -s

talon
BR 'talən, -z, -d
AM 'tælən, -z, -d

talus
BR 'teɪləs
AM 'teɪləs

Talybont
BR ,talɪ'bɒnt
AM ,tæli'bɑnt

Tal-y-bont
BR ,talɪ'bɒnt
AM ,tæli'bɑnt
WE ,talʌ'bɒnt

Tal-y-llyn
BR ,talɪ'ɬɪn, ,talɪ'lɪn
AM ,tæli'lɪn
WE ,talʌ'ɬɪn

TAM
BR tam
AM tæm

tam
BR tam, -z
AM tæm, -z

tamable
BR 'teɪməbl
AM 'teɪməbəl

tamale
BR tə'mɑːl|i, -ɪz
AM tə'mɑli, -z

tamandua
BR tə'mand(j)ʊə(r), tə'mandʒʊə(r), ,tamən'd(j)uːə(r), -z
AM tə'mændəwə, tə'mændʒəwə, -z

tamanoir
BR 'tamənwɑː(r), -z
AM ,tæmən'wɑr, -z

Tamar
BR 'teɪmɑː(r)
AM 'teɪmɑr

Tamara
BR tə'mɑːrə(r), 'tam(ə)rə(r)
AM tə'mɛrə, 'tæmərə

tamarack
BR 'tamərak, -s
AM 'tæm(ə),ræk, -s

tamari
BR tə'mɑːri
AM tə'mɑri

tamarillo
BR ,tamə'rɪləʊ, -z
AM ,tæmə'rɪloʊ, -z

tamarin
BR 'tam(ə)rɪn, -z
AM 'tæm(ə)rən, 'tæmə,rɪn, -z

tamarind
BR 'tam(ə)rɪnd, -z
AM 'tæm(ə)rənd, 'tæmə,rɪnd, -z

tamarisk
BR 'tam(ə)rɪsk, -s
AM 'tæm(ə)rəsk, 'tæmə,rɪsk, -s

tambala
BR tam'bɑːlə(r), -z
AM tɑm'bɑlə, -z

tamber
BR 'tambə(r), -z
AM 'tæmbər, -z

Tambo
BR 'tambəʊ
AM 'tæmboʊ

tambour
BR 'tambʊə(r), 'tambɔː(r), -z
AM 'tæm,bʊ(ə)r, -z

tamboura
BR tam'bʊərə(r), tam'bɔːrə(r), -z
AM tæm'bʊrə, -z

tambourin
BR 'tambərɪn, -z
AM ,tæmbə'rin, -z

tambourine
BR ,tambə'riːn, -z
AM ,tæmbə'rin, -z

tambourinist
BR ,tambə'riːnɪst, -s
AM ,tæmbə'rinɪst, -s

Tamburlaine
BR 'tambəːleɪn
AM 'tæmbər,leɪn

tame
BR teɪm, -z, -ɪŋ, -d
AM teɪm, -z, -ɪŋ, -d

tameability
BR ,teɪmə'bɪlɪti
AM ,teɪmə'bɪlɪdi

tameable
BR 'teɪməbl
AM 'teɪməbəl

tameableness
BR 'teɪməblnəs
AM 'teɪməbəlnəs

tamely
BR 'teɪmli
AM 'teɪmli

tameness
BR 'teɪmnɪs
AM 'teɪmnəs

tamer
BR 'teɪmə(r), -z
AM 'teɪmər, -z

Tamerlane
BR 'taməleɪn
AM 'tæmər,leɪn

Tamil
BR 'tam(ɪ)l, -z
AM 'tæməl, -z

Tamilian
BR tə'mɪlɪən
AM tə'mɪljən, tə'mɪliən

Tamil Nadu
BR ,tam(ɪ)l 'nɑːduː
AM ,tæməl nɑ'du

Tamla Motown
BR ,tamlə 'məʊtaʊn
AM ,tæmlə 'moʊ,taʊn

Tammany
BR 'taməni
AM 'tæməni

Tammie
BR 'tami
AM 'tæmi

tammy
BR 'tam|i, -ɪz
AM 'tæmi, -z

tam-o'-shanter
BR ,tamə'ʃantə(r), -z
AM 'tæmə,ʃæn(t)ər, -z

tamp
BR tam|p, -ps, -pɪŋ, -(p)t
AM tæm|p, -ps, -pɪŋ, -(p)t

Tampa
BR 'tampə(r)
AM 'tæmpə

tampan
BR 'tampan, -z
AM 'tæm,pæn, -z

tamper
BR 'tamp|ə(r), -əz, -(ə)rɪŋ, -əd
AM 'tæmp|ər, -ərz, -(ə)rɪŋ, -ərd

Tampere
BR 'tampərə(r)
AM 'tæmpərə

tamperer
BR 'tamp(ə)rə(r), -z
AM 'tæmp(ə)rər, -z

tampering
BR 'tamp(ə)rɪŋ, -z
AM 'tæmp(ə)rɪŋ, -z

tamper-proof
BR 'tampəpruːf
AM 'tæmpər,pruf

Tampico
BR tam'piːkəʊ
AM tæm'pi,koʊ

tampion
BR 'tampɪən, -z
AM 'tæmpiən, -z

tampon
BR 'tampɒn, 'tampən, -z
AM 'tæm,pɑn, -z

tamponade
BR 'tampə,neɪd, -z
AM ,tæmpə'neɪd, -z

tamponage
BR 'tampənɪdʒ
AM 'tæmpənɪdʒ

tam-tam
BR 'tamtam, -z
AM 'tæm,tæm, -z

Tamworth
BR 'tamwəθ, -s

AM 'tæm,wɑrθ, -s

tan
BR tan, -z, -ɪŋ, -d
AM tæn, -z, -ɪŋ, -d

tanager
BR 'tanədʒə(r), -z
AM 'tænədʒər, -z

Tanagra
BR 'tanəgrə(r), -z
AM 'tænəgrə, -z

Tánaiste
BR 'tɔːnɪʃt(ʃ)ə(r), 'tɑːnɪʃt(ʃ)ə(r)
AM 'tɑnɪʃt(ʃ)ə
IR 'taːnəsʲtʲə

Tananarive
BR ˌtanənə'riːv
AM ˌtænənə'riv

tanbark
BR 'tanbɑːk, -s
AM 'tæn,bɑrk, -s

Tancred
BR 'taŋkrɪd, 'taŋkrɛd
AM 'tæŋkrəd

tandem
BR 'tandəm, -z
AM 'tændəm, -z

tandoor
BR 'tandʊə(r), tan'dʊə(r), 'tandɔː(r), tan'dɔː(r), -z
AM tæn'dʊ(ə)r, -z

tandoori
BR tan'dʊər|i, tan'dɔːr|i, -ɪz
AM tæn'dʊri, -z

Tandy
BR 'tandi
AM 'tændi

tang
BR taŋ, -z
AM tæŋ, -z

tanga
BR 'taŋgə(r), -z
AM 'tæŋgə, -z

Tanganyika
BR ˌtaŋgən'jiːkə(r)
AM ˌtæŋgə'nikə

Tanganyikan
BR ˌtaŋgən'jiːkən, -z
AM ˌtæŋgə'nikən, -z

tangelo
BR 'tan(d)ʒələʊ, -z
AM 'tændʒə,loʊ, -z

tangency
BR 'tan(d)ʒ(ə)ns|i, -ɪz
AM 'tændʒənsi, -z

tangent
BR 'tan(d)ʒ(ə)nt, -s
AM 'tændʒənt, -s

tangential
BR tan'dʒɛn(t)ʃl
AM tæn'dʒɛn(t)ʃəl

tangentially
BR tan'dʒɛn(t)ʃl̩i, tan'dʒɛnʃəli
AM tæn'dʒɛn(t)ʃəli

tangerine
BR ˌtan(d)ʒə'riːn, -z
AM ˌtændʒə'rin, -z

tanghin
BR 'taŋgɪn, -z
AM 'tæŋgən, -z

tangibility
BR ˌtandʒɪ'bɪlɪti
AM ˌtændʒə'bɪlɨdi

tangible
BR 'tandʒɪbl
AM 'tændʒəbəl

tangibleness
BR 'tandʒɪblnəs
AM 'tændʒəbəlnəs

tangibly
BR 'tan(d)ʒɪbli
AM 'tændʒəbli

Tangier
BR tan'dʒɪə(r)
AM tæn'dʒɪ(ə)r

Tangiers
BR tan'dʒɪəz
AM tæn'dʒɪ(ə)rz

tanginess
BR 'taŋɪnɪs
AM 'tæŋinɨs

tangle
BR 'taŋg|l, -lz, -lɪŋ\-lɪŋ, -ld
AM 'tæŋg|əl, -əlz, -(ə)lɪŋ, -əld

Tanglewood
BR 'taŋglwʊd
AM 'tæŋgəl,wʊd

tangly
BR 'taŋl|i, -ɪə(r), -ɪɪst
AM 'tæŋli, 'tæŋg(ə)li, -ər, -ɨst

Tangmere
BR 'taŋmɪə(r)
AM 'tæŋ,mɪ(ə)r

tango
BR 'taŋgəʊ, -z, -ɪŋ, -d
AM 'tæŋgoʊ, -z, -ɪŋ, -d

tangram
BR 'tangram, -z
AM 'tæŋ,græm, 'tæn,græm, -z

tangy
BR 'taŋ|i, -ɪə(r), -ɪɪst
AM 'tæŋi, -ər, -ɨst

tanh
BR θæn, tanʃ, ˌtan'eɪtʃ
AM θæn, 'tænʃ, ˌtæn'eɪtʃ

Tania
BR 'tɑːnɪə(r), 'tanɪə(r)
AM 'tæniə, 'tɑniə

tanist
BR 'tanɪst, -s
AM 'tænəst, 'θɔnəst, 'θɑnəst, -s

tanistry
BR 'tanɪstri
AM 'tænəstri, 'θɔnəstri, 'θɑnəstri

tank
BR taŋ|k, -ks, -kɪŋ, -(k)t
AM tæŋ|k, -ks, -kɪŋ, -(k)t

tanka
BR 'taŋkə(r), 'tɑːŋkə(r), -z
AM 'tɑŋkə, -z

tankage
BR 'taŋk|ɪdʒ, -ɨdʒɪz
AM 'tæŋkɪdʒ, -ɪz

tankard
BR 'taŋkəd, -z
AM 'tæŋkərd, -z

tanker
BR 'taŋk|ə(r), -əz, -(ə)rɪŋ, -əd
AM 'tæŋkər, -z, -ɪŋ, -d

tankful
BR 'taŋkfʊl, -z
AM 'tæŋk,fʊl, -z

tankless
BR 'taŋkləs
AM 'tæŋkləs

tanksuit
BR 'taŋks(j)uːt, -s
AM 'tæŋk,sut, -s

tanktop
BR 'taŋktɒp, -s
AM 'tæŋk,tɑp, -s

tannable
BR 'tanəbl
AM 'tænəbəl

tannage
BR 'tan|ɪdʒ, -ɨdʒɪz
AM 'tænɪdʒ, -ɪz

tannate
BR 'taneɪt, -s
AM 'tæ,neɪt, -s

tanner
BR 'tanə(r), -z
AM 'tænər, -z

tannery
BR 'tan(ə)r|i, -ɪz
AM 'tænəri, -z

Tannhäuser
BR 'tan,hɔɪzə(r)
AM 'tæn,hɔɪzər

tannic
BR 'tanɪk
AM 'tænɪk

tannic acid
BR ˌtanɪk 'asɪd
AM ˌtænɪk 'æsəd

tannin
BR 'tanɪn
AM 'tænən

tannish
BR 'tanɪʃ
AM 'tænɪʃ

tannoy®
BR 'tanɔɪ, -z
AM 'tæ,nɔɪ, -z

Tanqueray
BR 'taŋkəreɪ, 'taŋk(ə)ri
AM 'tæŋkə,reɪ

tanrec
BR 'tanrɛk, -s
AM 'tænrɛk, -s

Tansey
BR 'tanzi
AM 'tænzi

tansy
BR 'tanz|i, -ɪz
AM 'tænzi, -z

tantalic
BR tan'talɪk
AM tæn'tælɪk

tantalisation
BR ˌtantəlʌɪ'zeɪʃn, ˌtantl̩ʌɪ'zeɪʃn
AM ˌtæn(t)l̩ə'zeɪʃən, ˌtæn(t)l,aɪ'zeɪʃən

tantalise
BR 'tantəlʌɪz, 'tantl̩ʌɪz, -ɪz, -ɪŋ, -d
AM 'tæn(t)l,aɪz, -ɪz, -ɪŋ, -d

tantaliser
BR 'tantəlʌɪzə(r), 'tantl̩ʌɪzə(r), -z
AM 'tæn(t)l,aɪzər, -z

tantalisingly
BR 'tantəlʌɪzɪŋli, 'tantl̩ʌɪzɪŋli
AM 'tæn(t)l,aɪzɪŋli

tantalite
BR 'tantəlʌɪt, 'tantl̩ʌɪt
AM 'tæn(t)l,aɪt

tantalization
BR ˌtantəlʌɪ'zeɪʃn, ˌtantl̩ʌɪ'zeɪʃn
AM ˌtæn(t)l̩ə'zeɪʃən, ˌtæn(t)l,aɪ'zeɪʃən

tantalize
BR 'tantəlʌɪz, 'tantl̩ʌɪz, -ɪz, -ɪŋ, -d
AM 'tæn(t)l,aɪz, -ɪz, -ɪŋ, -d

tantalizer
BR 'tantəlʌɪzə(r), 'tantl̩ʌɪzə(r), -z
AM 'tæn(t)l,aɪzər, -z

tantalizingly
BR 'tantəlʌɪzɪŋli, 'tantl̩ʌɪzɪŋli
AM 'tæn(t)l,aɪzɪŋli

tantalous
BR 'tantələs, 'tantl̩əs
AM 'tæn(t)l̩əs

tantalum
BR 'tantələm, 'tantl̩əm
AM 'tæn(t)l̩əm

tantalus
BR 'tantələs, 'tantl̩əs, -ɪz
AM 'tæn(t)l̩əs, -əz

tantamount
BR 'tantəmaʊnt
AM 'tæn(t)ə,maʊnt

tantivy
BR tan'tɪv|i, -ɪz
AM tæn'tɪvi, -z

tant mieux
BR ˌtõ ˈmjəː(r)
AM ˌtɑn ˈmjə

tant pis
BR ˌtõ ˈpiː
AM ˌtɑn ˈpi

tantra
BR ˈtantrə(r), -z
AM ˈtæntrə, -z

tantric
BR ˈtantrɪk
AM ˈtæntrɪk

tantrism
BR ˈtantrɪz(ə)m
AM ˈtænˌtrɪzəm

tantrist
BR ˈtantrɪst, -s
AM ˈtæntrəst, -s

tantrum
BR ˈtantrəm, -z
AM ˈtæntrəm, -z

Tanya
BR ˈtɑːnɪə(r), ˈtanɪə(r)
AM ˈtɑnjə, ˈtænjə

Tanzania
BR ˌtanzəˈniːə(r)
AM ˌtænzəˈniə

Tanzanian
BR ˌtanzəˈniːən, -z
AM ˌtænzəˈniən, -z

Tao
BR taʊ, ˈtɑːəʊ, -z
AM taʊ, -z

Taoiseach
BR ˈtiːʃək, ˈtiːʃəx
AM ˈtiʃək

Taoism
BR ˈtaʊɪz(ə)m, ˈtɑːəʊɪz(ə)m
AM ˈtaʊˌɪzəm

Taoist
BR ˈtaʊɪst, ˈtɑːəʊɪst, -s
AM ˈtaʊəst, -s

Taoistic
BR taʊˈɪstɪk, ˌtɑːəʊˈɪstɪk
AM taʊˈɪstɪk

Taormina
BR ˌtaʊəˈmiːnə(r)
AM ˌtaʊrˈminə

Taos
BR taʊs
AM ˈtɑˌoʊs

tap
BR tap, -s, -ɪŋ, -t
AM tæp, -s, -ɪŋ, -t

tapa
BR ˈtapə(r), ˈtɑːpə(r), -z
AM ˈtɑpə, -z

tap-dance
BR ˈtapdɑːns, ˈtapdans, -ɪz, -ɪŋ, -t
AM ˈtæpˌdæns, -əz, -ɪŋ, -t

tap-dancer
BR ˈtapˌdɑːnsə(r), ˈtapˌdansə(r), -z
AM ˈtæpˌdænsər, -z

tape
BR teɪp, -s, -ɪŋ, -t
AM teɪp, -s, -ɪŋ, -t

tapeable
BR ˈteɪpəbl
AM ˈteɪpəbəl

tapeless
BR ˈteɪplɨs
AM ˈteɪplɨs

tapelike
BR ˈteɪplʌɪk
AM ˈteɪpˌlaɪk

taper
BR ˈteɪp|ə(r), -əz, -(ə)rɪŋ, -əd
AM ˈteɪp|ər, -ərz, -(ə)rɪŋ, -ərd

taperecord
BR ˈteɪprɪˌkɔːd, -z, -ɪŋ, -ɨd
AM ˈteɪprəˌkɔ(ə)rd, -z, -ɪŋ, -əd

tapestry
BR ˈtapɨstr|i, -ɪz, -ɪd
AM ˈtæpəstri, -z, -d

tapeta
BR təˈpiːtə(r)
AM təˈpidə

tapetum
BR təˈpiːtəm, -z
AM təˈpidəm, -z

tapeworm
BR ˈteɪpwəːm, -z
AM ˈteɪpˌwərm, -z

tapioca
BR ˌtapɪˈəʊkə(r)
AM ˌtæpiˈoʊkə

tapir
BR ˈteɪp(ɪ)ə(r), -z
AM ˈteɪpər, -z

tapiroid
BR ˈteɪp(ɪ)ərɔɪd, -z
AM ˈteɪpəˌrɔɪd, -z

tapis
BR ˈtapi, ˈtapiː
AM ˈtɑpi, tɑˈpi

tapless
BR ˈtapləs
AM ˈtæpləs

Taplin
BR ˈtaplɪn
AM ˈtæplən

Taplow
BR ˈtapləʊ
AM ˈtæpˌloʊ

tapotement
BR təˈpəʊtm(ə)nt
AM təˈpoʊtmənt

Tapp
BR tap
AM tæp

tappable
BR ˈtapəbl
AM ˈtæpəbəl

tapper
BR ˈtapə(r), -z
AM ˈtæpər, -z

tappet
BR ˈtapɪt, -s
AM ˈtæpət, -s

tapping
BR ˈtapɪŋ, -z
AM ˈtæpɪŋ, -z

taproom
BR ˈtapruːm, ˈtaprʊm, -z
AM ˈtæpˌrum, ˈtæpˌrʊm, -z

taproot
BR ˈtapruːt, -s
AM ˈtæpˌrut, -s

Tapsell
BR ˈtapsl
AM ˈtæpsəl

tapster
BR ˈtapstə(r), -z
AM ˈtæpstər, -z

tap-tap
BR ˌtapˈtap, -s
AM ˈtæpˈtæp, -s

tapu
taboo
BR ˈtɑːpuː, -z, -ɪŋ, -d
AM ˈtɑˌpu, -z, -ɪŋ, -d

tap water
BR ˈtap ˌwɔːtə(r)
AM ˈtæp ˌwɑdər, + ˌwɔdər

taqueria
BR ˌtɑːkəˈriːə(r), -z
AM ˌtɑkəˈriə, -z

tar
BR tɑː(r), -z, -ɪŋ, -d
AM tɑr, -z, -ɪŋ, -d

Tara[1]
house in US
BR ˈtarə(r)
AM ˈtɛrə

Tara[2]
Ireland
BR ˈtɑːrə(r)
AM ˈtɑrə

taradiddle
BR ˈtarəˌdɪdl, ˌtarəˈdɪdl, -z
AM ˈtɛrəˌdɪdəl, -z

tarakihi
BR ˌtarəˈkiːhi, ˌtarəˈkiː, ˌtarəˈkiːhɪz\ˌtarəˈkiːz
AM ˌtɛrəˈkiˌhi, -z

taramasalata
BR ˌtarəməsəˈlɑːtə(r), təˌraməsəˈlɑːtə(r)
AM ˌtɛrəməsəˈlɑdə

taramosalata
BR ˌtarəməsəˈlɑːtə(r), təˌraməsəˈlɑːtə(r)
AM ˌtɛrəməsəˈlɑdə

Taranaki
BR ˌtarəˈnaki, ˌtarəˈnɑːki
AM ˌtɛrəˈnɑki

tarantass
BR ˌtarənˈtas, ˌtarn̩ˈtas, -ɪz
AM ˈtɑrənˌtɑs, -əz

tarantella
BR ˌtarənˈtɛlə(r), ˌtarn̩ˈtɛlə(r), -z
AM ˌtɛrənˈtɛlə, -z

tarantism
BR ˈtarəntɪz(ə)m, ˈtarn̩tɪz(ə)m
AM ˈtɛrənˌtɪzəm

tarantula
BR təˈrantjʊlə(r), təˈrantʃʊlə(r), təˈrantʃlə(r), -z
AM təˈræn(t)ʃələ, -z

taraxacum
BR təˈraksəkəm, -z
AM təˈræksəkəm, -z

Tarbert
BR ˈtɑːbət
AM ˈtɑrbərt

Tarbet
BR ˈtɑːbɪt
AM ˈtɑrbət

tarboosh
BR tɑːˈbuːʃ, -ɪz
AM tɑrˈbuʃ, tɑrˈbʊʃ, -əz

tarbrush
BR ˈtɑːbrʌʃ, -ɪz
AM ˈtɑrˌbrəʃ, -əz

Tarbuck
BR ˈtɑːbʌk
AM ˈtɑrˌbək

Tardenoisian
BR ˌtɑːdɪˈnɔɪzɪən
AM ˌtɑrdəˈnɔɪziən

tardigrade
BR ˈtɑːdɪgreɪd, -z
AM ˈtɑrdəˌgreɪd, -z

tardily
BR ˈtɑːdɪli
AM ˈtɑrdəli

tardiness
BR ˈtɑːdɪnɪs
AM ˈtɑrdinɪs

Tardis
BR ˈtɑːdɪs
AM ˈtɑrdəs

tardive dyskinesia
BR ˌtɑːdɪv ˌdɪskɪˈniːzɪə(r)
AM ˌtɑrdɪv ˌdɪskɪˈniziə, ˌdɪskɪˈniʒə

tardy
BR ˈtɑːd|i, -ɪə(r), -ɪɪst
AM ˈtɑrdi, -ər, -ɪst

tare
BR tɛː(r), -z
AM tɛ(ə)r, -z

target
BR ˈtɑːg|ɪt, -ɪts, -ɪtɪŋ, -ɪtɪd
AM ˈtɑrgə|t, -ts, -dɪŋ, -dəd

targetable
BR 'tɑːɡɪtəbl
AM 'tɑrɡədəbəl

Targum
BR 'tɑːɡəm, tɑː'ɡuːm, -z
AM 'tɑr,ɡʊm, 'tɑr,ɡum, -z

Targumist
BR 'tɑːɡʉmɪst, -s
AM 'tɑr,ɡʊməst, 'tɑr,ɡuməst, -s

Tarheel
BR 'tɑːhiːl, -z
AM 'tɑr,(h)il, -z

tariff
BR 'tarɪf, -s
AM 'tɛrəf, -s

Tariq
BR 'tarɪk
AM 'tɑrək

Tarka
BR 'tɑːkə(r)
AM 'tɑrkə

tarlatan
BR 'tɑːlətn, -z
AM 'tɑrlətn, -z

Tarleton
BR 'tɑːlt(ə)n
AM 'tɑrltən, 'tɑrletn

Tarmac®
BR 'tɑːmak
AM 'tɑr,mæk

tarmacadam
BR 'tɑːmə,kadəm
AM ˌtɑrmə'kædəm

tarn
BR tɑːn, -z
AM tɑrn, -z

tarnation
interjection
BR tɑː'neɪʃn
AM tɑr'neɪʃən

tarnish
BR 'tɑːn|ɪʃ, -ɪʃɪz, -ɪʃɪŋ, -ɪʃt
AM 'tɑrnɪʃ, -ɪz, -ɪŋ, -t

tarnishable
BR 'tɑːnɪʃəbl
AM 'tɑrnəʃəbəl

taro
BR 'tarəʊ, -z
AM 'tɛroʊ, -z

tarot
BR 'tarəʊ
AM 'tɛroʊ

tarp
BR tɑːp, -s
AM tɑrp, -s

tarpan
BR 'tɑːpan, -z
AM 'tɑr,pæn, -z

tarpaulin
BR tɑː'pɔːlɪn, -z
AM tɑr'pɔlən, 'tɑrpələn, tɑr'pɑlən, -z

Tarpeia
BR tɑː'piːə(r)
AM tɑr'piə

Tarpeian
BR tɑː'piːən
AM tɑr'peɪən

tarpon
BR 'tɑːp(ə)n, -z
AM 'tɑrpən, -z

Tarporley
BR 'tɑːpəli, 'tɑːpḷi
AM 'tɑrpərli

Tarquin
BR 'tɑːkwɪn
AM 'tɑrkwən

tarradiddle
BR 'tarə,dɪdl, ˌtarə'dɪdl, -z
AM ˌtɛrə,dɪdəl, -z

tarragon
BR 'tarəɡ(ə)n
AM 'tɛrə,ɡɑn, 'tɛrəɡən

Tarragona
BR ˌtarə'ɡɒnə(r)
AM ˌtɑrə'ɡoʊnə

Tarrasa
BR tə'rɑːsə(r)
AM tə'rɑsə

tarrier
BR 'tarɪə(r), -z
AM 'tɑriər, -z

tarriness
BR 'tɑːrɪnɪs
AM 'tɑrinɪs

tarry¹
covered with tar
BR 'tɑːr|i, -ɪə(r), -ɪɪst
AM 'tɑri, -ər, -ɪst

tarry²
wait
BR 'tar|i, -ɪz, -ɪɪŋ, -ɪd
AM 'tɛri, -z, -ɪŋ, -d

tarsal
BR 'tɑːsl, -z
AM 'tɑrsəl, -z

Tarshish
BR 'tɑːʃɪʃ
AM 'tɑrʃɪʃ

tarsi
BR 'tɑːsʌɪ
AM 'tɑr,saɪ

tarsia
BR 'tɑːsɪə(r)
AM 'tɑrsiə

tarsier
BR 'tɑːsɪə(r), -z
AM 'tɑrsiər, -z

Tarski
BR 'tɑːski
AM 'tɑrski

tarsus
BR 'tɑːsəs
AM 'tɑrsəs

tart
BR tɑːt, -s, -ɪŋ, -ɪd
AM tɑr|t, -ts, -dɪŋ, -dəd

tartan
BR 'tɑːt(ə)n, -z
AM 'tɑrtn, -z

tartar¹
deposit on teeth etc
BR 'tɑːtə(r), 'tɑːtɑː(r)
AM 'tɑrdər

tartar²
person
BR 'tɑːtə(r), -z
AM 'tɑrdər, -z

tartare
BR tɑː'tɑː(r)
AM tɑ(r)'tɑr

tartaric
BR tɑː'tarɪk
AM tɑr'tɛrɪk

tartaric acid
BR tɑːˌtarɪk 'asɪd
AM tɑrˌtɛrɪk 'æsəd

tartarise
BR 'tɑːtərʌɪz, -ɪz, -ɪŋ, -d
AM 'tɑrdə,raɪz, -ɪz, -ɪŋ, -d

tartarize
BR 'tɑːtərʌɪz, -ɪz, -ɪŋ, -d
AM 'tɑrdə,raɪz, -ɪz, -ɪŋ, -d

tartar sauce
BR ˌtɑːtə 'sɔːs, ˌtɑːtɑː +
AM 'tɑrdər ˌsɔs, 'tɑrdər ˌsɑs

Tartarus
BR 'tɑːt(ə)rəs
AM 'tɑrdərəs

Tartary
BR 'tɑːt(ə)ri
AM 'tɑrdəri

tartily
BR 'tɑːtɪli
AM 'tɑrdəli

tartiness
BR 'tɑːtɪnɪs
AM 'tɑrdinɪs

tartlet
BR 'tɑːtlɪt, -s
AM 'tɑrtlət, -s

tartly
BR 'tɑːtli
AM 'tɑrtli

tartness
BR 'tɑːtnəs
AM 'tɑrtnəs

tartrate
BR 'tɑːtreɪt, -s
AM 'tɑr,treɪt, -s

tartrazine
BR 'tɑːtrəziːn
AM 'tɑrtrə,zin, 'tɑrtrəzən

Tartuffe
BR (ˌ)tɑː'tuːf
AM ˌtɑr'tuf

tarty
BR 'tɑːt|i, -ɪə(r), -ɪɪst
AM 'tɑrdi, -ər, -ɪst

Tarzan
BR 'tɑːzn
AM 'tɑr,zæn, 'tɑrzən

Tashkent
BR ˌtaʃ'kɛnt
AM ˌtæʃ'kɛnt

task
BR tɑːsk, task, -s, -ɪŋ, -t
AM tæsk, -s, -ɪŋ, -t

Tasker
BR 'taskə(r), 'tɑːskə(r)
AM 'tæskər

taskmaster
BR 'tɑːsk,mɑːstə(r), 'task,mastə(r), -z
AM 'tæsk,mæstər, -z

taskmistress
BR 'tɑːsk,mɪstrɪs, 'task,mɪstrɪs, -ɪz
AM 'tæsk,mɪstrɪs, -ɪz

Tasman
BR 'tazmən
AM 'tæzmən

Tasmania
BR taz'meɪnɪə(r)
AM ˌtæz'meɪnjə, tæz'meɪniə

Tasmanian
BR taz'meɪnɪən, -z
AM tæz'meɪnjən, tæz'meɪniən, -z

tass
BR tas, -ɪz
AM tæs, -əz

tassa
BR 'tasə(r)
AM 'tɑsə

tassel
BR 'tasl, -z, -d
AM 'tæsəl, -z, -d

tassie
BR 'tas|i, -ɪz
AM 'tæsi, -z

Tasso
BR 'tasəʊ
AM 'tæsoʊ

taste
BR teɪst, -s, -ɪŋ, -ɪd
AM teɪst, -s, -ɪŋ, -ɪd

tasteable
BR 'teɪstəbl
AM 'teɪstəbəl

taste bud
BR 'teɪs(t) bʌd, -z
AM 'teɪs(t) ˌbəd, -z

tasteful
BR 'teɪs(t)f(ʊ)l
AM 'teɪs(t)fəl

tastefully
BR 'teɪs(t)fʊli, 'teɪs(t)fḷi
AM 'teɪs(t)fəli

tastefulness
BR 'teɪs(t)f(ʊ)lnəs
AM 'teɪs(t)fəlnəs

tasteless
BR 'teɪs(t)lɪs
AM 'teɪs(t)lɪs

tastelessly
BR 'teɪs(t)lɪsli

AM 'teɪs(t)lɪsli
tastelessness
BR 'teɪs(t)lɪsnɪs
AM 'teɪs(t)lɪsnɪs
taster
BR 'teɪstə(r), -z
AM 'teɪstər, -z
tastily
BR 'teɪstɨli
AM 'teɪstɨli
tastiness
BR 'teɪstɪnɪs
AM 'teɪstinɪs
tasting
BR 'teɪstɪŋ, -z
AM 'teɪstɪŋ, -z
tasty
BR 'teɪst|i, -ɪə(r), -ɪɪst
AM 'teɪsti, -ər, -ɪst
tat
BR tat, -s, -ɪŋ, -ɪd
AM tæ|t, -ts, -dɪŋ, -dəd
tata
BR ta'tɑː(r), tə'tɑː(r)
AM tɑ'tɑ
tatami
BR tə'tɑːm|i, ta'tɑːm|i, tɑː'tɑːm|i, -ɪz
AM tə'tɑmi, -z
Tatar
BR 'tɑːtə(r), -z
AM 'tɑdər, -z
Tatarstan
BR ˌtɑːtə'stɑːn, ˌtɑːtə'stan
AM 'tɑdərˌstæn
Tatchell
BR 'tatʃl
AM 'tætʃəl
Tate
BR teɪt
AM teɪt
tater
potato
BR 'teɪtə(r), -z
AM 'teɪdər, -z
Tatham
BR 'teɪθ(ə)m, 'teɪð(ə)m, 'tatəm
AM 'tædəm
Tati
BR 'tati
AM tɑ'ti
Tatiana
BR ˌtatɪ'ɑːnə(r)
AM ˌtɑdi'ɑnə
tatler
BR 'tatlə(r), -z
AM 'tædḷər, 'tætlər, -z
tatou
BR 'tatuː, -z
AM tə'tu, -z
Tatra
BR 'tɑːtrə(r), 'tatrə(r)
AM 'tætrə
Tatras
BR 'tɑːtrəs, 'tatrəs
AM 'tætrəz
tatter
BR 'tatə(r), -z, -d
AM 'tædər, -z, -d
tatterdemalion
BR ˌtatədɪ'meɪlɪən, -z
AM ˌtædərdə'meɪljən, ˌtædərdi'meɪljən, -z
tattersall[1]
BR 'tatəs(ɔː)l, -z
AM 'tædərˌsɔl, 'tædərˌsɑl, -z
tattersall[2]
BR 'tatəs(ɔː)l, -z
AM 'tædərˌsɔl, 'tædərˌsɑl, -z
tattery
BR 'tat(ə)ri
AM 'tædəri
tattie
potato
BR 'tat|i, -ɪz
AM 'tædi, -z
tattily
BR 'tatɪli
AM 'tædəli
tattiness
BR 'tatɪnɪs
AM 'tædinɪs
tattle
BR 'tat|l, -lz, -ḷɪŋ\-lɪŋ, -ld
AM 'tædəl, -z, -ɪŋ, -d
tattler
BR 'tatḷə(r), 'tatlə(r), -z
AM 'tædḷər, 'tætlər, -z
tattletale
BR 'tatlteɪl, -z
AM 'tædlˌteɪl, -z
Tatton
BR 'tatn
AM 'tætn
tattoo
BR tə'tuː, ta'tuː, -z, -ɪŋ, -d
AM tæ'tu, -z, -ɪŋ, -d
tattooer
BR tə'tuːə(r), ta'tuːə(r), -z
AM tæ'tuər, -z
tattooist
BR tə'tuːɪst, ta'tuːɪst, -s
AM tæ'tuəst, -s
tatty
BR 'tat|i, -ɪə(r), -ɪɪst
AM 'tædi, -ər, -ɪst
Tatum
BR 'teɪtəm
AM 'teɪdəm
tau
BR tɔː(r), taʊ
AM taʊ, tɔ
taught
BR tɔːt
AM tɔt, tɑt
taunt
BR tɔːnt, -s, -ɪŋ, -ɪd
AM tɔn|t, tɑn|t, -ts, -(t)ɪŋ, -(t)əd
taunter
BR 'tɔːntə(r), -z
AM 'tɔn(t)ər, 'tɑn(t)ər, -z
tauntingly
BR 'tɔːntɪŋli
AM 'tɔn(t)ɪŋli, 'tɑn(t)ɪŋli
Taunton
BR 'tɔːntən
AM 'tɔn(t)ən, 'tɑn(t)ən
Taunus
BR 'tɔːnəs, 'taʊnəs
AM 'tɔnəs, 'taʊnəs
taupe
BR təʊp
AM toʊp
Taupo
BR 'taʊpəʊ
AM 'taʊpoʊ
taupy
BR 'təʊpi
AM 'toʊpi
Tauranga
BR taʊ'raŋgə(r)
AM taʊ'rɑŋgə
Taurean
BR 'tɔːrɪən, tɔː'riːən, -z
AM 'tɔriən, tɔ'riən, -z
taurine[1]
amido-ethyl-sulphonic acid
BR 'tɔːriːn
AM 'tɔˌrin
taurine[2]
bovine
BR 'tɔːrʌɪn
AM 'tɔˌraɪn
tauromachy
BR tɔː'rɒmək|i, -ɪz
AM tɔ'rɑməki, -z
Taurus
BR 'tɔːrəs
AM 'tɔrəs
taut
BR tɔːt, -ə(r), -ɪst
AM tɔ|t, tɑ|t, -dər, -dəst
tauten
BR 'tɔːt|n, -nz, -ṇɪŋ\-nɪŋ, -nd
AM 'tɔtn, 'tɑtn, -z, -ɪŋ, -d
tautly
BR 'tɔːtli
AM 'tɔtli, 'tɑtli
tautness
BR 'tɔːtnəs
AM 'tɔtnəs, 'tɑtnəs
tautochrone
BR 'tɔːtəkrəʊn, -z
AM 'tɔdəˌkroʊn, 'tɑdəˌkroʊn, -z
tautog
BR tɔː'tɒg, -z
AM tɔ'tɔg, tɑ'tɑg, -z
tautologic
BR ˌtɔːtə'lɒdʒɪk
AM ˌtɔdl'ɑdʒɪk, ˌtɑdl'ɑdʒɪk
tautological
BR ˌtɔːtə'lɒdʒɪkl
AM ˌtɔdl'ɑdʒəkəl, ˌtɑdl'ɑdʒəkəl
tautologically
BR ˌtɔːtə'lɒdʒɪkli
AM ˌtɔdl'ɑdʒək(ə)li, ˌtɑdl'ɑdʒək(ə)li
tautologise
BR tɔː'tɒlədʒʌɪz, -ɪz, -ɪŋ, -d
AM tɔ'tɑləˌdʒaɪz, tɑ'tɑləˌdʒaɪz, -ɪz, -ɪŋ, -d
tautologist
BR tɔː'tɒlədʒɪst, -s
AM tɔ'tɑlədʒəst, tɑ'tɑlədʒəst, -s
tautologize
BR tɔː'tɒlədʒʌɪz, -ɪz, -ɪŋ, -d
AM tɔ'tɑləˌdʒaɪz, tɑ'tɑləˌdʒaɪz, -ɪz, -ɪŋ, -d
tautologous
BR tɔː'tɒləgəs
AM tɔ'tɑləgəs, tɑ'tɑləgəs
tautology
BR tɔː'tɒlədʒ|i, -ɪz
AM tɔ'tɑlədʒi, tɑ'tɑlədʒi, -z
tautomer
BR 'tɔːtəmə(r), -z
AM 'tɔdəmər, 'tɑdəmər, -z
tautomeric
BR ˌtɔːtə'mɛrɪk
AM ˌtɔdə'mɛrɪk, ˌtɑdə'mɛrɪk
tautomerism
BR tɔː'tɒmərɪz(ə)m
AM tɔ'tɑməˌrɪzəm, tɑ'tɑməˌrɪzəm
tautophony
BR tɔː'tɒfən|i, tɔː'tɒfṇi, -ɪz
AM tɔ'tɑfəni, tɑ'tɑfəni, -z
Tavare
BR 'tavəreɪ
AM ˌtævə'reɪ, 'tævəˌreɪ
Tavaré
BR 'tavəreɪ
AM ˌtævə'reɪ, 'tævəˌreɪ
tavern
BR 'tavn, -z
AM 'tævərn, -z
taverna
BR tə'vəːnə(r), -z
AM tə'vərnə, -z

Taverner
BR 'tavn̩ə(r), 'tavənə(r)
AM 'tævərnər

Taverners
BR 'tavn̩əz
AM 'tævərnərz

Tavistock
BR 'tavɪstɒk
AM 'tævəˌstɑk

taw
BR tɔː(r), -z, -ɪŋ, -d
AM tɔ, tɑ, -z, -ɪŋ, -d

tawa
BR 'tɑːwə(r)
AM 'tɑwə

tawdrily
BR 'tɔːdrɪli
AM 'tɔdrəli, 'tɑdrəli

tawdriness
BR 'tɔːdrɪnɪs
AM 'tɔdrinɨs, 'tɑdrinɨs

tawdry
BR 'tɔːdr|i, -ɪə(r), -ɪɪst
AM 'tɔdri, 'tɑdri, -ər, -ɨst

Tawe
river
BR 'taʊi
AM 'taʊi

tawer
BR 'tɔːə(r), -z
AM tɔ(ə)r, -z

tawniness
BR 'tɔːnɪnɪs
AM 'tɔninɨs, 'tɑninɨs

tawny
BR 'tɔːn|i, -ɪə(r), -ɪɪst
AM 'tɔni, 'tɑni, -ər, -ɨst

taws
BR tɔːz, -ɪz
AM tɔz, tɑz, -ɨz

tawse
BR tɔːz, -ɪz
AM tɔz, tɑz, -ɨz

tax
BR taks, -ɪz, -ɪŋ, -t
AM tæks, -əz, -ɪŋ, -t

taxa
BR 'taksə(r)
AM 'tæksə

taxability
BR ˌtaksə'bɪlɪti
AM ˌtæksə'bɪlɨdi

taxable
BR 'taksəbl
AM 'tæksəbəl

taxation
BR tak'seɪʃn
AM tæk'seɪʃən

tax-deductible
BR ˌtaksdɪ'dʌktɪbl
AM ˈtæksdə'dəktəbəl

tax-efficient
BR ˌtaksɪ'fɪʃnt
AM ˈtæksəˈfɪʃənt

taxer
BR 'taksə(r), -z
AM 'tæksər, -z

taxes
plural of taxis
BR 'taksiːz
AM 'tækˌsiz

taxi
BR 'taks|i, -ɪz, -ɪɪŋ, -ɪd
AM 'tæksi, -z, -ɪŋ, -d

taxicab
BR 'taksɪkab, -z
AM 'tæksiˌkæb, -z

taxidermal
BR ˌtaksɪ'dəːml
AM ˌtæksə'dərml

taxidermic
BR ˌtaksɪ'dəːmɪk
AM ˌtæksə'dərmɪk

taxidermist
BR 'taksɪdəːmɪst, tak'sɪdəmɪst, -s
AM 'tæksəˌdərməst, -s

taxidermy
BR 'taksɪdəːmi, tak'sɪdəmi
AM 'tæksəˌdərmi

taximeter
BR 'taksɪˌmiːtə(r), -z
AM 'tæksiˌmidər, -z

taxingly
BR 'taksɪŋli
AM 'tæksɪŋli

taxis
reflex
BR 'taksɪs
AM 'tæksəs

taxiway
BR 'taksɪweɪ, -z
AM 'tæksiˌweɪ, -z

taxless
BR 'taksləs
AM 'tæksləs

taxman
BR 'taksman
AM 'tæksˌmæn

taxmen
BR 'taksmɛn
AM 'tæksˌmɛn

taxol®
BR 'taksɒl
AM 'tæksɔl, 'tæksɑl

taxon
BR 'taksɒn
AM 'tækˌsɑn

taxonomic
BR ˌtaksə'nɒmɪk
AM ˌtæksə'nɑmɪk

taxonomical
BR ˌtaksə'nɒmɪkl
AM ˌtæksə'nɑməkəl

taxonomically
BR ˌtaksə'nɒmɪkli
AM ˈtæksə'nɑmək(ə)li

taxonomist
BR tak'sɒnəmɪst, -s
AM tæk'sɑnəməst, -s

taxonomy
BR tak'sɒnəm|i, -ɪz
AM tæk'sɑnəmi, -z

taxpayer
BR 'taksˌpeɪə(r), -z
AM 'tæksˌpeɪər, -z

taxpaying
BR 'taksˌpeɪɪŋ
AM 'tæksˌpeɪɪŋ

Tay
BR teɪ
AM teɪ

tayberry
BR 'teɪb(ə)r|i, -ɪz
AM 'teɪˌbɛri, 'teɪbəri, -z

Tayler
BR 'teɪlə(r)
AM 'teɪlər

Taylor
BR 'teɪlə(r)
AM 'teɪlər

tayra
BR 'tʌɪrə(r), -z
AM 'taɪrə, -z

Tay-Sachs
BR ˌteɪ'saks
AM ˌteɪ'sæks

Tayside
BR 'teɪsʌɪd
AM 'teɪˌsaɪd

tazza
BR 'tɑːtsə(r), -z
AM 'tɑtsə, -z

Tbilisi
BR ˌtɪbɪ'liːsi
AM ˌtəbə'lisi

Tblisi
BR ˌtɪbɪ'liːsi
AM ˌtəbə'lisi

Tchad
BR tʃad
AM tʃæd

Tchadian
BR 'tʃadɪən, -z
AM 'tʃædiən, -z

Tchaikovsky
BR tʃʌɪ'kɒfski, tʃʌɪ'kɒvzki
AM tʃaɪ'kɔfski, tʃaɪ'kɑfski, tʃaɪ'kaʊski

TD
BR ˌtiː'diː, -z
AM ˈti'di, -z

te
BR tiː
AM ti

tea
BR tiː, -z
AM ti, -z

teabag
BR 'tiːbag, -z
AM 'tiˌbæg, -z

teaball
BR 'tiːbɔːl, -z
AM 'tiˌbɔl, 'tiˌbɑl, -z

teabread
BR 'tiːbrɛd
AM 'tiˌbrɛd

teacake
BR 'tiːkeɪk, -s
AM 'tiˌkeɪk, -s

teach
BR tiːtʃ, -ɪz, -ɪŋ
AM titʃ, -əz, -ɪŋ

teachability
BR ˌtiːtʃə'bɪlɪti
AM ˌtitʃə'bɪlɨdi

teachable
BR 'tiːtʃəbl
AM 'titʃəbəl

teachableness
BR 'tiːtʃəblnəs
AM 'titʃəbəlnəs

teacher
BR 'tiːtʃə(r), -z
AM 'titʃər, -z

teacherly
BR 'tiːtʃəli
AM 'titʃərli

teach-in
BR 'tiːtʃɪn, -z
AM 'titʃˌɪn, -z

teaching
BR 'tiːtʃɪŋ, -z
AM 'titʃɪŋ, -z

teacup
BR 'tiːkʌp, -s
AM 'tiˌkəp, -s

teacupful
BR 'tiːkʌpfʊl, -z
AM 'tiˌkəpˌfʊl, -z

teacupsful
BR 'tiːkʌpsfʊl
AM 'tiˌkəpsˌfʊl

teagarden
BR 'tiːˌgɑːdn, -z
AM 'tiˌgɑrdən, -z

teahouse
BR 'tiːhaʊ|s, -zɪz
AM 'tiˌhaʊ|s, -zəz

teak
BR tiːk
AM tik

teakettle
BR 'tiːˌkɛtl, -z
AM 'tiˌkɛdəl, -z

teal
BR tiːl
AM til

tealeaf
BR 'tiːliːf
AM 'tiˌlif

tealeaves
BR 'tiːliːvz
AM 'tiˌlivz

team
BR tiːm, -z, -ɪŋ, -d
AM tim, -z, -ɪŋ, -d

teammate
BR 'tiːmmeɪt, -s
AM 'ti(m)ˌmeɪt, -s

teamster
BR 'tiːmstə(r), -z
AM 'timstər, -z

team-teaching
BR 'tiːmˌtiːtʃɪŋ, ˌtiːm'tiːtʃɪŋ
AM 'timˌtitʃɪŋ

teamwork
BR 'tiːmwəːk
AM 'timˌwərk

teapot
BR 'tiːpɒt, -s
AM 'tiˌpɑt, -s

teapoy
BR 'tiːpɔɪ, -z
AM 'tiˌpɔɪ, -z

tear[1]
crying
BR tɪə(r), -z
AM tɪ(ə)r, -z

tear[2]
rip
BR tɛː(r), -z, -ɪŋ
AM tɛ(ə)r, -z, -ɪŋ

tearable
BR 'tɛːrəbl
AM 'tɛrəbəl

tearaway
BR 'tɛːrəweɪ, -z
AM 'tɛrəˌweɪ, -z

teardrop
BR 'tɪədrɒp, -s
AM 'tɪrˌdrɑp, -s

tearer
BR 'tɛːrə(r), -z
AM 'tɛrər, -z

tearful
BR 'tɪəf(ʊ)l
AM 'tɪrfəl

tearfully
BR 'tɪəfʊli, 'tɪəfl̩i
AM 'tɪrfəli

tearfulness
BR 'tɪəf(ʊ)lnəs
AM 'tɪrfəlnəs

teargas
BR 'tɪəgas, -ɪz, -ɪŋ, -d
AM 'tɪrˌgæs, -əz, -ɪŋ, -d

tearjerker
BR 'tɪəˌdʒəːkə(r), -z
AM 'tɪrˌdʒərkər, -z

tear-jerking
BR 'tɪəˌdʒəːkɪŋ
AM 'tɪrˌdʒərkɪŋ

tearless
BR 'tɪələs
AM 'tɪrləs

tearlessly
BR 'tɪələsli
AM 'tɪrləsli

tearlessness
BR 'tɪələsnəs
AM 'tɪrləsnəs

tearlike
BR 'tɪəlʌɪk
AM 'tɪrˌlaɪk

tear-off
BR 'tɛːrɒf
AM 'tɛrˌɔf, 'tɛrˌɑf

tearoom
BR 'tiːruːm, 'tiːrʊm, -z
AM 'tiˌrum, 'tiˌrʊm, -z

tearstained
BR 'tɪəsteɪnd
AM 'tɪrˌsteɪnd

teary
BR 'tɪəri
AM 'tɪri

Teasdale
BR 'tiːzdeɪl
AM 'tizˌdeɪl

tease
BR tiːz, -ɪz, -ɪŋ, -d
AM tiz, -ɪz, -ɪŋ, -d

teasel
BR 'tiːz|l, -lz, -l̩ɪŋ\-lɪŋ, -ld
AM 'tiz|əl, -əlz, -(ə)lɪŋ, -əld

teaseler
BR 'tiːzl̩ə(r), 'tiːzlə(r), -z
AM 'tiz(ə)lər, -z

teaser
BR 'tiːzə(r), -z
AM 'tizər, -z

teaset
BR 'tiːsɛt, -s
AM 'tiˌsɛt, -s

teashop
BR 'tiːʃɒp, -s
AM 'tiˌʃɑp, -s

teasingly
BR 'tiːzɪŋli
AM 'tizɪŋli

Teasmade®
BR 'tiːzmeɪd
AM 'tizˌmeɪd

teaspoon
BR 'tiːspuːn, -z
AM 'tiˌspun, -z

teaspoonful
BR 'tiːspuːnfʊl, -z
AM 'tiˌspunˌfʊl, -z

teaspoonsful
BR 'tiːspuːnzfʊl
AM 'tiˌspunzˌfʊl

teat
BR tiːt, -s
AM tit, -s

tea table
BR 'tiː ˌteɪbl, -z
AM 'ti ˌteɪbəl, -z

teatime
BR 'tiːtʌɪm
AM 'tiˌtaɪm

teazel
BR 'tiːz|l, -lz, -l̩ɪŋ\-lɪŋ, -ld
AM 'tiz|əl, -əlz, -(ə)lɪŋ, -əld

teazle
BR 'tiːz|l, -lz, -l̩ɪŋ\-lɪŋ, -ld
AM 'tiz|əl, -əlz, -(ə)lɪŋ, -əld

Tebay
BR 'tiːbeɪ
AM 'tibeɪ

Tebbit
BR 'tɛbɪt
AM 'tɛbət

Tebbitt
BR 'tɛbɪt
AM 'tɛbət

tec
BR tɛk, -s
AM tɛk, -s

tech
BR tɛk
AM tɛk

techie
BR 'tɛk|i, -ɪz
AM 'tɛki, -z

techily
BR 'tɛtʃɪli
AM 'tɛtʃəli

techiness
BR 'tɛtʃɪnɪs
AM 'tɛtʃinɪs, 'tɛkinɪs

technetium
BR tɛk'niːʃ(ɪ)əm
AM tɛk'niʃ(i)əm

technic
BR 'tɛknɪk, -s
AM 'tɛknɪk, -s

technical
BR 'tɛknɪkl, -z
AM 'tɛknəkəl, -z

technicality
BR ˌtɛknɪ'kalɪt|i, -ɪz
AM ˌtɛknə'kælədi, -z

technically
BR 'tɛknɪkli
AM 'tɛknək(ə)li

technicalness
BR 'tɛknɪklnəs
AM 'tɛknəkəlnəs

technician
BR tɛk'nɪʃn, -z
AM tɛk'nɪʃən, -z

technicist
BR 'tɛknɪsɪst, -s
AM 'tɛknəsəst, -s

technicolor
BR 'tɛknɪˌkʌlə(r), -d
AM 'tɛknəˌkələr, -d

technicolour
BR 'tɛknɪˌkʌlə(r)
AM 'tɛknəˌkələr

technique
BR tɛk'niːk, -s
AM tɛk'nik, -s

techno
BR 'tɛknəʊ
AM 'tɛknoʊ

technobabble
BR 'tɛknə(ʊ)ˌbabl
AM 'tɛknoʊˌbæbəl

technocracy
BR tɛk'nɒkrəs|i, -ɪz
AM tɛk'nɑkrəsi, -z

technocrat
BR 'tɛknəkrat, -s
AM 'tɛknəˌkræt, -s

technocratic
BR ˌtɛknə'kratɪk
AM ˌtɛknə'krætɪk

technocratically
BR ˌtɛknə'kratɪkli
AM ˌtɛknə'krædək(ə)li

technological
BR ˌtɛknə'lɒdʒɪkl
AM ˌtɛknə'lɑdʒəkəl

technologically
BR ˌtɛknə'lɒdʒɪkli
AM ˌtɛknə'lɑdʒək(ə)li

technologist
BR tɛk'nɒlədʒɪst, -s
AM tɛk'nɑlədʒəst, -s

technology
BR tɛk'nɒlədʒ|i, -ɪz
AM tɛk'nɑlədʒi, -z

technophile
BR 'tɛknə(ʊ)fʌɪl, -z
AM 'tɛknəˌfaɪl, -z

technophobe
BR 'tɛknə(ʊ)fəʊb, -z
AM 'tɛknəˌfoʊb, -z

technophobia
BR ˌtɛknə(ʊ)'fəʊbɪə(r)
AM ˌtɛknə'foʊbiə

technophobic
BR ˌtɛknə(ʊ)'fəʊbɪk
AM ˌtɛknə'foʊbɪk

technospeak
BR 'tɛknə(ʊ)spiːk
AM 'tɛknəˌspik

techy
BR 'tɛtʃ|i, -ɪə(r), -ɪɪst
AM 'tɛtʃi, 'tɛki, -ər, -ɪst

Teck
BR tɛk
AM tɛk

tectonic
BR tɛk'tɒnɪk, -s
AM tɛk'tɑnɪk, -s

tectonically
BR tɛk'tɒnɪkli
AM tɛk'tɑnək(ə)li

tectorial
BR tɛk'tɔːrɪəl
AM tɛk'tɔriəl

tectrices
BR 'tɛktrɪsiːz
AM 'tɛktrəˌsiz

tectrix
BR 'tɛktrɪks, -ɪz
AM 'tɛkˌtrɪks, -ɪz

Tecumseh
BR tɪ'kʌmsə(r)
AM tə'kəmsə

Tecwyn
BR 'tɛkwɪn
AM 'tɛkwən

ted
BR tɛd, -z, -ɪŋ, -ɨd
AM tɛd, -z, -ɪŋ, -əd

tedder
BR 'tɛdə(r), -z
AM 'tɛdər, -z

Teddington
BR 'tɛdɪŋt(ə)n
AM 'tɛdɪŋtən

teddy
BR tɛd|i, -ɪz
AM tɛdi, -z

Te Deum
BR ˌtiː 'diːəm, ˌteɪ 'deɪəm, -z
AM teɪ 'deɪəm, ti +, -z

tedious
BR 'tiːdɪəs
AM 'tidiəs

tediously
BR 'tiːdɪəsli
AM 'tidiəsli

tediousness
BR 'tiːdɪəsnəs
AM 'tidiəsnəs

tedium
BR 'tiːdɪəm
AM 'tidiəm

tee
BR tiː, -z, -ɪŋ, -d
AM ti, -z, -ɪŋ, -d

tee-hee
BR ˌtiː'hiː, -z, -ɪŋ, -d
AM ˌti'hi, -z, -ɪŋ, -d

teem
BR tiːm, -z, -ɪŋ, -d
AM tim, -z, -ɪŋ, -d

teen
BR tiːn, -z
AM tin, -z

teenage
BR 'tiːneɪdʒ, -d
AM 'tiˌneɪdʒ, -d

teenager
BR 'tiːnˌeɪdʒə(r), -z
AM 'tiˌneɪdʒər, -z

teensy
BR 'tiːnz|i, -ɪɪst
AM 'tinsi, -ɪst

teensy-weensy
BR ˌtiːnzɪ'wiːnzi
AM 'tinsi'winsi

teeny
BR 'tiːn|i, -ɪɪst
AM 'tini, -ɪst

teenybopper
BR 'tiːnɪˌbɒpə(r), -z
AM 'tiniˌbɑpər, -z

teeny-weeny
BR ˌtiːnɪ'wiːni
AM 'tini'wini

teepee
BR 'tiːpiː, -z
AM 'tiˌpi, -z

Tees
BR tiːz
AM tiz

Teesdale
BR 'tiːzdeɪl
AM 'tizˌdeɪl

teeshirt
BR 'tiːʃəːt, -s
AM 'tiˌʃərt, -s

tee-square
BR 'tiːskwɛː(r), -z
AM 'tiˌskwɛ(ə)r, -z

Teesside
BR 'tiː(z)sʌɪd
AM 'ti(z)ˌsaɪd

teeter
BR 'tiːt|ə(r), -əz, -(ə)rɪŋ, -əd
AM 'tidər, -z, -ɪŋ, -d

teeterboard
BR 'tiːtəbɔːd, -z
AM 'tidərˌbɔ(ə)rd, -z

teeter-tatter
BR 'tiːtəˌtatə(r), -z
AM 'tidərˌtadər, -z

teeter-totter
BR 'tiːtəˌtɒtə(r), -z
AM 'tidərˌtadər, -z

teeth
BR tiːθ
AM tiθ

teethe
BR tiːð, -z, -ɪŋ, -d
AM tið, -z, -ɪŋ, -d

teething ring
BR 'tiːðɪŋ rɪŋ, -z
AM 'tiðɪŋ ˌrɪŋ, -z

teetotal
BR ˌtiː'təʊtl
AM 'tiˌtoʊdl

teetotaler
BR ˌtiː'təʊtlə(r), ˌtiː'təʊtḷə(r), -z
AM 'tiˌtoʊdḷər, -z

teetotalism
BR ˌtiː'təʊtḷɪz(ə)m
AM 'ti'toʊdlˌɪzəm

teetotaller
BR ˌtiː'təʊtlə(r), ˌtiː'təʊtḷə(r), -z
AM 'tiˌtoʊdḷər, -z

teetotally
BR ˌtiː'təʊtḷi, ˌtiː'təʊtəli
AM 'tiˌtoʊdḷi

teetotum
BR tiː'təʊtəm, -z
AM ti'toʊdəm, -z

teff
BR tɛf, -s
AM tɛf, -s

TEFL
BR 'tɛfl
AM 'tɛfəl

Teflon®
BR 'tɛflɒn
AM 'tɛfˌlɑn

teg
BR tɛg, -z
AM tɛg, -z

Tegucigalpa
BR ˌtɛgʊsɪ'galpə(r), tɪˌguːsɪ'galpə(r)
AM təˌgusə'gælpə

tegular
BR 'tɛgjʊlə(r)
AM 'tɛgjələr

tegularly
BR 'tɛgjʊləli
AM 'tɛgjələrli

tegument
BR 'tɛgjʊm(ə)nt, -s
AM 'tɛgjəmənt, -s

tegumental
BR ˌtɛgjʊ'mɛntl
AM ˌtɛgjə'mɛn(t)l

tegumentary
BR ˌtɛgjʊ'mɛnt(ə)ri
AM ˌtɛgjə'mɛn(t)əri

Teheran
BR ˌteɪ(ə)'rɑːn, ˌtɛ(ə)'rɑːn, ˌteɪ(ə)'ran, ˌtɛ(ə)'ran
AM ˌtɛə'ræn, ˌtɛə'rɑn

Tehran
BR ˌteɪ(ə)'rɑːn, ˌtɛ(ə)'rɑːn, ˌteɪ(ə)'ran, ˌtɛ(ə)'ran
AM ˌtɛə'ræn, ˌtɛə'rɑn

Teign
BR tiːn, tɪn
AM tin

Teignmouth
BR 'tɪnməθ, 'tiːnməθ
AM 'tinməθ

Teilhard de Chardin
BR ˌteɪɑː də 'ʃɑːdã, + 'ʃɑːdan
AM tɛˌjɑrd də ʃɑr'dɛn

Te Kanawa
BR ˌteɪ 'kɑːnəwə(r)
AM ˌteɪ 'kɑnəwə

teknonymous
BR tɛk'nɒnɪməs
AM tɛk'nɑnəməs

teknonymy
BR tɛk'nɒnɪmi
AM tɛk'nɑnəmi

tektite
BR 'tɛktʌɪt, -s
AM 'tɛkˌtaɪt, -s

telaesthesia
BR ˌtɛlɪs'θiːzɪə(r), ˌtɛlɪs'θiːʒə(r)
AM ˌtɛləsθiʒ(i)ə, ˌtɛləsθiziə

telaesthetic
BR ˌtɛləs'θɛtɪk
AM ˌtɛləs'θɛdɪk

telamon
BR 'tɛləmən, 'tɛləmɒn, -z
AM 'tɛləˌmɑn, -z

Tel Aviv
BR ˌtɛl ə'viːv
AM ˌtɛl ə'viv

tele
BR 'tɛl|i, -ɪz
AM 'tɛli, -z

tele-ad
BR 'tɛlɪad, -z
AM 'tɛliˌæd, -z

telebanking
BR 'tɛlɪˌbaŋkɪŋ
AM 'tɛləˌbæŋkɪŋ

telecamera
BR 'tɛlɪˌkam(ə)rə(r), -z
AM 'tɛləˌkæm(ə)rə, -z

telecast
BR 'tɛlɪkɑːst, 'tɛlɪkast, -s, -ɪŋ, -ɨd
AM 'tɛləˌkæst, -s, -ɪŋ, -əd

telecaster
BR 'tɛlɪˌkɑːstə(r), 'tɛlɪˌkastə(r), -z
AM 'tɛləˌkæstər, -z

telecine
BR 'tɛlɪˌsɪni
AM ˌtɛlə'sɪni

Telecom®
BR 'tɛlɪkɒm
AM 'tɛləˌkɑm

telecomms
BR 'tɛlɪkɒmz
AM 'tɛləˌkɑmz

telecommunication
BR ˌtɛlɪkəˌmjuːnɪ'keɪʃn, -z
AM ˌtɛləkəˌmjunə'keɪʃən, -z

telecommute
BR ˌtɛlɪkə'mjuːt, -s, -ɪŋ, -ɨd
AM ˌtɛləkə'mju|t, -ts, -dɪŋ, -dɨd

telecommuter
BR 'tɛlɪkəˌmjuːtə(r), -z
AM ˌtɛləkəˌmjudər, -z

telecoms
BR 'tɛlɪkɒmz
AM 'tɛləˌkɑmz

teleconference
BR ˌtɛlɪ'kɒnf(ə)rəns, ˌtɛlɪ'kɒnf(ə)rṇs, 'tɛlɪˌkɒnf(ə)rəns, 'tɛlɪˌkɒnf(ə)rṇs, -ɪz
AM 'tɛləˌkɑnf(ə)rəns, -əz

teleconferencing
BR ˌtɛlɪ'kɒnf(ə)rənsɪŋ, ˌtɛlɪ'kɒnf(ə)rṇsɪŋ, 'tɛlɪˌkɒnf(ə)rənsɪŋ, 'tɛlɪˌkɒnf(ə)rṇsɪŋ
AM 'tɛləˌkɑnf(ə)rənsɪŋ

telecottage
BR 'tɛlɪˌkɒt|ɪdʒ, -ɪdʒɪz, -ɪdʒɪŋ, -ɪdʒd
AM 'tɛləˌkɑdɪdʒ, -ɪz, -ɪŋ

telecourse
BR 'tɛlɪkɔːs, -ɪz
AM 'tɛləˌkɔ(ə)rs, -əz

teledu[1]
stinking badger
BR 'tɛlɨduː, -z
AM 'tɛlə,du, -z

teledu[2]
Welsh, television
BR tɪ'lɛdi
AM tə'lɛdi
WE te'ledi

tele-evangelism
BR ,tɛlɪɪ'van(d)ʒəl-ɪz(ə)m, ,tɛlɪɪ'van(d)ʒl̩ɪz(ə)m
AM ,tɛli'vændʒə,lɪzəm

tele-evangelist
BR ,tɛlɪɪ'van(d)ʒəlɪst, ,tɛlɪɪ'van(d)ʒl̩ɪst, -s
AM ,tɛli'vændʒələst, -s

telefacsimile
BR ,tɛlɪfak'sɪmɪl|i, ,tɛlɪfak'sɪml̩|i, -ɪz
AM ',tɛlə,fæk'sɪməli, -z

Telefax®
BR 'tɛlɪfaks, -ɨz, -ɪŋ, -t
AM 'tɛlə,fæks, -əz, -ɪŋ, -t

telefilm
BR 'tɛlɪfɪlm, -z
AM 'tɛlə,fɪlm, -z

telegenic
BR ,tɛlɪ'dʒɛnɪk
AM ,tɛlə'dʒɛnɪk

telegonic
BR ,tɛlɪ'gɒnɪk
AM ,tɛlə'gɑnɪk

telegony
BR tɪ'lɛgəni, tɪ'lɛgn̩i
AM tə'lɛgəni

telegram
BR 'tɛlɨgram, -z, -ɪŋ, -d
AM 'tɛlə,græm, -z, -ɪŋ, -d

telegraph
BR 'tɛlɨgrɑːf, 'tɛlɨgraf, -s, -ɪŋ, -t
AM 'tɛlə,græf, -s, -ɪŋ, -t

telegrapher
BR tɪ'lɛgrəfə(r), -z
AM tə'lɛgrəfər, 'tɛlə,græfər, -z

telegraphese
BR ,tɛlɨgrə'fiːz
AM ',tɛləgræ'fiz

telegraphic
BR ,tɛlɪ'grafɪk
AM ,tɛlə'græfɪk

telegraphically
BR ,tɛlɪ'grafɪkli
AM ,tɛlə'græfək(ə)li

telegraphist
BR tɪ'lɛgrəfɪst, -s
AM tə'lɛgrəfəst, 'tɛlə,græfəst, -s

telegraphy
BR tɪ'lɛgrəfi
AM tə'lɛgrəfi

Telegu
BR 'tɛlɨguː, -z
AM 'tɛlə,gu, -z

telekinesis
BR ,tɛlɨkʌɪ'niːsɪs, ,tɛlɨkɪ'niːsɪs
AM ,tɛlə'kɪnəsəs, ,tɛləkə'nisɪs

telekinetic
BR ,tɛlɨkʌɪ'nɛtɪk, ,tɛlɨkɪ'nɛtɪk
AM ',tɛləkə'nɛdɪk

Telemachus
BR tɪ'lɛməkəs
AM tə'lɛməkəs

Telemann
BR 'teɪləman, 'tɛləman
AM 'tɛlə,mɑn

telemark
BR 'tɛlɨmɑːk, -s
AM 'tɛlə,mɑrk, -s

telemarketer
BR 'tɛlɪ,mɑːkɪtə(r), -z
AM ',tɛlə',mɑrkədər, -z

telemarketing
BR 'tɛlɪ,mɑːkɪtɪŋ
AM ',tɛlə',mɑrkədɪŋ

telemessage
BR 'tɛlɪ,mɛs|ɪdʒ, -ɨdʒɨz
AM 'tɛlə,mɛsɪdʒ, -ɨz

telemeter
BR tɪ'lɛmɪt|ə(r), 'tɛlɪ,miːt|ə(r), -əz, -(ə)rɪŋ, -əd
AM 'tɛlə,midər, -z, -ɪŋ, -d

telemetric
BR ,tɛlɪ'mɛtrɪk
AM ,tɛlə'mɛtrɪk

telemetry
BR tɪ'lɛmɪtri
AM tə'lɛmətri

teleologic
BR ,tiːlɪə'lɒdʒɪk, ,tɛlɪə'lɒdʒɪk
AM ',tiliə'lɑdʒɪk ',tiliə-'lɑdʒɪk

teleological
BR ,tiːlɪə'lɒdʒɪkl, ,tɛlɪə'lɒdʒɪkl
AM ',tiliə'lɑdʒəkəl, ',tiliə'lɑdʒəkəl

teleologically
BR ,tiːlɪə'lɒdʒɪkli, ,tɛlɪə'lɒdʒɪkli
AM ',tiliə'lɑdʒək(ə)li, ',tɛliə'lɑdʒək(ə)li

teleologism
BR ,tiːlɪ'ɒlədʒɪz(ə)m, ,tɛlɪ'ɒlədʒɪz(ə)m
AM ,tili'ɑlə,dʒɪzəm, ,tɛli'ɑlə,dʒɪzəm

teleologist
BR ,tiːlɪ'ɒlədʒɪst, ,tɛlɪ'ɒlədʒɪst, -s
AM ,tili'ɑlədʒəst, ,tɛli'ɑlədʒəst, -s

teleology
BR ,tiːlɪ'ɒlədʒi, ,tɛlɪ'ɒlədʒi
AM ,tili'ɑlədʒi, ,tɛliə'ɑlədʒi

teleost
BR 'tiːlɪɒst, 'tɛlɪɒst, -s
AM 'tili,ɑst, 'tɛli,ɑst, -s

telepath
BR 'tɛlɪpaθ, -s
AM 'tɛləpæθ, -ðz\-θs

telepathic
BR ,tɛlɪ'paθɪk
AM ,tɛlə'pæθɪk

telepathically
BR ,tɛlɪ'paθɪkli
AM ,tɛlə'pæθək(ə)li

telepathise
BR tɪ'lɛpəθʌɪz, -ɨz, -ɪŋ, -d
AM tə'lɛpə,θaɪz, -ɨz, -ɪŋ, -d

telepathist
BR tɪ'lɛpəθɪst, -s
AM tə'lɛpəθəst, -s

telepathize
BR tɪ'lɛpə,θʌɪz, -ɨz, -ɪŋ, -d
AM tə'lɛpə,θaɪz, -ɨz, -ɪŋ, -d

telepathy
BR tɪ'lɛpəθi
AM tə'lɛpəθi

téléphérique
BR ,tɛlɪfə'riːk, -s
AM ,tɛləfə'rik, -s

telephone
BR 'tɛlɪfəʊn, -z, -ɪŋ, -d
AM 'tɛlə,foʊn, -z, -ɪŋ, -d

telephonic
BR ,tɛlɪ'fɒnɪk
AM ,tɛlə'fɑnɪk

telephonically
BR ,tɛlɪ'fɒnɪkli
AM ,tɛlə'fɑnək(ə)li

telephonist
BR tɪ'lɛfənɪst, tɪ'lɛfn̩ɪst, -s
AM 'tɛlə,foʊnəst, tə'lɛfənəst, -s

telephony
BR tɪ'lɛfəni, tɪ'lɛfn̩i
AM tə'lɛfəni, 'tɛlə,foʊni

telephoto
BR ,tɛlɪ'fəʊtəʊ
AM ,tɛlə'foʊdoʊ

telephotograph
BR ,tɛlɪ'fəʊtəgrɑːf, ,tɛlɪ'fəʊtəgraf, -s
AM ,tɛlə'foʊdə,græf, -s

telephotographic
BR ,tɛlɪ,fəʊtə'grafɪk
AM ',tɛlə,foʊdə'græfɪk

telephotographically
BR ,tɛlɪ,fəʊtə'grafɪkli
AM ',tɛlə,foʊdə'græfək(ə)li

telephotography
BR ,tɛlɪfə'tɒgrəfi
AM ,tɛləfə'tɑgrəfi

teleplay
BR 'tɛlɪpleɪ, -z
AM 'tɛlə,pleɪ, -z

telepoint
BR 'tɛlɪpɔɪnt, -s
AM 'tɛlə,pɔɪnt, -s

teleport
BR 'tɛlɪpɔːt, -s, -ɪŋ, -ɨd
AM 'tɛlə,pɔ(ə)rt, -ts, -,pɔrdɪŋ, -,pɔrdəd

teleportation
BR ,tɛlɪpɔː'teɪʃn, -z
AM ,tɛlə,pɔr'teɪʃən, -z

teleprinter
BR 'tɛlɪ,prɪntə(r), -z
AM 'tɛlə,prɪn(t)ər, -z

teleprompt
BR 'tɛlɪprɒm(p)t, -s
AM 'tɛlə,prɑm(p)t, -s

teleprompter
BR 'tɛlɪ,prɒm(p)tə(r), -z
AM 'tɛlə,prɑm(p)tər, -z

telerecord[1]
noun
BR 'tɛlɪ,rɛkɔːd, -z
AM 'tɛlə,rɛkərd, -z

telerecord[2]
verb
BR 'tɛlɪrɪ,kɔːd, ,tɛlɪrɪ'kɔːd, -z, -ɪŋ, -ɨd
AM ',tɛlərə'kɔ(ə)rd, -z, -ɪŋ, -ɨd

telerecording
noun
BR 'tɛlɪrɪ,kɔːdɪŋ, -z
AM 'tɛlərə',kɔrdɪŋ, -z

telergy
BR 'tɛləːdʒi
AM 'tɛlərdʒi

telesales
BR 'tɛlɪseɪlz
AM 'tɛlə,seɪlz

telescope
BR 'tɛlɪskəʊp, -s
AM 'tɛlə,skoʊp, -s

telescopic
BR ,tɛlɪ'skɒpɪk
AM ,tɛlə'skɑpɪk

telescopically
BR ,tɛlɪ'skɒpɪkli
AM ,tɛlə'skɑpək(ə)li

teleshopping
BR 'tɛlɪ,ʃɒpɪŋ
AM 'tɛlə,ʃɑpɪŋ

telesoftware
BR 'tɛlɪ,sɒftwɛː(r)
AM ,tɛlə'sɔf(t),wɛ(ə)r, ,tɛlə'sɑf(t),wɛ(ə)r

telesthesia
BR ,tɛlɪs'θiːzɪə(*r*), ,tɛlɪs'θiːʒə(*r*)
AM ,tɛlɪs'θiʒ(i)ə, ,tɛləsθiziə

telesthetic
BR ,tɛlɪs'θɛtɪk
AM ,tɛləs'θɛdɪk

Teletex®
BR ˈtɛlɪtɛks
AM ˈtɛləˌtɛks
teletext
BR ˈtɛlɪtɛkst
AM ˈtɛləˌtɛkst
telethon
BR ˈtɛlɪθɒn, -z
AM ˈtɛləˌθɑn, -z
teletype
BR ˈtɛlɪtʌɪp, -s, -ɪŋ, -t
AM ˈtɛləˌtaɪp, -s, -ɪŋ, -t
teletypewriter
BR ˌtɛlɪˈtʌɪprʌɪtə(r), -z
AM ˌtɛləˈtaɪpˌraɪdər, -z
televangelism
BR ˌtɛlɪˈvan(d)ʒəlɪz(ə)m, ˌtɛlɪˈvan(d)ʒl̩ɪz(ə)m
AM ˌtɛləˈvændʒəˌlɪzəm
televangelist
BR ˌtɛlɪˈvan(d)ʒəlɪst, ˌtɛlɪˈvan(d)ʒl̩ɪst, -s
AM ˌtɛləˈvændʒələst, -s
teleview
BR ˈtɛlɪvjuː, -z, -ɪŋ, -d
AM ˈtɛləˌvju, -z, -ɪŋ, -d
televiewer
BR ˈtɛlɪˌvjuːə(r), -z
AM ˈtɛləˌvjuər, -z
televisable
BR ˈtɛlɪvʌɪzəbl
AM ˈtɛləˌvaɪzəbəl
televise
BR ˈtɛlɪvʌɪz, -ɪz, -ɪŋ, -d
AM ˈtɛləˌvaɪz, -ɪz, -ɪŋ, -d
television
BR ˈtɛlɪˌvɪʒn, ˌtɛlɪˈvɪʒn, -z
AM ˈtɛləˌvɪʒən, -z
televisor
BR ˈtɛlɪvʌɪzə(r), -z
AM ˈtɛləˌvaɪzər, -z
televisual
BR ˌtɛlɪˈvɪʒʊ(ə)l, ˌtɛlɪˈvɪzjʊ(ə)l, ˌtɛlɪˈvɪʒ(ʉ)l, ˌtɛlɪˈvɪzj(ʉ)l
AM ˌtɛləˈvɪʒ(əw)əl
televisually
BR ˌtɛlɪˈvɪʒ(j)ʊəli, ˌtɛlɪˈvɪʒ(j)ʉli, ˌtɛlɪˈvɪzjʊəli, ˌtɛlɪˈvɪzjʉli
AM ˌtɛləˈvɪʒ(əw)əli
telework
BR ˈtɛlɪwəːk, -s, -ɪŋ, -t
AM ˈtɛləˌwərk, -s, -ɪŋ, -t
teleworker
BR ˈtɛlɪˌwəːkə(r), -z
AM ˈtɛləˌwərkər, -z
Telex
BR ˈtɛlɛks, -ɪz, -ɪŋ, -t
AM ˈtɛlɛks, -əz, -ɪŋ, -t
telfer
BR ˈtɛlfə(r), -z
AM ˈtɛlfər, -z
Telford
BR ˈtɛlfəd
AM ˈtɛlfərd
tell
BR tɛl, -z, -ɪŋ
AM tɛl, -z, -ɪŋ
tellable
BR ˈtɛləbl
AM ˈtɛləbəl
teller
BR ˈtɛlə(r), -z
AM ˈtɛlər, -z
tellership
BR ˈtɛləʃɪp, -s
AM ˈtɛlərˌʃɪp, -s
telling
BR ˈtɛlɪŋ, -z
AM ˈtɛlɪŋ, -z
tellingly
BR ˈtɛlɪŋli
AM ˈtɛlɪŋli
telling-off
BR ˌtɛlɪŋˈɒf
AM ˌtɛlɪŋˈɔf, ˌtɛlɪŋˈɑf
tellings-off
BR ˌtɛlɪŋzˈɒf
AM ˌtɛlɪŋzˈɔf, ˌtɛlɪŋzˈɑf
telltale
BR ˈtɛlteɪl, -z
AM ˈtɛlˌteɪl, -z
tellurate
BR ˈtɛljʊreɪt, -s
AM ˈtɛljəˌreɪt, -s
tellurian
BR tɛˈljʊərɪən, tɪˈljʊərɪən, tɛˈljɔːrɪən, tɪˈljɔːrɪən, -z
AM təˈl(j)ʊriən, -z
telluric
BR tɛˈljʊərɪk, tɪˈljʊərɪk, tɛˈljɔːrɪk, tɪˈljɔːrɪk
AM təˈl(j)ʊrɪk
telluride
BR ˈtɛljʊrʌɪd
AM ˈtɛljəˌraɪd
tellurite
BR ˈtɛljʊrʌɪt, -s
AM ˈtɛljəˌraɪt, -s
tellurium
BR tɛˈljʊərɪəm, tɪˈljʊərɪəm, tɛˈljɔːrɪəm, tɪˈljɔːrɪəm
AM təˈl(j)ʊriəm
tellurous
BR ˈtɛljʊrəs
AM ˈtɛljərəs
telly
BR ˈtɛl|i, -ɪz
AM ˈtɛli, -z
telnet
BR ˈtɛlnet, -s, -ɪŋ, -ɪd
AM ˈtɛlnɛ|t, -ts, -dɪŋ, -dɪd
teloi
BR ˈtɛlɔɪ
AM ˈtɛlɔɪ
telomere
BR ˈtiːləmɪə(r), ˈtɛləmɪə(r)
AM ˈtɛləmɪ(ə)r, ˈtiləmɪ(ə)r
telos
BR ˈtɛlɒs
AM ˈtɛlɔs, ˈtɛlɑs
telpher
BR ˈtɛlfə(r), -z
AM ˈtɛlfər, -z
telpherage
BR ˈtɛlf(ə)rɪdʒ
AM ˈtɛlfərɪdʒ
telson
BR ˈtɛlsn, -z
AM ˈtɛlsən, -z
Telstar®
BR ˈtɛlstɑː(r)
AM ˈtɛlˌstɑr
Telugu
BR ˈtɛlʊguː, -z
AM ˈtɛləˌgu, -z
temblor
BR tɛmˈblɔː(r), -z
AM ˈtɛmblər, ˈtɛmˌblɔ(ə)r, -z
temerarious
BR ˌtɛməˈrɛːrɪəs
AM ˌtɛməˈrɛriəs
temerity
BR tɪˈmɛrɪti
AM təˈmɛrədi
Temne
BR ˈtɛmn|iː, ˈtɪmn|iː, -ɪz
AM ˈtɛmni, ˈtɪmni, -z
temp
BR tɛm|p, -ps, -pɪŋ, -(p)t
AM tɛm|p, -ps, -pɪŋ, -(p)t
temper
BR ˈtɛmp|ə(r), -əz, -(ə)rɪŋ, -əd
AM ˈtɛmp|ər, -ərz, -(ə)rɪŋ, -ərd
tempera
BR ˈtɛmp(ə)rə(*r*)
AM ˈtɛmpərə
temperable
BR ˈtɛmp(ə)rəbl
AM ˈtɛmp(ə)rəbəl
temperament
BR ˈtɛmprəm(ə)nt, -s
AM ˈtɛmp(ə)rəmənt, -s
temperamental
BR ˌtɛmprəˈmɛntl
AM ˌtɛmp(ə)rəˈmɛn(t)l
temperamentally
BR ˌtɛmprəˈmɛntl̩i, ˌtɛmprəˈmɛntəli
AM ˌtɛmp(ə)rəˈmɛn(t)li
temperance
BR tɛmp(ə)rəns, ˈtɛmp(ə)rn̩s
AM ˈtɛmp(ə)rəns
temperate
BR ˈtɛmp(ə)rət
AM ˈtɛmp(ə)rət
temperately
BR ˈtɛmp(ə)rətli
AM ˈtɛmp(ə)rətli
temperateness
BR ˈtɛmp(ə)rətnəs
AM ˈtɛmp(ə)rətnəs
temperative
BR ˈtɛmp(ə)rətɪv
AM ˈtɛmp(ə)rədɪv
temperature
BR ˈtɛmprɪtʃə(r), -z
AM ˈtɛmpə(rə)tʃər, ˈtɛmp(ə)rəˌtʃʊ(ə)r, -z
temperedly
BR ˈtɛmpədli
AM ˈtɛmpərdli
temperer
BR ˈtɛmp(ə)rə(r), -z
AM ˈtɛmp(ə)rər, -z
Temperley
BR ˈtɛmpəli
AM ˈtɛmpərli
tempersome
BR ˈtɛmpəs(ə)m
AM ˈtɛmpərsəm
Temperton
BR ˈtɛmpət(ə)n
AM ˈtɛmpərtən
tempest
BR ˈtɛmpɪst, -s
AM ˈtɛmpəst, -s
tempestuous
BR tɛmˈpɛstʃʊəs, tɛmˈpɛstjʊəs
AM tɛmˈpɛstʃ(əw)əs
tempestuously
BR tɛmˈpɛstʃʊəsli, tɛmˈpɛstjʊəsli
AM tɛmˈpɛstʃ(əw)əsli
tempestuousness
BR tɛmˈpɛstʃʊəsnəs, tɛmˈpɛstjʊəsnəs
AM tɛmˈpɛstʃ(əw)əsnəs
tempi
BR ˈtɛmpiː
AM ˈtɛmpi
Templar
BR ˈtɛmplə(r), -z
AM ˈtɛmplər, -z
template
BR ˈtɛmpleɪt, ˈtɛmplɪt, -s
AM ˈtɛmˌpleɪt, ˈtɛmplət, -s
temple
BR ˈtɛmpl, -z
AM ˈtɛmpəl, -z
templet
BR ˈtɛmplɪt, -s
AM ˈtɛmplət, -s
Templeton
BR ˈtɛmplt(ə)n
AM ˈtɛmpəltən
tempo
BR ˈtɛmpəʊ, -z
AM ˈtɛmpoʊ, -z

tempora
BR 'tɛmp(ə)rə(r)
AM 'tɛmpərə

temporal
BR 'tɛmp(ə)rəl, 'tɛmp(ə)rl̩
AM 'tɛmp(ə)rəl

temporality
BR ˌtɛmpə'ralɨti
AM ˌtɛmpə'rælədi

temporally
BR 'tɛmp(ə)rəli, 'tɛmp(ə)rl̩i
AM 'tɛmp(ə)rəli

temporarily
BR 'tɛmp(ə)r(ər)ɨli
AM 'tɛmpəˌrɛrəli

temporariness
BR 'tɛmp(ə)r(ər)ɪnɨs
AM 'tɛmpəˌrɛrinɨs

temporary
BR 'tɛmp(ə)r(ər)|i, -ɪz
AM 'tɛmpəˌrɛri, -z

temporisation
BR ˌtɛmp(ə)rʌɪ'zeɪʃn
AM ˌtɛmpərə'zeɪʃən, ˌtɛmpəˌraɪ'zeɪʃən

temporise
BR 'tɛmpərʌɪz, -ɨz, -ɪŋ, -d
AM 'tɛmpəˌraɪz, -ɨz, -ɪŋ, -d

temporiser
BR 'tɛmpərʌɪzə(r), -z
AM 'tɛmpəˌraɪzər, -z

temporization
BR ˌtɛmp(ə)rʌɪ'zeɪʃn
AM ˌtɛmpərə'zeɪʃən, ˌtɛmpəˌraɪ'zeɪʃən

temporize
BR 'tɛmpərʌɪz, -ɨz, -ɪŋ, -d
AM 'tɛmpəˌraɪz, -ɨz, -ɪŋ, -d

temporizer
BR 'tɛmpərʌɪzə(r), -z
AM 'tɛmpəˌraɪzər, -z

tempt
BR tɛm(p)t, -s, -ɪŋ, -ɨd
AM tɛm(p)t, -s, -ɪŋ, -əd

temptability
BR ˌtɛm(p)tə'bɪlɨti
AM ˌtɛm(p)tə'bɪlɨdi

temptable
BR 'tɛm(p)təbl
AM 'tɛm(p)təbəl

temptation
BR 'tɛm(p)'teɪʃn, -z
AM tɛm(p)'teɪʃən, -z

tempter
BR 'tɛm(p)tə(r), -z
AM 'tɛm(p)tər, -z

tempting
BR 'tɛm(p)tɪŋ
AM 'tɛm(p)tɪŋ

temptingly
BR 'tɛm(p)tɪŋli
AM 'tɛm(p)tɪŋli

temptress
BR 'tɛm(p)trɪs, -ɨz
AM 'tɛm(p)trəs, -əz

tempura
BR tɛm'pʊərə(r), 'tɛmp(ə)rə(r)
AM tɛm'pʊrə, 'tɛmpərə

ten
BR tɛn, -z
AM tɛn, -z

tenability
BR ˌtɛnə'bɪlɨti
AM ˌtɛnə'bɪlɨdi

tenable
BR 'tɛnəbl
AM 'tɛnəbəl

tenableness
BR 'tɛnəblnəs
AM 'tɛnəbəlnəs

tenace
BR 'tɛneɪs, 'tɛnɪs, tɛ'neɪs, -ɨz
AM 'tɛˌn|eɪs, 'tɛn|əs, -eɪsɨz\-əsəz

tenacious
BR tɪ'neɪʃəs
AM tə'neɪʃəs

tenaciously
BR tɪ'neɪʃəsli
AM tə'neɪʃəsli

tenaciousness
BR tɪ'neɪʃəsnəs
AM tə'neɪʃəsnəs

tenacity
BR tɪ'nasɨti
AM tə'næsədi

tenacula
BR tɪ'nakjʉlə(r)
AM tə'nækjələ

tenaculum
BR tɪ'nakjʉləm
AM tə'nækjələm

tenancy
BR 'tɛnəns|i, -ɪz
AM 'tɛnənsi, -z

tenant
BR 'tɛnənt, -s
AM 'tɛnənt, -s

tenantable
BR 'tɛnəntəbl
AM 'tɛnən(t)əbəl

tenantless
BR 'tɛnəntləs
AM 'tɛnən(t)ləs

tenantry
BR 'tɛnəntri
AM 'tɛnəntri

Tenbury
BR 'tɛnb(ə)ri
AM 'tɛnˌbɛri

Tenby
BR 'tɛnbi
AM 'tɛnbi

tench
BR tɛn(t)ʃ, -ɨz
AM tɛn(t)ʃ, -əz

tend
BR tɛnd, -z, -ɪŋ, -ɨd
AM tɛnd, -z, -ɪŋ, -əd

tendance
BR 'tɛndəns
AM 'tɛndəns

tendencious
BR tɛn'dɛnʃəs
AM tɛn'dɛnʃəs

tendenciously
BR tɛn'dɛnʃəsli
AM tɛn'dɛnʃəsli

tendenciousness
BR tɛn'dɛnʃəsnəs
AM tɛn'dɛnʃəsnəs

tendency
BR 'tɛndəns|i, -ɪz
AM 'tɛndnsi, -z

tendentious
BR tɛn'dɛnʃəs
AM tɛn'dɛnʃəs

tendentiously
BR tɛn'dɛnʃəsli
AM tɛn'dɛnʃəsli

tendentiousness
BR tɛn'dɛnʃəsnəs
AM tɛn'dɛnʃəsnəs

tender
BR 'tɛnd|ə(r), -əz, -(ə)rɪŋ, -əd, -(ə)rə(r), -(ə)rɪst
AM 'tɛnd|ər, -ərz, -(ə)rɪŋ, -ərd, -ər, -əst

tenderer
BR 'tɛnd(ə)rə(r), -z
AM 'tɛnd(ə)rər, -z

tender-eyed
BR ˌtɛndər'ʌɪd
AM 'tɛndərˌaɪd

tenderfoot
BR 'tɛndəfʊt, -s
AM 'tɛndərˌfʊt, -s

tenderhearted
BR ˌtɛndə'hɑːtɪd
AM ˈtɛndərˈhɑrdəd

tenderheartedly
BR ˌtɛndə'hɑːtɪdli
AM ˈtɛndərˈhɑrdədli

tenderhearted-ness
BR ˌtɛndə'hɑːtɪdnɪs
AM ˈtɛndərˈhɑrdədnəs

tenderise
BR 'tɛndərʌɪz, -ɨz, -ɪŋ, -d
AM 'tɛndəˌraɪz, -ɨz, -ɪŋ, -d

tenderiser
BR 'tɛndərʌɪzə(r)
AM 'tɛndəˌraɪzər

tenderize
BR 'tɛndərʌɪz, -ɨz, -ɪŋ, -d
AM 'tɛndəˌraɪz, -ɨz, -ɪŋ, -d

tenderizer
BR 'tɛndərʌɪzə(r), -z
AM 'tɛndəˌraɪzər, -z

tenderloin
BR 'tɛndəlɔɪn, -z
AM 'tɛndərˌlɔɪn, -z

tenderly
BR 'tɛndəli
AM 'tɛndərli

tenderness
BR 'tɛndənəs
AM 'tɛndərnəs

tendinitis
BR ˌtɛndə'nʌɪtɪs
AM ˌtɛndə'naɪdɪs

tendinous
BR 'tɛndɪnəs
AM 'tɛndənəs

tendon
BR 'tɛndən, -z
AM 'tɛndən, -z

tendonitis
BR ˌtɛndə'nʌɪtɪs
AM ˌtɛndə'naɪdɪs

tendresse
BR tɒ̃'drɛs
AM tɛn'drɛs

tendril
BR 'tɛndr(ɨ)l, -z
AM 'tɛndrəl, -z

tenebrae
BR 'tɛnɨbriː, 'tɛnɨbreɪ
AM 'tɛnəˌbreɪ, 'tɛnəbri, 'tɛnəˌbraɪ

tenebrous
BR 'tɛnɨbrəs
AM 'tɛnəbrəs

Tenedos
BR 'tɛnɨdɒs
AM 'tɛnədɔs, 'tɛnədɑs

tenement
BR 'tɛnɪm(ə)nt, -s
AM 'tɛnəmənt, -s

tenemental
BR ˌtɛnɪ'mɛntl
AM ˌtɛnə'mɛn(t)l

tenementary
BR ˌtɛnɪ'mɛnt(ə)ri
AM ˌtɛnə'mɛn(t)əri

Tenerife
BR ˌtɛnə'riːf
AM ˌtɛnə'rɪf
SP tene'rife

tenesmus
BR tɪ'nɛzməs
AM tə'nɛzməs, tə'nɛzməs

tenet
BR 'tɛnɪt, -s
AM 'tɛnət, -s

tenfold
BR 'tɛnfəʊld
AM 'tɛnˌfoʊld

ten-gallon hat
BR ˌtɛnˌgalən 'hat, -s
AM 'tɛnˈgælən 'hæt, -s

Teng Hsiao-p'ing
BR ˌtɛŋ sɪaʊ'pɪŋ, + ʃaʊ'pɪŋ
AM 'tɛŋ ˌsiaʊ'pɪŋ

tenia
BR ˈtiːnɪə(r)
AM ˈtiniə
Teniers
BR ˈtɛnɪəz
AM ˈtɛniərz
tenioid
BR ˈtiːnɪɔɪd
AM ˈtiniˌɔɪd
Tenison
BR ˈtɛnɪs(ə)n
AM ˈtɛnəsən
Tenko
BR ˈtɛŋkəʊ
AM ˈtɛŋkoʊ
Tennant
BR ˈtɛnənt
AM ˈtɛnənt
tenné
BR ˈtɛni, -z
AM ˈtɛni, -z
tenner
BR ˈtɛnə(r), -z
AM ˈtɛnər, -z
Tennessean
BR ˌtɛnɪˈsiːən, -z
AM ˌtɛnəˈsiən, -z
Tennessee
BR ˌtɛnɪˈsiː
AM ˌtɛnəˈsi
Tennesseean
BR ˌtɛnɪˈsiːən, -z
AM ˌtɛnəˈsiən, -z
Tenniel
BR ˈtɛnɪəl
AM ˈtɛniəl
tennis
BR ˈtɛnɪs
AM ˈtɛnəs
Tennison
BR ˈtɛnɪs(ə)n
AM ˈtɛnəsən
tenno
BR ˈtɛnəʊ, -z
AM ˈtɛnoʊ, -z
tenny
BR ˈtɛn|i, -ɪz
AM ˈtɛni, -z
Tennyson
BR ˈtɛnɪs(ə)n
AM ˈtɛnəsən
Tennysonian
BR ˌtɛnɪˈsəʊnɪən
AM ˌtɛnəˈsoʊniən
Tenochtitlán
BR ˌtɛnɒtʃtɪˈtlɑːn
AM təˌnɑtʃtəˈtlɑn
tenon
BR ˈtɛnən, -z
AM ˈtɛnən, -z
tenoner
BR ˈtɛnənə(r), -z
AM ˈtɛnənər, -z
tenon-saw
BR ˈtɛnənsɔː(r), -z
AM ˈtɛnənˌsɔ, ˈtɛnənˌsɑ, -z

tenor
BR ˈtɛnə(r), -z
AM ˈtɛnər, -z
tenorist
BR ˈtɛnərɪst, -s
AM ˈtɛnərəst, -s
tenosynovitis
BR ˌtɛnəʊˌsʌɪnəˈvʌɪtɪs
AM ˌtɛnoʊˌsaɪnəˈvaɪdɪs
tenotomy
BR tɪˈnɒtəm|i, -ɪz
AM təˈnɑdəmi, -z
tenour
BR ˈtɛnə(r)
AM ˈtɛnər
tenpence
BR ˈtɛnpəns, -ɪz
AM ˈtɛnpəns, -əz
tenpenny
BR ˈtɛnpən|i, -ɪz
AM ˈtɛnˌpɛni, -z
tenpin
BR ˈtɛnpɪn, -z
AM ˈtɛnˌpɪn, -z
tenpin bowling
BR ˌtɛnpɪn ˈbəʊlɪŋ
AM ˈtɛnˌpɪn ˈboʊlɪŋ
tenrec
BR ˈtɛnrɛk, -s
AM ˈtɛnˌrɛk, -s
tense
BR tɛns, -ɪz, -ə(r), -ɪst
AM tɛns, -əz, -ər, -əst
tenseless
BR ˈtɛnsləs
AM ˈtɛnsləs
tensely
BR ˈtɛnsli
AM ˈtɛnsli
tenseness
BR ˈtɛnsnəs
AM ˈtɛnsnəs
tensile
BR ˈtɛnsʌɪl
AM ˈtɛnsəl, ˈtɛnˌsaɪl
tensility
BR tɛnˈsɪlɪti
AM tɛnˈsɪlɪdi
tensimeter
BR tɛnˈsɪmɪtə(r), -z
AM tɛnˈsɪmɪdər, -z
tension
BR ˈtɛnʃn, -z
AM ˈtɛnʃən, -z
tensional
BR ˈtɛnʃn̩(ə)l, ˈtɛnʃən(ə)l
AM ˈtɛnʃ(ə)nəl
tensionally
BR ˈtɛnʃn̩əli, ˈtɛnʃn̩li, ˈtɛnʃənl̩i, ˈtɛnʃ(ə)nəli
AM ˈtɛnʃ(ə)nəli
tensioner
BR ˈtɛnʃn̩ə(r), ˈtɛnʃənə(r), -z
AM ˈtɛnʃənər, -z

tensionless
BR ˈtɛnʃ(ə)nləs
AM ˈtɛnʃənləs
tensity
BR ˈtɛnsɪti
AM ˈtɛnsədi
tenson
BR ˈtɛnsn, -z
AM ˈtɛnsən, -z
tensor
BR ˈtɛnsə(r), -z
AM ˈtɛnsər, ˈtɛnˌsɔ(ə)r, -z
tensorial
BR tɛnˈsɔːrɪəl
AM tɛnˈsɔriəl
tent
BR tɛnt, -s, -ɪŋ, -ɪd
AM tɛn|t, -ts, -(t)ɪŋ, -(t)əd
tentacle
BR ˈtɛntəkl, -z, -d
AM ˈtɛn(t)əkəl, -z, -d
tentacular
BR tɛnˈtakjʊlə(r)
AM tɛnˈtækjələr
tentaculate
BR tɛnˈtakjʊlət
AM tɛnˈtækjələt
tentage
BR ˈtɛntɪdʒ
AM ˈtɛn(t)ɪdʒ
tentative
BR ˈtɛntətɪv, -z
AM ˈtɛn(t)ədɪv, -z
tentatively
BR ˈtɛntətɪvli
AM ˈtɛn(t)ədɪvli
tentativeness
BR ˈtɛntətɪvnɪs
AM ˈtɛn(t)ədɪvnɪs
tenter
BR ˈtɛntə(r), -z
AM ˈtɛn(t)ər, -z
Tenterden
BR ˈtɛntəd(ə)n
AM ˈtɛn(t)ərdən
tenterhook
BR ˈtɛntəhʊk, -s
AM ˈtɛn(t)ərˌ(h)ʊk, -s
tenth
BR tɛnθ, -s
AM tɛnθ, -s
tenthly
BR ˈtɛnθli
AM ˈtɛnθli
tenth-rate
BR ˌtɛnθˈreɪt
AM ˌtɛnθˈreɪt
tenuis
BR ˈtɛnjʊɪs, -ɪz
AM ˈtɛnjəwəs, -əz
tenuity
BR tɪˈnjuːɪti, tɛˈnjuːɪti
AM tɛˈn(j)uədi, təˈn(j)uədi

tenuous
BR ˈtɛnjʊəs
AM ˈtɛnjəwəs
tenuously
BR ˈtɛnjʊəsli
AM ˈtɛnjəwəsli
tenuousness
BR ˈtɛnjʊəsnəs
AM ˈtɛnjəwəsnəs
tenure
BR ˈtɛnjə(r), -d
AM ˈtɛnjər, -d
tenurial
BR tɛˈnjʊərɪəl, tɪˈnjʊərɪəl, tɛˈnjɔːrɪəl, tɪˈnjɔːrɪəl
AM tɛˈnjʊriəl
tenurially
BR tɛˈnjʊərɪəli, tɪˈnjʊərɪəli, tɛˈnjɔːrɪəli, tɪˈnjɔːrɪəli
AM tɛˈnjʊriəli, təˈnjʊriəli
tenuto
BR tɛˈnjuːtəʊ, tɪˈnjuːtəʊ, -z
AM tɛnudoʊ, -z
Tenzing Norgay
BR ˌtɛnzɪŋ ˈnɔːgeɪ
AM ˌtɛnzɪŋ ˈnɔrˌgeɪ
tenzon
BR ˈtɛnzn, -z
AM ˈtɛnzən, -z
teocalli
BR ˌtiːə(ʊ)ˈkal|i, -ɪz
AM ˌtioʊˈkɑli, -z
tepee
BR ˈtiːpiː, -z
AM ˈtiˌpi, -z
tephra
BR ˈtɛfrə(r), -z
AM ˈtɛfrə, -z
tepid
BR ˈtɛpɪd
AM ˈtɛpəd
tepidaria
BR ˌtɛpɪˈdɛːrɪə(r)
AM ˌtɛpəˈdɛriə
tepidarium
BR ˌtɛpɪˈdɛːrɪəm
AM ˌtɛpəˈdɛriəm
tepidity
BR tɛˈpɪdɪti, tɪˈpɪdɪti
AM təˈpɪdɪdi
tepidly
BR ˈtɛpɪdli
AM ˈtɛpədli
tepidness
BR ˈtɛpɪdnɪs
AM ˈtɛpədnəs
tequila
BR tɪˈkiːlə(r)
AM təˈkilə
terabyte
BR ˈtɛrəbʌɪt, -s
AM ˈtɛrəˌbaɪt, -s

teraflop
BR ˈtɛrəflɒp, -s
AM ˈtɛrəˌflɑp, -s

terai
BR təˈrʌɪ, -z
AM təˈraɪ, -z

terameter
BR ˈtɛrəˌmiːtə(r), -z
AM ˈtɛrəˌmidər, -z

terametre
BR ˈtɛrəˌmiːtə(r), -z
AM ˈtɛrəˌmidər, -z

teraph
BR ˈtɛrəf, -s
AM ˈtɛrəf, -s

teraphim
BR ˈtɛrəfɪm
AM ˈtɛrəfɪm

teratogen
BR tɛˈratədʒ(ə)n, tɪˈratədʒ(ə)n, ˈtɛrətədʒ(ə)n, -z
AM tɛˈrædədʒən, ˈtɛrədədʒən, -z

teratogenic
BR tɛˌratə(ʊ)ˈdʒɛnɪk, tɪˌratə(ʊ)ˈdʒɛnɪk, ˌtɛrətə(ʊ)ˈdʒɛnɪk
AM ˌtɛrədəˈdʒɛnɪk, ˌtɛrəˌtoʊˈdʒɛnɪk

teratogeny
BR ˌtɛrəˈtɒdʒɪni
AM ˌtɛrəˈtɑdʒəni

teratological
BR ˌtɛrətəˈlɒdʒɪkl
AM ˌtɛrədəˈlɑdʒəkəl

teratologist
BR ˌtɛrəˈtɒlədʒɪst, -s
AM ˌtɛrəˈtɑlədʒəst, -s

teratology
BR ˌtɛrəˈtɒlədʒi
AM ˌtɛrəˈtɑlədʒi

teratoma
BR ˌtɛrəˈtəʊmə(r), -z
AM ˌtɛrəˈtoʊmə, -z

teratomata
BR ˌtɛrəˈtəʊmətə(r)
AM ˌtɛrəˈtoʊmədə

terawatt
BR ˈtɛrəwɒt, -s
AM ˈtɛrəˌwɑt, -s

terbium
BR ˈtəːbɪəm
AM ˈtərbiəm

terce
BR təːs, -ɪz
AM tərs, -əz

tercel
BR ˈtəːsl, -z
AM ˈtərsəl, -z

tercentenary
BR ˌtəːsɛnˈtiːn(ə)r|i, ˌtəːs(ə)nˈtiːn(ə)r|i, ˌtəːsɛnˈtɛn(ə)r|i, ˌtəːs(ə)nˈtɛn(ə)r|i, -ɪz
AM ˌtərsənˈtɛnəri, ˌtɛrˈsɛntnˌɛri, -z

tercentennial
BR ˌtəːsɛnˈtɛnɪəl, ˌtəːs(ə)nˈtɛnɪəl, -z
AM ˌtɛrsənˈtɛniəl, ˌtɛrˌsɛnˈtɛniəl, -z

tercet
BR ˈtəːsɪt, -s
AM ˈtɛrsət, -s

terebinth
BR ˈtɛrɪbɪnθ, -s
AM ˈtɛrəˌbinθ, -s

terebinthine
BR ˌtɛrɪˈbɪnθʌɪn
AM ˌtɛrəˈbɪnθən

terebra
BR ˈtɛrɪbrə(r), tɪˈriːbrə(r)
AM ˈtɛrəbrə, təˈribrə

terebrae
BR ˈtɛrɪbriː, tɪˈriːbriː, ˈtɛrɪbreɪ, tɪˈriːbreɪ
AM ˈtɛrəbri, təˈribri, təˈriˌbraɪ, ˈtɛrəˌbraɪ

terebrant
BR ˈtɛrɪbr(ə)nt, tɪˈriːbr(ə)nt, -s
AM ˈtɛrəˌbrænt, təˈribrənt, -s

teredo
BR tɪˈriːdəʊ, tɛˈriːdəʊ, -z
AM tɛˈridoʊ, təˈridoʊ, -z

Terence
BR ˈtɛrəns, ˈtɛrn̩s
AM ˈtɛrəns

Teresa
BR tɪˈriːzə(r), tɪˈreɪzə(r), tɪˈriːsə(r), tɪˈreɪsə(r)
AM təˈrisə, təˈreɪsə, təˈrizə, təˈreɪzə

Terese
BR tɪˈriːz, tɪˈriːs, tɪˈreɪz, tɛˈreɪz
AM təˈrisə, təˈreɪsə, təˈrizə, təˈreɪzə

Teresina
BR ˌtɛrɪˈziːnə(r), ˌtɛrɪˈsiːnə(r)
AM ˌtɛrəˈsinə, ˌtɛrəˈzinə

terete
BR təˈriːt
AM ˈtɛˌrit

tergal
BR ˈtəːgl
AM ˈtərgəl

tergiversate
BR ˈtəːdʒɪvəseɪt, ˈtəːdʒɪˌvəːseɪt, -s, -ɪŋ, -ɪd
AM ˈtərdʒəvərˌseɪ|t, ˌtərdʒəˈvərˌseɪ|t, -ts, -dɪŋ, -dɪd

tergiversation
BR ˌtəːdʒɪvəˈseɪʃn
AM ˌtərdʒəvərˈseɪʃən

tergiversator
BR ˈtəːdʒɪvəˌseɪtə(r), -z
AM ˈtərdʒəvərˌseɪdər, ˌtərdʒəˈvərˌseɪdər, -z

teriyaki
BR ˌtɛrɪˈjɑːki, ˌtɛrɪˈjaki
AM ˌtɛriˈjɑki

term
BR təːm, -z, -ɪŋ, -d
AM tərm, -z, -ɪŋ, -d

termagant
BR ˈtəːməg(ə)nt, -s
AM ˈtərməgənt, -s

terminable
BR ˈtəːmɪnəbl
AM ˈtərmənəbəl

terminableness
BR ˈtəːmɪnəblnəs
AM ˈtərmənəbəlnəs

terminal
BR ˈtəːmɪnl, -z
AM ˈtərmənəl, -z

terminally
BR ˈtəːmɪnl̩i, ˈtəːmɪnəli
AM ˈtərmənəli

terminate
BR ˈtəːmɪneɪt, -s, -ɪŋ, -ɪd
AM ˈtərməˌneɪ|t, -ts, -dɪŋ, -dɪd

termination
BR ˌtəːmɪˈneɪʃn, -z
AM ˌtərməˈneɪʃən, -z

terminational
BR ˌtəːmɪˈneɪʃn̩(ə)l, ˌtəːmɪˈneɪʃən(ə)l
AM ˌtərməˈneɪʃ(ə)nəl

terminator
BR ˈtəːmɪneɪtə(r), -z
AM ˈtərməˌneɪdər, -z

termini
BR ˈtəːmɪnʌɪ
AM ˈtərməˌnaɪ, ˈtərməni

terminism
BR ˈtəːmɪnɪz(ə)m
AM ˈtərməˌnɪzəm

terminist
BR ˈtəːmɪnɪst, -s
AM ˈtərmənəst, -s

terminological
BR ˌtəːmɪnəˈlɒdʒɪkl
AM ˌtərmənəˈlɑdʒəkəl

terminologically
BR ˌtəːmɪnəˈlɒdʒɪkli
AM ˌtərmənəˈlɑdʒək(ə)li

terminologist
BR ˌtəːmɪˈnɒlədʒɪst, -s
AM ˌtərməˈnɑlədʒəst, -s

terminology
BR ˌtəːmɪˈnɒlədʒ|i, -ɪz
AM ˌtərməˈnɑlədʒi, -z

terminus
BR ˈtəːmɪnəs, -ɪz
AM ˈtərmənəs, -əz

termitaria
BR ˌtəːmɪˈtɛːrɪə(r)
AM ˌtərməˈtɛriə

termitarium
BR ˌtəːmɪˈtɛːrɪəm
AM ˌtərməˈtɛriəm

termitary
BR ˈtəːmɪt(ə)r|i, -ɪz
AM ˈtərməˌtɛri, -z

termite
BR ˈtəːmʌɪt, -s
AM ˈtərˌmaɪt, -s

termless
BR ˈtəːmləs
AM ˈtərmləs

termly
BR ˈtəːmli
AM ˈtərmli

termor
BR ˈtəːmə(r), -z
AM ˈtərmər, -z

tern
BR təːn, -z
AM tərn, -z

ternary
BR ˈtəːn(ə)r|i, -ɪz
AM ˈtərnəri, -z

ternate
BR ˈtəːnət, ˈtəːneɪt
AM ˈtərneɪt, ˈtərnət

ternately
BR ˈtəːnətli, ˈtəːneɪtli
AM ˈtərneɪtli, ˈtərnətli

terne
BR təːn
AM tərn

terne-plate
BR ˈtəːnpleɪt
AM ˈtərnˌpleɪt

terpene
BR ˈtəːpiːn, -z
AM ˈtərˌpin, -z

Terpsichore
BR ˌtəːpˈsɪk(ə)ri
AM ˌtərpˈsɪkəri

Terpsichorean
BR ˌtəːpsɪkəˈriːən, ˌtəːpsɪˈkɔːrɪən
AM ˌtərpˌsɪkəˈriən, ˌtərpsəkəˈriən

terra
BR ˈtɛrə(r)
AM ˈtɛrə

terra alba
BR ˌtɛrə(r) ˈalbə(r)
AM ˌtɛrə ˈælbə

terrace
BR ˈtɛrɪs, -ɪz, -ɪŋ, -t
AM ˈtɛrəs, -əz, -ɪŋ, -t

terracotta
BR ˌtɛrəˈkɒtə(r)
AM ˌtɛrəˈkɑdə

Terra del Fuego
BR ˌtɛrə dɛl fʊˈeɪgəʊ
AM ˌtɛrə dɛl fʊˈeɪgoʊ

terra firma
BR ˌtɛrə ˈfəːmə(r)

AM ˌtɛrə ˈfərmə

terrain
BR tɪˈreɪn, tɛˈreɪn, -z
AM təˈreɪn, tɛˈreɪn, -z

terra incognita
BR ˌtɛrə(r) ˌɪŋkɒɡˈniːtə(r), ɪŋˈkɒɡnɪtə(r)
AM ˌtɛrə ˌɪnˌkɑɡˈnidə, + ənˈkɑɡnədə

terramara
BR ˌtɛrəˈmɑːrə(r)
AM ˌtɛrəˈmɑrə

terramare
BR ˌtɛrəˈmɑːr|i, -ɪz
AM ˌtɛrəˈmɑri, -z

Terramycin®
BR ˌtɛrəˈmʌɪsɪn
AM ˌtɛrəˈmaɪsɪn

terrane
BR tɛˈreɪn, -z
AM təˈreɪn, -z

terrapin
BR ˈtɛrəpɪn, -z
AM ˈtɛrəˌpɪn, -z

terraria
BR tɛˈrɛːrɪə(r), tɪˈrɛːrɪə(r)
AM təˈrɛriə

terrarium
BR tɛˈrɛːrɪəm, tɪˈrɛːrɪəm
AM təˈrɛriəm

terra sigillata
BR ˌtɛrə ˌsɪdʒɪˈleɪtə(r)
AM ˌtɛrə ˌsɪdʒəˈlɑdə

terrazzo
BR tɛˈratsəʊ, tɪˈratsəʊ
AM təˈrɑzoʊ, təˈrɑtsoʊ

Terre Haute
BR ˌtɛrə ˈhəʊt
AM ˌtɛrə ˈhət

Terrell
BR ˈtɛrl̩
AM ˈtɛrəl, təˈrɛl

terrene
BR ˈtɛriːn, tɛˈriːn
AM təˈrin, ˈtɛˌrin

terreplein
BR ˈtɛːpleɪn, -z
AM ˈtɛrəˌpleɪn, -z

terrestrial
BR tɪˈrɛstrɪəl, tɛˈrɛstrɪəl, -z
AM təˈrɛstriəl, -z

terrestrially
BR tɪˈrɛstrɪəli, tɛˈrɛstrɪəli
AM təˈrɛstriəli

terret
BR ˈtɛrɪt, -s
AM ˈtɛrət, -s

terre-verte
BR ˌtɛːˈvɛːt
AM ˌtɛrˈvɛrt

terrible
BR ˈtɛrɪbl
AM ˈtɛrəbəl

terribleness
BR ˈtɛrɪblnəs
AM ˈtɛrəbəlnəs

terribly
BR ˈtɛrɪbli
AM ˈtɛrəbli

terricolous
BR tɛˈrɪkələs, tɛˈrɪkl̩əs
AM tɛˈrɪkələs, təˈrɪkələs

terrier
BR ˈtɛrɪə(r), -z
AM ˈtɛriər, -z

terrific
BR təˈrɪfɪk
AM təˈrɪfɪk

terrifically
BR təˈrɪfɪkli
AM təˈrɪfɪk(ə)li

terrifier
BR ˈtɛrɪfʌɪə(r), -z
AM ˈtɛrəˌfaɪər, -z

terrify
BR ˈtɛrɪfʌɪ, -z, -ɪŋ, -d
AM ˈtɛrəˌfaɪ, -z, -ɪŋ, -d

terrifyingly
BR ˈtɛrɪfʌɪɪŋli
AM ˈtɛrəˌfaɪɪŋli

terrigenous
BR tɛˈrɪdʒɪnəs
AM tɛˈrɪdʒənəs, təˈrɪdʒənəs

terrine
BR tɛˈriːn, təˈriːn, ˈtɛriːn, -z
AM təˈrin, tɛˈrin, -z

territ
BR ˈtɛrɪt, -s
AM ˈtɛrət, -s

territorial
BR ˌtɛrɪˈtɔːrɪəl, -z
AM ˌtɛrəˈtɔriəl, -z

territorialisation
BR ˌtɛrɪˌtɔːrɪəlʌɪˈzeɪʃn
AM ˌtɛrəˌtɔriələˈzeɪʃən, ˌtɛrəˌtɔriəˌlaɪˈzeɪʃən

territorialise
BR ˌtɛrɪˈtɔːrɪəlʌɪz, -ɪz, -ɪŋ, -d
AM ˌtɛrəˈtɔriəˌlaɪz, -ɪz, -ɪŋ, -d

territorialism
BR ˌtɛrɪˈtɔːrɪəlɪz(ə)m
AM ˌtɛrəˈtɔriəˌlɪzəm

territoriality
BR ˌtɛrɪˌtɔːrɪˈalɪti
AM ˌtɛrəˌtɔriˈælədi

territorialization
BR ˌtɛrɪˌtɔːrɪəlʌɪˈzeɪʃn
AM ˌtɛrəˌtɔriələˈzeɪʃən, ˌtɛrəˌtɔriəˌlaɪˈzeɪʃən

territorialize
BR ˌtɛrɪˈtɔːrɪəlʌɪz, -ɪz, -ɪŋ, -d
AM ˌtɛrəˈtɔriəˌlaɪz, -ɪz, -ɪŋ, -d

territorially
BR ˌtɛrɪˈtɔːrɪəli
AM ˌtɛrəˈtɔriəli

territory
BR ˈtɛrɪt(ə)r|i, -ɪz
AM ˈtɛrəˌtɔri, -z

terror
BR ˈtɛrə(r), -z
AM ˈtɛrər, -z

terrorisation
BR ˌtɛrərʌɪˈzeɪʃn
AM ˌtɛrərəˈzeɪʃən, ˌtɛrəˌraɪˈzeɪʃən

terrorise
BR ˈtɛrərʌɪz, -ɪz, -ɪŋ, -d
AM ˈtɛrəˌraɪz, -ɪz, -ɪŋ, -d

terroriser
BR ˈtɛrərʌɪzə(r), -z
AM ˈtɛrəˌraɪzər, -z

terrorism
BR ˈtɛrərɪz(ə)m
AM ˈtɛrəˌrɪzəm

terrorist
BR ˈtɛrərɪst, -s
AM ˈtɛrərəst, -s

terroristic
BR ˌtɛrəˈrɪstɪk
AM ˌtɛrəˈrɪstɪk

terroristically
BR ˌtɛrəˈrɪstɪkli
AM ˌtɛrəˈrɪstɪk(ə)li

terrorization
BR ˌtɛrərʌɪˈzeɪʃn
AM ˌtɛrərəˈzeɪʃən, ˌtɛrəˌraɪˈzeɪʃən

terrorize
BR ˈtɛrərʌɪz, -ɪz, -ɪŋ, -d
AM ˈtɛrəˌraɪz, -ɪz, -ɪŋ, -d

terrorizer
BR ˈtɛrərʌɪzə(r), -z
AM ˈtɛrəˌraɪzər, -z

terry
BR ˈtɛri
AM ˈtɛri

terse
BR təːs, -ə(r), -ɪst
AM tərs, -ər, -əst

tersely
BR ˈtəːsli
AM ˈtərsli

terseness
BR ˈtəːsnəs
AM ˈtərsnəs

tertian
BR ˈtəːʃn
AM ˈtərʃən

tertiary
BR ˈtəːʃ(ə)ri
AM ˈtərʃiˌɛri, ˈtərʃəri

tertium quid
BR ˌtəːʃɪəm ˈkwɪd, ˌtəːtɪəm +
AM ˌtərʃ(i)əm ˈkwɪd, ˌtərdiəm +

Tertius
BR ˈtəːʃ(ɪ)əs
AM ˈtərʃ(i)əs

Tertullian
BR təːˈtʌlɪən
AM tərˈtəljən, tərˈtəliən

tervalent
BR (ˌ)təːˈveɪlənt, (ˌ)təːˈveɪlnt
AM tərˈveɪlənt

terylene®
BR ˈtɛrɪliːn
AM ˈtɛrəˌlin

terza rima
BR ˌtəːtsə ˈriːmə(r), ˌtɛːtsə +
AM ˌtərtsə ˈrimə

terzetti
BR tɛːtˈsɛti, təːtˈsɛti
AM tərˈtsɛdi

terzetto
BR tɛːtˈsɛtəʊ, təːtˈsɛtəʊ, -z
AM tərˈtsɛdoʊ, -z

Tesco
BR ˈtɛskəʊ
AM ˈtɛskoʊ

TESL
BR ˈtɛsl
AM ˈtɛsəl

tesla
BR ˈtɛslə(r), -z
AM ˈtɛslə, -z

TESOL
BR ˈtɛsɒl
AM ˈtɛˌsɔl, ˈtiˌsɔl, ˈtɛˌsɑl, ˈtiˌsɑl

Tess
BR tɛs
AM tɛs

TESSA
BR ˈtɛsə(r)
AM ˈtɛsə

tessellate
BR ˈtɛsɪleɪt, -s, -ɪŋ, -ɪd
AM ˈtɛsəˌleɪ|t, -ts, -dɪŋ, -dɪd

tessellation
BR ˌtɛsɪˈleɪʃn, -z
AM ˌtɛsəˈleɪʃən, -z

tessera
BR ˈtɛs(ə)rə(r)
AM ˈtɛsərə

tesserae
BR ˈtɛs(ə)riː
AM ˈtɛsəˌraɪ, ˈtɛsəri

tesseral
BR ˈtɛs(ə)rəl, ˈtɛs(ə)rl̩
AM ˈtɛsərəl

tessitura
BR ˌtɛsɪˈt(j)ʊərə(r), -z
AM ˌtɛsəˈtʊrə, -z

test
BR tɛst, -s, -ɪŋ, -ɪd
AM tɛst, -s, -ɪŋ, -əd

testa
BR ˈtɛstə(r)
AM ˈtɛstə

testability
BR ˌtɛstəˈbɪlɪti
AM ˌtɛstəˈbɪlɪdi
testable
BR ˈtɛstəbl
AM ˈtɛstəbəl
testaceous
BR tɛˈsteɪʃəs
AM tɛˈsteɪʃəs
testacy
BR ˈtɛstəs|i, -ɪz
AM ˈtɛstəsi, -z
testae
BR ˈtɛstiː
AM ˈtɛsti, ˈtɛsˌtaɪ
testament
BR ˈtɛstəm(ə)nt, -s
AM ˈtɛstəmənt, -s
testamental
BR ˌtɛstəˈmɛntl
AM ˌtɛstəˈmɛn(t)l
testamentarily
BR ˌtɛstəˈmɛnt(ə)rɪli
AM ˌtɛstəˈmɛn(t)ərəli
testamentary
BR ˌtɛstəˈmɛnt(ə)ri
AM ˌtɛstəˈmɛn(t)əri
testamur
BR tɛˈsteɪmə(r), -z
AM tɛˈsteɪmər, -z
testate
BR ˈtɛsteɪt, ˈtɛstət
AM ˈtɛˌsteɪt, ˈtɛstət
testation
BR tɛˈsteɪʃn, -z
AM tɛˈsteɪʃən, -z
testator
BR tɛˈsteɪtə(r), -z
AM ˈtɛˌsteɪdər, -z
testatrices
BR tɛˈsteɪtrɪsiːz
AM tɛˈsteɪtrəˌsiz, ˌtɛstəˈtraɪˌsiz
testatrix
BR tɛˈsteɪtrɪks, -ɪz
AM ˈtɛˌsteɪˌtrɪks, tɛˈsteɪˌtrɪks, -ɪz
Test-Ban Treaty
BR ˈtɛs(t)ban ˌtriːti
AM ˈtɛs(t)ˌbæn ˌtridi
testee
BR tɛsˈtiː, -z
AM tɛsˈti, -z
testentry
BR ˈtɛstntr|i, -ɪz
AM ˈtɛstəntri, -z
tester
BR ˈtɛstə(r), -z
AM ˈtɛstər, -z
testes
BR ˈtɛstiːz
AM ˈtɛsˌtiz
testicle
BR ˈtɛstɪkl, -z
AM ˈtɛstəkəl, -z
testicular
BR tɛˈstɪkjʉlə(r)
AM tɛˈstɪkjələr
testiculate
BR tɛˈstɪkjʉlət
AM tɛˈstɪkjələt, tɛˈstɪkjəˌleɪt
testification
BR ˌtɛstɪfɪˈkeɪʃn, -z
AM ˌtɛstəfəˈkeɪʃən, -z
testifier
BR ˈtɛstɪfʌɪə(r), -z
AM ˈtɛstəˌfaɪər, -z
testify
BR ˈtɛstɪfʌɪ, -z, -ɪŋ, -d
AM ˈtɛstəˌfaɪ, -z, -ɪŋ, -d
testily
BR ˈtɛstɪli
AM ˈtɛstəli
testimonial
BR ˌtɛstɪˈməʊnɪəl, -z
AM ˌtɛstəˈmoʊniəl, -z
testimony
BR ˈtɛstɪmən|i, -ɪz
AM ˈtɛstəˌmoʊni, -z
testiness
BR ˈtɛstɪnɪs
AM ˈtɛstinɪs
testis
BR ˈtɛstɪs
AM ˈtɛstəs
testosterone
BR tɛˈstɒstərəʊn
AM tɛˈstɑstəˌroʊn
testudinal
BR tɛˈst(j)uːdɪnl, tɛˈstʃuːdɪnl
AM tɛˈst(j)udn̩l
testudines
BR tɛˈst(j)uːdɪniːz, tɛˈstʃuːdɪniːz
AM tɛˈst(j)udn̩ˌiz
testudo
BR tɛˈst(j)uːdəʊ, tɛˈstʃuːdəʊ, -z
AM tɛˈstudoʊ, -z
testy
BR ˈtɛst|i, -ɪə(r), -ɪɪst
AM ˈtɛsti, -iər, -ist
tetanic
BR tɪˈtanɪk, tɛˈtanɪk
AM tɛˈtænɪk
tetanically
BR tɪˈtanɪkli, tɛˈtanɪkli
AM tɛˈtænək(ə)li
tetanise
BR ˈtɛtənʌɪz, ˈtɛtn̩ʌɪz, -ɪz, -ɪŋ, -d
AM ˈtɛtnˌaɪz, -ɪz, -ɪŋ, -d
tetanize
BR ˈtɛtənʌɪz, ˈtɛtn̩ʌɪz, -ɪz, -ɪŋ, -d
AM ˈtɛtnˌaɪz, -ɪz, -ɪŋ, -d
tetanoid
BR ˈtɛtənɔɪd, ˈtɛtn̩ɔɪd
AM ˈtɛtnˌɔɪd
tetanus
BR ˈtɛtənəs, ˈtɛtn̩əs
AM ˈtɛtnəs, ˈtɛtn̩əs
tetany
BR ˈtɛtəni, ˈtɛtn̩i
AM ˈtɛtn̩i, ˈtɛtni
Tetbury
BR ˈtɛtb(ə)ri
AM ˈtɛtˌbɛri
tetchily
BR ˈtɛtʃɪli
AM ˈtɛtʃəli
tetchiness
BR ˈtɛtʃɪnɪs
AM ˈtɛtʃinɪs
tetchy
BR ˈtɛtʃ|i, -ɪə(r), -ɪɪst
AM ˈtɛtʃi, -ər, -ɪst
tête-à-tête
BR ˌteɪtɑːˈteɪt, ˌteɪtəˈteɪt, -s
AM ˈtɛdəˈtɛt, -s
tête-bêche
BR ˌtɛtˈbɛʃ, ˌteɪtˈbɛʃ
AM ˌtɛtˈbɛʃ
tether
BR ˈtɛð|ə(r), -əz, -(ə)rɪŋ, -əd
AM ˈtɛð|ər, -ərz, -(ə)rɪŋ, -ərd
Tethys
BR ˈtiːθɪs, ˈtɛθɪs
AM ˈtɛθəs
Tetley
BR ˈtɛtli
AM ˈtɛtli
Teton
BR ˈtiːtɒn, -z
AM ˈtiˌtɑn, -z
tetra
BR ˈtɛtrə(r)
AM ˈtɛtrə
tetrachloride
BR ˌtɛtrəˈklɔːrʌɪd
AM ˌtɛtrəˈklɔˌraɪd
tetrachloroethylene
BR ˌtɛtrəˌklɔːrəʊˈɛθɪliːn, ˌtɛtrəˌklɔːrəʊˈɛθl̩iːn
AM ˌtɛtrəˌklɔroʊˈɛθəˌlin
tetrachord
BR ˈtɛtrəkɔːd, -z
AM ˈtɛtrəˌkɔ(ə)rd, -z
tetracyclic
BR ˌtɛtrəˈsʌɪklɪk
AM ˌtɛtrəˈsaɪklɪk
tetracycline
BR ˌtɛtrəˈsʌɪkliːn, ˌtɛtrəˈsʌɪklɪn, -z
AM ˌtɛtrəˈsaɪˌklin, -z
tetrad
BR ˈtɛtrad, -z
AM ˈtɛˌtræd, -z
tetradactyl
BR ˌtɛtrəˈdakt(ɪ)l, -z
AM ˌtɛtrəˈdæktl, -z
tetradactylous
BR ˌtɛtrəˈdaktɪləs
AM ˌtɛtrəˈdæktələs
tetraethyl
BR ˌtɛtrə(r)ˈɛθ(ɪ)l, ˌtɛtrə(r)ˈɛθʌɪl, ˌtɛtrə(r)ˈiːθʌɪl
AM ˌtɛtrəˈɛθəl
tetragon
BR ˈtɛtrəg(ə)n, ˈtɛtrəgɒn, -z
AM ˈtɛtrəˌgɑn, -z
tetragonal
BR tɛˈtrag(ə)nl, tɪˈtrag(ə)nl
AM tɛˈtrægənəl
tetragonally
BR tɛˈtragənl̩i, tɛˈtragənəli, tɪˈtragənl̩i, tɪˈtragənəli
AM tɛˈtrægənəli
tetragram
BR ˈtɛtrəgram, -z
AM ˈtɛtrəˌgræm, -z
tetragrammaton
BR ˌtɛtrəˈgramət(ə)n, ˌtɛtrəˈgramətɒn
AM ˌtɛtrəˈgræməˌtɑn
tetragynous
BR tɛˈtradʒɪnəs, tɪˈtradʒɪnəs
AM tɛˈtrædʒənəs
tetrahedra
BR ˌtɛtrəˈhiːdrə(r)
AM ˌtɛtrəˈhidrə
tetrahedral
BR ˌtɛtrəˈhiːdr(ə)l
AM ˌtɛtrəˈhidrəl
tetrahedron
BR ˌtɛtrəˈhiːdr(ə)n, -z
AM ˌtɛtrəˈhidrən, -z
tetralogy
BR tɛˈtralədʒ|i, tɪˈtralədʒ|i, -ɪz
AM tɛˈtrɑlədʒi, -z
tetramerous
BR tɛˈtram(ə)rəs, tɪˈtram(ə)rəs
AM tɛˈtræmərəs
tetrameter
BR tɛˈtramɪtə(r), tɪˈtramɪtə(r), -z
AM tɛˈtræmədər, -z
tetramorph
BR ˈtɛtrəmɔːf, -s
AM ˈtɛtrəˌmɔ(ə)rf, -s
tetrandrous
BR tɛˈtrandrəs, tɪˈtrandrəs
AM tɛˈtrændrəs
tetraplegia
BR ˌtɛtrəˈpliːdʒ(ɪ)ə(r)
AM ˌtɛtrəˈpli(d)ʒ(i)ə
tetraplegic
BR ˌtɛtrəˈpliːdʒɪk, -s
AM ˌtɛtrəˈplidʒɪk, -s
tetraploid
BR ˈtɛtrəplɔɪd, -z
AM ˈtɛtrəˌplɔɪd, -z

tetrapod
BR ˈtɛtrəpɒd, -z
AM ˈtɛtrəˌpɑd, -z

tetrapodous
BR tɛˈtrapədəs, tɪˈtrapədəs
AM tɛˈtræpədəs

tetrapterous
BR tɛˈtrapt(ə)rəs, tɪˈtrapt(ə)rəs
AM tɛˈtræptərəs

tetrarch
BR ˈtɛtrɑːk, -s
AM ˈtɛˌtrɑrk, -s

tetrarchate
BR ˈtɛtrɑːkeɪt, -s
AM ˈtɛˌtrɑrˌkeɪt, -s

tetrarchical
BR tɛˈtrɑːkɨkl, tɪˈtrɑːkɨkl
AM təˈtrɑrkəkəl, tɛˈtrɑrkəkəl

tetrarchy
BR ˈtɛtrɑːk|i, -ɪz
AM ˈtɛˌtrɑrki, -z

tetrastich
BR ˈtɛtrəstɪk, -s
AM ˈtɛtrəˌstɪk, -s

tetrastyle
BR ˈtɛtrəstʌɪl, -z
AM ˈtɛtrəˌstaɪl, -z

tetrasyllabic
BR ˌtɛtrəsɪˈlabɪk
AM ˌtɛtrəsəˈlæbɪk

tetrasyllable
BR ˈtɛtrəˌsɪləbl, ˌtɛtrəˈsɪləbl, -z
AM ˌtɛtrəˈsɪləbəl, -z

tetrathlon
BR tɛˈtraθlən, tɪˈtraθlən, tɛˈtraθlɒn, tɪˈtraθlɒn, -z
AM təˈtræθˌlɑn, tɛˈtræθˌlɑn, -z

tetratomic
BR ˌtɛtrəˈtɒmɪk
AM ˌtɛtrəˈtɑmɪk

tetravalent
BR ˌtɛtrəˈveɪlənt, ˌtɛtrəˈveɪln̩t
AM ˌtɛtrəˈveɪlənt

Tetrazzini
BR ˌtɛtrəˈziːni
AM ˌtɛtrəˈzini

tetrode
BR ˈtɛtrəʊd, -z
AM ˈtɛˌtroʊd, -z

tetrodotoxin
BR ˌtɛtrə(ʊ)də(ʊ)ˈtɒksɪn
AM ˌtɛtroʊdoʊˈtɑksin

tetroxide
BR tɛˈtrɒksʌɪd, tɪˈtrɒksʌɪd
AM tɛˈtrɑkˌsaɪd

tetter
BR ˈtɛtə(r)
AM ˈtɛdər

Teuton
BR ˈtjuːt(ə)n, ˈtʃuːt(ə)n, -z
AM ˈt(j)utn, ˈt(j)uˌtɑn, -z

Teutonic
BR tjuːˈtɒnɪk, tʃuːˈtɒnɪk
AM t(j)uˈtɑnɪk

Teutonicism
BR tjuːˈtɒnɨsɪz(ə)m, tʃuːˈtɒnɨsɪz(ə)m
AM t(j)uˈtɑnəˌsɪzəm

Tevet
BR ˈtɛvɛt
AM teɪˈvɛt, ˈteɪˌvɛθ

Teviot
BR ˈtiːvɪət, ˈtɛvɪət
AM ˈtɛviət

Tewkesbury
BR ˈtjuːksb(ə)ri, ˈtʃuːksb(ə)ri
AM ˈt(j)uksˌbɛri

Tex
BR tɛks
AM tɛks

Texan
BR ˈtɛksn, -z
AM ˈtɛksən, -z

Texas
BR ˈtɛksəs
AM ˈtɛksəs

Texel
BR ˈtɛksl
AM ˈtɛksəl

Tex-Mex
BR ˌtɛksˈmɛks
AM ˈtɛksˈmɛks

text
BR tɛkst, -s
AM tɛkst, -s

textbook
BR ˈtɛks(t)bʊk, -s
AM ˈtɛks(t)ˌbʊk, -s

textbookish
BR ˈtɛks(t)bʊkɪʃ
AM ˈtɛks(t)ˌbʊkɪʃ

textile
BR ˈtɛkstʌɪl, -z
AM ˈtɛkˌstaɪl, -z

textless
BR ˈtɛks(t)ləs
AM ˈtɛks(t)ləs

textual
BR ˈtɛkstʃʊəl, ˈtɛkstʃ(ʉ)l, ˈtɛkstjʊəl, ˈtɛkstjʉl
AM ˈtɛk(st)ʃ(əw)əl

textualism
BR ˈtɛkstʃʊəlɪz(ə)m, ˈtɛkstʃʉlɪz(ə)m, ˈtɛkstʃl̩ɪz(ə)m, ˈtɛkstjʊəlɪz(ə)m, ˈtɛkstjʉlɪz(ə)m
AM ˈtɛk(st)ʃ(əw)əˌlɪzəm

textualist
BR ˈtɛkstʃʊəlɪst, ˈtɛkstʃʉlɪst, ˈtɛkstʃl̩ɪst, ˈtɛkstjʊəlɪst, ˈtɛkstjʉlɪst
AM ˈtɛk(st)ʃ(əw)ələst

textuality
BR ˌtɛkstʃʊˈalɪti, ˌtɛkstjʊˈalɪti
AM ˌtɛk(st)ʃəˈwælədi

textually
BR ˈtɛkstʃʊəli, ˈtɛkstʃʉli, ˈtɛkstʃl̩i, ˈtɛkstjʊəli, ˈtɛkstjʉli
AM ˈtɛk(st)ʃ(əw)əli

textural
BR ˈtɛkstʃ(ə)rəl, ˈtɛkstʃ(ə)rl̩
AM ˈtɛk(st)ʃərəl

texturally
BR ˈtɛkstʃ(ə)rəli, ˈtɛkstʃ(ə)rl̩i
AM ˈtɛk(st)ʃərəli

texture
BR ˈtɛkstʃə(r), -z, -d
AM ˈtɛk(st)ʃər, -z, -d

textureless
BR ˈtɛkstʃələs
AM ˈtɛk(st)ʃərləs

texturise
BR ˈtɛkstʃərʌɪz, -ɨz, -ɪŋ, -d
AM ˈtɛk(st)ʃəˌraɪz, -ɨz, -ɪŋ, -d

texturize
BR ˈtɛkstʃərʌɪz, -ɨz, -ɪŋ, -d
AM ˈtɛk(st)ʃəˌraɪz, -ɨz, -ɪŋ, -d

TGIF
BR ˌtiːdʒiːʌɪˈɛf
AM ˌtiˌdʒiˌaɪˈɛf

Thackeray
BR ˈθak(ə)ri, ˈθak(ə)reɪ
AM ˈθæk(ə)ri

Thaddeus
BR ˈθadɪəs
AM ˈθædiəs

Thai
BR tʌɪ, -z
AM taɪ, -z

Thailand
BR ˈtʌɪland, ˈtʌɪlənd
AM ˈtaɪˌlænd

Thailander
BR ˈtʌɪlandə(r), ˈtʌɪləndə(r), -z
AM ˈtaɪˌlændər, ˈtaɪləndər, -z

thalamic
BR θəˈlamɪk
AM θəˈlæmɪk

thalamus
BR ˈθaləməs
AM ˈθæləməs

thalassaemia
BR ˌθaləˈsiːmɪə(*r*)
AM ˌθæləˈsimiə

thalassemia
BR ˌθaləˈsiːmɪə(*r*)
AM ˌθæləˈsimiə

thalassic
BR θəˈlasɪk
AM θəˈlæsɪk

thalassotherapy
BR θəˌlasəʊˈθɛrəpi
AM ˈθæləˌsoʊˈθɛrəpi

thaler
BR ˈtɑːlə(r), -z
AM ˈtɑlər, -z

Thales
BR ˈθeɪliːz
AM ˈθeɪˌliz

Thalia
BR ˈθeɪlɪə(*r*), θəˈlʌɪə(*r*)
AM ˈθeɪljə, ˈθeɪliə

thalidomide
BR θəˈlɪdəmʌɪd
AM θəˈlɪdəˌmaɪd

thalli
BR ˈθalʌɪ, ˈθaliː
AM ˈθæli

thallic
BR ˈθalɪk
AM ˈθælɪk

thallium
BR ˈθalɪəm
AM ˈθæliəm

thalloid
BR ˈθalɔɪd
AM ˈθæˌlɔɪd

thallophyte
BR ˈθaləfʌɪt, -s
AM ˈθæləˌfaɪt, -s

thallous
BR ˈθaləs
AM ˈθæləs

thallus
BR ˈθaləs
AM ˈθæləs

thalweg
BR ˈtɑːlvɛg, ˈθɑːlvɛg, -z
AM ˈtælˌvɛg, -z

Thame
BR teɪm
AM teɪm, θeɪm

Thames[1]
in Connecticut
BR teɪmz, θeɪmz
AM teɪmz, θeɪmz

Thames[2]
in England, Canada, New Zealand
BR tɛmz
AM tɛmz

Thammuz
BR ˈtamʊz
AM ˈtɑmʊz

than[1]
strong form
BR ðan
AM ðæn

than[2]
weak form
BR ð(ə)n

AM ðən

thanage
BR 'θeɪnɪdʒ
AM 'θeɪnɪdʒ

thanatology
BR ˌθanə'tɒlədʒi
AM ˌθænə'tɑlədʒi

thane
BR θeɪn, -z
AM θeɪn, -z

thanedom
BR 'θeɪndəm, -z
AM 'θeɪndəm, -z

thaneship
BR 'θeɪnʃɪp, -s
AM 'θeɪnˌʃɪp, -s

Thanet
BR 'θanɪt
AM 'θænət

thank
BR θaŋ|k, -ks, -kɪŋ, -(k)t
AM θæŋ|k, -ks, -kɪŋ, -(k)t

thankful
BR 'θaŋkf(ʊ)l
AM 'θæŋkfəl

thankfully
BR 'θaŋkfʊli, 'θaŋkfḷi
AM 'θæŋkfəli

thankfulness
BR 'θaŋkf(ʊ)lnəs
AM 'θæŋkfəlnəs

thankless
BR 'θaŋkləs
AM 'θæŋkləs

thanklessly
BR 'θaŋkləsli
AM 'θæŋkləsli

thanklessness
BR 'θaŋkləsnəs
AM 'θæŋkləsnəs

thank-offering
BR 'θaŋkˌɒf(ə)rɪŋ, -z
AM 'θæŋkˌɔfərɪŋ, 'θæŋkˌɑfərɪŋ, -z

thanksgiving
BR ˌθaŋks'ɡɪvɪŋ, 'θaŋksˌɡɪvɪŋ, -z
AM ˌθæŋks'ɡɪvɪŋ, -z

thank you
BR 'θaŋk juː
AM 'θæŋk ˌju

thar
BR tɑː(r), -z
AM tɑr, -z

that[1]
demonstrative pronoun, adverb, determiner
BR ðat
AM ðæt

that[2]
relative pronoun, conjunction–strong form
BR ðat
AM ðæt

that[3]
relative pronoun, conjunction–weak form
BR ðət
AM ðət

thatch
BR θatʃ, -ɪz, -ɪŋ, -t
AM θætʃ, -əz, -ɪŋ, -t

thatcher
BR 'θatʃə(r), -z
AM 'θætʃər, -z

Thatcherism
BR 'θatʃ(ə)rɪz(ə)m
AM 'θætʃəˌrɪzəm

Thatcherite
BR 'θatʃərʌɪt, -s
AM 'θætʃəˌraɪt, -s

thaumatology
BR ˌθɔːmə'tɒlədʒi
AM ˌθɔmə'tɑlədʒi, ˌθɑmə'tɑlədʒi

thaumatrope
BR 'θɔːmətrəʊp, -s
AM 'θɔməˌtroʊp, 'θɑməˌtroʊp, -s

thaumaturge
BR 'θɔːmətəːdʒ, -ɪz
AM 'θɔməˌtərdʒ, 'θɑməˌtərdʒ, -əz

thaumaturgic
BR ˌθɔːmə'təːdʒɪk
AM ˌθɔmə'tərdʒɪk, ˌθɑmə'tərdʒɪk

thaumaturgical
BR ˌθɔːmə'təːdʒɪkl
AM ˌθɔmə'tərdʒəkəl, ˌθɑmə'tərdʒəkəl

thaumaturgist
BR 'θɔːmətəːdʒɪst, -s
AM 'θɔməˌtərdʒəst, 'θɑməˌtərdʒəst, -s

thaumaturgy
BR 'θɔːmətəːdʒi
AM 'θɔməˌtərdʒi, 'θɑməˌtərdʒi

thaw
BR θɔː(r), -z, -ɪŋ, -d
AM θɔ, θɑ, -z, -ɪŋ, -d

thawless
BR 'θɔːləs
AM 'θɔləs, 'θɑləs

THC
BR ˌtiːeɪtʃ'siː
AM ˌtiˌeɪtʃ'si

the[1]
strong form
BR ðiː
AM ði

the[2]
weak form before consonants
BR ðə
AM ð(ə)

the[3]
weak form before vowels
BR ðɪ, ðiː
AM ði

Thea
BR 'θiːə(r)
AM 'θiə

theandric
BR θiː'andrɪk
AM θi'ændrɪk

theanthropic
BR ˌθiːən'θrɒpɪk
AM ˌθiən'θrɑpɪk

thearchy
BR 'θiːɑːk|i, -ɪz
AM 'θiˌɑrki, -z

theater
BR 'θɪətə(r), -z
AM 'θiədər, -z

theatergoer
BR 'θɪətəˌɡəʊə(r), -z
AM 'θiədərˌɡoʊər, -z

theatergoing
BR 'θɪətəˌɡəʊɪŋ
AM 'θiədərˌɡoʊɪŋ

theater-in-the-round
BR ˌθɪət(ə)rɪnðə'raʊnd
AM ˌθiədərənðə'raʊnd

theatre
BR 'θɪətə(r), -z
AM 'θiədər, -z

theatregoer
BR 'θɪətəˌɡəʊə(r), -z
AM 'θiədərˌɡoʊər, -z

theatregoing
BR 'θɪətəˌɡəʊɪŋ
AM 'θiədərˌɡoʊɪŋ

theatre-in-the-round
BR ˌθɪət(ə)rɪnðə'raʊnd
AM ˌθiədərənðə'raʊnd

theatric
BR θɪ'atrɪk, -s
AM θi'ætrɪk, -s

theatrical
BR θɪ'atrɪkl, -z
AM θi'ætrəkəl, -z

theatricalisation
BR θɪˌatrɪkḷʌɪ'zeɪʃn, θɪˌatrɪkəlʌɪ'zeɪʃn
AM θiˌætrəkələ'zeɪʃən, θiˌætrəkəˌlaɪ'zeɪʃən

theatricalise
BR θɪ'atrɪkḷʌɪz, θɪ'atrɪkəlʌɪz, -ɪz, -ɪŋ, -d
AM θi'ætrəkəˌlaɪz, -ɪz, -ɪŋ, -d

theatricalism
BR θɪ'atrɪkḷɪz(ə)m, θɪ'atrɪkəlɪz(ə)m
AM θi'ætrəkəˌlɪzəm

theatricality
BR θɪˌatrɪ'kalɪti
AM θiˌætrə'kælədi

theatricalization
BR θɪˌatrɪkḷʌɪ'zeɪʃn, θɪˌatrɪkəlʌɪ'zeɪʃn
AM θiˌætrəkələ'zeɪʃən, θiˌætrəkəˌlaɪ'zeɪʃən

theatricalize
BR θɪ'atrɪkḷʌɪz, θɪ'atrɪkəlʌɪz, -ɪz, -ɪŋ, -d
AM θi'ætrəkəˌlaɪz, -ɪz, -ɪŋ, -d

theatrically
BR θɪ'atrɪkli
AM θi'ætrək(ə)li

Theban
BR 'θiːbn, -z
AM 'θibən, -z

thebe
BR 'θeɪbeɪ
AM 'tɛbɛ

Thebes
BR θiːbz
AM θibz

theca
BR 'θiːkə(r)
AM 'θikə

thecae
BR 'θiːsiː, 'θiːkiː
AM 'θiˌsi, 'θiki, 'θiˌsaɪ, 'θiˌkaɪ

thecate
BR 'θiːkeɪt, 'θiːkət
AM 'θiˌkeɪt

thé dansant
BR ˌteɪ ˌdɒ̃'sɒ̃, -z
AM ˌteɪ ˌdɑn'sɑn, -z

thee
BR ðiː
AM ði

theft
BR θɛft, -s
AM θɛft, -s

thegn
BR θeɪn, -z
AM θeɪn, -z

theine
BR 'θiːiːn, 'θiːɪn
AM 'θiˌin, 'θiɪn

their[1]
strong form
BR ðɛː(r)
AM ðɛ(ə)r

their[2]
weak form
BR ðə(r)
AM ðər

theirs
BR ðɛːz
AM ðɛ(ə)rz

theirselves
BR ðɛː'sɛlvz
AM ðɛr'sɛlvz

theism
BR 'θiːɪz(ə)m
AM 'θiˌɪzəm

theist
BR 'θiːɪst, -s
AM 'θiɪst, -s

theistic
BR θiː'ɪstɪk
AM θi'ɪstɪk

theistical
BR θiː'ɪstɪkl
AM θi'ɪstɪkəl
theistically
BR θiː'ɪstɪkli
AM θi'ɪstək(ə)li
Thelma
BR 'θɛlmə(r)
AM 'θɛlmə
Thelwall
BR 'θɛlwɔːl
AM 'θɛl,wɔl, 'θɛl,wɑl
Thelwell
BR 'θɛlw(ɛ)l
AM 'θɛl,wɛl
them[1]
strong form
BR ðɛm
AM ðɛm
them[2]
weak form
BR ð(ə)m
AM ðəm
thematic
BR θiː'matɪk, θɪ'matɪk, -s
AM θə'mædɪk, -s
thematically
BR θiː'matɪkli, θɪ'matɪkli
AM θə'mædək(ə)li
theme
BR θiːm, -z
AM θim, -z
Themistocles
BR θɪ'mɪstəkliːz, θɛ'mɪstəkliːz
AM θə'mɪstə,kliz
themself
BR ð(ə)m'sɛlf
AM ðəm'sɛlf, ðɛm'sɛlf
themselves
BR ð(ə)m'sɛlvz
AM ðəm'sɛlvz, ðɛm'sɛlvz
then
BR ðɛn
AM ðɛn
thenar
BR 'θiːnə(r), 'θiːnɑː(r), -z
AM 'θi,nɑr, -z
thence
BR ðɛns
AM ðɛns
thenceforth
BR ,ðɛns'fɔːθ
AM ,ðɛns'fɔ(ə)rθ
thenceforward
BR ,ðɛns'fɔːwəd
AM ,ðɛns'fɔrwərd
Theo
BR 'θiːəʊ
AM 'θioʊ
Theobald
BR 'θɪəbɔːld
AM ,θiə'bɔld, ,θiə'bɑld
theobromine
BR ,θɪə(ʊ)'brəʊmiːn, ,θɪə(ʊ)'brəʊmɪn
AM ,θiə'broʊ,min, ,θiə'broʊmən
theocentric
BR ,θiːə(ʊ)'sɛntrɪk
AM ,θioʊ'sɛntrɪk
theocentrism
BR ,θiːə(ʊ)'sɛntrɪz(ə)m
AM ,θioʊ'sɛn,trɪzəm
theocracy
BR θɪ'ɒkrəs|i, -ɪz
AM θi'ɑkrəsi, -z
theocrasy
BR 'θiːə,kreɪsi, θɪ'ɒkrəsi
AM θi'ɑkrəsi
theocrat
BR 'θɪəkrat, -s
AM 'θiə,kræt, -s
theocratic
BR ,θɪə'kratɪk
AM ,θiə'krædɪk
theocratically
BR ,θɪə'kratɪkli
AM ,θiə'krædək(ə)li
Theocritus
BR θɪ'ɒkrɪtəs
AM θi'ɑkrədəs
theodicean
BR θɪ,ɒdɪ'siːən
AM θi,ɑdə'siən
theodicy
BR θɪ'ɒdɪsi
AM θi'ɑdəsi
theodolite
BR θɪ'ɒdəlʌɪt, θɪ'ɒdl̩ʌɪt, -s
AM θi'ɑdə,laɪt, -s
theodolitic
BR θɪ,ɒdə'lɪtɪk, θɪ,ɒdl̩'ɪtɪk
AM θi,ɑdə'lɪdɪk
Theodora
BR ,θiːə'dɔːrə(r)
AM ,θiə'dɔrə
Theodorákis
BR ,θiːədə'rɑːkɪs, ,θiːədə'rakɪs
AM ,θiədə'rɑkəs
Theodore
BR 'θiːədɔː(r)
AM 'θiə,dɔ(ə)r
Theodoric
BR θɪ'ɒd(ə)rɪk
AM ,θi'ɑdərɪk
Theodosius
BR ,θiːə'dəʊsɪəs
AM ,θiə'doʊʃ(i)əs
theogonist
BR θɪ'ɒgənɪst, θɪ'ɒgn̩ɪst, -s
AM θi'ɑgənəst, -s
theogony
BR θɪ'ɒgən|i, θɪ'ɒgn̩i, -ɪz
AM θi'ɑgəni, -z
theologian
BR ,θiːə'ləʊdʒ(ə)n, ,θiːə'ləʊdʒɪən, -z
AM ,θiə'loʊdʒən, -z
theological
BR ,θiːə'lɒdʒɪkl
AM ,θiə'lɑdʒəkəl
theologically
BR ,θiːə'lɒdʒɪkli
AM ,θiə'lɑdʒək(ə)li
theologise
BR θɪ'ɒlədʒʌɪz, -ɪz, -ɪŋ, -d
AM θi'ɑlə,dʒaɪz, -ɪz, -ɪŋ, -d
theologist
BR θɪ'ɒlədʒɪst, -s
AM θi'ɑlədʒəst, -s
theologize
BR θɪ'ɒlədʒʌɪz, -ɪz, -ɪŋ, -d
AM θi'ɑlə,dʒaɪz, -ɪz, -ɪŋ, -d
theology
BR θɪ'ɒlədʒi
AM θi'ɑlədʒi
theomachy
BR θɪ'ɒmək|i, -ɪz
AM θi'ɑməki, -z
theomania
BR 'θɪə(ʊ),meɪnɪə(r)
AM ,θiə'meɪniə
theophany
BR θɪ'ɒfən|i, θɪ'ɒfn̩|i, -ɪz
AM θi'ɑfəni, -z
Theophilus
BR θɪ'ɒfɪləs, θɪ'ɒfl̩əs
AM θi'ɑfələs
theophoric
BR ,θiːə'fɒrɪk
AM ,θiə'fɔrɪk
Theophrastus
BR ,θiːə'frastəs
AM ,θiə'fræstəs
theophylline
BR ,θiːə'fɪliːn, ,θiːə'fɪlɪn
AM θi'ɑfələn, θiə'fɪlɪn
theorbist
BR θɪ'ɔːbɪst, -s
AM θi'ɔrbəst, -s
theorbo
BR θɪ'ɔːbəʊ, -z
AM θi'ɔrboʊ, -z
theorem
BR 'θɪərəm, -z
AM 'θiərəm, 'θɪrəm, -z
theorematic
BR ,θɪərə'matɪk
AM ,θiərə'mædɪk, ,θɪrə'mædɪk
theoretic
BR ,θɪə'rɛtɪk
AM ,θiə'rɛdɪk
theoretical
BR ,θɪə'rɛtɪkl
AM ,θiə'rɛdəkəl
theoretically
BR ,θɪə'rɛtɪkli
AM ,θiə'rɛdək(ə)li
theoretician
BR 'θɪərə'tɪʃn, -z
AM ,θiərə'tɪʃən, ,θɪrə'tɪʃən, -z
theorisation
BR ,θɪərʌɪ'zeɪʃn
AM ,θiərə'zeɪʃən, ,θiə,raɪ'zeɪʃən, ,θɪrə'zeɪʃən, ,θɪ,raɪ'zeɪʃən
theorise
BR 'θɪərʌɪz, -ɪz, -ɪŋ, -d
AM 'θiə,raɪz, 'θɪ,raɪz, -ɪz, -ɪŋ, -d
theoriser
BR 'θɪərʌɪzə(r)
AM 'θiə,raɪzər, 'θɪ,raɪzər
theorist
BR 'θɪərɪst, -s
AM 'θiərɪst, 'θɪrɪst, -s
theorization
BR ,θɪərʌɪ'zeɪʃn
AM ,θiərə'zeɪʃən, ,θiə,raɪ'zeɪʃən, ,θɪrə'zeɪʃən, ,θɪ,raɪ'zeɪʃən
theorize
BR 'θɪərʌɪz, -ɪz, -ɪŋ, -d
AM 'θiə,raɪz, 'θɪ,raɪz, -ɪz, -ɪŋ, -d
theorizer
BR 'θɪərʌɪzə(r), -z
AM 'θiə,raɪzər, 'θɪ,raɪzər, -z
theory
BR 'θɪər|i, -ɪz
AM 'θiəri, 'θɪri, -z
theosoph
BR 'θɪəsɒf, -s
AM 'θiə,sɑf, -s
theosopher
BR θɪ'ɒsəfə(r), -z
AM θi'ɑsəfər, -z
theosophic
BR ,θɪə'sɒfɪk
AM ,θiə'sɑfɪk
theosophical
BR ,θɪə'sɒfɪkl
AM ,θiə'sɑfəkəl
theosophically
BR ,θɪə'sɒfɪkli
AM ,θiə'sɑfək(ə)li
theosophise
BR θɪ'ɒsəfʌɪz, -ɪz, -ɪŋ, -d
AM θi'ɑsə,faɪz, -ɪz, -ɪŋ, -d
theosophism
BR θɪ'ɒsəfɪz(ə)m
AM θi'ɑsə,fɪzəm
theosophist
BR θɪ'ɒsəfɪst, -s
AM θi'ɑsəfəst, -s
theosophize
BR θɪ'ɒsəfʌɪz, -ɪz, -ɪŋ, -d

AM θi'ɑsəˌfaɪz, -ɨz, -ɪŋ, -d

theosophy
BR θɪ'ɒsəfi
AM θi'ɑsəfi

Thera
BR 'θɪərə(r)
AM 'θɪrə

therabouts
BR ˌðɛːrə'baʊts, 'ðɛːrəbaʊts
AM 'ðɛrəˌbaʊts, ˌðɛrə'baʊts

Theran
BR 'θɪərən
AM 'θɪrən

therapeutic
BR ˌθɛrə'pjuːtɪk, -s
AM ˌθɛrə'pjudɪk, -s

therapeutical
BR ˌθɛrə'pjuːtɨkl
AM ˌθɛrə'pjudəkəl

therapeutically
BR ˌθɛrə'pjuːtɨkli
AM ˌθɛrə'pjudək(ə)li

therapeutist
BR ˌθɛrə'pjuːtɪst, -s
AM ˌθɛrə'pjudəst, -s

therapist
BR 'θɛrəpɪst, -s
AM 'θɛrəpəst, -s

therapsid
BR θɛ'rapsɪd, θɪ'rapsɪd, -z
AM θə'ræpsɪd, -z

therapy
BR 'θɛrəp|i, -ɪz
AM 'θɛrəpi, -z

Theravada
BR ˌθɛrə'vɑːdə(r)
AM ˌθɛrə'vɑdə

there¹
strong form
BR ðɛː(r)
AM ðɛ(ə)r

there²
weak form
BR ðə(r)
AM ðər

thereabout
BR ˌðɛːrə'baʊt, 'ðɛːrəbaʊt, -s
AM 'ðɛrəˌbaʊt, ˌðɛrə'baʊt, -s

thereafter
BR ˌðɛːr'ɑːftə(r), ˌðɛːr'aftə(r)
AM ðɛ'ræftər

thereanent
BR ˌðɛːrə'nɛnt
AM ˌðɛrə'nɛnt

thereat
BR ˌðɛːr'at
AM ðɛ'ræt

thereby
BR ˌðɛː'bʌɪ, 'ðɛːbʌɪ
AM ðɛr'baɪ

therefor
for that
BR ˌðɛː'fɔː(r)
AM ˌðɛr'fɔ(ə)r

therefore
BR 'ðɛːfɔː(r)
AM 'ðɛrˌfɔ(ə)r

therefrom
BR ˌðɛː'frɒm
AM ðɛr'frɑm

therein
BR ˌðɛːr'ɪn
AM ðɛ'rɪn

thereinafter
BR ˌðɛːrɪn'ɑːftə(r), ˌðɛːrɪn'aftə(r)
AM ˈðɛrənˈæftər

thereinbefore
BR ˌðɛːrɪnbɪ'fɔː(r)
AM ˌðɛrənbə'fɔ(ə)r

thereinto
BR ˌðɛːr'ɪntuː
AM ˌðɛ'rɪnˌtu

theremin
BR 'θɛrəmɪn, -z
AM 'θɛrəmən, -z

thereof
BR ˌðɛːr'ɒv
AM ðɛ'rɑv

thereon
BR ˌðɛːr'ɒn
AM ðɛ'rɑn

thereout
BR ˌðɛːr'aʊt
AM ðɛ'raʊt

Theresa
BR tə'riːzə(r), tə'riːsə(r)
AM tə'risə, tə'reɪsə, tə'rizə, tə'reɪzə

therethrough
BR ˌðɛː'θruː
AM ðɛr'θru

thereto
BR ˌðɛː'tuː
AM ðɛr'tu

theretofore
BR ˌðɛːtʊ'fɔː(r)
AM ˌðɛrdə'fɔ(ə)r

thereunder
BR ˌðɛːr'ʌndə(r)
AM ðɛ'rəndər

thereunto
BR ˌðɛːr'ʌntuː, ˌðɛːrʌn'tuː
AM ðɛˌrən'tu

thereupon
BR ˌðɛːrə'pɒn, 'ðɛːrəpɒn
AM ˈðɛrəˌpɑn

therewith
BR ˌðɛː'wɪð
AM ðɛr'wɪð

therewithal
BR 'ðɛːwɪðɔːl, ˌðɛːwɪð'ɔːl
AM 'ðɛrwəˌθɔl, 'ðɛrwəˌðɔl, 'ðɛrwəˌθɑl, 'ðɛrwəˌðɑl

theriac
BR 'θɪərɪak, -s
AM 'θɪriˌæk, -s

therianthropic
BR ˌθɪərɪan'θrɒpɪk, ˌθɪərɪən'θrɒpɪk
AM ˈθɪriən'θrɑpɪk, ˈθɪriˌæn'θrɑpɪk

theriomorphic
BR ˌθɪərɪə(ʊ)'mɔːfɪk
AM ˈθɪriə'mɔrfɪk

therm
BR θəːm, -z
AM θərm, -z

thermae
BR 'θəːmiː
AM 'θərmi, 'θərˌmaɪ

thermal
BR 'θəːml, -z
AM 'θərməl, -z

thermalisation
BR ˌθəːml̩ʌɪ'zeɪʃn, ˌθəːməlʌɪ'zeɪʃn
AM ˌθərmələ'zeɪʃən, ˌθərməˌlaɪ'zeɪʃən

thermalise
BR 'θəːml̩ʌɪz, 'θəːməlʌɪz, -ɨz, -ɪŋ, -d
AM 'θərməˌlaɪz, -ɨz, -ɪŋ, -d

thermalization
BR ˌθəːml̩ʌɪ'zeɪʃn, ˌθəːməlʌɪ'zeɪʃn
AM ˌθərmələ'zeɪʃən, ˌθərməˌlaɪ'zeɪʃən

thermalize
BR 'θəːml̩ʌɪz, 'θəːməlʌɪz, -ɨz, -ɪŋ, -d
AM 'θərməˌlaɪz, -ɨz, -ɪŋ, -d

thermally
BR 'θəːml̩i, 'θəːməli
AM 'θərməli

thermic
BR 'θəːmɪk
AM 'θərmɪk

thermically
BR 'θəːmɨkli
AM 'θərmək(ə)li

thermidor
BR 'θəːmɨdɔː(r)
AM 'θərməˌdɔ(ə)r

thermion
BR 'θəːmɪən, 'θəːmɪɒn, -z
AM 'θərmˌaɪən, -z

thermionic
BR ˌθəːmɪ'ɒnɪk, -s
AM ˌθərmi'ɑnɪk, -s

thermistor
BR θəː'mɪstə(r), 'θəːmɪstə(r)
AM 'θərˌmɪstər, ˌθər'mɪstər

thermit
BR 'θəːmɪt
AM 'θərmət

thermite
BR 'θəːmʌɪt, -s
AM 'θərˌmaɪt, -s

thermochemical
BR ˌθəːməʊ'kɛmɨkl
AM ˌθərmoʊ'kɛməkəl

thermochemistry
BR ˌθəːməʊ'kɛmɨstri
AM ˌθərmoʊ'kɛməstri

thermocline
BR 'θəːmə(ʊ)klʌɪn
AM 'θərməˌklaɪn

thermocouple
BR 'θəːmə(ʊ)ˌkʌpl
AM 'θərməˌkəpəl

thermodynamic
BR ˌθəːmə(ʊ)dʌɪ'namɪk, -s
AM ˈθərmoʊˌdaɪ'næmɪk, -s

thermodynamical
BR ˌθəːmə(ʊ)dʌɪ'namɨkl
AM ˈθərmoʊˌdaɪ'næməkəl

thermodynamically
BR ˌθəːmə(ʊ)dʌɪ'namɨkli
AM ˈθərmoʊˌdaɪ'næmək(ə)li

thermodynamicist
BR ˌθəːmə(ʊ)dʌɪ'namɨsɪst, -s
AM ˈθərmoʊˌdaɪ'næməsəst, -s

thermoelectric
BR ˌθəːməʊɪ'lɛktrɪk
AM ˈθərmoʊə'lɛktrɪk, ˈθərmoʊˌi'lɛktrɪk

thermoelectrically
BR ˌθəːməʊɪ'lɛktrɨkli
AM ˈθərmoʊə'lɛktrək(ə)li, ˈθərmoʊˌi'lɛktrək(ə)li

thermoelectricity
BR ˌθəːməʊɪˌlɛk'trɪsɨti, ˌθəːməʊˌɛlɛk'trɪsɨti, ˌθəːməʊˌɛlɪk'trɪsɨti, ˌθəːməʊˌɪlɛk'trɪsɨti, ˌθəːməʊˌiːlɛk'trɪsɨti
AM ˈθərmoʊəˌlɛk'trɪsɨdi, ˈθərmoʊˌiˌlɛk'trɪsɨdi

thermogenesis
BR ˌθəːmə(ʊ)'dʒɛnɨsɪs
AM ˌθərmə'dʒɛnəsəs

thermogram
BR 'θəːməgram, -z
AM 'θərməˌgræm, -z

thermograph
BR 'θəːməgrɑːf, 'θəːməgraf, -s
AM 'θərməˌgræf, -s

thermographic
BR ˌθəːmə(ʊ)'grafɪk
AM ˌθərmə'græfɪk

thermography
BR θəː'mɒgrəfi
AM θər'mɑgrəfi

thermohaline
BR ˌθəːmə(ʊ)ˈheɪlʌɪn, ˌθəːmə(ʊ)ˈheɪliːn
AM ˌθərməˈheɪlin, ˌθərməˈheɪlaɪn

thermokarst
BR ˈθəːmə(ʊ)kɑːst
AM ˈθərməˌkɑrst

thermolabile
BR ˌθəːməʊˈleɪbʌɪl
AM ˌθərməˈleɪˌbaɪl, ˌθərməˈleɪbəl

thermoluminescence
BR ˌθəːməʊˌluːmɪˈnɛsns
AM ˌθərmoʊˌluməˈnɛsəns

thermoluminescent
BR ˌθəːməʊˌluːmɪˈnɛsnt
AM ˌθərmoʊˌluməˈnɛsənt

thermolysis
BR θəːˈmɒlɪsɪs
AM θərˈmɑləsəs

thermolytic
BR ˌθəːməˈlɪtɪk
AM ˌθərməˈlɪdɪk

thermometer
BR θəˈmɒmɪtə(r), -z
AM θərˈmɑmədər, -z

thermometric
BR ˌθəːməˈmɛtrɪk
AM ˌθərməˈmɛtrɪk

thermometrical
BR ˌθəːməˈmɛtrɪkl
AM ˌθərməˈmɛtrəkəl

thermometrically
BR ˌθəːməˈmɛtrɪkli
AM ˌθərməˈmɛtrək(ə)li

thermometry
BR θəˈmɒmɪtri
AM θərˈmɑmətri

thermonuclear
BR ˌθəːməʊˈnjuːklɪə(r)
AM ˌθərmoʊˈn(j)uklɪ(ə)r

thermophile
BR ˈθəːməfʌɪl, -z
AM ˈθərməˌfaɪl, -z

thermophilic
BR ˌθəːməˈfɪlɪk
AM ˌθərməˈfɪlɪk

thermopile
BR ˈθəːməpʌɪl, -z
AM ˈθərməˌpaɪl, -z

thermoplastic
BR ˌθəːməʊˈplastɪk, -s
AM ˌθərmoʊˈplæstɪk, -s

Thermopylae
BR θəˈmɒpɪliː, θəˈmɒpl̩iː, θəːˈmɒpɪliː, θəːˈmɒpl̩iː
AM θərˈmɑpəˌli

Thermos®
BR ˈθəːməs, -ɪz
AM ˈθərməs, -əz

thermoset
BR ˈθəːmə(ʊ)sɛt
AM ˈθərmoʊˌsɛt

thermosetting
BR ˈθəːməʊˌsɛtɪŋ
AM ˈθərmoʊˌsɛdɪŋ

thermosphere
BR ˈθəːməsfɪə(r)
AM ˈθərməˌsfɪ(ə)r

thermostable
BR ˌθəːməʊˈsteɪbl
AM ˈðərmoʊˌsteɪbəl

thermostat
BR ˈθəːməstat, -s
AM ˈθərməˌstæt, -s

thermostatic
BR ˌθəːmə(ʊ)ˈstatɪk
AM ˌθərməˈstædɪk

thermostatically
BR ˌθəːmə(ʊ)ˈstatɪkli
AM ˌθərməˈstædək(ə)li

thermotactic
BR ˌθəːmə(ʊ)ˈtaktɪk
AM ˌθərməˈtæktɪk

thermotaxic
BR ˌθəːmə(ʊ)ˈtaksɪk
AM ˌθərməˈtæksɪk

thermotaxis
BR ˌθəːmə(ʊ)ˈtaksɪs
AM ˌθərməˈtæksəs

thermotropic
BR ˌθəːməˈtrɒpɪk, ˌθəːməˈtrəʊpɪk
AM ˌθərməˈtrɑpɪk

thermotropism
BR ˌθəːmə(ʊ)ˈtrəʊpɪz(ə)m
AM ˌθərməˈtrɑˌpɪzəm

theropod
BR ˈθɪərəpɒd, -z
AM ˈθɪrəˌpɑd, -z

Theroux
BR θəˈruː
AM θəˈru

thesauri
BR θɪˈsɔːrʌɪ
AM θəˈsɔˌraɪ

thesaurus
BR θɪˈsɔːrəs, -ɪz
AM θəˈsɔrəs, -əz

these
BR ðiːz
AM ðiz

theses
BR ˈθiːsiːz
AM ˈθiˌsiz

Theseus
BR ˈθiːsɪəs, ˈθiːsjuːs
AM ˈθisiəs

thesis[1]
dissertation
BR ˈθiːsɪs
AM ˈθisɪs

thesis[2]
rhythm
BR ˈθɛsɪs
AM ˈθisɪs, ˈθɛsəs

thesp
BR θɛsp, -s
AM θɛsp, -s

thespian
BR ˈθɛspɪən, -z
AM ˈθɛspiən, -z

Thespis
BR ˈθɛspɪs
AM ˈθɛspəs

Thessalian
BR θɛˈseɪlɪən, θɪˈseɪlɪən, -z
AM θɛˈseɪljən, θɛˈseɪliən, -z

Thessalonian
BR ˌθɛsəˈləʊnɪən, -z
AM ˌθɛsəˈloʊniən, -z

Thessalonica
BR ˌθɛsəˈlɒnɪkə(*r*)
AM ˌθɛsəˈlɑnəkə

Thessaloníki
BR ˌθɛsələˈniːki
AM ˌθɛsələˈniki

Thessaly
BR ˈθɛsəli
AM ˈθɛsəli

theta
BR ˈθiːtə(*r*), -z
AM ˈθeɪdə, ˈθidə, -z

thetic
BR ˈθɛtɪk
AM ˈθɛdɪk

Thetis
BR ˈθɛtɪs, ˈθiːtɪs
AM ˈθidəs, ˈθɛdəs

theurgic
BR θɪˈəːdʒɪk
AM θiˈərdʒɪk

theurgical
BR θɪˈəːdʒɪkl
AM θiˈərdʒəkəl

theurgist
BR ˈθiːədʒɪst, -s
AM ˈθiərdʒəst, -s

theurgy
BR ˈθiːəːdʒi
AM ˈθiərdʒi

thew
BR θjuː, -z
AM θ(j)u, -z

they[1]
strong form
BR ðeɪ
AM ðeɪ

they[2]
weak form
BR ðeɪ
AM ðeɪ, ðɛ

they'd
BR ðeɪd
AM ðeɪd

they'll
BR ðeɪl
AM ðeɪl

they're
BR ðɛː(r)
AM ˈðeɪ(ə)r, ðɛ(ə)r

they've
BR ðeɪv
AM ðeɪv

thiamin
BR ˈθʌɪəmɪn
AM ˈθaɪəmən, ˈθaɪəˌmin

thiamine
BR ˈθʌɪəmiːn, ˈθʌɪəmɪn
AM ˈθaɪəmən, ˈθaɪəˌmin

thiazide
BR ˈθʌɪəzʌɪd, -z
AM ˈθaɪəˌzaɪd, -z

thiazole
BR θʌɪˈeɪzəʊl
AM ˈθaɪəˌzoʊl

thick
BR θɪk, -ə(r), -ɪst
AM θɪk, -ər, -ɪst

thick and thin
BR ˌθɪk (ə)n(d) ˈθɪn
AM ˌθɪk ən ˈθɪn

thicken
BR ˈθɪk|(ə)n, -(ə)nz, -n̩ɪŋ\-(ə)nɪŋ, -(ə)nd
AM ˈθɪk|ən, -ənz, -(ə)nɪŋ, -ənd

thickener
BR ˈθɪk(ə)nə(r), ˈθɪkn̩ə(r), -z
AM ˈθɪk(ə)nər, -z

thickening
BR ˈθɪk(ə)nɪŋ, ˈθɪkn̩ɪŋ, -z
AM ˈθɪk(ə)nɪŋ, -z

thicket
BR ˈθɪkɪt, -s
AM ˈθɪkɪt, -s

thickhead
BR ˈθɪkhɛd, -z
AM ˈθɪkˌ(h)ɛd, -z

thickheaded
BR ˌθɪkˈhɛdɪd
AM ˈθɪkˌhɛdəd

thickheadedness
BR ˌθɪkˈhɛdɪdnɪs
AM ˈθɪkˌhɛdədnəs

thickie
BR ˈθɪk|i, -ɪz
AM ˈθɪki, -z

thickish
BR ˈθɪkɪʃ
AM ˈθɪkɪʃ

thickly
BR ˈθɪkli
AM ˈθɪkli

thicknee
BR ˈθɪkniː, -z
AM ˈθɪkˌni, -z

thickness
BR ˈθɪknɪs, -ɪz, -ɪŋ, -t
AM ˈθɪknɪs, -ɪz, -ɪŋ, -t

thicknesser
BR ˈθɪknɪsə(r), -z
AM ˈθɪknɪsər, -z

thicko
BR 'θɪkəʊ, -z
AM 'θɪkoʊ, -z
thickset
BR ˌθɪk'sɛt
AM 'θɪkˌsɛt
thick-skinned
BR ˌθɪk'skɪnd
AM 'θɪkˌskɪnd
thick-skulled
BR ˌθɪk'skʌld
AM 'θɪkˌskəld
thick-witted
BR ˌθɪk'wɪtɨd
AM 'θɪkˌwɪdɨd
thief
BR θiːf
AM θif
thieve
BR θiːv, -z, -ɪŋ, -d
AM θiv, -z, -ɪŋ, -d
thievery
BR 'θiːv(ə)ri
AM 'θiv(ə)ri
thieves
BR θiːvz
AM θivz
thievish
BR 'θiːvɪʃ
AM 'θivɪʃ
thievishly
BR 'θiːvɨʃli
AM 'θivɨʃli
thievishness
BR 'θiːvɨʃnɨs
AM 'θivɨʃnɨs
thigh
BR θʌɪ, -z
AM θaɪ, -z
thighbone
BR 'θʌɪbəʊn, -z
AM 'θaɪˌboʊn, -z
thill
BR θɪl, -z
AM θɪl, -z
thiller
BR 'θɪlə(r), -z
AM 'θɪlər, -z
thimble
BR 'θɪmbl, -z
AM 'θɪmbəl, -z
thimbleful
BR 'θɪmblfʊl, -z
AM 'θɪmbəlˌfʊl, -z
thimblerig
BR 'θɪmblrɪɡ, -z, -ɪŋ, -d
AM 'θɪmbəlˌrɪɡ, -z, -ɪŋ, -d
thimblerigger
BR 'θɪmblˌrɪɡə(r), -z
AM 'θɪmbəlˌrɪɡər, -z
thimerosal
BR θʌɪ'mɛrəsal
AM θaɪ'mɛrəˌsæl
thin
BR θɪn, -z, -ɪŋ, -d, -ə(r), -ɨst
AM θɪn, -z, -ɪŋ, -d, -ər, -ɨst
thine
BR ðʌɪn
AM ðaɪn
thing
BR θɪŋ, -z
AM θɪŋ, -z
thingamabob
BR 'θɪŋəmɨbɒb, -z
AM 'θɪŋəm(ə)ˌbɑb, -z
thingamajig
BR 'θɪŋəmɨdʒɪɡ, -z
AM 'θɪŋəməˌdʒɪɡ, -z
thingambob
BR 'θɪŋəmbɒb, -z
AM 'θɪŋəmˌbɑb, -z
thingamy
BR 'θɪŋəm|i, -ɪz
AM 'θɪŋəmi, -z
thingum
BR 'θɪŋəm, -z
AM 'θɪŋəm, -z
thingumabob
BR 'θɪŋəmɨbɒb, -z
AM 'θɪŋəməˌbɑb, -z
thingumajig
BR 'θɪŋəmɨdʒɪɡ, -z
AM 'θɪŋəməˌdʒɪɡ, -z
thingummy
BR 'θɪŋəm|i, -ɪz
AM 'θɪŋəmi, -z
thingy
BR 'θɪŋ|i, -ɪz
AM 'θɪŋi, -z
think
BR θɪŋk, -s, -ɪŋ
AM θɪŋk, -s, -ɪŋ
thinkable
BR 'θɪŋkəbl
AM 'θɪŋkəbəl
thinker
BR 'θɪŋkə(r), -z
AM 'θɪŋkər, -z
think-tank
BR 'θɪŋktaŋk, -s
AM 'θɪŋkˌtæŋk, -s
thinly
BR 'θɪnli
AM 'θɪnli
thinner
BR 'θɪnə(r), -z
AM 'θɪnər, -z
thinness
BR 'θɪnnɨs
AM 'θɪ(n)nɨs
thinning
BR 'θɪnɪŋ, -z
AM 'θɪnɪŋ, -z
thinnish
BR 'θɪnɪʃ
AM 'θɪnɪʃ
thin-skinned
BR ˌθɪn'skɪnd
AM 'θɪnˌskɪnd
thio
BR 'θʌɪəʊ
AM 'θaɪoʊ
thiocyanate
BR ˌθʌɪəʊ'sʌɪəneɪt, -s
AM ˌθaɪə'saɪəneɪt, -s
thiol
BR 'θʌɪɒl
AM 'θaɪˌɔl, 'θaɪˌɑl
thionate
BR 'θʌɪəneɪt
AM 'θaɪəˌneɪt
thionyl
BR 'θʌɪənɪl
AM 'θaɪənɪl
thiopentone
BR ˌθʌɪə(ʊ)'pɛntəʊn
AM ˌθaɪə'pɛntoʊn
thiosulphate
BR ˌθɪə(ʊ)'sʌlfeɪt
AM ˌθiə'səlˌfeɪt
thiourea
BR ˌθʌɪəʊjʊ'riːə(r)
AM ˌθaɪoʊjə'riə
Thira
BR 'θɪərə(r)
AM 'θɪrə
third
BR θəːd, -z
AM θərd, -z
thirdhand
BR ˌθəːd'hand
AM ˌθərd'hænd
thirdly
BR 'θəːdli
AM 'θərdli
Thirlmere
BR 'θəːlmɪə(r)
AM 'θərlˌmɪ(ə)r
Thirsk
BR θəːsk
AM θərsk
thirst
BR θəːst, -s, -ɪŋ, -ɨd
AM θərst, -s, -ɪŋ, -əd
thirstily
BR 'θəːstɨli
AM 'θərstəli
thirstiness
BR 'θəːstɪnɨs
AM 'θərstinɨs
thirstless
BR 'θəːstləs
AM 'θərs(t)ləs
thirsty
BR 'θəːst|i, -ɪə(r), -ɪɨst
AM 'θərsti, -ər, -ɨst
thirteen
BR ˌθəː'tiːn
AM ˌθər'tin
thirteenth
BR ˌθəː'tiːnθ, -s
AM ˌθər'tinθ, -s
thirtieth
BR 'θəːtɪɨθ, -s
AM 'θərdiɨθ, -s
thirty
BR 'θəːt|i, -ɪz
AM 'θərdi, -z
thirtyfold
BR 'θəːtɪfəʊld
AM 'θərdiˌfoʊld
thirtysomething
BR 'θəːtɪˌsʌmθɪŋ, -z
AM 'θərdiˌsəmθɪŋ, -z
thirty-twomo
BR ˌθəːtɪ'tuːməʊ
AM ˌθərdi'tuˌmoʊ
this[1]
strong form
BR ðɪs
AM ðɪs
this[2]
weak form
BR ðɪs
AM ðəs
Thisbe
BR 'θɪzbi
AM 'θɪzbi
thistle
BR 'θɪsl, -z
AM 'θɪsəl, -z
thistledown
BR 'θɪsldaʊn
AM 'θɪsəlˌdaʊn
thistly
BR 'θɪsḷi, 'θɪsli
AM 'θɪs(ə)li
thither
BR 'ðɪðə(r)
AM 'ðɪðər
thitherto
BR ˌðɪðə'tuː
AM ˌðɪðərˌtu
thitherward
BR 'ðɪðəwəd, -z
AM 'ðɪðərwərd, -z
thixotropic
BR ˌθɪksə'trɒpɪk, ˌθɪksə'trəʊpɪk
AM ˌθɪksə'trɑpɪk
thixotropy
BR θɪk'sɒtrəpi
AM θɪk'sɑtrəpi
tho'
BR ðəʊ
AM ðoʊ
thole
BR θəʊl, -z
AM θoʊl, -z
tholepin
BR 'θəʊlpɪn, -z
AM 'θoʊlˌpɪn, -z
tholi
BR 'θəʊlʌɪ
AM 'θoʊˌlai
tholoi
BR 'θəʊlɔɪ
AM 'θoʊˌlɔɪ
tholos
BR 'θəʊlɒs, 'θɒlɒs
AM 'θoʊˌlɔs, 'θoʊˌlɑs
tholus
BR 'θəʊləs
AM 'θoʊləs

Thom
BR tɒm
AM tɑm
Thomas
BR 'tɒməs
AM 'tɑməs
Thomasina
BR ˌtɒmə'siːnə(r)
AM ˌtɑmə'sinə
Thomism
BR 'təʊmɪz(ə)m
AM 'toʊˌmɪzəm
Thomist
BR 'təʊmɪst, -s
AM 'toʊməst, -s
Thomistic
BR tə'mɪstɪk
AM tə'mɪstɪk
Thomistical
BR tə'mɪstɪkl
AM tə'mɪstəkəl
Thompson
BR 'tɒm(p)sn
AM 'tɑm(p)sən
Thomson
BR 'tɒmsn
AM 'tɑmsən
thong
BR θɒŋ, -z
AM θɔŋ, θɑŋ, -z
Thor
BR θɔː(r)
AM θɔ(ə)r
Thora
BR 'θɔːrə(r)
AM 'θɔrə
thoracal
BR 'θɔːrəkl
AM 'θɔrəkəl
thoraces
BR 'θɔːrəsiːz,
θɔː'reɪsiːz
AM 'θɔrəˌsiz
thoracic
BR θɔː'rasɪk, θə'rasɪk
AM θə'ræsɪk, θɔ'ræsɪk
thorax
BR 'θɔːraks, -ɪz
AM 'θɔˌræks, -ɪz
Thorazine®
BR 'θɔːrəziːn
AM 'θɔrəˌzin
Thorburn
BR 'θɔːbəːn
AM 'θɔrˌbərn
Thoreau
BR 'θɔːrəʊ, θɔː'rəʊ,
θə'rəʊ
AM θə'roʊ, θɔ'roʊ
thoria
BR 'θɔːrɪə(r)
AM 'θɔriə
thorite
BR 'θɔːrʌɪt
AM 'θɔˌraɪt
thorium
BR 'θɔːrɪəm
AM 'θɔriəm
thorn
BR θɔːn, -z
AM θɔ(ə)rn, -z
Thornaby
BR 'θɔːnəbi
AM 'θɔrnəbi
thornback
BR 'θɔːnbak, -s
AM 'θɔrnˌbæk, -s
thornbill
BR 'θɔːnbɪl, -z
AM 'θɔrnˌbɪl, -z
Thorndike
BR 'θɔːndʌɪk
AM 'θɔrnˌdaɪk
Thorne
BR θɔːn
AM θɔ(ə)rn
Thorner
BR 'θɔːnə(r)
AM 'θɔrnər
Thorneycroft
BR 'θɔːnɪkrɒft
AM 'θɔrniˌkrɔft
Thornhill
BR 'θɔːnhɪl
AM 'θɔrnˌ(h)ɪl
thornily
BR 'θɔːnɪli
AM 'θɔrnəli
thorniness
BR 'θɔːnɪnɪs
AM 'θɔrninɪs
thornless
BR 'θɔːnləs
AM 'θɔrnləs
Thornley
BR 'θɔːnli
AM 'θɔrnli
thornproof
BR 'θɔːnpruːf
AM 'θɔrnˌpruf
thorntail
BR 'θɔːnteɪl, -z
AM 'θɔrnˌteɪl, -z
Thornton
BR 'θɔːntən
AM 'θɔrn(t)n
thorny
BR 'θɔːn|i, -ɪə(r), -ɪɪst
AM 'θɔrni, -ər, -ɪst
Thorogood
BR 'θʌrəgʊd
AM 'θərəˌgʊd
thorough
BR 'θʌrə(r)
AM 'θərə, 'θəroʊ
thoroughbred
BR 'θʌrəbrɛd, -z
AM 'θərəˌbrɛd, -z
thoroughfare
BR 'θʌrəfɛː(r), -z
AM 'θərəˌfɛ(ə)r, -z
thoroughgoing
BR ˌθʌrə'gəʊɪŋ
AM 'θərəˌgoʊɪŋ
thoroughly
BR 'θʌrəli
AM 'θərəli, 'θəroʊli
thoroughness
BR 'θʌrənəs
AM 'θərənəs,
'θəroʊnəs
thorough-wax
BR 'θʌrəwaks
AM 'θərəˌwæks
thorow-wax
BR 'θʌrəwaks
AM 'θərəˌwæks
Thorp
BR θɔːp
AM θɔ(ə)rp
Thorpe
BR θɔːp
AM θɔ(ə)rp
those
BR ðəʊz
AM ðoʊz
Thoth
BR θəʊθ, təʊt, θɒθ
AM θɔθ, toʊt, θɑθ
thou
BR ðaʊ
AM ðaʊ
though
BR ðəʊ
AM ðoʊ
thought
BR θɔːt, -s
AM θɔt, θɑt, -s
thoughtful
BR 'θɔːtf(ʊ)l
AM 'θɔtfəl, 'θɑtfəl
thoughtfully
BR 'θɔːtfʊli, 'θɔːtfli
AM 'θɔtfəli, 'θɑtfəli
thoughtfulness
BR 'θɔːtf(ʊ)lnəs
AM 'θɔtfəlnəs,
'θɑtfəlnəs
thoughtless
BR 'θɔːtləs
AM 'θɔtləs, 'θɑtləs
thoughtlessly
BR 'θɔːtləsli
AM 'θɔtləsli, 'θɑtləsli
thoughtlessness
BR 'θɔːtləsnəs
AM 'θɔtləsnəs,
'θɑtləsnəs
thought-provoking
BR 'θɔːtprəˌvəʊkɪŋ
AM 'θɔtprəˌvoʊkɪŋ,
'θɑtprəˌvoʊkɪŋ
thousand
BR 'θaʊzn|d, -(d)z
AM 'θaʊzn(d), -z
thousandfold
BR 'θaʊzn(d)fəʊld
AM 'θaʊzn(d)ˌfoʊld
thousandth
BR 'θaʊzn(t)θ, -s
AM 'θaʊzn(t)θ, -s
Thrace
BR θreɪs
AM θreɪs
Thracian
BR 'θreɪʃn, -z
AM 'θreɪʃən, -z
thraldom
BR 'θrɔːldəm
AM 'θrɔldəm, 'θrɑldəm
thrall
BR θrɔːl
AM θrɔl, θrɑl
thralldom
BR 'θrɔːldəm
AM 'θrɔldəm, 'θrɑldəm
thrang
BR θraŋ
AM θræŋ
thrash
BR θraʃ, -ɪz, -ɪŋ, -t
AM θræʃ, -əz, -ɪŋ, -t
thrasher
BR 'θraʃə(r), -z
AM 'θræʃər, -z
thrashing
BR 'θraʃɪŋ, -z
AM 'θræʃɪŋ, -z
thrasonical
BR θrə'sɒnɪkl
AM θreɪ'sɑnəkəl
thrasonically
BR θrə'sɒnɪkli
AM θreɪ'sɑnək(ə)li
thrawn
BR θrɔːn
AM θrɔn, θrɑn
thread
BR θrɛd, -z, -ɪŋ, -ɪd
AM θrɛd, -z, -ɪŋ, -əd
threadbare
BR 'θrɛdbɛː(r)
AM 'θrɛdˌbɛ(ə)r
threader
BR 'θrɛdə(r), -z
AM 'θrɛdər, -z
threadfin
BR 'θrɛdfɪn, -z
AM 'θrɛdˌfɪn, -z
threadfish
BR 'θrɛdfɪʃ, -ɪz
AM 'θrɛdˌfɪʃ, -ɪz
threadlike
BR 'θrɛdlʌɪk
AM 'θrɛdˌlaɪk
Threadneedle
BR ˌθrɛd'niːdl,
'θrɛdˌniːdl
AM 'θrɛdˌnidəl
threadworm
BR 'θrɛdwəːm, -z
AM 'θrɛdˌwərm, -z
thready
BR 'θrɛd|i, -ɪə(r), -ɪɪst
AM 'θrɛdi, -ər, -ɪst
threat
BR θrɛt, -s

AM θrɛt, -s

threaten
BR 'θrɛt|n, -nz, -n̩ɪŋ\-nɪŋ, -nd
AM 'θrɛt|n, -nz, -n̩ɪŋ, -nd

threatener
BR 'θrɛtn̩ə(r), 'θrɛtnə(r), -z
AM 'θrɛtn̩ər, 'θrɛtnər, -z

threateningly
BR 'θrɛtn̩ɪŋli, 'θrɛtnɪŋli
AM 'θrɛtn̩ɪŋli, 'θrɛtnɪŋli

three
BR θriː, -z
AM θri, -z

three-bagger
BR ˌθriː'bagə(r), -z
AM ˌθri'bæɡər, -z

three-base hit
BR ˌθriːbeɪs 'hɪt, -s
AM 'θriˌbeɪs 'hɪt, -s

three-card trick
BR ˌθriːkɑːd 'trɪk, -s
AM 'θriˌkɑrd 'trɪk, -s

three-cornered
BR ˌθriː'kɔːnəd
AM 'θriˌkɔrnərd

three-D
BR ˌθriː'diː
AM 'θri'di

three-decker
BR ˌθriː'dɛkə(r), -z
AM 'θriˌdɛkər, -z

three-dimensional
BR ˌθriːdʌɪ'mɛnʃn̩(ə)l, ˌθriːdʌɪ'mɛnʃən(ə)l, ˌθriːdɪ'mɛnʃn̩(ə)l, ˌθriːdɪ'mɛnʃən(ə)l
AM ˌθridə'mɛn(t)ʃ(ə)nəl, ˌθriˌdaɪ'mɛn(t)ʃ(ə)nəl

threefold
BR 'θriːfəʊld, ˌθriː'fəʊld
AM 'θriˌfoʊld

three-handed
BR ˌθriː'handɪd
AM 'θriˌhændəd

three-legged
BR ˌθriː'lɛɡɪd
AM 'θriˌlɛɡəd

threeness
BR 'θriːnɪs
AM 'θrinɪs

threepence
BR 'θrɛp(ə)ns, -ɪz
AM 'θrɛpəns, 'θriˌpɛns, -əz

threepenny
BR 'θrɛp(ə)ni, 'θrɛpn̩i
AM 'θriˌpɛni

three-ply[1]
adjective
BR ˌθriː'plʌɪ, 'θriːplʌɪ
AM 'θriˌplaɪ

three-ply[2]
noun
BR 'θriːplʌɪ
AM 'θriˌplaɪ

three-point
BR ˌθriː'pɔɪnt
AM ˌθri'pɔɪnt

three-pointer
BR ˌθriː'pɔɪntə(r), -z
AM ˌθri'pɔɪn(t)ər, -z

three-point landing
BR ˌθriːpɔɪnt 'landɪŋ, -z
AM 'θriˌpɔɪnt 'lændɪŋ, -z

three-point turn
BR ˌθriːpɔɪn(t) 'təːn, -z
AM 'θriˌpɔɪn(t) 'tərn, -z

three-quarter
BR ˌθriː'kwɔːtə(r), -z
AM ˌθri'kwɔ(r)dər, -z

three R's
BR ˌθriː 'ɑːz
AM ˌθri 'ɑrz

threescore
BR ˌθriː'skɔː(r), -z
AM ˌθri'skɔ(ə)r, -z

threesome
BR 'θriːs(ə)m, -z
AM 'θrisəm, -z

three-way
BR ˌθriː'weɪ
AM 'θriˌweɪ

three-wheeler
BR ˌθriː'wiːlə(r), -z
AM ˌθri'(h)wilər, -z

Threlfall
BR 'θrɛlfɔːl
AM 'θrɛlˌfɔl, 'θrɛlˌfɑl

Threlkeld
BR 'θrɛlkɛld
AM 'θrɛlˌkɛl(d)

thremmatology
BR ˌθrɛmə'tɒlədʒi
AM ˌθrɛmə'tɑlədʒi

threnode
BR 'θrɛnəʊd, 'θriːnəʊd, -z
AM 'θriˌnoʊd, 'θrɛˌnoʊd, -z

threnodial
BR θrɪ'nəʊdɪəl
AM θrə'noʊdiəl

threnodic
BR θrɪ'nɒdɪk
AM θrə'nɑdɪk

threnodist
BR 'θrɛnədɪst, 'θriːnədɪst, -s
AM 'θrɛnədəst, -s

threnody
BR 'θrɛnəd|i, 'θriːnəd|i, -ɪz
AM 'θrɛnədi, -z

threonine
BR 'θrɪəniːn
AM 'θriəˌnin, 'θriənən

thresh
BR θrɛʃ, -ɪz, -ɪŋ, -t
AM θrɛʃ, -əz, -ɪŋ, -t

thresher
BR 'θrɛʃə(r), -z
AM 'θrɛʃər, -z

threshold
BR 'θrɛʃ(h)əʊld, -z
AM 'θrɛʃˌ(h)oʊld, -z

threw
BR θruː
AM θru

thrice
BR θrʌɪs
AM θraɪs

thrift
BR θrɪft, -s
AM θrɪft, -s

thriftily
BR 'θrɪftɨli
AM 'θrɪftɨli

thriftiness
BR 'θrɪftɪnɨs
AM 'θrɪftinɨs

thriftless
BR 'θrɪftlɨs
AM 'θrɪf(t)lɨs

thriftlessly
BR 'θrɪf(t)lɨsli
AM 'θrɪf(t)lɨsli

thriftlessness
BR 'θrɪftlɨsnɨs
AM 'θrɪf(t)lɨsnɨs

thrifty
BR 'θrɪft|i, -ɪə(r), -ɪɪst
AM 'θrɪfti, -ər, -ɨst

thrill
BR θrɪl, -z, -ɪŋ, -d
AM θrɪl, -z, -ɪŋ, -d

thriller
BR 'θrɪlə(r), -z
AM 'θrɪlər, -z

thrillingly
BR 'θrɪlɪŋli
AM 'θrɪlɪŋli

thrips
BR θrɪps
AM θrɪps

thrive
BR θrʌɪv, -z, -ɪŋ, -d
AM θraɪv, -z, -ɪŋ, -d

thriven
BR 'θrɪvn
AM 'θrɪvən

thro
BR θruː
AM θru

thro'
BR θruː
AM θru

throat
BR θrəʊt, -s
AM θroʊt, -s

throatily
BR 'θrəʊtɨli
AM 'θroʊdəli

throatiness
BR 'θrəʊtɪnɨs
AM 'θroʊdinɨs

throaty
BR 'θrəʊt|i, -ɪə(r), -ɪɪst
AM 'θroʊdi, -ər, -ɨst

throb
BR θrɒb, -z, -ɪŋ, -d
AM θrɑb, -z, -ɪŋ, -d

throe
BR θrəʊ, -z
AM θroʊ, -z

Throgmorton
BR 'θrɒɡmɔːtn, θrɒɡ'mɔːtn
AM 'θrɑɡˌmɔrtn

thrombi
BR 'θrɒmbʌɪ
AM 'θrɑmˌbaɪ

thrombin
BR 'θrɒmbɪn, -z
AM 'θrɑmbən, -z

thrombocyte
BR 'θrɒmbəsʌɪt, -s
AM 'θrɑmbəˌsaɪt, -s

thrombolysis
BR θrɒm'bɒlɨsɪs
AM ˌθrɑmbə'laɪsɪs

thrombose
BR 'θrɒmbəʊz, 'θrɒmbəʊs, θrɒm'bəʊz, θrɒm'bəʊs, -ɪz, -ɪŋ, -d
AM 'θrɑmˌboʊs, 'θrɑmˌboʊz, -əz, -ɪŋ, -d

thromboses
BR θrɒm'bəʊsiːz
AM θrɑm'boʊˌsiz

thrombosis
BR θrɒm'bəʊsɪs
AM θrɑm'boʊsəs

thrombotic
BR θrɒm'bɒtɪk
AM ˌθrɑm'bɑdɪk

thrombus
BR 'θrɒmbəs
AM 'θrɑmbəs

throne
BR θrəʊn, -z, -ɪŋ, -d
AM θroʊn, -z, -ɪŋ, -d

throneless
BR 'θrəʊnləs
AM 'θroʊnləs

throng
BR θrɒŋ, -z, -ɪŋ, -d
AM θrɔŋ, θrɑŋ, -z, -ɪŋ, -d

throstle
BR 'θrɒsl, -z
AM 'θrɔsəl, 'θrɑsəl, -z

throttle
BR 'θrɒt|l, -lz, -l̩ɪŋ\-lɪŋ, -ld
AM 'θrɑdəl, -z, -ɪŋ, -d

throttlehold
BR 'θrɒtlhəʊld
AM 'θrɑdlˌ(h)oʊld

throttler
BR 'θrɒtl̩ə(r), 'θrɒtlə(r), -z
AM 'θrɑdlər, 'θrɑtlər, -z

through
BR θruː
AM θru

throughout
BR θruː'aʊt, θrʊ'aʊt
AM θru'aʊt

throughput
BR 'θruːpʊt
AM 'θru,pʊt

throughway
BR 'θruːweɪ, -z
AM 'θru,weɪ, -z

throve
BR θrəʊv
AM θroʊv

throw
BR θrəʊ, -z, -ɪŋ
AM θroʊ, -z, -ɪŋ

throwable
BR 'θrəʊəbl
AM 'θroʊəbəl

throwaway
BR 'θrəʊəweɪ
AM 'θroʊə,weɪ

throwback
BR 'θrəʊbak, -s
AM 'θroʊ,bæk, -s

thrower
BR 'θrəʊə(r), -z
AM 'θroʊər, -z

throw-in
BR 'θrəʊɪn, -z
AM 'θroʊ,ɪn, -z

thrown
BR θrəʊn
AM θroʊn

throw-off
BR 'θrəʊɒf, -s
AM 'θroʊ,ɔf, 'θroʊ,ɑf, -s

throw-out
BR 'θrəʊaʊt, -s
AM 'θroʊ,aʊt, -s

throwster
BR 'θrəʊstə(r), -z
AM 'θroʊstər, -z

thru
BR θruː
AM θru

thrum
BR θrʌm, -z, -ɪŋ, -d
AM θrəm, -z, -ɪŋ, -d

thrummer
BR 'θrʌmə(r), -z
AM 'θrəmər, -z

thrummy
BR 'θrʌm|i, -ɪə(r), -ɪɪst
AM 'θrəmi, -ər, -ɨst

thrush
BR θrʌʃ, -ɪz
AM θrəʃ, -əz

thrust
BR θrʌst, -s, -ɪŋ
AM θrəst, -s, -ɪŋ

thruster
BR 'θrʌstə(r), -z
AM 'θrəstər, -z

thrutch
BR θrʌtʃ, -ɪz
AM θrətʃ, -əz

thruway
BR 'θruːweɪ, -z
AM 'θru,weɪ, -z

Thucydides
BR θjuː'sɪdɨdiːz
AM θu'sɪdi,diz

thud
BR θʌd, -z, -ɪŋ, -ɨd
AM θəd, -z, -ɪŋ, -əd

thuddingly
BR 'θʌdɪŋli
AM 'θədɪŋli

thug
BR θʌg, -z
AM θəg, -z

thuggee
BR θʌ'giː, 'θʌgiː
AM 'θəgi

thuggery
BR 'θʌg(ə)ri
AM 'θəgəri

thuggish
BR 'θʌgɪʃ
AM 'θəgɪʃ

thuggishly
BR 'θʌgɪʃli
AM 'θəgɪʃli

thuggishness
BR 'θʌgɪʃnɪs
AM 'θəgɪʃnɪs

thuggism
BR 'θʌgɪz(ə)m
AM 'θə,gɪzəm

thuja
BR 'θ(j)uːjə(*r*), 'θ(j)uːdʒə(*r*), -z
AM 'θujə, -z

Thule[1]
in classical geography
BR θjuːl, 'θ(j)uːli
AM 'tul(ə), θul

Thule[2]
in Greenland
BR 'tuːli, 'tuːlə(*r*)
AM 'tu,li

thulium
BR 'θjuːlɪəm
AM 'θ(j)uliəm

thumb
BR θʌm, -z, -ɪŋ, -d
AM θəm, -z, -ɪŋ, -d

thumbless
BR 'θʌmləs
AM 'θəmləs

thumbnail
BR 'θʌmneɪl
AM 'θəm,neɪl

thumbprint
BR 'θʌmprɪnt, -s
AM 'θəm,prɪnt, -s

thumbscrew
BR 'θʌmskruː, -z
AM 'θəm,skru, -z

thumbs-down
BR ,θʌmz'daʊn
AM ',θəmz'daʊn

thumbstall
BR 'θʌmstɔːl, -z
AM 'θəm,stɔl, 'θəm,stɑl, -z

thumbs-up
BR ,θʌmz'ʌp
AM ',θəmz'əp

thumbtack
BR 'θʌmtak, -s
AM 'θəm,tæk, -s

thump
BR θʌm|p, -ps, -pɪŋ, -(p)t
AM θəm|p, -ps, -pɪŋ, -(p)t

thumper
BR 'θʌmpə(r), -z
AM 'θəmpər, -z

thunder
BR 'θʌnd|ə(r), -əz, -(ə)rɪŋ, -əd
AM 'θənd|ər, -ərz, -(ə)rɪŋ, -ərd

thunderball
BR 'θʌndəbɔːl, -z
AM 'θəndər,bɔl, 'θəndər,bɑl, -z

Thunder Bay
BR ,θʌndə 'beɪ
AM ,θəndər 'beɪ

thunderbird
BR 'θʌndəbəːd, -z
AM 'θəndər,bərd, -z

thunderbolt
BR 'θʌndəbəʊlt, -s
AM 'θəndər,boʊlt, -s

thunderbox
BR 'θʌndəbɒks, -ɪz
AM 'θəndər,bɑks, -əz

thunderbug
BR 'θʌndəbʌg, -z
AM 'θəndər,bəg, -z

thunderclap
BR 'θʌndəklap, -s
AM 'θəndər,klæp, -s

thundercloud
BR 'θʌndəklaʊd, -z
AM 'θəndər,klaʊd, -z

thunderer
BR 'θʌnd(ə)rə(r), -z
AM 'θənd(ə)rər, -z

thunderflash
BR 'θʌndəflaʃ, -ɪz
AM 'θəndər,flæʃ, -əz

thunderfly
BR 'θʌndəflʌɪ, -z
AM 'θəndər,flaɪ, -z

thunderhead
BR 'θʌndəhɛd, -z
AM 'θəndər,(h)ɛd, -z

thunderiness
BR 'θʌnd(ə)rɪnɪs
AM 'θənd(ə)rinɪs

thundering
BR 'θʌnd(ə)rɪŋ, -z
AM 'θənd(ə)rɪŋ, -z

thunderingly
BR 'θʌnd(ə)rɪŋli
AM 'θənd(ə)rɪŋli

thunderless
BR 'θʌndələs
AM 'θəndərləs

thunderous
BR 'θʌnd(ə)rəs
AM 'θənd(ə)rəs

thunderously
BR 'θʌnd(ə)rəsli
AM 'θənd(ə)rəsli

thunderousness
BR 'θʌnd(ə)rəsnəs
AM 'θənd(ə)rəsnəs

thundershower
BR 'θʌndə,ʃaʊə(r), -z
AM 'θəndər,ʃaʊər, -z

thunderstorm
BR 'θʌndəstɔːm, -z
AM 'θəndər,stɔ(ə)rm, -z

thunderstruck
BR 'θʌndəstrʌk
AM 'θəndər,strək

thundery
BR 'θʌnd(ə)ri
AM 'θənd(ə)ri

thunk
BR θʌŋ|k, -ks, -kɪŋ, -(k)t
AM θəŋk, -s, -ɪŋ, -t

Thurber
BR 'θəːbə(r)
AM 'θərbər

Thurgau
BR 'tʊəgaʊ
AM 'tʊr,gaʊ

thurible
BR 'θjʊərɪbl, 'θjɔːrɪbl, -z
AM 'θ(j)ʊrəbəl, 'θərəbəl, -z

thurifer
BR 'θjʊərɪfə(r), 'θjɔːrɪfə(r), -z
AM 'θ(j)ʊrəfər, 'θərəfər, -z

thuriferous
BR θjʊ'rɪf(ə)rəs
AM θ(j)ʊ'rɪf(ə)rəs, θə'rɪf(ə)rəs

thurification
BR ,θjʊərɪfɪ'keɪʃn, ,θjɔːrɪfɪ'keɪʃn
AM ,θ(j)ʊrəfə'keɪʃən

Thuringia
BR θ(j)ʊ'rɪn(d)ʒɪə(*r*)
AM θʊ'rɪndʒ(i)ə

Thuringian
BR θ(j)ʊ'rɪn(d)ʒɪən, -z
AM θ(j)ʊ'rɪndʒ(i)ən, -z

Thurrock
BR 'θʌrək
AM 'θərək

Thursday
BR 'θəːzd|eɪ, 'θəːzd|i, -eɪz\-ɪz
AM 'θərz,deɪ, 'θərzdi, -z

Thurso
BR 'θəːsəʊ
AM 'θərsoʊ

Thurston
BR 'θəːst(ə)n
AM 'θərstən

thus
BR ðʌs
AM ðəs

thusly
BR 'ðʌsli
AM 'ðəsli

thuya
BR 'θuːjə(*r*), -z
AM 'θujə, -z

thwack
BR θwak, -s, -ɪŋ, -t
AM θwæk, -s, -ɪŋ, -t

Thwaite
BR θweɪt
AM θweɪt

thwart
BR θwɔːt, -s, -ɪŋ, -ɨd
AM θwɔ(ə)r|t, -ts, -dɪŋ, -dəd

thy
BR ðʌɪ
AM ðaɪ

Thyestean
BR θʌɪ'ɛstɪən
AM θaɪ'ɛstiən

Thyestes
BR θʌɪ'ɛstiːz
AM θaɪ'ɛstiz

thylacine
BR 'θʌɪləsʌɪn, 'θʌɪləsiːn , 'θʌɪləsɪn, -z
AM 'θaɪlə,saɪn, 'θaɪləsən, -z

thyme
BR tʌɪm
AM taɪm

thymi
BR 'θʌɪmʌɪ
AM 'θaɪ,maɪ

thymine
BR 'θʌɪmiːn
AM 'θaɪ,min, 'θaɪəmən

thymol
BR 'θʌɪmɒl
AM 'θaɪ,mɔl, 'θaɪ,mɑl

thymus
BR 'θʌɪməs, -ɪz
AM 'θaɪməs, -ɪz

thymy
BR 'tʌɪmi
AM 'taɪmi

thyratron
BR 'θʌɪrətrɒn, -z
AM 'θaɪrə,trɑn, -z

thyristor
BR θʌɪ'rɪstə(r), -z
AM θaɪ'rɪstər, -z

thyroid
BR 'θʌɪrɔɪd, -z
AM 'θaɪ,rɔɪd, -z

thyrotoxicosis
BR ,θʌɪrəʊ,tɒksɪ'kəʊsɪs
AM ,θaɪrə,tɑksə'koʊsəs

thyrotropin
BR ,θʌɪrə(ʊ)'trəʊpɪn
AM ,θaɪrə'troʊpɪn

thyroxine
BR θʌɪ'rɒksiːn
AM θaɪ'rɑksən, θaɪ'rɑk,sin

thyrsi
BR 'θəːsʌɪ
AM 'θər,saɪ

thyrsus
BR 'θəːsəs
AM 'θərsəs

Thysanoptera
BR ,θʌɪsə'nɒpt(ə)rə(*r*)
AM ,θaɪsə'nɑptərə

thysanopteran
BR ,θʌɪsə'nɒpt(ə)rən, ,θʌɪsə'nɒpt(ə)rn̩, -z
AM ,θaɪsə'nɑptərən, -z

thysanopterous
BR ,θʌɪsə'nɒpt(ə)rəs
AM ,θaɪsə'nɑptərəs

Thysanura
BR ,θʌɪsə'n(j)ʊərə(*r*)
AM ,θaɪsə'n(j)ʊrə

thysanuran
BR ,θʌɪsə'n(j)ʊərən, -z
AM ,θaɪsə'n(j)ʊrən, -z

thysanurous
BR ,θʌɪsə'n(j)ʊərəs
AM ,θaɪsə'n(j)ʊrəs

thyself
BR ðʌɪ'sɛlf
AM ðaɪ'sɛlf

Thyssen
BR 'tiːsn
AM 'tisən

ti
BR tiː
AM ti

Tia Maria®
BR ,tiːə mə'riːə(*r*), -z
AM ,tiə mə'riə, -z

Tiananmen Square
BR tɪ,anənmən 'skwɛː(r)
AM ti'ɛnə(n),mɛn 'skwɛ(ə)r

tiara
BR tɪ'ɑːrə(*r*), -z, -d
AM ti'ɛrə, ti'ɑrə, -z, -d

Tibbett
BR 'tɪbɪt
AM 'tɪbət

Tibbitts
BR 'tɪbɪts
AM 'tɪbəts

Tibbs
BR tɪbz
AM tɪbs

Tiber
BR 'tʌɪbə(r)
AM 'taɪbər

Tiberias
BR tʌɪ'bɪərɪas, tʌɪ'bɪərɪəs
AM taɪ'bɪriəs

Tiberius
BR tʌɪ'bɪərɪəs
AM taɪ'biriəs

Tibesti
BR tɪ'bɛsti
AM tə'bɛsti

Tibet
BR tɪ'bɛt
AM tə'bɛt

Tibetan
BR tɪ'bɛtn, -z
AM tə'bɛtn, -z

tibia
BR 'tɪbɪə(*r*), -z
AM 'tɪbiə, -z

tibiae
BR 'tɪbɪiː
AM 'tɪbi,i, 'tɪbi,aɪ

tibial
BR 'tɪbɪəl
AM 'tɪbiəl

tibiotarsi
BR ,tɪbɪəʊ'tɑːsʌɪ
AM ,tɪbioʊ'tɑr,saɪ

tibiotarsus
BR ,tɪbɪəʊ'tɑːsəs
AM ,tɪbioʊ'tɑrsəs

Tibullus
BR tɪ'bʊləs
AM tɪ'bʊləs

tic
BR tɪk, -s
AM tɪk, -s

tice
BR tʌɪs, -ɪz, -ɪŋ, -t
AM taɪs, -ɪz, -ɪŋ, -t

Tichborne
BR 'tɪtʃbɔːn
AM 'tɪtʃ,bɔ(ə)rn

Ticino
BR tɪ'tʃiːnəʊ
AM tɪ'tʃi,noʊ

tick
BR tɪk, -s, -ɪŋ, -t
AM tɪk, -s, -ɪŋ, -t

tick-bird
BR 'tɪkbəːd, -z
AM 'tɪk,bərd, -z

ticker
BR 'tɪkə(r), -z
AM 'tɪkər, -z

tickertape
BR 'tɪkəteɪp, -s
AM 'tɪkər,teɪp, -s

ticket
BR 'tɪk|ɪt, -ɪts, -ɨtɪŋ, -ɨtɨd
AM 'tɪkɨ|t, -ts, -dɪŋ, -dɨd

ticketless
BR 'tɪkɨtlɨs
AM 'tɪkɨtlɨs

ticket-of-leave man
BR ,tɪkɪtəv'liːv man
AM ,tɪkɨdə(v)'liv ,mæn

ticket-of-leave men
BR ,tɪkɪtəv'liːv mɛn
AM ,tɪkɨdə(v)'liv ,mɛn

tickety-boo
BR ,tɪkɨtɪ'buː
AM ,tɪkɨdi'bu

ticking
BR 'tɪkɪŋ, -z
AM 'tɪkɪŋ, -z

tickle
BR 'tɪk|l, -lz, -l̩ɪŋ\-lɪŋ, -ld
AM 'tɪk|əl, -əlz, -(ə)lɪŋ, -əld

tickler
BR 'tɪkl̩ə(r), 'tɪklə(r), -z
AM 'tɪk(ə)lər, -z

tickless
BR 'tɪklɨs
AM 'tɪklɨs

ticklish
BR 'tɪkl̩ɪʃ, 'tɪklɪʃ
AM 'tɪk(ə)lɪʃ

ticklishly
BR 'tɪkl̩ɪʃli, 'tɪklɪʃli
AM 'tɪk(ə)lɪʃli

ticklishness
BR 'tɪkl̩ɪʃnɪs, 'tɪklɪʃnɪs
AM 'tɪk(ə)lɪʃnɪs

tickly
BR 'tɪkl̩i, 'tɪkli
AM 'tɪk(ə)li

tickover
BR 'tɪk,əʊvə(r)
AM 'tɪk,oʊvər

tick-tack
BR 'tɪktak, -s
AM 'tɪk,tæk, -s

tick-tack-toe
BR ,tɪktak'təʊ
AM ,tɪk,tæk'toʊ

tick-tock
BR 'tɪktɒk, ,tɪk'tɒk, -s
AM 'tɪk,tɑk, -s

ticky-tacky
BR 'tɪkɪ,taki
AM 'tɪki,tæki

Ticonderoga
BR ,tʌɪkɒndə'rəʊgə(*r*), tʌɪ,kɒndə'rəʊgə(*r*)
AM ,taɪ,kɑndə'roʊgə

tic-tac
BR 'tɪktak
AM 'tɪk,tæk

tic-tac-toe
BR ˌtɪktak'təʊ
AM ˈˌtɪkˌtæk'toʊ
tidal
BR 'tʌɪdl
AM 'taɪdəl
tidally
BR 'tʌɪdḷi
AM 'taɪdli
tidbit
BR 'tɪdbɪt, -s
AM 'tɪdˌbɪt, -s
tiddledywink
BR 'tɪdldɪˌwɪŋk, -s
AM 'tɪdl(d)iˌwɪŋk, -s
tiddler
BR 'tɪdḷə(r), 'tɪdlə(r), -z
AM 'tɪd(ə)lər, -z
Tiddles
BR 'tɪdlz
AM 'tɪdəlz
tiddlewink
BR 'tɪdlɪwɪŋk, 'tɪdḷɪwɪŋk, -s
AM 'tɪdliˌwɪŋk, 'tɪdḷiˌwɪŋk, -s
tiddly
BR 'tɪdl|i, 'tɪdḷ|i, -ɪə(r), -ɪɨst
AM 'tɪdli, 'tɪdḷi, -ər, -ɨst
tiddlywink
BR 'tɪdlɪwɪŋk, 'tɪdḷɪwɪŋk, -s
AM 'tɪdliˌwɪŋk, 'tɪdḷiˌwɪŋk, -s
tide
BR tʌɪd, -z, -ɪŋ, -ɨd
AM taɪd, -z, -ɪŋ, -ɨd
tideland
BR 'tʌɪdland, -z
AM 'taɪdˌlænd, -z
tideless
BR 'tʌɪdlɨs
AM 'taɪdlɨs
tideline
BR 'tʌɪdlʌɪn, -z
AM 'taɪdˌlaɪn, -z
tidemark
BR 'tʌɪdmɑːk, -s
AM 'taɪdˌmark, -s
Tidenham
BR 'tɪdṇəm
AM 'tɪd(ə)nəm
Tideswell
BR 'tʌɪdzwɛl
AM 'taɪdzˌwɛl
tidewaiter
BR 'tʌɪdˌweɪtə(r), -z
AM 'taɪdˌweɪdər, -z
tidewater
BR 'tʌɪdˌwɔːtə(r)
AM 'taɪdˌwɔdər, 'taɪdˌwɑdər
tidewave
BR 'tʌɪdweɪv, -z
AM 'taɪdˌweɪv, -z
tideway
BR 'tʌɪdweɪ, -z
AM 'taɪdˌweɪ, -z
tidily
BR 'tʌɪdɨli
AM 'taɪdɨli
tidiness
BR 'tʌɪdɪnɨs
AM 'taɪdinɨs
tidings
BR 'tʌɪdɪŋz
AM 'taɪdɪŋz
Tidmarsh
BR 'tɪdmɑːʃ
AM 'tɪdˌmɑrʃ
tidy
BR 'tʌɪd|i, -ɪz, -ɪɪŋ, -ɪd, -ɪə(r), -ɪɨst
AM 'taɪdi, -z, -ɪŋ, -d, -ər, -ɨst
tie
BR tʌɪ, -z, -ɪŋ, -d
AM taɪ, -z, -ɪŋ, -d
tieback
BR 'tʌɪbak, -s
AM 'taɪˌbæk, -s
tiebreak
BR 'tʌɪbreɪk, -s
AM 'taɪˌbreɪk, -s
tie-breaker
BR 'tʌɪˌbreɪkə(r), -z
AM 'taɪˌbreɪkər, -z
tie-breaking
BR 'tʌɪˌbreɪkɪŋ
AM 'taɪˌbreɪkɪŋ
tie-dye
BR 'tʌɪdʌɪ, -z, -ɪŋ, -d
AM 'taɪˌdaɪ, -z, -ɪŋ, -d
tieless
BR 'tʌɪlɨs
AM 'taɪlɨs
Tientsin
BR ˌtjɛn'(t)sɪn
AM ti'ɛn(t)'sɪn
tiepin
BR 'tʌɪpɪn, -z
AM 'taɪˌpɪn, -z
Tiepolo
BR tɪ'ɛpələʊ, tɪ'ɛpḷəʊ
AM ti'ɛpəˌloʊ
tier[1]
a person who ties
BR 'tʌɪə(r), -z
AM 'taɪər, -z
tier[2]
layer, level
BR tɪə(r), -z, -d
AM tɪ(ə)r, -z, -d
tierce
BR tɪəs, -t
AM tɪ(ə)rs, -t
tiercel
BR 'tɪəsl, 'təːsl, -z
AM 'tɪ(ə)rsəl, -z
tiercet
BR 'tɪəsɪt, 'təːsɪt, -s
AM 'tɪrsət, -s
Tierney
BR 'tɪəni
AM 'tɪrni
Tierra del Fuego
BR tɪˌɛrə dɛl 'fweɪgəʊ, + f(j)ʊ'eɪgəʊ
AM ˌtiərə dɛl fʊ'eɪgoʊ
tiff
BR tɪf, -s
AM tɪf, -s
tiffany
BR 'tɪfəni, 'tɪfṇi
AM 'tɪfəni
tiffin
BR 'tɪfɪn
AM 'tɪfɪn
Tiflis
BR 'tɪflɪs
AM 'tɪflɨs, tə'flis
tig
BR tɪg, -z, -ɪŋ, -d
AM tɪg, -z, -ɪŋ, -d
tiger
BR 'tʌɪgə(r), -z
AM 'taɪgər, -z
tigerish
BR 'tʌɪg(ə)rɪʃ
AM 'taɪg(ə)rɪʃ
tigerishly
BR 'tʌɪg(ə)rɪʃli
AM 'taɪg(ə)rɪʃli
tiger moth
BR 'tʌɪgə mɒθ, ˌtʌɪgə 'mɒθ, -s
AM 'taɪgər ˌmɔθ, + ˌmɑθ, -s
Tigers
BR 'tʌɪgəz
AM 'taɪgərz
tiger's-eye
BR 'tʌɪgəzʌɪ
AM 'taɪgərzˌaɪ
tigerskin
BR 'tʌɪgəskɪn, -z
AM 'taɪgərˌskɪn, -z
Tighe
BR tʌɪ
AM taɪ
tight
BR tʌɪt, -s, -ə(r), -ɨst
AM taɪ|t, -ts, -dər, -dɨst
tighten
BR 'tʌɪt|n, -nz, -ṇɪŋ\-nɪŋ, -nd
AM 'taɪtn, -z, -ɪŋ, -d
tightener
BR 'tʌɪtṇə(r), 'tʌɪtnə(r), -z
AM ˌtaɪtṇər, ˌtaɪtnər, -z
tight-fisted
BR ˌtʌɪt'fɪstɨd
AM ˈˌtaɪtˈfɪstɨd
tight-fistedly
BR ˌtʌɪt'fɪstɨdli
AM ˈˌtaɪt'fɪstɨdli
tight-fistedness
BR ˌtʌɪt'fɪstɨdnɨs
AM ˈˌtaɪt'fɪstɨdnɨs
tightly
BR 'tʌɪtli
AM 'taɪtli
tightness
BR 'tʌɪtnɨs
AM 'taɪtnɨs
tightrope
BR 'tʌɪtrəʊp, -s
AM 'taɪtˌroʊp, -s
tightwad
BR 'tʌɪtwɒd, -z
AM 'taɪtˌwɑd, -z
Tiglath-pileser
BR ˌtɪglaθpʌɪ'liːzə(r), ˌtɪglaθpɪ'liːzə(r)
AM ˈˌtɪglæθpə'lizər
tiglic
BR 'tɪglɪk
AM 'tɪglɪk
tigon
BR 'tʌɪg(ə)n, 'tʌɪgɒn, -z
AM 'taɪgən, -z
Tigray
BR 'tɪgreɪ
AM tə'greɪ
Tigrayan
BR tɪ'greɪən, -z
AM tə'greɪən, -z
Tigre
BR 'tɪgreɪ
AM 'tigreɪ
Tigrean
BR tɪ'greɪən, -z
AM tə'greɪən, -z
tigress
BR 'tʌɪgrɪs, 'tʌɪgrɛs, -ɪz
AM 'taɪgrɨs, -ɨz
Tigrinya
BR tɪ'grɪnjə(r), tɪ'griːnjə(r)
AM tə'grɪnjə
Tigris
BR 'tʌɪgrɪs
AM 'taɪgrɨs
Tijuana
BR ˌtɪə'wɑːnə(r), tɪ'wɑːnə(r)
AM ˌtiə'wɑnə
SP ti'xwana
tike
BR tʌɪk, -s
AM taɪk, -s
tiki
BR 'tiːk|i, -ɪz
AM 'tiki, -z
tikka
BR 'tiːkə(r), 'tɪkə(r)
AM 'tɪkə
til
BR tɪl
AM tɪl
'til
BR tɪl
AM tɪl

tilapia
BR tɪˈlapɪə(r), tɪˈleɪpɪə(r), -z
AM təˈlɑpiə, -z

Tilburg
BR ˈtɪlbəːg
AM ˈtɪlˌbərg

tilbury
BR ˈtɪlb(ə)r|i, -ɪz
AM ˈtɪlˌbɛri, -z

Tilda
BR ˈtɪldə(r)
AM ˈtɪldə

tilde
BR ˈtɪld|ə(r), ˈtɪld|i, -ɪz
AM ˈtɪldə, -z

Tilden
BR ˈtɪld(ə)n
AM ˈtɪldən

tile
BR tʌɪl, -z, -ɪŋ, -d
AM taɪl, -z, -ɪŋ, -d

Tilehurst
BR ˈtʌɪlhəːst
AM ˈtaɪlˌ(h)ərst

tiler
BR ˈtʌɪlə(r), -z
AM ˈtaɪlər, -z

tiling
BR ˈtʌɪlɪŋ, -z
AM ˈtaɪlɪŋ, -z

till
BR tɪl, -z, -ɪŋ, -d
AM tɪl, -z, -ɪŋ, -d

tillable
BR ˈtɪləbl
AM ˈtɪləbəl

tillage
BR ˈtɪlɪdʒ
AM ˈtɪlɪdʒ

tiller
BR ˈtɪlə(r), -z, -ɪŋ, -d
AM ˈtɪlər, -z, -ɪŋ, -d

Tilley
BR ˈtɪli
AM ˈtɪli

Tilley lamp®
BR ˈtɪlɪ lamp, -s
AM ˈtɪli ˌlæmp, -s

Tillich
BR ˈtɪlɪk
AM ˈtɪlɪk

Tilly
BR ˈtɪli
AM ˈtɪli

Tilsit
BR ˈtɪlsɪt, ˈtɪlzɪt
AM ˈtɪlsɪt, ˈtɪlzɪt

tilt
BR tɪlt, -s, -ɪŋ, -ɨd
AM tɪlt, -s, -ɪŋ, -ɨd

tilter
BR ˈtɪltə(r), -z
AM ˈtɪltər, -z

tilth
BR tɪlθ
AM tɪlθ

tilt-hammer
BR ˈtɪltˌhamə(r), -z
AM ˈtɪltˌ(h)æmər, -z

tiltyard
BR ˈtɪltjɑːd, -z
AM ˈtɪltˌjɑrd, -z

Tim
BR tɪm
AM tɪm

Timaru
BR ˈtɪməruː
AM ˈtɪməˌru

timbal
BR ˈtɪmbl, -z
AM ˈtɪmbəl, -z

timbale
BR tamˈbɑːl, ˈtɪmbl, -z
AM ˈtɪmbəl, ˌtɪmˈbɑl, -z

timber
BR ˈtɪmb|ə(r), -əz, -(ə)rɪŋ, -əd
AM ˈtɪmb|ər, -ərz, -(ə)rɪŋ, -ərd

timberjack
BR ˈtɪmbədʒak, -s
AM ˈtɪmbərˌdʒæk, -s

Timberlake
BR ˈtɪmbəleɪk
AM ˈtɪmbərˌeɪk

timberland
BR ˈtɪmbəland, -z
AM ˈtɪmbərˌlænd, -z

timberline
BR ˈtɪmbəlʌɪn
AM ˈtɪmbərˌlaɪn

timberwork
BR ˈtɪmbəwəːk
AM ˈtɪmbərˌwərk

timbre
BR ˈtambə(r), ˈtɪmbə(r)
AM ˈtæmbər

timbrel
BR ˈtɪmbr(ə)l, -z
AM ˈtɪmbrəl, -z

Timbuctoo
BR ˌtɪmbʌkˈtuː
AM ˌtɪmbəkˈtu

Timbuktu
BR ˌtɪmbʌkˈtuː
AM ˌtɪmbəkˈtu

time
BR tʌɪm, -z, -ɪŋ, -d
AM taɪm, -z, -ɪŋ, -d

time-expired
BR ˌtʌɪmɪkˈspʌɪəd, ˌtʌɪmɛkˈspʌɪəd, ˈtʌɪmɪkˌspʌɪəd, ˈtʌɪmɛkˌspʌɪəd
AM ˈtaɪməkˌspaɪ(ə)rd

timekeeper
BR ˈtʌɪmˌkiːpə(r), -z
AM ˈtaɪmˌkipər, -z

timekeeping
BR ˈtʌɪmˌkiːpɪŋ
AM ˈtaɪmˌkipɪŋ

timeless
BR ˈtʌɪmlɨs
AM ˈtaɪmlɨs

timelessly
BR ˈtʌɪmlɨsli
AM ˈtaɪmlɨsli

timelessness
BR ˈtʌɪmlɨsnɨs
AM ˈtaɪmlɨsnɨs

timeliness
BR ˈtʌɪmlɪnɨs
AM ˈtaɪmlinɨs

timely
BR ˈtʌɪml|i, -ɪə(r), -ɪɪst
AM ˈtaɪmli, -ər, -ɨst

timeous
BR ˈtʌɪməs
AM ˈtaɪməs

timeously
BR ˈtʌɪməsli
AM ˈtaɪməsli

time-out
BR ˌtʌɪmˈaʊt, -s
AM ˌtaɪmˈaʊt, -s

timepiece
BR ˈtʌɪmpiːs, -ɨz
AM ˈtaɪmˌpis, -ɨz

timer
BR ˈtʌɪmə(r), -z
AM ˈtaɪmər, -z

Times
BR tʌɪmz
AM taɪmz

timesaving
BR ˈtʌɪmˌseɪvɪŋ
AM ˈtaɪmˌseɪvɪŋ

timescale
BR ˈtʌɪmskeɪl, -z
AM ˈtaɪmˌskeɪl, -z

timeserver
BR ˈtʌɪmˌsəːvə(r), -z
AM ˈtaɪmˌsərvər, -z

timeserving
BR ˈtʌɪmˌsəːvɪŋ
AM ˈtaɪmˌsərvɪŋ

timeshare
BR ˈtʌɪmʃɛː(r), -z
AM ˈtaɪmˌʃɛ(ə)r, -z

time-sharing
BR ˈtʌɪmˌʃɛːrɪŋ
AM ˈtaɪmˌʃɛrɪŋ

timesheet
BR ˈtʌɪmʃiːt, -s
AM ˈtaɪmˌʃit, -s

timetable
BR ˈtʌɪmˌteɪb|l, -lz, -l̩ɪŋ\-lɪŋ, -ld
AM ˈtaɪmˌteɪbəl, -əlz, -(ə)lɪŋ, -əld

timework
BR ˈtʌɪmwəːk
AM ˈtaɪmˌwərk

timeworker
BR ˈtʌɪmˌwəːkə(r), -z
AM ˈtaɪmˌwərkər, -z

timeworn
BR ˈtʌɪmwɔːn
AM ˈtaɪmˌwɔ(ə)rn

Timex®
BR ˈtʌɪmɛks
AM ˈtaɪˌmɛks

timid
BR ˈtɪmɪd
AM ˈtɪmɨd

timidity
BR tɪˈmɪdɨti
AM təˈmɪdɨdi

timidly
BR ˈtɪmɨdli
AM ˈtɪmɨdli

timidness
BR ˈtɪmɨdnɨs
AM ˈtɪmɨdnɨs

timing
BR ˈtʌɪmɪŋ, -z
AM ˈtaɪmɪŋ, -z

Timişoara
BR ˌtɪmɪˈʃwɑːrə(r)
AM ˌtimɪˈʃwɑrə

Timms
BR tɪmz
AM tɪmz

Timmy
BR ˈtɪmi
AM ˈtɪmi

timocracy
BR tɪˈmɒkrəs|i, -ɪz
AM təˈmɑkrəsi, -z

timocratic
BR ˌtɪməˈkratɪk
AM ˌtɪməˈkrædɪk

Timon
BR ˈtʌɪmən, ˈtʌɪmɒn
AM ˈtaɪmən

Timor
BR ˈtiːmɔː(r)
AM ˈtiˌmɔ(ə)r

Timorese
BR ˌtɪməˈriːz, ˌtiːmərˈiːz
AM ˌtɪməˈriz

timorous
BR ˈtɪm(ə)rəs
AM ˈtɪm(ə)rəs

timorously
BR ˈtɪm(ə)rəsli
AM ˈtɪm(ə)rəsli

timorousness
BR ˈtɪm(ə)rəsnəs
AM ˈtɪm(ə)rəsnəs

Timotei®
BR ˈtɪmәteɪ
AM ˈtɪməˌteɪ

timothy
BR ˈtɪməθi
AM ˈtɪməθi

timpani
BR ˈtɪmpəni
AM ˈtɪmpəni

timpanist
BR ˈtɪmpənɪst, -s
AM ˈtɪmpənəst, -s

Timpson
BR ˈtɪm(p)sn

AM ˈtɪm(p)sən
tin
BR tɪn, -z, -ɪŋ, -d
AM tɪn, -z, -ɪŋ, -d
tinamou
BR ˈtɪnəmuː, -z
AM ˈtɪnəˌmu, -z
tinctorial
BR tɪŋ(k)ˈtɔːrɪəl
AM tɪŋ(k)ˈtɔriəl
tincture
BR ˈtɪŋ(k)tʃ|ə(r), -əz, -(ə)rɪŋ, -əd
AM ˈtɪŋ(k)|(t)ʃər, -(t)ʃərz, -tʃərɪŋ\-ʃ(ə)rɪŋ, -(t)ʃərd
tindal
BR ˈtɪndl, -z
AM ˈtɪndəl, -z
Tindale
BR ˈtɪnd(eɪ)l
AM ˈtɪnˌdeɪl
Tindall
BR ˈtɪnd(ɔː)l
AM ˈtɪndəl
Tindell
BR ˈtɪnd(ɛ)l
AM ˈtɪndəl
tinder
BR ˈtɪndə(r)
AM ˈtɪndər
tinderbox
BR ˈtɪndəbɒks, -ɪz
AM ˈtɪndərˌbɑks, -əz
tindery
BR ˈtɪnd(ə)ri
AM ˈtɪndəri
tine
BR tʌɪn, -z, -d
AM taɪn, -z, -d
tinea
BR ˈtɪnɪə(r)
AM ˈtɪniə
tinfoil
BR ˈtɪnfɔɪl
AM ˈtɪnˌfɔɪl
ting
BR tɪŋ, -z, -ɪŋ, -d
AM tɪŋ, -z, -ɪŋ, -d
tinge
BR tɪn(d)ʒ, -ɪz, -ɪŋ, -d
AM tɪndʒ, -ɪz, -ɪŋ, -d
tingle
BR ˈtɪŋg|l, -lz, -l̩ɪŋ\-lɪŋ, -ld
AM ˈtɪŋg|əl, -əlz, -(ə)lɪŋ, -əld
tingly
BR ˈtɪŋl|i, ˈtɪŋgl̩|i, -ɪə(r), -ɪɪst
AM ˈtɪŋg(ə)li, -ər, -ɪst
Tingwall
BR ˈtɪŋw(ə)l, ˈtɪŋwɔːl
AM ˈtɪŋˌwɔl, ˈtɪŋˌwɑl
tinhorn
BR ˈtɪnhɔːn, -z
AM ˈtɪnˌ(h)ɔ(ə)rn, -z
tinily
BR ˈtʌɪnɨli
AM ˈtaɪnɨli
tininess
BR ˈtʌɪnɪnɨs
AM ˈtaɪninɨs
tinker
BR ˈtɪŋk|ə(r), -əz, -(ə)rɪŋ, -əd
AM ˈtɪŋk|ər, -ərz, -(ə)rɪŋ, -ərd
tinkerer
BR ˈtɪŋk(ə)rə(r), -z
AM ˈtɪŋk(ə)rər, -z
tinkering
BR ˈtɪŋk(ə)rɪŋ, -z
AM ˈtɪŋk(ə)rɪŋ, -z
tinkle
BR ˈtɪŋk|l, -lz, -l̩ɪŋ\-lɪŋ, -ld
AM ˈtɪŋk|əl, -əlz, -(ə)lɪŋ, -əld
tinkling
BR ˈtɪŋklɪŋ, ˈtɪŋkl̩ɪŋ, -z
AM ˈtɪŋk(ə)lɪŋ, -z
tinkly
BR ˈtɪŋkli, ˈtɪŋkl̩i
AM ˈtɪŋk(ə)li
tinner
BR ˈtɪnə(r), -z
AM ˈtɪnər, -z
tinnily
BR ˈtɪnɨli
AM ˈtɪnɨli
tinniness
BR ˈtɪnɪnɨs
AM ˈtɪninɨs
tinnitus
BR ˈtɪnɨtəs, tɨˈnʌɪtəs
AM ˈtɪnədəs
tinny
BR ˈtɪn|i, -ɪə(r), -ɪɪst
AM ˈtɪni, -ər, -ɪst
Tin Pan Alley
BR ˌtɪn pan ˈali
AM ˌtɪn ˌpæn ˈæli
tinpot
BR ˈtɪnpɒt
AM ˈtɪnˌpɑt
tinsel
BR ˈtɪnsl, -d
AM ˈtɪnsəl, -d
tinselly
BR ˈtɪnsl̩i
AM ˈtɪnsəli
Tinseltown
BR ˈtɪnsltaʊn
AM ˈtɪnsəlˌtaʊn
Tinsley
BR ˈtɪnzli
AM ˈtɪnzli
tinsmith
BR ˈtɪnsmɪθ, -s
AM ˈtɪnˌsmɪθ, -s
tinsnips
BR ˈtɪnsnɪps
AM ˈtɪnˌsnɪps
tinstone
BR ˈtɪnstəʊn
AM ˈtɪnˌstoʊn
tint
BR tɪnt, -s, -ɪŋ, -ɨd
AM tɪn|t, -ts, -(t)ɪŋ, -(t)əd
tintack
BR ˈtɪntak, -s
AM ˈtɪnˌtæk, -s
Tintagel
BR tɪnˈtadʒl
AM tɪnˈtædʒəl
tinter
BR ˈtɪntə(r), -z
AM ˈtɪn(t)ər, -z
Tintern
BR ˈtɪntən
AM ˈtɪn(t)ərn
tintinnabula
BR ˌtɪntɨˈnabjʉlə(r)
AM ˌtɪn(t)əˈnæbjələ
tintinnabular
BR ˌtɪntɨˈnabjʉlə(r)
AM ˌtɪn(t)əˈnæbjələr
tintinnabulary
BR ˌtɪntɨˈnabjʉləri
AM ˌtɪn(t)əˈnæbjəˌlɛri
tintinnabulation
BR ˌtɪntɨˌnabjʉˈleɪʃn, -z
AM ˌtɪn(t)əˌnæbjəˈleɪʃən, -z
tintinnabulous
BR ˌtɪntɨˈnabjʉləs
AM ˌtɪn(t)əˈnæbjələs
tintinnabulum
BR ˌtɪntɨˈnabjʉləm
AM ˌtɪn(t)əˈnæbjələm
Tintoretto
BR ˌtɪntəˈrɛtəʊ, -z
AM ˌtɪn(t)əˈrɛdoʊ, -z
tintype
BR ˈtɪntʌɪp
AM ˈtɪnˌtaɪp
tinware
BR ˈtɪnwɛː(r), -z
AM ˈtɪnˌwɛ(ə)r, -z
tiny
BR ˈtʌɪn|i, -ɪə(r), -ɪɪst
AM ˈtaɪni, -ər, -ɪst
Tío Pepe®
BR ˌtiːəʊ ˈpɛpi, + ˈpɛpeɪ
AM ˌtioʊ ˈpɛpɛ
tip
BR tɪp, -s, -ɪŋ, -t
AM tɪp, -s, -ɪŋ, -t
tip-and-run
BR ˌtɪp(ə)n(d)ˈrʌn
AM ˌtɪpənˈrən
tip-cart
BR ˈtɪpkɑːt, -s
AM ˈtɪpˌkɑrt, -s
tipcat
BR ˈtɪpkat
AM ˈtɪpˌkæt
tipless
BR ˈtɪplɨs
AM ˈtɪplɨs
tipper
BR ˈtɪpə(r), -z
AM ˈtɪpər, -z
Tipperary
BR ˌtɪpəˈrɛːri
AM ˌtɪpəˈrɛri
tippet
BR ˈtɪpɪt, -s
AM ˈtɪpɨt, -s
Tippett
BR ˈtɪpɪt
AM ˈtɪpɨt
Tipp-Ex®
BR ˈtɪpɛks, -ɪz, -ɪŋ, -t
AM ˈtɪˌpɛks, -əz, -ɪŋ, -t
tipple
BR ˈtɪp|l, -lz, -l̩ɪŋ\-lɪŋ, -ld
AM ˈtɪp|əl, -əlz, -(ə)lɪŋ, -əld
tippler
BR ˈtɪpl̩ə(r), ˈtɪplə(r), -z
AM ˈtɪp(ə)lər, -z
tippy
BR ˈtɪp|i, -ɪə(r), -ɪɪst
AM ˈtɪpi, -ər, -ɪst
tipsily
BR ˈtɪpsɨli
AM ˈtɪpsɨli
tipsiness
BR ˈtɪpsɪnɨs
AM ˈtɪpsinɨs
tipstaff
BR ˈtɪpstɑːf, ˈtɪpstaf, -s
AM ˈtɪpˌstæf, -s
tipstaves
BR ˈtɪpsteɪvz
AM ˈtɪpˌsteɪvz
tipster
BR ˈtɪpstə(r), -z
AM ˈtɪpstər, -z
tipsy
BR ˈtɪps|i, -ɪə(r), -ɪɪst
AM ˈtɪpsi, -ər, -ɪst
tipsy-cake
BR ˈtɪpsɪkeɪk, -s
AM ˈtɪpsiˌkeɪk, -s
tiptoe
BR ˈtɪptəʊ, -z, -ɪŋ, -d
AM ˈtɪpˌtoʊ, -z, -ɪŋ, -d
tiptop
BR ˌtɪpˈtɒp
AM ˈtɪpˈtɑp
tirade
BR tʌɪˈreɪd, tɨˈreɪd, -z
AM ˈtaɪˌreɪd, ˌtaɪˈreɪd, -z
tirailleur
BR ˌtɪrʌɪˈəː(r), -z
AM ˌtɪraɪˈ(j)ər, -z
tiramisu
BR ˌtɪrəmɨˈsuː
AM ˌtɪrəməˈsu

Tirana
BR tɪˈrɑːnə(*r*)
AM tɪˈrɑnə

Tiranë
BR tɪˈrɑːnə(*r*)
AM tɪˈrɑnə

tire
BR ˈtʌɪə(r), -z, -ɪŋ, -d
AM ˈtaɪ(ə)r, -z, -ɪŋ, -d

tiredly
BR ˈtʌɪədli
AM ˈtaɪ(ə)rdli

tiredness
BR ˈtʌɪədnəs
AM ˈtaɪ(ə)rdnəs

Tiree
BR tʌɪˈriː
AM taɪˈri

tire gauge
BR ˈtʌɪə geɪdʒ
AM ˈtaɪ(ə)r ˌgeɪdʒ

tireless
BR ˈtʌɪələs
AM ˈtaɪ(ə)rləs

tirelessly
BR ˈtʌɪələsli
AM ˈtaɪ(ə)rləsli

tirelessness
BR ˈtʌɪələsnəs
AM ˈtaɪ(ə)rləsnəs

Tiresias
BR tʌɪˈriːsɪəs, tʌɪˈriːsɪas
AM tɪˈrisiəs

tiresome
BR ˈtʌɪəs(ə)m
AM ˈtaɪ(ə)rsəm

tiresomely
BR ˈtʌɪəs(ə)mli
AM ˈtaɪ(ə)rsəmli

tiresomeness
BR ˈtʌɪəs(ə)mnəs
AM ˈtaɪ(ə)rsəmnəs

tiro
BR ˈtʌɪrəʊ, -z
AM ˈtaɪroʊ, -z

Tirol
BR tɪˈrəʊl, ˈtɪrəl, ˈtɪrl̩
AM təˈroʊl, ˈtɪˌroʊl

Tirpitz
BR ˈtəːpɪts
AM ˈtərpɪts

'tis
BR tɪz
AM tɪz

tisane
BR tɪˈzan, tiːˈzan, -z
AM təˈzæn, -z

Tishri
BR ˈtɪʃriː
AM ˈtɪʃri

Tisiphone
BR tɪˈsɪfəni, tɪˈsɪfn̩i, tʌɪˈsɪfəni, tʌɪˈsɪfn̩i
AM tɪˈsɪfəni

Tissot
BR ˈtiːsəʊ
AM təˈsoʊ

tissue
BR ˈtɪʃuː, ˈtɪsjuː, -z
AM ˈtɪʃu, -z

tit
BR tɪt, -s
AM tɪt, -s

titan
BR ˈtʌɪtn, -z
AM ˈtaɪtn, -z

titanate
BR ˈtʌɪtəneɪt, ˈtʌɪtn̩eɪt
AM ˈtaɪtnˌeɪt

Titaness
BR ˈtʌɪtn̩ɨs, ˌtʌɪtn̩ˈɛs, -ɨz
AM ˈtaɪtn̩ɨs, -ɨz

Titania
BR tɪˈtɑːnɪə(*r*), tɪˈteɪnɪə(*r*)
AM taɪˈteɪniə, təˈtɑniə

titanic
BR tʌɪˈtanɪk
AM taɪˈtænɪk

titanically
BR tʌɪˈtanɨkli
AM taɪˈtænək(ə)li

titanium
BR tʌɪˈteɪnɪəm, tɪˈteɪnɪəm
AM taɪˈteɪniəm, təˈteɪniəm

titbit
BR ˈtɪtbɪt, -s
AM ˈtɪtˌbɪt, -s

titch
BR tɪtʃ, -ɨz
AM tɪtʃ, -ɨz

titchiness
BR ˈtɪtʃɪnɨs
AM ˈtɪtʃinɨs

titchy
BR ˈtɪtʃ|i, -ɪə(r), -ɪɪst
AM ˈtɪtʃi, -ər, -ɨst

titer
BR ˈtʌɪtə(r), -z
AM ˈtaɪdər, -z

titfer
BR ˈtɪtfə(r), -z
AM ˈtɪtfər, -z

tit-for-tat
BR ˌtɪtfəˈtat
AM ˈtɪtfərˈtæt

tithable
BR ˈtʌɪðəbl
AM ˈtaɪðəbəl

tithe
BR tʌɪð, -z, -ɪŋ, -d
AM taɪð, -z, -ɪŋ, -d

tithing
BR ˈtʌɪðɪŋ, -z
AM ˈtaɪðɪŋ, -z

Tithonus
BR tɪˈθəʊnəs, tʌɪˈθəʊnəs
AM taɪˈθoʊnəs

titi¹
bird
BR ˈtiːtiː, -z
AM ˈtiˌti, -z

titi²
monkey
BR ˈtiːtiː, tɪˈtiː, -z
AM ˈtiˌti, təˈti, -z

titi³
tree
BR ˈtiːtiː, ˈtʌɪtʌɪ, -z
AM ˈtiˌti, ˈtaɪˌtaɪ, -z

Titian
BR ˈtɪʃn, -z
AM ˈtɪʃən, -z

Titicaca
BR ˌtɪtɪˈkɑːkɑː(*r*), ˌtɪtɪˈkɑːkə(*r*)
AM ˌtɪdiˈkɑkə

titillate
BR ˈtɪtɨleɪt, -s, -ɪŋ, -ɨd
AM ˈtɪdəˌleɪ|t, -ts, -dɪŋ, -dɨd

titillatingly
BR ˈtɪtɨleɪtɪŋli
AM ˈtɪdəˌleɪdɪŋli

titillation
BR ˌtɪtɨˈleɪʃn, -z
AM ˌtɪdəˈleɪʃən, -z

titivate
BR tɪtɨveɪt, -s, -ɪŋ, -ɨd
AM ˈtɪdəˌveɪ|t, -ts, -dɪŋ, -dɨd

titivation
BR ˌtɪtɨˈveɪʃn, -z
AM ˌtɪdəˈveɪʃən, -z

titlark
BR ˈtɪtlɑːk, -s
AM ˈtɪtˌlɑrk, -s

title
BR ˈtʌɪtl, -z, -d
AM ˈtaɪd(ə)l, -z, -d

titleholder
BR ˈtʌɪtlˌhəʊldə(r), -z
AM ˈtaɪdlˌ(h)oʊldər, -z

titling
BR ˈtʌɪtl̩ɪŋ, -z
AM ˈtaɪdlɪŋ, -z

Titmarsh
BR ˈtɪtmɑːʃ
AM ˈtɪtˌmɑrʃ

titmice
BR ˈtɪtmʌɪs
AM ˈtɪtˌmaɪs

titmouse
BR ˈtɪtmaʊs
AM ˈtɪtˌmaʊs

Titmus
BR ˈtɪtməs
AM ˈtɪtməs

Tito
BR ˈtiːtəʊ
AM ˈtidoʊ

Titograd
BR ˈtiːtə(ʊ)grad
AM ˈtidoʊˌgræd

Titoism
BR ˈtiːtəʊɪz(ə)m
AM ˈtidoʊˌɪzəm, ˈtidəˌwɪzəm

Titoist
BR ˈtiːtəʊɪst, -s
AM ˈtidoʊəst, ˈtidəwəst, -s

titrant
BR ˈtʌɪtr(ə)nt, -s
AM ˈtaɪtrənt, -s

titratable
BR tʌɪˈtreɪtəbl, ˈtʌɪtreɪtəbl, ˈtʌɪtrətəbl
AM ˈtaɪˌtreɪdəbl

titrate
BR tʌɪˈtreɪt, ˈtʌɪtreɪt, -s, -ɪŋ, -ɨd
AM ˈtaɪˌtreɪ|t, -ts, -dɪŋ, -dɨd

titration
BR tʌɪˈtreɪʃn, -z
AM ˌtaɪˈtreɪʃən, -z

titre
BR ˈtʌɪtə(r), -z
AM ˈtaɪdər, -z

titter
BR ˈtɪt|ə(r), -əz, -(ə)rɪŋ, -əd
AM ˈtɪdər, -z, -ɪŋ, -d

titterer
BR ˈtɪt(ə)rə(r), -z
AM ˈtɪdərər, -z

titteringly
BR ˌtɪt(ə)rɪŋli
AM ˈtɪdərɪŋli

tittivate
BR ˈtɪtɨveɪt, -s, -ɪŋ, -ɨd
AM ˈtɪdəˌveɪ|t, -ts, -dɪŋ, -dɨd

tittle
BR ˈtɪtl, -z
AM ˈtɪdəl, -z

tittlebat
BR ˈtɪtlbat, -s
AM ˈtɪdlˌbæt, -s

tittle-tattle
BR ˈtɪtlˌtatl
AM ˈtɪdəlˌtædəl

tittup
BR ˈtɪtəp, -s, -ɪŋ, -t
AM ˈtɪdəp, -s, -ɪŋ, -t

tittuppy
BR ˈtɪtəpi
AM ˈtɪdəpi

titty
BR ˈtɪt|i, -ɪz
AM ˈtɪdi, -z

titubation
BR ˌtɪtjʊˈbeɪʃn, ˌtɪtʃʊˈbeɪʃn
AM ˌtɪtʃəˈbeɪʃən

titular
BR ˈtɪtʃələ(r), ˈtɪtjələ(r)
AM ˈtɪtʃələr

titularly
BR ˈtɪtʃʉləli, ˈtɪtjʉləli
AM ˈtɪtʃələrli

Titus
BR ˈtʌɪtəs
AM ˈtaɪdəs

Tiverton
BR ˈtɪvət(ə)n
AM ˈtɪvərt(ə)n

Tivoli
BR ˈtɪvəli
AM ˈtɪvəli

tiz
BR tɪz
AM tɪz

Tizard
BR ˈtɪzɑːd, ˈtɪzəd
AM ˈtɪzərd

Tizer®
BR ˈtʌɪzə(r)
AM ˈtaɪzər

tizz
BR tɪz
AM tɪz

tizzy
BR ˈtɪz|i, -ɪz
AM ˈtɪzi, -z

T-joint
BR ˈtiːdʒɔɪnt, -s
AM ˈtiˌdʒɔɪnt, -s

T-junction
BR ˈtiːˌdʒʌŋ(k)ʃn, -z
AM ˈtiˌdʒəŋ(k)ʃən, -z

TKO
BR ˌtiːkeɪˈəʊ
AM ˌtiˌkeɪˈoʊ

Tlaxcala
BR tlɑːsˈkɑːlə(r)
AM tlɑˈskɑlə

Tlemcen
BR tlɛmˈsɛn
AM tlɛmˈsɛn

Tlingit
BR ˈtlɪŋgɪt, ˈtlɪŋkɪt, ˈklɪŋkɪt, -s
AM ˈtlɪŋ(g)ɪt, -s

tmesis
BR ˈtmiːsɪs, təˈmiːsɪs
AM təˈmisɪs

TNT
BR ˌtiːɛnˈtiː
AM ˌtiˌɛnˈti

to¹
adverb
BR tuː
AM tu

to²
preposition, strong form
BR tuː
AM tu

to³
preposition, weak form
BR tʉ
AM tə

toad
BR təʊd, -z
AM toʊd, -z

toadfish
BR ˈtəʊdfɪʃ, -ɪz
AM ˈtoʊdˌfɪʃ, -ɪz

toadflax
BR ˈtəʊdflaks
AM ˈtoʊdˌflæks

toad-in-the-hole
BR ˌtəʊdɪnðəˈhəʊl
AM ˌtoʊdənðəˈhoʊl

toadish
BR ˈtəʊdɪʃ
AM ˈtoʊdɪʃ

toadlet
BR ˈtəʊdlɪt, -s
AM ˈtoʊdlət, -s

toadlike
BR ˈtəʊdlʌɪk
AM ˈtoʊdˌlaɪk

toadstone
BR ˈtəʊdstəʊn, -z
AM ˈtoʊdˌstoʊn, -z

toadstool
BR ˈtəʊdstuːl, -z
AM ˈtoʊdˌstul, -z

toady
BR ˈtəʊd|i, -ɪz, -ɪɪŋ, -ɪd
AM ˈtoʊdi, -z, -ɪŋ, -d

toadyish
BR ˈtəʊdɪɪʃ
AM ˈtoʊdiɪʃ

toadyism
BR ˈtəʊdɪɪz(ə)m
AM ˈtoʊdiˌɪzəm

to-and-fro
BR ˌtuːən(d)ˈfrəʊ, ˌtuːn̩(d)ˈfrəʊ
AM ˌtuənˈfroʊ

toast
BR təʊst, -s, -ɪŋ, -ɪd
AM toʊst, -s, -ɪŋ, -əd

toaster
BR ˈtəʊstə(r), -z
AM ˈtoʊstər, -z

toastie
BR ˈtəʊst|i, -ɪz
AM ˈtoʊsti, -z

toastmaster
BR ˈtəʊs(t)ˌmɑːstə(r), ˈtəʊs(t)ˌmastə(r), -z
AM ˈtoʊs(t)ˌmæstər, -z

toastmistress
BR ˈtəʊs(t)ˌmɪstrɪs, -ɪz
AM ˈtoʊs(t)ˌmɪstrɪs, -ɪz

toastrack
BR ˈtəʊstrak, -s
AM ˈtoʊs(t)ˌræk, -s

toasty
BR ˈtəʊsti
AM ˈtoʊsti

tobacco
BR təˈbakəʊ, -z
AM təˈbækoʊ, -z

tobacconist
BR təˈbakənɪst, təˈbakn̩ɪst, -s
AM təˈbækənəst, -s

Tobagan
BR təˈbeɪg(ə)n, -z
AM təˈbeɪgən, -z

Tobago
BR təˈbeɪgəʊ
AM təˈbeɪgoʊ

Tobagonian
BR ˌtəʊbəˈgəʊnɪən, -z
AM ˌtoʊbəˈgoʊniən, -z

Tobermory
BR ˌtəʊbəʊˈmɔːri
AM ˌtoʊbəˈmɔri

Tobias
BR təˈbʌɪəs
AM təˈbaɪəs

Tobin
BR ˈtəʊbɪn
AM ˈtoʊbən

Tobit
BR ˈtəʊbɪt
AM ˈtoʊbət

Toblerone®
BR ˌtəʊbləʊˈrəʊn, ˈtəʊblərəʊn
AM ˌtoʊbləˈroʊn

toboggan
BR təˈbɒg|(ə)n, -(ə)nz, -ənɪŋ\-n̩ɪŋ, -(ə)nd
AM təˈbɑgən, -z, -ɪŋ, -d

tobogganer
BR təˈbɒgənə(r), təˈbɒgn̩ə(r), -z
AM təˈbɑgənər, -z

tobogganist
BR təˈbɒgənɪst, təˈbɒgn̩ɪst, -s
AM təˈbɑgənəst, -s

Tobruk
BR təˈbrʊk
AM təˈbrʊk

toby
BR ˈtəʊb|i, -ɪz
AM ˈtoʊbi, -z

toccata
BR təˈkɑːtə(r), -z
AM təˈkɑdə, -z

Toc H
BR ˌtɒk ˈeɪtʃ
AM ˌtɑk ˈeɪtʃ

Tocharian
BR təˈkɛːrɪən, tɒˈkɛːrɪən, təˈkɑːrɪən, tɒˈkɑːrɪən, -z
AM toʊˈkɛriən, -z

tocher
BR ˈtɒxə(r), ˈtɒkə(r), -z
AM ˈtɑkər, -z

tocopherol
BR tɒˈkɒfərɒl, təˈkɒfərɒl, -z
AM təˈkɑfəˌrɔl, təˈkɑfəˌroʊl, -z

Tocqueville
BR ˈtɒkvɪl, ˈtəʊkvɪl
AM ˈtoʊkˌvɪl

tocsin
BR ˈtɒksɪn, -z
AM ˈtɑksən, -z

tod
BR tɒd
AM tɑd

today
BR təˈdeɪ
AM təˈdeɪ

Todd
BR tɒd
AM tɑd

toddle
BR ˈtɒd|l, -lz, -l̩ɪŋ\-lɪŋ, -ld
AM ˈtɑd|əl, -əlz, -(ə)lɪŋ, -əld

toddler
BR ˈtɒdl̩ə(r), ˈtɒdlə(r), -z
AM ˈtɑd(ə)lər, ˈtɑdl̩ər, -z

toddlerhood
BR ˈtɒdl̩əhʊd, ˈtɒdləhʊd
AM ˈtɑdlərˌ(h)ʊd

toddy
BR ˈtɒdi
AM ˈtɑdi

todger
BR ˈtɒdʒə(r), -z
AM ˈtɑdʒər, -z

Todhunter
BR ˈtɒdˌhʌntə(r)
AM ˈtɑdˌ(h)ən(t)ər

Todmorden
BR ˈtɒdməd(ə)n
AM ˈtɑdˌmɔrdən

to-do
BR təˈduː
AM təˈdu

tody
BR ˈtəʊd|i, -ɪz
AM ˈtoʊdi, -z

toe
BR təʊ, -z, -ɪŋ, -d
AM toʊ, -z, -ɪŋ, -d

toea
BR ˈtɔɪə(r), -z
AM ˈtɔɪə, -z

toecap
BR ˈtəʊkap, -s
AM ˈtoʊˌkæp, -s

toehold
BR ˈtəʊhəʊld, -z
AM ˈtoʊˌhoʊld, -z

toeless
BR ˈtəʊləs
AM ˈtoʊləs

toenail
BR ˈtəʊneɪl, -z
AM ˈtoʊˌneɪl, -z

toey
BR ˈtəʊi
AM ˈtoʊi

toff
BR tɒf, -s
AM tɑf, -s
toffee
BR 'tɒf|i, -ɪz
AM 'tɔfi, 'tɑfi, -z
toffeeish
BR 'tɒfiɪʃ
AM 'tɔfiɪʃ, 'tɑfiɪʃ
toffee-nosed
BR 'tɒfɪnəʊzd, ˌtɒfɪ'nəʊzd
AM 'tɔfi,noʊzd, 'tɑfi,noʊzd
toft
BR tɒft, -s
AM tɔft, tɑft, -s
tofu
BR 'təʊfuː
AM ˌtoʊ'fu
tog
BR tɒg, -z, -ɪŋ, -d
AM tɑg, -z, -ɪŋ, -d
toga
BR 'təʊgə(*r*), -z, -d
AM 'toʊgə, -z, -d
together
BR tə'gɛðə(r)
AM tə'gɛðər
togetherness
BR tə'gɛðənəs
AM tə'gɛðərnəs
toggery
BR 'tɒg(ə)ri
AM 'tɑgəri
toggle
BR 'tɒgl, -z
AM 'tɑgəl, -z
Togo
BR 'təʊgəʊ
AM 'toʊgoʊ
Togolese
BR ˌtəʊgə'liːz
AM ˌtoʊgoʊ'liz, ˌtoʊgə'liz
toil
BR tɔɪl, -z, -ɪŋ, -d
AM tɔɪl, -z, -ɪŋ, -d
toile
BR twɑːl
AM twɑl
toiler
BR 'tɔɪlə(r), -z
AM 'tɔɪlər, -z
toilet
BR 'tɔɪlɪt, -s
AM 'tɔɪlɪt, -s
toiletry
BR 'tɔɪlɪtr|i, -ɪz
AM 'tɔɪlətri, -z
toilette
BR twɑː'lɛt, -s
AM twɑ'lɛt, -s
toilsome
BR 'tɔɪls(ə)m
AM 'tɔɪlsəm
toilsomely
BR 'tɔɪls(ə)mli
AM 'tɔɪlsəmli
toilsomeness
BR 'tɔɪls(ə)mnəs
AM 'tɔɪlsəmnəs
toilworn
BR 'tɔɪlwɔːn
AM 'tɔɪl,wɔ(ə)rn
toing and froing
BR ˌtuːɪŋ (ə)n(d) 'frəʊɪŋ, -z
AM ˌtuɪŋ ən 'froʊɪŋ, -z
toings and froings
BR ˌtuːɪŋz (ə)n(d) 'frəʊɪŋz
AM ˌtuɪŋz ən 'froʊɪŋz
Tojo
BR 'təʊdʒəʊ
AM 'toʊ,dʒoʊ
tokamak
BR 'təʊkəmak, -s
AM 'toʊkə,mæk, -s
tokay
BR tə(ʊ)'keɪ, 'təʊkeɪ, tɒ'keɪ, 'tɒkeɪ, -z
AM toʊ'keɪ, -z
toke
BR təʊk
AM toʊk
Tokelau
BR 'təʊkəlaʊ, 'tɒkəlaʊ
AM 'toʊkə,laʊ
token
BR 'təʊk(ə)n, -z
AM 'toʊkən, -z
tokenism
BR 'təʊkənɪz(ə)m, 'təʊkn̩ɪz(ə)m
AM 'toʊkə,nɪzəm
tokenist
BR 'təʊkənɪst, 'təʊkn̩ɪst
AM 'toʊkənəst
tokenistic
BR ˌtəʊkə'nɪstɪk, ˌtəʊkn'ɪstɪk
AM ˌtoʊkə'nɪstɪk
Tokharian
BR tə'kɑːrɪən, tɒ'kɑːrɪən, tə'kɛːrɪən, tɒ'kɛːrɪən
AM toʊ'kɛriən
Toklas
BR 'təʊkləs
AM 'toʊkləs
Tok Pisin
BR ˌtɒk 'pɪsɪn
AM ˌtɑk 'pɪsɪn
Tokugawa
BR ˌtəʊkʊ'gɑːwə(*r*)
AM ˌtoʊku'gawə
Tokyo
BR 'təʊkɪəʊ
AM 'toʊki,oʊ
tola
BR 'təʊlə(*r*), -z
AM 'toʊlə, -z
tolbooth
BR 'təʊlbuː|ð, 'tɒlbuː|ð, 'təʊlbuː|θ, 'tɒlbuː|θ, -ðz\-θs
AM 'toʊl,bu|θ, -θs\-ðz
tolbutamide
BR tɒl'bjuːtəmʌɪd
AM tɑl'bjudə,maɪd
told
BR təʊld
AM toʊld
Toledo[1]
place in Spain
BR tə'leɪdəʊ
AM tə'leɪdoʊ
Toledo[2]
place in US
BR tə'liːdəʊ
AM tə'lidoʊ
tolerability
BR ˌtɒl(ə)rə'bɪlɪti
AM ˌtɑl(ə)rə'bɪlɪdi
tolerable
BR 'tɒl(ə)rəbl
AM 'tɑl(ə)rəbəl, 'tɑlərbəl
tolerableness
BR 'tɒl(ə)rəblnəs
AM 'tɑl(ə)rəbəlnəs, 'tɑlərbəlnəs
tolerably
BR 'tɒl(ə)rəbli
AM 'tɑl(ə)rəbli, 'tɑlərbli
tolerance
BR 'tɒl(ə)rəns, 'tɒl(ə)rn̩s
AM 'tɑl(ə)rəns
tolerant
BR 'tɒl(ə)rənt, 'tɒl(ə)rn̩t
AM 'tɑl(ə)rənt
tolerantly
BR 'tɒl(ə)rəntli, 'tɒl(ə)rn̩tli
AM 'tɑl(ə)rən(t)li
tolerate
BR 'tɒləreɪt, -s, -ɪŋ, -ɪd
AM 'tɑlə,reɪ|t, -ts, -dɪŋ, -dɪd
toleration
BR ˌtɒlə'reɪʃn
AM ˌtɑlə'reɪʃən
tolerator
BR 'tɒləreɪtə(r), -z
AM 'tɑlə,reɪdər, -z
Tolima
BR tɒ'liːmə(*r*)
AM tə'limə
Tolkien
BR 'tɒlkiːn
AM 'toʊl,kin
toll
BR təʊl, -z, -ɪŋ, -d
AM toʊl, -z, -ɪŋ, -d
tollbooth
BR 'təʊlbuː|ð, 'tɒlbuː|ð, 'təʊlbuː|θ, 'tɒlbuː|θ, -ðz\-θs
AM 'toʊl,bu|θ, -θs\-ðz
tollbridge
BR 'təʊlbrɪdʒ, -ɪz
AM 'toʊl,brɪdʒ, -ɪz
Tolley
BR 'tɒli
AM 'tɑli
tollgate
BR 'təʊlgeɪt, -s
AM 'toʊl,geɪt, -s
tollhouse
BR 'təʊlhaʊ|s, -zɪz
AM 'toʊl,(h)aʊ|s, -zəz
tollroad
BR 'təʊlrəʊd, -z
AM 'toʊl,roʊd, -z
Tollund
BR 'tɒlənd
AM 'tɑlənd
tollway
BR 'təʊlweɪ, -z
AM 'toʊl,weɪ, -z
Tolpuddle
BR 'tɒl,pʌdl
AM 'tɑl,pədəl
Tolstoy
BR 'tɒlstɔɪ
AM 'toʊlz,tɔɪ
Toltec
BR 'tɒltɛk, -s
AM 'tɔl,tɛk, 'tɑl,tɛk, -s
Toltecan
BR tɒl'tɛk(ə)n, -z
AM tɔl'tɛkən, tɑl'tɛkən, -z
tolu
BR tɒ'luː, 'təʊluː
AM tə'lu, toʊ'lu
toluene
BR 'tɒljʊiːn
AM 'tɑlju,in
toluic
BR tɒ'ljuːɪk, tə'ljuːɪk
AM tə'luɪk, 'tɑljəwɪk
toluol
BR 'tɒljʊɒl
AM 'tɑljəwɔl, 'tɑljəwɑl
tom
BR tɒm, -z
AM tɑm, -z
tomahawk
BR 'tɒməhɔːk, -s
AM 'tɑmə,hɔk, 'tɑmə,hɑk, -s
tomalley
BR 'tɒmal|i, -ɪz
AM 'tɑm,æli, -z
tomatillo
BR ˌtɒmə'tɪl(j)əʊ, -z
AM ˌtoʊmə'ti(j)oʊ, -z
tomato
BR tə'mɑːtəʊ, -z
AM tə'meɪdoʊ, -z

tomatoey
BR tə'mɑːtəʊi
AM tə'meɪdoʊi

tomb
BR tuːm, -z
AM tum, -z

tombac
BR 'tɒmbak
AM 'tɑm,bæk

tombak
BR 'tɒmbak
AM 'tɑm,bæk

Tombaugh
BR 'tɒmbɔː(*r*)
AM 'tɑmbɔ, 'tɑmbɑ

tombola
BR tɒm'bəʊlə(*r*)
AM 'tɑmbələ

tombolo
BR tɒm'bəʊləʊ, -z
AM tɑm'boʊloʊ, -z

Tombouctou
BR ˌtɒmbʌk'tuː
AM ˌtɑmbək'tu

tomboy
BR 'tɒmbɔɪ, -z
AM 'tɑm,bɔɪ, -z

tomboyish
BR 'tɒmbɔɪɪʃ
AM 'tɑm,bɔɪɪʃ

tomboyishness
BR 'tɒmbɔɪɪʃnɪs
AM 'tɑmbɔɪɪʃnɪs

Tombs
BR tuːmz
AM tumz

tombstone
BR 'tuːmstəʊn, -z
AM 'tum,stoʊn, -z

tomcat
BR 'tɒmkat, -s
AM 'tɑm,kæt, -s

tome
BR təʊm, -z
AM toʊm, -z

tomenta
BR tə(ʊ)'mɛntə(*r*)
AM toʊ'mɛn(t)ə

tomentose
BR tə'mɛntəʊs,
'təʊm(ə)ntəʊs
AM toʊ'mɛntoʊs,
'toʊmən,toʊs

tomentous
BR tə'mɛntəs,
'təʊm(ə)ntəs
AM toʊ'mɛn(t)əs,
'toʊmən(t)əs

tomentum
BR tə(ʊ)'mɛntəm
AM toʊ'mɛn(t)əm

tomfool
BR ˌtɒm'fuːl, -z
AM 'tɑm'ful, -z

tomfoolery
BR (ˌ)tɒm'fuːl(ə)ri
AM tɑm'ful(ə)ri

Tomintoul
BR ˌtɒmɪn'tuːl,
ˌtɒmɪn'taʊl,
AM ˌtɑmən'taʊl,
ˌtɑmən'tul

Tomlin
BR 'tɒmlɪn
AM 'tɑmlən

Tomlinson
BR 'tɒmlɪns(ə)n
AM 'tɑmlənsən

tommy
BR 'tɒm|i, -ɪz
AM 'tɑmi, -z

tommyrot
BR 'tɒmɪrɒt, ˌtɒmɪ'rɒt
AM 'tɑmi,rɑt

tomogram
BR 'təʊməgram,
'tɒməgram, -z
AM 'toʊmə,græm, -z

tomograph
BR 'təʊməgrɑːf,
'təʊməgraf,
'tɒməgrɑːf, 'tɒməgraf,
-s
AM 'toʊmə,græf, -s

tomographic
BR ˌtəʊmə'grafɪk,
ˌtɒmə'grafɪk
AM ˌtoʊmə'græfɪk

tomography
BR tə(ʊ)'mɒgrəfi
AM toʊ'mɑgrəfi

Tomor
BR 'təʊmə(r)
AM 'toʊmər

tomorrow
BR tʊ'mɒrəʊ
AM tə'mɑroʊ,
tə'mɔroʊ

tompion
BR 'tɒmpɪən, -z
AM 'tɑmpiən, -z

Tompkins
BR 'tɒm(p)kɪnz
AM 'tɑm(p)kənz

Tompkinson
BR 'tɒm(p)kɪns(ə)n
AM 'tɑm(p)kənsən

tompot
BR 'tɒmpɒt, -s
AM 'tɑm,pɑt, -s

Toms
BR tɒmz
AM tɑmz

Tomsk
BR tɒmsk
AM tɑmsk

tomtit
BR 'tɒmtɪt, ˌtɒm'tɪt, -s
AM tɑm'tɪt, -s

tomtom
BR 'tɒmtɒm, -z
AM 'tɑm,tɑm, -z

ton¹
fashion
BR tõ, -z
AM tɔn, tɑn, -z

ton²
weight
BR tʌn, -z
AM tən, -z

tonal
BR 'təʊnl
AM 'toʊnəl

tonality
BR tə(ʊ)'nalɪt|i, -ɪz
AM toʊ'nælədi,
tə'nælədi, -z

tonally
BR 'təʊnl̩i, 'təʊnəli
AM 'toʊnəli

Tonbridge
BR 'tʌnbrɪdʒ
AM 'tən,brɪdʒ

tondi
BR 'tɒndi
AM 'tɑndi

tondo
BR 'tɒndəʊ
AM 'tɑndoʊ

tone
BR təʊn, -z, -ɪŋ, -d
AM toʊn, -z, -ɪŋ, -d

tonearm
BR 'təʊnɑːm, -z
AM 'toʊn,ɑrm, -z

toneburst
BR 'təʊnbəːst, -s
AM 'toʊn,bərst, -s

tone-deaf
BR ˌtəʊn'dɛf
AM 'toʊn,dɛf

toneless
BR 'təʊnləs
AM 'toʊnləs

tonelessly
BR 'təʊnləsli
AM 'toʊnləsli

tonelessness
BR 'təʊnləsnəs
AM 'toʊnləsnəs

toneme
BR 'təʊniːm, -z
AM 'toʊ,nim, -z

tonemic
BR tə(ʊ)'niːmɪk, -s
AM toʊ'nimɪk, -s

tonemically
BR tə(ʊ)'niːmɪkli
AM toʊ'nimək(ə)li

tonepad
BR 'təʊnpad, -z
AM 'toʊn,pæd, -z

toner
BR 'təʊnə(r), -z
AM 'toʊnər, -z

tone-row
BR 'təʊnrəʊ, -z
AM 'toʊn,roʊ, -z

tonetic
BR tə(ʊ)'nɛtɪk, -s
AM toʊ'nɛdɪk, -s

tonetically
BR tə(ʊ)'nɛtɪkli
AM toʊ'nɛdək(ə)li

tong
BR tɒŋ, -z
AM tɔŋ, tɑŋ, -z

tonga
BR 'tɒŋ(g)ə(*r*), -z
AM 'tɑŋgə, -z

Tongan
BR 'tɒŋ(g)ən, -z
AM 'tɑŋgən, -z

Tongariro
BR ˌtɒŋ(g)ə'riːrəʊ
AM ˌtɑŋgə'rɪroʊ

Tonge¹
placename
BR tɒŋ
AM tɔŋ, tɑŋ

Tonge²
surname
BR tɒŋ, tʌŋ, tɒn(d)ʒ
AM təŋ, tɔŋ, tɑŋ

tongkang
BR ˌtɒŋ'kaŋ, -z
AM ˌtɔŋ'kæŋ,
ˌtɑŋ'kæŋ, -z

tongue
BR tʌŋ, -z, -ɪŋ, -d
AM təŋ, -z, -ɪŋ, -d

tongue-and-groove
BR ˌtʌŋ(ə)n(d)'gruːv
AM 'təŋən'gruv

tongue-in-cheek
BR ˌtʌŋɪn'tʃiːk
AM 'təŋən'tʃik

tongue-lashing
BR 'tʌŋ,laʃɪŋ, -z
AM 'təŋ,læʃɪŋ, -z

tongueless
BR 'tʌŋləs
AM 'təŋləs

tongue-tie
BR 'tʌŋtʌɪ, -z, -d
AM 'təŋ,taɪ, -z, -d

tonguing
BR 'tʌŋɪŋ
AM 'təŋɪŋ

Toni
BR 'təʊni
AM 'toʊni

Tonia
BR 'təʊnɪə(*r*)
AM 'tɑnjə

tonic
BR 'tɒnɪk, -s
AM 'tɑnɪk, -s

tonically
BR 'tɒnɪkli
AM 'tɑnək(ə)li

tonicity
BR tə(ʊ)'nɪsɪt|i, -ɪz
AM toʊ'nɪsɪdi, -z

tonic sol-fa
BR ˌtɒnɪk sɒl'fɑː(*r*),
+ 'sɒlfɑː(*r*)

AM ˌtɑnɪk ˌsɔ(l)ˈfɑ

tonify
BR ˈtəʊnɪfʌɪ, -z, -ɪŋ, -d
AM ˈtoʊnəfaɪ, -z, -ɪn, -d

tonight
BR təˈnʌɪt
AM təˈnaɪt

tonish
BR ˈtəʊnɪʃ
AM ˈtoʊnɪʃ

Tonkin¹
surname
BR ˈtɒŋkɪn
AM ˈtɒŋkən

Tonkin²
Vietnam
BR ˌtɒnˈkɪn, ˌtɒŋˈkɪn
AM ˈtɑnˈkɪn, ˈtɑŋˈkɪn

Tonks
BR tɒŋks
AM tɔŋks, tɑŋks

ton-mile
BR ˈtʌnmʌɪl, ˌtʌnˈmʌɪl, -z
AM ˈtənˌmaɪl, -z

tonnage
BR ˈtʌn|ɪdʒ, -ɪdʒɪz
AM ˈtənɪdʒ, -ɪz

tonne
BR tʌn, -z
AM tən, -z

tonneau
BR ˈtɒnəʊ, -z
AM təˈnoʊ, ˈtɑnəʊ, -z

tonneaux
BR ˈtɒnəʊ(z)
AM təˈnoʊ, ˈtɑnoʊ

tonometer
BR tə(ʊ)ˈnɒmɪtə(r), -z
AM toʊˈnɑmədər, -z

tonsil
BR ˈtɒnsl, -z
AM ˈtɑnsəl, -z

tonsilitis
BR ˌtɒnsɪˈlʌɪtɪs, ˌtɒnslˈʌɪtɪs
AM ˌtɑnsəˈlaɪdɪs

tonsillar
BR ˈtɒnsɪlə(r), ˈtɒnsl̩ə(r)
AM ˈtɑnsələr

tonsillectomy
BR ˌtɒnsɪˈlɛktəm|i, ˌtɒnslˈɛktəm|i, -ɪz
AM ˌtɑnsəˈlɛktəmi, -z

tonsillitis
BR ˌtɒnsɪˈlʌɪtɪs, ˌtɒnslˈʌɪtɪs
AM ˌtɑnsəˈlaɪdɪs

tonsorial
BR tɒnˈsɔːrɪəl
AM tɑnˈsɔriəl

tonsure
BR ˈtɒnʃə(r), ˈtɒnsj(ʊ)ə(r), -z, -d
AM ˈtɑn(t)ʃər, -z, -d

tontine
BR ˈtɒntiːn, ˈtɒntʌɪn, tɒnˈtiːn
AM ˈtɑnˌtin

Tonto
BR ˈtɒntəʊ
AM ˈtɔn(t)oʊ, ˈtɑn(t)oʊ

Tonton Macoute
BR ˌtɒntɒn məˈkuːt, -s
AM ˈtɔnˌtɔn məˈkut, ˈtɑnˌtɑn məˈkut, -s

ton-up
BR ˈtʌnʌp, -s
AM ˈtənəp, -s

tonus
BR ˈtəʊnəs
AM ˈtoʊnəs

tony
BR ˈtəʊn|i, -ɪz
AM ˈtoʊni, -z

Tonypandy
BR ˌtɒnɪˈpandi
AM ˌtoniˈpændi, ˌtɑniˈpændi

Tonyrefail
BR ˌtɒnɪˈrɛvʌɪl
AM ˌtoniˈrɛvaɪl, ˌtɑniˈrɛvaɪl
WE ˌtɒnʌˈrevaɪl

too
BR tuː
AM tu

toodle-oo
BR ˌtuːdlˈuː
AM ˌtudəlˈu

toodle-pip
BR ˌtuːdlˈpɪp
AM ˌtudəlˈpɪp

Toogood
BR ˈtuːgʊd
AM ˈtuˌgʊd

took
BR tʊk
AM tʊk

tool
BR tuːl, -z, -ɪŋ, -d
AM tul, -z, -ɪŋ, -d

toolbox
BR ˈtuːlbɒks, -ɪz
AM ˈtulˌbɑks, -əz

toolchest
BR tuːltʃɛst, -s
AM ˈtulˌtʃɛst, -s

tooler
BR ˈtuːlə(r), -z
AM ˈtulər, -z

toolkit
BR ˈtuːlkɪt, -s
AM ˈtulˌkɪt, -s

toolmaker
BR ˈtuːlˌmeɪkə(r), -z
AM ˈtulˌmeɪkər, -z

toolmaking
BR ˈtuːlˌmeɪkɪŋ
AM ˈtulˌmeɪkɪŋ

toolroom
BR ˈtuːlruːm, ˈtuːlrʊm, -z
AM ˈtulˌrum, ˈtulˌrʊm, -z

toolshed
BR ˈtuːlʃɛd, -z
AM ˈtulˌʃɛd, -z

Toombs
BR tuːmz
AM tumz

toot
BR tuːt, -s, -ɪŋ, -ɨd
AM tu|t, -ts, -dɪŋ, -dəd

Tootal
BR ˈtuːtl
AM ˈtudl

tooter
BR ˈtuːtə(r), -z
AM ˈtudər, -z

tooth
BR tuːθ, -s, -ɪŋ, -t
AM tuθ, -s, -ɪŋ, -t

toothache
BR ˈtuːθeɪk, -s
AM ˈtuθˌeɪk, -s

tooth-billed
BR ˌtuːθˈbɪld
AM ˈtuθˌbɪld

toothbrush
BR ˈtuːθbrʌʃ, -ɪz
AM ˈtuθˌbrəʃ, -əz

toothcomb
BR ˈtuːθkəʊm, -z
AM ˈtuθˌkoʊm, -z

tooth-glass
BR ˈtuːθglɑːs, ˈtuːθglas, -ɪz
AM ˈtuθˌglæs, -əz

toothily
BR ˈtuːθɨli
AM ˈtuθəli

toothiness
BR ˈtuːθɪnɪs
AM ˈtuθinɪs

toothless
BR ˈtuːθləs
AM ˈtuθləs

toothlike
BR ˈtuːθlʌɪk
AM ˈtuθˌlaɪk

toothpaste
BR ˈtuːθpeɪst
AM ˈtuθˌpeɪst

toothpick
BR ˈtuːθpɪk, -s
AM ˈtuθˌpɪk, -s

toothsome
BR ˈtuːθs(ə)m
AM ˈtuθsəm

toothsomely
BR ˈtuːθs(ə)mli
AM ˈtuθsəmli

toothsomeness
BR ˈtuːθs(ə)mnəs
AM ˈtuθsəmnəs

toothwort
BR ˈtuːθwəːt, -s
AM ˈtuθwərt, ˈtuθwɔ(ə)rt, -s

toothy
BR ˈtuːθ|i, -ɪə(r), -ɪɪst
AM ˈtuθi, -ər, -ɪst

Tooting
BR ˈtuːtɪŋ
AM ˈtudɪŋ

tootle
BR ˈtuːt|l, -lz, -l̩ɪŋ\-lɪŋ, -ld
AM ˈtudəl, -z, -ɪŋ, -d

tootler
BR ˈtuːtl̩ə(r), ˈtuːtlə(r), -z
AM ˈtudlər, -z

too-too
BR ˈtuːtuː, ˌtuːˈtuː
AM ˈtuˌtu

tootsie
BR ˈtʊts|i, -ɪz
AM ˈtʊtsi, -z

tootsy
BR ˈtʊts|i, -ɪz
AM ˈtʊtsi, -z

Toowoomba
BR tʊˈwʊmbə(*r*)
AM təˈwʊmbə

top
BR tɒp, -s, -ɪŋ, -t
AM tɑp, -s, -ɪŋ, -t

topaz
BR ˈtəʊpaz, -ɪz
AM ˈtoʊˌpæz, -əz

topazolite
BR tə(ʊ)ˈpeɪzəlʌɪt
AM toʊˈpæzəˌlaɪt

topboot
BR ˈtɒpbuːt, -s
AM ˈtɑpˌbut, -s

topcoat
BR ˈtɒpkəʊt, -s
AM ˈtɑpˌkoʊt, -s

top-dress
verb
BR ˌtɒpˈdrɛs, -ɪz, -ɪŋ, -t
AM ˈtɑpˌdrɛs, -əz, -ɪŋ, -t

tope
BR təʊp, -s
AM toʊp, -s

topee
BR ˈtəʊpiː, -z
AM ˈtoʊpi, -z

Topeka
BR təˈpiːkə(*r*)
AM təˈpikə

toper
BR ˈtəʊpə(r), -z
AM ˈtoʊpər, -z

topgallant
BR ˈtɒpˌgalənt, ˈtɒpˌgaln̩t, təˈgalənt, təˈgaln̩t, -s
AM tɑpˈgælənt, ˈtɑpˌgælənt, təˈgælənt, -s

Topham
BR 'tɒp(ə)m
AM 'tɑpəm

top-hamper
BR 'tɒp,hampə(r)
AM 'tɑp,(h)æmpər

top-hatted
BR ,tɒp'hatɨd
AM 'tɑp'hædəd

top-heavily
BR ,tɒp'hɛvɨli
AM 'tɑp,(h)ɛvəli

top-heaviness
BR ,tɒp'hɛvɪnɨs
AM 'tɑp,(h)ɛvinɨs

top-heavy
BR ,tɒp'hɛvi
AM 'tɑp,(h)ɛvi

Tophet
BR 'təʊfɪt
AM 'toʊfət

tophi
BR 'təʊfʌɪ
AM 'toʊ,faɪ

tophus
BR 'təʊfəs
AM 'toʊfəs

topi
BR 'təʊpiː, -z
AM 'toʊpi, -z

topiarian
BR ,təʊpɪ'ɛːrɪən, -z
AM ,toʊpi'ɛriən, -z

topiarist
BR 'təʊpɪərɪst, -s
AM 'toʊpiərəst, -s

topiary
BR 'təʊpɪəri
AM 'toʊpi,ɛri

topic
BR 'tɒpɪk
AM 'tɑpɪk

topical
BR 'tɒpɨkl
AM 'tɑpəkəl

topicality
BR ,tɒpɪ'kalɨti
AM ,tɑpə'kælədi

topicalization
BR ,tɒpɨkl̩ʌɪ'zeɪʃn, ,tɒpɨkəlʌɪ'zeɪʃn
AM ,tɑpəkələ'zeɪʃən, ,tɑpəkə,laɪ'zeɪʃən

topicalize
BR 'tɒpɨkl̩ʌɪz, 'tɒpɨkəlʌɪz, -ɨz, -ɪŋ, -d
AM 'tɑpəkə,laɪz, -ɨz, -ɪŋ, -d

topically
BR 'tɒpɨkl̩i, 'tɒpɨk(ə)li
AM 'tɑpək(ə)li

topknot
BR 'tɒpnɒt, -s
AM 'tɑp,nɑt, -s

Toplady
BR 'tɒp,leɪdi
AM 'tɑp,leɪdi

topless
BR 'tɒpləs
AM 'tɑpləs

toplessness
BR 'tɒpləsnəs
AM 'tɑpləsnəs

toplofty
BR ,tɒp'lɒfti
AM 'tɑp,lɔfti, 'tɑp,lɑfti

topman
BR 'tɒpman
AM 'tɑp,mæn

topmast
BR 'tɒpmɑːst, 'tɒpmast, -s
AM 'tɑp,mæst, -s

topmen
BR 'tɒpmɛn
AM 'tɑp,mɛn

topmost
BR 'tɒpməʊst
AM 'tɑp,moʊst

topnotch
BR ,tɒp'nɒtʃ
AM 'tɑp'nɑtʃ

top-notcher
BR ,tɒp'nɒtʃə(r), -z
AM 'tɑp'nɑtʃər, -z

topo
BR 'tɒpəʊ, -z
AM 'tɑpoʊ, -z

topographer
BR tə'pɒgrəfə(r), tɒ'pɒgrəfə(r), -z
AM tə'pɑgrəfər, -z

topographic
BR ,tɒpə'grafɪk
AM ,tɑpə'græfɪk

topographical
BR ,tɒpə'grafɨkl
AM ,tɑpə'græfəkəl

topographically
BR ,tɒpə'grafɨkli
AM ,tɑpə'græfək(ə)li

topography
BR tə'pɒgrəfi, tɒ'pɒgrəfi
AM tə'pɑgrəfi

topoi
BR 'tɒpɔɪ
AM 'toʊ,pɔɪ

topological
BR ,tɒpə'lɒdʒɨkl
AM ,tɑpə'lɑdʒəkəl

topologically
BR ,tɒpə'lɒdʒɨkli
AM ,tɑpə'lɑdʒək(ə)li

topologist
BR tə'pɒlədʒɪst, tɒ'pɒlədʒɪst, -s
AM tə'pɑlədʒəst, -s

topology
BR tə'pɒlədʒi, tɒ'pɒlədʒi
AM tə'pɑlədʒi

Topolsky
BR tə'pɒlski
AM tə'pɔlski, tə'pɑlski

toponym
BR 'tɒpənɪm, -z
AM 'tɑpə,nɪm, -z

toponymic
BR ,tɒpə'nɪmɪk
AM ,tɑpə'nɪmɪk

toponymy
BR tə'pɒnəmi, tɒ'pɒnəmi
AM tə'pɑnəmi

topos
BR 'tɒpɒs
AM 'toʊ,poʊs

topper
BR 'tɒpə(r), -z
AM 'tɑpər, -z

topping
BR 'tɒpɪŋ, -z
AM 'tɑpɪŋ, -z

topple
BR 'tɒp|l, -lz, -l̩ɪŋ\-lɪŋ, -ld
AM 'tɑp|əl, -əlz, -(ə)lɪŋ, -əld

topsail
BR 'tɒpseɪl, 'tɒpsl, -z
AM 'tɑpsəl, 'tɑp,seɪl, -z

topside
BR 'tɒpsʌɪd
AM 'tɑp,saɪd

topslice
BR 'tɒpslʌɪs
AM 'tɑp,slaɪs

top-slicing
BR 'tɒp,slʌɪsɪŋ
AM 'tɑp,slaɪsɪŋ

topsoil
BR 'tɒpsɔɪl
AM 'tɑp,sɔɪl

topspin
BR 'tɒpspɪn
AM 'tɑp,spɪn

topstitch
BR 'tɒpstɪtʃ, -ɨz, -ɪŋ, -t
AM 'tɑp,stɪtʃ, -ɨz, -ɪŋ, -t

Topsy
BR 'tɒpsi
AM 'tɑpsi

topsy-turvily
BR ,tɒpsɪ'təːvɨli
AM ,tɑpsi'tərvəli

topsy-turviness
BR ,tɒpsɪ'təːvɪnɨs
AM ,tɑpsi'tərvinɨs

topsy-turvy
BR ,tɒpsɪ'təːvi
AM ,tɑpsi'tərvi

top-up
BR 'tɒpʌp, -s
AM 'tɑpəp, -s

toque
BR təʊk, -s
AM toʊk, -s

toquilla
BR tə(ʊ)'kiː(j)ə(r), -z
AM toʊ'ki(j)ə, -z

tor
BR tɔː(r), -z
AM tɔ(ə)r, -z

Torah
BR 'tɔːrə(r), 'təʊrə(r), ,tɔː'rɑː(r)
AM 'toʊrə, 'tɔrə

Torbay
BR ,tɔː'beɪ
AM ,tɔr'beɪ

torc
BR tɔːk, -s
AM tɔ(ə)rk, -s

torch
BR tɔːtʃ, -ɨz, -ɪŋ, -t
AM tɔrtʃ, -əz, -ɪŋ, -t

torch-bearer
BR 'tɔːtʃ,bɛːrə(r), -z
AM 'tɔrtʃ,bɛrər, -z

torchère
BR tɔː'ʃɛː(r), -z
AM tɔr'ʃɛ(ə)r, -z

torchlight
BR 'tɔːtʃlʌɪt
AM 'tɔrtʃ,laɪt

torchlit
BR 'tɔːtʃlɪt
AM 'tɔrtʃlɪt

torchon
BR 'tɔːʃɒn, 'tɔːʃ(ə)n, -z
AM 'tɔr,ʃɑn, -z

Tordoff
BR 'tɔːdɒf
AM 'tɔr,dɔf, 'tɔr,dɑf

tore
BR tɔː(r)
AM tɔ(ə)r

toreador
BR 'tɒrɪədɔː(r), -z
AM 'tɔriə,dɔ(ə)r, -z

torero
BR tə'rɛːrəʊ, -z
AM tə'rɛroʊ, -z

toreutic
BR tə'ruːtɪk, -s
AM tə'rudɪk, -s

Torfaen
BR tɔː'vʌɪn
AM ,tɔr'vaɪn

torgoch
BR 'tɔːgɒx, 'tɔːgɒk, -s
AM 'tɔr,gɑk, 'tɔr,goʊk, -s
WE tɔr'gɒx

tori
BR 'tɔːrʌɪ
AM 'tɔ,raɪ, 'toʊ,raɪ

toric
BR 'tɒrɪk, 'tɔːrɪk
AM 'tɔrɪk

torii
BR 'tɔːriː
AM 'tɔri,i

Torino
BR tə'riːnəʊ, tɒ'riːnəʊ
AM tə'rinoʊ

torment¹
noun
BR 'tɔːmɛnt, 'tɔːm(ə)nt, -s
AM 'tɔr,mɛnt, -s

torment²
verb
BR tɔː'mɛnt, -s, -ɪŋ, -ɨd
AM tɔr'mɛn|t, -ts, -(t)ɪŋ, -(t)əd

tormentedly
BR tɔː'mɛntɨdli
AM tɔr'mɛn(t)ədli

tormentil
BR 'tɔːm(ə)ntɪl, -z
AM 'tɔrmən,tɪl, -z

tormentingly
BR tɔː'mɛntɪŋli
AM tɔr'mɛn(t)ɪŋli

tormentor
BR tɔː'mɛntə(r), -z
AM tɔr'mɛn(t)ər, -z

torn
BR tɔːn
AM tɔ(ə)rn

tornadic
BR tɔː'nadɪk
AM tɔr'neɪdɪk, tɔr'nædɪk

tornado
BR tɔː'neɪdəʊ, -z
AM tɔr'neɪdoʊ, -z

Tornio
BR 'tɔːnɪəʊ
AM 'tɔrnioʊ

toroid
BR 'tɔːrɔɪd, -z
AM 'tɔr,ɔɪd, -z

toroidal
BR tɔː'rɔɪdl
AM ,tɔr'ɔɪdəl

toroidally
BR tɔː'rɔɪdḷi, tɔː'rɔɪdəli
AM ,tɔr'ɔɪd(ə)li

Toronto
BR tə'rɒntəʊ
AM tə'rɑn(t)oʊ, tə'rɔn(t)oʊ

torose
BR 'tɒrəʊs, 'tɔːrəʊs
AM 'tɔr,oʊs, 'tɔr,oʊz

torpedo
BR tɔː'piːdəʊ, -z, -ɪŋ, -d
AM tɔr'pidoʊ, -z, -ɪŋ, -d

torpefy
BR 'tɔːpɨfʌɪ, -z, -ɪŋ, -d
AM 'tɔrpə,faɪ, -z, -ɪŋ, -d

torpid
BR 'tɔːpɪd
AM 'tɔrpəd

torpidity
BR tɔː'pɪdɨti
AM tɔr'pɪdɨdi

torpidly
BR 'tɔːpɨdli
AM 'tɔrpədli

torpidness
BR 'tɔːpɪdnɨs
AM 'tɔrpədnəs

torpor
BR 'tɔːpə(r)
AM 'tɔrpər

torporific
BR ,tɔːpə'rɪfɪk
AM ,tɔrpə'rɪfɪk

torquate
BR 'tɔːkweɪt
AM 'tɔr,kweɪt

Torquay
BR ,tɔː'kiː
AM tɔr'ki

torque
BR tɔːk, -s, -ɪŋ, -t
AM tɔ(ə)rk, -s, -ɪŋ, -t

Torquemada
BR ,tɔːkwɪ'mɑːdə(r)
AM ,tɔrkə'mɑdə

torr
BR tɔː(r), -z
AM tɔ(ə)r, -z

Torrance
BR 'tɒrəns, 'tɒrn̩s
AM 'tɔrəns

torrefaction
BR ,tɒrɪ'fakʃn
AM ,tɔrə'fækʃən

torrefy
BR 'tɒrɪfʌɪ, -z, -ɪŋ, -d
AM 'tɔrə,faɪ, -z, -ɪŋ, -d

Torremolinos
BR ,tɒrɪmə'liːnɒs
AM ,tɔrəmə'linəs

torrent
BR 'tɒrənt, 'tɒrn̩t, -s
AM 'tɔrənt, -s

torrential
BR tə'rɛnʃl
AM tɔ'rɛn(t)ʃəl, tə'rɛn(t)ʃəl

torrentially
BR tə'rɛnʃḷi, tə'rɛnʃəli
AM tɔ'rɛn(t)ʃəli, tə'rɛn(t)ʃəli

Torres
BR 'tɒrɪs, 'tɒrɪz, 'tɔːrɪs, 'tɔːrɪz
AM 'tɔrəs, 'tɔr,ɛz

Torrez
BR 'tɒrɪs, 'tɒrɪz, 'tɔːrɪs, 'tɔːrɪz
AM 'tɔr,ɛz, 'tɔrəs

Torricelli
BR ,tɒrɪ'tʃɛli
AM ,tɔrə'tʃɛli

torrid
BR 'tɒrɪd
AM 'tɔrəd

torridity
BR tə'rɪdɨti
AM tə'rɪdɨdi

torridly
BR 'tɒrɨdli
AM 'tɔrədli

torridness
BR 'tɒrɨdnɨs
AM 'tɔrɪdnɨs

torse
BR tɔːs, -ɨz
AM tɔ(ə)rs, -əz

torsel
BR 'tɔːsl, -z
AM 'tɔrsəl, -z

Tórshavn
BR 'tɔːz,hɑːvn
AM 'tɔrs,hæv(ə)n
DAN 'toʌ's,hɑw'n

torsion
BR 'tɔːʃn
AM 'tɔrʃən

torsional
BR 'tɔːʃn̩(ə)l, 'tɔːʃən(ə)l
AM 'tɔrʃ(ə)nəl

torsionally
BR 'tɔːʃn̩əli, 'tɔːʃn̩li, 'tɔːʃənḷi, 'tɔːʃ(ə)nəli
AM 'tɔrʃ(ə)nəli

torsionless
BR 'tɔːʃnləs
AM 'tɔrʃənləs

torsk
BR tɔːsk, -s
AM tɔ(ə)rsk, -s

torso
BR 'tɔːsəʊ, -z
AM 'tɔrsoʊ, -z

tort
BR tɔːt, -s
AM tɔ(ə)rt, -s

torte
BR tɔːtə(r), tɔːt, 'tɔːtəz\tɔːts
AM tɔ(ə)rt, -s

Tortelier
BR tɔː'tɛlɪeɪ
AM tɔr,tɛli'eɪ
FR tɔʀtəlje

tortellini
BR ,tɔːtɪ'liːni, ,tɔːtl'iːni
AM ,tɔrdl'ini

tortelloni
BR ,tɔːtɪ'ləʊni, ,tɔːtl'əʊni
AM ,tɔrdl'oʊni

torten
BR 'tɔːtn
AM 'tɔrtən

tortfeasor
BR 'tɔːtfiːzə(r), ,tɔːt'fiːzə(r), -z
AM 'tɔrt,fizər, 'tɔrt,fi,zɔ(ə)r, -z

torticollis
BR ,tɔːtɪ'kɒlɪs
AM ,tɔrdə'kɑləs

tortilla
BR tɔː'tiːjə(r), -z
AM tɔr'ti(j)ə, -z

tortious
BR 'tɔːʃəs
AM 'tɔrʃəs

tortiously
BR 'tɔːʃəsli
AM 'tɔrʃəsli

tortoise
BR 'tɔːtəs, 'tɔːtɔɪs, 'tɔːtɔɪz, -ɨz
AM 'tɔrdəs, -əz

tortoise-like
BR 'tɔːtəslʌɪk, 'tɔːtɔɪslʌɪk, 'tɔːtɔɪzlʌɪk
AM 'tɔrdəs,laɪk

tortoiseshell
BR 'tɔːtəsʃɛl
AM 'tɔrdə(s),ʃɛl

Tortola
BR tɔː'təʊlə(r)
AM tɔr'toʊlə

tortrices
BR 'tɔːtrɪsiːz
AM 'tɔrtrə,siz

tortrix
BR 'tɔːtrɪks, -ɨz
AM 'tɔrtrɪks, -ɨz

tortuosity
BR ,tɔːtʃʊ'ɒsɨti, ,tɔːtjʊ'ɒsɨti
AM ,tɔrtʃə'wɑsədi

tortuous
BR 'tɔːtʃʊəs, 'tɔːtjʊəs
AM 'tɔrtʃ(əw)əs

tortuously
BR 'tɔːtʃʊəsli, 'tɔːtjʊəsli
AM 'tɔrtʃ(əw)əsli

tortuousness
BR 'tɔːtʃʊəsnəs, 'tɔːtjʊəsnəs
AM 'tɔrtʃ(əw)əsnəs

torturable
BR 'tɔːtʃ(ə)rəbl
AM 'tɔrtʃ(ə)rəbəl

torture
BR 'tɔːtʃ|ə(r), -əz, -(ə)rɪŋ, -əd
AM 'tɔrtʃ|ər, -ərz, -(ə)rɪŋ, -ərd

torturer
BR 'tɔːtʃ(ə)rə(r), -z
AM 'tɔrtʃ(ə)rər, -z

torturous
BR 'tɔːtʃ(ə)rəs
AM 'tɔrtʃ(ə)rəs

torturously
BR 'tɔːtʃ(ə)rəsli
AM 'tɔrtʃ(ə)rəsli

torula
BR 'tɒruːlə(r), 'tɒrjʊlə(r)
AM 'tɔr(j)ələ

torulae
BR 'tɒruːliː, 'tɒrjʊliː
AM 'tɔr(j)əli, 'tɔr(j)ə,laɪ

torus
BR 'tɔːrəs, -ɪz
AM 'tɔrəs, -əz

Torvill
BR 'tɔːvɪl
AM 'tɔrˌvɪl

Tory
BR 'tɔːr|i, -ɪz
AM 'tɔri, -z

Toryism
BR 'tɔːrɪɪz(ə)m
AM 'tɔriˌɪzəm

Toscana
BR tɒ'skɑːnə(r)
AM tɔ'skɑnə, tɑ'skɑnə

Toscanini
BR ˌtɒskə'niːni
AM ˌtɔskə'nini, ˌtɑskə'nini

tosh
BR tɒʃ
AM tɑʃ

Toshack
BR 'tɒʃak
AM 'tɔˌʃæk, 'tɑˌʃæk

Tosk
BR tɒsk, -s
AM tɑsk, -s

toss
BR tɒs, -ɪz, -ɪŋ, -t
AM tɔs, tɑs, -ɪz, -ɪŋ, -t

tosser
BR 'tɒsə(r), -z
AM 'tɔsər, 'tɑsər, -z

tosspot
BR 'tɒspɒt, -s
AM 'tɔsˌpɑt, 'tɑsˌpɑt, -s

toss-up
BR 'tɒsʌp, -s
AM 'tɔsəp, 'tɑsəp, -s

tostada
BR tɒ'stɑːdə(r), -z
AM tə'stɑdə, toʊ'stɑdə, -z

tostado
BR tɒ'stɑːdəʊ, -z
AM tə'stɑdoʊ, toʊ'stɑdoʊ, -z

tostone
BR tɒ'stəʊnʌɪ, -z
AM ˌtoʊ'stoʊneɪ, -z

tot
BR tɒt, -s, -ɪŋ, -ɪd
AM tɑ|t, -ts, -dɪŋ, -dəd

total
BR 'təʊt|l, -lz, -l̩ɪŋ\-lɪŋ, -ld
AM 'toʊdl, -z, -ɪŋ, -d

totalisation
BR ˌtəʊtl̩ʌɪ'zeɪʃn, ˌtəʊtəlʌɪ'zeɪʃn
AM ˌtoʊdlə'zeɪʃən, ˌtoʊdlˌaɪ'zeɪʃən

totalisator
BR 'təʊtl̩ʌɪˌzeɪtə(r), 'təʊtəlʌɪˌzeɪtə(r), -z
AM 'toʊdl̩əˌzeɪdər, -z

totalise
BR 'təʊtl̩ʌɪz, 'təʊtəlʌɪz, -ɪz, -ɪŋ, -d
AM 'toʊdlˌaɪz, -ɪz, -ɪŋ, -d

totaliser
BR 'təʊtl̩ʌɪzə(r), 'təʊtəlʌɪzə(r), -z
AM 'toʊdlˌaɪzər, -z

totalitarian
BR ˌtəʊtalɪ'tɛːrɪən, tə(ʊ)ˌtalɪ'tɛːrɪən
AM toʊˌtælə'tɛriən

totalitarianism
BR ˌtəʊtalɪ'tɛːrɪənɪz(ə)m, tə(ʊ)ˌtalɪ'tɛːrɪənɪz(ə)m
AM toʊˌtælə'tɛriəˌnɪzəm

totality
BR tə(ʊ)'talɪti
AM toʊ'tælədi

totalization
BR ˌtəʊtl̩ʌɪ'zeɪʃn, ˌtəʊtəlʌɪ'zeɪʃn
AM ˌtoʊdlə'zeɪʃən, ˌtoʊdlˌaɪ'zeɪʃən

totalizator
BR 'təʊtl̩ʌɪˌzeɪtə(r), 'təʊtəlʌɪˌzeɪtə(r), -z
AM 'toʊdl̩əˌzeɪdər, -z

totalize
BR 'təʊtl̩ʌɪz, 'təʊtəlʌɪz, -ɪz, -ɪŋ, -d
AM 'toʊdlˌaɪz, -ɪz, -ɪŋ, -d

totalizer
BR 'təʊtl̩ʌɪzə(r), 'təʊtəlʌɪzə(r), -z
AM 'toʊdlˌaɪzər, -z

totally
BR 'təʊtl̩i, 'təʊtəli
AM 'toʊdl̩i, 'toʊdli

totaquine
BR 'təʊtəkwiːn
AM 'toʊdəˌkwin

tote
BR təʊt, -s, -ɪŋ, -ɪd
AM toʊ|t, -ts, -dɪŋ, -dəd

totem
BR 'təʊtəm, -z
AM 'toʊdəm, -z

totemic
BR tə(ʊ)'tɛmɪk
AM toʊ'tɛmɪk

totemism
BR 'təʊtəmɪz(ə)m
AM 'toʊdəˌmɪzəm

totemist
BR 'təʊtəmɪst, -s
AM 'toʊdəməst, -s

totemistic
BR ˌtəʊtə'mɪstɪk
AM ˌtoʊdə'mɪstɪk

toter
BR 'təʊtə(r), -z
AM 'toʊdər, -z

t'other
BR 'tʌðə(r)
AM 'təðər

totipotent
BR təʊ'tɪpət(ə)nt
AM ˌtoʊdə'poʊtnt

Totnes
BR 'tɒtnɪs
AM 'tɔtnəs, 'tɑtnəs

toto
BR 'təʊtəʊ
AM 'toʊdoʊ, 'toʊˌtoʊ

Tottenham
BR 'tɒtn̩əm, 'tɒtnəm
AM 'tɑtn̩əm, 'tɑtnəm

totter
BR 'tɒt|ə(r), -əz, -(ə)rɪŋ, -əd
AM 'tɑdər, -z, -ɪŋ, -d

totterer
BR 'tɒt(ə)rə(r), -z
AM 'tɑdərər, -z

tottery
BR 'tɒt(ə)ri
AM 'tɑdəri

tottings-up
BR ˌtɒtɪŋz'ʌp
AM ˌtɑdɪŋz'əp

totting-up
BR ˌtɒtɪŋ'ʌp
AM ˌtɑdɪŋ'əp

totty
BR 'tɒti
AM 'tɑdi

toucan
BR 'tuːkən, 'tuːkan, -z
AM 'tuˌkæn, 'tuˌkɑn, -z

touch
BR tʌtʃ, -ɪz, -ɪŋ, -t
AM tətʃ, -ɪz, -ɪŋ, -t

touchable
BR 'tʌtʃəbl
AM 'tətʃəbəl

touch-and-go
BR ˌtʌtʃ(ə)n(d)'gəʊ
AM 'tətʃən'goʊ

touchback
BR 'tʌtʃbak, -s
AM 'tətʃˌbæk, -s

touchdown
BR 'tʌtʃdaʊn, -z
AM 'tətʃˌdaʊn, -z

touché
BR 'tuːʃeɪ, tuː'ʃeɪ
AM tu'ʃeɪ

toucher
BR 'tʌtʃə(r), -z
AM 'tətʃər, -z

touchily
BR 'tʌtʃɪli
AM 'tətʃəli

touchiness
BR 'tʌtʃɪnɪs
AM 'tətʃinɪs

touchingly
BR 'tʌtʃɪŋli
AM 'tətʃɪŋli

touchingness
BR 'tʌtʃɪŋnɪs
AM 'tətʃɪŋnɪs

touch-in-goal
BR 'tʌtʃɪngəʊl, -z
AM 'tʌtʃənˌgoʊl, -z

touchline
BR 'tʌtʃlʌɪn, -z
AM 'tətʃˌlaɪn, -z

touch-me-not
BR 'tʌtʃmɪnɒt, -s
AM ˈtətʃˌmi'nɑt, -s

touchpad
BR 'tʌtʃpad, -z
AM 'tətʃˌpæd, -z

touchpaper
BR 'tʌtʃˌpeɪpə(r)
AM 'tətʃˌpeɪpər

touchstone
BR 'tʌtʃstəʊn, -z
AM 'tətʃˌstoʊn, -z

touchwood
BR 'tʌtʃwʊd
AM 'tətʃˌwʊd

touchy
BR 'tʌtʃ|i, -ɪə(r), -ɪɪst
AM 'tətʃi, -ər, -ɪst

Tough[1]
Scottish place and surname
BR tuːx
AM tuk

Tough[2]
surname, except Scottish
BR tʌf
AM təf

tough
BR tʌf, -s, -ɪŋ, -t, -ə(r), -ɪst
AM təf, -s, -ɪŋ, -t, -ər, -əst

toughen
BR 'tʌf|n, -nz, -n̩ɪŋ\-nɪŋ, -nd
AM 'təf|ən, -ənz, -(ə)nɪŋ, -ənd

toughener
BR 'tʌfn̩ə(r), 'tʌfnə(r), -z
AM 'təf(ə)nər, -z

toughie
BR 'tʌf|i, -ɪz
AM 'təfi, -z

toughish
BR 'tʌfɪʃ
AM 'təfɪʃ

toughly
BR 'tʌfli
AM 'təfli

tough-minded
BR ˌtʌf'mʌɪndɪd
AM ˈtəfˈmaɪndɪd

tough-mindedness
BR ˌtʌf'mʌɪndɪdnɪs
AM ˈtəfˈmaɪn(d)ɪdnɪs

toughness
BR 'tʌfnəs
AM 'təfnəs

Toulon
BR tuː'lɔ̃

AM tu'lɔn, tu'lɑn
Toulouse
BR tuː'luːz, tʉ'luːz
AM tu'luz
Toulouse-Lautrec
BR tʉˌluːzlə(ʊ)'trɛk, ˌtuːluːzlə(ʊ)'trɛk
AM tʊˌlusˌlə'trɛk
toupée
BR 'tuːpeɪ, -z
AM tu'peɪ, -z
tour
BR tʊə(r), tɔː(r), -z, -ɪŋ, -d
AM tʊ(ə)r, -z, -ɪŋ, -d
touraco
BR 'tʊərəkəʊ, -z
AM 'tʊrəˌkoʊ, -z
tour de force
BR ˌtʊə də 'fɔːs, ˌtɔː +
AM ˈtʊr də 'fɔ(ə)rs
tourer
BR 'tʊərə(r), 'tɔːrə(r), -z
AM 'tʊrər, -z
touring car
BR 'tʊərɪŋ kɑː(r), 'tɔːrɪŋ +, -z
AM 'tərɪŋ ˌkɑr, -z
tourism
BR 'tʊərɪz(ə)m, 'tɔːrɪz(ə)m
AM 'tərɪzəm
tourist
BR 'tʊərɪst, 'tɔːrɪst, -s, -ɪd
AM 'tərəst, -s, -əd
touristic
BR tʊə'rɪstɪk, tɔː'rɪstɪk
AM tə'rɪstɪk
touristically
BR tʊə'rɪstɨkli, tɔː'rɪstɨkli
AM tə'rɪstɪk(ə)li
touristy
BR 'tʊərɪsti, 'tɔːrɪsti
AM 'tərəsti
tourmaline
BR 'tɔːməliːn, 'tʊəməliːn, -z
AM 'tʊrmələn, 'tʊrməˌlin, -z
Tournai
BR tʊə'neɪ
AM tʊr'neɪ
tournament
BR 'tʊənəm(ə)nt, 'tɔːnəm(ə)nt, 'təːnəm(ə)nt, -s
AM 'tərnəmənt, -s
tournedos
BR 'tʊənədəʊ, 'tɔːnədəʊ, 'təːnədəʊ, -z
AM ˈtʊrnəˈdoʊ, -z
tourney
BR 'tʊən|i, 'tɔːn|i, 'təːn|i, -ɪz
AM 'tərni, -z
tourniquet
BR 'tʊənɪkeɪ, 'tɔːnɪkeɪ, 'təːnɪkeɪ, -z
AM 'tərnəkət, -s
Tours
BR tʊə(r), tʊəz
AM tʊ(ə)r(z)
tours de force
BR ˌtʊə(z) də 'fɔːs, ˌtɔː(z) +
AM ˈtʊrz də 'fɔ(ə)rs
tousle
BR 'taʊz|l, -lz, -l̩ɪŋ, -ld
AM 'taʊz|əl, -əlz, -(ə)lɪŋ, -əld
tousle-haired
BR ˌtaʊzl'hɛːd
AM 'taʊzəlˌhɛ(ə)rd
tous-les-mois
BR ˌtuːleɪ'mwɑː(r), -z
AM ˌtulə'mwɑ, -z
tout
BR taʊt, -s, -ɪŋ, -ɪd
AM taʊ|t, -ts, -dɪŋ, -dəd
tout court
BR ˌtuː 'kɔː(r)
AM ˌtu 'kɔ(ə)r
tout de suite
BR ˌtuː də 'swiːt, ˌtuːt 'swiːt
AM ˌtut 'swit
tout ensemble
BR ˌtuːt ɒn'sɒmbl, + ɒ̃'sɒ̃bl
AM ˈtut ɑn'sɑmbəl
touter
BR 'taʊtə(r), -z
AM 'taʊdər, -z
tovarich
BR tə'vɑːrɪʃ, tɒ'vɑːrɪʃ, -ɪz
AM tə'vɑrɪ(t)ʃ, -ɪz
tovarish
BR tə'vɑːrɪʃ, tɒ'vɑːrɪʃ, -ɪz
AM tə'vɑrɪʃ, -ɪz
Tovey
BR 'təʊvi, 'tʌvi
AM 'toʊvi
tow
BR təʊ, -z, -ɪŋ, -d
AM toʊ, -z, -ɪŋ, -d
towable
BR 'təʊəbl
AM 'toʊəbəl
towage
BR 'təʊɪdʒ
AM 'toʊɪdʒ
toward
BR tə'wɔːd, -z
AM 'tɔ(ə)rd, t(ə)'wɔ(ə)rd, twɔ(ə)rd, -z
towardness
BR tə'wɔːdnəs
AM 'tɔrdnəs, 't(ə)wɔrdnəs
towbar
BR 'təʊbɑː(r), -z
AM 'toʊˌbɑr, -z
towboat
BR 'təʊbəʊt, -s
AM 'toʊˌboʊt, -s
Towcester
BR 'təʊstə(r)
AM 'toʊstər
towel
BR 'taʊ(ə)l, -z, -ɪŋ, -d
AM 'taʊ(ə)l, -z, -ɪŋ, -d
toweling
BR 'taʊ(ə)lɪŋ, -z
AM 'taʊ(ə)lɪŋ, -z
towelling
BR 'taʊ(ə)lɪŋ, -z
AM 'taʊ(ə)lɪŋ, -z
tower[1]
noun 'something that tows'
BR 'təʊə(r), -z
AM 'toʊər, -z
tower[2]
noun 'type of building', verb
BR 'taʊə(r), -z, -ɪŋ, -d
AM 'taʊ(ə)r, -z, -ɪŋ, -d
Towers
BR 'taʊəz
AM 'taʊərs
towery
BR 'taʊəri
AM 'taʊəri
towhead
BR 'təʊhɛd, -z
AM 'toʊˌhɛd, -z
tow-headed
BR ˌtəʊ'hɛdɪd
AM 'toʊˌ(h)ɛdəd
towhee
BR 'təʊhiː
AM 'toʊˌhi
towline
BR 'təʊlʌɪn, -z
AM 'toʊˌlaɪn, -z
town
BR taʊn, -z
AM taʊn, -z
town clerk
BR ˌtaʊn 'klɑːk, -s
AM ˌtaʊn 'klərk, -s
town crier
BR ˌtaʊn 'krʌɪə(r), -z
AM ˈtaʊn 'kraɪər, -z
Towne
BR taʊn
AM taʊn
townee
BR 'taʊn|i, -ɪz
AM taʊ'ni, -z
Townes
BR taʊnz
AM taʊnz
town hall
BR ˌtaʊn 'hɔːl, -z
AM ˈtaʊn 'hɔl, ˈtaʊn 'hɑl, -z
townhouse
BR 'taʊnhaʊ|s, -zɪz
AM 'taʊnˌ(h)aʊ|s, -zəz
townie
BR 'taʊn|i, -ɪz
AM 'taʊni, -z
townish
BR 'taʊnɪʃ
AM 'taʊnɪʃ
townless
BR 'taʊnləs
AM 'taʊnləs
townlet
BR 'taʊnlɨt, -s
AM 'taʊnlət, -s
Townley
BR 'taʊnli
AM 'taʊnli
town-major
BR 'taʊnˌmeɪdʒə(r), -z
AM 'taʊnˌmeɪdʒər, -z
townscape
BR 'taʊnskeɪp, -s
AM 'taʊnˌskeɪp, -s
Townsend
BR 'taʊnzɛnd
AM 'taʊnzˌɛnd
townsfolk
BR 'taʊnzfəʊk
AM 'taʊnzˌfoʊk
Townshend
BR 'taʊnzɛnd
AM 'taʊnzˌɛnd
township
BR 'taʊnʃɪp, -s
AM 'taʊnˌʃɪp, -s
townsman
BR 'taʊnzmən
AM 'taʊnzmən
townsmen
BR 'taʊnzmən
AM 'taʊnzmən
townspeople
BR 'taʊnzˌpiːpl
AM 'taʊnzˌpipəl
Townsville
BR 'taʊnzvɪl
AM 'taʊnzˌvɪl
townswoman
BR 'taʊnzˌwʊmən
AM 'taʊnzˌwʊmən
townswomen
BR 'taʊnzˌwɪmɪn
AM 'taʊnzˌwɪmɪn
Townswomen's Guild
BR ˌtaʊnzwɪmɪnz 'gɪld
AM 'taʊnzˌwɪmɪnz ˌgɪld
townward
BR 'taʊnwəd, -z
AM 'taʊnwərd, -z
towny
BR 'taʊn|i, -ɪz
AM 'taʊni, -z

towpath
BR 'təʊpɑːθ, 'təʊpaθ, 'təʊpɑːðz 'təʊpaðz 'təʊpaθs
AM 'toʊ,pæ|θ, -ðz\-θs

towplane
BR 'təʊpleɪn, -z
AM 'toʊ,pleɪn, -z

towrope
BR 'təʊrəʊp, -s
AM 'toʊ,roʊp, -s

Towy
BR 'taʊi
AM 'taʊi

towy
BR 'təʊi
AM 'toʊi

Towyn
BR 'taʊɪn
AM 'taʊən

toxaemia
BR tɒk'siːmɪə(r)
AM tɑk'simiə

toxaemic
BR tɒk'siːmɪk
AM tɑk'simɪk

toxaphene
BR 'tɒksəfiːn
AM 'tɑksə,fin

toxemia
BR tɒk'siːmɪə(r)
AM tɑk'simiə

toxemic
BR tɒk'siːmɪk
AM tɑk'simɪk

toxic
BR 'tɒksɪk
AM 'tɑksɪk

toxically
BR 'tɒksɪkli
AM 'tɑksək(ə)li

toxicant
BR 'tɒksɪk(ə)nt, -s
AM 'tɑksəkənt, -s

toxicity
BR tɒk'sɪsɪti
AM tɑk'sɪsədi

toxicological
BR ,tɒksɪkə'lɒdʒɪkl
AM ,tɑksəkə'lɑdʒəkəl

toxicologist
BR ,tɒksɪ'kɒlədʒɪst, -s
AM ,tɑksə'kɑlədʒəst, -s

toxicology
BR ,tɒksɪ'kɒlədʒi
AM ,tɑksə'kɑlədʒi

toxicomania
BR ,tɒksɪkə'meɪnɪə(r)
AM ,tɑksəkoʊ'meɪniə

toxigenic
BR ,tɒksɪ'dʒɛnɪk
AM ,tɑksə'dʒɛnɪk

toxigenicity
BR ,tɒksɪdʒə'nɪsɪti
AM ,tɑksədʒə'nɪsɪdi

toxin
BR 'tɒksɪn, -z
AM 'tɑksən, -z

toxocara
BR ,tɒksə'kɑːrə(r), -z
AM ,tɑksə'kɛrə, -z

toxocariasis
BR ,tɒksəkə'rʌɪəsɪs
AM ,tɑksəkə'raɪəsəs

toxophilite
BR tɒk'sɒfəlʌɪt, tɒk'sɒfl̩ʌɪt, -s
AM tɑk'sɑfə,laɪt, -s

toxophily
BR tɒk'sɒfɪli, tɒk'sɒfl̩i
AM tɑk'sɑfəli

toxoplasmosis
BR ,tɒksəʊplaz'məʊsɪs
AM ,tɑksə,plæz'moʊsɪs

Toxteth
BR 'tɒkstɛθ, 'tɒkstɪθ
AM 'tɑkstəθ

toy
BR tɔɪ, -z, -ɪŋ, -d
AM tɔɪ, -z, -ɪŋ, -d

Toyah
BR 'tɔɪə(r)
AM 'tɔɪə

toyboy
BR 'tɔɪbɔɪ, -z
AM 'tɔɪ,bɔɪ, -z

toylike
BR 'tɔɪlʌɪk
AM 'tɔɪ,laɪk

toymaker
BR 'tɔɪ,meɪkə(r), -z
AM 'tɔɪ,meɪkər, -z

Toynbee
BR 'tɔɪnbi
AM 'tɔɪnbi

Toyota®
BR tɔɪ'əʊtə(r), -z
AM tɔɪ'oʊdə, -z

toyshop
BR 'tɔɪʃɒp, -s
AM 'tɔɪ,ʃɑp, -s

toystore
BR 'tɔɪstɔː(r), -z
AM 'tɔɪ,stɔ(ə)r, -z

toytown
BR 'tɔɪtaʊn
AM 'tɔɪ,taʊn

Tozer
BR 'təʊzə(r)
AM 'toʊzər

T-piece
BR 'tiːpiːs, -ɪz
AM 'ti,pis, -ɪz

trabeate
BR 'treɪbɪeɪt
AM 'treɪbi,eɪt, 'treɪbiɪt

trabeation
BR ,treɪbɪ'eɪʃn
AM ,treɪbi'eɪʃən

trabecula
BR trə'bɛkjʊlə(r), -z
AM trə'bɛkjələ, -z

trabeculae
BR trə'bɛkjʊliː
AM trə'bɛkjəli, trə'bɛkjə,laɪ

trabecular
BR trə'bɛkjʊlə(r)
AM trə'bɛkjələr

trabeculate
BR trə'bɛkjʊlət
AM trə'bɛkjələt

tracasserie
BR trə'kas(ə)r|i, -ɪz
AM trə'kɑsə'ri, -z

trace
BR treɪs, -ɪz, -ɪŋ, -t
AM treɪs, -z, -ɪŋ, -t

traceability
BR ,treɪsə'bɪlɪti
AM ,treɪsə'bɪlɪdi

traceable
BR 'treɪsəbl
AM 'treɪsəbəl

traceableness
BR 'treɪsəblnəs
AM 'treɪsəbəlnəs

trace-horse
BR 'treɪshɔːs, -ɪz
AM 'treɪs,(h)ɔ(ə)rs, -əz

traceless
BR 'treɪslɪs
AM 'treɪslɪs

tracer
BR 'treɪsə(r), -z
AM 'treɪsər, -z

traceried
BR 'treɪs(ə)rɪd
AM 'treɪs(ə)rid

tracery
BR 'treɪs(ə)r|i, -ɪz
AM 'treɪs(ə)ri, -z

Tracey
BR 'treɪsi
AM 'treɪsi

trachea
BR trə'kiːə(r), 'treɪkɪə(r), -z
AM 'treɪkiə, -z

tracheae
BR trə'kiːiː, 'treɪkɪiː
AM 'treɪki,i, 'treɪki,aɪ

tracheal
BR 'treɪkɪəl, trə'kiːəl
AM trə'kiəl

tracheate
BR 'treɪkɪeɪt, trə'kiːeɪt
AM 'treɪkiɪt, 'treɪki,eɪt

tracheostomy
BR ,trakɪ'ɒstəm|i, -ɪz
AM ,treɪki'ɑstəmi, -z

tracheotomy
BR ,trakɪ'ɒtəm|i, -ɪz
AM ,treɪki'ɑdəmi, -z

trachoma
BR trə'kəʊmə(r)
AM trə'koʊmə

trachomatous
BR trə'kəʊmətəs
AM trə'koʊmədəs

trachyte
BR 'treɪkʌɪt, 'trakʌɪt, -s
AM 'treɪ,kaɪt, 'træ,kaɪt, -s

trachytic
BR trə'kɪtɪk
AM trə'kɪdɪk

tracing
BR 'treɪsɪŋ, -z
AM 'treɪsɪŋ, -z

track
BR trak, -s, -ɪŋ, -t
AM træk, -s, -ɪŋ, -t

trackage
BR 'trakɪdʒ
AM 'trækɪdʒ

track-and-field
BR ,trak(ə)n(d)'fiːld
AM ,trækən'fild

trackbed
BR 'trakbɛd, -z
AM 'træk,bɛd, -z

tracker
BR 'trakə(r), -z
AM 'trækər, -z

tracking
BR 'trakɪŋ, -z
AM 'trækɪŋ, -z

tracklayer
BR 'trak,leɪə(r), -z
AM 'træk,leɪər, -z

tracklaying
BR 'trak,leɪɪŋ
AM 'træk,leɪɪŋ

tracklement
BR 'traklm(ə)nt, -s
AM 'trækəlmənt, -s

trackless
BR 'trakləs
AM 'trækləs

tracklessness
BR 'trakləsnəs
AM 'trækləsnəs

trackman
BR 'trakmən, 'trakman
AM 'trækmən, 'træk,mæn

trackmen
BR 'trakmən, 'trakmɛn
AM 'trækmən, 'træk,mɛn

trackside
BR 'traksʌɪd
AM 'træk,saɪd

tracksuit
BR 'traks(j)uːt, -s, -ɪd
AM 'træk,su|t, -ts, -dəd

trackway
BR 'trakweɪ, -z
AM 'træk,weɪ, -z

tract
BR trakt, -s
AM træk|(t), -(t)s

tractability
BR ˌtraktəˈbɪlɪti
AM ˌtræktəˈbɪlɪdi

tractable
BR ˈtraktəbl
AM ˈtræktəbəl

tractableness
BR ˈtraktəblnəs
AM ˈtræktəbəlnəs

tractably
BR ˈtraktəbli
AM ˈtræktəbli

Tractarian
BR trakˈtɛːrɪən, -z
AM trækˈtɛriən, -z

tractarian
BR trakˈtɛːrɪən, -z
AM trækˈtɛriən, -z

Tractarianism
BR trakˈtɛːrɪənɪz(ə)m
AM trækˈtɛriəˌnɪzəm

tractate
BR ˈtrakteɪt, -s
AM ˈtrækˌteɪt, -s

traction
BR ˈtrakʃn
AM ˈtrækʃən

tractional
BR ˈtrakʃn̩(ə)l, ˈtrakʃən(ə)l
AM ˈtrækʃ(ə)nəl

tractive
BR ˈtraktɪv
AM ˈtræktɪv

tractor
BR ˈtraktə(r), -z
AM ˈtræktər, -z

tractorfeed
BR ˈtraktəfiːd
AM ˈtræktərˌfid

Tracy
BR ˈtreɪsi
AM ˈtreɪsi

trad
BR trad
AM træd

tradable
BR ˈtreɪdəbl
AM ˈtreɪdəbəl

trade
BR treɪd, -z, -ɪŋ, -ɪd
AM treɪd, -z, -ɪŋ, -ɪd

tradeable
BR ˈtreɪdəbl
AM ˈtreɪdəbəl

trademark
BR ˈtreɪdmɑːk, -s
AM ˈtreɪdˌmɑrk, -s

trader
BR ˈtreɪdə(r), -z
AM ˈtreɪdər, -z

tradescantia
BR ˌtradɪˈskantɪə(*r*)
AM ˌtrædəˈskæn(t)ʃ(i)ə, ˌtrædəˈskæn(t)iə

tradesman
BR ˈtreɪdzmən
AM ˈtreɪdzmən

tradesmen
BR ˈtreɪdzmən
AM ˈtreɪdzmən

tradespeople
BR ˈtreɪdzˌpiːpl
AM ˈtreɪdzˌpipəl

trades union
BR ˌtreɪdz ˈjuːnɪən, -z
AM ˈtreɪdz ˌjunjən, -z

trades unionism
BR ˌtreɪdz ˈjuːnɪənɪz(ə)m
AM ˈˌtreɪdz ˈjunjəˌnɪzəm

trades unionist
BR ˌtreɪdz ˈjuːnɪənɪst, -s
AM ˈˌtreɪdz ˈjunjənəst, -s

trade union
BR ˌtreɪd ˈjuːnɪən, -z
AM ˈtreɪd ˌjunjən, -z

trade unionism
BR ˌtreɪd ˈjuːnɪənɪz(ə)m
AM ˈˌtreɪd ˈjunjəˌnɪzəm

trade unionist
BR ˌtreɪd ˈjuːnɪənɪst, -s
AM ˈˌtreɪdˈjunjənəst, -s

trade-weighted
BR ˈtreɪdˌweɪtɪd
AM ˈtreɪdˌweɪdɪd

tradewind
BR ˈtreɪdwɪnd, -z
AM ˈtreɪdˌwɪnd, -z

tradition
BR trəˈdɪʃn, -z
AM trəˈdɪʃən, -z

traditional
BR trəˈdɪʃn̩(ə)l, trəˈdɪʃən(ə)l
AM trəˈdɪʃ(ə)nəl

traditionalism
BR trəˈdɪʃn̩əlɪz(ə)m, trəˈdɪʃn̩lɪz(ə)m, trəˈdɪʃənl̩ɪz(ə)m, trəˈdɪʃ(ə)nəlɪz(ə)m
AM trəˈdɪʃənlˌɪzəm, trəˈdɪʃnəˌlɪzəm

traditionalist
BR trəˈdɪʃn̩əlɪst, trəˈdɪʃn̩l̩ɪst, trəˈdɪʃənl̩ɪst, trəˈdɪʃ(ə)nəlɪst, -s
AM trəˈdɪʃənləst, trəˈdɪʃnələst, -s

traditionalistic
BR trəˌdɪʃn̩əˈlɪstɪk, trəˌdɪʃn̩lˈɪstɪk, trəˌdɪʃənlˈɪstɪk, trəˌdɪʃ(ə)nəˈlɪstɪk
AM trəˌdɪʃənlˈɪstɪk, trəˌdɪʃnəˈlɪstɪk

traditionally
BR trəˈdɪʃn̩əli, trəˈdɪʃn̩l̩i, trəˈdɪʃənl̩i, trəˈdɪʃ(ə)nəli
AM trəˈdɪʃ(ə)nəli

traditionary
BR trəˈdɪʃn̩(ə)ri
AM trəˈdɪʃəˌnɛri

traditionist
BR trəˈdɪʃn̩ɪst, trəˈdɪʃənɪst, -s
AM trəˈdɪʃənəst, -s

traditionless
BR trəˈdɪʃnləs
AM trəˈdɪʃənləs

traditor
BR ˈtradɪtə(r), -z
AM ˈtrædədər, -z

traditores
BR ˌtradɪˈtɔːriːz
AM ˌtrædəˈtɔˌriz

traduce
BR trəˈdjuːs, trəˈdʒuːs, -ɪz, -ɪŋ, -t
AM trəˈd(j)us, -əz, -ɪŋ, -t

traducement
BR trəˈdjuːsm(ə)nt, trəˈdʒuːsm(ə)nt
AM trəˈd(j)usmənt

traducer
BR trəˈdjuːsə(r), trəˈdʒuːsə(r), -z
AM trəˈd(j)usər, -z

traducian
BR trəˈdjuːsɪən, trəˈdjuːʃn, trəˈdʒuːsɪən, trəˈdʒuːʃn, -z
AM trəˈd(j)uʃən, -z

traducianism
BR trəˈdjuːsɪənɪz(ə)m, trəˈdjuːʃn̩ɪz(ə)m, trəˈdʒuːsɪənɪz(ə)m, trəˈdʒuːʃn̩ɪz(ə)m
AM trəˈd(j)uʃəˌnɪzəm

traducianist
BR trəˈdjuːsɪənɪst, trəˈdjuːʃn̩ɪst, trəˈdʒuːsɪənɪst, trəˈdʒuːʃn̩ɪst, -s
AM trəˈd(j)uʃənəst, -s

Trafalgar
BR trəˈfalgə(r), ˌtraflˈgɑː(r)
AM trəˈfælgər, trəˈfɔlgər, trəˈfɑlgər

traffic
BR ˈtraf|ɪk, -ɪks, -ɪkɪŋ, -ɪkt
AM ˈtræfɪk, -s, -ɪŋ, -t

trafficator
BR ˈtrafɪkeɪtə(r), -z
AM ˈtræfəˌkeɪdər, -z

trafficker
BR ˈtrafɪkə(r), -z
AM ˈtræfɪkər, -z

trafficless
BR ˈtrafɪklɪs
AM ˈtræfɪkləs

Trafford
BR ˈtrafəd
AM ˈtræfərd

tragacanth
BR ˈtragəkanθ
AM ˈtrægəˌkænθ

tragedian
BR trəˈdʒiːdɪən, -z
AM trəˈdʒidiən, -z

tragedienne
BR trəˌdʒiːdɪˈɛn, -z
AM trəˌdʒidiˈɛn, -z

tragedy
BR ˈtradʒɪd|i, -ɪz
AM ˈtrædʒədi, -z

tragi
BR ˈtreɪgʌɪ, ˈtreɪdʒʌɪ
AM ˈtreɪgaɪ, ˈtreɪdʒaɪ

tragic
BR ˈtradʒɪk
AM ˈtrædʒɪk

tragical
BR ˈtradʒɪkl
AM ˈtrædʒəkəl

tragically
BR ˈtradʒɪkli
AM ˈtrædʒək(ə)li

tragicomedy
BR ˌtradʒɪˈkɒmɪd|i, -ɪz
AM ˈˌtrædʒəˈkɑmədi, -z

tragicomic
BR ˌtradʒɪˈkɒmɪk
AM ˈˌtrædʒəˈkɑmɪk

tragicomical
BR ˌtradʒɪˈkɒmɪkl
AM ˈˌtrædʒəˈkɑməkəl

tragicomically
BR ˌtradʒɪˈkɒmɪkli
AM ˈˌtrædʒəˈkɑmək(ə)li

tragopan
BR ˈtragəpan, -z
AM ˈtrægəˌpæn, -z

tragus
BR ˈtreɪgəs
AM ˈtreɪgəs

Traherne
BR trəˈhəːn
AM trəˈhərn

trahison des clercs
BR ˌtrɑːɪˌzɒ̃ deɪ ˈklɛː(r)
AM treɪˌzɑn deɪ ˈklərk

trail
BR treɪl, -z, -ɪŋ, -d
AM treɪl, -z, -ɪŋ, -d

trailblazer
BR ˈtreɪlˌbleɪzə(r), -z
AM ˈtreɪlˌbleɪzər, -z

trailblazing
BR ˈtreɪlˌbleɪzɪŋ
AM ˈtreɪlˌbleɪzɪŋ

trailer
BR ˈtreɪlə(r), -z, -ɪŋ, -d
AM ˈtreɪlər, -z, -ɪŋ, -d

train
BR treɪn, -z, -ɪŋ, -d
AM treɪn, -z, -ɪŋ, -d

trainability
BR ˌtreɪnəˈbɪlɪti
AM ˌtreɪnəˈbɪlɨdi

trainable
BR ˈtreɪnəbl
AM ˈtreɪnəbəl

trainband
BR ˈtreɪnband, -z
AM ˈtreɪnˌbænd, -z

trainee
BR ˌtreɪˈniː, -z
AM ˌtreɪˈni, -z

traineeship
BR ˌtreɪˈniːʃɪp, -s
AM ˌtreɪˈniˌʃɪp, -s

trainer
BR ˈtreɪnə(r), -z
AM ˈtreɪnər, -z

trainless
BR ˈtreɪnlɪs
AM ˈtreɪnlɪs

trainload
BR ˈtreɪnləʊd, -z
AM ˈtreɪnˌloʊd, -z

trainman
BR ˈtreɪnman
AM ˈtreɪnˌmæn

trainmen
BR ˈtreɪnmɛn
AM ˈtreɪnˌmɛn

train-mile
BR ˈtreɪnmʌɪl, -z
AM ˈtreɪnˌmaɪl, -z

trainsick
BR ˈtreɪnsɪk
AM ˈtreɪnˌsɪk

trainsickness
BR ˈtreɪnˌsɪknɪs
AM ˈtreɪnˌsɪknɪs

traipse
BR treɪps, -ɪz, -ɪŋ, -t
AM treɪps, -ɪz, -ɪŋ, -t

trait
BR treɪ|(t), -z\-ts
AM treɪt, -s

traitor
BR ˈtreɪtə(r), -z
AM ˈtreɪdər, -z

traitorous
BR ˈtreɪt(ə)rəs
AM ˈtreɪdərəs, ˈtreɪtrəs

traitorously
BR ˈtreɪt(ə)rəsli
AM ˈtreɪdərəsli, ˈtreɪtrəsli

traitorousness
BR ˈtreɪt(ə)rəsnəs
AM ˈtreɪdərəsnəs, ˈtreɪtrəsnəs

traitress
BR ˈtreɪtrɪs, -ɪz
AM ˈtreɪdərəs, ˈtreɪtrɪs, -ɪz

Trajan
BR ˈtreɪdʒ(ə)n
AM ˈtreɪdʒən

trajectory
BR trəˈdʒɛkt(ə)r|i, -ɪz
AM trəˈdʒɛkt(ə)ri, -z

tra-la
BR trɑːˈlɑː(r), trəˈlɑː(r)
AM trəˈlɑ, ˈtrɑˈlɑ

Tralee
BR trəˈliː
AM trəˈli

tram
BR tram, -z
AM træm, -z

tramcar
BR ˈtramkɑː(r), -z
AM ˈtræmˌkɑr, -z

Traminer
BR trəˈmiːnə(r)
AM trəˈminər

tramline
BR ˈtramlʌɪn, -z
AM ˈtræmˌlaɪn, -z

trammel
BR ˈtram|l, -lz, -l̩ɪŋ\-əlɪŋ, -ld
AM ˈtræm|əl, -əlz, -(ə)lɪŋ, -əld

trammie
BR ˈtram|i, -ɪz
AM ˈtræmi, -z

tramontana
BR ˌtramɒnˈtɑːnə(r), -z
AM ˌtrɑmənˈtɑnə, -z

tramontane
BR trəˈmɒnteɪn, -z
AM trəˈmɑnˌteɪn, -z

tramp
BR tram|p, -ps, -pɪŋ, -(p)t
AM træmp, -s, -ɪŋ, -t

tramper
BR ˈtrampə(r), -z
AM ˈtræmpər, -z

trampish
BR ˈtrampɪʃ
AM ˈtræmpɪʃ

trample
BR ˈtramp|l, -lz, -l̩ɪŋ\-lɪŋ, -ld
AM ˈtræmp|əl, -əlz, -(ə)lɪŋ, -əld

trampler
BR ˈtramplə(r), ˈtrampl̩ə(r), -z
AM ˈtræmp(ə)lər, -z

trampoline
BR ˈtrampəliːn, ˌtrampəˈliːn, -z, -ɪŋ
AM ¦træmpəˈlin, -z, -ɪŋ

trampolinist
BR ˈtrampəliːnɪst, ˌtrampəˈliːnɪst, -s
AM ¦træmpəˈlinɪst, -s

tramway
BR ˈtramweɪ, -z
AM ˈtræmˌweɪ, -z

trance
BR trɑːns, trans, -ɪz
AM træns, -əz

tranche
BR trɑːn(t)ʃ, tran(t)ʃ, -ɪz
AM træn(t)ʃ, -əz

Tranmere
BR ˈtranmɪə(r)
AM ˈtrænˌmɪ(ə)r

tranny
BR ˈtran|i, -ɪz
AM ˈtræni, -z

tranquil
BR ˈtraŋkw(ɪ)l
AM ˈtræŋkwəl, ˈtrænkwəl

tranquilisation
BR ˌtraŋkwɪlʌɪˈzeɪʃn
AM ˌtræŋkwələˈzeɪʃən, ˌtrænkwələˈzeɪʃən, ˌtræŋkwəˌlaɪˈzeɪʃən, ˌtrænkwəˌlaɪˈzeɪʃən

tranquilise
BR ˈtraŋkwɪlʌɪz, -ɪz, -ɪŋ, -d
AM ˈtræŋkwəˌlaɪz, ˈtrænkwəˌlaɪz, -ɪz, -ɪŋ, -d

tranquiliser
BR ˈtraŋkwɪlʌɪzə(r), -z
AM ˈtræŋkwəˌlaɪzər, ˈtrænkwəˌlaɪzər, -z

tranquility
BR traŋˈkwɪlɪti
AM træŋˈkwɪlɨdi, trænˈkwɪlɨdi

tranquilization
BR ˌtraŋkwɪlʌɪˈzeɪʃn
AM ˌtræŋkwələˈzeɪʃən, ˌtrænkwələˈzeɪʃən, ˌtræŋkwəˌlaɪˈzeɪʃən, ˌtrænkwəˌlaɪˈzeɪʃən

tranquilize
BR ˈtraŋkwɪlʌɪz, -ɪz, -ɪŋ, -d
AM ˈtræŋkwəˌlaɪz, ˈtrænkwəˌlaɪz, -ɪz, -ɪŋ, -d

tranquilizer
BR ˈtraŋkwɪlʌɪzə(r), -z
AM ˈtræŋkwəˌlaɪzər, ˈtrænkwəˌlaɪzər, -z

tranquillisation
BR ˌtraŋkwɪlʌɪˈzeɪʃn
AM ˌtræŋkwələˈzeɪʃən, ˌtrænkwələˈzeɪʃən, ˌtræŋkwəˌlaɪˈzeɪʃən, ˌtrænkwəˌlaɪˈzeɪʃən

tranquillise
BR ˈtraŋkwɪlʌɪz, -ɪz, -ɪŋ, -d
AM ˈtræŋkwəˌlaɪz, ˈtrænkwəˌlaɪz, -ɪz, -ɪŋ, -d

tranquilliser
BR ˈtraŋkwɪlʌɪzə(r), -z
AM ˈtræŋkwəˌlaɪzər, ˈtrænkwəˌlaɪzər, -z

tranquillity
BR traŋˈkwɪlɪti
AM træŋˈkwɪlədi, trænˈkwɪlədi

tranquillization
BR ˌtraŋkwɪlʌɪˈzeɪʃn
AM ˌtræŋkwələˈzeɪʃən, ˌtrænkwələˈzeɪʃən, ˌtræŋkwəˌlaɪˈzeɪʃən, ˌtrænkwəˌlaɪˈzeɪʃən

tranquillize
BR ˈtraŋkwɪlʌɪz, -ɪz, -ɪŋ, -d
AM ˈtræŋkwəˌlaɪz, ˈtrænkwəˌlaɪz, -ɪz, -ɪŋ, -d

tranquillizer
BR ˈtraŋkwɪlʌɪzə(r), -z
AM ˈtræŋkwəˌlaɪzər, ˈtrænkwəˌlaɪzər, -z

tranquilly
BR ˈtraŋkwɪli, ˈtraŋkwl̩i
AM ˈtræŋkwəli, ˈtrænkwəli

transact
BR tranˈzakt, trɑːnˈzakt, tranˈsakt, trɑːnˈsakt, -s, -ɪŋ, -ɪd
AM trænˈzæk|(t), træn(t)ˈsæk|(t), -(t)s, -tɪŋ, -təd

transaction
BR tranˈzakʃn, trɑːnˈzakʃn, tranˈsakʃn, trɑːnˈsakʃn, -z
AM trænˈzækʃən, træn(t)ˈsækʃən, -z

transactional
BR tranˈzakʃn̩(ə)l, trɑːnˈzakʃn̩(ə)l, tranˈsakʃn̩(ə)l, trɑːnˈsakʃn̩(ə)l
AM trænˈzækʃ(ə)nəl, træn(t)ˈsækʃ(ə)nəl

transactionally
BR tranˈzakʃn̩əli, tranˈzakʃ(ə)nəli, trɑːnˈzakʃn̩əli, trɑːnˈzakʃ(ə)nəli, tranˈsakʃn̩əli, tranˈsakʃ(ə)nəli, trɑːnˈsakʃn̩əli, trɑːnˈsakʃ(ə)nəli
AM trænˈzækʃ(ə)nəli, træn(t)ˈsækʃ(ə)nəli

transactor
BR tranˈzaktə(r), trɑːnˈzaktə(r), tranˈsaktə(r), trɑːnˈsaktə(r), -z
AM ˌtrænˈzæktər, ˌtræn(t)ˈsæktər, -z

transalpine
BR (ˌ)tranzˈalpʌɪn, (ˌ)trɑːnzˈalpʌɪn, (ˌ)transˈalpʌɪn, (ˌ)trɑːnsˈalpʌɪn
AM ˌtrænˈzælpaɪn, ˌtræn(t)ˈsælpaɪn

transatlantic
BR ˌtranzətˈlantɪk, ˌtrɑːnzətˈlantɪk, ˌtransətˈlantɪk, ˌtrɑːnsətˈlantɪk
AM ˌtrænzətˈlæn(t)ɪk, ˌtræn(t)sətˈlæn(t)ɪk

transaxle
BR ˈtranzˌaksl, ˈtrɑːnzˌaksl, ˈtransˌaksl, ˈtrɑːnsˌaksl, -z
AM trænzˈæksəl, træn(t)sˈæksəl, -z

Transcaucasia
BR ˌtranzkɔːˈkeɪzɪə(r), ˌtranzkɔːˈkeɪʒə(r), ˌtrɑːnzkɔːˈkeɪzɪə(r), ˌtrɑːnzkɔːˈkeɪʒə(r), ˌtranskɔːˈkeɪzɪə(r), ˌtranskɔːˈkeɪʒə(r), ˌtrɑːnskɔːˈkeɪzɪə(r), ˌtrɑːnskɔːˈkeɪʒə(r)
AM ˌtrænzˌkɔˈkeɪʒə, ˌtræn(t)sˌkɔˈkeɪʒə, ˌtrænzˌkɑˈkeɪʒə, ˌtræn(t)sˌkɑˈkeɪʒə

Transcaucasian
BR ˌtranzkɔːˈkeɪzɪən, ˌtranzkɔːˈkeɪʒ(ə)n, ˌtrɑːnzkɔːˈkeɪzɪən, ˌtrɑːnzkɔːˈkeɪʒ(ə)n, ˌtranskɔːˈkeɪzɪən, ˌtranskɔːˈkeɪʒ(ə)n, ˌtrɑːnskɔːˈkeɪzɪən, ˌtrɑːnskɔːˈkeɪʒ(ə)n
AM ˌtrænzˌkɔˈkeɪʒən, ˌtræn(t)sˌkɔˈkeɪʒən, ˌtrænzˌkɑˈkeɪʒən, ˌtræn(t)sˌkɑˈkeɪʒən

transceiver
BR tranˈsiːvə(r), trɑːnˈsiːvə(r), -z
AM trænzˈsivər, træn(t)ˈsivər, -z

transcend
BR tranˈsɛnd, trɑːnˈsɛnd, -z, -ɪŋ, -ɨd
AM træn(t)ˈsɛnd, -z, -ɪŋ, -ɨd

transcendence
BR tranˈsɛnd(ə)ns, trɑːnˈsɛnd(ə)ns
AM træn(t)ˈsɛndəns

transcendency
BR tranˈsɛnd(ə)nsi, trɑːnˈsɛnd(ə)nsi
AM træn(t)ˈsɛndnsi

transcendent
BR tranˈsɛnd(ə)nt, trɑːnˈsɛnd(ə)nt
AM træn(t)ˈsɛndənt

transcendental
BR ˌtrans(ɛ)nˈdɛntl, ˌtrɑːns(ɛ)nˈdɛntl
AM ˌtrænˌ(t)sɛnˈdɛn(t)l, ˌtræn(t)snˈdɛn(t)l

transcendentalise
BR ˌtrans(ɛ)nˈdɛntl̩ʌɪz, ˌtrɑːns(ɛ)nˈdɛntl̩ʌɪz, -ɪz, -ɪŋ, -d
AM ˌtrænˌ(t)sɛnˈdɛn(t)l-ˌaɪz, ˌtræn(t)snˈdɛn(t)lˌaɪz, -ɪz, -ɪŋ, -d

transcendentalism¹
BR ˌtrans(ɛ)nˈdɛntl̩ɪz-(ə)m, ˌtrɑːns(ɛ)nˈdɛntl̩ɪz(ə)m
AM ˌtræn(t)ˌsɛnˈdɛn(t)l-ˌɪzəm, ˌtræn(t)snˈdɛn(t)lˌɪzəm

transcendentalism²
BR ˌtrans(ɛ)nˈdɛntl̩ɪz-(ə)m, ˌtrɑːns(ɛ)nˈdɛntl̩ɪz(ə)m
AM ˌtræn(t)ˌsɛnˈdɛn(t)l-ˌɪzəm, ˌtræn(t)snˈdɛn(t)lˌɪzəm

transcendentalist
BR ˌtrans(ɛ)nˈdɛntl̩ɪst, ˌtrɑːns(ɛ)nˈdɛntl̩ɪst, -s
AM ˌtræn(t)ˌsɛnˈdɛn(t)l-əst, ˌtræn(t)snˈdɛn(t)ləst, -s

transcendentalize
BR ˌtrans(ɛ)nˈdɛntl̩ʌɪz, ˌtrɑːns(ɛ)nˈdɛntl̩ʌɪz, -ɪz, -ɪŋ, -d
AM ˌtrænˌ(t)sɛnˈdɛn(t)l-ˌaɪz, ˌtræn(t)snˈdɛn(t)lˌaɪz, -ɪz, -ɪŋ, -d

transcendentally
BR ˌtrans(ɛ)nˈdɛntl̩i, ˌtrɑːns(ɛ)nˈdɛntl̩i
AM ˌtrænˌ(t)sɛnˈdɛn(t)li, træn(t)snˈdɛn(t)li

transcendently
BR tranˈsɛnd(ə)ntli, trɑːnˈsɛnd(ə)ntli
AM træn(t)ˈsɛndən(t)li

transcode
BR ˌtranzˈkəʊd, ˌtrɑːnzˈkəʊd, ˌtransˈkəʊd, ˌtrɑːnsˈkəʊd, -z, -ɪŋ, -ɨd
AM ˌtrænzˈkoʊd, ˌtræn(t)sˈkoʊd, -z, -ɪŋ, -əd

transcontinental
BR ˌtranzkɒntɪˈnɛntl, ˌtrɑːnzkɒntɪˈnɛntl, ˌtranskɒntɪˈnɛntl, ˌtrɑːnskɒntɪˈnɛntl
AM ¦trænzˌkɑntn¦ɛn(t)l, ¦træn(t)ˌskɑntn¦ɛn(t)l

transcontinentally
BR ˌtranzkɒntɪˈnɛntl̩i, ˌtrɑːnzkɒntɪˈnɛntl̩i, ˌtranskɒntɪˈnɛntl̩i, ˌtrɑːnskɒntɪˈnɛntl̩i
AM ¦trænzˌkɑntn¦ɛn(t)li, ¦træn(t)ˌskɑntn¦ɛn(t)li

transcribe
BR tranˈskrʌɪb, trɑːnˈskrʌɪb, -z, -ɪŋ, -d
AM træn(t)ˈskraɪb, -z, -ɪŋ, -d

transcriber
BR tranˈskrʌɪbə(r), trɑːnˈskrʌɪbə(r), -z
AM træn(t)ˈskraɪbər, -z

transcript
BR ˈtranskrɪpt, ˈtrɑːnskrɪpt, -s
AM ˈtrænzˌkrɪpt, ˈtræn(t)ˌskrɪpt, -s

transcription
BR tranˈskrɪpʃn, trɑːnˈskrɪpʃn, -z
AM træn(t)ˈskrɪpʃən, -z

transcriptional
BR tranˈskrɪpʃn̩(ə)l, trɑːnˈskrɪpʃn̩(ə)l
AM træn(t)ˈskrɪpʃ(ə)nəl

transcriptive
BR tranˈskrɪptɪv, trɑːnˈskrɪptɪv
AM ˈtrænzˌkrɪptɪv, ˈtræn(t)ˌskrɪptɪv

transcutaneous
BR ˌtranzkjʊˈteɪnɪəs, ˌtrɑːnzkjʊˈteɪnɪəs, ˌtranskjʊˈteɪnɪəs, ˌtrɑːnskjʊˈteɪnɪəs
AM ˌtræn(t)skjuˈteɪniəs, ˌtrænzkjuˈteɪniəs

transduce
BR tranzˈdjuːs, tranzˈdʒuːs, trɑːnzˈdjuːs, trɑːnzˈdʒuːs, transˈdjuːs, transˈdʒuːs, trɑːnsˈdjuːs, trɑːnsˈdʒuːs, -ɪz, -ɪŋ, -t
AM trænzˈd(j)us, træn(t)sˈd(j)us, -əz, -ɪŋ, -t

transducer
BR tranzˈdjuːsə(r), tranzˈdʒuːsə(r), trɑːnzˈdjuːsə(r), trɑːnzˈdʒuːsə(r), transˈdjuːsə(r), transˈdʒuːsə(r), trɑːnsˈdjuːsə(r), trɑːnsˈdʒuːsə(r), -z
AM trænzˈd(j)usər, træn(t)sˈd(j)usər, -z

transduction
BR ˌtranzˈdʌkʃn, ˌtrɑːnzˈdʌkʃn, ˌtransˈdʌkʃn, ˌtrɑːnsˈdʌkʃn
AM ˌtrænzˈdəkʃən, ˌtræn(t)sˈdəkʃən

transect
BR tranˈsɛkt, trɑːnˈsɛkt, -s, -ɪŋ, -ɨd
AM træn(t)ˈsɛk|(t), -(t)s, -tɪŋ, -təd

transection
BR tranˈsɛkʃn, trɑːnˈsɛkʃn, -z
AM træn(t)ˈsɛkʃən, -z

transept
BR ˈtransɛpt, ˈtrɑːnsɛpt, -s
AM ˈtræn(t)ˌsɛpt, -s

transeptal
BR tranˈsɛptl, trɑːnˈsɛptl
AM ˈtræn(t)ˌsɛptl

transexual
BR tran(s)ˈsɛkʃʊəl, tran(s)ˈsɛkʃ(ʉ)l, tran(s)ˈsɛksjʊ(ə)l, trɑːn(s)ˈsɛkʃʊəl, trɑːn(s)ˈsɛkʃ(ʉ)l, trɑːn(s)ˈsɛksjʊ(ə)l, tranzˈsɛkʃʊəl, tranzˈsɛkʃ(ʉ)l, tranzˈsɛksjʊ(ə)l, trɑːnzˈsɛkʃʊəl, trɑːnzˈsɛkʃ(ʉ)l, trɑːnzˈsɛksjʊ(ə)l, -z
AM ˌtræn(t)ˈsɛkʃ(əw)əl, -z

transexualism
BR ˌtran(z)ˈsɛkʃʊəl-ɪz(ə)m, ˌtran(z)ˈsɛkʃʉlɪz(ə)m, tran(z)ˈsɛkʃl̩ɪz(ə)m, ˌtran(z)ˈsɛksjʊ(ə)l-ɪz(ə)m, ˌtrɑːn(z)ˈsɛkʃʊəlɪz(ə)m, ˌtrɑːn(z)ˈsɛkʃʉlɪz(ə)m, trɑːn(z)ˈsɛkʃl̩ɪz(ə)m, ˌtrɑːn(z)ˈsɛksjʊ(ə)lɪz-(ə)m
AM ˌtræn(t)ˈsɛkʃ(əw)ə-ˌlɪzəm

transfer¹
noun
BR ˈtransfəː(r), ˈtrɑːnsfəː(r), ˈtranzfəː(r), ˈtrɑːnzfəː(r), -z
AM ˈtræn(t)sfər, -z

transfer²
verb
BR transˈfəː(r), trɑːnsˈfəː(r), ˈtransfəː(r), ˈtrɑːnsfəː(r), tranzˈfəː(r), trɑːnzˈfəː(r), ˈtranzfəː(r), ˈtrɑːnzfəː(r), -z, -ɪŋ, -d
AM træn(t)sˈfər, ˈtræn(t)sfər, -z, -ɪŋ, -d

transferability
BR transˌfəːrəˈbɪlɪti, ˌtransf(ə)rəˈbɪlɪti, trɑːnsˌfəːrəˈbɪlɪti,

ˌtrɑːnsf(ə)rəˈbɪlɨti, tranzˌfəːrəˈbɪlɨti, ˌtranzf(ə)rəˈbɪlɨti, trɑːnzˌfəːrəˈbɪlɨti, ˌtrɑːnzf(ə)rəˈbɪlɨti
AM ˌtræn(t)sfərəˈbɪlɨdi

transferable
BR transˈfəːrəbl, trɑːnsˈfəːrəbl, ˈtransf(ə)rəbl, ˈtrɑːnsf(ə)rəbl, tranzˈfəːrəbl, trɑːnzˈfəːrəbl, ˈtranzf(ə)rəbl, ˈtrɑːnzf(ə)rəbl
AM trænˈ(t)sˈfərəbəl, ˈtræn(t)sfərəbəl

transfer-book
BR ˈtransfəːbʊk, ˈtrɑːnsfəːbʊk, ˈtranzfəːbʊk, ˈtrɑːnzfəːbʊk, -s
AM ˈtræn(t)sfərˌbʊk, -s

transferee
BR ˌtransfəːˈriː, ˌtrɑːnsfəːˈriː, ˌtranzfəːˈriː, ˌtrɑːnzfəːˈriː, -z
AM ˌtræn(t)sfəˈri, -z

transference
BR ˈtransf(ə)rəns, ˈtransf(ə)rn̩s, ˈtrɑːnsf(ə)rəns, ˈtrɑːnsf(ə)rn̩s, ˈtranzf(ə)rəns, ˈtranzf(ə)rn̩s, ˈtrɑːnzf(ə)rəns, ˈtrɑːnzf(ə)rn̩s, -ɨz
AM trænˈ(t)sˈfərəns, ˈtræn(t)sfərəns, ˈtræn(t)sfrəns, -ɨz

transferor
BR transˈfəːrə(r), trɑːnsˈfəːrə(r), ˈtransfəːrə(r), ˈtrɑːnsfəːrə(r), tranzˈfəːrə(r), trɑːnzˈfəːrə(r), ˈtranzfəːrə(r), ˈtrɑːnzfəːrə(r), -z
AM træn(t)sˈfərər, ˈtræn(t)sfərər, -z

transfer-paper
BR ˈtransfəːˌpeɪpə(r), ˈtrɑːnsfəːˌpeɪpə(r), ˈtranzfəːˌpeɪpə(r), ˈtrɑːnzfəːˌpeɪpə(r), -z
AM ˈtræn(t)sfərˌpeɪpər, -z

transferral
BR transˈfəːrəl, trɑːnsˈfəːrəl, transˈfəːrl̩, trɑːnsˈfəːrl̩, tranzˈfəːrəl, trɑːnzˈfəːrəl, tranzˈfəːrl̩, trɑːnzˈfəːrl̩, -z
AM træn(t)sˈfərəl, ˈtræn(t)sfərəl, -z

transferrer
BR transˈfəːrə(r), trɑːnsˈfəːrə(r), ˈtransfəːrə(r), ˈtrɑːnsfəːrə(r), tranzˈfəːrə(r), trɑːnzˈfəːrə(r), ˈtranzfəːrə(r), ˈtrɑːnzfəːrə(r), -z
AM træn(t)sˈfərər, ˈtræn(t)sfərər, -z

transferrin
BR tranzˈfɛrɪn, transˈfɛrɪn, trɑːnzˈfɛrɪn, trɑːnsˈfɛrɪn
AM træn(t)sˈfɛrən

transfer RNA
BR ˈtransfəːr ˌɑːrɛnˈeɪ, ˌtrɑːnsfəːr +, ˈtranzfəː(r) +, ˈtrɑːnzfəː(r) +
AM ˈtræn(t)sfər ˌɑrˌɛnˈeɪ

transfiguration
BR ˌtransfɪgəˈreɪʃn, ˌtrɑːnsfɪgəˈreɪʃn, transˌfɪgəˈreɪʃn, trɑːnsˌfɪgəˈreɪʃn, ˌtranzfɪgəˈreɪʃn, ˌtrɑːnzfɪgəˈreɪʃn, tranzˌfɪgəˈreɪʃn, trɑːnzˌfɪgəˈreɪʃn, -z
AM træn(t)sˌfɪgjəˈreɪʃən, -z

transfigure
BR transˈfɪgə(r), trɑːnsˈfɪgə(r), tranzˈfɪgə(r), trɑːnzˈfɪgə(r), -z, -ɪŋ, -d
AM træn(t)sˈfɪgər, -z, -ɪŋ, -d

transfinite
BR tranzˈfʌɪnʌɪt, trɑːnzˈfʌɪnʌɪt, transˈfʌɪnʌɪt, trɑːnsˈfʌɪnʌɪt
AM træn(t)sˈfaɪˌnaɪt

transfix
BR transˈfɪks, trɑːnsˈfɪks, tranzˈfɪks, trɑːnzˈfɪks, -ɨz, -ɪŋ, -t
AM træn(t)sˈfɪks, -ɨz, -ɪŋ, -t

transfixion
BR transˈfɪkʃn, trɑːnsˈfɪkʃn, tranzˈfɪkʃn, trɑːnzˈfɪkʃn
AM træn(t)sˈfɪkʃən

transform
BR transˈfɔːm, trɑːnsˈfɔːm, tranzˈfɔːm, trɑːnzˈfɔːm, -z, -ɪŋ, -d
AM træn(t)sˈfɔ(ə)rm, -z, -ɪŋ, -d

transformable
BR transˈfɔːməbl, trɑːnsˈfɔːməbl, tranzˈfɔːməbl, trɑːnzˈfɔːməbl
AM træn(t)sˈfɔrməbəl

transformation
BR ˌtransfəˈmeɪʃn, ˌtrɑːnsfəˈmeɪʃn, ˌtranzfəˈmeɪʃn, ˌtrɑːnzfəˈmeɪʃn, -z
AM ˌtræn(t)sfərˈmeɪʃən, -z

transformational
BR ˌtransfəˈmeɪʃn̩(ə)l, ˌtrɑːnsfəˈmeɪʃn̩(ə)l, ˌtranzfəˈmeɪʃn̩(ə)l, ˌtrɑːnzfəˈmeɪʃn̩(ə)l
AM ˌtræn(t)sfərˈmeɪʃ(ə)nəl

transformationally
BR ˌtransfəˈmeɪʃn̩əli, ˌtransfəˈmeɪʃ(ə)nəli, ˌtrɑːnsfəˈmeɪʃn̩əli, ˌtrɑːnsfəˈmeɪʃənl̩i, ˌtrɑːnzfəˈmeɪʃ(ə)nəli, ˌtranzfəˈmeɪʃn̩əli, ˌtranzfəˈmeɪʃ(ə)nəli, ˌtrɑːnzfəˈmeɪʃn̩əli, ˌtrɑːnzfəˈmeɪʃ(ə)nəli
AM ˌtræn(t)sfərˈmeɪʃ(ə)nəli

transformative
BR transˈfɔːmətɪv, trɑːnsˈfɔːmətɪv, tranzˈfɔːmətɪv, trɑːnzˈfɔːmɪtɪv
AM træn(t)sˈfɔrmədɪv

transformer
BR transˈfɔːmə(r), trɑːnsˈfɔːmə(r), tranzˈfɔːmə(r), trɑːnzˈfɔːmə(r), -z
AM træn(t)sˈfɔrmər, -z

transfuse
BR transˈfjuːz, trɑːnsˈfjuːz, tranzˈfjuːz, trɑːnzˈfjuːz, -ɨz, -ɪŋ, -d
AM træn(t)sˈfjuz, -ɨz, -ɪŋ, -d

transfusion
BR transˈfjuːʒn, trɑːnsˈfjuːʃn, tranzˈfjuːʒn, trɑːnzˈfjuːʒn, -z
AM træn(t)sˈfjuʒən, -z

transgenic
BR tranzˈdʒɛnɪk, trɑːnzˈdʒɛnɪk, transˈdʒɛnɪk, trɑːnsˈdʒɛnɪk
AM trænzˈdʒɛnɪk, træn(t)sˈdʒɛnɪk

transgress
BR tranzˈgrɛs, trɑːnzˈgrɛs, transˈgrɛs, trɑːnsˈgrɛs, -ɨz, -ɪŋ, -t
AM trænzˈgrɛs, træn(t)sˈgrɛs, -əz, -ɪŋ, -t

transgression
BR tranzˈgrɛʃn, trɑːnzˈgrɛʃn, transˈgrɛʃn, trɑːnsˈgrɛʃn, -z
AM trænzˈgrɛʃən, træn(t)sˈgrɛʃən, -z

transgressional
BR tranzˈgrɛʃn̩(ə)l, trɑːnzˈgrɛʃn̩(ə)l, trɑːnzˈgrɛʃən(ə)l, trɑːnsˈgrɛʃn̩(ə)l
AM trænzˈgrɛʃ(ə)nəl, træn(t)sˈgrɛʃ(ə)nəl

transgressive
BR tranzˈgrɛsɪv, trɑːnzˈgrɛsɪv, transˈgrɛsɪv, trɑːnsˈgrɛsɪv
AM trænzˈgrɛsɪv, træn(t)sˈgrɛsɪv

transgressor
BR tranzˈgrɛsə(r), trɑːnzˈgrɛsə(r), transˈgrɛsə(r), trɑːnsˈgrɛsə(r), -z
AM trænzˈgrɛsər, træn(t)sˈgrɛsər, -z

tranship
BR transˈʃɪp, trɑːnsˈʃɪp, tranzˈʃɪp, trɑːnzˈʃɪp, -s, -ɪŋ, -t
AM ˌtræn(s)ˈʃɪp, -s, -ɪŋ, -t

transhipment
BR transˈʃɪpm(ə)nt, trɑːnsˈʃɪpm(ə)nt, tranzˈʃɪpm(ə)nt, trɑːnzˈʃɪpm(ə)nt, -s
AM ˌtræn(s)ˈʃɪpmənt, -s

transhumance
BR tranzˈhjuːməns, trɑːnzˈhjuːməns, transˈhjuːməns, trɑːnsˈhjuːməns
AM trænzˈ(h)jumənz, træn(t)sˈ(h)juməns

transience
BR ˈtranzɪəns, ˈtrɑːnzɪəns, ˈtransɪəns, ˈtrɑːnsɪəns
AM ˈtræn(t)ʃəns, ˈtrænʒəns

transiency
BR ˈtranzɪənsi, ˈtrɑːnzɪənsi, ˈtransɪənsi, ˈtrɑːnsɪənsi
AM ˈtræn(t)ʃənsi, ˈtrænʒənsi

transient
BR 'tranzɪənt, 'trɑːnzɪənt, 'transɪənt, 'trɑːnsɪənt, -s
AM 'træn(t)ʃənt, 'trænʒənt, -s

transiently
BR 'tranzɪəntli, 'trɑːnzɪəntli, 'transɪəntli, 'trɑːnsɪəntli
AM 'træn(t)ʃən(t)li, 'trænʒən(t)li

transientness
BR 'tranzɪəntnəs, 'trɑːnzɪəntnəs, 'transɪəntnəs, 'trɑːnsɪəntnəs
AM 'træn(t)ʃən(t)nəs, 'trænʒən(t)nəs

transilluminate
BR ˌtranzɪ'l(j)uːmɨneɪt, ˌtrɑːnzɪ'l(j)uːmɨneɪt, ˌtransɪ'l(j)uːmɨneɪt, ˌtrɑːnsɪ'l(j)uːmɨneɪt, -s, -ɪŋ, -ɨd
AM ˌtrænzə'lumə,neɪ|t, ˌtræn(t)sə'lumə,neɪ|t, -ts, -dɪŋ, -dɨd

transillumination
BR ˌtranzɪ,l(j)uːmɪ'neɪʃn, ˌtrɑːnzɪ,l(j)uːmɪ'neɪʃn, ˌtransɪ,l(j)uːmɪ'neɪʃn, ˌtrɑːnsɪ,l(j)uːmɪ'neɪʃn
AM ˌtrænzə,lumə'neɪʃən, ˌtræn(t)sə,lumə'neɪʃən

transire
BR tran'zʌɪə(r), trɑːn'zʌɪə(r), tran'sʌɪə(r), trɑːn'sʌɪə(r), tran'zʌɪri, trɑːn'zʌɪri, tran'sʌɪri, trɑːn'sʌɪri
AM træn'zaɪri

transires
BR tran'zʌɪəz, trɑːn'zʌɪəz, tran'sʌɪəz, trɑːn'sʌɪəz, tran'zʌɪrɪz, trɑːn'zʌɪrɪz, tran'sʌɪrɪz, trɑːn'sʌɪrɪz
AM træn'zaɪriz

transistor
BR tran'zɪstə(r), trɑːn'zɪstə(r), tran'sɪstə(r), trɑːn'sɪstə(r), -z
AM træn'zɪstər, -z

transistorisation
BR tran,zɪstərʌɪ'zeɪʃn, trɑːn,zɪstərʌɪ'zeɪʃn, tran,sɪstərʌɪ'zeɪʃn, trɑːn,sɪstərʌɪ'zeɪʃn
AM træn,zɪstərə'zeɪʃən, træn,zɪstə,raɪ'zeɪʃən

transistorise
BR tran'zɪstərʌɪz, trɑːn'zɪstərʌɪz, tran'sɪstərʌɪz, trɑːn'sɪstərʌɪz, -ɨz, -ɪŋ, -d
AM træn'zɪstə,raɪz, -ɨz, -ɪŋ, -d

transistorization
BR tran,zɪstərʌɪ'zeɪʃn, trɑːn,zɪstərʌɪ'zeɪʃn, tran,sɪstərʌɪ'zeɪʃn, trɑːn,sɪstərʌɪ'zeɪʃn
AM træn,zɪstərə'zeɪʃən, træn,zɪstə,raɪ'zeɪʃən

transistorize
BR tran'zɪstərʌɪz, trɑːn'zɪstərʌɪz, tran'sɪstərʌɪz, trɑːn'sɪstərʌɪz, -ɨz, -ɪŋ, -d
AM træn'zɪstə,raɪz, -ɨz, -ɪŋ, -d

transit
BR 'transɪt, 'trɑːnsɪt, 'tranzɪt, 'trɑːnzɪt, -s
AM 'trænzət, -s

transition
BR tran'zɪʃn, trɑːn'zɪʃn, tran'sɪʃn, trɑːn'sɪʃn, -z
AM træn'zɪʃən, -z

transitional
BR tran'zɪʃn̩(ə)l, trɑːn'zɪʃn̩(ə)l, tran'sɪʃn̩(ə)l, trɑːn'sɪʃn̩(ə)l
AM træn'zɪʃ(ə)nəl

transitionally
BR tran'zɪʃn̩əli, tran'zɪʃ(ə)nəli, trɑːn'zɪʃn̩əli, trɑːn'zɪʃ(ə)nəli, tran'sɪʃn̩əli, tran'sɪʃ(ə)nəli, trɑːn'sɪʃn̩əli, trɑːn'sɪʃ(ə)nəli
AM træn'zɪʃ(ə)nəli

transitionary
BR tran'zɪʃn̩(ə)ri, trɑːn'zɪʃn̩(ə)ri, tran'sɪʃn̩(ə)ri, trɑːn'sɪʃn̩(ə)ri
AM træn'zɪʃə,nɛri

transitive
BR 'tranzɨtɪv, 'trɑːnzɨtɪv, 'transɨtɪv, 'trɑːnsɨtɪv
AM 'trænzədɪv, 'træn(t)sədɪv

transitively
BR 'tranzɨtɨvli, 'trɑːnzɨtɨvli, 'transɨtɨvli, 'trɑːnsɨtɨvli
AM 'trænzədɨvli, 'træn(t)sədɨvli

transitiveness
BR 'tranzɨtɨvnɨs, 'trɑːnzɨtɨvnɨs, 'transɨtɨvnɨs, 'trɑːnsɨtɨvnɨs
AM 'trænzədɪvnɨs, 'træn(t)sədɪvnɨs

transitivity
BR ˌtranzɪ'tɪvɨti, ˌtrɑːnzɪ'tɪvɨti, ˌtransɪ'tɪvɨti, ˌtrɑːnsɪ'tɪvɨti
AM ˌtrænzə'tɪvɨdi, ˌtræn(t)sə'tɪvɨdi

transitorily
BR 'tranzɨt(ə)rɨli, 'trɑːnzɨt(ə)rɨli, 'transɨt(ə)rɨli, 'trɑːnsɨt(ə)rɨli
AM 'trænzə,tɔrəli, 'træn(t)sə,tɔrəli

transitoriness
BR 'tranzɨt(ə)rɪnɨs, 'trɑːnzɨt(ə)rɪnɨs, 'transɨt(ə)rɪnɨs, 'trɑːnsɨt(ə)rɪnɨs
AM 'trænzə,tɔrinɨs, 'træn(t)sə,tɔrinɨs

transitory
BR 'tranzɨt(ə)ri, 'trɑːnzɨt(ə)ri, 'transɨt(ə)ri, 'trɑːnsɨt(ə)ri
AM 'trænzə,tɔri, 'træn(t)sə,tɔri

Transjordan
BR (ˌ)tranz'dʒɔːdn, (ˌ)trɑːnz'dʒɔːdn, (ˌ)trans'dʒɔːdn, (ˌ)trɑːns'dʒɔːdn
AM trænz'dʒɔrdən

Transjordanian
BR ˌtranzdʒɔː'deɪnɪən, ˌtrɑːnzdʒɔː'deɪnɪən, ˌtransdʒɔː'deɪnɪən, ˌtrɑːnsdʒɔː'deɪnɪən, -z
AM ˌtrænz,dʒɔr'deɪniən, -z

Transkei
BR (ˌ)trans'kʌɪ, (ˌ)trɑːn'skʌɪ, (ˌ)tranz'kʌɪ, (ˌ)trɑːnz'kʌɪ
AM træn(t)'skaɪ

translatability
BR trans,leɪtə'bɪlɨti, trɑːns,leɪtə'bɪlɨti, tranz,leɪtə'bɪlɨti, trɑːnz,leɪtə'bɪlɨti
AM ˌtrænz,leɪdə'bɪlɨdi, ˌtræn(t)s,leɪdə'bɪlɨdi

translatable
BR trans'leɪtəbl, trɑːns'leɪtəbl, tranz'leɪtəbl, trɑːnz'leɪtəbl
AM trænz'leɪdəbəl, træn(t)s'leɪdəbəl

translate
BR trans'leɪt, trɑːns'leɪt, tranz'leɪt, trɑːnz'leɪt, -s, -ɪŋ, -ɨd
AM trænz'leɪ|t, træn(t)s'leɪ|t, -ts, -dɪŋ, -dɨd

translation
BR trans'leɪʃn, trɑːns'leɪʃn, tranz'leɪʃn, trɑːnz'leɪʃn, -z
AM trænz'leɪʃən, træn(t)s'leɪʃən, -z

translational
BR trans'leɪʃn̩(ə)l, trɑːns'leɪʃn̩(ə)l, tranz'leɪʃn̩(ə)l, trɑːnz'leɪʃn̩(ə)l
AM trænz'leɪʃ(ə)nəl, træn(t)s'leɪʃ(ə)nəl

translationally
BR trans'leɪʃn̩əli, trans'leɪʃ(ə)nəli, trɑːns'leɪʃn̩əli, trɑːns'leɪʃ(ə)nəli, tranz'leɪʃn̩əli, tranz'leɪʃ(ə)nəli, trɑːnz'leɪʃn̩əli, trɑːnz'leɪʃ(ə)nəli
AM trænz'leɪʃ(ə)nəli, træn(t)s'leɪʃ(ə)nəli

translator
BR trans'leɪtə(r), trɑːns'leɪtə(r), tranz'leɪtə(r), trɑːnz'leɪtə(r), -z
AM 'trænz,leɪdər, 'træn(t)s,leɪdər, -z

transliterate
BR trans'lɪtəreɪt, trɑːns'lɪtəreɪt, tranz'lɪtəreɪt, trɑːnz'lɪtəreɪt, -s, -ɪŋ, -ɨd
AM trænz'lɪdə,reɪ|t, træn(t)s'lɪdə,reɪ|t, -ts, -dɪŋ, -dɨd

transliteration
BR trans,lɪtə'reɪʃn, ˌtranslɪtə'reɪʃn, trɑːns,lɪtə'reɪʃn, ˌtrɑːnslɪtə'reɪʃn, tranz,lɪtə'reɪʃn, ˌtranzlɪtə'reɪʃn, trɑːnz,lɪtə'reɪʃn, ˌtrɑːnzlɪtə'reɪʃn, -z
AM trænz,lɪdə'reɪʃən, træn(t)s,lɪdə'reɪʃən, -z

transliterator
BR trans'lɪtəreɪtə(r), trɑːns'lɪtəreɪtə(r), tranz'lɪtəreɪtə(r), trɑːnz'lɪtəreɪtə(r), -z
AM trænz'lɪdə,reɪdər, træn(t)s'lɪdə,reɪdər, -z

translocate
BR ˌtransləʊ'keɪt, ˌtrɑːnsləʊ'keɪt, ˌtranzləʊ'keɪt, ˌtrɑːnzləʊ'keɪt, -s, -ɪŋ, -ɪd
AM trænz'loʊˌkeɪ|t, træn(t)s'loʊˌkeɪ|t, -ts, -dɪŋ, -dɪd

translocation
BR ˌtransləʊ'keɪʃn, ˌtrɑːnsləʊ'keɪʃn, ˌtranzləʊ'keɪʃn, ˌtrɑːnzləʊ'keɪʃn, -z
AM trænzˌloʊ'keɪʃən, træn(t)sˌloʊ'keɪʃən, -z

translucence
BR trans'luːsns, trɑːns'luːsns, tranz'luːsns, trɑːnz'luːsns
AM trænz'lusəns, træn(t)s'lusəns

translucency
BR trans'luːsnsi, trɑːns'luːsnsi, tranz'luːsnsi, trɑːnz'luːsnsi
AM trænz'lusənsi, træn(t)s'lusənsi

translucent
BR trans'luːsnt, trɑːns'luːsnt, tranz'luːsnt, trɑːnz'luːsnt
AM trænz'lusənt, træn(t)s'lusənt

translucently
BR trans'luːsntli, trɑːns'luːsntli, tranz'luːsntli, trɑːnz'luːsntli
AM trænz'lusn(t)li, træn(t)s'lusn(t)li

translunar
BR trans'luːnə(r), trɑːns'luːnə(r), tranz'luːnə(r), trɑːnz'luːnə(r)
AM ˌtrænz'lunər, ˌtræn(t)s'lunər

translunary
BR trans'luːn(ə)ri, trɑːns'luːn(ə)ri, tranz'luːn(ə)ri, trɑːnz'luːn(ə)ri
AM trænz'lunəri, træn(t)s'lunəri

transmarine
BR ˌtranzmə'riːn, ˌtrɑːnzmə'riːn, ˌtransmə'riːn, ˌtrɑːnsmə'riːn
AM ˌtrænzmə'rin, ˌtræn(t)smə'rin

transmigrant
BR tranz'mʌɪgr(ə)nt, trɑːnz'mʌɪgr(ə)nt, trans'mʌɪgr(ə)nt, trɑːns'mʌɪgr(ə)nt, -s
AM trænz'maɪgrənt, træn(t)s'maɪgrənt, -s

transmigrate
BR ˌtranzmʌɪ'greɪt, ˌtrɑːnzmʌɪ'greɪt, ˌtransmʌɪ'greɪt, ˌtrɑːnsmʌɪ'greɪt, -s, -ɪŋ, -ɪd
AM trænz'maɪˌgreɪ|t, træn(t)s'maɪˌgreɪ|t, -ts, -dɪŋ, -dɪd

transmigration
BR ˌtranzmʌɪ'greɪʃn, ˌtrɑːnzmʌɪ'greɪʃn, ˌtransmʌɪ'greɪʃn, ˌtrɑːnsmʌɪ'greɪʃn, -z
AM ˌtrænzˌmaɪ'greɪʃən, ˌtræn(t)sˌmaɪ'greɪʃən, -z

transmigrator
BR ˌtranzmʌɪ'greɪtə(r), ˌtrɑːnzmʌɪ'greɪtə(r), ˌtransmʌɪ'greɪtə(r), ˌtrɑːnsmʌɪ'greɪtə(r), -z
AM trænz'maɪˌgreɪdər, træn(t)s'maɪˌgreɪdər, -z

transmigratory
BR tranz'mʌɪgrət(ə)ri, ˌtranzmʌɪ'greɪt(ə)ri, trɑːnz'mʌɪgrət(ə)ri, ˌtrɑːnzmʌɪ'greɪt(ə)ri, trans'mʌɪgrət(ə)ri, ˌtransmʌɪ'greɪt(ə)ri, trɑːns'mʌɪgrət(ə)ri, ˌtrɑːnsmʌɪ'greɪt(ə)ri
AM trænz'maɪgrəˌtɔri, træn(t)s'maɪgrəˌtɔri

transmissibility
BR tranzˌmɪsɪ'bɪlɨti, ˌtranzmɪsɪ'bɪlɨti, trɑːnzˌmɪsɪ'bɪlɨti, ˌtrɑːnzmɪsɪ'bɪlɨti, transˌmɪsɪ'bɪlɨti, ˌtransmɪsɪ'bɪlɨti, trɑːnsˌmɪsɪ'bɪlɨti, ˌtrɑːnsmɪsɪ'bɪlɨti
AM trænzˌmɪsə'bɪlɨdi, træn(t)sˌmɪsə'bɪlɨdi

transmissible
BR tranz'mɪsɪbl, trɑːnz'mɪsɪbl, trans'mɪsɪbl, trɑːns'mɪsɪbl
AM trænz'mɪsəbəl, træn(t)s'mɪsəbəl

transmission
BR tranz'mɪʃn, trɑːnz'mɪʃn, trans'mɪʃn, trɑːns'mɪʃn, -z
AM trænz'mɪʃən, træn(t)s'mɪʃən, -z

transmissive
BR tranz'mɪsɪv, trɑːnz'mɪsɪv, trans'mɪsɪv, trɑːns'mɪsɪv
AM trænz'mɪsɪv, træn(t)s'mɪsɪv

transmit
BR tranz'mɪt, trɑːnz'mɪt, trans'mɪt, trɑːns'mɪt, -s, -ɪŋ, -ɪd
AM trænz'mɪ|t, træn(t)s'mɪ|t, -ts, -dɪŋ, -dɪd

transmittable
BR tranz'mɪtəbl, trɑːnz'mɪtəbl, trans'mɪtəbl, trɑːns'mɪtəbl
AM trænz'mɪdəbəl, træn(t)s'mɪdəbəl

transmittal
BR tranz'mɪtl, trɑːnz'mɪtl, trans'mɪtl, trɑːns'mɪtl, -z
AM trænz'mɪdl, træn(t)s'mɪdl, -z

transmitter
BR tranz'mɪtə(r), trɑːnz'mɪtə(r), trans'mɪtə(r), trɑːns'mɪtə(r), -z
AM trænz'mɪdər, træn(t)s'mɪdər, -z

transmogrification
BR tranzˌmɒgrɪfɪ'keɪʃn, ˌtranzmɒgrɪfɪ'keɪʃn, trɑːnzˌmɒgrɪfɪ'keɪʃn, ˌtrɑːnzmɒgrɪfɪ'keɪʃn, transˌmɒgrɪfɪ'keɪʃn, ˌtransmɒgrɪfɪ'keɪʃn, trɑːnsˌmɒgrɪfɪ'keɪʃn, ˌtrɑːnsmɒgrɪfɪ'keɪʃn
AM trænzˌmɑgrəfə'keɪʃən, træn(t)sˌmɑgrəfə'keɪʃən

transmogrify
BR tranz'mɒgrɪfʌɪ, trɑːnz'mɒgrɪfʌɪ, trans'mɒgrɪfʌɪ, trɑːns'mɒgrɪfʌɪ, -z, -ɪŋ, -d
AM trænz'mɑgrəˌfaɪ, træn(t)s'mɑgrəˌfaɪ, -z, -ɪŋ, -d

transmontane
BR tranz'mɒnteɪn, trɑːnz'mɒnteɪn, trans'mɒnteɪn, trɑːns'mɒnteɪn
AM trænz'mɑnˌteɪn, træn(t)s'mɑnˌteɪn

transmutability
BR tranzˌmjuːtə'bɪlɨti, ˌtranzmjuːtə'bɪlɨti, trɑːnzˌmjuːtə'bɪlɨti, ˌtrɑːnzmjuːtə'bɪlɨti, transˌmjuːtə'bɪlɨti, ˌtransmjuːtə'bɪlɨti, trɑːnsˌmjuːtə'bɪlɨti, ˌtrɑːnsmjuːtə'bɪlɨti:
AM trænzˌmjudə'bɪlɨdi, træn(t)sˌmjudə'bɪlɨdi

transmutable
BR tranz'mjuːtəbl, trɑːnz'mjuːtəbl, trans'mjuːtəbl, trɑːns'mjuːtəbl
AM trænz'mjudəbəl, træn(t)s'mjudəbəl

transmutation
BR ˌtranzmjuː'teɪʃn, ˌtranzmjʊ'teɪʃn, ˌtrɑːnzmjuː'teɪʃn, ˌtrɑːnzmjʊ'teɪʃn, ˌtransmjuː'teɪʃn, ˌtransmjʊ'teɪʃn, ˌtrɑːnsmjuː'teɪʃn, ˌtrɑːnsmjʊ'teɪʃn, -z
AM ˌtrænzmju'teɪʃən, ˌtræn(t)smju'teɪʃən, -z

transmutational
BR ˌtranzmjuː'teɪʃn̩(ə)l, ˌtranzmjʊ'teɪʃn̩(ə)l, ˌtrɑːnzmjuː'teɪʃn̩(ə)l, ˌtrɑːnzmjʊ'teɪʃn̩(ə)l, ˌtransmjuː'teɪʃn̩(ə)l, ˌtransmjʊ'teɪʃn̩(ə)l, ˌtrɑːnsmjuː'teɪʃn̩(ə)l, ˌtrɑːnsmjʊ'teɪʃn̩(ə)l
AM ˌtrænzmju'teɪʃ(ə)nəl, ˌtræn(t)smju'teɪʃ(ə)nəl

transmutationist
BR ˌtranzmjuː'teɪʃn̩ɪst, ˌtranzmjʊ'teɪʃn̩ɪst, ˌtrɑːnzmjuː'teɪʃn̩ɪst, ˌtrɑːnzmjʊ'teɪʃn̩ɪst, ˌtransmjuː'teɪʃn̩ɪst, ˌtransmjʊ'teɪʃn̩ɪst, ˌtrɑːnsmjuː'teɪʃn̩ɪst, ˌtrɑːnsmjʊ'teɪʃn̩ɪst, -s
AM ˌtrænzmju'teɪʃənəst, ˌtræn(t)smju'teɪʃənəst, -s

transmutative
BR tranz'mjuːtətɪv, trɑːnz'mjuːtətɪv, trans'mjuːtətɪv, trɑːns'mjuːtətɪv
AM trænz'mjudədɪv, træn(t)s'mjudədɪv

transmute
BR tranz'mjuːt, trɑːnz'mjuːt, trans'mjuːt, trɑːns'mjuːt, -s, -ɪŋ, -ɪd
AM trænz'mju|t, træn(t)s'mju|t, -ts, -dɪŋ, -dəd

transmuter
BR tranz'mjuːtə(r), trɑːnz'mjuːtə(r), trans'mjuːtə(r), trɑːns'mjuːtə(r), -z
AM trænz'mjudər, træn(t)s'mjudər, -z

transnational
BR tranz'naʃn̩(ə)l, trɑːnz'naʃn̩(ə)l, trans'naʃn̩(ə)l, trɑːns'naʃn̩(ə)l, -z
AM trænz'næʃ(ə)nəl, træn(t)s'næʃ(ə)nəl, -z

transoceanic
BR ˌtranzəʊʃɪ'anɪk, ˌtrɑːnzəʊʃɪ'anɪk, ˌtranzəʊsɪ'anɪk, ˌtrɑːnzəʊsɪ'anɪk, ˌtransəʊʃɪ'anɪk, ˌtrɑːnsəʊʃɪ'anɪk, ˌtransəʊsɪ'anɪk, ˌtrɑːnsəʊsɪ'anɪk
AM ˌtrænzoʊʃi'ænɪk

transom
BR trans(ə)m, -z, -d
AM 'træn(t)səm, -z, -d

transonic
BR tran'sɒnɪk, trɑːn'sɒnɪk
AM træn(t)'sɑnɪk

transpacific
BR ˌtranspə'sɪfɪk, ˌtrɑːnspə'sɪfɪk, ˌtranzpə'sɪfɪk, ˌtrɑːnzpə'sɪfɪk
AM ˌtræn(t)spə'sɪfɪk

transpadane
BR 'transpədeɪn, 'trɑːnspədeɪn, 'tranzpədeɪn, 'trɑːnzpədeɪn
AM 'træn(t)spəˌdeɪn, træn(t)s'peɪˌdeɪn

transparence
BR tran'sparəns, tran'sparn̩s, trɑːn'sparəns, trɑːn'sparn̩s, tran'spɛːrəns, tran'spɛːrn̩s, trɑːn'spɛːrəns, trɑːn'spɛːrn̩s
AM træn(t)'spɛrəns

transparency
BR tran'sparn̩s|i, trɑːn'sparn̩s|i, tran'spɛːrəns|i, trɑːn'spɛːrəns|i, -ɪz
AM træn(t)'spɛrənsi, -z

transparent
BR tran'sparn̩t, trɑːn'sparn̩t, tran'spɛːrn̩t, trɑːn'spɛːrn̩t
AM træn(t)'spɛrənt

transparently
BR tran'sparn̩tli, trɑːn'sparn̩tli, tran'spɛːrn̩tli, trɑːn'spɛːrn̩tli
AM træn(t)'spɛrən(t)li

transparentness
BR tran'sparn̩tnəs, trɑːn'sparn̩tnəs, tran'spɛːrn̩tnəs, trɑːn'spɛːrn̩tnəs
AM træn(t)'spɛrən(t)nəs

trans-Pennine
BR trans'pɛnʌɪn, trɑːns'pɛnʌɪn, tranz'pɛnʌɪn, trɑːnz'pɛnʌɪn
AM træn(t)s'pɛˌnaɪn

transpersonal
BR trans'pəːsn̩l, trans'pəːs(ə)nl, trɑːns'pəːsn̩l, trɑːns'pəːs(ə)nl, tranz'pəːsn̩l, tranz'pəːs(ə)nl, trɑːnz'pəːsn̩l, trɑːnz'pəːs(ə)nl
AM træn(t)s'pərs(ə)nəl

transpierce
BR trans'pɪəs, trɑːns'pɪəs, tranz'pɪəs, trɑːnz'pɪəs, -ɪz, -ɪŋ, -t
AM træn(t)s'pɪ(ə)rs, -əz, -ɪŋ, -t

transpirable
BR tran'spʌɪərəbl, trɑːn'spʌɪərəbl
AM træn(t)'spaɪ(ə)rəbəl, træn(t)'spaɪərbəl

transpiration
BR ˌtranspɪ'reɪʃn, ˌtrɑːnspɪ'reɪʃn
AM ˌtræn(t)spə'reɪʃən

transpiratory
BR tran'spʌɪrət(ə)ri, trɑːn'spʌɪrət(ə)ri
AM træn(t)'spaɪrəˌtɔri

transpire
BR tran'spʌɪə(r), trɑːn'spʌɪə(r), -z, -ɪŋ, -d
AM træn(t)'spaɪ(ə)r, -z, -ɪŋ, -d

transplant[1]
noun
BR 'transplɑːnt, 'trɑːnsplɑːnt, 'transplant, -s
AM 'træn(t)sˌplænt, -s

transplant[2]
verb
BR trans'plɑːnt, trɑːns'plɑːnt, trans'plant, -s, -ɪŋ, -ɪd
AM træn(t)s'plæn|t, -ts, -(t)ɪŋ, -(t)əd

transplantable
BR trans'plɑːntəbl, trɑːns'plɑːntəbl, trans'plantəbl
AM træn(t)s'plæn(t)əbəl

transplantation
BR ˌtransplɑːn'teɪʃn, ˌtrɑːnsplɑːn'teɪʃn, ˌtransplan'teɪʃn, -z
AM ˌtræn(t)sˌplæn'teɪʃən, -z

transplanter
BR trans'plɑːntə(r), trɑːns'plɑːntə(r), trans'plantə(r), -z
AM træn(t)s'plæn(t)ər, -z

transponder
BR tran'spɒndə(r), trɑːn'spɒndə(r), -z
AM træn(t)'spɑndər, -z

transpontine
BR trans'pɒntʌɪn, trɑːns'pɒntʌɪn, tranz'pɒntʌɪn, trɑːnz'pɒntʌɪn
AM træn(t)'spɑnˌtaɪn

transport[1]
noun
BR 'transpɔːt, 'trɑːnspɔːt, -s
AM 'træn(t)sˌpɔ(ə)rt, -s

transport[2]
verb
BR tran'spɔːt, trɑːn'spɔːt, -s, -ɪŋ, -ɪd
AM træn(t)s'pɔ(ə)rt, -ts, -'pɔrdɪŋ, -'pɔrdəd

transportability
BR tranˌspɔːtə'bɪlɪti, ˌtranspɔːtə'bɪlɪti, trɑːnˌspɔːtə'bɪlɪti, ˌtrɑːnspɔːtə'bɪlɪti
AM ˌtræn(t)sˌpɔrdə'bɪlɨdi

transportable
BR tran'spɔːtəbl, trɑːn'spɔːtəbl
AM træn(t)s'pɔrdəbəl

transportation
BR ˌtranspə'teɪʃn, ˌtranspɔː'teɪʃn, ˌtrɑːnspə'teɪʃn, ˌtrɑːnspɔː'teɪʃn
AM ˌtræn(t)spər'teɪʃən

transporter
BR tran'spɔːtə(r), trɑːn'spɔːtə(r), -z
AM træn(t)s'pɔrdər, -z

transposable
BR tran'spəʊzəbl, trɑːn'spəʊzəbl
AM træn(t)'spoʊzəbəl

transposal
BR tran'spəʊzl, trɑːn'spəʊzl
AM træn(t)'spoʊzəl

transpose
BR tran'spəʊz, trɑːn'spəʊz, -ɪz, -ɪŋ, -d
AM træn(t)'spoʊz, -ɨz, -ɪŋ, -d

transposer
BR tran'spəʊzə(r), trɑːn'spəʊzə(r), -z
AM træn(t)'spoʊzər, -z

transposition
BR ˌtranspə'zɪʃn, ˌtrɑːnspə'zɪʃn, ˌtranzpə'zɪʃn, ˌtrɑːnzpə'zɪʃn, -z
AM ˌtræn(t)spə'zɪʃən, -z

transpositional
BR ˌtranspə'zɪʃn̩(ə)l, ˌtrɑːnspə'zɪʃn̩(ə)l, ˌtranzpə'zɪʃn̩(ə)l, ˌtrɑːnzpə'zɪʃn̩(ə)l
AM ˌtræn(t)spə'zɪʃ(ə)nəl

transpositive
BR trans'pɒzɪtɪv, trɑːns'pɒzɪtɪv, tranz'spɒzɪtɪv, trɑːnz'pɒzɪtɪv
AM træn(t)'spɑzədɪv

transputer
BR tran'spjuːtə(r), trɑːn'spjuːtə(r), -z
AM træn(t)'spjudər, -z

transsexual
BR tran(s)'sɛkʃʊəl, tran(s)'sɛkʃ(ʉ)l, tran(s)'sɛksjʊ(ə)l, trɑːn(s)'sɛkʃʊəl, trɑːn(s)'sɛkʃ(ʉ)l, trɑːn(s)'sɛksjʊ(ə)l, tranz'sɛkʃʊəl, tranz'sɛkʃ(ʉ)l, tranz'sɛksjʊ(ə)l, trɑːnz'sɛkʃʊəl, trɑːnz'sɛkʃ(ʉ)l, trɑːnz'sɛksjʊ(ə)l, -z
AM træn(t)(s)'sɛkʃ(əw)əl, -z

transsexualism
BR tran(z)'sɛkʃʊəlɪz(ə)m, tran(z)'sɛkʃʉlɪz(ə)m, tran(z)'sɛkʃl̩ɪz(ə)m, tran(z)'sɛksjʊ(ə)lɪz(ə)m, trɑːn(z)'sɛkʃʊəlɪz(ə)m, trɑːn(z)'sɛkʃʉlɪz(ə)m, trɑːn(z)'sɛkʃl̩ɪz(ə)m, trɑːn(z)'sɛksjʊ(ə)lɪz(ə)m
AM træn(t)(s)'sɛkʃ(əw)əˌlɪzəm

transship
BR tran(s)'ʃɪp, trɑːn(s)'ʃɪp, tranz'ʃɪp, trɑːnz'ʃɪp, -s, -ɪŋ, -t
AM træn(t)(s)'ʃɪp, -s, -ɪŋ, -t

transshipment
BR tran(s)'ʃɪpm(ə)nt, trɑːn(s)'ʃɪpm(ə)nt, tranz'ʃɪpm(ə)nt, trɑːnz'ʃɪpm(ə)nt, -s
AM træn(t)(s)'ʃɪpmənt, -s

trans-Siberian
BR ˌtran(s)sʌɪ'bɪərɪən, ˌtrɑːn(s)sʌɪ'bɪərɪən,

ˌtranzsʌɪˈbɪərɪən, ˌtrɑːnzsʌɪˈbɪərɪən
AM ˌtræn(t)(s),saɪˈbɪriən

trans-sonic
BR tran(s)ˈsɒnɪk, trɑːn(s)ˈsɒnɪk, tranzˈsɒnɪk, trɑːnzˈsɒnɪk
AM træn(t)(s),sɑnɪk

transubstantiate
BR ˌtransəbˈstanʃɪeɪt, ˌtrɑːnsəbˈstanʃɪeɪt, ˌtransəbˈstansɪeɪt, ˌtrɑːnsəbˈstansɪeɪt, -s, -ɪŋ, -d
AM ˌtræn(t)səbˈstæn(t)ʃi,eɪ|t, -ts, -dɪŋ, -dɪd

transubstantiation
BR ˌtransəb,stanʃɪˈeɪʃn, ˌtrɑːnsəb,stanʃɪˈeɪʃn, ˌtransəb,stansɪˈeɪʃn, ˌtrɑːnsəb,stansɪˈeɪʃn
AM ˈtræn(t)səb,stæn(t)ʃiˈeɪʃən

transudation
BR ˌtransjʊˈdeɪʃn, ˌtrɑːnsjʊˈdeɪʃn, ˌtranzjʊˈdeɪʃn, ˌtrɑːnzjʊˈdeɪʃn
AM ˌtræn(t)səˈdeɪʃən

transudatory
BR tran(s)ˈsjuːdət(ə)ri, trɑːn(s)ˈsjuːdət(ə)ri, tranˈzjuːdət(ə)ri, trɑːnˈzjuːdət(ə)ri
AM træn(t)(s)ˈsudə,tɔri

transude
BR tranˈsjuːd, trɑːnˈsjuːd, tranˈzjuːd, trɑːnˈzjuːd, -z, -ɪŋ, -ɪd
AM træn(t)ˈs(j)ud, -z, -ɪŋ, -əd

transuranic
BR ˌtransjʊˈranɪk, ˌtrɑːnsjʊˈranɪk, ˌtranzjʊˈranɪk, ˌtrɑːnzjʊˈranɪk
AM ˌtræn(t)sjəˈrænɪk

Transvaal
BR ˈtranzvɑːl, ˈtrɑːnzvɑːl, (ˌ)tranzˈvɑːl, (ˌ)trɑːnzˈvɑːl, ˈtransvɑːl, ˈtrɑːnsvɑːl, (ˌ)transˈvɑːl, (ˌ)trɑːnsˈvɑːl
AM trænzˈvɑl

Transvaaler
BR ˈtranzvɑːlə(r), ˈtrɑːnzvɑːlə(r), (ˌ)tranzˈvɑːlə(r), (ˌ)trɑːnzˈvɑːlə(r), ˈtransvɑːlə(r), ˈtrɑːnsvɑːlə(r), (ˌ)transˈvɑːlə(r), (ˌ)trɑːnsˈvɑːlə(r), -z
AM trænzˈvɑlər, -z

transversal
BR tranzˈvəːsl, trɑːnzˈvəːsl, transˈvəːsl, trɑːnsˈvəːsl, -z
AM trænzˈvərsəl, træn(t)sˈvərsəl, -z

transversality
BR ˌtranzvəːˈsalɪti, ˌtrɑːnzvəːˈsalɪti, ˌtransvəːˈsalɪti, ˌtrɑːnsvəːˈsalɪti
AM ˌtrænzvərˈsælədi, ˌtræn(t)svərˈsælədi

transversally
BR (ˌ)tranzˈvəːsl̩i, (ˌ)trɑːnzˈvəːsl̩i, (ˌ)transˈvəːsl̩i, (ˌ)trɑːnsˈvəːsl̩i
AM trænzˈvərsəli, træn(t)sˈvərsəli

transverse
BR (ˌ)tranzˈvəːs, (ˌ)trɑːnzˈvəːs, (ˌ)transˈvəːs, (ˌ)trɑːnsˈvəːs
AM trænzˈvərs, træn(t)sˈvərs

transversely
BR (ˌ)tranzˈvəːsli, (ˌ)trɑːnzˈvəːsli, (ˌ)transˈvəːsli, (ˌ)trɑːnsˈvəːsli
AM trænzˈvərsli, træn(t)sˈvərsli

transvest
BR tranzˈvɛst, trɑːnzˈvɛst, transˈvɛst, trɑːnsˈvɛst, -s, -ɪŋ, -ɪd
AM trænzˈvɛst, træn(t)sˈvɛst, -s, -ɪŋ, -əd

transvestism
BR tranzˈvɛstɪz(ə)m, trɑːnzˈvɛstɪz(ə)m, transˈvɛstɪz(ə)m, trɑːnsˈvɛstɪz(ə)m
AM trænzˈvɛs,tɪzəm, træn(t)sˈvɛs,tɪzəm

transvestist
BR tranzˈvɛstɪst, trɑːnzˈvɛstɪst, transˈvɛstɪst, trɑːnsˈvɛstɪst, -s
AM trænzˈvɛstəst, træn(t)sˈvɛstəst, -s

transvestite
BR tranzˈvɛstʌɪt, trɑːnzˈvɛstʌɪt, transˈvɛstʌɪt, trɑːnsˈvɛstʌɪt, -s
AM trænzˈvɛs,taɪt, træn(t)sˈvɛs,taɪt, -s

Transworld
BR ˌtranzˈwəːld, ˌtrɑːnzˈwəːld, ˌtransˈwəːld, ˌtrɑːnsˈwəːld
AM ˌtrænzˈwərld, ˈtræn(t)sˈwərld

Transylvania
BR ˌtrans(ɪ)lˈveɪnɪə(r), ˌtrɑːns(ɪ)lˈveɪnɪə(r)
AM ˌtræn(t)səlˈveɪniə, ˌtræn(t)səlˈveɪnjə

Transylvanian
BR ˌtrans(ɪ)lˈveɪnɪən, ˌtrɑːns(ɪ)lˈveɪnɪən, -z
AM ˌtræn(t)səlˈveɪniən, ˌtræn(t)səlˈveɪnjən, -z

tranter
BR ˈtrantə(r), -z
AM ˈtræn(t)ər, -z

trap
BR trap, -s, -ɪŋ, -t
AM træp, -s, -ɪŋ, -t

trap-ball
BR ˈtrapbɔːl
AM ˈtræp,bɔl, ˈtræp,bɑl

trapdoor
BR ˌtrapˈdɔː(r), ˈtrapdɔː(r), -z
AM ˈtræp,dɔ(ə)r, -z

trapes
BR treɪps, -ɪz, -ɪŋ, -t
AM treɪps, -ɪz, -ɪŋ, -t

trapeze
BR trəˈpiːz, -ɪz
AM trəˈpiz, træˈpiz, -ɪz

trapezia
BR trəˈpiːzɪə(r)
AM trəˈpiziə

trapezium
BR trəˈpiːzɪəm, -z
AM trəˈpiziəm, -z

trapezoid
BR trəˈpiːzɔɪd, -z
AM ˈtræpə,zɔɪd, -z

trapezoidal
BR ˌtrapɪˈzɔɪdl
AM ˌtræpəˈzɔɪdəl

traplike
BR ˈtraplʌɪk
AM ˈtræp,laɪk

trappean
BR ˈtrapɪən
AM ˈtræpiən

trapper
BR ˈtrapə(r), -z
AM ˈtræpər, -z

trappings
BR ˈtrapɪŋz
AM ˈtræpɪŋz

Trappist
BR ˈtrapɪst, -s
AM ˈtræpəst, -s

Trappistine
BR ˈtrapɪstiːn
AM ˈtræpə,stin

trapse
BR treɪps, -ɪz, -ɪŋ, -t
AM treɪps, -ɪz, -ɪŋ, -t

trapshooter
BR ˈtrap,ʃuːtə(r), -z
AM ˈtræp,ʃudər, -z

trapshooting
BR ˈtrap,ʃuːtɪŋ
AM ˈtræp,ʃudɪŋ

trash
BR traʃ, -ɪz, -ɪŋ, -t
AM træʃ, -əz, -ɪŋ, -t

trashcan
BR ˈtraʃkan, -z
AM ˈtræʃ,kæn, -z

trashery
BR ˈtraʃ(ə)r|i, -ɪz
AM ˈtræʃəri, -z

trashily
BR ˈtraʃɪli
AM ˈtræʃəli

trashiness
BR ˈtraʃɪnɪs
AM ˈtræʃinɪs

trashman
BR ˈtraʃman
AM ˈtræʃ,mæn

trashmen
BR ˈtraʃmɛn
AM ˈtræʃ,mɛn

trashy
BR ˈtraʃ|i, -ɪə(r), -ɪɪst
AM ˈtræʃi, -ər, -ɪst

Trás-os-Montes
BR ˌtrɑːsəzˈmɒnteɪz
AM ˈtrɑsəzˈmɑn,teɪz
B PORT ˌtrɑsosˈmontʃis
L PORT ˌtrazuʒˈmõtəʃ

trass
BR tras
AM træs

trattoria
BR ˌtratəˈriːə(r), -z
AM ˌtrɑdəˈriə, -z

trauma
BR ˈtrɔːmə(r), ˈtraʊmə(r), -z
AM ˈtrɔmə, ˈtrɑmə, -z

traumata
BR ˈtrɔːmətə(r), ˈtraʊmətə(r)
AM ˈtrɔmədə, ˈtrɑmədə

traumatic
BR trɔːˈmatɪk, traʊˈmatɪk
AM trɔˈmædɪk, trəˈmædɪk, trɑˈmædɪk

traumatically
BR trɔːˈmatɪkli, traʊˈmatɪkli
AM trɔˈmædək(ə)li, trɑˈmædək(ə)li

traumatisation
BR ˌtrɔːmətʌɪˈzeɪʃn, ˌtraʊmətʌɪˈzeɪʃn
AM ˌtrɔmədəˈzeɪʃən, ˌtrɔmə,taɪˈzeɪʃən, ˌtrɑmədəˈzeɪʃən, ˌtrɑmə,taɪˈzeɪʃən

traumatise
BR 'trɔːmətʌɪz, 'traʊmətʌɪz, -ɨz, -ɪŋ, -d
AM 'trɔmə,taɪz, 'trɑmə,taɪz, -ɨz, -ɪŋ, -d

traumatism
BR 'trɔːmətɪz(ə)m, 'traʊmətɪz(ə)m
AM 'trɔmə,tɪzəm, 'trɑmə,tɪzəm

traumatization
BR ,trɔːmətʌɪ'zeɪʃn, ,traʊmətʌɪ'zeɪʃn
AM ,trɔmədə'zeɪʃən, ,trɔmə,taɪ'zeɪʃən, ,trɑmədə'zeɪʃən, ,trɑmə,taɪ'zeɪʃən

traumatize
BR 'trɔːmətʌɪz, 'traʊmətʌɪz, -ɨz, -ɪŋ, -d
AM 'trɔmə,taɪz, 'trɑmə,taɪz, -ɨz, -ɪŋ, -d

travail
BR 'traveɪl, -z, -ɪŋ, -d
AM trə'veɪ(ə)l, 'træ,veɪl, -z, -ɪŋ, -d

travel
BR 'trav|l, -lz, -l̩ɪŋ\-lɪŋ, -ld
AM 'træv|əl, -əlz, -(ə)lɪŋ, -əld

traveler
BR 'travl̩ə(r), 'travlə(r), -z
AM 'træv(ə)lər, -z

traveller
BR 'travl̩ə(r), 'travlə(r), -z
AM 'træv(ə)lər, -z

Travelodge®
BR 'travəlɒdʒ
AM 'trævə,lɑdʒ

travelog
BR 'travəlɒg, -z
AM 'trævə,lɔg, 'trævə,lɑg, -z

travelogue
BR 'travəlɒg, -z
AM 'trævə,lɔg, 'trævə,lɑg, -z

Travers
BR 'travəz
AM 'trævərs

traversable
BR 'travəsəbl, trə'vəːsəbl
AM trə'vərsəbəl

traversal
BR trə'vəːsl
AM trə'vərsəl

traverse
BR 'travəs, trə'vəːs, -ɨz, -ɪŋ, -t
AM trə'vərs, -əz, -ɪŋ, -t

traverser
BR 'travəsə(r), trə'vəːsə(r), -z
AM trə'vərsər, -z

travertine
BR 'travətiːn, -z
AM 'trævər,tin, -z

travesty
BR 'travɪst|i, -ɪz, -ɪɪŋ, -ɪd
AM 'trævəsti, -z, -ɪŋ, -d

Traviata
BR ,travɪ'ɑːtə(r)
AM ,trɑvi'ɑdə

Travis
BR 'travɪs
AM 'trævəs

travois[1]
singular
BR trə'vɔɪ, 'travɔɪ
AM 'træ,vɔɪ, trə'vɔɪ, trəv'wɑ

travois[2]
plural
BR trə'vɔɪz, 'travɔɪz
AM 'træ,vɔɪ(z), trə'vɔɪ(z), trəv'wɑ(z)

trawl
BR trɔːl, -z, -ɪŋ, -d
AM trɔl, trɑl, -z, -ɪŋ, -d

trawler
BR 'trɔːlə(r), -z
AM 'trɔlər, 'trɑlər, -z

trawlerman
BR 'trɔːləmən
AM 'trɔlərmən, 'trɑlərmən

trawlermen
BR 'trɔːləmən
AM 'trɔlərmən, 'trɑlərmən

Trawsfynydd
BR ,traʊs'vʌnɪð, ,traʊz'vʌnɪð
AM ,traʊs'vənəθ

tray
BR treɪ, -z
AM treɪ, -z

trayful
BR 'treɪfʊl, -z
AM 'treɪ,fʊl, -z

treacherous
BR 'trɛtʃ(ə)rəs
AM 'trɛtʃ(ə)rəs

treacherously
BR 'trɛtʃ(ə)rəsli
AM 'trɛtʃ(ə)rəsli

treacherousness
BR 'trɛtʃ(ə)rəsnəs
AM 'trɛtʃ(ə)rəsnəs

treachery
BR 'trɛtʃ(ə)r|i, -ɪz
AM 'trɛtʃ(ə)ri, -z

treacle
BR 'triːkl
AM 'trikəl

treacliness
BR 'triːkl̩ɪnɪs, 'triːklɪnɪs
AM 'trik(ə)linɪs

treacly
BR 'triːkl̩i, 'triːkli
AM 'trik(ə)li

Treacy
BR 'triːsi
AM 'trisi

tread
BR trɛd, -z, -ɪŋ, -ɨd
AM trɛd, -z, -ɪŋ, -əd

treader
BR 'trɛdə(r), -z
AM 'trɛdər, -z

treadle
BR 'trɛdl, -z
AM 'trɛdəl, -z

treadmill
BR 'trɛdmɪl, -z
AM 'trɛd,mɪl, -z

treadwheel
BR 'trɛdwiːl, -z
AM 'trɛd,(h)wil, -z

treason
BR 'triːzn, -z
AM 'trizn, -z

treasonable
BR 'triːzn̩əbl, 'triːz(ə)nəbl
AM 'trizn̩əbəl

treasonableness
BR 'triːzn̩əblnəs, 'triːz(ə)nəblnəs
AM 'trizn̩əbəlnəs

treasonably
BR 'triːzn̩əbli, 'triːz(ə)nəbli
AM 'triz(ə)nəbli

treasonous
BR 'triːzn̩əs, 'triːz(ə)nəs
AM 'trizn̩əs

treasure
BR 'trɛʒ|ə(r), -əz, -(ə)rɪŋ, -əd
AM 'trɛʒ|ər, -ərz, -(ə)rɪŋ, -ərd

treasurehouse
BR 'trɛʒəhaʊ|s, -zɪz
AM 'trɛʒər,(h)aʊ|s, -zəz

treasurer
BR 'trɛʒ(ə)rə(r), -z
AM 'trɛʒ(ə)rər, -z

treasurership
BR 'trɛʒ(ə)rəʃɪp, -s
AM 'trɛʒ(ə)rər,ʃɪp, -s

treasury
BR 'trɛʒ(ə)r|i, -ɪz
AM 'trɛʒ(ə)ri, -z

treat
BR triːt, -s, -ɪŋ, -ɨd
AM tri|t, -ts, -dɪŋ, -dɨd

treatable
BR 'triːtəbl
AM 'tridəbəl

treater
BR 'triːtə(r), -z
AM 'tridər, -z

treatise
BR 'triːtɪz, 'triːtɪs, -ɨz
AM 'tridɪs, -ɨz

treatment
BR 'triːtm(ə)nt, -s
AM 'tritmənt, -s

treaty
BR 'triːt|i, -ɪz
AM 'tridi, -z

Trebizond
BR 'trɛbɪzɒnd
AM 'trɛbɪ,zɑnd

treble
BR 'trɛb|l, -lz, -l̩ɪŋ\-lɪŋ, -ld
AM 'trɛbəl, -əlz, -(ə)lɪŋ, -əld

treble chance
BR ,trɛbl 'tʃɑːns, + 'tʃans
AM ,trɛbəl 'tʃæns

treble clef
BR ,trɛbl 'klɛf, -s
AM 'trɛbəl ,klɛf, -s

Treblinka
BR trɪ'blɪŋkə(r), trɛ'blɪŋkə(r)
AM trə'blɪŋkə, trɛ'blɪŋkə

trebly
BR 'trɛbli
AM 'trɛbli

Trebor
BR 'triːbɔː(r)
AM 'tribɔ(ə)r

trebuchet
BR 'trɛb(j)ʉʃɛt, -s
AM ,trɛb(j)ə'ʃɛt, -s

trecentist
BR treɪ'tʃɛntɪst, -s
AM treɪ'(t)ʃɛn(t)əst, -s

trecento
BR treɪ'tʃɛntəʊ
AM treɪ'(t)ʃɛn(t)oʊ
IT tre'tʃɛnto

Tredegar
BR trɪ'diːgə(r)
AM trə'digər

tree
BR triː, -z, -ɪŋ, -d
AM tri, -z, -ɪŋ, -d

treecreeper
BR 'triː,kriːpə(r), -z
AM 'tri,kripər, -z

treehouse
BR 'triːhaʊ|s, -zɪz
AM 'tri,haʊ|s, -zəz

treeless
BR 'triːlɪs
AM 'trilɪs

treelessness
BR 'triːlɪsnɪs
AM 'trilɪsnɪs

treeline
BR 'triːlʌɪn
AM 'tri,laɪn

treen
BR triːn
AM trin

treenail
BR 'triːneɪl, 'trɛnl, -z
AM 'tri,neɪl, 'trɛnl, -z

treetop
BR 'triːtɒp, -s
AM 'tri,tɑp, -s

trefa
BR 'treɪfə(r)
AM 'treɪfə

Trefgarne
BR 'trɛvgɑːn, 'trɛfgɑːn
AM 'trɛf,gɑrn

trefoil
BR 'trɛfɔɪl, 'triːfɔɪl, trɪ'fɔɪl, -z, -d
AM 'tri,fɔɪl, 'trɛ,fɔɪl, -z, -d

Trefusis
BR trɪ'fjuːsɪs
AM trə'fjusəs

Tregaron
BR trɪ'garən, trɪ'garn̩
AM trə'gɛrən

trehalose
BR 'triːhələʊs, trɪ'hɑːləʊs
AM 'tri(h)ə,loʊs

trek
BR trɛk, -s, -ɪŋ, -t
AM trɛk, -s, -ɪŋ, -t

trekker
BR 'trɛkə(r), -z
AM 'trɛkər, -z

Trelawney
BR trɪ'lɔːni
AM trə'lɔni, trə'lɑni

trellis
BR 'trɛlɪs, -ɪz, -t
AM 'trɛləs, -əz, -t

trellis-work
BR 'trɛlɪswəːk, -s
AM 'trɛləs,wərk, -s

Tremain
BR trɪ'meɪn
AM trə'meɪn

trematode
BR 'trɛmətəʊd, 'triːmətəʊd, -z
AM 'trɛmə,toʊd, 'trimə,toʊd, -z

tremble
BR 'trɛmbl, -z, -ɪŋ, -d
AM 'trɛmbəl, -əlz, -(ə)lɪŋ, -əld

trembler
BR 'trɛmblə(r), -z
AM 'trɛmb(ə)lər, -z

trembling
BR 'trɛmblɪŋ, -z
AM 'trɛmb(ə)lɪŋ, -z

tremblingly
BR 'trɛmblɪŋli
AM 'trɛmb(ə)lɪŋli

trembly
BR 'trɛmbli
AM 'trɛmb(ə)li

tremendous
BR trɪ'mɛndəs
AM trə'mɛndəs, tri'mɛndəs

tremendously
BR trɪ'mɛndəsli
AM trə'mɛndəsli, tri'mɛndəsli

tremendousness
BR trɪ'mɛndəsnəs
AM trə'mɛndəsnəs, tri'mɛndəsnəs

Tremlett
BR 'trɛmlɪt
AM 'trɛmlət

tremolo
BR 'trɛmələʊ, 'trɛml̩əʊ, -z
AM 'trɛmə,loʊ, -z

tremor
BR 'trɛmə(r), -z
AM 'trɛmər, -z

tremulant
BR 'trɛmjʉlənt, 'trɛmjʉln̩t
AM 'trɛmjələnt

tremulous
BR 'trɛmjʉləs
AM 'trɛmjələs

tremulously
BR 'trɛmjʉləsli
AM 'trɛmjələsli

tremulousness
BR 'trɛmjʉləsnəs
AM 'trɛmjələsnəs

trenail
BR 'triːneɪl, 'trɛnl, -z
AM 'tri,neɪl, 'trɛnl, -z

trench
BR trɛn(t)ʃ, -ɪz
AM trɛn(t)ʃ, -əz

trenchancy
BR 'trɛn(t)ʃ(ə)nsi
AM 'trɛn(t)ʃənsi

trenchant
BR 'trɛn(t)ʃ(ə)nt
AM 'trɛn(t)ʃənt

trenchantly
BR 'trɛn(t)ʃ(ə)n(t)li
AM 'trɛn(t)ʃəntli

Trenchard
BR 'trɛn(t)ʃɑːd, 'trɛn(t)ʃəd
AM 'trən(t)ʃərd

trencher
BR 'trɛn(t)ʃə(r), -z
AM 'trɛn(t)ʃər, -z

trencherman
BR 'trɛn(t)ʃəmən
AM 'trɛn(t)ʃərmən

trenchermen
BR 'trɛn(t)ʃəmən
AM 'trɛn(t)ʃərmən

trend
BR trɛnd, -z, -ɪŋ, -ɪd
AM trɛnd, -z, -ɪŋ, -əd

trendily
BR 'trɛndɪli
AM 'trɛndəli

trendiness
BR 'trɛndɪnɪs
AM 'trɛndinɨs

trendsetter
BR 'trɛnd,sɛtə(r), -z
AM 'trɛn(d),sɛdər, -z

trendsetting
BR 'trɛnd,sɛtɪŋ
AM 'trɛn(d),sɛdɪŋ

trendy
BR 'trɛnd|i, -ɪz, -ɪə(r), -ɪɪst
AM 'trɛndi, -z, -ər, -ɨst

Trent
BR trɛnt
AM trɛnt

trental
BR 'trɛntl, -z
AM 'trɛn(t)l, -z

trente-et-quarante
BR ,trɒ̃teɪka'rɒ̃t
AM ,trɑn(t)əkə'rɑnt

Trentham
BR 'trɛntəm
AM 'trɛn(t)əm

Trentino-Alto
BR trɛn,tiːnəʊ'altəʊ
AM trɛn,tinoʊ'ɑltoʊ

Trento
BR 'trɛntəʊ
AM 'trɛn(t)oʊ

Trenton
BR 'trɛnt(ə)n
AM 'trɛnt(ə)n

Treorchy
BR trɪ'ɔːki
AM tri'ɔrki

trepan
BR trɪ'pan, -z, -ɪŋ, -d
AM trə'pæn, tri'pæn, -z, -ɪŋ, -d

trepanation
BR ,trɛpə'neɪʃn, -z
AM ,trɛpə'neɪʃən, -z

trepang
BR trɪ'paŋ, -z
AM trə'pæŋ, tri'pæŋ, -z

trephination
BR ,trɛfɪ'neɪʃn
AM ,trɛfə'neɪʃən

trephine
BR trɪ'fiːn, trɪ'fʌɪn, -z, -ɪŋ, -d
AM 'tri,faɪn, -z, -ɪŋ, -d

trepidation
BR ,trɛpɪ'deɪʃn
AM ,trɛpə'deɪʃən

treponemata
BR ,trɛpə'niːmətə(r)
AM ,trɛpə'nimədə

treponeme
BR 'triːpəniːm, -z
AM 'trɛpənim, -z

treponima
BR ,trɛpə'niːmə(r)
AM ,trɛpə'nimə

Tresillian
BR trɪ'sɪlɪən
AM trə'sɪljən, trə'sɪliən

trespass
BR 'trɛspəs, -ɪz, -ɪŋ, -t
AM 'trɛspəs, 'trɛ,spæs, -əz, -ɪŋ, -t

trespasser
BR 'trɛspəsə(r), -z
AM 'trɛ,spæsər, 'trɛspəsər, -z

tress
BR trɛs, -ɪz
AM trɛs, -əz

tressure
BR 'trɛʃə(r), 'trɛs(j)ʊə(r), -z
AM 'trɛʃər, -z

tressy
BR 'trɛsi
AM 'trɛsi

trestle
BR 'trɛsl, -z
AM 'trɛsəl, -z

tret
BR trɛt, -s
AM trɛt, -s

Tretchikoff
BR 'trɛtʃɪkɒf
AM 'trɛtʃə,kɔf, 'trɛtʃə,kɑf

Trethowan
BR trɪ'θəʊən, trɪ'θaʊən
AM trə'θoʊən, trə'θaʊən

Tretyakov
BR 'trɛtjəkɒv
AM 'trɛtjə,kɔv, 'trɛtjə,kɑv
RUS trʲitʲji'kof

trevally
BR trɪ'val|i, -ɪz
AM trə'væli, -z

Trevelyan
BR trɪ'vɛlɪən, trɪ'vɪlɪən
AM trə'vɛljən, trə'vɛliən

Trevethick
BR trɪ'vɛθɪk
AM trə'vɛθɪk

Trevino
BR trɪ'viːnəʊ
AM trə'vinoʊ

Trevithick
BR trɪ'vɪθɪk
AM 'trə'vɪθɪk

Trevor
BR 'trɛvə(r)
AM 'trɛvər

trews
BR truːz
AM truz

trey
BR treɪ, -z
AM treɪ, -z

triable
BR 'trʌɪəbl
AM 'traɪəbəl

triacetate
BR trʌɪ'asɨteɪt, -s
AM traɪ'æsəˌteɪt, -s

triacid
BR trʌɪ'asɪd, -z
AM traɪ'æsəd, -z

triad
BR 'trʌɪad, -z
AM 'traɪˌæd, -z

triadelphous
BR ˌtrʌɪə'dɛlfəs
AM ˌtraɪə'dɛlfəs

triadic
BR trʌɪ'adɪk
AM traɪ'ædɪk

triadically
BR trʌɪ'adɨkli
AM traɪ'ædək(ə)li

triage
BR 'triːɑːʒ, 'trʌɪɑːʒ, 'triːɪdʒ, 'trʌɪɪdʒ
AM 'triɑʒ

trial
BR 'trʌɪəl, -z, -ɪŋ, -d
AM 'traɪ(ə)l, -z, -ɪŋ, -d

trial and error
BR ˌtrʌɪ(ə)l ən(d) 'ɛrə(r), + n̩(d) +
AM ˌtraɪ(ə)l ən 'ɛrər

trialist
BR 'trʌɪəlɪst, -s
AM 'traɪələst, -s

triallist
BR 'trʌɪəlɪst, -s
AM 'traɪələst, -s

trial marriage
BR ˌtrʌɪəl 'mar|ɪdʒ, -ɪdʒɪz
AM ¦træɪ(ə)l 'mɛrɪdʒ, -ɪz

trial run
BR ˌtrʌɪəl 'rʌn, -z
AM ¦traɪ(ə)l 'rən, -z

triandrous
BR trʌɪ'andrəs
AM traɪ'ændrəs

triangle
BR 'trʌɪaŋgl, 'trʌɪəŋgl, -z
AM 'traɪˌæŋgəl, -z

triangular
BR trʌɪ'aŋgjʉlə(r)
AM traɪ'æŋgjələr

triangularity
BR trʌɪˌaŋgjʉ'larɪti
AM traɪˌæŋgjə'lɛrədi

triangularly
BR trʌɪ'aŋgjʉləli
AM traɪ'æŋgjələrli

triangulate[1]
adjective
BR trʌɪ'aŋgjʉlət
AM traɪ'æŋgjələt

triangulate[2]
verb
BR trʌɪ'aŋgjʉleɪt, -s, -ɪŋ, -ɨd
AM traɪ'æŋgjəˌleɪ|t, -ts, -dɪŋ, -dɨd

triangulately
BR trʌɪ'aŋgjʉlətli
AM traɪ'æŋgjələtli

triangulation
BR trʌɪˌaŋgjʉ'leɪʃn, ˌtrʌɪaŋgjʉ'leɪʃn
AM ˌtraɪˌæŋgjə'leɪʃən

Trianon
BR 'triənɒn
AM 'triəˌnɑn

triantelope
BR trʌɪ'antɪləʊp, -s
AM traɪ'æn(t)əˌloʊp, -s

Trias
BR 'trʌɪas
AM 'traɪəs

Triassic
BR trʌɪ'asɪk
AM traɪ'æsɪk

triathlete
BR trʌɪ'aθliːt, -s
AM traɪ'æθ(ə)ˌlit, -s

triathlon
BR trʌɪ'aθlən, trʌɪ'aθlɒn, -z
AM traɪ'æθ(ə)lən, traɪ'æθ(ə)ˌlɑn, -z

triatomic
BR ˌtrʌɪə'tɒmɪk
AM ˌtraɪə'tɑmɪk

triaxial
BR trʌɪ'aksɪəl
AM traɪ'æksiəl

tribade
BR 'trɪbəd, -z
AM 'traɪbəd, trə'bɑd, -z

tribadism
BR 'trɪbədɪz(ə)m
AM 'trɪbəˌdɪzəm

tribal
BR 'trʌɪbl
AM 'traɪbəl

tribalism
BR 'trʌɪbəlɪz(ə)m, 'trʌɪbl̩ɪz(ə)m
AM 'traɪbəˌlɪzəm

tribalist
BR 'trʌɪbəlɪst, 'trʌɪbl̩ɪst, -s
AM 'traɪbələst, -s

tribalistic
BR ˌtrʌɪbə'lɪstɪk, ˌtrʌɪbl'ɪstɪk
AM ˌtraɪbə'lɪstɪk

tribally
BR 'trʌɪbəli, 'trʌɪbl̩i
AM 'trɪbəli

tribasic
BR trʌɪ'beɪsɪk
AM traɪ'beɪsɪk

tribe
BR trʌɪb, -z
AM traɪb, -z

tribesman
BR 'trʌɪbzmən
AM 'traɪbzmən

tribesmen
BR 'trʌɪbzmən
AM 'traɪbzmən

tribespeople
BR 'trʌɪbzˌpiːpl
AM 'traɪbzˌpipəl

tribeswoman
BR 'trʌɪbzˌwʊmən
AM 'traɪbzˌwʊmən

tribeswomen
BR 'trʌɪbzˌwɪmɪn
AM 'traɪbzˌwɪmɪn

triblet
BR 'trɪblɪt, -s
AM 'trɪblɪt, -s

triboelectricity
BR ˌtrʌɪbəʊɪˌlɛk'trɪsɨti, ˌtrʌɪbəʊˌɛlɛk'trɪsɨti, ˌtrʌɪbəʊˌɛlɪk'trɪsɨti, ˌtrʌɪbəʊˌɪlɛk'trɪsɨti, ˌtrʌɪbəʊˌiːlɛk'trɪsɨti
AM ¦traɪboʊələk'trɪsɨdi, ¦traɪboʊˌilək'trɪsɨdi

tribologist
BR trʌɪ'bɒlədʒɪst, -s
AM traɪ'bɑlədʒəst, -s

tribology
BR trʌɪ'bɒlədʒi
AM traɪ'bɑlədʒi

triboluminescence
BR ˌtrʌɪbəʊˌl(j)uːmɪ'nɛsns
AM ¦traɪboʊˌlumə'nɛsəns

triboluminescent
BR ˌtrʌɪbəʊˌl(j)uːmɪ'nɛsnt
AM ¦traɪboʊˌlumə'nɛsənt

tribometer
BR trʌɪ'bɒmɪtə(r), -z
AM traɪ'bɑmədər, -z

tribrach
BR 'trʌɪbrak, 'trɪbrak, -s
AM 'traɪˌbræk, -s

tribrachic
BR trʌɪ'brakɪk, trɪ'brakɪk
AM traɪ'brækɪk

tribulation
BR ˌtrɪbjʉ'leɪʃn
AM ˌtrɪbjə'leɪʃən

tribunal
BR trʌɪ'bjuːnl, -z
AM traɪ'bjunəl, trə'bjunəl, -z

tribunate
BR 'trɪbjʉnət, 'trɪbjʉneɪt, -s
AM 'trɪbjənət, 'trɪbjəˌneɪt, -s

tribune
BR 'trɪbjuːn, -z
AM 'trɪbjun, -z

tribuneship
BR 'trɪbjuːnʃɪp, -s
AM 'trɪbjunˌʃɪp, -s

tribunicial
BR ˌtrɪbjʉ'nɪʃl
AM ˌtrɪbjə'nɪʃəl

tribunician
BR ˌtrɪbjʉ'nɪʃn, -z
AM ˌtrɪbjə'nɪʃən, -z

tribunitial
BR ˌtrɪbjʉ'nɪʃl
AM ˌtrɪbjə'nɪʃəl

tributarily
BR 'trɪbjʉt(ə)rɨli
AM ˌtrɪbjə'tɛrəli

tributariness
BR 'trɪbjʉt(ə)rɪnɪs
AM 'trɪbjəˌtɛrinɨs

tributary
BR 'trɪbjʉt(ə)r|i, -ɪz
AM 'trɪbjəˌtɛri, -z

tribute
BR 'trɪbjuːt, -s
AM 'trɪbjut, -s

tricameral
BR (ˌ)trʌɪ'kam(ə)rəl, (ˌ)trʌɪ'kam(ə)rl̩
AM ˌtraɪ'kæm(ə)rəl

tricar
BR 'trʌɪkɑː(r), -z
AM 'traɪˌkɑr, -z

trice
BR trʌɪs
AM traɪs

Tricel®
BR 'trʌɪsɛl
AM 'traɪˌsɛl

tricentenary
BR ˌtrʌɪsɛn'tiːn(ə)r|i, ˌtrʌɪsɛn'tɛn(ə)r|i, trʌɪ'sɛntɪn(ə)r|i, -ɪz
AM traɪ'sɛn(t)əˌnɛri, traɪˌsɛn'tɛnəri, -z

triceps
BR 'trʌɪsɛps, -ɪz
AM 'traɪˌsɛps, -ɪz

triceratops
BR trʌɪ'sɛrətɒps
AM traɪ'sɛrəˌtɑps

trichiasis
BR trɪ'kʌɪəsɪs, ˌtrɪkɪ'eɪsɪs
AM trə'kaɪəsəs

trichina
BR trɪ'kʌɪnə(*r*), trɪ'kiːnə(*r*), -z
AM trə'kaɪnə, trə'kinə, -z

trichinae
BR trɪ'kʌɪniː, trɪ'kiːniː

AM trəˈkaɪni, trəˈkini

Trichinopoly
BR ˌtrɪtʃɪˈnɒpəli, ˌtrɪtʃɪˈnɒpl̩i
AM ˌtrɪkəˈnɑpəli

trichinosis
BR ˌtrɪkɪˈnəʊsɪs
AM ˌtrɪkəˈnoʊsəs

trichinous
BR ˈtrɪkɪnəs
AM ˈtrɪkənəs

trichloride
BR trʌɪˈklɔːrʌɪd, -z
AM traɪˈklɔˌraɪd, -z

trichloroethane
BR ˌtrʌɪklɔːrəʊˈiːθeɪn, trʌɪˌklɔːrəʊˈiːθeɪn
AM ¦traɪˌklɔroʊˈɛˌθeɪn

trichogenous
BR trɪˈkɒdʒɪnəs
AM trəˈkɑdʒənəs

trichological
BR ˌtrɪkəˈlɒdʒɪkl
AM ˌtrɪkəˈlɑdʒəkəl

trichologist
BR trɪˈkɒlədʒɪst, -s
AM trəˈkɑlədʒəst, -s

trichology
BR trɪˈkɒlədʒi
AM trəˈkɑlədʒi

trichome
BR ˈtrʌɪkəʊm, ˈtrɪkəʊm, -z
AM ˈtraɪˌkoʊm, ˈtrɪˌkoʊm, -z

trichomonad
BR ˌtrɪkə(ʊ)ˈmɒnad, -z
AM ˌtrɪkəˈmɑˌnæd, ˌtrɪkəˈmoʊˌnæd, -z

trichomoniasis
BR ˌtrɪkə(ʊ)mə(ʊ)ˈnʌɪəsɪs
AM ˌtrɪkəməˈnaɪəsəs

trichopathic
BR ˌtrɪkə(ʊ)ˈpaθɪk
AM ˌtrɪkəˈpæθɪk

trichopathy
BR trɪˈkɒpəθi
AM trəˈkɑpəθi

Trichoptera
BR trʌɪˈkɒpt(ə)rə(r)
AM traɪˈkɑptərə

trichopteran
BR trʌɪˈkɒpt(ə)rən, trʌɪˈkɒpt(ə)rn̩, -z
AM trəˈkɑptərən, -z

trichopterous
BR trʌɪˈkɒpt(ə)rəs
AM trəˈkɑpt(ə)rəs

trichord
BR ˈtrʌɪkɔːd, -z
AM ˈtraɪˌkɔ(ə)rd, -z

trichotomic
BR ˌtrʌɪkəˈtɒmɪk, ˌtrɪkəˈtɒmɪk
AM ˌtrɪkəˈtɑmɪk

trichotomise
BR trʌɪˈkɒtəmʌɪz, trɪˈkɒtəmʌɪz, -ɪz, -ɪŋ, -d
AM trəˈkɑdəˌmaɪz, ˌtraɪˈkɑdəˌmaɪz, -ɪz, -ɪŋ, -d

trichotomize
BR trʌɪˈkɒtəmʌɪz, trɪˈkɒtəmʌɪz, -ɪz, -ɪŋ, -d
AM trəˈkɑdəˌmaɪz, ˌtraɪˈkɑdəˌmaɪz, -ɪz, -ɪŋ, -d

trichotomous
BR trʌɪˈkɒtəməs, trɪˈkɒtəməs
AM trəˈkɑdəməs, ˌtraɪˈkɑdəməs

trichotomy
BR trʌɪˈkɒtəmi, trɪˈkɒtəmi
AM traɪˈkɑdəmi

trichroic
BR trʌɪˈkrəʊɪk
AM traɪˈkroʊɪk

trichroism
BR ˈtrʌɪkrəʊɪz(ə)m
AM ˈtraɪkrəˌwɪzəm

trichromatic
BR ˌtrʌɪkrə(ʊ)ˈmatɪk
AM ˌtraɪˌkroʊˈmædɪk

trichromatism
BR trʌɪˈkrəʊmətɪz(ə)m
AM ˌtraɪˈkroʊməˌtɪzəm

Tricia
BR ˈtrɪʃə(r)
AM ˈtrɪʃə

Tricity®
BR ˈtrɪsɪti
AM ˈtraɪˌsɪdi

tri-city
BR ˌtraɪˈsɪti, ˈtrʌɪˌsɪti
AM ˌtraɪˈsɪdi

trick
BR trɪk, -s, -ɪŋ, -t
AM trɪk, -s, -ɪŋ, -t

tricker
BR ˈtrɪkə(r), -z
AM ˈtrɪkər, -z

trickery
BR ˈtrɪk(ə)ri
AM ˈtrɪk(ə)ri

trickily
BR ˈtrɪkɪli
AM ˈtrɪkəli

trickiness
BR ˈtrɪkɪnɪs
AM ˈtrɪkinɪs

trickish
BR ˈtrɪkɪʃ
AM ˈtrɪkɪʃ

trickle
BR ˈtrɪk|l, -lz, -l̩ɪŋ\-lɪŋ, -ld
AM ˈtrɪk|əl, -əlz, -(ə)lɪŋ, -əld

trickler
BR ˈtrɪkl̩ə(r), ˈtrɪklə(r), -z
AM ˈtrɪk(ə)lər, -z

trickless
BR ˈtrɪklɪs
AM ˈtrɪklɪs

trickly
BR ˈtrɪkl̩i, ˈtrɪkli
AM ˈtrɪk(ə)li

trick-or-treat
BR ˌtrɪkɔːˈtriːt
AM ˌtrɪkərˈtrit

tricksily
BR ˈtrɪksɪli
AM ˈtrɪksəli

tricksiness
BR ˈtrɪksɪnɪs
AM ˈtrɪksinɪs

trickster
BR ˈtrɪkstə(r), -z
AM ˈtrɪkstər, -z

tricksy
BR ˈtrɪks|i, -ɪə(r), -ɪɪst
AM ˈtrɪksi, -ər, -ɪst

tricky
BR ˈtrɪk|i, -ɪə(r), -ɪɪst
AM ˈtrɪki, -ər, -ɪst

triclinia
BR trʌɪˈklɪnɪə(r), trɪˈklɪnɪə(r)
AM traɪˈkliniə

triclinic
BR trʌɪˈklɪnɪk
AM traɪˈklɪnɪk

triclinium
BR trʌɪˈklɪnɪəm, trɪˈklɪnɪəm
AM traɪˈkliniəm

tricolor
BR ˈtrɪkələ(r), ˈtrɪkl̩ə(r), ˈtrʌɪˌkʌlə(r), -z
AM ˈtraɪˌkələr, -z

tricolored
BR ˈtrʌɪˌkʌləd, ˌtrʌɪˈkʌləd
AM ˈtraɪˌkələrd

tricolour
BR ˈtrɪkələ(r), ˈtrɪkl̩ə(r), ˈtrʌɪˌkʌlə(r), -z
AM ˈtraɪˌkələr, -z

tricoloured
BR ˈtrʌɪˌkʌləd, ˌtrʌɪˈkʌləd
AM ˈtraɪˌkələrd

tricorn
BR ˈtrʌɪkɔːn, -z
AM ˈtraɪˌkɔ(ə)rn, -z

tricorne
BR ˈtrʌɪkɔːn, -z
AM ˈtraɪˌkɔ(ə)rn, -z

tricot
BR ˈtrɪkəʊ, ˈtriːkəʊ, -z
AM ˈtrikoʊ, -z

tricotyledonous
BR ˌtrʌɪkɒtɪˈliːdn̩əs, ˌtrʌɪkɒtlˈiːdn̩əs
AM ¦traɪˌkɑdəˈlidn̩əs

tricrotic
BR trʌɪˈkrɒtɪk
AM traɪˈkrɑdɪk

tricuspid
BR trʌɪˈkʌspɪd
AM traɪˈkəspəd

tricycle
BR ˈtrʌɪsɪkl, -z
AM ˈtraɪsɪkəl, ˈtraɪˌsɪkəl, -z

tricyclic
BR ˌtrʌɪˈsʌɪklɪk, ˌtrʌɪˈsɪklɪk
AM ˌtraɪˈsaɪklɪk, ˌtraɪˈsɪklɪk

tricyclist
BR ˈtrʌɪsɪklɪst, -s
AM ˈtraɪsɪklɪst, ˈtraɪˌsɪklɪst, -s

tridactyl
BR trʌɪˈdakt(ɪ)l
AM traɪˈdæktl

tridactylous
BR trʌɪˈdaktɪləs, trʌɪˈdaktl̩əs
AM traɪˈdæktələs

trident
BR ˈtrʌɪd(ə)nt, -s
AM ˈtraɪdnt, -s

tridentate
BR trʌɪˈdɛnteɪt
AM traɪˈdɛnˌteɪt

Tridentine
BR trʌɪˈdɛntʌɪn, trɪˈdɛntʌɪn
AM traɪˈdɛnˌtin, traɪˈdɛnˌtaɪn

tridigitate
BR trʌɪˈdɪdʒɪteɪt
AM traɪˈdɪdʒəˌteɪt

tridimensional
BR ˌtrʌɪdɪˈmɛnʃn̩(ə)l, ˌtrʌɪdɪˈmɛnʃən(ə)l, ˌtrʌɪdʌɪˈmɛnʃn̩(ə)l, ˌtrʌɪdʌɪˈmɛnʃən(ə)l
AM ˌtraɪdəˈmɛn(t)ʃ(ə)nəl

triduum
BR ˈtrɪdjʊəm, ˈtrʌɪdjʊəm
AM ˈtrɪdjəwəm, ˈtrɪdʒəwəm

tridymite
BR ˈtrɪdɪmʌɪt, -s
AM ˈtrɪdəˌmaɪt, -s

tried
BR trʌɪd
AM traɪd

triene
BR ˈtrʌɪiːn, -z
AM ˈtraɪin, -z

triennia
BR trʌɪˈɛnɪə(r)
AM traɪˈɛniə

triennial
BR trʌɪˈɛnɪəl
AM traɪˈɛniəl
triennially
BR trʌɪˈɛnɪəli
AM traɪˈɛniəli
triennium
BR trʌɪˈɛnɪəm, -z
AM traɪˈɛniəm, -z
Trier
BR ˈtrɪə(r)
AM ˈtrɪ(ə)r
trier
BR ˈtrʌɪə(r), -z
AM ˈtraɪər, -z
trierarchy
BR ˈtrʌɪərɑːk|i, -ɪz
AM ˈtraɪəˌrɑrki, -z
Trieste
BR trɪˈɛst
AM triˈɛst
IT triˈɛste
trifacial
BR trʌɪˈfeɪʃl
AM traɪˈfeɪʃəl
trifecta
BR trʌɪˈfɛktə(r)
AM traɪˈfɛktə
triffid
BR ˈtrɪfɪd, -z
AM ˈtrɪfɪd, -z
trifid
BR ˈtrʌɪfɪd
AM ˈtrifɪd
trifle
BR ˈtrʌɪf|l, -lz, -l̩ɪŋ\-lɪŋ, -ld
AM ˈtraɪf|əl, -əlz, -(ə)lɪŋ, -əld
trifler
BR ˈtrʌɪflə(r), ˈtrʌɪfl̩ə(r), -z
AM ˈtraɪf(ə)lər, -z
triflingly
BR ˈtrʌɪflɪŋli, ˈtrʌɪfl̩ɪŋli
AM ˈtraɪf(ə)lɪŋli
triflingness
BR ˈtrʌɪflɪŋnɪs, ˈtrʌɪfl̩ɪŋnɪs
AM ˈtraɪf(ə)lɪŋnɪs
trifocal
BR trʌɪˈfəʊkl, -z
AM ˈtraɪˌfoʊkəl, -z
trifoliate
BR trʌɪˈfəʊlɪət
AM traɪˈfoʊliət, traɪˈfoʊliˌeɪt
triforia
BR trʌɪˈfɔːrɪə(r)
AM traɪˈfɔriə
triforium
BR trʌɪˈfɔːrɪəm, -z
AM traɪˈfɔriəm, -z
triform
BR ˈtrʌɪfɔːm
AM ˈtraɪˌfɔ(ə)rm
trifurcate
BR ˈtrʌɪfəkeɪt, -s, -ɪŋ, -ɪd
AM ˈtraɪfərˌkeɪ|t, -ts, -dɪŋ, -dɪd
trig
BR trɪg, -z
AM trɪg, -z
trigamist
BR ˈtrɪgəmɪst, -s
AM ˈtrɪgəməst, -s
trigamous
BR ˈtrɪgəməs
AM ˈtrɪgəməs
trigamy
BR ˈtrɪgəmi
AM ˈtrɪgəmi
trigeminal
BR trʌɪˈdʒɛmɪnl
AM traɪˈdʒɛmənəl
trigemini
BR trʌɪˈdʒɛmɪnʌɪ
AM traɪˈdʒɛməˌnaɪ
trigeminus
BR trʌɪˈdʒɛmɪnəs
AM traɪˈdʒɛmənəs
trigger
BR ˈtrɪg|ə(r), -əz, -(ə)rɪŋ, -əd
AM ˈtrɪgər, -z, -ɪŋ, -d
triggerfish
BR ˈtrɪgəfɪʃ
AM ˈtrɪgərˌfɪʃ
triglyceride
BR trʌɪˈglɪsərʌɪd, -z
AM traɪˈglɪsəˌraɪd, -z
triglyph
BR ˈtrʌɪglɪf, -s
AM ˈtraɪˌglɪf, -s
triglyphic
BR trʌɪˈglɪfɪk
AM traɪˈglɪfɪk
triglyphical
BR trʌɪˈglɪfɪkl
AM traɪˈglɪfɪkəl
trigon
BR ˈtrʌɪg(ə)n, ˈtrʌɪgɒn, -z
AM ˈtraɪˌgɑn, -z
trigonal
BR ˈtrɪgənl
AM ˈtrɪgənəl
trigonally
BR ˈtrɪgənl̩i, ˈtrɪgənəli
AM ˈtrɪgənəli
trigoneutic
BR ˌtrʌɪgəˈnjuːtɪk
AM ˌtraɪgəˈn(j)udɪk
trigonometric
BR ˌtrɪgənəˈmɛtrɪk, ˌtrɪgn̩əˈmɛtrɪk
AM ¦trɪgənəˈmɛtrɪk
trigonometrical
BR ˌtrɪgənəˈmɛtrɪkl, ˌtrɪgn̩əˈmɛtrɪkl
AM ¦trɪgənəˈmɛtrəkəl
trigonometrically
BR ˌtrɪgənəˈmɛtrɪkli, ˌtrɪgn̩əˈmɛtrɪkli
AM ¦trɪgənəˈmɛtrək(ə)li
trigonometry
BR ˌtrɪgəˈnɒmɪtri
AM ˌtrɪgəˈnɑmətri
trigram
BR ˈtrʌɪgram, -z
AM ˈtraɪˌgræm, -z
trigraph
BR ˈtrʌɪgrɑːf, ˈtrʌɪgraf, -s
AM ˈtraɪˌgræf, -s
trigynous
BR ˈtrɪdʒɪnəs
AM ˈtrɪdʒɪnəs
trihedra
BR trʌɪˈhiːdrə(r), trʌɪˈhɛdrə(r)
AM traɪˈhidrə
trihedral
BR trʌɪˈhiːdr(ə)l, trʌɪˈhɛdr(ə)l
AM traɪˈhidrəl
trihedron
BR trʌɪˈhiːdrən, trʌɪˈhɛdrən, -z
AM traɪˈhidrən, -z
trihydric
BR trʌɪˈhʌɪdrɪk
AM traɪˈhaɪdrɪk
trijet
BR ˈtrʌɪdʒɛt, -s
AM ˈtraɪˌdʒɛt, -s
trike
BR trʌɪk, -s
AM traɪk, -s
trilabiate
BR trʌɪˈleɪbɪət
AM traɪˈleɪbiˌeɪt
trilaminar
BR trʌɪˈlamɪnə(r)
AM traɪˈlæmənər
trilateral
BR trʌɪˈlat(ə)rəl, trʌɪˈlat(ə)rl̩
AM traɪˈlædərəl, traɪˈlætrəl
trilaterally
BR trʌɪˈlat(ə)rəli, trʌɪˈlat(ə)rl̩i
AM traɪˈlædərəli, traɪˈlætrəli
trilateralness
BR trʌɪˈlat(ə)rəlnəs, trʌɪˈlat(ə)rl̩nəs
AM traɪˈlædərəlnəs, traɪˈlætrəlnəs
trilby
BR ˈtrɪlb|i, -ɪz, -d
AM ˈtrɪlbi, -z, -d
trilemma
BR trʌɪˈlɛmə(r), -z
AM traɪˈlɛmə, -z
trilinear
BR trʌɪˈlɪnɪə(r)
AM traɪˈlɪni(ə)r
trilingual
BR trʌɪˈlɪŋgw(ə)l
AM traɪˈlɪŋgwəl
trilingualism
BR trʌɪˈlɪŋgwəlɪz(ə)m, trʌɪˈlɪŋgwl̩ɪz(ə)m
AM traɪˈlɪŋgwəˌlɪzəm
triliteral
BR trʌɪˈlɪt(ə)rəl, trʌɪˈlɪt(ə)rl̩
AM traɪˈlɪdərəl, traɪˈlɪtrəl
trilith
BR ˈtrʌɪlɪθ, -s
AM ˈtraɪˌlɪθ, -s
trilithic
BR trʌɪˈlɪθɪk
AM traɪˈlɪθɪk
trilithon
BR ˈtrɪlɪθɒn, -z
AM ˈtrɪləˌθɑn, -z
trill
BR trɪl, -z, -ɪŋ, -d
AM trɪl, -z, -ɪŋ, -d
Trilling
BR ˈtrɪlɪŋ
AM ˈtrɪlɪŋ
trillion
BR ˈtrɪljən, -z
AM ˈtrɪljən, -z
trillionth
BR ˈtrɪljənθ
AM ˈtrɪljənθ
trillium
BR ˈtrɪlɪəm
AM ˈtrɪliəm
trilobate
BR trʌɪˈləʊbeɪt
AM ˈtraɪləˌbeɪt
trilobite
BR ˈtrʌɪlə(ʊ)bʌɪt, ˈtrɪlə(ʊ)bʌɪt, -s
AM ˈtraɪləˌbaɪt, ˈtrɪləˌbaɪt, -s
trilocular
BR trʌɪˈlɒkjʊlə(r)
AM traɪˈlɑkjələr
trilogy
BR ˈtrɪlədʒ|i, -ɪz
AM ˈtrɪlədʒi, -z
trim
BR trɪm, -z, -ɪŋ, -d
AM trɪm, -z, -ɪŋ, -d
trimaran
BR ˈtrʌɪməran, -z
AM ˈtraɪməˌræn, -z
Trimble
BR ˈtrɪmbl
AM ˈtrɪmbəl
trimer
BR ˈtrʌɪmə(r), -z
AM ˈtraɪmər, -z
trimeric
BR trʌɪˈmɛrɪk
AM traɪˈmɛrɪk
trimerous
BR ˈtrɪm(ə)rəs

AM 'trɪmərəs

trimester
BR trʌɪ'mɛstə(r), 'trʌɪmɛstə(r), -z
AM 'traɪˌmɛstər, -z

trimestral
BR trʌɪ'mɛstr(ə)l
AM traɪ'mɛstrəl

trimeter
BR 'trɪmɨtə(r), 'trʌɪˌmiːtə(r), -z
AM 'trɪmədər, -z

trimetric
BR trʌɪ'mɛtrɪk
AM traɪ'mɛtrɪk

trimetrical
BR trʌɪ'mɛtrɨkl
AM traɪ'mɛtrəkəl

trimly
BR 'trɪmli
AM 'trɪmli

trimmer
BR 'trɪmə(r), -z
AM 'trɪmər, -z

trimming
BR 'trɪmɪŋ, -z
AM 'trɪmɪŋ, -z

trimness
BR 'trɪmnɨs
AM 'trɪmnɪs

trimorphic
BR trʌɪ'mɔːfɪk
AM traɪ'mɔrfɪk

trimorphism
BR trʌɪ'mɔːfɪz(ə)m
AM traɪ'mɔrˌfɪzəm

trimorphous
BR trʌɪ'mɔːfəs
AM traɪ'mɔrfəs

Trimurti
BR trɪ'mʊəti
AM trɪ'mʊrdi

trinal
BR 'trʌɪnl
AM 'traɪnəl

Trincomalee
BR ˌtrɪŋkəmə'liː
AM ˌtrɪŋkəmə'li

trine
BR trʌɪn, -z
AM traɪn, -z

Tring
BR trɪŋ
AM trɪŋ

Trini
BR 'triːn|i, -ɪz
AM 'trini, -z

Trinian's
BR 'trɪnɪənz
AM 'trɪniənz

Trinidad
BR 'trɪnɨdad
AM 'trɪnəˌdæd

Trinidad and Tobago
BR 'trɪnɨdad (ə)n(d) tə'beɪgəʊ
AM 'trɪnədæd ən tə'beɪgoʊ

Trinidadian
BR ˌtrɪnɪ'dadɪən, -z
AM ˌtrɪnə'dædiən, ˌtrɪnə'deɪdiən, -z

Trinitarian
BR ˌtrɪnɪ'tɛːrɪən, -z
AM ˌtrɪnə'tɛriən, -z

Trinitarianism
BR ˌtrɪnɪ'tɛːrɪənɪz(ə)m
AM ˌtrɪnə'tɛriəˌnɪzəm

trinitrotoluene
BR ˌtrʌɪˌnʌɪtrəʊ'tɒljʊiːn
AM traɪˌnaɪtroʊ'tɑljəˌwin

trinitrotoluol
BR ˌtrʌɪˌnʌɪtrəʊ'tɒljʊɒl
AM traɪ¦naɪtroʊ'tɑljəˌwɔl, traɪˌnaɪtroʊ'tɑljəˌwɑl

trinity
BR 'trɪnɪt|i, -ɪz
AM 'trɪnɨdi, -z

trinket
BR 'trɪŋkɪt, -s
AM 'trɪŋkɪt, -s

trinketry
BR 'trɪŋkɨtri
AM 'trɪŋkɨtri

trinomial
BR trʌɪ'nəʊmɪəl
AM traɪ'noʊmiəl

trinomialism
BR trʌɪ'nəʊmɪəlɪz(ə)m
AM traɪ'noʊmiəˌlɪzəm

trio
BR 'triːəʊ, -z
AM 'trioʊ, -z

triode
BR 'trʌɪəʊd, -z
AM 'traɪˌoʊd, -z

trioecious
BR trʌɪ'iːʃəs
AM traɪ'iʃəs

triolet
BR 'triːə(ʊ)lɛt, 'trʌɪə(ʊ)lɛt, 'triːə(ʊ)lɨt, 'trʌɪə(ʊ)lɨt, -s
AM 'triələt, -s

trioxide
BR trʌɪ'ɒksʌɪd, -z
AM traɪ'ɑkˌsaɪd, -z

trip
BR trɪp, -s, -ɪŋ, -t
AM trɪp, -s, -ɪŋ, -t

tripartite
BR trʌɪ'pɑːtʌɪt
AM traɪ'pɑrˌtaɪt

tripartitely
BR trʌɪ'pɑːtʌɪtli
AM traɪ'pɑrˌtaɪtli

tripartition
BR ˌtrʌɪpɑː'tɪʃn
AM ˌtraɪpɑr'tɪʃən

tripe
BR trʌɪp
AM traɪp

tripetalous
BR trʌɪ'pɛtl̩əs, trʌɪ'pɛtələs
AM traɪ'pɛdləs

triphibious
BR trʌɪ'fɪbɪəs
AM traɪ'fibiəs

triphosphate
BR trʌɪ'fɒsfeɪt, -s
AM traɪ'fɑsˌfeɪt, -s

triphthong
BR 'trɪfθɒŋ, 'trɪpθɒŋ, -z
AM 'trɪfˌθɔŋ, 'trɪpˌθɔŋ, 'trɪfˌθɑŋ, 'trɪpˌθɑŋ, -z

triphthongal
BR ˌtrɪf'θɒŋgl, ˌtrɪp'θɒŋgl
AM trɪf'θɔŋ(g)əl, trɪp'θɔŋ(g)əl, trɪf'θɑŋ(g)əl, trɪp'θɑŋ(g)əl

triphyllous
BR trʌɪ'fɪləs
AM traɪ'fɪləs

tripinnate
BR trʌɪ'pɪneɪt, trʌɪ'pɪnɨt
AM traɪ'pɪˌneɪt, traɪ'pɪnɨt

Tripitaka
BR trɪ'pɪtəkə(r), ˌtrɪpɪ'tɑːkə(r)
AM ˌtrɪpi'tɑkə

triplane
BR 'trʌɪpleɪn, -z
AM 'traɪˌpleɪn, -z

triple
BR 'trɪp|l, -lz, -lɪŋ\-lɪŋ, -ld
AM 'trɪp|əl, -əlz, -(ə)lɪŋ, -əld

triple crown
BR ˌtrɪpl 'kraʊn, -z
AM ˌtrɪpəl 'kraʊn, -z

triple-header
BR ˌtrɪpl'hɛdə(r), -z
AM ¦trɪpəl'hɛdər, -z

triplet
BR 'trɪplɨt, -s
AM 'trɪplɨt, -s

triplex
BR 'trɪplɛks
AM 'trɪˌplɛks

triplicate[1]
noun, adjective
BR 'trɪplɨkət
AM 'trɪpləkət

triplicate[2]
verb
BR 'trɪplɨkeɪt, -s, -ɪŋ, -ɨd
AM 'trɪpləˌkeɪ|t, -ts, -dɪŋ, -dɨd

triplication
BR ˌtrɪplɪ'keɪʃn, -z
AM ˌtrɪplə'keɪʃən, -z

triplicity
BR trɪ'plɪsɪt|i, -ɪz
AM trɪ'plɪsɨdi, -z

triploid
BR 'trɪplɔɪd, -z
AM 'trɪplɔɪd, -z

triploidy
BR 'trɪplɔɪdi
AM 'trɪˌplɔɪdi

triply
BR 'trɪpli
AM 'trɪp(ə)li

tripmeter
BR 'trɪpˌmiːtə(r), -z
AM 'trɪpˌmidər, -z

tripod
BR 'trʌɪpɒd, -z
AM 'traɪˌpɑd, -z

tripodal
BR 'trɪpədl
AM traɪ'poʊdəl

tripoli
BR 'trɪpəl|i, 'trɪpl̩|i, -ɪz
AM 'trɪpəli, -z

Tripolis
BR 'trɪpəlɪs, 'trɪpl̩ɪs
AM 'trɪp(ə)ləs

Tripolitania
BR ˌtrɪpəlɪ'teɪnɪə(r), ˌtrɪpl̩ɪ'teɪnɪə(r), trɪˌpɒlɪ'teɪnɪə(r)
AM ˌtrɪpələ'teɪniə

Tripolitanian
BR ˌtrɪpəlɪ'teɪnɪən, ˌtrɪpl̩ɪ'teɪnɪən, trɪˌpɒlɪ'teɪnɪən, -z
AM ˌtrɪpələ'teɪniən, -z

tripos
BR 'trʌɪpɒs, -ɪz
AM 'traɪˌpɑs, -əz

Tripp
BR trɪp
AM trɪp

tripper
BR 'trɪpə(r), -z
AM 'trɪpər, -z

trippingly
BR 'trɪpɪŋli
AM 'trɪpɪŋli

trippy
BR 'trɪpi
AM 'trɪpi

triptych
BR 'trɪptɪk, -s
AM 'trɪptɪk, -s

triptyque
BR trɪp'tiːk, -s
AM trɪp'tik, 'trɪptɪk, -s

Tripura
BR 'trɪp(ʊ)rə(r)
AM 'trɪpʊrə

tripwire
BR 'trɪpˌwʌɪə(r), -z
AM 'trɪpˌwaɪ(ə)r, -z

triquetra
BR trʌɪ'kwiːtrə(r), trʌɪ'kwɛtrə(r), -z

AM traɪˈkwitrə, traɪˈkwɛtrə, -z
triquetrae
BR trʌɪˈkwiːtriː, trʌɪˈkwɛtriː
AM traɪˈkwitri, traɪˈkwɛtri, traɪˈkwitˌraɪ, traɪˈkwɛtˌraɪ
triquetral
BR trʌɪˈkwiːtr(ə)l, trʌɪˈkwɛtr(ə)l
AM traɪˈkwitrəl, traɪˈkwɛtrəl
triquetrous
BR trʌɪˈkwiːtrəs, trʌɪˈkwɛtrəs
AM traɪˈkwitrəs, traɪˈkwɛtrəs
trireme
BR ˈtrʌɪriːm, -z
AM ˈtraɪˌrim, -z
trisaccharide
BR trʌɪˈsakərʌɪd, -z
AM traɪˈsækəˌraɪd, -z
Trisagion
BR trɪˈsagɪən, trɪˈseɪgɪən, -z
AM triˈsægiən, -z
trisect
BR trʌɪˈsɛkt, -s, -ɪŋ, -ɨd
AM traɪˈsɛk|(t), -(t)s, -tɪŋ, -təd
trisection
BR trʌɪˈsɛkʃn, -z
AM traɪˈsɛkʃən, -z
trisector
BR trʌɪˈsɛktə(r), -z
AM traɪˈsɛktər, -z
Trish
BR trɪʃ
AM trɪʃ
Trisha
BR ˈtrɪʃə(r)
AM ˈtrɪʃə
trishaw
BR ˈtrʌɪʃɔː(r), -z
AM ˈtraɪˌʃɔ, ˈtraɪˌʃɑ, -z
triskelion
BR trɪˈskɛlɪən, trʌɪˈskɛlɪən, -z
AM traɪˈskɛliən, trəˈskɛliən, traɪˈskɛliˌɑn, trəˈskɛliˌɑn, -z
trismus
BR ˈtrɪzməs, -ɨz
AM ˈtrɪzməs, -ɨz
trisomy
BR ˈtrɪsəmi
AM ˈtrɪsɨmi
Tristan
BR ˈtrɪst(ə)n
AM ˈtrɪsˌtɑn, ˈtrɪstən
Tristan da Cunha
BR ˌtrɪst(ə)n də ˈkuːn(j)ə(r)
AM ˌtrɪstən də ˈkun(j)ə
Tri-Star
BR ˈtrʌɪstɑː(r)
AM ˈtraɪˌstɑr
triste
BR triːst
AM trist
tristesse
BR triːˈstɛs
AM triˈstɛs
tristichous
BR ˈtrɪstɨkəs
AM ˈtrɪstəkəs
tristigmatic
BR ˌtrʌɪstɪgˈmatɪk
AM ˌtrɪstɪgˈmædɪk
Tristram
BR ˈtrɪstrəm
AM ˈtrɪstrəm
tristylous
BR trʌɪˈstʌɪləs
AM traɪˈstaɪləs
trisulcate
BR trʌɪˈsʌlkeɪt
AM traɪˈsəlˌkeɪt
trisyllabic
BR ˌtrʌɪsɨˈlabɪk
AM ˌtraɪsəˈlæbɪk
trisyllabically
BR ˌtrʌɪsɨˈlabɨkli
AM ˌtraɪsəˈlæbək(ə)li
trisyllable
BR trʌɪˈsɪləbl, ˈtrʌɪˌsɪləbl, -z
AM traɪˈsɪləbəl, -z
tritagonist
BR trʌɪˈtagənɪst, trʌɪˈtagn̩ɪst, -s
AM traɪˈtægənəst, -s
tritanope
BR ˈtrɪtənəʊp, -s
AM ˈtrɪtnˌoʊp, -s
tritanopia
BR ˌtrɪtəˈnəʊpɪə(r)
AM ˌtrɪtnˈoʊpiə
trite
BR trʌɪt, -ə(r), -ɨst
AM traɪ|t, -dər, -dəst
tritely
BR ˈtrʌɪtli
AM ˈtraɪtli
triteness
BR ˈtrʌɪtnɨs
AM ˈtraɪtnəs
triternate
BR trʌɪˈtəːnət, trʌɪˈtəːneɪt
AM traɪˈtərneɪt, traɪˈtərnət
tritheism
BR ˈtrʌɪθɪɪz(ə)m, trʌɪˈθiːɪz(ə)m
AM traɪˈθiˌɪzəm
tritheist
BR ˈtrʌɪθɪɪst, trʌɪˈθiːɪst, -s
AM traɪˈθiɨst, -s
tritiate
BR ˈtrɪtɪeɪt, -s, -ɪŋ, -ɨd
AM ˈtrɪdiˌeɪ|t, ˈtrɪʃiˌeɪ|t, -ts, -dɪŋ, -dɨd
tritiation
BR ˌtrɪtɪˈeɪʃn
AM ˌtrɪʃiˈeɪʃən
triticale
BR ˌtrɪtɨˈkeɪli
AM ˌtrɪdɨˈkeɪli
tritium
BR ˈtrɪtɪəm
AM ˈtrɪdiəm
triton
BR ˈtrʌɪt(ə)n, -z
AM ˈtraɪtn, -z
tritone
BR ˈtrʌɪtəʊn, -z
AM ˈtraɪˌtoʊn, -z
triturable
BR ˈtrɪtjʊrəbl, ˈtrɪtʃ(ʊ)rəbl
AM ˈtrɪtʃərəbəl
triturate
BR ˈtrɪtjʊreɪt, ˈtrɪtʃʊreɪt, -s, -ɪŋ, -ɨd
AM ˈtrɪtʃəˌreɪ|t, -ts, -dɪŋ, -dɨd
trituration
BR ˌtrɪtjʊˈreɪʃn, ˌtrɪtʃʊˈreɪʃn
AM ˌtrɪtʃəˈreɪʃən
triturator
BR ˈtrɪtjʊreɪtə(r), ˈtrɪtʃʊreɪtə(r), -z
AM ˈtrɪtʃəˌreɪdər, -z
triumph
BR ˈtrʌɪəmf, ˈtrʌɪʌmf, -s, -ɪŋ, -t
AM ˈtraɪəmf, -s, -ɪŋ, -t
triumphal
BR trʌɪˈʌmfl
AM traɪˈəmfəl
triumphalism
BR trʌɪˈʌmfl̩ɪz(ə)m, trʌɪˈʌmfəlɪz(ə)m
AM traɪˈəmfəˌlɪzəm
triumphalist
BR trʌɪˈʌmfl̩ɪst, trʌɪˈʌmfəlɪst
AM traɪˈəmfələst
triumphally
BR trʌɪˈʌmfl̩i, trʌɪˈʌmfəli
AM traɪˈəmfəli
triumphant
BR trʌɪˈʌmf(ə)nt
AM traɪˈəmfənt
triumphantly
BR trʌɪˈʌmf(ə)ntli
AM traɪˈəmfən(t)li
triumvir
BR trʌɪˈʌmvə(r), ˈtrʌɪəmvə(r), -z
AM traɪˈəmvər, -z
triumviral
BR trʌɪˈʌmvɨrəl, trʌɪˈʌmvɨrl̩
AM traɪˈəmvərəl
triumvirate
BR trʌɪˈʌmvɨrət, -s
AM traɪˈəmvərət, traɪˈəmvəˌreɪt, -s
triune
BR ˈtrʌɪjuːn
AM ˈtraɪˌ(j)un
triunity
BR trʌɪˈjuːnɨt|i, -ɪz
AM traɪˈjunədi, -z
trivalency
BR (ˌ)trʌɪˈveɪləns|i, (ˌ)trʌɪˈveɪln̩s|i, -ɪz
AM traɪˈveɪlənsi, -z
trivalent
BR (ˌ)trʌɪˈveɪlənt, (ˌ)trʌɪˈveɪln̩t
AM trʌɪˈveɪlənt
trivet
BR ˈtrɪvɪt, -s
AM ˈtrɪvɨt, -s
trivia
BR ˈtrɪvɪə(r)
AM ˈtrɪviə
trivial
BR ˈtrɪvɪəl
AM ˈtrɪviəl
trivialisation
BR ˌtrɪvɪəlʌɪˈzeɪʃn
AM ˌtrɪviələˈzeɪʃən, ˌtrɪviəˌlaɪˈzeɪʃən
trivialise
BR ˈtrɪvɪəlʌɪz, -ɨz, -ɪŋ, -d
AM ˈtrɪviəˌlaɪz, -ɨz, -ɪŋ, -d
triviality
BR ˌtrɪvɪˈalɪt|i, -ɪz
AM ˌtrɪviˈælədi, -z
trivialization
BR ˌtrɪvɪəlʌɪˈzeɪʃn
AM ˌtrɪviələˈzeɪʃən, ˌtrɪviəˌlaɪˈzeɪʃən
trivialize
BR ˈtrɪvɪəlʌɪz, -ɨz, -ɪŋ, -d
AM ˈtrɪviəˌlaɪz, -ɨz, -ɪŋ, -d
trivially
BR ˈtrɪvɪəli
AM ˈtrɪviəli
trivialness
BR ˈtrɪvɪəlnəs
AM ˈtrɪviəlnəs
trivium
BR ˈtrɪvɪəm
AM ˈtrɪviəm
tri-weekly
BR (ˌ)trʌɪˈwiːkli
AM traɪˈwikli
Trixie
BR ˈtrɪksi
AM ˈtrɪksi
Troad
BR trəʊd
AM troʊd

Troas
BR 'trəʊas
AM 'troʊəs

Trobriand
BR 'trəʊbrɪənd, 'trəʊbrɪand
AM 'troʊˌbriɑnd

Trocadero
BR ˌtrɒkə'dɪərəʊ, ˌtrɒkə'dɛːrəʊ
AM ˌtrɑkə'dɛroʊ

trocar
BR 'trəʊkɑː(r), -z
AM 'troʊˌkɑr, -z

trochaic
BR trə(ʊ)'keɪɪk
AM troʊ'keɪɪk

trochal
BR 'trəʊkl
AM 'troʊkəl

trochanter
BR trə(ʊ)'kantə(r), -z
AM troʊ'kæn(t)ər, -z

troche
BR trəʊʃ, -z
AM 'troʊˌki, -z

trochee
BR 'trəʊkiː, -z
AM 'troʊˌki, -z

trochi
BR 'trəʊkʌɪ, 'trɒkʌɪ
AM 'troʊˌkaɪ

trochlea
BR 'trɒklɪə(r)
AM 'trɑkliə

trochleae
BR 'trɒklɪiː
AM 'trɑkliˌi, 'trɑkliˌaɪ

trochlear
BR 'trɒklɪə(r)
AM 'trɑkliər

trochoid
BR 'trəʊkɔɪd, -z
AM 'troʊˌkɔɪd, -z

trochoidal
BR trə(ʊ)'kɔɪdl
AM troʊ'kɔɪdəl

trochus
BR 'trəʊkəs, 'trɒkəs, -ɪz
AM 'troʊkəs, -əz

troctolite
BR 'trɒktəlʌɪt
AM 'trɑktəˌlaɪt

trod
BR trɒd
AM trɑd

trodden
BR 'trɒdn
AM 'trɑdən

trog
BR trɒg, -z
AM trɑg, -z

troglodyte
cave-dweller
BR 'trɒglədʌɪt, -s
AM 'trɑgləˌdaɪt, -s

troglodytes
wren
BR ˌtrɒglə'dʌɪtiːz
AM ˌtrɑglə'daɪˌtiz

troglodytic
BR ˌtrɒglə'dɪtɪk
AM ˌtrɑglə'dɪdɪk

troglodytical
BR ˌtrɒglə'dɪtɪkl
AM ˌtrɑglə'dɪdɪkəl

troglodytism
BR 'trɒglədʌɪtɪz(ə)m
AM 'trɑgləˌdaɪˌtɪzəm, 'trɑgləˌdaɪˌtɪzəm

trogon
BR 'trəʊgɒn, -z
AM 'troʊˌgɑn, -z

troika
BR 'trɔɪkə(r), -z
AM 'trɔɪkə, -z

troilism
BR 'trɔɪlɪz(ə)m
AM 'trɔɪˌlɪzəm

Troilus
BR 'trɔɪləs
AM 'trɔɪləs

Trojan
BR 'trəʊdʒ(ə)n, -z
AM 'troʊdʒən, -z

Trojan horse
BR ˌtrəʊdʒ(ə)n 'hɔːs, -ɪz
AM ¦troʊdʒən 'hɔ(ə)rs, -əz

troll[1]
noun
BR trɒl, trəʊl, -z
AM troʊl, -z

troll[2]
verb
BR trəʊl, trɒl, -z, -ɪŋ, -d
AM troʊl, -z, -ɪŋ, -d

troller
BR 'trəʊlə(r), 'trɒlə(r), -z
AM 'troʊlər, -z

trolley
BR 'trɒl|i, -ɪz
AM 'trɑli, -z

trolleybus
BR 'trɒlɪbʌs, -ɪz
AM 'trɑliˌbəs, -əz

trollop
BR 'trɒləp, -s
AM 'trɑləp, -s

Trollope
BR 'trɒləp
AM 'trɑləp

trollopish
BR 'trɒləpɪʃ
AM 'trɑləpɪʃ

trollopy
BR 'trɒləpi
AM 'trɑləpi

Tromans
BR 'trəʊmənz
AM 'troʊmənz

trombone
BR trɒm'bəʊn, -z
AM trɑm'boʊn, trəm'boʊn, -z

trombonist
BR trɒm'bəʊnɪst, -s
AM trɑm'boʊnəst, trəm'boʊnəst, -s

trommel
BR 'trɒml, -z
AM 'trɑməl, -z

tromometer
BR trə'mɒmɪtə(r), -z
AM trə'mɑmədər, -z

tromometric
BR ˌtrɒmə'mɛtrɪk
AM ˌtrɑmə'mɛtrɪk

tromp
BR trɒm|p, -ps, -pɪŋ, -(p)t
AM trɑmp, -s, -ɪŋ, -t

trompe
BR trɒmp, -s
AM trɑmp, -s

trompe l'œil
BR ˌtrɒ̃'plɔɪ, ˌtrɒm'plɔɪ
AM ˌtrɔm'plɔɪ

trona
BR 'trəʊnə(r)
AM 'troʊnə

tronc
BR trɒŋk, -s
AM trɑŋk, -s

Trondheim
BR 'trɒn(d)hʌɪm
AM 'trɑn(d),(h)aɪm
NO 'trunheim, 'tronheim

Troon
BR truːn
AM trun

troop
BR truːp, -s, -ɪŋ, -t
AM trup, -s, -ɪŋ, -t

trooper
BR 'truːpə(r), -z
AM 'trupər, -z

troopship
BR 'truːpʃɪp, -s
AM 'trupˌʃɪp, -s

tropaeola
BR trə(ʊ)'piːələ(r)
AM troʊ'piələ

tropaeolum
BR trə(ʊ)'piːələm, -z
AM troʊ'piələm, -z

trope
BR trəʊp, -s
AM troʊp, -s

trophic
BR 'trɒfɪk, 'trəʊfɪk
AM 'troʊfɪk

trophied
BR 'trəʊfɪd
AM 'troʊfid

trophoblast
BR 'trɒfə(ʊ)blɑːst, 'trɒfə(ʊ)blast, -s
AM 'trɑfəˌblæst, -s

trophoneuroses
BR ˌtrɒfəʊnjʊ'rəʊsiːz, ˌtrɒfəʊnjʊə'rəʊsiːz
AM ¦trɑfəˌn(j)u'roʊsiz, ¦trɑfən(j)ə'roʊsiz

trophoneurosis
BR ˌtrɒfəʊnjʊ'rəʊsɪs, ˌtrɒfəʊnjʊə'rəʊsɪs
AM ¦trɑfəˌn(j)u'roʊsəs, ¦trɑfən(j)ə'roʊsəz

trophy
BR 'trəʊf|i, -ɪz
AM 'troʊfi, -z

tropic
BR 'trɒpɪk, -s
AM 'trɑpɪk, -s

tropical
BR 'trɒpɪkl, -z
AM 'trɑpəkəl, -z

tropically
BR 'trɒpɪkli
AM 'trɑpək(ə)li

tropism
BR 'trəʊpɪz(ə)m
AM 'troʊˌpɪzəm

tropological
BR ˌtrɒpə'lɒdʒɪkl
AM ˌtrɑpə'lɑdʒəkəl

tropology
BR trə'pɒlədʒi
AM trə'pɑlədʒi

tropopause
BR 'trɒpəpɔːz
AM 'trɑpəˌpɔz, 'trɑpəˌpɑz

troposphere
BR 'trɒpəsfɪə(r)
AM 'trɑpəˌsfɪ(ə)r

tropospheric
BR ˌtrɒpə'sfɛrɪk
AM ˌtrɑpə'sfɛrɪk

troppo
BR 'trɒpəʊ
AM 'trɑpoʊ

Trossachs
BR 'trɒsəks
AM 'trɑsəks

trot
BR trɒt, -s, -ɪŋ, -ɪd
AM trɑ|t, -ts, -dɪŋ, -dəd

troth
BR trəʊθ, trɒθ
AM trɔθ, troʊθ, trɑθ

Trotsky
BR 'trɒtski
AM 'trɑtski

Trotskyism
BR 'trɒtskɪɪz(ə)m
AM 'trɑtskiˌɪzəm

Trotskyist
BR 'trɒtskɪɪst, -s
AM 'trɑtskiɪst, -s

Trotskyite
BR 'trɒtskɪʌɪt, -s
AM 'trɑtski,aɪt, -s

trotter
BR 'trɒtə(r), -z
AM 'trɑdər, -z

trotting race
BR 'trɒtɪŋ reɪs, -ɪz
AM 'trɑdɪŋ ,reɪs, -ɪz

trottoir
BR 'trɒtwɑː(r), -z
AM trɑ'twɑr, -z

trotyl
BR 'trəʊtɪl, 'trəʊtʌɪl
AM 'troʊdl

troubadour
BR 'truːbədɔː(r), 'truːbədʊə(r), -z
AM 'trubə,dɔ(ə)r, 'trubə,dʊ(ə)r, -z

trouble
BR 'trʌb|l, -lz, -l̩ɪŋ\-lɪŋ, -ld
AM 'trəbəl, -əlz, -(ə)lɪŋ, -əld

troublemaker
BR 'trʌbl,meɪkə(r), -z
AM 'trəbəl,meɪkər, -z

trouble-making
BR 'trʌbl,meɪkɪŋ
AM 'trəbəl,meɪkɪŋ

troubler
BR 'trʌblə(r), -z
AM 'trəb(ə)lər, -z

troubleshoot
BR 'trʌblʃuːt, -s, -ɪŋ
AM 'trəbəl,ʃu|t, -ts, -dɪŋ

troubleshooter
BR 'trʌbl,ʃuːtə(r), -z
AM 'trəbəl,ʃudər, -z

troubleshot
BR 'trʌblʃɒt
AM 'trəbəl,ʃɑt

troublesome
BR 'trʌbls(ə)m
AM 'trəbəlsəm

troublesomely
BR 'trʌbls(ə)mli
AM 'trəbəlsəmli

troublesomeness
BR 'trʌbls(ə)mnəs
AM 'trəbəlsəmnəs

troublous
BR 'trʌbləs
AM 'trəbləs

trough
BR trɒf, -s
AM trɔf, trɑf, -s

trounce
BR traʊns, -ɪz, -ɪŋ, -t
AM traʊns, -əz, -ɪŋ, -t

trouncer
BR 'traʊnsə(r), -z
AM 'traʊnsər, -z

troupe
BR truːp, -s
AM trup, -s

trouper
BR 'truːpə(r), -z
AM 'trupər, -z

trouser
BR 'traʊzə(r), -z, -d
AM 'traʊzər, -z, -d

trouserless
BR 'traʊzələs
AM 'traʊzərləs

trousseau
BR 'truːsəʊ, -z
AM 'tru,soʊ, ,tru'soʊ, -z

trousseaux
BR 'truːsəʊ(z)
AM 'tru,soʊ, ,tru'soʊ

trout
BR traʊt
AM traʊt

troutlet
BR 'traʊtlɪt, -s
AM 'traʊtlət, -s

troutling
BR 'traʊtlɪŋ, -z
AM 'traʊtlɪŋ, -z

trouty
BR 'traʊti
AM 'traʊdi

trouvaille
BR truː'vʌɪ\truː'vʌɪz
AM tru'vaɪ, -z

trouvère
BR truː'vɛː(r)\truː'vɛːz
AM tru'vɛ(ə)r, -z

trove
BR trəʊv
AM troʊv

trover
BR 'trəʊvə(r), -z
AM 'troʊvər, -z

trow
BR trəʊ, traʊ
AM troʊ

Trowbridge
BR 'trəʊbrɪdʒ
AM 'troʊ,brɪdʒ

trowel
BR 'traʊ(ə)l, -z, -ɪŋ, -d
AM 'traʊ(ə)l, -z, -ɪŋ, -d

Trowell
BR 'traʊ(ə)l, 'trəʊ(ə)l
AM 'traʊəl, 'troʊəl

troy
BR trɔɪ
AM trɔɪ

truancy
BR 'truːənsi
AM 'truənsi

truant
BR 'truːənt, -s, -ɪŋ, -ɪd
AM 'truənt, -s, -ɪŋ, -əd

Trubetskoy
BR trʊ'bɛtskɔɪ, ,truːbɛt'skɔɪ
AM trə'bɛt,skɔɪ

Trubshaw
BR 'trʌbʃɔː(r)
AM 'trəb,ʃɔ

truce
BR truːs, -ɪz
AM trus, -əz

truceless
BR 'truːsləs
AM 'trusləs

trucial
BR 'truːʃl
AM 'truʃəl

Trucial States
BR ,truːʃl 'steɪts
AM 'truʃəl ,steɪts

truck
BR trʌk, -s, -ɪŋ, -t
AM trək, -s, -ɪŋ, -t

truckage
BR 'trʌkɪdʒ
AM 'trəkɪdʒ

trucker
BR 'trʌkə(r), -z
AM 'trəkər, -z

truckie
BR 'trʌk|i, -ɪz
AM 'trəki, -z

truckle
BR 'trʌk|l, -lz, -l̩ɪŋ\-lɪŋ, -ld
AM 'trək|əl, -əlz, -(ə)lɪŋ, -əld

truckler
BR 'trʌkl̩ə(r), 'trʌklə(r), -z
AM 'trək(ə)lər, -z

truckload
BR 'trʌkləʊd, -z
AM 'trək,loʊd, -z

truculence
BR 'trʌkjʊləns, 'trʌkjʊl̩ns
AM 'trəkjələns

truculency
BR 'trʌkjʊlənsi, 'trʌkjʊl̩nsi
AM 'trəkjələnsi

truculent
BR 'trʌkjʊlənt, 'trʌkjʊl̩nt
AM 'trəkjələnt

truculently
BR 'trʌkjʊləntli, 'trʌkjʊl̩ntli
AM 'trəkjələn(t)li

Trudeau
BR 'truːdəʊ
AM tru'doʊ

trudge
BR trʌdʒ, -ɪz, -ɪŋ, -d
AM trədʒ, -əz, -ɪŋ, -d

trudgen
BR 'trʌdʒ(ə)n
AM 'trədʒən

trudger
BR 'trʌdʒə(r), -z
AM 'trədʒər, -z

Trudgill
BR 'trʌdgɪl
AM 'trəd,gɪl

Trudi
BR 'truːdi
AM 'trudi

Trudy
BR 'truːdi
AM 'trudi

true
BR truː, -z, -ɪŋ, -d, -ə(r), -ɪst
AM tru, -z, -ɪŋ, -d, -ər, -əst

true-blue
BR ,truː'bluː, -z
AM ',tru'blu, -z

trueish
BR 'truːɪʃ
AM 'truɪʃ

true-life
BR ,truː'lʌɪf
AM ',tru'laɪf

truelove
BR 'truːlʌv, ,truː'lʌv, -z
AM 'tru,ləv, -z

Trueman
BR 'truːmən
AM 'trumən

trueness
BR 'truːnəs
AM 'trunəs

Truffaut
BR 'truːfəʊ, 'truːfəʊ
AM trʊ'foʊ, 'trufoʊ

truffle
BR 'trʌfl, -z
AM 'trəfəl, -z

trug
BR trʌg, -z
AM trəg, -z

truism
BR 'truːɪz(ə)m, -z
AM 'tru,ɪzəm, -z

truistic
BR truː'ɪstɪk
AM tru'ɪstɪk

Trujillo
BR truː'hiːjəʊ
AM tru'hijoʊ

Truk
BR trʌk
AM trək

trull
BR trʌl, -z
AM trəl, -z

truly
BR 'truːli
AM 'truli

Truman
BR 'truːmən
AM 'trumən

Trumbull
BR 'trʌmbl
AM 'trəmbəl

trumeau
BR truː'məʊ, -z
AM tru'moʊ, -z

trumeaux
BR truː'məʊ(z)

AM tru'moʊ

trump
BR trʌm|p, -ps, -pɪŋ, -(p)t
AM trəm|p, -(p)s, -pɪŋ, -(p)t

trumped-up
BR ˌtrʌm(p)t'ʌp
AM ˌtrəm(p)t'əp

trumpery
BR 'trʌmp(ə)r|i, -ɪz
AM 'trəmp(ə)ri, -z

trumpet
BR 'trʌmp|ɪt, -ɪts, -ɨtɪŋ, -ɨtɨd
AM 'trəmpə|t, -ts, -dɪŋ, -dəd

trumpeter
BR 'trʌmpɨtə(r), -z
AM 'trəmpədər, -z

trumpeting
BR 'trʌmpɨtɪŋ, -z
AM 'trəmpədɪŋ, -z

trumpetless
BR 'trʌmpɨtlɨs
AM 'trəmpətləs

truncal
BR 'trʌŋkl
AM 'trəŋkəl

truncate
BR trʌŋ'keɪt, -s, -ɪŋ, -ɨd
AM 'trəŋˌkeɪ|t, -ts, -dɪŋ, -dɨd

truncately
BR trʌŋ'keɪtli
AM 'trəŋˌkeɪtli

truncation
BR trʌŋ'keɪʃn, -z
AM ˌtrəŋ'keɪʃən, -z

truncheon
BR 'trʌn(t)ʃ(ə)n, -z
AM 'trən(t)ʃən, -z

trundle
BR 'trʌnd|l, -lz, -l̩ɪŋ\-lɪŋ, -ld
AM 'trən|dəl, -dəlz, -(d)(ə)lɪŋ, -dəld

trunk
BR trʌŋk, -s
AM trəŋk, -s

trunkful
BR 'trʌŋkfʊl, -z
AM 'trəŋkˌfʊl, -z

trunking
BR 'trʌŋkɪŋ, -z
AM 'trəŋkɪŋ, -z

trunkless
BR 'trʌŋkləs
AM 'trəŋkləs

trunklike
BR 'trʌŋklʌɪk
AM 'trəŋkˌlaɪk

trunnel
BR 'trʌnl, -z, -d
AM 'trənəl, -z, -d

trunnion
BR 'trʌnjən, -z
AM 'trənjən, -z

Truro
BR 'trʊərəʊ
AM 'trʊˌroʊ

Truscott
BR 'trʌskɒt, 'trʌskət
AM 'trəsˌkɑt

truss
BR trʌs, -ɨz, -ɪŋ, -t
AM trəs, -əz, -ɪŋ, -t

trusser
BR 'trʌsə(r), -z
AM 'trəsər, -z

trust
BR trʌst, -s, -ɪŋ, -ɨd
AM trəst, -s, -ɪŋ, -əd

trustable
BR 'trʌstəbl
AM 'trəstəbəl

trustbuster
BR 'trʌs(t)ˌbʌstə(r), -z
AM 'trəs(t)ˌbəstər, -z

trustbusting
BR 'trʌs(t)ˌbʌstɪŋ
AM 'trəs(t)ˌbəstɪŋ

trustee
BR trʌ'stiː, trʌs'tiː, -z
AM trə'sti, -z

trusteeship
BR trʌ'stiːʃɪp, trʌs'tiːʃɪp, -s
AM trə'stiˌʃɪp, -s

truster
BR 'trʌstə(r), -z
AM 'trəstər, -z

trustful
BR trʌs(t)f(ʊ)l
AM 'trəs(t)fəl

trustfully
BR 'trʌs(t)fʊli, 'trʌs(t)fl̩i
AM 'trəs(t)fəli

trustfulness
BR 'trʌstf(ʊ)lnəs
AM 'trəs(t)fəlnəs

trustie
BR 'trʌst|i, -ɪz
AM 'trəsti, -z

trustily
BR 'trʌstɨli
AM 'trəstəli

trustiness
BR 'trʌstɪnɨs
AM 'trəstinɨs

trusting
BR 'trʌstɪŋ
AM 'trəstɪŋ

trustingly
BR 'trʌstɪŋli
AM 'trəstɪŋli

trustingness
BR 'trʌstɪŋnɨs
AM 'trəstɪŋnɨs

trustworthily
BR 'trʌs(t)ˌwəːðɨli
AM 'trəs(t)ˌwərðəli

trustworthiness
BR 'trʌs(t)ˌwəːðɪnɨs
AM 'trəs(t)ˌwərðinɨs

trustworthy
BR 'trʌs(t)ˌwəːði
AM 'trəs(t)ˌwərði

trusty
BR 'trʌst|i, -ɪz, -ɪə(r), -ɪɨst
AM 'trəsti, -z, -ər, -ɨst

truth
BR truː|θ, -ðz\-θs
AM tru|θ, -ðz\-θs

truthful
BR 'truːθf(ʊ)l
AM 'truθfəl

truthfully
BR 'truːθfʊli, 'truːθfl̩i
AM 'truθfəli

truthfulness
BR 'truːθf(ʊ)lnəs
AM 'truθfəlnəs

truthless
BR 'truːθləs
AM 'truθləs

try
BR trʌɪ, -z, -ɪŋ, -d
AM traɪ, -z, -ɪŋ, -d

Tryfan
BR 'trɪvn
AM 'trɪvən
WE 'trʌvan

tryingly
BR 'trʌɪɪŋli
AM 'traɪɪŋli

trypanosome
BR 'trɪpənəsəʊm, 'trɪpn̩əsəʊm, trɪ'panəsəʊm, -z
AM trə'pænəˌsoʊm, 'trɪpənəˌsoʊm, -z

trypanosomiasis
BR ˌtrɪpənə(ʊ)sə'mʌɪəsɪs, ˌtrɪpn̩ə(ʊ)sə'mʌɪəsɪs, trɪˌpanə(ʊ)sə'mʌɪəsɪs
AM trəˌpænəsoʊ'maɪəsɪs

trypsin
BR 'trɪpsɪn
AM 'trɪpsɪn

trypsinogen
BR trɪp'sɪnədʒ(ə)n
AM trɪp'sɪnədʒən, trɪp'sɪnəˌdʒɛn

tryptic
BR 'trɪptɪk
AM 'trɪptɪk

tryptophan
BR 'trɪptəfan
AM 'trɪptəˌfæn

trysail
BR 'trʌɪsl, 'trʌɪseɪl, -z
AM 'traɪsəl, 'traɪˌseɪl, -z

tryst
BR trɪst, -s, -ɪŋ, -ɨd
AM trɪst, -s, -ɪŋ, -ɨd

tryster
BR 'trɪstə(r), -z
AM 'trɪstər, -z

tsar
BR zɑː(r), tsɑː(r), -z
AM zɑr, tsɑr, -z

tsardom
BR 'zɑːdəm, 'tsɑːdəm, -z
AM 'zɑrdəm, 'tsɑrdəm, -z

tsarevich
BR 'zɑːrəvɪtʃ, 'tsɑːrəvɪtʃ, -ɨz
AM 'zɑrəˌvɪtʃ, 'tsɑrəˌvɪtʃ, -ɨz

tsarevitch
BR 'zɑːrəvɪtʃ, 'tsɑːrəvɪtʃ, -ɨz
AM 'zɑrəˌvɪtʃ, 'tsɑrəˌvɪtʃ, -ɨz

tsarevna
BR zɑː'rɛvnə(r), tsɑː'rɛvnə(r), 'zɑːrəvnə(r), 'tsɑːrəvnə(r), -z
AM 'zɑrəvnə, 'tsɑrəvnə, -z

tsarina
BR zɑː'riːnə(r), tsɑː'riːnə(r), -z
AM zɑ'rinə, tsɑ'rinə, -z

tsarism
BR 'zɑːrɪz(ə)m, 'tsɑːrɪz(ə)m
AM 'zɑˌrɪzəm, 'tsɑˌrɪzəm

tsarist
BR 'zɑːrɪst, 'tsɑːrɪst, -s
AM 'zɑrəst, 'tsɑrəst, -s

tsessebi
BR '(t)sɛsəb|i, tsɛ'seɪb|i, -ɪz
AM '(t)sɛsəbi, (t)sɛ'seɪbi, -z

tsetse
BR 't(s)ɛtsi
AM '(t)sitsi, '(t)sɛtsi

T-shirt
BR 'tiːʃəːt, -s
AM 'tiˌʃərt, -s

Tsinan
BR ˌtsiː'nan
AM ˈˌtsi'næn

Tsinghai
BR ˌtsɪŋ'hʌɪ
AM ˈˌtsɪŋ'haɪ

Tsitsikamma
BR ˌ(t)sɪtsɪ'kamə(r)
AM ˈˌ(t)sɪtsi'kɑmə

tsk
BR ǀ
AM ǀ

T-square
BR 'tiːskwɛː(r), -z
AM 'tiˌskwɛ(ə)r, -z

tsunami
BR (t)sʊ'nɑːm|i, -ɪz

AM (t)su'nɑmi, -z

Tsushima
BR (t)sʊ'ʃiːmə(r)
AM (t)sʊ'ʃimə

Tswana
BR 'tswɑːnə(r)
AM 'tswɑnə

TT
BR ˌtiː'tiː, -z
AM ˌti'ti, -z

t-test
BR 'tiːtɛst, -s
AM 'tiˌtɛst, -s

Tuareg
BR 'twɑːrɛɡ, -z
AM 'twɑˌrɛɡ, -z

tuatara
BR ˌtuːə'tɑːrə(r), -z
AM ˌtuə'tɑrə, -z

tub
BR tʌb, -z
AM təb, -z

tuba
BR 'tjuːbə(r), 'tʃuːbə(r), -z
AM 't(j)ubə, -z

tubal
BR 'tjuːbl, 'tʃuːbl
AM 't(j)ubəl

tubbable
BR 'tʌbəbl
AM 'təbəbəl

tubbiness
BR 'tʌbɪnɪs
AM 'təbinɪs

tubbish
BR 'tʌbɪʃ
AM 'təbɪʃ

tubby
BR 'tʌb|i, -ɪə(r), -ɪɪst
AM 'təbi, -ər, -ɪst

tubbyish
BR 'tʌbɪɪʃ
AM 'təbiɪʃ

tube
BR tjuːb, tʃuːb, -z
AM t(j)ub, -z

tubectomy
BR tjʊ'bɛktəm|i, tʃʊ'bɛktəm|i, -ɪz
AM t(j)u'bɛktəmi, -z

tubeless
BR 'tjuːbləs, 'tʃuːbləs
AM 't(j)ubləs

tubelike
BR 'tjuːblʌɪk, 'tʃuːblʌɪk
AM 't(j)ubˌlaɪk

tuber
BR 'tjuːbə(r), 'tʃuːbə(r), -z
AM 't(j)ubər, -z

tubercle
BR 'tjuːbəkl, 'tʃuːbəkl, -z
AM 't(j)ubərkəl, -z

tubercular
BR t(j)ʉ'bəːkjʉlə(r), tʃʉ'bəːkjʉlə(r)
AM tə'bərkjələr, t(j)u'bərkjələr

tuberculate
BR t(j)ʉ'bəːkjʉlət, tʃʉ'bəːkjʉlət
AM tə'bərkjəˌleɪt, t(j)u'bərkjəˌleɪt, tə'bərkjələt, t(j)u'bərkjələt

tuberculation
BR t(j)ʉˌbəːkjʉ'leɪʃn, tʃʉˌbəːkjʉ'leɪʃn
AM təˌbərkjə'leɪʃən, t(j)uˌbərkjə'leɪʃən

tuberculin
BR t(j)ʉ'bəːkjʉlɪn, tʃʉ'bəːkjʉlɪn
AM tə'bərkjələn, t(j)u'bərkjələn

tuberculin-tested
BR t(j)ʉˌbəːkjʉlɪn'tɛstɪd, tʃʉˌbəːkjʉlɪn'tɛstɪd
AM tə'bərkjələnˌtɛstəd, t(j)u'bərkjələnˌtɛstəd

tuberculosis
BR t(j)ʉˌbəːkjʉ'ləʊsɪs, tʃʉˌbəːkjʉ'ləʊsɪs
AM təˌbərkjə'loʊsəs, t(j)uˌbərkjə'loʊsəs

tuberculous
BR t(j)ʉ'bəːkjʉləs, tʃʉ'bəːkjʉləs
AM tə'bərkjələs, t(j)u'bərkjələs

tuberose
BR 'tjuːbərəʊz, 'tʃuːbərəʊz, -ɪz
AM 't(j)ubəˌroʊs, 't(j)ubəˌroʊz, -əz

tuberosity
BR ˌtjuːbə'rɒsɪti, ˌtʃuːbə'rɒsɪti
AM ˌt(j)ubə'rɑsədi

tuberous
BR 'tjuːb(ə)rəs, 'tʃuːb(ə)rəs
AM 't(j)ubərəs

tube worm
BR 'tjuːb wəːm, 'tʃuːb +, -z
AM 't(j)ub ˌwərm, -z

tubful
BR 'tʌbfʊl, -z
AM 'təbˌfʊl, -z

tubicolous
BR tjʉ'bɪkələs, tʃʉ'bɪkələs
AM t(j)u'bɪkələs

tubicorn
BR 'tjuːbɪkɔːn, 'tʃuːbɪkɔːn, -z
AM 't(j)ubəˌkɔ(ə)rn, -z

tubifex
BR 'tjuːbɪfɛks, 'tʃuːbɪfɛks
AM 't(j)ubəˌfɛks

tubiform
BR 'tjuːbɪfɔːm, 'tʃuːbɪfɔːm
AM 't(j)ubəˌfɔ(ə)rm

tubilingual
BR ˌtjuːbɪ'lɪŋɡw(ə)l, ˌtʃuːbɪ'lɪŋɡw(ə)l
AM tubɪ'lɪŋɡwəl

tubing
BR 'tjuːbɪŋ, 'tʃuːbɪŋ
AM 't(j)ubɪŋ

Tubman
BR 'tʌbmən
AM 'təbmən

tub-sized
BR 'tʌbsʌɪzd
AM 'təbˌsaɪzd

tubular
BR 'tjuːbjʉlə(r), 'tʃuːbjʉlə(r)
AM 't(j)ubjələr

tubule
BR 'tjuːbjuːl, 'tʃuːbjuːl, -z
AM 't(j)uˌbjul, -z

tubulous
BR 'tjuːbjʉləs, 'tʃuːbjʉləs
AM 't(j)ubjələs

tuck
BR tʌk, -s, -ɪŋ, -t
AM tək, -s, -ɪŋ, -t

tuckahoe
BR 'tʌkəhəʊ, -z
AM 'təkəˌhoʊ, -z

tuckbox
BR 'tʌkbɒks, -ɪz
AM 'təkˌbɑks, -əz

tucker
BR 'tʌkə(r), -z, -d
AM təkər, -z, -d

tuckerbag
BR 'tʌkəbaɡ, -z
AM 'təkərˌbæɡ, -z

tucket
BR 'tʌkɪt, -s
AM 'təkət, -s

tuckpoint
BR 'tʌkpɔɪnt, -s
AM 'təkˌpɔɪnt, -s

tuckshop
BR 'tʌkʃɒp, -s
AM 'təkˌʃɑp, -s

Tucson
BR 'tuːsɒn
AM 'tuˌsɑn

Tudor
BR 'tjuːdə(r), 'tʃuːdə(r)
AM 't(j)udər

Tudorbethan
BR ˌtjuːdə'biːθn, ˌtʃuːdə'biːθn
AM ˌt(j)udər'biθən

Tudoresque
BR ˌtjuːdər'ɛsk, ˌtʃuːdər'ɛsk
AM ˌt(j)udə'rɛsk

Tuesday
BR 'tjuːzd|eɪ, 'tʃuːzd|eɪ, 'tjuːzd|i, 'tʃuːzd|i, -eɪz\-ɪz
AM 't(j)uzˌdeɪ, 't(j)uzdi, -z

tufa
BR 'tjuːfə(r), 'tʃuːfə(r)
AM 't(j)ufə

tufaceous
BR tjʊ'feɪʃəs, tʃʊ'feɪʃəs
AM t(j)u'feɪʃəs

tuff
BR tʌf
AM təf

tuffaceous
BR tʌ'feɪʃəs
AM ˌtə'feɪʃəs

tuffet
BR 'tʌfɪt, -s
AM 'təfət, -s

Tuffnell
BR 'tʌfnl
AM 'təfnəl, 'təfˌnɛl

Tufnell
BR 'tʌfnl
AM 'təfnəl, 'təfˌnɛl

tuft
BR tʌft, -s, -ɪd
AM təft, -s, -əd

tuftiness
BR 'tʌftɪnɪs
AM 'təftinɪs

tufty
BR 'tʌfti
AM 'təfti

tug
BR tʌɡ, -z, -ɪŋ, -d
AM təɡ, -z, -ɪŋ, -d

tugboat
BR 'tʌɡbəʊt, -s
AM 'təɡˌboʊt, -s

Tugendhat
BR 'tuːɡ(ə)nhɑːt
AM 'tuɡənˌ(h)æt

tugger
BR 'tʌɡə(r), -z
AM 'təɡər, -z

tug-of-love
BR ˌtʌɡəv'lʌv
AM ˌtəɡə(v)'ləv

tug-of-war
BR ˌtʌɡə(v)'wɔː(r), -z
AM ˌtəɡə(v)'wɔ(ə)r, -z

tugrik
BR 'tuːɡriːk, -s
AM 'tuˌɡrik, -s

tui
BR 'tuː|i, -ɪz
AM 'tui, -z

Tuileries
BR 'twiːləri, 'twiːlərɪz
AM 'twiləri(z)

tuition
BR tju:ˈɪʃn, tʃu:ˈɪʃn
AM t(j)uˈɪʃən

tuitional
BR tju:ˈɪʃn̩(ə)l, tju:ˈɪʃən(ə)l, tʃu:ˈɪʃn̩(ə)l, tʃu:ˈɪʃən(ə)l
AM t(j)uˈɪʃ(ə)nəl

tuitionary
BR tju:ˈɪʃn̩(ə)ri, tʃu:ˈɪʃn̩(ə)ri
AM t(j)uˈɪʃəˌnɛri

Tula
BR ˈtu:lə(r)
AM ˈtulə

tularaemia
BR ˌt(j)u:ləˈri:mɪə(r)
AM ˌt(j)uləˈrimiə

tularaemic
BR ˌt(j)u:ləˈri:mɪk
AM ˌt(j)uləˈrimɪk

tularemia
BR ˌt(j)u:ləˈri:mɪə(r)
AM ˌt(j)uləˈrimiə

tularemic
BR ˌt(j)u:ləˈri:mɪk
AM ˌt(j)uləˈrimɪk

tulchan
BR ˈtʌlk(ə)n, ˈtʌlx(ə)n, -z
AM ˈtəlkən, -z

tulip
BR ˈtju:lɪp, ˈtʃu:lɪp, -s
AM ˈt(j)uləp, -s

tulipwood
BR ˈtju:lɪpwʊd, ˈtʃu:lɪpwʊd, -z
AM ˈt(j)uləpˌwʊd, -z

Tull
BR tʌl
AM təl

Tullamore
BR ˈtʌləmɔ:(r)
AM ˈtələˌmɔ(ə)r

tulle
BR tju:l, tʃu:l
AM tul

Tulloch
BR ˈtʌləx, ˈtʌlək
AM ˈtələk

Tully
BR ˈtʌli
AM ˈtəli

Tulsa
BR tʌlsə(r)
AM ˈtəlsə

Tulse Hill
BR ˌtʌls ˈhɪl
AM ˌtəls ˈhɪl

tum
BR tʌm, -z
AM təm, -z

tumble
BR ˈtʌmb|l, -lz, -l̩ɪŋ\-lɪŋ, -ld
AM ˈtəmbəl, -əlz, -(ə)lɪŋ, -əld

tumbledown
BR ˈtʌmbldaʊn
AM ˈtəmbəlˌdaʊn

tumble-drier
BR ˌtʌmblˈdrʌɪə(r), -z
AM ˈtəmbəlˌdraɪər, -z

tumble-dry
BR ˌtʌmblˈdrʌɪ, -z, -ɪŋ, -d
AM ˈtəmbəlˌdraɪ, -z, -ɪŋ, -d

tumble-dryer
BR ˌtʌmblˈdrʌɪə(r), -z
AM ˈtəmbəlˌdraɪər, -z

tumbler
BR ˈtʌmblə(r), -z
AM ˈtəmb(ə)lər, -z

tumblerful
BR ˈtʌmbləfʊl, -z
AM ˈtəmblərˌfʊl, -z

tumbleweed
BR ˈtʌmblwi:d, -z
AM ˈtəmbəlˌwid, -z

tumbrel
BR ˈtʌmbr(ɪ)l, -z
AM ˈtəmbrəl, -z

tumbril
BR ˈtʌmbr(ɪ)l, -z
AM ˈtəmbrəl, -z

tumefacient
BR ˌtju:mɪˈfeɪʃ(ə)nt, ˌtʃu:mɪˈfeɪʃ(ə)nt
AM ˌt(j)uməˈfeɪʃənt

tumefaction
BR ˌtju:mɪˈfakʃn, ˌtʃu:mɪˈfakʃn
AM ˌt(j)uməˈfækʃən

tumefy
BR ˈtju:mɪfʌɪ, ˈtʃu:mɪfʌɪ, -z, -ɪŋ, -d
AM ˈt(j)uməˌfaɪ, -z, -ɪŋ, -d

tumescence
BR tju:ˈmɛsns, tjʊˈmɛsns, tʃu:ˈmɛsns, tʃʊˈmɛsns
AM t(j)uˈmɛsəns

tumescent
BR tju:ˈmɛsnt, tjʊˈmɛsnt, tʃu:ˈmɛsnt, tʃʊˈmɛsnt
AM t(j)uˈmɛsənt

tumescently
BR tju:ˈmɛsntli, tjʊˈmɛsntli, tʃu:ˈmɛsntli, tʃʊˈmɛsntli
AM t(j)uˈmɛsn(t)li

tumid
BR ˈtju:mɪd, ˈtʃu:mɪd
AM ˈt(j)uməd

tumidity
BR tju:ˈmɪdɪti, tjʊˈmɪdɪti, tʃu:ˈmɪdɪti, tʃʊˈmɪdɪti
AM t(j)uˈmɪdɨdi

tumidly
BR ˈtju:mɪdli, ˈtʃu:mɪdli
AM ˈt(j)umədli

tumidness
BR tju:mɪdnɪs, tʃu:mɪdnɪs
AM ˈt(j)umədnəs

tummy
BR ˈtʌm|i, -ɪz
AM ˈtəmi, -z

tumor
BR ˈtju:mə(r), ˈtʃu:mə(r), -z, -əs
AM ˈt(j)umər, -z, -əs

tumorous
BR ˈtju:m(ə)rəs, ˈtʃu:m(ə)rəs
AM ˈt(j)umərəs

tumour
BR ˈtju:mə(r), ˈtʃu:mə(r), -z, -əs
AM ˈt(j)umər, -z, -əs

tump
BR tʌmp, -s
AM təmp, -s

tumtum
BR ˈtʌmtʌm, -z
AM ˈtəmˌtəm, -z

tumular
BR ˈtju:mjʊlə(r), ˈtʃu:mjʊlə(r)
AM ˈt(j)umjələr

tumuli
BR ˈtju:mjʊlʌɪ, ˈtʃu:mjʊlʌɪ
AM ˈt(j)umjəˌlaɪ

tumult
BR ˈtju:mʌlt, ˈtʃu:mʌlt, -s
AM ˈt(j)uˌməlt, -s

tumultuary
BR tjʊˈmʌltjʊəri, tʃʊˈmʌltʃʊəri
AM ˈt(j)uməlˌtʃʊɛri

tumultuous
BR tjʊˈmʌltjʊəs, tʃʊˈmʌltʃʊəs
AM t(j)uˈməltʃ(əw)əs, təˈməltʃ(əw)əs

tumultuously
BR tjʊˈmʌltjʊəsli, tʃʊˈmʌltʃʊəsli
AM t(j)uˈməltʃ(əw)əsli, təˈməltʃ(əw)əsli

tumultuousness
BR tjʊˈmʌltjʊəsnəs, tʃʊˈmʌltʃʊəsnəs
AM t(j)uˈməltʃ(əw)əs-nəs, təˈməltʃ(əw)əsnəs

tumulus
BR ˈtju:mjʊləs, ˈtʃu:mjʊləs, -ɪz
AM ˈt(j)umjələs, -əz

tun
BR tʌn, -z
AM tən, -z

tuna
BR ˈtju:nə(r), ˈtʃu:nə(r), -z
AM ˈtunə, -z

tunable
BR ˈtju:nəbl, ˈtʃu:nəbl
AM ˈt(j)unəbəl

Tunbridge Wells
BR ˌtʌnbrɪdʒ ˈwɛlz
AM ˈtənˌbrɪdʒ ˈwɛlz, ˈtəmˌbrɪdʒ +

tundish
BR ˈtʌndɪʃ, -ɪz
AM ˈtənˌdɪʃ, -ɪz

tundra
BR ˈtʌndrə(r)
AM ˈtəndrə

tune
BR tju:n, tʃu:n, -z, -ɪŋ, -d
AM t(j)un, -z, -ɪŋ, -d

tuneable
BR ˈtju:nəbl, ˈtʃu:nəbl
AM ˈt(j)unəbəl

tuneful
BR ˈtju:nf(ʊ)l, ˈtʃu:nf(ʊ)l
AM ˈt(j)unfəl

tunefully
BR ˈtju:nfʊli, ˈtju:nfl̩i, ˈtʃu:nfʊli, ˈtʃu:nfl̩i
AM ˈt(j)unfəli

tunefulness
BR ˈtju:nf(ʊ)lnəs, ˈtʃu:nf(ʊ)lnəs
AM ˈt(j)unfəlnəs

tuneless
BR ˈtju:nləs, ˈtʃu:nləs
AM ˈt(j)unləs

tunelessly
BR ˈtju:nləsli, ˈtʃu:nləsli
AM ˈt(j)unləsli

tunelessness
BR ˈtju:nləsnəs, ˈtʃu:nləsnəs
AM ˈt(j)unləsnəs

tuner
BR ˈtju:nə(r), ˈtʃu:nə(r), -z
AM ˈt(j)unər, -z

tung
BR tʌŋ, -z
AM təŋ, -z

tungstate
BR ˈtʌŋsteɪt, -s
AM ˈtəŋˌsteɪt, -s

tungsten
BR ˈtʌŋstən
AM ˈtəŋstən

tungstic
BR ˈtʌŋstɪk
AM ˈtəŋstɪk

tungstite
BR ˈtʌŋstʌɪt
AM ˈtəŋstaɪt

Tungus
BR 'tʊŋgʊs, tʊŋ'gu:z, -ɨz
AM 'təŋgəs, 'tʊŋ,gʊs, -əz

Tungusic
BR tʊŋ'gʊsɪk, tʊŋ'gu:zɪk
AM təŋ'gʊsɪk, tʊŋ'gʊsɪk

tunic
BR 'tju:nɪk, 'tʃu:nɪk, -s
AM 't(j)unɪk, -s

tunica
BR 'tju:nɨkə(r), 'tʃu:nɨkə(r)
AM 't(j)unəkə

tunicae
BR 'tju:nɨki:, 'tʃu:nɨki:
AM 't(j)unəki, 't(j)unə,kaɪ, 't(j)unəsi, 't(j)unə,saɪ

tunicate
BR 'tju:nɨkeɪt, 'tʃu:nɨkeɪt, -s, -ɪŋ, -ɨd
AM 't(j)unə,keɪ|t, -ts, -dɪŋ, -dɨd

tunicle
BR 'tju:nɨkl, 'tʃu:nɨkl, -z
AM 't(j)unəkəl, -z

tuning
BR 'tju:nɪŋ, 'tʃu:nɪŋ, -z
AM 't(j)unɪŋ, -z

Tunis
BR 'tju:nɪs, 'tʃu:nɪs
AM 'tunəs

Tunisia
BR tjʊ'nɪzɪə(r), tʃʊ'nɪzɪə(r)
AM tu'niʒə

Tunisian
BR tjʊ'nɪzɪən, tʃʊ'nɪzɪən, -z
AM tu'niʒən, -z

tunnel
BR 'tʌn|l, -lz, -l̩ɪŋ, -ld
AM 'tənəl, -z, -ɪŋ, -d

tunneler
BR 'tʌnl̩ə(r), -z
AM 'tənl̩ər, -z

tunneller
BR 'tʌnl̩ə(r), -z
AM 'tənl̩ər, -z

tunnel vision
BR ,tʌnl 'vɪʒn
AM 'tənəl ,vɪʒn

Tunney
BR 'tʌni
AM 'təni

Tunnicliff
BR 'tʌnɪklɪf
AM 'tənə,klɪf

Tunnicliffe
BR 'tʌnɪklɪf
AM 'tənə,klɪf

tunny
BR 'tʌn|i, -ɪz
AM 'təni, -z

Tuohy
BR 'tu:i
AM 'tui

tup
BR tʌp, -s, -ɪŋ, -t
AM təp, -s, -ɪŋ, -t

Tupamaro
BR ,t(j)u:pə'mɑ:rəʊ, ,t(j)u:pə'marəʊ, -z
AM ,tupə'mɑ,roʊ, -z

tupelo
BR 'tju:pələʊ, 'tʃu:pələʊ, -z
AM 't(j)upə,loʊ, -z

Tupi
BR 'tu:p|i, -ɪz
AM 'tu,pi, -z

tuppence
BR 'tʌp(ə)ns
AM 'təpəns

tuppenny
BR 'tʌp(ə)ni, 'tʌpn̩i
AM 'təpəni

tuppenny-ha'penny
BR 'tʌp(ə)nɪ'heɪp(ə)ni, 'tʌpn̩ɪ'heɪpn̩i
AM 'təpəni'heɪpəni

Tupperware®
BR 'tʌpəwɛ:(r)
AM 'təpər,wɛ(ə)r

tuque
BR tju:k, tʃu:k, -s
AM t(j)uk, -s

tu quoque
BR ,t(j)u: 'kwəʊkw|i, -ɪz
AM 't(j)u 'kwoʊkwi, -z

turaco
BR 'tʊərəkəʊ, -z
AM 't(j)ʊrə,koʊ, -z

Turandot
BR 't(j)ʊərəndɒt, 't(j)ʊərn̩dɒt
AM 't(j)ʊrən,doʊ

Turanian
BR tjʊ'reɪnɪən, tʃʊ'reɪnɪən, -z
AM t(j)ʊ'reɪniən, tə'reɪniən, -z

turban
BR 'tə:b(ə)n, -z, -d
AM 'tərbən, -z, -d

turbary
BR 'tə:b(ə)r|i, -ɪz
AM 'tərb(ə)ri, -z

turbellarian
BR ,tə:bə'lɛ:rɪən, -z
AM ,tərbə'lɛriən, -z

turbid
BR 'tə:bɪd
AM 'tərbəd

turbidity
BR tə:'bɪdɨti
AM tər'bɪdɨdi

turbidly
BR 'tə:bɪdli
AM 'tərbədli

turbidness
BR 'tə:bɪdnɪs
AM 'tərbɪdnɪs

turbinal
BR 'tə:bɪnl, 'tə:bn̩l
AM 'tərbənəl

turbinate
BR 'tə:bɪnət, 'tə:bn̩ət, 'tə:bɪneɪt
AM 'tərbənət, 'tərbə,neɪt

turbination
BR ,tə:bɪ'neɪʃn
AM ,tərbə'neɪʃən

turbine
BR 'tə:bʌɪn, 'tə:bɪn, -z
AM 'tərbən, 'tər,baɪn, -z

turbit
BR 'tə:bɪt, -s
AM 'tərbət, -s

turbo
BR 'tə:bəʊ, -z
AM 'tərboʊ, -z

turbocharge
BR 'tə:bə(ʊ)tʃɑ:dʒ, -ɨz, -ɪŋ, -d
AM 'tərboʊ,tʃɑrdʒ, -əz, -ɪŋ, -d

turbocharger
BR 'tə:bə(ʊ),tʃɑ:dʒə(r), -z
AM 'tərboʊ,tʃɑrdʒər, -z

turbocharging
BR 'tə:bə(ʊ),tʃɑ:dʒɪŋ
AM 'tərboʊ,tʃɑrdʒɪŋ

turbo-diesel
BR ,tə:bəʊ'di:zl, -z
AM ¦tərboʊ'dizəl, -z

turbofan
BR 'tə:bəʊfan, -z
AM 'tərboʊ,fæn, -z

turbojet
BR 'tə:bəʊdʒɛt, -s
AM 'tərboʊ,dʒɛt, -s

turboprop
BR 'tə:bəʊprɒp, -s
AM 'tərboʊ,prɑp, -s

turboshaft
BR 'tə:bəʊʃɑ:ft, 'tə:bəʊʃaft, -s
AM 'tərboʊ,ʃæft, -s

turbosupercharger
BR ,tə:bəʊ'su:pə,tʃɑ:dʒə(r), -z
AM ,tərboʊ'supər,tʃɑrdʒər, -z

turbot
BR 'tə:bət, -s
AM 'tərbət, -s

turbulence
BR 'tə:bjʉləns, 'tə:bjʉln̩s
AM 'tərbjələns

turbulent
BR 'tə:bjʉlənt, 'tə:bjʉln̩t
AM 'tərbjələnt

turbulently
BR 'tə:bjʉləntli, 'tə:bjʉln̩tli
AM 'tərbjələn(t)li

Turco
BR 'tə:kəʊ, -z
AM 'tərkoʊ, -z

Turcoman
BR 'tə:kəmən, 'tə:kəman, 'tə:kəmɑ:n, -z
AM 'tərkəmən, -z

Turcophile
BR 'tə:kə(ʊ)fʌɪl, -z
AM 'tərkə,faɪl, -z

Turcophobe
BR 'tə:kə(ʊ)fəʊb, -z
AM 'tərkə,foʊb, -z

turd
BR tə:d, -z
AM tərd, -z

turdoid
BR 'tə:dɔɪd
AM 'tər,dɔɪd

tureen
BR t(j)ʉ'ri:n, tʃʉ'ri:n, -z
AM tə'rin, t(j)ʊ'rin, -z

turf
BR tə:f, -s, -ɪŋ, -t
AM tərf, -s, -ɪŋ, -t

turfman
BR 'tə:fmən
AM 'tərfmən

turfmen
BR 'tə:fmən
AM 'tərfmən

turfy
BR 'tə:fi
AM 'tərfi

Turgenev
BR tʊə'geɪnjɛf, tə:'geɪnjɛf
AM tʊr'geɪ,njɛf

turgescence
BR tə:'dʒɛsns
AM ,tər'dʒɛsəns

turgescent
BR tə:'dʒɛsnt
AM tər'dʒɛsənt

turgid
BR 'tə:dʒɪd
AM 'tərdʒəd

turgidescence
BR ,tə:dʒɪ'dɛsns
AM ,tərdʒə'dɛsəns

turgidescent
BR ,tə:dʒɪ'dɛsnt
AM ,tərdʒə'dɛsənt

turgidity
BR tə:'dʒɪdɨti
AM tər'dʒɪdɨdi

turgidly
BR ˈtəːdʒɪdli
AM ˈtərdʒədli

turgidness
BR ˈtəːdʒɪdnɪs
AM ˈtərdʒɪdnɪs

turgor
BR ˈtəːɡə(r)
AM ˈtərɡər

Turin
BR tjʊˈrɪn, tjʊəˈrɪn, tʃʊˈrɪn, tʃʊəˈrɪn
AM ˈt(j)ʊrən

Turing
BR ˈtjʊərɪŋ, ˈtʃʊərɪŋ
AM ˈt(j)ʊrɪŋ

turion
BR ˈt(j)ʊərɪən, ˈtʃʊərɪən, -z
AM ˈt(j)ʊriən, ˈt(j)ʊriˌɑn, -z

Turk
BR təːk, -s
AM tərk, -s

Turkana
BR təːˈkɑːnə(r)
AM tərˈkɑnə

Turkestan
BR ˌtəːkɪˈstɑːn, ˌtəːkɪˈstan
AM ˈtərkəˌstæn

turkey
BR ˈtəːk|i, -ɪz
AM ˈtərki, -z

turkeycock
BR ˈtəːkɪkɒk, -s
AM ˈtərkiˌkɑk, -s

Turki
BR ˈtəːk|i, -ɪz
AM ˈtərki, -z

Turkic
BR ˈtəːkɪk
AM ˈtərkɪk

Turkish
BR ˈtəːkɪʃ
AM ˈtərkɪʃ

Turkistan
BR ˌtəːkɪˈstɑːn, ˌtəːkɪˈstan
AM ˈtərkəˌstæn

Turkmenistan
BR təːkˌmɛnɪˈstɑːn, təːkˌmɛnɪˈstan
AM tərkˈmɛnəˌstæn

Turkoman
BR ˈtəːkəmən, ˈtəːkəman, ˈtəːkəmɑːn, -z
AM ˈtərkəmən, -z

Turks and Caicos Islands
BR ˌtəːks (ə)n(d) ˈkeɪkɒs ˌʌɪlən(d)z
AM ˈtərks ən ˈkeɪkəs ˈaɪlən(d)z

Turku
BR ˈtʊəkuː
AM ˈtʊrˌku

turmeric
BR ˈtəːm(ə)rɪk
AM ˈtərmərɪk

turmoil
BR ˈtəːmɔɪl, -z
AM ˈtərˌmɔɪl, -z

turn
BR təːn, -z, -ɪŋ, -d
AM tərn, -z, -ɪŋ, -d

turnabout
BR ˈtəːnəbaʊt, -s
AM ˈtərnəˌbaʊt, -s

turnaround
BR ˈtəːnəraʊnd, -z
AM ˈtərnəˌraʊnd, -z

turnback
BR ˈtəːnbak, -s
AM ˈtərnˌbæk, -s

Turnberry
BR ˈtəːnb(ə)ri
AM ˈtərnˌbɛri

turnbuckle
BR ˈtəːnˌbʌkl, -z
AM ˈtərnˌbəkəl, -z

Turnbull
BR ˈtəːnbʊl
AM ˈtərnbəl

turncoat
BR ˈtəːnkəʊt, -s
AM ˈtərnˌkoʊt, -s

turncock
BR ˈtəːnkɒk, -s
AM ˈtərnˌkɑk, -s

turndown
BR ˈtəːndaʊn, -z
AM ˈtərnˌdaʊn, -z

turner
BR ˈtəːnə(r), -z
AM ˈtərnər, -z

turnery
BR ˈtəːn(ə)ri, -ɪz
AM ˈtərnəri, -z

turning
BR ˈtəːnɪŋ, -z
AM ˈtərnɪŋ, -z

turnip
BR ˈtəːnɪp, -s
AM ˈtərnəp, -s

turnipy
BR ˈtəːnɪpi
AM ˈtərnəpi

turnkey
BR ˈtəːnkiː, -z
AM ˈtərnˌki, -z

turnout
BR ˈtəːnaʊt, -s
AM ˈtərnˌaʊt, -s

turnover
BR ˈtəːnˌəʊvə(r), -z
AM ˈtərnˌoʊvər, -z

turnpike
BR ˈtəːnpʌɪk, -s
AM ˈtərnˌpaɪk, -s

turnround
BR ˈtəːnraʊnd, -z
AM ˈtərnˌraʊnd, -z

turnsick
BR ˈtəːnsɪk
AM ˈtərnˌsɪk

turnside
BR ˈtəːnsʌɪd
AM ˈtərnˌsaɪd

turnsole
BR ˈtəːnsəʊl, -z
AM ˈtərnˌsoʊl, -z

turnspike
BR ˈtəːnspʌɪk, -s
AM ˈtərnˌspaɪk, -s

turnspit
BR ˈtəːnspɪt, -s
AM ˈtərnˌspɪt, -s

turnstile
BR ˈtəːnstʌɪl, -z
AM ˈtərnˌstaɪl, -z

turnstone
BR ˈtəːnstəʊn, -z
AM ˈtərnˌstoʊn, -z

turntable
BR ˈtəːnˌteɪbl, -z
AM ˈtərnˌteɪbəl, -z

turnup
BR ˈtəːnʌp, -s
AM ˈtərnˌəp, -s

turpentine
BR ˈtəːp(ɪ)ntʌɪn
AM ˈtərpənˌtaɪn

turpeth
BR ˈtəːpəθ, -s
AM ˈtərpəθ, -s

Turpin
BR ˈtəːpɪn
AM ˈtərpən

turpitude
BR ˈtəːpɪtjuːd, ˈtəːpɪtʃuːd
AM ˈtərpəˌt(j)ud

turps
BR təːps
AM tərps

turquoise
BR ˈtəːkwɔɪz, ˈtəːkwɑːz
AM ˈtərˌk(w)ɔɪz

turret
BR ˈtʌrɪt, -s, -ɪd
AM ˈtərə|t, -ts, -dəd

turtle
BR ˈtəːtl, -z
AM ˈtərdəl, -z

turtledove
BR ˈtəːtldʌv, -z
AM ˈtərdlˌdəv, -z

turtleneck
BR ˈtəːtlnɛk, -s
AM ˈtərdlˌnɛk, -s

turtleshell
BR ˈtəːtlʃɛl
AM ˈtərdlˌʃɛl

Turton
BR ˈtəːtn
AM ˈtərtn

turves
BR təːvz
AM tərvz

Turvey
BR ˈtəːvi
AM ˈtərvi

Tuscan
BR ˈtʌsk(ə)n, -z
AM ˈtəskən, -z

Tuscany
BR ˈtʌskəni
AM ˈtəskəni

Tuscarora
BR ˌtʌskəˈrɔːrə(r)
AM ˌtəskəˈrɔrə

tush
BR tʌʃ, -ɪz
AM təʃ, tʊʃ, -əz

tusk
BR tʌsk, -s, -t
AM təsk, -s, -t

tusker
BR ˈtʌskə(r), -z
AM ˈtəskər, -z

tusky
BR ˈtʌski
AM ˈtəski

tussah
BR ˈtʌsə(r)
AM ˈtəsə

Tussaud's
BR tʊˈsɔːdz, tʊˈsəʊdz, ˈtuːsɔːdz, ˈtuːsəʊdz
AM tʊˈsoʊz

tusser
BR ˈtʌsə(r)
AM ˈtəsər

tussive
BR ˈtʌsɪv
AM ˈtəsɪv

tussle
BR tʌs|l, -lz, -l̩ɪŋ\-lɪŋ, -ld
AM ˈtəs|əl, -əlz, -(ə)lɪŋ, -əld

tussock
BR ˈtʌsək, -s
AM ˈtəsək, -s

tussocky
BR ˈtʌsəki
AM ˈtəsəki

tussore
BR ˈtʌsə(r), ˈtʌsɔː(r)
AM ˈtəˌsɔ(ə)r

tut[1]
interjection
BR ʇ, tʌt
AM tət

tut[2]
noun, verb
BR tʌt, -s, -ɪŋ, -ɪd
AM tə|t, -ts, -dɪŋ, -dəd

Tutankhamen
BR ˌtuːt(ə)nˈkɑːmən, ˌtuːtəŋˈkɑːmən
AM ˌtuˌtæŋˈkɑmən, ˌtətnˈkɑmən

Tutankhamun
BR ˌtuːt(ə)nˈkɑːmən, ˌtuːtəŋˈkɑːmən, ˌtuːtəŋkəˈmuːn

AM ˌtuˌtæŋˈkɑmən, ˌtətnˈkɑmən

tutee
BR ˌtjuːˈtiː, ˌtʃuːˈtiː, -z
AM t(j)uˈti, -z

tutelage
BR ˈtjuːtɨlɪdʒ, ˈtjuːtl̩ɪdʒ, ˈtʃuːtɨlɪdʒ, ˈtʃuːtl̩ɪdʒ
AM ˈt(j)udl̩ɪdʒ

tutelar
BR ˈtjuːtɨlə(r), ˈtjuːtl̩ə(r), ˈtʃuːtɨlə(r), ˈtʃuːtl̩ə(r)
AM ˈt(j)udl̩ər

tutelary
BR ˈtjuːtɨləri, ˈtjuːtl̩əri, ˈtʃuːtɨləri, ˈtʃuːtl̩əri
AM ˈt(j)udlˌɛri

tutenag
BR ˈtuːtɨnag
AM ˈtudəˌnæg

Tutin
BR ˈtjuːtɪn, ˈtʃuːtɪn
AM ˈt(j)udən

tutor
BR ˈtjuːt|ə(r), ˈtʃuːt|ə(r), -əz, -(ə)rɪŋ, -əd
AM ˈt(j)udər, -z, -ɪŋ, -d

tutorage
BR ˈtjuːt(ə)rɪdʒ, ˈtʃuːt(ə)rɪdʒ
AM ˈt(j)udərɪdʒ

tutoress
BR ˈtjuːt(ə)rɪs, ˈtʃuːt(ə)rɪs, -ɪz
AM ˈt(j)udərəs, ˈt(j)udəˌrɛs, -əz

tutorial
BR tjuːˈtɔːrɪəl, tjʊˈtɔːrɪəl, tʃuːˈtɔːrɪəl, tʃʊˈtɔːrɪəl, -z
AM t(j)uˈtɔriəl, -z

tutorially
BR tjuːˈtɔːrɪəli, tjʊˈtɔːrɪəli, tʃuːˈtɔːrɪəli, tʃʊˈtɔːrɪəli
AM t(j)uˈtɔriəli

tutorship
BR ˈtjuːtəʃɪp, ˈtʃuːtəʃɪp, -s
AM ˈt(j)udərˌʃɪp, -s

tutsan
BR ˈtʌtsən, -z
AM ˈtətsən, -z

Tutsi
BR ˈtʊtsi, ˈtuːtsi
AM ˈtutsi

tutti
BR ˈtʊti, ˈtuːti
AM ˈtudi

tutti-frutti
BR ˌtuːtɪˈfruːt|i, -ɪz
AM ˌtudiˈfrudi, -z

Tuttle
BR ˈtʌtl
AM ˈtədəl

tut-tut
BR ˌtʌtˈtʌt, -s, -ɪŋ, -ɨd
AM ˌtətˈtə|t, -ts, -dɪŋ, -dəd

tutty
BR ˈtʌti
AM ˈtədi

tutu
BR ˈtuːtuː, -z
AM ˈtuˌtu, -z

Tuva
BR ˈtuːvə(r)
AM ˈtuvə
RUS tuˈva

Tuvalu
BR tʊˈvɑːluː
AM təˈvɑlu

Tuvaluan
BR tʊˈvɑːlʊən, -z
AM təˈvɑluən, təˈvɑləwən, -z

tu-whit tu-whoo
BR tʉˌwɪt tʉˈwuː, -z
AM tuˈ(h)wɪt təˈ(h)wu, -z

tux
BR tʌks, -ɪz
AM təks, -ɪz

tuxedo
BR tʌkˈsiːdəʊ, -z
AM təkˈsidoʊ, -z

tuyère
BR ˈtuːˈjɛː(r), twiːˈjɛː(r), -z
AM tuˈjɛ(ə)r, twiˈjɛ(ə)r, -z

Twa
BR twɑː(r), -z
AM twɑ, -z

twaddle
BR ˈtwɒdl
AM ˈtwɑdəl

twaddler
BR ˈtwɒdl̩ə(r), -z
AM ˈtwɑd(ə)lər, -z

twaddly
BR ˈtwɒdl̩i
AM ˈtwɑdl̩i, ˈtwɑdli

twain
BR tweɪn
AM tweɪn

twang
BR twaŋ, -z, -ɪŋ, -d
AM twæŋ, -z, -ɪŋ, -d

twangle
BR ˈtwaŋg|l, -lz, -l̩ɪŋ\-lɪŋ, -ld
AM ˈtwæŋg|əl, -əlz, -(ə)lɪŋ, -əld

twangy
BR ˈtwaŋi
AM ˈtwæŋi

Twankey
BR ˈtwaŋki
AM ˈtwæŋki

Twanky
BR ˈtwaŋki
AM ˈtwæŋki

'twas
BR twɒz, twəz
AM twəz

twat
BR twɒt, twat, -s
AM twɑt, -s

twayblade
BR ˈtweɪbleɪd, -z
AM ˈtweɪˌbleɪd, -z

tweak
BR twiːk, -s, -ɪŋ, -t
AM twik, -s, -ɪŋ, -t

twee
BR twiː
AM twi

tweed
BR twiːd, -z
AM twid, -z

Tweeddale
BR ˈtwiːddeɪl
AM ˈtwi(d)ˌdeɪl

tweedily
BR ˈtwiːdɨli
AM ˈtwidɨli

tweediness
BR ˈtwiːdɪnɨs
AM ˈtwidinɨs

Tweedledee
BR ˌtwiːdlˈdiː
AM ˌtwidlˈdi

Tweedledum
BR ˌtwiːdlˈdʌm
AM ˌtwidlˈdəm

Tweedsmuir
BR ˈtwiːdzmjʊə(r), ˈtwiːdzmjɔː(r)
AM ˈtwidzˌmjʊ(ə)r

tweedy
BR ˈtwiːdi
AM ˈtwidi

tweely
BR ˈtwiːli
AM ˈtwili

'tween
BR twiːn
AM twin

'tween-decks
BR ˈtwiːndɛks
AM ˈtwinˌdɛks

tweeness
BR ˈtwiːnɨs
AM ˈtwinɨs

tweeny
BR ˈtwiːn|i, -ɪz
AM ˈtwini, -z

tweet
BR twiːt, -s, -ɪŋ, -ɨd
AM twi|t, -ts, -dɪŋ, -dɨd

tweeter
BR ˈtwiːtə(r), -z
AM ˈtwidər, -z

tweezer
BR ˈtwiːzə(r), -z, -ɪŋ, -d
AM ˈtwizər, -z, -ɪŋ, -d

twelfth
BR twɛlfθ, -s
AM twɛlf(θ), -s

Twelfth Day
BR ˌtwɛlfθ ˈdeɪ
AM ˈtwɛlf(θ) ˈdeɪ

twelfthly
BR ˈtwɛlfθli
AM ˈtwɛlf(θ)li, ˈtwɛlθli

Twelfth Night
BR ˌtwɛlfθ ˈnʌɪt
AM ˈtwɛlf(θ) ˈnaɪt

twelve
BR twɛlv
AM twɛlv

twelvefold
BR ˈtwɛlvfəʊld
AM ˈtwɛl(v)ˌfoʊld

twelvemo
BR ˈtwɛlvməʊ
AM ˈtwɛlvˌmoʊ

twelvemonth
BR ˈtwɛlvmʌnθ, -s
AM ˈtwɛlvˌmənθ, -s

twentieth
BR ˈtwɛntɪɨθ, -s
AM ˈtwɛn(t)iɨθ, -s

twenty
BR ˈtwɛnt|i, -ɪz
AM ˈtwɛn(t)i, -z

twenty-first
BR ˌtwɛntɪˈfəːst, -s
AM ˈtwɛn(t)iˈfərst, -s

twentyfold
BR ˈtwɛntɪfəʊld
AM ˈtwɛn(t)iˌfoʊld

twenty-fourmo
BR ˌtwɛntɪˈfɔːməʊ
AM ˈtwɛn(t)iˈfɔrˌmoʊ

twentysomething
BR ˈtwɛntɪˌsʌmθɪŋ, -z
AM ˈtwɛn(t)iˌsəmθɪŋ, -z

twenty-twenty
BR ˌtwɛntɪˈtwɛnti
AM ˈtwɛn(t)iˈtwɛn(t)i

'twere[1]
strong form
BR twəː(r)
AM twər

'twere[2]
weak form
BR twə(r)
AM twər

twerp
BR twəːp, -s
AM twərp, -s

Twi
BR twiː, -z
AM twi, -z

twibill
BR ˈtwʌɪbɪl, -z
AM ˈtwaɪˌbɪl, ˈtwaɪbəl, -z

twice
BR twʌɪs
AM twaɪs

twicer
BR ˈtwʌɪsə(r), -z
AM ˈtwaɪsər, -z

Twickenham
BR ˈtwɪkənəm, ˈtwɪkn̩əm
AM ˈtwɪkənəm

twiddle
BR ˈtwɪd|l, -lz, -l̩ɪŋ\-lɪŋ, -ld
AM ˈtwɪd|əl, -əlz, -(ə)lɪŋ, -əld

twiddler
BR ˈtwɪdl̩ə(r), ˈtwɪdlə(r), -z
AM ˈtwɪd(ə)lər, -z

twiddly
BR ˈtwɪdl̩i, ˈtwɪdli
AM ˈtwɪdl̩i, ˈtwɪdli

twig
BR twɪɡ, -z, -ɪŋ, -d
AM twɪɡ, -z, -ɪŋ, -d

twiggy
BR ˈtwɪɡi
AM ˈtwɪɡi

twilight
BR ˈtwʌɪlʌɪt
AM ˈtwaɪˌlaɪt

twilit
BR ˈtwʌɪlɪt
AM ˈtwaɪˌlɪt

twill
BR twɪl, -d
AM twɪl, -d

'twill
BR twɪl
AM twɪl

twin
BR twɪn, -z, -ɪŋ, -d
AM twɪn, -z, -ɪŋ, -d

twine
BR twʌɪn, -z, -ɪŋ, -d
AM twaɪn, -z, -ɪŋ, -d

twiner
BR ˈtwʌɪnə(r), -z
AM ˈtwaɪnər, -z

twinge
BR twɪn(d)ʒ, -ɪz, -ɪŋ, -d
AM twɪndʒ, -ɪz, -ɪŋ, -d

twi-night
BR ˈtwʌɪnʌɪt
AM ˈtwaɪˌnaɪt

Twining
BR ˈtwʌɪnɪŋ
AM ˈtwaɪnɪŋ

twink
BR twɪŋk, -s
AM twɪŋk, -s

twinkle
BR ˈtwɪŋk|l, -lz, -l̩ɪŋ\-lɪŋ, -ld
AM ˈtwɪŋk|əl, -əlz, -(ə)lɪŋ, -əld

twinkler
BR ˈtwɪŋklə(r), ˈtwɪŋkl̩ə(r), -z
AM ˈtwɪŋk(ə)lər, -z

twinkly
BR ˈtwɪŋkli, ˈtwɪŋkl̩i
AM ˈtwɪŋk(ə)li

twinning
BR ˈtwɪnɪŋ, -z
AM ˈtwɪnɪŋ, -z

twin-screw
BR ˌtwɪnˈskruː
AM ˈtwɪnˈskru

twinset
BR ˈtwɪnsɛt, -s
AM ˈtwɪnˌsɛt, -s

twin-size
BR ˈtwɪnsʌɪz
AM ˈtwɪnˌsaɪz

twintub
BR ˈtwɪntʌb, -z
AM ˈtwɪnˌtəb, -z

twirl
BR twəːl, -z, -ɪŋ, -d
AM twərl, -z, -ɪŋ, -d

twirler
BR ˈtwəːlə(r), -z
AM ˈtwərlər, -z

twirly
BR ˈtwəːli
AM ˈtwərli

twirp
BR twəːp, -s
AM twərp, -s

twist
BR twɪst, -s, -ɪŋ, -ɨd
AM twɪst, -s, -ɪŋ, -ɨd

twistable
BR ˈtwɪstəbl
AM ˈtwɪstəbəl

twister
BR ˈtwɪstə(r), -z
AM ˈtwɪstər, -z

twistily
BR ˈtwɪstɨli
AM ˈtwɪstɨli

twistiness
BR ˈtwɪstɪnɪs
AM ˈtwɪstinɪs

twisting
BR ˈtwɪstɪŋ, -z
AM ˈtwɪstɪŋ, -z

twisty
BR ˈtwɪst|i, -ɪə(r), -ɪɪst
AM ˈtwɪsti, -ər, -ɪst

twit
BR twɪt, -s, -ɪŋ, -ɨd
AM twɪ|t, -ts, -dɪŋ, -dɨd

twitch
BR twɪtʃ, -ɪz, -ɪŋ, -t
AM twɪtʃ, -ɪz, -ɪŋ, -t

twitcher
BR ˈtwɪtʃə(r), -z
AM ˈtwɪtʃər, -z

twitchily
BR ˈtwɪtʃɨli
AM ˈtwɪtʃɨli

twitchiness
BR ˈtwɪtʃɪnɪs
AM ˈtwɪtʃinɪs

twitchy
BR ˈtwɪtʃ|i, -ɪə(r), -ɪɪst
AM ˈtwɪtʃi, -ər, -ɪst

twite
BR twʌɪt, -s
AM twaɪt, -s

twitter
BR ˈtwɪt|ə(r), -əz, -(ə)rɪŋ, -əd
AM ˈtwɪdər, -z, -ɪŋ, -d

twitterer
BR ˈtwɪt(ə)rə(r), -z
AM ˈtwɪd(ə)rər, -z

twittery
BR ˈtwɪt(ə)ri
AM ˈtwɪdəri

twittish
BR ˈtwɪtɪʃ
AM ˈtwɪdɪʃ

'twixt
BR twɪkst
AM twɪkst

twizzle
BR ˈtwɪz|l, -lz, -l̩ɪŋ\-lɪŋ, -ld
AM ˈtwɪz|əl, -əlz, -(ə)lɪŋ, -əld

two
BR tuː
AM tu

two-a-penny
BR ˌtuːəˈpɛni
AM ˌtuəˈpɛni

two-bit
BR ˈtuːbɪt
AM ˈtuˌbɪt

two-by-four
BR ˌtuːbʌɪˈfɔː(r), ˌtuːbəˈfɔː(r), -z
AM ˈtuˌbaɪˌfɔ(ə)r, -z

two-dimensional
BR ˌtuːdʌɪˈmɛnʃn̩(ə)l, ˌtuːdʌɪˈmɛnʃən(ə)l, ˌtuːdɪˈmɛnʃn̩(ə)l, ˌtuːdɪˈmɛnʃən(ə)l
AM ˌtudəˈmɛn(t)ʃ(ə)nəl, ˌtudaɪˈmɛn(t)ʃ(ə)nəl

twofold
BR ˈtuːfəʊld
AM ˈtuˌfoʊld

Twohy
BR ˈtuːi
AM ˈtui

Twomey
BR ˈtuːmi
AM ˈtumi

twoness
BR ˈtuːnəs
AM ˈtunəs

twopence
BR ˈtʌp(ə)ns
AM ˈtəpəns

twopenny
BR ˈtʌpni, ˈtʌpn̩i
AM ˈtəpəni

twopenny-halfpenny
BR ˌtʌpnɪˈheɪpni, ˌtʌpn̩ɪˈheɪpn̩i
AM ˌtəpəniˈheɪpəni

twopennyworth
BR ˌtuːˈpɛnəθ, ˈtʌp(ə)nɪwəːθ, ˈtʌpn̩ɪwəːθ, ˈtʌp(ə)nɪwəθ, ˈtʌpn̩ɪwəθ
AM ˈtəpəniˌwərθ

two-piece[1]
adjective
BR ˌtuːˈpiːs
AM ˈtuˌpis

two-piece[2]
noun
BR ˈtuːpiːs, -ɪz
AM ˈtuˌpis, -ɪz

two-seater
BR ˌtuːˈsiːtə(r), -z
AM ˈtuˈsidər, -z

twosome
BR ˈtuːs(ə)m, -z
AM ˈtusəm, -z

two-timer
BR ˈtuːˌtʌɪmə(r), ˌtuːˈtʌɪmə(r), -z
AM ˈtuˌtaɪmər, -z

two-tone
BR ˈtuːtəʊn
AM ˈtuˌtoʊn

'twould[1]
it would, strong
BR twʊd
AM twʊd

'twould[2]
it would, weak
BR twəd
AM twəd

two-up
BR ˌtuːˈʌp
AM ˌtuˈəp

two-way
BR ˌtuːˈweɪ
AM ˈtuˈweɪ

two-wheeler
BR ˌtuːˈwiːlə(r), -z
AM ˈtuˈ(h)wilər, -z

twyer
BR ˈtwʌɪə(r), -z
AM ˈtwaɪər, -z

Twyford
BR ˈtwʌɪfəd
AM ˈtwaɪfərd

Tyburn
BR ˈtʌɪb(ə)n, ˈtʌɪbəːn
AM ˈtaɪbərn

Tyche
BR ˈtʌɪki
AM ˈtaɪki

tychism
BR ˈtʌɪkɪz(ə)m
AM ˈtaɪˌkɪzəm

tychist
BR ˈtʌɪkɪst, -s
AM ˈtaɪkɪst, -s

Tycho
BR 'tʌɪkəʊ
AM 'taɪkoʊ

Tychonian
BR tʌɪ'kəʊnɪən, -z
AM taɪ'koʊniən, -z

Tychonic
BR tʌɪ'kɒnɪk
AM taɪ'kɑnɪk

tycoon
BR tʌɪ'kuːn, -z
AM taɪ'kun, -z

Tye
BR tʌɪ
AM taɪ

tying
BR 'tʌɪɪŋ
AM 'taɪɪŋ

tyke
BR tʌɪk, -s
AM taɪk, -s

Tyldesley
BR 'tɪl(d)zli
AM 'tɪl(d)zli

Tyler
BR 'tʌɪlə(r)
AM 'taɪlər

tylopod
BR 'tʌɪləpɒd, -z
AM 'taɪlə,pɑd, -z

tylopodous
BR tʌɪ'lɒpədəs
AM taɪ'lɑpədəs

tympan
BR 'tɪmpən, -z
AM 'tɪmpən, -z

tympana
BR 'tɪmpənə(*r*)
AM 'tɪmpənə

tympani
BR 'tɪmpəni
AM 'tɪmpəni

tympanic
BR tɪm'panɪk
AM tɪm'pænɪk

tympanist
BR 'tɪmpənɪst, -s
AM 'tɪmpənəst, -s

tympanites
BR ,tɪmpə'nʌɪtiːz
AM ,tɪmpə'naɪdiz

tympanitic
BR ,tɪmpə'nɪtɪk
AM ,tɪmpə'nɪdɪk

tympanitis
BR ,tɪmpə'nʌɪtɨs
AM ,tɪmpə'naɪdɨs

tympanum
BR 'tɪmpənəm, -z
AM 'tɪmpənəm, -z

Tynan
BR 'tʌɪnən
AM 'taɪnən

Tyndale
BR 'tɪndl
AM 'tɪndl

Tyndall
BR 'tɪndl
AM 'tɪndl

Tyne
BR tʌɪn
AM taɪn

Tyne and Wear
BR ,tʌɪn ən(d) 'wɪə(r)
AM 'taɪn ən 'wɪ(ə)r

Tynemouth
BR 'tʌɪnmaʊθ
AM 'taɪn,maʊθ

Tyneside
BR 'tʌɪnsʌɪd
AM 'taɪn,saɪd

Tynesider
BR 'tʌɪn,sʌɪdə(r), -z
AM 'taɪn,saɪdər, -z

Tynwald
BR 'tɪnw(ə)ld,
'tʌɪnw(ə)ld
AM 'tɪnwəld, 'taɪnwəld

typal
BR 'tʌɪpl
AM 'taɪpəl

type
BR tʌɪp, -s, -ɪŋ, -t
AM taɪp, -s, -ɪŋ, -t

typebar
BR 'tʌɪpbɑː(r), -z
AM 'taɪp,bɑr, -z

typecast
BR 'tʌɪpkɑːst,
'tʌɪpkast, -s, -ɪŋ
AM 'taɪp,kæst, -s, -ɪŋ

typeface
BR 'tʌɪpfeɪs, -ɨz
AM 'taɪp,feɪs, -ɨz

typefounder
BR 'tʌɪp,faʊndə(r), -z
AM 'taɪp,faʊndər, -z

typescript
BR 'tʌɪpskrɪpt, -s
AM 'taɪp,skrɪpt, -s

typeset
BR 'tʌɪpsɛt, -s, -ɪŋ
AM 'taɪp,sɛ|t, -ts, -dɪŋ

typesetter
BR 'tʌɪp,sɛtə(r), -z
AM 'taɪp,sɛdər, -z

typesetting
BR 'tʌɪp,sɛtɪŋ
AM 'taɪp,sɛdɪŋ

typewriter
BR 'tʌɪp,rʌɪtə(r), -z
AM 'taɪp,raɪdər, -z

typewriting
BR 'tʌɪp,rʌɪtɪŋ
AM 'taɪp,raɪdɪŋ

typewritten
BR 'tʌɪp,rɪtn
AM 'taɪp,rɪtn

typhlitic
BR tɪf'lɪtɪk
AM tɪf'lɪdɪk

typhlitis
BR tɪf'lʌɪtɨs
AM tɪ'flaɪdɨs

typhoid
BR 'tʌɪfɔɪd
AM 'taɪ,fɔɪd

typhoidal
BR tʌɪ'fɔɪdl
AM taɪ'fɔɪdəl

typhonic
BR tʌɪ'fɒnɪk
AM taɪ'fɑnɪk

Typhoo®
BR ,tʌɪ'fuː
AM ,taɪ'fu

typhoon
BR tʌɪ'fuːn, -z
AM taɪ'fun, -z

typhous
BR 'tʌɪfəs
AM 'taɪfəs

typhus
BR 'tʌɪfəs
AM 'taɪfəs

typical
BR 'tɪpɨkl
AM 'tɪpɨkəl

typicality
BR ,tɪpɪ'kalɨti
AM ,tɪpə'kælədi

typically
BR 'tɪpɨkli
AM 'tɪpɨk(ə)li

typification
BR ,tɪpɨfɪ'keɪʃn, -z
AM ,tɪpəfə'keɪʃən, -z

typifier
BR 'tɪpɨfʌɪə(r), -z
AM 'tɪpə,faɪər, -z

typify
BR 'tɪpɨfʌɪ, -z, -ɪŋ, -d
AM 'tɪpə,faɪ, -z, -ɪŋ, -d

typist
BR 'tʌɪpɪst, -s
AM 'taɪpɪst, -s

typo
BR 'tʌɪpəʊ, -z
AM 'taɪ,poʊ, -z

typographer
BR tʌɪ'pɒgrəfə(r), -z
AM taɪ'pɑgrəfər, -z

typographic
BR ,tʌɪpə'grafɪk
AM ,taɪpə'græfɪk

typographical
BR ,tʌɪpə'grafɪkl
AM ,taɪpə'græfəkəl

typographically
BR ,tʌɪpə'grafɪkli
AM ,taɪpə'græfək(ə)li

typography
BR tʌɪ'pɒgrəfi
AM taɪ'pɑgrəfi

typological
BR ,tʌɪpə'lɒdʒɪkl
AM ,taɪpə'lɑdʒəkəl

typologist
BR tʌɪ'pɒlədʒɪst, -s
AM taɪ'pɑlədʒəst, -s

typology
BR tʌɪ'pɒlədʒi
AM taɪ'pɑlədʒi

typonym
BR 'tʌɪpənɪm, -z
AM 'taɪpə,nɪm, -z

Tyr
BR tɪə(r), tjʊə(r)
AM tɪ(ə)r

tyramine
BR 'tʌɪrəmiːn,
'tɪrəmiːn
AM 'taɪrə,min

tyrannical
BR tɨ'ranɨkl,
tʌɪ'ranɨkl
AM tə'rænəkəl

tyrannically
BR tɨ'ranɨkli,
tʌɪ'ranɨkli
AM tə'rænək(ə)li

tyrannicidal
BR tɨ,ranɪ'sʌɪdl,
tʌɪ,ranɪ'sʌɪdl
AM tə,rænə'saɪdəl

tyrannicide
BR tɨ'ranɨsʌɪd,
tʌɪ'ranɨsʌɪd, -z
AM tə'rænə,saɪd, -z

tyrannise
BR 'tɪrənʌɪz, 'tɪrn̩ʌɪz,
-ɨz, -ɪŋ, -d
AM 'tɪrə,naɪz, -ɨz, -ɪŋ, -d

tyrannize
BR 'tɪrənʌɪz, 'tɪrn̩ʌɪz,
-ɨz, -ɪŋ, -d
AM 'tɪrə,naɪz, -ɨz, -ɪŋ, -d

tyrannosaur
BR tɨ'ranəsɔː(r),
tʌɪ'ranəsɔː(r), -z
AM tə'rænə,sɔ(ə)r, -z

tyrannosauri
BR tɨ,ranə'sɔːrʌɪ,
tʌɪ,ranə'sɔːrʌɪ
AM tə,rænə'sɔ,raɪ

tyrannosaurus
BR tɨ,ranə'sɔːrəs,
tʌɪ,ranə'sɔːrəs, -ɨz
AM tə,rænə'sɔrəs, -əz

Tyrannosaurus Rex
BR tɨ,ranə,sɔːrəs 'rɛks,
tʌɪ,ranə,sɔːrəs +, -ɨz
AM tə,rænə'sɔrəs
'rɛks, -əz

tyrannous
BR 'tɪrənəs, 'tɪrn̩əs
AM 'tɪrənəs

tyrannously
BR 'tɪrənəsli, 'tɪrn̩əsli
AM 'tɪrənəsli

tyranny
BR 'tɪrən|i, 'tɪrn̩|i, -ɪz
AM 'tɪrəni, -z

tyrant
BR 'tʌɪrənt, 'tʌɪrn̩t, -s

AM 'taɪrənt, -s

tyre
BR 'tʌɪə(r), -z
AM 'taɪ(ə)r, -z

tyremark
BR 'tʌɪəmɑːk, -s
AM 'taɪ(ə)rˌmɑrk, -s

Tyrer
BR 'tʌɪrə(r)
AM 'taɪrər

Tyrian
BR 'tɪrɪən
AM 'tɪriən

tyro
BR 'tʌɪrəʊ, -z
AM 'taɪˌroʊ, -z

Tyrol
BR 'tɪrəl, 'tɪrl, tɪ'rəʊl
AM 'tɪrəl

Tyrolean
BR ˌtɪrə'liːən, tɪ'rəʊlɪən, -z
AM tə'roʊliən, -z

Tyrone[1]
forename
BR 'tʌɪrəʊn, tʌɪ'rəʊn
AM taɪ'roʊn

Tyrone[2]
Northern Ireland
BR tɪ'rəʊn
AM tə'roʊn

tyrosine
BR 'tʌɪrə(ʊ)siːn
AM 'taɪrəˌsin

tyrothricin
BR ˌtʌɪrə(ʊ)'θrʌɪsɪn
AM ˌtaɪrə'θraɪsɪn

Tyrrell
BR 'tɪrəl, 'tɪrl̩
AM 'tɪrəl

Tyrrhene
BR tɪ'riːn, -z
AM tə'rin, -z

Tyrrhenian
BR tɪ'riːnɪən, -z
AM tə'riniən, -z

Tyson
BR 'tʌɪsn
AM 'taɪsən

Tywyn
BR 'taʊɪn
AM 'taʊən

Tyzack
BR 'tʌɪzak, 'tɪzak
AM 'taɪzæk, 'tɪzæk

tzar
BR zɑː(r), tsɑː(r), -z
AM zɑr, tsɑr, -z

tzarevitch
BR 'zɑːrəvɪtʃ, 'tsɑːrəvɪtʃ, -ɪz
AM 'zɑrəˌvɪtʃ, 'tsɑrəˌvɪtʃ, -ɪz

tzarina
BR zɑː'riːnə(r), tsɑː'riːnə(r), -z
AM zɑ'rinə, tsɑ'rinə, -z

tzarist
BR 'zɑːrɪst, 'tsɑːrɪst, -s
AM 'zɑrəst, 'tsɑrəst, -s

tzatziki
BR (t)sat'siːki
AM (t)sɑt'siki

tzetze
BR 't(s)ɛtsi
AM '(t)sitsi, '(t)sɛtsi

tzigane
BR (t)sɪ'gɑːn, -z
AM (t)sɪ'gɑn, -z

Uu

u
BR juː, -z
AM ju, -z
U-2
BR ˌjuːˈtuː, -z
AM ˌjuˈtu, -z
UAW
BR ˌjuːeɪˈdʌbljuː
AM ˌjuˌeɪˈdəbəlˌju
Ubaid
BR uːˈbeɪd, uːˈbʌɪd
AM uˈbeɪd, uˈbaɪd
Ubange
BR ˌjuːˈbaŋgi
AM ˌjuˈbæŋgi
U-bend
BR ˈjuːbɛnd, -z
AM ˈjuˌbɛnd, -z
Übermensch
BR ˈuːbəmɛnʃ
AM ˈubərˌmɛn(t)ʃ
Übermenschen
BR ˈuːbəmɛnʃn
AM ˈubərˌmɛn(t)ʃən
UB40
BR ˌjuːbiːˈfɔːti
AM ˌjuˌbiˈfɔrdi
ubiety
BR juːˈbʌɪɨti, jʊˈbʌɪɨti
AM juˈbaɪədi
ubiquitarian
BR juːˌbɪkwɪˈtɛːrɪən, jʊˌbɪkwɪˈtɛːrɪən, -z
AM juˌbɪkwəˈtɛriən, -z
ubiquitarianism
BR juːˌbɪkwɪˈtɛːrɪənɪz(ə)m, jʊˌbɪkwɪˈtɛːrɪənɪz(ə)m
AM juˌbɪkwɪˈtɛriəˌnɪzəm
ubiquitous
BR juːˈbɪkwɪtəs, jʊˈbɪkwɪtəs
AM juˈbɪkwədəs
ubiquitously
BR juːˈbɪkwɪtəsli, jʊˈbɪkwɪtəsli
AM juˈbɪkwədəsli
ubiquitousness
BR juːˈbɪkwɪtəsnəs, jʊˈbɪkwɪtəsnəs
AM juˈbɪkwədəsnəs
ubiquity
BR juːˈbɪkwɪti, jʊˈbɪkwɪti
AM juˈbɪkwɨdi
U-boat
BR ˈjuːbəʊt, -s
AM ˈjuˌboʊt, -s
U-bolt
BR ˈjuːbəʊlt, -s
AM ˈjuˌboʊlt, -s
UCATT
BR ˈjuːkat
AM ˈjuˌkæt
UCCA
BR ˈʌkə(r), ˌjuːsiːsiːˈeɪ
AM ˌjuˌsiˌsiˈeɪ
Uccello
BR uːˈtʃɛləʊ
AM uˈtʃɛloʊ
Uckfield
BR ˈʌkfiːld
AM ˈəkˌfild
UCLA
BR ˌjuːsɪɛlˈeɪ
AM ˌjuˌsiˌɛlˈeɪ
udal
BR ˈjuːdl, -z
AM ˈjudəl, -z
Udall
BR ˈjuːdl, ˈjuːdɔːl
AM ˈjuˌdəl, ˈjuˌdɑl
udaller
BR ˈjuːdl̩ə(r), -z
AM ˈjudl̩ər, -z
udalman
BR ˈjuːdlmən
AM ˈjudlmən
udalmen
BR ˈjuːdlmən
AM ˈjudlmən
udder
BR ˈʌdə(r), -z, -d
AM ˈədər, -z, -d
UDI
BR ˌjuːdɪˈʌɪ
AM ˌjuˌdiˈaɪ
Udmurtia
BR ʊdˈmʊəʃə(r)
AM ʊdˈmʊrʃə
RUS udˈmurtʲijə
udometer
BR juːˈdɒmɪtə(r), jʊˈdɒmɪtə(r), -z
AM juˈdɑmədər, -z
UEFA
BR juːˈeɪfə(r)
AM juˈ(w)ɛfə
uey
BR ˈjuː|i, -ɪz
AM ˈjui, -z
Uffizi
BR (j)ʊˈfɪtsi, (j)ʊˈfiːtsi
AM juˈfitsi
UFO
BR ˈjuːfəʊ, ˌjuːɛfˈəʊ, -z
AM ˌjuˌɛfˈoʊ, -z
ufologist
BR juːˈfɒlədʒɪst, -s
AM juˈfɑlədʒəst, -s
ufology
BR juːˈfɒlədʒi
AM juˈfɑlədʒi
Uganda
BR juːˈgandə(r), jʊˈgandə(r)
AM juˈgændə
Ugandan
BR juːˈgandən, jʊˈgandən, -z
AM juˈgændən, -z
Ugaritic
adjective and noun
BR ˌuːgəˈrɪtɪk
AM ˌugəˈrɪdɪk
ugh!
BR ə(h), ʌx, ʊɸ
AM əg
ugli
BR ˈʌgl|i, -ɪz
AM ˈəgli, -z
uglification
BR ˌʌglɪfɪˈkeɪʃn
AM ˌəgləfəˈkeɪʃən
ugli fruit
BR ˈʌglɪ fruːt
AM ˈəgli ˌfrut
uglify
BR ˈʌglɪfʌɪ, -z, -ɪŋ, -d
AM ˈəgləˌfaɪ, -z, -ɪŋ, -d
uglily
BR ˈʌglɨli
AM ˈəgləli
ugliness
BR ˈʌglɪnɪs
AM ˈəglinɨs
ugly
BR ˈʌgl|i, -ɪə(r), -ɪɨst
AM ˈəgli, -ər, -ɨst
Ugrian
BR ˈ(j)uːgrɪən, -z
AM ˈ(j)ugriən, -z
Ugric
BR ˈ(j)uːgrɪk, -s
AM ˈ(j)ugrɪk, -s
UHF
BR ˌjuːeɪtʃˈɛf
AM ˌjuˌeɪtʃˈɛf
uh-huh
BR əˈhə(r), ʌˈhʌ(r)
AM əˈhə
uhlan
BR (j)uːˈlɑːn, (j)ʊˈlɑːn, -z
AM uˈlɑn, ˈ(j)ulən, -z
UHT
BR ˌjuːeɪtʃˈtiː
AM ˌjuˌeɪtʃˈti
Uighur
BR ˈwiːgʊə(r), -z
AM ˈwiˌgʊ(ə)r, -z
Uigur
BR ˈwiːgʊə(r), -z
AM ˈwiˌgʊ(ə)r, -z
Uist
BR ˈjuːɪst, -s
AM ˈjuɪst, -s
uitlander
BR ˈeɪtˌlandə(r), ˈɔɪtˌlandə(r), -z
AM ˈeɪtˌlændər, -z
ujamaa
BR ˌʊdʒəˈmɑː(r)
AM ˌudʒəˈmɑ
Ujjain
BR uːˈdʒeɪn
AM uˈdʒeɪn
UK
BR ˌjuːˈkeɪ
AM ˌjuˈkeɪ
ukase
BR juːˈkeɪz, juːˈkeɪs, -ɪz
AM juˈkeɪs, -ɪz
ukelele
BR ˌjuːkəˈleɪl|i, -ɪz
AM ˌjukəˈleɪli, -z
ukiyo-e
BR ˌuːkɪjəʊˈjeɪ
AM ˌukijoʊˈjeɪ
Ukraine
BR juːˈkreɪn, jʊˈkreɪn
AM juˈkreɪn, ˈjuˌkreɪn
RUS ukraˈinə
Ukrainian
BR juːˈkreɪnɪən, jʊˈkreɪnɪən, -z
AM juˈkreɪniən, -z
ukulele
BR ˌjuːkəˈleɪl|i, -ɪz
AM ˌjukəˈleɪli, -z
ulan
BR (j)uːˈlɑːn, (j)ʊˈlɑːn, -z
AM uˈlɑn, ˈ(j)ulən, -z
Ulan Bator
BR ʊˌlan baˈtɔː(r)
AM ʊˌlɑn ˌbɑˈtɔ(ə)r
Ulanova
BR jʊˈlanəvə(r)
AM jʊˈlɑnəvə
RUS uˈlanəvə
ulcer
BR ˈʌlsə(r), -z, -d
AM ˈəlsər, -z, -d
ulcerable
BR ˈʌls(ə)rəbl
AM ˈəlsərəbəl
ulcerate
BR ˈʌlsəreɪt, -s, -ɪŋ, -ɨd
AM ˈəlsəˌreɪ|t, -ts, -dɪŋ, -dɨd
ulceration
BR ˌʌlsəˈreɪʃn
AM ˌəlsəˈreɪʃən
ulcerative
BR ˈʌls(ə)rətɪv
AM ˈəlsərədɪv, ˈəlsəˌreɪdɪv
ulcerous
BR ˈʌls(ə)rəs
AM ˈəls(ə)rəs
ulema
BR ˈuːlɪmə(r), ˈuːlɪmɑː(r), ˌuːlɪˈmɑː(r), -z
AM ˈuləˌmɑ, -z
Ulfilas
BR ˈʊlfɪlas
AM ˈʊlfiˌlɑs
uliginose
BR juːˈlɪdʒɨnəʊs, jʊˈlɪdʒɨnəʊs

AM ju'lɪdʒəˌnoʊs, ju'lɪdʒəˌnoʊz

uliginous
BR juː'lɪdʒɪnəs, jʊ'lɪdʒɪnəs
AM ju'lɪdʒənəs

ullage
BR 'ʌlɪdʒ
AM 'əlɪdʒ

Ullapool
BR 'ʌləpuːl
AM 'ələˌpul

Ullman
BR 'ʊlmən, 'ʌlmən
AM 'əlmən, 'ʊlmən

Ullmann
BR 'ʊlmən, 'ʌlmən
AM 'əlmən, 'ʊlmən

Ulm
BR ʊlm
AM ʊlm

ulna
BR 'ʌlnə(r), -z
AM 'əlnə, -z

ulnae
BR 'ʌlniː
AM 'əlˌni, 'əlˌnaɪ

ulnar
BR 'ʌlnə(r)
AM 'əlnər

ulotrichan
BR juː'lɒtrɪk(ə)n, jʊ'lɒtrɪk(ə)n, -z
AM ju'lɑtrəkən, -z

ulotrichous
BR juː'lɒtrɪkəs, jʊ'lɒtrɪkəs
AM ju'lɑtrəkəs

Ulpian
BR 'ʌlpɪən
AM 'əlpiən

Ulster
BR 'ʌlstə(r), -z
AM 'əlstər, -z

Ulsterman
BR 'ʌlstəmən
AM 'əlstərmən

Ulstermen
BR 'ʌlstəmən
AM 'əlstərmən

Ulsterwoman
BR 'ʌlstəˌwʊmən
AM 'əlstərˌwʊmən

Ulsterwomen
BR 'ʌlstəˌwɪmɪn
AM 'əlstərˌwɪmɪn

ult
BR ʌlt
AM əlt

ulterior
BR ʌl'tɪərɪə(r)
AM əl'tɪriər

ulteriorly
BR ʌl'tɪərɪəli
AM əl'tɪriərli

ultima
BR 'ʌltɪmə(r)
AM 'əltəmə

ultimacy
BR 'ʌltɪməsi
AM 'əltəməsi

ultimata
BR ˌʌltɪ'meɪtə(r)
AM ˌəltə'meɪdə

ultimate
BR 'ʌltɪmət
AM 'əltəmət

ultimately
BR 'ʌltɪmətli
AM 'əltəmətli

ultimateness
BR 'ʌltɪmətnəs
AM 'əltəmətnəs

ultimatum
BR ˌʌltɪ'meɪtəm, -z
AM ˌəltə'meɪdəm, -z

ultimo
BR 'ʌltɪməʊ
AM 'əltəˌmoʊ

ultimogeniture
BR ˌʌltɪməʊ'dʒɛnɪtʃə(r), -z
AM ¦əltəˌmoʊ'dʒɛnəˌtʃʊ(ə)r, ¦əltəˌmoʊ'dʒɛnətʃər, -z

ultra
BR 'ʌltrə(r), -z
AM 'əltrə, -z

ultracentrifuge
BR ˌʌltrə'sɛntrɪfjuː(d)ʒ, -ɪz
AM ˌəltrə'sɛntrəˌfjudʒ, -əz

ultradian
BR ʌl'treɪdɪən
AM ˌəltrə'diən

ultraism
BR 'ʌltrəɪz(ə)m
AM 'əltrəˌɪzəm

ultramarine
BR ˌʌltrəmə'riːn
AM ˌəltrəmə'rin

ultramicroscope
BR ˌʌltrə'mʌɪkrəskəʊp, -s
AM ˌəltrə'maɪkrəˌskoʊp, -s

ultramicroscopic
BR ˌʌltrəˌmʌɪkrə'skɒpɪk
AM ¦əltrəˌmaɪkrə'skɑpɪk

ultramontane
BR ˌʌltrə'mɒnteɪn
AM ˌəltrəˌmɑn'teɪn

ultramontanism
BR ˌʌltrə'mɒntənɪz(ə)m
AM ˌəltrə'mɑn(t)əˌnɪzəm

ultramontanist
BR ˌʌltrə'mɒntənɪst, -s
AM ˌəltrə'mɑn(t)ənəst, -s

ultramundane
BR ˌʌltrə'mʌndeɪn
AM ˌəltrəˌmən'deɪn

ultrasonic
BR ˌʌltrə'sɒnɪk, -s
AM ˌəltrə'sɑnɪk, -s

ultrasonically
BR ˌʌltrə'sɒnɪkli
AM ˌəltrə'sɑnək(ə)li

ultrasound
BR 'ʌltrəsaʊnd
AM 'əltrəˌsaʊnd

ultrastructure
BR 'ʌltrəˌstrʌktʃə(r), -z
AM 'əltrəˌstrək(t)ʃər, -z

Ultrasuede®
BR 'ʌltrəˌsweɪd
AM 'əltrəˌsweɪd

ultraviolet
BR ˌʌltrə'vʌɪələt
AM ˌəltrə'vaɪələt

ultra vires
BR ˌʌltrə 'vʌɪriːz, + 'viːreɪz
AM ˌəltrə 'vaɪriz

ululant
BR 'juː(l)jʊlənt, 'ʌljʊlənt
AM 'ju(l)jələnt, 'əljələnt

ululate
BR 'juː(l)jʊleɪt, 'ʌljʊleɪt, -s, -ɪŋ, -ɪd
AM 'ju(l)jəˌleɪ|t, 'əljəˌleɪ|t, -ts, -dɪŋ, -dɪd

ululation
BR ˌjuː(l)jʊ'leɪʃn, ˌʌljʊ'leɪʃn, -z
AM ˌju(l)jə'leɪʃən, ˌəljə'leɪʃən, -z

Ulverston
BR 'ʌlvəst(ə)n
AM 'əlvərstən

Ulysses
BR 'juːlɪsiːz
AM ju'lɪsiz

um
BR (ə)m, ʌm
AM (ə)m

umbel
BR 'ʌmbl, -z
AM 'əmbəl, -z

umbellar
BR ʌm'bɛlə(r)
AM 'əmbələr

umbellate
BR 'ʌmbələt, 'ʌmbəleɪt
AM 'əmbələt, 'əmbəˌleɪt

umbellifer
BR ʌm'bɛlɪfə(r), -z
AM ˌəm'bɛləfər, -z

umbelliferae
BR ˌʌmbə'lɪfəriː
AM ˌəmbə'lɪfəri, ˌəmbə'lɪfəˌraɪ

umbelliferous
BR ˌʌmbə'lɪf(ə)rəs
AM ˌəmbə'lɪf(ə)rəs

umbellule
BR ʌm'bɛljuːl, -z
AM 'əmbəlˌjul, əm'bɛljul, -z

umber
BR 'ʌmbə(r), -z
AM 'əmbər, -z

umbilical
BR ʌm'bɪlɪkl, ˌʌmbɪ'lʌɪkl
AM ˌəm'bɪləkəl

umbilically
BR ʌm'bɪlɪkli
AM ˌəm'bɪlɪk(ə)li

umbilicate
BR ʌm'bɪlɪkət, ʌm'bɪlɪkeɪt
AM ˌəm'bɪləkət, ˌəm'bɪləˌkeɪt

umbilicus
BR ʌm'bɪlɪkəs, -ɪz
AM ˌəm'bɪlɪkəs, -əz

umble
BR 'ʌmbl, -z
AM 'əmbəl, -z

umbo
BR 'ʌmbəʊ, -z
AM 'əmboʊ, -z

umbonal
BR ʌm'bəʊnl
AM ˌəm'boʊnəl

umbonate
BR 'ʌmbənət, 'ʌmbəneɪt
AM 'əmbənət, 'əmbəˌneɪt

umbones
BR ʌm'bəʊniːz
AM ˌəm'boʊniz

umbra
BR 'ʌmbrə(r), -z
AM 'əmbrə, -z

umbrage
BR 'ʌmbrɪdʒ
AM 'əmbrɪdʒ

umbrageous
BR 'ʌmbrɪdʒəs
AM 'əmbrɪdʒəs

umbral
BR 'ʌmbr(ə)l
AM 'əmbrəl

umbrella
BR ʌm'brɛlə(r), -z
AM ˌəm'brɛlə, -z

umbrella-like
BR ʌm'brɛləlʌɪk
AM ˌəm'brɛləˌlaɪk

umbrette
BR ʌm'brɛt, -s
AM ˌəm'brɛt, -s

Umbria
BR 'ʌmbrɪə(r)

AM ˈəmbriə

Umbrian
BR ˈʌmbrɪən, -z
AM ˈəmbriən, -z

Umbriel
BR ˈʌmbrɪəl
AM ˈəmbriəl

umbriferous
BR ʌmˈbrɪf(ə)rəs
AM ˌəmˈbrɪf(ə)rəs

umiak
BR ˈuːmɪak, -s
AM ˈumiˌæk, -s

umlaut
BR ˈʊmlaʊt, -s
AM ˈʊmˌlaʊt, -s

ump
BR ʌmp, -s
AM əmp, -s

umph
BR ʌmf, ɵmf, hm
AM umf, ʊmf, əmf

umpirage
BR ˈʌmpʌɪrɪdʒ
AM ˈəmˌpaɪrɪdʒ

umpire
BR ˈʌmpʌɪə(r), -z, -ɪŋ, -d
AM ˈəmˌpaɪ(ə)r, -z, -ɪŋ, -d

umpireship
BR ˈʌmpʌɪəʃɪp, -s
AM ˈəmˌpaɪ(ə)rˌʃɪp, -s

umpteen
BR ˌʌm(p)ˈtiːn
AM ˌəm(p)ˌtin

umpteenth
BR ˌʌm(p)ˈtiːnθ
AM ˌəm(p)ˌtinθ

umpty
BR ˈʌm(p)ti
AM ˈəm(p)ti

UN
BR ˌjuːˈɛn
AM ˌjuˈɛn

'un
BR ən
AM ən

Una
BR ˈjuːnə(*r*)
AM ˈ(j)unə

unabashed
BR ˌʌnəˈbaʃt
AM ˌənəˈbæʃt

unabashedly
BR ˌʌnəˈbaʃɨdli
AM ˌənəˈbæʃədli

unabated
BR ˌʌnəˈbeɪtɨd
AM ˌənəˈbeɪdɨd

unabatedly
BR ˌʌnəˈbeɪtɨdli
AM ˌənəˈbeɪdɨdli

unable
BR ʌnˈeɪbl
AM ˌənˈeɪbəl

unabridged
BR ˌʌnəˈbrɪdʒd
AM ˌənəˈbrɪdʒd

unabsorbed
BR ˌʌnəbˈzɔːbd
AM ˌənəbˈzɔ(ə)rbd

unacademic
BR ˌʌnakəˈdɛmɪk
AM ˌənˌækəˈdɛmɪk

unaccented
BR ˌʌnəkˈsɛntɨd
AM ˌənˈækˌsɛn(t)əd

unacceptability
BR ˌʌnəkˌsɛptəˈbɪlɨti
AM ˌənəkˌsɛptəˈbɪlɨdi

unacceptable
BR ˌʌnəkˈsɛptəbl
AM ˌənəkˈsɛptəbəl

unacceptableness
BR ˌʌnəkˈsɛptəblnəs
AM ˌənəkˈsɛptəbəlnəs

unacceptably
BR ˌʌnəkˈsɛptəbli
AM ˌənəkˈsɛptəbli

unaccepted
BR ˌʌnəkˈsɛptɨd
AM ˌənəkˈsɛptəd

unacclaimed
BR ˌʌnəˈkleɪmd
AM ˌənəˈkleɪmd

unacclimatized
BR ˌʌnəˈklʌɪmətʌɪzd
AM ˌənəˈklaɪməˌtaɪzd

unaccommodated
BR ˌʌnəˈkɒmədeɪtɨd
AM ˌənəˈkɑməˌdeɪdɨd

unaccommodating
BR ˌʌnəˈkɒmədeɪtɪŋ
AM ˌənəˈkɑmədeɪdɪŋ

unaccompanied
BR ˌʌnəˈkʌmp(ə)nɪd
AM ˌənəˈkəmpənid

unaccomplished
BR ˌʌnəˈkʌmplɪʃt
AM ˌənəˈkɑmplɪʃt

unaccountability
BR ˌʌnəˌkaʊntəˈbɪlɨti
AM ˌənəˌkaʊn(t)əˈbɪlɨdi

unaccountable
BR ˌʌnəˈkaʊntəbl
AM ˌənəˈkaʊn(t)əbəl

unaccountable-ness
BR ˌʌnəˈkaʊntəblnəs
AM ˌənəˈkaʊn(t)əbəlnəs

unaccountably
BR ˌʌnəˈkaʊntəbli
AM ˌənəˈkaʊn(t)əbli

unaccounted
BR ˌʌnəˈkaʊntɨd
AM ˌənəˈkaʊn(t)əd

unaccustomed
BR ˌʌnəˈkʌstəmd
AM ˌənəˈkəstəmd

unaccustomedly
BR ˌʌnəˈkʌstəmdli
AM ˌənəˈkəstəmdli

unachievable
BR ˌʌnəˈtʃiːvəbl
AM ˌənəˈtʃivəbəl

unacknowledged
BR ˌʌnəkˈnɒlɪdʒd
AM ˌənəkˈnɑlɪdʒd

unacquainted
BR ˌʌnəˈkweɪntɨd
AM ˌənəˈkweɪn(t)ɨd

unadaptable
BR ˌʌnəˈdaptəbl
AM ˌənəˈdæptəbəl

unadapted
BR ˌʌnəˈdaptɨd
AM ˌənəˈdæptəd

unaddressed
BR ˌʌnəˈdrɛst
AM ˌənəˈdrɛst

unadjacent
BR ˌʌnəˈdʒeɪsnt
AM ˌənəˈdʒeɪsənt

unadjusted
BR ˌʌnəˈdʒʌstɨd
AM ˌənəˈdʒəstəd

unadmitted
BR ˌʌnədˈmɪtɨd
AM ˌənədˈmɪdɨd

unadopted
BR ˌʌnəˈdɒptɨd
AM ˌənəˈdɑpted

unadorned
BR ˌʌnəˈdɔːnd
AM ˌənəˈdɔ(ə)rnd

unadulterated
BR ˌʌnəˈdʌltəreɪtɨd
AM ˌənəˈdəltəˌreɪdɨd

unadventurous
BR ˌʌnədˈvɛntʃ(ə)rəs
AM ˌənədˈvɛntʃ(ə)rəs

unadventurously
BR ˌʌnədˈvɛntʃ(ə)rəsli
AM ˌənədˈvɛntʃ(ə)rəsli

unadvertised
BR ʌnˈadvətʌɪzd
AM ˌənˈædvərˌtaɪzd

unadvisable
BR ˌʌnədˈvʌɪzəbl
AM ˌənədˈvaɪzəbəl

unadvised
BR ˌʌnədˈvʌɪzd
AM ˌənədˈvaɪzd

unadvisedly
BR ˌʌnədˈvʌɪzɨdli
AM ˌənədˈvaɪzɨdli

unadvisedness
BR ˌʌnədˈvʌɪzɨdnɪs
AM ˌənədˈvaɪzɨdnɪs

unaesthetic
BR ˌʌniːsˈθɛtɪk, ˌʌnɪsˈθɛtɪk
AM ˌənəˈsθɛdɪk

unaffected
BR ˌʌnəˈfɛktɨd
AM ˌənəˈfɛktəd

unaffectedly
BR ˌʌnəˈfɛktɨdli
AM ˌənəˈfɛktədli

unaffectedness
BR ˌʌnəˈfɛktɨdnɪs
AM ˌənəˈfɛktədnəs

unaffectionate
BR ˌʌnəˈfɛkʃn̩ət, ˌʌnəˈfɛkʃənət
AM ˌənəˈfɛkʃənət

unaffiliated
BR ˌʌnəˈfɪlɪeɪtɨd
AM ˌənəˈfɪliˌeɪdɨd

unaffordable
BR ˌʌnəˈfɔːdəbl
AM ˌənəˈfɔrdəbəl

unafraid
BR ˌʌnəˈfreɪd
AM ˌənəˈfreɪd

unaggressive
BR ˌʌnəˈɡrɛsɪv
AM ˌənəˈɡrɛsɪv

unaided
BR (ˌ)ʌnˈeɪdɨd
AM ˌənˈeɪdɨd

unalarmed
BR ˌʌnəˈlɑːmd
AM ˌənəˈlɑrmd

unalienable
BR (ˌ)ʌnˈeɪlɪənəbl
AM ˌənˈeɪliənəbəl, ˌənˈeɪljənəbəl

unalienably
BR (ˌ)ʌnˈeɪlɪənəbli
AM ˌənˈeɪliənəbli, ˌənˈeɪljənəbli

unalienated
BR (ˌ)ʌnˈeɪlɪəneɪtɨd
AM ˌənˈeɪliəˌneɪdɨd, ˌənˈeɪljəˌneɪdɨd

unaligned
BR ˌʌnəˈlʌɪnd
AM ˌənəˈlaɪnd

unalike
BR ˌʌnəˈlʌɪk
AM ˌənəˈlaɪk

unalive
BR ˌʌnəˈlʌɪv
AM ˌənəˈlaɪv

unalleviated
BR ˌʌnəˈliːvɪeɪtɨd
AM ˌənəˈliviˌeɪdɨd

unallied
BR ˌʌnəˈlʌɪd
AM ˌənəˈlaɪd

unallocated
BR (ˌ)ʌnˈaləkeɪtɨd
AM ˌənˈæləˌkeɪdɨd

unallotted
BR ˌʌnəˈlɒtɨd
AM ˌənəˈlɑdəd

unallowable
BR ˌʌnəˈlaʊəbl
AM ˌənəˈlaʊəbəl

unalloyed
BR ˌʌnəˈlɔɪd
AM ˌənəˈlɔɪd

unalterable
BR (ˌ)ʌnˈɔːlt(ə)rəbl, (ˌ)ʌnˈɒlt(ə)rəbl

AM ˌənˈɔlt(ə)rəbəl, ˌənˈɑlt(ə)rəbəl

unalterableness
BR (ˌ)ʌnˈɔːlt(ə)rəblnəs, (ˌ)ʌnˈɒlt(ə)rəblnəs
AM ˌənˈɔlt(ə)rəbəlnəs, ˌənˈɑlt(ə)rəbəlnəs

unalterably
BR (ˌ)ʌnˈɔːlt(ə)rəbli, (ˌ)ʌnˈɒlt(ə)rəbli
AM ˌənˈɔlt(ə)rəbli, ˌənˈɑlt(ə)rəbli

unaltered
BR (ˌ)ʌnˈɔːltəd, (ˌ)ʌnˈɒltəd
AM ˌənˈɔltərd, ˌənˈɑltərd

unaltering
BR (ˌ)ʌnˈɔːlt(ə)rɪŋ, (ˌ)ʌnˈɒlt(ə)rɪŋ
AM ˌənˈɔlt(ə)rɪŋ, ˌənˈɑlt(ə)rɪŋ

unamazed
BR ˌʌnəˈmeɪzd
AM ˌənəˈmeɪzd

unambiguity
BR ˌʌnambɪˈgjuːɪti
AM ˌənˌæmbəˈgjuədi

unambiguous
BR ˌʌnamˈbɪgjʊəs
AM ˌənæmˈbɪgjəwəs

unambiguously
BR ˌʌnamˈbɪgjʊəsli
AM ˌənæmˈbɪgjəwəsli

unambitious
BR ˌʌnamˈbɪʃəs
AM ˌənæmˈbɪʃəs

unambitiously
BR ˌʌnamˈbɪʃəsli
AM ˌənæmˈbɪʃəsli

unambitiousness
BR ˌʌnamˈbɪʃəsnəs
AM ˌənæmˈbɪʃəsnəs

unambivalent
BR ˌʌnamˈbɪvələnt, ˌʌnamˈbɪvəlṇt, ˌʌnamˈbɪvḷ(ə)nt
AM ˌənəmˈbɪv(ə)lənt

unambivalently
BR ˌʌnəmˈbɪvələntli, ˌʌnamˈbɪvəlṇtli, ˌʌnamˈbɪvḷ(ə)ntli
AM ˌənəmˈbɪvələn(t)li

unamenable
BR ˌʌnəˈmiːnəbl
AM ˌənəˈminəbəl

unamended
BR ˌʌnəˈmɛndɪd
AM ˌənəˈmɛndəd

un-American
BR ˌʌnəˈmɛrɪk(ə)n
AM ˌənəˈmɛrəkən

un-Americanism
BR ˌʌnəˈmɛrɪkənɪz(ə)m, ˌʌnəˈmɛrɪkṇɪz(ə)m
AM ˌənəˈmɛrəkəˌnɪzəm

unamiable
BR (ˌ)ʌnˈeɪmɪəbl
AM ˌənˈeɪmiəbəl

unamplified
BR (ˌ)ʌnˈamplɪfʌɪd
AM ˌənˈæmpləˌfaɪd

unamused
BR ˌʌnəˈmjuːzd
AM ˌənəˈmjuzd

unamusing
BR ˌʌnəˈmjuːzɪŋ
AM ˌənəˈmjuzɪŋ

unanalysable
BR (ˌ)ʌnˈanəlʌɪzəbl, (ˌ)ʌnˈanḷʌɪzəbl
AM ˌənˈænəˌlaɪzəbəl

unanalysed
BR (ˌ)ʌnˈanəlʌɪzd, (ˌ)ʌnˈanḷʌɪzd
AM ˌənˈænəˌlaɪzd

unaneled
BR ˌʌnəˈniːld
AM ˌənəˈnild

unanimity
BR ˌjuːnəˈnɪmɪti
AM ˌjunəˈnɪmɪdi

unanimous
BR juːˈnanɪməs, jʊˈnanɪməs
AM juˈnænəməs

unanimously
BR juːˈnanɪməsli, jʊˈnanɪməsli
AM juˈnænəməsli

unanimousness
BR juːˈnanɪməsnəs, jʊˈnanɪməsnəs
AM juˈnænəməsnəs

unannounced
BR ˌʌnəˈnaʊnst
AM ˌənəˈnaʊnst

unanswerable
BR (ˌ)ʌnˈɑːns(ə)rəbl, (ˌ)ʌnˈans(ə)rəbl
AM ˌənˈæns(ə)rəbəl

unanswerable-ness
BR (ˌ)ʌnˈɑːns(ə)rəblnəs, (ˌ)ʌnˈans(ə)rəblnəs
AM ˌənˈæns(ə)rəbəlnəs

unanswerably
BR (ˌ)ʌnˈɑːns(ə)rəbli, (ˌ)ʌnˈans(ə)rəbli
AM ˌənˈæns(ə)rəbli

unanswered
BR (ˌ)ʌnˈɑːnsəd, (ˌ)ʌnˈansəd
AM ˌənˈænsərd

unanticipated
BR ˌʌnanˈtɪsɪpeɪtɪd
AM ˈənˌænˈtɪsəˌpeɪdɪd

unapologetic
BR ˌʌnəˌpɒləˈdʒɛtɪk
AM ˌənəˌpɑləˈdʒɛdɪk

unapologetically
BR ˌʌnəˌpɒləˈdʒɛtɪkli
AM ˌənəˌpɑləˈdʒɛdək(ə)li

unapostolic
BR ˌʌnapəˈstɒlɪk
AM ˌənæpəˈstɑlɪk

unapparent
BR ˌʌnəˈparənt, ˌʌnəˈparṇt
AM ˌənəˈpɛrənt

unappealable
BR ˌʌnəˈpiːləbl
AM ˌənəˈpiləbəl

unappealing
BR ˌʌnəˈpiːlɪŋ
AM ˌənəˈpilɪŋ

unappealingly
BR ˌʌnəˈpiːlɪŋli
AM ˌənəˈpilɪŋli

unappeasable
BR ˌʌnəˈpiːzəbl
AM ˌənəˈpizəbəl

unappeased
BR ˌʌnəˈpiːzd
AM ˌənəˈpizd

unappetising
BR (ˌ)ʌnˈapɪtʌɪzɪŋ
AM ˌənˈæpəˌtaɪzɪŋ

unappetisingly
BR (ˌ)ʌnˈapɪtʌɪzɪŋli
AM ˌənˈæpəˌtaɪzɪŋli

unappetizing
BR ˌʌnˈapɪtʌɪzɪŋ
AM ˌənˈæpəˌtaɪzɪŋ

unappetizingly
BR (ˌ)ʌnˈapɪtʌɪzɪŋli
AM ˌənˈæpəˌtaɪzɪŋli

unapplied
BR ˌʌnəˈplʌɪd
AM ˌənəˈplaɪd

unappreciable
BR ˌʌnəˈpriːʃ(ɪ)əbl
AM ˌənəˈpriʃ(i)əbəl

unappreciated
BR ˌʌnəˈpriːʃɪeɪtɪd
AM ˌənəˈpriʃiˌeɪdɪd

unappreciative
BR ˌʌnəˈpriːʃ(ɪ)ətɪv, ˌʌnəˈpriːsɪətɪv
AM ˌənəˈpriʃ(i)ədɪv

unapprehended
BR ˌʌnaprɪˈhɛndɪd
AM ˌənˌæprəˈhɛndəd

unapproachability
BR ˌʌnəˌprəʊtʃəˈbɪlɪti
AM ˌənəˌproʊtʃəˈbɪlɪdi

unapproachable
BR ˌʌnəˈprəʊtʃəbl
AM ˌənəˈproʊtʃəbəl

unapproachable-ness
BR ˌʌnəˈprəʊtʃəblnəs
AM ˌənəˈproʊtʃəbəlnəs

unapproachably
BR ˌʌnəˈprəʊtʃəbli
AM ˌənəˈproʊtʃəbli

unappropriated
BR ˌʌnəˈprəʊprɪeɪtɪd
AM ˌənəˈproʊpriˌeɪdɪd

unapproved
BR ˌʌnəˈpruːvd
AM ˌənəˈpruvd

unapt
BR (ˌ)ʌnˈapt
AM ˌənˈæpt

unaptly
BR (ˌ)ʌnˈaptli
AM ˌənˈæp(t)li

unaptness
BR (ˌ)ʌnˈap(t)nəs
AM ˌənˈæp(t)nəs

unarguable
BR (ˌ)ʌnˈɑːgjʊəbl
AM ˌənˈɑrgjəwəbəl

unarguably
BR (ˌ)ʌnˈɑːgjʊəbli
AM ˌənˈɑrgjəwəbli

unargued
BR (ˌ)ʌnˈɑːgjuːd
AM ˌənˈɑrgjud

unarm
BR (ˌ)ʌnˈɑːm, -z, -ɪŋ, -d
AM ˌənˈɑrm, -z, -ɪŋ, -d

unarmed
BR (ˌ)ʌnˈɑːmd
AM ˈənˈɑrmd

unarresting
BR ˌʌnəˈrɛstɪŋ
AM ˌənəˈrɛstɪŋ

unarrestingly
BR ˌʌnəˈrɛstɪŋli
AM ˌənəˈrɛstɪŋli

unarticulated
BR ˌʌnɑːˈtɪkjʊleɪtɪd
AM ˌənˌɑrˈtɪkjəˌleɪdɪd

unartistic
BR ˌʌnɑːˈtɪstɪk
AM ˌənɑrˈtɪstɪk

unartistically
BR ˌʌnɑːˈtɪstɪkli
AM ˌənɑrˈtɪstɪk(ə)li

unary
BR ˈjuːnəri
AM ˈjunəri

unascertainable
BR ˌʌnasəˈteɪnəbl
AM ˌənˌæsərˈteɪnəbəl

unascertainably
BR ˌʌnasəˈteɪnəbli
AM ˌənˌæsərˈteɪnəbli

unascertained
BR ˌʌnasəˈteɪnd
AM ˌənˌæsərˈteɪnd

unashamed
BR ˌʌnəˈʃeɪmd
AM ˌənəˈʃeɪmd

unashamedly
BR ˌʌnəˈʃeɪm(ɪ)dli
AM ˌənəˈʃeɪm(ɪ)dli

unashamedness
BR ˌʌnəˈʃeɪm(ɪ)dnɪs
AM ˌənəˈʃeɪm(ɪd)nɪs

unasked
BR (ˌ)ʌnˈɑːskt, (ˌ)ʌnˈaskt
AM ˌənˈæs(k)t

unasked-for
BR (ˌ)ʌnˈɑːsktfɔː(r), (ˌ)ʌnˈasktfɔː(r)

AM ˌən'æs(k)tˌfɔ(ə)r

unassailability
BR ˌʌnəˌseɪlə'bɪlɨti
AM ˌənəˌseɪlə'bɪlɨdi

unassailable
BR ˌʌnə'seɪləbl
AM ˌənə'seɪləbəl

unassailableness
BR ˌʌnə'seɪləblnəs
AM ˌənə'seɪləbəlnəs

unassailably
BR ˌʌnə'seɪləbli
AM ˌənə'seɪləbli

unassertive
BR ˌʌnə'səːtɪv
AM ˌənə'sərdɪv

unassertively
BR ˌʌnə'səːtɨvli
AM ˌənə'sərdɨvli

unassertiveness
BR ˌʌnə'səːtɨvnɨs
AM ˌənə'sərdɪvnɨs

unassignable
BR ˌʌnə'sʌɪnəbl
AM ˌənə'saɪnəbəl

unassigned
BR ˌʌnə'sʌɪnd
AM ˌənə'saɪnd

unassimilable
BR ˌʌnə'sɪmɨləbl
AM ˌənə'sɪmələbəl

unassimilated
BR ˌʌnə'sɪmɨleɪtɨd
AM ˌənə'sɪməˌleɪdɨd

unassisted
BR ˌʌnə'sɪstɨd
AM ˌənə'sɪstɨd

unassociated
BR ˌʌnə'səʊʃɪeɪtɨd, ˌʌnə'səʊsɪeɪtɨd
AM ˌənə'soʊʃiˌeɪdɨd, ˌənə'soʊsiˌeɪdɨd

unassuageable
BR ˌʌnə'sweɪdʒəbl
AM ˌənə'sweɪdʒəbəl

unassuaged
BR ˌʌnə'ʃweɪdʒd
AM ˌənə'sweɪdʒd

unassuming
BR ˌʌnə'sjuːmɪŋ
AM ˌənə's(j)umɪŋ

unassumingly
BR ˌʌnə'sjuːmɪŋli
AM ˌənə's(j)umɪŋli

unassumingness
BR ˌʌnə'sjuːmɪŋnɨs
AM ˌənə's(j)umɪŋnɨs

unatoned
BR ˌʌnə'təʊnd
AM ˌənə'toʊnd

unattached
BR ˌʌnə'tatʃt
AM ˌənə'tætʃt

unattackable
BR ˌʌnə'takəbl
AM ˌənə'tækəbəl

unattainable
BR ˌʌnə'teɪnəbl
AM ˌənə'teɪnəbəl

unattainableness
BR ˌʌnə'teɪnəblnəs
AM ˌənə'teɪnəbəlnəs

unattainably
BR ˌʌnə'teɪnəbli
AM ˌənə'teɪnəbli

unattained
BR ˌʌnə'teɪnd
AM ˌənə'teɪnd

unattempted
BR ˌʌnə'tɛm(p)tɨd
AM ˌənə'tɛm(p)təd

unattended
BR ˌʌnə'tɛndɨd
AM ˌənə'tɛndəd

unattested
BR ˌʌnə'tɛstɨd
AM ˌənə'tɛstəd

unattractive
BR ˌʌnə'traktɪv
AM ˌənə'træktɪv

unattractively
BR ˌʌnə'traktɨvli
AM ˌənə'træktɨvli

unattractiveness
BR ˌʌnə'traktɨvnɨs
AM ˌənə'træktɪvnɨs

unattributable
BR ˌʌnə'trɪbjʉtəbl
AM ˌənə'trɪbjədəbəl

unattributably
BR ˌʌnə'trɪbjʉtəbli
AM ˌənə'trɪbjədəbli

unattributed
BR ˌʌnə'trɪbjʉtɨd
AM ˌənə'trɪbjədəd

unau
BR 'juːnɔː(*r*), -z
AM 'jʊˌnaʊ, -z

unaudited
BR (ˌ)ʌn'ɔːdɨtɨd
AM ˌən'ɔdədəd, ˌən'ɑdədəd

unauthentic
BR ˌʌnɔː'θɛntɪk
AM ˌənɔ'θɛn(t)ɪk, ˌənɑ'θɛn(t)ɪk

unauthentically
BR ˌʌnɔː'θɛntɨkli
AM ˌənɔ'θɛn(t)ək(ə)li, ˌənɑ'θɛn(t)ək(ə)li

unauthenticated
BR ˌʌnɔː'θɛntɨkeɪtɨd
AM ˌənɔ'θɛn(t)əˌkeɪdɨd, ˌənɑ'θɛn(t)əˌkeɪdɨd

unauthorised
BR (ˌ)ʌn'ɔːθərʌɪzd
AM ˌən'ɔθəˌraɪzd, ˌən'ɑθəˌraɪzd

unauthorized
BR (ˌ)ʌn'ɔːθərʌɪzd
AM ˌən'ɔθəˌraɪzd, ˌən'ɑθəˌraɪzd

unavailability
BR ˌʌnəˌveɪlə'bɪlɨti
AM ˌənəˌveɪlə'bɪlɨdi

unavailable
BR ˌʌnə'veɪləbl
AM ˌənə'veɪləbəl

unavailableness
BR ˌʌnə'veɪləblnəs
AM ˌənə'veɪləbəlnəs

unavailing
BR ˌʌnə'veɪlɪŋ
AM ˌənə'veɪlɪŋ

unavailingly
BR ˌʌnə'veɪlɪŋli
AM ˌənə'veɪlɪŋli

unavenged
BR ˌʌnə'vɛn(d)ʒd
AM ˌənə'vɛndʒd

unavoidability
BR ˌʌnəˌvɔɪdə'bɪlɨti
AM ˌənəˌvɔɪdə'bɪlɨdi

unavoidable
BR ˌʌnə'vɔɪdəbl
AM ˌənə'vɔɪdəbəl

unavoidableness
BR ˌʌnə'vɔɪdəblnəs
AM ˌənə'vɔɪdəbəlnəs

unavoidably
BR ˌʌnə'vɔɪdəbli
AM ˌənə'vɔɪdəbli

unavowed
BR ˌʌnə'vaʊd
AM ˌənə'vaʊd

unawakened
BR ˌʌnə'weɪk(ə)nd
AM ˌənə'weɪkənd

unaware
BR ˌʌnə'wɛː(r), -z
AM ˌənə'wɛ(ə)r, -z

unawareness
BR ˌʌnə'wɛːnəs
AM ˌənə'wɛrnəs

unawares
BR ˌʌnə'wɛːz
AM ənə'wɛ(ə)rz

unawed
BR (ˌ)ʌn'ɔːd
AM ˌən'ɔd, ˌən'ɑd

unbackable
BR ˌʌn'bakəbl
AM ˌən'bækəbəl

unbacked
BR (ˌ)ʌn'bakt
AM ˌən'bækt

unbaked
BR (ˌ)ʌn'beɪkt
AM ən'beɪkt

unbalance
BR (ˌ)ʌn'baləns, (ˌ)ʌn'balṇs, -ɨz, -ɪŋ, -t
AM ˌən'bæləns, -əz, -ɪŋ, -t

unban
BR (ˌ)ʌn'ban, -z, -ɪŋ, -d
AM ˌən'bæn, -z, -ɪŋ, -d

unbaptised
BR ˌʌnbap'tʌɪzd
AM ˌən'bæpˌtaɪzd

unbaptized
BR ˌʌnbap'tʌɪzd
AM ˌən'bæpˌtaɪzd

unbar
BR ˌʌn'bɑː(r), -z, -ɪŋ, -d
AM ˌən'bɑr, -z, -ɪŋ, -d

unbearable
BR (ˌ)ʌn'bɛːrəbl
AM ˌən'bɛrəbəl

unbearableness
BR (ˌ)ʌn'bɛːrəblnəs
AM ˌən'bɛrəbəlnəs

unbearably
BR (ˌ)ʌn'bɛːrəbli
AM ˌən'bɛrəbli

unbeatable
BR (ˌ)ʌn'biːtəbl
AM ˌən'bidəbəl

unbeatably
BR (ˌ)ʌn'biːtəbli
AM ˌən'bidəbli

unbeaten
BR (ˌ)ʌn'biːtn
AM ˌən'bitn

unbeautiful
BR (ˌ)ʌn'bjuːtɨf(ʊ)l
AM ˌən'bjudəfəl

unbeautifully
BR (ˌ)ʌn'bjuːtɨfʊli, (ˌ)ʌn'bjuːtɨfḷi
AM ˌən'bjudəf(ə)li

unbecoming
BR ˌʌnbɪ'kʌmɪŋ
AM ˌənbə'kəmɪŋ

unbecomingly
BR ˌʌnbɪ'kʌmɪŋli
AM ˌənbə'kəmɪŋli

unbecomingness
BR ˌʌnbɪ'kʌmɪŋnɨs
AM ˌənbə'kəmɪŋnɨs

unbefitting
BR ˌʌnbɪ'fɪtɪŋ
AM ˌənbə'fɪdɪŋ

unbefittingly
BR ˌʌnbɪ'fɪtɪŋli
AM ˌənbə'fɪdɪŋli

unbefittingness
BR ˌʌnbɪ'fɪtɪŋnɨs
AM ˌənbə'fɪdɪŋnɨs

unbefriended
BR ˌʌnbɪ'frɛndɨd
AM ˌənbə'frɛndəd

unbegotten
BR ˌʌnbɪ'gɒtn
AM ˌənbə'gɑtn

unbeholden
BR ˌʌnbɪ'həʊldn
AM ˌənbə'hoʊldən

unbeknown
BR ˌʌnbɪ'nəʊn
AM ˌənbə'noʊn

unbeknownst
BR ˌʌnbɪ'nəʊnst
AM ˌənbəˌnoʊnst

unbelief
BR ˌʌnbɪ'liːf

AM ˌənbəˈlif

unbelievability
BR ˌʌnbɪˌliːvəˈbɪlɨti
AM ˌənbəˌlivəˈbɪlɨdi

unbelievable
BR ˌʌnbɪˈliːvəbl
AM ˌənbəˈlivəbəl

unbelievableness
BR ˌʌnbɪˈliːvəblnəs
AM ˌənbəˈlivəbəlnəs

unbelievably
BR ˌʌnbɪˈliːvəbli
AM ˌənbəˈlivəbli

unbelieved
BR ˌʌnbɪˈliːvd
AM ˌənbəˈlivd

unbeliever
BR ˌʌnbɪˈliːvə(r), -z
AM ˌənbəˈlivər, -z

unbelieving
BR ˌʌnbɪˈliːvɪŋ
AM ˌənbəˈlivɪŋ

unbelievingly
BR ˌʌnbɪˈliːvɪŋli
AM ˌənbəˈlivɪŋli

unbelievingness
BR ˌʌnbɨliːvɪŋnɨs
AM ˌənbɪˈlivɪŋnɨs

unbeloved
BR ˌʌnbɪˈlʌvɨd
AM ˌənbəˈləv(ə)d

unbelt
BR ˌʌnˈbɛlt, -s, -ɪŋ, -ɨd
AM ˌənˈbɛlt, -s, -ɪŋ, -əd

unbend
BR ˌʌnˈbɛnd, -z, -ɪŋ
AM ˌənˈbɛnd, -z, -ɪŋ

unbendingly
BR ˌʌnˈbɛndɪŋli
AM ˌənˈbɛndɪŋli

unbendingness
BR ˌʌnˈbɛndɪŋnɨs
AM ˌənˈbɛndɪŋnɨs

unbent
BR ˌʌnˈbɛnt
AM ˌənˈbɛnt

unbiased
BR ˌʌnˈbʌɪəst
AM ˌənˈbaɪəst

unbiblical
BR ˌʌnˈbɪblɨkl
AM ˌənˈbɪbləkəl

unbiddable
BR ˌʌnˈbɪdəbl
AM ˌənˈbɪdəbəl

unbidden
BR ˌʌnˈbɪdn
AM ˌənˈbɪdən

unbind
BR ˌʌnˈbʌɪnd, -z, -ɪŋ
AM ˌənˈbaɪnd, -z, -ɪŋ

unbirthday
BR ˌʌnˈbəːθdeɪ, -z
AM ¦ənˈbərθˌdeɪ, -z

unbleached
BR ˌʌnˈbliːtʃt
AM ˌənˈblitʃt

unblemished
BR (ˌ)ʌnˈblɛmɪʃt
AM ˌənˈblɛmɪʃt

unblended
BR ˌʌnˈblɛndɨd
AM ˌənˈblɛndəd

unblessed
BR ˌʌnˈblɛst
AM ˌənˈblɛst

unblest
BR ˌʌnˈblɛst
AM ˌənˈblɛst

unblinking
BR ˌʌnˈblɪŋkɪŋ
AM ˌənˈblɪŋkɪŋ

unblinkingly
BR ˌʌnˈblɪŋkɪŋli
AM ˌənˈblɪŋkɪŋli

unblock
BR ˌʌnˈblɒk, -s, -ɪŋ, -t
AM ˌənˈblɑk, -s, -ɪŋ, -t

unbloody
BR ˌʌnˈblʌdi
AM ˌənˈblədi

unblown
BR ˌʌnˈbləʊn
AM ˌənˈbloʊn

unblushing
BR ˌʌnˈblʌʃɪŋ
AM ˌənˈbləʃɪŋ

unblushingly
BR ˌʌnˈblʌʃɪŋli
AM ˌənˈbləʃɪŋli

unbolt
BR ˌʌnˈbəʊlt, -s, -ɪŋ, -ɨd
AM ˌənˈboʊlt, -s, -ɪŋ, -əd

unbonnet
BR ˌʌnˈbɒn|ɪt, -s, -ɨtɪŋ, -ɨtɨd
AM ˌənˈbɑnə|t, -ts, -dɪŋ, -dəd

unbookish
BR (ˌ)ʌnˈbʊkɪʃ
AM ˌənˈbʊkɪʃ

unboot
BR ˌʌnˈbuːt, -s, -ɪŋ, -ɨd
AM ˌənˈbu|t, -ts, -dɪŋ, -dəd

unborn
BR ˌʌnˈbɔːn
AM ˌənˈbɔ(ə)rn

unbosom
BR ˌʌnˈbʊz|(ə)m, -(ə)mz, -əmɪŋ\-m̩ɪŋ, -(ə)md
AM ˌənˈbʊzəm, -z, -ɪŋ, -d

unbothered
BR (ˌ)ʌnˈbɒðəd
AM ˌənˈbɑðərd

unbound
BR ˌʌnˈbaʊnd
AM ˌənˈbaʊnd

unbounded
BR (ˌ)ʌnˈbaʊndɨd
AM ˌənˈbaʊn(d)əd

unboundedly
BR (ˌ)ʌnˈbaʊndɨdli
AM ˌənˈbaʊn(d)ədli

unboundedness
BR (ˌ)ʌnˈbaʊndɨdnɨs
AM ˌənˈbaʊn(d)ədnəs

unbowed
BR ˌʌnˈbaʊd
AM ˌənˈbaʊd

unbrace
BR ˌʌnˈbreɪs, -ɨz, -ɪŋ, -t
AM ˌənˈbreɪs, -ɨz, -ɪŋ, -t

unbranded
BR (ˌ)ʌnˈbrandɨd
AM ˌənˈbrændəd

unbreachable
BR (ˌ)ʌnˈbriːtʃəbl
AM ˌənˈbritʃəbəl

unbreakable
BR (ˌ)ʌnˈbreɪkəbl
AM ˌənˈbreɪkəbəl

unbreakably
BR (ˌ)ʌnˈbreɪkəbli
AM ˌənˈbreɪkəbli

unbreathable
BR (ˌ)ʌnˈbriːðəbl
AM ˌənˈbriðəbəl

unbribable
BR (ˌ)ʌnˈbrʌɪbəbl
AM ˌənˈbraɪbəbəl

unbridgeable
BR (ˌ)ʌnˈbrɪdʒəbl
AM ˌənˈbrɪdʒəbəl

unbridle
BR (ˌ)ʌnˈbrʌɪd|l, -lz, -l̩ɪŋ\-lɪŋ, -ld
AM ˌənˈbraɪd|əl, -əlz, -(ə)lɪŋ, -əld

un-British
BR ˌʌnˈbrɪtɪʃ
AM ˌənˈbrɪdɪʃ

unbroken
BR (ˌ)ʌnˈbrəʊk(ə)n
AM ˌənˈbroʊkən

unbrokenly
BR (ˌ)ʌnˈbrəʊk(ə)nli
AM ˌənˈbroʊkənli

unbrokenness
BR (ˌ)ʌnˈbrəʊk(ə)nnəs
AM ˌənˈbroʊkə(n)nəs

unbrotherly
BR (ˌ)ʌnˈbrʌðəli
AM ˌənˈbrəðərli

unbruised
BR ˌʌnˈbruːzd
AM ˌənˈbruzd

unbrushed
BR ˌʌnˈbrʌʃt
AM ˌənˈbrəʃt

unbuckle
BR (ˌ)ʌnˈbʌk|l, -lz, -l̩ɪŋ\-lɪŋ, -ld
AM ˌənˈbək|əl, -əlz, -(ə)lɪŋ, -əld

unbuild
BR ˌʌnˈbɪld, -z, -ɪŋ
AM ˌənˈbɪld, -z, -ɪŋ

unbuilt
BR (ˌ)ʌnˈbɪlt
AM ˌənˈbɪlt

unbundle
BR (ˌ)ʌnˈbʌnd|l, -lz, -l̩ɪŋ\-lɪŋ, -ld
AM ˌənˈbən|dəl, -dəlz, -(d)(ə)lɪŋ, -dəld

unbundler
BR (ˌ)ʌnˈbʌndl̩ə(r), ˌʌnˈbʌndlə(r), -z
AM ˌənˈbən(də)lər, -z

unburden
BR (ˌ)ʌnˈbəːd|n, -nz, -n̩ɪŋ\-nɪŋ, -nd
AM ˌənˈbərdən, -z, -ɪŋ, -d

unburied
BR (ˌ)ʌnˈbɛrɪd
AM ˌənˈbɛrid

unburned
BR (ˌ)ʌnˈbəːnd
AM ˌənˈbərnd

unburnt
BR (ˌ)ʌnˈbəːnt
AM ˌənˈbərnt

unbury
BR (ˌ)ʌnˈbɛːr|i, -ɪz, -ɪɪŋ, -ɪd
AM ˌənˈbɛri, -z, -ɪŋ, -d

unbusinesslike
BR (ˌ)ʌnˈbɪznɨslʌɪk
AM ˌənˈbɪznɨsˌlaɪk

unbutton
BR ˌʌnˈbʌtn̩, -z, -ɪŋ, -d
AM ˌənˈbətn̩, -z, -ɪŋ, -d

uncage
BR ˌʌnˈkeɪdʒ, ˌʌŋˈkeɪdʒ, -ɨz, -ɪŋ, -d
AM ˌənˈkeɪdʒ, -ɨz, -ɪŋ, -d

uncalculated
BR (ˌ)ʌnˈkalkjʊleɪtɨd, (ˌ)ʌŋˈkalkjʊleɪtɨd
AM ˌənˈkælkjəˌleɪdɨd

uncalculating
BR (ˌ)ʌnˈkalkjʊleɪtɪŋ, (ˌ)ʌŋˈkalkjʊleɪtɪŋ
AM ˈənkælkjəˌleɪdɪŋ

uncalled
BR (ˌ)ʌnˈkɔːld, (ˌ)ʌŋˈkɔːld
AM ˌənˈkɔld, ˌənˈkɑld

uncalled-for
BR (ˌ)ʌnˈkɔːldfɔː(r), (ˌ)ʌŋˈkɔːldfɔː(r)
AM ˌənˈkɔldˌfɔ(ə)r, ˌənˈkɑldˌfɔ(ə)r

uncandid
BR (ˌ)ʌnˈkandɨd, (ˌ)ʌŋˈkandɨd
AM ˌənˈkændəd

uncannily
BR ʌnˈkanɨli, ʌŋˈkanɨli
AM ˌənˈkænəli

uncanniness
BR ʌnˈkanɪnɨs, ʌŋˈkanɪnɨs
AM ˌənˈkænɪnɨs

uncanny
BR ʌn'kan|i, ʌŋ'kan|i, -ɪə(r), -ɪɪst
AM ˌən'kæni, -ər, -ɪst

uncanonical
BR ˌʌnkə'nɒnɪkl, ˌʌŋkə'nɒnɪkl
AM ˌənkə'nɑnəkəl

uncanonically
BR ˌʌnkə'nɒnɪkli, ˌʌŋkə'nɒnɪkli
AM ˌənkə'nɑnək(ə)li

uncap
BR ˌʌn'kap, ˌʌŋ'kap, -s, -ɪŋ, -t
AM ˌən'kæp, -s, -ɪŋ, -t

uncared-for
BR (ˌ)ʌn'kɛːdfɔː(r), (ˌ)ʌŋ'kɛːdfɔː(r)
AM ˌən'kɛrdˌfɔ(ə)r

uncaring
BR (ˌ)ʌn'kɛːrɪŋ, (ˌ)ʌŋ'kɛːrɪŋ
AM ˌən'kɛrɪŋ

uncaringly
BR (ˌ)ʌn'kɛːrɪŋli, (ˌ)ʌŋ'kɛːrɪŋli
AM ˌən'kɛrɪŋli

uncarpeted
BR (ˌ)ʌn'kɑːpɪtɪd, (ˌ)ʌŋ'kɑːpɪtɪd
AM ˌən'kɑrpədəd

uncase
BR ˌʌn'keɪs, ˌʌŋ'keɪs, -ɪz, -ɪŋ, -t
AM ˌən'keɪs, -ɪz, -ɪŋ, -t

uncashed
BR (ˌ)ʌn'kaʃt, (ˌ)ʌŋ'kaʃt
AM ˌən'kæʃt

uncatchable
BR (ˌ)ʌn'katʃəbl, (ˌ)ʌŋ'katʃəbl
AM ˌən'kɛtʃəbəl

uncategorisable
BR ˌʌn'katɪgərʌɪzəbl, ˌʌŋ'katɪgərʌɪzəbl
AM ˌən'kædəgəˌraɪzəbəl

uncategorizable
BR ˌʌn'katɪgərʌɪzəbl, ˌʌŋ'katɪgərʌɪzəbl
AM ˌən'kædəgəˌraɪzəbəl

uncaught
BR (ˌ)ʌn'kɔːt, (ˌ)ʌŋ'kɔːt
AM ˌən'kɔt, ˌən'kɑt

uncaused
BR (ˌ)ʌn'kɔːzd, (ˌ)ʌŋ'kɔːzd
AM ˌən'kɔzd, ˌən'kɑzd

unceasing
BR (ˌ)ʌn'siːsɪŋ
AM ˌən'sisɪŋ

unceasingly
BR (ˌ)ʌn'siːsɪŋli
AM ˌən'sisɪŋli

uncelebrated
BR (ˌ)ʌn'sɛlɪbreɪtɪd
AM ˌən'sɛləˌbreɪdɪd

uncensored
BR (ˌ)ʌn'sɛnsəd
AM ˌən'sɛnsərd

uncensured
BR (ˌ)ʌn'sɛnʃəd
AM ˌən'sɛn(t)ʃərd

unceremonious
BR ˌʌnsɛrɪ'məʊnɪəs
AM ˌənsɛrə'moʊniəs

unceremoniously
BR ˌʌnsɛrɪ'məʊnɪəsli
AM ˌənsɛrə'moʊniəsli

unceremoniousness
BR ˌʌnsɛrɪ'məʊnɪəsnəs
AM ˌənsɛrə'moʊniəsnəs

uncertain
BR (ˌ)ʌn'səːtn
AM ˌən'sərtn

uncertainly
BR (ˌ)ʌn'səːtnli
AM ˌən'sərtnli

uncertainty
BR (ˌ)ʌn'səːtnt|i, -ɪz
AM ˌən'sərtn(t)i, -z

uncertificated
BR ˌʌnsə'tɪfɪkeɪtɪd
AM ˌənsər'tɪfəˌkeɪdɪd

uncertified
BR (ˌ)ʌn'səːtɪfʌɪd
AM ˌən'sərdəˌfaɪd

unchain
BR ˌʌn'tʃeɪn, -z, -ɪŋ, -d
AM ˌən'tʃeɪn, -z, -ɪŋ, -d

unchallengeable
BR (ˌ)ʌn'tʃalɪn(d)ʒəbl
AM ˌən'tʃæləndʒəbəl

unchallengeably
BR (ˌ)ʌn'tʃalɪn(d)ʒəbli
AM ˌən'tʃæləndʒəbli

unchallenged
BR (ˌ)ʌn'tʃalɪn(d)ʒd
AM ˌən'tʃæləndʒd

unchallenging
BR (ˌ)ʌn'tʃalɪn(d)ʒɪŋ
AM ˌən'tʃæləndʒɪŋ

unchangeability
BR ˌʌntʃeɪn(d)ʒə'bɪlɪti
AM ˌənˌtʃeɪndʒə'bɪlɪdi

unchangeable
BR (ˌ)ʌn'tʃeɪn(d)ʒəbl
AM ˌən'tʃeɪndʒəbəl

unchangeableness
BR (ˌ)ʌn'tʃeɪn(d)ʒəblnəs
AM ˌən'tʃeɪndʒəbəlnəs

unchangeably
BR (ˌ)ʌn'tʃeɪn(d)ʒəbli
AM ˌən'tʃeɪndʒəbli

unchanged
BR (ˌ)ʌn'tʃeɪn(d)ʒd
AM ˌən'tʃeɪndʒd

unchanging
BR (ˌ)ʌn'tʃeɪn(d)ʒɪŋ
AM ˌən'tʃeɪndʒɪŋ

unchangingly
BR (ˌ)ʌn'tʃeɪn(d)ʒɪŋli
AM ˌən'tʃeɪndʒɪŋli

unchangingness
BR (ˌ)ʌn'tʃeɪn(d)ʒɪŋnɪs
AM ˌən'tʃeɪndʒɪŋnɪs

unchaperoned
BR (ˌ)ʌn'ʃapərəʊnd
AM ˌən'ʃæpəˌroʊnd

uncharacteristic
BR ˌʌnkarəktə'rɪstɪk, ˌʌŋkarəktə'rɪstɪk
AM ˌənˌkɛrəktə'rɪstɪk

uncharacteristically
BR ˌʌnkarəktə'rɪstɪkli, ˌʌŋkarəktə'rɪstɪkli
AM ˌənˌkɛrəktə'rɪstɪk(ə)li

uncharged
BR ˌʌn'tʃɑːdʒd
AM ˌən'tʃɑrdʒd

uncharismatic
BR ˌʌnkarɪz'matɪk, ˌʌŋkarɪz'matɪk
AM ˌənˌkɛrəz'mædɪk

uncharitable
BR (ˌ)ʌn'tʃarɪtəbl
AM ˌən'tʃɛrədəbəl

uncharitableness
BR (ˌ)ʌn'tʃarɪtəblnəs
AM ˌən'tʃɛrədəbəlnəs

uncharitably
BR (ˌ)ʌn'tʃarɪtəbli
AM ˌən'tʃɛrədəbli

uncharming
BR ˌʌn'tʃɑːmɪŋ
AM ˌən'tʃɑrmɪŋ

uncharted
BR ˌʌn'tʃɑːtɪd
AM ˌən'tʃɑrdəd

unchartered
BR ˌʌn'tʃɑːtəd
AM ˌən'tʃɑrdərd

unchaste
BR ˌʌn'tʃeɪst
AM ˌən'tʃeɪst

unchastely
BR ˌʌn'tʃeɪs(t)li
AM ˌən'tʃeɪs(t)li

unchastened
BR (ˌ)ʌn'tʃeɪsnd
AM ˌən'tʃeɪsnd

unchasteness
BR ˌʌn'tʃeɪstnɪs
AM ˌən'tʃeɪs(t)nɪs

unchastity
BR ˌʌn'tʃastɪti
AM ˌən'tʃæstədi

unchecked
BR ˌʌn'tʃɛkt
AM ˌən'tʃɛkt

unchivalrous
BR (ˌ)ʌn'ʃɪvlrəs
AM ˌən'ʃɪvəlrəs

unchivalrously
BR (ˌ)ʌn'ʃɪvlrəsli
AM ˌən'ʃɪvəlrəsli

unchosen
BR (ˌ)ʌn'tʃəʊzn
AM ˌən'tʃoʊzn

unchristian
BR (ˌ)ʌn'krɪstʃ(ə)n
AM ˌən'krɪstʃən

unchristianly
BR (ˌ)ʌn'krɪstʃ(ə)nli
AM ˌən'krɪstʃənli

unchurch
BR ˌʌn'tʃəːtʃ, -ɪz, -ɪŋ, -t
AM ˌən'tʃərtʃ, -əz, -ɪŋ, -t

unci
BR 'ʌnsʌɪ
AM 'ənˌsaɪ

uncial
BR 'ʌnsɪəl, 'ʌnʃl, -z
AM 'ən(t)siəl, 'əntʃəl, -z

unciform
BR 'ʌnsɪfɔːm
AM 'ənsəˌfɔ(ə)rm

uncinate
BR 'ʌnsɪnət, 'ʌnsn̩ət, 'ʌnsɪneɪt
AM 'ənsənət, 'ənsəˌneɪt

uncircumcised
BR ˌʌn'səːkəmsʌɪzd
AM ˌən'sərkəmˌsaɪzd

uncircumcision
BR ˌʌnsəːkəm'sɪʒn
AM ˌənˌsərkəm'sɪʒən

uncircumscribed
BR ˌʌn'səːkəmskrʌɪbd
AM ˌən'sərkəmˌskraɪbd

uncivil
BR ˌʌn'sɪvl
AM ˌən'sɪvəl

uncivilised
BR (ˌ)ʌn'sɪvɪlʌɪzd, (ˌ)ʌn'sɪvl̩ʌɪzd
AM ˌən'sɪvəˌlaɪzd

uncivilized
BR (ˌ)ʌn'sɪvɪlʌɪzd, (ˌ)ʌn'sɪvl̩ʌɪzd
AM ˌən'sɪvəˌlaɪzd

uncivilly
BR ˌʌn'sɪvɪli
AM ˌən'sɪvəli

unclad
BR ˌʌn'klad, ˌʌŋ'klad
AM ˌən'klæd

unclaimed
BR ˌʌn'kleɪmd, ˌʌŋ'kleɪmd
AM ˌən'kleɪmd

unclasp
BR ˌʌn'klɑːsp, ˌʌn'klasp, ˌʌŋ'klɑːsp, ˌʌŋ'klasp, -s, -ɪŋ, -t
AM ˌən'klæsp, -s, -ɪŋ, -t

unclassifiable
BR (ˌ)ʌn'klasɪfʌɪəbl, (ˌ)ʌŋ'klasɪfʌɪəbl
AM ˌənˌklæsə'faɪəbəl

unclassified
BR (ˌ)ʌnˈklasɪfʌɪd, (ˌ)ʌŋˈklasɪfʌɪd
AM ˌənˈklæsəˌfaɪd

uncle
BR ˈʌŋkl, -z
AM ˈəŋkəl, -z

unclean
BR (ˌ)ʌnˈkliːn, (ˌ)ʌŋˈkliːn, -d
AM ˌənˈklin, -d

uncleanliness
BR (ˌ)ʌnˈklɛnlɪnɪs, (ˌ)ʌŋˈklɛnlɪnɪs
AM ˌənˈklɛnlinɪs

uncleanly[1]
adjective
BR (ˌ)ʌnˈklɛnli, (ˌ)ʌŋˈklɛnli
AM ˌənˈklɛnli

uncleanly[2]
adverb
BR (ˌ)ʌnˈkliːnli, (ˌ)ʌŋˈkliːnli
AM ˌənˈklinli

uncleanness
BR (ˌ)ʌnˈkliːnnɪs, (ˌ)ʌŋˈkliːnnɪs
AM ˌənˈklin(n)ɪs

uncleansed
BR (ˌ)ʌnˈklɛnzd, (ˌ)ʌŋˈklɛnzd
AM ˌənˈklɛnzd

unclear
BR ˌʌnˈklɪə(r), ˌʌŋˈklɪə(r), -d
AM ˌənˈklɪ(ə)r, -d

unclearly
BR ˌʌnˈklɪəli, ˌʌŋˈklɪəli
AM ˌənˈklɪrli

unclearness
BR ˌʌnˈklɪənəs, ˌʌŋˈklɪənəs
AM ˌənˈklɪrnəs

uncle-in-law
BR ˈʌŋklɪnˌlɔː(r)
AM ˈəŋkələnˌlɔ, ˈəŋkələnˌlɑ

unclench
BR ˌʌnˈklɛn(t)ʃ, ˌʌŋˈklɛn(t)ʃ, -ɪz, -ɪŋ, -t
AM ˌənˈklɛn(t)ʃ, -əz, -ɪŋ, -t

Uncle Sam
BR ˌʌŋkl ˈsam
AM ˌəŋkəl ˈsæm

uncles-in-law
BR ˈʌŋklzɪnˌlɔː(r), -z
AM ˈəŋkəlzənˌlɔ, ˈəŋkəlzənˌlɑ

Uncle Tom
BR ˌʌŋkl ˈtɒm, -z
AM ˌəŋkəl ˈtɑm, -z

unclimbable
BR ˌʌnˈklʌɪməbl, ˌʌŋˈklʌɪməbl
AM ˌənˈklaɪməbəl

unclimbed
BR ˌʌnˈklʌɪmd, ˌʌŋˈklʌɪmd
AM ˌənˈklaɪmd

unclinch
BR ˌʌnˈklɪn(t)ʃ, ˌʌŋˈklɪn(t)ʃ, -ɪz, -ɪŋ, -t
AM ˌənˈklɪn(t)ʃ, -ɪz, -ɪŋ, -t

unclip
BR ˌʌnˈklɪp, ˌʌŋˈklɪp, -s, -ɪŋ, -t
AM ˌənˈklɪp, -s, -ɪŋ, -t

uncloak
BR ˌʌnˈkləʊk, ˌʌŋˈkləʊk, -s, -ɪŋ, -t
AM ˌənˈkloʊk, -s, -ɪŋ, -t

unclog
BR ˌʌnˈklɒɡ, ˌʌŋˈklɒɡ, -z, -ɪŋ, -d
AM ˌənˈklɑɡ, -z, -ɪŋ, -d

unclose
BR ˌʌnˈkləʊz, ˌʌŋˈkləʊz, -ɪz, -ɪŋ, -d
AM ˌənˈkloʊz, -ɪz, -ɪŋ, -d

unclothe
BR ˌʌnˈkləʊð, ˌʌŋˈkləʊð, -z, -ɪŋ, -d
AM ˌənˈkloʊð, -z, -ɪŋ, -d

unclouded
BR (ˌ)ʌnˈklaʊdɪd, (ˌ)ʌŋˈklaʊdɪd
AM ˌənˈklaʊdəd

uncluttered
BR (ˌ)ʌnˈklʌtəd, (ˌ)ʌŋˈklʌtəd
AM ˌənˈklədərd

unco
BR ˈʌŋkəʊ, -z
AM ˈəŋkoʊ, -z

uncoded
BR (ˌ)ʌnˈkəʊdɪd, (ˌ)ʌŋˈkəʊdɪd
AM ˌənˈkoʊdəd

uncoil
BR ˌʌnˈkɔɪl, ˌʌŋˈkɔɪl, -z, -ɪŋ, -d
AM ˌənˈkɔɪl, -z, -ɪŋ, -d

uncollected
BR ˌʌnkəˈlɛktɪd, ˌʌŋkəˈlɛktɪd
AM ˌənkəˈlɛktəd

uncolored
BR (ˌ)ʌnˈkʌləd, (ˌ)ʌŋˈkʌləd
AM ˌənˈkələrd

uncoloured
BR (ˌ)ʌnˈkʌləd, (ˌ)ʌŋˈkʌləd
AM ˌənˈkələrd

uncombed
BR (ˌ)ʌnˈkəʊmd, (ˌ)ʌŋˈkəʊmd
AM ˌənˈkoʊmd

uncome-at-able
BR ˌʌnkʌmˈatəbl, ˌʌŋkʌmˈatəbl
AM ˌənˌkəmˈædəbəl

uncomely
BR ˌʌnˈkʌmli, ˌʌŋˈkʌmli
AM ˌənˈkəmli

uncomfortable
BR ʌnˈkʌmf(ə)təbl, ʌŋˈkʌmf(ə)təbl
AM ˌənˈkəmfərdəbəl, ˌənˈkəmftərbəl

uncomfortableness
BR ʌnˈkʌmf(ə)təblnəs, ʌŋˈkʌmf(ə)təblnəs
AM ˌənˈkəmfərdəbəlnəs, ˌənˈkəmftərbəlnəs

uncomfortably
BR ʌnˈkʌmf(ə)təbli, ʌŋˈkʌmf(ə)təbli
AM ˌənˈkəmfərdəbli, ˌənˈkəmftərbli

uncomforted
BR ˌʌnˈkʌmfətɪd, ˌʌŋˈkʌmfətɪd
AM ˌənˈkəmfərdəd

uncommercial
BR ˌʌnkəˈməːʃl, ˌʌŋkəˈməːʃl
AM ˌənkəˈmərʃəl

uncommercially
BR ˌʌnkəˈməːʃl̩i, ˌʌnkəˈməːʃəli, ˌʌŋkəˈməːʃl̩i, ˌʌŋkəˈməːʃəli
AM ˌənkəˈmərʃəli

uncommissioned
BR ˌʌnkəˈmɪʃnd, ˌʌŋkəˈmɪʃnd
AM ˌənkəˈmɪʃənd

uncommitted
BR ˌʌnkəˈmɪtɪd, ˌʌŋkəˈmɪtɪd
AM ˌənkəˈmɪdɪd

uncommon
BR (ˌ)ʌnˈkɒmən, (ˌ)ʌŋˈkɒmən
AM ˌənˈkɑmən

uncommonly
BR (ˌ)ʌnˈkɒmənli, (ˌ)ʌŋˈkɒmənli
AM ˌənˈkɑmənli

uncommonness
BR (ˌ)ʌnˈkɒmənnəs, (ˌ)ʌŋˈkɒmənnəs
AM ˌənˈkɑmə(n)nəs

uncommunicable
BR ˌʌnkəˈmjuːnɪkəbl, ˌʌŋkəˈmjuːnɪkəbl
AM ˌənkəˈmjunəkəbəl

uncommunicated
BR ˌʌnkəˈmjuːnɪkeɪtɪd, ˌʌŋkəˈmjuːnɪkeɪtɪd
AM ˌənkəˈmjunəˌkeɪdɪd

uncommunicative
BR ˌʌnkəˈmjuːnɪkətɪv, ˌʌŋkəˈmjuːnɪkətɪv
AM ˌənkəˈmjunəˌkeɪdɪv, ˌənkəˈmjunəkədɪv

uncommunicatively
BR ˌʌnkəˈmjuːnɪkətɪvli, ˌʌŋkəˈmjuːnɪkətɪvli
AM ˌənkəˈmjunəˌkeɪdɪvli, ˌənkəˈmjunəkədɪvli

uncommunicativeness
BR ˌʌnkəˈmjuːnɪkətɪvnɪs, ˌʌŋkəˈmjuːnɪkətɪvnɪs
AM ˌənkəˈmjunəˌkeɪdɪvnɪs, ˌənkəˈmjunəkədɪvnɪs

uncompanionable
BR ˌʌnkəmˈpanɪənəbl, ˌʌŋkəmˈpanɪənəbl
AM ˌənkəmˈpænjənəbəl

uncompensated
BR ˌʌnˈkʌmp(ɛ)nseɪtɪd, ˌʌŋˈkʌmp(ɛ)nseɪtɪd
AM ˌənˈkɑmpənˌseɪdɪd

uncompetitive
BR ˌʌnkəmˈpɛtɪtɪv, ˌʌŋkəmˈpɛtɪtɪv
AM ˌənkəmˈpɛdədɪv

uncompetitiveness
BR ˌʌnkəmˈpɛtɪtɪvnɪs, ˌʌŋkəmˈpɛtɪtɪvnɪs
AM ˌənkəmˈpɛdədɪvnɪs

uncomplaining
BR ˌʌnkəmˈpleɪnɪŋ, ˌʌŋkəmˈpleɪnɪŋ
AM ˌənkəmˈpleɪnɪŋ

uncomplainingly
BR ˌʌnkəmˈpleɪnɪŋli, ˌʌŋkəmˈpleɪnɪŋli
AM ˌənkəmˈpleɪnɪŋli

uncompleted
BR ˌʌnkəmˈpliːtɪd, ˌʌŋkəmˈpliːtɪd
AM ˌənkəmˈplidɪd

uncomplicated
BR ˌʌnˈkɒmplɪkeɪtɪd, ˌʌŋˈkɒmplɪkeɪtɪd
AM ˌənˈkɑmpləˌkeɪdɪd

uncomplimentary
BR ˌʌnkɒmplɪˈmɛnt(ə)ri, ˌʌŋkɒmplɪˈmɛnt(ə)ri
AM ˌənˌkɑmpləˈmɛn(t)əri

uncompounded
BR ˌʌnkəmˈpaʊndɪd, ˌʌŋkəmˈpaʊndɪd
AM ˌənkəmˈpaʊndəd

uncomprehended
BR ˌʌnkɒmprɪˈhɛndɪd, ˌʌŋkɒmprɪˈhɛndɪd
AM ˌənˌkɑmprəˈhɛndəd

uncomprehending
BR ˌʌnkɒmprɪˈhɛndɪŋ, ˌʌŋkɒmprɪˈhɛndɪŋ
AM ˌənˌkɑmprəˈhɛndɪŋ

uncomprehendingly
BR ˌʌnkɒmprɪˈhɛndɪŋli, ˌʌŋkɒmprɪˈhɛndɪŋli
AM ˌənˌkɑmprəˈhɛndɪŋli

uncomprehension
BR ˌʌnkɒmprɪˈhɛnʃn, ˌʌŋkɒmprɪˈhɛnʃn
AM ˌənˌkɑmprəˈhɛn(t)ʃən

uncompromising
BR ʌn'kɒmprəmʌɪzɪŋ, ʌŋ'kɒmprəmʌɪzɪŋ
AM ˌən'kɑmprəˌmaɪzɪŋ

uncompromisingly
BR ʌn'kɒmprəmʌɪzɪŋli, ʌŋ'kɒmprəmʌɪzɪŋli
AM ˌən'kɑmprəˌmaɪzɪŋ-li

uncompromising-ness
BR ʌn'kɒmprəmʌɪzɪŋ-nɨs, ʌŋ'kɒmprəmʌɪzɪŋnɨs
AM ˌən'kɑmprəˌmaɪzɪŋ-nɨs

unconcealed
BR ˌʌnkən'siːld, ˌʌŋkən'siːld
AM ˌənkən'sild

unconcern
BR ˌʌnkən'səːn, ˌʌŋkən'səːn, -d
AM ˌənkən'sərn, -d

unconcernedly
BR ˌʌnkən'səːnɨdli, ˌʌŋkən'səːnɨdli
AM ˌənkən'sərnədli

unconcluded
BR ˌʌnkən'kluːdɨd, ˌʌŋkən'kluːdɨd
AM ˌənkən'kludəd

unconditional
BR ˌʌnkən'dɪʃn̩(ə)l, ˌʌnkən'dɪʃən(ə)l, ˌʌŋkən'dɪʃn̩(ə)l, ˌʌŋkən'dɪʃən(ə)l
AM ˌənkən'dɪʃ(ə)nəl

unconditionality
BR ˌʌnkənˌdɪʃə'nalɨti, ˌʌŋkənˌdɪʃə'nalɨti
AM ˌənkənˌdɪʃə'nælədi

unconditionally
BR ˌʌnkən'dɪʃn̩əli, ˌʌnkən'dɪʃ(ə)nəli, ˌʌŋkən'dɪʃn̩əli, ˌʌŋkən'dɪʃ(ə)nəli
AM ˌənkən'dɪʃ(ə)nəli

unconditioned
BR ˌʌnkən'dɪʃnd, ˌʌŋkən'dɪʃnd
AM ˌənkən'dɪʃənd

unconfident
BR ʌn'kɒnfɨdnt, ˌʌŋ'kɒnfɨdnt
AM ˌən'kɑnfədənt

unconfined
BR ˌʌnkən'fʌɪnd, ˌʌŋkən'fʌɪnd
AM ˌənkən'faɪnd

unconfirmed
BR ˌʌnkən'fəːmd, ˌʌŋkən'fəːmd
AM ˌənkən'fərmd

unconformable
BR ˌʌnkən'fɔːməbl, ˌʌŋkən'fɔːməbl
AM ˌənkən'fɔrməbəl

unconformable-ness
BR ˌʌnkən'fɔːməblnəs, ˌʌŋkən'fɔːməblnəs
AM ˌənkən'fɔrməbəlnəs

unconformably
BR ˌʌnkən'fɔːməbli, ˌʌŋkən'fɔːməbli
AM ˌənkən'fɔrməbli

unconformity
BR ˌʌnkən'fɔːmɨti, ˌʌŋkən'fɔːmɨti
AM ˌənkən'fɔrmədi

uncongenial
BR ˌʌnkən'dʒiːnɪəl, ˌʌŋkən'dʒiːnɪəl
AM ˌənkən'dʒiniəl, ˌənkən'dʒinjəl

uncongenially
BR ˌʌnkən'dʒiːnɪəli, ˌʌŋkən'dʒiːnɪəli
AM ˌənkən'dʒiniəli, ˌənkən'dʒinjəli

uncongested
BR ˌʌnkən'dʒɛstɨd, ˌʌŋkən'dʒɛstɨd
AM ˌənkən'dʒɛstəd

unconjecturable
BR ˌʌnkən'dʒɛktʃ(ə)r-əbl, ˌʌŋkən'dʒɛktʃ(ə)rəbl
AM ˌənkən'dʒɛk(t)ʃ(ə)-rəbəl

unconnected
BR ˌʌnkə'nɛktɨd, ˌʌŋkə'nɛktɨd
AM ˌənkə'nɛktəd

unconnectedly
BR ˌʌnkə'nɛktɨdli, ˌʌŋkə'nɛktɨdli
AM ˌənkə'nɛktədli

unconnectedness
BR ˌʌnkə'nɛktɨdnɨs, ˌʌŋkə'nɛktɨdnɨs
AM ˌənkə'nɛktədnəs

unconquerable
BR ʌn'kɒŋk(ə)rəbl, ˌʌŋ'kɒŋk(ə)rəbl
AM ˌən'kɑŋk(ə)rəbəl

unconquerable-ness
BR ʌn'kɒŋk(ə)rəblnəs, ˌʌŋ'kɒŋk(ə)rəblnəs
AM ˌən'kɑŋk(ə)rəbəl-nəs

unconquerably
BR ʌn'kɒŋk(ə)rəbli, ˌʌŋ'kɒŋk(ə)rəbli
AM ˌən'kɑŋk(ə)rəbli

unconquered
BR ʌn'kɒŋkəd, ˌʌŋ'kɒŋkəd
AM ˌən'kɑŋkərd

unconscionable
BR ʌn'kɒnʃn̩əbl, ʌn'kɒnʃ(ə)nəbl, ʌŋ'kɒnʃn̩əbl, ʌŋ'kɒnʃ(ə)nəbl
AM ˌən'kɑnʃ(ə)nəbəl

unconscionable-ness
BR ʌn'kɒnʃn̩əblnəs, ʌn'kɒnʃ(ə)nəblnəs, ʌŋ'kɒnʃn̩əblnəs, ʌŋ'kɒnʃ(ə)nəblnəs
AM ˌən'kɑnʃ(ə)nəbəl-nəs

unconscionably
BR ʌn'kɒnʃn̩əbli, ʌn'kɒnʃ(ə)nəbli, ʌŋ'kɒnʃn̩əbli, ʌŋ'kɒnʃ(ə)nəbli
AM ˌən'kɑnʃ(ə)nəbli

unconscious
BR ʌn'kɒnʃəs, ʌŋ'kɒnʃəs
AM ˌən'kɑnʃəs

unconsciously
BR ʌn'kɒnʃəsli, ʌŋ'kɒnʃəsli
AM ˌən'kɑnʃəsli

unconsciousness
BR ʌn'kɒnʃəsnəs, ʌŋ'kɒnʃəsnəs
AM ˌən'kɑnʃəsnəs

unconsecrated
BR (ˌ)ʌn'kɒnsɨkreɪtɨd, (ˌ)ʌŋ'kɒnsɨkreɪtɨd
AM ˌən'kɑnsəˌkreɪdɨd

unconsenting
BR ˌʌnkən'sɛntɪŋ, ˌʌŋkən'sɛntɪŋ
AM ˌənkən'sɛn(t)ɪŋ

unconsidered
BR ˌʌnkən'sɪdəd, ˌʌŋkən'sɪdəd
AM ˌənkən'sɪdərd

unconsolable
BR ˌʌnkən'səʊləbl, ˌʌŋkən'səʊləbl
AM ˌənkən'soʊləbəl

unconsolably
BR ˌʌnkən'səʊləbli, ˌʌŋkən'səʊləbli
AM ˌənkən'soʊləbli

unconsolidated
BR ˌʌnkən'sɒlɨdeɪtɨd, ˌʌŋkən'sɒlɨdeɪtɨd
AM ˌənkən'sɑləˌdeɪdɨd

unconstitutional
BR ˌʌnkɒnstɪ'tjuːʃn̩(ə)l, ˌʌnkɒnstɪ'tʃuːʃn̩(ə)l, ˌʌŋkɒnstɪ'tjuːʃn̩(ə)l, ˌʌŋkɒnstɪ'tʃuːʃn̩(ə)l
AM ˌənˌkɑnstə't(j)uʃ(ə)-nəl

unconstitution-ality
BR ˌʌnkɒnstɪˌtjuːʃə-'nalɨti, ˌʌnkɒnstɪˌtʃuːʃə'nalɨti, ˌʌŋkɒnstɪˌtjuːʃə'nalɨti, ˌʌŋkɒnstɪˌtʃuːʃə'nalɨti
AM ˌənˌkɑnstəˌt(j)uʃə-'nælədi

unconstitutionally
BR ˌʌnkɒnstɪ'tjuːʃn̩əli, ˌʌnkɒnstɪ'tjuːʃ(ə)nəli, ˌʌnkɒnstɪ'tʃuːʃn̩əli, ˌʌnkɒnstɪ'tʃuːʃ(ə)nəli, ˌʌŋkɒnstɪ'tjuːʃn̩əli, ˌʌŋkɒnstɪ'tjuːʃ(ə)nəli, ˌʌŋkɒnstɪ'tʃuːʃn̩əli, ˌʌŋkɒnstɪ'tʃuːʃ(ə)nəli
AM ˌənˌkɑnstə't(j)uʃ(ə)-nəli

unconstrained
BR ˌʌnkən'streɪnd, ˌʌŋkən'streɪnd
AM ˌənkən'streɪnd

unconstrainedly
BR ˌʌnkən'streɪnɨdli, ˌʌŋkən'streɪnɨdli
AM ˌənkən'streɪnɨdli

unconstraint
BR ˌʌnkən'streɪnt, ˌʌŋkən'streɪnt
AM ˌənkən'streɪnt

unconstricted
BR ˌʌnkən'strɪktɨd, ˌʌŋkən'strɪktɨd
AM ˌənkən'strɪktɨd

unconstructive
BR ˌʌnkən'strʌktɪv, ˌʌŋkən'strʌktɪv
AM ˌənkən'strəktɪv

unconsulted
BR ˌʌnkən'sʌltɨd, ˌʌŋkən'sʌltɨd
AM ˌənkən'səltəd

unconsumed
BR ˌʌnkən'sjuːmd, ˌʌŋkən'sjuːmd
AM ˌənkən's(j)umd

unconsummated
BR ˌʌn'kɒnsjʉmeɪtɨd, ˌʌŋ'kɒnsjʉmeɪtɨd
AM ˌən'kɑns(j)əˌmeɪdɨd

uncontactable
BR ˌʌn'kɒntaktəbl, ˌʌŋ'kɒntaktəbl
AM ˌən'kɑnˌtæktəbəl

uncontainable
BR ˌʌnkən'teɪnəbl, ˌʌŋkən'teɪnəbl
AM ˌənkən'teɪnəbəl

uncontaminated
BR ˌʌnkən'tamɨneɪtɨd, ˌʌŋkən'tamɨneɪtɨd
AM ˌənkən'tæməˌneɪdɨd

uncontentious
BR ˌʌnkən'tɛnʃəs, ˌʌŋkən'tɛnʃəs
AM ˌənkən'tɛn(t)ʃəs

uncontentiously
BR ˌʌnkən'tɛnʃəsli, ˌʌŋkən'tɛnʃəsli
AM ˌənkən'tɛn(t)ʃəsli

uncontested
BR ˌʌnkən'tɛstɨd, ˌʌŋkən'tɛstɨd
AM ˌənkən'tɛstəd

uncontestedly
BR ˌʌnkənˈtɛstɨdli, ˌʌŋkənˈtɛstɨdli
AM ˌənkənˈtɛstədli

uncontradicted
BR ˌʌnkɒntrəˈdɪktɨd, ˌʌŋkɒntrəˈdɪktɨd
AM ˌənkɑntrəˈdɪktɨd

uncontrived
BR ˌʌnkənˈtrʌɪvd, ˌʌŋkənˈtrʌɪvd
AM ˌənkənˈtraɪvd

uncontrollable
BR ˌʌnkənˈtrəʊləbl, ˌʌŋkənˈtrəʊləbl
AM ˌənkənˈtroʊləbəl

uncontrollableness
BR ˌʌnkənˈtrəʊləblnəs, ˌʌŋkənˈtrəʊləblnəs
AM ˌənkənˈtroʊləbəlnəs

uncontrollably
BR ˌʌnkənˈtrəʊləbli, ˌʌŋkənˈtrəʊləbli
AM ˌənkənˈtroʊləbli

uncontrolled
BR ˌʌnkənˈtrəʊld, ˌʌŋkənˈtrəʊld
AM ˌənkənˈtroʊld

uncontrolledly
BR ˌʌnkənˈtrəʊlɨdli, ˌʌŋkənˈtrəʊlɨdli
AM ˌənkənˈtroʊlədli

uncontroversial
BR ˌʌnkɒntrəˈvəːʃl, ˌʌŋkɒntrəˈvəːʃl
AM ˌənˌkɑntrəˈvərʃəl, ˌənˌkɑntrəˈvərsiəl

uncontroversially
BR ˌʌnkɒntrəˈvəːʃl̩i, ˌʌnkɒntrəˈvəːʃəli, ˌʌŋkɒntrəˈvəːʃl̩i, ˌʌŋkɒntrəˈvəːʃəli
AM ˌənˌkɑntrəˈvərʃəli, ˌənˌkɑntrəˈvərsiəli

uncontroverted
BR ˌʌnkɒntrəˈvəːtɨd, ˌʌnˈkɒntrəvəːtɨd, ˌʌŋkɒntrəˈvəːtɨd, ˌʌŋˈkɒntrəvəːtɨd
AM ˌənˌkɑntrəˈvərdəd

uncontrovertible
BR ˌʌnkɒntrəˈvəːtɨbl, ˌʌŋkɒntrəˈvəːtɨbl
AM ˌənˌkɑntrəˈvərdəbəl

unconventional
BR ˌʌnkənˈvɛnʃn̩(ə)l, ˌʌnkənˈvɛnʃən(ə)l, ˌʌŋkənˈvɛnʃn̩(ə)l, ˌʌŋkənˈvɛnʃən(ə)l
AM ˌənkənˈvɛn(t)ʃ(ə)nəl

unconventionalism
BR ˌʌnkənˈvɛnʃn̩əlɪz(ə)m, ˌʌnkənˈvɛnʃ(ə)nəlɪz(ə)m, ˌʌŋkənˈvɛnʃn̩əlɪz(ə)m, ˌʌŋkənˈvɛnʃ(ə)nəlɪz(ə)m
AM ˌənkənˈvɛn(t)ʃənlˌɪzəm, ˌənkənˈvɛn(t)ʃnəˌlɪzəm

unconventionality
BR ˌʌnkənˌvɛnʃəˈnalɨti, ˌʌŋkənˌvɛnʃəˈnalɨti
AM ˌənkənˌvɛn(t)ʃəˈnælədi

unconventionally
BR ˌʌnkənˈvɛnʃn̩əli, ˌʌnkənˈvɛnʃ(ə)nəl̩i, ˌʌŋkənˈvɛnʃn̩əli, ˌʌŋkənˈvɛnʃ(ə)nəl̩i
AM ˌənkənˈvɛn(t)ʃ(ə)nəli

unconverted
BR ˌʌnkənˈvəːtɨd, ˌʌŋkənˈvəːtɨd
AM ˌənkənˈvərdəd

unconvertible
BR ˌʌnkənˈvəːtɨbl, ˌʌŋkənˈvəːtɨbl
AM ˌənkənˈvərdəbəl

unconvicted
BR ˌʌnkənˈvɪktɨd, ˌʌŋkənˈvɪktɨd
AM ˌənkənˈvɪktɨd

unconvinced
BR ˌʌnkənˈvɪnst, ˌʌŋkənˈvɪnst
AM ˌənkənˈvɪnst

unconvincing
BR ˌʌnkənˈvɪnsɪŋ, ˌʌŋkənˈvɪnsɪŋ
AM ˌənkənˈvɪnsɪŋ

unconvincingly
BR ˌʌnkənˈvɪnsɪŋli, ˌʌŋkənˈvɪnsɪŋli
AM ˌənkənˈvɪnsɪŋli

uncooked
BR ˌʌnˈkʊkt, ˌʌŋˈkʊkt
AM ˌənˈkʊkt

uncool
BR ˌʌnˈkuːl, ˌʌŋˈkuːl
AM ˌənˈkul

uncooperative
BR ˌʌnkəʊˈɒp(ə)rətɪv
AM ˌənkoʊˈɑp(ə)rədɪv

uncooperatively
BR ˌʌnkəʊˈɒp(ə)rətɨvli, ˌʌŋkəʊˈɒp(ə)rətɨvli
AM ˌənkoʊˈɑp(ə)rədɨvli

uncooperativeness
BR ˌʌnkəʊˈɒp(ə)rətɨvnɪs, ˌʌŋkəʊˈɒp(ə)rətɨvnɪs
AM ˌənkoʊˈɑp(ə)rədɪvnɪs

uncoordinated
BR ˌʌnkəʊˈɔːdɪneɪtɨd, ˌʌŋkəʊˈɔːdɪneɪtɨd
AM ˌənkoʊˈɔrdəˌneɪdɨd, ˌənkoʊˈɔrdnˌeɪdɨd

uncopiable
BR ˌʌnˈkɒpɪəbl, ˌʌŋˈkɒpɪəbl
AM ˌənˈkɑpiəbəl

uncord
BR ˌʌnˈkɔːd, ˌʌŋˈkɔːd, -z, -ɪŋ, -ɨd
AM ˌənˈkɔ(ə)rd, -z, -ɪŋ, -əd

uncordial
BR ˌʌnˈkɔːdɪəl, ˌʌŋˈkɔːdɪəl
AM ˌənˈkɔrdʒəl

uncork
BR ˌʌnˈkɔːk, ˌʌŋˈkɔːk, -s, -ɪŋ, -t
AM ˌənˈkɔ(ə)rk, -s, -ɪŋ, -t

uncorrected
BR ˌʌnkəˈrɛktɨd, ˌʌŋkəˈrɛktɨd
AM ˌənkəˈrɛktəd

uncorrelated
BR ˌʌnˈkɒrɪleɪtɨd, ˌʌŋˈkɒrɪleɪtɨd
AM ˌənˈkɔrəˌleɪdɨd

uncorroborated
BR ˌʌnkəˈrɒbəreɪtɨd, ˌʌŋkəˈrɒbəreɪtɨd
AM ˌənkəˈrɑbəˌreɪdɨd

uncorrupted
BR ˌʌnkəˈrʌptɨd, ˌʌŋkəˈrʌptɨd
AM ˌənkəˈrəptəd

uncorseted
BR ˌʌnˈkɔːsɪtɨd, ˌʌŋˈkɔːsɪtɨd
AM ˌənˈkɔrsədəd

uncountability
BR ˌʌnkaʊntəˈbɪlɨti, ˌʌŋkaʊntəˈbɪlɨti
AM ˌənkaʊn(t)əˈbɪlɨdi

uncountable
BR ˌʌnˈkaʊntəbl, ˌʌŋˈkaʊntəbl
AM ˌənˈkaʊn(t)əbəl

uncountably
BR ˌʌnˈkaʊntəbli, ˌʌŋˈkaʊntəbli
AM ˌənˈkaʊn(t)əbli

uncounted
BR (ˌ)ʌnˈkaʊntɨd, (ˌ)ʌŋˈkaʊntɨd
AM ˌənˈkaʊn(t)əd

uncouple
BR ˌʌnˈkʌp|l, ˌʌŋˈkʌp|l, -lz, -l̩ɪŋ\-lɪŋ, -ld
AM ˌənˈkəp|əl, -əlz, -(ə)lɪŋ, -əld

uncourtly
BR ˌʌnˈkɔːtli, ˌʌŋˈkɔːtli
AM ˌənˈkɔrtli

uncouth
BR ʌnˈkuːθ, ʌŋˈkuːθ
AM ˌənˈkuθ

uncouthly
BR ʌnˈkuːθli, ʌŋˈkuːθli
AM ˌənˈkuθli

uncouthness
BR ʌnˈkuːθnəs, ʌŋˈkuːθnəs
AM ˌənˈkuθnəs

uncovenanted
BR ˌʌnˈkʌvənəntɨd, ˌʌnˈkʌvn̩əntɨd, ˌʌŋˈkʌvənəntɨd, ˌʌŋˈkʌvn̩əntɨd
AM ˌənˈkəv(ə)nən(t)əd

uncover
BR (ˌ)ʌnˈkʌv|ə(r), (ˌ)ʌŋˈkʌv|ə(r), -əz, -(ə)rɪŋ, -əd
AM ˌənˈkəv|ər, -ərz, -(ə)rɪŋ, -ərd

uncrackable
BR (ˌ)ʌnˈkrakəbl, (ˌ)ʌŋˈkrakəbl
AM ˌənˈkrækəbəl

uncracked
BR ˌʌnˈkrakt, ˌʌŋˈkrakt
AM ˌənˈkrækt

uncreased
BR (ˌ)ʌnˈkriːst, (ˌ)ʌnˈkriːst
AM ˌənˈkrist

uncreate
BR ˌʌnkrɪˈeɪt, ˌʌŋkrɪˈeɪt, -s, -ɪŋ, -ɨd
AM ˌənˌkriˈeɪ|t, -ts, -dɪŋ, -dɨd

uncreative
BR ˌʌnkrɪˈeɪtɪv, ˌʌŋkrɪˈeɪtɪv
AM ˌənˌkriˈeɪdɪv

uncredited
BR (ˌ)ʌnˈkrɛdɪtɨd, (ˌ)ʌŋˈkrɛdɪtɨd
AM ˌənˈkrɛdədəd

uncritical
BR (ˌ)ʌnˈkrɪtɨkl, (ˌ)ʌŋˈkrɪtɨkl
AM ˌənˈkrɪdəkəl

uncritically
BR (ˌ)ʌnˈkrɪtɨkli, (ˌ)ʌŋˈkrɪtɨkli
AM ˌənˈkrɪdək(ə)li

uncropped
BR ˌʌnˈkrɒpt, ˌʌŋˈkrɒpt
AM ˌənˈkrɑpt

uncross
BR ˌʌnˈkrɒs, ˌʌŋˈkrɒs, -ɨz, -ɪŋ, -t
AM ˌənˈkrɔs, ˌənˈkrɑs, -əz, -ɪŋ, -t

uncrossable
BR ˌʌnˈkrɒsəbl, ˌʌŋˈkrɒsəbl
AM ˌənˈkrɔsəbəl, ˌənˈkrɑsəbəl

uncrowded
BR (ˌ)ʌnˈkraʊdɨd, (ˌ)ʌŋˈkraʊdɨd
AM ˌənˈkraʊdəd

uncrown
BR ˌʌnˈkraʊn, ˌʌŋˈkraʊn, -z, -ɪŋ, -d
AM ˌənˈkraʊn, -z, -ɪŋ, -d

uncrumpled
BR (ˌ)ʌnˈkrʌmpld, (ˌ)ʌŋˈkrʌmpld
AM ˌənˈkrəmpəld

uncrushable
BR (ˌ)ʌnˈkrʌʃəbl, (ˌ)ʌŋˈkrʌʃəbl
AM ˌənˈkrəʃəbəl

uncrushed
BR (ˌ)ʌnˈkrʌʃt, (ˌ)ʌŋˈkrʌʃt
AM ˌənˈkrəʃt

UNCTAD
BR ˈʌŋktad
AM ˈəŋkˌtæd

unction
BR ˈʌŋ(k)ʃn, -z
AM ˈəŋkʃən, -z

unctuous
BR ˈʌŋ(k)tjʊəs, ʌŋ(k)tʃʊəs
AM ˈəŋ(k)(t)ʃ(əw)əs

unctuously
BR ˈʌŋ(k)tjʊəsli, ʌŋ(k)tʃʊəsli
AM ˈəŋ(k)(t)ʃ(əw)əsli

unctuousness
BR ˈʌŋ(k)tjʊəsnəs, ʌŋ(k)tʃʊəsnəs
AM ˈəŋ(k)(t)ʃ(əw)əsnəs

unculled
BR ˌʌnˈkʌld, ˌʌŋˈkʌld
AM ˌənˈkəld

uncultivated
BR (ˌ)ʌnˈkʌltɪveɪtɪd, (ˌ)ʌŋˈkʌltɪveɪtɪd
AM ˌənˈkəltəˌveɪdɪd

uncultured
BR (ˌ)ʌnˈkʌltʃəd, (ˌ)ʌŋˈkʌltʃəd
AM ˌənˈkəltʃərd

uncurb
BR ˌʌnˈkəːb, ˌʌŋˈkəːb, -z, -ɪŋ, -d
AM ˌənˈkərb, -z, -ɪŋ, -d

uncured
BR ˌʌnˈkjʊəd, ˌʌŋˈkjʊəd, ˌʌnˈkjɔːd, ˌʌŋˈkjɔːd
AM ˌənˈkjʊ(ə)rd

uncurl
BR ˌʌnˈkəːl, ˌʌŋˈkəːl, -z, -ɪŋ, -d
AM ˌənˈkərl, -z, -ɪŋ, -d

uncurtailed
BR ˌʌnkəːˈteɪld, ˌʌŋkəːˈteɪld
AM ˌənkərˈteɪld

uncurtained
BR ˌʌnˈkəːtɪnd, ˌʌŋˈkəːtɪnd
AM ˌənˈkərtnd

uncus
BR ˈʌŋkəs
AM ˈəŋkəs

uncustomed
BR ˌʌnˈkʌstəmd, ˌʌŋˈkʌstəmd
AM ˌənˈkəstəmd

uncut
BR ˌʌnˈkʌt, ˌʌŋˈkʌt
AM ˌənˈkət

undamaged
BR ˌʌnˈdamɪdʒd
AM ˌənˈdæmɪdʒd

undamped
BR ˌʌnˈdam(p)t
AM ˌənˈdæm(p)t

undated
BR ˌʌnˈdeɪtɪd
AM ˌənˈdeɪdɪd

undaunted
BR (ˌ)ʌnˈdɔːntɪd
AM ˌənˈdɔn(t)əd, ˌənˈdɑn(t)əd

undauntedly
BR (ˌ)ʌnˈdɔːntɪdli
AM ˌənˈdɔn(t)ədli, ˌənˈdɑn(t)ədli

undauntedness
BR (ˌ)ʌnˈdɔːntɪdnɪs
AM ˌənˈdɔn(t)ədnəs, ˌənˈdɑn(t)ədnəs

undead
BR ʌnˈdɛd
AM ˌənˈdɛd

undealt
BR ʌnˈdɛlt
AM ˌənˈdɛlt

undecagon
BR ʌnˈdɛkəg(ə)n, ʌnˈdɛkəgɒn, -z
AM ˌənˈdɛkəˌgɑn, -z

undeceive
BR ˌʌndɪˈsiːv, -z, -ɪŋ, -d
AM ˌəndəˈsiv, ˌəndiˈsiv, -z, -ɪŋ, -d

undecidability
BR ˌʌndɪˌsʌɪdəˈbɪlɪti
AM ˌəndəˌsaɪdəˈbɪlɪdi, ˌəndiˌsaɪdəˈbɪlɪdi

undecidable
BR ˌʌndɪˈsʌɪdəbl
AM ˌəndəˈsaɪdəbəl, ˌəndiˈsaɪdəbəl

undecided
BR ˌʌndɪˈsʌɪdɪd
AM ˌəndəˈsaɪdɪd, ˌəndiˈsaɪdɪd

undecidedly
BR ˌʌndɪˈsʌɪdɪdli
AM ˌəndəˈsaɪdɪd, ˌəndiˈsaɪdɪdli

undecidedness
BR ˌʌndɪˈsʌɪdɪdnɪs
AM ˌəndəˈsaɪdɪdnɪs, ˌəndiˈsaɪdɪdnɪs

undecipherable
BR ˌʌndɪˈsʌɪf(ə)rəbl
AM ˌəndəˈsaɪf(ə)rəbəl, ˌəndiˈsaɪf(ə)rəbəl

undeciphered
BR ˌʌndɪˈsʌɪfəd
AM ˌəndəˈsaɪfərd, ˌəndiˈsaɪfərd

undeclared
BR ˌʌndɪˈklɛːd
AM ˌəndəˈklɛ(ə)rd, ˌəndiˈklɛ(ə)rd

undecodable
BR ˌʌndɪˈkəʊdəbl
AM ˌəndəˈkoʊdəbəl, ˌəndiˈkoʊdəbəl

undecorated
BR ˌʌnˈdɛkəreɪtɪd
AM ˌənˈdɛkəˌreɪdɪd

undefeated
BR ˌʌndɪˈfiːtɪd
AM ˌəndəˈfidɪd, ˌəndiˈfidɪd

undefended
BR ˌʌndɪˈfɛndɪd
AM ˌəndəˈfɛndəd, ˌəndiˈfɛndəd

undefiled
BR ˌʌndɪˈfʌɪld
AM ˌəndəˈfaɪld, ˌəndiˈfaɪld

undefinable
BR ˌʌndɪˈfʌɪnəbl
AM ˌəndəˈfaɪnəbəl, ˌəndiˈfaɪnəbəl

undefinably
BR ˌʌndɪˈfʌɪnəbli
AM ˌəndəˈfaɪnəbli, ˌəndiˈfaɪnəbli

undefined
BR ˌʌndɪˈfʌɪnd
AM ˌəndəˈfaɪnd, ˌəndiˈfaɪnd

undeflected
BR ˌʌndɪˈflɛktɪd
AM ˌəndəˈflɛktəd, ˌəndiˈflɛktəd

undeformed
BR ˌʌndɪˈfɔːmd
AM ˌəndəˈfɔ(ə)rmd, ˌəndiˈfɔ(ə)rmd

undelivered
BR ˌʌndɪˈlɪvəd
AM ˌəndəˈlɪvərd, ˌəndiˈlɪvərd

undemanding
BR ˌʌndɪˈmɑːndɪŋ, ˌʌndɪˈmandɪŋ
AM ˌəndəˈmændɪŋ, ˌəndiˈmændɪŋ

undemandingness
BR ˌʌndɪˈmɑːndɪŋnɪs, ˌʌndɪˈmandɪŋnɪs
AM ˌəndəˈmændɪŋnɪs, ˌəndiˈmændɪŋnɪs

undemocratic
BR ˌʌndɛməˈkratɪk
AM ˌənˌdɛməˈkrædɪk

undemocratically
BR ˌʌndɛməˈkratɪkli
AM ˌənˌdɛməˈkrædək(ə)li

undemonstrable
BR ˌʌndɪˈmɒnstrəbl, (ˌ)ʌnˈdɛmənstrəbl
AM ˌəndəˈmɑnstrəbəl, ˌəndiˈmɑnstrəbəl

undemonstrated
BR (ˌ)ʌnˈdɛmənstreɪtɪd
AM ˌənˈdɛmənˌstreɪdɪd

undemonstrative
BR ˌʌndɪˈmɒnstrətɪv
AM ˌəndəˈmɑnstrədɪv, ˌəndiˈmɑnstrədɪv

undemonstratively
BR ˌʌndɪˈmɒnstrətɪvli
AM ˌəndəˈmɑnstrədɪvli, ˌəndiˈmɑnstrədɪvli

undemonstrativeness
BR ˌʌndɪˈmɒnstrətɪvnɪs
AM ˌəndəˈmɑnstrədɪvnɪs, ˌəndiˈmɑnstrədɪvnɪs

undeniable
BR ˌʌndɪˈnʌɪəbl
AM ˌəndəˈnaɪəbəl, ˌəndiˈnaɪəbəl

undeniableness
BR ˌʌndɪˈnʌɪəblnəs
AM ˌəndəˈnaɪəbəlnəs, ˌəndiˈnaɪəbəlnəs

undeniably
BR ˌʌndɪˈnʌɪəbli
AM ˌəndəˈnaɪəbli, ˌəndiˈnaɪəbli

undenied
BR ˌʌndɪˈnʌɪd
AM ˌəndəˈnaɪd, ˌəndiˈnaɪd

undenominational
BR ˌʌndɪˌnɒmɪˈneɪʃn̩(ə)l, ˌʌndɪˌnɒmɪˈneɪʃən(ə)l
AM ˌəndəˌnɑməˈneɪʃ(ə)nəl, ˌəndiˌnɑməˈneɪʃ(ə)nəl

undented
BR (ˌ)ʌnˈdɛntɪd
AM ˌənˈdɛn(t)əd

undependable
BR ˌʌndɪˈpɛndəbl
AM ˌəndəˈpɛndəbəl, ˌəndiˈpɛndəbəl

under
BR ˈʌndə(r)
AM ˈəndər

underachieve
BR ˌʌnd(ə)rəˈtʃiːv, -z, -ɪŋ, -d
AM ˌəndərəˈtʃiv, -z, -ɪŋ, -d

underachievement
BR ˌʌnd(ə)rəˈtʃiːvm(ə)nt
AM ˌəndərəˈtʃivmənt

underachiever
BR ˌʌnd(ə)rəˈtʃiːvə(r), -z
AM ˌəndərəˈtʃivər, -z

underact
BR ˌʌndərˈakt, -s, -ɪŋ, -ɪd

AM ˌəndər'æk|(t), -(t)s, -tɪŋ, -təd
under-age
BR ˌʌndər'eɪdʒ
AM ˈəndər'eɪdʒ
underappreciated
BR ˌʌnd(ə)rə'priːʃɪeɪtɨd
AM ˌəndərə'priʃiˌeɪdɨd
underarm
BR 'ʌndərɑːm
AM 'əndərˌɑrm
underbelly
BR 'ʌndəˌbɛli
AM 'əndərˌbɛli
underbid
BR ˌʌndə'bɪd, -z, -ɪŋ
AM ˌəndər'bɪd, -z, -ɪŋ
underbidder
BR ˌʌndə'bɪdə(r), -z
AM ˈəndər'bɪdər, -z
underblanket
BR 'ʌndəˌblaŋkɪt, -s
AM 'əndərˌblæŋkət, -s
underbody
BR 'ʌndəˌbɒd|i, -ɪz
AM 'əndərˌbɑdi, -z
underbred
BR ˌʌndə'brɛd
AM ˌəndər'brɛd
underbrush
BR 'ʌndəbrʌʃ
AM 'əndərˌbrəʃ
undercapacity
BR ˌʌndəkə'pasɪti
AM ˈəndərkə'pæsədi
undercapitalised
BR ˌʌndə'kapɪtəlʌɪzd, ˌʌndə'kapɪtl̩ʌɪzd
AM ˌəndər'kæpədlˌaɪzd
undercapitalized
BR ˌʌndə'kapɪtəlʌɪzd, ˌʌndə'kapɪtl̩ʌɪzd
AM ˌəndər'kæpədlˌaɪzd
undercarriage
BR 'ʌndəˌkarɪdʒ
AM 'əndərˌkɛrɪdʒ
undercart
BR 'ʌndəkɑːt, -s
AM 'əndərˌkɑrt, -s
undercharge
BR ˌʌndə'tʃɑːdʒ, -ɪz, -ɪŋ, -d
AM ˌəndər'tʃɑrdʒ, -əz, -ɪŋ, -d
underclass
BR 'ʌndəklɑːs, 'ʌndəklas, -ɪz
AM 'əndərˌklæs, -əz
underclay
BR 'ʌndəkleɪ
AM 'əndərˌkleɪ
undercliff
BR 'ʌndəklɪf, -s
AM 'əndərˌklɪf, -s
underclothes
BR 'ʌndəkləʊ(ð)z
AM 'əndərˌkloʊ(ð)z
underclothing
BR 'ʌndəˌkləʊðɪŋ
AM 'əndərˌkloʊðɪŋ
undercoat
BR 'ʌndəkəʊt, -s, -ɪŋ, -ɨd
AM 'əndərˌkoʊ|t, -ts, -dɪŋ, -dəd
underconsumption
BR ˌʌndəkən'sʌm(p)ʃn
AM ˌəndərkən'səmpʃən
underconsumptionist
BR ˌʌndəkən'sʌm(p)ʃn̩ɪst, ˌʌndəkən'sʌm(p)ʃənɪst, -s
AM ˌəndərkən'səmpʃənəst, -s
undercook
BR ˌʌndə'kʊk, -s, -ɪŋ, -t
AM ˌəndər'kʊk, -s, -ɪŋ, -t
undercover
BR ˌʌndə'kʌvə(r)
AM ˌəndər'kəvər
undercroft
BR 'ʌndəkrɒft, -s
AM 'əndərˌkrɔft, 'əndərˌkrɑft, -s
undercurrent
BR 'ʌndəˌkʌrənt, 'ʌndəˌkʌrn̩t, -s
AM 'əndərˌkərənt, -s
undercut[1]
noun
BR 'ʌndəkʌt, -s
AM 'əndərˌkət, -s
undercut[2]
verb
BR ˌʌndə'kʌt, -s, -ɪŋ
AM ˌəndər'kə|t, -ts, -dɪŋ
underdeveloped
BR ˌʌndədɪ'vɛləpt
AM ˌəndərdə'vɛləpt, ˌəndərdi'vɛləpt
underdevelopment
BR ˌʌndədɪ'vɛləpm(ə)nt
AM ˌəndərdə'vɛləpmənt, ˌəndərdi'vɛləpmənt
underdid
BR ˌʌndə'dɪd
AM ˌəndər'dɪd
underdo
BR ˌʌndə'duː, -ɪŋ
AM ˌəndər'duː, -ɪŋ
underdoes
BR ˌʌndə'dʌz
AM ˌəndər'dəz
underdog
BR 'ʌndədɒg, -z
AM 'əndərˌdɔg, 'əndərˌdɑg, -z
underdone
BR ˌʌndə'dʌn
AM ˌəndər'dən
underdrainage
BR ˌʌndə'dreɪnɪdʒ
AM ˌəndər'dreɪnɪdʒ
underdrawers
plural noun
BR 'ʌndədrɔːz
AM 'əndərˌdrɔ(ə)rz
underdrawing
BR 'ʌndəˌdrɔː(r)ɪŋ
AM 'əndərˌdrɔɪŋ
underdress
BR ˌʌndə'drɛs, -ɪz, -ɪŋ, -t
AM ˌəndər'drɛs, -əz, -ɪŋ, -t
undereducated
BR ˌʌndər'ɛdjʊkeɪtɨd, ˌʌndər'ɛdʒʊkeɪtɨd
AM ˌəndər'ɛdʒəˌkeɪdɨd
underemphases
BR ˌʌndər'ɛmfəsiːz
AM ˌəndər'ɛmfəˌsiz
underemphasis
BR ˌʌndər'ɛmfəsɪs
AM ˌəndər'ɛmfəsəs
underemphasise
BR ˌʌndər'ɛmfəsʌɪz, -ɪz, -ɪŋ, -d
AM ˌəndər'ɛmfəˌsaɪz, -ɪz, -ɪŋ, -d
underemphasize
BR ˌʌndər'ɛmfəsʌɪz, -ɪz, -ɪŋ, -d
AM ˌəndər'ɛmfəˌsaɪz, -ɪz, -ɪŋ, -d
underemployed
BR ˌʌnd(ə)rɪm'plɔɪd
AM ˌəndərɛm'plɔɪd, ˌəndərəm'plɔɪd, ˌəndərɪm'plɔɪd
underemployment
BR ˌʌnd(ə)rɪm'plɔɪm(ə)nt
AM ˌəndərɛm'plɔɪmənt, ˌəndərəm'plɔɪmənt, ˌəndərɪm'plɔɪmənt
underequipped
BR ˌʌnd(ə)rɪ'kwɪpt
AM ˌəndərə'kwɪpt, ˌəndərˌi'kwɪpt
underestimate[1]
noun
BR ˌʌndər'ɛstɪmət, -s
AM ˌəndər'ɛstəmət, -s
underestimate[2]
verb
BR ˌʌndər'ɛstɪmeɪt, -s, -ɪŋ, -ɨd
AM ˌəndər'ɛstəˌmeɪ|t, -ts, -dɪŋ, -dɨd
underestimation
BR ˌʌndərˌɛstɪ'meɪʃn
AM ˌəndərˌɛstə'meɪʃən
underexploited
BR ˌʌnd(ə)rɪks'plɔɪtɨd
AM ˌəndərək'splɔɪdɨd
underexpose
BR ˌʌnd(ə)rɪk'spəʊz, -ɪz, -ɪŋ, -d
AM ˌəndərək'spoʊz, -əz, -ɪŋ, -d
underexposure
BR ˌʌnd(ə)rɪk'spəʊʒə(r), -z
AM ˌəndərək'spoʊʒər, -z
underfed
BR ˌʌndə'fɛd
AM ˌəndər'fɛd
underfelt
BR 'ʌndəfɛlt
AM 'əndərˌfɛlt
underfinanced
BR ˌʌndəfʌɪ'nanst, ˌʌndəfɪ'nanst
AM ˌəndər'faɪˌnænst, ˌəndərfə'nænst
underfinancing
BR ˌʌndəfʌɪ'nansɪŋ, ˌʌndəfɪ'nasnɪŋ
AM ˌəndər'faɪˌnænsɪŋ, ˌəndərfə'nænsɪŋ
under-fives
BR ˌʌndə'fʌɪvz, 'ʌndəfʌɪvz
AM ˈəndər'faɪvz
underfloor
BR ˌʌndə'flɔː(r)
AM 'əndərˌflɔ(ə)r
underflooring
BR 'ʌndəˌflɔːrɪŋ
AM 'əndərˌflɔrɪŋ
underflow
BR 'ʌndəfləʊ, -z
AM 'əndərˌfloʊ, -z
underfoot
BR ˌʌndə'fʊt
AM ˌəndər'fʊt
underframe
BR 'ʌndəfreɪm, -z
AM 'əndərˌfreɪm, -z
underfunded
BR ˌʌndə'fʌndɪd
AM ˌəndər'fəndəd
underfunding
BR ˌʌndə'fʌndɪŋ
AM ˌəndər'fəndɪŋ
underfur
BR 'ʌndəfəː(r)
AM 'əndərˌfər
under-gardener
BR 'ʌndəˌgɑːdnə(r), -z
AM 'əndərˌgɑrdn̩ər, 'əndərˌgɑrdnər, -z
undergarment
BR 'ʌndəˌgɑːm(ə)nt, -s
AM 'əndərˌgɑrmənt, -s
undergird
BR ˌʌndə'gəːd, -z, -ɪŋ, -ɨd
AM ˌəndər'gərd, -z, -ɪŋ, -əd
underglaze
BR 'ʌndəgleɪz
AM 'əndərˌgleɪz
undergo
BR ˌʌndə'gəʊ, -z, -ɪŋ
AM ˌəndər'goʊ, -z, -ɪŋ

undergone
BR ˌʌndəˈɡɒn
AM ˌəndərˈɡɔn, ˌəndərˈɡɑn

undergrad
BR ˈʌndəɡrad, ˌʌndəˈɡrad, -z
AM ˈəndərˌɡræd, -z

undergraduate
BR ˌʌndəˈɡradʒʊət, ˌʌndəˈɡradjʊət, -s
AM ˌəndərˈɡrædʒəwət, -s

underground¹
adjective
BR ˌʌndəˈɡraʊnd, ˈʌndəɡraʊnd
AM ˈəndə(r)ˌɡraʊnd

underground²
adverb
BR ˌʌndəˈɡraʊnd, ˈʌndəɡraʊnd
AM ¦əndərˈɡraʊnd

underground³
noun
BR ˈʌndəɡraʊnd
AM ˈəndərˌɡraʊnd

undergrowth
BR ˈʌndəɡrəʊθ
AM ˈəndərˌɡroʊθ

underhand
BR ˌʌndəˈhand
AM ˈəndərˌ(h)ænd

underhanded
BR ˌʌndəˈhandɪd
AM ¦əndərˈhæn(d)əd

underhandedly
BR ˌʌndəˈhandɪdli
AM ˌəndərˈhæn(d)ədli

underhandedness
BR ˌʌndəˈhandɪdnɪs
AM ˌəndərˈhæn(d)ədnəs

underheated
BR ˌʌndəˈhiːtɪd
AM ˌəndərˈhidɪd

Underhill
BR ˈʌndəhɪl
AM ˈəndərˌ(h)ɪl

underhung
BR ˌʌndəˈhʌŋ
AM ˌəndərˈhəŋ

underlain
BR ˌʌndəˈleɪn
AM ˌəndərˈleɪn

underlay¹
noun
BR ˈʌndəleɪ, -z
AM ˈəndərˌleɪ, -z

underlay²
verb
BR ˌʌndəˈleɪ, -z, -ɪŋ, -d
AM ˌəndərˈleɪ, -z, -ɪŋ, -d

underlease¹
noun
BR ˈʌndəliːs, -ɪz
AM ˈəndərˌlis, -ɪz

underlease²
verb
BR ˌʌndəˈliːs, -ɪz, -ɪŋ, -t
AM ˌəndərˈlis, -ɪz, -ɪŋ, -t

underlet
BR ˌʌndəˈlɛt, -s, -ɪŋ
AM ˌəndərˈlɛ|t, -ts, -dɪŋ

underlie
BR ˌʌndəˈlʌɪ, -z, -ɪŋ
AM ˌəndərˈlaɪ, -z, -ɪŋ

underline¹
noun
BR ˈʌndəlʌɪn, -z
AM ˈəndərˌlaɪn, -z

underline²
verb
BR ˌʌndəˈlʌɪn, -z, -ɪŋ, -d
AM ˈəndərˌlaɪn, -z, -ɪŋ, -d

underlinen
BR ˈʌndəˌlɪnɪn
AM ˈəndərˌlɪnɪn

underling
BR ˈʌndəlɪŋ, -z
AM ˈəndərlɪŋ, -z

underlip
BR ˈʌndəlɪp, -s
AM ˈəndərˌlɪp, -s

underlit
BR ˌʌndəˈlɪt
AM ¦əndərˈlɪt

under-manager
BR ˈʌndəˌmanɪdʒə(r), -z
AM ˈəndərˌmænədʒər, -z

undermanned
BR ˌʌndəˈmand
AM ˌəndərˈmænd

undermanning
BR ˌʌndəˈmanɪŋ
AM ˌəndərˈmænɪŋ

undermentioned
BR ˌʌndəˈmɛnʃnd
AM ˌəndərˈmɛn(t)ʃənd

undermine
BR ˌʌndəˈmʌɪn, -z, -ɪŋ, -d
AM ˌəndərˈmaɪn, -z, -ɪŋ, -d

underminer
BR ˌʌndəˈmʌɪnə(r), -z
AM ˈəndərˌmaɪnər, -z

underminingly
BR ˌʌndəˈmʌɪnɪŋli
AM ˌəndərˈmaɪnɪŋli

undermost
BR ˈʌndəməʊst
AM ˈəndərˌmoʊst

underneath
BR ˌʌndəˈniːθ
AM ˌəndərˈniθ

undernourished
BR ˌʌndəˈnʌrɪʃt
AM ˌəndərˈnərɪʃt

undernourishment
BR ˌʌndəˈnʌrɪʃm(ə)nt
AM ˌəndərˈnərɪʃmənt, ˌəndərˈnʊrɪʃmənt

under-occupancy
BR ˌʌndərˈɒkjʊp(ə)nsi
AM ˌəndərˈɑkjəpənsi

under-occupy
BR ˌʌndərˈɒkjʊpʌɪ, -z, -ɪŋ, -d
AM ˌəndərˈɑkjəˌpaɪ, -z, -ɪŋ, -d

underpaid
BR ˌʌndəˈpeɪd
AM ˌəndərˈpeɪd

underpainting
BR ˈʌndəˌpeɪntɪŋ
AM ˈəndərˌpeɪn(t)ɪŋ

underpants
BR ˈʌndəpan(t)s
AM ˈəndərˌpæn(t)s

underpart
BR ˈʌndəpɑːt, -s
AM ˈəndərˌpɑrt, -s

underpass
BR ˈʌndəpɑːs, ˈʌndəpas, -ɪz
AM ˈəndərˌpæs, -əz

underpay
BR ˌʌndəˈpeɪ, -z, -ɪŋ, -d
AM ˌəndərˈpeɪ, -z, -ɪŋ, -d

underpayment
BR ˌʌndəˈpeɪm(ə)nt, -s
AM ˌəndərˈpeɪmənt, -s

underperform
BR ˌʌndəpəˈfɔːm, -z, -ɪŋ, -d
AM ˌəndərpərˈfɔ(ə)rm, -z, -ɪŋ, -d

underperformance
BR ˌʌndəpəˈfɔːməns
AM ˌəndərpərˈfɔrməns

underpin
BR ˌʌndəˈpɪn, -z, -ɪŋ, -d
AM ˌəndərˈpɪn, -z, -ɪŋ, -d

underpinning
BR ˌʌndəˈpɪnɪŋ, ˈʌndəˌpɪnɪŋ, -z
AM ˈəndərˌpɪnɪŋ, -z

underplant
BR ˌʌndəˈplɑːnt, ˌʌndəˈplant, -s, -ɪŋ, -ɪd
AM ˌəndərˈplæn|t, -ts, -(t)ɪŋ, -(t)əd

underplay
verb
BR ˌʌndəˈpleɪ, -z, -ɪŋ, -d
AM ˌəndərˈpleɪ, -z, -ɪŋ, -d

underplot
BR ˈʌndəplɒt, -s
AM ˈəndərˌplɑt, -s

underpopulated
BR ˌʌndəˈpɒpjʊleɪtɪd
AM ˌəndərˈpɑpjəˌleɪdɪd

underpowered
BR ˌʌndəˈpaʊəd
AM ˌəndərˈpaʊərd

under-prepared
BR ˌʌndəprɪˈpɛːd
AM ˌəndərprəˈpɛ(ə)rd

underprice
BR ˌʌndəˈprʌɪs, -ɪz, -ɪŋ, -t
AM ˌəndərˈpraɪs, -ɪz, -ɪŋ, -t

underpriced
BR ˌʌndəˈprʌɪst
AM ˌəndərˈpraɪst

underprivileged
BR ˌʌndəˈprɪvɨlɪdʒd
AM ˌəndərˈprɪvɨlɪdʒd

underproduction
BR ˌʌndəprəˈdʌkʃn
AM ˌəndərprəˈdəkʃən

underproof
BR ˌʌndəˈpruːf
AM ˌəndərˈpruf

underprop
BR ˌʌndəˈprɒp, -s, -ɪŋ, -t
AM ˌəndərˈprɑp, -s, -ɪŋ, -t

under-provision
BR ˌʌndəprəˈvɪʒn
AM ˌəndərprəˈvɪʒən

underquote
BR ˌʌndəˈkwəʊt, -s, -ɪŋ, -ɪd
AM ˌəndərˈkwoʊ|t, -ts, -dɪŋ, -dəd

underrate
BR ˌʌndəˈreɪt, -s, -ɪŋ, -ɪd
AM ˌəndə(r)ˈreɪ|t, -ts, -dɪŋ, -dɪd

under-rehearsed
BR ˌʌndərɪˈhəːst
AM ˌəndə(r)rəˈhərst

under-report
BR ˌʌndərɪˈpɔːt, -s, -ɪŋ, -ɪd
AM ˌəndə(r)rəˈpɔ(ə)rt, -ts, -ˈpɔrdɪŋ, -ˈpɔrdəd

under-represented
BR ˌʌndəˌrɛprɪˈzɛntɪd
AM ˌəndə(r)ˌrɛprəˈzɛn(t)əd

under-resourced
BR ˌʌndərɪˈsɔːst
AM ˌəndə(r)ˈriˌsɔ(ə)rst, ˌəndə(r)rəˈsɔ(ə)rst

underripe
BR ˌʌndəˈrʌɪp
AM ˌəndə(r)ˈraɪp

underscore¹
noun
BR ˈʌndəskɔː(r), -z
AM ˈəndərˌskɔ(ə)r, -z

underscore²
verb
BR ˌʌndəˈskɔː(r), -z, -ɪŋ, -d
AM ˌəndərˈskɔ(ə)r, -z, -ɪŋ, -d

undersea
BR ˌʌndəˈsiː
AM ˌəndərˈsi

underseal¹
noun
BR 'ʌndəsiːl
AM 'əndərˌsil

underseal²
verb
BR ˌʌndə'siːl, -z, -ɪŋ, -d
AM ˌəndər'sil, -z, -ɪŋ, -d

undersecretary
BR ˌʌndə'sɛktrɨt(ə)r|i, ˌʌndə'sɛkrɨtɛr|i, -ɪz
AM ˌəndər'sekrəˌtɛri, -z

undersell
BR ˌʌndə'sɛl, -z, -ɪŋ
AM ˌəndər'sɛl, -z, -ɪŋ

underset
BR ˌʌndə'sɛt, -s, -ɪŋ
AM ˌəndər'sɛ|t, -ts, -dɪŋ

undersexed
BR ˌʌndə'sɛkst
AM ˌəndər'sɛkst

undersheet
BR 'ʌndəʃiːt, -s
AM 'əndərˌʃit, -s

under-sheriff
BR 'ʌndəˌʃɛrɪf, -s
AM 'əndərˌʃɛrəf, -s

undershirt
BR 'ʌndəʃəːt, -s
AM 'əndərˌʃərt, -s

undershoot
BR ˌʌndə'ʃuːt, -s, -ɪŋ
AM ˌəndər'ʃu|t, -ts, -dɪŋ

undershorts
BR 'ʌndəʃɔːts
AM 'əndərˌʃɔ(ə)rts

undershot
BR ˌʌndə'ʃɒt
AM ˌəndər'ʃɑt

undershrub
BR 'ʌndəʃrʌb, -z
AM 'əndərˌʃrəb, -z

underside
BR 'ʌndəsʌɪd, -z
AM 'əndərˌsaɪd, -z

undersign
BR ˌʌndə'sʌɪn, -z, -ɪŋ, -d
AM ˌəndər'saɪn, -z, -ɪŋ, -d

undersigned
noun
BR ˌʌndə'sʌɪnd, 'ʌndəsʌɪnd
AM 'əndərˌsaɪnd

undersize
BR ˌʌndə'sʌɪz
AM ¦əndər¦saɪz

undersized
BR ˌʌndə'sʌɪzd
AM ˌəndər'saɪzd

underskirt
BR 'ʌndəskəːt, -s
AM 'əndərˌskərt, -s

underslung
BR ˌʌndə'slʌŋ
AM ˌəndər'sləŋ

undersold
BR ˌʌndə'səʊld
AM ˌəndər'soʊld

undersow
BR ˌʌndə'səʊ, -z, -ɪŋ
AM ˌəndər'soʊ, -z, -ɪŋ

undersown
BR ˌʌndə'səʊn
AM ˌəndər'soʊn

underspend
BR ˌʌndə'spɛnd, -z, -ɪŋ
AM ˌəndər'spɛnd, -z, -ɪŋ

underspent
BR ˌʌndə'spɛnt
AM ˌəndər'spɛnt

understaffed
BR ˌʌndə'stɑːft, ˌʌndə'staft
AM ˌəndər'stæft

understaffing
BR ˌʌndə'stɑːfɪŋ, ˌʌndə'stafɪŋ
AM ˌəndər'stæfɪŋ

understairs
BR ˌʌndə'stɛːz
AM 'əndərˌstɛrz

understand
BR ˌʌndə'stand, -z, -ɪŋ
AM ˌəndər'stæn|d, -(d)z, -dɪŋ

understandability
BR ˌʌndəˌstandə'bɪlɨti
AM ˌəndərˌstændə'bɪlɨdi

understandable
BR ˌʌndə'standəbl
AM ˌəndər'stændəbəl

understandably
BR ˌʌndə'standəbli
AM ˌəndər'stændəbli

understander
BR ˌʌndə'standə(r), -z
AM ˌəndər'stændər, -z

understanding
BR ˌʌndə'standɪŋ, -z
AM ˌəndər'stændɪŋ, -z

understandingly
BR ˌʌndə'standɪŋli
AM ˌəndər'stændɪŋli

understate
BR ˌʌndə'steɪt, -s, -ɪŋ, -ɨd
AM ˌəndər'steɪ|t, -ts, -dɪŋ, -dɨd

understatement
BR ˌʌndə'steɪtm(ə)nt, 'ʌndəˌsteɪtm(ə)nt, -s
AM 'əndərˌsteɪtmənt, -s

understater
BR ˌʌndə'steɪtə(r), -z
AM 'əndərˌsteɪdər, -z

understeer¹
noun
BR 'ʌndəstɪə(r)
AM 'əndərˌstɪ(ə)r

understeer²
verb
BR ˌʌndə'stɪə(r), -z, -ɪŋ, -d
AM ˌəndər'stɪ(ə)r, -z, -ɪŋ, -d

understood
BR ˌʌndə'stʊd
AM ˌəndər'stʊd

understorey
BR 'ʌndəˌstɔːr|i, -ɪz
AM 'əndərˌstɔri, -z

understrapper
BR 'ʌndəˌstrapə(r), -z
AM 'əndərˌstræpər, -z

under-strength
BR ˌʌndə'strɛŋ(k)θ
AM ˌəndər'strɛŋθ

understudy
BR 'ʌndəˌstʌd|i, -ɪz, -ɪɪŋ, -ɪd
AM 'əndərˌstədi, -z, -ɪŋ, -d

undersubscribed
BR ˌʌndəsəb'skrʌɪbd
AM ˌəndərsəb'skraɪbd

undersurface
BR 'ʌndəˌsəːfɪs, -ɪz
AM 'əndərˌsərfəs, -əz

undertake
BR ˌʌndə'teɪk, -s, -ɪŋ
AM ˌəndər'teɪk, -s, -ɪŋ

undertaker¹
person who arranges funerals
BR 'ʌndəteɪkə(r), -z
AM 'əndərˌteɪkər, -z

undertaker²
person who undertakes something
BR ˌʌndə'teɪkə(r), -z
AM ˌəndər'teɪkər, -z

undertaking¹
arranging of funerals
BR 'ʌndəteɪkɪŋ
AM 'əndərˌteɪkɪŋ

undertaking²
something to be done
BR ˌʌndə'teɪkɪŋ, 'ʌndəteɪkɪŋ, -z
AM ˌəndər'teɪkɪŋ, -z

undertenancy
BR ˌʌndə'tɛnəns|i, 'ʌndəˌtɛnəns|i, -ɪz
AM ¦əndər'tɛnənsi, -z

undertenant
BR ˌʌndə'tɛnənt, 'ʌndəˌtɛnənt, -s
AM 'əndərˌtɛnənt, -s

under-the-counter
BR ˌʌndəðə'kaʊntə(r)
AM ¦əndərðə'kaʊn(t)ər

underthings
BR 'ʌndəθɪŋz
AM 'əndərˌθɪŋz

undertint
BR 'ʌndətɪnt, -s
AM 'əndərˌtɪnt, -s

undertone
BR 'ʌndətəʊn, -z
AM 'əndərˌtoʊn, -z

undertook
BR ˌʌndə'tʊk
AM ˌəndər'tʊk

undertow
BR 'ʌndətəʊ, -z
AM 'əndərˌtoʊ, -z

undertrained
BR ˌʌndə'treɪnd
AM ˌəndər'treɪnd

undertrick
BR 'ʌndətrɪk, -s
AM 'əndərˌtrɪk, -s

under-use
BR ˌʌndə'juːz, -ɨz, -ɪŋ, -d
AM ˌəndər'juz, -əz, -ɪŋ, -d

underused
BR ˌʌndə'juːzd
AM ˌəndər'juzd

under-utilisation
BR ˌʌndəˌjuːtɨlʌɪ'zeɪʃn, ˌʌndəˌjuːtl̩ʌɪ'zeɪʃn
AM ˌəndərˌjudl̩ə'zeɪʃən, ˌəndərˌjudlˌaɪ'zeɪʃən

under-utilise
BR ˌʌndə'juːtɨlʌɪz, ˌʌndə'juːtl̩ʌɪz, -ɨz, -ɪŋ, -d
AM ˌəndər'judlˌaɪz, -ɨz, -ɪŋ, -d

under-utilization
BR ˌʌndəˌjuːtɨlʌɪ'zeɪʃn, ˌʌndəˌjuːtl̩ʌɪ'zeɪʃn
AM ˌəndərˌjudl̩ə'zeɪʃən, ˌəndərˌjudlˌaɪ'zeɪʃən

under-utilize
BR ˌʌndə'juːtɨlʌɪz, ˌʌndə'juːtl̩ʌɪz, -ɨz, -ɪŋ, -d
AM ˌəndər'judlˌaɪz, -ɨz, -ɪŋ, -d

undervaluation
BR ˌʌndəˌvaljʊ'eɪʃn, -z
AM ˌəndərˌvæljə'weɪʃən, -z

undervalue
BR ˌʌndə'valj|uː, -uːz, -ʊɪŋ, -uːd
AM ˌəndər'væl|ju, -juz, -jəwɪŋ, -jud

undervest
BR 'ʌndəvɛst, -s
AM 'əndərˌvɛst, -s

underwater
BR ˌʌndə'wɔːtə(r)
AM ˌəndər'wɔdər, ˌəndər'wɑdər

underwear
BR 'ʌndəwɛː(r)
AM 'əndərˌwɛ(ə)r

underweight
BR ˌʌndə'weɪt

AM ˌəndər'weɪt

underwent
BR ˌʌndə'wɛnt
AM ˌəndər'wɛnt

underwhelm
BR ˌʌndə'wɛlm, -z, -ɪŋ, -d
AM ˌəndər'(h)wɛlm, -z, -ɪŋ, -d

underwing
BR 'ʌndəwɪŋ, -z
AM 'əndərˌwɪŋ, -z

underwire
BR 'ʌndəˌwʌɪə(r), -z
AM 'əndərˌwaɪ(ə)r, -z

underwired
BR ˌʌndə'wʌɪəd
AM ˌəndərˌwaɪ(ə)rd

underwood
BR 'ʌndəwʊd, -z
AM 'əndərˌwʊd, -z

underwork
BR 'ʌndəwəːk, -s, -ɪŋ, -t
AM ˌəndər'wərk, -s, -ɪŋ, -t

underworld
BR 'ʌndəwəːld
AM 'əndərˌwərld

underwrite
BR ˌʌndə'rʌɪt, 'ʌndərʌɪt, -s, -ɪŋ
AM ˌəndə(r)'raɪ|t, -ts, -dɪŋ

underwriter
BR 'ʌndəˌrʌɪtə(r), -z
AM 'əndə(r)ˌraɪdər, -z

underwritten
BR ˌʌndə'rɪtn, 'ʌndəˌrɪtn
AM ˌəndə(r)'rɪtn

undescended
BR ˌʌndɪ'sɛndɪd
AM ˌəndə'sɛndəd, ˌəndi'sɛndəd

undescribed
BR ˌʌndɪ'skrʌɪbd
AM ˌəndə'skraɪbd, ˌəndi'skraɪbd

undeserved
BR ˌʌndɪ'zəːvd
AM ˌəndə'zərvd, ˌəndi'zərvd

undeservedly
BR ˌʌndɪ'zəːvɪdli
AM ˌəndə'zərvədli, ˌəndi'zərvədli

undeservedness
BR ˌʌndɪ'zəːvɪdnɪs
AM ˌəndə'zərvədnəs, ˌəndi'zərvədnəs

undeserving
BR ˌʌndɪ'zəːvɪŋ
AM ˌəndə'zərvɪŋ, ˌəndi'zərvɪŋ

undeservingly
BR ˌʌndɪ'zəːvɪŋli
AM ˌəndə'zərvɪŋli, ˌəndi'zərvɪŋli

undesignated
BR (ˌ)ʌn'dɛzɪgneɪtɪd
AM ˌən'dɛzɪgˌneɪdɪd

undesigned
BR ˌʌndɪ'zʌɪnd
AM ˌəndə'zaɪnd, ˌəndi'zaɪnd

undesignedly
BR ˌʌndɪ'zʌɪnɪdli
AM ˌəndə'zaɪnɪdli, ˌəndi'zaɪnɪdli

undesirability
BR ˌʌndɪˌzʌɪərə'bɪlɪti
AM ˌəndəˌzaɪ(ə)rə'bɪlɪdi, ˌəndiˌzaɪ(ə)rə'bɪlɪdi

undesirable
BR ˌʌndɪ'zʌɪərəbl
AM ˌəndə'zaɪ(ə)rəbəl, ˌəndi'zaɪ(ə)rəbəl

undesirableness
BR ˌʌndɪ'zʌɪərəblnəs
AM ˌəndə'zaɪ(ə)rəbəlnəs, ˌəndi'zaɪ(ə)rəbəlnəs

undesirably
BR ˌʌndɪ'zʌɪərəbli
AM ˌəndə'zaɪ(ə)rəbli, ˌəndi'zaɪ(ə)rəbli

undesired
BR ˌʌndɪ'zʌɪəd
AM ˌəndə'zaɪ(ə)rd, ˌəndi'zaɪ(ə)rd

undesirous
BR ˌʌndɪ'zʌɪərəs
AM ˌəndə'zaɪ(ə)rəs

undetectability
BR ˌʌndɪˌtɛktə'bɪlɪti
AM ˌəndəˌtɛktə'bɪlɪdi, ˌəndiˌtɛktə'bɪlɪdi

undetectable
BR ˌʌndɪ'tɛktəbl
AM ˌəndə'tɛktəbəl, ˌəndi'tɛktəbəl

undetectably
BR ˌʌndɪ'tɛktəbli
AM ˌəndə'tɛktəbli, ˌəndi'tɛktəbli

undetected
BR ˌʌndɪ'tɛktɪd
AM ˌəndə'tɛktəd, ˌəndi'tɛktəd

undetermined
BR ˌʌndɪ'təːmɪnd
AM ˌəndə'tərmənd, ˌəndi'tərmənd

undeterred
BR ˌʌndɪ'təːd
AM ˌəndə'tərd, ˌəndi'tərd

undeveloped
BR ˌʌndɪ'vɛləpt
AM ˌəndə'vɛləpt, ˌəndi'vɛləpt

undeviating
BR (ˌ)ʌn'diːvɪeɪtɪŋ
AM ˌən'diviˌeɪdɪŋ

undeviatingly
BR (ˌ)ʌn'diːvɪeɪtɪŋli
AM ˌən'diviˌeɪdɪŋli

undiagnosed
BR (ˌ)ʌn'dʌɪəgnəʊzd, ˌʌndʌɪəg'nəʊzd
AM ˌənˌdaɪəg'noʊzd

undid
BR ʌn'dɪd
AM ˌən'dɪd

undies
BR 'ʌndɪz
AM 'əndiz

undifferentiated
BR ˌʌndɪfə'rɛnʃɪeɪtɪd
AM ˌənˌdɪfə'rɛnʃiˌeɪdɪd

undigested
BR ˌʌndʌɪ'dʒɛstɪd, ˌʌndɪ'dʒɛstɪd
AM ˌəndə'dʒɛstəd, ˌəndaɪ'dʒɛstəd

undignified
BR (ˌ)ʌn'dɪgnɪfʌɪd
AM ˌən'dɪgnəˌfaɪd

undiluted
BR ˌʌndʌɪ'l(j)uːtɪd, ˌʌndɪ'l(j)uːtɪd
AM ˌəndə'ludəd, ˌəndi'ludəd

undiminished
BR ˌʌndɪ'mɪnɪʃt
AM ˌəndə'mɪnɪʃt, ˌəndi'mɪnɪʃt

undimmed
BR (ˌ)ʌn'dɪmd
AM ˌən'dɪmd

undine
BR 'ʌndiːn, -z
AM 'ənˌdin, -z

undiplomatic
BR ˌʌndɪplə'matɪk
AM ˌənˌdɪplə'mædɪk

undiplomatically
BR ˌʌndɪplə'matɪkli
AM ˌənˌdɪplə'mædək(ə)li

undirected
BR ˌʌndɪ'rɛktɪd, ˌʌndʌɪ'rɛktɪd
AM ˌəndə'rɛktəd, ˌənˌdaɪ'rɛktəd

undiscerning
BR ˌʌndɪ'səːnɪŋ
AM ˌəndə'sərnɪŋ

undischarged
BR ˌʌndɪs'tʃɑːdʒd
AM ˌəndɪs'tʃɑrdʒd

undiscipline
BR ʌn'dɪsɪplɪn, -d
AM ˌən'dɪsəplən, -d

undisclosed
BR ˌʌndɪs'kləʊzd
AM ˌəndə'skloʊzd

undiscouraged
BR ˌʌndɪs'kʌrɪdʒd, ˌʌndɪ'skʌrɪdʒd
AM ˌəndə'skərədʒd

undiscoverable
BR ˌʌndɪ'skʌv(ə)rəbl
AM ˌəndə'skəv(ə)rəbəl

undiscoverably
BR ˌʌndɪ'skʌv(ə)rəbli
AM ˌəndə'skəv(ə)rəbli

undiscovered
BR ˌʌndɪ'skʌvəd
AM ˌəndə'skəvərd

undiscriminating
BR ˌʌndɪ'skrɪmɪneɪtɪŋ
AM ˌəndə'skrɪməˌneɪdɪŋ

undiscussed
BR ˌʌndɪ'skʌst
AM ˌəndə'skəst

undisguised
BR ˌʌndɪs'gʌɪzd
AM ˌəndɪs'gaɪzd

undisguisedly
BR ˌʌndɪs'gʌɪzɪdli
AM ˌəndɪs'gaɪzədli

undismayed
BR ˌʌndɪs'meɪd
AM ˌəndɪs'meɪd

undisposed
BR ˌʌndɪ'spəʊzd
AM ˌəndə'spoʊzd

undisputed
BR ˌʌndɪ'spjuːtɪd
AM ˌəndə'spjudəd

undissolved
BR ˌʌndɪ'zɒlvd
AM ˌəndə'zɑlvd

undistinguishable
BR ˌʌndɪ'stɪŋgwɪʃəbl
AM ˌəndə'stɪŋgwɪʃəbəl

undistinguished
BR ˌʌndɪ'stɪŋgwɪʃt
AM ˌəndə'stɪŋgwɪʃt

undistorted
BR ˌʌndɪ'stɔːtɪd
AM ˌəndə'stɔrdəd

undistracted
BR ˌʌndɪ'straktɪd
AM ˌəndə'stræktəd

undistributed
BR ˌʌndɪ'strɪbjʊtɪd
AM ˌəndə'strɪbjədəd

undisturbed
BR ˌʌndɪ'stəːbd
AM ˌəndə'stərbd

undivided
BR ˌʌndɪ'vʌɪdɪd
AM ˌəndə'vaɪdɪd

undivulged
BR ˌʌndʌɪ'vʌldʒd, ˌʌndɪ'vʌldʒd
AM ˌəndə'vəldʒd, ˌənˌdaɪ'vəldʒd

undo
BR (ˌ)ʌn'd|uː, -ʌz, -uːɪŋ
AM ˌən'd|u, -əz, -uɪŋ

undock
BR (ˌ)ʌn'dɒk, -s, -ɪŋ, -t
AM ˌən'dɑk, -s, -ɪŋ, -t

undocumented
BR (ˌ)ʌn'dɒkjʊmɛntɪd
AM ˌən'dɑkjəˌmɛn(t)əd

undogmatic
BR ˌʌndɒg'matɪk
AM ˌənˌdɔg'mædɪk, ˌənˌdɑg'mædɪk

undomesticated
BR ˌʌndəˈmɛstɨkeɪtɨd
AM ˌəndəˈmɛstəˌkeɪdɨd

undone
BR (ˌ)ʌnˈdʌn
AM ˌənˈdən

undoubtable
BR ʌnˈdaʊtəbl
AM ˌənˈdaʊdəbəl

undoubtably
BR ʌnˈdaʊtəbli
AM ˌənˈdaʊdəbli

undoubted
BR ʌnˈdaʊtɨd
AM ˌənˈdaʊdəd

undoubtedly
BR ʌnˈdaʊtɨdli
AM ˌənˈdaʊdədli

undoubting
BR ʌnˈdaʊtɪŋ
AM ˌənˈdaʊdɪŋ

undrained
BR (ˌ)ʌnˈdreɪnd
AM ˌənˈdreɪnd

undramatic
BR ˌʌndrəˈmatɪk
AM ˌəndrəˈmædɪk

undraped
BR (ˌ)ʌnˈdreɪpt
AM ˌənˈdreɪpt

undreamed
BR (ˌ)ʌnˈdriːmd
AM ˌənˈdrimd

undreamed-of
BR (ˌ)ʌnˈdriːmdɒv
AM ˌənˈdrimdəv

undreamt
BR (ˌ)ʌnˈdrɛm(p)t
AM ˌənˈdrɛmt

undreamt-of
BR (ˌ)ʌnˈdrɛm(p)tɒv
AM ˌənˈdrɛmtəv

undress
BR (ˌ)ʌnˈdrɛs, -ɪz, -ɪŋ, -t
AM ˌənˈdrɛs, -əz, -ɪŋ, -t

undrinkable
BR (ˌ)ʌnˈdrɪŋkəbl
AM ˌənˈdrɪŋkəbəl

undrivable
BR (ˌ)ʌnˈdrʌɪvəbl
AM ˌənˈdraɪvəbəl

undriveable
BR (ˌ)ʌnˈdrʌɪvəbl
AM ˌənˈdraɪvəbəl

UNDRO
BR ˈʌndrəʊ
AM ˈənˌdroʊ

undue
BR ˌʌnˈdjuː, ˌʌnˈdʒuː
AM ˌənˈd(j)u

undulant
BR ˈʌndjʊlənt, ˈʌndʒʊlənt
AM ˈəndʒələnt, ˈəndjələnt

undulate
BR ˈʌndjʊleɪt, ˈʌndʒʊleɪt, -s, -ɪŋ, -ɨd
AM ˈəndʒəˌleɪ|t, ˈəndjəˌleɪ|t, -ts, -dɪŋ, -dɨd

undulately
BR ˈʌndjʊlətli, ˈʌndʒʊlətli
AM ˈəndʒələtli, ˈəndjələtli

undulation
BR ˌʌndjʊˈleɪʃn, ˌʌndʒʊˈleɪʃn, -z
AM ˌəndʒəˈleɪʃən, ˌəndjəˈleɪʃən, -z

undulatory
BR ˈʌndjʊlət(ə)ri, ˈʌndʒʊlət(ə)ri, ˌʌndjʊˈleɪt(ə)ri, ˌʌndʒʊˈleɪt(ə)ri
AM ˈəndʒələˌtɔri, ˈəndjələˌtɔri

unduly
BR (ˌ)ʌnˈdjuːli, (ˌ)ʌnˈdʒuːli
AM ˌənˈd(j)uli

undutiful
BR (ˌ)ʌnˈdjuːtɪf(ʊ)l, (ˌ)ʌnˈdʒuːtɪf(ʊ)l
AM ˌənˈd(j)udəfəl

undutifully
BR (ˌ)ʌnˈdjuːtɪfʊli, (ˌ)ʌnˈdjuːtɪfl̩i, (ˌ)ʌnˈdʒuːtɪfʊli, (ˌ)ʌnˈdʒuːtɪfl̩i
AM ˌənˈd(j)udəf(ə)li

undutifulness
BR (ˌ)ʌnˈdjuːtɪf(ʊ)lnəs, (ˌ)ʌnˈdʒuːtɪf(ʊ)lnəs
AM ˌənˈd(j)udəfəlnəs

undy
BR ˈʌnd|i, -ɪz
AM ˈənd|i, -iz

undyed
BR (ˌ)ʌnˈdʌɪd
AM ˌənˈdaɪd

undying
BR (ˌ)ʌnˈdʌɪɪŋ
AM ˌənˈdaɪɪŋ

undyingly
BR (ˌ)ʌnˈdʌɪɪŋli
AM ˌənˈdaɪɪŋli

undynamic
BR ˌʌndʌɪˈnamɪk
AM ˌənˌdaɪˈnæmɪk

unearned
BR (ˌ)ʌnˈəːnd
AM ˌənˈərnd

unearth
BR (ˌ)ʌnˈəːθ, -s, -ɪŋ, -t
AM ˌənˈərθ, -s, -ɪŋ, -t

unearthliness
BR (ˌ)ʌnˈəːθlɪnɨs
AM ˌənˈərθlinɨs

unearthly
BR ʌnˈəːθli
AM ˌənˈərθli

unease
BR ʌnˈiːz
AM ˌənˈiz

uneasily
BR ʌnˈiːzɨli
AM ˌənˈizɨli

uneasiness
BR ʌnˈiːzɪnɨs
AM ˌənˈizinɨs

uneasy
BR ʌnˈiːz|i, -ɪə(r), -ɪɪst
AM ˌənˈizi, -ər, -ɨst

uneatable
BR (ˌ)ʌnˈiːtəbl
AM ˌənˈidəbəl

uneatableness
BR (ˌ)ʌnˈiːtəblnəs
AM ˌənˈidəbəlnəs

uneaten
BR (ˌ)ʌnˈiːtn
AM ˌənˈitn

uneconomic
BR ˌʌniːkəˈnɒmɪk, ˌʌnɛkəˈnɒmɪk
AM ˌənikəˈnɑmɪk, ˌənɛkəˈnɑmɪk

uneconomical
BR ˌʌniːkəˈnɒmɪkl, ˌʌnɛkəˈnɒmɪkl
AM ˌənikəˈnɑməkəl, ˌənɛkəˈnɑməkəl

uneconomically
BR ˌʌniːkəˈnɒmɪkli, ˌʌnɛkəˈnɒmɪkli
AM ˌənikəˈnɑmək(ə)li, ˌənɛkəˈnɑmək(ə)li

unedifying
BR ʌnˈɛdɪfʌɪɪŋ
AM ˌənˈɛdəˌfaɪɪŋ

unedifyingly
BR ʌnˈɛdɪfʌɪɪŋli
AM ˌənˈɛdəˌfaɪɪŋli

unedited
BR ˌʌnˈɛdɪtɨd
AM ˌənˈɛdədəd

uneducable
BR (ˌ)ʌnˈɛdjʊkəbl, (ˌ)ʌnˈɛdʒʊkəbl
AM ˌənˈɛdʒəkəbəl

uneducated
BR (ˌ)ʌnˈɛdjʊkeɪtɨd, (ˌ)ʌnˈɛdʒʊkeɪtɨd
AM ˌənˈɛdʒəˌkeɪdɨd

unelectable
BR ˌʌnɪˈlɛktəbl
AM ˌənəˈlɛktəbəl

unelected
BR ˌʌnɪˈlɛktɨd
AM ˌənəˈlɛktəd

unembarrassed
BR ˌʌnɪmˈbarəst
AM ˌənəmˈbɛrəst

unembellished
BR ˌʌnɪmˈbɛlɪʃt
AM ˌənəmˈbɛlɪʃt

unembittered
BR ˌʌnɪmˈbɪtəd
AM ˌənəmˈbɪdərd

unembroidered
BR ˌʌnɪmˈbrɔɪdəd
AM ˌənəmˈbrɔɪdərd

unemotional
BR ˌʌnɪˈməʊʃn̩(ə)l, ˌʌnɪˈməʊʃən(ə)l
AM ˌənəˈmoʊʃ(ə)nəl, ˌəniˈmoʊʃ(ə)nəl

unemotionally
BR ˌʌnɪˈməʊʃn̩əli, ˌʌnɪˈməʊʃn̩li, ˌʌnɪˈməʊʃənl̩i, ˌʌnɪˈməʊʃ(ə)nəli
AM ˌənəˈmoʊʃ(ə)nəli, ˌənˌiˈmoʊʃ(ə)nəli

unemphatic
BR ˌʌnɪmˈfatɪk, ˌʌnɛmˈfatɪk
AM ˌənəmˈfædɪk

unemphatically
BR ˌʌnɪmˈfatɪkli, ˌʌnɛmˈfatɪkli
AM ˌənəmˈfædək(ə)li

unemployability
BR ˌʌnɪmˌplɔɪəˈbɪlɪti, ˌʌnɛmˌplɔɪəˈbɪlɪti
AM ˌənəmplɔɪəˈbɪlɨdi

unemployable
BR ˌʌnɪmˈplɔɪəbl, ˌʌnɛmˈplɔɪəbl
AM ˌənəmˈplɔɪəbəl

unemployed
BR ˌʌnɪmˈplɔɪd, ˌʌnɛmˈplɔɪd
AM ˌənəmˈplɔɪd

unemployment
BR ˌʌnɪmˈplɔɪm(ə)nt, ˌʌnɛmˈplɔɪm(ə)nt
AM ˌənəmˈplɔɪmənt

unemptied
BR (ˌ)ʌnˈɛm(p)tɪd
AM ˌənˈɛm(p)tid

unenclosed
BR ˌʌnɪnˈkləʊzd, ˌʌnɛnˈkləʊzd
AM ˌənənˈkloʊzd

unencumbered
BR ˌʌnɪnˈkʌmbəd, ˌʌnɛnˈkʌmbəd
AM ˌənənˈkəmbərd

unendearing
BR ˌʌnɪnˈdɪərɪŋ, ˌʌnɛnˈdɪərɪŋ
AM ˌənənˈdɪrɪŋ

unending
BR ˌʌnˈɛndɪŋ
AM ˌənˈɛndɪŋ

unendingly
BR ˌʌnˈɛndɪŋli
AM ˌənˈɛndɪŋli

unendingness
BR ˌʌnˈɛndɪŋnɨs
AM ˌənˈɛndɪŋnɨs

unendowed
BR ˌʌnɪnˈdaʊd, ˌʌnɛnˈdaʊd
AM ˌənənˈdaʊd

unendurable
BR ˌʌnɪn'djʊərəbl, ˌʌnɪn'dʒʊərəbl, ˌʌnɪn'djɔːrəbl, ˌʌnɪn'dʒɔːrəbl
AM ˌənən'd(j)ʊrəbəl

unendurably
BR ˌʌnɪn'djʊərəbli, ˌʌnɪn'dʒʊərəbli, ˌʌnɪn'djɔːrəbli, ˌʌnɪn'dʒɔːrəbli
AM ˌənən'd(j)ʊrəbli

unenforceable
BR ˌʌnɪn'fɔːsəbl, ˌʌnɛn'fɔːsəbl
AM ˌənən'fɔrsəbəl

unenforced
BR ˌʌnɪn'fɔːst, ˌʌnɛn'fɔːst
AM ˌənən'fɔ(ə)rst

unengaged
BR ˌʌnɪn'geɪdʒd, ˌʌnɛn'geɪdʒd
AM ˌənən'geɪdʒd

un-English
BR (ˌ)ʌn'ɪŋlɪʃ
AM ˌən'ɪŋ(g)lɪʃ

unenjoyable
BR ˌʌnɪn'dʒɔɪəbl, ˌʌnɛn'dʒɔɪəbl
AM ˌənən'dʒɔɪəbəl

unenlightened
BR ˌʌnɪn'lʌɪtnd, ˌʌnɛn'lʌɪtnd
AM ˌənən'laɪtnd

unenlightening
BR ˌʌnɪn'lʌɪtn̩ɪŋ, ˌʌnɛn'lʌɪtn̩ɪŋ
AM ˌənən'laɪtn̩ɪŋ

unenterprising
BR ʌn'ɛntəprʌɪzɪŋ
AM ˌən'ɛn(t)ərˌpraɪzɪŋ

unenthusiastic
BR ˌʌnɪnˌθjuːzɪ'astɪk, ˌʌnɛnˌθjuːzɪ'astɪk
AM ˌənənˌθ(j)uzi'æstɪk

unenthusiastically
BR ˌʌnɪnˌθjuːzɪ'astɪkli, ˌʌnɛnˌθjuːzɪ'astɪkli
AM ˌənənˌθ(j)uzi'æstək(ə)li

unenviable
BR (ˌ)ʌn'ɛnvɪəbl
AM ˌən'ɛnviəbəl

unenviably
BR (ˌ)ʌn'ɛnvɪəbli
AM ˌən'ɛnviəbli

unenvied
BR (ˌ)ʌn'ɛnvɪd
AM ˌən'ɛnvid

unenvironmental
BR ˌʌnɪnˌvʌɪrən'mɛntl, ˌʌnɪnˌvʌɪrn̩'mɛntl, ˌʌnɛnˌvʌɪrən'mɛntl, ˌʌnɛnˌvʌɪrn̩'mɛntl
AM ˌənənˌvaɪrən'mɛn(t)l, ˌənənˌvaɪ(ə)rn'mɛn(t)l, ˌənɛnˌvaɪrən'mɛn(t)l, ˌənɛnˌvaɪ(ə)rn'mɛn(t)l

UNEP
BR 'juːnɛp
AM 'junɛp

unequable
BR (ˌ)ʌn'ɛkwəbl
AM ˌən'ɛkwəbəl

unequal
BR (ˌ)ʌn'iːkw(ə)l, -z, -d
AM ˌən'ikwəl, -z, -d

unequalise
BR (ˌ)ʌn'iːkwəlʌɪz, -ɪz, -ɪŋ, -d
AM ˌən'ikwəˌlaɪz, -ɪz, -ɪŋ, -d

unequalize
BR (ˌ)ʌn'iːkwəlʌɪz, -ɪz, -ɪŋ, -d
AM ˌən'ikwəˌlaɪz, -ɪz, -ɪŋ, -d

unequally
BR (ˌ)ʌn'iːkwəli, (ˌ)ʌn'iːkwl̩i
AM ˌən'ikwəli

unequalness
BR (ˌ)ʌn'iːkw(ə)lnəs
AM ˌən'ikwəlnəs

unequipped
BR ˌʌnɪ'kwɪpt
AM ˌənə'kwɪpt

unequitable
BR (ˌ)ʌn'ɛkwɪtəbl
AM ˌən'ɛkwədəbəl

unequitably
BR (ˌ)ʌn'ɛkwɪtəbli
AM ˌən'ɛkwədəbli

unequivocal
BR ˌʌnɪ'kwɪvəkl
AM ˌənə'kwɪvəkəl

unequivocally
BR ˌʌnɪ'kwɪvəkli
AM ˌənə'kwɪvək(ə)li

unequivocalness
BR ˌʌnɪ'kwɪvəklnəs
AM ˌənə'kwɪvəkəlnəs

unerring
BR (ˌ)ʌn'əːrɪŋ
AM ˌən'ɛrɪŋ

unerringly
BR (ˌ)ʌn'əːrɪŋli
AM ˌən'ɛrɪŋli

unerringness
BR (ˌ)ʌn'əːrɪŋnɪs
AM ˌən'ɛrɪŋnɪs

unescapable
BR ˌʌnɪ'skeɪpəbl
AM ˌənə'skeɪpəbəl

UNESCO
BR juː'nɛskəʊ, jʊ'nɛskəʊ
AM ju'nɛskoʊ

unescorted
BR ˌʌnɪ'skɔːtɪd
AM ˌənə'skɔrdəd, ˌən'ɛskɔrdəd

unessential
BR ˌʌnɪ'sɛnʃl
AM ˌənə'sɛn(t)ʃəl

unestablished
BR ˌʌnɪ'stablɪʃt
AM ˌənə'stæblɪʃt

unethical
BR (ˌ)ʌn'ɛθɪkl
AM ˌən'ɛθəkəl

unethically
BR (ˌ)ʌn'ɛθɪkli
AM ˌən'ɛθək(ə)li

uneven
BR (ˌ)ʌn'iːvn
AM ˌən'ivən

unevenly
BR (ˌ)ʌn'iːvnli
AM ˌən'ivənli

unevenness
BR (ˌ)ʌn'iːvnnəs
AM ˌən'ivə(n)nəs

uneventful
BR ˌʌnɪ'vɛntf(ʊ)l
AM ˌənə'vɛn(t)fəl

uneventfully
BR ˌʌnɪ'vɛntfəli, ˌʌnɪ'vɛntfl̩i
AM ˌənə'vɛn(t)fəli

uneventfulness
BR ˌʌnɪ'vɛntf(ʊ)lnəs
AM ˌənə'vɛn(t)fəlnəs

unexacting
BR ˌʌnɪg'zaktɪŋ, ˌʌnɛg'zaktɪŋ
AM ˌənəg'zæktɪŋ

unexamined
BR ˌʌnɪg'zamɪnd, ˌʌnɛg'zamɪnd
AM ˌənəg'zæmənd

unexampled
BR ˌʌnɪg'zɑːmpld, ˌʌnɪg'zampld, ˌʌnɛg'zɑːmpld, ˌʌnɛg'zampld
AM ˌənəg'zæmpəld

unexcavated
BR (ˌ)ʌn'ɛkskəveɪtɪd
AM ˌən'ɛkskəˌveɪdɪd

unexceptionable
BR ˌʌnɪk'sɛpʃn̩əbl, ˌʌnɪk'sɛpʃ(ə)nəbl, ˌʌnɛk'sɛpʃn̩əbl, ˌʌnɛk'sɛpʃ(ə)nəbl
AM ˌənək'sɛpʃ(ə)nəbəl

unexceptionableness
BR ˌʌnɪk'sɛpʃn̩əblnəs, ˌʌnɪk'sɛpʃ(ə)nəblnəs, ˌʌnɛk'sɛpʃn̩əblnəs, ˌʌnɛk'sɛpʃ(ə)nəblnəs
AM ˌənək'sɛpʃ(ə)nəbəlnəs

unexceptionably
BR ˌʌnɪk'sɛpʃn̩əbli, ˌʌnɪk'sɛpʃ(ə)nəbli, ˌʌnɛk'sɛpʃn̩əbli, ˌʌnɛk'sɛpʃ(ə)nəbli
AM ˌənək'sɛpʃ(ə)nəbli

unexceptional
BR ˌʌnɪk'sɛpʃn̩(ə)l, ˌʌnɪk'sɛpʃən(ə)l, ˌʌnɛk'sɛpʃn̩(ə)l, ˌʌnɛk'sɛpʃən(ə)l
AM ˌənək'sɛpʃ(ə)nəl

unexceptionally
BR ˌʌnɪk'sɛpʃn̩əli, ˌʌnɪk'sɛpʃ(ə)nəli, ˌʌnɛk'sɛpʃn̩əli, ˌʌnɛk'sɛpʃ(ə)nəli
AM ˌənək'sɛpʃ(ə)nəli

unexcitability
BR ˌʌnɪkˌsʌɪtə'bɪlɪti, ˌʌnɛkˌsʌɪtə'bɪlɪti
AM ˌənəkˌsaɪdə'bɪlɪdi

unexcitable
BR ˌʌnɪk'sʌɪtəbl, ˌʌnɛk'sʌɪtəbl
AM ˌənək'saɪdəbəl

unexciting
BR ˌʌnɪk'sʌɪtɪŋ, ˌʌnɛk'sʌɪtɪŋ
AM ˌənək'saɪdɪŋ

unexclusive
BR ˌʌnɪk'skluːsɪv, ˌʌnɛk'skluːsɪv
AM ˌənək'sklusɪv

unexecuted
BR (ˌ)ʌn'ɛksɪkjuːtɪd
AM ˌən'ɛksəˌkjudəd

unexhausted
BR ˌʌnɪg'zɔːstɪd, ˌʌnɛg'zɔːstɪd
AM ˌənəg'zɔstəd, ˌənəg'zɑstəd

unexpected
BR ˌʌnɪk'spɛktɪd, ˌʌnɛk'spɛktɪd
AM ˌənək'spɛktəd

unexpectedly
BR ˌʌnɪk'spɛktɪdli, ˌʌnɛk'spɛktɪdli
AM ˌənək'spɛktədli

unexpectedness
BR ˌʌnɪk'spɛktɪdnɪs, ˌʌnɛk'spɛktɪdnɪs
AM ˌənək'spɛktədnəs

unexpiated
BR (ˌ)ʌn'ɛkspɪeɪtɪd
AM ˌən'ɛkspiˌeɪdɪd

unexpired
BR ˌʌnɪk'spʌɪəd, ˌʌnɛk'spʌɪəd
AM ˌənək'spaɪ(ə)rd

unexplainable
BR ˌʌnɪk'spleɪnəbl, ˌʌnɛk'spleɪnəbl
AM ˌənək'spleɪnəbəl

unexplainably
BR ˌʌnɪk'spleɪnəbli, ˌʌnɛk'spleɪnəbli
AM ˌənək'spleɪnəbli

unexplained
BR ˌʌnɪk'spleɪnd, ˌʌnɛk'spleɪnd
AM ˌənək'spleɪnd

unexploded
BR ˌʌnɪk'spləʊdɪd, ˌʌnɛk'spləʊdɪd
AM ˌənɛk'sploʊdəd

unexploited
BR ˌʌnɪk'splɔɪtɪd, ˌʌnɛk'splɔɪtɪd
AM ˌənək'splɔɪdɪd

unexplored
BR ˌʌnɪk'splɔːd, ˌʌnɛk'splɔːd
AM ˌənək'splɔ(ə)rd

unexportable
BR ˌʌnɪk'spɔːtəbl, ˌʌnɛk'spɔːtəbl
AM ˌən'ɛkspɔrdəbəl, ˌənək'spɔrdəbəl

unexposed
BR ˌʌnɪk'spəʊzd, ˌʌnɛk'spəʊzd
AM ˌənək'spoʊzd

unexpressed
BR ˌʌnɪk'sprɛst, ˌʌnɛk'sprɛst
AM ˌənək'sprɛst

unexpressible
BR ˌʌnɪk'sprɛsɪbl, ˌʌnɛk'sprɛsɪbl
AM ˌənək'sprɛsəbəl

unexpressibly
BR ˌʌnɪk'sprɛsɪbli, ˌʌnɛk'sprɛsɪbli
AM ˌənək'sprɛsəbli

unexpressive
BR ˌʌnɪk'sprɛsɪv, ˌʌnɛk'sprɛsɪv
AM ˌənək'sprɛsɪv

unexpurgated
BR (ˌ)ʌn'ɛkspəgeɪtɪd
AM ˌən'ɛkspərˌgeɪdɪd

unfaceable
BR ˌʌn'feɪsəbl
AM ˌən'feɪsəbəl

unfaded
BR (ˌ)ʌn'feɪdɪd
AM ˌən'feɪdɪd

unfading
BR (ˌ)ʌn'feɪdɪŋ
AM ˌən'feɪdɪŋ

unfadingly
BR (ˌ)ʌn'feɪdɪŋli
AM ˌən'feɪdɪŋli

unfailing
BR ʌn'feɪlɪŋ
AM ˌən'feɪlɪŋ

unfailingly
BR ʌn'feɪlɪŋli
AM ˌən'feɪlɪŋli

unfailingness
BR ʌn'feɪlɪŋnɪs
AM ˌən'feɪlɪŋnɪs

unfair
BR (ˌ)ʌn'fɛː(r)
AM ˌən'fɛ(ə)r

unfairly
BR (ˌ)ʌn'fɛːli
AM ˌən'fɛrli

unfairness
BR (ˌ)ʌn'fɛːnəs
AM ˌən'fɛrnəs

unfaithful
BR (ˌ)ʌn'feɪθf(ʊ)l
AM ˌən'feɪθfəl

unfaithfully
BR (ˌ)ʌn'feɪθfʊli, (ˌ)ʌn'feɪθfl̩i
AM ˌən'feɪθfəli

unfaithfulness
BR (ˌ)ʌn'feɪθf(ʊ)lnəs
AM ˌən'feɪθfəlnəs

unfaltering
BR (ˌ)ʌn'fɔːlt(ə)rɪŋ, (ˌ)ʌn'fɒlt(ə)rɪŋ
AM ˌən'fɔlt(ə)rɪŋ, ˌən'fɑlt(ə)rɪŋ

unfalteringly
BR (ˌ)ʌn'fɔːlt(ə)rɪŋli, (ˌ)ʌn'fɒlt(ə)rɪŋli
AM ˌən'fɔlt(ə)rɪŋli, ˌən'fɑlt(ə)rɪŋli

unfamiliar
BR ˌʌnfə'mɪlɪə(r)
AM ˌənfə'mɪljər, ˌənfə'mɪliər

unfamiliarity
BR ˌʌnfəˌmɪlɪ'arɪti
AM ˌənfəˌmɪl'jɛrədi, ˌənfəˌmɪli'ɛrədi

unfancied
BR (ˌ)ʌn'fansɪd
AM ˌən'fænsid

unfashionable
BR (ˌ)ʌn'faʃ(ə)nəbl, (ˌ)ʌn'faʃn̩əbl
AM ˌən'fæʃ(ə)nəbəl

unfashionableness
BR (ˌ)ʌn'faʃ(ə)nəblnəs, (ˌ)ʌn'faʃn̩əblnəs
AM ˌən'fæʃ(ə)nəbəlnəs

unfashionably
BR (ˌ)ʌn'faʃ(ə)nəbli, (ˌ)ʌn'faʃn̩əbli
AM ˌən'fæʃ(ə)nəbli

unfashioned
BR (ˌ)ʌn'faʃnd
AM ˌən'fæʃənd

unfasten
BR (ˌ)ʌn'fɑːs|n, (ˌ)ʌn'fas|n, -nz, -n̩ɪŋ\-nɪŋ, -nd
AM ˌən'fæsn, -z, -ɪŋ, -d

unfathered
BR (ˌ)ʌn'fɑːðəd
AM ˌən'fɑðərd

unfatherliness
BR (ˌ)ʌn'fɑːðəlɪnɪs
AM ˌən'fɑðərlinɪs

unfatherly
BR (ˌ)ʌn'fɑːðəli
AM ˌən'fɑðərli

unfathomable
BR ʌn'faðəməbl, ʌn'faðm̩əbl
AM ˌən'fæθ(ə)məbəl

unfathomableness
BR ʌn'faðəməblnəs, ʌn'faðm̩əblnəs
AM ˌən'fæθ(ə)məbəlnəs

unfathomably
BR ʌn'faðəməbli, ʌn'faðm̩əbli
AM ˌən'fæθ(ə)məbli

unfathomed
BR (ˌ)ʌn'fað(ə)md
AM ˌən'fæðəmd

unfavorable
BR (ˌ)ʌn'feɪv(ə)rəbl
AM ˌən'feɪv(ə)r(ə)bəl

unfavorableness
BR (ˌ)ʌn'feɪv(ə)rəblnəs
AM ˌən'feɪv(ə)rəbəlnəs

unfavorably
BR (ˌ)ʌn'feɪv(ə)rəbli
AM ˌən'feɪv(ə)r(ə)bli

unfavorite
BR ˌʌn'feɪv(ə)rɪt
AM ˌən'feɪv(ə)rɪt

unfavourable
BR (ˌ)ʌn'feɪv(ə)rəbl
AM ˌən'feɪv(ə)r(ə)bəl

unfavourableness
BR (ˌ)ʌn'feɪv(ə)rəblnəs
AM ˌən'feɪv(ə)rəbəlnəs

unfavourably
BR (ˌ)ʌn'feɪv(ə)rəbli
AM ˌən'feɪv(ə)r(ə)bli

unfavourite
BR ˌʌn'feɪv(ə)rɪt
AM ˌən'feɪv(ə)rɪt

unfazed
BR (ˌ)ʌn'feɪzd
AM ˌən'feɪzd

unfeasibility
BR ˌʌnfiːzɪ'bɪlɪti
AM ˌənfizi'bɪlɪdi

unfeasible
BR (ˌ)ʌn'fiːzɪbl
AM ˌən'fizəbəl

unfeasibly
BR (ˌ)ʌn'fiːzɪbli
AM ˌən'fizəbli

unfed
BR ˌʌn'fɛd
AM ˌən'fɛd

unfeeling
BR ʌn'fiːlɪŋ
AM ˌən'filɪŋ

unfeelingly
BR ʌn'fiːlɪŋli
AM ˌən'filɪŋli

unfeelingness
BR ʌn'fiːlɪŋnɪs
AM ˌən'filɪŋnɪs

unfeigned
BR (ˌ)ʌn'feɪnd
AM ˌən'feɪnd

unfeignedly
BR ʌn'feɪnɪdli
AM ˌən'feɪnɪdli

unfelt
BR (ˌ)ʌn'fɛlt
AM ˌən'fɛlt

unfeminine
BR ˌʌn'fɛmɪnɪn
AM ˌən'fɛmənən

unfemininity
BR ˌʌnfɛmɪ'nɪnɪti
AM ˌənˌfɛmə'nɪnɪdi

unfenced
BR ˌʌn'fɛnst
AM ˌən'fɛnst

unfermented
BR ˌʌnfə'mɛntɪd
AM ˌənfər'mɛn(t)əd

unfertilised
BR ˌʌn'fəːtɪlʌɪzd, ˌʌn'fəːtl̩ʌɪzd
AM ˌən'fərdlˌaɪzd

unfertilized
BR ˌʌn'fəːtɪlʌɪzd, ˌʌn'fəːtl̩ʌɪzd
AM ˌən'fərdlˌaɪzd

unfetter
BR ˌʌn'fɛt|ə(r), -əz, -(ə)rɪŋ, -əd
AM ˌən'fɛdər, -z, -ɪŋ, -d

unfilial
BR ˌʌn'fɪlɪəl
AM ˌən'fɪliəl

unfilially
BR ˌʌn'fɪlɪəli
AM ˌən'fɪliəli, ˌən'fɪljəli

unfilled
BR (ˌ)ʌn'fɪld
AM ˌən'fɪld

unfiltered
BR ˌʌn'fɪltəd
AM ˌən'fɪltərd

unfinancial
BR ˌʌnfʌɪ'nanʃl, ˌʌnfɪ'nanʃl
AM ˌənˌfaɪ'næn(t)ʃəl, ˌənfə'næn(t)ʃəl

unfinished
BR (ˌ)ʌn'fɪnɪʃt
AM ˌən'fɪnɪʃt

unfit
BR (ˌ)ʌn'fɪt, -s, -ɪŋ, -ɪd
AM ˌən'fɪ|t, -ts, -dɪŋ, -dɪd

unfitly
BR (ˌ)ʌn'fɪtli
AM ˌən'fɪtli

unfitness
BR (ˌ)ʌn'fɪtnɪs
AM ˌən'fɪtnɪs

unfitted
BR (ˌ)ʌn'fɪtɪd
AM ˌən'fɪdɪd

unfitting
BR (ˌ)ʌn'fɪtɪŋ
AM ˌən'fɪdɪŋ

unfittingly
BR (ˌ)ʌn'fɪtɪŋli
AM ˌən'fɪdɪŋli

unfix
BR ˌʌn'fɪks, -ɪz, -ɪŋ, -t
AM ˌən'fɪks, -ɪz, -ɪŋ, -t

unflagging
BR (ˌ)ʌnˈflagɪŋ
AM ˌənˈflægɪŋ

unflaggingly
BR (ˌ)ʌnˈflagɪŋli
AM ˌənˈflægɪŋli

unflappability
BR ˌʌnflapəˈbɪlɨti
AM ˌənˌflæpəˈbɪlɨdi

unflappable
BR (ˌ)ʌnˈflapəbl
AM ˌənˈflæpəbəl

unflappably
BR (ˌ)ʌnˈflapəbli
AM ˌənˈflæpəbli

unflattering
BR (ˌ)ʌnˈflat(ə)rɪŋ
AM ˌənˈflædərɪŋ

unflatteringly
BR (ˌ)ʌnˈflat(ə)rɪŋli
AM ˌənˈflædərɪŋli

unflavored
BR ˌʌnˈfleɪvəd
AM ˌənˈfleɪvərd

unflavoured
BR ˌʌnˈfleɪvəd
AM ˌənˈfleɪvərd

unfledged
BR (ˌ)ʌnˈflɛdʒd
AM ˌənˈflɛdʒd

unfleshed
BR ˌʌnˈflɛʃt
AM ˌənˈflɛʃt

unflexed
BR ˌʌnˈflɛkst
AM ˌənˈflɛkst

unflickering
BR (ˌ)ʌnˈflɪk(ə)rɪŋ
AM ˌənˈflɪk(ə)rɪŋ

unflinching
BR (ˌ)ʌnˈflɪn(t)ʃɪŋ
AM ˌənˈflɪn(t)ʃɪŋ

unflinchingly
BR (ˌ)ʌnˈflɪn(t)ʃɪŋli
AM ˌənˈflɪn(t)ʃɪŋli

unflurried
BR (ˌ)ʌnˈflʌrɪd
AM ˌənˈflərid

unflustered
BR (ˌ)ʌnˈflʌstəd
AM ˌənˈfləstərd

unfocused
BR (ˌ)ʌnˈfəʊkəst
AM ˌənˈfoʊkəst

unfocussed
BR (ˌ)ʌnˈfəʊkəst
AM ˌənˈfoʊkəst

unfold
BR (ˌ)ʌnˈfəʊld, -z, -ɪŋ, -ɨd
AM ˌənˈfoʊld, -z, -ɪŋ, -əd

unfoldment
BR ʌnˈfəʊldm(ə)nt
AM ˌənˈfoʊldmənt

unforced
BR (ˌ)ʌnˈfɔːst
AM ˈənˈfɔ(ə)rst

unforcedly
BR ʌnˈfɔːsɨdli
AM ˌənˈfɔrsədli

unfordable
BR (ˌ)ʌnˈfɔːdəbl
AM ˌənˈfɔrdəbəl

unforecast
BR (ˌ)ʌnˈfɔːkɑːst, (ˌ)ʌnˈfɔːkast
AM ˌənˈfɔrˌkæst

unforeseeable
BR ˌʌnfɔːˈsiːəbl, ˌʌnfəˈsiːəbl
AM ˌənˌfɔrˈsiəbəl, ˌənfərˈsiəbəl

unforeseen
BR ˌʌnfɔːˈsiːn, ˌʌnfəˈsiːn
AM ˌənˌfɔrˈsin, ˌənfərˈsin

unforetold
BR ˌʌnfɔːˈtəʊld, ˌʌnfəˈtəʊld
AM ˌənˌfɔrˈtoʊld, ˌənfərˈtoʊld

unforgettable
BR ˌʌnfəˈgɛtəbl
AM ˌənfərˈgɛdəbəl

unforgettably
BR ˌʌnfəˈgɛtəbli
AM ˌənfərˈgɛdəbli

unforgivable
BR ˌʌnfəˈgɪvəbl
AM ˌənfərˈgɪvəbəl

unforgivably
BR ˌʌnfəˈgɪvəbli
AM ˌənfərˈgɪvəbli

unforgiveable
BR ˌʌnfəˈgɪvəbl
AM ˌənfərˈgɪvəbəl

unforgiveably
BR ˌʌnfəˈgɪvəbli
AM ˌənfərˈgɪvəbli

unforgiven
BR ˌʌnfəˈgɪvn
AM ˌənfərˈgɪvən

unforgiving
BR ˌʌnfəˈgɪvɪŋ
AM ˌənfərˈgɪvɪŋ

unforgivingly
BR ˌʌnfəˈgɪvɪŋli
AM ˌənfərˈgɪvɪŋli

unforgivingness
BR ˌʌnfəˈgɪvɪŋnɨs
AM ˌənfərˈgɪvɪŋnɨs

unforgotten
BR ˌʌnfəˈgɒtn
AM ˌənfərˈgɑtn

unformed
BR ˌʌnˈfɔːmd
AM ˌənˈfɔ(ə)rmd

unformulated
BR (ˌ)ʌnˈfɔːmjʉleɪtɨd
AM ˌənˈfɔrmjəˌleɪdɨd

unforthcoming
BR ˌʌnfɔːθˈkʌmɪŋ
AM ˌənfɔrθˈkəmɪŋ

unfortified
BR ˌʌnˈfɔːtɪfʌɪd
AM ˌənˈfɔrdəˌfaɪd

unfortunate
BR ʌnˈfɔːtʃn̩ət, ʌnˈfɔːtʃ(ə)nət, ʌnˈfɔːtjʉnət
AM ˌənˈfɔrtʃ(ə)nət

unfortunately
BR ʌnˈfɔːtʃn̩ətli, ʌnˈfɔːtʃ(ə)nətli, ʌnˈfɔːtjʉnətli
AM ˌənˈfɔrtʃ(ə)nətli

unfounded
BR (ˌ)ʌnˈfaʊndɨd
AM ˌənˈfaʊndəd

unfoundedly
BR (ˌ)ʌnˈfaʊndɨdli
AM ˌənˈfaʊndədli

unfoundedness
BR (ˌ)ʌnˈfaʊndɨdnɨs
AM ˌənˈfaʊndədnəs

unframed
BR ˌʌnˈfreɪmd
AM ˌənˈfreɪmd

unfree
BR ˌʌnˈfriː
AM ˌənˈfri

unfreedom
BR ˌʌnˈfriːdəm
AM ˌənˈfridəm

unfreeze
BR ˌʌnˈfriːz, -ɪz, -ɪŋ
AM ˌənˈfriz, -ɪz, -ɪŋ

unfrequented
BR ˌʌnfrɪˈkwɛntɨd, ˌʌnfriːˈkwɛntɨd
AM ˌənfriˈkwɛn(t)əd, ˌənˈfriˌkwɛn(t)əd

unfriended
BR ˌʌnˈfrɛndɨd
AM ˌənˈfrɛndəd

unfriendliness
BR (ˌ)ʌnˈfrɛn(d)lɪnɨs
AM ˌənˈfrɛn(d)linɨs

unfriendly
BR (ˌ)ʌnˈfrɛn(d)li
AM ˌənˈfrɛn(d)li

unfrightening
BR ˌʌnˈfrʌɪtn̩ɪŋ, ˌʌnˈfrʌɪtnɪŋ
AM ˌənˈfraɪtn̩ɪŋ, ˌənˈfraɪtnɪŋ

unfrock
BR ˌʌnˈfrɒk, -s, -ɪŋ, -t
AM ˌənˈfrɑk, -s, -ɪŋ, -t

unfroze
BR ˌʌnˈfrəʊz
AM ˌənˈfroʊz

unfrozen
BR ˌʌnˈfrəʊzn
AM ˌənˈfroʊzən

unfruitful
BR (ˌ)ʌnˈfruːtf(ʊ)l
AM ˌənˈfrutfəl

unfruitfully
BR (ˌ)ʌnˈfruːtfʊli, (ˌ)ʌnˈfruːtfl̩i
AM ˌənˈfrutfəli

unfruitfulness
BR (ˌ)ʌnˈfruːtf(ʊ)lnəs
AM ˌənˈfrutfəlnəs

unfuddled
BR ˌʌnˈfʌdld
AM ˌənˈfədld

unfulfillable
BR ˌʌnfʊlˈfɪləbl
AM ˌənfʊ(l)ˈfɪləbəl

unfulfilled
BR ˌʌnfʊlˈfɪld
AM ˌənfʊ(l)ˈfɪld

unfulfilling
BR ˌʌnfʊlˈfɪlɪŋ
AM ˌənfʊ(l)ˈfɪlɪŋ

unfunded
BR (ˌ)ʌnˈfʌndɨd
AM ˌənˈfəndəd

unfunnily
BR ˌʌnˈfʌnɨli
AM ˌənˈfənəli

unfunniness
BR ˌʌnˈfʌnɪnɨs
AM ˌənˈfəninɨs

unfunny
BR ˌʌnˈfʌni
AM ˈənˈfəni

unfurl
BR ˌʌnˈfəːl, -z, -ɪŋ, -d
AM ˌənˈfərl, -z, -ɪŋ, -d

unfurnished
BR (ˌ)ʌnˈfəːnɪʃt
AM ˌənˈfərnɪʃt

unfussily
BR ˌʌnˈfʌsɨli
AM ˌənˈfəsəli

unfussy
BR ˌʌnˈfʌsi
AM ˌənˈfəsi

ungainliness
BR (ˌ)ʌnˈgeɪnlɪnɨs, (ˌ)ʌŋˈgeɪnlɪnɨs
AM ˌənˈgeɪnlinɨs

ungainly
BR (ˌ)ʌnˈgeɪnli, (ˌ)ʌŋˈgeɪnli
AM ˌənˈgeɪnli

ungallant
BR (ˌ)ʌnˈgalənt, (ˌ)ʌnˈgalnt, (ˌ)ʌŋˈgalənt, (ˌ)ʌŋˈgalnt
AM ˌənˈgælənt

ungallantly
BR (ˌ)ʌnˈgaləntli, (ˌ)ʌnˈgalntli, (ˌ)ʌŋˈgaləntli, (ˌ)ʌŋˈgalntli
AM ˌənˈgælən(t)li

ungenerous
BR (ˌ)ʌnˈdʒɛn(ə)rəs
AM ˌənˈdʒɛn(ə)rəs

ungenerously
BR (ˌ)ʌnˈdʒɛn(ə)rəsli
AM ˌənˈdʒɛn(ə)rəsli

ungenerousness
BR (ˌ)ʌn'dʒɛn(ə)rəsnəs
AM ˌən'dʒɛn(ə)rəsnəs

ungenial
BR ˌʌn'dʒiːnɪəl
AM ˌən'dʒiniəl

ungentle
BR ˌʌn'dʒɛntl
AM ˌən'dʒɛn(t)əl

ungentlemanliness
BR ˌʌn'dʒɛntlmənlɪnɨs
AM ˌən'dʒɛn(t)lmənlinɨs

ungentlemanly
BR ˌʌn'dʒɛntlmənli
AM ˌən'dʒɛn(t)lmənli

ungentleness
BR ˌʌn'dʒɛntlnəs
AM ˌən'dʒɛn(t)lnəs

ungently
BR ˌʌn'dʒɛntli
AM ˌən'dʒɛn(t)li

un-get-at-able
BR ˌʌngɛt'atəbl, ˌʌŋgɛt'atəbl
AM ˌənˌgɛd'ædəbəl

ungifted
BR ˌʌn'gɪftɨd, ˌʌŋ'gɪftɨd
AM ˌən'gɪftɨd

ungilded
BR ˌʌn'gɪldɨd, ˌʌŋ'gɪldɨd
AM ˌən'gɪldɨd

ungird
BR ˌʌn'gəːd, ˌʌŋ'gəːd, -z, -ɪŋ, -ɨd
AM ˌən'gərd, -z, -ɪŋ, -əd

unglamorous
BR ˌʌn'glam(ə)rəs, ˌʌŋ'glam(ə)rəs
AM ˌən'glæm(ə)rəs

unglazed
BR ˌʌn'gleɪzd, ˌʌŋ'gleɪzd
AM ˌən'gleɪzd

ungloved
BR ˌʌn'glʌvd, ˌʌŋ'glʌvd
AM ˌən'gləvd

unglued
BR ˌʌn'gluːd, ˌʌŋ'gluːd
AM ˌən'glud

ungodliness
BR (ˌ)ʌn'gɒdlɪnɨs, (ˌ)ʌŋ'gɒdlɪnɨs
AM ˌən'gɑdlinɨs

ungodly
BR (ˌ)ʌn'gɒdli, (ˌ)ʌŋ'gɒdli
AM ˌən'gɑdli

ungovernability
BR ˌʌngʌv(ə)nə'bɪlɨti, ˌʌngʌvn̩ə'bɪlɨti, ʌnˌgʌv(ə)nə'bɪlɨti, ʌnˌgʌvn̩ə'bɪlɨti, ˌʌŋgʌv(ə)nə'bɪlɨti, ˌʌŋgʌvn̩ə'bɪlɨti, ʌŋˌgʌv(ə)nə'bɪlɨti, ʌŋˌgʌvn̩ə'bɪlɨti
AM ˌənˌgəvərnə'bɪlɨdi

ungovernable
BR (ˌ)ʌn'gʌv(ə)nəbl, (ˌ)ʌn'gʌvn̩əbl, (ˌ)ʌŋ'gʌv(ə)nəbl, (ˌ)ʌŋ'gʌvn̩əbl
AM ˌən'gəvərnəbəl

ungovernably
BR (ˌ)ʌn'gʌv(ə)nəbli, (ˌ)ʌn'gʌvn̩əbli, (ˌ)ʌŋ'gʌv(ə)nəbli, (ˌ)ʌŋ'gʌvn̩əbli
AM ˌən'gəvərnəbli

ungoverned
BR (ˌ)ʌn'gʌvnd, (ˌ)ʌŋ'gʌvnd
AM ˌən'gəvərnd

ungraceful
BR (ˌ)ʌn'greɪsf(ʊ)l, (ˌ)ʌŋ'greɪsf(ʊ)l
AM ˌən'greɪsfəl

ungracefully
BR (ˌ)ʌn'greɪsfʊli, (ˌ)ʌn'greɪsfl̩i, (ˌ)ʌŋ'greɪsfʊli, (ˌ)ʌŋ'greɪsfl̩i
AM ˌən'greɪsfəli

ungracefulness
BR (ˌ)ʌn'greɪsf(ʊ)lnəs, (ˌ)ʌŋ'greɪsf(ʊ)lnəs
AM ˌən'greɪsfəlnəs

ungracious
BR (ˌ)ʌn'greɪʃəs, (ˌ)ʌŋ'greɪʃəs
AM ˌən'greɪʃəs

ungraciously
BR (ˌ)ʌn'greɪʃəsli, (ˌ)ʌŋ'greɪʃəsli
AM ˌən'greɪʃəsli

ungraciousness
BR (ˌ)ʌn'greɪʃəsnəs, (ˌ)ʌŋ'greɪʃəsnəs
AM ˌən'greɪʃəsnəs

ungrammatical
BR ˌʌngrə'matɨkl, ˌʌŋgrə'matɨkl
AM ˌəngrə'mædəkəl

ungrammaticality
BR ˌʌngrəˌmatɪ'kalɨti, ˌʌŋgrəˌmatɪ'kalɨti
AM ˌəngrəˌmædə'kælədi

ungrammatically
BR ˌʌngrə'matɨkli, ˌʌŋgrə'matɨkli
AM ˌəngrə'mædək(ə)li

ungrammaticalness
BR ˌʌngrə'matɨklnəs, ˌʌŋgrə'matɨklnəs
AM ˌəngrə'mædəkəlnəs

ungraspable
BR (ˌ)ʌn'grɑːspəbl, (ˌ)ʌn'graspəbl, (ˌ)ʌŋ'grɑːspəbl, (ˌ)ʌŋ'graspəbl
AM ˌən'græspəbəl

ungrateful
BR (ˌ)ʌn'greɪtf(ʊ)l, (ˌ)ʌŋ'greɪtf(ʊ)l
AM ˌən'greɪtfəl

ungratefully
BR (ˌ)ʌn'greɪtfʊli, (ˌ)ʌn'greɪtfl̩i, (ˌ)ʌŋ'greɪtfʊli, (ˌ)ʌŋ'greɪtfl̩i
AM ˌən'greɪtfəli

ungratefulness
BR (ˌ)ʌn'greɪtf(ʊ)lnəs, (ˌ)ʌŋ'greɪtf(ʊ)lnəs
AM ˌən'greɪtfəlnəs

ungreen
BR ˌʌn'griːn, ˌʌŋ'griːn
AM ˌən'grin

ungrounded
BR (ˌ)ʌn'graʊndɨd, (ˌ)ʌŋ'graʊndɨd
AM ˌən'graʊndəd

ungrudging
BR (ˌ)ʌn'grʌdʒɪŋ, (ˌ)ʌŋ'grʌdʒɪŋ
AM ˌən'grədʒɪŋ

ungrudgingly
BR (ˌ)ʌn'grʌdʒɪŋli, (ˌ)ʌŋ'grʌdʒɪŋli
AM ˌən'grədʒɪŋli

ungual
BR 'ʌŋgw(ə)l, 'ʌŋgjʊəl
AM 'əŋgwəl

unguard
BR (ˌ)ʌn'gɑːd, (ˌ)ʌŋ'gɑːd, -z, -ɪŋ, -ɨd
AM ˌən'gɑrd, -z, -ɪŋ, -əd

unguardedly
BR (ˌ)ʌn'gɑːdɨdli, (ˌ)ʌŋ'gɑːdɨdli
AM ˌən'gɑrdədli

unguardedness
BR (ˌ)ʌn'gɑːdɨdnɨs, (ˌ)ʌŋ'gɑːdɨdnɨs
AM ˌən'gɑrdədnəs

unguent
BR 'ʌŋgwənt, 'ʌŋgjʊənt, -s
AM 'əŋgwənt, -s

unguessable
BR (ˌ)ʌn'gɛsəbl, (ˌ)ʌŋ'gɛsəbl
AM ˌən'gɛsəbəl

unguiculate
BR ˌʌn'gwɪkjʊlət, ˌʌŋ'gwɪkjʊlət
AM ˌən'gwɪkjəˌleɪt, ˌən'gwɪkjələt

unguided
BR (ˌ)ʌn'gʌɪdɨd, (ˌ)ʌŋ'gʌɪdɨd
AM ˌən'gaɪdɨd

unguis
BR 'ʌŋgwɪs, -ɪz
AM 'əŋgwɨs, -ɨz

ungula
BR 'ʌŋgjʊlə(r)
AM 'əŋgjələ

ungulae
BR 'ʌŋgjʊliː
AM 'əŋgjəli, 'əŋgjəˌlaɪ

ungulate
BR 'ʌŋgjʊlət, 'ʌŋgjʊleɪt, -s
AM 'əŋgjələt, 'əŋgjəˌleɪt, -s

ungum
BR ˌʌn'gʌm, ˌʌŋ'gʌm, -z, -ɪŋ, -d
AM ˌən'gəm, -z, -ɪŋ, -d

unhallowed
BR (ˌ)ʌn'haləʊd
AM ˌən'hæloʊd

unhampered
BR (ˌ)ʌn'hampəd
AM ˌən'hæmpərd

unhand
BR ˌʌn'hand, -z, -ɪŋ, -ɨd
AM ˌən'hænd, -z, -ɪŋ, -əd

unhandily
BR (ˌ)ʌn'handɨli
AM ˌən'hændəli

unhandiness
BR (ˌ)ʌn'handɪnɨs
AM ˌən'hændinɨs

unhandsome
BR ˌʌn'han(d)s(ə)m
AM ˌən'hæn(d)səm

unhandy
BR ˌʌn'handi
AM ˌən'hændi

unhang
BR ˌʌn'haŋ, -z, -ɪŋ
AM ˌən'hæŋ, -z, -ɪŋ

unhappily
BR (ˌ)ʌn'hapɨli
AM ˌən'hæpəli

unhappiness
BR (ˌ)ʌn'hapɪnɨs
AM ˌən'hæpinɨs

unhappy
BR (ˌ)ʌn'hapi
AM ˌən'hæpi

unharbour
BR ˌʌn'hɑːbə(r), -z, -ɪŋ, -d
AM ˌən'hɑrbər, -z, -ɪŋ, -d

unharmed
BR (ˌ)ʌn'hɑːmd
AM ˌən'hɑrmd

unharmful
BR (ˌ)ʌn'hɑːmf(ʊ)l
AM ˌən'hɑrmfəl

unharmonious
BR ˌʌnhɑː'məʊnɪəs
AM ˌənhɑr'moʊniəs

unharness
BR (ˌ)ʌn'hɑːnɪs, -ɪz, -ɪŋ, -t
AM ˌən'hɑrnəs, -əz, -ɪŋ, -t

unharvested
BR ˌʌn'hɑːvɪstɨd
AM ˌən'hɑrvəstəd

unhasp
BR ˌʌnˈhɑːsp, ˌʌnˈhasp, -s, -ɪŋ, -t
AM ˌənˈhæsp, -s, -ɪŋ, -t

unhatched
BR ˌʌnˈhatʃt
AM ˌənˈhætʃt

UNHCR
BR ˌjuːɛnˌeɪtʃsiːˈɑː(r)
AM ˌjuɛnˌeɪtʃsiˈɑr

unhealed
BR ˌʌnˈhiːld
AM ˌənˈhild

unhealthful
BR (ˌ)ʌnˈhɛlθf(ʊ)l
AM ˌənˈhɛlθfəl

unhealthfulness
BR (ˌ)ʌnˈhɛlθf(ʊ)lnəs
AM ˌənˈhɛlθfəlnəs

unhealthily
BR (ˌ)ʌnˈhɛlθɪli
AM ˌənˈhɛlθəli

unhealthiness
BR (ˌ)ʌnˈhɛlθɪnɪs
AM ˌənˈhɛlθinɪs

unhealthy
BR (ˌ)ʌnˈhɛlθ|i, -ɪə(r), -ɪɪst
AM ˌənˈhɛlθi, -ər, -ɪst

unheard
BR (ˌ)ʌnˈhəːd
AM ˌənˈhərd

unheard-of
BR (ˌ)ʌnˈhəːdɒv
AM ˌənˈhərdəv

unhearing
BR (ˌ)ʌnˈhɪərɪŋ
AM ˌənˈhɪrɪŋ

unheated
BR (ˌ)ʌnˈhiːtɪd
AM ˌənˈhidɪd

unhedged
BR ˌʌnˈhɛdʒd
AM ˌənˈhɛdʒd

unheeded
BR (ˌ)ʌnˈhiːdɪd
AM ˌənˈhidɪd

unheedful
BR (ˌ)ʌnˈhiːdf(ʊ)l
AM ˌənˈhidfəl

unheeding
BR (ˌ)ʌnˈhiːdɪŋ
AM ˌənˈhidɪŋ

unheedingly
BR (ˌ)ʌnˈhiːdɪŋli
AM ˌənˈhidɪŋli

unhelpful
BR ʌnˈhɛlpf(ʊ)l
AM ˌənˈhɛlpfəl

unhelpfully
BR ʌnˈhɛlpfʊli, ʌnˈhɛlpfl̩i
AM ˌənˈhɛlpfəli

unhelpfulness
BR ʌnˈhɛlpf(ʊ)lnəs
AM ˌənˈhɛlpfəlnəs

unheralded
BR (ˌ)ʌnˈhɛrəldɪd, (ˌ)ʌnˈhɛrl̩dɪd
AM ˌənˈhɛrəldəd

unheroic
BR ˌʌnhɪˈrəʊɪk
AM ˌənhəˈroʊɪk

unheroically
BR ˌʌnhɪˈrəʊɪkli
AM ˌənhəˈroʊək(ə)li

unhesitating
BR ʌnˈhɛzɪteɪtɪŋ
AM ˌənˈhɛzəˌteɪdɪŋ

unhesitatingly
BR ʌnˈhɛzɪteɪtɪŋli
AM ˌənˈhɛzəˌteɪdɪŋli

unhesitatingness
BR ʌnˈhɛzɪteɪtɪŋnɪs
AM ˌənˈhɛzəˌteɪdɪŋnɪs

unhidden
BR ʌnˈhɪdn
AM ˌənˈhɪdən

unhindered
BR ʌnˈhɪndəd
AM ˌənˈhɪndərd

unhinge
BR (ˌ)ʌnˈhɪn(d)ʒ, -ɪz, -ɪŋ, -d
AM ˌənˈhɪndʒ, -ɪz, -ɪŋ, -d

unhip
BR ˌʌnˈhɪp
AM ˈənˈhɪp

unhistoric
BR ˌʌnhɪˈstɒrɪk
AM ˌən(h)ɪˈstɔrɪk

unhistorical
BR ˌʌnhɪˈstɒrɪkl
AM ˌən(h)ɪˈstɔrəkəl

unhistorically
BR ˌʌnhɪˈstɒrɪkli
AM ˌən(h)ɪˈstɔrək(ə)li

unhitch
BR (ˌ)ʌnˈhɪtʃ, -ɪz, -ɪŋ, -t
AM ˌənˈhɪtʃ, -ɪz, -ɪŋ, -t

unholiness
BR (ˌ)ʌnˈhəʊlɪnɪs
AM ˌənˈhoʊlinɪs

unholy
BR (ˌ)ʌnˈhəʊli
AM ˌənˈhoʊli

unhonored
BR (ˌ)ʌnˈɒnəd
AM ˌənˈɑnərd

unhonoured
BR (ˌ)ʌnˈɒnəd
AM ˌənˈɑnərd

unhooded
BR (ˌ)ʌnˈhʊdɪd
AM ˌənˈhʊdəd

unhook
BR (ˌ)ʌnˈhʊk, -s, -ɪŋ, -t
AM ˌənˈhʊk, -s, -ɪŋ, -t

unhoped
BR (ˌ)ʌnˈhəʊpt
AM ˌənˈhoʊpt

unhoped-for
BR (ˌ)ʌnˈhəʊptfɔː(r)
AM ˌənˈhoʊp(t)ˌfɔ(ə)r

unhopeful
BR (ˌ)ʌnˈhəʊpf(ʊ)l
AM ˌənˈhoʊpfəl

unhorse
BR (ˌ)ʌnˈhɔːs, -ɪz, -ɪŋ, -t
AM ˌənˈhɔ(ə)rs, -əz, -ɪŋ, -t

unhouse
BR (ˌ)ʌnˈhaʊz, -ɪz, -ɪŋ, -d
AM ˌənˈhaʊz, -əz, -ɪŋ, -d

unhuman
BR ˌʌnˈhjuːmən
AM ˌənˈ(h)jumən

unhung
BR ˌʌnˈhʌŋ
AM ˌənˈhəŋ

unhurried
BR (ˌ)ʌnˈhʌrɪd
AM ˌənˈhərid

unhurriedly
BR (ˌ)ʌnˈhʌrɪdli
AM ˌənˈhəridli

unhurrying
BR (ˌ)ʌnˈhʌrɪɪŋ
AM ˌənˈhəriɪŋ

unhurt
BR (ˌ)ʌnˈhəːt
AM ˌənˈhərt

unhusk
BR ˌʌnˈhʌsk, -s, -ɪŋ, -t
AM ˌənˈhəsk, -s, -ɪŋ, -t

unhygienic
BR ˌʌnhʌɪˈdʒiːnɪk
AM ˌənhaɪˈdʒinɪk, ˌənhaɪˈdʒɛnɪk

unhygienically
BR ˌʌnhʌɪˈdʒiːnɪkli
AM ˌənhaɪˈdʒɛnək(ə)li, ˌənhaɪˈdʒinək(ə)li

unhyphenated
BR (ˌ)ʌnˈhʌɪfɪneɪtɪd
AM ˌənˈhaɪfəˌneɪdɪd

uni
BR ˈjuːn|i, -ɪz
AM ˈjuni, -z

Uniat
BR ˈjuːnɪat
AM ˈjuniˌæt, ˈjuniɪt, ˈjuniˌeɪt

Uniate
BR ˈjuːnɪət, ˈjuːnɪeɪt, -s
AM ˈjuniˌæt, ˈjuniɪt, ˈjuniˌeɪt, -s

uniaxial
BR ˌjuːnɪˈaksɪəl
AM ˌjuniˈæksiəl

uniaxially
BR ˌjuːnɪˈaksɪəli
AM ˌjuniˈæksiəli

unicameral
BR ˌjuːnɪˈkam(ə)rəl, ˌjuːnɪˈkam(ə)rl̩
AM ˌjunəˈkæm(ə)rəl

UNICEF
BR ˈjuːnɪsɛf
AM ˈjunəˌsɛf

unicellular
BR ˌjuːnɪˈsɛljʊlə(r)
AM ˌjunəˈsɛljələr

unicolor
BR ˌjuːnɪˈkʌlə(r), -d
AM ˈjunəˌkələr, -d

unicolour
BR ˌjuːnɪˈkʌlə(r), -d
AM ˈjunəˌkələr, -d

unicorn
BR ˈjuːnɪkɔːn, -z
AM ˈjunəˌkɔ(ə)rn, -z

unicuspid
BR ˌjuːnɪˈkʌspɪd, -z
AM ˌjunəˈkəspəd, -z

unicycle
BR ˈjuːnɪˌsʌɪkl, -z
AM ˈjunəˌsaɪkəl, -z

unicyclist
BR ˈjuːnɪˌsʌɪklɪst, -s
AM ˈjunəˌsaɪklɪst, -s

unidea'd
BR ˌʌnʌɪˈdɪəd
AM ˌənaɪˈdiəd

unideal
BR ˌʌnʌɪˈdɪəl, ˌʌnʌɪˈdiːəl
AM ˌənaɪˈdiəl

unidentifiable
BR ˌʌnʌɪˈdɛntɪfʌɪəbl
AM ˌənaɪˈdɛn(t)əˌfaɪəbəl

unidentified
BR ˌʌnʌɪˈdɛntɪfʌɪd
AM ˌənaɪˈdɛn(t)əˌfaɪd

unidimensional
BR ˌjuːnɪdʌɪˈmɛnʃn̩(ə)l, ˌjuːnɪdʌɪˈmɛnʃən(ə)l, ˌjuːnɪdɪˈmɛnʃn̩(ə)l, ˌjuːnɪdɪˈmɛnʃən(ə)l
AM ˌjunədəˈmɛn(t)ʃ(ə)nəl

unidiomatic
BR ˌʌnɪdɪəˈmatɪk
AM ˌənɪdiəˈmædɪk

unidirectional
BR ˌjuːnɪdʌɪˈrɛkʃn̩(ə)l, ˌjuːnɪdʌɪˈrɛkʃən(ə)l, ˌjuːnɪdɪˈrɛkʃn̩(ə)l, ˌjuːnɪdɪˈrɛkʃən(ə)l
AM ˌjunədəˈrɛkʃ(ə)nəl, ˌjunədaɪˈrɛkʃ(ə)nəl

unidirectionality
BR ˌjuːnɪdʌɪˌrɛkʃəˈnalɪti, ˌjuːnɪdɪˌrɛkʃəˈnalɪti
AM ˌjunədəˌrɛkʃəˈnælədi, ˌjunədaɪˌrɛkʃəˈnælədi

unidirectionally
BR ˌjuːnɪdʌɪˈrɛkʃn̩əli, ˌjuːnɪdʌɪˈrɛkʃn̩l̩i, ˌjuːnɪdʌɪˈrɛkʃənl̩i, ˌjuːnɪdʌɪˈrɛkʃ(ə)nəli, ˌjuːnɪdɪˈrɛkʃn̩əli, ˌjuːnɪdɪˈrɛkʃn̩l̩i, ˌjuːnɪdɪˈrɛkʃənl̩i, ˌjuːnɪdɪˈrɛkʃ(ə)nəli
AM ˌjunədəˈrɛkʃ(ə)nəli, ˌjunədaɪˈrɛkʃ(ə)nəli

UNIDO
BR 'juːnɪdəʊ
AM 'junəˌdoʊ

unifiable
BR 'juːnɪfʌɪəbl
AM ˌjunə'faɪəbəl

unification
BR ˌjuːnɪfɪ'keɪʃn
AM ˌjunəfə'keɪʃən

unificatory
BR ˌjuːnɪfɪ'keɪt(ə)ri, ˌjuːnɪ'fɪkət(ə)ri
AM ˌjunə'fɪkəˌtɔri

unifier
BR 'juːnɪfʌɪə(r), -z
AM 'junəˌfaɪər, -z

uniflow
BR 'juːnɪfləʊ
AM 'junəˌfloʊ

uniform
BR 'juːnɪfɔːm, -z
AM 'junəˌfɔ(ə)rm, -z

uniformitarian
BR ˌjuːnɪˌfɔːmɪ'tɛːrɪən, -z
AM ˌjunəˌfɔrmə'tɛriən, -z

uniformitarianism
BR ˌjuːnɪˌfɔːmɪ'tɛːrɪən-ɪz(ə)m
AM ˌjunəˌfɔrmə'tɛriən-ˌɪzəm

uniformity
BR ˌjuːnɪ'fɔːmɪti
AM ˌjunə'fɔrmədi

uniformly
BR 'juːnɪfɔːmli
AM 'junə'fɔrmli

unify
BR 'juːnɪfʌɪ, -z, -ɪŋ, -d
AM 'junəˌfaɪ, -z, -ɪŋ, -d

Unigate®
BR 'juːnɪgeɪt
AM 'junəˌgeɪt

unilateral
BR ˌjuːnɪ'lat(ə)rəl, ˌjuːnɪ'lat(ə)rl̩
AM ˌjunə'lædərəl

unilateralism
BR ˌjuːnɪ'lat(ə)rəl-ɪz(ə)m, ˌjuːnɪ'lat(ə)rl̩ɪz(ə)m
AM ˌjunə'lædərəˌlɪzəm

unilateralist
BR ˌjuːnɪ'lat(ə)rəlɪst, ˌjuːnɪ'lat(ə)rl̩ɪst, -s
AM ˌjunə'lædərələst, -s

unilaterally
BR ˌjuːnɪ'lat(ə)rəli, ˌjuːnɪ'lat(ə)rl̩i
AM ˌjunə'lædərəli

Unilever®
BR 'juːnɪˌliːvə(r)
AM 'junəˌlivər

unilingual
BR ˌjuːnɪ'lɪŋgw(ə)l
AM ˌjunə'lɪŋgwəl

unilingually
BR ˌjuːnɪ'lɪŋgwəli, ˌjuːnɪ'lɪŋgwl̩i
AM ˌjunə'lɪŋgwəli

uniliteral
BR ˌjuːnɪ'lɪt(ə)rəl, ˌjuːnɪ'lɪt(ə)rl̩
AM ˌjunə'lɪdərəl

unilluminated
BR ˌʌnɪ'l(j)uːmɪneɪtɪd
AM ˌənə'luməˌneɪdɪd

unilluminating
BR ˌʌnɪ'l(j)uːmɪneɪtɪŋ
AM ˌənə'luməˌneɪdɪŋ

unillustrated
BR (ˌ)ʌn'ɪləstreɪtɪd
AM ˌən'ɪləˌstreɪdɪd

unilocular
BR ˌjuːnɪ'lɒkjʉlə(r)
AM ˌjunə'lɑkjələr

unimaginable
BR ˌʌnɪ'madʒɪnəbl, ˌʌnɪ'madʒnəbl
AM ˌənə'mædʒ(ə)nəbəl

unimaginably
BR ˌʌnɪ'madʒɪnəbli, ˌʌnɪ'madʒnəbl
AM ˌənə'mædʒ(ə)nəbli

unimaginative
BR ˌʌnɪ'madʒɪnətɪv, ˌʌnɪ'madʒnətɪv
AM ˌənə'mædʒ(ə)nədɪv

unimaginatively
BR ˌʌnɪ'madʒɪnətɪvli, ˌʌnɪ'madʒnətɪvli
AM ˌənə'mædʒ(ə)nə-dɪvli

unimaginativeness
BR ˌʌnɪ'madʒɪnətɪvnɪs, ˌʌnɪ'madʒnətɪvnɪs
AM ˌənə'mædʒ(ə)nədɪv-nɪs

unimagined
BR ˌʌnɪ'madʒ(ɪ)nd
AM ˌənə'mædʒənd

unimpaired
BR ˌʌnɪm'pɛːd
AM ˌənəm'pɛ(ə)rd

unimparted
BR ˌʌnɪm'pɑːtɪd
AM ˌənəm'pɑrdəd

unimpassioned
BR ˌʌnɪm'paʃnd
AM ˌənəm'pæʃənd

unimpeachable
BR ˌʌnɪm'piːtʃəbl
AM ˌənəm'pitʃəbəl

unimpeachably
BR ˌʌnɪm'piːtʃəbli
AM ˌənəm'pitʃəbli

unimpeded
BR ˌʌnɪm'piːdɪd
AM ˌənəm'pidɪd

unimpededly
BR ˌʌnɪm'piːdɪdli
AM ˌənəm'pidɪdli

unimportance
BR ˌʌnɪm'pɔːt(ə)ns
AM ˌənəm'pɔrtns

unimportant
BR ˌʌnɪm'pɔːt(ə)nt
AM ˌənəm'pɔrtnt

unimposing
BR ˌʌnɪm'pəʊzɪŋ
AM ˌənəm'poʊzɪŋ

unimposingly
BR ˌʌnɪm'pəʊzɪŋli
AM ˌənəm'poʊzɪŋli

unimpressed
BR ˌʌnɪm'prɛst
AM ˌənəm'prɛst

unimpressionable
BR ˌʌnɪm'prɛʃ(ə)nəbl, ˌʌnɪm'prɛʃnəbl
AM ˌənəm'prɛʃ(ə)nəbəl

unimpressive
BR ˌʌnɪm'prɛsɪv
AM ˌənəm'prɛsɪv

unimpressively
BR ˌʌnɪm'prɛsɪvli
AM ˌənəm'prɛsɪvli

unimpressiveness
BR ˌʌnɪm'prɛsɪvnɪs
AM ˌənəm'prɛsɪvnɪs

unimproved
BR ˌʌnɪm'pruːvd
AM ˌənəm'pruvd

unimpugned
BR ˌʌnɪm'pjuːnd
AM ˌənəm'pjund

unincorporated
BR ˌʌnɪn'kɔːpəreɪtɪd
AM ˌənən'kɔrpəˌreɪdɪd, ˌənɪŋ'kɔrpəˌreɪdɪd

unindexed
BR ˌʌn'ɪndɛkst
AM ˌən'ɪnˌdɛkst

uninfected
BR ˌʌnɪn'fɛktɪd
AM ˌənən'fɛktəd

uninflamed
BR ˌʌnɪn'fleɪmd
AM ˌənən'fleɪmd

uninflammable
BR ˌʌnɪn'flaməbl
AM ˌənən'flæməbəl

uninflected
BR ˌʌnɪn'flɛktɪd
AM ˌənən'flɛktəd

uninfluenced
BR (ˌ)ʌn'ɪnflʊənst
AM ˌən'ɪnˌflʊənst

uninfluential
BR ˌʌnɪnflʊ'ɛnʃl
AM ˌənənˌflʊ'ɛn(t)ʃəl

uninformative
BR ˌʌnɪn'fɔːmətɪv
AM ˌənən'fɔrmədɪv

uninformed
BR ˌʌnɪn'fɔːmd
AM ˌənən'fɔ(ə)rmd

uninhabitable
BR ˌʌnɪn'habɪtəbl
AM ˌənən'hæbədəbəl

uninhabitableness
BR ˌʌnɪn'habɪtəbln-nəs
AM ˌənən'hæbədəbəlnəs

uninhabited
BR ˌʌnɪn'habɪtɪd
AM ˌənən'hæbədəd

uninhibited
BR ˌʌnɪn'hɪbɪtɪd
AM ˌənən'hɪbɪdɪd

uninhibitedly
BR ˌʌnɪn'hɪbɪtɪdli
AM ˌənən'hɪbɪdɪdli

uninhibitedness
BR ˌʌnɪn'hɪbɪtɪdnɪs
AM ˌənən'hɪbɪdɪdnɪs

uninitiated
BR ˌʌnɪ'nɪʃɪeɪtɪd
AM ˌənə'nɪʃiˌeɪdɪd

uninjured
BR (ˌ)ʌn'ɪn(d)ʒəd
AM ˌən'ɪndʒərd

uninspired
BR ˌʌnɪn'spʌɪəd
AM ˌənən'spaɪ(ə)rd

uninspiring
BR ˌʌnɪn'spʌɪərɪŋ
AM ˌənən'spaɪ(ə)rɪŋ

uninspiringly
BR ˌʌnɪn'spʌɪərɪŋli
AM ˌənən'spaɪ(ə)rɪŋli

uninstructed
BR ˌʌnɪn'strʌktɪd
AM ˌənən'strəktəd

uninsulated
BR (ˌ)ʌn'ɪnsjʉleɪtɪd
AM ˌən'ɪns(j)əˌleɪdɪd

uninsurable
BR ˌʌnɪn'ʃʊərəbl, ˌʌnɪn'ʃɔːrəbl
AM ˌənən'ʃʊrəbəl

uninsured
BR ˌʌnɪn'ʃʊəd, ˌʌnɪn'ʃɔːd
AM ˌənən'ʃʊ(ə)rd

unintegrated
BR (ˌ)ʌn'ɪntɪgreɪtɪd
AM ˌən'ɪn(t)əˌgreɪdɪd

unintellectual
BR ˌʌnɪntɪ'lɛktʃʊəl, ˌʌnɪntɪ'lɛktʃ(ʉ)l, ˌʌnɪntɪ'lɛktjʊəl, ˌʌnɪntɪ'lɛktjʉl
AM ˌənˌɪn(t)ə'lɛk(t)ʃ(əw)əl

unintelligent
BR ˌʌnɪn'tɛlɪdʒ(ə)nt
AM ˌənən'tɛlədʒənt

unintelligently
BR ˌʌnɪn'tɛlɪdʒ(ə)ntli
AM ˌənən'tɛlədʒən(t)li

unintelligibility
BR ˌʌnɪnˌtɛlɪdʒɪ'bɪlɪti
AM ˌənənˌtɛlədʒə'bɪlɪdi

unintelligible
BR ˌʌnɪn'tɛlɪdʒɪbl
AM ˌənən'tɛlədʒəbəl

unintelligibleness
BR ˌʌnɪnˈtɛlᵻdʒɪblnəs
AM ˌənənˈtɛlədʒəbəlnəs

unintelligibly
BR ˌʌnɪnˈtɛlᵻdʒɪbli
AM ˌənənˈtɛlədʒəbli

unintended
BR ˌʌnɪnˈtɛndᵻd
AM ˌənənˈtɛndəd

unintentional
BR ˌʌnɪnˈtɛnʃn̩(ə)l, ˌʌnɪnˈtɛnʃən(ə)l
AM ˌənənˈtɛn(t)ʃ(ə)nəl

unintentionally
BR ˌʌnɪnˈtɛnʃn̩əli, ˌʌnɪnˈtɛnʃn̩li, ˌʌnɪnˈtɛnʃənli, ˌʌnɪnˈtɛnʃ(ə)nəli
AM ˌənənˈtɛn(t)ʃ(ə)nəli

uninterested
BR (ˌ)ʌnˈɪntrɪstᵻd, (ˌ)ʌnˈɪnt(ə)rɛstᵻd
AM ˌənˈɪntrəstəd, ˌənˈɪn(t)ərəstəd, ˌənˈɪn(t)əˌrɛstəd

uninterestedly
BR (ˌ)ʌnˈɪntrɪstᵻdli, (ˌ)ʌnˈɪnt(ə)rɛstᵻdli
AM ˌənˈɪntrəstədli, ˌənˈɪn(t)ərəstədli, ˌənˈɪn(t)əˌrɛstədli

uninterestedness
BR (ˌ)ʌnˈɪntrɪstᵻdnᵻs, (ˌ)ʌnˈɪnt(ə)rɛstᵻdnᵻs
AM ˌənˈɪntrəstədnəs, ˌənˈɪn(t)ərəstədnəs, ˌənˈɪn(t)əˌrɛstədnəs

uninteresting
BR (ˌ)ʌnˈɪntrɪstɪŋ, (ˌ)ʌnˈɪnt(ə)rɛstɪŋ
AM ˌənˈɪntrəstɪŋ, ˌənˈɪn(t)ərəstɪŋ, ˌənˈɪn(t)əˌrɛstɪŋ

uninterestingly
BR (ˌ)ʌnˈɪntrɪstɪŋli, (ˌ)ʌnˈɪnt(ə)rɛstɪŋli
AM ˌənˈɪntrəstɪŋli, ˌənˈɪn(t)ərəstɪŋli, ˌənˈɪn(t)əˌrɛstɪŋli

uninterestingness
BR (ˌ)ʌnˈɪntrɪstɪŋnᵻs, (ˌ)ʌnˈɪnt(ə)rɛstɪŋnᵻs
AM ˌənˈɪntrəstɪŋnᵻs, ˌənˈɪn(t)ərəstɪŋnᵻs, ˌənˈɪn(t)əˌrɛstɪŋnᵻs

uninterpretable
BR ˌʌnɪnˈtəːprɪtəbl
AM ˌənənˈtərprədəbəl

uninterpreted
BR ˌʌnɪnˈtəːprɪtᵻd
AM ˌənənˈtərprədəd

uninterrupted
BR ˌʌnɪntəˈrʌptᵻd
AM ˌənˌɪn(t)əˈrəptəd

uninterruptedly
BR ˌʌnɪntəˈrʌptᵻdli
AM ˌənˌɪn(t)əˈrəptədli

uninterruptedness
BR ˌʌnɪntəˈrʌptᵻdnᵻs
AM ˌənˌɪn(t)əˈrəptədnəs

uninterruptible
BR ˌʌnɪntəˈrʌptᵻbl
AM ˌənˌɪn(t)əˈrəptəbəl

unintimidated
BR ˌʌnɪnˈtɪmᵻdeɪtᵻd
AM ˌənənˈtɪməˌdeɪdᵻd

uninucleate
BR ˌjuːnɪˈnjuːklɪeɪt
AM ˌjunəˈn(j)ukliᵻt

uninvented
BR ˌʌnɪnˈvɛntᵻd
AM ˌənənˈvɛn(t)əd

uninventive
BR ˌʌnɪnˈvɛntɪv
AM ˌənənˈvɛn(t)ɪv

uninventively
BR ˌʌnɪnˈvɛntᵻvli
AM ˌənənˈvɛn(t)ᵻvli

uninventiveness
BR ˌʌnɪnˈvɛntᵻvnᵻs
AM ˌənənˈvɛn(t)ɪvnᵻs

uninvested
BR ˌʌnɪnˈvɛstᵻd
AM ˌənənˈvɛstəd

uninvestigated
BR ˌʌnɪnˈvɛstᵻgeɪtᵻd
AM ˌənənˈvɛstəˌgeɪdᵻd

uninvited
BR ˌʌnɪnˈvʌɪtᵻd
AM ˌənənˈvaɪdᵻd

uninvitedly
BR ˌʌnɪnˈvʌɪtᵻdli
AM ˌənənˈvaɪdᵻdli

uninviting
BR ˌʌnɪnˈvʌɪtɪŋ
AM ˌənənˈvaɪdɪŋ

uninvitingly
BR ˌʌnɪnˈvʌɪtɪŋli
AM ˌənənˈvaɪdɪŋli

uninvoked
BR ʌnɪnˈvəʊkt
AM ˌənənˈvoʊkt

uninvolved
BR ˌʌnɪnˈvɒlvd
AM ˌənənˈvɑlvd

union
BR ˈjuːnɪən, -z
AM ˈjunjən, -z

union-bashing
BR ˈjuːnɪənˌbaʃɪŋ
AM ˈjunjənˌbæʃɪŋ

unionisation
BR ˌjuːnɪənʌɪˈzeɪʃn
AM ˌjunjənəˈzeɪʃən, ˌjunjəˌnaɪˈzeɪʃən

unionise
BR ˈjuːnɪənʌɪz, -ᵻz, -ɪŋ, -d
AM ˈjunjəˌnaɪz, -ᵻz, -ɪŋ, -d

un-ionised
BR ʌnˈʌɪənʌɪzd
AM ˌənˈaɪəˌnaɪzd

unionism
BR ˈjuːnɪənɪz(ə)m
AM ˈjunjəˌnɪzəm

unionist
BR ˈjuːnɪənɪst, -s
AM ˈjunjənəst, -s

unionistic
BR ˌjuːnɪəˈnɪstɪk
AM ˌjunjəˈnɪstɪk

unionization
BR ˌjuːnɪənʌɪˈzeɪʃn
AM ˌjunjənəˈzeɪʃən, ˌjunjəˌnaɪˈzeɪʃən

unionize
BR ˈjuːnɪənʌɪz, -ᵻz, -ɪŋ, -d
AM ˈjunjəˌnaɪz, -ᵻz, -ɪŋ, -d

un-ionized
BR ˌʌnˈʌɪənʌɪzd
AM ˌənˈaɪəˌnaɪzd

Union Jack
BR ˌjuːnɪən ˈdʒak, -s
AM ˈjunjən ˈdʒæk, -s

uniparous
BR juːˈnɪp(ə)rəs
AM juˈnɪp(ə)rəs

Unipart
BR ˈjuːnɪpɑːt
AM ˈjunəˌpɑrt

unipartite
BR ˌjuːnɪˈpɑːtʌɪt
AM ˌjunəˈpɑrˌtaɪt

uniped
BR ˈjuːnɪpɛd, -z
AM ˈjunəˌpɛd, -z

unipersonal
BR ˌjuːnɪˈpəːsn̩(ə)l
AM ˌjunəˈpərs(ə)nəl

uniplanar
BR ˌjuːnɪˈpleɪnə(r)
AM ˌjunəˈpleɪnər

unipod
BR ˈjuːnɪpɒd, -z
AM ˈjunəˌpɑd, -z

unipolar
BR ˌjuːnɪˈpəʊlə(r)
AM ˌjunəˈpoʊlər

unipolarity
BR ˌjuːnɪpə(ʊ)ˈlarᵻti
AM ˌjunəpəˈlɛrədi, ˌjunəˌpoʊˈlɛrədi

unique
BR juːˈniːk, jᵿˈniːk
AM juˈnik

uniquely
BR juːˈniːkli, jᵿˈniːkli
AM juˈnikli

uniqueness
BR juːˈniːknᵻs, jᵿˈniːknᵻs
AM juˈniknᵻs

unironed
BR (ˌ)ʌnˈʌɪənd
AM ˌənˈaɪ(ə)rnd

Uniroyal®
BR ˈjuːnɪˌrɔɪəl
AM ˈjunəˌrɔɪəl

uniserial
BR ˌjuːnɪˈsɪərɪəl
AM ˌjunɪˈsɪriəl

unisex
BR ˈjuːnɪsɛks
AM ˈjunəˌsɛks

unisexual
BR ˌjuːnɪˈsɛkʃʊəl, ˌjuːnɪˈsɛkʃ(ᵿ)l, ˌjuːnɪˈsɛksjʊ(ə)l
AM ˌjunəˈsɛkʃ(əw)əl

unisexuality
BR ˌjuːnɪˌsɛkʃʊˈalᵻti, ˌjuːnɪˌsɛksjʊˈalᵻti
AM ˌjunəˌsɛkʃəˈwælədi

unisexually
BR ˌjuːnɪˈsɛkʃʊəli, ˌjuːnɪˈsɛkʃᵿli, ˌjuːnɪˈsɛkʃl̩i, ˌjuːnɪˈsɛksjʊ(ə)li
AM ˌjunəˈsɛkʃ(əw)əli

UNISON
BR ˈjuːnᵻs(ə)n, ˈjuːnᵻz(ə)n
AM ˈjunəs(ə)n, ˈjunəz(ə)n

unison
BR ˈjuːnᵻs(ə)n, ˈjuːnᵻz(ə)n
AM ˈjunəs(ə)n, ˈjunəz(ə)n

unisonant
BR juːˈnɪsənənt, juːˈnɪsn̩ənt, jᵿˈnɪsənənt, jᵿˈnɪsn̩ənt
AM juˈnɪsənənt

unisonous
BR juːˈnɪsənəs, juːˈnɪsn̩əs, jᵿˈnɪsənəs, jᵿˈnɪsn̩əs
AM juˈnɪsənəs

unissued
BR (ˌ)ʌnˈɪʃ(j)uːd, (ˌ)ʌnˈɪsjuːd
AM ˌənˈɪʃ(j)ud

unit
BR ˈjuːnɪt, -s
AM ˈjunət, -s

UNITA
BR juːˈniːtə(*r*), jᵿˈniːtə(*r*)
AM juˈnidɑ

UNITAR
BR juːˈniːtɑː(r), jᵿˈniːtɑː(r), ˈjuːnɪtɑː(r)
AM ˈjunəˌtɑr

Unitarian
BR ˌjuːnᵻˈtɛːrɪən, -z
AM ˌjunəˈtɛriən, -z

Unitarianism
BR ˌjuːnᵻˈtɛːrɪənɪz(ə)m
AM ˌjunəˈtɛriəˌnɪzəm

unitarily
BR ˈjuːnᵻt(ə)rᵻli
AM ˈjunəˌtɛrəli

unitarity
BR ˌjuːnɪˈtarɪti
AM ˌjunəˈtɛrədi

unitary
BR ˈjuːnɪt(ə)ri
AM ˈjunəˌtɛri

unite
BR juːˈnʌɪt, jʊˈnʌɪt, -s, -ɪŋ, -ɪd
AM juˈnaɪ|t, -ts, -dɪŋ, -dɪd

unitedly
BR juːˈnʌɪtɪdli, jʊˈnʌɪtɪdli
AM juˈnaɪdɪdli

United Nations
BR jʊˌnʌɪtɪd ˈneɪʃnz
AM juˌnaɪdɪd ˈneɪʃənz

United States
BR jʊˌnʌɪtɪd ˈsteɪts
AM juˌnaɪdɪd ˈsteɪts

unitholder
BR ˈjuːnɪtˌhəʊldə(r), -z
AM ˈjunətˌ(h)oʊldər, -z

unitive
BR ˈjuːnɪtɪv
AM ˈjunədɪv

unitively
BR ˈjuːnɪtɪvli
AM ˈjunədɪvli

unitize
BR ˈjuːnɪtʌɪz, -ɪz, -ɪŋ, -d
AM ˈjunəˌtaɪz, -ɪz, -ɪŋ, -d

unit-linked
BR ˌjuːnɪtˈlɪŋ(k)t
AM ˈjunətˌlɪŋkt

unit trust
BR ˌjuːnɪt ˈtrʌst, -s
AM ˈjunə(t) ˌtrəst, -s

unity
BR ˈjuːnɪt|i, -ɪz
AM ˈjunədi, -z

Univac
BR ˈjuːnɪvak
AM ˈjunəˌvæk

univalent
BR ˌjuːnɪˈveɪlənt, ˌjuːnɪˈveɪln̩t, -s
AM ˌjunəˈveɪlənt, -s

univalve
BR ˈjuːnɪvalv, -z
AM ˈjunəˌvælv, -z

universal
BR ˌjuːnɪˈvəːsl
AM ˌjunəˈvərsəl

universalisability
BR ˌjuːnɪvəːsəlʌɪzəˈbɪlɪti, ˌjuːnɪvəːsl̩ʌɪzəˈbɪlɪti
AM ˌjunəˌvərsəˌlaɪzəˈbɪlɪdi

universalisation
BR ˌjuːnɪvəːsəlʌɪˈzeɪʃn, ˌjuːnɪvəːsl̩ʌɪˈzeɪʃn
AM ˌjunəˌvərsələˈzeɪʃən, ˌjunəˌvərsəˌlaɪˈzeɪʃən

universalise
BR ˌjuːnɪˈvəːsəlʌɪz, ˌjuːnɪˈvəːsl̩ʌɪz, -ɪz, -ɪŋ, -d
AM ˌjunəˈvərsəˌlaɪz, -ɪz, -ɪŋ, -d

universalism
BR ˌjuːnɪˈvəːsəlɪz(ə)m, ˌjuːnɪˈvəːsl̩ɪz(ə)m
AM ˌjunəˈvərsəˌlɪzəm

universalist
BR ˌjuːnɪˈvəːsəlɪst, ˌjuːnɪˈvəːsl̩ɪst, -s
AM ˌjunəˈvərsələst, -s

universalistic
BR ˌjuːnɪˌvəːsəˈlɪstɪk, ˌjuːnɪˌvəːsl̩ˈɪstɪk
AM ˌjunəˌvərsəˈlɪstɪk

universality
BR ˌjuːnɪvəːˈsalɪti
AM ˌjunəvərˈsælədi

universalizability
BR ˌjuːnɪvəːsəlʌɪzəˈbɪlɪti, ˌjuːnɪvəːsl̩ʌɪzəˈbɪlɪti
AM ˌjunəˌvərsəˌlaɪzəˈbɪlɪdi

universalization
BR ˌjuːnɪvəːsəlʌɪˈzeɪʃn, ˌjuːnɪvəːsl̩ʌɪˈzeɪʃn
AM ˌjunəˌvərsələˈzeɪʃən, ˌjunəˌvərsəˌlaɪˈzeɪʃən

universalize
BR ˌjuːnɪˈvəːsəlʌɪz, ˌjuːnɪˈvəːsl̩ʌɪz, -ɪz, -ɪŋ, -d
AM ˌjunəˈvərsəˌlaɪz, -ɪz, -ɪŋ, -d

universally
BR ˌjuːnɪˈvəːsl̩i, ˌjuːnɪˈvəːsəli
AM ˌjunəˈvərsəli

universe
BR ˈjuːnɪvəːs, -ɪz
AM ˈjunəvərs, -əz

university
BR ˌjuːnɪˈvəːsɪt|i, -ɪz
AM ˌjunəˈvərsədi, -z

univocal
BR ˌjuːnɪˈvəʊkl
AM ˌjunəˈvoʊkəl

univocality
BR ˌjuːnɪvəʊˈkalɪti
AM ˌjunəˌvoʊˈkælədi

univocally
BR ˌjuːnɪˈvəʊkl̩i, ˌjuːnɪˈvəʊkəli
AM ˌjunəˈvoʊkəli

UNIX®
BR ˈjuːnɪks
AM ˈjunɪks

unjaundiced
BR ˌʌnˈdʒɔːndɪst
AM ˌənˈdʒɔndəst, ˌənˈdʒɑndəst

unjoin
BR ˌʌnˈdʒɔɪn, -z, -ɪŋ, -d
AM ˌənˈdʒɔɪn, -z, -ɪŋ, -d

unjoint
BR ˌʌnˈdʒɔɪnt, -s, -ɪŋ, -ɪd
AM ˌənˈdʒɔɪn|t, -ts, -(t)ɪŋ, -(t)ɪd

unjust
BR ˌʌnˈdʒʌst
AM ˌənˈdʒəst

unjustifiable
BR (ˌ)ʌnˈdʒʌstɪfʌɪəbl, ˌʌndʒʌstɪˈfʌɪəbl
AM ˌənˌdʒəstəˈfaɪəbəl

unjustifiably
BR (ˌ)ʌnˈdʒʌstɪfʌɪəbli, ˌʌndʒʌstɪˈfʌɪəbli
AM ˌənˌdʒəstəˈfaɪəbli

unjustified
BR (ˌ)ʌnˈdʒʌstɪfʌɪd
AM ˌənˈdʒəstəˌfaɪd

unjustly
BR ˌʌnˈdʒʌstli
AM ˌənˈdʒəs(t)li

unjustness
BR ˌʌnˈdʒʌs(t)nəs
AM ˌənˈdʒəs(t)nəs

unkempt
BR ˌʌnˈkɛm(p)t
AM ˌənˈkɛm(p)t

unkemptly
BR ˌʌnˈkɛm(p)tli
AM ˌənˈkɛm(p)tli

unkemptness
BR ˌʌnˈkɛm(p)tnəs
AM ˌənˈkɛm(p)tnəs

unkept
BR ˌʌnˈkɛpt
AM ˌənˈkɛpt

unkillable
BR ˌʌnˈkɪləbl
AM ˌənˈkɪləbəl

unkind
BR ˌʌnˈkʌɪnd, -ə(r), -ɪst
AM ˌənˈkaɪnd, -ər, -ɪst

unkindly
BR ˌʌnˈkʌɪndli
AM ˌənˈkaɪn(d)li

unkindness
BR ˌʌnˈkʌɪn(d)nɪs
AM ˌənˈkaɪn(d)nɪs

unking
BR ˌʌnˈkɪŋ, -z, -ɪŋ, -d
AM ˌənˈkɪŋ, -z, -ɪŋ, -d

unkink
BR ˌʌnˈkɪŋ|k, -ks, -kɪŋ, -(k)t
AM ˌənˈkɪŋ|k, -ks, -kɪŋ, -(k)t

unkissed
BR ˌʌnˈkɪst
AM ˌənˈkɪst

unknit
BR ˌʌnˈnɪt, -s, -ɪŋ, -ɪd
AM ˌənˈnɪ|t, -ts, -dɪŋ, -dɪd

unknot
BR ˌʌnˈnɒt, -s, -ɪŋ, -ɪd
AM ˌənˈnɑ|t, -ts, -dɪŋ, -dəd

unknowable
BR (ˌ)ʌnˈnəʊəbl
AM ˌənˈnoʊəbəl

unknowing
BR (ˌ)ʌnˈnəʊɪŋ
AM ˌənˈnoʊɪŋ

unknowingly
BR (ˌ)ʌnˈnəʊɪŋli
AM ˌənˈnoʊɪŋli

unknowingness
BR (ˌ)ʌnˈnəʊɪŋnɪs
AM ˌənˈnoʊɪŋnɪs

unknown
BR (ˌ)ʌnˈnəʊn
AM ˌənˈnoʊn

unknownness
BR (ˌ)ʌnˈnəʊnnəs
AM ˌənˈnoʊ(n)nəs

unlabelled
BR ˌʌnˈleɪbld
AM ˌənˈleɪbəld

unlaboured
BR ˌʌnˈleɪbəd
AM ˌənˈleɪbərd

unlace
BR ˌʌnˈleɪs, -ɪz, -ɪŋ, -t
AM ˌənˈleɪs, -ɪz, -ɪŋ, -t

unlade
BR ˌʌnˈleɪd, -z, -ɪŋ, -ɪd
AM ˌənˈleɪd, -z, -ɪŋ, -ɪd

unladen
BR ˌʌnˈleɪdn
AM ˌənˈleɪdn

unladylike
BR ˌʌnˈleɪdɪlʌɪk
AM ˌənˈleɪdiˌlaɪk

unlaid
BR ˌʌnˈleɪd
AM ˌənˈleɪd

unlamented
BR ˌʌnləˈmɛntɪd
AM ˌənləˈmɛn(t)əd

unlash
BR ˌʌnˈlaʃ, -ɪz, -ɪŋ, -t
AM ˌənˈlæʃ, -əz, -ɪŋ, -t

unlatch
BR ˌʌnˈlatʃ, -ɪz, -ɪŋ, -t
AM ˌənˈlætʃ, -əz, -ɪŋ, -t

unlawful
BR (ˌ)ʌnˈlɔːf(ʊ)l
AM ˌənˈlɔfəl, ˌənˈlɑfəl

unlawfully
BR (ˌ)ʌnˈlɔːfʊli, (ˌ)ʌnˈlɔːfl̩i
AM ˌənˈlɔfəli, ˌənˈlɑfəli

unlawfulness
BR (ˌ)ʌnˈlɔːf(ʊ)lnəs
AM ˌənˈlɔfəlnəs, ˌənˈlɑfəlnəs

unlay
BR ˌʌnˈleɪ, -z, -ɪŋ
AM ˌənˈleɪ, -z, -ɪŋ

unleaded
BR ˌʌnˈlɛdɪd
AM ˌənˈlɛdəd

unlearn
BR ˌʌnˈləːn, -z, -ɪŋ, -t

AM ˌən'lərn, -z, -ɪŋ, -t
unlearned
adjective
BR ˌʌn'ləːnɪd
AM ˌən'lərn(ə)d
unlearnedly
BR ˌʌn'ləːnɪdli
AM ˌən'lərnədli
unlearnedness
BR ˌʌn'ləːnɪdnɪs
AM ˌən'lərnədnəs
unleash
BR (ˌ)ʌn'liːʃ, -ɪz, -ɪŋ, -t
AM ˌən'liʃ, -ɪz, -ɪŋ, -t
unleavened
BR ˌʌn'lɛvnd
AM ˌən'lɛvənd
unless
BR (ə)n'lɛs, ʌn'lɛs
AM ən'lɛs
unlet
BR ˌʌn'lɛt
AM ˌən'lɛt
unlettered
BR ˌʌn'lɛtəd
AM ˌən'lɛdərd
unliberated
BR ˌʌn'lɪbəreɪtɪd
AM ˌən'lɪbəˌreɪdɪd
unlicensed
BR (ˌ)ʌn'lʌɪsnst
AM ˌən'laɪsənst
unlighted
BR ˌʌn'lʌɪtɪd
AM ˌən'laɪdɪd
unlikable
BR (ˌ)ʌn'lʌɪkəbl
AM ˌən'laɪkəbəl
unlike
BR (ˌ)ʌn'lʌɪk
AM ¦ənˌlaɪk
unlikeable
BR (ˌ)ʌn'lʌɪkəbl
AM ˌən'laɪkəbəl
unlikelihood
BR (ˌ)ʌn'lʌɪklɪhʊd
AM ˌən'laɪkliˌhʊd
unlikeliness
BR (ˌ)ʌn'lʌɪklɪnɪs
AM ˌən'laɪklinɪs
unlikely
BR (ˌ)ʌn'lʌɪkli
AM ˌənˌlaɪkli
unlikeness
BR (ˌ)ʌn'lʌɪknɪs
AM ˌən'laɪknɪs
unlimited
BR ʌn'lɪmɪtɪd
AM ˌən'lɪmɪdɪd
unlimitedly
BR ʌn'lɪmɪtɪdli
AM ˌən'lɪmɪdɪdli
unlimitedness
BR ʌn'lɪmɪtɪdnɪs
AM ˌən'lɪmɪdɪdnɪs
unlined
BR (ˌ)ʌn'lʌɪnd
AM ˌən'laɪnd
unlink
BR ˌʌn'lɪŋ|k, -ks, -kɪŋ, -(k)t
AM ˌən'lɪŋ|k, -ks, -kɪŋ, -(k)t
unliquidated
BR ˌʌn'lɪkwɪdeɪtɪd
AM ˌən'lɪkwəˌdeɪdɪd
unlisted
BR (ˌ)ʌn'lɪstɪd
AM ˌən'lɪstɪd
unlistenable
BR ˌʌn'lɪsn̩əbl
AM ˌən'lɪsn̩əbəl, ˌən'lɪsnəbəl
unlit
BR ˌʌn'lɪt
AM ˌən'lɪt
unliterary
BR ˌʌn'lɪt(ə)rəri
AM ˌən'lɪtrəri, ˌən'lɪdəˌrɛri
unlivable
BR ˌʌn'lɪvəbl
AM ˌən'lɪvəbəl
unlived-in
BR (ˌ)ʌn'lɪvdɪn
AM ˌən'lɪvˌdɪn
unload
BR (ˌ)ʌn'ləʊd, -z, -ɪŋ, -ɪd
AM ˌən'loʊd, -z, -ɪŋ, -əd
unloader
BR (ˌ)ʌn'ləʊdə(r), -z
AM ˌən'loʊdər, -z
unlocatable
BR ˌʌnlə(ʊ)'keɪtəbl
AM ˌənˌloʊ'keɪdəbəl
unlocated
BR ˌʌnlə(ʊ)'keɪtɪd
AM ˌən'loʊˌkeɪdɪd
unlock
BR (ˌ)ʌn'lɒk, -s, -ɪŋ, -t
AM ˌən'lɑk, -s, -ɪŋ, -t
unlooked
BR (ˌ)ʌn'lʊkt
AM ˌən'lʊkt
unlooked-for
BR (ˌ)ʌn'lʊktfɔː(r)
AM ˌən'lʊktˌfɔ(ə)r
unloose
BR (ˌ)ʌn'luːs, -ɪz, -ɪŋ, -t
AM ˌən'lus, -əz, -ɪŋ, -t
unloosen
BR (ˌ)ʌn'luːs|n, -nz, -n̩ɪŋ\-nɪŋ, -nd
AM ˌən'lusən, -z, -ɪŋ, -d
unlovable
BR (ˌ)ʌn'lʌvəbl
AM ˌən'ləvəbəl
unloveable
BR (ˌ)ʌn'lʌvəbl
AM ˌən'ləvəbəl
unloved
BR (ˌ)ʌn'lʌvd
AM ˌən'ləvd
unloveliness
BR (ˌ)ʌn'lʌvlɪnɪs
AM ˌən'ləvlinɪs
unlovely
BR (ˌ)ʌn'lʌvli
AM ˌən'ləvli
unloving
BR (ˌ)ʌn'lʌvɪŋ
AM ˌən'ləvɪŋ
unlovingly
BR (ˌ)ʌn'lʌvɪŋli
AM ˌən'ləvɪŋli
unlovingness
BR (ˌ)ʌn'lʌvɪŋnɪs
AM ˌən'ləvɪŋnɪs
unluckily
BR (ˌ)ʌn'lʌkɪli
AM ˌən'ləkəli
unluckiness
BR (ˌ)ʌn'lʌkɪnɪs
AM ˌən'ləkinɪs
unlucky
BR (ˌ)ʌn'lʌk|i, -ɪə(r), -ɪɪst
AM ˌən'ləki, -ər, -ɪst
unmade
BR ˌʌn'meɪd
AM ˌən'meɪd
unmaidenly
BR ˌʌn'meɪdnli
AM ˌən'meɪdnli
unmake
BR ˌʌn'meɪk, -s, -ɪŋ
AM ˌən'meɪk, -s, -ɪŋ
unmalleable
BR ˌʌn'malɪəbl
AM ˌən'mæliəbəl, ˌən'mæl(j)əbəl
unman
BR ˌʌn'man, -z, -ɪŋ, -d
AM ˌən'mæn, -z, -ɪŋ, -d
unmanageable
BR (ˌ)ʌn'manɪdʒəbl
AM ˌən'mænədʒəbəl
unmanageableness
BR (ˌ)ʌn'manɪdʒəblnəs
AM ˌən'mænədʒəbəlnəs
unmanageably
BR (ˌ)ʌn'manɪdʒəbli
AM ˌən'mænədʒəbli
unmanaged
BR (ˌ)ʌn'manɪdʒd
AM ˌən'mænədʒd
unmaneuvrable
BR ˌʌnmə'nuːv(ə)rəbl
AM ˌənmə'n(j)uv(ə)rəbəl
unmanliness
BR (ˌ)ʌn'manlɪnɪs
AM ˌən'mænlinɪs
unmanly
BR (ˌ)ʌn'manli
AM ˌən'mænli
unmanned
BR ˌʌn'mand
AM ¦ənˌmænd
unmannered
BR ʌn'manəd
AM ˌən'mænərd
unmannerliness
BR ʌn'manəlɪnɪs
AM ˌən'mænərlinɪs
unmannerly
BR ʌn'manəli
AM ˌən'mænərli
unmanoeuvrable
BR ˌʌnmə'nuːv(ə)rəbl
AM ˌənmə'n(j)uv(ə)rəbəl
unmanured
BR ˌʌnmə'njʊəd, ˌʌnmə'njɔːd
AM ˌənmə'n(j)ʊ(ə)rd
unmapped
BR ˌʌn'mapt
AM ˌən'mæpt
unmarked
BR ˌʌn'mɑːkt
AM ¦ən'mɑrkt
unmarkedness
BR ˌʌn'mɑːkɪdnɪs
AM ˌən'mɑrkədnəs
unmarketable
BR ˌʌn'mɑːkɪtəbl
AM ˌən'mɑrkədəbəl
unmarred
BR ˌʌn'mɑːd
AM ˌən'mɑrd
unmarriageable
BR ˌʌn'marɪdʒəbl
AM ˌən'mɛrədʒəbəl
unmarried
BR ˌʌn'marɪd
AM ˌən'mɛrid
unmasculine
BR ˌʌn'maskjʉlɪn
AM ˌən'mæskjələn
unmask
BR ˌʌn'mɑːsk, ˌʌn'mask, -s, -ɪŋ, -t
AM ˌən'mæsk, -s, -ɪŋ, -t
unmasker
BR ˌʌn'mɑːskə(r), ˌʌn'maskə(r), -z
AM ˌən'mæskər, -z
unmatchable
BR ˌʌn'matʃəbl
AM ˌən'mætʃəbəl
unmatchably
BR ˌʌn'matʃəbli
AM ˌən'mætʃəbli
unmatched
BR ˌʌn'matʃt
AM ˌən'mætʃt
unmated
BR ˌʌn'meɪtɪd
AM ˌən'meɪdɪd
unmatured
BR ˌʌnmə'tʃʊəd, ˌʌnmə'tjʊəd, ˌʌnmə'tʃɔːd, ˌʌnmə'tjɔːd
AM ˌənmə'tʃərd, ˌənmə'tʃʊ(ə)rd

unmeaning
BR (ˌ)ʌnˈmiːnɪŋ
AM ˌənˈminɪŋ
unmeaningly
BR (ˌ)ʌnˈmiːnɪŋli
AM ˌənˈminɪŋli
unmeaningness
BR (ˌ)ʌnˈmiːnɪŋnɪs
AM ˌənˈminɪŋnɪs
unmeant
BR ˌʌnˈmɛnt
AM ˌənˈmɛnt
unmeasurable
BR (ˌ)ʌnˈmɛʒ(ə)rəbl
AM ˌənˈmɛʒ(ə)rəbəl, ˌənˈmɛʒərbəl
unmeasurably
BR (ˌ)ʌnˈmɛʒ(ə)rəbli
AM ˌənˈmɛʒ(ə)rəbli, ˌənˈmɛʒərbli
unmeasured
BR (ˌ)ʌnˈmɛʒəd
AM ˌənˈmɛʒərd
unmediated
BR ˌʌnˈmiːdɪeɪtɨd
AM ˌənˈmidiˌeɪdɨd
unmelodious
BR ˌʌnmɪˈləʊdɪəs
AM ˌənməˈloʊdiəs
unmelodiously
BR ˌʌnmɪˈləʊdɪəsli
AM ˌənməˈloʊdiəsli
unmelted
BR ˌʌnˈmɛltɨd
AM ˌənˈmɛltəd
unmemorable
BR ˌʌnˈmɛm(ə)rəbl
AM ˌənˈmɛm(ə)rəbəl, ˌənˈmɛmərbəl
unmemorably
BR ˌʌnˈmɛm(ə)rəbli
AM ˌənˈmɛm(ə)rəbli, ˌənˈmɛmərbli
unmended
BR ˌʌnˈmɛndɨd
AM ˌənˈmɛndəd
unmentionability
BR ʌnˌmɛnʃn̩əˈbɪlɪti, ʌnˌmɛnʃ(ə)nəˈbɪlɪti
AM ˌənˌmɛn(t)ʃ(ə)nəˈbɪlɨdi
unmentionable
BR ʌnˈmɛnʃn̩əbl, ʌnˈmɛnʃ(ə)nəbl, -z
AM ˌənˈmɛn(t)ʃ(ə)nəbəl, -z
unmentionableness
BR ʌnˈmɛnʃn̩əblnəs, ʌnˈmɛnʃ(ə)nəblnəs
AM ˌənˈmɛn(t)ʃ(ə)nəbəlnəs
unmentionably
BR ʌnˈmɛnʃn̩əbli, ʌnˈmɛnʃ(ə)nəbli
AM ˌənˈmɛn(t)ʃ(ə)nəbli
unmentioned
BR ʌnˈmɛnʃnd
AM ˌənˈmɛn(t)ʃənd
unmerchantable
BR ˌʌnˈməːtʃ(ə)ntəbl
AM ˌənˈmərtʃən(t)əbəl
unmerciful
BR ʌnˈməːsɪf(ʊ)l
AM ˌənˈmərsəfəl
unmercifully
BR ʌnˈməːsɪfʊli, ʌnˈməːsɪfl̩i
AM ˌənˈmərsəf(ə)li
unmercifulness
BR ʌnˈməːsɪf(ʊ)lnəs
AM ˌənˈmərsəfəlnəs
unmerited
BR (ˌ)ʌnˈmɛrɪtɨd
AM ˌənˈmɛrədəd
unmeritorious
BR ˌʌnmɛrɪˈtɔːrɪəs
AM ˌənˌmɛrəˈtɔriəs
unmet
BR ˌʌnˈmɛt
AM ˌənˈmɛt
unmetalled
BR ˌʌnˈmɛtld
AM ˌənˈmɛdld
unmethodical
BR ˌʌnmɪˈθɒdɪkl
AM ˌənməˈθɑdəkəl
unmethodically
BR ˌʌnmɪˈθɒdɪkli
AM ˌənməˈθɑdək(ə)li
unmetrical
BR ˌʌnˈmɛtrɪkl
AM ˌənˈmɛtrəkəl
unmilitary
BR ˌʌnˈmɪlɪt(ə)ri
AM ˌənˈmɪləˌtɛri
unmindful
BR (ˌ)ʌnˈmʌɪn(d)f(ʊ)l
AM ˌənˈmaɪndfəl
unmindfully
BR (ˌ)ʌnˈmʌɪn(d)fʊli, (ˌ)ʌnˈmʌɪn(d)fl̩i
AM ˌənˈmaɪn(d)fəli
unmindfulness
BR (ˌ)ʌnˈmʌɪn(d)f(ʊ)lnəs
AM ˌənˈmaɪn(d)fəlnəs
unmingled
BR ˌʌnˈmɪŋgld
AM ˌənˈmɪŋgəld
unmissable
BR ˌʌnˈmɪsəbl
AM ˌənˈmɪsəbəl
unmistakability
BR ˌʌnmɪˌsteɪkəˈbɪlɪti
AM ˌənməˌsteɪkəˈbɪlɨdi
unmistakable
BR ˌʌnmɪˈsteɪkəbl
AM ˌənməˈsteɪkəbəl
unmistakableness
BR ˌʌnmɪˈsteɪkəblnəs
AM ˌənməˈsteɪkəbəlnəs
unmistakably
BR ˌʌnmɪˈsteɪkəbli
AM ˌənməˈsteɪkəbli
unmistakeability
BR ˌʌnmɪˌsteɪkəˈbɪlɪti
AM ˌənməˌsteɪkəˈbɪlɨdi
unmistakeable
BR ˌʌnmɪˈsteɪkəbl
AM ˌənməˈsteɪkəbəl
unmistakeableness
BR ˌʌnmɪˈsteɪkəblnəs
AM ˌənməˈsteɪkəbəlnəs
unmistakeably
BR ˌʌnmɪˈsteɪkəbli
AM ˌənməˈsteɪkəbli
unmistaken
BR ˌʌnmɪˈsteɪk(ə)n
AM ˌənməˈsteɪkən
unmitigated
BR ʌnˈmɪtɪgeɪtɨd
AM ˌənˈmɪdəˌgeɪdɨd
unmitigatedly
BR ʌnˈmɪtɪgeɪtɨdli
AM ˌənˈmɪdəˌgeɪdɨdli
unmixed
BR ˌʌnˈmɪkst
AM ˌənˈmɪkst
unmodernised
BR ˌʌnˈmɒdənʌɪzd
AM ˌənˈmɑdərˌnaɪzd
unmodernized
BR ˌʌnˈmɒdənʌɪzd
AM ˌənˈmɑdərˌnaɪzd
unmodified
BR (ˌ)ʌnˈmɒdɪfʌɪd
AM ˌənˈmɑdəˌfaɪd
unmodulated
BR (ˌ)ʌnˈmɒdjʊleɪtɨd, (ˌ)ʌnˈmɒdʒʊleɪtɨd
AM ˌənˈmɑdʒəˌleɪdɨd
unmolested
BR ˌʌnməˈlɛstɨd
AM ˌənməˈlɛstəd
unmoor
BR ˌʌnˈmʊə(r), ˌʌnˈmɔː(r), -z, -ɪŋ, -d
AM ˌənˈmʊ|(ə)r, -(ə)rz, -rɪŋ, -(ə)rd
unmoral
BR ˌʌnˈmɒrəl, ˌʌnˈmɒrl̩
AM ˌənˈmɔrəl
unmorality
BR ˌʌnməˈralɪti
AM ˌənməˈrælədi
unmorally
BR ˌʌnˈmɒrəli, ˌʌnˈmɒrl̩i
AM ˌənˈmɔrəli
unmotherly
BR ˌʌnˈmʌðəli
AM ˌənˈməðərli
unmotivated
BR ˌʌnˈməʊtɪveɪtɨd
AM ˌənˈmoʊdəˌveɪdɨd
unmounted
BR ˌʌnˈmaʊntɨd
AM ˌənˈmaʊn(t)əd
unmourned
BR ˌʌnˈmɔːnd
AM ˌənˈmɔrnd
unmovable
BR (ˌ)ʌnˈmuːvəbl
AM ˌənˈmuvəbəl
unmoveable
BR (ˌ)ʌnˈmuːvəbl
AM ˌənˈmuvəbəl
unmoved
BR (ˌ)ʌnˈmuːvd
AM ˌənˈmuvd
unmoving
BR (ˌ)ʌnˈmuːvɪŋ
AM ˌənˈmuvɪŋ
unmown
BR ˌʌnˈməʊn
AM ˌənˈmoʊn
unmuffle
BR ˌʌnˈmʌf|l, -lz, -l̩ɪŋ\-lɪŋ, -ld
AM ˌənˈməf|əl, -əlz, -(ə)lɪŋ, -əld
unmurmuring
BR ˌʌnˈməːm(ə)rɪŋ
AM ˌənˈmərmərɪŋ
unmurmuringly
BR ˌʌnˈməːm(ə)rɪŋli
AM ˌənˈmərmərɪŋli
unmusical
BR ˌʌnˈmjuːzɪkl
AM ˌənˈmjuzəkəl
unmusicality
BR ˌʌnmjuːzɪˈkalɪti
AM ˌənˌmjuzəˈkælədi
unmusically
BR ˌʌnˈmjuːzɪkli
AM ˌənˈmjuzək(ə)li
unmusicalness
BR ˌʌnˈmjuːzɪklnɪs
AM ˌənˈmjuzəkəlnəs
unmutilated
BR ˌʌnˈmjuːtɪleɪtɨd
AM ˌənˈmjudəleɪdɨd
unmuzzle
BR ˌʌnˈmʌz|l, -lz, -l̩ɪŋ\-lɪŋ, -ld
AM ˌənˈməz|əl, -əlz, -(ə)lɪŋ, -əld
unnail
BR ˌʌnˈneɪl, -z, -ɪŋ, -d
AM ˌənˈneɪl, -z, -ɪŋ, -d
unnameable
BR ˌʌnˈneɪməbl
AM ˌənˈneɪməbəl
unnamed
BR ˌʌnˈneɪmd
AM ˌə(n)ˈneɪmd
unnational
BR ˌʌnˈnaʃn̩(ə)l, ˌʌnˈnaʃən(ə)l
AM ˌənˈnæʃ(ə)nəl
unnatural
BR (ˌ)ʌnˈnatʃ(ə)rəl, (ˌ)ʌnˈnatʃ(ə)rl̩
AM ˌənˈnætʃ(ə)rəl

unnaturally
BR (ˌ)ʌnˈnatʃ(ə)rəli, (ˌ)ʌnˈnatʃ(ə)rl̩i
AM ˌənˈnætʃ(ə)rəli
unnaturalness
BR (ˌ)ʌnˈnatʃ(ə)rəlnəs, (ˌ)ʌnˈnatʃ(ə)rl̩nəs
AM ˌənˈætʃ(ə)rəlnəs
unnavigability
BR ˌʌnnavɪgəˈbɪlɪti
AM ˌənˌnævəgəˈbɪlɪdi
unnavigable
BR ˌʌnˈnavɪgəbl
AM ˌənˈnævəgəbəl
unnecessarily
BR (ˌ)ʌnˈnɛsɪs(ə)rɪli, ˌʌnnɛsɪˈsɛrɪli
AM ˌənˌnɛsəˌsɛrəli
unnecessariness
BR (ˌ)ʌnˈnɛsɪs(ə)rɪnɪs
AM ˌənˈnɛsəˌsɛrinɪs
unnecessary
BR (ˌ)ʌnˈnɛsɪs(ə)ri, ˌʌnˈnɛsɪsɛri
AM ˌənˈnɛsəˌsɛri
unneeded
BR ˌʌnˈniːdɪd
AM ˌənˈnidɪd
unneighborliness
BR ˌʌnˈneɪbəlɪnɪs
AM ˌənˈneɪbərlinɪs
unneighborly
BR ˌʌnˈneɪbəli
AM ˌənˈneɪbərli
unneighbourliness
BR ˌʌnˈneɪbəlɪnɪs
AM ˌənˈneɪbərlinɪs
unneighbourly
BR ˌʌnˈneɪbəli
AM ˌənˈneɪbərli
unnerve
BR ˌʌnˈnəːv, -z, -ɪŋ, -d
AM ˌənˈnərv, -z, -ɪŋ, -d
unnervingly
BR ˌʌnˈnəːvɪŋli
AM ˌənˈnərvɪŋli
unnoticeable
BR (ˌ)ʌnˈnəʊtɪsəbl
AM ˌənˈnoʊdəsəbəl
unnoticeably
BR (ˌ)ʌnˈnəʊtɪsəbli
AM ˌənˈnoʊdəsəbli
unnoticed
BR (ˌ)ʌnˈnəʊtɪst
AM ˌənˈnoʊdəst
UNNRA
BR ˈʌnrə(*r*)
AM ˈənrə
unnumbered
BR ˌʌnˈnʌmbəd
AM ˌənˈnəmbərd
UNO
BR ˈjuːnəʊ
AM ˈjuˌnoʊ
Uno
card game
BR ˈuːnəʊ
AM ˈunoʊ
uno
number
BR ˈuːnəʊ
AM ˈunoʊ
unobjectionable
BR ˌʌnəbˈdʒɛkʃn̩əbl, ˌʌnəbˈdʒɛkʃ(ə)nəbl
AM ˌənəbˈdʒɛkʃ(ə)nəbəl
unobjectionableness
BR ˌʌnəbˈdʒɛkʃn̩əblnəs, ˌʌnəbˈdʒɛkʃ(ə)nəblnəs
AM ˌənəbˈdʒɛkʃ(ə)nəbəlnəs
unobjectionably
BR ˌʌnəbˈdʒɛkʃn̩əbli, ˌʌnəbˈdʒɛkʃ(ə)nəbli
AM ˌənəbˈdʒɛkʃ(ə)nəbli
unobliging
BR ˌʌnəˈblʌɪdʒɪŋ
AM ˌənəˈblaɪdʒɪŋ
unobscured
BR ˌʌnəbˈskjʊəd, ˌʌnəbˈskjɔːd
AM ˌənəbˈskjʊ(ə)rd
unobservable
BR ˌʌnəbˈzəːvəbl
AM ˌənəbˈzərvəbəl
unobservant
BR ˌʌnəbˈzəːv(ə)nt
AM ˌənəbˈzərvənt
unobservantly
BR ˌʌnəbˈzəːv(ə)ntli
AM ˌənəbˈzərvən(t)li
unobserved
BR ˌʌnəbˈzəːvd
AM ˌənəbˈzərvd
unobservedly
BR ˌʌnəbˈzəːvɪdli
AM ˌənəbˈzərvədli
unobstructed
BR ˌʌnəbˈstrʌktɪd
AM ˌənəbˈstrəktəd
unobtainable
BR ˌʌnəbˈteɪnəbl
AM ˌənəbˈteɪnəbəl
unobtainably
BR ˌʌnəbˈteɪnəbli
AM ˌənəbˈteɪnəbli
unobtrusive
BR ˌʌnəbˈtruːsɪv
AM ˌənəbˈtrusɪv
unobtrusively
BR ˌʌnəbˈtruːsɪvli
AM ˌənəbˈtrusɪvli
unobtrusiveness
BR ˌʌnəbˈtruːsɪvnɪs
AM ˌənəbˈtrusɪvnɪs
unoccupancy
BR (ˌ)ʌnˈɒkjʊp(ə)nsi
AM ˌənˈɑkjəpənsi
unoccupied
BR (ˌ)ʌnˈɒkjʊpʌɪd
AM ˌənˈɑkjəˌpaɪd
unoffended
BR ˌʌnəˈfɛndɪd
AM ˌənəˈfɛndəd
unoffending
BR ˌʌnəˈfɛndɪŋ
AM ˌənəˈfɛndɪŋ
unofficial
BR ˌʌnəˈfɪʃl
AM ˌənəˈfɪʃəl
unofficially
BR ˌʌnəˈfɪʃl̩i, ˌʌnəˈfɪʃəli
AM ˌənəˈfɪʃəli
unoiled
BR ˌʌnˈɔɪld
AM ˌənˈɔɪld
unopenable
BR ˌʌnˈəʊp(ə)nəbl, ˌʌnˈəʊpn̩əbl
AM ˌənˈoʊp(ə)nəbəl
unopened
BR ˌʌnˈəʊpnd
AM ˌənˈoʊpənd
unopposed
BR ˌʌnəˈpəʊzd
AM ˌənəˈpoʊzd
unordained
BR ˌʌnɔːˈdeɪnd
AM ˌənɔrˈdeɪnd
unordered
BR ˌʌnˈɔːdəd
AM ˌənˈɔrdərd
unordinary
BR ˌʌnˈɔːdɪn(ə)ri, ˌʌnˈɔːdn̩(ə)ri
AM ˌənˈɔrdn̩ˌɛri
unorganised
BR (ˌ)ʌnˈɔːgənʌɪzd, (ˌ)ʌnˈɔːgn̩ʌɪzd
AM ˌənˈɔrgəˌnaɪzd
unorganized
BR (ˌ)ʌnˈɔːgənʌɪzd, (ˌ)ʌnˈɔːgn̩ʌɪzd
AM ˌənˈɔrgəˌnaɪzd
unoriginal
BR ˌʌnəˈrɪdʒɪnl
AM ˌənəˈrɪdʒ(ə)nəl
unoriginality
BR ˌʌnəˌrɪdʒɪˈnalɪti
AM ˌənəˌrɪdʒəˈnælədi
unoriginally
BR ˌʌnəˈrɪdʒɪnl̩i, ˌʌnəˈrɪdʒɪnəli
AM ˌənəˈrɪdʒ(ə)nəli
unornamental
BR ˌʌnɔːnəˈmɛntl
AM ˌənˌɔrnəˈmɛn(t)l
unornamented
BR ˌʌnˈɔːnəmɛntɪd
AM ˌənˈɔrnəˌmɛn(t)əd
unorthodox
BR (ˌ)ʌnˈɔːθədɒks
AM ˌənˈɔrθəˌdɑks
unorthodoxly
BR (ˌ)ʌnˈɔːθədɒksli
AM ˌənˈɔrθəˌdɑksli
unorthodoxy
BR (ˌ)ʌnˈɔːθədɒksi
AM ˌənˈɔrθəˌdɑksi
unostentatious
BR ˌʌnɒstɛnˈteɪʃəs, ˌʌnɒst(ə)nˈteɪʃəs
AM ˌənˌɑst(ə)nˈteɪʃəs
unostentatiously
BR ˌʌnɒstɛnˈteɪʃəsli, ˌʌnɒst(ə)nˈteɪʃəsli
AM ˌənˌɑst(ə)nˈteɪʃəsli
unostentatiousness
BR ˌʌnɒstɛnˈteɪʃəsnəs, ˌʌnɒst(ə)nˈteɪʃəsnəs
AM ˌənˌɑst(ə)nˈteɪʃəsnəs
unowned
BR ˌʌnˈəʊnd
AM ˌənˈoʊnd
unoxidised
BR ˌʌnˈɒksɪdʌɪzd
AM ˌənˈɑksəˌdaɪzd
unoxidized
BR ˌʌnˈɒksɪdʌɪzd
AM ˌənˈɑksəˌdaɪzd
unpack
BR ˌʌnˈpak, -s, -ɪŋ, -t
AM ˌənˈpæk, -s, -ɪŋ, -t
unpacker
BR ˌʌnˈpakə(r), -z
AM ˌənˈpækər, -z
unpadded
BR ˌʌnˈpadɪd
AM ˌənˈpædəd
unpaged
BR ˌʌnˈpeɪdʒd
AM ˌənˈpeɪdʒd
unpaginated
BR ˌʌnˈpadʒɪneɪtɪd
AM ˌənˈpædʒəˌneɪdɪd
unpaid
BR ˌʌnˈpeɪd
AM ˌənˈpeɪd
unpainted
BR ˌʌnˈpeɪntɪd
AM ˌənˈpeɪn(t)ɪd
unpaired
BR ˌʌnˈpɛːd
AM ˌənˈpɛ(ə)rd
unpalatability
BR ˌʌnpalətəˈbɪlɪti
AM ˌənˌpælədəˈbɪlɪdi
unpalatable
BR (ˌ)ʌnˈpalətəbl
AM ˌənˈpælədəbəl
unpalatableness
BR (ˌ)ʌnˈpalətəblnəs
AM ˌənˈpælədəbəlnəs
unpalatably
BR (ˌ)ʌnˈpalətəbli
AM ˌənˈpælədəbli
unparalleled
BR (ˌ)ʌnˈparəlɛld
AM ˌənˈpɛrəˌlɛld
unpardonable
BR (ˌ)ʌnˈpɑːdn̩əbl, (ˌ)ʌnˈpɑːd(ə)nəbl
AM ˌənˈpɑrdn̩əbəl

unpardonableness
BR (ˌ)ʌnˈpɑːdn̩əblnəs, (ˌ)ʌnˈpɑːd(ə)nəblnəs
AM ˌənˈpɑrdn̩əbəlnəs

unpardonably
BR (ˌ)ʌnˈpɑːdn̩əbli, (ˌ)ʌnˈpɑːd(ə)nəbli
AM ˌənˈpɑrdn̩əbli

unparliamentary
BR ˌʌnpɑːləˈmɛnt(ə)ri
AM ˌənˌpɑrl(j)əˈmɛn(t)əri

unpasteurised
BR (ˌ)ʌnˈpɑːst(ʃ)ərʌɪzd, (ˌ)ʌnˈpast(ʃ)ərʌɪzd, (ˌ)ʌnˈpɑːstjərʌɪzd, (ˌ)ʌnˈpastjərʌɪzd
AM ˌənˈpæstʃəˌraɪzd, ˌənˈpæʃtʃəˌraɪzd, ˌənˈpæstəˌraɪzd

unpasteurized
BR (ˌ)ʌnˈpɑːst(ʃ)ərʌɪzd, (ˌ)ʌnˈpast(ʃ)ərʌɪzd, (ˌ)ʌnˈpɑːstjərʌɪzd, (ˌ)ʌnˈpastjərʌɪzd
AM ˌʌnˈpæstʃəˌraɪzd, ˌənˈpæʃtʃəˌraɪzd, ˌənˈpæstəˌraɪzd

unpatented
BR ˌʌnˈpat(ə)ntɨd, ˌʌnˈpeɪt(ə)ntɨd
AM ˌənˈpætn(t)əd

unpatriotic
BR ˌʌnpatrɪˈɒtɪk, ˌʌnpeɪtrɪˈɒtɪk
AM ˌənˌpeɪtriˈɑdɪk

unpatriotically
BR ˌʌnpatrɪˈɒtɨkli, ˌʌnpeɪtrɪˈɒtɨkli
AM ˌənˌpeɪtriˈɑdək(ə)li

unpatronising
BR ˌʌnˈpatrənʌɪzɪŋ
AM ˌənˈpeɪtrəˌnaɪzɪŋ, ˌənˈpætrəˌnaɪzɪŋ

unpatronizing
BR ˌʌnˈpatrənʌɪzɪŋ
AM ˌənˈpeɪtrəˌnaɪzɪŋ, ˌənˈpætrəˌnaɪzɪŋ

unpatterned
BR ˌʌnˈpat(ə)nd
AM ˌənˈpædərnd

unpaved
BR ˌʌnˈpeɪvd
AM ˌənˈpeɪvd

unpeaceful
BR ˌʌnˈpiːsf(ʊ)l
AM ˌənˈpisfəl

unpeeled
BR ˌʌnˈpiːld
AM ˌənˈpild

unpeg
BR ˌʌnˈpɛɡ, -z, -ɪŋ, -d
AM ˌənˈpɛɡ, -z, -ɪŋ, -d

unpenalised
BR ˌʌnˈpiːnəlʌɪzd, ˌʌnˈpiːnl̩ʌɪzd
AM ˌənˈpɛnlˌaɪzd, ˌənˈpinlˌaɪzd

unpenalized
BR ˌʌnˈpiːnəlʌɪzd, ˌʌnˈpiːnl̩ʌɪzd
AM ˌənˈpɛnlˌaɪzd, ˌənˈpinlˌaɪzd

unpeople
BR ˌʌnˈpiːpl, -z, -ɪŋ, -d
AM ˌənˈpipəl, -z, -ɪŋ, -d

unperceived
BR ˌʌnpəˈsiːvd
AM ˌənpərˈsivd

unperceptive
BR ˌʌnpəˈsɛptɪv
AM ˌənpərˈsɛptɪv

unperceptively
BR ˌʌnpəˈsɛptɨvli
AM ˌənpərˈsɛptɨvli

unperceptiveness
BR ˌʌnpəˈsɛptɨvnɪs
AM ˌənpərˈsɛptɪvnɪs

unperfected
BR ˌʌnpəˈfɛktɨd
AM ˌənpərˈfɛktəd

unperforated
BR (ˌ)ʌnˈpəːfəreɪtɨd
AM ˌənˈpərfəˌreɪdɨd

unperformed
BR ˌʌnpəˈfɔːmd
AM ˌənpərˈfɔrmd

unperfumed
BR ˌʌnˈpəːfjuːmd
AM ˌənˈpərˌfjumd, ˌənpərˈfjumd

unperson
BR ˌʌnˈpəːsn, -z
AM ˈˌənˌpərsən, -z

unpersuadable
BR ˌʌnpəˈsweɪdəbl
AM ˌənpərˈsweɪdəbəl

unpersuaded
BR ˌʌnpəˈsweɪdɪd
AM ˌənpərˈsweɪdɪd

unpersuasive
BR ˌʌnpəˈsweɪsɪv
AM ˌənpərˈsweɪsɪv

unpersuasively
BR ˌʌnpəˈsweɪsɨvli
AM ˌənpərˈsweɪsɨvli

unperturbed
BR ˌʌnpəˈtəːbd
AM ˌənpərˈtərbd

unperturbedly
BR ˌʌnpəˈtəːbɨdli
AM ˌənpərˈtərbədli

unphased
BR ˌʌnˈfeɪzd
AM ˌənˈfeɪzd

unphilosophic
BR ˌʌnfɪləˈsɒfɪk
AM ˌənˌfɪləˈsɑfɪk

unphilosophical
BR ˌʌnfɪləˈsɒfɨkl
AM ˌənˌfɪləˈsɑfəkəl

unphilosophically
BR ˌʌnfɪləˈsɒfɨkli
AM ˌənˌfɪləˈsɑfək(ə)li

unphysiological
BR ˌʌnfɪzɪəˈlɒdʒɨkl
AM ˌənˌfɪziəˈlɑdʒəkəl

unphysiologically
BR ˌʌnfɪzɪəˈlɒdʒɨkli
AM ˌənˌfɪziəˈlɑdʒək(ə)li

unpick
BR ˌʌnˈpɪk, -s, -ɪŋ, -t
AM ˌənˈpɪk, -s, -ɪŋ, -t

unpicturesque
BR ˌʌnpɪktʃəˈrɛsk
AM ˌənˌpɪk(t)ʃəˈrɛsk

unpierced
BR ˌʌnˈpɪəst
AM ˌənˈpɪ(ə)rst

unpin
BR ˌʌnˈpɪn, -z, -ɪŋ, -d
AM ˌənˈpɪn, -z, -ɪŋ, -d

unpitied
BR ˌʌnˈpɪtɪd
AM ˌənˈpɪdid

unpitying
BR ˌʌnˈpɪtɪɪŋ
AM ˌənˈpɪdiɪŋ

unpityingly
BR ˌʌnˈpɪtɪɪŋli
AM ˌənˈpɪdiɪŋli

unplaceable
BR ˌʌnˈpleɪsəbl
AM ˌənˈpleɪsəbəl

unplaced
BR ˌʌnˈpleɪst
AM ˌənˈpleɪst

unplait
BR ˌʌnˈplat, -s, -ɪŋ, -ɨd
AM ˌənˈplæ|t, -ts, -dɪŋ, -dəd

unplanned
BR ˌʌnˈpland
AM ˈˌənˈplænd

unplanted
BR ˌʌnˈplɑːntɨd, ˌʌnˈplantɨd
AM ˌənˈplæn(t)əd

unplastered
BR ˌʌnˈplɑːstəd, ˌʌnˈplastəd
AM ˌənˈplæstərd

unplasticised
BR ˌʌnˈplastɨsʌɪzd
AM ˌənˈplæstəˌsaɪzd

unplasticized
BR ˌʌnˈplastɨsʌɪzd
AM ˌənˈplæstəˌsaɪzd

unplausible
BR ˌʌnˈplɔːzɪbl
AM ˌənˈplɔzəbəl, ˌənˈplɑzəbəl

unplayable
BR (ˌ)ʌnˈpleɪəbl
AM ˌənˈpleɪəbəl

unplayably
BR (ˌ)ʌnˈpleɪəbli
AM ˌənˈpleɪəbli

unplayed
BR (ˌ)ʌnˈpleɪd
AM ˌənˈpleɪd

unpleasant
BR ʌnˈplɛznt
AM ˌənˈplɛznt

unpleasantly
BR ʌnˈplɛzntli
AM ˌənˈplɛzn(t)li

unpleasantness
BR ʌnˈplɛzntnəs
AM ˌənˈplɛzn(t)nəs

unpleasantry
BR (ˌ)ʌnˈplɛzntr|i, -ɪz
AM ˌənˈplɛzntri, -z

unpleasing
BR (ˌ)ʌnˈpliːzɪŋ
AM ˌənˈplizɪŋ

unpleasingly
BR ˌʌnˈpliːzɪŋli
AM ˌənˈplizɪŋli

unpleasurable
BR (ˌ)ʌnˈplɛʒ(ə)rəbl
AM ˌənˈplɛʒ(ə)r(ə)bəl

unpledged
BR ˌʌnˈplɛdʒd
AM ˌənˈplɛdʒd

unploughed
BR ˌʌnˈplaʊd
AM ˌənˈplaʊd

unplowed
BR ˌʌnˈplaʊd
AM ˌənˈplaʊd

unplucked
BR ˌʌnˈplʌkt
AM ˌənˈpləkt

unplug
BR ˌʌnˈplʌɡ, -z, -ɪŋ, -d
AM ˌənˈpləɡ, -z, -ɪŋ, -d

unplumbable
BR ˌʌnˈplʌməbl
AM ˌənˈpləməbəl

unplumbed
BR ˌʌnˈplʌmd
AM ˌənˈpləmd

unpoetic
BR ˌʌnpəʊˈɛtɪk
AM ˌənpoʊˈɛdɪk

unpoetical
BR ˌʌnpəʊˈɛtɨkl
AM ˌənpoʊˈɛdɪkəl

unpoetically
BR ˌʌnpəʊˈɛtɨkli
AM ˌənpoʊˈɛdək(ə)li

unpoeticalness
BR ˌʌnpəʊˈɛtɨklnəs
AM ˌənpoʊˈɛdɪkəlnəs

unpointed
BR ˌʌnˈpɔɪntɨd
AM ˌənˈpɔɪn(t)ɨd

unpolarised
BR ˌʌnˈpəʊlərʌɪzd
AM ˌənˈpoʊləˌraɪzd

unpolarized
BR ˌʌnˈpəʊlərʌɪzd
AM ˌənˈpoʊləˌraɪzd

unpolished
BR ˌʌnˈpɒlɪʃt
AM ˌənˈpɑlɪʃt

unpolitic
BR ˌʌnˈpɒlɪtɪk
AM ˌənˈpɑlədɪk

unpolitical
BR ˌʌnpəˈlɪtɪkl
AM ˌənpəˈlɪdɪkəl

unpolitically
BR ˌʌnpəˈlɪtɪkli
AM ˌənpəˈlɪdɪk(ə)li

unpolled
BR ˌʌnˈpəʊld
AM ˌənˈpoʊld

unpollinated
BR ˌʌnˈpɒlɪneɪtɪd
AM ˌənˈpɑləˌneɪdɪd

unpolluted
BR ˌʌnpəˈl(j)uːtɪd
AM ˌənpəˈludəd

unpompous
BR ˌʌnˈpɒmpəs
AM ˌənˈpɑmpəs

unpopular
BR (ˌ)ʌnˈpɒpjʊlə(r)
AM ˌənˈpɑpjələr

unpopularity
BR ˌʌnpɒpjʊˈlarɪti
AM ˌənpɑpjəˈlɛrədi

unpopularly
BR (ˌ)ʌnˈpɒpjʊləli
AM ˌənˈpɑpjələrli

unpopulated
BR ˌʌnˈpɒpjʊleɪtɪd
AM ˌənˈpɑpjəˌleɪdɪd

unposed
BR ˌʌnˈpəʊzd
AM ˌənˈpoʊzd

unpossessed
BR ˌʌnpəˈzɛst
AM ˌənpəˈzɛst

unposted
BR ˌʌnˈpəʊstɪd
AM ˌənˈpoʊstəd

unpowered
BR ˌʌnˈpaʊəd
AM ˌənˈpaʊərd

unpractical
BR (ˌ)ʌnˈpraktɪkl
AM ˌənˈpræktəkəl

unpracticality
BR ˌʌnpraktɪˈkalɪti
AM ˌənˌpræktəˈkælədi

unpractically
BR (ˌ)ʌnˈpraktɪkli
AM ˌənˈpræktək(ə)li

unpractised
BR (ˌ)ʌnˈpraktɪst
AM ˌənˈpræktəst

unprecedented
BR (ˌ)ʌnˈprɛsɪdɛntɪd, (ˌ)ʌnˈprɛsɪd(ə)ntɪd
AM ˌənˈprɛsəˌdɛn(t)əd

unprecedentedly
BR (ˌ)ʌnˈprɛsɪdɛntɪdli, (ˌ)ʌnˈprɛsɪd(ə)ntɪdli
AM ˌənˈprɛsəˌdɛn(t)ədli

unpredictability
BR ˌʌnprɪˌdɪktəˈbɪlɪti
AM ˌənprəˌdɪktəˈbɪlɪdi

unpredictable
BR ˌʌnprɪˈdɪktəbl
AM ˌənprəˈdɪktəbəl

unpredictableness
BR ˌʌnprɪˈdɪktəblnəs
AM ˌənprəˈdɪktəbəlnəs

unpredictably
BR ˌʌnprɪˈdɪktəbli
AM ˌənprəˈdɪktəbli

unpredicted
BR ˌʌnprɪˈdɪktɪd
AM ˌənprəˈdɪktɪd

unprejudiced
BR (ˌ)ʌnˈprɛdʒʊdɪst
AM ˌənˈprɛdʒədəst

unpremeditated
BR ˌʌnprɪˈmɛdɪteɪtɪd
AM ˌənprəˈmɛdəˌteɪdɪd, ˌənpriˈmɛdəˌteɪdɪd

unpremeditatedly
BR ˌʌnprɪˈmɛdɪteɪtɪdli
AM ˌənprəˈmɛdəˌteɪdɪdli, ˌənpriˈmɛdəˌteɪdɪdli

unprepared
BR ˌʌnprɪˈpɛːd
AM ˌənprəˈpɛ(ə)rd

unpreparedly
BR ˌʌnprɪˈpɛːrɪdli
AM ˌənprəˈpɛr(ə)dli

unpreparedness
BR ˌʌnprɪˈpɛːrɪdnɪs
AM ˌənprəˈpɛr(ə)dnəs

unprepossessing
BR ˌʌnpriːpəˈzɛsɪŋ
AM ˌənpripəˈzɛsɪŋ

unprescribed
BR ˌʌnprɪˈskrʌɪbd
AM ˌənprəˈskraɪbd

unpresentable
BR ˌʌnprɪˈzɛntəbl
AM ˌənprəˈzɛn(t)əbəl

unpressed
BR ˌʌnˈprɛst
AM ˌənˈprɛst

unpressurised
BR ˌʌnˈprɛʃərʌɪzd
AM ˌənˈprɛʃəˌraɪzd

unpressurized
BR ˌʌnˈprɛʃərʌɪzd
AM ˌənˈprɛʃəˌraɪzd

unpresuming
BR ˌʌnprɪˈzjuːmɪŋ
AM ˌənprəˈz(j)umɪŋ

unpresumptuous
BR ˌʌnprɪˈzʌm(p)tʃʊəs, ˌʌnprɪˈzʌm(p)tjʊəs
AM ˌənpriˈzəm(p)(t)ʃ(əw)əs, ˌənprəˈzəm(p)(t)ʃ(əw)əs

unpretending
BR ˌʌnprɪˈtɛndɪŋ
AM ˌənprəˈtɛndɪŋ

unpretendingly
BR ˌʌnprɪˈtɛndɪŋli
AM ˌənprəˈtɛndɪŋli

unpretendingness
BR ˌʌnprɪˈtɛndɪŋnɪs
AM ˌənprəˈtɛndɪŋnɪs

unpretentious
BR ˌʌnprɪˈtɛnʃəs
AM ˌənprəˈtɛn(t)ʃəs

unpretentiously
BR ˌʌnprɪˈtɛnʃəsli
AM ˌənprəˈtɛn(t)ʃəsli

unpretentiousness
BR ˌʌnprɪˈtɛnʃəsnəs
AM ˌənprəˈtɛn(t)ʃəsnəs

unpreventable
BR ˌʌnprɪˈvɛntəbl
AM ˌənprəˈvɛn(t)əbəl

unpriced
BR ˌʌnˈprʌɪst
AM ˌənˈpraɪst

unprimed
BR ˌʌnˈprʌɪmd
AM ˌənˈpraɪmd

unprincipled
BR (ˌ)ʌnˈprɪnsɪpld
AM ˌənˈprɪnsəpəld

unprincipledness
BR (ˌ)ʌnˈprɪnsɪpldnəs
AM ˌənˈprɪnsəpəldnəs

unprintable
BR (ˌ)ʌnˈprɪntəbl
AM ˌənˈprɪn(t)əbəl

unprintably
BR (ˌ)ʌnˈprɪntəbli
AM ˌənˈprɪn(t)əbli

unprinted
BR (ˌ)ʌnˈprɪntɪd
AM ˌənˈprɪn(t)ɪd

unprivileged
BR (ˌ)ʌnˈprɪv(ɪ)lɪdʒd, (ˌ)ʌnˈprɪvl̩ɪdʒd
AM ˌənˈprɪv(ə)lɪdʒd

unproblematic
BR ˌʌnprɒbləˈmatɪk
AM ˌənˌprɑbləˈmædɪk

unproblematically
BR ˌʌnprɒbləˈmatɪkli
AM ˌənˌprɑbləˈmædək(ə)li

unprocessed
BR ˌʌnˈprəʊsɛst
AM ˌənˈprɑˌsɛst

unproclaimed
BR ˌʌnprəˈkleɪmd
AM ˌənprəˈkleɪmd, ˌənˌproʊˈkleɪmd

unprocurable
BR ˌʌnprəˈkjʊərəbl, ˌʌnprəˈkjɔːrəbl
AM ˌənprəˈkjʊrəbəl

unproductive
BR ˌʌnprəˈdʌktɪv
AM ˌənprəˈdəktɪv

unproductively
BR ˌʌnprəˈdʌktɪvli
AM ˌənprəˈdəktɪvli

unproductiveness
BR ˌʌnprəˈdʌktɪvnɪs
AM ˌənprəˈdəktɪvnɪs

unprofessional
BR ˌʌnprəˈfɛʃn̩(ə)l, ˌʌnprəˈfɛʃən(ə)l
AM ˌənprəˈfɛʃ(ə)nəl

unprofessionalism
BR ˌʌnprəˈfɛʃn̩əlɪz(ə)m, ˌʌnprəˈfɛʃn̩lɪz(ə)m, ˌʌnprəˈfɛʃənl̩ɪz(ə)m, ˌʌnprəˈfɛʃ(ə)nəlɪz(ə)m
AM ˌənprəˈfɛʃənlˌɪzəm, ˌənprəˈfɛʃnəˌlɪzəm

unprofessionally
BR ˌʌnprəˈfɛʃn̩əli, ˌʌnprəˈfɛʃn̩l̩i, ˌʌnprəˈfɛʃənl̩i, ˌʌnprəˈfɛʃ(ə)nəli
AM ˌənprəˈfɛʃ(ə)nəli

unprofitable
BR (ˌ)ʌnˈprɒfɪtəbl
AM ˌənˈprɑfədəbəl

unprofitableness
BR (ˌ)ʌnˈprɒfɪtəblnəs
AM ˌənˈprɑfədəbəlnəs

unprofitably
BR (ˌ)ʌnˈprɒfɪtəbli
AM ˌənˈprɑfədəbli

unprogressive
BR ˌʌnprəˈgrɛsɪv
AM ˌənprəˈgrɛsɪv, ˌənproʊˈgrɛsɪv

unprohibited
BR ˌʌnprəˈhɪbɪtɪd
AM ˌənproʊˈhɪbɪdɪd

unpromising
BR (ˌ)ʌnˈprɒmɪsɪŋ
AM ˌənˈprɑməsɪŋ

unpromisingly
BR (ˌ)ʌnˈprʌmɪsɪŋli
AM ˌənˈprɑməsɪŋli

unprompted
BR (ˌ)ʌnˈprɒm(p)tɪd
AM ˌənˈprɑm(p)təd

unpronounceable
BR ˌʌnprəˈnaʊnsəbl
AM ˌənprəˈnaʊnsəbəl

unpronounceably
BR ˌʌnprəˈnaʊnsəbli
AM ˌənprəˈnaʊnsəbli

unpropertied
BR ˌʌnˈprɒpətɪd
AM ˌənˈprɑpərdid

unprophetic
BR ˌʌnprəˈfɛtɪk
AM ˌənprəˈfɛdɪk

unpropitious
BR ˌʌnprəˈpɪʃəs
AM ˌənprəˈpɪʃəs

unpropitiously
BR ˌʌnprəˈpɪʃəsli
AM ˌənprəˈpɪʃəsli

unpropitiousness
BR ˌʌnprəˈpɪʃəsnəs
AM ˌənprəˈpɪʃəsnəs

unprosperous
BR ˌʌnˈprɒsp(ə)rəs
AM ˌənˈprɑsp(ə)rəs

unprosperously
BR ˌʌnˈprɒsp(ə)rəsli
AM ˌənˈprɑsp(ə)rəsli
unprotected
BR ˌʌnprəˈtɛktɨd
AM ˌənprəˈtɛktəd
unprotectedness
BR ˌʌnprəˈtɛktɨdnɨs
AM ˌənprəˈtɛktədnəs
unprotesting
BR ˌʌnprəˈtɛstɪŋ
AM ˌənprəˈtɛstɪŋ, ˌənproʊˈtɛstɪŋ
unprotestingly
BR ˌʌnprəˈtɛstɪŋli
AM ˌənprəˈtɛstɪŋli, ˌənˌproʊˈtɛstɪŋli
unprovability
BR ˌʌnpruːvəˈbɪlɨti
AM ˌənˌpruvəˈbɪlɨdi
unprovable
BR ˌʌnˈpruːvəbl
AM ˌənˈpruvəbəl
unprovableness
BR ˌʌnˈpruːvəblnəs
AM ˌənˈpruvəbəlnəs
unproved
BR ˌʌnˈpruːvd
AM ˌənˈpruvd
unproven
BR ˌʌnˈpruːvn
AM ˌənˈpruvn
unprovided
BR ˌʌnprəˈvʌɪdɨd
AM ˌənprəˈvaɪdɨd
unprovocative
BR ˌʌnprəˈvɒkətɪv
AM ˌənprəˈvɑkədɪv
unprovoked
BR ˌʌnprəˈvəʊkt
AM ˌənprəˈvoʊkt
unpruned
BR ˌʌnˈpruːnd
AM ˌənˈprund
unpublicised
BR ˌʌnˈpʌblɨsʌɪzd
AM ˌənˈpəbləˌsaɪzd
unpublicized
BR ˌʌnˈpʌblɨsʌɪzd
AM ˌənˈpəbləˌsaɪzd
unpublishable
BR ˌʌnˈpʌblɨʃəbl
AM ˌənˈpəbləʃəbəl
unpublished
BR ˌʌnˈpʌblɪʃt
AM ˌənˈpəblɪʃt
unpunctual
BR (ˌ)ʌnˈpʌŋ(k)tʃʊəl, (ˌ)ʌnˈpʌŋ(k)tʃ(ʉ)l, (ˌ)ʌnˈpʌŋ(k)tjʉl
AM ˌənˈpəŋ(k)(t)ʃ(əw)əl
unpunctuality
BR ˌʌnpʌŋ(k)tʃʊˈalɨti, ˌʌnpʌŋ(k)tjʊˈalɨti
AM ˌənˌpəŋ(k)(t)ʃəˈwælədi
unpunctually
BR (ˌ)ʌnˈpʌŋ(k)tʃʊəli, (ˌ)ʌnˈpʌŋ(k)tʃʉli, (ˌ)ʌnˈpʌŋ(k)tʃl̩i, (ˌ)ʌnˈpʌŋ(k)tjʉli
AM ˌənˈpəŋ(k)(t)ʃ(əw)əli
unpunctuated
BR (ˌ)ʌnˈpʌŋ(k)tʃʉeɪtɨd, (ˌ)ʌnˈpʌŋ(k)tjʊeɪtɨd
AM ˌənˈpəŋ(k)(t)ʃəˌweɪdɨd
unpunishable
BR (ˌ)ʌnˈpʌnɨʃəbl
AM ˌənˈpənəʃəbəl
unpunished
BR (ˌ)ʌnˈpʌnɪʃt
AM ˌənˈpənɪʃt
unpurified
BR (ˌ)ʌnˈpjʊərɪfʌɪd, (ˌ)ʌnˈpjɔːrɪfʌɪd
AM ˌənˈpjʊrəˌfaɪd
unputdownable
BR ˌʌnpʊtˈdaʊnəbl
AM ˌənˌpʊtˈdaʊnəbəl
unqualified
BR ˌʌnˈkwɒlɨfʌɪd, ˌʌŋˈkwɒlɨfʌɪd
AM ˈənˈkwɔləˌfaɪd, ˈənˈkwɑləˌfaɪd
unquantifiable
BR (ˌ)ʌnˈkwɒntɨfʌɪəbl, (ˌ)ʌŋˈkwɒntɨfʌɪəbl
AM ˌənˌkwɑn(t)əˈfaɪəbəl
unquantified
BR (ˌ)ʌnˈkwɒntɨfʌɪd, (ˌ)ʌŋˈkwɒntɨfʌɪd
AM ˌənˈkwɑn(t)əˌfaɪd
unquenchable
BR (ˌ)ʌnˈkwɛn(t)ʃəbl, (ˌ)ʌŋˈkwɛn(t)ʃəbl
AM ˌənˈkwɛn(t)ʃəbəl
unquenchably
BR (ˌ)ʌnˈkwɛn(t)ʃəbli, (ˌ)ʌŋˈkwɛn(t)ʃəbli
AM ˌənˈkwɛn(t)ʃəbli
unquenched
BR ˌʌnˈkwɛn(t)ʃt, ˌʌŋˈkwɛn(t)ʃt
AM ˌənˈkwɛn(t)ʃt
unquestionability
BR (ˌ)ʌnˌkwɛstʃənəˈbɪlɨti, (ˌ)ʌŋˌkwɛstʃn̩əˈbɪlɨti
AM ˌənˈkwɛstʃənəˈbɪlɨdi, ˌənˈkwɛʃtʃənəˈbɪlɨdi
unquestionable
BR (ˌ)ʌnˈkwɛstʃənəbl, (ˌ)ʌnˈkwɛstʃn̩əbl, (ˌ)ʌŋˈkwɛstʃənəbl, (ˌ)ʌŋˈkwɛstʃn̩əbl
AM ˌənˈkwɛstʃənəbəl, ˌənˈkwɛʃtʃənəbəl
unquestionableness
BR (ˌ)ʌnˈkwɛstʃənəblnəs, (ˌ)ʌnˈkwɛstʃn̩əblnəs, (ˌ)ʌŋˈkwɛstʃənəblnəs, (ˌ)ʌŋˈkwɛstʃn̩əblnəs
AM ˌənˈkwɛstʃənəbəlnəs, ˌənˈkwɛʃtʃənəbəlnəs
unquestionably
BR (ˌ)ʌnˈkwɛstʃənəbli, (ˌ)ʌnˈkwɛstʃn̩əbli, (ˌ)ʌŋˈkwɛstʃənəbli, (ˌ)ʌŋˈkwɛstʃn̩əbli
AM ˌənˈkwɛstʃənəbli, ˌənˈkwɛʃtʃənəbli
unquestioned
BR (ˌ)ʌnˈkwɛstʃ(ə)nd, (ˌ)ʌŋˈkwɛstʃ(ə)nd
AM ˌənˈkwɛstʃənd, ˌənˈkwɛʃtʃənd
unquestioning
BR (ˌ)ʌnˈkwɛstʃənɪŋ, (ˌ)ʌnˈkwɛstʃn̩ɪŋ, (ˌ)ʌŋˈkwɛstʃənɪŋ, (ˌ)ʌŋˈkwɛstʃn̩ɪŋ
AM ˌənˈkwɛstʃənɪŋ, ˌənˈkwɛʃtʃənɪŋ
unquestioningly
BR (ˌ)ʌnˈkwɛstʃənɪŋli, (ˌ)ʌnˈkwɛstʃn̩ɪŋli, (ˌ)ʌŋˈkwɛstʃənɪŋli, (ˌ)ʌŋˈkwɛstʃn̩ɪŋli
AM ˌənˈkwɛstʃənɪŋli, ˌənˈkwɛʃtʃənɪŋli
unquiet
BR ˌʌnˈkwʌɪət, ˌʌŋˈkwʌɪət
AM ˌənˈkwaɪət
unquietly
BR ˌʌnˈkwʌɪətli, ˌʌŋˈkwʌɪətli
AM ˌənˈkwaɪətli
unquietness
BR ˌʌnˈkwʌɪətnəs, ˌʌŋˈkwʌɪətnəs
AM ˌənˈkwaɪətnəs
unquotable
BR ˌʌnˈkwəʊtəbl, ˌʌŋˈkwəʊtəbl
AM ˌənˈkwoʊdəbəl
unquote
BR ˌʌnˈkwəʊt, ˌʌŋˈkwəʊt
AM ˌənˈkwoʊt
unransomed
BR ˌʌnˈransəmd
AM ˌənˈrænsəmd
unrated
BR ˌʌnˈreɪtɨd
AM ˌənˈreɪdɨd
unratified
BR ˌʌnˈratɨfʌɪd
AM ˌənˈrædəˌfaɪd
unrationed
BR ˌʌnˈraʃnd
AM ˌənˈræʃənd, ˌənˈreɪʃənd
unravel
BR (ˌ)ʌnˈrav|l, -lz, -l̩ɪŋ\-(ə)lɪŋ, -ld
AM ˌənˈrævəl, -əlz, -(ə)lɪŋ, -əld
unreachable
BR (ˌ)ʌnˈriːtʃəbl
AM ˌənˈritʃəbəl
unreachableness
BR (ˌ)ʌnˈriːtʃəblnəs
AM ˌənˈritʃəbəlnəs
unreachably
BR (ˌ)ʌnˈriːtʃəbli
AM ˌənˈritʃəbli
unreached
BR (ˌ)ʌnˈriːtʃt
AM ˌənˈritʃt
unreactive
BR ˌʌnrɪˈaktɪv
AM ˌənriˈæktɪv
unread
BR ˌʌnˈrɛd
AM ˌənˈrɛd
unreadability
BR ʌnˌriːdəˈbɪlɨti
AM ˌənˌridəˈbɪlɨdi
unreadable
BR (ˌ)ʌnˈriːdəbl
AM ˌənˈridəbəl
unreadably
BR (ˌ)ʌnˈriːdəbli
AM ˌənˈridəbli
unreadily
BR (ˌ)ʌnˈrɛdɨli
AM ˌənˈrɛdəli
unreadiness
BR (ˌ)ʌnˈrɛdɪnɨs
AM ˌənˈrɛdinɨs
unready
BR ˌʌnˈrɛdi
AM ˌənˈrɛdi
unreal
BR (ˌ)ʌnˈrɪəl
AM ˌənˈri(ə)l
unrealisable
BR (ˌ)ʌnˈrɪəlʌɪzəbl
AM ˌənˌriəˈlaɪzəbəl
unrealised
BR (ˌ)ʌnˈrɪəlʌɪzd
AM ˌənˈriəˌlaɪzd
unrealism
BR (ˌ)ʌnˈrɪəlɪz(ə)m
AM ˌənˈriəˌlɪzəm
unrealistic
BR ˌʌnrɪəˈlɪstɪk
AM ˌənˌriəˈlɪstɪk
unrealistically
BR ˌʌnrɪəˈlɪstɪkli
AM ˌənˌriəˈlɪstɪk(ə)li
unreality
BR ˌʌnrɪˈalɨti
AM ˌənriˈælədi
unrealizable
BR (ˌ)ʌnˈrɪəlʌɪzəbl
AM ˌənˈriəˌlaɪzəbəl
unrealized
BR (ˌ)ʌnˈrɪəlʌɪzd
AM ˌənˈriəˌlaɪzd
unreally
BR ˌʌnˈrɪəli

AM ˌən'riəli
unreason
BR ˌʌn'riːzn, -d
AM ˌən'rizn, -d
unreasonable
BR (ˌ)ʌn'riːzn̩əbl, (ˌ)ʌn'riːz(ə)nəbl
AM ˌən'rizn̩əbəl, ˌən'riznəbəl
unreasonableness
BR (ˌ)ʌn'riːzn̩əblnəs, (ˌ)ʌn'riːz(ə)nəblnəs
AM ˌən'rizn̩əbəlnəs, ˌən'riznəbəlnəs
unreasonably
BR (ˌ)ʌn'riːzn̩əbli, (ˌ)ʌn'riːz(ə)nəbli
AM ˌən'rizn̩əbli, ˌən'riznəbli
unreasoning
BR (ˌ)ʌn'riːzn̩ɪŋ, (ˌ)ʌn'riːz(ə)nɪŋ
AM ˌən'rizn̩ɪŋ, ˌən'riznɪŋ
unreasoningly
BR (ˌ)ʌn'riːzn̩ɪŋli, (ˌ)ʌn'riːz(ə)nɪŋli
AM ˌən'rizn̩ɪŋli, ˌən'riznɪŋli
unrebelliousness
BR ˌʌnrɪ'bɛlɪəsnəs
AM ˌənrə'bɛljəsnəs, ˌənrə'bɛliəsnəs, ˌənri'bɛljəsnəs, ˌənri'bɛliəsnəs
unreceptive
BR ˌʌnrɪ'sɛptɪv
AM ˌənrə'sɛptɪv, ˌənri'sɛptɪv
unreciprocated
BR ˌʌnrɪ'sɪprəkeɪtɪd
AM ˌənrə'sɪprəˌkeɪdɪd, ˌənri'sɪprəˌkeɪdɪd
unreckoned
BR ˌʌn'rɛk(ə)nd
AM ˌən'rɛkənd
unreclaimed
BR ˌʌnrɪ'kleɪmd
AM ˌənrə'kleɪmd, ˌənri'kleɪmd
unrecognisable
BR (ˌ)ʌn'rɛkəgnʌɪzəbl, ˌʌnrɛkəg'nʌɪzəbl
AM ˌənˌrɛkəg'naɪzəbəl
unrecognisableness
BR ˌʌn'rɛkəgnʌɪzəblnəs, ˌʌnrɛkəg'nʌɪzəblnəs
AM ˌənˌrɛkəg'naɪzəbəlnəs
unrecognisably
BR ˌʌn'rɛkəgnʌɪzəbli, ˌʌnrɛkəg'nʌɪzəbli
AM ˌənˌrɛkəg'naɪzəbli
unrecognised
BR ˌʌn'rɛkəgnʌɪzd
AM ˌən'rɛkəgˌnaɪzd
unrecognizable
BR (ˌ)ʌn'rɛkəgnʌɪzəbl, ˌʌnrɛkəg'nʌɪzəbl
AM ˌənˌrɛkəg'naɪzəbəl
unrecognizableness
BR ˌʌn'rɛkəgnʌɪzəblnəs, ˌʌnrɛkəg'nʌɪzəblnəs
AM ˌənˌrɛkəg'naɪzəbəlnəs
unrecognizably
BR ˌʌn'rɛkəgnʌɪzəbli, ˌʌnrɛkəg'nʌɪzəbli
AM ˌənˌrɛkəg'naɪzəbli
unrecognized
BR ˌʌn'rɛkəgnʌɪzd
AM ˌən'rɛkəgˌnaɪzd
unrecompensed
BR ˌʌn'rɛkəmpɛnst
AM ˌən'rɛkəmˌpɛnst
unreconcilable
BR ˌʌn'rɛk(ə)nsʌɪləbl, ˌʌnrɛk(ə)n'sʌɪləbl
AM ˌənˌrɛkən'saɪləbəl
unreconciled
BR ˌʌn'rɛkənsʌɪld, ˌʌn'rɛk(ə)nsʌɪld
AM ˌən'rɛkənˌsaɪld
unreconstructed
BR ˌʌnriːkən'strʌktɪd
AM ˌənˌrikən'strəktəd
unrecordable
BR ˌʌnrɪ'kɔːdəbl
AM ˌənrə'kɔrdəbəl, ˌənri'kɔrdəbəl
unrecorded
BR ˌʌnrɪ'kɔːdɪd
AM ˌənrə'kɔrdəd, ˌənri'kɔrdəd
unrecovered
BR ˌʌnrɪ'kʌvəd
AM ˌənrə'kəvərd, ˌənri'kəvərd
unrectified
BR ˌʌn'rɛktɪfʌɪd
AM ˌən'rɛktəˌfaɪd
unredeemable
BR ˌʌnrɪ'diːməbl
AM ˌənrə'diməbəl, ˌənri'diməbəl
unredeemably
BR ˌʌnrɪ'diːməbli
AM ˌənrə'diməbli, ˌənri'diməbli
unredeemed
BR ˌʌnrɪ'diːmd
AM ˌənrə'dimd, ˌənri'dimd
unredressed
BR ˌʌnrɪ'drɛst
AM ˌənrə'drɛst, ˌənri'drɛst
unreel
BR ˌʌn'riːl, -z, -ɪŋ, -d
AM ˌən'ril, -z, -ɪŋ, -d
unrefined
BR ˌʌnrɪ'fʌɪnd
AM ˌənrə'faɪnd, ˌənri'faɪnd
unreflected
BR ˌʌnrɪ'flɛktɪd
AM ˌənrə'flɛktəd, ˌənri'flɛktəd
unreflecting
BR ˌʌnrɪ'flɛktɪŋ
AM ˌənrə'flɛktɪŋ, ˌənri'flɛktɪŋ
unreflectingly
BR ˌʌnrɪ'flɛktɪŋli
AM ˌənrə'flɛktɪŋli, ˌənri'flɛktɪŋli
unreflectingness
BR ˌʌnrɪ'flɛktɪŋnɪs
AM ˌənrə'flɛktɪŋnɪs, ˌənri'flɛktɪŋnɪs
unreflective
BR ˌʌnrɪ'flɛktɪv
AM ˌənrə'flɛktɪv, ˌənri'flɛktɪv
unreformed
BR ˌʌnrɪ'fɔːmd
AM ˌənrə'fɔ(ə)rmd, ˌənri'fɔ(ə)rmd
unrefreshed
BR ˌʌnrɪ'frɛʃt
AM ˌənrə'frɛʃt, ˌənri'frɛʃt
unrefuted
BR ˌʌnrɪ'fjuːtɪd
AM ˌənrə'fjudəd, ˌənri'fjudəd
unregarded
BR ˌʌnrɪ'gɑːdɪd
AM ˌənrə'gɑrdəd, ˌənri'gɑrdəd
unregeneracy
BR ˌʌnrɪdʒɛn(ə)rəsi
AM ˌənrə'dʒɛnərəsi, ˌənri'dʒɛnərəsi
unregenerate
BR ˌʌnrɪ'dʒɛn(ə)rət
AM ˌənrə'dʒɛnərət, ˌənri'dʒɛnərət
unregenerately
BR ˌʌnrɪ'dʒɛn(ə)rətli
AM ˌənrə'dʒɛnərətli, ˌənri'dʒɛnərətli
unregimented
BR (ˌ)ʌn'rɛdʒɪmɛntɪd
AM ˌən'rɛdʒəˌmɛn(t)əd
unregistered
BR (ˌ)ʌn'rɛdʒɪstəd
AM ˌən'rɛdʒəstərd
unregretted
BR ˌʌnrɪ'grɛtɪd
AM ˌənrə'grɛdəd, ˌənri'grɛdəd
unregulated
BR (ˌ)ʌn'rɛgjʊleɪtɪd
AM ˌən'rɛgjəˌleɪdɪd
unrehearsed
BR ˌʌnrɪ'həːst
AM ˌənrə'hərst, ˌənri'hərst
unrein
BR ˌʌn'reɪn, -z, -ɪŋ, -d
AM ˌən'reɪn, -z, -ɪŋ, -d
unreinforced
BR ˌʌnriːɪn'fɔːst
AM ˌənriɪn'fɔ(ə)rst
unrelated
BR ˌʌnrɪ'leɪtɪd
AM ˌənrə'leɪdɪd, ˌənri'leɪdɪd
unrelatedly
BR ˌʌnrɪ'leɪtɪdli
AM ˌənrə'leɪdɪdli, ˌənri'leɪdɪdli
unrelatedness
BR ˌʌnrɪ'leɪtɪdnɪs
AM ˌənrə'leɪdɪdnɪs, ˌənri'leɪdɪdnɪs
unrelaxed
BR ˌʌnrɪ'lakst
AM ˌənrə'lækst, ˌənri'lækst
unreleased
BR ˌʌnrɪ'liːst
AM ˌənrə'list, ˌənri'list
unrelenting
BR ˌʌnrɪ'lɛntɪŋ
AM ˌənrə'lɛn(t)ɪŋ, ˌənri'lɛn(t)ɪŋ
unrelentingly
BR ˌʌnrɪ'lɛntɪŋli
AM ˌənrə'lɛn(t)ɪŋli, ˌənri'lɛn(t)ɪŋli
unrelentingness
BR ˌʌnrɪ'lɛntɪŋnɪs
AM ˌənrə'lɛn(t)ɪŋnɪs, ˌənri'lɛn(t)ɪŋnɪs
unreliability
BR ˌʌnrɪˌlʌɪə'bɪlɪti
AM ˌənrəˌlaɪə'bɪlɪdi, ˌənriˌlaɪə'bɪlɪdi
unreliable
BR ˌʌnrɪ'lʌɪəbl
AM ˌənrə'laɪəbəl, ˌənri'laɪəbəl
unreliableness
BR ˌʌnrɪ'lʌɪəblnəs
AM ˌənrə'laɪəbəlnəs, ˌənri'laɪəbəlnəs
unreliably
BR ˌʌnrɪ'lʌɪəbli
AM ˌənrə'laɪəbli, ˌənri'laɪəbli
unrelieved
BR ˌʌnrɪ'liːvd
AM ˌənrə'livd, ˌənri'livd
unrelievedly
BR ˌʌnrɪ'liːvɪdli
AM ˌənrə'livɪdli, ˌənri'livɪdli
unreligious
BR ˌʌnrɪ'lɪdʒəs
AM ˌənrə'lɪdʒəs, ˌənri'lɪdʒəs
unremarkable
BR ˌʌnrɪ'mɑːkəbl

AM ˌənrəˈmɑrkəbəl, ˌənriˈmɑrkəbəl
unremarkably
BR ˌʌnrɪˈmɑːkəbli
AM ˌənrəˈmɑrkəbli, ˌənriˈmɑrkəbli
unremarked
BR ˌʌnrɪˈmɑːkt
AM ˌənrəˈmɑrkt, ˌənriˈmɑrkt
unremembered
BR ˌʌnrɪˈmɛmbəd
AM ˌənrəˈmɛmbərd, ˌənriˈmɛmbərd
unremitting
BR ˌʌnrɪˈmɪtɪŋ
AM ˌənrəˈmɪdɪŋ, ˌənriˈmɪdɪŋ
unremittingly
BR ˌʌnrɪˈmɪtɪŋli
AM ˌənrəˈmɪdɪŋli, ˌənriˈmɪdɪŋli
unremittingness
BR ˌʌnrɪˈmɪtɪŋnɨs
AM ˌənrəˈmɪdɪŋnɨs, ˌənriˈmɪdɪŋnɨs
unremorseful
BR ˌʌnrɪˈmɔːsf(ʊ)l
AM ˌənrəˈmɔrsfəl, ˌənriˈmɔrsfəl
unremorsefully
BR ˌʌnrɪˈmɔːsfʊli, ˌʌnrɪˈmɔːsfl̩i
AM ˌənrəˈmɔrsfəli, ˌənrəˈmɔrsfəli
unremovable
BR ˌʌnrɪˈmuːvəbl
AM ˌənrəˈmuvəbəl, ˌənriˈmuvəbəl
unremunerative
BR ˌʌnrɪˈmjuːn(ə)rətɪv
AM ˌənrəˈmjun(ə)rədɪv, ˌənriˈmjun(ə)rədɪv
unremuneratively
BR ˌʌnrɪˈmjuːn(ə)rətɪv-li
AM ˌənrəˈmjun(ə)rədɪv-li, ˌənriˈmjun(ə)rədɪvli
unremunerative-ness
BR ˌʌnrɪˈmjuːn(ə)rətɪv-nɨs
AM ˌənrəˈmjun(ə)rədɪv-nɨs, ˌənriˈmjun(ə)rədɪvnɨs
unrenewable
BR ˌʌnrɪˈnjuːəbl
AM ˌənrəˈn(j)uəbəl, ˌənriˈn(j)uəbəl
unrenewed
BR ˌʌnrɪˈnjuːd
AM ˌənrəˈn(j)ud, ˌənriˈn(j)ud
unrenounced
BR ˌʌnrɪˈnaʊnst
AM ˌənrəˈnaʊnst, ˌənriˈnaʊnst
unrepairable
BR ˌʌnrɪˈpɛːrəbl
AM ˌənrəˈpɛrəbəl, ˌənriˈpɛrəbəl
unrepaired
BR ˌʌnrɪˈpɛːd
AM ˌənrəˈpɛ(ə)rd, ˌənriˈpɛ(ə)rd
unrepealed
BR ˌʌnrɪˈpiːld
AM ˌənrəˈpild, ˌənriˈpild
unrepeatability
BR ˌʌnrɪˌpiːtəˈbɪlɨti
AM ˌənrəˌpidəˈbɪlɨdi, ˌənriˌpidəˈbɪlɨdi
unrepeatable
BR ˌʌnrɪˈpiːtəbl
AM ˌənrəˈpidəbəl, ˌənriˈpidəbəl
unrepeatably
BR ˌʌnrɪˈpiːtəbli
AM ˌənrəˈpidəbli, ˌənriˈpidəbli
unrepeated
BR ˌʌnrɪˈpiːtɨd
AM ˌənrəˈpidɨd, ˌənriˈpidɨd
unrepentant
BR ˌʌnrɪˈpɛntənt
AM ˌənrəˈpɛn(t)ənt, ˌənriˈpɛn(t)ənt
unrepentantly
BR ˌʌnrɪˈpɛntəntli
AM ˌənrəˈpɛn(t)ən(t)li, ˌənriˈpɛn(t)ən(t)li
unrepented
BR ˌʌnrɪˈpɛntɨd
AM ˌənrəˈpɛn(t)əd, ˌənriˈpɛn(t)əd
unreported
BR ˌʌnrɪˈpɔːtɨd
AM ˌənrəˈpɔrdəd, ˌənrəˈpɔrdəd
unrepresentative
BR ˌʌnrɛprɪˈzɛntətɪv
AM ˌənrɛprəˈzɛn(t)ədɪv
unrepresentative-ly
BR ˌʌnrɛprɪˈzɛntətɪvli
AM ˌənrɛprəˈzɛn(t)ədɪv-li
unrepresentative-ness
BR ˌʌnrɛprɪˈzɛntətɪvnɨs
AM ˌənrɛprəˈzɛn(t)ədɪv-nɨs
unrepresented
BR ˌʌnrɛprɪˈzɛntɨd, ˌʌnˈrɛprɨzɛntɨd
AM ˌənˌrɛprəˈzɛn(t)əd
unreproved
BR ˌʌnrɪˈpruːvd
AM ˌənrəˈpruvd, ˌənriˈpruvd
unrequested
BR ˌʌnrɪˈkwɛstɨd
AM ˌənrəˈkwɛstəd, ˌənriˈkwɛstəd
unrequited
BR ˌʌnrɪˈkwʌɪtɨd
AM ˌənrəˈkwaɪdɨd, ˌənriˈkwaɪdɨd
unrequitedly
BR ˌʌnrɪˈkwʌɪtɨdli
AM ˌənrəˈkwaɪdɨdli, ˌənriˈkwaɪdɨdli
unrequitedness
BR ˌʌnrɪˈkwʌɪtɨdnɨs
AM ˌənrəˈkwaɪdɨdnɨs, ˌənriˈkwaɪdɨdnɨs
unresearched
BR ˌʌnrɪˈsəːtʃt
AM ˌənrəˈsərtʃt, ˌənriˈsərtʃt
unreserve
BR ˌʌnrɪˈzəːv, -d
AM ˌənrəˈzərv, ˌənrəˈzərv, -d
unreservedly
BR ˌʌnrɪˈzəːvɨdli
AM ˌənrəˈzərvədli, ˌənriˈzərvədli
unreservedness
BR ˌʌnrɪˈzəːvɨdnɨs
AM ˌənrəˈzərvədnəs, ˌənriˈzərvədnəs
unresisted
BR ˌʌnrɪˈzɪstɨd
AM ˌənrəˈzɪstɨd, ˌənriˈzɪstɨd
unresistedly
BR ˌʌnrɪˈzɪstɨdli
AM ˌənrəˈzɪstɨdli, ˌənriˈzɪstɨdli
unresisting
BR ˌʌnrɪˈzɪstɪŋ
AM ˌənrəˈzɪstɪŋ, ˌənriˈzɪstɪŋ
unresistingly
BR ˌʌnrɪˈzɪstɪŋli
AM ˌənrəˈzɪstɪŋli, ˌənriˈzɪstɪŋli
unresistingness
BR ˌʌnrɪˈzɪstɪŋnɨs
AM ˌənrəˈzɪstɪŋnɨs, ˌənriˈzɪstɪŋnɨs
unresolvable
BR ˌʌnrɪˈzɒlvəbl
AM ˌənrəˈzɔlvəbəl, ˌənrəˈzɑlvəbəl, ˌənriˈzɔlvəbəl, ˌənriˈzɑlvəbəl
unresolved
BR ˌʌnrɪˈzɒlvd
AM ˌənrəˈzɔlvd, ˌənrəˈzɑlvd, ˌənriˈzɔlvd, ˌənriˈzɑlvd
unresolvedly
BR ˌʌnrɪˈzɒlvɨdli
AM ˌənrəˈzɔlvədli, ˌənrəˈzɑlvədli, ˌənriˈzɔlvədli, ˌənriˈzɑlvədli
unresolvedness
BR ˌʌnrɪˈzɒlvɨdnɨs
AM ˌənrəˈzɔlvədnəs, ˌənrəˈzɑlvədnəs, ˌənriˈzɔlvədnəs, ˌənriˈzɑlvədnəs
unresponsive
BR ˌʌnrɪˈspɒnsɪv
AM ˌənrəˈspɑnsɪv, ˌənriˈspɑnsɪv
unresponsively
BR ˌʌnrɪˈspɒnsɨvli
AM ˌənrəˈspɑnsɨvli, ˌənriˈspɑnsɨvli
unresponsiveness
BR ˌʌnrɪˈspɒnsɨvnɨs
AM ˌənrəˈspɑnsɪvnɨs, ˌənriˈspɑnsɪvnɨs
unrest
BR (ˌ)ʌnˈrɛst
AM ˌənˈrɛst
unrested
BR ˌʌnˈrɛstɨd
AM ˌənˈrɛstəd
unrestful
BR ˌʌnˈrɛs(t)f(ʊ)l
AM ˌənˈrɛs(t)fəl
unrestfully
BR ˌʌnˈrɛstfʊli, ˌʌnˈrɛstfl̩i
AM ˌənˈrɛs(t)fəli
unrestfulness
BR ˌʌnˈrɛs(t)f(ʊ)lnəs
AM ˌənˈrɛs(t)fəlnəs
unresting
BR ˌʌnˈrɛstɪŋ
AM ˌənˈrɛstɪŋ
unrestingly
BR ˌʌnˈrɛstɪŋli
AM ˌənˈrɛstɪŋli
unrestored
BR ˌʌnrɪˈstɔːd
AM ˌənrəˈstɔ(ə)rd, ˌənriˈstɔ(ə)rd
unrestrainable
BR ˌʌnrɪˈstreɪnəbl
AM ˌənrəˈstreɪnəbəl, ˌənriˈstreɪnəbəl
unrestrained
BR ˌʌnrɪˈstreɪnd
AM ˌənrəˈstreɪnd, ˌənriˈstreɪnd
unrestrainedly
BR ˌʌnrɪˈstreɪnɨdli
AM ˌənrəˈstreɪnɨdli, ˌənriˈstreɪnɨdli
unrestrainedness
BR ˌʌnrɪˈstreɪnɨdnɨs
AM ˌənrəˈstreɪnɨdnɨs, ˌənriˈstreɪnɨdnɨs
unrestraint
BR ˌʌnrɪˈstreɪnt
AM ˌənrəˈstreɪnt, ˌənriˈstreɪnt
unrestricted
BR ˌʌnrɪˈstrɪktɨd
AM ˌənrəˈstrɪktɨd, ˌənriˈstrɪktɨd

unrestrictedly
BR ˌʌnrɪˈstrɪktɨdli
AM ˌənrəˈstrɪktɨdli, ˌənriˈstrɪktɨdli

unrestrictedness
BR ˌʌnrɪˈstrɪktɨdnɨs
AM ˌənrəˈstrɪktɨdnɨs, ˌənriˈstrɪktɨdnɨs

unretentive
BR ˌʌnrɪˈtɛntɪv
AM ˌənrəˈtɛn(t)ɪv, ˌənriˈtɛn(t)ɪv

unretentively
BR ˌʌnrɪˈtɛntɨvli
AM ˌənrəˈtɛn(t)ɨvli, ˌənriˈtɛn(t)ɨvli

unretentiveness
BR ˌʌnrɪˈtɛntɨvnɨs
AM ˌənrəˈtɛn(t)ɪvnɨs, ˌənriˈtɛn(t)ɪvnɨs

unreturned
BR ˌʌnrɪˈtəːnd
AM ˌənrəˈtərnd, ˌənriˈtərnd

unrevealed
BR ˌʌnrɪˈviːld
AM ˌənrəˈvild, ˌənriˈvild

unrevealing
BR ˌʌnrɪˈviːlɪŋ
AM ˌənrəˈvilɪŋ, ˌənriˈvilɪŋ

unreversed
BR ˌʌnrɪˈvəːst
AM ˌənrəˈvərst, ˌənriˈvərst

unrevised
BR ˌʌnrɪˈvʌɪzd
AM ˌənrəˈvaɪzd, ˌənriˈvaɪzd

unrevoked
BR ˌʌnrɪˈvəʊkt
AM ˌənrəˈvoʊkt, ˌənriˈvoʊkt

unrevolutionary
BR ˌʌnrɛvəˈl(j)uːʃn̩(ə)ri
AM ˌənˌrɛvəˈl(j)uʃəˌnɛri

unrewarded
BR ˌʌnrɪˈwɔːdɨd
AM ˌənrəˈwɔrdəd, ˌənriˈwɔrdəd

unrewarding
BR ˌʌnrɪˈwɔːdɪŋ
AM ˌənrəˈwɔrdɪŋ, ˌənriˈwɔrdɪŋ

unrewardingly
BR ˌʌnrɪˈwɔːdɪŋli
AM ˌənrəˈwɔrdɪŋli, ˌənriˈwɔrdɪŋli

unrhymed
BR ˌʌnˈrʌɪmd
AM ˌənˈraɪmd

unrhythmical
BR ˌʌnˈrɪðmɪkl
AM ˌənˈrɪðmɪkəl

unrhythmically
BR ˌʌnˈrɪðmɪkli
AM ˌənˈrɪðmɪk(ə)li

unridable
BR (ˌ)ʌnˈrʌɪdəbl
AM ˌənˈraɪdəbəl

unridden
BR ˌʌnˈrɪdn
AM ˌənˈrɪdən

unriddle
BR ˌʌnˈrɪd|l, -lz, -l̩ɪŋ\-lɪŋ, -ld
AM ˌənˈrɪd|əl, -əlz, -(ə)lɪŋ, -əld

unriddler
BR ˌʌnˈrɪdl̩ə(r), ˌʌnˈrɪdlə(r), -z
AM ˌənˈrɪd(ə)lər, -z

unrideable
BR (ˌ)ʌnˈrʌɪdəbl
AM ˌənˈraɪdəbəl

unrig
BR ˌʌnˈrɪɡ, -z, -ɪŋ, -d
AM ˌənˈrɪɡ, -z, -ɪŋ, -d

unrighteous
BR (ˌ)ʌnˈrʌɪtʃəs
AM ˌənˈraɪtʃəs

unrighteously
BR (ˌ)ʌnˈrʌɪtʃəsli
AM ˌənˈraɪtʃəsli

unrighteousness
BR (ˌ)ʌnˈrʌɪtʃəsnəs
AM ˌənˈraɪtʃəsnəs

unrip
BR ˌʌnˈrɪp, -s, -ɪŋ, -t
AM ˌənˈrɪp, -s, -ɪŋ, -t

unripe
BR (ˌ)ʌnˈrʌɪp
AM ˌənˈraɪp

unripened
BR (ˌ)ʌnˈrʌɪpnd
AM ˌənˈraɪpənd

unripeness
BR (ˌ)ʌnˈrʌɪpnɨs
AM ˌənˈraɪpnɨs

unrisen
BR ˌʌnˈrɪzn
AM ˌənˈrɪzn

unrivalled
BR (ˌ)ʌnˈrʌɪvld
AM ˌənˈraɪvəld

unrivet
BR ˌʌnˈrɪv|ɪt, -ɪts, -ɨtɪŋ, -ɨtɨd
AM ˌənˈrɪvɨ|t, -ts, -dɪŋ, -dɨd

unroasted
BR (ˌ)ʌnˈrəʊstɨd
AM ˌənˈroʊstəd

unrobe
BR (ˌ)ʌnˈrəʊb, -z, -ɪŋ, -d
AM ˌənˈroʊb, -z, -ɪŋ, -d

unroll
BR (ˌ)ʌnˈrəʊl, -z, -ɪŋ, -d
AM ˌənˈroʊl, -z, -ɪŋ, -d

unromantic
BR ˌʌnrə(ʊ)ˈmantɪk
AM ˌənrəˈmæn(t)ɪk, ˌənroʊˈmæn(t)ɪk

unromantically
BR ˌʌnrə(ʊ)ˈmantɪkli
AM ˌənrəˈmæn(t)ək(ə)li, ˌənroʊˈmæn(t)ək(ə)li

unroof
BR ˌʌnˈruːf, ˌʌnˈrʊf, -s, -ɪŋ, -t
AM ˌənˈruf, ˌənˈrʊf, -s, -ɪŋ, -t

unroot
BR ˌʌnˈruːt, -s, -ɪŋ, -ɨd
AM ˌənˈru|t, ənˈrʊ|t, -ts, -dɪŋ, -dəd

unrope
BR ˌʌnˈrəʊp, -s, -ɪŋ, -t
AM ˌənˈroʊp, -s, -ɪŋ, -t

unrounded
BR ˌʌnˈraʊndɨd
AM ˌənˈraʊndəd

unrove
BR ˌʌnˈrəʊv
AM ˌənˈroʊv

unroyal
BR ˌʌnˈrɔɪəl
AM ˌənˈrɔɪəl

UNRRA
BR ˈʌnrə(r)
AM ˈənrə

unruffled
BR (ˌ)ʌnˈrʌfld
AM ˌənˈrəfəld

unruled
BR ˌʌnˈruːld
AM ˌənˈruld

unruliness
BR ʌnˈruːlɪnɨs
AM ˌənˈrulinɨs

unruly
BR ʌnˈruːli
AM ˌənˈruli

UNRWA
BR ˈʌnrə(r)
AM ˈənrə

unsackable
BR (ˌ)ʌnˈsakəbl
AM ˌənˈsækəbəl

unsaddle
BR (ˌ)ʌnˈsad|l, -lz, -l̩ɪŋ\-lɪŋ, -ld
AM ˌənˈsæd|əl, -əlz, -(ə)lɪŋ, -əld

unsafe
BR (ˌ)ʌnˈseɪf
AM ˌənˈseɪf

unsafely
BR (ˌ)ʌnˈseɪfli
AM ˌənˈseɪfli

unsafeness
BR (ˌ)ʌnˈseɪfnɨs
AM ˌənˈseɪfnɨs

unsaid
BR (ˌ)ʌnˈsɛd
AM ˌənˈsɛd

unsalability
BR ʌnˌseɪləˈbɪlɨti, ˌʌnseɪləˈbɪlɨti
AM ˌənˌseɪləˈbɪlɨdi

unsalable
BR (ˌ)ʌnˈseɪləbl
AM ˌənˈseɪləbəl

unsalableness
BR (ˌ)ʌnˈseɪləblnəs
AM ˌənˈseɪləbəlnəs

unsalaried
BR ˌʌnˈsalərɪd
AM ˌənˈsælərid

unsaleability
BR ʌnˌseɪləˈbɪlɨti, ˌʌnseɪləˈbɪlɨti
AM ˌənˌseɪləˈbɪlɨdi

unsaleable
BR ˌʌnˈseɪləbl
AM ˌənˈseɪləbəl

unsaleableness
BR (ˌ)ʌnˈseɪləblnəs
AM ˌənˈseɪləbəlnəs

unsalted
BR ˌʌnˈsɔːltɨd, ˌʌnˈsɒltɨd
AM ˌənˈsɔltəd, ˌənˈsɑltəd

unsalubrious
BR ˌʌnsəˈl(j)uːbrɪəs
AM ˌənsəˈl(j)ubriəs

unsalvageable
BR ˌʌnˈsalvɨdʒəbl
AM ˌənˈsælvədʒəbəl

unsanctified
BR ˌʌnˈsaŋ(k)tɨfʌɪd
AM ˌənˈsæŋ(k)təˌfaɪd

unsanctioned
BR ˌʌnˈsaŋ(k)ʃnd
AM ˌənˈsæŋkʃənd

unsanitary
BR ˌʌnˈsanɪt(ə)ri
AM ˌənˈsænəˌtɛri

unsatisfactorily
BR ˌʌnsatɪsˈfakt(ə)rɪli
AM ˌənˌsædəsˈfæktərəli

unsatisfactoriness
BR ˌʌnsatɪsˈfakt(ə)rɪnɪs
AM ˌənˌsædəsˈfæktərinɪs

unsatisfactory
BR ˌʌnsatɪsˈfakt(ə)ri
AM ˌənsædəsˈfæktəri

unsatisfied
BR (ˌ)ʌnˈsatɪsfʌɪd
AM ˌənˈsædəsˌfaɪd

unsatisfiedness
BR (ˌ)ʌnˈsatɪsfʌɪdnɪs
AM ˌənˈsædəsˌfaɪdnɪs

unsatisfying
BR (ˌ)ʌnˈsatɪsfʌɪɪŋ
AM ˌənˈsædəsˌfaɪɪŋ

unsatisfyingly
BR (ˌ)ʌnˈsatɪsfʌɪɪŋli
AM ˌənˈsædəsˌfaɪɪŋli

unsaturated
BR (ˌ)ʌnˈsatʃʉreɪtɪd, (ˌ)ʌnˈsatjʉreɪtɪd
AM ˌənˈsætʃəˌreɪdɪd

unsaturation
BR ˌʌnsatʃʊˈreɪʃn, ˌʌnsatjʊˈreɪʃn
AM ˌənˌsætʃəˈreɪʃən

unsaved
BR ˌʌnˈseɪvd
AM ˌənˈseɪvd

unsavorily
BR (ˌ)ʌnˈseɪv(ə)rɨli
AM ˌənˈseɪv(ə)rəli

unsavoriness
BR (ˌ)ʌnˈseɪv(ə)rɪnɨs
AM ˌənˈseɪv(ə)rinɨs

unsavory
BR (ˌ)ʌnˈseɪv(ə)ri
AM ˌənˈseɪv(ə)ri

unsavourily
BR (ˌ)ʌnˈseɪv(ə)rɨli
AM ˌənˈseɪv(ə)rəli

unsavouriness
BR (ˌ)ʌnˈseɪv(ə)rɪnɨs
AM ˌənˈseɪv(ə)rinɨs

unsavoury
BR (ˌ)ʌnˈseɪv(ə)ri
AM ˌənˈseɪv(ə)ri

unsay
BR ˌʌnˈs|eɪ, -ɛz, -eɪɪŋ, -ɛd
AM ˌənˈs|eɪ, -ɛz, -eɪɪŋ, -ɛd

unsayable
BR ˌʌnˈseɪəbl
AM ˌənˈseɪəbəl

unscalable
BR ˌʌnˈskeɪləbl
AM ˌənˈskeɪləbəl

unscaleable
BR ˌʌnˈskeɪləbl
AM ˌənˈskeɪləbəl

unscaled
BR ˌʌnˈskeɪld
AM ˌənˈskeɪld

unscarred
BR ˌʌnˈskɑːd
AM ˌənˈskɑrd

unscathed
BR (ˌ)ʌnˈskeɪðd
AM ˌənˈskeɪðd

unscented
BR ˌʌnˈsɛntɨd
AM ˌənˈsɛn(t)əd

unscheduled
BR ˌʌnˈʃɛdjʊld, ˌʌnˈʃɛdjuːld, ˌʌnˈskɛdʒʊld, ˌʌnˈʃɛdʒʊld, ˌʌnˈskɛdjʊld, ˌʌnˈskɛdjuːld
AM ˌənˈskɛdʒəld, ˌənˈskɛˌdʒʊld

unscholarliness
BR ˌʌnˈskɒləlɪnɨs
AM ˌənˈskɑlərlinɨs

unscholarly
BR ˌʌnˈskɒləli
AM ˌənˈskɑlərli

unschooled
BR ˌʌnˈskuːld
AM ˌənˈskuld

unscientific
BR ˌʌnsʌɪənˈtɪfɪk
AM ˌənsaɪənˈtɪfɪk

unscientifically
BR ˌʌnsʌɪənˈtɪfɨkli
AM ˌənsaɪənˈtɪfək(ə)li

unscramble
BR (ˌ)ʌnˈskramb|l, -lz, -lɪŋ\-lɪŋ, -ld
AM ˌənˈskræmb|əl, -əlz, -(ə)lɪŋ, -əld

unscrambler
BR (ˌ)ʌnˈskrambl̩ə(r), (ˌ)ʌnˈskramblə(r), -z
AM ˌənˈskræmb(ə)lər, -z

unscratched
BR (ˌ)ʌnˈskratʃt
AM ˌənˈskrætʃt

unscreened
BR ˌʌnˈskriːnd
AM ˌənˈskrind

unscrew
BR ˌʌnˈskruː, -z, -ɪŋ, -d
AM ˌənˈskru, -z, -ɪŋ, -d

unscripted
BR ˌʌnˈskrɪptɨd
AM ˌənˈskrɪptɨd

unscriptural
BR ˌʌnˈskrɪptʃ(ə)rəl, ˌʌnˈskrɪptʃ(ə)rl̩
AM ˌənˈskrɪptʃərəl, ˌənˈskrɪpʃ(ə)rəl

unscripturally
BR ˌʌnˈskrɪptʃ(ə)rəli, ˌʌnˈskrɪptʃ(ə)rl̩i
AM ˌənˈskrɪptʃərəli, ˌənˈskrɪpʃ(ə)rəli

unscrupulous
BR (ˌ)ʌnˈskruːpjʊləs
AM ˌənˈskrupjələs

unscrupulously
BR (ˌ)ʌnˈskruːpjʊləsli
AM ˌənˈskrupjələsli

unscrupulousness
BR (ˌ)ʌnˈskruːpjʊləsnəs
AM ˌənˈskrupjələsnəs

unseal
BR ˌʌnˈsiːl, -z, -ɪŋ, -d
AM ˌənˈsil, -z, -ɪŋ, -d

unsealed
BR ˌʌnˈsiːld
AM ˌənˈsild

unsearchable
BR (ˌ)ʌnˈsəːtʃəbl
AM ˌənˈsərtʃəbəl

unsearchableness
BR (ˌ)ʌnˈsəːtʃəblnəs
AM ˌənˈsərtʃəbəlnəs

unsearchably
BR (ˌ)ʌnˈsəːtʃəbli
AM ˌənˈsərtʃəbli

unsearched
BR ˌʌnˈsəːtʃt
AM ˌənˈsərtʃt

unseasonable
BR (ˌ)ʌnˈsiːzn̩əbl, (ˌ)ʌnˈsiːz(ə)nəbl
AM ˌənˈsizn̩əbəl, ˌənˈsiznəbəl

unseasonableness
BR (ˌ)ʌnˈsiːzn̩əblnəs, (ˌ)ʌnˈsiːz(ə)nəblnəs
AM ˌənˈsizn̩əbəlnəs, ˌənˈsiznəbəlnəs

unseasonably
BR (ˌ)ʌnˈsiːzn̩əbli, (ˌ)ʌnˈsiːz(ə)nəbli
AM ˌənˈsizn̩əbli, ˌənˈsiznəbli

unseasoned
BR ˌʌnˈsiːznd
AM ˌənˈsiznd

unseat
BR ˌʌnˈsiːt, -s, -ɪŋ, -ɨd
AM ˌənˈsi|t, -ts, -dɪŋ, -dɨd

unseaworthiness
BR (ˌ)ʌnˈsiːˌwəːðɪnɨs
AM ˌənˈsiˌwərðinɨs

unseaworthy
BR (ˌ)ʌnˈsiːˌwəːði
AM ˌənˈsiˌwərði

unseconded
BR ˌʌnˈsɛk(ə)ndɨd
AM ˌənˈsɛkəndəd

unsectarian
BR ˌʌnsɛkˈtɛːrɪən
AM ˌənˌsɛkˈtɛriən

unsecured
BR ˌʌnsɪˈkjʊəd, ˌʌnsɪˈkjɔːd
AM ˌənsəˈkjʊ(ə)rd

unseeable
BR ˌʌnˈsiːəbl
AM ˌənˈsiəbəl

unseeded
BR ˌʌnˈsiːdɨd
AM ˌənˈsidɨd

unseeing
BR ˌʌnˈsiːɪŋ
AM ˌənˈsiɪŋ

unseeingly
BR ˌʌnˈsiːɪŋli
AM ˌənˈsiɪŋli

unseemliness
BR ʌnˈsiːmlɪnɨs
AM ˌənˈsimlinɨs

unseemly
BR ʌnˈsiːmli
AM ˌənˈsimli

unseen
BR ˌʌnˈsiːn, -z
AM ˌənˈsin, -z

unsegregated
BR ˌʌnˈsɛgrɪgeɪtɨd
AM ˌənˈsɛgrəˌgeɪdɨd

unselect
BR ˌʌnsɪˈlɛkt
AM ˌənsəˈlɛk(t)

unselected
BR ˌʌnsɪˈlɛktɨd
AM ˌənsəˈlɛktəd

unselective
BR ˌʌnsɪˈlɛktɪv
AM ˌənsəˈlɛktɪv

unselfconscious
BR ˌʌnsɛlfˈkɒnʃəs
AM ˌənˌsɛlfˈkɑnʃəs

unselfconsciously
BR ˌʌnsɛlfˈkɒnʃəsli
AM ˌənˌsɛlfˈkɑnʃəsli

unselfconsciousness
BR ˌʌnsɛlfˈkɒnʃəsnəs
AM ˌənˌsɛlfˈkɑnʃəsnəs

unselfish
BR (ˌ)ʌnˈsɛlfɪʃ
AM ˌənˈsɛlfɪʃ

unselfishly
BR (ˌ)ʌnˈsɛlfɨʃli
AM ˌənˈsɛlfɨʃli

unselfishness
BR (ˌ)ʌnˈsɛlfɨʃnɨs
AM ˌənˈsɛlfɪʃnɨs

unsellable
BR ˌʌnˈsɛləbl
AM ˌənˈsɛləbəl

unsensational
BR ˌʌnsɛnˈseɪʃn̩(ə)l, ˌʌnsɛnˈseɪʃən(ə)l
AM ˌənsɛnˈseɪʃ(ə)nəl

unsensationally
BR ˌʌnsɛnˈseɪʃn̩əli, ˌʌnsɛnˈseɪʃn̩l̩i, ˌʌnsɛnˈseɪʃənl̩i, ˌʌnsɛnˈseɪʃ(ə)nəli
AM ˌənsɛnˈseɪʃ(ə)nəli

unsensitive
BR (ˌ)ʌnˈsɛnsɨtɪv
AM ˌənˈsɛnsədɪv

unsensitively
BR (ˌ)ʌnˈsɛnsɨtɨvli
AM ˌənˈsɛnsədɨvli

unsent
BR ˌʌnˈsɛnt
AM ˌənˈsɛnt

unsentimental
BR ˌʌnsɛntɪˈmɛntl
AM ˌənˌsɛn(t)əˈmɛn(t)l

unsentimentality
BR ˌʌnsɛntɪmɛnˈtalɨti, ˌʌnsɛntɪmənˈtalɨti
AM ¦ənˌsɛn(t)əˌmɛnˈtælədi, ¦ənˌsɛn(t)əmənˈtælədi

unsentimentally
BR ˌʌnsɛntɪˈmɛntl̩i
AM ˌənˌsɛn(t)əˈmɛn(t)li

unseparated
BR (ˌ)ʌnˈsɛpəreɪtɨd
AM ˌənˈsɛpəˌreɪdɨd

unserious
BR ˌʌnˈsɪərɪəs
AM ˌənˈsɪriəs

unserviceability
BR ʌnˌsəːvɪsəˈbɪlɨti
AM ˌənˌsərvəsəˈbɪlɨdi

unserviceable
BR (ˌ)ʌnˈsəːvɪsəbl
AM ˌənˈsərvəsəbəl
unset
BR ˌʌnˈsɛt
AM ˌənˈsɛt
unsettle
BR (ˌ)ʌnˈsɛt|l, -lz, -l̩ɪŋ\-lɪŋ, -ld
AM ˌənˈsɛ|dəl, -dlz, -dlɪŋ\-tlɪŋ, -dld
unsettledness
BR (ˌ)ʌnˈsɛtldnəs
AM ˌənˈsɛdldnəs
unsettlement
BR (ˌ)ʌnˈsɛtlm(ə)nt
AM ˌənˈsɛdlmənt
unsevered
BR ˌʌnˈsɛvəd
AM ˌənˈsɛvərd
unsewn
BR (ˌ)ʌnˈsəʊn
AM ˌənˈsoʊn
unsex
BR (ˌ)ʌnˈsɛks, -ɪz, -ɪŋ, -t
AM ˌənˈsɛks, -əz, -ɪŋ, -t
unsexy
BR ˌʌnˈsɛksi
AM ˌənˈsɛksi
unshackle
BR (ˌ)ʌnˈʃak|l, -lz, -l̩ɪŋ\-lɪŋ, -ld
AM ˌənˈʃæk|əl, -əlz, -(ə)lɪŋ, -əld
unshaded
BR ˌʌnˈʃeɪdɪd
AM ˌənˈʃeɪdɪd
unshakability
BR ʌnˌʃeɪkəˈbɪlɪti, ˌʌnʃeɪkəˈbɪlɪti
AM ˌənˌʃeɪkəˈbɪlɪdi
unshakable
BR ʌnˈʃeɪkəbl
AM ˌənˈʃeɪkəbəl
unshakably
BR ʌnˈʃeɪkəbli
AM ˌənˈʃeɪkəbli
unshakeability
BR ʌnˌʃeɪkəˈbɪlɪti, ˌʌnʃeɪkəˈbɪlɪti
AM ˌənˌʃeɪkəˈbɪlɪdi
unshakeable
BR ʌnˈʃeɪkəbl
AM ˌənˈʃeɪkəbəl
unshakeably
BR ʌnˈʃeɪkəbli
AM ˌənˈʃeɪkəbli
unshaken
BR (ˌ)ʌnˈʃeɪk(ə)n
AM ˌənˈʃeɪkən
unshakenly
BR (ˌ)ʌnˈʃeɪk(ə)nli
AM ˌənˈʃeɪkənli
unshapeliness
BR (ˌ)ʌnˈʃeɪplɪnɪs
AM ˌənˈʃeɪplinɪs
unshapely
BR (ˌ)ʌnˈʃeɪpli
AM ˌənˈʃeɪpli
unshared
BR ˌʌnˈʃɛːd
AM ˌənˈʃɛ(ə)rd
unsharp
BR ˌʌnˈʃɑːp
AM ˌənˈʃɑrp
unsharpened
BR (ˌ)ʌnˈʃɑːpnd
AM ˌənˈʃɑrpənd
unsharpness
BR ˌʌnˈʃɑːpnəs
AM ˌənˈʃɑrpnəs
unshaved
BR ˌʌnˈʃeɪvd
AM ˌənˈʃeɪvd
unshaven
BR ˌʌnˈʃeɪvn
AM ˌənˈʃeɪvən
unsheathe
BR (ˌ)ʌnˈʃiː|ð, (ˌ)ʌnˈʃiː|θ, -ðz\-θs, -ðɪŋ\-θɪŋ, -ðd\-θt
AM ˌənˈʃið, -z, -ɪŋ, -d
unshed
BR ˌʌnˈʃɛd
AM ˌənˈʃɛd
unshell
BR ˌʌnˈʃɛl, -z, -ɪŋ, -d
AM ˌənˈʃɛl, -z, -ɪŋ, -d
unsheltered
BR ˌʌnˈʃɛltəd
AM ˌənˈʃɛltərd
unshielded
BR ˌʌnˈʃiːldɪd
AM ˌənˈʃildɪd
unshiftable
BR ˌʌnˈʃɪftəbl
AM ˌənˈʃɪftəbəl
unshifted
BR ˌʌnˈʃɪftɪd
AM ˌənˈʃɪftɪd
unship
BR ˌʌnˈʃɪp, -s, -ɪŋ, -t
AM ˌənˈʃɪp, -s, -ɪŋ, -t
unshockability
BR ʌnˌʃɒkəˈbɪlɪti, ˌʌnʃɒkəˈbɪlɪti
AM ˌənˌʃɑkəˈbɪlɪdi
unshockable
BR ˌʌnˈʃɒkəbl
AM ˌənˈʃɑkəbəl
unshockably
BR ˌʌnˈʃɒkəbli
AM ˌənˈʃɑkəbli
unshod
BR ˌʌnˈʃɒd
AM ˌənˈʃɑd
unshorn
BR ˌʌnˈʃɔːn
AM ˌənˈʃɔ(ə)rn
unshrinkability
BR ʌnˌʃrɪŋkəˈbɪlɪti, ˌʌnʃrɪŋkəˈbɪlɪti
AM ˌənˌʃrɪŋkəˈbɪlɪdi
unshrinkable
BR (ˌ)ʌnˈʃrɪŋkəbl
AM ˌənˈʃrɪŋkəbəl
unshrinking
BR ʌnˈʃrɪŋkɪŋ
AM ˌənˈʃrɪŋkɪŋ
unshrinkingly
BR ʌnˈʃrɪŋkɪŋli
AM ˌənˈʃrɪŋkɪŋli
unshriven
BR ˌʌnˈʃrɪvn
AM ˌənˈʃrɪvən
unshut
BR ˌʌnˈʃʌt
AM ˌənˈʃət
unshuttered
BR ˌʌnˈʃʌtəd
AM ˌənˈʃədərd
unsighted
BR (ˌ)ʌnˈsʌɪtɪd
AM ˌənˈsaɪdɪd
unsightliness
BR ʌnˈsʌɪtlɪnɪs
AM ˌənˈsaɪtlinɪs
unsightly
BR ʌnˈsʌɪtl|i, -ɪə(r), -ɪɪst
AM ˌənˈsaɪtli, -ər, -ɪst
unsigned
BR ˌʌnˈsʌɪnd
AM ˌənˈsaɪnd
unsignposted
BR ˌʌnˈsʌɪnpəʊstɪd
AM ˌənˈsaɪnˌpoʊstəd
unsilenced
BR ˌʌnˈsʌɪlənst
AM ˌənˈsaɪlənst
unsimplified
BR (ˌ)ʌnˈsɪmplɪfʌɪd
AM ˌənˈsɪmpləˌfaɪd
unsinkability
BR ʌnˌsɪŋkəˈbɪlɪti, ˌʌnsɪŋkəˈbɪlɪti
AM ˌənˌsɪŋkəˈbɪlɪdi
unsinkable
BR (ˌ)ʌnˈsɪŋkəbl
AM ˌənˈsɪŋkəbəl
unsized
BR ˌʌnˈsʌɪzd
AM ˌənˈsaɪzd
unskilful
BR (ˌ)ʌnˈskɪlf(ʊ)l
AM ˌənˈskɪlfəl
unskilfully
BR (ˌ)ʌnˈskɪlfʊli, (ˌ)ʌnˈskɪlfl̩i
AM ˌənˈskɪlfəli
unskilfulness
BR (ˌ)ʌnˈskɪlf(ʊ)lnəs
AM ˌənˈskɪlfəlnəs
unskilled
BR ˌʌnˈskɪld
AM ˌənˈskɪld
unskimmed
BR ˌʌnˈskɪmd
AM ˌənˈskɪmd
unslakeable
BR (ˌ)ʌnˈsleɪkəbl
AM ˌənˈsleɪkəbəl
unslaked
BR ˌʌnˈsleɪkt
AM ˌənˈsleɪkt
unsleeping
BR (ˌ)ʌnˈsliːpɪŋ
AM ˌənˈslipɪŋ
unsleepingly
BR ʌnˈsliːpɪŋli
AM ˌənˈslipɪŋli
unsliced
BR ˌʌnˈslʌɪst
AM ˌənˈslaɪst
unsling
BR ˌʌnˈslɪŋ, -z, -ɪŋ
AM ˌənˈslɪŋ, -z, -ɪŋ
unslung
BR ˌʌnˈslʌŋ
AM ˌənˈsləŋ
unsmiling
BR (ˌ)ʌnˈsmʌɪlɪŋ
AM ˌənˈsmaɪlɪŋ
unsmilingly
BR (ˌ)ʌnˈsmʌɪlɪŋli
AM ˌənˈsmaɪlɪŋli
unsmilingness
BR (ˌ)ʌnˈsmʌɪlɪŋnɪs
AM ˌənˈsmaɪlɪŋnɪs
unsmoked
BR ˌʌnˈsməʊkt
AM ˌənˈsmoʊkt
unsmoothed
BR ˌʌnˈsmuːðd
AM ˌənˈsmuðd
unsnarl
BR ˌʌnˈsnɑːl, -z, -ɪŋ, -d
AM ˌənˈsnɑrl, -z, -ɪŋ, -d
unsoaked
BR ˌʌnˈsəʊkt
AM ˌənˈsoʊkt
unsociability
BR ʌnˌsəʊʃəˈbɪlɪti, ˌʌnsəʊʃəˈbɪlɪti
AM ˌənsoʊʃəˈbɪlɪdi
unsociable
BR (ˌ)ʌnˈsəʊʃəbl
AM ˌənˈsoʊʃəbəl
unsociableness
BR (ˌ)ʌnˈsəʊʃəblnəs
AM ˌənˈsoʊʃəbəlnəs
unsociably
BR (ˌ)ʌnˈsəʊʃəbli
AM ˌənˈsoʊʃəbli
unsocial
BR ˌʌnˈsəʊʃl
AM ˌənˈsoʊʃəl
unsocialist
BR ˌʌnˈsəʊʃl̩ɪst, ˌʌnˈsəʊʃəlɪst, -s
AM ˌənˈsoʊʃələst, -s
unsocially
BR ˌʌnˈsəʊʃl̩i, ˌʌnˈsəʊʃəli
AM ˌənˈsoʊʃəli

unsoftened
BR ˌʌnˈsɒfnd
AM ˌənˈsɔfənd, ˌənˈsɑfənd
unsoiled
BR ˌʌnˈsɔɪld
AM ˌənˈsɔɪld
unsold
BR ˌʌnˈsəʊld
AM ˌənˈsoʊld
unsolder
BR ˌʌnˈsɒld|ə(r), ˌʌnˈsəʊld|ə(r), -əz, -(ə)rɪŋ, -əd
AM ˌənˈsɑdər, -z, -ɪŋ, -d
unsoldierly
BR ˌʌnˈsəʊldʒəli
AM ˌənˈsoʊldʒərli
unsolicited
BR ˌʌnsəˈlɪsɪtɪd
AM ˌənsəˈlɪsɪdɪd
unsolicitedly
BR ˌʌnsəˈlɪsɪtɪdli
AM ˌənsəˈlɪsɪdɪdli
unsolvability
BR ʌnˌsɒlvəˈbɪlɪti, ˌʌnsɒlvəˈbɪlɪti
AM ˌənˌsɑlvəˈbɪlɪdi
unsolvable
BR ˌʌnˈsɒlvəbl
AM ˌənˈsɑlvəbəl
unsolvableness
BR ˌʌnˈsɒlvəblnəs
AM ˌənˈsɑlvəbəlnəs
unsolved
BR ˌʌnˈsɒlvd
AM ˌənˈsɑlvd
unsophisticated
BR ˌʌnsəˈfɪstɪkeɪtɪd
AM ˌənsəˈfɪstəˌkeɪdɪd
unsophisticatedly
BR ˌʌnsəˈfɪstɪkeɪtɪdli
AM ˌənsəˈfɪstəˌkeɪdɪdli
unsophisticatedness
BR ˌʌnsəˈfɪstɪkeɪtɪdnɪs
AM ˌənsəˈfɪstəˌkeɪdɪdnɪs
unsophistication
BR ˌʌnsəˌfɪstɪˈkeɪʃn
AM ˌənsəˌfɪstəˈkeɪʃən
unsorted
BR ˌʌnˈsɔːtɪd
AM ˌənˈsɔrdəd
unsought
BR ˌʌnˈsɔːt
AM ˌənˈsɔt, ˌənˈsɑt
unsound
BR ˌʌnˈsaʊnd
AM ˌənˈsaʊnd
unsounded
BR ˌʌnˈsaʊndɪd
AM ˌənˈsaʊndəd
unsoundly
BR ˌʌnˈsaʊndli
AM ˌənˈsaʊndli
unsoundness
BR ˌʌnˈsaʊn(d)nəs
AM ˌənˈsaʊn(d)nəs
unsoured
BR ˌʌnˈsaʊəd
AM ˌənˈsaʊ(ə)rd
unsown
BR ˌʌnˈsəʊn
AM ˌənˈsoʊn
unsparing
BR ʌnˈspɛːrɪŋ
AM ˌənˈspɛrɪŋ
unsparingly
BR ʌnˈspɛːrɪŋli
AM ˌənˈspɛrɪŋli
unsparingness
BR ʌnˈspɛːrɪŋnɪs
AM ˌənˈspɛrɪŋnɪs
unspeakable
BR ʌnˈspiːkəbl
AM ˌənˈspikəbəl
unspeakableness
BR ʌnˈspiːkəblnəs
AM ˌənˈspikəbəlnəs
unspeakably
BR ʌnˈspiːkəbli
AM ˌənˈspikəbli
unspeaking
BR (ˌ)ʌnˈspiːkɪŋ
AM ˌənˈspikɪŋ
unspecial
BR ˌʌnˈspɛʃl
AM ˌənˈspɛʃəl
unspecialised
BR (ˌ)ʌnˈspɛʃəlʌɪzd, (ˌ)ʌnˈspɛʃl̩ʌɪzd
AM ˌənˈspɛʃəˌlaɪzd
unspecialized
BR (ˌ)ʌnˈspɛʃəlʌɪzd, (ˌ)ʌnˈspɛʃl̩ʌɪzd
AM ˌənˈspɛʃəˌlaɪzd
unspecific
BR ˌʌnspɪˈsɪfɪk
AM ˌənspəˈsɪfɪk
unspecified
BR (ˌ)ʌnˈspɛsɪfʌɪd
AM ˌənˈspɛsəˌfaɪd
unspectacular
BR ˌʌnspɛkˈtakjʉlə(r)
AM ˌənˌspɛkˈtækjələr
unspectacularly
BR ˌʌnspɛkˈtakjʉləli
AM ˌənˌspɛkˈtækjələrli
unspent
BR ˌʌnˈspɛnt
AM ˌənˈspɛnt
unspilled
BR ˌʌnˈspɪld
AM ˌənˈspɪld
unspilt
BR ˌʌnˈspɪlt
AM ˌənˈspɪlt
unspiritual
BR ˌʌnˈspɪrɪtʃʊəl, ˌʌnˈspɪrɪtʃ(ʉ)l, ˌʌnˈspɪrɪtjʊəl, ˌʌnˈspɪrɪtjʉl
AM ˌənˈspɪrɪtʃ(əw)əl
unspirituality
BR ˌʌnspɪrɪtʃʊˈalɪti, ˌʌnspɪrɪtjʊˈalɪti
AM ˌənˌspɪrɪtʃ(ə)ˈwælədi
unspiritually
BR ˌʌnˈspɪrɪtʃʊəli, ˌʌnˈspɪrɪtʃʉli, ˌʌnˈspɪrɪtʃl̩i
AM ˌənˈspɪrɪtʃ(əw)əli
unspiritualness
BR ˌʌnˈspɪrɪtʃʊəlnəs, ˌʌnˈspɪrɪtʃ(ʉ)lnəs
AM ˌənˈspɪrɪtʃ(əw)əlnəs
unspoiled
BR ˌʌnˈspɔɪld, ˌʌnˈspɔɪlt
AM ˌənˈspɔɪld
unspoilt
BR ˌʌnˈspɔɪlt
AM ˌənˈspɔɪlt
unspoken
BR (ˌ)ʌnˈspəʊk(ə)n
AM ˌənˈspoʊkən
unsponsored
BR ˌʌnˈspɒnsəd
AM ˌənˈspɑnsərd
unsporting
BR ˌʌnˈspɔːtɪŋ
AM ˌənˈspɔrdɪŋ
unsportingly
BR (ˌ)ʌnˈspɔːtɪŋli
AM ˌənˈspɔrdɪŋli
unsportingness
BR (ˌ)ʌnˈspɔːtɪŋnɪs
AM ˌənˈspɔrdɪŋnɪs
unsportsmanlike
BR (ˌ)ʌnˈspɔːtsmənlʌɪk
AM ˌənˈspɔrtsmənˌlaɪk
unspotted
BR ˌʌnˈspɒtɪd
AM ˌənˈspɑdəd
unsprayed
BR ˌʌnˈspreɪd
AM ˌənˈspreɪd
unsprung
BR ˌʌnˈsprʌŋ
AM ˌənˈsprəŋ
Unst
BR ʌnst
AM ənst
unstable
BR (ˌ)ʌnˈsteɪbl
AM ˌənˈsteɪbəl
unstableness
BR (ˌ)ʌnˈsteɪblnəs
AM ˌənˈsteɪbəlnəs
unstably
BR (ˌ)ʌnˈsteɪbli
AM ˌənˈsteɪb(ə)li
unstaffed
BR ˌʌnˈstɑːft, ˌʌnˈstaft
AM ˌənˈstæft
unstained
BR ˌʌnˈsteɪnd
AM ˌənˈsteɪnd
unstall
BR ˌʌnˈstɔːl, -z, -ɪŋ, -d
AM ˌənˈstɔl, ˌənˈstɑl, -z, -ɪŋ, -d
unstamped
BR ˌʌnˈstam(p)t
AM ˌənˈstæm(p)t
unstandardised
BR ˌʌnˈstandədʌɪzd
AM ˌənˈstændərˌdaɪzd
unstandardized
BR ˌʌnˈstandədʌɪzd
AM ˌənˈstændərˌdaɪzd
unstarched
BR ˌʌnˈstɑːtʃt
AM ˌənˈstɑrtʃt
unstatable
BR ˌʌnˈsteɪtəbl
AM ˌənˈsteɪdəbəl
unstated
BR ˌʌnˈsteɪtɪd
AM ˌənˈsteɪdɪd
unstatesmanlike
BR (ˌ)ʌnˈsteɪtsmənlʌɪk
AM ˌənˈsteɪtsmənˌlaɪk
unstatutable
BR ˌʌnˈstatʃuːtəbl, ˌʌnˈstatjuːtəbl
AM ˌənˈstætʃudəbəl, ˌənˈstætʃədəbəl
unstatutably
BR ˌʌnˈstatʃuːtəbli, ˌʌnˈstatjuːtəbli
AM ˌənˈstætʃudəbli, ˌənˈstætʃədəbli
unsteadfast
BR ˌʌnˈstɛdfɑːst, ˌʌnˈstɛdfast
AM ˌənˈstɛdˌfæst
unsteadfastly
BR ˌʌnˈstɛdfɑːstli, ˌʌnˈstɛdfastli
AM ˌənˈstɛdˌfæst(l)i
unsteadfastness
BR ˌʌnˈstɛdfɑːs(t)nəs, ˌʌnˈstɛdfas(t)nəs
AM ˌənˈstɛdˌfæs(t)nəs
unsteadily
BR (ˌ)ʌnˈstɛdɪli
AM ˌənˈstɛdəli
unsteadiness
BR (ˌ)ʌnˈstɛdɪnɪs
AM ˌənˈstɛdinɪs
unsteady
BR (ˌ)ʌnˈstɛdi
AM ˌənˈstɛdi
unsterile
BR ˌʌnˈstɛrʌɪl
AM ˌənˈstɛrəl
unsterilely
BR ˌʌnˈstɛrʌɪlli
AM ˌənˈstɛrə(l)li
unsterilised
BR (ˌ)ʌnˈstɛrɪlʌɪzd
AM ˌənˈstɛrəˌlaɪzd
unsterilized
BR (ˌ)ʌnˈstɛrɪlʌɪzd
AM ˌənˈstɛrəˌlaɪzd

unstick
BR ˌʌnˈstɪk, -s, -ɪŋ
AM ˌənˈstɪk, -s, -ɪŋ
unstifled
BR ˌʌnˈstʌɪfld
AM ˌənˈstaɪfəld
unstimulated
BR ˌʌnˈstɪmjʉleɪtɪd
AM ˌənˈstɪmjəˌleɪdɪd
unstimulating
BR ˌʌnˈstɪmjʉleɪtɪŋ
AM ˌənˈstɪmjəˌleɪdɪŋ
unstinted
BR ʌnˈstɪntɪd
AM ˌənˈstɪn(t)ɪd
unstintedly
BR ʌnˈstɪntɪdli
AM ˌənˈstɪn(t)ɪdli
unstinting
BR ʌnˈstɪntɪŋ
AM ˌənˈstɪn(t)ɪŋ
unstintingly
BR ʌnˈstɪntɪŋli
AM ˌənˈstɪn(t)ɪŋli
unstirred
BR ˌʌnˈstəːd
AM ˌənˈstərd
unstitch
BR ˌʌnˈstɪtʃ, -ɪz, -ɪŋ, -t
AM ˌənˈstɪtʃ, -ɪz, -ɪŋ, -t
unstocked
BR (ˌ)ʌnˈstɒkt
AM ˌənˈstɑkt
unstockinged
BR ˌʌnˈstɒkɪŋd
AM ˌənˈstɑkɪŋd
unstop
BR ˌʌnˈstɒp, -s, -ɪŋ, -t
AM ˌənˈstɑp, -s, -ɪŋ, -t
unstoppability
BR ʌnˌstɒpəˈbɪlɪti, ˌʌnstɒpəˈbɪlɪti
AM ˌənˌstɑpəˈbɪlɪdi
unstoppable
BR (ˌ)ʌnˈstɒpəbl
AM ˌənˈstɑpəbəl
unstoppably
BR (ˌ)ʌnˈstɒpəbli
AM ˌənˈstɑpəbli
unstopper
BR (ˌ)ʌnˈstɒp|ə(r), -əz, -(ə)rɪŋ, -əd
AM ˌənˈstɑpər, -z, -ɪŋ, -d
unstrained
BR ˌʌnˈstreɪnd
AM ˌənˈstreɪnd
unstrap
BR ˌʌnˈstrap, -s, -ɪŋ, -t
AM ˌənˈstræp, -s, -ɪŋ, -t
unstratified
BR (ˌ)ʌnˈstratɪfʌɪd
AM ˌənˈstrædəˌfaɪd
unstreamed
BR ˌʌnˈstriːmd
AM ˌənˈstrimd
unstreamlined
BR (ˌ)ʌnˈstriːmlʌɪnd
AM ˌənˈstrimˌlaɪnd
unstrengthened
BR ˌʌnˈstrɛŋ(k)θnd
AM ˌənˈstrɛŋ(k)θənd
unstressed
BR ˌʌnˈstrɛst
AM ˌənˈstrɛst
unstretched
BR ˌʌnˈstrɛtʃt
AM ˌənˈstrɛtʃt
unstring
BR ˌʌnˈstrɪŋ, -z, -ɪŋ
AM ˌənˈstrɪŋ, -z, -ɪŋ
unstripped
BR ˌʌnˈstrɪpt
AM ˌənˈstrɪpt
unstructured
BR (ˌ)ʌnˈstrʌktʃəd
AM ˌənˈstrək(t)ʃərd
unstrung
BR ˌʌnˈstrʌŋ
AM ˌənˈstrəŋ
unstuck
BR ˌʌnˈstʌk
AM ˌənˈstək
unstudied
BR ˌʌnˈstʌdɪd
AM ˌənˈstədid
unstudiedly
BR ˌʌnˈstʌdɪdli
AM ˌənˈstədidli
unstuffed
BR ˌʌnˈstʌft
AM ˌənˈstəft
unstuffy
BR ˌʌnˈstʌfi
AM ˌənˈstəfi
unstylish
BR ˌʌnˈstʌɪlɪʃ
AM ˌənˈstaɪlɪʃ
unsubdued
BR ˌʌnsəbˈdjuːd, ˌʌnsəbˈdʒuːd
AM ˌənsəbˈd(j)ud
unsubjugated
BR ˌʌnˈsʌbdʒʉgeɪtɪd
AM ˌənˈsəbdʒəˌgeɪdɪd
unsubscribed
BR ˌʌnsəbˈskrʌɪbd
AM ˌənsəbˈskraɪbd
unsubsidised
BR ˌʌnˈsʌbsɪdʌɪzd
AM ˌənˈsəbsəˌdaɪzd
unsubsidized
BR ˌʌnˈsʌbsɪdʌɪzd
AM ˌənˈsəbsəˌdaɪzd
unsubstantial
BR ˌʌnsəbˈstanʃl
AM ˌənsəbˈstæn(t)ʃəl
unsubstantiality
BR ˌʌnsəbˌstanʃɪˈalɪti
AM ˌənsəbˌstæn(t)ʃiˈælədi
unsubstantially
BR ˌʌnsəbˈstanʃl̩i, ˌʌnsəbˈstanʃəli
AM ˌənsəbˈstæn(t)ʃəli
unsubstantiated
BR ˌʌnsəbˈstanʃɪeɪtɪd
AM ˌənsəbˈstæn(t)ʃiˌeɪdɪd
unsubtle
BR ˌʌnˈsʌtl
AM ˌənˈsədəl
unsubtly
BR ˌʌnˈsʌtl̩i
AM ˌənˈsəd(ə)li
unsuccess
BR ˌʌnsəkˈsɛs
AM ˌənsəkˈsɛs
unsuccessful
BR ˌʌnsəkˈsɛsf(ʉ)l
AM ˌənsəkˈsɛsfəl
unsuccessfully
BR ˌʌnsəkˈsɛsfʉli, ˌʌnsəkˈsɛsfl̩i
AM ˌənsəkˈsɛsfəli
unsuccessfulness
BR ˌʌnsəkˈsɛsf(ʉ)lnəs
AM ˌənsəkˈsɛsfəlnəs
unsugared
BR ˌʌnˈʃʊgəd
AM ˌənˈʃʊgərd
unsuggestive
BR ˌʌnsəˈdʒɛstɪv
AM ˌənsə(g)ˈdʒɛstɪv
unsuitability
BR ʌnˌs(j)uːtəˈbɪlɪti, ˌʌns(j)uːtəˈbɪlɪti
AM ˌənsudəˈbɪlɪdi
unsuitable
BR (ˌ)ʌnˈs(j)uːtəbl
AM ˌənˈsudəbəl
unsuitableness
BR (ˌ)ʌnˈs(j)uːtəblnəs
AM ˌənˈsudəbəlnəs
unsuitably
BR (ˌ)ʌnˈs(j)uːtəbli
AM ˌənˈsudəbli
unsuited
BR (ˌ)ʌnˈs(j)uːtɪd
AM ˌənˈsudəd
unsullied
BR ˌʌnˈsʌlɪd
AM ˌənˈsəlid
unsummoned
BR ˌʌnˈsʌmənd
AM ˌənˈsəmənd
unsung
BR ˌʌnˈsʌŋ
AM ˌənˈsəŋ
unsupervised
BR ˌʌnˈs(j)uːpəvʌɪzd
AM ˌənˈsupərˌvaɪzd
unsupplied
BR ˌʌnsəˈplʌɪd
AM ˌənsəˈplaɪd
unsupportable
BR ˌʌnsəˈpɔːtəbl
AM ˌənsəˈpɔrdəbəl
unsupportably
BR ˌʌnsəˈpɔːtəbli
AM ˌənsəˈpɔrdəbli
unsupported
BR ˌʌnsəˈpɔːtɪd
AM ˌənsəˈpɔrdəd
unsupportedly
BR ˌʌnsəˈpɔːtɪdli
AM ˌənsəˈpɔrdədli
unsupportive
BR ˌʌnsəˈpɔːtɪv
AM ˌənsəˈpɔrdɪv
unsuppressed
BR ˌʌnsəˈprɛst
AM ˌənsəˈprɛst
unsure
BR ˌʌnˈʃʊə(r), ˌʌnˈʃɔː(r)
AM ˌənˈʃʊ(ə)r
unsurely
BR ˌʌnˈʃʊəli, ˌʌnˈʃɔːli
AM ˌənˈʃʊrli
unsureness
BR ˌʌnˈʃʊənəs, ˌʌnˈʃɔːnəs
AM ˌənˈʃʊrnəs
unsurfaced
BR ˌʌnˈsəːfɪst
AM ˌənˈsərfəst
unsurmountable
BR ˌʌnsəˈmaʊntəbl
AM ˌənsərˈmaʊn(t)əbəl
unsurpassable
BR ˌʌnsəˈpɑːsəbl, ˌʌnsəˈpasəbl
AM ˌənsərˈpæsəbəl
unsurpassably
BR ˌʌnsəˈpɑːsəbli, ˌʌnsəˈpasəbli
AM ˌənsərˈpæsəbli
unsurpassed
BR ˌʌnsəˈpɑːst, ˌʌnsəˈpast
AM ˌənsərˈpæst
unsurprised
BR ˌʌnsəˈprʌɪzd
AM ˌənsə(r)ˈpraɪzd
unsurprising
BR ˌʌnsəˈprʌɪzɪŋ
AM ˌənsə(r)ˈpraɪzɪŋ
unsurprisingly
BR ˌʌnsəˈprʌɪzɪŋli
AM ˌənsə(r)ˈpraɪzɪŋli
unsurveyed
BR ˌʌnsəˈveɪd
AM ˌənsərˈveɪd
unsurvivable
BR ˌʌnsəˈvʌɪvəbl
AM ˌənsərˈvaɪvəbəl
unsusceptibility
BR ˌʌnsəˌsɛptɪˈbɪlɪti
AM ˌənsəˌsɛptəˈbɪlɪdi
unsusceptible
BR ˌʌnsəˈsɛptɪbl
AM ˌənsəˈsɛptəbəl
unsuspected
BR ˌʌnsəˈspɛktɪd
AM ˌənsəˈspɛktəd
unsuspectedly
BR ˌʌnsəˈspɛktɪdli

AM ˌənsəˈspɛktədli
unsuspecting
BR ˌʌnsəˈspɛktɪŋ
AM ˌənsəˈspɛktɪŋ
unsuspectingly
BR ˌʌnsəˈspɛktɪŋli
AM ˌənsəˈspɛktɪŋli
unsuspectingness
BR ˌʌnsəˈspɛktɪŋnɨs
AM ˌənsəˈspɛktɪŋnɨs
unsuspicious
BR ˌʌnsəˈspɪʃəs
AM ˌənsəˈspɪʃəs
unsuspiciously
BR ˌʌnsəˈspɪʃəsli
AM ˌənsəˈspɪʃəsli
unsuspiciousness
BR ˌʌnsəˈspɪʃəsnəs
AM ˌənsəˈspɪʃəsnəs
unsustainable
BR ˌʌnsəˈsteɪnəbl
AM ˌənsəˈsteɪnəbəl
unsustainably
BR ˌʌnsəˈsteɪnəbli
AM ˌənsəˈsteɪnəbli
unsustained
BR ˌʌnsəˈsteɪnd
AM ˌənsəˈsteɪnd
unswallowed
BR ˌʌnˈswɒləʊd
AM ˌənˈswɑloʊd
unswathe
BR ˌʌnˈsweɪð, -z, -ɪŋ, -d
AM ˌənˈsweɪð, -z, -ɪŋ, -d
unswayed
BR ˌʌnˈsweɪd
AM ˌənˈsweɪd
unsweetened
BR ˌʌnˈswiːtnd
AM ˌənˈswitnd
unswept
BR ˌʌnˈswɛpt
AM ˌənˈswɛpt
unswerving
BR (ˌ)ʌnˈswəːvɪŋ
AM ˌənˈswərvɪŋ
unswervingly
BR (ˌ)ʌnˈswəːvɪŋli
AM ˌənˈswərvɪŋli
unsworn
BR ˌʌnˈswɔːn
AM ˌənˈswɔ(ə)rn
Unsworth
BR ˈʌnzwəːθ, ˈʌnzwəθ
AM ˈənzˌwərθ
unsymmetrical
BR ˌʌnsɪˈmɛtrɪkl
AM ˌənsəˈmɛtrəkəl
unsymmetrically
BR ˌʌnsɪˈmɛtrɪkli
AM ˌənsəˈmɛtrək(ə)li
unsympathetic
BR ˌʌnsɪmpəˈθɛtɪk
AM ˌənsɪmpəˈθɛdɪk
unsympathetically
BR ˌʌnsɪmpəˈθɛtɪkli
AM ˌənˌsɪmpəˈθɛdək(ə)li
unsystematic
BR ˌʌnsɪstɪˈmatɪk
AM ˌənˌsɪstəˈmædɪk
unsystematically
BR ˌʌnsɪstɪˈmatɪkli
AM ˌənˌsɪstəˈmædək(ə)li
untack
BR ˌʌnˈtak, -s, -ɪŋ, -t
AM ˌənˈtæk, -s, -ɪŋ, -t
untainted
BR (ˌ)ʌnˈteɪntɨd
AM ˌənˈteɪn(t)ɨd
untaken
BR ˌʌnˈteɪk(ə)n
AM ˌənˈteɪkən
untalented
BR (ˌ)ʌnˈtaləntɨd
AM ˌənˈtæləntəd
untamable
BR ˌʌnˈteɪməbl
AM ˌənˈteɪməbəl
untameable
BR ˌʌnˈteɪməbl
AM ˌənˈteɪməbəl
untamed
BR ˌʌnˈteɪmd
AM ˌənˈteɪmd
untangle
BR (ˌ)ʌnˈtaŋɡ|l, -lz, -l̩ɪŋ\-lɪŋ, -ld
AM ˌənˈtæŋɡ|əl, -əlz, -(ə)lɪŋ, -əld
untanned
BR ˌʌnˈtand
AM ˌənˈtænd
untapped
BR ˌʌnˈtapt
AM ˌənˈtæpt
untarnished
BR (ˌ)ʌnˈtɑːnɪʃt
AM ˌənˈtɑrnɪʃt
untasted
BR ˌʌnˈteɪstɨd
AM ˌənˈteɪstɨd
untaught
BR ˌʌnˈtɔːt
AM ˌənˈtɔt, ˌənˈtɑt
untaxed
BR ˌʌnˈtakst
AM ˌənˈtækst
unteach
BR ˌʌnˈtiːtʃ, -ɨz, -ɪŋ
AM ˌənˈtitʃ, -ɨz, -ɪŋ
unteachable
BR (ˌ)ʌnˈtiːtʃəbl
AM ˌənˈtitʃəbəl
untearable
BR ˌʌnˈtɛːrəbl
AM ˌənˈtɛrəbəl
untechnical
BR ˌʌnˈtɛknɪkl
AM ˌənˈtɛknəkəl
untechnically
BR ˌʌnˈtɛknɪkli
AM ˌənˈtɛknək(ə)li
untempered
BR ˌʌnˈtɛmpəd
AM ˌənˈtɛmpərd
untempted
BR ˌʌnˈtɛm(p)tɨd
AM ˌənˈtɛm(p)təd
untenability
BR ʌnˌtɛnəˈbɪlɨti, ˌʌntɛnəˈbɪlɨti
AM ˌənˌtɛnəˈbɪlɨdi
untenable
BR (ˌ)ʌnˈtɛnəbl
AM ˌənˈtɛnəbəl
untenableness
BR (ˌ)ʌnˈtɛnəblnəs
AM ˌənˈtɛnəbəlnəs
untenably
BR (ˌ)ʌnˈtɛnəbli
AM ˌənˈtɛnəbli
untenanted
BR ˌʌnˈtɛnəntɨd
AM ˌənˈtɛnən(t)əd
untended
BR ˌʌnˈtɛndɨd
AM ˌənˈtɛndəd
untenured
BR ˌʌnˈtɛnjəd
AM ˌənˈtɛnjərd
Untermensch
BR ˈʊntəmɛnʃ
AM ˈʊntərˌmɛn(t)ʃ
Untermenschen
BR ˈʊntəˌmɛnʃn
AM ˈʊntərˌmɛn(t)ʃn
untestable
BR ˌʌnˈtɛstəbl
AM ˌənˈtɛstəbəl
untested
BR ˌʌnˈtɛstɨd
AM ˌənˈtɛstəd
untether
BR ˌʌnˈtɛð|ə(r), -əz, -(ə)rɪŋ, -əd
AM ˌənˈtɛðər, -z, -ɪŋ, -d
Unthank
BR ˈʌnθaŋk
AM ˈənˌθæŋk
unthanked
BR ˌʌnˈθaŋ(k)t
AM ˌənˈθæŋ(k)t
unthankful
BR (ˌ)ʌnˈθaŋkf(ʊ)l
AM ˌənˈθæŋkfəl
unthankfully
BR (ˌ)ʌnˈθaŋkfʊli, (ˌ)ʌnˈθaŋkfl̩i
AM ˌənˈθæŋkfəli
unthankfulness
BR (ˌ)ʌnˈθaŋkf(ʊ)lnəs
AM ˌənˈθæŋkfəlnəs
unthatched
BR ˌʌnˈθatʃt
AM ˌənˈθætʃt
untheological
BR ˌʌnθɪəˈlɒdʒɪkl
AM ˌənˌθiəˈlɑdʒəkəl
untheoretical
BR ˌʌnθɪəˈrɛtɪkl
AM ˌənˌθiəˈrɛdəkəl
untheorised
BR ˌʌnˈθɪərʌɪzd
AM ˌənˈθiəˌraɪzd
untheorized
BR ˌʌnˈθɪərʌɪzd
AM ˌənˈθiəˌraɪzd
unthickened
BR ˌʌnˈθɪknd
AM ˌənˈθɪkənd
unthink
BR ˌʌnˈθɪŋk, -s, -ɪŋ
AM ˌənˈθɪŋk, -s, -ɪŋ
unthinkability
BR ʌnˌθɪŋkəˈbɪlɨti, ˌʌnθɪŋkəˈbɪlɨti
AM ˌənˌθɪŋkəˈbɪlɨdi
unthinkable
BR ʌnˈθɪŋkəbl
AM ˌənˈθɪŋkəbəl
unthinkableness
BR ʌnˈθɪŋkəblnəs
AM ˌənˈθɪŋkəbəlnəs
unthinkably
BR ʌnˈθɪŋkəbli
AM ˌənˈθɪŋkəbli
unthinking
BR (ˌ)ʌnˈθɪŋkɪŋ
AM ˌənˈθɪŋkɪŋ
unthinkingly
BR (ˌ)ʌnˈθɪŋkɪŋli
AM ˌənˈθɪŋkɪŋli
unthinkingness
BR (ˌ)ʌnˈθɪŋkɪŋnɨs
AM ˌənˈθɪŋkɪŋnɨs
unthought
BR ˌʌnˈθɔːt
AM ˌənˈθɔt, ˌənˈθɑt
unthoughtful
BR (ˌ)ʌnˈθɔːtf(ʊ)l
AM ˌənˈθɔtfəl, ˌənˈθɑtfəl
unthoughtfully
BR (ˌ)ʌnˈθɔːtfʊli, (ˌ)ʌnˈθɔːtfl̩i
AM ˌənˈθɔtfəli, ˌənˈθɑtfəli
unthoughtfulness
BR (ˌ)ʌnˈθɔːtf(ʊ)lnəs
AM ˌənˈθɔtfəlnəs, ˌənˈθɑtfəlnəs
unthought-of
BR ʌnˈθɔːtɒv, ʌnˈθɔːtəv
AM ˌənˈθɔdəv, ˌənˈθɑdəv
unthought-out
BR ˌʌnθɔːtˈaʊt
AM ˌənˌθɔˈdaʊt, ˌənˌθɑˈdaʊt
unthread
BR ˌʌnˈθrɛd, -z, -ɪŋ, -ɨd
AM ˌənˈθrɛd, -z, -ɪŋ, -əd
unthreatened
BR ˌʌnˈθrɛtnd
AM ˌənˈθrɛtnd

unthreatening
BR ˌʌn'θrɛtn̩ɪŋ, ˌʌn'θrɛtnɪŋ
AM ˌən'θrɛtn̩ɪŋ, ˌən'θrɛtnɪŋ

unthreshed
BR ˌʌn'θrɛʃt
AM ˌən'θrɛʃt

unthriftily
BR (ˌ)ʌn'θrɪftɨli
AM ˌən'θrɪftɨli

unthriftiness
BR (ˌ)ʌn'θrɪftɪnɨs
AM ˌən'θrɪftinɨs

unthrifty
BR (ˌ)ʌn'θrɪfti
AM ˌən'θrɪfti

unthrone
BR ˌʌn'θrəʊn, -z, -ɪŋ, -d
AM ˌən'θroʊn, -z, -ɪŋ, -d

untidily
BR (ˌ)ʌn'tʌɪdɨli
AM ˌən'taɪdɨli

untidiness
BR (ˌ)ʌn'tʌɪdɪnɨs
AM ˌən'taɪdinɨs

untidy
BR (ˌ)ʌn'tʌɪd|i, -ɪz, -ɪɪŋ, -ɪd, -ɪə(r), -ɪɨst
AM ˌən'taɪdi, -z, -ɪŋ, -d, -ər, -ɨst

untie
BR ˌʌn'tʌɪ, -z, -ɪŋ, -d
AM ˌən'taɪ, -z, -ɪŋ, -d

until
BR (ə)n'tɪl, (ˌ)ʌn'tɪl
AM ˌən'tɪl, ən'tɪl

untilled
BR ˌʌn'tɪld
AM ˌən'tɪld

untimed
BR ˌʌn'tʌɪmd
AM ˈən'taɪmd

untimeliness
BR (ˌ)ʌn'tʌɪmlɪnɨs
AM ˌən'taɪmlinɨs

untimely
BR (ˌ)ʌn'tʌɪmli
AM ˌən'taɪmli

untinged
BR ˌʌn'tɪn(d)ʒd
AM ˌən'tɪndʒd

untipped
BR ˌʌn'tɪpt
AM ˌən'tɪpt

untired
BR (ˌ)ʌn'tʌɪəd
AM ˌən'taɪ(ə)rd

untiring
BR ʌn'tʌɪərɪŋ
AM ˌən'taɪ(ə)rɪŋ

untiringly
BR ʌn'tʌɪərɪŋli
AM ˌən'taɪ(ə)rɪŋli

untitled
BR ˌʌn'tʌɪtld
AM ˌən'taɪdld

unto
BR 'ʌntʊ, 'ʌntuː, 'ʌntə
AM 'əntə, 'əntu

untoasted
BR ˌʌn'təʊstɨd
AM ˌən'toʊstəd

untold
BR (ˌ)ʌn'təʊld
AM ˌən'toʊld

untouchability
BR ʌnˌtʌtʃə'bɪlɨti, ˌʌntʌtʃə'bɪlɨti
AM ˌənˌtətʃə'bɪlɨdi

untouchable
BR (ˌ)ʌn'tʌtʃəbl, -z
AM ˌən'tətʃəbəl, -z

untouchableness
BR ʌn'tʌtʃəblnəs
AM ˌən'tətʃəbəlnəs

untouched
BR (ˌ)ʌn'tʌtʃt
AM ˌən'tətʃt

untoward
BR ˌʌntə'wɔːd
AM ˌənˈto(ə)rd

untowardly
BR ˌʌntə'wɔːdli
AM ˌən'tɔrdli

untowardness
BR ˌʌntə'wɔːdnəs
AM ˌən'tɔrdnəs

untraceable
BR ˌʌn'treɪsəbl
AM ˌən'treɪsəbəl

untraceably
BR ˌʌn'treɪsəbli
AM ˌən'treɪsəbli

untraced
BR ˌʌn'treɪst
AM ˌən'treɪst

untracked
BR ˌʌn'trakt
AM ˌən'trækt

untraditional
BR ˌʌntrə'dɪʃn̩(ə)l, ˌʌntrə'dɪʃən(ə)l
AM ˌəntrə'dɪʃ(ə)nəl

untrainable
BR ˌʌn'treɪnəbl
AM ˌən'treɪnəbəl

untrained
BR (ˌ)ʌn'treɪnd
AM ˌən'treɪnd

untrammeled
BR (ˌ)ʌn'tramld
AM ˌən'træməld

untrammelled
BR (ˌ)ʌn'tramld
AM ˌən'træməld

untrampled
BR ˌʌn'trampld
AM ˌən'træmpəld

untransferable
BR ˌʌntrans'fəːrəbl, ˌʌntrɑːns'fəːrəbl, ˌʌntranz'fəːrəbl, ˌʌntrɑːnz'fəːrəbl, (ˌ)ʌn'transf(ə)rəbl, (ˌ)ʌn'trɑːnsf(ə)rəbl, (ˌ)ʌn'tranzf(ə)rəbl, (ˌ)ʌn'trɑːnzf(ə)rəbl
AM ˌən'træn(t)sf(ə)rəbəl, ˌən'træn(t)sfərbəl, ˌənˌtræn(t)s'fərəbəl

untransformed
BR ˌʌntrans'fɔːmd, ˌʌntrɑːns'fɔːmd, ˌʌntranz'fɔːmd, ˌʌntrɑːnz'fɔːmd
AM ˌəntræn(t)s'fɔrmd

untranslatability
BR ˌʌntransˌleɪtə'bɪlɨti, ˌʌntrɑːnsˌleɪtə'bɪlɨti, ˌʌntranzˌleɪtə'bɪlɨti, ˌʌntrɑːnzˌleɪtə'bɪlɨti
AM ˌənˌtræn(t)sˌleɪdə'bɪlɨdi, ˌənˌtrænzˌleɪdə'bɪlɨdi

untranslatable
BR ˌʌntrans'leɪtəbl, ˌʌntrɑːns'leɪtəbl, ˌʌntranz'leɪtəbl, ˌʌntrɑːnz'leɪtəbl
AM ˌən'træn(t)sˌleɪdəbəl, ˌən'trænzˌleɪdəbəl, ˌənˌtræn(t)s'leɪdəbəl, ˌənˌtrænz'leɪdəbəl

untranslatably
BR ˌʌntrans'leɪtəbli, ˌʌntrɑːns'leɪtəbli, ˌʌntranz'leɪtəbli, ˌʌntrɑːnz'leɪtəbli
AM ˌənˌtræn(t)s'leɪdəbli, ˌənˌtrænz'leɪdəbli

untranslated
BR ˌʌntrans'leɪtɨd, ˌʌntrɑːns'leɪtɨd, ˌʌntranz'leɪtɨd, ˌʌntrɑːnz'leɪtɨd
AM ˌən'træn(t)sˌleɪdɨd, ˌən'trænzˌleɪdɨd

untransmitted
BR ˌʌntranz'mɪtɨd, ˌʌntrɑːnz'mɪtɨd, ˌʌntrans'mɪtɨd, ˌʌntrɑːns'mɪtɨd
AM ˌəntrænz'mɪdɨd, ˌəntræn(t)s'mɪdɨd, ˌən'trænzˌmɪdɨd, ˌən'træn(t)sˌmɪdɨd

untransportable
BR ˌʌntran'spɔːtəbl, ˌʌntrɑːn'spɔːtəbl
AM ˌənˌtræn(t)s'pɔrdəbəl, ˌənˌtrænz'pɔrdəbəl

untravelled
BR (ˌ)ʌn'travld
AM ˌən'trævəld

untreatable
BR (ˌ)ʌn'triːtəbl
AM ˌən'tridəbəl

untreated
BR ˌʌn'triːtɨd
AM ˌən'tridɨd

untrendy
BR ˌʌn'trɛndi
AM ˌən'trɛndi

untried
BR ˌʌn'trʌɪd
AM ˌən'traɪd

untrimmed
BR ˌʌn'trɪmd
AM ˌən'trɪmd

untrodden
BR ˌʌn'trɒdn
AM ˌən'trɑdən

untroubled
BR (ˌ)ʌn'trʌbld
AM ˌən'trəbəld

untrue
BR (ˌ)ʌn'truː
AM ˈən'tru

untruly
BR ˌʌn'truːli
AM ˌən'truli

untruss
BR ˌʌn'trʌs, -ɨz, -ɪŋ, -t
AM ˌən'trəs, -əz, -ɪŋ, -t

untrusting
BR ˌʌn'trʌstɪŋ
AM ˌən'trəstɪŋ

untrustworthily
BR (ˌ)ʌn'trʌs(t)wəːðɨli
AM ˌən'trəs(t)ˌwərðəli

untrustworthiness
BR (ˌ)ʌn'trʌs(t)wəːðɪnɨs
AM ˌən'trəs(t)ˌwərðinɨs

untrustworthy
BR (ˌ)ʌn'trʌs(t)wəːði
AM ˌən'trəs(t)ˌwərði

untruth
BR (ˌ)ʌn'truː|θ, -ðz\-θs
AM ˌən'tru|θ, -ðz\-θs

untruthful
BR (ˌ)ʌn'truːθf(ʊ)l
AM ˌən'truθfəl

untruthfully
BR (ˌ)ʌn'truːθfʊli, (ˌ)ʌn'truːθfl̩i
AM ˌən'truθfəli

untruthfulness
BR (ˌ)ʌn'truːθf(ʊ)lnəs
AM ˌən'truθfəlnəs

untuck
BR ˌʌn'tʌk, -s, -ɪŋ, -t
AM ˌən'tək, -s, -ɪŋ, -t

untunable
BR ˌʌn'tjuːnəbl, ˌʌn'tʃuːnəbl
AM ˌən't(j)unəbəl

untuned
BR ˌʌn'tjuːnd, ˌʌn'tʃuːnd
AM ˌən't(j)und

untuneful
BR ˌʌn'tjuːnf(ʊ)l, ˌʌn'tʃuːnf(ʊ)l
AM ˌən't(j)unfəl

untunefully
BR ˌʌnˈtjuːnfʉli, ˌʌnˈtjuːnfl̩i, ˌʌnˈtʃuːnfʉli, ˌʌnˈtʃuːnfl̩i
AM ˌənˈt(j)unfəli

untunefulness
BR ˌʌnˈtjuːnf(ʊ)lnəs, ˌʌnˈtʃuːnf(ʊ)lnəs
AM ˌənˈt(j)unfəlnəs

unturned
BR ˌʌnˈtəːnd
AM ˌənˈtərnd

untutored
BR ˌʌnˈtjuːtəd, ʌnˈtʃuːtəd
AM ˌənˈt(j)udərd

untwine
BR (ˌ)ʌnˈtwʌɪn, -z, -ɪŋ, -d
AM ˌənˈtwaɪn, -z, -ɪŋ, -d

untwist
BR (ˌ)ʌnˈtwɪst, -s, -ɪŋ, -ɨd
AM ˌənˈtwɪst, -s, -ɪŋ, -ɨd

untying
BR (ˌ)ʌnˈtʌɪɪŋ
AM ˌənˈtaɪɪŋ

untypical
BR ˌʌnˈtɪpɨkl
AM ˌənˈtɪpɨkəl

untypically
BR ˌʌnˈtɪpɨkli
AM ˌənˈtɪpək(ə)li

unusable
BR (ˌ)ʌnˈjuːzəbl
AM ˌənˈjuzəbəl

unuseable
BR (ˌ)ʌnˈjuːzəbl
AM ˌənˈjuzəbəl

unused¹
not made use of
BR (ˌ)ʌnˈjuːzd
AM ˈənˈjuzd

unused²
unaccustomed
BR (ˌ)ʌnˈjuːst
AM ˌənˈjust

unusual
BR (ˌ)ʌnˈjuːʒʊəl, (ˌ)ʌnˈjuːʒ(ʊ)l
AM ˌənˈjuʒ(əw)əl

unusually
BR (ˌ)ʌnˈjuːʒʊəli, (ˌ)ʌnˈjuːʒʉli, (ˌ)ʌnˈjuːʒl̩i
AM ˌənˈjuʒ(əw)əli

unusualness
BR (ˌ)ʌnˈjuːʒʊəlnəs, (ˌ)ʌnˈjuːʒ(ʊ)lnəs
AM ˌənˈjuʒ(əw)əlnəs

unutterable
BR ʌnˈʌt(ə)rəbl
AM ˌənˈədərəbəl

unutterableness
BR ʌnˈʌt(ə)rəblnəs
AM ˌənˈədərəbəlnəs

unutterably
BR ʌnˈʌt(ə)rəbli
AM ˌənˈədərəbli

unuttered
BR ˌʌnˈʌtəd
AM ˌənˈədərd

unvaccinated
BR ˌʌnˈvaksɨneɪtɨd
AM ˌənˈvæksəˌneɪdɨd

unvalued
BR ˌʌnˈvaljuːd
AM ˌənˈvæljud

unvandalised
BR ˌʌnˈvandl̩ʌɪzd, ˌʌnˈvandəlʌɪzd
AM ˌənˈvændlˌaɪzd

unvandalized
BR ˌʌnˈvandl̩ʌɪzd, ˌʌnˈvandəlʌɪzd
AM ˌənˈvændlˌaɪzd

unvanquished
BR ˌʌnˈvaŋkwɪʃt
AM ˌənˈvæŋkwɪʃt

unvaried
BR ʌnˈvɛːrɪd
AM ˌənˈvɛrid

unvarnished
BR (ˌ)ʌnˈvɑːnɪʃt
AM ˌənˈvɑrnɪʃt

unvarying
BR ʌnˈvɛːrɪɪŋ
AM ˌənˈvɛriɪŋ

unvaryingly
BR ʌnˈvɛːrɪɪŋli
AM ˌənˈvɛriɪŋli

unvaryingness
BR ʌnˈvɛːrɪɪŋnɨs
AM ˌənˈvɛriɪŋnɨs

unveil
BR (ˌ)ʌnˈveɪl, -z, -ɪŋ, -d
AM ˌənˈveɪl, -z, -ɪŋ, -d

unvented
BR ˌʌnˈvɛntɨd
AM ˌənˈvɛn(t)əd

unventilated
BR (ˌ)ʌnˈvɛntɨleɪtɨd
AM ˌənˈvɛn(t)əˌleɪdɨd

unverifiable
BR (ˌ)ʌnˈvɛrɨfʌɪəbl
AM ˌənˌvɛrəˌfaɪəbəl

unverified
BR (ˌ)ʌnˈvɛrɨfʌɪd
AM ˌənˈvɛrəˌfaɪd

unversed
BR (ˌ)ʌnˈvəːst
AM ˌənˈvərst

unviability
BR ˌʌnvʌɪəˈbɪlɨti
AM ˌənˌvaɪəˈbɪlɨdi

unviable
BR ˌʌnˈvʌɪəbl
AM ˌənˈvaɪəbəl

unviolated
BR ˌʌnˈvʌɪəleɪtɨd
AM ˌənˈvaɪəˌleɪdɨd

unvisited
BR (ˌ)ʌnˈvɪzɨtɨd
AM ˌənˈvɪzɨdɨd

unvitiated
BR ˌʌnˈvɪʃɪeɪtɨd
AM ˌənˈvɪʃiˌeɪdɨd

unvoiced
BR ˌʌnˈvɔɪst
AM ˌənˈvɔɪst

unwaged
BR ˌʌnˈweɪdʒd
AM ˌənˈweɪdʒd

unwakened
BR ˌʌnˈweɪk(ə)nd
AM ˌənˈweɪkənd

unwalled
BR ˌʌnˈwɔːld
AM ˌənˈwɔld, ˌənˈwɑld

unwanted
BR (ˌ)ʌnˈwɒntɨd
AM ˌənˈwɑn(t)əd

unwarily
BR ʌnˈwɛːrɨli
AM ˌənˈwɛrəli

unwariness
BR ʌnˈwɛːrɪnɨs
AM ˌənˈwɛrinɨs

unwarlike
BR ˌʌnˈwɔːlʌɪk
AM ˌənˈwɔrˌlaɪk

unwarmed
BR ˌʌnˈwɔːmd
AM ˌənˈwɔ(ə)rmd

unwarned
BR ˌʌnˈwɔːnd
AM ˌənˈwɔ(ə)rnd

unwarrantable
BR ʌnˈwɒrəntəbl, ʌnˈwɒrn̩təbl
AM ˌənˈwɔrən(t)əbəl

unwarrantableness
BR ʌnˈwɒrəntəblnəs, ʌnˈwɒrn̩təblnəs
AM ˌənˈwɔrən(t)əbəlnəs

unwarrantably
BR ʌnˈwɒrəntəbli, ʌnˈwɒrn̩təbli
AM ˌənˈwɔrən(t)əbli

unwarranted
BR ʌnˈwɒrəntɨd, ʌnˈwɒrn̩tɨd
AM ˌənˈwɔrən(t)əd

unwary
BR (ˌ)ʌnˈwɛːri
AM ˌənˈwɛri

unwashed
BR ˌʌnˈwɒʃt
AM ˌənˈwɔʃt, ˌənˈwɑʃt

unwatchable
BR ˌʌnˈwɒtʃəbl
AM ˌənˈwɑtʃəbəl

unwatched
BR ˌʌnˈwɒtʃt
AM ˌənˈwɑtʃt

unwatchful
BR ˌʌnˈwɒtʃf(ʊ)l
AM ˌənˈwɑtʃfəl

unwatered
BR ˌʌnˈwɔːtəd
AM ˌənˈwɔdərd, ˌənˈwɑdərd

unwavering
BR ʌnˈweɪv(ə)rɪŋ
AM ˌənˈweɪv(ə)rɪŋ

unwaveringly
BR ʌnˈweɪv(ə)rɪŋli
AM ˌənˈweɪv(ə)rɪŋli

unwaxed
BR ˌʌnˈwakst
AM ˌənˈwækst

unweakened
BR (ˌ)ʌnˈwiːk(ə)nd
AM ˌənˈwikənd

unweaned
BR ˌʌnˈwiːnd
AM ˌənˈwind

unwearable
BR (ˌ)ʌnˈwɛːrəbl
AM ˌənˈwɛrəbəl

unwearied
BR ʌnˈwɪərɪd
AM ˌənˈwɪrid

unweariedly
BR ʌnˈwɪərɪdli
AM ˌənˈwɪridli

unweariedness
BR ʌnˈwɪərɪdnɨs
AM ˌənˈwɪridnɨs

unweary
BR ʌnˈwɪəri
AM ˌənˈwɪri

unwearying
BR ʌnˈwɪərɪɪŋ
AM ˌənˈwɪriɪŋ

unwearyingly
BR ʌnˈwɪərɪɪŋli
AM ˌənˈwɪriɪŋli

unwed
BR ˌʌnˈwɛd
AM ˌənˈwɛd

unwedded
BR ˌʌnˈwɛdɨd
AM ˌənˈwɛded

unweddedness
BR (ˌ)ʌnˈwɛdɨdnɨs
AM ˌənˈwɛdədnəs

unweeded
BR ˌʌnˈwiːdɨd
AM ˌənˈwidɨd

unweighed
BR ˌʌnˈweɪd
AM ˌənˈweɪd

unweight
BR ˌʌnˈweɪt, -s, -ɪŋ, -ɨd
AM ˌənˈweɪ|t, -ts, -dɪŋ, -dɨd

unwelcome
BR (ˌ)ʌnˈwɛlkəm, -ɪŋ, -d
AM ˌənˈwɛlkəm, -ɪŋ, -d

unwelcomely
BR (ˌ)ʌnˈwɛlkəmli
AM ˌənˈwɛlkəmli

unwelcomeness
BR (ˌ)ʌnˈwɛlkəmnəs
AM ˌənˈwɛlkəmnəs

unwell
BR (ˌ)ʌnˈwɛl
AM ˌənˈwɛl

unwept
BR ˌʌnˈwɛpt
AM ˌənˈwɛpt

unwetted
BR ˌʌnˈwɛtɨd
AM ˌənˈwɛdəd

unwhipped
BR ˌʌnˈwɪpt
AM ˌənˈ(h)wɪpt

unwhitened
BR ˌʌnˈwʌɪtnd
AM ˌənˈ(h)waɪtnd

unwholesome
BR (ˌ)ʌnˈhəʊls(ə)m
AM ˌənˈhoʊlsəm

unwholesomely
BR (ˌ)ʌnˈhəʊls(ə)mli
AM ˌənˈhoʊlsəmli

unwholesomeness
BR (ˌ)ʌnˈhəʊls(ə)mnəs
AM ˌənˈhoʊlsəmnəs

unwieldily
BR ʌnˈwiːldɨli
AM ˌənˈwi(ə)ldɨli

unwieldiness
BR ʌnˈwiːldɪnɨs
AM ˌənˈwi(ə)ldinɨs

unwieldy
BR ʌnˈwiːldi
AM ˌənˈwi(ə)ldi

unwilled
BR ˌʌnˈwɪld
AM ˌənˈwɪld

unwilling
BR ˌʌnˈwɪlɪŋ
AM ˌənˈwɪlɪŋ

unwillingly
BR ʌnˈwɪlɪŋli
AM ˌənˈwɪlɪŋli

unwillingness
BR ʌnˈwɪlɪŋnɨs
AM ˌənˈwɪlɪŋnɨs

Unwin
BR ˈʌnwɪn
AM ˈənwən

unwind
BR (ˌ)ʌnˈwʌɪnd, -z, -ɪŋ
AM ˌənˈwaɪnd, -z, -ɪŋ

unwinking
BR ˌʌnˈwɪŋkɪŋ
AM ˌənˈwɪŋkɪŋ

unwinkingly
BR ˌʌnˈwɪŋkɪŋli
AM ˌənˈwɪŋkɪŋli

unwinnable
BR ˌʌnˈwɪnəbl
AM ˌənˈwɪnəbəl

unwiped
BR ˌʌnˈwʌɪpt
AM ˌənˈwaɪpt

unwired
BR ˌʌnˈwʌɪəd
AM ˌənˈwaɪ(ə)rd

unwisdom
BR ˌʌnˈwɪzdəm
AM ˌənˈwɪzdəm

unwise
BR (ˌ)ʌnˈwʌɪz
AM ˌənˈwaɪz

unwisely
BR (ˌ)ʌnˈwʌɪzli
AM ˌənˈwaɪzli

unwish
BR ˌʌnˈwɪʃ, -ɨz, -ɪŋ, -t
AM ˌənˈwɪʃ, -ɨz, -ɪŋ, -t

unwithered
BR ˌʌnˈwɪðəd
AM ˌənˈwɪðərd

unwitnessed
BR ˌʌnˈwɪtnɨst
AM ˌənˈwɪtnɨst

unwitting
BR (ˌ)ʌnˈwɪtɪŋ
AM ˌənˈwɪdɪŋ

unwittingly
BR ʌnˈwɪtɪŋli
AM ˌənˈwɪdɪŋli

unwittingness
BR ʌnˈwɪtɪŋnɨs
AM ˌənˈwɪdɪŋnɨs

unwomanliness
BR (ˌ)ʌnˈwʊmənlɪnɨs
AM ˌənˈwʊmənlinɨs

unwomanly
BR (ˌ)ʌnˈwʊmənli
AM ˌənˈwʊmənli

unwonted
BR ʌnˈwəʊntɨd, ʌnˈwɒntɨd
AM ˌənˈwoʊn(t)əd, ˌənˈwɔn(t)əd, ˌənˈwɑn(t)əd

unwontedly
BR ʌnˈwəʊntɨdli, ʌnˈwɒntɨdli
AM ˌənˈwoʊn(t)ədli, ˌənˈwɔn(t)ədli, ˌənˈwɑn(t)ədli

unwontedness
BR ʌnˈwəʊntɨdnɨs, ʌnˈwɒntɨdnɨs
AM ˌənˈwoʊn(t)ədnɨs, ˌənˈwɔn(t)ədnəs, ˌənˈwɑn(t)ədnəs

unwooded
BR ˌʌnˈwʊdɨd
AM ˌənˈwʊdəd

unworkability
BR ʌnˌwəːkəˈbɪlɨti, ˌʌnwəːkəˈbɪlɨti
AM ˌənˌwərkəˈbɪlɨdi

unworkable
BR (ˌ)ʌnˈwəːkəbl
AM ˌənˈwərkəbəl

unworkableness
BR (ˌ)ʌnˈwəːkəblnəs
AM ˌənˈwərkəbəlnəs

unworkably
BR (ˌ)ʌnˈwəːkəbli
AM ˌənˈwərkəbli

unworked
BR ˌʌnˈwəːkt
AM ˌənˈwərkt

unworkmanlike
BR ˌʌnˈwəːkmənlʌɪk
AM ˌənˈwərkmənˌlaɪk

unworldliness
BR (ˌ)ʌnˈwəːldlɪnɨs
AM ˌənˈwərldlinɨs

unworldly
BR (ˌ)ʌnˈwəːldli
AM ˌənˈwərldli

unworn
BR ˌʌnˈwɔːn
AM ˌənˈwɔ(ə)rn

unworried
BR ˌʌnˈwʌrɪd
AM ˌənˈwərid

unworshipped
BR ˌʌnˈwəːʃɪpt
AM ˌənˈwərʃɪpt

unworthily
BR (ˌ)ʌnˈwəːðɨli
AM ˌənˈwərðəli

unworthiness
BR (ˌ)ʌnˈwəːðɪnɨs
AM ˌənˈwərðinɨs

unworthy
BR (ˌ)ʌnˈwəːði
AM ˌənˈwərði

unwound
BR ˌʌnˈwaʊnd
AM ˌənˈwaʊnd

unwounded
BR ˌʌnˈwuːndɨd
AM ˌənˈwundəd

unwoven
BR ˌʌnˈwəʊvn
AM ˌənˈwoʊvən

unwrap
BR (ˌ)ʌnˈrap, -s, -ɪŋ, -t
AM ˌənˈræp, -s, -ɪŋ, -t

unwrinkled
BR ˌʌnˈrɪŋkld
AM ˌənˈrɪŋkəld

unwritable
BR ˌʌnˈrʌɪtəbl
AM ˌənˈraɪdəbəl

unwritten
BR ˌʌnˈrɪtn
AM ˌənˈrɪtn

unwrought
BR ˌʌnˈrɔːt
AM ˌənˈrɔt, ˌənˈrɑt

unwrung
BR ˌʌnˈrʌŋ
AM ˌənˈrəŋ

unyielding
BR (ˌ)ʌnˈjiːldɪŋ
AM ˌənˈjildɪŋ

unyieldingly
BR (ˌ)ʌnˈjiːldɪŋli
AM ˌənˈjildɪŋli

unyieldingness
BR (ˌ)ʌnˈjiːldɪŋnɨs
AM ˌənˈjildɪŋnɨs

unyoke
BR (ˌ)ʌnˈjəʊk, -s, -ɪŋ, -t
AM ˌənˈjoʊk, -s, -ɪŋ, -t

unzip
BR ˌʌnˈzɪp, -s, -ɪŋ, -t
AM ˌənˈzɪp, -s, -ɪŋ, -t

up
BR ʌp
AM əp

up-anchor
BR ˌʌpˈaŋk|ə(r), -əz, -(ə)rɪŋ, -əd
AM ˈəpˈæŋkər, -z, -ɪŋ, -d

up-and-coming
BR ˌʌp(ə)n(d)ˈkʌmɪŋ
AM ˈəpənˈkəmɪŋ

up-and-over
BR ˌʌp(ə)n(d)ˈəʊvə(r)
AM ˈəpənˈoʊvər

up and running
BR ˌʌp (ə)n(d) ˈrʌnɪŋ
AM ˈəp ən ˈrənɪŋ

up-and-under
BR ˌʌp(ə)n(d)ˈʌndə(r), -z
AM ˈəpənˈəndər, -z

up-and-up
BR ˌʌp(ə)n(d)ˈʌp
AM ˈəpənˈəp

Upanishad
BR (j)uːˈpanɪʃad, (j)ʉˈpanɪʃad, -z
AM (j)ʊˈpænəˌʃæd, -z

upas
BR ˈjuːpəs, -ɨz
AM ˈjupəs, -əz

upas tree
BR ˈjuːpəs triː, -z
AM ˈjupəs ˌtri, -z

upbeat
BR ˈʌpbiːt, -s
AM ˈəpˌbit, -s

upbraid
BR ˌʌpˈbreɪd, -z, -ɪŋ, -ɨd
AM ˌəpˈbreɪd, -z, -ɪŋ, -ɨd

upbraiding
BR ˌʌpˈbreɪdɪŋ, -z
AM ˌəpˈbreɪdɪŋ, -z

upbringing
BR ˈʌpˌbrɪŋɪŋ
AM ˈəpˌbrɪŋɪŋ

upbuild
BR ˌʌpˈbɪld
AM ˌəpˈbɪld

upbuilt
BR ˌʌpˈbɪlt
AM ˌəpˈbɪlt

UPC
BR ˌjuːpiːˈsiː
AM ˌjuˌpiˈsi

upcast
BR ˈʌpkɑːst, ˈʌpkast, -s, -ɪŋ
AM ˈəpˌkæst, -s, -ɪŋ

upchuck
BR ˌʌp'tʃʌk, -s, -ɪŋ, -t
AM 'əpˌtʃək, -s, -ɪŋ, -t
upcoming
BR 'ʌpˌkʌmɪŋ
AM ˌəpˈkəmɪŋ
upcountry
BR ˌʌp'kʌntri
AM 'əpˌkəntri
upcurrent
BR 'ʌpˌkʌrənt, 'ʌpˌkʌrn̩t, -s
AM ˌəpˈkərənt, -s
update[1]
noun
BR 'ʌpdeɪt, -s
AM 'əpˌdeɪt, -s
update[2]
verb
BR ˌʌp'deɪt, -s, -ɪŋ, -ɪd
AM ˌəp'deɪ|t, -ts, -dɪŋ, -dɨd
updater
BR ˌʌp'deɪtə(r), -z
AM ˌəp'deɪdər, -z
Updike
BR 'ʌpdʌɪk
AM 'əpˌdaɪk
updraft
BR 'ʌpdrɑːft, 'ʌpdraft, -s
AM 'əpˌdræft, -s
updraught
BR 'ʌpdrɑːft, 'ʌpdraft, -s
AM 'əpˌdræft, -s
upend
BR ʌp'ɛnd, -z, -ɪŋ, -ɪd
AM ˌəp'ɛnd, -z, -ɪŋ, -əd
upfield
BR 'ʌpfiːld
AM ˌəpˈfild
upflow
BR 'ʌpfləʊ, -z
AM 'əpˌfloʊ, -z
upfold
BR 'ʌpfəʊld, -z
AM 'əpˌfoʊld, -z
up-front
BR ˌʌp'frʌnt
AM ˌəpˈfrənt
upgrade[1]
noun
BR 'ʌpgreɪd, -z
AM 'əpˌgreɪd, -z
upgrade[2]
verb
BR ˌʌp'greɪd, -z, -ɪŋ, -ɪd
AM ˌəpˈgreɪd, -z, -ɪŋ, -ɪd
upgradeable
BR ˌʌp'greɪdəbl
AM ˌəp'greɪdəbəl
upgrader
BR ˌʌp'greɪdə(r), -z
AM 'əpˌgreɪdər, -z
upgrowth
BR 'ʌpgrəʊθ, -s
AM 'əpˌgroʊθ, -s

uphaul
BR ˌʌp'hɔːl, -z
AM ˌəp'hɔl, ˌəp'hɑl, -z
upheaval
BR ʌp'hiːvl, -z
AM ˌəp'hivəl, -z
upheave
BR ˌʌp'hiːv, -z, -ɪŋ, -d
AM ˌəp'hiv, -z, -ɪŋ, -d
upheld
BR ʌp'hɛld
AM ˌəp'hɛld
uphill
BR ˌʌp'hɪl
AM ˌəp'hɪl
uphold
BR ʌp'həʊld, -z, -ɪŋ
AM ˌəp'hoʊld, -z, -ɪŋ
upholder
BR ʌp'həʊldə(r), -z
AM ˌəp'hoʊldər, -z
upholster
BR ʌp'həʊlst|ə(r), -əz, -(ə)rɪŋ, -əd
AM ˌəp'(h)oʊlst|ər, -ərz, -(ə)rɪŋ, -ərd
upholsterer
BR ʌp'həʊlst(ə)rə(r), -z
AM ˌəp'(h)oʊlst(ə)rər, -z
upholstery
BR ʌp'həʊlst(ə)ri
AM ˌəp'(h)oʊlst(ə)ri
UPI
BR ˌjuːpiː'ʌɪ
AM ˌjuˌpi'aɪ
Upjohn
BR 'ʌpdʒɒn
AM 'əpˌdʒɑn
upkeep
BR 'ʌpkiːp
AM 'əpˌkip
upland
BR 'ʌplənd, -z
AM 'əplənd, -z
uplift[1]
noun
BR 'ʌplɪft
AM 'əpˌlɪft
uplift[2]
verb
BR ʌp'lɪft, -s, -ɪŋ, -ɪd
AM ˌəpˈlɪft, -s, -ɪŋ, -ɪd
uplifter
BR ʌp'lɪftə(r), -z
AM ˌəpˈlɪftər, -z
uplighter
BR 'ʌpˌlʌɪtə(r), -z
AM 'əpˌlaɪdər, -z
upload
BR ˌʌp'ləʊd, -z, -ɪŋ, -ɪd
AM ˌəp'loʊd, -z, -ɪŋ, -əd
uplying
BR ˌʌp'lʌɪɪŋ
AM ˌəpˈlaɪɪŋ

upmarket
BR ˌʌp'mɑːkɪt
AM ˌəp'mɑrkət
upmost
BR 'ʌpməʊst
AM 'əpˌmoʊst
upon
BR ə'pɒn
AM ə'pɑn
upper
BR 'ʌpə(r)
AM 'əpər
uppercase
BR ˌʌpə'keɪs
AM ˌəpər'keɪs
upper-class
BR ˌʌpə'klɑːs, ˌʌpə'klas
AM ˌəpər'klæs
upperclassman
BR ˌʌpə'klɑːsmən, ˌʌpə'klasmən
AM ˌəpər'klæsmən
upperclassmen
BR ˌʌpə'klɑːsmən, ˌʌpə'klasmən
AM ˌəpər'klæsmən
uppercut
BR 'ʌpəkʌt, -s
AM 'əpərˌkət, -s
uppermost
BR 'ʌpəməʊst
AM 'əpərˌmoʊst
Upper Volta
BR ˌʌpə 'vɒltə(*r*)
AM ˌəpər 'vɔltə, ˌəpər 'voʊltə
Uppingham
BR 'ʌpɪŋəm
AM 'əpɪŋəm
uppish
BR 'ʌpɪʃ
AM 'əpɪʃ
uppishly
BR 'ʌpɨʃli
AM 'əpɪʃli
uppishness
BR 'ʌpɪʃnɨs
AM 'əpɪʃnɨs
uppity
BR 'ʌpɨti
AM 'əpədi
Uppsala
BR ʊp'sɑːlə(*r*), ʌp'sɑːlə(*r*), 'ʊpsɑːlə(*r*), 'ʌpsɑːlə(*r*)
AM 'ʊpsələ
SW 'əpsɑːla
upraise
BR ˌʌp'reɪz, -ɨz, -ɪŋ, -d
AM ˌəp'reɪz, -ɨz, -ɪŋ, -d
uprate
BR ˌʌp'reɪt, -s, -ɪŋ, -ɪd
AM ˌəp'reɪ|t, -ts, -dɪŋ, -dɪd
uprating
BR ˌʌp'reɪtɪŋ, -z

AM ˌəp'reɪdɪŋ, -z
upright
BR 'ʌprʌɪt, -s
AM 'əpˌraɪt, -s
uprightly
BR 'ʌprʌɪtli
AM 'əpˌraɪtli
uprightness
BR 'ʌprʌɪtnɨs
AM 'əpˌraɪtnɨs
uprise
verb
BR ˌʌp'rʌɪz, -z, -ɪŋ
AM ˌəp'raɪz, -z, -ɪŋ
uprisen
BR ˌʌp'rɪzn
AM ˌəp'rɪzn
uprising
BR 'ʌprʌɪzɪŋ, -z
AM 'əpˌraɪzɪŋ, -z
upriver
BR ˌʌp'rɪvə(r)
AM ˌəp'rɪvər
uproar
BR 'ʌprɔː(r), -z
AM 'əpˌrɔ(ə)r, -z
uproarious
BR ʌp'rɔːrɪəs
AM ˌəp'rɔriəs
uproariously
BR ʌp'rɔːrɪəsli
AM ˌəp'rɔriəsli
uproariousness
BR ʌp'rɔːrɪəsnəs
AM ˌəp'rɔriəsnəs
uproot
BR ˌʌp'ruːt, -s, -ɪŋ, -ɪd
AM ˌəp'ru|t, -ts, -dɪŋ, -dəd
uprooter
BR ˌʌp'ruːtə(r), -z
AM ˌəp'rudər, -z
uprose
BR ˌʌp'rəʊz
AM ˌəp'roʊz
uprush
BR 'ʌprʌʃ, -ɨz
AM 'əpˌrəʃ, -əz
ups-a-daisy
BR ˌʌpsə'deɪzi
AM 'əpsəˌdeɪsi, ˈəpsiˌdeɪsi
upscale
BR ˌʌp'skeɪl
AM ˌəpˌskeɪl
upset[1]
adjective
BR ˌʌp'sɛt
AM ˌəp'sɛt
upset[2]
noun
BR 'ʌpsɛt, -s
AM 'əpsət, -s
upset[3]
verb
BR ʌp'sɛt, -s, -ɪŋ
AM ˌəp'sɛ|t, -ts, -dɪŋ

upsetter
BR ʌp'sɛtə(r), -z
AM ˌəp'sɛdər, -z

upsettingly
BR ʌp'sɛtɪŋli
AM ˌəp'sɛdɪŋli

upshift
BR 'ʌpʃɪft, ˌʌp'ʃɪft, -s, -ɪŋ, -ɨd
AM 'əpˌʃɪft, -s, -ɪŋ, -ɨd

upshot
BR 'ʌpʃɒt
AM 'əpˌʃɑt

upside-down
BR ˌʌp'sʌɪ(d)'daʊn
AM ˌ'əpˌsaɪ(d)'daʊn

upsides
adverb
BR 'ʌpsʌɪdz
AM 'əpˌsaɪdz

upsilon
BR (j)uːp'sʌɪlən, 'juːpsɪlən, ʉp'sʌɪlən, -z
AM 'əpsəˌlɑn, '(j)ʊpsəˌlɑn, -z

upstage
BR ˌʌp'steɪdʒ, -ɪz, -ɪŋ, -d
AM ˌəp'steɪdʒ, -ɪz, -ɪŋ, -d

upstager
BR ˌʌp'steɪdʒə(r), -z
AM ˌəp'steɪdʒər, -z

upstair
adjective
BR ˌʌp'stɛː(r)
AM ˌ'əpˌstɛ(ə)r

upstairs
BR ˌʌp'stɛːz
AM ˌ'əpˌstɛ(ə)rz

upstanding
BR (ˌ)ʌp'standɪŋ
AM ˌəp'stændɪŋ

upstart
BR 'ʌpstɑːt, -s
AM 'əpˌstɑrt, -s

upstate
BR ˌʌp'steɪt
AM ˌ'əpˌsteɪt

upstater
BR ˌʌp'steɪtə(r), -z
AM ˌ'əpˌsteɪdər, -z

upstream
BR ˌʌp'striːm
AM ˌ'əp'strim

upstretched
BR ˌʌp'strɛtʃt
AM ˌ'əp'strɛtʃt

upstroke
BR 'ʌpstrəʊk, -s
AM 'əpˌstroʊk, -s

upsurge
BR 'ʌpsəːdʒ, -ɪz
AM 'əpˌsərdʒ, -əz

upswept
BR ˌʌp'swɛpt
AM ˌ'əp'swɛpt

upswing
BR 'ʌpswɪŋ, -z
AM 'əpˌswɪŋ, -z

upsy-daisy
BR ˌʌpsɪ'deɪzi
AM ˌ'əpsiˌ'deɪzi, ˌ'əpsəˌ'deɪzi

uptake
BR 'ʌpteɪk
AM 'əpˌteɪk

up-tempo
BR ˌʌp'tɛmpəʊ
AM ˌ'əp'tɛmpoʊ

upthrow
BR 'ʌpθrəʊ, -z
AM 'əpˌθroʊ, -z

upthrust
BR 'ʌpθrʌst, -s
AM 'əpˌθrəst, -s

uptight
BR ˌʌp'tʌɪt, 'ʌptʌɪt
AM ˌ'əp'taɪt

uptilt
BR ˌʌp'tɪlt, -s, -ɪŋ, -ɨd
AM 'əpˌtɪlt, -s, -ɪŋ, -ɨd

uptime
BR 'ʌptʌɪm
AM 'əpˌtaɪm

up-to-date
BR ˌʌptə'deɪt
AM ˌ'əptə'deɪt

Upton
BR 'ʌpt(ə)n
AM 'əptən

up-to-the-minute
BR ˌʌptəðə'mɪnɪt
AM ˌ'əptəðə'mɪnɪt

uptown
BR ˌʌp'taʊn
AM 'əpˌ'taʊn

uptowner
BR ˌʌp'taʊnə(r), -z
AM 'əp'taʊnər, -z

upturn
BR 'ʌptəːn, -z
AM 'əpˌtərn, -z

upturned
BR ˌʌp'təːnd
AM ˌ'əpˌ'tərnd

upward
BR 'ʌpwəd, -z
AM 'əpwərd, -z

upwardly
BR 'ʌpwədli
AM 'əpwərdli

upwarp
BR 'ʌpwɔːp, -s
AM 'əpˌwɔ(ə)rp, -s

upwell
BR ˌʌp'wɛl, -z, -ɪŋ, -d
AM ˌəp'wɛl, -z, -ɪŋ, -d

upwelling
BR ˌʌp'wɛlɪŋ
AM ˌ'əp'wɛlɪŋ

upwind
BR ˌʌp'wɪnd
AM ˌ'əp'wɪnd

Ur
BR əː(r)
AM ər

uracil
BR 'jʊərəsɪl, 'jɔːrəsɪl
AM 'jʊrəˌsɪl

uraei
BR jʊ'riːʌɪ
AM jʊ'riˌaɪ

uraemia
BR jʊ'riːmɪə(r)
AM jʊ'rimiə

uraemic
BR jʊ'riːmɪk
AM jʊ'rimɪk

uraeus
BR jʊ'riːəs
AM jʊ'riəs

Ural
BR 'jʊərəl, 'jʊərl̩, 'jɔːrəl, 'jɔːrl̩, -z
AM 'jʊrəl, -z

Ural-Altaic
BR ˌjʊərəlal'teɪɪk, ˌjʊərl̩al'teɪɪk, ˌjɔːrəlal'teɪɪk, ˌjɔːrl̩al'teɪɪk, -s
AM ˌ'jʊrəlˌæl'teɪɪk, -s

Uralic
BR jʊ'ralɪk, -s
AM jʊ'rælɪk, -s

Urania
BR jʊ'reɪnɪə(r)
AM jʊ'reɪniə

uranic
BR jʊ'ranɪk
AM jʊ'rænɪk

uranism
BR 'jʊərənɪz(ə)m, 'jʊərn̩ɪz(ə)m, 'jɔːrənɪz(ə)m, 'jɔːrn̩ɪz(ə)m
AM 'jʊrəˌnɪzəm

uranium
BR jʊ'reɪnɪəm
AM jʊ'reɪniəm, ju'reɪniəm

uranographer
BR ˌjʊərə'nɒgrəfə(r), ˌjɔːrə'nɒgrəfə(r), -z
AM ˌjʊrə'nɑgrəfər, -z

uranographic
BR ˌjʊərənə'grafɪk, ˌjɔːrənə'grafɪk
AM ˌjʊrənə'græfɪk

uranography
BR ˌjʊərə'nɒgrəfi, ˌjɔːrə'nɒgrəfi
AM ˌjʊrə'nɑgrəfi

uranometry
BR ˌjʊərə'nɒmɪtri, ˌjɔːrə'nɒmɪtri
AM ˌjʊrə'nɑmətri

uranous
BR 'jʊərənəs, 'jɔːrənəs
AM 'jʊrənəs, jʊ'reɪnəs

Uranus
BR 'jʊərənəs, 'jʊərn̩əs, 'jɔːrənəs, 'jɔːrn̩əs, jʊ'reɪnəs
AM 'jʊrənəs, jʊ'reɪnəs

urate
BR 'jʊəreɪt, 'jɔːreɪt, -s
AM 'jʊˌreɪt, -s

urban
BR 'əːb(ə)n
AM 'ərbən

urbane
BR əː'beɪn
AM ər'beɪn

urbanely
BR əː'beɪnli
AM ər'beɪnli

urbaneness
BR əː'beɪnnɪs
AM ər'beɪ(n)nɪs

urbanisation
BR ˌəːbənʌɪ'zeɪʃn, ˌəːbn̩ʌɪ'zeɪʃn
AM ˌərbənə'zeɪʃən, ˌərbəˌnaɪ'zeɪʃən

urbanise
BR 'əːbənʌɪz, 'əːbn̩ʌɪz, -ɪz, -ɪŋ, -d
AM 'ərbəˌnaɪz, -ɪz, -ɪŋ, -d

urbanism
BR 'əːbənɪz(ə)m, 'əːbn̩ɪz(ə)m
AM 'ərbəˌnɪzəm

urbanist
BR 'əːbənɪst, 'əːbn̩ɪst, -s
AM 'ərbənəst, -s

urbanite
BR 'əːbənʌɪt, 'əːbn̩ʌɪt, -s
AM 'ərbəˌnaɪt, -s

urbanity
BR əː'banɪti
AM ər'bænədi

urbanization
BR ˌəːbənʌɪ'zeɪʃn, ˌəːbn̩ʌɪ'zeɪʃn
AM ˌərbənə'zeɪʃən, ˌərbəˌnaɪ'zeɪʃən

urbanize
BR 'əːbənʌɪz, 'əːbn̩ʌɪz, -ɪz, -ɪŋ, -d
AM 'ərbəˌnaɪz, -ɪz, -ɪŋ, -d

urceolate
BR 'əːsɪələt, 'əːsɪəleɪt
AM ˌ'ər'siələt, ˌ'ər'siəˌleɪt

urchin
BR 'əːtʃɪn, -z
AM 'ərtʃən, -z

Urdu
BR 'ʊəduː, 'əːduː
AM 'ʊrdu, 'ərdu

Ure
BR 'jʊə(r)
AM 'jʊ(ə)r

urea
BR jʊ̈ˈriːə(r)
AM jʊˈriə

urea-formaldehyde
BR jʊ̈ˌriːəfɔːˈmaldɪhʌɪd
AM jʊˌriəˌfɔrˈmældəˌhaɪd

ureal
BR jʊ̈ˈriːəl
AM jʊˈriəl

uremia
BR jʊ̈ˈriːmɪə(r)
AM jʊˈrimiə

uremic
BR jʊ̈ˈriːmɪk
AM jʊˈrimɪk

ureter
BR jʊ̈ˈriːtə(r), ˈjʊərɪtə(r), -z
AM ˈjʊrədər, -z

ureteral
BR jʊ̈ˈriːt(ə)rəl, jʊ̈ˈriːt(ə)rl̩
AM jʊˈridərəl

ureteric
BR ˌjʊərɪˈtɛrɪk, jʊ̈ˈriːt(ə)rɪk, ˌjɔːrɪˈtɛrɪk
AM ˌjʊrəˈtɛrɪk

ureteritis
BR jʊ̈ˌriːtəˈrʌɪtɪs, ˌjʊərɪtəˈrʌɪtɪs, ˌjɔːrɪtəˈrʌɪtɪs
AM ˌjʊrədəˈraɪdɪs

ureterotomy
BR jʊ̈ˌriːtəˈrɒtəm|i, -ɪz
AM ˌjʊrədəˈrɑdəmi, -z

urethane
BR ˈjʊərɪθeɪn, ˈjɔːrɪθeɪn
AM ˈjʊrəˌθeɪn

urethra
BR jʊ̈ˈriːθrə(r), -z
AM jʊˈriθrə, -z

urethral
BR jʊ̈ˈriːθrəl, jʊ̈ˈriːθrl̩
AM jʊˈriθrəl

urethritis
BR ˌjʊərɪˈθrʌɪtɪs, ˌjɔːrɪˈθrʌɪtɪs
AM ˌjʊrəˈθraɪdɪs

urethrotomy
BR ˌjʊərɪˈθrɒtəm|i, ˌjɔːrɪˈθrɒtəm|i, -ɪz
AM ˌjʊrəˈθrɑdəmi, -z

Urey
BR ˈjʊəri
AM ˈ(j)ʊri

Urga
BR ˈəːgə(r)
AM ˈərgə

urge
BR əːdʒ, -ɪz, -ɪŋ, -d
AM ərdʒ, -əz, -ɪŋ, -d

urgency
BR ˈəːdʒ(ə)nsi
AM ˈərdʒənsi

urgent
BR ˈəːdʒ(ə)nt
AM ˈərdʒənt

urgently
BR ˈəːdʒ(ə)ntli
AM ˈərdʒən(t)li

urger
BR ˈəːdʒə(r), -z
AM ˈərdʒər, -z

urging
BR ˈəːdʒɪŋ, -z
AM ˈərdʒɪŋ, -z

Uriah
BR jʊ̈ˈrʌɪə(r)
AM jʊˈraɪə

uric
BR ˈjʊərɪk, ˈjɔːrɪk
AM ˈjʊrɪk

Uriel
BR ˈjʊərɪəl, ˈjɔːrɪəl
AM ˈjʊriəl, ˈjʊriˌɛl

urim
BR ˈjʊərɪm, ˈjɔːrɪm
AM ˈ(j)ʊrəm

urinal
BR jʊ̈ˈrʌɪnl, ˈjʊərɪnl, ˈjɔːrɪnl, -z
AM ˈjʊrənəl, -z

urinalyses
BR ˌjʊərɪˈnalɪsiːz, ˌjɔːrɪˈnalɪsiːz
AM ˌjʊrəˈnæləˌsiz

urinalysis
BR ˌjʊərɪˈnalɪsɪs, ˌjɔːrɪˈnalɪsɪs
AM ˌjʊrəˈnæləsəs

urinary
BR ˈjʊərɪn(ə)ri, ˈjɔːrɪn(ə)ri
AM ˈjʊrəˌnɛri

urinate
BR ˈjʊərɪneɪt, ˈjɔːrɪneɪt, -s, -ɪŋ, -ɪd
AM ˈjʊrəˌneɪ|t, -ts, -dɪŋ, -dɪd

urination
BR ˌjʊərɪˈneɪʃn, ˌjɔːrɪˈneɪʃn
AM ˌjʊrəˈneɪʃən

urine
BR ˈjʊərɪn, ˈjɔːrɪn
AM ˈjʊrən

urinous
BR ˈjʊərɪnəs, ˈjɔːrɪnəs
AM ˈjʊrənəs

Urmston
BR ˈəːmst(ə)n
AM ˈərmstən

urn
BR əːn, -z
AM ərn, -z

urnfield
BR ˈəːnfiːld, -z
AM ˈərnˌfild, -z

urnful
BR ˈəːnfʊl, -z
AM ˈərnˌfʊl, -z

urochord
BR ˈjʊərə(ʊ)kɔːd, ˈjɔːrə(ʊ)kɔːd, -z
AM ˈjʊrəˌkɔ(ə)rd, -z

urodele
BR ˈjʊərə(ʊ)diːl, ˈjɔːrə(ʊ)diːl, -z
AM ˈjʊrəˌdil, -z

urogenital
BR ˌjʊərə(ʊ)ˈdʒɛnɪtl, ˌjɔːrə(ʊ)ˈdʒɛnɪtl
AM ˌjʊroʊˈdʒɛnədl, ˌjʊrəˈdʒɛnədl

urolithiasis
BR ˌjʊərə(ʊ)lɪˈθʌɪəsɪs, ˌjɔːrə(ʊ)lɪˈθʌɪəsɪs
AM ˌjʊrələˈθaɪəsəs

urologic
BR ˌjʊərəˈlɒdʒɪk, ˌjɔːrəˈlɒdʒɪk
AM ˌjʊrəˈlɑdʒɪk

urologist
BR jʊ̈ˈrɒlədʒɪst, -s
AM jʊˈrɑlədʒəst, -s

urology
BR jʊ̈ˈrɒlədʒi
AM jʊˈrɑlədʒi

uropygium
BR ˌjʊərəˈpɪdʒɪəm, ˌjɔːrəˈpɪdʒɪəm, -z
AM ˌjʊrəˈpɪdʒiəm, -z

uroscopy
BR jʊ̈ˈrɒskəpi
AM jʊˈrɑskəpi

Urquhart
BR ˈəːkət
AM ˈərkət

Ursa
BR ˈəːsə(r)
AM ˈərsə

Ursa Major
BR ˌəːsə ˈmeɪdʒə(r)
AM ˌərsə ˈmeɪdʒər

Ursa Minor
BR ˌəːsə ˈmʌɪnə(r)
AM ˌərsə ˈmaɪnər

ursine
BR ˈəːsʌɪn
AM ˈərˌsin

Ursula
BR ˈəːsjʊ̈lə(r)
AM ˈərsələ

Ursuline
BR ˈəːsjʊ̈lʌɪn, -z
AM ˈərsələn, ˈərsəˌlin, ˈərsəˌlaɪn, -z

urticaria
BR ˌəːtɪˈkɛːrɪə(r)
AM ˌərdəˈkɛriə

urticate
BR ˈəːtɪkeɪt, -s, -ɪŋ, -ɪd
AM ˈərdəˌkeɪ|t, -ts, -dɪŋ, -dɪd

urtication
BR ˌəːtɪˈkeɪʃn
AM ˌərdəˈkeɪʃən

Uruguay
BR ˈjʊərəgwʌɪ, ˈjɔːrəgwʌɪ
AM ˈ(j)ʊrəˌgwaɪ
SP uruˈɣwaj

Uruguayan
BR ˌjʊərəˈgwʌɪən, ˌjɔːrəˈgwʌɪən, -z
AM ˌ(j)ʊrəˈgwaɪən, -z

Uruk
BR ˈʊrʊk
AM ˈʊrʊk

Urwin
BR ˈəːwɪn
AM ˈərwən

US
BR ˌjuːˈɛs
AM ˌjuˈɛs

us[1]
strong form
BR ʌs
AM əs

us[2]
weak form
BR əs, s
AM əs

USA
BR ˌjuːɛsˈeɪ
AM ˌjuˌɛsˈeɪ

usability
BR ˌjuːzəˈbɪlɪti
AM ˌjuzəˈbɪlɪdi

usable
BR ˈjuːzəbl
AM ˈjuzəbəl

usableness
BR ˈjuːzəblnəs
AM ˈjuzəbəlnəs

usage
BR ˈjuːs|ɪdʒ, ˈjuːz|ɪdʒ, -ɪdʒɪz
AM ˈjusɪdʒ, ˈjuzɪdʒ, -ɪz

usance
BR ˈjuːzns
AM ˈjuzəns

Usborne
BR ˈʌzbɔːn
AM ˈəzˌbɔ(ə)rn

USDAW
BR ˈʌzdɔː(r)
AM ˈəzˌdɔ

use[1]
noun
BR juːs, -ɪz
AM jus, -əz

use[2]
verb, make use of
BR juːz, -ɪz, -ɪŋ, -d
AM juz, -əz, -ɪŋ, -d

useability
BR ˌjuːzəˈbɪlɪti
AM ˌjuzəˈbɪlɪdi

useable
BR ˈjuːzəbl
AM ˈjuzəbəl

useableness
BR ˈjuːzəblnəs
AM ˈjuzəbəlnəs

used¹
adjective, accustomed
BR juːst
AM just

used²
adjective, not new, past tense of verb 'use'
BR juːzd
AM juzd

usedn't
BR ˈjuːsnt
AM ˈjusnt

useful
BR ˈjuːsf(ʊ)l
AM ˈjusfəl

usefully
BR ˈjuːsfʊli, ˈjuːsfl̩i
AM ˈjusfəli

usefulness
BR ˈjuːsf(ʊ)lnəs
AM ˈjusfəlnəs

useless
BR ˈjuːsləs
AM ˈjusləs

uselessly
BR ˈjuːsləsli
AM ˈjusləsli

uselessness
BR ˈjuːsləsnəs
AM ˈjusləsnəs

usen't
BR ˈjuːsnt
AM ˈjusnt

user
BR ˈjuːzə(r), -z
AM ˈjuzər, -z

user-friendliness
BR ˌjuːzəˈfrɛn(d)lɪnɪs
AM ˌjuzərˈfrɛn(d)linɪs

user-friendly
BR ˌjuːzəˈfrɛn(d)li
AM ˌjuzərˈfrɛn(d)li

ushabti
BR uːˈʃabt|i, -ɪz
AM (j)uˈʃæbti, -z

Ushant
BR ˈʌʃnt
AM ˈəʃənt

U-shaped
BR ˈjuːʃeɪpt
AM ˈjuˌʃeɪpt

usher
BR ˈʌʃ|ə(r), -əz, -(ə)rɪŋ, -əd
AM ˈəʃ|ər, -ərz, -(ə)rɪŋ, -ərd

usherette
BR ˌʌʃəˈrɛt, -s
AM ˌəʃəˈrɛt, -s

ushership
BR ˈʌʃəʃɪp, -s
AM ˈəʃərˌʃɪp, -s

USIA
BR ˌjuːɛsʌɪˈeɪ
AM ˌjuˌɛsˌaɪˈeɪ

Usk
BR ʌsk
AM əsk

USMC
BR ˌjuːɛsɛmˈsiː
AM ˌjuˌɛsˌɛmˈsi

USO
BR ˌjuːɛsˈəʊ
AM ˌjuˌɛsˈoʊ

USP
BR ˌjuːɛsˈpiː
AM ˌjuˌɛsˈpi

USPS
BR ˌjuːɛspiːˈɛs
AM ˌjuˌɛsˌpiˈɛs

usquebaugh
BR ˈʌskwɪbɔː(r)
AM ˈəskwəˌbɔ, ˈəskwəˌbɑ

USS
BR ˌjuːɛsˈɛs
AM ˌjuˌɛsˈɛs

USSR
BR ˌjuːɛsɛsˈɑː(r)
AM ˌjuˌɛsˌɛsˈɑr

Ustashe
BR ʊˈstɑːʃi
AM ʊˈstɑʃi

Ustinov
BR ˈjuːstɪnɒf, ˈjuːstɪnɒv
AM ˈjustəˌnɔf, ˈjustəˌnɔv, ˈjustəˌnɑf, ˈjustəˌnɑv
RUS uˈstʲinəf

usual
BR ˈjuːʒʊəl, ˈjuːʒ(ʊ)l
AM ˈjuʒ(əw)əl

usually
BR ˈjuːʒʊəli, ˈjuːʒʊli, ˈjuːʒl̩i
AM ˈjuʒ(əw)əli

usualness
BR ˈjuːʒʊəlnəs, ˈjuːʒ(ʊ)lnəs
AM ˈjuʒ(əw)əlnəs

usucaption
BR ˌjuːsjʊˈkapʃn, ˌjuːzjʊˈkapʃn
AM ˌjuzəˈkæpʃən, ˌjusəˈkæpʃən

usufruct
BR ˈjuːsjʊfrʌkt, ˈjuːzjʊfrʌkt, -s
AM ˈjuzəˌfrək|(t), ˈjusəˌfrək|(t), -(t)s

usufructuary
BR ˌjuːsjʊˈfrʌktjʊəri, ˌjuːzjʊˈfrʌktjʊəri, ˌjuːsjʊˈfrʌktʃ(ʊ)əri, ˌjuːzjʊˈfrʌktʃ(ʊ)əri, -ɪz
AM ˌjuzəˈfrək(t)ʃəˌwɛri, ˌjusəˈfrək(t)ʃəˌwɛri, -z

usurer
BR ˈjuːʒ(ə)rə(r), -z
AM ˈjuʒərər, -z

usurious
BR juːˈzjʊərɪəs, juːˈzjɔːrɪəs, juːˈʒʊərɪəs, juːˈʒɔːrɪəs
AM juˈʒʊriəs

usuriously
BR juːˈzjʊərɪəsli, juːˈzjɔːrɪəsli, juːˈʒʊərɪəsli, juːˈʒɔːrɪəsli
AM juˈʒʊriəsli

usuriousness
BR juːˈzjʊərɪəsnəs, juːˈzjɔːrɪəsnəs, juːˈʒʊərɪəsnəs, juːˈzjɔːrɪəsnəs, juːʒjɔːrɪəsnəs
AM juˈʒʊriəsnəs

usurp
BR juːˈzəːp, jʊˈzəːp, -s, -ɪŋ, -t
AM juˈsərp, -s, -ɪŋ, -t

usurpation
BR ˌjuːzəːˈpeɪʃn
AM ˌjusərˈpeɪʃən

usurper
BR juːˈzəːpə(r), jʊˈzəːpə(r), -z
AM juˈsərpər, -z

usury
BR ˈjuːʒ(ə)ri
AM ˈjuʒ(ə)ri

Utah
BR ˈjuːtɔː(r), ˈjuːtɑː(r)
AM ˈjuˌtɔ, ˈjuˌtɑ

Ute
BR juːt, -s
AM jut, -s

utensil
BR juːˈtɛns(ɪ)l, jʊˈtɛns(ɪ)l, -z
AM juˈtɛnsəl, -z

uteri
BR ˈjuːtərʌɪ
AM ˈjudəˌraɪ

uterine
BR ˈjuːtərʌɪn
AM ˈjudərən, ˈjudəˌraɪn

uteritis
BR ˌjuːtəˈrʌɪtɪs
AM ˌjudəˈraɪdɪs

uterus
BR ˈjuːt(ə)rəs, -ɪz
AM ˈjudərəs, -əz

utile
BR ˈjuːtʌɪl
AM ˈjudl, ˈjuˌtaɪl

utilisable
BR ˈjuːtɪlʌɪzəbl, ˈjuːtl̩ʌɪzəbl
AM ˌjudlˈaɪzəbəl

utilisation
BR ˌjuːtɪlʌɪˈzeɪʃn, ˌjuːtl̩ʌɪˈzeɪʃn
AM ˌjudləˈzeɪʃən, ˌjudlˌaɪˈzeɪʃən

utilise
BR ˈjuːtɪlʌɪz, ˈjuːtl̩ʌɪz, -ɪz, -ɪŋ, -d
AM ˈjudlˌaɪz, -ɪz, -ɪŋ, -d

utiliser
BR ˈjuːtɪlʌɪzə(r), ˈjuːtl̩ʌɪzə(r), -z
AM ˈjudlˌaɪzər, -z

utilitarian
BR ˌjuːtɪlɪˈtɛːrɪən, juːˌtɪlɪˈtɛːrɪən, jʊˌtɪlɪˈtɛːrɪən, -z
AM juˌtɪləˈtɛriən, -z

utilitarianism
BR ˌjuːtɪlɪˈtɛːrɪənɪz(ə)m, juːˌtɪlɪˈtɛːrɪənɪz(ə)m, jʊˌtɪlɪˈtɛːrɪənɪz(ə)m
AM juˌtɪləˈtɛriəˌnɪzəm

utility
BR juːˈtɪlɪt|i, jʊˈtɪlɪt|i, -ɪz
AM juˈtɪlɪdi, -z

utilizable
BR ˈjuːtɪlʌɪzəbl, ˈjuːtl̩ʌɪzəbl
AM ˌjudlˈaɪzəbəl

utilization
BR ˌjuːtɪlʌɪˈzeɪʃn, ˌjuːtl̩ʌɪˈzeɪʃn
AM ˌjudləˈzeɪʃən, ˌjudlˌaɪˈzeɪʃən

utilize
BR ˈjuːtɪlʌɪz, ˈjuːtl̩ʌɪz, -ɪz, -ɪŋ, -d
AM ˈjudlˌaɪz, -ɪz, -ɪŋ, -d

utilizer
BR ˈjuːtɪlʌɪzə(r), ˈjuːtl̩ʌɪzə(r), -z
AM ˈjudlˌaɪzər, -z

Utley
BR ˈʌtli
AM ˈətli

utmost
BR ˈʌtməʊst
AM ˈətˌmoʊst

utopia
BR juːˈtəʊpɪə(r), jʊˈtəʊpɪə(r), -z
AM juˈtoʊpiə, -z

Utopian
BR juːˈtəʊpɪən, jʊˈtəʊpɪən, -z
AM juˈtoʊpiən, -z

utopianism
BR juːˈtəʊpɪənɪz(ə)m, jʊˈtəʊpɪənɪz(ə)m
AM juˈtoʊpiəˌnɪzəm

Utrecht
BR juːˈtrɛkt, juːˈtrɛxt
AM ˈjuˌtrɛk(t)

utricle
BR ˈjuːtrɪkl, -z
AM ˈjutrəkəl, -z

utricular
BR jʊˈtrɪkjʊlə(r)
AM jəˈtrɪkjələr, juˈtrɪkjələr

Utrillo
BR jʊ'trɪləʊ
AM ʊ'trioʊ, ju'trɪloʊ
FR ytʀijo

Utsire
BR ʊt'sɪərə(r)
AM ʊt'sɪrə

Uttar Pradesh
BR ˌʊtə prə'dɛʃ
AM ˌʊtɑr prɑ'dɛʃ

utter
BR 'ʌt|ə(r), -əz, -(ə)rɪŋ, -əd
AM 'ədər, -z, -ɪŋ, -d

utterable
BR 'ʌt(ə)rəbl
AM 'ədərəbəl

utterance
BR 'ʌt(ə)rəns, 'ʌt(ə)rn̩s, -ɪz
AM 'ədərəns, -əz

utterer
BR 'ʌt(ə)rə(r), -z
AM 'ədərər, -z

utterly
BR 'ʌtəli
AM 'ədərli

uttermost
BR 'ʌtəməʊst
AM 'ədərˌmoʊst

utterness
BR 'ʌtənəs
AM 'ədərnəs

Uttley
BR 'ʌtli
AM 'ətli

Uttoxeter
BR jʊ'tɒksɪtə(r)
AM ju'tɑksədər

U-turn
BR 'juːtəːn, -z
AM 'juˌtərn, -z

uvea
BR 'juːvɪə(r), -z
AM 'juviə, -z

uvula
BR 'juːvjʉlə(r), -z
AM 'juvjələ, -z

uvulae
BR 'juːvjʉliː
AM 'juvjəli, 'juvjəˌlaɪ

uvular
BR 'juːvjʉlə(r)
AM 'juvjələr

UWIST
BR 'juːwɪst
AM 'juwɪst

Uxbridge
BR 'ʌksbrɪdʒ
AM 'əksˌbrɪdʒ

uxorial
BR ʌk'sɔːrɪəl
AM ək'zɔriəl, ək'sɔriəl

uxoricidal
BR ʌkˌsɔːrɪ'sʌɪdl
AM əkˌzɔrə'saɪdəl, əkˌsɔrə'saɪdəl

uxoricide
BR ʌk'sɔːrɪsʌɪd, -z
AM ək'zɔrəˌsaɪd, ək'sɔrəˌsaɪd, -z

uxorious
BR ʌk'sɔːrɪəs
AM ˌək'sɔriəs, ˌək'zɔriəs

uxoriously
BR ʌk'sɔːrɪəsli
AM ˌək'sɔriəsli, ˌək'zɔriəsli

uxoriousness
BR ʌk'sɔːrɪəsnəs
AM ˌək'sɔriəsnəs, ˌək'zɔriəsnəs

Uzbek
BR 'ʊzbɛk, 'ʌzbɛk, -s
AM 'ʊzˌbɛk, 'əzˌbɛk, -s

Uzbekistan
BR ʉzˌbɛkɪ'stɑːn, ʌzˌbɛkɪ'stɑːn, ʉzˌbɛkɪ'stan, ʌzˌbɛkɪ'stan
AM ʊz'bɛkəˌstæn, əz'bɛkəˌstæn

Uzi®
BR 'uːz|i, -ɪz
AM 'uzi, -z

Vv

v[1]
BR viː, -z
AM vi, -z

v[2]
versus
BR 'vəːsəs, viː
AM 'vərsəs, vi

Vaal
BR vɑːl
AM vɑl

Vaasa
BR 'vɑːsə(r)
AM 'vɑsə, 'vɑˌsɑ

vac
BR vak, -s, -ɪŋ, -t
AM væk, -s, -ɪŋ, -t

vacancy
BR 'veɪk(ə)ns|i, -ɪz
AM 'veɪkənsi, -z

vacant
BR 'veɪk(ə)nt
AM 'veɪkənt

vacantly
BR 'veɪk(ə)ntli
AM 'veɪkən(t)li

vacatable
BR və'keɪtəbl, veɪ'keɪtəbl
AM 'veɪˌkeɪdəbəl

vacate
BR və'keɪt, veɪ'keɪt, -s, -ɪŋ, -ɪd
AM 'veɪˌkeɪ|t, -ts, -dɪŋ, -dɪd

vacation
BR və'keɪʃn, veɪ'keɪʃn, -z, -ɪŋ, -d
AM veɪ'keɪʃən, və'keɪʃən, -z, -ɪŋ, -d

vacationer
BR və'keɪʃn̩ə(r), veɪ'keɪʃn̩ə(r), -z
AM veɪ'keɪʃənər, və'keɪʃənər, -z

vacationist
BR və'keɪʃn̩ɪst, veɪ'keɪʃn̩ɪst, -s
AM veɪ'keɪʃənəst, və'keɪʃənəst, -s

vaccinal
BR 'vaksɪnl
AM 'væksənəl

vaccinate
BR 'vaksɪneɪt, -s, -ɪŋ, -ɪd
AM 'væksəˌneɪ|t, -ts, -dɪŋ, -dɪd

vaccination
BR ˌvaksɪ'neɪʃn, -z
AM ˌvæksə'neɪʃən, -z

vaccinator
BR 'vaksɪneɪtə(r), -z
AM 'væksəˌneɪdər, -z

vaccine
BR 'vaksiːn, -z
AM væk'sin, -z

vaccinia
BR vak'sɪnɪə(r)
AM væk'sɪniə

vacillate
BR 'vasɪleɪt, -s, -ɪŋ, -ɪd
AM 'væsəˌleɪ|t, -ts, -dɪŋ, -dɪd

vacillation
BR ˌvasɪ'leɪʃn
AM ˌvæsə'leɪʃən

vacillator
BR 'vasɪleɪtə(r), -z
AM 'væsəˌleɪdər, -z

vacua
BR 'vakjʊə(r)
AM 'vækjəwə

vacuity
BR və'kjuːɪt|i, va'kjuːɪt|i, -ɪz
AM væ'kjuədi, və'kjuədi, -z

vacuolar
BR 'vakjʊələ(r)
AM ˌvækjʊ'oʊlər, 'vækjələr

vacuolation
BR ˌvakjʊə'leɪʃn, -z
AM ˌvækjə'leɪʃən, -z

vacuole
BR 'vakjʊəʊl, -z
AM 'vækjuˌoʊl, -z

vacuous
BR 'vakjʊəs
AM 'vækjəwəs

vacuously
BR 'vakjʊəsli
AM 'vækjəwəsli

vacuousness
BR 'vakjʊəsnəs
AM 'vækjəwəsnəs

vacuum
BR 'vakjuːm, -z, -ɪŋ, -d
AM 'vækˌjum, -z, -ɪŋ, -d

vade mecum
BR ˌvɑːdɪ 'meɪkəm, ˌveɪdɪ +, + 'miːkəm, -z
AM ˌveɪdi 'mikəm, ˌvɑdi +, -z

Vaduz
BR va'duːz, və'duːz
AM və'duz

vag
BR vag, -z, -ɪŋ, -d
AM væg, -z, -ɪŋ, -d

vagabond
BR 'vagəbɒnd, -z
AM 'vægəˌbɑnd, -z

vagabondage
BR 'vagəbɒndɪdʒ
AM 'vægəˌbɑndɪdʒ

vagal
BR 'veɪgl
AM 'veɪgəl

vagarious
BR və'gɛːrɪəs
AM və'gɛriəs, veɪ'gɛriəs

vagary
BR 'veɪg(ə)r|i, -ɪz
AM 'veɪgəri, -z

vagi
BR 'veɪdʒʌɪ, 'veɪgʌɪ
AM 'veɪˌgaɪ, 'veɪˌdʒaɪ

vagina
BR və'dʒʌɪnə(r), -z
AM və'dʒaɪnə, -z

vaginal
BR və'dʒʌɪnl
AM 'vædʒənəl

vaginally
BR və'dʒʌɪnl̩i
AM 'vædʒ(ə)nəli

vaginismus
BR ˌvadʒɪ'nɪzməs
AM ˌvædʒə'nɪzməs

vaginitis
BR ˌvadʒɪ'nʌɪtɪs
AM ˌvædʒə'naɪdɪs

vagotomy
BR veɪ'gɒtəm|i, -ɪz
AM veɪ'gɑdəmi, -z

vagrancy
BR 'veɪgr(ə)nsi
AM 'veɪgrənsi

vagrant
BR 'veɪgr(ə)nt, -s
AM 'veɪgrənt, -s

vagrantly
BR 'veɪgr(ə)ntli
AM 'veɪgrən(t)li

vague
BR veɪg, -ə(r), -ɪst
AM veɪg, -ər, -ɪst

vaguely
BR 'veɪgli
AM 'veɪgli

vagueness
BR 'veɪgnɪs
AM 'veɪgnɪs

vaguish
BR 'veɪgɪʃ
AM 'veɪgɪʃ

vagus
BR 'veɪgəs
AM 'veɪgəs

vail
BR veɪl, -z, -ɪŋ, -d
AM veɪl, -z, -ɪŋ, -d

vain
BR veɪn, -ə(r), -ɪst
AM veɪn, -ər, -ɪst

vainglorious
BR (ˌ)veɪn'glɔːrɪəs
AM ˌveɪn'glɔriəs

vaingloriously
BR (ˌ)veɪn'glɔːrɪəsli
AM ˌveɪn'glɔriəsli

vaingloriousness
BR (ˌ)veɪn'glɔːrɪəsnəs
AM ˌveɪn'glɔriəsnəs

vainglory
BR (ˌ)veɪn'glɔːri
AM 'veɪnˌglɔri

vainly
BR 'veɪnli
AM 'veɪnli

vainness
BR 'veɪnnɪs
AM 'veɪ(n)nɪs

vair
BR vɛː(r)
AM vɛ(ə)r

Vaishnava
BR 'vʌɪʃnəvə(r), -z
AM 'vɪʃnəvə, -z

Vaisya
BR 'vʌɪsjə(r), 'vʌɪʃjə(r), -z
AM 'vaɪsjə, -z

Vaizey
BR 'veɪzi
AM 'veɪzi

Val
BR val
AM væl

Valais
BR va'lɛ
AM vɑ'lɛ

valance
BR 'valəns, 'valn̩s, -ɪz
AM 'væləns, -əz

valanced
BR 'valənst, 'valn̩st
AM 'vælənst

Valda
BR 'valdə(r)
AM 'vɑldə

Valdemar
BR 'valdɪmɑː(r)
AM 'vɑldəˌmɑr

Valderma
BR val'dəːmə(r)
AM 'vɑldəmə

Valdez
BR val'diːz
AM vɑl'dɛz, vɑl'diz

vale
BR veɪl, -z
AM veɪl, -z

valediction
BR ˌvalɪ'dɪkʃn, -z
AM ˌvælə'dɪkʃən, -z

valedictorian
BR ˌvalɪdɪk'tɔːrɪən, -z
AM ˌvæləˌdɪk'tɔriən, -z

valedictory
BR ˌvalɪ'dɪkt(ə)ri
AM ˌvælə'dɪkt(ə)ri

valence
BR 'veɪləns, 'veɪln̩s, -ɪz
AM 'veɪləns, -əz

valencia
BR və'lɛnsɪə(r), -z

AM və'lɛn(t)siə, və'lɛntʃiə, -z

Valencian
BR və'lɛnsɪən
AM və'lɛn(t)siən, və'lɛn(t)ʃ(i)ən
SP ba'lenθja, ba'lensja

Valenciennes
BR ˌvalənsɪ'ɛn, ˌvaln̩sɪ'ɛn
AM ˌvælənsi'ɛn

valency
BR 'veɪləns|i, 'veɪln̩s|i, -ɪz
AM 'veɪlənsi, -z

valentine
BR 'valəntʌɪn, 'valn̩tʌɪn, -z
AM 'vælənˌtaɪn, -z

Valentinian
BR ˌvalən'tɪnɪən, ˌvaln̩'tɪnɪən
AM 'vælən'tɪniən

Valentino
BR ˌvalən'tiːnəʊ, ˌvaln̩'tiːnəʊ
AM ˌvælən'tinoʊ

Valera
BR və'lɛːrə(r), və'lɪərə(r)
AM və'lɛrə

valerate
BR 'valəreɪt, -s
AM 'væləˌreɪt, -s

valerian
BR və'lɪərɪən, və'lɛːrɪən, -z
AM və'lɪriən, və'lɛriən, -z

valeric
BR və'lɪərɪk, və'lɛːrɪk, və'lɛrɪk
AM və'lɛrɪk

Valerie
BR 'val(ə)ri
AM 'væl(ə)ri

Valéry
BR 'valəri
AM 'væləri

valet[1]
noun
BR 'val|ɪt, 'val|eɪ, -ɪts\-eɪz
AM væ'l|eɪ, 'vælə|t, -ts\-eɪz

valet[2]
verb
BR 'valɪt, -s, -ɪŋ, -ɪd
AM 'vælə|t, -ts, -dɪŋ, -dəd

valeta
BR və'liːtə(r), -z
AM və'lidə, -z

valetudinarian
BR ˌvalɪˌtjuːdɪ'nɛːrɪən, ˌvalɪˌtʃuːdɪ'nɛːrɪən, -z
AM ˌvæləˌt(j)udn'ɛriən, -z

valetudinarianism
BR ˌvalɪˌtjuːdɪ'nɛːrɪən-ɪz(ə)m, ˌvalɪˌtʃuːdɪ'nɛːrɪən-ɪz(ə)m
AM ˌvæləˌt(j)udn'ɛriə-ˌnɪzəm

valetudinary
BR ˌvalɪ'tjuːdɪn(ə)ri, ˌvalɪ'tʃuːdɪn(ə)ri
AM ˌvælə't(j)udnˌɛri

valgus
BR 'valgəs
AM 'vælgəs

Valhalla
BR val'halə(r)
AM væl'hælə, vɑl'hɑlə

valiant
BR 'valɪənt
AM 'væljənt

valiantly
BR 'valɪəntli
AM 'væljən(t)li

valid
BR 'valɪd
AM 'væləd

validate
BR 'valɪdeɪt, -s, -ɪŋ, -ɪd
AM 'væləˌdeɪ|t, -ts, -dɪŋ, -dɪd

validation
BR ˌvalɪ'deɪʃn
AM ˌvælə'deɪʃən

validity
BR və'lɪdɪti
AM və'lɪdɪdi

validly
BR 'valɪdli
AM 'vælədli

validness
BR 'valɪdnɪs
AM 'vælədnəs

valine
BR 'veɪliːn
AM 'væˌlin, 'veɪˌlin

valise
BR və'liːz, -ɪz
AM və'lis, -ɪz

valium
BR 'valɪəm
AM 'væliəm

Valkyrie
BR 'valkɪr|i, -ɪz
AM væl'kɪri, 'vælˌkɪri, -z

Vallance
BR 'valəns, 'valn̩s
AM 'væləns

Vallans
BR 'valəns, 'valn̩s
AM 'væləns

Valle Crucis
BR ˌvalɪ 'kruːsɪs
AM ˌvæli 'krusəs

vallecula
BR və'lɛkjʉlə(r), va'lɛkjʉlə(r)
AM və'lɛkjələ

valleculae
BR və'lɛkjʉliː, va'lɛkjʉliː
AM və'lɛkjəli, və'lɛkjəˌlaɪ

vallecular
BR və'lɛkjʉlə(r), va'lɛkjʉlə(r)
AM və'lɛkjələr

valleculate
BR və'lɛkjʉleɪt, va'lɛkjʉleɪt
AM və'lɛkjəˌleɪt

Valletta
BR və'lɛtə(r)
AM və'lɛdə

valley
BR 'val|i, -ɪz
AM 'væli, -z

vallum
BR 'valəm
AM 'væləm

Valois
BR 'valwɑː(r)
AM ˌvæl'wɑ, 'vælwɑ

Valona
BR və'ləʊnə(r)
AM və'loʊnə

valonia
BR və'ləʊnɪə(r)
AM və'loʊniə

valor
BR 'valə(r)
AM 'vælər

valorem
BR və'lɔːrɛm, və'lɔːrəm
AM və'lɔrəm

valorisation
BR ˌval(ə)rʌɪ'zeɪʃn
AM ˌvælərə'zeɪʃən, ˌvæləˌraɪ'zeɪʃən

valorise
BR 'valərʌɪz, -ɪz, -ɪŋ, -d
AM 'væləˌraɪz, -ɪz, -ɪŋ, -d

valorization
BR ˌval(ə)rʌɪ'zeɪʃn
AM ˌvælərə'zeɪʃən, ˌvæləˌraɪ'zeɪʃən

valorize
BR 'valərʌɪz, -ɪz, -ɪŋ, -d
AM 'væləˌraɪz, -ɪz, -ɪŋ, -d

valorous
BR 'val(ə)rəs
AM 'vælərəs

valorously
BR 'val(ə)rəsli
AM 'vælərəsli

valour
BR 'valə(r)
AM 'vælər

Valparaiso
BR ˌvalpə'rʌɪzəʊ
AM ˌvælpə'raɪˌzoʊ, ˌvælpə'reɪˌzoʊ
SP ˌbalpara'iso

valproic
BR val'prəʊɪk
AM væl'proʊɪk

valse
BR vɑːls, vals, vɔːls, -ɪz
AM vɑls, -əz

valuable
BR 'valjʉbl, 'valjʊəbl, -z
AM 'vælj(əw)əbəl, -z

valuably
BR 'valjʉbli, 'valjʊəbli
AM 'vælj(əw)əbli

valuate
BR 'valjʊeɪt, -s, -ɪŋ, -ɪd
AM 'væljəˌweɪ|t, -ts, -dɪŋ, -dɪd

valuation
BR ˌvaljʊ'eɪʃn, -z
AM ˌvæljə'weɪʃən, -z

valuator
BR 'valjʊeɪtə(r), -z
AM 'væljəˌweɪdər, -z

value
BR 'valjuː, -z, -ɪŋ, -d
AM 'vælju, -z, -əwɪŋ, -d

valueless
BR 'valjʉləs, 'valjuːləs
AM 'væljuləs

valuelessness
BR 'valjʊləsnəs, 'valjuːləsnəs
AM 'væljuləsnəs

valuer
BR 'valjʊə(r), -z
AM 'væljuər, -z

valuta
BR və'l(j)uːtə(r)
AM və'ludə

valvate
BR 'valveɪt
AM 'vælˌveɪt

valve
BR valv, -z, -d
AM vælv, -z, -d

valveless
BR 'valvləs
AM 'vælvləs

valvular
BR 'valvjʉlə(r)
AM 'vælvjələr

valvule
BR 'valvjuːl, -z
AM 'vælvˌjul, -z

valvulitis
BR ˌvalvjʉ'lʌɪtɪs
AM ˌvælvjə'laɪdɪs

vambrace
BR 'vambreɪs, -ɪz
AM 'væmˌbreɪs, -ɪz

vamoose
BR və'muːs, va'muːs, -ɪz, -ɪŋ, -t
AM væ'mus, və'mus, -əz, -ɪŋ, -t

vamp
BR vam|p, -ps, -pɪŋ, -(p)t
AM væmp, -s, -ɪŋ, -t

vampire
BR 'vampʌɪə(r), -z
AM 'væm,paɪ(ə)r, -z

vampiric
BR vam'pɪrɪk
AM væm'pɪrɪk

vampirism
BR 'vampʌɪərɪz(ə)m
AM 'væmpaɪ(ə),rɪzəm

vampish
BR 'vampɪʃ
AM 'væmpɪʃ

vamplate
BR 'vampleɪt, -s
AM 'væm,pleɪt, -s

vampy
BR 'vamp|i, -ɪə(r), -ɪɪst
AM 'væmpi, -ər, -ɪst

van
BR van, -z
AM væn, -z

vanadate
BR 'vanədeɪt, -s
AM 'vænə,deɪt, -s

vanadic
BR və'nadɪk, və'neɪdɪk
AM və'neɪdɪk, və'nædɪk

vanadium
BR və'neɪdɪəm
AM və'neɪdiəm

vanadous
BR 'vanədəs
AM və'nædəs, 'vænədəs

Van Allen
BR van 'alən
AM ,væn 'ælən

Vanbrugh
BR 'vanbrə(r)
AM 'vænbrə

Van Buren
BR van 'bjʊərən, + 'bjʊərn̩, + 'bjɔːrən, + 'bjɔːrn̩
AM ,væn 'bjʊrən

Vance
BR vans, vɑːns
AM væns

Vancouver
BR van'kuːvə(r), vaŋ'kuːvə(r)
AM væn'kuvər

Vanda
BR 'vandə(r)
AM 'vɑndə

vandal
BR 'vandl, -z
AM 'vændəl, -z

Vandalic
BR van'dalɪk
AM væn'dælɪk

vandalise
BR 'vandəlʌɪz, 'vandl̩ʌɪz, -ɪz, -ɪŋ, -d
AM 'vændl,aɪz, -ɪz, -ɪŋ, -d

vandalism
BR 'vandəlɪz(ə)m, 'vandl̩ɪz(ə)m
AM 'vændl,ɪzəm

vandalistic
BR ,vandə'lɪstɪk, ,vandl'ɪstɪk
AM ,vændə'lɪstɪk

vandalistically
BR ,vandə'lɪstɪkli, ,vandl̩'ɪstɪkli
AM ,vændə'lɪstək(ə)li

vandalize
BR 'vandəlʌɪz, 'vandl̩ʌɪz, -ɪz, -ɪŋ, -d
AM 'vændl,aɪz, -ɪz, -ɪŋ, -d

Van de Graaff
BR ,van də 'grɑːf, + 'graf
AM ,væn də 'grɑf

Vandenberg
BR 'vandənbəːg
AM 'vændən,bərg

Vanden Plas
BR ,vandən 'plas, + 'plɑːs
AM ,vændən 'plɑs

Vanderbilt
BR 'vandəbɪlt
AM 'vændər,bɪlt

Van der Post
BR ,van də 'pɒst, + 'pəʊst
AM ,væn dər 'poʊst

Van Der Rohe
BR ,van də 'rəʊə(r)
AM ,væn də(r) 'roʊə

van de Velde
BR ,van də 'vɛldə(r)
AM ,væn də 'vɛldə

Van Diemen's Land
BR ,van 'diːmənz land
AM ,væn 'dimənz ,lænd

Van Dyck
BR van 'dʌɪk
AM ,væn 'daɪk

vandyke
BR van'dʌɪk, -s
AM ,væn'daɪk, -s

vane
BR veɪn, -z, -d
AM veɪn, -z, -d

vaneless
BR 'veɪnlɪs
AM 'veɪnlɪs

Vanessa
BR və'nɛsə(r)
AM və'nɛsə

van Eyck
BR van 'ʌɪk
AM ,væn 'aɪk

vang
BR vaŋ, -z
AM væŋ, -z

van Gogh
BR van 'gɒf, vaŋ +, + 'gɒx, -s
AM ,væn 'goʊ, -s
DU vɑn 'xɔx

vanguard
BR 'vangɑːd, 'vaŋgɑːd, -z
AM 'væn,gɑrd, -z

vanilla
BR və'nɪlə(r), -z
AM və'nɪlə, -z

vanillin
BR və'nɪlɪn, 'vanɪlɪn, 'vanl̩ɪn
AM və'nɪlɪn, 'vænələn

vanish
BR 'van|ɪʃ, -ɪʃɪz, -ɪʃɪŋ, -ɪʃt
AM 'vænɪʃ, -ɪz, -ɪŋ, -t

vanitory
BR 'vanɪt(ə)ri
AM 'vænə,tɔri

vanity
BR 'vanɪt|i, -ɪz
AM 'vænədi, -z

vanload
BR 'vanləʊd, -z
AM 'væn,loʊd, -z

vanquish
BR 'vaŋkw|ɪʃ, -ɪʃɪz, -ɪʃɪŋ, -ɪʃt
AM 'væŋkwɪʃ, -ɪz, -ɪŋ, -t

vanquishable
BR 'vaŋkwɪʃəbl
AM 'væŋkwəʃəbəl

vanquisher
BR 'vaŋkwɪʃə(r), -z
AM 'væŋkwɪʃər, -z

Vansittart
BR van'sɪtət
AM ,væn'sɪdərt

vantage
BR 'vɑːntɪdʒ, 'vantɪdʒ
AM 'væn(t)ɪdʒ

vantagepoint
BR 'vɑːntɪdʒpɔɪnt, 'vantɪdʒpɔɪnt, -s
AM 'væn(t)ɪdʒ,pɔɪnt, -s

Vanuatu
BR ,vanʊ'ɑːtuː, ,vanʊ'atuː
AM ,vɑnʊ'ɑdu

Vanya
BR 'vɑːnjə(r), 'vanjə(r)
AM 'vɑnjə

vapid
BR 'vapɪd
AM 'væpəd

vapidity
BR va'pɪdɪti, və'pɪdɪti
AM və'pɪdɪdi

vapidly
BR 'vapɪdli
AM 'væpədli

vapidness
BR 'vapɪdnɪs
AM 'væpədnəs

vapor
BR 'veɪp|ə(r), -əz, -(ə)rɪŋ, -əd
AM 'veɪpər, -z, -ɪŋ, -d

vaporer
BR 'veɪp(ə)rə(r), -z
AM 'veɪpərər, -z

vaporetti
BR ,vapə'rɛtiː
AM ,veɪpə'rɛdi

vaporetto
BR ,vapə'rɛtəʊ, -z
AM ,veɪpə'rɛdoʊ, -z

vaporific
BR ,veɪpə'rɪfɪk
AM ,veɪpə'rɪfɪk

vaporiform
BR 'veɪp(ə)rɪfɔːm
AM veɪ'pɔrə,fɔ(ə)rm

vaporimeter
BR ,veɪpə'rɪmɪtə(r), -z
AM ,veɪpə'rɪmɪdər, -z

vaporisable
BR 'veɪp(ə)rʌɪzəbl
AM 'veɪpə,raɪzəbəl

vaporisation
BR ,veɪp(ə)rʌɪ'zeɪʃn
AM ,veɪpərə'zeɪʃən, ,veɪpə,raɪ'zeɪʃən

vaporise
BR 'veɪpərʌɪz, -ɪz, -ɪŋ, -d
AM 'veɪpə,raɪz, -ɪz, -ɪŋ, -d

vaporiser
BR 'veɪp(ə)rʌɪzə(r), -z
AM 'veɪpə,raɪzər, -z

vaporish
BR 'veɪp(ə)rɪʃ
AM 'veɪpərɪʃ

vaporizable
BR 'veɪp(ə)rʌɪzəbl
AM 'veɪpə,raɪzəbəl

vaporization
BR ,veɪp(ə)rʌɪ'zeɪʃn
AM ,veɪpərə'zeɪʃən, ,veɪpə,raɪ'zeɪʃən

vaporize
BR 'veɪpərʌɪz, -ɪz, -ɪŋ, -d
AM 'veɪpə,raɪz, -ɪz, -ɪŋ, -d

vaporizer
BR 'veɪp(ə)rʌɪzə(r), -z
AM 'veɪpə,raɪzər, -z

vaporous
BR 'veɪp(ə)rəs

AM 'veɪp(ə)rəs
vaporously
BR 'veɪp(ə)rəsli
AM 'veɪp(ə)rəsli
vaporousness
BR 'veɪp(ə)rəsnəs
AM 'veɪp(ə)rəsnəs
vapory
BR 'veɪp(ə)ri
AM 'veɪp(ə)ri
vapour
BR veɪp|ə(r), -əz, -(ə)rɪŋ, -əd
AM 'veɪpər, -z, -ɪŋ, -d
vapour-check
BR 'veɪpətʃɛk
AM 'veɪpər,tʃɛk
vapourer
BR 'veɪp(ə)rə(r)
AM 'veɪp(ə)rər
vapourish
BR 'veɪp(ə)rɪʃ
AM 'veɪp(ə)rɪʃ
vapoury
BR 'veɪp(ə)ri
AM 'veɪp(ə)ri
vaquero
BR və'kɛːrəʊ, va'kɛːrəʊ, -z
AM vɑ'kɛroʊ, -z
varactor
BR və'raktə(r), -z
AM 'vɛ,ræktər, -z
Varah
BR 'vɑːrə(r)
AM 'vɑrə
Varangian
BR və'ran(d)ʒɪən, -z
AM və'randʒiən, -z
Vardon
BR 'vɑːdn
AM 'vɑrdən
varec
BR 'varɛk
AM 'vɛrək
Varèse
BR və'rɛz
AM və'reɪz, və'rɛz
Vargas
BR 'vɑːgas, 'vɑːgəs
AM 'vɑrgəs
varia
BR 'vɛːrɪə(r)
AM 'vɛriə
variability
BR ,vɛːrɪə'bɪlɪti
AM ,vɛriə'bɪlɪdi
variable
BR 'vɛːrɪəbl, -z
AM 'vɛriəbəl, -z
variableness
BR 'vɛːrɪəblnəs
AM 'vɛriəbəlnəs
variably
BR 'vɛːrɪəbli
AM 'vɛriəbli
variance
BR 'vɛːrɪəns
AM 'vɛriəns
variant
BR 'vɛːrɪənt, -s
AM 'vɛriənt, -s
variate
BR 'vɛːrɪət, 'vɛːrɪeɪt, -s
AM 'vɛriət, -s
variation
BR ,vɛːrɪ'eɪʃn, -z
AM ,vɛri'eɪʃən, -z
variational
BR ,vɛːrɪ'eɪʃn̩(ə)l, ,vɛːrɪ'eɪʃən(ə)l
AM ,vɛri'eɪʃ(ə)nəl
variationally
BR ,vɛːrɪ'eɪʃn̩əli, ,vɛːrɪ'eɪʃn̩li, ,vɛːrɪ'eɪʃənl̩i, ,vɛːrɪ'eɪʃ(ə)nəli
AM ,vɛri'eɪʃ(ə)nəli
variationist
BR ,vɛːrɪ'eɪʃn̩ɪst, ,vɛːrɪ'eɪʃənɪst, -s
AM ,vɛri'eɪʃənəst, -s
varicella
BR ,varɪ'sɛlə(r)
AM ,vɛrə'sɛlə
varices
BR 'varɪsiːz, 'vɛːrɪsiːz
AM 'vɛrə,siz
varicocele
BR 'varɪkə(ʊ)siːl, -z
AM 'vɛrəkoʊ,sil, -z
varicolored
BR ,vɛːrɪ'kʌləd
AM 'vɛri,kələrd
varicoloured
BR ,vɛːrɪ'kʌləd
AM 'vɛri,kələrd
varicose
BR 'varɪkə(ʊ)s
AM 'vɛrə,koʊs, 'vɛrə,koʊz
varicosed
BR 'varɪkə(ʊ)st, 'varɪkəʊzd
AM 'vɛrə,koʊst, 'vɛrə,koʊzd
varicosity
BR ,varɪ'kɒsɪt|i, -ɪz
AM ,vɛrə'kɑsədi, -z
varied
BR 'vɛːrɪd
AM 'vɛrid
variedly
BR 'vɛːrɪdli
AM 'vɛridli
variegate
BR 'vɛːrɪəgeɪt, -s, -ɪŋ, -ɪd
AM 'vɛr(i)ə,geɪ|t, -ts, -dɪŋ, -dɪd
variegation
BR ,vɛːrɪə'geɪʃn, -z
AM ,vɛr(i)ə'geɪʃən, -z
varietal
BR və'rʌɪɪtl
AM və'raɪədl
varietally
BR və'rʌɪɪtl̩i, və'rʌɪɪtəli
AM və'raɪədli
varietist
BR və'rʌɪɪtɪst, -s
AM və'raɪədəst, -s
variety
BR və'rʌɪɪt|i, -ɪz
AM və'raɪədi, -z
varifocal
BR ,vɛːrɪ'fəʊkl, -z
AM ,vɛri'foʊkəl, -z
variform
BR 'vɛːrɪfɔːm
AM 'vɛrə,fɔ(ə)rm
variola
BR və'rʌɪələ(r)
AM və'raɪələ, ,vɛri'oʊlə
variolar
BR və'rʌɪələ(r)
AM və'rɪələr
variolate
BR 'vɛːrɪəleɪt
AM 'vɛriə,leɪt
variole
BR 'vɛːrɪəʊl, -z
AM 'vɛri,oʊl, -z
variolite
BR 'vɛːrɪəlʌɪt, -s
AM 'vɛriə,laɪt, -s
variolitic
BR ,vɛːrɪə'lɪtɪk
AM ,vɛriə'lɪdɪk
varioloid
BR 'vɛːrɪəlɔɪd, -z
AM 'vɛriə,lɔɪd, -z
variolous
BR 'vɛːrɪələs
AM 'vɛriələs
variometer
BR ,vɛːrɪ'ɒmɪtə(r), -z
AM ,vɛri'ɑmədər, -z
variorum
BR ,vɛːrɪ'ɔːrəm
AM ,vɛri'ɔrəm
various
BR 'vɛːrɪəs
AM 'vɛriəs
variously
BR 'vɛːrɪəsli
AM 'vɛriəsli
variousness
BR 'vɛːrɪəsnəs
AM 'vɛriəsnəs
varistor
BR (,)vɛː'rɪstə(r), və'rɪstə(r), -z
AM və'rɪstər, -z
varix
BR 'vɛːrɪks
AM 'vɛrɪks
varlet
BR 'vɑːlɪt, -s
AM 'vɑrlət, -s
varletry
BR 'vɑːlɪtri
AM 'vɑrlətri
Varley
BR 'vɑːli
AM 'vɑrli
varmint
BR 'vɑːmɪnt, -s
AM 'vɑrmənt, -s
varna
BR 'vɑːnə(r), -z
AM 'vɑrnə, -z
Varney
BR 'vɑːni
AM 'vɑrni
varnish
BR 'vɑːn|ɪʃ, -ɪʃɪz, -ɪʃɪŋ, -ɪʃt
AM 'vɑrnɪʃ, -ɪz, -ɪŋ, -t
varnisher
BR 'vɑːnɪʃə(r), -z
AM 'vɑrnɪʃər, -z
Varro
BR 'varəʊ
AM 'vɛroʊ
varsity
BR 'vɑːsɪt|i, -ɪz
AM 'vɑrsədi, -z
Varsovian
BR vɑː'səʊvɪən, -z
AM vɑr'soʊviən, -z
varsoviana
BR vɑː,səʊvɪ'ɑːnə(r), -z
AM vɑr,soʊvi'ɑnə, -z
varsovienne
BR vɑː,səʊvɪ'ɛn, -z
AM vɑr,soʊvi'ɛn, -z
varus
BR 'vɛːrəs, -ɪz
AM 'vɛrəs, -əz
varve
BR vɑːv, -z, -d
AM vɑrv, -z, -d
vary
BR 'vɛːr|i, -ɪz, -ɪɪŋ, -ɪd
AM 'vɛri, -z, -ɪŋ, -d
varyingly
BR 'vɛːrɪɪŋli
AM 'vɛriɪŋli
vas
BR vas
AM væs, væz
vasa deferentia
BR ,vasə ,dɛfə'rɛnʃ(ɪ)ə(r)
AM ,væsə ,dɛfə'rən(t)ʃ(i)ə
vasal
BR 'veɪsl, 'veɪzl
AM 'veɪsəl, 'veɪzəl
Vasari
BR və'sɑːri
AM və'sɑri

Vasco da Gama
BR ˌvaskəʊ də ˈɡɑːmə(r)
AM ˌvæskoʊ də ˈɡɑmə, ˌvɑskoʊ də ˈɡɑmə

vascula
BR ˈvaskjʉlə(r)
AM ˈvæskjələ

vascular
BR ˈvaskjʉlə(r)
AM ˈvæskjələr

vascularise
BR ˈvaskjʉlərʌɪz, -ɪz, -ɪŋ, -d
AM ˈvæskjələˌraɪz, -ɪz, -ɪŋ, -d

vascularity
BR ˌvaskjʉˈlarɪti
AM ˌvæskjəˈlɛrədi

vascularize
BR ˈvaskjʉlərʌɪz, -ɪz, -ɪŋ, -d
AM ˈvæskjələˌraɪz, -ɪz, -ɪŋ, -d

vascularly
BR ˈvaskjʉləli
AM ˈvæskjələrli

vasculum
BR ˈvaskjʉləm
AM ˈvæskjələm

vas deferens
BR ˌvas ˈdɛfərɛnz
AM ˌvæs ˈdɛfərənz, ˌvæs ˈdɛfəˌrɛnz, ˌvæz ˈdɛfərənz, ˌvæz ˈdɛfəˌrɛnz

vase
BR vɑːz, -ɪz
AM veɪs, veɪz, vɑz, -ɪz

vasectomise
BR vəˈsɛktəmʌɪz, -ɪz, -ɪŋ, -d
AM vəˈsɛktəˌmaɪz, -ɪz, -ɪŋ, -d

vasectomize
BR vəˈsɛktəmʌɪz, -ɪz, -ɪŋ, -d
AM vəˈsɛktəˌmaɪz, -ɪz, -ɪŋ, -d

vasectomy
BR vəˈsɛktəm|i, -ɪz
AM vəˈsɛktəmi, -z

vaseful
BR ˈvɑːzfʊl, -z
AM ˈveɪsˌfʊl, ˈveɪzˌfʊl, vɑzˌfʊl, -z

vaseline®
BR ˈvasɪliːn, ˈvasl̩iːn, ˌvasɪˈliːn, ˌvaslˈiːn, -z, -ɪŋ, -d
AM ˌvæsəˈlin, -z, -ɪŋ, -d

vasiform
BR ˈveɪzɪfɔːm
AM ˈveɪsəˌfɔ(ə)rm, ˈveɪzəˌfɔ(ə)rm, ˈvæsəˌfɔ(ə)rm, ˈvæzəˌfɔ(ə)rm

vasoactive
BR ˌveɪzəʊˈaktɪv
AM ˌveɪzoʊˈæktɪv

vasoconstriction
BR ˌveɪzəʊkənˈstrɪkʃn
AM ˌveɪzoʊkənˈstrɪkʃən

vasoconstrictive
BR ˌveɪzəʊkənˈstrɪktɪv
AM ˌveɪzoʊkənˈstrɪktɪv

vasoconstrictor
BR ˌveɪzəʊkənˈstrɪktə(r), -z
AM ˌveɪzoʊkənˈstrɪktər, -z

vasodilating
BR ˌveɪzəʊdʌɪˈleɪtɪŋ
AM ˌveɪzoʊˈdaɪˌleɪdɪŋ

vasodilation
BR ˌveɪzəʊdʌɪˈleɪʃn
AM ˌveɪzoʊˌdaɪˈleɪʃən

vasodilator
BR ˌveɪzəʊdʌɪˈleɪtə(r), -z
AM ˌveɪzoʊˈdaɪˌleɪdər, -z

vasomotor
BR ˌveɪzəʊˈməʊtə(r)
AM ˌveɪzoʊˈmoʊdər

vasopressin
BR ˌveɪzəʊˈprɛsɪn
AM ˌveɪzoʊˈprɛsən

Vásquez
BR ˈvaskwɛz
AM ˌvæsˈk(w)ɛz, ˈvæsˌk(w)ɛz
SP ˈbaskeθ, ˈbaskes

vassal
BR ˈvasl, -z
AM ˈvæsəl, -z

vassalage
BR ˈvasl̩ɪdʒ
AM ˈvæsəlɪdʒ

vast
BR vɑːst, vast, -ə(r), -ɪst
AM væst, -ər, -əst

vastation
BR vaˈsteɪʃn
AM vɑˈsteɪʃn

vastitude
BR ˈvɑːstɪtjuːd, ˈvɑːstɪtʃuːd, ˈvastɪtjuːd, ˈvastɪtʃuːd
AM ˈvæstəˌt(j)ud

vastly
BR ˈvɑːs(t)li, ˈvas(t)li
AM ˈvæs(t)li

vastness
BR ˈvɑːs(t)nəs, ˈvas(t)nəs, -ɪz
AM ˈvæs(t)nəs, -əz

VAT
BR ˌviːeɪˈtiː, vat
AM ˌviˌeɪˈti, væt

vat
BR vat, -s
AM væt, -s

Vatersay
BR ˈvatəseɪ
AM ˈvædərˌseɪ

VAT-free
BR ˌvatˈfriː
AM ˌvætˈfri

vatful
BR ˈvatfʊl, -z
AM ˈvætˌfʊl, -z

vatic
BR ˈvatɪk
AM ˈvædɪk

Vatican
BR ˈvatɪk(ə)n
AM ˈvædəkən

Vatican City
BR ˌvatɪk(ə)n ˈsɪti
AM ˌvædəkən ˈsɪdi

Vaticanism
BR ˈvatɪkənɪz(ə)m, ˈvatɪkn̩ɪz(ə)m
AM ˈvædəkəˌnɪzəm

Vaticanist
BR ˈvatɪkənɪst, ˈvatɪkn̩ɪst, -s
AM ˈvædəkənəst, -s

vaticinal
BR vaˈtɪsɪnl, vəˈtɪsɪnl, vaˈtɪsn̩l, vəˈtɪsn̩l
AM vəˈtɪsɪnəl

vaticinate
BR vaˈtɪsɪneɪt, vəˈtɪsɪneɪt, vaˈtɪsn̩eɪt, vəˈtɪsn̩eɪt, -s, -ɪŋ, -ɪd
AM vəˈtɪsn̩ˌeɪ|t, -ts, -dɪŋ, -dɪd

vaticination
BR vəˌtɪsɪˈneɪʃn, -z
AM vəˌtɪsn̩ˈeɪʃən, -z

vaticinator
BR vəˈtɪsɪneɪtə(r), vəˈtɪsn̩eɪtə(r), -z
AM vəˈtɪsəˌneɪdər, -z

vaticinatory
BR vəˈtɪsɪnət(ə)ri, vəˈtɪsn̩ət(ə)ri
AM vəˈtɪsn̩əˌtɔri

VAT-registered
BR vatˈrɛdʒɪstəd
AM ˌvætˈrɛdʒɪstərd

Vättern
BR ˈvatəːn
AM ˈvɛdərn
SW ˈvɛtɛn

vaudeville
BR ˈvɔːd(ə)vɪl, ˈvəʊd(ə)vɪl
AM ˈvɔd(ə)ˌvɪl, ˈvɔd(ə)vəl, ˈvɑd(ə)ˌvɪl, ˈvɑd(ə)vəl

vaudevillian
BR ˌvɔːd(ɪ)ˈvɪlɪən, ˌvəʊd(ɪ)ˈvɪlɪən, -z
AM ˌvɔd(ə)ˈvɪljən, ˌvɑd(ə)ˈvɪljən, ˌvɔd(ə)ˈvɪliən, ˌvɑd(ə)ˈvɪliən, -z

Vaudois
BR ˈvɔːdwɑː(r), ˈvəʊdwɑː(r), -z
AM vɔˈdwɑ, ˈvɔdwɑ, -z

Vaughan
BR vɔːn
AM vɔn, vɑn

Vaughan Williams
BR ˌvɔːn ˈwɪlɪəmz
AM ˌvɔn ˈwɪljəmz, ˌvɑn +, + ˈwɪliəmz

Vaughn
BR vɔːn
AM vɔn, vɑn

vault
BR vɔːlt, vɒlt, -s, -ɪŋ, -ɪd
AM vɔlt, vɑlt, -s, -ɪŋ, -əd

vaulter
BR ˈvɔːltə(r), ˈvɒltə(r), -z
AM ˈvɔltər, ˈvɑltər, -z

vaunt
BR vɔːnt, -s, -ɪŋ, -ɪd
AM vɔn|t, vɑn|t, -ts, -(t)ɪŋ, -(t)əd

vaunter
BR ˈvɔːntə(r), -z
AM ˈvɔn(t)ər, ˈvɑn(t)ər, -z

vauntingly
BR ˈvɔːntɪŋli
AM ˈvɔn(t)ɪŋli, ˈvɑn(t)ɪŋli

Vaux
BR vɔːks, vɒks, vəʊ
AM vɔks, vɑks

Vauxhall
BR ˈvɒks(h)ɔːl, -z
AM ˈvɔksˌ(h)ɔl, ˈvɑksˌ(h)ɑl, -z

vavasor
BR ˈvavəsɔː(r), ˈvavəsʊə(r), ˈvavəsə(r), -z
AM ˈvɑvəˌsɔ(ə)r, -z

vavasory
BR ˈvavəs(ə)r|i, -ɪz
AM ˈvɑvəˌsɔri, -z

vavasour
BR ˈvavəsɔː(r), ˈvavəsʊə(r), ˈvavəsə(r), -z
AM ˈvɑvəˌsɔ(ə)r, -z

Vavasseur
BR ˌvavəˈsəː(r)
AM ˌvɑvəˈsər

veal
BR viːl
AM vil

Veale
BR viːl
AM vil

vealy
BR ˈviːli
AM ˈvili

Veblen
BR ˈvɛblən

AM ˈvɛblən, ˈveɪblən

vector
BR ˈvɛktə(r), -z
AM ˈvɛktər, -z

vectorial
BR vɛkˈtɔːrɪəl
AM vɛkˈtɔriəl

vectorisation
BR ˌvɛkt(ə)rʌɪˈzeɪʃn
AM ˌvɛktərəˈzeɪʃən, ˌvɛktəˌraɪˈzeɪʃən

vectorise
BR ˈvɛktərʌɪz, -ɨz, -ɪŋ, -d
AM ˈvɛktəˌraɪz, -ɨz, -ɪŋ, -d

vectorization
BR ˌvɛkt(ə)rʌɪˈzeɪʃn
AM ˌvɛktərəˈzeɪʃən, ˌvɛktəˌraɪˈzeɪʃən

vectorize
BR ˈvɛktərʌɪz, -ɨz, -ɪŋ, -d
AM ˈvɛktəˌraɪz, -ɨz, -ɪŋ, -d

Veda
BR ˈveɪdə(*r*), ˈviːdə(*r*), -z
AM ˈveɪdə, ˈvidə, -z

Vedanta
BR vɪˈdɑːntə(*r*), vɛˈdɑːntə(*r*), vɪˈdantə(*r*), vɛˈdantə(*r*)
AM vəˈdɑn(t)ə

Vedantic
BR vɪˈdɑːntɪk, vɛˈdɑːntɪk, vɪˈdantɪk, vɛˈdantɪk
AM vəˈdɑn(t)ɪk

Vedantist
BR vɪˈdɑːntɪst, vɛˈdɑːntɪst, vɪˈdantɪst, vɛˈdantɪst, -s
AM vəˈdɑn(t)əst, -s

Vedda
BR ˈvɛdə(*r*), -z
AM ˈvɛdə, -z

vedette
BR vɪˈdɛt, -s
AM vəˈdɛt, -s

Vedic
BR ˈveɪdɪk, ˈviːdɪk
AM ˈveɪdɪk, ˈvidɪk

vee
BR viː, -z
AM vi, -z

veep
BR viːp, -s
AM vip, -s

veer
BR vɪə(r), -z, -ɪŋ, -d
AM vɪ(ə)r, -z, -ɪŋ, -d

veg
BR vɛdʒ, -ɨz
AM vɛdʒ, -əz

Vega
BR ˈviːgə(*r*), ˈveɪgə(*r*)
AM ˈveɪgə

vegan
BR ˈviːg(ə)n, -z
AM ˈvigən, ˈveɪgən, -z

veganism
BR ˈviːgənɪz(ə)m, ˈviːgn̩ɪz(ə)m
AM ˈvigənˌɪzəm, ˈveɪgənˌɪzəm

Vegeburger
BR ˈvɛdʒɪˌbəːgə(r), -z
AM ˈvɛdʒiˌbərgər, -z

Vegemite®
BR ˈvɛdʒɪmʌɪt
AM ˈvɛdʒəˌmaɪt

vegetable
BR ˈvɛdʒ(ɪ)təbl, -z
AM ˈvɛdʒtəbəl, ˈvɛdʒədəbəl, -z

vegetal
BR ˈvɛdʒɪtl
AM ˈvɛdʒədl

vegetarian
BR ˌvɛdʒɪˈtɛːrɪən, -z
AM ˌvɛdʒəˈtɛriən, -z

vegetarianism
BR ˌvɛdʒɪˈtɛːrɪənɪz(ə)m
AM ˌvɛdʒəˈtɛriəˌnɪzəm

vegetate
BR ˈvɛdʒɪteɪt, -s, -ɪŋ, -ɨd
AM ˈvɛdʒəˌteɪ|t, -ts, -dɪŋ, -dɨd

vegetation
BR ˌvɛdʒɪˈteɪʃn
AM ˌvɛdʒəˈteɪʃən

vegetational
BR ˌvɛdʒɪˈteɪʃn̩(ə)l, ˌvɛdʒɪˈteɪʃən(ə)l
AM ˌvɛdʒəˈteɪʃ(ə)nəl

vegetative
BR ˈvɛdʒɪtətɪv
AM ˈvɛdʒəˌteɪdɪv

vegetatively
BR ˈvɛdʒɪtətɨvli
AM ˈvɛdʒəˌteɪdɨvli

vegetativeness
BR ˈvɛdʒɪtətɨvnɨs
AM ˈvɛdʒəˌteɪdɪvnɨs

veggie
BR ˈvɛdʒ|i, -ɪz
AM ˈvɛdʒi, -z

vegie
BR ˈvɛdʒ|i, -ɪz
AM ˈvɛdʒi, -z

vehemence
BR ˈviːɪm(ə)ns
AM ˈvi(h)əməns

vehement
BR ˈviːɪm(ə)nt
AM ˈvi(h)əmənt

vehemently
BR ˈviːɪm(ə)ntli
AM ˈvi(h)əmən(t)li

vehicle
BR ˈviːɪkl, -z
AM ˈviˌhɪkəl, ˈviəkəl, -z

vehicular
BR vɪˈhɪkjʊlə(r), viːˈhɪkjʊlə(r)
AM viˈhɪkjələr

veil
BR veɪl, -z, -ɪŋ, -d
AM veɪl, -z, -ɪŋ, -d

veiling
BR ˈveɪlɪŋ, -z
AM ˈveɪlɪŋ, -z

veilless
BR ˈveɪllɨs
AM ˈveɪ(l)lɨs

vein
BR veɪn, -z, -ɪŋ, -d
AM veɪn, -z, -ɪŋ, -d

veinless
BR ˈveɪnlɨs
AM ˈveɪnləs

veinlet
BR ˈveɪnlɨt, -s
AM ˈveɪnlɨt, -s

veinlike
BR ˈveɪnlʌɪk
AM ˈveɪnˌlaɪk

veinstone
BR ˈveɪnstəʊn
AM ˈveɪnˌstoʊn

veiny
BR ˈveɪn|i, -ɪə(r), -ɪɪst
AM ˈveɪni, -ər, -ɨst

vela
BR ˈviːlə(*r*)
AM ˈvilə

velamen
BR vɪˈleɪmən
AM vəˈleɪmən

velamina
BR vɪˈlamɪnə(*r*)
AM vəˈlæmənə

velar
BR ˈviːlə(r), -z
AM ˈvilər, -z

velarization
BR ˌviːl(ə)rʌɪˈzeɪʃn, -z
AM ˌvilərəˈzeɪʃən, ˌviləˌraɪˈzeɪʃən, -z

velarize
BR ˈviːlərʌɪz, -ɨz, -ɪŋ, -d
AM ˈviləˌraɪz, -ɨz, -ɪŋ, -d

Velásquez
BR vɪˈlaskwɪz, vɛˈlaskwɪz, vɪˈlaskwɛz, vɛˈlaskwɛz
AM vəˈlɑsˌk(w)ɛz, vəˈlɑzˌk(w)ɛz
SP beˈlaskeθ, beˈlaskes

Velázquez
BR vɪˈlaskwɪz, vɛˈlaskwɪz, vɪˈlaskwɛz, vɛˈlaskwɛz
AM vəˈlɑsˌk(w)ɛz, vəˈlɑzˌk(w)ɛz
SP beˈlaθkeθ, beˈlaskes

velcro
BR ˈvɛlkrəʊ, -d
AM ˈvɛlˌkroʊ, -d

veld
BR vɛlt, fɛlt, -s
AM vɛlt, -s

veldskoen
BR ˈfɛltskuːn, ˈvɛltskuːn, -z
AM ˈvɛltˌskun, -z

veldt
BR vɛlt, fɛlt, -s
AM vɛlt, -s

veleta
BR vɪˈliːtə(*r*), -z
AM vəˈlidə, -z

velic
BR ˈviːlɪk
AM ˈvilɪk

velitation
BR ˌvɛlɪˈteɪʃn, -z
AM ˌvɛləˈteɪʃən, -z

velleity
BR vɛˈliːɪti, vəˈliːɪti
AM vəˈliɨdi, vɛˈliɨdi

vellum
BR ˈvɛləm
AM ˈvɛləm

Velma
BR ˈvɛlmə(*r*)
AM ˈvɛlmə

velocimeter
BR ˌvɛləˈsɪmɨtə(r), -z
AM ˌvɛləˈsɪmɪdər, -z

velocipede
BR vɪˈlɒsɪpiːd, -z
AM vəˈlɑsəˌpid, -z

velocipedist
BR vɪˈlɒsɪpiːdɪst, -s
AM vəˈlɑsəˌpidɨst, -s

velociraptor
BR vəˈlɒsɪraptə(r), -z
AM vəˈlɑsəˌræptər, -z

velocity
BR vɪˈlɒsɪt|i, -ɪz
AM vəˈlɑsədi, -z

velodrome
BR ˈvɛlədrəʊm, -z
AM ˈvɛləˌdroʊm, -z

velour
BR vəˈlʊə(r), vɛˈlʊə(r), vəˈlɔː(r), vɛˈlɔː(r), -z
AM vəˈlʊ(ə)r, -z

velours
BR vəˈlʊə(r), vɛˈlʊə(r), vəˈlɔː(r), vɛˈlɔː(r), -z
AM vəˈlʊ(ə)r, -z

velouté
BR vəˈluːteɪ, -z
AM vəˌluˈteɪ, -z

velum
BR ˈviːləm, -z
AM ˈviləm, -z

velutinous
BR vɪˈl(j)uːtɪnəs, vɛˈl(j)uːtɪnəs
AM vəˈlutn̩əs

velvet
BR ˈvɛlvɪt, -s
AM ˈvɛlvət, -s

velveted
BR ˈvɛlvɪtɪd
AM ˈvɛlvədəd

velveteen
BR ˌvɛlvɪˈtiːn, ˈvɛlvɪtiːn, -z
AM ˈvɛlvəˌtin, -z

velvety
BR ˈvɛlvɪti
AM ˈvɛlvədi

vena
BR ˈviːnə(r)
AM ˈvinə

Venables
BR ˈvɛnəblz
AM ˈvɛnəbəlz

vena cava
BR ˌviːnə ˈkeɪvə(r)
AM ˌvinə ˈkɑvə, ˌvinə ˈkeɪvə

venae
BR ˈviːniː
AM ˈvini, ˈviˌnaɪ

venae cavae
BR ˌviːniː ˈkeɪviː
AM ˌvini ˈkɑvi, ˌvini ˈkeɪvi, ˌvini ˈkɑˌvaɪ, ˌvini ˈkeɪˌvaɪ

venal
BR ˈviːnl
AM ˈvinəl

venality
BR viːˈnalɪti, vɪˈnalɪti
AM viˈnælədi, vəˈnælədi

venally
BR ˈviːnl̩i, ˈviːnəli
AM ˈvinəli

venation
BR vɪˈneɪʃn
AM viˈneɪʃən

venational
BR viːˈneɪʃn̩(ə)l, viːˈneɪʃən(ə)l, vɪˈneɪʃn̩(ə)l, vɪˈneɪʃən(ə)l
AM viˈneɪʃ(ə)nəl

vend
BR vɛnd, -z, -ɪŋ, -ɪd
AM vɛnd, -z, -ɪŋ, -əd

Venda
BR ˈvɛndə(r), -z
AM ˈvɛndə, -z

vendace
BR ˈvɛndɪs, ˈvɛndeɪs
AM ˈvɛndəs

Vendée
BR ˈvɒ̃deɪ
AM vɑnˈdeɪ

vendee
BR ˌvɛnˈdiː, -z
AM ˌvɛnˈdi, -z

vender
BR ˈvɛndə(r), -z
AM ˈvɛndər, -z

vendetta
BR vɛnˈdɛtə(r), -z
AM vɛnˈdɛdə, -z

vendeuse
BR vɒ̃ˈdəːz, -ɪz
AM vɑnˈdʊz, -əz

vendible
BR ˈvɛndɪbl, -z
AM ˈvɛndəbəl, -z

vendor
BR ˈvɛndɔː(r), ˈvɛndə(r), -z
AM ˈvɛndər, -z

vendue
BR vɛnˈdjuː, -z
AM vɛnˈd(j)u, -z

veneer
BR vɪˈnɪə(r), -z, -ɪŋ, -d
AM vəˈnɪ(ə)r, -z, -ɪŋ, -d

venepuncture
BR ˈvɛnɪˌpʌŋ(k)tʃə(r), ˈviːnɪˌpʌŋ(k)tʃə(r), -z
AM ˈvinəˌpəŋ(k)tʃər, -z

venerability
BR ˌvɛn(ə)rəˈbɪlɪti
AM ˌvɛn(ə)rəˈbɪlɨdi

venerable
BR ˈvɛn(ə)rəbl
AM ˈvɛnər(ə)bəl, ˈvɛnrəbəl

venerableness
BR ˈvɛn(ə)rəblnəs
AM ˈvɛnər(ə)bəlnəs, ˈvɛnrəbəlnəs

venerably
BR ˈvɛn(ə)rəbli
AM ˈvɛnər(ə)bli, ˈvɛnrəbli

venerate
BR ˈvɛnəreɪt, -s, -ɪŋ, -ɪd
AM ˈvɛnəˌreɪ|t, -ts, -dɪŋ, -dɪd

veneration
BR ˌvɛnəˈreɪʃn
AM ˌvɛnəˈreɪʃən

venerator
BR ˈvɛnəreɪtə(r), -z
AM ˈvɛnəˌreɪdər, -z

venereal
BR vɪˈnɪərɪəl
AM vəˈnɪriəl

venereally
BR vɪˈnɪərɪəli
AM vəˈnɪriəli

venereological
BR vɪˌnɪərɪəˈlɒdʒɪkl
AM vəˌnɪriəˈlɑdʒəkəl

venereologist
BR vɪˌnɪərɪˈɒlədʒɪst, -s
AM vəˌnɪriˈɑlədʒəst, -s

venereology
BR vɪˌnɪərɪˈɒlədʒi
AM vəˌnɪriˈɑlədʒi

venery
BR ˈvɛn(ə)ri, ˈviːn(ə)ri
AM ˈvɛnəri

venesection
BR ˌvɛnɪˈsɛkʃn, ˌviːnɪˈsɛkʃn, -z
AM ˈvinəˌsɛkʃən, -z

Venetia
BR vɪˈniːʃə(r)
AM vəˈniʃə

venetian
BR vɪˈniːʃn, -z, -d
AM vəˈniʃən, -z, -d

Veneto
BR vɪˈniːtəʊ
AM vəˈnɛdoʊ

Venezuela
BR ˌvɛnɪˈzweɪlə(r)
AM ˌvɛnəz(ə)ˈweɪlə
SP beneˈθwela, beneˈswela

Venezuelan
BR ˌvɛnɪˈzweɪlən, -z
AM ˌvɛnəz(ə)ˈweɪlən, -z

vengeance
BR ˈvɛn(d)ʒ(ə)nz
AM ˈvɛndʒəns

vengeful
BR ˈvɛn(d)ʒf(ʊ)l
AM ˈvɛndʒfəl

vengefully
BR ˈvɛn(d)ʒfʊli, ˈvɛn(d)ʒfl̩i
AM ˈvɛndʒfəli

vengefulness
BR ˈvɛn(d)ʒf(ʊ)lnəs
AM ˈvɛndʒfəlnəs

venial
BR ˈviːnɪəl
AM ˈviniəl, ˈvinjəl

veniality
BR ˌviːnɪˈalɪti
AM ˌviniˈælədi

venially
BR ˈviːnɪəli
AM ˈviniəli, ˈvinjəli

venialness
BR ˈviːnɪəlnəs
AM ˈviniəlnəs, ˈvinjəlnəs

Venice
BR ˈvɛnɪs
AM ˈvɛnəs

venipuncture
BR ˈvɛnɪˌpʌŋ(k)tʃə(r), ˈviːnɪˌpʌŋ(k)tʃə(r), -z
AM ˈvinəˌpəŋ(kt)ʃər, -z

venisection
BR ˌvɛnɪˈsɛkʃn, ˌviːnɪˈsɛkʃn, -z
AM ˈvinəˌsɛkʃən, -z

venison
BR ˈvɛnɪsn, ˈvɛnɪzn
AM ˈvɛnəsən, ˈvɛnəzn

Venite
BR vɪˈnʌɪt|i, vɪˈniːt|i, -ɪz
AM vəˈnaɪdi, vəˈnidi, -z

Venn diagram
BR ˈvɛn ˌdʌɪəgram, -z
AM ˈvɛn ˈdaɪəˌgræm, -z

Venner
BR ˈvɛnə(r)
AM ˈvɛnər

venom
BR ˈvɛnəm, -d
AM ˈvɛnəm, -d

venomous
BR ˈvɛnəməs
AM ˈvɛnəməs

venomously
BR ˈvɛnəməsli
AM ˈvɛnəməsli

venomousness
BR ˈvɛnəməsnəs
AM ˈvɛnəməsnəs

venose
BR ˈviːnəʊs
AM ˈviˌnoʊs, ˈviˌnoʊz

venosity
BR vɪˈnɒsɪti
AM vəˈnɑsədi, viˈnɑsədi

venous
BR ˈviːnəs
AM ˈvinəs

venously
BR ˈviːnəsli
AM ˈvinəsli

vent
BR vɛnt, -s, -ɪŋ, -ɪd
AM vɛn|t, -ts, -(t)ɪŋ, -(t)əd

ventage
BR ˈvɛnt|ɪdʒ, -ɪdʒɪz
AM ˈvɛn(t)ɪdʒ, -ɪz

Vent-Axia®
BR ˌvɛntˈaksɪə(r)
AM ˌvɛnˈtæksiə

vent-hole
BR ˈvɛnthəʊl, -z
AM ˈvɛntˌ(h)oʊl, -z

ventiduct
BR ˈvɛntɪdʌkt, -s
AM ˈvɛn(t)əˌdək|(t), -(t)s

ventifact
BR ˈvɛntɪfakt, -s
AM ˈvɛn(t)əˌfæk|(t), -(t)s

ventil
BR ˈvɛntɪl, -z
AM ˈvɛn(t)l, -z

ventilate
BR ˈvɛntɪleɪt, -s, -ɪŋ, -ɪd
AM ˈvɛn(t)əˌleɪ|t, -ts, -dɪŋ, -dɪd

ventilation
BR ˌvɛntɪˈleɪʃn
AM ˌvɛn(t)əˈleɪʃən

ventilative
BR ˈvɛntɪleɪtɪv
AM ˈvɛn(t)əˌleɪdɪv

ventilator
BR 'vɛntɪleɪtə(r), -z
AM 'vɛn(t)ə,leɪdər, -z

ventless
BR 'vɛntləs
AM 'vɛn(t)ləs

Ventnor
BR 'vɛntnə(r)
AM 'vɛntnər

Ventolin®
BR 'vɛntə(ʊ)lɪn
AM 'vɛn(t)ələn

ventouse
BR 'vɛntuːs, -ɪz
AM 'vɛn,tus, -əz

ventral
BR 'vɛntr(ə)l
AM 'vɛntrəl

ventrally
BR 'vɛntrəli, 'vɛntrḷi
AM 'vɛntrəli

ventre à terre
BR ,vɒ̃tr(ə) a 'tɛː(r)
AM ,vɑntrə ɑ 'tɛ(ə)r

ventricle
BR 'vɛntrɪkl, -z
AM 'vɛntrəkəl, -z

ventricose
BR 'vɛntrɪkəʊs
AM 'vɛntrə,koʊs,
'vɛntrə,koʊz

ventricular
BR vɛn'trɪkjʊlə(r)
AM vɛn'trɪkjələr

ventriloquial
BR ,vɛntrɪ'ləʊkwɪəl
AM ,vɛntrə'loʊkwiəl

ventriloquially
BR ,vɛntrɪ'ləʊkwɪəli
AM ,vɛntrə'loʊkwiəli

ventriloquise
BR vɛn'trɪləkwʌɪz, -ɪz,
-ɪŋ, -d
AM vɛn'trɪlə,kwaɪz,
-ɪz, -ɪŋ, -d

ventriloquism
BR vɛn'trɪləkwɪz(ə)m
AM vɛn'trɪlə,kwɪzəm

ventriloquist
BR vɛn'trɪləkwɪst, -s
AM vɛn'trɪləkwəst, -s

ventriloquistic
BR vɛn,trɪlə'kwɪstɪk
AM vɛn,trɪlə'kwɪstɪk

ventriloquize
BR vɛn'trɪləkwʌɪz, -ɪz,
-ɪŋ, -d
AM vɛn'trɪlə,kwaɪz,
-ɪz, -ɪŋ, -d

ventriloquous
BR vɛn'trɪləkwəs
AM vɛn'trɪləkwəs

ventriloquy
BR vɛn'trɪləkwi
AM vɛn'trɪləkwi

venture
BR 'vɛn(t)ʃ|ə(r), -əz,
-(ə)rɪŋ, -əd
AM 'vɛn(t)ʃər, -z, -ɪŋ, -d

venturer
BR 'vɛn(t)ʃ(ə)rə(r), -z
AM 'vɛn(t)ʃərər, -z

venturesome
BR 'vɛn(t)ʃəs(ə)m
AM 'vɛn(t)ʃərsəm

venturesomely
BR 'vɛn(t)ʃəs(ə)mli
AM 'vɛn(t)ʃərsəmli

venturesomeness
BR 'vɛn(t)ʃəs(ə)mnəs
AM 'vɛn(t)ʃərsəmnəs

venturi
BR vɛn'tjʊər|i,
vɛn'tʃʊər|i, -ɪz
AM vɛn't(ʃ)ʊri, -z

venturous
BR 'vɛn(t)ʃ(ə)rəs
AM 'vɛn(t)ʃ(ə)rəs

venturously
BR 'vɛn(t)ʃ(ə)rəsli
AM 'vɛn(t)ʃ(ə)rəsli

venturousness
BR 'vɛn(t)ʃ(ə)rəsnəs
AM 'vɛn(t)ʃ(ə)rəsnəs

venue
BR 'vɛnjuː, -z
AM 'vɛn,ju, -z

venule
BR 'vɛnjuːl, 'vɪnjuːl, -z
AM 'vɛn,jul, -z

Venus
BR 'viːnəs
AM 'vinəs

Venusian
BR vɪ'njuːzɪən,
vɪ'njuːsɪən, -z
AM və'n(j)usiən,
və'n(j)uʃ(i)ən, -z

Vera
BR 'vɪərə(*r*)
AM 'vɛrə, 'vɪrə

veracious
BR vɪ'reɪʃəs
AM və'reɪʃəs

veraciously
BR vɪ'reɪʃəsli
AM və'reɪʃəsli

veraciousness
BR vɪ'reɪʃəsnəs
AM və'reɪʃəsnəs

veracity
BR vɪ'rasɪti
AM və'ræsədi

Veracruz
BR ,vɪərə'kruːz,
,vɛrə'kruːz,
,vɛːrə'kruːz
AM ,vɛrə'kruz
SP ,bera'kruθ,
,bera'krus

veranda
BR və'randə(*r*), -z, -d
AM və'rændə, -z, -d

verandah
BR və'randə(*r*), -z
AM və'rændə, -z

veratrine
BR 'vɛrətriːn,
'vɛrətrɪn
AM 'vɛrə,trin,
'vɛrətrən

verb
BR vəːb, -z
AM vərb, -z

verbal
BR 'vəːbl
AM 'vərbəl

verbalisable
BR 'vəːbəlʌɪzəbl,
'vəːbḷʌɪzəbl
AM 'vərbə,laɪzəbəl

verbalisation
BR ,vəːbəlʌɪ'zeɪʃn,
,vəːbḷʌɪ'zeɪʃn, -z
AM ,vərbələ'zeɪʃən,
,vərbə,laɪ'zeɪʃən, -z

verbalise
BR 'vəːbəlʌɪz,
'vəːbḷʌɪz, -ɪz, -ɪŋ, -d
AM 'vərbə,laɪz, -ɪz, -ɪŋ,
-d

verbaliser
BR 'vəːbəlʌɪzə(r),
'vəːbḷʌɪzə(r), -z
AM 'vərbə,laɪzər, -z

verbalism
BR 'vəːbəlɪz(ə)m,
'vəːbḷɪz(ə)m
AM 'vərbə,lɪzəm

verbalist
BR 'vəːbəlɪst, 'vəːbḷɪst,
-s
AM 'vərbələst, -s

verbalistic
BR ,vəːbə'lɪstɪk,
,vəːbl'ɪstɪk
AM ,vərbə'lɪstɪk

verbalizable
BR 'vəːbəlʌɪzəbl,
'vəːbḷʌɪzəbl
AM 'vərbə,laɪzəbəl

verbalization
BR ,vəːbəlʌɪ'zeɪʃn,
,vəːbḷʌɪ'zeɪʃn, -z
AM ,vərbələ'zeɪʃən,
,vərbə,laɪ'zeɪʃən, -z

verbalize
BR 'vəːbəlʌɪz,
'vəːbḷʌɪz, -ɪz, -ɪŋ, -d
AM 'vərbə,laɪz, -ɪz, -ɪŋ,
-d

verbalizer
BR 'vəːbəlʌɪzə(r),
'vəːbḷʌɪzə(r), -z
AM 'vərbə,laɪzər, -z

verbally
BR 'vəːbḷi, 'vəːbəli
AM 'vərbəli

verbatim
BR vəː'beɪtɪm,
və'beɪtɪm
AM vər'beɪdɪm

verbena
BR vəː'biːnə(*r*),
və'biːnə(*r*), -z
AM vər'binə, -z

verbiage
BR 'vəːbɪɪdʒ
AM 'vərbiɪdʒ

verbose
BR vəː'bəʊs, və'bəʊs
AM vər'boʊs

verbosely
BR vəː'bəʊsli,
və'bəʊsli
AM vər'boʊsli

verboseness
BR vəː'bəʊsnəs,
və'bəʊsnəs
AM vər'boʊsnəs

verbosity
BR vəː'bɒsɪti, və'bɒsɪti
AM vər'bɑsədi

verboten
BR fə'bəʊtn, və'bəʊtn,
fɛː'bɔːtn
AM fər'boʊtn

verb. sap.
BR ,vəːb 'sap
AM ¦vərb 'sæp

Vercingetorix
BR ,vəːsɪn'gɛt(ə)rɪks,
,vəːsɪn'dʒɛt(ə)rɪks
AM ,vərsɪŋ'gɛdərɪks,
,vərsɪŋ'dʒɛdərɪks

verd
BR vəːd
AM vərd

verdancy
BR 'vəːdnsi
AM 'vərdnsi

verdant
BR 'vəːdnt
AM 'vərdnt

verd-antique
BR ,vəːdan'tiːk
AM ¦vər,dæn'tik

verdantly
BR 'vəːdntli
AM 'vərdn(t)li

verdelho
BR vəː'dɛljuː,
vəː'dɛljəʊ
AM vər'dɛljoʊ

verderer
BR 'vəːd(ə)rə(r), -z
AM 'vərdərər, -z

Verdi
BR 'vɛːdi
AM 'vɛrdi

Verdian
BR 'vɛːdɪən, -z
AM 'vɛrdiən, -z

verdict
BR 'vəːdɪkt, -s
AM 'vərdɪk|(t), -(t)s

verdigris
BR 'vəːdɪgriː(s)

AM ˈvərdəˌgris

verditer
BR ˈvəːdɪtə(r)
AM ˈvərdədər

Verdun
BR vəːˈdʌn
AM vərˈdən, ˈvərdn
FR vɛʀdœ̃

verdure
BR ˈvəːdʒə(r), ˈvəːdjə(r), -d
AM ˈvərdʒər, -d

verdurous
BR ˈvəːdʒ(ə)rəs, ˈvəːdjərəs
AM ˈvərdʒərəs

Vere
BR vɪə(r)
AM vɪ(ə)r

Vereeniging
BR vɪˈriːnɪgɪŋ
AM vəˈrinɪgɪŋ
AFK fərˈiənəxəŋ

verge
BR vəːdʒ, -ɪz, -ɪŋ, -d
AM vərdʒ, -əz, -ɪŋ, -d

vergence
BR ˈvəːdʒ(ə)ns
AM ˈvərdʒəns

verger
BR ˈvəːdʒə(r), -z
AM ˈvərdʒər, -z

vergership
BR ˈvəːdʒəʃɪp, -s
AM ˈvərdʒərˌʃɪp, -s

Vergil
BR ˈvəːdʒ(ɪ)l
AM ˈvərdʒəl

Vergilian
BR vəːˈdʒɪlɪən
AM vərˈdʒɪljən, vərˈdʒɪliən

verglas
BR ˈvɛːglɑː(*r*)
AM vɛrˈglɑ(s)

veridical
BR vɪˈrɪdɪkl
AM vəˈrɪdəkəl

veridicality
BR vɪˌrɪdɪˈkalɪti
AM vəˌrɪdəˈkælədi

veridically
BR vɪˈrɪdɪkli
AM vəˈrɪdək(ə)li

veriest
BR ˈvɛrɪɪst
AM ˈvɛriɪst

verifiable
BR ˈvɛrɪfʌɪəbl
AM ¦vɛrə¦faɪəbəl

verifiably
BR ˈvɛrɪfʌɪəbli
AM ¦vɛrə¦faɪəbli

verification
BR ˌvɛrɪfɪˈkeɪʃn
AM ˌvɛrəfəˈkeɪʃən

verifier
BR ˈvɛrɪfʌɪə(r)
AM ˈvɛrəˌfaɪər

verify
BR ˈvɛrɪfʌɪ, -z, -ɪŋ, -d
AM ˈvɛrəˌfaɪ, -z, -ɪŋ, -d

verily
BR ˈvɛrɪli
AM ˈvɛrəli

verisimilar
BR ˌvɛrɪˈsɪmɪlə(r), ˌvɛrɪˈsɪml̩ə(r)
AM ˌvɛrəˈsɪmələr

verisimilitude
BR ˌvɛrɪsɪˈmɪlɪtjuːd, ˌvɛrɪsɪˈmɪlɪtʃuːd
AM ˌvɛrəsəˈmɪləˌt(j)ud

verism
BR ˈvɛrɪz(ə)m
AM ˈvɛrɪzəm

verismo
BR vɛˈrɪzməʊ, -z
AM vəˈrɪzmoʊ, vɛˈrɪzmoʊ, -z

verist
BR ˈvɛrɪst, -s
AM ˈvɛrəst, -s

veristic
BR vɛˈrɪstɪk
AM vəˈrɪstɪk

veritable
BR ˈvɛrɪtəbl
AM ˈvɛrədəbəl

veritably
BR ˈvɛrɪtəbli
AM ˈvɛrədəbli

verity
BR ˈvɛrɪt|i, -ɪz
AM ˈvɛrədi, -z

verjuice
BR ˈvəːdʒuːs
AM ˈvərdʒəs

verkrampte
BR fəˈkram(p)tə(*r*), -z
AM fərˈkrɑm(p)tə, -z

Verlaine
BR vəˈleɪn, vɛːˈleɪn
AM vərˈleɪn

verligte
BR fəˈlɪktə(*r*), -z
AM vərˈlɪktə, -z

Vermeer
BR vəˈmɪə(r), vəːˈmɪə(r)
AM vərˈmɪ(ə)r
DU vərˈmeːr

vermeil
BR ˈvəːmeɪl, ˈvəːmɪl
AM ˈvərmɪl, ˈvərˌmeɪl, vərˈmeɪl

vermian
BR ˈvəːmɪən
AM ˈvərmiən

vermicelli
BR ˌvəːmɪˈsɛli, ˌvəːmɪˈtʃɛli
AM ˌvərməˈtʃɛli, ˌvərməˈsɛli

vermicide
BR ˈvəːmɪsʌɪd, -z
AM ˈvərməˌsaɪd, -z

vermicular
BR və(ː)ˈmɪkjʊlə(r)
AM vərˈmɪkjələr

vermiculate
BR və(ː)ˈmɪkjʊleɪt
AM vərˈmɪkjəˌleɪt

vermiculation
BR və(ː)ˌmɪkjʊˈleɪʃn
AM vərˌmɪkjəˈleɪʃən, -z

vermiculite
BR və(ː)ˈmɪkjʊlʌɪt, vəˈmɪkjʊlʌɪt
AM vərˈmɪkjəˌlaɪt

vermiform
BR ˈvəːmɪfɔːm
AM ˈvərməˌfɔ(ə)rm

vermifuge
BR ˈvəːmɪfjuː(d)ʒ, -ɪz
AM ˈvərməˌfjudʒ, -ɪz

vermilion
BR vəˈmɪlɪən
AM vərˈmɪljən, vərˈmɪliən

vermin
BR ˈvəːmɪn
AM ˈvərmən

verminate
BR ˈvəːmɪneɪt, -s, -ɪŋ, -ɪd
AM ˈvərməˌneɪ|t, -ts, -dɪŋ, -dɪd

vermination
BR ˌvəːmɪˈneɪʃn
AM ˌvərməˈneɪʃən

verminous
BR ˈvəːmɪnəs
AM ˈvərmənəs

verminously
BR ˈvəːmɪnəsli
AM ˈvərmənəsli

verminousness
BR ˈvəːmɪnəsnəs
AM ˈvərmənəsnəs

vermivorous
BR və(ː)ˈmɪv(ə)rəs
AM vərˈmɪv(ə)rəs

Vermont
BR vəˈmɒnt, vəːˈmɒnt
AM vərˈmɑnt

vermouth
BR ˈvəːməθ, və(ː)ˈmuːθ
AM vərˈmuθ

vernacular
BR vəˈnakjʊlə(r), -z
AM vərˈnækjələr, -z

vernacularise
BR vəˈnakjʊlərʌɪz, -ɪz, -ɪŋ, -d
AM vərˈnækjələˌraɪz, -ɪz, -ɪŋ, -d

vernacularism
BR vəˈnakjʊlərɪz(ə)m, -z
AM vərˈnækjələˌrɪzəm, -z

vernacularity
BR vəˌnakjʊˈlarɪti
AM vərˌnækjəˈlɛrədi

vernacularize
BR vəˈnakjʊlərʌɪz, -ɪz, -ɪŋ, -d
AM vərˈnækjələˌraɪz, -ɪz, -ɪŋ, -d

vernacularly
BR vəˈnakjʊləli
AM vərˈnækjələrli

vernal
BR ˈvəːnl
AM ˈvərnəl

vernalisation
BR ˌvəːnəlʌɪˈzeɪʃn, ˌvəːnl̩ʌɪˈzeɪʃn
AM ˌvərnl̩əˈzeɪʃən, ˌvərnl̩aɪˈzeɪʃən

vernalise
BR ˈvəːnəlʌɪz, ˈvəːnl̩ʌɪz, -ɪz, -ɪŋ, -d
AM ˈvərnlˌaɪz, -ɪz, -ɪŋ, -d

vernalization
BR ˌvəːnəlʌɪˈzeɪʃn, ˌvəːnl̩ʌɪˈzeɪʃn
AM ˌvərnl̩əˈzeɪʃən, ˌvərnl̩aɪˈzeɪʃən

vernalize
BR ˈvəːnəlʌɪz, ˈvəːnl̩ʌɪz, -ɪz, -ɪŋ, -d
AM ˈvərnlˌaɪz, -ɪz, -ɪŋ, -d

vernally
BR ˈvəːnl̩i, ˈvəːnəli
AM ˈvərnl̩i, ˈvərnəli

vernation
BR vəːˈneɪʃn
AM vərˈneɪʃən

Verne
BR vəːn
AM vərn

Verner
BR ˈvəːnə(r), ˈvɛːnə(r)
AM ˈvərnər

Verney
BR ˈvəːni
AM ˈvərni

vernicle
BR ˈvəːnɪkl, -z
AM ˈvərnəkəl, -z

vernier
BR ˈvəːnɪə(r), -z
AM ˈvərniər, -z

vernissage
BR ˌvɛːnɪˈsɑːʒ
AM ˌvərnɪˈsɑʒ

vernix
BR ˈvəːnɪks
AM ˈvərnɪks

Vernon
BR ˈvəːnən
AM ˈvərnən

Verny
BR ˈvəːni
AM ˈvərni

Verona
BR vɪ'rəʊnə(r)
AM və'roʊnə

veronal
BR 'vɛrənl, 'vɛrn̩l
AM 'vɛrə,nɔl, 'vɛrənl, 'vɛrə,nɑl, 'vɛrənəl

Veronese
BR ,vɛrə'neɪzi
AM ,vɛrə'neɪzi

veronica
BR vɨ'rɒnɨkə(r), -z
AM və'rɑnəkə, -z

veronique
BR ,vɛrə'niːk
AM ,vɛrə'nik

Verrazano
BR ,vɛrə'zɑːnəʊ
AM ,vɛrə'zɑnoʊ

verruca
BR vɨ'ruːkə(r), vɛ'ruːkə(r), -z
AM və'rukə, -z

verrucae
BR vɨ'ruːkiː, vɨ'ruːsiː, vɛ'ruːkiː, vɛ'ruːsiː
AM və'ruki, və'ru,kaɪ

verrucose
BR ,vɛrʊ'kəʊs, vɨ'ruːkəʊs, vɛ'ruːkəʊs
AM 'vɛr(j)ə,koʊs, 'vɛr(j)ə,koʊz

verrucous
BR vɨ'ruːkəs, vɛ'ruːkəs, 'vɛrʊkəs
AM və'rukəs, vɛ'rukəs

versa
BR 'vəːsə(r)
AM 'vərsə

Versailles
BR vɛː'sʌɪ, vəː'sʌɪ
AM vər'saɪ

versant
BR 'vəːsnt, -s
AM 'vərsənt, -s

versatile
BR 'vəːsətʌɪl
AM 'vərsədl

versatilely
BR 'vəːsətʌɪlli
AM 'vərsədl̩i

versatility
BR ,vəːsə'tɪlɨti
AM ,vərsə'tɪlɨdi

verse
BR vəːs, -ɨz, -t
AM vərs, -əz, -t

verselet
BR 'vəːslɨt, -s
AM 'vərslət, -s

verset
BR 'vəːsɪt, -s
AM 'vərsət, -s

versicle
BR 'vəːsɪkl, -z
AM 'vərsəkəl, -z

versicolored
BR ,vəːsɪ'kʌləd
AM 'vərsə,kələrd

versicoloured
BR ,vəːsɪ'kʌləd
AM 'vərsə,kələrd

versicular
BR və(ː)'sɪkjʊlə(r)
AM vər'sɪkjələr

versification
BR ,vəːsɪfɪ'keɪʃn
AM ,vərsəfə'keɪʃən

versifier
BR 'vəːsɪfʌɪə(r), -z
AM 'vərsə,faɪər, -z

versify
BR 'vəːsɪfʌɪ, -z, -ɪŋ, -d
AM 'vərsə,faɪ, -z, -ɪŋ, -d

versin
BR 'vəːsɪn, -z
AM 'vər,saɪn, -z

versine
BR 'vəːsʌɪn, -z
AM 'vər,saɪn, -z

version
BR 'vəːʃn, -z
AM 'vərʒən, -z

versional
BR 'vəːʃn̩(ə)l, 'vəːʃən(ə)l, 'vəːʒn̩(ə)l, 'vəːʒən(ə)l
AM 'vərʒ(ə)nəl

vers libre
BR ,vɛː 'liːbr(ər)
AM ,vɛr 'lɪbrə

verso
BR 'vəːsəʊ
AM 'vərsoʊ

verst
BR vəːst, -s
AM vərst, -s

versus
BR 'vəːsəs
AM 'vərsəs

vert
BR vəːt
AM vərt

vertebra
BR 'vəːtɪbrə(r)
AM 'vərdəbrə

vertebrae
BR 'vəːtɪbreɪ, 'vəːtɪbriː
AM 'vərdə,breɪ

vertebral
BR 'vəːtɪbr(ə)l
AM 'vərdəbrəl, vər'tibrəl

vertebrally
BR 'vəːtɪbrl̩i, 'vəːtɪbrəli
AM 'vərdəbrəli, vər'tibrəli

vertebrate
BR 'vəːtɪbrət, 'vəːtɪbreɪt, -s
AM 'vərdəbrət, 'vərdə,breɪt, -s

vertebration
BR ,vəːtɪ'breɪʃn
AM ,vərdə'breɪʃən

vertex
BR 'vəːtɛks, -ɨz
AM 'vər,tɛks, -əz

vertical
BR 'vəːtɨkl
AM 'vərdəkəl

verticalise
BR 'vəːtɨkl̩ʌɪz, -ɨz, -ɪŋ, -d
AM 'vərdəkə,laɪz, -ɨz, -ɪŋ, -d

verticality
BR ,vəːtɪ'kalɨti
AM ,vərdə'kælədi

verticalize
BR 'vəːtɨkl̩ʌɪz, -ɨz, -ɪŋ, -d
AM 'vərdəkə,laɪz, -ɨz, -ɪŋ, -d

vertically
BR 'vəːtɨkli, 'vəːtɨkl̩i
AM 'vərdək(ə)li

vertices
BR 'vəːtɨsiːz
AM 'vərdə,siz

verticil
BR 'vəːtɨsɪl, -z
AM 'vərdə,sɪl, -z

verticillate
BR vəː'tɪsɨlət, vəː'tɪsl̩ət, ,vəːtɪ'sɪlət
AM ,vərdə'sɪlət, vərdə'sɪleɪt

vertiginous
BR vəː'tɪdʒɪnəs, vəː'tɪdʒn̩əs
AM vər'tɪdʒənəs

vertiginously
BR vəː'tɪdʒɨnəsli, vəː'tɪgn̩əsli
AM vər'tɪdʒənəsli

vertigo
BR 'vəːtɨgəʊ
AM 'vərdəgoʊ

vertu
BR vəː'tuː
AM vər'tu

Verulamium
BR ,vɛr(j)ʊ'leɪmɪəm
AM ,vɛr(j)ə'leɪmiəm

vervain
BR 'vəːveɪn, -z
AM 'vər,veɪn, -z

verve
BR vəːv
AM vərv

vervet
BR 'vəːvɪt, -s
AM 'vərvət, -s

Verwoerd
BR fə'vʊət
AM fər'vʊ(ə)rt

very
BR 'vɛri
AM 'vɛri

Very light
BR 'vɪərɪ ,lʌɪt, 'vɛrɪ +, -s
AM 'vɪri ,laɪt, 'vɛri +, -s

Very pistol
BR 'vɪərɪ ,pɪstl, 'vɛrɪ +, -z
AM 'vɪri ,pɪstl, 'vɛri +, -z

Vesalius
BR vɪ'seɪlɪəs
AM və'seɪliəs

Vesey
BR 'viːzi
AM 'vizi

vesica
BR 'vɛsɪkə(r), 'viːsɪkə(r), vɪ'sʌɪkə(r), -z
AM və'sikə, və'saɪkə, 'vɛsəkə, -z

vesical
BR 'vɛsɪkl, 'viːsɪkl, vɪ'sʌɪkl
AM 'vɛsəkəl

vesicant
BR 'vɛsɪk(ə)nt, 'viːsɪk(ə)nt, vɪ'sʌɪk(ə)nt, -s
AM 'vɛsəkənt, -s

vesicate
BR 'vɛsɪkeɪt, -s, -ɪŋ, -ɨd
AM 'vɛsə,keɪ|t, -ts, -dɪŋ, -dɨd

vesication
BR ,vɛsɪ'keɪʃn, -z
AM ,vɛsə'keɪʃən, -z

vesicatory
BR 'vɛsɪkət(ə)ri
AM 'vɛsəkə,tɔri, və'sɪkə,tɔri

vesicle
BR 'vɛsɪkl, -z
AM 'vɛsəkəl, -z

vesicular
BR vɪ'sɪkjʊlə(r)
AM və'sɪkjələr

vesicularly
BR vɪ'sɪkjʊləli
AM və'sɪkjələrli

vesiculate
BR vɪ'sɪkjʊlət, vɪ'sɪkjʊleɪt
AM və'sɪkjə,leɪt, və'sɪkjələt

vesiculation
BR vɪ,sɪkjʊ'leɪʃn, -z
AM və,sɪkjə'leɪʃən, -z

Vespa®
BR 'vɛspə(r), -z
AM 'vɛspə, -z

Vespasian
BR vɛs'peɪʒn, vɛs'peɪzɪən
AM və'speɪʒ(i)ən, və'speɪziən

vesper
BR 'vɛspə(r), -z

AM ˈvɛspər, -z

vespertilionid
BR ˌvɛspətɪlɪˈɒnɪd
AM ˌvɛspərˌtɪliˈɑnɪd

vespertine
BR ˈvɛspətʌɪn
AM ˈvɛspərˌtin, ˈvɛspərˌtaɪn

vespiary
BR ˈvɛspɪər|i, -ɪz
AM ˈvɛspiˌɛri, -z

vespine
BR ˈvɛspʌɪn
AM ˈvɛˌspaɪn, ˈvɛspən

Vespucci
BR vɪˈspuːtʃi, vɛˈspuːtʃi
AM vəˈsputʃi, vɛˈsputʃi

vessel
BR ˈvɛsl, -z
AM ˈvɛsəl, -z

vest
BR vɛst, -s, -ɪŋ, -ɪd
AM vɛst, -s, -ɪŋ, -əd

vesta
BR ˈvɛstə(r), -z
AM ˈvɛstə, -z

vestal
BR ˈvɛstl, -z
AM ˈvɛstl, -z

vestee
BR ˌvɛˈstiː, -z
AM ˌvɛsˈti, -z

vestiary
BR ˈvɛstɪər|i, -ɪz
AM ˈvɛstiˌɛri, -z

vestibular
BR vɛˈstɪbjʊlə(r)
AM vəˈstɪbjələr, vɛˈstɪbjələr

vestibule
BR ˈvɛstɪbjuːl, -z
AM ˈvɛstəˌbjul, -z

vestige
BR ˈvɛst|ɪdʒ, -ɪdʒɪz
AM ˈvɛstɪdʒ, -ɪz

vestigial
BR vɛˈstɪdʒɪəl, vəˈstɪdʒɪəl, vɛˈstɪdʒ(ə)l, vəˈstɪdʒ(ə)l
AM vɛˈstɪdʒ(i)əl

vestigially
BR vɛˈstɪdʒɪəli, vəˈstɪdʒɪəli, vɛˈstɪdʒəli, vəˈstɪdʒəli, vɛˈstɪdʒli, vəˈstɪdʒli
AM vɛˈstɪdʒ(i)əli

vestiture
BR ˈvɛstɪtʃə(r), -z
AM ˈvɛstɪtʃər, ˈvɛstəˌtʃʊ(ə)r, -z

vestment
BR ˈvɛs(t)m(ə)nt, -s
AM ˈvɛs(t)mənt, -s

vestral
BR ˈvɛstr(ə)l
AM ˈvɛstrəl

vestry
BR ˈvɛstr|i, -ɪz
AM ˈvɛstri, -z

vestryman
BR ˈvɛstrɪmən
AM ˈvɛstrimən

vestrymen
BR ˈvɛstrɪmən
AM ˈvɛstrimən

vesture
BR ˈvɛstʃə(r), -z
AM ˈvɛstʃər, -z

Vesuvian
BR vɪˈsjuːvɪən
AM vəˈsuviən

Vesuvius
BR vɪˈsjuːvɪəs
AM vəˈsuviəs

vet
BR vɛt, -s, -ɪŋ, -ɪd
AM vɛ|t, -ts, -dɪŋ, -dəd

vetch
BR vɛtʃ, -ɪz
AM vɛtʃ, -əz

vetchling
BR ˈvɛtʃlɪŋ, -z
AM ˈvɛtʃlɪŋ, -z

vetchy
BR ˈvɛtʃi
AM ˈvɛtʃi

veteran
BR ˈvɛt(ə)rən, ˈvɛt(ə)rn̩, -z
AM ˈvɛdərən, ˈvɛtrən, -z

veterinarian
BR ˌvɛt(ə)rɪˈnɛːrɪən, -z
AM ˌvɛdərəˈnɛriən, ˌvɛtrəˈnɛriən, -z

veterinary
BR ˈvɛt(ə)rɪn(ə)ri
AM ˈvɛdərəˌnɛri, ˈvɛtrəˌnɛri

vetiver
BR ˈvɛtɪvə(r)
AM ˈvɛdəvər

veto
BR ˈviːtəʊ, -z, -ɪŋ, -d
AM ˈvidoʊ, ˈviˌtoʊ, -z, -ɪŋ, -d

vetoer
BR ˈviːtəʊə(r), -z
AM ˈvidoʊər, ˈviˌtoʊər, -z

vex
BR vɛks, -ɪz, -ɪŋ, -t
AM vɛks, -əz, -ɪŋ, -t

vexation
BR vɛkˈseɪʃn, -z
AM vɛkˈseɪʃən, -z

vexatious
BR vɛkˈseɪʃəs
AM vɛkˈseɪʃəs

vexatiously
BR vɛkˈseɪʃəsli
AM vɛkˈseɪʃəsli

vexatiousness
BR vɛkˈseɪʃəsnəs
AM vɛkˈseɪʃəsnəs

vexedly
BR ˈvɛksɪdli
AM ˈvɛksədli

vexer
BR ˈvɛksə(r), -z
AM ˈvɛksər, -z

vexilla
BR vɛkˈsɪlə(r)
AM vɛkˈsɪlə

vexillological
BR ˌvɛksɪləˈlɒdʒɪkl
AM ˌvɛksələˈlɑdʒəkəl

vexillologist
BR ˌvɛksɪˈlɒlədʒɪst, -s
AM ˌvɛksəˈlɑlədʒəst, -s

vexillology
BR ˌvɛksɪˈlɒlədʒi
AM ˌvɛksəˈlɑlədʒi

vexillum
BR vɛkˈsɪləm
AM vɛkˈsɪləm

vexingly
BR ˈvɛksɪŋli
AM ˈvɛksɪŋli

Vi
BR vʌɪ
AM vaɪ

via
BR ˈvʌɪə(r)
AM ˈviə, ˈvaɪə

viability
BR ˌvʌɪəˈbɪlɪti
AM ˌvaɪəˈbɪlɪdi

viable
BR ˈvʌɪəbl
AM ˈvaɪəbəl

viably
BR ˈvʌɪəbli
AM ˈvaɪəbli

Via Dolorosa
BR ˌviːə ˌdɒləˈrəʊsə(r)
AM ˌviə doʊlərˈoʊsə

viaduct
BR ˈvʌɪədʌkt, -s
AM ˈvaɪəˌdək(t), -(t)s

Viagra
BR vʌɪˈagrə(r)
AM vaɪˈægrə

vial
BR ˈvʌɪəl, -z
AM ˈvaɪ(ə)l, -z

vialful
BR ˈvʌɪəlfʊl, -z
AM ˈvaɪ(ə)lˌfʊl, -z

via media
BR ˌvʌɪə ˈmiːdɪə(r), ˌviːə +, + ˈmɛdɪə(r), + ˈmeɪdɪə(r)
AM ˌviə ˈmidiə, ˌvaɪə +, + ˈmeɪdiə

viand
BR ˈvʌɪənd, -z
AM ˈvaɪən|d, -(d)z

viatica
BR vʌɪˈatɪkə(r), vɪˈatɪkə(r)
AM vaɪˈædəkə

viaticum
BR vʌɪˈatɪkəm, vɪˈatɪkəm, -z
AM vaɪˈædəkəm, -z

vibes
BR vʌɪbz
AM vaɪbz

vibist
BR ˈvʌɪbɪst, -s
AM ˈvaɪbɪst, -s

vibracula
BR vʌɪˈbrakjʊlə(r)
AM vaɪˈbrækjələ

vibracular
BR vʌɪˈbrakjʊlə(r)
AM vaɪˈbrækjələr

vibraculum
BR vʌɪˈbrakjʊləm
AM vaɪˈbrækjələm

Vibram®
BR ˈvʌɪbram, ˈvʌɪbrəm
AM ˈvaɪˌbræm

vibrancy
BR ˈvʌɪbr(ə)nsi
AM ˈvaɪbrənsi

vibrant
BR ˈvʌɪbr(ə)nt
AM ˈvaɪbrənt

vibrantly
BR ˈvʌɪbr(ə)ntli
AM ˈvaɪbrən(t)li

vibraphone
BR ˈvʌɪbrəfəʊn, -z
AM ˈvaɪbrəˌfoʊn, -z

vibraphonist
BR ˈvʌɪbrəfəʊnɪst, -s
AM ˈvaɪbrəˌfoʊnəst, -s

vibrate
BR vʌɪˈbreɪt, -s, -ɪŋ, -ɪd
AM ˈvaɪˌbreɪ|t, -ts, -dɪŋ, -dɪd

vibratile
BR ˈvʌɪbrətʌɪl
AM ˈvaɪbrədl, ˈvaɪbrəˌtaɪl

vibration
BR vʌɪˈbreɪʃn, -z
AM vaɪˈbreɪʃən, -z

vibrational
BR vʌɪˈbreɪʃn̩(ə)l, vʌɪˈbreɪʃən(ə)l
AM vaɪˈbreɪʃ(ə)nəl

vibrative
BR ˈvʌɪbrətɪv
AM ˈvaɪbrədɪv

vibrato
BR vɪˈbrɑːtəʊ, -z
AM vəˈbrɑdoʊ, -z

vibrator
BR vʌɪ'breɪtə(r), -z
AM 'vaɪˌbreɪdər, -z

vibratory
BR 'vʌɪbrət(ə)ri,
vʌɪ'breɪt(ə)ri
AM 'vaɪbrəˌtɔri

vibrio
BR 'vɪbrɪəʊ, -z
AM 'vɪbrioʊ, -z

vibrissae
BR vʌɪ'brɪsiː
AM vaɪ'brɪsi,
vaɪ'brɪˌsaɪ

viburnum
BR vʌɪ'bəːnəm
AM vaɪ'bərnəm

Vic
BR vɪk
AM vɪk

vicar
BR 'vɪkə(r), -z
AM 'vɪkər, -z

vicarage
BR 'vɪk(ə)r|ɪdʒ, -ɨdʒɪz
AM 'vɪk(ə)rɪdʒ, -ɨz

vicarial
BR vɪ'kɛːrɪəl,
vʌɪ'kɛːrɪəl
AM vaɪ'kɛriəl,
və'kɛriəl

vicariate
BR vɪ'kɛːrɪət,
vʌɪ'kɛːrɪət, -s
AM və'kɛriət,
vaɪ'kɛriət,
vaɪ'kɛriˌeɪt,
və'kɛriˌeɪt, -s

vicarious
BR vɪ'kɛːrɪəs,
vʌɪ'kɛːrɪəs
AM və'kɛriəs,
vaɪ'kɛriəs

vicariously
BR vɪ'kɛːrɪəsli,
vʌɪ'kɛːrɪəsli
AM və'kɛriəsli,
vaɪ'kɛriəsli

vicariousness
BR vɪ'kɛːrɪəsnəs,
vʌɪ'kɛːrɪəsnəs
AM və'kɛriəsnəs,
vaɪ'kɛriəsnəs

vicarship
BR 'vɪkəʃɪp, -s
AM 'vɪkərˌʃɪp, -s

vice[1]
noun
BR vʌɪs, -ɨz
AM vaɪs, -ɨz

vice[2]
preposition
BR 'vʌɪsi, 'vʌɪsɪ
AM 'vaɪs(ə), 'vaɪs(i)

viceless
BR 'vʌɪslɪs
AM 'vaɪslɪs

vicelike
BR 'vʌɪslʌɪk
AM 'vaɪsˌlaɪk

vicennial
BR vʌɪ'sɛnɪəl
AM vaɪ'sɛniəl

viceregal
BR ˌvʌɪs'riːgl
AM ˌvaɪs'rigəl

viceregally
BR ˌvʌɪs'riːgḷi,
ˌvʌɪs'riːgəli
AM ˌvaɪs'rigəli

vicereine
BR ˌvʌɪs'reɪn,
'vʌɪsreɪn, -z
AM 'vaɪsˌreɪn, -z

viceroy
BR 'vʌɪsrɔɪ, -z
AM 'vaɪsˌrɔɪ, -z

viceroyal
BR ˌvʌɪs'rɔɪ(ə)l
AM ¦vaɪs'rɔɪəl

viceroyalty
BR ˌvʌɪs'rɔɪ(ə)lti
AM ¦vaɪs'rɔɪəlti

viceroyship
BR 'vʌɪsrɔɪʃɪp, -s
AM 'vaɪsˌrɔɪˌʃɪp, -s

vicesimal
BR vʌɪ'sɛsɪml
AM vaɪ'sɛsəml

vice versa
BR ˌvʌɪs(ɪ) 'vəːsə(r)
AM ¦vaɪs(ə) 'vərsə,
¦vaɪs(i) +

Vichy
BR 'vɪʃi
AM 'viʃi

vichyssoise
BR ˌvɪʃɪ'swɑːz
AM ¦viʃi¦swɑz,
¦vɪʃi¦swɑz

vicinage
BR 'vɪsɪn|ɪdʒ, -ɨdʒɪz
AM 'vɪsṇɪdʒ, -ɨz

vicinal
BR 'vɪsɪnl, 'vɪsṇl
AM 'vɪsənəl

vicinity
BR vɪ'sɪnɪti
AM və'sɪnɨdi, -z

vicious
BR 'vɪʃəs
AM 'vɪʃəs

viciously
BR 'vɪʃəsli
AM 'vɪʃəsli

viciousness
BR 'vɪʃəsnəs
AM 'vɪʃəsnəs

vicissitude
BR vɪ'sɪsɪtjuːd,
vɪ'sɪsɪtʃuːd,
vʌɪ'sɪsɪtjuːd,
vʌɪ'sɪsɪtʃuːd, -z
AM və'sɪsəˌt(j)ud, -z

vicissitudinous
BR vɪˌsɪsɪ'tjuːdɪnəs,
vɪˌsɪsɪ'tʃuːdɪnəs,
vʌɪˌsɪsɪ'tjuːdɪnəs,
vʌɪˌsɪsɪ'tʃuːdɪnəs
AM vəˌsɪsə't(j)udənəs

Vick
BR vɪk
AM vɪk

Vickers
BR 'vɪkəz
AM 'vɪkərz

Vickery
BR 'vɪk(ə)ri
AM 'vɪk(ə)ri

Vicki
BR 'vɪki
AM 'vɪki

Vickie
BR 'vɪki
AM 'vɪki

Vicksburg
BR 'vɪksbəːg
AM 'vɪksˌbərg

Vicky
BR 'vɪki
AM 'vɪki

Vico
BR 'vɪkəʊ
AM 'vikoʊ

vicomte
BR 'viːkɒ̃t, 'viːkɒmt
AM 'vaɪˌkɑnt

vicomtesse
BR ˌviːkɒ̃'tɛs,
ˌviːkɒn'tɛs
AM ¦vaɪ¦kaʊn(t)əs

victim
BR 'vɪktɪm, -z
AM 'vɪktɨm, -z

victimhood
BR 'vɪktɪmhʊd
AM 'vɪktɨmˌ(h)ʊd

victimisation
BR ˌvɪktɪmʌɪ'zeɪʃn
AM ˌvɪktəmə'zeɪʃən,
ˌvɪktəˌmaɪ'zeɪʃən

victimise
BR 'vɪktɪmʌɪz, -ɨz, -ɪŋ,
-d
AM 'vɪktəˌmaɪz, -ɨz, -ɪŋ,
-d

victimiser
BR 'vɪktɪmʌɪzə(r), -z
AM 'vɪktəˌmaɪzər, -z

victimization
BR ˌvɪktɪmʌɪ'zeɪʃn
AM ˌvɪktəmə'zeɪʃən,
ˌvɪktəˌmaɪ'zeɪʃən

victimize
BR 'vɪktɪmʌɪz, -ɨz, -ɪŋ,
-d
AM 'vɪktəˌmaɪz, -ɨz, -ɪŋ,
-d

victimizer
BR 'vɪktɪmʌɪzə(r), -z
AM 'vɪktəˌmaɪzər, -z

victimless
BR 'vɪktɪmlɪs
AM 'vɪktɨmlɨs

victimology
BR ˌvɪktɪ'mɒlədʒ|i, -ɪz
AM ˌvɪktə'mɑlədʒi, -z

victor
BR 'vɪktə(r), -z
AM 'vɪktər, -z

victoria
BR vɪk'tɔːrɪə(r), -z
AM vɪk'tɔriə, -z

Victorian
BR vɪk'tɔːrɪən, -z
AM vɪk'tɔriən, -z

Victoriana
BR vɪkˌtɔːrɪ'ɑːnə(r)
AM vɪkˌtɔri'ɑnə

Victorianism
BR vɪk'tɔːrɪənɪz(ə)m,
-z
AM vɪk'tɔriəˌnɪzəm, -z

victorious
BR vɪk'tɔːrɪəs
AM vɪk'tɔriəs

victoriously
BR vɪk'tɔːrɪəsli
AM vɪk'tɔriəsli

victoriousness
BR vɪk'tɔːrɪəsnəs
AM vɪk'tɔriəsnəs

victory
BR 'vɪkt(ə)r|i, -ɪz
AM 'vɪkt(ə)ri, -z

Victrola®
BR vɪk'trəʊlə(r)
AM vɪk'troʊlə

victual
BR 'vɪtl̩, -z, -ɪŋ, -d
AM 'vɪdl, -z, -ɪŋ, -d

victualler
BR 'vɪtl̩ə(r), -z
AM 'vɪdl̩ər, -z

victualless
BR 'vɪtl̩lɪs
AM 'vɪdl̩(l)ɪs

vicuna
BR vɪ'k(j)uːn(j)ə(r),
vʌɪ'k(j)uːn(j)ə(r), -z
AM vaɪ'k(j)unə,
və'k(j)unə, -z

vicuña
BR vɪ'k(j)uːn(j)ə(r),
vʌɪ'k(j)uːn(j)ə(r), -z
AM vaɪ'k(j)unə,
və'k(j)unə, -z

vid
video
BR vɪd, -z
AM vɪd, -z

Vidal
BR vɪ'dɑːl
AM və'dɑl

vide
BR 'vʌɪdi, 'vɪdi, 'viːdi,
'vɪdeɪ, 'viːdeɪ
AM 'vidi, 'videɪ

videlicet
BR vɪˈdiːlɪsɛt, vɪˈdiːlɪkɛt, vɪˈdeɪlɪsɛt, vɪˈdeɪlɪkɛt, vɪˈdɛlɪsɛt, vɪˈdɛlɪkɛt
AM vəˈdɛləˌsɛt, vəˈdɛləsət, vəˈdeɪləˌkɛt

video
BR ˈvɪdɪəʊ, -z, -ɪŋ, -d
AM ˈvɪdioʊ, -z, -ɪŋ, -d

videocassette
BR ˈvɪdɪəʊkəˌsɛt, -s
AM ˌvɪdioʊkəˈsɛt, -s

videoconferencing
BR ˌvɪdɪəʊˈkɒnf(ə)rənsɪŋ, ˌvɪdɪəʊˈkɒnf(ə)rn̩sɪŋ
AM ˌvɪdioʊˈkɑnf(ə)rənsɪŋ

videodisc
BR ˈvɪdɪəʊdɪsk, -s
AM ˈvɪdioʊˌdɪsk, -s

videodisk
BR ˈvɪdɪəʊdɪsk, -s
AM ˈvɪdioʊˌdɪsk, -s

video nasty
BR ˌvɪdɪəʊ ˈnɑːst|i, + ˈnast|i, -ɪz
AM ˌvɪdioʊ ˈnæsti, -z

videophile
BR ˈvɪdɪə(ʊ)fʌɪl, -z
AM ˈvɪdiəˌfaɪl, -z

videophone
BR ˈvɪdɪə(ʊ)fəʊn, -z
AM ˈvɪdioʊˌfoʊn, -z

videorecorder
BR ˈvɪdɪəʊrɪˌkɔːdə(r), -z
AM ˈvɪdioʊrəˌkɔrdər, -z

videorecording
BR ˈvɪdɪəʊrɪˌkɔːdɪŋ, -z
AM ˈvɪdioʊrəˌkɔrdɪŋ, -z

videotape
BR ˈvɪdɪə(ʊ)teɪp, -s, -ɪŋ, -t
AM ˈvɪdioʊˌteɪp, -s, -ɪŋ, -t

videotex
BR ˈvɪdɪə(ʊ)tɛks
AM ˈvɪdioʊˌtɛks

videotext
BR ˈvɪdɪə(ʊ)tɛkst
AM ˈvɪdioʊˌtɛkst

vidimus
BR ˈvʌɪdɪməs, -ɪz
AM ˈvɪdɪməs, ˈvaɪdɪməs, -əz

vie
BR vʌɪ, -z, -ɪŋ, -d
AM vaɪ, -z, -ɪŋ, -d

vielle
BR vɪˈɛl, -z
AM viˈɛl, -z

Vienna
BR vɪˈɛnə(*r*)
AM ˌviˈɛnə

Viennese
BR ˌviːəˈniːz
AM ˌviəˈniz

Vientiane
BR vjɛnˈtjɑːn, vɪˌɛntɪˈɑːn
AM vjɛnˈtjɑn, vɪˌɛntɪˈɑn

Vietcong
BR ˌvjɛtˈkɒŋ, vɪˌɛtˈkɒŋ
AM viˈɛtˈkɔŋ, ˈvjɛtˈkɔŋ, viˈɛtˈkɑŋ, ˈvjɛtˈkɑŋ

Vietminh
BR ˌvjɛtˈmɪn, vɪˌɛtˈmɪn
AM viˈɛtˈmɪn, ˈvjɛtˈmɪn

Vietnam
BR ˌvjɛtˈnam, vɪˌɛtˈnam
AM viˈɛtˈnɑm, vjɛtˈnɑm, viˈɛtˈnæm, vjɛtˈnæm

Vietnamese
BR ˌvjɛtnəˈmiːz, vɪˌɛtnəˈmiːz
AM viˌɛtnəˈmiz, ˌvjɛtnəˈmiz

vieux jeu
BR vjə ˈʒəː
AM vjə ˈʒə

view
BR vjuː, -z, -ɪŋ, -d
AM vju, -z, -ɪŋ, -d

viewable
BR ˈvjuːəbl
AM ˈvjuəbəl

viewdata
BR ˈvjuːˌdeɪtə(*r*), ˈvjuːˌdɑːtə(*r*)
AM ˈvjuˌdædə, ˈvjuˌdeɪdə

viewer
BR ˈvjuːə(r), -z
AM ˈvjuər, -z

viewership
BR ˈvjuːəʃɪp
AM ˈvjuərˌʃɪp

viewfinder
BR ˈvjuːˌfʌɪndə(r), -z
AM ˈvjuˌfaɪndər, -z

viewgraph
BR ˈvjuːgrɑːf, ˈvjuːgraf, -s
AM ˈvjuˌgræf, -s

viewing
BR ˈvjuːwɪŋ, -z
AM ˈvjuwɪŋ, -z

viewless
BR ˈvjuːləs
AM ˈvjuləs

viewpoint
BR ˈvjuːpɔɪnt, -s
AM ˈvjuˌpɔɪnt, -s

viewport
BR ˈvjuːpɔːt, -s
AM ˈvjuˌpɔ(ə)rt, -s

viewscreen
BR ˈvjuːskriːn, -z
AM ˈvjuˌskrin, -z

vigesimal
BR vʌɪˈdʒɛsɪml
AM vaɪˈdʒɛsəml

vigesimally
BR vʌɪˈdʒɛsɪmli, vʌɪˈdʒɛsɪməli
AM vaɪˈdʒɛsəmli

vigil
BR ˈvɪdʒ(ɪ)l, -z
AM ˈvɪdʒɪl, -z

vigilance
BR ˈvɪdʒɪləns, ˈvɪdʒɪln̩s, ˈvɪdʒl̩(ə)ns
AM ˈvɪdʒələns

vigilant
BR ˈvɪdʒɪlənt, ˈvɪdʒɪln̩t, ˈvɪdʒl̩(ə)nt
AM ˈvɪdʒələnt

vigilante
BR ˌvɪdʒɪˈlant|i, -ɪz
AM ˌvɪdʒəˈlæn(t)i, -z

vigilantism
BR ˌvɪdʒɪˈlantɪz(ə)m
AM ˌvɪdʒəˈlæn(t)(i)ˌɪzəm

vigilantly
BR ˈvɪdʒɪləntli, ˈvɪdʒɪln̩tli, ˈvɪdʒl̩(ə)ntli
AM ˈvɪdʒələn(t)li

vigneron
BR ˈviːnjərɒn, -z
AM ˌvɪnjəˈrɔn, ˌvɪnjəˈroʊn, -z

vignette
BR viːˈnjɛt, vɪˈnjɛt, -s
AM vɪnˈjɛt, -s

vignetter
BR viːˈnjɛtə(r), vɪˈnjɛtə(r), -z
AM vɪnˈjɛdər, -z

vignettist
BR viːˈnjɛtɪst, vɪˈnjɛtɪst, -s
AM vɪnˈjɛdəst, -s

Vignola
BR vɪˈnjəʊlə(*r*)
AM vɪnˈjoʊlə

Vigo
BR ˈviːgəʊ
AM ˈvigoʊ

vigor
BR ˈvɪgə(r)
AM ˈvɪgər

vigorish
BR ˈvɪg(ə)rɪʃ
AM ˈvɪgərɪʃ

vigorless
BR ˈvɪgələs
AM ˈvɪgərləs

vigoro
BR ˈvɪg(ə)rəʊ
AM ˈvɪgəˌroʊ

vigorous
BR ˈvɪg(ə)rəs
AM ˈvɪg(ə)rəs

vigorously
BR ˈvɪg(ə)rəsli
AM ˈvɪg(ə)rəsli

vigorousness
BR ˈvɪg(ə)rəsnəs
AM ˈvɪg(ə)rəsnəs

vigour
BR ˈvɪgə(r)
AM ˈvɪgər

vigourless
BR ˈvɪgələs
AM ˈvɪgərləs

vihara
BR vɪˈhɑːrə(*r*), -z
AM vəˈhɑrə, -z

vihuela
BR vɪˈ(h)weɪlə(*r*), -z
AM vɪˈ(h)weɪlə, -z

Viking
BR ˈvʌɪkɪŋ, -z
AM ˈvaɪkɪŋ, -z

Vikki
BR ˈvɪki
AM ˈvɪki

Vila
BR ˈviːlə(*r*)
AM ˈvilə

vilayet
BR vɪˈlɑːjɛt, -s
AM ˌviləˈjɛt, -s

vile
BR vʌɪl, -ə(r), -ɪst
AM vaɪl, -ər, -ɪst

Vileda
BR vʌɪˈliːdə(*r*)
AM vaɪˈlidə

vilely
BR ˈvʌɪlli
AM ˈvaɪ(l)li

vileness
BR ˈvʌɪlnɪs
AM ˈvaɪlnɪs

vilification
BR ˌvɪlɪfɪˈkeɪʃn
AM ˌvɪləfəˈkeɪʃən

vilifier
BR ˈvɪlɪfʌɪə(r), -z
AM ˈvɪləˌfaɪər, -z

vilify
BR ˈvɪlɪfʌɪ, -z, -ɪŋ, -d
AM ˈvɪləˌfaɪ, -z, -ɪŋ, -d

vill
BR vɪl, -z
AM vɪl, -z

Villa
Pancho
BR vɪˈlɑː(*r*), vɪˈjɑː(*r*)
AM ˈvijə
SP ˈbija

villa
BR ˈvɪlə(*r*), -z
AM ˈvɪlə, -z

village
BR ˈvɪl|ɪdʒ, -ɪdʒɪz
AM ˈvɪlɪdʒ, -ɪz

villager
BR ˈvɪlɪdʒə(r), -z
AM ˈvɪlɪdʒər, -z
villagey
BR ˈvɪlɪdʒi
AM ˈvɪlɪdʒi
villagisation
BR ˌvɪlɪdʒʌɪˈzeɪʃn
AM ˌvɪlɪdʒəˈzeɪʃən, ˌvɪlɪˌdʒaɪˈzeɪʃən
villagization
BR ˌvɪlɪdʒʌɪˈzeɪʃn
AM ˌvɪlɪdʒəˈzeɪʃən, ˌvɪlɪˌdʒaɪˈzeɪʃən
villain
BR ˈvɪlən, -z
AM ˈvɪlən, -z
villainess
BR ˈvɪlənɪs, -ɪz
AM ˈvɪlənəs, -əz
villainous
BR ˈvɪlənəs
AM ˈvɪlənəs
villainously
BR ˈvɪlənəsli
AM ˈvɪlənəsli
villainousness
BR ˈvɪlənəsnəs
AM ˈvɪlənəsnəs
villainy
BR ˈvɪlən|i, -ɪz
AM ˈvɪləni, -z
Villa-Lobos
BR ˌvɪləˈlɒbɒs, ˌvɪləˈləʊbɒs
AM ˈviləˈloʊˌboʊs
villanella
BR ˌvɪləˈnɛlə(r), -z
AM ˌvɪləˈnɛlə, -z
villanelle
BR ˌvɪləˈnɛl, -z
AM ˌvɪləˈnɛl, -z
villeggiatura
BR vɪˌlɛdʒ(ɪ)əˈt(j)ʊərə(r)
AM vəˌlɛdʒəˈtʊrə
villeggiature
BR vɪˌlɛdʒ(ɪ)əˈt(j)ʊəreɪ
AM vəˌlɛdʒəˈtʊreɪ
villein
BR ˈvɪlɪn, ˈvɪleɪn, -z
AM ˈvɪlɪn, vəˈleɪn, -z
villeinage
BR ˈvɪlɪnɪdʒ
AM ˈvɪlɪnɪdʒ, vəˈleɪnɪdʒ
villenage
BR ˈvɪlɪnɪdʒ
AM ˈvɪlɪnɪdʒ, vəˈleɪnɪdʒ
villi
BR ˈvɪlʌɪ
AM ˈviˌlaɪ, ˈvɪli
villiform
BR ˈvɪlɪfɔːm
AM ˈvɪlɪˌfɔ(ə)rm
Villon
BR viːˈjɒ̃
AM viˈjoʊn
villose
BR ˈvɪləʊs
AM ˈvɪˌloʊs, ˈvɪˌloʊz
villosity
BR vɪˈlɒsɪt|i, -ɪz
AM vəˈlɑsədi, -z
villous
BR ˈvɪləs
AM ˈvɪləs
villously
BR ˈvɪləsli
AM ˈvɪləsli
villus
BR ˈvɪləs
AM ˈvɪləs
Vilnius
BR ˈvɪlnɪəs
AM ˈvɪlniəs
vim
BR vɪm
AM vɪm
vimineous
BR vɪˈmɪnɪəs
AM vəˈmɪniəs
vin
BR vã, van
AM væn
vina
BR ˈviːnə(r), -z
AM ˈvinə, -z
vinaceous
BR vʌɪˈneɪʃəs, vɪˈneɪʃəs
AM vəˈneɪʃəs, vaɪˈneɪʃəs
vinaigrette
BR ˌvɪnɪˈgrɛt, -s
AM ˌvɪnəˈgrɛt, -s
vinca
BR ˈvɪŋkə(r), -z
AM ˈvɪŋkə, -z
Vince
BR vɪns
AM vɪns
Vincent
BR ˈvɪns(ə)nt
AM ˈvɪnsənt
Vinci
BR ˈvɪn(t)ʃi
AM ˈvɪn(t)ʃi
vincibility
BR ˌvɪnsɪˈbɪlɪti
AM ˌvɪnsəˈbɪlɪdi
vincible
BR ˈvɪnsɪbl
AM ˈvɪnsəbəl
vincula
BR ˈvɪŋkjʊlə(r)
AM ˈvɪŋkjələ
vinculum
BR ˈvɪŋkjʊləm, -z
AM ˈvɪŋkjələm, -z
vindaloo
BR ˌvɪndəˈluː, -z
AM ˌvɪndəˈlu, -z
vindicability
BR ˌvɪndɪkəˈbɪlɪti
AM ˌvɪndəkəˈbɪlɪdi
vindicable
BR ˈvɪndɪkəbl
AM ˈvɪndəkəbəl
vindicate
BR ˈvɪndɪkeɪt, -s, -ɪŋ, -ɪd
AM ˈvɪndəˌkeɪ|t, -ts, -dɪŋ, -dɪd
vindication
BR ˌvɪndɪˈkeɪʃn
AM ˌvɪndəˈkeɪʃən
vindicative
BR vɪnˈdɪkətɪv, ˈvɪndɪkeɪtɪv
AM vɪnˈdɪkədɪv, ˈvɪndəˌkeɪdɪv
vindicator
BR ˈvɪndɪkeɪtə(r), -z
AM ˈvɪndəˌkeɪdər, -z
vindicatory
BR vɪnˈdɪkət(ə)ri, ˈvɪndɪkeɪt(ə)ri
AM ˈvɪndəkəˌtɔri
vindictive
BR vɪnˈdɪktɪv
AM vinˈdɪktɪv
vindictively
BR vɪnˈdɪktɪvli
AM vinˈdɪktɪvli
vindictiveness
BR vɪnˈdɪktɪvnɪs
AM vinˈdɪktɪvnɪs
vine
BR vʌɪn, -z
AM vaɪn, -z
vine-dresser
BR ˈvʌɪnˌdrɛsə(r), -z
AM ˈvaɪnˌdrɛsər, -z
vine-dressing
BR ˈvʌɪnˌdrɛsɪŋ
AM ˈvaɪnˌdrɛsɪŋ
vinegar
BR ˈvɪnɪgə(r), -d
AM ˈvɪnəgər, -d
vinegarish
BR ˈvɪnɪg(ə)rɪʃ
AM ˈvɪnəg(ə)rɪʃ
vinegary
BR ˈvɪnɪg(ə)ri
AM ˈvɪnəg(ə)ri
Viner
BR ˈvʌɪnə(r)
AM ˈvaɪnər
vinery
BR ˈvʌɪn(ə)r|i, -ɪz
AM ˈvaɪnəri, -z
vinestock
BR ˈvʌɪnstɒk, -s
AM ˈvaɪnˌstɑk, -s
vineyard
BR ˈvɪnjəd, ˈvɪnjɑːd, -z
AM ˈvɪnjərd, -z
vingt-et-un
BR ˌvãteɪˈəːŋ, ˌvanteɪˈəːŋ, ˌvanteɪˈəːn
AM ˈvænteɪˈən
vinho verde
BR ˌviːnəʊ ˈvɛːd|i, -ɪz
AM ˈvɪnjoʊ ˈvərdi, -z
vinicultural
BR ˌvɪnɪˈkʌltʃ(ə)rəl, ˌvɪnɪˈkʌltʃ(ə)rl̩
AM ˌvɪnəˈkəltʃ(ə)rəl
viniculture
BR ˈvɪnɪˌkʌltʃə(r)
AM ˈvɪnəˌkəltʃər
viniculturist
BR ˌvɪnɪˈkʌltʃ(ə)rɪst, -s
AM ˌvɪnəˈkəltʃ(ə)rəst, -s
vinification
BR ˌvɪnɪfɪˈkeɪʃn
AM ˌvɪnəfəˈkeɪʃən
vinify
BR ˈvɪnɪfʌɪ, -z, -ɪŋ, -d
AM ˈvɪnəˌfaɪ, -z, -ɪŋ, -d
vining
BR ˈvʌɪnɪŋ
AM ˈvaɪnɪŋ
Vinland
BR ˈvɪnlənd, ˈvɪnland
AM ˈvɪnlənd
Vinney
BR ˈvɪni
AM ˈvɪni
Vinnitsa
BR ˈvɪnɪtsə(r)
AM ˈvɪnətsə
vino
BR ˈviːnəʊ, -z
AM ˈvinoʊ, -z
vin ordinaire
BR ˌvã ˌɔːdɪˈnɛː(r), ˌvan +, -z
AM ˈvæn ˌɔrdɪˈnɛ(ə)r, -z
vinosity
BR vʌɪˈnɒsɪti, vɪˈnɒsɪti
AM vəˈnɑsədi
vinous
BR ˈvʌɪnəs
AM ˈvaɪnəs
vin rosé
BR ˌvã ˈrəʊzeɪ, ˌvan +, -z
AM ˈvæn roʊˈzeɪ, -z
vint
BR vɪnt, -s, -ɪŋ, -ɪd
AM vɪn|t, -ts, -(t)ɪŋ, -(t)ɪd
vintage
BR ˈvɪnt|ɪdʒ, -ɪdʒɪz
AM ˈvɪn(t)ɪdʒ, -ɪz
vintager
BR ˈvɪntɪdʒə(r), -z
AM ˈvɪn(t)ɪdʒər, -z

vintner
BR ˈvɪntnə(r), -z
AM ˈvɪntnər, -z

viny
BR ˈvʌɪn|i, -ɪə(r), -ɪɪst
AM ˈvaɪni, -ər, -ɪst

vinyl
BR ˈvʌɪn(ɪ)l
AM ˈvaɪnl

viol
BR ˈvʌɪəl, -z
AM ˈvaɪ(ə)l, -z

Viola
BR ˈvʌɪələ(r), ˈvɪələ(r), vʌɪˈəʊlə(r)
AM viˈoʊlə

viola¹
flower
BR ˈvʌɪələ(r), ˈvɪələ(r), vʌɪˈəʊlə(r), -z
AM vaɪˈoʊlə, ˈvaɪələ, -z

viola²
musical instrument
BR vɪˈəʊlə(r), -z
AM viˈoʊlə, -z

violable
BR ˈvʌɪələbl
AM ˈvaɪələbəl

violaceous
BR ˌvʌɪəˈleɪʃəs
AM ˌvaɪəˈleɪʃəs

violate
BR ˈvʌɪəleɪt, -s, -ɪŋ, -ɪd
AM ˈvaɪəˌlaɪ|t, -ts, -dɪŋ, -dɪd

violation
BR ˌvʌɪəˈleɪʃn, -z
AM ˌvaɪəˈleɪʃən, -z

violator
BR ˈvʌɪəleɪtə(r), -z
AM ˈvaɪəˌleɪdər, -z

violence
BR ˈvʌɪələns, ˈvʌɪəlṇs
AM ˈvaɪ(ə)ləns

violent
BR ˈvʌɪələnt, ˈvʌɪəlṇt
AM ˈvaɪ(ə)lənt

violently
BR ˈvʌɪələntli, ˈvʌɪəlṇtli
AM ˈvaɪ(ə)lən(t)li

violet
BR ˈvʌɪəlɪt, -s
AM ˈvaɪ(ə)lət, -s

violin
BR ˌvʌɪəˈlɪn, -z
AM ˌvaɪəˈlɪn, -z

violinist
BR ˌvʌɪəˈlɪnɪst, -s
AM ˌvaɪəˈlɪnɪst, -s

violist
BR ˈvʌɪəlɪst, -s
AM viˈoʊləst, -s

violoncellist
BR ˌvʌɪələnˈtʃɛlɪst, -s
AM ˌvaɪələnˈtʃɛləst, -s

violoncello
BR ˌvʌɪələnˈtʃɛləʊ, -z
AM ˌvaɪələnˈtʃɛloʊ, -z

violone
BR ˈvʌɪələʊn, ˈviːələʊn, ˌviːəˈləʊneɪ, -z
AM ˌviəˈloʊˌneɪ, -z

VIP
BR ˌviːʌɪˈpiː, -z
AM ˌviˌaɪˈpi, -z

viper
BR ˈvʌɪpə(r), -z
AM ˈvaɪpər, -z

viperiform
BR ˈvʌɪp(ə)rɪfɔːm
AM ˈvaɪpərəˌfɔ(ə)rm

viperine
BR ˈvʌɪpərʌɪn
AM ˈvaɪpərən, ˈvaɪpəˌraɪn

viperish
BR ˈvʌɪp(ə)rɪʃ
AM ˈvaɪpərɪʃ

viper-like
BR ˈvʌɪpəlʌɪk
AM ˈvaɪpərˌlaɪk

viperous
BR ˈvʌɪp(ə)rəs
AM ˈvaɪp(ə)rəs

virago
BR vɪˈrɑːgəʊ, -z
AM vəˈrɑgoʊ, -z

viral
BR ˈvʌɪrəl, ˈvʌɪrḷ
AM ˈvaɪrəl

virally
BR ˈvʌɪrḷi, ˈvʌɪrəli
AM ˈvaɪrəli

virelay
BR ˈvɪrɪleɪ, -z
AM ˈvɪrəˌleɪ, -z

virement
BR ˈvʌɪəm(ə)nt, ˈvɪəmɒ̃, -s
AM ˈvɪrmɑn, -s

vireo
BR ˈvɪrɪəʊ, -z
AM ˈvɪrioʊ, -z

vires
BR ˈvʌɪriːz
AM ˈvaɪˌriz

virescence
BR vɪˈrɛsns, vʌɪˈrɛsns
AM vəˈrɛsns, vaɪˈrɛsəns

virescent
BR vɪˈrɛsnt, vʌɪˈrɛsnt
AM vəˈrɛsnt, vaɪˈrɛsənt

virgate
BR ˈvəːgət, ˈvəːgeɪt, -s
AM ˈvərgət, ˈvərˌgeɪt, -s

virger
BR ˈvəːdʒə(r), -z
AM ˈvərdʒər, -z

Virgil
BR ˈvəːdʒ(ɪ)l
AM ˈvərdʒəl

Virgilian
BR vəːˈdʒɪlɪən
AM vərˈdʒɪljən, vərˈdʒɪliən

virgin
BR ˈvəːdʒɪn, -z
AM ˈvərdʒən, -z

virginal
BR ˈvəːdʒɪnl, -z
AM ˈvərdʒənəl, -z

virginalist
BR ˈvəːdʒɪnḷɪst, -s
AM ˈvərdʒənləst, -s

virginally
BR ˈvəːdʒɪnḷi
AM ˈvərdʒ(ə)nəli

virginhood
BR ˈvəːdʒɪnhʊd
AM ˈvərdʒənˌ(h)ʊd

Virginia
BR vəˈdʒɪnɪə(r)
AM vərˈdʒɪnjə

Virginian
BR vəˈdʒɪnɪən, -z
AM vərˈdʒɪnjən, -z

virginibus puerisque
BR vəˌgɪnɪbəs p(j)ʊəˈrɪskwi, vəˌdʒɪnɪbəs
AM vərˌdʒɪnəbəs p(j)ʊəˈrɪsˌkwi

Virgin Islands
BR ˈvəːdʒɪn ˌʌɪlən(d)z
AM ˈvərdʒən ˈaɪlən(d)z

virginity
BR vəˈdʒɪnɪti, vəːˈdʒɪnɪti
AM vərˈdʒɪnɪdi

Virgo
BR ˈvəːgəʊ, -z
AM ˈvərgoʊ, -z

Virgoan
BR ˈvəːgəʊən, -z
AM ˈvərgoʊən, -z

virgule
BR ˈvəːgjuːl, -z
AM ˈvərˌgjul, -z

viridescence
BR ˌvɪrɪˈdɛsns
AM ˌvɪrəˈdɛsəns

viridescent
BR ˌvɪrɪˈdɛsnt
AM ˌvɪrəˈdɛsənt

viridian
BR vɪˈrɪdɪən
AM vəˈrɪdiən

viridity
BR vɪˈrɪdɪti
AM vəˈrɪdɪdi

virile
BR ˈvɪrʌɪl
AM ˈvɪrəl

virilism
BR ˈvɪrɪlɪz(ə)m
AM ˈvɪrəˌlɪzəm

virility
BR vɪˈrɪlɪti
AM vəˈrɪlɪdi

viroid
BR ˈvʌɪrɔɪd, ˈvɪrɔɪd, -z
AM ˈvaɪˌrɔɪd, -z

Virol
BR ˈvʌɪrɒl
AM ˈvaɪˌrɔl, ˈvaɪˌrɑl

virological
BR ˌvʌɪ(ə)rəˈlɒdʒɪkl
AM ˌvaɪrəˈlɑdʒəkəl

virologically
BR ˌvʌɪ(ə)rəˈlɒdʒɪkli
AM ˌvaɪrəˈlɑdʒək(ə)li

virologist
BR vʌɪˈrɒlədʒɪst, -s
AM vaɪˈrɑlədʒəst, -s

virology
BR vʌɪˈrɒlədʒi
AM vaɪˈrɑlədʒi

virtu
BR vəːˈtuː
AM vərˈtu

virtual
BR ˈvəːtʃʊəl, ˈvəːtʃ(ʉ)l, ˈvəːtjʊəl, ˈvəːtjʉl
AM ˈvərtʃ(əw)əl

virtuality
BR ˌvəːtʃʊˈalɪti, ˌvəːtjʊˈalɪti
AM ˌvərtʃəˈwælədi

virtually
BR ˈvəːtʃʊəli, ˈvəːtʃʉli, ˈvəːtʃḷi, ˈvəːtjʊəli, ˈvəːtjʉli
AM ˈvərtʃ(əw)əli

virtue
BR ˈvəːtʃuː, ˈvəːtjuː, -z
AM ˈvərtʃu, -z

virtueless
BR ˈvəːtʃuːləs, ˈvəːtjuːləs
AM ˈvərtʃuləs

virtuosic
BR ˌvəːtʃʊˈɒsɪk, ˌvəːtjʊˈɒsɪk
AM ˌvərtʃəˈwɑsɪk

virtuosity
BR ˌvəːtʃʊˈɒsɪti, ˌvəːtjʊˈɒsɪti
AM ˌvərtʃəˈwɑsədi

virtuoso
BR ˌvəːtʃʊˈəʊzəʊ, ˌvəːtʃʊˈəʊsəʊ, ˌvəːtjʊˈəʊzəʊ, ˌvəːtjʊˈəʊsəʊ, -z
AM ˌvərtʃəˈwoʊsoʊ, ˌvərtʃəˈwoʊzoʊ, -z

virtuosoship
BR ˌvəːtʃʊˈəʊzəʊʃɪp, ˌvəːtʃʊˈəʊsəʊʃɪp, ˌvəːtjʊˈəʊzəʊʃɪp, ˌvəːtjʊˈəʊsəʊʃɪp

AM ˌvərtʃəˈwoʊsoʊˌʃɪp, ˌvərtʃəˈwoʊzoʊˌʃɪp
virtuous
BR ˈvəːtʃʊəs, ˈvəːtjʊəs
AM ˈvərtʃ(əw)əs
virtuously
BR ˈvəːtʃʊəs, ˈvəːtjʊəsli
AM ˈvərtʃ(əw)əsli
virtuousness
BR ˈvəːtʃʊəsnəs, ˈvəːtjʊəsnəs
AM ˈvərtʃ(əw)əsnəs
virulence
BR ˈvɪr(j)ʉləns, ˈvɪr(j)ʉlṇs
AM ˈvɪr(j)ələns
virulent
BR ˈvɪr(j)ʉlənt, ˈvɪr(j)ʉlṇt
AM ˈvɪr(j)ələnt
virulently
BR ˈvɪr(j)ʉləntli, ˈvɪr(j)ʉlṇtli
AM ˈvɪr(j)ələn(t)li
virus
BR ˈvʌɪrəs, -ɪz
AM ˈvaɪrəs, -əz
vis
BR vɪs
AM vɪs
visa
BR ˈviːzə(r), -z
AM ˈvizə, -z
visage
BR ˈvɪz|ɪdʒ, -ɪdʒɪz, -ɪdʒd
AM ˈvɪzɪdʒ, -ɪz, -ɪdʒd
vis-à-vis
BR ˌviːzɑːˈviː, ˌviːzəˈviː
AM ˌvizəˈvi
Visby
BR ˈvɪzbi
AM ˈvɪzbi
viscacha
BR vɪˈskɑːtʃə(r), vɪˈskatʃə(r), -z
AM vɪˈskɑtʃə, -z
viscera
BR ˈvɪs(ə)rə(r)
AM ˈvɪsərə
visceral
BR ˈvɪs(ə)rəl, ˈvɪs(ə)rḷ
AM ˈvɪs(ə)rəl
viscerally
BR ˈvɪs(ə)rəli, ˈvɪs(ə)rḷi
AM ˈvɪs(ə)rəli
viscerotonic
BR ˌvɪs(ə)rəˈtɒnɪk
AM ˌvɪsərəˈtɑnɪk
viscid
BR ˈvɪsɪd
AM ˈvɪsɪd
viscidity
BR vɪˈsɪdɪti
AM vəˈsɪdɪdi
viscometer
BR vɪsˈkɒmɪtə(r), vɪˈskɒmɪtə(r), -z
AM vəˈskɑmədər, -z
viscometric
BR ˌvɪskəˈmɛtrɪk
AM ˌvɪskəˈmɛtrɪk
viscometrically
BR ˌvɪskəˈmɛtrɪkli
AM ˌvɪskəˈmɛtrək(ə)li
viscometry
BR vɪsˈkɒmɪtri, vɪˈskɒmɪtri
AM vəˈskɑmətri
Visconti
BR vɪˈskɒnti
AM vəˈskɑn(t)i
viscose
BR ˈvɪskəʊs, ˈvɪskəʊz
AM ˈvɪskoʊs, ˈvɪskoʊz
viscosimeter
BR ˌvɪskəˈsɪmɪtə(r), -z
AM ˌvɪskəˈsɪmɪdər, -z
viscosity
BR vɪˈskɒsɪti
AM ˌvɪsˈkɑsədi
viscount
BR ˈvʌɪkaʊnt, -s
AM ˈvaɪˌkaʊnt, -s
viscountcy
BR ˈvʌɪkaʊn(t)s|i, -ɪz
AM ˈvaɪˌkaʊn(t)si, -z
viscountess
BR ˈvʌɪkaʊntɪs, ˈvʌɪkaʊntɛs, -ɪz
AM ˈvaɪˌkaʊn(t)əs, -əz
viscountship
BR ˈvʌɪkaʊntʃɪp, -s
AM ˈvaɪˌkaʊntˌʃɪp, -s
viscounty
BR ˈvʌɪkaʊn(t)|i, -ɪz
AM ˈvaɪˌkaʊn(t)i, -z
viscous
BR ˈvɪskəs
AM ˈvɪskəs
viscously
BR ˈvɪskəsli
AM ˈvɪskəsli
viscousness
BR ˈvɪskəsnəs
AM ˈvɪskəsnəs
viscus
BR ˈvɪskəs
AM ˈvɪskəs
vise
BR vʌɪs, -ɪz
AM vaɪs, vaɪz, -ɪz
Vishnu
BR ˈvɪʃnuː
AM ˈvɪʃnu
Vishnuism
BR ˈvɪʃnuːɪz(ə)m, ˈvɪʃnʊɪz(ə)m
AM ˈvɪʃnuˌɪzəm, ˈvɪʃnəˌwɪzəm
Vishnuite
BR ˈvɪʃnuːʌɪt, ˈvɪʃnʊʌɪt, -s
AM ˈvɪʃnuˌaɪt, ˈvɪʃnəˌwaɪt, -s
visibility
BR ˌvɪzɪˈbɪlɪti
AM ˌvɪzəˈbɪlɪdi
visible
BR ˈvɪzɪbl
AM ˈvɪzəbəl
visibleness
BR ˈvɪzɪblnɪs
AM ˈvɪzəbəlnəs
visibly
BR ˈvɪzɪbli
AM ˈvɪzəbli
VisiCalc
BR ˈvɪzɪkalk
AM ˈvɪzɪˌkælk
Visigoth
BR ˈvɪzɪgɒθ, -s
AM ˈvɪzɪˌgɔθ, ˈvɪzɪˌgɑθ, -s
Visigothic
BR ˌvɪzɪˈgɒθɪk
AM ˌvɪzɪˈgɔθɪk, ˌvɪzɪˈgɑθɪk
vision
BR ˈvɪʒn, -z
AM ˈvɪʒən, -z
visional
BR ˈvɪʒṇ(ə)l, ˈvɪʒən(ə)l
AM ˈvɪʒ(ə)nəl
visionariness
BR ˈvɪʒṇ(ə)rɪnɪs
AM ˈvɪʒəˌnɛrinɪs
visionary
BR ˈvɪʒṇ(ə)r|i, -ɪz
AM ˈvɪʒəˌnɛri, -z
visionist
BR ˈvɪʒṇɪst, ˈvɪʒənɪst, -s
AM ˈvɪʒənəst, -s
visionless
BR ˈvɪʒnləs
AM ˈvɪʒənləs
visit
BR ˈvɪz|ɪt, -ɪts, -ɪtɪŋ, -ɪtɪd
AM ˈvɪzɪ|t, -ts, -dɪŋ, -dɪd
visitable
BR ˈvɪzɪtəbl
AM ˈvɪzɪdəbəl
visitant
BR ˈvɪzɪt(ə)nt, -s
AM ˈvɪzətnt, -s
visitation
BR ˌvɪzɪˈteɪʃn, -z
AM ˌvɪzəˈteɪʃən, -z
visitatorial
BR ˌvɪzɪtəˈtɔːrɪəl
AM ˌvɪzədəˈtɔriəl
visiting
BR ˈvɪzɪtɪŋ, -z
AM ˈvɪzɪdɪŋ, -z
visitor
BR ˈvɪzɪtə(r), -z
AM ˈvɪzɪdər, -z
visitorial
BR ˌvɪzɪˈtɔːrɪəl
AM ˌvɪzəˈtɔriəl
visna
BR ˈvɪznə(r)
AM ˈvɪznə
visor
BR ˈvʌɪzə(r), -z, -d
AM ˈvaɪzər, -z, -d
visorless
BR ˈvʌɪzələs
AM ˈvaɪzərləs
vista
BR ˈvɪstə(r), -z, -d
AM ˈvɪstə, -z, -d
Vistula
BR ˈvɪstjʉlə(r), ˈvɪstʃʉlə(r)
AM ˈvɪstʃələ
visual
BR ˈvɪʒʊ(ə)l, ˈvɪzjʊ(ə)l, ˈvɪʒ(ʉ)l, ˈvɪzj(ʉ)l
AM ˈvɪʒ(ə)wəl, ˈvɪʒəl
visualisable
BR ˈvɪʒjʉlʌɪzəbl, ˈvɪʒjʊəlʌɪzəbl, ˈvɪzjʉlʌɪzəbl, ˈvɪzjʊəlʌɪzəbl
AM ˈvɪʒ(ə)wəˌlaɪzəbəl, ˈvɪʒəˌlaɪzəbəl
visualisation
BR ˌvɪʒjʉlʌɪˈzeɪʃn, ˌvɪzjʉlʌɪˈzeɪʃn
AM ˌvɪʒələˈzeɪʃən, ˌvɪʒ(ə)wələˈzeɪʃən, ˌvɪʒəˌlaɪˈzeɪʃən, ˌvɪʒ(ə)wəˌlaɪˈzeɪʃən
visualise
BR ˈvɪʒjʉlʌɪz, ˈvɪʒjʊəlʌɪz, ˈvɪzjʉlʌɪz, ˈvɪzjʊəlʌɪz, -ɪz, -ɪŋ, -d
AM ˈvɪʒ(ə)wəˌlaɪz, ˈvɪʒəˌlaɪz, -ɪz, -ɪŋ, -d
visuality
BR ˌvɪʒjʊˈalɪti, ˌvɪzjʊˈalɪti
AM ˌvɪʒəˈwælədi
visualizable
BR ˈvɪʒjʉlʌɪzəbl, ˈvɪʒjʊəlʌɪzəbl, ˈvɪzjʉlʌɪzəbl, ˈvɪzjʊəlʌɪzəbl
AM ˈvɪʒ(ə)wəˌlaɪzəbəl, ˈvɪʒəˌlaɪzəbəl
visualization
BR ˌvɪʒjʉlʌɪˈzeɪʃn, ˌvɪzjʉlʌɪˈzeɪʃn
AM ˌvɪʒələˈzeɪʃən, ˌvɪʒ(ə)wələˈzeɪʃən, ˌvɪʒəˌlaɪˈzeɪʃən, ˌvɪʒ(ə)wəˌlaɪˈzeɪʃən
visualize
BR ˈvɪʒjʉlʌɪz, ˈvɪʒjʊəlʌɪz, ˈvɪzjʉlʌɪz, ˈvɪzjʊəlʌɪz, -ɪz, -ɪŋ, -d
AM ˈvɪʒ(ə)wəˌlaɪz, ˈvɪʒəˌlaɪz, -ɪz, -ɪŋ, -d

visually
BR 'vɪʒ(j)ʊəli, 'vɪʒ(j)ʉli, 'vɪzjʊəli, 'vɪzjʉli
AM 'vɪʒ(ə)wəli, 'vɪʒəli

vita
BR 'vi:tə(*r*), 'vʌɪtə(*r*), -z
AM 'vidə, -z

vitae
BR 'vi:tʌɪ
AM 'vidi, 'viˌtaɪ

vital
BR 'vʌɪtl, -z
AM 'vaɪdl, -z

vitalisation
BR ˌvʌɪtəlʌɪ'zeɪʃn, ˌvʌɪtl̩ʌɪ'zeɪʃn
AM ˌvaɪdl̩ə'zeɪʃən, ˌvaɪdlˌaɪ'zeɪʃən

vitalise
BR 'vʌɪtəlʌɪz, 'vʌɪtl̩ʌɪz, -ɨz, -ɪŋ, -d
AM 'vaɪdlˌaɪz, -ɨz, -ɪŋ, -d

vitalism
BR 'vʌɪtəlɪz(ə)m, 'vʌɪtl̩ɪz(ə)m
AM 'vaɪdlˌɪzəm

vitalist
BR 'vʌɪtəlɪst, 'vʌɪtl̩ɪst, -s
AM 'vaɪdl̩ɪst, -s

vitalistic
BR ˌvʌɪtə'lɪstɪk, ˌvʌɪtl'ɪstɪk
AM ˌvaɪdl'ɪstɪk

vitality
BR vʌɪ'talɨti
AM vaɪ'tælədi

vitalization
BR ˌvʌɪtəlʌɪ'zeɪʃn, ˌvʌɪtl̩ʌɪ'zeɪʃn
AM ˌvaɪdl̩ə'zeɪʃən, ˌvaɪdlˌaɪ'zeɪʃən

vitalize
BR 'vʌɪtəlʌɪz, 'vʌɪtl̩ʌɪz, -ɨz, -ɪŋ, -d
AM 'vaɪdlˌaɪz, -ɨz, -ɪŋ, -d

vitally
BR 'vʌɪtəli, 'vʌɪtl̩i
AM 'vaɪdl̩i

vitamin
BR 'vɪtəmɪn, 'vʌɪtəmɪn, -z
AM 'vaɪdəmən, -z

vitaminise
BR 'vɪtəmɨnʌɪz, 'vʌɪtəmɨnʌɪz, -ɨz, -ɪŋ, -d
AM 'vaɪdəməˌnaɪz, -ɨz, -ɪŋ, -d

vitaminize
BR 'vɪtəmɨnʌɪz, 'vʌɪtəmɨnʌɪz, -ɨz, -ɪŋ, -d
AM 'vaɪdəməˌnaɪz, -ɨz, -ɪŋ, -d

VitBe®
BR 'vɪtbi
AM 'vɪtbi

Vitebsk
BR vɪ'tɛbsk
AM vi'tɛbsk
RUS 'vʲitʲipsk

vitellary
BR 'vɪtl̩(ə)ri, vɪ'tɛl(ə)ri, vʌɪ'tɛl(ə)ri
AM və'tɛləri, 'vaɪdlˌɛri, 'vɪdlˌɛri, vaɪ'tɛləri

vitelli
BR vɪ'tɛlʌɪ, vʌɪ'tɛlʌɪ
AM və'tɛˌlaɪ, vaɪ'tɛˌlaɪ

vitellin
BR vɪ'tɛlɪn, vʌɪ'tɛlɪn
AM və'tɛlən, vaɪ'tɛlən

vitelline
BR vɪ'tɛlʌɪn, vʌɪ'tɛlʌɪn, vɪ'tɛlɪn, vʌɪ'tɛlɪn
AM və'tɛlən, vaɪ'tɛlən, vaɪ'tɛlin, və'tɛlin, vaɪ'tɛˌlaɪn, və'tɛˌlaɪn

Vitellius
BR vɪ'tɛlɪəs
AM və'tɛliəs

vitellus
BR vɪ'tɛləs, vʌɪ'tɛləs
AM və'tɛləs, vaɪ'tɛləs

vitiate
BR 'vɪʃɪeɪt, -s, -ɪŋ, -ɨd
AM 'vɪʃiˌeɪ|t, -ts, -dɪŋ, -dɨd

vitiation
BR ˌvɪʃɪ'eɪʃn
AM ˌvɪʃi'eɪʃən

vitiator
BR 'vɪʃɪeɪtə(r), -z
AM 'vɪʃiˌeɪdər, -z

viticultural
BR ˌvɪtɪ'kʌltʃ(ə)rəl, ˌvɪtɪ'kʌltʃ(ə)rl̩
AM ¦vɪdə¦kəltʃ(ə)rəl

viticulturally
BR ˌvɪtɪ'kʌltʃ(ə)rəli, ˌvɪtɪ'kʌltʃ(ə)rl̩i
AM ˌvɪdə'kəltʃərəli

viticulture
BR 'vɪtɪˌkʌltʃə(r)
AM 'vɪdəˌkəltʃər

viticulturist
BR ˌvɪtɪ'kʌltʃ(ə)rɪst, -s
AM ¦vɪdə¦kəltʃ(ə)rəst, -s

Viti Levu
BR ˌvɪtɪ 'leɪvu:, + 'lɛvu:
AM ˌvidi 'lɛˌvu

vitiligo
BR ˌvɪtɪ'lʌɪgəʊ
AM ˌvɪdɪ'laɪgoʊ

Vitoria
BR vɪ'tɔ:rɪə(*r*)
AM və'tɔriə

Vitosha
BR vɪ'təʊʃə(*r*)
AM və'toʊʃə

vitreous
BR 'vɪtrɪəs
AM 'vɪtriəs

vitreousness
BR 'vɪtrɪəsnəs
AM 'vɪtriəsnəs

vitrescence
BR vɪ'trɛsns
AM və'trɛsəns

vitrescent
BR vɪ'trɛsnt
AM və'trɛsənt

vitrifaction
BR ˌvɪtrɪ'fakʃn
AM ˌvɪtrə'fækʃən

vitrifiable
BR 'vɪtrɪfʌɪəbl, ˌvɪtrɪ'fʌɪəbl
AM ¦vɪtrə¦faɪəbəl

vitrification
BR ˌvɪtrɪfɪ'keɪʃn
AM ˌvɪtrəfə'keɪʃən

vitriform
BR 'vɪtrɪfɔ:m
AM 'vɪtrəˌfɔ(ə)rm

vitrify
BR 'vɪtrɪfʌɪ, -z, -ɪŋ, -d
AM 'vɪtrəˌfaɪ, -z, -ɪŋ, -d

vitriol
BR 'vɪtrɪəl, 'vɪtrɪɒl
AM 'vɪtriəl

vitriolic
BR ˌvɪtrɪ'ɒlɪk
AM ˌvɪtri'ɑlɪk

vitro
BR 'vi:trəʊ
AM 'vɪˌtroʊ

Vitruvian
BR vɪ'tru:vɪən
AM və'truviən

Vitruvius
BR vɪ'tru:vɪəs
AM və'truviəs

vitta
BR 'vɪtə(*r*)
AM 'vɪdə

vittae
BR 'vɪti:
AM 'vɪdi, 'vɪˌtaɪ

vittate
BR 'vɪteɪt
AM 'vɪˌteɪt

vituperate
BR vɪ'tju:pəreɪt, vʌɪ'tju:pəreɪt, vɪ'tʃu:pəreɪt, vʌɪ'tʃu:pəreɪt, -s, -ɪŋ, -ɨd
AM və't(j)upəˌreɪ|t, vaɪ't(j)upəˌreɪ|t, -ts, -dɪŋ, -dɨd

vituperation
BR vɪˌtju:pə'reɪʃn, vʌɪˌtju:pə'reɪʃn, vɪˌtʃu:pə'reɪʃn, vʌɪˌtʃu:pə'reɪʃn
AM vəˌt(j)upə'reɪʃən, vaɪˌt(j)upə'reɪʃən

vituperative
BR vɪ'tju:p(ə)rətɪv, vʌɪ'tju:p(ə)rətɪv, vɪ'tʃu:p(ə)rətɪv, vʌɪ'tʃu:p(ə)rətɪv
AM və't(j)upəˌreɪdɪv, vaɪ't(j)upəˌreɪdɪv, vaɪ't(j)up(ə)rədɪv, və't(j)up(ə)rədɪv

vituperatively
BR vɪ'tju:p(ə)rətɨvli, vʌɪ'tju:p(ə)rətɨvli, vɪ'tʃu:p(ə)rətɨvli, vʌɪ'tʃu:p(ə)rətɨvli
AM və't(j)upəˌreɪdɨvli, vaɪ't(j)upəˌreɪdɨvli, vaɪ't(j)up(ə)rədɨvli, və't(j)up(ə)rədɨvli

vituperator
BR vɪ'tju:pəreɪtə(r), vʌɪ'tju:pəreɪtə(r), vɪ'tʃu:pəreɪtə(r), vʌɪ'tʃu:pəreɪtə(r), -z
AM və't(j)upəˌreɪdər, vaɪ't(j)upəˌreɪdər, -z

Vitus
BR 'vʌɪtəs
AM 'vaɪdəs

Viv
BR vɪv
AM vɪv

viva![1]
interjection
BR 'vi:və(*r*)
AM 'vivə

viva[2]
spoken examination
BR 'vʌɪvə(r), -z
AM 'vaɪvə, -z

vivace
BR vɪ'vɑ:tʃi, vɪ'vɑ:tʃeɪ
AM vi'vɑˌtʃeɪ, vi'vɑˌtʃi

vivacious
BR vɪ'veɪʃəs
AM və'veɪʃəs

vivaciously
BR vɪ'veɪʃəsli
AM və'veɪʃəsli

vivaciousness
BR vɪ'veɪʃəsnəs
AM və'veɪʃəsnəs

vivacity
BR vɪ'vasɨti
AM və'væsədi

Vivaldi
BR vɪ'valdi
AM və'vɑldi

vivaria
BR vʌɪ'vɛ:rɪə(*r*), vɪ'vɛ:rɪə(*r*)
AM və'vɛriə, vaɪ'vɛriə

vivarium
BR vʌɪ'vɛ:rɪəm, vɪ'vɛ:rɪəm, -z
AM və'vɛriəm, vaɪ'vɛriəm, -z

vivat
BR 'vʌɪvat
AM 'viˌvæt, 'vaɪˌvæt

viva-voce
BR ˌvʌɪvə'vəʊtʃ|i, ˌviːvə'vəʊtʃ|i, ˌvʌɪvə'vəʊs|i, ˌviːvə'vəʊs|i, -ɪz, -ɪɪŋ, -ɪd
AM ˌvivə 'voʊtʃeɪ, ˌvaɪvə 'voʊsi, -z, -ɪŋ, -t

vivax
BR 'vʌɪvaks
AM 'vaɪˌvæks

viverrid
BR vɪ'vɛrɪd, vʌɪ'vɛrɪd, -z
AM vaɪ'vɛrəd, və'vɛrəd, -z

viverrine
BR vɪ'vɛrʌɪn, vʌɪ'vɛrʌɪn
AM vaɪ'vɛrən, və'vɛrən, vaɪ'vɛˌraɪn, və'vɛˌraɪn

vivers
BR 'vʌɪvəz
AM 'vaɪvərz

Vivian
BR 'vɪvɪən
AM 'vɪviən

vivid
BR 'vɪvɪd
AM 'vɪvɨd

vividly
BR 'vɪvɨdli
AM 'vɪvɨdli

vividness
BR 'vɪvɨdnɨs
AM 'vɪvɨdnɨs

Vivien
BR 'vɪvɪən
AM 'vɪviən

Vivienne
BR 'vɪvɪən, ˌvɪvɪ'ɛn
AM vɪvi'ɛn

vivification
BR ˌvɪvɨfɪ'keɪʃn
AM ˌvɪvəfə'keɪʃən

vivify
BR 'vɪvɨfʌɪ, -z, -ɪŋ, -d
AM 'vɪvəˌfaɪ, -z, -ɪŋ, -d

viviparity
BR ˌvɪvɪ'parɨti
AM ˌvɪvə'pɛrədi

viviparous
BR vɪ'vɪp(ə)rəs, vʌɪ'vɪp(ə)rəs
AM və'vɪp(ə)rəs

viviparously
BR vɪ'vɪp(ə)rəsli, vʌɪ'vɪpə(ə)rəsli
AM və'vɪp(ə)rəsli

viviparousness
BR vɪ'vɪp(ə)rəsnəs, vʌɪ'vɪp(ə)rəsnəs
AM və'vɪp(ə)rəsnəs

vivisect
BR 'vɪvɪsɛkt, -s, -ɪŋ, -ɨd
AM 'vɪvəˌsɛk|(t), -(t)s, -tɪŋ, -təd

vivisection
BR ˌvɪvɪ'sɛkʃn, 'vɪvɪsɛkʃn
AM ˌvɪvə'sɛkʃən

vivisectional
BR ˌvɪvɪ'sɛkʃn̩(ə)l, ˌvɪvɪ'sɛkʃən(ə)l
AM ˌvɪvə'sɛkʃ(ə)nəl

vivisectionist
BR ˌvɪvɪ'sɛkʃn̩ɪst, ˌvɪvɪ'sɛkʃənɪst, -s
AM ˌvɪvə'sɛkʃ(ə)nəst, -s

vivisector
BR 'vɪvɪsɛktə(r), -z
AM 'vɪvəˌsɛktər, -z

vivo
BR 'viːvəʊ
AM 'viˌvoʊ

vixen
BR 'vɪks(ə)n, -z
AM 'vɪksən, -z

vixenish
BR 'vɪksənɪʃ, 'vɪksn̩ɪʃ
AM 'vɪksənɪʃ

vixenly
BR 'vɪks(ə)nli
AM 'vɪksənli

Viyella®
BR vʌɪ'ɛlə(r)
AM ˌvaɪ'ɛlə

viz
BR vɪz
AM vɪz

vizard
BR 'vɪzəd, -z
AM 'vɪzərd, -z

vizcacha
BR vɪ'skɑːtʃə(r), vɪz'kɑːtʃə(r), vɪ'skatʃə(r), vɪz'katʃə(r), -z
AM və'skɑtʃə, -z

vizier
BR vɪ'zɪə(r), 'vɪzɪə(r), -z
AM və'zɪ(ə)r, -z

vizierate
BR vɪ'zɪərət, 'vɪzɪərət, vɪ'zɪəreɪt, 'vɪzɪəreɪt, -s
AM və'zɪrət, və'zɪˌreɪt, -s

vizierial
BR vɪ'zɪərɪəl
AM və'zɪriəl

viziership
BR vɪ'zɪəʃɪp, 'vɪzɪəʃɪp, -s
AM və'zɪrˌʃɪp, -s

vizor
BR 'vʌɪzə(r), -z
AM 'vaɪzər, -z

Vlach
BR vlɑːk, -s
AM vlɑk, vlæk, -s

Vlad
BR vlad
AM vlæd

Vladimir
BR 'vladɪmɪə(r)
AM 'vlædəˌmɪ(ə)r
RUS vla'dʲimʲir

Vladivostok
BR ˌvladɪ'vɒstɒk
AM ˌvlædə'vɑstɑk
RUS vlədʲiva'stok

vlei
BR fleɪ, vlʌɪ, -z
AM fleɪ, vleɪ, -z

Vlissingen
BR 'vlɪsɪŋən
AM 'vlɪsɪŋən

Vlorë
BR 'vlɔːrə(r)
AM 'vlɔrə

Vltava
BR 'v(ə)ltəvə(r)
AM 'vəldəvə

V-neck
BR 'viːnɛk, ˌviː'nɛk, -s, -t
AM 'viˌnɛk, -s, -t

vocab
BR 'vəʊkab, -z
AM 'voʊˌkæb, -z

vocable
BR 'vəʊkəbl, -z
AM 'voʊkəbəl, -z

vocabulary
BR və(ʊ)'kabjʉlər|i, -ɪz
AM voʊ'kæbjəˌlɛri, və'kæbjəˌlɛri, -z

vocal
BR 'vəʊkl
AM 'voʊkəl

vocalese
BR ˌvəʊkə'liːz, ˌvəʊkl'iːz
AM ˌvoʊkə'liz

vocalic
BR və(ʊ)'kalɪk
AM voʊ'kælɪk, və'kælɪk

vocalisation
BR ˌvəʊkəlʌɪ'zeɪʃn, ˌvəʊkl̩ʌɪ'zeɪʃn, -z
AM ˌvoʊkələ'zeɪʃən, ˌvoʊkəˌlaɪ'zeɪʃən, -z

vocalise
BR 'vəʊkəlʌɪz, 'vəʊkl̩ʌɪz, -ɨz, -ɪŋ, -d
AM 'voʊkəˌlaɪz, -ɨz, -ɪŋ, -d

vocaliser
BR 'vəʊkəlʌɪzə(r), 'vəʊkl̩ʌɪzə(r), -z
AM 'voʊkəˌlaɪzər, -z

vocalism
BR 'vəʊkəlɪz(ə)m, 'vəʊkl̩ɪz(ə)m, -z
AM 'voʊkəˌlɪzəm, -z

vocalist
BR 'vəʊkəlɪst, 'vəʊkl̩ɪst, -s
AM 'voʊkələst, -s

vocality
BR və(ʊ)'kalɨti
AM voʊ'kælədi

vocalization
BR ˌvəʊkəlʌɪ'zeɪʃn, ˌvəʊkl̩ʌɪ'zeɪʃn, -z
AM ˌvoʊkələ'zeɪʃən, ˌvoʊkəˌlaɪ'zeɪʃən, -z

vocalize
BR 'vəʊkəlʌɪz, 'vəʊkl̩ʌɪz, -ɨz, -ɪŋ, -d
AM 'voʊkəˌlaɪz, -ɨz, -ɪŋ, -d

vocalizer
BR 'vəʊkəlʌɪzə(r), 'vəʊkl̩ʌɪzə(r), -z
AM 'voʊkəˌlaɪzər, -z

vocally
BR 'vəʊkl̩i, 'vəʊkəli
AM 'voʊk(ə)li

vocation
BR və(ʊ)'keɪʃn, -z
AM voʊ'keɪʃən, -z

vocational
BR və(ʊ)'keɪʃn̩(ə)l, və(ʊ)'keɪʃən(ə)l
AM voʊ'keɪʃ(ə)nəl

vocationalise
BR və(ʊ)'keɪʃn̩əlʌɪz, və(ʊ)'keɪʃn̩l̩ʌɪz, və(ʊ)'keɪʃənl̩ʌɪz, və(ʊ)'keɪʃ(ə)nəlʌɪz, -ɨz, -ɪŋ, -d
AM voʊ'keɪʃ(ə)nəˌlaɪz, -ɨz, -ɪŋ, -d

vocationalism
BR və(ʊ)'keɪʃn̩əlɪz(ə)m, və(ʊ)'keɪʃn̩l̩ɪz(ə)m, və(ʊ)'keɪʃ(ə)nl̩ɪz(ə)m, və(ʊ)'keɪʃ(ə)nəlɪz(ə)m
AM voʊ'keɪʃ(ə)nəˌlɪzəm

vocationalize
BR və(ʊ)'keɪʃn̩əlʌɪz, və(ʊ)'keɪʃn̩l̩ʌɪz, və(ʊ)'keɪʃənl̩ʌɪz, və(ʊ)'keɪʃ(ə)nəlʌɪz, -ɨz, -ɪŋ, -d
AM voʊ'keɪʃ(ə)nəˌlaɪz, -ɨz, -ɪŋ, -d

vocationally
BR və(ʊ)'keɪʃn̩əli, və(ʊ)'keɪʃn̩l̩i, və(ʊ)'keɪʃənl̩i, və(ʊ)'keɪʃ(ə)nəli
AM voʊ'keɪʃ(ə)nəli

vocative
BR 'vɒkətɪv, -z
AM 'vɑkədɪv, -z

Voce
BR vəʊs

AM voʊs

vociferance
BR və(ʊ)'sɪf(ə)rəns, və(ʊ)'sɪf(ə)rn̩s
AM və'sɪfərəns

vociferant
BR və(ʊ)'sɪf(ə)rənt, və(ʊ)'sɪf(ə)rn̩t, -s
AM və'sɪfərənt, -s

vociferate
BR və(ʊ)'sɪfəreɪt, -s, -ɪŋ, -ɨd
AM və'sɪfə,reɪ|t, -ts, -dɪŋ, -dɨd

vociferation
BR və(ʊ),sɪfə'reɪʃn, -z
AM və,sɪfə'reɪʃən, -z

vociferator
BR və(ʊ)'sɪfəreɪtə(r), -z
AM və'sɪfə,reɪdər, -z

vociferous
BR və(ʊ)'sɪf(ə)rəs
AM və'sɪfərəs

vociferously
BR və(ʊ)'sɪf(ə)rəsli
AM və'sɪfərəsli

vociferousness
BR və(ʊ)'sɪf(ə)rəsnəs
AM və'sɪfərəsnəs

vocoder
BR ,vəʊ'kəʊdə(r), -z
AM 'voʊ,koʊdər, -z

vocoid
BR 'vəʊkɔɪd, -z
AM 'voʊ,kɔɪd, -z

Vodaphone®
BR 'vəʊdəfəʊn
AM 'voʊdə,foʊn

vodka
BR 'vɒdkə(r), -z
AM 'vɑdkə, -z

vodun
BR 'vəʊduːn
AM 'voʊdun

voe
BR vəʊ, -z
AM voʊ, -z

Vogel
BR 'vəʊgl
AM 'voʊgəl

vogue
BR vəʊg, -z
AM voʊg, -z

voguish
BR 'vəʊgɪʃ
AM 'voʊgɪʃ

voguishness
BR 'vəʊgɪʃnɨs
AM 'voʊgɪʃnɨs

voice
BR vɔɪs, -ɨz, -ɪŋ, -t
AM vɔɪs, -ɨz, -ɪŋ, -t

voiceful
BR 'vɔɪsf(ʊ)l
AM 'vɔɪsfəl

voiceless
BR 'vɔɪslɨs
AM 'vɔɪslɨs

voicelessly
BR 'vɔɪslɨsli
AM 'vɔɪslɨsli

voicelessness
BR 'vɔɪslɨsnɨs
AM 'vɔɪslɨsnɨs

voiceprint
BR 'vɔɪsprɪnt, -s
AM 'vɔɪs,prɪnt, -s

voicer
BR 'vɔɪsə(r), -z
AM 'vɔɪsər, -z

voicing
BR 'vɔɪsɪŋ, -z
AM 'vɔɪsɪŋ, -z

void
BR vɔɪd, -z, -ɪŋ, -ɨd
AM vɔɪd, -z, -ɪŋ, -ɨd

voidable
BR 'vɔɪdəbl
AM 'vɔɪdəbəl

voidance
BR 'vɔɪdns
AM 'vɔɪdəns

voidness
BR 'vɔɪdnɨs
AM 'vɔɪdnɨs

voilà
BR vwʌ'lɑː(r), vwʌ'la(r)
AM vwɑ'lɑ

voile
BR vɔɪl, vwɑːl
AM vɔɪl

vol
BR vɒl, -z
AM vɑl, -z

vol.
BR vɒl, -z
AM vɑl, -z

volant
BR 'vəʊlənt
AM 'voʊlənt

Volapük
BR 'vɒləpʊk, 'vɒləpuːk, 'vəʊləpʊk, 'vəʊləpuːk
AM 'voʊlə,pʊk, 'vɔlə,pʊk

volar
BR 'vəʊlə(r)
AM 'voʊlər

volatile[1]
adjective
BR 'vɒlətʌɪl
AM 'vɑlədl

volatile[2]
in 'sal volatile'
BR və'latɨli, və'latl̩i
AM və'lɑdli

volatileness
BR 'vɒlətʌɪlnɨs
AM 'vɑlədlnəs

volatilisable
BR və'latɨlʌɪzəbl, 'vɒlətɨlʌɪzəbl
AM 'vɑlədl,aɪzəbəl

volatilisation
BR və,latɨlʌɪ'zeɪʃn, ,vɒlətɨlʌɪ'zeɪʃn
AM ,vɑlədl̩ə'zeɪʃən, ,vɑlədl,aɪ'zeɪʃən

volatilise
BR və'latɨlʌɪz, 'vɒlətɨlʌɪz, -ɨz, -ɪŋ, -d
AM 'vɑlədl,aɪz, -ɨz, -ɪŋ, -d

volatility
BR ,vɒlə'tɪlɨti
AM ,vɑlə'tɪlɨdi

volatilizable
BR və'latɨlʌɪzəbl, 'vɒlətɨlʌɪzəbl
AM 'vɑlədl,aɪzəbəl

volatilization
BR və,latɨlʌɪ'zeɪʃn, ,vɒlətɨlʌɪ'zeɪʃn
AM ,vɑlədl̩ə'zeɪʃən, ,vɑlədl,aɪ'zeɪʃən

volatilize
BR və'latɨlʌɪz, 'vɒlətɨlʌɪz, -ɨz, -ɪŋ, -d
AM 'vɑlədl,aɪz, -ɨz, -ɪŋ, -d

vol-au-vent
BR 'vɒləvɒ̃, -z
AM ¦vɔlə¦vɑn, -z

volcanic
BR vɒl'kanɪk
AM vɔl'kænɪk, vɑl'kænɪk

volcanically
BR vɒl'kanɨkli
AM vɔl'kænək(ə)li, vɑl'kænək(ə)li

volcanicity
BR ,vɒlkə'nɪsɨti
AM ,vɔlkə'nɪsɨdi, ,vɑlkə'nɪsɨdi

volcanism
BR 'vɒlkənɪz(ə)m
AM 'vɔlkə,nɪzəm, 'vɑlkə,nɪzəm

volcano
BR vɒl'keɪnəʊ, -z
AM vɔl'keɪnoʊ, vɑl'keɪnoʊ, -z

volcanological
BR ,vɒlkənə'lɒdʒɨkl, ,vɒlkn̩ə'lɒdʒɨkl
AM ,vɔlkænl'ɑdʒəkəl, ,vɑlkænl'ɑdʒəkəl

volcanologist
BR ,vɒlkə'nɒlədʒɪst, -s
AM ,vɔlkə'nɑlədʒəst, ,vɑlkə'nɑlədʒəst, -s

volcanology
BR ,vɒlkə'nɒlədʒi
AM ,vɔlkə'nɑlədʒi, ,vɑlkə'nɑlədʒi

vole
BR vəʊl, -z
AM voʊl, -z

volet
BR 'vɒleɪ, -z
AM voʊ'leɪ, -z

Volga
BR 'vɒlgə(r)
AM 'voʊlgə

Volgograd
BR 'vɒlgəgrad
AM 'voʊlgə,græd
RUS vəlga'grat

volitant
BR 'vɒlɨt(ə)nt
AM 'vɑlədənt, 'vɑlətnt

volition
BR və'lɪʃn̩
AM voʊ'lɪʃən, və'lɪʃən

volitional
BR və'lɪʃn̩(ə)l, və'lɪʃən(ə)l
AM voʊ'lɪʃ(ə)nəl, və'lɪʃ(ə)nəl

volitionally
BR və'lɪʃn̩əli, və'lɪʃn̩l̩i, və'lɪʃənl̩i, və'lɪʃ(ə)nəli
AM və'lɪʃ(ə)nəli, voʊ'lɪʃ(ə)nəli

volitive
BR 'vɒlɨtɪv
AM 'vɑlədɪv

Volk[1]
German 'people'
BR fɒlk, vɒlk
AM fɔ(l)k, foʊ(l)k

Volk[2]
surname
BR vɒlk
AM voʊk

Völkerwanderung
BR 'fəːlkə,vɑːndərʊŋ
AM 'fəlkə(r),vɑndə,rʊŋ

Völkerwanderungen
BR 'fəːlkə,vɑːndərʊŋən
AM 'fəlkə(r),vɑndə,rʊŋən

völkisch
BR 'fəːlkɪʃ
AM 'fəlkɪʃ

Volkswagen®
BR 'vɒlks,wag(ə)n, 'fɒlks,vɑːg(ə)n, -z
AM 'voʊ(l)ks,wægən, 'voʊ(l)ks,wɑgən, -z

volley
BR 'vɒl|i, -ɪz, -ɪɪŋ, -ɪd
AM 'vɑli, -z, -ɪŋ, -d

volleyball
BR 'vɒlɪbɔːl
AM 'vɑli,bɔl, 'vɑli,bɑl

volleyer
BR 'vɒlɪə(r), -z
AM 'vɑliər, -z

Vólos
BR 'vəʊlɒs
AM 'voʊ,lɔs, 'voʊ,lɑs
GR 'vɔlɔs

volplane
BR 'vɒpleɪn, -z, -ɪŋ, -d
AM 'vɑlˌpleɪn, -z, -ɪŋ, -d

Volpone
BR vɒl'pəʊni
AM vɔl'pouni, voʊl'pouni

Volscian
BR 'vɒlskɪən, -z
AM 'vɑlʃən, -z

Volski
BR 'vɒlski, 'vɒlski:
AM 'vɔlski, 'vɑlski

volt
BR vəʊlt, vɒlt, -s
AM voʊlt, -s

Volta[1]
African lake and river
BR 'vɒltə(r)
AM 'voʊltə

Volta[2]
physicist
BR 'vəʊltə(r), 'vɒltə(r)
AM 'voʊltə

volta
BR 'vɒltə(r), -z
AM 'voʊltə, -z

voltage
BR 'vəʊlt|ɪdʒ, 'vɒlt|ɪdʒ, -ɪdʒɪz
AM 'voʊltɪdʒ, -ɪz

voltaic
BR vɒl'teɪɪk
AM vɑl'teɪɪk, voʊl'teɪɪk

Voltaire
BR vɒl'tɛː(r), 'vɒltɛː(r)
AM vɔl'tɛ(ə)r, vɑl'tɛ(ə)r

voltameter
BR vɒl'tamɪtə(r), -z
AM voʊl'tæmədər, -z

volte
BR vɒlt, vəʊlt, -s
AM 'vɑlt(ə), 'voʊlt(ə), -z

volte-face
BR ˌvɒlt'fɑːs, ˌvɒlt'fas, -ɪz
AM ˌvɑlt(ə)'fɑs, ˌvoʊlt(ə)'fɑs, -əz

voltmeter
BR 'vəʊltˌmiːtə(r), 'vɒltˌmiːtə(r), -z
AM 'voʊltˌmidər, -z

volubility
BR ˌvɒljʊ'bɪlɪti
AM ˌvɑljə'bɪlɪdi

voluble
BR 'vɒljʊbl
AM 'vɑljəbəl

volubleness
BR 'vɒljʊblnəs
AM 'vɑljəbəlnəs

volubly
BR 'vɒljʊbli
AM 'vɑljəbli

volume
BR 'vɒljuːm, -z, -d
AM 'vɑlˌjum, 'vɑljəm, -z, -d

volumetric
BR ˌvɒljʊ'mɛtrɪk
AM ˌvɑljə'mɛtrɪk

volumetrical
BR ˌvɒljʊ'mɛtrɪkl
AM ˌvɑljə'mɛtrəkəl

volumetrically
BR ˌvɒljʊ'mɛtrɪkli
AM ˌvɑljə'mɛtrək(ə)li

voluminosity
BR vəˌl(j)uːmɪ'nɒsɪti
AM vəˌl(j)umə'nɑsədi

voluminous
BR və'l(j)uːmɪnəs
AM və'l(j)umənəs

voluminously
BR və'l(j)uːmɪnəsli
AM və'l(j)umənəsli

voluminousness
BR və'l(j)uːmɪnəsnəs
AM və'l(j)umənəsnəs

voluntarily
BR 'vɒləntrɪli, 'vɒln̩trɪli
AM ˌvɑlən'tɛrəli

voluntariness
BR 'vɒləntrɪnɪs, 'vɒln̩trɪnɪs
AM ˌvɑlən'tɛrinɪs

voluntarism
BR 'vɒlənt(ə)rɪz(ə)m, 'vɒln̩t(ə)rɪz(ə)m
AM 'vɑlən(t)əˌrɪzəm

voluntarist
BR 'vɒlənt(ə)rɪst, 'vɒln̩t(ə)rɪst
AM 'vɑlən(t)ərəst

voluntary
BR 'vɒlənt(ə)r|i, vɒln̩t(ə)r|i, -ɪz
AM 'vɑlənˌtɛri, -z

voluntary-aided
BR ˌvɒlənt(ə)rɪ'eɪdɪd, ˌvɒln̩t(ə)rɪ'eɪdɪd
AM 'vɑlənˌtɛriˌeɪdɪd

voluntaryism
BR 'vɒlənt(ə)rɪɪz(ə)m, 'vɒln̩t(ə)rɪɪz(ə)m
AM 'vɑlənˌtɛriˌɪzəm

voluntaryist
BR 'vɒlənt(ə)rɪɪst, 'vɒln̩t(ə)rɪɪst, -s
AM 'vɑlənˌtɛriɪst, -s

volunteer
BR ˌvɒlən'tɪə(r), ˌvɒln̩'tɪə(r), -z, -ɪŋ, -d
AM ˌvɑlən'tɪ(ə)r, -z, -ɪŋ, -d

volunteerism
BR ˌvɒlən'tɪərɪz(ə)m, ˌvɒln̩'tɪərɪz(ə)m
AM ˌvɑlən'tɪ(ə)ˌrɪzəm

voluptuary
BR və'lʌptʃʊər|i, və'lʌptʃ(ʊ)r|i, və'lʌptjʊər|i, və'lʌptjʊr|i, -ɪz
AM və'ləp(t)ʃəˌwɛri, -z

voluptuous
BR və'lʌptʃʊəs, və'lʌptjʊəs
AM və'ləp(t)ʃ(əw)əs

voluptuously
BR və'lʌptʃʊəsli, və'lʌptjʊəsli
AM və'ləp(t)ʃ(əw)əsli

voluptuousness
BR və'lʌptʃʊəsnəs, və'lʌptjʊəsnəs
AM və'ləp(t)ʃ(əw)əsnəs

volute
BR və'l(j)uːt, -s, -ɪd
AM və'l(j)u|t, -ts, -dəd

voluted
BR və'l(j)uːtɪd
AM və'l(j)udəd

volution
BR və'l(j)uːʃn, -z
AM və'luʃən, -z

Volvo®
BR 'vɒlvəʊ, -z
AM 'vɔlˌvoʊ, 'vɑlˌvoʊ, -z

volvox
BR 'vɒlvɒks
AM 'vɑlˌvɑks

vomer
BR 'vəʊmə(r), -z
AM 'voʊmər, -z

vomit
BR 'vɒm|ɪt, -ɪts, -ɪtɪŋ, -ɪtɪd
AM 'vɑmə|t, -ts, -dɪŋ, -dəd

vomiter
BR 'vɒmɪtə(r), -z
AM 'vɑmədər, -z

vomitoria
BR ˌvɒmɪ'tɔːrɪə(r)
AM ˌvɑmə'tɔriə

vomitorium
BR ˌvɒmɪ'tɔːrɪəm
AM ˌvɑmə'tɔriəm

vomitory
BR 'vɒmɪt(ə)r|i, -ɪz
AM 'vɑməˌtɔri, -z

vomitus
BR 'vɒmɪtəs
AM 'vɑmədəs

von
BR vɒn, fɒn
AM vɑn

Vonnegut
BR 'vɒnɪgʌt
AM 'vɑnəgət

voodoo
BR 'vuːduː
AM 'vuˌdu

voodooism
BR 'vuːduːɪz(ə)m
AM 'vuˌduˌɪzəm

voodooist
BR 'vuːduːɪst, -s
AM 'vuˌduəst, -s

Voortrekker
BR 'fʊəˌtrɛkə(r), 'vʊəˌtrɛkə(r), 'fɔːˌtrɛkə(r), 'vɔːˌtrɛkə(r)
AM 'fʊrˌtrɛkər, 'fɔrˌtrɛkər, 'vʊrˌtrɛkər, 'vɔrˌtrɛkər

Vopo
BR 'fəʊpəʊ, -z
AM 'voʊˌpoʊ, -z

voracious
BR və'reɪʃəs
AM və'reɪʃəs

voraciously
BR və'reɪʃəsli
AM və'reɪʃəsli

voraciousness
BR və'reɪʃəsnəs
AM və'reɪʃəsnəs

voracity
BR və'rasɪti
AM və'ræsədi

Vorarlberg
BR 'fɔːrɑːlbəːg
AM 'fɔrˌɑrlˌbərg

Vorster
BR 'vɔːstə(r)
AM 'vɔrstər

vortex
BR 'vɔːtɛks, -ɪz
AM 'vɔrˌtɛks, -əz

vortex ring
BR 'vɔːtɛks rɪŋ, -z
AM 'vɔrˌtɛks ˌrɪŋ, -z

vortical
BR 'vɔːtɪkl
AM 'vɔrdəkəl

vortically
BR 'vɔːtɪkli
AM 'vɔrdək(ə)li

vorticella
BR ˌvɔːtɪ'sɛlə(r), -z
AM ˌvɔrdə'sɛlə, -z

vortices
BR 'vɔːtɪsiːz
AM 'vɔrdəˌsiz

vorticism
BR 'vɔːtɪsɪz(ə)m
AM 'vɔrdəˌsɪzəm

vorticist
BR 'vɔːtɪsɪst, -s
AM 'vɔrdəsəst, -s

vorticity
BR vɔː'tɪsɪti
AM vɔr'tɪsɪdi

vorticose
BR 'vɔːtɪkəʊs, ˌvɔːtɪ'kəʊs
AM 'vɔrdəˌkoʊs, 'vɔrdəˌkoʊz

vorticular
BR vɔː'tɪkjʊlə(r)
AM vɔr'tɪkjələr

Vortigern
BR 'vɔːtɪɡəːn, 'vɔːtɪɡ(ə)n, 'vɔːtɪdʒəːn, 'vɔːtɪdʒ(ə)n
AM 'vɔrdəˌɡərn

Vosburgh
BR 'vɒsb(ə)rə(r)
AM 'vɑsˌbərə

Vosene
BR 'vəʊziːn
AM 'voʊˌzin

Vosges
BR vəʊʒ
AM voʊʒ

Voss
BR vɒs
AM vɔs, vɑs

Vostok
BR 'vɒstɒk
AM 'vɑˌstɑk

votable
BR 'vəʊtəbl
AM 'voʊdəbəl

votaress
BR 'vəʊt(ə)rɪs, 'vəʊtərɛs, -ɪz
AM 'voʊdərɛs, -əz

votarist
BR 'vəʊt(ə)rɪst, -s
AM 'voʊdərəst, -s

votary
BR 'vəʊt(ə)r|i, -ɪz
AM 'voʊdəri, -z

vote
BR vəʊt, -s, -ɪŋ, -ɪd
AM voʊ|t, -ts, -dɪŋ, -dəd

voteless
BR 'vəʊtləs
AM 'voʊtləs

voter
BR 'vəʊtə(r), -z
AM 'voʊdər, -z

voting machine
BR 'vəʊtɪŋ məˌʃiːn, -z
AM 'voʊdɪŋ məˌʃin, -z

voting paper
BR 'vəʊtɪŋ ˌpeɪpə(r), -z
AM 'voʊdɪŋ ˌpeɪpər, -z

votive
BR 'vəʊtɪv
AM 'voʊdɪv

vouch
BR vaʊtʃ, -ɪz, -ɪŋ, -t
AM vaʊtʃ, -əz, -ɪŋ, -t

voucher
BR 'vaʊtʃə(r), -z
AM 'vaʊtʃər, -z

vouchsafe
BR (ˌ)vaʊtʃ'seɪf, -s, -ɪŋ, -t
AM vaʊtʃ'seɪf, 'vaʊtʃˌseɪf, -s, -ɪŋ, -t

voussoir
BR 'vuːswɑː(r), -z
AM vu'swɑr, -z

Vouvray
BR 'vuːvreɪ, -z
AM vu'vreɪ, -z

vow
BR vaʊ, -z, -ɪŋ, -d
AM vaʊ, -z, -ɪŋ, -d

vowel
BR 'vaʊəl, vaʊl, -z, -d
AM 'vaʊ(ə)l, -z, -d

vowelise
BR 'vaʊ(ə)lʌɪz, -ɪz, -ɪŋ, -d
AM 'vaʊəˌlaɪz, -ɪz, -ɪŋ, -d

vowelize
BR 'vaʊ(ə)lʌɪz, -ɪz, -ɪŋ, -d
AM 'vaʊəˌlaɪz, -ɪz, -ɪŋ, -d

vowelless
BR 'vaʊ(ə)lləs
AM 'vaʊ(ə)(l)ləs

vowelly
BR 'vaʊ(ə)lli
AM 'vaʊ(ə)li

vowel-point
BR 'vaʊ(ə)lpɔɪnt, -s
AM 'vaʊ(ə)lˌpɔɪnt, -s

Vowles
BR vəʊlz, vaʊlz
AM voʊlz, vaʊlz

vox angelica
BR ˌvɒks an'dʒɛlɪkə(r)
AM ˌvɑks æn'dʒɛlɪkə

vox humana
BR ˌvɒks hjuː'mɑːnə(r)
AM ˌvɑks (h)ju'mɑnə

vox pop
BR ˌvɒks 'pɒp, -s
AM ˌvɑks 'pɑp, -s

vox populi
BR ˌvɒks 'pɒpjʉliː, + 'pɒpjʉlʌɪ
AM ˌvɑks 'pɑpjəˌlaɪ

voyage
BR 'vɔɪ(ɪ)dʒ, vɔɪdʒ, -ɪz, -ɪŋ, -d
AM 'vɔɪ(ɪ)dʒ, -ɪz, -ɪŋ, -d

voyageable
BR 'vɔɪ(ɪ)dʒəbl
AM 'vɔɪ(ɪ)dʒəbəl

voyager
BR 'vɔɪ(ɪ)dʒə(r), -z
AM 'vɔɪ(ɪ)dʒər, -z

voyageur
BR ˌvwɑːjə'ʒəː(r), -z
AM ˌvwɑjə'ʒɛ(ə)r, -z

voyeur
BR (ˌ)vɔɪ'jəː(r), (ˌ)vwɑː'jəː(r), (ˌ)vwʌɪ'jəː(r), -z
AM vɔɪ'jər, -z

voyeurism
BR 'vɔɪjərɪz(ə)m, (ˌ)vɔɪ'(j)əːrɪz(ə)m, (ˌ)vwʌɪ'(j)əːrɪz(ə)m, (ˌ)vwɑː'jəːrɪz(ə)m
AM 'vɔɪjəˌrɪzəm

voyeuristic
BR ˌvɔɪə'rɪstɪk, ˌvwʌɪə'rɪstɪk, ˌvwɑːjə'rɪstɪk
AM ˌvɔɪjə'rɪstɪk

voyeuristically
BR ˌvɔɪə'rɪstɪkli, ˌvwʌɪə'rɪstɪkli, ˌvwɑːjə'rɪstɪkli
AM ˌvɔɪjə'rɪstək(ə)li

vraic
BR vreɪk
AM vreɪk

vroom
BR vruːm, -z, -ɪŋ, -d
AM vrum, -z, -ɪŋ, -d

vs
BR 'vəːsəs
AM 'vərsəs

V-sign
BR 'viːsʌɪn, -z
AM 'viˌsaɪn, -z

V/STOL
BR 'viːstɒl
AM 'viˌstɑl

VTOL
BR 'viːtɒl
AM 'viˌtɑl

vug
BR vʌɡ, -z
AM vəɡ, vʊɡ, -z

vuggy
BR 'vʌɡi
AM 'vəɡi, 'vʊɡi

vugular
BR 'vʌɡjʉlə(r)
AM 'vəɡjələr, 'vʊɡjələr

Vulcan
BR 'vʌlk(ə)n
AM 'vəlkən

Vulcanian
BR vʌl'keɪnɪən, -z
AM vəl'keɪniən, -z

vulcanic
BR vʌl'kanɪk
AM vəl'kænɪk

vulcanisable
BR 'vʌlkənʌɪzəbl
AM 'vəlkəˌnaɪzəbəl

vulcanisation
BR ˌvʌlkənʌɪ'zeɪʃn
AM ˌvəlkənə'zeɪʃən, ˌvəlkəˌnaɪ'zeɪʃən

vulcanise
BR 'vʌlkənʌɪz, -ɪz, -ɪŋ, -d
AM 'vəlkəˌnaɪz, -ɪz, -ɪŋ, -d

vulcaniser
BR 'vʌlkənʌɪzə(r), -z
AM 'vəlkəˌnaɪzər, -z

vulcanism
BR 'vʌlkənɪz(ə)m
AM 'vəlkəˌnɪzəm

Vulcanist
BR 'vʌlkənɪst, -s
AM 'vəlkənəst, -s

vulcanite
BR 'vʌlkənʌɪt
AM 'vəlkəˌnaɪt

vulcanizable
BR 'vʌlkənʌɪzəbl
AM 'vəlkəˌnaɪzəbəl

vulcanization
BR ˌvʌlkənʌɪ'zeɪʃn
AM ˌvəlkənə'zeɪʃən, ˌvəlkəˌnaɪ'zeɪʃən

vulcanize
BR 'vʌlkənʌɪz, -ɪz, -ɪŋ, -d
AM 'vəlkəˌnaɪz, -ɪz, -ɪŋ, -d

vulcanizer
BR 'vʌlkənʌɪzə(r), -z
AM 'vəlkəˌnaɪzər, -z

vulcanological
BR ˌvʌlkənə'lɒdʒɪkl, ˌvʌlkn̩ə'lɒdʒɪkl
AM ˌvəlkənə'lɑdʒəkəl

vulcanologist
BR ˌvʌlkə'nɒlədʒɪst, -s
AM ˌvəlkə'nɑlədʒəst, -s

vulcanology
BR ˌvʌlkə'nɒlədʒi
AM ˌvəlkə'nɑlədʒi

vulgar
BR 'vʌlɡə(r)
AM 'vəlɡər

vulgarian
BR vʌl'ɡɛːrɪən, -z
AM vəl'ɡɛriən, -z

vulgarisation
BR ˌvʌlɡ(ə)rʌɪ'zeɪʃn
AM ˌvəlɡərə'zeɪʃən, ˌvəlɡəˌraɪ'zeɪʃən

vulgarise
BR 'vʌlɡərʌɪz, -ɪz, -ɪŋ, -d
AM 'vəlɡəˌraɪz, -ɪz, -ɪŋ, -d

vulgarism
BR 'vʌlɡərɪz(ə)m, -z
AM 'vəlɡəˌrɪzəm, -z

vulgarity
BR vʌl'ɡarɪt|i, -ɪz
AM vəl'ɡɛrədi, -z

vulgarization
BR ˌvʌlɡ(ə)rʌɪ'zeɪʃn
AM ˌvəlɡərə'zeɪʃən, ˌvəlɡəˌraɪ'zeɪʃən

vulgarize
BR 'vʌlɡərʌɪz, -ɪz, -ɪŋ, -d
AM 'vəlɡəˌraɪz, -ɪz, -ɪŋ, -d

vulgarly
BR 'vʌlɡəli
AM 'vəlɡərli

vulgate
BR 'vʌlɡeɪt, 'vʌlɡət
AM 'vəlˌɡeɪt

vulnerability
BR ˌvʌln(ə)rə'bɪlɪti
AM ˌvəln(ə)rə'bɪlɪdi

vulnerable
BR ˈvʌln(ə)rəbl
AM ˈvəlnər(ə)bəl

vulnerableness
BR ˈvʌln(ə)rəblnəs
AM ˈvəlnər(ə)bəlnəs

vulnerably
BR ˈvʌln(ə)rəbli
AM ˈvəlnər(ə)bli

vulnerary
BR ˈvʌln(ə)rər|i, -ɪz
AM ˈvəlnəˌrɛri, -z

vulpine
BR ˈvʌlpʌɪn
AM ˈvəlˌpaɪn

vulture
BR ˈvʌltʃə(r), -z
AM ˈvəltʃər, -z

vulturine
BR ˈvʌltʃʊrʌɪn
AM ˈvəltʃərən

vulturish
BR ˈvʌltʃ(ə)rɪʃ
AM ˈvəltʃ(ə)rɪʃ

vulturous
BR ˈvʌltʃ(ə)rəs
AM ˈvəltʃ(ə)rəs

vulva
BR ˈvʌlvə(r), -z
AM ˈvəlvə, -z

vulval
BR ˈvʌlvl
AM ˈvəlvəl

vulvar
BR ˈvʌlvə(r)
AM ˈvəlvər

vulvitis
BR vʌlˈvʌɪtɪs
AM vəlˈvaɪdɪs

vying
BR ˈvʌɪɪŋ
AM ˈvaɪɪŋ

Vyrnwy
BR ˈvəːnwi
AM ˈvərnwi
WE ˈvʌrnwi

Vyvyan
BR ˈvɪvɪən
AM ˈvɪviən

Ww

w
BR ˈdʌbljuː, -z
AM ˈdəbəlˌju, -z

WAAF
BR waf, -s
AM wæf, -s

Waal
BR vɑːl
AM vɑl

Wabash
BR ˈwɔːbaʃ
AM ˈwɔˌbæʃ, ˈwɑˌbæʃ

WAC
BR wak, -s
AM wæk, -s

Wace
BR weɪs
AM wɑs, weɪs

wack
BR wak
AM wæk

wacke
BR ˈwakə(r), -z
AM ˈwækə, -z

wackily
BR ˈwakɨli
AM ˈwækəli

wackiness
BR ˈwakɪnɪs
AM ˈwækinɪs

wacko
BR ˈwakəʊ, -z
AM ˈwækoʊ, -z

wacky
BR ˈwak|i, -ɪə(r), -ɪɪst
AM ˈwæki, -ər, -ɪst

Waco
BR ˈweɪkəʊ
AM ˈweɪkoʊ

wad
BR wɒd, -z
AM wɑd, -z

wadable
BR ˈweɪdəbl
AM ˈweɪdəbəl

Waddell
BR wɒˈdɛl, wəˈdɛl
AM ˌwɑˈdɛl

wadding
BR ˈwɒdɪŋ
AM ˈwɑdɪŋ

Waddington
BR ˈwɒdɪŋt(ə)n
AM ˈwɑdɪŋtən

waddle
BR ˈwɒd|l, -lz, -l̩ɪŋ\-lɪŋ, -ld
AM ˈwɑd|əl, -əlz, -(ə)lɪŋ, -əld

waddler
BR ˈwɒdl̩ə(r), ˈwɒdlə(r), -z
AM ˈwɑd(ə)lər, -z

waddy
BR ˈwɒd|i, -ɪz
AM ˈwɑdi, -z

wade
BR weɪd, -z, -ɪŋ, -ɨd
AM weɪd, -z, -ɪŋ, -ɨd

wadeable
BR ˈweɪdəbl
AM ˈweɪdəbəl

Wadebridge
BR ˈweɪdbrɪdʒ
AM ˈweɪdˌbrɪdʒ

Wade-Giles
BR ˌweɪdˈdʒʌɪlz
AM ˌweɪdˈdʒaɪlz

wader
BR ˈweɪdə(r), -z
AM ˈweɪdər, -z

wadge
BR wɒdʒ, -ɨz
AM wɑdʒ, -əz

Wadham
BR ˈwɒdəm
AM ˈwɑdəm

wadi
BR ˈwɒd|i, -ɪz
AM ˈwɑdi, -z

Wadi Halfa
BR ˌwɒdɪ ˈhalfə(r)
AM ˌwɑdi ˈhɑlfə

Wadsworth
BR ˈwɒdzwəθ, ˈwɒdzwəːθ
AM ˈwɑdsˌwərθ

wady
BR ˈwɒd|i, -ɪz
AM ˈwɑdi, -z

WAF
BR waf, -s
AM wæf, -s

wafer
BR ˈweɪfə(r), -z
AM ˈweɪfər, -z

wafery
BR ˈweɪf(ə)ri
AM ˈweɪf(ə)ri

Waffen SS
BR ˌvɑːf(ə)n ˌɛsˈɛs, ˌvaf(ə)n +
AM ˈvɑfən ˌɛsˈɛs

waffle
BR ˈwɒf|l, -lz, -l̩ɪŋ\-lɪŋ, -ld
AM ˈwɑf|əl, -əlz, -(ə)lɪŋ, -əld

waffler
BR ˈwɒfl̩ə(r), ˈwɒflə(r), -z
AM ˈwɑf(ə)lər, -z

waffly
BR ˈwɒfl̩i, ˈwɒfli
AM ˈwɑf(ə)li

waft
BR wɑːft, wɒft, waft, -s, -ɪŋ, -ɨd
AM wɑft, -s, -ɪŋ, -əd

wag
BR wag, -z, -ɪŋ, -d
AM wæg, -z, -ɪŋ, -d

wage
BR weɪdʒ, -ɨz, -ɪŋ, -d
AM weɪdʒ, -ɨz, -ɪŋ, -d

wager
BR ˈweɪdʒ|ə(r), -əz, -(ə)rɪŋ, -əd
AM ˈweɪdʒər, -z, -ɪŋ, -d

Wagga Wagga
BR ˌwɒgə ˈwɒgə(r)
AM ˈwɑgə ˈwɑgə

waggery
BR ˈwag(ə)r|i, -ɪz
AM ˈwægəri, -z

waggish
BR ˈwagɪʃ
AM ˈwægɪʃ

waggishly
BR ˈwagɨʃli
AM ˈwægɨʃli

waggishness
BR ˈwagɪʃnɨs
AM ˈwægɪʃnɨs

waggle
BR ˈwag|l, -lz, -l̩ɪŋ\-lɪŋ, -ld
AM ˈwæg|əl, -əlz, -(ə)lɪŋ, -əld

waggly
BR ˈwagl̩i, ˈwagli
AM ˈwæg(ə)li

waggon
BR ˈwag(ə)n, -z
AM ˈwægən, -z

waggoner
BR ˈwagənə(r), ˈwagn̩ə(r)
AM ˈwægənər

waggonette
BR ˌwagəˈnɛt, -s
AM ˌwægəˈnɛt, -s

waggonful
BR ˈwag(ə)nfʊl
AM ˈwægənˌfʊl

waggonload
BR ˈwagənləʊd, -z
AM ˈwægənˌloʊd, -z

Wagnall
BR ˈwagnl
AM ˈwægnəl

Wagner[1]
English surname
BR ˈwagnə(r)
AM ˈwægnər

Wagner[2]
German surname
BR ˈvɑːgnə(r)
AM ˈvɑgnər

Wagnerian
BR vɑːgˈnɪərɪən, -z
AM vɑgˈnɛriən, -z

wagon
BR ˈwag(ə)n, -z
AM ˈwægən, -z

wagoner
BR ˈwagənə(r), ˈwagn̩ə(r), -z
AM ˈwægənər, -z

wagonette
BR ˌwagəˈnɛt, -s
AM ˌwægəˈnɛt, -s

wagonful
BR ˈwag(ə)nfʊl, -z
AM ˈwægənˌfʊl, -z

wagon-lit
BR ˌvagɒ̃ˈliː, ˌvagɒnˈliː, -z
AM ˈvɑgɔnˌli, -z

wagonload
BR ˈwag(ə)nləʊd, -z
AM ˈwægənˌloʊd, -z

wagtail
BR ˈwagteɪl, -z
AM ˈwægˌteɪl, -z

Wahabi
BR wəˈhɑːb|i, wɑːˈhɑːb|i, -ɪz
AM wəˈhɑbi, wɑˈhɑbi, -z

Wahhabi
BR wəˈhɑːb|i, wɑːˈhɑːb|i, -ɪz
AM wəˈhɑbi, wɑˈhɑbi, -z

wahine
BR wɑːˈhiːn|i, -ɪz
AM wɑˈhini, -z

wahoo
BR ˌwɑːˈhuː, wəˈhuː, -z
AM ˈwɑˈhu, -z

Wahran
BR wɑːˈrɑːn
AM wɑˈrɑn

wah-wah
BR ˈwɑːwɑː(r)
AM ˈwɑˈwɑ

waif
BR weɪf, -s
AM weɪf, -s

waifish
BR ˈweɪfɪʃ
AM ˈweɪfɪʃ

waif-like
BR ˈweɪflʌɪk
AM ˈweɪfˌlaɪk

Waikato
BR wʌɪˈkɑːtəʊ
AM ˈwaɪˌkɑdoʊ

Waikiki
BR ˌwʌɪkɪˈkiː, ˈwʌɪkɪkiː
AM ˌwaɪkiˈki

wail
BR weɪl, -z, -ɪŋ, -d
AM weɪl, -z, -ɪŋ, -d

wailer
BR ˈweɪlə(r), -z
AM ˈweɪlər, -z

wailful
BR 'weɪlf(ʊ)l
AM 'weɪlfəl
wailing
BR 'weɪlɪŋ, -z
AM 'weɪlɪŋ, -z
wailingly
BR 'weɪlɪŋli
AM 'weɪlɪŋli
wain
BR weɪn, -z
AM weɪn, -z
Waine
BR weɪn
AM weɪn
Wainfleet
BR 'weɪnfli:t
AM 'weɪn,flit
wainscot
BR 'weɪnskət, 'weɪnskɒt, -s, -ɪŋ
AM 'weɪn,skoʊ|t 'weɪnskə|t, 'weɪn,skɑ|t, -ts, -dɪŋ
wainwright
BR 'weɪnrʌɪt, -s
AM 'weɪnraɪt, -s
waist
BR weɪst, -s, -ɪd
AM weɪst, -s, -ɪd
waistband
BR 'weɪs(t)band, -z
AM 'weɪs(t),bænd, -z
waist-cloth
BR 'weɪs(t)klɒ|θ, -θs\-ðz
AM 'weɪs(t),klɔ|θ, 'weɪs(t),klɑ|θ, -θs\-ðz
waistcoat
BR 'weɪs(t)kəʊt, -s
AM 'weɪs(t),koʊt, -s
waisted
BR 'weɪstɪd
AM 'weɪstɪd
waistless
BR 'weɪstlɪs
AM 'weɪs(t)lɪs
waistline
BR 'weɪs(t)lʌɪn, -z
AM 'weɪs(t),laɪn, -z
wait
BR weɪt, -s, -ɪŋ, -ɪd
AM weɪ|t, -ts, -dɪŋ, -dɪd
Waite
BR weɪt
AM weɪt
waiter
BR 'weɪtə(r), -z
AM 'weɪdər, -z
Waites
BR weɪts
AM weɪts
waitress
BR 'weɪtrɪs, -ɪz, -ɪŋ
AM 'weɪtrɪs, -ɪz, -ɪŋ
Waitrose
BR 'weɪtrəʊz
AM 'weɪt,roʊz
waive
BR weɪv, -z, -ɪŋ, -d
AM weɪv, -z, -ɪŋ, -d
waiver
BR 'weɪvə(r), -z
AM 'weɪvər, -z
wake
BR weɪk, -s, -ɪŋ, -t
AM weɪk, -s, -ɪŋ, -t
Wakefield
BR 'weɪkfi:ld
AM 'weɪk,fild
wakeful
BR 'weɪkf(ʊ)l
AM 'weɪkfəl
wakefully
BR 'weɪkfʊli, 'weɪkfḷi
AM 'weɪkfəli
wakefulness
BR 'weɪkf(ʊ)lnəs
AM 'weɪkfəlnəs
Wakelin
BR 'weɪklɪn
AM 'weɪklɪn
waken
BR 'weɪk|(ə)n, -(ə)nz, -ṇɪŋ\-(ə)nɪŋ, -(ə)nd
AM 'weɪk|ən, -ənz, -(ə)nɪŋ, -ənd
waker
BR 'weɪkə(r), -z
AM 'weɪkər, -z
wake-robin
BR 'weɪk,rɒbɪn, -z
AM 'weɪk,rɑbən, -z
wakey-wakey
BR ,weɪkɪ'weɪki
AM 'weɪki'weɪki
Walach
BR 'wɒlək
AM 'wɑlək
Walachia
BR wɒ'leɪkɪə(*r*), wə'leɪkɪə(*r*)
AM wɑ'leɪkiə, wə'leɪkiən
Walachian
BR wɒ'leɪkɪən, wə'leɪkɪən, -z
AM wɑ'leɪkiən, wə'leɪkiən, -z
Walbrook
BR 'wɔ:lbrʊk, 'wɒlbrʊk
AM 'wɔl,brʊk, 'wɑl,brʊk
Walcot
BR 'wɔ:lkət, 'wɔ:lkɒt, 'wɒlkət, 'wɒlkɒt
AM 'wɔl,kɑt, 'wɑl,kɑt
Walcott
BR 'wɔ:lkət, 'wɔ:lkɒt, 'wɒlkət, 'wɒlkɒt
AM 'wɔl,kɑt, 'wɑl,kɑt
Waldegrave
BR 'wɔ:ld(ɪ)greɪv, 'wɒld(ɪ)greɪv, 'wɔ:lgreɪv
AM 'wɔl,greɪv, 'wɑl,greɪv
Waldemar
BR 'valdɪmɑ:(r), 'wɔ:ldɪmɑ:(r)
AM 'wɔldə,mɑr, 'wɑldə,mɑr
Walden
BR 'wɔ:ld(ə)n, 'wɒld(ə)n
AM 'wɔldən, 'wɑldən
Waldenses
BR wɔ:l'dɛnsi:z, wɒl'dɛnsi:z
AM wɔl'dɛnsiz, wɑl'dɛnsiz
Waldensian
BR wɔ:l'dɛnsɪən, wɒl'dɛnsɪən, -z
AM wɔl'dɛnsiən, wɑl'dɛnsiən, -z
Waldheim
BR 'vɑ:ldhʌɪm, 'valdhʌɪm
AM 'vɑld,(h)aɪm, 'wɔld,(h)aɪm
Waldo
BR 'wɔ:ldəʊ, 'wɒldəʊ
AM 'wɔl,doʊ, 'wɑl,doʊ
Waldorf
BR 'wɔ:ldɔ:f, 'wɒldɔ:f
AM 'wɔl,dɔ(ə)rf, 'wɑl,dɔ(ə)rf
Waldron
BR 'wɔ:ldr(ə)n, 'wɒldr(ə)n
AM 'wɔldrən, 'wɑldrən
wale
BR weɪl, -z, -ɪŋ, -d
AM weɪl, -z, -ɪŋ, -d
Wales
BR weɪlz
AM weɪlz
Waley
BR 'weɪli
AM 'weɪli
Walford
BR 'wɔ:lfəd, 'wɒlfəd
AM 'wɔlfərd, 'wɑlfərd
Walian
BR 'weɪlɪən, -z
AM 'weɪljən, 'weɪliən, -z
walk
BR wɔ:k, -s, -ɪŋ, -t
AM wɔk, wɑk, -s, -ɪŋ, -t
walkable
BR 'wɔ:kəbl
AM 'wɔkəbəl, 'wɑkəbəl
walkabout
BR 'wɔ:kəbaʊt, -s
AM 'wɔkə,baʊt, 'wɑkə,baʊt, -s
walkathon
BR 'wɔ:kəθɒn, -z
AM 'wɔkə,θɑn, 'wɑkə,θɑn, -z
walkaway
BR 'wɔ:kəweɪ, -z
AM 'wɔkə,weɪ, 'wɑkə,weɪ, -z
Walkden
BR 'wɔ:kdən
AM 'wɔkdən, 'wɑkdən
walker
BR 'wɔ:kə(r), -z
AM 'wɔkər, 'wɑkər, -z
walkies
BR 'wɔ:kɪz
AM 'wɔkiz, 'wɑkiz
walkie-talkie
BR ,wɔ:kɪ'tɔ:k|i, -ɪz
AM ',wɔki'tɔki, ',wɑki'tɑki, -z
walk-in
BR 'wɔ:kɪn, -z
AM 'wɔk,ɪn, 'wɑk,ɪn, -z
Walkman®
BR 'wɔ:kmən, -z
AM 'wɔk,mæn, 'wɔkmən, 'wɑk,mæn, 'wɑkmən, -z
walk-on
BR 'wɔ:kɒn, -z
AM 'wɔk,ɔn, 'wɑk,ɑn, -z
walkout
BR 'wɔ:kaʊt, -s
AM 'wɔk,aʊt, 'wɑk,aʊt, -s
walkover
BR 'wɔ:k,əʊvə(r), -z
AM 'wɔk,oʊvər, 'wɑk,oʊvər, -z
walk-through
BR 'wɔ:kθru:, -z
AM 'wɔk,θru, 'wɑk,θru, -z
walkup
BR 'wɔ:kʌp, -s
AM 'wɔk,əp, 'wɑk,əp, -s
walkway
BR 'wɔ:kweɪ, -z
AM 'wɔk,weɪ, 'wɑk,weɪ, -z
wall
BR wɔ:l, -z, -ɪŋ, -d
AM wɔl, wɑl, -z, -ɪŋ, -d
walla
BR 'wɒlə(*r*), -z
AM 'wɑlə, -z
wallaby
BR 'wɒləb|i, -ɪz
AM 'wɑləbi, -z
Wallace
BR 'wɒlɪs
AM 'wɔləs, 'wɑləs
Wallachia
BR wɒ'leɪkɪə(*r*), wə'leɪkɪə(*r*)
AM wɑ'leɪkiə, wə'leɪkiə

Wallachian
BR wɒˈleɪkɪən, wəˈleɪkɪən, -z
AM wɑˈleɪkiən, wəˈleɪkiən, -z

wallah
BR ˈwɒlə(*r*), -z
AM ˈwɑlə, -z

wallaroo
BR ˌwɒləˈruː, -z
AM ˌwɔləˈru, ˌwɑləˈru, -z

Wallasey
BR ˈwɒləsi
AM ˈwɔləsi, ˈwɑləsi

wallchart
BR ˈwɔːltʃɑːt, -s
AM ˈwɔlˌtʃɑrt, ˈwɑlˌtʃɑrt, -s

wallcovering
BR ˈwɔːlˌkʌv(ə)rɪŋ, -z
AM ˈwɔlˌkəv(ə)rɪŋ, ˈwɑlˌkəv(ə)rɪŋ, -z

Wallenberg
BR ˈwɒlənbəːg, ˈwɒln̩bəːg
AM ˈwɔlənˌbərg, ˈvɑlənˌbərg

Waller
BR ˈwɒlə(r)
AM ˈwɔlər, ˈwɑlər

wallet
BR ˈwɒlɪt, -s
AM ˈwɑlət, ˈwɔlət, -s

wall-eye
BR ˈwɔːlʌɪ, -z
AM ˈwɔlˌaɪ, ˈwɑlˌaɪ, -z

wall-eyed
BR ˌwɔːlˈʌɪd
AM ˈwɔlˌaɪd, ˈwɑlˌaɪd

wallflower
BR ˈwɔːlˌflaʊə(r), -z
AM ˈwɔlˌflaʊər, ˈwɑlˌflaʊər, -z

wall-hung
BR ˌwɔːlˈhʌŋ
AM ˈwɔlˌ(h)əŋ, ˈwɑlˌ(h)əŋ

Wallingford
BR ˈwɒlɪŋfəd
AM ˈwɔlɪŋfərd, ˈwɑlɪŋfərd

Wallis
BR ˈwɒlɪs
AM ˈwɔləs, ˈwɑləs

wall-less
BR ˈwɔːlləs
AM ˈwɔ(l)ləs, ˈwɑ(l)ləs

Wallonia
BR wɒˈləʊnɪə(*r*)
AM wəˈloʊniə, wɔˈloʊniə, wɑˈloʊniə

Walloon
BR wɒˈluːn, wəˈluːn, -z
AM wɑˈlun, wəˈlun, -z

wallop
BR ˈwɒləp, -s, -ɪŋ, -t
AM ˈwɑləp, -s, -ɪŋ, -t

walloper
BR ˈwɒləpə(r), -z
AM ˈwɑləpər, -z

wallow
BR ˈwɒləʊ, -z, -ɪŋ, -d
AM ˈwɑloʊ, -z, -ɪŋ, -d

wallower
BR ˈwɒləʊə(r), -z
AM ˈwɑləwər, -z

wallpaper
BR ˈwɔːlˌpeɪp|ə(r), -əz, -(ə)rɪŋ, -əd
AM ˈwɔlˌpeɪp|ər, ˈwɑlˌpeɪp|ər, -ərz, -(ə)rɪŋ, -ərd

wallplanner
BR ˈwɔːlˌplanə(r), -z
AM ˈwɔlˌplænər, ˈwɑlˌplænər, -z

Walls
BR wɔːlz
AM wɔlz, wɑlz

wally
BR ˈwɒl|i, -ɪz
AM ˈwɔli, ˈwɑli, -z

Walmesley
BR ˈwɔːmzli
AM ˈwɔmzli, ˈwɑmzli

Walmsley
BR ˈwɔːmzli
AM ˈwɔmzli, ˈwɑmzli

walnut
BR ˈwɔːlnʌt, -s
AM ˈwɔlˌnət, ˈwɑlˌnət, -s

Walpamur
BR ˈwɔːlpəmjʊə(r), ˈwɒlpəmjʊə(r)
AM ˈwɔlpəˌmjʊ(ə)r, ˈwɑlpəˌmjʊ(ə)r

Walpole
BR ˈwɔːlpəʊl, ˈwɒlpəʊl
AM ˈwɔlˌpoʊl, ˈwɑlˌpoʊl

Walpurgis
BR valˈpəːgɪs, valˈpʊəgɪs, vɑːlˈpəːgɪs, vɑːlˈpʊəgɪs
AM vɑlˈpʊrgəs

walrus
BR ˈwɔːlrəs, ˈwɔːlrʌs, ˈwɒlrəs, ˈwɒlrʌs, -ɪz
AM ˈwɔlrəs, ˈwɑlrəs, -əz

Walsall
BR ˈwɔːls(ɔː)l, ˈwɒls(ɔː)l, ˈwɔːsl
AM ˈwɔlˌsɔl, ˈwɑlˌsɑl

Walsh
BR wɔːlʃ, wɒlʃ
AM wɔlʃ, wɑlʃ

Walsham
BR ˈwɔːlʃəm, ˈwɒlʃəm
AM ˈwɔlʃəm, ˈwɑlʃəm

Walsingham[1]
place in UK
BR ˈwɔːlzɪŋəm, ˈwɒlzɪŋəm
AM ˈwɔlzɪŋəm, ˈwɑlzɪŋəm

Walsingham[2]
surname
BR ˈwɔːlsɪŋəm, ˈwɒlsɪŋəm
AM ˈwɔlzɪŋəm, ˈwɑlzɪŋəm

Walter
BR ˈwɔːltə(r), ˈwɒltə(r)
AM ˈwɔltər, ˈwɑltər

Walters
BR ˈwɔːltəz, ˈwɒltəz
AM ˈwɔltərz, ˈwɑltərz

Waltham
BR ˈwɔːlθəm, ˈwɒlθəm
AM ˈwɔlθəm, ˈwɑlθəm

Walthamstow
BR ˈwɔːlθəmstəʊ, ˈwɒlθəmstəʊ
AM ˈwɔlθəmˌstoʊ, ˈwɑlθəmˌstoʊ

Walton
BR ˈwɔːlt(ə)n, ˈwɒlt(ə)n
AM ˈwɔltən, ˈwɑltən

waltz
BR wɔːl(t)s, wɒl(t)s, -ɪz, -ɪŋ, -t
AM wɔl(t)s, wɑl(t)s, -əz, -ɪŋ, -t

waltzer
BR ˈwɔːl(t)sə(r), ˈwɒl(t)sə(r), -z
AM ˈwɔl(t)sər, ˈwɑl(t)sər, -z

Walvis Bay
BR ˌwɔːlvɪs ˈbeɪ
AM ˌwɔlvəs ˈbeɪ, ˌwɑlvəs ˈbeɪ

Walworth
BR ˈwɔːlwəːθ, ˈwɔːlwəθ, ˈwɒlwəːθ, ˈwɒlwəθ
AM ˈwɔlˌwərθ, ˈwɑlˌwərθ

wampum
BR ˈwɒmpəm
AM ˈwɑmpəm

WAN
wide area network
BR wan
AM wæn

wan
pale
BR wɒn, -ə(r), -ɪst
AM wɑn, -ər, -ɪst

Wanamaker
BR ˈwɒnəmeɪkə(r)
AM ˈwɑnəˌmeɪkər

wand
BR wɒnd, -z
AM wɑnd, -z

Wanda
BR ˈwɒndə(*r*)
AM ˈwɑndə

wander
BR ˈwɒnd|ə(r), -əz, -(ə)rɪŋ, -əd
AM ˈwɑnd|ər, -ərz, -(ə)rɪŋ, -ərd

wanderer
BR ˈwɒnd(ə)rə(r), -z
AM ˈwɑnd(ə)rər, -z

wandering
BR ˈwɒnd(ə)rɪŋ, -z
AM ˈwɑnd(ə)rɪŋ, -z

wanderlust
BR ˈwɒndəlʌst
AM ˈwɑndərˌləst

wanderoo
BR ˌwɒndəˈruː, -z
AM ˌwɑndəˈru, -z

wandoo
BR ˌwɒnˈduː, -z
AM ˌwɑnˈdu, -z

Wandsworth
BR ˈwɒn(d)zwəθ, ˈwɒn(d)zwəːθ
AM ˈwɑn(d)zˌwərθ

wane
BR weɪn, -z, -ɪŋ, -d
AM weɪn, -z, -ɪŋ, -d

waney
BR ˈweɪni
AM ˈweɪni

wang
BR waŋ, -z, -ɪŋ, -d
AM wæŋ, -z, -ɪŋ, -d

Wanganui
BR ˌwaŋəˈnuːi
AM ˌwaŋəˈnui

wangle
BR ˈwaŋg|l, -lz, -l̩ɪŋ\-lɪŋ, -ld
AM ˈwæŋg|əl, -əlz, -(ə)lɪŋ, -əld

wangler
BR ˈwaŋgl̩ə(r), ˈwaŋglə(r), -z
AM ˈwæŋ(ə)lər, -z

wank
BR waŋ|k, -ks, -kɪŋ, -(k)t
AM wæŋ|k, -ks, -kɪŋ, -(k)t

Wankel
BR ˈwaŋkl
AM ˈwæŋkəl

wanker
BR ˈwaŋkə(r), -z
AM ˈwæŋkər, -z

Wankie
BR ˈwaŋki
AM ˈwæŋki

wanky
BR ˈwaŋki
AM ˈwæŋki

wanly
BR ˈwɒnli
AM ˈwɑnli

wanna
want to
BR 'wɒnə(r)
AM 'wɑnə

wannabe
BR 'wɒnəbiː, -z
AM 'wɔnəbi, -z

wanness
BR 'wɒnnəs
AM 'wɑ(n)nəs

Wanstead
BR 'wɒnstɪd, 'wɒnstɛd
AM 'wɑn,stɛd

want
BR wɒnt, -s, -ɪŋ, -ɨd
AM wɑn|t, -ts, -(t)ɪŋ, -(t)əd

Wantage
BR 'wɒntɪdʒ
AM 'wɑn(t)ɪdʒ

wanter
BR 'wɒntə(r), -z
AM 'wɑn(t)ər, -z

wanton
BR 'wɒntən, -z
AM 'wɑn(t)ən, -z

wantonly
BR 'wɒntənli
AM 'wɑn(t)nli

wantonness
BR 'wɒntənnəs
AM 'wɑn(t)nnəs, 'wɑnt(n)nəs

wapentake
BR 'wɒp(ə)nteɪk, 'wap(ə)nteɪk, -s
AM 'wæpən,teɪk, 'wɑpən,teɪk, -s

wapiti
BR 'wɒpɪt|i, -ɪz
AM 'wɑpədi, -z

Wapping
BR 'wɒpɪŋ
AM 'wɑpɪŋ

war
BR wɔː(r), -z, -ɪŋ, -d
AM wɔ(ə)r, -z, -ɪŋ, -d

waratah
BR ˌwɒrə'tɑː(r), -z
AM ˌwɔrə'tɑ, -z

warb
BR wɔːb, -z
AM wɔ(ə)rb, -z

Warbeck
BR 'wɔːbɛk
AM 'wɔr,bɛk

warble
BR 'wɔːb|l, -lz, -l̩ɪŋ\-lɪŋ, -ld
AM 'wɔrbəl, -əlz, -(ə)lɪŋ, -əld

warbler
BR 'wɔːblə(r), -z
AM 'wɔrb(ə)lər, -z

Warboys
BR 'wɔːbɔɪz
AM 'wɔr,bɔɪz

Warburg
BR 'wɔːbəːg
AM 'wɔr,bərg

Warburton
BR 'wɔːbət(ə)n, 'wɔːˌbəːtn
AM 'wɔr,bərtən

warby
BR 'wɔːbi
AM 'wɔrbi

ward
BR wɔːd, -z, -ɪŋ, -ɨd
AM wɔ(ə)rd, -z, -ɪŋ, -əd

Wardell
BR wɔː'dɛl
AM ˌwɔr'dɛl

warden
BR 'wɔːdn, -z
AM 'wɔrdən, -z

wardenship
BR 'wɔːdnʃɪp, -s
AM 'wɔrdn,ʃɪp, -s

warder
BR 'wɔːdə(r), -z
AM 'wɔrdər, -z

Wardle
BR 'wɔːdl
AM 'wɔrdəl

Wardour
BR 'wɔːdə(r), 'wɔːdɔː(r)
AM 'wɔr,dɔ(ə)r

wardress
BR 'wɔːdrɪs, -ɨz
AM 'wɔrdrəs, -əz

wardrobe
BR 'wɔːdrəʊb, -z
AM 'wɔr,droʊb, -z

wardroom
BR 'wɔːdruːm, 'wɔːdrʊm, -z
AM 'wɔrd,rum, 'wɔrd,rʊm, -z

wardship
BR 'wɔːdʃɪp, -s
AM 'wɔrd,ʃɪp, -s

ware
BR wɛː(r), -z
AM 'wɛ(ə)r, -z

Wareham
BR 'wɛːrəm, 'wɛːrm̩
AM 'wɛrəm

warehouse
BR 'wɛːhaʊ|s, -zɨz, -zɪŋ, -zd
AM 'wɛr,(h)aʊ|s, -zəz, -zɪŋ, -zd

warehouseman
BR 'wɛːhaʊsmən
AM 'wɛr,(h)aʊsmən

warehousemen
BR 'wɛːhaʊsmən
AM 'wɛr,(h)aʊsmən

Wareing
BR 'wɛːrɪŋ
AM 'wɛrɪŋ

warfare
BR 'wɔːfɛː(r)
AM 'wɔr,fɛ(ə)r

warfarin
BR 'wɔːf(ə)rɪn
AM 'wɔrfərən

Wargrave
BR 'wɔːgreɪv
AM 'wɔr,greɪv

warhead
BR 'wɔːhɛd, -z
AM 'wɔr,(h)ɛd, -z

Warhol
BR 'wɔːhəʊl, 'wɔːhɒl
AM 'wɔr,(h)ɔl, 'wɔr,(h)ɑl

warhorse
BR 'wɔːhɔːs, -ɨz
AM 'wɔr,(h)ɔ(ə)rs, -əz

warily
BR 'wɛːrɪli
AM 'wɛrəli

wariness
BR 'wɛːrɪnɪs
AM 'wɛrinɨs

Waring
BR 'wɛːrɪŋ
AM 'wɛrɪŋ

Warkworth
BR 'wɔːkwəθ, 'wɔːkwəːθ
AM 'wɔrk,wərθ

Warley
BR 'wɔːli
AM 'wɔrli

warlike
BR 'wɔːlʌɪk
AM 'wɔr,laɪk

warlock
BR 'wɔːlɒk, -s
AM 'wɔr,lɑk, -s

warlord
BR 'wɔːlɔːd, -z
AM 'wɔr,lɔ(ə)rd, -z

warm
BR wɔːm, -z, -ɪŋ, -d, -ə(r), -ɨst
AM 'wɔ(ə)rm, -z, -ɪŋ, -d, -ər, -əst

warm-blooded
BR ˌwɔːm'blʌdɪd
AM ˌwɔrm'blədəd

warm-bloodedness
BR ˌwɔːm'blʌdɪdnɨs
AM ˈwɔrm'blədədnəs

warmed-over
BR ˌwɔːmd'əʊvə(r)
AM ˈwɔrmd'oʊvər

warmed-up
BR ˌwɔːmd'ʌp
AM ˌwɔrmd'əp

warmer
BR 'wɔːmə(r), -z
AM 'wɔrmər, -z

warm-hearted
BR ˌwɔːm'hɑːtɪd
AM ˈwɔrmˈhɑrdəd

warm-heartedly
BR ˌwɔːm'hɑːtɪdli
AM ˈwɔrmˈhɑrdədli

warm-heartedness
BR ˌwɔːm'hɑːtɪdnɨs
AM ˈwɔrmˈhɑrdədnəs

Warminster
BR 'wɔːmɪnstə(r)
AM 'wɔr,mɪnstər

warmish
BR 'wɔːmɪʃ
AM 'wɔrmɪʃ

warmly
BR 'wɔːmli
AM 'wɔrmli

warmness
BR 'wɔːmnəs
AM 'wɔrmnəs

warmonger
BR 'wɔːˌmʌŋg|ə(r), -əz, -ərɪŋ
AM 'wɔr,mɑŋgər, 'wɔr,məŋgər, -z, -ɪŋ

warmth
BR wɔːmθ
AM 'wɔrmθ

warm-up
BR 'wɔːmʌp, -s
AM 'wɔrməp, -s

warn
BR wɔːn, -z, -ɪŋ, -d
AM wɔ(ə)rn, -z, -ɪŋ, -d

warner
BR 'wɔːnə(r), -z
AM 'wɔrnər, -z

warning
BR 'wɔːnɪŋ, -z
AM 'wɔrnɪŋ, -z

warningly
BR 'wɔːnɪŋli
AM 'wɔrnɪŋli

Warnock
BR 'wɔːnɒk
AM 'wɔrnək

warp
BR wɔːp, -s, -ɪŋ, -t
AM wɔ(ə)rp, -s, -ɪŋ, -t

warpage
BR 'wɔːpɪdʒ
AM 'wɔrpɪdʒ

warpaint
BR 'wɔːpeɪnt
AM 'wɔr,peɪnt

warpath
BR 'wɔːpɑːθ, 'wɔːpaθ
AM 'wɔr,pæθ

warper
BR 'wɔːpə(r), -z
AM 'wɔrpər, -z

warplane
BR 'wɔːpleɪn, -z
AM 'wɔr,pleɪn, -z

warragal
BR 'wɒrəgl, -z
AM 'wɔrəgəl, -z

warrant
BR 'wɒrənt, 'wɒrn̩t, -s, -ɪŋ, -ɪd
AM 'wɔrən|t, -ts, -(t)ɪŋ, -(t)əd

warrantable
BR 'wɒrəntəbl, 'wɒrn̩təbl
AM 'wɔrən(t)əbəl

warrantableness
BR 'wɒrəntəblnəs, 'wɒrn̩təblnəs
AM 'wɔrən(t)əbəlnəs

warrantably
BR 'wɒrəntəbli, 'wɒrn̩təbli
AM 'wɔrən(t)əbli

warrantee
BR ˌwɒrən'tiː, ˌwɒrn̩'tiː, -z
AM ˌwɔrən'ti, -z

warranter
BR 'wɒrəntə(r), 'wɒrn̩tə(r), -z
AM 'wɔrən(t)ər, -z

warrantor
BR ˌwɒrən'tɔː(r), ˌwɒrn̩'tɔː(r), 'wɒrəntɔː(r), 'wɒrn̩tɔː(r), -z
AM 'wɔrən(t)ər, -z

warranty
BR 'wɒrənt|i, 'wɒrn̩t|i, -ɪz
AM 'wɔrən(t)i, -z

warren
BR 'wɒrən, 'wɒrn̩, -z
AM 'wɔrən, -z

Warrender
BR 'wɒrɨndə(r)
AM 'wɔrəndər

warrener
BR 'wɒrənə(r), 'wɒrn̩ə(r), -z
AM 'wɔrənər, -z

warrigal
BR 'wɒrɪgl, -z
AM 'wɔrəgəl, -z

Warrington
BR 'wɒrɪŋt(ə)n
AM 'wɔrɪŋtən

warrior
BR 'wɒrɪə(r), -z
AM 'wɔriər, -z

Warsaw
BR 'wɔːsɔː(*r*)
AM 'wɔrˌsɔ

warship
BR 'wɔːʃɪp, -s
AM 'wɔrˌʃɪp, -s

Warsop
BR 'wɔːsɒp
AM 'wɔrsəp

Warspite
BR 'wɔːspʌɪt
AM 'wɔrˌspaɪt

wart
BR wɔːt, -s
AM wɔ(ə)rt, -s

Wartburg
BR 'wɔːtbəːg, 'vɑːtbəːg
AM 'wɔrtˌbərg

warthog
BR 'wɔːthɒg, -z
AM 'wɔrtˌ(h)ɔg, 'wɑrtˌ(h)ɑg, -z

wartime
BR 'wɔːtʌɪm
AM 'wɔrˌtaɪm

Warton
BR 'wɔːtn
AM 'wɔrtən

wartorn
BR 'wɔːtɔːn
AM 'wɔrˌtɔ(ə)rn

warty
BR 'wɔːt|i, -ɪə(r), -ɪɪst
AM 'wɔrdi, -ər, -ɪst

Warwick[1]
in UK, place and surname
BR 'wɒrɪk
AM 'wɔr(w)ɪk

Warwick[2]
in US, place and surname
BR 'wɔːwɪk
AM 'wɔr(w)ɪk

Warwickshire
BR 'wɒrɪkʃ(ɪ)ə(r)
AM 'wɔr(w)əkˌʃɪ(ə)r

warworn
BR 'wɔːwɔːn
AM 'wɔrˌwɔ(ə)rn

wary
BR 'wɛːr|i, -ɪə(r), -ɪɪst
AM 'wɛri, -ər, -ɪst

was[1]
strong form
BR wɒz
AM wəz

was[2]
weak form
BR wəz
AM wəz

Wasatch
BR 'wɔːsatʃ
AM 'wɔˌsætʃ, 'wɑˌsætʃ

wash
BR wɒʃ, -ɪz, -ɪŋ, -t
AM wɔʃ, wɑʃ, -əz, -ɪŋ, -t

washability
BR ˌwɒʃə'bɪlɪti
AM ˌwɔʃə'bɪlɨdi, ˌwɑʃə'bɪlɨdi

washable
BR 'wɒʃəbl
AM 'wɔʃəbəl, 'wɑʃəbəl

wash-and-wear
BR ˌwɒʃ(ə)n(d)'wɛː(r)
AM ¦wɔʃən'wɛ(ə)r, ¦wɑʃən'wɛ(ə)r

washbag
BR 'wɒʃbag, -z
AM 'wɔʃˌbæg, 'wɑʃˌbæg, -z

washbasin
BR 'wɒʃˌbeɪsn, -z
AM 'wɔʃˌbeɪsn, 'wɑʃˌbeɪsn, -z

washboard
BR 'wɒʃbɔːd, -z
AM 'wɔʃˌbɔ(ə)rd, 'wɑʃˌbɔ(ə)rd, -z

Washbourn
BR 'wɒʃbɔːn
AM 'wɔʃˌbɔ(ə)rn, 'wɑʃˌbɔ(ə)rn

Washbourne
BR 'wɒʃbɔːn
AM 'wɔʃˌbɔ(ə)rn, 'wɑʃˌbɔ(ə)rn

washbowl
BR 'wɒʃbəʊl, -z
AM 'wɔʃˌboʊl, 'wɑʃˌboʊl, -z

Washbrook
BR 'wɒʃbrʊk
AM 'wɔʃˌbrʊk, 'wɑʃˌbrʊk

Washburn
BR 'wɒʃbəːn
AM 'wɔʃˌbərn, 'wɑʃˌbərn

washcloth
BR 'wɒʃklɒ|θ, -θs\-ðz
AM 'wɔʃˌklɔθ, 'wɑʃˌklɑ|θ, -θs\-ðz

washday
BR 'wɒʃdeɪ, -z
AM 'wɔʃˌdeɪ, 'wɑʃˌdeɪ, -z

washed out
BR ˌwɒʃt 'aʊt
AM ¦wɔʃt 'aʊt, ¦wɑʃt +

washed up
BR ˌwɒʃt 'ʌp
AM ¦wɔʃt 'əp, ¦wɑʃt +

washer
BR 'wɒʃə(r), -z
AM 'wɔʃər, 'wɑʃər, -z

washer/dryer
BR ˌwɒʃə'drʌɪə(r), -z
AM ¦wɔʃər'draɪər, ¦wɑʃər'draɪər, -z

washerman
BR 'wɒʃəmən
AM 'wɔʃərmən, 'wɑʃərmən

washermen
BR 'wɒʃəmən
AM 'wɔʃərmən, 'wɑʃərmən

washerwoman
BR 'wɒʃəˌwʊmən
AM 'wɔʃərˌwʊmən, 'wɑʃərˌwʊmən

washerwomen
BR 'wɒʃəˌwɪmɪn
AM 'wɔʃərˌwɪmɨn, 'wɑʃərˌwɪmɨn

washery
BR 'wɒʃ(ə)r|i, -ɪz
AM 'wɔʃəri, 'wɑʃəri, -z

washeteria
BR ˌwɒʃə'tɪərɪə(*r*), -z
AM ˌwɔʃə'tɪriə, ˌwɑʃə'tɪ(ə)riə, -z

wash-hand basin
BR 'wɒʃhan(d) ˌbeɪsn, -z
AM 'wɔʃˌ(h)ænd ˌbeɪsn, 'wɑʃˌ(h)ænd +, -z

washhouse
BR 'wɒʃhaʊ|s, -zɪz
AM 'wɔʃˌ(h)aʊ|s, 'wɑʃˌ(h)aʊ|s, -zəz

Washington
BR 'wɒʃɪŋt(ə)n
AM 'wɔʃɪŋtən, 'wɑʃɪŋtən

Washingtonian
BR ˌwɒʃɪŋ'təʊnɪən
AM ˌwɔʃɪŋ'toʊniən, ˌwɑʃɪŋ'toʊniən

washing-up
BR ˌwɒʃɪŋ'ʌp
AM ¦wɔʃɪŋ'əp, ¦wɑʃɪŋ'əp

washland
BR 'wɒʃland, -z
AM 'wɔʃˌlænd, 'wɑʃˌlænd, -z

washout
BR 'wɒʃaʊt, -s
AM 'wɔʃˌaʊt, 'wɑʃˌaʊt, -s

washroom
BR 'wɒʃruːm, 'wɒʃrʊm, -z
AM 'wɔʃˌrum, 'wɔʃˌrʊm, 'wɑʃˌrum, 'wɑʃˌrʊm, -z

washstand
BR 'wɒʃstand, -z
AM 'wɔʃˌstænd, 'wɑʃˌstænd, -z

washtub
BR 'wɒʃtʌb, -z
AM 'wɔʃˌtəb, 'wɑʃˌtəb, -z

wash-up
BR 'wɒʃʌp
AM 'wɔʃəp, 'wɑʃəp

wash/wipe
BR ˌwɒʃ'wʌɪp
AM 'wɔʃ'waɪp, 'wɑʃ'waɪp

washy
BR 'wɒʃ|i, -ɪə(r), -ɪɪst
AM 'wɔʃi, 'wɑʃi, -ər, -ɪst

wasn't
BR 'wɒznt
AM 'wəznt

WASP
BR wɒsp, -s
AM wɑsp, -s

wasp
BR wɒsp, -s
AM wɑsp, -s

waspie
BR 'wɒsp|i, -ɪz
AM 'wɑspi, -z

waspish
BR 'wɒspɪʃ
AM 'wɑspɪʃ

waspishly
BR 'wɒspɨʃli
AM 'wɑspɨʃli

waspishness
BR 'wɒspɨʃnɨs
AM 'wɑspɪʃnɪs

wasplike
BR 'wɒsplʌɪk
AM 'wɑsp,laɪk

waspy
BR 'wɒspi
AM 'wɑspi

wassail
BR 'wɒseɪl, 'wɒsl̩, -z, -ɪŋ
AM 'wɑ,seɪl, 'wɑsəl, -z, -ɪŋ

wassail-bowl
BR 'wɒseɪlbəʊl, 'wɒslbəʊl, -z
AM 'wɑ,seɪl,boʊl, 'wɑsəl,boʊl, -z

wassail-cup
BR 'wɒseɪlkʌp, 'wɒslkʌp, -s
AM 'wɑ,seɪl,kəp, 'wɑsəl,kəp, -s

wassailer
BR 'wɒseɪlə(r), 'wɒsl̩ə(r), -z
AM 'wɑ,seɪlər, 'wɑsələr, -z

wast[1]
strong form
BR wɒst
AM wɔst, wɑst

wast[2]
weak form
BR wəst
AM wəst

wastable
BR 'weɪstəbl
AM 'weɪstəbəl

wastage
BR 'weɪstɪdʒ
AM 'weɪstɪdʒ

waste
BR weɪst, -s, -ɪŋ, -ɨd
AM weɪst, -s, -ɪŋ, -ɨd

wastebasket
BR 'weɪs(t),bɑːskɪt, 'weɪs(t),baskɪt, -s
AM 'weɪs(t),bæskət, -s

wasteful
BR 'weɪstf(ʊ)l
AM 'weɪs(t)fəl

wastefully
BR 'weɪstfʊli, 'weɪstfl̩i
AM 'weɪs(t)fəli

wastefulness
BR 'weɪstf(ʊ)lnəs
AM 'weɪs(t)fəlnəs

wasteland
BR 'weɪs(t)land, -z
AM 'weɪs(t),lænd, -z

wasteless
BR 'weɪstlɨs
AM 'weɪs(t)lɨs

waster
BR 'weɪstə(r), -z
AM 'weɪstər, -z

wastrel
BR 'weɪstr(ə)l, -z
AM 'weɪstrəl, 'wɑstrəl, -z

Wastwater
BR 'wɒst,wɔːtə(r)
AM 'wɑs(t),wɔdər, 'wɑs(t),wɑdər

Wat
BR wɒt
AM wɑt

watch
BR wɒtʃ, -ɪz, -ɪŋ, -t
AM wɑtʃ, -əz, -ɪŋ, -t

watchable
BR 'wɒtʃəbl
AM 'wɑtʃəbəl

watchband
BR 'wɒtʃband, -z
AM 'wɑtʃ,bænd, -z

watchcase
BR 'wɒtʃkeɪs, -ɨz
AM 'wɑtʃ,keɪs, -ɨz

watchchain
BR 'wɒtʃtʃeɪn, -z
AM 'wɑtʃ,tʃeɪn, -z

watchdog
BR 'wɒtʃdɒg, -z
AM 'wɑtʃ,dɑg, -z

watcher
BR 'wɒtʃə(r), -z
AM 'wɑtʃər, -z

Watchet
BR 'wɒtʃɪt
AM 'wɑtʃət

watchfire
BR 'wɒtʃ,fʌɪə(r), -z
AM 'wɑtʃ,faɪ(ə)r, -z

watchful
BR 'wɒtʃf(ʊ)l
AM 'wɑtʃfəl

watchfully
BR 'wɒtʃfʊli, 'wɒtʃfl̩i
AM 'wɑtʃfəli

watchfulness
BR 'wɒtʃf(ʊ)lnəs
AM 'wɑtʃfəlnəs

watch-glass
BR 'wɒtʃglɑːs, 'wɒtʃglas, -ɨz
AM 'wɑtʃ,glæs, -əz

watchkeeper
BR 'wɒtʃ,kiːpə(r), -z
AM 'wɑtʃ,kipər, -z

watchmaker
BR 'wɒtʃ,meɪkə(r), -z
AM 'wɑtʃ,meɪkər, -z

watchmaking
BR 'wɒtʃ,meɪkɪŋ
AM 'wɑtʃmeɪkɪŋ

watchman
BR 'wɒtʃmən
AM 'wɑtʃmən

watchmen
BR 'wɒtʃmən
AM 'wɑtʃmən

watchnight
BR 'wɒtʃnʌɪt
AM 'wɑtʃ,naɪt

watchspring
BR 'wɒtʃsprɪŋ, -z
AM 'wɑtʃ,(s)prɪŋ, -z

watchstrap
BR 'wɒtʃstrap, -s
AM 'wɑtʃ,(s)træp, -s

watchtower
BR 'wɒtʃ,taʊə(r), -z
AM 'wɑtʃ,taʊər, -z

watchword
BR 'wɒtʃwəːd, -z
AM 'wɑtʃ,wərd, -z

Watendlath
BR wɒ'tɛndləθ
AM wɑ'tɛn(d)ləθ

water
BR 'wɔːt|ə(r), -əz, -(ə)rɪŋ, -əd
AM 'wɔdər, 'wɑdər, -z, -ɪŋ, -d

waterbed
BR 'wɔːtəbɛd, -z
AM 'wɔdər,bɛd, 'wɑdər,bɛd, -z

waterbird
BR 'wɔːtəbəːd, -z
AM 'wɔdər,bərd, 'wɑdər,bərd, -z

waterborne
BR 'wɔːtəbɔːn
AM 'wɔdər,bɔ(ə)rn, 'wɑdər,bɔ(ə)rn

waterbrash
BR 'wɔːtəbraʃ
AM 'wɔdər,bræʃ, 'wɑdər,bræʃ

watercolor
BR 'wɔːtə,kʌlə(r), -z
AM 'wɔdər,kələr, 'wɑdər,kələr, -z

watercolorist
BR 'wɔːtə,kʌl(ə)rɪst, -s
AM 'wɔdər,kələrəst, 'wɑdər,kələrəst, -s

watercolour
BR 'wɔːtə,kʌlə(r), -z
AM 'wɔdər,kələr, 'wɑdər,kələr, -z

watercolourist
BR 'wɔːtə,kʌl(ə)rɪst, -s
AM 'wɔdər,kələrəst, 'wɑdər,kələrəst, -s

watercourse
BR 'wɔːtəkɔːs, -ɨz
AM 'wɔdər,kɔ(ə)rs, 'wɑdər,kɔ(ə)rs, -əz

watercraft
BR 'wɔːtəkrɑːft, 'wɔːtəkraft, -s
AM 'wɔdər,kræft, 'wɑdər,kræft, -s

watercress
BR 'wɔːtəkrɛs
AM 'wɔdər,krɛs, 'wɑdər,krɛs

waterer
BR 'wɔːt(ə)rə(r), -z
AM 'wɔdərər, 'wɑdərər, -z

waterfall
BR 'wɔːtəfɔːl, -z
AM 'wɔdər,fɔl, 'wɑdər,fɑl, -z

Waterford
BR 'wɔːtəfəd
AM 'wɔdərfərd, 'wɑdərfərd

waterfowl
BR 'wɔːtəfaʊl
AM 'wɔdər,faʊl, 'wɑdər,faʊl

waterfront
BR 'wɔːtəfrʌnt, -s
AM 'wɔdər,frənt, 'wɑdər,frənt, -s

watergate
BR 'wɔːtəgeɪt, -s
AM 'wɔdər,geɪt, 'wɑdər,geɪt, -s

waterhole
BR 'wɔːtəhəʊl, -z
AM 'wɔdər,(h)oʊl, 'wɑdər,(h)oʊl, -z

Waterhouse
BR 'wɔːtəhaʊs
AM 'wɔdər,(h)aʊs, 'wɑdər,(h)aʊs

wateriness
BR 'wɔːt(ə)rɪnɪs
AM 'wɔdərinɨs, 'wɑdərinɨs

watering
BR 'wɔːt(ə)rɪŋ, -z
AM 'wɔdərɪŋ, 'wɔdərɪŋ, -z

waterless
BR 'wɔːtələs
AM 'wɔdərləs, 'wɑdərləs

waterline
BR 'wɔːtəlʌɪn, -z
AM 'wɔdər,laɪn, 'wɑdər,laɪn, -z

waterlogged
BR 'wɔːtəlɒgd
AM 'wɔdər,lɔgd, 'wɑdər,lɔgd

Waterloo
BR ˌwɔːtəˈluː
AM ˌwɔdərˈlu, ˌwɑdərˈlu

waterman
BR ˈwɔːtəmən
AM ˈwɔdərmən, ˈwɑdərmən

watermark
BR ˈwɔːtəmɑːk, -s
AM ˈwɔdərˌmɑrk, ˈwɑdərˌmɑrk, -s

watermelon
BR ˈwɔːtəˌmɛlən, -z
AM ˈwɔdərˌmɛlən, ˈwɑdərˌmɛlən, -z

watermen
BR ˈwɔːtəmən
AM ˈwɔdərmən, ˈwɑdərmən

watermill
BR ˈwɔːtəmɪl, -z
AM ˈwɔdərˌmɪl, ˈwɑdərˌmɪl, -z

waterpower
BR ˈwɔːtəˌpaʊə(r)
AM ˈwɔdərˌpaʊər, ˈwɑdərˌpaʊər

waterproof
BR ˈwɔːtəpruːf, -s, -ɪŋ, -t
AM ˈwɔdərˌpruf, ˈwɑdərˌpruf, -s, -ɪŋ, -t

waterproofer
BR ˈwɔːtəpruːfə(r), -z
AM ˈwɔdərˌprufər, ˈwɑdərˌprufər, -z

waterproofness
BR ˈwɔːtəpruːfnəs
AM ˈwɔdərˌprufnəs, ˈwɑdərˌprufnəs

water-repellant
BR ˌwɔːtərɪˈpɛlənt, ˌwɔːtərɪˈpɛln̩t, ˈwɔːtərɪˌpɛlənt, ˈwɔːtərɪˌpɛln̩t
AM ˈwɔdə(r)rəˌpɛlənt, ˈwɑdə(r)rəˌpɛlənt

water-repellency
BR ˌwɔːtərɪˈpɛlənsi, ˌwɔːtərɪˈpɛln̩si, ˈwɔːtərɪˌpɛlənsi, ˈwɔːtərɪˌpɛln̩si
AM ˈwɔdə(r)rəˌpɛlənsi, ˈwɑdə(r)rəˌpɛlənsi

water-repellent
BR ˌwɔːtərɪˈpɛlənt, ˌwɔːtərɪˈpɛln̩t, ˈwɔːtərɪˌpɛlənt, ˈwɔːtərɪˌpɛln̩t
AM ˈwɔdə(r)rəˌpɛlənt, ˈwɑdə(r)rəˌpɛlənt

water-resistance
BR ˌwɔːtərɪˈzɪst(ə)ns, ˈwɔːtərɪˌzɪst(ə)ns
AM ˈwɔdə(r)rəˌzɪstəns, ˈwɑdə(r)rəˌzɪstəns

water-resistant
BR ˌwɔːtərɪˈzɪst(ə)nt, ˈwɔːtərɪˌzɪst(ə)nt
AM ˈwɔdə(r)rəˌzɪstənt, ˈwɑdə(r)rəˌzɪstənt

Waters
BR ˈwɔːtəz
AM ˈwɔdərz, ˈwɑdərz

watershed
BR ˈwɔːtəʃɛd, -z
AM ˈwɔdərˌʃɛd, ˈwɑdərˌʃɛd, -z

waterside
BR ˈwɔːtəsʌɪd
AM ˈwɔdərˌsaɪd, ˈwɑdərˌsaɪd

water-soluble
BR ˌwɔːtəˈsɒljʊbl
AM ˈwɔdərˌsɑl(j)əbəl, ˈwɑdərˌsɑl(j)əbəl

Waterson
BR ˈwɔːtəs(ə)n
AM ˈwɔdərsən, ˈwɑdərsən

watersport
BR ˈwɔːtəspɔːt, -s
AM ˈwɔdərˌspɔ(ə)rt, ˈwɑdərˌspɔ(ə)rt, -s

waterspout
BR ˈwɔːtəspaʊt, -s
AM ˈwɔdərˌspaʊt, ˈwɑdərˌspaʊt, -s

watertight
BR ˈwɔːtətʌɪt
AM ˈwɔdərˌtaɪt, ˈwɑdərˌtaɪt

waterway
BR ˈwɔːtəweɪ, -z
AM ˈwɔdərˌweɪ, ˈwɑdərˌweɪ, -z

waterweed
BR ˈwɔːtəwiːd, -z
AM ˈwɔdərˌwid, ˈwɑdərˌwid, -z

waterwheel
BR ˈwɔːtəwiːl, -z
AM ˈwɔdərˌ(h)wil, ˈwɑdərˌ(h)wil, -z

waterwings
BR ˈwɔːtəwɪŋz
AM ˈwɔdərˌwɪŋz, ˈwɑdərˌwɪŋz

waterworks
BR ˈwɔːtəwəːks
AM ˈwɔdərˌwərks, ˈwɑdərˌwərks

watery
BR ˈwɔːt(ə)ri
AM ˈwɔdəri, ˈwɑdəri

Wates
BR weɪts
AM weɪts

Watford
BR ˈwɒtfəd
AM ˈwɑtfərd

Wath
BR wɒθ
AM wɑθ

Watkin
BR ˈwɒtkɪn
AM ˈwɑtkən

Watkins
BR ˈwɒtkɪnz
AM ˈwɑtkənz

Watkinson
BR ˈwɒtkɪns(ə)n
AM ˈwɑtkənsən

Watling Street
BR ˈwɒtlɪŋ striːt
AM ˌwɑtlɪŋ ˌstrit

Watney
BR ˈwɒtni
AM ˈwɑtni

WATS line
BR ˈwɒts lʌɪn
AM ˈwɑts ˌlaɪn

Watson
BR ˈwɒtsn
AM ˈwɑtsən

watsonia
BR wɒtˈsəʊnɪə(*r*), -z
AM wɑtˈsoʊniə, -z

Watson-Watt
BR ˌwɒtsnˈwɒt
AM ˌwɑtsənˈwɑt

Watt
BR wɒt
AM wɑt

watt
BR wɒt, -s
AM wɑt, -s

wattage
BR ˈwɒtɪdʒ
AM ˈwɑdɪdʒ

Watteau
BR ˈwɒtəʊ
AM wɑˈtoʊ

watt-hour
BR ˌwɒtˈaʊə(r), -z
AM ˈwɑdˌaʊər, -z

wattle
BR ˈwɒtl, -z, -d
AM ˈwɑdəl, -z, -d

wattlebird
BR ˈwɒtlbəːd, -z
AM ˈwɑdlˌbərd, -z

wattmeter
BR ˈwɒtˌmiːtə(r), -z
AM ˈwɑtˌmidər, -z

Watts
BR wɒts
AM wɑts

Watusi
BR wəˈtuːs|i, wɑːˈtuːs|i, -ɪz
AM wɑˈtusi, -z

Watutsi
BR wəˈtʊtsi, wɑːˈtʊtsi
AM wɑˈtutsi

Waugh
BR wɔː(*r*)
AM wɔ

waul
BR wɔːl, -z, -ɪŋ, -d
AM wɔl, wɑl, -z, -ɪŋ, -d

wave
BR weɪv, -z, -ɪŋ, -d
AM weɪv, -z, -ɪŋ, -d

waveband
BR ˈweɪvband, -z
AM ˈweɪvˌbænd, -z

waveform
BR ˈweɪvfɔːm
AM ˈweɪvˌfɔ(ə)rm

wavefront
BR ˈweɪvfrʌnt, -s
AM ˈweɪvˌfrənt, -s

waveguide
BR ˈweɪvgʌɪd, -z
AM ˈweɪvˌgaɪd, -z

wavelength
BR ˈweɪvlɛŋ(k)θ, -s
AM ˌweɪvˌlɛŋ(k)θ, -s

waveless
BR ˈweɪvlɨs
AM ˈweɪvlɨs

wavelet
BR ˈweɪvlɨt, -s
AM ˈweɪvlɨt, -s

wavelike
BR ˈweɪvlʌɪk
AM ˈweɪvˌlaɪk

waver
BR ˈweɪv|ə(r), -əz, -(ə)rɪŋ, -əd
AM ˈweɪv|ər, -ərz, -(ə)rɪŋ, -ərd

waverer
BR ˈweɪv(ə)rə(r), -z
AM ˈweɪv(ə)rər, -z

waveringly
BR ˈweɪv(ə)rɪŋli
AM ˈweɪv(ə)rɪŋli

wavery
BR ˈweɪv(ə)ri
AM ˈweɪv(ə)ri

wavetop
BR ˈweɪvtɒp, -s
AM ˈweɪvˌtɑp, -s

wavily
BR ˈweɪvɨli
AM ˈweɪvɨli

waviness
BR ˈweɪvɪnɨs
AM ˈweɪvinɨs

wavy
BR ˈweɪv|i, -ɪə(r), -ɪɪst
AM ˈweɪvi, -ər, -ɨst

wa-wa
BR ˈwɑːwɑː(*r*), -z
AM ˈwɑˈwɑ, -z

wawl
BR wɔːl, -z, -ɪŋ, -d
AM wɔl, wɑl, -z, -ɪŋ, -d

wax
BR waks, -ɪz, -ɪŋ, -t
AM wæks, -əz, -ɪŋ, -t

waxberry
BR ˈwaksb(ə)r|i, -ɪz
AM ˈwæksˌbɛri, -z

waxbill
BR ˈwaksbɪl, -z

AM 'wæks,bɪl, -z
waxcloth
BR 'waksklɒ|θ, -θs\-ðz
AM 'wæks,klɔ|θ, 'wæks,klɑ|θ, -θs\-ðz
waxen
BR 'waksn
AM 'wæksən
waxer
BR 'waksə(r), -z
AM 'wæksər, -z
waxily
BR 'waksɨli
AM 'wæksəli
waxiness
BR 'waksɪnɨs
AM 'wæksinɨs
waxing
BR 'waksɪŋ, -z
AM 'wæksɪŋ, -z
wax-light
BR 'wakslʌɪt, -s
AM 'wæks,laɪt, -s
wax-like
BR 'wakslʌɪk
AM 'wæks,laɪk
waxplant
BR 'waksplɑːnt, 'waksplant, -s
AM 'wæks,plænt, -s
waxwing
BR 'wakswɪŋ, -z
AM 'wæks,wɪŋ, -z
waxwork
BR 'wakswəːk, -s
AM 'wæks,wərk, -s
waxy
BR 'waks|i, -ɪə(r), -ɪɨst
AM 'wæksi, -ər, -ɨst
way
BR weɪ, -z
AM weɪ, -z
wayback
BR 'weɪbak
AM 'weɪ,bæk
waybill
BR 'weɪbɪl, -z
AM 'weɪ,bɪl, -z
waybread
BR 'weɪbrɛd, -z
AM 'weɪ,brɛd, -z
wayfarer
BR 'weɪ,fɛːrə(r), -z
AM 'weɪ,fɛrər, -z
wayfaring
BR 'weɪ,fɛːrɪŋ
AM 'weɪ,fɛrɪŋ
Wayland
BR 'weɪlənd
AM 'weɪlənd
waylay
BR ,weɪ'leɪ, -z, -ɪŋ, -d
AM 'weɪ,leɪ, -z, -ɪŋ, -d
waylayer
BR ,weɪ'leɪə(r), -z
AM 'weɪ,leɪər, -z
wayleave
BR 'weɪliːv, -z
AM 'weɪ,liv, -z
waymark
BR 'weɪmɑːk, -s, -ɪŋ, -t
AM 'weɪ,mɑrk, -s, -ɪŋ, -t
waymarker
BR 'weɪ,mɑːkə(r), -z
AM 'weɪ,mɑrkər, -z
Wayne
BR weɪn
AM weɪn
way-out
BR ,weɪ'aʊt
AM ¦weɪ'aʊt
waypoint
BR 'weɪpɔɪnt, -s
AM 'weɪ,pɔɪnt, -s
wayside
BR 'weɪsʌɪd
AM 'weɪ,saɪd
wayward
BR 'weɪwəd
AM 'weɪwərd
waywardly
BR 'weɪwədli
AM 'weɪwərdli
waywardness
BR 'weɪwədnəs
AM 'weɪwərdnəs
way-worn
BR 'weɪwɔːn
AM 'weɪ,wɔ(ə)rn
wayzgoose
BR 'weɪzguːs, -ɨz
AM 'weɪz,gus, -əz
wazzock
BR 'wazək, -s
AM 'wɑzək, -s
WC
BR ,dʌbljuː'siː, -z
AM ,dəbəlju'si, -z
we¹
strong form
BR wiː
AM wi
we²
weak form
BR wɪ
AM wɪ
weak
BR wiːk, -ə(r), -ɨst
AM wik, -ər, -ɨst
weaken
BR 'wiːk|(ə)n, -(ə)nz, -n̩ɪŋ\-(ə)nɪŋ, -(ə)nd
AM 'wik|ən, -ənz, -(ə)nɪŋ, -ənd
weakener
BR 'wiːk(ə)nə(r), 'wiːkn̩ə(r), -z
AM 'wik(ə)nər, -z
weakfish
BR 'wiːkfɪʃ, -ɨz
AM 'wik,fɪʃ, -ɨz
weakish
BR 'wiːkɪʃ
AM 'wikɪʃ
weak-kneed
BR ,wiːk'niːd
AM 'wik¦nid
weakliness
BR 'wiːklɪnɨs
AM 'wiklinɨs
weakling
BR 'wiːklɪŋ, -z
AM 'wiklɪŋ, -z
weakly
BR 'wiːkl|i, -ɪə(r), -ɪɨst
AM 'wikli, -ər, -ɨst
weakness
BR 'wiːknɨs, -ɨz
AM 'wiknɨs, -ɨz
weak-willed
BR ,wiːk'wɪld
AM ¦wik¦wɪld
weal
BR wiːl, -z
AM wil, -z
weald
BR wiːld, -z
AM wild, -z
wealden
BR 'wiːld(ə)n
AM 'wildən
Wealdstone
BR 'wiːl(d)stəʊn
AM 'wil(d),stoʊn
wealth
BR wɛlθ, -s
AM wɛlθ, -s
wealthily
BR 'wɛlθɨli
AM 'wɛlθəli
wealthiness
BR 'wɛlθɪnɨs
AM 'wɛlθinɨs
wealthy
BR 'wɛlθ|i, -ɪə(r), -ɪɨst
AM 'wɛlθi, -ər, -ɨst
wean
BR wiːn, -z, -ɪŋ, -d
AM win, -z, -ɪŋ, -d
weaner
BR 'wiːnə(r), -z
AM 'winər, -z
weanling
BR 'wiːnlɪŋ, -z
AM 'winlɪŋ, -z
weapon
BR 'wɛp(ə)n, -z, -d
AM 'wɛpən, -z, -d
weaponless
BR 'wɛp(ə)nləs
AM 'wɛpənləs
weaponry
BR 'wɛp(ə)nri
AM 'wɛpənri
Wear
river etc
BR wɪə(r)
AM wɪ(ə)r
wear
BR wɛː(r), -z, -ɪŋ
AM wɛ(ə)r, -z, -ɪŋ
wearability
BR ,wɛːrə'bɪlɨti
AM ,wɛrə'bɪlɨdi
wearable
BR 'wɛːrəbl
AM 'wɛrəbəl
wear-and-tear
BR ,wɛːrən(d)'tɛː(r), ,wɛːrn̩(d)'tɛː(r)
AM ¦wɛrən'tɛ(ə)r
wearer
BR 'wɛːrə(r), -z
AM 'wɛrər, -z
weariless
BR 'wɪərɪlɨs
AM 'wɪrilɨs
wearily
BR 'wɪərɨli
AM 'wɪrɨli
weariness
BR 'wɪərɪnɨs
AM 'wɪrinɨs
wearing
BR 'wɛːrɪŋ
AM 'wɛrɪŋ
wearingly
BR 'wɛːrɪŋli
AM 'wɛrɪŋli
wearisome
BR 'wɪərɪs(ə)m
AM 'wɪrisəm
wearisomely
BR 'wɪərɪs(ə)mli
AM 'wɪrisəmli
wearisomeness
BR 'wɪərɪs(ə)mnəs
AM 'wɪrisəmnəs
Wearmouth
BR 'wɪəmaʊθ
AM 'wɪr,maʊθ, 'wɪrməθ
Wearside
BR 'wɪəsʌɪd
AM 'wɪr,saɪd
weary
BR 'wɪər|i, -ɪz, -ɪɪŋ, -ɪd, -ɪə(r), -ɪɨst
AM 'wɪri, -z, -ɪŋ, -d, -ər, -ɨst
wearyingly
BR 'wɪərɪɪŋli
AM 'wɪriɪŋli
weasel
BR 'wiːzl, -z
AM 'wizəl, -z
weaselly
BR 'wiːzl̩i
AM 'wiz(ə)li
weather
BR 'wɛð|ə(r), -əz, -(ə)rɪŋ, -əd
AM 'wɛð|ər, -ərz, -(ə)rɪŋ, -ərd
Weatherall
BR 'wɛð(ə)rɔːl, 'wɛð(ə)rl̩

AM ˈwɛðərˌɔl, ˈwɛðərˌɑl

weatherbeaten
BR ˈwɛðəˌbiːtn
AM ˈwɛðərˌbitn

weatherboard
BR ˈwɛðəbɔːd, -z, -ɪŋ
AM ˈwɛðərˌbɔ(ə)rd, -z, -ɪŋ

weatherbound
BR ˈwɛðəbaʊnd
AM ˈwɛðərˌbaʊnd

weathercock
BR ˈwɛðəkɒk, -s
AM ˈwɛðərˌkɑk, -s

weather eye
BR ˌwɛðər ˈʌɪ, ˈwɛðər ʌɪ
AM ˈwɛðər ˌaɪ

weathergirl
BR ˈwɛðəgəːl, -z
AM ˈwɛðərˌgərl, -z

weatherglass
BR ˈwɛðəglɑːs, ˈwɛðəglas, -ɪz
AM ˈwɛðərˌglæs, -əz

Weatherhead
BR ˈwɛðəhɛd
AM ˈwɛðərˌ(h)ɛd

weatherize
BR ˈwɛðərʌɪz, -ɪz, -ɪŋ, -d
AM ˈwɛðəˌraɪz, -ɪz, -ɪŋ, -d

weatherliness
BR ˈwɛðəlɪnɪs
AM ˈwɛðərlinɪs

weatherly
BR ˈwɛðəli
AM ˈwɛðərli

weatherman
BR ˈwɛðəman
AM ˈwɛðərˌmæn

weathermen
BR ˈwɛðəmɛn
AM ˈwɛðərˌmɛn

weathermost
BR ˈwɛðəməʊst
AM ˈwɛðərˌmoʊst

weatherproof
BR ˈwɛðəpruːf, -s, -ɪŋ, -t
AM ˈwɛðərˌpruf, -s, -ɪŋ, -t

weatherstrip
BR ˈwɛðəːstrɪp, -s, -ɪŋ, -t
AM ˈwɛðərˌstrɪp, -s, -ɪŋ, -t

weathertight
BR ˈwɛðətʌɪt
AM ˈwɛðərˌtaɪt

weathervane
BR ˈwɛðəveɪn, -z
AM ˈwɛðərˌveɪn, -z

weatherworn
BR ˈwɛðəwɔːn
AM ˈwɛðərˌwɔ(ə)rn

weave
BR wiːv, -z, -ɪŋ
AM wiv, -z, -ɪŋ

weaver
BR ˈwiːvə(r), -z
AM ˈwivər, -z

weaverbird
BR ˈwiːvəbəːd, -z
AM ˈwivərˌbərd, -z

weaving
BR ˈwiːvɪŋ, -z
AM ˈwivɪŋ, -z

web
BR wɛb, -z, -ɪŋ, -d
AM wɛb, -z, -ɪŋ, -d

Webb
BR wɛb
AM wɛb

Webber
BR ˈwɛbə(r)
AM ˈwɛbər

webby
BR ˈwɛbi
AM ˈwɛbi

Weber[1]
composer, physicist
BR ˈveɪbə(r)
AM ˈveɪbər

Weber[2]
English surname
BR ˈwɛbə(r), ˈwiːbə(r), ˈweɪbə(r)
AM ˈwɛbər

weber
BR ˈveɪbə(r), -z
AM ˈwɛbər, -z

web-footed
BR ˌwɛbˈfʊtɪd
AM ˈwɛbˌfʊdəd

Webley®
BR ˈwɛbli
AM ˈwɛbli

Webster
BR ˈwɛbstə(r)
AM ˈwɛbstər

web-toed
BR ˌwɛbˈtəʊd
AM ˈwɛbˌtoʊd

wed
BR wɛd, -z, -ɪŋ, -ɪd
AM wɛd, -z, -ɪŋ, -əd

we'd
BR wiːd
AM wid

Weddell
BR ˈwɛdl
AM ˈwɛdəl

wedding
BR ˈwɛdɪŋ, -z
AM ˈwɛdɪŋ, -z

Wedekind
BR ˈweɪdəkɪnd
AM ˈweɪdəˌkɪnd

wedge
BR wɛdʒ, -ɪz, -ɪŋ, -d
AM wɛdʒ, -əz, -ɪŋ, -d

wedgelike
BR ˈwɛdʒlʌɪk
AM ˈwɛdʒˌlaɪk

wedge-shaped
BR ˈwɛdʒʃeɪpt, ˌwɛdʒˈʃeɪpt
AM ˈwɛdʒˌʃeɪpt

wedgewise
BR ˈwɛdʒwʌɪz
AM ˈwɛdʒˌwaɪz

Wedgewood
BR ˈwɛdʒwʊd
AM ˈwɛdʒˌwʊd

wedgie
BR ˈwɛdʒ|i, -ɪz
AM ˈwɛdʒi, -z

Wedgwood
BR ˈwɛdʒwʊd
AM ˈwɛdʒˌwʊd

wedlock
BR ˈwɛdlɒk
AM ˈwɛdˌlɑk

Wednesbury
BR ˈwɛnzb(ə)ri
AM ˈwɛnzˌbɛri

Wednesday
BR ˈwɛnzd|eɪ, ˈwɛnzd|i, -eɪz\-ɪz
AM ˈwɛnzˌdeɪ, ˈwɛnzdi, -z

Wednesfield
BR ˈwɛnzfiːld
AM ˈwɛnzˌfild

wee
BR wiː, -z, -ɪŋ, -d
AM wi, -z, -ɪŋ, -d

weed
BR wiːd, -z, -ɪŋ, -ɪd
AM wid, -z, -ɪŋ, -ɪd

weeder
BR ˈwiːdə(r), -z
AM ˈwidər, -z

weediness
BR ˈwiːdɪnɪs
AM ˈwidinɪs

weedkiller
BR ˈwiːdˌkɪlə(r), -z
AM ˈwidˌkɪlər, -z

weedless
BR ˈwiːdlɪs
AM ˈwidlɪs

Weedon
BR ˈwiːdn
AM ˈwidən

weedy
BR ˈwiːd|i, -ɪə(r), -ɪɪst
AM ˈwidi, -ər, -ɪst

Wee Free
BR ˌwiː ˈfriː, -z
AM ˌwi ˈfri, -z

week
BR wiːk, -s
AM wik, -s

weekday
BR ˈwiːkdeɪ, -z
AM ˈwikˌdeɪ, -z

weekend
BR ˌwiːkˈɛnd, ˈwiːkɛnd, -z
AM ˈwɪkˌɛnd, -z

weekender
BR ˌwiːkˈɛndə(r), -z
AM ˈwikˌɛndər, -z

Weekes
BR wiːks
AM wiks

Weekley
BR ˈwiːkli
AM ˈwikli

week-long
BR ˈwiːklɒŋ, ˌwiːkˈlɒŋ
AM ˌwikˌlɔŋ, ˌwikˌlɑŋ

weekly
BR ˈwiːkl|i, -ɪz
AM ˈwikli, -z

weeknight
BR ˈwiːknʌɪt, -s
AM ˈwikˌnaɪt, -s

Weeks
BR wiːks
AM wiks

ween
BR wiːn, -z, -ɪŋ, -d
AM win, -z, -ɪŋ, -d

weenie
BR ˈwiːn|i, -ɪz
AM ˈwini, -z

weeny
BR ˈwiːn|i, -ɪz, -ɪə(r), -ɪɪst
AM ˈwini, -z, -ər, -ɪst

weeny-bopper
BR ˈwiːnɪˌbɒpə(r), -z
AM ˈwiniˌbɑpər, -z

weep
BR wiːp, -s, -ɪŋ
AM wip, -s, -ɪŋ

weeper
BR ˈwiːpə(r), -z
AM ˈwipər, -z

weepie
BR ˈwiːp|i, -ɪz
AM ˈwipi, -z

weepily
BR ˈwiːpɪli
AM ˈwipɪli

weepiness
BR ˈwiːpɪnɪs
AM ˈwipinɪs

weepingly
BR ˈwiːpɪŋli
AM ˈwipɪŋli

weepy
BR ˈwiːp|i, -ɪz, -ɪə(r), -ɪɪst
AM ˈwipi, -z, -ər, -ɪst

Weetabix®
BR ˈwiːtəbɪks
AM ˈwidəˌbɪks

weever
BR ˈwiːvə(r), -z
AM ˈwivər, -z

weevil
BR ˈwiːv(ɪ)l, -z
AM ˈwivəl, -z

weevily
BR ˈwiːvɪli, ˈwiːvl̩i

AM ˈwivɨli

weewee
BR ˈwiːwiː, -z, -ɪŋ, -d
AM ˈwiˌwi, -z, -ɪŋ, -d

weft
BR wɛft
AM wɛft

Wehrmacht
BR ˈvɛːmɑːkt, ˈvɛːmɑːxt
AM ˈwɛrˌmɑkt

Wei
BR weɪ
AM weɪ

Weidenfeld
BR ˈvʌɪdnfɛlt
AM ˈwaɪdənˌfɛld, ˈvaɪdənˌfɛld

weigh
BR weɪ, -z, -ɪŋ, -d
AM weɪ, -z, -ɪŋ, -d

weighable
BR ˈweɪəbl
AM ˈweɪəbəl

weighbridge
BR ˈweɪbrɪdʒ, -ɨz
AM ˈweɪˌbrɪdʒ, -ɨz

Weighell
BR wiːl, ˈweɪəl, weɪl
AM ˈweɪəl

weigher
BR ˈweɪə(r), -z
AM ˈweɪər, -z

weigh-in
BR ˈweɪɪn, -z
AM ˈweɪˌɪn, -z

weight
BR weɪt, -s, -ɪŋ, -ɨd
AM weɪ|t, -ts, -dɪŋ, -dɨd

weightily
BR ˈweɪtɨli
AM ˈweɪdɨli

weightiness
BR ˈweɪtɪnɨs
AM ˈweɪdinɨs

weighting
BR ˈweɪtɪŋ, -z
AM ˈweɪdɪŋ, -z

weightless
BR ˈweɪtlɨs
AM ˈweɪtlɨs

weightlessly
BR ˈweɪtlɨsli
AM ˈweɪtlɨsli

weightlessness
BR ˈweɪtlɨsnɨs
AM ˈweɪtlɨsnɨs

weightlifter
BR ˈweɪtˌlɪftə(r), -z
AM ˈweɪtˌlɪftər, -z

weightlifting
BR ˈweɪtˌlɪftɪŋ
AM ˈweɪtˌlɪftɪŋ

weight loss
BR ˈweɪt lɒs
AM ˈweɪt ˌlɔs, ˈweɪt ˌlɑs

Weightwatchers®
BR ˈweɪtˌwɒtʃəz
AM ˈweɪtˌwɑtʃərz

weighty
BR ˈweɪt|i, -ɪə(r), -ɪɨst
AM ˈweɪdi, -ər, -ɨst

Weil
BR vʌɪl, wiːl
AM vaɪl, waɪl

Weill
BR vʌɪl, wiːl
AM vaɪl, waɪl

Weimar
BR ˈvʌɪmɑː(r)
AM ˈvaɪˌmɑr

Weimaraner
BR ˈvʌɪmərɑːnə(r), ˈwʌɪmərɑːnə(r), ˌvʌɪməˈrɑːnə(r), ˌwʌɪməˈrɑːnə(r), -z
AM ˈwaɪməˌrɑnər, -z

Weinberger
BR ˈwʌɪnbəːgə(r)
AM ˈwaɪnˌbərgər

Weiner
BR ˈvʌɪnə(r)
AM ˈwaɪnər

Weinstock
BR ˈwʌɪnstɒk
AM ˈwaɪnˌstɑk

weir
BR wɪə(r), -z
AM wɪ(ə)r, -z

weird
BR wɪəd, -ə(r), -ɨst
AM wɪ(ə)rd, -ər, -ɨst

weirdie
BR ˈwɪəd|i, -ɪz
AM ˈwɪrdi, -z

weirdly
BR ˈwɪədli
AM ˈwɪrdli

weirdness
BR ˈwɪədnəs
AM ˈwɪrdnəs

weirdo
BR ˈwɪədəʊ, -z
AM ˈwɪrdoʊ, -z

Weismann
BR ˈvʌɪsmən
AM ˈwaɪsmən

Weismannism
BR ˈvʌɪsmənɪz(ə)m
AM ˈwaɪsməˌnɪzəm

Weiss
BR vʌɪs, weɪs
AM waɪs, vaɪs

Weissmuller
BR ˈwʌɪsˌmʊlə(r)
AM ˈwaɪsˌmʊlər

Weizmann
BR ˈvʌɪtsmən
AM ˈvaɪtsmən

weka
BR ˈwɛkə(r), -z
AM ˈwɛkə, -z

welch
BR wɛl(t)ʃ, -ɨz, -ɪŋ, -t
AM wɛl(t)ʃ, -əz, -ɪŋ, -t

welcome
BR ˈwɛlkəm, -z, -ɪŋ, -d
AM ˈwɛlkəm, -z, -ɪŋ, -d

welcomely
BR ˈwɛlkəmli
AM ˈwɛlkəmli

welcomeness
BR ˈwɛlkəmnəs
AM ˈwɛlkəmnəs

welcomer
BR ˈwɛlkəmə(r), -z
AM ˈwɛlkəmər, -z

welcomingly
BR ˈwɛlkəmɪŋli
AM ˈwɛlkəmɪŋli

weld
BR wɛld, -z, -ɪŋ, -ɨd
AM wɛld, -z, -ɪŋ, -əd

weldability
BR ˌwɛldəˈbɪlɨti
AM ˌwɛldəˈbɪlɨdi

weldable
BR ˈwɛldəbl
AM ˈwɛldəbəl

welder
BR ˈwɛldə(r), -z
AM ˈwɛldər, -z

Weldon
BR ˈwɛld(ə)n
AM ˈwɛldən

welfare
BR ˈwɛlfɛː(r)
AM ˈwɛlˌfɛ(ə)r

welfare state
BR ˌwɛlfɛː ˈsteɪt, -s
AM ˈwɛlfɛr ˌsteɪt, -s

welfarism
BR ˈwɛlfərɪz(ə)m, ˈwɛlfɛːrɪz(ə)m
AM ˈwɛlˌfɛrˌɪzəm

welfarist
BR ˈwɛlfərɪst, ˈwɛlfɛːrɪst, -s
AM ˈwɛlˌfɛrəst, -s

Welford
BR ˈwɛlfəd
AM ˈwɛlfərd

welkin
BR ˈwɛlkɪn
AM ˈwɛlkən

well
BR wɛl, -z, -ɪŋ, -d
AM wɛl, -z, -ɪŋ, -d

we'll[1]
strong form
BR wiːl
AM wiːl

we'll[2]
weak form
BR wɪl
AM wəl

Welland
BR ˈwɛlənd
AM ˈwɛlənd

wellbeing
BR ˈwɛlbiɪŋ
AM ˌwɛlˈbiɪŋ

Wellbeloved
BR ˈwɛlbɨlʌvd
AM ˈwɛlbəˌləvd

Wellcome
BR ˈwɛlkəm
AM ˈwɛlkəm

well deck
BR ˈwɛl dɛk, -s
AM ˈwɛl ˌdɛk, -s

well-dressing
BR ˈwɛlˌdrɛsɪŋ, -z
AM ˌwɛlˈdrɛsɪŋ, -z

Weller
BR ˈwɛlə(r)
AM ˈwɛlər

Welles
BR wɛlz
AM wɛlz

Wellesbourne
BR ˈwɛlzbɔːn
AM ˈwɛlzˌbɔ(ə)rn

Wellesley
BR ˈwɛlzli
AM ˈwɛlzli

wellhead
BR ˈwɛlhɛd, -z
AM ˈwɛlˌ(h)ɛd, -z

wellie
BR ˈwɛl|i, -ɪz
AM ˈwɛli, -z

Wellingborough
BR ˈwɛlɪŋb(ə)rə(r)
AM ˈwɛlɪŋˌbərə

wellington
BR ˈwɛlɪŋt(ə)n, -z
AM ˈwɛlɪŋtən, -z

wellness
BR ˈwɛlnəs
AM ˈwɛlnəs

Wells
BR wɛlz
AM wɛlz

wellspring
BR ˈwɛlsprɪŋ, -z
AM ˈwɛlˌsprɪŋ, -z

well-to-do
BR ˌwɛltəˈduː
AM ˌwɛldəˈdu

well-wisher
BR ˈwɛlˌwɪʃə(r), -z
AM ˈwɛlˌwɪʃər, -z

welly
BR ˈwɛl|i, -ɪz
AM ˈwɛli, -z

welsh
BR wɛlʃ, -ɨz, -ɪŋ, -t
AM wɛlʃ, -əz, -ɪŋ, -t

welsher
BR ˈwɛlʃə(r), -z
AM ˈwɛlʃər, -z

Welshman
BR ˈwɛlʃmən
AM ˈwɛlʃmən

Welshmen
BR ˈwɛlʃmən
AM ˈwɛlʃmən
Welshness
BR ˈwɛlʃnəs
AM ˈwɛlʃnəs
Welshpool
BR ˈwɛlʃpuːl
AM ˈwɛlʃˌpul
welsh rarebit
BR ˌwɛlʃ ˈrɛːbɪt, + ˈrabɪt
AM ˌwɛlʃ ˈrɛrˌbɪt
Welshwoman
BR ˈwɛlʃˌwʊmən
AM ˈwɛlʃˌwʊmən
Welshwomen
BR ˈwɛlʃˌwɪmɪn
AM ˈwɛlʃˌwɪmɨn
welt
BR wɛlt, -s, -ɪŋ, -ɨd
AM wɛlt, -s, -ɪŋ, -əd
Weltanschauung
BR ˈvɛltanˌʃaʊʊŋ, ˈvɛlt(ə)nˌʃaʊʊŋ
AM ˈwɛltˈɑnˌʃaʊʊŋ
Weltanschauungen
BR ˈvɛltanˌʃaʊʊŋən, ˈvɛlt(ə)nˌʃaʊʊŋən
AM ˈwɛltˈɑnˌʃaʊʊŋən
welter
BR ˈwɛlt|ə(r), -əz, -(ə)rɪŋ, -əd
AM ˈwɛlt|ər, -ərz, -(ə)rɪŋ, -ərd
welterweight
BR ˈwɛltəweɪt, -s
AM ˈwɛltərˌweɪt, -s
Weltschmerz
BR ˈvɛltˌʃməːts
AM ˈwɛltˌʃmərts
Welty
BR ˈwɛlti
AM ˈwɛlti
Welwyn
BR ˈwɛlɪn
AM ˈwɛlwən
Wem
BR wɛm
AM wɛm
Wembley
BR ˈwɛmbli
AM ˈwɛmbli
Wemyss
BR wiːmz
AM wimz
wen
BR wɛn, -z
AM wɛn, -z
Wenceslas
BR ˈwɛnsɪsləs, ˈwɛnsɪslas
AM ˈwɛnsəsˌlɑs
wench
BR wɛn(t)ʃ, -ɨz, -ɪŋ, -t
AM wɛn(t)ʃ, -əz, -ɪŋ, -t
wencher
BR ˈwɛn(t)ʃə(r), -z
AM ˈwɛn(t)ʃər, -z
wend
BR wɛnd, -z, -ɪŋ, -ɨd
AM wɛnd, -z, -ɪŋ, -əd
Wenda
BR ˈwɛndə(r)
AM ˈwɛndə
Wendell
BR ˈwɛndl
AM ˈwɛndəl, ˌwɛnˈdɛl
Wendic
BR ˈwɛndɪk
AM ˈwɛndɪk
Wendish
BR ˈwɛndɪʃ
AM ˈwɛndɪʃ
Wendover
BR ˈwɛndəʊvə(r)
AM ˈwɛnˌdoʊvər
Wendy
BR ˈwɛndi
AM ˈwɛndi
Wenham
BR ˈwɛnəm
AM ˈwɛnəm
Wenlock Edge
BR ˌwɛnlɒk ˈɛdʒ
AM ˌwɛnlɑk ˈɛdʒ
Wensleydale
BR ˈwɛnzlɪdeɪl, -z
AM ˈwɛnzliˌdeɪl, -z
Wensum
BR ˈwɛnsəm, ˈwɛnsm̩
AM ˈwɛnsəm
went
BR wɛnt
AM wɛnt
wentletrap
BR ˈwɛntltrap, -s
AM ˈwɛn(t)lˌtræp, -s
Wentworth
BR ˈwɛntw(ə)θ
AM ˈwɛntˌwərθ
Wenvoe
BR ˈwɛnvəʊ
AM ˈwɛnvoʊ
Weobley
BR ˈwɛbli
AM ˈwɛbli
wept
BR wɛpt
AM wɛpt
were
BR wəː(r)
AM wər
we're[1]
strong form
BR wɪə(r)
AM wɪ(ə)r
we're[2]
weak form
BR wə(r)
AM wər
weren't
BR wəːnt
AM wər(ə)nt
werewolf
BR ˈwɛːwʊlf, ˈwɪəwʊlf
AM ˈwɛrˌwʊlf
werewolves
BR ˈwɛːwʊlvz, ˈwɪəwʊlvz
AM ˈwɛrˌwʊlvz
wergeld
BR ˈwəːɡɛld, ˈwɛːɡɛld, ˈwɪəɡɛld
AM ˈwɛrˌɡɛld, ˈwɪrˌɡɛld
wergild
BR ˈwəːɡɪld, ˈwɛːɡɪld, ˈwɪəɡɪld
AM ˈwɛrˌɡɪld, ˈwɪrˌɡɪld
Werner
BR ˈwəːnə(r), ˈvəːnə(r)
AM ˈwərnər, ˈvərnər
wert[1]
strong form
BR wəːt
AM wərt
wert[2]
weak form
BR wət
AM wərt
Weser
BR ˈveɪzə(r)
AM ˈweɪzər, ˈweɪsər
Wesker
BR ˈwɛskə(r)
AM ˈwɛskər
Wesley
BR ˈwɛzli, ˈwɛsli
AM ˈwɛzli, ˈwɛsli
Wesleyan
BR ˈwɛzlɪən, ˈwɛslɪən, -z
AM ˈwɛsliən, ˈwɛzliən, -z
Wesleyanism
BR ˈwɛzlɪənɪz(ə)m, ˈwɛslɪənɪz(ə)m
AM ˈwɛsliəˌnɪzəm, ˈwɛzliəˌnɪzəm
Wessex
BR ˈwɛsɪks
AM ˈwɛsəks
Wesson
BR ˈwɛsn
AM ˈwɛsən
west
BR wɛst
AM wɛst
westabout
BR ˈwɛstəbaʊt
AM ˈwɛstəbaʊt
westbound
BR ˈwɛs(t)baʊnd
AM ˈwɛs(t)ˌbaʊnd
West Bromwich
BR ˌwɛs(t) ˈbrɒmɪdʒ
AM ˌwɛs(t) ˈbrɑm(w)ɪtʃ
Westbury
BR ˈwɛs(t)b(ə)ri
AM ˈwɛs(t)ˌbɛri
Westclox
BR ˈwɛs(t)klɒks
AM ˈwɛs(t)ˌklɑks
Westcott
BR ˈwɛs(t)kət, ˈwɛs(t)kɒt
AM ˈwɛs(t)ˌkɑt, ˈwɛs(t)kət
West Country
BR ˈwɛs(t) ˌkʌntri
AM ˈwɛs(t) ˌkəntri
West Countryman
BR ˌwɛs(t) ˈkʌntrɪmən
AM ˈwɛs(t) ˌkəntrimən
West Countrymen
BR ˌwɛs(t) ˈkʌntrɪmən
AM ˈwɛs(t) ˌkəntrimən
wester
BR ˈwɛst|ə(r), -əz, -(ə)rɪŋ, -əd
AM ˈwɛstər, -z, -ɪŋ, -d
Westerham
BR ˈwɛst(ə)rəm, ˈwɛst(ə)rm̩
AM ˈwɛstərəm
westerly
BR ˈwɛstəl|i, -ɪz
AM ˈwɛstərli, -z
western
BR ˈwɛst(ə)n, -z
AM ˈwɛstərn, -z
westerner
BR ˈwɛstənə(r), ˈwɛstn̩ə(r), -z
AM ˈwɛstərnər, -z
westernisation
BR ˌwɛstənʌɪˈzeɪʃn, ˌwɛstn̩ʌɪˈzeɪʃn
AM ˌwɛstərnəˈzeɪʃən, ˌwɛstərˌnaɪˈzeɪʃən
westernise
BR ˈwɛstənʌɪz, ˈwɛstn̩ʌɪz, -ɨz, -ɪŋ, -d
AM ˈwɛstərˌnaɪz, -ɨz, -ɪŋ, -d
westerniser
BR ˈwɛstənʌɪzə(r), ˈwɛstn̩ʌɪzə(r), -z
AM ˈwɛstərˌnaɪzər, -z
westernization
BR ˌwɛstənʌɪˈzeɪʃn, ˌwɛstn̩ʌɪˈzeɪʃn
AM ˌwɛstərnəˈzeɪʃən, ˌwɛstərˌnaɪˈzeɪʃən
westernize
BR ˈwɛstənʌɪz, ˈwɛstn̩ʌɪz, -ɨz, -ɪŋ, -d
AM ˈwɛstərˌnaɪz, -ɨz, -ɪŋ, -d
westernizer
BR ˈwɛstənʌɪzə(r), ˈwɛstn̩ʌɪzə(r), -z
AM ˈwɛstərˌnaɪzər, -z
westernmost
BR ˈwɛstənməʊst, ˈwɛstnməʊst

AM 'wɛstərn,moʊst

Westfield
BR 'wɛs(t)fi:ld
AM 'wɛs(t),fild

Westgate
BR 'wɛs(t)geɪt
AM 'wɛs(t),geɪt

westing
BR 'wɛstɪŋ, -z
AM 'wɛstɪŋ, -z

Westinghouse
BR 'wɛstɪŋhaʊs
AM 'wɛstɪŋ,(h)aʊs

Westland
BR 'wɛs(t)lənd
AM 'wɛs(t)lənd

Westmeath
BR ,wɛs(t)'mi:θ
AM ,wɛs(t)'miθ

Westminster
BR 'wɛs(t)mɪnstə(r), ,wɛs(t)'mɪnstə(r)
AM ¦wɛs(t)¦mɪnstər

Westmorland[1]
in Kansas and Pennsylvania, USA
BR ,wɛs(t)'mɔ:lənd
AM ,wɛs(t)'mɔrlənd

Westmorland[2]
in UK and in Virginia, USA
BR 'wɛs(t)mələnd
AM 'wɛs(t)mərlənd

Westmorland[3]
surname
BR 'wɛs(t),mɔ:lənd
AM ,wɛs(t)'mɔrlənd

west-northwest[1]
BR ,wɛs(t)nɔ:θ'wɛst
AM ¦wɛs(t),nɔrθ'wɛst

west-northwest[2]
nautical use
BR ,wɛs(t)nɔ:'wɛst
AM ¦wɛs(t),nɔr'wɛst

Weston
BR 'wɛst(ə)n
AM 'wɛstən

Weston-super-Mare
BR ,wɛst(ə)n,s(j)u:pə'mɛ:(r)
AM ,wɛstən,s(j)upər'mɛ(ə)r

Westphalia
BR wɛs(t)'feɪlɪə(*r*)
AM ,wɛs(t)'feɪljə, ,wɛs(t)'feɪliə

Westphalian
BR wɛs(t)'feɪlɪən, -z
AM ,wɛs(t)'feɪljən, ,wɛs(t)'feɪliən, -z

west-southwest[1]
BR ,wɛs(t)saʊθ'wɛst
AM ¦wɛs(t),saʊθ'wɛst

west-southwest[2]
nautical use
BR ,wɛs(t)saʊ'wɛst
AM ¦wɛs(t),saʊ'wɛst

westward
BR 'wɛstwəd, -z
AM 'wɛs(t)wərd, -z

westwardly
BR 'wɛstwədli
AM 'wɛs(t)wərdli

Westwood
BR 'wɛs(t)wʊd
AM 'wɛs(t),wʊd

wet
BR wɛt, -s, -ɪŋ, -ɨd, -ə(r), -ɨst
AM wɛ|t, -ts, -dɪŋ, -dɨd, -dər, -dəst

wet-and-dry
BR ,wɛt(ə)n(d)'drʌɪ
AM ¦wɛdən'draɪ, ¦wɛtn'draɪ

wetback
BR 'wɛtbak, -s
AM 'wɛt,bæk, -s

wether
BR 'wɛðə(r), -z
AM 'wɛðər, -z

Wetherall
BR 'wɛð(ə)rɔ:l, 'wɛð(ə)rl̩
AM 'wɛðər,ɔl, 'wɛðər,ɑl

Wetherby
BR 'wɛðəbi
AM 'wɛðərbi

wetland
BR 'wɛtland, 'wɛtlənd, -z
AM 'wɛt,lænd, 'wɛtlənd, -z

wetlook
BR 'wɛtlʊk
AM 'wɛt,lʊk

wetly
BR 'wɛtli
AM 'wɛtli

wetness
BR 'wɛtnəs
AM 'wɛtnəs

wet-nurse
BR 'wɛtnə:s, -ɨz, -ɪŋ, -t
AM 'wɛt,nərs, -əz, -ɪŋ, -t

wetsuit
BR 'wɛts(j)u:t, -s
AM 'wɛt,sut, -s

wettable
BR 'wɛtəbl
AM 'wɛdəbəl

wetting
BR 'wɛtɪŋ, -z
AM 'wɛdɪŋ, -z

wettish
BR 'wɛtɪʃ
AM 'wɛdɪʃ

wetware
BR 'wɛtwɛ:(r)
AM 'wɛt,wɛ(ə)r

wet-weather
BR ,wɛt'wɛðə(r)
AM 'wɛt¦wɛðər

we've[1]
strong form
BR wi:v
AM wiv

we've[2]
weak form
BR wɪv
AM wiv

Wexford
BR 'wɛksfəd
AM 'wɛksfərd

wey
BR weɪ, -z
AM weɪ, -z

Weybridge
BR 'weɪbrɪdʒ
AM 'weɪ,brɪdʒ

Weymouth
BR 'weɪməθ
AM 'weɪməθ

whack
BR wak, -s, -ɪŋ, -t
AM (h)wæk, -s, -ɪŋ, -t

whacker
BR 'wakə(r), -z
AM '(h)wækər, -z

whacking
BR 'wakɪŋ, -z
AM '(h)wækɪŋ, -z

whacko
BR ,wak'əʊ
AM 'wækoʊ

whacky
BR 'waki
AM 'wæki

whale
BR weɪl, -z, -ɪŋ
AM (h)weɪl, -z, -ɪŋ

whaleback
BR 'weɪlbak, -s
AM '(h)weɪl,bæk, -s

whaleboat
BR 'weɪlbəʊt, -s
AM '(h)weɪl,boʊt, -s

whalebone
BR 'weɪlbəʊn
AM '(h)weɪl,boʊn

whale-oil
BR 'weɪlɔɪl
AM '(h)weɪl,ɔɪl

whaler
BR 'weɪlə(r), -z
AM '(h)weɪlər, -z

whale-watching
BR 'weɪl,wɒtʃɪŋ
AM ''(h)weɪl,wɑtʃɪŋ

Whaley
BR 'weɪli
AM '(h)weɪli

whaling-master
BR 'weɪlɪŋ,mɑ:stə(r), 'weɪlɪŋ,mastə(r), -z
AM '(h)weɪlɪŋ,mæstər, -z

Whalley
BR 'wɒli, 'wɔ:li, 'weɪli
AM '(h)weɪli, '(h)wɔli, '(h)wɑli

Whalley Range
BR ,wɒlɪ 'reɪn(d)ʒ
AM '(h)wɔli ,reɪndʒ, '(h)wɑli ,reɪndʒ

wham
BR wam
AM (h)wæm

whammy
BR 'wam|i, -ɪz
AM '(h)wæmi, -z

whang
BR waŋ, -z
AM (h)wæŋ, -z

Whangarei
BR ,waŋə'reɪ
AM ,(h)wɑŋə'reɪ

whangee
BR ,waŋ'(g)i:, -z
AM (h)wæŋ'gi, -z

whap
BR wɒp
AM (h)wæp

whare
BR 'wɒr|i, -ɪz
AM '(h)wɑ,reɪ, -z

wharf
BR wɔ:f
AM (h)wɔ(ə)rf

wharfage
BR wɔ:fɪdʒ
AM '(h)wɔrfɪdʒ

Wharfe
BR wɔ:f
AM (h)wɔ(ə)rf

Wharfedale
BR 'wɔ:fdeɪl
AM '(h)wɔrf,deɪl

wharfie
BR 'wɔ:f|i, -ɪz
AM '(h)wɔrfi, -z

wharfinger
BR 'wɔ:fɪn(d)ʒə(r), -z
AM '(h)wɔrfəndʒər, -z

Wharton
BR 'wɔ:tn
AM '(h)wɔrtən

wharves
BR wɔ:vz
AM (h)wɔ(ə)rvz

what
BR wɒt
AM (h)wət

whate'er
BR wɒt'ɛ:(r), wət'ɛ:(r)
AM (h)wə'tɛ(ə)r

whatever
BR wɒt'ɛvə(r), wət'ɛvə(r)
AM (h)wət'ɛvər, '(h)wədɛvər

Whatmough
BR 'wɒtməʊ, 'wɒtmʌf
AM '(h)wətmoʊ

whatnot
BR 'wɒtnɒt, -s

AM '(h)wət,nɑt, -s

what's-her-name
BR 'wɒtsəneɪm
AM '(h)wətsər,neɪm

what's-his-name
BR 'wɒtsɪzneɪm
AM '(h)wətsɪz,neɪm

whatsit
BR 'wɒtsɪt, -s
AM '(h)wətsɪt, -s

what's it
BR 'wɒts ɪt, -s
AM '(h)wəts ɪt, -s

what's-its-name
BR 'wɒtsɪtsneɪm
AM '(h)wətsɪts,neɪm

whatsoe'er
BR ,wɒtsəʊ'ɛː(r)
AM ,(h)wətsoʊ'ɛ(ə)r

whatsoever
BR ,wɒtsəʊ'ɛvə(r)
AM ,(h)wətsoʊ'ɛvər

what-you-may-call-it
BR 'wɒtʃəmə,kɔːlɪt, 'wɒdʒəmə,kɔːlɪt
AM '(h)wətʃəmə,kɔlɪt, '(h)wətʃəmə,kɑlɪt

whaup
BR wɔːp, -s
AM (h)wɑp, -s

wheal
BR wiːl, -z, -ɪŋ, -d
AM (h)wil, -z, -ɪŋ, -d

wheat
BR wiːt
AM (h)wit

wheat cake
BR 'wiːt keɪk, -s
AM '(h)wit ,keɪk, -s

Wheatcroft
BR 'wiːtkrɒft
AM '(h)wit,krɔft, '(h)wit,krɑft

wheatear
BR 'wiːtɪə(r), -z
AM 'wid,ɪ(ə)r, -z

wheaten
BR 'wiːtn
AM '(h)witn

wheatgerm
BR 'wiːtdʒəːm
AM '(h)wit,dʒərm

wheatgrass
BR 'wiːtgrɑːs, 'wiːtgras
AM '(h)wit,græs

Wheathampstead
BR 'wiːt(ə)mstɛd, 'wiːt(ə)mstɪd, 'wɛtəmstɛd, 'wɛtəmstɪd
AM '(h)widəm,stɛd, '(h)wɛdəm,stɛd

Wheatley
BR 'wiːtli
AM '(h)witli

wheatmeal
BR 'wiːtmiːl
AM '(h)wit,mil

wheatsheaf
BR 'wiːtʃiːf
AM '(h)wit,ʃif

wheatsheaves
BR 'wiːtʃiːvz
AM '(h)wit,ʃivz

Wheatstone
BR 'wiːtstəʊn
AM '(h)wit,stoʊn

whee
BR wiː
AM (h)wi

wheedle
BR 'wiːd|l, -lz, -l̩ɪŋ\-lɪŋ, -ld
AM '(h)wid|əl, -əlz, -(ə)lɪŋ, -əld

wheedler
BR 'wiːdl̩ə(r), 'wiːdlə(r), -z
AM '(h)wid(ə)lər, -z

wheedlingly
BR 'wiːdl̩ɪŋli, 'wiːdlɪŋli
AM '(h)widlɪŋli

wheel
BR wiːl, -z, -ɪŋ, -d
AM (h)wil, -z, -ɪŋ, -d

wheelbarrow
BR 'wiːl,barəʊ, -z
AM '(h)wil,bɛroʊ, -z

wheelbase
BR 'wiːlbeɪs, -ɪz
AM '(h)wil,beɪs, -ɪz

wheelchair
BR 'wiːltʃɛː(r), -z
AM '(h)wil,tʃɛ(ə)r, -z

wheel-clamp
BR 'wiːlklam|p, -ps, -pɪŋ, -(p)t
AM '(h)wil,klæm|p, -(p)s, -pɪŋ, -(p)t

wheeler
BR 'wiːlə(r), -z
AM '(h)wilər, -z

wheeler-dealer
BR ,wiːlə'diːlə(r), -z
AM ',(h)wilər'dilər, -z

wheeler-dealing
BR ,wiːlə'diːlɪŋ
AM ',(h)wilɪŋ'dilɪŋ

wheelhouse
BR 'wiːlhaʊ|s, -zɪz
AM '(h)wil,(h)aʊ|s, -zəz

wheelie
BR 'wiːl|i, -ɪz
AM '(h)wili, -z

wheeling
BR 'wiːlɪŋ, -z
AM '(h)wilɪŋ, -z

wheelless
BR 'wiːllɪs
AM '(h)wi(l)lɪs

wheelman
BR 'wiːlman
AM '(h)wil,mæn

wheelmen
BR 'wiːlmɛn
AM '(h)wil,mɛn

wheelright
BR 'wiːlrʌɪt, -s
AM '(h)wil,raɪt, -s

wheelslip
BR 'wiːlslɪp
AM '(h)wil,slɪp

wheelsman
BR 'wiːlzmən
AM '(h)wilzmən

wheelsmen
BR 'wiːlzmən
AM '(h)wilzmən

wheelspin
BR 'wiːlspɪn
AM '(h)wil,spɪn

wheelwright
BR 'wiːlrʌɪt, -s
AM '(h)wil,raɪt, -s

Wheen
BR wiːn
AM (h)win

wheeze
BR wiːz, -ɪz, -ɪŋ, -d
AM (h)wiz, -ɪz, -ɪŋ, -d

wheezer
BR 'wiːzə(r), -z
AM '(h)wizər, -z

wheezily
BR 'wiːzɪli
AM '(h)wizɪli

wheeziness
BR 'wiːzɪnɪs
AM '(h)wizinɪs

wheezingly
BR 'wiːzɪŋli
AM '(h)wizɪŋli

wheezy
BR 'wiːz|i, -ɪə(r), -ɪɪst
AM '(h)wizi, -ər, -ɪst

Whelan
BR 'wiːlən
AM '(h)weɪlən, '(h)wilən

whelk
BR wɛlk, -s
AM (h)wɛlk, -s

whelp
BR wɛlp, -s
AM (h)wɛlp, -s

when
BR wɛn
AM (h)wɛn

whence
BR wɛns
AM (h)wɛns

whencesoever
BR ,wɛns(s)əʊ'ɛvə(r)
AM ',(h)wɛn(s)soʊ'ɛvər

whene'er
BR wə'nɛː(r), wɛ'nɛː(r)
AM (h)wə'nɛ(ə)r, (h)wɛ'nɛ(ə)r

whenever
BR wə'nɛvə(r), wɛ'nɛvə(r)
AM (h)wə'nɛvər, (h)wɛ'nɛvər

whensoe'er
BR ,wɛnsəʊ'ɛː(r)
AM ',(h)wɛnsoʊ'ɛ(ə)r

whensoever
BR ,wɛnsəʊ'ɛvə(r)
AM ',(h)wɛnsoʊ'ɛvər

where
BR wɛː(r)
AM (h)wɛ(ə)r

whereabouts[1]
adverb
BR ,wɛːrə'baʊts, 'wɛːrəbaʊts
AM ',(h)wɛrə'baʊts

whereabouts[2]
noun
BR 'wɛːrəbaʊts
AM '(h)wɛrə,baʊts

whereafter
BR wər'ɑːftə(r), wɛːr'ɑːftə(r), wɛr'ɑːftə(r), wər'aftə(r), wɛːr'aftə(r), wɛr'aftə(r)
AM (h)wə'ræftər, (h)wɛ'ræftər

whereas
BR wər'az, wɛːr'az, wɛr'az
AM (h)wə'ræz, (h)wɛ'ræz

whereat
BR wər'at, wɛːr'at, wɛr'at
AM (h)wə'ræt, (h)wɛ'ræt

whereby
BR wɛː'bʌɪ
AM (h)wɛr'baɪ

where'er
BR wɛːr'ɛː(r)
AM (h)wɛ'rɛ(ə)r

wherefore
BR 'wɛːfɔː(r), -z
AM '(h)wɛr,fɔ(ə)r, -z

wherefrom
BR wɛː'frɒm
AM ,(h)wɛr'frəm

wherein
BR wər'ɪn, wɛː'rɪn, wɛr'ɪn
AM (h)wɛ'rɪn

whereof
BR wər'ɒv, wɛːr'ɒv, wɛr'ɒv
AM (h)wɛ'rəv, (h)wɛ'rɑv

whereon
BR wər'ɒn, wɛː'rɒn, wɛr'ɒn

AM (h)wɛ'rɑn

wheresoe'er
BR ˌwɛːsəʊ'ɛː(r)
AM ˌ(h)wɛrsoʊ'ɛ(ə)r

wheresoever
BR ˌwɛːsəʊ'ɛvə(r)
AM ˌ(h)wɛrsoʊ'ɛvər

whereto
BR wɛː'tuː
AM (h)wɛr'to

whereupon
BR ˌwɛːrə'pɒn
AM ˌ(h)wɛrə'pɑn

wherever
BR wər'ɛvə(r), wɛːr'ɛvə(r), wɛr'ɛvə(r)
AM (h)wə'rɛvər, (h)wɛ'rɛvər

wherewith
BR wɛː'wɪð
AM (h)wɛr'wɪð, (h)wɛr'wɪθ

wherewithal[1]
adverb
BR ˌwɛːwɪ'ðɔːl, 'wɛːwɪðɔːl
AM '(h)wɛrwəˌðɔl, '(h)wɛrwəˌθɔl, '(h)wɛrwəˌðɑl, '(h)wɛrwəˌθɑl

wherewithal[2]
noun
BR 'wɛːwɪðɔːl
AM '(h)wɛrwəˌðɔl, '(h)wɛrwəˌθɔl, '(h)wɛrwəˌðɑl, '(h)wɛrwəˌθɑl

Whernside
BR 'wəːnsʌɪd
AM '(h)wərnˌsaɪd

wherry
BR 'wɛr|i, -ɪz
AM '(h)wɛri, -z

wherryman
BR 'wɛrɪmən
AM '(h)wɛrimən

wherrymen
BR 'wɛrɪmən
AM '(h)wɛrimən

whet
BR wɛt, -s, -ɪŋ, -ɪd
AM (h)wɛt, -s, -ɪŋ, -əd

whether
BR 'wɛðə(r)
AM '(h)wɛðər

whetstone
BR 'wɛtstəʊn, -z
AM '(h)wɛtˌstoʊn, -z

whetter
BR 'wɛtə(r), -z
AM '(h)wɛdər, -z

whew
BR h(w)juː
AM h(w)ju

Whewell
BR 'hjuː(ə)l
AM 'hju(ə)l

whey
BR weɪ
AM (h)weɪ

which
BR wɪtʃ
AM (h)wɪtʃ

whichever
BR wɪtʃ'ɛvə(r)
AM ˌ(h)wɪ'tʃɛvər

whichsoever
BR ˌwɪtʃsəʊ'ɛvə(r)
AM ¦(h)wɪtʃsoʊ'ɛvər

whicker
BR 'wɪk|ə(r), -əz, -(ə)rɪŋ, -əd
AM '(h)wɪkər, -z, -ɪŋ, -d

whidah
BR 'wɪdə(*r*), -z
AM '(h)wɪdə, -z

whiff
BR wɪf, -s, -ɪŋ, -t
AM (h)wɪf, -s, -ɪŋ, -t

whiffiness
BR 'wɪfɪnɪs
AM 'wɪfinɪs

whiffle
BR 'wɪf|l, -lz, -lɪŋ\-lɪŋ, -ld
AM '(h)wɪfəl, -əlz, -(ə)lɪŋ, -əld

whiffler
BR 'wɪfḷə(r), 'wɪflə(r), -z
AM '(h)wɪf(ə)lər, -z

whiffletree
BR 'wɪfltriː, -z
AM '(h)wɪfəlˌtri, -z

whiffy
BR 'wɪf|i, -ɪə(r), -ɪɪst
AM '(h)wɪfi, -ər, -ɪst

Whig
BR wɪg, -z
AM (h)wɪg, -z

whiggery
BR 'wɪg(ə)ri
AM '(h)wɪgəri

whiggish
BR 'wɪgɪʃ
AM '(h)wɪgɪʃ

whiggishness
BR 'wɪgɪʃnɪs
AM '(h)wɪgɪʃnɪs

whiggism
BR 'wɪgɪz(ə)m
AM '(h)wɪgˌɪzəm

while
BR wʌɪl, -z, -ɪŋ, -d
AM (h)waɪl, -z, -ɪŋ, -d

whilom
BR 'wʌɪləm
AM '(h)waɪləm

whilst
BR wʌɪlst
AM (h)waɪlst

whim
BR wɪm, -z
AM (h)wɪm, -z

whimbrel
BR 'wɪmbr(ə)l, -z
AM '(h)wɪmbrəl, -z

whimper
BR 'wɪmp|ə(r), -əz, -(ə)rɪŋ, -əd
AM (h)wɪmp|ər, -ərz, -(ə)rɪŋ, -ərd

whimperer
BR 'wɪmp(ə)rə(r), -z
AM '(h)wɪmp(ə)rər, -z

whimpering
BR 'wɪmp(ə)rɪŋ, -z
AM '(h)wɪmp(ə)rɪŋ, -z

whimperingly
BR 'wɪmp(ə)rɪŋli
AM '(h)wɪmp(ə)rɪŋli

whimsey
BR 'wɪmz|i, -ɪz
AM '(h)wɪmzi, -z

whimsical
BR 'wɪmzɪkl
AM '(h)wɪmzɪkəl

whimsicality
BR ˌwɪmzɪ'kalɪti
AM ˌ(h)wɪmzə'kælədi

whimsically
BR 'wɪmzɪkli
AM '(h)wɪmzɪk(ə)li

whimsicalness
BR 'wɪmzɪklnəs
AM '(h)wɪmzɪkəlnəs

whimsy
BR 'wɪmz|i, -ɪz
AM '(h)wɪmzi, -z

whim-wham
BR 'wɪmwam, -z
AM '(h)wɪmˌ(h)wæm, -z

whin
BR wɪn
AM (h)wɪn

whinchat
BR 'wɪntʃat, -s
AM '(h)wɪnˌtʃæt, -s

whine
BR wʌɪn, -z, -ɪŋ, -d
AM (h)waɪn, -z, -ɪŋ, -d

whiner
BR 'wʌɪnə(r), -z
AM '(h)waɪnər, -z

whinge
BR wɪn(d)ʒ, -ɪz, -ɪŋ, -d
AM (h)wɪndʒ, -ɪz, -ɪŋ, -d

whingeingly
BR 'wɪn(d)ʒɪŋli
AM '(h)wɪndʒɪŋli

whinger
BR 'wɪn(d)ʒə(r), -z
AM '(h)wɪndʒər, -z

whingey
BR 'wɪn(d)ʒi
AM '(h)wɪndʒi

whingingly
BR 'wɪn(d)ʒɪŋli
AM '(h)wɪndʒɪŋli

whingy
BR 'wɪn(d)ʒi
AM '(h)wɪndʒi

whiningly
BR 'wʌɪnɪŋli
AM '(h)waɪnɪŋli

whinny
BR wɪn|i, -ɪz, -ɪɪŋ, -ɪd
AM '(h)wɪni, -z, -ɪŋ, -d

whinsill
BR 'wɪnsɪl, -z
AM '(h)wɪnˌsɪl, -z

whinstone
BR 'wɪnstəʊn
AM '(h)wɪnˌstoʊn

whiny
BR 'wʌɪn|i, -ɪə(r), -ɪɪst
AM '(h)waɪni, -ər, -ɪst

whip
BR wɪp, -s, -ɪŋ, -t
AM (h)wɪp, -s, -ɪŋ, -t

whipcord
BR 'wɪpkɔːd
AM '(h)wɪpˌkɔ(ə)rd

whipcracking
BR 'wɪpˌkrakɪŋ
AM '(h)wɪpˌkrækɪŋ

whip hand
BR ˌwɪp 'hand
AM '(h)wɪp ˌ(h)ænd

whiplash
BR 'wɪplaʃ
AM '(h)wɪpˌlaʃ

whipless
BR 'wɪplɪs
AM '(h)wɪplɪs

whipper
BR 'wɪpə(r), -z
AM '(h)wɪpər, -z

whipper-in
BR ˌwɪpər'ɪn
AM '(h)wɪpə'rɪn

whippers-in
BR ˌwɪpəz'ɪn
AM '(h)wɪpərz'ɪn

whippersnapper
BR 'wɪpəˌsnapə(r), -z
AM '(h)wɪpərˌsnæpər, -z

whippet
BR wɪpɪt, -s
AM '(h)wɪpɪt, -s

whippiness
BR 'wɪpɪnɪs
AM '(h)wɪpinɪs

whipping
BR 'wɪpɪŋ, -z
AM '(h)wɪpɪŋ, -z

whippletree
BR 'wɪpltriː, -z
AM '(h)wɪpəlˌtri, -z

whippoorwill
BR 'wɪpəwɪl, -z
AM '(h)wɪpərˌwɪl, -z

whippy
BR 'wɪpi
AM '(h)wɪpi

whip-round
BR ˈwɪpraʊnd, -z
AM ˈ(h)wɪpˌraʊnd, -z

whipsaw
BR ˈwɪpsɔː(r), -z
AM ˈ(h)wɪpˌsɔ, ˈ(h)wɪpˌsɑ, -z

Whipsnade
BR ˈwɪpsneɪd
AM ˈ(h)wɪpˌsneɪd

whipster
BR ˈwɪpstə(r), -z
AM ˈ(h)wɪpstər, -z

whipstock
BR ˈwɪpstɒk, -s
AM ˈ(h)wɪpˌstɑk, -s

whipworm
BR ˈwɪpwəːm, -z
AM ˈ(h)wɪpˌwərm, -z

whir
BR wəː(r), -z, -ɪŋ, -d
AM (h)wər, -z, -ɪŋ, -d

whirl
BR wəːl, -z, -ɪŋ, -d
AM (h)wərl, -z, -ɪŋ, -d

whirler
BR ˈwəːlə(r), -z
AM ˈ(h)wərlər, -z

whirligig
BR ˈwəːlɪɡɪɡ, -z
AM ˈ(h)wərliˌɡɪɡ, -z

whirlingly
BR ˈwəːlɪŋli
AM ˈ(h)wərlɪŋli

whirlpool
BR ˈwəːlpuːl, -z
AM ˈ(h)wərlˌpul, -z

whirlwind
BR ˈwəːlwɪnd, -z
AM ˈ(h)wərlˌwɪnd, -z

whirlybird
BR ˈwəːlɪbəːd, -z
AM ˈ(h)wərliˌbərd, -z

whirr
BR wəː(r), -z, -ɪŋ, -d
AM (h)wər, -z, -ɪŋ, -d

whisht
BR (h)wɪʃt
AM (h)wɪʃt

whisk
BR wɪsk, -s, -ɪŋ, -t
AM (h)wɪsk, -s, -ɪŋ, -t

Whiskas®
BR ˈwɪskəz
AM ˈ(h)wɪskəz

whiskbroom
BR ˈwɪs(k)bruːm, -z
AM ˈ(h)wɪs(k)ˌbrum, ˈ(h)wɪs(k)ˌbrʊm, -z

whisker
BR ˈwɪskə(r), -z, -d
AM ˈ(h)wɪskər, -z, -d

whiskery
BR ˈwɪsk(ə)ri
AM ˈ(h)wɪskəri

whiskey
BR ˈwɪsk|i, -ɪz
AM ˈ(h)wɪski, -z

whisky
BR ˈwɪsk|i, -ɪz
AM ˈ(h)wɪski, -z

whisper
BR ˈwɪsp|ə(r), -əz, -(ə)rɪŋ, -əd
AM ˈ(h)wɪsp|ər, -ərz, -(ə)rɪŋ, -ərd

whisperer
BR ˈwɪsp(ə)rə(r), -z
AM ˈ(h)wɪsp(ə)rər, -z

whispering
BR ˈwɪsp(ə)rɪŋ, -z
AM ˈ(h)wɪsp(ə)rɪŋ, -z

whist
BR wɪst
AM (h)wɪst

whistle
BR ˈwɪs|l, -lz, -l̩ɪŋ\-lɪŋ, -ld
AM ˈ(h)wɪs|əl, -əlz, -(ə)lɪŋ, -əld

whistler
BR ˈwɪsl̩ə(r), ˈwɪslə(r), -z
AM ˈ(h)wɪs(ə)lər, -z

Whistlerian
BR wɪˈslɪərɪən
AM (h)wɪˈslɪriən

whistle-stop
BR ˈwɪslstɒp
AM ˈ(h)wɪsəlˌstɑp

whit
BR wɪt
AM (h)wɪt

Whitaker
BR ˈwɪtəkə(r)
AM ˈ(h)wɪdəkər

Whitbread
BR ˈwɪtbrɛd
AM ˈ(h)wɪtˌbrɛd

Whitby
BR ˈwɪtbi
AM ˈ(h)wɪtbi

Whitchurch
BR ˈwɪttʃəːtʃ
AM ˈ(h)wɪt(t)ʃərtʃ

Whitcut
BR ˈwɪtkʌt
AM ˈ(h)wɪtkət

Whitcutt
BR ˈwɪtkʌt
AM ˈ(h)wɪtkət

white
BR wʌɪt, -s, -ɪŋ, -ə(r), -ɨst
AM (h)waɪ|t, -ts, -dɪŋ, -dər, -dəst

whitebait
BR ˈwʌɪtbeɪt
AM ˈ(h)waɪtˌbeɪt

whitebeam
BR ˈwʌɪtbiːm, -z
AM ˈ(h)waɪtˌbim, -z

whiteboard
BR ˈwʌɪtbɔːd, -z
AM ˈwaɪtˌbɔ(ə)rd, -z

whitecap
BR ˈwʌɪtkap, -s
AM ˈ(h)waɪtˌkæp, -s

Whitechapel
BR ˈwʌɪtˌtʃapl
AM ˈ(h)waɪtˌtʃæpəl

white-collar
BR ˌwʌɪtˈkɒlə(r)
AM ˌ(h)waɪtˈkɑlər

whitecurrant
BR ˈwʌɪtˌkʌrənt, ˈwʌɪtˌkʌrn̩t, -s
AM ˈ(h)waɪtˌkərənt, -s

whited sepulchre
BR ˌwʌɪtɨd ˈsɛp(ə)lkə(r), -z
AM ˌ(h)waɪdɨd ˈsɛpəlkər, -z

white-eye
BR ˈwʌɪtʌɪ, -z
AM ˈ(h)waɪdˌaɪ, -z

whiteface
BR ˈwʌɪtfeɪs, -ɨz
AM ˈ(h)waɪtˌfeɪs, -ɨz

whitefaced
BR ˌwʌɪtˈfeɪst
AM ˈ(h)waɪtˌfeɪst

Whitefield
BR ˈwʌɪtfiːld, ˈwɪtfiːld
AM ˈ(h)waɪtˌfild

whitefish
BR ˈwʌɪtfɪʃ
AM ˈ(h)waɪtˌfɪʃ

whitefly
BR ˈwʌɪtflʌɪ, -z
AM ˈ(h)waɪtˌflaɪ, -z

Whitefriars
BR ˈwʌɪtˌfrʌɪəz
AM ˈ(h)waɪtˌfraɪərz

Whitehall
BR ˈwʌɪthɔːl, ˌwʌɪtˈhɔːl
AM ˈ(h)waɪtˌ(h)ɔl, ˈ(h)waɪtˌ(h)ɑl

Whitehaven
BR ˈwʌɪtˌheɪvn
AM ˈ(h)waɪtˌ(h)eɪvən

whitehead
BR ˈwʌɪthɛd, -z
AM ˈ(h)waɪtˌ(h)ɛd, ˈ(h)waɪt(h)ɛd, -z

Whitehorn
BR ˈwʌɪthɔːn
AM ˈ(h)waɪtˌ(h)ɔ(ə)rn

Whitehorse
BR ˈwʌɪthɔːs
AM ˈ(h)waɪtˌ(h)ɔ(ə)rs

Whitehouse
BR ˈwʌɪthaʊs
AM ˈ(h)waɪtˌ(h)aʊs

White House
BR ˈwʌɪt haʊs
AM ˈ(h)waɪt ˌ(h)aʊs

Whitelaw
BR ˈwʌɪtlɔː(r)
AM ˈ(h)waɪtˌlɔ, ˈ(h)waɪtˌlɑ

Whiteley
BR ˈwʌɪtli
AM ˈ(h)waɪtli

whitely
BR ˈwʌɪtli
AM ˈ(h)waɪtli

white man
BR ˈwʌɪt man
AM ˈ(h)waɪt ˌmæn

white men
BR ˈwʌɪt mɛn
AM ˈ(h)waɪt ˌmɛn

whiten
BR ˈwʌɪt|n, -nz, -n̩ɪŋ\-nɪŋ, -nd
AM ˈ(h)waɪtn, -z, -ɪŋ, -d

whitener
BR ˈwʌɪtn̩ə(r), ˈwʌɪtnə(r), -z
AM ˈ(h)wətn̩ər, -z

whiteness
BR ˈwʌɪtnɨs
AM ˈ(h)waɪtnɨs

white-out
BR ˈwʌɪtaʊt, -s
AM ˈ(h)waɪtˌaʊt, -s

whitesmith
BR ˈwʌɪtsmɪθ, -s
AM ˈ(h)waɪtˌsmɪθ, -s

white-tail
BR ˈwʌɪtteɪl, -z, -d
AM ˈ(h)waɪtˌteɪl, -z, -d

whitethorn
BR ˈwʌɪtθɔːn, -z
AM ˈ(h)waɪtˌθɔ(ə)rn, -z

whitethroat
BR ˈwʌɪtθrəʊt, -s
AM ˈ(h)waɪtˌθroʊt, -s

whitewall
BR ˈwʌɪtwɔːl, -z
AM ˈ(h)waɪtˌwɔl, ˈ(h)waɪtˌwɑl, -z

whitewash
BR ˈwʌɪtwɒʃ, -ɨz, -ɪŋ, -t
AM ˈ(h)waɪtˌwɔʃ, ˈ(h)waɪtˌwɑʃ, -əz, -ɪŋ, -t

whitewasher
BR ˈwʌɪtwɒʃə(r), -z
AM ˈ(h)waɪtˌwɔʃər, ˈ(h)waɪtˌwɑʃər, -z

Whitewater
BR ˈwʌɪtˌwɔːtə(r)
AM ˈ(h)waɪtˌwɔdər, ˈ(h)waɪtˌwɑdər

whitewood
BR ˈwʌɪtwʊd
AM ˈ(h)waɪtˌwʊd

whitey
BR ˈwʌɪt|i, -ɪz
AM ˈ(h)waɪdi, -z

Whitfield
BR ˈwɪtfiːld
AM ˈ(h)wɪtˌfild

Whitgift
BR 'wɪtgɪft
AM '(h)wɪt,gɪft
whither
BR 'wɪðə(r)
AM '(h)wɪðər
whithersoever
BR ,wɪðəsəʊ'ɛvə(r)
AM ,(h)wɪðərsoʊ'ɛvər
whitherward
BR 'wɪðəwəd
AM '(h)wɪðərwərd
whiting
BR 'wʌɪtɪŋ
AM '(h)waɪdɪŋ
whitish
BR 'wʌɪtɪʃ
AM '(h)waɪdɪʃ
whitishness
BR 'wʌɪtɪʃnɨs
AM '(h)waɪdɪʃnɨs
Whitlam
BR 'wɪtləm
AM '(h)wɪtləm
whitleather
BR 'wɪt,lɛðə(r)
AM '(h)wɪt,lɛðər
Whitley
BR 'wɪtli
AM '(h)wɪtli
Whitlock
BR 'wɪtlɒk
AM '(h)wɪt,lɑk
whitlow
BR 'wɪtləʊ, -z
AM '(h)wɪt,loʊ, -z
Whitman
BR 'wɪtmən
AM '(h)wɪtmən
Whitmore
BR 'wɪtmɔː(r)
AM '(h)wɪt,mɔ(ə)r
Whitney
BR 'wɪtni
AM '(h)wɪtni
Whitstable
BR 'wɪtstəbl
AM '(h)wɪtstəbəl
Whitsun
BR 'wɪtsn, -z
AM '(h)wɪtsən, -z
Whit Sunday
BR ,wɪt 'sʌnd|eɪ, + 'sʌnd|i, -eɪz\-ɪz
AM ¦(h)wɪt 'sən,deɪ, + 'səndi, -z
Whitsuntide
BR 'wɪtsntʌɪd, -z
AM '(h)wɪtsən,taɪd, -z
Whittaker
BR 'wɪtəkə(r)
AM '(h)wɪdəkər
Whittier
BR 'wɪtɪə(r)
AM '(h)wɪdiər
Whittington
BR 'wɪtɪŋt(ə)n
AM '(h)wɪdɪŋtən
whittle
BR 'wɪt|l, -lz, -l̩ɪŋ\-lɪŋ, -ld
AM '(h)wɪdəl, -z, -ɪŋ, -d
Whitty
BR 'wɪti
AM '(h)wɪdi
Whitworth
BR 'wɪtwəːθ, 'wɪtwəθ
AM '(h)wɪt,wərθ
whity
BR 'wʌɪt|i, -ɪz
AM '(h)waɪdi, -z
whiz
BR wɪz, -ɨz, -ɪŋ, -d
AM (h)wɪz, -ɨz, -ɪŋ, -d
whiz-bang
BR 'wɪzbaŋ, -z
AM '(h)wɪz,bæŋ, -z
whizkid
BR 'wɪzkɪd, -z
AM '(h)wɪz,kɪd, -z
whizz
BR wɪz, -ɨz, -ɪŋ, -d
AM (h)wɪz, -ɨz, -ɪŋ, -d
whizzbang
BR 'wɪzbaŋ, -z
AM '(h)wɪz,bæŋ, -z
whizzer
BR 'wɪzə(r), -z
AM '(h)wɪzər, -z
whizz-kid
BR 'wɪzkɪd, -z
AM '(h)wɪz,kɪd, -z
whizzo
BR 'wɪzəʊ
AM '(h)wɪ,zoʊ
WHO
BR ,dʌbljʊeɪtʃ'əʊ
AM ,dəbəlju,eɪtʃ'oʊ
who
BR huː
AM hu
whoa!
BR wəʊ
AM (h)woʊ
who'd¹
strong form, who had, who would
BR huːd
AM hud
who'd²
weak form, who had, who would
BR hʊd
AM hʊd
whodunit
BR ,huː'dʌnɪt, -s
AM hu'dənət, -s
whodunnit
BR ,huː'dʌnɪt, -s
AM hu'dənət, -s
whoe'er
BR huː'ɛː(r), hʊ'ɛː(r)
AM hu'ɛ(ə)r
whoever
BR huː'ɛvə(r), hʊ'ɛvə(r)
AM hu'ɛvər
whole
BR həʊl
AM hoʊl
wholefood
BR 'həʊlfuːd, -z
AM 'hoʊl,fud, -z
wholegrain
BR 'həʊlgreɪn, -z
AM ¦hoʊl¦greɪn, -z
wholehearted
BR ,həʊl'hɑːtɪd
AM ¦hoʊl¦hardəd
wholeheartedly
BR ,həʊl'hɑːtɪdli
AM ¦hoʊl¦hardədli
wholeheartedness
BR ,həʊl'hɑːtɪdnɨs
AM ¦hoʊl¦hardədnəs
whole-life insurance
BR ,həʊllʌɪf ɪn'ʃʊərəns, + ɪn'ʃʊərn̩s, + ɪn'ʃɔːrəns, + ɪn'ʃɔːrn̩s
AM ¦hoʊl'laɪf ɪn,ʃʊrəns
wholely
BR 'həʊlli
AM 'hoʊ(l)li
wholemeal
BR 'həʊlmiːl
AM ¦hoʊl'mil
wholeness
BR 'həʊlnəs
AM 'hoʊlnəs
wholesale
BR 'həʊlseɪl
AM 'hoʊl,seɪl
wholesaler
BR 'həʊlseɪlə(r), -z
AM 'hoʊl,seɪlər, -z
wholesome
BR 'həʊls(ə)m
AM 'hoʊlsəm
wholesomely
BR 'həʊls(ə)mli
AM 'hoʊlsəmli
wholesomeness
BR 'həʊls(ə)mnəs
AM 'hoʊlsəmnəs
whole-time
BR 'həʊltʌɪm
AM 'hoʊl,taɪm
wholewheat
BR 'həʊlwiːt
AM ¦hoʊl'wit
wholism
BR 'həʊlɪz(ə)m
AM 'hoʊl,ɪzəm
wholly
BR 'həʊlli
AM 'hoʊ(l)li
whom¹
strong form
BR huːm
AM hum
whom²
weak form
BR hʊm
AM hʊm
whomever
BR huːm'ɛvə(r)
AM hum'ɛvər
whomp
BR wɒmp, -s
AM (h)wɔmp, (h)wɑmp, -s
whomso
BR 'huːmsəʊ
AM 'humsoʊ
whomsoever
BR ,huːmsəʊ'ɛvə(r)
AM ,humsoʊ'ɛvər
whoop
BR wuːp, huːp, -s, -ɪŋ, -t
AM (h)wup, hup, -s, -ɪŋ, -t
whoopee¹
interjection
BR wʊ'piː
AM (h)wu'pi
whoopee²
noun
BR 'wʊpiː
AM '(h)wupi
whooper
BR 'wuːpə(r), 'huːpə(r), -z
AM '(h)wupər, 'hupər, -z
whooping cough
BR 'huːpɪŋ kɒf
AM 'hupɪŋ ,kɔf, + ,kɑf
whoopla
BR 'huːplɑː(r)
AM 'h(w)up,lɑ
whoops
BR wʊps, wuːps
AM (h)wups, (h)wʊps
whoosh
BR wʊʃ, wuːʃ, -ɨz, -ɪŋ, -t
AM (h)wuʃ, (h)wʊʃ, -ɨz, -ɪŋ, -t
whop
BR wɒp, -s, -ɪŋ, -t
AM (h)wɑp, -s, -ɪŋ, -t
whopper
BR 'wɒpə(r), -z
AM '(h)wɑpər, -z
whore
BR hɔː(r), -z, -ɪŋ, -d
AM hɔ(ə)r, -z, -ɪŋ, -d
who're
BR 'huːə(r), hʊə(r)
AM 'huər, 'hʊ(ə)r
whoredom
BR 'hɔːdəm
AM 'hɔrdəm
whorehouse
BR 'hɔːhaʊ|s, -zɪz

AM 'hɔr,(h)aʊ|s, -zəz

whoremaster
BR 'hɔː,mɑːstə(r), 'hɔː,mastə(r), -z
AM 'hɔr,mæstər, -z

whoremonger
BR 'hɔː,mʌŋgə(r), -z
AM 'hɔr,mɑŋgər, 'hɔr,məŋgər, -z

whorer
BR 'hɔːrə(r), -z
AM 'hɔrər, -z

whoreson
BR 'hɔːsn
AM 'hɔrsən

Whorf
BR wɔːf
AM (h)wɔ(ə)rf

whorish
BR 'hɔːrɪʃ
AM 'hɔrɪʃ

whorishly
BR 'hɔːrɨʃli
AM 'hɔrɨʃli

whorishness
BR 'hɔːrɨʃnɨs
AM 'hɔrɪʃnɨs

whorl
BR wəːl, -z, -d
AM (h)wɔ(ə)rl, -z, -d

whortleberry
BR 'wəːtl,bɛr|i, 'wəːtlb(ə)r|i, -ɪz
AM '(h)wərdl,bɛri, -z

who's
BR huːz
AM huz

whose
BR huːz
AM huz

whosesoever
BR ˌhuːzsəʊ'ɛvə(r)
AM ˌhuz,soʊ'ɛvər

whoso
BR 'huːsəʊ
AM 'hu,soʊ

whosoever
BR ˌhuːsəʊ'ɛvə(r), 'huːsəʊɛvə(r)
AM ˌhusoʊ'ɛvər

Who's Who
BR ˌhuːz 'huː, -z
AM ˌhuz'hu, -z

who've
BR huːv
AM huv

whump
BR wʌmp, -s, -ɪŋ, -t
AM (h)wəmp, -s, -ɪŋ, -t

why
BR wʌɪ
AM (h)waɪ

Whyalla
BR wʌɪ'alə(r)
AM (h)waɪ'ælə

whydah
BR 'wɪdə(r), -z
AM '(h)wɪdə, -z

Whymper
BR 'wɪmpə(r)
AM '(h)wɪmpər

Whyte
BR wʌɪt
AM (h)waɪt

Whythorne
BR 'wʌɪthɔːn
AM '(h)waɪt,(h)ɔ(ə)rn

wibbly-wobbly
BR ˌwɪblɪ'wɒbli
AM 'wɪbli'wɑbli

Wibsey
BR 'wɪbsi, 'wɪbzi
AM 'wɪbsi, 'wɪbzi

Wicca
BR 'wɪkə(r)
AM 'wɪkə

Wiccan
BR 'wɪk(ə)n
AM 'wɪkən

Wichita
BR 'wɪtʃɨtɔː(r)
AM 'wɪtʃə,tɑ

Wichnor
BR 'wɪtʃnɔː(r), 'wɪtʃnə(r)
AM 'wɪtʃnər

wick
BR wɪk, -s
AM wɪk, -s

wicked
BR 'wɪk|ɪd, -ɨdɪst
AM 'wɪkɨd, -ɨst

wickedly
BR 'wɪkɨdli
AM 'wɪkɨdli

wickedness
BR 'wɪkɨdnɨs
AM 'wɪkɨdnɨs

Wicken
BR 'wɪk(ɨ)n
AM 'wɪkən

wicker
BR 'wɪkə(r)
AM 'wɪkər

wickerwork
BR 'wɪkəwəːk
AM 'wɪkər,wərk

wicket
BR 'wɪkɪt, -s
AM 'wɪkɨt, -s

wicketkeeper
BR 'wɪkɪt,kiːpə(r), -z
AM 'wɪkɨt,kipər, -z

wicketkeeping
BR 'wɪkɪt,kiːpɪŋ
AM 'wɪkɨt,kipɪŋ

wicket-taker
BR 'wɪkɪt,teɪkə(r), -z
AM 'wɪkɨt,teɪkər, -z

wicket-taking
BR 'wɪkɪt,teɪkɪŋ
AM 'wɪkɨt,teɪkɪŋ

Wickham
BR 'wɪkəm
AM 'wɪkəm

wickiup
BR 'wɪkɪʌp, -s
AM 'wɪki,əp, -s

Wicklow
BR 'wɪkləʊ
AM 'wɪkloʊ

Wicks
BR wɪks
AM wɪks

Widdecombe
BR 'wɪdɨkəm
AM 'wɪdəkəm

widdershins
BR 'wɪdəʃɪnz
AM 'wɪdər,ʃɪnz

Widdicombe
BR 'wɪdɨkəm
AM 'wɪdəkəm

Widdowson
BR 'wɪdə(ʊ)sn
AM 'wɪdəsən

wide
BR wʌɪd, -ə(r), -ɨst
AM waɪd, -ər, -ɨst

wide-angle
BR ˌwʌɪd'aŋgl
AM ˌwaɪd'æŋgəl

wideawake
BR ˌwʌɪdə'weɪk, -s
AM ˌwaɪdə'weɪk, -s

Widecombe
BR 'wɪdɨkəm
AM 'wɪdəkəm

widely
BR 'wʌɪdli
AM 'waɪdli

widemouth
BR 'wʌɪdmaʊθ
AM 'waɪd,maʊθ

widemouthed
BR ˌwʌɪd'maʊðd, ˌwʌɪd'maʊθt
AM 'waɪd,maʊθ(t)

widen
BR 'wʌɪd|n, -nz, -n̩ɪŋ\-nɪŋ, -nd
AM 'waɪdən, -z, -ɪŋ, -d

widener
BR 'wʌɪdn̩ə(r), 'wʌɪdnə(r), -z
AM 'waɪdn̩ər, 'waɪdnər, -z

wideness
BR 'wʌɪdnɨs
AM 'wʌɪdnɨs

widening
BR 'wʌɪdn̩ɪŋ, 'wʌɪdnɪŋ, -z
AM 'waɪdn̩ɪŋ, 'waɪdnɪŋ, -z

widespread
BR 'wʌɪdsprɛd, ˌwʌɪd'sprɛd
AM ˌwaɪd'sprɛd

widgeon
BR 'wɪdʒ(ɨ)n, -z
AM 'wɪdʒən, -z

widget
BR 'wɪdʒɪt, -s
AM 'wɪdʒɨt, -s

widgie
BR 'wɪdʒ|i, -ɪz
AM 'wɪdʒi, -z

widish
BR 'wʌɪdɪʃ
AM 'waɪdɪʃ

Widlake
BR 'wɪdleɪk
AM 'wɪd,leɪk

Widmark
BR 'wɪdmɑːk
AM 'wɪd,mɑrk

Widnes
BR 'wɪdnɨs
AM 'wɪdnəs

widow
BR 'wɪdəʊ, -z, -ɪŋ, -d
AM 'wɪdoʊ, -z, -ɪŋ, -d

widow-bird
BR 'wɪdəʊbəːd, -z
AM 'wɪdoʊ,bərd, -z

widower
BR 'wɪdəʊə(r), -z
AM 'wɪdoʊər, -z

widowhood
BR 'wɪdəʊhʊd
AM 'wɪdoʊ,(h)ʊd

widow-maker
BR 'wɪdə(ʊ),meɪkə(r), -z
AM 'wɪdoʊ,meɪkər, -z

width
BR wɪdθ, wɪtθ, -s
AM wɪdθ, -s

widthways
BR 'wɪdθweɪz, 'wɪtθweɪz
AM 'wɪ(d)θ,weɪz, 'wɪð,weɪz

widthwise
BR 'wɪdθwʌɪz, 'wɪtθwʌɪz
AM 'wɪ(d)θ,waɪz, 'wɪð,waɪz

Wieland
BR 'wiːlənd
AM 'wilənd

wield
BR wiːld, -z, -ɪŋ, -ɨd
AM wild, -z, -ɪŋ, -ɨd

wielder
BR 'wiːldə(r), -z
AM 'wildər, -z

wieldy
BR 'wiːldi
AM 'wildi

wiener
BR 'wiːnə(r), -z
AM 'winər, -z

Wiener schnitzel
BR ˌwiːnə 'ʃnɪtsl
AM 'winər ˌʃnɪtsəl

wienie
BR ˈwiːn|i, -ɪz
AM ˈwini, -z

Wiesbaden
BR ˈviːsˌbɑːdn
AM ˈwisbɑdən, ˈvisbɑdən

Wiesel
BR ˈviːsl
AM ˈvisəl

Wiesenthal
BR ˈviːzntɑːl
AM ˈwizənˌtɑl, ˈwizənˌθɑl

wife
BR wʌɪf
AM waɪf

wifehood
BR ˈwʌɪfhʊd
AM ˈwaɪfˌ(h)ʊd

wifeless
BR ˈwʌɪflɨs
AM ˈwaɪflɨs

wifelike
BR ˈwʌɪflʌɪk
AM ˈwaɪfˌlaɪk

wifeliness
BR ˈwʌɪflɪnɨs
AM ˈwaɪflinɨs

wifely
BR ˈwʌɪfli
AM ˈwaɪfli

wife-swapping
BR ˈwʌɪfˌswɒpɪŋ
AM ˈwaɪfˌswɑpɪŋ

wifish
BR ˈwʌɪfɪʃ
AM ˈwaɪfɪʃ

wig
BR wɪɡ, -z, -d
AM wɪɡ, -z, -d

Wigan
BR ˈwɪɡ(ə)n
AM ˈwɪɡən

wigeon
BR ˈwɪdʒ(ɨ)n, -z
AM ˈwɪdʒən, -z

Wiggin
BR ˈwɪɡɪn
AM ˈwɪɡɨn

wigging
BR ˈwɪɡɪŋ, -z
AM ˈwɪɡɪŋ, -z

Wiggins
BR ˈwɪɡɪnz
AM ˈwɪɡɨnz

wiggle
BR ˈwɪɡ|l, -lz, -l̩ɪŋ\-lɪŋ, -ld
AM ˈwɪɡ|əl, -əlz, -(ə)lɪŋ, -əld

wiggler
BR ˈwɪɡl̩ə(r), ˈwɪɡlə(r), -z
AM ˈwɪɡ(ə)lər, -z

Wigglesworth
BR ˈwɪɡlzwəːθ, ˈwɪɡlzwəθ
AM ˈwɪɡəlzˌwərθ

wiggly
BR ˈwɪɡl̩i, ˈwɪɡli
AM ˈwɪɡ(ə)li

wight
BR wʌɪt, -s
AM waɪt, -s

Wigley
BR ˈwɪɡli
AM ˈwɪɡli

Wigmore
BR ˈwɪɡmɔː(r)
AM ˈwɪɡˌmɔ(ə)r

Wigram
BR ˈwɪɡrəm
AM ˈwɪɡrəm

Wigton
BR ˈwɪɡt(ə)n
AM ˈwɪɡtən

Wigtownshire
BR ˈwɪɡt(ə)nʃ(ɪ)ə(r)
AM ˈwɪɡtənʃɪ(ə)r

wigwag
BR ˈwɪɡwaɡ, -z, -ɪŋ, -d
AM ˈwɪɡˌwæɡ, -z, -ɪŋ, -d

wigwam
BR ˈwɪɡwam, -z
AM ˈwɪˌɡwɑm, -z

Wilberforce
BR ˈwɪlbəfɔːs
AM ˈwɪlbərˌfɔ(ə)rs

Wilbert
BR ˈwɪlbət
AM ˈwɪlbərt

Wilbraham
BR ˈwɪlbrəhəm, ˈwɪlbrəm
AM ˈwɪlbrəm, ˈwɪlbrəˌhæm

Wilbur
BR ˈwɪlbə(r)
AM ˈwɪlbər

Wilby
BR ˈwɪlbi
AM ˈwɪlbi

wilco
BR ˈwɪlkəʊ
AM ˈwɪlkoʊ

Wilcock
BR ˈwɪlkɒk
AM ˈwɪlˌkɑk

Wilcocks
BR ˈwɪlkɒks
AM ˈwɪlˌkɑks

Wilcox
BR ˈwɪlkɒks
AM ˈwɪlˌkɑks

Wilcoxon
BR ˈwɪlkɒksn
AM ˈwɪlˌkɑksən

wild
BR wʌɪld, -z, -ə(r), -ɨst
AM waɪld, -z, -ər, -ɨst

Wildblood
BR ˈwʌɪl(d)blʌd
AM ˈwaɪl(d)ˌblʊd

wild card
BR ˈwʌɪl(d) kɑːd, -z
AM ˈwaɪl(d) ˌkɑrd, -z

wildcat
BR ˈwʌɪl(d)kat
AM ˈwaɪl(d)ˌkæt

Wilde
BR wʌɪld
AM waɪld

wildebeest
BR ˈwɪldɨbiːst, -s
AM ˈwɪldəˌbist, -s

Wildenstein
BR ˈwɪld(ə)nstʌɪn
AM ˈwɪldənˌstaɪn

Wilder
BR ˈwʌɪldə(r)
AM ˈwaɪldər

wilder
bewilder
BR ˈwɪld|ə(r), -əz, -(ə)rɪŋ, -əd
AM ˈwɪldər, -z, -ɪŋ, -d

wilderness
BR ˈwɪldənəs, -ɨz
AM ˈwɪldərnəs, -əz

wild-eyed
BR ˌwʌɪldˈʌɪd
AM ˈwaɪldˌaɪd

wildfire
BR ˈwʌɪl(d)fʌɪə(r)
AM ˈwaɪl(d)ˌfaɪ(ə)r

wildfowl
BR ˈwʌɪl(d)faʊl
AM ˈwaɪl(d)ˌfaʊl

wildfowler
BR ˈwʌɪl(d)faʊlə(r), -z
AM ˈwaɪl(d)ˌfaʊlər, -z

wildfowling
BR ˈwʌɪl(d)faʊlɪŋ
AM ˈwaɪl(d)ˌfaʊlɪŋ

wild-goose chase
BR ˌwʌɪl(d)ˈɡuːs tʃeɪs, -ɨz
AM ˌwaɪl(d)ˈɡus ˌtʃeɪs, -ɨz

wilding
BR ˈwʌɪldɪŋ, -z
AM ˈwaɪldɪŋ, -z

wildish
BR ˈwʌɪldɪʃ
AM ˈwaɪldɪʃ

wildlife
BR ˈwʌɪl(d)lʌɪf
AM ˈwaɪl(d)ˌlaɪf

wildly
BR ˈwʌɪldli
AM ˈwaɪl(d)li

wildness
BR ˈwʌɪldnɨs
AM ˈwaɪl(d)nɨs

wildwood
BR ˈwʌɪldwʊd, -z
AM ˈwaɪl(d)ˌwʊd, -z

wile
BR wʌɪl, -z, -ɪŋ, -d
AM waɪl, -z, -ɪŋ, -d

Wiley
BR ˈwʌɪli
AM ˈwaɪli

Wilf
BR wɪlf
AM wɪlf

Wilford
BR ˈwɪlfəd
AM ˈwɪlfərd

Wilfred
BR ˈwɪlfrɪd
AM ˈwɪlfrɨd

Wilfrid
BR ˈwɪlfrɪd
AM ˈwɪlfrɨd

wilful
BR ˈwɪlf(ʊ)l
AM ˈwɪlfəl

wilfully
BR ˈwɪlfʊli, ˈwɪlfl̩i
AM ˈwɪlfəli

wilfulness
BR ˈwɪlf(ʊ)lnəs
AM ˈwɪlfəlnəs

wilga
BR ˈwɪlɡə(r), -z
AM ˈwɪlɡə, -z

Wilhelmina
BR ˌwɪlhɛlˈmiːnə(r), ˌwɪlhəlˈmiːnə(r)
AM ˌwɪləlˈminə

Wilhelmshaven
BR ˈwɪlhɛlmzˌhɑːvn, ˈwɪlhɛlmzˌhɑːfn
AM ˈwɪlˌ(h)ɛlmzˌhɑvən

wilily
BR ˈwʌɪlɪli
AM ˈwaɪlɨli

wiliness
BR ˈwʌɪlɪnɨs
AM ˈwaɪlinɨs

Wilkerson
BR ˈwɪlkəs(ə)n
AM ˈwɪlkərsən

Wilkes
BR wɪlks
AM wɪlks

Wilkie
BR ˈwɪlki
AM ˈwɪlki

Wilkins
BR ˈwɪlkɪnz
AM ˈwɪlkɨnz

Wilkinson
BR ˈwɪlkɪns(ə)n
AM ˈwɪlkɨnsən

will
BR wɪl, -z, -ɪŋ, -d
AM wɪl, -z, -ɪŋ, -d

Willa
BR ˈwɪlə(r)
AM ˈwɪlə

Willard
BR 'wɪlɑːd
AM 'wɪlərd

Willcock
BR 'wɪlkɒk
AM 'wɪlˌkɑk

Willcocks
BR 'wɪlkɒks
AM 'wɪlˌkɑks

Willcox
BR 'wɪlkɒks
AM 'wɪlˌkɑks

Willemstadt
BR 'wɪləmstat
AM 'wɪləmˌstɑt, 'wɪləmˌʃtɑt

Willenhall
BR 'wɪlənhɔːl
AM 'wɪlənˌ(h)ɔl, 'wɪlənˌ(h)ɑl

willer
BR 'wɪlə(r), -z
AM 'wɪlər, -z

Willesden
BR 'wɪlzdən
AM 'wɪlzdən

willet
BR 'wɪlɨt, -s
AM 'wɪlɨt, -s

Willetts
BR 'wɪlɨts
AM 'wɪlɨts

Willey
BR 'wɪli
AM 'wɪli

willful
BR 'wɪlf(ʊ)l
AM 'wɪlfəl

willfully
BR 'wɪlfʊli, 'wɪlfl̩i
AM 'wɪlfəli

willfulness
BR 'wɪlf(ʊ)lnəs
AM 'wɪlfəlnəs

William
BR 'wɪljəm
AM 'wɪljəm, 'wɪliəm

Williams
BR 'wɪljəmz
AM 'wɪljəmz, 'wɪliəmz

Williamsburg
BR 'wɪljəmzbəːg
AM 'wɪljəmzˌbərg, 'wɪliəmzˌbərg

Williamson
BR 'wɪljəms(ə)n
AM 'wɪljəmsən, 'wɪliəmsən

willie
BR 'wɪl|i, -ɪz
AM 'wɪli, -z

willing
BR 'wɪlɪŋ
AM 'wɪlɪŋ

willingly
BR 'wɪlɪŋli
AM 'wɪlɪŋli

willingness
BR 'wɪlɪŋnɨs
AM 'wɪlɪŋnɨs

Willis
BR 'wɪlɪs
AM 'wɪlɪs

will-less
BR 'wɪllɨs
AM 'wɪ(l)lɨs

Willmott
BR 'wɪlmɒt
AM 'wɪlˌmɑt

will-o'-the-wisp
BR ˌwɪləðə'wɪsp, -s
AM 'wɪləðə'wɪsp, -s

Willoughby
BR 'wɪləbi
AM 'wɪləbi

willow
BR 'wɪləʊ, -z
AM 'wɪloʊ, -z

willowherb
BR ˌwɪləʊhəːb
AM 'wɪloʊˌərb

willowy
BR 'wɪləʊi
AM 'wɪloʊi

willpower
BR 'wɪlˌpaʊə(r)
AM 'wɪlˌpaʊər

Wills
BR wɪlz
AM wɪlz

willy
BR 'wɪl|i, -ɪz
AM 'wɪli, -z

willy-nilly
BR ˌwɪlɪ'nɪli
AM 'wɪli'nɪli

willy-willy
BR 'wɪlɪˌwɪl|i, -ɪz
AM 'wɪli'wɪli, -z

Wilma
BR 'wɪlmə(r)
AM 'wɪlmə

Wilmcote
BR 'wɪlmkəʊt
AM 'wɪlmˌkoʊt

Wilmer
BR 'wɪlmə(r)
AM 'wɪlmər

Wilmington
BR 'wɪlmɪŋt(ə)n
AM 'wɪlmɪŋtən

Wilmot
BR 'wɪlmɒt
AM 'wɪlˌmɑt

Wilmott
BR 'wɪlmɒt
AM 'wɪlˌmɑt

Wilmslow
BR 'wɪlmzləʊ
AM 'wɪlmzloʊ

Wilsher
BR 'wɪlʃə(r)
AM 'wɪlʃər

Wilson
BR 'wɪlsn
AM 'wɪlsən

Wilsonian
BR wɪl'səʊnɪən
AM wɪl'soʊniən

wilt
BR wɪlt, -s, -ɪŋ, -ɨd
AM wɪlt, -s, -ɪŋ, -ɨd

Wilton
BR 'wɪltn, -z
AM 'wɪltən, -z

Wilts.
BR wɪlts
AM wɪlts

Wiltshire
BR 'wɪltʃ(ɪ)ə(r)
AM 'wɪltʃɪ(ə)r

wily
BR 'wʌɪl|i, -ɪə(r), -ɪɨst
AM 'waɪli, -ər, -ɨst

wimble
BR 'wɪmbl, -z
AM 'wɪmbəl, -z

Wimbledon
BR 'wɪmbld(ə)n
AM 'wɪmbəldən

Wimborne
BR 'wɪmbɔːn
AM 'wɪmˌbɔ(ə)rn

Wimbourne
BR 'wɪmbɔːn
AM 'wɪmˌbɔ(ə)rn

Wimbush
BR 'wɪmbʊʃ
AM 'wɪmbəʃ

Wimoweh
BR 'wɪməweɪ
AM 'wɪməˌweɪ

wimp
BR wɪmp, -s
AM wɪmp, -s

wimpish
BR 'wɪmpɪʃ
AM 'wɪmpɪʃ

wimpishly
BR 'wɪmpɨʃli
AM 'wɪmpɨʃli

wimpishness
BR 'wɪmpɨʃnɨs
AM 'wɪmpɪʃnɨs

wimple
BR 'wɪmpl, -z
AM 'wɪmpəl, -z

Wimpole
BR 'wɪmpəʊl
AM 'wɪmˌpoʊl

wimpy
BR 'wɪmp|i, -ɪə(r), -ɪɨst
AM 'wɪmpi, -ər, -ɨst

win
BR wɪn, -z, -ɪŋ
AM wɪn, -z, -ɪŋ

Winalot®
BR 'wɪnəlɒt
AM 'wɪnəˌlɑt

Wincanton
BR wɪn'kantən
AM wɪn'kæn(t)ən

Wincarnis
BR wɪn'kɑːnɪs
AM wɪn'kɑrnəs

wince
BR wɪns, -ɨz, -ɪŋ, -t
AM wɪns, -ɨz, -ɪŋ, -t

wincer
BR 'wɪnsə(r), -z
AM 'wɪnsər, -z

wincey
BR 'wɪns|i, -ɪz
AM 'wɪnsi, -z

winceyette
BR ˌwɪnsɪ'ɛt
AM ˌwɪnsi'ɛt

winch[1]
BR wɪn(t)ʃ, -ɨz, -ɪŋ, -t
AM wɪn(t)ʃ, -ɨz, -ɪŋ, -t

winch[2]
BR wɪn(t)ʃ, -ɨz, -ɪŋ, -t
AM wɪn(t)ʃ, -ɨz, -ɪŋ, -t

Winchelsea
BR 'wɪn(t)ʃlsiː
AM 'wɪn(t)ʃəlˌsi

wincher
BR 'wɪn(t)ʃə(r), -z
AM 'wɪn(t)ʃər, -z

winchester
BR 'wɪntʃɪstə(r), 'wɪntʃɛstə(r), -z
AM 'wɪnˌtʃɛstər, -z

Winchmore
BR 'wɪn(t)ʃmɔː(r)
AM 'wɪn(t)ʃˌmɔ(ə)r

wincingly
BR 'wɪnsɪŋli
AM 'wɪnsɪŋli

Winckelmann
BR 'wɪŋklman
AM 'wɪŋkəlmən

wind[1]
verb make breathless, noun air
BR wɪnd, -z, -ɪŋ, -ɨd
AM wɪnd, -z, -ɪŋ, -ɨd

wind[2]
verb turn, blow
BR wʌɪnd, -z, -ɪŋ
AM waɪnd, -z, -ɪŋ

windage
BR 'wɪnd|ɪdʒ, -ɨdʒɨz
AM 'wɪndɪdʒ, -ɨz

Windaus
BR 'vɪndaʊs
AM 'vɪndaʊs

windbag
BR 'wɪn(d)bag, -z
AM 'wɪn(d)ˌbæg, -z

windblown
BR 'wɪn(d)bləʊn
AM 'wɪn(d)ˌbloʊn

windbound
BR 'wɪn(d)baʊnd
AM 'wɪn(d)ˌbaʊnd

windbreak
BR ˈwɪn(d)breɪk, -s
AM ˈwɪn(d)ˌbreɪk, -s

Windbreaker®
BR ˈwɪn(d)ˌbreɪkə(r), -z
AM ˈwɪn(d)ˌbreɪkər, -z

windburn
BR ˈwɪn(d)bəːn, -d
AM ˈwɪn(d)ˌbərn, -d

windcheater
BR ˈwɪn(d)ˌtʃiːtə(r), -z
AM ˈwɪn(d)ˌtʃidər, -z

windchill
BR ˈwɪn(d)tʃɪl
AM ˈwɪn(d)ˌtʃɪl

windcone
BR ˈwɪn(d)kəʊn, -z
AM ˈwɪn(d)ˌkoʊn, -z

wind-down
BR ˈwʌɪn(d)daʊn, -z
AM ˈwaɪn(d)ˌdaʊn, -z

winder
BR ˈwʌɪndə(r), -z
AM ˈwaɪndər, -z

Windermere
BR ˈwɪndəmɪə(r)
AM ˈwɪndərˌmɪ(ə)r

windfall
BR ˈwɪn(d)fɔːl, -z
AM ˈwɪn(d)ˌfɔl, ˈwɪn(d)ˌfɑl, -z

windfarm
BR ˈwɪn(d)fɑːm, -z
AM ˈwɪn(d)fɑrm, -z

windflower
BR ˈwɪn(d)ˌflaʊə(r), -z
AM ˈwɪn(d)ˌflaʊər, -z

Windhoek
BR ˈwɪndhʊk, ˈvɪnthʊk
AM ˈwɪn(d)ˌ(h)ʊk

windhover
BR ˈwɪndˌhɒvə(r), -z
AM ˈwɪn(d)ˌ(h)əvər, -z

windily
BR ˈwɪndɨli
AM ˈwɪndɨli

windiness
BR ˈwɪndɪnɨs
AM ˈwɪndinɨs

windjammer
BR ˈwɪn(d)ˌdʒamə(r), -z
AM ˈwɪn(d)ˌdʒæmər, -z

windlass
BR ˈwɪndləs, -ɪz
AM ˈwɪn(d)ləs, -əz

Windlesham
BR ˈwɪndlʃ(ə)m
AM ˈwɪndlʃəm

windless
BR ˈwɪndlɨs
AM ˈwɪn(d)lɨs

windlestraw
BR ˈwɪndlstrɔː(r), -z
AM ˈwɪndlˌstrɔ, ˈwɪndlˌstrɑ, -z

windmill
BR ˈwɪn(d)mɪl, -z
AM ˈwɪn(d)ˌmɪl, -z

Windolene®
BR ˈwɪndə(ʊ)liːn
AM ˈwɪndəˌlin

window
BR ˈwɪndəʊ, -z, -ɪŋ, -d
AM ˈwɪndoʊ, -z, -ɪŋ, -d

windowless
BR ˈwɪndə(ʊ)ləs
AM ˈwɪndoʊləs

windowpane
BR ˈwɪndə(ʊ)peɪn, -z
AM ˈwɪndoʊˌpeɪn, -z

windowseat
BR ˈwɪndə(ʊ)siːt, -s
AM ˈwɪndoʊˌsit, -s

window-shop
BR ˈwɪndəʊʃɒp, -s, -ɪŋ, -t
AM ˈwɪndoʊˌʃɑp, -s, -ɪŋ, -t

window-shopper
BR ˈwɪndəʊˌʃɒpə(r), -z
AM ˈwɪndoʊˌʃɑpər, -z

windowsill
BR ˈwɪndə(ʊ)sɪl, -z
AM ˈwɪndoʊˌsɪl, -z

windpipe
BR ˈwɪn(d)pʌɪp, -s
AM ˈwɪn(d)ˌpaɪp, -s

windproof
BR ˈwɪn(d)pruːf
AM ˈwɪn(d)ˌprʊf

windrow
BR ˈwɪn(d)rəʊ, -z
AM ˈwɪn(d)ˌroʊ, -z

Windrush
BR ˈwɪndrʌʃ
AM ˈwɪn(d)ˌrəʃ

windsail
BR ˈwɪn(d)sl, ˈwɪn(d)seɪl
AM ˈwɪn(d)ˌseɪl, ˈwɪn(d)səl

Windscale
BR ˈwɪn(d)skeɪl
AM ˈwɪn(d)ˌskeɪl

windscreen
BR ˈwɪn(d)skriːn, -z
AM ˈwɪn(d)ˌskrin, -z

windshield
BR ˈwɪn(d)ʃiːld, -z
AM ˈwɪn(d)ˌʃild, -z

windsock
BR ˈwɪn(d)sɒk, -s
AM ˈwɪn(d)ˌsɑk, -s

Windsor
BR ˈwɪnzə(r)
AM ˈwɪnzər

windstorm
BR ˈwɪn(d)stɔːm, -z
AM ˈwɪn(d)ˌstɔ(ə)rm, -z

windsurf
BR ˈwɪn(d)səːf, -s, -ɪŋ, -t
AM ˈwɪn(d)ˌsərf, -s, -ɪŋ, -t

windsurfer
BR ˈwɪn(d)ˌsəːfə(r), -z
AM ˈwɪn(d)ˌsərfər, -z

windswept
BR ˈwɪn(d)swɛpt
AM ˈwɪn(d)ˌswɛpt

wind-up
BR ˈwʌɪndʌp, -s
AM ˈwaɪndəp, -s

windward
BR ˈwɪndwəd
AM ˈwɪn(d)wərd

windy
BR ˈwɪnd|i, -ɪə(r), -ɪɨst
AM ˈwɪndi, -ər, -ɨst

wine
BR wʌɪn, -z, -ɪŋ, -d
AM waɪn, -z, -ɪŋ, -d

wineberry
BR ˈwʌɪnb(ə)r|i, -ɪz
AM ˈwaɪnˌbɛri, -z

winebibber
BR ˈwʌɪnˌbɪbə(r), -z
AM ˈwaɪnˌbɪbər, -z

winebibbing
BR ˈwʌɪnˌbɪbɪŋ
AM ˈwaɪnˌbɪbɪŋ

wineglass
BR ˈwʌɪnglɑːs, ˈwʌɪnglas, -ɪz
AM ˈwaɪnˌglæs, -ɪz

wineglassful
BR ˈwʌɪnglɑːsfʊl, ˈwʌɪnglasfʊl, -z
AM ˈwaɪnˌglæsˌfʊl, -z

winegrower
BR ˈwʌɪnˌgrəʊə(r), -z
AM ˈwaɪnˌgroʊər, -z

wineless
BR ˈwʌɪnlɨs
AM ˈwaɪnlɨs

winemaker
BR ˈwʌɪnˌmeɪkə(r), -z
AM ˈwaɪnˌmeɪkər, -z

winemaking
BR ˈwʌɪnˌmeɪkɪŋ
AM ˈwaɪnˌmeɪkɪŋ

winepress
BR ˈwʌɪnprɛs, -ɪz
AM ˈwaɪnˌprɛs, -əz

winery
BR ˈwʌɪn(ə)r|i, -ɪz
AM ˈwaɪn(ə)ri, -z

wineskin
BR ˈwʌɪnskɪn, -z
AM ˈwaɪnˌskɪn, -z

Winfield
BR ˈwɪnfiːld
AM ˈwɪnˌfild

Winford
BR ˈwɪnfəd
AM ˈwɪnfərd

Winfred
BR ˈwɪnfrɪd
AM ˈwɪnˌfrɛd

Winfrith
BR ˈwɪnfrɪθ
AM ˈwɪnˌfrɪθ

wing
BR wɪŋ, -z, -ɪŋ, -d
AM wɪŋ, -z, -ɪŋ, -d

Wingate
BR ˈwɪngeɪt, ˈwɪŋgeɪt
AM ˈwɪnˌgeɪt

wingback
BR ˈwɪŋbak, -s
AM ˈwɪŋˌbæk, -s

wingding
BR ˈwɪŋdɪŋ, -z
AM ˈwɪŋˌdɪŋ, -z

winge
BR wɪn(d)ʒ, -ɪz, -ɪŋ, -d
AM (h)wɪndʒ, -ɪz, -ɪŋ, -d

winged[1]
with wings
BR wɪŋd
AM wɪŋd

winged[2]
with wings, old poetic form
BR ˈwɪŋɪd
AM ˈwɪŋɪd

winger[1]
complainer
BR ˈwɪn(d)ʒə(r), -z
AM ˈwɪndʒər, -z

winger[2]
player etc
BR ˈwɪŋə(r), -z
AM ˈwɪŋər, -z

Wingfield
BR ˈwɪŋfiːld
AM ˈwɪŋˌfild

wing forward
BR ˌwɪŋ ˈfɔːwəd, -z
AM ˈwɪŋ ˈfɔrwərd, -z

wing-half
BR ˌwɪŋˈhɑːf, -s
AM ˈwɪŋˌ(h)æf, -s

wingless
BR ˈwɪŋlɨs
AM ˈwɪŋlɨs

winglet
BR ˈwɪŋlɨt, -s
AM ˈwɪŋlɨt, -s

winglike
BR ˈwɪŋlʌɪk
AM ˈwɪŋˌlaɪk

wingman
BR ˈwɪŋman
AM ˈwɪŋˌmæn

wingmen
BR ˈwɪŋmɛn
AM ˈwɪŋˌmɛn

wingnut
BR ˈwɪŋnʌt, -s
AM ˈwɪŋˌnət, -s

wingover
BR ˈwɪŋˌəʊvə(r), -z

AM ˈwɪŋˌoʊvər, -z
wingspan
BR ˈwɪŋspan, -z
AM ˈwɪŋˌspæn, -z
wingspread
BR ˈwɪŋsprɛd
AM ˈwɪŋˌsprɛd
wingtip
BR ˈwɪŋtɪp, -s
AM ˈwɪŋˌtɪp, -s
Winifred
BR ˈwɪnɨfrɪd
AM ˈwɪnifrəd
wink
BR wɪŋ|k, -ks, -kɪŋ, -(k)t
AM wɪŋ|k, -ks, -kɪŋ, -(k)t
winker
BR ˈwɪŋkə(r), -z
AM ˈwɪŋkər, -z
winkle
BR ˈwɪŋk|l, -lz, -ḷɪŋ\-lɪŋ, -ld
AM ˈwɪŋkəl, -əlz, -(ə)lɪŋ, -əld
winklehawk
BR ˈwɪŋklhɔːk, -s
AM ˈwɪŋkəlˌ(h)ɔk, ˈwɪŋkəlˌ(h)ɑk, -s
winkler
BR ˈwɪŋklə(r), ˈwɪŋkḷə(r), -z
AM ˈwɪŋk(ə)lər, -z
winless
BR ˈwɪnlɨs
AM ˈwɪnlɨs
winnable
BR ˈwɪnəbl
AM ˈwɪnəbəl
Winnebago
BR ˌwɪnɨˈbeɪgəʊ, -z
AM ˌwɪnəˈbeɪgoʊ, -z
winner
BR ˈwɪnə(r), -z
AM ˈwɪnər, -z
Winnie
BR ˈwɪni
AM ˈwɪni
Winnie-the-Pooh
BR ˌwɪniðəˈpuː
AM ˈwɪniðəˈpu
winning
BR ˈwɪnɪŋ, -z, -ɨst
AM ˈwɪnɪŋ, -z, -ɨst
winningly
BR ˈwɪnɪŋli
AM ˈwɪnɪŋli
winningness
BR ˈwɪnɪŋnɨs
AM ˈwɪnɪŋnɨs
Winnipeg
BR ˈwɪnɪpɛg
AM ˈwɪnəˌpɛg
winnow
BR ˈwɪnəʊ, -z, -ɪŋ, -d
AM ˈwɪnoʊ, -z, -ɪŋ, -d
winnower
BR ˈwɪnəʊə(r), -z
AM ˈwɪnəwər, -z
wino
BR ˈwʌɪnəʊ, -z
AM ˈwaɪˌnoʊ, -z
Winona
BR wɪˈnəʊnə(r)
AM wɪˈnoʊnə, waɪˈnoʊnə
Winslow
BR ˈwɪnzləʊ
AM ˈwɪnzloʊ
winsome
BR ˈwɪns(ə)m
AM ˈwɪnsəm
winsomely
BR ˈwɪns(ə)mli
AM ˈwɪnsəmli
winsomeness
BR ˈwɪns(ə)mnəs
AM ˈwɪnsəmnəs
Winstanley
BR wɪnˈstanli, ˈwɪnst(ə)nli
AM ˈwɪnstənli, wɪnˈstænli
Winston
BR ˈwɪnst(ə)n
AM ˈwɪnstən
winter
BR ˈwɪnt|ə(r), -əz, -(ə)rɪŋ, -əd
AM ˈwɪn|(t)ər, -(t)ərz, -(t)ərɪŋ\-trɪŋ, -(t)ərd
Winterbotham
BR ˈwɪntəˌbɒtəm
AM ˈwɪn(t)ərˌbɑdəm
Winterbottom
BR ˈwɪntəˌbɒtəm
AM ˈwɪn(t)ərˌbɑdəm
Winterbourn
BR ˈwɪntəbɔːn
AM ˈwɪn(t)ərˌbɔ(ə)rn
Winterbourne
BR ˈwɪntəbɔːn
AM ˈwɪn(t)ərˌbɔ(ə)rn
winterer
BR ˈwɪnt(ə)rə(r), -z
AM ˈwɪn(t)ərər, ˈwɪntrər, -z
wintergreen
BR ˈwɪntəgriːn
AM ˈwɪn(t)ərˌgrin
winterisation
BR ˌwɪnt(ə)rʌɪˈzeɪʃn
AM ˌwɪn(t)ərəˈzeɪʃən, ˌwɪn(t)əˌraɪˈzeɪʃən, ˌwɪntrəˈzeɪʃən
winterise
BR ˈwɪntərʌɪz, -ɨz, -ɪŋ, -d
AM ˈwɪn(t)ərˌaɪz, -ɨz, -ɪŋ, -d
winterization
BR ˌwɪnt(ə)rʌɪˈzeɪʃn
AM ˌwɪn(t)ərəˈzeɪʃən, ˌwɪn(t)əˌraɪˈzeɪʃən, ˌwɪntrəˈzeɪʃən
winterize
BR ˈwɪntərʌɪz, -ɨz, -ɪŋ, -d
AM ˈwɪn(t)ərˌaɪz, -ɨz, -ɪŋ, -d
winterless
BR ˈwɪntələs
AM ˈwɪn(t)ərləs
winterly
BR ˈwɪntəli
AM ˈwɪn(t)ərli
Winters
BR ˈwɪntəz
AM ˈwɪn(t)ərz
wintertime
BR ˈwɪntətʌɪm
AM ˈwɪn(t)ərˌtaɪm
Winterton
BR ˈwɪntət(ə)n
AM ˈwɪn(t)ərtən
wintery
BR ˈwɪnt(ə)ri
AM ˈwɪntri, ˈwɪnəri
Winthrop
BR ˈwɪnθrɒp, ˈwɪnθrəp
AM ˈwɪnθrəp
Winton
BR ˈwɪntən
AM ˈwɪn(t)ən
Wintour
BR ˈwɪntə(r)
AM ˈwɪn(t)ər
wintrily
BR ˈwɪntrɨli
AM ˈwɪntrɨli
wintriness
BR ˈwɪntrɪnɨs
AM ˈwɪntrinɨs
wintry
BR ˈwɪntri
AM ˈwɪntri
winy
BR ˈwʌɪn|i, -ɪə(r), -ɪɪst
AM ˈwaɪni, -ər, -ɨst
wipe
BR wʌɪp, -s, -ɪŋ, -t
AM waɪp, -s, -ɪŋ, -t
wipeable
BR ˈwʌɪpəbl
AM ˈwaɪpəbəl
wipeout
BR ˈwʌɪpaʊt, -s
AM ˈwaɪpˌaʊt, -s
wiper
BR ˈwʌɪpə(r), -z
AM ˈwaɪpər, -z
WIPO
BR ˈwʌɪpəʊ
AM ˈwaɪˌpoʊ
wire
BR ˈwʌɪə(r), -z, -ɪŋ, -d
AM ˈwaɪ(ə)r, -z, -ɪŋ, -d
wiredraw
BR ˈwʌɪədrɔː(r), -z, -ɪŋ
AM ˈwaɪ(ə)rˌdrɔ, ˈwaɪ(ə)rˌdrɑ, -z, -ɪŋ
wiredrawn
BR ˈwʌɪədrɔːn
AM ˈwaɪ(ə)rˌdrɔn, ˈwaɪ(ə)rˌdrɑn
wiredrew
BR ˈwʌɪədruː
AM ˈwaɪ(ə)rˌdru
wireless
BR ˈwʌɪələs, -ɨz
AM ˈwaɪ(ə)rləs, -əz
wireman
BR ˈwʌɪəman
AM ˈwaɪ(ə)rˌmæn
wiremen
BR ˈwʌɪəmɛn
AM ˈwaɪ(ə)rˌmɛn
wirepuller
BR ˈwʌɪəˌpʊlə(r), -z
AM ˈwaɪ(ə)rˌpʊlər, -z
wirepulling
BR ˈwʌɪəˌpʊlɪŋ
AM ˈwaɪ(ə)rˌpʊlɪŋ
wirer
BR ˈwʌɪərə(r), -z
AM ˈwaɪ(ə)rər, -z
wireworm
BR ˈwʌɪəwəːm, -z
AM ˈwaɪ(ə)rˌwərm, -z
wirily
BR ˈwʌɪərɨli
AM ˈwaɪrɨli
wiriness
BR ˈwʌɪərɪnɨs
AM ˈwaɪrinɨs
wiring
BR ˈwʌɪərɪŋ
AM ˈwaɪ(ə)rɪŋ
Wirksworth
BR ˈwəːkswəθ, ˈwəːkswəːθ
AM ˈwərksˌwərθ
Wirral
BR ˈwɪrəl, ˈwɪrḷ
AM ˈwɪrəl
wiry
BR ˈwʌɪər|i, -ɪə(r), -ɪɪst
AM ˈwaɪ(ə)ri, -ər, -ɨst
Wisbech
BR ˈwɪzbiːtʃ
AM ˈwɪzˌbitʃ
Wisconsin
BR wɪˈskɒnsɪn
AM wəˈskɑnsən
Wisden
BR ˈwɪzd(ə)n
AM ˈwɪzdən
wisdom
BR ˈwɪzdəm
AM ˈwɪzdəm
wise
BR wʌɪz, -ə(r), -ɨst
AM waɪz, -ər, -ɨst
wiseacre
BR ˈwʌɪzˌeɪkə(r), -z
AM ˈwaɪzˌeɪkər, -z

wiseass
BR 'wʌɪzas, -ɪz
AM 'waɪ,zæs, -ɪz

wisecrack
BR 'wʌɪzkrak, -s, -ɪŋ, -t
AM 'waɪz,kræk, -s, -ɪŋ, -t

wisecracker
BR 'wʌɪz,krakə(r), -z
AM 'waɪz,krækər, -z

wisely
BR 'wʌɪzli
AM 'waɪzli

Wiseman
BR 'wʌɪzmən
AM 'waɪzmən

wisenheimer
BR 'wʌɪz(ə)n,hʌɪmə(r), -z
AM 'waɪzən,(h)aɪmər, -z

wisent
BR 'viːzɛnt, 'viːz(ə)nt, 'wiːzɛnt, 'wiːz(ə)nt, -s
AM 'vi,zɛnt, 'wi,zɛnt, -s

wish
BR wɪʃ, -ɪz, -ɪŋ, -t
AM wɪʃ, -ɪz, -ɪŋ, -t

Wishart
BR 'wɪʃət
AM 'wɪʃərt

Wishaw
BR 'wɪʃɔː(r)
AM 'wɪ,ʃɔ, 'wɪ,ʃɑ

wishbone
BR 'wɪʃbəʊn, -z
AM 'wɪʃ,boʊn, -z

wisher
BR 'wɪʃə(r), -z
AM 'wɪʃər, -z

wishful
BR 'wɪʃf(ʊ)l
AM 'wɪʃfəl

wish-fulfilling
BR 'wɪʃfʊl,fɪlɪŋ
AM 'wɪʃfə(l),fɪlɪŋ

wish-fulfillment
BR 'wɪʃfʊl,fɪlm(ə)nt
AM 'wɪʃfə(l),fɪlmənt

wish-fulfilment
BR 'wɪʃfʊl,fɪlm(ə)nt
AM 'wɪʃfə(l),fɪlmənt

wishfully
BR 'wɪʃfʊli, 'wɪʃfl̩i
AM 'wɪʃfəli

wishfulness
BR 'wɪʃf(ʊ)lnəs
AM 'wɪʃfəlnəs

wishing-well
BR 'wɪʃɪŋwɛl, -z
AM 'wɪʃɪŋ,wɛl, -z

wish-list
BR 'wɪʃlɪst, -s
AM 'wɪʃ,lɪst, -s

wish-wash
BR 'wɪʃwɒʃ, -ɪz
AM 'wɪʃ,wɔʃ, 'wɪʃ,wɑʃ, -əz

wishy-washy
BR 'wɪʃɪ,wɒʃi, ,wɪʃɪ'wɒʃi
AM ¦wɪʃi¦wɔʃi, 'wɪʃi¦wɑʃi

Wisley
BR 'wɪzli
AM 'wɪzli

wisp
BR wɪsp, -s
AM wɪsp, -s

Wispa®
BR 'wɪspə(r)
AM 'wɪspə

wispily
BR 'wɪspɨli
AM 'wɪspɨli

wispiness
BR 'wɪspɪnɪs
AM 'wɪspinɨs

wispy
BR 'wɪspi
AM 'wɪspi

wist
BR wɪst
AM wɪst

wistaria
BR wɪ'stɪərɪə(r)
AM wə'stɪriə, wə'stɛriə

wisteria
BR wɪ'stɪərɪə(r)
AM wə'stɪriə

wistful
BR wɪs(t)f(ʊ)l
AM 'wɪs(t)fəl

wistfully
BR 'wɪs(t)fʊli, 'wɪs(t)fl̩i
AM 'wɪs(t)fəli

wistfulness
BR 'wɪs(t)f(ʊ)lnəs
AM 'wɪs(t)fəlnəs

Wiston
BR 'wɪst(ə)n, 'wɪsn
AM 'wɪstən

wit
BR wɪt, -s
AM wɪt, -s

witan
BR 'wɪtən
AM 'wɪ,tɑn

witch
BR wɪtʃ, -ɪz, -ɪŋ
AM wɪtʃ, -ɪz, -ɪŋ

witchcraft
BR 'wɪtʃkrɑːft, 'wɪtʃkraft
AM ,wɪtʃ,kræft

witchdoctor
BR 'wɪtʃ,dɒktə(r), -z
AM 'wɪtʃ,dɑktər, -z

witchelm
BR 'wɪtʃɛlm, -z
AM 'wɪtʃ,ɛlm, -z

witchery
BR 'wɪtʃ(ə)ri
AM 'wɪtʃəri

witchetty
BR 'wɪtʃɪt|i, -ɪz
AM 'wɪtʃɨdi, -z

witch hazel
BR 'wɪtʃ ,heɪzl, -z
AM 'wɪtʃ ,(h)eɪzəl, -z

witch-hunt
BR 'wɪtʃhʌnt, -s
AM 'wɪtʃ,(h)ənt, -s

witchlike
BR 'wɪtʃlʌɪk
AM 'wɪtʃ,laɪk

witenagemot
BR 'wɪtɨnəjə,məʊt, 'wɪtn̩əjə,məʊt, 'wɪtɨnəgɪ,məʊt, 'wɪtn̩əgɪ,məʊt, -s
AM 'wɪtn̩əgə,moʊt, -s

with
BR wɪð
AM wɪð, wɪθ

withal
BR wɪð'ɔːl
AM wə'ðɔl, wə'θɔl, wə'ðɑl, wə'θɑl

Witham
BR 'wɪð(ə)m
AM 'wɪðəm

withdraw
BR wɪð'drɔː(r), wɪθ'drɔː(r), -z, -ɪŋ
AM wɪð'drɔ, wɪθ'drɔ, wɪð'drɑ, wɪθ'drɑ, -z, -ɪŋ

withdrawal
BR wɪð'drɔː(r)əl, wɪð'drɔː(r)l̩, wɪθ'drɔː(r)əl, wɪθ'drɔː(r)l̩, -z
AM wɪð'drɔ(ə)l, wɪθ'drɔ(ə)l, wɪð'drɑ(ə)l, wɪθ'drɑ(ə)l, -z

withdrawer
BR wɪð'drɔː(r)ə(r), wɪθ'drɔː(r)ə(r), -z
AM wɪð'drɔ(w)ər, wɪθ'drɔ(w)ər, wɪð'drɑ(w)ər, wɪθ'drɑ(w)ər, -z

withdrawn
BR wɪð'drɔːn, wɪθ'drɔːn
AM wɪð'drɔn, wɪθ'drɔn, wɪð'drɑn, wɪθ'drɑn

withdrew
BR wɪð'druː, wɪθ'druː
AM wɪð'dru, wɪθ'dru

withe
BR wɪθ, wɪð, wʌɪð, wɪθs\wɪðz\wʌɪðz
AM wɪ|θ, wɪ|ð, -θs\-ðz

wither
BR 'wɪð|ə(r), -əz, -(ə)rɪŋ, -əd
AM 'wɪð|ər, -ərz, -(ə)rɪŋ, -ərd

witheringly
BR 'wɪð(ə)rɪŋli
AM 'wɪðərɪŋli

Withernsea
BR 'wɪðnsiː
AM 'wɪðərn,si

withers
BR 'wɪðəz
AM 'wɪðərz

withershins
BR 'wɪðəʃɪnz
AM 'wɪðər,ʃɪnz

withheld
BR wɪð'hɛld, wɪθ'hɛld
AM wɪθ'(h)ɛld, wɪð'(h)ɛld

withhold
BR wɪð'həʊld, wɪθ'həʊld, -z, -ɪŋ
AM wɪθ'(h)oʊld, wɪð'(h)oʊld, -z, -ɪŋ

withholder
BR wɪð'həʊldə(r), wɪθ'həʊldə(r), -z
AM wɪθ'(h)oʊldər, wɪð'(h)oʊldər, -z

within
BR wɪð'ɪn
AM wə'ðɪn, wə'θɪn

Withington
BR 'wɪðɪŋt(ə)n
AM 'wɪðɪŋtən, 'wɪθɪŋtən

with-it
BR 'wɪðɪt
AM 'wɪðɨt, 'wɪθɨt

without
BR wɪð'aʊt
AM wə'ðaʊt, wə'θaʊt

with-profits
BR wɪð'prɒfɪts
AM wɪθ'prɑfəts, wɪð'prɑfəts

withstand
BR wɪð'stand, wɪθ'stand, -z, -ɪŋ
AM wɪθ'stænd, wɪð'stænd, -z, -ɪŋ

withstander
BR wɪð'standə(r), wɪθ'standə(r), -z
AM wɪθ'stændər, wɪð'stændər, -z

withstood
BR wɪð'stʊd, wɪθ'stʊd
AM wɪθ'stʊd, wɪð'stʊd

withy
BR 'wɪð|i, -ɪz
AM 'wɪði, 'wɪθi, -z

witless
BR 'wɪtlɪs
AM 'wɪtlɨs

witlessly
BR 'wɪtlɨsli
AM 'wɪtlɨsli
witlessness
BR 'wɪtlɨsnɨs
AM 'wɪtlɨsnɨs
Witley
BR 'wɪtli
AM 'wɪtli
witling
BR 'wɪtlɪŋ, -z
AM 'wɪtlɪŋ, -z
witloof
BR 'wɪtlu:f
AM 'wɪt,luf
witness
BR 'wɪtnɨs, -ɨz, -ɪŋ, -t
AM 'wɪtnɨs, -ɨz, -ɪŋ, -t
Witney
BR 'wɪtni
AM 'wɪtni
Witt
BR wɪt
AM wɪt
Wittenberg
BR 'wɪtnbə:g
AM 'wɪtn,bərg
witter
BR 'wɪt|ə(r), -əz, -(ə)rɪŋ, -əd
AM 'wɪd|ər, -z, -ɪŋ, -d
witterer
BR 'wɪt(ə)rə(r), -z
AM 'wɪdərər, -z
wittering
BR 'wɪt(ə)rɪŋ, -z
AM 'wɪdərɪŋ, -z
Wittgenstein
BR 'vɪtg(ə)nstʌɪn, 'vɪtg(ə)nʃtʌɪn
AM 'vɪtgən,staɪn, 'vɪtgən,ʃtaɪn
witticism
BR 'wɪtɨsɪz(ə)m, -z
AM 'wɪdə,sɪzəm, -z
wittily
BR 'wɪtɨli
AM 'wɪdɨli
wittiness
BR 'wɪtɪnɨs
AM 'wɪdinɨs
witting
BR 'wɪtɪŋ
AM 'wɪdɪŋ
wittingly
BR 'wɪtɪŋli
AM 'wɪdɪŋli
Witton
BR 'wɪtn
AM 'wɪtn
witty
BR 'wɪt|i, -ɪə(r), -ɪɪst
AM 'wɪdi, -ər, -ɨst
Witwatersrand
BR wɪt'wɔ:təzrand
AM ,wɪt'wɔdərz,rænd, ,wɪt'wadərz,rænd
AFK vət'vɑ:tərs,rant
wive
BR wʌɪv, -z, -ɪŋ, -d
AM waɪv, -z, -ɪŋ, -d
Wiveliscombe
BR 'wɪvəlɪskəm, 'wɪlskəm
AM 'wɪvələskəm
Wivelsfield
BR 'wɪvlzfi:ld
AM 'wɪvəlz,fild
Wivenhoe
BR 'wɪvnhəʊ
AM 'wɪvən,hoʊ
wivern
BR 'wʌɪv(ə:)n, -z
AM 'waɪvərn, -z
wives
BR wʌɪvz
AM waɪvz
wiz
BR wɪz
AM wɪz
wizard
BR 'wɪzəd, -z
AM 'wɪzərd, -z
wizardly
BR 'wɪzədli
AM 'wɪzərdli
wizardry
BR 'wɪzədri
AM 'wɪzərdri
wizened
BR 'wɪznd
AM 'wɪzənd, 'waɪzənd
wizzo
BR 'wɪzəʊ, wɪ'zəʊ
AM 'wɪzoʊ
wo
BR wəʊ
AM woʊ
woad
BR wəʊd
AM woʊd
wobbegong
BR 'wɒbɪgɒŋ, -z
AM 'wabə,gɔŋ, 'wabə,gɑŋ, -z
wobble
BR 'wɒb|l, -lz, -l̩ɪŋ\-lɪŋ, -ld
AM 'wabəl, -əlz, -(ə)lɪŋ, -əld
wobble-board
BR 'wɒblbɔ:d, -z
AM 'wabəl,bɔ(ə)rd, -z
wobbler
BR 'wɒbl̩ə(r), 'wɒblə(r), -z
AM 'wab(ə)lər, -z
wobbliness
BR 'wɒbl̩ɪnɨs, 'wɒblɪnɨs
AM 'wab(ə)linɨs
wobbly
BR 'wɒbl̩|i, wɒbl|i, -ɪə(r), -ɪɪst
AM 'wab(ə)li, -ər, -ɨst
Wobegon
BR 'wəʊbɪgɒn
AM 'woʊbə,gɔn, 'woʊbə,gɑn
Woburn
BR 'wəʊbə:n, 'wəʊb(ə)n, 'wu:bə:n, 'wu:b(ə)n
AM 'woʊ,bərn
Wodehouse
BR 'wʊdhaʊs
AM 'wʊd,(h)aʊs
Woden
BR 'wəʊdn
AM 'woʊdən
wodge
BR wɒdʒ, -ɨz
AM wadʒ, -əz
woe
BR wəʊ, -z
AM woʊ, -z
woebegone
BR 'wəʊbɪgɒn
AM 'woʊbə,gɔn, 'woʊbə,gɑn
woeful
BR 'wəʊf(ʊ)l
AM 'woʊfəl
woefully
BR 'wəʊfʊli, 'wəʊfl̩i
AM 'woʊfəli
woefulness
BR 'wəʊf(ʊ)lnəs
AM 'woʊfəlnəs
wog
BR wɒg, -z
AM wag, -z
Wogan
BR 'wəʊg(ə)n
AM 'woʊgən
woggle
BR 'wɒgl, -z
AM 'wagəl, -z
wok
BR wɒk, -s
AM wak, -s
woke
BR wəʊk
AM woʊk
woken
BR 'wəʊk(ə)n
AM 'woʊkən
Woking
BR 'wəʊkɪŋ
AM 'woʊkɪŋ
Wokingham
BR 'wəʊkɪŋəm
AM 'woʊkɪŋəm
wold
BR wəʊld, -z
AM woʊld, -z
Wolf[1]
English name
BR wʊlf
AM wʊlf
Wolf[2]
German name
BR vɒlf
AM vɔlf
wolf
BR wʊlf, -s, -ɪŋ, -t
AM wʊlf, -s, -ɪŋ, -t
wolfcub
BR 'wʊlfkʌb, -z
AM 'wʊlf,kəb, -z
Wolfe
BR wʊlf
AM wʊlf
Wolfenden
BR 'wʊlfndən
AM 'wʊlfəndən
Wolff
BR wʊlf
AM wʊlf
Wolfgang
BR 'wʊlfgaŋ
AM 'wʊlf,gæŋ
wolfhound
BR 'wʊlfhaʊnd, -z
AM 'wʊlf,(h)aʊnd, -z
wolfish
BR 'wʊlfɪʃ
AM 'wʊlfɪʃ
wolfishly
BR 'wʊlfɨʃli
AM 'wʊlfɨʃli
wolfishness
BR 'wʊlfɨʃnɨs
AM 'wʊlfɪʃnɨs
Wolfit
BR 'wʊlfɪt
AM 'wʊlfət
wolf-like
BR 'wʊlflʌɪk
AM 'wʊlf,laɪk
wolf-man
BR 'wʊlfman
AM 'wʊlf,mæn
wolf-men
BR 'wʊlfmɛn
AM 'wʊlf,mɛn
wolfram
BR 'wʊlfrəm
AM 'wʊlfrəm
wolframite
BR 'wʊlfrəmʌɪt
AM 'wʊlfrə,maɪt
wolfsbane
BR 'wʊlfsbeɪn
AM 'wʊlfs,beɪn
wolfskin
BR 'wʊlfskɪn, -z
AM 'wʊlf,skɪn, -z
wolf's-milk
BR 'wʊlfsmɪlk
AM 'wʊlfs,mɪlk
Wolfson
BR 'wʊlfsn
AM 'wʊlfsən
Wollaston
BR 'wʊləst(ə)n
AM 'wʊləstən

Wollongong
BR ˈwʊlənɡɒŋ, ˈwʊləŋɡɒŋ
AM ˈwʊlənɡɔŋ, ˈwʊlənɡɑŋ

Wollstonecraft
BR ˈwʊlstnkrɑːft, ˈwʊlstnkraft
AM ˈwʊlstənˌkræft

Wolof
BR ˈwɒlɒf
AM ˈwoʊˌlɑf

Wolseley
BR ˈwʊlzli
AM ˈwʊlzli

Wolsey
BR ˈwʊlzi
AM ˈwʊlzi

Wolsingham
BR ˈwʊlzɪŋəm
AM ˈwʊlzɪŋəm

Wolstenholme
BR ˈwʊlst(ə)nhəʊm
AM ˈwʊlstənˌ(h)oʊm

Wolverhampton
BR ˌwʊlvəˈham(p)t(ə)n
AM ˈwʊlvərˌ(h)æm(p)tən

wolverine
BR ˈwʊlvəriːn, -z
AM ˌwʊlvəˈrin, -z

Wolverton
BR ˈwʊlvət(ə)n
AM ˈwʊlvərtən

wolves
BR wʊlvz
AM wʊlvz

woman
BR ˈwʊmən
AM ˈwʊmən

womanhood
BR ˈwʊmənhʊd
AM ˈwʊmənˌ(h)ʊd

womanise
BR ˈwʊmənʌɪz, -ɨz, -ɪŋ, -d
AM ˈwʊməˌnaɪz, -ɨz, -ɪŋ, -d

womaniser
BR ˈwʊmənʌɪzə(r), -z
AM ˈwʊməˌnaɪzər, -z

womanish
BR ˈwʊmənɪʃ
AM ˈwʊmənɪʃ

womanishly
BR ˈwʊmənɨʃli
AM ˈwʊmənɨʃli

womanishness
BR ˈwʊmənɪʃnɪs
AM ˈwʊmənɪʃnɪs

womanize
BR ˈwʊmənʌɪz, -ɨz, -ɪŋ, -d
AM ˈwʊməˌnaɪz, -ɨz, -ɪŋ, -d

womanizer
BR ˈwʊmənʌɪzə(r), -z
AM ˈwʊməˌnaɪzər, -z

womankind
BR ˈwʊmənkʌɪnd
AM ˈwʊmənˌkaɪnd

womanless
BR ˈwʊmənləs
AM ˈwʊmənləs

womanlike
BR ˈwʊmənlʌɪk
AM ˈwʊmənˌlaɪk

womanliness
BR ˈwʊmənlɪnɪs
AM ˈwʊmənlinɨs

womanly
BR ˈwʊmənli
AM ˈwʊmənli

womb
BR wuːm, -z
AM wum, -z

wombat
BR ˈwɒmbat, -s
AM ˈwɑmˌbæt, -s

womb-like
BR ˈwuːmlʌɪk
AM ˈwumˌlaɪk

Wombwell
BR ˈwʊmw(ɛ)l, ˈwuːmw(ɛ)l
AM ˈwʊmˌwɛl

women
BR ˈwɪmɪn
AM ˈwɪmɨn

womenfolk
BR ˈwɪmɪnfəʊk
AM ˈwɪmɨnˌfoʊk

womenkind
BR ˈwɪmɪnkʌɪnd
AM ˈwɪmɨnˌkaɪnd

women's lib
BR ˌwɪmɪnz ˈlɪb
AM ˈwɪmɨnz ˈlɪb

women's libber
BR ˌwɪmɪnz ˈlɪbə(r), -z
AM ˈwɪmɨnz ˈlɪbər, -z

womenswear
BR ˈwɪmɪnzwɛː(r)
AM ˈwɪmɨnzˌwɛ(ə)r

won[1]
BR wʌn
AM wən

won[2]
currency
BR wɒn
AM wɑn

wonder
BR ˈwʌnd|ə(r), -əz, -(ə)rɪŋ, -əd
AM ˈwənd|ər, -ərz, -(ə)rɪŋ, -ərd

wonderer
BR ˈwʌnd(ə)rə(r), -z
AM ˈwənd(ə)rər, -z

wonderful
BR ˈwʌndəf(ʊ)l
AM ˈwəndərfəl

wonderfully
BR ˈwʌndəfʊli, ˈwʌndəfl̩i
AM ˈwəndərf(ə)li

wonderfulness
BR ˈwʌndəf(ʊ)lnəs
AM ˈwəndərfəlnəs

wondering
BR ˈwʌnd(ə)rɪŋ, -z
AM ˈwənd(ə)rɪŋ, -z

wonderingly
BR ˈwʌnd(ə)rɪŋli
AM ˈwənd(ə)rɪŋli

wonderland
BR ˈwʌndəland
AM ˈwəndərˌlænd

wonderment
BR ˈwʌndəm(ə)nt
AM ˈwəndərmənt

wondrous
BR ˈwʌndrəs
AM ˈwəndrəs

wondrously
BR ˈwʌndrəsli
AM ˈwəndrəsli

wondrousness
BR ˈwʌndrəsnəs
AM ˈwəndrəsnəs

Wong
BR wɒŋ
AM wɔŋ, wɑŋ

wonkily
BR ˈwɒŋkɨli
AM ˈwɑŋkəli

wonkiness
BR ˈwɒŋkɪnɪs
AM ˈwɑŋkinɨs

wonky
BR ˈwɒŋk|i, -ɪə(r), -ɪɪst
AM ˈwɑŋki, -ər, -ɨst

wont
BR wəʊnt, wɒnt
AM wɔnt, woʊnt, wɑnt

won't
BR wəʊnt
AM woʊnt

wonted
BR ˈwəʊntɨd, ˈwɒntɨd
AM ˈwɔn(t)əd, ˈwoʊn(t)əd, ˈwɑn(t)əd

wonton
BR ˌwɒnˈtɒn, -z
AM ˈwɑnˌtɑn, -z

woo
BR wuː, -z, -ɪŋ, -d
AM wu, -z, -ɪŋ, -d

wooable
BR ˈwuːəbl
AM ˈwuəbəl

wood
BR wʊd, -z
AM wʊd, -z

Woodall
BR ˈwʊdɔːl
AM ˈwʊdˌɔl, ˈwʊdˌɑl

Woodard
BR ˈwʊdɑːd
AM ˈwʊdərd

woodbind
BR ˈwʊdbʌɪnd, -z
AM ˈwʊdˌbaɪnd, -z

woodbine
BR ˈwʊdbʌɪn, -z
AM ˈwʊdˌbaɪn, -z

woodblock
BR ˈwʊdblɒk, -s
AM ˈwʊdˌblɑk, -s

Woodbridge
BR ˈwʊdbrɪdʒ
AM ˈwʊdˌbrɪdʒ

woodcarver
BR ˈwʊdˌkɑːvə(r), -z
AM ˈwʊdˌkɑrvər, -z

woodcarving
BR ˈwʊdˌkɑːvɪŋ, -z
AM ˈwʊdˌkɑrvɪŋ, -z

woodchip
BR ˈwʊdtʃɪp, -s
AM ˈwʊdˌtʃɪp, -s

woodchopper
BR ˈwʊdˌtʃɒpə(r), -z
AM ˈwʊdˌtʃɑpər, -z

woodchuck
BR ˈwʊdtʃʌk, -s
AM ˈwʊdˌtʃək, -s

woodcock
BR ˈwʊdkɒk, -s
AM ˈwʊdˌkɑk, -s

woodcraft
BR ˈwʊdkrɑːft, ˈwʊdkraft
AM ˈwʊdˌkræft

woodcut
BR ˈwʊdkʌt, -s
AM ˈwʊdˌkət, -s

woodcutter
BR ˈwʊdˌkʌtə(r), -z
AM ˈwʊdˌkədər, -z

woodcutting
BR ˈwʊdˌkʌtɪŋ
AM ˈwʊdˌkədɪŋ

wooded
BR ˈwʊdɨd
AM ˈwʊdəd

wooden
BR ˈwʊdn
AM ˈwʊdən

woodenhead
BR ˈwʊdnhɛd, -z
AM ˈwʊdnˌ(h)ɛd, -z

woodenheaded
BR ˌwʊdnˈhɛdɨd
AM ˈwʊdnˌhɛdəd

wooden-headedness
BR ˌwʊdnˈhɛdɨdnɨs
AM ˈwʊdnˌhɛdədnəs

woodenly
BR ˈwʊdnli
AM ˈwʊdnli

woodenness
BR ˈwʊdnnəs
AM ˈwʊdn(n)əs

Woodford
BR ˈwʊdfəd
AM ˈwʊdfərd

woodgrouse
BR ˈwʊdɡraʊs
AM ˈwʊdˌɡraʊs
Woodhall
BR ˈwʊdhɔːl
AM ˈwʊdˌ(h)ɔl, ˈwʊdˌ(h)ɑl
Woodhead
BR ˈwʊdhɛd
AM ˈwʊdˌ(h)ɛd
Woodhouse
BR ˈwʊdhaʊs
AM ˈwʊdˌ(h)aʊs
woodiness
BR ˈwʊdɪnɪs
AM ˈwʊdinɨs
woodland
BR ˈwʊdlənd, -z
AM ˈwʊdlənd, -z
woodlander
BR ˈwʊdləndə(r), -z
AM ˈwʊdləndər, -z
woodlark
BR ˈwʊdlɑːk, -s
AM ˈwʊdˌlɑrk, -s
Woodlesford
BR ˈwʊdlzfəd
AM ˈwʊdəlzfərd
woodless
BR ˈwʊdləs
AM ˈwʊdləs
Woodley
BR ˈwʊdli
AM ˈwʊdli
woodlice
BR ˈwʊdlʌɪs
AM ˈwʊdˌlaɪs
woodlot
BR ˈwʊdlɒt, -s
AM ˈwʊdˌlɑt, -s
woodlouse
BR ˈwʊdlaʊs
AM ˈwʊdˌlaʊs
woodman
BR ˈwʊdmən
AM ˈwʊdmən
woodmen
BR ˈwʊdmən
AM ˈwʊdmən
woodnote
BR ˈwʊdnəʊt, -s
AM ˈwʊdˌnoʊt, -s
woodpecker
BR ˈwʊdˌpɛkə(r), -z
AM ˈwʊdˌpɛkər, -z
woodpie
BR ˈwʊdpʌɪ, -z
AM ˈwʊdˌpaɪ, -z
woodpigeon
BR ˈwʊdˌpɪdʒ(ɨ)n, -z
AM ˈwʊdˌpɪdʒən, -z
woodpile
BR ˈwʊdpʌɪl, -z
AM ˈwʊdˌpaɪl, -z
Woodrow
BR ˈwʊdrəʊ
AM ˈwʊdroʊ

woodruff
BR ˈwʊdrʌf, -s
AM ˈwʊdrəf, -s
woodrush
BR ˈwʊdrʌʃ, -ɪz
AM ˈwʊdˌrəʃ, -əz
Woods
BR wʊdz
AM wʊdz
woodscrew
BR ˈwʊdskruː, -z
AM ˈwʊdˌskru, -z
woodshed
BR ˈwʊdʃɛd, -z
AM ˈwʊdˌʃɛd, -z
woodsman
BR ˈwʊdzmən
AM ˈwʊdzmən
woodsmen
BR ˈwʊdzmən
AM ˈwʊdzmən
woodsmoke
BR ˈwʊdsməʊk
AM ˈwʊdˌsmoʊk
Woodstock
BR ˈwʊdstɒk
AM ˈwʊdˌstɑk
woodsy
BR ˈwʊdz|i, -ɪə(r), -ɪɪst
AM ˈwʊdzi, -ər, -ɨst
woodturner
BR ˈwʊdˌtəːnə(r), -z
AM ˈwʊdˌtərnər, -z
woodturning
BR ˈwʊdˌtəːnɪŋ
AM ˈwʊdˌtərnɪŋ
Woodward
BR ˈwʊdwəd
AM ˈwʊdwərd
woodwasp
BR ˈwʊdwɒsp, -s
AM ˈwʊdˌwɑsp, -s
woodwind
BR ˈwʊdwɪnd
AM ˈwʊdˌwɪnd
woodwork
BR ˈwʊdwəːk
AM ˈwʊdˌwərk
woodworker
BR ˈwʊdˌwəːkə(r), -z
AM ˈwʊdˌwərkər, -z
woodworking
BR ˈwʊdˌwəːkɪŋ
AM ˈwʊdˌwərkɪŋ
woodworm
BR ˈwʊdwəːm
AM ˈwʊdˌwərm
woody
BR ˈwʊd|i, -ɪə(r), -ɪɪst
AM ˈwʊdi, -ər, -ɨst
woodyard
BR ˈwʊdjɑːd, -z
AM ˈwʊdˌjɑrd, -z
wooer
BR ˈwuːə(r), -z
AM ˈwuər, -z

woof[1]
dog's bark
BR wʊf
AM wʊf, wuf
woof[2]
weaving
BR wuːf, -s
AM wʊf, wuf, -s
woofer
BR ˈwuːfə(r), ˈwʊfə(r), -z
AM ˈwʊfər, -z
Woofferton
BR ˈwʊfət(ə)n
AM ˈwʊfərtən
Wookey
BR ˈwʊki
AM ˈwʊki
wool
BR wʊl, -z
AM wʊl, -z
Woolacombe
BR ˈwʊləkəm
AM ˈwʊləkəm
Woolard
BR ˈwʊlɑːd
AM ˈwʊlərd
Wooldridge
BR ˈwʊldrɪdʒ
AM ˈwʊlˌrɪdʒ
woolen
BR ˈwʊlən, -z
AM ˈwʊlən, -z
Wooler
BR ˈwʊlə(r)
AM ˈwʊlər
Woolf
BR wʊlf
AM wʊlf
woolgathering
BR ˈwʊlˌɡað(ə)rɪŋ
AM ˈwʊlˌɡæð(ə)rɪŋ
Woollard
BR ˈwʊlɑːd
AM ˈwʊlərd
woollen
BR ˈwʊlən, -z
AM ˈwʊlən, -z
Woolley
BR ˈwʊli
AM ˈwʊli
wool-like
BR ˈwʊllʌɪk
AM ˈwʊlˌlaɪk
woolliness
BR ˈwʊlɪnɪs
AM ˈwʊlinɨs
woolly
BR ˈwʊl|i, -ɪz, -ɪə(r), -ɪɪst
AM ˈwʊli, -z, -ər, -ɨst
woolly-bear
BR ˈwʊlɪbɛː(r), -z
AM ˈwʊliˌbɛ(ə)r, -z
woolly-headed
BR ˌwʊlɪˈhɛdɪd
AM ˌwʊliˈhɛdəd

woolpack
BR ˈwʊlpak, -s
AM ˈwʊlˌpæk, -s
woolsack
BR ˈwʊlsak, -s
AM ˈwʊlˌsæk, -s
woolsey
BR ˈwʊlzi
AM ˈwʊlzi
woolshed
BR ˈwʊlʃɛd, -z
AM ˈwʊlˌʃɛd, -z
Woolwich
BR ˈwʊlɪdʒ, ˈwʊlɪtʃ
AM ˈwʊlˌwɪtʃ
Woolworth
BR ˈwʊlwəθ, ˈwʊlwəːθ, -s
AM ˈwʊlˌwərθ, -s
woomera
BR ˈwʊm(ə)rə(r), ˈwuːm(ə)rə(r), -z
AM ˈwumərə, -z
woops
BR wʊps
AM wʊps, wups
woosh
BR wʊʃ, -ɪz, -ɪŋ, -t
AM wʊʃ, -əz, -ɪŋ, -t
Woosnam
BR ˈwuːznəm
AM ˈwuznəm
Wooster
BR ˈwʊstə(r), ˈwuːstə(r)
AM ˈwʊstər, ˈwustər
Wooten
BR ˈwʊtn
AM ˈwʊtn
Wootton
BR ˈwʊtn
AM ˈwʊtn
woozily
BR ˈwuːzɪli
AM ˈwuzəli
wooziness
BR ˈwuːzɪnɪs
AM ˈwuzinɨs
woozy
BR ˈwuːz|i, -ɪə(r), -ɪɪst
AM ˈwuzi, -ər, -ɨst
wop
BR wɒp, -s
AM wɑp, -s
Worcester
BR ˈwʊstə(r)
AM ˈwʊstər
Worcestershire
BR ˈwʊstəʃ(ɪ)ə(r)
AM ˈwʊstərʃɪ(ə)r
word
BR wəːd, -z, -ɪŋ, -ɨd
AM wərd, -z, -ɪŋ, -əd
wordage
BR ˈwəːdɪdʒ
AM ˈwərdɪdʒ

wordbook
BR 'wəːdbʊk, -s
AM 'wərd,bʊk, -s

wordfinder
BR 'wəːd,fʌɪndə(r), -z
AM 'wərd,faɪndər, -z

word for word
BR ,wəːd fə 'wəːd
AM 'wərd fər 'wərd

wordily
BR 'wəːdɪli
AM 'wərdəli

wordiness
BR 'wəːdɪnɪs
AM 'wərdinɪs

wording
BR 'wəːdɪŋ, -z
AM 'wərdɪŋ, -z

wordless
BR 'wəːdləs
AM 'wərdləs

wordlessly
BR 'wəːdləsli
AM 'wərdləsli

wordlessness
BR 'wəːdləsnəs
AM 'wərdləsnəs

word-perfect
BR ,wəːd'pəːfɪkt
AM ¦wərd'pərfək(t)

wordplay
BR 'wəːdpleɪ
AM 'wərd,pleɪ

wordsearch
BR 'wəːdsəːtʃ, -ɪz
AM 'wərd,sərtʃ, -əz

wordsmith
BR 'wəːdsmɪθ, -s
AM 'wərd,smɪθ, -s

WordStar
BR 'wəːdstɑː(r)
AM 'wərd,stɑr

Wordsworth
BR 'wəːdzwəθ, 'wəːdzwəːθ
AM 'wərdz,wərθ

Wordsworthian
BR ,wəːdz'wəːðɪən
AM ,wərdz'wərθiən

wordy
BR 'wəːd|i, -ɪə(r), -ɪɪst
AM 'wərdi, -ər, -ɪst

wore
BR wɔː(r)
AM wɔ(ə)r

work
BR wəːk, -s, -ɪŋ, -t
AM wərk, -s, -ɪŋ, -t

workability
BR ,wəːkə'bɪlɪti
AM ,wərkə'bɪlɪdi

workable
BR 'wəːkəbl
AM 'wərkəbəl

workableness
BR 'wəːkəblnəs
AM 'wərkəbəlnəs

workably
BR 'wəːkəbli
AM 'wərkəbli

workaday
BR 'wəːkədeɪ
AM 'wərkə,deɪ

workaholic
BR ,wəːkə'hɒlɪk, -s
AM ¦wərkə'hɔlɪk, ¦wərkə'hɑlɪk, -s

workbasket
BR 'wəːk,bɑːskɪt, 'wəːk,baskɪt, -s
AM 'wərk,bæskət, -s

workbench
BR 'wəːkbɛn(t)ʃ, -ɪz
AM 'wərk,bɛn(t)ʃ, -əz

workboat
BR 'wəːkbəʊt, -s
AM 'wərk,boʊt, -s

workbook
BR 'wəːkbʊk, -s
AM 'wərk,bʊk, -s

workbox
BR 'wəːkbɒks, -ɪz
AM 'wərk,bɑks, -əz

workday
BR 'wəːkdeɪ, -z
AM 'wərk,deɪ, -z

worker
BR 'wəːkə(r), -z
AM 'wərkər, -z

workfare
BR 'wəːkfɛː(r)
AM 'wərk,fɛ(ə)r

workforce
BR 'wəːkfɔːs
AM 'wərk,fɔ(ə)rs

workhorse
BR 'wəːkhɔːs, -ɪz
AM 'wərk,(h)ɔ(ə)rs, -əz

workhouse
BR 'wəːkhaʊ|s, -zɪz
AM 'wərk,(h)aʊ|s, -zəz

working
BR 'wəːkɪŋ, -z
AM 'wərkɪŋ, -z

Workington
BR 'wəːkɪŋt(ə)n
AM 'wərkɪŋtən

workless
BR 'wəːkləs
AM 'wərkləs

workload
BR 'wəːkləʊd, -z
AM 'wərk,loʊd, -z

workman
BR 'wəːkmən
AM 'wərkmən

workmanlike
BR wəːkmənlʌɪk
AM 'wərkmən,laɪk

workmanship
BR 'wəːkmənʃɪp
AM 'wərkmən,ʃɪp

workmate
BR 'wəːkmeɪt, -s
AM 'wərk,meɪt, -s

workmen
BR 'wəːkmən
AM 'wərkmən

workout
BR 'wəːkaʊt, -s
AM 'wərk,aʊt, -s

workpeople
BR 'wəːk,piːpl
AM 'wərk,pipəl

workpiece
BR 'wəːkpiːs, -ɪz
AM 'wərk,pis, -ɪz

workplace
BR 'wəːkpleɪs, -ɪz
AM 'wərk,pleɪs, -ɪz

workroom
BR 'wəːkruːm, 'wəːkrʊm, -z
AM 'wərk,rum, 'wərk,rʊm, -z

worksharing
BR 'wəːk,ʃɛːrɪŋ
AM 'wərk,ʃɛrɪŋ

worksheet
BR 'wəːkʃiːt, -s
AM 'wərk,ʃit, -s

workshop
BR 'wəːkʃɒp, -s
AM 'wərk,ʃɑp, -s

workshy
BR 'wəːkʃʌɪ
AM 'wərk,ʃaɪ

worksite
BR 'wəːksʌɪt, -s
AM 'wərk,saɪt, -s

Worksop
BR 'wəːksɒp
AM 'wərk,sɑp

workspace
BR 'wəːkspeɪs, -ɪz
AM 'wərk,speɪs, -ɪz

workstation
BR 'wəːk,steɪʃn, -z
AM 'wərk,steɪʃən, -z

worktop
BR 'wəːktɒp, -s
AM 'wərk,tɑp, -s

work-to-rule
BR ,wəːktʊ'ruːl, -z
AM 'wərktə'rul, -z

workwear
BR 'wəːkwɛː(r)
AM 'wərk,wɛ(ə)r

workweek
BR 'wəːkwiːk, -s
AM 'wərk,wik, -s

workwoman
BR 'wəːk,wʊmən
AM 'wərk,wʊmən

workwomen
BR 'wəːk,wɪmɪn
AM 'wərk,wɪmɪn

world
BR wəːld, -z
AM wər(ə)ld, -z

World Cup
BR 'wəːl(d) kʌp
AM ¦wər(ə)l(d) 'kəp

worlde
BR 'wəːld(i)
AM 'wər(ə)ld(i)

worldliness
BR 'wəːldlɪnɪs
AM 'wər(ə)l(d)linɪs

worldling
BR 'wəːldlɪŋ, -z
AM 'wər(ə)l(d)lɪŋ, -z

worldly
BR 'wəːldl|i, -ɪə(r), -ɪɪst
AM 'wər(ə)l(d)li, -ər, -ɪst

worldview
BR ,wəːld'vjuː, -z
AM ¦wər(ə)l(d)¦vju, -z

worldwide
BR ,wəːl(d)'wʌɪd
AM ¦wər(ə)l(d)¦waɪd

worm
BR wəːm, -z, -ɪŋ, -d
AM wərm, -z, -ɪŋ, -d

Wormald
BR 'wəːmld
AM 'wərməld

worm-cast
BR 'wəːmkɑːst, 'wəːmkast, -s
AM 'wərm,kæst, -s

wormer
BR 'wəːmə(r), -z
AM 'wərmər, -z

wormhole
BR 'wəːmhəʊl, -z
AM 'wərm,(h)oʊl, -z

worminess
BR 'wəːmɪnɪs
AM 'wərminɪs

wormlike
BR 'wəːmlʌɪk
AM 'wərm,laɪk

Wormold
BR 'wəːməʊld, 'wəːmld
AM 'wərməld, 'wər,moʊld

Worms
BR wəːmz, vɔːmz
AM wərmz
GER vɔrmz

wormseed
BR 'wəːmsiːd, -z
AM 'wərm,sid, -z

wormwood
BR 'wəːmwʊd
AM 'wərm,wʊd

wormy
BR 'wəːm|i, -ɪə(r), -ɪɪst
AM 'wərmi, -ər, -ɪst

worn
BR wɔːn
AM wɔ(ə)rn

Worrall
BR 'wɒrəl, 'wɒrl̩

AM ˈwɔrəl

worriedly
BR ˈwʌrɪdli
AM ˈwəridli

worrier
BR ˈwʌrɪə(r), -z
AM ˈwəriər, -z

worriment
BR ˈwʌrɪm(ə)nt
AM ˈwərimənt

worrisome
BR ˈwʌrɪs(ə)m
AM ˈwəriˌsəm

worrisomely
BR ˈwʌrɪs(ə)mli
AM ˈwəriˌsəmli

worrit
BR ˈwʌr|ɪt, -ɪts, -ɪtɪŋ, -ɪtɪd
AM ˈwərə|t, -ts, -dɪŋ, -dəd

worry
BR ˈwʌr|i, -ɪz, -ɪɪŋ, -ɪd
AM ˈwəri, -z, -ɪŋ, -d

worryingly
BR ˈwʌrɪɪŋli
AM ˈwəriɪŋli

worrywart
BR ˈwʌrɪwɔːt, -s
AM ˈwəriˌwɔ(ə)rt, -s

worse
BR wəːs
AM wərs

worsen
BR ˈwəːs|n, -nz, -nɪŋ\-n̩ɪŋ, -nd
AM ˈwərsən, -z, -ɪŋ, -d

worship
BR ˈwəːʃ|ɪp, -ɪps, -ɪpɪŋ, -ɪpt
AM ˈwərʃəp, -s, -ɪŋ, -t

worshipable
BR ˈwəːʃɪpəbl
AM ˈwərʃəpəbəl

worshiper
BR ˈwəːʃɪpə(r), -z
AM ˈwərʃəpər, -z

worshipful
BR ˈwəːʃɪpf(ʊ)l
AM ˈwərʃəpfəl

worshipfully
BR ˈwəːʃɪpfʊli, ˈwəːʃɪpfl̩i
AM ˈwərʃɪpf(ə)li

worshipfulness
BR ˈwəːʃɪpf(ʊ)lnəs
AM ˈwərʃɪpfəlnəs

worshipper
BR ˈwəːʃɪpə(r), -z
AM ˈwərʃəpər, -z

Worsley
BR ˈwəːsli, ˈwəːzli
AM ˈwərzli

Worsnip
BR ˈwəːsnɪp
AM ˈwərsnəp

worst
BR wəːst
AM wərst

worsted¹
noun
BR ˈwʊstɪd
AM ˈwʊstəd, ˈwərstəd

worsted²
past tense, adjective, from 'worse'
BR ˈwəːstɪd
AM ˈwərstəd

Worsthorne
BR ˈwəːsθɔːn
AM ˈwərsˌθɔ(ə)rn

wort
BR wəːt, -s
AM wərt, wɔ(ə)rt, -s

worth
BR wəːθ
AM wərθ

worthily
BR ˈwəːðɪli
AM ˈwərðəli

worthiness
BR ˈwəːðɪnɪs
AM ˈwərðinɪs

Worthing
BR ˈwəːðɪŋ
AM ˈwərðɪŋ

Worthington
BR ˈwəːðɪŋt(ə)n
AM ˈwərðɪŋtən

worthless
BR ˈwəːθləs
AM ˈwərθləs

worthlessly
BR ˈwəːθləsli
AM ˈwərθləsli

worthlessness
BR ˈwəːθləsnəs
AM ˈwərθləsnəs

worthwhile
BR ˌwəːθˈwʌɪl
AM ˈˌwərθˈ(h)waɪl

worthwhileness
BR ˌwəːθˈwʌɪlnɪs
AM ˈˌwərθˈ(h)waɪlnɪs

worthy
BR ˈwəːð|i, -ɪz, -ɪə(r), -ɪɪst
AM ˈwərði, -z, -ər, -ɪst

Wortley
BR ˈwəːtli
AM ˈwərtli

wot
BR wɒt
AM wɑt

wotcha
BR ˈwɒtʃə(r)
AM ˈwɑtʃə

wotcher
BR ˈwɒtʃə(r)
AM ˈwɑtʃər

Wotton
BR ˈwʊtn, ˈwɒtn
AM ˈwɑtn

would¹
strong form
BR wʊd
AM wʊd

would²
weak form
BR wəd, (ə)d
AM wəd, (ə)d

would-be
BR ˈwʊdbiː, ˈwʊdbɪ
AM ˈwʊdˌbi

wouldn't
BR ˈwʊdnt
AM ˈwʊdnt

wouldst
BR wʊdst, wʊtst
AM wʊdst, wʊtst

wound¹
injury, injure
BR wuːnd, -z, -ɪŋ, -ɪd
AM wund, -z, -ɪŋ, -ɪd

wound²
past tense, adjective, from wind
BR waʊnd
AM waʊnd

Wounded Knee
BR ˌwuːndɪd ˈniː
AM ˌwundəd ˈni

woundedness
BR ˈwuːndɪdnɪs
AM ˈwundədnəs

wounding
BR ˈwuːndɪŋ, -z
AM ˈwundɪŋ, -z

woundingly
BR ˈwuːndɪŋli
AM ˈwundɪŋli

woundless
BR ˈwuːndləs
AM ˈwun(d)ləs

woundwort
BR ˈwuːndwəːt, -s
AM ˈwundˌwərt, ˈwundˌwɔ(ə)rt, -s

wove
BR wəʊv
AM woʊv

woven
BR ˈwəʊvn
AM ˈwoʊvən

wow
BR waʊ, -z, -ɪŋ, -d
AM waʊ, -z, -ɪŋ, -d

wowser
BR ˈwaʊzə(r), -z
AM ˈwaʊzər, -z

WRAC
BR rak, -s
AM ræk, -s

wrack
BR rak, -s
AM ræk, -s

WRAF
BR raf, -s
AM ræf, -s

wraggle-taggle
BR ˌraglˈtagl
AM ˈˌrægəlˌtægəl

wraith
BR reɪθ, -s
AM reɪθ, -s

wraithlike
BR ˈreɪθlʌɪk
AM ˈreɪθˌlaɪk

Wrangel
BR ˈraŋgl
AM ˈræŋgəl

wrangle
BR ˈraŋg|l, -lz, -l̩ɪŋ\-lɪŋ, -ld
AM ˈræŋg|əl, -əlz, -(ə)lɪŋ, -əld

wrangler
BR ˈraŋglə(r), -z
AM ˈræŋg(ə)lər, -z

wrangling
BR ˈraŋglɪŋ, ˈraŋgl̩ɪŋ, -z
AM ˈræŋg(ə)lɪŋ, -z

wrap
BR rap, -s, -ɪŋ, -t
AM ræp, -s, -ɪŋ, -t

wraparound
BR ˈrapəraʊnd
AM ˈræpəˌraʊnd

wrappage
BR ˈrapɪdʒ
AM ˈræpɪdʒ

wrapper
BR ˈrapə(r), -z
AM ˈræpər, -z

wrapping
BR ˈrapɪŋ, -z
AM ˈræpɪŋ, -z

wrapround
BR ˈrapraʊnd, -z
AM ˈræpˌraʊnd, -z

wrasse
BR ras, -ɪz
AM ræs, -əz

wrath
BR rɒθ
AM ræθ

wrathful
BR ˈrɒθf(ʊ)l
AM ˈræθfəl

wrathfully
BR ˈrɒθfʊli, ˈrɒθfl̩i
AM ˈræθfəli

wrathfulness
BR ˈrɒθf(ʊ)lnəs
AM ˈræθfəlnəs

wrathy
BR ˈrɒθi
AM ˈræθi

Wray
BR reɪ
AM reɪ

wreak
BR riːk, -s, -ɪŋ, -t
AM rik, -s, -ɪŋ, -t

wreaker
BR 'ri:kə(r), -z
AM 'rikər, -z

wreath
BR ri:|θ, -ðz\-θs
AM ri|θ, -ðz\-θs

wreathe
BR ri:ð, -z, -ɪŋ, -d
AM rið, -z, -ɪŋ, -d

wreck
BR rɛk, -s, -ɪŋ, -t
AM rɛk, -s, -ɪŋ, -t

wreckage
BR 'rɛkɪdʒ
AM 'rɛkɪdʒ

wrecker
BR 'rɛkə(r), -z
AM 'rɛkər, -z

Wrekin
BR 'ri:kɪn
AM 'rikɪn

wren
BR rɛn, -z
AM rɛn, -z

wrench
BR rɛn(t)ʃ, -ɨz, -ɪŋ, -t
AM rɛn(t)ʃ, -əz, -ɪŋ, -t

wrentit
BR 'rɛntɪt, -s
AM 'rɛn,tɪt, -s

wrest
BR rɛst, -s, -ɪŋ, -ɨd
AM rɛst, -s, -ɪŋ, -əd

wrest-block
BR 'rɛs(t)blɒk, -s
AM 'rɛs(t),blɑk, -s

wrestle
BR 'rɛs|l, -lz, -l̩ɪŋ\-lɪŋ, -ld
AM 'rɛs|əl, -əlz, -(ə)lɪŋ, -əld

wrestler
BR 'rɛslə(r), 'rɛsl̩ə(r), -z
AM 'rɛs(ə)lər, -z

wrestling
BR 'rɛslɪŋ, 'rɛsl̩ɪŋ, -z
AM 'rɛs(ə)lɪŋ, -z

wrest-pin
BR 'rɛs(t)pɪn, -z
AM 'rɛs(t),pɪn, -z

wretch
BR rɛtʃ, -ɨz
AM rɛtʃ, -əz

wretched
BR 'rɛtʃɨd
AM 'rɛtʃəd

wretchedly
BR 'rɛtʃɨdli
AM 'rɛtʃədli

wretchedness
BR 'rɛtʃɨdnɨs
AM 'rɛtʃədnəs

Wrexham
BR 'rɛks(ə)m
AM 'rɛksəm

wrick
BR rɪk, -s, -ɪŋ, -t
AM rɪk, -s, -ɪŋ, -t

wriggle
BR 'rɪg|l, -lz, -l̩ɪŋ\-lɪŋ, -ld
AM 'rɪg|əl, -əlz, -(ə)lɪŋ, -əld

wriggler
BR 'rɪgl̩ə(r), 'rɪglə(r), -z
AM 'rɪg(ə)lər, -z

wriggly
BR 'rɪgl̩i, 'rɪgl|i, -ɪə(r), -ɪɪst
AM 'rɪg(ə)li, -ər, -ɨst

wright
BR rʌɪt, -s
AM raɪt, -s

Wrighton
BR 'rʌɪtn
AM 'raɪtn

Wrigley
BR 'rɪgli
AM 'rɪgli

wrily
BR 'rʌɪli
AM 'raɪli

wring
BR rɪŋ, -z, -ɪŋ
AM rɪŋ, -z, -ɪŋ

wringer
BR 'rɪŋə(r), -z
AM 'rɪŋər, -z

wrinkle
BR 'rɪŋk|l, -lz, -l̩ɪŋ\-lɪŋ, -ld
AM 'rɪŋk|əl, -əlz, -(ə)lɪŋ, -əld

wrinkliness
BR 'rɪŋklɪnɨs
AM 'rɪŋk(ə)linɨs

wrinkly
BR 'rɪŋkl|i, -ɪz
AM 'rɪŋk(ə)li, -z

wrist
BR rɪst, -s
AM rɪst, -s

wristband
BR 'rɪs(t)band, -z
AM 'rɪs(t),bænd, -z

wristlet
BR 'rɪs(t)lɪt, -s
AM 'rɪs(t)lət, -s

wristwatch
BR 'rɪs(t)wɒtʃ, -ɨz
AM 'rɪs(t),wɑtʃ, -əz

wristy
BR 'rɪsti
AM 'rɪsti

writ
BR rɪt, -s
AM rɪt, -s

writable
BR 'rʌɪtəbl
AM 'raɪdəbəl

write
BR rʌɪt, -s, -ɪŋ
AM raɪ|t, -ts, -dɪŋ

writer
BR 'rʌɪtə(r), -z
AM 'raɪdər, -z

writerly
BR 'rʌɪtəli
AM 'raɪdərli

writhe
BR rʌɪð, -z, -ɪŋ, -d
AM raɪð, -z, -ɪŋ, -d

writhing
BR 'rʌɪðɪŋ, -z
AM 'raɪðɪŋ, -z

writing
BR 'rʌɪtɪŋ, -z
AM 'raɪdɪŋ, -z

written
BR 'rɪtn
AM 'rɪtn

WRNS
BR rɛnz
AM rɛnz

Wrocław
BR 'vrɒtslɑ:v, 'vrɒtslav
AM '(v)rɔ(t)slɑf, '(v)rɑ(t)slɑv
POL 'vrɒtswav

wrong
BR rɒŋ, -z, -ɪŋ, -d
AM rɔŋ, rɑŋ, -z, -ɪŋ, -d

wrongdoer
BR 'rɒŋ,du:ə(r), -z
AM 'rɔŋ,duər, 'rɑŋ,duər, -z

wrongdoing
BR 'rɒŋ,du:ɪŋ, ,rɒŋ'du:ɪŋ
AM 'rɔŋ,duɪŋ, 'rɑŋ,duɪŋ

wronger
BR 'rɒŋə(r), -z
AM 'rɔŋgər, 'rɑŋgər, -z

wrong-foot
BR ,rɒŋ'fʊt, -s, -ɪŋ, -ɨd
AM ,rɔn'fʊ|t, ,rɑŋ'fʊ|t, -ts, -dɪŋ, -dəd

wrong-footed
BR ,rɒŋ'fʊtɨd
AM ,rɔŋ'fʊdəd, ,rɑŋ'fʊdəd

wrongful
BR 'rɒŋf(ʊ)l
AM 'rɔŋfəl, 'rɑŋfəl

wrongfully
BR 'rɒŋfʊli, 'rɒŋfl̩i
AM 'rɔŋfəli, 'rɑŋfəli

wrongfulness
BR 'rɒŋf(ʊ)lnəs
AM 'rɔŋfəlnəs, 'rɑŋfəlnəs

wrong-headed
BR ,rɒŋ'hɛdɨd
AM ¦rɔŋ¦hɛdəd, ¦rɑŋ¦hɛdəd

wrong-headedly
BR ,rɒŋ'hɛdɨdli
AM ¦rɔŋ¦hɛdədli, ¦rɑŋ¦hɛdədli

wrong-headedness
BR ,rɒŋ'hɛdɨdnɨs
AM ¦rɔŋ¦hɛdədnəs, ¦rɑŋ¦hɛdədnəs

wrongly
BR 'rɒŋli
AM 'rɔŋli, 'rɑŋli

wrongness
BR 'rɒŋnəs
AM 'rɔŋnəs, 'rɑŋnəs

wrong'un
BR 'rɒŋən, -z
AM 'rɔŋən, 'rɑŋən, -z

wrote
BR rəʊt
AM roʊt

wroth
BR rəʊθ, rɒθ
AM rɔθ, rɑθ

wrought
BR rɔ:t
AM rɔt, rɑt

wrought-iron
BR ,rɔ:t'ʌɪən
AM ¦rɔt¦aɪ(ə)rn, ¦rɑt¦aɪ(ə)rn

Wroxeter
BR 'rɒksɪtə(r)
AM 'rɑksədər

Wroxham
BR 'rɒks(ə)m
AM 'rɑksəm

wrung
BR rʌŋ, -z
AM rəŋ, -z

WRVS
BR ,dʌbljʊɑ:vi:'ɛs
AM ,dəbəlju,ɑr,vi'ɛs

wry
BR rʌɪ, -ə(r), -ɨst
AM raɪ, -ər, -ɨst

wrybill
BR 'rʌɪbɪl, -z
AM 'raɪ,bɪl, -z

wryly
BR 'rʌɪli
AM 'raɪli

wry-mouth
BR 'rʌɪmaʊθ, -s
AM 'raɪ,maʊθ, -s

wry-mouthed
BR ,rʌɪ'maʊðd, ,rʌɪ'maʊθt
AM 'raɪ,maʊθt

wryneck
BR 'rʌɪnɛk, -s
AM 'raɪ,nɛk, -s

wryness
BR 'rʌɪnɨs
AM 'raɪnɨs

Wu
BR wu:

AM wu

Wuhan
BR ˌwuːˈhan
AM ˈwuˈhæn

Wulfila
BR ˈwʊlfɪlə(*r*)
AM ˈwʊlfələ

Wulfrun
BR ˈwʊlfrən, ˈwʊlfrn̩
AM ˈwʊlfˌrən

Wulstan
BR ˈwʊlst(ə)n
AM ˈwʊlstən

wunderkind
BR ˈwʊndəkɪnd, -z
AM ˈwʊndərˌkɪnd, -z

Wuppertal
BR ˈvʊpətɑːl, ˈwʊpətɑːl
AM ˈwʊpərˌtɑl,
ˈvupərˌtɑl

Wurlitzer®
BR ˈwəːlɪtsə(r), -z
AM ˈwərˌlɪtsər, -z

wurst
BR wəːst, wʊəst, vʊəst
AM wərst, wʊ(ə)rst

Württemberg
BR ˈvəːtəmbəːg,
ˈwəːtəmbəːg
AM ˈwərtəmˌbərg,
ˈvərtəmˌbərg
GER ˈvʏrtm̩bɛrk

Würzburg
BR ˈvəːtsbəːg,
ˈwəːtsbəːg
AM ˈwərtsˌbərg,
ˈvərtsˌbərg
GER ˈvʏrtsbʊrk

wu-wei
BR ˌwuːˈweɪ
AM ˈwuˈweɪ

Wyandot
BR ˈwʌɪəndɒt
AM ˈwaɪənˌdɑt

Wyandotte
BR ˈwʌɪəndɒt
AM ˈwaɪənˌdɑt

Wyatt
BR ˈwʌɪət
AM ˈwaɪət

wych alder
BR ˈwɪtʃ ˌɔːldə(r),
+ ˌɒldə(r), -z
AM ˈwɪtʃ ˌɔldər, ˈwɪtʃ
ˌɑldər, -z

wychelm
BR ˈwɪtʃɛlm, -z
AM ˈwɪˌtʃɛlm, -z

Wycherley
BR ˈwɪtʃəli
AM ˈwɪtʃərli

wych-hazel
BR ˈwɪtʃˌheɪzl, -z
AM ˈwɪtʃˌ(h)eɪzəl, -z

Wychwood
BR ˈwɪtʃwʊd
AM ˈwɪtʃˌwʊd

Wyclif
BR ˈwɪklɪf
AM ˈwɪklɪf

Wycliffe
BR ˈwɪklɪf
AM ˈwɪklɪf

Wycombe
BR ˈwɪkəm
AM ˈwɪkəm

Wye
BR wʌɪ
AM waɪ

Wyke
BR wʌɪk
AM waɪk

Wykehamist
BR ˈwɪkəmɪst, -s
AM ˈwɪkəməst, -s

Wyld
BR wʌɪld
AM waɪld

Wylde
BR wʌɪld
AM waɪld

Wylfa
BR ˈwɪlvə(*r*)
AM ˈwɪlfə

Wylie
BR ˈwʌɪli
AM ˈwaɪli

Wyllie
BR ˈwʌɪli
AM ˈwaɪli

Wylye
BR ˈwʌɪli
AM ˈwaɪli

Wyman
BR ˈwʌɪmən
AM ˈwaɪmən

Wymondham[1]
Leicestershire, UK
BR ˈwʌɪməndəm
AM ˈwaɪməndem

Wymondham[2]
Norfolk, UK
BR ˈwɪməndəm,
ˈwɪndəm
AM ˈwɪməndəm,
ˈwɪndəm

Wyn
BR wɪn
AM wɪn

wynd
BR wʌɪnd, -z
AM waɪnd, -z

Wyndham
BR ˈwɪndəm
AM ˈwɪndəm

Wynford
BR ˈwɪnfəd
AM ˈwɪnfərd

Wynn
BR wɪn
AM wɪn

Wynne
BR wɪn
AM wɪn

Wyoming
BR wʌɪˈəʊmɪŋ
AM waɪˈoʊmɪŋ

Wyre
BR ˈwʌɪə(r)
AM ˈwaɪ(ə)r

WYSIWYG
BR ˈwɪzɪwɪg
AM ˈwɪziˌwɪg

Wystan
BR ˈwɪst(ə)n
AM ˈwɪstən

Wythenshawe
BR ˈwɪðnʃɔː(*r*)
AM ˈwɪðənˌʃɔ

wyvern
BR ˈwʌɪvəːn, ˈwʌɪvn, -z
AM ˈwaɪvərn, -z

Xx

x
BR ɛks, -ɪz
AM ɛks, -əz

Xanadu
BR 'zanədu:
AM 'zænə,du

xanthate
BR 'zanθeɪt, -s
AM 'zæn,θeɪt, -s

Xanthe
BR 'zanθi
AM 'zænθi

xanthic
BR 'zanθɪk
AM 'zænθɪk

xanthine
BR 'zanθi:n
AM 'zænθin, 'zænθən

Xanthippe
BR zan'θɪpi, zan'tɪpi
AM zæn'θɪpi, zæn'tɪpi

xanthoma
BR zan'θəʊmə(r), -z
AM zæn'θoʊmə, -z

xanthomata
BR zan'θəʊmətə(r), -z
AM zæn'θoʊmədə, -z

xanthophyll
BR 'zanθə(ʊ)fɪl
AM 'zænθə,fɪl

Xantippe
BR zan'tɪpi
AM zæn'tɪpi

Xavier
BR 'zeɪvɪə(r), 'zavɪə(r)
AM 'zeɪviər, 'zeɪvjər

x-axes
BR 'ɛks,aksi:z
AM 'ɛks,æksiz

x-axis
BR 'ɛks,aksɪs
AM 'ɛks,æksəs

xebec
BR 'zi:bɛk, 'zeɪbɛk, -s
AM 'zi,bɛk, -s

xenia
BR 'zi:nɪə(r), 'zɛnɪə(r)
AM 'ziniə

Xenix
BR 'zi:nɪks
AM 'zinɪks

xenogamous
BR zɛ'nɒgəməs, zi:'nɒgəməs, zɪ'nɒgəməs
AM zə'nɑgəməs

xenogamy
BR zɛ'nɒgəmi, zi:'nɒgəmi, zɪ'nɒgəmi
AM zə'nɑgəmi

xenograft
BR 'zɛnə(ʊ)grɑ:ft, 'zɛnə(ʊ)graft, -s
AM 'zɛnə,græft, -s

xenolith
BR 'zɛnəlɪθ, -s
AM 'zɛnə,lɪθ, -s

xenon
BR 'zi:nɒn, 'zɛnɒn
AM 'zi,nɑn

Xenophanes
BR zɛ'nɒfəni:z, zɪ'nɒfəni:z
AM zə'nɑfə,niz

xenophile
BR 'zɛnəfʌɪl, -z
AM 'zinə,faɪl, 'zɛnə,faɪl, -z

xenophobe
BR 'zɛnəfəʊb, -z
AM 'zinə,foʊb, 'zɛnə,foʊb, -z

xenophobia
BR ,zɛnə'fəʊbɪə(r)
AM ,zinə'foʊbiə, ,zɛnə'foʊbiə

xenophobic
BR ,zɛnə'fəʊbɪk
AM ,zinə'foʊbɪk, ,zɛnə'foʊbɪk

Xenophon
BR 'zɛnəfɒn
AM 'zɛnə,fɑn

xenotropic
BR ,zɛnə(ʊ)'trɒpɪk, ,zɛnə(ʊ)'trəʊpɪk
AM ,zinə'trɑpɪk

xeranthemum
BR zɪ'ranθɪməm, -z
AM zə'rænθəməm, -z

xeric
BR 'zɪərɪk
AM 'zɛrɪk

xeroderma
BR ,zɪərə(ʊ)'də:mə(r)
AM ,zɪrə'dərmə

xerograph
BR 'zɪərə(ʊ)grɑ:f, 'zɪərə(ʊ)graf, -s
AM 'zɪrə,græf, -s

xerographic
BR ,zɪərə(ʊ)'grafɪk
AM ,zɪrə'græfɪk

xerographically
BR ,zɪərə(ʊ)'grafɪkli
AM ,zɪrə'græfək(ə)li

xerography
BR zɪə'rɒgrəfi, zɛ'rɒgrəfi, zɪ'rɒgrəfi
AM ,zɪr'ɑgrəfi

xerophile
BR 'zɪərə(ʊ)fʌɪl, -z
AM 'zɪrə,faɪl, -z

xerophilous
BR zɪə'rɒfɪləs, zɛ'rɒfɪləs, zɪ'rɒfɪləs
AM zə'rɑfələs

xerophyte
BR 'zɪərə(ʊ)fʌɪt, -s
AM 'zɪrə,faɪt, -s

xerox
BR 'zɪərɒks, 'zɛrɒks, -ɪz, -ɪŋ, -t
AM 'zi,rɑks, 'zɪ,rɑks, -əz, -ɪŋ, -t

Xerxes
BR 'zə:ksi:z
AM 'zər,ksiz

Xhosa
BR 'kɔ:sə(r), 'kəʊsə(r), 'kɔ:zə(r), 'kəʊzə(r)
AM 'koʊsə, 'kɔsə, 'kɑsə

xi
BR (k)sʌɪ, (g)zʌɪ, -z
AM zaɪ, ksaɪ, -z

Xian
BR ʃan
AM ʃæn

Ximenes
BR 'zɪmɪni:z
AM 'zɪmɪniz

Xingtai
BR ,ʃɪŋ'tʌɪ
AM 'ʃɪŋ'taɪ

Xining
BR ,ʃi:'nɪŋ
AM 'ʃɪ'nɪŋ

Xinjiang
BR ,ʃɪn'dʒ(ɪ)aŋ
AM 'ʃɪn'dʒæŋ

Xiphias
BR 'zɪfɪəs
AM 'zɪfiəs

xiphisterna
BR ,zɪfɪ'stə:nə(r)
AM ,zɪfə'stərnə

xiphisternum
BR ,zɪfɪ'stə:nəm, -z
AM ,zɪfə'stərnəm, -z

xiphoid
BR 'zɪfɔɪd
AM 'zaɪ,fɔɪd, 'zɪ,fɔɪd

Xizang
BR ,ʃi:'zaŋ
AM 'ʃɪ'zæŋ

Xmas
BR 'krɪsməs, 'ɛksməs, -ɪz
AM 'krɪsməs, 'ɛksməs, -əz

xoana
BR 'zəʊənə(r)
AM 'zoʊənə

xoanon
BR 'zəʊənɒn
AM 'zoʊə,nɑn

X-rated
BR ,ɛks'reɪtɪd
AM ,ɛks,reɪdɪd

X-ray
BR 'ɛksreɪ, -z, -ɪŋ, -d
AM 'ɛks,reɪ, -z, -ɪŋ, -d

Xuzhou
BR ,ʃu:'dʒəʊ
AM 'ʃu'dʒoʊ

xylem
BR 'zʌɪləm
AM 'zaɪləm

xylene
BR 'zʌɪli:n
AM 'zaɪ,lin

xylocarp
BR 'zʌɪlə(ʊ)kɑ:p, -s
AM 'zaɪlə,kɑrp, -s

xylocarpous
BR ,zʌɪlə(ʊ)'kɑ:pəs
AM ,zaɪlə'kɑrpəs

xylograph
BR 'zʌɪləgrɑ:f, 'zʌɪləgraf, -s
AM 'zaɪlə,græf, -s

xylographer
BR zʌɪ'lɒgrəfə(r), -z
AM zaɪ'lɑgrəfər, -z

xylography
BR zʌɪ'lɒgrəfi
AM ,zaɪ'lɑgrəfi

xylonite
BR 'zʌɪlənʌɪt
AM 'zaɪlə,naɪt

xylophagous
BR zʌɪ'lɒfəgəs
AM zaɪ'lɑfəgəs

xylophone
BR 'zʌɪləfəʊn, -z
AM 'zaɪlə,foʊn, -z

xylophonic
BR ,zʌɪlə'fɒnɪk
AM ,zaɪlə'fɑnɪk

xylophonist
BR zʌɪ'lɒfənɪst, zʌɪ'lɒfn̩ɪst, 'zʌɪləfəʊnɪst, -s
AM 'zaɪlə,foʊnəst, -s

xylose
BR 'zʌɪləʊz, 'zʌɪləʊs
AM 'zaɪ,loʊs, 'zaɪ,loʊz

xysti
BR 'zɪstʌɪ
AM 'zɪs,taɪ

xystus
BR 'zɪstəs
AM 'zɪstəs

Yy

y
BR wʌɪ, -z
AM waɪ, -z

yabber
BR 'jab|ə(r), -əz, -(ə)rɪŋ, -əd
AM 'jæbər, -z, -ɪŋ, -d

yabbie
BR 'jab|i, -ɪz
AM 'jæbi, -z

yabby
BR 'jab|i, -ɪz
AM 'jæbi, -z

yacht
BR jɒt, -s, -ɪŋ
AM jɑt, -s, -ɪŋ

yachtie
BR 'jɒt|i, -ɪz
AM 'jɑdi, -z

yachtsman
BR 'jɒtsmən
AM 'jɑtsmən

yachtsmen
BR 'jɒtsmən
AM 'jɑtsmən

yachtswoman
BR 'jɒts,wʊmən
AM 'jɑts,wʊmən

yachtswomen
BR 'jɒts,wɪmɪn
AM 'jɑts,wɪmɪn

yack
BR jak, -s, -ɪŋ, -t
AM jæk, -s, -ɪŋ, -t

yacka
BR 'jakə(r)
AM 'jækə

yacker
BR 'jakə(r)
AM 'jækər

yackety-yack
BR ,jakətɪ'jak
AM 'jækədi'jæk

yadda-yadda
BR 'jadəjadə
AM 'jɑdə'jɑdə

yaffle
BR 'jafl, -z
AM 'jæfəl, -z

Yafo
BR 'jɑːfəʊ
AM 'jɑfoʊ

YAG
BR jag
AM jæg

yager
BR 'jeɪgə(r), -z
AM 'jeɪgər, -z

Yagi antenna
BR 'jɑːgɪ ən,tɛnə(r), -z
AM 'jɑgi ən'tɛnə, -z

yah
BR jɑː(r)
AM jɑ

yahoo
BR 'jɑːhuː, jə'huː, -z
AM 'jɑ,hu, -z

Yahveh
BR 'jɑːveɪ
AM 'jɑ,veɪ

Yahvist
BR 'jɑːvɪst, -s
AM 'jɑvəst, -s

Yahweh
BR 'jɑːweɪ
AM 'jɑ,weɪ

Yahwist
BR 'jɑːwɪst, -s
AM 'jɑwəst, -s

yak
BR jak, -s
AM jæk, -s

Yakima
BR 'jakɪmə(r)
AM 'jækəmə

yakka
BR 'jakə(r)
AM 'jækə

yakker
BR 'jakə(r), -z
AM 'jækər, -z

Yakut
BR ja'kʊt, -s
AM jæ'kʊt, -s

Yakutia
BR ja'kʊtɪə(r)
AM jæ'kuʃə

Yakutsk
BR jə'kʊtsk, ja'kʊtsk, jɑː'kʊtsk
AM jə'kʊ(t)sk, jæ'kʊ(t)sk

yakuza
BR jɑː'kuːzə(r), jə'kuːzə(r)
AM jɑ'kuzə

Yale
BR jeɪl
AM jeɪl

Yalta
BR 'jaltə(r), 'jɒltə(r), 'jɔːltə(r)
AM 'jɑltə

Yalu
BR 'jaluː
AM 'jɑ,lu

yam
BR jam, -z
AM jæm, -z

Yama
BR 'jɑːmə(r)
AM 'jɑmə

Yamaha
BR 'jaməhɑː(r), -z
AM 'jɑmə,hɑ, -z

Yamamoto
BR ,jamə'məʊtəʊ
AM ,jɑmə'moʊdoʊ

yammer
BR 'jam|ə(r), -əz, -(ə)rɪŋ, -əd
AM 'jæmər, -z, -ɪŋ, -d

Yamoussoukro
BR ,jamʊ'suːkrəʊ
AM ,jɑmə'su,kroʊ

Yancheng
BR ,jan'tʃɛŋ
AM 'jæn'tʃɛŋ

yandy
BR 'jand|i, -ɪz, -ɪŋ, -d
AM 'jændi, -z, -ɪŋ, -d

yang
BR jaŋ
AM jæŋ

Yangshao
BR ,jaŋ'ʃaʊ
AM 'jæŋk'ʃaʊ

Yangtse
BR 'jaŋ(k)tsi, 'jaŋsi
AM 'jɑŋk'(t)si

Yangtze
BR 'jaŋ(k)tsi, 'jaŋsi
AM 'jɑŋk'(t)si

yank
BR jaŋ|k, -ks, -kɪŋ, -(k)t
AM jæŋ|k, -ks, -kɪŋ, -(k)t

Yankee
BR 'jaŋk|i, -ɪz
AM 'jæŋki, -z

Yankee Doodle
BR ,jaŋkɪ 'duːdl
AM 'jæŋki 'dudəl

Yanomami
BR ,janə'mɑːmi
AM ,jɑnə'mɑmi

Yantai
BR ,jan'tʌɪ
AM 'jæn'taɪ

yantra
BR 'jantrə(r), -z
AM 'jæntrə, -z

Yaoundé
BR jɑː'ʊndeɪ, jaʊ'ʊndeɪ
AM ,jaʊn'deɪ

yap
BR jap, -s, -ɪŋ, -t
AM jæp, -s, -ɪŋ, -t

yapok
BR jə'pɒk, -s
AM jə'pɑk, -s

yapp
BR jap, -s
AM jæp, -s

yapper
BR 'japə(r), -z
AM 'jæpər, -z

yappy
BR 'jap|i, -ɪə(r), -ɪɪst
AM 'jæpi, -ər, -ɪst

yarborough
BR 'jɑːb(ə)rə(r), -z
AM 'jɑr,b(ə)rə, -z

yard
BR jɑːd, -z
AM jɑrd, -z

yardage
BR 'jɑːdɪdʒ
AM 'jɑrdɪdʒ

yardarm
BR 'jɑːdɑːm, -z
AM 'jɑrd,ɑrm, -z

yardbird
BR 'jɑːdbəːd, -z
AM 'jɑrd,bərd, -z

Yardie
BR 'jɑːd|i, -ɪz
AM 'jɑrdi, -z

Yardley
BR 'jɑːdli
AM 'jɑrdli

yardline
BR 'jɑːdlʌɪn, -z
AM 'jɑrd,laɪn, -z

yardman
BR 'jɑːdman
AM 'jɑrd,mæn

yardmaster
BR 'jɑːdmɑːstə(r), 'jɑːdmastə(r), -z
AM 'jɑrd,mæstər, -z

yardmen
BR 'jɑːdmɛn
AM 'jɑrd,mɛn

yardstick
BR 'jɑːdstɪk, -s
AM 'jɑrd,stɪk, -s

Yarm
BR jɑːm
AM jɑrm

Yarmouth
BR 'jɑːməθ
AM 'jɑrməθ

yarmulka
BR 'jɑːm(ʉ)lkə(r), -z
AM 'jɑməlkə, -z

yarmulke
BR 'jɑːm(ʉ)lkə(r), -z
AM 'jɑməlkə, -z

yarn
BR jɑːn, -z, -ɪŋ, -d
AM jɑrn, -z, -ɪŋ, -d

yarran
BR 'jarən, -z
AM 'jɛrən, -z

yarrow
BR 'jarəʊ, -z
AM 'jæroʊ, -z

Yarwood
BR 'jɑːwʊd
AM 'jɑr,wʊd

yashmak
BR 'jaʃmak, -s
AM jɑʃ'mɑk, 'jæʃ,mæk, -s

Yasmin
BR 'jazmɪn, 'jasmɪn
AM 'jæzmən

yataghan
BR 'jatəg(ə)n, -z

AM 'jædəgən, 'jædə,gæn, -z

Yates
BR jeɪts
AM jeɪts

yatter
BR 'jat|ə(r), -əz, -(ə)rɪŋ, -əd
AM 'jædər, -z, -ɪŋ, -d

yaupon
BR 'jɔːpɒn
AM 'jɔ,pɔn, 'jɑ,pɑn

yaw
BR jɔː(*r*), -z, -ɪŋ, -d
AM jɔ, jɑ, -z, -ɪŋ, -d

yawl
BR jɔːl, -z
AM jɔl, jɑl, -z

yawn
BR jɔːn, -z, -ɪŋ, -d
AM jɔn, jɑn, -z, -ɪŋ, -d

yawner
BR 'jɔːnə(r), -z
AM 'jɔnər, 'jɑnər, -z

yawningly
BR 'jɔːnɪŋli
AM 'jɔnɪŋli, 'jɑnɪŋli

yawp
BR jɔːp, -s, -ɪŋ, -t
AM jɔp, jɑp, -s, -ɪŋ, -t

yawper
BR 'jɔːpə(r), -z
AM 'jɔpər, 'jɑpər, -z

yaws
BR jɔːz
AM jɔz, jɑz

y-axes
BR 'wʌɪ,aksiːz
AM 'waɪ,æksiz

y-axis
BR 'wʌɪ,aksɪs
AM 'waɪ,æksəs

Yayoi
BR 'jɑːjɔɪ
AM 'jɑ,jɔɪ

yclept
BR ɪ'klɛpt
AM ɪ'klɛpt

ye
BR jiː
AM ji

yea
BR jeɪ
AM jeɪ

Yeadon[1]
placename, UK
BR 'jiːdn
AM 'jidən

Yeadon[2]
placename, USA
BR 'jeɪdn
AM 'jeɪdən

Yeadon[3]
surname
BR 'jiːdn, 'jɛdn, 'jeɪdn
AM 'jidən, 'jeɪdən

Yeadon[4]
placename, US
BR 'jeɪdn
AM 'jeɪdən

yeah
BR jɛː(*r*), jɛ(*r*)
AM jɛ(ə), jæ(ə)

yean
BR jiːn, -z, -ɪŋ, -d
AM jin, -z, -ɪŋ, -d

yeanling
BR 'jiːnlɪŋ, -z
AM 'jinlɪŋ, -z

year
BR jɪə(r), jəː(r), -z
AM jɪ(ə)r, -z

yearbook
BR 'jɪəbʊk, 'jəːbʊk, -s
AM 'jɪr,bʊk, -s

yearling
BR 'jɪəlɪŋ, 'jəːlɪŋ, -z
AM 'jɪrlɪŋ, -z

yearlong
BR ,jɪə'lɒŋ, ,jəː'lɒŋ
AM 'jɪr'lɔŋ, 'jɪr'lɑŋ

yearly
BR 'jɪəli, 'jəːli
AM 'jɪrli

yearn
BR jəːn, -z, -ɪŋ, -d
AM jərn, -z, -ɪŋ, -d

yearner
BR 'jəːnə(r), -z
AM 'jərnər, -z

yearning
BR 'jəːnɪŋ, -z
AM 'jərnɪŋ, -z

yearningly
BR 'jəːnɪŋli
AM 'jərnɪŋli

yeast
BR jiːst
AM jist

yeastily
BR 'jiːstɨli
AM 'jistɨli

yeastiness
BR 'jiːstɪnɨs
AM 'jistinɨs

yeastless
BR 'jiːstlɨs
AM 'jis(t)lɨs

yeastlike
BR 'jiːstlʌɪk
AM 'jis(t),laɪk

yeasty
BR 'jiːsti
AM 'jisti

Yeates
BR jeɪts
AM jeɪts

Yeats
BR jeɪts
AM jeɪts

Yeatsian
BR 'jeɪtsɪən
AM 'jeɪtsiən

yecch
BR jɛk, jɛx
AM jək, jɛk

yech
BR jɛk, jɛx
AM jək, jɛk

yegg
BR jɛg, -z
AM jɛg, -z

Yehudi
BR jɪ'huːdi, jɛ'huːdi
AM jə'hudi

Yekaterinburg
BR jɪ'kat(ə)rɪnbəːg
AM jə'kætrən,bərg
RUS jikatʲirʲinʲburk

yell
BR jɛl, -z, -ɪŋ, -d
AM jɛl, -z, -ɪŋ, -d

Yelland
BR 'jɛlənd
AM 'jɛlənd

yellow
BR 'jɛləʊ, -z, -ɪŋ, -d, -ə(r), -ɨst
AM 'jɛl|oʊ, -oʊz, -əwɪŋ, -oʊd, -əwər, -əwəst

yellowback
BR 'jɛlə(ʊ)bak, -s
AM 'jɛloʊ,bæk, -s

yellow-bellied
BR ,jɛlə(ʊ)'bɛlɪd
AM 'jɛloʊ,bɛlid

yellow-belly
BR 'jɛlə(ʊ),bɛl|i, -ɪz
AM 'jɛloʊ,bɛli, -z

yellow-bill
BR 'jɛlə(ʊ)bɪl
AM 'jɛloʊ,bɪl

yellow fever
BR 'jɛləʊ ,fiːvə(r), ,jɛləʊ 'fiːvə(r)
AM ,jɛloʊ 'fivər

yellowfin
BR 'jɛlə(ʊ)fɪn, -z
AM 'jɛloʊ,fɪn, -z

yellowhammer
BR 'jɛlə(ʊ),hamə(r), -z
AM 'jɛloʊ,hæmər, -z

yellowish
BR 'jɛləʊɪʃ
AM 'jɛləwɪʃ

Yellowknife
BR 'jɛlə(ʊ)nʌɪf
AM 'jɛloʊ,naɪf

yellowlegs
BR 'jɛlə(ʊ)lɛgz
AM 'jɛloʊ,lɛgz

yellowness
BR 'jɛlə(ʊ)nəs
AM 'jɛloʊnəs

Yellowstone
BR 'jɛlə(ʊ)stəʊn
AM 'jɛloʊ,stoʊn

yellowy
BR 'jɛləʊi
AM 'jɛləwi

yelp
BR jɛlp, -s, -ɪŋ, -t
AM jɛlp, -s, -ɪŋ, -t

yelper
BR 'jɛlpə(r), -z
AM 'jɛlpər, -z

Yeltsin
BR 'jɛltsɪn
AM 'jɛltsən

Yelverton
BR 'jɛlvət(ə)n
AM 'jɛlvərtən

Yemen
BR 'jɛmən
AM 'jɛmən

Yemeni
BR 'jɛmən|i, -ɪz
AM 'jɛməni, -z

yen
BR jɛn, -z
AM jɛn, -z

Yen-cheng
BR ,jɛn'tʃɛŋ
AM 'jɛn'tʃɛŋ

Yenisey
BR ,jɛnɪ'seɪ
AM ,jɛni'seɪ

yeoman
BR 'jəʊmən
AM 'joʊmən

yeomanly
BR 'jəʊmənli
AM 'joʊmənli

yeomanry
BR 'jəʊmənri
AM 'joʊmənri

Yeomans
BR 'jəʊmənz
AM 'joʊmənz

yeomen
BR 'jəʊmən
AM 'joʊmən

Yeovil
BR 'jəʊv(ɪ)l
AM 'joʊvəl

yep
BR jɛp
AM jɛp

yerba buena
BR ,jəːbə 'bweɪnə(*r*)
AM ,jərbə 'bweɪnə

yerba maté
BR ,jəːbə 'mateɪ, + 'mɑːteɪ
AM ,jərbə 'mɑ,teɪ

Yerevan
BR ,jɛrə'van
AM ,jɛrə'vɑn

Yerkes
BR 'jəːkɪz
AM 'jərkiz

yes
BR jɛs
AM jɛs

yeshiva
BR jə'ʃiːvə(r), -z
AM jə'ʃivə, jə'ʃɪvə, -z

yesterday
BR 'jɛstəd|eɪ, 'jɛstəd|i, -eɪz\-ɪz
AM 'jɛstər,deɪ, 'jɛstərdi, -z

yestereve
BR 'jɛstəriːv
AM 'jɛstər,iv

yestermorn
BR 'jɛstəmɔːn
AM 'jɛstər,mɔ(ə)rn

yesternight
BR 'jɛstənʌɪt
AM 'jɛstər,naɪt

yesteryear
BR 'jɛstəjɪə(r), 'jɛstəjəː(r)
AM 'jɛstər,jɪ(ə)r

yet
BR jɛt
AM jɛt

yeti
BR 'jɛt|i, -ɪz
AM 'jɛdi, 'jeɪdi, -z

Yevtushenko
BR ,jɛvtʊ'ʃɛŋkəʊ
AM ,jɛvtə'ʃɛŋ,koʊ
RUS jiftu'ʃenkə

yew
BR juː, -z
AM ju, -z

Y-fronts®
BR 'wʌɪfrʌnts
AM 'waɪ,frən(t)s

Ygdrasil
BR 'ɪgdrəsɪl
AM 'ɪgdrəsəl

Yggdrasil
BR 'ɪgdrəsɪl
AM 'ɪgdrəsəl

yid
BR jɪd, -z
AM jɪd, -z

Yiddish
BR 'jɪdɪʃ
AM 'jɪdɪʃ

Yiddisher
BR 'jɪdɪʃə(r), -z
AM 'jɪdɪʃər, -z

Yiddishism
BR 'jɪdɪʃɪz(ə)m, -z
AM 'jɪdə,ʃɪzəm, -z

yield
BR jiːld, -z, -ɪŋ, -ɪd
AM jild, -z, -ɪŋ, -ɪd

yielder
BR 'jiːldə(r), -z
AM 'jildər, -z

yielding
BR 'jiːldɪŋ
AM 'jildɪŋ

yieldingly
BR 'jiːldɪŋli
AM 'jildɪŋli

yieldingness
BR 'jiːldɪŋnɪs
AM 'jildɪŋnɪs

yikes
BR jʌɪks
AM jaɪks

yin
BR jɪn
AM jɪn

Yinchuan
BR ,jɪn'tʃwɑːn
AM 'jɪn'tʃwɑn

yip
BR jɪp, -s, -ɪŋ, -t
AM jɪp, -s, -ɪŋ, -t

yippee
BR jɪ'piː
AM 'jɪpi, ,jɪ'pi

ylang-ylang
BR ,iːlaŋ'iːlaŋ, -z
AM ,ilɑŋ'ilɑŋ, -z

YMCA
BR ,wʌɪɛmsiː'eɪ
AM ,waɪ,ɛm,si'eɪ

Ymir
BR 'ɪmɪə(r)
AM 'i,mɪ(ə)r

Ynys
BR 'ʌnɪs
AM 'ɪnɪs

Ynys-ddu
BR ,ʌnɪs'ðiː, ,ʌnɪs'diː
AM ,ɪnɪs'ði

Ynysybwl
BR ,ʌnɪsə'bʊl
AM ,ɪnɪs'bʊl

yo
BR jəʊ
AM joʊ

yob
BR jɒb, -z
AM jɑb, -z

yobbish
BR 'jɒbɪʃ
AM 'jɑbɪʃ

yobbishly
BR 'jɒbɪʃli
AM 'jɑbɪʃli

yobbishness
BR 'jɒbɪʃnɪs
AM 'jɑbɪʃnɪs

yobbo
BR 'jɒbəʊ, -z
AM 'jɑboʊ, -z

yobo
BR 'jɒbəʊ, -z
AM 'jɑboʊ, -z

yod
BR jɒd, -z
AM jɑd, -z

yodel
BR 'jəʊd|l, -lz, -l̩ɪŋ\-lɪŋ, -ld
AM 'joʊd|əl, -əlz, -(ə)lɪŋ, -əld

yodeler
BR 'jəʊdl̩ə(r), 'jəʊdlə(r), -z
AM 'joʊdl̩ər, 'joʊdlər, -z

yodeller
BR 'jəʊdl̩ə(r), 'jəʊdlə(r), -z
AM 'joʊdl̩ər, 'joʊdlər, -z

Yoder
BR 'jəʊdə(r)
AM 'joʊdər

yoga
BR 'jəʊgə(r)
AM 'joʊgə

yogh
BR jɒg, -z
AM joʊg, -z

yoghourt
BR 'jɒgət, -s
AM 'joʊgərt, -s

yoghurt
BR 'jɒgət, -s
AM 'joʊgərt, -s

yogi
BR 'jəʊg|i, -ɪz
AM 'joʊgi, -z

yogic
BR 'jəʊgɪk
AM 'joʊgɪk

yogism
BR 'jəʊgɪz(ə)m
AM 'joʊ,gɪzəm

yogurt
BR 'jɒgət, -s
AM 'joʊgərt, -s

yo-heave-ho
BR ,jəʊhiːv'həʊ
AM ',joʊ,hiv'hoʊ

yohimbe
BR jə(ʊ)'hɪmbeɪ
AM joʊ'hɪmbeɪ

yohimbine
BR jə(ʊ)'hɪmbiːn
AM joʊ'hɪmbin

yo-ho
BR ,jəʊ'həʊ
AM ,joʊ'hoʊ

yo-ho-ho
BR ,jəʊhəʊ'həʊ
AM ',joʊ',hoʊ'hoʊ

yoicks
BR jɔɪks
AM jɔɪks

yoke
BR jəʊk, -s, -ɪŋ, -t
AM joʊk, -s, -ɪŋ, -t

yokel
BR 'jəʊkl, -z
AM 'joʊkəl, -z

Yokohama
BR ,jəʊkə'hɑːmə(r)
AM ,joʊkə'hɑmə

yokozuna
BR ,jəʊkə'zuːnə(r)
AM ,joʊkə'zunə

Yolanda
BR jə(ʊ)'landə(r)
AM joʊ'lændə

yolk
BR jəʊk, -s, -t
AM joʊk, -s, -t

yolkless
BR 'jəʊkləs
AM 'joʊkləs

yolky
BR 'jəʊki
AM 'joʊki

Yom Kippur
BR ,jɒm kɪ'pʊə(r), + kɪ'pɔː(r), + 'kɪpə(r)
AM ,joʊm 'kɪpər, 'jom kɪ'pʊ(ə)r, ,jɑm 'kɪpər, 'jɑm kɪ'pʊ(ə)r

yomp
BR jɒm|p, -(p)s, -pɪŋ, -(p)t
AM jɑm|p, -ps, -pɪŋ, -(p)t

yon
BR jɒn
AM jɑn

yond
BR jɒnd
AM jɑnd

yonder
BR 'jɒndə(r)
AM 'jɑndər

Yonge
BR jʌŋ
AM jəŋ

yoni
BR 'jəʊni
AM 'joʊni

Yonkers
BR 'jɒŋkəz
AM 'jɑŋkərz

yonks
BR jɒŋks
AM jɑŋks

yoof
youth
BR juːf
AM juf

yoo-hoo
BR 'juːhuː, ,juː'huː
AM 'ju,hu

yore
BR jɔː(r)
AM jɔ(ə)r

Yorick
BR 'jɒrɪk
AM 'jɔrək

york¹
BR jɔːk, -s, -ɪŋ, -t
AM jɔ(ə)rk, -s, -ɪŋ, -t

york²
BR jɔːk, -s, -ɪŋ, -t

AM jɔ(ə)rk, -s, -ɪŋ, -t

Yorke
BR jɔːk
AM jɔ(ə)rk

yorker
BR 'jɔːkə(r), -z
AM 'jɔrkər, -z

Yorkist
BR 'jɔːkɪst, -s
AM 'jɔrkəst, -s

Yorkshire
BR 'jɔːkʃ(ɪ)ə(r)
AM 'jɔrkʃɪ(ə)r

Yorkshireman
BR 'jɔːkʃəmən
AM 'jɔrkʃɪrmən

Yorkshiremen
BR 'jɔːkʃəmən
AM 'jɔrkʃɪrmən

Yorkshirewoman
BR 'jɔːkʃə,wʊmən
AM 'jɔrkʃɪr,wʊmən

Yorkshirewomen
BR 'jɔːkʃə,wɪmɪn
AM 'jɔrkʃɪr,wɪmɪn

Yorktown
BR 'jɔːktaʊn
AM 'jɔrk,taʊn

Yoruba
BR 'jɒrʉbə(r)
AM 'jɔrəbə

Yosemite
BR jə(ʊ)'sɛmɪti
AM joʊ'sɛmədi

you[1]
strong form
BR juː
AM ju

you[2]
weak form
BR jə
AM jə

you-all
BR ,juː'ɔːl, jɔːl
AM 'ju,ɔl, jɔl

you'd
BR juːd
AM jud

Youel
BR 'juː(ə)l
AM 'ju(ə)l

Youell
BR 'juːəl, juːl
AM 'ju(ə)l

Youens
BR 'juːɪnz
AM 'juənz

you-know-what
BR ,juːnəʊ'wɒt, -s
AM 'ju,noʊ,(h)wɑt, -s

you-know-who
BR ,juːnəʊ'huː
AM 'ju,noʊ,hu

you'll
BR juːl
AM jul

young
BR jʌŋ, -gə(r), -gɪst
AM jəŋ, -ər, -əst

Younger
BR 'jʌŋgə(r)
AM 'jəŋgər

Younghusband
BR 'jʌŋ,hʌzb(ə)nd
AM 'jəŋ,(h)əzbənd

youngish
BR 'jʌŋɪʃ
AM 'jəŋɪʃ

youngling
BR 'jʌŋlɪŋ, -z
AM 'jəŋlɪŋ, -z

youngster
BR 'jʌŋ(k)stə(r), -z
AM 'jəŋztər, 'jəŋ(k)stər, -z

Youngstown
BR 'jʌŋztaʊn
AM 'jəŋz,taʊn

younker
BR 'jʌŋkə(r), -z
AM 'jəŋkər, -z

your[1]
strong form
BR jɔː(r), jʊə(r)
AM jɔ(ə)r, jʊ(ə)r

your[2]
weak form
BR jə(r)
AM jər

you're
BR jʊə(r)
AM jʊ(ə)r, jɔ(ə)r, jər

yours
BR jɔːz, jʊəz
AM jɔ(ə)rz, jʊ(ə)rz, jərz

yourself
BR jɔː'sɛlf, jʊə'sɛlf, jə'sɛlf
AM jɔr'sɛlf, jʊr'sɛlf, jər'sɛlf

yourselves
BR jɔː'sɛlvz, jʊə'sɛlvz, jə'sɛlvz
AM jɔr'sɛlvz, jʊr'sɛlvz, jər'sɛlvz

youse
BR juːz
AM juz

youth
BR juː|θ, -ðz
AM ju|θ, -θs\-ðz

youthful
BR 'juːθf(ʉ)l
AM 'juθfəl

youthfully
BR 'juːθfʉli, 'juːθfl̩i
AM 'juθfəli

youthfulness
BR 'juːθf(ʉ)lnəs
AM 'juθfəlnəs

youth hostel
BR 'juːθ ,hɒst|l, -lz, -l̩ɪŋ\-əlɪŋ, -ld
AM 'juθ ,(h)ɑstl, -z, -ɪŋ, -d

youth hosteller
BR 'juːθ ,hɒstl̩ə(r), + ,hɒstələ(r), -z
AM 'juθ ,(h)ɑs(t)lər, + ,(h)ɑstələr, -z

you've[1]
strong form
BR juːv
AM juv

you've[2]
weak form
BR jəv
AM jəv

yowl
BR jaʊl, -z, -ɪŋ, -d
AM jaʊl, -z, -ɪŋ, -d

yo-yo®
BR 'jəʊjəʊ, -z, -ɪŋ, -d
AM 'joʊ,joʊ, -z, -ɪŋ, -d

Ypres
BR 'iːpr(ər)
AM 'iprə

Ystalyfera
BR ,ʌstələ'vɛrə(r), ,ʌstl̩ə'vɛrə(r)
AM ,ɪstələ'vɛrə
WE ,ʌstala'vera

Ystrad
BR 'ʌstrəd
AM 'ɪstrəd

Ystradgynlais
BR ,ʌstrə(d)'gʌnlʌɪs
AM ,ɪstrə'gɪn,laɪs

Ystwyth
BR 'ʌstwɪθ
AM 'ɪstwɪθ

ytterbium
BR ɪ'təːbɪəm
AM ɪ'tərbiəm

yttrium
BR 'ɪtrɪəm
AM 'ɪtriəm

yuan
BR juː'ɑːn, juː'an
AM 'ju'ɑn

Yucatán
BR ,jʊkə'tɑːn, ,jʊkə'tan
AM ,jukə'tæn, ,jukə'tɑn

yucca
BR 'jʌkə(r), -z
AM 'jəkə, -z

yuck
BR jʌk
AM jək

yuckiness
BR 'jʌkɪnɪs
AM 'jəkinɨs

yucky
BR 'jʌk|i, -ɪə(r), -ɪɪst
AM 'jəki, -ər, -ɨst

Yudkin
BR 'juːdkɪn
AM 'judkən

Yugo
BR 'juːgəʊ
AM 'ju,goʊ

Yugoslav
BR 'juːgə(ʊ)slɑːv, -z
AM 'jugoʊ,slɑv, 'jugə,slɑv, -z

Yugoslavia
BR ,juːgə(ʊ)'slɑːvɪə(r)
AM ,jugoʊ'slɑviə, ,jugə'slɑviə

Yugoslavian
BR ,juːgə(ʊ)'slɑːvɪən, -z
AM ,jugoʊ'slɑviən, ,jugə'slɑviən, -z

Yuit
BR 'juːɪt, -s
AM 'juət, -s

yuk
BR jʌk
AM jək

yukkiness
BR 'jʌkɪnɪs
AM 'jəkinɨs

yukky
BR 'jʌk|i, -ɪə(r), -ɪɪst
AM 'jəki, -ər, -ɨst

Yukon
BR 'juːkɒn
AM 'ju,kɑn

yule
BR juːl
AM jul

yule log
BR 'juːl lɒg, -z
AM 'jul ,lɑg, 'jul ,lɔg, -z

Yuletide
BR 'juːltʌɪd
AM 'jul,taɪd

yum
BR jʌm
AM jəm

yummy
BR 'jʌm|i, -ɪə(r), -ɪɪst
AM 'jəmi, -ər, -ɨst

yum-yum
BR ,jʌm'jʌm
AM ,jəm'jəm

Yunnan
BR juː'nan
AM ju'næn

yup
BR jʌp, -s
AM jəp, -s

Yupik
BR 'juːpɪk
AM 'ju,pɪk

yuppie
BR 'jʌp|i, -ɪz
AM 'jəpi, -z

yuppiedom
BR 'jʌpɪdəm
AM 'jəpi,dəm

yuppification
BR ˌjʌpɪfɪˈkeɪʃn
AM ˌjəpəfəˈkeɪʃən

yuppify
BR ˈjʌpɪfʌɪ, -z, -ɪŋ, -d
AM ˈjəpəˌfaɪ, -z, -ɪŋ, -d

yuppy
BR ˈjʌp|i, -ɪz
AM ˈjəpi, -z

yurt
BR jəːt, -s
AM jərt, -s

Yves
BR iːv
AM iv(z)

Yvette
BR ɪˈvɛt
AM ɪˈvɛt

Yvonne
BR ɪˈvɒn
AM ɪˈvɔn, ɪˈvɑn

YWCA
BR ˌwʌɪˌdʌbljʊˌsiːˈeɪ
AM ˌwaɪˌdəbəljuˌsiˈeɪ

Zz

z
BR zɛd, -z
AM zi, -z
zabaglione
BR ˌzablˈjəʊni, ˌzabalˈjəʊni
AM ˌzɑbəlˈjoʊni
Zacatecas
BR ˌzakəˈteɪkəs
AM ˌzɑkəˈteɪkəs
Zacchaeus
BR zəˈkiːəs
AM zəˈkijəs
Zachariah
BR ˌzakəˈrʌɪə(r)
AM zækəˈraɪə
Zachary
BR ˈzak(ə)ri
AM ˈzæk(ə)ri
Zack
BR zak
AM zæk
Zadok
BR ˈzeɪdɒk
AM ˈzeɪˌdɑk
zaffer
BR ˈzafə(r)
AM ˈzæfər
zaffre
BR ˈzafə(r)
AM ˈzæfər
zag
BR zag, -z
AM zæg, -z
Zagazig
BR ˈzagəzɪg
AM ˈzægəˌzɪg
Zagreb
BR ˈzɑːgrɛb
AM ˈzɑˌgrɛb
zaibatsu
BR zʌɪˈbatsuː
AM zaɪˈbɑtsu
Zaïre
BR (ˌ)zʌɪˈɪə(r), (ˌ)zɑːˈɪə(r)
AM ˌzɑˈɪ(ə)r
Zaïrean
BR zʌɪˈɪərɪən, zɑːˈɪərɪən, -z
AM zaɪˈɪriən, -z
Zairian
BR zʌɪˈɪərɪən, zɑːˈɪərɪən, -z
AM zaɪˈɪriən, -z
zakat
BR zəˈkɑːt
AM zɑˈkɑt
Zakopane
BR ˌzakəˈpɑːni
AM ˈzɑkəˌpeɪn, ˌzɑkəˈpɑni
POL ˌzakɒˈpanɛ
Zambesi
BR zamˈbiːzi
AM zæmˈbizi
Zambezi
BR zamˈbiːzi
AM zæmˈbizi
Zambia
BR ˈzambɪə(r)
AM ˈzæmbiə
Zambian
BR ˈzambɪən, -z
AM ˈzæmbiən, -z
Zamboanga
BR ˌzambəʊˈaŋgə(r)
AM ˌzæmboʊˈæŋgə
Zamboni
BR zamˈbəʊni
AM ˌzæmˈboʊni
zamindar
BR zəˈmiːndɑː(r), -z
AM ˈzæmənˌdɑr, -z
zander
BR ˈzandə(r), -z
AM ˈzændər, -z
Zandra
BR ˈzɑːndrə(r), ˈzandrə(r)
AM ˈzændrə
Zane
BR zeɪn
AM zeɪn
zanily
BR ˈzeɪnɨli
AM ˈzeɪnɨli
zaniness
BR ˈzeɪnɪnɨs
AM ˈzeɪninɨs
Zanskar
BR ˈzanskɑː(r)
AM ˈzænˌskɑr
Zanskari
BR zanˈskɑːr|i, -ɪz
AM zænˈskɑri, zænˈskɛri, -z
Zante
BR ˈzanti
AM ˈzæn(t)i
ZANU
BR ˈzɑːnuː, ˈzanuː
AM ˈzæˌnu
Zanuck
BR ˈzanək
AM ˈzænək
zany
BR ˈzeɪn|i, -ɪə(r), -ɪɨst
AM ˈzeɪni, -ər, -ɨst
Zanzibar
BR ˈzanzɪbɑː(r), ˌzanzɪˈbɑː(r)
AM ˈzænzəˌbɑr
Zanzibari
BR ˌzanzɪˈbɑːr|i, -ɪz
AM ˌzænzəˈbɑri, -z
Zaozhuang
BR ˌzaʊˈʒwaŋ
AM ˈzaʊˈʒwɑŋ
zap
BR zap, -s, -ɪŋ, -t
AM zæp, -s, -ɪŋ, -t
Zapata
BR zəˈpɑːtə(r)
AM zəˈpɑdə
zapateado
BR ˌzɑːpətrˈɑːdəʊ, zaˌpatrˈɑːdəʊ, -z
AM ˌzɑpədiˈɑdoʊ, -z
Zapotec
BR ˈzapətɛk, ˈzɑːpətɛk, -s
AM ˈzɑpəˌtɛk, -s
Zappa
BR ˈzapə(r)
AM ˈzæpə
zappy
BR ˈzap|i, -ɪə(r), -ɪɨst
AM ˈzæpi, -ər, -ɨst
ZAPU
BR ˈzɑːpuː, ˈzapuː
AM ˈzæˌpu
Zaqaziq
BR ˈzakəzɪk
AM ˈzɑkəˌzɪk
Zara
BR ˈzɑːrə(r)
AM ˈzɑrə
Zaragoza
BR ˌzarəˈgɒsə(r)
AM ˌzɑrəˈgɔsə, ˌzɑrəˈgɑsə
SP θaraˈɣoθa, saraˈɣosa
Zarathustra
BR ˌzarəˈθuːstrə(r)
AM ˌzɛrəˈθustrə
Zarathustrian
BR ˌzarəˈθuːstrɪən, -z
AM ˌzɛrəˈθustriən, -z
zareba
BR zəˈriːbə(r), -z
AM zəˈribə, -z
Zaria
BR ˈzɑːrɪə(r)
AM ˈzɑriə
zariba
BR zəˈriːbə(r), -z
AM zəˈribə, -z
Zarqa
BR ˈzɑːkə(r)
AM ˈzɑrkə
zarzuela
BR zɑːˈzweɪlə(r), -z
AM zɑrˈzweɪlə, -z
zax
BR zaks, -ɪz
AM zæks, -əz
z-axes
BR ˈzɛdˌaksiːz
AM ˈziˌæksiz
z-axis
BR ˈzɛdˌaksɪs
AM ˈziˌæksɪs
zazen
BR zɑːˈzɛn
AM zɑˈzɛn
Z-bend
BR ˈzɛdbɛnd, -z
AM ˈziˌbɛnd, -z
zeal
BR ziːl
AM zil
Zealand
BR ˈziːlənd
AM ˈzilənd
zealot
BR ˈzɛlət, -s
AM ˈzɛlət, -s
zealotry
BR ˈzɛlətri
AM ˈzɛlətri
zealous
BR ˈzɛləs
AM ˈzɛləs
zealously
BR ˈzɛləsli
AM ˈzɛləsli
zealousness
BR ˈzɛləsnəs
AM ˈzɛləsnəs
zebec
BR ˈziːbɛk, -s
AM ˈziˌbɛk, -s
zebeck
BR ˈziːbɛk, -s
AM ˈziˌbɛk, -s
Zebedee
BR ˈzɛbɨdiː
AM ˈzɛbəˌdi
zebra
BR ˈzɛbrə(r), ˈziːbrə(r), -z
AM ˈzibrə, -z
zebrine
BR ˈzɛbrʌɪn, ˈziːbrʌɪn
AM ˈziˌbraɪn, ˈzibrən
zebu
BR ˈziːb(j)uː, -z
AM ˈziˌb(j)u, -z
Zebulon
BR ˈzɛbjʉlən, zɛˈbjuːlən
AM ˈzɛbjələn, ˈzɛbjəˌlɑn
Zech.
BR zɛk
AM zɛk
Zechariah
BR ˌzɛkəˈrʌɪə(r)
AM ˌzɛkəˈraɪə
zed
BR zɛd, -z
AM zɛd, -z
Zedekiah
BR ˌzɛdɪˈkʌɪə(r)
AM ˌzɛdəˈkaɪə
zedoary
BR ˈzɛdəʊər|i, -ɪz
AM ˈzɛdoʊˌɛr|i, -z

zee
BR ziː, -z
AM zi, -z

Zeebrugge
BR ˌzeɪˈbrʊɡə(r), ˌziːˈbrʊɡə(r), ˈzeɪˌbrʊɡə(r), ˈziːˌbrʊɡə(r)
AM ˈziˌbrʊɡə
FL ˈzeːbrəxə

Zeeland
BR ˈziːlənd
AM ˈzilənd
DU ˈzeːlɑnt

Zeffirelli
BR ˌzɛfɪˈrɛli
AM ˌzɛfəˈrɛli

zein
BR ˈziːɪn
AM ˈziɪn

Zeiss
BR zʌɪs
AM zaɪs

Zeitgeist
BR ˈzʌɪtɡʌɪst
AM ˈzaɪtˌɡaɪst

zek
BR zɛk, -s
AM zɛk, -s

Zelda
BR ˈzɛldə(r)
AM ˈzɛldə

Zelotes
BR zɪˈləʊtiːz, zɛˈləʊtiːz
AM zəˈloʊdiz

zemindar
BR zəˈmiːndɑː(r), -z
AM ˈzɛmənˌdɑr, -z

zemstvo
BR ˈzɛmstvəʊ, -z
AM ˈzɛmstvoʊ, -z
RUS ˈzʲemstvə

Zen
BR zɛn
AM zɛn

Zena
BR ˈziːnə(r)
AM ˈzinə

zenana
BR zɪˈnɑːnə(r), -z
AM zəˈnɑnə, -z

Zend
BR zɛnd, -z
AM zɛnd, -z

Zend-Avesta
BR ˌzɛndəˈvɛstə(r)
AM ˈzɛndəˈvɛstə

Zener diode
BR ˌziːnə ˈdʌɪəʊd, ˌzɛnə +, -z
AM ˈzinər ˌdaɪoʊd, -z

Zenist
BR ˈzɛnɪst, -s
AM ˈzɛnɪst, -s

zenith
BR ˈzɛnɪθ, ˈziːnɪθ, -s
AM ˈzinɨθ, -s

zenithal
BR ˈzɛnɪθl, ˈziːnɪθl
AM ˈzinɨθəl

Zeno
BR ˈziːnəʊ
AM ˈzinoʊ

Zenobia
BR zɪˈnəʊbɪə(r)
AM zəˈnoʊbiə

zeolite
BR ˈziːəlʌɪt, -s
AM ˈziəˌlaɪt, -s

zeolitic
BR ˌziːəˈlɪtɪk
AM ˌziəˈlɪdɪk

Zephaniah
BR ˌzɛfəˈnʌɪə(r)
AM ˌzɛfəˈnaɪə

zephyr
BR ˈzɛfə(r), -z
AM ˈzɛfər, -z

Zephyrus
BR ˈzɛf(ɪ)rəs
AM ˈzɛf(ə)rəs

zeppelin
BR ˈzɛpəlɪn, ˈzɛplɪn, -z
AM ˈzɛp(ə)lən, -z

Zermatt
BR ˈzəːmat
AM ˈzərmɑt

zero
BR ˈzɪərəʊ, -z, -ɪŋ, -d
AM ˈzɪroʊ, ˈziroʊ, -z, -ɪŋ, -d

zeroth
BR ˈzɪərəʊθ
AM ˈzɪroʊθ, ˈziroʊθ

zest
BR zɛst
AM zɛst

zester
BR ˈzɛstə(r), -z
AM ˈzɛstər, -z

zestful
BR ˈzɛs(t)tf(ʊ)l
AM ˈzɛs(t)fəl

zestfully
BR ˈzɛs(t)fʊli, ˈzɛs(t)fl̩i
AM ˈzɛs(t)fəli

zestfulness
BR ˈzɛs(t)f(ʊ)lnəs
AM ˈzɛs(t)fəlnəs

zestiness
BR ˈzɛstɪnɪs
AM ˈzɛstinɨs

zesty
BR ˈzɛst|i, -ɪə(r), -ɪɪst
AM ˈzɛsti, -ər, -ɪst

zeta
BR ˈziːtə(r)
AM ˈzeɪdə

zetetic
BR zɪˈtɛtɪk
AM zəˈtɛdɪk

Zetland
BR ˈzɛtlənd
AM ˈzɛtlənd

zeugma
BR ˈz(j)uːɡmə(r)
AM ˈzuɡmə

zeugmatic
BR z(j)uːɡˈmatɪk
AM zuɡˈmædɪk

Zeus
BR z(j)uːs
AM zus

Zeuxis
BR ˈz(j)uːksɪs
AM ˈz(j)uksəs

Zhang
BR dʒaŋ
AM dʒæŋ

Zhanjiang
BR ˌʒanˈdʒ(ɪ)aŋ
AM ˈʒænˈdʒæŋ

Zhdanov
BR ˈʒdɑːnɒv, ˈʒdanɒv
AM ˈʒdɑˌnɔv, ˈʒdɑˌnɑv

Zhengzhou
BR ˌʒɛŋˈʒəʊ
AM ˈʒɛŋˈʒu

Zhenjiang
BR ˌʒɛnˈdʒ(ɪ)aŋ
AM ˈʒɛnˈdʒ(i)æŋ

Zhivago
BR ʒɪˈvɑːɡəʊ
AM ˌʒɪˈvɑɡoʊ

zho
BR zəʊ, -z
AM zoʊ, -z

Zhongshan
BR ˌʒɒŋˈʃan
AM ˈʒɔŋˈʃæn, ˈʒɑŋˈʃæn

Zhou
BR dʒəʊ
AM dʒoʊ

Zhukov
BR ˈʒuːkɒv, ˈʒuːkɒf
AM ˈʒukɔv, ˈʒukɔf, ˈʒukɑv, ˈʒukɑf

Zia
BR ˈzɪə(r)
AM ˈziə

zibet
BR ˈzɪbɪt, -s
AM ˈzɪbɨt, -s

zibeth
BR ˈzɪbɪθ, -s
AM ˈzɪbɨθ, -s

Ziegfeld
BR ˈziːɡfɛld
AM ˈziɡˌfɛld

Ziegler
BR ˈziːɡlə(r)
AM ˈziɡlər, ˈzɪɡlər

ziff
BR zɪf, -s
AM zɪf, -s

ziggurat
BR ˈzɪɡʊrat, -s
AM ˈzɪɡəˌræt, -s

zigzag
BR ˈzɪɡzaɡ, -z, -ɪŋ, -d
AM ˈzɪɡˌzæɡ, -z, -ɪŋ, -d

zilch
BR zɪltʃ
AM zɪltʃ

zillah
BR ˈzɪlə(r), -z
AM ˈzɪlə, -z

zillion
BR ˈzɪljən, -z
AM ˈzɪljən, -z

zillionth
BR ˈzɪljənθ, -s
AM ˈzɪljənθ, -s

Zimbabwe
BR zɪmˈbɑːbwi, zɪmˈbabwi, zɪmˈbɑːbweɪ, zɪmˈbabweɪ
AM zɪmˈbɑbˌweɪ

Zimbabwean
BR zɪmˈbɑːbwɪən, zɪmˈbabwɪən, zɪmˈbɑːbweɪən, zɪmˈbabweɪən, -z
AM zɪmˈbɑbˌweɪən, -z

zimmer
BR ˈzɪmə(r), -z
AM ˈzɪmər, -z

Zimmerman
BR ˈzɪmәmәn
AM ˈzɪmərmən

zinc
BR zɪŋk
AM zɪŋk

zinco
BR ˈzɪŋkəʊ, -z, -ɪŋ, -d
AM ˈzɪŋkoʊ, -z, -ɪŋ, -d

zincograph
BR ˈzɪŋkəɡrɑːf, ˈzɪŋkəɡraf, -s
AM ˈzɪŋkəˌɡræf, -s

zincography
BR zɪŋˈkɒɡrəfi
AM zɪŋˈkɑɡrəfi

zincotype
BR ˈzɪŋkətʌɪp, -s
AM ˈzɪŋkəˌtaɪp, -s

zincy
BR ˈzɪŋki
AM ˈzɪŋki

zinfandel
BR ˈzɪnf(ə)ndɛl, ˌzɪnf(ə)nˈdɛl, -z
AM ˈzɪnfənˌdɛl, -z

zing
BR zɪŋ
AM zɪŋ

zingari
BR ˈ(d)zɪŋɡəriː
AM ˈ(d)zɪŋ(ɡ)əri

zingaro
BR ˈ(d)zɪŋɡərəʊ
AM ˈ(d)zɪŋ(ɡ)əˌroʊ

zinger
BR ˈzɪŋə(r), -z
AM ˈzɪŋər, -z

zingy
BR ˈzɪŋ|i, -ɪə(r), -ɪɪst
AM ˈzɪŋi, -ər, -ɪst

Zinjanthropus
BR zɪnˈdʒanθrəpəs
AM ˌzɪnˈdʒanθrəpəs

zinnia
BR ˈzɪnɪə(r), -z
AM ˈzɪniə, -z

Zion
BR ˈzʌɪən
AM ˈzaɪən

Zionism
BR ˈzʌɪənɪz(ə)m
AM ˈzaɪəˌnɪzəm

Zionist
BR ˈzʌɪənɪst, -s
AM ˈzaɪənəst, -s

zip
BR zɪp, -s, -ɪŋ, -t
AM zɪp, -s, -ɪŋ, -t

zip-code
BR ˈzɪpkəʊd, -z
AM ˈzɪpˌkoʊd, -z

zip-fastener
BR ˌzɪpˈfɑːsn̩ə(r),
ˌzɪpˈfɑːsnə(r),
ˌzɪpˈfasn̩ə(r),
ˌzɪpˈfasnə(r), -z
AM ˈzɪpˌfæsnər, -z

zip-lock
BR ˈzɪplɒk
AM ˈzɪpˌlɑk

zip-on
BR ˈzɪpɒn, -z
AM ˈzɪpˌɑn, -z

zipper
BR ˈzɪpə(r), -z, -ɪŋ, -d
AM ˈzɪpər, -z, -ɪŋ, -d

zippily
BR ˈzɪpɨli
AM ˈzɪpɨli

zippiness
BR ˈzɪpɪnɨs
AM ˈzɪpinɪs

zippy
BR ˈzɪp|i, -ɪə(r), -ɪɪst
AM ˈzɪpi, -ər, -ɪst

zip-up
BR ˈzɪpʌp, -s
AM ˈzɪpəp, -s

zircon
BR ˈzəːkɒn
AM ˈzərˌkɑn

zirconia
BR zəːˈkəʊnɪə(r)
AM zərˈkoʊniə

zirconium
BR zəːˈkəʊnɪəm
AM zərˈkoʊniəm

zit
BR zɪt, -s
AM zɪt, -s

zither
BR ˈzɪðə(r), -z
AM ˈzɪðər, ˈzɪθər, -z

zitherist
BR ˈzɪð(ə)rɪst, -s
AM ˈzɪðərəst, ˈzɪθərəst,
-s

zizz
BR zɪz
AM zɪz

złoty
BR ˈzlɒt|i, -ɪz
AM ˈzlɔdi, ˈzlɑdi, -z
POL ˈzwɔti

zodiac
BR ˈzəʊdɪak
AM ˈzoʊdiˌæk, -s

zodiacal
BR zə(ʊ)ˈdʌɪəkl
AM zoʊˈdaɪəkəl

Zoë
BR ˈzəʊi
AM ˈzoʊi

zoetrope
BR ˈzəʊɪtrəʊp
AM ˈzoʊəˌtroʊp

Zoffany
BR ˈzɒfəni, ˈzɒfn̩i
AM ˈzɔfəni, ˈzɑfəni

Zog
BR zɒg
AM zɑg

zoic
BR ˈzəʊɪk
AM ˈzoʊɪk

zoisite
BR ˈzɔɪsʌɪt
AM ˈzɔɪˌsaɪt

Zola
BR ˈzəʊlə(r)
AM ˈzoʊlə, ˌzoʊˈlɑ

zollverein
BR ˈtsɒlfərʌɪn,
ˈzɒlfərʌɪn, -z
AM ˈtsɔlfəˌraɪn,
ˈzɔlfəˌraɪn, -z

Zomba
BR ˈzɒmbə(r)
AM ˈzɑmbə

zombi
BR ˈzɒmb|i, -ɪz
AM ˈzɑmbi, -z

zombie
BR ˈzɒmb|i, -ɪz
AM ˈzɑmbi, -z

zonal
BR ˈzəʊnl
AM ˈzoʊnəl

zonally
BR ˈzəʊnl̩i
AM ˈzoʊnəli

zonary
BR ˈzəʊn(ə)ri
AM ˈzoʊnəri

zonate
BR ˈzəʊneɪt
AM ˈzoʊˌneɪt

zonation
BR zəʊˈneɪʃn, -z
AM zoʊˈneɪʃən, -z

zonda
BR ˈzɒndə(r), -z
AM ˈzɔndə, ˈzɑndə, -z

zone
BR zəʊn, -z, -ɪŋ, -d
AM zoʊn, -z, -ɪŋ, -d

zonk
BR zɒŋ|k, -ks, -kɪŋ,
-(k)t
AM zɔŋ|k, zɑŋ|k, -ks,
-kɪŋ, -(k)t

Zonta
BR ˈzɒntə(r)
AM ˈzɑn(t)ə

Zontian
BR ˈzɒntɪən
AM ˈzɑn(t)iən

zoo
BR zuː, -z
AM zu, -z

zoogeographic
BR ˌzuːə(ʊ)ˌdʒiːəˈgrafɪk,
ˌzəʊə(ʊ)ˌdʒiːəˈgrafɪk,
ˌzuːdʒɪəˈgrafɪk
AM ˌzuəˌdʒiəˈgræfɪk,
ˌzoʊəˌdʒiəˈgræfɪk

zoogeographical
BR ˌzuːə(ʊ)ˌdʒiːəˈgraf-
ɪkl,
ˌzəʊə(ʊ)ˌdʒiːəˈgrafɪkl
AM ˌzuəˌdʒiəˈgræfəkəl,
ˌzoʊəˌdʒiəˈgræfəkəl

zoogeographically
BR ˌzuːə(ʊ)ˌdʒiːəˈgraf-
ɪkli,
ˌzəʊə(ʊ)ˌdʒiːəˈgrafɪkli,
ˌzuːdʒɪəˈgrafɪkli
AM ˌzuəˌdʒiəˈgræfək(ə)li,
ˌzoʊəˌdʒiəˈgræfək(ə)li

zoogeography
BR ˌzuːə(ʊ)dʒɪˈɒgrəfi,
ˌzəʊə(ʊ)dʒɪˈɒgrəfi,
ˌzuːdʒɪˈɒgrəfi,
ˌzuːəʊˈdʒɒgrəfi,
ˌzəʊəʊˈdʒɒgrəfi,
ˌzuːˈdʒɒgrəfi
AM ˌzuəˌdʒiˈɑgrəfi,
ˌzoʊəˌdʒiˈɑgrəfi

zoography
BR zuːˈɒgrəfi,
zəʊˈɒgrəfi
AM zuˈɑgrəfi,
zoʊˈɑgrəfi

zooid
BR ˈzuːɔɪd, ˈzəʊɔɪd,
ˈzuːɪd, -z
AM ˈzuˌɔɪd, ˈzoʊˌɔɪd, -z

zooidal
BR zuːˈɔɪdl, zəʊˈɔɪdl,
ˈzuːɪdl
AM ˌzuˈɔɪdəl, ˌzoʊˈɔɪdəl

zookeeper
BR ˈzuːˌkiːpə(r), -z
AM ˈzuˌkipər, -z

zoolatry
BR zuːˈɒlətri,
zəʊˈɒlətri
AM zuˈɑlətri,
zoʊˈɑlətri

zoological
BR ˌzuːəˈlɒdʒɪkl,
ˌzəʊəˈlɒdʒɪkl
AM ˌzuəˈlɑdʒəkəl,
ˌzoʊəˈlɑdʒəkəl

zoologically
BR ˌzuːəˈlɒdʒɪkli,
ˌzəʊəˈlɒdʒɪkli
AM ˌzuəˈlɑdʒək(ə)li,
ˌzoʊəˈlɑdʒək(ə)li

zoologist
BR zuːˈɒlədʒɪst,
zəʊˈɒlədʒɪst, -s
AM zuˈɑlədʒəst,
zoʊˈɑlədʒəst, -s

zoology
BR zuːˈɒlədʒi,
zəʊˈɒlədʒi
AM zuˈɑlədʒi,
zoʊˈɑlədʒi

zoom
BR zuːm, -z, -ɪŋ, -d
AM zum, -z, -ɪŋ, -d

zoomancy
BR ˈzuːəˌmansi,
ˈzəʊəˌmansi
AM ˈzuəˌmænsi,
ˈzoʊəˌmænsi

zoometry
BR zuːˈɒmɪtri,
zəʊˈɒmɪtri
AM zuˈɑmətri,
zoʊˈɑmətri

zoom lens
BR ˌzuːm ˈlɛnz, ˈzuːm
lɛnz, -ɪz
AM ˈzum ˈlɛnz, -əz

zoomorphic
BR ˌzuːə(ʊ)ˈmɔːfɪk,
ˌzəʊə(ʊ)ˈmɔːfɪk,
zuːˈmɔːfɪk
AM ˌzu(ə)ˈmɔrfɪk,
ˌzoʊ(ə)ˈmɔrfɪk

zoomorphism
BR ˌzuːə(ʊ)ˈmɔːfɪz(ə)m,
ˌzəʊə(ʊ)ˈmɔːfɪz(ə)m
AM ˌzu(ə)ˈmɔrˌfɪzəm,
ˌzoʊ(ə)ˈmɔrˌfɪzəm

zoonoses
BR ˌzuːəˈnəʊsiːz,
ˌzəʊəˈnəʊsiːz,
zuːˈnəʊsiːz
AM zuˈnoʊsiz,
zoʊˈnoʊsiz

zoonosis
BR ˌzuːəˈnəʊsɪs,
ˌzəʊəˈnəʊsɪs,
zuːˈnəʊsɪs
AM zuˈnoʊsəs,
zoʊˈnoʊsəs

zoophyte
BR ˈzuːəfʌɪt, ˈzəʊəfʌɪt,
ˈzuːfʌɪt, -s
AM ˈzu(ə)ˌfaɪt,
ˈzoʊ(ə)ˌfaɪt, -s

zoophytic
BR ˌzuːəˈfɪtɪk, ˌzəʊəˈfɪtɪk, zuːˈfɪtɪk
AM ˌzuəˈfɪdɪk, ˌzoʊəˈfɪdɪk

zooplankton
BR ˈzuːə(ʊ)ˌplaŋ(k)tən, ˈzəʊə(ʊ)ˌplaŋ(k)tən, ˈzuːˌplaŋ(k)tən
AM ˈzuəˌplæŋktən, ˈzoʊəˌplæŋktən

zoospore
BR ˈzuːə(ʊ)spɔː(r), ˈzəʊə(ʊ)spɔː(r), ˈzuːspɔː(r), -z
AM ˈzuəˌspɔ(ə)r, ˈzoʊəˌspɔ(ə)r, -z

zoosporic
BR ˌzuːə(ʊ)ˈspɔːrɪk, ˌzəʊə(ʊ)ˈspɔːrɪk, zuːˈspɔːrɪk
AM ˌzuəˈspɔrɪk, ˌzoʊəˈspɔrɪk

zootomy
BR zuːˈɒtəmi, zəʊˈɒtəmi
AM zuˈɑdəmi, zoʊˈɑdəmi

zoot suit
BR ˈzuːt suːt, -s
AM ˈzut ˌsut, -s

Zora
BR ˈzɔːrə(r)
AM ˈzɔrə

Zorah
BR ˈzɔːrə(r)
AM ˈzɔrə

zorbing
BR ˈzɔːbɪŋ
AM ˈzɔrbɪŋ

zori
BR ˈzɔːr|i, ˈzɒr|i, -ɪz
AM ˈzɔri, -z

zoril
BR ˈzɒrɪl, -z
AM ˈzɔrəl, -z

zorilla
BR zɒˈrɪlə(r), zəˈrɪlə(r), -z
AM zəˈrɪlə, -z

Zoroaster
BR ˌzɒrəʊˈastə(r), ˈzɒrəʊastə(r)
AM ˌzɔroʊˈæstər

Zoroastrian
BR ˌzɒrəʊˈastrɪən, -z
AM ˌzɔroʊˈæstriən, -z

Zoroastrianism
BR ˌzɒrəʊˈastrɪənɪz(ə)m
AM ˌzɔroʊˈæstriəˌnɪzəm

zoster
BR ˈzɒstə(r)
AM ˈzɑstər

Zouave
BR zʊˈɑːv, ˈzuːɑːv, zwɑːv, -z
AM ʒuˈɑv, ʒwɑv, -z

zouk
BR zuːk
AM zuk

zounds
BR zaʊndz, zuːndz
AM zaʊndz

Zsa Zsa
BR ˈʒɑː ʒɑː
AM ˈʒɑ ˌʒɑ

Z score
BR ˈzɛd skɔː(r), -z
AM ˈzi ˌskɔ(ə)r, -z

Zubes
BR z(j)uːbz
AM z(j)ubz

zucchetto
BR tsʊˈkɛtəʊ, zʊˈkɛtəʊ, -z
AM (t)suˈkɛdoʊ, zuˈkɛdoʊ, -z

zucchini
BR zʊˈkiːn|i, -ɪz
AM zuˈkini, -z

Zuckerman
BR ˈzʊkəmən
AM ˈzəkərmən

zugzwang
BR ˈzuːgzwaŋ, ˈzʌgzwaŋ, ˈtsʊktsvɑːŋ, -z
AM ˈzəgˌzwæŋ, ˈtsugˌtsvæŋ, -z

Zuider Zee
BR ˌzʌɪdə ˈziː
AM ˌzaɪdər ˈzi

Zuleika
BR zʊˈleɪkə(r), zʊˈlʌɪkə(r), zʊˈliːkə(r)
AM zuˈlaɪkə, zuˈlikə

Zulu
BR ˈzuːluː, -z
AM ˈzulu, -z

Zululand
BR ˈzuːluːland, ˈzuːlʊland
AM ˈzuluˌlænd

Zürich
BR ˈz(j)ʊərɪk
AM ˈzurɪk
GER ˈtsyːrɪç

zwieback
BR ˈzwiːbak, ˈtsviːbak, ˈtsviːbɑːk, -s
AM ˈswiˌbæk, -s

Zwingli
BR ˈzwɪŋgli
AM ˈswɪŋli

Zwinglian
BR ˈzwɪŋglɪən, -z
AM ˈ(t)swɪŋliən, -z

zwitterion
BR ˈzwɪtərˌʌɪən, ˈtsvɪtərˌʌɪən, -z
AM ˈ(t)swɪdərˌaɪən, -z

Zwolle
BR ˈzwɒlə(r)
AM ˈzwɔlə, ˈzwɑlə
DU ˈzvɔlə

Zworykin
BR ˈzwɔːrɪkɪn
AM ˈzwɔrəkən

zydeco
BR ˈzʌɪdɪkəʊ
AM ˈzaɪdəˌkoʊ

zygodactyl
BR ˌzʌɪgə(ʊ)ˈdakt(ɪ)l, ˌzɪgə(ʊ)ˈdakt(ɪ)l, -z
AM ˌzaɪgoʊˈdæktl, -z

zygodactylous
BR ˌzʌɪgə(ʊ)ˈdaktɪləs, ˌzɪgə(ʊ)ˈdaktɪləs
AM ˌzaɪgoʊˈdæktl̩əs

zygoma
BR zʌɪˈgəʊmə(r), zɪˈgəʊmə(r), -z
AM zaɪˈgoʊmə, -z

zygomata
BR zʌɪˈgəʊmətə(r), zɪˈgəʊmətə(r)
AM zaɪˈgoʊmədə

zygomatic
BR ˌzʌɪgə(ʊ)ˈmatɪk, ˌzɪgə(ʊ)ˈmatɪk
AM ˌzaɪgəˈmædɪk

zygomorphic
BR ˌzʌɪgə(ʊ)ˈmɔːfɪk, ˌzɪgə(ʊ)ˈmɔːfɪk
AM ˌzaɪgəˈmɔrfɪk

zygomorphous
BR ˌzʌɪgəˈmɔːfəs, ˌzɪgəˈmɔːfəs
AM ˌzaɪgəˈmɔrfəs

zygosis
BR zʌɪˈgəʊsɪs, zɪˈgəʊsɪs
AM zaɪˈgoʊsəs

zygospore
BR ˈzʌɪgə(ʊ)spɔː(r), ˈzɪgə(ʊ)spɔː(r), -z
AM ˈzaɪgəˌspɔ(ə)r, -z

zygote
BR ˈzʌɪgəʊt, -s
AM ˈzaɪˌgoʊt, -s

zygotene
BR ˈzʌɪgətiːn, ˈzɪgətiːn
AM ˈzaɪgəˌtin

zygotic
BR zʌɪˈgɒtɪk
AM zaɪˈgɑdɪk

zygotically
BR zʌɪˈgɒtɪkli, zɪˈgɒtɪkli
AM zaɪˈgɑdək(ə)li

zymase
BR ˈzʌɪmeɪs, ˈzʌɪmeɪz
AM ˈzaɪˌmeɪs, ˈzaɪˌmeɪz

zymological
BR ˌzʌɪməˈlɒdʒɪkl
AM ˌzaɪməˈlɑdʒəkəl

zymologist
BR zʌɪˈmɒlədʒɪst, -s
AM zaɪˈmɑlədʒəst, -s

zymology
BR zʌɪˈmɒlədʒi
AM zaɪˈmɑlədʒi

zymosis
BR zʌɪˈməʊsɪs
AM zaɪˈmoʊsəs

zymotic
BR zʌɪˈmɒtɪk
AM zaɪˈmɑdɪk

zymotically
BR zʌɪˈmɒtɪkli
AM zaɪˈmɑdək(ə)li

zymurgy
BR ˈzʌɪˌməːdʒi
AM ˈzaɪˌmərdʒi

zzz
BR zː
AM z